A COMMENTARY

CRITICAL, EXPERIMENTAL, AND PRACTICAL

ON THE

OLD AND NEW TESTAMENTS
by
ROBERT JAMIESON,
A. R. FAUSSET,
and
DAVID BROWN

VOLUME THREE

PART ONE
MATTHEW — JOHN

PART TWO
ACTS — ROMANS

by DAVID BROWN

PART THREE
I CORINTHIANS — REVELATION

by A. R. FAUSSET

WILLIAM B. EERDMANS PUBLISHING COMPANY
GRAND RAPIDS, MICHIGAN

Library of Congress Cataloging in Publication Data
Jamieson, Robert, 1802–1880.
    A commentary, critical, experimental, and practical,
on the Old and New Testaments.
    CONTENTS: v. 1. pt. 1. Jamieson, R. Genesis-
Deuteronomy. pt. 2. Jamieson, R. Joshua-Esther.—
v. 2. pt. 1. Fausset, A. R. Job-Isaiah. pt. 2.
Fausset, A. R. Jeremiah-Malachi.—v. 3. pt. 1.
Brown, D. Matthew-John. pt. 2. Brown, D. Acts-Romans.
pt. 3. Fausset, A. R. 1 Corinthians-Revelation.
    1. Bible—Commentaries. I. Fausset, Andrew Robert,
1821–1910. II. Brown, David, 1803–1897. III. Title.
BS491.J3   1973   220.7   73–14988
ISBN 0–8028–2158–8

Reprinted, April 1993

PHOTOLITHOPRINTED BY EERDMANS PRINTING COMPANY
GRAND RAPIDS, MICHIGAN, UNITED STATES OF AMERICA

PART ONE
MATTHEW — JOHN

INTRODUCTION TO THE GOSPELS.

A THOROUGHLY critical Introduction to the Gospels is rather for a separate Treatise than for the Preface to such a Volume as this. Happily, if amongst the biblical works with which our language is now enriched one complete and satisfactory Treatise on this subject, adapted to the present state of research and of thought, is scarcely yet within the reach of the mere English reader, the materials for it are abundant.

In what follows we can do little more than indicate the proper line of investigation, state briefly the leading facts on the different branches of the subject, and draw the conclusions which these justify and demand.

When we enter on a critical examination of any work of ancient literature, we have first to discover its *value;* next, to ascertain its *integrity*, or the purity in which its text has come down to us; and finally, to determine its *meaning.* Applying this to the Four Gospels, our first inquiries must be *Apologetical;* our second *Critical;* our third *Exegetical.*

By the Value of any ancient book we mean both its literary and its intrinsic value: that is to say, its genuineness on the one hand, and on the other, its intrinsic worth. A work is 'genuine' when it is the production of the person it is ascribed to, or, if it be anonymous, when it belongs to the period in which it professes to have been written, and has been composed in the circumstances alleged or presumed. When it is otherwise, it is 'spurious,' or a forgery. Of this latter nature are some treatises once ascribed to Plato, for example, and several of the Apocryphal books both of the Old and New Testaments. But some spurious works may possess considerable intrinsic worth —such as the Apocryphal books of Wisdom and Ecclesiasticus (as it is called) —while there are hundreds of genuine works, in every branch of literature, which are altogether worthless. It will be necessary, therefore, to inquire into the value, in both senses, of our Four Gospels. And this inquiry must be conducted on the same general principles as an inquiry into the value of any other literary production. But before we begin, let us well understand what is at stake.

The Fourfold Gospel is the central portion of Divine Revelation. Into it, as a Reservoir, all the foregoing revelations pour their full tide, and out of it, as a Fountain, flow all subsequent revelations. In other parts of Scripture we hear Christ by the hearing of the ear; but here our eye seeth Him. Elsewhere we see Him through a glass darkly; but here, face to face. The orthodox Fathers of the Church well understood this peculiar feature of the

Gospels, and expressed it emphatically by their usages—some of them questionable, others almost childish. Nor did the heretical sects differ from them in this; the best proof of which is, that nearly all the heresies of the first four or five centuries turned upon the Person of Christ as represented in the Gospels. As to the heathen enemies of Christianity, their determined opposition was directed against the facts regarding Christ recorded in the Gospels. And it is the same still. The battle of Christianity, and with it of all Revealed Religion, must be fought on the field of the Fourfold Gospel. If its Credibility and Divine Authority cannot be made good—if we must give way to some who would despoil us of its miracles, or to others who, under the insidious name of 'the higher criticism,' would weaken its historical claims—all Christianity is undermined, and will sooner or later dissolve in our hands. But so long as the Gospels maintain their place in the enlightened convictions of the Church, as the Divine record of God manifest in the flesh, believers, reassured, will put to flight the armies of the aliens.

'I will arrange,' says *Michaelis*, who may be called the father of the modern criticism of the New Testament, whose learning and research were vast and various, and whose tendencies, certainly, were in the direction rather of scepticism than of credulity—' I will arrange under their several heads the reasons which may induce a critic to suspect a work to be spurious:—

'1. When doubts have been made from its first appearance in the world whether it proceeded from the author to whom it is ascribed. 2. When the immediate friends of the pretended author, who were able to decide upon the subject, have denied it to be his production. 3. When a long series of years has elapsed after his death, in which the book was unknown, and in which it must unavoidably have been mentioned and quoted had it really existed. 4. When the style is different from that of his other writings, or, in case no other remain, different from that which might reasonably be expected. 5. When events are recorded which happened later than the time of the pretended author. 6. When opinions are advanced which contradict those he is known to maintain in his other writings; though this latter argument *alone* leads to no positive conclusion'—for reasons which need not be here quoted.[*] ' Now, of all these grounds for denying a work to be genuine, not one,' adds this author, ' can be applied with justice to the New Testament.' But we must not take this upon his or any man's testimony. We must make it good for ourselves. What, then, are the facts of this case?

In one of the most important chapters of his 'Ecclesiastical History'[†] *Eusebius*, who wrote in the fourth century, reports the judgment of the Christian Church, from the beginning up to his time, on the books of the New Testament which claimed to be canonical. And as his testimony on such matters of fact is of the utmost weight, let us, in the first place, listen to it.[‡] He divides

---

[*] Introd., vol. i. page 27.   [†] E. H., iii. 25.
[‡] We the rather call attention to this important testimony, because, from an incidental but very

all the books claiming to be canonical writings of the New Testament into three classes:

The *acknowledged* (Τὰ ὁμολογούμενα),

The *disputed* (Τὰ ἀντιλεγόμενα),

The *spurious* (Τὰ νόθα).

The first of these divisions embraces no fewer than *twenty-one* out of the *twenty-seven* books of the New Testament, or four-fifths of the whole collection. Of these twenty-one books Eusebius testifies that they had all along been received in the Christian Church, without any dispute, as canonical books of the New Testament. Of the remaining six—on what grounds, to what extent, and with what justice they were 'disputed'—we shall speak when we come to them in the Commentary. But what we wish here to mention is that, in the list of the twenty-one undisputed, always and universally acknowledged books, the first place is assigned to those which, by way of distinction from all the rest, Eusebius styles ' *The Holy Quaternion of the Gospels.*' *

Important, however, as this testimony is, we cannot allow it to decide the question. What, we have still to ask, are the facts of the case? The more we investigate these, the more evident will it appear that the Genuineness of the Four Gospels is attested by a mass of evidence, external and internal, altogether unparalleled and quite overpowering. No work of classical antiquity, even the most undoubted, is half so well attested, or can lay claim, one might say, to a tithe of the evidence which the Gospels possess.

It will greatly facilitate our inquiries to bear in mind the following fact: 'It is,' to use the words of Olshausen, 'wholly a peculiar circumstance in the history of the Gospels, and one which goes a great way to sustain their genuineness, that *we nowhere find, in any writer of any part of the ancient world, any indication that only a single one of the four Gospels was in use,*

interesting fact, the testimony of any intelligent and impartial historian writing when he did was of far more value than it would have been in an earlier age. In the last of the Pagan persecutions, under Diocletian (which burst forth in the year 303), an order was issued—for the first time since Christianity had been persecuted at all—'that the Scriptures should be destroyed by fire.' This order was instigated by a bitter antagonist of the Gospel, who well knew that so long as the sacred writings of the Christians remained Christianity would continue to live, and the Church, though exterminated, would spring up afresh. What was the effect? While many preferred death to the surrender of their dearest treasures, others (who were called *traditores*), unable to face the consequences of resisting, yielded them up. But as some of the proconsuls, anxious to save the Christians, were willing to seize any books which they might resign into their hands in place of the New Testament, some gave them the writings of heretics, and those reckoned among the 'spurious' writings of the New Testament; and as the 'traditors' of the canonical books were subjected to severe ecclesiastical discipline, while these latter were subjected to none at all, the question was thus raised, *as it had never been before*—it being now a matter of life and death—'What are the Genuine Scriptures of the New Testament?' Certain it is that this whole question, by the time of Eusebius—that is, by the end of the third and beginning of the fourth century—had assumed a more scientific form than it had ever done before. Not that the conclusions then arrived at differed from the beliefs of the previous age—the reverse was the case—but that what had all along been held by the Church with little definite expression was now put with the precision which we observe in the chapter of Eusebius above referred to.

* Ἡ ἁγία τῶν εὐαγγελίων τετρακτύς.

*or ever known to exist separately. All possessed the entire collection of the four Gospels.'** Hence the current name by which they were known, as one work —'THE GOSPEL.' †

Ascending upwards to the age of the apostles, it is needless to begin so late as the age of *Councils*. It is enough here to say that in the very first General Council which was held under Constantine—that of Nicæa (A. D. 325)—though no catalogue of the books of Scripture was drawn up, because this was no subject of dispute, the Gospels were referred to on both sides of the Arian controversy, as they were by all the orthodox Fathers of that age who wrote against the Arian heresy, as of undisputed canonical and divine authority. But passing from this, the external evidence for the genuineness of the Gospels may be ranged under the four following heads:—

FIRST, The evidence of the ANCIENT VERSIONS, of which it is enough here to notice the two earliest and most venerable: The original SYRIAC (commonly called the *Peshito*) and the Old LATIN (which used to be called the *Itala*, or the *Italic*); the one prepared for the use of the Oriental portion of the Christian community; the other for the use of the Latin-speaking Christians of North Africa, and generally of the West. Whatever differences of opinion exist among critics as to the precise age of these venerable Versions of the New Testament, it is almost unanimously agreed that they both belong either to the latter half of the second century or the beginning of the third. And if so, it is obvious that the books of the New Testament which are found in those Versions must have been familiar to both the Eastern and the Western Churches, and been recognized by them, *long before those Versions were made*— which carries us back to a period not much later than the death of the Apostle John. Well, in both those earliest Versions the Four Gospels, it is almost unnecessary to say, occupy the first place.

SECOND, The evidence of individual CHRISTIAN WRITERS, both *orthodox* and *heretical*. Of the former we name the following:—

1. *Origen* (A. D. 184 or 185-253): of Egyptian birth; the greatest scholar and the first thoroughly biblical critic that the Church produced. He may be said to have spent his life in biblical inquiries; he examined MSS., observed, compared, and weighed various readings; he defended Christianity against acute enemies, and explained it to Christians themselves, and was of too independent a mind not to form his own judgment and speak out his convictions on the books of the New Testament. Well, not only did this great Father publish commentaries on the Gospels, as on other parts of Scripture, but he has in several of his extant writings given lists of the canonical Scriptures, in all of which the Four Gospels stand first among the books of the New Testament. And never does he drop a word from which it could be inferred that a doubt existed, either then or at any former period, as to the genuine and canonical character of those books.

2. *Tertullian* (as early at least as about A. D. 160-220): born at Carthage;

* 'Commentary on the Gospels' Introd. (*Clark*). † Τὸ εὐαγγέλιον.

the most ancient of the Latin Fathers; the first great light of the African Church, and the most original, forcible, and, in his own peculiar style, the most eloquent of the Latin Fathers, until Augustin rose to eclipse all others. In the fourth of his books against the heretic Marcion—who rejected all the Gospels but that of Luke, and mutilated even that—he rests his whole case upon the notorious fact that not only Luke, entire as we have it, but the other three Gospels of Matthew, Mark, and John, had the unbroken testimony of all the churches either founded by the apostles or in ecclesiastical fellowship with them,—in other words, of the whole catholic Church; and so confident is he that an appeal on this subject to all the churches would be at once responded to, that he narrows the whole question to this one—of known and undeniable fact.* Such statements, so near the apostolic age, cannot but be felt to possess immense weight.

3. *Clement* of Alexandria (nearly contemporary with Tertullian): assistant to Pantænus, who, if not the first, was the second head of the celebrated catechetical school of Alexandria—a seminary which, though it seems to have embraced a lower department for the training of catechumens, was chiefly a school of theological teaching; and if it had not St. Mark, according to the tradition, for its founder, was at least of high antiquity. Pantænus and he seem to have taught jointly till 211, when Clement became its head—dying about two years thereafter. Only four of his writings are extant; but these are of great value, partly as illustrating the peculiar type of theological thought which reigned then at Alexandria, and partly for the facts to which they incidentally bear witness. In a fragment of one of his works,† which Eusebius has preserved,‡ he gives the tradition (says Eusebius) regarding the order of the Gospels, derived from the earliest presbyters (which we need not here repeat), and says that John, finally perceiving that all which pertained to the *body* (τὰ σωματικὰ), or the outward life of Christ, had been sufficiently recorded, being invited by his friends, and moved by the Spirit, composed a *spiritual* Gospel (πνευματικὸν εὐαγγέλιον). This testimony to the apostolic antiquity and genuineness of the Gospels is that not only of an early Presbyter but a Divinity teacher, in the highest repute over the entire Church; of one who not only taught according to what had been handed down in the Alexandrian school from the beginning, but had travelled, as he himself tells us, in Greece, Italy, and various parts of the East, studying under superior masters, and weighing the information he received from all sources. And his method of establishing the authority of the Gospels was the same with Tertullian's, asserting nothing on his own judgment—for the age of historical criticism had not then come—but sending us back to the earliest antiquity, giving no hint that there ever had been the least diversity of opinion on the subject.

4. The *Muratorian Fragment* (as it is called): an anonymous Latin fragment on the Canon of the New Testament, so called as having been discovered in the Ambrosian Library at Milan, and first published by Muratori in his 'Antiquities of Mediæval Italy' (1740), who ascribed it to Caius, a well-known Presbyter of the

* Adv. Marc. c. 2 and 5.   † Entitled, 'Ὑποτυπώσεις (' *Outlines*').   ‡ E. H. vi. 14.

Roman Church, about the close of the second century. Though this has been disputed, it is agreed by all who have critically examined the Fragment that it belonged either to the latter part of the second, or at latest the very beginning of the third century.* If we place its composition between the years 160 or 170 and 200, we shall probably be near the truth. The Latin is that of one who hardly knew the elements of the language, and abounds in Greek idioms; confirming his connection with the Roman Church at a time when Greek, not Latin, was used at Rome. Be the writer who he may, he simply states the current view of the Church of his own day regarding the Canon of the New Testament—that is, a century or so after the death of the Apostle John. The half sentence with which the Fragment begins is unintelligible. But we gather from what immediately follows that the writer had begun to enumerate the books of the New Testament, and had just said that of the Four Gospels Matthew and Mark were the first in order; for he immediately adds that 'the third book of the Gospel† is that according to Luke. . . . The fourth of the Gospels is that of John,' &c. After describing, according to the current tradition, how John was induced to undertake this work, the Fragment proceeds to enumerate the other books of the New Testament; and after naming all the 'acknowledged' books (ὁμολογούμενα), it passes straight to the 'spurious' (νόθα), 'which cannot be received into the catholic Church, for it is not fit that gall should be mingled with honey.' ‡ While this writer simply reports the judgment of the Church in his own day—high antiquity certainly—on the books of the New Testament, he drops no hint of any difference of opinion having ever been entertained.

5, *Irenæus*—perhaps the most important witness of all, as being, until Origen appeared, the most textual and expository of the earlier Fathers. He was a disciple of Polycarp, Bishop of Smyrna, and succeeded Pothinus as Bishop of Lyons in the year 177, when that venerable man suffered martyrdom at the age of ninety or upwards. Of his works, only his Five Books 'Against Heresies' are extant, and with the exception of the first book and fragments of the others, these exist only in a Latin Version, which, however, was probably almost contemporary with the original Greek. In his third book (c. 1) occurs an important passage which, besides the Latin version of it, Eusebius has preserved to us in the original Greek. In this passage, while giving an account of each of the Gospels, this disciple of Polycarp, less than a century after the death of the Apostle John, speaks of our four Gospels (and we know them to be ours

---

* The late venerable Dr. Routh, who, in the second edition of his *Reliquiæ Sacræ*, has printed this Fragment, and appended to it some forty pages of valuable Latin Annotations, is of opinion that if not written soon after the middle of the second century, it must have been at least before its close. This opinion is founded on an allusion which the Fragment makes to Hermas's having 'very recently in our times (*nuperrime temporibus nostris*) written at Rome the book called "The Shepherd," during the Episcopate of his (Hermas's) brother Pius.' Now the date of Pius's Episcopate ranges from 142-157. And though *Hug* has given some ingenious reasons for assigning it a rather later date, even he ascribes it to the beginning of the third century.

† *Evangelii*, τοῦ Εὐαγγελίου.

‡ *Quæ in catholicam ecclesiam recipi non potest (possunt): fel enim cum melle misceri non congruit.*

because he quotes them so largely and verbally) as not only the genuine productions of two of the apostles and of the constant companions of two other apostles, but as the very teaching of Christ Himself; and this not as an opinion of his own, but as matter of undisputed fact. In another chapter of this same book (c. 11) occurs a grand passage, the original Greek of which has been happily recovered since the date of the early editions of the work. 'Nor,' says this Father, 'can there be more Gospels in number, nor yet fewer than these [four]. For as there are four quarters of the world which we inhabit, and four presiding spirits,* and the Church is diffused over the whole earth, and the pillar and foundation of the Church is the Gospel and the Spirit of life, on the same principle has the Church four pillars, breathing everywhere incorruption, and kindling in men new warmth. Whence it is evident that the Word, the Artificer of all things, who sitteth upon the Cherubim and keepeth all things in order, hath given us the Gospel in a four-fold kind, but informed by one Spirit.' † After giving the symbolic signification of the lion, the calf, the man, and the eagle—which made up the form of the Cherub—he continues: 'And with these harmonize the Gospels, whereon Christ sitteth' [that is, sitteth enthroned, as on the Cherubim, Ezek. i. 26—a grand idea]. After expatiating on the cherubic characteristics of each Gospel, he concludes thus: 'And these things being so, foolish and ignorant, yea, and daring, are all they [heretics] who set aside the idea (or plan) of the Gospel, bringing in either more or fewer Gospels than those we have specified; some, that they may seem to have discovered more than the truth, others, that they may set aside ‡ God's arrangements.'

Now, we make nothing of all that Irenæus says about the figures of the Cherubim; for that part of his statement is no matter of fact, but purely of speculation—ingenious, indeed, and beautiful, and like his conjecture as to "the number of the beast,"§ echoed not only by the ancient Church but by many moderns. But the fact on which Irenæus bases this speculation, which he states as a thing familiarly known and recognized in the Church—that there were not only four harmonious divinely inspired Gospels, neither more nor fewer, but this by a Divine arrangement—this is the important point. And this is stated by one between whom and the Apostle John there was but one link—Polycarp.

6. *Papias*, Bishop of Hierapolis (in Phrygia), and a disciple of John—but whether of the apostle or of a presbyter of that name, is not certain. He flourished somewhere about the year 110, 115, or 116; and he devoted himself chiefly to the collecting of every scrap of tradition which he could pick up regarding our Lord and his apostles. Some of these are silly enough, verifying the well-known opinion of Eusebius regarding him as a man of slender judgment.‖ Yet in matters of fact his testimony is not to be despised, and Eusebius himself (three chapters before) commends him in that respect. His writings are lost;

* καθολικά, *principales:*—probably ἀρχεῖα (*Stieren*).
† ἔδωκεν ἡμῖν τετράμορφον τὸ εὐαγγέλιον, ἑνὶ δὲ πνεύματι συνεχόμενον.   ‡ ἀθετήσωσι.
§ "666" = λατεῖνος (Rev. xiii. 18).
‖ σφόδρα γάρ τοι σμικρὸς ὢν τὸν νοῦν.' E. H. iii. 39.

but Eusebius, in whose time they were extant, tells us that he made express mention in them of the Evangelists, and how they wrote their Gospels.

Over against this *Hexapla* of express witnesses to the genuineness of the Gospels, we might place another, of those who, without expressly naming them, refer beyond all doubt to them, and are as valid, and some of them no less valuable witnesses, than the former. Ascending up from Irenæus towards the apostolic age, the latest we need quote, and the most important, is—

1. *Justin* Martyr. Though a Greek by descent, his family had settled at Flavia Neapolis, near the site of the ancient Sichem or Sychar, and there he was born (as he tells us in his first Apology, addressed at Rome to Antoninus Pius). Whether he was born so late as 103 (according to Cave), or as early as 89 (as Fabricius and Grabe judge)—some seven years before the last survivor of the apostles died—we cannot be wrong in placing his birth (with *Westcott*) about the close of the first century, or quite near the time of John's decease. His writings are all extant in the original Greek; and what renders his testimony of peculiar importance is the immense quantity of references which he makes to the facts of our Lord's life and teaching—so many and so explicit that even if the Four Gospels had perished we might construct a tolerably accurate summary of their principal contents from Justin's writings. All this, however, he draws from what he calls 'Memoirs of the Apostles,'* which, until the beginning of this century, was always understood to mean our Gospel History. The *Tübingen* critics have tried hard to show that the reference is not to it, but to shorter narratives which were in wide circulation before our Gospels appeared. But this hypothesis has been shown to rest on narrow and untenable grounds, while the positive evidence that it is our Gospels that Justin quotes from is most convincing (though there appear to have been some passages in the copies he used which are not now extant).† Here, then, we have large portions of the Gospels quoted or referred to in the works of a Christian philosopher and martyr, writing less than fifty years after the death of the Apostle John; and as this was probably about twenty years after his conversion to Christianity, and not a hint is given in any of his writings that doubts of the genuineness of the History to which he refers had been known or heard of among Christians, we are thus carried up, in a manner singularly convincing, to the very age of the apostles.

2. The anonymous and very interesting *Epistle to Diognetus:* written in a classical style of Greek, which has with good reason been assigned to the close of Trajan's reign, or about the year 117. This letter leaves no doubt that the writer of it was acquainted with the First and Fourth Gospels, and with the Epistles. We cannot doubt, therefore, that had he had occasion to refer to the other two Gospels, we should have had evidence that he knew them too.

This brings us, in our ascent towards the apostles, to the Apostolic Fathers,

---

* Ἀπομνημονεύματα τῶν Ἀποστόλων.

† No one has handled this subject more searchingly, candidly, and convincingly than *Westcott*, pages 126-201. If we might venture to obtrude our own judgment, founded on an examination of Justin's writings many years ago, it would be altogether in the same direction.

as they are termed, or such of the disciples and companions of the apostles as have left works behind them. Of these, the latest we name in point of time is—

3. *Polycarp*, Bishop of Smyrna, who heroically suffered martyrdom for his Lord at a great age. 'Eighty and six years have I served Christ,' said he to the Proconsul. Whether we take this to mean simply that he had been a Christian all that time—which, if he suffered under M. Antoninus, about the year 166, would make his conversion to have happened about A.D. 80—or whether we take it to refer to the duration of his services as a minister of Christ, which is not probable, it is beyond doubt that he was a disciple of the Apostle John, and may have seen other apostles and many who saw the Lord Himself; and some have thought that "the angel of the church in Smyrna," to whom our Lord directed the second of His Apocalyptic Epistles (Rev. ii. 8), was no other than this Polycarp. Well, this most venerable and apostolic bishop wrote several letters, only one of which remains—his Epistle to the Philippians—truly a precious relic, supposed by Lardner to have been written about the year 108. It contains more references to the New Testament than was customary in such early writings, though they are interwoven with his own language rather than expressly quoted; and these show beyond doubt that this Asiatic bishop, whose life and ministry were like a prolongation of the beloved disciple's, was familiar with the Gospels and the Epistles of the New Testament. Still ascending upwards, we come to—

4. *Ignatius*, Bishop of Antioch, whose ordination is placed by Eusebius in the year 69, after the death of the Apostles Peter and Paul at Rome. In this case he was doubtless acquainted with some of the apostles; and Chrysostom says he conversed familiarly with them, and was perfectly acquainted with their doctrine. He suffered martyrdom, under Trajan, about the year 107, though, according to others, a few years later. The extant writings of this bishop consist of seven Epistles, though several others, now admitted to be spurious, were ascribed to him. We have nothing to do here with the intensely interesting and much litigated question, whether the longer or the shorter Recension of these Epistles be the genuine one (by which questions of ecclesiastical antiquity are considerably affected, and which, after much learned controversy, the Syriac version of them recently discovered and edited by Dr. Cureton would seem to have set at rest in favour of the shorter). The question for us here is, What testimony does this martyr-bishop, who preceded even Polycarp, bear to the New Testament? The brief answer is, that his references to the Gospels and the Epistles of Paul are numerous and explicit,—a fact the importance of which, in one so very near the apostles themselves, cannot be over-estimated.

5. *Barnabas*, who has left an extant Greek Epistle, though part of it existed only in the Old Latin version, until quite recently, when the indefatigable *Tischendorf* discovered that it existed entire in the precious *Codex Sinaiticus*, which he brought from the convent of St. Catherine, at mount Sinai, and has now given to the world. Whether he was the very Barnabas, "the son of consolation," who was Paul's companion in missionary travel, or another of the same name—about

which even yet there is not entire unanimity among scholars—he certainly belonged to the apostolic age; and as his Epistle gives plain evidence that he was acquainted both with the Gospels and the Epistles of the New Testament, this is one more link in the chain of evidence.

We pass by *Hermas*, who has left a work entitled 'The Shepherd'[*]—fragments of which are also in the *Codex Sinaiticus*—and whom many have taken to be the same Hermas to whom Paul sends a salutation (Rom. xvi. 14); because there is reason to think he was a somewhat later person, though his testimony is quite as clear as the former; and we are now brought to the most ancient relic of apostolic antiquity, next to the books of the New Testament themselves. We mean the Epistle of—

6. *Clement*, Bishop of Rome. Without doubt he is the very person of whom Paul says, "With Clement also, and other my fellow-labourers, whose names are in the book of life" (Phil. iv. 3). A number of writings have been palmed upon this Clement; but all these are now rejected as spurious—even what is called his Second Epistle to the Corinthians. One Epistle to the Corinthians only is universally regarded as the genuine production of this Clement, written in the name of his own Roman church, to aid in composing the dissensions which had again sprung up in that church. Its date cannot be later than the year 90, while some think it earlier. Well, his references to the Epistles of the New Testament, as well as to the Old Testament, are numerous; and though his subject did not lead him so directly to the Gospels, the three or four passages which bore the most upon his point are quoted, and with such explicitness, as the words of the Lord Jesus, that it is quite clear he had the Gospels before him just as we have them.

Thus have we the unbroken testimony of the orthodox Fathers of the Church to the genuineness of the Gospels,—in two chains of evidence, each consisting of six links, reaching up to the apostles themselves. They are not all that might have been quoted, but they clearly prove—according to the ordinary rules of literary evidence—that those original Documents of the Christian Faith were the genuine productions of their reputed authors. But this evidence is confirmed by—

THIRD, The testimony borne by HERETICAL CHRISTIANS in their controversies with the orthodox. We can afford room here only for two of these, both within the first two centuries.

1. *Tatian:* an Assyrian convert to Christianity, who, on coming to Rome, met with Justin, and who, after the martyrdom of that Christian philosopher (about 164 to 167), continued his work at Rome with some success. Being of a restless turn, he began to introduce novelties, and returning to the East he put himself at the head of a sect called the Encratites, about the year 172. His only remaining work is an Oration against the Gentiles. But we refer merely to one exceedingly interesting fact regarding his literary activity, which is preserved by Eusebius. This Tatian, he says[†] 'having put together[‡] a certain combination and collection of the Gospels,[§] I know not how, called this the Diatessaron,[||] which is still in the hands of some.' Now, as Eusebius had

---

[*] ὁ Ποιμήν.　　　　　　[†] E. H. iv. 29.　　　　　　[‡] συνθείς.
[§] τῶν εὐαγγελίων.　　　　[||] τὸ διὰ τεσσάρων.

just said that Tatian's sect 'made use of the Law, the Prophets, and *the Gospels*,* there can be no doubt that it is our own Four Gospels which he says Tatian wove into one continuous narrative. And that this Diatessaron, though it wanted the genealogies of Matthew and Luke, came immediately into great repute, even in the orthodox Church, is evident from two interesting facts. One, stated by Assemani (Biblioth. Orient.), is, that Ephraem the Syrian, who flourished some centuries after Tatian, issued a commentary on this Diatessaron. The other, and still more interesting fact, is, that in the diocese over which Theodoret presided, in the fifth century, this Diatessaron seems actually to have superseded the Gospels themselves in the public worship of the churches. 'I have met,' says Theodoret, 'with above two hundred of these books, which were in use in our churches,—all which I took away and laid aside in a parcel, placing in their room the Gospels of the four Evangelists.' From this it is perfectly evident, not only that the orthodox Church had the same Four Gospels that we have, little more than seventy years after the death of the Apostle John, but that the heretical sect of which Tatian was the head used the same Gospels; and when Theodoret charges his Diatessaron with leaving out the genealogies, that is only an additional evidence that in other respects it differed not from the orthodox copies.

2. *Marcion*, who preceded Tatian by about thirty years—flourishing somewhere between the years 130 and 144. From a strong antipathy to everything that seemed to savour of Judaism in Christianity, he rejected all the Gospels except Luke's, and cut down even it to suit his own ideas. The Tübingen critics, Baur † and Ritschl, ‡ made a desperate attempt —which Eichhorn had made before them—to show that Marcion's was the original Gospel from which that of Luke was derived. But the torture of internal, and the defiance of all external evidence by which alone this monstrous position was made plausible is now almost universally admitted among the scholars of Germany; and such ingenuity of negative and destructive criticism has met there with the fate which it deserved, although in this country the more critical Unitarians still entrench themselves in it. Extravagant, however, as were Marcion's claims for his own Gospel, he not only gained many followers, but impressed his own critical spirit upon them, and drew forth replies from Irenæus and Tertullian. From these, and fragments of Marcion's own statements, we find that he accused all the apostles except Paul of altering and corrupting the original Gospel. Tertullian challenged Marcion to produce a copy of the original Gospel, with historical attestation of its being handed down as such from the beginning. But he only met this challenge by alleging that as the corruption took place in apostolic times, and was perpetrated by apostles themselves, it was impossible to do so—which, as Tertullian rejoins, was only to throw the blame upon our Lord Himself for choosing such apostles. But besides this, when he begins to assign his reasons

---

* τοῖς εὐαγγελίοις.   † 'Kritische Untersuchungen,' 1847,
‡ 'Das Evang. Marcions u. d., kanonische Evang. Lucas,' 1846.

for rejecting all but his own mutilated Gospel of Luke, we find them purely subjective or doctrinal. In other words, he rejected the rest, not because it was not historically attested, but because it taught what he was not prepared to believe. And thus Marcionism, by its unhistorical and capricious formation of an Evangelical canon of its own (we have not required to advert to the Epistolary part of it), and by its inability, when challenged, to produce such attestations as the true canon possessed, only acted as a foil to show the more clearly on what a firm historical foundation the true canon of the New Testament had all along rested.

Fourth, If the Heathen Authors who attempted to write down Christianity were obliged to admit the genuineness of its sacred books, they must surely be regarded as beyond question. Now there are two such, whose writings were unfortunately destroyed through the mistaken zeal of the Christian emperors, for had they survived they would have been of great service to the Christian cause. We refer to Celsus, who wrote against Christianity in the latter part of the second century, and Porphyry, who lived a century later.

1. *Porphyry* was a man of great critical sagacity, and, living in Syria, was well acquainted with the Old Testament, examined it critically, and made acute objections to the book of Daniel, for instance, on critical and philological grounds So well qualified was he to speak to the genuineness of the New Testament books, that, as Michaelis says, every real friend of Christ would gladly give the works of a pious Father to rescue his writings from the flames. 'He possessed' says this critic, 'every advantage which natural abilities or great political situation could afford for discovering whether the New Testament was a genuine work of the Apostles and Evangelists, or whether it was imposed upon the world after the decease of its pretended authors. But no trace of this suspicion is anywhere to be found, nor did it ever occur to Porphyry to suppose that it was spurious.' And again he asks, 'Is it credible, then, that so sagacious an inquirer could have failed to discover a forgery with respect to the New Testament, had a forgery existed; a discovery which would have given him the completest triumph, by striking a mortal blow at the religion which he attempted to destroy?'*

2. *Celsus's* work against Christianity, entitled 'The True Word,'† was answered by Origen in the middle of the third century; and as he speaks of the author as long since dead, he may have issued it somewhere about the year 180 or 190. Happily, Origen has quoted from it so largely that we can hardly doubt he has preserved at least its more important statements and reasonings. Though he quotes none of the New Testament books by name, no one who studies his references to it can doubt that the Gospels from which he draws his arguments are our Gospels. Indeed, he makes a merit of drawing from the Christians' own writings, and says he has no need to go beyond them, since their own weapons were enough to destroy them. He denominates the Evangelical writings 'The

---

* Introd. i. pages 42-44. † ' Ἀληθὴς Λόγος.

Gospel,'* and refers to circumstances peculiar to each of the Gospels, showing that he had them all four before him. No testimony to the genuineness of those writings can be more satisfactory than this.

This surely is a chain of *external* evidence perfectly irrefragable. Accordingly, up to the beginning of the present century, no doubts as to the genuineness of the Four Gospels had ever arisen within the bosom of the Christian Church. Till then these had all come *from without*—from the dark regions of infidelity and scepticism. But in Germany, during the last thirty years of the last century, a spirit of rationalism had been gradually creeping over its Professors and clergy, which, like the dry rot, penetrated the whole fabric of its theology. This is not the place to write the melancholy workings and products of that spirit. But it is the place to notice one of the directions which it took, and still, in one form or another, takes. The celebrated Eichhorn, the successor of Michaelis at Göttingen, in his 'Introduction to the New Testament' (1804-1814), while admitting the Credibility of the Gospel *History*, maintained that there are no traces of our *Gospels* before the end of the second or beginning of the third century, when, out of the many different and discrepant narratives of this kind which were then in circulation, the Church deemed it necessary to select the most credible and best adapted for general use, and accordingly pitched upon four, which from that time have been acknowledged in the Church as the authentic Gospel History. Why Eichhorn fixed upon the end of the second and beginning of the third century as the time by which the Gospels must have been adopted, will be obvious after what we have stated about Irenæus's testimony to the universal reception of the Gospels in his day.

The most crushing answer to this assertion has been given by Professor Norton.† We could wish to have found room for at least the principal portion of this reply, which is very valuable for its own sake. Suffice it to say, that from the nature of the case the thing supposed is shown to be impossible; that even if it could have happened, or anything like it, there must of necessity have remained some historical traces of it; but that as there are absolutely none, it is against all the principles of historical evidence to assume and affirm it.

Other modes of destroying the credit of the Gospels have been successively and perseveringly tried in Germany, only to be first refuted and then abandoned, or to fall into neglect—such as the theory of Strauss, and that of Baur and the Tübingen school. Schleiermacher's method of handling them—which, while admitting their substantial truth, regards them as well-meaning but in many respects confused and inaccurate efforts to exhibit the Life of Jesus, and out of which it is the part of the ' higher criticism ' to construct the *true* History—is more subtle, and has told to too large an extent upon many otherwise sound and able scholars.

On the score of external evidence, then, the Four Gospels stand on an immoveable foundation of continuous, unbroken, historic attestation.

* τὸ Εὐαγγέλιον.　　　　　　　　† Genuineness, &c., vol. i. pages 19-35.

But mere external evidence for the Genuineness of such books as the Gospels, however unanswerable, is not all that we have a right to expect. The very nature of the case is such that we cannot rest—and, we will venture to say, ought not to rest—satisfied without *internal* evidence also. By this we mean not what are called the Internal Evidences of Christianity, or the Nature of the *Religion* itself. We shall advert to that by and by. But our present point is with the *Books* which constitute the primary Documents of our Faith; and of these we say that, after finding them attested to us from without by irrefragable evidence, we naturally, and even irresistibly, feel impelled to inquire what internal marks of genuineness they present. But here we find it impossible to separate the Genuineness of the books from the Credibility of the History; for, from the nature of the case, the vindication of the writings, as those of their reputed authors, will go far to authenticate what they relate.

Observe, then, first of all, the *language* of these narratives. It is Greek, indeed, but Jewish Greek; bearing the nearest resemblance to the Greek of the Septuagint, yet differing even from it; such Greek, in fact, as (we may say with Michaelis *) could not have been written a hundred and twenty years after Christ. For after that period there were hardly any Jewish converts to Christianity—any, at least, who became preachers or writers; and none but a Jewish convert *could* have written these narratives. Mark the style of the Greek Apostolical Fathers: not one of them writes in such a style as that of the Gospels, nor, we may safely say, could have done so.† Thus, these narratives must of necessity have been written within the three quarters of that one century which intervened between the ascension of Christ and the time when the peculiar language in which they are couched could no longer be written by any one. But that is just to say that they could only have been written in the apostolic age itself, which extended to the close of the first century.‡

Observe, next, the *style* of these productions. It is that of uneducated, yet sensible men, perfectly artless and unpolished, such as you expect from the publican on the shore of the Galilean lake, who gives his name to the First Gospel, and the fisherman on the same lake from whom the Fourth receives its name. If there be any exception, it ought to be in the Third Gospel, professing, as it does, to be from the pen of a physician, and one who, if we may judge from his other treatise—the Acts of the Apostles—must have seen something of the world. Accordingly, while the prevailing character of Luke's Gospel is that of all the rest—Jewish Greek—there are portions of it, and of the Acts also, which are written in a quite classic style.

But far more decisive of the genuineness of the Gospels are the innumerable

---

* Introd.; i. 47.

† This remark is still more applicable to the Clementine Homilies, a romantic yet important production of the latter part of the second century, written in the name of the apostolical Clement of Rome.

‡ This is a *kind* of argument the peculiar force of which will be felt with ever-growing strength in proportion as we familiarize ourselves with the Greek of the Gospels, on the one hand, and on the ether with the Greek of the Apostolic Fathers.

allusions which they incidentally make to the geography and topography of Palestine, the mixed political condition of the people, their manners and customs, religious principles, observances, and prejudices, the sects and parties into which they were divided, &c. Had these narratives been spurious productions of a later time, after Jerusalem was destroyed and the Jews dispersed, or constructed at a distance out of but a few fragments of truth, their authors would have either taken care to make as few allusions as possible of the kind we have noticed, or they would have infallibly discovered their own fraud. In fact, it is hardly possible to avoid detection in fraudulent histories which go into any degree of detail. Anachronisms are almost invariably committed, either in fact or in style; and the latter are fully more difficult to avoid than the former. Well, our Gospels, steeped as they are in all manner of allusions—every particular narrative which they contain being full of them—have supplied the severest test of their own truth. And how do they stand that test? Everything is in keeping—such a difficulty as that about the *taxing*, for example, in Luke ii., only revealing the undisputed accuracy of the rest. There is a pre-raphaelite minuteness and accuracy of detail which it is a perfect delight to trace, attesting them to all candid readers, in whose minds they are vivified afresh at every reading. Who has not been struck with those inimitable touches of character by which the Pharisees and the Sadducees, with the rivalry that subsisted between them, are depicted or chiselled to the life—not to speak of the Samaritans, differing from and disliked by both; the allusions to the different members of the Herod family, with the account of the Baptist's death, so strikingly agreeing with that of Josephus; and all that we meet with in every page of the Gospels, and which burn these incomparable narratives into the memory and imagination of every reader? Some allusions are of such a kind that their minute accuracy only appears on investigation, but which, when pointed out, are at once felt to be astonishing and beautiful. For a mass of these we must refer the reader to such writers as *Lardner, Michaelis*, and *Hug*.

There is a class of internal evidences of genuineness of a peculiar but irresistible nature,—what are called *Undesigned Coincidences* between the different Gospels. That the Four Gospels were not drawn up by one writer, nor by any number of writers acting in concert, is perfectly evident on the slightest examination of them. Remarkable as their agreement is, their differences and apparent contradictions—some of them exceedingly difficult to explain—put it beyond all doubt that they are independent productions of different pens. And yet there occur a number of coincidences, at those points where they travel over the same ground or cross each other's path, which, while manifestly undesigned, are strikingly confirmatory of the coinciding narratives. And the more trivial the circumstance about which the undesigned coincidence occurs, so much the more convincing, of course, is it as a mark of genuineness and truth in the different records.*

* One example may here be given merely to illustrate, to those to whom the remark may be new,

But there is one internal mark of genuineness in the writings, and at the same time of truth in the things written, which is beyond every other—*the Story itself* which these Documents tell. It could not by possibility have been told by any forger, designing to palm off a composition of his own as the authentic records of eye and ear-witnesses of the things related; whether we view him as inventing the whole, or only dressing up a few fragments of truth in the way which we find done in these narratives. Who could have invented such a Character and such a History as that of the Christ of these Gospels? Every one whose intellectual judgment and moral sense have not been miserably warped, must see that in order to be *written* it must first have been *real*. Nor let it be said that as many such narratives were afloat in the early Christian ages, the Four we now have may fairly be regarded as just specimens of the religiously inventive turn of that age. For while the existence of those many narratives shows beyond doubt that they all rest on the basis of a real historical Christ, the still extant remains of such productions—of the Apocryphal Gospels, we mean—are so childish, extravagant, and contradictory, as only to act as a foil to our Gospels. We shall have occasion to recur to this subject; and in the Commentary we have once and again adverted to it. Here we shall only observe, that these apocryphal fragments seem to have been providentially preserved just to show that those Four Gospels, which the Church unanimously and from the first acknowledged, were THE Gospel History, whose truth was to carry its own evidence and extinguish every rival.

Thus is the internal evidence of the Genuineness of the Four Gospels as complete and resistless as the external. Both together constitute a mass of evidence such as no other book in existence can lay claim to; and we hesitate not to say, that he who resists this evidence ought not to believe in the genuineness of any literary production of older date than the generation in which he lives.

There still, however, remain some points to be disposed of. The character of the writers is a point of much interest. If they were not wilful impostors or designing knaves—and the time has gone by when that needs to be disproved—they must be regarded as honest men; for there is no medium. It is needless to ask whether any one would fly in the face of all his known interests, and persist in doing so, with a knavish purpose—whether the Evangelists, having neither

the nature of the thing intended. In the First Gospel it is said (Matt. xxvi. 67), "Then did they spit in His face, and buffeted Him; and others smote Him with the palms of their hands, saying, *Prophesy unto us, thou Christ, Who is he that smote thee?*" Had we no other information than what is conveyed in this Gospel, or the Second, or the Fourth Gospel, we should never have been able to account for one who struck another asking the person struck to point out who did it. But in the Third Gospel the difficulty vanishes; for there (Luke xxii. 64) we read that it was after "the men that held Jesus had *blindfolded* Him" that they asked Him to point out who had smitten Him. In the present Commentary several such coincidences are pointed out (as in the remarks on Mark viii. 9, page 169). But the reader who would wish to pursue this subject, the line of which was first suggested by Paley in his 'Horæ Paulinæ,' is referred to Dr. Blunt's 'Undesigned Coincidences,' &c.— although considerable deduction must be made for some of his examples which are weak, and others which are more than doubtful.

pecuniary advantage nor literary reputation to gain by putting forth as true what they knew to be false; and belonging as they did to a party whose testimony to what they record exposed them to ridicule, reproach, loss of property, and death itself—whether they can be believed to have deliberately done that very thing, and four of them independently. But it is not needless to call attention to the peculiar character of the History itself, in so far as it bears upon such a theory. The Evangelists represent the Person whose Story they tell as brought into the world with no attractions, and born only to suffering from the first; as passing the first thirty years of a life destined to great things, in perfect obscurity, and emerging into public life only to encounter opposition from the leading spirits of the nation; as raising comparatively few constant followers, deserted about the middle of His brief career by a considerable number even of these, frequently misunderstood by the selectest band of His attendants, one of whom betrayed Him at last to His enemies, while another, to save himself from danger, swore that he knew nothing about Him; as arraigned before the highest council of the nation, and by it condemned to die, and after being treated with every species of contumely, handed over to the civil authority, which, after some feeble efforts to save Him, yielded Him up to crucifixion; as led forth to execution, nailed to a cross, and uplifted between two malefactors, with every circumstance of ignominy; as covered with the derision of all classes of the spectators, and at length dying and being buried; and, though rising again, yet appearing no more in public, but after forty days' seclusion from every eye, with the exception of occasional manifestations to His handful of adherents, leaving the world altogether for heaven; His disciples having the task committed to them of telling all this to the world, and making it the basis of a religious community over the whole earth. Is such a story, either in its substance or in its details, what a designing person would invent? Who can doubt that in the hands of a dishonest writer, the whole would have assumed a different, and in most of its particulars an opposite, complexion? We speak not of the precepts inculcated and the sins condemned, such as it is inconceivable that any writer should have put into the mouth of a Teacher whose life, as written by him, was known to be fictitious, or in the main unreal. Such transcendent morality could not by possibility have come, either more or less, from a dishonest writer. It *must* have been Reality before it became History.

But even after the thorough honesty of the Evangelists has been admitted, there are still some points to be cleared up. Had they the requisite information? Are they telling us what they had immediate access to know, or giving us information received at second or third hand, or further off? Every reader of the Gospels can answer this question. The First and Fourth of the Evangelists were two of the Twelve whom Christ selected to be constantly with Him, on purpose to be able, from their own eyes and ears, to report all that He did and said; and as for the other two, it is enough at present to say, that their narratives so perfectly agree in all main particulars with those of Matthew and John, that if the History as told by the First and Fourth be authentic, the same History as told by the Second and Third cannot consistently be rejected. Indeed, a mere glance at the narratives themselves is sufficient to show that they are given on the authority of those who saw and heard what they report. Who, for example, can doubt that the whole scene of Lazarus's sickness, death, and resurrection is recorded by an eye and ear-witness? and the resurrection of Jairus' daughter, and of the widow of Nain's son; the storms on the sea of Galilee, when Jesus and His disciples were on it, and His walking on that sea; the feeding of the five and of the four thousand:—are not all these related with a circumstantiality and an artlessness which bespeak the presence, in the Record, of parties to the scenes themselves? Still more, perhaps, is this felt in such narratives as that of the triumphal Entry into Jerusalem, the Last Supper, Gethsemane, the Betrayal, Apprehension, Trial, Crucifixion, and Burial; the scenes of the Resurrection-day, the subsequent Appearances and the eventual Ascension, in the sight of the disciples, into heaven. Each and all of these are related in a way which would defy invention, had the things never happened, or even had it been intended merely to dress up a meagre outline of fact with imaginary circumstances.

But we must look a little deeper into the History itself, or the Tale it tells. The existence of the Four Gospels, supposing the History unreal, would involve three distinct moral impossibilities. First, The conception of such a character as the Christ of the Gospels; next, the construction of the Narrative, considered as a literary task, so as to keep up the character throughout, and never let it down—to make the great Actor in all its scenes neither to say nor to do aught that is incongruous or out of keeping; finally, that not one person should do all this, nor two, nor three, but four persons, and all independently of each other, or without any collusion (as is manifest on the face of the narratives)—so as that the Story told by all four should be one and the same Story, and the success in telling it should be equal in all, while yet each narrator should have peculiarities and attractions of his own. Add to this, that one of these four astonishing writers was an untutored fisherman, another a publican, on the Galilean shore, a third the companion of another of those fishermen of Galilee; and that only one of these had any pretensions to literary culture; and that with the exception of him—if even with that exception—none of them had written a line, of a literary nature, before. When all this is considered, the moral impossibility of four such narratives coming from four such hands—not to say, if it was in the main untrue, but even if it was more or less an invention of their own—is complete and overwhelming.

Consider only for a moment what those four men have done. They have written the History of One to whom they all give the name of Jesus, because, as divinely announced, He was to be a *Saviour from sin*. Keeping this perpetually in view, they all agree in representing Him as bone of our bone, flesh of our flesh, man as we are men; yet free from all the moral imperfections by which other characters are stained; subject to every innocent infirmity of our nature, yet morally spotless. And what is particularly worthy of notice, it never appears to be their professed *object* to teach this, or teach anything at all. They are not *preaching* Histories: they tell their tale, an unvarnished tale, leaving the facts to speak for themselves. Even the Fourth Gospel, which differs from the other three in being of a *reflective* character, is so in a way which in nowise interferes with the remark just made. But the *Human* in Christ is not more manifest on every page than the *Divine*. We state this quite broadly and generally here—not requiring to do more for our immediate purpose. And what we say is, that in His claiming equality with the Father, and speaking and acting in a vast number of particulars in a way which could not fail to suggest the conviction that this, and no other, was His meaning, our Evangelists have to do with a Character altogether unique and totally unmanageable, save in the Record of a *real life*. No human ingenuity could have hidden the art, if art had had to be put in requisition at all, in the construction of such a life. At some places or other the writers would infallibly have discovered themselves. If, indeed, the story had been of a very vague and general character, we might conceive of its being passably executed. But no such History is that of the Gospels. The Evangelists carry the Person whose life they write through a multitude of the most *novel*, the most *complicated*, the most *testing* scenes conceivable—scenes such as had never before been dreamt of. They have undertaken to represent Him as so speaking, so acting—in a word, so conducting Himself throughout—that the readers of their Histories may be convinced, as they were, that this Jesus is the Son of God, and believing, may have life through His name. In doing this, need we say that they had no model whatever to guide them—no literary work, and no known example, to give them the least hint *how* to make the subject of their History speak and act so as never to be out of keeping either with real Humanity or with proper Deity.

But the strength of the case only grows upon us as we proceed. The Four Gospels only record with the pen what had been proclaimed by the lips of Christ's followers from the fiftieth day after His resurrection, without intermission, in the streets of Jerusalem, and in all the most public parts of the country where the scenes of the History are alleged to have taken place. The followers of Jesus neither waited till the whole affair was likely to be forgotten, nor went away to distant lands to be beyond the reach of detection. But they told their Tale in the very spots where it occurred, and while every circumstance was quite fresh and warm in the public mind. Even this might be conceived possible consistently with invention, provided the things related had been of so *trifling* a nature that nobody cared to sift them, or of so *private* a nature that few could be supposed privy to them, or of so *abstract and unimpassioned* a nature as to encounter no formidable prejudices and be fitted to produce no great changes. But the facts reported were of the most public and patent nature; they were of the most vivid and startling character; they were in the teeth of every existing prejudice; they were fitted to destroy the whole edifice of the existing Judaism; they were of a nature to revolutionize, so far as embraced, the religious views of all mankind. It would be ridiculous to suppose that such a Tale should stir no public interest, and be for any time let alone. If the whole thing was a falsehood, or even in its leading particulars false, it could not have lived a month. If true, and yet the Jewish community unprepared to submit to it, we may be quite sure that attempts would immediately be made to put the witnesses and preachers of it down. Such attempts we know *were* made, and that within the first day or two, but all in vain. The Story was credited, and the believers of it increased by thousands every day in Jerusalem itself. The first and most splendid triumphs of the Story of a Crucified, Risen, and Glorified Saviour were achieved in the very spots to which, and over the very people to whom, they could point as the scenes and the witnesses of the transactions which they reported—transactions the chief of which were but a few weeks old when the preachers first stood in the streets of the capital to proclaim it, and on the truth or falsehood of which the whole nation could with perfect certainty pronounce. But—to try every supposition— it is conceivable that the written Documents of our Faith, though faulty—that the character which they depict, though defective—might, if well executed on the whole, escape detection, provided they were subjected to little criticism, or criticism on narrow or false principles. But these Four Documents—*multiplied* as no writings ever were, *translated* into other tongues as no writings ever were, *commented on* as no writings ever were, *sifted* untiringly, by foes to destroy and by friends to defend them, for sixteen or seventeen centuries, as no writings ever were—must, if untrue, have been torn into ten thousand pieces long ere now, and ceased to obtain any credit or exercise any influence. But these Four Produc- tions—which may all be read through in a few hours—live still, and sit enthroned on the faith and affection of the most cultivated portion of the human race, and most of all of those who have shown that they understand the principles and laws of evidence, and are quite competent to detect literary fraud, who have no motive whatever for maintaining the credit of any falsehood, and who, from pure conviction of the truth of this History, profound admiration of its glorious Sub- ject, and gratitude to Him for what He hath done for them, have dedicated all their gifts to the study of this History, and their lives to the propagation of its facts among their fellow-men. Nor is it a barren faith which the Christian world reposes in this unique History. This Story of Jesus has penetrated to the core of that commanding portion of the human family which we call Christendom, has permeated its whole manifold life—its intellectual, moral, social, political, religious life—and has revolutionized and ennobled it. Paganism is dead; Judaism is dead; Mohammedanism is dead; the various intermediate speculations of restless and proud minds, if they cannot be said to be dead, con- stitute no substantive Religion at all, and never will nor can crystallize into any- thing worthy of that name, on which a living soul can repose and a dying man may build hope for a future state. Christianity alone lives. It lives not, indeed, an undisturbed life. Transcendental philosophies, rationalistic criticism, materialistic science, and political theories for the advancement of the human species, bred of materialism, are at this hour in full activity. But this History

—with the preceding and following portions of the Bible that do but minister to t—has not only stood its ground, but seen nearly every successive form of antagonism to its grave. Fresh forms of hostility succeed, because the spirit of enmity to Revelation and all divine authority, that gives them birth, still lives. But since nearly every imaginable form of hostility to Revelation has already run its course, while Biblical Christianity is only fresher and mightier than ever, we have in this a sure pledge of its undying vitality. For every new speculation in philosophy, for every new discovery in science, for every new development in the life of nations, Christianity shows itself prepared;—to grapple with and overcome it, if false and deadly; to own it, to regulate it, to ride on the top of it, if sound and salutary. It superannuates and supersedes whatever stands in its way; itself never superannuated, but eternally young. It is the vital element of modern society, and the very spirit of progress. It is the salt of the earth; it is the light of the world. It has its points of real difficulty—in criticism, in doctrine, even in form, considered as a Documentary Revelation. On all these sides it will continue to be assailed so long as enmity to whatever is Divine remains among men, and has leave to speak out. Nor will such things cease to stumble even some "who believe and know the truth." But as the efforts of its adversaries prove bootless, the hearts of its leal disciples get reassured. The difficulties remain where they were, and "that which is crooked" we find, with the wise king of Israel, "cannot be made straight." But on every side we behold shattered systems—and, alas! the wreck of noble minds who commit themselves to them. "Come and behold the works of the Lord, what desolations He hath wrought in the earth." Outside of Christianity we find no harbour of refuge for our tossed and weary souls, but here we enjoy deep and settled repose. And thus, as we survey historically the vicissitudes through which the Gospel has come, from the first day until now, is the uncorrupted heart, as by a method of exhaustion, "shut up unto the Faith," exclaiming, as it enters this haven of rest, "Lord, to whom shall we go? Thou hast the words of Eternal Life."

On the subject of *Miracles*, as a preliminary objection to the reception of the Gospel History, this is not the place to enter. One might have thought that since the days of *Hume* this objection had been sufficiently disposed of. In so far as it drew forth an astonishing amount of beautiful investigation and important illustration on the subject of human testimony, one may be pleased at the extraordinary attention which that objection attracted. At the same time we are free to confess to something akin to shame at the panic it created, the anxiety which some writers have shown in dealing with it, and the elaborateness and even metaphysical subtlety of some of the ablest replies to it—as if it involved some real difficulty. The possibility of a miracle (and the possibility of authenticating it) is, in our view, simply a question of Theism or Atheism. If there be no God, there can be no miracle, in any proper sense of the term. But if there be, 'the laws of nature' are but His own method of rule in His own physical creation.

Whether He has at any time, and in certain given cases, for ends higher than the physical creation, acted otherwise than according to these 'laws'—that men might be startled into the recognition of His own presence, and constrained to receive truths of eternal moment as an immediate message from Himself—must be purely a matter of *evidence*. And if this evidence be in its own nature convincing, and to the candid mind overwhelming, it is not to be weakened by difficulties as to the possibility of such Divine Intervention, which, explain them as men will, have their rise only in the atheistic spirit. It is a grief to us to observe these difficulties obtruded anew upon the Christian world, not by professed infidels, but by ordained ministers of the Church of Christ in our land—the victims of a wretched Naturalism, which, while clinging to the sentiment, or what they call the spirit of Christianity, is impatient of the Supernatural in every form. There seems to be a growing party, including some learned clergy, who, like an extinct school in Germany, flatter themselves that they can retain their belief in the Bible in general, and in the Gospels in particular, while they sit loose to all that is miraculous or, in the strict sense, supernatural in it. No doubt this phase of scepticism, like others, will pass away. It is an inclined plane, and we know the terminus of those who venture on it. Meanwhile, we add our testimony, in various parts of this Commentary, to that of all other thorough students of the Gospels, that they must be accepted entire, or entire rejected, as, like the Saviour's own tunic, "without seam, woven from the top throughout."

This naturally suggests the subject of *Inspiration*, on which it will be proper to say a closing word or two.

Every thoughtful reader of the Gospels must at times have asked himself how the Evangelists were able to report as they have done so much of what our Lord said and did, with all those circumstances and incidents which so much affect the sense and design of it. As mere *memory* would plainly have been inadequate to the production of such narratives, there remains but one other explanation of them. Some *prompting* from above—enabling the Evangelists to reproduce the scenes and circumstances, discourses and actions, as we have them—is irresistibly suggested to the mind as the only adequate explanation of those four unique compositions called The Gospels. Yet so little can one safely rely on mere conjecture or theory in such a case, that had we no explicit information in the narratives themselves as to the source of their proper authority, we should never have felt satisfied that we had solved the problem. But happily that information we have, and the solidity which it imparts to our faith in these Four Gospels, and by consequence in the rest of the Scripture, is complete and reassuring.

"These things have I spoken unto you," said Jesus to His disciples, in the upper room, the night before He suffered, "being yet present with you. But the Comforter, which is the Holy Ghost, Whom the Father will send in My name, He shall teach you all things, and bring all things to your remembrance, whatsoever I have said unto you."* So imperfectly did the

* John xiv. 25, 26.

apostles apprehend what Jesus said to them, that they could not be expected to remember it even as it was spoken; for nothing is harder than to recall with precision any but the briefest statement, if it be not comprehended. But while Jesus here promises to send them a Prompter from heaven, it was not to recall His teaching simply as it fell on their ears from His lips. This would have left them the same half-instructed and bewildered, weak and timid men, as before— all unfit to evangelize the world, either by their preaching or their writings. But the Spirit was to *teach* as well as *remind* them—to *reproduce the whole teaching of Christ*, not as they understood it, but *as He meant it to be understood*. Thus have we here a double promise, that through the agency of the Holy Ghost the whole teaching of Christ should stand up in the minds of His disciples, when He was gone from them, in all its *entireness*, as at first *uttered*, and in all its vast *significance*, as by Him *intended*. Before the close of this same Discourse our Lord announces an extension even of this great office of the Spirit. They were not able to take in all that he had to tell them. He had accordingly expressed much in but a seminal form, and some things He could hardly be said to have spoken at all. But when the Spirit should come, on His departure to the Father, He should "guide them into *all the truth*," filling up whatever was wanting to their *complete apprehension of the mind of Christ*. On these great promises rests the CREDIBILITY—in the highest sense of that term—OF THE GOSPEL HISTORY, and so its DIVINE AUTHORITY.*

We have here said that the Credibility of the Gospel History, in the lofty sense guaranteed by our Lord's promise, gives it Divine Authority. We sometimes hear the Inspiration of the Gospels spoken of as if it were something distinct from the character of the History itself. But the Gospels possess no *separate* element of Inspiration—separate, that is, from their strict Historical accuracy in the lofty sense above explained. And the best proof that this accuracy is such as attaches to no human composition whatever, will be found in the Gospels themselves, which, while evincing their own Inspiration, determine also the nature of that Inspiration. Each Gospel has its own broad, indelible characteristics; yet each tells the same Tale, travelling on its own line. And not only is the History the same, but amidst not inconsiderable diversity of representation in minor details, the success of each in bringing out the One Historical Result is equal; each contributes something towards the complete conception of the Great Subject, and so may be said to be indispensable to the others; and all together—amidst partially unharmonizable diversities in subordinate features of the Narrative—constitute in four-fold perfection the True History of the Saviour of the World. Like the four seasons of the year, each is welcome and each beautiful in its turn. We read them again and again, and yet again, and never tire of them. Try this upon the most accurate and exalted history that ever came from a merely human pen. Read it twice or thrice you may; four or five times, not so likely; but oftener, never. It gets flat, stale, and unprofitable. The best do so. But these peerless Histories never **do.**

* See the Commentary on John xiv. 25, 26.

Millions read them and re-read them. Still they are as fresh as the first day. New wonders appear in them, and still new. Men comment upon them, and people read with endless interest every sensible, elevated, warm commentary on them. But the text itself rises above all, and keeps above all. In our most enlarged, most heavenly frames of mind, these incomparable Documents are ever above us. And who that weighs this will not be ready to say, with the most entire conviction, that these Four Histories "came not in old time by the will of man, but holy men of God wrote them"—from personal knowledge, no doubt, and the materials they possessed, but still, in the use of that knowledge and those materials, wrote them—"as they were moved by the Holy Ghost." Yes; and while they have defied hostile criticism, and will for ever baffle all attempts to break them down, they minister alike to the rudest and the most refined, who open their souls to the reception of their testimony, light and life, daily nutriment and strength for work, joy unspeakable and full of glory;—nor will they cease to do this until that which is perfect is come, when that which is in part shall be done away.

THE GOSPEL ACCORDING TO MATTHEW.

THE *author* of this Gospel was a publican or tax-gatherer, residing at Capernaum, on the western shore of the sea of Galilee. As to his identity with the "Levi" of the Second and Third Gospels, and other particulars, see on Matt. ix. 9. Hardly anything is known of his apostolic labours. That, after preaching to his countrymen in Palestine, he went to the East, is the general testimony of antiquity; but the precise scene or scenes of his ministry cannot be determined. That he died a natural death may be concluded from the belief of the best-informed of the Fathers, that of the apostles only three, James the greater, Peter, and Paul, suffered martyrdom. That the first Gospel was written by this apostle is the testimony of all antiquity.

For the *date* of this Gospel we have only internal evidence, and that far from decisive. Accordingly, opinion is much divided. That it was the first issued of all the Gospels was universally believed. Hence, although in the order of the Gospels, those by the two apostles were placed first in the oldest MSS. of the Old Latin version, while in all the Greek MSS., with scarcely an exception, the order is the same as in our Bibles, the Gospel according to Matthew is *in every case* placed first. And as this Gospel is of all the four the one which bears the most evident marks of having been prepared and constructed with a special view to the Jews—who certainly first required a written Gospel, and would be the first to make use of it—there can be no doubt that it was issued before any of the others. That it was written before the destruction of Jerusalem is equally certain; for, when he reports our Lord's prophecy of that awful event, on coming to the warning about "the abomination of desolation" which they should "see standing in the holy place," he interposes (contrary to his invariable practice, which is to *relate* without *remark*) a call to his readers to read intelligently—"Whoso readeth, let him understand" (Matt. xxiv. 15)—a call to attend to the divine signal for flight, which could be intended only for those who lived before the event.* But how long before that event this Gospel was written is not so clear. Some internal evidences seem to imply a very early date. Since the Jewish Christians were, for five or six years, exposed to persecution from their own countrymen—until the Jews, being persecuted by the Romans, had to look to themselves—it is not likely (it is argued) that they should be left so long without some written Gospel to reassure and sustain them, and Matthew's Gospel was eminently fitted for that purpose. But the digests to which Luke refers in his Introduction (see on Luke i. 1-4, with the Remarks at the close of that Section) would be sufficient for a time, especially as the living voice of the "eye-witnesses and ministers of the word" was yet sounding abroad. Other considerations in favour of a very early date—such as the tender way in which the author seems studiously to speak of Herod Antipas, as if still reigning, and his writing of Pilate apparently as if still in power—appear to have no foundation in fact, and cannot therefore be made the ground of reasoning as to the date of this Gospel. Its Hebraic structure and hue, though they prove, as we think, that this Gospel must have been published at a period considerably anterior to the destruction of Jerusalem, are no evidence in favour of so early a date as A. D. 37 or 38—according to some of the Fathers, and, of the moderns, *Tillemont, Townson, Owen, Birks, Tregelles*. On the other hand, the date suggested by the statement of Irenæus

* Hug, page 316.

(iii. 1), that Matthew put forth his Gospel while Peter and Paul were at Rome preaching and founding the Church—or after A. D. 60—though probably the majority of critics are in favour of it, would seem rather too late, especially as the Second and Third Gospels, which were doubtless published, as well as this one, before the destruction of Jerusalem, had still to be issued. Certainly, such statements as the following, "Wherefore that field is called the field of blood *unto this day;*" "And this saying is commonly reported among the Jews *until this day*" (Matt. xxvii. 8, and xxviii. 15), bespeak a date considerably later than the events recorded. We incline, therefore, to a date intermediate between the earlier and the later dates assigned to this Gospel, without pretending to greater precision.

We have adverted to the strikingly Jewish character and colouring of this Gospel. The facts which it selects, the points to which it gives prominence, the cast of thought and phraseology—all bespeak the Jewish point of view *from* which it was written and *to* which it was directed. This has been noticed from the beginning, and is universally acknowledged. It is of the greatest consequence to the right interpretation of it; but the tendency among some even of the best of the Germans to infer, from this special design of the First Gospel, a certain laxity on the part of the Evangelist in the treatment of his facts must be guarded against.

But by far the most interesting and important point connected with this Gospel is the *language* in which it was written. It is believed by a formidable number of critics that this Gospel was originally written in what is loosely called Hebrew, but more correctly *Aramaic*, or *Syro-Chaldaic*, the native tongue of the country at the time of our Lord; and that the Greek Matthew which we now possess is a translation of that work, either by the Evangelist himself or some unknown hand. The evidence on which this opinion is grounded is wholly external. But it has been deemed conclusive by *Grotius, Michaelis*, (and his translator) *Marsh, Townson, Campbell, Olshausen, Greswell, Meyer, Ebrard, Lange, Davidson, Cureton, Tregelles, Webster and Wilkinson*, &c. The evidence referred to is the following:—

(1.) *Papias* (of whom see page ix.) is reported by Irenæus, Eusebius, &c., to have stated, in a lost work of his, that 'Matthew drew up the oracles (meaning his Gospel) in the Hebrew dialect (or tongue),* and every one interpreted them as he was able.' (2.) *Irenæus* says, 'Matthew, among the Hebrews, put forth a written Gospel in their own tongue.'† (3.) *Pantænus* is said by Eusebius (E. H. v. 10) to have gone to the Indians,‡ and there, as 'is reported,'§ to have 'found the Gospel of Matthew, which had been in the hands of some there who knew Christ before his arrival; to whom the Apostle Bartholomew is said to have preached, leaving them this writing of Matthew in Hebrew letters,‖ which they kept till the time referred to.' Jerome,¶ who gives substantially the same report, adds that, 'on his return to Alexandria, Pantænus brought it with him.' (4.) *Origen* says, according to the report of Eusebius,** that 'the first Gospel was written by him who once was a publican but afterwards an apostle of Jesus Christ, Matthew, and that, having drawn it up in Hebrew letters,†† he issued it for the Jewish believers.' (5.) *Eusebius's* own statement is that 'Matthew, having first preached the Gospel to the Hebrews, when about to go to others, also delivered [to them] in writing the Gospel according to him (Matthew), in the native tongue.'* (6.) *Jerome* (later in the fourth century) says† that 'Matthew first composed a Gospel of Christ in Judæa for the benefit of the Jewish believers, in the Hebrew tongue and character. Who afterwards translated it into Greek is not sufficiently certain. Moreover, that very Hebrew Gospel is in the Library of Cæsarea, which Pamphilus the martyr collected with the greatest diligence. I myself also translated it, with permission of the Nazarenes, who make use of that volume in Berœa, a town of Syria.' And again, he speaks of the Gospel used by the Nazarenes and Ebionites, 'which we recently translated from Hebrew into Greek, and which is by most called the authentic Gospel of Matthew.'‡ (7.) *Epiphanius*, in the same fourth century, says § regarding the Nazarenes and Ebionites, that what they call the Gospel according to the Hebrews was just the original, in the Hebrew tongue and character, of Matthew's Gospel.

This chain of testimony is certainly formidable, especially as it is unbroken, there being no external testimony to the contrary. But when closely examined, it will not, we believe, be found to bear the weight laid upon it. There is the strongest reason to suspect that most of the preceding testimonies are, after all, but one testimony—that of Papias—repeated from hand to hand. Irenæus, at least, who had the greatest regard for all that Papias wrote, as he must have seen his statement on this subject, and says nothing himself in addition to what Papias had said before him, in all probability just echoed it from him. As to Origen, the following circumstances are very suspicious: that the report comes to us only through Eusebius; that, as reported by him, Origen is not said to have ascertained it as a fact in consequence of investigations made by himself on so important a subject, but merely to have learnt it by tradition;‖ it is not said he had ever seen, or made it his business to search out, this Gospel—which, considering the energy with which he prosecuted such biblical inquiries, is somewhat surprising if he ever stated what Eusebius reports; it is not said even that he believed in the tradition, but merely that it had reached him. But more than this: in his extant commentaries on Matthew, Origen speaks of the Greek of it as if it were the only and the original Matthew, reasoning on the Greek word rendered in the Lord's Prayer "daily" (ἐπιούσιος) as one formed by the Evangelists themselves; and in several places he refers to "the Gospel according to the Hebrews" as a work known to be in existence—but only if one chose to use it for *illustration*, not as having any *authority*. This is enough of itself to throw doubt over the whole tradition. The Pantænus-story wears a very mythical air. Eusebius merely says that he was *said* to have gone tô India, and there *said* to have found a Hebrew Matthew; and Jerome, who just echoes Eusebius, adds only that he was *said* to have brought it home with him to Alexandria. That he went to India (or probably southern Arabia) is likely enough. But without inquiring too critically into the Indian part of the story, if Pantænus valued it so highly as to bring it home with him, why do we hear nothing of it after that? Either, then, he brought home no such Gospel, or if he did, it was found, on further examination, too worthless to be even spoken about, much less published as Matthew's original. As to Eusebius, the probability is, that what he says was designed to express, not so much the result of his own critical judgment as what he had learnt, and the rather as elsewhere he speaks of the Greek

---

* πατρίῳ γλώττῃ γραφῇ. † In his Comment on Matt. xii. 13.
‡ Vocatur a plerisque Matthæi authenticum. § Hær. xxx. 3. ‖ ὡς ἐν παραδόσει μαθών.

Matthew as if it were the original and only Gospel according to Matthew. Before referring to the testimony of Jerome and Epiphanius, which is more independent, let us inquire for a moment what is the value of that of Papias, on which most of the others appear to us to lean. We stay not to ask what *can* be the meaning of that strange clause, that 'every one interpreted this Hebrew Gospel of Matthew as he was able.' We accept it as a fact, that Papias did report that Matthew wrote his Gospel in Hebrew. Now, if this report had involved no exercise of *discrimination*, we should attach great weight to it; for a man of slender judgment, if honest, earnest, industrious, and successful as a collector of facts—all which even Eusebius vouches for—is entitled to deference. But it so happens that the very point now in question, so far from being a simple matter of fact, required a careful discrimination of the true from the false, the genuine from the spurious. Those Nazarenes and Ebionites were no other than the Judaizing party in the Christian Church, who were kept within its bosom so long as the apostles lived, but thereafter broke away, and became two distinct though closely allied heretical sects. That they had a Hebrew Gospel—which they confidently affirmed to be the original of the Gospel according to Matthew, which each of these sects modified according to its own ideas, and which was variously called the Gospel according to the Hebrews, according to the Twelve Apostles, and the Gospel of Peter—admits of no doubt. And as there was a total separation between them and the catholic Church, and individuals belonging to each only occasionally met, it may easily be supposed that this assertion of the Nazarenes and Ebionites regarding the original of the First Gospel would find its way into the orthodox pale, and give rise to the supposition that as the First Gospel was manifestly designed in the first instance for Jewish Christians, and of all the four was the best adapted to them, it was first drawn up in the vernacular language, and that so the Nazarene and Ebionite tradition might have some foundation in truth. We do not affirm that this was the case. But as we find Jerome and Epiphanius both expressing their belief in it, and Jerome going the length of translating this Nazarene and Ebionite Gospel into Greek, *as being the original* of Matthew's Gospel, we are not able to resist the inference that some confusion on this subject did very early get into the Church; and if it existed as early as the time of Papias, *he* at least was not the man to extricate and give us the precise truth. In a matter about which Jerome and Epiphanius write with some degree of obscurity (for so much will be allowed by the most strenuous upholders of a Hebrew original), we are not entitled to build much on anything so very brief from the pen of Papias. As to Jerome's translation of this Hebrew Gospel, different conclusions have been drawn from his way of speaking of it at different times. One thing is very suspicious. It is not now extant—indeed, he seems never to have published it; and without going into the disputes raised by his language, when we put the few fragments of it still remaining —differing considerably from the canonical Matthew—over against the fact that Jerome's version never properly saw the light, we may safely conclude that he placed no reliance upon the work, and regarded it, at most, in the light of a literary curiosity rather than a valuable instrument of interpretation, which, on his first supposition, that it was the original of Matthew's Gospel, it surely would have proved.

In a word, and leaving out of view all the suspicious things attaching to the testimonies we have adduced in favour of a Hebrew original of our First Gospel, who can readily bring himself to believe that if such Hebrew original of the Gospel according to Matthew was in existence for nearly four centuries, the orthodox Church would have allowed it to go out of their own hands almost from the first, and that this treasure was preserved exclusively among a contemptible body of Judaizing heretics, who at length melted away altogether, and their Gospel with them?

Now, how stand the facts as to our Greek Gospel? We have not a tittle of historical evidence that it is a *Translation*, either by Matthew himself or any one else. When referred to, it is invariably as the work of Matthew the publican and apostle, just as the other Gospels are ascribed to their respective authors. This Greek Gospel was from the first received by the Church as an integral part of the one Quadriform GOSPEL. And while the Fathers often advert to the two Gospels which we have from apostles, and the two which we have from men not apostles—in order to show that as that of Mark leans so entirely on Peter, and that of Luke on Paul, so these are really no less apostolical than the other two—though we attach less weight to this circumstance than they did, we cannot but think it striking that, in thus speaking, they never drop a hint that the full apostolic authority of the Greek Matthew had ever been questioned on the ground of its not being the *original*. Further, not a trace can be discovered in this Gospel itself of its being a Translation. Michaelis tried to detect, and fancied that he had succeeded in detecting, one or two such. Other Germans since, and Davidson and Cureton amongst ourselves, have made the same attempt. But the entire failure of all such attempts is now generally admitted, and candid advocates of a Hebrew original are quite ready to own that none such are to be found, and that but for external testimony no one would have imagined that the Greek was not the original. This they regard as showing how perfectly the translation has been executed. But those who know best what translating from one language into another is, will be the readiest to own that this is tantamount to giving up the question. This Gospel proclaims its own originality in a number of striking points; such as its manner of quoting from the Old Testament, and its phraseology in some peculiar cases. The length to which these observations have already extended precludes our going into detail here. But the close *verbal coincidences* of our Greek Matthew with the next two Gospels must not be quite passed over. There are but two possible ways of explaining this. Either the translator, sacrificing verbal fidelity in his Version, intentionally conformed certain parts of his author's work to the Second and Third Gospels—in which case it can hardly be called Matthew's Gospel at all—or our Greek Matthew is itself the original.

Moved by these considerations, some advocates of a Hebrew original have adopted the theory of *a double original;* the external testimony, they think, requiring us to believe in a Hebrew original, while internal evidence is decisive in favour of the originality of the Greek. This theory is espoused by *Guericke, Olshausen, Thiersch, Townson, Tregelles,* &c. But, besides that this looks too like an artificial theory, invented to solve a difficulty, it is utterly void of historical support. There is not a vestige of testimony to support it in Christian antiquity. This ought to be decisive against it.

It remains, then, that our Greek Matthew is the original of that Gospel, and that no other original ever existed. It is greatly to the credit of Dean *Alford,* that after maintaining, in the first edition of his 'Greek Testament' the theory of a Hebrew original; he thus expresses himself in the second and subsequent editions: 'On the whole, then, I find myself constrained to abandon the view maintained in my first edition, and to adopt that of a Greek original.'

One argument on the other side, on which not a little reliance has been placed, we have purposely left unnoticed till now, believing that the determination of the main question does not depend upon the point which it raises. It has been **very** confidently affirmed that the Greek language was not sufficiently understood by the Jews of Palestine, when Matthew published his Gospel, to make it at all probable that he would write a Gospel for their benefit in the first instance in that language. Now, as this merely alleges the improbability of a Greek original, it is enough to place against it the evidence already adduced, which is positive, in favour of the sole originality of our Greek Matthew. It is indeed a question how far the Greek language was understood in Palestine at the time referred to. But we advise the reader not to be drawn into that question as essential to the settlement of the other one. It is an element in it, no doubt, but not an essential element. There are extremes on both sides of it. The old idea, that our Lord hardly ever spoke anything but Syro-Chaldaic, is now pretty nearly exploded. Many, however, will not go the length, on the other side, of Hug* and Roberts.† For ourselves, though we believe that our Lord, in all the more public scenes of His ministry, spoke in Greek, all we think it necessary here to say is, that there is no ground to believe that Greek was so little understood in Palestine as to make it improbable that Matthew would write his Gospel exclusively in that language—so improbable as to outweigh the evidence that he did so. And when we think of the number of Digests or short narratives of the principal facts of our Lord's History, which we know from Luke (i. 1-4) were floating about for some time before he wrote his Gospel, of which he speaks by no means disrespectfully, and most of which would be in the mother tongue, we can have no doubt that the Jewish Christians and the Jews of Palestine generally would have from the first reliable written matter sufficient to supply every necessary requirement, until the publican-apostle should leisurely draw up the First of the Four Gospels in a language to them not a strange tongue, while to the rest of the world it was *the* language in which the entire Quadriform Gospel was to be for all time enshrined. The following among others hold to this view, of the sole originality of the Greek Matthew:—*Erasmus, Calvin, Beza, Lightfoot, Wetstein, Lardner, Hug, Fritzsche, Credner, de Wette, Stuart, da Costa, Fairbairn, Roberts.*

On two other questions regarding this Gospel it would have been desirable to say something had not our available space been already exhausted:—The *characteristics,* both in language and matter, by which it is distinguished from the other three; and its *relation to the Second and Third Gospels.* On the latter of these topics —whether one or more of the Evangelists made use of the materials of the other Gospels, and if so, which of the Evangelists drew from which—the opinions are just as numerous as the possibilities of the case, every conceivable way of it having one or more who plead for it. The most popular opinion until within a pretty recent period, and in this country, perhaps, the most popular still, is that the Second Evangelist availed himself more or less of the materials of the First Gospel, and the Third of the materials of both the First and Second Gospels. Here we can but state our own belief, that each of the First Three Evangelists wrote independently of both the others; while the Fourth, familiar with the First Three, wrote to supplement them, and, even where he travels along the same line, wrote quite independently of them. This judgment we express, with all deference for those who think otherwise, as the result of a pretty close study of each of the Gospels in immediate juxtaposition and comparison with the others. On

---

* Introduction, pages 326, &c.　　　　　　　† Discussions, pages 25, &c.

the former of the two topics noticed, the linguistic peculiarities of each of the Gospels have been handled most closely and ably by *Credner*,* of whose results a good summary will be found in Davidson.† The other peculiarities of the Gospels have been most felicitously and beautifully brought out by *da Costa*,‡ to whom we must simply refer the reader.

THE GOSPEL ACCORDING TO MARK.

THAT the Second Gospel was written by Mark is universally agreed; though by what Mark, not so. The great majority of critics take the writer to be "John whose surname was Mark," of whom we read in the Acts, and who was "sister's son to Barnabas" (Col. iv. 10). But no reason whatever is assigned for this opinion, for which the tradition, though ancient, is not uniform; and one cannot but wonder how it is so easily taken for granted by *Wetstein*,§ *Hug, Meyer, Ebrard, Lange, Ellicott, Davidson, Tregelles*, &c. *Alford* goes the length of saying it 'has been universally believed that he was the same person with the John Mark of the Gospels.' But *Grotius* thought differently, and so did *Schleiermacher, Campbell, Burton*, and *da Costa;* and the grounds on which it is concluded that they were two different persons appear to us quite unanswerable. 'Of John, surnamed Mark,' says Campbell,‖ 'one of the first things we learn is, that he attended Paul and Barnabas in their apostolical journeys, when these two travelled together (Acts xii. 25; xiii. 5). And when afterwards there arose a dispute between them concerning him, insomuch that they separated, Mark accompanied his uncle Barnabas, and Silas attended Paul. When Paul was reconciled to Mark, which was probably soon after, we find Paul again employing Mark's assistance, recommending him, and giving him a very honourable testimony (Col. iv. 10; 2 Tim. iv. 11; Phil. 24). But we hear not a syllable of his attending Peter as his minister, or assisting him in any capacity'—although, as we shall presently see, no tradition is more ancient, more uniform, and better sustained by internal evidence, than that Mark, in his Gospel, was but 'the interpreter of Peter,' who, at the close of his first Epistle, speaks of him as 'Marcus my son' (1 Pet. v. 13), that is, without doubt, his son in the Gospel—converted to Christ through his instrumentality. And when we consider how little the Apostles Peter and Paul were together—how seldom they even met—how different were their tendencies, and how separate their spheres of labour, is there not, in the absence of all evidence of the fact, something approaching to violence in the supposition that the same Mark was the intimate associate of both? 'In brief,' adds Campbell, 'the accounts given of Paul's attendant, and those of Peter's interpreter, concur in nothing but the name, Mark or Marcus; too slight a circumstance to conclude the sameness of the person from, especially when we consider how common the name was at Rome, and how customary it was for the Jews in that age to assume some Roman name when they went thither.'

---

* Einleitung, u. s. w.   † Introduction.

‡ 'Four Witnesses,' in which, however, there are a few things we cannot concur in.

§ Who says, 'Nihil vetat quominus simpliciter, cum *Victore* et *Theophylacto* hunc eundem Marcum intelligamus, quoties illius nomen in Actis et Epistolis reperimus.'

‖ Preface to Mark's Gospel.

Regarding the Evangelist Mark, then, as another person from Paul's companion in travel, all we know of his personal history is that he was a convert, as we have seen, of the Apostle Peter. But as to his Gospel, the tradition regarding Peter's hand in it is so ancient, so uniform, and so remarkably confirmed by internal evidence, that we must regard it as an established fact. 'Mark,' says *Papias* (according to the testimony of Eusebius) 'becoming *the interpreter of Peter*,* wrote accurately, though not in order, whatever he remembered of what was either said or done by Christ; for he was neither a hearer of the Lord nor a follower of Him, but afterwards, as I said, [he was a follower] of Peter, who arranged the discourses for use, but not according to the order in which they were uttered by the Lord.' To the same effect *Irenæus:* 'Matthew published a Gospel while Peter and Paul were preaching and founding the Church at Rome; and after their departure (or decease)†, Mark, *the disciple and interpreter of Peter*,‡ he also gave forth to us in writing the things which were preached by Peter.'§ And *Clement* of Alexandria is still more specific, in a passage preserved to us by Eusebius:|| 'Peter, having publicly preached the word at Rome, and spoken forth the Gospel by the Spirit, many of those present exhorted Mark, as *having long been a follower of his*, and remembering what he had said, to write what had been spoken; and that having prepared the Gospel, he delivered it to those who had asked him for it; which, when Peter came to the knowledge of, he neither decidedly forbade nor encouraged him.' *Eusebius's* own testimony, however, from other accounts, is rather different:¶ that Peter's hearers were so penetrated by his preaching that they gave Mark, as being *a follower of Peter*, no rest till he consented to write his Gospel, as a memorial of his oral teaching; and 'that the apostle, when he knew by the revelation of the Spirit what had been done, was delighted with the zeal of those men, and sanctioned the reading of the writing (that is, of this Gospel of Mark) in the churches.' And giving in another of his works a similar statement, he says that 'Peter, from excess of humility, did not think himself qualified to write the Gospel; but Mark, his acquaintance and pupil, is said to have recorded his relations of the actings of Jesus. And Peter testifies these things of himself; for all things that are recorded by Mark are said to be memoirs of Peter's discourses.' It is needless to go further—to *Origen*, who says Mark composed his Gospel 'as Peter guided' or 'directed him, who, in his catholic Epistle, calls him his son,' &c.; and to *Jerome*, who but echoes Eusebius.

This, certainly, is a remarkable chain of testimony; which, confirmed as it is by such striking internal evidence, may be regarded as establishing the fact that the Second Gospel was drawn up mostly from materials furnished by Peter. In *da Costa's* 'Four Witnesses' the reader will find this internal evidence detailed at length, though all the examples are not equally convincing. But if he will refer to our remarks on Mark i. 36; xi. 20-21; xiii. 3; xvi. 7; Luke xix. 32; xxii. 34, he will have evidence enough of a *Petrine* hand in this Gospel.

It remains only to advert, in a word or two, to the *readers* for whom this Gospel was, in the first instance, designed, and the *date* of it. That it was not for *Jews* but *Gentiles*, is evident from the great number of explanations of Jewish usages, opinions, and places, which to a Jew would at that time have been superfluous, but were highly needful to a Gentile. We can here but refer to ch. ii. 18; vii. 3, 4; xii. 18; xiii. 3;

---

* ἑρμηνευτὴς Πέτρου γενόμενος, E. H. iii. 39.
‡ ὁ μαθητὴς καὶ ἑρμηνευτὴς Πέτρου.
¶ E. H. vi. 14

† μετὰ δὲ τὴν τοιουτῶν ἔξοδον.
§ Adv. Hær. iii. 1.
¶ E. H. ii. 15.

xiv. 12; xv. 42, for examples of these. Regarding the date of this Gospel—about which nothing certain is known—if the tradition reported by Irenæus can be relied on, that it was written at Rome, 'after the departure of Peter and Paul,' and if by that word 'departure'* we are to understand their *death*, we may date it somewhere between the years 64 and 68; but in all likelihood this is too late. It is probably nearer the truth to date it eight or ten years earlier.

THE GOSPEL ACCORDING TO LUKE.

THE writer of this Gospel is universally allowed to have been Lucas,† though he is not expressly named either in the Gospel or in the Acts. From Col. iv. 14 we learn that he was a "physician;" and by comparing that verse with verses 10, 11—in which the apostle enumerates all those of the circumcision who were then with him, but does not mention Luke, though he immediately afterwards sends a salutation from him—we gather that Luke was not a born Jew. Possibly he was a freed man (*libertinus*), as the Romans devolved the healing art on persons of this class and on their slaves, as an occupation beneath themselves. His intimate acquaintance with Jewish customs, and his facility in Hebraic Greek, seem to show that he was an early convert to the Jewish Faith; and this is curiously confirmed by Acts xxi. 27-29, where we find the Jews enraged at Paul's supposed introduction of Greeks into the temple, because they had seen "Trophimus the Ephesian" with him; and as we know that Luke was with Paul on that occasion, it would seem that they had taken him for a Jew, as they made no mention of him. On the other hand, his fluency in classical Greek confirms his Gentile origin. The time when he joined Paul's company is clearly indicated in the Acts by his changing (at ch. xvi. 10) from the third person singular ("he") to the first person plural ("we"). From that time he hardly ever left the apostle till near the period of his martyrdom (2 Tim. iv. 11). Eusebius makes him a native of Antioch. If so, he would have every advantage for cultivating the literature of Greece, and such medical knowledge as was then possessed. That he died a natural death is generally agreed among the ancients; Gregory Nazianzen alone affirming that he died a martyr.

The *time* and *place* of the publication of his Gospel are alike uncertain. But we can approximate to it. It must at any rate have been issued before the Acts, for there the 'Gospel' is expressly referred to as the same author's "former treatise" (Acts i. 1). Now the book of the Acts was not published for two whole years after Paul's arrival as a prisoner at Rome, for it concludes with a reference to this period; but probably it was published soon after that, which would appear to have been early in the year 63. Before that time, then, we have reason to believe that the Gospel of Luke was in circulation, though the majority of critics make it later. If we date it somewhere between A. D. 50 and 60, we shall probably be near the truth; but nearer it we cannot with any certainty come. Conjectures as to the place of publication are too uncertain to be mentioned here.

That it was addressed, in the first instance, to Gentile *readers*, is beyond doubt.

---

* ἔξοδος.   † Λουκᾶς, an abbreviated form of Λουκανός, as *Silas* of *Silvanus*.

This is no more, as Davidson remarks, than was to have been expected from the companion of an 'apostle of the Gentiles,' who had witnessed marvellous changes in the condition of many heathens by the reception of the Gospel.* But the explanations in his Gospel of things known to every Jew, and which could only be intended for Gentile readers, make this quite plain—see ch. i. 26; iv. 31; viii. 26; xxi. 37; xxii. 1; xxiv. 13. A number of other minute particulars, both of things inserted and of things omitted, confirm the conclusion that it was Gentiles whom this Evangelist had in the first instance in view.

We have already adverted to the classical *style* of Greek which this Evangelist writes—just what might have been expected from an educated Greek and travelled physician. But we have also observed that along with this he shows a wonderful flexibility of style; so much so, that when he comes to relate transactions wholly Jewish, where the speakers and actors and incidents are all Jewish, he writes in such Jewish Greek as one would do who had never been out of Palestine, or mixed with any but Jews. In *da Costa's* 'Four Witnesses' will be found some traces of 'the beloved *physician*' in this Gospel. But far more striking and important are the traces in it of his intimate connection with the apostle of the Gentiles. That one who was so long and so constantly in the society of that master-mind has in such a work as this shown no traces of that connection, no stamp of that mind, is hardly to be believed. Writers of Introductions seem not to see it, and take no notice of it. But those who look into the interior of it will soon discover evidences enough in it of a *Pauline* cast of mind. Referring for a number of details to *da Costa*, we notice here only two examples. In 1 Cor. xi. 23 Paul ascribes to an express revelation from Christ Himself the account of the Institution of the Lord's Supper which he there gives. Now, if we find this account differing in small yet striking particulars from the accounts given by Matthew and Mark, but agreeing to the letter with Luke's account, it can hardly admit of a doubt that the one had it from the other; and in that case, of course, it was Luke that had it from Paul. Now Matthew and Mark both say of the Cup, "This is my blood of the New Testament;" while Paul and Luke say, in identical terms, "This cup is the New Testament in My blood." Further, Luke says, "Likewise also the cup *after supper*, saying," &c.; while Paul says, "After the same manner He took the cup *when He had supped*, saying," &c.: whereas neither Matthew nor Mark mention that this was after supper. But still more striking is another point of coincidence in this case. Matthew and Mark both say of the Bread merely this: "Take, eat; this is My body:" whereas Paul says, "Take, eat; this is My Body, *which is broken for you*," and Luke, "This is My Body, *which is given for you*." And while Paul adds the precious clause, "THIS DO IN REMEMBRANCE OF ME," Luke does the same, in identical terms. How can one who reflects on this resist the conviction of a Pauline stamp in this Gospel? The other proof of this to which we ask the reader's attention is in the fact that Paul, in enumerating the parties by whom Christ was seen after His resurrection, begins, singularly enough, with *Peter*—"And that He rose again the third day according to the Scriptures: and that He was seen of *Cephas*, then of the Twelve" (1 Cor. xv. 4, 5) —coupled with the remarkable fact, that Luke is the only one of the Evangelists who mentions that Christ appeared to Peter at all. When the disciples had returned from Emmaus to tell their brethren how the Lord had appeared to them in the way, and how

---

* Introduction, page 186.

He had made Himself known to them in the breaking of bread, they were met, as Luke relates, ere they had time to utter a word, with this wonderful piece of news, "The Lord is risen indeed, and hath appeared to *Simon*" (Luke xxiv. 34).

Other points connected with this Gospel will be adverted to in the Commentary.

THE GOSPEL ACCORDING TO JOHN.

THE author of the Fourth Gospel was the younger of the two sons of Zebedee, a fisherman on the sea of Galilee, who resided at Bethsaida, where were born Peter and Andrew his brother, and Philip also. His mother's name was Salome, who, though not without her imperfections (Matt. xx. 20, &c.), was one of those dear and honoured women who accompanied the Lord on one of His preaching circuits through Galilee, ministering to His bodily wants; who followed Him to the cross, and bought sweet spices to anoint Him after His burial, but, on bringing them to the grave, on the morning of the First Day of the week, found their loving services gloriously superseded by His resurrection ere they arrived. His father, Zebedee, appears to have been in good circumstances, owning a vessel of his own and having hired servants (Mark i. 20). Our Evangelist, whose occupation was that of a fisherman with his father, was beyond doubt a disciple of the Baptist, and one of the two who had the first interview with Jesus. He was called while engaged at his secular occupation (see on Matt. iv. 21, 22), and again on a memorable occasion (see on Luke v. 1-11), and finally chosen as one of the Twelve Apostles (see on Matt. x. 2, 4, with the Remarks at the close of that Section). He was the youngest of the Twelve—the "Benjamin," as *da Costa* calls him—and he and James his brother were named in the native tongue, by Him who knew the heart, "Boanerges," which the Evangelist Mark (iii. 17) explains to mean "Sons of thunder;" no doubt from their natural *vehemence* of character. They and Peter constituted that select triumvirate of whom we have spoken on Luke ix. 28. But the highest honour bestowed on this disciple was his being admitted to the bosom-place with his Lord at the table, as "the disciple whom Jesus loved" (John xiii. 23; xx. 2; xxi. 7, 20, 24), and to have committed to him by the dying Redeemer the care of His mother (xix. 26, 27). There can be no reasonable doubt that this distinction was due to a sympathy with His own spirit and mind on the part of John which the all-penetrating Eye of their common Master beheld in none of the rest; and although this probably never seen either in his life or in his ministry by his fellow-apostles, it is brought wonderfully out in his writings, which, in Christ-like spirituality, heavenliness, and love, surpass, we may freely say, all the other inspired writings.

After the effusion of the Spirit on the day of Pentecost, we find him in constant but silent company with Peter, the great spokesman and actor in the infant Church until the accession of Paul. While his love to the Lord Jesus drew him spontaneously to the side of His eminent servant, and his chastened vehemence made him ready to stand courageously by him, and suffer with him, in all that his testimony to Jesus might cost him, his modest humility, as the youngest of all the apostles, made him an admiring listener and faithful supporter of his brother apostle rather than a speaker or separate actor. Ecclesiastical history is uniform in testifying that John went to Asia Minor—but it is next to certain that this could not have been till after the death both of Peter and Paul—

that he resided at Ephesus, whence, as from a centre, he superintended the churches of that region, paying them occasional visits, and that he long survived the other apostles. Whether the mother of Jesus died before this, or went with John to Ephesus, where she died and was buried, is not agreed. One or two anecdotes of his later days have been handed down by tradition, one at least bearing marks of reasonable probability. But it is not necessary to give them here. In the reign of Domitian (A. D. 81-96) he was banished to "the isle that is called Patmos" (a small rocky and then almost uninhabited island in the Ægean sea), "for the word of God and for the testimony of Jesus Christ" (Rev. i. 9). Irenæus and Eusebius say that this took place about the end of Domitian's reign.[*] That he was thrown into a cauldron of boiling oil, and miraculously delivered, is one of those legends which, though reported by Tertullian and Jerome, is entitled to no credit. His return from exile took place during the brief but tolerant reign of Nerva: he died at Ephesus in the reign of Trajan,[†] at an age above 90, according to some; according to others, 100; and even 120, according to others still. The intermediate number is generally regarded as probably the nearest to the truth.

As to the *date* of this Gospel, the arguments for its having been composed before the destruction of Jerusalem (though relied on by some superior critics) are of the slenderest nature: such as the expression in ch. v. 2, "there *is* at Jerusalem, by the sheep gate, a pool," &c.—as to which see remark on that verse; and there being no allusion to Peter's martyrdom as having occurred, according to the prediction in ch. xxi. 18—a thing too well known to require mention. That it was composed long after the destruction of Jerusalem, and after the decease of all the other apostles, is next to certain, though the precise time cannot be determined. Probably it was before his banishment, however; and if we date it between the years 90 and 94, we shall probably be pretty near the truth.

As to the *readers* for whom it was more immediately designed, that they were Gentiles we might naturally presume from the lateness of the date; but the multitude of explanations of things familiar to every Jew puts this beyond all question.

No doubt was ever thrown upon the genuineness and authenticity of this Gospel till about the close of the last century, nor were these embodied in any formal attack upon it till *Bretschneider*, in 1820, issued his famous treatise,[‡] the conclusions of which he afterwards was candid enough to admit had been satisfactorily disproved. To advert to these would be as painful as unnecessary; consisting as they mostly do of assertions regarding the Discourses of our Lord recorded in this Gospel which are revolting to every spiritual mind. The Tübingen school did their best, on their peculiar mode of reasoning, to galvanize into fresh life this theory of the post-Joannean date of the Fourth Gospel; and some Unitarian critics in this country still cling to it. But to use the striking language of *van Osterzee* regarding similar speculations on the Third Gospel, 'Behold, the feet of them that shall carry it out dead are already at the door' (Acts v. 9). Is there one mind of the least elevation of spiritual discernment that does not see in this Gospel marks of historical truth and a surpassing glory such as none of the other Gospels possess, brightly as they too attest their own verity; and who will not be ready to say that if not historically true, and true *just as it stands*, it never could have been by mortal man composed or conceived?

Of the peculiarities of this Gospel we note here only two. The one is its *reflective*

---

* Eus. E. H. iii. 18.   † Eus. E. H. iii. 23.
‡ Probabilia de Evangelii et Epistolarum Joannis Apostoli Indole et Origine.

character. While the others are purely *narrative*, the Fourth Evangelist 'pauses, as it were, at every turn,' as *da Costa* says, 'at one time to give a reason, at another to fix the attention, to deduce consequences, or make applications, or to give utterance to the language of praise.'* See ch. ii. 20, 21; ii. 23-25; iv. 1, 2; vii. 37-39; xi. 12, 13; xi. 49-52; xxi. 18, 19, 22, 23. The other peculiarity of this Gospel is its *supplementary* character. By this, in the present instance, we mean something more than the studiousness with which he omits many most important particulars in our Lord's history, for no conceivable reason but that they were already familiar as household words to all his readers, through the three preceding Gospels, and his substituting in place of these an immense quantity of the richest matter not found in the other Gospels. We refer here more particularly to the *nature* of the additions which distinguish this Gospel; particularly the notices of the different passovers which occurred during our Lord's public ministry, and the record of His teaching at Jerusalem, without which it is not too much to say that we could have had but a most imperfect conception either of the duration of His ministry or of the plan of it. But another feature of these additions is quite as noticeable and not less important. 'We find,' to use again the words of *da Costa*, slightly abridged, 'only six of our Lord's miracles recorded in this Gospel, but these are all of the most remarkable kind, and surpass the rest in depth, specialty of application, and fulness of meaning. Of these six we find only one in the other three Gospels—the multiplication of the loaves. That miracle chiefly, it would seem, on account of the important instructions of which it furnished the occasion (ch. vi.), is here recorded anew. The five other tokens of Divine power are distinguished from among the many recorded in the three other Gospels, by their furnishing a still higher display of power and command over the ordinary laws and course of nature. Thus we find recorded here the first of all the miracles that Jesus wrought—the changing of water into wine (ch. ii.), the cure of the nobleman's son *at a distance* (ch. iv.); of the numerous cures of the lame and the paralytic by the word of Jesus, only one—of the man impotent for *thirty and eight years* (ch. v.); of the many cures of the blind, one only—of the man *born blind* (ch. ix.); the restoration of Lazarus, not from a death-bed, like Jairus' daughter, nor from a bier, like the widow of Nain's son, but *from the grave*, and after lying there four days, and there sinking into corruption (ch. xi.); and lastly, after His resurrection, the miraculous draught of fishes on the sea of Tiberias, (ch. xxi.) But these are all recorded chiefly to give occasion for the record of those astonishing Discourses and Conversations, alike with friends and with foes, with His disciples and with the multitude, which they drew forth.'†

Other illustrations of the peculiarities of this Gospel will occur, and other points connected with it be adverted to, in the course of the Commentary.

* 'Four Witnesses,' page 234.   † 'Four Witnesses,' pages 238, 239.

SOURCES OF AUTHORITY FOR THE TEXT OF THE GOSPELS.

THESE are ancient MANUSCRIPTS of the text; ancient VERSIONS of the text; and CITATIONS from the text, or the Versions of it, in the works of the ancient ecclesiastical writers. Of these three sources, the *Manuscripts* of the text itself are, of course, of primary authority; the *Versions* come next, but only in so far as we may gather from them what they included or excluded from the text, and what readings of the text they recognized; and the *Citations*, so far as they discover to us the text which the writers acknowledged.

The Manuscripts of the Gospels now known to exist, in whole or in part, amount to nearly a *Thousand*—which can be said of no other ancient work whatever. These are divided into two classes: *Uncial* Manuscripts, or those written in what we call capital letters; and *Cursive* Manuscripts, or those written in what are called small or running hand. The former are, of course, of older date than the latter. Uncial characters continued to be employed in the manuscripts of the New Testament from the fourth down to about the tenth century; cursive letters came into use in the tenth century, or perhaps a little earlier, and continued till the invention of printing. In the present Commentary, *Uncial* Manuscripts are denoted by the large capitals—MSS.; *Cursive*, by the small capitals—MSS.

On the palæographic principles on which the age and general value of New Testament manuscripts are approximately determined there is now a pretty general agreement among those who have devoted special attention to this interesting subject; the best proof of which is, that in the results arrived at there is scarcely any difference, and in the few cases where a difference exists it hardly exceeds half a century. Of course, high probability is all that can be attained, except where the date is expressly given, which it hardly ever is, and in none of the older manuscripts.

No known manuscript contains the New Testament entire, except the recently discovered, and now published, *Codex Sinaiticus;* and it is important to know what portions are wanting in any manuscript, lest the want of reference to it in a statement of evidence for or against a particular reading should be thought to decide, when it does not, how that manuscript read in such a case.

The Uncial MSS. are denoted by the capital letters of the Roman Alphabet, with a few additions from the Greek and Hebrew alphabets; the Cursive MSS., by numbers, and, in the case of some recently collated, by small letters.

For a full description of these and the ancient Versions, we must refer the reader to *Tregelles's* Volume of Horne's 'Introduction to the Scriptures,' and *Scrivener's* 'Introduction to the Criticism of the New Testament.' A shorter account of them will be found in *Tischendorf's* 'Synopsis Evangelica.'

The oldest MSS. which are comparatively entire are the five following :—

Name.	Probable Date.	Where Deposited.
א—CODEX SINAITICUS, ...4th century, ...Imperial Library of St. Petersburg.*		
B—CODEX VATICANUS, ...4th century, ...Vatican Library, Rome.†		

* The romantic history of the discovery of this precious treasure is given by the discoverer himself, and all its peculiarities are carefully described in the Prolegomena to the New Testament part of it, newly published under his editorial care, in splendid royal quarto, entitled NOVUM 'TESTAMENTUM SINAITICUM' . . . Ex Codice Sinaitico . . . AEN. FRID. CONST. TISCHENDORF. Lips., 1863. The most remarkable fact regarding this MS., in connection with its great antiquity, is its being *entire.*

† This MS., in the original hand, *goes no further than* Heb. ix. 14 (καθα): all the rest is in a

A—CODEX ALEXANDRINUS, ...5th century,...British Museum, London. *
C—CODEX EPHRAEMI (*rescriptus*), ...5th century,...Imperial Library, Paris. †
D—CODEX BEZÆ (or CANTABRIGIENSIS), 6th century,...Cambridge Library. ‡

The following are a few Fragments of MSS. which, from their antiquity—being all of date *prior to the seventh century*—are of greater value than those of later date :—

N—CODEX PURPUREUS; end of 6th or beginning of 7th century: Twelve Leaves of the Gospels—of which four are in the British Museum (J of *Tischendorf*); six in the Vatican Library (T of *Tischendorf*); and two in the Imperial Library of Vienna (N of *Tischendorf*).

Z—CODEX DUBLINENSIS (*rescriptus*); 6th century: Dublin University Library, containing the greater part of the First Gospel.

{T
{Tˢ —CODEX BORGIANUS; 5th century: Propaganda Library, Rome. A few leaves of the Third and Fourth Gospels in Greek and Thebaic (or Sahidic). Tˢ (*Fragmentum Woideanum*) appears to be part of the same MS.

{P—CODEX GUELPHERBYTANUS A} 6th century. These are two palimpsests or rescripts (over
{Q——————————————— B} which other works have been written), in the Ducal Library of Wolfenbüttel.

R—CODEX NITRIANUS; 6th century: British Museum. A considerable part of the Third Gospel.
FRAGMENTA TISCHENDORFIANA; mostly of 5th century: a number of very short fragments.

Of the later Uncials the following three are regarded by *Tregelles* as of not much inferior value to the five oldest §:—

L—CODEX REGIUS; about 8th century: Imperial Library, Paris.
X—CODEX MONACENSIS; end of 9th or beginning of 10th century: University Library, Munich
Δ—CODEX SANGALLENSIS; 9th century: Monastic Library, St. Gall.

The following, though of somewhat less value, are, along with any of the oldest class, important links in a chain of evidence :—

E—CODEX BASILEENSIS; 8th century: Basle Library.
F—CODEX BOREELI; 9th or 10th century: Utrecht Library.
{G—CODEX SEIDELII A} 9th or 10th century: {A is in the British Museum;
{H——————— B}   {B in the Hamburg Library.
K—CODEX CYPRIUS; 9th century: Imperial Library, Paris.
M—CODEX CAMPIANUS; end of 9th, or beginning of 10th century: Imperial Library, Paris.
S—CODEX VATICANUS (No. 354 ‖); A. D. 949 ¶: Vatican Library, Rome.

very late hand, and useless, therefore, for critical purposes. It has at length been published, with permission of the Papal authorities, but so uncritically that, even as re-edited, we cannot always be sure what belongs exclusively to the first hand, and what is by a second hand, which about the 8th century retouched it.

* This MS. *commences in the middle of* Matt. xxv. 6; and wants part of three chapters in John, ch. vi. 50—viii 52. It was published, in letters resembling the original characters, in 1786.

† So called from a Greek version of some of the works of Ephraem the Syrian having been (according to the barbarous practice of the middle ages) written over it. Though the original writing has been by chemical processes recovered, it is a pity that so valuable a MS. has so many gaps—so many indeed, and in so many places, that it is impossible to enumerate them here. They will be found enumerated in *Tischendorf*, *Tregelles*, and *Scrivener*.

‡ This MS. receives its name from its having been presented by *Beza* to the *Cambridge* University. It contains only the Gospels and Acts, though the Catholic Epistles at least were once in it. It is a Græco-Latin MS., the Greek being on the left page, the Latin on the right. Its very singular character has occasioned much discussion and diversity of opinion.

§ In consequence, chiefly, of their agreeing so frequently with B, where B differs from A. But as A in such cases has generally all, or nearly all, the other MSS. on its side, this is equivalent to such a preference for B, with its few supporters, over A, with its many, as only a fuller collation than has yet been made will warrant.

‖ The No. of this MS. in the Vatican Library is given, to distinguish it from B, which is called Cod. Vat., No. 1209.

¶ This date is given in the MS. itself.

U—Codex Nanianus; 9th or 10th century: Library of St. Mark's, Venice.
V—Codex Mosquensis; 9th century: Library of Holy Synod, Moscow.

A few Fragments of this later class will complete these lists of Uncials:—

Ξ—Codex Zacynthius; 8th or 9th century: Library of British and Foreign Bible Society—
Edited by *Tregelles.*
O—Fragmentum Mosquense: Library of Holy Synod, Moscow.
Wᵃ—Two Leaves of Luke;   8th century: Imperial Library, Paris.
Wᵇ—————— John;   do.   Tübingen.
Wᶜ—Three Leaves of Mark and Luke;   do.   St. Gall.
Y—Codex Barberini; 8th century: Barberini Library, Rome.

Of the many hundreds of extant Cursive Manuscripts only a very few are as yet *known* to possess much critical value. Of these we name only the following, with the *numbers* by which they are distinguished:—

1. *Codex Basileensis;* 10th century: Basle Library. It closely resembles B, L, and others of that class.
2. *Codex Colbertinus;* 11th century: Imperial Library, Paris. It resembles B, D, L, more than any other of the Cursives.
3. *Codex Leicestrensis;* 14th century: Town Council Library of Leicester. Its text is very remarkable.

Of the ancient Versions of the New Testament the following are the most important for critical purposes:—

1. The Syriac Versions. Of these the three principal are,—
   (1). The *Peshito* Syriac (as it is called); probably the oldest Version of the New Testament. It may be regarded as belonging to the *second century*, (see p. vi.)
   (2). The *Curetonian* Syriac; discovered by Dr. Cureton amongst the Syriac treasures of the British Museum, and edited by him in 1858: a version of great antiquity, though later, in all probability, than the Peshito.
   (3.) The *Philoxenian* or *Harclean* Syriac: a version originally made for *Philoxenus*, Bishop of Mabug (or Hierapolis), near the beginning of the 6th century, and about a century afterwards critically revised by Thomas of *Harkel*, who rendered the original with excessive literality, which, however, gives it, in the opinion of *Tregelles*, greater critical value than either of the other Syriac versions.
   (4). The *Jerusalem* Syriac; of which but one MS. is known to exist: it is in a very peculiar dialect, more Chaldee than Syriac; and from its resemblance to the dialect of the *Jerusalem* Targum, has its distinctive name. Whether it belongs to the 5th or 6th century is not agreed. But many of its readings resemble those of B and D. *It is the only Syriac book which contains John* vii. 53—viii. 11 (The Woman taken in Adultery).

It is needless to refer to what is called the *Karkaphensian*, of which very little is known, save that it closely resembles the Peshito; and a fragment nearly resembling the Jerusalem Syriac, which *Tischendorf*, who assigns it to the 5th century, brought from the East to St. Petersburg.

2. The Latin Versions. Of these there are two, or rather but one and a revision of it.
   (1.) The *Old Latin.* Critics are now generally agreed that instead of there being many, there was but one such Version, and that this venerable Version was made in North Africa for the use of the Latin-speaking Christians; and though opinions differ as to the exact date, the probability is that it belongs to the *second century*, and if not older, or as old, cannot be of much later date than the Peshito.
   Of this Version upwards of twenty Manuscripts are extant, denoted by the small Italic letters *a, b, c,* &c.

(2.) *Jerome's Revision* of the same, or the *Vulgate;* executed at the request of Damasus, Bishop of Rome, on account of the confounding variety of readings, many of them manifest corruptions, which had crept into the current copies of the Old Latin. The Gospels were published A. D. 384, and the rest afterwards. This work took some three centuries entirely to supersede the Old, when it got the name of *Vulgata*. The Clementine Vulgate, alone recognized in the Church of Rome, differs to a considerable extent from the same Version as left by Jerome, of which, happily, we have some valuable Manuscripts—the best of which is the *Codex Amiatinus*, in the Laurentian Library at Florence, executed, there is reason to believe, in the *sixth century*. The high value of the true Vulgate for critical purposes, not only above the Old Latin, but intrinsically, is now generally recognized.

3. The EGYPTIAN VERSIONS. Of these there are two; the one designed for the Christians of *Upper*, the other for those of *Lower* Egypt.

(1.) The *Memphitic* Version, or that used by the Christians of Lower Egypt, whose capital was *Memphis*. It used to be called the Coptic, when no other was known to exist; but as that did not designate the region to which it belonged, but rather the Upper region, it is now better named as above. It belongs, at least portions of it, probably to the *fifth century*.

(2.) The *Thebaic* Version, or that used by the Christians of Upper Egypt, of which *Thebes* was the capital. Fragments only of this Version now exist; but there is every reason to believe that it is more ancient than the Memphitic, as the Christians of Upper Egypt, early in the *fourth century* appear to have been acquainted with the New Testament, though even the clergy were ignorant of Greek and knew only their own tongue.

4. The GOTHIC VERSION, made about the middle of the fourth century. The *Codex Argenteus*, containing Fragments of the Gospels, discovered in the 17th century, and now in the University Library at Upsala in Sweden, is a precious treasure, whose date is the *fifth*, or early in the *sixth* century. This and other Fragments, since discovered, have been published more than once.

5. The ARMENIAN VERSION of the *fifth* century.

It is needless to come further down for critical purposes.

To give a list of the ancient ecclesiastical writers whose *citations* from the New Testament are of chief importance for critical purposes would hardly be desirable here. Those who have opportunity may consult the works to which we have referred for an account of the MSS. and Versions; and a little familiarity with the references in critical editions of the New Testament will soon give all the information that is needed by the general student.

The three critical editions of the Greek Testament to which continual reference is made in the Commentary, for the settlement of the Text, are the following:—

1. NOVUM TESTAMENTUM GRÆCE ET LATINE: CAROLUS LACHMANNUS Recensuit, *Philip. Butmannus* Ph. T. Græcæ Lectionis Auctoritates apposuit, 1842-1850.

2. NOVUM TESTAMENTUM GRÆCE: Ad Antiquos Testes denuo Recensuit, Apparatum Criticum omni studio perfectum Apposuit, Commentationem Isagogicam Protexuit ÆNOTH. FRID. CONST. TISCHENDORF. *Editio Septima*, 1859.

3. THE GREEK NEW TESTAMENT: SAM. PRID. TREGELLES, LL.D. Part I., Matthew and Mark, 1857. Part II., Luke and John, 1860.

WORKS QUOTED OR REFERRED TO IN THIS VOLUME.

ALEXANDER (Joseph Addison, D.D.)—The Gospel according to Matthew Explained, 1861.
——————— The Gospel according to St. Mark Explained, 1859.

ALFORD (Henry, D.D.)—The Greek Testament, with a Critically Revised Text, &c., and a Critical and Exegetical Commentary. Third Edition. Vol. i., 1856.

BAUR (Dr. F. Chr.)—Kritische Untersuchungen ü die Kanononischen Evangelien, 1847.

BENGELII (Joh. Alb.)—Gnomon Novi Testamenti. Tom. i. Ed Tertia, 1835.

BEZA (Theod.)—Novum Testamentum. Interpretatio et Annotationes, 1698.

BIRKS (Rev. T. R.)—Horæ Evangelicæ, &c., 1852.

BLOOMFIELD (S. T., D.D.)—The Greek Testament, with English Notes, Critical, Philological, and Explanatory. Eighth Edition. Vol. i., 1850.

BLUNT (J. J., B.D.)—Undesigned Coincidences in the Writings of the Old and New Testaments, an Argument for their Veracity. Fourth Edition, 1853.

CALVINI (Joan.) in Nov. Test. Commentarii, Vol. i. ii. In Harmoniam ex Matth., Marc, et Luca, Compositam. Ed. Tholuck, 1833.
——————— Vol. iii. In Evangelium Joannis, 1833.

CAMPBELL (George, D.D.)—The Four Gospels, Translated from the Greek, with Preliminary Dissertations and Notes. 3 Vols , 1821.

Da COSTA (Dr. Isaac)—The Four Witnesses. Being a Harmony of the Gospels on a New Principle. Translated by D. D. Scott, Esq., 1851.

DAVIDSON (Dr. Sam.)—Introduction to the New Testament. Vol i., The Four Gospels. 1848.

EBRARD (Dr. J. H. A.)—Wissenchaftliche Kritik der Evangelischen Geschichte, 2te Auflage, 1850.

ELLICOTT (Bp. C. J.)—Historical Lectures on the Life of our Lord Jesus Christ. First Edition, 1860.

EUSEBIUS (Pamph.)—Historiæ Ecclesiasticæ, Gr. 3 Vols., 8vo, 1827—1840.

FAIRBAIRN (Patrick, D.D.)—Hermeneutical Manual, &c. 1858.

FRITZSCHE (C. F. A.)—Evangelium Matthæi recens. et cum Commentariis Perpetuis ed. 1826.
——————— Evangelium Marci, &c., 1830.

GROTII (Hug.)—Annotationes in Libros Evangeliorum, 1641.

GRESWELL (Edw., B.D.)—Dissertations upon the Principles and Arrangement of an Harmony of the Gospels. Second Edition. 4 Vols., 1837.

HALL (Bp. Joseph)—Contemplations on the Historical Passages of the Old and New Testaments. 3 Vols., 1749. The Gospels. Vol. iii.

HUG.—Introduction to the New Testament. Translated by Fosdick, &c., 1836.

LANGE (Dr. J. P.)—Theolog. Homil. Bibelwerk: Matt.—Johannes, 1857—1859. 3 Vols. The Same, Translated as far as Luke. (Clark.) The Gospels of St. Matthew and St. Mark, from the German of Dr. J. P. Lange. 3 Vols. The Gospel of St. Luke, from the German of Dr. J. J. Van Osterzee. 2 Vols. Das Evang. nach Joannes, von Dr. J. P. Lange, 1860.

LAMPE (F. A.) Commentarius . . . Evangelii sec. Joannem, 3 Vol. 4to, 1727.

LARDNER (Nath., D. D.)—Works, 10 Vols., 1838: especially The Credibility of the Gospel History.

LIGHTFOOT (John, D.D.)—Works, Vol. xi., Hebrew and Talmudical Exercitations upon the Gospels of St. Matthew and St. Mark; and Vol. xii., Hebrew and Talmudical Exercitations upon the Gospels of St. Luke and St. John. 1823.

LÜCKE (Dr. Fr.)—Commentar über das Evangelium des Johannes. Dritte Auflage, 1840—1843.

LUTHARDT (Chr. E.)—Das Joanneische Evangelium, u. s. w., 1852, 1853.

MALDONATI (Joan.)—Commentarii in Quatuor Evangelistas. 2 Tom., 1853, 1854.

MEYER (Dr. H. A. W.)—Kritisch Exegetischer Kommentar über das Neue Testament. Matth., 1853; Marcus u. Lukas, 1855; Johann. 1852.

MICHAELIS (J. D.)—Introduction to the New Testament, Translated by Bishop Herbert Marsh. Fourth Edition. 6 Vols., 1823.

MIDDLETON (Bishop T. F.)—The Doctrine of the Greek Article applied to the Criticism and Illustration of the New Testament. Edited by Rose, 1841.

NEANDER (Dr. Aug.)—The Life of Jesus Christ, &c. Translated by M'Lintock and Blumenthal, 1851.

NORTON (Prof. Andrew)—The Evidences of the Genuineness of the Gospels. 2 Vols. Second Edition, 1847.

OLSHAUSEN (Dr. Herm.)—Biblical Commentary on the Gospels, from the German. (*Clark.*) 4 Vols.

RITSCHL (Dr. A.)—Evangelium Marcions u. das Kanonische Evangelium des Lukas, 1846.

ROBERTS (Rev. A.)—Discussions on the Gospels, 1862.

ROBINSON (Dr. Edw.)—Biblical Researches in Palestine, &c. Second Edition. 3 Vols., 1851.

———— Harmony of the Four Gospels in Greek, with Explanatory Notes, 1845. The same in English, edited for the Tract Society (by Rev. Dr. Davies).

ROUTH (Dr. M. J.)—Reliquiæ Sacræ, &c. Ed. Altera. 4 Vols., 1846.

SCHLEIERMACHER (Dr. Fr.)—Critical Essay on the Gospel of St. Luke, with Critical Introduction by the Translator, 1825.

SCRIVENER (Rev. F. H.)—Plain Introduction to the Criticism of the New Testament, 1861.

———— Supplement to the Authorized English Version of the New Testament, &c., 1845.

STANLEY (A. P.)—Sinai and Palestine, &c. First Edition, 1856.

STIER (Dr. Rud.)—The Words of the Lord Jesus. 8 Vols. Translated. (*Clark.*)

THOLUCK (Dr. Aug.)—Commentary on the Sermon on the Mount. Translated from the Fourth German Edition. (*Clark.*) 1860.

———— Commentary on the Gospel of St. John. Translated from the last German Edition. (*Clark.*) 1860.

TISCHENDORF (Dr. Fr. Const.)—Synopsis Evangelica, &c., 1854.

TRENCH (Rich. Chen.)—Notes on the Parables of our Lord. Sixth Edition, 1855.

———— Notes on the Miracles of our Lord. Fifth Edition, 1856.

———— Synonyms of the New Testament, &c. First Edition, 1854.

WEBSTER (W. F.) AND WILKINSON (W. F.)—The Greek Testament, with Notes, Grammatical and Exegetical. Vol. i., 1855.

WESTCOTT (Brooke Foss)—General Survey of the History of the Canon of the New Testament during the First Four Centuries, 1855.

De WETTE (Dr. N. M. L.)—Kurtzgefasstes Exegetisches Handbuch zum Neuen Testament, Matth., 1845; Lukas und Markus, 1846; Johann., 1852.

WIESELER (K.)—Chronologische Synopse der vier Evangelien, 1843.

WINER (Dr. G. B.) Grammar of the New Testament Diction. Translated from the Sixth German Edition. (*Clark.*) 2 Vols., 1859.

The Works of the principal Greek and Latin Fathers.

N.B.—In references to the Psalms, the verses are given, for the convenience of ordinary readers, as in our English version, where it differs from the Hebrew.

THE GOSPEL ACCORDING TO

ST. MATTHEW.

1 THE book of the *a*generation of Jesus Christ, *b*the son of David, *c*the son of Abraham.

2 Abraham begat Isaac; and Isaac begat Jacob; and Jacob begat Judas

3 and his brethren; and Judas begat Phares and Zara of Thamar; and

4 *d*Phares begat Esrom; and Esrom begat Aram; and Aram begat Amina-

5 dab; and Aminadab begat *e*Naasson; and Naasson begat Salmon; and Salmon begat Booz of *f*Rachab; and Booz begat Obed of Ruth; and

6 Obed begat Jesse; and *g*Jesse begat David the king;

And David *h*the king begat Solomon of her *that had been the wife* of

7 Urias; and *i*Solomon begat Roboam; and Roboam begat Abia; and Abia

8 begat Asa; and Asa begat Josaphat; and Josaphat begat Joram; and

A. M. 4000.

CHAP. 1.
a Luke 3. 23.
b Ps. 132. 11.
Isa. 11. 1.
Acts 2. 30.
c Gal. 3. 16.
d Ruth 4. 18.
e Num. 1. 7.
f Jos. 6. 22.
Heb. 11. 31.
g 1 Sam.16. 1.
h 2 Sam.12.24.
i 1 Chr. 3. 10.

CHAP. I. Verses 1-17.—GENEALOGY OF CHRIST. (= Luke iii. 23-38.)

1. The book of the generation—an expression purely Jewish; meaning, 'Table of the genealogy.' In Gen. v. 1 the same expression occurs in this sense [ספר תולדת, which the LXX. translate by our phrase here—βίβλος γενέσεως]. We have here, then, the title, not of this whole Gospel of Matthew, but only of the first seventeen verses. **of Jesus Christ.** For the meaning of these glorious words, see on *v.* 21 and on *v.* 16. "Jesus," the name given to our Lord at His circumcision (Luke ii. 21), was that by which He was familiarly known while on earth. The word "Christ"—though applied to Him as a proper name by the angel who announced His birth to the shepherds (Luke ii. 11), and once or twice used in this sense by our Lord Himself (ch. xxiii. 8, 10; Mark ix. 41)—only began to be so used by others about the very close of His earthly career (ch. xxvi. 68; xxvii. 17). The full form, "Jesus Christ," though once used by Himself in His Intercessory Prayer (John xvii. 3), was never used by others till after His ascension and the formation of churches in His name. Its use, then, in the opening words of this Gospel (and in *v.* 17, 18) is in the style of the late period when our Evangelist wrote, rather than of the events he was going to record. **the son of David, the son of Abraham.** As Abraham was the *first* from whose family it was predicted that Messiah should spring (Gen. xxii. 18), so David was the *last.* To a Jewish reader, accordingly, these behoved to be the two great starting-points of any true genealogy of the promised Messiah; and thus this opening verse, as it stamps the first Gospel as one peculiarly Jewish, would at once tend to conciliate the writer's people. From the nearest of those two fathers came that familiar name of the promised Messiah, "the son of David" (Luke xx. 41), which was applied to Jesus, either in devout acknowledgment of His rightful claim to it (ch. ix. 27; xx. 31), or in the way of insinuating inquiry whether such were the case (see on John iv. 29; ch. xii. 23).

2. Abraham begat Isaac; and Isaac begat Jacob; and Jacob begat Judas and his brethren. Only the fourth son of Jacob is here named, as it was from his loins that Messiah was to spring (Gen. xlix. 10). **3. And Judas begat Phares and Zara of Thamar; and Phares begat Esrom; and Esrom begat Aram; 4. And Aram begat Aminadab; and Aminadab begat Naasson; and Naasson begat Salmon; 5. And Salmon begat Booz of Rachab; and Booz

begat Obed of Ruth; and Obed begat Jesse; 6. And Jesse begat David the king; and David the king begat Solomon of her of Urias.** [The words, "that had been the wife," introduced by our translators, only weaken the delicate brevity of our Evangelist—ἐκ τῆς τοῦ Οὐρίου]. Four women are here introduced: two of them Gentiles by birth—*Rahab* and *Ruth;* and three of them with a blot at their names in the Old Testament—*Thamar, Rahab,* and *Bath-sheba.* This feature in the present genealogy—herein differing from that given by Luke—comes well from him who styles himself in his list of the Twelve, what none of the other lists do, "Matthew *the publican;*" as if thereby to hold forth, at the very outset, the unsearchable riches of that grace which could not only fetch in "them that are afar off," but reach down even to "publicans and harlots," and raise them to "sit with the princes of his people." David is here twice emphatically styled "David the king" (for the MS. authority against the repetition is insufficient), as not only the first of that royal line from which Messiah was to descend, but the one king of all that line from 'which the throne that Messiah was to occupy took its name—"the throne of David." The angel Gabriel, in announcing Him to His virgin-mother, calls it "the throne of David His father," sinking all the intermediate kings of that line, as having no importance save as links to connect the first and the last king of Israel as father and son. It will be observed that Rahab is here represented as the great-great-grandmother of David (see Ruth iv. 20-22; and 1 Chr. ii. 11-15)—a thing not beyond possibility indeed, but extremely improbable, there being about four centuries between them. There can hardly be a doubt that one or two intermediate links are omitted. (See on *v.* 17, and Remarks 1. and 2. at the end of this section.)

7. And Solomon begat Roboam; and Roboam begat Abia; and Abia begat Asa; 8. And Asa begat Josaphat; and Josaphat begat Joram; and Joram begat Ozias (or Uzziah). Three kings are here omitted—*Ahaziah, Joash,* and *Amaziah* (1 Chr. iii. 11, 12). Some omissions behoved to be made, to compress the whole into three fourteens (v. 17). The reason why these, rather than other names, are omitted must be sought in *religious* considerations—either in the connection of those kings with the house of Ahab (as *Lightfoot, Ebrard,* and *Alford* view it); in their slender right to be regarded as true links in the

9 Joram begat Ozias; and Ozias begat Joatham; and Joatham begat Achaz;
10 and Achaz begat Ezekias; and ^jEzekias begat Manasses; and Manasses
11 begat Amon; and Amon begat Josias; and ¹Josias begat Jechonias. and
    his brethren, about the time they were ^k carried away to Babylon:
12 And after they were brought to Babylon, Jechonias begat Salathiel;
13 and Salathiel begat ¹Zorobabel; and Zorobabel begat Abiud; and Abiud
14 begat Eliakim; and Eliakim begat Azor; and Azor begat Sadoc; and
15 Sadoc begat Achim; and Achim begat Eliud; and Eliud begat Eleazar;
16 and Eleazar begat Matthan; and Matthan begat Jacob; and Jacob begat
    Joseph the husband of Mary, of whom was born ^m Jesus who is called Christ.
17 So all the generations from Abraham to David *are* fourteen generations;

A. M. 4000.

j 2 Ki. 20. 21.
1 Some read, Josias begat Jakim, and Jakim begat Jechonias.
k 2 Ki. 25. 11.
Jer. 27. 20.
l Ezra 3. 2.
Hag. 1. 1.
m Gen. 3. 15.
Isa. 9. 6.

theocratic chain (as *Lange* takes it); or in some similar disqualification. **9. And Ozias begat Joatham; and Joatham begat Achaz; and Achaz begat Ezekias; 10. And Ezekias begat Manasses; and Manasses begat Amon; and Amon begat Josias; 11. And Josias begat Jechonias and his brethren.** Jechoniah was Josiah's grandson, being the son of Jehoiakim, Josiah's second son (1 Chr. iii. 15); but Jehoiakim might well be sunk in such a catalogue, being a mere puppet in the hands of the king of Egypt (2 Chr. xxxvi. 4). The "brethren" of Jechonias here evidently mean his uncles—the chief of whom, Mattaniah or Zedekiah, who came to the throne (2 Kin. xxiv. 17), is, in 2 Chr. xxxvi. 10, called "his brother," as well as here. **about the time they were carried away to Babylon** [ἐπὶ τῆς μετοικεσίας]—literally, 'of their migration,' for the Jews avoided the word 'captivity' [αἰχμαλωσία] as too bitter a recollection, and our Evangelist studiously respects the national feeling.

12. And after they were brought to ('after the migration of') **Babylon, Jechonias begat Salathiel.** So 1 Chr. iii. 17. Nor does this contradict Jer. xxii. 30, "Thus saith the Lord, Write ye this man (Coniah, or Jechoniah) childless;" for what follows explains in what sense this was meant—"for no man of his seed shall prosper, sitting upon the throne of David." He *was* to have seed, but no *reigning* child. **and Salathiel** (or Shealtiel) **begat Zorobabel.** So Ezra iii. 2; Neh. xii. 1; Hag. i. 1. But it would appear from 1 Chr. iii. 19 that Zerubbabel was Salathiel's grandson, being the son of Pedaiah, whose name, for some reason unknown, is omitted. **13-15. And Zorobabel begat Abiud, &c.** None of these names are found in the Old Testament; but they were doubtless taken from the public or family registers, which the Jews carefully kept, and their accuracy was never challenged. **16. And Jacob begat Joseph, the husband of Mary, of whom was born Jesus.** From this it is clear that the genealogy here given is not that of Mary, but of Joseph; nor has this ever been questioned. And yet it is here studiously proclaimed that Joseph was not the natural, but only the legal father of our Lord. His birth of a virgin was known only to a few; but the acknowledged descent of his legal father from David secured that the descent of Jesus Himself from David should never be questioned. See on *v.* 20. **who is called Christ** [Χριστός]—from the Hebrew [מָשִׁיחַ], both signifying 'anointed.' It is applied in the Old Testament to the *kings* (1 Sam. xxiv. 6, 10); to the *priests* (Lev. iv. 5, 16, &c.); and to the *prophets* (1 Kin. xix. 16)—these all being anointed with oil, the symbol of the needful spiritual gifts, to consecrate them to their respective offices; and it was applied, in its most sublime and comprehensive sense, to the promised Deliverer, inasmuch as He was to be

consecrated to an office embracing all three by the immeasurable anointing of the Holy Ghost (Isa. lxi. 1; compare Joh. iii. 34). **17. So all the generations from Abraham to David are fourteen generations; and from David until the carrying away (or migration) into Babylon are fourteen generations; and from the carrying away into ('the migration of') Babylon unto Christ are fourteen generations.** That is, the whole may be conveniently divided into three fourteens, each embracing one marked era, and each ending with a notable event, in the Israelitish annals. Such artificial aids to memory were familiar to the Jews, and much larger gaps than those here are found in some of the Old Testament genealogies. In Ezra vii. 1-5 no fewer than six generations of the priesthood are omitted, as will appear by comparing it with 1 Chr. vi. 3-15. It will be observed that the last of the three divisions of fourteen appears to contain only thirteen distinct names, including Jesus as the last. *Lange* thinks that this was meant as a tacit hint that *Mary* was to be supplied, as the thirteenth link of this last chain, as it is impossible to conceive that the Evangelist could have made any mistake in the matter. But there is a simpler way of accounting for it. As the Evangelist himself (*v.* 17) reckons David twice—as the last of the first fourteen and the first of the second—so, if we reckon the second fourteen to end with Josiah, who was coeval with the "carrying away into captivity" (*v.* 11), and the third to begin with Jechoniah, it will be found that this last division, as well as the other two, embraces fourteen names, including that of our Lord.

Remarks. — 1. When superficial readers ask what can be the use of those long, dry catalogues of names which fill whole chapters of the Old Testament, they may be referred to this and the corresponding genealogy in Luke for one very sufficient answer. They enable us, in some measure, to trace the golden thread which connects our Lord with David, Abraham, and Adam, according to the flesh, and so make good one of His claims to the Messiahship. The links in the chain of those two genealogies which we *can* test by the corresponding tables of the Old Testament serve to verify those which must be received on their own sole authority. And that this is thoroughly reliable is manifest, both because these catalogues would not have been published at a time when, if inaccurate, they could easily have been refuted by reference to the well-known family and public registers; and because there is not a particle of evidence that they were ever questioned, much less invalidated. 2. That there should be difficulty in these genealogies is not surprising, considering, first, the want of sufficient materials of comparison; second, the double or triple names given to the same persons; third, the intermediate names omitted; fourth, the name of *sons* given to

2

and from David until the carrying away into Babylon *are* fourteen generations; and from the carrying away into Babylon unto Christ *are* fourteen generations.

18   Now the [n]birth of Jesus Christ was on this wise: When as his mother Mary was espoused to Joseph, before they came together, she was

19   found with child of the Holy Ghost.   Then Joseph her husband, being a just *man,* and not willing [o]to make her a public example, was minded to

20   put her away privily.   But while he thought on these things, behold, the angel of the Lord appeared unto him in a dream, saying, Joseph, thou son of David, fear not to take unto thee Mary thy wife; [p]for that which is

21   [2]conceived in her is of the Holy Ghost.   And she shall bring forth a son, and thou shalt call his name [3]Jesus; for [q]he shall save his people from

22   their sins.   (Now all this was done, that [r]it might be fulfilled which was

23   spoken of the Lord by the prophet, saying, Behold, [s]a virgin shall be

A. M. 4000.
[n] Luke 1. 27.
Gal. 4. 4.
Heb. 10. 5.
[o]. Deut. 24. 1.
[p] Luke 1. 35.
[2] begotten.
[3] That is,
Saviour.
[q] Gen. 49. 10.
Jer. 33. 16.
Dan. 9. 24.
Acts 5. 31.
Heb. 7. 25.
1 John 3. 5.
Rev. 1. 5.
[r] Heb. 6. 18.
[s] Isa. 7. 14.

those who were only in the direct line of descent, and of *brothers* to those who were only collaterally related; and, finally, the Levirate law, by which one is called the son, not of his actual, but of his Levirate father (see Deut. xxv. 5, 6; Luke xx. 28). From these causes great perplexity and much discussion have arisen, nor is it possible to solve every difficulty.   So much, however, is clear as to make it "evident that our Lord sprang out of Juda" (Heb. vii. 14), and was "the Seed of the woman" "who should bruise the Serpent's head."   (For a beautiful remark of *Olshausen's* on this whole subject, see on Luke's genealogy, ch. iii., at the close.) To a Jewish Christian how delightful it must have been, and to any unprejudiced Jew how conciliatory, to find themselves, in the very first section of this Gospel, so entirely at home, and to see even the more external lines of their ancient economy converging upon Jesus of Nazareth as its proper goal; but this only to pave the way for the exhibition of that same Jesus, in the sequel of this Gospel, in a still deeper relation to the old economy—as the very "Travail of its soul, its Satisfaction!"

18-25.—BIRTH OF CHRIST.

18. Now the birth of Jesus Christ [*Tischendorf* and *Tregelles* read 'the birth of Christ;' a very ancient reading, but otherwise most insufficiently attested.]   **was on this wise,** or 'thus:' **When as his mother Mary was espoused** [μνηστευθείσης] —rather, 'betrothed'—**to Joseph, before they came together, she was found** (or discovered to be) **with child of the Holy Ghost.**   It was, of course, the fact only that was discovered: the explanation of the fact here given is the Evangelist's own.   That the Holy Ghost is a living, conscious Person is plainly implied here, and is elsewhere clearly taught (Acts v. 3, 4, &c.); and that, in the unity of the Godhead, He is distinct both from the Father and the Son, is taught with equal distinctness (Matt. xxviii. 19; 2 Cor. xiii. 14). On the Miraculous Conception of our Lord, see on Luke i. 35.   **19. Then Joseph her husband:** compare ver. 20, "Mary, thy wife."   Betrothal was, in Jewish law, valid marriage.   In giving Mary up, therefore, Joseph had to take legal steps to effect the separation.   **being a just man, and not willing to make her a public example**—or 'to expose her' (see Deut. xxii. 23, 24)—**was minded to put her away privily** ('privately')—by giving her the required writing of divorcement (Deut. xxiv. 1), in presence only of two or three witnesses, and without cause assigned, instead of having her before a magistrate.   That some communication had passed between him and his betrothed, directly or indirectly, on the subject, after she returned from her three months' visit to Elizabeth, can hardly be doubted.   Nor does the purpose to divorce her necessarily imply disbelief, on Joseph's part, of the explanation given him.   Even supposing him to have yielded to it some reverential assent—and the Evangelist seems to convey as much, by ascribing the proposal to screen her to the *justice* of his character—he might think it altogether unsuitable and incongruous in such circumstances to follow out the marriage.   **20. But while he thought on these things.** Who would not feel for him after receiving such intelligence, and before receiving any light from above?   As he brooded over the matter alone, in the stillness of the night, his domestic prospects darkened and his happiness blasted for life, his mind slowly making itself up to the painful step, yet planning how to do it in the way least offensive—at the last extremity the Lord Himself interposes.   **behold, the angel of the Lord appeared to him in a dream, saying, Joseph, son of David.**   This style of address was doubtless advisedly chosen to remind him of what all the families of David's line so eagerly coveted, and thus it would prepare him for the marvellous announcement which was to follow. **fear not to take unto thee Mary thy wife:** *q. d.,* 'Though a dark cloud now overhangs this relationship, it is unsullied still.' **for that which is conceived** ['begotten,' γεννηθὲν] **in her is of the Holy Ghost.   21. And she shall bring forth a son.**   Observe, it is not said, 'she shall bear *thee* a son,' as was said to Zacharias of his wife Elizabeth (Luke i. 13). **and thou** (as his legal father) **shalt call his name JESUS** [Ἰησοῦν]—from the Hebrew יְהוֹשׁוּעַ, *Jehoshua,* Num. xiii. 16; or, as after the captivity it was contracted, יֵשׁוּעַ, *Jeshua,* Neh. vii. 7]; meaning 'Jehovah the Saviour;' in Greek JESUS—to the awakened and anxious sinner sweetest and most fragrant of all names, expressing so melodiously and briefly His whole saving office and work!   **for he shall save** [αὐτὸς γὰρ σώσει].   The "He" is here emphatic—'He it is that shall save:' He personally, and by personal acts (as *Webster and Wilkinson* express it).   **his people**—the lost sheep of the house of Israel, in the first instance; for they were the only people He then had.   But, on the breaking down of the middle wall of partition, the saved people embraced the "redeemed unto God by His blood out of every kindred and people and tongue and nation.   **from their sins**—in the most comprehensive sense of salvation from sin (Rev. i. 5; Eph. v. 25-27.)   **22. Now all this was done, that it might be fulfilled which was spoken of the Lord by the prophet** (Isa. vii. 14), **saying, 23. Behold, a virgin**—it should be 'the virgin' [ἡ

3

with child, and shall bring forth a son, and [4]they shall call his name
24 Emmanuel, which, being interpreted, is, *(God with us.)* Then Joseph,
being raised from sleep, did as the angel of the Lord had bidden him,
25 and took unto him his wife; and knew her not till she had brought forth
"her first-born son: and he called his name JESUS.

2 NOW when *Jesus was born in Bethlehem of Judea, in the days of
Herod the king, behold, there came wise men *b*from the east to Jerusalem,
2 saying, *c*Where is he that is born King of the Jews? for we have seen *d*his
3 star in the east, and are come to worship him. When Herod the king had

A. M. 4000.

[4] Or, his
name shall
be called.
t Isa. 9. 6.
" Ex. 13. 2.

CHAP. 2.
a Dan. 9. 24.
b 1 Ki. 4. 30.,
c Luke 2. 11.
d Num.24.17.

παρθένος, exactly as in the Hebrew, הָעַלְמָה]; meaning that particular virgin destined to this unparalleled distinction. **shall be with child, and shall
bring forth a son, and they shall call his name
Emmanuel [**עִמָּנוּ אֵל, *nobiscum-Deus*]**, which, being
interpreted, is, God with us.** Not that He was to
have this for a proper name (like "Jesus"), but that
He should come to be known *in this character*, as
God manifested in the flesh, and the living bond
of holy and most intimate fellowship between God
and men from henceforth and for ever. **24. Then
Joseph, being raised from sleep** (and all his difficulties now removed), **did as the angel of the
Lord had bidden him, and took unto him his wife.**
With what deep and reverential joy would this
now be done on his part; and what balm would
this minister to his betrothed one, who had till
now lain under suspicions of all others the most
trying to a chaste and holy woman—suspicions, too,
arising from what, though to her an honour unparalleled, was to all around her wholly unknown!
**25. And knew her not till she had brought forth
her first-born son.** [τὸν πρωτότοκον. *Lachmann,
Tischendorf,* and *Tregelles,* on certainly ancient,
but, as we think, insufficient authority, exclude
τὸν πρωτότοκον from the text here, though inserting it in Luke ii. 7, where it is undisputed. Here
they read simply υἱοῦ—'till she had brought forth
a son.'] **and he called his name JESUS.** The
word "till" does not necessarily imply that they
lived on a different footing afterwards (as will be
evident from the use of the same word in 1 Sam.
xv. 35; 2 Sam. vi. 23; Matt. xii. 20); nor does the
word "first-born" decide the much disputed question, whether Mary had any children to Joseph
after the birth of Christ; for, as *Lightfoot* says,
'The law, in speaking of the first-born, regarded
not whether any were born *after.* or no, but only
that none were born before.' (See on ch. xiii.
55, 56.)

Remarks.—1. Was ever faith more tried than
the Virgin's, when for no fault of hers, but in
consequence of an act of God Himself, her conjugal relation to Joseph was allowed to be all but
snapped asunder by a legal divorce? Yet how
glorious was the reward with which her constancy
and patience were at length crowned! And is
not this one of the great laws of God's procedure towards his believing people? Abraham was
allowed to do all but sacrifice Isaac (Gen. xxii.);
the last year of the predicted Babylonish captivity
had arrived ere any signs of deliverance appeared
(Dan. ix. 1, 2); the massacre of all the Jews in
Persia had all but taken place (Esth. vii. viii.);
Peter, under Herod Agrippa, was all but brought
forth for execution (Acts xii.); Paul was all but
assassinated by a band of Jewish enemies (Acts
xxiii.); Luther all but fell a sacrifice to the machinations of his enemies (1521); and so in cases
innumerable since,—of all which it may be said,
as in the song of Moses, "The Lord shall judge
His people, and repent Himself for His servants,
when He seeth that their power is gone" (Deut. xxxii.

36). 2. What divine wisdom was there in the
arrangement by which our Lord was born of a
betrothed virgin, thus effectually providing against
the reproach of illegitimacy, and securing for His
Infancy an honourable protection! "This also
cometh forth from the Lord of hosts, who is wonderful in counsel and excellent in working" (Isa.
xxviii. 29).

CHAP. II. 1-12.—VISIT OF THE MAGI TO JERU-
SALEM AND BETHLEHEM.

*The Wise Men reach Jerusalem—The Sanhe-
drim, on Herod's demand, pronounce Bethlehem
to be Messiah's predicted Birth-place* (1-6). **1. Now
when Jesus was born in Bethlehem of Judea**—so
called to distinguish it from another Bethlehem
in the tribe of Zebulun, near the sea of Galilee
(Jos. xix. 15): called also *Beth-lehem-judah,* as
being in that tribe (Jud. xvii. 7); and *Ephrath*
(Gen. xxxv. 16); and combining both, *Beth-lehem
Ephratah* (Mic. v. 2). It lay about six miles
south-west of Jerusalem. But how came Joseph
and Mary to remove thither from Nazareth, the
place of their residence? Not of their own accord,
and certainly not with the view of fulfilling the
prophecy regarding Messiah's birth-place; nay,
they stayed at Nazareth till it was almost too late
for Mary to travel with safety; nor would they
have stirred from it at all, had not an order
which left them no choice forced them to the
appointed place. A high hand was in all these
movements. (See on Luke ii. 1-6.) **in the days
of Herod the king**—styled the Great; son of Antipater, an *Edomite,* made king by the Romans.
Thus was "the sceptre departing from Judah"
(Gen. xlix. 10), a sign that Messiah was now at
hand. As Herod is known to have died in the
year of Rome 750, in the fourth year before the
commencement of our Christian era, the birth of
Christ must be dated four years before the date
usually assigned to it, even if He was born within
the year of Herod's death, as it is next to certain
that he was. **there came wise men** [μάγοι] lit.,
'Magi' or 'Magians;' probably of the learned class
who cultivated astrology and kindred sciences.
Balaam's prophecy (Num. xxiv. 17), and perhaps
Daniel's (ch. ix. 24, &c.), might have come down
to them by tradition; but nothing definite is
known of them. **from the east**—but whether
from Arabia, Persia, or Mesopotamia is uncertain. **to Jerusalem**—as the Jewish metropolis.
**2. Saying, Where is he that is born King of
the Jews?** From this it would seem they were
not themselves Jews. (Compare the language
of the Roman governor, John xviii. 33, and of
the Roman soldiers, ch. xxvii. 29, with the
very different language of the Jews themselves,
ch. xxvii. 42, &c.) The Roman historians, *Suetonius* and *Tacitus,* bear witness to an expectation,
prevalent in the East, that out of Judea should
arise a sovereign of the world. **for we have seen
his star in the east.** Much has been written on
the subject of this star; but from all that is here
said it is perhaps safest to regard it as simply a

4

4 heard *these things*, he was troubled, and all Jerusalem with him. And
  when he had gathered all [e]the chief priests and [f]scribes of the people

5 together, [g]he demanded of them where Christ should be born. And
  they said unto him, In Bethlehem of Judea: for thus it is written by the

6 prophet, And [h]thou, Bethlehem, *in* the land of Juda, art not the least
  among the princes of Juda: for out of thee shall come a Governor, [i]that

7 shall [1]rule my people Israel. Then Herod, when he had privily called
  the wise men, enquired of them diligently what time the star appeared.

8 And he sent them to Bethlehem, and said, Go and search diligently for
  the young child; and when ye have found *him*, bring me word again,

9 that I may come and worship him also. When they had heard the king,

A. M. 4000.
[e] Ps. 2. 1.
[f] 2 Chr. 34. 13.
Ezra 7. 6, 11, 12.
[g] Mal. 2. 7. John 3. 10.
[h] Mic. 5. 2. John 7. 42.
[i] Rev. 2. 27. Gen. 49. 10. Nu. 24. 19.
1 Or, feed. Isa. 40. 11.

luminous meteor, which appeared under special laws and for a special purpose. **and are come to worship him**—'to do Him homage,' as the word [προσκυνῆσαι] signifies; the nature of that homage depending on the circumstances of the case. That not civil but religious homage is meant here is plain from the whole strain of the narrative, and particularly *v.* 11. Doubtless these simple strangers expected all Jerusalem to be full of its new-born King, and the time, place, and circumstances of His birth to be familiar to every one. Little would they think that the first announcement of His birth would come from themselves, and still less could they anticipate the startling, instead of transporting, effect which it would produce—else they would probably have sought their information regarding His birth-place in some other quarter. But God overruled it to draw forth a noble testimony to the predicted birth-place of Messiah from the highest ecclesiastical authority in the nation. **3. When Herod the king heard these things, he was troubled**—viewing this as a danger to his own throne: perhaps his guilty conscience also suggested other grounds of fear. **and all Jerusalem with him**—from a dread of revolutionary commotions, and perhaps also of Herod's rage. **4. And when he had gathered all the chief priests and scribes of the people together.** The class of the "*chief priests*" included the high priest for the time being, together with all who had previously filled this office; for though the then head of the Aaronic family was the only rightful high priest, the Romans removed them at pleasure, to make way for creatures of their own. In this class probably were included also the heads of the four-and-twenty courses of the priests. The "*scribes*" were at first merely transcribers of the law and synagogue-readers; afterwards interpreters of the law, both civil and religious, and so both lawyers and divines. The first of these classes, a proportion of the second, and "*the elders*"—that is, as *Lightfoot* thinks, 'those elders of the laity that were not of the Levitical tribe,' constituted the supreme council of the nation, called the *Sanhedrim*, the members of which, at their full complement, were seventy-two. That this was the council which Herod now convened is most probable, from the solemnity of the occasion; for though the elders are not mentioned we find a similar omission where all three were certainly meant (cf. ch. xxvi. 59; xxvii. 1). As *Meyer* says, it was all the theologians of the nation whom Herod convened, because it was a theological response that he wanted. **he demanded of them**—as the authorized interpreters of Scripture—**where Christ** [ὁ Χριστὸς]—'the Messiah'—**should be born**—according to prophecy. **5. And they said unto him, In Bethlehem of Judea** —a prompt and involuntary testimony from the highest tribunal; which yet at length condemned Him to die. **for thus it is written by the prophet** (Mic. v. 2). **6. And thou, Bethlehem, [in] the land**

of Juda—the "in" being familiarly left out, as we say, 'London, Middlesex'—**art not the least among the princes of Juda: for out of thee shall come a Governor, &c.** This quotation, though differing verbally, agrees substantially with the Hebrew and LXX. For says the prophet, "Though thou be little, yet out of thee shall come the Ruler"—this honour more than compensating for its natural insignificance; while our Evangelist, by a lively turn, makes him say, "Thou art *not the least: for out of thee shall come a Governor*"—this distinction lifting it from the lowest to the highest rank. The "thousands of Juda," in the prophet, mean the subordinate divisions of the tribe: our Evangelist, instead of these, merely names the "princes" or heads of these families, including the districts which they occupied. **that shall rule** [ποιμανεῖ]—or 'feed,' as in the margin—**my people Israel.** In the Old Testament, kings are, by a beautiful figure, styled "shepherds" (Ezek. xxxiv. &c.) The classical writers use the same figure. The pastoral rule of Jehovah and Messiah over His people is a representation pervading all Scripture, and rich in import. (See Ps. xxiii.; Isa. xl. 11; Ezek. xxxvii. 24; John x. 11; Rev. vii. 17). That this prophecy of Micah referred to the Messiah, was admitted by the ancient Rabbins.

The Wise Men, despatched to Bethlehem by Herod to see the Babe, and bring him word, make a Religious Offering to the Infant King, but, divinely warned, return home by another way (7-12). **7. Then Herod, when he had privily called the wise men.** Herod has so far succeeded in his murderous design: he has tracked the spot where lies his victim, an unconscious babe. But he has another point to fix—the date of His birth—without which he might still miss his mark. The one he had got from the Sanhedrim: the other he will have from the sages; but secretly, lest his object should be suspected and defeated. So he **enquired of them diligently** [ἠκρίβωσε]—rather, 'precisely' —**what time the star appeared**—presuming that this would be the best clue to the age of the child. The unsuspecting strangers tell him all. And now he thinks he is succeeding to a wish, and shall speedily clutch his victim; for at so early an age as they indicate, He would not likely have been removed from the place of his birth. Yet he is wary. He sends them as messengers from himself, and bids them come to *him*, that he may follow their pious example. **8. And he sent them to Bethlehem, and said, Go and search diligently** [ἀκριβῶς ἐξετάσατε]—'search out carefully'—**for the young child; and when ye have found him, bring me word again, that I may come and worship him also.** The cunning and bloody hypocrite! Yet this royal mandate would meantime serve as a safe-conduct to the strangers. **9. When they had heard the king, they departed.** But where were ye, O Jewish ecclesiastics, ye chief priests and

they departed; and, lo, the star, which they saw in the east, went before
10 them, till it came and stood over where the young child was. When
11 they saw the star, they rejoiced with exceeding great joy. And when
they were come into the house, they saw the young child with · Mary his
mother, and fell down and *ʲ*worshipped him: and when they had opened
their treasures, they ²presented unto him gifts; gold, and frankincense,
12 and myrrh. And being warned of God *ᵏ*in a dream that they should
not return to Herod, they departed into their own country another way.

A. M. 4000.

ʲ Ps. 2. 12.
Ps. 95. 6.
John 5. 23.
Acts 10. 26.
Rev. 19. 10.
² Or, offered.
Ps. 22. 29.
Ps. 72. 10.
ᵏ ch. 1. 20.

scribes of the people? Ye could tell Herod where Christ should be born, and could hear of these strangers from the far East that the Desire of all nations had actually come: but I do not see you trooping to Bethlehem—I find these devout strangers journeying thither all alone. Yet God ordered this too, lest the news should be blabbed, and reach the tyrant's ears, ere the Babe could be placed beyond his reach. Thus are the very errors and crimes and cold indifference of men all overruled. **and, lo, the star, which they saw in the east** —implying apparently that it had disappeared in the interval—**went before them, and stood over where the young child was.** Surely this could hardly be but by a luminous meteor, and not very high. **10. When they saw the star, they rejoiced with exceeding great joy** [ἐχάρησαν χαρὰν μεγάλην σφόδρα]. The language is very strong, expressing exuberant transport.. **11. And when they were come into the house**—not the stable; for as soon as Bethlehem was emptied of its strangers, they would have no difficulty in finding a dwelling-house. **they saw.** The received text has "found" [εὖρον]; but here our translators rightly depart from it, for it has no authority. **the young child with Mary his mother.** The blessed Babe is naturally mentioned first, then the mother; but Joseph, though doubtless present, is not noticed, as being but the head of the house. **and fell down and worshipped him.** Clearly this was no civil homage to a petty Jewish king, whom these star-guided strangers came so far, and enquired so eagerly, and rejoiced with such exceeding joy to pay, but a lofty spiritual homage. The next clause confirms this. **and when they had opened their treasures, they presented** —rather, 'offered'—**unto him gifts** [προσήνεγκαν αὐτῷ δῶρα]. This expression, used frequently in the Old Testament of the oblations presented to God, is in the New Testament employed seven times, and always in a *religious* sense of *offerings to God.* Beyond doubt, therefore, we are to understand the presentation of these gifts by the Magi as *a religious offering.* **gold, frankincense, and myrrh.** Visits were seldom paid to sovereigns without a present (1 Ki. x. 2, &c.): compare Ps. lxxii. 10, 11, 15; Isa. lx. 3, 6. "Frankincense" was an aromatic used in sacrificial offerings; "myrrh" was used in perfuming ointments. These, with the gold which they presented, seem to show that the offerers were persons in affluent circumstances. That the gold was presented to the infant King in token of His royalty; the frankincense in token of His divinity, and the myrrh, of his sufferings; or that they were designed to express His divine and human natures; or that the prophetical, priestly, and kingly offices of Christ are to be seen in these gifts; or that they were the offerings of three individuals respectively, each of them kings, the very names of whom tradition has handed down;—all these are, at the best, precarious suppositions. But that the feelings of these devout givers are to be seen in the richness of their gifts, and that the gold, at least, would be highly serviceable to the parents of the blessed Babe in their unexpected journey to Egypt and stay there—thus much at least admits of no dis-

pute. **12. And being warned of God in a dream that they should not return to Herod, they departed** [ἀνεχώρησαν]—or 'withdrew'—**to their own country another way.** What a surprise would this vision be to the sages, just as they were preparing to carry the glad news of what they had seen to the *pious* king! But the Lord knew the bloody old tyrant better than to let him see their face again.

Remarks.—1. As in the first chapter of this Gospel Christ's genealogy and His birth of the Virgin show that salvation is of the *Jews*, so the visit of these eastern Magi, in the second chapter, exhibits the interest of the *Gentile* world in Christ. And as the genealogical tree of the first chapter is bright on the Jewish side, while the Gentile side is pitch-dark, so in the second chapter the picture is reversed — the Gentile world presenting the bright, while unbelieving Israel presents the dark side, as *Lange* well observes. 2. How differently was the birth of Christ regarded by different parties! While the shepherds, Simeon and Anna, with as many as waited for the consolation of Israel, hailed it with joy, and these eastern sages, attracted from afar, hied them to Jerusalem to do homage to the new-born King, the cruel tyrant that sat upon the throne of Israel, the temporizing and turbulent priesthood, and the fickle, frivolous multitude, were only startled and troubled at the announcement. Thus is it in every age, as old Simeon said, that "the thoughts of many hearts might be revealed" (Luke ii. 35). 3. We have here a striking illustration of the important distinction between the civil and the ecclesiastical functions, and of the signal services which each may render to the other. While the religious liberties of the Church are under the protection of the civil power, it will be the wisdom of the State, instead of intermeddling with ecclesiastical functions, to refer questions affecting religion to those who are its proper representatives, as Herod did in this case. 4. What a commentary is furnished by this narrative on such sayings as these: "Many shall come from the east and west, and shall sit down with Abraham, and Isaac, and Jacob, in the kingdom of heaven; but the children of the kingdom shall be cast out;" "The last shall be first, and the first last;" "I am found of them that sought me not;" but "I have stretched out my hands all day long to a disobedient and gainsaying people" (Matt. viii. 11, 12; xx. 16; Rom. xi. 20, 21). Here, in the city of divine solemnities, the seat of a divinely instituted worship, we see unbelief and religious indifference reigning not only among the chosen people, but among the consecrated ecclesiastics; while from distant heathenism come devout and eager enquirers after the new-born King of Israel. Yea, here we see persons directing others to Christ who show no readiness to enquire after Him themselves. 5. How gloriously does God serve Himself, not only of those who themselves have no such intention, but of those whose only intention is to thwart His purposes! The Word had been made flesh, but in poverty rather than riches—meanness than ma-

6

13 And when they were departed, behold, the angel of the Lord appeareth to Joseph in a dream, saying, Arise, and take the young child and his mother, and flee into Egypt, and be thou there until I bring thee word:

14 for Herod will seek the young child to destroy him. When he arose, he took the young child and his mother by night, and departed into Egypt;

15 and was there until the death of Herod: that it might be fulfilled which was spoken of the Lord by the prophet, saying, Out *of Egypt have I called my son:

A. M. 4000.

Gen. 20. 6, 7.
Gen. 27. 19.
Gen. 31. 24.
Job 33. 15.
Dan. 2. 19.
l Ex. 4. 22.
Num. 24. 8.
Hos. 2. 15.
Hos. 11. 1.

---

jesty. It was fitting, then, that some public seal should be set upon Him. Accordingly, as His birth-place had been explicitly foretold by the ancient prophets, He will have this proclaimed by lips all unconscious of what they were attesting, lips beyond all suspicion—by the greatest and most august assembly of the Church's rulers—that His Son, in being born at Bethlehem, had come into the world at the right place. And whereas Herod's purpose in convening this grave synod and despatching the sages to Bethlehem, was dark and murderous—only to scent out his victim—he was herein but God's puny instrument for obtaining a glorious testimony in behalf of His Son, and procuring Him the homage of these honourable representatives of the heathen world. 6. See here the importance of the written Word, and of an intelligent acquaintance and familiarity with it; but yet how compatible this is with a total absence of the spirit and life of it; or, as *Lange* quaintly expresses it, 'the value of life-less Bible learning, and the worthlessness of the lifeless Bible-learned.' 7. How glorious is that faith which triumphs over all visible appearances! To the expectations of these eastern visitors "the house" at Bethlehem would be not a little disappointing. Yet "when they saw the child"—differing in nothing to the outward eye from any other babe—"they fell down and worshipped Him." That Babe was reverend and majestic in their eyes. 'This baseness (as *Bishop Hall* says) hath bred wonder, not contempt: they well knew the star could not lie.' Even so in every age, the more unaided by visible probabilities, and the more it triumphs over all that to sense would seem irrational, the nobler faith is. 8. How beautiful is natural knowledge when it leads, as in these sages, to Christ! But what sadder spectacle is there than towering attainments in science and philosophy, accumulating, as we have seen in our own day, to extreme old age, and attracting the homage of the world, yet conjoined with blank irreligion, and going out at length in atheistic silence as to all that is supernatural! 9. How grand is the providence which concealed both from the sages and from the parents of our Lord all suspicion of Herod's designs, until the divine purposes in this visit were all attained! The Magi, on reaching the capital, are allowed to visit the king in his palace; and on a *religious* mission from the king himself they hie them to Bethlehem. Haunted by no suspicions of foul play, they have free scope for their joy at the star, and for their rapture at the sight of the child. And they are about to return to Herod ere they get the warning to return by another way. Thus on their part, and to the very last, all is unalloyed satisfaction. Joseph and Mary, too, left in the same blessed ignorance, are free to wonder and exult at the visit of the Magi—possibly also to anticipate an introduction to Herod, and honour at his court. But this stage reached, the veil is lifted, and the king is revealed to both parties as a murderer in disguise. Both are warned off without delay, and not a moment is lost. While the wise men withdraw to their

own country by another way, the same "night" Joseph and Mary, with the blessed Babe, are off to Egypt. "O the depth of the riches both of the wisdom and knowledge of God! how unsearchable are His judgments and His ways past finding out! For of Him, and through Him, and to Him, are all things: to Whom be glory for ever. Amen." (Rom. xi. 33, 36.)

13-25.—THE FLIGHT INTO EGYPT—THE MASSACRE AT BETHLEHEM—THE RETURN OF JOSEPH AND MARY WITH THE BABE, AFTER HEROD'S DEATH, AND THEIR SETTLEMENT AT NAZARETH. (= Luke ii. 39.)

The Flight into Egypt. (13-15.) **13. And when they were departed, behold, the angel of the Lord appeareth to Joseph in a dream, saying, Arise, and take the young child and his mother.** Observe this form of expression, repeated in the next verse—another indirect hint that Joseph was no more than the Child's *guardian*. Indeed, personally considered, Joseph has no spiritual significance, and very little place at all, in the Gospel history. **and flee into Egypt**—which being near, as *Alford* says, and a Roman province independent of Herod, and much inhabited by Jews, was an easy and convenient refuge. Ah! blessed Saviour, on what a chequered career hast Thou entered here below! At Thy birth there was no room for Thee in the inn; and now all Judea is too hot for Thee. How soon has the sword begun to pierce through the Virgin's soul! (Luke ii. 35.) How early does she taste the reception which this mysterious Child of her's is to meet with in the world! And whither is He sent? To "the house of bondage"? Well, it once was that. But Egypt was a house of refuge before it was a house of bondage, and now it has but returned to its first use. **and be thou there until I bring thee word: for Herod will seek the young child to destroy him.** The word [μέλλει] implies that the action was already in progress, though incomplete. Herod's murderous purpose was formed ere the Magi set out for Bethlehem. **14. When he arose, he took the young child and his mother by night**—doubtless the same night—**and departed into Egypt; 15. And was there until the death of Herod**—which took place not very long after this of a horrible disease; the details of which will be found in *Josephus* (Antt. xvii. 6. 1, 5, 7, 8), **that it might be fulfilled which was spoken of the Lord by the prophet, saying** (Hos. xi. 1), **Out of Egypt have I called my son.** Our Evangelist here quotes directly from the Hebrew, warily departing from the LXX., which renders the words, 'From Egypt have I recalled his children' [τὰ τέκνα αὐτοῦ], meaning Israel's children. The prophet is reminding his people how dear Israel was to God in the days of his youth; how Moses was bidden say to Pharaoh, "Thus saith the Lord, Israel is my *son*, my first-born: and I say unto thee, Let *my* son go, that he may serve me: and if thou refuse to let him go, behold, I will slay *thy* son, even thy first-born" (Ex. iv. 22, 23); how, when Pharaoh refused, God, having slain all *his* first-born, "called his own son out of Egypt," by a stroke of high-handed power

16 Then Herod, when he saw that he was mocked of the wise men, was exceeding wroth, and sent forth, and slew all the children that were in Bethlehem, and in all the coasts thereof, from two years old and under, according to the time which he had diligently enquired of the wise men.
17 Then was fulfilled that which was spoken by [m]Jeremy the prophet, saying,
18 In Rama was there a voice heard, lamentation, and weeping, and great mourning, Rachel weeping *for* her children, and would not be comforted, because they are not.
19 But when [n]Herod was dead, behold, an [o]angel of the Lord appeareth in
20 a dream to Joseph in Egypt, saying, [p]Arise, and take the young child and

A. M. 4000.
[m]Jer. 31. 15.
[n]Ps. 76. 10.
Isa. 51. 12.
Dan. 8. 25;
11. 45.
[o]ch. 5. 13;
1. 20.
Ps. 139. 7.
Jer. 30. 10.
Ez. 11. 16.
[p]Pro. 3. 5, 6.

and love. Viewing the words in this light, even if our Evangelist had not applied them to the recall from Egypt of God's own beloved, Only-begotten Son, the application would have been irresistibly made by all who have learnt to pierce beneath the surface to the deeper relations which Christ bears to His people, and both to God; and who are accustomed to trace the analogy of God's treatment of each respectively. **16. Then Herod, &c.** As Deborah sang of the mother of Sisera, "She looked out at a window, and cried through the lattice, Why is his chariot so long in coming? why tarry the wheels of his chariots? Have they not sped?" so Herod wonders that his messengers, with pious zeal, are not hastening with the news that all is ready to receive him as a worshipper. What can be keeping them? Have they missed their way? Has any disaster befallen them? At length his patience is exhausted. He makes his enquiries, and finds they are already far beyond his reach on their way home. **when he saw that he was mocked** [ἐνεπαίχθη]—'was trifled with'—**of the wise men.** No, Herod, thou art not mocked of the wise men, but of a Higher than they. He that sitteth in the heavens doth laugh at thee; the Lord hath thee in derision. He disappointeth the devices of the crafty, so that their hands cannot perform their enterprise. He taketh the wise in their own craftiness, and the counsel of the froward is carried headlong. (Ps. ii. 4; Job v. 12, 13.) That blessed Babe shall die indeed, but not by thy hand. As He afterwards told that son of thine —as cunning and as unscrupulous as thyself— when the Pharisees warned Him to depart, for *Herod would seek to kill Him*—"Go ye, and tell that *fox*, Behold, I cast out devils, and I do cures to-day and to-morrow, and the third day I shall be perfected. Nevertheless I must walk to-day, and to-morrow, and the day following: for it cannot be that a prophet perish out of Jerusalem" (Luke xiii. 32, 33). Bitter satire! **was exceeding wroth.** To be made a fool of is what none like, and proud kings cannot stand. Herod burns with rage, and is like a wild bull in a net. So he **sent forth a band** of hired murderers, **and slew all the** [male] **children** [πάντας τοὺς παῖδας] **that were in Bethlehem, and in all the coasts,** or 'environs,' thereof, **from two years old and under, according to the time which he had diligently**—'carefully' —**enquired of the wise men.** In this ferocious step Herod was like himself—as crafty as cruel. He takes a large sweep, not to miss his mark. He thinks this will surely embrace his victim. And so it had, if He had been there. But He is gone. Heaven and earth shall sooner pass away than thou shalt have that Babe into thy hands. Therefore, Herod, thou must be content to want Him; to fill up the cup of thy bitter mortifications, already full enough—until thou die not less of a broken heart than of a loathsome and excruciating disease. Why, ask sceptics and sceptical critics, is not this massacre, if it really occurred, recorded by Jose-

phus, who is minute enough in detailing the cruelties of Herod? To this the answer is not difficult. If we consider how small a town Bethlehem was, it is not likely there would be many male children in it from two years old and under; and when we think of the number of fouler atrocities which Josephus has recorded of him, it is unreasonable to make anything of his silence on this. **17. Then was fulfilled that which was spoken by Jeremy the prophet, saying** (Jer. xxxi. 15—from which the quotation differs but verbally), **18. In Rama was there a voice heard, lamentation, and weeping, and great mourning, Rachel weeping for her children, and would not be comforted, because they are not.** These words, as they stand in Jeremiah, undoubtedly relate to the Babylonish captivity. Rachel, the mother of Joseph and Benjamin, was buried in the neighbourhood of Bethlehem (Gen. xxxv. 19), where her sepulchre is still shown. She is figuratively represented as rising from the tomb and uttering a double lament for the loss of her children—first, by a bitter captivity, and now by a bloody death. And a foul deed it was. O ye mothers of Bethlehem, methinks I hear you asking why your innocent babes should be the ram caught in the thicket, whilst Isaac escapes. I cannot tell you; but one thing I know, that ye shall, some of you, live to see a day when that Babe of Bethlehem shall be Himself the Ram, caught in another sort of thicket, in order that your babes may escape a worse doom than they now endure. And if these babes of yours be now in glory, through the dear might of that blessed Babe, will they not deem it their honour that the tyrant's rage was exhausted upon themselves instead of their Infant Lord? (See *Keble's* exquisite Hymn, entitled, "The Holy Innocents," on the appropriate words, "These were redeemed from among men, being the *first-fruits* unto God and to the Lamb," Rev. xiv. 4.) **19. But when Herod was dead**—Miserable Herod! Thou thoughtest thyself safe from a dreaded Rival; but it was He only that was safe from thee; and thou hast not long enjoyed even this fancied security. See on v. 15. **behold, an angel of the Lord.** Our translators, somewhat capriciously, render the same expression [ἄγγελος Κυρίου] "*the* angel of the Lord," ch. i. 20; ii. 13; and "*an* angel of the Lord," as here. As the same angel appears to have been employed on all these high occasions—and most likely he to whom in Luke is given the name of "Gabriel," ch. i. 19, 26—perhaps it should, in every instance except the first, be rendered "*the* angel." **appeareth in a dream to Joseph in Egypt. 20. Saying, Arise, and take the young child and his mother, and go into the land of Israel**—not to the land of Judea, for he was afterward expressly warned not to settle there, nor to Galilee, for he only went thither when he found it unsafe to settle in Judea, but to "the land of Israel," in its most general sense; meaning the Holy Land at large—the particular province being not as yet indicated.

8

his mother, and go into the land of Israel: for they are dead which
21 sought the young child's life. And he arose, and took the young child
22 and his mother, and came into the land of Israel. But when he heard
that Archelaus did reign in Judea in the room of his father Herod, he
was afraid to go thither: notwithstanding, being warned of God in a
23 dream, he turned aside *q*into the parts of Galilee: and he came and
dwelt in a city *r*called Nazareth: that it might be fulfilled *s*which was
spoken by the prophets, He shall be called a [3]Nazarene.

A. M. 4000.

q ch. 3. 13.
Luke 2. 39.
r John 1. 45.
s Jud. 13. 5.
[3] That is,
Branch, or,
Separated
one.
Num. 6. 2.

So Joseph and the Virgin had, like Abraham, to "go out, not knowing whither they went," till they should receive further direction. **for they are dead which sought the young child's life**—a common expression in most languages where only one is meant, who here is Herod. But the words are taken from the strikingly analogous case in Ex. iv. 19, which probably suggested the plural here; and where the command is given to Moses to return *to* Egypt for the same reason that the Greater than Moses was now ordered to be brought back *from* it—the death of him who sought his life. Herod died in the seventieth year of his age, and thirty-seventh of his reign. **21. And he arose, and took the young child and his mother, and came into the land of Israel**—intending, as is plain from what follows, to return to Bethlehem of Judea, there, no doubt, to rear the Infant King, as at His own royal city, until the time should come when they would expect Him to occupy Jerusalem, "the city of the Great King." **22. But when he heard that Archelaus did reign in Judea in the room of his father Herod.** Archelaus succeeded to Judea, Samaria, and Idumea; but Augustus refused him the title of *king* till it should be seen how he conducted himself; giving him only the title of *Ethnarch* (*Joseph.* Antt. xvii., 11, 4). Above this, however, he never rose. The people, indeed, recognized him as his father's successor; and so it is here said that he "*reigned* in the room of his father Herod." But, after ten years' defiance of the Jewish law and cruel tyranny, the people lodged heavy complaints against him, and the emperor banished him to Vienne in Gaul, reducing Judea again to a Roman province. Then "the sceptre" clean "departed from Judah." **he was afraid to go thither**—and no wonder, for the reason just mentioned. **notwithstanding**—or more simply, 'but'—**being warned of God in a dream, he turned aside** [ἀνεχώρησεν]—'withdrew'—**into the parts of Galilee**, or the Galilean parts. The whole country west of the Jordan was at this time, as is well known, divided into three provinces—GALILEE being the northern, JUDEA the southern, and SAMARIA the central province. The province of Galilee was under the jurisdiction of Herod Antipas, the brother of Archelaus, his father having left him that and Perea, on the east side of the Jordan, as his share of the kingdom, with the title of *tetrarch*, which Augustus confirmed. Though crafty and licentious, according to *Josephus*—precisely what the Gospel History shows him to be (see on Mark vi. 14-30, and on Luke xiii. 31-35)—he was of a less cruel disposition than Archelaus; and Nazareth being a good way off from the seat of government, and considerably secluded, it was safer to settle there. **23. And he came and dwelt in a city called Nazareth**—a small town in Lower Galilee, lying in the territory of the tribe of Zebulon, and about equally distant from the Mediterranean sea on the west and the sea of Galilee on the east. 'The town of Nazareth (says *Dr. Robinson*) lies upon the western side of a narrow oblong basin, extending, from S.S.W. to N.N.E., perhaps about twenty minutes in length

by eight or ten in breadth. The houses stand on the lower part of the slope of the western hill, which rises steep and high above them, and is crowned by a Wely, or saint's tomb, called Neby Ismaïl. After breakfast I walked out alone to the top of this western hill above Nazareth. Here, quite unexpectedly, a glorious prospect opened on the view. The air was perfectly clear and serene; and I shall never forget the impression I received as the enchanting panorama burst suddenly upon me. There lay the magnificent plain of Esdraelon, or at least all its western part; on the left was seen the round top of Tabor over the intervening hills, with portions of the little Hermon and Gilboa, and the opposite mountains of Samaria, from Jenin westwards to the lower hills extending towards Carmel. Then came the long line of Carmel itself. In the west lay the Mediterranean gleaming in the morning sun. Below, on the north, was spread out another of the beautiful plains of northern Palestine, called el-Buttauf. Farther towards the right is a sea of hills and mountains; backward lay the higher ones beyond the lake of Tiberias; and in the northeast lay the majestic Hermon with its icy crown. I remained for some hours upon this spot, lost in the contemplation of the wide prospect, and of the events connected with the scenes around. In the village below the Saviour of the world had passed His childhood. He must often have visited the fountain near which we had pitched our tent; His feet must frequently have wandered over the adjacent hills; and His eyes, doubtless, have gazed upon the splendid prospect from this very spot. Here the Prince of peace looked down upon the plain where the din of battles so often had rolled, and the garments of the warrior been dyed in blood; and He looked out, too, upon that sea over which the swift ships were to bear the tidings of His salvation to nations and to continents then unknown. How has the moral aspect of things been changed! Battles and bloodshed have indeed not ceased to desolate this unhappy country, and gross darkness now covers the people; but from this region a light went forth which has enlightened the world and unveiled new climes; and now the rays of that light begin to be reflected back from distant isles and continents, to illuminate anew the darkened land where it first sprung up.' *N. B.* If, from Luke ii. 39, one would conclude that the parents of Jesus brought Him straight back to Nazareth after His presentation in the temple—as if there had been no visit of the Magi, no flight to Egypt, no stay there, and no purpose on returning to settle again at Bethlehem—one might, from our Evangelist's way of speaking here, equally conclude that the parents of our Lord had never been at Nazareth until now. Did we know exactly the sources from which the matter of each of the Gospels was drawn up, or the mode in which these were used, this apparent discrepancy would probably disappear at once. In neither case is there any inaccuracy. At the same time it is difficult, with these facts before us, to conceive that

3 IN those days came ^aJohn the Baptist, preaching ^bin the wilder-
2 ness of Judea, and saying, Repent ye: for ^cthe kingdom of heaven is at
3 hand. For this is he that was spoken of by the prophet Esaias, saying,

A. D. 26.
^a Mal. 3. 1.
^b Jos. 14. 10.
^c Dan. 2. 44.

either of these two Evangelists wrote his Gospel with the other's before him—though many think this a precarious inference. **that it might be fulfilled which was spoken by the prophets, He shall be called a Nazarene** [Ναζωραῖος]—better, perhaps, 'Nazarene.' The best explanation of the origin of this name appears to be that which traces it to the word *netzer* [נֵצֶר], in Isa. xi. 1—the small *'twig,' 'sprout,'* or *'sucker,'* which the prophet there says "shall come forth from the stem (or rather 'stump') of Jesse, the branch which should fructify [יִפְרֶה] from his roots." The little town of Nazareth —mentioned neither in the Old Testament nor in *Josephus*—was probably so called from its insignificance—a weak twig in contrast to a stately tree; and a special contempt seemed to rest upon it— "Can any good thing come out of Nazareth?" (John i. 46)—over and above the general contempt in which all Galilee was held, from the number of Gentiles that settled in the upper territories of it, and, in the estimation of the Jews, debased it. Thus, in the providential arrangement by which our Lord was brought up at the insignificant and opprobrious town called *Nazareth*, there was involved, first, a local humiliation; next, an allusion to Isaiah's prediction of His lowly, twig-like upspringing from the branchless, dried-up stump of Jesse; and yet further, a standing memorial of that humiliation which "the prophets," in a number of the most striking predictions, had attached to the Messiah.

Remarks.—1. In the sleepless watch which the providence of God kept over His Son when a helpless Babe, and the ministry of angels so busily employed in directing all His movements, we see a lively picture of that over-canopies and secures and directs that Church which is His body. "No man ever yet hated his own flesh; but nourisheth and cherisheth it, even as the Lord the Church: for we are members of His body, of His flesh, and of His bones" (Eph. v. 29, 30). 2. Didst Thou spend all but thirty years, blessed Jesus, in the obscurity of a place whose very name afterwards brought opprobrium upon Thee? And should not this reconcile us to like humiliation for Thy sake; and all the more, as we are sure that like as Thou didst thereafter emerge into glorious manifestation, so do Thy servants shine out of obscurity, and make even the world to see that God is with them of a truth, and that at length, "if we suffer with Him, we shall also reign with Him."

CHAP. III. 1-12.—PREACHING AND MINISTRY OF JOHN. (= Mark i. 1-8; Luke iii. 1-18.) For the proper introduction to this section, we must go to—

Luke iii. 1, 2. Here, as *Bengel* well observes, the curtain of the New Testament is, as it were, drawn up, and the greatest of all epochs of the Church commences. Even our Lord's own age is determined by it (v. 23). No such elaborate chronological precision is to be found elsewhere in the New Testament, and it comes fitly from him who claims it as the peculiar recommendation of his Gospel, that 'he had traced down all things with precision from the very first' (ch. i. 3). Here evidently commences his proper narrative. V. 1. "Now in the fifteenth year of the reign of Tiberius Cæsar"—not the fifteenth from his full accession on the death of Augustus, but from the period when he was associated with him in the govern-

ment of the empire, three years earlier, about the end of the year of Rome 779, or about four years before the usual reckoning. "Pontius Pilate being governor of Judea." His proper title was *Procurator*, but with more than the usual powers of that office. After holding it for about ten years, he was summoned to Rome to answer to charges brought against him; but ere he arrived Tiberius died (A.D. 35), and soon after miserable Pilate committed suicide. "and Herod being tetrarch of Galilee (see on Mark vi. 14), and his brother Philip"—a very different and very superior Philip to the one whose name was *Herod Philip*, and whose wife, Herodias, went to live with Herod Antipas (see on Mark vi. 17)—"tetrarch of Iturea"—lying to the north-east of Palestine, and so called from *Itur* or *Jetur*, Ishmael's son (1 Chr. i. 31), and anciently belonging to the half-tribe of Manasseh. "and of the region of Trachonitis"—lying farther to the north-east, between Iturea and Damascus; a rocky district infested by robbers, and committed by Augustus to Herod the Great to keep in order. "and Lysanias the tetrarch of Abilene"—still more to the north-east; so called, says *Robinson*, from *Abila*, eighteen miles from Damascus. V. 2. "Annas and Caiaphas being the high priests." The former, though deposed, retained much of his influence, and, probably, as *Sagan* or deputy, exercised much of the power of the high priesthood along with Caiaphas his son-in-law (John xviii. 13; Acts iv. 6). In David's time both Zadok and Abiathar acted as high priests (2 Sam. xv. 35), and it seems to have been the fixed practice to have two (2 Ki. xxv. 18). "the word of God came unto John the son of Zacharias in the wilderness." Such a way of speaking is never once used when speaking of Jesus, because He was himself *The Living Word;* whereas to all merely creature-messengers of God, the word they spake was a foreign element. See on John iii. 31, and *Remark* 5 at the close of that Section. We are now prepared for the opening words of Matthew.

1. **In those days**—of Christ's secluded life at Nazareth, where the last chapter left Him. **came John the Baptist, preaching**—about six months before his Master. **in the wilderness of Judea**—the desert valley of the Jordan, thinly peopled and bare in pasture, a little north of Jerusalem. 2. **And saying, Repent ye.** Though the word [μετανοεῖτε] strictly denotes a *change of mind*, it has respect here, and wherever it is used in connection with salvation, primarily to that *sense of sin* which leads the sinner to flee from the wrath to come, to look for relief only from above, and eagerly to fall in with the provided remedy. (See on Acts xx. 21.) **for the kingdom of heaven is at hand.** This sublime phrase [ἡ βασιλεία τῶν οὐρανῶν=מַלְכוּת הַשָּׁמַיִם], used in none of the other Gospels, occurs in this peculiarly Jewish Gospel nearly thirty times; and being suggested by Daniel's grand vision of the Son of Man coming in the clouds of heaven to the Ancient of days, to receive His Investiture in a world-wide kingdom (Dan. vii. 13, 14), it was fitted at once both to meet the national expectations and to turn them into the right channel. A kingdom for which *repentance* was the proper preparation behoved to be essentially spiritual. Deliverance from sin, the great blessing of Christ's kingdom (ch. i. 21), can be valued by those only to whom sin is a burden (ch. ix. 12). John's great work, accordingly, was

10

^dThe voice of one crying in the wilderness, ^ePrepare ye the way of the
4 Lord, make his paths straight. And ^fthe same John ^ghad his raiment
of camel's hair, and a leathern girdle about his loins; and his meat
was ^hlocusts and wild ⁱhoney.

5   Then went out to him Jerusalem, and all Judea, and all the region round
6 about Jordan, and ^jwere baptized of him in Jordan, confessing their sins.
7 But when he saw many of the Pharisees and Sadducees come to his baptism, he said unto them, O generation of vipers, who hath warned you to
8 flee from ^kthe wrath to come? Bring forth therefore fruits meet for

A. D. 26.
d Isa. 40. 3.
Luke 3. 4.
e Luke 1. 76.
f Mark 1. 6.
g 2 Ki. 1. 8.
Zech. 13. 4.
h Lev. 11. 22.
i 1 Sam.14.25.
j Acts 19. 4.
k Rom. 5. 9.
1 Thes.1.10.

to awaken this feeling, and hold out the hope of a speedy and precious remedy. **3. For this is he that was spoken of by the prophet Esaias, saying** (ch. xi. 3), **The voice of one crying in the wilderness** (see on John i. 23, and on Luke iii. 2)—the scene of his ministry corresponding to its rough nature. **Prepare ye the way of the Lord, make his paths straight.** This prediction is quoted in all the four Gospels, showing that it was regarded as a great outstanding one, and the predicted fore-runner as the connecting link between the old and the new economies. Like the great ones of the earth, the Prince of peace was to have His imme-diate approach proclaimed and His way prepared; and the call here—taking it generally—is a call to put out of the way whatever would obstruct His progress and hinder His complete triumph, whether those hindrances were public or personal, outward or inward. In Luke (iii. 5, 6) the quotation is thus continued: "Every valley shall be filled, and every mountain and hill shall be brought low; and the crooked shall be made straight, and the rough ways shall be made smooth; and all flesh shall see the salvation of God." Levelling and smoothing are here the obvious figures whose sense is conveyed in the first words of the procla-mation—"*Prepare ye the way of the Lord.*" The idea is, that every obstruction shall be so removed as to reveal to the whole world the Salvation of God in Him whose name is the "Saviour." (Com-pare Ps. xcviii. 3; Isa. xi. 10; xlix. 6; lii. 10; Luke ii. 31, 32; Acts xiii. 47.) **4. And the same John had his raiment of camel's hair**—that is, woven of it—**and a leathern girdle about his loins**—the prophetic dress of Elijah (2 Ki. i. 8; and see Zech. xiii. 4). **and his meat was locusts**—the great well-known eastern locust, a food of the poor (Lev. xi. 22). **and wild honey**—made by wild bees (1 Sam. xiv. 25, 26). This dress and diet, with the shrill cry in the wilderness, would recall the stern days of Elijah.

5. Then went out to him Jerusalem, and all Judea, and all the region round about Jordan. From the metropolitan centre to the extremities of the Judean province the cry of this great preacher of repentance and herald of the approach-ing Messiah brought trooping penitents and eager expectants. **6. And were baptized of him in Jor-dan, confessing**—probably confessing aloud [ἐξομο-λογούμενοι]—**their sins.** This baptism was at once a public seal of their felt need of deliverance from sin, of their expectation of the coming Deliverer, and of their readiness to welcome Him when He appeared. The baptism itself startled, and was in-tended to startle them. They were familiar enough with the *baptism of proselytes* from heathenism; but this *baptism of Jews* themselves was quite new and strange to them. **7. But when he saw many of the Pharisees and Sadducees come to his baptism** (on these sects, and what they represented, see *Remark* 2. at the close of this Section), **he said unto them**—astonished at such a spectacle—**O generation of vipers** [Γεννήματα ἐχιδνῶν]—'Viper-brood;' expressing the deadly influence of both

sects alike upon the community. Mutually and entirely antagonistic as were their religious prin-ciples and spirit, the stern prophet charges both alike with being the poisoners of the nation's re-ligious principles. In ch. xii. 34, and xxiii. 33, this strong language of the Baptist is anew applied by the faithful and true Witness to the Pharisees specifically—the only party that had zeal enough actively to diffuse this poison. **who hath warned you** [ὑπέδειξεν]—'given you the hint,' as the idea is —**to flee from the wrath to come?**—'What can have brought *you* hither?' John more than sus-pected it was not so much their own spiritual anxi-eties as the popularity of his movement that had drawn them thither. What an expression is this, "The wrath to come!" [ἡ μέλλουσα ὀργή.] God's "wrath," in Scripture, is His righteous displeasure against sin, and consequently against all in whose skirts sin is found, arising out of the essential and eternal opposition of His nature to all moral evil. This is called "the *coming* wrath," not as being wholly future—see remark on the verb [μέλλω], on ch. ii. 13—for as a merited sentence it lies on the sinner already, and its effects, both inward and out-ward, are to some extent experienced even now—but because the impenitent sinner will not, until "the judgment of the great day," be concluded under it, will not have sentence publicly and irre-vocably passed upon him, will not have it discharged upon him and experience its effects without mix-ture and without hope. In this view of it, it is a wrath *wholly* to come—as is implied in the notice-ably different form of the expression employed by the apostle in 1 Thes. i. 10 [ἡ ὀργὴ ἡ ἐρχομένη]. Not that even true penitents came to John's bap-tism with all these views of "the wrath to come." But what he says is, that this was the *real import of the step* itself, and so much is implied in the use of the aorist [φυγεῖν]. In this view of it, how strik-ing is the word he employs to express that step—*fleeing* from it—as of one who, beholding a tide of fiery wrath rolling rapidly towards him, sees in instant flight his only escape! **8. Bring forth therefore fruits** [καρποὺς]—but the true reading clearly is 'fruit' [καρπόν]—**meet for repentance**—that is, such fruit as *befits* a true penitent. John, not being gifted with a knowledge of the human heart, like a true minister of righteousness and lover of souls, here directs them how to evidence and carry out their repentance, supposing it genu-ine; and in the following verses warns them of their danger in case it were not. **9. And think not to say within yourselves, We have Abraham to our father**—that pillow on which the nation so fatally reposed, that rock on which at length it split. (John viii. 33, 39, 53, &c.) **for I say unto you, that God is able of these stones to raise up children unto Abraham**—*q. d.*, 'Flatter not yourselves with the fond delusion that God stands in need of you, to make good his promise of a seed to Abraham; for I tell you that, though you were all to perish, God is able to raise up a seed to Abraham out of those stones as He was to take Abraham him-self out of the rock whence he was hewn, out of the

9 repentance: and think not to say within yourselves, We 'have Abraham
to *our* father: for I say unto you, that God is able of these stones to
10 raise up children unto Abraham.　And now also the ax is laid unto the
root of the trees: *ᵐ*therefore every tree which bringeth not forth good
11 fruit is hewn down, and cast into the fire.　I *ⁿ*indeed baptize you with
water unto repentance: but he that cometh after me is mightier than I,
whose shoes I am not worthy to bear: *°*he shall baptize you with the

A. D. 26.

ˡ John 8. 33.
Acts 13. 26.
ᵐ ch. 7. 19.
John 15. 6.
ⁿ Mark 1. 8.
Luke 3. 16.
° Isa. 4. 4.
Mal. 3. 2.

hole of the pit whence he was digged' (Isa li. 1.)
Though the stern speaker may have pointed as
he spake to the pebbles of the bare clay hills that
lay around (so *Stanley's* "Sinai and Palestine"), it
was clearly the calling of the *Gentiles*—at that time
stone-dead in their sins, and quite as unconscious
of it—into the room of unbelieving and disinherited
Israel that he meant thus to indicate. (See ch.
xxi. 43; Rom. xi. 20, 30.) **10. And now also** ['Ήδη
δὲ καὶ]—'And even already'—**the ax is laid unto**
[κεῖται]—'lieth at'—**the root of the trees**—as it were
ready to strike; an expressive figure of impending
judgment, only to be averted in the way next described. **therefore every tree which bringeth not
forth good fruit is hewn down, and cast into the
fire.** Language so personal and individual as this
can scarcely be understood of any national judgment like the approaching destruction of Jerusalem, with the breaking up of the Jewish polity
and the extrusion of the chosen people from their
peculiar privileges which followed it; though this
would serve as the dark shadow, cast before, of a
more terrible retribution to come. The "fire,"
which in another verse is called "unquenchable,"
can be no other than that future "torment" of the
impenitent, whose "smoke ascendeth up for ever
and ever," and which by the Judge Himself is
styled "everlasting punishment" (Matt. xxv. 46).
What a strength, too, of just indignation is in that
word "cast" or "flung into the fire!" [βάλλεται].
The Third Gospel here adds the following important particulars, Luke iii. 10-16: *V.* 10. "And
the people"—rather, 'the multitudes' [οἱ ὄχλοι]—
"asked him, saying, What shall we do then?"—
that is, to show the sincerity of our repentance.
V. 11. "He answereth and saith unto them, He
that hath two coats, let him impart to him that
hath none; and he that hath meat"—'provisions,' 'victuals' [βρώματα]—"let him do likewise." This is directed against the reigning
avarice and selfishness. (Compare the corresponding precepts of the Sermon on the Mount, ch.
v. 40-42.) *V.* 12. "Then came also the publicans
to be baptized, and said unto him, Master," or
'Teacher' [Διδάσκαλε], "what shall we do?"—
in what special way is the genuineness of our repentance to be manifested? *V.* 13. "And he said
unto them, Exact no more than that which is appointed you." This is directed against that extortion which made the publicans a by-word. (See
on ch. v. 46; and on Luke xv. 1.) *V.* 14. "And
the soldiers"—rather, 'And soldiers' [στρατευ-
όμενοι]—the word means 'soldiers on active duty'—
"likewise demanded (or asked) of him, saying,
And what shall we do? And he said unto them,
Do violence to," or 'Intimidate' [διασείσητε], "no
man." The word signifies to 'shake thoroughly,'
and refers probably to the extorting of money or
other property. "neither accuse any falsely"—by
acting as informers vexatiously on frivolous or false
pretexts—"and be content with your wages," or
'rations' [τοῖς ὀψωνίοις ὑμῶν]. We may take this,
say *Webster and Wilkinson,* as a warning against
mutiny, which the officers attempted to suppress
by largesses and donations. And thus the "fruits"
which would evidence their repentance were just
resistance to the reigning sins—particularly of the

class to which the penitent belonged—and the
manifestation of an opposite spirit. *V.* 15. "And
as the people were in expectation"—in a state of
excitement, looking for something new—"and all
men mused in their hearts of John, whether he
were the Christ, or not" [μήποτε αὐτὸς εἴη ὁ Χρισ-
τὸς]—rather, 'whether he himself might be the
Christ.' The structure of this clause implies that
they could hardly think it, but yet could not help
asking themselves whether it might not be; showing both how successful he had been in awakening
the expectation of Messiah's immediate appearing,
and the high estimation, and even reverence, which
his own character commanded. *V.* 16. "John answered"—either to that deputation from Jerusalem, of which we read in John i. 19, &c., or on some
other occasion, to remove impressions derogatory
to his blessed Master, which he knew to be taking
hold of the popular mind—" saying unto them all"
—in solemn protestation: (We now return to the
First Gospel.)
**11. I indeed baptize you with water unto re-
pentance** (see on *v.* 6): **but he that cometh
after me is mightier than I.** In Mark and Luke
this is more emphatic—"But there cometh the
Mightier than I" [ἔρχεται δὲ ὁ ἰσχυρότερός μου].
whose shoes, or 'sandals' [ὑποδήματα], **I am not
worthy to bear.** The sandals were tied and un-
tied, and borne about by the meanest servants.
he shall baptize you [Αὐτὸς]—the emphatic "He;"
'He it is,' to the exclusion of all others 'that shall
baptize you.' **with the Holy Ghost.** 'So far from
entertaining such a thought as laying claim to the
honours of Messiahship, the meanest services I can
render to that "Mightier than I that is coming
after me" are too high an honour for me; I am but
the servant, but the Master is coming; I administer but the outward symbol of purification; His it
is, as His sole prerogative, to dispense the inward
reality.' Beautiful spirit, distinguishing this servant of Christ throughout! **and with fire.** To
take this as a distinct baptism from that of the
Spirit—a baptism of the impenitent with hell-fire
—is exceedingly unnatural. Yet this was the view
of *Origen* among the Fathers; and among moderns,
of *Neander, Meyer, de Wette,* and *Lange.* Nor is it
much better to refer it to the fire of the great day,
by which the earth and the works that are therein
shall be burned up. Clearly, as we think, it is but
the *fiery* character of the Spirit's operations upon
the soul—searching, consuming, refining, sublimat-
ing—as nearly all good interpreters understand
the words. And thus, in two successive clauses,
the two most familiar emblems—*water* and *fire*—are
employed to set forth the same purifying operations
of the Holy Ghost upon the soul. **12. Whose** [win-
nowing] **fan is in his hand**—ready for use. This is
no other than the preaching of the Gospel, even
now beginning, the effect of which would be to
separate the solid from the spiritually worthless,
as wheat, by the winnowing fan, from the chaff.
(Compare the similar representation in Mal. iii. 1-
3.) **and he will throughly purge** [διακαθαριεῖ] **his**
[threshing] **floor**—that is, the visible Church. **and
gather his wheat**—His true-hearted saints; so
called for their solid worth (cf. Amos ix. 9; Luke
xxii. 31). **into the garner**—"the kingdom of their

12 Holy Ghost, and *with* fire: whose [p]fan *is* in his hand, and he will
throughly purge his floor, and gather his wheat into the garner; but he
will [q]burn up the chaff with unquenchable fire.

A. D. 26.

[p] Mal. 3. 3.
[q] Mal. 4. 1. ch. 13. 30.

Father," as this "garner" or "barn" [ἀποθήκη] is beautifully explained by our Lord in the parable of the Wheat and the Tares (ch. xiii. 30, 43). **but he will burn up the chaff**—empty, worthless professors of religion, void of all solid religious principle and character (see Ps. i. 4). **with unquenchable fire.** Singular is the strength of this apparent contradiction of figures:—to be burnt up, but with a fire that is unquenchable; the one expressing the *utter destruction* of all that constitutes one's true life, the other the *continued consciousness of existence* in that awful condition.

Luke adds the following important particulars, iii. 18-20: *V.* 18. "And many other things in his exhortation preached he unto the people," showing that we have here but an abstract of his teaching. Besides what we read in John i. 29, 33, 34; iii. 27-36; the incidental allusion to His having taught His disciples to pray (Luke xi. 1)—of which not a word is said elsewhere—shows how varied His teaching was. *V.* 19. "But Herod the tetrarch, being reproved by him for Herodias his brother Philip's wife, and for all the evils which Herod had done." In this last clause we have an important fact, here only mentioned, showing how *thorough-going* was the fidelity of the Baptist to his royal hearer, and how strong must have been the workings of conscience in that slave of passion when, notwithstanding such plainness, he "did many things, and heard John gladly" (Mark vi. 20). *V.* 20. "Added yet this above all, that he shut up John in prison." This imprisonment of John, however, did not take place for some time after this; and it is here recorded merely because the Evangelist did not intend to recur to his history till he had occasion to relate the message which he sent to Christ from his prison at Machærus (Luke vii. 18, &c.).

Remarks.—1. If the view we have given of the import of John's ministry be correct, it has its counterpart in the divine procedure towards each individual believer. In the transition of the Church from Moses to Christ—from the Law to the Gospel—the ministry of the forerunner was expressly provided, in order to bear in upon the national conscience the sense of sin, and shut it up to the coming Deliverer. The dispensation even of the Law itself was introduced, we are told, for the same purpose—merely as a transition-stage from Adam to Christ. "The Law *entered*," says the apostle—'entered incidentally' or 'parenthetically' [παρεισῆλθεν]—"that the offence might abound" (see on Rom. v. 20). The promulgation of the Law was no primary or essential feature of the divine plan. It "was added" [προσετέθη] (Gal. iii. 19) for a subordinate purpose—the more fully to reveal the evil that had been done by Adam, and the need and glory of the remedy by Christ. Thus, as in every age God has provided special means for making the need of salvation, and the value of His Son as a Saviour, felt on a wide scale by the obtuse conscience, so in the history of every believer it will be found that the cordial reception of Christ, as all his salvation and all his desire, has been preceded by some *forerunning* dispensation of mercy; in some cases lengthened and slow, in others brief and rapid—in some operating perceptibly enough, in others all unconsciously—but in every case real and necessary, as "a schoolmaster, to bring us unto Christ." 2. The Pharisees and Sadducees were not *sects*, in the modern sense of that term—holding no ecclesiastical fellowship with each other—but rather *schools* or *parties*, antagonistic both in principle and feeling. The Pharisees were the zealots of outward, literal, legal Judaism—not, however, as represented in Scripture, but as interpreted, or rather perverted, by the traditions which had from age to age grown up around it, penetrated to its core, and eaten into its life. The Sadducees, occupying sceptical or rationalistic ground, were, of course, anti-traditional; but they went much further, limiting their canon of Scripture—in effect if not professedly—to the Pentateuch, and explaining away almost everything supernatural even in it. The Essenes were a sect, it would appear, in the modern sense of the term; and so, not coming across the Evangelical territory, the Gospels are silent regarding them. Their religious system appears to have been a compound of Oriental, Alexandrian, and Jewish elements, while a peculiar ritualism in practice and asceticism in spirit kept them very much by themselves. In these religious divisions of the Jews at this time, we have but the representatives for the time being of abiding and outstanding forms of religious thought—of that traditionary *formalism*, that sceptical *rationalism*, and that separative *mysticism*, which, with various modifications in kind and degree, divide among themselves the unwholesome thinking and feeling of Christendom at this day. And just as then, so still, the medicine which will alone heal the Church visible, and make it "white and ruddy" with spiritual health and vigour, lies in those three notes of the Baptist's teaching—"Flee from the wrath to come;" "Behold the Lamb of God which taketh away the sin of the world;" "He shall baptize you with the Holy Ghost and with fire!" 3. In times of religious awakening, the most unpromising classes are sometimes found making a religious profession. But, whatever just suspicions this may awaken, where the change is not very marked, let not the preacher repel any who even seem to be turning to the Lord, but, like the Baptist, temper his faithful warnings with encouragements and directions. 4. How sharp is the contrast here drawn between all mere human agency in the salvation of men and that of the Master of whom John here speaks. When John, the greatest of all the prophets, says of his own agency, "I indeed baptize you with water unto repentance," he manifestly means not only that this was all he could do towards their salvation, but that it was all *outside* work; he could not work repentance in them, nor deposit in their hearts one grain of true grace. When, therefore, he adds, "He that cometh after me is mightier than I; He shall baptize you with the Holy Ghost, and with fire," beyond doubt he means to teach not only that Christ could do what he could not, but that it was His sole prerogative to do it—as "the Mightier than he" (Mark i. 7; Luke iii. 16)—imparting the inner element, of which water-baptism was but the outward sign, and giving it a glorious, fiery efficacy in the heart. No wonder that at the thought of this difference John should say, "Whose shoes' latchet I am not worthy to bear"—language very offensive if we could suppose it meant of any mere *creature*, however gifted and honoured of God, but most fit and proper regarding *Emmanuel*, "God with us." 5. As the saving operations of the Holy Ghost are here first mentioned in the New Testament, so His precise relation to Christ in the economy of

13   Then cometh Jesus ^rfrom Galilee to Jordan unto John, to be baptized of
14 him. But John forbade him, saying, I have need to be baptized of thee,
15 and comest thou to me? And Jesus answering said unto him, Suffer *it to*
    be so now; for thus it becometh us to ^sfulfil all righteousness. Then he
16 suffered him. And ^tJesus, when he was baptized, went up straightway

A. D. 26.
^r ch. 2. 22.
^s Dan. 9. 24.
^t Mark 1. 10.
Luke 3. 21.

---

salvation is here distinctly taught—that He is *Christ's Agent,* carrying into effect *in* men all that He did *for* men. 6. The vengeance here denounced against impenitence under all this spiritual culture best exhibits the guilt of it—"Every tree, therefore, which bringeth not forth good fruit is hewn down, and cast into the fire." "Be instructed, then, O Jerusalem, lest my soul depart from thee."

13-17.—Baptism of Christ, and Descent of the Spirit upon Him immediately thereafter. (= Mark i. 9-11; Luke iii. 21, 22; John i. 31-34.)

Baptism of Christ (13-15). **13. Then cometh Jesus from Galilee to Jordan unto John, to be baptized of him.** Moses rashly anticipated the Divine call to deliver his people, and for this was fain to flee the house of bondage, and wait in obscurity for forty years more (Ex. ii. 11, &c.). But so this Greater than Moses. All but thirty years had He now spent in privacy at Nazareth, gradually ripening for His public work, and calmly awaiting the time appointed of the Father. Now it had arrived; and this movement from Galilee to Jordan is the step, doubtless, of deepest interest to all heaven since that first one which brought Him into the world. Luke (iii. 21) has this important addition—"Now *when all the people were baptized,* it came to pass, that Jesus being baptized," &c.—implying that Jesus waited till all other applicants for baptism that day had been disposed of, ere He stepped forward, that He might not seem to be merely one of the crowd. Thus, as He rode into Jerusalem upon an ass "whereon yet never man sat" (Luke xix. 30), and lay in a sepulchre "wherein was never man yet laid" (John xix. 41), so in His baptism too He would be "separate from sinners." **14. But John forbade him** [διεκώλυεν] —rather, 'was [in the act of] hindering him,' or 'attempting to hinder him'—**saying, I have need to be baptized of thee, and comest thou to me?** (How John came to recognize Him, when he says he knew Him not, see on John i. 31-34.) The emphasis of this most remarkable speech lies all in the pronouns ['Εγὼ ὑπὸ σοῦ . . . καὶ σὺ . . . πρός με]: 'What! Shall the Master come for baptism to the servant—the sinless Saviour to a sinner?' That thus much is in the Baptist's words will be clearly seen if it be observed that he evidently regarded Jesus as *Himself needing no purification,* but rather *qualified to impart it to those who did.* And do not all his other testimonies to Christ fully bear out this sense of the words? But it were a pity if, in the glory of this testimony to Christ, we should miss the beautiful spirit in which it was borne—'Lord, must *I* baptize *Thee?* Can I bring myself to do such a thing?'—reminding us of Peter's exclamation at the supper-table, "Lord, dost Thou wash my feet?" while it has nothing of the false humility and presumption which dictated Peter's next speech, "Thou shalt never wash my feet" (John xiii. 6, 8). **15. And Jesus answering said unto him, Suffer it to be so now** ['Αφες ἄρτι]—'Let it pass for the present' (*Webster and Wilkinson*); *q. d.*, 'Thou recoilest, and no wonder, for the seeming incongruity is startling; but in the present case do as thou art bidden.' **for thus it becometh us**—"*us,*" not in the sense of 'me and thee,' or 'men in general,'

but as in John iii. 11. **to fulfil all righteousness** [πᾶσαν δικαιοσύνην]. If this be rendered, with *Scrivener,* 'every ordinance,' or, with *Campbell,* 'every institution,' the meaning is obvious enough; and the same sense is brought out by "all righteousness," or compliance with everything enjoined, baptism included. Indeed, if this be the meaning, our version perhaps best brings out the force of the opening word "Thus" [οὕτως]. But we incline to think that our Lord meant more than this. The import of Circumcision and of Baptism seems to be radically the same. And if our remarks on the circumcision of our Lord (on Luke ii. 21-24) are well founded, He would seem to have said, 'Thus do I impledge myself to the whole righteousness of the Law—thus symbolically do enter on and engage to fulfil it all.' Let the thoughtful reader weigh this. **Then he suffered him**—with true humility, yielding to higher authority than his own impressions of propriety.

Descent of the Spirit upon the Baptized Redeemer (16, 17). **16. And Jesus, when he was baptized, went up straightway out of** [ἀπὸ]—rather, 'from'—**the water.** Mark has "out of the water" [ἐκ]. **and** —adds Luke (iii. 21), "while He was praying"—a grand piece of information. Can there be a doubt about the burden of that prayer; a prayer sent up, probably, while yet in the water—His blessed head suffused with the baptismal element; a prayer continued likely as He stepped out of the stream, and again stood upon the dry ground? The work before Him, the needed and expected Spirit to rest upon Him for it, and the glory He would then put upon the Father that sent Him—would not these fill His breast, and find silent vent in such form as this?—'Lo, I come; I delight to do thy will, O God. Father, glorify thy name. Show me a token for good. Let the Spirit of the Lord God come upon me, and I will preach the Gospel to the poor, and heal the broken-hearted, and send forth judgment unto victory.' Whilst He was yet speaking—lo, **the heavens were opened.** Mark says, sublimely, "He saw the heavens cleaving" [σχιζομένους]. **and he saw the Spirit of God descending**—that is, He only, with the exception of His honoured servant, as He tells us Himself, John 1. 32-34; the by-standers apparently seeing nothing. **like a dove, and lighting upon him.** Luke says, "in a bodily shape" (iii. 22); that is, the blessed Spirit, assuming the corporeal form of a dove, descended thus upon His sacred head. But why in this form? The Scripture use of this emblem will be our best guide here. "My dove, *my undefiled* is one," says the Song (vi. 9). This is chaste purity. Again, "Be ye *harmless* as doves," says Christ Himself (Matt. x. 16). This is the same thing, in the form of inoffensiveness towards men. "A conscience void of offence toward God and toward men" (Acts xxiv. 16) expresses both. Further, when we read in the Song (ii. 14), "O my dove, that art in the *clefts* of the rock, in the *secret places* of the stairs (see Isa. lx. 8), let me see thy countenance, let me hear thy voice; for sweet is thy voice, and thy countenance is comely"—it is shrinking modesty, meekness, gentleness, that is thus charmingly depicted. In a word—not to allude to the historical emblem of the dove that flew back to the ark, bearing in its

out of the water: and, lo, the heavens were opened unto him, and he saw

17 "the Spirit of God descending like a dove, and lighting upon him: and 'lo a voice from heaven, saying, This "is my beloved Son, in whom I am well pleased.

4   THEN was ^aJesus led up of ^bthe Spirit into the wilderness to be

A. D. 26.	
^u Isa. 11. 2.	
^v John 12. 28.	
^w Ps. 2. 7.	
^a Mark 1. 12.	
^b 1 Ki. 18. 12.	

mouth the olive leaf of *peace* (Gen. viii. 11)—when we read (Ps. lxviii. 13), "Ye shall be as the wings of a dove covered with silver, and her feathers with yellow gold," it is *beauteousness* that is thus held forth. And was not such that "Holy, harmless, undefiled One," the "Separate from sinners?" "Thou art fairer than the children of men; grace is poured into Thy lips; therefore God hath blessed Thee for ever!" But the fourth Gospel gives us one more piece of information here, on the authority of one who saw and testified of it: "John bare record, saying, I saw the Spirit descending from heaven like a dove, and IT ABODE UPON HIM" [καὶ ἔμεινεν ἐπ' αὐτόν]. And lest we should think that this was an accidental thing, he adds that this last particular was expressly given him as part of the sign by which he was to recognize and identify Him as the Son of God: "And I knew Him not: but He that sent me to baptize with water, the same said unto me, Upon whom thou shalt see the Spirit descending AND REMAINING ON HIM [καὶ μένον ἐπ' αὐτόν], the same is He which baptizeth with the Holy Ghost. And I saw, and bare record that this is the Son of God" (John i. 32-34). And when with this we compare the predicted descent of the Spirit upon Messiah (Isa. xi. 2), "And *the Spirit of the Lord shall rest upon him*" [נָחָה, ἀναπαύσεται], we cannot doubt that it was this permanent and perfect resting of the Holy Ghost upon the Son of God—now and henceforward in His *official* capacity—that was here visibly manifested. **17. And lo a voice from heaven, saying, This is**—Mark and Luke give it in the direct form, "Thou art"—**my beloved Son, in whom I am well pleased** [εὐδόκησα]. The verb is put in the aorist to express absolute complacency, once and for ever felt towards Him. The English here, at least to modern ears, is scarcely strong enough. 'I delight' comes the nearest, perhaps, to that ineffable *complacency* which is manifestly intended; and this is the rather to be preferred, as it would immediately carry the thoughts back to that august Messianic prophecy to which the voice from heaven plainly alluded (Isa. xlii. 1), "Behold my Servant, whom I uphold; mine Elect, IN WHOM MY SOUL DELIGHTETH" [רָצְתָה]. Nor are the words which follow to be overlooked, "I have put my Spirit upon Him; He shall bring forth judgment to the Gentiles." (The LXX. pervert this, as they do most of the Messianic predictions, interpolating the word "Jacob," and applying it to the Jews.) Was this voice heard by the by-standers? From Matthew's form of it, one might suppose it so designed; but it would appear that it was not, and 'probably John only heard and saw anything peculiar about that great baptism. Accordingly, the words "Hear ye Him" are not added, as at the Transfiguration.

Remarks.—1. Here we have three of the most astonishing things which eye could behold and ear hear. *First,* We have Jesus formally entered and articled to His Father, contracted and engaged, going voluntarily under the yoke, and by a public deed sealed over to obedience. *Next,* We have Him consecrated and anointed with the Holy Ghost above measure (John iii. 34); and thus thoroughly furnished, divinely equipped for the work given Him to do. *Thirdly,* We have Him divinely attested by Him who knew Him best and

cannot lie; and thus publicly inaugurated, formally installed in all the authority of His mediatorial office, as the Son of God in the flesh, and the Object of His Father's absolute complacency. 2. That the Holy Ghost, whose supernatural agency formed the human nature of Christ, and sanctified it from the womb, was a stranger to the breast of Jesus until now that He descended upon Him at His baptism, is not for a moment to be conceived. The whole analogy of Scripture, on the work of the Spirit and of sanctification, leads to the conclusion that as He "grew in favour with God and man," from infancy to youth, and from youth to manhood, His moral beauty, His spiritual loveliness, His faultless excellence, was enstamped and developed from stage to stage by the gentle yet efficacious energy of the Holy Ghost; though only at His full maturity was He capable of all that fulness which He then received. To use the words of *Olshausen,* 'Even the pure offspring of the Spirit needed the anointing of the Spirit; and it was only when His human nature had grown strong enough for the support of the fulness of the Spirit that it remained stationary, and fully endowed with power from above.' Knowing, therefore, as we do, that at His baptism He passed out of private into public life, we can have no doubt that the descent of the Spirit upon Christ at His baptism was for *official* purposes. But in this we include His whole public work—life, character, spirit, carriage, actings, endurances, everything that constituted and manifested Him to be the pure, inoffensive, gentle, beauteous "DOVE"—all this was of the Spirit of the Lord that "*rested*"—that "*abode*"—upon Him. How well may the Church now sing, "God, thy God, hath anointed Thee with the oil of gladness above thy fellows. All thy garments smell of myrrh, and aloes, and cassia, out of the ivory palaces, whereby they have made Thee glad!" (Ps. xlv. 7, 8.) 3. Here, in the baptism of our blessed Head, we find ourselves in the presence at once of THE FATHER, THE SON, and THE HOLY GHOST, into whose adorable name we are baptized (ch. xxviii. 19). The early Fathers of the Church were struck with this, and often advert to it. 'Go to Jordan,' said *Augustin* to the heretic Marcion, 'and thou shalt see the Trinity' [*I ad Jordanem et videbis Trinitatem*]. Nor is it to be overlooked, as *Lange* remarks, that as it is at Christ's own baptism that we have the first distinct revelation of the doctrine of the Trinity, so it is at the institution of baptism for His Church that this doctrine brightens into full glory.

CHAP. IV. 1-11.—TEMPTATION OF CHRIST. (= Mark i. 12, 13; Luke iv. 1-13.)

1. Then [Τότε]—an indefinite note of sequence. But Mark's word (i. 12) fixes what we should have presumed was meant, that it was "immediately" [εὐθὺς] after His baptism; and with this agrees the statement of Luke (iv. 1). **was Jesus led up** [ἀνήχθη] —*i. e.,* from the low Jordan valley to some more elevated spot. **of the Spirit**—that blessed Spirit immediately before spoken of as descending upon Him at His baptism, and abiding upon Him. Luke, connecting these two scenes, as if the one were but the sequel of the other, says, "Jesus, being full of the Holy Ghost, returned from Jordan, and was led," &c. Mark's expression has a startling sharpness about it—"Immediately the Spirit driveth

2 ᶜtempted of the devil. And when he had ᵈfasted forty days and forty nights, he was afterward an hungered.

3 And when the tempter came to him, he said, If thou be the Son of God,

4 command that these stones be made bread. But he answered and said, ᵉIt

A. D. 27.

ᶜ Heb. 4. 15.
ᵈ Ex. 34. 28.

ᵉ Eph. 6. 17.

Him" [ἐκβάλλει], 'putteth,' or 'hurrieth, Him forth,' or 'impelleth Him.' (See the same word in Mark i. 43; v. 40; Matt. ix. 25; xiii. 52; John x. 4.) The thought thus strongly expressed is the mighty constraining impulse of the Spirit under which He went; while Matthew's more gentle expression, "was led up," intimates how purely voluntary on His own part this action was. **into the wilderness**—probably the wild Judean desert. The particular spot which tradition has fixed upon has hence got the name of *Quarantana* or *Quarantaria*, from the forty days,—'an almost perpendicular wall of rock twelve or fifteen hundred feet above the plain.' —*Robinson's* Palestine. The supposition of those who incline to place the Temptation amongst the mountains of Moab is, we think, very improbable. **to be tempted** [πειρασθῆναι]. The Greek word [πειράζειν] means simply to *try* or make proof of; and when ascribed to God in His dealings with men, it means, and can mean no more than this. Thus, Gen. xxii. 1, "It came to pass that God did tempt Abraham," or put his faith to a severe proof. (See Deut. viii. 2.) But for the most part in Scripture the word is used in a bad sense, and means to entice, solicit, or provoke to sin. Hence the name here given to the wicked one—"the tempter" (*v.* 3). Accordingly, "to be tempted" here is to be understood both ways. The Spirit conducted Him into the wilderness simply to have His faith *tried;* but as the agent in this trial was to be the wicked one, whose whole object would be to seduce Him from His allegiance to God, it was a *temptation* in the bad sense of the term. The unworthy inference which some would draw from this is energetically repelled by an apostle (Jas. i. 13-17). **of the devil.** The word [διάβολος] signifies a slanderer—one who casts imputations upon another. Hence that other name given him (Rev. xii. 10), "The accuser of the brethren, who accuseth them before our God day and night." Mark (i. 13) says, "He was forty days tempted of *Satan*" [שָׂטָן], a word signifying an *adversary*, one who lies in wait for, or sets himself in opposition to another. These and other names of the same fallen spirit point to different features in his character or operations. What was the high design of this? First, as we judge, to give our Lord a taste of what lay before Him in the work He had undertaken; next, to make trial of the glorious furniture for it which He had just received; further, to give Him encouragement, by the victory now to be won, to go forward spoiling principalities and powers, until at length He should make a show of them openly, triumphing over them in His Cross; that the tempter, too, might get a taste, at the very outset, of the new kind of material in *Man* which he would find he had here to deal with; finally, that He might acquire experimental ability "to succour them that are tempted" (Heb. ii. 18). The temptation evidently embraced two stages: the one continuing throughout the forty days' fast; the other, at the conclusion of that period. First Stage: **2. And when he had fasted forty days and forty nights.** Luke says, "When they were quite ended [συντελεσθεισῶν], **he was afterward** [ὕστερον] an hungered—evidently implying that the sensation of hunger was unfelt during all the forty days; coming on only at their close. So it was apparently with Moses (Ex. xxxiv. 28) and

Elijah (1 Ki. xix. 8) for the same period. (The ὕστερον in Luke iv. 2 has scarcely sufficient authority, and was probably introduced from Matthew.) A supernatural power of endurance was of course imparted to the body; but this probably operated through a natural law—the absorption of the Redeemer's spirit in the dread conflict with the tempter. (See on Acts ix. 9.) Had we only this Gospel, we should suppose the temptation did not begin till after this. But it is clear, from Mark's statement that "He was in the wilderness forty days tempted of Satan," and Luke's "being forty days tempted of the devil," that there was a forty days' temptation *before* the three specific temptations afterwards recorded. And this is what we have called the First Stage. What the precise nature and object of the forty days' temptation was is not recorded. But two things seem plain enough. First, the tempter had utterly failed of his object, else it had not been renewed; and the terms in which he opens his second attack imply as much. But further, the tempter's whole object during the forty days evidently was to get Him to distrust the heavenly testimony borne to Him at His baptism as THE SON OF GOD—to persuade Him to regard it as but a splendid illusion—and, generally, to dislodge from His breast the consciousness of His Sonship. With what plausibility the events of His previous history from the beginning would be urged upon Him in support of this temptation it is easy to imagine. And it makes much in support of this view of the forty days' temptation, that the particulars of it are not recorded; for how the details of such a purely internal struggle could be recorded it is hard to see. If this be correct, how naturally does the SECOND STAGE of the temptation open! In Mark's brief notice of the temptation there is one expressive particular not given either by Matthew or by Luke—that "He was with the wild beasts," no doubt to add terror to solitude, and aggravate the horrors of the whole scene.

3. And when the tempter came to him. Evidently we have here a new scene. **he said, If thou be the Son of God, command that these stones be made bread** [ἄρτοι]—rather, 'loaves,' answering to "stones" in the plural; whereas Luke, having said, "Command this stone," in the singular, adds, "that it be made bread" [ἄρτος] in the singular. The sensation of hunger, unfelt during all the forty days, seems now to have come on in all its keenness—no doubt to open a door to the tempter, of which he is not slow to avail himself: *q. d.*, 'Thou still clingest to that vainglorious confidence, that thou art the Son of God, carried away by those illusory scenes at the Jordan. Thou wast born in a stable—but thou art the Son of God! hurried off to Egypt for fear of Herod's wrath—but thou art the Son of God! a carpenter's roof supplied thee with a home, and, in the obscurity of a despicable town of Galilee thou hast spent thirty years—yet still thou art the Son of God; and a voice from heaven, it seems, proclaimed it in thine ears at the Jordan! Be it so; but after *that*, surely thy days of obscurity and trial should have an end. Why linger for weeks in this desert, wandering among the wild beasts and craggy rocks, unhonoured, unattended, unpitied, ready to starve for want of the necessaries of life? Is this befitting "the Son of God?" At the bidding of

16

is written, Man *f* shall not live by bread alone, but by every word that proceedeth out of the mouth of God.

5 Then the devil taketh him up *g* into the holy city, and setteth him
6 on a pinnacle of the temple, and saith unto him, If thou be the Son of God, cast thyself down: for it is written, He *h* shall give his angels charge concerning thee; and in *their* hands they shall bear thee up, lest at any
7 time thou dash thy foot against a stone. Jesus said unto him, It is written again, Thou *i* shalt not tempt the Lord thy God.
8 Again, the devil taketh him up into an exceeding high mountain, and

A. D. 27.

f Deut. 8. 3.
g Neh. 11. 1.
   Isa. 48. 2;
   52. 1.
h Ps. 91. 11.
   Heb. 1. 14.
i Ex. 17. 2, 7.
   Num. 14. 22.
   Deut. 6. 16.
   Mal. 3. 15.

"the Son of God" sure those stones shall all be turned into loaves, and in a moment present an abundant repast?' **4. But he answered and said, It is written** (Deut. viii. 3), **Man shall not live by bread alone**—more emphatically, as in the Greek, 'Not by bread alone shall man live'—**but by every word that proceedeth out of the mouth of God.** Of all passages in Old Testament scripture, none could have been pitched upon more apposite, perhaps not one so apposite, to our Lord's purpose. 'The Lord led thee (said Moses to Israel, at the close of their journeyings) these forty years in the wilderness, to humble thee, and to prove thee, to know what was in thine heart, whether thou wouldest keep his commandments, or no. And he humbled thee, and suffered thee to hunger, and fed thee with manna, which thou knewest not, neither did thy fathers know; that he might make thee know that man doth not live by bread only," &c. 'Now, if Israel spent, not forty days, but forty years in a waste, howling wilderness, where there were no means of human subsistence, not starving, but divinely provided for, on purpose to prove to every age that human support depends not upon bread, but upon God's unfailing word of promise and pledge of all needful providential care, am I, distrusting this word of God, and despairing of relief, to take the law into my own hand? True, the Son of God is able enough to turn stones into bread: but what the Son of God is able to do is not the present question, but what is *Man's duty* under want of the necessaries of life. And as Israel's condition in the wilderness did not justify their unbelieving murmurings and frequent desperation, so neither would mine warrant the exercise of the power of the Son of God in snatching despairingly at unwarranted relief. As man, therefore, I will await divine supply, nothing doubting that at the fitting time it will arrive.' The *second* temptation in this Gospel is in Luke's the *third*. That Matthew's order is the right one will appear, we think, pretty clearly in the sequel. **5. Then the devil taketh him up** [παραλαμβάνει] —rather, 'conducteth him'—**into the holy city**— so called (as in Isa. xlviii. 2; Neh. xi. 1) from its being "the city of the Great King," the seat of the temple, the metropolis of all Jewish worship. **and setteth him on a pinnacle** [τὸ πτερύγιον]— rather, 'the pinnacle'—**of the temple**—a certain well-known projection. Whether this refer to the highest summit of the temple [the κορυφή], which bristled with golden spikes (*Joseph.* Antt. v. 5, 6); or whether it refer to another peak, on Herod's royal portico, overhanging the ravine of Kedron, at the valley of Hinnom—an immense tower built on the very edge of this precipice, from the top of which dizzy height Josephus says one could not look to the bottom (*Antt.* xv. 11, 5)—is not certain; but the latter is probably meant. **6. And saith unto him, If thou be the Son of God.** As this temptation starts with the same point as the first—our Lord's determination not to be disputed out of His Sonship—it seems to us clear that the one came directly after the other; and as the remaining

temptation shows that the hope of carrying that point was abandoned, and all was staked upon a desperate venture, we think that remaining temptation is thus shown to be the last; as will appear still more when we come to it. **cast thyself down** ("from hence," Luke iv. 9): **for it is written** (Ps. xci. 11, 12). 'But what is this I see?' exclaims stately *Bishop Hall*, 'Satan himself with a Bible under his arm and a text in his mouth!' Doubtless the tempter, having felt the power of God's word in the former temptation, was eager to try the effect of it from his own mouth (2 Cor. xi. 14). **He shall give his angels charge concerning thee; and in**—rather, 'on' [ἐπί]—**their hands they shall bear thee up, lest at any time thou dash thy foot against a stone.** The quotation is precisely as it stands in the Hebrew and LXX., save that after the first clause the words, "to keep thee in all thy ways," is here omitted. Not a few good expositors have thought that this omission was intentional, to conceal the fact that this would *not* have been one of "His ways," that is, of duty. But as our Lord's reply makes no allusion to this, but seizes on the great principle involved in the promise quoted; so when we look at the promise itself, it is plain that the sense of it is precisely the same whether the clause in question be inserted or not. **7. Jesus said unto him, It is written again** (Deut. vi. 16)—*q. d.*, 'True, it is so written, and on that promise I implicitly rely; but in using it there is another scripture which must not be forgotten, **Thou shalt not tempt the Lord thy God.** Preservation in danger is divinely pledged: shall I then *create* danger, either to put the promised security sceptically to the proof, or wantonly to demand a display of it? That were to "tempt the Lord my God," which, being expressly forbidden, would forfeit the right to expect preservation.'

8. Again, the devil taketh him up—'conducteth him,' as before—**into,** or 'unto,' **an exceeding high mountain, and showeth him all the kingdoms of the world, and the glory of them.** Luke (iv. 5) adds the important clause, "in a moment of time;" a clause which seems to furnish a key to the true meaning. That a scene was presented to our Lord's natural eye seems plainly expressed. But to limit this to the most extensive scene which the natural eye could take in, is to give a sense to the expression, "all the kingdoms of the world," quite violent. It remains, then, to gather from the expression, "in a moment of time"—which manifestly is intended to intimate some supernatural operation—that it was permitted to the tempter to extend preternaturally for a moment our Lord's range of vision, and throw a "glory" or glitter over the scene of vision; a thing not inconsistent with the analogy of other scriptural statements regarding the permitted operations of the wicked one. In this case, the "exceeding height" of the "mountain" from which this sight was beheld would favour the effect intended to be produced. **9. And saith unto him, All these things will I give thee**—"and the glory of them," adds Luke. But

9 showeth him all the kingdoms of the world, and the glory of them; and
  saith unto him, All these things will I give thee, if thou wilt fall down
10 and worship me. Then saith Jesus unto him, Get thee hence, Satan: for
  it is written, *j*Thou shalt worship the Lord thy God, and him only shalt

A. D. 27.

j Deut. 6. 13;
10. 20.
Jos. 24. 14.
1 Sam. 7. 3.

Matthew having already said that this was "showed Him," did not need to repeat it here. Luke (iv. 6) adds these other very important clauses, here omitted—"for that is," or 'has been,' "delivered unto me, and to whomsoever I will I give it." Was this wholly false? That were not like Satan's usual policy, which is to insinuate his lies under cover of some truth. What truth, then, is there here? We answer, Is not Satan thrice called by our Lord Himself, "the prince of this world?" (John xii. 31; xiv. 30; xvi. 11;) does not the apostle call him "the God of this world?" (2 Cor. iv. 4;) and still further, is it not said that Christ came to destroy by His death "him that *hath the power of death,* that is, the devil?" (Heb. ii. 14.) No doubt these passages only express men's voluntary subjection to the rule of the wicked one while they live, and his power to surround death to them, when it comes, with all the terrors of the wages of sin. But as this is a real and terrible sway, so all Scripture represents men as righteously sold under it. In this sense he speaks what is not devoid of truth, when he says, "All this is delivered unto me." But how does he deliver this "to whomsoever he will?" As employing whomsoever he pleases of his willing subjects in keeping men under his power. In this case his offer to our Lord was that of a *deputed* supremacy commensurate with his own, though as *his gift* and for *his ends.* **if thou wilt fall down** and **worship me.** This was the sole, but monstrous condition. No Scripture, it will be observed, is quoted now, because none could be found to support so blasphemous a claim. In fact, he has ceased now to present his temptations under the mask of piety, and stands out unblushingly as the rival of God Himself in his claims on the homage of men. Despairing of success as an angel of light, he throws off all disguise, and with a splendid bribe solicits divine honour. This again shows that we are now at the last of the temptations, and that Matthew's order is the true one. **10. Then saith Jesus unto him, Get thee hence, Satan.** (The evidence for the *insertion* here of the words ὀπίσω μου—'behind me,'—and the *omission* of them in Luke iv. 8, is nearly equal; but perhaps the received text in both places has slightly the better support.) Since the tempter has now thrown off the mask, and stands forth in his true character, our Lord no longer deals with him as a pretended friend and pious counsellor, but calls him by his right name—His knowledge of which from the outset He had carefully concealed till now—and orders him off. This is the final and conclusive evidence, as we think, that Matthew's must be the right order of the temptations. For who can well conceive of the tempter's returning to the assault after this, in the pious character again, and hoping still to dislodge the consciousness of His Sonship; while our Lord must in that case be supposed to quote Scripture to one He had called the Devil to his face—thus throwing His pearls before worse than swine? **for it is written** (Deut. vi. 13): Thus does our Lord part with Satan on the rock of Scripture, **Thou shalt worship.** In the Hebrew and LXX. it is, "Thou shalt *fear;*" but as the sense is the same, so "worship" is here used to show emphatically that what the tempter claimed was precisely what God had forbidden. **the Lord thy God, and him only shalt thou serve.** The word "serve" [λατρεύσεις], in the second clause, is one never

used by the LXX. of any but *religious* service; and in this sense exclusively is it used in the New Testament, as we find it here. Once more the word "only," in the second clause—not expressed in the Hebrew and LXX.—is here added to bring out emphatically the *negative* and *prohibitory* feature of the command. (See Gal. iii. 10 for a similar supplement of the word "all," in a quotation from Deut. xxvii. 26.) 11. **Then the devil leaveth him.** Luke says, "And when the devil had exhausted"—or, 'quite ended' [συντελέσας], as in Luke iv. 2—"every [mode of] temptation [πάντα πειρασμόν], he departed from him till a season" [ἄχρι καιροῦ]. The definite "season" here indicated is expressly referred to by our Lord in John xiv. 30, and Luke xxii. 52, 53. **and, behold, angels came and ministered unto him**—or supplied Him with food, as the same expression means in Mark i. 31, and Luke viii. 3. Thus did angels to Elijah (1 Ki. xix. 5-8). Excellent critics think that they ministered, not food only, but supernatural support and cheer also. But this would be the natural *effect* rather than the direct *object* of the visit, which was plainly what we have expressed. And after having refused to claim the *illegitimate* ministration of angels in His behalf, O with what deep joy would He accept their services when sent, unasked, at the close of all this Temptation, direct from Him whom He had so gloriously honoured! What "angels' food" would this repast be to Him; and as He partook of it, might not a Voice from heaven be heard again, by any who could read the Father's mind, 'Said I not well, This is my beloved Son, in whom I am well pleased!'

Remarks.—1. After such an exalted scene as that of the Baptism, the Descent of the Spirit, and the Voice from heaven, and before entering on His public ministry, this long period of solitude would doubtless be to Jesus a precious interval for calmly pondering His whole past history, and deliberately weighing the momentous future that lay before Him. So would Moses feel his forty years' seclusion in Midian, far from the glitter and pomp of an Egyptian court, and before entering on the eventful career which awaited him on his return. So would Elijah, after the grandeur of the Carmel scene, feel his forty days' solitary journey to Horeb, the mount of God. So would the beloved disciple feel his Patmos exile, after a long apostolic life, short and uneventful though his after career was. So, doubtless, Luther felt his ten months' retreat in the castle of Wartburg to be, after four years of exciting and incessant warfare with the Romish perverters of the Gospel, and before entering afresh on a career which has changed the whole face of European Christendom. And so will such periods, whether longer or shorter, ever be felt by God's faithful people, when in His providence they are called to pass through them. 2. Sharp temptations, as they often follow seasons of high communion, so are they often preparatives for the highest work. 3. What a contrast does Christ here present to Adam! Adam was tempted in a paradise, and yet fell: Christ was tempted in a wilderness, and yet stood. Adam, in a state of innocence, was surrounded by the beasts of the field, all tame and submissive to their lord: Christ, in a fallen world, had the wild beasts raging around him, and only supernaturally restrained. In Adam we see man easily and quickly falling without a

18

11 thou serve. Then the devil *k* leaveth him; and, behold, *l* angels came and ministered unto him.

A. D. 27.

k Jas. 4. 7.
l Heb. 1. 14.

single incentive to evil save the tempter's insinuations: in Christ we see man standing encircled by all that is terrific, and harassed by long-continued, varied, and most subtle attacks from the tempter. 4. Deep is the disquietude which many Christians suffer from finding themselves subject to internal temptations to sin, both continuous and vehement. It staggers them to find that, without any external solicitations, they are tempted so frequently, and at times so violently, that as by a tempest they are ready to be carried away, and in a moment make shipwreck of faith and of a good conscience. Surely, they think, this can only be accounted for but by some depth and virulence of corruption never reached by the grace of God, and inconsistent with that delight in the law of God after the inward man which is characteristic of His children. But here we see, in the holy One of God, an example of solicitations to sin purely internal, for aught that we can perceive, continued throughout the long period of forty days. The *source* of them, it is true, was all external to the Redeemer's soul—they were from the devil solely—but the sphere of them was wholly internal; and it is impossible to doubt that, in order to their being temptations at all, there must have been permitted a vivid presentation by the tempter, to the mind of Jesus, of all that was adverse to His claims—so vivid, indeed, as to make entire and continued resistance a fruit of pure faith. And though probably no temptation of any strength and duration passes over the spirit of a Christian without finding some echo, however faint, and leaving some stain, however slight, the Example here presented should satisfy us that it is neither the duration nor the violence of our temptations—though they come as "fiery darts" (Eph. vi. 16) thick as hail—that tells the state of the heart before God, but *how they are met*. 5. It has long been a prevalent opinion that the three temptations here recorded were addressed to what the beloved disciple calls (1 John ii. 16) "the lust of the flesh (the first one), the lust of the eyes (Luke's second one), and the pride of life" (Luke's third one). Others also, as *Ellicott*, think they were addressed respectively to that three-fold division of our nature (1 Thes. v. 23)—the "body, soul, and spirit," in the same order. Whether this does not presuppose Luke's order of the temptations to be the right one, contrary to what we have endeavoured to show, we need not enquire. But too much should not be made of such things. One thing is certain, that after so long trying our Lord without success, and then proceeding to solicit Him from *without*, the tempter would leave no avenue to desire, either bodily or mental, unassailed; and so we may rest assured that He "was *in all points* tempted like as we are." The first temptation was to *distrust the providential care of God*—on the double plea that 'it had not come to the rescue in time of need,' and that 'He had the remedy in His own hands, and so need not be at a moment's loss.' This is repelled, not by denying His power to relieve Himself, but by holding up the sinfulness of distrusting God, which that would imply, and the duty, even in the most straitened circumstances, of unshaken confidence in God's word of promise, which is man's true life. O what a word is this for the multitudes of God's children who at times are at their wit's end for the things that are needful for the body—things easily to be had, could they but dare to snatch at them unlawfully, but which seem divinely with-

held from them at the very time when they appear most indispensable! The second temptation was to just the opposite of distrust (and this may further show that it *was* the second)—to *presumption* or a *wanton appeal to promised safety*, by creating the danger against which that safety is divinely pledged. And O how many err here! adventuring themselves where they have no warrant to expect protection, and there, exercising a misplaced confidence, are left to suffer the consequences of their presumption. The last temptation is addressed to the principle of *ambition*, which makes us accessible to the lust of possessions, grandeur, and power. These, to a boundless extent, and in all their glitter, are held forth to Jesus as His own, on one single condition—that He will do homage for them to another than God; which was but another way of saying, 'if thou wilt transfer thine allegiance from God to the devil.' It is just the case, then, which our Lord Himself afterwards put to His disciples, "What shall it profit a man if he should gain the whole world, and lose his own soul? Or what shall a man give in exchange for his soul?" And how many are there, naming the name of Christ, who, when, not the whole world, but a very fractional part of it, lies open before them as even likely to become theirs, on the single condition of selling their conscience to what they know to be sinful, give way, and incur the dreadful penalty; instead of resolutely saying, with Joseph, "How can I do this great wickedness, and sin against God," or, with a Greater than Joseph here, "Get thee behind me, Satan, for it is written, Thou shalt worship the Lord thy God, and Him only shalt thou serve." We thus see, however, that within the limits of this temptation-scene—however it be arranged and viewed—all the forms of human temptation were, in *principle*, experienced by "the Man Christ Jesus," and accordingly that "He was tempted in all points like as we are, yet without sin." 6. That the second stage of the Temptation was purely internal as well as the first—which is the theory of some otherwise sound critics, especially of Germany—is at variance with the obvious meaning of the text; creates greater difficulties than those it is intended to remove; is suggested by a spirit of subjective criticism which would explain away other external facts of the Evangelical History as well as this; and is rejected by nearly all orthodox interpreters, as well as repudiated by the simple-minded reader of the narrative. 7. What a testimony to the *divine authority of the Old Testament* have we here! Three quotations are made from it by our Lord—two of them from "the law," and one from "the Psalms"—all introduced by the simple formula, "*It is written*," as divinely settling the question of human duty in the cases referred to; while elsewhere, in quoting from the remaining division of the Old Testament—"the Prophets"—the same formula is employed by our Lord, "*It is written*," (Matt. xxi. 13, &c.) Nor will the theory of 'accommodation to the current views of the time'—as if that would justify an erroneous interpretation of the Old Testament to serve a present purpose—be of any service here. For here our Lord is not contending with the Jews, nor even in their presence, but with the foul tempter alone. Let any one take the trouble to collect and arrange our Lord's quotations from the Old Testament, and indirect references to it, and he will be constrained to admit either that the Old Testament is of divine authority, as a record of

19

12 Now ^{m}when Jesus had heard that John was ^{1}cast into prison, he
13 departed into Galilee; and leaving Nazareth, he came and dwelt in
Capernaum, which is upon the sea coast, in the borders of Zabulon and

A. D. 31.

^{m} Luke 3. 20.
^{1} Or, deliver-
ed up.

truth and directory of duty, because the Faithful and True Witness so regarded it, or if it be not, that Christ Himself was not above the erroneous views of the time and the people to which He belonged, and in regard tô the true character of the Old Testament was simply mistaken: a conclusion which some in our day who call themselves Christians have not shrunk from insinuating. 8. See how one may most effectually resist the devil. "The whole armour of God" is indeed to be used; but particularly "the sword of the Spirit, which is the Word of God"—so called because it is the Spirit that gives that Word living power, as God's own testimony, in the heart. As His divine and authoritative directory in duty against all the assaults of the tempter, Jesus wielded that sword of the Spirit with resistless power. To this secret of successful resistance the beloved disciple alludes when he says, "I have written unto you, young men, because ye are strong, and the Word of God abideth in you, and ye have overcome the wicked one" (1 John ii. 14). But 9. This presupposes, not only that the Scriptures are not impiously and cruelly withheld from the tempted children of God, but that they "search" them, and "meditate in them day and night." We have seen how remarkably apposite as well as ready was our Lord's use of Scripture; but this must have arisen from His constant study of it and experimental application of it to His own uses, both in the daily occupations of His previous life, and in the view of all that lay before Him. Nor will the tempted children of God find the Scriptures to be the ready sword of the Spirit in the hour of assault otherwise than their Lord did; but thus "resist the devil, and he will flee from you" (Jas. iv. 7): "Whom resist *stedfast in the faith*, knowing that the same afflictions are accomplished in your brethren that are in the world" (1 Pet. v. 9). 10. Let not God's dear children suffer themselves to be despoiled, by the tempter, of the sense of that high relationship. It is their strength as well as joy, not less really, though on a vastly lower scale, than it was their Lord's. 11. What can be more glorious, to those who see in Christ the only begotten of the Father, than the sense which Christ had, during all this temptation, of His standing, as *Man*, under the very same law of duty as His "brethren!" When tempted to supply His wants as man, by putting forth His power as the Son of God, He refused, because it was written that "MAN doth not live by bread only, but by every word of God," Again, when tempted to cast Himself down from the pinnacle of the temple, because the saints—even as many as "made the most High their habitation"—were under the charge of God's angels, He declined, because it was written, "Thou (meaning God's people, whether collectively or individually) shalt not tempt the Lord thy God." 'I therefore refuse to tempt the Lord *my* God.' Finally, when solicited, by a splendid bribe, to fall down and worship the tempter, He indignantly ordered him off with that scripture, "Thou shalt worship the Lord thy God, and Him only shalt thou serve." Evidently, Christ read that command as *addressed to Himself* as man; and on the rock of adoring subjection to the Lord as His God He is found standing at the close of this whole Temptation-scene. How identical with our entire tempted life does our Lord thus show His own to be! And what vividness and force does this give to the assurance that "in that He

Himself hath suffered, being tempted, He is able also to succour them that are tempted!" (Heb. ii. 18.) This way of viewing our Lord's victory over the tempter is far more natural and satisfactory than the quaint conceit of the Fathers, that our Lord, 'by His divinity, caught the tempter on the hook of His humanity.' Not but that there is a truth couched under it. But it is too much in the line of a vicious separation, in His actions, of the one nature from the other, in which they indulged, and is apt to make His human life and obedience appear fantastic and unreal. His personal divinity secured to Him that operation of the Spirit in virtue of which He was born the Holy Thing, and that continued action of the Spirit in virtue of which His holy humanity was gradually developed into the maturity and beauty of holy manhood; but when the Spirit descended upon Him at His baptism, it was for His whole official work; and in this, the very first scene of it, and one so precious, He overcame throughout as man, through the power of the Holy Ghost—His Godhead being the security that He should not and could not fail. 12. Henceforth there is no mention of Satan making any formal assault upon our Lord until the night before He suffered. Nor did he come then, as he did now, to try directly to seduce Him from His fidelity to God; but in the way of compassing His death, and by the hands of those whose part it was, if He were the Son of God, to acknowledge His claims. Once before, indeed, He said to Peter, "Get thee behind me, Satan" (Matt. xvi. 22, 23)—as if He had descried the tempter again stealthily approaching Him in the person of Peter, to make Him shrink from dying. And again, when the Greeks expressed their wish to see Him, He spoke mysteriously of His hour having come, and had a kind of agony by anticipation; but after it was over, He exclaimed, "Now is the judgment of this world; now shall the prince of this world be cast out" (John xii. 20-31)—as if, in the momentary struggle with the horrors of His final "hour," He had descried the tempter holding up this as his master-stroke for at length accomplishing His overthrow, but at the same time got a glimpse of the glorious victory over Satan which this final stroke of his policy was to prove. These, however, were but tentative approaches of the adversary. After the last supper, and ere they had risen from the table, our Lord said, "Henceforth [ἔτι] I will not talk much with you: for the *prince of this world cometh, and hath nothing in me*" (John xiv. 30); as if the moment of his "coming" were just at hand. At length, when in the garden they drew near to take Him, He said, "When I was daily with you in the temple, ye stretched forth no hands against me: *but this is* your hour, and *the power of darkness*" (Luke xxii. 52, 53). The tempter had "departed from Him till a season," and this at length is it. Not but that he was in everything that tried our Lord's stedfastness from first to last. But his formal and outstanding efforts against our Lord were at the *outset* and at the *close* of His career, and, as we have seen, of a very different nature the one from the other. Blessed Saviour, look upon our tempted condition here below; and what time the enemy cometh in upon us like a flood, by Thy good Spirit help us to tread in Thy footsteps: so shall we be more than conquerors through Him that loved us!

12-25.—CHRIST BEGINS HIS GALILEAN MINISTRY

20

14 Nephthalim: that it might be fulfilled which was spoken by Esaias the | A. D. 31.
15 prophet, saying, The ⁿland of Zabulon, and the land of Nephthalim, *by* the | ⁿ Isa. 9. 1, 2.

—CALLING OF PETER AND ANDREW, JAMES AND JOHN—HIS FIRST GALILEAN CIRCUIT. (= Mark i. 14-20, 35-39; Luke iv. 14, 15.)

There is here a notable gap in the History, which but for the fourth Gospel we should never have discovered. From the former Gospels we should have been apt to draw three inferences, which from the fourth one we know to be erroneous: First, that our Lord awaited the close of John's ministry, by his arrest and imprisonment, before beginning His own; next, that there was but a brief interval between the baptism of our Lord and the imprisonment of John; and further, that our Lord not only opened His work in Galilee, but never ministered out of it, and never visited Jerusalem at all nor kept a Passover till He went thither to become "our Passover, sacrificed for us." The fourth Gospel alone gives the true succession of events; not only recording those important openings of our Lord's public work which preceded the Baptist's imprisonment—extending to the end of the third chapter—but so specifying the Passovers which occurred during our Lord's ministry as to enable us to line off, with a large measure of certainty, the events of the first three Gospels according to the successive Passovers which they embraced. *Eusebius,* the ecclesiastical historian, who, early in the fourth century, gave much attention to this subject, in noticing these features of the Evangelical Records, says (iii. 24) that John wrote his Gospel at the entreaty of those who knew the important materials he possessed, and filled up what is wanting in the first three Gospels. Why it was reserved for the fourth Gospel, published at so late a period, to supply such important particulars in the Life of Christ, it is not easy to conjecture with any probability. It may be, that though not unacquainted with the general facts, they were not furnished with reliable details. But one thing may be affirmed with tolerable certainty, that as our Lord's teaching at Jerusalem was of a depth and grandeur scarcely so well adapted to the prevailing character of the first three Gospels, but altogether congenial to the fourth; and as the bare mention of the successive Passovers, without any account of the transactions and discourses they gave rise to, would have served little purpose in the first three Gospels, there may have been no way of preserving the unity and consistency of each Gospel, so as to furnish by means of them all the precious information we get from them, save by the plan on which they are actually constructed.

Entry into Galilee (12-17). **12. Now when Jesus had heard that John was cast into prison** [παρεδόθη]—more simply, 'was delivered up;' as recorded in ch. xiv. 3-5; Mark vi. 17-20; Luke iii. 19, 20—**he departed**—rather, 'withdrew' [ἀνεχώρησεν]—**into Galilee**—as recorded, in its proper place, in John iv. 1-3. **13. And leaving** [καταλιπὼν] **Nazareth.** The prevalent opinion is, that this refers to a *first* visit to Nazareth after His baptism, whose details are given by Luke (iv. 16, &c.); a *second* visit being that detailed by our Evangelist (ch. xiii. 54-58), and by Mark (ch. vi. 1-6). But to us there seem all but insuperable difficulties in the supposition of two visits to Nazareth after His baptism; and on the grounds stated on Luke iv. 16, &c., we think that the *one only* visit to Nazareth is that recorded by Matthew (xiii.), Mark (vi.), and Luke (iv.) But how, in that case, are we to take the word "*leaving* Nazareth*" here? We answer, just as the

same word is used in Acts xxi. 3, "Now when we had sighted [ἀναφάναντες] Cyprus, and *left* it [καταλιπόντες] on the left, we sailed unto Syria," &c.—that is, without entering Cyprus at all, but merely 'sighting' it, as the nautical phrase is, they steered south-east of it, leaving it on the north-west. So here, what we understand the Evangelist to say is, that Jesus, on His return to Galilee, did not, as might have been expected, make Nazareth the place of His stated residence, but "leaving (or passing by) Nazareth, **he came and dwelt in Capernaum, which is upon the sea coast** [K. τὴν παραθαλασσίαν]—'maritime Capernaum,' on the north-west shore of the sea of Galilee; but the precise spot is unknown. (See on ch. xi. 23.) Our Lord seems to have chosen it for several reasons. Four or five of the Twelve lived there; it had a considerable and mixed population, securing some freedom from that intense bigotry which even to this day characterizes all places where Jews in large numbers dwell nearly alone; it was centrical, so that not only on the approach of the annual festivals did large numbers pass through it or near it, but on any occasion multitudes could easily be collected about it; and for crossing and recrossing the lake, which our Lord had so often occasion to do, no place could be more convenient. But one other high reason for the choice of Capernaum remains to be mentioned, the only one specified by our Evangelist. **in the borders of Zabulon and Nephthalim**—the one lying to the west of the sea of Galilee, the other to the north of it; but the precise boundaries cannot now be traced out. **14. That it might be fulfilled which was spoken by Esaias the prophet** (ch. ix. 1, 2, or, as in *Heb.*, ch. viii. 23, and ix. 1), **saying, 15. The land of Zabulon, and the land of Nephthalim, [by] the way of the sea**—the coast skirting the sea of Galilee westward—**beyond Jordan**—a phrase commonly meaning eastward of Jordan; but here and in several places it means westward of the Jordan. The word [πέραν] seems to have got the general meaning of 'the other side;' the nature of the case determining which side that was. **Galilee of the Gentiles**—so called from its position, which made it 'the frontier' between the Holy Land and the external world. While Ephraim and Judah, as *Stanley* says, were separated from the world by the Jordan-valley on one side and the hostile Philistines on another, the northern tribes were in the direct highway of all the invaders from the north, in unbroken communication with the promiscuous races who have always occupied the heights of Lebanon, and in close and peaceful alliance with the most commercial nation of the ancient world—the Phœnicians. Twenty of the cities of Galilee were actually annexed by Solomon to the adjacent kingdom of Tyre, and formed, with their territory, the "boundary" or "offscouring" ("Gebul" or "Cabul") of the two dominions—at a later time still known by the general name of "the boundaries ("coasts" or "borders") of Tyre and Sidon." In the first great transportation of the Jewish population, Naphthali and Galilee suffered the same fate as the trans-Jordanic tribes before Ephraim or Judah had been molested (2 Ki. xv. 29). In the time of the Christian era this original disadvantage of their position was still felt; the speech of the Galileans "bewrayed them" by its uncouth pronunciation (Matt. xxvi. 73); and their distance from the seats of government and civilization at Jeru-

16 way of the sea, beyond Jordan, Galilee of the Gentiles: the [o]people which
sat in darkness saw great light; and to them which sat in the region and
17 shadow of death light is sprung up. From [p]that time Jesus began to
preach, and to say, [q]Repent: for the kingdom of heaven is at hand.
18 And [r]Jesus, walking by the sea of Galilee, saw two brethren, Simon
[s]called Peter, and Andrew his brother, casting a net into the sea: for
19 they were fishers. And he saith unto them, Follow me, and [t]I will make
20 you fishers of men. And [u]they straightway left *their* nets, and followed
21 him. And [v]going on from thence, he saw other two brethren, James *the
son* of Zebedee, and John his brother, in a ship with Zebedee their father,
22 mending their nets; and he called them. And they immediately left
the ship and their father, and followed him.

A. D. 31.

[o] Isa. 42. 7. Luke 2. 32.
[p] Mark 1. 14.
[q] ch. 10. 7.
[r] Mark 1. 16.
[s] Matt. 16.18. John 1. 42.
[t] Ezek. 47.10. Luke 5. 10.
[u] ch. 10.37,38. Mark 10.28. Luke 18. 28. Gal. 1. 16.
[v] Mark 1. 19. Luke 5. 10.

salem and Cæsarea gave them their character for turbulence or independence, according as it was viewed by their friends or their enemies. **16. The people which sat in darkness saw great light; and to them which sat in the region and shadow of death light is sprung up.** [This is rendered pretty closely from the Hebrew—not at all from the LXX., as usual, which here goes quite aside from the original.] The prophetic strain to which these words belong commences with Isa. vii., to which ch. vi. is introductory, and goes down to the end of ch. xii., which hymns the spirit of that whole strain of prophecy. It belongs to the reign of Ahaz, and turns upon the combined efforts of the two neighbouring kingdoms of Syria and Israel to crush Judah. In these critical circumstances Judah and her king were, by their ungodliness, provoking the Lord to sell them into the hands of their enemies. What, then, is the burden of this prophetic strain, on to the passage here quoted? First, Judah shall not, cannot perish, because IMMANUEL, the Virgin's Son, is to come forth from his loins. Next, One of the invaders shall soon perish, and the kingdom of neither be enlarged. Further, While the Lord will be the Sanctuary of such as confide in these promises and await their fulfilment, He will drive to confusion, darkness, and despair the vast multitude of the nation who despised His oracles, and, in their anxiety and distress, betook themselves to the lying oracles of the heathen. This carries us down to the end of the eighth chapter. At the opening of the ninth chapter a sudden light is seen breaking in upon one particular part of the country, the part which was to suffer most in these wars and devastations —"the land of Zebulun, and the land of Naphtali, the way of the sea, beyond Jordan, Galilee of the Gentiles." The rest of the prophecy stretches over both the Assyrian and the Chaldean captivities, and terminates in the glorious Messianic prophecy of ch. xi., and the choral hymn of ch. xii. Well, this is the point seized on by our Evangelist. By Messiah's taking up His abode in those very regions of Galilee, and shedding His glorious light upon them, this prediction, he says, of the evangelical prophet was now fulfilled; and if it was not thus fulfilled, we may confidently affirm it was not fulfilled in any age of the Jewish economy, and has received no fulfilment at all. Even the most rationalistic critics have difficulty in explaining it in any other way. **17. From that time Jesus began to preach, and to say, Repent: for the kingdom of heaven is at hand.** Thus did our Lord not only take up the strain, but give forth the identical summons of His honoured forerunner. Our Lord sometimes speaks of the new kingdom as already come—in His own Person and ministry; but the *economy* of it was only "at hand" [ἤγγικεν] until the blood of the cross was shed, and the Spirit on the day of Pentecost opened the fountain for sin and for uncleanness to the world at large.

Calling of Peter and Andrew, James and John (18-22). **18. And Jesus, walking.** (The word "Jesus" here appears not to belong to the text, but to have been introduced from those portions of it which were transcribed to be used as Church Lessons; where it was naturally introduced as a connecting word at the commencement of a Lesson.) **by the sea of Galilee, saw two brethren, Simon called Peter**—for the reason mentioned in ch. xvi. 18—**and Andrew his brother, casting a net into the sea: for they were fishers. 19. And he saith unto them, Follow me**—rather, as the same expression is rendered in Mark, "Come ye after me" [Δεῦτε ὀπίσω μου]—**and I will make you fishers of men** —raising them from a lower to a higher *fishing*, as David was from a lower to a higher *feeding* (Ps. lxxviii. 70-72). **20. And they straightway left their nets, and followed him. 21. And going on from thence, he saw other two brethren, James the son of Zebedee, and John his brother, in a ship** [ἐν τῷ πλοίῳ]—rather, 'in the ship,' their fishing boat—**with Zebedee their father, mending their nets; and he called them. 22. And they immediately left the ship and their father.** Mark adds an important clause: "They left their father Zebedee in the ship with the *hired servants;*" showing that the family were in easy circumstances. **and followed him.** Two harmonistic questions here arise. *First*, Was this the same calling with that recorded in John i. 35-42? Clearly not. For, 1. That call was given while Jesus was yet in Judea: this, after His return to Galilee. 2. Here, Christ calls Andrew: there, Andrew solicits an interview with Christ. 3. Here, Andrew and Peter are called together: there, Andrew having been called, with an unnamed disciple, who was clearly the beloved disciple (see on John i. 40), goes and fetches Peter his brother to Christ, who then calls him. 4. Here, John is called along with James his brother: there, John is called along with Andrew, after having at their own request had an interview with Jesus; no mention being made of James, whose call, if it then took place, would not likely have been passed over by his own brother. Thus far nearly all are agreed. But on the *next* question opinion is divided—Was this the same calling as that recorded in Luke v. 1-11? Many able critics think so. But the following considerations are to us decisive against it. First, Here, the four are called separately, in pairs: in Luke, all together. Next, In Luke, after a glorious miracle: here, the one pair are casting their net, the other are mending theirs. Further, Here, our Lord had made no public appearance in Galilee,

23 And Jesus went about all Galilee, teaching *ʷ*in their synagogues, and preaching the gospel of the kingdom, and healing all manner of sickness 24 and all manner of disease among the people. And his *ˣ*fame went throughout all Syria: and they brought unto him all sick people that were taken with divers diseases and torments, and those which were possessed with devils, and those which were lunatic, and those that had 25 the palsy; and he healed them. And there followed him *ʸ*great multitudes of people from Galilee, and *from* Decapolis, and *from* Jerusalem, and *from* Judea, and *from* beyond Jordan.

A. D. 31.
ʷ ch. 9. 35.
Mark 1. 21, 39.
Luke 4. 15.
ˣ Isa. 52. 13.
Mark 1. 28.
Luke 4. 14.
ʸ Gen. 49. 10.
Isa. 55. 5.
ch. 19. 2.
Mark 3. 7.

and so had gathered none around Him; He is walking solitarily by the shores of the lake when He accosts the two pairs of fishermen: in Luke, "the multitude [τὸν ὄχλον] are lying upon Him [ἐπικεῖσθαι αὐτῷ], and hearing the word of God, as He stands by the lake of Gennesaret"—a state of things implying a somewhat advanced stage of His early ministry, and some popular enthusiasm. Regarding these successive callings, see on Luke v. i.

First Galilean Circuit (23-25). **23. And Jesus went about all Galilee, teaching in their synagogues.** These were houses of local worship. It cannot be proved that they existed before the Babylonish captivity; but as they began to be erected soon after it, probably the idea was suggested by the religious inconveniences to which the captives had been subjected. In our Lord's time, the rule was to have one wherever ten learned men, or professed students of the law, resided; and they extended to Syria, Asia Minor, Greece, and most places of the dispersion. The larger towns had several, and in Jerusalem the number approached 500. In point of officers and mode of worship, the Christian congregations were modelled after the synagogue. **and preaching the gospel**—'proclaiming the glad tidings' **of the kingdom, and healing all manner of sickness** [πᾶσαν νόσον]—'every disease'—**and all manner of disease** [πᾶσαν μαλακίαν]—'every complaint.' The word means any incipient malady causing 'softness.' **among the people. 24. And his fame went throughout all Syria**—reaching first to that part of it adjacent to Galilee, called Syrophenicia (Mark vii. 26), and thence extending far and wide. **and they brought unto him all sick people** [τοὺς κακῶς ἔχοντας]—' all that were ailing' or 'unwell.' [those] **that were taken**—for this is a distinct class, not an explanation of the "unwell" class, as our translators understood it: **with divers diseases and torments**—that is, acute disorders; **and those which were possessed with devils** [δαιμονιζομένους]—'that were demonized' or 'possessed with demons.' On this subject, see Remark 4 below. **and those which were lunatic** [σεληνιαζομένους]—'moon-struck'—**and those that had the palsy** [παραλυτικοὺς]—'paralytics,' a word not naturalized when our version was made—**and he healed them.** These healings were at once His credentials and illustrations of "the glad tidings" which He proclaimed. After reading this account of our Lord's first preaching tour, can we wonder at what follows? **25. And there followed him great multitudes of people from Galilee, and from Decapolis**—a region lying to the east of the Jordan, so called as containing ten cities, founded and chiefly inhabited by Greek settlers. **and from Jerusalem, and from beyond Jordan**—meaning from Perea. Thus not only was all Palestine upheaved, but all the adjacent regions. But the more immediate object for which this is here mentioned is, to give the reader some idea both of the vast concourse and of the varied complexion of eager attendants upon the great Preacher, to whom

the astonishing Discourse of the next three chapters was addressed. On the importance which our Lord Himself. attached to this first preaching circuit, and the preparation which He made for it, see on Mark i. 35-39.

Remarks. — 1. When, in the prophetic strain regarding Emmanuel, we read that a great light was to irradiate certain specified parts of Palestine—the most disturbed and devastated in the early wars of the Jews, and in after times the most mixed and the least esteemed—and when, in the Gospel History, we find our Lord taking up His stated abode in those very regions, as every way the most suited to His purposes, while at the same time it furnished the bright fulfilment of Isaiah's prophecy—can we refrain from exclaiming, "This also must have come forth from the Lord of hosts, who is wonderful in counsel, and excellent in working"? 2. What marvellous power over the hearts of men must Jesus have possessed, when, on the utterance of those few now familiar words, "Follow Me"—"Come ye after Me," men instantly obeyed, leaving all behind them! But is His power to captivate men's hearts, with a word or two from the lips of His servants, less now that He "has ascended on high, and led captivity captive, and received gifts for men, yea for the rebellious also, that the Lord God might dwell among them"? 3. Did the Prince of preachers not only "teach in the synagogues," the regular places of public worship, but under the open canopy of heaven proclaim the glad tidings to the crowds that gathered around Him, whom no synagogue would have held, and not a few of whom would probably never have heard Him in a synagogue? And shall those who profess to be the followers of Christ account all open-air preaching disorderly and fanatical, or at least regard it as irregular, unnecessary, and inexpedient in a Christian country and a settled state of the Church? When the apostle says to Timothy, "Preach the word; be instant in season, *out of season*" [εὐκαίρως, ἀκαίρως, 2 Tim. iv. 2], does he not enjoin it at what are called *canonical* hours and at uncanonical too? And is not the same principle applicable to what may be called canonical places? These are good, but every other place where crowds can be collected to hear the glad tidings is good also; especially if such would not likely be reached in any other way, and if the uncanonical, abnormal way of it should be fitted, at any particular period, to arrest the attention of those who, in the regular places of worship, have become listless and indifferent to eternal things. 4. It is remarkable, as *Campbell* observes in an acute Dissertation, vi. l., that in the New Testament men are never said to be possessed with the *devil* or with devils [διάβολος], but always with a *demon* or demons [δαίμων], but much more frequently δαιμόνιον], or to be *demonized* [δαιμονίζεσθαι]. On the other hand, the ordinary operations of the wicked one —even in their most extreme and malignant forms—are invariably ascribed to the "*devil*"

23

5   AND seeing the multitudes, [a]he went up into a mountain: and when
2   he was set, his disciples came unto him: and he opened his mouth, and
    taught them, saying,

A. D. 31.

[a] Mark 3. 13.
Luke 6. 12.

himself or to "*Satan*." Thus Satan "filled the heart" of Ananias (Acts v. 3); men are said to be "taken captive by the devil [διαβόλου] at his will" (2 Tim. ii. 26); unregenerate men are the children of the devil (1 John iii. 10); Satan entered into Judas (John xiii. 27); and he is called by our Lord Himself (John vi. 70) "a devil" [διάβολος]. It is impossible that a distinction so invariably observed throughout the New Testament should be without a meaning; but, whatever it be, it is lost to the English reader, as our translators have in both cases used the term "devil." It is true that we have our Lord's own authority for viewing this whole mysterious agency of *demons* as belonging to the kingdom of *Satan* (ch. xii. 24-29), and set in motion, as truly as his own more immediate operations on the souls of men, for his destructive ends. But some notable features in his general policy are undoubtedly intended by the marked distinction of terms observed in the New Testament. One thing comes out of it clearly enough—that these possessions were something totally different from the ordinary operations of the devil on the souls of men; otherwise the distinction would be unintelligible. And that they are not to be confounded with any mere bodily disease—as lunacy or epilepsy—is evident, both from their being expressly distinguished from all such in this very passage, and from the personal intelligence, intentions, and actions ascribed to them in the New Testament. Deeply mysterious is such agency; and one cannot but enquire what may have been the reason why such amazing activity and virulence were allowed it during our Lord's sojourn upon earth. The answer to this, at least, is not difficult. For if all his miracles were designed to illustrate the *character* of His mission; and if "For this purpose the Son of God was manifested, that He might destroy the works of the devil" (1 John iii. 8), there can be no doubt that it was to make this destruction all the more manifest and illustrious that the enemy was allowed such terrific swing at that period. And thus might we imagine it said to the great Enemy from above, with respect to that mighty power allowed him at this time—"Even for this same purpose have I raised thee up, that I might show my power in thee, and that my name might be declared throughout all the earth" (Rom. ix. 17). On the *impurity* so often ascribed to evil spirits in the Gospels, it is impossible to enter here; but perhaps it may be intended to express, not so much anything in human sensuality peculiarly diabolical, as the general vileness or loathsomeness of the character in which these evil spirits revel. But the whole subject is one of difficulty. **5.** But the illustrative design of our Lord's miracles takes wider range than this. His miraculous cures were all of a purely beneficent nature, rolling away one or other of the varied evils brought in by the fall, and in no instance inflicting any. And when we find Himself saying, "The Son of Man is not come to destroy men's lives, but to *save* them" (Luke ix. 56), does He not teach us to behold in all His miraculous cures a faint manifestation of THE HEALING SAVIOUR, in the highest sense of that office? [Compare Exod. xv. 26, "Jehovah that healeth thee"—יְהֹוָה רֹפְאֶךָ.] **6.** *Lange* justly notices here an important difference between the ministry of John and that of our Lord; the one being stationary, the other moving from place to

place—the *diffusive* character of the Gospel thus peering forth at the very outset in the movements of the Great Preacher. And we may add, that the glorious ordinance of preaching could not have been more illustriously inaugurated.

CHAP. V–VII. SERMON ON THE MOUNT.
When surrounded by multitudes of eager listeners, of every class and from all quarters, and solemnly seated on a mountain on purpose to teach them for the first time the great leading principles of His kingdom, why, it may be asked, did our Lord not discourse to them in such strains as these:—"God so loved the world, that He gave His only begotten Son, that whosoever believeth in Him should not perish, but have everlasting life;" "Come unto me, all ye that labour and are heavy laden, and I will give you rest," &c.? While the absence of such sayings from this His first great Discourse startles some to whom they are all-precious, it emboldens others to think that evangelical Christians make too much of them, if not entirely misconceive them. But since the Jewish mind had been long systematically perverted on the subject of human *duty*, and consequently of *sin* by the breach of it, and under such teaching had grown obtuse, unspiritual, and self-satisfied, it was the dictate of wisdom first to lay broad and deep the foundations of all revealed truth and duty, and hold forth the great principles of true and acceptable righteousness, in sharp contrast with the false teaching to which the people were in bondage. At the same time this Discourse is by no means so exclusively ethical as many suppose. On the contrary, though avoiding all evangelical *details*, at so early a stage of His public teaching, our Lord holds forth, from beginning to end of this Discourse, the great *principles* of evangelical and spiritual religion; and it will be found to breathe a spirit entirely in harmony with the subsequent portions of the New Testament.
That this is the *same Discourse* with that in Luke vi. 17 to 49—only reported more fully by Matthew, and less fully, as well as with considerable variation, by Luke—is the opinion of many very able critics (of the Greek commentators; of *Calvin, Grotius, Maldonatus*—who stands almost alone among Romish commentators; and of most moderns, as *Tholuck, Meyer, De Wette, Tischendorf, Stier, Wieseler, Robinson*). The prevailing opinion of these critics is, that Luke's is the original form of the Discourse, to which Matthew has added a number of sayings, uttered on other occasions, in order to give at one view the great outlines of our Lord's ethical teaching. But that they are *two distinct Discourses*—the one delivered about the close of His first missionary tour, and the other after a second such tour and the solemn choice of the Twelve—is the judgment of others who have given much attention to such matters (of most Romish commentators, including *Erasmus;* and among the moderns, of *Lange, Greswell, Birks, Webster and Wilkinson*. The question is left undecided by *Alford*). *Augustin's* opinion—that they were both delivered on one occasion, Matthew's on the mountain, and to the disciples; Luke's in the plain, and to the promiscuous multitude—is so clumsy and artificial as hardly to deserve notice. To us the weight of argument appears to lie with those who think them two separate Discourses. It seems hard to conceive that Matthew should have put

24

3 Blessed ^b*are* the poor in spirit: for theirs is the kingdom of heaven.
4 5 Blessed ^c*are* they that mourn: for they shall be comforted. Blessed

A. D. 31.

b Ps. 51. 17.
c 2 Cor. 1. 7.

this Discourse before his own calling, if it was not uttered till long after, and was spoken in his own hearing as one of the newly-chosen Twelve. Add to this, that Matthew introduces his Discourse amidst very definite markings of time, which fix it to our Lord's first preaching tour; while that of Luke, which is expressly said to have been delivered immediately after the choice of the Twelve, could not have been spoken till long after the time noted by Matthew. It is hard, too, to see how either Discourse can well be regarded as the expansion or contraction of the other. And as it is beyond dispute that our Lord repeated some of His weightier sayings in different forms, and with varied applications, it ought not to surprise us that, after the lapse of perhaps a year—when, having spent a whole night on the hill in prayer to God, and set the Twelve apart, He found Himself surrounded by crowds of people, few of whom probably had heard the Sermon on the Mount, and fewer still remembered much of it—He should go over again its principal points, with just as much sameness as to show their enduring gravity, but at the same time with that difference which shows His exhaustless fertility as the great Prophet of the Church.

CHAP. V. 1-16.—THE BEATITUDES, AND THEIR BEARING UPON THE WORLD.

1. And seeing the multitudes—those mentioned in ch. iv. 25—**he went up into a mountain** [εἰς τὸ ὄρος]—one of the dozen mountains which *Robinson* says there are in the vicinity of the sea of Galilee, any one of them answering about equally well to the occasion. So charming is the whole landscape that the descriptions of it, from *Josephus* downwards (*J. W.*, iv. 10, 8), are apt to be thought a little coloured. **and when he was set**—'had sat' or 'seated Himself' [καθίσαντος αὐτοῦ]—**his disciples came unto him**—already a large circle, more or less attracted and subdued by His preaching and miracles, in addition to the smaller band of devoted adherents. Though the latter only answered to the subjects of His kingdom, described in this Discourse, there were drawn from time to time into this inner circle souls from the outer one, who, by the power of His matchless word, were constrained to forsake their all for the Lord Jesus. **2. And he opened his mouth**—a solemn way of arousing the reader's attention, and preparing him for something weighty (Job iii. 1; Acts viii. 35; x. 34)—**and taught them, saying, 3. Blessed, &c.** Of the two words which our translators render "blessed," the one here used [μακάριοι] points more to what is *inward*, and so might be rendered "happy," in a lofty sense; while the other [εὐλογημένοι] denotes rather what comes to us *from without* (as Matt. xxv. 34). But the distinction is not always nicely carried out. One Hebrew word [אַשְׁרֵי] expresses both.

On these precious Beatitudes, observe that though eight in number, there are here but *seven* distinct features of character. The eighth one—the "persecuted for righteousness' sake"—denotes merely the possessors of the seven preceding features, on account of which it is that they are persecuted (2 Tim. iii. 12). Accordingly, instead of any distinct promise to this class, we have merely a repetition of the first promise. This has been noticed by several critics, who by the *sevenfold* character thus set forth have rightly observed that a *complete* character is meant to be depicted, and by the *sevenfold* blessedness attached to it, a *perfect* blessedness is intended.

Observe, again, that the language in which these beatitudes are couched is purposely fetched from the Old Testament, to show that the new kingdom is but the old in a new form; while the characters described are but the varied forms of that *spirituality* which was the essence of real religion all along, but had well-nigh disappeared under corrupt teaching. Further, the things here promised, far from being mere arbitrary rewards, will be found in each case to grow out of the characters to which they are attached, and in their completed form are but the appropriate coronation of them. Once more, as "the kingdom of heaven," which is the first and the last thing here promised, has two stages—a present and a future, an initial and a consummate stage—so the fulfilment of each of these promises has two stages—a present and a future, a partial and a perfect stage.

3. Blessed are the poor in spirit. All familiar with Old Testament phraseology know how frequently God's true people are styled "the poor" [עֲנִיִּים]—the 'oppressed,' 'afflicted,' 'miserable'—"the needy" [אֶבְיוֹנִים], or both together (as in Ps. xl. 17; Isa. xli. 17). The explanation of this lies in the fact that it is generally "the poor of this world" who are "rich in faith" (Jas. ii. 5; cf. 2 Cor. vi. 10, and Rev. ii. 9); while it is often "the ungodly" who "prosper in the world" (Ps. lxxiii. 12). Accordingly, in Luke (vi. 20, 21), it seems to be this class—the literally "poor" and "hungry"—that are specially addressed. But since God's people are in so many places styled "the poor" and "the needy," with no evident reference to their temporal circumstances (as in Ps. lxviii. 10; lxix. 29-33; cxxxii. 15; Isa. lxi. 1; lxvi. 2), it is plainly a *frame of mind* which those terms are meant to express. Accordingly, our translators sometimes render such words "the humble" (Ps. x. 12, 17), "the meek" (Ps. xxii. 26), "the lowly" (Prov. iii. 34), as having no reference to outward circumstances. But here the explanatory words, "in spirit" [τῷ πνεύματι], fix the sense to 'those who in their deepest consciousness realize their entire need' (cf. the *Gr.* of Luke x. 21; John xi. 33; xiii. 21; Acts xx. 22; Rom. xii. 11; 1 Cor. v. 3; Phil. iii). This self-emptying conviction, that 'before God we are void of everything,' lies at the foundation of all spiritual excellence, according to the teaching of Scripture. Without it we are inaccessible to the riches of Christ: with it we are in the fitting state for receiving all spiritual supplies (Rev. iii. 17, 18; Matt. ix. 12, 13). **for theirs is the kingdom of heaven.** [Our translators rightly disregard the plural—τῶν οὐρανῶν—here, as it is merely a literal rendering of הַשָּׁמַיִם, which has no singular.] See on ch. iii. 2 The poor in spirit not only shall have—they already have—the kingdom. The very sense of their poverty is begun riches. While others "walk in a vain show" [בְּצֶלֶם]—'in a shadow,' 'an image'—in an unreal world, taking a false view of themselves and all around them—the poor in spirit are rich in the knowledge of their real case. Having courage to look this in the face, and own it guilelessly, they feel strong in the assurance that "unto the upright there ariseth light in the darkness" (Ps. cxii. 4); and soon it breaks forth as the morning. God wants nothing from us as the price of His saving gifts; we have but to feel our universal destitution, and cast ourselves upon His compassion

6 *d are* the meek: for *e* they shall inherit the earth. Blessed *are* they which do hunger and thirst after righteousness: *f* for they shall be filled.

A. D. 31.

d Ps. 37. 11.
e Rom. 4. 13.
f Isa. 65. 13.

(Job xxxiii. 27, 28; 1 John i. 9). So the poor in spirit are enriched with the fulness of Christ, which is the kingdom in substance; and when He shall say to them from His great white throne, "Come, ye blessed of my Father, inherit the kingdom *prepared* for you," He will invite them merely to the full enjoyment of an already possessed inheritance. **4. Blessed are they that mourn: for they shall be comforted.** [*Lachmann, Tischendorf*, and *Tregelles* place this verse after *v.* 5, but on evidence decidedly inferior, in our judgment, to that for the received order. And certainly the order of the *ideas* is in favour of the common arrangement; while in Isa. lxi. 1, and Luke iv. 18, the "mourners" come immediately after the "poor."] This "mourning" must not be taken loosely for that feeling which is wrung from men under pressure of the ills of life, nor yet strictly for sorrow on account of committed sins. Evidently it is that entire feeling which the sense of our spiritual poverty begets; and so the second beatitude is but the complement of the first. The one is the intellectual, the other the emotional aspect of the same thing. It is poverty of spirit that says, "I am undone;" and it is the mourning which this causes that makes it break forth in the form of a lamentation—"Woe is me, for I am undone." Hence this class are termed "mourners *in Zion*," or, as we might express it, religious mourners, in sharp contrast with all other sorts (Isa. lxi. 1-3; lxvi. 2). Religion, according to the Bible, is neither a set of intellectual convictions nor a bundle of emotional feelings, but a compound of both, the former giving birth to the latter. Thus closely do the first two beatitudes cohere. The mourners shall be "comforted." Even now they get beauty for ashes, the oil of joy for mourning, the garment of praise for the spirit of heaviness. Sowing in tears, they reap even here in joy. Still all present comfort, even the best, is partial, interrupted, short-lived. But the days of our mourning shall soon be ended, and then God shall wipe away all tears from our eyes. Then, in the fullest sense, shall the mourners be "comforted." **5. Blessed are the meek: for they shall inherit the earth.** This promise to the meek is but a repetition of Ps. xxxvii. 11; only the word which our Evangelist renders "the meek," [οἱ πραεῖς] after the LXX. is the same which we have found so often translated "the poor" [עֲנָוִים], showing how closely allied these two features of character are. It is impossible, indeed, that "the poor in spirit" and "the mourners" in Zion should not at the same time be "meek;" that is to say, persons of a lowly and gentle carriage. How fitting, at least, it is that they should be so, may be seen by the following touching appeal: "Put them in mind to be subject to principalities and powers, to obey magistrates, to be ready to every good work, to speak evil of no man, to be no brawlers, *but gentle, showing all meekness unto all men:* FOR WE OURSELVES WERE ONCE [ποτὲ] FOOLISH, disobedient, deceived, serving divers lusts and pleasures. ... But after that the kindness and love of God our Saviour toward man appeared, ... according to His mercy He saved us," &c. (Titus iii. 1-7.) But He who had no such affecting reasons for manifesting this beautiful carriage, said, nevertheless, of Himself, "Take My yoke upon you, and learn of Me; for I am meek and lowly in heart: and ye

shall find rest unto your souls" (Matt. xi. 29); and the apostle besought one of the churches by "the meekness and gentleness of Christ" (2 Cor. x. 1). In what esteem this is held by Him who seeth not as man seeth, we may learn from 1 Pet. iii. 4, where the true adorning is said to be that of "a meek and quiet spirit, which in the sight of God is of great price." Towards men this disposition is the opposite of high-mindedness, and a quarrelsome and revengeful spirit; it "rather takes wrong, and suffers itself to be defrauded" (1 Cor. vi. 7); it "avenges not itself, but rather gives place unto wrath" (Rom. xii. 19); like the meek One, "when reviled, it reviles not again; when it suffers, it threatens not; but commits itself to Him that judgeth righteously" (1 Pet. ii. 19-22). "The earth" [τὴν γῆν = הָאָרֶץ or אֶרֶץ] which the meek are to inherit might be rendered "the land"—bringing out the more immediate reference to Canaan as the promised land, the secure possession of which was to the Old Testament saints the evidence and manifestation of God's favour resting on them, and the ideal of all true and abiding blessedness. Even in the Psalm from which these words are taken the promise to the meek is not held forth as an arbitrary reward, but as having a kind of natural fulfilment. When they delight themselves in the Lord, He gives them the desires of their heart: When they commit their way to Him, He brings it to pass; bringing forth their righteousness as the light, and their judgment as the noon-day: The little that they have, even when despoiled of their rights, is better than the riches of many wicked, &c. (Ps. xxxvii.) All things, in short, are theirs—in the possession of that favour which is life, and of those rights which belong to them as the children of God—whether the world, or life, or death, or things present, or things to come; all are theirs (1 Cor. iii. 21, 22); and at length, overcoming, they "inherit all things" (Rev. xxi. 7). Thus are the meek the only rightful occupants of a foot of ground or a crust of bread here, and heirs of all coming things. **6. Blessed are they which do hunger and thirst after righteousness** [τὴν δικαιοσύνην = צְדָקָה]: **for they shall be filled** [χορτασθήσονται]—'shall be saturated.' 'From this verse,' says *Tholuck*, 'the reference to the Old Testament background ceases.' Surprising! On the contrary, none of these beatitudes is more manifestly dug out of the rich mine of the Old Testament. Indeed, how could any one who found in the Old Testament "the poor in spirit," and "the mourners in Zion," doubt that he would also find those same characters also *craving* that righteousness which they feel and mourn their want of? But what is the precise meaning of "righteousness" here? Lutheran expositors, and some of our own, seem to have a hankering after that more restricted sense of the term in which it is used with reference to the sinner's justification before God. (See Jer. xxiii. 6; Isa. xlv. 24; Rom. iv. 6; 2 Cor. v. 21.) But, in so comprehensive a saying as this, it is clearly to be taken—as in *v.* 10 also—in a much wider sense, as denoting that spiritual and entire conformity to the law of God, under the want of which the saints groan, and the possession of which constitutes the only true saintship. The Old Testament dwells much on this righteousness, as that which alone God regards with approbation (Ps. xi. 7;

26

7 8 Blessed *are* the merciful: *g*for they shall obtain mercy. Blessed
9 *h are* the pure in heart: for *i*they shall see God. Blessed *are* *j*the
peacemakers: for they shall be called the children of God.

g Ps. 41. 1.
h Heb. 12. 14.
i 1 Cor. 13.12.
Heb. 12. 14.

---

xxiii. 3; cvi. 3; Pro. xii. 28; xvi. 31; Isa. lxiv. 5, &c.) As hunger and thirst are the keenest of our appetites, our Lord, by employing this figure here, plainly means 'those whose deepest cravings are after spiritual blessings.' And in the Old Testament we find this craving variously expressed:— "Hearken unto me, ye that follow after righteousness, ye that seek the Lord" (Isa. li. 1); "I have waited for thy salvation, O Lord," exclaimed dying Jacob (Gen. xlix. 18); "My soul," says the sweet Psalmist, "breaketh for the longing that it hath unto thy judgments at all times" (Ps. cxix. 20); and in similar breathings does he give vent to his deepest longings in that and other Psalms. Well, our Lord just takes up here this blessed frame of mind, representing it as the surest pledge of the coveted supplies, as it is the best preparative, and indeed itself the beginning of them. "They shall be saturated," He says; they shall not only have what they so highly value and long to possess, but they shall have their fill of it. Not here, however. Even in the Old Testament this was well understood. "Deliver me," says the Psalmist, in language which, beyond all doubt, stretches beyond the present scene, "from men of the world, which have their portion in this life: As for me, I shall behold thy face in righteousness: I shall be satisfied, when I awake, with thy likeness" (Ps. xvii. 13-15).

The foregoing beatitudes—the first four—represent the saints rather as *conscious of their need of salvation*, and acting suitably to that character, than as *possessed of it*. The next three are of a different kind—representing the saints as *having now found salvation*, and conducting themselves accordingly.

7. Blessed are the merciful [ἐλεήμονες = רַחֲמָנִים]: **for they shall obtain mercy.** Beautiful is the connection between this and the preceding beatitude. The one has a natural tendency to beget the other. As for the words, they seem directly fetched from Ps. xviii. 25, "With the merciful thou wilt show thyself merciful." Not that our mercifulness comes absolutely first. On the contrary, our Lord Himself expressly teaches us that God's method is to awaken in us compassion towards our fellow-men by His own exercise of it, in so stupendous a way and measure, towards ourselves. In the parable of the unmerciful debtor, the servant to whom his lord forgave ten thousand talents was naturally expected to exercise the small measure of the same compassion required for forgiving his fellow-servant's debt of a hundred pence; and it is only when, instead of this, he relentlessly imprisoned him till he should pay it up, that his lord's indignation was roused, and he who was designed for a vessel of mercy is treated as a vessel of wrath (Matt. xviii. 23-35; and see ch. v. 23, 24; vi. 15; Jas. ii. 13). 'According to the view given in Scripture,' says *Trench* most justly, 'the Christian stands in a middle point, between a mercy received and a mercy yet needed. Sometimes the first is urged upon him as an argument for showing mercy—"forgiving one another, as Christ forgave you" (Col. iii. 13; Eph. iv. 32); sometimes the last—"Blessed are the merciful: for they shall obtain mercy;" "Forgive, and ye shall be forgiven" (Luke vi. 37; Jas. v. 9). And thus, while he is ever to look back on the mercy received as the source and motive of the mercy which he shows, he also looks forward to the mercy which he yet needs, and which he is assured that the merciful—according to what *Bengel* beautifully calls the *benigna talio* (the gracious requital) of the kingdom of God—shall receive, as a new provocation to its abundant exercise.' The foretastes and beginnings of this judicial recompense are richly experienced here below: its perfection is reserved for that day when, from His great white throne, the King shall say, "Come, ye blessed of my Father, inherit the kingdom prepared for you from the foundation of the world; for I was an hungered, and thirsty, and a stranger, and naked, and sick, and in prison, and ye ministered unto me." Yes, thus He acted towards us while on earth, even laying down His life for us; and He will not, He cannot disown, in the merciful, the image of Himself. **8. Blessed are the pure in heart** [οἱ καθαροὶ τῇ καρδίᾳ = בָּרֵי לֵבָב, Ps. xxiv. 4; lxxiii. l]: **for they shall see God.** Here, too, we are on Old Testament ground. There the difference between outward and inward purity, and the acceptableness of the latter only in the sight of God, is everywhere taught. Nor is the 'vision of God' strange to the Old Testament; and though it was an understood thing that this was not possible in the present life (Exod. xxxiii. 20; and cf. Job xix. 26, 27; Isa. vi. 5), yet spiritually it was known and felt to be the privilege of the saints even here, (Gen. v. 24; vi. 9; xvii. 1; xlviii. 15; Ps. xxvii. 4; xxxvi. 9; lxiii. 2; Isa. xxxviii. 3, 11, &c.) But O, with what grand simplicity, brevity, and power is this great fundamental truth here expressed! And in what striking contrast would such teaching appear to that which was then current, in which exclusive attention was paid to ceremonial purification and external morality? This heart-purity begins in a "heart sprinkled from an evil conscience," or a "conscience purged from dead works" (Heb. x. 22; ix. 14; and see Acts xv. 9); and this also is taught in the Old Testament (Ps. xxxii. 1, 2; cf. Rom. iv. 5-8; and Isa. vi. 5-8). The conscience thus purged—the heart thus sprinkled—there is light within wherewith to see God. "If we say that we have fellowship with Him, and walk in darkness, we lie, and do not the truth: but if we walk in the light, as He is in the light, we have fellowship one with the other" [μετ' ἀλλήλων]—He with us and we with Him—"and the blood of Jesus Christ His Son cleanseth us"—us who have this fellowship, and who, without such continual cleansing, would soon lose it again—"from all sin" (1 John i. 6, 7). "Whosoever sinneth hath not seen Him, neither known Him" (1 John iii. 6); "He that doeth evil hath not seen God" (3 John 11). The inward vision thus clarified, and the whole inner man in sympathy with God, each looks upon the other with complacency and joy, and we are "changed into the same image from glory to glory." But the full and beatific vision of God is reserved for that time to which the Psalmist stretches his views—"As for me, I shall behold Thy face in righteousness: I shall be satisfied, when I awake with Thy likeness" (Ps. xvii. 15). Then shall His servants serve Him: and they shall see His face; and His name shall be in their foreheads (Rev. xxii. 3, 4). They shall see Him as He is (1 John iii. 2). But, says the apostle, expressing the converse of this beatitude—"Follow holiness, without which no man shall see the Lord" (Heb.

10 Blessed ^k *are* they which are persecuted for righteousness' .sake: for
11 theirs is the kingdom of heaven. Blessed are ye when *men* shall
revile you, and persecute *you,* and shall say all manner of evil against
12 you ¹ falsely, for my sake. Rejoice, and be exceeding glad; for great
is your reward in heaven: for so persecuted they the prophets which
were before you.

A. D. 31.

k Mark 10. 30.
Luke 6. 22,
23.
2 Cor. 4. 17.
2 Tim. 2. 12.
1 Pet. 3. 14.
1 lying.

xii. 14). **9. Blessed are the peacemakers** [εἰρηνο-
ποιοί = שְׁלוֹם יֹצֵר, Pro. xii. 20]—who not only
study peace, but diffuse it—**for they shall be
called the children**—'shall be called sons'—**of God**
[υἱοὶ Θεοῦ]. Of all these beatitudes this is the only
one which could hardly be expected to find its
definite ground in the Old Testament; for that
most glorious character of God, the likeness of
which appears in the peacemakers, had yet to be
revealed. His glorious name, indeed—as "The
Lord, the Lord God, merciful and gracious, long-
suffering, and abundant in goodness and truth,
forgiving iniquity and transgression and sin"—
had been proclaimed in a very imposing manner
(Exod. xxxiv. 6), and manifested in action with
affecting frequency and variety in the long course
of the ancient economy. And we have undeniable
evidence that the saints of that economy felt its
transforming and ennobling influence on their own
character. But it was not till Christ "made peace
by the blood of the cross" that God could manifest Himself as "the God of peace, that brought
again from the dead our Lord Jesus, that great
Shepherd of the sheep, through the blood of the
everlasting covenant" (Heb. xiii. 20)—could reveal
Himself as "in Christ reconciling the world unto
Himself, not imputing their trespasses unto them,"
and hold Himself forth in the astonishing attitude
of beseeching men to be "reconciled to Himself"
(2 Cor. v. 19, 20). When this reconciliation actually takes place, and one has "peace with God
through our Lord Jesus Christ"—even "the peace
of God which passeth all understanding"—the
peace-receivers become transformed into peace-
diffusers. God is thus seen reflected in them;
and by the family likeness these peacemakers
are recognized as the children of God.

In now coming to the eighth, or supplementary
beatitude, it will be seen that all that the saints
are *in themselves* has been already described, in
seven features of character; that number indicating *completeness* of delineation. The last feature, accordingly, is a passive one, representing
the treatment that the characters already described
may expect from the world. He who shall one
day fix the destiny of all men here pronounces
certain characters "blessed;" but He ends by
forewarning them that the world's estimation
and treatment of them will be the reverse of His.
**10. Blessed are they which are persecuted for
righteousness' sake, &c.** How entirely this final
beatitude has its ground in the Old Testament,
is evident from the concluding words, where the
encouragement held out to endure such persecutions consists in its being but a continuation of
what was experienced by the Old Testament
servants of God. But how, it may be asked,
could such beautiful features of character provoke persecution? To this the following answers
should suffice: "Every one that doeth evil hateth
the light, neither cometh to the light, lest his deeds
should be reproved." "The world cannot hate
you; but me it hateth, because I testify of it, that
the works thereof are evil." "If ye were of the
world, the world would love his own: but because ye are not of the world, but I have chosen
you out of the world, therefore the world hateth

you." "There is yet one man (said wicked Ahab
to good Jehoshaphat), by whom we may enquire
of the Lord: but I hate him; for he never prophesied good unto me, but always evil" (John iii. 20;
vii. 7; xv. 19; 2 Chr. xviii. 7). But more particularly, the seven characters here described are
all in the teeth of the spirit of the world, insomuch
that such hearers of this Discourse as breathed
that spirit must have been startled, and had
their whole system of thought and action rudely
dashed. Poverty of spirit runs counter to the
pride of men's heart; a pensive disposition, in
the view of one's universal deficiences before God,
is ill relished by the callous, indifferent, laughing, self-satisfied world; a meek and quiet spirit,
taking wrong, is regarded as pusillanimous, and
rasps against the proud, resentful spirit of the
world; that craving after spiritual blessings rebukes but too unpleasantly the lust of the flesh,
the lust of the eye, and the pride of life; so does a
merciful spirit the hardheartedness of the world;
purity of heart contrasts painfully with painted
hypocrisy; and the peacemaker cannot easily be
endured by the contentious, quarrelsome world.
Thus does "righteousness" come to be "persecuted." But blessed are they who, in spite of
this, dare to be righteous. **for theirs is the
kingdom of heaven.** As this was the reward
promised to the poor in spirit—the leading one of
these seven beatitudes—of course it is the proper
portion of such as are persecuted for exemplifying them. **11. Blessed are ye when men shall
revile you**—or abuse you to your face, in opposition to backbiting. (See Mark xv. 32.) **and
persecute you, and shall say all manner of evil
against you falsely** [*Tischendorf*—on quite insufficient evidence, we think—omits this last word
ψευδόμενοι : *Tregelles*, however, retains it. Even
though it had not been expressed, it would of
course have been implied.] **for my sake.** Observe this. He had before said, "for righteousness' sake." Here He identifies Himself and His
cause with that of righteousness, binding up the
cause of righteousness in the world with the
reception of Himself. Would Moses, or David,
or Isaiah, or Paul have so expressed themselves?
Never. Doubtless they suffered for righteousness'
sake. But to have called this "their sake,"
would, as every one feels, have been very unbecoming. Whereas He that speaks, being Righteousness incarnate (see Mark i. 24; Acts iii. 14; Rev.
iii. 7), when He so speaks, speaks only like Himself. **12. Rejoice, and be exceeding glad**—'exult'
[ἀγαλλιᾶσθε]. In the corresponding passage of
Luke (vi. 22, 23), where every indignity trying to
flesh and blood is held forth as the probable
lot of such as were faithful to Him, the word is
even stronger than here, "leap" [σκιρτήσατε], as
if He would have their inward transport to overpower and absorb the sense of all these affronts
and sufferings; nor will anything else do it. **for
great is your reward in heaven: for so persecuted they the prophets which were before you:**
—*q. d.*, 'You do but serve yourselves heirs to their
character and sufferings, and the reward will be
common.'

13-16. We have here the practical application

13   Ye are the salt of the earth: but if the salt have lost his savour, wherewith shall it be salted? it is thenceforth good for nothing, but to
14 be cast out, and to be trodden under foot of men. Ye *ᵗ*are the light of
15 the world. A city that is set on an hill cannot be hid. Neither do men light a candle, and put it under a ²bushel, but on a candlestick; and it
16 giveth light unto all that are in the house. Let your light so shine before

A. D. 31.
ᶦ Pro. 4. 13. Phil. 2. 15.
² modius. It contained nearly a peck.

of the foregoing principles to those disciples who sat listening to them, and to their successors in all time. Our Lord, though he began by pronouncing certain *characters* to be blessed—without express reference to any of His hearers—does not close the beatitudes without intimating that such characters were in existence, and that already they were before Him. Accordingly, from characters He comes to *persons* possessing them, saying, "Blessed are ye when men shall revile you," &c. And now, continuing this mode of direct personal address, He startles those humble, unknown men by pronouncing them the exalted benefactors of their whole species. 13. **Ye are the salt of the earth**—to preserve it from corruption, to season its insipidity, to freshen and sweeten it. The value of salt for these purposes is abundantly referred to by classical writers as well as in Scripture; and hence its symbolical significance in the religious offerings as well as of those without as of those within the pale of revealed religion. In Scripture, mankind, under the unrestrained workings of their own evil nature, are represented as entirely corrupt. Thus, before the flood (Gen. vi. 11, 12); after the flood (Gen. viii. 21); in the days of David (Ps. xiv. 2, 3); in the days of Isaiah (Isa. i. 5, 6); and in the days of Paul (Eph. ii. 1-3; see also Job xiv. 4; xv. 15, 16; John iii. 6; compared with Rom. viii. 8; Titus iii. 2, 3). The remedy for this, says our Lord here, is the active presence of His disciples among their fellows. The character and principles of Christians, brought into close contact with it, are designed to arrest the festering corruption of humanity and season its insipidity. But how, it may be asked, are Christians to do this office for their fellow-men, if their righteousness only exasperate them, and recoil, in every form of persecution, upon themselves? The answer is, That is but the first and partial effect of their Christianity upon the world: though the great proportion would dislike and reject the truth, a small but noble band would receive and hold it fast; and in the struggle that would ensue, one and another even of the opposing party would come over to His ranks, and at length the Gospel would carry all before it. **but if the salt have lost his savour** [μωρανθῇ]—'become unsavoury' or 'insipid;' losing its saline or salting property. The meaning is, If that Christianity on which the health of the world depends, does in any age, region, or individual, exist only in *name*, or if it contain not those *saving elements* for want of which the world languishes, **wherewith shall it be salted?**—how shall the salting qualities be restored to it? (Cf. Mark ix. 50.) Whether salt ever does lose its saline property—about which there is a difference of opinion—is a question of no moment here. The point of the case lies in the supposition—that *if it should lose it*, the consequence would be as here described. So with Christians. The question is not, Can, or do, the saints ever totally lose that grace which makes them a blessing to their fellow-men? But, What is to be the issue of that Christianity which is found wanting in those elements which can alone stay the corruption and season the tastelessness of an all-pervading carnality? The restoration or non-

restoration of *grace*, or true living Christianity, to those who have lost it, has, in our judgment, nothing at all to do here. The question is not, If a man lose his grace, how shall *that grace* be restored to him? but, Since living Christianity is the only "salt of the earth," if men lose that, *what else* can supply its place? What follows is the appalling answer to this question. **it is thenceforth good for nothing, but to be cast out**—a figurative expression of indignant exclusion from the kingdom of God (cf. ch. viii. 12; xxii. 13; John vi. 37; ix. 34). **and to be trodden under foot of men**—expressive of contempt and scorn. It is not the mere want of a certain character, but the want of it in those whose *profession* and *appearance* were fitted to beget expectation of finding it. 14. **Ye are the light of the world** [τὸ φῶς τοῦ κόσμου]. This being the distinctive title which our Lord appropriates to Himself (John viii. 12; ix. 5; and see John i. 4, 9; iii. 19; xii. 35, 36)—a title expressly said to be unsuitable even to the highest of all the prophets (John i. 8)—it must be applied here by our Lord to His disciples only as they shine with His light upon the world, in virtue of His Spirit dwelling in them, and the same mind being in them which was also in Christ Jesus. Nor are Christians anywhere else so called. Nay, as if to avoid the august title which the Master has appropriated to Himself, Christians are said to "shine"—not as "lights," as our translators render it, but—"as *luminaries* [φωστῆρες] in the world" (Phil. ii. 15); and the Baptist is said to have been "the burning and shining"—not "light," as in our translation, but—"*lamp*" [λύχνος] of his day (John v. 35). Let it be observed, too, that while the two figures of salt and sunlight both express the same function of Christians—their blessed influence on their fellow-men—they each set this forth under a different aspect. Salt operates *internally*, in the mass with which it comes in contact; the sunlight operates *externally*, irradiating all that it reaches. Hence Christians are warily styled "the salt of the *earth*"—with reference to the masses of mankind with whom they are expected to mix; but "the light of the *world*"—with reference to the vast and variegated surface which feels its fructifying and gladdening radiance. The same distinction is observable in the second pair of those seven parables which our Lord spoke from the Galilean lake—that of the "mustard seed," which grew to be a great overshadowing tree, answering to the sunlight which invests the world, and that of the "leaven," which a woman took and, like the salt, *hid* in three measures of meal, till the whole was leavened (ch. xiii. 31-33). **A city that is set on an hill cannot be hid**—nor can it be supposed to have been so built except to be seen by many eyes. 15. **Neither do men light a candle**—or 'lamp' [λύχνον]—**and put it under a bushel**—a dry measure—**but on a candlestick**—rather, 'under the bushel, but on the lamp-stand' [ὑπὸ τὸν μόδιον, ἀλλ' ἐπὶ τὴν λυχνίαν]. The article is inserted in both cases to express the familiarity of every one with those household utensils. **and it giveth light** [λάμπει]—'shineth'—**unto all that are in the house.** 16. **Let your light so shine before men, that they may see your good works, and glorify your**

29

men, that ^m they may see your good works, and glorify ⁿyour Father which is in heaven.

17 Think ^onot that I am come to destroy the Law, or the Prophets: I am
18 not come to destroy, but to fulfil. For verily I say unto you, ^pTill heaven and earth pass, one jot or one tittle shall in no wise pass from the law,

A. D. 31.

^m 1 Pet. 2. 12.
ⁿ John 15. 8.
1 Cor. 14. 25.
^o Dan. 9. 24.
^p Luke 16. 17.

Father which is in heaven. As nobody lights a lamp only to cover it up, but places it so conspicuously as to give light to all who need light, so Christians, being the light of the world, instead of hiding their light, are so to hold it forth before men that they may see what a life the disciples of Christ lead, and seeing this, may glorify their Father for so redeeming, transforming, and ennobling earth's sinful children, and opening to themselves the way to like redemption and transformation.

Remarks.—1. All-precious though the doctrines of the Gospel be, since the proper appreciation and cordial reception of them depends upon a previous preparation of the heart—especially, on the soul's being thoroughly emptied of its own fancied excellences, and made painfully alive to its spiritual necessities—it will be the wisdom of all Christian preachers to imitate the Great Preacher here, in laying first the foundation of this frame. 2. The theology of the Old Testament, when stripped of its accidents and reduced to its essence, is one with that of the New: it is spiritual; it is evangelical. 3. The earthly and the heavenly stages of the kingdom of God are essentially one; the former preparing the way for the latter, and opening naturally into it, as the commencing and consummating stages of the same condition. Thus the connection between them, far from being arbitrary, is inherent. 4. How entirely contrary to the spirit and design of Christianity is that monkish seclusion from society and ascetic solitude which, attractive though it be to a morbid spirituality, is just to do the very thing which our Lord here represents as against the nature of the Christian calling, and rendering observance of His injunctions here impossible. If even a lamp is not lighted to be put under a bushel, but placed conspicuously for the very purpose of giving light to all within reach of its rays, how much less is the sun placed in the heavens in order that men on the earth may walk in darkness? Even so, says our Lord, instead of hiding the light of your Christianity from the dark world around you, bring it out into the view of men, on purpose to let them see it. Much more plainly does this come out in the other figure. As salt must come into actual contact with what is to be seasoned by it, so must Christians, instead of standing at a distance from their fellows, come into contact with them, on purpose to communicate to them their own qualities. Nor does our Lord think it necessary to guard against confounding this with the spirit of religious ostentation, of which He treats sufficiently in the following chapter; for what follows is quite enough to prevent any such perversion of His language: "that they may see your good works, and glorify your Father which is in heaven"—not 'see how much superior you are to them,' but 'see what an astonishing change He can work by the Gospel upon men ·of every·class.' Thus, God is deprived of the testimony He expects from His redeemed and transformed people, when, instead of manifesting before their fellows what He hath wrought for their souls, they shut themselves up—whether systematically or otherwise—or habitually retire within themselves. But, 5. Not by the preaching or publication of

mere *truths*, are Christians to bear down the opposition and effect the conversion of their fellow-men. Not thus is their light to "shine before men." But it is so to shine that men "may *see their good works*, and (so) glorify their Father which is in heaven." In other words, while it is Christianity which is to carry all before it, it is not the Christianity of books, nor even of mere preaching—much less of an empty profession—but the Christianity of *life*. "YE (whom I have been pronouncing blessed, as possessors of a blessed character) are the light of the world." Yes: It is humility, not as preached, but as practised; it is contrition, not as depicted, not as inculcated, but as exemplified; it is meekness manifested; it is spiritual aspiration, not as enjoined, but as beheld in men on whose whole carriage may be seen written *Excelsior;* it is mercy embodied; it is heart-purity in flesh and blood; it is peace incarnate. This many-sided manifestation of a divine life in men, mixing with their fellows, and of like passions with their fellows, is the divinely ordained specific for arresting the progress of human corruption, diffusing health and sweetness through it, and irradiating it with the fructifying and gladdening beams of heavenly light.

17-48.—IDENTITY OF THESE PRINCIPLES WITH THOSE OF THE ANCIENT ECONOMY, IN CONTRAST WITH THE REIGNING TRADITIONAL TEACHING.

Exposition of Principles (17-20). **17.** **Think not that I am come**—'that I came' [ἠλθον] **to destroy the Law, or the Prophets**—that is, 'the authority and principles of the Old Testament.' (On the phrase, see ch. vii. 12; xxii. 40; Luke xvi. 16; Acts xiii. 15.) This general way of taking the phrase is much better than understanding "the Law" and "the Prophets" separately, and enquiring, as many good critics do, in what sense our Lord could be supposed to meditate the subversion of each. To the various classes of His hearers, who might view such supposed abrogation of the Law and the Prophets with very different feelings, our Lord's announcement would, in effect, be such as this—'Ye who "tremble at the word of the Lord," *fear* not that I am going to sweep the foundations from under your feet: Ye restless and revolutionary spirits, *hope* not that I am going to head any revolutionary movement: And ye who hypocritically affect great reverence for the Law and the Prophets, *pretend* not to find anything in my teaching derogatory to God's living oracles.' **I am not come to destroy, but to fulfil.** 'Not to subvert, abrogate, or annul, but to establish the Law and the Prophets—to unfold them, to embody them in living form, and to enshrine them in the reverence, affection, and character of men, am I come.' **18. For verily I say unto you** ['Αμὴν = ןֵמָא—λέγω ὑμῖν]. Here, for the first time, does that august expression occur in our Lord's recorded teaching, with which we have grown so familiar as hardly to reflect on its full import. It is the expression, manifestly, of *supreme legislative authority;* and as the subject in connection with which it is uttered is the Moral Law, no higher claim to an authority *strictly divine* could be advanced. For when we observe how jealously Jehovah asserts it as His exclusive prerogative to give law to men

19 till all be fulfilled. Whosoever *q* therefore shall break one of these least commandments, and shall teach men so, he shall be called the least in the kingdom of heaven : but whosoever shall do and teach *them,* the same

20 shall be called great in the kingdom of heaven. For I say unto you, That except your righteousness shall exceed *r the righteousness* of the scribes and Pharisees, ye shall in no case enter into the kingdom of heaven.

21 Ye have heard that it was said [3] by them of old time, *s* Thou shalt not

A. D. 31.

q Jas. 2. 10.
    Gal. 3. 10.
r Rom. 10. 3.
    2 Cor. 5. 17.
    Phil. 3. 9.
[3] Or, to them.
s Ex. 20. 13.
    2 Sam. 20. 18.
    Job 8. 8.

(Lev. xviii. 1-5; xix. 37; xxvi. 1-4, 13-16, &c.), such language as this of our Lord will appear totally unsuitable, and indeed abhorrent, from any creature-lips. When the Baptist's words—"I say unto you" (ch. iii. 9)—are compared with those of his Master here, the difference of the two cases will be at once apparent. **Till heaven and earth pass.** Though even the Old Testament announces the ultimate "perdition of the heavens and the earth," in contrast with the immutability of Jehovah (Ps. cii. 24-27), the prevalent representation of the heavens and the earth in Scripture, when employed as a popular figure, is that of their *stability* (Ps. cxix. 89-91; Eccl. i. 4; Jer. xxxiii. 25, 26). It is the enduring stability, then, of the great truths and principles, moral and spiritual, of the Old Testament Revelation which our Lord thus expresses. **one jot** [ἰῶτα]—the smallest of the Hebrew letters—**or one tittle** [κεραία]—one of those little strokes by which alone some of the Hebrew letters are distinguished from others like them—**shall in no wise pass from the law, till all be fulfilled.** The meaning is, that 'not so much as the smallest loss of authority or vitality shall ever come over the law.' The expression, "till all be fulfilled," is much the same in meaning as 'it *shall* be had in undiminished and enduring honour, from its greatest to its least requirements.' Again, this general way of viewing our Lord's words here seems far preferable to that *doctrinal* understanding of them which would require us to determine the different kinds of "fulfilment" which the *moral* and the *ceremonial* parts of it were to have. **19. Whosoever therefore shall break** [λύσῃ]—rather, 'dissolve,' 'annul,' or 'make invalid'—**one of these least commandments**—an expression equivalent to 'one of the least of these commandments'—**and shall teach men so**—referring to the Pharisees and their teaching, as is plain from the next verse, but of course embracing all similar schools and teaching in the Christian Church—**he shall be called the least in the kingdom of heaven.** As the thing spoken of is not the practical breaking, or disobeying, of the law, but annulling, or enervating its obligation by a vicious system of interpretation, and teaching others to do the same; so the thing threatened is not exclusion from heaven, and still less the lowest place in it, but a degraded and contemptuous position in the present stage of the kingdom of God. In other words, 'they shall be reduced, by the retributive providence that overtakes them, to the same condition of dishonour to which, by their system and their teaching, they have brought down those eternal principles of God's law.' **but whosoever shall do and teach them**—whose principles and teaching go to exalt the authority and honour of God's law, in its lowest as well as highest requirements—**the same shall be called great in the kingdom of heaven**—'shall, by that providence which watches over the honour of God's moral administration, be raised to the same position of authority and honour to which they exalt the law.' **20. For I say unto you, That except your righteousness**

shall exceed the righteousness of the scribes and Pharisees. For the characteristics of the Pharisaic school, see on ch. iii. 1-12, Remark 2. But the superiority to the Pharisaic righteousness here required is plainly in *kind,* not *degree;* for all Scripture teaches that entrance into God's kingdom, whether in its present or future stage, depends, not on the degree of our excellence in anything, but solely on our having the character itself which God demands. Our righteousness, then—if it is to contrast with the *outward* and *formal* righteousness of the scribes and Pharisees—must be *inward, vital, spiritual.* Some, indeed, of the scribes and Pharisees themselves might have the very righteousness here demanded; but our Lord is speaking, not of persons, but of the *system* they represented and taught. **ye shall in no case enter into the kingdom of heaven.** If this refer, as in the preceding verse, rather to the earthly stage of this kingdom, the meaning is, that without a righteousness exceeding that of the Pharisees, we cannot be members of it at all, save in name. This was no new doctrine (Rom. ii. 28, 29; ix. 6; Phil. iii. 3). But our Lord's teaching here stretches beyond the present scene, to that everlasting stage of the kingdom, where without "purity of heart" none "shall see God."

The spirituality of the true righteousness, in contrast with that of the Scribes and Pharisees, illustrated from the Sixth Commandment (21-26). **21. Ye have heard that it was said by them of old time** [ἐρρήθη—a better authorized form than ἐρρέθη—τοῖς ἀρχαίοις]—or, as in the margin, 'to them of old time.' Which of these translations is the right one has been much controverted. Either of them is grammatically defensible, though the latter—"to the ancients"—is more consistent with New Testament usage (see the *Greek* of Rom. ix. 12, 26; Rev. vi. 11; ix. 4); and most critics decide in favour of it. But it is not a question of Greek only. Nearly all who would translate "to the ancients" take the speaker of the words quoted to be *Moses in the law;* "the ancients" to be *the people* to whom Moses gave the law; and the intention of our Lord here to be to contrast His own teaching, more or less, with that of Moses; either as opposed to it—as some go the length of affirming—or at least as modifying, enlarging, elevating it. But who can reasonably imagine such a thing, just after the most solemn and emphatic proclamation of the perpetuity of the law, and the honour and glory in which it was to be held under the new economy? To us it seems as plain as possible that our Lord's one object is to contrast the traditional perversions of the law with the true sense of it as expounded by Himself. A few of those who assent to this still think that "to the ancients" is the only legitimate translation of the words; understanding that our Lord is reporting what had been said to the ancients, not by Moses, but by the perverters of his law. We do not object to this; but we incline to think (with *Beza,* and after him with *Fritzsche, Olshausen, Stier,* and *Bloomfield*) that "by the ancients" must have been what our Lord meant

22 kill; and whosoever shall kill shall be in danger of the judgment: but
I say unto you, That ᵗwhosoever is angry with his brother without a
cause shall be in danger of the judgment: and whosoever shall say to his
brother, ⁴Raca! shall be in danger of the council: but whosoever shall
23 say, Thou ⁵fool! shall be in danger of hell fire. Therefore, if thou bring
thy gift to the altar, and there rememberest that thy brother hath ought
24 against thee; leave ᵘthere thy gift before the altar, and go thy way;
first be reconciled to thy brother, and then come and offer thy gift.

A. D. 31.
t 1 John 3.15.
4 That is, vain fellow.
5 Or, graceless wretch. John 8. 44.
Acts 13. 10.
u Job 42. 8.

here, referring to the corrupt teachers rather than the perverted people. **Thou shalt not kill:**—*q. d.,* 'This being all that the law requires, whosoever has imbrued his hands in his brother's blood, but he only, is guilty of a breach of this commandment;' **and whosoever shall kill shall be in danger of**—'liable to' [ἔνοχος] **the judgment**—that is, of the sentence of those inferior courts of judicature which were established in all the principal towns, in compliance with Deut. xvi. 16. Thus was this commandment reduced, from a holy law of the heart-searching God, to a mere criminal statute, taking cognizance only of outward actions, such as that which we read in Exod. xxi. 12; Lev. xxiv. 17. **22. But I say unto you.** Mark the authoritative tone in which—as Himself the Lawgiver and Judge—Christ now gives the true sense, and explains the deep reach, of the commandment. **That whosoever is angry with his brother without a cause** [εἰκῇ. Most recent critical editors either wholly exclude, or place within brackets, as of doubtful authority, the word εἰκῇ. External authority, however, preponderates in its favour. On the internal evidence opinions differ; some thinking it got in to soften the apparent harshness of the precept, while others think it was left out of some MSS. and early versions from jealousy at anything which looked like an attempt to dilute the strength of our Lord's teaching. But however we decide as to the *text*, we must restrict our *interpretation* to 'causeless anger.'] **shall be in danger of the judgment: and whosoever shall say to his brother, Raca!** [Ρακὰ = רֵקָא, 'brainless'] **shall be in danger of the council** [τῷ συνεδρίῳ]: **but whosoever shall say, Thou fool!** [Μωρὲ = נָבָל] **shall be in danger of hell fire** [εἰς τὴν γέενναν—a word formed from הִנֹּם ﬠֵ֫, or 'valley of Hinnom']. It is unreasonable to deny, as *Alexander* does, that three degrees of punishment are here meant to be expressed, and to say that it is but a threefold expression of one and the same thing. But Romish expositors greatly err in taking the first two—"the judgment" and "the council"—to refer to degrees of *temporal* punishment with which lesser sins were to be visited under the Gospel, and only the last—"hell fire"—to refer to the future life. All three clearly refer to *divine retribution*, and that alone, for breaches of this commandment; though this is expressed by an *allusion* to Jewish tribunals. The "judgment," as already explained, was the lowest of these; the "council," or 'Sanhedrim'—which sat at Jerusalem—was the highest; while the word used for "hell fire" contains an allusion to the "valley of the son of Hinnom" (Josh. xviii. 16). In this valley the Jews, when steeped in idolatry, went the length of burning their children to Moloch "on the high places of Tophet" [תֹּ֫פֶת, Jer. vii. 31] —in consequence of which good Josiah defiled it, to prevent the repetition of such abominations (2 Ki. xxiii. 10); and from that time forward, if we may believe the Jewish writers, a fire was kept burning in it to consume the carrion, and all kinds

of impurities, that collected about the capital. Certain it is, that while the final punishment of the wicked is described in the Old Testament by allusions to this valley of Tophet or Hinnom (Isa. xxx. 33; lxvi. 24), our Lord Himself describes the same by merely quoting these terrific descriptions of the evangelical prophet (Mark ix. 43-48). What precise degrees of unholy feeling towards our brother are indicated by the words "Raca" and "fool" it would be as useless as it is vain to enquire. Every age and every country has its modes of expressing such things; and, no doubt, our Lord seized on the then current phraseology of unholy disrespect and contempt, merely to express and condemn the different degrees of such feeling when brought out in words, as He had immediately before condemned the feeling itself. In fact, so little are we to make of mere *words*, apart from the feeling which they express, that as *anger* is expressly said to have been borne by our Lord towards His enemies, though mixed with "grief for the hardness of their hearts" (Mark iii. 5), and as the apostle teaches us that there is an anger which is not sinful (Eph. iv. 26); so in the Epistle of James (ii. 20) we find the words, "O vain" or 'empty' man [ὦ ἄνθρωπε κενέ]; and our Lord Himself applies the very word "fools" [μωροί] twice in one breath to the blind guides of the people (ch. xxiii. 17, 19)—although, in both cases, it is to *false reasoners* rather than persons that such words are applied. The spirit, then, of the whole statement may be thus given—'For ages ye have been taught that the sixth commandment, for example, is broken only by the murderer, to pass sentence upon whom is the proper business of the recognized tribunals: but I say unto you that it is broken even by causeless anger, which is but hatred in the bud, as hatred is incipient murder (1 John iii. 15); and if by the feelings, much more by those *words* in which all ill feeling, from the slightest to the most envenomed, are wont to be cast upon a brother: and just as there are gradations in human courts of judicature, and in the sentences which they pronounce according to the degrees of criminality, so will the judicial treatment of all the breakers of this commandment at the divine tribunal be according to their real criminality before the heart-searching Judge.' O what holy teaching is this! **23. Therefore**—to apply the foregoing, and show its paramount importance—**if thou bring thy gift to the altar, and there rememberest that thy brother hath aught** —of just complaint **against thee; 24. Leave there thy gift before the altar, and go thy way; first be reconciled to thy brother** [διαλλάγηθι τῷ ἀδελφῷ]. The meaning evidently is—not, 'dismiss from thine own breast all ill-feeling,' but, 'get thy brother to dismiss from his mind all grudge against thee.' **and then come and offer thy gift.** 'The picture,' says *Tholuck*, 'is drawn from life. It transports us to the moment when the Israelite, having brought his sacrifice to the court of the Israelites, awaited the instant when the priest would approach to receive it at his hands.

25 Agree ^vwith thine adversary quickly, whiles ^wthou art in the way with him; lest at any time the adversary deliver thee to the judge, and the
26 judge deliver thee to the officer, and thou be cast into prison. Verily I say unto thee, Thou ^xshalt by no means come out thence, till thou hast paid the uttermost farthing.
27 Ye have heard that it was said by them of old time, Thou shalt not
28 commit adultery: but I say unto you, That whosoever looketh ^yon a woman to lust after her hath committed adultery with her already in his

A. D. 31.
^v Job 22. 21.
Pro. 25. 8.
Heb. 3. 7.
^wPs. 32. 6.
Isa. 55. 6.
^x 2 Thes. 1. 9.
^y Gen. 34. 2.
Pro. 6. 25.
Eph. 5. 5.

He waits with his gift at the rails which separate the place where he stands from the court of the priests, into which his offering will presently be taken, there to be slain by the priest, and by him presented upon the altar of sacrifice.' It is at this solemn moment, when about to cast himself upon divine mercy, and seek in his offering a seal of divine forgiveness, that the offerer is supposed, all at once, to remember that some brother has a just cause of complaint against him through breach of this commandment in one or other of the ways just indicated. What then? Is he to say, As soon as I have offered this gift I will go straight to my brother, and make it up with him? Nay; but before another step is taken—even before the offering is presented—this reconciliation is to be sought, though the gift have to be left unoffered before the altar. The converse of the truth here taught is very strikingly expressed in Mark xi. 25, 26. "And *when ye stand praying* (in the very act), forgive, if ye have aught (of just complaint) against any; that your Father also which is in heaven may forgive you your trespasses. But if ye do not forgive, neither will your Father which is in heaven forgive you." Hence the beautiful practice of the early Church, to see that all differences amongst brethren and sisters in Christ were made up, in the spirit of love, before going to the Holy Communion; and the Church of England has a rubrical direction to this effect in her Communion service. Certainly, if this be the highest act of worship on earth, such reconciliation—though obligatory on all other occasions of worship—must be peculiarly so then. **25. Agree with thine adversary** [ἀντιδίκῳ]—thine opponent in a matter cognizable by law, **quickly, whiles thou art in the way with him**—"to the magistrate," as in Luke xii. 58; **lest at any time** [μήποτε]—here, rather, 'lest at all,' or simply 'lest' the adversary **deliver thee to the judge, and the judge**—having pronounced thee in the wrong, **deliver thee to the officer**—the official whose business it is to see the sentence carried into-effect, **and thou be cast into prison. 26. Verily I say unto thee, Thou shalt by no means come out thence, till thou hast paid the uttermost farthing** [κοδράντην = *quadrantem*]; a fractional Roman coin, to which our "farthing" answers sufficiently well. That our Lord meant here merely to give a piece of prudential advice to his hearers, to keep out of the hands of the law and its officials by settling all disputes with one another privately, is not for a moment to be supposed, though there are critics of a school low enough to suggest this. The concluding words—"Verily I say unto thee, Thou shalt by no means come out," &c.—manifestly show that though the *language* is drawn from human disputes and legal procedure, He is dealing with a higher than any human quarrel, a higher than any human tribunal, a higher than any human and temporal sentence. In this view of the words—in which nearly all critics worthy of the name agree—the spirit of them may be thus expressed:—'In expounding the sixth com-

33

mandment, I have spoken of offences between man and man; reminding you that the offender has another party to deal with besides him whom he has wronged on earth, and assuring you that all worship offered to the Searcher of hearts by one who knows that a brother has just cause of complaint against him, and yet takes no steps to remove it, is vain: But I cannot pass from this subject without reminding you of One whose cause of complaint against you is far more deadly than any that man can have against man; and since with that Adversary you are already on the way to judgment, it will be your wisdom to make up the quarrel without delay, lest sentence of condemnation be pronounced upon you, and then will execution straightway follow, from the effects of which you shall never escape as long as any remnant of the offence remains unexpiated.' It will be observed that as the *principle* on which we are to "agree" with this "Adversary" is not here specified, and the precise *nature* of the retribution that is to light upon the despisers of this warning is not to be gathered from the mere use of the word "prison;" so, the *remedilessness* of the punishment is not in so many words expressed, and still less is its actual *cessation* taught. The language on all these points is designedly general; but it may safely be said that the *unending duration* of future punishment —elsewhere so clearly and awfully expressed by our Lord Himself, as in verses 29 and 30, and Mark ix. 43, 48—is the only doctrine with which His language here quite naturally and fully accords. (Compare ch. xviii. 30, 34.)

The same subject illustrated from the Seventh Commandment (27-32). **27. Ye have heard that it was said.** The words [τοῖς ἀρχαίοις] "by," or "to them of old time," in this verse are insufficiently supported, and probably were not in the original text. **Thou shalt not commit adultery.** Interpreting this seventh, as they did the sixth commandment, the traditional perverters of the law restricted the breach of it to *acts* of criminal intercourse between, or with, married persons exclusively. Our Lord now dissipates such delusions. **28. But I say unto you, That whosoever looketh on a woman to lust after her** [πρὸς τό]—with the intent to do so, as the same expression is used in ch. vi. 1; or, with the full consent of his will, to feed thereby his unholy desires. **hath committed adultery with her already in his heart.** We are not to suppose, from the word here used— "adultery"—that our Lord means to restrict the breach of this commandment to married persons, or to criminal intercourse with such. The expressions, "*whosoever* looketh," and "looketh upon a *woman*," seem clearly to extend the range of this commandment to all forms of impurity, and the counsels which follow—as they most certainly were intended for all, whether married or unmarried—seem to confirm this. As in dealing with the sixth commandment our Lord first expounds it, and then in the four following verses applies His exposition, so here, He first expounds the seventh commandment, and then in

29 heart.　And ^zif thy right eye ⁶offend thee, pluck it out, and cast *it* from thee: for it is profitable for thee that one of thy members should perish,

30 and not *that* thy whole body should be cast into hell.　And if thy right hand offend thee, cut it off, and cast *it* from thee: for it is profitable for thee that one of thy members should perish, and not *that* thy whole body should be cast into hell.

31　It hath been said, ^aWhosoever shall put away his wife, let him give

32 her a writing of divorcement: but I say unto you, That ^bwhosoever shall put away his wife, saving for the cause of fornication, causeth her to commit adultery: and whosoever shall marry her that is divorced committeth adultery.

33　Again, ye have heard that it hath been said ⁷by them of old time, ^cThou shalt not forswear thyself, but ^dshalt perform unto the Lord thine

34 oaths: but I say unto you, ^eSwear not at all: neither by heaven; for it

A. D. 31.

^z Mark 9. 43.
⁶ Or, do cause thee to offend.
Ps. 119. 37.
^a Deut. 24. 1.
Jer. 3. 1.
Mark 10. 2.
^b Rom. 7. 3.
1 Cor. 7. 10.
7 to the an-cients.
^c Ex. 20. 7.
Lev. 19. 12.
Num. 30. 2.
^d Deut. 23. 23.
^e Jas. 5. 12.

the four following verses applies His exposition. **29. And if thy right eye**—the readier and the dearer of the two, **offend thee** [σκανδαλίζει σε]—be [a σκανδάληθρον] a 'trap-spring,' or, as in the New Testament, be 'an occasion of stumbling' to thee, **pluck it out, and cast it from thee**—implying a certain indignant promptitude, heedless of whatever cost to feeling the act may involve.　Of course, it is not *the eye simply* of which our Lord speaks—as if execution were to be done upon the bodily organ—though there have been fanatical ascetics who have both advocated and practised this, showing a very low apprehension of spiritual things—but *the offending eye*, or the eye considered as the occasion of sin; and consequently, only the *sinful exercise* of the organ which is meant.　For as one might put out his eyes without in the least quenching the lust to which they ministered, so, "if thine eye be single, thy whole body shall be full of light," and, when directed by a holy mind, becomes an "instrument of righteousness unto God."　At the same time, just as by cutting off a hand, or plucking out an eye, the *power* of acting and of seeing would be destroyed, our Lord certainly means that we are to *strike at the root* of such unholy dispositions, as well as cut off the occasions which tend to stimulate them. **for it is profitable for thee that one of thy members should perish, and not that thy whole body should be cast into hell.** He who despises the warning to "cast from him," with indignant promptitude, an offending member, will find his whole body "cast," with a retributive promptitude of indignation, "into hell."　Sharp language this, from the lips of Love incarnate! **30. And if thy right hand**—the organ of *action*, to which the eye excites, **offend thee, cut it off, and cast it from thee: for it is profitable, &c.** See on *v.* 29.　The repetition, in identical terms, of such stern truths and awful lessons seems characteristic of our Lord's manner of teaching.　Compare Mark ix. 43-48.

31. It hath been said. This shortened form **was** perhaps intentional, to mark a transition from the commandments of the Decalogue to a civil enactment on the subject of Divorce, quoted from Deut. xxiv. 1.　The law of Divorce—according to its strictness or laxity—has so intimate a bearing upon purity in the married life, that nothing could be more natural than to pass from the seventh commandment to the loose views on that subject then current.　**Whosoever shall put away his wife, let him give her a writing of divorcement**—a legal check upon reckless and tyrannical separation.　The one legitimate ground of divorce allowed by the enactment just quoted **was** "**some uncleanness**" [עֶרְוַת דָּבָר, ἄσχημον

πρᾶγμα]—in other words, conjugal infidelity.　But while one school of interpreters (that of Shammai) explained this quite correctly, as prohibiting divorce in every case save that of adultery, another school (that of Hillel) stretched the expression so far as to include everything in the wife offensive or disagreeable to the husband—a view of the law too well fitted to minister to caprice and depraved inclination not to find extensive favour.　And, indeed, to this day the Jews allow divorces on the most frivolous pretexts.　It was to meet this that our Lord uttered what follows: **32. But I say unto you, That whosoever shall put away his wife, saving for the cause of fornication, causeth her to commit adultery**—that is, drives her into it, in case she marries again; **and whosoever shall marry her that is divorced**—for anything short of conjugal infidelity, **committeth adultery**—for if the commandment is broken by the one party, it must be by the other also.　But see on chap. xix. 4-9. Whether the innocent party, after a just divorce, may lawfully marry again, is not treated of here. The Church of Rome says, No; but the Greek and Protestant Churches allow it.

Same subject illustrated from the Third Commandment (33-37). **33. Again, ye have heard that it hath been said by them of old time, Thou shalt not forswear thyself.** These are not the precise words of Exod. xx. 7; but they express all that it was currently understood to condemn, namely, false swearing (Lev. xix. 12, &c.)　This is plain from what follows. **But I say unto you, Swear not at all.** That this was meant to condemn swearing of every kind and on every occasion—as the Society of Friends and some other ultra-moralists allege—is not for a moment to be thought.　For even Jehovah is said once and again to have sworn by Himself; and our Lord certainly answered upon oath to a question put to Him by the high priest; and the apostle several times, and in the most solemn language, takes God to witness that He spoke and wrote the truth; and it is inconceivable that our Lord should here have quoted the precept about not forswearing ourselves but performing to the Lord our oaths, only to give a precept of His own directly in the teeth of it. Evidently, it is 'swearing in common intercourse and on frivolous occasions' that is here meant. Frivolous oaths were indeed severely condemned in the teaching of the times.　But so narrow was the circle of them that a man might swear, says *Lightfoot*, a hundred thousand times and yet not be guilty of vain swearing.　Hardly anything was regarded as an oath if only the name of God were not in it; just as among ourselves, as *Trench* well

34

35 is *f* God's throne: nor by the earth; for it is his footstool: neither by
36 Jerusalem; for it is the city of the great King. Neither shalt thou swear
37 by thy head, because thou canst not make one hair white or black. But
g let your communication be, Yea, yea; Nay, nay: for whatsoever is more
than these cometh of evil.

38   Ye have heard that it hath been said, An *h* eye for an eye, and a tooth
39 for a tooth: but I say unto you, *i* That ye resist not evil; *j* but whosoever
40 shall smite thee on thy right cheek, turn to him the other also.   And if
any man will sue thee at the law, and take away thy coat, let him have
41 *thy* cloak also.   And whosoever *k* shall compel thee to go a mile, go with
42 him twain.   Give to him that asketh thee, and from *l* him that would
borrow of thee turn not thou away.

A. D. 31.
f Isa. 66. 1.
g 1 Cor. 1. 17-20.
Col. 4. 6.
Jas. 5. 12.
h Lev. 24. 20.
i Pro. 20. 22.
Rom. 12. 17.
1 Cor. 6. 7.
1 Thes. 5. 15.
1 Pet. 3. 9.
j Isa. 50. 6.
k Mark 15. 21.
l Deut. 15. 8.

remarks, a certain lingering reverence for the name of God leads to cutting off portions of His name, or uttering sounds nearly resembling it, or substituting the name of some heathen deity, in profane exclamations or asseverations. Against all this our Lord now speaks decisively; teaching His audience that every oath carries an appeal to God, whether named or not. **neither by heaven; for it is God's throne: 35. Nor by the earth; for it is his footstool** (quoting Isa. lxvi. 1): **neither by Jerusalem; for it is the city of the great King** (quoting Ps. xlviii. 2). **36. Neither shalt thou swear by thy head, because thou canst not make one hair white or black.** In the other oaths specified, God's name was profaned quite as really as if His name had been uttered, because it was instantly *suggested* by the mention of "His "throne," His "footstool," His "city." But in swearing by our own *head* and the like, the objection lies in their being 'beyond our control,' and therefore profanely assumed to have a stability which they have not. **37. But let your communication**—'your word' [λόγος], in ordinary intercourse, **be, Yea, yea; Nay, nay:**—'Let a simple *Yes* and *No* suffice, in affirming the truth or the untruth of anything. (See Jas. v. 12, and 2 Cor. i. 17, 18.) **for whatsoever is more than these cometh of evil** [ἐκ τοῦ πονηροῦ]—not 'of the evil One;' though an equally correct rendering of the words, and one which some expositors prefer. It is true that all evil in our world is originally of the devil, that it forms a kingdom at the head of which he sits, and that, in every manifestation of it he has an active part. But any reference to this here seems unnatural [cf. τῷ πονηρῷ, v. 39], and the allusion to this passage in the Epistle of James (v. 12) seems to show that this is not the sense of it—"Let your yea be yea; and your nay, nay; *lest ye fall into condemnation.*" The untruthfulness of our corrupt nature shows itself not only in the tendency to deviate from the strict truth, but in the disposition to suspect others of doing the same; and as this is not diminished, but rather aggravated, by the habit of confirming what we say by an oath, we thus run the risk of having all reverence for God's holy name, and even for strict truth, destroyed in our hearts, and so "fall into condemnation." The practice of going beyond Yes and No, in affirmations and denials—as if our word for it were not enough, and we expected others to question it—springs from that vicious root of untruthfulness which is only aggravated by the very effort to clear ourselves of the suspicion of it. And just as swearing to the truth of what we say begets the disposition it is designed to remove, so the love and reign of truth in the breasts of Christ's disciples reveals itself so plainly even to those who themselves cannot be trusted, that their simple Yes and No come soon to be more relied on than the most solemn asseverations of

others. Thus does the grace of our Lord Jesus Christ, like a tree cast into the bitter waters of human corruption, heal and sweeten them.
Same Subject—Retaliation (38-42). We have here the converse of the preceding lessons. They were *negative:* these are *positive.* **38. Ye have heard that it hath been said** (Exod. xxi. 23-25; Lev. xxiv. 19, 20; Deut. xix. 21), **An eye for an eye, and a tooth for a tooth**—that is, whatever penalty was regarded as a proper equivalent for these. This law of retribution—designed to take vengeance out of the hands of private persons, and commit it to the magistrate—was abused in the opposite way to the commandments of the Decalogue. While they were reduced to the level of civil enactments, this judicial regulation was held to be a warrant for taking redress into their own hands, contrary to the injunctions of the Old Testament itself (Prov. xx. 22; xxiv. 29). **39. But I say unto you, That ye resist not evil; but whosoever shall smite thee on thy right cheek, turn to him the other also.** Our Lord's own meek, yet dignified bearing, when smitten rudely on the cheek (John xviii. 22, 23), and *not* literally presenting the other, is the best comment on these words. It is the preparedness, after one indignity, not to invite but to submit meekly to another, without retaliation, which this strong language is meant to convey. **40. And if any man will sue thee at the law, and take away thy coat** [χιτῶνα]—the inner garment; in pledge for a debt (Exod. xxii. 26, 27)—**let him have thy cloak also** [ἱμάτιον]—the outer and more costly garment. This overcoat was not allowed to be retained over-night as a pledge from the poor, because they used it for a bed-covering. **41. And whosoever shall compel thee to go a mile, go with him twain**—an allusion, probably, to the practice of the Romans and some eastern nations, who, when Government-despatches had to be forwarded, obliged the people not only to furnish horses and carriages, but to give personal attendance, often at great inconvenience, when required. But the thing here demanded is a readiness to submit to unreasonable demands of whatever kind, rather than raise quarrels, with all the evils resulting from them. What follows is a beautiful extension of this precept. **42. Give to him that asketh thee.** The sense of *unreasonable* asking is here implied (cf. Luke vi. 30). **and from him that would borrow of thee turn not thou away.** Though the word [δανείζομαι in Med.] signifies classically 'to have money lent to one on security,' or 'with interest,' yet as this was not the original sense of the word, and as usury was forbidden among the Jews (Exod. xxii. 25, &c.), it is doubtless simple borrowing which our Lord here means, as indeed the whole strain of the exhortation implies. This shows that such counsels as "Owe no man anything" (Rom. xiii. 8) are not to be taken absolutely; else the Scripture commen-

43   Ye have heard that it hath been said, Thou *ᵐ*shalt love thy neighbour,
44 *ⁿ*and hate thine enemy: but I say unto you, *ᵒ*Love your enemies, bless
them that curse you, do good to them that hate you, and pray *ᵖ*for them
45 which despitefully use you, and persecute you; that ye may be the
children of your Father which is in heaven: for he maketh his sun to
rise on the evil and on the good, and sendeth rain on the just and on the
46 unjust.   For *�q*if ye love them which love you, what reward have ye? do
47 not even the publicans the same?   And if ye salute your brethren only,

A. D. 31.
ᵐ Lev. 19. 18.
ⁿ Deut. 23. 6.
ᵒ Pro. 25. 21.
Rom. 12. 14.
ᵖ Luke 23. 34.
Acts 7. 60.
1 Cor. 4. 12.
1 Pet. 2. 23.
q Luke 6. 32.

dations of the righteous for "lending" to his necessitous brother (Ps. xxxvii. 26; cxii. 5; Luke vi. 37) would have no application. **turn not thou away**—a graphic expression of unfeeling refusal to relieve a brother in extremity.

Same Subject—Love to Enemies (43-48). **43. Ye have heard that it hath been said** (Lev. xix. 18), **Thou shalt love thy neighbour.** To this the corrupt teachers added, **and hate thine enemy**—as if the one were a legitimate inference from the other, instead of being a detestable gloss, as *Bengel* indignantly calls it. *Lightfoot* quotes some of the cursed maxims inculcated by those traditionists regarding the proper treatment of all Gentiles. No wonder that the Romans charged the Jews with hatred of the human race. **44. But I say unto you, Love your enemies.** The word [ἀγαπᾶν] here used denotes *moral* love, as distinguished from the other word [φιλεῖν], which expresses *personal* affection. Usually, the former denotes 'complacency in the character' of the person loved; but here it denotes the benignant, compassionate outgoing of desire for another's good. [**bless them that curse you, do good to them that hate you**], **and pray for them which despitefully use you, and persecute you.** [The two bracketed clauses are omitted here by recent editors, who think them borrowed from Luke vi. 27, 28; but the evidence on both sides is pretty equally balanced.] The best commentary on these matchless counsels is the bright example of Him who gave them. (See 1 Pet. ii. 21-24; and cf. Rom. xii. 20, 21; 1 Cor. iv. 12; 1 Pet. iii. 9.) But though such precepts were never before expressed—perhaps not even conceived—with such breadth, precision, and sharpness as here, our Lord is here only the incomparable Interpreter of a law in force from the beginning; and this is the only satisfactory view of the entire strain of this Discourse. **45. That ye may be the children**—'that ye may be sons' [υἱοὶ]—**of your Father which is in heaven.** The meaning is, 'that ye may show yourselves to be such by *resembling* Him (cf. v. 9 and Eph. v. 1). **for he maketh his sun**—'your Father's sun.' Well might *Bengel* exclaim, 'Magnificent appellation!'—**to rise on the evil and on the good, and sendeth rain on the just and on the unjust**—rather [without the article], 'on evil and good, and on just and unjust.' When we find God's own procedure held up for imitation in the law, and much more in the prophets (Lev. xix. 2; xx. 26; and cf. 1 Pet. i. 15, 16), we may see that the principle of this surprising verse was nothing new: but the form of it certainly is that of One who spake as never man spake. **46. For if ye love them which love you, what reward have ye? do not even the publicans the same?** [τὸ αὐτό. The reading οὕτως has perhaps slightly the better support.] The publicans, as collectors of taxes due to the Roman government, were even on this account obnoxious to the Jews, who sat uneasy under a foreign yoke, and disliked whatever brought this unpleasantly before them. But the extortion practised by this class made them hateful to the community, who in their current speech ranked

them with "harlots." Nor does our Lord scruple to speak of them as others did, which we may be sure He never would if it had been calumnious. The meaning, then, is, 'In loving those who love you, there is no evidence of superior principle: the worst of men will do this: even a publican will go that length.' **47. And if ye salute your brethren only**—of the same nation and religion with yourselves—**what do ye more [than others]?** [τί περισσόν]—'what do ye uncommon' or 'extraordinary?' that is, wherein do ye *excel?* **do not even the publicans so?** The true reading here appears to be, 'Do not even the heathens the same?' [ἐθνικοί.] Cf. ch. xviii. 17, where the excommunicated person is said to be "as an heathen man and a publican." **48. Be ye therefore** ['Ἔσεσθε οὖν]—rather, 'Ye shall therefore be,' or 'Ye are therefore to be,' as My disciples and in My kingdom—**perfect** [τέλειοι], or 'complete.' Manifestly, our Lord here speaks, not of *degrees* of excellence, but of the *kind* of excellence which was to distinguish His disciples and characterize His kingdom. When therefore He adds, **even as your Father which is in heaven is perfect,** He refers to that full-orbed glorious completeness which is in the great Divine Model, "their Father which is in heaven." ['Your heavenly Father'—οὐράνιος—is here the preferable reading.]

Remarks.—1. In the light of this Section what shall we think of those low views of the Old Testament which have long been current in Germany, even among the most distinguished theologians and critics, and which from them have passed over to this country and across the Atlantic; poisoning some otherwise well affected to evangelical truth, and introducing a principle of laxity into their whole Biblical system? Not to speak of our Lord's solemn asseverations of the enduring authority of "the Law and the Prophets," and the honour in which they were to be held in His kingdom: who can read with intelligence, impartiality, and reverential docility, the illustrations which our Lord here gives of the spirituality and breadth of the ancient law, in opposition to the detestable perversions of it under which His hearers had grown up, without perceiving that instead of supplanting or even modifying it—which some excellent critics have too hastily conceded—the highest position towards the ancient law which our Lord here assumes, is that of its supreme and authoritative Interpreter? It is only the glorious comprehensiveness, the pure spirituality, the self-evidencing truth, and the heavenly radiance of His interpretations of the law —transcending, it is true, everything which we read in the Old Testament—that has deceived many into the notion that we have here a more or less *new code of morals;* a thing as contrary to a sound exposition of this Section as derogatory to the honour of God's ancient law. And if this is not to be endured, much less the Romish notion that all our Lord's teachings here are but 'evangelical counsels' (*consilia evangelica*), or counsels of perfection—not obligatory upon any, but the more meritorious in those who can work them-

48 what do ye more *than others?* do not even the publicans so? Be ʳye therefore perfect, even ˢas your Father which is in heaven is perfect.

A. D. 31.
ʳ Gen. 17. 1.
ˢ Eph. 5. 1.

selves up to them. 2. After reading such spiritual and searching expositions of the law, with what force is the apostolic inference borne in upon the awakened conscience, "Therefore by the deeds of the law there shall no flesh be justified in His sight: for by the law is the knowledge of sin"! (Rom. iii. 20.) The whole doctrinal system, indeed, of the Epistle to the Romans is seminally contained in the Gospels; but this truth in particular is written here as with a sunbeam. And yet, there are those who take refuge, from the pretended severity of the Pauline doctrine, in the Sermon on the Mount—as if it were of a milder type. We have ourselves heard the Jews chanting in the synagogue the praises of the law, while rejecting Him who alone can deliver them from the curse of it; but what better are those called Christians who turn away from the Pauline doctrine of Justification to that teaching from the Mount which, but for this Pauline doctrine the awakened conscience cannot abide—a teaching which, but for salvation by free grace, makes us feel ourselves standing under a very different Mount from that of the Beatitudes, beneath whose thunderings, and lightnings, and earthquakes, and voices the people exclaimed, "Let not God speak with us, lest we die" (Exod. xx. 19). Now this, without doubt, was what our Lord in the first instance sought to produce by so constructing His Sermon on the Mount. Accordingly, 3. Who that weighs the faint exposition we have given of the holy teaching of this Section, can fail to see the wisdom with which our Lord selected this line of thought for the first formal proclamation of the principles of His kingdom, rather than anything more definite regarding the "Lamb of God" which was to "take away the sin of the world"? While this would have been of little avail to such a motley assemblage, "alive without the law" and "at ease in Zion," nothing could be better fitted to dash vain expectations from Him of support to the reigning ideas; to rouse to anxious thought as many as were prepared to give Him even a respectful hearing; and to humble to the dust the thoroughly awakened, and create in them longings after further light and solid rest to their troubled souls. 4. When will Christians strive in earnest, as one man, to carry out the law of love, in respect of 'causeless anger,' here laid down? That little of it is to be seen at present is but too manifest; but that, if resolutely and habitually exemplified, it would astonish and impress the world around them more than all other arguments in favour of Christianity, who can doubt? O brother—sister—in Christ, blush, first of all, that thy Lord hath spoken to thee from the Mount so much in vain, and hath hitherto gotten so little testimony from thee. Then, on thy knees, pledge thyself to Him anew, and in strength divine make it thy daily business, whether in the quiet walks of domestic intercourse, or in the busy haunts of a more public calling, to exemplify the law of love here expounded. Nor, if thou hast broken it, despair or rest contented; but quickly repair, at any cost to feeling, the wrong thou hast hastily done to a brother, whether by unwarrantable anger in thy heart, or by unmerited and unbecoming rudeness of speech. Failing this, every act of worship offered to the Searcher of hearts will be vain (Ps. lxvi. 18), and should rather be interrupted till thou hast come to one with thy brother, than performed with a guilty conscience. (See Job xlii. 8.) 5. In vain do Romanists plead for the

sacrifice of the mass, and some Protestants for "altars" in the Christian Church, from the "gifts brought to the altar," to which our Lord alludes in this Section. Spoken to Jews while the temple service was in full force, such language was altogether natural; it was most intelligible; it was life-like. But how far such things would or would not remain under an economy which was to supersede the Jewish, must be decided, not by such phraseology occurring here, but by other considerations altogether. 6. When we see how naturally our Lord rose, in His teaching, from disputes between man and man to the great controversy between man and God (v. 25, 26), it should be our study to imitate such spirituality—even in ordinary intercourse, but much more in teaching—and to make the immediate settlement of the great question of *peace with God* the paramount subject of all we say and teach on eternal things. 7. The sense in which our Lord here uses the phrase "*be reconciled*" [διαλλάγηθι, v. 24], is to be carefully noted, as the expression has been laid hold of to subvert the proper doctrine of the Atonement. It has been confidently affirmed that God is nowhere said to be reconciled to us as if any change were needed, or possible, in the Unchangeable One towards men—but always we are said to be reconciled to God. In proof of this we are referred to 2 Cor. v. 18-20—"All things are of God, who hath reconciled *us to Himself* by Jesus Christ. God was in Christ, reconciling *the world unto Himself* . . . Now then . . . we pray you, in Christ's stead, be *ye reconciled to God*." But since our Lord, in this Sermon on the Mount, when He requires the offending party to '*be reconciled to his offended brother*,' plainly means—not that the offender is to get rid of the cause of offence in his own breast, or to banish all doubts of his brother's willingness to forgive him—but that he is to take steps towards obtaining his brother's forgiveness, or getting his brother's just displeasure against himself removed; so in the words quoted from the Epistle to the Corinthians, the world's reconciliation to God by Jesus Christ, as a thing already accomplished—which is the great fact that the Gospel ministry is appointed to publish—cannot possibly mean any change which has come over the world's views of God: it can only mean the altered view of the world which God takes in consequence of Christ's death; or, to speak more properly, a new relation in which He stands to it *as reconciled through that death;* and it is when we "set to our seal that this is true," that we "are reconciled to God," for it must take effect on both sides. 8. If we would avoid sin we must cut off the occasions of it. This obvious rule solves a great many casuistical questions, as to how far Christians may warrantably go to this place and that, or join in this amusement and that. It is not enough to show that there is no express divine prohibition of them. If what the eyes see, and the hands handle, is found to suck one into the vortex of sin, it is no more to be indulged at such expense than if we should pluck them out, and cut them off, and cast them from us. A hard saying this, some will say. But a harder still, our Lord would answer, if I tell you those eyes and hands will otherwise drag you down to hell. No soft, silken teaching is this; and yet it is the teaching of Him to whom some affect to retreat as that of 'the meek and lowly Jesus,' from what they deem the harsh notes of the apostle of the Gentiles. To such one would be disposed to say, "Jesus I know, and Paul I know, but who are ye?" (Acts

6   TAKE heed that ye do not your [1]alms before men, to be seen of them; otherwise ye have no reward [2]of your Father which is in heaven.

2   Therefore, *a* when thou doest *thine* alms, [3]do not sound a trumpet before thee, as the hypocrites do in the synagogues and in the streets, that they may have glory of men. Verily I say unto you, They have

3 their reward. But when thou doest alms, let not thy left hand know

4 what thy right hand doeth; that thine alms may be in secret: and thy Father which seeth in secret himself shall reward thee openly.

A. D. 31.
1 Or, righteousness.
2 Or, with.
a Rom. 12. 8.
3 Or, cause not a trumpet to be sounded.

---

xix. 15). 9. What sanctity is stamped upon the married life by our Lord's teaching here, especially when taken in connection with His teaching on the subject of purity in general! (*vv.* 28-32). 10. By cutting off all swearing in ordinary intercourse, with what sacredness is lawful swearing invested; especially when the presence of God, as the Avenger of falsehood, is seen to be invoked even when not expressly named! 11. Were simple truth to be so reverend in the eyes, and dear to the heart of every genuine disciple of Christ, that all around them were constrained to regard their "Yes" and "No" as far more to be trusted than the most solemn asseverations of others, what a testimony would thus be borne to Him to whom they owe their all! And why should it not be universally so! But, 12. What shall we say to the concluding expositions of this Section? To what a God-like height—not only of forbearance with those who wrong us, and submission to unreasonable demands, but of well-doing to the uttermost in return for ill-doing of the worst—does Jesus teach His disciples to rise! They are not to deem it enough to be as good as others, or up to the current standard, or 'neighbour-like.' As "the light of the world" and "the salt of the earth," their walk is to be a model for others, as their Heavenly Father Himself is to be their Model. (See Col. iii. 14; 1 John iv. 16.) Does any ingenuous disciple ask, But how is this to be attained and carried out? Let him hear the answer from the same blessed lips, "I say unto you, Ask, and it shall be given you; seek, and ye shall find; knock, and it shall be opened unto you: for if ye, being evil, know how to give good gifts unto your children, how much more shall your heavenly Father give the Holy Spirit to them that ask Him?' (Luke xi. 9, 13). And if we do but think that it was when we were *enemies* that we ourselves were reconciled to God by the death of His Son (Rom. v. 10), can we choose but extend that love to any enemies, even the greatest, that we may have among our fellow-men?

CHAP. VI. SERMON ON THE MOUNT—*continued.*

1-18.—FURTHER ILLUSTRATION OF THE RIGHTEOUSNESS OF THE KINGDOM—ITS UNOSTENTATIOUSNESS.

General Caution against Ostentation in Religious Duties (1). **1. Take heed that ye do not your alms** [ἐλεημοσύνην]. But the true reading seems clearly to be 'your righteousness' [δικαιοσύνην]. The external authority for both readings is pretty nearly equal; but internal evidence is decidedly in favour of 'righteousness.' The subject of the second verse being 'almsgiving,' that word—so like the other in Greek—might easily be substituted for it by the copyist: whereas the opposite would not be so likely. But it is still more in favour of "righteousness," that if we so read the first verse, it then becomes a general heading for this whole Section of the Discourse, inculcating unostentatiousness in *all* deeds of righteousness —Almsgiving, Prayer, and Fasting being, in that case, but selected examples of this righteous-

ness; whereas, if we read "Do not your *alms*," &c., this first verse will have no reference but to that one point. By "righteousness," in this case, we are to understand that same righteousness of the kingdom of heaven, whose leading features—in opposition to traditional perversions of it—it is the great object of this Discourse to open up; that righteousness of which the Lord says, "Except your righteousness shall exceed the righteousness of the Scribes and Pharisees, ye shall in no case enter into the kingdom of heaven" (ch. v. 20). To "*do*" this righteousness, was an old and well understood expression. Thus, "Blessed is he that doeth righteousness [חֲשֵׂי, עֹשׂה, ποιοῦντες δικαιοσύνην] at all times" (Ps. cvi. 3). It refers to the *actings* of righteousness in the life—the outgoings of the gracious nature—of which our Lord afterwards said to His disciples," "Herein is my Father glorified, that ye bear much fruit: so shall ye be my disciples" (John xv. 8). **before men, to be seen of them** [πρὸς τὸ θεαθῆναι αὐτοῖς]—'with the view' or 'intention of being beheld of them.' See the same expression in ch. v. 28. True, He had required them to let their light so shine before men that they might see their good works, and glorify their Father which is in heaven (ch. v. 16). But this is quite consistent with not making a display of our righteousness for self-glorification. In fact, the doing of the former necessarily implies our *not* doing the latter. **otherwise ye have no reward of your Father which is in heaven.** When all duty is done to God—as primarily enjoining and finally judging of it—He will take care that it be duly recognized; but when done purely for ostentation, God cannot own it, nor is His judgment of it even thought of —God accepts only what is done to Himself. So much for the general principle. Now follow three illustrations of it.

Almsgiving (2-4). **2. Therefore, when thou doest thine alms, do not sound a trumpet before thee.** The expression is to be taken figuratively for *blazoning* it. Hence our expression to 'trumpet.' **as the hypocrites do.** This word [ὑποκριτὴς]—of such frequent occurrence in Scripture, signifying primarily 'one who acts a part'—denotes one who either *pretends* to be what he is not (as here), or *dissembles* what he really is (as in Luke xii. 1, 2). **in the synagogues and in the streets**—the places of religious and of secular resort—that **they may have glory of men. Verily I say unto you.** In such august expressions, it is the Lawgiver and Judge Himself that we hear speaking to us. **They have their reward.** All they wanted was human applause, and they have it—and with it, all they will ever get. **3. But when thou doest alms, let not thy left hand know what thy right hand doeth.** 'So far from making a display of it, dwell not on it even in thine own thoughts, lest it minister to spiritual pride.' **4. That thine alms may be in secret, and thy Father which seeth in secret [Himself] shall reward thee openly.** The word "Himself" [αὐτὸς] appears to be an unauthorized addition to the text, which the sense no doubt suggested. See 1 Tim. v. 25; Rom. ii. 16; 1 Cor. iv. 5.

5   And when thou *b*prayest, thou shalt not be as the hypocrites *are:* for they love to pray standing in the synagogues and in the corners of the streets, that they may be seen of men. Verily I say unto you, They
6 have their reward. But thou, when thou prayest, enter into thy closet, and when thou hast shut thy door, pray to thy Father which is in secret;
7 and thy Father *c*which seeth in secret shall reward thee openly. But when ye pray, *d*use not vain repetitions, as the heathen *do:* *e*for they
8 think that they shall be heard for their much speaking. Be not ye therefore like unto them: for your *f*Father knoweth what things ye

A. D. 31.

b Jer. 29. 12.
Luke 18. 1.
John 16. 24.
c Jer. 17. 10.
d Eccl. 5. 2.
Dan. 9. 18,
19.
ch. 26.39,42,
44.
e 1 Ki. 18. 26.
f Ps. 139. 2.

Prayer (5, 6). **5. And when thou prayest** [προσ-εύχῃ], thou shalt—or, according to the preferable reading, '**when ye pray** [προσεύχησθε] ye shall' **not be as the hypocrites are: for they love to pray standing in the synagogues and in the corners of the streets** (see on *v.* 2), **that they may be seen of men. Verily I say unto you, They have, &c.** The *standing* posture in prayer was the ancient practice, alike in the Jewish and in the early Christian Church, as is well known to the learned. But of course this conspicuous posture opened the way for the ostentatious. **6. But thou, when thou prayest, enter into thy closet** [ταμεῖον, a 'store-house'—here, a 'place of retirement'], **and when thou hast shut thy door, pray to thy Father which is in secret; and thy Father which seeth in secret shall reward thee openly.** Of course it is not the simple publicity of prayer which is here condemned. It may be offered in any circumstances, however open, if not prompted by the spirit of ostentation, but dictated by the great ends of prayer itself. It is the *retiring* character of true prayer which is here taught.
Supplementary Directions, and Model-Prayer (7-15). **7. But when ye pray, use not vain repetitions** [μὴ βαττολογήσητε]. 'Babble not' would be a better rendering, both for the form of the word—which in both languages is intended to imitate the sound—and for the sense, which expresses not so much the repetition of the same words as a senseless multiplication of them; as appears from what follows. **as the heathen do: for they think that they shall be heard for their much speaking.** This method of heathen devotion is still observed by Hindu and Mohammedan devotees. With the Jews, says *Lightfoot,* it was a maxim, that 'Every one who multiplies prayer is heard.' In the Church of Rome, not only is it carried to a shameless extent, but, as *Tholuck* justly observes, the very Prayer which our Lord gave as an antidote to vain repetitions is the most abused to this superstitious end; the number of times it is repeated counting for so much more merit. Is not this just that character-istic feature of heathen devotion which our Lord here condemns? But praying much, and using at times the same words, is *not* here condemned, and has the example of our Lord Himself in its favour. **8. Be not ye therefore like unto them: for your Father knoweth what things ye have need of before ye ask him**—and so needs not to be *informed* of our wants, any more than to be *roused* to attend to them by our incessant speaking. What a view of God is here given, in sharp contrast with the gods of the heathen! But let it be carefully noted that it is not as *the general Father of Mankind* that our Lord says, "Your Father" knoweth what ye need before ye ask it; for it is not men, as such, that He is addressing in this Discourse, but His own disciples—the poor in spirit, the mourners, the meek, hungry and thirsty souls, the merciful, the pure in heart, the peacemakers, who allow themselves to have all manner of evil said against them for the Son

of Man's sake—in short, the new-born children of God, who, making their Father's interests their own, are here assured that their Father, in return, makes their interests His, and needs neither to be told nor to be reminded of their wants. Yet He will have His children pray to Him, and links all His promised supplies to their petitions for them; thus encouraging us to draw near and keep near to Him, to talk and walk with Him, to open our every case to Him, and assure our-selves that asking we shall receive—thus seeking we shall find—thus knocking it shall be opened to us. **9. After this manner** [Οὕτως]—more simply, 'Thus,' **therefore pray ye.** The "ye" [ὑμεῖς] is emphatic here, in contrast with the heathen prayers. That this matchless prayer was given not only as a *model*, but as a *form*, might be concluded from its very nature. Did it consist only of hints or directions for prayer, it could only be used as a directory; but seeing it is an actual prayer—designed, indeed, to show how much real prayer could be compressed into the fewest words, but still, as a prayer, only the more incomparable for that—it is strange that there should be a doubt whether we ought to pray that very prayer. Surely the words with which it is introduced, in the second utterance and varied form of it which we have in Luke xi. 2, ought to set this at rest: "When ye pray, *say* [λέγετε], Our Father." Nevertheless, since the se-cond form of it varies considerably from the first, and since no example of its actual use, or express quotation of its phraseology, occurs in the sequel of the New Testament, we are to guard against a superstitious use of it. How early this began to appear in the Church-services, and to what an extent it was afterwards carried, is known to every one versed in Church History. Nor has the spirit which bred this abuse quite departed from some branches of the Protestant Church, though the opposite and equally condemnable extreme is to be found in other branches of it.
Model-Prayer (9-13). According to the Latin fathers and the Lutheran Church, the petitions of the Lord's Prayer are *seven* in number; according to the Greek fathers, the Reformed Church, and the Westminster divines, they are only *six;* the two last being regarded—we think, less correctly—as one. The first three petitions have to do ex-clusively with GOD: "*Thy* name be hallowed"—"*Thy* kingdom come"—"*Thy* will be done." And they occur in a *descending* scale—from Himself down to the manifestation of Himself in His king-dom; and from His kingdom to the entire subjec-tion of its subjects, or the complete doing of His will. The remaining four petitions have to do with OURSELVES: "Give *us* our bread"—"For-give *us* our debts"—"Lead *us* not into tempta-tion"—"Deliver *us* from evil." But these latter petitions occur in an *ascending* scale—from our bodily wants of every day up to our final deliver-ance from all evil.
Invocation: **Our Father which art in heaven.** In the former clause we express His nearness to

9 have need of before ye ask him. After this manner therefore pray ye:
10 *⁹Our* Father which art in heaven, *ʰ*Hallowed be thy name. Thy
11 kingdom come. Thy will be done in earth, *ⁱas it is* in heaven. Give

A. D. 31.

ᵍ Luke 11. 2.
ʰ Isa. 6. 3.
ⁱ Ps. 103. 20.

us; in the latter, His distance from us. (See Eccl. v. 2; Isa. lxvi. 1.) Holy, loving familiarity suggests the one; awful reverence the other. In calling Him "Father," we express a relationship we have all known and felt surrounding us even from our infancy; but in calling Him our Father "who art in heaven," we contrast Him with the fathers we all have here below, and so raise our souls to that "heaven" where He dwells, and that Majesty and Glory which are there as in their proper home. These first words of the Lord's Prayer—this Invocation with which it opens—what a brightness and warmth does it throw over the whole prayer, and into what a serene region does it introduce the praying believer, the child of God, as he thus approaches Him! It is true that the paternal relationship of God to His people is by no means strange to the Old Testament. (See Deut. xxxii. 6; Ps. ciii. 13; Isa. lxiii. 16; Jer. iii. 4, 19; Mal. i. 6; ii. 10.) But these are only glimpses—the "back parts" (Exod. xxxiii. 23), if we may so say, in comparison with the "open face" of our Father revealed in Jesus. (See on 2 Cor. iii. 18.) Nor is it too much to say, that the view which our Lord gives, throughout this His very first lengthened discourse, of "our Father in heaven," beggars all that was ever taught, even in God's own Word, or conceived before by His saints, on this subject.

First Petition: **Hallowed be** [ἁγιασθήτω]—that is, 'Be held in reverence'—*regarded* and *treated* as holy. **thy name.** God's name means 'Himself as revealed and manifested.' Everywhere in Scripture God defines and marks off the faith and love and reverence and obedience He will have from men by the disclosures which He makes to them of what He is; both to shut out false conceptions of Him, and to make all their devotion take the shape and hue of His own teaching. Too much attention cannot be paid to this.

Second Petition: **10. Thy kingdom come.** The kingdom of God is that moral and spiritual kingdom which the God of grace is setting up in this fallen world, whose subjects consist of as many as have been brought into hearty subjection to His gracious sceptre, and of which His Son Jesus is the glorious Head. In the inward reality of it, this kingdom existed ever since there were men who "walked with God" (Gen. v. 24), and "waited for His salvation" (Gen. xlix. 18); who were "continually with Him, holden by His right hand" (Ps. lxxiii. 23), and who, even in the valley of the shadow of death, feared no evil, when He was with them (Ps. xxiii. 4). When Messiah Himself appeared, it was, as a visible kingdom, "at hand." His death laid the deep foundations of it—His ascension on high, "leading captivity captive and receiving gifts for men, yea, for the rebellious, that the Lord God might dwell among them," and the Pentecostal effusion of the Spirit, by which those gifts for men descended upon the rebellious, and the Lord God was beheld, in the persons of thousands upon thousands "dwelling" among men—was a glorious "coming" of this kingdom. But it is still to come, and this petition, "Thy kingdom come," must not cease to ascend so long as one subject of it remains to be brought in. But does not this prayer stretch further forward—to "the glory to be revealed," or that stage of the kingdom called "the everlasting kingdom of our Lord and Saviour Jesus Christ"? (2 Pet. i. 11). Not directly, perhaps,

since the petition that follows this—"Thy will be done in earth, as it is in heaven"—would then bring us back to this present state of imperfection. Still, the mind refuses to be so bounded by stages and degrees, and in the act of praying "Thy kingdom come," it irresistibly stretches the wings of its faith, and longing, and joyous expectation out to the final and glorious consummation of the kingdom of God.

Third Petition: **Thy will be done in earth, as it is in heaven**—or, as the same words are rendered in Luke, 'as in heaven, so upon earth'—as *cheerfully,* as *constantly,* as *perfectly.* But some will ask, Will this ever be? We answer, If the "new heavens and new earth" are to be just our present material system purified by fire and transfigured, of course it will. But we incline to think that the aspiration which we are taught in this beautiful petition to breathe forth has no direct reference to any such *organic* fulfilment, and is only the spontaneous and resistless longing of the renewed soul—put into words—to see the whole inhabited earth in entire conformity to the will of God. It asks not if ever it shall be—or if ever it can be—in order to pray this prayer. It *must* have its holy yearnings breathed forth, and this is just the bold yet simple expression of them. Nor is the Old Testament without prayers which come very near to this, (Ps. vii. 9; lxvii.; lxxii. 19; &c.)

Fourth Petition: **11. Give us this day our daily bread.** The compound word here rendered "daily" [ἐπιούσιος] occurs nowhere else, either in classical or sacred Greek, and so must be interpreted by the analogy of its component parts. But on this critics are divided. To those who would understand it to mean, "Give us this day the bread of to-morrow" —as if the sense thus slid into that of Luke, "Give us *day by day*" (as *Bengel, Meyer,* &c.)—it may be answered that the sense thus brought out is scarcely intelligible, if not something less; that the expression "bread of to-morrow" is not at all the same as bread "from day to day," and that, so understood, it would seem to contradict *v.* 34. The great majority of the best critics [taking the word to be compounded of οὐσία, '*substance,*' or 'being'] understand by it the 'staff of *life,*' 'the bread of *subsistence;*' and so the sense will be, 'Give us this day the bread which this day's necessities require.' In this case, the rendering of our authorized version (after the *Vulgate, Luther,* and some of the best modern critics)—"our daily bread"—is, in sense, accurate enough. (See Prov. xxx. 8.) Among commentators, there was early shown an inclination to understand this as a prayer for the heavenly bread, or spiritual nourishment; and in this they have been followed by many superior expositors, even down to our own times. But as this is quite unnatural, so it deprives the Christian of one of the sweetest of his privileges—to cast his bodily wants, in this short prayer, by one simple petition, upon his heavenly Father. No doubt the spiritual mind will, from "the meat that perisheth," naturally rise in thought to "that meat which endureth to everlasting life." But let it be enough that the petition about bodily wants irresistibly *suggests* a higher petition; and let us not rob ourselves—out of a morbid spirituality—of our one petition in this prayer for that bodily provision which the immediate sequel of this discourse shows that our heavenly Father has so much at heart. In limiting our petitions, however, to provision *for the*

40

12 us this day our *ʲ*daily bread. And forgive us our debts, as we
13 forgive our debtors. And *ᵏ*lead us not into temptation, but deliver

A. D. 31.
ʲ Job 23. 12.
ᵏ 1 Cor. 10.13.

day, what a spirit of child-like dependence does the Lord both demand and beget!

Fifth Petition. **12. And forgive us our debts.** A vitally important view of sin this—as an offence against God demanding reparation to His dishonoured claims upon our absolute subjection. As the debtor in the creditor's hands, so is the sinner in the hands of God. This idea of sin had indeed come up before in this Discourse—in the warning to agree with our adversary quickly, in case of sentence being passed upon us, adjudging us to payment of the last farthing, and to imprisonment till then (ch. v. 25, 26). And it comes up once and again in our Lord's subsequent teaching—as in the parable of the Creditor and his two debtors (Luke vii. 41, &c.), and in the parable of the Unmerciful debtor, (ch. xviii. 23, &c.) But by embodying it in this brief Model of acceptable prayer, and as the first of three petitions more or less bearing upon sin, our Lord teaches us, in the most emphatic manner conceivable, to regard this view of sin as the primary and fundamental one. Answering to this is the "forgiveness" which it directs us to seek—not the removal from our own hearts of the stain of sin, nor yet the removal of our just dread of God's anger, or of unworthy suspicions of His love, which is all that some tell us we have to care about —but the removal from God's own mind of His displeasure against us on account of sin, or, to retain the figure, the wiping or crossing out from His "book of remembrance" of all entries against us on this account. **as we forgive our debtors**—the same view of sin as before; only now transferred to the region of offences given and received between man and man. After what has been said on ch. v. 7, it will not be thought that our Lord here teaches that our exercise of forgiveness towards our offending fellow-men absolutely precedes and is the proper ground of God's forgiveness of us. His whole teaching, indeed—as of all Scripture—is the reverse of this. But as no one can reasonably imagine himself to be the object of Divine forgiveness who is deliberately and habitually unforgiving towards his fellow-men, so it is a beautiful provision to make our right to ask and expect daily forgiveness of our daily shortcomings, and our final absolution and acquittal at the great day of admission into the kingdom, dependent upon our consciousness of a forgiving disposition towards our fellows, and our preparedness to protest before the Searcher of hearts that we do actually forgive them. (See Mark xi. 25, 26.) God sees His own image reflected in His forgiving children; but to ask God for what we ourselves refuse to men, is to insult Him. So much stress does our Lord put upon this, that immediately after the close of this Prayer, it is the one point in it which He comes back upon (*vv.* 14, 15), for the purpose of solemnly assuring us that the Divine procedure in this matter of forgiveness will be exactly what our own is.

Sixth Petition: **13. And lead us not into temptation.** He who honestly seeks, and has the assurance of, forgiveness for past sin, will strive to avoid committing it for the future. But conscious that "when we would do good evil is present with us," we are taught to offer this sixth petition, which comes naturally close upon the preceding, and flows, indeed, instinctively from it in the hearts of all earnest Christians. There is some difficulty in the form of the petition, as it is certain that God does bring His people—as He did Abraham, and Christ Himself—into circumstances both fitted and designed to try them, or test the strength of their faith. Some meet this by regarding the petition as simply an humble expression of self-distrust and instinctive shrinking from danger; but this seems too weak. Others take it as a prayer against yielding to temptation, and so equivalent to a prayer for 'support and deliverance when we are tempted;' but this seems to go beyond the precise thing intended. We incline to take it as a prayer against being *drawn* or *sucked, of our own will,* into temptation, to which the word here used [εἰσενέγκῃς] seems to lend some countenance—'Introduce us not.' This view, while it does not put into our mouths a prayer against being tempted—which is more than the Divine procedure would seem to warrant—does not, on the other hand, change the sense of the petition into one for support *under* temptation, which the words will hardly bear; but it gives us a subject for prayer, in regard to temptation, most *definite,* and of all others most *needful.* It was precisely this which Peter needed to ask, but did not ask, when—of his own accord, and in spite of difficulties—he pressed for entrance into the palace-hall of the high priest, and where, once sucked into the scene and atmosphere of temptation, he fell so foully. And if so, does it not seem pretty clear that this was exactly what our Lord meant His disciples to pray against when he said in the garden—"Watch and pray, that ye *enter not into* temptation" [ἵνα μὴ εἰσέλθητε εἰς πειρασμόν]? (ch. xxvi. 41).

Seventh Petition: **But deliver us from evil.** We can see no good reason for regarding this as but the second half of the sixth petition. With far better ground might the second and third petitions be regarded as one. The "but" [ἀλλὰ] connecting the two petitions is an insufficient reason for regarding them as one, though enough to show that the one thought naturally follows close upon the other. As the expression "from evil" [ἀπὸ τοῦ πονηροῦ] may be equally well rendered 'from the evil one,' a number of superior critics think the devil is intended, especially from its following close upon the subject of "temptation." But the comprehensive character of these brief petitions, and the place which this one occupies, as that on which all our desires die away, seems to us against so contracted a view of it. Nor can there be a reasonable doubt that the apostle, in some of the last sentences which he penned before he was brought forth to suffer for his Lord, alludes to this very petition in the language of calm assurance—"And the Lord shall deliver me from every evil work (compare the Greek of the two passages), and will preserve me unto his heavenly kingdom" (2 Tim. iv. 18). This final petition, then, is only rightly grasped when regarded as a prayer for deliverance from all evil of whatever kind—not only from sin, but from all its consequences—fully and finally. Fitly, then, are our prayers ended with this. For what can we desire which this does not carry with it? [**For thine is the kingdom, and the power, and the glory, for ever. Amen.**—If any reliance is to be placed on external evidence, this doxology, we think, can hardly be considered part of the original text. It is wanting in all the most ancient MSS.; it is wanting in the *Old Latin* version and in the *Vulgate:* the former mounting up to about the middle of the second century, and the latter being a revision of it in the fourth century by *Jerome,* a most reverential and conservative as well as able and impartial critic. As might be expected from this,

¹us from evil: For thine is the kingdom, and the power, and the glory,
14 for ever. Amen. For ᵐif ye forgive men their trespasses, your hea-
15 venly Father will also forgive you: but ⁿif ye forgive not men their
trespasses, neither will your Father forgive your trespasses.
16 Moreover, °when ye fast, be not, as the hypocrites, of a sad countenance: for they disfigure their faces, that they may appear unto men to
17 fast. Verily I say unto you, They have their reward. But thou, when
18 thou fastest, anoint thine head, and wash thy face; that thou appear
not unto men to fast, but unto thy Father which is in secret: and thy
Father, which seeth in secret, shall reward thee openly.

A. D. 31.

ⁱ John 17. 15,
ᵐ Mark 11.25;
Eph. 4. 32.
Col. 3. 13.
ⁿ ch. 18. 35.
Jas. 2. 13.
° 2 Sam. 12.16.
Neh. 1. 4.
Esth. 4. 16.
Ps. 35. 13.
Ps. 69. 10.
Isa. 58. 5.

it is passed by in silence by the earliest Latin fathers; but even the Greek commentators, when expounding this Prayer, pass by the doxology. On the other hand, it is found in a majority of MSS., though not the oldest; it is found in all the Syriac versions, even the Peshito—dating probably as early as the second century—although this version wants the "Amen," which the doxology, if genuine, could hardly have wanted; it is found in the *Sahidic* or *Thebaic* version made for the Christians of Upper Egypt, possibly as early as the Old Latin; and it is found in perhaps most of the later versions. On a review of the evidence, the strong probability, we think, is that it was no part of the original text. Not that our Lord could be supposed to direct that this or any prayer should close thus abruptly. But as, ever since David's exuberant doxology in 1 Chr. xxix. 11, the Jewish prayers had become rich in such doxologies (as may be seen in all their Liturgies), perhaps our Lord designedly left this model of prayer to be concluded more or less fully as circumstances might direct. This would account for the fact, that this doxology is variously given even in those MSS. and versions that have it, while some which omit it have the "Amen." On the whole, while we may in this way account for its finding its way into the venerable Peshito-Syriac and Old Latin versions, perhaps from the margins of some MSS., though not in the original text, it is very hard to conceive how it should have been allowed to drop out of all the most ancient MSS. if it was originally in the sacred text.]

14. For if ye forgive men, &c.: 15. But if ye forgive not, &c. See on *v.* 12.

Fasting (16-18). Having concluded His supplementary directions on the subject of Prayer with this divine Pattern, our Lord now returns to the subject of *Unostentatiousness* in our deeds of righteousness, in order to give one more illustration of it, in the matter of Fasting. **16. Moreover, when ye fast**—referring, probably, to private and voluntary fasting, which was to be regulated by each individual for himself; though in spirit it would apply to any fast. **be not, as the hypocrites, of a sad countenance: for they disfigure their faces** —[ἀφανίζουσιν]—lit., 'make unseen;' very well rendered "disfigure." They went about with a slovenly appearance, and ashes sprinkled on their head. **that they may appear unto men to fast.** It was not the *deed*, but *reputation* for the deed which they sought; and with this view those hypocrites multiplied their fasts. And are the exhausting fasts of the Church of Rome, and of Romanizing Protestants, free from this taint? **Verily I say unto you, They have their reward. 17. But thou, when thou fastest, anoint thine head, and wash thy face**—as the Jews did, except when mourning (Dan. x. 3); so that the meaning is, 'Appear as usual'—appear so as to attract no notice. **18. That thou appear not unto men to fast, but unto thy Father which is in secret: and thy Father, which seeth in secret, shall reward**

thee [openly] [ἐν τῷ φανερῷ]. The "openly" seems evidently a later addition to the text of this verse from *vv.* 4, 7, though of course the idea is implied.

Remarks. — 1. We have here one of many proofs that the whole teaching of the Epistles of the New Testament is seminally contained in the Gospels. When the apostle bids servants obey their masters, "not with eye-service, as menpleasers; but *in singleness of heart, fearing God*" (Col. iii. 22), what is this but the great precept of this Section, to "do our righteousness"—whatsoever we do in word or deed—*to the Lord alone?* Not that we are to be indifferent to men's observations on our conduct—quite the reverse—for servants are exhorted so to carry themselves towards their masters as to "please them well in all things" (Tit. ii. 9). But just as the supreme authority for all duty, and the final 'judgment on all we do in respect of it, lies with God, so in simple obedience to Him must all duty be done, and to His judicial procedure upon it must all be referred. 2. As nothing is more hateful to God, and beneath the true dignity of His children, than an ostentatious way of performing any duty—while a retiring spirit, and an absorbing desire to please God in all we do, is as beautiful in itself as it is in the Divine eye—so at the great day this will be signally manifested, when "they that despise Him shall be lightly esteemed," and as "having had their reward," shall be "sent empty away;" whereas "them that honour Him He will honour" by "rewarding them openly." 3. What power and warmth is there in the brevity of those prayers which are offered by God's dear children to a Father who wants no information from them, and no stimulus to attend to them, though with equal love and wisdom He has linked all His supplies to their confiding petitions! What "babbling" would this spirit effectually disperse, and what a glorious contrast would it present, not only to the prayers of "the heathen," but to the heathenish prayers which one too often hears from professedly Christian lips! 4. Surely it is not for nothing that the first three Petitions in the Model-Prayer have respect to GOD; and that not till we have exhausted the uttermost desires of the gracious soul for His glory are we directed to seek anything for OURSELVES. This was very early observed by the devout students of this Prayer, and has been often, but cannot be too often, pointed out. The inference is obvious, but weighty—that God must have the first place, as in our prayers, so in the desires of our heart (Ps. lxxiii. 25, 26). 5. Are not the fountains of the *missionary spirit* opened by the first three Petitions of this incomparable Prayer; and must not its living waters spring up into everlasting life within us the other we pour them forth from the bottom of our hearts? Can he who says daily, "Hallowed be Thy name," hear that name "continually every day blasphemed," without trying to "come to the help of the Lord against the mighty"? Can he who ceases not to say, "Thy

19 Lay [p]not up for yourselves treasures upon earth, where moth and rust
20 doth corrupt, and where thieves break through and steal: but [q]lay up
for yourselves treasures in heaven, where neither moth nor rust doth
21 corrupt, and where thieves do not break through nor steal: for where
22 your treasure is, there will your heart be also. The [r]light of the body is
the eye: if therefore thine eye be single, thy whole body shall be full of

A. D. 31.

[p] Pro. 23. 4. 1 Tim. 6. 17. Heb. 13. 5.
[q] 1 Tim. 6. 19. 1 Pet. 1. 4.
[r] Luke 11. 34.

kingdom come; Thy will be done in earth, as it is in heaven," know that the kingdom of God's enemy embraces, even in this nineteenth century of the Christian era, a majority of the earth's population, and that even where God's kingdom is set visibly up, and where it is had in greatest honour, His will is yet far, O how far! from being done as it is in heaven—and not feel his spirit stirred within him, remembering that to His own disciples did the Master, ere he took His flight for glory, commit the evangelization of the world, and that the curse of Meroz (Jud. v. 23) rests upon those who come not to the help of the Lord, to the help of the Lord against the mighty? 6. Dear to all the children of God should be the fourth petition of this matchless prayer—in its proper literal sense—because it teaches them that this body, which God thus cares for, is of value in His esteem: because, if they be needy, it gives them "cords of a man, and bands of love," to draw them to the fountain of plenty, and calms their anxious spirits with the assurance that the needed supply will not be withheld; and if they be not needy, but blessed with plenty, it teaches them consideration and compassion for those whose case is the reverse, and identifies them with such—constraining them to feel that for the gift, and the continuance of their abundance, they are as dependent upon their Father in heaven as are the poorest of their brethren for their scanty means. 7. By directing God's children to say daily, "Forgive us our debts," our Lord rebukes not only those perfectionists who say that as believers "they have no sin" (1 John i. 8), but those who, without going this length, deem it so the privilege of believers to *have* forgiveness, that to *ask* it is unbelief. Were this really the case, who that knows the plagues of his own heart would not think it a pity, and would not irresistibly break through the restraint, for the very privilege of crying, "Forgive us our debts"? But that it is not the case, this petition plainly shows. It is true that "he that is washed needeth not save to wash his feet, but is clean every whit;" but it is just this exceptive "washing of the feet," the felt need of which daily makes it such a necessity and such a privilege to say daily, "Forgive us our debts." (See on John xiii. 10.) 8. O how much hypocrisy is there in multitudes of worshippers, who protest before the Searcher of hearts that they "forgive their debtors!" And if we have just so much forgiveness of God as we ourselves extend to men, may not this be at least one explanation of the inability of some real Christians to attain to the joy of God's salvation? 9. How strange it is that any real Christians, after saying, "Lead us not into temptation," should deliberately adventure themselves into scenes which not only they ought to know are trying to Christian principle, but from which they themselves have already suffered! It is not enough that what is transacted is not intrinsically sinful. Whatever is found by experience to wound the conscience, or even greatly endanger its purity, ought to be eschewed by all who cry daily from the heart, "Lead us not into temptation." 10. How precious is the closing petition of this Model-Prayer—"But deliver us from evil"! lifting the soul into a region of superiority to evil, even while yet in the midst of it, encouraging it to stretch the neck of its expectation beyond it all, and assuring it, as its believing aspirations are dying away, that the time is drawing nigh when it shall bid an eternal adieu to the last remnant and memorial of it.

19-34.—CONCLUDING ILLUSTRATIONS OF THE RIGHTEOUSNESS OF THE KINGDOM—HEAVENLY-MINDEDNESS AND FILIAL CONFIDENCE.

19. Lay not up for yourselves—or hoard not—**treasures upon earth, where moth** [σὴς = סָס]—a 'clothes-moth.' Eastern treasures, consisting partly in costly dresses stored up (Job xxvii. 16), were liable to be consumed by moths (Job xiii. 28; Isa. l. 9; li. 8). In Jas. v. 2 there is an evident reference to our Lord's words here. **and rust** [βρῶσις]—any 'eating into' or 'consuming;' here, probably, 'wear-and-tear.' **doth corrupt** [ἀφανίζει]—'cause to disappear.' By this reference to moth and rust our Lord would teach how *perishable* are such earthly treasures. **and where thieves break through and steal.** Treasures these, how *precarious!* **20. But lay up for yourselves treasures in heaven.** The language in Luke (xii. 33) is very bold—"Sell that ye have, and give alms; provide yourselves bags which wax not old, a treasure in the heavens that faileth not," &c. **where neither moth nor rust doth corrupt, and where thieves do not break through nor steal.** Treasures these, *imperishable* and *unassailable!* (Compare Col. iii. 2.) **21. For where your treasure is**—that which ye value most, **there will your heart be also.** ['Thy treasure—thy heart' is probably the true reading here: 'your,' in Luke xii. 34, from which it seems to have come in here.] Obvious though this maxim be, by what multitudes who profess to bow to the teaching of Christ is it practically disregarded! 'What a man loves,' says *Luther*, quoted by *Tholuck*, 'that is his God. For he carries it in his heart, he goes about with it night and day, he sleeps and wakes with it; be it what it may—wealth or pelf, pleasure or renown.' But because "laying up" is not in itself sinful, nay, in some cases enjoined (2 Cor. xii. 14), and honest industry and sagacious enterprise are usually rewarded with prosperity, many flatter themselves that all is right between them and God while their closest attention, anxiety, zeal, and time are exhausted upon these earthly pursuits. To put this right, our Lord adds what follows, in which there is profound practical wisdom. **22. The light**—rather, 'The lamp' [λύχνος]—**of the body is the eye: if therefore thine eye be single** [ἁπλοῦς]—'simple,' 'clear.' As applied to the outward eye, this means general soundness; particularly, not looking two ways. Here, as also in classical Greek, it is used figuratively to denote the simplicity of the mind's eye, singleness of purpose, looking right at its object, as opposed to having two ends in view. (See Pro. iv. 25-27.) **thy whole body shall be full of light** [φωτεινὸν]—'illuminated.' As with the bodily vision, the man who looks with a good, sound eye walks in light, seeing every object clear; so a simple and persistent purpose to serve and please God in everything will make the whole character consistent and bright. **23. But if thine eye be evil** [πονηρὸς]—'distem-

23 light. But if thine eye be evil, thy whole body shall be full of darkness. If therefore the light that is in thee be darkness, *how great *is* that dark-
24 ness! No *man can serve two masters: for either he will hate the one, and love the other; or else he will hold to the one, and despise the other.
25 *Ye cannot serve God and mammon. Therefore I say unto you, ⁴Take no thought for your life, what ye shall eat, or what ye shall drink; nor yet for your body, what ye shall put on. Is not the life more than meat,
26 and the body than raiment? Behold *the fowls of the air: for they sow not, neither do they reap, nor gather into barns; yet your heavenly
27 Father feedeth them. Are ye not much better than they? Which of you,

A. D. 31.
* Rom. 1. 21,
2 Cor. 4. 4.
t Luke 16. 13.
⁎ Gal. 1. 10.
1 Tim. 6.17.
⁴ Be not anxiously careful.
Ps. 55. 22.
Phil. 4. 6.
ᵛ Job 38. 41.
Ps. 147. 9.

---

pered,' or, as we should say, If we have got a *bad* eye [cf. Prov. xxiii. 6, "an evil eye," רַע עַיִן]. **thy whole body shall be full of darkness** [σκο-τεινὸν]—'darkened.' As a vitiated eye, or an eye that looks not straight and full at its object, sees nothing as it is, so a mind and heart divided between heaven and earth is all dark. **If there-fore the light that is in thee** [not λύχνος now, but φῶς, 'light'] **be darkness, how great is that dark-ness!** As the conscience is the regulative faculty, and a man's inward purpose, scope, aim in life, determines his character—if these be not simple and heavenward, but distorted and double, what must all the other faculties and principles of our nature be which take their direction and character from these, and what must the whole man and the whole life be, but a mass of darkness? In Luke (xi. 36) the converse of this statement very strik-ingly expresses what pure, beautiful, broad per-ceptions the *clarity of the inward eye* imparts : "If thy whole body therefore be full of light, having no part dark, the whole shall be full of light, as the bright shining of a candle doth give thee light." But now for the application of this. **24. No man can serve** [δουλεύειν]. The word means to 'belong wholly and be entirely under command to,' **two masters: for either he will hate the one, and love the other; or else he will hold to the one, and despise the other.** Even if the two masters be of one character and have but one object, the servant must *take law* from one or other: though he may do what is agree-able to both, he cannot, in the nature of the thing, be *servant* to more than one. Much less if, as in the present case, their interests are quite different, and even conflicting. In this case, if our affections be in the service of the one—if we "love the one"—we must of necessity "hate the other;" if we determine resolutely to "hold to the one," we must at the same time disregard, and, if he insist on his claims upon us, even "despise the other." **Ye cannot serve God and mammon.** The word "mamon"—better written with one *m* — is a foreign one, whose precise de-rivation cannot certainly be determined, though the most probable one gives it the sense of 'what one trusts in.' Here, there can be no doubt it is used for *riches*, considered as an idol-master, or god of the heart. The service of this god and the true God together is here, with a kind of indignant curtness, pronounced impossible. But since the teaching of the preceding verses might seem to endanger our falling short of what is requisite for the present life, and so being left destitute, our Lord now comes to speak to that point. **25. Therefore I say unto you, Take no thought** [μὴ μεριμνᾶτε] — 'Be not solicitous.' The English word "thought," when our version was made, expressed this idea of 'solicitude,' 'anxious concern' it,—as may be seen in any old English classic; and in the same sense it is used in I Sam. ix, 5, &c. But this sense of the word

has now nearly gone out, and so the mere English reader is apt to be perplexed. *Thought* or fore-thought, for temporal things—in the sense of reflection, consideration—is required alike by Scripture and common sense. It is that anxious solicitude, that carking care, which springs from unbelieving doubts and misgivings, which alone is here condemned. (See Phil. iv. 6.) **for your life, what ye shall eat, or what ye shall drink; nor yet for your body, what ye shall put on.** In Luke (xii. 29) our Lord adds, 'neither be ye un-settled' [μετεωρίζεσθε]—not "of doubtful mind," as in our version. When "careful (or 'full of care') about nothing," but committing all in prayer and supplication with thanksgiving unto God, the apostle assures us that "the peace of God, which passeth all understanding, shall keep our hearts and minds [νοήματα] in Christ Jesus" (Phil. iv. 6, 7); that is, shall guard both our feelings and our thoughts from undue agitation, and keep them in a holy calm. But when we commit our whole temporal condition to the wit of our own minds, we get into that "unsettled" state against which our Lord exhorts His dis-ciples. **Is not the life more than meat**—or 'food' [τροφῆς], **and the body than raiment?** If God, then, give and keep up the greater—the life, the body—will He withhold the less, food to sustain life and raiment to clothe the body? **26. Behold the fowls of the air**—in *v.* 28, 'observe well' [καταμάθετε], and in Luke xii. 24, "con-sider" [κατανοήσατε]—so as to learn wisdom from them. **for they sow not, neither do they reap, nor gather into barns; yet your heavenly Father feedeth them. Are ye not much better than they?**—nobler in yourselves and dearer to God. The argument here is from the greater to the less; but how rich in detail! The brute creation—void of reason—are incapable of sowing, reaping, and storing; yet your heavenly Father suffers them not helplessly to perish, but sustains them without any of those processes: Will He see, then, His own children using all the means which reason dictates for procuring the things need-ful for the body—looking up to Himself at every step—and yet leave them to starve? **27. Which of you, by taking thought** ('anxious solicitude'), **can add one cubit unto his stature** [ἡλικίαν]? "Stature" can hardly be the thing intended here: first, because the subject is the *prolongation of life,* by the supply of its necessaries of food and cloth-ing; and next, because no one would dream of adding a cubit—or a foot and a half—to his stature, while in the corresponding passage in Luke (xii. 25, 26), the thing intended is represented as "that thing which is *least*." But if we take the word in its primary sense of 'age' (for 'stature' is but a secondary sense) the idea will be this, 'Which of you, however anxiously you vex your-selves about it, can add so much as a step to the length of your life's journey?' To compare the length of life to measures of this nature is not

44

28 by taking thought, can add one cubit unto his stature? And why take
ye thought for raiment? Consider the lilies of the field, how they grow:
29 they toil not, neither do they spin: and yet I say unto you, That even
30 Solomon in all his glory was not arrayed like one of these. Wherefore, if
God so clothe the grass of the field, which to-day is, and to-morrow is
cast into the oven, *shall he* not much more *clothe* you, O ye of little faith?
31 Therefore take no thought, saying, What shall we eat? or, What shall
32 we drink? or, Wherewithal shall we be clothed? (For after all these
things do the Gentiles seek:) for *w*your heavenly Father knoweth that ye
33 have need of all these things. But *x*seek ye first the kingdom of God,
and his righteousness; *y*and all these things shall be added unto you.
34 Take therefore no *5*thought for the morrow: for the morrow shall take
thought for the things of itself. Sufficient unto the day *is* the evil
thereof.

A. D. 31.
w Ps. 23. 1.
Phil. 4. 19.
z 1 Ki. 3. 13.
Ps. 34. 9.
Ps. 37. 25.
Mark 10.30.
Luke 12. 31.
Rom. 8. 32.
1 Tim. 4. 8.
y Ps. 34. 9, 10.
ch. 19. 29.
Mark 10.30.
Luke 18.29,
30.
Rom. 8. 32.
5 anxious
thought.

foreign to the language of Scripture, (cf. Ps. xxxix. 5; 2 Tim. iv. 7, &c.) So understood, the meaning is clear and the connection natural. In this the best critics now agree. **28. And why take ye thought for raiment? Consider** ('observe well') **the lilies of the field, how they grow: they toil not**—as men, planting and preparing the flax, **neither do they spin**—as women: **29. And yet I say unto you, That even Solomon in all his glory was not arrayed like one of these.** What incomparable teaching!—best left in its own transparent clearness and rich simplicity. **30. Wherefore, if God so clothe the grass**—the 'herbage' [χόρτον]—**of the field, which to-day is, and to-morrow is cast into the oven**—wild flowers cut with the grass, withering by the heat, and used for fuel. (See Jas. i. 11.) **shall he not much more clothe you, O ye of little faith?** The argument here is something fresh. 'Gorgeous as is the array of the flowers that deck the fields, surpassing all artificial human grandeur, it is for but a brief moment; you are ravished with it to-day, and to-morrow it is gone; your own hands have seized and cast it into the oven: Shall, then, God's children, so dear to Him, and instinct with a life that cannot die, be left naked?' He does not say, Shall they not be more beauteously arrayed? but, Shall He not much more *clothe* them? that being all He will have them regard as secured to them (cf. Heb. xiii. 5). The expression, 'Little-faithed ones' [ὀλιγόπιστοι], which our Lord applies once and again to His disciples (ch. viii. 26; xiv. 31; xvi. 8), can hardly be regarded as rebuking any actual manifestations of unbelief at that early period, and before such an audience. It is His way of gently chiding the *spirit* of unbelief, so natural even to the best, who are surrounded by a world of sense, and of kindling a generous desire to shake it off. **31. Therefore take no thought** ('solicitude'), **saying, What shall we eat? or, What shall we drink? or, Wherewithal shall we be clothed? 32. (For after all these things do the Gentiles seek)** [ἐπιζητεῖ]—rather, 'pursue.' Knowing nothing definitely beyond the present life to kindle their aspirations and engage their supreme attention, the heathen naturally pursue present objects as their chief, their only good. To what an elevation above these does Jesus here lift His disciples! **for your heavenly Father knoweth that ye have need of all these things.** How precious this word! Food and raiment are pronounced *needful* to God's children; and He who could say, "No man knoweth the Father but the Son, and he to whomsoever the Son will reveal Him" (ch. xi. 27), says with an authority which none but Himself could claim, "Your heavenly Father *knoweth* that ye have
need of all these things." Will not that suffice you, O ye needy ones of the household of faith? **33. But seek ye first the kingdom of God, and his righteousness; and all these things shall be added unto you.** This is the great summing up. Strictly speaking, it has to do only with the subject of the present Section—the right state of the heart with reference to heavenly and earthly things; but being couched in the form of a brief general directory, it is so comprehensive in its grasp as to embrace the whole subject of this Discourse. And, as if to make this the more evident, the two key-notes of this great Sermon seem purposely struck in it—"the KINGDOM" and "the RIGHTEOUSNESS" of the kingdom—as the grand objects, in the supreme pursuit of which all things needful for the present life will be added to us. The precise sense of every word in this golden verse should be carefully weighed. *"The kingdom of God"* is the primary subject of the Sermon on the Mount—that kingdom which the God of heaven is erecting in this fallen world, within which are all the spiritually recovered and inwardly subject portion of the family of Adam, under Messiah as its divine Head and King. *"The righteousness thereof"* is the character of all such, so amply described and variously illustrated in the foregoing portions of this Discourse. The *"seeking"* of these is the making them the object of supreme choice and pursuit; and the seeking of them *"first"* is the seeking of them before and above all else. The *"all these things"* which shall in that case be added to us are just the "all these things" which the last words of the preceding verse assured us "our heavenly Father knoweth that we have need of;" that is, all we require for the present life. And when our Lord says they shall be *"added,"* it is implied, as a matter of course, that the seekers of the kingdom and its righteousness shall have these as their proper and primary portion; the rest being their gracious reward for *not* seeking them. (See an illustration of the principle of this in 2 Chr. i. 11, 12.) What follows is but a reduction of this great general direction into a practical and ready form for daily use. **34. Take therefore no thought** ('anxious care') **for the morrow: for the morrow shall take thought for the things of itself** (or, according to other authorities, 'for itself')—shall have its own causes of anxiety. **Sufficient unto the day is the evil thereof.** An admirable practical maxim, and better rendered in our version than in almost any other, not excepting the preceding English ones. Every day brings its own cares; and to anticipate is only to double them.

Remarks.—1. Worldly-mindedness is as insidious as it is destructive to spirituality in the Christian,

7 JUDGE *a*"not, that ye be not judged. For with what judgment ye
2 judge, ye shall be judged: *b*and with what measure ye mete, it shall be
3 measured to you again. And *c*why beholdest thou the mote that is in
thy brother's eye, but considerest not the beam that is in thine own eye?
4 Or how wilt thou say to thy brother, Let me pull out the mote out of
5 thine eye; and, behold, a beam *is* in thine own eye? Thou hypocrite,

A. D. 31.
CHAP. 7.
a Rom. 2. 1.
Rom. 14. 3.
Jas. 4. 11.
b Mark 4. 24.
Luke 6. 38.
c Luke 6. 41.

The innocence of secular occupations is the plea on which inordinate attention to them is permitted to steal away the heart. And thus it is that the care of this world, and the deceitfulness of riches, and the pleasures of this life—silently but surely—choke the word, and no fruit is brought to perfection (see on Mark iv. 7). 2. What vanity and folly might be written over the life of many persons in high repute for religion; made up as it is of a long struggle to solve an impossible problem—how to serve two masters! But this is not the worst of their case. For, 3. This dividedness of heart vitiates and darkens their whole inner man; making them strangers to that glorious light which irradiates the path of the just, whose one aim in life is to serve and glorify their Father who is in heaven. 4. Since the whole animal and vegetable creation—so liberally fed and so gorgeously clad—is silently, perpetually, and charmingly preaching to the children of God the duty of confidence in their Father who is in heaven, what a noble field of devout study do these kingdoms of nature open up to us; and what a monstrous misuse of this study is made by those who study themselves into an Atheistic Naturalism, which not only makes the laws of nature their sole object of pursuit, but drearily rests in them as the ultimate account of all physical things! 5. In this Discourse we find our Lord telling us what "the heathen" do, that He may teach us how differently He expected His own disciples to do. The heathen "babble" their prayers, and the heathen pursue this present world as their all. But if so, O how many heathen are there in the visible Christian Church; and what a heathenish formality in devotion and secularity in the business of life do too many of the children of God suffer to invade and to mar the spirituality, and liberty, and joy, and strength of their Christian life! 6. As honesty is the best policy, so spirituality of mind in the prosecution of the business of life is the true secret of all real temporal prosperity. "The blessing of the Lord it maketh rich; and he addeth no sorrow with it" (Prov. x. 22)—not, He addeth no sorrow with the blessing; but none with the riches—whereas unblest riches are full of sorrow. 7. Let it never be forgotten that our Lord here condemns is not *attention* to business, nor any amount or range of *thought* on the subject of it which may be necessary for its most successful prosecution; but only such attention to it as is due exclusively to heavenly things, and cannot possibly be given to both; and such *anxiety* of mind about the means of life as springs from distrust of God, and corrodes the heart, while it does not in the least advance the object we have in view. Nor is riches spoken against here, but only the setting of the heart upon them, which the poor may do and the rich not. (See Ps. lxii. 10; 1 Tim. vi. 17-19.)

CHAP. VII. SERMON ON THE MOUNT—*concluded.*

1-12.—MISCELLANEOUS SUPPLEMENTARY COUNSELS. That these verses are entirely supplementary is the simplest and most natural view of them. All attempts to make out any evident connection with the immediately preceding context are, in our judgment, forced. But, though supple-

mentary, these counsels are far from being of subordinate importance. On the contrary, they involve some of the most delicate and vital duties of the Christian life. In the vivid form in which they are here presented, perhaps they could not have been introduced with the same effect under any of the foregoing heads; but they spring out of the same great principles, and are but other forms and manifestations of the same evangelical "righteousness."

Censorious Judgment (1-5). **1. Judge not, that ye be not judged.** To "judge" here [κρίνειν] does not exactly mean to pronounce condemnatory judgment [κατακρίνειν]; nor does it refer to simple judging at all, whether favourable or the reverse. The context makes it clear that the thing here condemned is that disposition to look unfavourably on the character and actions of others, which leads invariably to the pronouncing of rash, unjust, and unlovely judgments upon them. No doubt it is the judgments so pronounced which are here spoken of; but what our Lord aims at is the spirit out of which they spring. Provided we eschew this unlovely spirit, we are not only warranted to sit in judgment upon a brother's character and actions, but, in the exercise of a necessary discrimination, are often constrained to do so for our own guidance. It is the violation of the law of love involved in the exercise of a censorious disposition which alone is here condemned. And the argument against it—"that ye be not judged"—confirms this: 'that your own character and actions be not pronounced upon with the like severity;' that is, at the great day. **2. For with what judgment ye judge, ye shall be judged: and with what measure ye mete**—whatever standard of judgment ye apply to others, it shall be measured to you [again] [ἀντιμετρηθήσεται. The ἀντι—'again,' or 'in return'—which belongs to the corresponding passage in Luke vi. 38, has hardly any support here; though of course it is implied.] This proverbial maxim is used by our Lord in other connections—as in Mark iv. 24, and with a slightly different application in Luke vi. 38—as a great principle in the divine administration. Untender judgment of others will be judicially returned upon ourselves, in the day when God shall judge the secrets of men by Jesus Christ. But, as in many other cases under the divine administration, such harsh judgment gets self-punished even here. For people shrink from contact with those who systematically deal out harsh judgment upon others—naturally concluding that they themselves may be the next victims—and feel impelled in self-defence, when exposed to it, to roll back upon the assailant his own censures. 3. **And why beholdest thou the mote** [κάρφος]—'splinter;' here very well rendered "mote," denoting any small fault. **that is in thy brother's eye, but considerest not the beam** [δοκόν] **that is in thine own eye?**—denoting the much greater fault which we overlook in ourselves. **4. Or how wilt thou say to thy brother, Let me pull out the mote out of thine eye; and, behold, a beam is in thine own eye? 5. Thou hypocrite** ['Υποκριτά]—'Hypocrite!' **first cast out the beam out of thine own eye; and then shalt thou see clearly to cast out the mote out of**

first cast out the beam out of thine own eye; and then shalt thou see clearly to cast out the mote out of thy brother's eye.

6   Give ^dnot that which is holy unto the dogs, neither cast ye your pearls before swine, lest they trample them under their feet, and turn again and rend you.

7   Ask, ^eand it shall be given you; seek, and ye shall find; knock, and
8 it shall be opened unto you: for ^fevery one that asketh receiveth; and he that seeketh findeth; and to him that knocketh it shall be
9 opened. Or what man is there of you, whom if his son ask bread, will
10 he give him a stone? or if he ask a fish, will he give him a serpent?
11 If ye then, being evil, know how to give good gifts unto your children, how much ^gmore shall your Father which is in heaven give good things to them that ask him!
12   Therefore all things ^hwhatsoever ye would that men should do to you, do ye even so to them: for ⁱthis is the Law and the Prophets.

A. D. 31.

^d Pro. 9. 7, 8.
Pro. 23. 9.
Acts 13. 45.
^e ch. 21. 22.
Mark 11. 24.
John 15. 7.
Jas. 1. 5, 6.
1 John 3. 22.
^f Pro. 8. 17.
Jer. 29. 12.
Jon. 2. 2.
Jon. 3. 8-10.
^g Isa. 49. 15.
Rom. 8. 32.
^h Luke 6. 31.
ⁱ Lev. 19. 18.
Rom. 13. 8.
Gal. 5. 14.
1 Tim. 1. 5.

thy brother's eye. Our Lord uses a most hyperbolical, but not unfamiliar figure, to express the monstrous inconsistency of this conduct. The "hypocrisy" which, not without indignation, He charges it with, consists in the pretence of a zealous and compassionate charity, which cannot possibly be real in one who suffers worse faults to lie uncorrected in himself. He only is fit to be a reprover of others who jealously and severely judges himself. Such persons will not only be slow to undertake the office of censor on their neighbours, but, when constrained in faithfulness to deal with them, will make it evident that they do it with *reluctance* and not satisfaction, with *moderation* and not exaggeration, with *love* and not harshness.

Prostitution of Holy Things (6). The opposite extreme to that of censoriousness is here condemned—want of discrimination of character. **6. Give not that which is holy unto the dogs**—savage or snarling haters of truth and righteousness. **neither cast ye your pearls before swine** —the impure or coarse, who are incapable of appreciating the priceless jewels of Christianity. In the East dogs are wilder and more gregarious, and, feeding on carrion and garbage, are coarser and fiercer than the same animals in the West. Dogs and swine, besides being ceremonially unclean, were peculiarly repulsive to the Jews, and indeed to the ancients generally. **lest they trample them under their feet**—as swine do—and **turn again and rend you**—as dogs do. Religion is brought into contempt, and its professors insulted, when it is forced upon those who cannot value it and will not have it. But while the indiscriminately zealous have need of this caution, let us be on our guard against too readily setting our neighbours down as dogs and swine, and excusing ourselves from endeavouring to do them good on this poor plea.

Prayer (7-11). Enough, one might think, had been said on this subject in ch. vi. 5-15. But the difficulty of the foregoing duties seems to have recalled the subject, and this gives it quite a new turn. 'How shall we ever be able to carry out such precepts as these, of tender, holy, yet discriminating love?' might the humble disciple enquire. 'Go to God with it,' is our Lord's reply; but He expresses this with a fulness which leaves nothing to be desired, urging now not only confidence, but importunity in prayer. **7. Ask, and it shall be given you; seek, and ye shall find; knock, and it shall be opened unto you.** Though there seems evidently a climax here, expressive of more and more importunity, yet each of these terms used presents what we desire

of God in a different light. We *ask* for what we *wish;* we *seek* for what we *miss;* we *knock* for that from which we feel ourselves *shut out.* Answering to this threefold representation is the triple assurance of success to our believing efforts. 'But ah!' might some humble disciple say, 'I cannot persuade myself that *I* have any interest with God.' To meet this, our Lord repeats the triple assurance he had just given, but in such a form as to silence every such complaint. **8. For every one that asketh receiveth; and he that seeketh findeth; and to him that knocketh it shall be opened.** Of course, it is presumed that he asks aright—that is, in faith—and with an honest purpose to make use of what he receives. "If any of you lack wisdom, let him ask of God. But let him ask in faith, nothing wavering (undecided whether to be altogether on the Lord's side). For he that wavereth is like a wave of the sea driven with the wind and tossed. For *let not that man think that he shall receive any thing of the Lord*" (Jas. i. 5-7). Hence, "Ye ask, and receive not, because ye ask amiss, that ye may consume it upon your lusts" (Jas. iv. 3). **9. Or what man is there of you, whom if his son ask bread** [ἄρτον] —'a loaf,' will he give him a stone?—round and smooth like such a loaf or cake as was much in use, but only to mock him. **10. Or if he ask a fish, will he give him a serpent?**—like it, indeed, but only to sting him. **11. If ye then, being evil, know how to give good gifts unto your children, how much more shall your Father which is in heaven give good things to them that ask him!** Bad as our fallen nature is, the *father* in us is not extinguished. What a heart, then, must the Father of all fathers have towards His pleading children! In the corresponding passage in Luke (see on xi. 13), instead of "good things," our Lord asks whether He will not much more give *the Holy Spirit* to them that ask Him. At this early stage of His ministry, and before such an audience, He seems to avoid such sharp doctrinal teaching as was more accordant with His plan at the riper stage indicated in Luke, and in addressing His own disciples exclusively.

Golden Rule (12). **12. Therefore**—to say all in one word—**all things whatsoever ye would that men should do to you, do ye even so** [οὕτως]— the same thing or in the same way, **to them: for this is the Law and the Prophets.** 'This is the substance of all relative duty; all Scripture in a nutshell.' Incomparable summary! How well called "the royal law"! (Jas. ii. 8; cf. Rom. xiii. 9). It is true that similar maxims are found floating in the writings of the cultivated Greeks and Romans, and naturally enough in the Rabbinical

13   Enter *ʲ*ye in at the strait gate: *ᵏ*for wide *is* the gate, and broad *is* the way, that leadeth to destruction, and many there be which go in thereat:
14   ¹because strait *is* the gate, and narrow *is* the way, which leadeth unto life, and few there be that find it.

A. D. 31.
ʲ Luke 9. 23.
Luke 13. 24.
ᵏ 1 John 5. 19.
1 Or, how.

writings. But so expressed as it is here—in immediate connection with, and as the sum of *such* duties as had been just enjoined, and such principles as had been before taught—it is to be found nowhere else. And the best commentary upon this fact is, that never till our Lord came down thus to teach did men effectually and widely exemplify it in their practice. The precise sense of the maxim is best referred to common sense. It is not, of course, what—in our wayward, capricious, grasping moods —we should *wish* that men would do to us, that we are to hold ourselves bound to do to them; but only what—in the exercise of an impartial judgment, and putting ourselves in their place—we consider it reasonable that they should do to us, that we are to do to them.

Remarks.—1. How grievous is it to think to what an extent, in spite of our Lord's injunctions and warnings here, censoriousness prevails, not only amongst the mass of professing Christians, but even among the undoubted children of God! Of two or more motives by which any action or course may have been prompted, and only one of which is wrong, how readily do many Christians—in a spirit the reverse of love—fasten upon the wrong one, without any evidence, but merely on presumption! And even after they have discovered themselves to have wronged their neighbour—perhaps a brother or sister in Christ—by imputing to them motives to which they find they were strangers, instead of grieving over such want of love (Prov. x. 12; 1 Pet. iv. 8), and guarding against it for the future, are they not as ready again to do the same thing? We speak not of such snarling dispositions as seem incapable of looking upon any person or action but unfavourably—of which one meets with unhappy specimens in some whom one would fain include among the sincere disciples of Christ. But we refer to a too prevalent tendency in many who are above this. Let such think whether, at the great day, they would like to have their own harsh measure meted out to themselves; let them remember to what a small extent one is able to enter into the circumstances of another; let them consider whether in any given case, they are called on to pronounce a judgment at all; and if they think they are, let it be with reluctance and regret that an unfavourable judgment is pronounced; and let full weight be given to extenuating circumstances. As the law of love demands all this, so shall we find, at the great day, that we have our own merciful measure meted out to ourselves. But after all, 2. Self-knowledge will be the best preservative against a censorious disposition. He who knows how often his own motives would be misunderstood, if judged in every case from first appearances, will not be ready to judge thus of his neighbour's; nor will he who is conscious of his own uprightness, even when he has been betrayed into something wrong, be ready to put the worst construction even upon what cannot be defended. And as the censorious get self-punished even here, so a considerate, kind, charitable way of looking at the character and actions of others is rewarded with general respect, esteem, and confidence. 3. Christian zeal must be tempered with discretion. No love to the souls of men can oblige a Christian to thrust divine truth upon ears that will not listen to it, that will but loathe it, and are only irritated to keener hatred by efforts made to force it on them. (See Prov. ix. 7, 8; xiv. 7;

xxiii. 9, &c.) And yet how few are there so virulent that love cannot approach them and persevering love cannot subdue them! Discernment of character is indeed indispensable for hopefully giving "that which is holy" to those who are strangers to it, and offering safely our "pearls" to the needy. But He who said to obstinate and scornful Jerusalem, "How often would I have gathered thy children, and ye would not"—He who has, even for ages, "stretched out His hands all day long to a disobedient and gainsaying people!"—will not have us too readily to despair of our fellow-men, and cease from endeavouring to win them to the truth. And surely, when we remember what forbearance we ourselves have needed and experienced, and how hopeless some of us once were, we should not be over-hasty in turning even from the obstinate opponents of truth and righteousness as "dogs" and "swine," whom to meddle with is equally bootless and perilous. 4. Delicate and difficult as are the duties enjoined in this Section, demanding a high tone and involving habitual self-command, the disciple of Christ has an unfailing resource in his Father which is in heaven, to whom there is free access by prayer for all, and no believing application is made in vain. 5. Had the *universal depravity* of our nature not been an understood and acknowledged truth, it is difficult to see how our Lord could have expressed Himself as He does in the 11th verse of this chapter, nor can the full force of His reasoning be felt on any other principle. For this is it: 'The natural affection of human parents towards their children has to struggle through the *evil* which every child of Adam brings with him into the world, and carries about with him to his dying day; and yet, in spite of this, what parent is there whose heart does not yearn over his own child, or is able to resist his reasonable pleadings? But your heavenly Father has no evil in His nature to struggle with; and has a heart towards His children, compared with which the affections of all the parents that ever did, do, or shall exist, though they were blended into one mighty affection, is not even as a drop to the ocean: How much more, then, will He give good gifts to His pleading children!' What an argument this for faith to plead upon!

13-29.—CONCLUSION AND EFFECT OF THE SERMON ON THE MOUNT. We have here the application of the whole preceding Discourse.

Conclusion of the Sermon on the Mount (13-27). "The righteousness of the kingdom," so amply described, both in principle and in detail, would be seen to involve *self-sacrifice* at every step. Multitudes would never face this. But it must be faced, else the consequences will be fatal. This would divide all within the sound of these truths into two classes: the many, who will follow the path of ease and self-indulgence—end where it might; and the few, who, bent on eternal safety above everything else, take the way that leads to it—at whatever cost. This gives occasion to the two opening verses of this application. 13. **Enter ye in at the strait gate**—as if hardly wide enough to admit one at all. This expresses the difficulty of the first right step in religion, involving, as it does, a triumph over all our natural inclinations. Hence the still stronger expression in Luke (xiii. 24), "Strive [ἀγωνίζεσθε] to enter in at the strait gate." **for wide is the gate—easily**

15   Beware *l*of false prophets, *m*which come to you in sheep's clothing, but
16 inwardly they are *n*ravening wolves.   Ye shall know them by their fruits.
17 *o*Do men gather grapes of thorns, or figs of thistles?   Even so *p*every
good tree bringeth forth good fruit; but a corrupt tree bringeth forth
18 evil fruit.   A good tree cannot bring forth evil fruit, neither *can* a cor-
19 rupt tree bring forth good fruit.   Every tree that bringeth not forth good
20 fruit is hewn down, and cast into the fire.   Wherefore by their fruits ye
shall know them.
21   Not every one that saith unto me, *q*Lord, Lord, shall enter into the
kingdom of heaven; but he that doeth the will of my Father which is in
22 heaven.   Many will say to me in that day, Lord, Lord, have we *r*not
prophesied in thy name? and in thy name have cast out devils? and in

A. D. 31.

l Deut. 13. 3.
   Jer. 23. 16.
   Rom. 16. 17.
m Mic. 3. 5.
   2 Tim. 3. 5.
n Acts 20. 29.
o Luke 6. 43.
p Jer. 11. 19.
q Hos. 8. 2.
   Acts 19. 13.
   Rom. 2. 13.
   Jas. 1. 22.
r Num. 24. 4.
   John 11. 51.
   1 Cor. 13. 2.

entered—and broad is the way—easily trodden—that leadeth to destruction, and—thus lured—many there be which go in thereat: **14. Because strait is the gate, and narrow is the way, which leadeth unto life**—in other words, the whole course is as difficult as the first step; and (so it comes to pass that) **few there be that find it.** The recommendation of the broad way is the ease with which it is trodden and the abundance of company to be found in it. It is sailing with a fair wind and a favourable tide. The natural inclinations are not crossed, and fears of the issue, if not easily hushed, are in the long run effectually subdued. The one disadvantage of this course is its end—it "leadeth to destruction." The great Teacher says it, and says it as "One having authority." To the supposed injustice or harshness of this He never once adverts. He leaves it to be inferred that such a course righteously, naturally, necessarily so ends. But whether men see this or no, here He lays down the law of the kingdom, and leaves it with us. As to the other way, the disadvantage of it lies in its narrowness and solitude. Its very first step involves a revolution in our whole purposes and plans for life, and a surrender of all that is dear to natural inclination, while all that follows is but a repetition of the first great act of self-sacrifice. No wonder, then, that few find and few are found in it. But it has one advantage—it "leadeth unto life." Some critics take "the gate" here, not for the first, but the last step in religion; since gates seldom open into roads, but roads usually terminate in a gate, leading straight to a mansion. But as this would make our Lord's words to have a very inverted and unnatural form as they stand, it is better, with the majority of critics, to view them as we have done. [The reading in *v*. 14, of Tí for "Οτι—'How strait!'—preferred by *Tregelles*—is, we think, with *Tischendorf*, to be disapproved.]

But since such teaching would be as unpopular as the way itself, our Lord next forewarns His hearers that preachers of smooth things—the true heirs and representatives of the false prophets of old—would be rife enough in the new kingdom. **15. Beware** [Προσέχετε δὲ]—'But beware' **of false prophets**—that is, of teachers coming as authorized expounders of the mind of God and guides to heaven. (See Acts xx. 29, 30; 2 Pet. ii. 1, 2.) **which come to you in sheep's clothing** —with a bland, gentle, plausible exterior; persuading you that the gate is not strait nor the way narrow, and that to teach so is illiberal and bigoted—precisely what the old prophets did (Ezek. xiii. 1-10, 22). **but inwardly they are ravening wolves**—bent on devouring the flock for their own ends (2 Cor. xi. 2, 3, 13-15). **16. Ye shall know them by their fruits**—not their doctrines—as many of the elder interpreters and some later ones explain

it—for that corresponds to the tree itself; but the practical effect of their teaching, which is the proper fruit of the tree. **Do men gather grapes of thorns** [ἀκανθῶν]—any kind of prickly plant, **or figs of thistles?** [τριβόλων]—a three-pronged variety. The general sense is obvious—Every tree bears its own fruit. **17. Even so every good tree bringeth forth good fruit; but a corrupt tree bringeth forth evil fruit. 18. A good tree cannot bring forth evil fruit, neither can a corrupt tree bring forth good fruit.** Obvious as is the truth here expressed in different forms—that the heart determines and is the only proper interpreter of the actions of our life—no one who knows how the Church of Rome makes a merit of actions, quite apart from the motives that prompt them, and how the same tendency manifests itself from time to time even among Protestant Christians, can think it too obvious to be insisted on by the teachers of divine truth. Here follows a wholesome digression. **19. Every tree that bringeth not forth good fruit is hewn down, and cast into the fire.** See on ch. iii. 10. **20. Wherefore by their fruits ye shall know them:**—*q. d.,* 'But the point I now press is not so much the end of such, as the means of detecting them; and this, as already said, is their fruits.' The hypocrisy of teachers now leads to a solemn warning against religious hypocrisy in general.

21. Not every one that saith unto me, Lord, Lord—the reduplication of the title "Lord" denoting zeal in according it to Christ (see Mark xiv. 45). Yet our Lord claims and expects this of all His disciples, as when He washed their feet, "Ye call me Master and Lord: and ye say well; for so I am" (John xiii. 13). **shall enter into the kingdom of heaven; but he that doeth the will of my Father which is in heaven**—that will which it had been the great object of this Discourse to set forth. Yet our Lord says warily, not 'the will of *your* Father,' but "of *My* Father;" thus claiming a relationship to His Father with which His disciples might not intermeddle, and which He never lets down. And He so speaks here, to give authority to His asseverations. But now He rises higher still—not formally *announcing* Himself as the Judge, but intimating what men will say to Him, and He to them, *when* He sits as their final judge. **22. Many will say to me in that day** [בַּיּוֹם הַהוּא]. What day? It is emphatically unnamed. But it is the day to which He had just referred, when men shall "enter" or not enter "into the kingdom of heaven." (See a similar way of speaking of "that day" in 2 Tim. i. 12; iv. 8). Lord, Lord. The reiteration denotes surprise. 'What, Lord? How is this? Are *we* to be disowned?' **have we not prophesied**—or 'publicly taught.' As one of the special gifts of the Spirit in the early Church, it has the sense of 'inspired and authoritative teaching,'

49

23 thy name done many wonderful works? And then will I profess unto them, I never knew you: ^sdepart from me, ye that work iniquity.

24 Therefore, ^twhosoever heareth these sayings of mine, and doeth them,

25 I will liken him unto a wise man, which built his house upon a rock: and ^uthe rain descended, and the floods came, and the winds blew, and beat upon that house; and ^vit fell not: for it was founded upon a rock.

26 And every one that heareth these sayings of mine, and doeth them not, shall be likened unto a foolish man, which built his house upon the sand:

27 and the rain descended, and the floods came, and the winds blew, and beat upon that house; and it fell: ^wand great was the fall of it.

28 And it came to pass, when Jesus had ended these sayings, ^xthe people

29 were astónished at his doctrine: for ^yhe taught them as *one* having authority, and not as the scribes.

A. D. 31.
^s Ps. 5. 5.
Ps. 6. 8.
ch. 25. 41.
^t Luke 6. 47.
^u Acts 14. 22.
2 Tim. 3. 12.
^v 2 Tim. 2. 19.
1 Pet. 1. 5.
^w Heb. 10. 31.
2 Pet. 2. 20.
^x ch. 13. 54.
Mark 1. 22.
Mark 6. 2.
Luke 4. 32.
^y Isa. 50. 4.
John 7. 46.

and is ranked next to the apostleship. (See 1 Cor. xii. 28; Eph. iv. 11.) In this sense it is used here, as appears from what follows. **in thy name?**—or, 'to thy name,' and so in the two following clauses [τῷ σῷ ὀνόματι, only here and in Mark ix. 38]—'having reference to Thy name as the sole power in which we did it.' **and in thy name have cast out devils? and in thy name done many wonderful works?**—or 'miracles' [δυνάμεις]. These are selected as three examples of the highest services rendered to the Christian cause, and through the power of Christ's own name, invoked for that purpose; Himself, too, responding to the call. And the threefold repetition of the question, each time in the same form, expresses in the liveliest manner the astonishment of the speakers at the view now taken of them. **23. And then will I profess unto them,** [ὁμολογήσω]—or, 'openly proclaim'—tearing off the mask—**I never knew you.** What they claimed—intimacy with Christ—is just what He repudiates, and with a certain scornful dignity. 'Our acquaintance was not broken off—there never was any.' **depart from me** (cf. ch. xxv. 41). The connection here gives these words an awful significance. They claimed intimacy with Christ, and in the corresponding passage, Luke xiii. 26, are represented as having gone out and in with Him on familiar terms. 'So much the worse for you,' He replies: 'I bore with that long enough; but now—begone!' **ye that work iniquity**—not 'that *wrought* iniquity;' for they are represented as fresh from the scenes and acts of it as they stand before the Judge. (See on the almost identical, but even more vivid and awful, description of the scene in Luke xiii. 24-27.) That the apostle alludes to these very words in 2 Tim. ii. 19, there can hardly be any doubt—"Nevertheless the foundation of God standeth sure, having this seal, The Lord *knoweth* them that are His. And, let every one that nameth the *name* of Christ depart from *iniquity*."

24. Therefore—to bring this Discourse to a close, **whosoever heareth these sayings of mine, and doeth them.** See Jas. i. 22, which seems a plain allusion to these words; also Luke xi. 28; Rom. ii. 13; 1 John iii. 7. **I will liken him unto a wise man** [ἀνδρὶ φρονίμῳ]—a shrewd, prudent, provident man, **which built his house upon a rock**—the rock of true discipleship, or genuine subjection to Christ. **25. And the rain**—from above—**descended, and the floods**—from below—**came** [ποταμοί], **and the winds**—sweeping across—**blew, and**—thus from every direction—**beat upon that house; and it fell not: for it was founded upon a rock.** See 1 John ii. 17. **26. And every one that heareth these sayings of mine**—in the attitude of discipleship, **and doeth them** not, **shall be likened unto**

a foolish man, which built his house upon the sand—denoting a loose foundation—that of an empty profession and mere external services. **27. And the rain descended, and the floods came, and the winds blew, and beat upon** [προσέκοψαν]—or 'struck against' that house; **and it fell: and great was the fall of it**—terrible the ruin! How lively must this imagery have been to an audience accustomed to the fierceness of an Eastern tempest, and the suddenness and completeness with which it sweeps everything unsteady before it!

Effect of the Sermon on the Mount (28-29). **28. And it came to pass, when Jesus had ended these sayings, the people were astonished at his doctrine**—rather, 'His teaching' [διδαχῇ], for the reference is to the manner of it quite as much as to the matter, or rather more so. **29. For he taught them as [one] having authority.** The word "one," which our translators have here inserted, only weakens the statement. **and not as the scribes.** The consciousness of divine authority, as Lawgiver, Expounder, and Judge, so beamed through His teaching, that the scribes' teaching could not but appear drivelling in such a light.

Remarks.—1. Let the disciples of Christ beware of obliterating the distinction between the "broad" and the "narrow" way; and neither be carried away by the plausibilities of that 'liberal' school of preachers and writers whose aim is to refine away the distinguishing peculiarities of the two classes, nor be ashamed of the fidelity which holds them up in bold, clear, sharp outline. It is easy to run down the latter class as narrow bigots, and cry up the former as sensible and large-minded. But He, Whom none claiming the Christian name dare call narrow or harsh, concludes this incomparable Discourse with the assurance that there are but two great courses—the one ending in "life," the other in "destruction;" that the easy one is the fatal, the difficult the only safe way; and that true wisdom lies in eschewing the former and making choice of the latter. Genuine, out-and-out discipleship yields its devout assent to this, and casts in its lot with all that teach it, however despised; stopping its ears to the preachers of smooth things, charm they never so wisely. 2. While corrupt teaching is followed, sooner or later, by corresponding practice, the *immediate* effects are often, to all appearance, the reverse. There is often a simplicity, an earnestness, an absorption in the objects at which they aim, in preachers who are conscious that they have peculiar ideas to lodge in the minds of their hearers; and there are other subtle elements in the popularity of some, who, by widening the strait gate and broadening the narrow way, win to religious

8 WHEN he was come down from the mountain, great multitudes followed him.

2   And, ^abehold, there came a leper and worshipped him, saying, Lord,
3 if thou wilt, thou canst make me clean. And Jesus put forth *his* hand, and touched him, saying, I will; be thou clean. And immediately his

A. D. 31.

CHAP. 8.
^a Mark 1. 40.
Luke 5. 12.
2 Ki. 5. 1.
2 Chr. 26. 19.

thought and earnestness not a few who otherwise would in all probability have remained strangers to both. But when we see clearly the character of such teaching, let us never doubt what its ultimate issue must be, and, in spite of all present appearances, and in answer to all charges of bigotry, let us be ready, with our Master, to exclaim, "Do men gather grapes of thorns, or figs of thistles?" 3. The light in which our Lord presents Himself in the closing words of this Discourse has a grandeur, on supposition of His proper personal Divinity, which must commend itself to every devout, reflecting mind; whereas, if we regard Him as a mere creature, they are so dishonouring to God as to be repulsive in the last degree to all who are jealous for His glory. The dialogue form in which the appeals at the great day are said to be made to Him, and rejected by Him—though expressive, it may be, of nothing more than the principles and feelings of both parties towards each other, which will then be brought out—places our Lord Himself in a light wholly incompatible with anything which Scripture warrants a *creature* to assume. Not only does it exhibit Him as the Judge, but it represents all moral and religious duties as terminating in *Him*, and the blissful or blighted future of men as turning upon their doing or not doing all to Him. In perfect, yet awful accordance with this is the sentence—"DEPART FROM ME"—as if separation from HIM were death and hell. If the Speaker were a mere creature, no language can express the mingled absurdity and profanity of such assumptions; but if He was the Word, who at the beginning was with God and was God, and if thus rich He for our sakes only became poor, then all that He says here is worthy of Himself, and shines in its own lustre. See Remark 2 at the close of the corresponding Section (Luke xiii. 23-30). 4. While most persons within the pale of the Christian Church are ready to admit that, not professed, but proved subjection to the Father of our Lord Jesus Christ—not lip, but life service—will avail "in that day," it is not so readily admitted and felt that services such as "prophesying in Christ's name, and in His name casting out devils, and in His name doing many miracles"—or, what in later ages correspond to these, eloquent and successful preaching—even to the deliverance of souls from the thraldom of sin and Satan; learned contributions to theological literature; great exertions for the diffusion of Christianity and the vindication of religious liberty; and princely donations for either or both of these—may all be rendered in honour of Christ, while the heart is not subjected to Him, and the life is a contradiction to His precepts. What need, then, have we to tremble at the closing words of this great Discourse; and, "Let every one that nameth the name of Christ depart from iniquity"! See Remark 1 at the close of the corresponding Section (Luke xiii. 23-30). 5. Is there not something awful in the astonishment and dismay with which the inconsistent disciples of the Lord Jesus are here represented as receiving their sentence at the great day? What a light does it throw upon the extent to which men may be the victims of self-deception, and the awful inveteracy of it—

as if nothing would open their eyes but the Judge's own sentence: "I never knew you: depart from me"! Well may one, on rising from the study of this solemn close to the Sermon on the Mount, exclaim with Bunyan, in the closing words of his immortal 'Pilgrim,' 'THEN I SAW THAT THERE WAS A WAY TO HELL EVEN FROM THE GATES OF HEAVEN.'

CHAP. VIII. 1-4.—HEALING OF A LEPER. (= Mark i. 40-45; Luke v. 12-16.)

The time of this miracle seems too definitely fixed here to admit of our placing it where it stands in Mark and Luke, in whose Gospels no such precise note of time is given.

1. [And] When he was come down from the mountain, great multitudes followed him. 2. And, behold, there came a leper—"a man full of leprosy," says Luke, v. 12. Much has been written on this disease of leprosy, but certain points remain still doubtful. All that needs be said here is, that it was a cutaneous disease, of a loathsome, diffusive, and, there is reason to believe, when thoroughly pronounced, incurable character; that though in its distinctive features it is still found in several countries—as Arabia, Egypt, and South Africa—it prevailed, in the form of what is called white leprosy, to an unusual extent, and from a very early period, among the Hebrews; and that it thus furnished to the whole nation a familiar and affecting symbol of SIN, considered as (1) *loathsome*, (2) *spreading*, (3) *incurable.* And while the ceremonial ordinances for detection and cleansing prescribed in this case by the law of Moses (Lev. xiii., xiv.) held forth a coming remedy "for sin and for uncleanness" (Ps. li. 7; 2 Ki. v. 1, 7, 10, 13, 14), the numerous cases of leprosy with which our Lord came in contact, and the glorious cures of them which He wrought, were a fitting manifestation of the work which He came to accomplish. In this view, it deserves to be noticed that the first of our Lord's miracles of healing recorded by Matthew is this cure of a leper. **and worshipped him**—in what sense we shall presently see. Mark says (i. 40), he came, "beseeching and kneeling to Him," and Luke says (v. 12), "he fell on his face." **saying, Lord, if thou wilt, thou canst make me clean.** As this is the only cure of leprosy recorded by all the three first Evangelists, it was probably the first case of the kind; and if so, this leper's faith in the power of Christ must have been formed in him by what he had heard of His other cures. And how striking a faith is it! He does not say he *believed* Him able, but with a brevity expressive of a confidence that knew no doubt, he says simply, "Thou canst" [δύνασαι]. But of Christ's willingness to heal him he was not so sure. It needed more knowledge of Jesus than he could be supposed to have to assure him of that. But one thing he was sure of, that He had but to "will" it. This shows with what "worship" of Christ this leper fell on his face before him. Clear theological knowledge of the Person of Christ was not then possessed even by those who were most with Him and nearest to Him. Much less could full insight into all that we know of the Only begotten of the Father be expected of this leper. But he who at that moment felt and owned that to heal an incurable disease needed but the *fiat* of the Person who

51

4 leprosy was cleansed. And Jesus saith unto him, [b]See thou tell no man; but go thy way, show thyself to the priest, and offer the gift that [c]Moses commanded, for a testimony unto them.

5 And [d]when Jesus was entered into Capernaum, there came unto him

6 a centurion, beseeching him, and saying, Lord, my servant lieth at

7 home sick of the palsy, grievously tormented. And Jesus saith unto him,

8 I will come and heal him. The centurion answered and said, Lord, I [e]am not worthy that thou shouldest come under my roof: but [f]speak the word

9 only, and my servant shall be healed. For I am a man under authority, having soldiers under me: and I say to this *man*, Go, and he goeth; and to another, Come, and he cometh; and to my servant, Do this, and he

10 doeth *it*. When Jesus heard *it*, he marvelled, and said to them that followed, Verily I say unto you, I have not found so great faith, no, not in

11 Israel. And I say unto you, That [g]many shall come from the east and west, and shall sit down with Abraham, and Isaac, and Jacob, in the

A. D. 31.

[b] ch. 9. 30.
Mark 5. 43.
[c] Lev. 14. 3.
Luke 5. 14.
[d] Luke 7. 1.
[e] Luke 15. 19.
[f] Ps. 33. 9.
Ps. 107. 20.
[g] Gen. 12. 3.
Isa. 2, 2, 3.
Isa. 11. 10.
Mal. 1. 11.
Luke 13. 29.
Acts 10. 45.
Acts 11. 18.
Acts 14. 27.
Rom. 15. 9.
Eph. 3. 6.

---

stood before him, had assuredly that very faith in the germ which now casts its crown before Him that loved us, and would at any time die for His blessed name. **3. And Jesus** [or 'He,' according to another reading]—"moved with compassion," says Mark (i. 41); a precious addition, **put forth his hand, and touched him.** Such a touch occasioned ceremonial defilement (Lev. v. 3); even as the leper's coming near enough for contact was against the Levitical regulations (Lev. xiii. 46). But as the man's faith told him there would be no case for such regulations if the cure he hoped to experience should be accomplished, so He who had healing in His wings transcended all such statutes. **saying, I will; be thou clean** [Θέλω, καθαρίσθητι]. How majestic those two words! By not assuring the man of His *power* to heal him, He delightfully sets His seal to the man's previous confession of that power; and by assuring him of the one thing of which he had any doubt, and for which he waited—His *will* to do it—He makes a claim as divine as the cure which immediately followed it. **And immediately his leprosy was cleansed.** Mark, more emphatic, says (i. 42), "And as soon as He had spoken, immediately the leprosy departed from him, and he was cleansed"—as perfectly as instantaneously. What a contrast this to modern pretended cures! **4. And Jesus** ("straitly charged him, and forthwith sent him away," Mark i. 43, and) **saith unto him, See thou tell no man.** A hard condition this would seem to a grateful heart, whose natural language, in such a case, is, "Come, hear, all ye that fear God, and I will declare what He hath done for my soul" (Ps. lxvi. 16). We shall presently see the reason for it. **but go thy way, show thyself to the priest, and offer the gift that Moses commanded** (Lev. xiv.), **for a testimony unto them**—a palpable witness that the Great Healer had indeed come, and that "God had visited His people." What the sequel was, our Evangelist says not; but Mark thus gives it (i. 45): "But he went out, and began to publish it much, and to blaze abroad the matter, insomuch that Jesus could no more openly enter into the city, but was without in desert places: and they came to Him from every quarter." Thus—by an over-zealous, though most natural and not very culpable, infringement of the injunction to keep the matter quiet—was our Lord, to some extent, thwarted in His movements. As His whole course was sublimely noiseless (ch. xii. 19), so we find Him repeatedly taking steps to prevent matters coming prematurely to a crisis with Him. (But see on Mark v. 19, 20.) "And He withdrew Himself," adds Luke (v. 16), "into the wilderness, and prayed;" retreating from the popular excite-

ment into the secret place of the Most High, and thus coming forth as dew upon the mown grass, and as showers that water the earth (Ps. lxxii. 6). And this is the secret both of strength and of sweetness in the servants and followers of Christ in every age.

Remarks.—1. It is, at least, a pleasing thought, that this first healed leper was none other than he who within a few days of his Lord's death, under the familiar name of "Simon the leper," made Him a supper at Bethany in his own house. (See on Mark xiv. 3.) And if so, is it not refreshing to think that he who so early experienced the healing power and grace of Jesus, and abode true and grateful to Him throughout, should have had the privilege of ministering to him at His loved retreat of Bethany when the hour of His last sufferings was so near at hand? 2. How gloriously is the absolute authority of Christ to heal or not, just as He "will," both owned by this leper and claimed by Himself! And as the cure instantaneously followed the expression of that will, how bright is the attestation of Heaven thus given to the Personal Divinity of the Lord Jesus! (Compare Ps. xxxiii. 9; Gen. i. 3, &c.) 3. Would those who groan under the leprosy of sin obtain a glorious cure? Let them but honour the power of Christ as did this poor leper, adding to this a confidence in His "will" which the leper could not be expected to reach; and they will not be disappointed. 4. Our own sense of propriety is never to be carried out in opposition to commanded duty. The strange command of Christ would seem to this healed leper to be more honoured in the breach than in the observance. In blazing abroad his cure, he would seem to himself to be simply obeying a resistless and holy impulse; and but for the injunction, in this particular case, to do the very opposite, he would have acted most laudably. But after receiving a command to keep silence, the part of duty was not to judge of it, but to obey it. As he was no competent judge of the reasons which dictated the command, so he ought to have "brought into captivity every thought to the *obedience* of Christ;" and thus should we act in every such case. 5. Healed lepers, not now required to keep silence, let the love of Christ constrain you to sing forth the honour of His name, and make His praise glorious: so will the sense of it habitually retain its freshness and warmth.

5-13.—HEALING OF THE CENTURION'S SERVANT. (= Luke vii. 1-10.) This incident belongs to a later stage. For the exposition, see on **Luke vii. 1-10.**

12 kingdom of heaven: but [h]the children of the kingdom [i]shall be cast
out into outer darkness: there shall be weeping and gnashing of teeth.
13 And Jesus said unto the centurion, Go thy way; and as thou hast
believed, *so* be it done unto thee. And his servant was healed in the
self-same hour.
14 And [j]when Jesus was come into Peter's house, he saw [k]his wife's mother
15 laid, and sick of a fever. And he touched her hand, and the fever left
her: and she arose, and ministered unto them.
16 When [l]the even was come, they brought unto him many that were
possessed with devils: and he cast out the spirits with *his* word, and
17 healed all that were sick: that it might be fulfilled which was spoken by
Esaias the prophet, saying, Himself [m]took our infirmities, and bare *our*
sicknesses.
18 Now when Jesus saw great multitudes about him, he gave command-
19 ment to depart unto the other side. And [n]a certain scribe came, and said
20 unto him, Master, I will follow thee whithersoever thou goest. And
Jesus saith unto him, The foxes have holes, and the birds of the air *have*
21 nests; but [o]the Son of man hath not where to lay *his* head. And [p] another of his disciples said unto him, Lord, [q]suffer me first to go and bury
22 my father. But Jesus said unto him, Follow me; and let [r]the dead bury
their dead.

A. D. 31.

[h] ch. 21. 43.
[i] ch. 13. 42. ch. 22. 13. ch. 24. 51. ch. 25. 30. Luke 13. 28. 2 Pet. 2. 17. Jude 13.
[j] Mark 1. 29. Luke 4. 38.
[k] 1 Cor. 9. 5.
[l] Mark 1. 32. Luke 4. 40.
[m] Isa. 53. 4. 1 Pet. 2. 24.
[n] Luke 9. 57.
[o] Ps. 22. 6. Ps. 40. 17. Ps. 69. 29. Luke 2. 7, 12. Luke 8. 3. John 1. 10. 11.
[p] Luke 9. 59.
[q] 1 Ki. 19. 20.
[r] Eph. 2. 1.

14-17.—HEALING OF PETER'S MOTHER-IN-LAW, AND MANY OTHERS. (=Mark i. 29-34; Luke iv. 38-41.) For the exposition, see on Mark i. 29-34.

18-22.—INCIDENTS ILLUSTRATIVE OF DISCIPLESHIP. (= Luke ix. 57-62.)

The incidents here are two: in the corresponding passage of Luke they are three. Here they are introduced before the mission of the Twelve; in Luke, when our Lord was making preparation for His final journey to Jerusalem. But to conclude from this, as some good critics do, as *Bengel*, *Ellicott*, &c., that one of these incidents at least occurred twice—which led to the mention of the others at the two different times—is too artificial. Taking them, then, as one set of occurrences, the question arises, Whether are they recorded by Matthew or by Luke in their proper place? *Neander*, *Schleiermacher*, and *Olshausen* adhere to Luke's order; while *Meyer*, *de Wette*, and *Lange* prefer that of Matthew. Probably the first incident is here in its right place. But as the command, in the second incident, to preach the kingdom of God, would scarcely have been given at so early a period, it is likely that it and the third incident have their true place in Luke. Taking these three incidents, then, up here, we have—

I. *The Rash or Precipitate Disciple* (19, 20). **19. And a certain scribe came, and said unto him, Master, I will follow thee whithersoever thou goest. 20. And Jesus saith unto him, The foxes have holes, and the birds of the air have nests; but the Son of man hath not where to lay his head.** Few as there were of the scribes who attached themselves to Jesus, it would appear, from his calling Him 'Teacher' [Διδάσκαλε], that this one was a "disciple" in that looser sense of the word in which it is applied to the crowds who flocked after Him, with more or less conviction that His claims were well founded. But from the answer which he received we are led to infer that there was more of transient emotion—of temporary impulse—than of intelligent principle in the speech. The preaching of Christ had riveted and charmed him; his heart had swelled; his enthusiasm had been kindled; and in this state of mind he will go anywhere with Him, and feels impelled to tell Him so. 'Wilt thou?' replies the Lord Jesus, 'Knowest thou Whom thou art pledging thyself to follow, and whither haply He may lead thee? No warm home, no downy pillow has He for thee: He has them not for Himself. The foxes are not without their holes, nor do the birds of the air want their nests; but the Son of man has to depend on the hospitality of others, and borrow the pillow whereon He lays His head.' How affecting is this reply! And yet He rejects not this man's offer, nor refuses him the liberty to follow Him. Only He will have him know what he is doing, and 'count the cost.' He will have him weigh well the real nature and the strength of his attachment, whether it be such as will abide in the day of trial. If so, he will be right welcome, for Christ puts none away. But it seems too plain that in this case that had not been done. And so we have called this The Rash or Precipitate Disciple.

II. *The Procrastinating or Entangled Disciple* (21, 22). As this is more fully given in Luke, we must take both together. "And He said unto another of his disciples, Follow me. But he said," **Lord, suffer me first to go and bury my father. But Jesus said unto him, Follow me; and let the dead bury their dead**—or, as more definitely in Luke, "Let the dead bury their dead: but go thou and preach the kingdom of God." This disciple did not, like the former, volunteer his services, but is called by the Lord Jesus, not only to follow, but to preach Him. And he is quite willing; only he is not ready just yet. "Lord, I *will;* but"—'There is a difficulty in the way just now; but that once removed, I am Thine.' What now is this difficulty? Was his father actually dead—lying a corpse—having only to be buried? Impossible. As it was the practice, as noticed on Luke vii. 12, to bury on the day of death, it is not very likely that this disciple would have been here at all if his father had just breathed his last; nor would the Lord, if He was there, have hindered him discharging the last duties of a son to a father. No doubt it was the common case of a son having a frail or aged father, not likely to live long, whose head he thinks it his duty to see under the ground ere he goes abroad. 'This aged father of mine will soon be removed; and if I

23 And when he was entered into a ship, his disciples followed him.
24 And, 'behold, there arose a great tempest in the sea, insomuch that the
25 ship was covered with the waves: but he was asleep. And his disciples
26 came to *him*, and awoke him, saying, Lord, save us: we perish. And he
  saith unto them, Why 'are ye fearful, O ye of little faith? Then "he
  arose, and rebuked the winds and the sea; and there was a great calm.
27 But the men marvelled, saying, What manner of man is this, that even
  the winds and the sea obey him!

A. D. 31.
* Mark 4. 37.
Luke 8. 23.
t Phil 4. 6.
u Job 38.8-11.
Ps. 65. 7.
Ps. 89. 9.
Ps. 93. 4.
Ps. 104. 3.
Ps. 107. 29.

might but delay till I see him decently interred, I should then be free to preach the kingdom of God wherever duty might call me.' This view of the case will explain the curt reply, "Let the dead bury their dead: but go thou and preach the kingdom of God." Like all the other paradoxical sayings of our Lord, the key to it is the different senses—a higher and a lower—in which the same word "dead" is used: 'There are two kingdoms of God in existence upon earth; the kingdom of nature, and the kingdom of grace: To the one kingdom all the children of this world, even the most ungodly, are fully alive; to the other, only the children of light: The reigning irreligion consists not in indifference to the common humanities of social life, but to things spiritual and eternal: Fear not, therefore, that your father will in your absence be neglected, and that when he breathes his last there will not be relatives and friends ready enough to do to him the last offices of kindness. Your wish to discharge these yourself is natural, and to be allowed to do it a privilege not lightly to be foregone. But the Kingdom of God lies now all neglected and needy: Its more exalted character few discern; to its paramount claims few are alive; and to "preach" it fewer still are qualified and called: But thou art: The Lord therefore hath need of thee: Leave, then, those claims of nature, high though they be, to those who are dead to the still higher claims of the kingdom of grace, which God is now erecting upon earth—Let the dead bury their dead: but go thou and preach the Kingdom of God.' And so have we here the genuine, but Procrastinating or Entangled Disciple. The next case is recorded only by Luke:

III. *The Irresolute or Wavering Disciple* (Luke ix. 61, 62). 61. "And another also said, Lord, I will follow thee; but let me first go bid them farewell which are at home at my house. 62. And Jesus said unto him, No man, having put his hand to the plough, and looking back, is fit for the kingdom of God." But for the very different replies given, we should hardly have discerned the difference between this and the second case: the one man called, indeed, and the other volunteering, as did the first; but both seemingly alike willing, and only having a difficulty in their way just at that moment. But, by help of what is said respectively to each, we perceive the great difference between the two cases. From the warning given against "looking back," it is evident that this man's discipleship was not yet *thorough*, his separation from the world not entire. It is not a case of *going* back, but of *looking* back; and as there is here a manifest reference to the case of "Lot's wife" (Gen. xix. 26; and see on Luke xvii. 32), we see that it is not *actual return* to the world that we have here to deal with, but a *reluctance to break with it*. The figure of putting one's hand to the plough and looking back is an exceedingly vivid one, and to an agricultural people most impressive. As ploughing requires an eye intent on the furrow to be made, and is marred the instant one turns about, so will they

come short of salvation who prosecute the work of God with a distracted attention, a divided heart. The reference may be chiefly to ministers; but the application at least is general. As the image seems plainly to have been suggested by the case of Elijah and Elisha, a difficulty may be raised, requiring a moment's attention. When Elijah cast his mantle about Elisha—which the youth quite understood to mean appointing him his successor, he was ploughing with twelve yoke of oxen, the last pair held by himself. Leaving his oxen, he ran after the prophet, and said, "Let me, I pray thee, kiss my father and my mother, and [then] I will follow thee." Was this said *in the same spirit* with the same speech uttered by our disciple? Let us see. "And Elijah said unto him, Go back again: for what have I done to thee." Commentators take this to mean that Elijah had really done nothing to hinder him from going on with all his ordinary duties. But to us it seems clear that Elijah's intention was to try what manner of spirit the youth was of:—'Kiss thy father and mother? And why not? By all means, go home and stay with them; for what have I done to thee? I did but throw a mantle about thee; but what of that?' If this was his meaning, Elisha thoroughly apprehended and nobly met it. "He returned back from him, and took a yoke of oxen, and slew them, and boiled their flesh with the instruments of the oxen [the wood of his ploughing implements], and gave unto the people, and they did eat: then he arose, and went after Elijah, and ministered unto him" (1 Ki. xix. 19-21). We know not if even his father and mother had time to be called to this hasty feast. But this much is plain, that, though in affluent circumstances, he gave up his lower calling, with all its prospects, for the higher, and at that time perilous office to which he was called. What now is the bearing of these two cases? Did Elisha do wrong in bidding them farewell with whom he was associated in his earthly calling? Or, if not, would this disciple have done wrong if he had done the same thing, and in the same spirit, with Elisha? Clearly not. Elisha's doing it proved that he could *with safety* do it; and our Lord's warning is not against bidding them farewell which were at home at his house, but against the probable *fatal consequences* of that step; lest the embraces of earthly relationship should prove too strong for him, and he should never return to follow Christ. Accordingly, we have called this the Irresolute or Wavering Disciple.

Remarks.—1. Rash or precipitate discipleship is scarcely to be looked for in times of spiritual death in lethargic conditions of the Church. The man who said he would follow Christ wherever He went had doubtless had his enthusiasm kindled, as we have said, by Christ's matchless preaching, though possibly also by the sight of His miracles. Even so an earnest, warm, rousing ministry, or a season of unusual awakening, stirring the most thoughtless, calls forth the enthusiasm of not a few, particularly among the young and ardent, who resolve—perhaps with tears of joy—that

54

28 And *ᵛ*when he was come to the other side, into the country of the
Gergesenes, there met him two possessed with devils, coming out of the
29 tombs, exceeding fierce, so that no man might pass by that way. And,
behold, they cried out, saying, What *ʷ*have we to do with thee, Jesus,
thou Son of God? art thou come hither to torment us before the time?
30 And there was a good way off from them an herd of many *ˣ*swine feeding.
31 So the devils *ʸ*besought him, saying, If thou cast us out, suffer us to go
32 away into the herd of swine. And he said unto them, Go. And when
they were come out, they went into the herd of swine: and, behold, the
whole herd of swine ran violently down a steep place into the sea, and
33 perished in the waters. And they that kept them fled, and went their
ways into the city, and told every thing, and what was befallen to the
34 possessed of the devils. And, behold, the whole city came out to meet
Jesus: and when they saw him, they *ᶻ*besought *him* that he would depart
out of their coasts.

9 AND he entered into a ship, and passed over, *ᵃ*and came into his own
2 city. And, *ᵇ*behold, they brought to him a man sick of the palsy,
lying on a bed: *ᶜ*and Jesus, seeing their faith, said unto the sick of the
3 palsy, Son, be of good cheer; *ᵈ*thy sins be forgiven thee. And, behold,
certain of the scribes said within themselves, This *man* blasphemeth.

A. D. 31.

ᵛ Mark 5. 1.
ʷ 2 Sam. 16. 10.
2 Sam. 19. 22.
Joel 3. 4.
Mark 1. 24.
Mark 5. 7.
Luke 4. 34.
2 Pet. 2. 4.
ˣ Deut. 14. 8.
ʸ Phil. 2. 10.
ᶻ Deut. 5. 25.
1 Ki. 17. 18.
Luke 5. 8.
Acts 16. 39.

CHAP. 9.
ᵃ ch. 4. 13.
ᵇ Mark 2. 3.
Luke 5. 8.
ᶜ ch. 8. 10.
ᵈ Ps. 32, 1. 2.
Luke 5. 20.
Rom. 4. 6-8.
Rom. 5. 11.
Eph. 1. 7.

they will henceforth abandon the world and follow Christ. "Yet have they not root in themselves, but endure *for a while;* for when tribulation or persecution ariseth because of the word,
presently they are stumbled." They want depth
of solid conviction. Their spiritual necessities
and danger have never led them to flee from the
wrath to come. Their faith in Christ, then, and
joy in the Gospel being but superficial, it gives
way in the day of trial. The thing which such
require is to 'count the cost;' and while rejoicing
to see men, in a time of general awakening, drinking in the truth, melted under it, and giving in
their accession to Christ, let them see to it that
they "break up their fallow ground, and sow not
among thorns." 2. How many real disciples are
not ready disciples. The Lord hath need of them,
and they are heartily desirous of serving Him—
"*but.*" They will do this and that—*but:* they
will go hither or thither when called to do so—
but. There is a difficulty in the way just now.
As soon as that is out of the way they are ready.
But what if the work required of them can only
be done just now—cannot stand still till their difficulty is removed? What if, ere that is out of the
way, their disposition to go has evaporated, or, if
still there, has no field—"help having come from
another quarter"? Young ministers are wanted
as missionaries abroad, and young, ardent, female
disciples, who are wanted as helps meet for them,
both hesitate. 'But for those aged parents, I
would gladly go; but till their head is beneath the
ground I am not free.' By that time, however, they
are neither so in love with the work, nor is the
field open to them. While the harvest is so plenteous and the labourers so few, let those who hear
the Macedonian cry, "Come over and help us,"
beware of allowing secular obstacles, however formidable, to arrest the impulse to obey the summons. Beyond all doubt it is owing to this, among
other things, that the commission, "Go, make disciples of all nations," remains still to so vast an
extent unexecuted—eighteen centuries since it
was given forth. 3. The best illustration of the
danger of "looking back," after having "put our
hand to the plough," is the case of those converts
from Hinduism, whose parents, when apprised of
their intention to be baptized, travel to the mission-house, and plead, with tears and threats, that

they will not take a step so fatal. Failing by this
means to shake their resolution, they at length
submit to their hard fate; only requesting that
before they undergo the rite which is to sever
them for ever from home, they will pay them one
parting visit—to "bid them farewell which are at
home at their house." It seems but reasonable.
To refuse it looks like gratuitously wounding parental feeling. 'Well, I will go; but my heart is
with you, my spiritual fathers, and soon I will rejoin you.' He goes—*but never returns.* How many
promising converts have thus been lost to Christianity, to the anguish of dear missionaries, travailing in birth till Christ be formed in the heathen,
and to their own undoing! And though some have,
after again conforming to heathenism, been filled
with such remorse, that, like Peter when he denied his Lord, they have gone out and wept bitterly, and, after severe and protracted struggles,
have returned to be more resolute followers of
Christ than ever, what seas of trouble does this
"looking back" cost them! and how very few are
such cases compared to the many that "make
shipwreck of faith and of a good conscience"!
"Let him that thinketh he standeth take heed
lest he fall."

23-27.—JESUS, CROSSING THE SEA OF GALILEE,
MIRACULOUSLY STILLS A TEMPEST. (= Mark iv.
35-41; Luke viii. 22-25.) For the exposition, see
on Mark iv. 35-41.

28-34.—JESUS HEALS THE GERGESENE DEMO
NIACS. (= Mark v. 1-20; Luke viii. 26-39.) For
the exposition, see on Mark v. 1-20.

CHAP. IX. 1-8.—HEALING OF A PARALYTIC.
(= Mark ii. 1-12; Luke v. 17-26.) This incident
appears to follow next in order of time to the cure
of the leper (ch. viii. 1-4). For the exposition,
see on Mark ii. 1-12.

9-13.—MATTHEW'S CALL AND FEAST. (=Mark
ii. 14-17; Luke v. 27-32.)

The Call of Matthew (9). 9. **And as Jesus passed
forth from thence**—that is, from the scene of the
paralytic's cure in Capernaum, towards the shore
of the sea of Galilee, on which that town lay.
Mark, as usual, pictures the scene in more detail,
thus (ii. 13): "And He went forth again by the
sea-side; and all the multitude resorted unto
Him, and He taught them" [ἐδίδασκεν αὐτοὺς]
—or, 'kept teaching them.' "And as he passed

4 And Jesus, ^eknowing their thoughts, said, Wherefore think ye evil in
5 your hearts? For whether is easier to say, *Thy* sins be forgiven thee; or
6 to say, Arise, and walk? But that ye may know that ^fthe Son of man
hath power on earth to forgive sins, (then saith he to the sick of the
7 palsy,) Arise, take up thy bed, and go unto thine house. And he arose,
8 and departed to his house. But when the multitudes saw *it*, they marvelled, and glorified God, which had given such power unto men.
9 And ^gas Jesus passed forth from thence, he saw a man, named
Matthew, sitting at the receipt of custom: and he saith unto him, Follow me. And he arose, and followed him.
10 And ^hit came to pass, as Jesus sat at meat in the house, behold, many
11 publicans and sinners came and sat down with him and his disciples. And
when the Pharisees saw *it*, they said unto his disciples, Why eateth your
12 Master with ⁱpublicans and ^jsinners? But when Jesus heard *that*, he said
unto them, They that be whole need not a physician, but they that are sick.
13 But go ye and learn what *that* meaneth, I ^kwill have mercy, and not sacrifice: for I am not come to call the righteous, ^lbut sinners to repentance.

A. D. 31.
^e Ps. 139. 2.
ch. 12. 25.
Mark 12.15.
^f Luke 5. 21.
Acts 5. 31.
2 Cor. 2. 10.
^g Mark 2. 14.
Luke 5. 27.
^h Mark 2. 15.
Luke 5. 29.
ⁱ Luke 5. 30.
Luke 15. 2.
Luke 19. 7.
Gal. 2. 5.
^j Gal. 2. 15.
Eph. 2. 12.
^k Pro. 21. 3.
Hos. 6. 6.
Mic. 6. 6.
^l 1 Tim. 1.15.
1 John 3. 5.

by," he saw a man, named Matthew — the writer of this precious Gospel, who here, with singular modesty and brevity, relates the story of his own calling. In Mark and Luke he is called *Levi* [Λευεί, or, according to the preferable reading, Λευείν], which seems to have been his family name. In their lists of the twelve apostles, however, Mark and Luke give him the name of Matthew, which seems to have been the name by which he was known as a disciple. While he himself sinks his family name, he is careful not to sink his occupation, the obnoxious associations with which he would place over against the grace that called him from it, and made him an apostle. (See on ch. x. 3.) Mark alone tells us (ii. 14) that he was "the son of Alpheus"—the same, probably, with the father of James the less. From this and other considerations it is pretty certain that he must at least have heard of our Lord before this meeting. Unnecessary doubts, even from an early period, have been raised about the identity of Levi and Matthew. No English jury, with the evidence before them which we have in the Gospels, would hesitate in giving in a unanimous verdict of identity. sitting at the receipt of custom —as a publican, which Luke (v. 27) calls him. It means the place of receipt, the toll-house or booth in which the collector sat. Being in this case by the sea-side, it might be the ferry-tax, for the transit of persons and goods across the lake, which he collected. (See on ch. v. 46.) and he saith unto him, Follow me. Witching words these, from the lips of Him who never employed them without giving them resistless efficacy in the hearts of those they were spoken to. And he "left all" (Luke v. 28), arose and followed him.
The Feast (10-13). 10. And it came to pass, as Jesus sat at meat in the house. The modesty of our Evangelist signally appears here. Luke says (v. 29) that "Levi made Him *a great feast*," or 'reception' [δοχὴν μεγάλην], while Matthew merely says, "He sat at meat;" and Mark and Luke say that it was in Levi's "own house," while Matthew merely says, "He sat at meat *in the house*." Whether this feast was made now, or not till afterwards, is a point of some importance in the order of events, and not agreed among harmonists The probability is that it did not take place till a considerable time afterwards. For Matthew, who ought surely to know what took place while his Lord was speaking at his own table, tells us that the visit of Jairus, the ruler of the synagogue, occurred at that moment (v. 18). But we

know from Mark and Luke that this visit of Jairus did not take place till after our Lord's return, at a later period, from the country of the Gadarenes. (See Mark v. 21, &c., and Luke viii. 40, &c.) We conclude, therefore, that the feast was not made in the novelty of his discipleship, but after Matthew had had time to be somewhat established in the faith; when, returning to Capernaum, his compassion for old friends, of his own calling and character, led him to gather them together that they might have an opportunity of hearing the gracious words which proceeded out of His Master's mouth, if haply they might experience a like change. behold, many publicans and sinners—Luke says, "a great company" (v. 29), came and sat down with him and his disciples. In all such cases the word rendered 'sat' is 'reclined,' in allusion to the ancient mode of lying on couches at meals. 11. And when the Pharisees—"and scribes," add Mark and Luke. saw it, they "murmured" or 'muttered,' says Luke (v. 30), and said unto his disciples—not venturing to put their question to Jesus Himself. Why eateth your Master with publicans and sinners? (See on Luke xv. 2.) 12. But when Jesus heard [that], he said unto them —to the Pharisees and scribes; addressing Himself to them, though they had shrunk from addressing Him. They that be whole need not a physician, but they that are sick—*q.d.*, 'Ye deem yourselves whole; My mission, therefore, is not to you: The physician's business is with the sick; therefore eat I with publicans and sinners.' O, what myriads of broken hearts, of sin-sick souls, have been bound up by this matchless saying! 13. But go ye and learn what that meaneth (Hos. vi. 6), I will have mercy, and not sacrifice—that is, the one rather than the other. "Sacrifice," the chief part of the ceremonial law, is here put for a religion of literal adherence to mere rules; while "Mercy" expresses such compassion for the fallen as seeks to lift them up. The duty of keeping aloof from the polluted, in the sense of "having no fellowship with the unfruitful works of darkness," is obvious enough; but to understand this as prohibiting such intercourse with them as is necessary to their recovery, is to abuse it. This was what these pharisaical religionists did, and this is what our Lord here exposes. for I am not come to call the righteous, but sinners [to repentance]. The words enclosed in brackets are of doubtful authority here, and more than doubtful authority in Mark ii. 17; but in Luke v. 32 they are undisputed. We have here just the former statement

14   Then came to him the disciples of John, saying, [m]Why do we and the
15 Pharisees fast oft, but thy disciples fast not? And Jesus said unto them,
Can [n]the children of the bride-chamber mourn, as long as the bridegroom
is with them? but the days will come, when the bridegroom shall be
16 taken from them, and [o]then shall they fast. No man putteth a piece
of [1]new cloth unto an old garment; for that which is put in to fill it up
17 taketh from the garment, and the rent is made worse. Neither do men
put new wine into old bottles; else the bottles break, and the wine
runneth out, and the bottles perish: but they put new wine into new
bottles, and both are preserved.
18   While [p]he spake these things unto them, behold, there came a certain
ruler, and worshipped him, saying, My daughter is even now dead: but
19 come and lay thy hand upon her, and she shall live. And Jesus arose,
and followed him, and *so did* his disciples.
20   And, [q]behold, a woman, which was diseased with an issue of blood
twelve years, came behind *him*, and touched the hem of his garment:
21 For she said within herself, If I may but touch his garment, I shall be
22 whole. But Jesus turned him about; and when he saw her, he said,
Daughter, be of good comfort; [r]thy faith hath made thee whole. And
the woman was made whole from that hour.
23   And [s]when Jesus came into the ruler's house, and saw [t]the minstrels
24 and the people making a noise, he said unto them, [u]Give place; for the
25 maid is not dead, but sleepeth. And they laughed him to scorn. But
when the people were put forth, he went in, and took her by the hand,
26 and the maid arose. And [2]the fame hereof went abroad into all that
land.
27   And when Jesus departed thence, two blind men followed him, crying,

A. D. 31.
[m] Mark 2. 18.
Luke 5. 33.
Luke 18. 12.
[n] Luke 24.13.
John 3. 29.
John 16. 6.
Acts 1. 10.
[o] Acts 13. 2.
Acts 14. 23.
1 Cor. 7. 5.
1 Or, raw, or, unwrought cloth.
[p] Mark 5. 22.
Luke 8. 41.
[q] Lev. 15. 25.
Mark 5. 25.
Luke 8. 43.
[r] Mark 10.52.
Luke 7. 50.
Luke 8. 48.
Luke 17. 19.
Luke 18.42.
Acts 14. 9.
Heb. 4. 2.
[s] Mark 5. 38.
Luke 8. 51.
[t] 2 Chr.35.25.
[u] 1 Ki. 17. 18-24.
Acts. 9. 40.
Acts 20. 10.
2 Or, this fame.
Isa. 52. 13.

stripped of its figure. "The righteous" are the whole; "sinners," the sick. When Christ "called" the latter, as He did Matthew, and probably some of those publicans and sinners whom he had invited to meet with Him, it was to heal them of their spiritual maladies, or save their souls: "The righteous," like those miserable, self-satisfied Pharisees, "He sent empty away."

Remarks.—1. How glorious is the grace which not only saves the chief of sinners, but places one of a proverbially sunken class among "the princes of His people"! (See on ch. i. 3, 5, 6.) 2. How delightful is it to trace the deep humility with which this disciple ever after carried himself—whether in the Genealogy which he gives of His Master, to which reference has just been made; or in avoiding, in the record of his own calling, what was to his own credit; or in noting, in his catalogue of the Twelve, as none of the other New Testament writers do, the justly branded class out of which he had been called. (See on ch. x. 3.) 3. But let us not fail to observe the compassion with which he sought to fetch in his old associates to the circle of the saved, "that they also might have fellowship with him" in the love of Jesus. There is no more certain evidence of genuine repentance and true discipleship than this. (See Ps li. 12, 13; Luke xxii. 32, second clause.) 4. How grievously do they err, and pervert the simple, who represent the object of Christ's mission to have been merely to furnish a code of sound morality, or establish spirituality of worship, or certify the doctrine of the resurrection, or the like. He came to heal the sick soul, to raise the sunken, to save sinners; to bring back to God the vilest prodigals, and beautify them with salvation. Such as want Him not for this He passes by; they are not His patients, and they get nothing from Him.

They may laud the purity and loftiness of His teaching and example; but they are strangers to Him as "the Balm in Gilead and the Physician there."

14-17.—DISCOURSE ON FASTING. (= Mark ii. 18-22; Luke v. 33-39.) As this Discourse is recorded by all the three first Evangelists immediately after their account of Matthew's Call and Feast, there can be no doubt that it was delivered on that occasion. For the exposition of this important Discourse, see on Luke v. 33-39, where it is given most fully.

18-26.—THE WOMAN WITH THE ISSUE OF BLOOD HEALED.—THE DAUGHTER OF JAIRUS RAISED TO LIFE (= Luke viii. 40-56; Mark v. 21-43.) For the exposition, see on Mark v. 21-43.

27-34.—TWO BLIND MEN, AND A DUMB DEMONIAC, HEALED. These two miracles are recorded by Matthew alone.

Two Blind Men Healed (27-31). **27. And when Jesus departed thence, two blind men followed him**—hearing, doubtless, as in a later case is expressed, "that Jesus passed by" (ch. xx. 30), **crying, and saying, Thou Son of David, have mercy on us.** It is remarkable that in the only other recorded case in which the blind applied to Jesus for their sight, and obtained it, they addressed Him, over and over again, by this one Messianic title, so well known—"Son of David" (ch. xx. 30). Can there be a doubt that their faith fastened on such great Messianic promises as this, "Then the eyes of the blind shall be opened"? &c. (Isa. xxxv. 5); and if so, this appeal to Him, as the Consolation of Israel, to do His predicted office, would fall with great weight upon the ears of Jesus. **28. And when he was come into the house.** To try their faith and patience, He seems to have made them no answer. But **the blind men came to Him**—which, no doubt, was what He desired, **and Jesus saith unto them, Believe ye that I**

28 and saying, *^{v}Thou* son of David, have mercy on us. And when he was
come into the house, the blind men came to him: and Jesus saith unto
them, Believe ye that I am able to do this? They said unto him, Yea,
29 Lord. Then touched he their eyes, saying, According to your faith be it
30 unto you. And *^{w}their* eyes were opened: and Jesus straitly charged
31 them, saying, *^{x}See that* no man know *it*. But *^{y}they*, when they were
departed, spread abroad his fame in all that country.
32 As *^{z}they* went out, behold, they brought to him a dumb man pos-
33 sessed with a devil. And when the devil was cast out, the dumb spake:
34 and the multitudes marvelled, saying, It was never so seen in Israel. But
the Pharisees said, He casteth out devils through the prince of the devils.
35 And *^{a}Jesus* went about all the cities and villages, teaching in their
synagogues, and preaching the gospel of the kingdom, and healing
every sickness and every disease, among the people.

A. D. 31.

^{v} ch. 15. 22.
ch. 20. 30.
Mark 9. 22.
Mark 10.47.
Luke 17. 13.
Luke 18.38.
John 7. 42.
^{w} Ps. 146. 8.
John 9. 7, 26.
^{x} Luke 5. 14.
^{y} Mark 7. 36.
^{z} ch. 12. 22.
Mark 9. 17.
Luke 11.14.
^{a} Mark 6. 6.
. Luke 13.22.

am able to do this? They said unto him, Yea,
Lord. Doubtless our Lord's design was not only
to put their faith to the test by this question, but
to deepen it, to raise their expectation of a cure,
and so prepare them to receive it; and the cordial
acknowledgment, so touchingly simple, which they
immediately made to Him of His power to heal
them, shows how entirely that object was gained.
**29. Then touched he their eyes, saying, Accord-
ing to your faith be it unto you**—not, Receive a
cure *proportioned* to your faith, but, Receive this
cure as *granted to* your faith. Thus would they
carry about with them, in their restored vision, a
gracious seal of the faith which drew it from their
compassionate Lord.   **30. And their eyes were
opened: and Jesus straitly charged them.** The
expression is very strong [ἐνεβριμήσατο αὐτοῖς],
denoting great earnestness. **31. But they, when
they were departed, spread abroad his fame in
all that country.** (See on ch. viii. 4, and Remark
4 on that Section.)

A Dumb Demoniac Healed (32-34).   **32. As they
went out, behold, they brought to him a dumb
man possessed with a devil** [δαιμονιζόμενον]—'demonized.' The dumbness was not natural, but was
the effect of the possession.   **33. And when the
devil**—or 'demon'—**was cast out, the dumb spake.**
The particulars in this case are not given; the
object being simply to record the instantaneous restoration of the natural faculties, on the removal of
the malignant oppression of them, the form which
the popular astonishment took, and the very different effect of it upon another class. **and the
multitudes marvelled, saying, It was never so
seen in Israel**—referring, probably, not to this
case only, but to all those miraculous displays of
healing power which seemed to promise a new era
in the history of Israel. Probably they meant by
this language to indicate, as far as they thought it
safe to do so, their inclination to regard Him as
the promised Messiah. **34. But the Pharisees
said, He casteth out devils through the prince
of the devils**—'the demons through the prince of
the demons.' This seems to be the first muttering
of a theory of such miracles which soon became a
fixed mode of calumniating them—a theory which
would be ridiculous if it were not melancholy, as
an outburst of the darkest malignity. (See on ch.
xii. 24, &c.)

Remarks.—1. So manifestly were these bodily
cures designed to set forth analogous operations
of grace on the soul, that in the case of opening
the eyes of the blind, our Lord, before performing it, in one notable instance, expressly announced the higher design of it, saying, "As
long as I am in the world, I am the light of the
world" (John ix. 5).   Nor would it have been

possible beforehand to tell with certainty whether
the predictions of such glorious miracles (for
example, in Isa. xxxv. 5, 6; xlii. 7)—as inaugu-
rating and distinguishing the Messianic economy
—were designed to be understood literally, or
spiritually, or both. Hence, we are to regard
all such incidents as are here recorded as having
higher aspects and bearings than any that terminate on the body; and on the same principle,
the honour which our Lord here put upon the
faith and patience of these blind men may surely
be reckoned on by all who sigh to be "turned by
Him from darkness to light, and from the power
of Satan unto God." 2. How differently are the
same operations and events regarded by the unsophisticated and the prejudiced! 'More light,'
is the cry of many besides these prejudiced Pharisees. But what they want is more simplicity
and godly sincerity, the stifling of which leaves
the soul a prey to the darkest passions.

35—X. 5.—THIRD GALILEAN CIRCUIT—MISSION
OF THE TWELVE APOSTLES. As the Mission of the
Twelve supposes the previous Choice of them—of
which our Evangelist gives no account, and which
did not take place till a later stage of our Lord's
public life—it is introduced here out of its proper
place, which is after what is recorded in Luke vi.
12-19.

Third Galilean Circuit (35)—and probably the
last. **35. And Jesus went about all the cities
and villages, teaching in their synagogues, and
preaching the gospel of the kingdom, and healing every sickness and every disease, [among the
people].** The bracketed words are of more than
doubtful authority here, and were probably introduced from ch. iv. 23. The language here is so
identical with that used in describing the first circuit (ch. iv. 23), that we may presume the work
done on both occasions was much the same. It
was just a further preparation of the soil, and a
fresh sowing of the precious seed. (See on ch. iv.
23.) To these fruitful journeyings of the Redeemer, "with healing in His wings," Peter no
doubt alludes, when, in his address to the household of Cornelius, he spoke of "How God
anointed Jesus of Nazareth with the Holy Ghost
and with power: who *went about* doing good
[διῆλθεν εὐεργετῶν], and healing all that were
oppressed of the devil: for God was with Him"
(Acts x. 38).

*Jesus, Compassionating the Multitudes, Asks
Prayer for Help* (36-38). He had now returned
from His preaching and healing circuit, and the
result, as at the close of the first one, was the
gathering of a vast and motley multitude around
Him. After a whole night spent in prayer, He
had called His more immediate disciples, and

36 But when he saw the multitudes, he was moved with compassion on them, because they ³fainted, and were scattered abroad, as sheep having
37 no shepherd. Then saith he unto his disciples, ᵇThe harvest truly *is*
38 plenteous, but the labourers *are* few; pray ᶜye therefore the Lord of the harvest, that he will send forth labourers into his harvest.

10 AND ᵃwhen he had called unto *him* his twelve disciples, he gave them power ¹*against* unclean spirits, to cast them out, and to heal all manner of sickness, and all manner of disease.
2 Now the names of the twelve apostles are these; The first, Simon, ᵇwho is called Peter, and Andrew his brother; James *the son* of Zebedee,
3 and John his brother; Philip, and Bartholomew; Thomas, and Matthew the publican; James *the son* of Alpheus, and Lebbeus, whose surname
4 was ²Thaddeus; Simon ᶜthe Canaanite, and Judas ᵈIscariot, who also betrayed him.

A. D. 31.

³ Or, were tired and lay down.
ᵇ Luke 10. 2.
John 4. 35.
ᶜ Acts 13. 2.
Acts 20. 28.
1 Cor. 12. 28.

CHAP. 10.
ᵃ Mark 3. 13.
Mark 6. 7.
1 Or, over.
ᵇ John 1. 42.
² Or, Judas.
Jude 1.
ᶜ Acts 1. 13.
ᵈ John 13. 26.

from them had solemnly chosen the Twelve; then, coming down from the mountain, on which this was transacted, to the multitudes that waited for Him below, He had addressed to them—as we take it—that Discourse which bears so strong a resemblance to the Sermon on the Mount that many critics take it to be the same. (See on Luke vi. 12-49; and on Matt. v., Introductory Remarks.) Soon after this, it should seem, the multitudes still hanging on Him, Jesus is touched with their wretched and helpless condition, and acts as is now to be described. **36. But when he saw the multitudes, he was moved with compassion on them, because they fainted** [ἦσαν ἐκλελυμμένοι]. This reading, however, has hardly any authority at all. The true reading doubtless is, 'were harassed' [ἦσαν ἐσκυλμένοι], **and were scattered abroad** [ἐῤῥιμμένοι]—rather, 'lying about,' 'abandoned,' or 'neglected' **—as sheep having no shepherd**—their pitiable condition as wearied and couching under bodily fatigue, a vast disorganized mass, being but a faint picture of their wretchedness as the victims of Pharisaic guidance; their souls uncared for, yet drawn after and hanging upon Him. This moved the Redeemer's compassion. **37. Then saith he unto his disciples, The harvest truly is plenteous.** His eye doubtless rested immediately on the Jewish field, but this he saw widening into the vast field of "the world" (ch. xiii. 38), teeming with souls having to be gathered to Him. **but the labourers**—men divinely qualified and called to gather them in—**are few; 38. Pray ye therefore the Lord of the harvest**—the great Lord and Proprietor of all. Compare John xv. 1—"I am the true Vine, and my Father is the Husbandman." **that he will send forth labourers into his harvest.** The word [ἐκβάλῃ] properly means 'thrust forth;' but this emphatic sense disappears in some places, as in *v*. 25, and John x. 4—"When He *putteth forth* His own sheep." (See on ch. iv. 1.)

CHAP. X. 1-5.—*Mission of the Twelve Apostles.* (= Mark vi. 7-13; Luke ix. 1-6.) The last three verses of ch. ix. form the proper introduction to the Mission of the Twelve; as is evident from the remarkable fact that the Mission of the Seventy was prefaced by the very same words. (See on Luke x. 2.) **1. And when he had called unto him his twelve disciples, he gave them power** [ἐξουσίαν]. The word signifies both 'power,' and 'authority' or 'right.' Even if it were not evident that here both ideas are included, we find both words expressly used in the parallel passage of Luke (ix. 1)—"He gave them power and authority" [δύναμιν καὶ ἐξουσίαν]—in other words, He both *qualified* and

authorized them—**against**—or 'over'—**unclean spirits, to cast them out, and to heal all manner of sickness, and all manner of disease.**
2. **Now the names of the twelve apostles are these.** The other Evangelists enumerate the Twelve in immediate connection with their appointment (Mark iii. 13-19; Luke vi. 13-16). But our Evangelist, not intending to record the appointment, but only the Mission of the Twelve, gives their names here. And as in the Acts (i. 13) we have a list of the Eleven who met daily in the upper room with the other disciples after their Master's ascension until the day of Pentecost, we have four catalogues in all for comparison. **The first, Simon, who is called Peter** (see on John i. 42), **and Andrew his brother; James the son of Zebedee, and John his brother**—named after James, as the younger of the two. 3. **Philip, and Bartholomew.** That this person is the same with "Nathanael of Cana in Galilee," is justly concluded for the three following reasons: First, because Bartholomew [= בַּר תַּלְמַי, or 'son of Ptolomy'] is not so properly a name as a family surname; next, because not only in this list, but in Mark's and Luke's, he follows the name of "Philip," who was the instrument of bringing Nathanael first to Jesus (John i. 45); and again, when our Lord, after His resurrection, appeared at the sea of Tiberias, "Nathanael of Cana in Galilee" is mentioned along with six others, all of them apostles, as being present (John xxi. 2). **Matthew the publican.** In none of the four lists of the Twelve is this apostle so branded but in his own one, as if he would have all to know how deep a debtor he had been to his Lord. (See on ch. i. 3, 5, 6; and ix. 9, and Remark 2 on that Section.) **James the son of Alpheus** [= חַלְפִּי]—the same person apparently who is called *Cleopas* or *Clopas* (Luke xxiv. 18; John xix. 25); and as he was the husband of Mary, sister to the Virgin, James the less must have been our Lord's cousin. **and Lebbeus, whose surname was Thaddeus**—the same, without doubt, as "Judas the brother of James," mentioned in both the lists of Luke (vi. 16; Acts i. 13), while no one of the name of Lebbeus or Thaddeus is so. It is he who in John (xiv. 22) is sweetly called "Judas, not Iscariot." That he was the author of the Catholic Epistle of "Jude," and not "the Lord's brother" (ch. xiii. 55), unless these be the same, is most likely. **4. Simon the Canaanite**; rather 'Kananite' [Κανανίτης], but better still, 'the Zealot' [Ζηλωτής], as he is called in Luke vi. 15, where the original term should not, have been retained as in our version ("Simon, called Zelotes"), but rendered 'Simon, called the Zelot.' The word "Kananite" is just the Aramaic, or Syro-Chaldaic, term for 'Zealot' [Heb.

59

	A. D. 31.
5 These twelve Jesus sent forth, and commanded them, saying, Go not into the way of the Gentiles, and into *any* city of ᶜthe Samaritans enter	ᶜ 2 Ki. 17. 24.

אָנֵק, 'jealous' or 'zealous'—Chald. וָאנֵק]. Probably before his acquaintance with Jesus, he belonged to the sect of the Zealots, who bound themselves, as a sort of voluntary ecclesiastical police, to see that the law was not broken with impunity. and **Judas Iscariot**—that is, Judas of Kerioth, a town of Judah (Josh. xv. 25); so called to distinguish him from "Judas the brother of James" (Luke vi. 16). who also betrayed him—a note of infamy attached to his name in all the catalogues of the Twelve.

Remarks.—1. As the reapers of every harvest are appointed by the proprietor of the field, so the labourers whom God will own in "His harvest" are of His own appointing, and to be sought of Him by prayer (ch. ix. 38). Even the Lord Jesus spent a whole night in prayer to God before selecting the Twelve Apostles (Luke vi. 12, 13). But just as in that case the Redeemer followed up His prayer by action, so must we. If to take action for providing preachers without asking them from God be the spirit of naturalism, to cry to God for preachers and do nothing to provide them, is mere fanaticism; but to do both, with full assurance that each is indispensable for its own purposes, and necessary to make the other available—this is to tread in the very footsteps of Christ. In every age and every land the nature of the steps requisite on our part to procure and prepare the proper labourers will vary; but our action in this matter is not superseded by divine interpositions. The Lord indeed will not bind Himself to employ none on whom no human preparation has been bestowed; and facts prove that to disown the labours of all on whom the stamp of an organized Church has not been affixed, would be to fight against God. But to make such exceptional cases determine the Church's line of procedure, in so solemn a matter as the Gospel ministry, would be short-sighted and ruinous. On the other hand, as the tendency of all churches is to depend upon its own measures for providing qualified preachers of the everlasting Gospel, it will be our true wisdom to drink in the spirit of the Master's teaching here—that the Lord appoints His own labourers, and for this thing must be entreated of us to do it for us; remembering that whatever be the gifts which men bring to the work of the ministry, and whatever their external success in it, unless they be of God's own selecting and appointing, they have no right to be there, and are liable at the last to hear from the lips of the Lord of the harvest those awful words, "I never knew you." 2. Did the Redeemer, as He beheld the multitudes harassed and abandoned, like shepherdless sheep, have compassion upon them, and go out in thought to the vastness of the harvest to be gathered in and the fewness of the labourers to do it; and did He call the attention of His disciples to this affecting state of things, that they might enter into His own mind about it, and, like Himself, carry the matter to God for relief? Then, what a model-attitude for ourselves is here held up before us! Were the churches, and all the true followers of Christ, to direct their eye steadily upon the spiritually wretched and necessitous condition of the world, till their eye affected their heart, and the cry of faith went up from it to God, to send forth labourers into His harvest, how speedily would the answer come, and in how rich a form! Nor would it be confined to the direct object of their prayer. For He, whose

own very attitude in the days of His flesh would thus be reflected by His believing people, would set the seal of His complacency upon them in a thousand ways—drying up the fountains of dissension and separation and weakness amongst themselves, and drawing them into love and concord and strength, to the astonishment of a surrounding world. Blessed Jesus, shall not this consummation be realized at length? "My soul breaketh for the longing that it hath at all times" to see this great sight, which we cannot doubt will be fulfilled in its season. On the choice of the apostles, we observe, 3. That the number *Twelve* was fixed on to correspond with the number of the tribes of Israel, as is evident from ch. xix. 28; as the number of *Seventy*, to go on a subsequent mission (Luke x. 1), had certainly a reference to the seventy elders of Israel, on whom the Spirit of the Lord was made to rest, that they might bear along with Moses the burden of administration (Num. xi. 16, 17, 25). 4. The relationship existing among those Twelve is one of the most remarkable facts. There were no fewer than three pairs of brothers among them: Andrew and Peter; James and John; James the less and Judas, or Lebbæus, or Simon the Zealot—not to speak of the peculiar tie which bound Bartholomew, or Nathanael, to Philip, and the common tie that bound them all together as disciples—probably the most devoted and advanced—of John the Baptist, and as drawn mostly from the same locality. Reasons for all this may easily be imagined; but we here leave the fact to speak for itself. 5. Our Evangelist enumerates the Twelve in couples, with evident allusion to their being sent on this mission "by two and two" (Mark vi. 7). 6. In all the first three lists the names are arranged in three quaternions, or divisions of four each. Nor can it be doubted that this has reference to some distribution of them by the Lord Himself; for in all of them *Philip* stands first in the second quaternion—as in the third, *James the son of Alphæus.* 7. The first quaternion evidently stood highest in order. Peter and James and John, who constituted a sacred trio in some of the leading events of our Lord's public life, were at the head of all; Andrew being associated with them, to make up the first quaternion, not only as being Peter's brother, but as having been the first to "bring him to Jesus" (John i. 41, 42). In the lists of Matthew and Luke he stands next after Peter, from connection with him; while in the other two lists the sacred trio stand first, the name of Andrew completing that quaternion. 8. When our Evangelist says, "The *first,* Simon"—without assigning a number to any of the rest—while in the other three lists his name stands first, as it does here, the evident design is to hold forth his prominence amongst the Twelve: not as having any authority above the rest—for not a vestige of this appears in the New Testament—but as marking the use which His Lord made of him above any of the rest; for which his qualifications, in spite of failings, stand out on almost every page of the Gospel History, and in the earlier portion of the Acts of the Apostles. 9. With the exception of the four first names, the rest are almost unknown in the New Testament; and the slight variety with which they are arranged in the several lists shows the little prominence with which they were regarded for the purposes of this History. 10. In all the catalogues the

6 ye not: but *f*go rather to the *g*lost sheep of the house of Israel.

7 And *h*as ye go, preach, saying, The kingdom of heaven is at hand.

8 Heal the sick, cleanse the lepers, raise the dead, cast out devils: freely ye

9 have received, freely give. ³Provide neither gold, nor silver, nor brass in

10 your purses, nor scrip for *your* journey, neither two coats, neither shoes,

11 nor yet ⁴staves; ⁱfor the workman is worthy of his meat. And into

    whatsoever city or town ye shall enter, enquire who in it is worthy;

12 and there abide till ye go thence. And when ye come into an house,

13 salute it. And if the house be worthy, let your peace come upon it:

A. D. 31.

f Acts 13. 46.
g Isa. 53. 6.
    Rom. 11. 1.
h Luke 9. 2.
³ Or. Get.
    1 Sam. 9. 7.
⁴ a staff.
ⁱ Luke 10. 7.
1 Cor. 9. 7.
1 Tim. 5.18.

name of *Judas* not only stands last, but "*traitor*" is added to it as a brand of abhorrence; and so revolting were the associations connected with his name, that the beloved disciple, in recording a deeply interesting question put at the last supper by Judas to his Lord, hastens to explain, in a sweet parenthesis, that it was "*not* Iscariot" that he meant (John xiv. 22). 11. How terrific is the warning which the case of Judas holds forth to the ministers of Christ, not to trust in any gifts, any offices, any services, any success, as sure evidence of divine acceptance, apart from that "holiness without which no man shall see the Lord"!

5-42.—THE TWELVE RECEIVE THEIR INSTRUCTIONS. This Directory divides itself into three distinct parts. The *first* part—extending from *vv.* 5 to 15—contains directions for the brief and temporary mission on which they were now going forth, with respect to the places they were to go to, the works they were to do, the message they were to bear, and the manner in which they were to conduct themselves. The *second* part—extending from *vv.* 16 to 23—contains directions of no such limited and temporary nature, but opens out into the permanent exercise of the Gospel ministry. The *third* part—extending from *vv.* 24 to 42 —is of wider application still, reaching not only to the ministry of the Gospel in every age, but to the service of Christ in the widest sense. *It is a strong confirmation of this threefold division, that each part closes with the words,* "VERILY I SAY UNTO YOU" (*vv.* 15, 23, 42).

Directions for the Present Mission (5-15). **5.** These twelve Jesus sent forth, and commanded them, saying, Go not into the way of the Gentiles, and into any city of the Samaritans enter ye not. The Samaritans were Gentiles by blood; but being the descendants of those whom the king of Assyria had transported from the East to supply the place of the ten tribes carried captive, they had adopted the religion of the Jews, though with admixtures of their own; and, as the nearest neighbours of the Jews, they occupied a place intermediate between them and the Gentiles. Accordingly, when this prohibition was to be taken off, on the effusion of the Spirit at Pentecost, the apostles were told that they should be Christ's witnesses first "in Jerusalem, and in all Judea," then "in Samaria," and lastly, "unto the uttermost part of the earth" (Acts i. 8). **6. But go rather to the lost sheep of the house of Israel.** Until Christ's death, which broke down the middle wall of partition (Eph. ii. 14), the Gospel commission was to the Jews only, who, though the visible people of God, were "lost sheep," not merely in the sense in which all sinners are (Isa. liii. 6; 1 Pet. ii. 25; with Luke xix. 10), but as abandoned and left to wander from the right way by faithless shepherds, (Jer. l. 6, 17; Ezek. xxxiv. 2-6, &c.) **7. And as ye go, preach, saying, The kingdom of heaven is at hand.** (See on ch. iii. 2.) **8. Heal the sick, cleanse the lepers, [raise the dead,] cast out devils.** [The bracketed clause—

"raise the dead"—is wanting in so many MSS. and ancient versions that *Tischendorf* and others omit it altogether, as having found its way into this verse from ch. xi. 5. *Griesbach, Lachmann,* and *Tregelles* insert it, putting it before the words "cleanse the lepers," which, if it be genuine, is its right place. But it seems very improbable that our Lord imparted at so early a period this highest of all forms of supernatural power.] Here we have the first communication of supernatural power by Christ Himself to his followers—thus anticipating the gifts of Pentecost. And right royally does he dispense it. **freely ye have received, freely give.** Divine saying, divinely said! (cf. Deut. xv. 10, 11; Acts iii. 6)—an apple of gold in a setting of silver (Prov. xxv. 11). It reminds us of that other golden saying of our Lord, rescued from oblivion by Paul, "It is more blessed to give than to receive" (Acts xx. 35). Who can estimate what the world owes to such sayings, and with what beautiful foliage and rich fruit such seeds have covered, and will yet cover, this earth! **9. Provide neither gold, nor silver, nor brass in** [εἰs]—'for' **your purses** [ζώναs]—lit., 'your belts,' in which they kept their money. **10. Nor scrip for your journey** —the wallet used by travellers for holding provisions—**neither two coats** [χιτῶναs]—or tunics, worn next the skin. The meaning is, Take no change of dress, no additional articles. **neither shoes** —that is, change of them—**nor yet staves.** The received text here has 'a staff' [ῥάβδον], but our version follows another reading [ῥάβδουs], 'staves,' which is found in the received text of Luke (ix. 3). The true reading, however, evidently is 'a staff'— meaning, that they were not to procure even thus much expressly for this missionary journey, but to go with what they had. No doubt it was the misunderstanding of this that gave rise to the reading "staves" in so many MSS. Even if this reading were genuine, it could not mean 'more than one;' for who, as *Alford* well asks, would think of taking a spare staff? **for the workman is worthy of his meat** [τροφῆs]—his 'food' or 'maintenance;' a principle which, being universally recognized in secular affairs, is here authoritatively applied to the services of the Lord's workmen, and by Paul repeatedly and touchingly employed in his appeals to the churches (Rom. xv. 27; 1 Cor. ix. 11; Gal. vi. 6), and once as "Scripture" (1 Tim. v. 18). **11. And into whatsoever city or town** [πόλιν ἢ κώμην]—'town or village' **ye enter** [carefully] **enquire** [ἐξετάσατε] **who in it is worthy**—or 'meet' to entertain such messengers; not in point of rank, of course, but of congenial disposition. **and there abide till ye go thence**—not shifting about, as if discontented, but returning the welcome given them with a courteous, contented, accommodating disposition. **12. And when ye come into an house** —or 'the house' [τὴν οἰκίαν], but it means not the worthy house, but the house ye first enter, to try if it be worthy. **salute it**—show it the usual civilities. **13. And if the house be worthy**—

14 but if it be not worthy, let your peace return to you. And whosoever
shall not receive you, nor hear your words, when ye depart out of that
15 house or city, *shake off the dust of your feet. Verily I say unto you,
It shall be more tolerable for the land of Sodom and Gomorrha in the
day of judgment, than for that city.
16   Behold, I send you forth as sheep in the midst of wolves: *be ye there-
17 fore wise as serpents, and 5 harmless as doves. But beware of men; for
they will deliver you up to the councils, and *they will scourge you in
18 their synagogues: and *ye shall be brought before governors and kings
19 for my sake, for a testimony against them and the Gentiles. But when
they deliver you up, take no thought how or what ye shall speak: for *it
20 shall be given you in that same hour what ye shall speak. For *it is not
ye that speak, but the Spirit of your Father which speaketh in you.
21 And *the brother shall deliver up the brother to death, and the father
the child: and the children shall rise up against *their* parents, and cause
22 them to be put to death. And ye shall be hated of all *men* for my name's

A. D. 31.
j Neh. 5. 13.
Acts 13. 51.
Acts 18. 6.
Acts 20. 26.
27.
k Gen. 3. 1.
Luke 21. 15.
Rom. 16.19.
Eph. 5. 15.
5 Or, simple.
1 Cor. 14.20.
l Acts 5. 40.
m Acts 12. 1.
Acts 24. 10.
n Ex. 4. 12.
Jer. 1. 7.
o 2 Sam. 23. 2.
Acts 4. 8.
Acts 6. 10.
p Mic. 7. 6.

showing this by giving you a welcome—**let your peace come upon it.** This is best explained by the injunction to the Seventy, "And into whatsoever house ye enter, first say, Peace be to this house" (Luke x. 5). This was the ancient salutation of the East, and it prevails to this day. But from the lips of Christ and his messengers, it means something far higher, both in the gift and the giving of it, than in the current salutation. (See on John xiv. 27.) **but if it be not worthy, let your peace return to you.** If your peace finds a shut instead of an open door in the heart of any household, take it back to yourselves, who know how to value it, and it will taste the sweeter to you for having been offered, even though rejected. **14. And whosoever shall not receive you, nor hear your words, when ye depart out of that house or city**—for possibly a whole town might not furnish one "worthy", **shake off the dust of your feet** —"for a testimony against them," as Mark and Luke add. By this symbolical action they vividly shook themselves from all *connection* with such, and all *responsibility* for the guilt of rejecting them and their message. Such symbolical actions were common in ancient times, even among others than the Jews, as strikingly appears in Pilate (ch. xxvii. 24). And even to this day it prevails in the East. **15. Verily I say unto you, It shall be more tolerable—more bearable, for Sodom and Gomorrah in the day of judgment, than for that city.** Those cities of the plain, which were given to the flames for their loathsome impurities, shall be treated as less criminal, we are here taught, than those places which, though morally respectable, reject the Gospel message and affront those that bear it.

Directions for the Future and Permanent Exercise of the Christian Ministry (16-23). **16. Behold, I send you forth.** The "I" here [Εγώ] is emphatic, holding up Himself as the Fountain of the Gospel ministry, as He is also the Great Burden of it. **as sheep**—defenceless, **in the midst of wolves** —ready to make a prey of you (John x. 12). To be left exposed, as sheep to wolves, would have been startling enough; but that the sheep should be *sent* among the wolves would sound strange indeed. No wonder this announcement begins with the exclamation, "Behold." **be ye therefore wise as serpents, and harmless as doves.** Wonderful combination this! Alone, the wisdom of the serpent is mere cunning, and the harmlessness of the dove little better than weakness: but in combination, the wisdom of the serpent would save them from unnecessary ex-

posure to danger; the harmlessness of the dove, from sinful expedients to escape it. In the apostolic age of Christianity, how harmoniously were these qualities displayed! Instead of the fanatical thirst for martyrdom, to which a later age gave birth, there was a manly combination of unflinching zeal and calm discretion, before which nothing was able to stand. **17. But beware of men; for they will deliver you up to the councils** [συνέδρια]—the local courts, used here for civil magistrates in general. **and they will scourge you in their synagogues.** By this is meant persecution at the hands of the ecclesiastics. **18. And ye shall be brought before governors**—or provincial rulers, **and kings**—the highest tribunals—**for my sake, for a testimony against them** [αὐτοῖς]—rather, 'to them,' in order to bear testimony to the truth and its glorious effects—**and [to] the Gentiles**—a hint that their message would not long be confined to the lost sheep of the house of Israel. The Acts of the Apostles are the best commentary on these warnings. **19. But when they deliver you up, take no thought**—'be not solicitous' or 'anxious' [μὴ μεριμνήσητε]. (See on ch. vi. 25.) **how or what ye shall speak**—that is, either in what *manner* ye shall make your defence, or of what *matter* it shall consist—**for it shall be given you in that same hour what ye shall speak.** (See Exod. iv. 12; Jer. i. 7.) **20. For it is not ye that speak, but the Spirit of your Father which speaketh in you.** How remarkably this has been verified, the whole history of persecution thrillingly proclaims—from the Acts of the Apostles to the latest martyrology. **21. And the brother shall deliver up the brother to death, and the father the child: and the children shall rise up against their parents, and cause them to be put to death**—for example, by lodging informations against them with the authorities. The deep and virulent hostility of the old nature and life to the new—as of Belial to Christ —was to issue in awful wrenches of the dearest ties; and the disciples, in the prospect of their cause and themselves being launched upon society, are here prepared for the worst. **22. And ye shall be hated of all men for my name's sake.** The universality of this hatred would make it evident to them, that since it would not be owing to any temporary excitement, local virulence, or personal prejudice, on the part of their enemies, so no amount of discretion on their part, consistent with entire fidelity to the truth, would avail to stifle that enmity—though it might soften its violence, and in some cases avert the outward

23 sake: ⁹but he that endureth to the end shall be saved. But ʳwhen they persecute you in this city, flee ye into another: for verily I say unto you, Ye
shall not ⁶have gone over the cities of Israel, till ˢthe Son of man be come.
24　The disciple is not above *his* master, nor the servant above his
25 lord. It is enough for the disciple that he be as his master, and
the servant as his lord. If they have called the master of the house
⁷Beelzebub, how much more *shall they call* them of his household?
26 Fear them not therefore: for there is nothing covered, that shall not be
27 revealed; and hid, that shall not be known. What I tell you in darkness, *that* speak ye in light: and what ye hear in the ear, *that* preach
28 ye upon the house-tops. And ᵗfear not them which kill the body, but
are not able to kill the soul: but rather fear him which is able to destroy
29 both soul and body in hell. Are not two sparrows sold for a ⁸farthing?

A. D. 31.

⁹ Dan. 12. 12.
Gal. 6. 9.
ʳ Acts 14. 6.
⁶ Or, end,
or, finish.
ˢ ch. 16. 28.
Acts 2. 1.
⁷ Beelzebul.
ᵗ Isa. 8. 12.
1 Pet. 3. 14.
⁸ Halfpenny
farthing,
the tenth
part of
the Roman
penny.

manifestations of it. **but he that endureth to the
end shall be saved**—a great saying, repeated, in
connection with similar warnings, in the prophecy
of the destruction of Jerusalem (ch. xxiv. 13); and
often reiterated by the apostle as a warning
against "drawing back unto perdition." (Heb.
iii. 6, 13; vi. 4-6; x. 23, 26-29, 38, 39; &c.) As
"drawing back unto perdition" is merely the
palpable evidence of the want of "root" from the
first in the Christian profession (Luke viii. 13), so
"enduring to the end" is just the proper evidence
of its reality and solidity. **23. But when they
persecute you in this city, flee ye into another**
[εἰς τὴν ἄλλην]—'into the other.' This, though
applicable to all time, and exemplified by our
Lord Himself once and again, had special reference to the brief opportunities which Israel was
to have of "knowing the time of his visitation."
for verily I say unto you—what will startle you,
but at the same time show you the solemnity of
your mission, and the need of economizing the
time for it—**Ye shall not have gone over** [οὐ μὴ
τελέσητε]—'Ye shall in nowise have completed'
the cities of Israel, till the Son of man be come.
To understand this—as *Lange* and others do—in
the first instance, of Christ's own peregrinations,
as if He had said, 'Waste not your time upon
hostile places, for I myself will be after you ere
your work be over'—seems almost trifling. "The
coming of the Son of man" has a fixed doctrinal
sense, here referring immediately to the crisis of
Israel's history as the visible kingdom of God,
when Christ was to come and judge it; when
"the wrath would come upon it to the uttermost;" and when, on the ruins of Jerusalem and
the old economy, He would establish His own
kingdom. This, in the uniform language of Scripture, is more immediately "the coming of the Son
of man." "the day of vengeance of our God" (ch.
xvi. 28; xxiv. 27, 34; with Heb. x. 25; Jas. v.
7-9)—but only as being such a lively anticipation of
His Second Coming for vengeance and deliverance.
So understood, it is parallel with ch. xxiv. 14 (on
which see).
　*Directions for the Service of Christ in its widest
sense* (24-42). **Ye disciple is not above his
master** [διδάσκαλον]—'teacher,' **nor the servant
above his lord**—another maxim which our Lord
repeats in various connections (Luke vi. 40; John
xiii. 16; xv. 20). **25. It is enough for the disciple that he be as his Master, and the servant
as his Lord. If they have called the master
of the house Beelzebub.** All the Greek MSS.
write "Beelzebul," which undoubtedly is the
right form of this word. The other reading came
in no doubt from the Old Testament "Baalzebub,"
the god of Ekron (2 Ki. i. 2), which it was designed to express. As all idolatry was regarded

as devil-worship (Lev. xvii. 7; Deut. xxxii. 17;
Ps. cvi. 37; 1 Cor. x. 20), so there seems to have
been something peculiarly Satanic about the worship of this hateful god, which caused his name
to be a synonym of Satan. Though we nowhere
read that our Lord was actually called "Beelzebul," He was charged with being in league with
Satan under that hateful name (ch. xii. 24, 26),
and more than once Himself was charged with
"having a devil" or "demon" (Mark iii. 30; John
vii. 20; viii. 48). Here it is used to denote the
most opprobrious language which could be applied
by one to another. **how much more [shall they
call] them of his household?** [οἰκιακοὺς]—'the inmates.' Three relations in which Christ stands
to His people are here mentioned: He is their
Teacher—they His disciples; He is their Lord—
they His servants; He is the Master of the household—they its inmates. In all these relations,
He says here, He and they are so bound up together that they cannot look to fare better than
He, and should think it enough if they are no
worse. **26. Fear them not therefore: for there
is nothing covered, that shall not be revealed;
and hid, that shall not be known:**—*q. d.,* 'There
is no use, and no need, of concealing anything;
right and wrong, truth and error, are about to
come into open and deadly collision; and the day
is coming when all hidden things shall be disclosed, everything seen as it is, and every one
have his due' (1 Cor. iv. 5). **27. What I tell you
in darkness**—in the privacy of a teaching for
which men are not yet ripe—**that speak ye in
the light**—for when ye go forth all will be ready—
**and what ye hear in the ear, that preach ye upon
the house-tops:**—Give free and fearless utterance to all that I have taught you while yet
with you. *Objection:* But this may cost us our
life? *Answer:* It may, but there their power
ends: **28. And fear not them which kill the
body, but are not able to kill the soul.** In Luke
xii. 4, "and after that have no more that they
can do." **but rather fear him**—in Luke this
is peculiarly solemn, "I will forewarn you whom
ye shall fear," even Him **which is able to
destroy both soul and body in hell.** A decisive
proof this that there is a hell for the body as
well as the soul in the eternal world; in other
words, that the torment that awaits the lost will
have elements of suffering adapted to the *material*
as well as the spiritual part of our nature, both
of which, we are assured, will exist for ever. In
the corresponding warning contained in Luke,
Jesus calls His disciples "My friends," as if He
had felt that such sufferings constituted a bond
of peculiar tenderness between Him and them.
29. Are not two sparrows sold for a farthing?
In Luke (xii. 6) it is "Five sparrows for two

30 and one of them shall not fall on the ground without your Father. But
31 [u]the very hairs of your head are all numbered. Fear ye not therefore,
32 ye are of more value than many sparrows. Whosoever [v]therefore shall
    confess me before men, [w]him will I confess also before my Father which
33 is in heaven. But [x]whosoever shall deny me before men, him will I
34 also deny before my Father which is in heaven. Think not that I am
    come to send peace on earth: I came not to send peace, but a sword.
35 For I am come to set a man at variance [y]against his father, and the
    daughter against her mother, and the daughter-in-law against her
36 mother-in-law. And a man's foes *shall be* they of his own household.
37 He that loveth father or mother more than me, is not worthy of me; and
38 he that loveth son or daughter more than me, is not worthy of me. And
    he that taketh not his cross, and followeth after me, is not worthy of me.
39 He [z]that findeth his life shall lose it: and he that loseth his life for my
40 sake shall find it. He that receiveth you, receiveth me; and he that
41 receiveth me, receiveth him that sent me. He [a]that receiveth a prophet
    in the name of a prophet shall receive a prophet's reward; and he that
    receiveth a righteous man in the name of a righteous man shall receive

A. D. 31.

[u] Acts 27. 31.
[v] Ps. 119. 46.
    Rom. 10. 9.
    1 Tim. 6. 12,
    13.
    Rev. 2. 13.
[w] 1 Sam. 2. 30.
    ch. 25. 34.
    Rev 3. 5.
[x] ch. 26. 70-75.
    Mark 8. 38.
    Luke 9. 26.
    Luke 12. 9.
    2 Tim. 2. 12.
[y] Mic. 7. 6.
    ch. 24. 10.
    Mark 13. 12.
[z] ch. 16. 25.
    Luke 17. 33.
    John 12. 25.
    Rev. 2. 10.
[a] 1 Ki. 17. 10.
    2 Ki. 4. 8.

farthings;" so that, if the purchaser took two farthings' worth, he got one in addition—of such small value were they. **and one of them shall not fall on the ground**—exhausted or killed—**without your Father**—"Not one of them is forgotten before God," as it is in Luke. 30. **But the very hairs of your head are all numbered.** See Luke xxi. 18, (and compare for the language 1 Sam. xiv. 45; Acts xxvii. 34). **Fear ye not therefore, ye are of more value than many sparrows.** Was ever language of such simplicity felt to carry such weight as this does? But here lies much of the charm and power of our Lord's teaching. 32. **Whosoever therefore shall confess me before men**—"despising the shame", **him will I confess also before my Father which is in heaven**—I will not be ashamed of him, but will own him before the most august of all assemblies. 33. **But whosoever shall deny me before men, him will I also deny before my Father which is in heaven**—before that same assembly: 'He shall have from Me his own treatment of Me on the earth.' But see on ch. xvi. 27. 34. **Think not that I am come to send peace on earth: I came not to send peace, but a sword**—strife, discord, conflict; deadly opposition between eternally hostile principles, penetrating into and rending asunder the dearest ties. 35. **For I am come to set a man at variance against his father, and the daughter against her mother, and the daughter-in-law against her mother-in-law.** See on Luke xii. 51-53. 36. **And a man's foes shall be they of his own household.** This saying, which is quoted, as is the whole verse, from Mic. vii. 6, is but an extension of the Psalmist's complaint, Ps. xli. 9; lv. 12-14, which had its most affecting illustration in the treason of Judas against our Lord Himself (John xiii. 18; Matt. xxvi. 48-50). Hence would arise the necessity of a choice between Christ and the nearest relations, which would put them to the severest test. 37. **He that loveth father or mother more than me, is not worthy of me; and he that loveth son or daughter more than me, is not worthy of me.** Compare Deut. xxxiii. 9. As the preference of the one would, in the case supposed, necessitate the abandonment of the other, our Lord here, with a sublime, yet awful self-respect, asserts His own claims to supreme affection. 38. **And he that taketh not his cross, and followeth after me, is not worthy of me**—a saying which our Lord

once and again emphatically reiterates (ch. xvi. 24; Luke ix. 23; xiv. 27). We have become so accustomed to this expression—"taking up one's cross"—in the sense of 'being prepared for trials in general for Christ's sake,' that we are apt to lose sight of its primary and proper sense here—'a preparedness to go forth even to crucifixion,' as when our Lord had to bear His own cross on His way to Calvary—a saying the more remarkable as our Lord had not as yet given a hint that He would die this death, nor was crucifixion a Jewish mode of capital punishment. 39. **He that findeth his life shall lose it: and he that loseth his life for my sake shall find it**—another of those pregnant sayings which our Lord so often reiterates (ch. xvi. 25; Luke xvii. 33; John xii. 25). The pith of such paradoxical maxims depends on the double sense attached to the word "life"—a lower and a higher, the natural and the spiritual, the temporal and eternal. An entire sacrifice of the lower, with all its relationships and interests—or, which is the same thing, a willingness to make it—is indispensable to the preservation of the higher life; and he who cannot bring himself to surrender the one for the sake of the other shall eventually lose both. 40. **He that receiveth**—or 'entertaineth' you, **receiveth me; and he that receiveth me, receiveth him that sent me.** As the treatment which an ambassador receives is understood and regarded as expressing the light in which he that sends him is viewed, so, says our Lord here, 'Your authority is mine, as mine is my Father's.' 41. **He that receiveth a prophet**—one divinely commissioned to deliver a message from heaven. Predicting future events was no necessary part of a prophet's office, especially as the word is used in the New Testament. **in the name of a prophet**—for his office' sake and love to his Master. (See 2 Kings iv. 9, 10.) **shall receive a prophet's reward.** What an encouragement to those who are *not* prophets! (See 3 John 5-8.) **and he that receiveth a righteous man in the name of a righteous man**—from sympathy with his character and esteem for himself as such, **shall receive a righteous man's reward**—for he must himself have the seed of righteousness who has any real sympathy with it and complacency in him who possesses it. 42. **And whosoever shall give to drink unto one of these little ones.** Beautiful epithet! originally taken from Zech. xiii. 7. The reference is to their

64

42 a righteous man's reward. And *b*whosoever shall give to drink unto one of these little ones a cup of cold *water* only in the name of a disciple, verily I say unto you, *c*he shall in no wise lose his reward.

11 AND it came to pass, when Jesus had made an end of commanding his twelve disciples, he departed thence, to teach and to preach in their cities.

A. D. 31.

b ch. 25. 40.
Mark 9. 42.
Heb. 6. 10.
c Prov. 24. 14.
Luke 6. 35.

lowliness in spirit, their littleness in the eyes of an undiscerning world, while high in Heaven's esteem. **a cup of cold water only**—meaning, the smallest service, **in the name of a disciple**—or, as it is in Mark (ix. 41), because ye are Christ's [Χριστοῦ ἐστέ]: from love to Me, and to him from his connection with Me, **verily I say unto you, he shall in no wise lose his reward.** There is here a descending climax—"a prophet," "a righteous man," "a little one;" signifying that however low we come down in our services to those that are Christ's, all that is done for His sake, and that bears the stamp of love to His blessed name, shall be divinely appreciated and owned and rewarded.

Remarks.—1. It is a manifest abuse of the directions here given for this first, hasty and temporary, mission (*vv.* 5-15), to take them as a general Directory for the missionaries of Christ in all time and under all circumstances. The cessation of those miraculous credentials with which the Twelve were furnished for this present Mission, might surely convince Christian men that the directions for such a mission were not intended to be literally followed by the missionaries of the Cross in all time. Even our Lord Himself did not act on the strict letter of these directions, having for needful uses, as *Luther* (in *Stier*) quaintly says—"money, bag, and bread-baskets too." It is true that one or two servants of Christ, in the course of an age, are found, who, in a spirit of entire self-abnegation, consecrate themselves to works of Christian philanthropy without wealth or other ordinary resources, and yet not only obtain enough to maintain them in their work, but the means of extending it beyond all anticipation, and that for a long series of years, or even a life-time. But the interest and admiration which such cases draw forth throughout the Christian world shows them to be exceptional illustrations of answer to prayer, and childlike confidence in working the work of God, rather than the normal character of the work of His kingdom. At the same time, the servants of Christ will do well to imbibe the *spirit* of these first directions—in simplicity of purpose and superiority to fastidious concern about their personal comfort; in energy also, and alacrity in prosecuting their work: taking as their motto that golden maxim, "Freely ye have received, freely give;" yet "not casting their pearls before swine," but acting on the principle that the rejection of their message is an affront put upon their Master, rather than themselves. 2. Though the vast change which the Gospel has produced upon Christendom is apt to make men think that our Lord's statements, here and elsewhere, of the universal hatred with which Christians would be regarded, have become inapplicable, we are never to forget that the hostility He speaks of is a hostility of *unchangeable principles;* and that although the unfaithfulness and timidity of Christians, on the one hand, may so compromise or keep in the background those principles which the world hates, or on the other hand, the world itself may from various causes be restrained from manifesting that hatred, yet, whenever and wherever the light and the darkness, Christ and Belial, are brought face to face in vivid juxtaposition, there will the eternal

and irreconcileable opposition of the one to the other appear. 3. How vastly greater would be the influence of Christians upon the world around them if they were more studious to combine the wisdom of the serpent with the harmlessness of the dove! We have Christians and Christian ministers who pride themselves upon their knowledge of the world, and the shrewdness with which they conduct themselves in it; while the simplicity of the dove is almost entirely in abeyance. Even the world can discern this, and, discerning it, despise those who to all appearance are no better than others, and yet pretend to be so. But on the other hand, there are Christians and Christian ministers who have the harmlessness of the dove, but being totally void of the wisdom of the serpent, carry no weight, and even expose themselves and their cause to the contempt of the world. O that the followers of the Lamb would lay this to heart! 4. What weighty inducements to suffer unflinchingly for the Gospel's sake are here provided! Such as do so are no worse off than their Master, and may rest assured of His sympathy and support, in a furnace which in His own case was heated seven times. And what though their life should be taken from them for Jesus' sake? The power of their enemies ceases there; whereas He whose wrath they incur by selling their conscience to save life is able to cast both soul and body into hell-fire. (See on Mark ix. 43-48.) God's suffering children are unspeakably dear to Him; their every trial in His service is full before Him; and their courage in confessing the name of Jesus will be rewarded by the confession of their name amidst the solemnities and the splendours of the great day: whereas a faithless denial of Christ here will be followed by the indignant and open denial of such by the Judge from His great white throne. 5. When Jesus here demands of His followers a love beyond all that is found in the tenderest relations of life, and pronounces all who withhold this to be unworthy of Him, He makes a claim which, on the part of any mere creature, would be wicked and intolerable, and in Him who honoured the Father as no other on earth ever did, is not to be imagined, if He had not been "the Fellow of the Lord of Hosts." 6. It is an abuse of the duty of *disinterestedness* in religion to condemn all reference to our own future safety and blessedness as a motive of action. For what have we here, as the conclusion of this lofty Directory, but an encouragement to entertain His servants, and welcome His people, and do offices of kindness, however small, to the humblest of His disciples, by the emphatic assurance that not the lowest of such offices shall go unrewarded? And shall not Christians be stimulated to lay themselves thus out for Him to whom they owe their all?

CHAP. XI. 1-19.—THE IMPRISONED BAPTIST'S MESSAGE TO HIS MASTER—THE REPLY, AND DISCOURSE, ON THE DEPARTURE OF THE MESSENGERS, REGARDING JOHN AND HIS MISSION. (=Luke vii. 18-35.)

1. And it came to pass, when Jesus had made an end of commanding his—rather, 'the' **twelve disciples, he departed thence to teach and to preach in their cities.** This was scarcely a fourth

2　Now *a*when John had heard *b*in the prison the works of Christ, he sent
3　two of his disciples, and said unto him, Art thou *c*he that should come,
4　or do we look for another?　Jesus answered and said unto them, Go and
5　show John again those things which ye do hear and see: the *d*blind receive their sight, and the lame walk, the lepers are cleansed, and the
deaf hear, the dead are raised up, and the *e*poor have the Gospel preached
6　to them.　And blessed is *he*, whosoever shall not be *f*offended in me.
7　And *g*as they departed, Jesus began to say unto the multitudes concerning John, What went ye out into the wilderness to see?　A reed
8　shaken with the wind?　But what went ye out for to see?　A man clothed
in soft raiment?　Behold, they that wear soft *clothing* are in kings'
9　houses.　But what went ye out for to see?　A prophet? yea, I say unto
10　you, *h*and more than a prophet.　For this is *he*, of whom it is written,
*i*Behold, I send my messenger before thy face, which shall prepare thy
11　way before thee.　Verily I say unto you, Among them that are born of
women there hath not risen a greater than John the Baptist; notwithstanding he that is least in the kingdom of heaven is greater than he.
12　And *j*from the days of John the Baptist until now the kingdom of
13　heaven ¹suffereth violence, and the violent take it by force.　For *k*all
14　the Prophets and the Law prophesied until John.　And if ye will receive
15　*it*, this is *l*Elias, which was for to come.　He *m*that hath ears to hear,
16　let him hear.　But *n*whereunto shall I liken this generation?　It is like
17　unto children sitting in the markets, and calling unto their fellows, and
saying, We have piped unto you, and ye have not danced; we have
18　mourned unto you, and ye have not lamented.　For John came neither
19　eating nor drinking, and they say, He hath a devil.　The Son of man
came eating and drinking, and they say, Behold a man gluttonous, and
a wine-bibber, *o*a friend of publicans and sinners.　*p*But Wisdom is justified of her children.
20　Then *q*began he to upbraid the cities wherein most of his mighty works
21　were done, because they repented not: Woe unto thee, Chorazin! woe
unto thee, Bethsaida! for if the mighty works which were done in you
had been done in Tyre and Sidon, they would have repented long ago

A. D. 31.

a Luke 7. 18.
b ch. 14. 3.
c Gen. 49. 10.
　Num. 24. 17.
　Dan. 9. 24.
　Mal. 3. 1-3.
d Isa. 29. 18.
　Isa. 35. 4.
　Isa. 42. 7.
e Ps. 22. 26.
　Isa. 61. 1.
　Luke 4. 18.
　Jas. 2. 5.
f Isa. 8. 14.
　ch. 13. 57.
　ch. 24. 10.
　ch. 26. 31.
　Rom. 9. 32.
　1 Cor. 1. 23.
　1 Cor. 2. 14.
　Gal. 5. 11.
　1 Pet. 2. 8.
g Luke 7. 24.
h Luke 1. 76.
i Mal. 3. 1.
　Mark 1. 2.
j Luke 16. 16.
1 Or, is got-
　ten by
　force, and
　they that
　thrust
　men.
k Mal. 4. 6.
l Mal. 4. 5.
　ch. 17. 12.
　Luke 1. 17.
　John 1. 23.
m Rev. 2. 7.
n Luke 7. 31.
o ch. 9. 10.
p Phil. 2. 15.
q Luke 10. 13.

circuit—if we may judge from the less formal way in which it is expressed—but, perhaps, a set of visits paid to certain places, either not reached at all, or too rapidly passed through before, in order to fill up the time till the return of the Twelve. As to their labours, nothing is said of them by our Evangelist.　But Luke (ix. 6) says, "They departed, and went through the towns" [κώμας], or 'villages,' "preaching the Gospel, and healing everywhere."　Mark (vi. 12, 13), as usual, is more explicit: "And they went out, and preached that men should repent.　And they cast out many devils (or 'demons'), and anointed with oil many that were sick, and healed them."　Though this "anointing with oil" was not mentioned in our Lord's instructions—at least in any of the records of them—we know it to have been practised long after this in the apostolic Church (see Jas. v. 14, and compare Mark vi. 12, 13)—not *medicinally*, but as a sign of the healing virtue which was com-municated by their hands, and a symbol of some-thing still more precious.　It was *unction*, indeed, but, as *Bengel* remarks, it was something very different from what Romanists call *extreme unction*.　He adds, what is very probable, that they do not appear to have carried the oil about with them, but, as the Jews used oil as a medicine, to have employed it just as they found it with the sick, in their own higher way.

2. Now when John had heard in the prison.
66

For the account of this imprisonment, see on Mark vi. 17-20.　**the works of Christ, he sent, &c.**　On the whole passage, see on Luke vii. 18-35.

20-30.—OUTBURST OF FEELING, SUGGESTED TO THE MIND OF JESUS BY THE RESULT OF HIS LABOURS IN GALILEE.

The connection of this with what goes before it, and the similarity of its tone, makes it evident, we think, that it was delivered on the same occa-sion, and that it is but a new and more compre-hensive series of reflections in the same strain. **20. Then began he to upbraid the cities wherein most of his mighty works were done, because they repented not: 21. Woe unto thee, Chora-zin!**—not elsewhere mentioned, but it must have lain near Capernaum.　**woe unto thee, Bethsaida!** [בֵּית and צַיְד, 'hunting' or 'fishing-house'—'a fish-ing station']—on the western side of the sea of Galilee, and to the north of Capernaum; the birth-place of three of the apostles—the brothers Andrew and Peter, and Philip.　These two cities appear to be singled out to denote the whole region in which they lay—a region favoured with the Redeemer's presence, teaching, and works above every other.　**for if the mighty works** [αἱ δυνά-μεις]—'the miracles' **which were done in you had been done in Tyre and Sidon**—ancient and celebrated commercial cities, on the north-eastern shores of the Mediterranean sea, lying north of Palestine, and the latter the northern-most.　As their wealth and prosperity engendered

22 ʳin sackcloth and ashes. But I say unto you, It shall be more tolerable
23 for Tyre and Sidon at the day of judgment, than for you. And thou,
    Capernaum, ˢwhich art exalted unto heaven, shalt be brought down to
    hell: for if the mighty works, which have been done in thee, had been
24 done in Sodom, it would have remained until this day. But I say unto
    you, That it shall be more tolerable for the land of Sodom in the
    day of judgment, than for thee.
25   At that time Jesus answered and said, I thank thee, O Father, Lord of
    heaven and earth, because ᵗthou hast hid these things from the wise and
26 prudent, and hast revealed them unto babes. Even so, Father; for so it
27 seemed good in thy sight. All ᵘthings are delivered unto me of my
    Father: and no man knoweth the Son, but the Father; ᵛneither knoweth
    any man the Father, save the Son, and *he* to whomsoever the Son will

A. D. 31.

ʳ Job 13. 6.
Jon. 3. 8.
ˢ Isa. 14. 12.
Lam. 2. 1.
ᵗ Ps. 8. 2.
1 Cor. 1. 27.
1 Cor. 2.7,8.
2 Cor. 3. 14.
ᵘ ch. 28. 18.
Luke 10. 22.
John 3. 35.
1 Cor. 15.27.
Eph. 1. 21.
ᵛ John 1. 18.
John 6. 46.
John 10. 15.

luxury and its concomitant evils—irreligion and moral degeneracy—their overthrow was repeatedly foretold in ancient prophecy, and once and again fulfilled by victorious enemies. Yet they were rebuilt, and at this time were in a flourishing condition. **they would have repented long ago in sackcloth and ashes.** Remarkable language, showing that they had done less violence to conscience, and so, in God's sight, were less criminal than the region here spoken of. **22. But I say unto you, It shall be more tolerable**—more 'endurable,' **for Tyre and Sidon at the day of judgment, than for you. 23. And thou, Capernaum** (see on ch. iv. 13), **which art exalted unto heaven.** Not even of Chorazin and Bethsaida is this said. For since at Capernaum Jesus had His stated abode during the whole period of His public life which He spent in Galilee, it was *the most favoured spot upon earth*, the most exalted in privilege. **shalt be brought down to hell: for if the mighty works, which have been done in thee, had been done in Sodom**—destroyed for its pollutions, **it would have remained until this day**—having done no such violence to conscience, and so incurred unspeakably less guilt. **24. But I say unto you, That it shall be more tolerable for the land of Sodom in the day of judgment, than for thee.** 'It has been indeed,' says *Dr. Stanley*, 'more tolerable, in one sense, in the day of its earthly judgment, for the land of Sodom than for Capernaum: for the name, and perhaps even the remains, of Sodom are still to be found on the shores of the Dead Sea; whilst that of Capernaum has, on the Lake of Gennesareth, been utterly lost.' But the judgment of which our Lord here speaks is still future; a judgment not on material cities, but their responsible inhabitants—a judgment final and irretrievable.

25. At that time Jesus answered and said. We are not to understand by this, that the previous discourse had been concluded; and that this is a record only of something said about the same period. For the connection is most close, and the word "answered"—which, when there is no one to answer, refers to something just before said, or rising in the mind of the speaker in consequence of something said—confirms this. What Jesus here "answered" evidently was the melancholy results of His ministry, lamented over in the foregoing verses. It is as if He had said, 'Yes; but there is a brighter side of the picture: even in those who have rejected the message of eternal life, it is the pride of their own hearts only which has blinded them, and the glory of the truth does but the more appear in their inability to receive it: Nor have all rejected it even here; souls thirsting for salvation have drawn water with joy from the wells of salvation; the weary

have found rest; the hungry have been filled with good things, while the rich have been sent empty away.' **I thank thee** ['Ἐξομολογοῦμαί σοι]—rather, 'I assent to thee.' But this is not strong enough. The idea of '*full*' or 'cordial' concurrence is conveyed by the preposition ['Εξ]. The thing expressed is adoring acquiescence, holy satisfaction with that law of the divine procedure about to be mentioned. And as, when He afterwards uttered the same words, He "exulted in spirit" (see on Luke x. 21), probably He did the same now, though not recorded. **O Father, Lord of heaven and earth.** He so styles His Father here, to signify that from Him of right emanate all such high arrangements. **because thou hast hid these things**—the knowledge of these saving truths—**from the wise and prudent** [σοφῶν καὶ συνετῶν]. The former of these terms points to the men who pride themselves upon their speculative or philosophical attainments; the latter to the men of worldly shrewdness—the clever, the sharp-witted, the men of affairs. The distinction is a natural one, and was well understood. (See 1 Cor. i. 19; &c.) But why had the Father hid from such the things that belonged to their peace, and why did Jesus so emphatically set His seal to this arrangement? Because it is not for the offending and revolted to speak or to speculate, but to listen to Him from whom we have broken loose, that we may learn whether there be any recovery for us at all; and if there be, on what principles—of what nature—to what ends. To bring our own "wisdom and prudence" to such questions is impertinent and presumptuous; and if the truth regarding them, or the glory of it, be "hid" from us, it is but a fitting retribution, to which all the right-minded will set their seal along with Jesus. But, **Thou hast revealed them unto babes**—to babe-like men; men of unassuming docility, men who, conscious that they know nothing, and have no right to sit in judgment on the things that belong to their peace, determine simply to "hear what God the Lord will speak." Such are well called "babes." (See Heb. v. 13; 1 Cor. xiii. 11; xiv. 20; &c.) **26. Even so, Father; for so it seemed good** [εὐδοκία] —the emphatic and chosen term for expressing any object of divine complacency; whether Christ Himself (see on ch. iii. 17) or God's gracious eternal arrangements (see on Phil. ii. 13)—**in thy sight.** This is just a sublime echo of the foregoing words; as if Jesus, when He uttered them, had paused to reflect on it, and as if the glory of it—not so much in the light of its own reasonableness as of God's absolute will that so it should be—had filled His soul. **27. All things are delivered unto me of my Father.** He does not say, They are *revealed*—as to one who knew them not, and

28 reveal *him.* Come unto me, all *ye* that labour and are heavy laden, and
29 I will give you rest. Take my yoke upon you, *ʷ*and learn of me;
for I am meek and *ˣ*lowly in heart: and *ʸ*ye shall find rest unto your
30 souls. For *ᶻ*my yoke *is* easy, and my burden is light.

A. D. 31.

ʷ 1 John 2. 6.
ˣ Zech. 9. 9.
ʸ Jer. 6. 16.
ᶻ 1 John 5. 3.

---

was an entire stranger to them save as they were discovered to him—but, They are 'delivered over' [παρεδόθη], or 'committed,' to me of my Father; meaning the whole administration of the kingdom of grace. So in John iii. 35, "The Father loveth the Son, and hath given all things into His hand" (see on that verse). But though the "all things" in both these passages refer properly to the kingdom of grace, they of course include all things necessary to the full execution of that trust—that is, *unlimited* power. (So ch. xxviii. 18; John xvii. 2; Eph. i. 22.) **and no man knoweth the Son, but the Father; neither knoweth any man the Father, save the Son, and he to whomsoever the Son will**—or 'willeth' [βούληται] to **reveal him.** What a saying is this, that 'the Father and the Son are mutually and exclusively known to each other!' A higher claim to equality with the Father cannot be conceived. Either, then, we have here one of the most revolting assumptions ever uttered, or the proper Divinity of Christ should to Christians be beyond dispute. 'But alas for me!' may some burdened soul, sighing for relief, here exclaim. If it be thus with us, what can any poor creature do but lie down in passive despair, unless he could dare to hope that *he* may be one of the favoured class ' to whom the Son is willing to reveal the Father'? But nay. This testimony to the sovereignty of that gracious "will," on which alone men's salvation depends, is designed but to reveal the source and enhance the glory of it when once imparted—not to paralyze or shut the soul up in despair. Hear, accordingly, what follows: **28. Come unto me, all ye that labour and are heavy laden, and I will give you rest.** Incomparable, ravishing sounds these—if ever such were heard in this weary, groaning world! What gentleness, what sweetness is there in the very style of the invitation —'Hither to Me' [Δεῦτε πρός Mε]: and in the words, 'All ye that toil and are burdened' [οἱ κοπιῶντες καὶ πεφορτισμένοι], the universal wretchedness of man is depicted, on both its sides—the *active* and the *passive* forms of it. **29. Take my yoke upon you**—the yoke of subjection to Jesus—**and learn of me; for I am meek and lowly in heart: and ye shall find rest unto your souls.** As Christ's willingness to empty Himself to the uttermost of His Father's requirements was the spring of ineffable repose to His own spirit, so in the same track does He invite all to follow Him, with the assurance of the same experience. **30. For my yoke is easy, and my burden is light.** Matchless paradox, even amongst the paradoxically couched maxims in which our Lord delights! That rest which the soul experiences, when once safe under Christ's wing, makes all yokes easy, all burdens light. *Remarks.*—1. Perhaps in no Section of this wonderful History is the veil so fully lifted from the Redeemer's soul, and His inmost thoughts and deepest emotions more affectingly disclosed, than here. When we think how much more profound and acute must have been His sensibilities than any other's—from the unsullied purity of His nature and the vast reach of His perceptions—we may understand, in some degree, what "a Man of sorrows" He must have been, and how "acquainted with grief"—to see His Person slighted, His errand misapprehended, and His message

rejected, in the very region on which He bestowed the most of His presence and the richest of His labours. Even in ancient prophecy we find Him exclaiming, "I have laboured in vain, I have spent My strength for nought and in vain;" and falling back upon this affecting consolation, that there was One that knew Him, and was the Judge of His doings:—"Yet surely my judgment is with the Lord, and my work with my God" (Isa. xlix. 4). But, as we turn to the bright side of the picture, who can fathom the depth of that exultant complacency with which His eye rested upon those "babes" into whose souls streamed the light of God's salvation, and with which He set His seal to that law of the divine procedure in virtue of which this was done, while from the self-sufficient it was hidden! And after thus seeming to wrap Himself and His Father up from all human penetration, save of some favoured class, what ineffable joy must it have been to His heart to disabuse the anxious of such a thought, by giving forth that most wonderful of all invitations, "Come unto Me!" &c. These are some of the lights and shadows of the Redeemer's life on earth; and what a reality do they impart to the Evangelical Narrative—what resistless attraction, what heavenly sanctity! 2. Let those who, under the richest ministrations of the word of life, "repent not," but live on unrenewed in the spirit of their minds, remember the doom of the cities of Galilee—executed in part, but in its most dread elements yet to come—and rest assured that at the judgment-day the degree of guilt will be estimated, not by the flagrancy of outward transgression, but by the degree of violence habitually offered to the voice of conscience—the extent to which light is quenched and conviction stifled. (See on Luke xii. 47, 48.) Ah! blighted Chorazin, Bethsaida, Capernaum—who, and more particularly what pastor, can wander over that region somewhere in which ye once basked in the very sunshine of Heaven's light, as no other spots on earth ever did, and not enter thrillingly into the poet's soliloquy,—

" These days are past—Bethsaida, where?
  Chorazin, where art thou?
His tent the wild Arab pitches there,
  The wild reed shades thy brow.

" Tell me, ye mouldering fragments, tell,
  Was the Saviour's city here?
Lifted to heaven, has it sunk to hell,
  With none to shed a tear?

" Ah! would my flock from thee might learn
  How days of grace will flee;
How all an offered Christ who spurn
  Shall mourn at last like thee."—M'CHEYNE.

3. If it be true that "no man knoweth the Son but the Father," how unreasonable is it to measure the statements of Scripture regarding the Person and work of Christ by the limited standard of human apprehension—rejecting, modifying, or explaining away whatever we are unable fully to comprehend, even though clearly expressed in the oracles of God! Nay, in the light of what our Lord here says of it, are not the difficulties just what might have been expected? 4. Let those who set the sovereignty of divine grace in opposition to the freedom and responsibility of the human will —rejecting now the one and now the other, as if they were irreconcileable—take the rebuke

12   AT that time *a* Jesus went on the sabbath day through the corn; and
his disciples were an hungered, and began to pluck the ears of corn, and
2 to eat. But when the Pharisees saw *it*, they said unto him, Behold, thy
3 disciples do that which is not lawful to do upon the sabbath day. But
he said unto them, Have ye not read *b* what David did, when he was an
4 hungered, and they that were with him; how he entered into the house

A. D. 31.

CHAP. 12.
a Deut. 23. 25.
Mark 2. 23.
Luke 6. 1.
b Ex. 25. 30.
1 Sam. 21. 6.

which our Lord here gives them. For while
nowhere is there a more explicit declaration than
here of the one doctrine—That the saving knowledge of the Father depends absolutely on the
sovereign "will" of the Son to impart it; yet
nowhere is there a brighter utterance of the other
also—That this knowledge, and the rest it brings,
is open to all who will come to Christ for it, and
that all who sigh for rest unto their souls are
freely invited, and will be cordially welcomed,
under Christ's wing. 5. But Whose voice do I
hear in this incomparable Invitation? Moses was
the divinely commissioned lawgiver of Israel, but
I do not find him speaking so; nor did the chiefest of the apostles presume to speak so. But that
is saying little. For no human lips ever ventured
to come within any measurable approach to such
language. We could fancy one saying—We might
say it and have said it ourselves—'Come, and I
will show you where rest is to be found.' But
here the words are, "COME UNTO ME, AND I WILL
GIVE YOU REST." To give repose even to one
weary, burdened soul—much more to all of every
age and every land—what mortal ever undertook
this? what creature is able to do it? But here
is One who undertakes it, and is conscious that He
has power to do it. It is the voice of my Beloved.
It is not the syren voice of the Tempter, coming
to steal away our hearts from the living God—it
would be that, if the spokesman were a creature—
but it is the Only begotten of the Father, full
of grace and truth; and in calling so lovingly,
"Come hither to ME," He is but wooing us back
to that blessed Bosom of the Father, that original and proper home of the heart, from which
it is our misery that we were ever estranged. 6.
As the source of all unrest is estrangement from
God, so the secret of true and abiding repose is
that of the prodigal, who, when at length he came
to say, "I will arise and go to my Father," straightway "arose and went." But as Jesus is the way,
and the truth, and the life of this return, so in
subjection to Jesus—as Himself was in absolute
subjection to His Father—is the heart's true rest.
When "the love of Christ constrains us to live
not unto ourselves, but unto Him who died for
us, and rose again;" when we enter into His
meekness and lowliness of heart who "made
Himself" of no reputation," and "pleased not
Himself" in anything, but His Father in everything—then, and only then, shall we find rest
unto our souls. Whereas those who chafe with
restless discontent and ambition and self-seeking
are "like the troubled sea when it cannot rest,
whose waters cast up mire and dirt." 7. Although the Fathers of the Church were not wrong
in calling the Fourth Gospel, 'the *spiritual* Gospel [τὸ πνευματικὸν], in contradistinction to the
First Three, which they called 'the corporeal'
ones [τὰ σωματικά]—striving thus to express
the immensely higher platform of vision to
which the Fourth lifts us—yet is it the same
glorious Object who is held in all the Four; and
while the Fourth enshrines some of its most divine and spiritual teachings in a framework of
exquisitely concrete historical fact, the First
Three rise at times—as Matthew here, and Luke
in the corresponding passage (x. 21, 22)—into a

region of pure Joannean thought; insomuch that
on reading the last six verses of this Section, we
seem to be reading out of the 'spiritual' Gospel.
In fact, it is all corporeal and all spiritual; only,
the one side was committed peculiarly to the
First Three Evangelists, "by the same Spirit;"
the other, to the Fourth Evangelist, "by the
same Spirit"—"but all these worketh that one
and the self-same Spirit, dividing to every man
severally as He will."

CHAP. XII. 1-8.—PLUCKING CORN-EARS ON
THE SABBATH DAY. (= Mark ii. 23-28; Luke vi.
1-5.)

The season of the year when this occurred is
determined by the event itself. Ripe corn-ears
are only found in the fields just before harvest.
The barley harvest seems clearly intended here,
at the close of our March and beginning of our
April. It coincided with the Passover-season, as
the wheat harvest with Pentecost. But in Luke
(vi. 1) we have a still more definite note of time, if
we could be certain of the meaning of the peculiar term which he employs to express it. "It
came to pass (he says) on the sabbath, which was
the *first-second* [σαββάτω δευτεροπρώτω]—for that
is the proper rendering of the word, and not "the
second sabbath after the first," as in our version.
Of the various conjectures what this may mean,
that of *Scaliger* is the most approved, and, as we
think, the freest from difficulty, namely, 'the
first sabbath after the second day of the Passover;' that is, the first of the seven sabbaths
which were to be reckoned from the second day of
the Passover, which was itself a sabbath, until
the next feast, the feast of Pentecost (Lev. xxiii.
15, 16; Deut. xvi. 9, 10). In this case, the day
meant by the Evangelist is the first of those seven
sabbaths intervening between Passover and Pentecost. And if we are right in regarding the
"feast" mentioned in John v. 1 as a *Passover*, and
consequently the second during our Lord's public
ministry (see on that passage), this plucking of the
ears of corn must have occurred immediately after
the scene and the Discourse recorded in John
v., which, doubtless, would induce our Lord to
hasten His departure for the north, to avoid the
wrath of the Pharisees, which He had kindled at
Jerusalem. Here, accordingly, we find Him in
the fields—on His way probably to Galilee. **1. At
that time Jesus went on the sabbath day
through the corn**—"the corn fields" (Mark ii. 23;
Luke vi. 1). **and his disciples were an hungered**
—not as one may be before his regular meals; but
evidently from shortness of provisions; for Jesus
defends their plucking the corn-ears and eating
them on the plea of *necessity*. **and began to pluck
the ears of corn, and to eat**—"rubbing them
in their hands" (Luke vi. 1). **2. But when the
Pharisees saw it, they said unto him, Behold,
thy disciples do that which is not lawful to do
upon the sabbath day.** The act itself was expressly permitted (Deut. xxiii. 25). But as being
"servile work," which was prohibited on the
sabbath day, it was regarded as sinful. **3. But he
said unto them, Have ye not read**—or as Mark
has it, "Have ye never read"—**what David did**
(1 Sam. xxi. 1-6), **when he was an hungered, and
they that were with him; 4. How he entered into**

of God, and did eat *c*the showbread, which was not lawful for him to eat,
5 neither for them which were with him, *d*but only for the priests? Or
   have ye not read in the *e*Law, how that on the sabbath days the priests
6 in the temple profane the sabbath, and are blameless? But I say unto
7 you, That in this place is *one f*greater than the temple. But if ye had
   known what *this* meaneth, I *g*will have mercy, and not sacrifice, ye would
8 not have condemned the guiltless. For the *h*Son of man is Lord even
   of the sabbath day.
9   And *i*when he was departed thence, he went into their synagogue:
10 And, behold, there was a man which had *his* hand withered. And they
   asked him, saying, *j*Is it lawful to heal on the sabbath days? that they

A. D. 31.

c Ex. 25. 30.
Lev. 24. 5.
d Ex. 29. 32.
Lev. 8. 31.
e Num. 28. 9.
John 7. 22.
f 2 Chr. 6. 18.
Hag. 2. 7, 9.
g Hos. 6. 6.
h Dan. 7. 13.
i Mark 3. 1.
j Luke 13. 14.
Luke 14. 3.

the house of God, and did eat the showbread, which was not lawful for him to eat, neither for them which were with him, but only for the priests? No example could be more apposite than this. The man after God's own heart, of whom the Jews ever boasted, when suffering in God's cause and straitened for provisions, asked and obtained from the high priest what, according to the law, it was illegal for any one save the priests to touch. Mark (ii. 26) says this occurred "in the days of Abiathar the high priest." But this means not during his high priesthood—for it was under that of his father Ahimelech—but simply, in his time. Ahimelech was soon succeeded by Abiathar, whose connection with David, and prominence during his reign, may account for his name, rather than his father's, being here introduced. Yet there is not a little confusion in what is said of these priests in different parts of the Old Testament. Thus he is called both the son and the father of Ahimelech (1 Sam. xxii. 20; 2 Sam. viii. 17); and Ahimelech is called Ahiah (1 Sam. xiv. 3), and Abimelech (1 Chr. xviii. 16). **5. Or have ye not read in the Law, how that on the sabbath days the priests in the temple profane the sabbath**—by doing "servile work,"—**and are blameless?** The double offerings required on the sabbath day (Num. xxviii. 9) could not be presented, and the new-baked showbread (Lev. xxiv. 5; 1 Chr. ix. 32) could not be prepared and presented every sabbath morning, without a good deal of servile work on the part of the priests; not to speak of circumcision, which, when the child's eighth day happened to fall on a sabbath, had to be performed by the priests on that day. (See on John vii. 22, 23.) **6. But I say unto you, That in this place is one greater [μείζων] than the temple**—or rather, according to the reading which is best supported [μεῖζον], 'something greater.' The argument stands thus: 'The ordinary rules for the observance of the sabbath give way before the requirements of the temple; but there are rights here before which the temple itself must give way.' Thus indirectly, but not the less decidedly, does our Lord put in His own claims to consideration in this question—claims to be presently put in even more nakedly. **7. But if ye had known what [this] meaneth, I will have mercy, and not sacrifice,** (Hos. vi. 6; Mic. vi. 6-8, &c.) See on ch. ix. 13. **ye would not have condemned the guiltless:—***q. d.,* 'Had ye understood the great principle of all religion, which the Scripture everywhere recognizes—that ceremonial observances must give way before moral duties, and particularly the necessities of nature—ye would have refrained from these captious complaints against men who in this matter are blameless.' But our Lord added a specific application of this great principle to the law of the sabbath, preserved only in Mark: "And he said unto them, the sabbath was made for man, and not man for

the sabbath" (Mark ii. 27). A glorious and far-reaching maxim, alike for the permanent establishment of the sabbath and the true freedom of its observance. **8. For the Son of man is Lord [even] of the sabbath day.** [The bracketed word "even"—καὶ—should not be in the text, as the overwhelming weight of authority against it shows.] In what sense now is the Son of man Lord of the sabbath day? Not surely to abolish it—that surely were a strange lordship, especially just after saying that it was made or instituted [ἐγένετο] for MAN—but to *own* it, to *interpret* it, to *preside over* it, and to *ennoble* it, by merging it in "the Lord's Day" (Rev. i. 10), breathing into it an air of liberty and love necessarily unknown before, and thus making it the nearest resemblance to the eternal sabbatism.

Remarks.—1. How affecting are the glimpses, of which this is one, which the Gospel History furnishes of the straitened circumstances into which once and again our Lord found Himself in the discharge of His public work! Doubtless, He whose is every beast of the forest, and the cattle upon a thousand hills, could have easily and simply supplied Him, or sent "twelve legions of angels" to minister to Him. But He did not; partly, that we might know how "poor He who was rich for our sakes became, that we through His poverty might be rich," and partly, no doubt, to give Him an experimental taste of His people's and His servants' straits, and thus assure them of His sympathy with them, and ability to succour them. 2. How valuable is an intelligent and ready familiarity with Scripture, when beset by the temptations of Satan (see on ch. iv. 3, &c.) and the cavils of captious men! 3. How miserable a thing is a slavish adherence to the letter of Scripture, which usually the closer it is occasions only a wider departure from its spirit! 4. How can the teaching of this Section be made to agree with the theory of the temporary and local character of the sabbath-law, and its abrogation under the Gospel? (See on Rom. xiv. 6.)

9-21. THE HEALING OF A WITHERED HAND ON THE SABBATH DAY, AND RETIREMENT OF JESUS TO AVOID DANGER. (=Mark iii. 1-12; Luke vi. 6-11.)

Healing of a Withered Hand (9-14). **9. And when he was departed thence**—but "on another sabbath" (Luke vi. 6), **he went into their synagogue**—"and taught." He had now, no doubt, arrived in Galilee; but this, it would appear, did not occur at Capernaum, for after it was over He "withdrew Himself," it is said, "*to the sea*" (Mark iii. 7), whereas Capernaum was *at* the sea. **10. And, behold, there was a man which had his hand withered**—disabled by paralysis (as 1 Kings xiii. 4). It was his right hand, as Luke graphically notes. **And they asked him, saying, Is it lawful to heal on the sabbath days? that they might accuse him.** Matthew and Luke say

11 might accuse him. And he said unto them, What man shall there be
among you that shall have one sheep, and ^kif it fall into a pit on the

12 sabbath day, will he not lay hold on it, and lift *it* out? How much then
is a man better than a sheep? Wherefore it is lawful to do well on the

13 sabbath days. Then saith he to the man, Stretch forth thine hand.
And he stretched *it* forth; and it was restored whole, like as the other.

14 Then ^lthe Pharisees went out, and ¹held a council against him, how
they might destroy him.

15 But when Jesus ^mknew *it*, ⁿhe withdrew himself from thence: and

16 great multitudes followed him, and he healed them all; and charged

17 them that they should not make him known: that ^oit might be fulfilled

18 which was spoken by Esaias the prophet, saying, Behold ^pmy servant,
whom I have chosen; my beloved, in whom my soul is well pleased: I
will put ^qmy Spirit upon him, and he shall show judgment to the Gen-

19 tiles. He shall not strive, nor cry; neither shall any man hear his voice

20 in the streets. A ^rbruised reed shall he not break, and smoking flax

A. D. 31.
k Ex. 23. 4.
Deut. 22. 4.
l Mark 3. 6.
Luke 6. 11.
John 5. 18.
John 10. 39.
John 11. 53.
1 Or. took counsel
m Heb. 4. 13.
Ps. 139. 2.
n Mark 3. 7.
o Num. 23.19.
Isa. 49. 5, 6.
Isa. 52. 13.
p Isa. 42. 1.
ch. 3. 16.
q Isa. 61. 1.
ch. 11. 28.
r Isa. 40. 11.

they "watched Him whether He would heal on the sabbath day." They were now come the length of dogging His steps, to collect materials for a charge of impiety against Him. It is probable that it was to their *thoughts* rather than their words that Jesus addressed Himself in what follows. 11. **And he said unto them, What man shall there be among you that shall have one sheep, and if it fall into a pit on the sabbath day, will he not lay hold on it, and lift it out? 12. How much then is a man better than a sheep?** Resistless appeal! "A righteous man regardeth the life of his beast" (Prov. xii. 10), and would instinctively rescue it from death or suffering on the sabbath day; how much more his nobler fellow-man. But the reasoning, as given in the other two Gospels, is singularly striking: "But He knew their thoughts, and said to the man which had the withered hand, Rise up, and stand forth in the midst. And he arose and stood forth. Then said Jesus unto them, I will ask you one thing; Is it lawful on the sabbath days to do good, or to do evil? to save life or to destroy it?" (Luke vi. 8, 9) or as in Mark (iii. 4) "to kill?" He thus shuts them up to this startling alternative: 'Not to do good, when it is in the power of our hand to do it, is to do evil; not to save life, when we can, is to kill'—and must the letter of the sabbath-rest be kept at this expense? This unexpected thrust shut their mouths. By this great ethical principle our Lord, we see, held Himself bound, as Man. But here we must turn to Mark, whose graphic details make the second Gospel so exceedingly precious. "When He had looked round about on them with anger, being grieved for the hardness of their hearts, He saith unto the man" (Mark iii. 5). This is one of the very few passages in the Gospel History which reveal our Lord's *feelings*. How holy this anger was, appears from the "grief" which mingled with it at "the hardness of their hearts." 13. **Then saith he to the man, Stretch forth thine hand. And he stretched it forth**—the power to obey going forth with the word of command. **and it was restored whole, like as the other.** The poor man, having faith in this wonderful Healer—which no doubt the whole scene would singularly help to strengthen—disregarded the proud and venomous Pharisees, and thus gloriously put them to shame. 14. **Then the Pharisees went out, and held a council against him, how they might destroy him.** This is the first explicit mention of their murderous designs against our Lord. Luke (vi. 11) says "they were

filled with madness, and communed one with another what they might do to Jesus." But their doubt was not, *whether* to get rid of Him, but *how* to compass it. Mark (iii. 6), as usual, is more definite: "The Pharisees went forth, and straightway took counsel with the Herodians against Him, how they might destroy Him." These Herodians were supporters of Herod's dynasty, created by Cæsar—a political rather than religious party. The Pharisees regarded them as untrue to their religion and country. But here we see them combining together against Christ, as a common enemy. So on a subsequent occasion, Matt. xxii. 15, 16.

Jesus Retires to Avoid Danger (15-21). 15. **But when Jesus knew it, he withdrew himself from thence**—whither, our Evangelist says not; but Mark (iii. 7) says "it was *to the sea*"—to some distance, no doubt, from the scene of the miracle, the madness, and the plotting just recorded. **and great multitudes followed him, and he healed them all.** Mark gives the following interesting details: "A great multitude from Galilee followed Him, and from Judea, and from Jerusalem, and from Idumea, and from beyond Jordan; and they about Tyre and Sidon, a great multitude, when they had heard what great things he did, came unto Him. And he spake to His disciples, that a small ship"—or 'wherry' [πλοιάριον—"should wait on Him because of the multitude, lest they should throng Him. For He had healed many; insomuch that they pressed upon Him for to touch Him, as many as had plagues. And unclean spirits, when they saw Him, fell down before Him, and cried, saying, Thou art the Son of God. And He straitly charged them that they should not make Him known" (Mark iii. 7-12). How glorious this extorted homage to the Son of God! But as this was not the time, so neither were they the fitting preachers, as *Bengel* says. (See on Mark i. 25, and cf. Jas. ii. 19.) Coming back now to our Evangelist: after saying "He healed them all," he continues, 16. **And charged them**—the healed —**that they should not make him known.** (See on ch. viii. 4.) 17. **That it might be fulfilled which was spoken by Esaias the prophet, saying** (Isa. xlii. 1), 18. **Behold my servant, whom I have chosen; my beloved, in whom my soul is well pleased: I will put my Spirit upon him, and he shall show judgment to the Gentiles.** 19. **He shall not strive, nor cry; neither shall any man hear his voice in the streets.** 20. **A bruised reed shall he not break, and smoking flax shall he not quench, till he send forth judgment unto victory**—"unto truth," says the

21 shall he not quench, till he send forth judgment unto victory. And in his name shall the Gentiles trust.

22 Then [s]was brought unto him one possessed with a devil, blind and dumb: and he healed him, insomuch that the blind and dumb both

23 spake and saw. And all the people were amazed; and said, Is not this

A. D. 31.
[s] ch. 9. 32.
Mark 3. 11.
Mark 9. 17.
Luke 11. 14.

Hebrew original, and the LXX. also. But our Evangelist merely seizes the spirit, instead of the letter of the prediction in this point. The grandeur and completeness of Messiah's victories would prove, it seems, not more wonderful than the unobtrusive noiselessness with which they were to be achieved. And whereas one rough touch will break a bruised reed, and quench the flickering, smoking flax, His it should be, with matchless tenderness, love, and skill, to lift up the meek, to strengthen the weak hands and confirm the feeble knees, to comfort all that mourn, to say to them that are of a fearful heart, Be strong, fear not. **21. And in his name shall the Gentiles trust.** Part of His present audience were Gentiles —from Tyre and Sidon—first-fruits of the great Gentile harvest, contemplated in the prophecy.

Remarks.—1. Did Christians habitually act on the great principle by which our Lord held Himself bound—that to neglect any opportunity of doing good is to do evil—what a different face would the Church, and society, and even the world at large, soon put on! And shall not we who write, and we who read or hear these things, strive prayerfully for ourselves to act upon it? 2. What a picture of finely-balanced sensibilities have we in the emotions of "anger" and "grief" which the conduct of the Pharisees on this occasion kindled in the bosom of Jesus! It is possible, we see, to "be angry and sin not" (Eph. iv. 26); but first, the anger must be causeless (see on ch. v. 22); and next, even though just, nay, though demanded by the occasion, as in the present case, that anger is never sinless, unless when "grief" for what kindles the "anger" mingles with and tempers it. 3. In the remarkable command, to stretch forth a withered hand, we have an illustration of such seemingly unreasonable calls as these: "Prophesy upon these bones, and say unto them, O ye dry bones, hear the word of the Lord" (Ezek. xxxvii. 4); "Incline your ear, and come unto me: hear, and your soul shall live" (Isa. lv. 3); "Awake thou that sleepest, and arise from the dead, and Christ shall give thee light" (Eph. v. 14). To ask dry bones to hear and live, and call upon the dead to listen and live, and demand from the impotent an exercise of power—there is apparent mockery in all this. Yet as the dry bones, in the vision, when prophesied to as commanded, did hear and obey; and the withered hand found power to extend itself—even so, it is no vain thing to say to the dead in sin, "Hear, and your soul shall live." Your "wise and prudent" (see on ch. xi. 25), will demonstrate to you, that one or other of these things must be false:—'either they are *not* dead, or, if they be, they can't hear; and if they hear, you need not add "and your soul shall live," for they are alive already.' But if the narrative of this Section be not a fable, all such reasoning is false; and as long as the Gospel History lives, this narrative will stand out at once as a directory and as a glorious encouragement, to preach to the dead in sin as the divinely appointed means of summoning them into life. 4. Determined prejudice against the truth is only irritated by additional evidence. Of this the whole conduct of the Pharisees towards our Lord forms one varied, vivid, and affecting illustration. 5. If the enemies of the truth, notwithstanding their mutual jealousies and discords, find it easy to unite and co-operate against the truth which they feel a common interest in crushing, how shameful is it that Christians should allow their petty differences to prevent combined action for the advancement of their common Christianity! 6. The predicted noiselessness of Messiah's footsteps, and the gentleness of His dealings with feeble and tender souls, opens up a great general principle of moral and spiritual strength. This was grandly illustrated to Elijah. Standing on Mount Horeb, the Lord passed by, while a great and strong wind rent the mountains, and brake in pieces the rocks before him; but the Lord was not in the *wind:* and after the wind an earthquake; but the Lord was not in the *earthquake:* and after the earthquake a fire; but the Lord was not in the *fire:* and after the fire, *a still small voice:* And it was so, when Elijah heard it, that he wrapped his face in his mantle (1 Ki. xix. 11-13). Yes, in that still small voice the prophet felt the immediate presence of God, as he had not done in the wind, nor in the earthquake, nor in the fire. True power is quiet. Even "a *soft* answer turneth away wrath" (Prov. xv. 1); and how grand—though all noiseless and imperceptible—is the growth of the animal and vegetable world! Let the servants of Christ, then, not estimate the value of the work done in His service by the sound of their movements and the noise of the machinery, but by the steady silent purpose and the persistent activity with which they prosecute the work given them to do.

22-37.—A BLIND AND DUMB DEMONIAC HEALED, AND REPLY TO THE MALIGNANT EXPLANATION PUT UPON IT. (=Mark iii. 20-30; Luke xi. 14-23.)

The precise time of this Section is uncertain. Judging from the statements with which Mark introduces it, we should conclude that it was when our Lord's popularity was approaching its zenith, and so, before the feeding of the five thousand. But, on the other hand, the advanced state of the charges brought against our Lord, and the plainness of His warnings and denunciations in reply, seem to favour the later period at which Luke introduces it. "And the multitude," says Mark (iii. 20, 21), "cometh together again," referring back to the immense gathering which Mark had before recorded (ch. ii. 2)—"so that they could not so much as eat bread. And when His friends" [οἱ παρ' αὐτοῦ]—or rather, 'relatives,' as appears from verse 31, and see on ch. xii. 46—"heard of it, they went out to lay hold on Him: for they said, He is beside Himself" [ἐξέστη]. Compare 2 Cor. v. 13, "For whether we be beside ourselves [ἐξέστημεν], it is *to God*."

22. Then was brought unto him one possessed with a devil—or 'a demonized person' [δαιμονίζομενος]—**blind and dumb: and he healed him, insomuch that the blind and dumb both spake and saw. 23. And all the people were amazed, and said, Is not this the son of David?** [Μήτι οὗτός ἐστιν ὁ υἱὸς Δαβίβ?] The form of the interrogative requires this to be rendered, 'Is this the Son of David?' And as questions put in this form (in Greek) suppose doubt, and expect rather a negative answer, the meaning is, 'Can it possibly be?'—the people thus indicating their secret impression that this *must* be He; yet saving them-

24 ᵗthe son of David? But ᵘwhen the Pharisees heard *it*, they said, This *fellow* doth not cast out devils, but by ²Beelzebub the prince of the devils.

25 And Jesus ᵛknew their thoughts, and said unto them, Every kingdom divided against itself is brought to desolation; and every city or house

26 divided against itself shall not stand: and if Satan cast out Satan, he

27 is divided against himself; how shall then his kingdom stand? And if I by Beelzebub cast out devils, by whom do your children cast

28 *them* out? therefore they shall be your judges. But if I cast out devils by the Spirit of God, then ʷthe kingdom of God is come unto

29 you. Or ˣelse how can one enter into a strong man's house, and spoil his goods, except he first bind the strong man? and then he

30 will spoil his house. He that is not with me is against me; and

31 he that gathereth not with me scattereth abroad. Wherefore I say unto you, ʸAll manner of sin and blasphemy shall be forgiven unto men : ᶻbut the blasphemy *against* the *Holy* Ghost shall not be forgiven unto

32 men. And whosoever ᵃspeaketh a word against the Son of man, ᵇit shall be forgiven him: but whosoever speaketh against the Holy Ghost, it shall not be forgiven him, neither in this world, neither in the *world* to

A. D. 31.

ᵗ Rom. 9. 5.
ᵘ Mark 3. 22.
² Beelzebul.
ᵛ ch. 9. 4.
   John 2. 25.
   Rev. 2. 23.
ʷDan. 2. 44.
   Dan. 7. 14.
   Luke 1. 33.
   Luke 11. 20.
   Luke 17. 20.
   Heb. 12. 28.
ˣ Isa. 49. 24.
ʸ Mark 3. 28.
   Luke 12. 10.
   Heb. 10. 26.
   1 John 5. 16.
ᶻ Acts 7. 51.
   Heb. 6. 4.
ᵃ ch. 11. 19.
   ch. 13. 55.
   John 7. 12.
ᵇ 1 Tim. 1. 13.

selves from the wrath of the ecclesiastics, which a direct assertion of it would have brought upon them. (See on a similar question in John iv. 29; and on the phrase, "Son of David," on ch. ix. 27.) **24. But when the Pharisees heard it.** Mark (iii. 22) says "the scribes which came down from Jerusalem;" so that this had been a hostile party of the ecclesiastics, who had come all the way from Jerusalem to collect materials for a charge against Him. (See on *v.* 14.) **they said, This fellow** [Οὗτος]—an expression of contempt—**doth not cast out devils, but by Beelzebub**—rather, Beelzebul (see on ch. x. 25)—**the prince of the devils.** Two things are here implied—first, that the bitterest enemies of our Lord were unable to deny the reality of His miracles; and next, that they believed in an *organized infernal kingdom of evil*, under one chief. This belief would be of small consequence, had not our Lord set His seal to it; but this He immediately does. Stung by the unsophisticated testimony of "all the people," they had no way of holding out against His claims, but by the desperate shift of ascribing His miracles to Satan. **25. And Jesus knew their thoughts**—"called them" (Mark iii. 23), **and said unto them, Every kingdom divided against itself is brought to desolation; and every city or house**—that is, household—**divided against itself shall not stand: 26. And if Satan cast out Satan, he is divided against himself; how shall then his kingdom stand?** The argument here is irresistible: 'No organized society can stand—whether kingdom, city, or household—when turned against itself; such intestine war is suicidal: But the works I do are destructive of Satan's kingdom: That I should be in league with Satan, therefore, is incredible and absurd.' **27. And if I by Beelzebub cast out devils, by whom do your children**—'your sons' [υἱοί] meaning here, the 'disciples' or pupils of the Pharisees, who were so termed after the familiar language of the Old Testament in speaking of the sons of the prophets. (1 Ki. xx. 35; 2 Ki. ii. 3, &c.) Our Lord here seems to admit that such works were wrought by them; in which case the Pharisees stood self-condemned, as expressed in Luke (xi. 19), "Therefore shall they be your judges." **28. But if I cast out devils by the Spirit of God.** In Luke (xi. 20) it is, "with (or 'by') the finger of God." This latter expression is just a figurative way of representing the *power* of God, while the former tells us the *living Personal*

Agent made use of by the Lord Jesus in every exercise of that power. **then**—"no doubt" (Luke xi. 20)—**the kingdom of God is come unto you** [ἐφ' ὑμᾶς]—rather 'upon you,' as the same expression is rendered in Luke:—*q. d.*, 'If this expulsion of Satan is, and can be, by no other than the Spirit of God, then is his Destroyer already in the midst of you, and that kingdom which is destined to supplant his, is already rising on its ruins.' **29. Or else how can one enter into a**—or rather, 'the'—**strong man's house, and spoil his goods, except he first bind the strong man? and then he will spoil his house. 30. He that is not with me is against me; and he that gathereth not with me scattereth abroad.** On this important parable, in connection with the corresponding one, *vv.* 43-45, see on Luke xi. 21-26. **31. Wherefore I say unto you, All manner of sin and blasphemy shall be forgiven unto men.** The word "blasphemy" [βλασφημία] properly signifies 'detraction' or 'slander.' In the New Testament it is applied, as it is here, to vituperation directed against God as well as against men; and in this sense it is to be understood as an aggravated form of sin. Well, says our Lord, all sin—whether in its ordinary or its more aggravated forms—shall find forgiveness with God. Accordingly, in Mark (iii. 28) the language is still stronger: "All sins shall be forgiven unto the sons of men, and blasphemies wherewith soever they shall blaspheme." There is no sin whatever, it seems, of which it may be said, 'That is not a pardonable sin.' This glorious assurance is not to be limited by what follows; but, on the contrary, what follows is to be explained by this. **but the blasphemy against the Holy Ghost shall not be forgiven unto men. 32. And whosoever speaketh a word against the Son of man, it shall be forgiven him: but whosoever speaketh against the Holy Ghost, it shall not be forgiven him, neither in this world, neither in the world to come.** In Mark the language is awfully strong, "hath never forgiveness, but is in danger of eternal damnation" [κρίσεως]—or rather, according to what appears to be the preferable, though very unusual reading, 'in danger of eternal guilt' [ἁμαρτήματος]—a guilt which he will underlie for ever. Mark has the important addition (*v.* 30), "Because they said, He hath an unclean spirit." (See on ch. x. 25). What, then, is this sin against the Holy Ghost—the unpardonable sin? One thing is clear: Its

73

33 come. Either make the tree good, and ^chis fruit good; or else make the tree corrupt, and his fruit corrupt: for the tree is known by *his* fruit.

34 O ^dgeneration of vipers, how can ye, being evil, speak good things? ^efor

35 out of the abundance of the heart the mouth speaketh. A good man, out of the good treasure of the heart, bringeth forth good things: and an evil man, out of the evil treasure, bringeth forth evil things.

36 But I say unto you, That every ^fidle word that men shall speak, they

37 shall give account thereof in the day of judgment. For by thy words thou shalt be justified, and by thy words thou shalt be condemned.

A. D. 31.
^c ch. 7. 17.
Luke 6. 43.
^d ch. 3. 7.
ch. 23. 33.
Luke 3. 7.
John 8. 44.
1 John 3. 10.
^e Luke 6. 45.
^f Eccl. 12. 14.
Eph. 5. 4.
Rev. 20. 12.

unpardonableness cannot arise from anything in the nature of the sin itself; for that would be a naked contradiction to the emphatic declaration of verse 31st, that all manner of sin is pardonable. And what is this but the fundamental truth of the Gospel? (See Acts xiii. 38, 39; Rom. iii. 22, 24; 1 John i. 7; &c.) Then, again, when it is said (*v.* 32), that to speak against or blaspheme the Son of man is pardonable, but the blasphemy against the Holy Ghost is not pardonable, it is not to be conceived that this arises from any greater sanctity in the one blessed Person than the other. These remarks so narrow the question, that the true sense of our Lord's words seem to disclose themselves at once. It is a contrast between slandering "the Son of man" *in His veiled condition and unfinished work*—which might be done "ignorantly, in unbelief" (1 Tim. i. 13), and slandering the same blessed Person after the blaze of glory which *the Holy Ghost* was soon to throw around His claims, and in the full knowledge of all that. This would be to slander Him with eyes open, or to do it "presumptuously." To blaspheme Christ in the former condition—when even the apostles stumbled at many things—left them still open to conviction on fuller light; but to blaspheme Him in the latter condition would be to hate the light the clearer it became, and resolutely to shut it out; which, of course, precludes salvation. (See on Heb. x. 26-29.) The Pharisees had not as yet done this; but in charging Jesus with being in league with hell they were displaying beforehand a malignant determination to shut their eyes to all evidence, and so, *bordering upon*, and *in spirit* committing the unpardonable sin. **33. Either make the tree good, &c. O generation of vipers** (see on ch. iii. 7), **how can ye, being evil, speak good things? for out of the abundance of the heart the mouth speaketh**—a principle obvious enough, yet of deepest significance and vast application. In Luke vi. 45 we find it uttered as part of the Discourse delivered after the choice of the apostles. **35. A good man, out of the good treasure of the heart, bringeth** [ἐκβάλλει] — ' or putteth' **forth good things: and an evil man, out of the evil treasure, bringeth**—or 'putteth' **forth evil things.** The word 'putteth' indicates the spontaneousness of what comes from the heart; for it is out of the *abundance* of the heart that the mouth speaketh. We have here a new application of a former saying (see on ch. vii. 16-20). Here, the sentiment is, 'There are but two kingdoms, interests, parties—with the proper workings of each: If I promote the one, I cannot belong to the other; but they that set themselves in wilful opposition to the kingdom of light openly proclaim to what other kingdom they belong. As for you, in what ye have now uttered ye have but revealed the venomous malignity of your hearts.' **36. But I say unto you, That every idle word that men shall speak, they shall give account thereof in the day of judgment.** They might say, 'It was nothing; we meant no evil; we merely threw out a supposition, as one way of accounting for the miracle we

witnessed; if it will not stand, let it go; why make so much of it, and bear down with such severity for it?' Jesus replies, 'It was not nothing, and at the great day will not be treated as nothing: Words, as the index of the heart, however idle they may seem, will be taken account of, whether good or bad, in estimating character in the day of judgment.'

Remarks.—1. Instead of wondering that our Lord should have been thought "beside Himself," by those who were honestly unable to sympathize with, or even to comprehend, His exalted views, His compassionate feelings, His gracious errand, and the preciousness of the time allotted for the execution of it, this is precisely what we might have expected from those who "judged after the flesh." Nor is it any wonder, if those who tread the most in His steps are similarly misunderstood and misrepresented. (See on 2 Cor. v. 13.) 2. When we see the vast organized unseen kingdom of evil, though full of contradiction and division within itself, so tremendously harmonious in its opposition to truth and righteousness, what a consolation is it to know that "for this purpose the Son of God was manifested, that he might destroy the works of the devil" (1 John iii. 8), subvert his kingdom, and utterly bruise the serpent's head (Gen. iii. 15)! 3. Let scoffers of Christianity tremble. For, if they tread under foot the Son of God, and do despite unto the Spirit of grace, "there remaineth no more sacrifice for sins," and nothing more to be done by the Spirit of grace (Heb. x. 26-29); and having poured contempt upon the uttermost provisions of Heaven for their restoration to eternal life, they shut themselves up by their own act and deed, and, with their eyes open, to irremediable ruin. But 4. How distressing is it, on the other hand, to find tender consciences making themselves miserable with the apprehension that the guilt of the unpardonable sin lies upon them? If this arise, as in many cases it does, from a morbid state of the nervous system, acting on a religious temperament, the remedy lies beyond the limits of this Exposition. But if it be the fruit of inaccurate conceptions of Bible teaching, surely a dispassionate consideration of verses 31, 32 of the present Section, as above expounded, ought to dissipate such apprehensions. And if the language of 1 John v. 16, 17, should seem still to present some difficulty (see on those verses)—let not the plain sense of the great catholic statements of Scripture be stripped of their value by the supposed meaning of some isolated and obscure passage; but, in spite of all such obscurities, let the trembling sinner assure himself of this, that "*all* manner of sin and blasphemy shall be forgiven unto men," and that "the blood of Jesus Christ, God's Son, cleanseth from *all* sin."

38-50.—A SIGN DEMANDED, AND THE REPLY—HIS MOTHER AND BRETHREN SEEK TO SPEAK WITH HIM, AND THE ANSWER. (= Luke xi. 16, 24-36; Mark iii. 31-35; Luke viii. 19-21.)

A Sign demanded, and the Reply (38-45). **The**

38   Then *g*certain of the scribes and of the Pharisees answered, saying,
39 Master, we would see a sign from thee. But he answered and said unto
them, An evil and *h*adulterous generation seeketh after a sign; and there
40 shall no sign be given to it, but the sign of the prophet Jonas: For
*i*as Jonas was three days and three nights in the whale's belly, so
shall the Son of man be three days and three nights in the heart
41 of the earth. The *j*men of Nineve shall rise in judgment with this
generation, and *k*shall condemn it: *l*because they repented at the preach-
42 ing of Jonas; and, behold, *m*a greater than Jonas *is* here. The *n*queen
of the south shall rise up in the judgment with this generation, and shall
condemn it: for she came from the uttermost parts of the earth to hear
the wisdom of Solomon; and, behold, a *o*greater than Solomon *is* here.
43   When *p*the unclean spirit is gone out of a man, *q*he walketh through dry
44 places, seeking rest, and findeth none. Then he saith, I will return into
my house from whence I came out; and when he is come, he findeth *it*
45 empty, swept, and garnished. Then *r*goeth he, and taketh with himself
seven other spirits more wicked than himself, and they enter in and
dwell there: and *s*the last *state* of that man is worse than the first.
Even so shall it be also unto this wicked generation.

A. D. 31.

g ch. 16. 1.
Mark 8. 11.
Luke 11. 16.
John 2. 18.
1 Cor. 1. 22.
h Isa. 57. 3.
Mark 8. 38.
John 4. 48.
i Jon. 1. 17.
j Luke 11. 32.
k Jer. 3. 11.
Ezek. 16.51.
l Jon. 3. 5.
m Isa. 9. 6.
Rom. 9. 5.
n 1 Ki. 10. 1.
2 Chr. 9. 1.
o Col. 2. 2, 3.
p Luke 11.24.
q Job 1. 7.
1 Pet. 5. 8.
r Isa. 66. 3, 4.
s Heb. 6. 4.
Heb. 10. 26.

occasion of this Section was manifestly the same with that of the preceding. **38. Then certain of the scribes and of the Pharisees answered, saying, Master** [Διδάσκαλε]—'Teacher,' equivalent to 'Rabbi'—**we would see a sign from thee**—"a sign from heaven" (Luke xi. 16); something of an immediate and decisive nature, to show, not that his miracles were *real*—that they seemed willing to concede—but that they were from above, not from beneath. These were not the same class with those who charged Him with being in league with Satan (as we see from Luke xi. 15, 16); but as the spirit of both was similar, the tone of severe rebuke is continued. **39. But he answered and said unto them**—"when the people were gathered thick together" (Luke xi. 29), **An evil and adulterous generation**. This latter expression is best explained by Jer. iii. 20, "Surely as a wife treacherously departeth from her husband, so have ye dealt treacherously with me, O house of Israel, saith the Lord." For this was the relationship in which He stood to the covenant people—"I am married unto you" (Jer. iii. 14). **seeketh after a sign**. In the eye of Jesus this class were but the spokesmen of their generation, the exponents of the reigning spirit of unbelief. **and there shall no sign be given to it, but the sign of the prophet Jonas: 40. For as Jonas was**—"a sign unto the Ninevites, so shall also the Son of man be to this generation" (Luke xi. 30). For as Jonas was **three days and three nights in the whale's belly** (Jon. i. 17), **so shall the Son of man be three days and three nights in the heart of the earth.** This was the second public announcement of His resurrection three days after His death. (For the first, see John ii. 19.) Jonah's case was analogous to this, as being a signal judgment of God; reversed in three days; and followed by a glorious mission to the Gentiles. The expression "in the heart of the earth," suggested by the expression of Jonah with respect to the sea (ii. 3, in LXX.), means simply the grave, but this considered as the most emphatic expression of real and total entombment. The period during which He was to lie in the grave is here expressed in round numbers, according to the Jewish way of speaking, which was to regard any part of a day, however small, included within a period of days, as a full day. (See 1 Sam. xxx. 12, 13; Esth. iv. 16; v. 1; Matt. xxvii. 63, 64; &c.) **41. The men of Nineve**

shall rise in judgment with this generation, and shall condemn it: because they repented at the preaching of Jonas; and, behold, a greater than Jonas is here. The Ninevites, though heathens, repented at a man's preaching; while they, God's covenant people, repented not at the preaching of the Son of God—whose supreme dignity is rather implied here than expressed. **42. The queen of the south shall rise up in the judgment with this generation, and shall condemn it: for she came from the uttermost parts of the earth to hear the wisdom of Solomon; and, behold, a greater than Solomon is here.** The queen of Sheba—a tract in Arabia, near the shores of the Red Sea—came from a remote country, "south" of Judea, to hear the wisdom of a mere man, though a gifted one, and was transported with wonder at what she saw and heard (1 Ki. x. 1-9). They, when a Greater than Solomon had come *to them*, despised and rejected, slighted and slandered Him.

43-45. When the unclean spirit is gone out of a man, &c. On this important parable, in connection with the corresponding one —*v.* 29—see on Luke xi. 21-26.

A charming little incident, given only in Luke xi. 27, 28, seems to have its proper place here. "And it came to pass, as He spake these things, a certain woman of the company" [ἐκ τοῦ ὄχλου]—'out of the crowd,' "lifted up her voice and said unto Him, Blessed is the womb that bare thee, and the paps which Thou hast sucked." With true womanly feeling, she envies the mother of such a wonderful Teacher. And a higher and better than she had said as much before her (see on Luke i. 28). 42. How does our Lord, then, treat it? He is far from condemning it. He only holds up as "blessed rather" another class: "But he said, Yea rather, blessed are they that hear the word of God, and keep it"—in other words, the humblest real saint of God. How utterly alien is this sentiment from the teaching of the Church of Rome, which would doubtless excommunicate any one of its members that dared to talk in such a strain!

His Mother and Brethren Seek to Speak with Him, and the Answer (46-50). **46. While he yet talked to the people, behold, his mother and his brethren** (see on ch. xiii. 55, 56) **stood without, desiring to speak with him**—"and could not come

46 While he yet talked to the people, behold, *this* mother and *his*
47 brethren stood without, desiring to speak with him. Then one said unto
him, Behold, thy mother and thy brethren stand without, desiring to
48 speak with thee. But he answered and said unto him that told him,
49 Who is my mother? and who are my brethren? And he stretched forth
his hand toward his disciples, and said, Behold my mother and my
50 brethren! For *whosoever* shall do the will of my Father which is in
heaven, the same is my brother, and sister, and mother.

13 THE same day went Jesus out of the house, *and* sat by the sea-side.
2 And *great* multitudes were gathered together unto him, so that *he*
went into a ship, and sat; and the whole multitude stood on the shore.
3 And he spake many things unto them in parables, saying,
4 Behold, a sower went forth to sow: and when he sowed, some *seeds* fell
5 by the way-side, and the fowls came and devoured them up: some fell

A. D. 31.

t Mark 3. 31.
Luke 8. 19.
u Mark 6. 3.
John 2. 12.
John 7. 3, 5.
Acts 1. 14.
1 Cor. 9. 5.
Gal. 1. 19.
v John 15. 14.
Gal. 5. 6.
Gal. 6. 15.
Col. 3. 11.
Heb. 2. 11.

CHAP. 13.
a Mark 4. 1.
b Luke 8, 4.
c Luke 5. 3.

at Him for the press" (Luke viii. 19). For what purpose these came, we learn from Mark iii. 20, 21. In His zeal and ardour He seemed indifferent both to food and repose, and "they went to lay hold of Him" as one "beside himself." Mark says graphically, "And the multitude sat about Him" [περὶ αὐτόν]—or 'around Him.' 47. Then **one said unto him, Behold, thy mother and thy brethren stand without, desiring to speak with thee. 48. But he answered and said unto him that told him, Who is my mother? and who are my brethren?** Absorbed in the awful warnings He was pouring forth, He felt this to be an unseasonable interruption, fitted to dissipate the impression made upon the large audience—such an interruption as duty to the nearest relatives did not require Him to give way to. But instead of a direct rebuke, He seizes on the incident to convey a sublime lesson, expressed in a style of inimitable condescension. **49. And he stretched forth his hand toward his disciples.** How graphic is this! It is the language evidently of an eye-witness. **and said, Behold my mother and my brethren! 50. For whosoever shall do the will of my Father which is in heaven, the same is my brother, and sister, and mother:**—*q. d.,* 'There stand here the members of a family transcending and surviving this of earth: Filial subjection to the will of my Father in heaven is the indissoluble bond of union between Me and all its members; and whosoever enters this hallowed circle becomes to Me brother, and sister, and mother!'

Remarks.—1. What strange revelations will the day of judgment make, particularly as to the relative character of some of the most, and some of the least, favoured of the human family! (*vv.* 41-42.) Verily "the last shall be first, and the first last." 2. When the demands of even the nearest and dearest relatives, urging on us only that attention to our personal interests or comforts which in other circumstances would be natural and proper, are seen to interfere with some present work of God, let the spirit of our Lord's example here be our guiding principle, rather than the suggestions of nature. 3. How glorious is the thought that there is a family even upon earth of which the Son of God holds Himself a part; a family, the loving bond and reigning principle of which is subjection to the Father of our Lord Jesus Christ, and so embracing high and low, rude and refined, bond and free, of every kindred and every age that have tasted that the Lord is gracious; a family whose members can at once understand each other and take sweetest counsel together, though meeting for the first time from the ends of the earth—while with their nearest relatives, who are but the chil-

dren of this world, they have no sympathy in such things; a family which death cannot break up, but only transfer to their Father's house! Did Christians but habitually realize and act upon this, as did their blessed Master, what would be the effect upon the Church and upon the world!

CHAP. XIII. 1-52.—JESUS TEACHES BY PARABLES. (= Mark iv. 1-34; Luke viii. 4-18; xiii. 18-20.)

Introduction (1-3). **1. The same day went Jesus out of the house, and sat by the sea-[side]. 2. And great multitudes were gathered together unto him, so that he went into a ship**—the article in the received text wants authority—**and sat; and the whole multitude stood on the shore.** How graphic this picture—no doubt from the pen of an eye-witness, himself impressed with the scene! It was "the same day" on which the foregoing solemn discourse was delivered, when His kindred thought Him "beside Himself" for His indifference to food and repose—that same day, retiring to the sea-shore of Galilee, and there seating Himself, perhaps for coolness and rest, the crowds again flock around Him, and He is fain to push off from them, in the boat usually kept in readiness for Him; yet only to begin, without waiting to rest, a new course of teaching by parables to the eager multitudes that lined the shore. To the parables of our Lord there is nothing in all language to be compared, for simplicity, grace, fulness, and variety of spiritual teaching. They are adapted to all classes and stages of advancement, being understood by each according to the measure of his spiritual capacity. **3. And he spake many things unto them in parables, saying, &c.**

These parables are SEVEN in number; and it is not a little remarkable that while this is the *sacred number,* the first FOUR of them were spoken to the mixed multitude, while the remaining THREE were spoken to the Twelve in private—these divisions, *four* and *three,* being themselves notable in the symbolical arithmetic of Scripture. Another thing remarkable in the structure of these parables is, that while the first of the Seven—that of the Sower—is of the nature of an Introduction to the whole, the remaining Six consist of *three pairs*—the Second and Seventh, the Third and Fourth, and the Fifth and Sixth, corresponding to each other; each pair setting forth the same general truths, but with a certain diversity of aspect. All this can hardly be accidental.

First Parable: THE SOWER (3-9, 18-23). This Parable may be entitled, THE EFFECT OF THE WORD DEPENDENT ON THE STATE OF THE HEART. For the exposition of this parable, see on Mark iv. 1-9, 14-20.

upon [d]stony places, where they had not much earth; and forthwith they
6 sprung up, because they had no deepness of earth: and when the sun was up, they were scorched; and because they had no [e]root, they withered
7 away: and some fell among thorns; and the thorns sprung up and
8 choked them: but other fell into good ground, and brought forth fruit,
9 some [f]an hundred-fold, some sixty-fold, some thirty-fold. Who [g]hath ears to hear, let him hear.
10 And the disciples came, and said unto him, Why speakest thou unto
11 them in parables? He answered and said unto them, Because [h]it is given unto you to know the mysteries of the kingdom of heaven, but to
12 them it is not given. For [i]whosoever hath, to him shall be given, and he shall have more abundance; but whosoever hath not, from him shall
13 be taken away even that he hath. Therefore speak I to them in parables: because they seeing, see not; and hearing, they hear not;
14 neither do they understand. And in them is fulfilled the prophecy of Esaias, which saith, [j]By hearing ye shall hear, and shall not understand;
15 and seeing ye shall see, and shall not perceive: for this people's heart is waxed gross, and *their* ears [k]are dull of hearing, and their eyes they have closed; lest at any time they should see with *their* eyes, and hear with *their* ears, and should understand with *their* heart, and should be
16 converted, and I should heal them. But [l]blessed *are* your eyes, for they

A. D. 31.
d Ezek. 11.19.
e Col. 2. 7.
f Gen. 26. 12.
g Mark 4. 9.
h ch. 11. 25.
ch. 16. 17.
Mark 4. 11.
1 Cor. 2. 10.
1 John 2.27.
Col. 1. 26.
i Mark 4. 25.
Luke 8. 18.
Luke 19. 26.
j Isa. 6. 9.
Ezek. 12. 2.
Mark 4. 12.
Luke 8. 10.
John 12. 40.
Acts 28. 26, 27.
Rom. 11. 8.
2 Cor. 3. 14.
k Heb. 5. 11.
l ch. 16. 17.
Luke 10. 23, 24.
John 20. 29.

Reason for Teaching in Parables (10-17). **10. And the disciples came, and said unto him—** "they that were with Him, when they were alone" (Mark iv. 10)—**Why speakest thou unto them in parables?** Though before this He had couched some things in the parabolic form, for more vivid illustration, it would appear that He now, for the first time, formally employed this method of teaching. **11. He answered and said unto them, Because it is given unto you to know the mysteries of the kingdom of heaven.** The word "mysteries" [μυστήρια] in Scripture is not used in its classical sense—of 'religious secrets,' nor yet of 'things incomprehensible, or in their own nature difficult to be understood'—but in the sense of 'things of purely divine revelation,' and, usually, 'things darkly announced under the ancient economy, and during all that period darkly understood, but fully published under the Gospel' (1 Cor. ii. 6-10; Eph. iii. 3-6, 8, 9). "The mysteries of the kingdom of heaven," then, mean those glorious Gospel truths which at that time only the more advanced disciples could appreciate, and they but partially. **but to them it is not given.** (See on ch. xi. 25.) Parables serve the double purpose of *revealing* and *concealing*; presenting 'the mysteries of the kingdom' to those who know and relish them, though in never so small a degree, in a new and attractive light; but to those who are insensible to spiritual things yielding only, as so many tales, some temporary entertainment. **12. For whosoever hath** —that is, keeps; as a thing which he values, **to him shall be given, and he shall have more abundance**—he will be rewarded by an increase of what he so much prizes; **but whosoever hath not**—who lets this go or lie unused, as a thing on which he sets no value—**from him shall be taken away even that he hath**—or as it is in Luke (viii. 18), "what he seemeth to have" [ὃ δοκεῖ ἔχειν], or 'thinketh he hath.' This is a principle of immense importance, and, like other weighty sayings, appears to have been uttered by our Lord on more than one occasion, and in different connections. (See on ch. xxv. 9.) As a great ethical principle, we see it in operation everywhere, under the general law of *habit;* in virtue of which moral principles become stronger by exercise, while by disuse, or the exercise of their contraries, they wax weaker, and at length expire. The same principle reigns in the intellectual world, and even in the animal—if not in the vegetable also—as the facts of physiology sufficiently prove. Here, however, it is viewed as a divine ordination, as a judicial retribution in continual operation under the divine administration. **13. Therefore speak I to them in parables**—which our Lord, be it observed, did not begin to do till His miracles were malignantly ascribed to Satan. **because they seeing, see not.** They "saw," for the light shone on them as never light shone before; but they "saw not," for they closed their eyes. **and hearing, they hear not; neither do they understand.** They "heard," for He taught them who "spake as never man spake;" but they "heard not," for they took nothing in, apprehending not the soul-penetrating, life-giving words addressed to them.. In Mark and Luke, what is here expressed as a human fact is represented as the fulfilment of a divine purpose—"that seeing they may see, and not perceive," &c. The explanation of this lies in the statement of the foregoing verse—that, by a fixed law of the divine administration, the duty men voluntarily refuse to do, and in point of fact do not do, they at length become morally incapable of doing. **14. And in them is fulfilled** [ἀναπληροῦται]—rather, 'is fulfilling,' or is receiving its fulfilment—**the prophecy of Esaias, which saith** (Isa. vi. 9, 10—here quoted according to the LXX.), **By hearing ye shall hear, and shall not understand, &c. 15. For this people's heart is waxed gross . . . and their eyes they have closed; lest at any time they should see . . . and hear . . . and should understand . . . and should be converted, and I should heal them.** They were thus judicially sealed up under the darkness and obduracy which they deliberately preferred to the light and healing which Jesus brought nigh to them. **16. But blessed are your eyes, for they see; and your ears, for they hear:**—*q. d.*, 'Happy ye, whose eyes and ears, voluntarily and gladly opened, are drinking in the light divine.' **17. For verily I say unto you, That many prophets and righteous**

17 see; and your ears, for they hear. For verily I say unto you, *m* That many prophets and righteous *men* have desired to see *those things* which ye see, and have not seen *them;* and to hear *those things* which ye hear, and have not heard *them.*

18 Hear *n* ye therefore the parable of the sower. When any one hear-
19 eth the word of the kingdom, and understandeth *it* not, then cometh *o* the wicked *one,* and catcheth away that which was sown in his heart.
20 This is he which received seed by the way-side. But he that received the seed into stony places, the same is he that heareth the word, and
21 anon *p* with joy receiveth it: yet hath he not root in himself, but dureth for a while; for when tribulation or persecution ariseth because
22 of the word, by and by *q* he is offended. He *r* also that received seed *s* among the thorns is he that heareth the word; and the care of this world, and the deceitfulness of riches, choke the word, and he becometh
23 unfruitful. But he that received seed into the good ground is he that heareth the word, and understandeth *it;* which also beareth fruit, and bringeth forth, some an hundred-fold, some sixty, some thirty.

24 Another parable put he forth unto them, saying, The kingdom of
25 heaven is likened unto a man which sowed good seed in his field: but while men slept, *t* his enemy came and sowed tares among the wheat, and
26 went his way. But when the blade was sprung up, and brought forth
27 fruit, then appeared the tares also. So the servants of the householder came and said unto him, Sir, didst not thou sow good seed in thy field?
28 from whence then hath it tares? He said unto them, An enemy hath done this. The servants said unto him, Wilt thou then that we go and
29 gather them up? But he said, Nay; lest, while ye gather up the tares,
30 ye root up also the wheat with them. Let both grow together until the harvest: and in the time of harvest I will say to the reapers, Gather ye together first the tares, and bind them in bundles to burn them; but *u* gather the wheat into my barn.

31 Another parable put he forth unto them, saying, *v* The kingdom of heaven is like to a grain of mustard seed, which a man took, and sowed
32 in his field: which indeed is the least of all seeds; but when it is grown, it is the greatest among herbs, and becometh a tree, so that the birds of the air come and lodge in the branches thereof.

33 Another *w* parable spake he unto them; The kingdom of heaven is like unto leaven, which a woman took and hid in three [1] measures of meal, till the whole was leavened.

34 All these things spake Jesus unto the multitude in parables; and
35 without a parable spake he not unto them: that it might be fulfilled which was spoken by the prophet, saying, *x* I will open my mouth in parables; *y* I will utter things which have been kept secret from the foundation of the world.

A. D. 31.
m Luke 10. 24.
John 8. 56.
Eph. 3. 5.
Heb. 11. 13.
1 Pet. 1. 10.
n Mark 4. 14.
Luke 8. 11.
o Mark 4. 15.
Luke 8. 12.
2 Cor. 2. 11.
p Isa. 58. 2.
Ezek. 33.31.
Mark 4. 16.
John 5. 35.
Acts 8. 13.
q ch. 11. 6.
2 Tim. 1. 15.
r ch. 19. 23.
Mark 10.23.
Luke 18. 24.
1 Tim. 6. 9.
2 Tim. 4. 10.
s Jer. 4. 3.
t Luke 10. 19.
2 Cor. 11.13-15.
1 Pet. 5. 8.
u ch. 3. 12.
ch. 24. 31.
Luke 3. 17.
1 Thes. 4. 17.
2 Thes. 2. 1.
v Isa. 2. 2, 3.
Mic. 4. 1.
Mark 4. 30.
Luke 13. 18.
2 Pet. 3. 18.
w Luke 13. 20.
1 The word in the Greek is a measure containing about a peck and a half, wanting a little more than a pint.
x Ps. 78. 2.
y Ps. 49. 4.
Am. 3. 7.
Rom. 16.25.
1 Cor. 2. 7.
Eph. 3. 9.
Col. 1. 26.

men have desired [ἐπεθύμησαν]—rather, 'coveted,' to see those things which ye see, and have not seen them; and to hear those things which ye hear, and have not heard them. Not only were the disciples blessed above the blinded just spoken of, but favoured above the most honoured and the best that lived under the old economy, who had but glimpses of the things of the new kingdom, just sufficient to kindle in them desires not to be fulfilled to any in their day. In Luke x. 23, 24, where the same saying is repeated on the return of the Seventy—the words, instead of "many prophets and righteous men," are "many prophets *and kings;*" for several of the Old Testament saints were kings.

Second and Seventh Parables, or *First Pair:* THE WHEAT AND THE TARES, and THE GOOD AND BAD FISH (24-30; 36-43; and 47-50). The subject of both these Parables—which teach the same truth, with a slight diversity of aspect—is THE MIXED CHARACTER OF THE KINGDOM IN ITS PRESENT STATE, AND THE FINAL ABSOLUTE SEPARATION OF THE TWO CLASSES.

The Tares and the Wheat (24-30, 36-43). **24.** Another parable put he forth unto them, saying, The kingdom of heaven is likened unto a man which sowed good seed in his field. Happily for us, these exquisite parables are, with like charming simplicity and clearness, expounded to us by the Great Preacher Himself. Accordingly, we pass to *vv.* 36-38. Then Jesus sent the multitude away, and went into the house: and his disciples came unto him, saying, Declare unto us the parable of the tares of the field. He answered and

36   Then Jesus sent the multitude away, and went into the house: and his disciples came unto him, saying, Declare unto us the parable of the
37 tares of the field.   He answered and said unto them, He that *z*soweth
38 the good seed is the Son of man; the *a*field is the world; the good seed are the children of the kingdom; but the tares are *b*the children of the
39 wicked *one;* the enemy that sowed them is the devil; *c*the harvest is
40 the end of the world; and the reapers are the angels. As therefore the tares are gathered and burned in the fire; so shall it be in the end of
41 this world. The Son of man shall send forth his angels, *d*and they shall gather out of his kingdom all [2]things that offend, and them which do
42 iniquity, and *e*shall cast them into a furnace of fire: there shall be
43 wailing and gnashing of teeth. Then *f*shall the righteous shine forth as

A. D. 31.
z Isa. 61. 1.
a ch. 24. 14.
Luke 24. 47.
b Gen. 3. 13.
Acts 13. 10.
c Joel 3. 13.
Rev. 14. 15.
d 2 Pet. 2. 1,2
2 Or,
scandals.
e Rev. 19. 20.
Rev. 20. 10.
f Dan. 12. 3.
1 Cor. 15.42.

said unto them, He that soweth the good seed is the Son of man (see on John i. 52); the field is the world; the good seed are the children of the kingdom. In the parable of the Sower, "the seed is the word of God" (Luke viii. 11). But here that word has been received into the heart, and has converted him that received it into a new creature, a "child of the kingdom," according to that saying of James (i. 18), "Of His own will begat He us with the word of truth, that we should be a kind of first-fruits of His creatures." It is worthy of notice that this vast field of the world is here said to be *Christ's own*—"His field," says the parable. (See Ps. ii. 8.) 25. But while men slept, his enemy came and sowed tares among the wheat, and went his way. 38. The tares are the children of the wicked one. As this sowing could only be "while men slept," no blame seems intended, and certainly none is charged upon "the servants:" it is probably just the dress of the parable. 39. The enemy that sowed them is the devil—emphatically "*His* enemy" (*v.* 25). See Gen. iii. 15; 1 John iii. 8. By "tares" [ζιζάνια] is meant, not what in our husbandry is so called, but some noxious plant, probably *darnel.* "The tares are the children of the wicked one;" and by their being sown "among the wheat",is meant their being deposited within the territory of the visible Church. As they resemble the children of the kingdom, so they are produced, it seems, by a similar process of "sowing"—the seeds of evil being scattered and lodging in the soil of those hearts upon which falls the seed of the word. The enemy, after sowing his "tares," "went his way" —his dark work soon done, but taking time to develop its true character. 26. But when the blade was sprung up, and brought forth fruit, then appeared the tares also—the growth in both cases running parallel, as antagonistic principles are seen to do. 27. So the servants of the householder came—that is, Christ's ministers— and said unto him, Sir, didst not thou sow good seed in thy field? from whence then hath it tares? This well expresses the surprise, disappointment, and anxiety of Christ's faithful servants and people, at the discovery of "false brethren" among the members of the Church. 28. He said unto them, An enemy hath done this. Kind words these from a good Husbandman, honourably clearing His faithful servants of the wrong done to His field. The servants said unto him, Wilt thou then that we go and gather them up? Compare with this the question of James and John (Luke ix. 54), "Lord, wilt thou that we command fire to come down from heaven and consume" those Samaritans? In this kind of zeal there is usually a large mixture of carnal heat. (See Jas. i. 20.) 29. But he said, Nay—'It will be done in due time, but not now, nor is it your business.' lest, while ye gather up the tares, ye root up

also the wheat with them. Nothing could more clearly or forcibly teach the difficulty of distinguishing the two classes, and the high probability that in the attempt to do so these will be confounded. 30, 39. Let both grow together—that is, in the visible Church—until the harvest—till the one have ripened for full salvation, the other for destruction. The harvest is the end of the world [συντελεία τοῦ αἰῶνος]—the period of Christ's second coming, and of the judicial separation of the righteous and the wicked. Till then, no attempt is to be made to effect such separation. But to stretch this so far as to justify allowing openly scandalous persons to remain in the communion of the Church, is to wrest the teaching of this parable to other than its proper design, and go in the teeth of apostolic injunctions (1 Cor. v). and in the time of harvest I will say to the reapers. And the reapers are the angels. But whose angels are they? "The Son of man shall send forth HIS angels" (*v.* 41). Compare 1 Pet. iii. 22—"Who is gone into heaven, and is on the right hand of God; angels and authorities and powers being made subject unto Him." Gather ye together first the tares, and bind them in bundles to burn them—"in the fire" (*v.* 40)—but gather the wheat into my barn. Christ, as the Judge, will separate the two classes (as in ch. xxv. 32). It will be observed that the tares are burned *before* the wheat is housed; in the exposition of the parable (*vv.* 41, 43) the same order is observed; and the same in ch. xxv. 46—as if, in some literal sense, "with thine eyes shalt thou behold and see the reward of the wicked" (Ps. xci. 8). 41. The Son of man shall send forth his angels, and they shall gather out of his kingdom—to which they never really belonged. They usurped their place and name and outward privileges; but "the ungodly shall not stand in the judgment, nor sinners [abide] in the congregation of the righteous" (Ps. i. 5). all things that offend [πάντα τὰ σκάνδαλα]—all those who have proved a stumbling-block to others, and them which do iniquity. The former class, as the worst, are mentioned first. 42. And shall cast them into a furnace—rather, 'the furnace' of fire: there shall be wailing and gnashing of teeth. What terrific strength of language—the "casting" or "flinging" expressive of indignation, abhorrence, contempt (cf. Ps. ix. 17; Dan. xii. 2); "the furnace of fire" denoting the fierceness of the torment; the "wailing" signifying the anguish this causes; while the "gnashing of teeth" is a graphic way of expressing the despair in which its remedilessness issues (see on ch. viii. 12)! 43. Then shall the righteous shine forth as the sun in the kingdom of their Father—as if they had been under a cloud during their present association with ungodly pretenders to their character, and claimants of their privileges, and obstructors

the sun in the kingdom of their Father. Who hath ears to hear, let him hear.

44 Again, the kingdom of heaven is like unto treasure hid in a field; the which when a man hath found, he hideth, and for joy thereof goeth and *g*selleth all that he hath, and *h*buyeth that field.

45 Again, the kingdom of heaven is like unto a merchant-man seeking
46 goodly pearls: who, when he had found *i*one pearl of great price, went and sold all that he had, and bought it.

A. D. 31.
g ch. 19. 27.
Phil. 3. 7.
h Pro. 23. 23.
Isa. 55. 1.
ch. 25. 9.
Rev. 3. 18.
i Pro. 2. 4.
Pro. 3. 14.
Pro. 8. 10.

of their course. Who hath ears to hear, let him hear. (See on Mark iv. 9.)

The Good and Bad Fish (47-50). The object of this brief parable is the same with that of the Tares and Wheat. But as its details are fewer, so its teaching is less rich and varied. **47. Again, the kingdom of heaven is like unto a net, that was cast into the sea, and gathered of every kind.** The word here rendered "net" [σαγήνη] signifies, a large *drag-net*, which draws everything after it, suffering nothing to escape, as distinguished from 'a *casting-net*' [ἀμφίβληστρον, and δίκτυον], Mark i. 16, 18. The far-reaching efficacy of the Gospel is thus denoted. This Gospel net "gathered of every kind," meaning every variety of character. **48. Which, when it was full, they drew to shore**—for the separation will not be made till the number of the elect is accomplished—**and sat down**—expressing the deliberateness with which the judicial separation will at length be made—**and gathered the good into vessels, but cast the bad away** [τὰ δὲ σαπρὰ]—lit., 'the rotten,' but here meaning, 'the foul' or 'worthless' fish; corresponding to the "tares" of the other parable. **49. So shall it be at the end of the world: the angels shall come forth, and sever the wicked from among the just, 50. And shall cast them into the furnace of fire: there shall be wailing and gnashing of teeth.** See on verse 42. We have said that each of these two parables holds forth the same truth under a slight diversity of aspect. What is that diversity? First, the *bad*, in the former parable, are represented as vile seed sown amongst the wheat by the enemy of souls; in the latter, as foul fish drawn forth out of the great sea of human beings by the Gospel net itself. Both are important truths—that the Gospel draws within its pale, and into the communion of the visible Church, multitudes who are Christians only in name; and that the injury thus done to the Church on earth is to be traced to the wicked one. But further, while the former parable gives chief prominence to the present mixture of good and bad, in the latter, the prominence is given to the future separation of the two classes.

Remarks.—1. These two parables teach clearly the vanity of expecting a perfectly pure Church in the present state, or before Christ comes. In the latter parable, it is the Gospel net itself that gathers the bad as well as the good; and as it is by this tie that they get and keep their connection with the Church, we cannot expect so to cast that net as to draw in the good only. But, on the other hand, as the presence of tares among the wheat, in the former parable, is ascribed to the enemy of the Church and her Lord, it follows that, in so far as we *encourage* the entrance of such into the communion of the Church, we do the devil's work. Thus does this parable give as little encouragement to *laxity* as to a utopian *purism* in church-discipline. 2. When the servants, in the former parable, ask liberty to pull up the tares, that the growth of the wheat may not suffer from their presence, and that liberty is denied them, does not this rebuke *intolerance* in religion, on pretence of purging out heresy? 3. How grand is the view here given by the Great Preacher of His own majesty, as *Bengel* remarks! The field of the world into which the seed of the kingdom is cast is "*His field*" (v. 24); the angels who do the work of separation at the end of the world are "*His angels;*" and as it is "the Son of man that sends them forth," so in "gathering out of *His kingdom* all things that offend, and them which do iniquity," they do but obey His commands (vv. 30, 41.) 4. The Scripture nowhere holds out the expectation of a Millennium in which there will be none but regenerate men on the earth, in flesh and blood—or, in the language of our parable, in which the earth will be one field of wheat without any tares. It would seem to follow that there are but two great stages of Humanity under the Gospel: the present *mixed* state, and the future, final, absolutely *unmixed* condition; the Millennial era being, in that case, but a continuation of the present condition—vastly superior, indeed, and with much less mixture than we now see, but—not *essentially* differing from it, and so, having no place in this parable at all. The proper place of the Millennium, in these parables, is in the next pair. 5. Do those who talk so much of "the meekness and gentleness of Christ," as if that were the one feature of His character, set their seal to the sharp lines of His teaching in these two parables—on the subject of the tares as "the children of the wicked one," and "the enemy that sows them" being "the devil;" as to the "furnace of fire" prepared for them, the "casting" or "flinging" of them into the furnace, which that gentle Lamb of God shall demand of His angels, and the "wailing and gnashing of teeth" in which this will end? O, if men but knew it, it is just the gentleness of the Lamb which explains the eventual "wrath of the Lamb."

Third and Fourth Parables, or *Second Pair:* THE MUSTARD SEED and THE LEAVEN (31-33). The subject of both these parables, as of the first pair, is the same, but under a slight diversity of aspect: namely, THE GROWTH OF THE KINGDOM, FROM THE SMALLEST BEGINNINGS TO ULTIMATE UNIVERSALITY.

The Mustard Seed (31, 32). **31. Another parable put he forth unto them, saying, The kingdom of heaven is like to a grain of mustard seed, which a man took, and sowed in his field: 32. Which indeed is the least of all seeds**—not absolutely, but popularly and proverbially, as in Luke xvii. 6, "If ye had faith as a grain of mustard seed," that is, 'never so little faith.' but when it is grown, it is the greatest among herbs--not absolutely, but in relation to the small size of the seed, and in warm latitudes proverbially great. **and becometh a tree, so that the birds of the air come and lodge in the branches thereof.** This is added, no doubt, to express the *amplitude* of the tree. But as this seed has a hot, fiery vigour, gives out its best virtues when bruised, and is grateful to the taste of birds, which are accordingly attracted to

47 Again, the kingdom of heaven is like unto a net, that was cast into
48 the sea, and gathered of every kind: which, when it was full, they
drew to shore, and sat down, and gathered the good into vessels, but cast
49 the bad away. So shall it be at the end of the world: the angels shall
50 come forth, and *j*sever the wicked from among the just, and shall cast
them into the furnace of fire: there shall be wailing and gnashing of
teeth.

A. D. 31.

j Mal. 3. 18.
ch. 22. 12-14.
ch. 25. 5-12.
ch. 25. 33.
2 Thes. 1. 7-
10.
Rev. 20. 12-
15.

its branches both for shelter and food, is it straining the parable, asks *Trench*, to suppose that,
besides the wonderful *growth* of His kingdom, our
Lord selected this seed to illustrate further the
shelter, repose, and *blessedness* it is destined to
afford to the nations of the world?

The Leaven (33). **33. Another parable spake he
unto them; The kingdom of heaven is like unto
leaven, which a woman took and hid in three
measures of meal, till the whole was leavened.**
This parable, while it teaches the same general
truth as the foregoing one, holds forth, perhaps,
rather the *inward* growth of the kingdom, while
"the Mustard Seed" seems to point chiefly to the
outward. It being a woman's work to knead, it
seems a refinement to say that "the woman" here
represents *the Church,* as the instrument of de-
positing the leaven. Nor does it yield much satisfaction to understand the "three measures of
meal" of that threefold division of our nature
into "spirit, soul, and body," alluded to in 1
Thes. v. 23, or of the threefold partition of the
world among the three sons of Noah (Gen. x. 32),
as some do. It yields more real satisfaction to
see in this brief parable just the *all-penetrating*
and *assimilating* quality of the Gospel, by virtue
of which it will yet mould all institutions and
tribes of men, and exhibit over the whole earth
one "Kingdom of our Lord and of His Christ."
(See on Rev. xi. 15.)

**34. All these things spake Jesus unto the mul-
titude in parables; and without a parable spake
he not unto them**—that is, on this occasion; refraining not only from all naked discourse, but
even from all interpretation of these parables to
the mixed multitude. **35. That it might be fulfilled which was spoken by the prophet, saying** (Ps. lxxviii. 2, nearly as in LXX.), **I will open
my mouth in parables; I will utter things which
have been kept secret from the foundation of
the world.** Though the Psalm seems to contain
only a summary of Israelitish *history,* the Psalmist
himself calls it "a parable," and "dark sayings
from of old" [מִנִּי־קֶדֶם, *ἀπ' ἀρχῆς*]—as containing,
underneath the history, truths for all time, not fully
brought to light till the Gospel-day.

Remarks.—1. Those who maintain that the Millennial era will be organically different from the
present Gospel dispensation, and denounce as unscriptural the notion that the one will be but the
universal triumph of the other, will find it hard to
interpret the parables of the Mustard Seed and
the Leaven on any other principle. The gradual
growth of the Christian tree until the world be
overshadowed by its wide-spreading branches—
the silent operation of the Gospel on the mass of
mankind, until the whole be leavened —these are
representations of what the Gospel is designed
to do, which it will be hard to reconcile to the
belief that the world is not to be Christianized
before Christ's Second Coming; that Christendom
is to wax worse and worse, and be at its worst condition, when He comes; and that not till after
He appears the second time, without sin, unto
salvation, will the Millennium commence and a
universal Christianity be seen upon the earth.

That those gigantic superstitions, and spiritual
tyrannies, and hideous corruptions, which have
for ages supplanted and well-nigh crushed out
a pure Christianity in some of the fairest portions of Christendom, will not disappear without
a struggle, and that in this sense the blessed
Millennial era will be ushered in *convulsively,* we
may well believe, and Scripture prophecy is abundant and clear in such details. But in the light
of such grand divisions as are presented to us in
the parables of the Tares and Wheat and of the
Good Fish and Bad—between the present mixed
and the future unmixed condition of Humanity,
all such minor divisions disappear; and the representations of the parables of the Mustard Seed
and the Leaven are seen to stretch from the commencement of the Christian era, *unbroken,* into
and through and on to the termination of the
Millennial era. But 2. It were a pity if these
parables were used merely for adjusting our views
of the kingdom of Christ. They cheer the servants of Christ, when planting the standard of the
Cross on new ground, with the assurance of ultimate triumph; when exposed to crushing persecution, with assurances of final victory; and when
gaining little ground on the heathen world, while
old forms of corrupted Christianity seem never to
yield, with the certainty that the time to favour
Zion is coming, even the set time, and the kingdom and dominion, and the greatness of the
kingdom under the whole heaven shall be given
unto the saints of the Most High, and the kingdoms of this world shall become the Kingdom of
our Lord and of His Christ.

Fifth and Sixth Parables, or *Third Pair:* THE
HIDDEN TREASURE and THE PEARL OF GREAT
PRICE (44-46). The subject of this last Pair, as of
the two former, is the same, but also under a
slight diversity of aspect: namely,

THE PRICELESS VALUE OF THE BLESSINGS OF
THE KINGDOM. And while the one parable represents the Kingdom as *found without seeking,* the
other holds forth the Kingdom as *sought and
found.*

The Hidden Treasure (44-46). **44. Again, the
kingdom of heaven is like unto treasure hid in
a field**—no uncommon thing in unsettled and half-
civilized countries, even now as well as in ancient
times, when there was no other way of securing it
from the rapacity of neighbours or marauders.
(Jer. xli. 8; Job iii. 21; Prov. ii. 4.) **the which
when a man hath found**—that is, unexpectedly
found—**he hideth, and for joy thereof**—on perceiving what a treasure he had lighted on, passing
the worth of all he possessed, **goeth and selleth
all that he hath, and buyeth that field**—in which
case, by Jewish law, the treasure would become
his own.

The Pearl of Great Price (45, 46). **45. Again, the
kingdom of heaven is like unto a merchant-
man, seeking goodly pearls: 46. Who, when he
had found one pearl of great price, went and
sold all that he had, and bought it.** The one
pearl of great price, instead of being found by
accident, as in the former case, is found by one
whose *business* it is to seek for such, and who finds

51   Jesus saith unto them, Have ye understood all these things? They
52 say unto him, Yea, Lord. Then said he unto them, Therefore every
scribe *which is* instructed unto the kingdom of heaven, is like unto a
man *that is* an householder which bringeth forth out of his treasure
k things new and old.

53   And it came to pass, *that*, when Jesus had finished these parables, he
54 departed thence. And *l*when he was come into his own country, he
taught them in their synagogue, insomuch that they were astonished,
and said, Whence hath this *man* this wisdom, and *these* mighty works?
55 Is *m*not this the carpenter's son? is not his mother called Mary? and *n*his
56 brethren, *o*James, and Joses, and Simon, and Judas? and his sisters, are

A. D. 31.

k Song 7. 13.
l Deut. 18.15.
ch. 2. 23.
Mark 6. 1.
Luke 4. 16.
John 1. 11.
m Isa. 49. 7.
Isa. 53. 2, 3.
Mark 6. 3.
Luke 3. 23.
John 6. 42.
n ch. 12. 46.
o Mark 15. 40.

it just in the way of *searching* for such treasures. But in both cases the surpassing value of the treasure is alike recognized, and in both all is parted with for it.

51. Jesus saith unto them—that is, to the Twelve. He had spoken the first *four* in the hearing of the mixed multitude : the last *three* He reserved till, on the dismissal of the mixed audience, He and the Twelve were alone, (*v.* 36, &c.) **Have ye understood all these things? They say unto him, Yea, Lord. 52. Then said he unto them, Therefore**—or as we should say, Well, then, **every scribe**—or Christian teacher ; here so called from that well-known class among the Jews. (See ch. xxiii. 34.) **which is instructed unto the kingdom of heaven**—himself taught in the mysteries of the Gospel which he has to teach to others, **is like unto a man that is an householder which bringeth forth**—'turneth' or 'dealeth out' [ἐκβάλλει]—**out of his treasure**—his store of divine truth, **things new and old**—old truths in ever new forms, aspects, applications, and with ever new illustrations.

Remarks.—1. The truths taught in the third pair of these parables—the Hidden Treasure and the Pearl of Great Price—are these: that the blessings of Christ's kingdom are of incomparable value ; that they only truly deem them so who are prepared to part with all for them ; and that while some find Christ without seeking Him, others find Him as the result of long and anxious search. Of the *former* sort, Messiah Himself says, "I was found of them that sought me not ; I was made manifest unto them that asked not after me." (Isa. lxv. i.; Rom. x. 20.) Such was the woman of Samaria (John iv.); such was Matthew the publican (ch. ix. 9); such was Zaccheus the publican (Luke xix. 1-10); such was the thief on the cross (Luke xxiii. 39-43); such was the man born blind (John ix.); and such was Saul of Tarsus, (Acts ix.) Of the *latter* sort it is said, "Ye shall seek me, and find me, when ye shall search for me with all your heart" (Jer. xxix. 13). Such was Nathanael (John i. 45-49), and many others of whom we read in the New Testament. Of the former sort were nearly all who were called from among the Gentiles, as are the fruits of missions still in heathen lands : of the latter sort were probably most of John's disciples who went from him to His Master, and generally, "all who in Jerusalem looked for Redemption" and "waited for the Consolation of Israel" (Luke ii. 25, 38); and to them must be added all now in Christian lands reared in the knowledge of Christ, taught to seek Him early, yet often long of finding Him. 2. Those who find Christ without seeking Him have usually the liveliest joy—the joy of a blessed surprise; while those who find Him after long and anxious search have usually the deepest apprehensions of His value. It will be observed that the "joy" of discovery is only in the former

parable—as if to express, not the *value* set upon the treasure, but the *unexpectedness* of it. On this principle, there was "more joy" over the unexpected return of the Prodigal Son than over the son who had been with his father all his days. (Luke xv.) Yet not less, but more profound is the sense of Christ's preciousness, when found after lengthened and weary search, which has deepened the sense of wretchedness without Him and the craving of the soul after Him.

53-58.—How Jesus was Regarded by His Relatives. (= Mark vi. 1-6; Luke iv. 16-30.)
53. And it came to pass, that, when Jesus had finished these parables, he departed thence. 54. And when he was come into his own country—that is, *Nazareth ;* as is plain from Mark vi. 1. See on John iv. 43, where also the same phrase occurs. This, according to the majority of Harmonists, was the *second* of *two* visits which our Lord paid to Nazareth during His public ministry; but in our view it was His *first* and *only* visit to it. See on ch. iv. 13; and for the reasons, see on Luke iv. 16-30. **he taught them in their synagogue, insomuch that they were astonished, and said, Whence hath this man this wisdom, and these mighty works?** —'these miracles' [δυνάμεις]. These surely are not like the questions of people who had asked precisely the same questions before, who from astonishment had proceeded to rage, and in their rage had hurried Him out of the synagogue, and away to the brow of the hill whereon their city was built, to thrust Him down headlong, and who had been foiled even in that object by His passing through the midst of them, and going His way. But see on Luke iv. 16, &c. **55. Is not this the carpenter's son?** In Mark (vi. 3) the question is, "Is not this the carpenter?" In all likelihood, our Lord, during His stay under the roof of His earthly parents, wrought along with His legal father. **is not his mother called Mary?**—'Do we not know all about His parentage? Has He not grown up in the midst of us? Are not all His relatives our own townsfolk? Whence, then, such wisdom and such miracles?' These particulars of our Lord's *human* history constitute the most valuable testimony, first, to His true and real humanity—for they prove that during all His first thirty years His townsmen had discovered nothing about Him different from other men; secondly, to the divine character of His mission—for these Nazarenes proclaim both the unparalleled character of His teaching and the reality and glory of His miracles, as transcending human ability; and thirdly, to His wonderful humility and self-denial—in that when He was such as they now saw Him to be, He yet never gave any indications of it for thirty years, because "His hour was not yet come." **and his brethren, James, and Joses, and Simon, and Judas? 56. And his sisters, are they not all with us? Whence then**

they not all with us? Whence then hath this *man* all these things?
57 And they [p] were offended in him. But Jesus said unto them, [q] A prophet is not without honour, save in his own country, and in his own house.
58 And [r] he did not many mighty works there, because of their unbelief.
14 AT that time [a] Herod the tetrarch heard of the fame of Jesus, and
2 said unto his servants, This is John the Baptist: he is risen from the dead; and therefore mighty works [1] do show forth themselves in him.
3 For [b] Herod had laid hold on John, and bound him, and put *him* in
4 prison for Herodias' sake, his brother Philip's wife. For John said unto
5 him, [c] It is not lawful for thee to have her. And when he would have put him to death, he feared the multitude, [d] because they counted him
6 as a prophet. But when Herod's [e] birthday was kept, the daughter of
7 Herodias danced [2] before them, and pleased Herod. Whereupon he pro-
8 mised with an oath to give her whatsoever she would ask. And she, being before instructed of her mother, said, Give me here John Bap-
9 tist's head in a charger. And the king was sorry: [f] nevertheless, for the oath's sake, and them which sat with him at meat, he commanded
10 *it* to be given *her*. And he sent, and beheaded John in the prison.
11 And his head was brought in a charger, and given to the damsel: and
12 she brought *it* to her mother. And his disciples came, and took up the body, and buried it, and went and told Jesus.
13 When [g] Jesus heard *of it*, he departed thence by ship into a desert

A. D. 31.

[p] Ps. 22. 6.
ch. 11. 6.
[q] Luke 4. 24.
John 4. 44.
[r] Heb. 3. 19.
Heb. 4. 2.

CHAP. 14.
[a] Mark 6. 14.
Luke 9. 7.
[1] Or, are wrought by him.
[b] Pro. 10. 17.
Pro. 15. 10.
[c] Lev. 18. 16.
Lev. 20. 21.
[d] ch. 21. 26.
Luke 20. 6.
[e] Gen. 40. 20.
[2] in the midst.
[f] Titus 1. 16.
[g] ch. 10 23.
ch 12. 15.
Mark 6. 32.
Luke 9. 10.
John 6. 1, 2.

---

hath this [man] all these things? An exceedingly difficult question here arises—What were these "brethren" and "sisters" to Jesus? Were they, *First*, His full brothers and sisters? or, *Secondly*, Were they his step-brothers and step-sisters, children of Joseph by a former marriage? or, *Thirdly*, Were they His cousins, according to a common way of speaking among the Jews respecting persons of collateral descent? On this subject an immense deal has been written; nor are opinions yet by any means agreed. For the second opinion there is no ground but a vague tradition, arising probably from the wish for some such explanation. The first opinion undoubtedly suits the text best in all the places where the parties are certainly referred to (ch. xii. 46, and its parallels, Mark iii. 31, and Luke viii. 19; our present passage, and its parallel, Mark vi. 3; John ii. 12; vii. 3, 5, 10; Acts i. 14). But, in addition to other objections, many of the best interpreters, thinking it in the last degree improbable that our Lord, when hanging on the cross, would have committed His mother to John if He had had full brothers of His own then alive, prefer the third opinion; although, on the other hand, it is not to be doubted that our Lord might have good reasons for entrusting the guardianship of His doubly widowed mother to the beloved disciple in preference even to full brothers of His own. Thus dubiously we prefer to leave this vexed question, encompassed as it is with difficulties. As to the names here mentioned, the *first* of them, "JAMES," is afterwards called "the Lord's brother" (see on Gal. i. 19), but is perhaps not to be confounded with "James the son of Alpheus," one of the Twelve, though many think their identity beyond dispute. This question also is one of considerable difficulty, and not without importance; since the James who occupies so prominent a place in the Church of Jerusalem, in the latter part of the Acts, was apparently the apostle, but is by many regarded as "the Lord's brother," while others think their identity best suits all the statements. The *second* of those here named, "JOSES" (or Joseph), who must not be confounded with "Joseph called Barsabas, who was surnamed Justus" (Acts i. 23); and the *third*

here named, "SIMON," is not to be confounded with Simon the Kananite or Zealot (see on ch. x. 4). These three are nowhere else mentioned in the New Testament. The *fourth* and last-named, "JUDAS," can hardly be identical with the apostle of that name—though the brothers of both were of the name of "James"—nor (unless the two be identical, was this Judas) with the author of the catholic Epistle so called. **57. And they were offended in him. But Jesus said unto them, A prophet is not without honour, save in his own country, and in his own house. 58. And he did not many mighty works there, because of their unbelief**—"save that He laid His hands on a few sick folk, and healed them" (Mark vi. 5). See on Luke iv. 16-30, and Remarks at the close of that Section.

CHAP. XIV. 1-12.—HEROD THINKS JESUS A RESURRECTION OF THE MURDERED BAPTIST— ACCOUNT OF HIS IMPRISONMENT AND DEATH. (= Mark vi. 14-29; Luke ix. 7-9.)

The time of this alarm of Herod Antipas appears to have been during the mission of the Twelve, and shortly after the Baptist—who had lain in prison for probably more than a year—had been cruelly put to death.

Herod's Theory of the Works of Christ (1, 2). **1. At that time Herod the tetrarch**—Herod Antipas, one of the three sons of Herod the Great, and own brother of Archelaus (ch. ii. 22), who ruled as *Ethnarch* over Galilee and Perea. **heard of the fame of Jesus**—"for His name was spread abroad" (Mark vi. 14). **2. And said unto his servants**—his counsellors or court-ministers, **This is John the Baptist: he is risen from the dead; and therefore mighty works do show forth themselves in him.** The murdered prophet haunted his guilty breast like a spectre, and seemed to him alive again and clothed with unearthly powers in the person of Jesus.

Account of the Baptist's Imprisonment and Death (3-12). For the exposition of this portion, see on Mark vi. 17-29.

12-21.—HEARING OF THE BAPTIST'S DEATH, JESUS CROSSES THE LAKE WITH THE TWELVE, AND MIRACULOUSLY FEEDS FIVE THOUSAND.

place apart: and when the people had heard *thereof,* they followed him on foot out of the cities.

14 And Jesus went forth, and saw a great multitude, and [h]was moved with compassion toward them, and he healed their sick.

15 And when it was evening, his disciples came to him, saying, This is a desert place, and the time is now past; send the multitude away, that

16 they may go into the villages, and buy themselves victuals. But Jesus

17 said unto them, They need not depart; [i]give ye them to eat. And they

18 say unto him, We have here but five loaves, and two fishes. He said,

19 Bring them hither to me. And he commanded the multitude to sit down on the grass, and took the five loaves, and the two fishes, and, looking up to heaven, [j]he blessed, and brake, and gave the loaves to *his*

20 disciples, and the disciples to the multitude. And they did all eat, and were filled: and they took up of the fragments that remained twelve

21 baskets full. And they that had eaten were about five thousand men, besides women and children.

22 And straightway Jesus constrained his disciples to get into a ship, and to go before him unto the other side, while he sent the multitudes away.

23 And [k]when he had sent the multitudes away, he went up into a mountain apart to pray: [l]and when the evening was come, he was there alone.

24 But the ship was now in the midst of the sea, tossed with waves: for the

25 wind was contrary. And in the fourth watch of the night Jesus went

26 unto them, walking on the sea. And when the disciples saw him [m]walking on the sea, they were troubled, saying, It is a spirit: and they cried

27 out for fear. But straightway Jesus spake unto them, saying, Be of

28 good cheer: it is I; be not afraid. And Peter answered him and said,

29 Lord, if it be thou, bid me come unto thee on the water. And he said, Come. And when Peter was come down out of the ship, he walked on

30 the water, to go to Jesus. But when he saw the wind [3]boisterous, he was afraid; and, beginning to sink, he cried, saying, Lord, save me!

31 And immediately Jesus stretched forth *his* hand, and caught him, and said unto him, O thou of little faith, wherefore [n]didst thou

32 doubt? And when they were come into the ship, the [o]wind ceased.

33 Then they that were in the ship came and worshipped him, saying, Of a truth thou [p]art the Son of God.

34 And [q]when they were gone over, they came into the land of Gennesaret.

35 And when the men of that place had knowledge of him, they sent out into all that country round about, and brought unto him all that were

36 diseased; and besought him that they might only touch the hem of his garment: and [r]as many as touched were made perfectly whole.

15 THEN [a]came to Jesus scribes and Pharisees, which were of Jerusalem,

2 saying, Why [b]do thy disciples transgress [c]the tradition of the elders? for

A. D. 31.
[h] ch. 9. 36.
Heb. 2. 17.
Heb. 4. 15.
Heb. 5. 2.
[i] 2 Ki. 4. 42, 43.
Luke 3. 11.
John 13. 29.
2 Cor. 8. 2, 3.
[j] ch. 15 36.
ch. 26. 26.
Mark 8. 6.
Luke 22.19.
John 6. 11, 23.
Acts 27. 35.
[k] ch. 6. 6.
ch. 26. 36.
Mark 6. 46.
Luke 6. 12.
Acts 6. 4.
[l] John 6. 16.
[m] Job 7. 19.
Job 9. 8.
Ps. 39. 13.
Ps. 73. 19.
Isa. 43. 16.
Lam. 3. 3,8.
[3] Or, strong.
[n] ch. 8. 26.
ch. 16. 8.
Jas. 1. 6.
[o] Ps. 107. 29.
Mark 4. 41.
Mark 6. 5.
John 6. 21.
[p] Ps. 2. 7.
Mark 1. 1.
ch. 16. 16.
ch. 26. 63.
Luke 4. 41.
John 1. 49.
John 6. 69.
John 11. 27.
[q] Mark 6. 53.
[r] ch. 9. 20.
Mark 3. 10.
Luke 6. 19.
Acts 19. 12.
CHAP. 15.
[a] Mark 7. 1.
[b] Mark 7. 5.
[c] Gal. 1. 14.
Col. 2. 8.

(= Mark vi. 30-44; Luke ix. 10-17; John vi. 1-14.) For the exposition of this Section—one of the very few where all the four Evangelists run parallel—see on Mark vi. 30-44.

22-36.—JESUS CROSSES TO THE WESTERN SIDE OF THE LAKE WALKING ON THE SEA—INCIDENTS ON LANDING. (= Mark vi. 45; John vi. 15-24.) For the exposition, see on John vi. 15-24.

CHAP. XV. 1-20.—DISCOURSE ON CEREMONIAL POLLUTION. (= Mark vii. 1-23.) The time of this Section was after that Passover which was nigh at hand when our Lord fed the five thousand (John vi. 4)—the third Passover, as we take it, since His public ministry began, but which He did not keep at Jerusalem for the reason mentioned in John vii. 1.

1. Then came to Jesus scribes and Pharisees, which were of [ἀπό]—or 'from' Jerusalem. Mark says they "came from" it; a deputation probably

sent from the capital expressly to watch Him. As He had not come to them at the last Passover, which they had reckoned on, they now come to Him. "And," says Mark, "when they saw some of His disciples eat bread with defiled, that is to say, with unwashen, hands"—hands not ceremonially cleansed by washing—"they found fault. For the Pharisees, and all the Jews, except they wash their hands oft" [πυγμῇ]—lit., 'in' or 'with the fist;' that is, probably, washing the one hand by the use of the other—though some understand it, with our version, in the sense of 'diligently,' 'sedulously'—"eat not, holding the tradition of the elders;" acting religiously according to the custom handed down to them. "And when they come from the market" [Καὶ ἀπὸ ἀγορᾶς]—'And after market;' after any common business, or attending a court of justice, where the Jews, as *Webster and Wil-*

3 they wash not their hands when they eat bread. But he answered and said unto them, Why do ye also transgress the commandment of God by
4 your tradition? For God commanded, saying, *d*Honour thy father and mother: and, *e*He that curseth father or mother, let him die the death.
5 But ye say, Whosoever shall say to *his* father or *his* mother, *f It is* a gift,
6 by whatsoever thou mightest be profited by me; and honour not his father or his mother, *he shall be free.* Thus have ye made the com-
7 mandment of God of none effect by your tradition. Ye *g*hypocrites,
8 well did Esaias prophesy of you, saying, This *h*people draweth nigh unto me with their mouth, and honoureth me with *their* lips; but their heart
9 is far from me. But in vain they do worship me, *i*teaching *for* doctrines the commandments of men.
10 And *j*he called the multitude, and said unto them, Hear, and under-
11 stand: not *k*that which goeth into the mouth defileth a man; but that which cometh out of the mouth, this defileth a man.
12 Then came his disciples, and said unto him, Knowest thou that the
13 Pharisees were offended, after they heard this saying? But he answered and said, *l*Every plant, which my heavenly Father hath not planted,

A. D. 32
d Ex. 20. 12.
Lev. 19. 3.
Deut. 5. 16.
Pro. 23. 22.
e Ex. 21. 17.
Lev. 20. 9.
Deut. 27.16.
Pro. 20. 20.
Pro. 30. 17.
f Mark 7. 11.
g Mark 7. 6.
h Isa. 29. 13.
Ezek. 33 31.
i Isa. 29. 13.
Col. 2. 18.
Titus 1. 14.
j Mark 7. 14.
k Acts 10. 15.
Rom. 14.14.
1 Tim. 4. 4.
Titus 1. 15.
l John 15. 2.
1 Cor. 3. 12.

kinson remark, after their subjection to the Romans, were especially exposed to intercourse and contact with heathens —"except they wash, they eat not. And many other things there be, which they have received to hold, as the washing of cups and pots, brazen vessels and tables" [κλινῶν]— rather 'couches,' such as were used at meals, which probably were merely *sprinkled* for ceremonial purposes. "Then the Pharisees and scribes asked Him," **saying, 2. Why do thy disciples transgress the tradition of the elders? for they wash not their hands when they eat bread. 3. But he answered and said unto them, Why do ye also transgress the commandment of God by your tradition?** The charge is retorted with startling power: 'The tradition they transgress is but *man's*, and is itself the occasion of heavy transgression, undermining the authority of *God's law.*' **4. For God commanded, saying** (Exod. xx. 12; &c.), **Honour thy father and mother: and** (Exod. xxi. 17; &c.), **He that curseth father or mother, let him die the death. 5. But ye say, Whosoever shall say to his father or his mother, It is a gift** [Δῶρου]—or simply, 'A gift!' In Mark it is, "Corban!" [קָרְבָּן]—that is, 'An oblation!' meaning, any unbloody offering or gift dedicated to sacred uses. **by whatsoever thou mightest be profited by me; 6. And honour not his father or his mother, [he shall be free]**—*q. d.*, 'It is true, father—mother—that by giving to thee this, which I now present, thou mightest be profited by me; but I have gifted it to pious uses, and therefore, at whatever cost to thee, I am not now at liberty to alienate any portion of it.' "And," it is added in Mark, "ye suffer him no more to do aught for his father or his mother." To dedicate property to God is indeed lawful and laudable, but not at the expense of filial duty. **Thus have ye made the commandment of God of none effect** [ἠκυρώσατε]—'cancelled' or 'nullified' it—**by your tradition. 7. Ye hypocrites, well did Esaias prophesy of you, saying** (Isa. xxix. 13), **8. This people draweth nigh unto me with their mouth, and honoureth me with their lips; but their heart is far from me. 9. But in vain they do worship me, teaching for doctrines the commandments of men.** By putting the commandments of men on a level with the divine requirements, *their whole worship was rendered vain*—a principle of deep moment in the service of God. "For," it is added in Mark vii. 8, "laying aside the commandment of God, ye hold the tradition of men, as the washing of pots and cups; and many other such like things ye do." [*Tregelles* brackets all the words after "men" in this verse as of doubtful authority; but we see no ground for this: *Tischendorf* inserts the whole as in the received text.] The drivelling nature of their multitudinous observances is here pointedly exposed, in contrast with the manly observance of "the commandment of God;" and when our Lord says, "Many other such like things ye do," it is implied that He had but given a specimen of the hideous treatment which the divine law received, and the grasping disposition which, under the mask of piety, was manifested by the ecclesiastics of that day. **10. And he called the multitude, and said unto them.** The foregoing dialogue, though in the people's hearing, was between Jesus and the pharisaic cavillers, whose object was to disparage Him with the people. But Jesus, having put them down, turns to the multitude, who at this time were prepared to drink in everything He said, and with admirable plainness, strength, and brevity lays down the great principle of real pollution, by which a world of bondage and uneasiness of conscience would be dissipated in a moment, and the sense of sin be reserved for deviations from the holy and eternal law of God. Hear and understand: **11. Not that which goeth into the mouth defileth a man; but that which cometh out of the mouth, this defileth a man.** This is expressed even more emphatically in Mark (vii. 15, 16), and it is there added, "If any man have ears to hear, let him hear." [*Tregelles* brackets this little verse here, as wanting in some good MSS.; but *Tischendorf*, we think rightly, gives it as in the received text.] As in ch. xiii. 9, this so oft-repeated saying seems designed to call attention to the *fundamental* and *universal* character of the truth it refers to. **12. Then came his disciples, and said unto him, Knowest thou that the Pharisees were offended, after they heard this saying?** They had given vent to their irritation, and perhaps threats, not to our Lord Himself, from whom they seem to have slunk away, but to some of the disciples, who report it to their Master. **13. But he answered and said, Every plant, which my heavenly Father hath not planted, shall be rooted up.** 'They are offended, are they? Heed it not: their corrupt teaching is already doomed; the Garden of the Lord upon earth, too

14 shall be rooted up. Let ^mthem alone: ⁿthey be blind leaders of the
blind. And if the blind lead the blind, both shall fall into the
15 ditch. Then ^oanswered Peter and said unto him, Declare unto us this
16 parable. And Jesus said, ^pAre ye also yet without understanding?
17 Do not ye yet understand, that ^qwhatsoever entereth in at the mouth
18 goeth into the belly, and is cast out into the draught? But ^rthose
things which proceed out of the mouth come forth from the heart; and
19 they defile the man. For ^sout of the heart proceed evil thoughts,
20 murders, adulteries, fornications, thefts, false witness, blasphemies: these
are *the things* which defile a man: but to eat with unwashen hands
defileth not a man.
21   Then Jesus went thence, and departed into the coasts of Tyre and
22 Sidon. And, behold, a woman of Canaan came out of the same coasts,
and cried unto him, saying, Have mercy on me, O Lord, *thou* son of
23 David; my daughter is grievously vexed with a devil. But he answered

A. D. 32.
^m Hos. 4. 14, 17.
ⁿ Isa. 9. 16.
Mal. 2. 8.
ch. 23. 16.
Luke 6. 39.
^o Mark 7. 17.
^p ch. 16. 9.
Mark 7. 18.
^q 1 Cor. 6. 13.
^r Pro. 6. 12.
ch. 12. 34.
Jas. 3. 6.
^s Gen. 6. 5.
Gen. 8. 21.
Pro. 6. 14.
Jer. 17. 9.
Mark 7. 21.

long cumbered with their presence, shall yet be purged of them and their accursed system; yea, and whatsoever is not of the planting of My heavenly Father, the great Husbandman (John xv. 1), shall share the same fate.' **14. Let them alone: they be blind leaders of the blind. And if the blind lead the blind, both shall fall into the ditch.** Striking expression of the ruinous effects of erroneous teaching! **15. Then answered Peter and said unto him**—"when He was entered into the house from the people," says Mark—**Declare unto us this parable. 16. And Jesus said, Are ye also yet without understanding?** Slowness of spiritual apprehension in His genuine disciples grieves the Saviour: from others He expects no better (ch. xiii. 11). **17, 18. Do not ye yet understand, that whatsoever entereth in at the mouth, &c.** Familiar though these sayings have now become, what freedom from bondage to outward things do they proclaim, on the one hand, and on the other, how searching is the truth which they express—that nothing which enters from without can really defile us; and that only the evil that is in the heart, that is allowed to stir there, to rise up in thought and affection, and to flow forth in voluntary action, really defiles a man! **19. For out of the heart proceed evil thoughts** [διαλογισμοὶ πονηροὶ]—'evil reasonings;' referring here more immediately to those corrupt reasonings which had stealthily introduced and gradually reared up that hideous fabric of tradition which at length practically nullified the unchangeable principles of the moral law. But the statement is far broader than this, namely, that the first shape which the evil that is in the heart takes, when it begins actively to stir, is that of 'considerations' or 'reasonings' on certain suggested actions. **murders, adulteries, fornications, thefts, false witness, blasphemies** [βλασφημίαι]—'detractions,' whether directed against God or man: here the reference seems to be to the latter. Mark adds, "covetousnesses" [πλεονεξίαι]—or desires after more; "wickednesses"[πονηρίαι]—here meaning, perhaps, 'malignities' of various form; "deceit, lasciviousness" [ἀσέλγεια]—meaning, 'excess' or 'enormity' of any kind, though by later writers restricted to lewdness; "an evil eye"—meaning, all looks or glances of envy, jealousy, or ill-will towards a neighbour; "pride, foolishness" [ἀφροσύνη]—in the Old Testament sense of "folly;" that is, criminal senselessness, the folly of the *heart.* How appalling is this black catalogue! **20. These are the things which defile a man: but to eat with unwashen hands defileth not a man.** Thus does our Lord sum up this whole searching Discourse.

Remarks.—1. There is a *principle* at the bottom of such traditional practices as are here exposed, without the knowledge of which we cannot rightly improve the teaching of our Lord on the subject. Be it observed, then, that the practices here referred to, though based only on "the tradition of the elders," might seem, even to conscientious Israelites, in the highest degree laudable. It was a ceremonial economy they lived under; and as one principal design of this economy was to *teach the difference between clean and unclean by external symbols*, it was natural to think that *the more vividly and variously* they could bring this before their own minds, the more would they be falling in with the spirit and following out the design of that economy. Such are the plausibilities by which most of the symbolical features of the Romish ritual are defended. Nor is it merely as acts of will-worship, without divine warrant, that they are to be condemned, but as tending to *weaken the sense of divine authority for what* is *commanded by mixing it up with what is purely human*, though originally introduced with the best intentions. Examples of this deep principle will readily occur —such as the effect, everywhere seen, of observing a multitude of saints' days in weakening the sense of the paramount claims of "the Lord's Day." 2. When we read here of the detestable pretexts under which those Jewish ecclesiastics suffered no more their deluded followers, when once they had them committed to some rash pledge, "to do aught for their father or mother," who can help thinking of the clergy of the Church of Rome, who have served themselves heirs to the worst features of Rabbinical Judaism? 3. If it be true that to multiply human devices for strengthening the force of religious principles in the life tends to draw the attention so far off from the divine law enjoining duty, and to rivet it upon the human device for securing obedience to it, may it not be worthy of the consideration of Christians whether, when sin is committed in spite of these devices, the breach of their own pledges is not apt to trouble them more than that of the divine law, which they were designed to fortify? But we would not press this too far; and there certainly are cases where evil habits, when inveterate, require restraints which in other cases are superfluous. It is to the former only that we refer. 4. If nothing outward can *defile*, it is obvious that nothing purely outward can *sanctify*—as the Church of Rome teaches that *Sacraments*, for example, do of themselves ['*ex opere operato*']. "God is a Spirit, and they that worship Him must worship Him in spirit and in truth."

21-23.—THE WOMAN OF CANAAN AND HER

her not a word. And his disciples came and besought him, saying, Send

24 her away; for she crieth after us. But he answered and said, [t]I am not

25 sent but unto the lost sheep of the house of Israel. Then came she and

26 worshipped him, saying, Lord, help me! But he answered and said, It

27 is not meet to take the children's bread, and to cast it to [u]dogs. And she said, Truth, Lord: yet the dogs eat of the crumbs which fall from

28 their master's table. Then Jesus answered and said unto her, O woman, great is thy faith: be it unto thee even as thou wilt. And her daughter was made whole from that very hour.

29 And [v]Jesus departed from thence, and came nigh [w]unto the sea of

30 Galilee; and went up into a mountain, and sat down there. And [x]great multitudes came unto him, having with them those that were lame, blind, dumb, maimed, and many others, and cast them down at Jesus'

31 feet; and he healed them: insomuch that the multitude wondered, when they saw the dumb to speak, the maimed to be whole, the lame to walk, and the blind to see: and they glorified the God of Israel.

32 Then [y]Jesus called his disciples unto him, and said, I [z]have compassion on the multitude, because they continue with me now three days, and have nothing to eat: and I will not send them away fasting, lest they

33 faint in the way. And [a]his disciples say unto him, Whence should we have so much bread in the wilderness as to fill so great a multitude?

34 And Jesus saith unto them, How many loaves have ye? And they said,

35 Seven, and a few little fishes. And he commanded the multitude to sit

36 down on the ground. And [b]he took the seven loaves and the fishes, and [c]gave thanks, and brake them, and gave to his disciples, and the disciples

37 to the multitude. And they did all eat, and were filled: and they took

38 up of the broken meat that was left seven baskets full. And they that did eat were four thousand men, besides women and children.

39 And [d]he sent away the multitude, and took ship, and came into the coasts of Magdala.

16 THE [a]Pharisees also with the Sadducees came, and tempting desired

2 him that he would show them a sign from heaven. He answered and said unto them, When it is evening, ye say, It will be fair weather; for

3 the sky is red: and in the morning, It will be foul weather to-day; for the sky is red and lowring. O ye hypocrites, ye can discern the face of

4 the sky; but can ye not discern the [b]signs of the times? A [c]wicked and adulterous generation seeketh after a sign; and there shall no sign be given unto it, but the sign of the prophet Jonas. And he left them, and departed.

5 And [d]when his disciples were come to the other side, they had for-

6 gotten to take bread. Then Jesus said unto them, [e]Take heed and

7 beware of the leaven of the Pharisees and of the Sadducees. And they reasoned among themselves, saying, It is because we have taken

8 no bread. Which when Jesus perceived, he said unto them, O ye of little faith, why reason ye among yourselves, because ye have brought

9 no bread? Do [f]ye not yet understand, neither remember the five loaves

10 of the five thousand, and how many baskets ye took up? Neither [g]the seven loaves of the four thousand, and how many baskets ye took up?

11 How is it that ye do not understand that I spake it not to you concerning bread, that ye should beware of the leaven of the Pharisees and of the

12 Sadducees? Then understood they how that he bade them not beware

---

A. D. 31.

[t] Isa. 53. 6.
ch. 10. 5, 6.
Acts 3. 25, 26.
Acts 13. 46.
Rom. 15. 8.
[u] ch. 7. 6.
Eph. 2. 12.
Phil. 3. 2.
[v] Mark 7. 31
[w] ch. 4. 18
John 6.1,23.
Mark 1. 16.
[x] Isa. 35. 5, 6.
ch. 11. 5.
Luke 7. 22.
[y] Mark 8. 1.
[z] Ps. 86. 15.
Ps. 103. 13.
Ps. 111. 4.
Mark 1. 41.
Heb. 2. 17.
Heb. 4. 15.
Heb. 5. 2.
[a] Num.11.21, 22.
2 Ki. 4. 43.
[b] ch. 14. 19.
[c] Deut. 8. 10.
1 Sam. 9.13.
Ps. 104. 28.
Luke 22.19.
[d] Mark 8. 10.

CHAP. 16.
[a] ch. 12. 38.
Mark 8. 11.
Luke 11. 16.
Luke 12. 54-56.
1 Cor. 1. 22.
[b] Gen. 49. 10.
Isa. 7. 14.
Isa. 11. 1.
Isa. 42. 1.
Ezek. 21.27.
Dan. 9. 24.
Mic. 5. 2.
Hag. 2. 7.
Mal. 3. 1.
[c] ch. 12. 39.
[d] ch. 15. 39.
Mark 8. 14.
[e] ch. 7. 15.
ch. 24. 4.
Luke 12. 1.
Rom. 16.17, 18.
Eph. 5. 6.
Col. 2. 8.
Phil. 3. 2.
2 Pet. 3. 17.
[f] ch. 14. 17.
ch. 15.16,17.
John 6. 9.
Rev. 2. 23.
[g] ch. 15. 34.

DAUGHTER. For the exposition, see on Mark vii. 24-30.

29-39.—MIRACLES OF HEALING—FOUR THOUSAND MIRACULOUSLY FED. For the exposition, see on Mark vii. 31—viii. 10.

CHAP. XVI. 1-12.—A SIGN FROM HEAVEN

SOUGHT AND REFUSED—CAUTION AGAINST THE LEAVEN OF THE PHARISEES AND SADDUCEES. For the exposition, see on Mark viii. 11-21.

13-28.—PETER'S NOBLE CONFESSION OF CHRIST, AND THE BENEDICTION PRONOUNCED UPON HIM—CHRIST'S FIRST EXPLICIT ANNOUNCEMENT OF HIS

of the leaven of bread, but of the doctrine of the Pharisees and of the Sadducees.

13 When Jesus came into the coasts of Cesarea Philippi, he asked his
14 disciples, saying, *h*Whom do men say that I the Son of man am? And they said, *i*Some *say that thou art* John the Baptist; some, *j*Elias; and
15 others, Jeremias, or one of the prophets. He saith unto them, But
16 whom say ye that I am? And Simon Peter answered and said, Thou
17 *k*art the Christ, the Son of the living God. And Jesus answered and said unto him, Blessed art thou, Simon Bar-jona: *l*for flesh and blood hath

A. D. 32.

h Dan. 7. 13.
Mark 8. 27.
Luke 9. 18.
i ch. 14. 2.
Luke 9. 7,8,
9.
j Mal. 4. 5.
k Ps. 2. 7.
ch. 14. 33.
l Eph. 2. 8.

APPROACHING SUFFERINGS, DEATH, AND RESURRECTION—HIS REBUKE OF PETER AND WARNING TO ALL THE TWELVE. (= Mark viii. 27; ix. 1; Luke ix. 18-27.) The time of this Section—which is beyond doubt, and will presently be mentioned —is of immense importance, and throws a touching interest around the incidents which it records. *Peter's Confession and the Benediction pronounced upon him* (13-20). **13. When Jesus came into the coasts** [τὰ μέρη]—'the parts;' that is, the territory or region: in Mark (viii. 27) it is "the towns" or 'villages' [κώμας]. **of Cesarea Philippi.** It lay at the foot of mount Lebanon, near the sources of the Jordan, in the territory of Dan, and at the north-east extremity of Palestine. It was originally called *Panium* (from a cavern in its neighbourhood dedicated to the god *Pan*) and *Paneas.* Philip, the tetrarch, the only good son of Herod the Great, in whose dominions Paneas lay, having beautified and enlarged it, changed its name to *Cesarea*, in honour of the Roman emperor, and added *Philippi* after his own name, to distinguish it from the other Cesarea (Acts x. 1) on the north-east coast of the Mediterranean sea. (*Joseph.* Antt. xv. 10, 3; xviii. 2, 1.) This quiet and distant retreat Jesus appears to have sought, with the view of talking over with the Twelve the fruit of His past labours, and breaking to them for the first time the sad intelligence of His approaching death. **he asked his disciples**—"by the way," says Mark (viii. 27), and "as He was alone praying," says Luke (ix. 18)—**saying, Whom**—or more grammatically, "Who" **do men say that I the Son of man am?** [or, 'that the Son of man is'—recent editors omitting here the με of Mark and Luke; though the evidence seems pretty nearly balanced]—*q. d.*, 'What are the views generally entertained of Me, the Son of man, after going up and down among them so long?' He had now closed the first great stage of His ministry, and was just entering on the last dark one. His spirit, burdened, sought relief in retirement, not only from the multitude, but even for a season from the Twelve. He retreated into "the secret place of the Most High," pouring out His soul "in supplications and prayers, with strong crying and tears" (Heb. v. 7). On rejoining His disciples, and as they were pursuing their quiet journey, He asked them this question. **14. And they said, Some say that thou art John the Baptist**—risen from the dead. So that Herod Antipas was not singular in his surmise (ch. xiv. 1, 2). **some, Elias** —cf. Mark vi. 15. **and others, Jeremias.** Was this theory suggested by a supposed resemblance between the "Man of Sorrows" and 'the weeping prophet?' **or one of the prophets**—or, as Luke (ix. 8) expresses it, "that one of the old prophets is risen again." In another report of the popular opinions which Mark (vi. 15) gives us, it is thus expressed, "That it is a prophet, [or] as one of the prophets" [the word "or"—ἤ—is wanting in authority]:—in other words, That he was a prophetical person, resembling those of old. **15. He saith**

unto them, **But whom**—rather, "Who" **say ye that I am?** He had never put this question before, but the crisis He was reaching made it fitting that He should now have it from them. We may suppose this to be one of those moments of which the prophet says, in His name, "Then I said, I have laboured in vain; I have spent my strength for nought, and in vain" (Isa. xlix. 4): Lo, these three years I come seeking fruit on this fig tree; and what is it? As the result of all, I am taken for John the Baptist, for Elias, for Jeremias, for one of the prophets. Yet some there are that have beheld My glory, the glory as of the Only begotten of the Father, and I shall hear their voice, for it is sweet. **16. And Simon Peter answered and said, Thou art the Christ, the Son of the living God.** He does not say, 'Scribes and Pharisees, rulers and people, are all perplexed; and shall we, unlettered fishermen, presume to decide?' But feeling the light of his Master's glory shining in his soul, he breaks forth—not in a tame, prosaic acknowledgment, '*I believe that thou art*,' &c.—but in the language of adoration—such as one uses in worship, "THOU ART THE CHRIST, THE SON OF THE LIVING GOD!" He first owns Him the promised *Messiah* (see on ch. i. 16); then he rises higher, echoing the voice from heaven— "This is my beloved Son, in whom I am well pleased;" and in the important addition— "Son of the LIVING GOD,"—he recognizes the essential and eternal life of God as in this His Son —though doubtless without that distinct perception afterwards vouchsafed. **17. And Jesus answered and said unto him, Blessed art thou.** Though it is not to be doubted that Peter, in this noble testimony to Christ, only expressed the conviction of all the Twelve, yet since he alone seems to have had clear enough apprehensions to put that conviction in proper and suitable words, and courage enough to speak them out, and readiness enough to do this at the right time—so he only, of all the Twelve, seems to have met the present want, and communicated to the saddened soul of the Redeemer at the critical moment that balm which was needed to cheer and refresh it. Nor is Jesus above giving indication of the deep satisfaction which this speech yielded Him, and hastening to respond to it by a signal acknowledgment of Peter in return. **Simon Bar-jona** [בַּר יוֹנָה] —or, 'son of Jona' (John i. 42) or Jonas (John xxi. 15). This name, denoting his humble fleshly extraction, seems to have been purposely here mentioned, to contrast the more vividly with the spiritual elevation to which divine illumination had raised him. **for flesh and blood hath not revealed it unto thee**—'This is not the fruit of human teaching.' **but my Father which is in heaven.** In speaking of God, Jesus, it is to be observed, never calls Him, "Our Father" (see on John xx. 17), but either '*your* Father'—when He would encourage His timid believing ones with the assurance that He was theirs, and teach themselves to call Him so—or, as here, "My Father," to signify some peculiar action or aspect

18 not revealed *it* unto thee, but [m]my Father which is in heaven. And I
say also unto thee, That [n]thou art Peter, and [o]upon this rock I will
build my church; and [p]the gates of hell shall not prevail against it.
19 And [q]I will give unto thee the keys of the kingdom of heaven: and
whatsoever thou shalt bind on earth shall be bound in heaven; and
20 whatsoever thou shalt loose on earth shall be loosed in heaven. Then
charged he his disciples that they should tell no man that he was Jesus
the Christ.
21 From that time forth began Jesus to show unto his disciples, how that
he must go unto Jerusalem, and suffer many things of the elders and
chief priests and scribes, and be killed, and be raised again the third day.
22 Then Peter took him, and began to rebuke him, saying, [1]Be it far from
23 thee, Lord: this shall not be unto thee. But he turned, and said unto
Peter, Get thee behind me, Satan: [r]thou art an offence unto me; for
thou savourest not the things that be of God, but those that be of men.

A. D. 32.

[m] 1 Cor. 2. 10. Gal. 1. 16.
[n] John 1. 42.
[o] Isa. 28. 16. 1 Cor. 3. 11. Eph. 2. 20. Rev. 21. 14.
[p] Isa. 54. 17.
[q] John 20. 23.
[1] Pity thyself.
[r] Gen. 3. 1-6, 17. ch. 4. 10. Mark 8. 33. Luke 4. 8. Rom. 8. 7. 2 Cor. 11. 14, 15.

of Him as "the God and Father of our Lord Jesus Christ." **18. And I say also unto thee** [Κἀγὼ δὲ σοὶ λέγω]:—*q. d.*, 'As thou hast borne such testimony to Me, even so in return do I to thee;' **That thou art Peter.** At his first calling, this new name was announced to him as an honour *afterwards* to be conferred on him (John i. 43). Now he gets it, with an explanation of what it was meant to convey. **and upon this rock.** As "Peter" and "Rock" are one word in the dialect familiarly spoken by our Lord—the Aramaic or Syro-Chaldaic, which was the mother tongue of the country—this exalted *play upon the word* [כֵּיפָא] Κηφᾶς, John i. 43] can be fully seen only in languages which have one word for both. Even in the Greek it is imperfectly represented [σὺ εἶ Πέτρος, καὶ ἐπὶ ταύτῃ τῇ πέτρᾳ]. In French, as *Webster and Wilkinson* remark, it is perfect, *Pierre—pierre.* **I will build my church**—not on the man Simon Bar-jona; but on him as the heaven-taught Confessor of such a faith. "My Church," says our Lord, calling the Church HIS OWN; a magnificent expression, remarks *Bengel*, regarding Himself—nowhere else occurring in the Gospels. See on ch. xiii. 24-30, 36-43, Remark 3. **and the gates of hell** [ᾅδου]—'of Hades,' or, the unseen world; meaning, the gates of Death: in other words, 'It shall never perish.' Some explain it of 'the assaults of the powers of darkness;' but though that expresses a glorious truth, probably the former is the sense here. **19. And I will give unto thee the keys of the kingdom of heaven**—the kingdom of God about to be set up on earth—**and whatsoever thou shalt bind on earth shall be bound in heaven; and whatsoever thou shalt loose on earth shall be loosed in heaven.** Whatever this mean, it was soon expressly *extended to all the apostles* (ch. xviii. 18); so that the claim of supreme authority in the Church, made for Peter by the Church of Rome, and then arrogated to themselves by the Popes as the legitimate successors of St. Peter, is baseless and impudent. As first in confessing Christ, Peter got this commission before the rest; and with these "keys," on the day of Pentecost, he first "opened the door of faith" to the *Jews*, and then, in the person of Cornelius, he was honoured to do the same to the *Gentiles.* Hence, in the lists of the apostles, Peter is always first named. See on ch. xviii. 18. One thing is clear, that not in all the New Testament is there the vestige of any authority either claimed or exercised by Peter, or conceded to him, above the rest of the apostles—a thing conclusive against the Romish claims in behalf of that apostle. See on ch. x. 1-5, Remark 8. **20. Then charged he his disciples that they should tell no man that he was Jesus the Christ.** Now that He had been so explicit, they might naturally think the time come for giving it out openly; but here they are told it had not.

Announcement of His approaching Death, and Rebuke of Peter (21-28). The occasion here is evidently the same. **21. From that time forth began Jesus to show unto his disciples**—that is, with an *explicitness and frequency* He had never observed before, **how that he must go unto Jerusalem, and suffer many things** ("and be rejected," Matt. and Mark) **of the elders and chief priests and scribes**—not as before, merely by not receiving Him, but by formal deeds—**and be killed, and be raised again the third day.** Mark (viii. 32) adds, that "He spake that saying openly" [παῤῥησίᾳ]—'explicitly,' or 'without disguise.' **22. Then Peter took him** [aside], apart from the rest; presuming on the distinction just conferred on him; showing how *unexpected* and *distasteful* to them all was the announcement. **and began to rebuke him**—affectionately, yet with a certain generous indignation, to chide him. **saying, Be it far from thee, Lord: this shall not be unto thee**—*i. e.*, 'If I can help it;' the same spirit that prompted him in the garden to draw the sword in His behalf (John xviii. 10). **23. But he turned, and said**—in the hearing of the rest; for Mark (viii. 33) expressly says, "When He had turned about and looked on His disciples, He rebuked Peter;" perceiving that he had but boldly uttered what others felt, and that the check was needed by them also. **Get thee behind me, Satan**—the same words as He had addressed to the Tempter (Luke iv. 8); for He felt in it a Satanic lure, a whisper from hell, to move Him from His purpose to suffer. So He shook off the Serpent, then coiling around Him, and "felt no harm" (Acts xxviii. 5). How quickly has the "rock" turned to a devil! The fruit of divine teaching the Lord delighted to honour in Peter; but the mouthpiece of hell, which he had in a moment of forgetfulness become, the Lord shook off with horror. **thou art an offence** [σκάνδαλον]—'a stumbling-block' **unto me:** 'Thou playest the Tempter, casting a stumbling-block in my way to the Cross. Could it succeed, where wert thou? and how should the Serpent's head be bruised?' **for thou savourest not** [οὐ φρονεῖς]—'thou thinkest not'—**the things that be of God, but those that be of men.** 'Thou art carried away by human views of the way of setting up Messiah's kingdom, quite contrary to those of God.' This was kindly said, not to take off the sharp edge of the

24 Then *said Jesus unto his disciples, If any *man* will come after me, let
25 him deny himself, and take up his cross, and follow me. For whosoever
will save his life shall lose it: and whosoever will lose his life for my
26 sake shall find it. For what is a man profited, if he shall gain the
whole world, and lose his own soul? or 'what shall a man give in
27 exchange for his soul? For the Son of man shall come in the glory of
his Father "with his angels; *and then he shall reward every man
28 according to his works. Verily I say unto you, There be some standing
here which shall not taste of death, till they see the Son of man coming
in his "kingdom.

A. D. 32.	
* Acts 14. 22.	
1 Thes. 3. 3.	
2 Tim. 3. 12.	
t Ps. 49. 7, 8.	
" Dan. 7. 10.	
Zech. 14. 5.	
Jude 14.	
* Jer. 17. 10.	
Rom. 2. 6.	
2 Cor. 5. 10.	
1 Pet. 1. 17.	
" Mark 9. 1.	

rebuke, but to explain and justify it, as it was evident Peter knew not what was in the bosom of his rash speech. **24. Then said Jesus unto his disciples.** Mark (viii. 34) says, "When He had called the people unto Him, with His disciples also, He said unto them"—turning the rebuke of one into a warning to all. **If any man will come after me, let him deny himself, and take up his cross, and follow me. 25. For whosoever will save** [θέλη σῶσαι]—'is minded to save,' or bent on saving, **his life shall lose it: and whosoever will lose his life for my sake shall find it.** See on ch. x. 38, 39. 'A suffering and dying Messiah liketh you ill; but what if His servants shall meet the same fate? They may not; but who follows Me must be prepared for the worst.' **26. For what is a man profited, if he shall gain the whole world, and lose** [ζημιωθῆ]—or 'forfeit' **his own soul? or what shall a man give in exchange for his soul?** Instead of these weighty words, which we find in Mark also, it is thus expressed in Luke: "If he gain the whole world, and lose himself, or be cast away" [ἑαυτὸν δὲ ἀπολέσας ἢ ζημιωθείς], or better, 'If he gain the whole world, and destroy or forfeit himself.' How awful is the stake as here set forth! If a man makes the present world—in its various forms of riches, honours, pleasures, and such like—the object of supreme pursuit, be it that he gains the world; yet along with it he forfeits his own soul. Not that any ever did, or ever will gain the whole world—a very small portion of it, indeed, falls to the lot of the most successful of the world's votaries—but to make the extravagant concession, that by giving himself entirely up to it, a man gains the whole world; yet, setting over against this gain the forfeiture of his soul—necessarily following the surrender of his whole heart to the world—what is he profited? But, if not the whole world, yet possibly something else may be conceived as an equivalent for the soul. Well, what is it?—"Or what shall a man give in exchange for his soul?" Thus, in language the weightiest, because the simplest, does our Lord shut up His hearers, and all who shall read these words to the end of the world, to the priceless value to every man of his own soul. In Mark and Luke the following words are added: "Whosoever therefore shall be ashamed of Me and of My words"—'shall be ashamed of belonging to Me, and ashamed of My Gospel,' "in this adulterous and sinful generation" (see on ch. xii. 39), "of him shall the Son of man be ashamed when He cometh in the glory of His Father, with the holy angels" (Mark viii. 38; Luke ix. 26). He will render back to that man his own treatment, disowning him before the most august of all assemblies, and putting him to "*shame* and everlasting *contempt*" (Dan. xii. 2). 'O shame,' exclaims *Bengel*, 'to be put to shame before God, Christ, and angels!' The sense of *shame* is founded on our love of *reputation*, which causes instinctive aversion to what is fitted to lower it, and was given us as a preserva-

tive from all that is properly *shameful*. To be lost *to shame*, is to be nearly past hope. (Zeph. iii. 5; Jer. vi. 15; iii. 3.) But when Christ and "His words" are unpopular, the same instinctive desire to *stand well with others* begets that temptation to be ashamed of Him which only the 'expulsive power' of a higher affection can effectually counteract. **27. For the Son of man shall come in the glory of his Father with his angels**—in the splendour of His Father's authority and with all His angelic ministers, ready to execute His pleasure; **and then he shall reward, &c. 28. Verily I say unto you, There be some standing here** [τινες τῶν ὧδε ἑστηκότων]—'some of those standing here,' **which shall not taste of death, till they see the Son of man coming in his kingdom**—or, as in Mark (ix. 1), "till they see the kingdom of God come with power;" or, as in Luke (ix. 27), more simply still, "till they see the kingdom of God." The reference, beyond doubt, is to the firm establishment and victorious progress, in the life-time of some then present, of that new Kingdom of Christ, which was destined to work the greatest of all changes on this earth, and be the grand pledge of His final coming in glory.

Remarks.—1. The distraction and indecision of the public mind on the great vital questions of Religion will be no excuse for the want of definite convictions on the part either of the educated or the illiterate on such momentous matters. On the contrary, it is just when such distraction and indecision are greatest that the Lord Jesus expects firm conviction and decision on the part of His true friends, and values it most. 2. The testimony here borne, in our Lord's commendation of Peter, to the reality of an inward divine teaching, distinct from the outward communication of divine truth, is very precious. For Peter had enjoyed the outward teaching of the Son of God Himself. But since many others had done this to no saving effect, the Lord expressly ascribes the difference between Peter and them to supernatural illumination. 3. When the Lord has any eminent work to do in His kingdom, He always finds the fitting instruments to do it; and yet, how different, usually, from those He might have been expected to select! Who would have thought that a humble Galilean fisherman would be chosen, and found qualified, to do what at that time was the highest work for Christ, to lay the foundations of the Church—opening the door of faith to the Jews first, and thereafter to the Gentiles? But this is God's way—to choose the foolish things of the world to confound the wise, and the weak things of the world to confound the mighty, and base things of the world, and things which are despised, yea, and things which are not, to bring to nought the things that are: that no flesh should glory in His presence (1 Cor. i. 27-29). 4. In the words of commendation and reward here addressed to Peter we have a striking example of the extremes to be avoided in the interpretation of

17 AND *after six days Jesus taketh Peter, James, and John his brother,
2 and bringeth them up into an high mountain apart, and was transfigured
before them; and his face did shine as the sun, and his raiment was
3 white as the light. And, behold, there appeared unto them Moses *b*and
4 Elias talking with him. Then answered Peter, and said unto Jesus,
Lord, it is good for us to be here: if thou wilt, let us make here three
5 tabernacles; one for thee, and one for Moses, and one for Elias. While
*c*he yet spake, behold, a bright cloud overshadowed them: and behold
a voice out of the cloud, which said, *d*This is my beloved Son, *e*in
6 whom I am well pleased; *f*hear ye him. And *g*when the disciples
7 heard *it*, they fell on their face, and were sore afraid. And Jesus came
8 and touched them, and said, Arise, and be not afraid. And when they
9 had lifted up their eyes, they saw no man, save Jesus only.
9 And as they came down from the mountain, Jesus charged them,
saying, Tell the vision to no man, until the Son of man be risen again
10 from the dead. And his disciples asked him, saying, Why *h*then say
11 the scribes that Elias must first come? And Jesus answered and said
12 unto them, Elias truly shall first come, and restore *i*all things. But *j*I
say unto you, That Elias is come already, and they knew him not, but
have *k*done unto him whatsoever they listed. Likewise shall also the
13 Son of man suffer of them. Then the disciples understood that he
spake unto them of John the Baptist.
14 And *l*when they were come to the multitude, there came to him a
15 *certain* man, kneeling down to him, and saying, Lord, have mercy on my

A. D. 32.
CHAP. 17.
a Mark 9. 2.
Luke 9. 28.
b Rom. 3. 21.
c 2 Pet. 1. 17.
d ch. 3. 17.
Mark 1. 11.
Luke 3. 22.
Luke 9. 35.
John 3. 16, 35.
John 5. 20.
e Isa. 42. 1.
f Deut. 18.15.
Acts 3. 22.
Heb. 12. 25.
g 2 Pet. 1. 18.
h Mal. 4. 5.
ch. 11. 14.
ch. 27. 47-49.
Mark 9. 11.
i John 1. 21, 25.
j Mal. 4. 6.
Luke 1. 16.
Acts 3. 21.
j Mark 9. 12.
k ch. 14. 3.
l Mark 9. 14.
Luke 9. 37.

Scripture. While Romanists and Romanizers build upon this a distinction in favour of Peter, in which none else, even of the Twelve, were destined to share, able Protestants have gone to the opposite extreme, of denying that our Lord, in speaking of "that rock on which He was to build His Church," had any reference to Peter at all; and take the rock to mean either the Speaker Himself, or at least the fundamental truth regarding Him which Peter had just uttered—that He was "the Christ, the Son of the living God." But as in that case the manifest play upon the word "rock," which the name of Peter was designed to express, would be lost, so we do not lose the truth for which these Protestant interpreters contend by admitting that Peter himself is intended in this announcement, provided it be understood that it was not as the man "Simon, son of Jonas," that anything was to be built upon Peter, but on Peter as the man of most distinguished faith in Jesus as the Christ, the Son of the living God. Thus, while the plain sense of the passage is preserved, the truth expressed is according to Scripture. 5. How hard is it even for eminent Christians to stand high commendation without forgetting themselves! (See on Luke xxii. 31, &c.; and see 2 Cor. xii. 7.) Peter, it is to be feared, must have been carried somewhat off his feet by the encomium pronounced upon him—even though his superiority was expressly ascribed to Grace—ere he could have been betrayed into the presumption of taking his Master to task. 6. How deeply instructive is the sharp distinction which Christ here draws between the things that be of God and those that be of men, and how severe the rebuke administered to Peter for judging of the one by the standard of the other! If the things of God be hid from "the wise and prudent" (see on ch. xi. 25), can we wonder that when God's own children make use of the world's wisdom and prudence to measure His ways, they should misjudge and run against them? And yet, so plausible is this worldly wisdom, that when, having fallen into un-

spiritual conceptions of the things of God, Christians throw stumbling-blocks before those servants of Christ who are more devoted than themselves, they fancy they are only checking a too fiery zeal, and arresting proceedings which are injudicious and hurtful; while our Lord here teaches us that they are but tools of Satan! 7. Let the example of Jesus, in not only resenting and repelling all such suggestions as tended to arrest His onward career, but even when they came from His most eminent disciple, tracing them with horror to their proper source in the dark Enemy of man's salvation, stand out before us as our perfect Model in all such cases. 8. In times of severe persecution, and in prospect of suffering in any shape for the sake of the Gospel, it will be our wisdom, and be found a tower of strength, calmly to weigh both issues—the gain and the loss of each course. And to be prepared for the worst, it will be well to put the best of the world's gain over against the worst of Christ's service. Put the gain of the whole world against only one loss—the loss of the soul—and the loss of everything in this world, friends, goods, liberty, life itself, against only one gain—the gain of the soul. Then let us ask ourselves, in the sight of conscience and God, and an eternity of bliss or woe, With which side lies the advantage? And to make the answer to this question the more certain and the more impressive, let us habitually summon up before us the scene here presented to us by Him who is to be Himself the Judge—the great assize, the parties at the bar, the open acknowledgment and acquittal of the one, the disavowal and condemnation of the other, and the eternal issues. So shall we feel ourselves driven out of the denial of that blessed Name, and shut up and shut in to Christ and the fearless confession of His truth and grace, come what may.
CHAP. XVII. 1-13.—JESUS IS TRANSFIGURED—CONVERSATION ABOUT ELIAS. (=Mark ix. 2-13; Luke ix. 28-36.) For the exposition, see on Luke ix. 28-36.
14-23.—HEALING OF A DEMONIAC BOY—SECOND

son: for he is lunatic, and sore vexed: for ofttimes he falleth into the
16 fire, and oft into the water. And I brought him to thy disciples, and
17 they could not cure him. Then Jesus answered and said, O faithless
and perverse generation, how long shall I be with you! how long shall I
18 suffer you! Bring him hither to me. And Jesus rebuked the devil;
and he departed out of him: and the child was cured from that very
19 hour. Then came the disciples to Jesus apart, and said, Why could
20 not we cast him out? And Jesus said unto them, Because of your
unbelief: for verily I say unto you, If ᵐye have faith as a grain of
mustard seed, ye shall say unto this mountain, Remove hence to yonder
place; and it shall remove; and nothing shall be impossible unto you.
21 Howbeit this kind goeth not out but by prayer and fasting.
22   And ⁿwhile they abode in Galilee, Jesus said unto them, The Son of
23 man shall be betrayed into the hands of men; and °they shall kill him,
and the third day he shall be raised again. And they were exceeding
sorry.
24   And when they were come to Capernaum, they that received ¹tribute
25 *money* came to Peter, and said, Doth not your master pay tribute? He
saith, Yes. And when he was come into the house, Jesus prevented
him, saying, What thinkest thou, Simon? of whom do the kings of the
earth take custom or tribute? of their own children, or of strangers?

A. D. 32.	
ᵐ ch. 21. 21.	
Mark 11.23.	
Luke 17. 6.	
1 Cor. 12. 9.	
1 Cor. 13. 2.	
ⁿ ch. 16. 21.	
ch. 20. 17.	
Mark 8. 31.	
Mark 9. 30, 31.	
Mark 10.33.	
Luke 9. 22.	
Luke 18. 31.	
Luke 24. 6, 7.	
° Ps. 22.15,22.	
Isa. 53. 7,10-12.	
Dan. 9. 26.	
Mark 9. 33.	
1 Cor.15.3,4.	
¹ didrachma, in value fifteenpence.	
Ex. 30. 13.	
Ex. 38. 26.	

EXPLICIT ANNOUNCEMENT BY OUR LORD OF HIS APPROACHING DEATH AND RESURRECTION. (= Mark ix. 14-32; Luke ix. 37-45.) The time of this Section is sufficiently denoted by the events which all the narratives show to have immediately preceded it—the first explicit announcement of His death, and the transfiguration—both being between his third and his fourth and last Passover,

Healing of the Demoniac and Lunatic Boy (14-21). For the exposition of this portion, see on Mark ix. 14-32.

Second Announcement of His Death (22, 23). **22. And while they abode in Galilee, Jesus said unto them.** Mark (ix. 30), as usual, is very precise here: "And they departed thence"—that is, from the scene of the last miracle—"and passed through Galilee; and He would not that any man should know it." So this was not a preaching, but a private, journey through Galilee. Indeed, His public ministry in Galilee was now all but concluded. Though He sent out the Seventy after this to preach and heal, Himself was little more in public there, and He was soon to bid it a final adieu. Till this hour arrived He was chiefly occupied with the Twelve, preparing them for the coming events. **The Son of man shall be betrayed into the hands of men; 23. And they shall kill him, and the third day he shall be raised again. And they were exceeding sorry.** Though the shock would not be so great as at the first announcement (ch. xvi. 21, 22), their "sorrow" would not be the less, but probably the greater, the deeper the intelligence went down into their hearts, and a new wave dashing upon them by this repetition of the heavy tidings. Accordingly, Luke (ix. 43, 44), connecting it with the scene of the miracle just recorded, and the teaching which arose out of it—or possibly with all His recent teaching—says our Lord forewarned the Twelve that they would soon stand in need of all that teaching: "But while they wondered every one at all things which Jesus did, He said unto His disciples, Let these sayings sink down into your ears; for the Son of Man shall be delivered, &c.:" 'Be not carried off your feet by the grandeur you have lately seen in Me, but

remember what I have told you, and now tell you again, that that Sun in whose beams ye now rejoice is soon to set in midnight gloom.' Remarkable is the antithesis in those words of our Lord, preserved in all the three Narratives—"The Son of *man* shall be betrayed into the hands of *men*." He adds (*v.* 45) that "they understood not this saying, and it was hid from them, that they perceived it not"—for the plainest statements, when they encounter long-continued and obstinate prejudices, are seen through a distorting and dulling medium—"and were afraid to ask Him;" deterred partly by the air of lofty sadness with which doubtless these sayings were uttered, and on which they would be reluctant to break in, and partly by the fear of laying themselves open to rebuke for their shallowness and timidity. How artless is all this!

For Remarks on this Section, see on Mark ix. 14-32, at the close of that Section.

24-27.—THE TRIBUTE MONEY.
The time of this Section is evidently in immediate succession to that of the preceding one. The brief but most pregnant incident which it records is given by our Evangelist alone—for whom, no doubt, it would have a peculiar interest, from its relation to his own town and his own familiar lake. **24. And when they were come to Capernaum, they that received tribute money** [τὰ δίδραχμα]—'the double drachma;' a sum equal to two Attic drachmas, and corresponding to the Jewish "half-shekel," payable, towards the maintenance of the Temple and its services, by every male Jew of twenty years old and upwards. For the origin of this annual tax, see Exod. xxx. 13, 14; 2 Chr. xxiv. 6, 9. Thus, it will be observed, it was not a civil, but *an ecclesiastical tax.* The tax mentioned in the next verse was a civil one. The whole teaching of this very remarkable scene depends upon this distinction. **came to Peter**—at whose house Jesus probably resided while at Capernaum. This explains several things in the narrative. **and said, Doth not your master pay tribute?** The question seems to imply that the payment of this tax was *voluntary*, but *expected;* or what, in modern phrase, would be called a 'voluntary assessment.' **25. He**

26 Peter saith unto him, Of strangers. Jesus saith unto him, Then are the
27 children free. Notwithstanding, lest we **should offend them, go thou
to the sea, and cast an hook, and take up the fish that first cometh
up; and when thou hast opened his mouth, thou shalt find ²a piece
of money: that take, and give unto them for me and thee.

18 AT *^a*the same time came the disciples unto Jesus, saying, Who is
2 the greatest in the kingdom of heaven? And Jesus called a little child
3 unto him, and set him in the midst of them, and said, Verily I say
unto you, *^b*Except ye be converted, and become as little children, ye
4 shall not enter into the kingdom of heaven. Whosoever *^c*therefore shall
humble himself as this little child, the same is greatest in the kingdom
5 of heaven. And *^d*whoso shall receive one such little child in my name
6 receiveth me. But whoso shall offend one of these little ones which
believe in me, it were better for him that a millstone were hanged about
his neck, and *that* he were drowned in the depth of the sea.
7 Woe unto the world because of offences! for *^e*it must needs be that

A. D. 32.

p Mark 12. 17.
1 Cor. 10. 32.
2 Or, a
stater. It
is in value
2s. 6d. after
5s. the
ounce.

CHAP. 18.
a Mark 9. 33.
    Luke 9. 46.
b Ps. 131. 2.
    Mark 10. 14.
    Luke 18. 16.
c Ps. 57. 15.
. Ps. 66. 2.
d ch. 10 42.
e Luke 17. 1.
    1 Cor. 11. 19.

---

saith, Yes—*q. d.*, 'To be sure He does;' as if eager to remove even the suspicion of the contrary. If Peter knew—as surely he did—that there was at this time no money in the bag, this reply must be regarded as a great act of faith in his Master. **And when he was come into the house**—Peter's, **Jesus prevented him** [προέφθασεν αὐτὸν]—'anticipated him;' according to the old sense of the word "prevent," **saying, What thinkest thou, Simon?**—using his family name for familiarity, **of whom do the kings of the earth take custom** [τέλη]—meaning custom on goods exported or imported—**or tribute?** [κῆνσον, from the Latin word *census*]—meaning the poll-tax, payable to the Romans by every one whose name was in the 'census.' This, therefore, it will be observed, was strictly *a civil tax*. **of their own children, or of strangers** [ἀλλοτρίων]? This cannot mean 'foreigners,' from whom sovereigns certainly do not raise taxes, but 'those who are not of their own family,' that is, their subjects. **26. Peter saith unto him, Of strangers**—or, 'Of those not their children.' **Jesus saith unto him, Then are the children free.** By "the children" our Lord cannot here mean Himself and the Twelve together, in some loose sense of their near relationship to God as their common Father. For besides that our Lord never once mixes Himself up with His disciples in speaking of their relation to God, but ever studiously keeps His relation and theirs apart (see, for example, on the last words of this chapter)—this would be to teach the right of believers to exemption from the dues required for sacred services, in the teeth of all that Paul teaches and that He Himself indicates throughout. He can refer here, then, only to Himself; using the word "children" evidently in order to express the general principle observed by sovereigns, who do not draw taxes from their own children, and thus convey the truth respecting His own exemption the more strikingly:—*q. d.*, 'If the sovereign's own family be exempt, you know the inference in My case;' or to express it more nakedly than Jesus thought needful and fitting: 'This is a tax for upholding My Father's house: As His Son, then, that tax is not due by Me—I AM FREE.' **27. Notwithstanding, lest we should offend**—or 'stumble'—**them**—all ignorant as they are of My relation to the Lord of the Temple, and should misconstrue a claim to exemption into indifference to His honour who dwells in it, **go thou to the sea**—Capernaum, it will be remembered, lay on the sea of Galilee, **and cast an hook, and take up the fish that first cometh up; and when thou hast opened his mouth, thou**

shalt find a piece of money [στατῆρα]—'a stater.' So it should have been rendered, and not indefinitely, as in our version; for the coin **was an** Attic silver coin, equal to two of the fore-mentioned "didrachms" of half-a-shekel's value, and so, was the exact sum required for both. Accordingly, the Lord adds, **that take, and give unto them for me and thee** [ἀντὶ ἐμοῦ καὶ σοῦ]—lit., 'instead of Me and thee;' perhaps because the payment was a *redemption of the person* paid for (Exod. xxx. 12)—in which view Jesus certainly was "free." If the house was Peter's, this will account for payment being provided on this occasion, not for all the Twelve, but only for him and His Lord. Observe, our Lord does not say "for us," but "for Me and thee;" thus distinguishing the Exempted One and His non-exempted disciple. (See on John xx. 17.)

Remarks.—1. A stronger claim to essential Divinity than our Lord in this scene at Capernaum advances—as "own Son" of the Lord of the Temple—cannot well be conceived. Either, therefore, the teaching of the Lord Jesus was systematically subversive of the prerogatives of Him who will not give His glory to another, or He was the Fellow of the Lord of hosts. But the former cannot be true, attested as Jesus was in every imaginable way by His Father in heaven: His claim, then, to supreme personal Divinity, ought with Christians to be beyond dispute, and is so with all who deserve the name—who would die sooner than surrender it, and with whose loftiest joys and hopes it is inseparably bound up. 2. What manifold wonders are there in the one miracle of this Section! The exact sum required was found in a fish's mouth; Jesus showed that He knew this; this very fish came to the spot where Peter's hook was to be cast, and at the very time when it was cast; that fish took that hook, retained it till drawn to land, and there yielded up the needed coin! And yet, 3. Amidst such wealth of divine resources—lo, the Lord's whole means of temporal subsistence at this time appear to have been exhausted! "Ye know the grace of our Lord Jesus Christ"—but *do ye know it*, O my readers?— "that though He was rich, yet for your sakes He became poor, that ye through his poverty might be rich!" (2 Cor. viii. 9).

CHAP. XVIII. 1-9.—STRIFE AMONG THE TWELVE WHO SHOULD BE GREATEST IN THE KINGDOM OF HEAVEN, WITH RELATIVE TEACHING. (=Mark ix. 33-50; Luke ix. 46-50.) For the exposition, see on Mark ix. 33-50.

10-35.—FURTHER TEACHING ON THE SAME

offences come; but *f* woe to that man by whom the offence cometh!

8 Wherefore *g* if thy hand or thy foot offend thee, cut them off, and cast *them* from thee: it is better for thee to enter into life halt or maimed, rather than having two hands or two feet to be cast into everlasting fire.

9 And if thine eye offend thee, pluck it out, and cast *it* from thee: it is better for thee to enter into life with one eye, rather than having two eyes to be cast into hell fire.

10 Take heed that ye despise not one of these little ones; for I say unto you, That in heaven *h* their angels do always *i* behold the face of my

11 Father which is in heaven. For the Son of man is come to save that

12 which was lost. How *j* think ye? If a man have an hundred sheep, and one of them be gone astray, doth he not leave the ninety and nine, and goeth into the mountains, and seeketh that which is gone astray?

13 And if so be that he find it, verily I say unto you, He rejoiceth more of

14 that *sheep*, than of the ninety and nine which went not astray. Even so it is not the will of your Father which is in heaven, that one of these little ones should perish.

15 Moreover, *k* if thy brother shall trespass against thee, go and tell him his fault between thee and him alone: if he shall hear thee, *l* thou hast

16 gained thy brother. But if he will not hear *thee, then* take with thee one or two more, that in *m* the mouth of two or three witnesses every

17 word may be established. And if he shall neglect to hear them, tell *it* unto *n* the church: but if he neglect to hear the church, let him be unto thee as an *o* heathen man and a publican.

18 Verily I say unto you, *p* Whatsoever ye shall bind on earth shall be

A. D. 32.
f ch. 26. 24.
g Deut. 13. 6.
ch. 5. 29, 30.
ch. 14. 3, 4.
Mark 9. 43.
Luke 14. 26.
Luke 18. 22.
h Ps. 34. 7.
Zech. 13. 7.
Heb. 1. 14.
i Esth. 1. 14.
Luke 1. 19.
j Luke 15. 4.
k Lev. 19. 17.
Luke 17. 3.
l Jas. 5. 20.
1 Pet. 3. 1.
m Num. 35. 30.
Deut. 17. 6.
Deut. 19. 15.
1 Ki. 21. 13.
John 8. 17.
2 Cor. 13. 1.
Heb. 10. 28.
1 John 5. 7, 8.
Rev. 11. 3.
n 1 Tim. 5. 20.
o Rom. 16. 17.
1 Cor. 5. 9.
2 John 10.
p John 20. 23.

SUBJECT, INCLUDING THE PARABLE OF THE UN- MERCIFUL DEBTOR.

Same Subject (10-20). **10. Take heed that ye de- spise**—'stumble'—**not one of these little ones; for I say unto you, That in heaven their angels do always behold the face of my Father which is in heaven.** A difficult verse; but perhaps the fol- lowing may be more than an illustration:—Among men, those who nurse and rear the royal children, however humble in themselves, are allowed free entrance with their charge, and a degree of famil- iarity which even the highest state-ministers dare not assume. Probably our Lord means that, in virtue of their charge over His disciples (Heb. i. 13; John i. 51), the angels have *errands* to the throne, a *welcome* there, and a *dear familiarity* in dealing with "His Father which is in heaven," which on their own matters they could not assume (See on John v. 1-47, Remark 1, at the close of that Section.) **11. For the Son of man is come to save that which was**—or 'is'—**lost.** A golden saying, once and again repeated in different forms. Here the connection seems to be, 'Since the whole object and errand of the Son of Man into the world is to save the lost, take heed lest, by causing 'offences, ye lose the saved.' That this is the idea intended we may gather from verse 14. **12, 13. How think ye? If a man have an hundred sheep, and one of them be gone astray,** &c. This is another of those pregnant sayings which our Lord uttered more than once. See on the de- lightful parable of the lost sheep in Luke xv. 4-7. Only the object *there* is to show what the good Shepherd will do, when even one of His sheep is lost, to *find* it; *here* the object is to show, when found, how reluctant He is to *lose* it. Accordingly, it is added, *v.* 14. **Even so it is not the will of your Father which is in heaven, that one of these little ones should perish.** How, then, can He but visit for those "offences" which endanger the souls of these little ones!

15. Moreover, if thy brother shall trespass against thee, go and tell him his fault between thee and him alone: if he shall hear thee, thou hast gained thy brother. **16. But if he will not hear thee, then take with thee one or two more, that in the mouth of two or three witnesses every word may be established.** (Deut. xvii. 6; xix. 15.) **17. And if he shall neglect to hear them, tell it unto the church: but if he neglect to hear the church, let him be unto thee as an heathen man and a publican.** Probably our Lord has reference still to the late dispute, Who should be the greatest? After the rebuke—so gentle and captivating, yet so dignified and divine—under which they would doubtless be smarting, perhaps each would be saying, It was not *I* that began it, it was not I that threw out unworthy and irritating insinuations against my brethren. Be it so, says our Lord; but as such things will often arise, I will direct you how to proceed. *First*, Neither harbour a grudge against your offending brother, nor break forth upon him in presence of the un- believing, but take him aside, show him his fault, and if he own and make reparation for it, you have done more service to him than even justice to yourself. *Next*, If this fail, take two or three to witness how just your complaint is, and how brotherly your spirit in dealing with him. *Again*, If this fail, bring him before the church or congre- gation to which both belong. *Lastly*, If even this fail, regard him as no longer a brother Christian, but as one "without"—as the Jews did Gentiles and Publicans. **18. Verily I say unto you, Whatsoever ye shall bind on earth shall be bound in heaven; and whatsoever ye shall loose on earth shall be loosed in heaven.** Here, what had been granted but a short time before to Peter only (see on ch. xvi. 16) is plainly extended to all the Twelve; so that whatever it means, it means nothing peculiar to Peter, far less to his pretended successors at Rome. It has to do with admission to and rejection from the membership of the Church. But see on John

bound in heaven; and whatsoever ye shall loose on earth shall be loosed
19 in heaven. Again ^{*q*}I say unto you, That if two of you shall agree on earth as touching any thing that they shall ask, ^{*r*}it shall be done for
20 them of my Father which is in heaven. For where two or three are gathered together in my name, ^{*s*}there am I in the midst of them.
21 Then came Peter to him, and said, Lord, how oft shall my brother sin
22 against me, and I forgive him? ^{*t*}till seven times? Jesus saith unto him, I say not unto thee, Until seven times; ^{*u*}but, Until seventy times seven.
23 Therefore is the kingdom of heaven likened unto a certain king, which
24 would take account of his servants. And when he had begun to reckon,
25 one was brought unto him, which owed him ten thousand ¹talents: but forasmuch as he had not to pay, his lord commanded him ^{*v*}to be sold, and his wife and children, and all that he had, and payment to be made.
26 The servant therefore fell down, and ²worshipped him, saying, Lord, have

A. D. 32.
q ch. 5. 24.
r Jas. 5. 16.
s Ezek. 48.35.
t Luke 17. 4.
u Col. 3. 13.
1 A talent is 750 ounces of silver, which after five shillings the ounce is 187*l* 10s.
v 2 Ki. 4. 1.
2 Or, besought him.

xx. 23. **19. Again I say unto you, That if two of you shall agree on earth as touching any thing that they shall ask, it shall be done for of my Father which is in heaven. 20. For where two or three are gathered together in** [or 'unto' —εἰς] **my name, there am I in the midst of them.** On this passage—so full of sublime encouragement to Christian union in action and in prayer—observe, first, the connection in which it stands. Our Lord had been speaking of church-meetings, before which the obstinate perversity of a brother was, in the last resort, to be brought, and whose decision was to be final—such honour does the Lord of the Church put upon its lawful assemblies. But not these assemblies only does He deign to countenance and honour. For even two uniting to bring any matter before Him shall find that they are not alone, for My Father is with them, says Jesus. Next, observe the *premium here put upon union in prayer.* As this cannot exist with fewer than two, so by letting it down so low as that number, He gives the utmost conceivable encouragement to union in this exercise. But what kind of union? Not an agreement merely to pray in concert, but to pray *for some definite thing.* "As touching anything which they shall ask," says our Lord anything they shall agree to ask in concert. At the same time, it is plain He had certain things at that moment in His eye, as most fitting and needful subjects for such concerted prayer. The Twelve had been "falling out by the way" about the miserable question of precedence in their Master's kingdom, and this, as it stirred their corruptions, had given rise—or at least was in danger of giving rise—to "offences" perilous to their souls. The Lord Himself had been directing them how to deal with one another about such matters. "But now shows He unto them a more excellent way." Let them bring all such matters—yea, and everything whatsoever by which either their own loving relationship to each other, or the good of His kingdom at large, might be affected—to their Father in heaven; and if they be but agreed in petitioning Him about that thing, it shall be done for them of His Father which is in heaven. But further, it is not merely union in prayer for the same thing—for that might be with very jarring ideas of the thing to be desired—but it is to symphonious prayer [as the word signifies—συμφωνήσωσιν], to prayer by kindred spirits, members of one family, servants of one Lord, constrained by the same love, fighting under one banner, cheered by assurances of the same victory; a living and loving union, whose voice in the Divine ear is as the sound of many waters. Accordingly, what they ask "*on earth*" is done for

them, says Jesus, "of my Father which is *in heaven.*" Not for nothing does He say, "of MY FATHER"—not "YOUR FATHER;" as is evident from what follows: "For where two or three are gathered together *unto my name*"—the "My" is emphatic [εἰς τὸ ἐμὸν ὄνομα] "*there am I* in the midst of them." As His name would prove a spell to draw together many clusters of His dear disciples, so if there should be but two or three, that will attract Himself down into the midst of them; and related as He is to both the parties, the petitioners and the Petitioned—to the one on earth by the tie of His assumed flesh, and to the other in heaven by the tie of His eternal Spirit—their symphonious prayers on earth would thrill upwards through Him to heaven, be carried by Him into the holiest of all, and so reach the Throne. Thus will He be the living Conductor of the prayer upward and the answer downward.

Parable of the Unmerciful Debtor (21-35). **21. Then came Peter to him, and said, Lord, how oft shall my brother sin against me, and I forgive him?** In the recent dispute, Peter had probably been an object of special envy, and his forwardness in continually answering for all the rest would likely be cast up to him—and if so, probably by Judas—notwithstanding his Master's commendations. And as such insinuations were perhaps made once and again, he wished to know how often and how long he was to stand it. **till seven times?** This being the sacred and complete number, perhaps his meaning was, Is there to be a limit at which the needful forbearance will be *full?* **22. Jesus saith unto him, I say not unto thee, Until seven times; but, Until seventy times seven** —that is, so long as it shall be needed and sought: you are never to come to the point of refusing forgiveness sincerely asked. (See on Luke xvii. 3, 4.) **23. Therefore—**'with reference to this matter,' **is the kingdom of heaven likened unto a certain king, which would take account of his servants** —or, would scrutinize the accounts of his revenue-collectors. **24. And when he had begun to reckon, one was brought unto him, which owed him ten thousand talents.** If *Attic* talents are here meant, 10,000 of them would amount to above *a million and a half* sterling; if Jewish talents, to a much larger sum. **25. But forasmuch as he had not to pay, his lord commanded him to be sold, and his wife and children, and all that he had, and payment to be made.** (See 2 Ki. iv. 1; Neh. v. 8; Lev. xxv. 39.) **26. The servant therefore fell down, and worshipped him—**or did humble obeisance to him, saying, Lord, have patience with me, and I will pay thee all. This was just an acknowledgment of the justice of the claim made against

27 patience with me, and I will pay thee all.   Then the lord of that servant
was moved with compassion, and loosed him, and forgave him the debt.
28 But the same servant went out, and found one of his fellow-servants,
which owed him an hundred ³pence; and he laid hands on him, and took
29 *him* by the throat, saying, Pay me that thou owest.   And his fellow-
servant fell down at his feet, and besought him, saying, Have patience
30 with me, and I will pay thee all.   And he would not; but went and cast
31 him into prison, till he should pay the debt.   So when his fellow-servants saw what was done, they were very sorry, and came and told unto
32 their lord all that was done.   Then his lord, after that he had called him,
said unto him, O thou wicked servant, I forgave thee all that debt,
33 because thou desiredst me: shouldest ʷnot thou also have had compassion
34 on thy fellow-servant, even as I had pity on thee?   And his lord was
wroth, and delivered him to the tormentors, till he should pay all that
35 was due unto him.   So ˣlikewise shall my heavenly Father do also unto
you, if ye from your hearts forgive not every one his brother their
trespasses.

A. D. 32.

³ The Ro-
man penny
is the
eighth part
of an
ounce,
which after
five shil-
lings the
ounce is
seven-
pence
halfpenny.
ch. 20. 2.
ʷ Eph. 4. 32.
Eph. 5. 2.
Col. 3. 13.
ˣ Pro. 21. 13.
ch. 6. 12.
Mark 11.26.
Jas. 2. 13.

him, and a piteous imploration of mercy. **27. Then
the lord of that servant was moved with compassion, and loosed him, and forgave him the debt.**
Payment being hopeless, the Master is, first,
moved with compassion; next, liberates his debtor
from prison; and then cancels the debt freely.
**28. But the same servant went out, and found
one of his fellow-servants.** Mark the difference
here. The first case is that of master and servant; in this case, both are on a footing of equality.
(See *v.* 33, below.) **which owed him an hundred
pence.** If Jewish money is intended, this debt
was to the other less than *one to a million.* **and
he laid hands on him, and took him by the
throat** [κρατήσας αὐτὸν ἔπνιγε]—'he seized and
throttled him,' **saying, Pay me that thou owest.**
Mark the mercilessness even of the tone. **29. And
his fellow-servant fell down at his feet, and besought him, saying, Have patience with me, and
I will pay thee all.** The same attitude, and the
same words which drew compassion from his master are here employed towards himself by his fellow-servant. **30. And he would not; but went and
cast him into prison, till he should pay the debt.
31. So when his fellow-servants saw what was
done, they were very sorry, and came and told
unto their lord all that was done.** Jesus here
vividly conveys the intolerable injustice and impudence which even the servants saw in this act,
on the part of one so recently laid under the
heaviest obligations to their common master. **32.
Then his lord, after that he had called him, said
unto him, O thou wicked servant, I forgave thee all
that debt, because thou desiredst me: 33. Shouldest not thou also have had compassion on thy
fellow-servant, even as I had pity on thee?** Before bringing down his vengeance upon him, he
calmly points out to him how shamefully unreasonable and heartless his conduct was ; which would
give the punishment inflicted on him a double sting.
**34. And his lord was wroth, and delivered him to
the tormentors** [βασανισταῖς]—more than *jailers ;*
denoting the severity of the treatment which he
thought such a case demanded. **till he should
pay all that was due unto him. 35. So likewise**
[Οὕτως καὶ]—in this *spirit,* or on this principle,
**shall my heavenly Father do also unto you, if
ye from your hearts forgive not every one his
brother their trespasses.**
Remarks.—1. When we think how Jesus here
speaks of God's "little ones"—how dear, He tells
us, even one of them is to His Father, and what
perdition to them lies in the bosom of those

"offences" which are apt to spring up amongst
them—how incredible would it appear, if we did
not see it with our eyes, that Christians should
think so little of falling out on the merest trifles,
and insist so rancorously on their own point in
every argument! See on Mark ix. 33-50, and Remark 1 there; and compare Rom. xiv. 13-17, where
our Lord's teaching on this subject seems to have
been in the apostle's eye. Ours rather be the Good
Shepherd's jealous care to recover His sheep when
lost, and keep them when found! 2. How delightful is the truth—here and elsewhere taught
in Scripture—that God's dear children are committed by Him, during their sojourn here, to the
guardianship of angels! Whatever may be the
meaning of the remarkable expression, "*their
angels*"—whether it be designed to teach us that
each child of God is under the special care of one
particular angel, a doctrine in which, notwithstanding Romish abuses, we can see nothing
unscriptural; or whether it mean no more than
simply 'the angelic guardians of believers'—the
information communicated here only, that they
do always behold the face of Christ's Father in
heaven, is surely designed to teach us how dear to
God and how high in His favour each of them is,
when even their guardians have uninterrupted
and familiar access to their Father on their
account. Children of God, brighten up, when ye
hear this. But O, have a care how ye think and
speak and act, under such high guardianship!
3. How much unlovely feeling among Christians
would disappear under the treatment here enjoined! Many misunderstandings melt away
under a quiet brotherly expostulation with the
offending party: failing this, the affectionate and
faithful dealings of two or three more—still in
private—might be expected to have more weight:
and if even an appeal, in the last resort, to the
body of Christians to which both belonged, should
fail to bring an offending party to reason, the
matter would but require to end there, and
Christian fellowship with the refractory member
henceforth to cease. 4. The opening and shutting
of the doors of Christian fellowship—in other
words, Church Discipline—is an ordinance of the
Church's Living Head, whose sanction is pledged
to the faithful exercise of it, in accordance with
His word. 5. What sublime encouragement to
concerted prayer among Christians, for definite
objects, have we in this Section. And should not
Christians prove their Lord now herewith, if He
will not open to them the windows of heaven, and

19 AND it came to pass, *ᵃthat* when Jesus had finished these sayings, he departed from Galilee, and came into the coasts of Judea beyond Jordan;

2 and *ᵇ*great multitudes followed him; and he healed them there.

3 The Pharisees also came unto him, tempting him, and saying unto

4 him, Is it lawful for a man to put away his wife for *every cause?* And he answered and said unto them, Have ye not read, *ᶜthat* he which made

5 *them* at the beginning made them male and female, and said, *ᵈ*For this cause shall a man leave father and mother, and shall cleave to his wife:

6 and *ᵉ*they twain shall be one flesh? Wherefore they are no more twain, but one flesh. What therefore God hath joined together, let not man put asunder.

7 They say unto him, *ᶠ*Why did Moses then command to give a writing

8 of divorcement, and to put her away? He saith unto them, Moses because of the hardness of your hearts suffered you to put away your

A. D. 32.

CHAP. 19.
ᵃ Mark 10. 1.
John 10. 40.
ᵇ ch. 12. 15.
ch. 15. 20.
Mark 6. 55.
ᶜ Gen. 1. 27.
Gen. 5. 2.
Mal. 2. 15.
ᵈ Gen. 2. 24.
Mark 10. 5.
9.
Eph. 5. 31.
ᵉ 1 Cor. 6. 16.
1 Cor. 7. 2.
ᶠ Deut. 24. 1.
ch. 5. 31.

---

pour them out a blessing that there shall not be room enough to receive it? 6. When we read our Lord's injunctions here to stretch our forbearance with brethren to the utmost, can we but blush to think how little it is done, especially in the light of that other saying of His—"Ye are my friends, if ye do whatsoever I command you"? (John xv. 14). Let us hear the apostle. "Put on therefore, as the elect of God, holy and beloved, bowels of mercies, kindness, humbleness of mind, meekness, long-suffering; forbearing one another, and forgiving one another, if any man have a quarrel against any: even as Christ forgave you, so also do ye. And above all these things put on charity, which is the bond of perfectness. And let the peace of God rule in your hearts, to the which also ye are called in one body; and be ye thankful" (Col. iii. 12-15). 7. Let the grand evangelical principle on which turns the beautiful parable of the Unmerciful Debtor be written as in letters of gold and hung up before every Christian eye—that *God's forgiveness of our vast debts to Him precedes our forgiveness of the petty debts we owe to one another;* that this is that which *begets in us the forgiving disposition;* and that it *furnishes us with the grand model of forgiving Mercy which we have to copy.* 8. When our Lord represents the king in the parable as cancelling the free pardon of the relentless debtor, and again shutting him up in prison till he should pay all that he owed; and when He then says, "So shall My heavenly Father do also unto you, if ye from your hearts forgive not every one his brother their trespasses"—we must not understand Him to teach that such literal reversals of pardon do actually take place in God's treatment of His pardoned children—for that, we take it, is but the dress of the parable—but simply, that *on this principle* God will deal, in the matter of forgiveness, with unforgiving men; and so, we have here just a repetition—in the form of a parable—of the truth expressed in ch. vi. 15, and elsewhere, that "if we forgive not men their trespasses, neither will our heavenly Father forgive our trespasses."

CHAP. XIX. 1-12.—FINAL DEPARTURE FROM GALILEE—DIVORCE. (= Mark x. 1-12; Luke ix. 51.)
Farewell to Galilee. 1. **And it came to pass, that when Jesus had finished these sayings, he departed from Galilee.** This marks a very solemn period in our Lord's public ministry. So slightly is it touched here, and in the corresponding passage of Mark (x. 1), that few readers probably note it as the Redeemer's *Farewell to Galilee,* which however it was. See on the sublime statement of Luke (ix. 51), which relates to the same transition-stage in the progress of our Lord's work. **and came**

into the coasts—or 'boundaries'—**of Judea beyond Jordan**—that is, to the further, or east side of the Jordan, into Perea, the dominions of Herod Antipas. But though one might conclude from our Evangelist that our Lord went straight from the one region to the other, we know from the other Gospels that a considerable time elapsed between the departure from the one and the arrival at the other, during which many of the most important events in our Lord's public life occurred—probably a large part of what is recorded in Luke ix. 51, onwards to ch. xviii. 15, and part of John vii. 2—xi. 54. 2. **And great multitudes followed him; and he healed them there.** Mark says further (x. 1), that "as He was wont, He taught them there." What we now have on the subject of Divorce is some of that teaching.

Divorce (3-12). 3. **The Pharisees also came unto him, tempting him, and saying unto him, Is it lawful for a man to put away his wife for every cause?** Two rival schools (as we saw on ch. v. 31) were divided on this question—a delicate one, as de Wette pertinently remarks, in the dominions of Herod Antipas. 4. **And he answered and said unto them, Have ye not read, that he which made them at the beginning made them male and female**—or better, perhaps, 'He that made them made them from the beginning a male and a female.' 5. **And said, For this cause**—to follow out this divine appointment, **shall a man leave father and mother, and shall cleave to his wife: and they twain shall be one flesh? 6. Wherefore they are no more twain, but one flesh. What therefore God hath joined together, let not man put asunder.** Jesus here sends them back to the original constitution of man as one pair, a male and a female; to their marriage, as such, by divine appointment; and to the purpose of God, expressed by the sacred historian, that in all time one man and one woman should by marriage become one flesh—so to continue as long as both are in the flesh. This being *God's* constitution, let not *man* break it up by causeless divorces.

7. **They say unto him, Why did Moses then command to give a writing of divorcement, and to put her away? 8. He saith unto them, Moses**—as a civil lawgiver, **because of [πρὸς τὴν]**—or 'having respect to' the hardness of your hearts—looking to your low moral state, and your inability to endure the strictness of the original law, **suffered you to put away your wives**—tolerated a relaxation of the strictness of the marriage bond—not as approving of it, but to prevent still greater evils. **but from the beginning it was not so.** This is repeated, in order to impress upon His audience the temporary and purely civil character of this Mosaic relaxation. 9. **And I say**

9 wives: but *g*from the beginning it was not so. And *h*I say unto you, Whosoever shall put away his wife, except *it be* for fornication, and shall marry another, committeth adultery; and whoso marrieth her which is put away doth commit adultery.

10 His disciples say unto him, *i*If the case of the man be so with *his* wife,
11 it is not good to marry. But he said unto them, *j*All *men* cannot receive
12 this saying, save *they* to whom it is given. For there are some eunuchs, which were so born from *their* mother's womb; and there are some eunuchs, which were made eunuchs of men; and *k*there be eunuchs, which have made themselves eunuchs for the kingdom of heaven's sake. He that is able to receive *it*, let him receive *it*.

13 Then *l*were there brought unto him little children, that he should put
14 *his* hands on them, and pray: and the disciples rebuked them. But Jesus said, Suffer little children, and forbid them not, to come unto me;
15 for of *m*such is the kingdom of heaven. And he laid *his* hands on them, and departed thence.

16 And, behold, one came and said unto him, *n*Good Master, what *o*good
17 thing shall I do, that I may have eternal life? And he said unto him, Why callest thou me good? *there is* none good but one, *that is*, God:
18 but if thou wilt enter into life, keep the commandments. He saith unto him, Which? Jesus said, Thou *p*shalt do no murder, Thou shalt not commit adultery, Thou shalt not steal, Thou shalt not bear false witness,
19 Honour *q*thy father and *thy* mother; and, *r*Thou shalt love thy neighbour
20 as thyself. The young man saith unto him, All these things have I kept
21 from my youth up: what lack I yet? Jesus said unto him, If thou wilt be perfect, *s*go *and* sell that thou hast, and give to the poor, and thou
22 shalt have treasure in heaven; and come *and* follow me. But when the young man heard that saying, he went away sorrowful: for he had great possessions.
23 Then said Jesus unto his disciples, Verily I say unto you, That *t*a rich
24 man shall hardly enter into the kingdom of heaven. And again I say

A. D. 33.

g Jer. 6. 16.
h ch. 5. 32.
Mark 10.11.
Luke 16. 18.
1 Cor. 7. 10, 11.
i Gen. 2. 18.
Pro.5.15-19.
Pro. 21. 19.
1 Cor. 7. 1, 2, 8.
1 Tim. 4. 3.
1 Tim. 5.11-15.
j 1 Cor. 7. 2, 7, 9, 17.
k 1 Cor. 7. 32, 34.
1 Cor. 9. 5, 15.
l Mark 10.13.
Luke 18.15.
m ch. 18. 3.
1 Pet. 2. 1, 2.
n Luke 10.25.
o Rom. 9. 31.
p Exod.20.13.
Deut. 5. 17.
q ch. 15. 4.
r Lev. 19. 18.
Rom. 13. 9.
Gal. 5. 14.
Jas. 2. 8.
s Luke 12.33.
Luke 16. 9.
Acts 2. 45.
Acts 4. 34.
1 Tim. 6,18.
t 1 Cor. 1. 26.
1 Tim. 6. 9.

unto you, Whosoever shall put away his wife, except, &c.; and whoso marrieth her which is put away doth commit adultery. See on ch. v. 32. [*Tregelles* brackets this last clause, as of doubtful authority—but without sufficient reason, as we think. *Tischendorf* inserts it, as in the received text.]

10. His disciples say unto him, If the case of the man be so with his wife, it is not good to marry:—*q. d.*, 'In this view of marriage, surely it must prove a snare rather than a blessing, and had better be avoided altogether.' 11. But he said unto them, All men cannot receive this saying, save they to whom it is given:—*q. d.*, 'That the unmarried state is better, is a saying not for every one, and indeed only for such as it is divinely intended for.' But who are these? they would naturally ask; and this our Lord proceeds to tell them in three particulars. 12. For there are some eunuchs, which were so born from their mother's womb—persons constitutionally either incapable of or indisposed to marriage; and there are some eunuchs, which were made eunuchs of men—persons rendered incapable by others; and there be eunuchs, which have made themselves eunuchs for the kingdom of heaven's sake—persons who, to do God's work better, deliberately choose this state. Such was Paul (1 Cor. vii. 7). He that is able to receive it, let him receive it—'He who feels this to be his proper vocation, let him embrace it;' which, of course, is as much as to say—'he only.' Thus, all is left free in this matter.

Remarks.—1. If the sanctity of the marriage-tie,

as the fountain of all social well-being, is to be upheld among men, it must be by basing it on the original divine institution of it; nor will those relaxations of it which corrupt ingenuity introduces and defends be effectually checked but by reverting, as our Lord here does, to the great primary character and design of it as established at the beginning. 2. Let those who reverence the authority of Christ mark the divine authority which He ascribes to the Old Testament in general, and to the books of Moses in particular, in the settlement of all questions of divine truth and human duty (*vv.* 4, 5); nor let us fail to observe the important distinction which He draws between things commanded and things permitted—between things tolerated for a time, and regulated by civil enactment, to keep the barriers of social morality from being quite broken down, and the enduring sanctities of the great moral law (*vv.* 8, 9). 3. When our Lord holds forth the single life as designed for and suited to certain specific classes, let Christians understand that, while their own plan and condition of life should be regulated by higher considerations than mere inclination or personal advantage, they are not to lay down rules for others, but let each decide for himself, as to his own Master he standeth or falleth. For he that in these things serveth Christ is acceptable to God and approved of men.

13-15.—LITTLE CHILDREN BROUGHT TO CHRIST. (= Mark x. 13-16; Luke xviii. 15-17.) For the exposition, see on Luke xviii. 15-17.

16-30.—THE RICH YOUNG RULER. (= Mark x. 17-31; Luke xviii. 18-30.) For the exposition, see on Luke xviii. 18-30.

unto you, It is easier for a camel to go through the eye of a needle, than
25 for a rich man to enter into the kingdom of God. When his disciples
heard *it*, they were exceedingly amazed, saying, Who then can be saved?
26 But Jesus beheld *them*, and said unto them, With men this is impossible;
but with "God all things are possible.
27   Then *answered Peter and said unto him, Behold, *w*we have forsaken
28 all, and followed thee; what shall we have therefore? And Jesus said
unto them, Verily I say unto you, That ye which have followed me, in
*x*the regeneration, when the Son of man shall sit in the throne of his
glory, *y*ye also shall sit upon twelve thrones, judging the twelve tribes of
29 Israel. And every one that hath forsaken houses, or brethren, or sisters,
or father, or mother, or wife, or children, or lands, for my name's sake,
30 shall receive an hundredfold, and shall inherit everlasting life. But *z*many
that are first shall be last; and the last *shall be* first.

20   FOR the kingdom of heaven is like unto a man *that is* an householder,
which went out early in the morning to hire labourers into his vineyard.
2 And when he had agreed with the labourers for a ¹penny a day, he sent
3 them into his vineyard. And he went out about the third hour, and saw
4 others standing idle in the market-place, and said unto them, Go ye
also into the vineyard, and whatsoever is right I will give you. And
5 they went their way. Again he went out about the sixth and ninth hour,
6 and did likewise. And about the eleventh hour he went out, and found
others standing idle, and saith unto them, Why stand ye here all the day
7 idle? They say unto him, Because no man hath hired us. He saith unto
them, Go ye also into the vineyard; and whatsoever is right, *that* shall
8 ye receive. So when "even was come, the lord of the vineyard saith unto
his steward, Call the labourers, and give them *their* hire, beginning from
9 the last unto the first. And when they came that *were hired* about the
10 eleventh hour, they received every man a penny. But when the first

A. D. 33.

"Gen. 18. 14.
Job 42. 2.
Jer. 32. 17.
Zech. 8. 6.
Mark 10.27.
v Mark 10.28.
*w*Deut. 33. 9.
ch. 4. 20.
ch. 9. 9.
Mark 1. 17-20.
Mark 2. 14.
Luke 5. 11.
Luke 14.33.
Luke 18.28.
z 2 Cor. 5. 17.
y Luke 22. 28.
1 Cor. 6. 2,3.
Rev. 2. 26.
s ch. 20. 16.
Mark 10.31.

CHAP. 20.
¹ The Roman penny is the eighth part of an ounce, whichafter five shillings the ounce is sevenpence halfpenny.
a Acts 17. 31.
1Thes.4.16.

CHAP. XX. 1-16.—PARABLE OF THE LABOUR-
ERS IN THE VINEYARD.
    This parable, recorded only by Matthew, is
closely connected with the end of ch. xix., being
spoken with reference to Peter's question, How it
should fare with those who, like himself, had left
all for Christ? It is designed to show that while
they would be richly rewarded, a certain equity
would still be observed towards *later* converts and
workmen in His service. **1. For the kingdom of
heaven is like unto a man that is an householder, which went out early in the morning to
hire labourers into his vineyard.** The figure of
a Vineyard, to represent the rearing of souls for
heaven, the culture required and provided for
that purpose, and the care and pains which God
takes in that whole matter, is familiar to every
reader of the Bible. (Ps. lxxx. 8-16; Isa. v. 1-7;
Jer. ii. 21; Luke xx. 9-16; John xv. 1-8.) At
vintage-time, as *Webster and Wilkinson* remark,
labour was scarce, and masters were obliged to be
early in the market to secure it. Perhaps the
pressing nature of the work of the Gospel, and the
comparative paucity of labourers, may be incidentally suggested, ch. ix. 37, 38. The "labourers," as
in ch. ix. 38, are first, the *official* servants of the
Church, but after them and along with them *all*
the servants of Christ, whom he has laid under
the weightiest obligation to work in His service.
**2. And when he had agreed with the labourers
for a penny** [δηναρίου]—a usual day's hire (the
amount of which will be found in the margin
of our Bibles), **he sent them into his vineyard. 3. And he went out about the third hour**
—about nine o'clock, or after a fourth of the
working day had expired: the day of twelve

hours was reckoned from six to six. **and saw
others standing idle** [ἀργοὺς]—'unemployed—**in
the market-place, 4. And said unto them, Go ye
also into the vineyard; and whatsoever is right**
[δίκαιον]—'just,' 'equitable,' in proportion to their
time—**I will give you. And they went their way.
5. Again he went out about the sixth and ninth
hour**—about noon, and about three o'clock afternoon—**and did likewise**—hiring and sending into his
vineyard fresh labourers each time. **6. And about
the eleventh hour**—but one hour before the close
of the working day; a most unusual hour both
for offering and engaging—**and found others standing idle, and saith, Why stand ye here all the day
idle? 7. They say unto him, Because no man hath
hired us. He saith unto them, Go ye also into the
vineyard; and whatsoever is right, that shall ye
receive.** Of course they had not been there, or
not been disposed to offer themselves at the proper
time; but as they were now willing, and the day
was not over, and "yet there was room," they also
are engaged, and on similar terms with all the rest.
8. So when even was come—that is, the reckon-
ing-time between masters and labourers (see Deut.
xxiv. 15); pointing to the day of final account—**the
lord of the vineyard saith unto his steward**—
answering to Christ Himself, represented "as a
Son over His own house" (Heb. iii. 6; see Matt.
xi. 27; John iii. 35; v. 27), **Call the labourers, and
give them their hire, beginning from the last unto
the first.** Remarkable direction this—'last hired,
first paid.' **9. And when they came that were
hired about the eleventh hour, they received every
man a penny**—a full day's wages. **10. But when
the first came, they supposed that they should
have received more.** This is that calculating,

came, they supposed that they should have received more; and they like-
11 wise received every man a penny. And when they had received *it*, they
12 murmured against the goodman of the house, saying, These last [2]have
wrought *but* one hour, and thou hast made them equal unto us, which
13 have borne the burden and heat of the day. But he answered one of
them, and said, Friend, I do thee no wrong: didst not thou agree with
14 me for a penny? Take *that* thine *is*, and go thy way: I will give unto
15 this last even as unto thee. Is [b]it not lawful for me to do what I will
16 with mine own? [c]Is thine eye evil, because I am good? So [d]the last
shall be first, and the first last: [e]for many be called, but few chosen.

A. D. 33.

[2] Or, have continued one hour only.
[b] Rom. 9. 21.
[c] Deut. 15. 9. Pro. 23. 6.
Jon. 4. 1.
ch. 6. 23.
[d] ch. 19. 30.
[e] ch. 22. 14.
Luke 14. 24.

mercenary spirit which had peeped out—though perhaps very slightly—in Peter's question (ch. xix. 27), and which this parable was designed once for all to put down among the servants of Christ. **11. And when they had received it, they murmured against the goodman of the house** [οἰκοδεσπότου] —rather, 'the householder,' the word being the same as in verse 1. **12. Saying, These last have wrought [but] one hour, and thou hast made them equal unto us, which have borne the burden and heat**—'the burning heat' [καύσωνα] **of the day**—who have wrought not only longer but during a more trying period of the day. **13. But he answered one of them**—doubtless the spokesman of the complaining party—**and said, Friend, I do thee no wrong: didst not thou agree with me for a penny? 14. Take that thine is, and go thy way: I will give unto this last even as unto thee. 15. Is it not lawful for me to do what I will with mine own? Is thine eye evil, because I am good?**—*q. d.*, 'You appeal to *justice*, and by that your mouth is shut; for the sum you agreed for is paid you: Your case being disposed of, with the terms I make with other labourers you have nothing to do; and to grudge the benevolence shown to others, when by your own admission you have been honourably dealt with, is both unworthy envy of your neighbour, and discontent with the goodness that engaged and rewarded you in his service at all.' **16. So the last shall be first, and the first last:**—*q. d.*, 'Take heed lest by indulging the spirit of these "murmurers" at the "penny" given to the last hired, ye miss your own penny, though first in the vineyard; while the consciousness of having come in so late may inspire these last with such a humble frame, and such admiration of the grace that has hired and rewarded them at all, as will put them into the foremost place in the end.' **for many be called, but few chosen.** This is another of our Lord's terse and pregnant sayings, more than once uttered in different connections. (See ch. xix. 30; xxii. 14.) The "calling" of which the New Testament almost invariably speaks is what divines call *effectual* calling, carrying with it a supernatural operation on the will to secure its consent. But that cannot be the meaning of it here; the "called" being emphatically distinguished from the "chosen." It can only mean here the 'invited.' And so the sense is, Many receive the invitations of the Gospel whom God has never "chosen to salvation through sanctification of the Spirit and belief of the truth" (2 Thes. ii. 13). But what, it may be asked, has this to do with the subject of our parable? Probably this—to teach us that men who have wrought in Christ's service all their days may, by the spirit which they manifest at the last, make it too evident that, as between God and their own souls, they never were chosen workmen at all.

Taking the parable thus, the difficulties which have divided so many commentators seem to melt

away, and its general teaching may be expressed in the following

Remarks.—1. True Christianity is a life of active service rendered to Christ, whose love, as soon as one has tasted that the Lord is gracious, constrains him to live not unto himself, but unto Him that died for him and rose again. 2. Though we might well deem it a privilege to work for Christ without fee or reward, yet is our Father pleased to attach rewards—not of merit, of course, but of pure grace, as all rewards to those who once were sinners must be—to faithful working in His vineyard. 3. Although the Lord may surely "do what He will with His own," and so His rewards must be regarded as all flowing from His own sovereign will, yet there is a certain equity stamped upon them in relation to each other. That true attachment to Christ, and that fidelity in His service which is common to all chosen labourers in His vineyard—this is acknowledged by a reward common to all alike; and only those services in which Christians differ from each other in self-sacrificing devotedness are distinguished by special rewards corresponding with their character. And thus, while aspiring to those special rewards to distinguished Christians which are promised at the close of ch. xix., we are never to forget that there are gracious rewards common to all the true servants of Christ. 4. How unreasonable and ungrateful are those who, not contented with being called into the service of Christ—itself a high privilege—and graciously rewarded for all they do, envy their fellow-servants, and reflect upon their common Master, for seeming to do to others more than is consistent with justice to themselves. Such was the spirit of the elder brother in the parable of the Prodigal Son (Luke xv). Those men who appeal to God's justice will find their mouth closed in the day that He deals with them. 5. Let those who, conscious of having come in *late*, are afraid lest neither themselves nor their offers of service should be accepted at all, be encouraged by the assurance which this parable holds forth, that as long as the working-day of life and the present state of the kingdom of grace lasts, so long will the great Householder be found looking out for fresh labourers in His vineyard, and so long will He be ready to receive the offers and engage the services of all that are prepared to yield themselves to Him. 6. What strange revelations will the day of final reckoning make—discovering some that came latest in, and were least accounted of, amongst the first in the ranks of heaven; and some that were earliest in, and stood the highest in Christian estimation, among the last and lowest in the ranks of heaven; and some not amongst them at all who were of greatest note in the Church below! "Nevertheless, the foundation of God standeth sure, having this seal, The Lord knoweth them that are His; and, Let every one that nameth the name of Christ depart from iniquity" (2 Tim. ii. 19).

17 And *f*Jesus going up to Jerusalem took the twelve disciples apart in
18 the way, and said unto them, behold, *g*we go up to Jerusalem; and the
Son of man shall be betrayed unto the chief priests and unto the scribes,
19 and they shall condemn him to death, and *h*shall deliver him to the
Gentiles to mock, and to scourge, and to crucify *him:* and the third day
he shall rise again.
20 Then *i*came to him *j*the mother of Zebedee's *k*children with her sons,
21 worshipping *him*, and desiring a certain thing of him. And he said unto
her, What wilt thou? She saith unto him, Grant that these my two sons
*l*may sit, the one on thy right hand, and the other on the left, in thy
22 kingdom. But Jesus answered and said, Ye know not what ye ask. Are
ye able to drink of the *m*cup that I shall drink of, and to be baptized
with *n*the baptism that I am baptized with? They say unto him, We are
23 able. And he saith unto them, *o*Ye shall drink indeed of my cup, and
be baptized with the baptism that I am baptized with: but to sit on my
right hand, and on my left, is not mine to *p*give, but *it shall be given to
them* for whom it is prepared of my Father.
24 And *q*when the ten heard *it*, they were moved with indignation against
25 the two brethren. But Jesus called them *unto him*, and said, Ye know
that the princes of the Gentiles exercise dominion over them, and they
26 that are great exercise authority upon them. But *r*it shall not be so
among you: but whosoever *s*will be great among you, let him be your
27 minister; and *t*whosoever will be chief among you, let him be your
28 servant: even *u*as the Son of man came not to be ministered unto, *v*but
to minister, and to *w*give his life a ransom *x*for many.
29 And *y*as they departed from Jericho, a great multitude followed him.
30 And, behold, *z*two blind men sitting by the way-side, when they heard
that Jesus passed by, cried out, saying, Have mercy on us, O Lord, *thou*
31 son of David! And the multitude rebuked them, because they should
hold their peace: but they cried the more, saying, Have mercy on us, O
32 Lord, *thou* son of David! And Jesus stood still, and called them, and
33 said, What will ye that I shall do unto you? They say unto him, Lord,
34 that our eyes may be opened. So Jesus had *a*compassion *on them*, and
touched their eyes; and immediately their eyes received sight, and they
followed him.

21 AND *a*when they drew nigh unto Jerusalem, and were come to Beth-
2 phage, unto *b*the mount of Olives, then sent Jesus two disciples, saying
unto them, Go into the village over against you, and straightway ye shall
find an ass tied, and a colt with her: loose *them*, and bring *them* unto me.
3 And if any *man* say ought unto you, ye shall say, The *c*Lord hath *d*need
4 of them; and straightway he will send them. (All this was done, that
5 it might be fulfilled which was spoken by the prophet, saying, Tell *e*ye
the daughter of Sion, Behold, thy King cometh unto thee, meek, and
6 sitting upon an ass, and a colt the foal of an ass.) And *f*the disciples
7 went, and did as Jesus commanded them, and brought the ass, and the
8 colt, and put *g*on them their clothes, and they set *him* thereon. And a
very great multitude spread their garments in the way; *h*others cut down
9 branches from the trees, and strawed *them* in the way. And the multitudes that went before, and that followed, cried, saying, *i*Hosanna to the

A. D. 33.
f John 12. 12.
g ch. 16. 21.
h ch. 27. 2.
John 18. 28.
Acts 3. 13.
i Mark 10.35.
j ch. 27. 56.
Mark 15.40.
k ch. 4. 21.
l ch. 19. 28.
Jas. 4. 3.
*m*ch. 26. 39.
Mark 14.36.
John 18. 11.
*n*Luke 12. 50.
o Acts 12. 2.
Rom. 8. 17.
2 Cor. 1. 7.
Rev. 1. 9.
p ch. 25. 34.
q Luke 22. 24.
r 1 Pet. 5. 3.
s ch. 23. 11.
Mark 9. 35.
Mark 10.43.
t ch. 18. 4.
u John 13. 4.
Phil. 2. 7.
v Luke 22. 27.
John 13. 14.
w Isa. 53. 10.
Dan. 9. 24.
John 11. 51.
1 Tim. 2. 6.
Tit. 2. 14.
1 Pet. 1. 19.
x ch. 26. 28.
Rom. 5. 15.
Heb. 9. 28.
y Mark 10.46.
Luke 18. 35.
z ch. 9. 27.
a Ps. 145. 8.
Heb. 4. 15.

CHAP. 21.
a Mark 11. 1.
Luke 19. 29.
b Zec. 14. 4.
c Ps. 24. 1.
d 2 Cor. 8. 9.
e 1 Ki. 1. 33.
Isa. 62. 11.
Zec. 9. 9.
f Mark 11. 4.
g 2 Ki. 9. 13.
h Lev. 23. 40.
John 12. 13.
i Ps. 118. 25.
ch. 22. 42.
Mark 12.35-37.
Luke 18.38.
Rom. 1. 3.

But that is not all the teaching of this parable; for, as *Olshausen* finely says, the parables are like many-sided precious stones, cut so as to cast their lustre in more than one direction.
17-28.—THIRD EXPLICIT ANNOUNCEMENT OF HIS APPROACHING SUFFERINGS, DEATH, AND RESURRECTION—THE AMBITIOUS REQUEST OF JAMES AND JOHN, AND THE REPLY. (= Mark

x. 32-45; Luke xviii. 31-34.) For the exposition, see on Mark x. 32-45.
29-34.—TWO BLIND MEN HEALED. (= Mark x. 46-52; Luke xviii. 35-43.) For the exposition, see on Luke xviii. 35-43.
CHAP. XXI. 1-9.—CHRIST'S TRIUMPHAL ENTRY INTO JERUSALEM ON THE FIRST DAY OF THE WEEK. (= Mark xi. 1-11; Luke xix. 29-40; John

son of David! *^j*Blessed *is* he that cometh in the name of the Lord! Hosanna in the highest!

10 And *^k*when he was come into Jerusalem, all the city was moved, saying,

11 Who is this? And the multitude said, This is Jesus the *^l*prophet of Nazareth of Galilee.

12 And *^m*Jesus went into the temple of God, and cast out all them that sold and bought in the temple, and overthrew the tables of the *^n*money-

13 changers, and the seats of them that sold doves, and said unto them, It is written, *^o*My house shall be called the house of prayer; but *^p*ye have

14 made it a den of thieves. And *^q*the blind and the lame came to him in

15 the temple; and he healed them. And when the chief priests and scribes saw the wonderful things that he did, and the children crying in the temple, and saying, Hosanna to *^r*the son of David; they were sore dis-

16 pleased, and said unto him, Hearest thou what these say? And Jesus saith unto them, Yea; have ye never read, *^s*Out of the mouth of babes

17 and sucklings thou hast perfected praise? And he left them, and went out of the city into *^t*Bethany; and he lodged there.

18 Now in the morning, as he returned into the city, he hungered.

19 And when he saw ^1a fig tree in the way, he came to it, and found nothing thereon, but leaves only, and said unto it, Let no fruit grow on thee henceforward for ever. And presently the fig tree withered away.

20 And when the disciples saw *it*, they marvelled, saying, How soon is

21 the fig tree withered away! Jesus answered and said unto them, Verily I say unto you, *^u*If ye have faith, and *^v*doubt not, ye shall not only do this *which is done* to the fig tree, *^w*but also if ye shall say unto this mountain, Be thou removed, and be thou cast into the sea; it shall be

22 done. And *^x*all things, whatsoever ye shall ask in prayer, believing, ye shall receive.

23 And *^y*when he was come into the temple, the chief priests and the elders of the people came unto him as he was teaching, and *^z*said, By what authority doest thou these things? and who gave thee this au-

24 thority? And *^a*Jesus answered and said unto them, I also will ask you one thing, which if ye tell me, I in like wise will tell you by what author-

25 ity I do these things. The baptism of John, whence was it? from heaven, or of men? And they reasoned with themselves, saying, If we shall say, From heaven; he will say unto us, Why did ye not then be-

26 lieve him? But if we shall say, Of men; we fear the people; *^b*for all

A. D. 33.
^j ch. 23. 39.
^k Mark 11.15.
Luke 19. 45.
John 12. 13.
^l John 6. 14.
^m Mal. 3. 1, 2.
Mark 11.11.
John 2. 15.
^n Deut. 14.25.
^o Isa. 56. 7.
^p Jer. 7. 11.
Mark 11.17.
Luke 19.46.
^q Isa. 35. 5.
ch. 9. 35.
ch. 11. 4, 5.
Acts 3. 1-9.
Acts 10. 38.
^r Isa. 11. 1.
ch. 22. 42.
John 7. 42.
^s Ps. 8. 2.
ch. 11. 25.
^t Mark 11.11.
John 11. 18.
1 one fig tree.
^u ch. 17. 20.
Luke 17. 6.
^v Jas. 1. 6.
^w 1 Cor. 13. 2.
^x ch. 7. 7.
Mark 11.24.
Luke 11. 9.
Jas. 5. 16.
1 John 3.22.
1 John 5.14.
^y Luke 20.21.
^z Ex. 2. 14.
Acts 4. 7.
Acts 7. 27.
^a Job 5. 13.
^b ch. 14. 5.
Luke 20. 6.
Mark 6. 20.
John 5. 35.
John 10. 41, 42.

xii. 12-19.) For the exposition of this majestic scene—recorded, as will be seen, by all the Evangelists—see on Luke xix. 29-40.

10-22.—STIR ABOUT HIM IN THE CITY—SECOND CLEANSING OF THE TEMPLE, AND MIRACLES THERE—GLORIOUS VINDICATION OF THE CHILDREN'S TESTIMONY—THE BARREN FIG TREE CURSED, WITH LESSONS FROM IT. (= Mark xi. 11-26; Luke xix. 45-48.) For the exposition, see Luke xix. after *v.* 44; and on Mark xi. 12-26.

23-46.—THE AUTHORITY OF JESUS QUESTIONED, AND THE REPLY—THE PARABLES OF THE TWO SONS, AND OF THE WICKED HUSBANDMEN. (= Mark xi. 27—xii. 12; Luke xx. 1-19.)

Now commences, as *Alford* remarks, that series of parables and discourses of our Lord with His enemies, in which He develops, more completely than ever before, His hostility to their hypocrisy and iniquity: and so they are stirred up to compass His death.

The Authority of Jesus Questioned, and the Reply (23-27). **23.** And when he was come into the temple, the chief priests and the elders of the people came unto him as he was teaching, and said, By what authority doest thou these things?— referring particularly to the expulsion of the buyers and sellers from the temple. and who gave thee this authority? **24.** And Jesus answered and said unto them, I also will ask you one thing, which if ye tell me, I in like wise will tell you by what authority I do these things. **25.** The baptism of John—meaning, his whole mission and ministry, of which baptism was the proper character, whence was it? from heaven, or of men? What wisdom there was in this way of meeting their question, will best appear by their reply. And they reasoned with themselves, saying, If we shall say, From heaven; he will say unto us, Why did ye not then believe him?— 'Why did ye not believe the testimony which he bore to Me, as the promised and expected Messiah?' for that was the burden of his whole testimony. **26.** But if we shall say, Of men; we fear the people [τὸν ὄχλον]—rather the multitude. In Luke (xx. 6) it is, "all the people will stone us" [καταλιθάσει]—'stone us to death.' for all hold John as a prophet. Crooked, cringing hypocrites! No wonder Jesus gave you no answer. **27.** And they answered Jesus, and said, We cannot tell. Evidently their difficulty was, how to

27 hold John as a prophet. And they answered Jesus, and said, We cannot tell. And he said unto them, Neither tell I you by what authority I do these things.

28 But what think ye? A *certain* man had two sons; and he came to
29 the first, and said, Son, go work to-day in my vineyard. He answered
30 and said, I will not: but afterward *c* he repented, and went. And he came to the second, and said likewise. And he answered and said, I *go*,
31 sir; and went not. Whether of them twain did the will of *his* father? They say unto him, The first. Jesus saith unto them, Verily I say unto you, That the publicans and the harlots go into the kingdom of God be-
32 fore you. For *d* John came unto you in the way of righteousness, and ye believed him not: but *e* the publicans and the harlots believed him: and ye, when ye had seen *it*, repented not afterward, that ye might believe him.

33 Hear another parable: There was a certain householder, *f* which planted a vineyard, and hedged it round about, and digged a winepress in it, and built a tower, and let it out to husbandmen, and *g* went into a
34 far country: and when the time of the fruit drew near, he sent his servants to the husbandmen, *h* that they might receive the fruits of it.

A. D. 33.
c ch. 3. 2.
2 Chr.33.19.
Isa. 1. 16.
Isa. 55. 6, 7.
Ezek. 18.28.
Dan. 4. 34-37.
Jonah 3. 2.
Luke 15.18.
Acts 26. 20.
Eph. 2.1-10.
d Isa. 35. 8.
Jer. 6. 16.
ch. 3. 1.
Luke3.8-13.
e Luke 3. 12.
f Ps. 80. 9.
Song 8. 11.
Isa. 5. 1.
Jer. 2. 21.
Mark 12. 1.
Luke 20. 9.
g ch. 25. 14.
h Song 8. 11.

answer, so as neither to shake their determination to reject the claims of Christ nor damage their reputation with the people. For the truth itself they cared nothing whatever. **And he said unto them, Neither tell I you by what authority I do these things.** What composure and dignity of wisdom does our Lord here display, as He turns their question upon themselves, and, while revealing His knowledge of their hypocrisy, closes their mouths! Taking advantage of the surprise, silence, and awe, produced by this reply, our Lord followed it immediately up by the two following parables.

Parable of the Two Sons (28-32). **28. But what think ye? A certain man had two sons; and he came to the first, and said, Son, go work to-day in my vineyard**—for true religion is a practical thing, a "bringing forth fruit unto God." **29. He answered and said, I will not.** *Trench* notices the rudeness of this answer, and the total absence of any attempt to excuse such disobedience, both characteristic; representing careless, reckless sinners, resisting God to His face. **but afterward he repented, and went. 30. And he came to the second, and said likewise. And he answered and said, I** [go], **sir** [Ἐγώ κύριε]—'I, sir.' The emphatic "I," here, denotes the self-righteous complacency which says, "God, I thank thee that *I* am not as other men" (Luke xviii. 11). **and went not.** *He* did not "afterward repent" and refuse to go; for there was here no *intention* to go. It is the class that "say and do not" (ch. xxiii. 3)—a falseness more abominable to God, says *Stier*, than any "I will not." **31. Whether of them twain did the will of his Father? They say unto him, The first.** [Instead of ὁ πρῶτος, "the first," *Tregelles* reads ὁ ὕστερος, 'the latter,' contrary not only to the manifest sense of the parable, but to the decided preponderance, as we think, of MS. authority. *Tischendorf* adheres to the received text.] Now comes the application. **Jesus saith unto them, Verily I say unto you, That the publicans and the harlots go**—or 'are going;' even now entering, while ye hold back. **into the kingdom of God before you.** The publicans and the harlots were the first son, who, when told to work in the Lord's vineyard, said, I will not; but afterwards repented and went. Their early life was a flat and flagrant refusal to do what they were commanded; it was one continued rebellion against the authority of God. "The chief priests and the elders of the people," with whom our Lord was now speaking, were the second son, who said, I go, Sir, but went not. They were early called, and all their life long professed obedience to God, but never rendered it; their life was one of continued disobedience. **32. For John came unto you in the way of righteousness**—that is, 'calling you to repentance;' as Noah is styled "a preacher of righteousness" (2 Pet. ii. 5), when like the Baptist he warned the old world to "flee from the wrath to come." **and ye believed him not.** "They did not reject him;" nay, they "were willing for a season to rejoice in his light" (John v. 35): but they would not receive his testimony to Jesus. **but the publicans and the harlots believed him.** Of the publicans this is twice expressly recorded, Luke iii. 12; vii. 29. Of the harlots, then, the same may be taken for granted, though the fact is not expressly recorded. These outcasts gladly believed the testimony of John to the coming Saviour, and so hastened to Jesus when He came. See Luke vii. 37; xv. 1, &c. **and ye, when ye had seen it, repented not afterward, that ye might believe him.** Instead of being "provoked to jealousy" by their example, ye have seen them flocking to the Saviour and getting to heaven, unmoved.

Parable of the Wicked Husbandmen (33-46). **33. Hear another parable: There was a certain householder, which planted a vineyard.** See on Luke xiii. 6. **and hedged it round about, and digged a winepress in it, and built a tower.** These details are taken, as is the basis of the parable itself, from that beautiful parable of Isa. v. 1-7, in order to fix down the application and sustain it by Old Testament authority. **and let it out to husbandmen.** These are just the ordinary spiritual guides of the people, under whose care and culture the fruits of righteousness are expected to spring up. **and went into a far country**—"for a long time" (Luke xx. 9), leaving the vineyard to the laws of the spiritual husbandry during the whole time of the Jewish economy. On this phraseology, see on Mark iv. 26. **34. And when the time of the fruit drew near, he sent his servants to the husbandmen.** By these "servants" are meant the prophets and other extraordinary messengers, raised up from time to time. See on ch. xxiii. 37. **that they might receive**

35 And [i]the husbandmen took his servants, and beat one, and killed
36 another, and stoned another. Again, he sent other servants more than
37 the first; and they did unto them likewise. But last of all [j]he sent unto
38 them his son, saying, They will reverence my son. But when the husbandmen saw the son, they said among themselves, [k]This is the heir;
39 [l]come, let us kill him, and let us seize on his inheritance. And [m]they
40 caught him, and cast *him* out of the vineyard, and slew *him*. When the
   Lord therefore of the vineyard cometh, what will he do unto those hus-
41 bandmen? They [n]say unto him, [o]He will miserably destroy those
   wicked men, [p]and will let out *his* vineyard unto other husbandmen,
42 which shall render him the fruits in their seasons. Jesus saith unto them,
   [q]Did ye never read in the Scriptures, The stone which the builders rejected, the same is become the head of the corner: this is the Lord's
43 doing, and it is [r]marvellous in our eyes? Therefore say I unto you,
   [s]The kingdom of God shall be taken from you, and given to a nation
44 bringing forth the fruits thereof. And whosoever [t]shall fall on this stone
   shall be broken: but on whomsoever it shall fall, [u]it will grind him to
   powder.

A. D. 33.

[i] 2 Chr. 24. 21.
    2 Chr. 36. 16.
[j] Gal. 4. 4.
[k] Ps. 2. 8.
[l] Ps. 2. 2.
    John 11. 53.
    Acts 4. 27.
[m] Acts 2. 23.
[n] Luke 20. 16.
[o] Deut. 4. 26.
[p] Acts 13. 46.
    Rom. 9. 1.
[q] Ps 118. 22.
    Isa. 28. 16.
    Mark 12. 10.
    Acts 4. 11.
[r] 1 Tim. 3. 16.
[s] ch. 8. 12.
[t] Isa. 8. 14.
    Zec. 12. 3.
[u] Isa. 60. 12.
    Dan. 2. 44.

the fruits of it. See again on Luke xiii. 6. **35. And the husbandmen took his servants, and beat one**—see Jer. xxxvii. 15; xxxviii. 6. **and killed another**—see Jer. xxvi. 20-23. **and stoned another**—see 2 Chr. xxiv. 21. Compare with this whole verse ch. xxiii. 37, where our Lord reiterates these 'charges in the most melting strain. **36. Again, he sent other servants more than the first; and they did unto them likewise**—see 2 Kings xvii. 13; 2 Chr. xxxvi. 15, 16; Neh. ix. 26. **37. But last of all he sent unto them his son, saying, They will reverence my son.** In Mark (xii. 6) this is most touchingly expressed: "Having yet therefore one son, His well-beloved, He sent Him also last unto them, saying, They will reverence my son." Luke's version of it too (xx. 13) is striking: "Then said the lord of the vineyard, What shall I do? I will send my beloved son: it may be they will reverence Him when they see Him." Who does not see that our Lord here severs Himself, by the sharpest line of demarcation, from all merely *human* messengers, and claims for Himself *Sonship* in its loftiest sense? (Compare Heb. i. 3-6.) The expression, "*It may be* they will reverence my son," is designed to teach the almost unimaginable guilt of *not* reverentially welcoming God's Son. **38. But when the husbandmen saw the son, they said among themselves**—compare Gen. xxxvii. 18-20; John xi. 47-53, **This is the heir.** Sublime expression this of the great truth, that God's inheritance was destined for, and in due time is to come into the possession of, His own Son *in our nature* (Heb. i. 2). **come, let us kill him, and let us seize on his inheritance**—that so, from mere *servants*, we may become *lords*. This is the deep aim of the depraved heart; this is emphatically "the root of all evil." **39. And they caught him, and cast him out of the vineyard**—compare Heb. xiii. 11-13 ("without the gate—without the camp"); 1 Ki. xxi. 13; John xix. 17, **and slew him. 40. When the lord therefore of the vineyard cometh.** This represents 'the settling time,' which, in the case of the Jewish ecclesiastics, was that judicial trial of the nation and its leaders which issued in the destruction of their whole state. **what will he do unto those husbandmen? 41. They say unto him, He will miserably destroy those wicked men** [κακοὺς κακῶς]—an emphatic alliteration not easily conveyed in English: 'He will badly destroy those bad men.' or 'miserably destroy those miser-

able men,' is something like it, **and will let out his vineyard unto other husbandmen, which shall render him the fruits in their seasons.** If this answer was given by the Pharisees, to whom our Lord addressed the parable, they thus unwittingly pronounced their own condemnation; as did David to Nathan the prophet (2 Sam. xii. 5-7), and Simon the Pharisee to our Lord, (Luke vii. 43, &c.) But if it was given, as the two other Evangelists agree in representing it, by our Lord Himself, and the explicitness of the answer would seem to favour that supposition, then we can better explain the exclamation of the Pharisees which followed it, in Luke's report—"And when they heard it, they said, God forbid"—His whole meaning now bursting upon them. **42. Jesus saith unto them, Did ye never read in the Scriptures** (Ps. cxviii. 22, 23), **The stone which the builders rejected, the same is become the head of the corner: this is the Lord's doing, and it is marvellous in our eyes?** A bright Messianic prophecy, which reappears in various forms (Isa. xxviii. 16, &c.), and was made glorious use of by Peter before the Sanhedrim (Acts iv. 11). He recurs to it in his first Epistle (1 Pet. ii. 4-6). **43. Therefore say I unto you, The kingdom of God**—God's visible Kingdom, or Church, upon earth, which up to this time stood in the seed of Abraham, **shall be taken from you, and given to a nation bringing forth the fruits thereof**—that is, the great Evangelical community of the faithful, which, after the extrusion of the Jewish nation, would consist chiefly of Gentiles, until "all Israel should be saved" (Rom. xi. 25, 26). This vastly important statement is given by Matthew only. **44. And whosoever shall fall on this stone shall be broken: but on whomsoever it shall fall, it will grind him to powder.** The Kingdom of God is here a Temple, in the erection of which *a certain stone*, rejected as unsuitable by the spiritual builders, is, by the great Lord of the House, made the key-stone of the whole. On that Stone the builders were now "falling" and being "broken" (Isa. viii. 15). They were sustaining great spiritual hurt; but soon that Stone should "fall upon *them*" and "grind them to powder" (Dan. ii. 34, 35; Zec. xii. 3)—in their *corporate* capacity, in the tremendous destruction of Jerusalem, but *personally*, as unbelievers, in a more awful sense still.
    45. And when the chief priests and Pharisees had heard his parables—referring to that of the

45   And when the chief priests and Pharisees had heard his parables, they
46   perceived that he spake of them.   But when they sought to lay hands on
him, they feared the multitude, because they ^vtook him for a prophet.
22   AND Jesus answered ^aand spake unto them again by parables, and
2   said, The kingdom of heaven is like unto a certain king, which made a

A. D. 33.
^v Luke 7. 16.
CHAP. 22.
^a Luke 14.16.
Rev. 19. 7,9.

Two Sons and this one of the Wicked Husband-men, they perceived that he spake of them. 46. But when they sought to lay hands on him—which Luke (xx. 19) says they did "the same hour," hardly able to restrain their rage, they **feared the multitude**—rather 'the multitudes' [τοὺς ὄχλους], because they **took him for a prophet** —just as they feared to say John's baptism was of men, because the masses took him for a prophet (v. 26.) Miserable creatures! So, for this time, "they left Him and went their way" (Mark xii. 12).

Remarks.—1. Though argument be thrown away upon those who are resolved not to believe, the wisdom that can silence them and thus obtain a hearing for weighty truths and solemn warnings, is truly enviable. In this our Lord was incomparable, and He hath herein, as in all else, left us an example that we should follow His steps. 2. The self-righteousness of the Pharisees, which scorn-fully rejected the salvation of the Gospel, and the conscious unworthiness of the publicans and sinners, which thankfully embraced it, reappear from age to age as types of character. Wherever the Gospel is faithfully preached and earnestly pressed, the self-satisfied religious professors show the old reluctance to receive it on the same foot-ing with the profligate; while these great sin-ners, conscious that they deeply need it, and cannot dare to hope for it on the footing of merit, gladly hail it as a message of free grace. 3. A purely democratic form of the Church seems in-consistent with the representations of our Lord in this Section—in which official men are supposed, to whom the Great Proprietor of the vineyard "lets it out," and to whom He will naturally look that they should render Him of its fruits. And though the language of parables is not to be stretched beyond the lessons which they may naturally be supposed intended to teach, it is diffi-cult to make anything out of the parable of the Wicked Husbandmen—at least as regards the Christian Church—on anything short of the above view. 4. Though our Lord—to meet the charge of setting Himself up against God, by the loftiness of His claims—represents Himself invariably as the Father's commissioned Servant in every step of His work; yet, in relation to other servants and messengers of God, He is careful so to sever Him-self from them all, that there may be no danger of His being confounded with them—holding Him-self forth as the Son, Only and Well-beloved (Mark xii. 6), in the sense of a *relationship of na-ture* not to be mistaken, a relationship manifestly implying proper Personal Divinity. 5. The dis-inheriting of Israel after the flesh, and the substi-tution or surrogation of the Gentiles in their place, must not be misunderstood. As Gentiles were not absolutely excluded from the Church of God under the Jewish economy, so neither are Jews now shut out from the Church of Christ. All that we are taught is, that as it was the purpose of God to constitute the seed of Abraham of old to be His visible people, so now, for their unfaithfulness to the great trust com-mitted to them, it has been transferred to the Gentiles, from amongst whom, accordingly God is now taking out a people for His name. When, therefore, we are assured that the time is com-

ing when "all Israel shall be saved" (Rom. xi. 26), that cannot mean merely that they will drop into the Christian Church individually from time to time—for that they have been doing all along, and have never ceased to do—but that they shall be *nationally* re-engrafted into their own olive tree, not now to the exclusion of the Gentiles, but to constitute along with them one universal Church of God upon earth. (See on Rom. xi. 22-24, 26, 28.) 6. "If some of the branches be broken off, and thou," O Gentile, "being a wild olive tree, wert graffed in among them, and with them partakest of the root and fatness of the olive tree; boast not against the branches. Thou wilt say, The branches were broken off, that I might be graffed in. Well; be-cause of unbelief they were broken off, and thou standest by faith. Be not highminded, but fear: for if God spared not the natural branches, take heed lest He also spare not thee. Behold there-fore the goodness and severity of God: on them which fell, severity; but toward thee, goodness, if thou continue in His goodness: otherwise thou also shalt be cut off" (Rom. xi. 17, 19-22). Nor is this a mere threatening *in case* of Gentile unbelief; for Scripture prophecy too clearly intimates, that at that great crisis in the history of Christendom when "all Israel shall be saved," a vast portion of the Gentile Church shall be found equally un-faithful to the trust committed to them with Israel of old, and will be judged accordingly. "Where-fore, let him that thinketh he standeth take heed lest he fall."

CHAP. XXII. 1-14.—PARABLE OF THE MAR-RIAGE OF THE KING'S SON.

This is a different parable from that of the Great Supper, in Luke xiv. 15, &c., and is recorded by Matthew alone. 1. And Jesus answered and spake unto them again by parables, and said, 2. The kingdom of heaven is like unto a certain king, which made a marriage for his son. 'In this parable,' as *Trench* admirably remarks, 'we see how the Lord is revealing Himself in ever clearer light as the central Person of the kingdom, giving here a far plainer hint than in the last parable of the nobility of His descent. There He was indeed the Son, the only and beloved one (Mark xii. 6), of the Householder; but here His race is royal, and He appears as Himself at once the King and the King's Son. (Ps. lxxii. 1.) The last was a parable of the Old Testament history; and Christ is rather the last and greatest of the line of its prophets and teachers than the Founder of a new kingdom. In that, God appears *demanding* some-thing *from* men; in this, a parable of grace, God appears more as *giving* something *to* them. Thus, as often, the two complete each other; this taking up the matter where the other left it.' The "mar-riage" of Jehovah to His people Israel was familiar to Jewish ears; and in Ps. xlv. this marriage is seen consummated in the Person of Messiah 'THE KING,' Himself addressed as 'GOD' and yet as anointed by 'HIS GOD' with the oil of gladness above His fellows.' These apparent contradic-tories (see on Luke xx. 41-44) are resolved in this parable; and Jesus, in claiming to be this King's Son, *serves Himself Heir to all that the pro-phets and sweet singers of Israel held forth as to Jehovah's ineffably near and endearing union to His*

3 marriage for his son, and sent forth his servants to call them that were
4 bidden to the wedding: and they would not come. Again, he sent forth other servants, saying, Tell them which are bidden, Behold, I have prepared my dinner: *b*my oxen and *my* fatlings *are* killed, and all things
5 *are* ready: come unto the marriage. But they *c*made light of *it*, and
6 went their ways, one to his farm, another to his merchandise: and *d*the remnant took his servants, and entreated *them* spitefully, and slew *them*.
7 But when the king heard *thereof*, he was wroth: and he sent forth *e*his
8 armies, and destroyed those murderers, and burned up their city. Then saith he to his servants, The wedding is ready, but they which were
9 bidden were not *f*worthy. Go ye therefore into the highways, and as
10 many as ye shall find, bid to the marriage. So those servants went out into the highways, and *g*gathered together all as many as they found,
11 both bad and good: and the wedding was furnished with guests. And when the king came in to see the guests, he saw there a man *h*which had

A. D. 33.

b Pro. 9. 2.
c Ps. 81. 11.
d 1 Thes. 2.14, 15.
e Isa. 10. 5-7. Jer. 51. 20-23.
Dan. 9. 26.
Luke 19. 27.
f ch. 10. 11.
Luke 20. 35.
Acts 13. 46.
g ch. 13. 38.
h 2 Cor. 5. 3.
Eph. 4. 24.
Col. 3.10,12.
Rev. 3. 4.
Rev. 16. 15.
Rev. 19. 8.

---

people. But observe carefully, that THE BRIDE does not come into view in this parable; its design being to teach certain truths under the figure of *guests* at a wedding *feast*, and the want of a wedding *garment*, which would not have harmonized with the introduction of the Bride. *And sent forth his servants*—representing all preachers of the Gospel, *to call them that were bidden* —here meaning the Jews, who were "bidden," from the first choice of them onwards through every summons addressed to them by the prophets to hold themselves in readiness for the appearing of their King. *to the wedding*—or the marriage festivities, when the preparations were all concluded. *and they would not come*—as the issue of the whole ministry of the Baptist, our Lord Himself, and His apostles thereafter, too sadly showed. *4. Again, he sent forth other servants, saying, Tell them which are bidden, Behold, I have prepared my dinner: my oxen and my fatlings are killed, and all things are ready: come unto the marriage.* This points to those Gospel calls *after* Christ's death, resurrection, ascension, and effusion of the Spirit, to which the parable could not directly allude, but when only it could be said, with strict propriety, "that all things were ready." Compare 1 Cor. v. 7, 8, "Christ our passover is sacrificed for us; therefore, let us keep the feast:" also John vi. 51, "I am the living bread which came down from heaven: if any man eat of this bread, he shall live for ever: and the bread which I will give is my flesh, which I will give for the life of the world." *5. But they made light of it, and went their ways, one to his farm, another to his merchandise: 6. And the remnant took his servants, and entreated them spitefully* [ὕβρισαν]—'insulted them,' *and slew them*. These are two different classes of unbelievers; the one simply *indifferent;* the other absolutely *hostile*—the one, contemptuous *scorners;* the other, bitter *persecutors*. *7. But when the king* —the Great God, who is the Father of our Lord Jesus Christ, *heard thereof*. [*Tregelles*, with not sufficient warrant, as we think, omits the word ἀκούσας. *Tischendorf* retains it.] *he was wroth* —at the affront put both on His Son, and on Himself who had deigned to invite them. *and he sent forth his armies*. The *Romans* are here styled God's armies, just as the Assyrian is styled "the rod of His anger" (Isa. x. 5), as being the executors of His judicial vengeance. *and destroyed those murderers*—and in what vast numbers did they do it! *and burned up their city*. Ah! Jerusalem, once "the city of the Great King" (Ps. xlviii. 2), and even up al-

most to this time (ch. v. 35); but now it is *"their city"*—just as our Lord, a day or two after this, said of the temple, where God had so long dwelt, "Behold *your* house is left unto you desolate" (ch. xxiii. 38)! Compare Luke xix. 43, 44. 8. *Then saith he to his servants, The wedding is ready, but they which were bidden were not worthy*—for how should those be deemed worthy to sit down at His table who had affronted Him by their treatment of His gracious invitation? 9. *Go ye therefore into the highways*—the great outlets and thoroughfares, whether of town or country, where human beings are to be found, *and as many as ye shall find bid to the marriage*—that is, just as they are. 10. *So those servants went out into the highways, and gathered together all as many as they found, both bad and good*— that is, without making any distinction between open sinners and the morally correct. The Gospel call fetched in Jews, Samaritans, and outlying heathen alike. Thus far the parable answers to that of 'the Great Supper,' Luke xiv. 16, &c. But the distinguishing feature of our parable is what follows: 11. *And when the king came in to see the guests.* Solemn expression this, of that *omniscient inspection of every professed disciple of the Lord Jesus* from age to age, in virtue of which his true character will hereafter be judicially proclaimed! *he saw there a man*. This shows that it is the judgment of *individuals* which is intended in this latter part of the parable: the first part represents rather *national* judgment. *which had not on a wedding garment*. The language here is drawn from the following remarkable passage in Zeph. i. 7, 8:— "Hold thy peace at the presence of the Lord God; for the day of the Lord is at hand: for the Lord hath prepared a sacrifice, He hath bid His guests. And it shall come to pass in the day of the Lord's sacrifice, that I will punish the princes, and the king's children, and all such as are clothed with strange apparel." The custom in the East of presenting festival garments (See Gen. xlv. 22; 2 Ki. v. 22), even though not clearly proved, is certainly presupposed here. It undoubtedly means something which they bring not of their own— for how could they have any such dress who were gathered in from the highways indiscriminately?— but which they *receive* as their appropriate dress. And what can that be but what is meant by "putting on the Lord Jesus" as "THE LORD OUR RIGHTEOUSNESS"? (See Ps. xlv. 13, 14.) Nor could such language be strange to those in whose ears had so long resounded those words of prophetic joy:— "1 will greatly rejoice in the Lord, my soul shall be

12 not on a wedding garment: and he saith unto him, Friend, how camest thou in hither not having a wedding garment? And he *i*was speechless.

13 Then said the king to the servants, Bind him hand and foot, and take him away, and cast *him* *j*into outer darkness; there shall be weeping and

14 gnashing of teeth. For *k*many are called, but few *are* chosen.

15 Then *l*went the Pharisees, and took counsel how they might entangle

16 him in *his* talk. And they sent out unto him their disciples with the Herodians, saying, Master, we know that thou art true, and teachest the way of God in truth, neither carest thou for any *man;* for thou regardest

17 not the person of men. Tell us therefore, What thinkest thou? Is it

18 lawful to give tribute unto Cesar, or not? But Jesus perceived their

19 wickedness, and said, Why tempt ye me, *ye* hypocrites? Show me the

20 tribute money. And they brought unto him a ¹penny. And he saith

21 unto them, Whose *is* this image and ²superscription? They say unto him, Cesar's. Then saith he unto them, *m*Render therefore unto Cesar the things which are Cesar's; and unto God the things that are God's.

22 When they had heard *these words*, they *n*marvelled, and left him, and went their way.

23 The *o*same day came to him the Sadducees, *p*which say that there is

24 no resurrection, and asked him, saying, Master, *q*Moses said, If a man die, having no children, his brother shall marry his wife, and raise up

A. D. 33.

i Rom 3. 19.
j ch. 8. 12.
k ch. 20. 16.
l Mark 12. 13.
Luke 20. 20.
¹ In value seven-pence half-penny.
ch. 20. 2.
² Or, inscription.
m ch. 17. 25.
Luke 23. 2.
Rom. 13. 7.
n Job 5. 13.
o ch. 3. 7.
ch. 16. 6.
Mark 12. 18.
Luke 20. 27.
Acts 4. 1.
Acts 5. 17.
p Acts 23. 8.
1 Cor. 15.12.
2 Tim. 2.17.
q Gen. 38. 8.
Deut. 25. 6.

---

joyful in my God; for He hath clothed me with the garments of salvation, He hath covered me with the robe of righteousness, as a bridegroom decketh himself with ornaments, and as a bride adorneth herself with her jewels" (Isa. lxi. 10). **12. And he saith unto him, Friend, how camest thou in hither not having a wedding garment? And he was speechless**—being self-condemned. **13. Then said the king to the servants**—the angelic ministers of divine vengeance (as in ch. xiii. 41). **Bind him hand and foot**—putting it out of his power to resist, **and take him away, and cast him into outer darkness;** [εἰς τὸ σκότος τὸ ἐξώτερον]. So ch. viii. 12; xxv. 30. The expression is emphatic—'The darkness which is outside.' To be '*outside*' at all—or, in the language of Rev. xxii. 15, to be '*without*' the heavenly city [ἔξω], excluded from its joyous nuptials and gladsome festivities—is sad enough of itself, without anything else. But to find themselves not only excluded from the brightness and glory and joy and felicity of the kingdom above, but thrust into a region of "darkness," with all its horrors, this is the dismal retribution here announced, that awaits the unworthy at the great day. [there] [ἐκεῖ]—in that region and condition, **shall be weeping and gnashing of teeth.** See on ch. xiii. 42. **14. For many are called, but few are chosen.** So ch. xix. 30. See on ch. xx. 16.

Remarks.—1. What claim to supreme Divinity brighter and more precious than our Lord here advances can be conceived? Observe the succession of ideas, as unfolded in the Old Testament, and how Jesus places Himself in the centre of them. First, all the gracious relations which Jehovah is represented as sustaining to His people culminate in the intimate and endearing one of a marriage-union (Jer. iii. 14; Hos. ii. 16; &c). But next, when the nuptial-song of this high union is sung, in the Forty-fifth Psalm, we find it to celebrate a union, not directly and immediately between *Jehovah* and the Church, but between *Messiah* and the Church; yet a Messiah who, while anointed *of God* with the oil of gladness above His fellows, is addressed in the Psalm as *Himself God:* so that it is just Jehovah in the Person of Messiah "the King" who in that nuptial-song is cele-

107

brated as taking the Church to be His Bride. But this is not all; for in other predictions this Divine Messiah is expressly called the *Son of God* (Ps. ii. 7, 12; compare Prov. xxx. 4; Dan. iii. 25). Such being the representations of the Old Testament, what does Jesus here but serve Himself Heir to them, holding Himself forth as Himself *the King's Son* of Old Testament prophecy, as the Anointed King in whose Person Jehovah was to marry His people to Himself, and whose nuptials are celebrated in the lofty Messianic Psalm to which we have adverted? 2. As in the parable of the Great Supper (Luke xiv.), so here, it is not those who have all along basked in the sunshine of religious privileges who are the readiest to embrace the Gospel call, but the very opposite classes. And is it not so still? 3. The terrible destruction which fell upon Jerusalem, and the breaking up and dispersion and wretchedness of the nation which ensued, and continues to this hour—what a warning are they of that vengeance of God which awaits the despisers of His Son! 4. Though sinners are invited to Christ as they are, and salvation is "without money and without price," we are "accepted" only "in the Beloved" (Eph. i. 6); if there be "no condemnation," it is "to them that are *in Christ Jesus*" (Rom. viii. 1). These are they that have "put on the Lord Jesus" (Rom. xiii. 14; Gal. iii. 27). This is to have the wedding garment. 5. Though we may deceive not only others but ourselves, there is an Eye which comes in expressly to see the guests; the one thing He looks for is that wedding garment; and amongst myriads of persons, all professing to be His, He can discern even one who is not. 6. No moral or religious excellences will compensate for the absence of this wedding garment. If we have not put on the Lord Jesus, if we are not "in Christ Jesus," our doom is sealed; and what a doom—to be cast indignantly and without the power of resistance into outer darkness, where there shall be weeping and gnashing of teeth! Oh! do men really believe that this doom awaits those who, however exemplary in other respects, venture to present themselves before God *out of Christ?*

15-40.—ENTANGLING QUESTIONS ABOUT TRIBUTE, THE RESURRECTION, AND THE GREAT COM-

25 seed unto his brother. Now there were with us seven brethren: and the
first, when he had married a wife, deceased, and, having no issue, left his
26 wife unto his brother: likewise the second also, and the third, unto the
27, [3] seventh. And last of all the woman died also. Therefore in the
28 resurrection whose wife shall she be of the seven? for they all had her.
29 Jesus answered and said unto them, Ye do err, [r] not knowing the
30 Scriptures, nor the power of God. For in the resurrection they neither
marry, nor are given in marriage, but [s] are as the angels of God in heaven.
31 But as touching the resurrection of the dead, have ye not read that
32 which was spoken unto you by God, saying, I [t] am the God of Abraham,
and the God of Isaac, and the God of Jacob? God is not the God of
33 the dead, but of the living. And when the multitude heard *this*, they
[u] were astonished at his doctrine.
34 But when the Pharisees had heard that he had put the Sadducees to
35 silence, they were gathered together. Then one of them, *which was* [v] a
36 lawyer, asked *him a question*, tempting him, and saying, Master, which
37 *is* the great commandment in the law? Jesus said unto him, [w] Thou
shalt love the Lord thy God with all thy heart, and with all thy soul,
38 and with all thy mind. This is the first and great commandment.
39 And the second *is* like unto it, [x] Thou shalt love thy neighbour as thyself.
40 On [y] these two commandments hang all the Law and the Prophets.
41 While [z] the Pharisees were gathered together, Jesus asked them,
42 saying, What think ye of Christ? whose son is he? They say unto him,
43 *The son* of David. He saith unto them, How then doth David [a] in spirit
44 call him Lord, saying, The [b] LORD said unto my Lord, Sit thou on my
45 right hand, till I make thine enemies thy footstool? If David then call
46 him Lord, how is he his son? And [c] no man was able to answer him a
word; neither durst any *man* from that day forth ask him any more
questions.

23 THEN spake Jesus to the multitude, and to his disciples, saying, [a] The
2, scribes and the Pharisees sit in Moses' seat: all therefore whatsoever
3 they bid you observe, *that* observe and do; but do not ye after their
4 works: for [b] they say, and do not. For [c] they bind heavy burdens
and grievous to be borne, and lay *them* on men's shoulders; but they
5 *themselves* will not move them with one of their fingers. But [d] all their

A. D. 33.
[3] seven.
[r] John 20. 9.
[s] Ps. 103. 20.
Zec. 3. 7.
ch. 13. 43.
1 Cor. 7. 29.
1 John 3. 2.
[t] Ex. 3. 6, 16.
Mark 12.26.
Luke 20. 37.
Acts 7. 32.
Heb. 11. 16.
[u] ch. 7. 28.
[v] Luke 10. 25.
[w] Deut. 6. 5.
Deut. 10.12.
Deut. 30. 6.
Pro. 23. 26.
[x] Lev. 19. 18.
ch. 19. 19.
Mark 12.31.
Rom. 13. 9.
Gal. 5. 14.
Jas. 2. 8.
[y] ch. 7. 12.
1 Tim 1. 5.
[z] Mark 12.35.
Luke 20. 41.
[a] 2 Sam. 23.2.
Acts 2. 30.
2 Pet. 1. 21.
[b] Ps. 110. 1.
Acts 2. 31.
1 Cor. 15.25.
Heb. 1. 13.
Heb. 10. 12.
[c] Luke 14. 6.
CHAP. 23.
[a] Neh. 8. 4,8.
Mal. 2. 7.
[b] Rom. 2. 19.
[c] Luke 11.46.
Acts 15. 10.
Gal. 6. 13.
[d] ch. 6. 1, 2.

MANDMENT, WITH THE REPLIES. (= Mark xii.
13-34; Luke xx. 20-40.) For the exposition, see on
Mark xii. 13-34.
   41-46.—CHRIST BAFFLES THE PHARISEES BY A
QUESTION ABOUT DAVID AND MESSIAH. (= Mark
xii. 35-37; Luke xx. 41-44.) For the exposition, see
on Mark xii. 35-37.
   CHAP. XXIII. 1-39.—DENUNCIATION OF THE
SCRIBES AND PHARISEES—LAMENTATION OVER
JERUSALEM, AND FAREWELL TO THE TEMPLE.
(= Mark xii. 38-40; Luke xx. 45-47.) For this
long and terrible discourse we are indebted,
with the exception of a few verses in Mark and
Luke, to Matthew alone. But as it is only an
extended repetition of denunciations uttered
not long before at the table of a Pharisee, and
recorded by Luke (xi. 37-54), we may take both
together in the exposition.
   Denunciation of the Scribes and Pharisees (1-36).
The first twelve verses were addressed more immediately to the disciples, the rest to the scribes
and Pharisees.
   1. **Then spake Jesus to the multitude** [ὄχλοις]—
'to the multitudes,' **and to his disciples, 2. Saying, The scribes and the Pharisees sit.** The Jewish teachers *stood* to read, but *sat* to expound the
Scriptures, as will be seen by comparing Luke
iv. 16 with *v.* 20. **in Moses' seat**—that is, as in-

terpreters of the law given by Moses. **3. All
therefore**—that is, all which, as *sitting in that seat*
and teaching *out of that law*, **they bid you observe, that observe and do.** The word "therefore" is thus, it will be seen, of great importance,
as limiting those injunctions which He would have
them obey to what they fetched from the law
itself. In requiring implicit obedience to such
injunctions, He would have them to recognize
the authority with which they taught over and
above the obligation of the law itself—an important principle truly; but He who denounced
the traditions of such teachers (ch. xv. 3) cannot have meant here to throw His shield over
these. It is remarked by *Webster and Wilkinson*
that the warning to *beware* of the scribes is
given by Mark and Luke without any qualification; the charge to *respect* and *obey* them being
reported by Matthew alone, indicating for whom
this Gospel was especially written, and the writer's
desire to conciliate the Jews. **4. For they bind
heavy burdens and grievous to be borne, and lay
them on men's shoulders; but they themselves
will not move them**—"touch them not" (Luke
xi. 46), **with one of their fingers**—referring not so
much to the irksomeness of the legal rites, though
they were irksome enough (Acts xv. 10), as to the
heartless rigour with which they were enforced,

works they do for to be seen of men: 'they make broad their phylac-
6 teries, and enlarge the borders of their garments, and *f*love the uppermost
7 rooms at feasts, and the chief seats in the synagogues, and greetings in
8 the markets, and to be called of men, Rabbi, Rabbi. But *g*be not ye
called Rabbi: for one is your Master, *even* Christ; and all ye are brethren.
9 And call no *man* your father upon the earth: *h*for one is your Father,
10 which is in heaven. Neither be ye called masters: for one is your Master,
11 *even* Christ. But *i*he that is greatest among you shall be your servant.
12 And *j*whosoever shall exalt himself shall be abased; and he that shall
humble himself shall be exalted.
13 But *k*woe unto you, scribes and Pharisees, hypocrites! for ye shut up
the kingdom of heaven against men: for ye neither go in *yourselves*,
14 neither suffer ye them that are entering to go in. Woe unto you, scribes
and Pharisees, hypocrites! *l*for ye devour widows' houses, and for a pretence make long prayer: therefore ye shall receive the greater damnation.
15 Woe unto you, scribes and Pharisees, hypocrites! for ye compass sea and
land to make one proselyte; and when he is made, ye make him two-
16 fold more the child of hell than yourselves. Woe unto you, *m*ye blind
guides, which say, *n*Whosoever shall swear by the temple, it is nothing;
but whosoever shall swear by the gold of the temple, he is a debtor!
17 *Ye* fools, and blind! for whether is greater, the gold, *o*or the temple that

A. D. 33.

e Num. 15.38.
Deut. 22.12.
f Mark 12.33.
Luke 20.46.
g Jas. 3. 1.
h Mal. 1. 6.
Rom. 8. 14-
17.
i ch. 20. 26.
j Job 22. 29.
Pro. 15. 33.
Pro. 29. 23.
Dan. 4. 37.
Luke 14. 11.
Luke 18.14.
Jas. 4. 6.
1 Pet. 5. 5.
k Luke 11. 52.
l Ezek. 22. 25.
Mark 12.40.
Luke 20. 47.
2 Tim. 3. 6.
Titus 1. 11.
m Isa. 56. 10.
ch. 15. 14.
n ch. 5. 33.
o Ex. 30. 29.

and by men of shameless inconsistency. **5. But
all their works they do for to be seen of men.**
Whatever good they do, or zeal they show, has
but one motive—human applause. **they make
broad their phylacteries**—strips of parchment
with Scripture-texts on them, worn on the forehead, arm, and side, in time of prayer. **and
enlarge the borders of their garments**—fringes
of their upper garments (Num. xv. 37-40). **6.
And love the uppermost rooms.** The word
"room" is now obsolete in the sense here intended. It should be 'the uppermost place' [πρω-
τοκλισίαν], that is, the place of highest honour.
at feasts, and the chief seats in the synagogues.
See on Luke xiv. 7, 8. **7. And greetings in the
markets, and to be called of men, Rabbi, Rabbi.**
It is the *spirit* rather than the *letter* of this that
must be pressed; though the violation of the letter, springing from spiritual pride, has done incalculable evil in the Church of Christ. The reiteration of the word "Rabbi" shows how it tickled
the ear and fed the spiritual pride of those ecclesiastics. [*Tregelles* improperly, as we think, omits
the repetition, but *Tischendorf* does not.] **8. But
be not ye called Rabbi: for one is your Master**
[Καθηγητὴς]—'your Guide, your Teacher,' even
**Christ; and all ye are brethren. 9. And call no
man your father upon the earth: for one is your
Father, which is in heaven. 10. Neither be ye
called masters: for one is your Master, even
Christ.** To construe these injunctions into a condemnation of every title by which church rulers
may be distinguished from the flock which they
rule, is virtually to condemn that rule itself; and
accordingly the same persons do both—but against
the whole strain of the New Testament and sound
Christian judgment. But when we have guarded
ourselves against these extremes, let us see to it
that we retain the full spirit of this warning
against that itch for ecclesiastical superiority
which has been the bane and the scandal of
Christ's ministers in every age. (On the use of
the word "Christ" here, see on ch. i. 1.) **11. But
he that is greatest among you shall be your
servant.** This plainly means, 'shall show that he
is so by becoming your servant;' as in ch. xx. 27,
compared with Mark x. 44. **12. And whosoever**

shall exalt himself shall be abased; and he that
shall humble himself shall be exalted.** See on
Luke xviii. 14.
What follows was addressed more immediately
to the scribes and Pharisees. **13. But woe unto
you, scribes and Pharisees, hypocrites! for ye shut
up the kingdom of heaven against men: for ye
neither go in [yourselves], neither suffer ye them
that are entering to go in.** Here they are charged
with *shutting heaven* against men: in Luke xi. 52,
they are charged with what was worse, *taking away
the key*—"the key of knowledge"—which means, not
the key to open knowledge, but knowledge as the
only key to open heaven. A right knowledge of
God's revealed word is eternal life, as our Lord
says (John xvii. 3, and v. 39); but this they took
away from the people, substituting for it their
wretched traditions. **14. Woe unto you, scribes
and Pharisees, hypocrites! for ye devour widows'
houses, and for a pretence make long prayer:
therefore ye shall receive the greater damnation.**
Taking advantage of the helpless condition and
confiding character of "widows," they contrived
to obtain possession of their property, while by
their "long prayers" they made them believe they
were raised far above "filthy lucre." So much
"the greater damnation" awaits them. What a
life-like description of the Romish clergy, the true
successors of those scribes! **15. Woe unto you,
scribes and Pharisees, hypocrites! for ye compass
sea and land to make one proselyte**—from heathenism. We have evidence of this in *Josephus*.
**and when he is made, ye make him two-fold more
the child of hell than yourselves**—condemned, for
the hypocrisy he would learn to practice, both by
the religion he left and that he embraced. **16.
Woe unto you, ye blind guides.** Striking expression
this of the ruinous effects of erroneous teaching.
Our Lord, here and in some following verses, condemns the subtle distinctions they made as to the
sanctity of oaths, distinctions invented only to
promote their own avaricious purposes. **which**
say, **Whosoever shall swear by the temple, it is
nothing**—he has incurred no debt, **but whosoever
shall swear by the gold of the temple**—meaning
not the gold that adorned the temple itself, but the
Corban, set apart for sacred uses (see on ch. xv. 5),

18 sanctifieth the gold? And, Whosoever shall swear by the altar, it is nothing; but whosoever sweareth by the gift that is upon it, he is [1]guilty.

19 *Ye* fools, and blind! for whether *is* greater, the gift, or [p]the altar that

20 sanctifieth the gift? Whoso therefore shall swear by the altar, sweareth

21 by it, and by all things thereon. And whoso shall swear by the temple,

22 sweareth by it, and by [q]him that dwelleth therein. And he that shall swear by heaven, sweareth by [r]the throne of God, and by him that sitteth therecn.

23   Woe unto you, scribes and Pharisees, hypocrites! [s]for ye pay tithe of mint and [2]anise and cummin, and [t]have omitted the weightier *matters* of the law, judgment, mercy, and faith: these ought ye to have done,

24 and not to leave the other undone. *Ye* blind guides, which strain at a

25 gnat, and swallow a camel. Woe unto you, scribes and Pharisees, hypocrites! [u]for ye make clean the outside of the cup and of the platter, but

26 within they are full of extortion and excess. *Thou* blind Pharisee, cleanse first that *which* [v]*is* within the cup and platter, that the outside of them may be clean also.

27   Woe unto you, scribes and Pharisees, hypocrites! [w]for ye are like unto whited sepulchres, which indeed appear beautiful outward, but are within

Marginal references:

A. D. 33.

[1] Or, debtor, or, bound.
[p] Ex. 29. 37.
[q] 1 Ki. 8. 13.
2 Chr. 6. 2.
Ps. 26. 8.
Ps. 132. 14.
[r] ch. 5. 34.
Ps. 11. 4.
Acts 7. 49.
[s] Luke 11. 42.
[2] anethon, dill.
[t] 1 Sam. 15. 22.
Hos. 6. 6.
Mic. 6. 8.
[u] Mark 7. 4.
Luke 11. 39.
[v] Isa. 55. 7.
Jer. 4. 14.
Ezek. 18. 31.
Luke 6. 45.
Titus 1. 15.
[w] Acts 23. 3.

---

he is a debtor!—that is, it is no longer his own, even though the necessities of a parent might require it. We know who the successors of these men are. **17. Ye fools, and blind! for whether is greater, the gold, or the temple that sanctifieth the gold? And, Whosoever shall swear by the gift that is upon it, he is guilty** [ὀφείλει]. It should have been rendered, "he is a debtor," as in *v.* 16. **19. Ye fools, and blind! for whether is greater, the gift, or the altar that sanctifieth the gift?** (See Exod. xxix. 37.) **20-22. Whoso therefore shall swear by the altar, . . . And . . . by the temple, . . . And . . . by heaven,** &c. See on Matt. v. 33-37.

23. Woe unto you, scribes and Pharisees, hypocrites! for ye pay tithe of mint and anise—rather 'dill,' as in margin [ἄνηθον], **and cummin.** In Luke (xi. 42) it is "and rue, and all manner of herbs." They grounded this practice on Lev. xxvii. 30, which they interpreted rigidly. Our Lord purposely names the most trifling products of the earth, as examples of what they punctiliously exacted the tenth of. **and have omitted the weightier matters of the law, judgment, mercy, and faith.** In Luke (xi. 42) it is, "judgment, mercy, and the love of God"—the expression being probably varied by our Lord Himself on the two different occasions. In both His reference is to Mic. vi. 6-8, where the prophet makes all acceptable religion to consist of three elements—"doing justly, loving mercy, and walking humbly with our God;" which third element pre-supposes and comprehends both the "faith" of Matthew and the "love" of Luke. See on Mark xii. 29, 32, 33. The same tendency to merge greater duties in less besets even the children of God; but *it is the characteristic of hypocrites.* **these ought ye to have done, and not to leave the other undone.** There is no need for one set of duties to jostle out another; but it is to be carefully noted that of the *greater* duties our Lord says, "Ye ought to have done" them, while of the *lesser* He merely says, "Ye ought not to leave them undone." **24. Ye blind guides, which strain at a gnat.** The proper rendering—as in the older English translations, and perhaps our own as it came from the translators' hands—evidently is, 'strain out.' It was the custom, says *Trench*, of the stricter Jews to strain their wine, vinegar, and other potables through

linen or gauze, lest unawares they should drink down some little unclean insect therein, and thus transgress (Lev. xi. 20, 23, 41, 42)—just as the Budhists do now in Ceylon and Hindostan—and to this custom of theirs our Lord here refers. **and swallow a camel**—the largest animal the Jews knew, as the "gnat" was the smallest: both were by the law *unclean.* **25. Woe unto you, scribes and Pharisees, hypocrites! for ye make clean the outside of the cup and of the platter, but within they are full of extortion** [ἁρπαγῆς]. In Luke (xi. 39) the same word is rendered "ravening," that is, 'rapacity.' **and excess. 26. Thou blind Pharisee, cleanse first that which is within the cup and platter, that the outside of them may be clean also.** In Luke (xi. 40) it is, "Ye fools, did not he that made that which is without make that which is within also?"—'He to whom belongs the outer life, and of right demands its subjection to Himself, is the inner man less His?' A remarkable example this of our Lord's power of drawing the most striking illustrations of great truths from the most familiar objects and incidents in life. To these words, recorded by Luke, He adds the following, involving a principle of immense value: "But rather give alms of such things as ye have, and behold, all things are clean unto you" (Luke xi. 41). As the greed of these hypocrites was one of the most prominent features of their character (Luke xvi. 14), our Lord bids them exemplify the opposite character, and then their *outside,* ruled by this, would be beautiful in the eye of God, and their meals would be eaten with clean hands, though never so fouled with the business of this worky world. (See Eccl. ix. 7).

27. Woe unto you, scribes and Pharisees, hypocrites! for ye are like whited (or 'white-washed') **sepulchres** (cf. Acts xxiii. 3). The process of white-washing the sepulchres, as *Lightfoot* says, was performed on a certain day every year, not for ceremonial cleansing, but, as the following words seem rather to imply, to beautify them. **which indeed appear beautiful outward, but are within full of dead men's bones, and** of all uncleanness. What a powerful way of conveying the charge, that with all their fair show their hearts were full of corruption! (Cf. Ps. v. 9; Rom. iii. 13.) But our Lord, stripping off the figure, next holds up their iniquity in naked colours: **28. Even so ye also outwardly appear**

28 full of dead *men's* bones, and of all uncleanness. Even so ye also outwardly appear righteous unto men, but within ye are full of hypocrisy
29 and iniquity. Woe unto you, scribes and Pharisees, hypocrites! because
ye build the tombs of the prophets, and garnish the sepulchres of the
30 righteous, and say, If we had been in the days of our fathers, we would
31 not have been partakers with them in the blood of the prophets. Wherefore ye be witnesses unto yourselves, that *ˣ*ye are the children of them
32 which killed the prophets. Fill *ʸ*ye up then the measure of your fathers.
33 *Ye* serpents, *ye ᶻ*generation of vipers, how can ye escape the damnation
34 of hell? Wherefore, *ᵃ*behold, I send unto you prophets, and wise men,
and scribes: and *some ᵇ*of them ye shall kill and crucify; and *ᶜsome* of
them shall ye scourge in your synagogues, and persecute *them* from city
35 to city: that *ᵈ*upon you may come all the righteous blood shed upon the
earth, *ᵉ*from the blood of righteous Abel unto the blood of Zacharias son
36 of Barachias, whom ye slew between the temple and the altar. Verily I
say unto you, All these things shall come upon this generation.
37 O Jerusalem, Jerusalem, *thou* that killest the prophets, and stonest
them which are sent unto thee, how often would I *ᶠ*have gathered thy
children together, even as a hen gathereth her chickens under *her* wings

A. D. 33.

ˣ Acts 7. 51.
1 Thes 2.15.
ʸ Gen. 15. 16.
Num.32.14.
Zec. 5. 6-11.
1 Thes.2.16.
ᶻ ch. 3. 7.
ch. 12. 34.
Luke 3. 7.
ᵃ ch. 21. 34.
Luke 11. 49.
Acts 11. 27.
Acts 13. 1.
Acts 15. 32.
Rev. 11. 10.
ᵇ Acts 5. 40.
Acts 7. 58.
Acts 22. 19.
ᶜ 2 Cor.11.24.
ᵈ Rev. 18. 24.
ᵉ Gen. 4. 8.
1 John 3.12.
ᶠ Deut. 32.11.

righteous unto men, but within ye are full of
hypocrisy and iniquity. 29-31. Woe unto you,
. . . hypocrites! ye build the tombs of the prophets, . . . And say, If we had been in the
days of our fathers, we would not, &c. Wherefore ye be witnesses unto yourselves, that ye are
the children of them which killed the prophets
—that is, 'ye be witnesses that ye have inherited, and voluntarily served yourselves heirs to,
the truth-hating, prophet-killing, spirit of your
fathers.' Out of pretended respect and honour,
they repaired and beautified the sepulchres of the
prophets, and with whining hypocrisy said, "If
we had been in their days, how differently should
we have treated these prophets?" while all the
time they were witnesses to themselves that they
were the children of them that killed the prophets,
convicting themselves daily of as exact a resemblance in spirit and character to the very classes
over whose deeds they pretended to mourn, as child
to parent. In Luke xi. 44 our Lord gives another
turn to this figure of a grave: "Ye are as graves
which appear not, and the men that walk over
them are not aware of them." As one might unconsciously walk over a grave concealed from view,
and thus contract ceremonial defilement, so the
plausible exterior of the Pharisees kept people
from perceiving the pollution they contracted from
coming in contact with such corrupt characters.
32. Fill ye up then the measure of your fathers.
33. Ye serpents, ye generation of vipers, how can
ye escape the damnation of hell? In thus, at
the end of His ministry, recalling the words of
the Baptist at the outset of his, our Lord would
seem to intimate that the only difference between
their condemnation now and then was, that now
they were ripe for their doom, which they were
not then. 34. Wherefore, behold, I send unto
you prophets, and wise men, and scribes ['Εγὼ
ἀποστέλλω]. The *I* here is emphatic: 'I am sending,' that is, 'am about to send.' In Luke xi. 49,
the variation is remarkable: "Therefore also, said
the wisdom of God, I will send them," &c. What
precisely is meant by "the wisdom of God" here,
is somewhat difficult to determine. To us it appears to be simply an announcement of a purpose
of the Divine Wisdom, in the high style of ancient
prophecy, to send a last set of messengers whom
the people would reject, and, rejecting, would fill
up the cup of their iniquity. But, whereas in

Luke it is 'I, the Wisdom of God, will send them,'
in Matthew it is 'I, Jesus, am sending them,'
language only befitting the one Sender of all the
prophets, the Lord God of Israel now in the flesh.
They are evidently Evangelical messengers, but
called by the familiar Jewish names of "prophets, wise men, and scribes," whose counterparts
were the inspired and gifted servants of the Lord
Jesus; for in Luke (xi. 49) it is "prophets and
apostles." **And some of them ye shall kill and
crucify; and some scourge, . . . and persecute
. . . 35. That upon you may come all the
righteous blood shed upon the earth, from the
blood of righteous Abel unto the blood of Zacharias son of Barachias, whom ye slew between the
temple and the altar.** As there is no record of
any fresh murder answering to this description,
probably the allusion is not to any recent murder,
but to 2 Chr. xxiv. 20-22, as the *last recorded* and
most suitable case for illustration. And as Zacharias' last words were, "The Lord *require it,*" so they
are here warned that of that generation it should
be *required.* **36. Verily I say unto you, All these
things shall come upon this generation.** As it
was only in the last generation of them that "the
iniquity of the Amorites was full" (Gen. xv. 16),
and then the abominations of ages were at once
completely and awfully avenged, so the iniquity of
Israel was allowed to accumulate from age to age
till in that generation it came to the full, and the
whole collected vengeance of Heaven broke at once
over its devoted head. In the first French Revolution the same awful principle was exemplified,
and *Christendom has not done with it yet.*

*Lamentation over Jerusalem, and Farewell to
the Temple* (37-39). **37. O Jerusalem, Jerusalem,
thou that killest the prophets, and stonest
them which are sent unto thee, how often
would I have gathered thy children together,
even as a hen gathereth her chickens under
her wings, and ye would not!** How ineffably
grand and melting is this apostrophe! It is the
very heart of God pouring itself forth through
human flesh and speech. It is this incarnation of
the innermost life and love of Deity, pleading with
men, bleeding for them, and ascending only to
open His arms to them and win them back by the
power of this Story of matchless love, that has
conquered the world, that will yet "draw all men
unto Him," and beautify and ennoble Humanity

38 and ye would not! Behold, your house is left unto you desolate.
39 For I say unto you, *^g*Ye shall not see me henceforth, till ye shall say, *^h*Blessed *is* he that cometh in the name of the Lord.

A. D. 33.

^g Pro. 1. 26.
^h Ps. 118. 26.

itself! "Jerusalem" here does not mean the mere city or its inhabitants; nor is it to be viewed merely as the metropolis of the *nation*, but as the *centre of their religious life*,—"the city of their solemnities, whither the tribes went up, to give thanks unto the name of the Lord;" and at this moment it was full of them. It is the whole family of God, then, which is here apostrophized, by a name dear to every Jew, recalling to him all that was distinctive and precious in his religion. The intense feeling that sought vent in this utterance comes out first in the redoubling of the opening word—"Jerusalem, Jerusalem!" but, next, in the picture of it which He draws—"that killest the prophets, and stonest them which are sent unto thee!"—not content with spurning God's messages of mercy, that canst not suffer even the messengers to live! (See 2 Chr. xxxvi. 15, 16; Neh. ix. 26; Matt. v. 12; xxi. 35-39; xxiii. 29-32; Acts vii. 51-54, 57-59.) When He adds, "How often would I have gathered thee!" He refers surely to something beyond the six or seven times that He visited and taught in Jerusalem while on earth. No doubt it points to "the prophets," whom they "killed," to "them that were sent unto her," whom they "stoned;" for, says Peter, it was "the Spirit of Christ which was in them that did testify beforehand the sufferings of Christ and the following glories" [τὰς μετὰ ταῦτα δόξας, 1 Pet. i. 11]. He it was that "sent unto them all His servants the prophets, rising early and sending them, saying, Oh, do not this abominable thing that I hate!" (Jer. xliv. 4). In His divine and eternal nature, as *Olshausen* says, He was the Prophet of the prophets. But whom would He have gathered so often? "Thee," truth-hating, mercy-spurning, prophet-killing Jerusalem—how often would I have gathered *Thee!* Compare with this that affecting clause in the great ministerial commission, "that repentance and remission of sins should be preached in His name among all nations, *beginning at Jerusalem!*" (Luke xxiv. 47). What encouragement to the heart-broken at their own long-continued and obstinate rebellion! But we have not yet got at the whole heart of this utterance. I would have gathered thee, He says, "even as a hen gathereth her chickens under her wings." Was ever imagery so homely invested with such grace and such sublimity as this, at our Lord's touch? And yet how exquisite the figure itself—of protection, rest, warmth, and all manner of conscious well-being in those poor, defenceless, dependent little creatures, as they creep under and feel themselves overshadowed by the capacious and kindly wing of the mother-bird! If, wandering beyond hearing of her peculiar call, they are overtaken by a storm or attacked by an enemy, what can they do but in the one case droop and die, and in the other submit to be torn in pieces? But if they can reach in time their place of safety, under the mother's wing, in vain will any enemy try to drag them thence. For rising into strength, kindling into fury, and forgetting herself entirely in her young, she will let the last drop of her blood be shed out and perish in defence of her precious charge, rather than yield them to an enemy's talons. How significant all this of what Jesus is and does for men! Under His great Mediatorial wing would He have "gathered" Israel. For the figure, see Deut. xxxii. 10-12; Ruth ii. 12; Ps. xvii. 8; xxxvi. 7; lxi. 4; lxiii. 7; xci. 4; Isa. xxxi. 5; Mal. iv. 2. The ancient rabbins had a beautiful expression for proselytes from the heathen—that they had 'come under the wings of the Shechinah.' For this last word, see on *v.* 38. But what was the result of all this tender and mighty love? The answer is, "And ye would not." (See Neh. ix. 26; Ps. lxxxi. 11, 13; Isa. vi. 9, 10; xxviii. 12; xxx. 8, 9, 15; xlix. 4; liii. 1; with John xii. 37-40.) O mysterious word! mysterious the resistance of such patient Love—mysterious the liberty of self-undoing! The awful dignity of the *will*, as here expressed, might make the ears to tingle. **38.** **Behold, your house**—the Temple, beyond all doubt; but *their* house now, not *the Lord's.* See on ch. xxii. 7. **is left unto you desolate** [ἔρημος]—'deserted;' that is, of its Divine Inhabitant. But who is that? Hear the next words: **39.** **For I say unto you**—and these were *His last words* to the impenitent nation: see opening remarks on Mark xiii.—**Ye shall not see me henceforth.** What? Does Jesus mean that He was Himself the Lord of the temple, and that it became "deserted" when HE finally left it? It is even so. Now is thy fate sealed, O Jerusalem, for the glory is departed from thee! That glory, once visible in the holy of holies, over the mercy-seat, when on the day of atonement the blood of typical expiation was sprinkled on it and in front of it—called by the Jews the *Shechinah*, or the *Dwelling* [שְׁכִינָה], as being the visible pavilion of Jehovah—that glory, which Isaiah (ch. vi.) saw in vision, the beloved disciple says was *the glory of Christ* (John xii. 41). Though it was never visible in the second temple, Haggai foretold that " *the glory of that latter house should be greater than of the former*" (ch. ii. 9), because "the Lord whom they sought was suddenly to come to His temple" (Mal. iii. 1), not in a mere bright cloud, but enshrined in living Humanity! Yet brief as well as "sudden" was the manifestation to be: for the words He was now uttering were to be HIS VERY LAST within its precincts. **till ye shall say, Blessed is he that cometh in the name of the Lord:** that is, till those "Hosannas to the Son of David" with which the multitude had welcomed Him into the city—instead of "sore displeasing the chief priests and scribes" (ch. xxi. 15)—should break forth from the whole nation, as their glad acclaim to their once pierced but now acknowledged Messiah. That such a time will come is clear from Zec. xii. 10; Rom. xi. 26; 2 Cor. iii. 15, 16, &c. In what sense they shall then "see Him," may be gathered from Zec. ii. 10-13; Ezek. xxxvii. 23-28; xxxix. 28, 29, &c.

Remarks.—1. Though the proceedings of church rulers have no intrinsic validity against the truth of God, they have a divine sanction, and as such are to be reverenced, when their sole object is to maintain, unfold, and enforce the word of God (*vv.* 2, 3). 2. Humility and brotherly love, and that supreme attachment to CHRIST which will beget and strengthen both these, are the glory and stability of the Christian ministry; but when the ministers of religion, seeking the fleece rather than the flock, abandon themselves to pride and self-seeking, they not only reveal their own hypocrisy, but bring their office into contempt. What sad illustrations of this does history furnish! If the Jewish ecclesiastics are faithfully, and not too darkly, depicted in this Section, what language would adequately describe their Romish successors, who, with far clearer light, have exceeded them in every detestable feature of their charac-

24 AND ^aJesus went out, and departed from the temple: and his dis-
2 ciples came to *him,* for to show him the buildings of the temple. And
Jesus said unto them, See ye not all these things? Verily I say unto
you, There ^bshall not be left here one stone upon another, that shall not
be thrown down.
3   And as he sat upon the mount of Olives, the disciples came unto
him privately, saying, ^cTell us, when shall these things be? and what

A. D. 33.

CHAP. 24.
^a Mark 13. 1.
Luke 21. 5.
^b 1 Ki. 9. 7.
Jer. 5. 10.
Jer. 26. 18.
Mic. 3. 12.
^c 1 Thes. 5. 1.

---

ter? 3. As "evil men and seducers wax worse and worse, deceiving and being deceived" (2 Tim. iii. 13), and treasure up unto themselves wrath against the day of wrath (Rom. ii. 5); so over and above the partial retribution which often overtakes them individually, there are outstanding accounts left to be settled with them as a class, which accumulate from time to time—sometimes for ages—and are at length, "in the day of visitation," awfully brought up against them and settled, by an exercise of collective and crushing vengeance (*vv.* 31-36). This terrific but righteous law of the divine administration has been illustrated at different times on a scale of no little magnitude; but perhaps its most appalling illustration is yet to come (see Dan. vii. 9-14; 2 Thes. ii. 7-12; Rev. xi. 15-18; xvii. 14; xviii. 5-8, 24). 4. What a combination of withering denunciation and weeping lamentation do we find here—as if the intensity of the Redeemer's holy emotions, in their most vivid contrast, had only found full vent at this last visit to Jerusalem, and in this *His last public address to the impenitent nation!* And if the verses which conclude this chapter were indeed His last words to them, as it is evident they were (see opening remarks on Mark xiii.), how worthy were they of Him, and of the awful occasion, and how pregnant with warning to every such favoured region:—

JERUSALEM.

Jerusalem! Jerusalem! enthroned once on high,   [sky!
Thou favour'd home of God on earth, thou heaven below the
Now brought to bondage with thy sons, a curse and grief to
Jerusalem! Jerusalem! our tears shall flow for thee.   [see,

Oh! hadst thou known thy day of grace, and flock'd beneath
  the wing
Of Him who called thee lovingly, thine own anointed King,
Then had the tribes of all the world gone up thy pomp to see,
And glory dwelt within thy gates, and all thy sons been free!

" And who art thou that mournest me?" replied the ruin gray,
" And fear'st not rather that thyself may prove a castaway?
I am a dried and abject branch,—my place is given to thee;
But woe to ev'ry barren graft of thy wild olive tree!

"Our day of grace is sunk in night, our time of mercy spent,
For heavy was my children's crime, and strange their punish-
  ment;
Yet gaze not idly on our fall, but, sinner, warned be,—
Who spared not His chosen seed may send His wrath on thee!

"Our day of grace is sunk in night, thy noon is in its prime;
Oh, turn and seek thy Saviour's face in this accepted time!
So, Gentile, may Jerusalem a lesson prove to thee,
And in the New Jerusalem thy home for ever be!"—HEBER.

5. Ye that are ready to despair of salvation, when ye think of your obstinate and long-continued rebellion against light and love, truth and grace —yea, bloody persecutors, '*Jerusalem-sinners*'— come hither, and suffer me to plead with you. Listen once more to the Friend of sinners. "O Jerusalem, Jerusalem," says He, "that killest the prophets, and stonest them that are sent unto thee, how often would I have gathered thee!" And would He not have gathered them even then, whilst He was yet speaking? Verily He would, "*but they would not.*" That was all the hindrance: there was none, none at all, in Him. If thou, then, art of their mind, there is indeed no help, no hope, for thee: but if thou only *wilt* be made whole—

'Jesus ready stands to save thee,
  Full of pity, love, and power:
    He is able,
  He is willing, ask no more.'

6. The doctrine of Scripture regarding man's *will* embraces the following points:—First, that whether men are to be saved or lost hinges entirely upon their own will. "Whosoever *will* [ὁ θέλων], let him take the water of life freely" (Rev. xxii. 17). "I would have gathered you, and ye *would* not" [οὐκ ἠθελήσατε]. This great truth must not be qualified or explained away. Next, the will of man is utterly indisposed and disabled from yielding itself to Christ. "No man can come to Me, except the Father which hath sent Me draw him" (John vi. 44). And hence, finally, when the will is effectually gained, and salvation thus obtained, it is in consequence of a divine operation upon it. "It is God that worketh in you, both to *will* and to do" of His good pleasure (Phil. ii. 13). Nor is this to be modified or attenuated in the least. The result of all is, that when a soul is undone, it is self-destroyed; but when surrendered to Christ and saved, it is purely of grace (Hos. xiii. 9). That self-surrender to Christ which secures its salvation is as purely voluntary as the rejection of Him which is fatal to unbelievers; but never is this done till God "worketh in us to will" it. How this is effected, consistently with the entire freedom of the human will, we shall never know—here below, at least. But it is a pitiful thing for men, who see the same principle of divine operation on the free will of man in the ordinary administration of the world, to pitch the one of these against the other in the matter of salvation: Pelagians and Semi-pelagians, of different name, denying the *grace* which alone ever gains the consent of man's will to salvation in Christ Jesus; and ultra-Calvinists, denying the entire freedom of that *will* which in one class rejects Christ and is undone, and in another embraces Him and lives for ever. With what awful dignity and responsibility is the human will invested by these words of Christ, "I would have gathered you, but—ye would not;" and by those other words of the same Lips, now glorified and enthroned, "Behold, I stand at the door, and knock: if any man hear my voice, and *open the door,* I will come in to him, and will sup with him, and he with Me"! (Rev. iii. 20). But when we have opened our willing hearts to this glorious and full-handed Saviour, our resistless language is, "By the grace of God I am what I am" (1 Cor. xv. 10). 7. What a day will that be when those whom Christ solicited so long in vain "shall look on Him whom they have pierced, and mourn for Him as one mourneth for his only son, and be in bitterness for Him as one that is in bitterness for his first-born!" What acclamations of "Hosanna to the Son of David" will those be that come from the lips of Abraham's seed that once cried, "Crucify Him, crucify Him"! No wonder that the apostle asks, "What shall the receiving of them be but life from the dead?" (Rom. xi. 15). The Lord hasten it in its time.

CHAP. XXIV. 1-51.—CHRIST'S PROPHECY OF
THE DESTRUCTION OF JERUSALEM, AND WARN-

4 *shall be* the sign of thy coming, and of the end of the world? And
Jesus answered and said unto them, Take [d]heed that no man deceive
5 you. For [e]many shall come in my name, saying, I am Christ; and shall
6 deceive many. And ye shall hear of wars and rumours of wars: see
that ye be not troubled: for all *these things* must come to pass, but the
7 end is not yet. For [f]nation shall rise against nation, and kingdom
against kingdom: and there shall be famines, and pestilences, and
8 earthquakes, in divers places. All these *are* the beginning of sorrows.
9 Then [g]shall they deliver you up to be afflicted, and shall kill you: and
10 ye shall be hated of all nations for my name's sake. And then shall
many [h]be offended, and shall betray one another, and shall hate one
11 another. And [i]many false prophets shall rise, and [j]shall deceive many.
12 And because iniquity shall abound, the love of many shall wax cold.
13 But [k]he that shall endure unto the end, the same shall be saved.
14 And this gospel of the kingdom [l]shall be preached in all the world for a
witness unto all nations; and then shall the end come.
15   When ye therefore shall see the abomination of desolation, spoken of
by Daniel [m]the prophet, stand in the holy place, ([n]whoso readeth, let
16 him understand,) then let them which be in Judea flee into the moun-
17 tains: let him which is on the house-top not come down to take any
18 thing out of his house: neither let him which is in the field return back
19 to take his clothes. And woe unto them that are with child, and to
20 them that give suck, in those days! But pray ye that your flight be not
21 in the winter, neither on the sabbath day: for [o]then shall be great tribulation, such as was not since the beginning of the world to this time,
22 no, nor ever shall be. And except those days should be shortened, there
should no flesh be saved: [p]but for the elect's sake those days shall be
23 shortened. Then if any man shall say unto you, Lo, here *is* Christ, or
24 there; believe *it* not. For [q]there shall arise false Christs, and false prophets, and shall show great signs and wonders; insomuch that, [r]if *it were*
25 possible, they shall deceive the very elect. Behold, I have told you
26 before. Wherefore, if they shall say unto you, Behold, he is in the
desert; go not forth: behold, *he is* in the secret chambers; believe *it* not.
27 For as the lightning cometh out of the east, and shineth even unto the
28 west; so shall also the coming of the Son of man be. For [s]wheresoever
the carcase is, there will the eagles be gathered together.
29   Immediately [t]after the tribulation of those days [u]shall the sun be
darkened, and the moon shall not give her light, and the stars shall fall
30 from heaven, and the powers of the heavens shall be shaken: and [v]then
shall appear the sign of the Son of man in heaven: [w]and then shall all
the tribes of the earth mourn, [x]and they shall see the Son of man coming
31 in the clouds of heaven with power and great glory. And [y]he shall send
his angels [1]with a great sound of a trumpet, and they shall gather
together his elect from the four winds, from one end of heaven to the
other.
32   Now learn [z]a parable of the fig tree: When his branch is yet tender,
33 and putteth forth leaves, ye know that summer *is* nigh: so likewise ye,
when ye shall see all these things, know that [2]it is near, *even* at the
34 doors. Verily I say unto you, [a]This generation shall not pass, till all
35 these things be fulfilled. Heaven [b]and earth shall pass away, but my
words shall not pass away.
36   But [c]of that day and hour knoweth no *man*, no, not the angels of
37 heaven, [d]but my Father only. But as the days of Noe *were*, so shall

A. D. 33.
[d] Eph. 5. 6.
2 Thes. 2. 3.
1 John 4. 1.
[e] Jer. 14. 14.
Jer. 23. 21.
John 5. 43.
[f] Isa. 19. 2.
Hag. 2. 22.
Zec. 14. 13.
[g] Acts 4. 2, 3.
Acts 7. 59.
Acts 12. 1.
[h] 2 Tim. 1. 15.
[i] Acts 20. 29.
2 Cor. 11.13.
2 Pet. 2. 1.
[j] 1 Tim. 4. 1.
[k] Heb. 3. 6.
[l] Rom. 10.18.
[m] Dan. 9. 27.
Dan. 12. 11.
[n] Dan. 9. 23.
[o] Dan. 12. 1.
Joel 1. 2.
Joel 2. 2.
[p] Isa. 65. 8, 9.
Zec. 14. 2,3.
[q] Deut. 13. 1.
2 Thes. 2. 9.
Rev. 13. 13.
[r] Rom. 8. 28.
2 Tim. 2.19.
1 Pet. 1. 5.
[s] Job 39. 30.
[t] Dan. 7. 11.
[u] Isa. 13. 10.
Ezek. 32. 7.
Acts 2. 20.
Rev. 6. 12.
[v] Dan. 7. 13.
[w] Zec. 12. 12.
[x] Rev. 1. 7.
[y] 1 Cor. 15.52.
1 Thes.4.16.
[1] Or. with a trumpet, and a **great** voice.
[z] Luke 21.29.
[2] Or, he.
Jas. 5. 9.
[a] ch. 16. 28.
ch. 23. 36.
[b] Ps. 102. 26, 27.
Isa. 34. 4.
Isa. 51. 6.
Jer. 31. 35.
ch. 5. 18.
Mark 13.31.
Luke 21.33.
Heb. 1. 11.
2 Pet. 3. 7-12.
Rev. 6. 14.
[c] Acts 1. 7.
1 Thes. 5. 2.
2 Pet. 3. 10.
[d] Zec. 14. 7.

38 also the coming of the Son of man be. For *as in the days that were before the flood they were eating and drinking, marrying and giving in
39 marriage, until the day that Noe entered into the ark, and knew not until the flood came, and took them all away; so shall also the coming
40 of the Son of man be. Then shall two be in the field; the one shall be
41 taken, and the other left. Two *women shall be* grinding at the mill; the one shall be taken, and the other left.
42 Watch therefore; for ye know not what hour your Lord doth come.
43 But *f* know this, that if the goodman of the house had known in what watch the thief would come, he would have watched, and would not
44 have suffered his house to be broken up. Therefore be ye also ready:
45 for in such an hour as ye think not the Son of man cometh. Who *g* then is a faithful and wise servant, whom his lord hath made ruler over his
46 household, to give them meat in due season? Blessed *h is* that servant
47 whom his lord when he cometh shall find so doing. Verily I say unto
48 you, That he shall make him ruler over all his goods. But and if that
49 evil servant shall say in his heart, My lord delayeth his coming; and shall begin to smite *his* fellow-servants, and to eat and drink with the
50 drunken; the lord of that servant shall come in a day when he looketh
51 not for *him*, and in an hour that he is not aware of, and shall ³cut him asunder, and appoint *him* *i* his portion with the hypocrites: there shall be weeping and gnashing of teeth.

25 THEN shall the kingdom of heaven be likened unto ten virgins, which
2 took their lamps, and went forth to meet *a* the bridegroom. And *b* five
3 of them were wise, and five *were* foolish. They that *were* foolish took their
4 lamps, and took *c* no oil with them: but the wise took oil in their vessels

A. D. 33.	
c Gen. 6. 3.	
Gen. 7. 1.	
Luke 17. 26.	
1 Pet. 3. 20.	
f Mark 13. 33,	
36.	
1 Thes. 5. 6.	
Rev. 3. 3.	
Rev. 16. 15.	
g 1 Cor. 4. 2.	
Heb. 3. 5.	
h ch. 25. 34.	
1 Tim. 4. 7,	
8.	
Rev. 16. 15.	
³ Or, cut him	
off.	
i Ps. 11. 6.	
ch. 25. 30.	
Luke 12. 46·	
CHAP. 25.	
a John 3. 29.	
Eph. 5. 29.	
Rev. 19. 7.	
Rev. 21. 2,	
9.	
b ch. 13. 47.	
ch. 22. 10.	
c Isa. 29. 13.	
Ezra 33. 30-	
32.	
2 Tim. 3. 5.	
Titus 1. 16.	

CHAP. XXV. 1-13.— PARABLE OF THE TEN VIRGINS. This and the following parable are in Matthew alone.

1. Then—at the time referred to at the close of the preceding chapter, the time of the Lord's Second Coming to reward His faithful servants and take vengeance on the faithless. *Then* shall the kingdom of heaven be likened unto ten virgins, which took their lamps, and went forth to meet the bridegroom. This supplies a key to the parable, whose object is, in the main, the same as that of the last parable—to illustrate *the vigilant and expectant attitude of faith*, in respect of which believers are described as "they that look for Him" (Heb. ix. 28), and "love His appearing" (2 Tim. iv. 8). In the last parable it was that of servants waiting for their absent Lord; in this it is that of virgin-attendants on a Bride, whose duty it was to go forth at night with lamps, and be ready on the appearance of the Bridegroom to conduct the Bride to his house, and go in with him to the marriage. This entire and beautiful change of figure brings out the lesson of the former parable in quite a new light. But let it be observed that, just as in the parable of the Marriage Supper, so in this—the *Bride* does not come into view at all in this parable; the *Virgins* and the *Bridegroom* holding forth all the intended instruction: nor could believers be represented both as Bride and Bridal Attendants without incongruity. **2. And five of them were wise, and five were foolish.** They are not distinguished into good and bad, as *Trench* observes, but into "wise" and "foolish" —just as in Matt. vii. 25-27, those who reared their house for eternity are distinguished into "wise" and "foolish builders;" because in both cases a certain degree of good will towards the truth is assumed. To make anything of the equal number of both classes would, we think, be precarious, save to warn us how large a portion of those who, up to the last, so nearly resemble those that love

Christ's appearing will be disowned by Him when He comes. **3. They that were foolish took their lamps, and took no oil with them: 4. But the wise took oil in their vessels with their lamps.** What are these "lamps" and this "oil?" Many answers have been given. But since the foolish as well as the wise took their lamps and went forth with them to meet the bridegroom, these lighted lamps, and this advance a certain way in company with the wise, must denote that Christian profession which is common to all who bear the Christian name; while the insufficiency of this without something else, of which they never possessed themselves, shows that "the foolish" mean those who, with all that is common to them with real Christians, *lack the essential preparation for meeting Christ*. Then, since the wisdom of "the wise" consisted in their taking with them lamps a supply of oil in their vessels, keeping their lamps burning till the Bridegroom came, and so fitting them to go in with Him to the marriage—this supply of oil must mean that *inward reality of grace* which alone will stand when He appeareth whose eyes are as a flame of fire. But this is too general; for it cannot be for nothing that this inward grace is here set forth by the familiar symbol of *oil*, by which the *Spirit of all grace* is so constantly represented in Scripture. Beyond all doubt, this was what was symbolized by that precious anointing oil with which Aaron and his sons were consecrated to the priestly office (Exod. xxx. 23-25, 30); by "the oil of gladness above His fellows" with which Messiah was to be anointed (Ps. xlv. 7; Heb. i. 9), even as it is expressly said, that "God giveth not the Spirit by measure unto Him" (John iii. 34); and by the bowl full of golden oil, in Zechariah's vision, which, receiving its supplies from the two olive-trees on either side of it, poured it through seven golden pipes into the golden lamp-stand, to keep it continually burning bright (Zec. iv.)—for

5 with their lamps. While the bridegroom tarried, ^dthey all slumbered
6 and slept. And at midnight ^ethere was a cry made, Behold, the bride-
7 groom cometh; go ye out to meet him. Then all those virgins arose,
8 and trimmed their ^flamps. And the foolish said unto the wise, Give
9 us of your oil; for our lamps are ¹gone out. But the wise answered,
saying, *Not so;* lest there be not enough for us and you : but go ye rather
10 to them that sell, and buy for yourselves. And while they went to buy,
the bridegroom came; and they that were ready went in with him to

A. D. 33.

d 1 Thes. 5. 6.
e ch. 24. 31.
1 Thes. 4. 16.
2 Thes. 1. 7-
10.
Jude 14. 15.
f Luke 12. 35.
1 Or, going
out.

the prophet is expressly told that it was to pro-claim the great truth, "Not by might, nor by power, but by MY SPIRIT, saith the Lord of hosts [shall this temple be built]. Who art thou, O great mountain [of opposition to this issue]? Be-fore Zerubbabel thou shalt become a plain [or, be swept out of the way], and he shall bring forth the head-stone [of the temple], with shoutings [crying], GRACE, GRACE unto it." This supply of oil, then, representing that inward grace which distinguishes the wise, must denote, more particu-larly, that "supply of the Spirit of Jesus Christ," which, as it is the source of the new spiritual life at the first, is the secret of its *enduring* character. Everything *short of this* may be possessed by "the foolish;" while it is the possession of this that makes "the wise" to be "ready" when the Bridegroom appears, and fit to "go in with Him to the marriage." Just so in the parable of the Sower, the stony ground hearers, "having no deepness of earth" and "no root in them-selves," though they spring up and get even into ear, never ripen, while they in the good ground bear the precious grain. **5. While the bride-groom tarried.** So in ch. xxiv. 48, "My Lord delayeth His coming;" and so Peter says sublimely of the ascended Saviour, "Whom the heaven must receive until the times of restitution of all things" (Acts iii. 21, and compare Luke xix. 11, 12). Christ "tarries," among other reasons, to try the faith and patience of His people. **they all slumbered and slept**—the wise as well as the foolish. The word "slumbered" [ἐνύσταξαν] signifies, simply, 'nodded,' or, 'became drowsy;' while the word "slept" [ἐκάθευδον] is the usual word for 'lying down to sleep:' denoting two stages of spiritual declension—first, that half-in-voluntary lethargy or drowsiness which is apt to steal over one who falls into inactivity; and then a conscious, deliberate yielding to it, after a little vain resistance. Such was the state alike of the wise and the foolish virgins, even till the cry of the Bridegroom's approach awoke them. So like-wise in the parable of the Importunate Widow: "When the Son of man cometh, shall He find faith on the earth?" (Luke xviii. 8). **6. And at midnight**—that is, the time when the Bridegroom will be least expected; for "the day of the Lord so cometh as a thief in the night" (1 Thes. v. 2), **there was a cry made, Behold, the bridegroom cometh; go ye out to meet him**—that is, 'Be ready to welcome Him.' **7. Then all those virgins arose, and trimmed their lamps**—the foolish virgins as well as the wise. How very long do both parties seem the same—almost to the moment of decision! Looking at the mere form of the parable, it is evident that the folly of "the foolish" consisted not in having no oil at all; for they must have had oil enough in their lamps to keep them burning up to this moment: their folly consisted in not making provision against its *exhaustion*, by taking with their lamp an *oil-vessel* wherewith to replenish their lamp from time to time, and so have it burn-ing until the bridegroom should come. Are we, then—with some even superior expositors—to

conclude that the foolish virgins must represent true Christians as well as the wise, since only true Christians have the Spirit; and that the difference between the two classes consists only in the one having the necessary watchfulness which the other wants? Certainly not. Since the parable was designed to hold forth the prepared and the unprepared to meet Christ at His coming, and how the unprepared might, up to the very last, be confounded with the prepared—the structure of the parable behoved to accommodate itself to this, by making the lamps of the foolish to burn, as well as those of the wise, up to a certain point of time, and only then to discover their inability to burn on for want of a fresh supply of oil. But this is evidently just a *structural device;* and the real difference between the two classes who profess to love the Lord's appearing is a *radical* one—the possession by the one class of *an enduring principle of spiritual life,* and the want of it by the other. **8. And the foolish said unto the wise, Give us of your oil; for our lamps are gone out [σβέν-νυνται]**—rather, as in the margin, 'are going out;' for oil will not light an extinguished lamp, though it will keep a burning one from going out. Ah! now at length they have discovered not only their own folly, but the wisdom of the other class, and they do homage to it. They did not perhaps despise them before, but they thought them right-eous overmuch; now they are forced, with bitter mortification, to wish they were like them. **9. But the wise answered, [Not so]; lest there be not enough for us and you.** The words "Not so," it will be seen, are not in the original, where the reply is very elliptical [Μήποτε οὐκ ἀρκέσῃ ἡμῖν καὶ ὑμῖν]—'In case there be not enough for us and you.' A truly wise answer this. 'And what, then, if we shall share it with you? Why, both will be undone.' **but go ye rather to them that sell, and buy for yourselves.** Here again it would be straining the parable beyond its legiti-mate design to make it teach that men may get salvation even after they are supposed and required to have it already gotten. It is merely a friendly way of reminding them of the proper way of ob-taining the needed and precious article, with a cer-tain reflection on them for having it now to seek. Also, when the parable speaks of "selling" and "buying" that valuable article, it means simply, 'Go, get it in the only legitimate way.' And yet the word "buy" is significant; for we are else-where bidden "buy wine and milk without money and without price," and "buy of Christ gold tried in the fire," &c. (Isa. lv. 1; Rev. iii. 18). Now, since what we pay the demanded price for becomes thereby *our own property,* the salvation which we thus take gratuitously at God's hands, being bought in His own sense of that word, becomes ours there-by in inalienable possession. (Compare, for the language, Prov. xxiii. 23; Matt. xiii. 44.) **10. And while they went to buy, the bridegroom came; and they that were ready went in with him to the marriage: and the door was shut.** They are sensible of their past folly; they have taken good advice: they are in the act of getting

116

11 the marriage: and the *g*door was shut. Afterward came also the other
12 virgins, saying, *h*Lord, Lord, open to us. But he answered and said,
13 Verily I say unto you, *i*I know you not. Watch *j*therefore; for ye know
neither the day nor the hour wherein the Son of man cometh.

A. D. 33.
g Luke 13. 25.
h ch. 7. 21.
i Ps. 5. 5.
j ch. 24. 42.

what alone they lacked: a very little more, and they also are ready. But the Bridegroom comes: the ready are admitted; "the door is shut," and they are undone. How graphic and appalling this picture of *almost saved—but lost!* **11.** **Afterward came also the other virgins, saying, Lord, Lord, open to us.** In ch. vii. 22 this reiteration of the name was an exclamation rather of surprise: here it is a piteous cry of urgency, bordering on despair. Ah! now at length their eyes are wide open, and they realize all the consequences of their past folly. **12. But he answered and said, Verily I say unto you, I know you not.** The attempt to establish a difference between "I know you not" here, and "I never knew you" in ch. vii. 23—as if this were gentler, and so implied a milder fate, reserved for "the foolish" of this parable—is to be resisted, though advocated by such critics as *Olshausen, Stier,* and *Alford.* Besides being inconsistent with the general tenor of such language, and particularly the solemn moral of the whole (*v.* 13), it is a *kind* of criticism which tampers with some of the most awful warnings regarding the future. If it be asked why unworthy guests were admitted to the marriage of the King's Son, in a former parable, and the foolish virgins are excluded in this one, we may answer, in the admirable words of *Gerhard,* quoted by *Trench,* that those festivities are celebrated in this life, in the Church militant; these at the last day, in the Church triumphant: to those, even they are admitted who are not adorned with the wedding-garment; but to these, only they to whom it is granted to be arrayed in fine linen clean and white, which is the righteousness of saints (Rev. xix. 8): to those, men are called by the trumpet of the Gospel; to these by the trumpet of the Archangel: to those, who enters may go out from them, or be cast out; who is once introduced to these never goes out, nor is cast out, from them any more: wherefore it is said, "The door is shut." **13. Watch therefore; for ye know neither the day nor the hour [wherein the Son of man cometh.]** This, the moral or practical lesson of the whole parable, needs no comment. [The evidence against the genuineness, in this verse, of the words enclosed in brackets is decisive. They seem to have been first copied, exactly as they stand in ch. xxiv. 44, into what are called *Lectionaries,* or portions of Scripture transcribed to be read as Church Lessons—in all of which these words are found—in order to avoid the apparent abruptness with which the verse otherwise closes, and then to have found their way into a tolerable number of MSS. and versions. But the abruptness is more apparent than real; and the event itself being supposed, the uncertainty ascribed simply to "the day and the hour" has something striking and emphatic in it.]

Remarks.—1. So essential a feature of the Christian character, according to the New Testament, is looking for Christ's Second Appearing, that both real and apparent disciples are here described as "going forth to meet Him." And so everywhere. It is "to them that *look for Him*" that "He will appear the second time, without sin, unto salvation" (Heb. ix. 28); it is to "them that *love His appearing*" that "He will give a crown of righteousness at that day" (2 Tim. iv. 8); to His servants, His parting word, on "going to the far country," is, "Occupy *till I come*" (Luke xix. 13); communicants

at His table, "as often as they eat this bread and drink this cup, do show forth the Lord's death *till He come*" (1 Cor. xi. 26); and, when the Thessalonians turned to God from idols, it was, on the one hand, "to serve the living God, and," on the other, "to *wait for His Son from heaven*" (1 Thess. i. 9, 10). No expectation of the Latter-Day glory —no, nor preparedness to die, ought to take the place, or is fitted to produce the effects, of this love of Christ's appearing and waiting for Him from heaven, which lifts the soul into its highest attitude and dress for heaven, carrying every other scriptural expectation along with it. But 2. It should be carefully observed that it was not the want of expectation that the bridegroom would come that constituted the folly of "the foolish," but their not having any provision for meeting him in case he should tarry. The burning lamp represents the state of readiness. But whereas the lamps of the foolish, though burning at the first, went out ere the bridegroom came, this is to signify that the class intended are such as have no real preparedness to meet Christ at all. On the other hand, lively expectation of Christ's coming, up to the time of His arrival, is so far from being the distinguishing mark of the wise, that even these wise virgins, as well as the foolish, first sank into a lethargic state, and then yielded themselves up to sleep. Were they shut out, then? Nay. At the time of deepest sleep, a warning cry was kindly sent them, loud enough to rouse the foolish and the wise alike; both now set themselves to meet the bridegroom; and then did it become manifest that the wisdom of the wise and the folly of the foolish lay, not in the one *expecting the coming* which the other did not, but in the one having from the very outset a *provision for meeting* the bridegroom, *however long he might tarry,* while the provision of the other was but temporary, and so failed in the time of need. We make these observations because those who expect the Second Coming of Christ *before* the Millennium have made a use of this parable, against such as think this expectation unscriptural, which appears to us to distort its proper teaching. The love of their Lord's appearing is certainly not confined to those who take the former of these views; and perhaps they might do well to consider whether it be not possible to substitute this expectation for that enduring principle of spiritual life in Christ Jesus which is the grand and never-wanting preparation for meeting Him, however long He may tarry. But we deprecate controversy here among the loving expectants of a common Lord. Our sole object is to get at the actual teaching of our blessed Master, and gently to brush away what we think has been obtruded upon it. 3. How appalling it is to think of the nearness to final salvation and heaven's fruition in the presence of Christ to which some may attain, and yet miss it! But see on ch. vii. 13-29, Remark 5, at the close of that Section. 4. The way to secure ourselves against being found *wrong at the last* is to get *right at the first.* The wisdom of the wise virgins lay in their taking along with their lamps, from the time they first went forth to meet the bridegroom, *a supply of oil* that should keep their lamps burning however long he might tarry: the foolish virgins, by their not doing so, showed that they *began with inadequate preparation against the future.*

14 For [k]*the kingdom of heaven is* [l]as a man travelling into a far country,
15 *who* called his own servants, and delivered unto them his goods. And unto one he gave five [2]talents, to another two, and to another one; [m]to every man according to his several ability; and straightway took his
16 journey. Then he that had received the five talents went and [n]traded
17 with the same, and made *them* other five talents. And likewise he that
18 *had received* two, he also gained other two. But he that had received
19 one went and digged in the earth, and [o]hid his lord's money. After a long time the lord of those servants cometh, and reckoneth with them.
20 And so he that had received five talents came and brought other five talents, saying, Lord, thou deliveredst unto me five talents: behold, I

A. D. 33.

[k] Luke 19. 12.
[l] ch. 21. 33.
Mark 13. 34.
Luke 19. 12,
13.
[2] A talent is
187l. 10s.
[m] Rom. 12. 6.
1 Cor. 12. 7.
Eph. 4. 11.
[n] Pro. 3. 14.
1 Pet. 4. 10.
[o] Phil. 2. 21.

They never were right, and the issue only brought out what was their radical mistake all along. 5. Nothing will avail for meeting Christ in peace but that unction from the Holy One, of which it is said, "If any man have not the Spirit of Christ, he is none of His" (Rom. viii. 9): "But the anointing which ye have received of Him abideth in you, and ye need not that any man teach you: but as the same anointing teacheth you all things, and is truth, and is no lie, and even as it hath taught you, ye shall abide in Him" (1 John ii. 27). 6. We have here a lively illustration of the great truth, that what is *saving* cannot be imparted by one man to another (*v.* 9). "The just shall live by his (own) faith" (Hab. ii. 4). "If thou be wise," says the wisest of men, "thou shalt be wise for thyself; but if thou scornest, thou alone shalt bear it" (Pro. ix. 12). "Let every man prove his own work, and then shall he have rejoicing in himself, and not in another: for every man shall bear his own burden" (Gal. vi. 4, 5). 7. Though such as love their Lord's appearing—when through His long tarrying they have sunk into a lethargic state, and even surrendered themselves to sleep—may have only to "trim their lamps" when the cry of His coming is heard, there being a supply of oil within them sufficient to brighten them up, it is a sad and shameful thing they should have this to do. As these slumbers are dishonouring to the heavenly Bridegroom, so they are the bane of the soul, paralyzing it for all good. "Therefore, let us not sleep, as do others, but let us watch and be sober; putting on the breast-plate of faith and hope, and for an helmet the hope of salvation." And as for others, when they shall be saying, Peace and safety, then sudden destruction shall come upon them, as travail upon a woman with child, and they shall not escape.

14-30.—PARABLE OF THE TALENTS. This parable, while closely resembling it, is yet a different one from that of THE POUNDS, in Luke xix. 11-27; though *Calvin, Olshausen, Meyer,* &c., identify them—but not *de Wette* and *Neander.* For the difference between the two parables, see the opening remarks on that of The Pounds. While—as *Trench* observes with his usual felicity—'the virgins were represented as *waiting* for their Lord, we have the servants *working* for Him: there the *inward spiritual life* of the faithful was described; here his *external activity.* It is not, therefore, without good reason that they appear in their actual order—that of the Virgins first, and of the Talents following—since it is the sole condition of a profitable outward activity for the Kingdom of God, that the life of God be diligently maintained within the heart.'

14. For [the kingdom of heaven is] as a man. The ellipsis is better supplied by our translators in the corresponding passage of Mark (xiii. 34), "[For the Son of man is] as a man," &c., travelling into a far country [ἀποδημῶν]—or more sim-

ply, 'going abroad.' The idea of long "tarrying" is certainly implied here, since it is expressed in *v.* 19. who called his own servants, and delivered unto them his goods. Between master and slaves this was not uncommon in ancient times. Christ's "servants" here mean all who, by their Christian profession, stand in the relation to Him of entire subjection. His "goods" mean all their gifts and endowments, whether original or acquired, natural or spiritual. As all that slaves have belongs to their master, so Christ has a claim to everything which belongs to His people, everything which may be turned to good, and He demands its appropriation to His service; or, viewing it otherwise, they first offer it up to Him, as being "not their own, but bought with a price" (1 Cor. vi. 19, 20), and He "delivers it to them" again to be put to use in His service. 15. And unto one he gave five talents, to another two, and to another one. While the *proportion of gifts* is different in each, the same *fidelity* is required of all, and equally rewarded. And thus there is perfect equity. to every man according to his several ability—his natural capacity as enlisted in Christ's service, and his opportunities in providence for employing the gifts bestowed on him. and straightway took his journey. Compare ch. xxi. 33, where the same departure is ascribed to God, after setting up the ancient economy. In both cases, it denotes the leaving of men to the action of all those spiritual laws and influences of Heaven under which they have been graciously placed for their own salvation and the advancement of their Lord's kingdom. 16. Then he that had received the five talents went and traded with the same [εἰργάσατο]—expressive of the activity which he put forth, and the labour he bestowed. and made them other five talents. 17. And likewise he that had received two [τὰ δύο]—rather, 'the two'—he also gained other two—each doubling what he received, and therefore *both equally faithful.* 18. But he that had received one went and digged in the earth, and hid his lord's money—not misspending, but simply making no use of it. Nay, his action seems that of one anxious that the gift should not be misused or lost, but ready to be returned, just as he got it. 19. After a long time the lord of those servants cometh and reckoneth with them. That any one—within the life-time of the apostles at least—with such words before them, should think that Jesus had given any reason to expect His Second Appearing within that period, would seem strange, did we not know the tendency of enthusiastic, ill-regulated love of His appearing ever to take this turn. 20. And so he that had received five talents came and brought other five talents, saying, Lord, thou deliveredst unto me five talents: behold, I have gained besides them five talents more. How beautifully does this illustrate what the beloved disciple says of "boldness in the

118

21 have gained besides them five talents more. His lord said unto him, Well done, *thou* good and faithful servant: thou hast been faithful over a few things, *P*I will make thee ruler over many things: enter thou into 22 *q*the joy of thy lord. He also that had received two talents came and said, Lord, thou deliveredst unto me two talents: behold, I have gained 23 two other talents besides them. His lord said unto him, Well done, good and faithful servant: thou hast been faithful over a few things, I will make thee ruler over many things: enter thou into the joy of thy 24 lord. Then he which had received the one talent came and said, Lord, I knew thee that thou art an hard man, reaping where thou hast not sown, 25 and gathering where thou hast not strawed: and I was afraid, and went 26 and hid thy talent in the earth: lo, *there* thou hast *that is* thine. His lord answered and said unto him, *Thou* wicked and slothful servant, thou knewest that I reap where I sowed not, and gather where I have 27 not strawed; thou oughtest therefore to have put my money to the exchangers, and *then* at my coming I should have received mine own 28 with usury. Take therefore the talent from him, and give *it* unto him 29 which hath ten talents. For *r*unto every one that hath shall be given, and he shall have abundance: but from him that hath not shall be taken 30 away even that which he hath. And cast ye the unprofitable servant into outer darkness: there shall be weeping and gnashing of teeth.

A. D. 33.

P ch. 10. 40, 42.
ch. 24. 47.
ch. 25. 34, 40.
Mark 8. 35.
Mark 13. 13.
Luke 12. 44.
Luke 22. 29, 30.
John 12. 25.
2 Tim. 4. 7, 8.
Rev. 2. 10, 26-28.
Rev. 3. 21.
Rev. 21. 7.
q Acts 2. 28.
Heb. 12. 2.
2 Tim. 2. 12.
1 Pet. 1. 8.
r Luke 8. 18.
John 15. 2.
1 Cor. 15. 10.
2 Cor. 6. 1.

day of judgment," and his desire that "when He shall appear we may have confidence, and not be ashamed before Him at His coming"! (1 John iv. 17; ii. 28). **21. His lord said unto him, Well done** [Εὖ]—a single word, not of bare satisfaction, but of warm and delighted commendation. And from what Lips! **good and faithful servant: thou hast been faithful over a few things, I will make thee ruler over many things: enter thou into the joy of thy lord. 22. He also that had received two talents came and said, Lord, thou deliveredst unto me two talents: behold, I have gained two other talents besides them. 23. His lord said unto him, Well done, good and faithful servant: thou hast been faithful over a few things, I will make thee ruler over many things.** *Both are commended in the same terms, and the reward of both is precisely the same.* (See on *v.* 15.) Observe also the contrasts: 'Thou hast been faithful as a *servant;* now be a *ruler*—thou hast been *entrusted* with a *few* things; now have *dominion* over *many* things.' **enter thou into the joy of thy lord**—thy Lord's own joy. (See John xv. 11; Heb. xii. 2.) **24. Then he which had received the one talent came and said, Lord, I knew thee that thou art an hard**—or 'harsh,' **man** [σκληρός]. The word in Luke (xix. 21) is "austere" [αὐστηρός]. **reaping where thou hast not sown, and gathering where thou hast not strawed.** The sense is obvious: 'I knew thou wast one whom it was impossible to serve, one whom nothing would please; exacting what was impracticable, and dissatisfied with what was attainable.' Thus do men secretly think of God as a hard Master, and virtually throw on Him the blame of their fruitlessness. **25. And I was afraid**—of making matters worse by meddling with it at all. **and went and hid thy talent in the earth.** This depicts the conduct of all those who shut up their gifts from the active service of Christ, without actually prostituting them to unworthy uses. Fitly, therefore, may it, at least, comprehend those, to whom *Trench* refers, who, in the early Church, pleaded that they had enough to do with their own souls, and were afraid of losing them in trying to save others; and so, instead of being the salt of the earth, thought rather of

keeping their own saltness, by withdrawing sometimes into caves and wildernesses, from all those active ministries of love by which they might have served their brethren. **lo, there thou hast that is thine. 26. His lord answered and said unto him, Thou wicked and slothful servant.** "Wicked" or "bad" [Πονηρὲ] means 'false-hearted,' as opposed to the others, who are emphatically styled "*good* servants." The addition of "slothful" [ὀκνηρὲ] is to mark the precise nature of his wickedness: it consisted, it seems, not in his doing anything *against*, but simply nothing *for* his master. **Thou knewest that I reap where I sowed not, and gather where I have not strawed.** He takes the servant's own account of his demands, as expressing graphically enough, not the "*hardness*" which he had basely imputed to him, but simply his demand of '*a profitable return for the gift entrusted.*' **27. thou oughtest therefore to have put my money to the exchangers** [τοῖς τραπεζίταις]—or, 'the bankers,' **and then at my coming I should have received mine own with usury** [τόκῳ]—or 'interest.' **28. Take therefore the talent from him, and give it unto him which hath ten talents. 29. For unto every one that hath shall be given, &c.** See on ch. xiii. 12. **30. And cast ye**—'cast ye out' [ἐκβάλλετε, but the true reading is ἐκβάλετε]. **the unprofitable servant** [ἀχρεῖον]—'the useless servant,' that does his Master no service, **into outer darkness**—'the darkness which is outside.' On this expression see on ch. xxii. 13. **there shall be weeping and gnashing of teeth.** See on ch. xiii. 42.

Remarks.—1. Christ's voice in this parable is not, as in the former one, ' *Wait* for your Lord'—' *Love* His appearing'—but, as in that of the Pounds (Luke xix. 13), "*Occupy* till I come." Blessed is that servant whom His Lord, when He cometh, shall find—not *watching*, as in the former parable—but *working*. 2. How interesting is the view here given of the relation in which every Christian stands to Christ. Not only are they all "servants of Jesus Christ," but all that distinguishes each of them from all the rest—in natural capacity and in acquirements, in providential position, influence, means, and opportunities—all

31　　When *the Son of man shall come in his glory, and all the holy angels
32　with him, then shall he sit upon the throne of his glory: and *before him
　　　shall be gathered all nations: and "he shall separate them one from
33　another, as a shepherd divideth *his* sheep from the goats: and he shall
　　　set the sheep on his right hand, but the goats on the left.
34　　Then shall the King say unto them on his right hand, Come, ye blessed
　　　of my Father, *inherit the kingdom *prepared for you from the founda-

A. D. 33.

* Zec. 14. 5.
　Acts 1. 11.
* Rom. 14. 10.
　2 Cor. 5. 10.
* Ezek. 20. 38.
　ch. 13. 49.
* Rom. 8. 17.
* 1 Cor. 2. 9.

are Christ's; rendered up to Him by them first, with their body and their spirit, which are His by purchase (1 Cor. vi. 19, 20), and then given back by Him to them to be employed in His service. Hence that diversity in the proportion of talents which this parable represents the Master as committing respectively to each of His servants. But 3. Since it is neither the *amount* nor the *nature* of the work done which this parable represents as rewarded, but the *fidelity* shown in the doing of it, the possessor of two talents has an equal reward—proportionably to what was committed to him—with the possessor of five. And thus it is that the most exalted in intellectual gifts, or wealth, or opportunity—though consecrating all these in beautiful fidelity to Christ—may be found occupying no higher position in the kingdom above than the lowest in all these respects, who have shown equal fidelity to the common Master. And thus may we use the language of an apostle in a wider sense than that more immediately intended—" Let the brother of low degree rejoice in that he is exalted, but the rich in that he is made low; because as the flower of the grass he shall pass away" (Jas. i. 9, 10). 4. To be "cast out" at the great day, it is not necessary that we prostitute our powers to a life of positive wickedness: it is enough that our Christianity be merely negative, that we do nothing for Christ, that we are found to have been *unprofitable*, or *useless* servants of the Lord Jesus. But, ah! is it indeed so? Then what numbers are there within the Christian pale whose doom this seals—their life perfectly unexceptionable, and their frame apparently devout, yet negative Christians, and nothing more! But is not the principle on which such shall be condemned most reasonable? If Jesus has a *people* upon earth whom He deigns to call His "mothers and sisters and brothers," and those who claim the Christian name know them not and treat them with cold indifference; if He has a *cause* upon earth which is dear to Him, requiring the services of all His people, and such persons ignore it, and never lend a helping-hand to it—how should they expect Him to recognize and reward them at the great day? But there is something more than righteous disavowal and rejection here. There is "indignation and wrath, tribulation and anguish," in the treatment here awarded to the profitless servant. "Cast ye—thrust ye—fling ye out the useless servant into outer darkness; there shall be weeping and gnashing of teeth." 5. The truth expressed in the taking of the talent from the unprofitable servant and giving it to him that had the ten talents—if we are to view it, as it would seem we should, with reference to the *future* state—is somewhat difficult to conceive. But as it is just as difficult to conceive of it in relation even to the present state, perhaps nothing more is meant by it than this, that while the useless servants shall be *judicially incapacitated* from ever rendering that service to Christ which once they might have done, the faithful servants of the Lord Jesus shall richly "supply their lack of service."

120

31-46. THE LAST JUDGMENT. The close connection between this sublime scene—peculiar to Matthew—and the two preceding parables is too obvious to need pointing out. **31. When the Son of man shall come in his glory**—His *personal* glory, and all the holy angels with him. See Deut. xxxiii. 2; Dan. vii. 9, 10; Jude 14; with Heb. i. 6; 1 Pet. iii. 22. [*Lachmann, Tischendorf,* and *Tregelles* omit the word ἄγιοι—"holy"—but, as we read the authorities, it is to be retained as genuine.] then shall he sit upon the throne of his glory—the glory of His *judicial authority.* **32. And before him shall be gathered all nations** [πάντα τὰ ἔθνη]—or, 'all the nations.' That this should be understood to mean the *heathen nations,* or all *except* believers in Christ, will seem amazing to any simple reader. Yet this is the exposition of *Olshausen, Stier, Keil, Alford* (though latterly with some diffidence), and of a number, though not all, of those who hold that Christ will come the Second Time before the Millennium, and that the saints will be caught up to meet Him in the air before His Appearing. Their chief argument is, the impossibility of any that ever knew the Lord Jesus wondering, at the Judgment Day, that they should be thought to have done—or left undone—anything "unto Christ." To that we shall advert when we come to it. But here we may just say, that if this scene do not describe a personal, public, final judgment on men, according to the treatment they have given to Christ—and consequently men within the Christian pale—we shall have to consider again whether our Lord's teaching on the greatest themes of human interest does indeed possess that incomparable simplicity and transparency of meaning which, by universal consent, has been ascribed to it. If it be said, But how can this be the General Judgment, if only those within the Christian pale be embraced by it?—we answer, What is here described, as it certainly does not meet the case of all the family of Adam, is of course *so far* not general. But we have no right to conclude that the whole "Judgment of the great day" will be limited to the points of view here presented. Other explanations will come up in the course of our exposition and following Remarks. and he shall separate them—now for the first time; the two classes having been mingled all along up to this awful moment—as a shepherd divideth his sheep from the goats (see Ezek. xxxiv. 17.) **33. And he shall set the sheep on his right hand**—the side of honour (1 Ki. ii. 19; Ps. xlv. 9; cx. 1, &c.)—but the goats on the left—the side consequently of dishonour. **34. Then shall the King.** Magnificent title, here for the first and only time, save in parabolical language, given to Himself by the Lord Jesus, and that on the eve of his deepest humiliation! It is to intimate that in then addressing the heirs of the kingdom *He will put on all His regal majesty.* say unto them on his right hand, Come [Δεῦτε]—the same sweet word with which He had so long invited all the weary and heavy laden to come unto Him for rest. Now it is addressed exclusively to such as *have* come and found

35 tion of the world: for ^xI was an hungered, and ye gave me meat: I was thirsty, and ye gave me drink: ^yI was a stranger, and ye took me in:

36 naked, ^zand ye clothed me: I was sick, and ye visited me: ^aI was in

37 prison, and ye came unto me. Then shall the righteous answer him, saying, Lord, when saw we thee an hungered, and fed *thee?* or thirsty, and

38 gave *thee* drink? When saw we thee a stranger, and took *thee* in? or

39 naked, and clothed *thee?* Or when saw we thee sick, or in prison, and

40 came unto thee? And the King shall answer and say unto them, Verily I say unto you, ^bInasmuch as ye have done *it* unto one of the least of these my brethren, ye have done *it* unto me.

41 Then shall he say also unto them on the left hand, ^cDepart from me, ye cursed, into ^deverlasting fire, prepared for ^ethe devil and his angels:

A. D. 33.

^x Isa. 58. 7.
Ezek. 18. 7.
2 Tim. 1.16.
Jas. 1. 27.
^y Heb. 13. 2.
3 John 5.
^z Jas. 2. 15.
^a 2 Tim. 1.16.
^b Pro. 14. 31.
Pro. 19. 17.
Heb. 6. 10.
^c Ps. 6. 8.
^d ch. 13. 40.
^e 2 Pet. 2. 4.
Jude 6.

---

rest. It is still "Come," and to "rest" too; but to rest in a higher style, and in another region. **ye blessed of my Father, inherit the kingdom prepared for you from the foundation of the world.** The whole story of this their blessedness is given by the apostle, in words which seem but an expansion of these: "Blessed be the God and Father of our Lord Jesus Christ, who hath blessed us with all spiritual blessings in heavenly places in Christ; according as He hath chosen us in Him before the foundation of the world, that we should be holy and without blame before Him in love." They were chosen from everlasting to the possession and enjoyment of all spiritual blessings in Christ, and so chosen in order to be holy and blameless in love. This is the holy love whose practical manifestations the King is about to recount in detail; and thus we see that their whole life of love to Christ is the fruit of an eternal purpose of love to them in Christ. **35. For I was an hungered, and ye gave me meat: . . . thirsty, and ye gave me drink: . . . a stranger, and ye took me in: 36. Naked, and ye clothed me: . . . sick, and ye visited me: . . . prison, and ye came unto me. 37-39. Then shall the righteous answer him, saying, Lord, when saw we thee an hungered, and fed thee? &c. 40. And the King shall answer and say unto them, Verily I say unto you, Inasmuch as ye have done it unto one of the least of these my brethren, ye have done it unto me.** Astonishing dialogue this between the King, from the Throne of His glory, and His wondering people! 'I was an hungered, and ye gave Me meat,' &c.—'Not we,' they reply, 'We never did that, Lord: We were born out of due time, and enjoyed not the privilege of ministering unto Thee.' 'But ye did it to these My brethren, now beside you, when cast upon your love.' 'Truth, Lord, but was that doing it to Thee? Thy name was indeed dear to us, and we thought it an honour too great to suffer shame for it. When among the destitute and distressed we discerned any of the household of faith, we will not deny that our hearts leapt within us at the discovery, and when their knock came to our dwelling, "our bowels were moved," as though "our Beloved Himself had put in His hand by the hole of the door." Sweet was the fellowship we had with them, as if we had "entertained angels unawares;" all difference between giver and receiver somehow melted away under the beams of that love of Thine which knit us together; nay rather, as they left us with gratitude for our poor givings, we seemed the debtors—not they. But, Lord, were we all that time in company with Thee?' 'Yes, that scene was all with Me,' replies the King—'Me in the disguise of My poor ones. The door shut against Me by others was opened by you'—"Ye took Me in."

121

Apprehended and imprisoned by the enemies of the truth, ye whom the truth had made free sought Me out diligently and found Me; visiting Me in My lonely cell at the risk of your own lives, and cheering My solitude: ye gave Me a coat, for I shivered; and then I felt warm. With cups of cold water ye moistened My parched lips; when famished with hunger ye supplied Me with crusts, and My spirit revived—"YE DID IT UNTO ME." What thoughts crowd upon us as we listen to such a description of the scenes of the Last Judgment! And in the light of this view of the heavenly Dialogue, how bald and wretched, not to say unscriptural, is that view of it to which we referred at the outset, which makes it a Dialogue between Christ and *heathens* who never heard of His name, and of course never felt any stirrings of His love in their hearts! To us it seems a poor, superficial objection to the *Christian* view of this scene, that Christians could never be supposed to ask such questions as the "blessed of Christ's Father" are made to ask here. If there were any difficulty in explaining this, the difficulty of the other view is such as to make it, at least, insufferable. But there is no real difficulty. The surprise expressed is not at their being told that they acted from love to Christ, but that *Christ Himself* was the *Personal Object* of all their deeds:—that they found *Him* hungry, and supplied Him with food; that they brought water to *Him,* and slaked His thirst; that seeing *Him* naked and shivering, they put warm clothing upon Him, paid *Him* visits when lying in prison for the truth, and sat by *His* bedside when laid down with sickness. This, this is the astonishing interpretation which Jesus says "the King" will give to them of their own actions here below. And will any Christian reply, 'How could this astonish them? Does not every Christian know that He does these very things, when He does them at all, just as they are here represented? Nay, rather, is it conceivable that they should *not* be astonished, and almost doubt their own ears, to hear such an account of their own actions upon earth from the lips of the Judge? And remember, that Judge has come in His glory, and now sits upon the Throne of His glory, and all the holy angels are with Him; and that it is from those glorified Lips that the words come forth, 'Ye did all this unto ME.' O can we imagine such a word addressed to *ourselves,* and then fancy ourselves replying, 'Of course we did—To whom else did we anything? It must be others than we that are addressed, who never knew, in all their good deeds, what they were about'? Rather, can we imagine ourselves not overpowered with astonishment, and scarcely able to credit the testimony borne to us by the King?

41. Then shall he say also unto them on the

42 for I was an hungered, and ye gave me no meat: I was thirsty, and ye
43 gave me no drink: I was a stranger, and ye took me not in: naked, and
44 ye clothed me not: sick, and in prison, and ye visited me not. Then shall
they also answer him, saying, Lord, when saw we thee an hungered, or
athirst, or a stranger, or naked, or sick, or in prison, and did not minister
45 unto thee? Then shall he answer them, saying, Verily I say unto you,
f Inasmuch as ye did *it* not to one of the least of these, ye did *it* not to
46 me. And *g* these shall go away into everlasting punishment: but the
righteous into life *h* eternal.

A. D. 33.

f Pro. 14. 31.
Pro. 17. 5.
Zec. 2. 8.
Acts 9. 5.
g Dan. 12. 2.
John 5. 29.
Rom. 2. 7.
Rev. 20. 10,
15.
h Rev. 3. 21.
Rev. 7. 15.

left hand, Depart from me, ye cursed, into everlasting fire, prepared for the devil and his angels: 42, 43. For I was an hungered, and ye gave me no meat, &c. 44. Then shall they also answer him, saying, Lord, when saw we thee an hungered, &c., and did not minister unto thee? 45. Then shall he answer them, saying, Verily I say unto you, Inasmuch as ye did it not to one of the least of these, ye did it not to me. ' As for you on the left hand, ye did nothing for Me. I came to you also, but ye knew Me not; ye had neither warm affections nor kind deeds to bestow upon Me: I was as one despised in your eyes.' 'In *our* eyes, Lord? We never saw Thee before, and never, sure, behaved we so to Thee.' 'But thus ye treated these little ones that believe in Me and now stand on My right hand. In the disguise of these poor members of Mine I came soliciting your pity, but ye shut up your bowels of compassion from Me: I asked relief, but ye had none to give Me. Take back therefore your own coldness, your own contemptuous distance: Ye bid Me away from your presence, and now I bid you from Mine—*Depart from Me, ye cursed!*' 46. **And these shall go away**—these "cursed" ones. Sentence, it should seem, was first *pronounced*—in the hearing of the wicked—upon the *righteous*, who thereupon sit as assessors in the judgment upon the wicked (1 Cor. vi. 2); but sentence is first *executed*, it should seem, upon the *wicked*, in the sight of the righteous—whose glory will thus not be beheld by the wicked, while *their* descent into "their own place" will be witnessed by the righteous, as *Bengel* notes. **into everlasting punishment** [κόλασιν αἰώνιον]—or, as in v. 41, "everlasting fire, prepared for the devil and his angels." Compare ch. xiii. 42; 2 Thes. i. 9, &c. This is said to be "prepared for the devil and his angels," because they were "first in transgression." But both have one doom, because one unholy character. See on Mark i. 21-39, Remark 1. **but the righteous into life eternal** [ζωὴν αἰώνιον]—'life everlasting.' The word in both clauses, being in the original the same, should have been the same in the translation also. Thus the decisions of this awful day will be final, irreversible, unending. "The Lord grant," to both the writer and his readers, "that they may find mercy of the Lord in THAT DAY!" (2 Tim.i. 18).

Remarks.—1. What claims does "the Son of Man" here put forward for Himself! He is to come in His own glory; all the holy angels are to come with Him; He is to take his seat on the Throne, and that the Throne of His own glory; all nations are to be gathered before Him; the awful separation of the two great classes is to be His doing; the word of *decision* on both—"Ye blessed!" "Ye cursed!" and the word of *command* to the one, "Come!" to the other, "Depart!"—'To the Kingdom!' 'To the flames!'—all this is to be His doing. But most astonishing of all, *The blissful or blighted eternity of each one of both classes is suspended upon his treatment of Him*—is made to turn upon those mysterious ministrations from age to age to the Lord of glory, disguised in the persons of those who love His Name: 'Ye did thus and thus unto Me—Come, ye blessed! Ye did it not to Me—Depart, ye cursed!' In that "ME" lies an emphasis, the strength of which only the scene itself and its everlasting issues will disclose. Verily, "GOD IS JUDGE HIMSELF" (Ps. l. 6); but it is *God in flesh*, God in One who is "not ashamed to call us BRETHREN." 2. What a *practical* character is here stamped upon Christ's service! It is not, 'Ye had it in your hearts,' but 'Ye DID it with your hands.' It is the love of Christ in the heart rushing to the eyes, ears, hands, feet—going in search of Him, hastening to embrace and to cherish Him, as He wanders through this bleak and cheerless world in His persecuted *cause* and needy *people*. O what has this done, and what will it yet do, to bless and to beautify this fallen world! Lo! He casts His entire cause in the earth upon the love of His people. His own poverty was to have an end, but His Church in its poverty was to take His place. His Personal conflict "finished," that of His *cause* was then only to begin. *The whole Story of His necessities and endurances from the world was to be repeated in the Church,* which was to "fill up *that which was behind of the afflictions* of Christ" (Col. i 24). And what condescension is there in identifying Himself with "THE LEAST of His brethren," holding Himself to be the Person to whom anything whatever is done that is done to the humblest and the meanest of them. Nor let it be overlooked, as *Webster and Wilkinson* beautifully remark, that the assistance to the sick and imprisoned here is not *healing* and *release*, which only few could render, but just that which all could bestow—*visitation, sympathy, attention.* (See Exod. ii. 11; 1 Ki. xvii. 10-15; Jer. xxx. 7-13; Acts xvi. 15; 2 Tim. i. 16-18; 3 John 5-8.) 3. Here also, as in the former parable, we are taught that a life of positive wickedness is not necessary to rejection at the great day. It is enough that, according to the former parable, we do nothing for Christ; and according to the present one, that we recognize Him not in His cause and people, and do not to them as would be due to Himself, if Personally present, suffering and dependent. And will not this set the eyes and ears of those who love Him astir to seek Him out, and catch His tones—in the thin disguises in which He still deigns to walk amongst us—and make us tremble at the thought of turning Him away from our door, or passing Him by on the other side? Perhaps JAMES MONTGOMERY'S charming comment on this scene may help us here:—

> A poor wayfaring man of grief
> Hath often crossed me in my way,
> Who asked so humbly for relief
> That I could never answer, "Nay:"
> I had not power to ask his name,
> Whither he went or whence he came,
> Yet was there something in his eye
> That won my love, I knew not why.

26 AND it came to pass, when Jesus had finished all these sayings, he
2 said unto his disciples, ye "know that after two days is *the feast of* the
passover, and the Son of man is betrayed to be crucified.

3   Then [b]assembled together the chief priests, and the scribes, and the
elders of the people, unto the palace of the high priest, who was called
4 Caiaphas, and consulted that they might take Jesus by subtilty, and
5 kill *him*. But they said, Not on the feast *day*, lest there be an uproar
among the people.

6   Now [c]when Jesus was in [d]Bethany, in the house of Simon the leper,
7 there came unto him a woman having an alabaster box of very precious
8 ointment, and poured *it* on his head, as he sat *at meat*. But [e]when his
disciples saw *it*, they had indignation, saying, To what purpose *is* this
9 waste? For this ointment might have been sold for much, and given to
10 the poor. When Jesus understood *it*, he said unto them, Why trouble
11 ye the woman? for she hath wrought a good work upon me. For [f]ye
12 have the poor always with you; but [g]me ye have not always. For in
that she hath poured this ointment on my body, she did *it* for my
13 burial. Verily I say unto you, [h]Wheresoever this gospel shall be
preached in the whole world, *there* shall also this, that this woman hath
done, be told for a memorial of her.

14   Then [i]one of the twelve, called Judas [j]Iscariot, went unto the chief
15 priests, and said *unto them*, [k]What will ye give me, and I will deliver
him unto you? And they covenanted with him for thirty pieces of
16 silver. And from that time he sought opportunity to betray him.

17   Now [l]the first *day* of the *feast of* unleavened bread the disciples came
to Jesus, saying unto him, Where wilt thou that we prepare for thee to
18 eat the passover? And he said, Go into the city to such a man, and say
unto him, The Master saith, My time is at hand; I will keep the passover
19 at thy house with my disciples. And the disciples did as Jesus had
appointed them; and they made ready the passover.

20   Now when the even was come, he sat down with the twelve.
21 And as they did eat, he said, Verily I say unto you, That one of you
22 shall betray me. And they were exceeding sorrowful, and began every
23 one of them to say unto him, Lord, is it I? And he answered and said,
[m]He that dippeth *his* hand with me in the dish, the same shall betray

A. D. 33.

CHAP. 26.
[a] Mark 14. 1.
Luke 22. 1.
John 13. 1.
[b] Ps. 2. 2.
John 11. 47.
Acts 4. 25.
[c] Mark 14. 3.
John 11. 1.
2
John 12. 3.
[d] ch. 21. 17.
[e] John 12. 4.
[f] Deut. 15.11.
Pro. 22. 2.
Mark 14. 7.
John 12. 8.
[g] ch. 18. 20.
John 8. 2L
John 13. 33.
John 14. 19.
John 16. 5,
28.
John 17. 11.
Acts 3. 21.
Acts 19. 11.
[h] Mark 13.10.
Luke 24.47.
Rom. 1. 8.
Rom. 10.18.
Col. 1. 6.
23.
1 Tim. 2. 6.
[i] Mark 14.10.
Luke 22. 3.
John 13. 2.
[j] ch. 10. 4.
[k] Zec. 11. 12.
ch. 27. 3.
[l] Ex. 12. 6.
Lev. 23. 5,
6.
[m] Ps. 41. 9.
Luke 22. 21.
John 13. 18.

Once, when my scanty meal was spread,
He entered;—not a word he spake;—
Just perishing for want of bread;
"HUNGRY, AND   I gave him all; he blest it, brake,
YE FED ME."   And ate,—but gave me part again
Mine was an angel's portion then,
For while I fed with eager haste
That crust was manna to my taste.

I spied him where a fountain burst
Clear from the rock; his strength was gone;
The heedless water mocked his thirst,
"THIRSTY, AND   He heard it, saw it hurrying on:
YE GAVE ME   I ran to raise the sufferer up;
DRINK."   Thrice from the stream he drained my cup,
Dipt, and returned it running o'er:
I drank, and never thirsted more.

"A STRANGER,   'Twas night; the floods were out; it blew
AND YE TOOK   A winter hurricane aloof;
ME IN."   I heard his voice abroad, and flew
To bid him welcome to my roof.
"NAKED, AND   I warm'd, I cloth'd, I cheer'd my guest;
YE CLOTHED   Laid him on my own couch to rest;
ME."   Then made the hearth my bed, and seem'd
In Eden's garden while I dream'd.

Stript, wounded, beaten, nigh to death,
I found him by the highway-side;
"SICK, AND YE   Revived his spirit, and supplied
VISITED ME."   Wine, oil, refreshment: he was heal'd.
I had myself a wound conceal'd,
But from that hour forgot the smart,
And peace bound up my broken heart.

In prison I saw him next, condemn'd
To meet a traitor's doom at morn;
The tide of lying tongues I stemm'd,
"IN PRISON,   And honour'd him 'midst shame and scorn:
AND YE CAME   My friendship's utmost zeal to try,
UNTO ME."   He ask'd if I for Him would die:
The flesh was weak, my blood ran chill,
But the free spirit cried, "I will."

Then in a moment to my view
The stranger darted from disguise
The tokens in his hands I knew,
My Saviour stood before mine eyes:
He spake, and my poor name He nam'd;
"Of Me thou hast not been asham'd
These deeds shall thy memorial be;
Fear not, thou didst them unto Me."

4. If the concluding words of this chapter, expressly intended to teach the duration of future
bliss and future woe—personal and conscious—do
not proclaim them to be both alike unending,
what words, supposing our Lord *meant* to teach
this, could possibly do it? And shall we venture—
on the strength of our own notions of what is just
or worthy of God—to tamper with His teaching of
Whom the Father hath said, "This is My Beloved
Son, in Whom I am well pleased: HEAR HIM"?

CHAP. XXVI. 1-16.—CHRIST'S FINAL AN-
NOUNCEMENT OF HIS DEATH, AS NOW WITHIN
TWO DAYS, AND THE SIMULTANEOUS CONSPIRACY

24 me. The Son of man goeth [n]as it is written of him: but [o]woe unto that man by whom the Son of man is betrayed! it had been good for that
25 man if he had not been born. Then Judas, which betrayed him, answered and said, Master, is it I? He said unto him, Thou hast said.
26 And as they were eating, [p]Jesus took bread, and [1]blessed *it*, and brake *it*, and gave *it* to the disciples, and said, Take, eat; this [q]is my body.
27 And he took the cup, and gave thanks, and gave *it* to them, saying,
28 Drink ye all of it; for [r]this is my blood [s]of the new testament, which is
29 shed [t]for many for the remission of sins. But I say unto you, I will not drink henceforth of this fruit of the vine, [u]until that day when I drink it new with you in my Father's kingdom.
30 And [v]when they had sung an [2]hymn, they went out into the mount
31 of Olives. Then saith Jesus unto them, [w]All ye shall [x]be offended because of me this night: for it is written, [y]I will smite the Shepherd,
32 and the sheep of the flock shall be scattered abroad. But after I am
33 risen again, [z]I will go before you into Galilee. Peter answered and said unto him, Though all *men* shall be offended because of thee, *yet* will I
34 never be offended. Jesus said unto him, [a]Verily I say unto thee, That
35 this night, before the cock crow, thou shalt deny me thrice. Peter said unto him, Though I should die with thee, yet will I not deny thee. Likewise also said all the disciples.
36 Then [b]cometh Jesus with them unto a place called Gethsemane, and
37 saith unto the disciples, Sit ye here, while I go and pray yonder. And he took with him Peter and [c]the two sons of Zebedee, and began to be
38 sorrowful and very heavy. Then saith he unto them, [d]My soul is exceeding sorrowful, even unto death: tarry ye here, and [e]watch with
39 me. And he went a little farther, and fell on his face, and [f]prayed, saying, [g]O my Father, if it be possible, [h]let this cup pass from me:
40 nevertheless [i]not as I will, but as thou *wilt*. And he cometh unto the disciples, and findeth them asleep, and saith unto Peter, What! could ye
41 not watch with me one hour? Watch [j]and pray, that ye enter not into
42 temptation: the spirit indeed *is* willing, but the flesh *is* weak. He went away again the second time, and prayed, saying, O my Father, if this cup may not pass away from me, except I drink it, thy will be done.
43 And he came and found them asleep again: for their eyes were heavy.
44 And he left them, and went away again, and prayed the third time,
45 saying the same words. Then cometh he to his disciples, and saith unto them, Sleep on now, and take *your* rest: behold, the hour is at hand,
46 and the Son of man is betrayed into the hands of sinners. Rise, let us be going: behold, he is at hand that doth betray me.
47 And [k]while he yet spake, lo, Judas, one of the twelve, came, and with him a great multitude with swords and staves, from the chief priests and
48 elders of the people. Now he that betrayed him gave them a sign, say-
49 ing, Whomsoever I shall kiss, that same is he: hold him fast. And forthwith he came to Jesus, and said, Hail, Master! [l]and kissed him.
50 And Jesus said unto him, [3]Friend, wherefore art thou come? Then came
51 they, and laid hands on Jesus, and took him. And, behold, [m]one of

A. D. 33.

[n] Gen. 3. 15.
Ps. 22. 1.
Isa. 53. 1.
Dan. 9. 26.
Acts 26. 22.
1 Cor. 15. 3.
[o] John 17.12.
[p] 1 Cor. 11.23.
[1] Many Greek copies have, gave thanks.
Mark 6. 41.
[q] Or, represents.
1 Cor. 10. 4.
1 Cor. 10.16.
[r] Ex. 24. 8.
Lev. 17. 11.
[s] Jer. 31. 31.
[t] Rom. 5. 15.
Heb. 9. 22.
[u] Acts 10. 41.
[v] Mark 14.26.
[2] Or, psalm.
[w] John 16.32.
[x] ch. 11. 6.
[y] Zec. 13. 7.
[z] ch. 28. 7.
Mark 16. 7.
[a] Luke 22.34.
John 13.38.
[b] John 18. 1.
[c] ch. 4. 21.
[d] John 12. 27.
[e] 1 Pet. 5. 8.
[f] Mark 14.36.
Luke 22.42.
Heb. 5. 7.
[g] John 12. 27.
[h] ch. 20. 22.
John 18. 11.
[i] 2Sam.15.26.
John 5. 30.
John 6. 38.
Phil. 2. 8.
[j] Mark 13.33.
Mark 14.38.
Luke 22. 40.
1 Cor. 16.13.
[k] Mark 14. 43.
Luke 22.47.
John 18. 3.
Acts 1. 16.
[l] 2 Sam. 20.9.
[3] Companion.
Ps. 41. 9.
Ps. 55. 13.
[m] John 18.10.

OF THE JEWISH AUTHORITIES TO COMPASS IT— THE ANOINTING AT BETHANY—JUDAS AGREES WITH THE CHIEF PRIESTS TO BETRAY HIS LORD. (= Mark xiv. 1-11; Luke xxii. 1-6; John xii. 1-11.) For the exposition, see on Mark xiv. 1-11.

17-30.—PREPARATION FOR AND LAST CELEBRATION OF THE PASSOVER, ANNOUNCEMENT OF THE TRAITOR, AND INSTITUTION OF THE SUPPER. (= Mark xiv. 12-26; Luke xxii. 7-23; John xiii. 1-3, 10, 11, 18-30.) For the exposition, see on Luke xxii. 7-23.

31-35.—THE DESERTION OF JESUS BY HIS DISCIPLES, AND THE FALL OF PETER FORETOLD. (= Mark xiv. 27-31; Luke xxii. 31-46; John xiii. 36-38.) For the exposition, see on Luke xxii. 31-38.

36-46.—THE AGONY IN THE GARDEN. (= Mark xiv. 32-42; Luke xxii. 39-46.) For the exposition, see on Luke xxii. 39-46.

47-56.—BETRAYAL AND APPREHENSION OF JESUS —FLIGHT OF HIS DISCIPLES. (= Mark xiv. 43-52; Luke xxii. 47-54; John xviii. 1-12.) For the exposition, see on John xviii. 1-12.

them which were with Jesus stretched out *his* hand, and drew his sword,
52 and struck a servant of the high priest, and smote off his ear. Then
said Jesus unto him, *n*Put up again thy sword into his place: *o*for all
53 they that take the sword shall perish with the sword. Thinkest thou that
I cannot now pray to my Father, and he shall presently give me *p*more
54 than twelve legions of angels? But how then shall *q*the Scriptures be
fulfilled, that thus it must be?
55 In that same hour said Jesus to the multitudes, Are ye come out as
against a thief with swords and staves for to take me? I sat daily with
56 you teaching in the temple, and ye laid no hold on me. But all this was
done, that the *r*scriptures of the prophets might be fulfilled. Then *s*all
the disciples forsook him, and fled.
57 And *t*they that had laid hold on Jesus led *him* away to Caiaphas the
58 high priest, where the scribes and the elders were assembled. But Peter
followed him afar off unto the high priest's palace, and went in, and sat
59 with the servants, to see the end. Now the chief priests, and elders, and
all the council, sought false witness against Jesus, to put him to death;
60 but found none: yea, though *u*many false witnesses came, *yet* found they
61 none. At the last came *v*two false witnesses, and said, This *fellow* said,
*w*I am able to destroy the temple of God, and to build it in three days.
62 And the high priest arose, and said unto him, Answerest thou nothing?
63 what *is it which* these witness against thee? But *x*Jesus held his peace.
And the high priest answered and said unto him, *y*I adjure thee by the
living God, that thou tell us whether thou be the Christ, the Son of God.
64 Jesus saith unto him, Thou hast said: nevertheless, I say unto you,
*z*Hereafter shall ye see the Son of man *a*sitting on the right hand of
65 power, and coming in the clouds of heaven. Then the high priest *b*rent
his clothes, saying, He hath spoken blasphemy; what further need have
66 we of witnesses? behold, now ye have heard his blasphemy. What think
67 ye? They answered and said, *c*He is guilty of death. Then *d*did they
spit in his face, and buffeted him; and *e*others smote *him* with *4*the
68 palms of their hands, saying, *f*Prophesy unto us, thou Christ, Who is he
that smote thee?
69 Now Peter sat without in the palace: and a damsel came unto him,
70 saying, Thou also wast with Jesus of Galilee. But he denied before
71 *them* all, saying, I know not what thou sayest. And when he was gone
out into the porch, another *maid* saw him, and said unto them that
72 were there, This *fellow* was also with Jesus of Nazareth. And again he
73 denied with an oath, I do not know the man. And after a while came
unto *him* they that stood by, and said to Peter, Surely thou also art *one*
74 of them; for thy speech bewrayeth thee. Then began he to curse and to
swear, *saying,* I know not the man. And immediately the cock crew.
75 And Peter remembered the word of Jesus, which said unto him, Before
the cock crow, thou shalt deny me thrice. And he went out, and *g*wept
bitterly.

27 WHEN the morning was come, *a*all the chief priests and elders of
2 the people took counsel against Jesus to put him to death: and when
they had bound him, they led *him* away, and *b*delivered him to Pontius
Pilate the governor.
3 Then *c*Judas, which had betrayed him, when he saw that he was

Marginal references:

A. D. 33.
n 1 Cor. 4. 12.
o Gen. 9. 6.
Rev. 13. 10.
p 2 Ki. 6. 17.
Ps. 91. 11.
Dan. 7. 10.
q Isa. 53. 7.
Dan. 9. 26.
r Lam. 4. 20.
s John 18. 15.
t Mark 14.53.
Luke 22. 54.
u 1 Ki. 21. 10.
Ps. 27. 12.
v Deut. 19.15.
w ch. 27. 40.
John 2. 19.
x Isa. 53. 7.
ch. 27. 12.
y Lev. 5. 1.
1Sam.14.24.
z Ps. 110. 1.
Dan. 7. 13.
John 1. 51.
Rom. 14 10.
1 Thes.4.16.
Rev. 1. 7.
a Ps. 110. 1.
Acts 7. 55.
b 2 Ki. 18. 37.
2 Ki. 19. 1.
c Lev. 24. 16.
John 19. 7.
d Isa. 50. 6.
Isa. 53. 3.
ch. 27. 30.
Mark 14.65.
Luke 18.32.
e Mic. 5. 1.
Luke 22.63.
4 Or, rods.
f Mark 14.65.
g 2Sam.12.13.
Zec. 12. 10.
Rom. 7. 18-20.
1 Cor. 4. 7.
2 Cor. 7. 10.
Gal. 6. 1.

CHAP. 27.
a Ps. 2. 2.
Mark 15. 1.
Luke 22.66.
Luke 23. 1.
John 18. 28.
b ch. 20. 19.
Acts 3. 13.
1 Thes.2.14.
c Job 20. 5.
ch. 26. 14.
Mark 14.10,
11, 43-46.
Luke 22. 2-6, 47, 48.
2 Cor. 7. 10.

57-75.—JESUS ARRAIGNED BEFORE THE SANHE-
DRIM, CONDEMNED TO DIE, AND SHAMEFULLY
ENTREATED—THE FALL OF PETER. (= Mark
xiv. 53-72; Luke xxii. 54-71; John xviii. 13-18,
24-27.) For the exposition, see on Mark xiv. 53-72.
CHAP. XXVII. 1-10.—JESUS LED AWAY TO
PILATE—REMORSE AND SUICIDE OF JUDAS. (=
Mark xv. 1; Luke xxiii. 1; John xviii. 28.)
125

Jesus Led Away to Pilate (1-2). For the exposition of this portion, see on John xviii. 28, &c.
Remorse and Suicide of Judas (3-10). This portion is peculiar to Matthew. On the progress of
guilt in the traitor, see on Mark xiv. 1-11, Remark
8; and on John xiii. 21-30.
3. Then Judas, which had betrayed him, when
he saw that he was condemned. The condemna-

condemned, repented himself, and brought again the thirty pieces of
4 silver to the chief priests and elders, saying, I have sinned in that I have
betrayed the innocent blood. And they said, What *is that* to us? see
5 thou *to that.* And he cast down the pieces of silver in the temple, *d* and
6 departed, and went and hanged himself. And the chief priests took the
silver pieces, and said, It is not lawful for to put them into the treasury,
7 because it is the price of blood. And they took counsel, and bought
8 with them the potter's field, to bury strangers in. Wherefore that field
9 was called, The field of blood, unto this day. Then was fulfilled that
which was spoken by Jeremy the prophet, saying, *e* And they took the
thirty pieces of silver, the price of him that was valued, [1] whom they of
10 the children of Israel did value, and gave them for the potter's field,
as the Lord appointed me.

A. D. 33.

d 1 Sam. 31.
4, 5.
2 Sam. 17. 23.
Job. 2. 9.
Job. 7. 15.
Ps. 55, 23.
Acts 1. 18.
e Zec. 11. 12,
13.
ch. 26. 15.
1 Or, whom
they
bought of
the chil-
dren of
Israel.

tion, even though not unexpected, might well fill
him with horror. But perhaps this unhappy man
expected that, while he got the bribe, the Lord
would miraculously escape, as He had once and
again done before, out of His enemies' power; and
if so, his remorse would come upon him with all
the greater keenness. **repented himself**—but, as
the issue too sadly showed, it was "the sorrow of
the world, which worketh death" (2 Cor. vii. 10).
**and brought again the thirty pieces of silver to
the chief priests and elders.** A remarkable illustration of the power of an awakened conscience.
A short time before, the promise of this sordid pelf
was temptation enough to his covetous heart to
outweigh the most overwhelming obligations of
duty and love; now, the possession of it so lashes
him that he cannot use it, cannot even keep it!
**4. Saying, I have sinned in that I have betrayed
the innocent blood.** What a testimony this to
Jesus! Judas had been with Him in all circumstances for three years; his post, as treasurer to
Him and the Twelve (John xii. 6), gave him peculiar
opportunity of watching the spirit, disposition, and
habits of his Master; while his covetous nature and
thievish practices would incline him to dark and
suspicious, rather than frank and generous, interpretations of all that He said and did. If, then,
he could have fastened on one questionable feature
in all that he had so long witnessed, we may be
sure that no such speech as this would ever have
escaped his lips, nor would he have been so stung
with remorse as not to be able to keep the money
and survive his crime. **And they said, What is
that to us? see thou to that**:—'Guilty or innocent is nothing to us: We have him now—
begone!' Was ever speech more hellish uttered?
5. And he cast down the pieces of silver. The
sarcastic, diabolical reply which he had got, in
place of the sympathy which perhaps he expected,
would deepen his remorse into an agony. **in the
temple** [ἐν τῷ ναῷ]—the temple proper, commonly
called 'the sanctuary,' or 'the holy place,' into
which only the priests might enter. How is
this to be explained? Perhaps he flung the
money in after them. But thus were fulfilled
the words of the prophet—"I cast them to
the potter in the house of the Lord" (Zec. xi. 13).
and departed, and went and hanged himself.
See, for the details, on Acts i. 18. **6. And the
chief priests took the silver pieces, and said,
It is not lawful for to put them into the
treasury** [κορβανᾶν]—'the *Corban*,' or chest containing the money dedicated to sacred purposes
(see on ch. xv. 5)—**because it is the price of
blood.** How scrupulous now! But those punctilious scruples made them unconsciously fulfil the
Scripture. **7. And they took counsel, and bought
with them the potter's field, to bury strangers in.**

**8. Wherefore that field was called, The field of
blood, unto this day. 9. Then was fulfilled that
which was spoken by Jeremy the prophet, saying**
(Zec. xi. 12, 13), **And they took the thirty pieces
of silver, the price of him that was valued, whom
they of the children of Israel did value, 10. And
gave them for the potter's field, as the Lord appointed me.** Never was a complicated prophecy,
otherwise hopelessly dark, more marvellously fulfilled. Various conjectures have been formed to
account for Matthew's ascribing to Jeremiah a
prophecy found in the book of Zechariah. But
since with this book he was plainly familiar, having quoted one of its most remarkable prophecies
of Christ but a few chapters before (ch. xxi. 4, 5),
the question is one more of critical interest than
real importance. Perhaps the true explanation is
the following, from *Lightfoot*:—'Jeremiah of old
had the first place among the prophets, and hereby
he comes to be mentioned above all the rest in ch.
xvi. 14; because he stood first in the volume of the
prophets (as he proves from the learned *David
Kimchi*) therefore he is first named. When, therefore, Matthew produceth a text of Zechariah under
the name of Jeremy, he only cites the words of the
volume of the prophets under his name who stood
first in the volume of the prophets. Of which sort
is that also of our Saviour (Luke xxiv. 44), "All
things must be fulfilled which are written of me
in the Law, and the Prophets, and the Psalms,"
or the Book of Hagiographa, in which the Psalms
were placed first.'

Remarks.—1. The mastery acquired by the passions is, probably in every case, gradual. In the
case of Judas—the most appalling on record—it
must have been very gradual; otherwise it is incredible that he should have been such a constant and
promising follower of our Lord as to be admitted
by Him into the number of the Twelve, and that
he should not only have been allowed to remain
within that sacred circle to the last, but have
remained undiscovered in his true character to
the Eleven till after he had sold his Master, and
even within an hour of his consummated treason.
What a lesson does this read to the self-confident,
to resist the beginnings of sinful indulgence! 2.
The love of money, when it becomes the ruling passion, blinds—as does every other passion—the mind
of its victim, which is only to be opened by some
unexpected and disappointing event. 3. The true
character of repentance is determined neither by
its sincerity nor by its bitterness, but by the *views*
under which it is wrought. Judas and Peter repented, it should seem, with equal sincerity and
equal pungency, of what they had done. But the
one "went and hanged himself;" the other "went
out and wept bitterly." Whence this difference?
The one, under the sense of his guilt, had nothing

11 And Jesus stood before the governor: and *f* the governor asked him, saying, Art thou the King of the Jews? And Jesus said unto him, *g* Thou
12 sayest. And when he was accused of the chief priests and elders, *h* he
13 answered nothing. Then said Pilate unto him, *i* Hearest thou not how
14 many things they witness against thee? And he answered him to never a word; insomuch that the governor marvelled greatly.
15 Now *j* at *that* feast the governor was wont to release unto the people a
16 prisoner, whom they would. And they had then a notable prisoner,
17 called Barabbas. Therefore, when they were gathered together, Pilate said unto them, Whom will ye that I release unto you? Barabbas, or
18 Jesus which is called Christ? For he knew that for *k* envy they had delivered him.
19 When he was set down on the judgment seat, his wife sent unto him, saying, Have thou nothing to do with that just man: for I have suffered many things this day in *l* a dream because of him.
20 But *m* the chief priests and elders persuaded the multitude that they
21 should ask Barabbas, and destroy Jesus. The governor answered and said unto them, Whether of the twain will ye that I release unto you?
22 They said, Barabbas. Pilate saith unto them, What shall I do then with Jesus which is called Christ? *They* all say unto him, Let him be cruci-
23 fied. And the governor said, Why, what evil hath he done? But they
24 cried out the more, saying, Let him be crucified. When Pilate saw that he could prevail nothing, but *that* rather a tumult was made, he *n* took water, and washed *his* hands before the multitude, saying, I am innocent
25 of the blood of this just person: see ye *to it.* Then answered all the
26 people, and said, *o* His blood *be* on us, and on our children. Then released he Barabbas unto them: and when *p* he had scourged Jesus, he delivered *him* to be crucified.
27 Then the soldiers of the governor took Jesus into the *2* common hall,
28 and gathered unto him the whole band *of soldiers.* And they stripped
29 him, and *q* put on him a scarlet robe. And *r* when they had platted a crown of thorns, they put *it* upon his head, and a reed in his right hand: and they bowed the knee before him, and mocked him, saying, Hail,
30 King of the Jews! And *s* they spit upon him, and took the reed, and

A. D. 33.

f Mark 15. 2.
Luke 23. 3.
John 18. 33.
g John 18.37.
1 Tim. 6.13.
h Isa. 53. 7.
ch. 26. 63.
John 19. 9.
1 Pet 2. 23.
i ch. 26. 62.
John 19. 10.
j Mark 15. 6.
Luke 23. 17.
John 18. 39.
k Acts 7. 9.
l Job 33. 15.
m Mark 15.11.
Luke 23. 18.
John 18.40.
Acts 3. 14.
n Deut. 21. 6.
o Deut. 19.10.
Jos. 2. 19.
1 Ki. 2. 32.
2 Sam. 1.16.
p Isa. 53. 5.
Mark 15.15.
John 19. 1.
2 Or,
governor's
house.
q Luke 23. 11.
r Ps. 35.15,16.
Ps. 69. 19.
Isa. 49. 7.
Isa. 53. 3.
Jer. 20. 7.
Heb. 12.2 3.
s Job 30. 10.
Isa. 50. 6.
Isa. 52. 14.
Mark 15.19.
Luke 18.32.
33.

to fall back upon; and deeming pardon for such a wretch utterly hopeless, and unable to live without it, he hasted to terminate with his own hand a life of insupportable misery. The other, having done a deed which might well have made him incapable of ever again looking his Lord in the face, nevertheless turned toward Him his guilty eyes, when, lo! the Eye of his wounded Lord, glancing from the hall of judgment full down upon himself, with a grief and a tenderness that told their own tale, shot right into his heart, and brought from it a flood of penitential tears! In the one case we have natural principles working themselves out to deadly effect; in the other, we see grace working repentance unto salvation, not to be repented of. 4. What a vivid illustration have we here of the reality of supernatural illumination and the divine truth of the Scriptures, as also of the consistency of the divine arrangements with the liberty of the human will in executing them! Here we have a prophet, five centuries before the birth of Christ, personating Messiah, in bidding the Jewish authorities give him his price, if they thought good, and if not, to forbear; whereupon they weigh him for his price the exact sum agreed upon between Judas and the chief priests for the sale of his Lord—thirty pieces of silver. Then, the Lord bids him cast this to the *potter;* adding, with sublime satire, "A goodly price that I was prized at of them!" Whereupon

he takes the 'thirty pieces of silver, and casts them to the potter in the house of the Lord' (Zec. xi. 12, 13). Now, each of these acts was so unessential to the main business, that they might have been quite different from what they were, without in the least affecting it. Our Lord might have been identified and apprehended without being betrayed by one of His apostles; for the plan was first suggested to the authorities by Judas offering, for a consideration, to do it. And when agreed to, the sum offered and accepted might have been more or less than that actually agreed on. But so it was, that of their own accord they bargained with Judas for precisely the predicted thirty pieces of silver. Nor was this all. For, as the consciences of those holy hypocrites would have been hurt by putting the price of blood into the treasury, and therefore it must be put to some pious use, they resolve to buy with it "the *potter's* field" as a burial-ground for strangers—thus again unconsciously, and with marvellous minuteness, fulfilling a prediction five centuries old, and so setting a double seal on the Messiahship of Jesus!

11-26.—JESUS AGAIN BEFORE PILATE—HE SEEKS TO RELEASE HIM, BUT AT LENGTH DELIVERS HIM TO BE CRUCIFIED. (= Mark xv. 1-15; Luke xxiii. 1-25; John xviii 28-40.) For the exposition, see on Luke xxiii. 1-25, and on John xviii. 28-40.

27-33.—JESUS, SCORNFULLY AND CRUELLY ENTREATED OF THE SOLDIERS, IS LED AWAY TO BE

31 ^tsmote him on the head. And after that they had mocked him, they took the robe off from him, and put his own raiment on him, ^uand led him away to crucify *him*.

32 And ^vas they came out, ^wthey found a man of Cyrene, Simon by name:

33 him they compelled to bear his cross. And when they were come unto

34 a place called Golgotha, that is to say, A place of a skull, they ^xgave him vinegar to drink mingled with gall: and when he had tasted *thereof*,

35 he would not drink. And they crucified him, and parted his garments, casting lots: that it might be fulfilled which was spoken by the prophet, They ^yparted my garments among them, and upon my

36 vesture did they cast lots. And sitting down they watched him there;

37 and set up over his head his accusation written, THIS IS JESUS THE

38 KING OF THE JEWS. Then ^zwere there two thieves crucified with him; one on the right hand, and another on the left.

39, And ^athey that passed by reviled him, wagging their heads, and

40 saying, ^bThou that destroyest the temple, and buildest *it* in three days, save thyself. If thou be the Son of God, come down from the cross.

41 Likewise also the chief priests, mocking *him*, with the scribes and elders,

42 said, He saved others; himself he cannot save. If he be the King of Israel, let him now come down from the cross, and we will believe him.

43 He ^ctrusted in God; let him deliver him now, if he will have him: for

44 he said, I am the Son of God. The ^dthieves also, which were crucified with him, cast the same in his teeth.

45 Now ^efrom the sixth hour there was darkness over all the land unto

46 the ninth hour. And about the ninth hour ^fJesus cried with a loud voice, saying, Eli! Eli! lama sabachthani? that is to say, ^gMy God! My

47 God! why hast thou forsaken me? Some of them that stood there, when

48 they heard *that*, said, This *man* calleth for Elias. And straightway one of them ran, and took a sponge, ^hand filled *it* with vinegar, and put *it* on

49 a reed, and gave him to drink. The rest said, Let be, let us see whether Elias will come to save him.

50 Jesus, when he had cried again with a loud voice, yielded up the ghost.

51 And, behold, ⁱthe veil of the temple was rent in twain from the top

A. D. 33.
t Mic. 5. 1.
Mark 15.19.
Luke 22.63.
u Isa. 53. 7.
ch. 20. 19.
ch. 21. 39.
John 19. 16.
17.
v Num. 15.35.
1 Ki. 21. 13.
Acts 7. 58.
Heb. 13. 12.
w Mark 15.21.
x Ps. 22. 18.
Ps. 69. 21.
Mark 15.23.
John 19. 28
30.
y Ps. 22. 18.
z Isa. 53. 12.
Mark 15.27.
Luke 23.32.
John 19.18.
a Ps. 22. 7.
Ps. 109. 25.
b ch. 26. 61.
John 2. 19.
c Ps. 22. 8.
d Luke 23.39.
e Isa. 50. 3.
Amos 8. 9.
f Heb. 5. 7.
g Ps. 22. 1.
h Ps. 69. 21.
John 19. 29.
i Ex. 26. 31.
2 Chr. 3. 14.
Mark 15.38.
Luke 23. 45.
Eph. 2. 14.
18.
Heb. 6. 19.
Heb. 10. 19.
20.

CRUCIFIED. (= Mark xv. 16-22; Luke xxiii. 26-31; John xix. 2, 17.) For the exposition, see on Mark xv. 16-22.

34-50.—CRUCIFIXION AND DEATH OF THE LORD JESUS. (= Mark xv. 25-37; Luke xxiii. 33-46; John xix. 18-30.) For the exposition, see on John xix. 18-30.

51-66.—SIGNS AND CIRCUMSTANCES FOLLOWING THE DEATH OF THE LORD JESUS—HE IS TAKEN DOWN FROM THE CROSS, AND BURIED—THE SEPULCHRE IS GUARDED. (= Mark xv. 38-47; Luke xxiii. 47-56; John xix. 31-42.)

The Veil Rent (51). **51. And, behold, the veil of the temple was rent in twain from the top to the bottom.** This was the thick and gorgeously wrought veil which was hung between the "holy place" and the "holiest of all," shutting out all access to the presence of God as manifested "from above the mercyseat and from between the cherubim:"—"the Holy Ghost this signifying, that the way into the holiest of all was *not yet* made manifest" (Heb. ix. 8). Into this holiest of all none might enter, not even the high priest, save once a year, on the great day of atonement, and then only with the blood of atonement in his hands, which he sprinkled "upon and before the mercyseat seven times" (Lev. xvi. 14)—to signify that *access for sinners to a holy God is only through atoning blood.* But as they had only the blood of bulls and of goats, which could not take away

sins (Heb. x. 4), during all the long ages that preceded the death of Christ, the thick veil remained; the blood of bulls and of goats continued to be shed and sprinkled; and once a year access to God through an atoning sacrifice was vouchsafed—*in a picture,* or rather, was *dramatically represented,* in those symbolical actions—nothing more. But *now,* the one atoning Sacrifice being provided in the precious blood of Christ, access to this holy God could no longer be denied; and so the moment the Victim expired on the altar, that thick veil which for so many ages had been the dread symbol of *separation between God and guilty men* was, without a hand touching it, mysteriously "rent in twain from top to bottom:"—"the Holy Ghost this signifying, that the way into the holiest of all was NOW made manifest!" How emphatic the statement, "*from top to bottom;*" as if to say, Come boldly now to the Throne of Grace; *the veil is clean gone;* the Mercyseat stands open to the gaze of sinners, and the way to it is sprinkled with the blood of Him—"who through the eternal Spirit hath offered Himself without spot to God"! Before, it was death *to go in,* now it is *death to stay out.* See more on this glorious subject on Heb. x. 19-22.

An Earthquake—The Rocks Rent—The Graves Opened, that the Saints which slept in them might Come Forth after their Lord's Resurrection (51-53). **51. and the earth did quake.** From what follows

52 to the bottom; and ʲthe earth did quake, and the rocks rent; and the
graves were opened; ᵏand many bodies of the saints which slept arose,
53 And came out of the graves after his resurrection, and went into the holy
city, and appeared unto many.
54   Now ˡwhen the centurion, and they that were with him watching
Jesus, saw the earthquake, and those things that were done, they feared
greatly, saying, Truly this was the Son of God.
55   And many women were there beholding afar off, ᵐwhich followed
56 Jesus from Galilee, ministering unto him: among ⁿwhich was Mary
Magdalene, and Mary the mother of James and Joses, and the mother
of Zebedee's children.
57   When ᵒthe even was come, there came a rich man of Arimathea, named
58 Joseph, who also himself was Jesus' disciple: he went to Pilate, and
begged the body of Jesus. Then Pilate commanded the body to be
59 delivered. And when Joseph had taken the body, he wrapped it in a
60 clean linen cloth, and ᵖlaid it in his own new tomb, which he had hewn
out in the rock: and he rolled a great stone to the door of the sepulchre,

A. D. 33.
ʲ Ex. 19. 18.
Ps. 18. 7.
Mic. 1. 3, 4.
Nah. 1. 5.
Hab. 3. 10.
ᵏ Ps. 68. 20.
Dan. 12. 2.
1 Cor. 11. 30.
1 Cor. 15 57.
ˡ Ex. 20.18,19.
Deut. 22.31.
Mark 15. 39.
Luke 23. 47.
ᵐ Luke 8. 2.
Luke 23. 27,
28, 48, 49.
ⁿ Mark 15. 40.
ᵒ Mark 15.42.
Luke 23. 50.
John 19. 38.
ᵖ Isa. 53. 9.

it would seem that this earthquake was local, having for its object the rending of the rocks and the opening of the graves. **and the rocks rent** ('were rent')—the physical creation thus sublimely proclaiming, at the bidding of its Maker, the *concussion* which at that moment was taking place in the moral world at the most critical moment of its history. Extraordinary rents and fissures have been observed in the rocks near this spot. **52. And the graves were opened; and many bodies of the saints which slept arose, 53. And came out of the graves after his resurrection.** These sleeping saints (see on 1 Thes. iv. 14) were Old Testament believers, who—according to the usual punctuation in our version—were quickened into resurrection-life at the moment of their Lord's death, but lay in their graves till His resurrection, when they came forth. But it is far more natural, as we think, and consonant with other scriptures, to understand that only the graves were opened, probably by the earthquake, at our Lord's death, and this only in preparation for the subsequent exit of those who slept in them, when the Spirit of life should enter into them from their risen Lord, and along with Him they should come forth, trophies of His victory over the grave. Thus, in the opening of the graves at the moment of the Redeemer's expiring, there was a glorious symbolical proclamation that the Death which had just taken place had "swallowed up death in victory;" and whereas the saints that slept in them were awakened only by their risen Lord, to accompany Him out of the tomb, it was fitting that "the Prince of Life" "should be *the First* that should rise from the dead" (Acts xxvi. 23; 1 Cor. xv. 20, 23; Col. i. 18; Rev. i. 5). **and went into the holy city**—that city where He, in virtue of whose resurrection they were now alive, had been condemned, **and appeared unto many**—that there might be undeniable evidence of their own resurrection first, and through it of their Lord's. Thus, while it was not deemed fitting that He Himself should appear again in Jerusalem, save to the disciples, provision was made that the fact of His resurrection should be left in no doubt. It must be observed, however, that the resurrection of these sleeping saints was not like those of the widow of Nain's son, of Jairus' daughter, of Lazarus, and of the man who "revived and stood upon his feet," on his dead body touching the bones of Elisha (2 Ki. xiii. 21)—which were mere temporary recallings of the departed spirit to the *mortal* body, to be followed by a final departure of

it "till the trumpet shall sound." But this was a resurrection *once for all, to life everlasting;* and so there is no room to doubt that they went to glory with their Lord, as bright trophies of His victory over death.
The Centurion's Testimony (54). **54. Now when the centurion**—the military superintendent of the execution, **and they that were with him watching Jesus, saw the earthquake**—or felt it and witnessed its effects, **and those things that were done**—reflecting upon the entire transaction, **they feared greatly**—convinced of the presence of a Divine Hand, **saying, Truly this was the Son of God.** There cannot be a reasonable doubt that this expression was used in the Jewish sense, and that it points to the claim which Jesus made to be the Son of God, and on which His condemnation expressly turned. The meaning, then, clearly is, that He must have been what He professed to be; in other words, that He was no impostor. There was no medium between those two. See, on the similar testimony of the penitent thief—"This man hath done nothing amiss"—on Luke xxiii. 41.
The Galilean Women (55, 56). **55. And many women were there beholding afar off, which followed Jesus** [ἡκολούθησαν]. The sense here would be better brought out by the use of the pluperfect, 'which had followed Jesus,' **from Galilee, ministering unto him.** As these dear women had ministered to Him during His glorious missionary tours *in* Galilee (see on Luke viii. 1-3), so from this statement it should seem that they accompanied Him and ministered to His wants *from* Galilee on His final journey to Jerusalem. **56. Among which was Mary Magdalene** (see on Luke viii. 2), **and Mary the mother of James and Joses**—the wife of Cleophas, or rather Clopas, and sister of the Virgin (John xix. 25). See on ch. xii. 55, 56. **and the mother of Zebedee's children**—that is, Salome: compare Mark xv. 40. All this about the women is mentioned for the sake of what is afterwards to be related of their purchasing spices to anoint their Lord's body.
The Taking Down from the Cross and the Burial (57-60). For the exposition of this portion, see on John xix. 38-42.
The Women mark the Sacred Spot, that they might recognize it on coming thither to Anoint the Body (61). **61. And there was Mary Magdalene, and the other Mary**—"the mother of James and Joses," mentioned before (v. 56), **sitting over against the sepulchre.** See on Mark xvi. 1.

61 and departed. And there was Mary Magdalene, and the other Mary, sitting over against the sepulchre.

62 Now the next day, that followed the day of the preparation, the chief

63 priests and Pharisees came together unto Pilate, saying, Sir, we remember that *q* that deceiver said, while he was yet alive, After *r* three days

64 I will rise again. Command therefore that the sepulchre be made sure until the third day, lest his disciples come by night, and steal him away, and say unto the people, He is risen from the dead: so the last error

65 shall be worse than the first. Pilate said unto them, Ye have a watch:

66 go your way, make *it* as sure as ye can. So they went, and made the sepulchre sure, *s* sealing the stone, and setting a watch.

A. D. 33.
q Ps. 2. 1–6.
Acts 4. 27, 28.
2 Cor. 6. 8.
r ch. 16. 21.
ch. 17. 23.
ch. 20. 19.
ch. 26. 61.
Mark 8. 31.
Mark 10. 34.
Luke 9. 22.
Luke 18. 33.
s Dan. 6. 17.

The Sepulchre Guarded (62-66). **62. Now the next day, that followed the day of the preparation**—that is, after six o'clock of our *Saturday* evening. The crucifixion took place on the *Friday*, and all was not over till shortly before sunset, when the Jewish Sabbath commenced; and "that sabbath day was an high day" (John xix. 31), being the first day of the feast of Unleavened Bread. That day being over at six on Saturday evening, they hastened to take their measures. **the chief priests and Pharisees came together unto Pilate, 63. Saying, Sir, we remember that that deceiver**—Never, remarks *Bengel*, will you find the heads of the people calling Jesus by His own name. And yet here there is betrayed a certain uneasiness, which one almost fancies they only tried to stifle in their own minds, as well as crush in Pilate's, in case he should have any lurking suspicion that he had done wrong in yielding to them. **said, while he was yet alive.** Important testimony this, from the lips of His bitterest enemies, to *the reality of Christ's death;* the cornerstone of the whole Christian religion. **After three days**—which, according to the customary Jewish way of reckoning, need signify no more than 'after the commencement of the third day.' **I will rise again** [ἐγείρομαι]—'I rise,' in the present tense, thus reporting not only the *fact* that this prediction of His had reached their ears, but that they understood Him to look forward *confidently* to its occurring on the very day named. **64. Command therefore that the sepulchre be made sure**—by a Roman guard, **until the third day**—after which, if He still lay in the grave, the imposture of His claims would be manifest to all. **lest his disciples come by night, and steal him away, and say unto the people, He is risen from the dead.** [The word νυκτὸς, 'by night,' appears by the authorities not to belong to the genuine text here, and was probably introduced from ch. xxviii. 13.] Did they really fear this? **so the last error shall be worse than the first**—the imposture of His pretended resurrection worse than that of His pretended Messiahship. **65. Pilate said unto them, Ye have a watch.** The guards had already acted under orders of the Sanhedrim, with Pilate's consent; but probably they were not clear about employing them as a night-watch without Pilate's express authority. **go your way, make it as sure as ye can** [ὡς οἴδατε]—'as ye know how,' or in the way ye deem securest. Though there may be no irony in this speech, it evidently insinuated that *if* the event should be contrary to their wish, it would not be for want of sufficient human appliances to prevent it. **66. So they went, and made the sepulchre sure, sealing the stone**—which Mark (xvi. 4) says was "very great," **and setting a watch**—to guard it. What more could man do? But while they are trying to prevent the resurrection of the Prince of Life, God makes use of

130

their precautions for His own ends. Their stone-covered, seal-secured sepulchre shall preserve the sleeping dust of the Son of God free from all indignities, in undisturbed, sublime repose; while their watch shall be His guard of honour until the angels shall come to take their place!

Remarks.—1. How grandly was the true nature of Christ's death proclaimed by the rending of the veil at the moment when it took place! He was "by wicked hands," indeed, "crucified and slain." He died, it is true, a glorious example of suffering "for righteousness' sake." Yet not these, nor any other explanations of His death, however correct in themselves, furnish the true key to the divine intent of it. But if the temple and its services were the centre and soul of the Church's instituted worship under the ancient economy; if that portion of the temple which was the holiest of all, and the symbol of God's dwelling place among men, was shut to every Israelite by a thick veil through which it was death to pass, and was accessible to His high-priestly representative only on that one day of the year when he carried within the veil *the blood of atonement*, and sprinkled it upon and before that mercyseat which represented the Throne of God; if on that one occasion, and *upon that one action*, in all the year, Jehovah manifested Himself in visible glory, as a God graciously present with sinful men, and accepting the persons and services of sinful worshippers—thus symbolically proclaiming that without the shedding of blood there was no remission, and without remission, no access to God, and no acceptable worship—while yet it was manifest that the only blood which ever was shed upon the Jewish altar, and sprinkled upon the mercyseat had no atoning virtue in it at all, and so could not, and never did take away sin; and finally, if after all this teaching of the ancient economy up to the moment of Christ's death, as to the *necessity* and yet the *absence* of atoning blood, it came to pass that at the moment when Christ died—without a hand touching it—the thick veil of the Temple was rent in twain *from the top to the bottom*, and so the holiest was thrown open: who can fail to see that this was done by a Divine Hand, in order to teach, even by the naked eye, that the true atoning Victim had now been slain, and that, having put away sin by the sacrifice of Himself—having finished the transgression, and made an end of sins, and made reconciliation for iniquity, and brought in everlasting righteousness, and sealed up the vision and prophecy, He had anointed the holy of holies (Dan. ix. 24), in order that not the high priest only, but every believer, not once a year, but at all times, might have boldness to enter by the blood of Jesus, by the new and living way which He hath consecrated for us through the veil, that is to say, His own flesh" (Heb. x. 19, 20). Nor is it possible to give any tolerable explanation of this rending of

28 IN the *a*end of the sabbath, as it began to dawn toward the first *day* of the week, came Mary Magdalene *b*and the other Mary to see the 2 sepulchre. And, behold, there ¹was a great earthquake: for *c*the angel of the Lord descended from heaven, and came and rolled back the stone

A. D. 33.

a Mark 16. 1.
b ch. 27. 56.
1 had been.
c Mark 16. 5.

the veil at Christ's death, if its sacrificial, atoning character be denied or explained away. To talk of its signifying the breaking down of the wall of partition between Jew and Gentile, as some do, is altogether wide of the mark. For the veil was intended to shut out, not Gentiles, but *Jews themselves*, from the presence of God; and the liberty to pass through it once, but once only, with atoning blood, both showed what alone would remove that veil for any worshipper, and the absence of that one thing so long as the veil remained. And thus the great doctrine of the sacrificial design and atoning efficacy of the death of Christ was proclaimed in the most expressive symbolical language at the moment when it took place. 2. Do Christians sufficiently recognize *the fact*, that sin is "put away" as a ground of exclusion from the favour of God; so that the most guilty on the face of the earth, believing this, has "boldness to enter in by the blood of Jesus" to *perfect reconciliation*. As no worshipper was holy enough to have right to go within that veil which shut out the guilty under the law, so no worshipper is sinful enough to be shut out from the holiest of all who will enter it by the blood of Jesus. As all were shut out alike under the law, so all are alike free to enter under the Gospel. This is that *present* salvation which Christ's servants are honoured to preach to every sinner, the faith of which sets the conscience free, and overcomes the world; but want of the clear apprehension of which keeps multitudes of sincere Christians all their lifetime subject to bondage. 3. What a grand testimony did the rending of the rocks and the opening of the graves at the moment of Christ's death bear to the subserviency of all nature to the purposes of Redemption! As when He walked the earth all nature was at His bidding, so now at His Death—which was the reconciliation of Heaven, the life of the dead, the knell of the kingdom of darkness, and Paradise regained— Nature felt the deed, and heaved sympathetic. 4. How beautifully does the resurrection of those sleeping saints of the Old Testament, by virtue of Christ's resurrection—that they might grace with their presence His exit from the tomb —proclaim the unity of the Church of the redeemed under every economy, and the fact that, whether they lived before or live after Christ, it is 'because He lives that they live also!' 5. How remarkable is it to find a heathen officer— who probably knew little or nothing of Christ save the charge on which He was condemned to die, that "He made Himself the Son of God"—unable to resist the evidence which the scenes of Calvary furnished of His innocence, and consequently of the truth of His claims, little as he would understand what they were; while those who had been trained to the study of the Scriptures, and had been favoured with overpowering evidence of the claims of Jesus to be the Hope of Israel, were His bloody murderers! 6. How precious to Christians should be those testimonies to the reality of Christ's death which even His enemies unconsciously bore, since on this depends the reality of His resurrection, and on both of these hang all that is dear to God's children! So little did they doubt of His death, that their only fear—whether real or pretended—was that His disciples would come and steal away His dead body, and pretend that He had risen from the dead. Then, having

got what they wanted from Pilate—full power to see to the sealing of the stone and the placing of a military guard to watch it till the third day —they thus themselves unconsciously attested the reality of the resurrection which, on the morning of the third day took place, when, in spite of all their precautions, the sepulchre was found empty, and the grave-clothes lying disposed in grand orderliness, as they had been laid calmly aside when no longer needed! 7. Have we not here one of the most striking commentaries imaginable on those words of the Psalmist, "Surely the wrath of man shall praise thee: the remainder of wrath shalt thou restrain"? (Ps. lxxvi. 10). For as the death of Christ, which the wrath of man procured, was infinitely to the praise of God, and the "remainder of that wrath" might have extended to the infliction of indignities even upon the dead body, had it been exposed, it pleased God to put it into the heart of Pilate to give the body for interment into the hands of Jesus' friends, and so to "restrain the remainder" of His enemies' wrath that they themselves sealed up the grave and set the military guard over it— thus securing its sacred repose till the appointed hour of release. O the depth of the riches, both of the wisdom and knowledge of God! How unsearchable are His judgments, and His ways past finding out! 8. How sweet should be the grave to Christ's sleeping saints! Might we not hear Him saying to them beforehand, "Fear not to go down into Egypt; for I will go down with you, and I will surely bring you up again"? And indeed He has gone down, and lain in as cold, and dark, and narrow, and repulsive a bed as any of you, O believers, will ever be called to lie down in; and has He not sweetened the clods of the valley —or haply, the great deep—as a perfumed bed for you to lie down in?

CHAP. XXVIII. 1-15.—GLORIOUS ANGELIC ANNOUNCEMENT ON THE FIRST DAY OF THE WEEK, THAT CHRIST IS RISEN—HIS APPEARANCE TO THE WOMEN—THE GUARDS BRIBED TO GIVE A FALSE ACCOUNT OF THE RESURRECTION. (= Mark xvi. 1-8; Luke xxiv. 1-8; John xx. i.)

The Resurrection Announced to the Women (1-8). 1. **In the end of the sabbath, as it began to dawn** [ὀψὲ δὲ σαββάτων, ἐπιφωσκούσῃ]—' After the Sabbath, as it grew toward daylight.' **toward the first day of the week**. Luke (xxiv. 1) has it, "very early in the morning" [ὄρθρου βαθέος, but the true reading is βαθέως]—properly, 'at the first appearance of day-break;' and corresponding with this, John (xx. 1) says, "when it was yet dark." See on Mark xvi. 2. Not an hour, it would seem, was lost by those dear lovers of the Lord Jesus. **came Mary Magdalene and the other Mary**—"the mother of James and Joses" (see on ch. xxvii. 56, 61), **to see the sepulchre**—with a view to the anointing of the body, for which they had made all their preparations. See on Mark xvi. 1. 2. **And, behold, there was**—that is, there had been, before the arrival of the women, **a great earthquake: for the angel of the Lord descended from heaven, and came and rolled back the stone from the door, and sat upon it.** And this was the state of things when the women drew near. Some judicious critics think all this was transacted while the women were approaching; but the view we have given, which is the prevalent

3 from the door, and sat upon it. His *d*countenance was like lightning,
4 and his raiment white as snow: and for fear of him the keepers did
5 shake, and became as dead *men*. And the angel answered and said unto
the women, 'Fear not ye; for I know that ye seek Jesus, which was
6 crucified. He is not here; for he is risen, *f*as he said. Come, see the
7 place where the Lord lay: and go quickly, and tell his disciples that he
is risen from the dead; and, behold, he *g*goeth before you into Galilee;
8 there shall ye see him: lo, I have told you. And they departed quickly
from the sepulchre with fear and great joy, and did run to bring his
disciples word.
9 And as they went to tell his disciples, behold, *h*Jesus met them, saying,
All hail! And they came and held him by the feet, and worshipped
10 him. Then said Jesus unto them, Be not afraid: go tell *i*my brethren
that they go into Galilee, and there shall they see me.
11 Now when they were going, behold, some of the watch came into the
city, and showed unto the chief priests all the things that were done.
12 And when they were assembled with the elders, and had taken counsel,
13 they gave large money unto the soldiers, saying, Say ye, His disciples
14 came by night, and stole him *away* while we slept. And if this come to

A. D. 33.

d Dan. 10. 6.
ch. 17. 2.
Rev. 10. 1.
Rev. 18. 1.
e Isa. 35. 4.
Dan. 10. 12.
Mark 16. 6.
Luke 1. 12.
Heb. 1. 14.
Rev. 1. 17.
f ch. 12. 40.
ch. 16. 21.
ch. 17. 23.
ch. 20. 19.
Mark 8. 31.
g ch. 26. 32.
Mark 16. 7.
h Mark 16. 9.
John 20. 14.
Rev. 1. 17,
18.
i Rom. 8. 29.
Heb. 2. 11.

one, seems the more natural. All this august preparation—recorded by Matthew alone—bespoke the grandeur of the exit which was to follow. The angel sat upon the huge stone, to overawe, with the lightning-lustre that darted from him, the Roman guard, and do honour to his rising Lord. **3. His countenance** [ἰδέα]—or, ' appearance,' was **like lightning, and his raiment white as snow**—the one expressing the *glory*, the other the *purity* of the celestial abode from which he came. **4. And for fear of him the keepers did shake, and became as dead men**. Is the sepulchre "sure" now, O ye chief priests? He that sitteth in the heavens doth 'laugh at you. **5. And the angel answered and said unto the women, Fear not ye** [Μὴ φοβεῖσθε ὑμεῖς]. The "ye" here is emphatic, to contrast their case with that of the guards. 'Let those puny creatures, sent to keep the Living One among the dead, for fear of Me shake and become as dead men (*v.* 4); but ye that have come hither on another errand, fear not ye.' **for I know that ye seek Jesus, which was crucified** [τὸν ἐσταυρωμένου]—'Jesus the Crucified.' **6. He is not here; for he is risen, as he said.** See on Luke xxiv. 5-7. **Come** [Δεῦτε], as in ch. xi. 28, **see the place where the Lord lay.** Charming invitation! 'Come, see the spot where the Lord of glory lay: now it is an empty grave: He lies not, but He *lay* there. Come, feast your eyes on it!' But see on John xx. 12; and Remarks below. **7. And go quickly, and tell his disciples.** For a precious addition to this, see on Mark xvi. 7. **that he is risen from the dead; and, behold, he goeth before you into Galilee**—to which those women belonged (ch. xxvii. 55). **there shall ye see him.** This must refer to those more public manifestations of Himself to large numbers of disciples at once, which He vouchsafed only in Galilee; for individually He was seen of some of those very women almost immediately after this (*v.* 9, 10). **lo, I have told you.** Behold, ye have this word from the world of light! **8. And they departed quickly.** Mark (xvi. 8) says "they fled" **from the sepulchre with fear and great joy.** How natural this combination of feelings! See on a similar statement of Mark xvi. 11. **and did run to bring his disciples word.** "Neither said they anything to any man [by the way]; for they were afraid" (Mark xvi. 8).

Appearance to the Women (9, 10). This appearance is recorded only by Matthew. **9. And as they**

went to tell his disciples, behold, Jesus met them, saying, All hail! [Χαίρετε]—the usual salute, but from the lips of Jesus bearing a higher signification. **And they came and held him by the feet.** How truly womanly! **and worshipped him. 10. Then said Jesus unto them, Be not afraid.** What dear associations would these familiar words—now uttered in a higher style, but by the same Lips—bring rushing back to their recollection! **go tell my brethren that they go into Galilee, and there shall they see me.** The brethren here meant must have been His brethren after the flesh (ch. xiii. 55); for His brethren in the higher sense (see on John xx. 17) had several meetings with Him at Jerusalem *before* he went to Galilee, which they would have missed if they had been the persons ordered to Galilee to meet Him.

The Guards Bribed (11-15). The whole of this important portion is peculiar to Matthew. **11. Now when they were going**—while the women were on their way to deliver to His brethren the message of their risen Lord, **behold, some of the watch came into the city, and showed unto the chief priests all the things that were done.** Simple, unsophisticated soldiers! How could ye imagine that such a tale as ye had to tell would not at once commend itself to your sacred employers? Had they doubted this for a moment, would they have ventured to go near them, knowing it was death to a Roman soldier to be proved asleep when on guard? and of course that was the only other explanation of the case. **12. And when they were assembled with the elders.** But Joseph at least was absent; Gamaliel probably also; and perhaps others. **and had taken counsel, they gave large money unto the soldiers.** It would need a good deal; but the whole case of the Jewish authorities was now at stake. With what contempt must these soldiers have regarded the Jewish ecclesiastics! **13. Saying, Say ye, His disciples came by night, and stole him away while we slept**—which, as we have observed, was a capital offence for soldiers on guard. **14. And if this come to the governor's ears** [ἐὰν ἀκουσθῇ τοῦτο ἐπὶ τοῦ ἡγεμόνος]—rather, 'If this come before the governor;' that is, not in the way of mere report, but for judicial investigation. **we will persuade him, and secure you** [ἡμεῖς πείσομεν αὐτόν, καὶ ὑμᾶς ἀμερίμνους ποιήσομεν]. The "we" and the "you" are emphatic here—'We

15 the governor's ears, we will persuade him, and secure you. So they took
the money, and did as they were taught: and this saying is commonly
reported among the Jews until this day.

16   Then the *j*eleven disciples went away into Galilee, into a mountain

A. D. 33.
j Mark 16. 14.
John 6. 70.
Acts 1. 13.
1 Cor. 15. 5.

shall [take care to] persuade him and keep you
from trouble,' or 'save you harmless.' The grammatical form of this clause [ἐὰν ἀκουσθῇ . . πεί-
σομεν] implies that the thing supposed was expected to happen. The meaning then is, 'If this
come before the governor—as it likely will—we
shall see to it that,' &c. The "persuasion" of
Pilate meant, doubtless, quieting him by a bribe,
which we know otherwise he was by no means
above taking (like Felix afterwards, Acts xxiv. 26).
15. So they took the money, and did as they were
taught—thus consenting to brand themselves with
infamy—and this saying is commonly reported
among the Jews until this day—to the date of the
publication of this Gospel. The wonder is that
so clumsy and incredible a story lasted so long.
But those who are resolved *not* to come to the
light will catch at straws. *Justin Martyr,* who
flourished about A.D. 170, says, in his 'Dialogue
with Trypho the Jew,' that the Jews dispersed
the story by means of special messengers sent to
every country.

Remarks.—1. If the Crucifixion and Burial of
the Son of God were the most stupendous manifestations of self-sacrifice, His Resurrection was
no less grand a vindication of His character
and claims—rolling away the reproach of the
Cross, revealing His Personal dignity, and putting
the crown upon His whole claims. (See Rom. i.
4). As His own Self bare our sins in His own
body on the tree (1 Pet. ii. 24), and so was "made
a curse for us" (Gal. iii. 13), His resurrection was
a public proclamation that He had now made an
end of sin, and brought in everlasting righteousness (Dan. ix. 24). And how august was this
proclamation! While His enemies were watching the hours, in hope that the third day might
see Him still in the tomb, and His loving disciples were almost in despair of ever beholding
Him again, lo! the ground heaves sublime, an
angel, bright as lightning and clad in raiment of
snowy white, descends from heaven, rolls the
huge sealed stone from the door of the sepulchre,
and takes his seat upon it as a guard of honour
from heaven; while the keepers for fear of him
are shaking and crouching as dead men. *What
then took place, none of the Four sacred Narra-
tors has dared to describe,* or rather, none of
them knew. All that we need to know they do
record—that when the women arrived, the grave
was empty, and speedily Jesus Himself stood
before them in resurrection-life and love! What
a glorious Gospel-voice issues from these facts!
O, if even the guiltiest sinner on the face of the
earth would but draw near, might he not hear a
voice saying to him, "He is not here; for He has
risen, as He said. Come, see the place where the
Lord lay;" and as he looks into this open grave,
shall he not hear the Risen One Himself whispering to him, "Peace be unto thee," and as He says
this "showing him His hands and His side," in
evidence of the price paid for the remission of
sins? 3. How delightful a subject of contemplation is the ministry of angels, especially in connection with Christ Himself, and most of all in
connection with this scene of His resurrection;
where we not only find them hovering around the
Person of Jesus, as their own adored Lord, but
showing the liveliest interest in every detail, and
the tenderest care for the disciples of their Lord!

And what is this but a specimen of what they feel
and do towards "the heirs of salvation" of every
quality, every age, every clime? 4. If anything
were needed to complete the proof of the reality of
Christ's resurrection, it would be the silliness of
the explanation which the guards were bribed to
give of it. That a whole guard should go to sleep
on their watch at all, was not very likely; that
they should do it in a case like this, where there
was such anxiety on the part of the authorities
that the grave should remain undisturbed, was in
the last degree improbable; but—even if it could
be supposed that so many disciples should come to
the grave as would suffice to break the seal, roll
back the huge stone, and carry off the body—that
the guards should all sleep soundly enough and
long enough to admit of all this tedious and noisy
work being gone through at their very side without
being awoke, and done too so leisurely, that the
very grave clothes—which would naturally have
been kept upon the body, if only to aid them in
bearing the heavy burden—should be found carefully folded and orderly disposed within the
tomb:—all this *will not believe* even by credulity
itself, and could not have been credited even at
the first, though it might suit those who were
determined to resist the Redeemer's claims to
pretend that they believed it. And the best proof
that it was not believed is, that within a few
weeks of this time, and in the very place where
the imposture of a pretended resurrection—if it
really was such—could most easily have been detected, thousands upon thousands, many of whom
had been implicated in His death, came trooping
into the ranks of the risen Saviour, resting their
whole salvation upon the belief of His Resurrection. Now, therefore, is Christ risen from the
dead, and become the First-Fruits of His sleeping
people! 5. Let believers take the full comfort of
that blessed assurance, that "as Jesus died and
rose again, even so them also which sleep in Jesus
will God bring with Him" (1 Thes. iv. 14). "But
each [ἕκαστος] in his own order, Christ the first-
fruits, afterwards they that are Christ's at His
coming" (1 Cor. xv. 23). 6. The Resurrection of
Christ—as it brought resurrection-life not only
to believers in their persons, but to the cause of
truth and righteousness in the earth—should animate the Church, in its seasons of deepest depression, with assurances of resurrection, and encourage
it to sing such "songs in the night" as these: *"After
two days will He revive us; in the third day He will
raise us up, and we shall live in His sight."* *"I
shall not die, but live, and declare the works of
the Lord"* (Hos. vi. 2; Ps. cxviii. 17).

16-20.—JESUS MEETS WITH THE DISCIPLES ON A
MOUNTAIN IN GALILEE, AND GIVES FORTH THE
GREAT COMMISSION. **16. Then the eleven disciples went away into Galilee**—but certainly
not before the second week after the resurrection,
and probably somewhat later. **into a mountain**
[τὸ ὄρος], **where Jesus had appointed them.** It
should have been rendered 'the mountain,' meaning some certain mountain which He had named
to them—probably the night before He suffered,
when He said, "After I am risen, I will go before
you into Galilee" (ch. xxvi. 32; Mark xiv. 28).
What it was can only be conjectured; but of the
two between which opinions are divided—the Mount
of the Beatitudes or Mount Tabor—the former is

17 where Jesus had appointed them. And when they saw him, they worshipped him: but some doubted.

18 And Jesus came and spake unto them, saying, *k* All power is given unto

much the more probable, from its nearness to the sea of Tiberias, where last before this the Narrative tells us that He met and dined with seven of them. (John xxi. 1, &c.) That the interview here recorded was the same with that referred to in one place only—1 Cor. xv. 6—when "He was seen of above five hundred brethren at once; of whom the greater part remained unto that day, though some were fallen asleep," is now the opinion of the ablest students of the Evangelical History. Nothing can account for such a number as five hundred assembling at one spot but the expectation of some promised manifestation of their risen Lord; and the promise before His resurrection, twice repeated after it, best explains this immense gathering. **17. And when they saw him, they worshipped him: but some doubted**—certainly none of "the Eleven," after what took place at previous interviews in Jerusalem. But if the five hundred were now present, we may well believe this of some of them.

18. And Jesus came and spake unto them, saying, All power is given unto me in heaven and in earth. 19. Go ye therefore, and teach all nations [μαθητεύσατε]—rather, 'make disciples of all nations;' for "teaching," in the more usual sense of that word, comes in afterwards, and is expressed by a different term. **baptizing them in the name** [εἰς τὸ ὄνομα]. It should be, 'into the name:' as in 1 Cor. x. 2, "And were all baptized unto (or rather 'into') Moses" [εἰς τὸν Μωσῆν]; and Gal. iii. 27, "For as many of you as have been baptized *into* Christ" [εἰς Χριστόν]. **of the Father, and of the Son, and of the Holy Ghost; 20. Teaching them** [Διδάσκοντες]. This is teaching in the more usual sense of the term; or instructing the converted and baptized disciples. **to observe all things whatsoever I have commanded you: and, lo, I.** The "*I*" [Εγὼ] here is emphatic. It is enough that *I* am with you alway [πάσας τὰς ἡμέρας]—'all the days;' that is, till making converts, baptizing, and building them up by Christian instruction, shall be no more. **even unto the end of the world** [αἰῶνος]. **Amen.** [On the difference between the words αἰὼν and κόσμος, see on Heb. i. 2.] This glorious Commission embraces two primary departments, the *Missionary* and the *Pastoral*, with two sublime and comprehensive *Encouragements* to undertake and go through with them.

First, The MISSIONARY department (*v.* 18): "Go, make disciples of all nations." In the corresponding passage of Mark (xvi. 15) it is, "Go ye into all the world, and preach the Gospel to every creature." The only difference is, that in this passage the *sphere*, in its world-wide compass and its universality of *objects*, is more fully and definitely expressed; while in the former the great *aim* and certain *result* is delightfully expressed in the command to "make disciples of all nations." 'Go, conquer the world for Me; carry the glad tidings into all lands and to every ear, and deem not this work at an end till all nations shall have embraced the Gospel and enrolled themselves My disciples.' Now, Was all this meant to be done by the Eleven men nearest to Him of the multitude then crowding around the risen Redeemer? Impossible. Was it to be done even in their lifetime? Surely not. In that little band Jesus virtually addressed Himself to all who, in every age, should take up from them the same work. Before the eyes of the Church's risen Head were spread out, in those Eleven men,

all His servants of every age; and one and all of them received His commission at that moment. Well, what next? Set the seal of visible discipleship upon the converts, by "baptizing them into the name," that is, into the whole fulness of the grace "of the Father, and of the Son, and of the Holy Ghost," as belonging to them who believe. (See on 2 Cor. xiii. 14.) This done, the Missionary department of your work, which in its own nature is temporary, must merge in another, which is permanent. This is,

Second, The PASTORAL department (*v.* 20): "Teach them"—teach these baptized members of the Church visible—"to observe all things whatsoever I have commanded you," My apostles, during the three years ye have been with Me. What must have been the feelings which such a Commission awakened! 'WE conquer the world for Thee, Lord, who have scarce conquered our own misgivings—we, fishermen of Galilee, with no letters, no means, no influence over the humblest creature? Nay, Lord, do not mock us.' 'I mock you not, nor send you a warfare on your own charges. For'—Here we are brought to

Third, The ENCOURAGEMENTS to undertake and go through with this work. These are two; one in the van, the other in the rear of the Commission itself.

First Encouragement: "All power in *heaven*"— the whole power of Heaven's love and wisdom and strength, "and all power in *earth*"—power over all persons, all passions, all principles, all movements—to bend them to this one high object, the evangelization of the world: All this "is *given unto Me*," as the risen Lord of all, to be *by Me placed at your command*—"Go ye therefore." But there remains a

Second Encouragement—which will be best taken up in the Remarks below—"And lo! I am with you all the days"—not only to perpetuity, but without one day's interruption, "even to the end of the world." The "Amen" is of doubtful genuineness in this place. If, however, it belongs to the text it is the Evangelist's own closing word.

Remarks.—1. In this Great Commission we have the permanent institution of the Gospel Ministry, in both its departments, the Missionary and the Pastoral—the one for fetching in, the other for building up—together with Baptism, the link of connection and point of transition from the one to the other. The Missionary department, it is true, merges in every case in the Pastoral, as soon as the converts are baptized into visible discipleship; yet since the servants of Christ are commanded to "go into all the world, and preach the Gospel to every creature," it follows that so long as there is an inhabited spot unreached, or a human being outside the pale of visible discipleship, so long will the Missionary department of the Christian ministry abide in the Church as a divine institution. As for the Pastoral office, it is manifest that as the children of believers will require to be trained in the truth, and the members of the Church to be taught, not only to know, but to observe, all that Christ commanded, there can be no cessation of it so long as the Church itself continues in the flesh, or before Christ comes in glory. 2. But we have here also something for the Church's private members as well as for its ministers. Are they to deem themselves exempt from all concern in this matter? Nay, is it not certain that just as all ministers are to trace their commission to this Great

134

19 me in heaven and in earth. Go ye therefore, and [2] teach all nations, baptizing them in the name of the Father, and of the Son, and of the Holy

A. D. 33.

[2] Or, make disciples.

Commission, so the whole Church, from age to age, should regard itself as here virtually addressed in its own sphere, and summoned forth to *co-operate* with its ministers, to *aid* its ministers, to *encourage* its ministers in the doing of this missionary and pastoral work to the world's end? 3. We must have a care not unduly to narrow that direction regarding the Pastoral instruction of the disciples —"Teach them to observe all things whatsoever I have commanded you," the Twelve. For some talk of Christ as the only Lawgiver of Christians, to the exclusion of the Old Testament, as authoritative for Christians; while some would exclude, in this sense, all the New Testament save the Evangelical Records of our Lord's own teaching. But does not our Lord Himself set His seal on the Old Testament Scriptures at large as the Word of God and the Record of eternal life? And what are all the subsequent portions of the New Testament but the development of Christ's own teaching by those on whom, for that very end, He set the seal of His own authority? Thus may our Lord be said virtually to have referred His servants to the entire Scripture as their body of instructions. Still it may be asked, Is there nothing peculiar in all those things whatsoever Christ commanded the Twelve, that He should refer the pastors of the flock for their instructions in every age specifically to that as their grand repository? Undoubtedly there is; for as all that preceded Christ pointed forward to Him, and all that follows His teaching refers back to it, so His personal teaching is the incarnation and vitalization, the maturity and perfection of all divine teaching, to which all else in Scripture is to be referred, and in the light of which all else is to be studied and apprehended. 4. What an all-comprehensive encouragement to the continued discharge of even the most difficult and trying duties embraced in this Commission is found in the closing words of it! Thus:—

'Feel ye your utter incompetency to undertake the work? Lo! *I am with you*, to furnish you for it; for all power in heaven and in earth is Mine. Fear ye for the safety of the cause, amidst the indifference and the hatred of a world that crucified your Lord? Be of good cheer: *I am with you*, who have overcome the world. Dare ye not to hope that the world will fall before you? It is Mine by promise—the heathen for My inheritance, the uttermost parts of the earth for My possession; and to conquer and to keep it by your agency, all power in heaven and in earth is given unto Me and by Me made over to you.

'Dread ye the exhaustion of My patience or power, amidst oft-recurring seasons of difficulty, despondency and danger, and the dreary length of time it will take to bring all nations to the obedience of faith, and to build them up unto life eternal? Lo! I am with you *always*, to whom *all* power in heaven and in earth is given for your behoof.'

'Truth, Lord'—perhaps ye will still say—'this pledge to be with us to perpetuity is indeed cheering; but may there not be *intervals of withdrawal*, to be followed, no doubt, by seasons of certain return, but enough, in the meantime, to fill us with anxiety, on whose shoulders Thou art laying the whole weight of Thy cause in the earth?' 'Nay, have ye not marked those words of Mine, "Lo! I am with you," not only to perpetuity, but " *all the days*"—without any break—"even unto the end of the world."' What more could they, or the servants of Christ in any age, desire or imagine of encourage-

ment to fulfil this blessed Commission? 5. Is it necessary to ask any intelligent reader whether such a Commission could have issued from the lips of one who knew himself to be a mere creature? Would "all power in heaven and in earth" be *given away* to a creature, by Him who will not give His glory to another? or if this were conceivable, could it be *lodged in* a creature, or *wielded by* a creature? And whereas it is here said to be *given* to Christ, that is only in conformity with the whole economy of Redemption and the uniform language of the New Testament, which represents the Son as sent and furnished by the Father, in order to bring men back, as prodigal children, to their Father's love. But while the Son thus honours the Father, the Father requires, in return, "that all men should honour the Son even as they honour the Father." 6. If there is one inference from the language of this Great Commission more obvious than another, it is this, that Jesus would have Himself regarded by His servants in every age as *sole Master in His own House.* Are they to make disciples of all nations? It is disciples *to Him.* Are they to set the seal of visible discipleship upon them? It is to bind them over only the more effectually *to Him.* Are they to teach the converts thus made and thus sealed? It is to observe all things whatsoever HE has *commanded* them. Want they support and encouragement in all the branches of this work? They are to derive it from this twofold consideration, that all the resources of heaven and earth are, for their benefit, given *unto Him*, and that *He is with them* alway, even unto the end of the world. Thus are they to transact, each with the other—no other third party coming in between them. Hence, whatever understanding or arrangement they may deem it lawful and expedient to. come to with the civil powers in matters ecclesiastical, they are to stipulate for perfect *freedom to carry out all their Master's requirements;* nor dare they abridge themselves of one iota of this liberty for any temporal consideration whatever. 7. We have here the secret of the Church's poverty during long ages of its past history, and of the world's present condition, to so appalling an extent estranged from the Christian pale. The Church has neglected the Missionary, and corrupted the Pastoral, department of its great Commission. For long ages the missionary energy of the Church had either ceased, or expended itself chiefly on efforts to extend the ghostly authority of Papal Rome; and when at the Reformation-period it sprang forth in such glorious rejuvenescence, instead of sending forth its healing waters into the vast deserts of heathenism, making the wilderness and the solitary place to rejoice, it kept them pent up within its own narrow boundaries till they stank and bred the pestilence of rancorous controversy and deadly heresy and every evil. And then did the Pastoral work languish, thousands upon thousands fell away from all observance of Christian ordinances, and within the bosom of Christendom infidelity and irreligion spread apace, while real Christianity came to a very low ebb. Nor could aught else be expected of such unfaithfulness to the Church's Head. Neglecting either branch of this great Commission, neither the *Power* nor the *Presence* promised dare be expected. But going forth in faith to both alike, the conquest of the world to Christ—as it might have been achieved long ago, but for the Church's unbelief, selfishness, apathy, corruption, division—so it will be achieved,

20 Ghost; teaching them to observe all things whatsoever I have commanded you: and, lo, *I am with you alway, even* unto the end of the world. Amen.

A. D. 33.

i Acts 18. 19.
Rev. 22. 21.

when, through the Spirit poured upon it from on high, it shall become "fair as the moon, clear as the sun, and terrible as an army with banners" (Song vi. 10). 8. In concluding this First Portion of our Fourfold Gospel, who that has followed our humble efforts to display a little of its riches does not feel it to be as treasure hid in a field, the which, when a man hath found, he hideth, and for joy thereof goeth and selleth all that he hath and buyeth that field? The good Lord lodge its contents in the hearts both of the writer and his readers!

136

THE GOSPEL ACCORDING TO

ST. MARK.

1 THE beginning of the gospel of Jesus Christ, ^athe Son of God;
2 as it is written in the Prophets, ^bBehold, I send my messenger before
3 thy face, which shall prepare thy way before thee. The ^cvoice of one
   crying in the wilderness, Prepare ye the way of the Lord, make his paths
4 straight. John did baptize in the wilderness, and preach the baptism of
5 repentance ¹for the remission of sins. And there went out unto him all
   the land of Judea, and they of Jerusalem, and were all baptized of him
6 in the river of Jordan, confessing their sins. And John was clothed with
   camel's hair, and with a girdle of a skin about his loins; and he did eat
7 ^dlocusts and wild honey; and preached, saying, ^eThere cometh one
   mightier than I after me, the latchet of whose shoes I am not worthy to
8 stoop down and unloose. I ^findeed have baptized you with water; but
   he shall baptize you ^gwith the Holy Ghost.
9   And ^hit came to pass in those days, that Jesus came from Nazareth
10 of Galilee, and was baptized of John in Jordan. And ⁱstraightway com-
    ing up out of the water, he saw the heavens ²opened, and the Spirit like
11 a dove descending upon him: and there came a voice from heaven, say-
    ing, ^jThou art my beloved Son, in whom I am well pleased.
12   And ^kimmediately the Spirit driveth him into the wilderness.

A. D. 26.
ending.

CHAP. 1.
^a Ps. 2. 7.
Luke 1. 35.
John 1. 34.
Rom. 8. 3.
1 John 4. 15.
^b Mal. 3. 1.
^c Isa. 40. 3.
Luke 3. 4.
John 1. 15,
23.
1 Or, unto.
^d Lev. 11. 22.
^e Acts 13. 25.
^f Acts 11. 16.
Acts 19. 4.
^g Isa. 44. 3.
^h Matt. 3. 13.
ⁱ John 1. 32.
² Or, cloven,
or, rent.
^j Ps. 2. 7.
^k Matt. 4. 1.

CHAP. I. 1-8.—THE PREACHING AND BAPTISM OF JOHN. (= Matt. iii. 1-12; Luke iii. 1-18.)
1. The beginning of the gospel of Jesus Christ, the Son of God. By the "Gospel" of Jesus Christ here is evidently meant the blessed Story which our Evangelist is about to tell of His Life, Ministry, Death, Resurrection and Glorification, and of the begun Gathering of Believers in His Name. The abruptness with which he announces his subject, and the energetic brevity with which, passing by all preceding events, he hastens over the ministry of John and records the Baptism and Temptation of Jesus—as if impatient to come to the Public Life of the Lord of glory—have often been noticed as characteristic of this Gospel; a Gospel whose direct, practical power and singularly vivid setting impart to it a preciousness peculiar to itself. What strikes every one is, that though the briefest of all the Gospels, this is in some of the principal scenes of our Lord's history the fullest. But what is not so obvious is, that wherever the finer and subtler feelings of humanity, or the deeper and more peculiar hues of our Lord's character were brought out, these, though they should be lightly passed over by all the other Evangelists, are sure to be found here, and in touches of such quiet delicacy and power, that though scarce observed by the cursory reader, they leave indelible impressions upon all the thoughtful, and furnish a key to much that is in the other Gospels.
These few opening words of the Second Gospel are enough to show, that though it was the purpose of this Evangelist to record chiefly the outward and palpable facts of our Lord's public life, he recognized in Him, in common with the Fourth Evangelist, the glory of the Only begotten of the Father. **2. As it is written in** the Prophets (Mal. iii. 1; and Isa. xl. 3), **Behold, I send my messenger before thy face, which shall prepare thy way before thee. 3. The voice of one crying in the wilderness, Prepare ye the way of the Lord, make his paths straight.** The second of these quotations is given by Matthew and Luke in the same connection, but they reserve the former quotation till they have occasion to return to the Baptist, after his imprisonment (Matt. xi. 10; Luke vii. 27). [Instead of the words, "as it is written in the Prophets," there is weighty evidence in favour of the following reading: 'As it is written in Isaiah the prophet.' This reading is adopted by all the latest critical editors. If it be the true one, it is to be explained thus—that of the two quotations, the one from Malachi is but a later development of the great primary one in Isaiah, from which the whole prophetical matter here quoted takes its name. But the received text is quoted by *Irenæus*, before the end of the second century, and the evidence in its favour is greater in *amount*, if not in weight. The chief objection to it is, that if this was the true reading, it is difficult to see how the other one could have got in at all; whereas, if it be not the true reading, it is very easy to see how it found its way into the text, as it removes the startling difficulty of a prophecy beginning with the words of Malachi being ascribed to Isaiah.] For the exposition, see on Matt. iii. 1-6, 11.
9-11.—BAPTISM OF CHRIST, AND DESCENT OF THE SPIRIT UPON HIM IMMEDIATELY THEREAFTER. (= Matt. iii. 13-17; Luke iii. 21, 22.) For the exposition, see on Matt. iii. 13-17.
12, 13.—TEMPTATION OF CHRIST. (= Matt. iv. 1-11; Luke iv. 1-13.) For the exposition, see on Matt. iv. 1-11.

13 And he was there in the wilderness forty days, tempted of Satan; and was with the wild beasts; [i]and the angels ministered unto him.

14 Now after that John was put in prison, Jesus came into Galilee,

15 [m]preaching the gospel of the kingdom of God, and saying, [n]The time is fulfilled, and the kingdom of God is at hand: repent ye, and believe the Gospel.

16 Now [o]as he walked by the sea of Galilee, he saw Simon, and Andrew

17 his brother casting a net into the sea: for they were fishers. And Jesus said unto them, Come ye after me, and I will make you to become fishers

18 of men. And straightway [p]they forsook their nets, and followed him.

19 And [q]when he had gone a little farther thence, he saw James the *son* of Zebedee, and John his brother, who also were in the ship mending their

20 nets. And straightway he called them: and they left their father Zebedee in the ship with the hired servants, and went after him.

21 And [r]they went into Capernaum; and straightway on the sabbath day

22 he entered into the synagogue, and taught. And [s]they were astonished at his doctrine: for he taught them as one that had authority, and not

23 as the scribes. And [t]there was in their synagogue a man with an unclean

24 spirit; and he cried out, saying, Let *us* alone; [u]what have we to do with thee, thou Jesus of Nazareth? art thou come to destroy us? I know

25 thee who thou art, the [v]Holy One of God. And Jesus rebuked him,

26 saying, Hold thy peace, and come out of him. And when the unclean spirit [w]had torn him, and cried with a loud voice, he came out of him.

A. D. 31.
[i] Matt. 4. 11.
1 Tim. 3.16.
[m] Matt. 4. 23.
[n] Ps. 110. 3.
Dan. 2. 44.
Dan. 9. 25.
Gal. 4. 4.
Eph. 1. 10.
[o] Matt. 4. 18.
Luke 5. 4.
John 1. 35-44.
[p] Matt. 19.27.
Luke 5. 11.
[q] Matt. 4. 21.
[r] Matt. 4. 13.
Luke 4. 31.
[s] Matt. 7. 28.
[t] Luke 4. 33.
[u] Matt. 8. 29.
ch 5. 7.
Luke 4. 34.
Luke 8. 28.
John 2. 4.
[v] Ps. 16. 10.
Luke 4. 34.
Acts 2. 31.
Jas. 2. 19.
[w] ch. 9. 20.

14-20.—CHRIST BEGINS HIS GALILEAN MINISTRY —CALLING OF SIMON AND ANDREW, JAMES AND JOHN. See on Matt. iv. 12-22. **21-39.—HEALING OF A DEMONIAC IN THE SYNAGOGUE OF CAPERNAUM, AND THEREAFTER OF SIMON'S MOTHER-IN-LAW AND MANY OTHERS—JESUS, NEXT DAY, IS FOUND IN A SOLITARY PLACE AT MORNING PRAYERS, AND IS ENTREATED TO RETURN, BUT DECLINES, AND GOES FORTH ON HIS FIRST MISSIONARY CIRCUIT.** (= Luke iv. 31-44; Matt. viii. 14-17; iv. 23-25.) **21. And they went into Capernaum**—see on Matt. iv. 13—and **straightway on the sabbath day he entered into the synagogue, and taught** [τοῖς σάββασιν]. This should have been rendered, 'straightway on the sabbaths He entered into the synagogue and taught,' or 'continued to teach.' The meaning is, that as He began this practice on the very first Sabbath after coming to settle at Capernaum, so He continued it regularly thereafter. **22. And they were astonished at his doctrine**—or 'teaching' [διδαχῇ]—referring quite as much to the manner as the matter of it. **for he taught them as one that had authority, and not as the scribes.** See on Matt. vii. 28, 29. **23. And there was in their synagogue a man with** (lit., 'in') **an unclean spirit**—that is, so entirely under demoniacal power that his personality was sunk for the time in that of the spirit. The frequency with which this character of 'impurity' is ascribed to evil spirits—some twenty times in the Gospels—is not to be overlooked. For more on this subject, see on Matt. iv. 12-25, Remark 4. **and he cried out, 24. Saying, Let [us] alone**—or rather, perhaps, 'ah!' expressive of mingled *astonishment* and *terror*. [The exclamation Ἔα is probably not here the imperative of the verb ἐᾶν, to 'permit'—as the *Vulgate* in Luke iv. 34, *Luther*, and our own version take it, or, at least, had ceased to be so regarded—but an interjection=אֲהָה, Jud. vi. 22, &c.] **what have we to do with thee** [Τί ἡμῖν καὶ σοί=מַה־לִּי וְלָךְ] —an expression of frequent occurrence in the Old Testament, (1 Ki. xvii. 18; 2 Ki. iii. 13; 2 Chr.

xxxv. 21, &c.) It denotes '*entire separation of interests:*'—*q. d.*, 'Thou and we have nothing in common: we want not Thee; what wouldst thou with us?' For the analogous application of it by our Lord to His mother, see on John ii. 4. **[thou] Jesus of Nazareth?**—'Jesus, Nazarene!' an epithet originally given to express contempt, but soon adopted as the current designation by those who held our Lord in honour (Luke xviii. 37; Mark xvi. 6; Acts ii. 22)—**art thou come to destroy us?** In the case of the Gadarene demoniac the question was, "Art thou come hither to torment us before the time?" (Matt. viii. 29). Themselves tormentors and destroyers of their victims, they discern in Jesus their own destined Tormentor and Destroyer, anticipating and dreading what they know and feel to be awaiting them! Conscious, too, that their power was but permitted and temporary, and perceiving in Him, perhaps, the Woman's Seed that was to bruise the head and destroy the works of the devil, they regard His approach to them on this occasion as a signal to let go their grasp of this miserable victim. **I know thee who thou art, the Holy One of God.** This and other even more glorious testimonies to our Lord were given, as we know, with no good will, but in hope that by the acceptance of them He might appear to the people to be in league with evil spirits—a calumny which His enemies were ready enough to throw out against Him. But a Wiser than either was here, who invariably rejected and silenced the testimonies that came to Him from beneath, and thus was able to rebut the imputations of His enemies against Him (Matt. xii. 24-30). The expression, "Holy One of God," seems evidently taken from that Messianic Psalm (xvi. 10), in which He is styled "Thine Holy One" [τὸν ὅσιόν σου, קְדוֹשֶׁךָ—in קְרְ]. **25. And Jesus rebuked him, saying, Hold thy peace, and come out of him.** A glorious word of command. *Bengel* remarks that it was only the testimony borne to Himself which our Lord meant to silence. That he should afterwards cry out for fear or rage (*v.* 26) He would right willingly permit. **26. And when the unclean**

138

27 And they were all amazed, insomuch that they questioned among themselves, saying, What thing is this? what new doctrine *is* this? for with authority commandeth he even the unclean spirits, and they do obey
28 him. And immediately his fame spread abroad throughout all the region round about Galilee.
29 And *ˣ*forthwith, when they were come out of the synagogue, they entered into the house of Simon and Andrew, with James and John.
30 But Simon's wife's mother lay sick of a fever, and anon they tell him of
31 her. And he came and took her by the hand, and lifted her up; and *ʸ*immediately the fever left her, and she ministered unto them.
32 And *ᶻ*at even, when the sun did set, they brought unto him all that
33 were diseased, and them that were possessed with devils. And all the
34 city was gathered together at the door. And he healed many that were sick of divers diseases, and cast out many devils; and *ᵃ*suffered not the devils ³to speak, because they knew him.
35 And *ᵇ*in the morning, rising up a great while before day, he went out,

A. D. 31.

ˣ Matt. 8. 14.
Luke 4 33.
ʸ Ps. 103. 3.
ᶻ Luke 4. 40.
ᵃ Matt. 8. 16.
ch. 3, 12.
Luke 4. 41.
Acts 16. 17,
18.
³ Or, to say
that they
knew him.
ᵇ Ps. 5. 3.
Ps. 109. 4.
ch. 6. 46.
Luke 4. 42.
John 4. 34.
Eph. 6. 18.
Heb. 5. 7.

spirit had torn him. Luke (iv. 35) says, "When he had thrown him in the midst." Malignant cruelty—just showing what he *would* have done, if permitted to go further: it was a last fling ! **and cried with a loud voice**—the voice of enforced submission and despair—**he came out of him.** Luke (iv. 35) adds, "and hurt him not." Thus impotent were the malignity and rage of the impure spirit when under the restraint of "the Stronger than the strong one armed" (Luke xi. 21, 22). **27. And they were all amazed, insomuch that they questioned among themselves, saying, What thing is this ? what new doctrine** ('teaching') **is this ? for with authority commandeth he even the unclean spirits, and they do obey him.** The audience, rightly apprehending that the miracle was wrought to illustrate the teaching and display the character and glory of the Teacher, begin by asking what novel kind of teaching this could be, which was so marvellously attested. [The various reading which the latest editors prefer here—τί ἐστιν τοῦτο; διδαχὴ καινὴ κατ᾽ ἐξουσίαν καὶ τοῖς πνεύμασιν . . . αὐτῷ; κ. τ. λ.—has too slender support, we think, and is harsh.] **28. And immediately his fame spread abroad throughout all the region round about Galilee** [ὅλην τὴν περίχωρον τῆς Γ.]—rather, 'the whole region of Galilee;' though some, as *Meyer* and *Ellicott*, explain it of the country surrounding Galilee. **29. And forthwith, when they were come out of the synagogue**—so also in Luke iv. 38, **they entered into the house of Simon and Andrew, with James and John.** The mention of these four—which is peculiar to Mark—is the first of those traces of Peter's hand in this Gospel, of which we shall come to many more. (See Introduction.) The house being his, and the disease and cure so nearly affecting himself, it is interesting to observe this minute specification of the number and names of the witnesses; interesting also as the first occasion on which the sacred triumvirate of Peter and James and John are selected from amongst the rest, to be a threefold cord of testimony to certain events in their Lord's life (see on ch. v. 37)—Andrew being present on this occasion, as the occurrence took place in his own house. **30. But Simon's wife's mother lay sick of a fever,** Luke, as was natural in "the beloved *physician*" (Col. iv. 14), describes it professionally; calling it a "great fever" [πυρετῷ μεγάλῳ], and thus distinguishing it from that lighter kind which the Greek physicians were wont to call "small fevers," as *Galen*, quoted by *Wetstein*, tells us. **and anon**—or 'immediately'
139

they tell him of her—naturally hoping that His compassion and power towards one of His own disciples would not be less signally displayed than towards the demonized stranger in the synagogue. **31. And he came and took her by the hand**—rather, 'And advancing, He took her,' &c.—[προσελθὼν κ. τ. λ]. The beloved physician again is very specific: "And He stood over her" [ἐπιστὰς ἐπάνω αὐτῆς, Luke iv. 39]. **and lifted her up.** This act of condescension, much felt doubtless by Peter, is recorded only by Mark. **and immediately the fever left her, and she ministered unto them**—preparing their Sabbathmeal; in token both of the perfectness and immediateness of the cure, and of her gratitude to the glorious Healer.
32. And at even, when the sun did set—so Matt. viii. 16. Luke (iv. 40) says it was setting [δύνοντος]. **they brought unto him all that were diseased, and them that were possessed with devils**—'the demonized.' From Luke xiii. 14 we see how unlawful they would have deemed it to bring their sick to Jesus for a cure during the Sabbath hours. They waited, therefore, till these were over, and then brought them in crowds. Our Lord afterwards took repeated occasion to teach the people by example, even at the risk of His own life, how superstitious a straining of the Sabbath-rest this was. **33. And all the city was gathered together at the door**—of Peter's house; that is, the sick and those who brought them, and the wondering spectators. This bespeaks the presence of an eye-witness, and is one of those lively specimens of word-painting so frequent in this Gospel. **34. And he healed many that were sick of divers diseases, and cast out many devils.** In Matt. viii. 16 it is said, "He cast out the spirits with His word ;" or rather, 'with a word' [λόγῳ]—a word of command. **and suffered not the devils to speak, because they knew him.** Evidently they *would* have spoken, if permitted, proclaiming His Messiahship in such terms as in the synagogue; but once in one day, and that testimony immediately silenced, was enough. See on *v.* 24. After this account of His miracles of healing, we have in Matt. viii. 17 this pregnant quotation, "That it might be fulfilled which was spoken by Esaias the prophet, saying (liii. 4), Himself took our infirmities, and bare our sicknesses." On this pregnant quotation, see Remark 2 below.
35. And in the morning—that is, of the day after this remarkable Sabbath; or, *on the First day of the week.* His choosing this day to inaugurate

36 and departed into a solitary place, and ^cthere prayed. And Simon and
37 they that were with him followed after him. And when they had found
38 him, they said unto him, All *men* seek for thee. And he said unto them,
     ^dLet us go into the next towns, that I may preach there also : for ^ethere-
39 fore came I forth. And ^fhe preached in their synagogues throughout all
     Galilee, and ^gcast out devils.

A. D. 31.

^c Heb. 5. 7.
^d Luke 4. 43.
^e Isa. 61. 1.
     John 16. 28.
^f Matt. 4. 23.
^g Gen. 3. 15.

a new and glorious stage of His public work, should be noted by the reader. **rising up a great while before day** [πρωῒ ἔννυχον or ἔννυχα λίαν]—'while it was yet night,' or long before daybreak, **he went out**—from Peter's house, where He slept, all unperceived, **and departed into a solitary place, and there prayed** [προσηύχετο]—or, 'continued in prayer.' He was about to begin His first preaching and healing Circuit; and as on similar solemn occasions (Luke v. 16; vi. 12; ix. 18, 28, 29; Mark vi. 46), He spends some time in special prayer, doubtless with a view to it. What would one not give to have been, during the stillness of those grey morning-hours, within hearing—not of His "strong crying and tears," for He had scarce arrived at the stage for that—but of His calm, exalted anticipations of the work which lay immediately before Him, and the outpourings of His soul about it into the bosom of Him that sent Him! 'The Spirit of the Lord God is upon Me, because the Lord hath anointed Me to preach the Gospel to the poor; and I am going to heal the broken-hearted, to preach deliverance to the captives, and recovering of sight to the blind, to set at liberty them that are bruised, to preach the acceptable year of the Lord. Now, Lord, let it be seen that grace is poured into These lips, and that God hath blessed Me for ever: Here am I, send Me: I must work the works of Him that sent Me while it is day; and, lo, I come! I delight to do Thy will, O My God: yea, Thy law is within My heart.' He had doubtless enjoyed some uninterrupted hours of such communings with His heavenly Father ere His friends from Capernaum arrived in search of Him. As for them, they doubtless expected, after such a day of miracles, that the next day would witness similar manifestations. When morning came, Peter, loath to break in upon the repose of his glorious Guest, would await His appearance beyond the usual hour; but at length, wondering at the stillness, and gently coming to see where the Lord lay, he finds it—like the sepulchre afterwards—empty! Speedily a party is made up to go in search of Him, Peter naturally leading the way. **36. And Simon and they that were with him followed after him** [κατεδίωξαν]—rather, 'pressed after Him.' Luke (iv. 42) says, "The multitudes sought after Him" [οἱ ὄχλοι ἐπεζήτουν αὐτόν]: but this would be a party from the town. Mark, having his information from Peter himself, speaks only of what related directly to him. "They that were with him" would probably be Andrew his brother, James and John, with a few other choice brethren. **37. And when they had found him**—evidently after some search. [The reading adopted here by *Tischendorf* and *Tregelles*—καὶ εὗρον αὐτὸν καὶ λέγουσιν, 'And they found Him and said'—seems to us without sufficient evidence.] **they said unto him, All men seek for thee.** By this time, "the multitudes" who, according to Luke, "sought after Him"—and who, on going to Peter's house, and there learning that Peter and a few more were gone in search of Him, had set out on the same errand—would have arrived, and "came unto Him and stayed Him, that He should not depart from them" (Luke iv. 42); all now urging His return to their impatient townsmen. **38. And he said**

unto them, Let us go—or, according to another reading, ' Let us go elsewhere' [though the word ἀλλαχοῦ, added by *Tischendorf* and *Tregelles*, has scarcely sufficient authority]. **into the next towns** [εἰς τὰς ἐχομένας κωμοπόλεις]—rather, 'unto the neighbouring village-towns;' meaning those places intermediate between towns and villages, with which the western side of the sea of Galilee was studded. **that I may preach there also: for therefore came I forth**—not from Capernaum, as *De Wette* miserably interprets, nor from His privacy in the desert place, as *Meyer*, no better; but from the Father. Compare John xvi. 28, "I came forth from the Father, and am come into the world," &c.—another proof, by the way, that the lofty phraseology of the Fourth Gospel was not unknown to the authors of the others, though their design and point of view are different. The language in which our Lord's reply is given by Luke (iv. 43) expresses the high necessity under which, in this as in every other step of His work, He acted—"I must preach the kingdom of God to other cities also; for therefore" [εἰς τοῦτο]—or, ' to this end'—"am I sent." An act of self-denial it doubtless was, to resist such pleadings to return to Capernaum. But there were overmastering considerations on the other side.

Remarks.—1. How terrific is the consciousness in evil spirits, when brought into the presence of Christ, of a total opposition of feelings and separation of interests between them and Him! But how grand is their sense of impotence and subjection, and the expression of this, which His presence wrings out from them! Knowing full well that He and they cannot dwell together, they expect, on His approach to them, a summons to quit, and, haunted by their guilty fears, they wonder if the judgment of the great day be coming on them before its time. How analogous is this to the feelings of the wicked and ungodly among men—opening up glimpses of that dreadful oneness in fundamental character between the two parties, which explains the final sentence, "Depart from Me, ye cursed, into everlasting fire, *prepared for the devil and his angels*"! (Matt. xxv. 41). 2. The remarkable words which the first Evangelist quotes from Isa. liii. 4—"HIMSELF TOOK OUR INFIRMITIES AND BARE OUR SICKNESSES"—involve two difficulties, the patient study of which, however, will be rewarded by deeper conceptions of the work of Christ. First, the prediction is applied, in 1 Pet. ii. 24, to Christ's "bearing our *sins* in His own body on the tree," whereas here it is applied to the removal of *bodily maladies*. Again, the Evangelist seems to view the diseases which our Lord cured as only transferred from the patients to Himself. But both difficulties find their explanation in that profound and comprehensive view of our Lord's redeeming work which a careful study of Scripture reveals. When He took our nature upon Him and made it His own, He identified Himself with its sin and curse, that He might roll them away on the cross (2 Cor. v. 21), and felt all the maladies and ills that sin had inflicted on humanity as His own; His great *conscience* drinking in the sense of that sin of which Himself knew none, and His mighty *heart* feeling all the ills He saw

40 And ^hthere came a leper to him, beseeching him, and kneeling down to him, and saying unto him, If thou wilt, thou canst ⁱmake me clean.

41 And Jesus, ^jmoved with compassion, put forth *his* hand, and touched

42 him, and saith unto him, I will; be thou clean. And as soon as he had spoken, immediately the leprosy departed from him, and he was

43 cleansed. And he straitly charged him, and forthwith sent him away;

44 And saith unto him, See thou say nothing to any man: but go thy way, show thyself to the priest, and offer for thy cleansing those things ^kwhich

45 Moses commanded, for a testimony unto them. But ^lhe went out, and began to publish *it* much, and to blaze abroad the matter, insomuch that Jesus could no more openly enter into the city, but was without in desert places: ^mand they came to him from every quarter.

2 AND again ^ahe entered into Capernaum after *some* days; and it was

2 noised that he was in the house. And straightway many were gathered together, insomuch that there was no room to receive *them*, no, not so

3 much as about the door: and he ^bpreached the word unto them. And they come unto him, bringing one sick of the palsy, which was borne of

4 four. And when they could not come nigh unto him for the press, they

A. D. 31.

^h Matt. 8. 2.
Luke 5. 12.
ⁱ Gen. 18. 14.
Jer. 32. 17.
^j Heb. 2. 17.
Heb. 4. 15.
^k Lev. 14. 3, 4, 10.
Luke 5. 14.
^l Luke 5. 15.
^m ch. 2. 13.

CHAP. 2.
^a Matt. 9. 1.
Luke 5. 18.
^b Isa. 61. 1.
Matt. 5. 2.
ch. 6. 34.
Luke 8. 1.
Acts 8. 25.
Rom. 10. 8.
Eph. 2. 17.
Heb. 2. 3.

---

around Him as attaching to Himself. And as we have already seen that His whole ministry of healing, as respects the body, was but a visible exhibition and illustration of His mission "to destroy the works of the devil," so the eye which rightly apprehends the visible miracle, piercing downwards, will discover the deeper and more spiritual aspect of it as a portion of the Redeemer's work, and see the sin-bearing Lamb of God Himself, the Bearer, in this sense, of every ill of sinful humanity that He cured. But the subject is fitter for devout thought than adequate expression. **3.** Did Jesus, ere He started on His first missionary tour, "rising up a great while before it was day," steal away unperceived even by those under whose roof He slept, and hieing Him to a solitary spot, there spend the morning hours in still communion with His Father, no doubt about the work that lay before Him? And will not His servants learn of Him not only to sanctify their whole work by prayer, but to set apart special seasons of communion with God before entering on its greater stages, or any important step of it, and for this end to withdraw as much as possible into undisturbed solitude? **4.** When we find our Lord, from the very outset of His ministry, acting on that great principle enunciated by Himself, "I must work the works of Him that sent me while it is day: the night cometh when no man can work" (John ix. 4); and actuated by this principle, disregarding the demands of wearied nature and the solicitations of friends, what an example is thus furnished to His ministers in every age, of self-denial and devotion to their work! Oh, if the Lord of the harvest would but thrust forth *such* labourers into his harvest, what work might we not see done! **5.** What an affecting contrast does Capernaum here present to its final condition! Ravished with the wonderful works and the matchless teaching of Him who had taken up His abode amongst them, they are loath to part with Him; and while the Gadarenes prayed Him to depart out of their coasts, they are fain to stay Him, that He should not depart from them. And if our Lord declined to settle in Nazareth, and even to do there the mighty works which He did at Capernaum, because of the disrespect with which He was regarded in the place where He had been brought up, how grateful to His feelings would be this early welcome at Capernaum! But, alas! in them was fulfilled that great law of the divine

kingdom, "Many that are first shall be last." What a warning is this to similarly favoured spots! 40-45.—HEALING OF A LEPER. (= Matt. viii. 1-4; Luke v. 12-16.) For the exposition, see on Matt. viii. 1-4.

CHAP. II. 1-12.—HEALING OF A PARALYTIC. (= Matt. ix. 1-8; Luke v. 17-26.) This incident, as remarked on Matt. ix. 1, appears to follow next in order of time after the cure of the Leper (ch. i. 40-45). **1. And again he entered into Capernaum**—"His own city" (Matt. ix. 1), **and it was noised that he was in the house**—no doubt of Simon Peter (ch. i. 29). **2. And straightway many were gathered together, insomuch that there was no room to receive them, no, not so much as about the door.** This is one of Mark's graphic touches. No doubt in this case, as the scene occurred at his informant's own door, these details are the vivid recollections of that honoured disciple. **and he preached the word unto them**—that is, in-doors; but in the hearing, doubtless, of the multitude that pressed around. Had He gone forth, as He naturally would, the paralytic's faith would have had no such opportunity to display itself. Luke (v. 17) furnishes an additional and very important incident in the scene—as follows: "And it came to pass on a certain day, as He was teaching, that there were Pharisees and doctors of the law sitting by, which were come out of every town," or 'village' [κώμης]," of Galilee, and Judea, and Jerusalem." This was the highest testimony yet borne to our Lord's growing influence, and the necessity increasingly felt by the ecclesiastics throughout the country of coming to some definite judgment regarding Him. "And the power of the Lord was [present] to heal them" [ἦν εἰς τὸ ἰᾶσθαι αὐτοὺς] —or, 'was [efficacious] to heal them,' that is, the sick that were brought before Him. So that the miracle that is now to be described was only the most glorious and worthy to be recorded of many then performed; and what made it so was doubtless the faith which was manifested in connection with it, and the proclamation of the forgiveness of the patient's sins that immediately preceded it. **3. And they come unto him**—that is, towards the house where He was, **bringing one sick of the palsy**—"lying on a bed" (Matt. ix. 2), **which was borne of four**—a graphic particular of Mark only. **4. And when they could not come nigh unto him for the press**—or, as in Luke,

141

uncovered the roof where he was: and when they had broken *it* up, they
5 let down the bed wherein the sick of the palsy lay. When Jesus *c*saw
their faith, he said unto the sick of the palsy, *d*Son, thy sins be forgiven
6 thee. But there were certain of the scribes sitting there, and reasoning
7 in their hearts, Why doth this *man* thus speak blasphemies? *e*who can
8 forgive sins but God only? And immediately *f*when Jesus perceived in
his spirit that they so reasoned within themselves, he said unto them,
9 Why reason ye these things in your hearts? Whether *g*is it easier to say
to the sick of the palsy, *Thy* sins be forgiven thee; or to say, Arise, and
10 take up thy bed, and walk? But that ye may know that *h*the Son of
man hath power on earth to forgive sins, (he saith to the sick of the
11 palsy,) I say unto thee, Arise, and take up thy bed, and go thy way into
12 thine house. And *i*immediately he arose, took up the bed, and went
forth before them all; insomuch that they were all amazed, and glorified
God, saying, We never saw it on this fashion.

A. D. 31.
c Gen. 22. 12.
Heb. 4. 13.
d Ps. 103. 3.
Isa. 53 11.
e Job 14. 4.
Ps. 130. 4.
Isa. 43. 25.
Rom. 8. 33.
f 1 Sam. 16.7.
1 Chr 29.17.
Ps 7. 9.
Ps. 139. 1.
Jer. 17. 10.
Matt. 9. 4.
Heb 4. 13.
g Matt. 9. 5.
h Isa. 53. 11.
Dan. 7. 13.
i Ps. 33. 9.

"when they could not find by what way they might bring him in because of the multitude," **they** "went upon the house-top"—the flat or terrace-roof, universal in eastern houses—and **uncovered the roof where he was: and when they had broken it up, they let down the bed** [κράββατον]—or portable couch, **wherein the sick of the palsy lay.** Luke says, they "let him down through the tiling with his couch into the midst before Jesus." Their whole object was to *bring the patient into the presence of Jesus;* and this not being possible in the ordinary way, for the multitude that surrounded Him, they took the very unusual method here described of accomplishing their object, and succeeded. Several explanations have been given of the way in which this was done; but unless we knew the precise plan of the house, and the part of it from which Jesus taught—which may have been a quadrangle or open court, within the buildings of which Peter's house was one, or a gallery covered by a verandah —it is impossible to determine precisely how the thing was done. One thing, however, is clear, that we have both the accounts from an eye-witness. **5. When Jesus saw their faith.** It is remarkable that all the three narratives call it "*their* faith" which Jesus saw. That the patient himself had faith, we know from the proclamation of his forgiveness, which Jesus made before all; and we should have been apt to conclude that his four friends bore him to Jesus merely out of benevolent compliance with the urgent entreaties of the poor sufferer. But here we learn, not only that his bearers had the same faith with himself, but that Jesus marked it as a faith which was not to be defeated—a faith victorious over all difficulties. This was the faith for which He was ever on the watch, and which He never saw without marking, and, in those who needed anything from Him, richly rewarding. **he said unto the sick of the palsy, Son,** "be of good cheer" (Matt. ix. 2), **thy sins be forgiven thee** [ἀφέωνται σοί αἱ ἁμαρτίαι]. By the word "be," our translators perhaps meant "are," as in Luke (v. 20). For it is not a command to his sins to depart, but an authoritative proclamation of the man's pardoned state as a believer. And yet, as the Pharisees understood our Lord to be *dispensing* pardon by this saying, and Jesus not only acknowledges that they were right, but founds His whole argument upon the correctness of it, we must regard the saying as a royal proclamation of the man's forgiveness by Him to whom it belonged to dispense it; nor could such a style of address be justified on any lower supposition. (See on Luke vii. 41. &c.) **6. But there were**

certain of the scribes—"and the Pharisees" (Luke v. 21), **sitting there**—those Jewish ecclesiastics who, as Luke told us, "were come out of every village of Galilee, and Judea, and Jerusalem," to make their observations upon this wonderful Person, in anything but a teachable spirit, though as yet their venomous and murderous feeling had not showed itself; **and reasoning in their hearts, 7. Why doth this man thus speak blasphemies? who can forgive sins but God only?** In this second question they expressed a great truth. (See Isa. xliii. 25; Mic. vii. 18; Exod. xxxiv. 6, 7, &c.) Nor was their first question altogether unnatural, though in our Lord's sole case it was unfounded. That a man, to all appearance like one of themselves, should claim authority and power to forgive sins, they could not, on the first blush of it, but regard as in the last degree startling; nor were they entitled even to weigh such a claim, as worthy of a hearing, save on supposition of resistless evidence afforded by Him in support of the claim. Accordingly, our Lord deals with them as men entitled to such evidence, and supplies it; at the same time chiding them for rashness, in drawing harsh conclusions regarding Himself. **8. And immediately when Jesus perceived in his spirit that they so reasoned within themselves, he said unto them, Why reason ye these things**—or, as in Matthew, "Wherefore think ye evil" **in your hearts? 9. Whether is it easier to say to the sick of the palsy, Thy sins be (or 'are') forgiven thee; or to say, Arise, and take up thy bed, and walk?** 'Is it easier to command away disease than to bid away sin? If, then, I do the one, which you can see, know thus that I have done the other, which you cannot see.' **10. But that ye may know that the Son of man hath power on earth to forgive sins**—'that forgiving power dwells in the Person of this Man, and is exercised by Him while on this earth and going out and in with you'—(**he saith to the sick of the palsy,) 11. I say unto thee, Arise, and take up thy bed, and go thy way into thine house.** This taking up the portable couch, and walking home with it, was designed to prove the completeness of the cure. **12. And immediately he arose, took up the bed.** 'Sweet saying!' says *Bengel* · 'The bed had borne the man: now the man bore the bed.' **and went forth before them all**—proclaiming by that act to the multitude, whose wondering eyes would follow Him as He pressed through them, that He who could work such a glorious miracle of healing, must indeed "have power on earth to forgive sins." **insomuch that they were all amazed, and glorified God, saying, We never saw it on this**

13 And [j]he went forth again by the sea-side; and all the multitude
14 resorted unto him, and he taught them. And [k]as he passed by, he
saw Levi the *son* of Alpheus sitting [l]at the receipt of custom, and said
15 unto him, Follow me. And he arose and followed him. And [l]it came
to pass, that, as Jesus sat at meat in his house, many publicans and
sinners sat also together with Jesus and his disciples: for there were
16 many, and they followed him. And when [m]the scribes and Pharisees
saw him eat with publicans and sinners, they said unto his disciples,
How is it that he eateth and drinketh with publicans and sinners?
17 When Jesus heard *it*, he saith unto them, [n]They that are whole have
no need of the physician, but they that are sick: I came not to call
the righteous, but sinners to repentance.
18 And [o]the disciples of John and of the Pharisees used to fast: and
they come and say unto him, Why do the disciples of John and of the
19 Pharisees fast, but thy disciples fast not? And Jesus said unto them,
Can the children of [p]the bride-chamber fast while the bridegroom is
with them? as long as they have [q]the bridegroom with them, they
20 cannot fast. But the days will come, when the bridegroom shall be
21 taken away from them, and then shall they fast in those days. No
man also seweth a piece of [2]new cloth on an old garment; else the new
piece that filled it up taketh away from the old, and the rent is made
22 worse. And no man putteth new wine into old bottles; else the new
wine doth burst the bottles, and the wine is spilled, and the bottles will
be marred: but new wine must be put into new bottles.
23 And [r]it came to pass, that he went through the corn fields on the
sabbath day; and his disciples began, as they went, [s]to pluck the ears of
24 corn. And the Pharisees said unto him, Behold, why do they on the
25 sabbath day that which is not lawful? And he said unto them, Have ye
never read [t]what David did, when he had need, and was an hungered,
26 he, and they that were with him?· How he went into the house of God
in the days of Abiathar the high priest, and did eat the showbread,
[u]which is not lawful to eat but for the priests, and gave also to them
27 which were with him? And he said unto them, The sabbath was made
28 for man, and not man for the sabbath: therefore [v]the Son of man is Lord
also of the sabbath.
3 AND [a]he entered again into the synagogue; and there was a man
2 there which had a withered hand. And they watched him, whether he
3 would heal him on the sabbath day; that they might accuse him. And

A. D. 31.

[j] Matt. 9. 9.
[k] Luke 5. 27.
[l] Or, at the place where the custom was received.
[l] Matt. 9. 10.
[m] Isa. 65. 5.
[n] Matt. 9. 12, 13.
Matt. 18.11.
Luke 5. 31, 32.
[o] Luke 15. 7, 29.
Luke 16 15.
Luke 19. 10.
1 Tim. 1. 15.
[o] Matt. 9. 14.
Luke 5 33.
[p] Song 1. 4.
[q] Ps. 45.
Isa. 54. 5.
Matt 22. 2
John 3. 29.
2 Cor. 11. 2.
Eph. 5. 25, 32.
Fev. 19. 7.
Rev. 21. 1.
[2] Or, raw, or, un-wrought.
[r] Matt. 12. 1.
Luke 6. 1.
[s] Deut. 23.25.
[t] 1 Sam. 21.6.
[u] Ex. 25. 30.
Ex. 29. 32, 33.
[v] Matt. 12. 8.
Eph. 1. 20, 21.
1 Pet. 3. 22.

CHAP. 3.
[a] Matt. 12. 9.
Luke 6. 6.

fashion [οὕτως]—'never saw it thus,' or,as we say, 'never saw the like.' In Luke (v. 26) it is, "We have seen strange (or 'unexpected') things [παράδοξα] to-day"—referring both to the miracles wrought and the forgiveness of sins pronounced by Human Lips. In Matthew (ix. 8) it is, "They marvelled, and glorified God, which had given such power unto men." At forgiving power they wondered not, but that a man, to all appearance like one of themselves, should possess it!

Remarks.—1. Was it not a blessed deed those four did, to bring a patient to the Great Physician? But may not this be done many ways still? And how encouraging is the notice which Jesus took, not only of the patient's, but of his bearers' faith! 2. What a lesson does the extraordinary determination of these believing bearers of the paralytic teach us, to let no obstacles stand in the way of our reaching Jesus, either for ourselves or for those dear to us! 3. How does the supreme Divinity of the Lord Jesus shine forth here, in the authority and power to forgive sins, even as the Son of Man upon earth, which He first put forth and then demonstrated that He possessed! and the

half-suppressed horror which filled those ecclesiastics who were spectators of the scene, as they heard from Human Lips what it was the sole prerogative of God to utter, when we connect with it the evidence which Jesus gave them of the justice of His claim, only crowns the proof which this scene furnishes of the Divine glory of Christ. 4. If even on earth, or in the depth of His humiliation, the Son of Man had power to forgive sins, shall we doubt His "ability to save to the uttermost," now that He is set down at the right hand of the Majesty on high?

13-17.—LEVI'S (OR MATTHEW'S) CALL AND FEAST. (= Matt. ix. 9-13; Luke v. 27-32.) For the exposition, see on Matt. ix. 9-13.

18-22.—DISCOURSE ON FASTING. (= Matt. ix. 14-17; Luke v. 33-39.) For the exposition, see on Luke v. 33-39.

23-28.—PLUCKING CORN-EARS ON THE SABBATH DAY. (=Matt. xii. 1-8; Luke vi. 1-5.) For the exposition, see on Matt. xii. 1-8.

CHAP. III. 1-12.—THE HEALING OF A WITHERED HAND ON THE SABBATH DAY, AND RETIREMENT OF JESUS TO AVOID DANGER. (=Matt. xii.

143

4 he saith unto the man which had the withered hand, ¹Stand forth. And
he saith unto them, Is it lawful to do good on the sabbath days, or to do
5 evil? to save life, or to kill? But they held their peace. And when he
had looked round about on them with ᵇanger, being grieved for the
²hardness of their hearts, he saith unto the man, Stretch forth thine
hand. And he stretched *it* out: and his hand was restored whole as the
6 other. And ᶜthe Pharisees went forth, and straightway took counsel
with ᵈthe Herodians against him, how they might destroy him.
7 But Jesus withdrew himself with his disciples to the sea: and a great
8 multitude from Galilee followed him, ᵉand from Judea, and from Jerusalem, and from Idumea, and *from* beyond Jordan; and they about Tyre
and Sidon, a great multitude, when they had heard what great things
9 he did, came unto him. And he spake to his disciples, that a small
ship should wait on him because of the multitude, lest they should
10 throng him: for he had healed many; insomuch that they ³pressed upon
11 him for to touch him, as many as had plagues. And ᶠunclean spirits,
when they saw him, fell down before him, and cried, saying, ᵍThou art
12 the Son of God. And ʰhe straitly charged them that they should not
make him known.
13 And ⁱhe goeth up into a mountain, and calleth *unto him* whom he
14 would: and they came unto him. And he ordained twelve, that they
15 should be with him, and that he might send them forth to preach, and
16 to have power to heal sicknesses, and to cast out devils. And Simon ʲhe
17 surnamed Peter; and James the *son* of Zebedee, and John the brother of
James; (and he surnamed them Boanerges, which is, ᵏThe sons of
18 thunder;) and Andrew, and Philip, and Bartholomew, and Matthew, and
Thomas, and James the *son* of Alpheus, and ˡThaddeus, and Simon the
19 Canaanite, and Judas Iscariot, which also betrayed him. And they went
⁴into an house.
20 And the multitude cometh together again, ᵐso that they could not so
21 much as eat bread. And when his ⁵friends heard *of it*, they went out to
22 lay hold on him: for they said, He is beside himself. And the scribes
which came down from Jerusalem said, ⁿHe hath Beelzebub, and by the
23 prince of the devils casteth he out devils. And ᵒhe called them *unto*
him, and said unto them in parables, How can Satan cast out Satan?
24 And if a kingdom be divided against itself, that kingdom cannot
25 stand. And if a house be divided against itself, that house cannot stand.
26 And if Satan rise up against himself, and be divided, he cannot stand,
27 but hath an end. No ᵖman can enter into a strong man's house, and
spoil his goods, except he will first bind the strong man; and then
28 he will spoil his house. Verily ᑫI say unto you, All sins shall be
forgiven unto the sons of men, and blasphemies wherewith soever they
29 shall blaspheme; but he that shall blaspheme against the Holy Ghost
30 hath ʳnever forgiveness, but is in danger of eternal damnation: because
they said, He hath an unclean spirit.
31 There ˢcame then his brethren and his mother, and, standing without,
32 sent unto him, calling him. And the multitude sat about him; and
they said unto him, Behold, ᵗthy mother and thy brethren without seek
33 for thee. And he answered them, saying, Who is my mother, or my
34 brethren? And he looked round about on them which sat about him,
35 and said, ᵘBehold my mother and my brethren! For whosoever shall
do the will of God, the same is my brother, and my sister, and mother.

A. D. 31.

¹ Arise, stand forth in the midst. Dan. 6. 10. Phil. 1. 14.
ᵇ Ps. 69. 9. Ps. 119. 139.
² Or, blindness.
ᶜ Matt 12.14.
ᵈ Matt. 22.16.
ᵉ Luke 6. 17.
³ Or, rushed.
ᶠ ch. 1. 23. Luke 4. 41.
ᵍ Acts 16. 17. Matt. 14.33. ch. 1. 1.
ʰ ch. 1. 25,34. Matt. 12.16.
ⁱ Matt. 10. 1. Luke 6. 12. Luke 9. 1.
ʲ John 1. 42.
ᵏ Isa. 58. 1.
ˡ Jude 1.
⁴ Or, home.
ᵐ ch. 6. 31.
⁵ Or, kinsmen.
John 7. 5. John 10. 20.
ⁿ Matt. 9. 34. Matt. 10.25. Luke 11. 15. John 7. 20. John 8. 48, 52.
John 10. 22.
ᵒ Matt. 12.25. Luke 11. 17-23.
ᵖ Isa. 49. 24. Matt. 12.29.
ᑫ Matt. 12.31. Luke 12.10. Heb. 6. 4-8. Heb. 10. 26-31. 1 John 5.16.
ʳ Matt. 25.46. ch. 12. 40. Acts 7. 51. 2 Thes. 1. 9. Heb. 6. 4. Jude 7. 13.
ˢ Matt.12.46. Luke 8. 19.
ᵗ Matt. 13.55. ch. 6. 3. John 7. 3
ᵘ Deut. 33. 9. Song 4.9,10. Matt. 25.40-45. Rom. 8. 29. Heb. 2. 11.

9-21; Luke vi. 6-11.) For the exposition, see on Matt. xii. 9-21.
13-19.—THE TWELVE APOSTLES CHOSEN. For the exposition, see on Luke vi. 12-19.
20-30.—JESUS IS CHARGED WITH MADNESS AND DEMONIACAL POSSESSION—HIS REPLY. (=Matt. xii. 22-37; Luke xi. 14-26.) For the exposition, see on Matt. xii. 22-37, and on Luke xi. 21-26.
31-35.—HIS MOTHER AND BRETHREN SEEK TO SPEAK WITH HIM, AND THE REPLY. (=Matt.

4 AND ^ahe began again to teach by the sea-side: and there was gathered unto him a great multitude, so that he entered into a ship, and sat in 2 the sea; and the whole multitude was by the sea on the land. And he taught them many things by parables, and said unto them 3 in his doctrine, ^bHearken; Behold, there went out a sower to sow: 4 and it came to pass, as he sowed, some fell by the way-side, and the fowls 5 of the air came and devoured it up. And some fell on stony ground, where it had not much earth; and immediately it sprang up, because it 6 had no depth of earth: but when the sun was up, it was scorched; and 7 because it had no root, it withered away. And some ^cfell among thorns, 8 and the thorns grew up, and choked it, and it yielded no fruit. And other fell on good ground, and did yield fruit that sprang up and increased; and brought forth, some thirty, and some sixty, and some an 9 hundred. And he said unto them, He that hath ears to hear, let him hear.

A. D. 31.

CHAP. 4.
^a Matt. 13. 1.
ch. 2. 13.
Luke 8. 4.
^b Deut. 4. 1.
Ps. 34. 11.
Ps. 45. 10.
Pro. 7. 24.
Pro. 8. 32.
Isa. 55. 1.
Acts 2. 14.
Jas. 2. 5.
^c Gen. 3. 18.
Jer. 4. 3.
Luke 8. 7.
John 15. 5.
1 Tim. 6. 9.
Col. 1. 6.

---

xii. 46-50; Luke viii. 19-21.) For the exposition, see on Matt. xii. 46-50.

CHAP. IV. 1-29.—PARABLE OF THE SOWER—REASON FOR TEACHING IN PARABLES—PARABLES OF THE SEED GROWING WE KNOW NOT HOW, AND OF THE MUSTARD SEED. (= Matt. xiii. 1-23, 31, 32; Luke viii. 4-18.)

1. And he began again to teach by the sea-side: and there was gathered unto him a great multitude—or, according to another well-supported reading, 'a mighty,' or 'immense multitude' [ὄχλος πλεῖστος], **so that he entered into a ship** [εἰς τὸ πλοῖον]—rather, 'into the ship,' meaning the one mentioned in ch. iii. 9. (See on Matt. xii. 15.) **and sat in the sea; and the whole multitude was by the sea on the land**—crowded on the sea-shore to listen to Him. See on Matt. xiii. 1, 2. **2. And he taught them many things by parables, and said unto them in his doctrine** [διδαχῇ]—or 'teaching.'

Parable of the Sower (3-9, 13-20). After this parable is recorded, the Evangelist says, *v.* 10. And when he was alone, they that were about him with the twelve—probably those who followed Him most closely and were firmest in discipleship, next to the Twelve. **asked of him the parable.** The reply would seem to intimate that this parable of the Sower was of that fundamental, comprehensive, and introductory character which we have assigned to it (see on Matt. xiii. 1). **13. And he said unto them, Know ye not this parable? and how then will ye know all parables?** Probably this was said not so much in the spirit of rebuke, as to call their attention to the exposition of it which He was about to give, and so train them to the right apprehension of His future parables. As in the parables which we have endeavoured to explain in Matt. xiii., we shall take this parable and the Lord's own exposition of the different parts of it together.

The SOWER, the SEED, and the SOIL. **3. Hearken; Behold, there went out a sower to sow.** What means this? **14. The sower. soweth the word**—or, as in Luke (viii. 11), "Now the parable is this: The seed is *the word of God*." But who is "the sower?" This is not expressed here, because if "the word of God" be the seed, every scatterer of that precious seed must be regarded as a sower. It is true that in the parable of the Tares it is said, "He that soweth the good seed is the Son of Man," as "He that soweth the tares is the devil"(Matt. xiii. 37, 38). But these are only the great unseen parties, struggling in this world for the possession of man. Each of these has his agents among men themselves; and Christ's agents in the sowing of the good seed are the *preachers* of the

word. Thus, as in all the cases about to be described, the Sower is the same, and the seed is the same, while the result is entirely different, the whole difference must lie in the *soils*, which mean the *different states of the human heart*. And so, the great general lesson held forth in this parable of the Sower is, That however faithful the preacher, and how pure soever his message, *the effect of the preaching of the word depends upon the state of the hearer's heart*. Now follow the cases.

First Case: THE WAY-SIDE. **4. And it came to pass, as he sowed, some fell by the way-side**—by the side of the hard path through the field, where the soil was not broken up: **and the fowls** [of the air] **came and devoured it up** [τοῦ οὐρανοῦ is wanting in support]. Not only could the seed not get beneath the surface, but "it was trodden down" (Luke viii. 5), and afterwards picked up and devoured by the fowls. What means this? **15. And these are they by the way-side, where the word is sown; but, when they have heard, Satan cometh immediately, and taketh away the word that was sown in their hearts** — or, more fully, Matt. xiii. 19, "When any one heareth the word of the kingdom, and understandeth it not, then cometh the wicked one, and catcheth away that which was sown in his heart." The great truth here taught is, that *Hearts all unbroken and hard are no fit soil for saving truth.* They apprehend it not (Matt. xiii. 19), as God's means of restoring them to Himself; it penetrates not, makes no impression, but lies loosely on the surface of the heart, till the wicked one—afraid of losing a victim by his "believing to salvation," Luke viii. 12)—finds some frivolous subject by whose greater attractions to draw off the attention, and straightway it is gone. Of how many hearers of the word is this the graphic but painful history!

Second Case: THE STONY, or rather, ROCKY GROUND. **5. And some fell on stony ground, where it had not much earth** [τὸ πετρῶδες]— 'the rocky ground;' in Matthew (xiii. 5), 'the rocky places' [τὰ πετρώδη]; in Luke, 'the rock' [τὴν πέτραν]. The thing intended is, not ground with stones in it, which would not prevent the roots striking downward, but ground where a quite thin surface of earth covers a rock. What means this? **16. And these are they likewise which are sown on stony ground; who, when they have heard the word, immediately receive it with gladness; 17. And have no root in themselves, and so endure but for a time: afterward, when affliction or persecution ariseth for the word's sake, immediately they are offended.** "Immediately" the seed in such case "springs

145

10 And ^dwhen he was alone, they that were about him with the twelve
11 asked of him the parable. And he said unto them, Unto you it is given
    to know ^ethe mystery of the kingdom of God: but unto ^fthem that are
12 without, all *these* things are done in parables: that ^gseeing they may see,
    and not perceive; and hearing they may hear, and not understand; lest
    at any time they should be converted, and *their* sins should be forgiven
13 them. And he said unto them, Know ye not this parable? and
14 how then will ye know all parables? The ^hsower soweth the word.
15 And these are they by the way-side, where the word is sown; but, when
    they have heard, ⁱSatan cometh immediately, and taketh away the word
16 that was sown in their hearts. And these are they likewise which are
    sown on stony ground; who, when they have heard the word, immediately
17 receive it with gladness; and have ^jno root in themselves, and so endure
    but for a time: afterward, when affliction or persecution ariseth for the
18 word's sake, immediately they are offended. And these are they which
19 are sown among thorns; such as hear the word, and the cares of this

A. D. 31.

^d Pro. 2. 1.
Pro. 4. 7.
Pro. 13. 20.
Matt. 13.10.
Luke 8. 9.
^e 1 Cor. 2. 10.
^f 1 Cor. 1. 18.
1 Cor. 5. 12.
^g Isa. 6. 9.
Isa. 44. 18.
Jer. 5. 21.
Matt. 13.14.
^h Matt. 13.19.
Eph. 3. 8.
1 Pet. 1. 23,
25.
ⁱ 2 Cor. 2. 11.
2 Cor. 4. 4.
1 Pet. 5. 8.
^j Job 27. 10

up"—all the quicker from the shallowness of the soil—"because it has no depth of earth." But the sun, beating on it, as quickly scorches and withers it up, "because it has no root" (*v.* 6), and "lacks moisture" (Luke viii. 6). The great truth here taught is that *Hearts superficially impressed are apt to receive the truth with readiness, and even with joy* (Luke viii. 13); *but the heat of tribulation or persecution because of the word, or the trials which their new profession brings upon them quickly dries up their relish for the truth, and withers all the hasty promise of fruit which they showed.* Such disappointing issues of a faithful and awakening ministry—alas, how frequent are they!

Third Case: THE THORNY GROUND. 7. And some fell among thorns, and the thorns grew up, and choked it, and it yielded no fruit. This case is that of ground not thoroughly cleaned of the thistles, &c.; which, rising above the good seed, "choke" or "smother" it, excluding light and air, and drawing away the moisture and richness of the soil. Hence it "becomes unfruitful" (Matt. xiii. 22); it grows, but its growth is checked, and it never ripens. The evil here is neither a hard nor a shallow soil—there is *softness* enough, and *depth* enough; but it is the existence in it of what draws all the moisture and richness of the soil away to itself, and so *starves the plant.* What now are these "thorns"? 18. And these are they which are sown among thorns; such as hear the word, 19. And the cares of this world, and the deceitfulness of riches, and the lusts of other things entering in—or "the pleasures of this life" (Luke viii. 14), choke the word, and it becometh unfruitful. First, "The cares of this world"—anxious, unrelaxing attention to the business of this present life; second, "The deceitfulness of riches"—of those riches which are the fruit of this worldly "care;" third, "The pleasures of this life," or "the lusts of other things entering in" —the enjoyments, in themselves it may be innocent, which worldly prosperity enables one to indulge. These "*choke*" or "*smother*" the word; drawing off so much of one's attention, absorbing so much of one's interest, and using up so much of one's time, that only the dregs of these remain for spiritual things, and a fagged, hurried, and heartless formalism is at length all the religion of such persons. What a vivid picture is this of the mournful condition of many, especially in great commercial countries, who once promised much fruit! "They bring no fruit *to perfection*"

(Luke viii. 14); indicating how much *growth* there may be, in the early stages of such a case, and *promise* of fruit—which after all never *ripens.*

Fourth Case: THE GOOD GROUND. 8. And other fell on good ground, and did yield fruit that sprang up and increased; and brought forth, some thirty, and some sixty, and some an hundred. The goodness of this last soil consists in its qualities being precisely the reverse of the other three soils: from its softness and tenderness, receiving and cherishing the seed; from its depth, allowing it to take firm root, and not quickly losing its moisture; and from its cleanness, giving its whole vigour and sap to the plant. In such a soil the seed "brings forth fruit," in all different degrees of profusion, according to the measure in which the soil possesses those qualities. So 20. And these are they which are sown on good ground; such as hear the word, and receive it, and bring forth fruit, some thirty-fold, some sixty, and some an hundred. A heart soft and tender, stirred to its depths on the great things of eternity, and jealously guarded from worldly engrossments, such only is the "*honest and good heart*" (Luke viii. 15), which "*keeps*" [κατέχουσι]—that is, "*retains*" the seed of the word, and bears fruit just in proportion as it is such a heart. Such "bring forth fruit with *patience*" (*v.* 15), or continuance, 'enduring to the end;' in contrast with those in whom the word is "choked" and brings no fruit *to perfection.* The "thirty-fold" is designed to express the *lowest* degree of fruitfulness; the "hundred-fold" the *highest;* and the "sixty-fold" the *intermediate* degrees of fruitfulness. As 'a hundred-fold,' though not unexampled (Gen. xxvi. 12), is a rare return in the natural husbandry, so the highest degrees of spiritual fruitfulness are too seldom witnessed. The closing words of this introductory parable seem designed to call attention to the *fundamental* and *universal* character of it. 9. And he said unto them, He that hath ears to hear, let him hear.

Reason for Teaching in Parables (11, 12). 11, 12. And he said unto them, Unto you it is given to know the mystery of the kingdom of God: but unto them, &c. See on Matt. xiii. 10-17. 21. And he said unto them, Is a candle—or 'lamp,' [ὁ λύχνος]—brought to be put under a bushel, or under a bed? and not to be set on a candlestick?—"that they which enter in may see the light" (Luke viii. 16). See on Matt. v. 15, of which this is nearly a repetition. 22. For there is nothing hid, which shall not be manifested;

world, [k]and the deceitfulness of riches, and the lusts of other things
20 entering in, choke the word, and it becometh unfruitful. And these are
they which are sown on good [l]ground; such as hear the word, and receive
it, and bring forth fruit, some thirty-fold, some sixty, and some an
hundred.

21 And [m]he said unto them, Is a candle brought to be put under a
22 [1]bushel, or under a bed? and not to be set on a candlestick? For [n]there
is nothing hid, which shall not be manifested; neither was any thing kept
23 secret, but that it should come abroad. If [o]any man have ears to hear,
24 let him hear. And he saith unto them, [p]Take heed what ye hear: [q]with
what measure ye mete, it shall be measured to you; and unto you that
25 hear shall more be given. For [r]he that hath, to him shall be given; and
he that hath not, from him shall be taken even that which he hath.

26 And he said, [s]So is the kingdom of God, as if a man should cast seed
27 into the ground; and should sleep, and rise night and day, and the seed
28 should spring and grow up, he knoweth not how. For the earth bringeth
forth fruit of himself; first the blade, then the ear, after that the full
29 corn in the ear. But when the fruit is [2]brought forth, immediately [t]he
putteth in the sickle, because the harvest is come.

30 And he said, [u]Whereunto shall we liken the kingdom of God? or with
31 what comparison shall we compare it? *It is* like a grain of mustard seed,
which, when it is sown in the earth, is less than all the seeds that be in
32 the earth: but when it is sown, it [v]groweth up, and becometh greater
than all herbs, and shooteth out great branches; so that the fowls of the
air may lodge under the shadow of it.

33 And [w]with many such parables spake he the word unto them, as they
34 were able to hear *it*. But without a parable spake he not unto them:
and when they were alone, he expounded all things to his disciples.

A. D. 31.

[k] Ps. 52. 7.
Pro. 23. 5.
Eccl. 5. 13.
[l] Rom. 7. 4.
2 Cor. 5. 17.
2 Pet. 1. 4.
[m] Matt. 5. 15.
Luke 8. 16.
Luke 11.33.
[1] The word
in the
original
signifieth
a less mea-
sure, as
Matt. 5. 15.
[n] Matt. 10.26.
[o] Matt. 11.15.
[p] 1 John 4. 1.
[q] Matt. 7. 2.
[r] Matt. 13.12.
[s] Matt. 13.24.
[2] Or, ripe.
Eph. 4. 13.
[t] Rev. 14. 15.
[u] Matt. 13.31.
Luke 13.18.
Acts 2. 41.
Acts 4. 4.
Acts 5. 14.
Acts 19. 20.
[v] Mal. 1. 11.
Rev. 11. 15.
[w] Matt. 13.34.
John 16.12.

---

neither was any thing kept secret, but that it should come abroad. See on Matt. x. 26, 27; but the connection there and here is slightly different. Here the idea seems to be this:—'I have privately expounded to you these great truths, but only that ye may proclaim them publicly; and if ye will not, others will. For these are not designed for secrecy. They are imparted to be diffused abroad, and they shall be so; yea, a time is coming when the most hidden things shall be brought to light.' 23. If any man have ears to hear, let him hear. This for the second time on the same subject (see on *v*. 9). 24. And he saith unto them, Take heed what ye hear [τί]. In Luke (viii. 18) it is, "Take heed how ye hear" [πῶς]. The one implies the other, but both precepts are very weighty. with what measure ye mete, it shall be measured to you. See on Matt. vii. 2. and unto you that hear—that is, thankfully, teachably, profitably, shall more be given. 25. For he that hath, to him shall be given; and he that hath not, from him shall be taken even that which he hath—or "seemeth to have," or 'thinketh he hath' [ὃ δοκεῖ ἔχειν]. See on Matt. xiii. 12. This "having" and "thinking he hath" are not different; for when it hangs loosely upon him, and is not appropriated to its proper ends and uses, it both *is* and *is not* his.

Parable of the Seed Growing We Know Not How (26-29). This beautiful parable is peculiar to Mark. Its design is to teach the *Imperceptible Growth* of the word sown in the heart, from its earliest stage of development to the ripest fruits of practical righteousness. 26. And he said, So is the kingdom of God, as if a man should cast seed into the ground; 27. And should sleep, and rise night and day—go about his other ordinary occupations, leaving it to the well-known laws of vegetation

under the genial influences of heaven. This is the sense of "the earth bringing forth fruit *of herself*," in the next verse. and the seed should spring and grow up, he knoweth not how. 28. For the earth bringeth forth fruit of herself; first the blade, then the ear, after that the full corn in the ear. Beautiful allusion to the succession of similar stages, though not definitely-marked periods, in the Christian life, and generally in the kingdom of God. 29. But when the fruit is brought forth—to maturity, immediately he putteth in the sickle, because the harvest is come. This charmingly points to the transition from the earthly to the heavenly condition of the Christian and the Church.

Parable of the Mustard Seed (30-32). For the exposition of this Portion, see on Matt. xiii. 31, 32. 33. And with many such parables spake he the word unto them, as they were able to hear it. Had this been said in the corresponding passage of Matthew, we should have concluded that what that Evangelist recorded was but a specimen of other parables spoken on the same occasion. But Matthew (xiii. 34) says, "All *these* things spake Jesus unto the multitude in parables;" and as Mark records only some of the parables which Matthew gives, we are warranted to infer that the "many such parables" alluded to here mean no more than the full complement of them which we find in Matthew. 34. But without a parable spake he not unto them. See on Matt. xiii. 34. and when they were alone, he expounded all things to his disciples. See on *v*. 22.

Remarks.—1. In the parable of the Sower, we have an illustration of the principle that our Lord's parables illustrate only certain features of a subject, and that though others *may* be added as accessory and subsidiary, no conclusions are to

35   And [x]the same day, when the even was come, he saith unto them, | A. D. 31.
36   Let us pass over unto the other side.   And when they had sent away | [x] Isa. 42. 4.

be drawn as to those features of the subject which are not in the parable at all. (See on Matt. xxii. 2, &c., xxv. 1, where, though the subject in both is a *marriage*, the *Bride* appears in neither.) Thus, the one point in this parable is the *diversity of the soils*, as affecting the result of the sowing. To make this the clearer, the *sower* and the *seed* are here supposed to be the same in all. But were one to infer from this that the preacher and his doctrine are of no importance, or of less moment than the state of the heart on which the word lights, he would fall into that spurious style of interpretation which has misled not a few. 2. Perhaps our Lord's own ministry furnishes the most striking illustration of this Parable of the Sower. Look first at Chorazin, Bethsaida, Capernaum, Jerusalem—what a hard *Way-side* did they present to the precious seed that fell upon it—yielding, with few exceptions, not only no fruit, but not so much as one green blade! Turn next to him who said to Him, "Lord, I will follow thee whithersoever thou goest," and the crowds that followed Him with wonder and heard Him with joy, and cast in their lot with Him—until the uncompromising severity of His teaching, or the privations and the obloquy they had to suffer, or the prospect of a deadly conflict with the world, stumbled them, and then they went back, and walked no more with Him: this was the *Rocky Ground*. As for the *Thorny Ground*—not hard, like the way-side; nor shallow, like the rocky ground; but soft enough and deep enough; in which, therefore the good seed sprang up, and promised fruit, and *would have ripened* but for the thorns which were allowed to spring up and choke the plant—this kind of hearers had scarcely time to develop themselves ere the Lord Himself was taken from them. But *Judas*—in so far as he bade so fair as a disciple as to be taken into the number of the Twelve, and went forth with the rest of the apostles on their preaching-tour, and in every other thing acted so faithfully to all appearance as to inspire no suspicion of his false-heartedness up to the very night of his treason—perhaps he may be taken as one of a class which, but for one or more predominant sins, cherished till they become resistless, *would have borne fruit* unto life eternal. Of honest and good hearts there were but too few to cheer the heart of the Great Sower. But the Eleven certainly were such, and "as many as received Him, to whom He gave power to become sons of God;" and them He deigned to call "His brother, and sister, and mother." As to the varying fruitfulness of these, Peter and John might perhaps be taken as examples of the "some who brought forth an hundred-fold;" Andrew, and Nathanael (or Bartholomew), and Matthew, and Thomas, and it may be others, sixty-fold; and the rest thirty. But from age to age these diversified characters are developed; and some more in one, some in another. There are periods of such spiritual death in the Church, that its whole territory presents to the spiritual eye the aspect of one vast Way-side, with but here and there, at wide distances, a green spot. There are periods of intense religious excitement, in which, as if all were Rocky ground, the sower's heart is gladdened by the quick up-springing of an immense breadth of beautiful green "blade," as if the Latter Day of υ iversal turning to the Lord were about to daw ; and a goodly portion of it comes into "ear;" but of "the full corn

in the ear," scarce any is there to reward the reaper's toil. And there are periods of high orthodox belief, fair religious profession, and universally proper outward Christianity, in which the all-engrossing pursuit of wealth in the walks of untiring industry, and the carnal indulgences to which outward prosperity ministers, starve the soul and suffer no spiritual fruit to come "to perfection." These are the Thorny-ground periods. Of Good-ground periods have there been any? In a partial sense there certainly have; but on any great scale it is rather to be expected in the Times of Refreshing which are coming upon the earth, than referred to as an experienced fact. Perhaps every congregation furnishes some of all these classes; but would to God we could see more of the last! 3. What encouragement may not be fetched from the parable of the *imperceptible growth* of the good seed! It is slow; it is gradual; it is unseen—alike in the natural and the spiritual kingdom. Hence the wisdom of early sowing, and long patience, and cheerful expectancy. 4. Illustrative preaching has here the highest example. Not more attractive than instructive is this style of preaching; and the parables of our Lord are incomparable models of both. If there be such a thing in perfection as "apples of gold in a framework of silver," these are they. It is true that to excel in this style requires an original capacity, with which every preacher is not gifted. But the systematic observation of nature and of human life, with continual reference to spiritual things, will do a good deal to aid the most unapt, while luxuriant fancies, which are apt to overpower with their illustrations the thing illustrated, have quite as much need of pruning. For both classes of mind the careful study of that grand simplicity and freedom, and freshness and elegance, and whatever else there be, which combine to render our Lord's parables indescribably perfect, both in the truths they convey and the mode of conveying them, would be a fruitful exercise. 5. The command to take heed *what* we hear is to be taken as a hint supplementary to the parable of the Sower, and is just on that account the more worthy of attention. For since the quality of the seed sown had nothing to do with the design of that parable —it being supposed in all the cases to be good seed—a supplementary caution to look well to "what" we hear, as well as "how," must have been intended to teach us that, in point of fact, the doctrine taught requires as much attention as the right frame of mind in listening to it. For in respect of both, "the word which we hear, the same shall judge us at the last day."

35—V. 20.—JESUS, CROSSING THE SEA OF GALILEE, MIRACULOUSLY STILLS A TEMPEST—HE CURES THE DEMONIAC OF GADARA. (= Matt. viii. 23-34; Luke viii. 22-39.)

The time of this Section is very definitely marked by our Evangelist, and by him alone, in the opening words.

Jesus Stills a Tempest on the Sea of Galilee (35-41). **35. And the same day**—on which He spoke the memorable parables of the preceding Section, and of Matt. xiii., **when the even was come**. See on ch. vi. 35. This must have been the earlier evening—what we should call the afternoon—since after all that passed on the other side, when He returned to the west side, the people were waiting for Him in great numbers (*v.* 21; Luke viii. 40). **he saith unto them, Let us pass over unto the other side**—to the east side of the Lake, to grapple

the multitude, they took him even as he was in the ship. And there
37 were also with him other little ships. And there arose a great storm of
38 wind, and the waves beat into the ship, so that it was now full. And he
was in the hinder part of the ship, asleep on a pillow: and they awake
39 him, and say unto him, Master, carest thou not that we perish? And
he arose, and ʸrebuked the wind, and said unto the sea, Peace, be still.
40 And the wind ceased, and there was a great calm. And he said unto
41 them, Why are ye so fearful? how is it that ye have no faith? And
they ᶻfeared exceedingly, and said one to another, What manner of man
is this, that even the wind and the sea obey him?
5   AND ᵃthey came over unto the other side of the sea, into the country
2 of the Gadarenes. And when he was come out of the ship, immediately

A. D. 31.

ᵛ Job 28. 11.
Job 38. 11.
Ps. 29. 10.
Ps. 65. 5, 7.
Ps. 89. 9.
Ps. 93. 4.
Ps. 107. 23-
29.
Ps. 135. 5, 6.
Nah. 1. 4.
ᶻ Ps. 33. 8, 9.

CHAP. 5.
ᵃ Matt. 8. 28.
Luke 8. 26.

with a desperate case of possession, and set the captive free, and to give the Gadarenes an opportunity of hearing the message of salvation, amid the wonder which that marvellous cure was fitted to awaken and the awe which the subsequent events could not but strike into them. **36. And when they had sent away the multitude, they took him even as he was in the ship**—that is, without any preparation, and without so much as leaving the vessel, out of which He had been all day teaching. **And there were also with him other little ships**—with passengers, probably, wishing to accompany Him. **37. And there arose a great storm of wind** [λαῖλαψ ἀνέμου]—'a tempest of wind.' To such sudden squalls the sea of Galilee is very liable from its position, in a deep basin, skirted on the east by lofty mountain-ranges, while on the west the hills are intersected by narrow gorges through which the wind sweeps across the lake, and raises its waters with great rapidity into a storm. **and the waves beat into the ship** [ἐπέβαλλεν εἰς τὸ πλοῖον]—'kept beating' or 'pitching on the ship,' **so that it was now full** [ὥστε αὐτὸ ἤδη γεμίζεσθαι]—rather, 'so that it was already filling.' In Matt. (viii. 24), "insomuch that the ship was covered with the waves;" but this is too strong. It should be, 'so that the ship was getting covered by the waves' [ὥστε τὸ πλοῖον καλύπτεσθαι]. So we must translate the word used in Luke (viii. 23)—not as in our version—"And there came down a storm on the lake, and they were filled [with water]"—but 'they were getting filled' [συνεπληροῦντο], that is, those who sailed; meaning, of course, that their ship was so. **38. And he was in the hinder**—or stern, **part of the ship, asleep on a pillow** [ἐπὶ τὸ προσκεφάλαιον]—either a place in the vessel made to receive the head, or a cushion for the head to rest on. It was evening; and after the fatigues of a busy day of teaching under the hot sun, having nothing to do while crossing the lake, He sinks into a deep sleep, which even this tempest raging around and tossing the little vessel did not disturb. **and they awake him, and say unto him, Master** [Διδάσκαλε]—or 'Teacher.' In Luke (viii. 24) this is doubled—in token of their life-and-death-earnestness—"Master, Master" ['Επιστάτα, 'Επιστάτα]. **carest thou not that we perish?** Unbelief and fear made them sadly forget their place, to speak so. Luke has it, "Lord, save us, we perish." When those accustomed to fish upon that deep thus spake, the danger must have been imminent. They say nothing of what would become of *Him*, if they perished; nor think whether, if He could not perish, it was likely He would let this happen to them: but they hardly knew what they said. **39. And he arose, and rebuked the wind**—"and the raging of the water" (Luke viii. 24), **and said unto the sea, Peace, be still**—two sublime words of command, from a Master to His servants, the elements [Σιώπα, πεφίμωσο]. **And the wind ceased, and there was a great calm.** The sudden hushing of the wind would not at once have calmed the sea, whose commotion would have settled only after a considerable time. But the word of command was given to both elements at once. **40. And he said unto them, Why are ye so fearful?** There is a natural apprehension under danger; but there was unbelief in their fear. It is worthy of notice how considerately the Lord defers this rebuke till He had first removed the danger, in the midst of which they would not have been in a state to listen to anything. **how is it that ye have no faith?**—next to none, or none in present exercise. In Luke it is, "Why are ye fearful, O ye of little faith?" *Faith* they had, for they applied to Christ for relief; but *little*, for they were afraid, though Christ was in the ship. Faith dispels fear, but only in proportion to its strength. **41. And they feared exceedingly**—were struck with deep awe, **and said one to another, What manner of man is this, that even the wind and the sea obey him?**—'What is this? Israel has all along been singing of JEHOVAH, "Thou rulest the raging of the sea: when the waves thereof arise, Thou stillest them"! "The Lord on high is mightier than the noise of many waters, yea, than the mighty waves of the sea"! (Ps. lxxxix. 9; xciii. 4). But, lo, in this very boat of ours is One of our own flesh and blood, who with His word of command hath done the same! Exhausted with the fatigues of the day, He was but a moment ago in a deep sleep, undisturbed by the howling tempest, and we had to awake Him with the cry of our terror; but rising at our call, His majesty was felt by the raging elements, for they were instantly hushed—'WHAT MANNER OF MAN IS THIS?"'

CHAP. V. *Glorious Cure of the Gadarene Demoniac* (1-20). **1. And they came over unto the other side of the sea, into the country of the Gadarenes.** [*Lachmann, Tischendorf,* and *Tregelles* read here and in the corresponding passage of Luke (viii. 26) "Gerasenes"—Γερασηνῶν—on ancient, but not, as we think, sufficient authority to displace the received reading. In Matthew (viii. 28) the received reading, "Gergesenes," would seem the true one, and not "Gerasenes" with *Lachmann,* nor "Gadarenes" with *Tischendorf* and *Tregelles.* While the MS. evidence for it is satisfactory, some recent geographical discoveries seem to favour it. *Gadara* perhaps denoted the general locality. *Josephus* (Antt. xvii. 11. 4) speaks of it as the chief city of Perea, and a Greek city. It or its suburbs lay on the southern shore of the lake on the east side. Possibly the reading "Gergesenes," which seems a corrupted form of "Gadarenes," originated in that tract of country being still called after the "Girgashites" of ancient Canaan.] **2.**

149

3 there met him out of the tombs a man with an unclean spirit, who had
his dwelling among the tombs; and no man could bind him, no, not
4 with chains: because that he had been often bound with fetters and
chains, and the chains had been plucked asunder by him, and the
5 fetters broken in pieces: neither could any *man* tame him. And always,
night and day, he was in the mountains, and in the tombs, crying, and
6 cutting himself with stones. But when he saw Jesus afar off, he ran and
7 *b*worshipped him, and cried with a loud voice, What have I to
do with thee, Jesus, *thou* Son of the most high God? I adjure thee by
8 God, that thou torment me not. (For he said unto him, Come out of
9 the man, *thou* unclean spirit.) And he asked him, What *is* thy name?
10 And he answered, saying, My name *is* Legion: for we are many. And
he besought him much that he would not send them away out of the
11 country. Now there was there, nigh unto the mountains, a great herd
12 of *c*swine feeding. And all the devils besought him, saying, Send us
13 into the swine, that we may enter into them. And forthwith Jesus
*d*gave them leave. And the unclean spirits went out, and entered into

A. D. 31.
b Ps. 66. 3.
Acts 16. 17.
Phil. 2. 10,
11.
Jas. 2. 19.
c Lev. 11. 7.
Deut. 14. 8.
Isa. 65. 4.
Isa. 6 i. 3.
Matt. 8. 30.
Luke 8. 32.
d 1 Ki. 22. 22.
Job 1. 12.
Job 2. 6.
Job 12. 16
Matt. 28.18.
Luke 4. 36.
Eph. 1. 20,
23.
Col. 2. 10.
Heb. 2. 8.

And when he was come out of the ship, immediately (see *v.* 6) **there met him a man with an unclean spirit**—"which had devils (or 'demons') long time" (Luke viii. 27). In Matthew (viii. 28), "there met Him two men possessed with devils." Though there be no discrepancy between these two statements—more than between two witnesses, one of whom testifies to something done by one person, while the other affirms that there were two—it is difficult to see how the principal details here given could apply to more than one case. 3. **Who had his dwelling among the tombs.** Luke says, "He ware no clothes, neither abode in any house." These tombs were hewn out of the rocky caves of the locality, and served for shelters and lurking-places (Luke viii. 26). **and no man could bind him, no, not with chains: 4. Because that he had been often bound with fetters and chains, and the chains had been plucked asunder by him, and the fetters broken in pieces.** Luke says (viii. 29) that "often times it (the unclean spirit) had caught him;" and after mentioning how they had vainly tried to bind him with chains and fetters, because "he brake the bands," he adds, "and was driven of the devil (or 'demon') into the wilderness." The dark tyrant-power by which he was held clothed him with superhuman strength, and made him scorn restraint. Matthew (viii. 28) says he was "exceeding fierce, so that no man might pass by that way." He was the terror of the whole locality. 5. **And always, night and day, he was in the mountains, and in the tombs, crying, and cutting himself with stones.** Terrible as he was to others, he himself endured untold misery, which sought relief in tears and self-inflicted torture. 6. **But when he saw Jesus afar off, he ran and worshipped him**—not with the spontaneous alacrity which says to Jesus, "Draw me, we will *run* after thee," but inwardly compelled, with terrific rapidity, before the Judge, to receive sentence of expulsion. 7. **And cried with a loud voice, What have I to do with thee, Jesus, Son of the most high God? I adjure thee by God, that thou torment me not**—or, as in Matt. viii. 29, "Art thou come to torment us before the time?" See on ch. i. 24. Behold the *tormentor* anticipating, dreading, and entreating exemption from *torment!* In Christ they discern their destined Tormentor; the time, they know, is fixed, and they feel as if it were come already! (Jas. ii. 19). 8. **(For he said unto him**—that is, before the unclean spirit cried out, **Come out of the man, unclean spirit!)** Ordinarily, obedi-

ence to a command of this nature was immediate. But here, a certain delay is permitted, the more signally to manifest the power of Christ and accomplish his purposes. 9. **And he asked him, What is thy name?** The object of this question was to extort an acknowledgment of the virulence of demoniacal power by which this victim was enthralled. **And he answered, saying, My name is Legion: for we are many**—or, as in Luke, "because many devils (or 'demons') were entered into him." A legion, in the Roman army, amounted, at its full complement, to six thousand; but here the word is used, as such words with us, and even this one, for an indefinitely large number—large enough however to rush, as soon as permission was given, into two thousand swine and destroy them. 10. **And he besought him much that he would not send them away out of the country.** The entreaty, it will be observed, was made by *one* spirit, but in behalf of *many*—"*he* besought Him not to send *them*," &c.—just as in the former verse, "*he* answered *we* are many." But what do they mean by entreating so earnestly not to be ordered out of the country? Their next petition (*v.* 12) will make that clear enough. 11. **Now there was there, nigh unto the mountains** [πρὸς τὰ ὄρη]—rather, 'to the mountain' [πρὸς τῷ ὄρει], according to what is clearly the true reading. In Matt. viii. 30 they are said to have been "a good way off." But these expressions, far from being inconsistent, only confirm, by their precision, the minute accuracy of the narrative. **a great herd of swine feeding.** There can hardly be any doubt that the owners of these were Jews, since to them our Lord had now come to proffer His services. This will explain what follows. 12. **And all the devils besought him, saying**—"if thou cast us out" (Matt. viii. 31), **Send us into the swine, that we may enter into them.** Had they spoken out all their mind, perhaps this would have been it: 'If we must quit our hold of this man, suffer us to continue our work of mischief in another form, that by entering these swine and thus destroying the people's property, we may steel their hearts against Thee !' 13. **And forthwith Jesus gave them leave.** In Matthew this is given with majestic brevity—"Go !" The owners, if Jews, drove an illegal trade; if heathens, they insulted the national religion: in either case the permission was just. **And the unclean spirits went out** (of the man), **and entered into the swine: and the herd ran violently**—or 'rushed' [ὥρμησεν] **down a steep place**—'down the hanging cliff' [κατὰ

150

the swine: and the herd ran violently down a steep place into the sea,
14 (they were about two thousand,) and were choked in the sea. And
    they that fed the swine fled, and told *it* in the city, and in the country.
15 And they went out to see what it was that was done. And they come
    to Jesus, and see him that was possessed with the devil, and had the
    legion, sitting, and clothed, and *e*in his right mind: and they were afraid.
16 And they that saw *it* told them how it befell to him that was possessed
17 with the devil, and *also* concerning the swine. And *f*they began to pray
18 him to depart out of their coasts. And when he was come into the
    ship, he *g*that had been possessed with the devil prayed him that he
19 might be with him. Howbeit Jesus suffered him not, but saith unto
    him, Go home to thy friends, and tell them how great things the

A. D. 31.
e Rom. 16. 20.
1 John 3. 8.
f Gen. 26. 16.
Deut. 5. 25.
1 Ki. 17. 18.
Job 21. 14.
Matt. 8. 34.
ch. 1. 24.
Acts 16. 39.
1 Cor. 2. 14.
g Ps. 116. 12.
Luke 8. 38.
Luke 17. 15,
17.

τοῦ κρημνοῦ], **into the sea (they were about two thousand.)** The number of them is given by our graphic Evangelist alone. **and were choked in the sea**—or "perished in the waters" (Matt. viii. 32). **14. And they that fed the swine fled, and told it**—"told everything, and what was befallen to the possessed of the devils" (Matt. viii. 33), **in the city, and in the country. And they went out to see what it was that was done.** Thus had they the evidence both of the herdsmen and of their own senses to the reality of both miracles. **15. And they come to Jesus.** Matthew (viii. 34) says, "Behold, the whole city came out to meet Jesus." **and see him that was possessed with the devil**—'the demonized person' [τὸν δαιμονιζόμενον], **and had the legion, sitting**—"at the feet of Jesus," adds Luke (viii. 35); in contrast with his former *wild* and *wandering* habits, **and clothed.** As our Evangelist had not told us that he "ware no clothes," the meaning of this statement could only have been conjectured but for "the beloved physician" (Luke viii. 27), who supplies the missing piece of information here. This is a striking case of what are called *Undesigned Coincidences* amongst the different Evangelists; one of them taking a thing for granted, as familiarly known at the time, but which we should never have known but for one or more of the others, and without the knowledge of which some of their statements would be unintelligible. The clothing which the poor man would feel the want of, the moment his consciousness returned to him, was doubtless supplied to him by some of the Twelve. **and in his right mind**—but now, O in what a lofty sense! (Compare an analogous, though a different kind of case, Dan. iv. 34-37.) **and they were afraid.** Had this been *awe* only, it had been natural enough; but other feelings, alas! of a darker kind, soon showed themselves. **16. And they that saw it told them how it befell to him that was possessed with the devil** ('the demonized person') **and also concerning the swine.** Thus had they the double testimony of the herdsmen and their own senses. **17. And they began to pray him to depart out of their coasts.** Was it the owners only of the valuable property now lost to them that did this? Alas, no! For Luke (viii. 37) says, "Then the whole multitude of the country of the Gadarenes round about besought Him to depart from them; for they were taken [or 'seized' —συνείχοντο] with great fear" The evil spirits had thus, alas! their object. Irritated, the people could not suffer His presence: yet awestruck, they dared not order Him off: so they entreat Him to withdraw, and—He takes them at their word. **18. And when he was come into the ship, he that had been possessed with the devil** ['he that had been demonized'—the word is not now δαιμονιζόμενος, but δαιμονισθείς]

prayed him that he might be with him—the grateful heart, fresh from the hands of demons, clinging to its wondrous Benefactor. How exquisitely natural! **19. Howbeit Jesus suffered him not, but saith unto him, Go home to thy friends, and tell them how great things the Lord hath done for thee, and hath had compassion on thee.** To be a missionary for Christ, in the region where he was so well known and so long dreaded, was a far nobler calling than to follow Him where nobody had ever heard of Him, and where other trophies not less illustrious could be raised by the same power and grace. **20. And he departed, and began to publish**—not only among his friends, to whom Jesus more immediately sent him, but **in Decapolis**—so called, as being a region of ten cities. (See on Matt. iv. 25.) **how great things Jesus had done for him: and all men did marvel.** Throughout that considerable region did this monument of mercy proclaim his new-found Lord; and some, it is to be hoped, did more than "marvel."

Remarks—1. Nowhere, perhaps, in all the Gospel History does the true Humanity and proper Divinity of the one Lord Jesus Christ come out in sharper, brighter, and, if we might so say, more pre-raphaelite outline than in this Section. Behold here the Prince of preachers. He has finished those glorious parables which He spoke from His boat to the multitudes that lined the shore. The people are dismissed; but though early evening has come, He rests not, but bids the Twelve put out to sea, as He has work to do on the other side. They push off, accordingly, for the eastern side; but have not gone very far when one of those storms to which the lake is subject, but of more than usual violence, arises; and the fishermen, who knew well the element they were on, expecting that their little wherry would upset and send them to the bottom, hasten to their Master. As for Him, the fatigues of the day have come upon Him; and having other occupation awaiting Him at Gadara, He has retired to the stern-end of the vessel, to give Himself up, during the passage across, to balmy sleep. So deep is that sleep, that neither howling winds nor dashing waves break in upon it; and in this profound repose the disciples find Him, when in their extremity they come to Him for help. What a picture of innocent Humanity! Why did they disturb Him? Why were they so fearful? Was it possible that *He* should perish? or—"with Christ in the vessel"—could they? How was it that they had no faith? They were but training. Their faith as yet was but as a grain of mustard seed. But He shall do a thing now that will help it forward. He wakens up at their call; and He who but a moment before was in profound unconsciousness, under the care of His Father, looks around Him and just

15]

20 Lord hath done for thee, and hath had compassion on thee. And he departed, and *h* began to publish in Decapolis how great things Jesus had done for him: and all *men* did marvel.

A. D. 31.

h Ex. 15. 2.
Isa. 63. 7.

gives the word of command, and the raging elements are hushed into an immediate calm. This sleeping and waking Man, it seems, is the Lord of nature. It feels its Maker's presence, it hears His voice, it bows instant submission! The men marvel, but He does not. He is walking amongst His own works, and in commanding them He is breathing His proper element. 'What aileth you?' He exclaims, with sublime placidity amidst their perturbation: 'Have I been so long time with you, and yet ye have not known Me? I have stilled this tempest with a word: Doth that amaze you? Ye shall see greater things than these.' And now they are at the eastern side. But who is that who, descrying Him from a distance as He steps ashore, runs to Him, as if eager to embrace Him? It is a poor victim of Demoniacal malignity. The case is one of unusual virulence and protracted suffering. But the hour of deliverance has at length arrived. Demons, in frightful number, yet all marshalled obediently under one master-spirit, combine to inflict upon their victim all the evil he seems capable of suffering, in mind and in body. But the Lord of devils, stepping forth from that boat, has summoned them to His presence, and in their human victim they stand before Him. Ere they are made to quit their hold, they are forced to tell their number, and while uttering a reluctant testimony to the glory of their destined Tormentor whom they see before them, they are constrained to avow that they have not a spark of sympathy with Him, and utter forth their dread of Him, as if the day of their final doom had come. But with all this—the malignity of their nature nothing abated—they ask permission, if they must quit the higher victim, to take possession of victims of another kind, thereby to gain the same end on even a larger scale and to more fatal purpose. What a spectacle is this! That legion of spirits that were able to defy all the power of men to restrain and to tame their victim, behold them now crouching before one Man, who had never been in that region before, trembling as in the presence of their Judge, conscious that His word, whatever it be, must be law to them, and meekly petitioning, as servants of a master, to be allowed to enter a lower class of victims on letting go their long-secure prey! But the majesty of that word "Go!"—what conscious power over the whole kingdom of darkness does it display! Then their instant obedience, the perfect liberation of the poor demoniac, and the rage and rout with which they rushed upon the creatures they had selected to destroy—all at the word of this Man, newly arrived on the shores of Gadara! But this display of power and majesty Divine was crowned and irradiated by the grace which brought the grateful captive, now set free, to the feet of his Deliverer. What a spectacle was that, on which the eye of all heaven might have rested with wonder—the wild creature, "driven of the devil into the wilderness," whom no man could tame, "sitting at the feet of Jesus;" the man who walked naked, and was not ashamed—like our first parents in Paradise, but, ah! for how different a reason—now "clothed;" the frightful maniac, now "in his right mind," and in an attitude of mute admiration and gratitude and love, at his great Deliverer's feet! Blessed Saviour—fairer than the children of men, yet Thyself the Son of Man—we worship Thee, and yet are not afraid to come near unto Thee: we fall down before Thee, yet we embrace Thee. The Word is God, but the Word has been made flesh and dwells, and will for ever dwell, among us; and of Thy fulness have all we received, who have tasted that Thou art gracious, and grace for grace! 2. Observe the complicated evil which the powers of darkness inflicted on their victim. They deprived him of the exercise of his rational powers; they so lashed his spirit that he could not suffer even a garment upon his body, but went naked, and could not endure the sight of living men and social comfort, but dwelt among the tombs, as if the sepulchral gloom had a mysterious congeniality with the wretchedness of his spirit; they allowed him not a moment's repose even there, for "*always, night and day*, he was in the mountains and in the tombs, crying"—his ceaseless misery venting itself in wild wailing cries; nay, so intolerable was his mental torture, that he "kept cutting himself with stones!"—the *natural* explanation of which seems to be, that one in this state is fain to draw off his feelings from the *mind*, when its anguish grows unendurable, by trying to make the *body*, thus lacerated and smarting, to bear its own share. One other feature of the evil, thus diabolically inflicted, is very significant—"No man could tame him; for he had been often bound with fetters and chains, and the chains had been plucked asunder by him, and the fetters broken in pieces!" And now, suppose ye that this man was a sinner above all sinners, because he suffered such things? Nay (see Luke xiii. 2, 3); but thus was it designed that on the theatre of the *body* we should see affectingly exhibited what the powers of darkness are, when uncontrolled, and what men have to expect from them when once given into their hand! Human *reason* they cannot abide, for it is a light shining full upon their own darkness. Human *liberty*, which is one with *law*, in its highest state—"the perfect *law* of *liberty*"—this they hate, substituting for it a wild anarchy, that can submit to no rational control. Human *peace* they cannot endure, for they have lost their own—"There is no peace to the wicked." For the same reason, human *comfort*, in any the least and lowest of its forms, they will never leave, if they can take it away. And over the howlings and self-inflicted tortures of their maddened victims they sing the dance of death, saying to all their complaints and appeals for sympathy, with the chief priests to Judas, "What is that to us? see thou to that!" 3. Is it so? Then, O the blessedness of being delivered from the power of darkness, and "translated into the Kingdom of God's dear Son"! (Col. i. 13). Till then we are as helpless captives of "the rulers of the darkness of this world, the spirit that now worketh in the children of disobedience," as was this poor demoniac before Jesus came to him. The strong man armed guardeth his palace, and his goods are in peace, until the Stronger than he doth come upon him, and taketh from him all his armour, dividing his spoil (Luke xi. 21, 22). It is a deadly struggle between Heaven and Hell for the possession of man. Only, since Demoniacal possession deprives its victims of their personal consciousness, rational considerations are not in the least instrumental to their deliverance, which must come by a sheer act of divine power; whereas the *soul* is rescued from the tyranny of Satan by the eyes of the understanding being divinely opened to see its wretched condition and descry the remedy, and the heart being drawn

21 And *when Jesus was passed over again by ship unto the other side,
22 much people gathered unto him: and he was nigh unto the sea. And,
*behold, there cometh one of the rulers of the synagogue, Jairus by name;
23 and when he saw him, he fell at his feet, and besought him greatly, saying,
My little daughter lieth at the point of death: *I pray thee,* come and
24 lay thy hands on her, that she may be healed; and she shall live. And
Jesus went with him; and much people followed him, and thronged
him.
25 And a certain woman, *k*which had an issue of blood twelve years,
26 and had suffered many things of many physicians, and had spent all that
27 she had, and *l*was nothing bettered, but rather grew worse, when she had

A. D. 31.

i Gen. 49.10.
Matt. 9. 1.
Luke 8. 37.
j Matt. 9. 18.
Luke 8. 40.
Luke 8.14.
Acts 13. 15.
Acts 18. 8,
17.
k Lev. 15. 25.
Matt. 9.20.
Luke 8. 43.
l Ps. 108. 12.

willingly to embrace it. "The God of this world hath blinded the minds of them that believe not, lest the light of the glorious Gospel of Christ, who is the image of God, should shine unto them. But God, who commanded the light to shine out of darkness, shines in our hearts, to give the light of the knowledge of the glory of God in the face of Jesus Christ" (2 Cor. iv. 4, 6). Thus are we, in our deliverance from the power of Satan and of sin, sweetly voluntary, while the deliverance itself is as truly divine as when Jesus uttered His majestic "Go" to the demons of darkness and the demoniac was freed. 4. In this grateful soul's petition to be with Jesus, we see the clinging feeling of all Christ's freed-men towards Himself; while in his departure, when Jesus suggested something better, and in his itinerary through Decapolis with the story of his deliverance, himself a living story of the grace and power of the Lord Jesus, we may read these words:—*The liberated believer a missionary for Christ!* 5. As Christ took those wretched Gadarenes at their word, when they besought Him to depart out of their coasts, so it is to be feared He still does to not a few who, when He comes to them in mercy, bid Him away. Will not awakened sinners dread this, and welcome Him whilst it is called To-day?

21-43.—THE DAUGHTER OF JAIRUS RAISED TO LIFE—THE WOMAN WITH AN ISSUE OF BLOOD HEALED. (= Matt. ix. 18-26; Luke viii. 41-56.) The occasion of this scene will appear presently.

Jairus' Daughter (21-24). 21. And when Jesus was passed over again by ship unto the other side—from the Gadarene side of the lake, where He had parted with the healed demoniac, to the west side, at Capernaum — much people gathered unto him—who "gladly received Him; for they were all waiting for Him" (Luke viii. 40). The abundant teaching of that day (ch. iv. 1, &c., and Matt. xiii.) had only whetted the people's appetite; and disappointed, as would seem, that He had left them in the evening to cross the lake, they remain hanging about the beach, having got a hint, probably through some of His disciples, that He would be back the same evening. Perhaps they witnessed at a distance the sudden calming of the tempest. The tide of our Lord's popularity was now fast rising. and he was nigh unto the sea. 22. And, behold, there cometh one of the rulers of the synagogue—of which class there were but few who believed in Jesus (John vii. 48). One would suppose from this that the ruler had been with the multitude on the shore, anxiously awaiting the return of Jesus, and immediately on His arrival had accosted Him as here related. But Matthew (ix. 18) tells us that the ruler came to Him while He was in the act of speaking at his own table on the subject of fasting; and as we must suppose that this converted publican ought to know what took place on that memorable occasion when he made a feast to his

Lord, we conclude that here the right order is indicated by the First Evangelist alone. Jairus by name ['Ιάειρος]—or 'Jaeirus.' It is the same name as *Jair,* in the Old Testament (Num. xxxii. 41; Jud. x. 3; Esth. ii. 5). and when he saw him, he fell at his feet—in Matthew (ix. 18), "worshipped Him." The meaning is the same in both. 23. And besought him greatly, saying, My little daughter [θυγάτριον]. Luke (viii. 42) says, "He had one only daughter, about twelve years of age." According to a well-known rabbin, quoted by *Lightfoot,* a daughter, till she had completed her twelfth year, was called 'little,' or 'a little maid;' after that, ' a young woman.' lieth at the point of death. Matthew gives it thus: "My daughter is even now dead" [ἄρτι ἐτελεύτησεν]—'has just expired.' The news of her death reached the father after the cure of the woman with the issue of blood; but Matthew's brief account gives only the *result,* as in the case of the centurion's servant, (Matt. viii. 5, &c.) come and lay thy hands on her, that she may be healed; .and she shall live [ζήσεται]—or, 'that she may be healed and live' [ζήσῃ], according to a fully preferable reading. In one of the class to which this man belonged, so steeped in prejudice, such faith would imply more than in others.

The Woman with an Issue of Blood Healed (24-34). 24. And Jesus went with him; and much people followed him, and thronged him [συνέθλιβον]. The word in Luke is stronger [συνέπνιγον]—'choked,' 'stifled Him.' 25. And a certain woman, which had an issue of blood twelve years, 26. And had suffered many things of many physicians [πολλὰ παθοῦσα]. The expression perhaps does not necessarily refer to the suffering she endured under medical treatment, but to the much varied treatment which she underwent. and had spent all that she had, and was nothing bettered, but rather grew worse. Pitiable case, and affectingly aggravated; emblem of our natural state as fallen creatures (Ezek. xvi. 5, 6), and illustrating the worse than vanity of all human remedies for spiritual maladies (Hos. v. 13). The higher design of all our Lord's miracles of healing irresistibly suggests this way of viewing the present case, the propriety of which will still more appear as we proceed. 27. When she had heard of Jesus, came. This was the right experiment at last. What had she "heard of Jesus"? No doubt it was His marvellous cures she had heard of; and the hearing of these, in connection with her bitter experience of the vanity of applying to any other, had been blessed to the kindling in her soul of a firm confidence that He who had so willingly wrought such cures on others was able and would not refuse to heal her also. in the press behind—shrinking, yet seeking, and touched his garment. According to the ceremonial law, the touch of any one having the disease which this woman had would have defiled the person touched. Some think that the

28 heard of Jesus, came in the press behind, and ^mtouched his garment. For
29 she said, If I may touch but his clothes, I shall be whole. And ⁿstraight-
way the fountain of her blood was dried up; and she felt in *her* body that
30 she was healed of that plague. And Jesus, immediately knowing in
himself that ^ovirtue had gone out of him, turned him about in the press,
31 and said, Who touched my clothes? And his disciples said unto him,
Thou seest the multitude thronging thee, and sayest thou, Who touched
32 me? And he looked round about to see her that had done this thing.
33 But the woman, fearing and trembling, knowing what was done in her,
34 came and fell down before him, and told him all the truth. And he said
unto her, Daughter, ^pthy faith hath made thee whole; go in peace, and
be whole of thy plague.
35 While ^qhe yet spake, there came from the ruler of the synagogue's
house certain which said, Thy daughter is dead: why troublest thou the
36 Master any further? As soon as Jesus heard the word that was spoken,
he saith unto the ruler of the synagogue, ^rBe not afraid, only believe.
37 And he suffered no man to follow him, save Peter, and James, and John
38 the brother of James. And he cometh to the house of the ruler of the
synagogue, and seeth the tumult, and them that wept and wailed greatly.

A. D. 31.
^m ch. 3. 10.
Acts 5. 15.
Acts 19. 12.
ⁿ Ex. 15. 26.
Luke 6. 19.
Luke 8. 46.
^o Luke 6. 19.
Luke 8. 46.
^p Matt. 9. 22.
ch. 10. 52.
Luke 7. 50.
Luke 8. 48.
Luke 17.19.
Luke 18. 42.
Acts 14. 9.
^q Luke 8 49.
^r 2 Chr.20.20.
Ps. 103. 13.
Matt. 9. 23,
29.
Matt. 17.20.
Luke 8. 50.
John 11. 25,
40.

recollection of this may account for her stealthily approaching Him in the crowd behind, and touching but the hem of His garment. But there was an instinct in the faith which brought her to Jesus, which taught her, that if that touch could set her free from the defiling disease itself, it was impossible to communicate defilement to Him, and that this wondrous Healer must be above such laws. **28. For she said**—"within herself" (Matt. ix. 21), **If I may touch but his clothes, I shall be whole**—that is, if I may but *come in contact* with this glorious Healer *at all.* Remarkable faith this! **29. And straightway the fountain of her blood was dried up.** Not only was "her issue of blood stanched" (Luke viii. 44), but the cause of it was thoroughly removed, insomuch that by her bodily sensations she immediately knew herself perfectly cured. **and she felt in her body that she was healed of that plague. 30. And Jesus, immediately knowing in himself that virtue**—or 'efficacy' [δύναμιν]—**had gone out of him.** He was conscious of the forth-going of His healing power, which was not—as in prophets and apostles—something *foreign to Himself* and imparted merely, but what He had *dwelling within Him* as "His own fulness." **turned him about in the press**—'or crowd' [ἐν τῷ ὄχλῳ]—**and said, Who touched my clothes? 31. And his disciples said unto him.** Luke says (viii. 45), "When all denied, Peter and they that were with Him, said, Master" ['Επιστάτα], **Thou seest the multitude thronging thee, and sayest thou, Who touched me?** 'Askest thou, Lord, who touched Thee? Rather ask who touched Thee *not* in such a throng.' "And Jesus said, Somebody hath touched me"—'a certain person hath touched Me ["Ηψατό μου τίς], "for I perceive that virtue is gone out of Me" (Luke viii. 46). Yes, the multitude "*thronged* and *pressed* Him"—they *jostled against* Him, but all *involuntarily;* they were merely *carried along;* but one, one only—"a certain person—TOUCHED HIM," with the conscious, voluntary, dependent touch of faith, reaching forth its hand expressly to have contact with Him. This and this only Jesus acknowledges and seeks out. Even so, as *Augustin* long ago said, *multitudes still come similarly close to Christ in the means of grace, but all to no purpose, being only sucked into the crowd.* The voluntary, living contact of faith is that electric conductor which alone draws virtue out of Him.

32. And he looked round about to see her that had done this thing—not for the purpose of summoning forth a culprit, but, as we shall presently see, to obtain from the healed one a testimony to what He had done for her. **33. But the woman, fearing and trembling, knowing what was done in her**—alarmed, as a humble, shrinking female would naturally be, at the necessity of so public an exposure of herself, yet conscious that she had a tale to tell which would speak for her. **came and fell down before him, and told him all the truth.** In Luke (viii. 47) it is, "When the woman saw that she was not hid, she came trembling, and falling down before Him, she declared unto Him before all the people for what cause she had touched Him, and how she was healed immediately." This, though it tried the modesty of the believing woman, was just what Christ wanted in dragging her forth, her public testimony to the facts of her case—the disease with her abortive efforts at a cure, and the instantaneous and perfect relief which her touching the Great Healer had brought her. **34. And he said unto her, Daughter**—"be of good comfort" (Luke viii. 48), **thy faith hath made thee whole; go in peace, and be whole of thy plague.** Though healed as soon as she believed, it seemed to her a stolen cure—she feared to acknowledge it. Jesus therefore sets His royal seal upon it. But what a glorious dismissal from the lips of Him who is "our Peace" is that, "Go in peace!"

Jairus' Daughter Raised to Life (35-43). **35. While he yet spake, there came from the ruler of the synagogue's house certain which said, Thy daughter is dead: why troublest thou the Master**—'the Teacher' [τὸν Διδάσκαλον]—**any further? 36. As soon as Jesus heard the word that was spoken, he saith unto the ruler of the synagogue, Be not afraid, only believe.** Jesus knowing how the heart of the agonized father would sink at the tidings, and the reflections at the *delay* which would be apt to rise in his mind, hastens to reassure him, and in His accustomed style; "Be not afraid, only believe"—words of unchanging preciousness and power! How vividly do such incidents bring out Christ's knowledge of the human heart and tender sympathy! (Heb. iv. 15). **37. And he suffered no man to follow him, save Peter, and James, and John the brother of James.** See on ch. i. 29. **38. And he cometh—**rather 'they

39 And when he was come in, he saith unto them, Why make ye this ado,
40 and weep? the damsel is not dead, but *sleepeth. And they laughed
him to scorn. ᵗBut when he had put them all out, he taketh the father
and the mother of the damsel, and them that were with him, and entereth
41 in where the damsel was lying. And he took the damsel by the hand,
and said unto her, Talitha cumi; which is, being interpreted, Damsel, I
42 say unto thee, arise. And ᵘstraightway the damsel arose, and walked;
for she was *of the age* of twelve years. And they were astonished with a
43 great astonishment. And ᵛhe charged them straitly that no man should
know it; and commanded that something should be given her to eat.

A D. 31.

* John 11.11.
Acts 20. 10.
1 Cor. 1I.
30.
1 Thes.4.14.
1 Thes.5.10.
ᵗ Acts 9. 40.
ᵘ Ps. 33. 9.
ᵛ Matt. 12.16.
Matt. 17. 9.
ch. 3. 12.
Luke 5. 14.

come' [ἔρχονται has much better support than ἔρχεται]—to the house of the ruler of the synagogue, and seeth the tumult, and them that wept and wailed greatly—" the minstrels and the people making a noise" (Matt. ix. 23)—lamenting for the dead. (See 2 Chr. xxxv. 25; Jer. ix. 20, Am. v. 16.) 39. And when he was come in, he saith unto them, Why make ye this ado, and weep? the damsel is not dead, but sleepeth—so brief her state of death as to be more like a short sleep. 40. And they laughed him to scorn [κατεγέλων αὐτοῦ]—rather, simply, 'laughed at Him'—"knowing that she was dead" (Luke viii. 53); an important testimony this to the reality of her death. But when he had put them all out. The word is strong [ἐκβαλὼν]—'when he had put,' or 'turned them all out;' meaning all those who were making this noise, and any others that may have been there from sympathy, that only those might be present who were most nearly concerned, and those whom He had Himself brought as witnesses of the great act about to be done. he taketh the father and the mother of the damsel, and them that were with him (Peter, and James, and John), and entereth in where the damsel was lying. 41. And he took the damsel by the hand—as He did Peter's mother-in-law (ch. i. 31)—and said unto her, Talitha cumi. The words are Aramaic, or Syro-Chaldaic, the then language of Palestine. Mark loves to give such wonderful words just as they were spoken. See ch. vii. 34; xiv. 36. [' Cūm' is evidently the true reading, being the popular form of the other, to which it has been corrected as the more accurate form =טַלְיְתָא קוּמִי]. 42. And straightway the damsel [τὸ κοράσιον]. The word here is different from that in vv. 39, 40, 41 [τὸ παιδίον], and signifies 'young maiden,' or ' little girl.' arose, and walked—a vivid touch evidently from an eye-witness—for she was of the age of twelve years. And they were astonished with a great astonishment [ἐξέστησαν ἐκστάσει μεγάλῃ]. The language here is the strongest. 43. And he charged them straitly—or strictly, that no man should know it. The only reason we can assign for this is His desire not to let the public feeling regarding Him come too precipitately to a crisis. and commanded that something should be given her to eat—in token of perfect restoration.

Remarks.—1. Burdened soul, wearied and wasted with an inward malady which has baffled every human specific, and forced thee to say from bitter experience of those who have recommended change of air and scene, business, pleasure, travel, and the like—' Miserable comforters are ye all, forgers of lies, physicians of no value!' hast thou not "heard of Jesus"—what miracles of healing, what wonders of transformation He has wrought in some of the most obstinate and hopeless cases; opening blind eyes, casting out devils, cleansing lepers, making the lame man to leap as an hart, and the tongue of the dumb to sing? Bring thy case to Him at last, and doubt not His power to

bring thee a perfect cure who said to such as Thou, "They that be whole need not a physician: I came not to call the righteous, but sinners." But thou art afraid to show thyself, lest they who knew thy reckless life should say of thee jeeringly, Is Saul also among the prophets? Come, then, in the press behind, and do but touch Him, and thou shalt instantly feel the virtue that has gone out of Him. It needeth not a close embrace, or vehement handling, or much ado. It is *living contact*, the simple *touch of faith*, that fetches out the healing virtue. And it will tell its own tale. Thou shalt know the difference between Christ and all other healers; and when Jesus calls for thy testimony to His power and grace, thou shalt have something to say, thou shalt have a tale to tell, which will glorify His name and be His desired reward; thou shalt be fain to say, "Come, all ye that fear God, and I will declare what He hath done for my soul." 2. Dumb debtors to healing mercy, be rebuked by the narrative of the Lord's procedure towards this healed woman. He suffered her not, as doubtless she would have preferred, to depart in silence, to pour out her secret thanksgivings, or at some private meeting to testify her love to Jesus. He would have her, in spite of her shrinking modesty, to come forward before all and declare what she had done and how she had sped. Thus, in her own way, was she a preacher of Christ. And such witness will He have from all His saved ones. "If thou shalt *confess with thy mouth* the Lord Jesus, and believe in thine heart that God hath raised Him from the dead, thou shalt be saved." 3. Amidst the multitudes who crowd—with no spiritual desires and to no saving purpose—around the Saviour, in the services of His house and the profession of His name, He discerns the timid, tremulous touch of faith in even one believing soul, and is conscious of the healing virtue which that touch has drawn resistlessly forth from Him. What encouragement this to such as fear that their worthless feelings and poor exercises will have no interest for Him; and what a warning to those who, without wanting anything from Him, suffer themselves to be sucked into the current of those who follow Him and crowd about Him—not to set any store by this, as if it would draw more of Christ's regard towards them at the great day than if they had never heard of His name. (See on Luke xiii. 26, 27.) For see how, taking no notice of all that thronged Him and pressed upon Him on this occasion, He exclaimed of this humble, believing woman, "Some *one* hath touched Me." 4. If the Lord Jesus was so tender and considerate of human feelings as to anticipate this believing ruler's regret that by being so slow of coming to him his darling child had been allowed to die—bidding him, "Fear not, only believe"—just as He had before quelled the storm ere He rebuked the unbelief of His disciples in the view of it (see on *v.* 24)—we may rest well assured that on the right hand of the Majesty in the heavens

6 AND [a]he went out from thence, and came into his own country; and
2 his disciples follow him. And when the sabbath day was come, he began
to teach in the synagogue: and many hearing *him* were astonished,
saying, [b]From whence hath this *man* these things? and what wisdom *is*
this which is given unto him, that even such mighty works are wrought
3 by his hands? Is [c]not this the carpenter, the son of Mary, [d]the brother
of James, and Joses, and of Juda, and Simon? and are not his sisters
4 here with us? And they [e]were offended at him. But Jesus said unto
them, [f]A prophet is not without honour, but in his own country, and
5 among his own kin, and in his own house. And [g]he could there do no
mighty work, save that he laid his hands upon a few sick folk, and healed
6 *them*. And [h]he marvelled because of their unbelief. [i]And he went
round about the villages, teaching.
7 And [j]he called *unto him* the twelve, and began to send them forth by
8 two and two; and gave them power over unclean spirits; and commanded
them that they should take nothing for *their* journey, save a staff only;
9 no scrip, no bread, no [1]money in *their* purse: but [k]be shod with sandals;
10 and not put on two coats. And [l]he said unto them, In what place soever
11 ye enter into an house, there abide till ye depart from that place. And
[m]whosoever shall not receive you, nor hear you, when ye depart thence,
shake [n]off the dust under your feet for a testimony against them. [o]Verily
I say unto you, It shall be more tolerable for Sodom [2]and Gomorrha in
12 the day of judgment, than for that city. And they went out, and
13 preached that men should repent. And they cast out many devils, [p]and
anointed with oil many that were sick, and healed *them*.
14 And [q]king Herod heard *of him;* (for his name was spread abroad:) and
he said, That John the Baptist was risen from the dead, and therefore
15 mighty works do show forth themselves in him. Others [r]said, That it is
Elias. And others said, That it is a prophet, or as one of the prophets.
16 But [s]when Herod heard *thereof*, he said, It is John, whom I beheaded:
he is risen from the dead.
17 For Herod himself had sent forth and laid hold upon John, and

A. D. 31.

CHAP. 6.
[a] Matt. 13.54.
[b] John 6. 42.
[c] Isa. 53. 2, 3.
[d] Matt. 12.46.
[e] Matt. 11. 6.
[f] Matt. 13.57.
[g] Gen. 19. 22.
[h] Isa. 59. 1, 2, 16.
[i] Matt. 9. 35.
[j] Matt. 10. 1.
[1] The word signifieth a piece of brass money, in value somewhat less than a farthing, Matt. 10. 9: but here it is taken in general for money.
Luke 9. 3.
[k] Acts 12. 8.
[l] Matt. 10.11. Luke 9. 4.
[m] Matt. 10.14. Luke 10.10.
[n] Acts 13. 51.
[o] Heb. 10. 31.
[2] or.
[p] Jas. 5. 14.
[q] Matt. 14. 1. Luke 9. 7.
[r] Matt 16.14. ch 8. 28.
[s] Luke 3. 19.

"we have not an High Priest which cannot be touched with the feeling of our infirmities," and that still, as in the days of His flesh, "He will not break the bruised reed." 5. Of the three resuscitations to life, recorded in the Gospel History, it is worthy of notice that one was *newly dead*—Jairus' daughter; another, *on his way to the grave*—the widow of Nain's son; and the third—Lazarus—was *dead four days*, was in his grave, insomuch that his sister said, "By this time he stinketh:" as if to teach us that it matters not how long we have lain in the state of death—whether three or four score years in spiritual death, or thousands of years in death temporal—the Spirit of life in Christ Jesus is as able to quicken us at one stage as at another. "Said I not unto thee, that, if thou wouldest believe, thou shouldest see the glory of God? I am the Resurrection and the Life: he that believeth in Me, though he were dead, yet shall he live: and he that liveth and believeth in Me shall never die." 6. Though when the classical writers (euphemistically) liken death to a sleep, we may please ourselves with the hope that the gleams of a future state were never quite extinguished in the heathen mind, it is only in the light of this incomparable Gospel History, interpreted by the teaching of the Pentecostal Gift, that faith hears Jesus saying of every dead believer of the one sex, "The damsel is not dead, but sleepeth," and of the other, "Our friend Lazarus sleepeth; but I go, that I may awake him out of sleep."

CHAP. VI. 1-6.—CHRIST REJECTED AT NAZARETH. (= Matt. xiii. 54-58; Luke iv. 16-30.) For the exposition, see on Luke iv. 16-30.
7-13.—MISSION OF THE TWELVE APOSTLES. (= Matt. x. 1, 5-15; Luke ix. 1-6.) For the exposition, see on Matt. x. 1, 5-15.
14-29.—HEROD THINKS JESUS A RESURRECTION OF THE MURDERED BAPTIST—ACCOUNT OF HIS DEATH. (= Matt. xiv. 1-12; Luke ix. 7-9.)
Herod's View of Christ (14-16). **14. And king Herod**—that is, Herod Antipas, one of the three sons of Herod the Great, and own brother of Archelaus (Matt. ii. 22), who ruled as *Ethnarch* over Galilee and Perea. **heard of him; (for his name was spread abroad:) and he said**—"unto his servants" (Matt. xiv. 2), his councillors or court-ministers, **That John the Baptist was risen from the dead, and therefore mighty works do show forth themselves in him.** The murdered prophet haunted his guilty breast like a spectre, and seemed to him alive again and clothed with unearthly powers, in the person of Jesus. **15. Others said, That it is Elias. And others, That it is a prophet, or as one of the prophets.** See on Matt. xvi. 14. **16. But when Herod heard thereof, he said, It is John, whom I beheaded: he is risen from the dead.** [αὐτὸς]—'Himself has risen;' as if the innocence and sanctity of his faithful reprover had not suffered that he should lie long dead.
Account of the Baptist's Imprisonment and Death (17-29). **17. For Herod himself had sent forth, and laid hold upon John, and bound him**

bound him in prison for Herodias' sake, his brother Philip's wife;
18 for he had married her. For John had said unto Herod, *t* It is not
19 lawful for thee to have thy brother's wife. Therefore Herodias had
3 a quarrel against him, and would have killed him; but she could not:
20 for Herod *u* feared John, knowing that he was a just man and an holy,
and *4* observed him; and when he heard him, he did many things,
21 and heard him gladly. And *v* when a convenient day was come, that
Herod, *w* on his birth day, made a supper to his lords, high captains, and
22 chief *estates* of Galilee; and when *x* the daughter of the said Herodias
came in, and danced, and pleased Herod and them that sat with him,
the king said unto the damsel, Ask of me whatsoever thou wilt, and I
23 will give *it* thee. And he sware unto her, *y* Whatsoever thou shalt ask
24 of me, I will give *it* thee, unto the half of my kingdom. And she went
forth, and said unto her mother, What shall I ask? And she said, The
25 *z* head of John the Baptist. And she came in straightway with haste
unto the king, and asked, saying, I will that thou give me by and by in
26 a charger the head of John the Baptist. And the king was exceeding
sorry; *yet* for his oath's sake, and for their sakes which sat with him, he
27 would not reject her. And immediately the king sent *5* an executioner,

A. D. 32.
t Lev. 18. 16.
Lev. 20. 21.
2 Sam. 12.7.
Dan. 5. 22,
23.
Eph. 5. 11.
2 Tim. 4. 2.
Heb. 13. 4.
3 Or. an inward grudge.
u Matt. 14. 5.
Matt. 21.26.
4 Or. kept him, or, saved him.
v Matt. 14. 6.
w Gen. 40. 20.
x Esth. 1. 11, 12
y Esth. 5. 3,6.
z Pro. 12. 10.
5 Or, one of his guard.

in prison—in the castle of Machærus, near the southern extremity of Herod's dominions, and adjoining the Dead Sea. (*Joseph.* Antt. xviii. 5, 2). **for Herodias' sake.** She was the grand-daughter of Herod the Great. **his brother Philip's wife**—and therefore the niece of both brothers. This Philip, however, was not the tetrarch of that name mentioned in Luke iii. 1 (see there), but one whose distinctive name was 'Herod Philip,' another son of Herod the Great, who was disinherited by his father. Herod Antipas's own wife was the daughter of Aretas, king of Arabia; but he prevailed on Herodias, his half-brother Philip's wife, to forsake her husband and live with him, on condition, says *Josephus* (Antt. xviii. 5,1), that he should put away his own wife. This involved him afterwards in war with Aretas, who totally defeated him and destroyed his army, from the effects of which he was never able to recover himself. **18. For John had said unto Herod, It is not lawful for thee to have thy brother's wife.** Noble fidelity! It was not lawful, because Herod's wife and Herodias' husband were both living; and further, because the parties were within the forbidden degrees of consanguinity (see Lev. xx. 21); Herodias being the daughter of Aristobulus, the brother of both Herod and Philip (*Joseph.* xviii. 5, 4). **19. Therefore Herodias had a quarrel against him** [ἐνεῖχεν αὐτῷ]—rather, as in the margin, 'had a grudge against him.' Probably she was too proud to speak to him: still less would she quarrel with him, **and would have killed him; but she could not: 20 For Herod feared John**—but, as *Bengel* notes, John feared not Herod. **knowing that he was a just man and an holy.** Compare the case of Elijah with Ahab, after the murder of Naboth (1 Ki. xxi. 20). **and observed him** [συνετήρει αὐτὸν]—rather, as in the margin, 'kept' or 'saved him:' that is, from the wicked designs of Herodias, who had been watching for some pretext to get Herod entangled and committed to despatch him. **and when he heard him, he did many things**—many good things under the influence of the Baptist on his conscience; **and heard him gladly**—a striking statement this, for which we are indebted to our graphic Evangelist alone; illustrating the working of contrary principles in the slaves of passion. But this only shows how far Herodias must have wrought upon him, as Jezebel upon Ahab, that he should at length agree to what his

awakened conscience kept him long from executing. **21. And when a convenient day** (for the purposes of Herodias) **was come, that Herod** [γενομένης ἡμέρας εὐκαίρου, ὅτε]—rather, 'A convenient day being come, when Herod,' **on his birth day, made a supper to his lords, high captains and chief [estates] of Galilee.** This graphic minuteness of detail adds much to the interest of the tragic narrative. **22. And when the daughter of the said Herodias**—that is, her daughter by her proper husband, Herod Philip: Her name was Salome, (*Joseph.* Ib.) **came in, and danced, and pleased Herod and them that sat with him, the king said unto the damsel** [κορασίῳ]—'the girl.' (See on ch. v. 42.) **Ask of me whatsoever thou wilt, and I will give it thee. 23. And he**—the king, so called, but only by courtesy (see on *v.* 14)—**sware unto her, Whatsoever thou shalt ask of me, unto the half of my kingdom.** Those in whom passion and luxury have destroyed self-command will in a capricious moment say and do what in their cool moments they bitterly regret. **24. And she went forth, and said unto her mother, What shall I ask? And she said, The head of John the Baptist.** Abandoned women are more shameless and heartless than men. The Baptist's fidelity marred the pleasures of Herodias, and this was too good an opportunity of getting rid of him to let slip. **25. And she came in straightway with haste unto the king, and asked, saying, I will that thou give me by and by** [ἐξ αὐτῆς]—rather, 'at once,' **in a charger**—or large flat 'trencher' [πίνακι]—**the head of John the Baptist. 26. And the king was exceeding sorry.** With his feelings regarding John, and the truths which so told upon his conscience from that preacher's lips, and after so often and carefully saving him from his paramour's rage, it must have been very galling to find himself at length entrapped by his own rash folly. **yet for his oath's sake.** See how men of no principle, but troublesome conscience, will stick at breaking a rash oath, while yielding to the commission of the worst crimes! **and for their sakes which sat with him**—under the influence of that false shame, which could not brook being thought to be troubled with religious or moral scruples. To how many has this proved a fatal snare! **he would not reject her. 27. And immediately the king sent an executioner** [σπεκουλάτωρα—the true

and commanded his head to be brought: and he went and beheaded him 28 in the prison, and brought his head in a charger, and gave it to the 29 damsel: and the damsel gave it to her mother.   And when his disciples heard *of it*, they came and *ª*took up his corpse, and laid it in a tomb.

reading is evidently σπεκουλάτορα]—one of the guards in attendance.   The word is Roman, denoting one of the Imperial guard. **and commanded his head to be brought: and he went and beheaded him in the prison**—after, it would seem, more than twelve months' imprisonment. Blessed martyr.   Dark and cheerless was the end reserved for thee; but now thou hast thy Master's benediction, "Blessed is he whosoever shall not be offended in Me" (Matt. xi. 6), and hast found the life thou gavest away (Matt. x. 39).   But where are they in whose skirts is found thy blood? **28. And brought thy head in a charger, and gave it to the damsel: and the damsel gave it to her mother.** Herodias did not shed the blood of the stern reprover; she only got it done, and then gloated over it, as it streamed from the trunkless head.   The striking analogy to this in the Church of Rome will be noticed in Remark 3, below. **29. And when his disciples heard of it**—that is, the Baptist's own disciples, **they came and took up his corpse, and laid it in a tomb**—"and went and told Jesus" (Matt. xiv. 12).   If these disciples had, up to this time, stood apart from Him, as adherents of John (Matt. xi. 2), perhaps they now came to Jesus, not without some secret reflection on Him for His seeming neglect of their master: but perhaps, too, as orphans, to cast in their lot henceforth with the Lord's disciples.   How Jesus felt, or what He said, on receiving this intelligence, is not recorded; but He of whom it was said, as He stood by the grave of His friend Lazarus, "Jesus wept," was not likely to receive such intelligence without deep emotion.   And one reason why He might not be unwilling that a small body of John's disciples should cling to him to the last, might be to provide some attached friends who should do for his precious body, on a small scale, what was afterwards to be done for His own.

Remarks—1. The truth of the Gospel History is strikingly illustrated in this Section.   Had the Life of Christ which it contains been a literary invention, instead of a historical reality, the last thing probably which the writers would have thought of would have been to terminate the life of His honoured forerunner in the way here recorded.   When we read it, we at once feel that, to be written, it must have been real.   But we turn to the Jewish historian, and in his Antiquities of his nation we find precisely the same account of the Baptist's character, his fidelity to Herod, and his death, which is here given—with just this difference, that *Josephus*, as might be expected, presents rather the public bearings of this event, while our Evangelists treat it solely with reference to the Baptist's connection with his blessed Master. Thus each throws light upon the other. 2. When men in power connect themselves, whether by marriage or otherwise, with unprincipled women, they usually become their tools, and are not unfrequently dragged by them to ruin.   Illustrations of this are furnished by history, from the days of that accursed Jezebel, who first drew Ahab into the commission of treason against the God of Israel and the murder of his own subjects, and then hurried him to destruction; and of Herodias, who was the means of imbruing the hands of Herod Antipas in the blood of the saintly Baptist, and

was the occasion of that war which proved so fatal to him, down to pretty modern times. And might not the working of the same passions to similar issues be seen in the history of less exalted persons, if only it were written?   A warning this, surely, against such unhallowed unions. 3. When we read of Herodias, how she shed, not with her own hand nor by her own immediate order, the blood of this faithful witness for the truth, but only got it done by the secular arm, and how she then gloated over it—we can hardly help thinking that, when the harlot-Church was depicted by the apocalyptic seer, as a "woman drunken with the blood of the saints, and with the blood of the martyrs of Jesus" (Rev. xvii. 6), this bloody adulteress, Herodias, must have sat for her picture.   For the apocalyptic woman does not herself shed the blood of saints or martyrs, nor order them to be slain; it is "the beast"—the secular power of apostate Christendom—that makes war against the saints, the faithful witnesses for the truth, and overcomes them, and kills them (Rev. xi. 7; xiii. 7).   But yet the "woman" rides this beast, seen as a scarlet-coloured, or bloody, beast (Rev. xvii. 6); the secular power acting according to her dictates, in ridding her of those hateful witnesses against her abominations as a horse obeys his rider; while she herself is represented as drunken with their blood—revelling in her freedom from their withering rebukes.   Can so vivid and deep an analogy be quite accidental? 4. Fidelity in testifying against sin, though sometimes rewarded here, is not unfrequently allowed to be borne at the cost of temporal interests, liberty, and even life itself.   How easily could He who healed the sick, cleansed the lepers, opened blind eyes, and raised even the dead to life, have interposed for the rescue of His true-hearted servant from the rage of Herodias, that he should not have been deprived of his liberty, and at least that his precious life should be spared!   But He did not do it.   Instead of this He suffered His public career to be closed by arrest and imprisonment; and after lying long in prison, and without any light as to his prospects—in answer to a deputation which he sent expressly from his prison —He allowed him to seal his testimony with his blood in that gloomy cell, with none to comfort him, and none to witness the deed but the bloody executioner, as if to proclaim to his servants in all time what He had bidden the messengers say to himself, "Blessed is he whosoever shall not be offended in Me."   How noble was the answer of the three Hebrew youths to King Nebuchadnezzar, when he threatened them with the burning fiery furnace if they would not fall down and worship the golden image which he had set up—"If it be so, our God whom we serve is able to deliver us from the burning fiery furnace; and he will deliver us out of thine hand, O king. *But if not,* be it known unto thee, O king, that we will not serve thy gods," &c. (Dan. iii. 17, 18).   They had full confidence that deliverance would be vouchsafed for the honour of Jehovah's name.   But they might in that be mistaken; He might not see it fit to interpose; and "*if not,*" then they were prepared to burn for Him: but that, deliverance or none, they were resolved not to sin.   And that is the spirit in which all Christ's servants should take up their

30   And ^bthe apostles gathered themselves together unto Jesus, and told him all things, both what they had done, and what they had taught.

31 And ^che said unto them, Come ye yourselves apart into a desert place, and rest a while: for ^dthere were many coming and going, and they had

32 no leisure so much as to eat. And they departed into a desert place by ship privately.

33   And the people saw them departing, and many knew him, and ran afoot thither out of all cities, and outwent them, and came together

34 unto him. And ^eJesus, when he came out, saw much people, and was moved with compassion toward them, because they were as sheep not having a shepherd: and ^fhe began to teach them many things.

35   And ^gwhen the day was now far spent, his disciples came unto him,

36 and said, This is a desert place, and now the time *is* far passed: send

A. D. 32.
b Luke 9. 10.
c Matt. 14.13.
John 6. 1.
d ch. 3. 20.
e Ps. 86. 15.
Ps 111. 4.
Ps. 145. 8.
Matt. 9. 36.
Matt. 14.14.
Heb. 4. 15.
Heb. 5. 2.
f Isa. 54. 13.
Isa. 61. 1.
Luke 9. 11.
g Matt. 14.15.
Luke 9. 12.

---

cross; prepared to be nailed to it, if necessary, which it may or may not be—they cannot tell—rather than prove faithless to the Lord Jesus.

30-56.—THE TWELVE, ON THEIR RETURN, HAV-ING REPORTED THE SUCCESS OF THEIR MISSION, JESUS CROSSES THE SEA OF GALILEE WITH THEM, TEACHES THE PEOPLE, AND MIRACULOUSLY FEEDS THEM TO THE NUMBER OF FIVE THOUSAND—HE SENDS HIS DISCIPLES BY SHIP AGAIN TO THE WES-TERN SIDE, WHILE HIMSELF RETURNS AFTER-WARDS WALKING ON THE SEA—INCIDENTS ON LANDING. (=Matt. xiv. 13-36; Luke ix. 10-17; John vi. 1-24.)

Here, for the first time, all the four streams of sa-cred text run parallel. The occasion, and all the cir-cumstances of this grand Section are thus brought before us with a vividness quite remarkable.

Five Thousand Miraculously Fed (30-44). 30. **And the apostles gathered themselves together** —probably at Capernaum, on returning from their mission (*vv.* 7-13)—**and told him all things, both what they had done, and what they had taught. 31. And he said, Come ye yourselves apart into a desert place, and rest a while: for there were many coming and going, and they had no leisure so much as to eat.** Observe the various reasons He had for crossing to the other side. First, Matthew (xiv. 13) says, that "when Jesus heard" of the murder of His faithful forerunner—from those attached disciples of his who had taken up his body and laid it in a sepulchre (see on *v.* 29)—"He departed by ship into a desert place apart;" either to avoid some apprehended consequences to Himself, arising from the Baptist's death (Matt. x. 23), or more probably to be able to indulge in those feelings which that affecting event had doubtless awakened, and to which the bustle of the multitude around Him was very unfavourable. Next, since He must have heard the report of the Twelve with the deepest interest, and probably with something of the emotion which He experi-enced on the return of the Seventy (see on Luke x. 17-22), He sought privacy for undisturbed reflection on this begun preaching and progress of His kingdom. Once more, He was wearied with the multitude of "comers and goers"—depriving Him even of leisure enough to take His food—and wanted *rest:* "Come ye yourselves apart into a desert place, and rest a while," &c. Under the com-bined influence of all these considerations, our Lord sought this change. **32. And they departed into a desert place by ship privately**—"over the sea of Galilee, which is the sea of Tiberias," says John (vi. 1), the only one of the Evangelists who so fully describes it; the others having written when their readers were supposed to know something of it, while the last wrote for those at a greater distance of time and place. This "desert place" is more

definitely described by Luke (ix. 10) as "belonging to the city called Bethsaida." This must not be confounded with the town so called on the western side of the lake (see on Matt. xi. 21). This town lay on its north-eastern side, near where the Jordan empties itself into it; in Gaulonitis, out of the dominions of Herod Antipas, and within the dominions of Philip the Tetrarch (Luke iii. 1), who raised it from a village to a city, and called it *Julias*, in honour of Julia, the daughter of Augus-tus (*Joseph.* Antt. xviii. 2, 1).

33. And the people—'the multitudes' [οἱ ὄχλοι] **saw them departing, and many knew him.** The true reading would seem to be: 'And many saw them departing, and knew or recognized [them]'— [Καὶ εἶδον αὐτοὺς ὑπάγοντας καὶ ἐπέγνωσαν πολλοί], **and ran afoot** [πεζῇ]. Here, perhaps, it should be rendered 'by land'—running round by the head of the lake, and taking one of the fords of the river, so as to meet Jesus, who was crossing with the Twelve by ship. **thither out of all cities, and outwent them**—got before them, **and came together unto him.** How exceedingly graphic is this! every touch of it betokening the presence of an eye-witness. John (vi. 3) says, that "Jesus went up into a mountain"—somewhere in that hilly range, the green table-land which skirts the eastern side of the lake. **34. And Jesus, when he came out of the ship** [ἐξελθών]—'having gone on shore.' **saw much people**—'a great multitude' [πολὺν ὄχλον], **and was moved with compassion toward them, because they were as sheep not having a shepherd: and he began to teach them many things.** At the sight of the multitudes who had followed Him by land and even got before Him, He was so moved, as was His wont in such cases, with compassion, because they were like shepherdless sheep, as to forego both privacy and rest that He might minister to them. Here we have an important piece of information from the Fourth Evangelist (John vi. 4), "And the passover, a feast of the Jews, was nigh"—rather, 'Now the passover, the feast of the Jews [ἡ ἑορτή], was nigh.' This accounts for the multi-tudes that now crowded around Him. They were on their way to keep that festival at Jerusalem. But Jesus did not go up to this festival, as John expressly tells us (ch. vii. 1)—remaining in Galilee, because the ruling Jews sought to kill Him. **35. And when the day was now far spent**—"be-gan to wear away" or 'decline,' says Luke (ix. 12), [κλίνειν]. Matthew (xiv. 15) says, "when it was evening;" and yet he mentions a later evening of the same day (*v.* 23). This earlier evening began at three o'clock P.M.; the later began at sunset. **his disciples came unto him, and said, This is a desert place, and now the time is far passed:**

them away, that they may go into the country round about, and into the villages, and buy themselves bread: for they have nothing to eat.

37 He answered and said unto them, Give ye them to eat. And they say unto him, *h* Shall we go and buy two hundred [6]pennyworth of bread, and

38 give them to eat? He saith unto them, How many loaves have ye? go

39 and see. And when they knew, they say, *i* Five, and two fishes. And he commanded them to make all sit down [7]by companies upon the

40 green grass. And they sat down in ranks, by hundreds, and by fifties.

41 And when he had taken the five loaves and the two fishes, he looked up to heaven, and *j* blessed, and brake the loaves, and gave *them* to his disciples

42 to set before them; and the two fishes divided he among them all. And

43 they did all eat, and were filled. And they took up twelve baskets full of

44 the fragments, and of the fishes. And they that did eat of the loaves were about five thousand men.

45 And *k* straightway he constrained his disciples to get into the ship, and to go to the other side before [8]unto Bethsaida, while he sent away the

Right margin references:
A. D. 32.
h Num. 11. 13, 22.
[6] The Roman penny is sevenpence halfpenny. Matt. 18 28.
i Matt. 14. 17. Matt. 15. 34.
[7] banquets, banquets. 1 Cor. 14. 40.
j 1 Sam. 9. 13. Matt. 26. 26.
k Matt. 14. 22. John 6. 17.
[8] Or, over against Bethsaida.

---

36. Send them away, that they may go into the country round about, and into the villages, and buy themselves bread: for they have nothing to eat. John tells us (vi. 5, 6) that "Jesus said to Philip, Whence shall we buy bread, that these may eat? (And this He said to prove him: for He Himself knew what He would do.)" The subject may have been introduced by some remark of the disciples; but the precise order and form of what was said by each can hardly be gathered with precision, nor is it of any importance. **37. He answered and said unto them,** "They need not depart" (Matt. xiv. 16), **Give ye them to eat**—doubtless said to prepare them for what was to follow. **And they say unto him, Shall we go and buy two hundred pennyworth of bread, and give them to eat?** "Philip answered Him, Two hundred pennyworth of bread is not sufficient for them, that every one of them may take a little" (John vi. 7). **38. He saith unto them, How many loaves have ye? go and see. And when they knew, they say, Five, and two fishes.** John is more precise and full. "One of his disciples, Andrew, Simon Peter's brother, saith unto Him, There is a lad here which hath five barley loaves and two small fishes: but what are they among so many?" (John vi. 8, 9). Probably this was the whole stock of provisions then at the command of the disciples —no more than enough for one meal to them—and entrusted for the time to this lad. "He said, Bring them hither to me" (Matt. xiv. 18). **39. And he commanded them to make all sit down by companies upon the green grass** [ἐπὶ τῷ χλωρῷ χόρτῳ]—or 'green hay;' the rank grass of those bushy wastes. For, as John (vi. 10) notes, "there was much grass [χόρτος] in the place." **40. And they sat down in ranks, by hundreds, and by fifties.** Doubtless this was to show at a glance the number fed, and to enable all to witness in an orderly manner this glorious miracle. **41. And when he had taken the five loaves and the two fishes, he looked up to heaven.** Thus would the most distant of them see distinctly what He was doing. **and blessed** [εὐλόγησε]. John says, "And when He had given thanks" [εὐχαριστήσας]. The sense is the same. This thanksgiving for the meat, and benediction of it as the food of thousands, was the crisis of the miracle. **and brake the loaves, and gave them to his disciples to set before them**—thus virtually holding forth these men as His future ministers. **and the two fishes divided he among them all. 42. And they did all eat, and were**

filled. All the four Evangelists mention this; and John (vi. 11) adds, "and likewise of the fishes, as much as they would"—to show that vast as was the multitude, and scanty the provisions, the meal to each and all of them was a plentiful one. "When they were filled, He said unto His disciples, Gather up the fragments that remain, that nothing be lost" (John vi. 12). This was designed to bring out the whole extent of the miracle. **43. And they took up twelve baskets full of the fragments, and of the fishes.** "Therefore (says John vi. 13), they gathered them together, and filled twelve baskets with the fragments of the five barley loaves, which remained over and above unto them that had eaten." The article here rendered "baskets" [κόφινοι] in all the four narratives was part of the luggage taken by Jews on a journey—to carry, it is said, both their provisions and hay to sleep on, that they might not have to depend on Gentiles, and so run the risk of ceremonial pollution. In this we have a striking corroboration of the truth of the four narratives. Internal evidence renders it clear, we think, that the first three Evangelists wrote independently of each other, though the fourth must have seen all the others. But here, each of the first three Evangelists uses the same word to express the apparently insignificant circumstance, that the baskets employed to gather up the fragments were of the kind which even the Roman satirist, *Juvenal*, knew by the name of *cophïnus;* while in both the narratives of the feeding of the Four Thousand the baskets used are expressly said to have been of the kind called *spuris*. (See on ch. viii. 19, 20.) **44. And they that did eat of the loaves were [about] five thousand men**—"besides women and children" (Matt. xiv. 21). Of these, however, there would probably not be many; as only the males were obliged to go to the approaching festival. [The word "about"—ὡσεί—should be omitted here, as quite void of authority; but in the other three Gospels it certainly belongs to the genuine text.]

Jesus Re-crosses to the Western side of the Lake, Walking on the Sea (45-56). One very important particular given by John alone (vi. 15) introduces this portion: "When Jesus therefore perceived that they would take Him by force, to make Him a king, He departed again into a mountain Himself alone." **45. And straightway he constrained his disciples to get into the ship, and to go to the other side before—Him—unto Bethsaida**—Bethsaida of Galilee (John xii. 21). John says they "went over the sea towards Capernaum"—the wind, probably,

46 people. And when he had sent them away, *he departed into a mountain to pray.

47 And when even was come, the ship was in the midst of the sea, and
48 he alone on the land. And he saw them toiling in rowing; for the wind was contrary unto them: and about the fourth watch of the night he cometh unto them, walking upon the sea, and would have passed by
49 them. But when they saw him walking upon the sea, they supposed it
50 had been a spirit, and cried out: for they all saw him, and were troubled. And immediately he talked with them, and saith unto them, *m*Be of good cheer: it is I; be not afraid.

A. D. 32.

l ch. 1. 35.
Matt. 6. 6.
Matt. 14. 22.
Luke 6. 12.
John 6. 15.
1 Pet. 2. 21.
m Ps. 23. 4.
Isa 43. 2.
Matt. 14. 27.
Luke 20. 19.
Luke 24. 38.
John 6. 19.

occasioning this slight deviation from the direction of Bethsaida. **while he sent away the people** [τόν ὄχλον]—'the multitude.' His object in this was to put an end to the misdirected excitement in His favour (John vi. 15), into which the disciples themselves may have been somewhat drawn. The word "constrained" [ἠνάγκασεν] implies reluctance on their part, perhaps from unwillingness to part with their Master and embark at night, leaving Him alone on the mountain. **46. And when he had sent them away, he departed into a mountain to pray**—thus at length getting that privacy and rest which He had vainly sought during the earlier part of the day; opportunity also to pour out His soul in connection with the extraordinary excitement in His favour that evening—which appears to have marked the zenith of His reputation, for it began to decline the very next day; and a place whence He might watch the disciples on the lake, pray for them in their extremity, and observe the right time for coming to them, in a new manifestation of His glory, on the sea. **47. And when even was come**—the later evening (see on *v.* 35). It had come even when the disciples embarked (Matt. xiv. 23 John vi. 16). **the ship was in the midst of the sea, and he alone on the land.** John says (vi. 17), "It was now dark, and Jesus was not come to them." Perhaps they made no great effort to push across at first, having a lingering hope that their Master would yet join them, and so allowed the darkness to come on. "And the sea arose (adds the beloved disciple, vi. 18), by reason of a great wind that blew." **48. And he saw them toiling in rowing; for the wind was contrary unto them**—putting forth all their strength to buffet the waves and bear on against a head-wind, but to little effect. He "saw" this from His mountain-top, and through the darkness of the night, for His heart was all with them: yet would He not go to their relief till His own time came. **and about the fourth watch of the night.** The Jews, who used to divide the night into three watches, latterly adopted the Roman division into four watches, as here. So that, at the rate of three hours to each, the fourth watch, reckoning from six P.M., would be three o'clock in the morning. "So when they had rowed about five and twenty or thirty furlongs" (John vi. 19)—rather more than half-way across. The lake is about seven miles broad at its widest part. So that in eight or nine hours they had only made some three and a-half miles. By this time, therefore, they must have been in a state of exhaustion and despondency bordering on despair; and now at length, having tried them long enough, **he cometh unto them, walking upon the sea**—"and drawing nigh unto the ship" (John vi. 19), **and would have passed by them**—but only in the sense of Luke xxiv. 28; Gen. xxxii. 26: compare Gen. xviii. 3, 5; xlii. 7. **49. But when they saw him walking upon the sea, they sup**-

posed **it had been a spirit, and cried out**—"for fear" (Matt. xiv. 26). He would appear to them at first like a dark moving speck upon the waters; then as a human figure; but in the dark tempestuous sky, and not dreaming that it could be their Lord, they take it for a spirit. Compare Luke xxiv. 37. **50. For they all saw him, and were troubled. And immediately he talked with them, and saith unto them, Be of good cheer: it is I; be not afraid.** There is something in these two little words—given by Matthew, Mark, and John—"'Tis I" ['Εγώ εἰμι—'I AM'], which from the mouth that spake it and the circumstances in which it was uttered, passes the power of language to express. Here were they in the midst of a raging sea, their little bark the sport of the elements, and with just enough of light to descry an object on the waters which only aggravated their fears. But Jesus deems it enough to dispel all apprehension to let them know that *He was there.* From other lips that "I am" would have merely meant that the person speaking was such a one and not another person. That, surely, would have done little to calm the fears of men expecting every minute, it may be, to go to the bottom. But spoken by One who at that moment was "treading upon the waves of the sea," and was about to hush the raging elements with His word, what was it but the Voice which cried of old in the ears of Israel, even from the days of Moses, "I AM;" "I, EVEN I, AM HE!" Compare John xviii. 5, 6; viii. 58. Now, that word is "made flesh, and dwells among us," uttering itself from beside us in dear familiar tones—"It is the Voice of my Beloved!" How far was this apprehended by these frightened disciples? There was one, we know, in the boat who outstripped all the rest in susceptibility to such sublime appeals. It was not the deep-toned writer of the Fourth Gospel, who, though he lived to soar beyond all the apostles, was as yet too young for prominence, and all unripe. It was Simon-Barjonas.

Here follows a very remarkable and instructive episode, recorded by Matthew alone:—

Peter ventures to Walk upon the Sea (Matt. xiv. 28-32). 28. "And Peter answered Him, and said, Lord, If it be Thou [εἰ Σύ εἶ—'If Thou art'—responding to his Lord's "I am"], bid me come unto thee on the water;" not '*let* me,' but 'give me the word of *command*' [κελευσόν με πρὸς Σε ἐλθεῖν ἐπὶ τὰ ὕδατα]—'command,' or 'order me to come unto Thee upon the waters.' 29. "And He said, Come." Sublime word, issuing from One conscious of power over the raging element, to bid it serve both Himself and whomsoever else He pleased! "And when Peter was come down out of the ship, he walked upon the water"—'waters' [ὕδατα]—"to come to Jesus." 'It was a bold spirit,' says *Bp. Hall,* 'that could wish it; more bold that could act it—not fearing either the softness or the roughness of that uncouth passage.' 30. "But when he saw the wind boisterous, he was afraid; and

51 And he went up unto them into the ship; and the wind ceased: and they were sore amazed in themselves beyond measure, and wondered.

52 For ⁿ they considered not *the miracle* of the loaves: for their °heart was hardened.

53 And ᵖ when they had passed over, they came into the land of Genne-

54 saret, and drew to the shore. And when they were come out of the ship,

55 straightway they knew him, and ran through that whole region round about, and began to carry about in beds those that were sick, where they

A. D. 32.

ⁿ ch. 8. 17.
Luke 24.25.
° Jer. 17. 9.
ch. 3. 5.
ch. 16. 14.
Rom. 8. 7.
ᵖ Matt. 14.34.
Luke 5. 1.
John 6. 24.

beginning to sink, he cried, saying, Lord, save me." The wind was as boisterous before, but Peter "*saw*" it not; seeing only the power of Christ, in the lively exercise of faith. Now he "*sees*" the fury of the elements, and immediately the power of Christ to bear him up fades before his view, and this makes him "afraid"—as how could he be otherwise, without any *felt* power to keep him up? He then "begins to sink;" and finally, conscious that his experiment had failed, he casts himself, in a sort of desperate confidence, upon his "Lord" for deliverance! 31. "And immediately Jesus stretched forth His hand, and caught him, and said unto him, O thou of little faith, wherefore didst thou doubt?" *This rebuke was not administered while Peter was sinking, nor till Christ had taken him by the hand;* first re-invigorating his faith and then with it enabling him again to walk upon the crested wave. Bootless else had been this loving reproof, which owns the *faith* that had ventured on the deep upon the bare word of Christ, but asks why that *distrust* which so quickly marred it? 32. "And when they were come into the ship (Jesus and Peter), the wind ceased."

51. And he went up unto them into the ship. John (vi. 21) says, "Then they willingly received him into the ship" [Ἤθελον οὖν λαβεῖν αὐτὸν]—or rather, 'Then were they willing to receive Him' (with reference to their previous terror); but implying also a glad welcome, their first fears now converted into wonder and delight. "And immediately," adds the beloved disciple, "they were at the land whither they went" [εἰς ἦν ὑπῆγον], or 'were bound.' This additional miracle, for as such it is manifestly related, is recorded by the Fourth Evangelist alone. As the storm was suddenly calmed, so the little bark—propelled by the secret power of the Lord of nature now sailing in it—glided through the now unruffled waters, and, while they were wrapt in wonder at what had happened, not heeding their rapid motion, *was found* at port, to their still further surprise.

> "Then are they glad, because at rest
> And quiet now they be;
> So to the haven He them brings
> Which they desired to see."

Matthew (xiv. 33) says, "Then they that were in the ship came (that is, ere they got to land) and worshipped him, saying, Of a truth Thou art the Son of God." But our Evangelist is wonderfully striking. **and the wind ceased: and they were sore amazed in themselves beyond measure, and wondered.** The Evangelist seems hardly to find language strong enough to express their astonishment. [*Tregelles*, on too slight authority, omits altogether the clause, καὶ ἐθαύμαζον—"and wondered"—and brackets the phrase, ἐκ περισσοῦ—": beyond measure,"as of doubtful genuineness; but *Tischendorf* does neither.] **52. For they considered not the miracle of the loaves: for their heart was hardened.** What a singular statement! The meaning seems to be that if they had but "considered (or reflected upon) the miracle of the loaves," wrought but a few hours before, they would

have *wondered at nothing* which He might do within the whole circle of power and grace.

Incidents on Landing (53-56). The details here are given with a rich vividness quite peculiar to this charming Gospel. **53. And when they had passed over, they came into the land of Gennesaret**—from which the lake sometimes takes its name, stretching along its western shore. Capernaum was their landing-place (John vi. 24, 25). **and drew to the shore** [προσωρμίσθησαν]—a nautical phrase, nowhere else used in the New Testament. **54. And when they were come out of the ship, straightway they knew him—**"immediately they recognized Him;" that is, the people did. **55. And ran through that whole region round about, and began to carry about in beds those that were sick, where they heard he was.** At this period of our Lord's ministry the popular enthusiasm in His favour was at its height. **56. And whithersoever he entered, into villages, or cities, or country, they laid the sick in the streets, and besought him that they might touch if it were but the border of his garment—**having heard, no doubt, of what the woman with the issue of blood experienced on doing so (ch. v. 25-29), and perhaps of other unrecorded cases of the same nature. **and as many as touched [him]—**or 'it'—the border of His garment, **were made whole.** All this they *continued* to do and to experience while our Lord was in that region [as is implied in the imperfect tenses here employed—εἰσεπορεύετο, ἐτίθουν, παρεκάλουν, ἐσώζοντο]. The *time* corresponds to that mentioned (John vii. 1), when He "walked in Galilee," instead of appearing in Jerusalem at the Passover, "because the Jews," that is, *the rulers*, "sought to kill Him"—while *the people* sought to enthrone Him!

Remarks. — 1. What devout and thoughtful reader can have followed the graphic details of this wonderful Section without hearing the tread of Divinity in the footstep and voice, and beholding it in the hands and eyes of that warm, living, tender Humanity whose movements are here recorded? While yet on the western side of the lake, the Twelve return to Him and report the success of their missionary tour. Almost simultaneously with this, tidings reach Him of the foul murder and decent burial of His loving and faithful forerunner. He would fain get alone with the Twelve, after such moving events, but cannot, for the crowds that kept moving about Him. So He bids the Twelve put across to the eastern side, to "rest a while." But the people, dismayed at the sight of His departure, and having no boats, run round by the head of the lake, hastily cross the river, and observing the direction in which His boat made for the land, were there before Him. He pities them as shepherdless sheep, and instead of putting them away, preaches to them, until the decline of the day warns Him to think of the meat that perisheth as now needful for them. The Twelve were for dispersing them in search of victuals, but He bids them supply them with these themselves. But how can they? Let them see what they can

56 heard he was. And whithersoever he entered, into villages, or cities, or country, they laid the sick in the streets, and besought him that they ⁹might touch if it were but the border of his garment: and as many as touched ⁹him were made whole.

A. D. 32.

⁹ Matt 9. 20.
Luke 8. 44.
Acts 5. 15.
⁹ Or, it

muster. The exact quantity in hand is given with precision by all the four Evangelists. The barley loaves—they are five; and the small fishes, two. But what will these do? They will suffice. Direction is given to make the vast multitude sit down on the rank green grass in orderly form, by hundreds and by fifties. It is done, and He stands forth, we might conceive, within an outer semicircle of thirty hundreds, and an inner semicircle of forty fifties; the women and children by themselves, it may be in groups, still nearer the glorious Provider. All eyes are now fastened upon Him as He took up the five loaves and the two fishes, and looking up to heaven, blessed them as Heaven's bountiful provision for that whole multitude, and then gave them to the Twelve to distribute amongst them. Who can imagine the wonder that would sit upon every countenance, as the thought shot across them, How is this handful to feed even one of the fifties, not to speak of the hundreds? But as they found it passed by the Twelve from rank to rank unexhausted, and the last man, and woman, and child of them fed to the full, and the *leavings*, both of the loaves and of the fishes, greatly more than the whole provision at the first—the baskets filled with these being twelve, and the number fed five thousand, besides women and children—what must they have thought, if they thought at all? It is true, we have faint precursors of this glorious miracle in the doings of *Elijah* (1 Ki. xvii. 14-16), and still more of *Elisha* (2 Ki. iv. 1-7, 42-44); but besides the inferiority of the things done, those prophets acted ever as *servants*, saying, "Thus saith the Lord," when they announced the miracles they were to perform; whereas, the one feature which most struck all who came in contact with Jesus was the air of *Personal authority* with which He ever taught and wrought His miracles, thus standing confessed before the devout and penetrating eye as the *Incarnate Lord of Nature:*

' Here may we sit and dream
Over the heavenly theme,
Till to our soul the former days return;
Till on the grassy bed
Where thousands once He fed,
The world's incarnate Maker we discern."—KEBLE

But the scene changes. The transported multitude, in a frenzy of enthusiasm, are consulting together how they are to hasten His Installation in the regal rights of "the King of Israel," which they now plainly saw Him to be. (What a testimony, by the way, is this to the reality of the miracle—the testimony of five thousand participants of the fruit of the miracle !) They have taken no action, but "knowing their thoughts," He quickly disperses them; and retiring for the night to a solitary mountain-top, overlooking the sea, He there pours out His great soul in prayer, watching at the same time the gathering tempest and the weary struggle of the disciples—whom He made to put out reluctantly to sea without Him—with the contrary wind and the beating waves; until, after some eight hours' trial of them in these perilous circumstances, He rises, descends to the sea, and walks to them, cresting the roaring billows; and when the sight of His dim figure only aggravates their terror and makes them cry out for fear, He bids them be calm and confident, *for it was He*—Himself as unmoved as on dry land and under a serene sky. This reassures them; insomuch that Peter thinks even he would be safe upon the

great deep if only JESUS would order him to come to Him upon it. He does it; and for a moment—as he looks to HIM only—the watery element, obedient to its Lord, bears him up. But looking to the angry roar of the wind, as it whisked up the sea, he is ready to be swallowed up, and cries for help to the mighty Lord of the deep, who gives him His hand and steps with him into the ship, when at His presence the storm immediately ceases, and ere they have time to pour forth their astonishment they are in port. The thing which is so amazing here is scarcely so much the absolute *command* which Jesus shows over the elements of nature in all their rage, as *His own perfect ease*, whether in riding upon them or keeping His poor disciple from being swallowed up of them, and gently chiding him for having any fear of the elements so long as HE was with him. Not all the chanting of the Old Testament over Jehovah's power to "raise the stormy wind which lifteth up the waves," and then to "make the storm a calm, so that the waves thereof are still" (Ps. cvii. 25-29, &c.) makes such an impression upon the mind, as the concrete manifestation of it in this sublime narrative. In the one, we hear of Him by the hearing of the ear; in the other, our eye seeth Him. It is like the difference between shadow and substance. Indeed, the one may be regarded as the incarnation of the other. 2. Since all Christ's miracles had a deeper significance than that which appears on the surface of them, we cannot doubt that the multiplication of the loaves, which was one of the most stupendous, has its profound meaning also. We may say, indeed, that as this multitude had made such exertions and sacrifices to be with Jesus and drink in His wonderful teaching, and were not sent empty away, but got more than they expected—even the meat that perisheth, when they seemed to look only for that which endureth to everlasting life—so if we "seek first the kingdom of God and His righteousness, all these things will be added unto us." But this and similar lessons hardly reach the depth of this subject, much less exhaust it. As the Lord Jesus multiplied on this occasion the meat that perisheth, so is the meat that endureth to everlasting life capable of indefinite multiplication. Look at the Scriptures at large; look at the glorious Gospel History; look at this one stupendous Section of it. In bulk, how little is it—like the five barley loaves and the two small fishes it tells of. But what thousands upon thousands has it fed, and will it feed, in every age, in every land of Christendom, to the world's end ! And is this true only of inspired Scripture? There, we may say, it is Christ Himself that ministers the bread of life. But just as Elijah and Elisha did something of the same kind—though on a small scale, and with a humble acknowledgment that they were but *servants*, or instruments in the hand of the Lord—so have the ministers of the Lord Jesus been privileged, from a little portion of "the oracles of God," to feed the souls of thousands, and that so richly as to leave baskets of fragments unconsumed. Nor can the writer refrain from testifying to all who read these lines, what a feast of fat things he has found daily for himself as he passed from Section to Section of this wonderful History, exhilarating him amidst the considerable labour which this work involves; nor can he wish anything better for his readers than

163

7 THEN ^acame together unto him the Pharisees, and certain of the
2 scribes, which came from Jerusalem. And when they saw some of his
disciples eat bread with ¹defiled (that is to say, with unwashen) hands,
3 they found fault. (For the Pharisees, and all the Jews, except they wash
4 *their* hands ²oft, eat not, holding the tradition of the elders. And *when
they come* from the market, except they wash, they eat not. And many
other things there be which they have received to hold, *as* the washing of
5 cups, and ³pots, brasen vessels, and of ⁴tables.) Then ^bthe Pharisees
and scribes asked him, Why walk not thy disciples according to the
6 tradition of the elders, but eat bread with unwashen hands? He answered
and said unto them, Well hath Esaias prophesied of you hypocrites, as it
is written, ^cThis people honoureth me with *their* lips, but their heart is
7 far from me. Howbeit in vain do they worship me, teaching *for* doctrines
8 the commandments of men. For, laying aside the commandment of God,
ye hold the tradition of men, *as* the washing of pots and cups: and many
9 other such like things ye do. And he said unto them, Full well ye
⁵reject the commandment of God, that ye may keep your own tradition.
10 For Moses said, ^dHonour thy father and thy mother; and, ^eWhoso
11 curseth father or mother, let him die the death: but ye say, If a man
shall say to his father or mother, *It is* ^fCorban, (that is to say, a gift,)
12 by whatsoever thou mightest be profited by me; *he shall be free.* And
13 ye suffer him no more to do ought for his father or his mother; making

A. D. 32.

CHAP. 7.
^a Matt. 15. 1.
1 Or,
  common.
² with the
  fist, or,
  diligently.
  Theophy-
  lact, up to
  the elbow.
3 Sextarius
  is about a
  pint and a
  half.
4 Or, beds.
^b Matt. 15. 2.
^c Isa. 29. 13.
  Matt. 15. 8.
5 Or, frus-
  trate.
^d Ex 20. 12.
  Deut. 5 16.
^e Ex. 21. 17.
  Lev. 20. 9.
  Pro 20. 20.
^f Matt. 15. 5.
  Matt. 23. 18.
1 Tim. 5. 8.

that they also may have fellowship with him, for truly his fellowship in this bread of life has been with the Father and with His Son Jesus Christ. 3. In these poor disciples, after this day of wonders, we have a picture of the blindness of the best of us ofttimes to the divine purposes and our own mercies. How reluctant were they to put out to sea without their Master; but had He not stayed behind, they had missed—and along with them the Church in all time had missed—the one manifestation of His glory which He saw fit to give in that majestic form, of walking upon the sea, and that too when the waves thereof roared by reason of a mighty wind. Doubtless, when they urged Him to come with them, if He would not let them spend the night with Him on the eastern side, He would assure them that He was *coming after them*. But how little would they dream of what He meant! Anxiously and often would they look back, to see if they could descry any other wherry by which He might have set sail at a later hour; and when, after eight hours' beating against the storm, they found themselves, ere the morning light dawned on them, alone and helpless in the midst of the sea, how would they say one to another, 'O that we had not parted from Him! Would that He were here! When that storm arose as we crossed with Him to the country of the Gadarenes, though He was fast asleep in the stern-end of the ship, how quickly, on our awaking Him, did He hush the winds and calm the sea, even with one word of command; but now, alas, we are alone!' At length they descry a dark object. What can it be? It draws nearer and nearer them; their fears arise; now it is near enough to convince them that it is a living form, in quest of *them*. And what can a living, moving form upon the waters be but a spectre? and what can a spectre want with them? At length, as it approaches them, they shriek out for fear. And yet this is their Beloved, and this is their Friend—so eagerly longed for, but at length despaired of! Thus do we often miscall our chiefest mercies; not only thinking them distant when they are near, but thinking the best the worst. Yes, Jesus was with them all the while, though they knew it not. His heart followed

them with His eye, as the storm gathered; though in body far away, in spirit He was with them, giving command to the furious elements to be to them as was the burning fiery furnace to the Hebrew youths when they were in it, and the lions when Daniel was in their den—to do them no hurt. He pitied them as He "saw them toiling in rowing," but for their own sake He would not come to them till the right time. But O what words were those with which He calmed their fears—"Be of good cheer: it is I; be not afraid"! The re-assuring word was that central one "*I*" ['Εγώ]; and after what they had seen of His glory but a few hours before, in addition to all their past experience, what a fulness of relief would be to them wrapt up in that one little word "*I!*" And what else need even we, tossed, and O how often! upon a tempestuous sea—at one time of doubts and fears, at another, of difficulties and wants, at another, of sorrows and sufferings—"toiling in rowing" to beat our way out of them: What need we, to stay our souls when all these waves and billows are going over us, and to cheer us with songs in the night, but to hear that Voice so loving, so divine, "Be of good cheer: IT IS I; be not afraid"! 4. When sure of a divine warrant, what may not faith venture on, and so long as our eye is directed to a present Saviour, what dangers may we not surmount? But when, like Peter, we direct our eye to the raging element, and "see the wind boisterous," fear takes the place of faith; and beginning to sink, our only safety lies in casting our critical case upon Him whose are all the elements of nature and providence and grace. Happy then are we, if we can feel that warm fleshly Hand which caught sinking Peter and immediately ascended with him into the ship! For then are we at once in the haven of rest.

'Thou Framer of the light and dark,
  Steer through the tempest thine own ark;
  Amid the howling wintry sea
  We are in port if we have Thee!'—KEBLE.

CHAP. VII. 1-23.—DISCOURSE ON CEREMONIAL POLLUTION. (= Matt. xv. 1-20.) For the exposition, see on Matt. xv. 1-20.
24-37.—THE SYROPHENICIAN WOMAN AND HER

the word of God of none effect through your tradition, which ye have delivered: and many such like things do ye.

14 And when he had called all the people *unto him*, he said unto them,

15 Hearken unto me every one *of you*, and understand: there is *g*nothing from without a man, that entering into him can defile him: but the

16 things which come out of him, those are they that defile the man. If *h*any man have ears to hear, let him hear.

17 And *i*when he was entered into the house from the people, his disciples

18 asked him concerning the parable. And he saith unto them, Are ye so without understanding also? Do ye not perceive, that whatsoever thing

19 from without entereth into the man, *it* cannot defile him; because it entereth not into his heart, but into the belly, and goeth out into the

20 draught, purging all meats? And he said, That which cometh out of

21 the man, that defileth the man. For *j*from within, out of the heart of

22 men, proceed evil thoughts, adulteries, fornications, murders, thefts, *6*covetousness, wickedness, deceit, lasciviousness, an evil eye, blasphemy,

23 pride, foolishness: all these evil things come from within, and defile the man.

24 And *k*from thence he arose, and went into the borders of Tyre and Sidon, and entered into an house, and would have no man know *it:* but

25 he could not be hid. For a *certain* woman, whose young daughter had

26 an unclean spirit, heard of him, and came and fell at his feet: the woman was a *7*Greek, a Syrophenician by nation; and she besought him that he would cast forth the devil out of her daughter.

27 But Jesus said unto her, Let *l*the children first be filled: for it is not

A. D. 32.
g Acts 10. 14,
15.
Rom 14.17.
1 Cor. 8. 8.
1 Tim. 4. 4.
Titus 1. 15.
h Matt 11.15.
i Matt. 15.15.
j Gen. 6. 5.,
Gen. 8. 21.
Matt 15.19.
Acts 8. 22
Gal. 5. 19.
6 covetous-
nesses.
wicked-
nesses.
k Matt. 15.21.
7 Or,
Gentile.
Isa. 49. 12.
Gal. 3 28.
Col. 3. 11.
l Matt 7. 6.
Matt. 10. 5,
6.
Matt. 15.26-
28.
Acts 13. 46.
Acts 22. 21.
Rom. 9. 4.
Eph. 2. 12.

DAUGHTER—A DEAF AND DUMB MAN HEALED. (= Matt. xv. 21-31.)

The Syrophenician Woman and her Daughter (24-30). The first words of this narrative show that the incident followed, in point of time, immediately on what precedes it. **24. And from thence he arose, and went into, or 'unto' the borders of Tyre and Sidon**—the two great Phenician seaports, but here denoting the territory generally, to the frontiers of which Jesus now came. But did Jesus actually enter this heathen territory? The whole narrative, we think, proceeds upon the supposition that He did. His immediate object seems to have been to avoid the wrath of the Pharisees at the withering exposure He had just made of their traditional religion. **and entered into an house, and would have no man know it**—because He had not come there to minister to heathens. But though not "*sent* but to the lost sheep of the house of Israel" (Matt. xv. 24), He hindered not the lost sheep of the vast Gentile world from coming to Him, nor put them away when they did come—as this incident was designed to show. **but he could not be hid.** Christ's fame had early spread from Galilee to this very region (ch. iii. 8; Luke vi. 17). **25. For a certain woman, whose young daughter had an unclean spirit**—or, in Matthew, 'was badly demonized' [κακῶς δαιμονίζεται], **heard of him**—one wonders how; but distress is quick of hearing; **and fell at his feet: 26. The woman was a Greek** ['Ελληνίς]— that is, 'a Gentile,' as in the margin; **a Syrophenician by nation**—so called as inhabiting the Phenician tract of Syria. *Juvenal* uses the same term, as was remarked by *Justin Martyr* and *Tertullian.* Matthew calls her "a woman of Canaan"—a more intelligible description to his Jewish readers (cf. Jud. i. 30, 32, 33). **and she besought him that he would cast forth the devil out of her daughter**—"She cried unto him, saying, Have mercy on me, O Lord, Son of David: my daughter is grievously vexed with a devil" (Matt. 165

xv. 22). Thus, though no Israelite herself, she salutes Him as Israel's promised Messiah. Here we must go to Matt. xv. 23-25, for some important links in the dialogue omitted by our Evangelist. 23. "But He answered her not a word." The design of this was first, perhaps, to show that He was not *sent* to such as she. He had said expressly to the Twelve, "Go not into the way of the Gentiles" (Matt. x. 5); and being now amongst them Himself, He would, for consistency's sake, let it be seen that He had not gone thither for *missionary* purposes. Therefore He not only kept silence, but had actually left the house and—as will presently appear—was proceeding on His way back, when this woman accosted Him. But another reason for keeping silence plainly was to try and to whet her faith, patience, and perseverance. And it had the desired effect: "She *cried after them*," which shows that He was already on His way from the place. "And His disciples came and besought Him, saying, Send her away; for she crieth after us." They thought her troublesome with her importunate cries, just as they did the people who brought young children to be blessed of Him, and they ask their Lord to "send her away," that is, to grant her request and be rid of her; for we gather from His reply that they meant to solicit favour for her, though not for her sake so much as their own. 24. "But He answered and said, I am not sent but unto the lost sheep of the house of Israel"—a speech evidently intended for the disciples themselves, to satisfy them that, though the grace He was about to show to this Gentile believer was *beyond His strict* commission, He had not gone *spontaneously* to dispense it. Yet did even this speech open a gleam of hope, could she have discerned it. For thus might she have spoken: 'I am not SENT, did He say? Truth, Lord, Thou comest not hither in quest of *us*, but I come in quest of *Thee*; and must I go empty away? So did not the woman of Samaria, whom when Thou foundest her on Thy way

28 meet to take the children's bread, and to cast *it* unto the dogs. And she answered and said unto him, Yes, Lord: yet the dogs under the
29 table eat of the children's crumbs. And he said unto her, For this
30 saying go thy way; the devil is gone out of thy daughter. And when she was come to her house, she found *ᵐ*the devil gone out, and her daughter laid upon the bed.
31 And *ⁿ*again, departing from the coasts of Tyre and Sidon, he came unto the sea of Galilee, through the midst of the coasts of Decapolis.
32 And they bring unto him one that was deaf, and had an impediment
33 in his speech; and they beseech him to put his hand upon him. And *°*he took him aside from the multitude, and put his fingers into his ears, and

A. D. 32.

ᵐ Jos. 21. 45.
Matt. 9. 29.
ch. 9. 23.
1 John 3. 8.
ⁿ Matt. 15.29.
° 1 Ki. 17. 19-22.
2 Ki. 4. 4-6.
2 Ki. 11. 24.
Matt. 4. 25.
ch. 5. 20.
ch. 5. 40.
ch. 8. 23.

to Galilee, Thou sentest away to make many rich!' But this our poor Syrophenician could not attain to. What, then, can she answer to such a speech? Nothing. She has reached her lowest depth, her darkest moment; she will just utter her last cry: 25. "Then came she and worshipped Him, saying, Lord, help me!" This appeal, so artless, wrung from the depths of a believing heart, and reminding us of the Publican's "God be merciful to me a sinner," moved the Redeemer at last to break silence—but in what style?

Here we return to our own Evangelist. **27. But Jesus said unto her, Let the children first be filled.** 'Is there hope for me here?' 'Filled FIRST?' 'Then my turn, it seems, *is* coming!—but then, "The CHILDREN first?" Ah! when, on that rule, shall my turn ever come?' But ere she has time for these ponderings of His word, another word comes to supplement it. **for it is not meet to take the children's bread, and to cast it unto the dogs.** Is this the death of her hopes? Nay, but it is life from the dead. Out of the eater shall come forth meat (Jud. xiv. 14). At evening time it shall be light (Zec. xiv. 7). 'Ha! I have it now. Had He kept silence, what could I have done but go unblest? but He hath spoken, and the victory is mine.' **28. And she answered and said unto him, Yes, Lord**—or, as the same word [Nαὶ] is rendered in Matt. xv. 27, "Truth, Lord," **yet the dogs eat of the children's crumbs**—"which fall from their master's table" (Matt.) 'I thank Thee, O blessed One, for that word! That's my whole case. Not of the children? True. A dog? True also: *Yet* the dogs under the table are allowed to eat of the children's crumbs—the droppings from their master's full table: Give me that, and I am content: One crumb of power and grace from Thy table shall cast the devil out of my daughter.' O what lightning quickness, what reach of instinctive ingenuity, do we behold in this heathen woman! **29. And he said unto her**—"O woman, great is thy faith" (Matt. xv. 28.) As *Bengel* beautifully remarks, Jesus "marvelled" only at two things—*faith* and *unbelief* (see on Luke vii. 9). **For this saying go thy way; the devil is gone out of thy daughter.** That moment the deed was done. **30. And when she was come to her house, she found the devil gone out, and her daughter laid upon the bed.** But Matthew is more specific: "And her daughter was made whole from that very hour." The wonderfulness of this case in all its features has been felt in every age of the Church, and the balm it has administered, and will yet administer, to millions will be known only in that day that shall reveal the secrets of all hearts.

Deaf and Dumb Man Healed (31-37). **31. And again, departing from the coasts of Tyre and Sidon, he came unto the sea of Galilee**—or, according to what has very strong claims to be regarded as the true text here, 'And again, departing from the coasts of Tyre, He came through Sidon [δὶα

Σιδῶνος] to the sea of Galilee.' The MSS. in favour of this reading, though not the most numerous, are weighty, while the versions agreeing with it are among the most ancient; and all the best critical editors and commentators adopt it. In this case we must understand that our Lord, having once gone out of the Holy Land the length of Tyre, proceeded as far north as Sidon, though without ministering, so far as appears, in those parts, and then bent His steps in a south-easterly direction. There is certainly a difficulty in the supposition of so long a *detour* without any missionary object; and some may think this sufficient to cast the balance in favour of the received reading. Be this as it may, on returning from these coasts of Tyre, He passed **through the midst of the coasts**—or frontiers—**of Decapolis**—crossing the Jordan, therefore, and approaching the lake on its east side. Here Matthew, who omits the details of the cure of this deaf and dumb man, introduces some particulars, from which we learn that it was only one of a great number. "And Jesus," says that Evangelist (xv. 29-31), "departed from thence, and came nigh unto the sea of Galilee, and went up into a mountain"—the mountain-range bounding the lake on the north-east, in Decapolis: "And great multitudes came unto Him, having with them lame, blind, dumb, maimed" [κυλλοὺς]—not 'mutilated,' which is but a secondary sense of the word, but 'deformed'—"and many others, and cast them down at Jesus' feet; and he healed them: insomuch that the multitude"—'the multitudes' [τοὺς ὄχλους]—"wondered, when they saw the dumb to speak, the maimed to be whole, the lame to walk, and the blind to see: and they glorified the God of Israel"—who, after so long and dreary an absence of visible manifestation, had returned to bless His people as of old (compare Luke vii. 16). Beyond this it is not clear from the Evangelist's language that the people saw into the claims of Jesus. Well, of these cases Mark here singles out one, whose cure had something peculiar in it. **32. And they bring unto him one that was deaf, and had an impediment in his speech; and they beseech him to put his hand upon him.** In their eagerness they appear to have been somewhat too officious. Though usually doing as here suggested, He will deal with this case in His own way. **33. And he took him aside from the multitude**—as in another case He "took the blind man by the hand and led him out of the town" (ch. viii. 23), probably to fix his undistracted attention on Himself and, by means of certain actions He was about to do, to awaken and direct his attention to the proper source of relief. **and put his fingers into his ears.** As his indistinct articulation arose from his deafness, our Lord addresses Himself to this first. To the impotent man He said, "Wilt thou be made whole?" to the blind men, "What will ye that I shall do unto you?" and "Believe ye that I am able to do this?"

34 he *P*spit, and touched his tongue; and, *q*looking up to heaven, *r*he sighed,
35 and saith unto him, Ephphatha, that is, Be opened. And *s*straightway
his ears were opened, and the string of his tongue was loosed, and he
36 spake plain. And *t*he charged them that they should tell no man: but
the more he charged them, so much the more a great deal they published
37 *it;* and were beyond measure astonished, saying, He hath done all things
well: he maketh both the deaf to hear, and the dumb to speak.

A. D. 32.

P ch. 8. 23.
John 9. 6.
q ch. 6. 41.
John 11. 41.
r John 11. 33, 38.
s Ps. 33. 9.
t Isa. 42. 2.

(John v. 6; Matt. xx. 32; ix. 28). But as this patient could *hear* nothing, our Lord substitutes symbolical actions upon each of the organs affected. **and he spit and touched his tongue**—moistening the man's parched tongue with saliva from His own mouth, as if to lubricate the organ or facilitate its free motion; thus indicating the source of the healing virtue to be His own person. (For similar actions, see ch. viii. 23; John ix. 6.) **34. And looking up to heaven**—ever acknowledging His Father, even while the Healing was seen to flow from Himself (see on John v. 19), **he sighed**—'over the wreck,' says *Trench*, 'which sin had brought about, and the malice of the devil in deforming the fair features of God's original creation.' But, we take it, there was a yet more painful impression of that "evil thing and bitter" whence all our ills have sprung, and which, when Himself took our infirmities and bare our sicknesses" (Matt. viii. 17), became mysteriously His own.

> 'In thought of these His brows benign,
> Not even in healing, cloudless shine.'—KEBLE.

and saith unto him, Ephphatha, that is, Be opened. Our Evangelist, as remarked on ch. v. 41, loves to give such wonderful words just as they were spoken. **35. And straightway his ears were opened.** This is mentioned first, as the source of the other derangement. **and the string of his tongue was loosed, and he spake plain.** The cure was thus alike instantaneous and perfect. **36. And he charged them that they should tell no man.** Into this very region He had sent the man out of whom had been cast the legion of devils, to proclaim "what the Lord had done for him" (ch. v. 19). Now He will have them "tell no man." But in the former case there was no danger of obstructing His ministry by "blazing the matter" (ch. i. 45), as He Himself had left the region; whereas now He was sojourning in it. **but the more he charged them, so much the more a great deal they published it.** They could not be restrained; nay, the prohibition seemed only to whet their determination to publish His fame. **37. And were beyond measure astonished, saying, He hath done all things well**—reminding us, says *Trench*, of the words of the first creation (Gen. i. 31, LXX.), upon which we are thus not unsuitably thrown back, for Christ's work is in the truest sense "a new creation." **he maketh both the deaf to hear, and the dumb to speak**—"and they glorified the God of Israel" (Matt. xv. 31). See on *v.* 31 of this chapter.

Remarks.—1. The Syrophenician woman had never witnessed any of Christ's miracles, nor seen His face, but she had "heard of Him." Like the woman with the issue of blood (ch. v. 27), she had heard of His wondrous cures, particularly how He cast out devils; and she probably said within herself, O that He would but come hither, or I could come to Him—which her circumstances did not permit. But now He is within reach, and though desiring concealment, she finds Him out, and implores a cure for her grievously demonized daughter. Instead of immediately meeting her faith, He keeps a mysterious silence; nay, leaves

her, and suffers her to cry after Him without uttering a word. Does she now give it up, muttering to herself as she leaves Him, 'It's a false report—He can't do it?' Nay, His silence only redoubles her entreaties, and His withdrawal does but draw her after Him. The disciples—ever studying their Master's ease, rather than penetrating into His deep designs—suggest whether, as she was "troubling Him," it might not be better to throw a cure to her, so to speak, and get rid of her, lest, like the importunate widow, "by her continual coming she weary" Him. His reply seemed to extinguish all hope. "I am not sent but to the lost sheep of the house of Israel." Is not this very like breaking the bruised reed, and quenching the smoking flax? But the bruised reed shall not break, the smoking flax shall not go out. There is a tenacity in her faith which refuses to give up. It seems to hear a voice saying to her—

> 'Know the darkest part of night
> Is before the dawn of light;
> Press along, you're going right,
> Try, try again.'

At His feet she casts herself, with a despairing cry, "Lord, help me!"—as strong in the confidence of His *power*, as now, at the very weakest, of His *willingness*, to give relief. But even as to that willingness, while she clings to hope against hope, what a word does He at length utter— "Let the children first be filled: for it is not meet to take the children's bread, and to cast it unto the dogs." Worse and worse. But her faith is too keen not to see her advantage. That faith of hers is ingenious. 'The children's bread! Ah, yes! that is too good for me. Thou art right, Lord. To take the children's bread, and cast it to a heathen dog like me, is what I dare not ask. It is the dogs' portion only that I ask—the crumbs that fall from the Master's table—from Thy fulness even a crumb is more than sufficient.' Who can wonder at the wonder even of Jesus at this, and His inability any longer to hold out against her? The woman with the issue of blood heard of Jesus, as did this Syrophenician woman, and from the mere report conceived a noble faith in His power to heal her. But that woman was a Jewess, nursed amid religious opportunities and fed on the oracles of God. This woman was born a heathen, and reared under all the disadvantages of a pagan creed. With that woman it was short work: with this one it was tough and trying. Like Jacob of old, she wept and made supplication unto Him; yea, she had power over the Angel, and prevailed. And this has been written for the generations following, that men may say, "I will not let Thee go except Thou bless me." 2. We have in this case an example of that *cross* procedure which Jesus was wont to observe when He only wished to train and draw forth and be gained over by persevering faith. And certainly, never was the invincible tenacity of living faith more touchingly and beautifully educed than here. But for His knowledge where it would all end, that tender, great Heart would

8 IN those days "the multitude being very great, and having nothing to
2 eat, Jesus called his disciples *unto him,* and saith unto them, I have
^bcompassion on the multitude, because they have now been with me
3 three days, and have nothing to eat: and if I send them away fasting to
their own houses, they will faint by the way: for divers of them came
4 from far. And his disciples answered him, From whence ^ccan a man
5 satisfy these *men* with bread here in the wilderness? And^{·d}he asked
6 them, How many loaves have ye? And they said, Seven. And he commanded the people to sit down on the ground: and he took the seven
loaves, and ^egave thanks, and brake, and gave to his disciples to set
7 before *them;* and they did set *them* before the people. And they had a
few small fishes: and he ^fblessed, and commanded to set them also before
8 *them.* So they did eat, and were filled: and they took up of the broken
9 *meat* that was left seven baskets. And they that had eaten were about
four thousand: and he sent them away.

A. D. 32.

CHAP. 8.
^a Matt. 15.32.
^b Ps. 145. 9.
Heb. 3. 17.
Heb. 4. 15.
^c Num.11.21,
22.
2 Ki. 4. 42,
43.
2 Ki. 7. 2.
ch. 6. 52.
^d Matt. 15.34.
ch. 6. 38.
^e Deut. 8. 10.
ch. 6. 41-44.
1 Tim. 4. 4,
5.
^f Matt. 14.19.
ch 6. 41.

never have stood such a melting importunity of true faith, nor have endured to speak to her as He did. And shall we not learn from such cases how to interpret His procedure, when our Joseph "speaks roughly" to His brethren, and seems to treat them so, and yet all the while it is if He would seek where to weep, and He only waits for the right moment for making Himself known unto them? 3. When we read that Jesus sighed over the case of this deaf and dumb man, and groaned and wept over the grave of Lazarus, we have faint glimpses of feelings the depth of which we shall never fathom, and the whole meaning of which it is hard to take in, but of which we know enough to assure us that all the ills that flesh is heir to, and the one root of them—sin—He made His own. And now that He has put away sin by the sacrifice of Himself, and so provided for the rolling away of the complicated ills that have come in its train, He sits in heaven to reap the fruits of Redemption, with all His rich experience of human ill. Shall we not, then, "come boldly to the throne of grace, that we may obtain mercy, and find grace to help in time of need? For we have not an High Priest which cannot be touched by the feeling of our infirmities, but was in all points tempted like as we are, yet without sin."

CHAP. VIII. 1-26.—FOUR THOUSAND MIRA-CULOUSLY FED—A SIGN FROM HEAVEN SOUGHT AND REFUSED—THE LEAVEN OF THE PHARISEES AND SADDUCEES—A BLIND MAN AT BETHSAIDA RESTORED TO SIGHT. (= Matt. xv. 32—xvi. 12.) This Section of miscellaneous matter evidently follows the preceding one in point of time, as will be seen by observing how it is introduced by Matthew.

Feeding of the Four Thousand (1-9). **1. In those days the multitude being very great, and having nothing to eat, Jesus called his disciples unto him, and saith unto them, 2. I have compassion on the multitude** — an expression of that deep emotion in the Redeemer's heart which always preceded some remarkable interposition for relief. (See Matt. xiv. 14; xx. 34; Mark i. 41; Luke vii. 13; also Matt. ix. 36, before the mission of the Twelve: compare Jud. ii. 18; x. 16.) **because they have now been with me,** in constant attend-ance, **three days, and have nothing to eat: 3. And if I send them away fasting to their own houses, they will faint by the way: for divers of them came from far.** In their eagerness they seem not to have thought of the need of provisions for such a length of time; but the Lord thought of it. In Matt. (xv. 32) it is, "I will not send them away fasting" [ἀπολῦσαι αὐτοὺς νήστεις οὐ θέλω]

—or rather, 'To send them away fasting I am un-willing.' **4. And his disciples answered him, From whence can a man satisfy these men with bread here in the wilderness?** Though the question here is the same as when He fed the five thousand, they evidently *now* meant no more by it than that *they* had not the means of feeding the multitude; modestly leaving the Lord to decide what was to be done. And this will the more appear from His not now trying them, as before, by saying, "They need not depart, give ye them to eat;" but simply asking what they had, and then giving His directions. **5. And he asked them, How many loaves have ye? And they said, Seven.** It was important in this case, as in the former, that the precise number of the loaves should be brought out. Thus also does the distinctness of the two miracles appear. **6. And he commanded the people to sit down on the ground: and he took the seven loaves, and gave thanks, and brake, and gave to his disciples to set before them; and they did set them before the people** [τῷ ὄχλῳ—'the multitude.' **7. And they had a few small fishes: and he blessed, and com-manded to set them also before them. 8. So they did eat, and were filled: and they took up of the broken meat**—or 'fragments' [κλασμάτων], that **was left seven baskets. 9. And they that had eaten were about four thousand: and he sent them away.** Had not our Lord distinctly referred, in this very chapter and in two successive sentences to the feeding of the Five and of the Four Thousand, as two distinct miracles, many critics would have insisted that they were but two different represen-tations of one and the same miracle, as they do of the two expulsions of the buyers and sellers from the temple, at the beginning and end of our Lord's ministry. But even in spite of what our Lord says, it is painful to find such men as *Neander* endeavouring to identify the two miracles. The localities, though both on the eastern side of the lake, were different: the time was different: the preceding and following circumstances were differ-ent: the period during which the people continued fasting was different—in the one case not one en-tire day, in the other three days: the number fed was different—five thousand in the one case, in the other four thousand: the number of the loaves was different—five in the one case, in the other seven: the number of the fishes in the one case is definitely stated by all the four Evangelists—two; in the other case both give them indefinitely—"a few small fishes" [ἰχθύδια ὀλίγα]: in the one case the multitude were commanded to sit down "upon the green grass;" in the other, "on the ground" [ἐπὶ τῆς γῆς]: in the one case the number of the

10　And *g*straightway he entered into a ship with his disciples, and came
11　into the parts of Dalmanutha.　And *h*the Pharisees came forth, and began
　　to question with him, seeking of him a sign from heaven, tempting him.
12　And he sighed deeply in his spirit, and saith, Why doth this generation
　　seek after a sign?　Verily I say unto you, There shall no sign be given
13　unto this generation.　And he left them, and, entering into the ship
　　again, departed to the other side.
14　Now *i the disciples* had forgotten to take bread, neither had they in the
15　ship with them more than one loaf.　And *j*he charged them, saying, Take
　　heed, beware of the leaven of the Pharisees, and *of* the leaven of Herod.
16　And they reasoned among themselves, saying, *It is* *k*because we have no

A. D. 32
g Matt. 15 39.
h Matt 12.38.
　 Matt. 16. 1.
　 Matt. 19. 3.
　 ch 2. 16.
　 Luke 11.53.
　 John 6. 30.
i Matt. 16. 5.
j Num.27.19.
　 1 Chr. 28. 9.
　 Luke 12. 1.
　 1 Cor. 5. 7.
k Matt. 16. 7.

---

baskets taken up filled with the fragments was twelve; in the other seven: but more than all, perhaps, because apparently quite incidental, in the one case the name given to the kind of baskets used is the same in all the four narratives—the *cophinus* (see on ch. vi. 43); in the other case the name given to the kind of baskets used, while it is the same in both the narratives, is quite different—the *spuris* [σπυρίς], a basket large enough to hold a man's body, for Paul was let down in one of these from the wall of Damascus [ἐν σπυρίδι], (Acts ix. 25). It might be added, that in the one case the people, in a frenzy of enthusiasm, would have taken Him by force to make Him a king; in the other case no such excitement is recorded. In view of these things, who could have believed that these were one and the same miracle, even if the Lord Himself had not expressly distinguished them?

Sign from Heaven Sought (10-13). **10. And straightway he entered into a ship** [εἰς τὸ πλοῖον] —'into the ship,' or 'embarked,' **with his disciples, and came into the parts of Dalmanutha.** In Matthew (xv. 39) it is "the coasts of Magdala." [For this word *Tischendorf, Tregelles*, and others read 'Magadan'—Μαγαδάν—on weighty, but not, as we think, preponderating authority. It is indeed easier to see how "Magadan"—a place of which nobody seems ever to have known anything—should have been changed into the now pretty well identified "Magdala," than how the known place should have been changed into one totally unknown. But the authorities do not seem to authorize this change in the text.] Magdala and Dalmanutha were both on the western shore of the lake, and probably not far apart. From the former the surname "Magdalenē" was probably taken, to denote the residence of one of the Maries. Dalmanutha may have been a village, but it cannot now be identified with certainty. **11. And the Pharisees came forth, and began to question with him, seeking of him a sign from heaven, tempting him**—not in the least desiring evidence for their conviction, but hoping to entrap Him. The first part of the answer is given in Matthew alone (xvi. 2, 3): "He answered and said unto them, When it is evening, ye say, It will be fair weather: for the sky is red. And in the morning, It will be foul weather to day: for the sky is red and lowring"—'sullen' or 'gloomy' [στυγνάζων]. "Hypocrites! ye can discern the face of the sky; but can ye not discern the signs of the times?" The same simplicity of purpose and careful observation of the symptoms of approaching events which they showed in common things would enable them to "discern the signs of the times"—or rather "seasons," to which the prophets pointed for the manifestation of the Messiah. The sceptre had departed from Judah; Daniel's seventy weeks were expiring, &c.; and many other significant indications of the close of

the old economy, and preparations for a freer and more comprehensive one, might have been discerned. But all was lost upon them. **12. And he sighed deeply in his spirit** [ἀναστενάξας τῷ πνεύματι αὐτοῦ]. The language is very strong. These glimpses into the interior of the Redeemer's heart, in which our Evangelist abounds, are more precious than rubies. The state of the Pharisaic heart, which prompted this desire for a fresh sign, went to His very soul. **and saith, Why doth this generation**—"this wicked and adulterous generation" (Matt. xvi. 4), **seek after a sign?**—when they have had such abundant evidence already? **There shall no sign be given unto this generation** [εἰ δοθήσεται]—lit., 'If there shall be given to this generation a sign;' a Jewish way of expressing a solemn and peremptory determination to the contrary, (compare Heb. iv. 5; Ps. xcv. 11, marg.) 'A generation incapable of appreciating such demonstrations shall not be gratified with them.' In Matt. xvi. 4, He added, "but the sign of the prophet Jonas." See on Matt. xii. 39, 40. **13. And he left them**—no doubt with tokens of displeasure, **and entering into the ship again, departed to the other side.**

The Leaven of the Pharisees and Sadducees (14-21). **14. Now the disciples had forgotten to take bread, neither had they in the ship with them more than one loaf.** This is another example of that graphic circumstantiality which gives such a charm to this briefest of the four Gospels. The circumstance of the "one loaf" only remaining, as *Webster and Wilkinson* remark, was more suggestive of their Master's recent miracles than the entire absence of provisions. **15. And he charged them, saying, Take heed, beware of the leaven of the Pharisees**—"and of the Sadducees" (Matt. xvi. 6), **and of the leaven of Herod.** The teaching or "doctrine" (Matt. xvi. 12) of the Pharisees and of the Sadducees was quite different, but both were equally pernicious; and the Herodians, though rather a political party, were equally envenomed against our Lord's spiritual teaching. See on Matt. xii. 11. The *penetrating* and *diffusive* quality of leaven, for good or bad, is the ground of the comparison. **16. And they reasoned among themselves, saying, It is because we have no bread.** But a little ago He was tried with the obduracy of the Pharisees; now He is tried with the obtuseness of His own disciples. The *nine* questions following each other in rapid succession (*vv.* 17-21), show how deeply He was hurt at this want of spiritual apprehension, and worse still, their low thoughts of Him, as if He would utter so solemn a warning on so petty a subject. It will be seen, however—from the very form of their conjecture, "It is because *we* have no bread," and our Lord's astonishment that they should not by that time have known better what He took up His attention with—that He ever left *the whole care for His own temporal wants to the Twelve*: that He did this so

17 bread. And when Jesus knew *it*, he saith unto them, Why reason ye
because ye have no bread? 'perceive ye not yet, neither understand?
18 have ye your heart yet hardened? Having eyes, see ye not? and having
19 ears, hear ye not? and do ye not remember? When *m* I brake the five
loaves among five thousand, how many baskets full of fragments took ye
20 up? They say unto him, Twelve. And *n* when the seven among four
thousand, how many baskets full of fragments took ye up? And they said,
21 Seven. And he said unto them, How is it °that ye do not understand?
22   And he cometh to Bethsaida; and they bring a blind man unto him,
23 and besought him to touch him. And he took the blind man by the
hand, and led him out of the town; and when *p* he had spit on his eyes,
24 and put his hands upon him, he asked him if he saw ought. And he
25 looked up, and said, I see men as trees, walking. After that he put *his*
hands again upon his eyes, and made him look up: and he was restored,
26 and saw every man clearly. And he sent him away to his house, saying,
Neither go into the town, *q* nor tell *it* to any in the town.

A. D. 32.

i Isa. 63. 17.
Matt. 15.17.
Matt. 16. 8.
9.
ch. 6. 52.
ch. 16. 14.
Luke 24. 25
Heb. 5. 11.
12.
m Matt. 24.20.
ch. 6. 43.
Luke 9. 17.
John 6. 13.
n Matt. 15.37.
° Ps. 94. 8.
ch. 6. 52.
John 14. 9.
p ch. 7. 33.
q Matt. 8. 4.
ch 5. 43.

entirely, that finding they were reduced to their last loaf they felt as if unworthy of such a trust, and could not think but that the same thought was in their Lord's mind which was pressing upon their own; but that in this they were so far wrong that it hurt His feelings—sharp just in proportion to His love—that such a thought of Him should have entered their minds! Who that, like angels, "desire to look into these things" will not prize such glimpses above gold? 17. **And when Jesus knew it, he saith unto them, Why reason ye because ye have no bread? perceive ye not yet, neither understand? have ye your heart yet hardened?** How strong an expression to use of true-hearted disciples! See on ch. vi. 52. 18. **Having eyes, see ye not? and having ears, hear ye not?** See on Matt. xiii. 13. **and do ye not remember?** 19. **When I brake the five loaves among**—'the'—**five thousand, how many baskets** [κοφίνους] **full of fragments took ye up? They say unto him, Twelve.** 20. **And when the seven among**—'the'—**four thousand, how many baskets** [σπυρίδων] **full of fragments took ye up? And they said, Seven.** 21. **And he said unto them, How is it that ye do not understand?**—'do not understand that the warning I gave you could not have been prompted by any such petty consideration as the want of loaves in your scrip?' Profuse as were our Lord's miracles, we see from this that they were not wrought at random, but that He carefully noted their minutest details, and desired that this should be done by those who witnessed, as doubtless by all who read the record of them. Even the different kind of baskets used at the two miraculous feedings, so carefully noted in the two narratives, are here also referred to; the one smaller, of which there were twelve, the other much larger, of which there were seven. *Blind Man at Bethsaida Restored to Sight* (22-26). 22. **And he cometh to Bethsaida**—Bethsaida-Julias, on the north-east side of the lake, whence after this He proceeded to Cesarea Philippi (*v.* 27)—**and they bring a blind man unto him, and besought him to touch him.** See on ch. vii. 32. 23. **And he took the blind man by the hand, and led him out of the town.** Of the deaf and dumb man it is merely said that "He took him aside" (ch. vii. 33); but this blind man He *led by the hand* out of the town, doing it Himself rather than employing another—great humility, exclaims *Bengel!*—that He might gain his confidence and raise his expectation. **and when he had spit on his eyes**—the organ affected. See on ch. vii. 33. **and put his hands upon him,**

he asked him if he saw ought. 24. **And he looked up, and said, I see men as trees, walking.** This is one of the cases in which one edition of what is called the received text differs from another. That which is decidedly the best supported, and has also internal evidence on its side is this: 'I see men; for I see [them] as trees walking' [βλέπω τοὺς ἀνθρώπους, ὅτι ὡς δένδρα ὁρῶ περιπατοῦντας]— that is, he could distinguish them from trees only by their motion; a minute mark of truth in the narrative, as *Alford* observes, describing how human objects had appeared to him during that gradual failing of sight which had ended in blindness. 25. **After that he put his hands again upon his eyes, and made him look up: and he was restored, and saw every man clearly.** Perhaps the one operation perfectly restored the *eyes*, while the other imparted immediately the *faculty of using them*. It is the only recorded example of a *progressive* cure, and it certainly illustrates similar methods in the spiritual kingdom. Of the four recorded cases of sight restored, all the patients save one either *came* or *were brought* to the Physician. In the case of the man born blind, *the Physician came* to the patient. So some seek and find Christ; of others He is found who seek Him not. See on Matt. xiii. 44-46, Remark 1. 26. **And he sent him away to his house, saying, Neither go into the town, nor tell it to any in the town.** Besides the usual reasons against going about "blazing the matter," retirement in this case would be salutary to himself.

Remarks.—1. When our Lord was about to open the ears and loose the tongue of the deaf man who had an impediment in his speech, our Evangelist says that He looked up to heaven and *sighed* (ch. vii. 34); but when He had to reply to the captious petulance which sought of Him, amidst a profusion of signs, a sign from heaven, he says He *sighed deeply in His spirit*. Nor can we wonder. For if the spectacle of what sin had done affected Him deeply, how much more deeply would sin itself affect Him, when exhibited in so trying a form! And occurring, as such things now did, almost daily, what a touching commentary do they furnish on the prophetic account of Him as "a Man of sorrows, and acquainted with grief"! 2. When men apply to religion none of the ordinary principles of judgment and action, it shows itself to be with them but an empty creed or an outward ritual, neither acceptable to God nor profitable to themselves. But when it becomes a nature and a life, we learn to bring all our natural judgment,

27   And *Jesus went out, and his disciples, into the towns of Cesarea Philippi: and by the way he asked his disciples, saying unto them,
28   Whom do men say that I am?   And they answered, *John the Baptist:
29   but some *say*, Elias; and others, One of the prophets.   And he saith unto them, But whom say ye that I am?   And Peter answereth and saith
30   unto him, *Thou art the Christ.   And *he charged them that they should tell no man of him.
31   And *he began to teach them, that the Son of man must suffer many things, and be rejected of the elders, and *of* the chief priests, and scribes,
32   and be killed, and after three days rise again.   And he spake that saying
33   openly.   And Peter took him, and began to rebuke him.   But when he had turned about, and looked on his disciples, he rebuked Peter, saying, Get thee behind me, Satan: *for thou savourest not the things that be of God, but the things that be of men.
34   And when he had called the people *unto him*, with his disciples also, he said unto them, *Whosoever will come after me, let him deny himself,
35   and take up his cross, and follow me.   For *whosoever will save his life shall lose it; but whosoever shall lose his life for my sake and the
36   Gospel's, the same shall save it.   For what shall it profit a man, if he
37   shall gain the whole world, and lose his own soul?   Or what shall a man
38   give in exchange for his soul?   Whosoever *therefore shall be ashamed of me and of my words in this adulterous and sinful generation, of him also shall the Son of man be ashamed, when he cometh in the glory of his Father with the holy angels.

9   AND he said unto them, *Verily I say unto you, That there be some of them that stand here, which shall not taste of death, till they have seen *the kingdom of God come with power.
2   And *after six days Jesus taketh *with him* Peter, and James, and John, and leadeth them up into an high mountain apart by themselves: and he
3   was transfigured before them.   And his raiment became shining, exceeding
4   *white as snow; so as no fuller on earth can white them.   And there appeared unto them Elias with Moses: and they were talking with Jesus.
5   And Peter answered and said to Jesus, Master, it is good for us to be here: and let us make three tabernacles; one for thee, and one for Moses,
6   and one for Elias.   For he wist not what to say; for they were sore afraid.
7   And there was *a cloud that overshadowed them: and a voice came out
8   of the cloud, saying, This is my beloved Son: hear *him.   And suddenly, when they had looked round about, they saw no man any more, save Jesus only with themselves.

A. D. 32.

Matt. 16.13.
Luke 9. 18.
*Matt. 14. 2.
*Matt. 16. 6.
John 1. 41. 49.
John 6. 69.
John 11.27.
Acts 8. 37.
Acts 9. 20.
1 John 4.15.
*Matt. 16.20.
*Matt. 16.21.
Matt. 17.22.
Luke 9. 22.
*Rom. 8. 7.
1 Cor. 2. 14.
*Matt. 10.38.
Matt. 16.24.
Luke 9. 23.
Luke 14.27.
Gal. 5. 24.
Gal. 6. 14.
*John 12 25.
Rev. 12. 11.
*Matt. 10.33.
Luke 9. 26.
Luke 12. 9.
Rom. 1, 16.
2 Tim. 1. 8.
2 Tim. 2.12.
1 John 2.23.

CHAP. 9.
*Matt 16.28.
Luke 9. 27.
*Matt. 24.30.
Matt. 25.31.
Luke 22. 18.
Heb. 2. 8, 9.
*Matt. 17. 1.
Luke 9. 28.
d Dan. 7. 9.
Matt. 28. 3.
*Ex. 40. 34.
Isa. 42. 1.
2 Pet. 1. 17.
*Heb. 1. 1, 2.
Heb. 2. 3.
Heb. 12. 25, 26.

---

worldly sagacity, ordinary shrewdness, and growing experience to bear upon religious matters; and thus our entire life acquires a unity—having to do now with things temporal, and now with things spiritual and eternal, but in both cases alike governed by the same principles and directed to the same ends. And yet, how often do even the children of God incur that rebuke of their Lord, that they can discern the signs of change in the material, mercantile, or political atmosphere, but are dull in their perceptions of what is passing, and in their ability to forecast what is coming, in the moral, religious, or spiritual world! 3. If the Redeemer was tried with enemies, He had not a little to bear from time to time even from His own chosen Twelve. How little did they comprehend much that He said to them; how unworthy of Him were many of the thoughts which they imagined to be passing through His mind; and how petty the motives by which they supposed Him to be actuated! How admirable is the long-suffering patience which bore with both! But is the need for this patience yet ended? Not to speak

of the world's enmity to Him, His truth, His cause, His people, which time certainly has not changed, is there not much still in His own people, the endurance of which, when rightly apprehended, is matter of wonder? 4. As our Lord seems purposely to have varied His mode of healing the maladies that came before Him—having respect, doubtless, to the nature of each case—so is the history of every soul that is healed of its deadly malady by the Great Physician different, probably, from that of every other: some, in particular, being healed quickly, others slowly; some apparently by one word, others by successive steps. But as in all the result is one, so the hand of one mighty, gracious Healer is to be seen alike in all.

27-38.—PETER'S NOBLE CONFESSION OF CHRIST—OUR LORD'S FIRST EXPLICIT ANNOUNCEMENT OF HIS APPROACHING SUFFERINGS, DEATH, AND RESURRECTION—HIS REBUKE OF PETER, AND WARNING TO ALL THE TWELVE. (= Matt. xvi. 13-27; Luke ix. 18-26.) For the exposition, see on Matt. xvi. 13-23.
CHAP. IX. 1-13.—JESUS IS TRANSFIGURED—

9   And *g*as they came down from the mountain, he charged them that they should tell no man what things they had seen, till the Son of man
10 were risen from the dead. And they kept that saying with themselves, questioning one with another what the rising from the dead should
11 mean. And they asked him, saying, Why say the scribes *h*that Elias
12 must first come? And. he answered and told them, Elias verily cometh first, and restoreth all things; and *i*how it is written of the Son of man,
13 that he must suffer many things, and *j*be set at nought. But I say unto you, That *k*Elias is indeed come, and they have done unto him whatsoever they listed, as it is written of him.
14   And *l*when he came to *his* disciples, he saw a great multitude about
15 them, and the scribes questioning with them. And straightway all the people, when they beheld him, were greatly amazed, and running to *him*
16 saluted him. And he asked the scribes, What question ye ¹with them?
17 And *m*one of the multitude answered and said, Master, I have brought
18 unto thee my son, which hath a dumb spirit: and wheresoever he taketh him, he ²teareth him; and he foameth, and gnasheth with his teeth, and pineth away: and I spake to thy disciples that they should cast him out;
19 and they could not. He answereth him, and saith, O faithless generation, how long shall I be with you? how long shall I suffer you? Bring him

A. D. 32.
g Matt. 17. 9.
h Mal. 4. 5.
Matt. 17.10.
i Gen. 3. 15.
Num. 21. 9.
Ps. 22. 6.
Isa. 50. 6.
Isa. 53. 2.
Dan. 9. 26.
Zec. 13. 7.
John 3. 14.
j Luke 23.11.
Phil. 2. 7.
k Matt.11.14.
Matt. 17.12.
Luke 1. 17.
l Matt. 17.14.
Luke 9. 37.
1 Or, among yourselves?
m Matt 17 14
Luke 9. 33.
2 Or, dasheth him.

CONVERSATION ABOUT ELIAS. (= Matt. xvi. 28—xvii. 13; Luke ix, 27-36.) For the exposition, see on Luke ix. 27-36.

14-32.—HEALING OF A DEMONIAC BOY—SECOND EXPLICIT ANNOUNCEMENT OF HIS APPROACHING DEATH AND RESURRECTION. (= Matt. xvii. 14-23; Luke ix. 37-45.)

Healing of the Demoniac Boy (14-29). **14. And when he came to his disciples, he saw a great multitude about them, and the scribes questioning with them.** This was "on the next day, when they were come down from the hill" (Luke ix. 37). The Transfiguration appears to have taken place at night. In the morning, as He came down from the hill on which it took place—with Peter, and James, and John—on approaching the other nine, He found them surrounded by a great multitude, and the scribes disputing or discussing with them. No doubt these cavillers were twitting the apostles of Jesus with their inability to cure the demoniac boy of whom we are presently to hear, and insinuating doubts even of their Master's ability to do it; while they, zealous for their Master's honour, would no doubt refer to His past miracles in proof of the contrary. **15. And straightway all the people**—'the multitude' [ὁ ὄχλος], **when they beheld him, were greatly amazed** [ἐξεθαμβήθη]—or 'were astounded'—**and running to him saluted him.** The singularly strong expression of surprise, the sudden arrest of the discussion, and the rush of the multitude towards Him, can be accounted for by nothing less than something amazing in His appearance. There can hardly be any doubt that *His countenance still retained traces of His transfiguration-glory.* (See Exod. xxxiv. 29, 30.) So *Bengel, De Wette, Meyer, Trench, Alford.* No wonder, if this was the case, that they not only ran to Him, but saluted Him. Our Lord, however, takes no notice of what had attracted them, and probably it gradually faded away as He drew near; but addressing Himself to the scribes, He demands the subject of their discussion, ready to meet them where they had pressed hard upon His half-instructed, and as yet timid apostles. **16. And he asked the scribes, What question ye with them?** Ere they had time to reply, the father of the boy, whose case had occasioned the dispute, himself steps forward and answers the question; telling a piteous tale of deafness, and dumbness, and fits of epilepsy—ending with this, that the disciples, though entreated, could not perform the cure. **17. And one of the multitude answered and said, Master, I have brought unto thee my son**—"mine only child" (Luke ix. 38), **which hath a dumb spirit**—a spirit whose operation had the effect of rendering his victim speechless, and deaf also (v. 25). In Matthew's report of the speech (xvii. 15), the father says "he is lunatic;" this being another and most distressing effect of the possession. **18. And wheresoever he taketh him, he teareth him; and he foameth, and gnasheth with his teeth, and pineth away** [ξηραίνεται]—rather, 'becomes withered,' 'dried up,' or 'paralyzed;' as the same word is everywhere else rendered in the New Testament. Some additional particulars are given by Luke, and by our Evangelist below. "Lo," says he in Luke ix. 39, "a spirit taketh him, and he suddenly crieth out; and it teareth him that he foameth again, and bruising him hardly (or with difficulty) departeth from him." **and I spake to thy disciples that they should cast him out; and they could not.** Our Lord replies to the father by a severe rebuke to the disciples. As if wounded at the exposure before such a multitude, of the weakness of His disciples' faith, which doubtless He felt as a reflection on Himself, He puts them to the blush before all, but in language fitted only to raise expectation of what Himself would do. **19. He answereth him, and saith, O faithless generation**—"and perverse," or 'perverted' [διεστραμμένη] (Matt. xvii. 17; Luke ix. 41), **how long shall I be with you? how long shall I suffer you?**—language implying that it was a shame to them to want the faith necessary to perform this cure, and that it needed some patience to put up with them. It is to us surprising that some interpreters, as *Chrysostom* and *Calvin*, should represent this rebuke as addressed, not to the disciples at all, but to the scribes who disputed with them. Nor does it much, if at all, mend the matter to view it as addressed to both, as most expositors seem to do. With *Bengel, de Wette,* and *Meyer,* we regard it as addressed directly to the nine apostles who were unable to expel this evil spirit. And though, in ascribing this inability to their 'want of faith' and the 'perverted turn of mind' which they had drunk in with their early training, the rebuke

172

20 unto me. And they brought him unto him: and when [n]he saw him, straightway the spirit tare him; and he fell on the ground, and wallowed
21 foaming. And he asked his father, How long is it ago since this came
22 unto him? And he said, Of a child. And ofttimes it hath cast him into the fire, and into the waters, to destroy him: but if thou canst do
23 any thing, have compassion on us, and help us. Jesus said unto him,
24 [o]If thou canst believe, all things *are* possible to him that believeth. And straightway the father of the child cried out, and said with tears, Lord, I
25 believe; [p]help thou mine unbelief. When Jesus saw that the people came running together, he [q]rebuked the foul spirit, saying unto him, *Thou* dumb and deaf spirit, I charge thee, come out of him, and enter no
26 more into him. And *the spirit* cried, and rent him sore, and came out

A. D. 32.
[n] ch. 1. 26.
Luke 9. 42.
[o] 2 Chr. 20 20.
Matt. 17.20.
ch. 11. 23.
Luke 17. 6.
John 11.40.
Acts 14. 9.
[p] Phil. 1. 29.
2 Thes. 1. 3, 11.
Heb. 12. 2.
[q] Acts 10 38.
1 John 3. 8.

would undoubtedly apply, with vastly greater force, to those who twitted the poor disciples with their inability; it would be to change the whole nature of the rebuke to suppose it addressed to those who had *no faith at all*, and were *wholly perverted*. It was because faith sufficient for curing this youth was to have been expected of the disciples, and because they should by that time have got rid of the perversity in which they had been reared, that Jesus exposes them thus before the rest. And who does not see that this was fitted, more than anything else, to impress upon the bystanders the severe loftiness of the training He was giving to the Twelve, and the unsophisticated footing He was on with them? **Bring him unto me.** The order to bring the patient to Him was instantly obeyed; when, lo! as if conscious of the presence of his divine Tormentor, and expecting to be made to quit, the foul spirit rages and is furious, determined to die hard, doing all the mischief he can to this poor child while yet within his grasp. **20. And they brought him unto him: and when he saw him, straightway the spirit tare him.** Just as the man with the legion of demons, "when he *saw* Jesus, ran and worshipped Him" (ch. v. 6), so this demon, *when he saw Him*, immediately "tare him." The feeling of terror and rage was the same in both cases. **and he fell on the ground, and wallowed foaming.** Still Jesus does nothing, but keeps conversing with the father about the case—partly to have its desperate features told out by him who knew them best, in the hearing of the spectators; partly to let its virulence have time to show itself; and partly to deepen the exercise of the father's soul, to draw out his faith, and thus to prepare both him and the bystanders for what He was to do. **21. And he asked his father, How long is it ago since this came unto him? And he said, Of a child. 22. And ofttimes it hath cast him into the fire, and into the waters, to destroy him.** Having told briefly the affecting features of the case, the poor father, half dispirited by the failure of the disciples and the aggravated virulence of the malady itself in presence of their Master, yet encouraged too by what he had heard of Christ, by the severe rebuke He had given to His disciples for not having faith enough to cure the boy, and by the dignity with which He had ordered him to be brought to Him—in this mixed state of mind, he closes his description of the case with these touching words: **but if thou canst do any thing, have compassion on us, and help us**—"us," says the father; for it was a sore family affliction. Compare the language of the Syrophenician woman regarding her daughter, "Lord, help *me*." Still, nothing is done; the man is but *struggling into faith;* it must come a step farther. But he had to do with Him who breaks not the bruised reed, and who knew how to inspire what He demanded. The man had said to Him, "*If*

Thou canst do;" **23. Jesus**—retorting upon him, **said unto him, If thou canst believe:** The man had said, "If Thou canst do *any thing;*" Jesus replies, **all things are possible to him that believeth**—'My doing all depends on thy believing.' To impress this still more, He redoubles upon the believing: "If thou canst believe, all things are possible to him that believeth." Thus the Lord helps the birth of faith in that struggling soul; and now, though with pain and sore travail, it comes to the birth, as *Trench*, borrowing from *Olshausen*, expresses it. Seeing the case stood still, waiting not upon the Lord's power but his own faith, the man becomes immediately conscious of conflicting principles, and rises into one of the noblest utterances on record. **24. And straightway the father of the child cried out, and said with tears, Lord, I believe; help thou mine unbelief.**—*q. d.*, "'Tis useless concealing from Thee, O Thou mysterious, mighty Healer, the unbelief that still struggles in this heart of mine; but that heart bears me witness that I do believe in Thee; and if distrust still remains, I disown it, I wrestle with it, I seek help from Thee against it.' Two things are very remarkable here: First, *The felt and owned presence of unbelief,* which only the strength of the man's faith could have so revealed to his own consciousness. Second, *His appeal to Christ for help against his felt unbelief*—a feature in the case quite unparalleled, and showing, more than all protestations could have done, the insight he had attained into the existence of *a power in Christ more glorious than any he had besought for his poor child.* The work was done; and as the commotion and confusion in the crowd was now increasing, Jesus at once, as Lord of spirits, gives the word of command to the dumb and deaf spirit to be gone, never again to return to his victim. **25. When Jesus saw that the people came running together, he rebuked the foul spirit, saying unto him, Dumb and deaf spirit, I charge thee, come out of him, and enter no more into him. 26. And the spirit cried, and rent him sore, and came out of him: and he was as one dead; insomuch that many said, He is dead.** The malignant, cruel spirit, now conscious that his time was come, gathers up his whole strength, with intent by a last stroke to kill his victim, and had nearly succeeded. But the Lord of life was there; the Healer of all maladies, the Friend of sinners, the Seed of the woman, "the Stronger than the strong man armed," was there. The very faith which Christ declared to be enough for everything being now found, it was not possible that the serpent should prevail. Fearfully is he permitted to bruise the *heel*, as in this case; but his own *head* shall go for it—his works shall be destroyed (1 John iii. 8). **27. But Jesus took him by the hand, and lifted him up; and he arose.**

of him: and he was as one dead; insomuch that many said, He is dead.
27 But Jesus took him by the hand, and lifted him up; and he arose.
28 And 'when he was come into the house, his disciples asked him
29 privately, Why could not we cast him out? And he said unto them,
This kind can come forth by nothing but by prayer and fasting.
30 And they departed thence, and passed through Galilee; and he would
31 not that any man should know *it*. For 'he taught his disciples, and said
unto them, The Son of man is delivered into the hands of men, and they
shall kill him; and after that he is killed, he shall rise the third day.
32 But they understood not that saying, and were afraid to ask him.

A. D. 32.
^r Matt. 17. 19.
^s Matt. 17. 22.
ch 8. 31.
Luke 9. 44.
Luke 22. 24,
44, 46.
John 2. 19.
John 3. 14.
John 10. 18.
Acts 2. 23,
24.
2 Tim. 2. 2.

28. And when he was come into the house, his disciples asked him privately, Why could not we cast him out? 29. And he said unto them, This kind can come forth by nothing but by prayer and fasting—that is, as nearly all good interpreters are agreed, 'this kind of evil spirits cannot be expelled,' or 'so desperate a case of demoniacal possession cannot be cured, but by prayer and fasting.' But since the Lord Himself says that His disciples could not fast while He was with them, perhaps this was designed, as *Alford* hints, for their after guidance—unless we take it as but a definite way of expressing the general truth, that great and difficult duties require special preparation and self-denial. But the answer to their question, as given by Matthew (xvii.), is more full: "And Jesus said unto them, Because of your unbelief" [ἀπιστίαν. *Tregelles*, on insufficient authority, as we think, substitutes what appears to be a mere interpretation—ὀλιγοπιστίαν, 'because of your little faith.' *Tischendorf* adheres to the received text.] "For verily I say unto you, If ye have faith as a grain of mustard seed, ye shall say unto this mountain, Remove hence to yonder place, and it shall remove; and nothing shall be impossible unto you" (*v.* 20). See on Mark xi. 23. "Howbeit this kind goeth not out but by prayer and fasting" (*v.* 21): that is, though nothing is impossible to faith, yet such a height of faith as is requisite for such triumphs is not to be reached either in a moment or without effort—either with God in prayer or with ourselves in self-denying exercises. Luke (ix. 43) adds, "And they were all amazed at the mighty power of God" [ἐπὶ τῇ μεγαλειότητι τοῦ θεοῦ]—'at the majesty' or 'mightiness of God,' in this last miracle, in the transfiguration, &c.; or, at the *divine grandeur* of Christ rising upon them daily.

Second Explicit Announcement of His Approaching Death and Resurrection (30-32). **30. And they departed thence, and passed** [παρεπορεύοντο]—'were passing along' **through Galilee; and he would not that any man should know it.** By comparing Matt. xvii. 22, 23, and Luke ix. 43, 44, with this, we gather, that as our Lord's reason for going through Galilee more privately than usual on this occasion, was to reiterate to them the announcement which had so shocked them at the first mention of it, and thus familiarize them with it by little and little, so this was His reason for enjoining silence upon them as to their present movements. **31. For he taught his disciples, and said unto them**—"Let these sayings sink down into your ears" (Luke ix. 44); not what had been passing between them as to His grandeur, but what He was now to utter, "for" **The Son of man is delivered** [παραδίδοται]. The use of the present tense expresses how near at hand He would have them to consider it. As *Bengel* says, steps were already in course of being taken to bring it about. **into the hands of men.** This remarkable anti-

thesis—"the Son of *man* shall be delivered into the hands of *men*"—it is worthy of notice, is in all the three Evangelists. **and they shall kill him**:—*q. d.*, 'Be not carried off your feet by all that grandeur of Mine which ye have lately witnessed, but bear in mind what I have already told you and now distinctly repeat, that that Sun in whose beams ye now rejoice is soon to set in midnight gloom.' **and after he is killed, he shall rise the third day. 32. But they understood not that saying**—"and it was hid from them, [so] that they perceived it not" (Luke ix. 45), **and were afraid to ask him.** Their most cherished ideas were so completely dashed by such announcements, that they were afraid of laying themselves open to rebuke by asking Him any questions. But "they were exceeding sorry" (Matt. xvii. 23). While the other Evangelists, as *Webster and Wilkinson* remark, notice their ignorance and their fear, St. Matthew, who was one of them, retains a vivid recollection of their sorrow.

Remarks.—1. When the keen-edged rebuke which our Lord administers to his apostles (*v.* 19, and Matt. xvii. 17) is compared with the almost identical language of Jehovah Himself to His ancient people, on an occasion of the deepest provocation (Num. xiv. 11, 27), who can help coming to the conclusion, that He regarded Himself as occupying the same position towards His disciples which the Lord God of Israel did towards His people of old? Let this be weighed. And it tends greatly to confirm this, that never once do we find anything approaching to a rebuke of them, or a correction of mistake in them or any others, for attributing *too much* to Him or conceiving of Him *too loftily*. Here, as everywhere else, it is the reverse. He takes with every charge of His "making Himself equal with God," and what He says in reply is but designed to make that good. Here, He is hurt at His disciples because their confidence in His power to aid them, even when at a distance from them, was not such as to enable them to grapple successfully even with one of the most desperate manifestations of diabolical power. 2. Our Lord thinks such attachment to Him and confidence in Him as is found in all genuine disciples from the first, is not enough. As there are degrees in this—from the lowest to the highest, from the infancy to the manhood of faith—so He takes it ill when His people either make no progress, or inadequate progress; when, "for the time they ought to be teachers, they have need that one teach them" (Heb. v. 12); when they do not "grow in grace, and in the knowledge of our Lord and Saviour Jesus Christ" (2 Pet. iii. 18). 3. How often have we to remark that distress and extremity in honest hearts does more towards a right appreciation of the glory of Christ than all teaching without it! (See, for example, on Luke vii. 36-50; xxiii. 39-43.) Here is a man who, without any of the advantages of the Twelve, but out of the depths of his anguish,

33　And ʰhe came to Capernaum: and, being in the house, he asked them,
34　What was it that ye disputed among yourselves by the way? But they
　　held their peace: ᵘfor by the way they had disputed among themselves,
35　who *should be* the greatest. And he sat down, and called the twelve, and
　　saith unto them, ᵛIf any man desire to be first, *the same* shall be last of
36　all, and servant of all. And ʷhe took a child, and set him in the midst
　　of them: and when he had taken him in his arms, he said unto them,
37　Whosoever shall receive one of such children in my name, receiveth me:
　　ˣand whosoever shall receive me, receiveth not me, but him that sent me.
38　And ʸJohn answered him, saying, Master, we saw one casting out

A. D. 32.
ᵗ Matt. 18. 1.
Luke 9. 46.
ᵘ Pro. 13. 10.
ᵛ Matt. 20. 26,
27.
ch. 10. 43.
ʷ Matt. 18. 2.
ch. 10. 16.
ˣ Matt. 10. 40.
Luke 9. 48.
ʸ Num. 11. 28.
Luke 9. 49.

utters a speech more glorifying to Christ than all which they ever expressed during the days of His flesh—protesting his faith in the Lord Jesus, but in the same breath beseeching Him for help against his unbelief! To be conscious at once both of faith and of unbelief; to take the part of the one against the other; yet to feel the unbelief, though disowned and struggled against, to be strong and obstinate, while his faith was feeble and ready to be overpowered, and so to "cry out" even "with tears" for help against that cursed unbelief—this is such a wonderful speech, that, all things considered, the like of it is not to be found. The nearest to it is that prayer of the apostles to the Lord, "Increase our faith" (Luke xvii. 5). But besides that this was uttered by *apostles,* whose advantages were vastly greater than this man's, it was said *a good while after* the scene here recorded, and was evidently but an echo, or rather an adaptation of it. So that this man's cry may be said to have supplied the apostles themselves with a new idea, nay perhaps with a new view altogether of the power of Christ. And is it not true still, that "there are last which shall be first"? 4. Signal triumphs in the kingdom of grace are not to be won by an easy faith, or by stationary, slothful, self-indulgent believers: they are to be achieved only by much nearness to God and denial of ourselves. As to "fasting," if the question be, Whether and how far is it an evangelical duty? there is a preliminary question, What is its proper object? Evidently the mortification of the flesh; and generally, the counteracting of all earthly, sensual, grovelling tendencies, which eat out the heart of our spirituality. Hence it follows, that whatever abstinence from food is observed *without any reference to this object,* and for its own sake, is nothing but "bodily exercise" (1 Tim. iv. 8); and whatsoever abstinence is found by experience to have an exhausting, stupefying effect upon the spirit itself, is, so far as it is so, of the same nature. The true fasting is the opposite of "surfeiting" (Luke xxi. 34), which destroys all elasticity of spirit and all vigour of thought and feeling. And while Christians should habitually keep themselves far from this, by being sparing rather than otherwise in the satisfaction of their appetites, the lesson here taught us is that there are sometimes duties to be done and victories to be achieved, which demand even more than ordinary nearness to God in prayer, and more than ordinary denial of ourselves.

33-50.—Strife among the Twelve who should be Greatest in the Kingdom of Heaven, with Relative Teaching—Incidental Rebuke of John for Exclusiveness. (=Matt. xviii. 1-9; Luke ix. 46-50.)

Strife among the Twelve, with Relative Teaching (33-37). **33. And he came to Capernaum: and, being in the house, he asked them, What was it that ye disputed among yourselves by the way?** From this we gather that after the painful communication He had made to them, the Redeemer had

allowed them to travel so much of the way by themselves;.partly, no doubt, that He might have privacy for Himself to dwell on what lay before Him, and partly that they might be induced to weigh together and prepare themselves for the terrible events which He had announced to them. But if so, how different was their occupation! **34. But they held their peace: for by the way they had disputed among themselves, who should be the greatest.** From Matt. xviii. 1 we should infer that the subject was introduced, not by our Lord, but by the disciples themselves, who came and asked Jesus who should be greatest. Perhaps one or two of them first referred the matter to Jesus, who put them off till they should all be assembled together at Capernaum. He had all the while "perceived the thought of their heart" (Luke ix. 47); but now that they were all together "in the house," He questions them about it, and they are put to the blush, conscious of the *temper* towards each other which it had kindled. This raised the whole question afresh, and at this point our Evangelist takes it up. The subject was suggested by the recent announcement of the Kingdom (Matt. xvi. 19-28), the transfiguration of their Master, and especially the preference given to three of them at that scene. **35. And he sat down, and called the twelve, and saith unto them, If any man desire to be first, the same shall be last of all, and servant of all**—that is, 'let him be' such; he must be prepared to take the last and lowest place. See on ch. x. 42-45. **36. And he took a child** [παιδίον] —'a little child' (Matt. xviii. 2); but the word is the same in both places, as also in Luke ix. 47. **and set him in the midst of them: and when he had taken him in his arms.** This beautiful trait is mentioned by our Evangelist alone. **he said unto them.** Here we must go to Matthew (xviii. 3, 4) for the first part of this answer:—"Verily I say unto you, except ye be converted, and become as little children, ye shall not enter into the kingdom of Heaven:"—*q. d.,* 'Conversion must be thorough; not only must the heart be turned to God in general, and from earthly to heavenly things, but in particular, except ye be converted from that carnal ambition which still rankles within you, into that freedom from all such feelings which ye see in this child, ye have neither part nor lot in the kingdom at all; and he who in this feature has most of the child, is highest there.' Whosoever, therefore, shall "humble himself as this little child, the same is greatest in the kingdom of heaven;" "for he that is (willing to be) least among you all, the same shall be great" (Luke ix. 48). And **Whosoever shall receive one of such children**—so manifesting the spirit unconsciously displayed by this child, **in my name**—from love to Me, **receiveth me; and whosoever shall receive me, receiveth not me, but him that sent me.** See on Matt. x. 40.

Incidental Rebuke of John for Exclusiveness (38-41). **38. And John answered him, saying, Master, we saw one casting out devils in thy**

devils in thy name, and he followeth not us: and we forbade him,
39 because he followeth not us. But Jesus said, Forbid him not: [z]for
there is no man which shall do a miracle in my name, that can lightly
40 speak evil of me. For [a]he that is not against us is on our part.
41 For [b]whosoever shall give you a cup of water to drink in my name,
because ye belong to Christ, verily I say unto you, he shall not lose his
reward.
42 And [c]whosoever shall offend one of *these* little ones that believe in me,
it is better for him that a millstone were hanged about his neck, and he
43 were cast into the sea. And if thy hand [3]offend thee, cut it off: it is
better for thee to enter into life maimed, than having two hands to go
44 into hell, into the fire that never shall be quenched; where [d]their worm
45 dieth not, and the fire is not quenched. And if thy foot offend thee, cut
it off: it is better for thee to enter halt into life, than having two feet to
46 be cast into hell, into the fire that never shall be quenched; where their
47 worm dieth not, and the fire is not quenched. And if thine eye [4]offend
thee, [e]pluck it out: it is better for thee to enter into the kingdom of God
48 with one eye, than having two eyes to be cast into hell-fire; where their

A. D. 32.

[z] 1 Cor. 12. 3.
[a] Matt. 12.30.
    Luke 11.23.
[b] Matt. 10.42.
    Matt. 25. 40.
[c] Matt. 18. 6.
    Luke 17. 1.
[3] Or, cause
    thee to
    offend.
    Deut. 13. 6.
    Matt. 5. 29.
    Matt. 18. 8.
    Col. 3. 5.
    Heb. 12. 1.
[d] Isa. 66. 24.
    2 Thes. 1. 9.
[4] Or, cause
    thee to
    offend.
[e] Rom. 8. 13.
    Gal. 5. 24.

name, and he followeth not us: and we forbade him, because he followeth not us. The link of connection here with the foregoing context lies, we apprehend, in the emphatic words which our Lord had just uttered, "in My name." 'O,' interposes John—young, warm, but not sufficiently apprehending Christ's teaching in these matters—'that reminds me of something that we have just done, and we should like to know if we did right. We saw one casting out devils "*in Thy name*," and we forbade him, because he followeth not us. Were we right, or were we wrong?' Answer—'Ye were wrong.' 'But we did it because he followeth not us?' 'No matter.' **39. But Jesus said, Forbid him not: for there is no man which shall do a miracle in my name, that can lightly [τ αχ ὺ]—or, 'soon,' that is, 'readily,' speak evil of me. 40. For he that is not against us is on our part.** Two principles of immense importance are here laid down: 'First, No one will readily speak evil of Me who has the faith to do a miracle in My name; and Second, If such a person cannot be supposed to be *against* us, ye are to hold him *for* us.' Let it be carefully observed that our Lord does not say this man should *not* have "followed them," nor yet that it was indifferent whether he did or not; but simply teaches how such a person was to be regarded, *although he did not*—namely, as a reverer of His name and a promoter of His cause. **41. For whosoever shall give you a cup of water to drink in my name, because ye belong to Christ, verily I say unto you, he shall not lose his reward.** See on Matt. x. 42.

Continuation of Teaching suggested by the Disciples' Strife (42-50). What follows appears to have no connection with the incidental reproof of John, immediately preceding. As that had interrupted some important teaching, our Lord hastens back from it, as if no such interruption had occurred. **42. And whosoever shall offend [σκανδαλίσῃ] one of these little ones that believe in me**—or, shall cause them to stumble; referring probably to the effect which such unsavoury disputes as they had held would have upon the inquiring and hopeful who came in contact with them, leading to the belief that after all they were no better than others. **It is better for him that a millstone were hanged about his neck.** The word here is simply 'millstone' [λίθος μυλικὸς], without expressing of which kind. But in Matt. xviii. 6, it is the 'ass-turned' kind [μύλος ὀνικὸς], far heavier than the small

hand-mill turned by female slaves, as in Luke xvii. 35. It is of course the same which is meant here. **and he were cast into the sea**—meaning, that if by such a death that stumbling were prevented, and so its eternal consequences averted, it would be a happy thing for them. Here follows a striking verse in Matt. xviii. 7. "Woe unto the world because of offences!"—'There will be stumblings and falls and loss of souls enough from the world's treatment of disciples, without any addition from you: dreadful will be its doom in consequence; see that ye share not in it.' "For it must needs be that offences come; but woe to that man by whom the offence cometh!" 'The struggle between light and darkness will inevitably cause stumblings, but not less guilty is he who wilfully makes any to stumble.' **43. And if thy hand offend thee, cut it off: it is better for thee to enter into life maimed, than having two hands to go into hell.** See on Matt. v. 29, 30, and Remark 8 on that Section. The only difference between the words there and here is, that there they refer to impure inclinations; here, to an ambitious disposition, an irascible or quarrelsome temper, and the like: and the injunction is, to strike at the root of such dispositions and cut off the occasions of them. **into the fire that never shall be quenched; 44. Where their worm dieth not, and the fire is not quenched. 45. And if thy foot offend thee, cut it off: it is better for thee to enter halt into life, than having two feet to be cast into hell.** See, as above, on Matt. v. 29, 30, and Remark 8 there. **into the fire that never shall be quenched; 46. Where their worm dieth not, and the fire is not quenched. 47. And if thine eye offend thee, pluck it out: it is better for thee to enter into the kingdom of God with one eye, than having two eyes to be cast into hell-fire; 48. Where their worm dieth not, and the fire is not quenched.** [We cannot but regret that the words of the 48th verse—which in the received text are thrice repeated, with a thrilling and deeply rhythmical effect—are in *Tischendorf's* text excluded in *vv.* 44 and 46, as being genuine only in *v.* 48; while *Tregelles* brackets them, as of doubtful genuineness. The MSS. by whose authority they are guided in this case are of formidable weight; but those in favour of the received text are far more numerous, and one (A) equal perhaps in value to the most ancient; while the authority of the most ancient and best versions is de-

49 worm dieth not, and the fire is not quenched. For every one shall be
salted with fire, and *f* every sacrifice shall be salted with salt.
50   Salt *g is* good; but if the salt have lost his saltness, wherewith will ye
season it? Have *h* salt in yourselves, and *i* have peace one with another.

A. D. 32.

f Lev. 2. 13.
g Luke 14 34.
h Eph. 4. 29.
i Rom. 12.18.

cidedly in favour of the received text. To us it seems not difficult to see how, though genuine, the repetition should have been excluded by copyists, to avoid an apparent tautology and to conform the text to that of Matthew, but very difficult to see how, if not genuine, it should have found its way into so many ancient MSS. *Lachmann* adheres to the received text, and even *Fritzsche* contends for it; while *Alford* says the triple repetition gives sublimity, and leaves no doubt of the discourse having been thus uttered *verbatim.*] See on Matt. v. 30; and on the words "hell" [γέεννα] and "hell-fire," or 'the hell of fire' [ἡ γέεννα τοῦ πυρὸς]; see on Matt. v. 22. The "unquenchableness" of this fire has already been brought before us (see on Matt. iii. 12); and the awfully vivid idea of an undying worm, everlastingly consuming an unconsumable body, is taken from the closing words of the Evangelical prophet (Isa. lxvi. 24), which seem to have furnished the later Jewish Church with its current phraseology on the subject of future punishment (see *Lightfoot*). **49. For every one shall be salted with fire, and every sacrifice shall be salted with salt.** [It is surprising that *Tregelles* should bracket the last clause, as doubtful—against very preponderating authority, and nearly all critics.] A difficult verse, on which much has been written —some of it to little purpose. "Every one" probably means, 'Every follower of mine;' and the "fire" with which he "must be salted" probably means 'a fiery trial' to season him, (Compare Mal. iii. 2, &c.) The reference to salting the sacrifice is of course to that maxim of the Levitical law, that every acceptable sacrifice must be sprinkled with salt, to express symbolically its soundness, sweetness, wholesomeness, acceptability. But as it had to be *roasted* first, we have here the further idea of a salting with fire. In this case, "every sacrifice," in the next clause, will mean, 'Every one who would be found an acceptable offering to God;' and thus the whole verse may perhaps be paraphrased as follows: 'Every disciple of Mine shall have a fiery trial to undergo, and every one who would be found an odour of a sweet smell, a sacrifice acceptable and well-pleasing to God, must have such a *salting*, like the Levitical sacrifices.' Another, but, as it seems to us, far-fetched as well as harsh, interpretation—suggested first, we believe, by *Michaelis*, and adopted by *Alexander*—takes the "every sacrifice which must be salted with fire" to mean those who are "cast into hell," and the *preservative* effect of this salting to refer to the preservation of the lost not only *in* but *by means of* the fire of hell. Their reason for this is that the other interpretation changes the meaning of the "fire," and the characters too, from the lost to the saved, in these verses. But as our Lord confessedly ends His discourse with the case of His own true disciples, the transition to them in the preceding verse is perfectly natural; whereas to apply the preservative salt of the sacrifice to the preserving quality of hell-fire, is equally contrary to the symbolical sense of salt and the Scripture representations of future torment. Our Lord has still in His eye the unseemly jarrings which had arisen among the Twelve, the peril to themselves of allowing any indulgence to such passions, and the severe self-sacrifice which salvation would cost them.

50. Salt is good; but if the salt have lost his saltness—its power to season what it is brought into contact with, **wherewith will ye season it?** How is this property to be restored? See on Matt. v. 13. **Have salt in yourselves**—'See to it that ye retain in yourselves those precious qualities that will make you a blessing to one another, and to all around you;' and—with respect to the miserable strife out of which all this discourse has sprung, in one concluding word—**have peace one with another.** This is repeated in 1 Thess. **v. 13.**

Remarks.—1. How little suffices to stir unholy jealousies and strifes, even in genuine disciples of the Lord Jesus and loving friends! In the present case they were occasioned, it would seem, by the recent extraordinary manifestations of their Master's glory, opening up to the half-instructed minds of the Twelve the prospect of earthly elevation, coupled with the preference shown to three of them on several occasions, and particularly to one; stirring the jealousy of the rest, and leading probably to insinuations that they were taking too much upon them—which, in the case of the two sons of Zebedee, was probably not quite groundless. The traitor, at least, though his real character had not yet come out, would probably be ready enough to resent any appearances of presumption among the rest. The flame, thus kindled, would soon spread; and this journey to Capernaum—probably their last in company with their blessed Master, who left them to travel part of the way by themselves—was embittered by dissensions which would leave a sting behind them for many a day! And did not the scene between Paul and Barnabas at Antioch, though of a very different nature, show how easily the holiest and dearest fellowships may be interrupted by miserable misunderstandings? See on Acts xv. 37-40; and on Matt. xviii. 10-35, Remark 1. 2. Of all the forms in which the great Evangelical Lesson is taught by our Lord—'that Humility is the entrance-gate into the kingdom of heaven, and that the humblest here is the highest there'— none is more captivating than this, under the lowly roof in Capernaum, when, surrounded by the Twelve and with a little child in His arms, He answered their question, Which of them should be greatest in the kingdom of heaven, by saying, 'He that is likest this unassuming child.' And what a Religion is that, at the foundation of which lies this divine principle! What a contrast to all that Paganism taught! Some bright manifestations were given of it under the ancient economy (Gen. xiii. 8, 9; Num. xii. 3; Ps. cxxxi. 1, 2, &c.), and some sublime expressions of it occur in the Old Testament, (Ps. xviii. 27; cxiii. 5, 6; cxlvii. 3-6; Isa. lvii. 15; Isa. lxvi. 1, 2, &c.) Nor could it well be otherwise, since the Religion of Israel was that of Christ in the bud, and the Old Testament Scriptures are the oracles of God (Rom. iii. 2). But as the Son of God Himself was the Incarnation of Humility, so it was reserved for Him to teach as well as exemplify it as before it had never been, nor ever again will be. See on ch. x. 42-45. 3. Alas, that with such lessons before them, the spirit of pride should have such free scope among the followers of Christ; that in particular the pride ecclesiastic should have become proverbial; and that so few who name the

177

10 AND *ª*he arose from thence, and cometh into the coasts of Judea by the farther side of Jordan: and the people resort unto him again: and, as he was wont, he taught them again.

2 And *ᵇ*the Pharisees came to him, and asked him, Is it lawful for a man

3 to put away *his* wife? tempting him. And he answered and said unto

4 them, What did Moses command you? And they said, *ᶜ*Moses suffered

5 to write a bill of divorcement, and to put *her* away. And Jesus answered and said unto them, For *ᵈ*the hardness of your heart he wrote you this

6 precept: but from the beginning of the creation God *ᵉ*made them male

7 and female. For *ᶠ*this cause shall a man leave his father and mother,

8 and cleave to his wife; and they twain shall be one flesh: so then they

9 are no more twain, but one flesh. What therefore God hath joined together, let no man put asunder.

10 And in the house his disciples asked him again of the same *matter.*

A. D. 33.
CHAP. 10.
ª Matt. 19. 1.
John 10.40.
John 11. 7.
ᵇ Matt. 19. 3.
ᶜ Deut. 24. 1.
Matt. 5. 31.
Matt. 19. 7.
ᵈ Deut. 9. 6.
Acts 13. 18.
ᵉ Gen. 1. 27.
Gen. 2. 20-23.
Gen. 5 2.
ᶠ Gen. 2. 24.
1 Cor. 6. 16.
Eph. 5. 31.

name of Christ should be distinguished for lowliness of mind! 4. The disposition which prompted John to forbid the man who cast out devils in Christ's name and yet followed not with Him and the Twelve, was extremely natural. Whether he was one of that small band of John's disciples who did not attach themselves to Christ's company but yet seem to have believed in Him, or whether, though a believer in Jesus, he had found some inconveniences in attending him statedly and so did not do it, we cannot tell. Though it is likely enough that he ought to have joined the company of Christ, the man had not seen his way to that himself. But the first question with John should have been, Have I any right to decide that point for him, or to judge him by my standard? 'You had not,' says our Lord. But further, 'Supposing the man does wrong in not following with us, is it right in me to forbid him, on that account, to cast out devils in my Master's name?' 'It was not,' says Christ. 'The deed itself was a good deed; it helped to destroy the works of the devil; and the Name in which this was done was that at which devils tremble. Thus far, then, the man was My servant, doing My work, and doing it not the less effectually and beneficially that he "followeth not us:" that is a question between him and Me; a question involving more points than you are aware of or able to deal with; a question with which you have nothing to do: Let such alone.' How instructive is this, and how condemning! Surely it condemns not only those horrible attempts *by force* to shut up all within one visible pale of discipleship, which have deluged Christendom with blood in Christ's name, but the same spirit in its milder form of proud ecclesiastic scowl upon all who "after the form which they call 'a sect' [*αἵρεσιν*] do so worship the God of their fathers" (see on Acts xxiv. 14). Visible unity in Christ's Church is indeed devoutly to be wished, and the want of it is cause enough of just sorrow and humiliation. But this is not the way to bring it about. It is not to be thought that the various ranks into which the Church of Christ is divided are all equally right in being what and where they are, if only they be sincere in their own convictions. But, right or wrong, they are as much entitled to exercise and act upon their conscientious judgment as we are, and to their own Master, in so doing, they stand or fall. It is the duty, and should be felt as the privilege, of all Christ's servants to rejoice in the promotion of His kingdom and cause by those they would wish, but cannot bring, within their own pale. Nor will anything contribute so much to bring Christians visibly together as just this

joy at each other's success, although separate in the meantime; while on the other hand rancorous jealousies in behalf of our own sectional interests are the very thing to narrow these interests still further, and to shrivel ourselves. What a noble spirit did Moses display when the Spirit descended upon the seventy elders, and they prophesied and did not cease. Besides these the Spirit had come upon two men, who remained in the camp prophesying, *and did not join the seventy.* Whereupon there ran a zealous youth to Moses, saying, Eldad and Medad do prophesy in the camp; and even Joshua said, My lord Moses, forbid them. But what was the reply of the great leader of Israel? "Enviest thou for my sake? Would God that all the Lord's people were prophets, and that the Lord would pour out His Spirit upon them!" (Num. xi. 24-29). 5. The word "*hell*" thrice repeated here in the same breath is tremendous enough in itself; but how awful does it sound from the lips of *Love Incarnate!* And when to this He adds, thrice over in the same terms, "where their worm dieth not, and the fire is not quenched"—words enough to make both the ears of every one that heareth them to tingle—what shall be thought of the mawkish sentimentalism which condemns all such language in the mouths of His servants, as inconsistent with what they presume to call 'the religion of the meek and lowly Jesus?' Why, it is just the apostle who breathed most of His Master's love whose Epistles express what would be thought the harshest things against vital error and those who hold it. It is love to men, not hatred, that prompts such severity against what will inevitably ruin them. 6. Who that has any regard for the teaching of Christ can venture, in the face of these verses (42-48), to limit the duration of future torment? See on Matt. xxv. 31-46, Remark 4. 7. As Christians are to present themselves a living sacrifice to God, so when the sacrifice has had the fire applied to it, and stood the fire, it is an odour of a sweet smell, a sacrifice acceptable and well-pleasing to God. But let them not think that the only fiery trial they have to stand is persecution *from without.* The numberless things that tend to stir their corruptions, even in their intercourse with each other, constitute an almost daily trial, and sometimes fiery enough. Then it is that a living Christianity, subduing corruption and overcoming evil with good, shows its value. This is the true *salt of the sacrifice.* "Let your speech," says the apostle—and the same applies to every other feature of the Christian character—"be alway *with grace,*" or to speak sacrificially, "*seasoned with salt* that ye may know how ye ought to answer every man" (Col. iv. 6).

CHAP. X. 1-12.—FINAL DEPARTURE FROM

11 And he saith unto them, ^{*g*}Whosoever shall put away his wife, and marry
12 another, committeth adultery against her. And if a woman shall put away her husband, and be married to another, she committeth adultery.
13 And ^{*h*}they brought young children to him, that he should touch them:
14 and *his* disciples rebuked those that brought *them*. But when Jesus saw *it*, he was much displeased, and said unto them, Suffer the little children to come unto me, and forbid them not: for ^{*i*}of such is the kingdom of God.
15 Verily I say unto you, ^{*j*}Whosoever shall not receive the kingdom of God
16 as a little child, he shall not enter therein. And he ^{*k*}took them up in his arms, put *his* hands upon them, and blessed them.
17 And ^{*l*}when he was gone forth into the way, there came one running, and kneeled to him, and asked him, Good Master, what shall I do that I
18 may inherit eternal life? And Jesus said unto him, Why callest thou
19 me good? *there is* none good but one, *that is*, God. Thou knowest the commandments, ^{*m*}Do not commit adultery, Do not kill, Do not steal, Do
20 not bear false witness, Defraud not, Honour thy father and mother. And he answered and said unto him, Master, all these have I observed from
21 my youth. Then Jesus, beholding him, loved him, and said unto him, One thing thou lackest: go thy way, sell ^{*n*}whatsoever thou hast, and give to the poor, and thou shalt have treasure ^{*o*}in heaven: and come, take up
22 the ^{*p*}cross, and follow me. And he was sad at that saying, and went away grieved: for he had great possessions.
23 And ^{*q*}Jesus looked round about, and saith unto his disciples, How
24 hardly shall they that have riches enter into the kingdom of God! And the disciples were astonished at his words. But Jesus answereth again, and saith unto them, Children, how hard is it for them ^{*r*}that trust in
25 riches to enter into the kingdom of God! It is easier for a camel to go through the eye of a needle, than for a rich man to enter into the
26 kingdom of God. And they were astonished out of measure, saying
27 among themselves, Who then can be saved? And Jesus, looking upon them, saith, With men *it is* impossible, but not with God: for ^{*s*}with God all things are possible.
28 Then ^{*t*}Peter began to say unto him, Lo, we have left all, and have
29 followed thee. And Jesus answered and said, Verily I say unto you, There is no man that hath left house, or brethren, or sisters, or father, or
30 mother, or wife, or children, or lands, for my sake, and the Gospel's, but ^{*u*}he shall receive an hundred-fold now in this time, houses, and brethren, and sisters, and mothers, and children, and lands, ^{*v*}with persecutions;
31 and in the world to come eternal life. But ^{*w*}many *that are* first shall be last; and the last first.
32 And ^{*x*}they were in the way going up to Jerusalem; and Jesus went before them: and they were amazed; and as they followed, they were

A. D. 33.
g Matt. 5. 32.
Matt. 19. 9.
Luke 16.18.
Rom. 7. 3.
h Matt. 19.13.
Luke 18.15.
i 1 Cor. 14.20.
j Matt. 18. 3.
k Isa. 40. 11.
l Matt. 19.16.
Luke 18.18.
m Ex. 20.
Rom. 13. 9.
Jas. 2. 11.
n Acts 2. 44.
1 Tim. 6.18.
o Matt. 6. 19, 20.
Matt. 19.21.
Luke 12.33.
Luke 16. 9.
p Acts 14. 22.
2 Tim. 3.12.
q Matt. 19.23.
Luke 18.24.
r Job 31. 24.
Ps. 17. 14.
Ps. 52. 7.
Ps. 62. 10.
1 Tim. 6.17.
s Jer. 32. 17.
Matt. 19.26.
Luke 1. 37.
Heb. 7. 25.
t Matt. 19.27.
Luke 18.28.
u 2 Chr. 25. 9.
Ps. 19. 11.
Luke 18.30.
v Matt. 5. 11, 12.
John 16.22, 23.
Acts 14. 22.
Rom. 5. 3.
1 Thes. 3.3.
2 Tim. 3.12.
Heb. 12. 6.
1 Pet. 4. 12-16.
w Matt. 19.30.
Matt. 20.16.
Luke 13.30.
x Matt. 20.17.
Luke 18.31.

GALILEE—DIVORCE. (= Matt. xix. 1-12; Luke ix. 51.) For the exposition, see on Matt. xix. 1-12.

13-16.—LITTLE CHILDREN BROUGHT TO CHRIST. (= Matt. xix. 13-15; Luke xviii. 15-17.) For the exposition, see on Luke xviii. 15-17.

17-31.—THE RICH YOUNG RULER. (= Matt. xix. 16-30; Luke xviii. 18-30.) For the exposition, see on Luke xviii. 18-30.

32-45.—THIRD EXPLICIT AND STILL FULLER ANNOUNCEMENT OF HIS APPROACHING SUFFERINGS, DEATH, AND RESURRECTION—THE AMBITIOUS REQUEST OF JAMES AND JOHN, AND THE REPLY. (= Matt. xx. 17-28; Luke xviii. 31-34.)

Third Announcement of His approaching Sufferings, Death, and Resurrection (32-34). **32. And they were in the way**—or on the road, **going up to Jerusalem**—in Perea, and probably somewhere between Ephraim and Jericho, on the farther side

of the Jordan, and to the north-east of Jerusalem. **and Jesus went before them**—as *Grotius* says, in the style of an intrepid Leader. **and they were amazed** [ἐθαμβοῦντο]—or 'struck with astonishment' at His courage in advancing to certain death. **and as they followed, they were afraid**—for their own safety. These artless, life-like touches—not only from an eye-witness, but one whom the noble carriage of the Master struck with wonder and awe—are peculiar to Mark, and give the second Gospel a charm all its own; making us feel as if we ourselves were in the midst of the scenes it describes. Well might the poet exclaim,

'The Saviour, what a noble flame
Was kindled in His breast,
When, hasting to Jerusalem,
He march'd before the rest!'—COWPER.

And he took again the twelve—referring to His

afraid. ʸAnd he took again the twelve, and began to tell them what
33 things should happen unto him, *saying,* Behold, we go up to Jerusalem;
and the Son of man shall be delivered unto the chief priests, and unto
the scribes; and they shall condemn him to death, and shall deliver him
34 to the Gentiles: and they shall ᶻmock him, and shall scourge him, and
shall spit upon him, and shall kill him: and the third day he shall rise
again.
35 And James and John, the sons of Zebedee, come unto him, saying,
Master, we would that thou shouldest do for us whatsoever we shall
36 desire. And he said unto them, What would ye that I should do for you?
37 They said unto him, Grant unto us that we may sit, one on thy right
38 hand, and the other on thy left hand, in thy glory. But Jesus said unto
them, Ye know not what ye ask: can ye drink of the cup that I drink
39 of? and be baptized with the baptism that I am baptized with? And
they said unto him, We can. And Jesus said unto them, ᵃYe shall
indeed drink of the cup that I drink of; and with the baptism that I am

A. D. 33.
ʸ Matt. 11.35.
Matt. 13.12.
ch. 4. 34.
ch. 8. 31.
ch. 9. 31.
Luke 9. 22.
Luke 18.31.
ᶻ Ps. 22. 6-8.
Isa. 53. 3.
Matt 27.27.
Luke 22.63.
Luke 23. 11.
John 19. 2.
ᵃ Matt 10.25.
ch. 14. 36.
John 15.20.
John 17.14.
Acts 12. 2.
Col. 1. 24.
Rev. 1. 9.

previous announcements on this sad subject. **and
began to tell them what things should happen
unto him** [τὰ μέλλοντα αὐτῷ συμβαίνειν]—'were
going to befall Him.' The word expresses something already begun but not brought to a head,
rather than something wholly future. 33. **Saying, Behold, we go up to Jerusalem**—for the
last time, **and**—"all things that are written by
the prophets concerning the Son of man shall be
accomplished" (Luke xviii. 31). **the Son of
man shall be delivered unto the chief priests,
and unto the scribes; and they shall condemn
him to death, and shall deliver him to the
Gentiles.** This is the first express statement that
the Gentiles would combine with the Jews in His
death; the two grand divisions of the human race
for whom He died thus taking part in crucifying
the Lord of Glory, as *Webster and Wilkinson* observe. 34. **And they shall mock him, and shall
scourge him, and shall spit upon him, and shall
kill him: and the third day he shall rise again.**
Singularly explicit as this announcement was, Luke
(xviii. 34) says " they understood none of these
things: and this saying was hid from them, neither
knew they the things which were spoken." The
meaning of the words they could be at no loss to
understand, but their import in relation to His
Messianic kingdom they could not penetrate;
the whole prediction being right in the teeth
of their preconceived notions. That they should
have clung so tenaciously to the popular notion of
an *unsuffering* Messiah, may surprise us; but it
gives inexpressible weight to their after-testimony
to a suffering and dying Saviour.
*Ambitious Request of James and John—The
Reply* (35-45). 35. **And James and John, the sons
of Zebedee, come unto him, saying.** Matthew
(xx. 20) says their "mother came to Him with
her sons, worshipping Him and desiring," &c.
(Compare Matt. xxvii. 56, with Mark xv. 40.)
Salome was her name (ch. xvi. 1). We cannot
be sure with which of the parties the movement
originated; but as our Lord, even in Matthew's
account, addresses Himself to James and John,
making no account of the mother, it is likely the
mother was merely set on by them. The thought
was doubtless suggested to her sons by the recent
promise to the Twelve of "thrones to sit on,
when the Son of man should sit on the throne
of His glory" (Matt. xix. 28); but after the reproof so lately given them (ch. ix. 33, &c.), they
get their mother to speak for them. **Master, we
would that thou shouldest do for us whatsoever
we shall desire**—thus cautiously approaching the
180

subject. 36. **And he said unto them, What would
ye that I should do for you?** Though well aware
what was their mind and their mother's, our
Lord will have the unseemly petition uttered
before all. 37. **They said unto him, Grant unto
us that we may sit, one on thy right hand, and
the other on thy left hand, in thy glory**—that
is, Assign to us the two places of highest honour
in the coming kingdom. The semblance of a plea
for so presumptuous a request might possibly have
been drawn from the fact that one of the two
usually leaned on the breast of Jesus, or sat next
Him at meals, while the other was one of the
favoured three. 38. **But Jesus said unto them,
Ye know not what ye ask.** How gentle the
reply to such a request, preferred at such a
time, after the sad announcement just made!
can ye drink of the cup that I drink of? To
'drink of a cup' is in Scripture a figure for getting one's fill either of good (Ps. xvi. 5; xxiii.
5; cxvi. 13; Jer. xvi. 7) or of ill (Ps. lxxv. 8;
John xviii. 11; Rev. xiv. 10). Here it is the cup
of suffering. **and be baptized with the baptism
that I am baptized with?** (Compare, for the language, Ps. xlii. 7.) The object of this question
seems to have been to try how far those two men
were *capable* of the dignity to which they aspired;
and this on the principle that he who is able to
suffer most for His sake will be the nearest to
Him in His kingdom. 39. **And they said unto
him, We can.** Here we see them owning their
mother's petition for them as their own; and
doubtless they were perfectly sincere in professing their willingness to follow their Master to
any suffering He might have to endure. Well,
and they shall have to do it. As for *James,* he
was the first of the apostles who was honoured,
and showed himself able, to be baptized with his
Master's baptism of blood (Acts xii. 1, 2); while
John, after going through all the persecutions to
which the infant Church was exposed from the
Jews, and sharing in the struggles and sufferings
occasioned by the first triumphs of the Gospel
among the Gentiles, lived to be the victim, after
all the rest had got to glory, of a bitter persecution in the evening of his days, for the word of
God and for the testimony of Jesus Christ. Yes,
they were dear believers and blessed men, in spite
of this unworthy ambition, and their Lord knew
it; and perhaps the foresight of what they would
have to pass through, and the courageous testimony He would yet receive from them, was
the cause of that gentleness which we cannot
but wonder at in His reproof. **And Jesus said**

40 baptized withal shall ye be baptized: but to sit on my right hand and on my left hand is not mine to give; but *it shall be given* [b]*to them* for whom it is prepared.

41 And [e]when the ten heard *it*, they began to be much displeased with

42 James and John. But Jesus called them *to him*, and saith unto them, [d]Ye know that they which [1]are accounted to rule over the Gentiles exercise lordship over them; and their great ones exercise authority upon them.

43 But [e]so shall it not be among you: but whosoever will be great among

44 you, shall be your minister; and whosoever of you will be the chiefest,

45 shall be servant of all. For even [f]the Son of man came not to be ministered unto, but to minister, and to [g]give his life a ransom for many.

A. D. 33.

[b] Jas. 4. 3.
[c] Matt. 20. 24.
[d] Luke 22. 25.
[1] Or, think good.
[e] ch. 9. 35.
  Luke 9. 48.
[f] John 13. 14.
  Phil. 2. 7.
  Heb. 5. 8.
[g] Isa. 53. 10.
  Dan. 9. 24, 26.

---

unto them, **Ye shall indeed drink of the cup that I drink of; and with the baptism that I am baptized withal shall ye be baptized.** No doubt this prediction, when their sufferings at length came upon them, cheered them with the assurance, not that they would sit on His right and left hand—for of that thought they would be heartily ashamed—but that "if they suffered with Him, they should be also glorified together." **40. But to sit on my right hand and on my left hand is not mine to give; but [it shall be given to them] for whom** [ἀλλ' οἷς] **it is prepared**—"of my Father" (Matt. xx. 23). The supplement which our translators have inserted is approved by some good interpreters, and the proper sense of the word rendered "but" [ἀλλὰ] is certainly in favour of it. But besides that it makes the statement too elliptical—leaving too many words to be supplied—it seems to make our Lord repudiate the right to assign to each of His people his place in the kingdom of glory; a thing which He nowhere else does, but rather the contrary. It is true that He says their place is "prepared for them by His Father." But that is true of their admission to heaven at all; and yet from His great white throne Jesus will Himself adjudicate the kingdom, and authoritatively invite into it those on His right hand, calling them the "blessed of His Father:" so little inconsistency is there between the eternal choice of them by His Father, and that public adjudication of them, not only to heaven in general, but each to his own position in it, which all Scripture assigns to Christ. The true rendering, then, of this clause, we take it, is this: 'But to sit on My right hand and on My left hand is not Mine to give, save to them for whom it is prepared.' [The use of ἀλλὰ in this sense, as equivalent to εἰ μή, occurs in ch. ix. 8, "They saw no man any more *save* Jesus only"—ἀλλὰ τὸν Ἰησοῦν. And the very words of our Evangelist, ἀλλ' οἷς, occur in this sense in Matt. xix. 11]. When therefore He says, "It is not mine to give" the meaning is, 'I cannot give it as a *favour* to whomsoever I *please*, or on a principle of *favouritism:* it belongs exclusively to those for whom it is prepared,' &c. And if this be His meaning, it will be seen how far our Lord is from disclaiming the right to assign to each his proper place in His Kingdom; that on the contrary, He expressly asserts it, merely announcing that the principle of distribution is quite different from what these petitioners supposed. Our Lord, it will be observed, does not *deny* the petition of James and John, or say they shall *not* occupy the place in His kingdom which they now improperly sought:—for aught we know, *that may be their true place.* All we are sure of is, that their asking it was displeasing to Him "to whom all judgment is committed," and so was not fitted to gain their object, but just the reverse. (See what is taught in Luke xiv. 8-11.) One at least of these brethren, as

Alford strikingly remarks, saw on the right and on the left hand of their Lord, as He hung upon the tree, the crucified thieves; and bitter indeed must have been the remembrance of this ambitious prayer at that moment. **41. And when the ten heard it, they began to be much displeased with James and John**—or "were moved with indignation," as the same word [ἀγανακτεῖν] is rendered in Matt. xx. 24. The expression "*began* to be," which is of frequent occurrence in the Gospels, means that more passed than is expressed, and that we have but the result. And can we blame the ten for the indignation which they felt? Yet there was probably a spice of the old spirit of rivalry in it, which in spite of our Lord's recent lengthened, diversified, and most solemn warnings against it, had not ceased to stir in their breasts. **42. But Jesus called them to him, and saith unto them, Ye know that they which are accounted to rule**—are recognized or acknowledged as rulers, **over the Gentiles exercise lordship over them; and their great ones exercise authority upon them**—as superiors exercising an acknowledged authority over inferiors. **43. But so shall it not be among you: but whosoever will be great among you, shall be your minister** [διάκονος]—a subordinate servant. **44. And whosoever of you will be the chiefest**—or 'first' [πρῶτος], **shall be**—that is, 'let him be,' or 'shall be he who is prepared to be' **servant of all** [δοῦλος]—one in the lowest condition of service. **45. For even the Son of man came not to be ministered unto, but to minister, and to give his life a ransom for**—or, 'instead of'—**many** [λύτρον ἀντὶ πολλῶν]:—*q. d.,* 'In the kingdom about to be set up this primitive shall have no place. All my servants shall there be equal; and the only "greatness" known to it shall be the greatness of humility and devotedness to the service of others. He that goes down the deepest in these services of self-denying humility shall rise the highest and hold the "chiefest" place in that kingdom; even as the Son of man, whose abasement and self-sacrifice for others, transcending all, gives Him of right a place above all! As "the Word in the beginning with God," He *was* ministered unto; and as the risen Redeemer in our nature He now *is* ministered unto, "angels and authorities and powers being made subject unto Him" (1 Pet. iii. 22); but not for this came He hither. The Served of all came to be the Servant of all; and His last act was the grandest Service ever beheld by the universe of God—"HE GAVE HIS LIFE A RANSOM FOR MANY!" "Many" is here to be taken, not in contrast with *few* or with *all*, but in opposition to' *one*—the one Son of man for the many sinners.

Remarks.—1. When we read of Jesus, on His last journey from Galilee to Jerusalem, going before the Twelve, with a courage which amazed and

46   And [h] they came to Jericho: and as he went out of Jericho with his
disciples and a great number of people, blind Bartimeus, the son of Timeus,
47 sat by the highway-side begging.   And when he heard that it was Jesus
of Nazareth, he began to cry out, and say, Jesus, *thou* [i] son of David, have
48 mercy on me.   And many charged him that he should hold his peace:
but he cried the more a great deal, *Thou* son of David, have mercy on
49 me.   And Jesus stood still, and commanded him to be called.   And they
call the blind man, saying unto him, Be of good comfort, rise; he calleth
50 thee.   And he, casting away his garment, rose, and came to Jesus.
51 And Jesus answered and said unto him, What wilt thou that I should
do unto thee?   The blind man said unto him, Lord, that I might receive
52 my sight.   And Jesus said unto him, Go thy way; thy faith hath [2] made
thee whole.   And immediately [j] he received his sight, and followed Jesus
in the way.
11   AND [a] when they came nigh to Jerusalem, unto Bethphage and
Bethany, at the mount of [b] Olives, he sendeth forth two of his disciples,
2 and saith unto them, Go your way into the village over against you: and
as soon as ye be entered into it, ye shall find a colt tied, whereon never
3 man sat; loose him, and bring *him*.   And if any man say unto you, Why
do ye this? say ye that [c] the Lord hath need of him; and straightway he
4 will send him hither.   And they went their way, and found the colt tied
by the door without in a place where two ways met; and they loose him.
5 And certain of them that stood there said unto them, What do ye, loosing
6 the colt?   And they said unto them even as Jesus had commanded: and
7 they let them go.   And they brought the colt to Jesus, and cast their
8 garments on him; [d] and he sat upon him.   And [e] many spread their garments in the way; and others cut down branches off the trees, and
9 strawed *them* in the way.   And they that went before, and they that
followed, cried, saying, [f] Hosanna!   Blessed *is* he that cometh in the

A. D. 33.

[h] Matt. 20. 29.
Luke 18. 35.
[i] Isa. 11. 1.
Jer. 23. 5, 6.
Rom. 1. 3.
Rev. 22. 16.
[2] Or, *saved*
thee.
Matt. 9. 22.
[j] Isa. 29. 18.
Isa. 32. 3.
Isa. 35. 5.
Isa. 42. 6, 7.
Isa. 43. 8.
Acts 26. 18.

CHAP. 11.
[a] Matt. 21. 1.
Luke 19. 29.
John 12. 14.
[b] Zec. 14. 4.
Matt. 24. 3.
John 8. 1.
Acts 1. 12.
[c] Ps. 24. 1.
Acts 10. 36.
Heb. 1. 3.
Heb. 2. 7-9.
[d] 1 Ki. 1. 33.
Zec. 9. 9.
[e] Matt. 21. 8.
[f] Ps. 118. 26.
Isa 62. 11.
Matt. 21. 9.
Matt. 23. 39.
Luke 19. 37.
38.
John 12. 13.

terrified them, it were well that we searched
into the hidden springs of this, so far as we have
scriptural light to guide us.   Turning then to
that glorious Messianic prediction, in the 50th
of Isaiah, we find Him saying, "The Lord God
hath given me the tongue of the learned, that I
should know how to speak a word in season to
Him that is weary: He wakeneth morning by
morning; He wakeneth mine ear to hear as the
learned (or 'as an instructed person').   The Lord
God hath opened mine ear, and I was not rebellious,
neither turned away back.   I gave my back to
the smiters, and my cheeks to them that plucked
off the hair: I hid not my face from shame
and spitting.   For the Lord God will help me;
therefore shall I not be confounded: therefore
have I *set my face like a flint*, and I know that
I shall not be ashamed," &c. (*vv.* 4-7).   Here He
speaks as if He went each successive morning
to His Father, to receive His instructions for the
work of each day; so that when He either spake
a word in season to a weary soul, or showed
unflinching courage in encountering opposition,
or, as here, marched to the rude mockeries and
cruel sufferings which awaited Him, with His
"face set like a flint, knowing that He should
not be ashamed," it was not mere impassive Godhead that did it, but the Son of man, keenly
sensitive to shame and suffering, and only rising
above them through the power of an all-subduing
devotion to the great end of His mission into
the world, and this, too, fed by daily communion
with His Father in heaven.   Thus is He to His
people the perfect Model of self-devotion to the
work given them to do.   2. How hard it is for
even the plainest truths to penetrate through

prejudice, we see once and again in these disciples
of the Lord Jesus.   The third Evangelist seems
unable to say strongly enough how entirely hidden
from them at that time was the *sense* of those
exceeding plain statements in which our Lord
now, for the third time, announced what lay before
Him.   And though this added prodigious, and, to
the simple-hearted, irresistible weight to their subsequent testimony in behalf of a suffering, dying,
and rising Messiah—now so incomprehensible to
them—it teaches to us a lesson, of which we have
as much need as they, to guard against allowing
prepossessions and prejudices to thicken around
us and shut out from our mind the clearest truth.
3. When the indignation of the ten was kindled
against James and John for their offensive petition,
how admirable was the wisdom of their Lord
which then interposed, checking the hot quarrel
which doubtless would have broken out at that
moment, by calling them all equally around Him
and opening to them calmly the relation in which
they were to stand, and the spirit they were to
cherish to each other in the future work of His
kingdom, holding forth Himself as the sublime
Model both for their feeling and for their acting!
4. The *sacrificial* and *vicarious* nature of Christ's
death is here expressed by Himself (*v.* 45) as
plainly as the *manner* of His death is foretold a
few verses before.   And to say that this was merely
in accommodation to Jewish ideas, is to dishonour
the teaching of our Lord, and degrade Judaism
to a level with the rites of Paganism.

46-52.—BLIND BARTIMEUS HEALED. (= Matt.
xx. 29-34; Luke xviii. 35-43.)   For the exposition,
see on Luke xviii. 35-43.

CHAP. XI. 1-11.—CHRIST'S TRIUMPHAL ENTRY

10 name of the Lord! Blessed *be* the kingdom of our father David, that cometh in the name of the Lord! *g*Hosanna in the highest!

11 And *h*Jesus entered into Jerusalem, and into the temple: and when he had looked round about upon all things, and now the even-tide was come, he went out unto Bethany with the twelve.

12 And *i*on the morrow, when they were come from Bethany, he was hungry:

13 and *j*seeing a fig tree afar off having leaves, he came, if haply he might find any thing thereon: and when he came to it, he found

14 nothing but leaves; for the time of figs was not *yet.* And Jesus answered and said unto it, No man eat fruit of thee hereafter for ever. And his disciples heard *it.*

15 And *k*they come to Jerusalem: and Jesus went into the temple, and began to cast out them that sold and bought in the temple, and overthrew the tables of the money-changers, and the seats of them that sold

16 doves; and would not suffer that any man should carry *any* vessel

17 through the temple. And he taught, saying unto them, Is it not written, *l*My house shall be called *1*of all nations the house of prayer? but *m*ye

18 have made it a den of thieves. And *n*the scribes and chief priests heard *it,* and sought how they might destroy him: for they feared him, because

19 all *o*the people was astonished at his doctrine. And when even was come, he went out of the city.

20 And *p*in the morning, as they passed by, they saw the fig tree dried

A. D. 33.

g Ps. 148. 1.
h Matt. 21.12.
i Matt. 21.18.
j Matt. 21.19.
k Matt. 21.12.
Luke 19.45.
John 2. 14.
l Isa. 56. 7.
Isa. 60. 7.
Zec. 2. 11.
1 Or, an house of prayer for all nations?
m Jer. 7. 11.
Hos. 12. 7.
John 2. 16.
n Matt. 21.45, 46
Luke 19.47.
o Matt. 7. 28.
ch. 1. 22.
Luke 4. 32.
p Matt. 21.19.
John 15. 6.
Heb. 6. 8.
Jude 12.

INTO JERUSALEM, ON THE FIRST DAY OF THE WEEK. (= Matt. xxi. 1-9; Luke xix. 29-40; John xii. 12. 19.) For the exposition of this majestic scene—recorded, as will be seen, by all the Evangelists—see on Luke xix. 29-40.

11-26.—THE BARREN FIG TREE CURSED, WITH LESSONS FROM IT—SECOND CLEANSING OF THE TEMPLE, ON THE SECOND AND THIRD DAYS OF THE WEEK. (= Matt. xxi. 12-22; Luke xix. 45-48.)

11. And Jesus entered - into Jerusalem, and into the temple: and when he had looked round about upon—or 'surveyed' all things, and now the even-tide was come, he went out unto Bethany with the twelve. Thus briefly does our Evangelist dispose of this His first day in Jerusalem, after the triumphal entry. Nor do the Third and Fourth Gospels give us more light. But from Matthew (xxi. 10, 11, 14-16) we learn some additional and precious particulars, for which see on Luke xix. 45-48. It was not now safe for the Lord to sleep in the City, nor, from the day of His Triumphal Entry, did He pass one night in it, save the last fatal one.

The Barren Fig Tree Cursed (12-14). 12. And on the morrow. The Triumphal Entry being on the First day of the week, this following day was Monday. when they were come from Bethany—"in the morning" (Matt. xxi. 18)—he was hungry. How was that? Had He stolen forth from that dear roof at Bethany to the "mountain to pray, and continued all night in prayer to God?" (Luke vi. 12); or, "in the morning," as on a former occasion, "risen up a great while before day, and departed into a solitary place, and there prayed" (Mark i. 35); not breaking His fast thereafter, but bending His steps straight for the city, that He might "work the works of Him that sent Him while it was day"? (John ix. 4). We know not, though one lingers upon and loves to trace out the every movement of that life of wonders. One thing, however, we are sure of—it was *real bodily hunger* which He now sought to allay by the fruit of this fig tree, "if haply He might find any thing thereon;" not a mere *scene* for the purpose of teaching a lesson, as some early heretics maintained, and some still

seem virtually to hold. 13. And seeing a fig tree. (In Matt. xxi. 19, it is 'one fig tree' [μίαν], but the sense is the same as here, 'a certain fig tree' [= τινα], as in Matt. viii. 19, &c.) Bethphage, which adjoined Bethany, derives its name from its being a *fig-region* [בֵּית־פַגֵּא]—'House of figs.' afar off having leaves—and therefore promising fruit, which in the case of figs comes before the leaves. he came, if haply he might find any thing thereon: and when he came to it, he found nothing but leaves; for the time of figs was not [yet]. What the precise import of this explanation is, interpreters are not agreed. Perhaps all that is meant is, that as the proper fig season had not arrived, no fruit would have been expected even of this tree but for the leaves which it had, which were in this case prematurely and unnaturally developed. 14. And Jesus answered and said unto it, No man eat fruit of thee hereafter for ever. That word did not *make* the tree barren, but sealed it up in its own barrenness. See on Matt. xiii. 13-15. And his disciples heard it—and marked the saying. This is introduced as a connecting link, to explain what was afterwards to be said on the subject, as the narrative has to proceed to the other transactions of this day.

Second Cleansing of the Temple (15-18). For the exposition of this portion, see on Luke xix. 45-48.

Lessons from the Cursing of the Fig Tree (20-26). 20. And in the morning—of Tuesday, the third day of the week: He had slept, as during all this week, at Bethany. as they passed by—going into Jerusalem again, they saw the fig tree dried up from the roots—no partial blight, leaving life in the root; but it was now dead, root and branch. In Matt. xxi. 19, it is said it withered away as soon as it was cursed. But the full blight had not appeared probably at once; and in the dusk perhaps, as they returned to Bethany, they had not observed it. The precision with which Mark distinguishes the days is not observed by Matthew, intent only on holding up the truths which the incident was designed to teach. In Matthew the whole is represented as taking place at once, just as the two stages of Jairus' daughter—dying and dead—are represented by him as one. The only

183

21 up from the roots. And Peter calling to remembrance saith unto him,
22 Master, behold, the fig tree which thou cursedst is withered away. And
23 Jesus answering saith unto them, [2]Have faith in God. For [q]verily I say
unto you, That whosoever shall say unto this mountain, Be thou removed,
and be thou cast into the sea; and shall not doubt in his heart, but shall
believe that those things which he saith shall come to pass; he shall have
24 whatsoever he saith. Therefore I say unto you, [r]What things soever ye
desire, when ye pray, believe that ye receive *them,* and ye shall have *them.*
25 And when ye stand praying, [s]forgive, if ye have ought against any; that
your Father also which is in heaven may forgive you your trespasses.
26 But [t]if ye do not forgive, neither will your Father which is in heaven
forgive your trespasses.
27 And they come again to Jerusalem: and [u]as he was walking in the
temple, there come to him the chief priests, and the scribes, and the

A. D. 33.

[2] Or, Have the faith of God.

[q] Matt. 17. 20. Matt. 21. 21. Luke 17. 6.

[r] Luke 11. 9. John 14. 13. John 15. 7. John 16. 24. Jas. 1. 5, 6.

[s] Matt. 6. 14. Col. 3. 13. Eph. 4. 32.

[t] Matt. 18. 35.

[u] Matt 21. 23. Luke 20. 1.

difference is between a more summary and a more detailed narrative, each of which only confirms the other. **21. And Peter calling to remembrance saith unto him**—satisfied that a miracle so very peculiar, a miracle, not of *blessing*, as all his other miracles, but of *cursing*, could not have been wrought but with some higher reference, and fully expecting to hear something weighty on the subject: **Master, behold, the fig tree which thou cursedst is withered away**—so connecting the two things as to show that he traced the death of the tree entirely to the curse of his Lord. Matthew (xxi. 20) gives this simply as a general exclamation of surprise by the disciples "how soon" the blight had taken effect. **22. And Jesus answering saith unto them, Have faith in God. 23. For verily I say unto you, That whosoever shall say unto this mountain, Be thou removed, and be thou cast into the sea; and shall not doubt in his heart, but shall believe that those things which he saith shall come to pass; he shall have whatsoever he saith.** Here is the lesson now. From the nature of the case supposed—that they might wish a mountain removed and cast into the sea, a thing far removed from anything which they could be thought actually to desire—it is plain that not physical but moral obstacles to the progress of His kingdom were in the Redeemer's view, and that what He designed to teach was the great lesson, that *no obstacle should be able to stand before a confiding faith in God.* **24. Therefore I say unto you, What things soever ye desire, when ye pray, believe that ye receive them, and ye shall have them.** This verse only *generalizes* the assurance of the former verse; which seems to show that it was designed for the special encouragement of *evangelistic* and *missionary* efforts, while this is a directory for prevailing *prayer in general.* **25. And when ye stand praying, forgive, if ye have aught against any; that your Father also which is in heaven may forgive you your trespasses. 26. But if ye do not forgive, neither will your Father which is in heaven forgive your trespasses.** This is repeated from the Sermon on the Mount (see on Matt. vi. 14, 15); to remind them that if this was necessary to the acceptableness of *all* prayer, much more *when great things were to be asked and confidently expected.* [*Tischendorf* excludes *v.* 26 from his text, on what appears to us very insufficient evidence. He thinks it borrowed from Matt. vi. 15. *Tregelles* also excludes it; but *Lachmann* retains it. Of critical commentators, though *Fritzsche* brackets it and inclines against it, *Meyer* and *Alford* defend it, and *De Wette* is in favour of it.]

Remarks.—1. Needless difficulties have been raised, and indifferent solutions of them offered, on the subject of our Lord's expecting fruit from the fig tree when He must have known there was none. But the same difficulty may be raised about the structure of the parable of the Barren Fig Tree, in which it is said that the great Husbandman "came and sought fruit thereon, and found none" (Luke xiii. 6). The same difficulty may be raised about almost every human thought, feeling, and action of our Lord—that if He possessed Divine knowledge and infinite power, such thoughts, feelings, and actions could not have been real. Nay, such difficulties may be raised about the reality of human freedom and responsibility, if it be true that everything is under the supreme direction of the Lord of all. Let us have done with such vain speculations, which every well-regulated mind sees to involve no difficulty at all, though the principle which lies at the bottom of them is beyond the reach of the human mind at present—possibly beyond all finite comprehension. 2. Was there not another fig tree to which Christ came—not once only, but "lo, those three years—seeking fruit and finding none"? (See on Luke xiii. 6-9.) How really, how continuously, how keenly, He hungered for *that* fruit, is best understood by His lamentation over it—"How often would I have gathered thee, and ye would not!" (Matt. xxiii. 37). And is not this repeated from age to age? Well, just as the fig tree which Christ cursed was *dried* up from the roots long before it was *pulled* up by the roots, so was it with Israel, of whom Jesus said, whilst He was yet alive, "but *now* the things that belong to thy peace are hid from thine eyes;" and yet it was long after that before "the wrath came upon them to the uttermost." And so it is to be feared that many are blighted before they are cut down and cast into the fire, and that there may be a definite time when the curse is pronounced, when the transition takes place, and when the withering process begins, never to be arrested. (See Ezek. xvii. 24.) O that men were wise, that they understood these things, that they would consider their latter end! 3. What glorious encouragement to evangelistic and missionary effort is here held forth! And has not the promise of *v.* 23 been so abundantly fulfilled in past history as to put to flight all our fears about the future? Certainly when one thinks of the "mountains" that have already been "removed and cast into the sea" by the victorious faith of Christ's disciples—the towering paganisms of the old world which have fallen before the Church of Christ—we may well exclaim of the gigantic Indian superstitions, with the hoar of entire millenniums upon them, and of all other obstacles whatever to the triumphs of the Cross, "*Who art thou, O great mountain? Before Zerubbabel thou shalt become a plain*" (Zec. iv. 7).

27-33.—The Authority of Jesus Questioned

	A. D. 33.
28 elders, and say unto him, By what authority doest thou these things?	
29 and who gave thee this authority to do these things? And Jesus	³ Or, thing.
answered and said unto them, I will also ask of you one ³ question, and	ᵛ Matt. 3. 6.
30 answer me, and I will tell you by what authority I do these things. The	Matt. 14. 6.
31 baptism of John, was *it* from heaven, or of men? answer me. And they	ch. 6. 20.
reasoned with themselves, saying, If we shall say, From heaven; he will	ʷ Job 5. 13.
32 say, Why then did ye not believe him? But if we shall say, Of men;	Ps. 9. 15.
they feared the people: for ᵛall *men* counted John, that he was a prophet	Ps. 33. 10.
33 indeed. And they answered and said unto Jesus, We cannot tell. And	Pro. 26. 4,5.
Jesus answering saith unto them, ʷNeither do I tell you by what authority	Matt. 16. 4.
I do these things.	1 Cor. 3. 19.
	CHAP. 12.
12 AND ᵃhe began to speak unto them by parables. A *certain* man	ᵃ Ps. 80. 8.
planted a vineyard, and set an hedge about *it*, and digged *a place for*	Song 8. 11.
the winefat, and built a tower, and let it out to husbandmen, and went	Isa. 5. 1.
2 into a far country. And at the season he sent to the husbandmen a	Jer. 2. 21.
servant, that he might receive from the husbandmen of the fruit of the	Matt. 21.33.
3 vineyard. And they caught *him*, and beat him, and sent *him* away	Luke 20. 9.
4 empty. And again he sent unto them another servant; and at him they	ᵇ 2 Chr. 24.14.
cast stones, and wounded *him* in the head, and sent *him* away shamefully	2 Chr. 36.16.
5 handled. And again he sent another; and him they killed, and many	Neh. 9. 26.
6 others; beating some, and ᵇkilling some. Having yet therefore one son,	Acts 7. 52.
ᶜhis well-beloved, he sent him also last unto them, saying, They will	1 Thes.2,15.
7 reverence my son. But those husbandmen said among themselves, This	Heb. 11. 36.
is ᵈthe heir; come, let us kill him, and the inheritance shall be ours.	ᶜ Ps. 2. 7.
8 And they took him, and ᵉkilled *him*, and cast *him* out of the vineyard.	Matt. 1. 23.
9 What shall therefore the lord of the vineyard do? He will come and	Rom. 8. 3.
10 destroy the husbandmen, and ᶠwill give the vineyard unto others. And	Gal. 4. 4.
have ye not read this scripture; The ᵍstone which the builders rejected	1 John 4. 9.
11 is become the head of the corner: this was the Lord's doing, and ʰit is	1 John 5. 11,
marvellous in our eyes?	12.
12 And ⁱthey sought to lay hold on him, but feared the people; for they	ᵈ Ps 2. 8.
knew that he had spoken the parable against them: and they left him,	Heb. 1. 2.
and went their way.	Acts 4. 27.
13 And ʲthey send unto him certain of the Pharisees and of the Herodians,	ᵉ Acts 2. 23.
to catch him in *his* words.	ᶠ Acts 28. 23,
14 And when they were come, they say unto him, Master, we know	23.
that thou art true, and carest for no man; for thou regardest not the	ᵍ Ps. 118. 22.
person of men, but teachest the way of God in truth: Is it lawful to give	Matt. 21.42.
15 tribute to Cesar, or not? Shall we give, or shall we not give? But he,	Luke 20.17,
knowing their hypocrisy, said unto them, Why tempt ye me? bring me	18.
	Rom. 9. 33.
	Eph. 2. 20.
	1 Pet. 2. 7,8.
	ʰ 1 Tim. 3.16.
	ⁱ Matt.21.45,
	46.
	ch. 11. 18.
	John 7. 25,
	30, 44.
	ʲ Matt.22.15.
	Luke 20.20.

—HIS REPLY. (=Matt. xxi. 23-27; Luke xx. 1-8.) For the exposition, see on Matt. xxi. 23-27.

CHAP. XII. 1-12.—PARABLE OF THE WICKED HUSBANDMEN. (Matt. xxi. 33-46; Luke xx. 9-18.) For the exposition, see on Matt. xxi. 33-46.

13-40.—ENTANGLING QUESTIONS ABOUT TRIBUTE, THE RESURRECTION, AND THE GREAT COMMANDMENT, WITH THE REPLIES—CHRIST BAFFLES THE PHARISEES BY A QUESTION ABOUT DAVID, AND DENOUNCES THE SCRIBES. (=Matt. xxii. 15-46; Luke xx. 20-47.) The time of this Section appears to be still the third day of Christ's last week —Tuesday. Matthew introduces the subject by saying (xxii. 15), "Then went the Pharisees and took counsel how they might entangle Him in His talk."

13. **And they send unto him certain of the Pharisees**—"their disciples," says Matthew; probably young and zealous scholars in that hardening school. **and of the Herodians.** See on Matt. xxii. 16. In Luke xx. 20 these willing tools

are called "spies, which should feign themselves just (or 'righteous') men, that they might take hold of His words, that so they might deliver Him unto the power and authority of the governor." Their plan, then, was to entrap Him into some expression which might be construed into disaffection to the Roman government; the Pharisees themselves being notoriously discontented with the Roman yoke.

Tribute to Cesar (14-17). **14. And when they were come, they say unto him, Master**—or 'teacher' [Διδάσκαλε]—**we know that thou art true, and carest for no man; for thou regardest not the person of men, but teachest the way of God in truth.** By such flattery—though they said only the truth—they hoped to throw Him off His guard. **Is it lawful to give tribute** [κῆνσον] **to Cesar, or not?** It was the civil poll-tax paid by all enrolled in the 'Census.' See on Matt. xvii. 25. **15. Shall we give, or shall we not give? But he, knowing their hypocrisy** [ὑπό-

16 a [1]penny that I may see *it*. And they brought *it*. And he saith unto them, Whose *is* this image and superscription? And they said unto him,
17 Cesar's. And Jesus answering said unto them, Render to Cesar the things that are Cesar's, and to God the things that are God's. And they marvelled at him.
18   Then [k]come unto him the Sadducees, which [l]say there is no resurrec-
19 tion; and they asked him, saying, Master, [m]Moses wrote unto us, If a man's brother die, and leave *his* wife *behind him*, and leave no children, that his brother should take his wife, and raise up seed unto his brother.
20 Now there were seven brethren: and the first took a wife, and dying left
21 no seed. And the second took her, and died, neither left he any seed:
22 and the third likewise. And the seven had her, and left no seed: last of
23 all the woman died also. In the resurrection therefore, when they shall
24 rise, whose wife shall she be of them? for the seven had her to wife. And Jesus answering said unto them, Do ye not therefore err, because ye know
25 not [n]the Scriptures, neither [o]the power of God? For when they shall rise from the dead, they neither marry, nor are given in marriage; but
26 [p]are as the angels which are in heaven. And as touching the dead, that they rise; have ye not read in the book of Moses, how in the bush God spake unto him, saying, [q]I *am* the God of Abraham, and the God of
27 Isaac, and the God of Jacob? He is not the God of the dead, but the God of the living: ye therefore do greatly err.

A. D. 33.

[1] In value sevenpence halfpenny.
[k] Matt. 22.23. Luke 20.27.
[l] Acts 23. 8. 1 Cor.15.12.
[m] Gen. 38. 8. Deut. 25. 5. Ruth 4. 5.
[n] Dan. 12. 2. Hos. 6. 2. 1 Tim. 1, 7. 2 Pet. 1. 19.
[o] Luke 1. 37. Rom. 4. 17. Eph. 1. 19, 20. Heb. 11.16.
[p] Matt.22.30. Luke 20.35, 36. 1 Cor. 7. 29. 1 Cor. 15.42, 49, 52. Heb. 12. 22, 23.
[q] Ex. 3. 6.

κρισιν]—"their wickedness" [πονηρίαν] Matt. xxii. 18; "their craftiness" [πανουργίαν] Luke xx. 23. The malignity of their hearts took the form of craft, pretending what they did not feel—an anxious desire to be guided aright in a matter which to a scrupulous few might seem a question of some difficulty. Seeing perfectly through this, He said unto them, Why tempt ye me?—"hypocrites!" bring me a penny [δηνάριον], that I may see it—or "the tribute money" (Matt. xxii. 19). 16. And they brought it. And he saith unto them, Whose is this image [εἰκὼν]—stamped upon the coin, and superscription? [ἐπιγραφή]—the words encircling it on the obverse side. And they said unto him, Cesar's. 17. And Jesus answering said unto them, Render to Cesar the things that are Cesar's. Putting it in this general form, it was impossible for sedition itself to dispute it, and yet it dissolved the snare. and to God the things that are God's. How much is there in this profound but to them startling addition to the maxim, and how incomparable is the whole for fulness, brevity, clearness, weight! and they marvelled at him—"at His answer, and held their peace" (Luke xx. 26), "and left Him, and went their way" (Matt. xxii. 22).

The Resurrection (18-27). 18. Then come unto him the Sadducees, which say there is no resurrection—"neither angel nor spirit" (Acts xxiii. 7). They were the materialists of the day. See on Acts xxiii. 7. and they asked him, saying, 19-22. Master, Moses wrote unto us (Deut. xxv. 5), If a man's brother die, and leave his wife behind him, &c. . . . And the seven had her, and left no seed: last of all the woman died also. 23. In the resurrection therefore [when they shall rise]. The clause in brackets is of doubtful authority, and *Tregelles* omits it; but *Lachmann* and *Tischendorf* retain it. whose wife shall she be of them? for the seven had her to wife. 24. And Jesus answering said unto them, Do ye not therefore err, because ye know not the Scriptures —regarding the future state, neither the power of God?—before which a thousand such difficulties vanish. 25. For when they shall rise from the dead, they neither marry, nor are given in mar-

riage—"neither can they die any more" (Luke xx. 36). Marriage is ordained to perpetuate the human family; but as there will be no breaches by death in the future state, this ordinance will cease. but are as the angels which are in heaven. In Luke it is "equal unto the angels" [ἰσάγγελοι]: but as the subject is death and resurrection, we are not warranted to extend the equality here taught beyond the one point—the *immortality* of their nature. A beautiful clause is added in Luke—"and are the children of God" —not in respect of *character*, which is not here spoken of, but of *nature*—"being the children of the resurrection," as rising to an undecaying existence (Rom. viii. 21, 23), and so being the children of their Father's immortality (1 Tim. vi. 16). 26. And as touching the dead, that they rise; have ye not read in the book of Moses—"even Moses" (Luke xx. 37), whom they had just quoted for the purpose of entangling Him, how in the bush God spake unto him [ἐπὶ τοῦ βάτου]—either 'at the bush,' as the same expression is rendered in Luke xx. 37, that is, when he was there; or 'in the (section of his history regarding the) bush.' The structure of our verse suggests the latter sense, which is not unusual. saying (Exod. iii. 6), I am the God of Abraham, and the God of Isaac, and the God of Jacob? 27. He is not the God of the dead, but [the God] of the living [ὁ Θεὸς νεκρῶν ἀλλὰ Θεὸς ζώντων]—not 'the God of dead but [the God] of living persons.' The word in brackets is almost certainly an addition to the genuine text, and critical editors exclude it. "For all live unto Him" [αὐτῷ] Luke xx. 38—'in His view,' or 'in His estimation.' This last statement—found only in Luke—though adding nothing to the argument, is an important additional illustration. It is true, indeed, that to God no human being is dead or ever will be, but all mankind sustain an abiding conscious relation to Him; but the "all" here mean "those who shall be accounted worthy to obtain that world." These sustain a gracious covenant-relation to God which cannot be dissolved. (Compare Rom. vi. 10, 11.) In this sense our Lord affirms that for Moses to call the Lord the "GOD" of His patriarchal servants, if at that

28 And ʳone of the scribes came, and having heard them reasoning together, and perceiving that he had answered them well, asked him, 29 Which is the first commandment of all? And Jesus answered him, The first of all the commandments *is*, ˢHear, O Israel; The Lord our God is 30 one Lord: and thou shalt love the Lord thy God with all thy heart, and with all thy soul, and with all thy mind, and with all thy strength. This 31 *is* the first commandment. And the second *is* like, *namely* this, Thou ᵗshalt love thy neighbour as thyself. There is none other commandment

A. D. 33.

ʳ Matt. 22.35.
ˢ Deut. 6. 4.
  Pro. 23. 26.
  Luke 10.27.
ᵗ Lev. 19 18.
  Rom. 13. 9.
  1 Cor. 13. 1.
  Gal. 5. 14.
  Jas. 2. 8.

---

moment they had no existence, would be unworthy of Him. He "would be *ashamed* to be called their God, if He had not prepared for them a city" (Heb. xi. 16). It was concluded by some of the early Fathers, from our Lord's resting His proof of the Resurrection on such a passage as this, instead of quoting some much clearer testimonies of the Old Testament, that the Sadducees, to whom this was addressed, acknowledged the authority of no part of the Old Testament but the Pentateuch; and this opinion has held its ground even till now. But as there is no ground for it in the New Testament, so *Josephus* is silent upon it; merely saying that they rejected the Pharisaic traditions. It was because the Pentateuch was regarded by all classes as the fundamental source of the Hebrew Religion, and all the succeeding books of the Old Testament but as developments of it, that our Lord would show that even there the doctrine of the Resurrection was taught. And all the rather does He select this passage, as being not a bare annunciation of the doctrine in question, but as expressive of that glorious truth *out of which the Resurrection springs.* "And when the multitude heard this (says Matt. xxii. 33), they were astonished at His doctrine." "Then (adds Luke xx. 39, 40) certain of the scribes answering said, Master"—'Teacher' [Διδάσκαλε], "thou hast well said"—enjoying His victory over the Sadducees. "And after that they durst not ask Him any [question at all]"—neither party could; both being for the time utterly foiled.

The Great Commandment (28-34). "But when the Pharisees had heard that He had put the Sadducees to silence, they were gathered together" (Matt. xxii. 34). **28. And one of the scribes** [γραμματέων]—"a lawyer" [νομικὸς], says Matthew (xxii. 35); that is, a teacher of the law, **came, and having heard them reasoning, and perceiving that he had answered them well, asked him**—manifestly in no bad spirit. When Matthew therefore says he came "tempting," or "trying him," as one of the Pharisaic party who seemed to enjoy the defeat He had given to the Sadducees, we may suppose that though somewhat priding himself upon his insight into the law, and not indisposed to measure his knowledge with One in whom he had not yet learned to believe, he was nevertheless an honest-hearted, fair disputant. **Which is the first commandment of all?**—first in importance; the primary, leading commandment, the most fundamental one. This was a question which, with some others, divided the Jewish teachers into rival schools. Our Lord's answer is in a strain of respect very different from what He showed to cavillers—ever observing His own direction, "Give not that which is holy to the dogs, neither cast ye your pearls before swine; lest they trample them under their feet, and turn again and rend you" (Matt. vii. 6). **29. And Jesus answered him, The first of all the commandments is.** The readings here vary considerably. *Tischendorf* and *Tregelles* read simply [Πρώτη ἐστὶν] 'the first is;' and they are followed by *Meyer* and *Alford.* But though the authority for the precise form of the

received text is slender, a form almost identical with it seems to have most weight of authority. Our Lord here gives His explicit sanction to the distinction between commandments of a more *fundamental* and *primary* character, and commandments of a more *dependent* and *subordinate* nature; a distinction of which it is confidently asserted by a certain class of critics that the Jews knew nothing, that our Lord and his apostles nowhere lay down, and which has been invented by Christian divines. (Compare Matt. xxiii. 23.) **Hear, O Israel; the Lord our God is one Lord.** This every devout Jew recited twice every day, and the Jews do it to this day; thus keeping up the great ancient national protest against the polytheisms and pantheisms of the heathen-world: it is the great utterance of the national faith in One Living and Personal God—"ONE JEHOVAH!" **30. And thou shalt love the Lord thy God with all thy heart, and with all thy soul, and with all thy mind, and with all thy strength. This is the first commandment. 31. And the second is like, namely this, Thou shalt love thy neighbour as thyself. There is none other commandment greater than these.** As every word here is of the deepest and most precious import, we must take it in all its details. **30. And thou shalt.** We have here the language of *law*, expressive of God's *claims.* What then are we here bound down to do? One word is made to express it. And what a word! Had the essence of the divine law consisted in *deeds*, it could not possibly have been expressed in a single word; for no one deed is comprehensive of all others embraced in the law. But as it consists in *an affection of the soul*, one word suffices to express it—but only one. *Fear*, though due to God and enjoined by Him, is *limited* in its sphere and *distant* in character. *Trust, Hope*, and the like, though essential features of a right state of heart towards God, are called into action only by *personal necessity*, and so are—in a good sense, it is true, but still are properly—*selfish* affections; that is to say, they have respect to *our own well-being.* But LOVE is an *all-inclusive* affection, embracing not only every other affection proper to its Object, but all that is proper to be *done* to its Object; for as love spontaneously seeks to please its Object, so, in the case of men to God, it is the native well-spring of a voluntary obedience. It is, besides, the most *personal* of all affections. One may fear an *event*, one may hope for an *event*, one may rejoice in an *event*; but one can love only a *Person.* It is the *tenderest*, the most *unselfish*, the most *divine* of all affections. Such, then, is the affection in which the essence of the divine law is declared to consist—**Thou shalt love.** We now come to the glorious Object of that demanded affection. **Thou shalt love the Lord, thy God**—that is, Jehovah, the Self-Existent One, who has revealed Himself as the "I AM," and there is "*none else;*" who, though by his name JEHOVAH apparently at an unapproachable distance from His finite creatures, yet bears to *Thee* a real and definite relationship, out of which arises *His claim* and *Thy duty*—of LOVE. But with what are we to love Him? Four things

32 greater than these. And the scribe said unto him, Well, Master, thou hast said the truth: for there is one God; ^uand there is none other but
33 he: And to love him with all the heart, and with all the understanding, and with all the soul, and with all the strength, and to love *his* neighbour
34 as himself, ^vis more than all whole burnt offerings and sacrifices. And when Jesus saw that he answered discreetly, he said unto him, Thou art not far from the kingdom of God. ^wAnd no man after that durst ask him *any question.*
35 And ^xJesus answered and said, while he taught in the temple, How say

A. D. 33.

^u Deut. 4. 39.
Isa. 45. 6,14.
Isa. 46. 9.
1 Cor. 8.4,6.
^v 1 Sam. 15. 22.
Hos. 6. 6.
Mic. 6. 6.
^w Matt. 22.46.
^x Luke 20.41.

are here specified. First, "Thou shalt love the Lord thy God" **with thy heart.** This sometimes means 'the whole inner man' (as Prov. iv. 23): but that cannot be meant here; for then the other three particulars would be superfluous. Very often it means 'our emotional nature'—the seat of *feeling* as distinguished from our intellectual nature or the seat of *thought,* commonly called the "mind" (as in Phil. iv. 7). But neither can this be the sense of it here; for here the heart is distinguished both from the "mind" and the "soul." The "heart," then, must here mean the *sincerity* of both the thoughts and the feelings; in other words, '*uprightness*' or '*true-heartedness,*' as opposed to a *hypocritical* or *divided* affection. [So the word—לֵב and καρδία—is used in Gen. xx. 6; Heb. x. 22; and see particularly Jer. iii. 10.] But next, "Thou shalt love the Lord thy God" **with thy soul.** This is designed to command our emotional nature: 'Thou shalt put *feeling* or *warmth* into thine affection.' Further, "Thou shalt love the Lord thy God" **with thy mind.** This commands our intellectual nature: 'Thou shalt put *intelligence* into thine affection'— in opposition to a blind devotion, or mere devoteeism. Lastly, "Thou shalt love the Lord thy God" **with thy strength.** This commands our energies: 'Thou shalt put *intensity* into thine affection' —"Do it with thy might" (Eccl. ix. 10). Taking these four things together, the command of the Law is, 'Thou shalt love the Lord thy God *with all thy powers*—with a *sincere,* a *fervid,* an *intelligent,* an *energetic* love.' But this is not all that the Law demands. God will have all these qualities in their most perfect exercise. "Thou shalt love the Lord thy God," says the Law, "with *all* thy heart," or, with perfect sincerity; "Thou shalt love the Lord thy God with *all* thy soul," or, with the utmost fervour; "Thou shalt love the Lord thy God with *all* thy mind," or, in the fullest exercise of an enlightened reason; and "Thou shalt love the Lord thy God with *all* thy strength," or, with the whole energy of our being! So much for the First Commandment. **31. And the second is like**—"unto it" (Matt. xxii. 39); as demanding the same affection, and only the extension of it, in its proper measure, to the creatures of Him whom we thus love—our *brethren* in the participation of the same nature, and *neighbours,* as connected with us by ties that render each dependent upon and necessary to the other. **Thou shalt love thy neighbour as thyself.** Now, as we are not to love ourselves supremely, this is virtually a command, **in** the first place, *not* to love our neighbour with all our heart and soul and mind and strength. And thus it is a condemnation of the idolatry of the creature. Our supreme and uttermost affection is to be reserved for God. But as *sincerely* as ourselves we are to love all mankind, and with *the same readiness to do and suffer for them* as we should reasonably desire them to show to us. The golden rule (Matt. vii. 12) is here our best interpreter of the nature and extent of these claims. **There is**

none other commandment greater than these— or, as in Matt. xxii. 40, "On these two commandments hang all the Law and the Prophets" (see on Matt. v. 17). It is as if He had said, 'This is all Scripture in a nutshell; the whole law of human duty in a portable, pocket form.' Indeed, it is so *simple* that a child may understand it, so *brief* that all may remember it, so *comprehensive* as to embrace all possible cases. And from its very nature it is *unchangeable.* It is inconceivable that God should require from his rational creatures anything *less,* or in substance anything *else,* under any *dispensation,* in any *world,* at any *period* throughout eternal duration. He cannot but claim this—all this—alike in *heaven,* in *earth,* and in *hell! And* this incomparable summary of the Divine Law belonged to *the Jewish Religion!* As it shines in its own self-evidencing splendour, so it reveals its own true source. The Religion from which the world has received it could be none other than a *God-given Religion.* **32. And the scribe said unto him, Well, Master**—'Teacher' [Διδάσκαλε], **thou hast said the truth: for there is one [God]; and there is none other but he.** The genuine text here seems clearly to have been, "There is one," without the word [Θεός] "God;" and so nearly all critical editors and expositors read. **33. And to love him with all the heart, and with all the understanding, and with all the soul, and with all the strength, and to love his neighbour as himself, is more than all whole burnt offerings and sacrifices**—more, that is, than all positive institutions; thereby showing insight into the essential difference between what is *moral* and in its own nature *unchangeable,* and what is obligatory only *because enjoined* and only *so long as enjoined.* **34. And when Jesus saw that he answered discreetly** [νουνεχῶς] — rather, 'intelligently,' or 'sensibly;' not only in a good spirit, but with a promising measure of insight into spiritual things, **he said unto him, Thou art not far from the kingdom of God**—for he had but *to follow out a little further* what he seemed sincerely to own, to find his way into the kingdom. He needed only the experience of another eminent scribe who at a later period said, "We know that *the law is spiritual,* but *I am carnal,* sold under sin;" who exclaimed, "O wretched man that I am! Who shall deliver me?" but who added, "I thank God through Jesus Christ!" (Rom. vii. 14, 24, 25). Perhaps among the "great company of the priests" and other Jewish ecclesiastics who "were obedient to the faith," almost immediately after the day of Pentecost (Acts vi. 7) this upright lawyer was one. But for all his nearness to the Kingdom of God, it may be he never entered it. **And no man after that durst ask any question**— all feeling that they were no match for Him, and that it was vain to enter the lists with Him.

Christ Baffles the Pharisees regarding David (35-37). **35. And Jesus answered and said, while he taught in the temple**—and "while the Pharisees were gathered together" (Matt. xxii. 41).

188

36 the scribes that Christ is the son of David? For David himself said ʸby the Holy Ghost, ᶻThe LORD said to my Lord, Sit thou on my right hand,
37 till I make thine enemies thy footstool. David therefore himself calleth him Lord; and ᵃwhence is he *then* his son? And the common people heard him gladly.
38   And ᵇhe said unto them in his doctrine, ᶜBeware of the scribes, which love to go in long clothing, and ᵈ*love* salutations in the market-places,
39 and the chief seats in the synagogues, and the uppermost rooms at feasts;
40 which ᵉdevour widows' houses, and for a pretence make long prayers: these shall receive greater damnation.

A. D. 33.
ʸ 2 Sam. 23.2.
2 Tim. 3.16.
ᶻ Ps. 110. 1.
1 Cor.15.25.
Heb. 1. 13.
ᵃ Rom. 1. 3.
Rom. 9. 5.
ᵇ ch. 4. 2.
ᶜ Matt. 23.1.
Luke 20.46.
ᵈ Luke 11.43.
ᵉ Matt.23.14.

How say the scribes that Christ is the son of David?—How come they to give it out, that Messiah is to be the son of David? In Matthew, Jesus asks them, "What think ye of Christ?" or of the promised and expected Messiah? "Whose son is He (to be)? They say unto Him, The son of David." The sense is the same. "He saith unto them, How then doth David in spirit call Him Lord?" (Matt. xxii. 42, 43). **36. For David himself said by the Holy Ghost** (Ps. cx. 1), **The Lord said to my Lord, Sit thou on my right hand, till I make thine enemies thy footstool. 37. David therefore himself calleth him Lord; and whence is he then his son?** There is but one solution of this difficulty. Messiah is at once inferior to David as his · son according to the flesh, and superior to him as the Lord of a kingdom of which David is himself a subject, not the sovereign. The Human and Divine natures of Christ, and the spirituality of His kingdom—of which the highest earthly sovereigns are honoured if they be counted worthy to be its subjects—furnish the only key to this puzzle. **And the common people** [ὁ πολὺς ὄχλος]—or, 'the immense crowd,' **heard him gladly.** "And no man was able to answer Him a word; neither durst any man from that day forth ask Him any more questions" (Matt. xxii. 46).

The Scribes Denounced (38-40). **38. And he said unto them in his doctrine** [ἐν τῇ διδαχῇ αὐτοῦ]— rather, 'in His teaching;' implying that this was but a specimen of an extended Discourse, which Matthew gives in full (ch. xxiii.) Luke says (xx. 45) this was "in the audience of all the people said unto his disciples." [The reading, 'unto them'— πρὸς αὐτοὺς—which *Tischendorf* adopts there is ill supported: *Lachmann* and *Tregelles* take the received text.] **Beware of the scribes, which love**—or 'like' [ϑελόντων] **to go in long clothing** (see on Matt. xxiii. 5), **and [love] salutations in the market-places, 39. And the chief seats in the synagogues, and the uppermost rooms**, or positions, **at feasts.** See on this love of distinction, Luke xiv. 7; and on Matt. vi. 5. **40. Which devour widows' houses, and for a pretence make long prayers: these shall receive greater damnation.** They took advantage of their helpless condition and confiding character, to obtain possession of their property, while by their "long prayers" they made them believe they were raised far above "filthy lucre." So much the "greater damnation" awaited them. (Compare Matt. xxiii. 33). A life-like description this of the Romish clergy, the true successors of "the scribes."

Remarks.—1. What an exalted illustration does our Lord's example here afford of His own direction to the Twelve and His servants in every age, "Behold, I send you forth as sheep among wolves: be ye therefore wise as serpents and harmless as doves"! And shall not we, the deeper we drink into His spirit, approach the nearer to that match-

less wisdom with which, in the midst of "wolves" hungry for their prey, He not only avoided their snares but put them to silence and shame; with wise speech, even as by well-doing, putting to silence the ignorance of foolish men? 2. The things of Cesar and the things of God—or things civil and things sacred—are essentially distinct, though quite harmonious. Neither may overlap or intrude itself into the sphere of the other. In the things of God we may not take law from men (Acts iv. 19; v. 29); while in honouring and obeying Cesar in his own sphere, we are rendering obedience to God Himself (Rom. xiii. 1, 2, 5). 3. In matters which lie entirely beyond the present sphere—as the Resurrection of the dead—the authority of "the Scriptures" must decide everything; and all difficulties arising out of their teaching on this and kindred subjects must be referred, as here, to "the power of God." A seasonable directory this in our day, when physical difficulties in the way of any corporeal resurrection of the dead have well-nigh annihilated the faith of it in the minds of many scientific Christians. While "the Scriptures" must be the sole rule of faith with Christians on this subject, let us learn to refer every difficulty in the way of believing its testimony to "the power of God" to accomplish whatever He promises. So much for the doctrine of the Resurrection generally. As to the difficulty with which the Sadducees plied our Lord—the difficulty of adjusting, in the resurrection-state, the relationships of the present life —His reply not only dissolves it, but opens to us some beautiful glimpses into the heavenly state. The Sadducean difficulty proceeded on the supposition that the marriage-relations of the present life would require to reappear in the resurrection-state, if there was to be any. This was but one of those gross conceptions of the future life to which some minds seem prone. As marriage is designed to supply the waste of human life here which death creates, it can have no place in a state where there is no death. The future life of the children of God, as it will be sinless, so will be deathless. This supposes new and higher laws stamped upon their physical system, to which the purer and higher element in which they are to move will be adapted. In respect of this undecaying life they will be on a level with the angels, and a faint reflection of their Father's own immortality. Yet there is an extreme on the other side to be guarded against, of so attenuating our ideas of the resurrection-state as to amount to scarcely more than the immortality of the *soul*. Were this all, the resurrection of the dead would have no meaning at all. It is the *body* only which does or can rise from the dead; and however "spiritual" the resurrection-body is to be (1 Cor. xv, 44), it must be a body still, and therefore possessed of all the essential characteristics of a body. Never let us lose hold of this truth, one of the brightest and most distinguishing of the Christian verities. 3. What a light is here thrown upon the historical

189

41   And *ʲ*Jesus sat over against the treasury, and beheld how the people cast money into the *ᵍ*treasury: and many that were rich cast in much.

A. D. 33.
ʲ Luke 21. 1.
ᵍ 2 Ki. 12. 9.

truth and inspiration of the Pentateuch! On any lower supposition, it is incredible that our Lord should have rested the divine authority of the doctrine of the Resurrection upon such words as He has quoted from it; and when, in His subsequent question about David, He quotes the 110th Psalm as what David said "in spirit" or "by the Holy Ghost," and throughout all His teaching refers to every portion of the Old Testament Scriptures as of equal divine authority, we must set our seal also to that great truth, if we would not charge our Lord either with inability to rise above the errors of His age or with unworthy accommodation to them, knowing them to be errors. 4. Our Lord's selection of an implied evidence of the resurrection in the Pentateuch, in preference to a direct proof which He might have found in the prophets, is worthy of note, not as showing His wish to confine Himself to the Pentateuch, but as encouraging us to penetrate beneath the surface of Scripture, and, in particular, to take God's own words in their most comprehensive sense. When the Lord said to Moses, "I am the God of Abraham, and the God of Isaac, and the God of Jacob," He might seem to mean no more than that He had neither forgotten nor grown indifferent to the promises which He made, some centuries before, to those patriarchs, whose God He *was* when they were alive. But as our Lord read, and would have us to read, those words, they were an assurance to Moses that He and the patriarchs, dead though they were, sustained the same relation still, and that as "all (of them) lived to Him," He held Himself under pledge to them; and in now sending Moses to redeem their children from Egypt and bring them to the promised land, He was but fulfilling His engagements to the patriarchs themselves, as living and not dead men. To superficial readers this may seem, if not far-fetched, yet not the most cogent reasoning. But the views which it opens up of the indissoluble relation that God sustains to His redeemed—which death cannot for a moment interrupt, much less destroy or impair (John xi. 25, 26)—as they necessarily imply a resurrection of the dead, will be deemed by all deeper thinkers to be as cogent in point of argument as they are precious in themselves. In fact, the strongest arguments for a Future State in the Old Testament are derived, not so much from explicit statements—which however are not wanting—as from the essentially indestructible character of those relations and intercourses which the saints sustained to God, and the consciousness of this which the saints themselves seemed to feel; as if they took it for granted rather than reasoned it out, or even reflected upon it. 5. The intelligent reader of the New Testament will not fail to perceive that "life" in the future world is never once ascribed to the wicked as their portion, even though a life of misery. That they will "rise" as well as the righteous, is explicitly declared; but never "from the dead" [ἐκ νεκρῶν]—as if they would rise to *live:* They "rise to the resurrection of *damnation*" (John v. 29), even as in the Old Testament they are said to "awake to shame and everlasting contempt" (Dan. xii. 2). But the word "life," as expressive of the future state, is invariably reserved for the condition of the saints. Hence, when our Lord here says, "For all live unto Him," we might conclude, even although the connection did not make it clear, that He meant 'all His saints'—all the dead that die in the Lord—and

they only. 6. How unscriptural as well as gloomy is the doctrine of *the sleep of the soul* between death and the resurrection! The argument of our Lord here for the resurrection of the patriarchs, and consequently of the saints in general, is founded on their being *even now alive.* Yes; and not only are their souls in conscious life, but as God is the God of themselves—the embodied Abraham and Isaac and Jacob—"though worms have destroyed their bodies, yet in their flesh must they see God," in order to be their full selves again, and get in full the promised inheritance. Sweet consolation this "concerning them which are asleep, that we sorrow not, even as others which have no hope." They are not dead. They have but fallen asleep. Their souls are still awake; "for all live unto Him." And as to their sleeping dust, "If we believe that Jesus died and rose again, even so them also which sleep in Jesus will God bring with Him" (1 Thess. iv. 13, 14). 7. In the light of the Great Commandment, what shall we think of those who talk of the Pentateuch as but fragments of the early Jewish literature, and this as embodying none but narrow and rude ideas of Religion, suited to a gross age of the world, but not worthy to give law to the religious thinking of all time? Whether we compare the religious and ethical views opened up in that Commandment with the best religious thinking to be found outside the pale of Judaism during any period whatever before Christ; or compare it with the light which the teaching of Christ has shed upon Religion, and with the most advanced ideas of the present time—the peerless perfection of this monument of the Mosaic Religion stands equally forth before the unsophisticated, reflecting mind, as evidence of its *supernatural* origin and *revealed* character. And just as the deeper view of those words of the Pentateuch, "I am the God of Abraham, and the God of Isaac, and the God of Jacob," suggest the continued life and ultimate resurrection of those patriarchs, so does the deeper study of the Great Commandment, like a "schoolmaster, bring us unto Christ, that we may be justified by faith." For who, in the view of its requirements, must not exclaim, "By the deeds of the law there shall no flesh be justified in His sight; for by the law is the knowledge of sin;" but "Christ hath redeemed us from the curse of the law, being made a curse for us;" and this redemption, or rather "the love of Christ" which prompted it, "constraineth us to live no longer to ourselves, but to Him who died for us and rose again." And thus is the Law reinstated in its rightful place in our hearts; and, despairing of life through the Great Commandment, the life which we fetch out of Christ's death is a life of real, loving, acceptable obedience to that Great Commandment. O the depth of the riches both of the wisdom and knowledge of God, in that wonderful invention! 8. The doctrine of the two natures—the Divine and the Human—in the one Person of Christ, is the only key to the satisfactory solution of many enigmas in Scripture, of which that which our Lord propounded to the scribes regarding David was but one. Accordingly, none who repudiate this doctrine have been able to retain their hold of almost any of the cardinal doctrines of Scripture, nor have held firmly even by the Scriptures themselves, of which this may be called the chief corner stone—elect, precious.

41-44.—THE WIDOW'S TWO MITES. (= Luke xxi. 1-4.) For the exposition, see on Luke xxi. 1-4.

42 And there came a certain poor widow, and she threw in two [3]mites,
43 which make a farthing. And he called *unto him* his disciples, and saith
  unto them, Verily I say unto you, That [h]this poor widow hath cast more
44 in than all they which have cast into the treasury: for all *they* did cast
  in of their abundance; but she of her want did cast in all that she had,
  [i]*even* all her living.

13 AND [a]as he went out of the temple, one of his disciples saith unto
  him, Master, see what manner of stones and what buildings *are here!*
2 And Jesus answering said unto him, Seest thou these great buildings?
  [b]there shall not be left one stone upon another, that shall not be thrown
  down.
3 And as he sat upon the mount of Olives, over against the temple, Peter
4 and James and John and Andrew asked him privately, Tell [c]us, when
  shall these things be? and what *shall be* the sign when all these things
  shall be fulfilled?
5 And Jesus answering them began to say, [d]Take heed lest any *man*
6 deceive you: for many shall come in my name, saying, I am *Christ;*
7 and shall deceive many. And when ye shall hear of wars and rumours
  of wars, be ye not troubled: for *such things* must needs be; but

A. D. 33.

[3] It is the seventh part of one piece of that brass money.
[h] 2 Cor. 8. 12.
[i] 1 John 3.17.

CHAP. 13.
[a] Matt. 24. 1.
Luke 25. 1.
[b] 1 Ki. 9. 7.
2 Chr 7. 20.
Jer. 26. 18.
Mic. 3. 12.
Luke 19.44.
[c] Dan. 12. 6.
Matt. 24. 3.
Luke 21. 7.
John 21.22.
[d] Jer. 29. 8.
Matt. 24. 5.
Luke 21. 8.
Eph. 5. 6.

CHAP. XIII. 1-37.—CHRIST'S PROPHECY OF THE DESTRUCTION OF JERUSALEM, AND WARNINGS SUGGESTED BY IT TO PREPARE FOR HIS SECOND COMING. (= Matt. xxiv. 1-51; Luke xxi. 5-36.)

Jesus had uttered all His mind against the Jewish ecclesiastics, exposing their character with withering plainness, and denouncing, in language of awful severity, the judgments of God against them for that unfaithfulness to their trust which was bringing ruin upon the nation. He had closed this His last public Discourse (Matt. xxiii.) by a passionate Lamentation over Jerusalem, and a solemn Farewell to the Temple. "And (says Matthew, xxiv. 1) Jesus went out, and departed from the temple"—never more to re-enter its precincts, or open His mouth in public teaching. *With this act ended His public ministry.* As He withdrew, says *Olshausen,* the gracious presence of God left the sanctuary; and the Temple, with all its service, and the whole theocratic constitution, was given over to destruction. What immediately followed is, as usual, most minutely and graphically described by our Evangelist.

1. And as he went out of the temple, one of his disciples saith unto him. The other Evangelists are less definite. "As some spake," says Luke: "His disciples came to Him," says Matthew. Doubtless it was the speech of one, the mouth-piece, likely, of others. Master—'Teacher' [Διδάσκαλε], see what manner of stones and what buildings are here!—wondering, probably, how so massive a pile could be overthrown, as seemed implied in our Lord's last words regarding it. *Josephus,* who gives a minute account of the wonderful structure, speaks of stones forty cubits long (Jewish War, v. 5. 1.), and says the pillars supporting the porches were twenty-five cubits high, all of one stone, and that the whitest marble (Ib., v. 5. 2). Six days' battering at the walls, during the siege, made no impression upon them (Ib., vi. 4. 1.) Some of the under-building, yet remaining, and other works, are probably as old as the first temple. 2. And Jesus answering said unto him, Seest thou these great buildings? 'Ye call my attention to these things? I have seen them. Ye point to their massive and durable appearance: now listen to their fate.' there shall not be left—"left here" (Matt. xxiv. 2). [*Tregelles* adds ὧδε—"here"—in Mark also,

on authority of some weight; but we think *Tischendorf* right in adhering to the received text here]. one stone upon another, that shall not be thrown down. Titus ordered the whole city and temple to be demolished (*Joseph. J. W.,* vii. l. 1.); Eleazar wished they had all died before seeing that holy city destroyed by enemies' hands, and before the temple was so profanely *dug up.* (Ib. vii. 8. 7.)

3. And as he sat upon the mount of Olives, over against the temple. On their way from Jerusalem to Bethany they would cross mount Olivet; on its summit He seats Himself, over against the temple, having the city all spread out under His eye. How graphically is this set before us by our Evangelist. Peter and James and John and Andrew asked him privately. The other Evangelists tell us merely that "the disciples" did so. But Mark not only says it was four of them, but names them; and they were the first *quaternion* of the Twelve. See on Matt. x. 1-5, Remarks 6 and 7. 4. Tell us, when shall these things be? and what shall be the sign when all these things shall be fulfilled?—"and what shall be the sign of thy coming, and of the end of the world?" [συντελείας τοῦ αἰῶνος]. They no doubt looked upon the date of all these things as one and the same, and their notions of the things themselves were as confused as of the times of them. Our Lord takes His own way of meeting their questions.

Prophecies of the Destruction of Jerusalem (5-31). 5. And Jesus answering them. [The words ἀποκριθεὶς αὐτοῖς are, without reason, we think, excluded from the text by *Tischendorf* and *Tregelles. Lachmann* inserts them.] began to say, Take heed lest any man deceive you: 6. For many shall come in my name, saying, I am [Christ] (see Matt. xxiv. 5)—"and the time draweth nigh" (Luke xxi. 8); that is, the time of the kingdom in its full splendour. and shall deceive many. "Go ye not therefore after them" (Luke xxi. 8). The reference here seems not to be to pretended Messiahs, deceiving those who rejected the claims of Jesus, of whom indeed there were plenty—for our Lord is addressing His own genuine disciples—but to persons pretending to be Jesus Himself, returned in glory to take possession of His kingdom. This gives peculiar force to the words, "Go ye not therefore after them." 7. And when ye shall hear of

8 [e]the end *shall* not *be* yet. For nation shall rise against nation, and kingdom against kingdom; and there shall be earthquakes in divers places, and there shall be famines and troubles. These *are* the beginnings of [1]sorrows.

9 But [f]take heed to yourselves: for they shall deliver you up to councils; and in the synagogues ye shall be beaten: and ye shall be brought before

10 rulers and kings for my sake, for a testimony against them. And [g]the gospel must first be published among all nations. But [h]when they shall

11 lead *you*, and deliver you up, take no thought beforehand what ye shall speak, neither do ye premeditate; but whatsoever shall be given you in that hour, that speak ye: for it is not ye that speak, [i]but the Holy

12 Ghost. Now [j]the brother shall betray the brother to death, and the father the son; and children shall rise up against *their* parents, and shall

13 cause them to be put to death. And ye shall be hated of all *men* for my name's sake: but [k]he that shall endure unto the end, the same shall be saved.

14 But [l]when ye shall see the abomination of desolation, [m]spoken of by Daniel the prophet, standing where it ought not, (let him that readeth

15 understand,) then let [n]them that be in Judea flee to the mountains: and

A. D. 33.
[e] Jer. 4. 27.
Jer. 5. 10.
1 The word in the original importeth the pains of a woman in travail.
[f] Matt. 10. 17. Rev. 2. 10.
[g] Matt. 24. 14. Rom. 10. 18.
[h] Ex. 24. 12. Luke 12. 11.
[i] Acts 2. 4. Acts 4. 8, 31.
[j] Mic. 7. 6. Luke 21. 16.
[k] Dan. 12. 12. 2 Tim 4. 7, 8.
[l] Matt. 24. 15.
[m] Dan. 9. 27.
[n] Luke 21. 21.

wars and rumours of wars, be ye not troubled—see on *v.* 13, and compare Isa. viii. 11-14, **for such things must needs be; but the end shall not be yet.** In Luke (xxi. 9), "the end is not by and by" [εὐθέως] or 'immediately.' Worse must come before all is over. 8. For nation shall rise against nation, and kingdom against kingdom; and there shall be earthquakes in divers places, and there shall be famines and troubles. These are the beginnings of sorrows [ὠδίνων]—'of travail-pangs,' to which heavy calamities are compared. (See Jer. iv. 31, &c.) The annals of *Tacitus* tell us how the Roman world was convulsed, before the destruction of Jerusalem, by rival claimants of the imperial purple. **9. But take heed to yourselves: for**—"before all these things" (Luke xxi. 12); that is, before these public calamities come, **they shall deliver you up to councils; and in the synagogues ye shall be beaten.** These refer to *ecclesiastical* proceedings against them. **and ye shall be brought before rulers and kings**—before *civil* tribunals next, **for my sake, for a testimony against them**—rather 'unto them' [εἰς μαρτύριον αὐτοῖς]—to give you an opportunity of bearing testimony to Me before them. In the Acts of the Apostles we have the best commentary on this announcement. (Compare Matt. x. 17, 18.) **10. And the gospel must first be published among all nations**—"for a witness, and then shall the end come" (Matt. xxiv. 14). God never sends judgment without previous warning; and there can be no doubt that the Jews, already dispersed over most known countries, had nearly all heard the Gospel "as a witness," before the end of the Jewish state. The same principle was repeated and will repeat itself to *"the* end." **11. But when they shall lead you, and deliver you up, take no thought beforehand** [μὴ προμεριμνᾶτε]—'be not anxious beforehand,' **what ye shall speak, neither do ye premeditate:** 'Be not filled with apprehension, in the prospect of such public appearances for Me, lest ye should bring discredit upon My name, nor think it necessary to prepare beforehand what ye are to say.' **but whatsoever shall be given you in that hour, that speak ye: for it is not ye that speak, but the Holy Ghost.** See on Matt. x. 19, 20. **12. Now the brother shall betray the brother to death, and the father the son; and children shall rise up against their parents, and shall cause them to be put to death. 13. And ye shall be hated of all**

men for my name's sake. Matthew (xxiv. 12) adds this important intimation: "And because iniquity shall abound, the love of many" [τῶν πολλῶν]—'of the many,' or 'of the most;' that is, of the generality of professed disciples—"shall wax cold." Sad illustrations of the effect of abounding iniquity in cooling the love even of faithful disciples we have in the *Epistle of James,* written about the period here referred to, and too frequently ever since. **but he that shall endure unto the end, the same shall be saved.** See on Matt. x. 21, 22; and compare Heb. x. 38, 39, which is a manifest allusion to these words of Christ; also Rev. ii. 10. Luke adds these re-assuring words: "But there shall not an hair of your heads perish" (xxi. 18). Our Lord had just said (Luke xxi. 16) that they should be *put to death;* showing that this precious promise is far above immunity from mere bodily harm, and furnishing a key to the right interpretation of Ps. xci., and such like. **14. But when ye shall see**—"Jerusalem compassed by armies" [στρατοπέδων]—'by encamped armies;' in other words, when ye shall see it *besieged,* and **the abomination of desolation** [τὸ βδέλυγμα τῆς ἐρημώσεως], **spoken of by Daniel the prophet, standing where it ought not**—that is, as explained in Matthew (xxiv. 15), "standing in the holy place." **(let him that readeth**—readeth that prophecy, **understand.)** That "the abomination of desolation" here alluded to was intended to point to the Roman ensigns, as the symbols of an idolatrous, and so unclean Pagan power, may be gathered by comparing what Luke says in the corresponding verse (xxi. 20); and commentators are agreed on it. It is worthy of notice, as confirming this interpretation, that in 1 Macc. i. 54—which, though Apocryphal *Scripture,* is authentic *history*—the expression of Daniel is applied to the idolatrous profanation of the Jewish altar by Antiochus Epiphanes. **then let them that be in Judea flee to the mountains.** The ecclesiastical historian, *Eusebius,* early in the fourth century, tells us that the Christians fled to *Pella,* at the northern extremity of Perea, being "prophetically directed"—perhaps by some prophetic intimation more explicit than this, which would be their chart—and that thus they escaped the predicted calamities by which the nation was overwhelmed. **15. And let him that is on the house-top not go down into the house, neither**

let him that is on the house-top not go down into the house, neither
16 enter *therein*, to take any thing out of his house: and let him that
is in the field not turn back again for to take up his garment.
17 But [o]woe to them that are with child, and to them that give suck,
18 in those days! And pray ye that your flight be not in the winter.
19 For [p]*in* those days shall be affliction, such as was not from the beginning
20 of the creation which God created unto this time, neither shall be. And
except that the Lord had shortened those days, no flesh should be saved:
but for the elect's sake, whom he hath chosen, he hath shortened the
21 days. And [q]then, if any man shall say to you, Lo, here *is* Christ; or, lo,
22 *he is* there; believe *him* not: for false Christs and false prophets shall
rise, and shall show signs and wonders, to seduce, [r]if *it were* possible,
23 even the elect. But [s]take ye heed: behold, I have foretold you all
things.

A. D. 33.

[o] Luke 23.29.
[p] Deut.28.15. Dan. 9. 26. Dan. 12. 1. Joel 2. 2. Matt.24.21.
[q] Luke 17.23. Luke 21. 8.
[r] Rom. 8. 28-39. 1 Pet. 1. 5. 1 John 2.19, 26, 27.
[s] Matt. 7. 15. Luke 21. 8, 34. 2 Pet. 3. 17.

enter therein, to take any thing out of his house:—that is, let him take the outside flight of steps from the roof to the ground; a graphic way of denoting the extreme urgency of the case, and the danger of being tempted, by the desire to save his property, to delay till escape should become impossible. **16. And let him that is in the field not turn back again for to take up his garment. 17. But woe to them**—or, 'alas for them,' **that are with child, and to them that give suck in those days**—in consequence of the aggravated suffering which those conditions would involve. **18. And pray ye that your flight be not in the winter**—making escape perilous, or tempting you to delay your flight. Matthew (xxiv. 20) adds, "neither on the sabbath day," when, from fear of a breach of its sacred rest, they might be induced to remain. **19. For in those days shall be affliction, such as was not from the beginning of the creation which God created unto this time, neither shall be.** Such language is not unusual in the Old Testament with reference to tremendous calamities. But it is matter of literal fact, that there was crowded into the period of the Jewish War an amount and complication of suffering perhaps unparalleled; as the narrative of *Josephus*, examined closely and arranged under different heads, would show. **20. And except that the Lord had shortened those days, no flesh**—that is, no human life—**should be saved: but for the elect's sake, whom he hath chosen, he hath shortened the days.** But for this merciful "shortening," brought about by a remarkable concurrence of causes, the whole nation would have perished, in which there yet remained a remnant to be afterwards gathered out. This portion of the prophecy closes, in Luke, with the following vivid and important glance at the subsequent fortunes of the chosen people: "And they shall fall by the sword, and shall be led away captive into all nations: and Jerusalem shall be trodden down of the Gentiles, until the times of the Gentiles be fulfilled" (Luke xxi. 24). The language as well as the idea of this remarkable statement is taken from Dan. viii. 10, 13. What, then, is its import here? It implies, first, that a time is coming when Jerusalem shall cease to be "trodden down of the Gentiles;" which it was then by Pagan, and since and till now is by Mohammedan unbelievers: and next, it implies that the period when this treading down of Jerusalem by the Gentiles is to cease will be when "the times of the Gentiles are fulfilled" or 'completed.' But what does this mean? We may gather the meaning of it from Rom. xi., in which the divine purposes and procedure towards the chosen people from first to last are treated in detail. In *v.* 25 of that chapter, these words of our Lord are thus reproduced: "For I would not, brethren, that ye should be ignorant of this mystery, lest ye should be wise in your own conceits; that blindness in part is happened to Israel, until the fulness of the Gentiles be come in." See the exposition of that verse, from which it will appear that—"till the fulness of the Gentiles be come in"—or, in our Lord's phraseology, "till the times of the Gentiles be fulfilled"—does not mean 'till the general conversion of the world to Christ,' but 'till the Gentiles have had their *full time* of that place in the Church which the Jews had before them.' After that period of *Gentilism*, as before of *Judaism*, "Jerusalem" and Israel, no longer "trodden down by the Gentiles" but "grafted into their own olive tree," shall constitute, with the believing Gentiles, one Church of God, and fill the whole earth. What a bright vista does this open up! **21. And then, if any man shall say to you, Lo, here is Christ; or, lo, [he is] there; believe him not.** So Luke xvii. 23. **22. For false Christs and false prophets shall rise, and shall show signs and wonders.** No one can read *Josephus'* account of what took place before the destruction of Jerusalem without seeing how strikingly this was fulfilled. **to seduce, if it were possible, even the elect**—implying that this, though all *but* done, will prove impossible. What a precious assurance! (Compare 2 Thess. ii. 9-12.) **23. But take ye heed: behold, I have foretold you all things.** He had just told them that the seduction of the elect would prove impossible; but since this would be all but accomplished, He bids them be on their guard, as the proper means of averting that catastrophe. In Matthew (xxiv. 26-28) we have some additional particulars: "Wherefore, if they shall say unto you, Behold, He is in the desert; go not forth: behold, He is in the secret chambers; believe it not. For as the lightning cometh out of the east, and shineth even unto the west; so shall also the coming of the Son of man be." See on Luke xvii. 23, 24. "For wheresoever the carcase is, there will the eagles be gathered together." See on Luke xvii. 37.

The preceding portion of this prophecy is by all interpreters applied to the destruction of Jerusalem by the Romans. But on the portion that follows some of the most eminent expositors are divided; one class of them considering that our Lord here makes an abrupt transition to the period and the events of His Second Personal Coming and the great Day of Judgment; while another class think there is no evidence of such transition, and that the subject is still the judicial vengeance on Jerusalem, ending not only in the destruction of the city and temple, but in the breaking up of the entire polity, civil and ecclesiastical, of which Jerusalem

24 But ‘in those days, after that tribulation, the sun shall be darkened, and
25 the moon shall not give her light, and the stars of heaven shall fall, and
26 the powers that are in heaven shall be shaken. And “then shall they see

A. D. 33.
‘ Dan. 7. 10.
“ Dan. 7. 13.

was the centre. From the remarkable analogy, however, which subsists between those two events, they admit that the language gradually swells into what is much more descriptive of the events of Christ's Personal Coming and the final Judgment than of the destruction of Jerusalem; and in the concluding warnings most of this latter class see an exclusive reference to the Personal Coming of the Lord to judgment. For the following reasons we judge that this latter is the correct view of the Prophecy. FIRST, the connection between the two parts of the prophecy is that of *immediate sequence of time.* In Matt. xxiv. 29 it is said, "Immediately after [Εὐθέως δὲ μετὰ] the tribulation of those days"—shall all the following things happen. What can be plainer than that the one set of events was to happen in close succession after the other? Whereas, on the other supposition, they were to be so far from happening "immediately" after the others, that after eighteen centuries the time for them has not even yet come. The inconvenience of this is felt to be so great, that "the tribulation of those days" is taken to mean, not the calamities which issued in the destruction of Jerusalem at all, but the tribulation which is to usher in the Personal Coming of Christ and the Judgment of the great day. But though this *might* do, as an exposition of the words of Matthew, the words of Mark (xiii. 24) seem in flat contradiction to it: "But in those days, after *that* tribulation" emphatically [μετὰ τὴν Ϡλίψιν ἐκείνην]. How can this possibly mean any tribulation but the one just described? And were we to try the other sense of it, how very unnatural is it—after reading a minute account of the tribulations which were to bring on the destruction of Jerusalem, and then that "immediately after the tribulation of those days" certain other events are to happen — to understand this to mean, 'Immediately after the tribulation of another and far distant day, a tribulation not here to be described at all, shall occur the following events!' What object could there be for alluding so abruptly to "the tribulation of those days," if that tribulation was not to be described at all, but only something which was to happen *after* it? But, SECONDLY, at the conclusion of the second part of this prophecy, our Lord says (v. 30), "Verily I say unto you, that this generation shall not pass away till all these things be done," or "fulfilled" (as in Matt. xxiv. 34; Luke xxi. 32). This, on the face of it, is so decisive that those who think the second half of the Prophecy refers to the Second Coming of Christ and the Final Judgment are obliged to translate the words [ἡ γενεὰ αὕτη]. 'This (Jewish) *nation,*' or 'This (human) *race* shall not pass away,' &c. But besides that this is quite contrary to the usage of the word—just think how inept a sense is brought out by translating 'this race;' for who could require to be told that the human family would not have passed away before certain events occurred which were to befall the human race? and how pointless is the other sense, that the Jewish *nation* would not be extinct before those events! Whereas, if we understand the words in their natural sense—that the generation then running should see all those predictions fulfilled—all is intelligible, deeply important, and according to literal fact. But the exposition will throw further light upon this question.

24. But in those days, after that tribulation— "Immediately after the tribulation of those days"

(Matt. xxiv. 29); see introductory remarks on this latter portion of the prophecy, the sun shall be darkened, and the moon shall not give her light. 25. And the stars of heaven shall fall— "and upon the earth distress of nations, with perplexity; the sea and the waves roaring; men's hearts failing them for fear, and for looking after those things which are coming on the earth" (Luke xxi. 25, 26). and the powers that are in heaven shall be shaken. Though the grandeur of this language carries the mind over the head of all periods but that of Christ's Second Coming, nearly every expression will be found used of the Lord's coming in terrible national judgments: as of Babylon (Isa. xiii. 9-13); of Idumea (Isa. xxxiv. 1, 2, 4, 8-10); of Egypt (Ezek. xxxii. 7, 8): compare also Ps. xviii. 7-15; Isa. xxiv. 1, 17-19; Joel ii. 10, 11, &c. We cannot therefore consider the mere strength of this language a proof that it refers exclusively or primarily to the precursors of the final day, though of course in "*that day*" it will have its most awful fulfilment. 26. And then shall they see the Son of man coming in the clouds with great power and glory. In Matt. xxiv. 30, this is given most fully: "And then shall appear the sign of the Son of man in heaven; and then shall all the tribes of the earth mourn, and they shall see the Son of man," &c. That this language finds its highest interpretation in the Second Personal Coming of Christ, is most certain. But the question is, whether that be the primary sense of it as it stands here? Now, if the reader will turn to Dan. vii. 13, 14, and connect with it the preceding verses, he will find, we think, the true key to our Lord's meaning here. There the powers that oppressed the Church—symbolized by rapacious wild beasts—are summoned to the bar of the great God, who as the Ancient of days seats Himself, with His assessors, on a burning Throne; thousand thousands ministering to Him, and ten thousand times ten thousand standing before Him. "The judgment is set, and the books are opened." Who that is guided by the *mere words* would doubt that this is a description of the Final Judgment? And yet nothing is clearer than that it is *not*, but a description of a vast *temporal* judgment, upon organized bodies of men, for their incurable hostility to the kingdom of God upon earth. Well, after the doom of these has been pronounced and executed, and room thus prepared for the unobstructed development of the kingdom of God over the earth, what follows? "I saw in the night visions, and, behold, one like THE SON OF MAN came with the clouds of heaven, and came to the Ancient of days, and they (the angelic attendants) brought Him near before Him." For what purpose? To receive investiture in the kingdom, which, as Messiah, of right belonged to Him. Accordingly, it is added, "And there was given Him dominion, and glory, and a kingdom, that all peoples, nations, and languages should serve Him: His dominion is an everlasting dominion, which shall not pass away, and His kingdom that which shall not be destroyed." Comparing this with our Lord's words, He seems to us, by "the Son of man (on which phrase, see on John i. 51) coming in the clouds with great power and glory," to mean, that when judicial vengeance shall once have been executed upon Jerusalem, and the ground thus cleared for the unobstructed establishment of His own kingdom, His true regal claims and rights would be visibly

27 the Son of man coming in the clouds with great power and glory. And then shall he send his angels, and shall gather together his elect from the four winds, from the uttermost part of the earth to the uttermost part of heaven.

28 Now learn a parable of the fig tree; When her branch is yet tender,
29 and putteth forth leaves, ye know that summer is near: so ye, in like manner, when ye shall see these things come to pass, know that it is nigh,
30 *even* at the doors. Verily I say unto you, that this generation shall not
31 pass, till all these things be done. Heaven and earth shall pass away; but my *°*words shall not pass away.
32 But of that day and *that* hour knoweth no man, no, not the angels which are in heaven, neither the Son, but the Father.

A. D. 33.
° Num. 23.19.
Jos. 23. 14, 15.
Ps. 19. 7.
Ps. 102. 26.
Ps. 119. 89.
Isa. 40. 8.
Isa. 46. 10.
Isa. 51. 6.
Zec. 1. 6.
Luke 21.33.
2 Tim. 2.13.
Titus 1. 2.

---

and gloriously asserted and manifested. See on Luke ix. 28 (with its parallels in Matthew and Mark), in which nearly the same language is employed, and where it can hardly be understood of anything else than *the full and free establishment of the kingdom of Christ on the destruction of Jerusalem.* But what is that "sign of the Son of man in heaven"? Interpreters are not agreed. But as before Christ came to destroy Jerusalem some appalling portents were seen in the air, so before His Personal appearing it is likely that something *analogous* will be witnessed, though of what nature it would be vain to conjecture. **27. And then shall he send his angels**—"with a great sound of a trumpet" (Matt. xxiv. 31), and **shall gather together his elect from the four winds, from the uttermost part of the earth to the uttermost part of heaven.** As the tribes of Israel were anciently gathered together by sound of trumpet (Exod. xix. 13, 16, 19; Lev. xxiii. 24; Ps. lxxxi. 3-5), so any mighty gathering of God's people, by divine command, is represented as collected by sound of trumpet (Isa. xxvii. 13; compare Rev. xi. 15); and the ministry of angels, employed in all the great operations of Providence, is here held forth as the agency by which the present assembling of the elect is to be accomplished. *Lightfoot* thus explains it: 'When Jerusalem shall be reduced to ashes, and that wicked nation cut off and rejected, then shall the Son of man send His ministers with the trumpet of the Gospel, and they shall gather His elect of the several nations, from the four corners of heaven: so that God shall not want a Church, although that ancient people of His be rejected and cast off; but that ancient Jewish Church being destroyed, a new Church shall be called out of the Gentiles.' But though something like this appears to be the primary sense of the verse, in relation to the destruction of Jerusalem, no one can fail to see that the language swells beyond any gathering of the human family into a Church upon earth, and forces the thoughts onward to that gathering of the Church "at the last trump," to meet the Lord in the air, which is to wind up the present scene. Still, this is not, in our judgment, the *direct* subject of the prediction; for the next verse limits the whole prediction to the generation then existing.
28. Now learn a parable of the fig tree ['Aπò δὲ τῆς συκῆς μάθετε τὴν παραβολήν]—' Now from the fig tree learn the parable,' or the high lesson which this teaches: **When her branch is yet tender, and putteth forth leaves** [τὰ φύλλα]—' its leaves,' ye **know that summer is near: 29. So ye, in like manner, when ye shall see these things come to pass** [γινόμενα]—rather, ' coming to pass,' **know that it**—"the kingdom of God" (Luke xxi. 31), **is nigh, even at the doors**—that is, the full manifestation of it; for till then it admitted of no full

195

development. In Luke (xxi. 28) the following words precede these: "And when these things begin to come to pass, then look up, and lift up your heads; for your redemption draweth nigh"— their redemption, in the first instance certainly, from Jewish oppression (1 Thess. ii. 14-16; Luke xi. 52): but in the highest sense of these words, redemption from all the oppressions and miseries of the present state at the Second Appearing of the Lord Jesus. **30. Verily I say unto you, that this generation shall not pass till all these things be done**—or "fulfilled" (Matt. xxiv. 34; Luke xxi. 32). See introductory remarks on this second half of the prophecy. Whether we take this to mean that the whole would be fulfilled within the limits of the generation then current, or, according to a usual way of speaking, that the generation then existing would not pass away without seeing a *begun* fulfilment of this prediction, the facts entirely correspond. For either the whole was fulfilled in the destruction accomplished by Titus, as many think; or if we stretch it out, according to others, till the thorough dispersion of the Jews a little later, under Adrian, every requirement of our Lord's words seems to be met. **31. Heaven |and earth shall pass away; but my words shall not pass away**—the strongest possible expression of the divine authority by which He spake; not as Moses or Paul might have said of their own inspiration, for such language would be unsuitable in any merely human mouth.
Warnings to Prepare for the Coming of Christ Suggested by the foregoing Prophecy (32-37). It will be observed that, in the foregoing prophecy, as our Lord approaches the crisis of the day of vengeance on Jerusalem, and redemption for the Church—at which stage the analogy between that and the day of final vengeance and redemption waxes more striking—His language rises and swells beyond all temporal and partial vengeance, beyond all earthly deliverances and enlargements, and ushers us resistlessly into the scenes of the final day. Accordingly, in these six concluding verses it is manifest that preparation for "THAT DAY" is what our Lord designs to inculcate.
32. But of that day and that hour—that is, the precise time, **knoweth no man** [οὐδεὶς]—lit., 'no one,' **no, not the angels which are in heaven, neither the Son, but the Father.** This very remarkable statement regarding "the Son" is peculiar to Mark. Whether it means that the Son was *not at that time in possession of the knowledge* referred to, or simply that it was not *among the things which He had received to communicate*—has been matter of much controversy even amongst the firmest believers in the proper Divinity of Christ. In the latter sense it was taken by some of the most eminent of the ancient Fathers, and by *Luther*, *Melancthon*, and most of the elder Lutherans; and it is so taken by *Bengel, Lange, Webster and Wilkin-*

33   Take ^wye heed, watch and pray: for ye know not when the time is.

34   *For ^xthe Son of man is* as a man taking a far journey, who left his house, and gave authority to his servants, and to every man his work, and com-

35 manded the porter to watch.   Watch ^yye therefore; for ye know not when the master of the house cometh, at even, or at midnight, or at the

36 cock-crowing, or in the morning; lest, coming suddenly, he find you

37 sleeping.   And what I say unto you I say unto all, Watch.

A. D. 33.
^w Matt. 24. 42.
Luke 12. 40.
Rom. 13. 11.
^x Matt. 24. 45.
Matt. 25. 14.
^y Matt. 24. 42, 44.
Rev. 3. 3.

son. Chrysostom and others understood it to mean that *as Man* our Lord was ignorant of this. It is taken literally by *Calvin, Grotius, de Wette, Meyer, Fritzsche, Stier, Alford,* and *Alexander.* Beyond all doubt, as the word "knoweth" [οἶδεν] in this verse is the well-known word for the knowledge of any fact, this latter sense is the one we should naturally put upon the statement; namely, that our Lord did not at that time know the day and hour of His own Second Coming. But *the nature of the case*—meaning by this the speaker, His subject, and the probable design of the statement in question—is always allowed to have its weight in determining the sense of any doubtful utterance. What, then, is the nature of this case? First, The Speaker was One who, from the time when He entered on His public ministry, spoke ever, acted ever, as One *from whom nothing was hid;* and *to Whom was committed the whole administration of the Kingdom of God* from first to last; nor when Peter ascribed *omniscience* to Him (John xxi. 17), can He be supposed to have pointed to any enlargement of the sphere of His Lord's knowledge since His resurrection, or to aught save what he had witnessed of Him "in the days of His flesh." Second, There seems nothing so peculiar in the knowledge of *the precise time of His Second Coming*, much less of *the destruction of Jerusalem*, more than of other things which we are certain that our Lord knew at that time, that *it* should be kept from Him, while those other things were all full before His view. We are ill judges indeed of such matters, but we are obliged to give this consideration some weight. So far as we may presume to judge, there was no benefit to the disciples to be gained by the concealment from *Him*—as certainly there could be no danger to Himself from the knowledge—of the precise time of His coming. But, Third, When we have familiarized ourselves with our Lord's way of speaking of His communications to men, we shall perhaps obtain a key to this remarkable saying of His. Thus: "And what He hath seen and heard, that He testifieth;" "I speak to the world those things that I have heard of Him;" "The Father which sent me, He gave me a commandment what I should say and what I should speak" (John iii. 32; viii. 26; xii. 49). And in a remarkable prophecy (Isa. l. 4) to which we have already adverted (see on ch. x. 32-45, Remark 1)—in which beyond doubt He is the Speaker—He represents Himself as receiving His instructions daily, being each morning instructed what to communicate for that day. In this view, as the precise time of His coming was certainly not in His instructions; as He had not "*seen* and *heard*" it, and so could not "testify" it; as He had no communication from His Father on that subject—might He not, in this sense, after saying that neither men nor angels knew it, add that *Himself knew it not*, without the danger of lowering, even in the minds of any of His half-instructed disciples, the impression of His Omniscience, which every fresh communication to them only tended to deepen? What recommends this opinion is not any inconsistency in the opposite view with the supreme Divinity of Christ. That view might

quite well be maintained, if only there appeared sufficient ground for it. But while the one argument in its favour is the natural sense of the words;—a very strong argument, however, we are constrained to admit—everything else which one is accustomed to take into account, in weighing the sense of a doubtful saying, is in favour of a *modified* sense of the words in question.

Here follow, in Matt. xxiv. 37-41, some additional particulars: 37. "But as the days of Noe were, so shall also the coming of the Son of man be. 38. For as in the days that were before the flood they were eating and drinking, marrying and giving in marriage, until the day that Noe entered into the ark, 39. And knew not until the flood came, and took them all away; so shall also the coming of the Son of Man be" (see on Luke xvii. 26, 27). 40. "Then shall two (men) be in the field"—at their ordinary work—"the one shall be taken, and the other left. 41. Two women shall be grinding at the mill (see on Mark ix. 42); the one shall be taken, and the other left"—the children of this world and the children of light mingled to the last. See on Luke xvii. 34-36.

33. Take ye heed, watch and pray: for ye know not when the time is. 34. [For the Son of man is] as a man taking a far journey, who left his house, and gave authority to his servants, and to every man his work. The idea thus far is similar to that in the opening part of the parable of the talents (Matt. xxv. 14,15). **and commanded the porter** [τῷ θυρωρῷ]—or 'the gate-keeper,' **to watch**—pointing to the official duty of the ministers of religion to give warning of approaching danger to the people. **35. Watch ye therefore; for ye know not when the master of the house cometh, at even, or at midnight, or at the cock-crowing, or in the morning**—an allusion to the four Roman watches of the night. **36. Lest, coming suddenly, he find you sleeping.** See on Luke xii. 35-40, 42-46. **37. And what I say unto you**—this Discourse, it will be remembered, was delivered in private, **I say unto all, Watch**—anticipating and requiring the diffusion of His teaching by them amongst all His disciples, and its perpetuation through all time.

The closing words of the Discourse, as given by Luke, xxi. 34-36, are remarkable. "And take heed to yourselves, lest at any time your hearts be overcharged" [βαρυνθῶσιν], or 'weighted down,' "with surfeiting" [κραιπάλη]—'debauchery,' or its effects; "and drunkenness"—meaning all animal excesses, which quench spirituality; "and cares of this life"—engrossing the interest, absorbing the attention, and so choking spirituality: "and so that day come upon you unawares. For as a snare"—a trap catching them when least expecting it—"shall it come on all them that dwell on the face of the whole earth. Watch ye therefore, and pray always"—the two great duties which, in prospect of trial, are always enjoined—"that ye may be accounted worthy to escape all these things that shall come to pass, and to stand before the Son of man." These warnings, though suggested by the need of preparedness for the tremen-

196

14 AFTER [a] two days was *the feast of* the passover, and of unleavened bread: and the chief priests and the scribes sought how they might take

dous calamities approaching, and the total wreck of the existing state of things, have reference to a Coming of another kind, for judicial Vengeance of another nature and on a grander and more awful scale—not ecclesiastical or political but *personal*, not temporal but *eternal*—when all safety and blessedness will be found to lie in being able to "STAND BEFORE THE SON OF MAN" in the glory of His Personal appearing.

The nine concluding verses of Matthew's account (ch. xxiv. 43-51) are peculiar to that Gospel, but are in the same strain of warning to prepare for His Second Coming and the Final Judgment. "But know this, that if the goodman of the house had known in what watch the thief would come, he would have watched, and would not have suffered his house to be broken up. Therefore be ye also ready: for in such an hour as ye think not the Son of man cometh. Who then is a faithful and wise servant, whom his lord hath made ruler over his household, to give them meat in due season? Blessed is that servant whom his lord when he cometh shall find so doing. Verily I say unto you, That he shall make him ruler over all his goods. But and if that evil servant shall say in his heart, My lord delayeth his coming; and shall begin to smite his fellow-servants, and to eat and drink with the drunken; the lord of that servant shall come in a day when he looketh not for him, and in an hour that he is not aware of. And shall cut him asunder, and appoint him his portion with the hypocrites: there shall be weeping and gnashing of teeth." On this whole passage, see on Luke xii. 35-40, 42-46, which is almost identical with it; and on the last words, see on Matt. xiii. 42.

In Luke's account (xxi. 37, 38) the following brief summary is given of our Lord's proceedings until the fifth day (or the Thursday) of His last week: "And in the daytime" [τὰς ἡμέρας]— 'during the days'— "He was teaching in the temple; and at night" [τὰς νύκτας]—'during the nights'—"He went out and abode in the mount that is called the mount of Olives"—that is, at Bethany.

Remarks.—1. In the destruction of Jerusalem, and the utter extinction of all that the Jews prided themselves in, on the one hand; and in the preservation, on the other, of the little flock of Christ's disciples, and their secure establishment and gradual diffusion, as now the only visible kingdom of God upon earth—we see an appalling illustration of those great principles of the Divine Government: "Yet a little while, and the wicked shall not be: yea, thou shall diligently consider his place, and it shall not be. But the meek shall inherit the earth; and shall delight themselves in the abundance of peace." "Behold, the day cometh that shall burn as an oven; and all the proud, yea, and all that do wickedly, shall be stubble: and the day that cometh shall burn them up, saith the Lord of Hosts, that it shall leave them neither root nor branch. But unto you that fear my name shall the Sun of Righteousness arise, with healing in His wings; and ye shall go forth, and grow up as calves of the stall." "Every plant which my heavenly Father hath not planted shall be rooted up." (Ps. xxxvii. 10, 11; Mal. iv. 1, 2; Matt. xv. 13.) Every spiritual edifice that is not built of living stones has the rot in it, and will sooner or later crumble down. Like the house built upon the sand, the storm of divine indignation will sweep it away. *He only that doeth*

the will of God abideth for ever (1 John ii. 17). "Well; because of unbelief they were broken off, and thou standest by faith. Be not high-minded, but fear: for if God spared not the natural branches, take heed lest He also spare not thee" (Rom. xi. 20, 21). 2. We here see the falsity of that shallow view of prophecy which used to be so generally accepted, and even yet is advocated by too many who speak contemptuously of all study of unfulfilled prophecy—that it was designed exclusively for the benefit of those who live *after* its fulfilment, to confirm their faith in the inspiration by which it was uttered, and generally, in the Religion of which it forms a part. Certainly this was not the primary object of our Lord's prophecy of the destruction of Jerusalem; for throughout He gives it forth expressly as a directory *in prospect of it,* for the guidance of those who heard it. "Take heed lest any man deceive you: for many shall come in my name, &c. And when ye shall hear of wars and rumours of wars, be not troubled. When ye shall see the abomination, spoken of by Daniel the prophet, standing where it ought not, (LET HIM THAT READETH UNDERSTAND,) then let them which be in Judea flee, &c. False Christs and false prophets shall rise, and shall show signs and wonders, to seduce, if it were possible, even the elect. But take heed: *behold, I have foretold you all things.* Now learn a parable of the fig tree: . . So ye, in like manner, *when ye shall see these things come to pass, know that it is nigh, even at the doors."* And if this prophecy was intended directly for those who lived *before* its fulfilment, why not others? Even the darkest prophecy—the Apocalypse—bears on its face throughout a reference to those who should live, not after, but before its accomplishment—to forewarn them of coming dangers, to indicate at least the general nature of them, to prepare and animate them to encounter these, and to assure them of the ultimate safety and triumph of Christ's cause and the glorious reward awaiting the steadfast followers of the Lamb. It is the rashness and dogmatism of the students of prophecy, and the fantastic principles which have often been applied to the interpretation of it, that have scared away sensible Christians and grave theologians from this study, despairing of success. But let us take heed of being thus spoiled of so precious a portion of our Scripture inheritance; missing the blessing pronounced on those who read and keep what is written in prophecy (Rev. i. 3), and disobeying our Lord's own solemn injunction: "*Whoso readeth let him understand"* (*v.* 14). **3.** As temperance in animal indulgences is indispensable to that wakefulness and elevation of spirit which fits us for welcoming Christ when He comes, so that spirit of excess which goes to the utmost lawful indulgence wars against the soul, leaving it a prey to surprises even the most fatal (Luke xxi. 34-36; 1 Cor. ix. 27; 1 Pet. ii. 11). 4. In whatever providential events Christ may come to us (Rev. iii. 3; xvi. 15)—even in the summons to "depart and be with Him, which is far better"—it is to His Personal Appearing the second time, without sin unto salvation," that the hearts of believers must ever supremely rise; nor is it a healthy state of soul to stop short of this—as most certainly it is not scriptural. Let us, then, "love His appearing."

CHAP. XIV. 1-11.—THE CONSPIRACY OF THE JEWISH AUTHORITIES TO PUT JESUS TO DEATH—THE SUPPER AND THE ANOINTING AT BETHANY—

2 him by craft, and put *him* to death. But they said, Not on the feast day, lest there be an uproar of the people.

JUDAS AGREES WITH THE CHIEF PRIESTS TO BETRAY HIS LORD. (= Matt. xxvi. 1-16; Luke xxii. 1-6; John xii. 1-11.) The events of this Section appear to have occurred on the fourth day of the Redeemer's Last Week—the *Wednesday*.

Conspiracy of the Jewish Authorities to. Put Jesus to Death (1, 2). **1. After two days was the feast of the passover, and of unleavened bread.** The meaning is, that two days after what is about to be mentioned the Passover would arrive; in other words, what follows occurred two days *before* the feast. **and the chief priests and the scribes sought how they might take him by craft, and put him to death.** From Matthew's fuller account (ch xxvi.) we learn that our Lord announced this to the Twelve as follows, being the first announcement to them of the precise time : "And it came to pass, when Jesus had finished all these sayings"—referring to the contents of ch. xxiv., xxv., which He delivered to His disciples; His public ministry being now closed : from His *prophetical* He is now passing into His *Priestly* office, although all along Himself took our infirmities and bare our sicknesses—"He said unto His disciples, Ye know that after two days is [the feast of] the Passover, and the Son of man is betrayed to be crucified." The *first* and the *last* steps of his final sufferings are brought together in this brief announcement of all that was to take place. The *Passover* [τὸ πάσχα = חֶסֶּפ] was the first and the chief of the three great annual festivals, commemorative of the redemption of God's people from Egypt, through the sprinkling of the blood of a lamb divinely appointed to be slain for that end; the destroying angel, "when he saw the blood, *passing over*" the Israelitish houses, on which that blood was seen, when he came to destroy all the first-born in the land of Egypt (Exod. xii.)—bright typical foreshadowing of the great Sacrifice, and the Redemption effected thereby. Accordingly, "by the determinate counsel and foreknowledge of God, who is wonderful in counsel and excellent in working," it was so ordered that precisely at the Passover-season, "Christ our Passover should be sacrificed for us." On the day following the Passover commenced "the feast of unleavened bread" [τὰ ἄζυμα], so called because for seven days only unleavened bread was to be eaten (Exod. xii. 18-20). See on 1 Cor. v. 6-8. We are further told by Matthew (xxvi. 3) that the consultation was held in the palace of Caiaphas the high priest, between the chief priests, [the scribes], and the elders of the people, how "they might take Jesus by subtlety and kill Him." [The words καὶ οἱ γραμματεῖς are probably not genuine here. *Tischendorf* and *Tregelles* exclude them. It is likely they were introduced from Matthew and Luke.] **2. But they said, Not on the feast** [day]—rather, 'not during the feast' [ἐν τῇ ἑορτῇ]; not until the seven days of unleavened bread should be over. **lest there be an uproar of the people.** In consequence of the vast influx of strangers, embracing all the male population of the land who had reached a certain age, there were within the walls of Jerusalem at this festival some two millions of people; and in their excited state, the danger of tumult and bloodshed among "the people," who for the most part took Jesus for a prophet, was extreme. (See *Joseph.* Antt. xx. 5. 3.) What plan, if any, these ecclesiastics fixed upon for seizing our Lord, does not appear. But the proposal of Judas being at once

and eagerly gone into, it is probable they were till then at some loss for a plan sufficiently quiet and yet effectual. So, just at the feast time shall it be done; the unexpected offer of Judas relieving them of their fears. Thus, as *Bengel* remarks, did the divine counsel take effect.

The Supper and the Anointing at Bethany Six Days before the Passover (3-9). The time of this part of the narrative, as we shall presently see, is *four days before* what has just been related. Had it been part of the regular train of events which our Evangelist designed to record, he would probably have inserted it in its proper place, before the conspiracy of the Jewish authorities. But having come to the treason of Judas, he seems to have gone back upon this scene as what probably gave immediate occasion to the awful deed. The best introduction to it we have in the Fourth Gospel.

John xii. 1, 2.—"Then Jesus, six days before the Passover, came to Bethany" (see on Luke xix. 29)—that is, on the sixth day before it; probably after sunset on *Friday* evening, or the commencement of the Jewish *Sabbath* that preceded the Passover : "where Lazarus was which had been dead, whom He raised from the dead. There they made Him a supper"—in what house is not here stated; but the first two Evangelists expressly tell us it was "in the house of Simon the leper" (Matt. xxvi. 6; Mark xiv. 3). But for this statement, we should have taken it for granted that the same occurred in the house of Lazarus. At the same time, as Martha served (John xii. 2), he was probably some near relative of her family. Who this "Simon the leper" was, is quite unknown. A leper at that time, while entertaining guests at his own table, he could not have been, as this would have been contrary to the Jewish law. But he *had been* one, perhaps long one, and so came to be best known by his old name, "Simon the leper.". And just as Matthew, long after he was transformed into "an apostle of Jesus Christ," continued to call himself what none of the other Evangelists do, "Matthew the publican;" so, perhaps, this healed leper, after the Saviour had cleansed him, and won his heart—healing soul and body together—felt it pleasant to be known ever after as "Simon the leper:" and just as Matthew, again, "made Him a great feast in his own house," this Simon, out of the fulness of a grateful heart, made Him this supper. And what if he was that very leper whose case is the first recorded in the Gospel History, who, immediately after the Sermon on the Mount," as Jesus descended from the hill on which it was delivered, came running and kneeling to Him, saying, "Lord, if thou wilt, thou canst make me clean," and whose leprosy immediately departed from him, when the Lord said, "I will; be thou clean"! (See on Matt. viii. 1-4.) The time when this supper was made to Jesus was affecting. As it was His last visit to His quiet and loved retreat at Bethany, so He honoured it by making it His longest. He made it His nightly home during His final week; going thence daily into the city, but never sleeping there. And, says the beloved disciple, "Martha served." Active, busy, but true-hearted, Martha is here at her proper vocation—serving her Lord. A blessed employment. She got a gentle check once when so engaged, though not for so doing. But there is no rebuke here; nay, it seems recorded here as her privilege that she served. Service to Christ there must be; somebody must do it; and Martha on this occasion was the honoured servant; "but

3   And *b*being in Bethany, in the house of Simon the leper, as he sat at meat, there came a woman having an alabaster box of ointment of [1]spikenard very precious; and she brake the box, and poured *it* on his
4   head.   And there were some that had indignation within themselves, and
5   said, Why was this waste of the ointment made? for it might have been sold for more than three hundred *c*pence, and have been given to the
6   poor.   And they murmured against her.   And Jesus said, Let her alone;
7   why trouble ye her? she hath wrought a good work on me.   For *d*ye have the poor with you always, and whensoever ye will ye may do them
8   good: but me ye have not always.   She hath done what she could: she
9   is come aforehand to anoint my body to the burying.   Verily I say unto you, Wheresoever this gospel shall be preached throughout the whole world, *this* also that she hath done shall be spoken of for a memorial of her.
10   And *e*Judas Iscariot, one of the twelve, went unto the chief priests, to

A. D. 33.

b Matt. 26. 6.
Luke 7. 37.
John 12. 1,
3.

1 Or, pure
nard, or,
liquid
nard.

c Matt.18.28.
John 6. 7.
d Deut.15.11.
Pro. 22. 2.
Matt.26.11.
Matt. 25.35.
John 12. 8.
2 Cor. 9. 13.
e Matt.26.14.
John 13. 2,
30.

Lazarus," says John, "was one of them that sat at the table with him"—a trophy of his Master's resurrection-power and glory. So much for John's introduction to the scene. Let us now return to our own narrative:
3. And being in Bethany, in the house of Simon the leper, as he sat at meat, there came a woman. It was "Mary," as we learn from John xii. 3. **having an alabaster box of ointment of spikenard** [νάρδου]—pure *nard*, a celebrated aromatic. (See Cant. i. 12.) **very precious** —"very costly" (John xii. 3), **and she brake the box, and poured it on his head**—"and anointed," adds John, "the feet of Jesus, and wiped His feet with her hair: and the house was filled with the odour of the ointment." The only use of this was to refresh and exhilarate—a grateful compliment in the East; amidst the closeness of a heated atmosphere, with many guests at a feast. Such was the form in which Mary's love to Christ, at so much cost to herself, poured itself out. **4. And there were some that had indignation within themselves, and said.** Matthew says (xxvi. 8), "But when His disciples saw it, they had indignation, saying." The spokesman, however, was none of the true-hearted Eleven—as we learn from John (xii. 4): "Then saith one of His disciples, Judas Iscariot, Simon's son, which should betray Him." Doubtless the thought stirred first in his breast, and issued from his base lips; and some of the rest, ignorant of his true character and feelings, and carried away by his plausible speech, might for the moment feel some chagrin at the apparent waste. **Why was this waste of the ointment made? 5. For it might have been sold for more than three hundred pence**—between nine and ten pounds sterling, **and have been given to the poor. And they murmured against her.** "This he said," remarks John, and the remark is of exceeding importance, "not that he cared for the poor; but because he was a thief, and had the bag" [τὸ γλωσσόκομον]—the scrip or treasure-chest; "and bare what was put therein" [ἐβάσταζεν]—not 'bare it off' by theft, as some understand it. It is true that he did this; but the expression means simply that he had charge of it and its contents, or was treasurer to Jesus and the Twelve. What a remarkable arrangement was this, by which an avaricious and dishonest person was not only taken into the number of the Twelve, but entrusted with the custody of their little property! The purposes which this served are obvious enough; but it is farther noticeable, that the remotest hint was never given to the Eleven of his true character, nor did the dis-
199

ciples most favoured with the intimacy of Jesus ever suspect him, till a few minutes before he voluntarily separated himself from their company —for ever! **6. And Jesus said, Let her alone; why trouble ye her? she hath wrought a good work on me.** It was good in itself, and so was acceptable to Christ; it was eminently seasonable, and so more acceptable still; and it was "what she could," and so most acceptable of all. **7. For ye have the poor with you always**—referring to Deut. xv. 11, **and whensoever ye will ye may do them good: but me ye have not always**—a gentle hint of His approaching departure, by One who knew the worth of His own presence. **8. She hath done what she could**—a noble testimony, embodying a principle of immense importance. **she is come aforehand to anoint my body to the burying**—or, as in John (xii. 7), "Against the day of my burying hath she kept this." Not that she, dear heart, thought of His burial, much less reserved any of her nard to anoint her dead Lord. But as the time was so near at hand when that office would have to be performed, *and she was not to have that privilege even after the spices were brought for the purpose* (ch. xvi. 1), He lovingly *regards it as done now.* **9. Verily I say unto you, Wheresoever this gospel shall be preached throughout the whole world, this also that she hath done shall be spoken of for a memorial of her.** 'In the act of love done to Him,' says *Olshausen* beautifully, 'she has erected to herself an eternal monument, as lasting as the Gospel, the eternal Word of God. From generation to generation this remarkable prophecy of the Lord has been fulfilled; and even we, in explaining this saying of the Redeemer, of necessity contribute to its accomplishment.' 'Who but Himself,' asks *Stier*, 'had the power to ensure to any work of man, even if resounding in His own time through the whole earth, an imperishable remembrance in the stream of history? Behold once more here the majesty of His royal judicial supremacy in the government of the world, in this "Verily I say unto you."'
10. And Judas Iscariot, one of the twelve, went unto the chief priests, to betray him unto them—that is, to make his proposals, and to bargain with them, as appears from Matthew's fuller statement (ch. xxvi.), which says, he "went unto the chief priests, and said, What will ye give me, and I will deliver Him unto you? And they covenanted with him for thirty pieces of silver" (*v.* 15). The thirty pieces of silver were thirty shekels, the fine paid for man or maid-servant accidentally killed (Exod. xxi. 32), and equal to between four and five pounds sterling

11 betray him unto them. And when they heard *it*, they were glad, and promised to give him *ᶠ*money. And he sought how he might conveniently betray him.

A. D. 33.

ᶠ Zec. 11. 12.
1 Tim. 6. 10.

—"a *goodly* price that I was prized at of them"! (Zec. xi. 13). **11. And when they heard it, they were glad, and promised to give him money.** Matthew alone records the precise sum, because a remarkable and complicated prophecy, which he was afterwards to refer to, was fulfilled by it. **And he sought how he might conveniently betray him** —or, as more fully given in Luke (xxii. 6), "And he promised, and sought opportunity to betray Him unto them in the absence of the multitude." That he should avoid an "uproar" or 'riot' among the people, which probably was made an essential condition by the Jewish authorities, was thus assented to by the traitor; into whom, says Luke (xxii. 3), "Satan entered," to put him upon this hellish deed.

Remarks. — 1. Among the 'undesigned coincidences' in the narratives of the Four Evangelists which so strongly confirm their truth, not the least striking are the representations given of the respective characters of Martha and Mary by the Third and Fourth Evangelists. While in Luke we have a scene omitted by John, in which the active services of Martha and the placid affection, the passive docility, of Mary come strikingly out (see on Luke x. 38-42), we have in John (xii. 1, &c.) a very different scene, omitted by Luke, in which, nevertheless, the same characteristics appear. Martha serves, while Mary diffuses over her Lord the odour of her love, in the costly ointment which she spent upon Him. What are these but different rays from one bright historic Reality? 2. In this feast, beheld in its inner character, may we not see on a small scale something like what is from age to age realized in the kingdom of grace? Here is the Redeemer surrounded by the varied trophies of His grace. First, we have Simon the leper—the healed man; next, Lazarus—the risen man; and here is the man that leaned on Jesus' breast, nearest to his Lord—type of seraphic affection; and that other "son of thunder," James, the brother of John, who was honoured to drink of his Lord's cup, and be baptized with the baptism which He was baptized withal—the man of impulsive but robust devotion to Christ; and here was blessed Simon Bar-jona—the man of commanding energy—first among the Twelve; and all the diversified types of Christian character, as exemplified in the rest: But, lo! in the midst of these, and one of their number, was "a devil"—type of that traitorous spirit from which probably the Christian Church has hardly ever been quite free. But woman also is here represented— redeemed womanhood; and in its two great types—active and passive, or doing and feeling. And yet there was doing in both, and feeling in both; although the hands were the characteristic in the one case, the heart in the other. And what would the Church and the world be without both? Active service laid the foundations of the infant Church, and has ever since diffused and preserved it; active service has rolled back the tide of corruption when it had settled over the Church, and restored its evangelical character; and the active services of woman have been in every age of quickened Christianity as precious as they have been beautiful. But it is the service of love which Christ values. Love to Christ transfigures the humblest services. All, indeed, who have themselves a heart value its least outgoings above the most costly mechanical performances; but how does it endear the Saviour

to us to find Himself endorsing that principle, as His own standard in judging of character and deeds!

> 'What though in poor and humble guise
> Thou here didst sojourn cottage-born?
> Yet from thy glory in the skies
> Our earthly gold thou dost not scorn.
> For Love delights to bring her best,
> And where Love is, that offering evermore is blest.

> 'Love on the Saviour's dying head
> Her spikenard drops unblam'd may pour,
> May mount His cross and wrap Him dead
> In spices from the golden shore,' &c.—KEBLE.

3. Works of *utility* are never to be set in opposition to the promptings of self-sacrificing *love*, and the sincerity of those who do so is to be suspected. What a number of starving families might those "three hundred pence" have cheered (would Judas exclaim, if time had been allowed him to enlarge upon this waste)! In like manner, under the mask of concern for the poor at home, how many excuse themselves from all care of the perishing heathen abroad! The bad source of such complaints and the insincerity of such excuses may reasonably be suspected. 4. Amidst conflicting duties, that which our hand presently findeth to do is to be preferred to that which can be done at any time. "Ye have the poor always with you; but Me ye have not always." 5. The Lord Jesus has an exalted consciousness of the worth of His own presence with His people, and will have them alive to it too. There is, indeed, a sense in which He is with them always, even to the world's end (Matt. xxviii. 20). But there are special opportunities of which it may be said, "Me ye have not always;" and it is the part of wisdom to avail ourselves of these while we have them, even though it should interfere with duties, which, however important, are of such a nature that opportunities for doing them never cease. 6. To those who are oppressed with the little they can do for Christ, what unspeakable consolation is there in that testimony borne to Mary, "She hath done what she could"! Not the poorest and humblest of Christ's loving followers but may, on this principle, rise as high in the esteem of Christ as the wealthiest and those who move in the widest spheres of Christian usefulness. "If there be first a willing mind, it is accepted according to what a man hath, and not according to what he hath not" (2 Cor. viii. 12). On this delightful subject, see also on Luke xxi. 1-4, with Remarks at the close of that Section. 7. As Jesus beheld in spirit the universal diffusion of His Gospel, while His lowest depth of humiliation was only approaching, so He regarded the facts of His earthly History as constituting the substance of "this Gospel," and the proclamation of them as just the "preaching of this Gospel." Not that preachers are to confine themselves to a bare narration of these facts, but that they are to make their whole preaching revolve around them as its grand centre, and derive from them its proper vitality; all that goes before this in the Bible being but the *preparation* for them, and all that follows but the *sequel.* 8. The crime of Judas is too apt to be viewed as something exceptional in character and atrocity. But the study of its different stages is fitted to dissipate that delusion. First, *Covetousness* being his master-passion, the Lord suffered it to reveal itself and gather strength, by entrusting him with "the bag" (John xii. 6), as treasurer to Himself and the Twelve. Next, in the dis-

12   And *g* the first day of unleavened bread, when they [2] killed the passover, his disciples said unto him, Where wilt thou that we go and prepare that
13 thou mayest eat the passover?   And he sendeth forth two of his disciples, and saith unto them, Go ye into the city, and there shall meet you a man
14 bearing a pitcher of water: follow him.   And wheresoever he shall go in, say ye to the goodman of the house, The Master saith, Where is the
15 guest-chamber, where I shall eat *h* the passover with my disciples?   And he will show you a large upper room furnished *and* prepared: there make
16 ready for us.   And his disciples went forth, and came into the city, and found as he had said unto them: and they made ready the passover.
17   And *i* in the evening he cometh with the twelve.   And as they sat and
18 did eat, Jesus said, Verily I say unto you, One of you which eateth with
19 me shall betray me.   And they began to be sorrowful, and to say unto
20 him one by one, *Is* it I? and another *said, Is* it I?   And he answered and said unto them, *It is* one of the twelve, that dippeth with me in the
21 dish.   The *j* Son of man indeed goeth, as it is written of him: but woe to that man by whom the Son of man is betrayed! good were it for that man if he had never been born.
22   And *k* as they did eat, Jesus took bread, and blessed, and brake *it,* and
23 gave to them, and said, Take, eat: this [3] is my body.   And he took the cup, and when he had given thanks, he gave *it* to them: and they all
24 drank of it.   And he said unto them, This is *l* my blood of the new
25 testament, which is shed for many.   Verily I say unto you, I will drink no more of the fruit of the vine, until that day that I drink it new in the kingdom of God.
26   And *m* when they had sung an [4] hymn, they went out into the mount of
27 Olives.   And *n* Jesus saith unto them, All ye shall be offended because of me this night: for it is written, *o* I will smite the Shepherd, and the sheep

A. D. 33.

g Luke 22. 7.
[2] Or,
   sacrificed.
h Ex. 12. 6.
Lev. 23. 5.
i Matt. 26. 20.
Luke 22. 14.
John 13. 21.
j Gen. 23. 15.
Isa. 53. 1-12.
Dan. 9. 26.
Zec. 13. 7.
Matt. 26. 24.
Luke 22. 22.
k Matt. 26. 26.
Luke 22. 19.
1 Cor. 11. 23.
[3] Or,
   represents.
1 Cor. 10. 4, 16.
l Ex. 24. 8.
Zec. 9. 11.
1 Cor. 11. 25.
Heb. 9. 14.
m Matt. 26. 30.
[4] Or, psalm.
n Matt. 26. 31.
Luke 22. 31, 32.
John 16. 31, 32.
1 Tim. 4. 16.
o Isa. 53. 2-10.
Dan. 9. 26.
Zec. 13. 7.

---

charge of that most sacred trust, he began to pilfer, and became "a thief," appropriating the store from time to time to his own use. Then Satan, walking about seeking whom he might devour, and seeing this door standing wide open, determined to enter by it; but cautiously (2 Cor. ii. 11)— at first merely "putting it into his heart to betray him" (John xiii. 2), or whispering to him the thought that by this means he might enrich himself, and that possibly, when the danger became extreme, He who had wrought so many miracles, might miraculously extricate Himself. The next stage was the conversion of that thought into the settled purpose to do it; to which we may well suppose he would be loath to come till something occurred to fix it. That something, we apprehend, was what took place at the house of Simon the leper; from which he probably withdrew with a chagrin which was perhaps all that was now wanted to decide him. Still starting back, however, or mercifully held back for some time, the determination to carry it into immediate effect was not consummated, it would appear, till, sitting at the Paschal supper, "*Satan entered into him,*" John xiii. 27; and conscience, now effectually stifled, only rose, after the deed, to drive him to despair. O, what warnings do these facts sound forth to every one! Could the traitor but be permitted to send a messenger from "his own place" (Acts i. 25) to warn the living—as the rich man in the parable wished that Lazarus might be to his five brethren—with what a piercing cry would he utter these words, "They that will be rich fall into temptation and a snare, and into many foolish and hurtful lusts, which drown men in destruction and perdition. For the love of money is the root of all evil; which while some coveted after, they have erred from the faith, and

pierced themselves through with many sorrows." "Your adversary the devil, as a roaring lion, walketh about, seeking whom he may devour: whom resist steadfast in the faith." "Resist the devil, and he will flee from you." (1 Tim. vi. 9, 10; 1 Pet. v. 8, 9; Jas. iv. 7.) 9. How sublime is the self-possession with which Jesus, four days after this scene at Bethany, announced to the Twelve that in two days more He should be betrayed to be crucified! At that very moment, perhaps, the Jewish authorities were assembled in the palace of the high priest, consulting together how they might do it; and Judas, who had stolen away from the rest of the Twelve, and got admission to the Council, was just concluding his bargain, perhaps, when He to whose mind every step of the process lay open, disclosed to His true-hearted ones the near-approaching consummation. What a study have we here: on the one hand, of incomparable placidity in One of acutest sensibility; and on the other, of the harmonious working of man's perfectly free will, and the determinate counsel and foreknowledge of God that what men freely resolve on and do shall come to pass for His own high ends! "For *of* Him, and *through* Him, and *to* Him, are all things: to Whom be glory for ever. Amen." (See on Rom. xi. 36.)

12-26.—PREPARATION FOR, AND LAST CELEBRATION OF, THE PASSOVER—ANNOUNCEMENT OF THE TRAITOR—INSTITUTION OF THE SUPPER. (= Matt. xxvi. 17-30; Luke xxii. 7-23, 39; John xiii. 21-30.) For the exposition, see on Luke xxii. 7-23, 39; and on John xiii. 10, 11, 18, 19, 21-30.

27-31.—THE DESERTION OF JESUS BY HIS DISCIPLES, AND THE FALL OF PETER, FORETOLD. (= Matt. xxvi. 31-35; Luke xxii. 31-38; John xiii. 36-38.) For the exposition, see on Luke xxii. 31-46.

| | A. D. 33. |

28 shall be scattered. But *p*after that I am risen, I will go before you into
29 Galilee. But *q*Peter said unto him, Although all shall be offended, yet
30 *will* not I. And Jesus saith unto him, Verily I say unto thee, That this day, *even* in this night, before the cock crow twice, thou shalt deny me
31 thrice. But he spake the more vehemently, If I should die with thee, I will not deny thee in any wise. Likewise also said they all.
32 And *r*they came to a place which was named Gethsemane: and he
33 saith to his disciples, Sit ye here, while *s*I shall pray. And he taketh with him Peter and James and John, and began to be sore amazed, and
34 to be very heavy; and saith unto them, *t*My soul is exceeding sorrowful
35 unto death: tarry ye here, and watch. And he went forward a little, and fell on the ground, and prayed that, if it were possible, the hour
36 might pass from him. And he said, *u*Abba, Father, *v*all things *are* possible unto thee; take away this cup from me: *w*nevertheless not what
37 I will, but what thou wilt. And he cometh, and findeth them sleeping, and saith unto Peter, Simon, sleepest thou? couldest not thou watch one
38 hour? Watch ye and pray, lest ye enter into temptation. *x*The spirit
39 truly *is* ready, but the flesh *is* weak. And again he went away, and
40 prayed, and spake the same words. And when he returned, he found them asleep again, (for their eyes were heavy,) neither wist they what to
41 answer him. And he cometh the third time, and saith unto them, Sleep on now, and take *your* rest: it is enough, *y*the hour is come; behold, the
42 Son of man is betrayed into the hands of sinners. Rise *z*up, let us go; lo, he that betrayeth me is at hand.
43 And *a*immediately, while he yet spake, cometh Judas, one of the twelve, and with him a great multitude with swords and staves, from the
44 chief priests and the scribes and the elders. And he that betrayed him had given them a token, saying, Whomsoever I shall kiss, that same is he;
45 take him, and lead *him* away safely. And as soon as he was come, he goeth straightway to him, and saith, [5]Master, master; and *b*kissed him.
46 And they laid their hands on him, and took him.
47 And one of them that stood by drew a sword, and smote a servant of
48 the high priest, and cut off his ear. And *c*Jesus answered and said unto them, Are ye come out, as against a thief, with swords and *with* staves to
49 take me? I was daily with you in the temple teaching, and ye took me
50 not: but *d*the Scriptures must be fulfilled. And *e*they all forsook him,
51 and fled. And there followed him a certain young man, having a linen cloth cast about *his* naked *body;* and the young men laid hold on him:
52 And he left the linen cloth, and fled from them naked.

A. D. 33.

p Matt. 16.21. Matt. 26.32. Matt. 28. 7, 10-16. ch. 16. 7. John 21. 1. 1 Cor. 15. 4-6.
q Matt. 26.33, 34. Luke 22.33, 34. John 13.37, 38.
r Matt. 26.36. Luke 22.39. John 18. 1.
s Heb 5. 7.
t John 12.27.
u Rom. 8. 15. Gal. 4. 6.
v Heb. 5. 7.
w John 5. :0. John 6. 38.
x Rom. 7. 23. Gal. 5. 17.
y John 13. 1.
z Matt. 26.46. John 18. 1, 2.
a Matt. 26.47. Luke 22.47. John 18. 3.
[5] Rabbi, Rabbi. Matt 23.10. John 20.16.
b 2 Sam. 20.9.
c Matt. 26.55. Luke 22.52.
d Ps. 22. 6. Isa 53. 7. Dan. 9. 26. Luke 22.37. Luke 24.44.
e Job 19. 13, 14. Ps. 38. 11. Ps. 88. 8. John 16.32.

32-42.—THE AGONY IN THE GARDEN. (=Matt. xxvi. 36-46; Luke xxii. 39-46.) For the exposition, see on Luke xxii. 39-46.

43-52.—BETRAYAL AND APPREHENSION OF JESUS —FLIGHT OF HIS DISCIPLES. (= Matt. xxvi. 47-56; Luke xxii. 47-53; John xviii. 1-12.) For the exposition, see on John xviii. 1-12.

53-72.—JESUS ARRAIGNED BEFORE THE SANHE-DRIM, CONDEMNED TO DIE, AND SHAMEFULLY EN-TREATED—THE FALL OF PETER. (=Matt. xxvi. 57-75; Luke xxii. 54-71; John xviii. 13-18, 24-27.)

Had we only the first three Gospels, we should have concluded that our Lord was led immediately to Caiaphas, and had before the Council. But as the Sanhedrim could hardly have been brought together at the dead hour of night—by which time our Lord was in the hands of the officers sent to take Him—and as it was only "as soon as it was day" that the Council met (Luke xxii. 66), we should have had some difficulty in knowing what was done with Him during those intervening hours. In the fourth Gospel, however, all this is cleared up, and a very important addi-

tion to our information is made (John xviii. 13, 14, 19-24). Let us endeavour to trace the events in the true order of succession, and in the detail supplied by a comparison of all the four streams of text.

Jesus is brought privately before Annas, the Father-in-law of Caiaphas (John xviii. 13, 14). 13. "And they led Him away to Annas first; for he was father-in-law to Caiaphas, which was the high priest that same year." This successful Annas, as *Ellicott* remarks, was appointed high priest by Quirinus A.D. 12, and after holding the office for several years, was deposed by Valerius Gratus, Pilate's predecessor in the procuratorship of Judea, (*Joseph.* Antt. xviii. 2. 1, &c.) He appears, however, to have possessed vast influence, having obtained the high priesthood, not only for his son Eleazar, and his son-in-law Caiaphas, but subsequently for four other sons, under the last of whom James, the brother of our Lord, was put to death (Ib. xx. 9. 1). It is thus highly probable that, besides having the title of "high priest" merely as one who had filled the office, he to a great degree

53 And ʲthey led Jesus away to the high priest: and with him were
54 assembled all the chief priests and the elders and the scribes. And Peter
followed him afar off, even into the palace of the high priest: and he sat
with the servants, and warmed himself at the fire.

A. D. 33.

ʲ Matt. 26. 67.
Luke 22. 54.
John 18. 13.

---

retained the powers he had formerly exercised, and came to be regarded practically as a kind of rightful high priest. 14. "Now Caiaphas was he which gave counsel to the Jews, that it was expedient that one man should die for the people." See on John xi. 50. What passed between Annas and our Lord during this interval the beloved disciple reserves till he has related the beginning of Peter's fall. To this, then, as recorded by our own Evangelist, let us meanwhile listen.

Peter obtains Access within the Quadrangle of the High Priest's Residence, and Warms Himself at the Fire (53, 54). **53. And they led Jesus away to the high priest: and with him were assembled** [συνέρχονται αὐτῷ]—or rather, 'there gathered together unto him,' **all the chief priests and the elders and the scribes.** It was then a full and formal meeting of the Sanhedrim. Now, as the first three Evangelists place all Peter's denials of his Lord after this, we should naturally conclude that they took place *while our Lord stood before the Sanhedrim*. But besides that the natural impression is that the scene around the fire took place *over-night*, the *second crowing of the cock*, if we are to credit ancient writers, would occur about the beginning of the fourth watch, or between three and four in the morning. By that time, however, the Council had probably convened, being warned, perhaps, that they were to prepare for being called at any hour of the morning, should the Prisoner be successfully secured. If this be correct, it is pretty certain that only the *last* of Peter's three denials would take place while our Lord was under trial before the Sanhedrim. One thing more may require explanation. If our Lord had to be transferred from the residence of Annas to that of Caiaphas, one is apt to wonder that there is no mention of His being marched from the one to the other. But the building, in all likelihood, was one and the same; in which case He would merely have to be taken, perhaps across the court, from one chamber to another. **54. And Peter followed him afar off, even into** [ἀπο μακρόθεν ἕως ἔσω]—or 'from afar, even to the interior of,' **the palace of the high priest** [εἰς τὴν αὐλήν]. 'An Oriental house,' says *Robinson*, 'is usually built around a quadrangular interior court; into which there is a passage (sometimes arched) through the front part of the house, closed next the street by a heavy folding gate, with a smaller wicket for single persons, kept by a porter. The interior court, often paved or flagged, and open to the sky, is the *hall* [αὐλή], which our translators have rendered "palace," where the attendants made a fire; and the passage beneath the front of the house, from the street to this court, is the *porch* [προαύλιον, Mark xiv. 68, or πυλών, Matt. xxvi. 71]. The place where Jesus stood before the high priest may have been an open room, or place of audience on the ground-floor, in the rear or on one side of the court; such rooms, open in front, being customary. It was close upon the court, for Jesus heard all that was going on around the fire, and turned and looked upon Peter (Luke xxii. 61).'

In the fourth Gospel we have an extremely graphic description of the way in which Peter obtained access within the court or hall of the high priest (John xviii. 15, 16): "And Simon Peter followed Jesus." Natural though this was, and safe enough had he only "watched and prayed

203

that he might not enter into temptation" as his Master bade him (Matt. xxvi. 41)—it was in his case a fatal step. "And so did another (rather 'the other') disciple." This was the beloved disciple himself, no doubt. "That disciple was known unto the high priest (see on John xviii. 15), and went in with Jesus into the palace of the high priest. But Peter stood at the door without"—by a preconcerted arrangement with his friend, till he should procure access for him. "Then went out that other disciple, which was known unto the high priest, and spake unto her that kept the door, and brought in Peter." The *naturalness* of these small details is not unworthy of notice. This other disciple having first made good his own entrance, on the score of acquaintance with the High Priest, goes forth again, now as a privileged person, to make interest for Peter's admission. But thus our poor disciple is in the coils of the serpent.

54. And he sat with the servants, and warmed himself at the fire. The graphic details, here omitted, are supplied in the other Gospels. John xviii. 18, "And the servants and officers stood there (that is, in the hall, within the quadrangle, open to the sky), who had made a fire of coals" [ἀνθρακιάν], or 'charcoal' (in a brazier probably), "for it was cold." John alone of all the Evangelists mentions the *material*, and the *coldness* of the night, as *Webster and Wilkinson* remark. The elevated situation of Jerusalem, observes *Tholuck*, renders it so cold about Easter, as to make a watch-fire at night indispensable. "And Peter stood with them and warmed himself." "He went in (says Matt. xxvi. 58), and sat with the servants *to see the end.*" These two minute statements throw an interesting light on each other. His wishing to "see the end," or issue of these proceedings, was what led him into the palace, for he evidently feared the worst. But once in, the serpent-coil is drawn closer; it is a cold night, and why should not he take advantage of the fire as well as others? Besides, in the talk of the crowd about the all-engrossing topic, he may pick up something which he would like to hear. Poor Peter! But now, let us leave him warming himself at the fire, and listening to the hum of talk about this strange case by which the subordinate officials, passing to and fro and crowding around the fire in this open court, would while away the time; and, following what appears the order of the Evangelical Narrative, let us turn to Peter's Lord.

Jesus is Interrogated by Annas—His Dignified Reply—Is Treated with Indignity by one of the Officials—His Meek Rebuke (John xviii. 19-23). We have seen that it is only the Fourth Evangelist who tells us that our Lord was sent to Annas first, over-night, until the Sanhedrim could be got together at earliest dawn. We have now, in the same Gospel, the deeply instructive scene that passed during this non-official interview. 19. "The high priest [Annas] then asked Jesus of His disciples and of His doctrine"—probably to entrap Him into some statements which might be used against Him at the trial. From our Lord's answer it would seem that "His disciples" were understood to be some secret party. 20. "Jesus answered him, I spake openly to the world"—compare ch. vii. 4. He speaks of His public teaching as now a past thing—as now all over [ἐλάλησα]. "I ever

55 And *the chief priests and all the council sought for witness against
56 Jesus to put him to death; and *found none: for many bare *false witness
57 against him, but their witness agreed not together. And there arose cer-

A. D. 33.

9 Matt 26. 59.
h Dan. 6. 4.
i Ps. 35. 11.

taught in the synagogue and in the temple, whither the Jews always resort," courting publicity, though with sublime noiselessness, "and in secret have I said nothing" [ἐλάλησα οὐδὲν] — rather, 'spake I nothing;' that is, nothing different from what He taught in public; all His private communications with the Twelve being but explanations and developments of His public teaching. (Compare Isa. xlv. 19; xlviii. 16). 21. "Why askest thou Me? ask them which heard Me what I have said to them" [ἐλάλησα] — rather, 'what I said unto them:' "behold, they know what I said." From this mode of replying, it is evident that our Lord saw the attempt to draw Him into self-crimination, and resented it by falling back upon the right of every accused party to have some charge laid against Him by competent witnesses. 22. "And when He had thus spoken, one of the officers which stood by struck Jesus with the palm of his hand, saying, Answerest thou the high priest so?" (see Isa. l. 6). It would seem, from Acts xxiii. 2, that this summary and undignified way of punishing what was deemed insolence in the accused had the sanction even of the high priests themselves. 23. "Jesus answered him, If I have spoken evil" [ἐλάλησα] — rather, 'If I spoke evil,' in reply to the high priest, "bear witness of the evil; but if well, why smitest thou Me?" He does not say, 'if *not* evil,' as if His reply had been merely unobjectionable; but "if *well*," which seems to challenge something altogether fitting in the remonstrance He had addressed to the high priest. From our Lord's procedure here, by the way, it is evident enough that His own precept in the Sermon on the Mount—that when smitten on the one cheek we are to turn to the smiter the other also (Matt. v. 39)—is not to be taken to the letter.

Annas Sends Jesus to Caiaphas (24). 24. "[Now] Annas had sent Him bound unto Caiaphas the high priest." [The particle "Now"—οὖν—though in the *Elzevir*, is not in the *Stephanic* form of the received text, and is rejected by most critics as wanting authority, and even by those who understand the verse as our translators did: the evidence for it is considerable; but it is rather stronger against it. *Lachmann* prints it in his text; *Tregelles* brackets it; but *Tischendorf* excludes it, and *Alford* follows him—concluding, as we think, rightly from the variations between οὖν and δὲ in the MSS. that it crept in as a connecting particle.] On the meaning of this verse there is much diversity of opinion; and according as we understand it will be the conclusion we come to, whether there was but *one hearing* of our Lord before Annas and Caiaphas together, or whether, according to the view we have given above, there were *two hearings*—a preliminary and informal one before Annas, and a formal and official one before Caiaphas and the Sanhedrim. If our translators have given the right sense of the verse, there was but one hearing before Caiaphas; and then this 24th verse is to be read as a *parenthesis*, merely supplementing what was said in *v.* 13. This is the view of *Calvin, Beza, Grotius, Bengel, de Wette, Meyer, Lücke, Tholuck*. But there are decided objections to this view. First, We cannot but think that the *natural* sense of the whole passage, embracing *vv.* 13, 14 and 19-24, is that of a preliminary non-official hearing before "Annas first," the particulars of which are accordingly recorded; and then of a transference of our Lord from Annas to Caiaphas. Second, On

the other view, it is not easy to see why the Evangelist should not have inserted *v.* 24 immediately after *v.* 13; or rather, how he could well have done otherwise. As it stands, it is not only quite out of its proper place, but comes in most perplexingly. Whereas, if we take it as a simple statement of fact, that after Annas had finished his interview with Jesus, as recorded in *vv.* 19-23, he transferred Him to Caiaphas to be formally tried, all is clear and natural. Third, The pluperfect sense "*had sent*" is in the translation only; the sense of the original word [ἀπέστειλεν] being simply 'sent.' And though there are cases where the aorist here used has the sense of an English pluperfect, this sense is not to be put upon it unless it be obvious and indisputable. Here that is so far from being the case, that the pluperfect 'had sent' is rather an unwarrantable *interpretation* than a simple *translation* of the word; informing the reader that, *according to the view of our translators*, our Lord "had been" sent to Caiaphas *before* the interview just recorded by the Evangelist; whereas, if we translate the verse literally—"Annas *sent* Him bound unto Caiaphas the high priest"—we get just the information we expect, that Annas, having merely '*precognosced*' the prisoner, hoping to draw something out of Him, "sent Him to Caiaphas" to be formally tried before the proper tribunal. This is the view of *Chrysostom* and *Augustin* among the Fathers; and of the moderns, of *Olshausen, Schleiermacher, Neander, Ebrard, Wieseler, Lange, Luthardt*. This brings us back to the text of our second Gospel, and in it to—

The Judicial Trial and Condemnation of the Lord Jesus by the Sanhedrim (55-64). But let the reader observe, that though this is introduced by the Evangelist before any of the denials of Peter are recorded, we have given reasons for concluding that probably *the first two denials* took place while our Lord was with Annas, and the last only during the trial before the Sanhedrim.

55. And the chief priests and all the council sought for witness against Jesus to put him to death: Matthew (xxvi. 59) says they "sought *false* witness." They knew they could find nothing valid; but having their Prisoner to bring before Pilate, they behoved to *make a case*. **and found none**—none that would suit their purpose, or make a decent ground of charge before Pilate. **56. For many bare false witness against him.** From their debasing themselves to "*seek*" them, we are led to infer that they were *bribed* to bear false witness; though there are never wanting sycophants enough, ready to sell themselves for nought, if they may but get a smile from those above them: see a similar scene in Acts vi. 11-14. How is one reminded here of that complaint, "False witnesses did rise up: they laid to my charge things that I knew not!" (Ps. xxxv. 11). **but their witness agreed not together.** If even *two* of them had been agreed, it would have been greedily enough laid hold of, as all that the law insisted upon even in capital cases (Deut. xvii. 6). But even in this they failed. One cannot but admire the providence which secured this result; since, on the one hand, it seems astonishing that those unscrupulous prosecutors and their ready tools should so bungle a business in which they felt their whole interests bound up, and, on the other hand, if they *had* succeeded in making even a plausible case, the effect on the progress of the Gospel might for a time have been injurious. But

58 tain, and bare false witness against him, saying, We heard him say, *ʲ*I will destroy this temple that is made with hands, and within three days I will
59 build another made without hands. But neither so did their witness agree
60 together. And *ᵏ*the high priest stood up in the midst, and asked Jesus, saying, Answerest thou nothing? what *is it which* these witness against
61 thee? But *ˡ*he held his peace, and answered nothing. *ᵐ*Again the high priest asked him, and said unto him, Art thou the Christ, the Son of
62 the Blessed? And Jesus said, I am: *ⁿ*and ye shall see the Son of man sitting on the right hand of power, and coming in the clouds of heaven.

A. D. 33.

ʲ ch. 15. 29.
John 2. 19.
ᵏ Matt. 26. 62.
ˡ Isa 53. 7.
1 Pet. 2. 23.
ᵐ Matt. 26. 63.
ⁿ Matt. 24. 30.
Matt. 26. 64.
Luke 22. 69.
Acts 1. 11.

at the very time when His enemies were saying, "God hath forsaken Him; persecute and take Him; for there is none to deliver Him" (Ps. lxxi. 11), He whose Witness He was and whose work He was doing was keeping Him as the apple of His eye, and while He was making the wrath of man to praise Him, was restraining the remainder of that wrath (Ps. lxxvi. 10). **57. And there arose certain, and bare false witness against him.** Matthew (xxvi. 60) is more precise here: "*At the last* came two false witnesses." As no two had before agreed in anything, they felt it necessary to secure a duplicate testimony to something, but they were long of succeeding. And what was it, when at length it was brought forward? **saying, 58. We heard him say, I will destroy this temple that is made with hands, and within three days I will build another made without hands.** On this charge, observe, first, that eager as His enemies were to find criminal matter against our Lord, they had to go back to the outset of His ministry, His first visit to Jerusalem, more than three years before this. In all that He said and did after that, though ever increasing in boldness, they could find nothing: Next, that even then, they fix only on one speech, of two or three words, which they dared to adduce against Him: Further, they most manifestly pervert the speech of our Lord. We say not this because in Mark's form of it, it differs from the report of the words given by the Fourth Evangelist (John ii. 18-22)—the only one of the Evangelists who reports it at all, or mentions even any visit paid by our Lord to Jerusalem before his last—but because the one report bears truth, and the other falsehood, on its face. When our Lord said on that occasion, "Destroy this temple, and in three days I will raise it up," they *might*, for a moment, have understood Him to refer to the temple out of whose courts He had swept the buyers and sellers. But *after* they had expressed their astonishment at His words, in that sense of them, and reasoned upon the time it had taken to rear the temple as it then stood, since *no answer* to this appears to have been given by our Lord, it is hardly conceivable that they should continue in the persuasion that this was really His meaning. But finally, even if the more ignorant among them had done so, it is next to certain that *the ecclesiastics,* who were *the prosecutors* in this case, *did not believe that this was His meaning.* For, in less than three days after this, they went to Pilate, saying, "Sir, we remember that that deceiver said, while he was yet alive, *after three days I will rise again*" (Matt. xxvii. 63). Now what utterance of Christ, known to his enemies, *could* this refer to, if not to this very saying about destroying and rearing up the temple? And if so, it puts it beyond a doubt that by this time, at least, they were perfectly aware that our Lord's words referred to *His death by their hands and His resurrection by His own.* But this is confirmed by the next verse. **59. But neither so did their witness agree together—** that is, not even as to so brief a speech, consisting

205

of but a few words, was there such a concurrence in their mode of reporting it as to make out a decent case. In such a charge *everything depended on the very terms alleged to have been used.* For every one must see that a very slight turn, either way, given to such words, would make them either something like *indictable matter,* or else *a ridiculous ground for a criminal charge*—would either give them a colourable pretext for the charge of impiety which they were bent on making out, or else make the whole saying appear, on the worst view that could be taken of it, as merely some mystical or empty boast. **60. And the high priest stood up in the midst, and asked Jesus, saying, Answerest thou nothing? what is it which these witness against thee?** Clearly, they felt that *their case had failed,* and by this artful question the high priest hoped to get *from his own mouth* what they had in vain tried to obtain from their false and contradictory witnesses. But in this, too, they failed. **61. But he held his peace, and answered nothing.** This must have nonplussed them. But they were not to be easily baulked of their object. **Again the high priest**—arose (Matt. xxvi. 62), matters having now come to a crisis, and **asked him, and said unto him, Art thou the Christ, the Son of the Blessed?** Why our Lord should have answered this question, when He was silent as to the former, we might not have quite seen, but for Matthew, who says (xxvi. 63) that the high priest *put Him upon solemn oath,* saying, "I adjure thee by the living God, that thou tell us whether thou be the Christ, the Son of God." Such an adjuration was understood to render an answer legally necessary (Lev. v. 1). **62. And Jesus said, I am**—or, as in Matt. xxvi. 64, "Thou hast said [it]." In Luke, however (xxii. 70), the answer, "Ye say that I am" ['Υμεῖς λέγετε, ὅτι ἐγώ εἰμι], should be rendered—as *de Wette, Meyer, Ellicott,* and the best critics agree that the preposition requires —'Ye say [it], for I am [so].' Some words, however, were spoken by our Lord before giving His answer to this solemn question. These are recorded by Luke alone (xxii. 67, 68): "Art thou the Christ (they asked)? tell us. And He said unto them, If I tell you, ye will not believe: and if I also ask"—or 'interrogate' [ἐρωτήσω] "you, ye will not answer me, nor let me go." This seems to have been uttered before giving His direct answer, as a calm remonstrance and dignified protest against the prejudgment of His case and the unfairness of their mode of procedure. But now let us hear the rest of the answer, in which the conscious majesty of Jesus breaks forth from behind the dark cloud which overhung Him as He stood before the Council: **and** (in that character) **ye shall see the Son of man sitting on the right hand of power, and coming in the clouds of heaven.** In Matthew (xxvi. 64) a slightly different but interesting turn is given to it by one word: "Thou hast said [it]: nevertheless"—We prefer this sense of the word [πλήν] to 'besides,' which some recent critics decide for—"I say

63 Then the high priest rent his clothes, and saith, What need we any
64 further witnesses? ye have heard °the blasphemy: what think ye? And
they all condemned him to be guilty of death.

65   And some began to ᵖspit on him, and to cover his face, and to buffet
him, and to say unto him, Prophesy: and the servants did strike him
with the palms of their hands.

A. D. 33.

° Lev. 24. 16.
1 Ki. 21. 9,
13.
Acts 6. 13.
ᵖ Isa. 50. 6.
Isa. 53. 3.

unto you, Hereafter shall ye see the Son of man sit on the right hand of power, and coming in the clouds of heaven:" 'I know the scorn with which ye are ready to meet such an avowal: To your eyes, which are but eyes of flesh, there stands at this bar only a mortal like yourselves, and he at the mercy of the ecclesiastical and civil authorities: *Nevertheless*, a day is coming when ye shall see another sight: those eyes, which now gaze on me with proud disdain, shall see this very prisoner at the right hand of the Majesty on high, and coming in the clouds of heaven. Then shall the Judged One be revealed as the Judge, and His judges in this chamber appear at His august tribunal: then shall the *unrighteous* judges be *impartially* judged; and while they are wishing that they had never been born, He for whom they now watch as their Victim shall be greeted with the hallelujahs of heaven and the welcome of Him that sitteth upon the Throne!' The word rendered "hereafter" [ἀπ᾽ἄρτι] means, not 'at some future time' (as now "hereafter" commonly does), but what the English word originally signified, 'after here,' 'after now,' or 'from this time.' Accordingly, in Luke xxii. 69, the words used [ἀπὸ τοῦ νῦν] mean 'from now.' So that though the reference we have given it to the day of His glorious Second Appearing is too obvious to admit of doubt, He would, by using the expression, 'From this time,' convey the important thought which He had before expressed, immediately after the traitor left the Supper-table to do his dark work, "*Now* is the Son of Man glorified" (John xiii. 31). At this moment, and by this speech, did He "witness *the* good confession" [τὴν καλὴν ὁμολογίαν], emphatically and properly, as the apostle says, 1 Tim. vi. 13. Our translators render the words there, "Who *before* Pontius Pilate witnessed," referring it to the admission of His being a *King*, in the presence of Cesar's own chief representative. But it should be rendered, as *Luther* renders it, and as the best interpreters now understand it, 'Who *under* Pontius Pilate witnessed, &c. [Compare the sense of ἐπί τινος in such passages as Matt. i. 11; Mark ii. 26; Luke iii. 2; Acts xi. 28; as also in the Apostles' Creed— "suffered *under* Pontius Pilate."] In this view of it, the apostle is referring not to what our Lord confessed *before* Pilate—which, though noble, was not of such primary importance—but to that sublime confession which, under Pilate's administration, He witnessed before the only competent tribunal on such occasions, the Supreme Ecclesiastical Council of God's chosen nation, that He was THE MESSIAH, and THE SON OF THE BLESSED ONE; in the former word owning His Supreme *Official*, in the latter His Supreme *Personal* Dignity. **63. Then the high priest rent his clothes.** On this expression of *horror at blasphemy*, see 2 Ki. xviii. 37. **and saith, What need we any further witnesses? 64. Ye have heard the blasphemy.** (See John x. 33.) In Luke (xxii. 71), "For we ourselves have heard of his own mouth"—an affectation of religious horror. **what think ye?** 'Say what the verdict is to be.' **And they all condemned him to be guilty of death**—or of a capital crime, which *blasphemy* against God was according to the Jewish law (Lev. xxiv. 16). Yet *not absolutely all; for*

Joseph of Arimathea, "a good man and a just," was one of that Council, and '*he was not a consenting party* to the counsel and deed of them,' for that is the strict sense of the words of Luke xxiii. 50, 51 [οὐκ ἦν συγκατατεθειμένος τῇ βουλῇ καὶ τῇ πράξει αὐτῶν]. Probably he absented himself, and *Nicodemus* also, from this meeting of the Council, the temper of which they would know too well to expect their voice to be listened to; and in that case, the words of our Evangelist are to be taken strictly, that, without one dissentient voice, "all [present] condemned Him to be guilty of death."

The Blessed One is now Shamefully Entreated (65). Every word here must be carefully observed, and the several accounts put together, that we may lose none of the awful indignities about to be described. **65. And some began to spit on him**—or, as in Matt. xxvi. 67, "to spit in [or 'into'—εἰς] His face." Luke (xxii. 63) says in addition, "And the men that held Jesus mocked Him"—or cast their jeers at Him. **and to cover his face** [περικαλύπτειν]—or 'to blindfold him' (as in Luke xxii. 64), **and to buffet him** [κολαφίζειν]. Luke's word, which is rendered "smote Him" (xxii. 63), is a stronger one [δέροντες], conveying an idea for which we have an exact equivalent in English, but one too colloquial to be inserted here. **and [began] to say unto him, Prophesy.** In Matt. xxvi. 68 this is given more fully: "Prophesy unto us, thou Christ, Who is he that smote thee?" The sarcastic fling at Him as "*the Christ*," and the demand of Him in this character to name the unseen perpetrator of the blows inflicted on Him, was in them as infamous as to Him it must have been, and was intended to be, stinging. **and the servants did strike him with the palms of their hands** — or "struck Him on the face" (Luke xxii. 64). Ah! Well did He say prophetically, in that Messianic prediction which we have often referred to, "I gave my back to the smiters, and my cheeks to them that plucked off the hair: I hid not my face from shame and spitting"! (Isa. l. 6). "And many other things blasphemously spake they against Him" (Luke xxii. 65). This general statement is important, as showing that virulent and varied as were the *recorded* affronts put upon Him, they are but a *small specimen* of what He endured on that dark occasion.

But this brings us back to our poor disciple, now fairly within the coils of the serpent. It is extremely difficult so to piece together the several charges thrown against Peter, and his replies, as perfectly to harmonize and exhaust the four streams of text. But the following, in which the best critics concur, comes as near to it, perhaps, as we shall succeed in getting. Nothing could better show how independently of each other the Evangelists must have written, than the almost hopeless difficulty of putting all the accounts of Peter's denials into their exact order, so as to make one harmonious record out of them. But the circumstantial differences are just of that nature which is so well understood in sifting a mass of complicated evidence on a public trial, which, instead of throwing doubt over them, only confirms the more strongly the truth of the facts reported.

66   And ^qas Peter was beneath in the palace, there cometh one of the maids
67 of the high priest: and when she saw Peter warming himself, she looked
68 upon him, and said, And thou also wast with Jesus of Nazareth. But he
      denied, saying, I know not, neither understand I what thou sayest. And
69 he went out into the porch; and the cock crew. And ^ra maid saw him

A. D. 33.

^q Matt. 26. 58,
69.
Luke 22. 55.
^r Matt. 26. 71.
Luke 22. 58.

Peter's FIRST DENIAL *of his Lord* (66-68). **66. And as Peter was beneath in the palace.** This little word *"beneath"* [κάτω]—one of our Evangelist's graphic touches—is most important for the right understanding of what we may call the topography of the scene. We must take it in connection with Matthew's word (xxvi. 69). "Now Peter sat *without* [ἔξω] in the palace"—or quadrangular court, in the centre of which the fire would be burning; and crowding around and buzzing about it would be the menials and others who had been admitted within the court. At the upper end of this court, probably, would be the memorable chamber in which the trial was held—*open to the court*, likely, and *not far from the fire* (as we gather from Luke xxii. 61), but *on a higher level;* for (as our verse says) the court, with Peter in it, was "beneath" it. The ascent to the Council-chamber was perhaps by a short flight of steps. If the reader will bear this explanation in mind, he will find the intensely interesting details which follow more intelligible. **there cometh one of the maids of the high priest**—"the damsel that kept the door" (John xviii. 17). The Jews seem to have employed women as porters of their doors (Acts xii. 13). **67. And when she saw Peter warming himself, she looked upon him.** Luke (xxii. 56) is here more graphic; "But a certain maid beheld him as he sat by the fire" [πρὸς τὸ φῶς]—literally, 'by the *light*,' which, shining full upon him, revealed him to the girl—"and earnestly looked upon him" [καὶ ἀτενίσασα αὐτῷ]—or, 'fixed her gaze upon him.' His demeanour and timidity, which must have attracted notice, as so generally happens, 'leading,' says *Olshausen*, 'to the recognition of him.' **and said, And thou also wast with Jesus of Nazareth**—'with Jesus the Nazarene,' or, "with Jesus of Galilee" (Matt. xxvi. 69). The *sense* of this is given in John's report of it (xviii. 17), "Art not thou also one of this man's disciples?" that is, thou as well as "that other disciple," whom she knew to be one, but did not challenge, perceiving that he was a privileged person. In Luke (xxii. 56) it is given as a remark made by the maid to one of the bystanders—"this man was also with Him." If so expressed in Peter's hearing—drawing upon him the eyes of every one that heard it (as we know it did, Matt. xxvi. 70), and compelling him to answer to it—that would explain the different forms of the report naturally enough. But in such a case this is of no real importance. **68. But he denied**—"before all" (Matt. xxvi. 70). **saying, I know not, neither understand I what thou sayest**—in Luke, "I know Him not." **And he went out into the porch** [τὸ προαύλιον]—the vestibule leading to the street—no doubt finding the fire-place too *hot* for him; possibly also with the hope of escaping—but that was not to be, and perhaps he dreaded that too. Doubtless, by this time his mind would be getting into a sea of commotion, and would fluctuate every moment in its resolves. **AND THE COCK CREW.** See on Luke xxii. 34. This, then, was the First Denial. *Peter's* SECOND DENIAL *of his Lord* (69, 70). There is here a verbal difference among the Evangelists, which, without some information which has been withheld, cannot be quite extricated. **69. And a maid saw him again**—or, 'a girl'

[ἡ παιδίσκη]. It might be rendered 'the girl;' but this would not necessarily mean the same one as before, but might, and probably does, mean just the female who had charge of the door or gate near which Peter now was. Accordingly, in Matt. xxvi. 71, she is expressly called "another [maid]" [ἄλλη]. But in Luke it is a *male* servant: "And after a little while (from the time of the first denial) another"—that is, as the word signifies, 'another male' servant [ἕτερος]. But there is no real difficulty, as the challenge, probably, after being made by one was reiterated by another. Accordingly, in John, it is "*They* said therefore unto him," &c., as if more than one challenged him at once. **and began to say to them that stood by, This is one of them**—or, as in Matt. xxvi. 71—"This [fellow] was also with Jesus the Nazarene" [τοῦ Ναζωραίου]. **70. And he denied it again.** In Luke, "Man, I am not." But worst of all in Matthew—"And again he denied with an oath, I do not know the man." (xxvi. 72). This was the Second Denial, more vehement, alas! than the first.

Peter's THIRD DENIAL *of His Lord* (70-72). **70. And a little after**—"about the space of one hour after" (Luke xxii. 59), **they that stood by said again to Peter, Surely thou art one of them: for thou art a Galilean, and thy speech agreeth thereto**—"bewrayeth (or 'discovereth') thee" (Matt. xxvi. 73). In Luke it is "Another confidently affirmed, saying, Of a truth this [fellow] also was with him; for he is a Galilean." The Galilean dialect had a more *Syrian* cast than that of Judea. *If Peter had held his peace*, this peculiarity had not been observed; but hoping, probably, to put them off the scent by joining in the *fireside-talk*, he only thus discovered himself. The Fourth Gospel is particularly interesting here: "One of the servants of the high priest, being his kinsman (or kinsman to him) whose ear Peter cut off, saith, Did not I see thee in the garden with Him?" (John xviii. 26). No doubt his relationship to Malchus drew his attention to the man who had smitten him, and this enabled him to identify Peter. 'Sad reprisals!' exclaims *Bengel*. Thus everything tended to identify him as a disciple of the Prisoner—his being introduced into the interior by one who was known to be a disciple, as the maid who kept the gate could testify; the recognition of him by the girl at the fire, as one whom she had seen in His company; his broad guttural Galilean dialect; and there being one present who recognized him as the man who, at the moment of the prisoner's apprehension, struck a blow with his sword at a relative of his own. Poor Peter! Thou art caught in thine own toils; but like a wild bull in a net, thou wilt toss and rage, filling up the measure of thy terrible declension by one more denial of thy Lord, and that the foulest of all. **71. But he began to curse** [ἀναθεματίζειν]—'to anathematize,' or wish himself accursed if what he was now to say was not true, **and to swear**—or to take a solemn oath, **saying, I know not this man of whom ye speak. 72. And THE SECOND TIME THE COCK CREW.** The other three Evangelists, who mention but one crowing of the cock—and that not the first, but the second and last one of Mark—all say the cock crew "immediately," but Luke says, "Im-

70 again, and began to say to them that stood by, This is *one* of them. And he denied it again. ^sAnd a little after, they that stood by said again to Peter, Surely thou art *one* of them: ^tfor thou art a Galilean, and thy

A. D. 33.
^s Matt 26.73.
^t Acts 2. 7.

mediately, while he yet spake, the cock crew" (xxii. 60). Alas!—But now comes the wonderful sequel.

The Redeemer's Look upon Peter, and Peter's Bitter Tears (72; Luke xxii. 61, 62). It has been observed that while the beloved disciple is the only one of the four Evangelists who does not record the repentance of Peter, he is the only one of the four who records the affecting and most beautiful scene of his complete restoration. (John xxi. 15-17.)

Luke xxii. 61: "And the Lord turned and looked upon Peter." How? it will be asked. We answer, From the chamber in which the trial was going on, in the direction of the court where Peter then stood—in the way already explained. See on ch. xiv. 66. Our Second Evangelist makes no mention of this look, but dwells on the warning of his Lord about the double crowing of the cock, which would announce his triple fall, as what rushed stingingly to his recollection and made him dissolve in tears. **And Peter called to mind the word that Jesus said unto him, Before the cock crow twice, thou shalt deny me thrice. And when he thought thereon, he wept.** To the same effect is the statement of the First Evangelist (Matt. xxvi. 75), save that like "the beloved physician," he notices the "bitterness" of the weeping. The most precious link, however, in the whole chain of circumstances in this scene is beyond doubt that "look" of deepest, tenderest import reported by Luke alone. Who can tell what lightning flashes of wounded love and piercing reproach shot from that "look" through the eye of Peter into his heart! "And Peter remembered the word of the Lord, how He had said unto him, Before the cock crow, thou shalt deny Me thrice. And Peter went out and wept bitterly." How different from the sequel of Judas's act! Doubtless the hearts of the two men towards the Saviour were perfectly different from the first; and the treason of Judas was but the consummation of the wretched man's resistance of the blaze of light in the midst of which he had lived for three years, while Peter's denial was but a momentary obscuration of the heavenly light and love to his Master which ruled his life. But the immediate cause of the blessed revulsion which made Peter "weep bitterly" was, beyond all doubt, this heart-piercing "look" which his Lord gave him. And remembering the Saviour's own words at the table, "Simon, Simon, Satan hath desired to have you, that he may sift you as wheat; *but I prayed for thee, that thy faith fail not,*" may we not say that *this prayer fetched down all that there was in that "look"* to pierce and break the heart of Peter, to keep it from despair, to work in it "repentance unto salvation not to be repented of," and at length, under other healing touches, to "restore his soul"? (See on Mark xvi. 7.)

Remarks.—1. The demeanour of the Blessed One before Annas first, and then before Caiaphas and the Sanhedrim, is best left to speak its own mingled meekness and dignity. *We*, at least, are not able to say aught—beyond what has come out in the exposition—that would not run the risk of weakening the impression which the Evangelical Narrative itself leaves on every devout and thoughtful mind. But the reader may be asked to observe the *wisdom* which to Annas speaks, but before the Sanhedrim keeps silence while the witnesses against Him are uttering their lies and con-

tradictions. In the former case, silence might have been liable to misconstruction; and the opportunity which the questions of Annas about "His disciples and His doctrine" afforded, of appealing to the *openness* of all His movements from first to last, was too important not to be embraced: whereas, in the latter case, the silence which He preserved—while the false witnesses were stultifying themselves and the case was breaking down of itself the further they proceeded—was the most dignified, and to His envenomed judges most stinging reply to them. It was only when, in despair of evidence save from His own mouth, the high priest demanded of Him on solemn oath to say whether He were the Christ, the Son of the Blessed, and the moment had thus arrived when it was right and fitting in itself, and according to the law, that He should "witness" the "good confession," that He broke silence accordingly—and in how exalted terms! 2. Perhaps the best commentary on the Sixth Petition of the Lord's Prayer —"Lead us not into temptation"—is to be found in the conduct of Peter, and the circumstances in which he found himself, after our Lord warned him to "pray that he might not enter into temptation." See on Matt. vi. 13, and Remark 9 at the close of that Section. The explicit announcement that all the Eleven should be stumbled in Him and scattered that very night, might have staggered him; but it did not. The still more explicit announcement addressed immediately to Peter, that Satan had sought and obtained them all—to the extent of being permitted to sift them as wheat—but as to Peter in particular, that He had prayed for *him*, that his faith might not fail, was fitted, surely, to drive home upon his conscience a sense of more than ordinary danger, and more than ordinary need to watch and pray; but it did not. Above all, the appalling announcement, that—instead of the certainty of his standing, even if all the rest should fall, and of his readiness to go to prison and to death for his blessed Master—the cock should not crow twice before he had thrice denied that he knew Him, was fitted, one should think, to dash the confidence of the most self-confident believer; but it made no impression upon Peter. Once more, in the Garden his Lord found him sleeping, along with the other two, in the midst of His agony and bloody sweat; and He chided him for his inability to watch with Him one hour on that occasion. He gave him and the rest a last warning, almost immediately before Judas and the officers approached to take Him, to "watch and pray, that they entered not into temptation." But how did he take it? Why, he insisted on admission within that fatal quadrangle, which from that time he would never forget. We wonder not at his eagerness to learn all that was going on within that court; but one who had been so warned of what he would do that very night should have kept far away from a spot which must have seemed, even to himself, the most likely to prove the fatal one. The coil of the serpent, however, was insensibly but surely drawing him in, and he was getting, by his own act and deed, sucked into the vortex—"led into temptation." Through the influence of "that disciple who was known to the high priest," the door which was shut to the eager crowd was opened to him. No doubt he now thought all was right, and congratulated himself on his good fortune. He lounges about, pre-

71 speech agreeth *thereto.* But ᵃhe began to curse and to swear, *saying,* I
72 know not this man of whom ye speak. And the second time the cock
crew. And Peter called to mind the word that Jesus said unto him,

A. D. 33.

ᵃ Pro. 29. 25.
1 Cor.10.12.

tending indifference or the mere general curiosity of others. But it is bitterly cold, and an inviting fire is blazing in the court. He will join the knot that is clustering around it—perhaps he will pick up some of the current talk about the Prisoner, the trial, and its probable issue. He has got close to the fire, and a seat too—so near, that his countenance is lighted up by the blazing fuel. He has now gained his end, and in so cold a night how comfortable he feels—"*till a dart strikes through his liver*"/ (Pro. vii. 22, 23.) O, if this true-hearted and noble disciple had but retained the spirit which prompted him to say, along with others, of the unnamed traitor that sat at the Supper-Table, "Lord, Is it I?" (see on John xiii. 21-25)—if he had watched and gone to his knees, when his Master was on His, agonizing in the Garden, his danger had not been so great, even within the court of the high priest. *There,* indeed, *he had no business to be,* considering the sad prediction which hung over him—this, in fact, was what sold him into the enemy's hands. But, if we could have supposed him sitting at that fire in a "watching and praying" spirit, the challenge of him by the maid, as one who had been "with Jesus the Nazarene," had drawn forth a "good confession." And what though he had had to "go to prison and to death for His sake"? it had been but what he was undoubtedly prepared for as he sat at the Supper-Table, and what he afterwards did cheerfully in point of fact. But he was caught without his armour. The fear of man now brought a snare (Pro. xxix. 25). His locks were shorn. The secret of his great strength was gone, and he had become weak as other men. O, let these mournful facts pierce the ears of the children of God, and let them listen to One who knows them better than they do themselves, when He warns them to "watch and pray, that they enter not into temptation." 3. See how the tendency of all sin is to aggravate as well as multiply itself. Peter's first fall naturally led to his second, and his second to his third; each denial of his Lord being now felt as but one and the same act—as only the keeping up of the character which he would regret that he had been driven to assume, but, once assumed, needed to keep up for consistency's sake. 'The deed was done, and could not be undone—he must now go through with it.' But merely to reiterate, even in a different form, his first denial, would not do for the second, nor the second for the third, if he was to be believed. He must exaggerate his denials; he must repudiate his Master in such a style that people would be forced to say, We *must* be mistaken—that man *cannot* be a disciple, so unlike all we have ever heard of His character and teaching. So Peter at length comes to "anathematize" himself if he should be uttering a lie in ignoring the Nazarene, and solemnly "swears" that he knows nothing of Him. Nor, although there was about an hour's interval between the first and the second denials, is there any reason to suppose that he had begun to give way, or seriously meditated confessing his Lord within that court. His mind, from the first moment that he fell before the maid, would be in a burning fever—his one object being to avoid detection; and this would keep the warning about the cock-crowing from ever coming up to his recollection; for it is expressly said that it was only after his last denial and the immediate crowing of the cock,

that "Peter remembered" his Lord's warning. Well, these details will not have been recorded in vain, if they convince believers that, besides the danger of the strongest giving way, there is no length in defection to which they may not quickly go, when once that has been done. Times of persecution, especially when unto death, have furnished sad enough evidence that Peter's case was no abnormal one; that he acted only according to the stable laws of the human mind and heart in such circumstances, and only illustrated the laws of the Kingdom of God as to the sources of weakness and of strength; and that in similar circumstances the children of God in every age, when like him they flatter themselves, in spite of warnings, that they will never be moved, will act a similar part. 4. Secret things indeed belong unto the Lord our God, but those which are revealed unto us and to our children for ever (Deut. xxix. 29). We intrude not into those things which we have not seen, vainly puffed up by our fleshly mind (Col. ii. 18); but the few glimpses with which Scripture favours us of what is passing on the subject of men's eternal interests in the unseen world are of too vital a nature to be overlooked. In the book of Job we have revelations to which there is a manifest allusion in our Lord's warning to Peter, and without which it could not perhaps be fully understood. The all-seeing Judge is seen surrounded by His angelic assessors on human affairs, and Satan presents himself among them. "Whence comest thou?" the Lord says. "From going to and fro in the earth, and walking up and down in it," is the reply—watching men's actions, studying their character, seeking whom he might devour. 'In these roamings, hast thou seen My servant Job (asks the Lord), a saint above all saints on the earth?' 'O yes (is the reply), I have seen him, and weighed his religion too: 'Tis easy for him to be religious, with a divine hedge about him, and laden with prosperity. But only let me have him, that I may sift him as wheat, and we shall soon see what becomes of his religion. Why, touch but his substance, and he will curse Thee to Thy face.' 'Behold, he is in thine hand (is the divine response), to sift him to the uttermost; only upon his person lay not a hand.' So Satan goes forth, strips him of substance and family at once, leaving him only a wife worse than none, who did but aid the tempter's purposes. Observe now the result. "So Job arose and rent his mantle, and shaved his head, and fell upon the ground, and worshipped, and said, Naked came I out of my mother's womb, and naked shall I return thither: The Lord gave, and the Lord hath taken away; blessed be the name of the Lord. In all this Job sinned not, nor charged God foolishly." But the enemy of men's souls is not to be easily foiled. He has missed his mark once, to be sure; but the next time he will succeed. He mistook the patriarch's weak point. Now, however, he is sure of it. Again he enters the councils of heaven, is questioned as before, and rebuked, in language unspeakably comforting to the tempted, for moving the Lord to destroy His dear saint without cause. 'Not without cause (replies the tempter): Skin for skin; yea, all that a man hath will he give for his life: suffer me once more to sift him as wheat, and it will be seen what chaff his religion is.' 'Then, behold, he is in thine hand, to smite his person even as thou wilt; only save his life.' So Satan

Before the cock crow twice, thou shalt deny me thrice. And *ᵛ*when he thought thereon, he wept.

A. D. 33.

ᵛ 2 Cor. 7. 10.

went forth, and did his worst; the body of this saint is now a mass of running sores; he sits among the ashes, scraping himself with a potsherd; while his heartless wife advises him to have done with this at once, by sending up to God such a curse upon Him for His cruelty as would bring down a bolt of vengeance, and end his sufferings with his life. Now hear the noble reply: "Thou speakest as one of the foolish women speaketh. What? Shall we receive good at the hand of God, and shall we not receive evil? In all this did not Job sin with his lips." He is seen to be wheat and no chaff, and the enemy disappears from the stage. This now is what our Lord alludes to in His warning at the Supper-Table. Satan, still at his old work, had demanded to have these poor disciples, to sift them too; and he had gotten them—in that sense and to that extent. [The reader is requested to refer to the remarks on the sense of the word ἐξητήσατο, Luke xxii. 31.] But while that transaction was going on in the unseen world, a counteraction, in the case of Peter, was proceeding at the same time. He whom the Father heareth alway "prayed for Peter that his faith might not fail." And (as implied in the tenses of the verbs employed—see the remarks on the above passage) when the one action was *completed*, so was the other—the bane and the antidote going together. Poor Peter! Little thinkest thou what is passing between heaven and hell about thee, and thy one source of safety. That thou gottest that "look" of wounded love from thy suffering Lord; that thy heart, pierced by it, was not driven to despair; that the warning of the triple denial and the double cock-crowing did not send thee after the traitor, by the nearest road to "his own place:" what was all this due to but to that "*prayer* for thee, that thy faith fail not"? Now, for the first time, thou knowest the meaning of that word "fail." Perhaps it deluded thee into the persuasion that thou wouldst not give way at all, and thou wert thyself confident enough of that. Now thou knowest by sad experience what "shipwreck of faith and of a good conscience" thou hadst made, but that the means of preventing it were fetched down by the great Intercessor's "prayer." 5. If Christ's praying for Peter, even in the days of His flesh here below, availed so much, what a glorious efficacy must attach to His pleadings for them that are dear to Him within the veil? For here, His proper work was to give His life a Ransom for them: there, to sue out the fruit of His travail in their behalf. But along with these intercessions, are there no such "looks" now cast upon His poor fallen ones, such as He darted upon Peter, just when he had gone down to his lowest depth in shameful repudiation of Him? Let the fallen and recovered children of God answer that question. 6. What light does this last thought, in connection with Christ's special prayer in behalf of Peter, cast upon the eternal safety of believers? "While I was with them in the world I kept them in Thy name: those that Thou hast given Me I kept [δέδωκας—ἐφύλαξα], and none of them is lost but the son of perdition, that the Scripture might be fulfilled. But now I am no more in the world, but these are in the world, and I come to Thee: Holy Father, keep through thine own name those whom Thou hast given Me, that they may be one as We are" (John xvii. 11, 12). 7. If prayer on the part of Christ for His people is so essential to their safety, shall their own prayer for it be less

so? He who said, "*I prayed* for thee," said also, "Watch and pray ye, that ye enter not into temptation." And who that verily believes that Jesus within the veil is praying for *him* that his faith fail not, can choose but cry, "Hold Thou me up, and I shall be safe"? 8. Was it while those false witnesses were rising up against Thee, blessed Saviour, and laying to Thy charge things that Thou knewest not, that Thou didst cast towards Peter that soul-piercing "look"? Or was it in the midst of those heart-rending indignities, at the reading of which one almost covers his face, and the calm endurance of which must have filled even heaven with wonder—was it during one of those dreadful moments when they were proceeding to blindfold that blessed Face, that Thou lookedst full on Thy poor disciple with that never-to-be-forgotten look? I know not. But I can well believe that no indignities from enemies wounded Thee at that hour like that which was done unto Thee by thine own familiar friend and dear disciple, and that this quite absorbed the sense of that. And if in heaven He *feels* the slight put upon Him by those who will not suffer Him to "gather" them, shall He not feel even more acutely (if the word may be allowed) "the wounds wherewith He is wounded in the house of His friends"? 9. In reviewing the contents of this Section, who can be insensible to the self-evidencing reality which is stamped upon the facts of it, both in their general bearing and in their minute details! What mere inventor of a Story would have so used the powerful influence of Annas as to hand over the Prisoner to him first, relating what passed between them in the dead of night, ere the Council could be got together for the formal trial? And who would have thought of making Him answer with *silence* the lies and contradictions of the witnesses against Him; when these failed to make any decent charge, bringing forward at the last two more, only to neutralize each other by the inconsistency of their statements; and, when all failed, and the high priest in despair had to put it to Him on oath to say if He were the Christ, the Son of the Blessed, *then* drawing from Him a sublime affirmative? The condemnation and the indignities which followed would be natural enough; but the particulars now enumerated lie quite beyond the range of conceivable fiction. But far more so are the details of Peter's denials. That the most eminent of the Eleven should be made to inflict on his Master the deepest wound, and this in the hour of greatest apparent weakness, when a Prisoner in the hands of His enemies—is unlike enough the work of fiction. But those minute details — the "following Him from afar" [ἀπὸ μακρόθεν]; the introduction into the quadrangle through the influence of "that disciple who was known to the high priest;" the cold night, and the blazing fire, and the clustering of the menials and others around it, with Peter among them, and the detection of him by a maid, through the reflection of the fire-light on his countenance, the first denial in that moment of surprise, and the crowing of the cock; his uneasy removal "out into the porch," the second denial, more emphatic than the first, and then the last and foulest, and the second cock-crowing; but beyond every other thought that would never occur to an inventor, that "look upon Peter" by his wounded Lord, and that rush of recollection which brought the sad warning at the Supper-Table fresh to view, and

210

15 AND ^astraightway in the morning the chief priests held a consultation with the elders and scribes and the whole council, and bound Jesus, and

2 carried *him* away, and delivered *him* to Pilate. And ^bPilate asked him, Art thou the King of the Jews? And he answering said unto

3 him, ^cThou sayest *it*. And the chief priests accused him of many

4 things: but ^dhe answered nothing. And ^ePilate asked him again, saying, Answerest thou nothing? behold how many things they witness against

5 thee. But ^fJesus yet answered nothing; so that Pilate marvelled.

6 Now ^gat *that* feast he released unto them one prisoner, whomsoever

7 they desired. And there was *one* named Barabbas, *which lay* bound with them that had made insurrection with him, who had committed murder

8 in the insurrection. And the multitude, crying aloud, began to desire

9 *him to do* as he had ever done unto them. But Pilate answered them,

10 saying, Will ye that I release unto you the King of the Jews? For he

11 knew that the chief priests had delivered him for ^henvy. But ⁱthe chief priests moved the people, that he should rather release Barabbas

12 unto them. And Pilate answered and said again unto them, What will ye then that I shall do *unto him* whom ye call ^jthe King of

13 the Jews? And they cried out again, Crucify him. Then Pilate said

14 unto them, Why, what evil hath he done? And they cried out the more

15 exceedingly, Crucify him. And *so* Pilate, ^kwilling to content the people, released Barabbas unto them, and delivered Jesus, when he had scourged *him*, to be crucified.

16 And the soldiers led him away into the hall called Pretorium; and

17 they call together the whole band. And· they clothed him with purple,

18 and platted a crown of thorns, and put it about his *head*, and began to

19 salute him, Hail, King of the Jews! And they smote him on the head with a reed, and did spit upon him, and bowing *their* knees worshipped

20 him. And when they had mocked him, they took off the purple from him, and put his own clothes on him, and led him out to crucify him.

21 And ^lthey compel one Simon a Cyrenian, who passed by, coming out of the country, the father of Alexander ^mand Rufus, to bear his cross.

22 And ⁿthey bring him unto the place Golgotha, which is, being inter-

23 preted, The place of a skull. And they gave him ^oto drink wine

24 mingled with myrrh: but he received *it* not. And when they had crucified him, they ^pparted his garments, casting lots upon them, what

25 every man should take. And ^qit was the third hour, and they crucified

26 him. And ^rthe superscription of his accusation was written over, THE

27 KING OF THE JEWS. And with him they crucify two thieves; the

28 one on his right hand, and the other on his left. And the scripture was fulfilled, which saith, ^sAnd he was numbered with the transgressors.

29 And ^tthey that passed by railed on him, wagging their heads, and saying,

30 Ah! thou ^uthat destroyest the temple, and buildest *it* in three days, save

A. D. 33.

CHAP. 15.
^a Ps. 2. 2.
Matt. 21.38.
Matt. 27. 1.
Luke 22. 66.
Luke 23. 1.
John 18.28.
Acts 3. 13.
Acts 4. 26.
^b Matt. 27.11.
^c 1 Tim. 6.13.
^d 1 Pet. 2. 23.
^e Matt. 27.13.
^f Isa. 53. 7.
John 19. 9.
^g Matt. 27.15.
Luke 23.17.
John 18.39.
^h Acts 7.9,51.
1 John 3.12.
ⁱ Matt. 27.20.
Acts 3. 14.
^j Jer. 23. 5, 6.
Mic. 5. 2.
^k Pro. 29. 25.
^l Matt. 27.32.
Luke 23.26.
^m Rom. 16.13.
ⁿ John 19.17.
Acts 7. 58.
Heb. 13. 12.
^o Ps. 69. 21.
^p Ps. 22. 18.
Matt. 27.35,
36.
Luke 23.34.
John 19.23,
24.
^q Matt. 27.45.
Luke 23.44.
John 19.14.
^r Deut. 23. 5.
Ps. 76. 10.
Pro. 21. 1.
Isa. 10. 7.
Isa. 46. 10.
Matt. 27.37.
^s Isa. 53. 12.
Luke 22.37.
^t Ps. 22. 7.
Ps. 35. 15,
16.
Matt. 9. 24.
Luke 16.14.
^u ch. 14. 58.
John 2. 19.

his "going out and weeping bitterly,"—who that reads all this with unsophisticated intelligence, can doubt its reality, or fail to feel as if himself had been in the midst of it all? But what puts the crown upon the self-evidencing truth of all this is, that we have four Records of it, so harmonious as to be manifestly but different reports of the same transactions, yet differing to such an extent in minute details, that hostile criticism has tried to make out a case of irreconcilable contradiction, which has staggered some—while the most friendly and loving criticism has not been able to remove all difficulties. This at least shows that none of them wrote to prop up the statements of the others, and that the facts of the Gospel History are bound together by a fourfold cord that cannot be broken. Thanks, then, be unto God for this inestimable treasure, but above all for the Unspeakable Gift of Whom it tells its wondrous Tale—a Tale as new while we now write as when the Evangelists themselves were holding the pen—a Tale, like the new song, that will never grow old!

CHAP. XV. 1-20.—JESUS IS BROUGHT BEFORE PILATE—AT A SECOND HEARING, PILATE, AFTER SEEKING TO RELEASE HIM, DELIVERS HIM UP—AFTER BEING CRUELLY ENTREATED, HE IS LED AWAY TO BE CRUCIFIED. (= Matt. xxvi. 1, 2,11-31; Luke xxiii. 1-6, 13-25; John xviii. 28-xix. 16.) For the exposition, see on John xviii. 28-xix. 16.

21-37.—CRUCIFIXION AND DEATH OF THE LORD JESUS. (= Matt. xxvii. 32-50; Luke xxiii. 26-46; John xix. 17-30.) For the exposition, see on John xix. 17-30.

31 thyself, and come down from the cross. Likewise also the chief priests mocking said among themselves with the scribes, He saved others; him-
32 self he cannot save. Let Christ the King of Israel descend now from the cross, that we may see and believe. And *ᵛ*they that were crucified with him reviled him.
33 And *ʷ*when the sixth hour was come, there was darkness over the
34 whole land until the ninth hour. And at the ninth hour Jesus cried with a loud voice, saying, *ˣ*Eloi! Eloi! lama sabachthani? which is,
35 being interpreted, My God! my God! why hast thou forsaken me? And some of them that stood by, when they heard *it*, said, Behold, he calleth
36 Elias. And *ʸ*one ran and filled a sponge full of vinegar, and put *it* on a reed, and *ᶻ*gave him to drink, saying, Let alone; let us see whether Elias will come to take him down.
37, And *ᵃ*Jesus cried with a loud voice, and gave up the ghost. And
38 *ᵇ*the veil of the temple was rent in twain from the top to the bottom.
39 And *ᶜ*when the centurion, which stood over against him, saw that he so cried out, and gave up the ghost, he said, Truly this man was the Son of
40 God. There *ᵈ*were also women looking on afar *ᵉ*off: among whom was Mary Magdalene, and Mary the mother of James the less and of Joses,
41 and Salome; (who also, when he was in Galilee, followed *ᶠ*him, and ministered unto him;) and many other women which came up with him unto Jerusalem.
42 And *ᵍ*now when the even was come, because it was the preparation,
43 that is, the day before the sabbath, Joseph of Arimathea, an honourable counsellor, which also *ʰ*waited for the kingdom of God, came, and went
44 in boldly unto Pilate, and craved the body of Jesus. And Pilate marvelled if he were already dead: and, calling *unto him* the centurion, he
45 asked him whether he had been any while dead. And when he knew *it*
46 of the centurion, he gave the body to Joseph. And *ⁱ*he bought fine linen, and took him down, and wrapped him in the linen, and laid him in a sepulchre which was hewn out of a rock, and rolled a stone unto the
47 door of the sepulchre. And Mary Magdalene and Mary *the mother* of Joses beheld where he was laid.

16 AND *ᵃ*when the sabbath was past, Mary Magdalene, and Mary the *mother* of James, and Salome, *ᵇ*had bought sweet spices, that they might
2 come and anoint him. And *ᶜ*very early in the morning, the first *day*
3 of the week, they came unto the sepulchre at the rising of the sun. And they said among themselves, Who shall roll us away the stone from the
4 door of the sepulchre? And when they looked, they saw that the stone

A. D. 33.
Matt. 27.44.
Luke 23.39.
Heb. 12. 3.
1 Pet. 2. 23.
Luke 23.44.
Ps. 22. 1.
Matt. 27.46.
Heb. 5. 7.
Matt. 27.48.
John 19.29.
Ps. 69. 21.
Matt. 27.50.
Luke 23.46.
John 19. 30.
Ex. 26. 31.
Ex. 40. 20, 21.
2 Chr. 3. 14.
Matt. 27. 51-53.
Luke 23.45.
Heb. 4. 14-16.
Heb. 6. 19.
Heb. 9.3-12.
Heb. 10. 19.
Deut. 32.31.
Matt. 27.54.
Ps. 38. 11.
Matt. 27.55, 56.
Luke 23.49.
John 19.26, 27.
Ps. 38. 11.
Luke 8. 2.
John 19 38.
Ps. 25. 2.
Ps. 27. 14.
Isa. 8. 16.
Lam. 3. 25, 26.
Luke 2. 25.
Isa. 53. 9.
CHAP. 16.
Matt. 28. 1.
Luke 23. 56.
Matt. 28. 1.
Luke 24. 1.
John 20. 1.

38-47.—SIGNS AND CIRCUMSTANCES FOLLOWING THE DEATH OF THE LORD JESUS—HE IS TAKEN DOWN FROM THE CROSS AND BURIED—THE SEPULCHRE IS GUARDED. (= Matt. xxvii. 51-66; Luke xxiii. 45, 47-56; John xix. 31-42.) For the exposition, see on Matt. xxvii. 51-56; and on John xix. 31-42.

CHAP. XVI. 1-20.—ANGELIC ANNOUNCEMENT TO THE WOMEN ON THE FIRST DAY OF THE WEEK, THAT CHRIST IS RISEN—HIS APPEARANCES AFTER HIS RESURRECTION—HIS ASCENSION —TRIUMPHANT PROCLAMATION OF HIS GOSPEL. (= Matt. xxviii. 1-10, 16-20; Luke xxiv. 1-51; John xx. 1, 2, 11-29.)

The Resurrection Announced to the Women (1-8). **1. And when the sabbath was past**—that is, at sunset of our Saturday, **Mary Magdalene**—see on Luke viii. 2, and **Mary the Mother of James** —James the Less (see on ch. xv. 40), **and Salome** —the mother of Zebedee's sons (compare ch. xv. 40 with Matt. xxvii. 56), **had bought sweet spices, that they might come and anoint him.** The word is simply 'bought' [ἠγόρασαν]. But our

translators are perhaps right in rendering it here 'had bought,' since it would appear, from Luke xxiii. 56, that they had purchased them immediately after the Crucifixion, on the *Friday* evening, during the short interval that remained to them before sunset, when the Sabbath rest began; and that they had only deferred using them to anoint the body till the Sabbath rest should be over. On this "anointing," see on John xix. 40. **2. And very early in the morning**—see on Matt. xxviii. 1, **the first day of the week, they came unto the sepulchre at the rising of the sun**—not quite literally, but 'at earliest dawn;' according to a way of speaking not uncommon, and occurring sometimes in the Old Testament. Thus our Lord rose on the third day; having lain in the grave part of Friday, the whole of Saturday, and part of the following First day. **3. And they said among themselves**—as they were approaching the sacred spot, **Who shall roll us away the stone from the door of the sepulchre? 4. And when they looked, they saw that the stone was rolled away: for it was very great.**

5 was rolled away: for it was very great. And ^dentering into the sepulchre, they saw a young man sitting on the right side, clothed in a
6 long white garment; and they were affrighted. And ^ehe saith unto them, Be not affrighted : Ye seek Jesus of Nazareth, which was crucified:
7 he is ^frisen; he is not here: behold the place where they laid him. But go your way, tell his disciples and Peter that he goeth before you into
8 Galilee: there shall ye see him, ^gas he said unto you. And they went out quickly, and fled from the sepulchre; for they trembled and were amazed: ^hneither said they any thing to any *man;* for they were afraid.
9   Now when *Jesus* was risen early the first *day* of the week, ⁱhe appeared

A. D. 33.	
d Luke 24. 3.	
John 20. 8.	
e Matt. 28. 5.	
f ch. 10. 34.	
John 2. 19.	
1 Cor. 15. 3-7.	
g Matt. 26.32.	
Matt 28.10, 16, 17.	
ch. 14. 28.	
h Matt. 28. 8.	
i John 20. 14.	

This last clause is added, both to account for their wonder how with such a stone on it the grave was to be laid open for them, and to call attention to the power which had rolled it away. Though it was too great for themselves to remove, and without that their spices had been useless, they come notwithstanding; discussing their difficulty, yet undeterred by it. On reaching it they find their difficulty gone—the stone already rolled away by an unseen hand. *And are there no others who, when advancing to duty in the face of appalling difficulties, find their stone also rolled away?* 5. **And entering into the sepulchre, they saw a young man.** In Matt. xxviii. 2, he is called " the angel of the Lord;" but here he is described as he appeared to the eye, in the bloom of a life that knows no decay. In Matthew he is represented as sitting on the stone *outside* the sepulchre; but since even there he says, "*Come,* see the place where the Lord lay" (xxviii. 6), he seems, as *Alford* says, to have gone in with them from without; only awaiting their arrival to accompany them into the hallowed spot, and instruct them about it. **sitting on the right side**—having respect to the position in which His Lord had lain there. This trait is peculiar to Mark; but compare Luke i. 11. **clothed in a long white garment.** On its *length,* see Isa. vi. 1; and on its *whiteness,* see on Matt. xxviii. 3. **and they were affrighted** [ἐξεθαμβήθησαν]. 6. **And he saith unto them, Be not affrighted** [Μὴ ἐκθαμβεῖσθε]—a stronger word than " Fear not" [μὴ φοβεῖσθε] in Matthew. **Ye seek Jesus of Nazareth, which was crucified** [τὸν Ναζαρηνὸν, τὸν ἐσταυρωμένον]—'the Nazarene, the Crucified.' **he is risen; he is not here.** See on Luke xxiv. 5, 6. **behold the place where they laid him.** See on Matt. xxviii. 6. 7. **But go your way, tell his disciples and Peter.** This Second Gospel, being drawn up—as all the earliest tradition states— *under the eye of Peter,* or from materials chiefly furnished by him, there is something deeply affecting in the preservation of this little clause by Mark alone, and in the clause itself, which it is impossible not to connect with the cloud under which Peter lay in the eyes of the Eleven, not to say in his own also. Doubtless the "look" of Jesus and the "bitter weeping" which followed upon it (Luke xxii. 61, 62) contained all the materials of a settlement and a reconciliation. But such wounds are not easily healed; and this was but the first of a series of medicinal touches, the rest of which will follow anon. **that he goeth before you into Galilee: there shall ye see him, as he said unto you.** See on Matt. xxviii. 7. 8. **And they went out quickly, and fled from the sepulchre; for they trembled and were amazed** [εἶχε δὲ αὐτὰς τρόμος καὶ ἔκστασις]—' for tremor and amazement seized them.' **neither said they any thing to any man; for they were afraid.** How intensely natural and simple is this!

Appearances of Jesus After His Resurrection

(9-18). [All the verses of this chapter, from the 9th to the end, are regarded by *Griesbach, Tischendorf,* and *Tregelles* as no part of the original text of this Gospel, but as added by a later hand: Because, first, they are wanting in B and ℵ—the well-known *Vatican* and the recently discovered *Sinaitic,* being the oldest MSS. yet known; in one copy of the *Old Latin* Version; in some copies of the Armenian Version; and in an Arabic Lectionary or Church Lesson; while a few of the Cursive or later MSS. of this Gospel have the verses with marks indicative of doubt as to their genuineness: Again, because *Eusebius* and *Jerome*—most competent witnesses and judges, of the fourth century— pronounce against them, affirming that the genuine text of this Gospel ended with verse 8: And further, because the style of this portion so differs from the rest of this Gospel as to suggest a different author; while the variations in the text itself are just ground of suspicion. For these reasons, *Meyer, Fritzsche, Alford,* and other critical commentators, decide against the passage. But these reasons seem to us totally insufficient to counterbalance the evidence in favour of the verses in question. First, they are found in *all* the Uncial or earlier Greek MSS., except the two above-mentioned—including A, or the Alexandrian MS., which is admitted to be not more than fifty years later than the two oldest, and of scarcely less, if indeed of any less, authority; in one or two MSS. in which they are not found, a space is left to show that something is wanting—not large enough, indeed, to contain the verses, but this probably only to save space; nor do the variations in the text exceed those in some passages whose genuineness is admitted: They are found in *all* the Cursive or later Greek MSS.: They are found in all the most ancient Versions: They are quoted by *Irenæus,* and so must have been known in the *second* century; by one father at least in the *third* century, and by two or three in the *fourth,* as part of this Gospel. The argument from difference of style is exceedingly slender—confined to a few words and phrases, which vary, as every one knows, in different writings of the same author and even different portions of the same writing, with the varying aspects of the subject and the writer's emotions. That so carefully constructed a Narrative as that of this Gospel terminated with the words, "for they were afraid"—ἐφοβοῦντο γάρ— is what one wonders that any can bring themselves to believe. Accordingly, *Lachmann* inserts it as part of his text; and *de Wette, Hug,* and *Lange* in Germany, with *Ellicott* and *Scrivener* among ourselves, defend it. The conjecture of some recent critics, that it may have been added by the Evangelist himself, after the copies first issued had been for some time in circulation, is too far-fetched to be entitled to consideration.]

9. **Now when Jesus was risen early the first day of the week, he appeared first to Mary Magdalene,**

10 first to Mary Magdalene, [j] out of whom he had cast seven devils. *And* she went and told them that had been with him, as they mourned and
11 wept. And [k] they, when they had heard that he was alive, and had been seen of her, believed not.
12 After that he appeared in another form unto two of them, as they
13 walked, and went into the country. And they went and told *it* unto the residue : neither believed they them.
14 Afterward [l] he appeared unto the eleven as they sat [1] at meat, and upbraided them with their unbelief and hardness of heart, because they believed not them which had seen him after he was risen.
15 And [m] he said unto them, Go ye into all the world, [n] and preach the
16 Gospel to every creature. He [o] that believeth and is baptized shall be
17 saved; [p] but he that believeth not shall be damned. And these signs shall follow them that believe : [q] In my name shall they cast out devils;
18 [r] they shall speak with new tongues: they [s] shall take up serpents; and if they drink any deadly thing, it shall not hurt them; [t] they shall lay hands on the sick, and they shall recover.
19 So then, [u] after the Lord had spoken unto them, he was [v] received up
20 into heaven, and [w] sat on the right hand of God. And they went forth, and preached every where, the Lord working with *them*, and [x] confirming the word with signs following. Amen.

A. D. 33.

[j] Luke 8. 2.
[k] Luke 24. 11.
[l] Luke 24. 36.
1 Cor. 15. 5.
[1] Or,
together.
[m] John 15.16.
[n] Col. 1. 23.
[o] John 3. 18, 36.
[p] John 12. 48.
[q] Luke 10. 17.
[r] Acts 2. 4.
1 Cor. 12.10, 28.
[s] Acts 28. 5.
[t] Acts 9. 17.
Jas. 5. 14.
[u] Acts 1. 2, 3.
[v] Luke 24.51.
[w] Ps. 110. 1.
Acts 7. 55.
Heb. 1. 3.
Rev. 3. 21.
[x] Acts 14. 3.
1 Cor. 2. 4, 5.

---

out of whom he had cast seven devils. There is some difficulty here, and different ways of removing it have been adopted. She had gone with the other women to the sepulchre (*v.* 1), parting from them, perhaps, before their interview with the angel, and on finding Peter and John she had come with them back to the spot; and it was at this second visit, it would seem, that Jesus appeared to this Mary, as detailed in John xx. 11-18. *To a woman was this honour given to be the first that saw the risen Redeemer; and that woman was* NOT *his virgin-mother.* 10. **And she went and told them that had been with him, as they mourned and wept. 11. And they, when they had heard that he was alive, and had been seen of her, believed not.** This, which is once and again repeated of them all, is most important in its bearing on their subsequent testimony to His resurrection, at the risk of life itself. **12. After that he appeared in another form** (compare Luke xxiv. 16) **unto two of them, as they walked, and went into the country.** The reference here, of course, is to His manifestation to the two disciples going to Emmaus, so exquisitely told by the third Evangelist (see on Luke xxiv. 13, &c.). **12. And they went and told it unto the residue: neither believed they them.** **14. Afterward he appeared unto the eleven as they sat at meat, and upbraided them with their unbelief and hardness of heart, because they believed not them which had seen him after he was risen. 15. And he said unto them, Go ye into all the world, and preach the Gospel to every creature.** See on John xx. 19-23; and on Luke xxiv. 36-49. **16. He that believeth and is baptized.** Baptism is here put for the external signature of the inner faith of the heart, just as " confessing with the mouth " is in Rom. x. 10; and there also as here this *outward* manifestation, once mentioned as the proper fruit

214

of faith, is not repeated in what follows (Rom. x. 11). **shall be saved; but he that believeth not shall be damned.** These awful issues of the reception or rejection of the Gospel, though often recorded in other connections, are given in this connection only by Mark. **17. And these signs shall follow them that believe: In my name shall they cast out devils; they shall speak with new tongues; 18. They shall take up serpents; and if they drink any deadly thing, it shall not hurt them; they shall lay hands on the sick, and they shall recover.** These two verses also are peculiar to Mark.

The Ascension and Triumphant Proclamation of the Gospel thereafter (19-20). **19. So then, after the Lord**—an epithet applied to Jesus by this Evangelist only in the two concluding verses, when He comes to His glorious Ascension and its subsequent fruits. It is most frequent in Luke. **had spoken unto them, he was received up into heaven.** See on Luke xxiv. 50, 51. **and sat on the right hand of God.** This great truth is here only related as a fact in the Gospel History. In that exalted attitude He appeared to Stephen (Acts vii. 55, 56); and it is thereafter perpetually referred to as His proper condition in glory. **20. And they went forth, and preached every where, the Lord working with them, and confirming the word with signs following. Amen.** We have in this closing verse a most important link of connection with the Acts of the Apostles, where He who directed all the movements of the infant Church is perpetually styled "THE LORD;" thus illustrating His own promise for the founding and building up of the Church, "LO, I AM WITH YOU alway!"

For Remarks on this Section, see those on the corresponding Section of the First Gospel—Matt. xxviii. 1-15.

1 FORASMUCH as many have taken in hand to set forth in order a
declaration of *a*those things which are most surely believed among
2 us, even *b*as they delivered them unto us, which *c*from the beginning
3 were eye-witnesses, and ministers of the word; it *d*seemed good to me
also, having had perfect understanding of all things from the very first,
4 to write unto thee *e*in order, most *f*excellent Theophilus, that *g*thou
mightest know the certainty of those things, wherein thou hast been
instructed.
5 THERE was, *h*in the days of Herod the king of Judea, a certain priest
named Zacharias, *i*of the course of Abia: and his wife *was* of the
6 daughters of Aaron, and her name *was* Elisabeth. And they were
both *j*righteous before God, walking in all the commandments and
7 ordinances of the Lord blameless. And they had no child, because
that Elisabeth was barren; and they both were *now* well stricken in
years.
8 And it came to pass, that, while he executed the priest's office before

A. M. 4000.

CHAP. 1.
a John 20. 31.
Acts 1. 1-3.
1 Tim. 3.16.
b Heb. 2. 3.
1 Pet. 5. 1.
2 Pet. 1. 16.
1 John 1. 1.
c John 15.27.
d 1 Cor. 7. 40.
e Acts 11. 4.
f Acts 1. 1.
g John 20. 31.
h Matt. 2. 1.
i 1 Chr.24.19.
Neh. 12. 4.
j 1 Ki. 9. 4.
2 Ki. 20. 3.
Ps. 119. 6.
2 Cor. 1. 12.

CHAP. I. 1-17.—INTRODUCTION—ANNOUNCE-
MENT OF THE FORERUNNER.
Introduction (1-4). **1. Forasmuch as many have
taken in hand to set forth in order a declaration** [ἐπεχείρησαν ἀνατάξασθαι διήγησιν]—'have
undertaken to draw up a narrative,' **of those
things which are most surely believed** [τῶν
πεπληροφορημένων] among us—not 'believed confidently,' but 'believed on sure grounds.' So the
word "surely" is used by our translators in Prov.
x. 9, "He that walketh uprightly walketh *surely*."
**2. Even as they delivered them unto us, which
from the beginning** [ἀπ᾽ ἀρχῆς]—that is, of Christ's
ministry, **were eye-witnesses, and ministers of
the word** [αὐτόπται καὶ ὑπηρέται τοῦ λόγου].
Though it would not be strictly proper to understand "the word" here of Christ Himself—since
only John applies to Him this exalted title, and
He seems never to have been actually so denomi-
nated—yet since the term rendered "ministers"
[ὑπηρέται] denotes the servants of a *person*, it must
refer to those apostles of the Lord Jesus, who, in
proclaiming everywhere that word which they had
heard from His own lips, acted as *His* servants.
**3. It seemed good to me also, having had perfect
understanding of** [παρηκολουθηκότι]—rather, 'having closely followed,' or 'traced along' **all things
from the very first** [ἄνωθεν πᾶσιν ἀκριβῶς]—'all
things with precision from the earliest;' referring
particularly to the precious incidents of his first
two chapters, for which we are indebted to this
Evangelist alone, **to write unto thee in order**
[καθεξῆς = ἐφεξῆς]—*i. e., consecutively;* probably
in contrast with the disjointed productions he
had just referred to. But we need not take
this as a claim to rigid chronological accuracy
in the arrangement of his materials (as some
able Harmonists insist that we should do); a
claim which, on a comparison of this with the
other Gospels, it would be difficult in every case
to make good. **most excellent** [κράτιστε] **Theophilus.** As the term here applied to Theophilus
was given to Felix and Festus, the Roman governors (Acts xxiii. 26; xxiv. 3; xxvi. 25), he
probably occupied some similar official position.

4. That thou mightest know—'know thoroughly'
[ἐπιγνῷς]—**the certainty of those things wherein
thou hast been instructed** [κατηχήθης]—'orally
instructed;' *i. e.,* as a catechumen, or candidate
for Christian baptism.
**5. There was, in the days of Herod the king
of Judea** (see on Matt. ii. 1), **a certain priest
named Zacharias, of the course of Abia**—or
Abijah, the eighth of the twenty-four courses
or orders into which David divided the priests
(1 Chr. xxiv. 1, 4, 10). Of these courses only
four returned after the captivity (Ezra ii. 36-
39), which were again divided into twenty-
four courses, retaining the ancient name and
the original order; and each of these took the
whole Temple-service for a week. **and his wife
was of the daughters of Aaron.** Though the
priests, says *Lightfoot*, might marry into any tribe,
it was most commendable of all to marry one
of the priests' line. **and her name was Elisabeth.**
6. And they were both righteous—not merely virtuous before men, but righteous **before God** who
searcheth the heart. What that comprehended is
next explained. **walking**—a familiar biblical term
denoting the habitual tenor of one's life, (Ps. i. 1,
&c.) **in all the commandments and ordinances
of the Lord**—the one denoting the *moral*, the other
the *ceremonial* precepts of the law—a distinction
which it is falsely alleged that the ancient Jews
were strangers to (see on Mark xii. 33; and see
Ezek. xi. 20; Heb. ix. 1). **blameless**—irreproachable. **7. And they had no child, because that
Elisabeth was barren; and they both were now
well stricken in years.** This quiet couple have
one trial. Almost every one has some crook in
his lot; but here it was a link in the great chain
of the divine purposes. As with Abraham and
Sarah before Isaac was given; with Elkanah and
Hannah before Samuel was granted them; and
with Manoah and his wife before Samson was
born; so here with Zacharias and Elisabeth before the Forerunner was bestowed—in each case,
doubtless, to make the gift more prized, and raise
high expectations from it.
8. And it came to pass, that, while he executed

9 God *k*in the order of his course, according to the custom of the priest's office, his lot was *l*to burn incense when he went into the temple of the
10 Lord.   And *m*the whole multitude of the people were praying without
11 at the time of incense.   And there appeared unto him an angel of the
12 Lord standing on the right side of the altar of incense.   And when
13 Zacharias saw *him*, *n*he was troubled, and fear fell upon him.   But the angel said unto him, Fear not, Zacharias: for *o*thy prayer is heard; and thy wife Elisabeth shall bear thee a son, and thou shalt call his name
14 John.   And thou shalt have joy and gladness; and many shall rejoice
15 at his birth.   For he shall be *p*great in the sight of the Lord, and *q*shall drink neither wine nor strong drink; and he shall be filled with the

A. M. 4000.

k 2 Chr. 8. 14.
l Ex. 30. 7. 8.
m Lev. 16. 17.
n Dan. 10. 8.
Acts 10. 4.
Rev. 1. 17.
o Gen. 25. 21.
1 Sam. 1. 19.
p Matt. 11. 11.
John 5. 35.
q Num. 6. 3.
Jud. 13. 4.
ch. 7. 33.

the priest's office before God in the order of his course, 9. According to the custom of the priest's office, his lot was to burn incense when he went into the temple. The part assigned to each priest during his week of service was decided by lot. Three were employed at the offering of incense: to remove the ashes of the former service; to bring in and place on the golden altar the pan filled with hot burning coals taken from the altar of burnt offering; and to sprinkle the incense on the hot coals, and, while the smoke of it ascended, to make intercession for the people. This was the most distinguished part of the service (Rev. viii. 3), and this was what fell to the lot of Zacharias at this time [*Lightfoot*]. 10. And the whole multitude of the people were praying without—outside the court fronting the temple, where stood the altar of burnt offering; the men and women worshipping in separate courts, but the altar visible to all. at the time of incense—which was offered twice every day, along with the morning and evening sacrifice, at the third and ninth hours (or 9 A.M. and 3 P.M.)—a beautiful symbol, first of *the acceptableness of the sacrifice* which was then burning on the altar of burnt offering, with coals from which the incense laid on the golden altar was burnt (Lev. xvi. 12, 13); but next, of the *acceptableness of themselves and all their services*, as "living sacrifices" presented daily to God. Hence the language of Ps. cxli. 2, "Let my prayer come up before thee as incense, and the lifting up of my hands as the evening sacrifice;" and see Gen. viii. 3, 4. That the acceptableness of this *incense-offering* depended on the *expiatory* virtue pre-supposed in the *burnt offering*, and pointed to the Lamb of God that taketh away the sin of the world, is clear from Isa. vi. 6, 7, where the symbolic action of touching the prophet's lips with a live coal from off the altar is interpreted to mean the "taking away of his iniquity, and the purging of his sin," in order that his lips might be clean to speak for God. 11. And there appeared unto him an angel of the Lord—not while at home, but in the act of discharging his sacerdotal duties; yet not when engaged *outside*, at the altar of burnt offering, but during his week of inside-service, and so while *alone* with God. It is impossible not to observe here a minuteness of providential arrangement, proclaiming in every detail the hand of Him who is "wonderful in counsel and excellent in working." standing—the attitude of service, on the right side of the altar of incense—*i. e.*, the south side, between the golden altar and the candlestick or lamp-stand; Zacharias being on the north side, and fronting the altar as he offered the incense. Why did the angel appear on the right side? Because, say some, the right was regarded as the favourable side [*Schöttgen*, and *Wetstein* in *Meyer*]. See Matt. xxv. 33; and cf. Mark xvi. 5. But perhaps it was only to make the object more visible. 12. And when Zach-

arias saw him, he was troubled—'discomposed,' and fear fell upon him. And what wonder? The unseen world is so veiled from us, and so different from ours in its nature and laws, that when in any of its features it breaks in unexpectedly upon mortals, it cannot but startle and appal them, as it did Daniel (Dan. x. 7, 8, 17), and the beloved disciple in Patmos (Rev. i. 17). 'He that had wont to live and serve in presence of the Master was now astonished at the presence of the servant. So much difference is there betwixt our faith and our senses, that the apprehension of the presence of the God of spirits by faith goes down sweetly with us, whereas the sensible apprehension of an angel dismays us. Holy Zachary, that had wont to live by faith, thought he should die when his sense began to be set on work. It was the weakness of him that served at the altar without horror, to be daunted with the face of his fellow-servant' (*Bp. Hall.*) 13. But the angel said unto him, Fear not. Thus by two familiar, endeared, exhilarating words, was the silence of four centuries broken, and thus unexpectedly, yet all noiselessly, was the curtain of a stupendous and enduring Economy in this world's history at once drawn up! And was it not worth all the terror which Zacharias experienced to be greeted with so gladsome a salutation! It is God's prerogative, indeed, to dispel our fears—"Thou drewest near (sings Jeremiah) in the day that I called upon Thee; Thou saidst, Fear not" (Lam. iii. 57)—but angels, we see, are privileged to convey the message from heaven; nay, all who have themselves been divinely cheered are bidden "Say to them that are of a fearful heart, Be strong, fear not" (Isa. xxxv. 4). Zacharias! How sweet is it to hear the name of this lowly mortal man sounded forth by an exalted messenger from the very presence-chamber of the Most High! Does it not bring vividly before us the nearness of heaven to earth, God's intimate knowledge of those who serve Him here below, and the tender interest which He takes in them? for thy prayer is heard —doubtless for *offspring*, which, by some presentiment, perhaps, he had even till now been kept from quite despairing of. and thy wife Elisabeth shall bear thee a son, and thou shalt call his name John [=יוֹחָנָן=יְהוֹחָנָן]—the "Johanan" so frequent in the Old Testament, meaning Jehovah's gracious gift. 14. And thou shalt have joy and gladness—'exultation,' and many shall rejoice —*i. e.*, shall have cause to rejoice at his birth— through whose ministry they were "turned to the Lord their God." 15. For he shall be great in the sight of the Lord—*i. e.*, great *officially* beyond all the prophets that went before him (as is evident from Matt. xi. 11). In personal character John was indeed among the greatest of men; but it is the supereminent dignity of his office, as Messiah's Forerunner, that is here meant. and shall drink neither wine nor strong drink

16 Holy Ghost, ᵣeven from his mother's womb. And ˢmany of the children
17 of Israel shall he turn to the Lord their God. And ᵗhe shall go before
him in the spirit and power of Elias, to turn the hearts of the fathers to
the children, and the disobedient ¹to the wisdom of the just; to make
ready a people prepared for ᵘthe Lord.

A. M. 4000.
ᵣ Jer. 1. 5.
ˢ Mal. 4. 5,6.
ᵗ Matt. 11.14.
1 Or, by.
ᵘ Isa. 40. 3.

—that is, he shall be a *Nazarite*, or 'separated one.' See Num. vi. 1, &c. As the leper was the living symbol of *sin*, so was the Nazarite of *holiness:* nothing inflaming was to cross his lips; no razor was to come on his head; no ceremonial defilement was to be contracted. Thus was he to be ceremonially "holy to the Lord all the days of his separation." In ordinary cases this separation was voluntary and temporary: we read of three only who were Nazarites from the womb—*Samson* (Jud. xiii. 7), *Samuel* (1 Sam. i. 11), and here *John Baptist.* It was fitting that the utmost severity of legal consecration should be in the Forerunner. In Christ Himself we see the REALITY and PERFECTION of the Nazarite without the symbol, which perished in that living realization of it. "Such an high priest became us, who is holy, harmless, undefiled, SEPARATE FROM SINNERS" (Heb. vii. 26). **and he shall be filled with the Holy Ghost** (see Matt. i. 18), **even from his mother's womb**—a holy vessel for future service. This is never said of the supernatural endowments of ungodly men; and indeed of John it is expressly said that he "did no miracle" (John x. 41). Nor can the reference be to inspiration, for this does not appear to have come on John till his public ministry commenced, when "the word of God came to John the son of Zacharias in the wilderness" (Luke iii. 2). It is *sanctification from the womb*—a truth of high import in personal Christianity, of weighty bearing on the standing of the infants of believers in the Church of God, and ministering precious encouragement to religious parents. **16. And many of the children of Israel shall he turn to the Lord their God. 17. And he shall go before him**—*i. e.*, before "the Lord their God" just spoken of; showing that Messiah, before whom John was to go, as a *herald* to announce his approach and as a *pioneer* to prepare his way, was to be "the Lord God of Israel" manifested in the flesh (Isa. xl. 3; Mal. iii. 1). So *Calvin, Olshausen*, &c. **in the spirit and power of Elias**—*i. e.*, after the model of that distinguished reformer, and with like success, in "turning hearts." Strikingly indeed did John resemble Elias: both fell on evil times; both witnessed fearlessly for God; neither was much seen save in the direct exercise of their ministry; both were at the head of schools of disciples; the result of the ministry of both might be expressed in the same terms—"*many* (not all, nor even the majority, but still many) of the children of Israel did they turn to the Lord their God." **to turn the hearts of the fathers to the children** This, if taken literally, with *Meyer* and others, denotes the restoration of parental fidelity, the decay of which is certainly the beginning of religious and social corruption. In this case it is just one prominent feature of the coming revival put for the whole. But the next clause, **and the disobedient to the wisdom of the just**—which seems designed to give the sense of the preceding one, rather suggests a *figurative* meaning: 'He shall bring back the ancient spirit of the nation to their degenerate children.' So *Calvin, Bengel*, &c. Thus prayed Elijah, "Lord God of Abraham, Isaac, and Israel, hear me, that this people may know that thou art the Lord God, and that thou hast *turned their heart back again*" (1 Ki. xviii. 36, 37). **to make ready a people prepared for the Lord**

[ἐτοιμάσαι Κυρίῳ λαὸν κατεσκευασμένον]—rather, 'to make ready for the Lord a prepared people;' prepared, that is, to welcome Him. Such preparation for welcoming the Lord is required, not only in every age, but in every soul.

Remarks.—1. Works such as Jesus wrought and Teaching such as poured from His lips, as He walked up and down Judea and Galilee, in the days of His flesh, could not but be carried on the wings of the wind, especially after He rose from the dead, ascended up into heaven, and at the Pentecostal festival made His handful of adherents proclaim, in the tongues of all the nationalities then assembled at Jerusalem, the wonderful works of God. These Jewish strangers and proselytes would carry them to their homes, and the first preachers —and every Christian would be more or less a preacher—would tell the tale to all who had ears to hear them. Of such astonishing tidings eager listeners would take notes; and digests, more or less full, would be put into circulation. For lack of better, such summaries would be read aloud at prayer-meetings and other small assemblies of Christians; and of these a few would be pretty full, and, on the whole, pretty correct narratives of the Life, Acts, and Sayings of Christ. To such it is that our Evangelist here refers, and in terms of studied respect, as narratives of what was 'on sure grounds believed among Christians, and drawn up from the testimony of eye-witnesses and ministers of the word.' But when he adds that it seemed good to him also, having traced down all things with exactness from its first rise, to write a consecutive History, he virtually claims, by this Gospel of his own, to supersede all these narratives. Accordingly, while not one of them has survived the wreck of time, this and the other canonical Gospels live, and shall live, the only worthy vehicles of those life-bringing facts which have made all things new. Apocryphal or spurious gospels—such as sprang up in swarms at a later period to feed a prurient curiosity and minister to the taste of those who could not rise to the tone of the canonical Gospels—have *not* altogether perished: but those well-meant and substantially correct narratives here referred to, used only while better were not to be had, were by tacit consent allowed to merge in the four peerless documents which, as one Gospel, have from age to age, even from the very time of their publication, and with astonishing unanimity, been accepted as the written Charter of all Christianity. 2. The diversity which obtains among these Four Gospels is as beautiful a feature of them as their inner harmony. Each has an invaluable character of its own which the others want. And although a comparison of the four different streams of narration with each other, with the view of tracing out the unity of incident and discourse, and so shaping out as perfectly as possible *The Life of Jesus*, has been the laudable, and delightful, and fruitful occupation of biblical students in every age; one cannot but feel, the longer he studies these matchless productions, that every detail of them is so much fresher just *where it lies* than in any combination of them into one, that every such attempt as Tatian's DIATESSARON (about A.D. 170), and that of Professor White of Oxford (1803)—that is, one continuous History woven out of the text of the

18 And Zacharias said unto the angel, Whereby ^vshall I know this? for
19 I am an old man, and my wife well stricken in years. And the angel
answering said unto him, I am ^wGabriel, that stand in the presence of
God; and am sent to speak unto thee, and to show thee these glad
20 tidings. And, behold, ^xthou shalt be dumb, and not able to speak,
until the day that these things shall be performed, because thou believest
21 not my words, which shall be fulfilled in their season. And the people
^ywaited for Zacharias, and marvelled that he tarried so long in the
22 temple. And when he came out, he could not speak unto them: and
they perceived that he had seen a vision in the temple; for he beckoned
unto them, and remained speechless.
23 And it came to pass, that, as soon as the ^zdays of his ministration
24 were accomplished, he departed to his own house. And after those days
25 his wife Elisabeth conceived, and hid herself five months, saying, Thus
hath the Lord dealt with me in the days wherein he looked on *me*, to
^atake away my reproach among men.
26 And in the sixth month the angel Gabriel was sent from God unto a

A. M. 4000.
^v Gen. 15. 8.
Gen. 17. 17.
Gen. 18. 12.
Jud. 6. 36.
Isa. 38. 22.
^w Dan. 8. 16.
Dan. 9. 21.
Matt. 18. 10.
Heb. 1. 14.
^x Ex. 4. 11.
Ezek. 3. 26
Ezek. 24. 27
ch. 1. 62.
^y Num. 6. 23.
Lev. 9. 22.
^z 2 Ki. 11. 5.
1 Chr. 9. 25
^a Gen. 30. 23.
1 Sam. 1. 6.
Isa. 4. 1.
Isa. 54. 1.

Four Gospels—is a mistake. Let that river, the streams whereof make glad the city of God, flow, like the river that watered the garden of Eden, in its four crystal streams and in their own native beds, until that which is perfect is come, when that which is in part shall be done away. 3. How beautiful is the spectacle of husband and wife, in advancing years, when "joint-heirs [συγκληρονόμοι] of the grace of life," and "their prayers [together] are not hindered" (1 Pet. iii. 7) by misunderstandings or inconsistencies! (*vv.* 7, 13). 4. When God has any special blessing in store for His people, He usually creates in them a longing for it, and yet withholds it from them till all hope of it is dying within them. By this He makes the blessing, when at length it comes, the more surprising and the more welcome, an object of deeper interest and dearer delight (*v.* 7). 5. The most cheering visitations of Heaven are wont to come to us in the discharge of duty. It was when Elijah *"still went on and talked"* with Elisha, who was to succeed him in office, that the chariots and horses of fire appeared to take him up to heaven (2 Ki. ii. 11): more gloriously still—when Jesus had led His disciples out "as far as to Bethany, and lifted up His hands and blessed them—it came to pass, *while He blessed them*, He was parted from them, and carried up into heaven" (Luke xxiv. 50, 51). So here, it was "while Zacharias was executing the priest's office in the order of his course, burning incense in the temple of the Lord, and the whole multitude of the people were praying without," that the angel of the Lord appeared to him with the glad announcement of a son who should usher in and prepare the way of Christ Himself (*vv.* 8-11). 6. If the heart is ready to sink when the thin partitions between heaven and earth are, even in a small degree, rent asunder, how re-assuring is it to find such exceptional visitations only confirming the teaching of Moses and the prophets, and strengthening the expectations built upon them! (*vv.* 13-17).

18-38.—UNBELIEF AND PUNISHMENT OF ZACHARIAS—ANNUNCIATION OF CHRIST, AND FAITH OF HIS VIRGIN-MOTHER.

Unbelief and Punishment of Zacharias (18-25). **18. And Zacharias said unto the angel, Whereby** [κατὰ τί] **shall I know this? for I am an old man, and my wife well stricken in years.** Had such a promise never been made and fulfilled before, the unbelief of Zacharias would have been more easily accounted for, and less sinful. But

when the like promise was made to Abraham, at a more advanced age, "he staggered not at the promise of God through unbelief, but was strong in faith, giving glory to God" (Rom. iv. 20). "Through faith Sara herself also received strength to conceive seed, and was delivered of a child when she was past age, because she judged Him faithful who had promised" (Heb. xi. 11). As God is glorified by implicit confidence in His promises—and just in proportion to the natural obstacles in the way of their fulfilment—so unbelief like that of Zacharias here is regarded as a dishonour put upon His word, and resented accordingly. **19. And the angel answering said unto him, I am Gabriel** —'man of God' [גַּבְרִיאֵל]. He appeared to Daniel, and at the same time of incense (Dan. ix. 21); to Mary also he was sent (*v.* 26). **that stand in the presence of God**—as His attendant (cf. 1 Ki. xvii. 1) **and am sent to speak unto thee, and to show thee these glad tidings. 20. And, behold, thou shalt be dumb** —'speechless' [σιωπῶν]—**until the day that these things shall be performed, because thou believest not my words, which shall be fulfilled in their season.** He asked for a sign, and now he got one. **21. And the people waited for Zacharias**—to receive from him the usual benediction (Num. vi. 23-27). **and marvelled that he tarried so long in the temple.** It was not usual to tarry long, lest it should be thought vengeance had stricken the people's representative for something wrong. (*Lightfoot*). **22. And when he came out, he could not speak unto them: and they perceived that he had seen a vision in the temple; for he beckoned unto them**—by some motion of his hands and eyes, signifying what had happened, **and remained speechless**—'dumb' [κωφός], and deaf also, as appears from *v.* 62. **23. And it came to pass, that, as soon as the days of his ministration were accomplished, he departed to his own house. 24. And Elisabeth conceived, and hid herself five months**—that is, till the event was put beyond doubt. **saying, 25. Thus hath the Lord dealt with me in the days wherein he looked on me, to take away my reproach among men.** There was. here more than true womanly simplicity and gratitude to the Lord for the gift of offspring. She has respect to the *manner* in which that reproach was to be taken away, in connection with the great Hope of Israel.

Annunciation of Christ, and Faith of His Virgin-Mother (26-38). The curtain of the first scene of this wonderful story has dropt, but only to rise again and disclose a scene of surpassing sacredness

27 city of Galilee, named Nazareth, to a *ᵇ*virgin espoused to a man whose
name was Joseph, of the house of David; and the virgin's name *was*
Mary.

28　　And the angel came in unto her, and said, Hail! *thou that art* ²highly
29 favoured, the Lord *is* with thee: blessed *art* thou among women! And
when she saw *him*, she was troubled at his saying, and cast in her mind
30 what manner of salutation this should be. And the angel said unto
31 her, Fear not, Mary; for thou hast found favour with God. And,
*ᶜ*behold, thou shalt conceive in thy womb; and bring forth a son, and
32 shalt call his name JESUS. He shall be *ᵈ*great, and shall be called the
Son of the Highest: and *ᵉ*the Lord God shall give unto him the throne
33 of his father David: and *ᶠ*he shall reign over the house of Jacob for ever;
34 and of his kingdom there shall be no end. Then said Mary unto the
35 angel, How shall this be, seeing I know not a man? And the angel
answered and said unto her, The Holy Ghost shall come upon thee, and
the power of the Highest shall overshadow thee: therefore also that holy

A. M. 4000.

ᵇ Isa. 7. 14.
Matt. 1. 18.
² Or,
graciously
accepted,
or, much
graced.
ᶜ Gal. 4. 4.
ᵈ 1 Tim. 6.15.
Phil. 2. 10.
ᵉ 2 Sam. 7.11.
Ps. 132. 11.
Isa. 9. 6, 7.
Isa. 16. 5.
Jer. 23. 5.
ᶠ Dan. 2. 44.
Dan. 7. 14.
Oba. 21.
Mic. 4. 7.
John 12.34.

and delicacy, simplicity and grandeur. **26. And in the sixth month** of Elisabeth's conception **the angel Gabriel was sent from God.** I could envy thee, O Gabriel, these most exalted of all errands. But I remember that true greatness lies, not in the dignity of our calling, but in the right discharge of its duties—not in the loftiness of our talents, but in the use we make of them. **unto a city named Nazareth.** "Can any good thing come out of Nazareth?" asked the guileless Nathanael, having respect to its proverbially bad name. But the Lord selects His own places as well as persons. **27. To a virgin espoused**—rather 'betrothed' [μεμνηστευμένην] **to a man whose name was Joseph, of the house of David.** See on Matt. i. 16. **and the virgin's name was Mary** [=מִרְיָם]—equivalent to *Miriam* in the Old Testament.

28. And the angel came in unto her, and said, Hail! highly favoured—a word [κεχαριτωμένη] only once used elsewhere (Eph. i. 6, "made accepted"). That our translators have given the right sense of it here seems plain not only from the import of verbs of that termination, but from the next clause, **the Lord is with thee**, and *v.* 30, "Thou hast found favour with God." The Vulgate's mistaken rendering—"full of grace" [*gratiâ plena*]—has been taken abundant advantage of by the Romish Church. As the mother of our Lord, she was indeed "the most blessed among women;" but His own reply to the woman who once said this to Himself (see on ch. xi. 27, 28) is enough to teach us that this blessedness of His virgin-mother is not to be mixed up or confounded with her personal character—high as no doubt that was. **blessed art thou among women!** This clause is excluded from the text here by *Tischendorf*, and *Tregelles* brackets it as of doubtful authority, though admitted to be without question in *v.* 42. *Alford* excludes it from his text, and *Meyer* pronounces against it. But the authority in favour of the clause here also is immensely preponderating. *Lachmann* inserts it. The expression, "Blessed among women," is Old Testament language for "Most blessed of women." **29. And when she saw him, she was troubled, &c. 30. And the angel said unto her, Fear not, &c. 31. And, behold, thou shalt conceive in thy womb, and bring forth a son, and shalt call his name JESUS.** See on Matt. i. 21-23. **32, 33. He shall be great, &c.** The whole of this magnificent announcement is purposely couched in almost the terms of Isaiah's sublime prediction (Isa. ix. 6). **He shall be great.** Of His Forerunner too it had been said by the same Gabriel, "He

shall be great;" but it was immediately added, "in the sight of the Lord"—an explanation highly suitable in the case of a *mere servant*, but omitted, with evident purpose, in the present case. Indeed, the words that follow, **and shall be called the Son of the Highest**—or, "of the Most High" [υἱὸς ὑψίστου = בֶּן-עֶלְיוֹן], would have forbidden such an explanation, as altogether unsuitable here. And is there one reader of unsophisticated and teachable spirit who can take these last words as designed to express a merely figurative relation of a creature to God? But see on John v. 18; and on Rom. viii. 32. **33. And he shall reign over the house of Jacob**—God's visible people, who then stood in Jacob's descendants, but soon to take in all the families of the earth who should come under the Redeemer's ample wing; **and of his kingdom there shall be no end.** The perpetuity of Messiah's kingdom, stretching even into eternity, was one of its brightest prophetic features. See 2 Sam. vii. 13; Ps. lxxii. 5, 7, 17; lxxxix. 36, &c.; Dan. ii. 44; vii. 13, 14. **34. Then said Mary, How shall this be, seeing I know not a man?** There was here none of the unbelief of Zacharias. On the contrary, taking the fact for granted, the simple import of the question seems to be—*On what principle is* this to be, so contrary to the hitherto unbroken law of human generation? Accordingly, instead of reproof, she receives an explanation on that very point, and in mysterious detail. **35. And the angel answered and said unto her, The Holy Ghost shall come upon thee** (see on Matt. i. 18), **and the power of the Highest**—the immediate energy of the Godhead, conveyed by the Holy Ghost, **shall overshadow thee.** What exquisite delicacy is there in the use of this word, suggesting how gentle, while yet efficacious, would be this power, and its mysterious secrecy too, as if withdrawn by a cloud from human scrutiny—as *Calvin* hints. **therefore also that holy thing which shall be born [of thee]** [τὸ γεννώμενον ἅγιον] —an expression denoting the singularity and consequent sanctity of this birth. The words "of thee" [ἐκ σου] are wanting in the best MSS., and even in the received text as printed by *Stephens* and the *Elzevirs*. **shall be called the Son of God.** That Christ is the Son of God in His Divine and eternal nature is clear from all the New Testament; yet here we see that Sonship efflorescing into human and palpable manifestation by His being born, through "the power of the Highest," an Infant of days. We must neither think of a double Sonship—a divine and a human—as some

36 thing which shall be born of thee shall be called the *g*Son of God. And, behold, thy cousin Elisabeth, she hath also conceived a son in her old
37 age: and this is the sixth month with her, who was called barren. For
38 *h*with God nothing shall be impossible. And Mary said, Behold the handmaid of the Lord; be it unto me according to thy word. And the angel departed from her.
39 And Mary arose in those days, and went into the hill country with
40 haste, *i*into a city of Juda; and entered into the house of Zacharias, and
41 saluted Elisabeth. And it came to pass, that, when Elisabeth heard the salutation of Mary, the babe leaped in her womb; and Elisabeth was
42 filled *j*with the Holy Ghost; and she spake out with a loud voice, and said, *k*Blessed *art* thou among women, and blessed *is* the fruit of thy
43 womb. And whence *is* this to me, that the mother of my Lord should

A. M. 4000.

g Matt. 14. 33.
Matt. 26. 63.
Mark 1. 1.
John 1. 34.
John 20. 31.
Acts 8. 37.
Rom. 1. 4.
h Gen. 18. 14.
Jer. 32. 17.
Zec. 8. 6.
Rom. 4. 21.
i Jos. 21. 9.
j Acts 6. 3.
Eph. 5. 18.
Rev. 1. 10.
k Jud. 5. 24.

do, harshly and groundlessly, nor yet deny what is here plainly expressed, the connection between His human birth and His proper personal Sonship. **36. And, behold, thy cousin**—rather, 'relative' [συγγενὶς]; for how nearly they were related the word does not decide. Though Elisabeth was of the tribe of Levi and Mary of Judah, as will afterwards appear, they might still be related, as intermarriage among the tribes was permitted. **she hath also conceived a son in her old age: and this is the sixth month with her, who was called barren.** This was to Mary an *unsought* sign, in reward of a faith so simple; and what a contrast to the demanded sign which unbelieving Zacharias got! **37. For with God nothing shall be impossible**—reminding her, for her encouragement, of what had been said to Abraham in like case (Gen. xviii. 14). The future tense here employed [ἀδυνατήσει], "shall be impossible," is designed to express an enduring principle—*q. d.*, 'With God nothing ever has been nor ever shall be impossible.' **38. And Mary said, Behold the handmaid of the Lord; be it unto me according to thy word.** Marvellous faith, in the teeth of natural law, and in a matter which to one betrothed and already in law the wife of one of the royal line, fitted to inspire feelings in the last degree painful and embarrassing! Meet vessel for such a treasure!

Remarks.—The reflections most naturally suggested by this Section are best conveyed by the blessed Virgin herself, in the exalted Hymn which she uttered under the roof of Elisabeth. But such as she could not express may here be indicated. 1. The language in which the angel conveyed to the Virgin the mode in which her Offspring was to come into the world is nearly as remarkable as the event itself. It is too far removed from ordinary phraseology, and, considering the low state of tone and feeling then prevalent—which is well reflected in the apocryphal gospels of a somewhat later date—too lofty in its delicate simplicity to admit of any doubt that it is the very phraseology employed by the angel. And when it is remembered how every word and turn of expression in this most remarkable verse—containing all the information we possess on this subject—has been scrutinized by friends and foes in every age, and compared with all we otherwise know of the Person and Character of Jesus of Nazareth; and that not a word or shade of thought in it has been found unsuitable to the occasion, but everything in keeping with circumstances of surpassing sacredness and delicacy, what a character of *divine authority* does it stamp upon this Third Gospel! 2. The information given us in this verse furnishes the only adequate key to the sinless life of the Virgin's Son. As the facts of His recorded History show Him to have been throughout the "Undefiled and Separate from

sinners," so we have here the root of it all, in that operation of the Holy Ghost which after His birth had merely to be continued as an indwelling energy, in order to develop all that was seminally there from the first.

39-56.—VISIT OF MARY TO ELISABETH. This is the third scene in the great Story of Redemption, beautifully knitting up the two former.
39. And Mary arose in those days, and went into the hill country—a mountain-range, running north to south from the one extremity of Palestine to the other, in a parallel course to the Jordan, and nearly dividing the country in two. It is the most striking of all the physical features of the country. In Judea this "hill country" stands well out from the flat parts around it, and it was thither that Mary hied her. **with haste**—the haste, not of trepidation, but of transport, not only at the wonderful announcement she had to make to her relative, but at the scarcely less astonishing news she expected to receive from her of her own condition. **into a city of Juda.** Writing in the first instance to Gentiles, it was not necessary to be more particular; but without doubt the city was Hebron: see Jos. xx. 7; xxi. 11. **40. And entered into the house of Zacharias, and saluted Elisabeth**—now returned from her seclusion (*v.* 24). **41. And it came to pass, that, when Elisabeth heard the salutation, the babe leaped in her womb.** That this was like nothing of the same kind which she had felt before, and with which mothers are familiar, is plain from *v.* 44: nor does Elisabeth ascribe to it merely an extraordinary character; she describes it, and this when "filled with the Holy Ghost," as a sympathetic emotion of the unconscious babe at the presence of her and his Lord. **and Elisabeth was filled with the Holy Ghost; 42. And she spake out.** This word [ἀνεφώνησε] is often used classically of persons who burst into poetic exclamations: **with a loud voice, and said, Blessed art thou among women**—that is, most blessed of all women, **and blessed is the fruit of thy womb.** In the case of Mary, there was, as yet, no visible evidence that she had even conceived, nor does she appear to have had time to communicate to Elisabeth the tidings she came to bring her. But the rapt spirit of this honoured woman sees all as already accomplished. **43. And whence is this to me, that the mother of my Lord should come to me?** What beautiful superiority to *envy* have we here? High as was the distinction conferred upon herself, Elisabeth loses sight of it altogether, in presence of one more honoured still; upon whom, and on her unborn Babe, in an ecstasy of inspiration, she pronounces a benediction, feeling it to be a wonder unaccountable that "the mother of her Lord should come to *her.*" 'Turn this as we will,' says *Olshausen,* 'we shall never

44 come to me? For, lo, as soon as the voice of thy salutation sounded in
45 mine ears, the babe leaped in my womb for joy. And blessed *is* she
   [3]that believed: for there shall be a performance of those things which
46 were told her from the Lord. And Mary said,
    [l]My soul doth magnify the Lord,
47 And my spirit hath rejoiced in God my Saviour.
48 For [m]he hath regarded the low estate of his handmaiden:
    For, behold, from henceforth [n] all generations shall call me blessed.
49 For he that is mighty hath done to me great things;
    And holy *is* his name.
50 And [o]his mercy *is* on them that fear him
    From generation to generation.
51 He [p]hath showed strength with his arm:
    [q]He hath scattered the proud in the imagination of their hearts.
52 He [r]hath put down the mighty from *their* seats,
    And exalted them of low degree.
53 He [s]hath filled the hungry with good things;
    And the rich he hath sent empty away.
54 He hath holpen his servant Israel, [t]in remembrance of *his* mercy,
55 As [u]he spake to our fathers, to Abraham, and to his seed for ever.
56   And Mary abode with her about three months, and returned to her
    own house.

A. M. 4000.
[3] Or, which believed that there.
[l] 1 Sam. 2. 1.
[m] 1 Sam. 1.11.
Ps. 138. 6.
[n] Mal. 3, 12.
ch. 11. 27.
[o] Gen. 17. 7.
Ex. 20. 6.
Ps. 85. 9.
Ps. 118. 4.
Ps. 145. 19.
Ps. 147. 11.
Mal. 3. 16-18.
Rev. 19. 5.
[p] Ps. 98. 1.
Ps. 118. 15.
[q] Ps. 33. 10.
1 Pet. 5. 5.
[r] 1 Sam. 2. 6.
Ps. 113. 6.
[s] Ps. 34. 10.
[t] Ps. 98. 3.
Jer. 31 3,20.
[u] Gen. 17. 19.
Gal. 3. 16.

be able to see the propriety of calling an unborn child "Lord," but by supposing Elisabeth, like the prophets of old, enlightened to perceive the Messiah's *Divine nature.*' Cf. ch. xx. 42; John xx. 28. **44. For, lo, as soon, &c.. 45. And blessed is she that believed: for** [ὅτι] **there shall be a performance of those things which were told her from the Lord**—or, rather, perhaps (as in *marg.*) "Blessed is she that believed that there shall be a performance," &c. But the word will bear either sense. This is an additional benediction on the Virgin for her implicit faith, in tacit and delicate contrast with her own husband. **46. And Mary said**—Magnificent canticle! in which the strain of Hannah's ancient song, in like circumstances, is caught up, and just slightly modified and sublimed. Is it unnatural to suppose that the spirit of the blessed Virgin had been drawn beforehand into mysterious sympathy with the ideas and the tone of this hymn, so that when the life and fire of inspiration penetrated her whole soul it spontaneously swept the chords of this song, enriching the Hymnal of the Church with that spirit-stirring canticle which has resounded ever since from its temple walls? In both songs those holy women—filled with wonder to behold "the proud, the mighty, the rich," passed by, and, in their persons, the lowliest chosen to usher in the greatest events—sing of this as being no exceptional movement but a great law of the kingdom of God, by which He delights to "put down the mighty from their seats, and exalt them of low degree." In both songs the strain dies away on CHRIST: in Hannah's, under the name of "Jehovah's King," to whom, through all His line from David onwards to Himself, He will "give strength," and as His "Anointed," whose horn He will exalt (1 Sam. ii. 10); in the Virgin's song, it is as the "Help" promised to Israel by all the prophets. **My soul doth magnify the Lord, 47. And my spirit**—or, "all that is within me" (Ps. ciii. 1), **hath rejoiced in God my Saviour.** Mary never dreamt, we see, of her 'own immaculate conception' —to use the offensive language of the Romanists— any more than of her own immaculate life. **48. For**

he hath regarded the low estate of his handmaiden—for the family of David was now very low in Israel (as predicted, Isa. xi. 1). **for, behold, from henceforth all generations shall call me blessed.** In spirit, her eye stretching into all succeeding time, and beholding the blessed fruits of Messiah's benign and universal sceptre, her heart is overpowered with the honour in which herself shall be held in every succeeding age, as having been selected to give Him birth. **49-53. For he that is mighty hath done to me great things . . . 50. And his mercy is on them that fear him from generation to generation. 51. He hath showed strength with his arm . . . 52. He hath put down the mighty . . . 53. He hath filled the hungry, &c.** [The *aorists* here—ἐποίησεν, down to ἐξαπέστειλεν—express a general principle, as seen in a succession of single examples; according to a known, though peculiar application of that tense.] Mary here recognizes, in God's procedure towards herself—in His passing by all those families and individuals whom He might have been expected to select for such an honour, and pitching upon one so insignificant as herself—one of the greatest laws of His kingdom in overpowering operation, (cf. ch. xiv. 11; xviii. 14, &c.) **54. He hath holpen his servant Israel, in remembrance of his mercy.** Cf. Ps. lxxxix. 19, "I have laid *help* on One that is mighty." **55. (As he spake to our fathers)**—*These words should be read as a parenthesis*, **to Abraham**—that is, in remembrance of His mercy to Abraham, **and to his seed for ever.** See on *v.* 33, and cf. Mic. vii. 20; Ps. xcviii. 3.

56. And Mary abode with her about three months—that is, till there should be visible evidence of the fulfilment of the promise regarding her, **and returned to her own house**—at Nazareth. She had not yet been taken home by Joseph; but that was the next, or fourth, scene in this divine History. See on Matt. i. 18-25, where alone it is recorded.

Remarks.—1. 'Only the meeting of saints in heaven,' as *Bishop Hall* well remarks, 'can parallel the meeting of these two cousins: the two wonders of the world are met under one

57 Now Elisabeth's full time came that she should be delivered; and
58 she brought forth a son. And her neighbours and her cousins heard
how the Lord had showed great mercy upon her; and they rejoiced
with her.

59 And it came to pass, that *ᵛon the eighth day they came to circumcise
the child; and they called him Zacharias, after the name of his father.
60 And his mother answered and said, Not *so;* but he shall be called John.
61 And they said unto her, There is none of thy kindred that is called by
62 this name. And they made signs to his father, how he would have him
63 called. And he asked for a writing table, and wrote, saying, His name
64 is John. And they marvelled all. And his mouth was opened im-
65 mediately, and his tongue *loosed,* and he spake, and praised God. And
fear came on all that dwelt round about them: and all these ⁴sayings
66 were noised abroad throughout all the hill country of Judea. And
all they that heard *them* ʷlaid *them* up in their hearts, saying, What
manner of child shall this be! And ˣthe hand of the Lord was with
him.

67 And his father Zacharias ʸwas filled with the Holy Ghost, and prophesied, saying,

A. M. 4000.
ᵛ Gen. 17. 12.
Gen. 21. 4.
Lev. 12. 3.
ch. 2. 21.
Acts 7. 8.
Phil. 3. 5.
4 Or, things.
ʷ Gen. 37. 11.
Dan. 7. 28.
ch. 2. 19.
ch. 9. 44.
ˣ Gen. 39. 2.
Jud. 13. 24.
1 Sam. 2.18.
1Sam.16.18.
1 Ki. 18. 46.
Ps. 80. 17.
Ps. 89. 21.
Acts 11. 21.
ʸ Num.11,25.
2 Sam. 23.2.
2 Chr.20.14.
Joel 2. 28.
2 Pet. 1. 21.

roof, and congratulate their mutual happiness.' 2. What an honoured roof was that which for the period of three months overarched those holy women, whose progeny—though the one was but the herald of the other—have made the world new! And yet not a trace of it is now to be seen, nor can it even be known, save by inference, what "city of Juda" is meant to which the Virgin hied her to visit her relative. This remark, applicable to most of the so-called 'holy places,' not only rebukes the childish superstition of the Greek and Latin Churches, which have built convents at nearly all these places, and filled them with lazy monks, whose monotonous and dreary services are designed to commemorate the events of which they were the scenes, but may also suggest matter for useful reflection to a class of Protestants whose religion is not free from the same tincture. 3. How beautiful does womanhood appear in the light of the foregoing scenes—the grace of God making the "spices" of modesty, simplicity, and religious susceptibility, which are the characteristics of the sex, so charmingly to "flow out!" And yet these are but premonitions of what we shall meet with throughout all this History of Him to whom woman owes not only the common salvation but the recovery of her proper relation to the other sex. 4. 'How should our hearts leap within us,' to use again the words of *Bishop Hall,* 'when the Son of God vouchsafes to come into the secret of our souls, not to visit us, but to dwell with us, to dwell in us!'

57-80.—BIRTH, CIRCUMCISION, AND NAMING OF THE FORERUNNER—SONG OF ZACHARIAS, AND PROGRESS OF THE CHILD.

Birth, Circumcision, and Naming of the Forerunner (57-66). **57. Now Elisabeth's full time came . . . and she brought forth a son. 58. And her neighbours . . . rejoiced with her. 59. And it came to pass, that on the eighth day they came to circumcise the child.** The law which required circumcision to be performed on the eighth day (Gen. xvii. 12) was so strictly observed, that it was done even on the Sabbath if it fell on that day; although it was of the nature of servile work, which on the Sabbath day was prohibited. See John vii. 22, 23; and Phil. iii. 5. **and they called him** [ἐκάλουν]—rather, 'were calling,' that is, 'were going to call him' **Zacharias.** The naming

222

of children at baptism has its origin in this Jewish custom at circumcision (Gen. xxi. 3, 4; ch. ii. 21), and the names of Abram and Sarai were changed at its first performance (Gen. xvii. 5, 15). **after the name of his father. 60-63. And his mother answered and said, Not so; but he shall be called John . . . And they made signs to his father, how he would have him called**—showing that he was deaf as well as dumb. **And he asked for a writing table, and wrote, saying, His name is John. And they marvelled all**—at his concurring with his wife in giving to the child a name so new in the family; not knowing of any communication between them on the subject. **64. And his mouth was opened immediately, and his tongue loosed** —on his thus showing how entirely the unbelief for which he had been struck dumb had passed away. Probably it ceased immediately on his receiving the *sign,* so different from what he expected; and as the truth of the promise became palpable in Elisabeth, and was so gloriously confirmed during the visit of Mary, it would ripen doubtless into full assurance. But the words of the angel behoved to be fulfilled to the letter, "Thou shalt be dumb *until the day that these things shall be performed;*" and since one of these things was "*Thou shalt call his name John,*" it was fitting that not before, but "immediately" upon his doing this, his mouth should be opened. **and he spake, and praised God.** The song in which he did this being long, the Evangelist postpones it till he has recorded the effect which these strange doings produced upon the neighbourhood. **65. And fear** —or a religious awe, **came on all that dwelt round about them**—under the conviction that God's hand was specially in these events (cf. ch. v. 26; vii. 16): **and all these sayings were noised abroad throughout all the hill country of Judea. 66. And all they that heard them laid them up in their hearts, saying, What manner of child shall this be!** Yet there is every reason to believe that long ere John appeared in public all these things were forgotten, nor were recalled even after that by his wonderful success. **And the hand of the Lord was with him**—by special tokens marking him out as destined to some great work (cf. I Ki. xviii. 46; 2 Ki. iii. 15; Acts xi. 21).

67. And Zacharias was filled with the Holy Ghost, and prophesied—or, spake by inspiration, according to the Scripture sense of that term. It

68   Blessed *be* the Lord God of Israel;
     For he hath visited and redeemed his people,
69   And hath raised up an horn of salvation for us
     In the house of his servant David;
70   As *²*he spake by the mouth of his holy prophets,
     Which have been since the world began;
71   That we should be saved from our enemies,
     And from the hand of all that hate us;
72   To *ᵃ*perform the mercy *promised* to our fathers,
     And to remember his holy covenant,
73   The *ᵇ*oath which he sware to our father Abraham,
74   That he would grant unto us,
     That we, being delivered out of the hand of our enemies,
     Might *ᶜ*serve him without fear,
75   In *ᵈ*holiness and righteousness before him, all the days of our life.
76   And thou, child, shalt be called the Prophet of the Highest:
     For *ᵉ*thou shalt go before the face of the Lord to prepare his ways:
77   To give knowledge of salvation unto his people,
     *⁵*By the remission of their sins,

A. M. 4000.
ᶻ Jer. 23. 5.
Jer. 30. 10.
Dan. 9. 24.
Acts 3. 21.
Rom. 1. 2.
ᵃ Gen. 12. 3.
Lev. 26. 42.
Ps 93. 3.
Acts 3. 25.
ᵇ Gen. 12. 3.
Heb. 6. 13.
ᶜ Rom. 6. 18.
Heb. 9. 14.
ᵈ Jer. 32. 39.
Eph. 4. 24.
2 Thes. 2. 13.
2 Tim. 1. 9.
Titus 2. 12.
1 Pet. 1. 15.
2 Pet. 1. 4.
ᵉ Isa. 40. 3.
Mal 3. 1.
Matt 11. 10.
⁵ Or, for.

did not necessarily include the prediction of future events, though here it certainly did. **saying,**
68. Blessed. There is not a word in this noble burst of divine song about his own relationship to this child, nor about the child at all, till it has expended itself upon Christ. Like rapt Elisabeth, Zacharias loses sight entirely of self in the glory of a Greater than both. **be the Lord God of Israel**—the ancient covenant-God of the peculiar people; **for he hath visited and redeemed**—that is, visited in order to redeem **his people**—returning to His own after long absence, and now for the first time breaking the silence of centuries. In the Old Testament God is said to "visit" chiefly for *judgment*, in the New Testament for *mercy*. Zacharias—looking from the Israelitish point of view—would as yet have but imperfect apprehensions of the design of this "visit" and the nature of this "redemption." But though, when he sang of "salvation from our enemies, and from the hand of all that hated us," the *lower* and more *outward* sense would naturally occur first to Zacharias as a devout Jew, his words are equally adapted, when viewed in the light of a loftier and more comprehensive kingdom of God, to convey the most spiritual conceptions of the redemption that is in Christ Jesus. (But see on *v.* 77.) **69. And hath raised up an horn of salvation for us**—that is, a 'strength of salvation,' or 'a mighty salvation;' meaning the Saviour Himself, whom Simeon in his song calls "Thy Salvation" (ch. ii. 30). The metaphor is taken from those animals whose strength lies in their horns, and was familiar in the Psalmody of the agricultural Jews, (Ps. cxxxii. 17; lxxv. 10; xviii. 2, &c.) **in the house of his servant David.** *This shows that Mary must have been of the royal line,* independent of Joseph—of whom Zacharias could not know that after this he would recognize his legal connection with Mary. The Davidic genealogy of the Messiah, as it was one of the most prominent of His predicted characteristics, and one by which the Jews were warranted and prepared to test the pretensions of any claimant of that office who should arise, so it is here emphatically sung of as fulfilled in the unborn Offspring of the blessed Virgin. **70. As he spake by the mouth of his holy prophets, which have been since the world began**—or, from the earliest period. **71. That we should be saved from our enemies, and from**

the hand of all that hate us; **72. To perform the mercy promised to our fathers, and to remember his holy covenant, 73. The oath which he sware to our father Abraham.** The whole work of Messiah, and the kingdom He was to establish on the earth, are represented here as a mercy promised, and pledged on oath, to Abraham and his seed, to be at an appointed period—"the fulness of time"—gloriously made good. Hence, not only *"grace,"* or the thing promised, but *"truth,"* or fidelity to the promise, are said to "come by Jesus Christ" (see on John i. 14, 16, 17). **74. That he would grant unto us, that we, being delivered out of the hand of our enemies, might serve him without fear, 75. In holiness and righteousness before him, all the days of our life.** How rich and comprehensive is the view here given of Messiah's work! First, the grand *purpose* of redemption—"that we should serve Him," that is, "the Lord God of Israel" (*v.* 68): the word [λατρεύειν] signifies *religious* service, and points to the priesthood of believers under the New Testament (Heb. xiii. 10, 15). Second, the *nature* of this service—"in holiness and righteousness before Him"—or, in His presence (cf. Ps. lvi. 13). Third, its *freedom*—"being delivered out of the hand of our enemies." Fourth, its *fearlessness*—"might serve Him without fear." Fifth, its *duration*—"all our days." [The words τῆς ζωῆς are quite wanting in authority.]
76-79. Here are the dying echoes of this song: and very beautiful are these closing notes—like the setting sun, shorn indeed of its noon-tide radiance, but skirting the horizon with a wavy and quivering light, as of molten gold—on which the eye delights to gaze, till it disappears from the view. The song passes not here from Christ to John, but only from Christ direct, to Christ as heralded by his Forerunner. **76. And thou, child**—not, 'thou, my son,' for this child's relation to himself was lost in his relation to a Greater than either; **shalt be called the Prophet of the Highest: for thou shalt go before the face of the Lord**—that is, "before the face of the Most High." As this epithet is in Scripture applied to the supreme God, it is inconceivable that Inspiration should here so plainly apply it to Christ, if He were not "over all, God blessed for ever" (Rom. ix. 5). **77. To give knowledge of salvation.** To sound the note of a needed and provided salvation—now at the

78 Through the ⁶tender mercy of our God,
    Whereby the ⁷dayspring from on high hath visited us,
79 To ᶠgive light to them that sit in darkness and *in* the shadow of death,
    To guide our feet into the way of peace.
80   And the child grew, and waxed strong in spirit, and was in the deserts
    till the day of his showing unto Israel.

2   AND it came to pass in those days, that there went out a decree from
2 Cesar Augustus, that all the world should be ¹taxed. (*And* this taxing
3 was first made when Cyrenius was governor of Syria.) And all went to

Marginal notes:
A. M. 4000.
⁶ Or, bowels of the mercy.
⁷ Or, sunrising.
ᶠ Isa. 9. 2.
CHAP. 2.
¹ Or, enrolled in order to be taxed.

---

door—was the noble, the distinguishing office of the Forerunner. **by**—rather, 'in' **the remission of their sins** [ἐν ἀφέσει ἀμαρτιῶν αὐτῶν]—this remission being, not the way, but rather the primary element of salvation (cf. 1 John ii. 12). This view of salvation throws great light upon the *Jewish* language of verses 71 and 74, about "deliverance from enemies," stamping an undeniably *spiritual* character upon it. **78. Through the tender mercy of our God**—which is, and must be, the sole spring of all salvation for sinners; **whereby the dayspring from on high hath visited us.** This may mean either Christ Himself, as "the Sun of Righteousness," arising on a dark world (so *Calvin, Beza, Grotius, de Wette, Olshausen,* &c., understand it), or the glorious light which He sheds: the sense is the same. **79. To give light to them that sit in darkness and in the shadow**—rather, 'in the darkness and shadow' **of death**—meaning, 'in the most utter darkness.' So this expression should always be understood in the Old Testament, from which it is taken. Even in Ps. xxiii. 4, its application to the *dying hour* is but one, though certainly the most resistless and delightful, application of a great comprehensive truth—that believers have no reason to fear the most unrelieved darkness through which, in the mysterious providence of "the Lord their Shepherd," they may be called to pass. **to guide our feet into the way of peace.** Christianity is distinguished from all other religions, not only in bringing to men *what* the troubled spirit most needs—"peace," even "the peace of God, which passeth all understanding"—but in opening up the one only "*way* of peace."

80. And the child grew, and waxed strong [ηὔξανεν καὶ ἐκραταιοῦτο] **in spirit.** The grammatical tenses here employed denote the continuance of the action—'kept growing (that is, bodily) and waxing strong in spirit,' or in mental development. **and was in the deserts**—probably "the wilderness of Judea," whence we find him issuing on his entrance into public life (Matt. iii. 1). **till the day of his showing unto Israel**—or of his presenting himself before the nation as Messiah's Forerunner. Retiring into this wilderness in early life, in the true Nazarite spirit, and there free from rabbinical influences and alone with God, his spirit would be educated, like Moses in the desert of Sinai, for his future high vocation.

Remarks.—1. While to the believing Gentiles—"aliens from the commonwealth of Israel, and strangers from the covenants of promise"—the Gospel came with all the freshness of an overpowering novelty; it came to the devout Israelite with all the charm of ancient and oft-repeated promises at length fulfilled, of hopes, divinely kindled but long deferred, in the end unexpectedly realized. It is this latter view of the Gospel which reigns in Zacharias' noble song, in which God is seen 'mindful of His grace and truth' to the house of Israel, accomplishing the high objects of the ancient economy, and introducing His people into the blessedness of a realized

224

salvation, and the dignity of a free and fearless service of their covenant-God. 2. The "Fearlessness" of the Christian life is no less emphatically celebrated here (*v.* 74) than its priestly sanctity and enduring character (*v.* 75): but is this a leading and manifest feature in our current Christianity? 3. If "the remission of our sins" be the primary element of our salvation (*v.* 77), why is it that there are so many of God's dear children who "through fear of death are all their lifetime subject to bondage"? For if "the sting of death be [unpardoned] sin," what else than the sense of forgiveness can dissolve that fear? And surely it cannot be God's will that His children should have to meet the last enemy without that weapon which effectually disarms him. 4. Seasons of comparative retirement have usually preceded and proved a precious preparative for great public usefulness: for example, Moses' sojourn in Midian; the Baptist's stay in the Judean desert (*v.* 80); our Lord's own privacy at Nazareth; Paul's three years in Arabia; Luther's ten month's seclusion at Wartburg; and Zwingli's two years and a half at Einsiedeln.

CHAP. II. 1–7.—THE BIRTH OF CHRIST.
1. And it came to pass in those days—a general reference to the foregoing transactions, particularly the birth of John, which preceded that of our Lord by about six months (ch. i. 26). **that there went out a decree from Cesar Augustus**—the first of the Roman emperors—**that all the world**—that is, the Roman empire; so called as being now virtually world-wide. **should be taxed**—or 'enrolled,' or 'register themselves.' **2. (And this taxing was first made when Cyrenius was governor of Syria)**—a very perplexing verse, inasmuch as Cyrenius, or Quirinus, appears not to have been governor of Syria for about ten years after the birth of Christ, and the taxing under his administration was what led to the insurrection alluded to in Acts v. 37 (cf. *Joseph.* Antt. xviii. 1. 1). That Augustus took steps towards introducing uniform taxation throughout the empire, has been proved beyond dispute (by *Savigny,* the highest authority on the Roman law); and candid critics, even of sceptical tendency, are forced to allow that no such glaring anachronism as the words, on the first blush of them, seem to imply, was likely to be fallen into by a writer so minutely accurate on Roman affairs as our Evangelist shows himself, in the Acts, to be. Some superior scholars would render the words thus: 'This registration was *previous to* Cyrenius being governor of Syria.' In this case, of course, the difficulty vanishes. But, as this is a very precarious sense of the word [πρώτη], it is better, with others, to understand the Evangelist to mean; that though the registration was now ordered with a view to the taxation, the taxing itself—an obnoxious measure in Palestine—was not carried out till the time of Quirinus. **3. And all went to be taxed, every one into his own city**—*i.e.*, the city of his *extraction*, according to the Jewish custom; not of his *abode*, which was the usual Roman method. **4. And Joseph also went up from Galilee, out of the**

4 be taxed, every one into his own city. And Joseph also went up from Galilee, out of the city of Nazareth, into Judea, unto *a*the city of David, which is called Bethlehem, (*b*because he was of the house and lineage of
5 David,) to be taxed with Mary his espoused wife, being great with child.
6 And so it was, that, while they were there, the days were accomplished
7 that she should be delivered. And *c*she brought forth her first-born son, and wrapped him in swaddling clothes, and laid him in *d*a manger; because there was no room for them in the inn.

A. M. 4000.

a 1 Sam. 16. 1.
Mic. 5. 2.
John 7. 42.
b Matt. 1. 16.
ch. 1. 27.
c Matt. 1. 25.
Gal. 4. 4.
d Isa. 53. 2.
2 Cor. 4. 4.

city of Nazareth, into Judea, unto the city of David, which is called Bethlehem, (because he was of the house and lineage of David.) The transfer from the one province to the other, and from the one city to the other, is carefully noted. **5. To be taxed with Mary his espoused**—'betrothed' **wife.** She had sometime before this been taken home by Joseph (see on Matt. i. 18-24); but she is so called here, perhaps, for the reason mentioned in Matt. i. 25. **being great with child.** Not only does Joseph, as being of the royal line, go to Bethlehem (1 Sam. xvi. 1), but Mary too; not from choice, surely, in her tender condition. It is possible that in this they simply followed the Roman method, of the wife accompanying the husband; but the more likely reason would seem to be that she herself was of the family of David.

6. And so it was, that, while they were there, the days were accomplished that she should be delivered. Mary had up to this time been living at the wrong place for Messiah's birth. A little longer stay at Nazareth, and the prophecy of His birth at Bethlehem would have failed. But, lo! with no intention on her part—much less on the part of Cesar Augustus—to fulfil the prophecy, she is brought from Nazareth to Bethlehem, and at that very nick of time her period for delivery arrives. **7. And she brought forth her first-born son** (see on Matt. i. 25), **and wrapped him in swaddling clothes, and laid him**—that is, the mother herself did so. Had she then none to assist her in such circumstances? All we can say is, it would seem so. **in a manger**—or crib, in which was placed the horses' food, **because there was no room for them in the inn**—a square erection, open inside, where travellers put up, and whose back parts were used as stables. The ancient tradition, that our Lord was born in a grotto or cave, is quite consistent with this, the country being rocky. In Mary's condition the journey would be a slow one, and ere they arrived the inn would be pre-occupied—affecting anticipation of the reception He was throughout to meet with (John i. 11).

> ' Wrapt in His swaddling bands,
> And in His manger laid,
> The hope and glory of all lands
> Is come to the world's aid.
> No peaceful home upon His cradle smiled,
> Guests rudely went and came where slept the royal Child.'
>   KEBLE.

But some 'guests went and came,' *not* 'rudely,' but reverently. God sent visitors of His own to pay court to the new-born King.

Remarks.—1. Cesar Augustus had his own ends to serve in causing steps to be taken for a general census of his kingdom. But God had ends in it too, and infinitely higher. Augustus must bring Joseph and Mary to Bethlehem, and bring them just before the time for the Virgin's delivery, that the mark of His Son's birth-place, which He had set up seven centuries before, might not be missed. Even so must Pharaoh dream, that Joseph might be summoned from prison to read it; and dream such a dream as required Joseph's elevation to be governor of all Egypt, in order to the fulfilment

of divine predictions (Gen. xl., &c.); and king Ahasuerus must pass a sleepless night, and beguile the weary hours with the chronicles of the kingdom, and read there of his obligations to Mordecai for the preservation of his life, in order that at the moment when he was to be sacrificed he might be lifted into a position to save his whole people (Esth. vi.); and Belshazzar must dream, and his dream must pass from him, and the wise men of Babylon must be required both to tell and to interpret it on pain of death, and all of them fail, in order that Daniel, by doing both, might be promoted along with his companions, for the present good and ultimate deliverance of his people, (Dan. ii., &c.) 2. In the Roman edict, which brought the Jews of Palestine to their several tribal towns, we see one of the badges of their lost independence. The splendour of the theocracy was now going fast down: but this was doubtless divinely ordered, that the new glory of Messiah's kingdom, which it dimly shadowed forth, might the more strikingly appear. 3. Our Evangelist simply records the fact, that the new-born Babe of Bethlehem was laid in a manger, because there was no room for them in the inn; leaving his readers from age to age to their own reflections on so stupendous a dispensation. 'Thou camest,' exclaims *Bp. Hall*, 'to Thine own, and Thine own received thee not: how can it trouble us to be rejected of the world, which is not ours?'

8-20.—ANGELIC ANNUNCIATION TO THE SHEPHERDS OF THE SAVIOUR'S BIRTH—THEIR VISIT TO THE NEW-BORN BABE.

Annunciation to the Shepherds (8-14). **8. And there were in the same country shepherds abiding in the field**—staying there, probably in huts or tents, **keeping watch** [φυλάσσοντες φυλακὰς τῆς νυκτὸς]—rather, 'keeping the night watches,' or taking their turn of watching **by night.** From this most critics, since *Lightfoot*, conclude that the time which, since the fourth century, has been ecclesiastically fixed upon for the celebration of Christ's birth—the 25th of December, or the midst of the rain season—cannot be the true time, as the shepherds drove their flocks about the spring or passover time out to the fields, and remained out with them all summer, under cover of huts or tents, returning with them late in the autumn. But recent travellers tell us that in the end of December, after the rains, the flowers come again into bloom, and the flocks again issue forth. The nature of the seasons in Palestine could hardly have been unknown to those who fixed upon the present Christmas-period: the difficulty, therefore, is perhaps more imaginary than real. But leaving this question undecided, another of some interest may be asked—Were these shepherds chosen to have the first sight of the blessed Babe without any respect to their own state of mind? That, at least, is not God's way. No doubt, as *Olshausen* remarks, they were, like Simeon (*v.* 25), among the waiters for the Consolation of Israel; and if the simplicity of their rustic minds, their quiet occupation, the stillness of the midnight hours, and the amplitude of the deep

8   And there were in the same country shepherds abiding in the field,
9 keeping [2]watch over their flock by night. And, lo, the angel of the
Lord came upon them, and the glory of the Lord shone round about
10 them; and they were sore afraid. And the angel said unto them, Fear
not; for, behold, I bring you good tidings of great joy, [e]which shall be
11 to all people. For [f]unto you is born this day, in the city of David, a
12 Saviour, [g]which is Christ the Lord. And this *shall be* a sign unto you;
Ye shall find the babe wrapped in swaddling clothes, lying in a manger.
13 And [h]suddenly there was with the angel a multitude of the heavenly
14 host praising God, and saying, Glory to God in the highest, and on
earth peace, good will toward men.

A. M. 4000.
[2] Or, the night watches.
[e] Gen. 12. 3. Col. 1. 23.
[f] Isa. 9. 6. Matt. 1. 21 Gal. 4. 4. 2 Tim. 1. 9. 1 John 4.14.
[g] Phil. 2. 11.
[h] Gen. 28. 12. Ps. 103. 20.

blue vault above them for the heavenly music which was to fill their ear, pointed them out as fit recipients for the first tidings of an Infant Saviour, the congenial meditations and conversations by which, we may suppose, they would beguile the tedious hours would perfect their preparation for the unexpected visit. Thus was Nathanael engaged, all alone but not unseen, under the fig tree, in unconscious preparation for his first interview with Jesus. (See on John i. 48.) So was the rapt seer on his lonely rock "in the spirit on the Lord's day," little thinking that this was his preparation for hearing behind him the trumpet-voice of the Son of Man, (Rev. i. 10, &c.) But if the shepherds in his immediate neighbourhood had the *first*, the sages from afar had the *next* sight of the new-born King. Even so still, simplicity first, science next, finds its way to Christ. Whom,

'In quiet ever and in shade
Shepherd and Sage may find;
They who have bowed untaught to Nature's sway,
And they who follow Truth along her star-pav'd way.'
KEBLE.

9. And, lo, the angel of the Lord came upon them, and the glory of the Lord—'the brightness or glory which is represented as encompassing all heavenly visions,' to use the words of *Olshausen*, **and they were sore afraid.** See on ch. i. 12. **10. And the angel said unto them, Fear not** (see on ch. i. 13); **for, behold, I bring you good tidings of great joy, which shall be to all people** [παντὶ τῷ λαῷ]—or rather, 'to the whole people;' meaning the chosen people of Israel, but only to be by them afterwards extended to the whole world, as a message of "good will to *men*" (*v.* 14). **11. For unto you is born this day, in the city of David, a Saviour, which is Christ the Lord.** Every word here contains transporting intelligence from heaven. For whom provided? "To *you*"—shepherds, Israel, mankind. Who is provided? "A SAVIOUR." What is He? "CHRIST THE LORD." How introduced into the world? He "is *born*"—as said the prophet, "Unto us a child is born" (Isa. ix. 6); "the Word was made flesh" (John i. 14). When? "*This Day*." Where? "*In the city of David*." In the predicted line, and at the predicted spot, where prophecy bade us look for Him and faith accordingly expected Him. How dear to us should be these historical moorings of our faith, with the loss of which all historical Christianity vanishes! By means of them how many have been kept from making shipwreck, and have attained to a certain admiration of Christ, ere yet they have fully "beheld His glory"! Nor does the angel say that One is born who *shall be* a Saviour, but He "is *born* a Saviour;" adding, "which is CHRIST THE LORD." 'Magnificent appellation!' exclaims devout *Bengel*. *Alford* notices that these words come together nowhere else, and sees no way of understanding this "Lord" but as corresponding to the Hebrew word

JEHOVAH. **12. And this shall be a sign** [τὸ σημεῖον] —'the sign,' **unto you; Ye shall find the babe** [βρέφος]—'a Babe.' Pity that our translators so often insert the definite article where it is emphatically wanting in the original, and omit it where in the original it is emphatically inserted. **wrapped in swaddling clothes, lying in a manger.** Here the article, though existing in the received text, ought not to be there, having but weak authority: our translators, therefore, are right here. The sign, it seems, was to consist solely in the overpowering *contrast* between the lofty things just said of Him and the lowly condition in which they would find Him. 'Him whose goings forth have been from of old, from everlasting, ye shall find a Babe: Whom the heaven of heavens cannot contain ye shall find "wrapped in swaddling bands and lying in a manger!"' Thus early were those amazing contrasts, which are His chosen style, held forth. (See 2 Cor. viii. 9.) **13. And suddenly**—as if eager to break in as soon as the last words of the wonderful tidings had dropped from their fellow's lips, **there was with the angel**—not in place of him; for he retires not, and is only joined by others, come to seal and to celebrate the tidings which he was honoured first to announce, **a multitude of the heavenly host**—or 'army;' 'An army,' as *Bengel* quaintly remarks, 'celebrating peace!' come down to let it be known here how this great event is regarded in heaven: **praising God, and saying, 14. Glory to God in the highest, and on earth peace, good will toward men**—brief but transporting hymn, not only in articulate human speech for our behoof, but in tunable measure, in the form of a Hebrew parallelism of two complete members, and a third one, as we take it, only explaining and amplifying the second, and so without the connecting "and." The "glory to God" which the new-born Saviour was to bring is the first note of this exalted hymn, and was sounded forth probably by one detachment of the choir. To this answers the "peace on earth," of which He was to be the Prince (Isa. ix. 6), probably sung responsively by a second detachment of the celestial choir; while quick follows the glad echo of this note— "good will to men"—by a third detachment, we may suppose, of these angelic choristers. Thus:—
First division of the celestial choir—
"GLORY TO GOD IN THE HIGHEST."
Second——
"AND ON EARTH PEACE."
Third——
"GOOD WILL TO MEN."
Peace with God is the grand necessity of a fallen world. To bring in this, in whose train comes all other peace worthy of the name, was the prime errand of the Saviour to this earth. This effected, Heaven's whole "good will to men" or the Divine complacency [εὐδοκία, cf. Eph. i. 5, 9; Phil. ii. 13, &c.] descends now on a new footing to rest upon men, even as upon the Son Himself, "in

15   And it came to pass, as the angels were gone away from them into heaven, [3]the shepherds said one to another, [4]Let us now go even unto Bethlehem, and see this thing which is come to pass, which the Lord
16 hath made known unto us.   And they came with haste, and found Mary
17 and Joseph, and the babe lying in a manger.   And when they had seen *it*, they made known abroad the saying which was told them concerning
18 this child.   And all they that heard *it* wondered at those things which
19 were told them by the shepherds.   But [j]Mary kept all these things, and
20 pondered *them* in her heart.   And the shepherds returned, glorifying and praising God for all the things that they had heard and seen, as it was told unto them.

A. M. 4000.
[3] The men the shepherds.
[4] Ex. 3. 3. Ps. 111. 2. Matt. 2. 1. Matt.12 42. John 20. 1-10.
[j] Gen. 37. 11. 1Sam.21.12. Pro. 4. 4. Hos. 14. 9.

whom God is well pleased" [εὐδόκησα, Matt. iii. 17]. *Bengel* notices that they say not 'glory to God in heaven,'—but using a rare expression—"in the highest" heavens [ἐν ὑψίστοις], whither angels aspire not (Heb. i. 3, 4). [The reading, 'to men of good will'—ἐν ἀνθρώποις εὐδοκίας—is introduced into the text by *Tischendorf* and *Tregelles*, after *Lachmann*—on the authority of the Alexandrian and Beza MSS. (A and D); but chiefly on the strength of the Latin versions, and from the difficulty of accounting for so uncommon a reading occurring at all if not genuine. In this case the sense will still be agreeable to Scripture doctrine—'to men of (His, that is, God's) good will,' or the objects of the Divine complacency; not as the Romish Church, after the Vulgate, take it to mean, 'to men of good disposition.' But the great preponderance of MSS. and versions is in favour of the received reading; nor will the objections to it, as spoiling the rhythm, appear the least force in the view we have given of it above, but just the reverse. *De Wette, Meyer, Alford,* and *van Osterzee,* are decidedly in favour of the received reading.]

Visit of the Shepherds to the New-born Babe (15-20). **15. And it came to pass, as the angels were gone away from them into heaven, the shepherds** [οἱ ἄνθρωποι οἱ ποιμένες]—'the men, the shepherds,' in contrast with the angelic party, **said one to another, Let us now go even unto Bethlehem, and see this thing which is come to pass, which the Lord hath made known unto us.** Lovely simplicity of devoutness and faith this! They say not, Let us go and see if this be true—for they have no misgivings—but, "Let us go and see this thing *which is come to pass,* which the Lord hath *made known unto us.*" Does not this confirm the view we have given (on *v.* 8) of the previous character of these humble shepherds? Nor are they taken up with the angels, the glory that invested them, and the lofty strains with which they filled the air. It is the Wonder itself, the Babe of Bethlehem, that absorbs these devout shepherds. **16. And they came with haste** (see on ch. i. 39; Matt. xxviii. 8), **and found Mary** —'mysteriously guided,' says *Olshausen,* 'to the right place through the obscurity of the night,' **and Joseph, and the babe lying in a manger** — [ἐν τῇ φάτνῃ] 'the manger,' of which the angel had told them. **17. And when they had seen it, they made known abroad the saying which was told them concerning this child**—that is, as is evident from *v.* 20, before they left the neighbourhood. And so they were, as *Bengel* remarks, the first evangelists; having, indeed, no commission, but feeling with Peter and John, "We cannot but speak the things which we have seen and heard." **18. And all they that heard it wondered at those things which were told them by the shepherds. 19. But Mary kept all these things, and pondered**—or 'revolved' **them in her heart**—

seeking to gather from them, in combination, what light she could as to the future of this wondrous Babe of hers. **20. And the shepherds returned, glorifying and praising God for all the things that they had heard and seen, as it was told unto them.** The word for "praising" [αἰνοῦντες] —used of the song of the angels (*v.* 13), and in ch. xix. 37, and xxiv. 53—would lead us to suppose that theirs was a song too, and perhaps some canticle from the Psalter; meet vehicle for the swelling emotions of their simple hearts at what "they had seen and heard."

Remarks.—1. Not in the busy hum of day, but in the profound stillness of night, came these heavenly visitants to the shepherds of Bethlehem. So came the Lord to Abraham (Gen. xv.); and once and again to Jacob, (Gen. xxviii.; xxxii.; xlvi. 2, &c.) It was in the night season that Jesus Himself was transfigured on the mount. And who can tell what visits of Heaven were paid Him when He spent whole nights alone in prayer? See Ps. iv. 4; lxiii. 6; cxix. 55, 62, 147, 148; Isa. xxvi. 9; Job xxxv. 10.

> 'Sun of my soul, Thou Saviour dear,
> It is not night if Thou be near:
> O may no earth-born cloud arise
> To hide Thee from thy servant's eyes.
>
> 'Abide with me from morn till eve,
> For without Thee I cannot live:
> Abide with me when night is nigh,
> For without Thee I cannot die.'—KEBLE.

2. What a view of heaven is here disclosed to us! As it teems with angels (cf. Deut. xxxiii. 2; 1 Ki. xxii. 19; Ps. lxviii. 17; ciii. 20, 21; cxlviii. 2; Dan. vii. 10; Matt. xxvi. 53; xxv. 31; Rev. v. 11), all orderly, harmonious, and vocal, so their uniting principle, the soul of all their harmony, the Object of their chiefest wonder and transport, is the Word made flesh, the Saviour born in the city of David, Christ the Lord. Accordingly, as Moses and Elias, when they appeared in glory on the mount of transfiguration and talked with Him, "spake of His decease which He should accomplish at Jerusalem" (Luke ix. 31); so we are told that "these things the angels desire to look into" (1 Pet. i. 12); and among the wonders of the Incarnation, this is said to be one, that He "was seen of angels" (1 Tim. iii. 16). Is this our element upon earth? Would our sudden transportation to heaven bring us to "our own company" (Acts iv. 23), and "our own place"—as Judas went to his? (Acts i. 25). By this may all men know whether they be travelling thither. 3. If we would thoroughly sympathize with heaven in its views of Salvation, and be prepared at once to unite in its music, we must take the elements of which salvation consists as heaven here presents them to us. As the "peace on earth" of which they sing—expounded by that "good will to men" which is its abiding result— means God's own peace, or His "reconciling the

21 And [k]when eight days were accomplished for the circumcising of the child, his name was called [l]JESUS, which was so named of the angel before he was conceived in the womb.

22 And when [m]the days of her purification according to the law of Moses were accomplished, they brought him to Jerusalem, to present *him* to

A. M. 4000.

[k] Gen. 17. 12.
Lev. 12. 3.
Phil. 2. 8.
[l] Matt. 1. 21.
[m] Lev. 12. 2.

world unto Himself by Jesus Christ," we must regard this as the proper spring of all peace between man and man that is thoroughly solid and lasting. And even in experiencing, exemplifying, and diffusing this, let that "glory to God in the highest" which is due on account of the birth into our world of the Prince of peace, and for all that He has done to unite earth to heaven and man to man, be uppermost and first in all our thoughts, affections, and praises. 4. What wondrous contrasts are those shepherds of Bethlehem invited to contemplate—the Lord of glory, a Babe; Christ the Lord, born; the Son of the Highest, wrapped in swaddling bands and lying in a manger! Yet what was this but a foretaste of like overpowering contrasts of Infinite and finite, Divine and human, Fulness and want, Life and death, throughout all His after-history upon earth? "Ye know the grace of our Lord Jesus Christ, that though He was rich, yet for your sakes He became poor, that ye through His poverty might be rich" (2 Cor. viii. 9). Nor is the Church which He hath purchased with His own blood and erected upon earth a stranger to analogous contrasts. 5. When the Evangelist says, "It came to pass, as the angels *were gone away* from them into heaven," we are reminded that this was but a momentary visit—sweet but short. Like their Master, they "ascended up where they were before," even as the shepherds returned—to their flocks. But the time is coming when they and we shall dwell together. And so shall we all and ever be with the Lord. 6. Our Evangelist tells us that the shepherds "found Mary and Joseph, and the Babe lying in a manger." But he does *not* tell us what passed between the visitors and the visited in that rude birth-place of the Son of God. Apocryphal gospels would probably manufacture information enough on such topics, and gaping readers would greedily enough drink it in. But the silences of Scripture are as grand and reverend as its disclosures. In this light, when we merely read in the next verse, "And when they had seen [it], they made known abroad the saying that was told them concerning this Child," we feel that there is a Wisdom presiding over these incomparable Narratives, alike in the dropping as in the drawing of the veil, which fills the soul with ever-growing satisfaction. 7. The shepherds, not lifted off their feet, "returned"—"glorifying and praising God," indeed, but still returned—to their proper business. So Jesus Himself, at twelve years of age, after sitting in the temple among the doctors, and filling all with astonishment at His understanding and His answers, "went down with His parents, and came to Nazareth, and was subject unto them" (*v.* 51). Thus should it ever be; and O what a heaven upon earth would this hallowing of earthly occupations and interests and joys and sorrows by heavenly intercourses make!

21-24.—CIRCUMCISION OF THE INFANT SAVIOUR —PURIFICATION OF THE VIRGIN-MOTHER—PRESENTATION OF THE BABE IN THE TEMPLE. *Circumcision of the Infant Saviour* (21). **21. And when eight days were accomplished** (see on ch. i. 59) **for the circumcising of the child**—'for circumcising Him' is the better supported reading, **his name was called JESUS, which was so named of the angel before he was conceived,**

&c. Circumcision was a symbolical and bloody removal of the body of sin (Col. ii. 11, 13; cf. Deut. x. 16; Jer. iv. 4; Rom. ii. 29). But as if to proclaim, in the very act of performing this rite, that there was no body of sin to be removed in His case, but rather that He was the destined Remover of it from others, the name JESUS, in obedience to express command from heaven, was given Him at His circumcision, and given Him *"because,"* as said the angel, "He shall save His people from their sins" (Matt. i. 21). So significant was this, that His circumciser, had he been fully aware of what he was doing, might have said to Him, as John afterwards did, "I have need to be circumcised of Thee, and comest Thou to me?" and the answer, in this case as in that, would doubtless have been, "Suffer it to be so now: for thus it becometh us to fulfil all righteousness" (Matt. iii. 14, 15). Still, the circumcision of Christ had a profound bearing on His own work. For since he that is "circumcised is a debtor to do the whole law" (Gal. v. 3), the circumcised Saviour thus bore about with Him, in His very flesh, the seal of a voluntary *obligation* to do the whole law—by Him only possible in the flesh, since the fall. But further, as it was only to "redeem (from its curse) them that were under the law," that He submitted at all to be "made under the law" (Gal. iv. 4, 5; iii. 13), the obedience to which Jesus was bound over was purely a *redeeming* obedience, or the obedience of a "Saviour." Once more, as it was only by being made a curse for us that Christ could redeem us from the curse of the law (Gal. iii. 13), the circumcision of Christ is to be regarded as a virtual *pledge to die;* a pledge not only to yield obedience in general, but to be "obedient unto death, even the death of the cross" (Phil. ii. 8).

> 'Like sacrificial wine
> Pour'd on a victim's head
> Are those few precious drops of thine
> Now first to offering led.'—KEBLE.

Purification of the Virgin-Mother and Presentation of the Babe in the Temple (22-24). **22. And when the days of her purification.** This reading [αὐτῆς] has hardly any support at all. All the best and most ancient MSS. and versions read 'their purification' [αὐτῶν]—which some late transcribers had been afraid to write. But whether this is to be understood of mother and Babe together, or of Joseph and Mary, as the parents, the great fact that "we are shapen in iniquity, and in sin by our mothers conceived," which the Levitical rite was designed to proclaim, had no real place, and so could only be symbolically taught, in the present case; since "that which was conceived in the Virgin was of the Holy Ghost," and Joseph was only the Babe's legal father. **according to the law of Moses were accomplished.** The days of purification, in the case of a male child, were forty in all (Lev. xii. 2, 4): **they brought him to Jerusalem, to present him to the Lord.** All the first-born males had been claimed as "holy to the Lord," or set apart to sacred uses, in memory of the deliverance of the first-born of Israel from destruction in Egypt, through the sprinkling of blood (Exod. xiii. 2). In lieu of these, however, one whole tribe, that of Levi, was accepted, and set apart to occu-

23 the Lord; (as it is written in the law of the Lord, Every [n]male that
24 openeth the womb shall be called holy to the Lord;) and to offer a
sacrifice according to that which is said in the law of the Lord, A pair
of turtle doves, or two young pigeons.
25 And, behold, there was a man in Jerusalem, whose name *was* Simeon;
and the same man *was* just and devout, [o]waiting for the consolation of
26 Israel: and the Holy Ghost was upon him. And it was revealed unto
him by the Holy Ghost, that he should not [p]see death, before he had
27 seen the Lord's Christ. And he came by [q]the Spirit into the temple:
and when the parents brought in the child Jesus, to do for him after

A. M. 4000.
[n] Ex. 13. 2.
Ex. 22. 29.
Num. 3. 13.
[o] Isa. 40. 1.
Mark 15. 43.
[p] Ps. 89. 48.
Heb. 11. 5.
[q] Acts 8. 29.
Acts 10. 19.
Acts 16. 7.
Rev. 1. 10.
Rev. 17. 3.

pations exclusively sacred (Num. iii. 11-38);
and whereas there were fewer Levites than
first-born of all Israel on the first reckoning,
each of these supernumerary first-born was to
be redeemed by the payment of five shekels,
but not without being "*presented* [publicly]
unto the Lord," in token of His rightful claim
to them and their service. (Num. iii. 44-47;
xviii. 15-16). It was in obedience to this "law of
Moses," that the Virgin presented her Babe unto
the Lord, 'in the east gate of the court called
Nicanor's Gate, where herself would be sprinkled
by the priest with the blood of her sacrifice'
[*Lightfoot*]. By that Babe, in due time, we were
to be redeemed, "not with corruptible things as
silver and gold, but with the precious blood of
Christ" (1 Pet. i. 18, 19); and the consuming of the
mother's burnt offering, and the sprinkling of her
with the blood of her sin offering, were to find
their abiding realization in the "living sacrifice"
of the Christian mother herself, in the fulness of a
"heart sprinkled from an evil conscience" by
"the blood which cleanseth from all sin." 23. (As
it is written in the law of the Lord, Every male
that openeth the womb shall be called holy to
the Lord;) 24. And to offer a sacrifice according
to that which is said in the law of the Lord,
A pair of turtle doves, or two young pigeons.
The proper sacrifice was a lamb for a burnt
offering, and a turtle-dove or young pigeon for a
sin offering. But if a lamb could not be afforded,
the mother was to bring two turtle-doves or two
young pigeons; and if even this was beyond the
family means, then a portion of fine flour, but
without the usual fragrant accompaniments of oil
and frankincense, because it represented a sin
offering (Lev. xii. 6-8; v. 7-11). From this we gather
that our Lord's parents were in poor circumstances (2 Cor. viii. 9), and yet not in abject
poverty; as they neither brought the lamb, nor
availed themselves of the provision for the poorest, but presented the intermediate offering of
"a pair of turtle-doves, or two young pigeons."
Remarks.—1. We have here the first example
of that double aspect of Christ's conformity to
the law which characterized it throughout.
Viewed simply in the light of obedience—and
obedience in the highest sense voluntary, and
faultlessly perfect—it is for men the model-obe-
dience: He hath left us an example that we
should follow His steps (1 Pet. ii. 21). But as He
was made under the law only to redeem them that
were under the law, His obedience was more than
voluntary—it was strictly *self-imposed* obedience;
and since it is by the obedience of this One that
the many are made righteous (Rom. v. 19), it
had throughout, and in every part of it, a *substitutionary* character, which made it altogether unique.
As it was *human* obedience, it is our glorious
exemplar: but as it is *mediatorial* obedience—
strictly self-imposed and vicarious—a stranger
doth not intermeddle with it. Thus, Christ is at
229

once imitable and inimitable; and—paradoxical
though it may sound—it is just the inimitable
character of Christ's obedience that puts us in a
condition to look at it in its imitable character,
with the humble but confident assurance that we
shall be able to follow His steps. 2. That He
who was rich should for our sakes have become,
in the very circumstances of His birth, so poor
that His parents should not have been able to
afford a lamb for a burnt offering on His presentation in the temple—is singularly affecting; but
that this poverty was not so abject as to awaken
the emotion of *pity*—is one of those marks of
Wisdom in the arrangement even of the comparatively trivial circumstances of His history,
which bespeak the Divine presence in it all,
stamp the Evangelical Record with the seal of
truth, and call forth devout admiration.

25-39.—SIMEON AND ANNA RECOGNIZE THE
INFANT SAVIOUR IN THE TEMPLE—THE RETURN
TO NAZARETH, AND ADVANCEMENT OF THE CHILD
JESUS.

Simeon's Recognition of the Infant Saviour (25-35).
25. And, behold, there was a man in Jerusalem,
whose name was Simeon. The attempts that
have been made to identify this Simeon with a
famous man of the same name, but who died long
before, and with the father of Gamaliel, who bore
that name, are quite precarious. The name was a
common one. and the same man was just—upright
in his moral character, and devout—of a religious
frame of spirit, waiting for the consolation of
Israel—or, for the Messiah; a beautiful and pregnant title of the promised Saviour: and the Holy
Ghost was upon him—supernaturally. Thus was
the Spirit, after a dreary absence of nearly four
hundred years, returning to the Church, to quicken
expectation and prepare for coming events. 26.
And it was revealed unto him by the Holy Ghost,
that he should not see death before he had seen
the Lord's Christ. *Bengel* notices the 'sweet antithesis' here between the two sights—his "seeing
the Lord's Christ" ere he should "see death."
How would the one sight gild the gloom of the
other! He was probably by this time advanced
in years. 27. And he came by the Spirit into the
temple—the Spirit guiding him, all unconsciously,
to the temple at the very moment when the Virgin
was about to present the Infant to the Lord. Let
it here be observed, once for all, that whenever
the priests are said to go, or come, into "the
temple," as in ch. i. 9, the word always used [ὁ
ναός] is that which denotes the *temple proper*, into
which none might enter save the priests; and
never is this word used when our Lord, or any *not*
of the priestly family, is said to go into the temple:
in such case the word used [τὸ ἱερόν] is one of
wider signification, denoting any place *within the
sacred precincts.* So here of Simeon. and when
the parents brought in the child Jesus, to do for
him after the custom of the law, 28. Then took
he him up in his arms—the same Spirit that drew

28 the custom of the law, then took he him up in his arms, and blessed God, and said,

29 Lord, ^rnow lettest thou thy servant depart
In peace, according to thy word:

30 For mine eyes ^shave seen thy salvation,

31 Which thou hast prepared before the face of all people;

32 A ^tlight to lighten the Gentiles,
And the glory of thy people Israel.

33 And Joseph and his mother marvelled at those things which were

34 spoken of him. And Simeon blessed them, and said unto Mary his mother, Behold, this *child* is set for the ^ufall and rising again of many

35 in Israel: and for ^va sign which shall be spoken against; (yea, ^wa sword shall pierce through thy own soul also,) that ^xthe thoughts of many hearts may be revealed.

36 And there was one Anna, ^ya prophetess, the daughter of Phanuel, of the tribe of Aser: she was of a great age, and had lived with an husband

37 seven years from her virginity; and she *was* a widow of about fourscore and four years, which departed not from the temple, but served *God* with

A. M. 4000.
^r Gen. 46. 30.
1 Cor.15.54.
Phil. 1. 23.
Rev. 14. 13.
^s Isa. 52. 10.
Acts 4. 12.
^t Isa. 9. 2.
Acts 13. 47.
^u Isa. 8. 14.
Hos. 14. 9.
Rom. 9. 32.
1 Cor. 1. 23.
2 Cor. 2. 16.
1 Pet. 2.7,8.
^v Matt.11.19.
Acts 28. 22.
1 Pet. 2. 12.
1 Pet. 4. 14.
^w Ps. 42. 10.
John 19. 25.
^x 1 Cor 11.19.
^y Ex. 15. 20.

him thither revealing to him at once the glory of that blessed Babe. Now, since all that he uttered might as well have been simply *pronounced over* the Child, there is to be seen in this act of taking Him into his arms a most affecting, personal, and, so to speak, palpable appropriation of this new-born, unconscious, helpless Babe, as "all his salvation and all his desire," which it were a pity we should miss. **and blessed God, and said, 29. Lord.** The word is 'Master' [Δέσποτα], a word but rarely used in the New Testament, and never but to mark emphatically the sovereign rights of Him who is so styled, as Proprietor of the persons or things meant. Here it is selected with peculiar propriety, when the aged saint, feeling that his last object in wishing to live had now been attained, only awaited his Master's word of command to "depart." **now lettest thou thy servant depart in peace, according to thy word.** Most readers probably take this to be a prayer for permission to depart, not observing that "lettest Thou" is just 'Thou art letting,' or 'permitting thy servant to depart.' It had been clearer as well as more literal thus—"Lord, now art Thou releasing Thy servant"—a placid, reverential intimation that having now "seen the Lord's Christ," his time, divinely indicated, for "seeing death" had arrived, and he was ready to go. **30. For mine eyes have seen thy salvation.** How many saw this Child, nay the full-grown "Man, Christ Jesus," who never saw in Him "God's Salvation!" This estimate of Simeon's was an act of pure faith. While gazing upon that Infant, borne in his own arms, he "beheld His glory." In another view it was prior *faith* rewarded by present *sight*. **31. Which thou hast prepared before the face of all people** [πάντων τῶν λαῶν]—' of all the peoples,' or mankind at large. **32. A light to lighten the Gentiles**—then in thick darkness, **and the glory of thy people Israel**—already Thine, and now, in the believing portion of it, to be more gloriously so than ever. It will be observed that this 'swan-like song,' bidding an eternal farewell to this terrestrial life,' to use the words of *Olshausen*, takes a more comprehensive view of the kingdom of Christ than that of Zacharias (cf. ch. i. 68-79), though the kingdom they sing of is one.
33. And Joseph and his mother—or, according to what is probably the true reading here, 'And his father and mother,' marvelled at those things which were spoken of him—each successive recognition of the glory of this Babe filling

them with fresh wonder. **34. And Simeon blessed them**—the parents, **and said unto Mary his mother, Behold, this child is set** [κεῖται]—'lieth,' or, 'is appointed:' compare Isa. xxviii. 16, "Behold, I *lay* in Zion," &c. Perhaps, this Infant's lying in his own arms at that moment suggested this sublime allusion. **for the fall and rising again of many in Israel: and for a sign which shall be spoken against.** If the latter of these two expressions refer to the determined rejecters of Christ, perhaps the former refers, not to two classes—one "falling" from a higher to a lower, the other "rising" from a lower to a higher state—but to one and the same class of persons, who after "falling," through inability to discern the glory of Christ in the days of His flesh, "rose again" when, after the effusion of the Spirit at Pentecost, a new light dawned upon their minds. The like treatment do the claims of Christ experience from age to age. **35. Yea, a sword shall pierce through thy own soul also.** 'Blessed though thou art among women, thou shalt have thine own deep share of the struggles and sufferings which this Babe is to occasion'—pointing not only to the obloquy to which He would be exposed through life, to those agonies of His on the cross which she was to witness, and to her own desolate condition thereafter, but perhaps also to dreadful alternations of faith and unbelief, of hope and fear regarding Him which she should have to pass through: **that the thoughts of many hearts may be revealed**—for men's views and decisions regarding Christ are a mirror in which the very thoughts of their hearts are seen.
Anna's Recognition of the Infant Saviour (36-38). **36. And there was one Anna**—or Hannah, **a prophetess**—another sign that "the last times" in which God was to "pour out His Spirit upon all flesh" were at the door, **the daughter of Phanuel, of the tribe of Aser**—one of the ten tribes, of whom many were not carried captive, and not a few, particularly of this very tribe, re-united themselves to Judah after the return from Babylon (2 Chr. xxx. 11). The distinction of tribes, though practically destroyed by the captivity, was well enough known up to their final dispersion (Rom. xi. 1; Heb. vii. 14); nor even now is it entirely lost. **she was of a great age, and had lived with an husband seven years from her virginity. 37. And she was a widow of about fourscore and four years.** If this mean that she had been 84 years in a state of widow-

38 fastings and prayers *night and day. And she coming in that instant gave thanks likewise unto the Lord, and spake of him to all them that "looked for redemption in ⁴Jerusalem.

39 And when they had performed all things according to the law of the

40 Lord, they returned into Galilee, to their own city Nazareth. And the child grew, and waxed strong in spirit, filled with wisdom; and the grace of God was upon him.

A. M. 4000.

* Acts 26. 7.
1 Tim. 5. 5.
ᵃ Lam. 3. 25,
26.
Mark 15.43.
ch. 24. 21.
⁴ Or, Israel.

---

hood, then, since her married life extended to seven years, she could not now have been less than 103 years old, even though she had married at the age of twelve, the earliest marriageable age of Jewish females. But probably the meaning is that her whole present age was 84, of which there had been but seven years of a married life. **which departed not from the temple**—that is, at any of the stated hours of day-service, and was found there even during the night-services of the temple-watchmen (see Ps. cxxxiv. 1, 2); **but served God**—the word here used denotes religious services, **with fastings and prayers night and day.** It is this statement about Anna that appears to have suggested to the apostle his description of the "widow indeed and desolate," that she "trusteth in God, and continueth in supplications and prayers night and day" (1 Tim. v. 5). **38. And she coming in that instant** [ἐπιστᾶσα]—rather, 'standing by' or 'presenting herself;' for she had been there already. When Simeon's testimony to the blessed Babe was dying away, she was ready to take it up. **gave thanks likewise unto the Lord** [ἀνθωμολογεῖτο] —rather, 'gave thanks in turn,' or responsively to Simeon, **and spake of him to all them that looked for redemption in Jerusalem.** [The reading, adopted by recent critics, 'the redemption of Jerusalem,' has not, as we think, sufficient authority. The meaning appears to be, 'She spake of Him to all them in Jerusalem that were looking for redemption,' meaning, the expectants of Messiah who were then in the city. Saying in effect—In that Babe are wrapt up all your expectations. If this took place at the hour of prayer, it would account, as *Alford* remarks, for her having such an audience as the words imply.

Return to Nazareth and Advancement of the Child Jesus (39, 40). **39. And when they had performed all things according to the law of the Lord, they returned into Galilee, to their own** **city Nazareth.** Are we to conclude from this that the parents of Jesus went straight back to Nazareth from these temple scenes, and that the visit of the Magi, the flight into Egypt, and the return thence, recorded by Matthew (ch. ii.), all took place *before* the presentation of the Babe in the temple? So some think, but in our judgment very unnaturally. To us it seems far more natural to suppose that the presentation in the temple took place during the residence of the parents at Bethlehem, where they appear at first to have thought it their duty henceforth to reside (see on Matt. ii. 22). In this case all that is recorded by Luke in the preceding verses was over before the Magi arrived in Jerusalem. Nor is there any difficulty in Luke's saying here, that "when they had performed all that they returned to Galilee." If, indeed, we had no account of any intermediate transactions, we should of course conclude that they went *straight* from Jerusalem to Nazareth. But if we have reason to believe that the whole transactions of Matt. ii. occurred in the interval, we have only to conclude that our Evangelist, having no information to communicate to his readers between those events, just passes them by. A precisely similar, and at least equally important, omission by Matthew himself occurs at ch. iv. 12 (on which see

note). **40. And the child grew, and waxed strong in spirit**—His mental development keeping pace with His bodily: **filled with wisdom**—yet a fulness ever enlarging with His capacity to receive it; **and the grace of God**—the divine favour, **was upon him**—resting upon Him, manifestly and increasingly. Compare *v.* 52. [*Tischendorf* and *Tregelles* omit πνεύματι—" in spirit," but, as we think, on insufficient authority.]

Remarks.—1. Now began to be fulfilled that beautiful prediction—uttered as an encouragement to rebuild the temple after the captivity — "I will fill this house with glory, saith the Lord of Hosts: the glory of this latter house shall be greater than of the former, saith the Lord of Hosts; and in this place will I give peace, saith the Lord of Hosts" (Hag. ii. 7, 9). The peculiar glory of the first temple was wholly wanting in the second. "The ark of the covenant, overlaid round about with gold, wherein was the golden pot that had manna, and Aaron's rod that budded, and the tables of the covenant, and over it the cherubim of glory shadowing the mercy seat" —all these had been lost, and the impossibility of recovering them was keenly felt. By what other "glory" was the second temple to eclipse the first? Not certainly by its architectural and ornamental beauty; and if not, what greater glory had it than the first, save this only, that the Lord of the temple in human flesh came into it, bringing peace? 2. By what glorious premonitions of future greatness was the Infancy of Christ distinguished—fitted to arrest the attention, and to quicken the expectation, and to direct the views of all who were waiting for the Consolation of Israel! 3. To be prepared to welcome death as the peaceful release of a servant by his divine Master, in the conscious enjoyment of His salvation, is the frame of all others most befitting the aged saint. 4. The reception or rejection of Christ is in every age the great test of real character. 5. How richly rewarded was Anna for the assiduousness with which she attended all the temple-services! Not only was she privileged in consequence to behold the Infant Saviour, and to give public thanks to the Lord for so precious a gift, but she got an audience of devout worshippers to hear her, to whom, as expectants of the coming Redemption, she spake of Him, proclaiming Him the Hope and Consolation of Israel. 6. How beautiful is age when mellowed, as in Simeon and Anna, by a devout and heavenly spirit, and gladdened with the joy of God's salvation! 7. Those whose hearts are full of Christ will hardly be able to refrain, whether they be male or female, from speaking of Him to others, as did Anna here.

41-52.—FIRST CONSCIOUS VISIT OF JESUS TO JERUSALEM—RETURN TO NAZARETH, SUBJECTION TO HIS PARENTS, AND GRADUAL ADVANCEMENT. After following with rapt interest the minute details of the Redeemer's Birth and Infancy, one is loath to see the curtain suddenly drop, to be but once raised, and disclose but one brief scene, before His thirtieth year. How curiosity yearns for more, may be seen by the puerile and degrading information regarding the boyhood of Jesus, with which some of the

41   Now his parents went to Jerusalem every ^byear at the feast of the
42 passover. And when he was twelve years old, they went up to Jerusalem after the custom of the feast.
43   And when they had fulfilled the days, as they returned, the child Jesus tarried behind in Jerusalem; and Joseph and his mother knew not *of it*.
44 But they, supposing him to have been in the company, went a day's jour-
45 ney; and they sought him among *their* kinsfolk and acquaintance. And when they found him not, they turned back again to Jerusalem, seeking him.
46   And it came to pass, that after three days they found him in the temple, sitting in the midst of the doctors, ^cboth hearing them, and

A. M. 4000.
b Ex. 12. 14.
Ex. 23. 14-17.
Ex. 34. 23.
Lev. 23. 5.
Deut. 12. 5, 7, 11.
Deut. 16. 1.
1 Sam. 1. 3, 21.
c Isa. 49. 1, 2.
Isa. 50. 4.

apocryphal Gospels pandered to the vicious taste of that class of Christians for which they were written. What a contrast to these are our Four Gospels, whose *historical chastity*, as *Olshausen* well says, chiefly discovers their divine character. As all great and heroic characters, whether of ancient or of modern times, have furnished glimpses in early life of their commanding future, so it was meet, perhaps, that something of this nature should distinguish the Youth of Jesus. One incident is given: one, to show what budding glory, the glory of the Only Begotten of the Father, lay concealed for nearly thirty years under a lowly Nazarene roof; and but one, that the life of secret *preparation* and patient *waiting* for public work might not draw off that attention which should be engrossed with the work itself, and that edification might be imparted rather than curiosity fed. In this view of it, let us reverently approach that most wonderful scene, of our Lord's first visit to Jerusalem, since the time that He was carried thither a Babe hanging upon His mother's breast.

First Conscious Visit to Jerusalem (41-50). **41. Now his parents went** [ἐπορεύοντο]—'were wont' or, 'used to go' **to Jerusalem every year at the feast of the passover.** Though the males only were required to go up to Jerusalem at the three annual festivals (Exod. xxiii. 14-17), devout women, when family duties permitted, went also. So did Hannah (1 Sam. i. 7), and, as here appears, the mother of Jesus. **42. And when he was twelve years old, they went up to Jerusalem after the custom of the feast.** At the age of twelve every Jewish boy was styled 'a son of the law;' being then put under a course of instruction, and trained to fasting and attendance on public worship, besides being set to learn a trade. About this age the young of both sexes have been in use to appear before the bishop for confirmation, where this rite is practised; and at this age, in Scotland, they were regarded as *examinable* by the minister for the first time—so uniform has been the view of the Church, both Jewish and Christian, that about the age of twelve the mind is capable of a higher discipline than before. At this age, then, our Lord is taken up for the first time to Jerusalem, at the Passover-season, the chief of the three annual festivals. But, O, with what thoughts and feelings must this Youth have gone up! Long ere He beheld it, He had doubtless "loved the habitation of God's house, and the place where His honour dwelt" (Ps. xxvi. 8); a love nourished, we may be sure, by that "word hid in His heart," with which in after life He showed so perfect a familiarity. As the time for His first visit approached, could one's ear have caught the breathings of His young soul, he might have heard Him whispering, "As the hart panteth after the water brooks, so panteth my soul after Thee, O God. The Lord loveth the gates of Zion more than all the dwellings of Jacob. I was glad when they said unto me, Let us go into the house of the Lord. Our feet shall stand within thy gates, O Jerusalem"! (Ps. xlii. 1; lxxxvii. 2; cxxii. 1, 2). On catching the first view of "the city of their solemnities," and high above all in it, "the place of God's rest," we hear Him saying to Himself, "Beautiful for situation, the joy of the whole earth, is Mount Zion, on the sides of the north, the city of the great King. Out of Zion, the perfection of beauty, God hath shined" (Ps. xlviii. 2; l. 2). Of His feelings or actions during all the seven days of the feast, not a word is said. As a devout Child, in company with His parents, He would go through the services, keeping His thoughts to Himself; but methinks I hear Him, after the sublime services of that feast, saying to Himself, "He brought me to the banqueting house, and His banner over me was love. I sat down under His shadow with great delight, and His fruit was sweet to my taste" (Song ii. 3, 4). **43. And when they had fulfilled the days**—the seven days of the festival; **as they returned.** Yes, they had to return. For if the duties of life must give place to worship, worship in its turn must give place to them. *Jerusalem* is good; but *Nazareth* is good too. Let him then who neglects the one, on pretext of attending to the other, ponder this scene. Work and Worship serve to relieve each other, and beautifully alternate. **the child Jesus tarried behind in Jerusalem; and Joseph and his mother knew not of it.** Accustomed to the discretion and obedience of the lad, as *Olshausen* says, they might be thrown off their guard. **44. But they, supposing him to have been in the company** [ἐν τῇ συνοδίᾳ]—'the travelling-company,' **went a day's journey; and they sought him among their kinsfolk and acquaintance.** On these sacred journeys whole villages and districts travelled in groups together, partly for protection, partly for company; and as the well-disposed would beguile the tediousness of the way by good discourse, to which the Child Jesus would be no silent listener, they expect to find Him in such a group. **45. And when they found him not, they turned back again to Jerusalem, seeking him. 46. And it came to pass, that after three days they found him.** Do you inquire how he subsisted all this time? I do not. This is one of those impertinences which we should avoid indulging. The spurious gospels, we daresay, would tell their readers all that: how everybody vied with his neighbour who should have Him to keep, and how angels came and fed Him with nectar, or how He needed neither food nor sleep, and so on. But where God has dropt the veil, let us not seek to raise it. Well, they found Him. Where? Not gazing on the architecture of the sacred metropolis, or studying its forms of busy life, but **in the temple**—not of course in the "sanctuary" [τῷ ναῷ], as in ch. i. 9, to which only the priests had access (see on *v.* 27), but in some one of the en-

47 asking them questions. And [d]all that heard him were astonished at his
48 understanding and answers. And when they saw him, they were amazed: and his mother said unto him, Son, why hast thou thus dealt with us?
49 behold, thy father and I have sought thee sorrowing. And he said unto them, How is it that ye sought me? wist ye not that I must be about
50 [e]my Father's business? And [f]they understood not the saying which he spake unto them.
51 And he went down with them, and came to Nazareth, and was subject unto them: but his mother [g]kept all these sayings in her heart.
52 And Jesus [h]increased in wisdom and [5]stature, and in favour with God and man.

A. M. 4000.
[d] Matt. 7. 28.
Mark 1. 22.
John 7. 15.
[e] Matt.21.12.
John 2. 16.
John 4. 34.
John 8. 29.
[f] ch. 9. 45.
ch. 18. 34.
[g] Gen. 37. 11.
Dan. 7. 28.
[h] 1 Sam. 2.26.
[5] Or, age.

closures around it, where the rabbins, or "doctors," taught their scholars. **sitting in the midst of the doctors, both hearing them, and asking them questions.** The method of question and answer was the customary form of rabbinical teaching; teacher and learner becoming by turns questioner and answerer, as may be seen from their extant works. This would give full scope for all that "astonished them in His understanding and answers." Not that He assumed the office of *teaching*—"His hour" for that "was not yet come," and His furniture for that was not complete; for He had yet to "increase in wisdom" as well as "stature" (*v.* 52). In fact, the beauty of Christ's example lies very much in His never at one stage of His life anticipating the duties of another. All would be in the style and manner of a learner, "opening His mouth and panting—His soul breaking for the longing that it had unto God's judgments at all times," and now more than ever before, when finding Himself for the first time in His Father's house. Still there would be in His *questions* far more than in their *answers;* and, if we may take the frivolous interrogatories with which they afterwards plied Him—about the woman that had seven husbands and such like—as a specimen of their present drivelling questions, perhaps we shall not greatly err, if we suppose that the "questions," which He now "asked them" in return, were just the germs of those pregnant questions with which He astonished and silenced them in after years:—"*What think ye of Christ?*—*Whose Son is He? If David call him Lord, how is he then his son?*"—"*Which is the first and great commandment?*"—"*Who is my neighbour?*" **47. And all that heard him were astonished at his understanding and answers.** This confirms what we have said above, that while His "*answers*" to their questions made His attitude appear throughout to be that of a *learner*, "His understanding" peered forth to the amazement of all. **48. And when they saw him, they were amazed: and his mother said unto him, Son, why hast thou thus dealt with us? behold, thy father and I have sought thee sorrowing.** Probably this was said, not before the group, but in private. **49. And he said unto them, How is it that ye sought me? wist (knew) ye not that I must be about my Father's business** [ἐν τοῖς τοῦ Πατρός μου]. These, as THE FIRST RECORDED WORDS OF CHRIST, have a peculiar interest, over and above their intrinsic preciousness. They are somewhat elliptical. The meaning may be, as our translators have taken it, 'about my Father's affairs' or 'business' [*sc.* πράγμασιν]. So *Calvin, Beza, Maldonat, de Wette, Alford, Stier, van Oosterzee,* &c. Or the sense may be, 'in my Father's house' [*sc.* οἰκήμασιν, or δώμασιν]. This latter shade of meaning, besides being the primary one, includes the former. So most of the fathers and of the moderns, *Erasmus,Grotius, Bengel, Olshausen, Meyer,*

Trench, Webster and Wilkinson. In His Father's house Jesus felt Himself at home, breathing His own proper air, and His words convey a gentle rebuke of their obtuseness in requiring Him to *explain this.* 'Once here, thought ye I should so readily hasten away? Let ordinary worshippers be content to keep the feast and be gone; but is this all ye have learnt of Me?' Methinks we are here let into the holy privacies of Nazareth; for sure what He says they *should* have known He must have given them *ground* to know. She tells Him of the sorrow with which *His father* and she had sought Him. He speaks of *no father but one,* saying, in effect, 'My Father has *not* been seeking Me; I have been with Him all this time; the King hath brought me into His chambers: His left hand is under my head, and His right hand doth embrace Me (Song i. 4; ii. 6). How is it that ye do not understand (Mark viii. 21)?' **50. And they understood not the saying which he spake unto them.** Probably He had never *said* so much to them, and so they were confounded; though it was but the true interpretation of many things which they had seen and heard from Him at home. We have an example of this way of speaking in John xiv. 4, 5, where the disciples are presumed to know more than had been told them in so many words.

Return to Nazareth, Subjection to His Parents, and gradual Advancement (51-52). **51. And he went down with them, and came to Nazareth, and was subject unto them,** &c. This is added lest it should be thought that He now threw off the filial yoke, and became henceforth His own master, and theirs too. The marvel of such condescension as this verse records lies in its coming after such a scene, and such an assertion of His higher Sonship; and the words are evidently meant to convey this. **but his mother kept all these sayings in her heart.** *N.B.* After this it will be observed that *Joseph entirely disappears* from the Sacred Narrative. Henceforth, it is always "His mother and His brethren." From this it is inferred, that before the next appearance of our Lord in the History Joseph had *died.* Having now served the double end of being the protector of our Lord's Virgin-mother, and affording Himself the opportunity of presenting a matchless pattern of subjection to both parents, he is silently withdrawn from the stage.

52. And Jesus increased in wisdom and stature. So our translators have rendered the word [ἡλικία], with *Beza, Grotius, Bengel, Meyer.* But it may be rendered 'age'; and so the *Vulgate, Erasmus, Calvin, de Wette, Olshausen, Alford, Webster and Wilkinson, van Oosterzee,* and the best interpreters. Probably this latter idea is the one intended; as filling up, by a general expression, the long interval until the age at which He emerged from this mysterious privacy. **and in favour with God and man.** (See on *v.* 40.) This is all the record we

3 NOW in the fifteenth year of the reign of Tiberius Cesar, Pontius Pilate being governor of Judea, and Herod being tetrarch of Galilee, and his brother Philip tetrarch of Iturea and of the region of Trachonitis,

2 and Lysanias the tetrarch of Abilene, Annas *a* and Caiaphas being the high priests, the word of God came unto John the son of Zacharias in the wilderness.

3 And *b* he came into all the country about Jordan, preaching the baptism

4 of repentance *c* for the remission of sins; as it is written in the book of the words of Esaias the prophet, saying, *d* The voice of one crying in the wilderness, Prepare ye the way of the Lord, make his paths straight.

5 Every valley shall be filled, and every mountain and hill shall be brought low; and the crooked shall be made straight, and the rough

6 ways *shall be* made smooth; and *e* all flesh shall see the salvation of

7 God. Then said he to the multitude that came forth to be baptized of him, *f* O generation of vipers, who hath warned you to flee from the

8 wrath to come? Bring *g* forth therefore fruits [1] worthy of repentance, and begin not to say within yourselves, We have Abraham to *our* father: for I say unto you, That God is able of these stones to raise

9 up children unto Abraham. And now also the ax is laid unto the root

A. D. 26.

CHAP. 3.
a John 11.49.
John 18.13.
Acts 4. 6.
b Mal. 4. 6.
Matt. 3. 1.
Mark 1. 4.
Acts 13. 24.
Acts 19. 4.
c ch. 1. 77.
d Isa. 40. 3.
Matt. 3. 3.
Mark 1. 3.
John 1. 23.
e Ps. 98. 2.
Isa. 52. 10.
f Matt. 3. 7.
g Isa. 1. 16.
Ezek. 18.27.
Acts 26. 20.
2 Cor. 7. 10.
Heb. 6. 7.
[1] Or, meet for.

---

have of the next eighteen years of that wondrous life.

Remarks.—1. Those who love the habitation of God's house and the place where His honour dwelleth, will not be ready to take advantage of permitted absence from it, but, like the mother of Jesus, be found there at all stated seasons when necessary duties allow. 2. The children of Christian parents are the children of the Church; they should be early taught to feel this, and—like the Child Jesus—trained to early attendance on its public ordinances and more private arrangements for instruction and edification. 3. One of the most decisive marks of early piety is a delight in the gates of Zion. And if we cannot attain to all that was in the mind of Jesus, when in language so remarkable He gently rebuked His earthly parents for their anxiety on His account (*v.* 49), let us imbibe and manifest the spirit of His words. 4. Let us realize the glorious identity with ourselves of the Infant Saviour, the Child, the Youth, the Man, Christ Jesus. 5. What an overpowering Example of filial obedience have we here! That the Child Jesus, so long as He *was* a Child, should be subject to His parents, though He was Lord of all, is not so wonderful; but that after His glory broke forth so amazingly in his Father's house, He still "went down with them to Nazareth, and was subject unto them;" continuing so, as we cannot doubt, until, at the appointed time, He emerged into public life—this is that marvel of filial obedience which even angels cannot but desire to look into. 6. Is it asked how "that holy thing," which was born of the Virgin, the sinless Seed of the woman, could increase "in wisdom, and in favour with God and man"? This is but to ask how He could become an Infant of days at all, and go through the successive stages of human life, up to full-grown manhood. But a simple illustration may perhaps aid our conceptions. Suppose a number of golden vessels, from the smallest conceivable size up to the largest, all filled to the brim with pure water, clear as crystal, so full that the least drop added to any one of them would make it to run over. Of all these vessels alike it may be said that they are quite full; and yet there is, in point of fact, less in the smallest than the largest, and each of them has less in it than in the next larger one. Such was Jesus. The golden vessels of all different sizes are His human nature

at each successive period of His life up to the age of thirty, when He came to full maturity; and the crystal-clear water in them is the holy excellences and graces with which He was filled. He was never otherwise than full of these to the whole measure of His capacity. His understanding was ever as full as it could hold of intelligence and wisdom; His heart ever as full as it could hold of grace. But as it could hold more and more the further He advanced, so He might be said to become more and more lovely, more and more attractive, as He advanced, and so to "increase in favour with God and man." True, the favour of men was afterwards turned into frown and rage, when His fidelity irritated their corruption and dashed their expectations. But at this early period, there being nothing in Him to prejudice them against Him, His ever-unfolding loveliness could not fail to be increasingly attractive to all who observed it. 6. See the patience of Jesus, who, though doubtless conscious of His high destination, yet waited thirty years, not only for the entire development and maturity of all His powers and graces, but for the appointed time of His public appearance. Not so Moses, who, burning with the consciousness of his divine destination to deliver Israel, waited not his full time and the manifest call to act, but took this into his own hand, and was punished for it by having forty years longer to wait, far from the scene of his future work. Yet such patient waiting has unspeakable reliefs and consolations. The conviction that the best things ever take the longest to come to maturity would doubtless minister quiet satisfaction. But besides this, what seasons of tranquil meditation over the lively oracles, and holy fellowship with His Father; what inlettings, on the one hand, of light, and love, and power from on high, and on the other, what outgoings of filial supplication, freedom, love, joy, and what glad consecration to the work before Him, would these last eighteen years of His private life embrace! And would they not "seem but a few days" when thus spent, however ardently He might long to be more directly "about His Father's business."

CHAP. III. 1-20.—PREACHING, BAPTISM, AND IMPRISONMENT OF JOHN. (=Matt. iii. 1-12; Mark i. 1-8.) For the exposition, see on Matt. iii. 1-12.

21, 22.—BAPTISM OF CHRIST, AND DESCENT OF THE SPIRIT UPON HIM IMMEDIATELY THEREAFTER. (=Matt. iii. 13-17; Mark i. 9-11; John

of the trees: [h]every tree therefore which bringeth not forth good fruit is hewn down, and cast into the fire.

10, And the people asked him, saying, What [i]shall we do then? He
11 answereth and saith unto them, He [j]that hath two coats, let him impart to him that hath none; and he that hath meat, let him do likewise.
12 Then [k]came also publicans to be baptized, and said unto him, Master,
13 what shall we do? And he said unto them, [l]Exact no more than that
14 which is appointed you. And the soldiers likewise demanded of him, saying, And what shall we do? And he said unto them, [2]Do violence to no man, [m]neither accuse *any* falsely; and be content with your [3]wages.

15 And as the people were [4]in expectation, and all men [5]mused in their
16 hearts of John, whether he were the Christ, or not; John answered, saying unto *them* all, I [n]indeed baptize you with water; but one mightier than I cometh, the latchet of whose shoes I am not worthy to unloose:
17 he shall baptize you with [o]the Holy Ghost and with fire: whose fan *is* in his hand, and he will throughly purge his floor, and [p]will gather the wheat into his garner; but the chaff he will burn with fire unquenchable.
18 And many other things in his exhortation preached he unto the people.
19 But [q]Herod the tetrarch, being reproved by him for Herodias his
20 brother Philip's wife, and for all the evils which Herod had done, added yet this above all, that he shut up John in prison.

21 Now when all the people were baptized, [r]it came to pass, that Jesus
22 also being baptized, and praying, the heaven was opened, and the Holy Ghost descended in a bodily shape like a dove upon him, and a voice came [s]from heaven, which said, Thou art my beloved Son; in thee I am well pleased.

23 And Jesus himself began to be [t]about thirty years of age, being (as
24 was supposed) the [u]son of Joseph, which was *the* [6]son of Heli, which was *the son* of Matthat, which was *the son* of Levi, which was *the son* of
25 Melchi, which was *the son* of Janna, which was *the son* of Joseph, which was *the son* of Mattathias, which was *the son* of Amos, which was *the son*
26 of Naum, which was *the son* of Esli, which was *the son* of Nagge, which was *the son* of Maath, which was *the son* of Mattathias, which was *the son*
27 of Semei, which was *the son* of Joseph, which was *the son* of Juda, which was *the son* of Joanna, which was *the son* of Rhesa, which was *the son* of [7]Zorobabel, which was *the son* of Salathiel, which was *the son* of Neri,
28 which was *the son* of Melchi, which was *the son* of Addi, which was *the son* of Cosam, which was *the son* of Elmodam, which was *the son* of Er.

A. D. 26.

h Matt. r. 19.
  John 15.2,6.
i Acts 2. 37.
j 2 Cor. 8. 14.
  1 Tim. 6 18.
  Jas. 2. 15.
  1 John 3.17.
k Matt.21.32.
l Mic. 6. 8.
  ch. 19. 8.
2 Or, put no man in fear.
m Ex. 23. 1.
  Lev. 19. 11.
3 Or, allowance.
4 Or. in suspense.
5 Or, reasoned. or, debated.
n Matt. 3. 11.
o 1 Cor.12.13
p Mic. 4. 12.
q Pro. 28. 15, 16.
  Matt. 1!. 2.
  Matt. 14. 3.
  Mark 6. 17.
r Matt. 3. 13.
  John 1. 32.
s 2 Pet. 1. 17.
t Num. 4. 3, 35, 39, 47.
u Matt. 13.55.
  John 6. 42.
6 Son-in-law.
7 It is uncertain whether Zorobabel and Salathiel are the same as those mentioned in Matt. 1. 12, 13, and 1 Chr. 3. 17, 19.

i. 31-34.) For the exposition, see on Matt. iii. 13-17.

23-38.—GENEALOGY OF CHRIST. (= Matt. i. 1-18.)

23. And Jesus himself began to be about thirty years of age [ὡσεὶ ἐτῶν τριάκοντα ἀρχόμενος]—or, 'was about entering on His thirtieth year.' So our translators have taken the word, and so *Calvin, Beza, Bloomfield, Webster and Wilkinson;* but 'was about thirty years of age when He began [His ministry]' makes better Greek, and is probably the true sense. So *Bengel, Olshausen, de Wette, Meyer, Alford,* &c. At this age the priests entered on their office (Num. iv. 3), and the commencement of the ministry both of our Lord and His Forerunner appears to have been fixed on this principle. **being (as was supposed) the son of Joseph.** By this expression the Evangelist reminds his readers of His miraculous conception by the Virgin, and His being thus only the *legal* son of Joseph. **which was the son of Heli, &c.** Have we in this genealogical table the line of *Joseph* again, as in Matthew; or is this the line of *Mary?*

235

—a point on which there has been great difference of opinion and much acute discussion. Those who take the *former* opinion contend that it is the natural sense of this verse, and that no other would have been thought of but for its supposed improbability and the uncertainty which it seems to throw over our Lord's real descent. But it is liable to another difficulty, viz., that in this case Matthew makes "*Jacob,*" while Luke makes "*Heli,*" to be Joseph's father; and though the same person had often more than one name, we ought not to resort to that supposition, in such a case as this, without necessity. And then, though the descent of Mary from David would be liable to no real doubt, even though we had no table of her line preserved to us (see, for example, ch. i. 32, and on ch. ii. 4), still it does seem unlikely—we say not incredible—that two genealogies of our Lord should be preserved to us, neither of which gives his *real* descent. Those who take the *latter* opinion, that we have here the line of *Mary,* as in Matthew that of *Joseph*—here his *real,* there his *reputed* line—explain the statement about Joseph, that he was "*the son of*

29 which was *the son* of Jose, which was *the son* of Eliezer, which was *the son*
30 of Jorim, which was *the son* of Matthat, which was *the son* of Levi, which was *the son* of Simeon, which was *the son* of Juda, which was *the son* of
31 Joseph, which was *the son* of Jonan, which was *the son* of Eliakim, which was *the son* of Melea, which was *the son* of Menan, which was *the son* of Mattatha, which was *the son* of *ᵛ*Nathan, which *ʷ*was *the son* of David,
32 which *ˣ*was *the son* of Jesse, which was *the son* of Obed, which was *the son* of Booz, which was *the son* of Salmon, which was *the son* of Naasson,
33 which was *the son* of Aminadab, which was *the son* of Aram, which was *the son* of Esrom, which was *the son* of Phares, which was *the son* of Juda,
34 which was *the son* of Jacob, which was *the son* of Isaac, which was *the son* of Abraham, *ʸ*which was *the son* of Thara, which was *the son* of Nachor,
35 which was *the son* of Saruch, which was *the son* of Ragau, which was *the son* of Phalec, which was *the son* of Heber, which was *the son* of Sala,
36 which *ᶻ*was *the son* of Cainan, which was *the son* of Arphaxad, *ᵃ*which was *the son* of Sem, which was *the son* of Noe, which was *the son* of
37 Lamech, which was *the son* of Mathusala, which was *the son* of Enoch, which was *the son* of Jared, which was *the son* of Maleleel, which was *the*
38 son of Cainan, which was *the son* of Enos, which was *the son* of Seth, which was *the son* of Adam, *ᵇ*which was *the son* of God.

4 AND *ᵃ*Jesus, being full of the Holy Ghost, returned from Jordan, and
2 *ᵇ*was led by the Spirit into the wilderness, being forty days *ᶜ*tempted of the devil. And *ᵈ*in those days he did eat nothing: and when they
3 were ended, he afterward hungered. And the devil said unto him, If thou be the Son of God, command this stone that it be made bread.
4 And Jesus answered him, saying, *ᵉ*It is written, That man shall not live
5 by bread alone, but by every word of God. And the devil, taking him up into an high mountain, showed unto him all the kingdoms of the
6 world in a moment of time. And the devil said unto him, All this power will I give thee, and the glory of them: for *ᶠ*that is delivered unto
7 me; and to whomsoever I will I give it. If thou therefore wilt ¹worship
8 me, all shall be thine. And Jesus answered and said unto him, Get thee behind me, Satan: *ᵍ*for it is written, Thou shalt worship the Lord thy
9 God, and him only shalt thou serve. And *ʰ*he brought him to Jerusalem, and set him on a pinnacle of the temple, and said unto him, If thou be
10 the Son of God, cast *ⁱ*thyself down from hence: for *ʲ*it is written, He
11 shall give his angels charge over thee, to keep thee; and in *their* hands they shall bear thee up, lest at any time thou dash thy foot against a

A. D. 30.

ᵛ Zec. 12. 12.
ʷ 2 Sam. 5.14.
1 Chr. 3. 5.
ˣ Ruth 4. 18
1Sam.17.58.
1 Chr. 2. 10.
Ps. 72. 20.
Isa. 11. 1, 2.
Matt. 1.3-6.
Acts 13. 22, 23.
ʸ Gen. 11. 24, 26.
ᶻ Gen. 11. 12.
ᵃ Gen. 5. 6.
Gen. 11. 10.
ᵇ Gen. 1. 26, 27.
Gen. 2. 7.
Gen. 5. 1, 2.
Isa. 64. 8.

CHAP. 4.
ᵃ Isa. 11. 2.
Isa 61. 1.
Matt. 4. 1.
Mark 1. 12.
John 1. 33.
John 3. 34.
ᵇ ch. 2. 27.
ᶜ Gen. 3. 15.
Heb 2. 18.
Heb. 4 15.
ᵈ Ex. 34. 28.
1 Ki. 19. 8.
ᵉ Deut. 8. 3.
Eph 6. 17.
ᶠ John 12 31.
John 14.30.
Rev. 13.2,7.
1 Or, fall down before me.
ᵍ Deut. 6. 13.
Deut. 10 20.
ʰ Matt. 4. 5.
ⁱ Matt. 8. 29.
Rom. 1. 4.
1 Pet. 5. 8.
ʲ Ps. 91. 11.

Heli," to mean that he was his *son-in-law*, as being the husband of his daughter Mary (so in Ruth i. 11, 12), and believe that Joseph's name is only introduced instead of Mary's, in conformity with the Jewish custom in such tables. Perhaps this view is attended with fewest difficulties, as it certainly is the best supported. However we decide, it is a satisfaction to know that not a doubt was thrown out by the bitterest of the early enemies of Christianity as to *our Lord's real descent from David.* On comparing the two genealogies, it will be observed that Matthew, writing more immediately for *Jews*, deemed it enough to show that the Saviour was sprung from Abraham and David; whereas Luke, writing more immediately for *Gentiles*, traces the descent back to Adam, the parent stock of the whole human family, thus showing Him to be the promised "Seed of the woman." Without going into the various questions raised by this and the corresponding genealogical line in the First Gospel, we merely quote the following striking remarks of *Olshausen*.—'The possibility of constructing such a table, comprising a period of thousands of years,

in an uninterrupted line from father to son, of a family that dwelt for a long time in the utmost retirement, would be inexplicable, had not the members of this line been endowed with *a thread* by which they could extricate themselves from the many families into which every tribe and branch was again subdivided, and thus hold fast and know *the* member that was destined to continue the lineage. This thread was the hope that Messiah would be born of the race of Abraham and David. The ardent desire to behold Him and be partakers of His mercy and glory suffered not the attention to be exhausted through a period embracing thousands of years. Thus the member destined to continue the lineage, whenever doubtful, became easily distinguishable, awakening the hope of a final fulfilment, and keeping it alive until it was consummated.'

For general Remarks on this Section, see on Matt. i. 1-17, Remarks 1 and 2.

CHAP. IV. 1-15.—TEMPTATION OF CHRIST: BEGINNING OF HIS GALILEAN MINISTRY. (= Matt. iv. 1-25; Mark i. 12-20, 35-39.) For the exposition, see on Matt. iv. 1-25, and Mark i. 35-39.

12 stone. And Jesus answering said unto him, It ^kis said, Thou shalt not
13 tempt the Lord thy God. And when the devil had ended all the temptation, he ^ldeparted from him ^mfor a season.
14 And ⁿJesus returned in the power of the Spirit into ^oGalilee: and
15 there went out a fame of him through all the region round about. And he taught in their synagogues, being ^pglorified of all.
16 And he came to ^qNazareth, where he had been brought up: and, as his custom was, ^rhe went into the synagogue on the sabbath day, and

A. D. 30.

k Deut. 6. 16.
l Jas. 4. 7.
m John 14.30.
n Matt. 4. 12.
o Acts 10. 37.
p Isa. 52. 13.
q Matt. 2. 23.
  Mark 6. 1.
r Acts 13. 14.

16-30. — CHRIST'S REJECTION AT NAZARETH. (= Matt. xiii. 54-58; Mark vi. 1-6.) As observed on Matt. iv. 13, the prevalent opinion has always been that our Lord paid two visits to Nazareth: the first being that recorded here; the second that recorded in Matt. xiii. 54-58, and Mark vi. 1-6. This is maintained on the following grounds:— First, The most natural sense of the words in Matt. iv. 13, "And leaving Nazareth, He came down and dwelt in Capernaum," is that He then paid a visit to it, though the particulars of it are not given. In this case the visit recorded in ch. xiii. 54-58 must be a second visit. Next the visit recorded in Luke bears on its face to have been made at the outset of our Lord's ministry, if not the very first opening of it; whereas that recorded in Matt. xiii. and in Mark vi. is evidently one paid at a somewhat advanced period of His ministry. Further, at the visit recorded by Luke, our Lord appears to have wrought no miracles; whereas it is expressly said that at the visit recorded in Mark He did work some miracles. Once more it is alleged of the wonder expressed by the Nazarenes at our Lord's teaching, that the language is noticeably different in Luke and in Mark. In reply to this, we observe: First, That as none of the Evangelists record more than one public visit to Nazareth, so we have shown in our exposition of Matt. iv. 13, that it is not necessary to infer from that verse that our Lord actually visited Nazareth at that time. Thus are we left free to decide the question—of one or two visits—on internal evidence alone. Secondly, The unparalleled violence with which the Nazarenes treated our Lord, at the visit recorded by Luke, suits far better with a somewhat advanced period of His ministry than with the very opening scene of it, or any very near its commencement. Thirdly, The visit, accordingly, recorded by Luke, though it reads at first like the opening scene of our Lord's ministry, gives evidence, on closer inspection, of its having occurred at a somewhat advanced period. The challenge which they would be ready to throw out to Him, and which He here meets, was *that He ought to work among His Nazarene townsmen as wonderful miracles as had made His stay at Capernaum so illustrious.* Does not this prove not only that His ministry did not begin at Nazareth, but that He had stayed so long away from it after His public ministry began, that the Nazarenes were irritated at the slight thus put upon them, and would be ready to insinuate that He was afraid to face them? Fourthly, Supposing our Lord to have framed His own procedure according to the instructions which He gave to His disciples —"Give not that which is holy unto the dogs, neither cast ye your pearls before swine;" and "When they persecute you in one city, flee ye into another" (Matt. vii. 6; x. 23)—it is in the last degree improbable that He would again expose Himself to those who had, at a former visit, rushed upon Him and thrust Him out of their city, and attempted to hurl Him down a precipice to kill Him; and though, if recorded, it is of course to be believed, the evidence of the

fact would require to be much clearer than we think it is to warrant the conclusion that He actually did so. Fifthly, If our Lord did pay a second public visit to Nazareth, we might expect, in the record of it, some allusion to the first; or, if that be not necessary, it is surely reasonable to suppose that the impression made upon the Nazarenes, and the observations that fell from them would differ somewhat at least from those produced by the first visit. But, instead of this, not only do we find the impression produced upon them by the visit recorded by Matthew (xiii.) and by Mark (vi.), to be just what might have been expected from such a people on hearing Him *for the first time;* but we find their remarks to be identical with those recorded by Luke as made at *his* visit. Who can readily believe this of two distinct visits? Can anything be more unnatural than to suppose that after these Nazarenes had attempted the life of our Lord, and been disappointed of their object at one visit, they should at a subsequent one express their surprise at His teaching precisely in the terms they had before employed, and just as if they had never heard him before? As for the attempts to show that the questions are not put so strongly in Matthew and Mark, as they are in Luke (see *Birks'* "Horæ Evangelicæ"), it is astonishing to us that this should be urged— so devoid of all plausibility does it appear. The one argument of real force in favour of two visits is, that at the visit recorded by Mark (which is the same as that of Matthew) our Lord is expressly said to have wrought miracles, while it would seem that at that of Luke He wrought none. But the very way in which Mark records those miracles suggests its own explanation: "He could there do no mighty work" [δύναμιν], or, "*He could there do no miracle,* save that He laid His hands upon a few sick folk, and healed them" (Mark vi. 5)—suggesting that the unbelief of the Nazarenes tied up His hands, so to speak, from any display of His miraculous power. But as that unbelief evidently refers to what was displayed *in public,* so the inability is clearly an inability, in the face of that unbelief, to give any manifestation *in the synagogue,* or *in public,* of His miraculous power, as He did in the synagogue of Capernaum and elsewhere. Hence His "laying His hands on a few sick folk," being expressly recorded as *exceptional,* had been done in private, and in all likelihood before His public appearance in the synagogue had kindled the popular rage, and made it impossible. If this be correct, the demand of the Nazarenes for miracles and our Lord's refusal of them, as recorded by Luke, is quite consistent with the statement of what He wrought as given in Mark. A striking confirmation of the conclusion we have formed on this question will be found in the exposition of John iv. 43, 44, and Remark 1 at the close of that Section.

16. **And he came to Nazareth, where he had been brought up, and, as his custom was** [κατὰ τὸ εἰωθὸς αὐτῷ]—compare Acts xvii. 2, **he went into the synagogue on the sabbath day, and stood up**

17 stood up for to read. And there was delivered unto him the book of the
prophet Esaias. And when he had opened the book, he found the place
18 where it was written, The *Spirit of the Lord *is* upon me, because he
hath anointed me to preach the Gospel to the poor; he hath sent me
to heal the broken-hearted, to preach deliverance to the captives, and
19 recovering of sight to the blind, to set at liberty them that are bruised, to
20 preach the *acceptable year of the Lord. And he closed the book, and
he gave *it* again to the minister, and sat down. And the eyes of all
21 them that were in the synagogue were fastened on him. And he began
22 to say unto them, This day is this scripture fulfilled in your ears. And
all bare him witness, and *wondered at the gracious words which proceeded out of his mouth. And they said, Is *not this Joseph's son?
23 And he said unto them, Ye will surely say unto me this proverb,
Physician, heal thyself: whatsoever we have heard done in *Capernaum,
24 do also here in *thy country. And he said, Verily I say unto you, No

A. D. 30.
* Ps. 45. 7.
Isa. 11. 2-5.
Isa. 42. 1.
Isa. 50. 4.
Isa. 59. 21.
Dan. 9. 24.
t Lev. 25. 8.
2 Cor. 6. 2.
u Ps. 45. 2.
Pro. 10. 32.
Matt.13.54.
Mark 6. 2.
ch. 2. 47.
v John 6. 42.
w Matt. 4. 13.
Matt. 11.23.
x Matt. 13.54.
Mark 6. 1.

for to read. Does this read like the opening of our
Lord's public ministry? Does it not expressly tell
us, on the contrary, that His ministry had already
continued long enough to acquire a certain uniformity of procedure on the Sabbath days? As
others besides Rabbins were allowed to address
the congregation (see Acts xiii. 15), our Lord took
advantage of that liberty. **17. And there was
delivered unto him the book of the prophet Esaias.
And when he had opened the book, he found the
place where it was written** (Isa. lxi. 1, 2). There
is no sufficient ground for supposing that our Lord
fixed upon the *portion for the day*. The language
used rather implies the contrary—that it was a
portion selected by Himself for the occasion. **18.
The Spirit of the Lord is upon me, because—**or
'*inasmuch as*' [οὗ ἕνεκεν]—**he hath anointed me
to preach the Gospel to the poor; he hath sent me
to heal the broken-hearted, to preach deliverance
to the captives, and recovering of sight to the
blind, to set at liberty them that are bruised,
19. To preach the acceptable—**or '*accepted*' [τὸ
δεκτὸν]—**year of the Lord.** To have fixed on any
portion relating to His *sufferings* (as Isa. liii.) would
have been unsuitable at that early stage of His
ministry. But He selects a passage announcing
the sublime object of His whole mission, its Divine
character, and His special endowments for it; expressed in the first person, and so singularly adapted
to the first opening of the mouth in His prophetic
capacity, that it seems as if made expressly for the
occasion when He first opened His mouth where
He had been brought up. It is from the well-
known section of Isaiah's prophecies whose burden
is that mysterious "SERVANT OF THE LORD" [עֶבֶד
יְהֹוָה], despised of man, abhorred of the nation, but
before whom kings on seeing Him are to arise, and
princes to worship; in visage more marred than
any man, and his form than the sons of men, yet
sprinkling many nations; labouring seemingly in
vain, and spending His strength for nought and in
vain, yet Jehovah's Servant to raise up the tribes
of Jacob, and be His Salvation to the ends of the
earth, (Isa. xlix., &c.) The quotation is chiefly
from the Septuagint version, used, it would
seem, in the synagogues. **acceptable year—**an
allusion to the Jubilee year (Lev. xxv. 10), a
year of universal *release* for person and property. See also Isa. xlix. 8; 2 Cor. vi. 2. As
the maladies under which humanity groans are
here set forth under the names of *poverty,
broken-heartedness, bondage, blindness, bruisedness,*
(or *crushedness*), so Christ announces Himself, in
the act of reading it, as the glorious HEALER of all
these maladies; stopping the quotation just before
it comes to "the day of vengeance," which was

only to come on the rejecters of His message
(John iii. 17). The first words, "THE SPIRIT of
THE LORD is upon ME,"have been noticed since
the days of the Church Fathers, as an illustrious
example of *Father, Son, and Holy Ghost* being
exhibited as in distinct yet harmonious action in
the scheme of salvation. **20. And he closed the
book, and he gave it again to the minister—**the
Chazan or synagogue-officer. **And the eyes of all
them that were in the synagogue were fastened
on him—**astounded at His putting in such Messianic claims; for that, they saw, was what He
meant. **21. And he began to say unto them—**
language implying that only the substance, or
even the general drift, of His address is here
given. **This day is this scripture fulfilled in
your ears.** The Evangelist means to say in a
word, that His whole address was just a detailed application to Himself of this, and perhaps other like prophecies. **22. And all bare him
witness, and wondered at the gracious words
which proceeded out of his mouth** [ἐπὶ τοῖς
λόγοις τῆς χάριτος]—'the words of grace,' referring
to the richness of His matter and the sweetness of
his manner (Ps. xlv. 2). **And they said, Is not this
Joseph's son?** See on Matt. xiii. 54-56. They knew
He had received no rabbinical education, and
could not imagine how one who had gone in and
out amongst them, as one of themselves, during
all his boyhood and youth, up to within a short
time before, could be the predicted Servant
of the Lord who was to speak comfort to all
mourners, to bring healing for all human maladies, and be, in fact, the Consolation of Israel.
23. And he said unto them, Ye will surely [πάντως]
—'Ye will no doubt' **say unto me this proverb,
Physician, heal thyself—**not unlike our proverb,
'Charity begins at home.' **whatsoever we have
heard done in Capernaum, do also here in thy
country.** 'Strange rumours have reached our ears
of thy doings at Capernaum; but if such power resides in thee to cure the ills of humanity, why has
none of it yet come nearer home, and why is all
this alleged power reserved for strangers?' His
choice of Capernaum as a place of residence since
entering on public life was, it seems, already well
known at Nazareth; and when He did come
thither, that he should give no displays of his
power when distant places were ringing with
His fame wounded their pride. He had indeed "laid His hands on a few sick folk, and
healed them" (Mark vi. 5); but this, as we have
said, seems to have been done quite privately—
the general unbelief precluding anything more
open. **24. And he said, Verily I say unto you.
No prophet is accepted in his own country,**

25 prophet ^{y} is accepted in his own country. But I tell you of a truth, ^{z} many widows were in Israel in the days of Elias, when the heaven was shut up three years and six months, when great famine was throughout

26 all the land; but unto none of them was Elias sent, save unto Sarepta,

27 *a city* of Sidon, unto a woman *that was* a widow. And ^{a} many lepers were in Israel in the time of Eliseus the prophet; and none of them was cleansed, saving Naaman the Syrian.

28 And all they in the synagogue, when they heard these things, were

29 filled with wrath, and rose up, and thrust him out of the city, and led him unto the ^{2} brow of the hill whereon their city was built, that they

30 might cast him down headlong. But he ^{b} passing through the midst of them went his way,

A. D. 30.

y Matt. 13.57.
Mark 6. 4.
John 4. 44.
Acts 22. 3,
18-22.
z 1 Ki. 17. 9.
1 Ki. 18. 1.
Jas. 5. 17.
a 2 Ki. 5. 14.
2 Or. edge.
b John 8. 59.
John 10. 39.
John 18. 6,
7.
Acts 12. 18.

In Mark vi. 4, "A prophet is not without honour, but in his own country, and among his own kin, and in his own house." He replies to one proverb by another equally familiar, which we express in rougher forms, such as, 'Too much familiarity breeds contempt.' Our Lord's long residence in Nazareth merely as a townsman had made Him *too common*, incapacitating them for appreciating Him as others did who were *less familiar with His every-day demeanour in private life*. A most important principle, to which the wise will pay due regard. **25. But I tell you of a truth, many widows were in Israel in the days of Elias, when the heaven was shut up three years and six months.** So Jas. v. 17, including perhaps the six months *after the last fall of rain*, when there would be little or none at any rate; whereas in 1 Ki. xviii. 1, which says the rain returned "in the third year," that period is probably not reckoned. **when great famine was throughout all the land; 26. But unto none of them was Elias sent, save** [εἰ μή]—rather, 'but only,' as the same phrase means in Mark xiii. 32, **unto Sarepta**—or "Zarephath" (1 Ki. xvii. 9), far beyond the northern border of Palestine, and near to Sidon (see Mark vii. 24): **unto a woman that was a widow.** Passing by all the famishing widows in Israel, the prophet was sent to one who was not an Israelite at all. **27. And many lepers were in Israel in the time of Eliseus**—or Elisha, **the prophet; and none of them was cleansed, saving** [εἰ μή again]—rather, 'but only' Naaman the Syrian. Thus, in defending the course which He had taken in passing by the place and the people that might be supposed to have the greatest claim on Him, our Lord falls back upon the well-known examples of Elijah and Elisha, whose miraculous power—passing by those who were *near*—expended itself on those *at a distance*, yea on *heathens;* 'these being,' to use the words of *Stier*, 'the two great prophets who stand at the commencement of prophetic antiquity, and whose miracles strikingly prefigured those of our Lord. As He intended like them to feed the poor and cleanse the lepers, He points to these *miracles of mercy*, and not to the *fire* from heaven and the *bears* that tore the mockers.' **28. And all they in the synagogue, when they heard these things, were filled with wrath**—maddened at the severity with which it reflected upon them, and at those allusions to the *heathen* which brought such a storm of violence afterwards on His apostle at Jerusalem (Acts xxii. 21, 22): **29. And rose up**—breaking up the service irreverently and rushing forth, **and thrust him out of the city**—with violence, as a prisoner in their hands. **and led him unto the brow of the hill whereon their city was built.** Nazareth, though not built on the ridge of a hill, is in part surrounded by one to the west, having several such precipices. It was a mode of capital punishment not unusual in ancient times

239

among the Jews (see 2 Chr. xxv. 12; 2 Ki. ix. 33), the Romans, and others; and to this day examples of it occur in the East. This was the first open insult which the Son of God received, and it came from "them of His own household"! (Matt. x. 36). **30. But he passing through the midst of them went his way**—evidently in a miraculous manner, though perhaps quite noiselessly, leading them to wonder afterwards what spell could have come over them that they allowed Him to escape. Escapes, however, remarkably similar and beyond dispute, in times of persecution, stand on record.

Remarks.—1. Was there ever a more appalling illustration of human depravity than the treatment which the Lord Jesus received from His Nazarene townsmen? Real provocation there was none. Demonstrations of His miraculous power they had no right to demand; and if without these they declined to believe in Him, they had their liberty to do so unchallenged. He knew them too well to indulge them with bootless displays of His divine power; and by an all usion to the Lord's sovereign procedure in ancient times, in dispensing His compassion to whom He would, and quite differently from what might have been expected, He indicated to them intelligibly enough why He declined to do at Nazareth what He had done exuberantly at Capernaum. But, as if to compensate for this, and gain them otherwise, if that were possible, He seems to have spoken in their synagogue with even more than His usual suavity and grace; insomuch that "all bore Him witness, and wondered at the gracious words which proceeded out of His mouth." Yet all was in vain. Nor were they contented with venting their rage in malignant speeches; but, unable to restrain themselves, they broke through the sanctities of public worship and the decencies of ordinary life, and like lions roaring for their prey they rushed upon Him to destroy Him. After this, we may indeed wonder the less at the question, "Can any good thing come out of Nazareth?" But instead of contenting ourselves with ascribing such procedure to the exceptional perversity of the Nazarene character, we shall do well to inquire whether there be not in it a revelation of human malignity, which hateth the light, neither cometh to the light, lest its deeds should be reproved, and which, if it would speak out its mind on the Redeemer's gracious approach to it, would say, "What have we to do with Thee, Jesus, thou Son of God most High? We know Thee who thou art; the Holy One of God"! 2. Did the Lord Jesus become so common amongst His Nazarene townsmen, with whom He had mingled in the ordinary intercourse of society during His early life, that they were unable to take in His divine claims when at length presented to them with matchless benignity and grace? Then must there be a deep principle in the proverb by which

31 And *came down to Capernaum, a city of Galilee, and taught them on	A. D. 30.
32 the sabbath days. And they were astonished at his doctrine: *d*for his	*c* Matt. 4. 13. Mark 1. 21.
33 word was with power. And *e*in the synagogue there was a man	*d* Matt. 7. 28, 29.
which had a spirit of an unclean devil, and cried out with a loud voice,	Tit. 2. 15.
34 saying, ³Let *us* alone; what have we to do with thee, *thou* Jesus of	*e* Mark 1. 23.
Nazareth? art thou come to destroy us? I know thee who thou art; *f*the	3 Or. away.
35 Holy One of God. And Jesus rebuked him, saying, Hold thy peace, and	*f* Ps. 16. 10. Isa. 49. 7.
come out of him. And when the devil had thrown him in the midst, he	Dan. 9. 24.
36 came out of him, and hurt him not. And they were all amazed, and	ch. 1. 35.
spake among themselves, saying, What a word *is* this! for with authority	Acts 2. 31.
37 and power he commandeth the unclean spirits, and they come out. And	Ac s 4. 37.
*g*the fame of him went out into every place of the country round about.	*g* Ps. 72. 8. Mic. 5. 4.
38 And *h*he arose out of the synagogue, and entered into Simon's house.	*h* Matt. 8. 14.
And Simon's wife's mother was taken with a great fever; and they	Mark 1. 29. 1 Cor. 9. 5.
39 besought him for her. And he stood over her, and *i*rebuked the fever;	*i* Ps. 103. 3.
and it left her. And immediately she arose and ministered unto them.	ch. 8. 24.
40 Now *j*when the sun was setting, all they that had any sick with divers	*j* Matt. 8. 16. Mark 1. 32.
diseases brought them unto him; and he laid his hands on every one of	*k* Mark 1. 34.
41 them, and healed them. And *k*devils also came out of many, crying	Mark 3. 11.

He explains it, "A prophet is not without honour, but in his own country, and among his own kin, and in his own house." As if He had said, 'The nearer the vision, the less the attraction.' We must not descend so low as to recall our own analogous maxims; but in fact, almost every language has such sayings, showing that there is a principle in it, everywhere arresting attention. In the case of mere showy virtues, there is no difficulty in explaining it. It is merely this, that nearer inspection discovers the tinsel which distance concealed. The difficulty is to account for the ordinary intercourses of life destroying, or at least blunting, the charm of real excellence, and in this case taking down, in the eyes of His Nazarene townsmen, even the matchless excellences of the Lord Jesus. In all other cases there is an element which cannot be taken into account here. There are foibles of character invisible at a distance, which the familiarities of ordinary life never fail to reveal. But if it be asked on what principle, common to the Holy One of God with all other men, the fact in question is to be accounted for, perhaps two things may explain it. As novelty charms, so that to which we are accustomed has one charm less, however intrinsically worthy of admiration. But in addition to this, there is such a tendency to dissociate loftiness of spirit from the ordinary functions and intercourses of life, that if the one be seen without the other it is likely to be appreciated at its full value; whereas, when associated with languor and want, waste and dust, and the consequent necessity of eating and drinking, sleeping and waking, and such like, then that loftiness of spirit is apt to be less lofty in our esteem, and we say in our hearts, 'After all, they are much like other people'—as if in such things they could or ought to be otherwise. This, however, would be a small matter, if it did not intrude itself into the spiritual domain. But there also its operation is painfully felt, occasioning a false and unholy separation between natural and spiritual, human and divine, earthly and heavenly things. 'Is not this the carpenter's son? Is not his mother called Mary? And his brothers —James and Joses and Simon and Judas—don't we all know them? Haven't we done business with them? Haven't they been in our houses? and this Jesus himself, have we not seen Him in boyhood and youth moving about amongst

us? Can this be He of whom Moses and all the prophets wrote? Can this be He who is sent to heal the broken-hearted, and comfort all that mourn? Incredible!' Nor can it be doubted that a nearer view of Him than even ordinary Nazarenes could have was the very thing that stumbled His own "brethren," who for a while, we are told, "did not believe in Him," and that made even the whole family think He was "beside Himself" (Mark iii. 21). Well, if these things be so, let Christians learn wisdom from it. Recognizing the principle which lies at the bottom of the proverb quoted by our Lord, it will be their wisdom, with Him, to bring their character and principles to bear rather upon *strangers* than upon those to whom they have become too familiar in the ordinary walks of life; for the rare exceptions to this only prove the rule. On the other hand, let Christians beware of being too slow to recognize eminent graces and gifts in those whom they have known very intimately *before* these discovered themselves. 3. As we read that Jesus, when about to be hurled down a precipice, glided through the midst of them and went His way, we perhaps think only of His own peculiar resources for self-preservation. But when we remember how He only refused to avail Himself wantonly of the promise rehearsed to Him by the Tempter, "He shall give His angels charge over Thee, to keep Thee in all Thy ways; and in their hands they shall bear Thee up, lest at any time Thou dash Thy foot against a stone," may we not suppose that the unseen ministry of angels, now if ever legitimately available, had something to do with the marvellous preservation of Jesus on this occasion? Nor can it well be doubted that their interposition in similar ways since in behalf of "the heirs of salvation" (Heb. i. 14) is the secret of the many and marvellous escapes of such which are on record.

31-44.—HEALING OF A DEMONIAC IN THE SYNAGOGUE OF CAPERNAUM, AND THEREAFTER OF SIMON'S MOTHER-IN-LAW AND MANY OTHERS— NEXT DAY, JESUS IS FOUND IN A SOLITARY PLACE, AND IS ENTREATED TO RETURN, BUT DECLINES, AND GOES FORTH ON HIS FIRST MISSIONARY CIRCUIT. (= Matt. viii. 14-17; iv. 23-25; Mark i. 29-39.) For the exposition of this Section —embracing, as appears, the first recorded transactions of our Lord on the Sabbath day in Galilee,

out, and saying, Thou art Christ, the Son of God. And *ʲ*he, rebuking *them*, suffered them not ⁴ to speak: for they knew that he was Christ.

42 And *ᵐ* when it was day, he departed and went into a desert place.; and the people sought him, and came unto him, and stayed him, that he
43 should not depart from them. And he said unto them, *ⁿ* I must preach
44 the kingdom of God to other cities also: for therefore am I sent. And *°* he preached in the synagogues of Galilee.

5 AND *ᵃ* it came to pass, that, as the people pressed upon him to hear
2 the word of God, he stood by the lake of Gennesaret, and saw two ships standing by the lake: but the fishermen were gone out of them, and were
3 washing *their* nets. And he entered into one of the ships, which was Simon's, and prayed him that he would thrust out a little from the land. And he sat down, and taught the people out of the ship.
4 Now when he had left speaking, he said unto Simon, *ᵇ* Launch out into
5 the deep, and let down your nets for a draught. And Simon answering said unto him, Master, we have toiled all the night, and have taken
6 nothing: nevertheless at thy word I will let down the net. And when they had this done, they inclosed a great multitude of fishes: and their
7 net brake. And they beckoned unto *their* partners, which were in the other ship, that they should come and help them. And they came, and
8 filled both the ships, so that they began to sink. When Simon Peter saw *it*, he fell down at Jesus' knees, saying, *ᶜ* Depart from me; for I am a
9 sinful man, O Lord. For he was astonished, and all that were with him,
10 at the draught of the fishes which they had taken: and so *was* also James and John, the sons of Zebedee, which were partners with Simon. And Jesus said unto Simon, Fear not; *ᵈ* from henceforth thou shalt catch
11 men. And when they had brought their ships to land, *ᵉ* they forsook all, and followed him.

ʲ Mark 1. 25, 34.
4 Or, to say that they knew him to be Christ
ᵐ Mark 1. 35.
ⁿ Mark 1. 14, 15.
Acts 10. 38.
Rom. 15. 8.
° Mark 1. 39.

CHAP. 5.
ᵃ Matt. 4. 18.
Mark 1. 16.
ch. 12. 1.
ᵇ John 21. 6.
ᶜ Ex. 20. 19.
Jud. 13. 22.
1 Sam. 6.20.
2 Sam. 6. 9.
1 Ki. 17. 18.
1 Chr. 13.12.
Job 42. 5, 6.
Dan. 8. 17.
ᵈ Ezek. 47. 9, 10.
Matt. 4. 19.
Mark 1. 17.
ᵉ Matt. 4. 20.
Matt.19.27.
Mark 1. 18.
ch. 18. 28.
Phil. 3. 7,8.

and those of the following morning—see on Mark i. 29-39; and on Matt. iv. 23-25.

CHAP. V. 1-11.—MIRACULOUS DRAUGHT OF FISHES, AND CALL OF PETER, JAMES, AND JOHN. In our exposition of Matt. iv. 18-22, we have shown, as it appears to us, that this was quite a different occasion from that, and consequently that the calling of the disciples there and here recorded were different callings. This one, as we take it, was neither their first call, recorded in John i. 35-42; nor their second, recorded in Matt. iv. 18-22; but their *third* and last before their appointment to the apostleship. These calls are to be viewed as progressive stages in their preparation for the great work before them, and something similar is observable in the providential preparation of other eminent servants of Christ for the work to which they are destined. **1. And it came to pass, that, as the people pressed upon him** [ἐπικεῖσθαι]—lit., 'lay upon Him' to hear **the word of God, he stood by the lake of Gennesaret, 2, 3. And saw two ships, &c.** And he entered into one of the ships, which **was Simon's** . . . And he sat down, and taught **the people out of the ship**—as in Matt. xiii. 2. **4. Now when he had left speaking, he said unto Simon, Launch out into the deep, and let down your nets for a draught**—munificent recompense for the use of his boat ! **5. And Simon answering said unto him, Master** ['Ἐπιστάτα]—betokening not surely a first acquaintance, but a relationship already formed. **we have toiled all night**—the usual time of fishing then (John xxi. 3), and even now. **and have taken nothing: nevertheless at thy word I will let down the net.** Peter, as a fisherman, knew how hopeless it was to "let down his net" again at that time, save as a mere act of faith, "at His word" of command,

which carried in it, as it ever does, assurance of success. This is a further proof that he must have been already and for some time a follower of Christ. **6. And when they had this done, they inclosed a great multitude of fishes: and their net brake** [διερρήγνυτο]. This should have been rendered, 'was breaking,' or 'was beginning to break;' for evidently it did not break. **7. And they beckoned unto their partners which were in the other ship, that they should come and help them. And they came, and filled both the ships, so that they began to sink** [βυθίζεσθαι]—'were sinking,' or 'were beginning to sink.' **8. When Simon Peter saw it, he fell down at Jesus' knees, saying, Depart from me; for I am a sinful man, O Lord.** Did Peter then wish Christ to leave him? Verily no. His all was wrapt up in Him. (See John vi. 68.) 'Twas rather, 'Woe is me, Lord! How shall I abide this blaze of glory? A sinner such as I am is not fit company for Thee.' Compare Isa. vi. 5. **9, 10. For he was astonished, and all that were with him . . . And Jesus said unto Simon, Fear not.** This shows that the Lord read Peter's speech very differently from many learned and well-meaning commentators on it. **from henceforth**—marking a new stage in their connection with Christ. **thou shalt catch men.** 'What wilt thou think, Simon, overwhelmed by this draught of fishes, when I shall bring to thy net what will dim all this glory?' **11. And when they had brought their ships to land, they forsook all and followed him.** They did this before (Matt. iv. 20); now they do it again: and yet after the Crucifixion they are at their boats once more (John xxi. 3). In such a business this is easily conceivable. After Pentecost, however, they appear to have finally abandoned their secular calling.

241

12 And *ʲ*it came to pass, when he was in a certain city, behold a man full of leprosy; who, seeing Jesus, fell on *his* face, and besought him, saying,
13 Lord, if thou wilt, thou canst *ᵍ*make me clean. And he put forth *his* hand, and touched him, saying, I will: be thou clean. And immediately
14 the leprosy departed from him. And *ʰ*he charged him to tell no man: but go, and show thyself to the priest, and offer for thy cleansing,
15 *ⁱ*according as Moses commanded, for a testimony unto them. But so much the more went there a fame abroad of him: and *ʲ*great multitudes came together to hear, and to be healed by him of their infirmities.
16 And *ᵏ*he withdrew himself into the wilderness, and prayed.
17 And it came to pass on a certain day, as he was teaching, that there were Pharisees and doctors of the law sitting by, which were come out of every town of Galilee, and Judea, and Jerusalem: and the power of the
18 Lord was *present* to heal them. And, *ˡ*behold, men brought in a bed a man which was taken with a palsy: and they sought *means* to bring
19 him in, and to lay *him* before him. And when they could not find by what *way* they might bring him in because of the multitude, they went upon the housetop, and let him down through the tiling with *his* couch
20 into the midst before Jesus. And when he saw their *ᵐ*faith, he said
21 unto him, Man, *ⁿ*thy sins are forgiven thee. And *ᵒ*the scribes and the Pharisees began to reason, saying, Who is this which speaketh blasphemies?

A. D. 31.

ʲ Matt. 8. 2.
Mark 1. 40.
ᵍ Gen. 18. 14.
Jer. 32. 17, 27.
Matt. 8.8 9.
Matt 9. 28.
Mark 9. 22-24.
ʰ Matt. 8. 4.
ⁱ Lev. 13. 1.
Lev. 14. 4,10, 21, 22.
ʲ Matt 4. 25.
Mark 3. 7.
ch. 12. 1.
ch. 14. 25.
John 6. 2.
ᵏ Mark 14.23.
Mark 6. 46.
ˡ Matt. 9. 2.
Mark 2. 3.
ᵐ Rev. 2. 23.
ⁿ Acts 5. 31.
ᵒ Matt. 9. 3.
Mark 2 6.7.

Remarks.—1. Did Jesus give His disciples this miraculous draught of fishes after they had toiled all the previous night and caught nothing? Did He do the same thing after His resurrection in precisely similar circumstances? Did He heal the impotent man at the pool of Bethesda, who had endured his infirmity thirty and eight years, but not till he had long vainly endeavoured to obtain a cure by stepping into the pool? In a word, Did He let the woman endure her issue of blood twelve years, and spend all that she had upon physicians, only to find herself worse instead of better, before she found instant healing under His wings? Let us not doubt that "all these things happened unto them for ensamples, and are written for our admonition on whom the ends of the world are come," to the intent we should not doubt that at evening time it shall be light, that God *will* hear His own elect that cry unto Him day and night, though He hold out long, as if deaf to them. 2. If the exclamation of Peter, "Depart from me, for I am a sinful man, O Lord," be compared with that of Isaiah, when the thrice-Holy One was revealed to him in his temple-vision, "Woe is me! for I am undone; because I am a man of unclean lips . . . for mine eyes have seen the King the Lord of hosts" (Isa. vi. 5), can any right-thinking mind fail to see that such a speech, if from one creature to another, ought to have been met as Paul met the attempts of the Lycaonians to do sacrifice to him and Barnabas, when he ran in among them, exclaiming with horror—"Sirs, why do ye these things? We also are men of like passions with you, and preach unto you that ye should turn from these vanities unto the living God" (Acts xiv. 14, 15); and that when Jesus, instead of rebuking it, only comforted His trembling disciple with the assurance that wonders far surpassing what he had just witnessed would follow his own labours, He set His seal to views of His Person and character, which only the Word made flesh was entitled to accept? In fact, the more highly they deemed of Him, ever the more grateful it seemed to be to the Redeemer's spirit. Never did they pain Him by manifesting too lofty conceptions of Him. 3. 'Simon,' says *Bishop Hall* most admirably, 'doth not greedily fall upon

so unexpected and profitable a booty, but he turns his eyes from the draught to Himself, from the act to the Author, acknowledging vileness in the one, in the other majesty: "Go from me, Lord, for I am a sinful man." It had been a pity the honest fisher should have been taken at his word. O Simon, thy Saviour is come into thine own ship to call thee, to call others by thee, unto blessedness; and dost thou say, "Lord, go from me?" as if the patient should say to the physician, Depart from me, for I am sick. [But] it was the voice of astonishment, not of dislike; the voice of humility, not of discontentment: yea, because thou art a sinful man, therefore hath thy Saviour need to come to thee, to stay with thee; and because thou art humble in the acknowledgement of thy sinfulness, therefore Christ delights to abide with thee, and will call thee to abide with Him. No man ever fared the worse for abasing himself to his God. Christ hath left many a soul for froward and unkind usage; never any for the disparagement of itself, and entreaties of humility. Simon could not devise how to hold Christ faster than by thus suing Him to be gone, than by thus pleading his unworthiness.' 4. Did Jesus teach Simon to regard the ingathering of souls to Himself by the Gospel as transcending all physical miracles? O that the ministers of the everlasting Gospel would rise to such a view of their calling, and travail in birth until Christ be formed in men's souls! But it is not they only whom Christ's words to Peter are fitted to stimulate. "He that winneth souls is wise" (Prov. xi. 30)—be he who he may. "They that be wise shall shine as the brightness of the firmament; and they"—whoever they be—"that turn many to righteousness as the stars for ever and ever" (Dan. xii. 3). "Brethren, if any of you do err from the truth, and *one* convert him"—no matter who—"let him know that he which converteth the sinner from the error of his way shall save a soul from death, and shall hide a multitude of sins" (Jas. v. 19, 20).

12-16.—HEALING OF A LEPER. (=Matt. viii. 1-4; Mark i. 40-45.) For the exposition, see on Matt. viii. 1-4.

17-26.—HEALING OF A PARALYTIC. (=Matt. ix.

22 ^pWho can forgive sins but God alone? But when Jesus perceived their thoughts, he answering said unto them, What reason ye in your hearts?
23 Whether is easier to say, Thy sins be forgiven thee; or to say, Rise up
24 and walk? But that ye may know that ^qthe Son of man hath power upon earth to forgive sins, (he said unto the sick of the palsy,) I say unto thee, Arise, and take up thy couch, and go unto thine house.
25 And immediately he rose up before them, and took up that whereon he
26 lay, and departed to his own house, ^rglorifying God. And they were all amazed, and they glorified God, and were filled with fear, saying, We have seen strange things to-day.
27 And ^safter these things he went forth, and saw a publican, named Levi, sitting at the receipt of custom: and he said unto him, Follow me.
28, And he left all, rose up, and followed him. And ^tLevi made him a great
29 feast in his own house: and ^uthere was a great company of publicans and
30 of others that sat down with them. But their scribes and Pharisees murmured against his disciples, saying, Why do ye eat and drink with
31 publicans and sinners? And Jesus answering said unto them, They that
32 are whole need not a physician; but they that are sick. I ^vcame not to call the righteous, but sinners to repentance.
33 And they said unto him, ^wWhy do the disciples of John fast often, and make prayers, and likewise *the disciples* of the Pharisees; but thine
34 eat and drink? And he said unto them, Can ye make the children of the
35 bride-chamber fast while the ^xbridegroom is with them? But the days will come, when the bridegroom shall ^ybe taken away from them, and
36 then shall they ^zfast in those days. And ^ahe spake also a parable unto them; No man putteth a piece of a new garment upon an old: if otherwise, then both the new maketh a rent, and the piece that was *taken* out
37 of the new agreeth not with the old. And no man putteth new wine into old bottles; else the new wine will burst the bottles, and be spilled, and
38 the bottles shall perish. But new wine must be put into new bottles;
39 and both are preserved. No man also having drunk old *wine* straightway desireth new; for he saith, The old is better.

A. D. 31.

^p Ex. 34. 7.
^f s. 32. 5.
Ps. 103. 3.
Isa. 1. 18.
Isa. 43. 25.
Dan. 9. 9.
^q Isa. 53. 11.
Matt. 9. 6.
Matt. 28. 18.
John 5. 22, 23.
Acts 5. 31.
Col. 3. 13.
^r Ps. 103. 1.
^s Matt. 9. 9.
Mark 2. 13, 14.
^t Matt. 9. 10.
Mark 2. 15.
^u ch. 15. 1.
^v Matt. 9. 13.
1 Tim. 1. 15.
^w Matt. 9. 14.
Mark 2. 18.
^x Matt. 22. 2.
ch. 14.16-23.
2 Cor. 11. 2.
Rev. 19. 7.
Rev. 21. 2.
^y Dan. 9. 26.
Zec. 13. 7.
John 7. 33.
^a Matt. 6. 16, 17.
Acts 13. 2,3.
1 Cor. 7. 5.
2 Cor. 6.4,5.
2 Cor. 11.27.
^a Matt. 9. 16, 17.
Mark 2. 21, 22.

1-8; Mark ii. 1-12.) For the exposition, see on Mark ii. 1-12.
27-32.—LEVI'S (OR MATTHEW'S) CALL AND FEAST. (= Matt. ix. 9-13; Mark ii. 14-17.) For the exposition, see on Matt. ix. 9-13.
33-39.—DISCOURSE ON FASTING. (= Matt.ix.14-17; Mark ii. 18-22.) As this discourse is recorded by all the three first Evangelists immediately after their account of the Feast which Matthew made to his Lord, there can be no doubt that it was delivered on that occasion.

Mark introduces the subject thus (ii. 18): "And the disciples of John and of the Pharisees used to fast." These disciples of John, who seem not to have statedly followed Jesus, occupied a position intermediate between the Pharisaic life and that to which Jesus trained His own disciples; further advanced than the one, not so far advanced as the other. "And they come and say unto him"—or, according to our Evangelist, to whose narrative we now come, they brought their difficulty to Him through our Lord's own disciples. **33. And they said unto him, Why do the disciples of John fast often, and make prayers, and likewise the disciples of the Pharisees?** These seem to have fasted twice in the week (Luke xviii. 12), besides the prescribed seasons, but thine eat and drink —or, as in Matt. and Mark, "thy disciples fast not?" **34. And he said unto them, Can ye make the children of the bride-chamber**—the bridal attendants, **fast while the bridegroom is with them?** Glorious title for Jesus to take to Him-

self! The Old Testament is full of this conjugal tie between Jehovah and His people, to be realized in Messiah. See on Matt. xxii. 2, and Remark 1 on that Section; and compare John iii. 29. **35. But the days will come** [Ἐλεύσονται δὲ ἡμέραι]—rather, 'But days will come,' **when the bridegroom shall be taken away from them**— a delicate and affecting allusion to coming events, and the grief with which these would fill the disciples, **and then shall they fast in those days**—*q.d.*, 'In My presence such exercises were unseemly: when bereft of Me, they will have time enough and cause enough.' **36. And he spake also a parable unto them; No man putteth a piece of a new garment upon an old.** In Matthew and Mark the word employed [ἀγνάφου] signifies 'uncarded,' 'unfulled,' or 'undressed' cloth, which, as it is apt to shrink when wetted, would rend the old cloth to which it was sewed: **if otherwise**—if he *will* do so unwise a thing, **then both the new maketh a rent, and the piece that was taken out of the new agreeth not with the old. 37. And no man putteth new wine into old bottles** [ἀσκοὺς]— 'wine-skins.' They were made usually of goatskins, and of course would be liable to burst in the case supposed: **else** [εἰ δέ μήγε, again]—if he do such a thing, **the new wine will burst the bottles, and be spilled, and the bottles shall perish. 38. But new wine must be put into new bottles; and both are preserved. 39. No man also having drunk old wine straightway desireth new; for he saith, The old is better.** These are just examples of *incon-*

6 AND ^ait came to pass, on the second sabbath after the first, that he went through the corn fields; and his disciples plucked the ears of corn,

2 and did eat, rubbing *them* in *their* hands. And certain of the Pharisees said unto them, ^bWhy do ye that which is not lawful to do on the

3 sabbath days? And Jesus answering them said, Have ye not read so much as this, ^cwhat David did, when himself was an hungered, and they

4 which were with him; how he went into the house of God, and did take and eat the showbread, and gave also to them that were with him;

5 ^dwhich it is not lawful to eat but for the priests alone? And he said unto them, That the Son of man is Lord also of the sabbath.

6 And ^eit came to pass also on another sabbath, that he entered into the synagogue and taught: and there was a man whose right hand was

7 withered. And the scribes and Pharisees watched him, whether he would heal on the sabbath day; that they might find an accusation against

8 him. But he ^fknew their thoughts, and said to the man which had the withered hand, Rise up, and stand forth in the midst. And he arose and

9 stood forth. Then said Jesus unto them, I will ask you one thing; ^gIs it lawful on the sabbath days to do good, or to do evil? to save life, or to

10 destroy *it?* And looking round about upon them all, he said unto the man, Stretch forth thy hand. And he did so: and his hand was restored

11 whole as the other. And they were filled with madness; and communed one with another what they might do to Jesus.

A. D. 31.
CHAP. 6.
^a Matt. 12. 1.
Mark 2. 23.
^b Ex. 20. 10.
Matt. 12. 2.
Matt. 15. 2.
Mark 7. 2.
^c 1 Sam. 21.6.
^d Ex. 29.23,33.
Lev. 24. 9.
^e Matt. 12. 9.
Mark 3. 1.
ch. 13. 14.
ch. 14. 3.
John 9. 16.
^f 1 Sam. 16.7.
ch. 5. 22.
John 2. 24, 25.
John 6. 64.
John 21.17.
Acts 1. 24.
Rev. 2. 23.
^g Matt. 12.12, 13.
Mark 3. 4.
ch. 14. 3.
John 7. 23.

gruities in common things. As men's good sense leads them to avoid these in ordinary life, so are there analogous incongruities in spiritual things which the wise will shun. But what has this to do with the question about fasting? Much every way. The genius of the old economy—of whose *sadness* and *bondage* "fasting" might be taken as the symbol—was quite different from that of the new, whose characteristic is *freedom* and *joy:* the one of these, then, was not to be mixed up with the other. As, in the one case adduced for illustration, "the rent is made worse," and in the other "the new wine is spilled," so 'by a mongrel mixture of the ascetic ritualism of the old with the spiritual freedom of the new economy both are disfigured and destroyed.' The parable about preferring the old wine to the new, which is peculiar to our Gospel, has been variously interpreted. But the "new wine" seems plainly to be the evangelical freedom which Christ was introducing; and "the old," the opposite spirit of Judaism: men long accustomed to the latter could not be expected "straightway," or all at once, to take a liking for the former:—*q. d.*, 'These inquiries about the difference between My disciples, and the Pharisees, and even John's ways of living, are not surprising; they are the effect of *a natural revulsion against sudden change*, which time will cure; *the new wine will itself in time become old, and so acquire all the added charms of antiquity.'*

Remarks.—1. There may seem to be some inconsistency between the freedom and joy which our Lord here indirectly teaches to be characteristic of the new economy, and that sadness at His departure in Person from the Church which He intimates would be the proper feeling of all that love Him during the present state. But the two are quite consistent. We may sorrow for one thing and rejoice for another, even at the same time. The one, indeed, will necessarily chasten the other; and so it is here. The liberty wherewith Christ hath made us free is a well-spring of resistless and commanded joy; nor is this a jot abated, but only chastened and refined, by the widowed feeling of Christ's absence. But neither is this sense of Christ's absence the less real and sad that we are taught to "rejoice in

the Lord alway, " "Whom having not seen we love, in whom believing we rejoice with joy unspeakable and full of glory," in the assurance that "when He who is our Life shall appear, we also shall appear with Him in glory." 2. In all transition-states of the Church, or of any section of it, from the worse to the better, two classes appear among the true-hearted, representing two extremes. In the one, the *conservative* element prevails; in the other, the *progressive*. The one, sympathizing with the movement, are yet afraid of its going too fast and too far: the other are impatient of half-measures. The sympathy of the one class with what is good in the movement is almost neutralized and lost by their apprehension of the evil that is likely to attend the change: the sympathy of the other class with it is so commanding, that they are blind to danger, and have no patience with that caution which seems to them only timidity and trimming. There are dangers on both sides. Of many who shrink in the day of trial, when one bold step would land them safely on the right side, it may be said, "The children are brought to the birth, and there is not strength to bring forth." To many reckless reformers, who mar their own work, it may be said, "Be not righteous overmuch, neither make thyself overwise: why shouldest thou destroy thyself?" Our Lord's teaching here, while it has a voice to those who unreasonably cling to what is antiquated, speaks still more clearly to those hasty reformers who have no patience with the timidity of their weaker brethren. What a gift to the Church, in times of life from the dead, are even a few men endued with the wisdom to steer the ship between those two rocks!

CHAP. VI. 1-5.—Plucking Corn-Ears on the Sabbath Day. (= Matt. xii. 1-8; Mark ii. 23-28.) For the exposition, see on Matt. xii. 1-8.

6-11.—The Healing of a Withered Hand. (= Matt. xii. 9-14; Mark iii. 1-6.) For the exposition, see on Matt. xii. 9-14.

12-49.—The Twelve Apostles Chosen—Gathering Multitudes and Glorious Healings—The Sermon in the Plain (or Level Place). (= Matt. x. 2-4; v.—vii.; Mark iii. 13-19.)

12 And ^hit came to pass in those days, that he went out into a mountain
13 to pray, and continued all night in prayer to God. And when it was day, he called *unto him* his disciples: ⁱand of them he chose twelve,
14 whom also he named Apostles; Simon, (^jwhom he also named Peter,) and Andrew his brother, James and John, Philip and Bartholomew,
15 Matthew and Thomas, James the *son* of Alpheus, and Simon called
16 Zelotes, and Judas ^k*the brother* of James, and Judas Iscariot, which also was the traitor.
17 And he came down with them, and stood in the plain, and the company of his disciples, ^land a great multitude of people out of all Judea and Jerusalem, and from the sea coast of Tyre and Sidon,
18 which came to hear him, and to be healed of their diseases; and they
19 that were vexed with unclean spirits: and they were healed. And the whole multitude ^msought to touch him: for ⁿthere went virtue out of him, and healed *them* all.
20 And he lifted up his eyes on his disciples, and said, ^oBlessed *be ye*
21 poor: for yours is the kingdom of God. Blessed ^p*are ye* that hunger now: for ye shall be filled. ^qBlessed *are ye* that weep now: for ye shall
22 laugh. Blessed ^rare ye when men shall hate you, and when they ^sshall separate you *from their company*, and shall reproach *you*, and cast out your

A. D. 31.	
h	Matt. 14. 23.
i	Matt. 10. 1.
j	John 1. 42.
k	John 14. 22.
	Acts 1. 13.
	Jude 1.
l	Matt. 4. 25.
	Mark 3. 7.
m	Matt. 14. 36.
n	Mark 5. 30.
	ch. 8. 46.
o	Matt. 5. 3.
	Matt. 11. 5.
	Acts 14. 22.
	Jas. 2. 5.
p	Isa. 55. 1.
	1 Cor. 4. 11.
q	Isa. 61. 3.
	Rev. 7. 14-17.
r	Matt. 5. 11.
	1 Pet. 2. 19.
	1 Pet. 3. 14.
	1 Pet. 4. 14.
s	John 16. 2.

Our Lord has now reached the most important period in His public ministry, when His Twelve Apostles have to be chosen; and it is done with a solemnity corresponding to the weighty issues involved in it.

The Twelve Chosen (12-16). **12. And it came to pass in those days, that he went out**—probably from Capernaum, **and continued all night in prayer to God. 13. And when it was day, he called unto him his disciples: and of them he chose twelve, whom also he named apostles** [ἀποστόλους]—'sent,' or 'commissioned;' as if to put upon the very name by which they were in all future time to be known the seal of their Master's appointment. The work with which the day began shows what had been the burden of this whole night's devotions. As He directed His disciples to pray for "labourers" just before sending themselves forth (see on Matt. ix. 35—x. 5, Remarks 1 and 2), so here we find the Lord Himself in prolonged communion with His Father in preparation for the solemn appointment of those men who were to give birth to His Church, and from whom the world in all time was to take a new mould. How instructive is this! They appear all to have been first selected from amongst those who had been disciples of John the Baptist (see Acts i. 21, 22), as probably the most advanced or the most teachable; with a view also, no doubt, to diversity of gifts. And after watching the steadiness with which they had followed Him, the progress they had made in the knowledge of the truth, and their preparedness to enter the higher school to which they were now to be advanced, He solemnly "ordained" [ἐποίησεν], or 'constituted' these Twelve men, "that they should be with Him" (Mark iii. 14) as a Family, and enjoy His most private fellowship, as none of His other followers were permitted to do. By this they would not only hear much more from Him, and have it impressed upon them as it could not else have been, but catch His spirit, and take on a stamp which, when He was removed from them, and they had to prosecute His work, would bring their Master Himself to the recollection of His enemies. (See on Acts iv. 13.) **14-16. Simon, &c.** See on Matt. x. 1-4.

Gathering Multitudes and Glorious Healings (17-19). **17. And he came down with them, and**

stood in the plain [ἐπὶ τόπου πεδινοῦ]—or, 'on a level place;' that is, probably on some level plat below the mountain, while the listening multitudes lay beneath Him on what was more strictly "the plain." **and the company of his disciples**—the outer circle of His stated followers, **and a great multitude . . . which came to hear him, and to be healed of their diseases; 18. And they that were vexed with unclean spirits: and they were healed. 19. And the whole multitude sought to touch him: for there went virtue** [δύναμις]—or healing 'efficacy'—compare Mark v. 30, **out of him, and healed them all** [ἰᾶτο]—or 'kept healing,' denoting successive acts of mercy, 'till it went over "*all*" that needed it. There is something unusually grand in this touch of description, giving to the reader the impression of a more than usual exuberance of His majesty and grace in this succession of healings, which made itself felt among all the vast multitude.

Sermon in the Plain or Level Place (20-49). **20. And he lifted up his eyes on his disciples, and said.** Referring to our ample comments on the Sermon on the Mount (Matt. v.-vii.), we here only note a few things suggested by the present form of the Discourse, which could not be so properly taken up under the other form of it. **Blessed be ye poor: for yours is the kingdom of God. 21. Blessed are ye that hunger now: for ye shall be filled.** In the Sermon on the Mount the benediction is pronounced upon the "poor *in spirit*" and those who "hunger and thirst *after righteousness*." Here it is simply on the "poor" and the "hungry now." In this form of the Discourse, then, our Lord seems to have had in view "*the poor of this world*, rich in faith, and heirs of the kingdom which God hath promised to them that love Him," as these very beatitudes are paraphrased by James (ii. 5). **Blessed are ye that weep now: for ye shall laugh** [γελάσατε]. How charming is the liveliness of this word, to express what in Matthew is calmly set forth by the word "comfort!" **22. Blessed are ye when men shall hate you, and when they shall separate you [from their company]** [ἀφορίσωσιν]—whether from Church-fellowship, by excommunication, or from their social circles—both hard to flesh and blood. **and shall reproach you, and cast out your name as evil, for the Son of**

23 name as evil, for the Son of man's sake. Rejoice 'ye in that day, and leap for joy: for, behold, your reward *is* great in heaven: for "in the like
24 manner did their fathers unto the prophets. But °woe unto you that
25 are rich! for ye "have received your consolation. Woe *unto you that are full! for ye shall hunger. *Woe unto you that laugh now! for ye
26 shall mourn and weep. Woe *unto you when all men shall speak well of you! for so did their fathers to the false prophets.
27 But "I say unto you which hear, Love your enemies, do good to them
28 which hate you, bless them that curse you, and *pray for them which
29 despitefully use you. And °unto him that smiteth thee on the *one* cheek offer also the other; *and him that taketh away thy cloak forbid not *to*
30 *take thy* coat also. Give °to every man that asketh of thee; and of him
31 that taketh away thy goods ask *them* not again. And *as ye would that
32 men should do to you, do ye also to them likewise. For *if ye love them which love you, what thank have ye? for sinners also love those that
33 love them. And if ye do good to them which do good to you, what
34 thank have ye? for sinners also do even the same. And *if ye lend *to* *them* of whom ye hope to receive, what thank have ye? for sinners also
35 lend to sinners, to receive as much again. But love ye your enemies, and do good, and 'lend, hoping for nothing again'; and your reward shall be great, and *ye shall be the children of the Highest: for *he is kind
36 unto the unthankful and *to* the evil. Be 'ye therefore merciful, as your
37 Father also is merciful. Judge *not, and ye shall not be judged: condemn not, and ye shall not be condemned: forgive, and ye shall be
38 forgiven: give, "and it shall be given unto you; good measure, pressed down, and shaken together, and running over, shall men give into your °bosom. For *with the same measure that ye mete withal it shall be measured to you again.
39 And he spake a parable unto them: Can *the blind lead the blind?
40 shall they not both fall into the ditch? The 'disciple is not above his master: but every one ¹that is perfect shall be as his master.
41 And *why beholdest thou the mote that is in thy brother's eye, but
42 perceivest not the beam that is in thine own eye? Either how canst thou say to thy brother, Brother, let me pull out the mote that is in thine eye, when thou thyself beholdest not the beam that is in thine own eye? Thou hypocrite, 'cast out first the beam out of thine own eye, and then shalt thou see clearly to pull out the mote that is in thy brother's eye.

A. D. 31.
t Acts 5. 41.
Col. 1. 24.
Jas. 1. 2.
u Acts 7. 51.
v Amos 6. 1.
ch. 12. 21.
Jas. 5. 1.
w Matt. 6. 2.
ch. 16. 25.
x Isa. 65. 13.
y Pro. 14. 13.
z John 15. 19.
1 John 4. 5.
a Ex. 23. 4.
Pro. 25. 2.
Matt. 5. 44.
Rom. 12.20.
b ch. 23. 34.
Acts 7. 60.
c Matt. 5. 39
d 1 Cor. 6. 7.
e Deut. 15. 7.
Pro. 3. 27.
Pro. 21. 26.
Matt. 5. 42.
f Matt. 7. 12.
Phil. 4. 8.
g Matt. 5. 46.
h Matt. 5. 42.
i Lev. 25. 35.
Ps. 37. 26.
j Matt. 5. 45.
1 John 3. 1.
k Acts 14. 17.
l Matt. 5. 48.
Eph. 5. 1, 2.
m Matt. 7. 1.
n Pro. 19. 17.
o Ps. 79. 12.
p Matt. 7. 2.
q Matt.15.14.
r Matt. 10.24.
1 Or, shall be perfected as his master.
s Matt. 7. 3.
t Pro. 18. 17

man's sake. Compare the following: "Being reviled, we bless; being persecuted, we suffer it; being defamed, we entreat; we are made as the filth of the world, and are the offscouring of all things unto this day" (1 Cor. iv. 12, 13). Observe the language of our Lord in regard to the cause of all this ill treatment "For the Son of man's sake," says He in *v.* 22: "For My sake," says He in Matt. v. 11: "For righteousness' sake," says He in the immediately preceding *v.* 10. *Thus does Christ bind up the cause of Righteousness in the world with the reception of Himself.* 23. Rejoice ye in that day, and leap [for joy] [σκιρτήσατε] —a livelier word than even "be exceeding glad," or 'exult' in Matt. v. 12; for, behold, your reward is great in heaven: for in the like manner did their fathers unto the prophets. As five of the benedictions in the Sermon on the Mount are omitted in this Discourse, so now follow four *woes* not to be found there. And yet, being but the opposites of the benedictions pronounced, they need hardly any illustration. 24. But woe unto you that are rich! for ye have received your consolation. 25. Woe unto you that are full! for ye shall hunger—your inward craving strong as ever, but the materials of satisfaction for ever gone. Woe unto you that laugh now! for ye shall mourn and weep—who have all your good things and joyous feelings *here* and *now*, in perishable objects. See on ch. xvi. 25. 26. Woe unto you when all men shall speak well of you! for so did their fathers to the false prophets—paying court to them because they flattered them with peace when there was no peace. See Mic. ii. 11. For the principle of this woe and its proper limits, see John xv. 19.

37, 38. Judge not, and ye shall not be judged: condemn not . . . forgive . . . give, and it shall be given unto you; good measure, pressed down, &c. It will be observed, on comparing this with Matt. vii. 1, 2, that here it is much fuller and more graphic. 39. And he spake a parable unto them: Can the blind lead the blind? shall they not both fall into the ditch? This is not in the Sermon on the Mount; but it is recorded by Matthew in another and very striking connection (ch. xv. 14). 40. The disciple is not above his master: but every one that is perfect shall be as his master—*q. d.,* 'The disciple's aim is to come up to his master, and he

43 For "a good tree bringeth not forth corrupt fruit: neither doth a corrupt
44 tree bring forth good fruit. For "every tree is known by his own fruit.
For of thorns men do not gather figs, nor of a bramble bush gather they
45 ²grapes. A "good man out of the good treasure of his heart bringeth
forth that which is good; and an evil man out of the evil treasure of his
heart bringeth forth that which is evil: for of the abundance of the heart
his mouth speaketh.
46 And "why call ye me, Lord, Lord, and do not the things which I say?
47 Whosoever "cometh to me, and heareth my sayings, and doeth them, I
48 will show you to whom he is like: he is like a man which built an house,
and digged deep, and laid the foundation on a rock: and when 'the
flood arose, the stream beat vehemently upon that house, and could not
49 shake it; for it was founded upon "a rock. But he that heareth, and
doeth not, is like a man that without a foundation built an house upon
the earth; against which the stream did beat vehemently, and immediately it fell; and ᵇthe ruin of that house was great.

7 NOW when he had ended all his sayings in the audience of the people,
2 "he entered into Capernaum. And a certain centurion's servant, who
3 was dear unto him, was sick, and ready to die. And when he heard of
Jesus, he sent unto him the elders of the Jews, beseeching him that he
4 would come and heal his servant. And when they came to Jesus, they
besought him instantly, saying, That he was worthy for whom he should
5 do this: for he loveth our nation, and he hath built us a synagogue.
6 Then Jesus went with them.
And when he was now not far from the house, the centurion sent

A. D. 31
ᵘ Matt. 7. 16.
Gal. 6. 19,
23.
2 Tim. 3. 1-2.
ᵛ Matt. 12. 33.
² A grape.
ʷ Rom. 8. 5-8.
ˣ Mal. 1. 6.
Matt. 25. 11.
ch. 13. 25.
Rom. 2. 13.
Jas. 1. 22.
ʸ Matt. 7 24.
ᶻ Acts 14. 22.
2 Tim. 3. 12.
ᵃ Ps. 125. 1.
2 Tim. 2. 19.
1 Pet. 1. 5.
Jude 1.
ᵇ Job 8. 13.
Heb. 10. 29-
31.
2 Pet. 2. 20,
21.

CHAP. 7.
ᵃ Matt. 8. 5.
Matt. 27 54.
ch. 23. 47.
Acts 10. 1. 2.
Acts 23. 26.
Acts 23. 17.

thinks himself complete when he does so: if ye
then be but blind leaders of the blind, the perfection of your training will be but the certain and
complete ruin of both."

For Remarks on this Section, see those on the
Sermon on the Mount generally, and particularly
on the portions of it with which this Discourse
corresponds.

CHAP. VII. 1-10.—HEALING OF THE CENTU-
RION'S SERVANT. (= Matt. viii. 5-13.) The time
of this scene seems to have been just after the
preceding Discourse; the healing of the Leper
(Matt. viii. 1-4, and Mark i. 40-45) only intervening—on the way, probably, from the Mount
to Capernaum.

1. **Now when he had ended all his sayings in
the audience of the people, he entered into
Capernaum. 2. And a certain centurion's servant, who was dear unto him, was sick, and
ready to die.** These centurions were Roman
officers, so called from being captains over a
hundred soldiers. Though a heathen by birth and
early training, he had become acquainted with the
Jewish Religion probably either while quartered
at Capernaum or in some other Galilean town;
although there were so many proselytes to the
Jewish Religion in all the principal Greek and
Roman cities that he might have embraced the
true Faith even before his arrival in the Holy Land.
The same may be said of Cornelius (Acts x. 1).
His character appears here in the most beautiful
light. The value which he set upon this dying
servant and his anxiety for his recovery—as if he
had been his own son—is the first feature in it;
for, as *Bp. Hall* observes, he is unworthy to be
well served who will not sometimes wait upon his
followers. This servant was "sick of the palsy,
grievously tormented" (Matt. viii. 6). 3. **And
when he heard of Jesus**—like the woman with
the issue of blood (Mark v. 27), and the Syrophenician woman (Mark vii. 25). **he sent unto him
the elders** [πρεσβυτέρους]—rather 'elders' **of the**

Jews. His reason for this is best given in his own
words of profound humility: "wherefore neither
thought I myself worthy to come unto Thee"
(*v.* 7). Matthew represents him as coming himself
(viii. 5, 6): but this is only as James and John are
said to have petitioned their Lord (Mark x. 35),
when they got their mother to do it for them
(Matt. xx. 20); and as Jesus made and baptized
more disciples than John, though Jesus Himself
baptized not, but His disciples (John iv. 1, 2); and
as Pilate scourged Jesus (John xix. 1), when he
ordered it to be done. **beseeching him that he
would come and heal his servant. 4. And when
they came to Jesus, they besought him instantly**
[σπουδαίως]—or 'in haste,' **saying, That he was
worthy for whom he should do this: 5. for he
loveth our nation, and he hath built us a
synagogue.** These elders content not themselves
with delivering the humble petition of the centurion himself, but urge their own arguments in
support of it. And how precious is the testimony
they bear to this devout soldier; all the more so
as coming from persons who were themselves
probably strangers to the principle from which he
acted. "He loveth our nation," they say; for he
had found, in his happy experience, as our Lord
said to the woman of Samaria, that "Salvation is
of the Jews" (John iv. 22); "and (they add) he
hath built us a synagogue" [καὶ τὴν συναγωγὴν
αὐτὸς ᾠκοδόμησεν ἡμῖν]—'and himself built us
the synagogue;' rebuilding the synagogue of the
place at his own sole expense. His love to the
Jews took this appropriate and somewhat costly
form. He would leave a monument in Capernaum
of the debt he owed to the God of Israel by providing for His worship and the comfort of His
worshippers. If "a good name is better than
precious ointment" (Eccl. vii. 1), this military
proselyte certainly had it. **6. Then Jesus went
with them.**
**And when he was now not far from the
house, the centurion sent friends to him. This**

247

friends to him, saying unto him, Lord, trouble not thyself; for I am not
7 worthy that thou shouldest enter under my roof: wherefore neither thought
I myself worthy to come unto thee: *b*but say in a word, and my servant
8 shall be healed. For I also am a man set under authority, having under
me soldiers; and I say unto ¹one, Go, and he goeth; and to another,
Come, and he cometh; and to my servant, Do this, and he doeth *it.*
9 When Jesus heard these things, he marvelled at him, and turned him
about, and said unto the people that followed him, I say unto you, I
10 have not found so great faith, no, not in *c*Israel. And they that were
sent, returning to the house, found the servant whole that had been
sick.

A. D. 31.

1 This man,
b Ex. 15. 16.
Deut. 32. 39.
1 Sam. 2. 6.
Ps. 33. 9.
Ps. 107. 20.
Mark 1. 27.
ch. 4. 36.
ch. 5. 13.
* Ps. 147. 19.
Matt 9. 33.
Rom. 3.1,2.
Rom. 9. 4.

was a second message; and here again, what Matthew represents as said to our Lord by the centurion himself is by Luke, who is more specific and full, put into the mouth of the centurion's friends. **saying unto him, Lord, trouble not thyself; for I am not worthy that thou shouldest enter under my roof.** What deep humility! **7. Wherefore neither thought I myself worthy to come unto thee: but say in a word.** In Matthew it is "but speak the word only" [ἀλλὰ μόνον εἰπὲ λόγον]—or more expressively, 'but speak only a word.' **and my servant shall be healed.** No such faith as this had been before displayed. **8. For I also am a man set under authority, having under me soldiers; and I say unto one, Go, and he goeth; and to another, Come, and he cometh; and to my servant, Do this, and he doeth it**—*q. d.,* 'I know both to obey and command: though but a subaltern, my orders are implicitly obeyed: Shall not diseases, then, obey their Lord, and at His word be gone?' **9. When Jesus heard these things, he marvelled at him.** As *Bengel* hints, Jesus marvelled but at two things—*faith* (as here) and *unbelief* (Mark vi. 6): at the one, considering the general blindness in spiritual things; at the other, considering the light that shone around all who were privileged to hear Him and behold His works. But the unprecedented faith of this heathen convert could not fail to fill His soul with peculiar admiration. **and turned him about, and said unto the people that followed him**—Jews, no doubt, **I have not found so great faith, no, not in Israel**—among the chosen people; this Gentile outstripping all the children of the covenant. A most important addition to this statement is given by Matthew (viii. 11, 12), who wrote specially for the Jews: "And I say unto you, that many shall come from the east and west"—from all parts of the heathen world—"and shall sit down" [ἀνακλιθήσονται]—'shall recline,' as at a feast, "with Abraham, and Isaac, and Jacob"—the fathers of the ancient covenant: Luke, reporting a solemn repetition of these words on a later occasion (ch. xiii. 28-30), adds, "and all the prophets;" "in the kingdom of heaven:" "but the children of the kingdom"—born to its privileges, but void of faith, "shall be cast out into outer darkness," the darkness outside the banqueting-house; "there (or in this outside-region) shall be weeping and gnashing of teeth"—the one expressive of *anguish*, the other of *despair.* **10. And they that were sent, returning to the house, found the servant whole that had been sick.** In Matthew we read, "And Jesus said unto the centurion, Go thy way: and as thou hast believed, so be it done unto thee. And his servant was healed the self-same hour" (Matt. viii. 13), teaching, that as in these *bodily* diseases, so in the salvation of the *soul,* all hinges on *faith.* No doubt this was conveyed to him in the form of a message through the "friends" that brought the

second message. Whether Jesus now visited this centurion we are not informed.

Remarks.—1. How devoutly would this centurion, as he thought of the Providence that brought him into contact with the chosen people, and thus turned his heathen darkness into light, exclaim with the sweet Psalmist of Israel, "The lines are fallen unto me in pleasant places; yea, I have a goodly heritage"! (Ps. xvi. 6). And Cornelius also (Acts x. 1, &c.); and Lydia (Acts xvi. 14). And by what wonderful providences have hundreds and thousands since then been brought, as by accident and through circumstances the most trivial, into contact with the truth which has set them free! But, perhaps, if we knew all, it would be found that in every case it is in a way perfectly casual and all unexpected that the ear first hears effectually the loving Voice which says, "Look unto me, and be saved." And if so, what materials will this afford for wonder in heaven, when the whole story of each one's life will stand up before his view distinct and vivid; and what a fund of blissful intercourse will be thus provided, when the redeemed will, as we may reasonably believe, exchange with each other their past experience, as each says to the other, "Come, all ye that fear God, and I will declare what He hath done for my soul!"

'When this passing world is done,
When has sunk yon glaring sun,
When we stand with Christ in glory,
Looking o'er life's finished story,
Then, Lord, shall I fully know—
Not till then, how much I owe.'—M'CHEYNE.

2. Bright as was the radiance which shone from the Old Testament upon this mind that had been reared in Pagan darkness, it rested not there, but was only guided by it to Him of whom Moses, in the law, and the Prophets did write. Nor was his a hesitating or superficial faith. Capernaum being the place of Christ's stated residence while in Galilee, this devout officer seems to have not only heard His public addresses, but made himself sufficiently acquainted with the wonders of His gracious hand to have every doubt as to His claims removed, and a profound conviction implanted in his mind of His Divine dignity. When, therefore, he has need of His interposition, he applies for it with undoubting confidence, "beseeching Him to come and heal His Servant." But he shrinks from a personal application as "unworthy to come to Him;" and though he had petitioned Jesus to come and heal his servant, he sends again to say that it was too much honour to him that He should come under his roof, but that since one word of command from Him would suffice, he would be content with that. What wonderful faith is this for a convert from heathenism to reach! The arguments by which he illustrates the power of Jesus to order diseases to be gone—as servants in entire subjection to their Master and Lord—are singularly expressive of a

11　And it came to pass the day after, that he went into a city called
12　Nain; and many of his disciples went with him, and much people.　Now
when he came nigh to the gate of the city, behold, there was a dead man
carried out, the only son of his mother, and she was a widow: and much
13　people of the city was with her.　And when the Lord saw her, he *d*had
14　compassion on her, and said unto her, Weep not.　And he came and
touched the ²bier: and they that bare *him* stood still.　And he said,
15　Young man, I say unto thee, *e*Arise.　And he that was dead sat up, and
16　began to speak.　And he delivered him to his mother.　And there came
a fear on all: and they glorified God, saying, *f*That a great prophet is
17　risen up among us; and, *g*That God hath visited his people.　And this
rumour of him went forth throughout all Judea, and throughout all the
region round about.

A. D. 31.

d Lam. 3. 32.
John 11.33, 35.
Heb. 2. 17.
Heb. 4. 15.
2 Or, coffin.
e ch. 8. 54.
John 11.43.
Acts 9. 40.
Rom. 4. 17.
f ch. 24 19.
John 4. 19.
John 6. 14.
John 9. 17.
g ch. 1. 68.
ch. 19. 44.

faith in the sovereignty of Christ over the elements of nature and the forces of life to which nothing was impossible.　And when we "see how faith wrought with his works (in loving God's nation and building them a synagogue), and by works his faith was made perfect;" and when we observe how all this anxiety of his was not like that of Jairus for the life of an only *daughter* (ch. viii. 42), nor like that of the nobleman for his *son* (John iv. 47), but for a *servant* that was dear to him, can we wonder that Jesus should say, "I have not found so great faith, no, not in Israel"?　3. If the Lord Jesus had been a mere creature, could He have suffered such views of Him to pass uncorrected?　But instead of this—as on every other occasion—*the more exalted were men's views of Him, ever the more grateful it was to His spirit.*　See on ch. v. 1-11, Remark 2.　4. There is too good reason to fear that those very elders of the Jews who besought Jesus to come and heal the Centurion's servant, and enforced their petition so well, had themselves none of the centurion's faith in the Lord Jesus.　Our Lord's words seem to imply as much.　And when He says that this centurion was, after all, but one of a class which, from the most distant and unpromising spots, would occupy the highest places and be in the most favoured company in the kingdom of heaven—while those that had been nursed in the arms and dandled upon the knees and had sucked the breasts of God's lawgivers and prophets, and basked in the sunshine of supernatural truth and divine ordinances, without any inward transformation, would be thrust out, and found weltering in anguish and despair—what a warning does it utter to the religiously favoured, and what encouragement does it hold out to work hopefully amongst the heathen abroad and the outcasts at home, that "there are first which shall be last, and there are last which shall be first!"

11-17.—THE WIDOW OF NAIN'S SON RAISED TO LIFE.　This incident is peculiar to our Evangelist, and its occurrence in Luke's Gospel alone illustrates that charming characteristic of it—its liking for those scenes, circumstances, and sayings of Jesus which manifest His *human tenderness, compassion, and grace.*　The time is expressly stated in the opening words.

11. And it came to pass the day after—that is, the day after He had healed the centurion's servant, that he went into a city called Nain —a small village not elsewhere mentioned in Scripture, and only this once probably visited by our Lord: it lay a little to the south of mount Tabor, about twelve miles from Capernaum.　and many of his disciples went with him, and much people [ὄχλος πολύς]—'a great multitude.'　12. Now when he came nigh to the gate of

the city, behold, there was a dead man carried out [ἐξεκομίζετο]—in the act of being so.　Dead bodies, being ceremonially unclean, were not allowed to be buried within the cities—though the kings of David's house were buried in the city of David—and the funeral was usually on the same day as the death.　the only son of his mother, and she was a widow—affecting particulars, and told with delightful simplicity.　13. And when the Lord saw her.　This sublime appellation of Jesus—"the Lord"—is more usual, as *Bengel* notes, with Luke and John than Matthew, while Mark holds the mean.　he had compassion on her, and said unto her, Weep not.　What consolation to thousands of the bereaved has this single verse carried from age to age!　14. And he came and touched the bier—no doubt with a look and manner which said, Stand still.　and they that bare him stood still.　And he said, Young man, I say unto thee, Arise.　15. And he that was dead sat up—the bier [σορὸς] was an open one, and began to speak—evidencing that he was both alive and well.　And he delivered him to his mother.　What mingled majesty and grace shines here!　Behold, the Resurrection and the Life in human flesh, with a word of command, bringing back life to the dead body, and Incarnate Compassion putting forth its absolute power to dry a widow's tears.　16. And there came a fear on all—a religious awe, and they glorified God, saying, That a great prophet is risen up among us; and, That God hath visited his people—after long absence, more than bringing back the days of Elijah and Elisha.　For they, though they raised the dead, did so *laboriously;* Jesus immediately, and with a word: they confessedly as servants and creatures, by a power *not their own;* Jesus by that inherent "virtue," which "went out of Him," in every cure which He wrought.　Compare 1 Ki. xvii. 17-24; 2 Ki. iv. 32-37; and see on Mark v. 30.　17. And this rumour of him went forth throughout all Judea, and throughout all the region round about.

For Remark on this Section, see on Mark v. 21-43, Remark 5.

18-35.—THE IMPRISONED BAPTIST'S MESSAGE TO HIS MASTER—THE REPLY, AND DISCOURSE REGARDING JOHN AND HIS MISSION, ON THE DEPARTURE OF THE MESSENGERS (=Matt. xi. 2-19.)　For the circumstances of the Baptist's imprisonment, see on Mark vi. 17-20.

He had now lain in prison probably a full year, far away from the scene of his Master's labours.　But his faithful disciples appear from time to time to have kept him informed of them.　At length the tidings they brought him, including no doubt those of the resurrection of the widow of Nain's son from the dead, appear to have determined the lonely prisoner to take a step

18, And [h] the disciples of John showed him of all these things. And John

19 calling *unto him* two of his disciples, sent *them* to Jesus, saying, Art thou

20 [i] he that should come? or look we for another? When the men were come unto him, they said, John Baptist hath sent us unto thee, saying,

21 Art thou he that should come? or look we for another? And in the same hour he cured many of *their* infirmities and plagues, and of evil

22 spirits; and unto many *that were* blind he gave sight. Then [j] Jesus answering said unto them, Go your way, and tell John what things ye have seen and heard; [k] how that the blind see, the lame walk, the lepers are cleansed, the deaf hear, the dead are raised, [l] to the poor the Gospel

23 is preached. And blessed is *he*, whosoever shall not be offended in me.

24 And [m] when the messengers of John were departed, he began to speak unto the people concerning John, What went ye out into the wilderness

25 for to see? A reed shaken with the wind? But what went ye out for to see? A man clothed in soft raiment? Behold, they which are gorgeously

26 apparelled, and live delicately, are in kings' courts. But what went ye

A. D. 31.

[h] Matt. 11. 2.
[i] Ezek. 21. 27.
Ezek 34. 23, 29.
Dan. 9. 24-26.
Mic. 5. 2.
Hag. 2. 7.
Zec. 9. 9.
Mal. 3. 1-3.
[j] Matt. 11. 5.
[k] Isa. 29. 18.
Isa. 35. 5.
Isa. 42. 6.
Acts 26. 18.
[l] Isa. 61. 1.
Zeph. 3. 12.
ch. 4. 18.
Jas. 2. 5.
[m] Matt. 11. 7.

---

which probably he had often thought of, but till now shrunk from. **18. And the disciples of John showed him of all these things. 19. And John calling unto him two of his disciples** [δύο τινὰς]—'two certain disciples;' that is, two picked, trusty ones. [In Matt. xi., instead of δύο, *Lachmann, Tischendorf, and Tregelles,* on certainly powerful evidence, print διὰ—'sent by his disciples.' *Fritzsche* and *Alford* follow them in their text; and *Meyer* and *de Wette* approve of the change. But as the external evidence is not overpowering, so there is, in our judgment, the strongest internal evidence against it, and in favour of the received reading, which differs only by a letter and a half from the other reading.] **sent them to Jesus, saying, Art thou he that should come? or look we for another? 20. When the men were come unto him, they said, John Baptist hath sent us unto thee, saying, Art thou he that should come? or look we for another?** Was this a question of doubt as to the Messiahship of his Lord, as Rationalists are fain to represent it? Impossible, from all we know of him. Was it then purely for the satisfaction of his disciples, as some expositors, more concerned for the Baptist's reputation than for simple and natural interpretation, take it? Obviously not. The whole strain of our Lord's reply shows that it was designed for John himself. Clearly it was a message of *impatience,* and almost of *desperation.* It seemed, no doubt, hard to him that his Master should let him lie so long in prison for his fidelity —useless to his Master's cause and a comparative stranger to His proceedings—after having been honoured to announce and introduce Him to His work and to the people. And since the wonders of His hand seemed only to increase in glory as He advanced, and it could not but be easy for Him who preached deliverance to the captives, and the opening of the prison to them that were bound, to put it into the heart of Herod to set him at liberty, or to effect his liberation in spite of him, he at length determines to see if, through a message from the prison by his disciples, he cannot get Him to speak out His mind, and at least set his own at rest. This, we take it, was the real object of his message. The message itself, indeed, was far from a proper one. It was peevish; it was presumptuous; it was all but desperate. He had got depressed; he was losing heart; his spirit was clouded; Heaven's sweet light had, to some extent, departed from him; and this message was the consequence. As it was announced that he should come in the spirit and power of Elijah,

so we find him treading in that prophet's steps rather more than was desirable (see 1 Ki. xix. 1-4). **21. And in the same hour**—no doubt expressly with a view to its being reported to John, **he cured many of their infirmities and plagues, and of evil spirits; and unto many that were blind he gave sight** [ἐχαρίσατο τὸ βλέπειν]—'granted [the gift of] sight.' **22. Then Jesus answering said unto them, Go your way, and tell John what things ye have seen and heard.** No doubt along with the miracles which they "saw," they would "hear" those magic words with which He rolled away the maladies that came before Him. Nor would He fail to drop some other words of grace, fitted to impress the minds of the messengers, and, when reported, to cheer the spirit of their lonely master. **how that the blind see, the lame walk, the lepers are cleansed, the deaf hear, the dead are raised.** As the article is wanting in each of these clauses, the sense would be better perceived by the English reader thus, though scarcely tunable enough: 'Blind persons are seeing, lame people are walking, leprous persons are getting cleansed, deaf people are hearing, dead persons are being raised,' **to the poor the Gospel is preached** [εὐαγγελίζονται] —or 'is [in course of] being preached;' alluding to the great Messianic prediction, as it was uttered and appropriated by Himself at Nazareth, "The Spirit of the Lord is upon me, because He hath anointed me to preach the Gospel to the *poor.*" **23. And blessed is he, whosoever shall not be offended in me.** 'Let these things convince him that My hand is not shortened that it cannot save; but blessed is he who can take Me with just as much light as to his future lot as is vouchsafed to him.' This was all the reply that the messengers received. Not a ray of light is cast on his prospects, nor a word of commendation uttered while his disciples are present; he must die in simple faith, and as a martyr to his fidelity. But no sooner are they gone, than Jesus breaks forth into a glorious commendation of him.

24. And when the messengers of John were departed, he began to speak unto the people concerning John, What went ye out into the wilderness for to see? A reed shaken with the wind? —'a man driven about by every gust of popular opinion, and uttering an uncertain sound? Such is not John.' **25. But what went ye out for to see? A man clothed in soft raiment?**—'a self-indulgent, courtly preacher? Such was not John.' **Behold, they which are gorgeously apparelled, and live delicately, are in kings' courts.** 'If that be the

250

out for to see? A prophet? Yea, I say unto you, and much more than
27 a prophet. This is *he* of whom it is written, "Behold, I send my mes-
28 senger before thy face, which shall prepare thy way before thee. For I
say unto you, Among those that are born of women there is not a greater
prophet than John the Baptist: but he that is least in the kingdom of
God is greater than he.

29 And all the people that heard *him*, and the publicans, justified God,
30 °being baptized with the baptism of John. But the Pharisees and lawyers
³rejected ᴾthe counsel of God ⁴against themselves, being not baptized of
him.

31 And the Lord said, ᵠWhereunto then shall I liken the men of this
32 generation? and to what are they like? They are like unto children
sitting in the market-place, and calling one to another, and saying, We
have piped unto you, and ye have not danced; we have mourned to you,
33 and ye have not wept. For ʳJohn the Baptist came neither eating bread

A. D. 31.	
ⁿ Isa. 40. 3.	
Mal. 3. 1.	
Mal. 4. 5.	
ch. 1. 16, 17.	
76.	
ᵒ Matt. 3. 5.	
ch. 3. 12.	
₃ Or. frus-	
trated.	
ᴾ Acts 20. 27.	
₄ Or. within	
them-	
selves.	
ᵠ Lam. 2. 13.	
Matt. 11.16.	
Mark 4. 30.	
ʳ Matt. 3. 4.	
Mark 1. 6.	
ch. 1. 15.	

man ye wanted, ye must go in quest of him to royal palaces.' **26. But what went ye out for to see? A prophet?**—a faithful straightforward utterer of the testimony given to him to bear? **Yea, I say unto you, and much more than a prophet.** 'If that was what ye flocked to the wilderness to see in John, then ye have not been disappointed; for he is that, and much more than that.' **27. This is he of whom it is written** (Mal. iii. 1), **Behold, I send my messenger before thy face, which shall prepare thy way before thee.** See on Mark i. 3; and on Luke i. 17. 'There were many prophets, but only one Forerunner of the Lord's Christ; and this is he.' **28. For I say unto you, Among those that are born of women there is not—** "there hath not risen" (Matt. xi. 11) **a greater prophet than John the Baptist: but he that is least in the kingdom of God is greater than he.** The point of comparison is manifestly not personal character; for as it could hardly be said that in this respect he excelled every human being that preceded him, so it would be absurd to say that he was outstripped by the least advanced of the disciples of Christ. It is of his official *standing* or *position* in the economy of grace that our Lord is speaking. In that respect he was above all that ever went before him, inasmuch as he was the last and most honoured of the Old Testament prophets, and stood on the very edge of the new economy, though belonging to the old: but for this very reason, the humblest member of the new economy was *in advance of him.* In Matt. xi. 12-15, we have the following important additions:—"And from the days of John the Baptist until now the kingdom of heaven suffereth violence, and the violent take it by force" [βιάζεται, καὶ βιασταὶ ἁρπάζουσιν αὐτήν]; 'is being forced, and violent persons are seizing it.' The sense of these remarkable words is best seen in the form in which they were afterwards repeated, as preserved by our Evangelist alone (Luke xvi. 16): "The law and the prophets were until John"—who stood midway between the old economy of the law and the prophets and the new; above the one, but below the other—" since that time the kingdom of God is preached, and every man presseth into it" [εἰς αὐτὴν βιάζεται], or ' is forcing his way into it.' The idea is that of a *rush* for something unexpectedly and transportingly brought within their reach. In the one passage the *struggle* to obtain entrance is the prominent idea; in the other and later one it is the *multitude* that were thus pressing or forcing their way in. And what our Lord says of John in both places is that his ministry constituted the honourable point of transition from the one state of things to the other. "For,"

251

to continue Matthew's additions to this Discourse, "all the prophets and the law prophesied until John. And if ye will receive it, this is Elias, which was for to come. He that hath ears to hear, let him hear." They expected the literal Elijah the Tishbite to reappear before the coming of Messiah; misinterpreting the closing words of the prophet Malachi (iv. 5), and misled by the LXX., which rendered it, "Behold, I send you Elijah *the Tishbite*." But our Lord here tells them plainly that this promised messenger was no other than John the Baptist of whom he had been speaking; although, knowing that this would be a startling and not very welcome announcement to those who confidently looked for the reappearance of the ancient prophet himself from heaven, He first says it was intended *for those who could take it in,* and then calls the attention of all who had ears to hear it to what he had said. Coming back now to our own Evangelist,
29. And all the people that heard [him] [ἀκούσας] —rather, 'on hearing [this],' **and the publicans, justified God, being baptized** [βαπτισθέντες]—rather, 'having been baptized' **with the baptism of John. 30. But the Pharisees and lawyers rejected the counsel of God against themselves, being not—** or rather, 'not having been' **baptized of him—** a striking remark of the Evangelist himself on the different effects produced by our Lord's testimony to John. The spirit of it is, that all those of the audience who had surrendered themselves to the great preparatory ministry of John, and submitted themselves to his Baptism—including the publicans, amongst whom there had been a considerable awakening—were grateful for this encomium on one to whom they owed so much, and gave glory to God for such a gift, through whom they had been led to Him who now spake to them (ch. i. 16, 17); whereas the Pharisees and lawyers, true to themselves in having refused the Baptism of John, now set at nought the merciful design of God in the Saviour Himself, to their own undoing.
31. [And the Lord said], Whereunto then shall I liken the men of this generation? and to what are they like? [The introductory words of this verse—Εἶπεν δὲ ὁ Κύριος—have scarcely any authority at all, and were evidently no part of the original text. They were added probably at first to some Church Lesson, to introduce what follows, and thence found their way into the text.] **32-35. They are like unto children . . . saying, We have piped . . . and ye have not danced . . . mourned . . . and ye have not wept. For John . . . came neither eating . . . nor drinking . . . and ye say, He hath a devil. The Son of man**

34 nor drinking wine; and ye say, He hath a devil. The Son of man is come eating and drinking; and ye say, Behold a gluttonous man, and a 35 wine-bibber, a friend of publicans and sinners! But *Wisdom is justified of all her children.

A. D. 31.

* Hos. 14. 9.
Matt 11. 19.
1 Cor. 1. 23, 24.

is come eating and drinking; and ye say, Behold a gluttonous man . . . a friend of publicans and sinners! But Wisdom is justified of all her children. As cross, capricious children, invited by their playmates to join them in their amusements, will play with them neither at weddings nor at funerals (juvenile imitations of the joyous and mournful scenes of life), so that generation rejected both John and his Master: the one because he was too unsocial—as if under some dark demoniacal influence; the other, because he was too much the reverse, lax in his habits, and consorting with the lowest classes of society. But the children of Wisdom recognize and honour her whether in the austere garb of the Baptist or in the more attractive style of his Master, whether in the Law or in the Gospel, whether in rags or in royalty; as it is written, "The full soul loatheth an honeycomb: but to the hungry soul every bitter thing is sweet" (Prov. xxvii. 7).

Remarks.—1. Among the internal evidences of the truth of the Gospel History, none is more striking, and to an unsophisticated mind more resistless, than the view which it gives of John the Baptist. Who, in the first place, would not have expected that the ministry of the Forerunner should cease as soon as that of his Master commenced; and yet it did not, but both continued for some time the same work of preaching and baptizing. Next, who would not have expected that the disciples of John would all attach themselves to his Master, especially after what he said when questioned on that subject? (John iii. 25-36). And yet, to the very last, there was a company known by the name of "John's disciples," who not only remained with him, but followed a more austere rule of life than the disciples of Jesus Himself, a mode of life suited to the man who seems never to have mixed in general society, but kept himself, in a great measure, secluded; and only when John was beheaded, and by his affectionate and faithful disciples decently interred, do this class seem to have joined themselves to Jesus in a body. Then, Christ's not only letting John be imprisoned, but lie in prison so long without even a message of sympathy being sent him; and, after the patience of the lonely prisoner was well-nigh worn out, and all the more tried by the tidings that reached him of Christ's triumphant career, when he sent a message to his Master, couched in terms almost of desperation, that he should receive no other answer than that the tidings that had reached him of his Master's glory were true to the full, and that blessed was he who did not allow himself to be staggered and stumbled at Him—all this is the very reverse of anything one would expect. But further still, that while uttering not one word in commendation of John in the hearing of his disciples, the reporting of which might have lifted up his depressed spirit, our Lord should, as soon as they were gone, break forth into a lofty encomium on his character and office—who would have expected Him to act so? Finally, that He should allow him to be beheaded, to gratify a base woman, and when tidings of this were brought to Jesus by his sorrowing disciples, that not a word should be uttered by Him on the subject:—these things, which surprise and almost perplex us as *facts*, it is impossible to conceive of as pure *inven-*

tions; being the very opposite of all that the history of such inventions would lead us to expect. But, 2. When we come to deal with them *as* facts, we see in them but vivid illustrations of certain features of the Divine procedure for which we ought to be prepared. When the three Hebrew youths were threatened with the burning fiery furnace if they would not worship Nebuchadnezzar's golden idol, they expressed their full conviction that the God they served both could and would deliver them; but even should they be mistaken in this expectation, they were still resolved rather to suffer than to sin. And they suffered not. But John did. He had indeed counted the cost, but he had it to pay. 'Wilt thou be faithful even unto death?' was the question, and his spirit answered, Yes. 'Canst thou lie in prison unrescued, and even uncheered, save by the light thou already hast, and at length in a moment be despatched by those whom thy fidelity hath stung to the quick?' To this also his true heart doubtless bowed, though the trying question was never explicitly submitted to him. And such is what thousands of the martyrs of Jesus have undergone for His name. Nor can we doubt that this very record of the Lord's procedure towards the Baptist has soothed many a one when called to pass through a like dreary period of comfortless suffering, ending in death, for Jesus' sake. And may we not please ourselves with the thought that, like as the words wrung from the Saviour Himself in Gethsemane—"O my Father, if it be possible, let this cup pass from me"—were followed by the placid words, "Father, into thy hands I commend my spirit;" so the deep depression which prompted the question, "Art Thou He that should come, or look we for another?" was followed by a serene contentment and placid hope which might thus sing its pensive song, and only be interrupted by the murderer with his bloody axe?—

> 'God moves in a mysterious way
>   His wonders to perform:
> He plants His footsteps in the sea,
>   And rides upon the storm.
>
> 'Deep in unfathomable mines
>   Of never-failing skill,
> He treasures up His bright designs,
>   And works His sovereign will.
>
> 'His purposes will ripen fast,
>   Unfolding every hour;
> The bud may have a bitter taste,
>   But sweet will be the flower.'—COWPER.

3. As when John the Baptist ushered in an era of new light and liberty in the kingdom of God, "every man pressed into it;" so there have been periods in the history of the Church ever since, in which a light and a freedom altogether unwonted have been infused into the Christian ministry, or men have been raised up outside the regular ministry, but gifted specially for special work, and particularly for rousing the impenitent to flee from the coming wrath and lay hold on eternal life, whose labours God designs to bless to the shaking of the dry bones and the turning of many to righteousness. Publicans and sinners—the most unlikely classes—are then to be seen flocking to Christ; while scribes and Pharisees—the respectably religious and the formal amongst the ministers of the Gospel—stand aloof,

36   And 'one of the Pharisees desired him that he would eat with him. And he went into the Pharisee's house, and sat down to meat.

37   And, behold, a "woman in the city, which was a sinner, when she knew that *Jesus* sat at meat in the Pharisee's house, brought an alabaster box

38   of ointment, and stood at his feet behind "*him* weeping, and began to wash his feet with tears, and did wipe *them* with the hairs of her head,

39   and kissed his feet, and anointed *them* with the ointment. Now when the Pharisee which had bidden him saw *it*, he spake within himself,

A. D. 31.

ᵗ Matt. 26 6.
Mark 14. 3.
John 11. 2.
ᵘ ch. 8. 2.
John 9. 24.
ᵛ Zec. 12. 10.
Rom. 5. 20.
1 Tim. 1.15.
· 16.

and cannot easily conceal their dislike at what they deem irregularities, and fanaticism, and dangers. At such a time it will be the part of the simple-hearted and the wise to hail, on the one hand, the ingathering of souls to Christ, however it be effected, and, on the other hand, by prudent and kindly guidance of it, to keep so glorious a work from being marred by human folly. 4. Is it not extraordinary that, after our Lord's most explicit declaration here, that John the Baptist was *the* Elias that prophecy taught the Church to look for before the coming of Messiah, there are Christian students of prophecy who affirm that the Jews were quite right in expecting the literal Elijah from heaven; and who, while admitting that John was *an* Elias, sent to announce the *first* coming of Christ, maintain that the prophecy will only be properly fulfilled in the coming of the Tishbite himself to prepare men for His *second* coming? The thing to be condemned here is not so much the extravagance of the expectation itself, which, the more one thinks of it, will appear the more extravagant, but the manifest distortion which it puts upon our Lord's words, and the violence which it does to the prophecy. But all this comes of an out-and-out literalism in the interpretation of prophecy, which in some cases brings out conclusions, not only very harsh, but scarcely consistent with the principle itself. 5. When men want an excuse for rejecting or disregarding the grace of the Gospel, they easily find it. And there are none more ready and common than those arising out of something objectionable in the mode of presenting the truth. One preacher is too austere; another too free: one is too long; another too short: one is too sentimental; another too hard. Nothing pleases; nobody quite suits them. But O, when the soul is hungry, how welcome is God's solid truth, Christ's precious Gospel, however it comes! And so "Wisdom is justified of her children," who know her, hail her, clasp her to their bosom, however humbly clad; while those who do otherwise only show themselves to be "full souls," to whom even an honey-comb is distasteful—"the whole, who need not the Physician" and prize Him not.

36-50. THE WOMAN THAT WAS A SINNER, AND SIMON THE PHARISEE. This exquisite scene is peculiar to Luke. The time is quite uncertain. Perhaps it is introduced here as being suggested by "the publicans" and others of similar character, whom the preceding Section brought before us as welcoming Christ, while "the Pharisees and lawyers rejected the counsel of God against themselves" (vv. 29, 30).

36. And one of the Pharisees desired—or 're-quested' him that he would eat with him. And he went into the Pharisee's house, and sat down to meat. This Pharisee seems to have been in a state of mind regarding Jesus intermediate between that of the few who, like Nicodemus, were led to believe on Him, and of the overwhelming majority who regarded Him with suspicion from the first, which soon grew into deadly dislike. We shall see that, though not free from cold suspicion, He

was desirous of a closer acquaintance with our Lord, under the impression that He might perhaps at least be a prophet. And our Lord, knowing the opportunity it would afford Him of receiving the love of a remarkable convert from the worst class of society, and expounding the great principles of saving truth, accepts His invitation.

37. And, behold, a woman in the city—what city is not known: it may have been Capernaum, which was a sinner—who had led a profligate life. But *there is no ground whatever for the prevalent notion that this woman was Mary Magdalene* (see on ch. viii. 2); nor do we know what her name was. It may have been concealed from motives of delicacy; but indeed the names of very few women are given in the Gospels. when she knew that Jesus sat at meat in the Pharisee's house, brought an alabaster box of ointment—a perfume-vessel, in some cases very costly, as we know from John xii. 5. If the ointment, as *Alford* suggests, had been an accessory to her unhallowed work of sin, the offering of it as here described has a tender interest; but there is no certainty of that. 38. And stood at his feet behind him weeping—the posture at meals being a reclining one, with the feet out behind, and began—or proceeded to wash his feet with tears. The word here translated "wash" [βρέχειν] signifies to 'bathe' or 'bedew.' and did wipe them with the hairs of her head—the long tresses of that hair on which before she had bestowed too much attention. Had she come for such a purpose, she had not been at a loss for a towel. But tears do not come at will, especially in such plenty. No, they were quite involuntary, pouring down in a flood upon His naked feet, as she bent down to kiss them; and deeming them rather fouled than washed by this, she hastened to wipe them off with the only towel she had, the long tresses of her own hair, with which, as *Stier* observes, slaves were wont to wash their masters' feet. and kissed his feet [κατεφίλει]. The word signifies to 'caress,' or 'kiss tenderly and repeatedly'—which *v.* 45 shows to be the meaning here. What prompted all this? He who knew her heart tells·us it was *much love, springing from a sense of much forgiveness.* Where she had met with Christ before, or what words of His had brought life to her dead heart and a sense of Divine pardon to her guilty soul, we know not. But probably she was of the crowd of "publicans and *sinners*" whom incarnate Compassion drew so often around Him, and heard from His lips some of those words such as never man spake, "Come unto me, all ye that labour," &c. No personal interview had up to this time taken place between them; but she could keep her feelings no longer to herself, and having found her way to Him (and entered along with him, *v.* 45), they burst forth in this surpassing, yet most art less style, as if her whole soul would go out to Him. 39. Now when the Pharisee which had bidden him saw it. Up to this time He seems to have formed no definite opinion of our Lord, and invited him apparently to obtain materials for a judgment. he spake within himself, saying, This man, if he were a prophet—one

253

saying, *w*"This man, if he were a prophet, would have known who and what manner of woman *this is* that toucheth him; for she is a sinner.

40 And Jesus answering said unto him, Simon, I have somewhat to say

41 unto thee. And he saith, Master, say on. There was a certain creditor which had two debtors: the one owed five hundred *x*pence, and the other

42 fifty. And when they had nothing to pay, he frankly *y*forgave them

43 both. Tell me therefore, which of them will love him most? Simon answered and said, I suppose that *he* to whom he forgave most. And he

44 said unto him, Thou hast rightly judged. And he turned to the woman, and said unto Simon, Seest thou this woman? I entered into thine house, thou gavest me no *z*water for my feet: but she hath washed my feet with

45 tears, and wiped *them* with the hairs of her head. Thou gavest me no *a*kiss: but this woman since the time I came in hath not ceased to kiss

46 my feet. My *b*head with oil thou didst not anoint: but this woman hath

47 anointed my feet with ointment. Wherefore *c*I say unto thee, Her sins, which are many, are forgiven; for she loved much: but to whom little is

48 forgiven, *the same* loveth little. And he said unto her, *d*Thy sins are

49 forgiven. And they that sat at meat with him began to say within

A. D. 31.

w ch. 15. 2.
x Matt. 18. 28.
y Isa. 1. 18.
Isa. 43. 25.
Isa. 44. 22.
z Gen. 18. 4.
1 Tim. 5. 10.
a 1 Cor. 16. 20.
2 Cor. 13. 12.
b Ps. 23. 5.
Eccl. 9. 8.
1 John 2. 20, 27.
c 1 Tim. 1. 14.
d Matt. 9. 2.
Mark 2. 5.
ch. 5. 20.
Acts 13. 38, 39.
Rom. 4. 6-8.
Col. 1. 12-14.

possessed of supernatural knowledge. The form of expression here employed is to this effect—'If he were a prophet—but that he cannot be,' [εἰ ἦν προφήτης] **would have known who and what manner of woman this is that toucheth him; for she is a sinner.** 'I have now discovered this man: If he were what he gives himself forth to be, he would not have suffered a wretch like this to come near him; but plainly he knows nothing about her, and therefore he can be no prophet.' Not so fast, Simon; thou hast not seen through thy Guest yet, but He hath seen through thee. Too courteous to expose him nakedly at his own table, He couches His home-thrusts, like Nathan with David, in the first instance under the veil of a parable, and makes him pronounce both the woman's vindication and his own condemnation; and then he lifts the veil.

40, 41. And Jesus answering said unto him, Simon . . . There was a certain creditor which had two debtors: the one owed five hundred pence, the other fifty. 42. And when they had nothing to pay, he frankly forgave them both. Tell me therefore, which of them will love him most? 43. Simon answered and said, I suppose he to whom he forgave most. And he said unto him, Thou hast rightly judged. Now for the unexpected and pungent application. The two debtors are the woman and Simon; the criminality of the one was *ten times* that of the other—or in the proportion of *five hundred* to *fifty;* but both being equally insolvent, both are with equal frankness forgiven; and Simon is made to own that the greatest debtor to forgiving mercy will cling to her Divine Benefactor with the deepest gratitude. Does our Lord then admit that Simon and the woman were both truly forgiven persons? Let us see. **44. And he turned to the woman, and said unto Simon, Seest thou this woman? I entered into thine house, thou gavest me no water for my feet**—'a compliment from a host to his guest which love surely would have prompted; but I got it not: Was there much love in that? *Was there any?*' **but she hath washed my feet with tears, and wiped them with the hairs of her head.** Dear penitent! Thy tears fell faster and fuller than thou thoughtest endurable on those blessed feet, and thou didst hasten to wipe them off, as if they had been a stain: but to Him who forgave thee all that debt, the water from those weeping eyes of thine is more precious than would crystal streams from fountains

in the Pharisee's house have been; for they welled forth from a bursting heart. That, indeed, was 'much love.' Again, **45. Thou gavest me no kiss**—of salutation. 'How much love was there here? *Any at all?*' **but this woman since the time I came in hath not ceased to kiss my feet.** She would, in so doing, both hide her head, and get her womanly feelings in a womanly way all expressed. That indeed was 'much love.' But once more, **46. My head with oil thou didst not anoint: but this woman hath anointed my feet with ointment.** The double contrast is here to be observed—between *his* not anointing the *head* and *her* anointing the *feet;* and between his withholding even common *olive* oil for the higher purpose, and her expending that precious *aromatic balsam* for the humbler. *What evidence did the one afford of any feeling which forgiveness prompts? But what beautiful evidence of this did the other furnish!* Our Lord speaks this with delicate politeness, as if *hurt* at these inattentions of His host, which though not *invariably* shown to guests, were the customary marks of studied respect and regard. The inference is plain—*Only one of the debtors was really forgiven,* though in the first instance, to give room for the play of withheld feeling, the forgiveness of both is supposed in the parable. Our Lord now confines Himself to the woman's case. **47. Wherefore I say unto thee, Her sins, which are many, are forgiven** [ἀφέωνται αἱ ἁμαρτίαι αὐτῆς αἱ πολλαί]—'those many sins of hers are forgiven.' As He had acknowledged before how deep was her debt, so now He reiterates it: her sins were indeed many; her guilt was of a deep dye; but in terms the most solemn He proclaims it all cancelled. **for she loved much.** The "for" here [ὅτι] is plainly *evidential,* and means, 'inasmuch as' or 'seeing that.' Her love was not the *cause,* but the *proof* of her forgiveness; as is evident from the whole structure of the parable. **but to whom little is forgiven, the same loveth little**—a delicately ironical intimation of there being *no love* in the present case, and so *no forgiveness.* **48. And he said unto her, Thy sins are forgiven**—an unsought assurance of what she had felt, indeed, in the simple appropriation to herself of the first words of grace which she had heard—we know not where—but how precious, now that those blessed Lips addressed it to herself! **49. And they that sat at meat with him began to say within themselves** [ἐν ἑαυτοῖς]—or, 'among themselves.' **Who is this**

254

50 themselves, 'Who is this that forgiveth sins also? And he said to the woman, ' Thy faith hath saved thee; go in peace.

A. D. 31.
a Isa. 53. 3.
j Matt. 9. 22.

that forgiveth sins also? 50. And he said to the woman, Thy faith hath saved thee; go in peace. No wonder they were startled to hear One who was reclining at the same couch, and partaking of the same hospitalities with themselves, assume the awful prerogative of 'even forgiving sins.' But so far from receding from this claim, or softening it down, our Lord only repeats it, with two precious additions: one, announcing what was the secret of the "forgiveness" she had experienced, and which carried "salvation" in its bosom—her "faith;" the other, a glorious dismissal of her in that "peace" which she had already felt, but is now assured she has His full warrant to enjoy! The expression, "in peace," is literally "into peace" [εἰς εἰρήνην]—'into the assured and abiding enjoyment of the peace of a pardoned state.'

Remarks.—1. What a glorious exhibition of the grace of the Gospel have we in this Section? A woman of the class of profligates casually hears the Lord Jesus pour forth some of those wonderful words of majesty and grace, which dropped as an honey-comb. They pierce her heart; but, as they wound, they heal. Abandoned of men, she is not forsaken of God. Hers, she had thought, was a lost case; but the prodigal, she finds, has a Father still. She will arise and go to Him; and as she goes He meets her, and falls on her neck and kisses her. Light breaks into her soul, as she revolves what she heard from those Lips that spake as never man spake, and draws from them the joyful assurance of Divine reconciliation for the chief of sinners, and the peace of a pardoned state. She cannot rest; she must see that wonderful One again, and testify to Him what He hath done for her soul. She inquires after His movements, as if she would say with the Spouse, "Tell me, O Thou whom my soul loveth, where Thou feedest, for why should I be as one that turneth aside by the flocks of Thy companions?" She learns where He is, and follows in His train till she finds herself at His feet behind Him at the Pharisee's table. At the sight of Him, her head is waters and her eyes a fountain of tears, which drop copiously on those beautiful feet. What a spectacle, which even angels might desire—and doubtless did—to look into! But, how differently is it regarded by one at least at that table! Simon the Pharisee thinks it conclusive evidence against the claims of his Guest, that He should permit such a thing to be done to Him by such a person. So the matter shall be expounded, the woman vindicated, and the Pharisee's suspicions courteously yet pointedly rebuked. And what a rich statement of Gospel truth is here conveyed in a few words. Though there be degrees of guilt, yet insolvency—or inability to wipe out the dishonour done to God by sin—is common to all sinners alike. The debtors are sinners, and sin is a debt incurred to Heaven. The debtor of "five hundred" represents the one extreme of them; the debtor of "fifty" the other—those at the bottom and those at the top of the scale of sinners, the greatest and the least sinners, the profligate and the respectable, the publicans and the Pharisees. A great difference there is between these. But it is a difference only of degree; for of both debtors alike it is said that they had nothing to pay. They were both alike insolvent. The debtor of "fifty" could no more pay his fifty than the debtor of five hundred her's. The least sinner is insolvent; the greatest is no more. "There is no difference,

255

for all have sinned, and come short of the glory of God." But when they had nothing to pay, the Creditor frankly forgave them both. The least sinner, to have peace with God and get to heaven, needs a frank forgiveness, and the greatest needs only that. Reputable Simon must be saved on the same terms with this once profligate and still despised woman; and she, now that she has tasted that the Lord is gracious, is on a level with every other pardoned believer. "Such *were* some of you: but ye are washed, but ye are sanctified, but ye are justified, in the name of the Lord Jesus, and by the Spirit of our God" (1 Cor. vi. 11). But the working of this doctrine of Grace comes out here as beautifully as the doctrine itself. Love to its Divine Benefactor, reigning in the heart of the pardoned believer, is seen seeking Him, finding Him, broken down at the sight of Him, embracing His very feet, and pouring out its intensest emotions in the most expressive form. Even so, "the love of Christ constraineth us . . . to live not unto ourselves, but unto Him that died for us and rose again." It casts its crown at His feet. It lives for Him; and, if required, it lays down its life for Him. Thus, what law could not do love does, writing the law in the heart. But, now, turning from the sinner to the Saviour, 2. In what light does this Section exhibit Christ? He plainly represents Himself here as the great Creditor to Whom is owing that debt, and Whose it is to cancel it. For, observe His argument. 'The more forgiveness, the greater the debtor's love to his generous Creditor.' Such is the general principle laid down by Simon and approved by Christ. Well, then, says our Lord, let the conduct of these two be tried by this test. So He proceeds, by the woman's treatment of Himself, to show how much she loved Him, and consequently how much forgiveness she felt that she had received from Him; and by the Pharisee's treatment of Him, to show what an absence of the feeling of love to Him there was, and consequently of the sense of forgiveness. The more that the structure and application of the parable of this Section is studied, the more will the intelligent reader be struck with the high claim which our Lord here puts forth—a claim which would never have entered into the mind of a mere creature, with reference to the Person to whom sin lays us under obligation, and whose prerogative accordingly it is with royal "frankness" to remit the debt. Should any hesitate about the force of this indirect—but just on that account the more striking—argument for the proper Divinity of Christ, let him look on to the close of this Section, where he will find the Lord Jesus putting forth His royal prerogative of publicly *pronouncing* that forgiveness which had been already *experienced;* and when it was manifest to His fellow-guests that He was assuming a Divine prerogative, and it seemed nothing short of blasphemy that one who reclined at the same table and partook of the same hospitalities with themselves, should speak and act *as God,* He not only did not correct them by retreating out of the supposed claim, but reiterated the august language, and with even increased majesty and grace: "Thy faith hath saved thee, Go in peace!" Let the Person of Christ be studied in the light of these facts. 3. How cheering is it to be assured that love gives beauty and value, in the eye of Christ, to every the least act of His genuine people! But on this subject,

8 AND it came to pass afterward, that he went throughout every city and village, preaching and showing the glad tidings of the kingdom of

2 God: and the twelve *were* with him, and *"certain women, which had been healed of evil spirits and infirmities, Mary called Magdalene, *"out of

3 whom went seven devils, and Joanna the wife of Chuza Herod's steward, and Susanna, and many others, which ministered unto him of their substance.

4 And *"when much people were gathered together, and were come to

5 him out of every city, he spake by a parable: A sower went out to sow his seed: and as he sowed, some fell by the way-side; and it was trodden

A. D. 31.
CHAP. 8.
a Matt. 27.55, 56.
Mark 15.40, 41.
Mark 16. 1.
ch. 23. 27.
John 19.25.
Acts 1. 14.
b Mark 16. 9.
c Matt. 13. 2.
Mark 4. 1.

see on Mark xiv. 1-11, Remark 2. 4. As this woman came not for the purpose of shedding tears, so neither did she come to get an assurance from Jesus of her pardon and reconciliation. But as the evidences of the change that had passed upon her flowed forth, the balm of a pronounced acceptance was poured in. And thus do the most delightful assurances of our forgiveness usually spring up unsought, in the midst of active duty and warm affections; while they fly from those who hunt for them in the interior of an anxious heart, and not finding them there go mourning and weak for want of them.

CHAP. VIII. 1-3.—JESUS MAKES A SECOND GALILEAN CIRCUIT WITH THE TWELVE AND CERTAIN MINISTERING WOMEN. This exquisite Section is peculiar to Luke. It seems to follow, in point of time, the events of the preceding chapter. **1. And it came to pass afterward, that he went** [καὶ αὐτὸς διώδευε]—'that He travelled about,' or 'made a progress.' The "He" is emphatic here. **throughout every city and village** [κατὰ πόλιν καὶ κώμην]—'through town and village,' **preaching and showing the glad tidings of the kingdom of God**—the Prince of itinerant preachers scattering far and wide the seed of the Kingdom: **and the twelve were with him, 2. And certain women, which had been healed of evil spirits and infirmities**—on whom He had the double claim of having brought healing to their bodies and new life to their souls. Drawn to Him by an attraction more than magnetic, they accompany Him on this tour as His *almoners*—ministering unto Him of their substance. **Mary called Magdalene** [Μαγδαληνή]—probably 'of Magdala,' as to which see on Mark viii. 10, **out of whom went** [ἐξεληλύθει]—rather, 'had gone,' **seven devils.** The same thing being said in Mark xvi. 9, it seems plain that this was what distinguished her amongst the Maries. It is a great wrong to this female to identify her with the once profligate, though afterwards marvellously changed, woman who is the subject of the preceding Section (ch. vii. 37, &c.), and to call all such penitents *Magdalenes.* The mistake has arisen from confounding unhappy demoniacal possession with the conscious entertainment of diabolic impurity, or supposing the one to have been inflicted as a punishment for the other—for which there is not the least scriptural ground. See on ch. xiii. 1-9, Remark 2, at the close of that Section. **3. And Joanna the wife of Chuza Herod's steward.** If the steward of such a godless, cruel, and licentious sovereign as Herod Antipas (see on Mark vi. 14, &c.) differed greatly from himself, his post would be no easy or enviable one. That he was a disciple of Christ is very improbable, though he might be favourably disposed towards Him. But what we know not of him, and may fear he wanted, we are sure his wife possessed. Healed either of "evil spirits" or of some one of the "infirmities" here referred to—the ordinary diseases of humanity—she joins

in the Saviour's train of grateful, clinging followers. **and Susanna.** Of her we know nothing but the name, and that in this one place only; but her services on this memorable occasion have immortalized her name—"Wheresoever this Gospel shall be preached throughout the whole world, this also that she hath done," in ministering to the Lord of her substance on this Galilean tour, "shall be spoken of as a memorial of her" (Mark xiv. 9). **and many others** [καὶ ἕτεραι πολλαὶ]—that is, 'many other healed women,' **which ministered unto him**—rather, according to the better supported reading, 'unto them;' that is, to the Lord and the Twelve.

Remarks.—1. What a train have we here! all ministering to the Lord of their substance, and He allowing them to do it, and subsisting upon it. Blessed Saviour! It melts us to see Thee living upon the love of Thy ransomed people. That they bring Thee their poor offerings we wonder not. Thou hast sown unto them spiritual things, and they think it, as well they might, a small thing that Thou shouldst reap their carnal things (1 Cor. ix. 11). But dost Thou take it at their hand, and subsist upon it? "O the depth of the riches"—of this poverty of His! Very noble are the words of *Olshausen* upon this scene: 'He who was the support of the spiritual life of His people disdained not to be supported by them in the body. He was not ashamed to penetrate so far into the depths of poverty as to live upon the alms of love. He only fed others miraculously: for Himself, He lived upon the love of His people. He gave all things to men His brethren, and received all things from them, enjoying thereby the pure blessing of love; which is then only perfect when it is at the same time both giving and receiving. Who could invent such things as these? *It was necessary to live in this manner that it might be so recorded.*' See more on this exalted subject, on ch. xix. 28-44, Remark 2, at the close of that Section. But 2. May not His loving people, and particularly those of the tender clinging sex, still accompany Him as He goes from land to land preaching, by His servants, and showing the glad tidings of the kingdom of God? and may they not minister to Him of their substance by sustaining and cheering these agents of His? Verily they may; and they do. "Inasmuch as ye have done it unto the least of these My brethren, ye have done it unto Me." Yes, as He is with them "alway, even unto the end of the world," in preaching and showing the glad tidings of the kingdom of God, even so, as many as are with the faithful workers of this work, and helpful to them in it, are accompanying Him and ministering to Him of their substance. But see on Matt. xxv. 31-46, concluding Remarks.

4-18.—PARABLE OF THE SOWER. (=Matt. xiii. 1-23; Mark iv. 1-23.) For the exposition, see on Mark iv. 1-23.

19-21.—HIS MOTHER AND BRETHREN SEEK TO

6 down, and the fowls of the air devoured it. And some fell upon a rock; and as soon as it was sprung up, it withered away, because it lacked

7 moisture. And some fell among thorns; and the thorns sprang up with

8 it, and choked it. And other fell on good ground, and sprang up, and bare fruit an hundred-fold. And when he had said these things, he cried, He that hath ears to hear, let him hear.

9 And [d]his disciples asked him, saying, What might this parable be?

10 And he said, Unto you it is given to know the mysteries of the kingdom of God: but to others in parables; [e]that seeing they might not see, and

11 hearing they might not understand. Now [f]the parable is this: The

12 [g]seed is the word of God. Those by [h]the way-side are they that hear; then cometh [i]the devil, and taketh away the word out of their hearts,

13 lest they should believe and be saved. They on the rock *are they*, which, when they hear, receive the word with joy; and these have no root,

14 which for a while believe, and in time of temptation fall away. And that which fell among thorns are they, which, when they have heard, go forth, and are choked with cares [j]and riches and pleasures of *this* life,

15 and bring no fruit to perfection. But that on the good ground are they, which in an honest and good heart, having heard the word, keep *it*, and [k]bring forth fruit with patience.

16 No [l]man, when he hath lighted a candle, covereth it with a vessel, or putteth *it* under a bed; but setteth *it* on a candlestick, that they which

17 enter in may see the light. For [m]nothing is secret that shall not be made manifest; neither *any thing* hid that shall not be known and

18 come abroad. Take heed therefore how ye hear: [n]for whosoever hath, to him shall be given; and whosoever hath not, from him shall be taken even that which he [1]seemeth to have.

19 Then [o]came to him *his* mother and his brethren, and could not come

20 at him for the press. And it was told him *by certain*, which said, Thy

21 mother and thy brethren stand without, desiring to see thee. And he answered and said unto them, My mother and my brethren are these which hear the word of God, and do it.

22 Now [p]it came to pass on a certain day, that he went into a ship with his disciples: and he said unto them, Let us go over unto the other side

23 of the lake. And they launched forth. But as they sailed he fell asleep: and there came down a storm of wind on the lake; and they were filled

24 *with water*, and were in jeopardy. And they came to him, and awoke him, saying, Master, master, we perish! Then he [q]arose, and rebuked the wind and the raging of the water: and they ceased, and there was a

25 calm. And he said unto them, Where is your faith? And they being [r]afraid wondered, saying one to another, What manner of man is this! for he commandeth even the winds and water, and they obey him.

26 And [s]they arrived at the country of the Gadarenes, which is over

27 against Galilee. And when he went forth to land, there met him out of the city a certain man, which had devils long time, and ware no clothes,

28 neither abode in *any* house, but in the tombs. When he saw Jesus, he [t]cried out, and fell down before him, and with a loud voice said, What have I to do with thee, Jesus, *thou* Son of God most high? I beseech

29 thee, torment me not. (For he had commanded the unclean spirit to come out of the man. For oftentimes it had caught him: and he was kept bound with chains and in fetters; and he brake the bands, and was

30 driven of the devil into the wilderness.) And Jesus asked him, saying, What is thy name? And he said, Legion: because many devils were

A. D. 31.

[d] Matt. 13.10.
Mark 4. 10.
[e] Isa. 6. 9.
Mark 4. 12.
[f] Matt 13.18.
Mark 4. 14.
[g] Mark 4. 14.
Acts 20. 27.
32.
1 Cor. 3.6,7,
9-12.
Jas. 1. 21.
1 Pet. 1. 23.
[h] Jas. 1.23,24.
[i] 2 Cor. 2. 11.
2 Cor. 4. 3.
2 Thes. 2.
10.
1 Pet. 5. 8.
[j] Matt 19 23.
1 Tim. 6. 9,
10.
2 Tim. 4.10.
[k] Eph. 2. 4.
2 Pet.1.5-10.
[l] Matt. 5. 15.
Mark 4. 21.
ch. 11. 33.
Phil. 2. 15,
16.
[m] Matt.10.26.
ch. 12. 2.
[n] Matt. 13.12.
Matt. 25.29.
Mark 4. 25.
ch. 19. 26.
John 15. 2.
Rev. 22. 11.
1 Or., think-
eth that he
hath.
[o] Matt.12.46.
Matt.13.55.
Mark 3. 31.
John 7. 5.
Acts 1. 14.
1 Cor. 9. 5.
Gal. 1. 19.
[p] Matt. 8., 23.
Mark 4. 35.
[q] Job 28. 11.
Job 38. 11.
Ps. 29. 10.
Ps. 46. 1.
Ps. 65. 7.
Ps. 89. 9.
Ps. 93. 4.
Ps. 107. 29.
Ps. 135. 6.
Nah. 1. 4.
[r] Ps. 33. 8, 9.
Mark 4. 41.
Mark 6. 51.
[s] Matt. 8. 28.
Mark 5. 1.
[t] Acts 16. 16,
17.
Phil. 2. 10,
11.

SPEAK WITH HIM, AND THE REPLY. (=Matt. xii. 46-50; Mark iii. 31-35.) For the exposition, see on Matt. xii. 46-50.

22-39.—JESUS, CROSSING THE SEA OF GALILEE,

MIRACULOUSLY STILLS A TEMPEST—HE CURES THE DEMONIAC OF GADARA. (=Matt. viii. 23-34; Mark iv. 35—v. 20.) For the exposition, see on Mark iv. 35—v. 20.

257

31 entered into him. And they besought him that he would not command them to go out ᵘinto the deep.

32 And there was there an herd ᵛof many swine feeding on the mountain: and they besought him that he would suffer them to enter into them.

33 And ᵂhe suffered them. Then went the devils out of the man, and entered into the swine: and the herd ran violently down a steep place

34 into the lake, and were choked. When they that fed *them* saw what was done, they fled, and went and told *it* in the city, and in the country.

35 Then they went out to see what was done: and came to Jesus, and found the man out of whom the devils were departed, sitting at the feet

36 of Jesus, clothed, ˣand in his right mind: and they were afraid. They also which saw *it* told them by what means he that was possessed of the devils was healed.

37 Then ʸthe whole multitude of the country of the Gadarenes round about besought ᶻhim to depart from them; for they were taken with great fear.

38 And he went up into the ship, and returned back again. Now ᵃthe man out of whom the devils were departed besought him that he might be

39 with him: but Jesus sent him away, saying, Return to thine own house, and show how great things God hath done unto thee. And he went his way, and published throughout the whole city how great things Jesus had done unto him.

40 And it came to pass, that, when Jesus was returned, the people *gladly*

41 received him: for they were all waiting for him. And, ᵇbehold, there came a man named Jairus, and he was a ruler of the synagogue: and he fell down at Jesus' feet, and besought him that he would come into his

42 house: for he had one only daughter, about twelve years of age, and she lay a-dying. But as he went the people thronged him.

43 And ᶜa woman, having an issue of blood twelve years, which had spent

44 all her living upon physicians, neither could be healed of any, came behind *him*, and ᵈtouched the border of his garment: and immediately

45 her issue of blood stanched. And Jesus said, Who touched me? When all denied, Peter and they that were with him said, Master, the multitude

46 throng thee and press *thee*, and sayest thou, Who touched me? And Jesus said, Somebody hath touched me: for I perceive that ᵉvirtue is

47 gone out of me. And when the woman saw that she was not hid, she came trembling, and falling down before him, she declared unto him before all the people for what cause she had touched him, and how she

48 was healed immediately. And he said unto her, Daughter, be of good comfort: thy faith hath made thee whole; go in peace.

49 While ᶠhe yet spake, there cometh one from the ruler of the synagogue's *house*, saying to him, Thy daughter is dead; trouble not the Master.

50 But when Jesus heard *it*, he answered him, saying, Fear not: ᵍbelieve

51 only, and she shall be made whole. And when he came into the house, he suffered no man to go in, save Peter and James and John, and the

52 father and the mother of the maiden. And all wept, and bewailed her:

53 but he said, Weep not; she is not dead, ʰbut sleepeth. And they

54 laughed him to scorn, knowing that she was dead. And he put them

55 all out, and took her by the hand, and called, saying, Maid, ⁱarise. And her spirit came again, and she arose straightway: and he commanded to

56 give her meat. And her parents were astonished: but he ʲcharged them that they should tell no man what was done.

9 THEN ᵃhe called his twelve disciples together, and ᵇgave them power

2 and authority over all devils, and to cure diseases. And ᶜhe sent them

A. D. 31.

ᵘ Rev. 20. 3.
ᵛ Lev. 11. 7.
  Deut. 14. 8.
ᵂ Job 1. 12.
  Job 12. 16.
  Rev. 20. 7.
ˣ 1 John 3. 8.
  Rom. 10.20.
ʸ Matt. 8. 34.
ᶻ Deut. 5. 25.
  1 Sam.6.20.
  1 Sam. 16.4.
  2 Sam. 6. 8,
  9.
  Job 21. 14.
  Matt. 8. 34.
  Mark 1. 24.
  Mark 5. 17.
  ch. 4. 34.
  ch. 5. 8.
  Acts 16. 39.
  1 Cor. 2. 14.
ᵃ Ps. 103. 1.
  Ps. 116. 12.
  Mark 5. 18.
  ch. 18. 43.
ᵇ Matt. 9. 18.
  Mark 5. 22.
ᶜ Lev. 15. 25.
  Matt. 9. 20.
  Mark 5. 25.
ᵈ Deut. 22.12
  Mark 5. 27,
  28.
  Mark 6. 56.
  Acts 5. 15.
  Acts 19. 12.
ᵉ Mark 5. 30.
  ch. 6. 17.
  ch. 6. 19.
ᶠ Mark 5. 35.
ᵍ 2 Chr.20 20.
  Isa. 1. 10.
  Mark 9. 23.
  Mark 11.22-
  24.
  John 11. 25,
  40.
ʰ John 11. 11,
  13.
ⁱ ch. 7. 14.
  John 11. 43.
  Acts 9. 40.
ʲ Matt. 8. 4.
  Matt. 9. 30.
  Mark 5. 43.

CHAP. 9.
ᵃ Matt. 10. 1.
  Mark 3. 13.
  Mark 6. 7.
ᵇ John 14. 12.
  Acts 3. 6.
ᶜ Matt. 10. 7,
  8.
  Mark 6. 12.
  ch. 10. 1, 9.
  Tit. 1. 9.
  Tit. 2. 12,
  14.

40-56.—RE-CROSSING THE LAKE, THE DAUGHTER OF JAIRUS IS RAISED TO LIFE, AND THE WOMAN WITH THE ISSUE OF BLOOD IS HEALED. (=Matt. ix. 18-26; Mark v. 21-43.) For the exposition, see on Mark v. 21-43.   CHAP. IX. 1-6.—MISSION OF THE TWELVE

3 to preach the kingdom of God, and to heal the sick. And [d]he said unto
them, Take nothing for *your* journey, neither staves, nor scrip, neither
4 bread, neither money; neither have two coats apiece. And [e]whatsoever
5 house ye enter into, there abide, and thence depart. And [f]whosoever
will not receive you, when ye go out of that city, [g]shake off the very dust
6 from your feet for a testimony against them. And [h]they departed, and
went through the towns, preaching the Gospel, and healing every where.
7 Now [i]Herod the tetrarch heard of all that was done by him: and he
was perplexed, because that it was said of some, that John was risen from
8 the dead, and of some, that Elias had appeared; and of others, that
9 one of the old prophets was risen again. And Herod said, John have I
beheaded: but who is this of whom I hear such things? And [j]he desired
to see him.
10 And [k]the apostles, when they were returned, told him all that they had
done. And [l]he took them, and went aside privately into a desert place
11 belonging to the city called Bethsaida. And the people, when they knew
it, followed him: and he received them, and spake unto them of the
kingdom of God, and healed them that had need of healing.
12 And [m]when the day began to wear away, then came the twelve, and
said unto him, Send the multitude away, that they may go into the
towns and country round about, and lodge, and get victuals: for we are
13 here in a desert place. But he said unto them, [n]Give ye them to eat.
And they said, [o]We have no more but five loaves and two fishes; except
14 we should go and buy meat for all this people. (For they were about five
thousand men.) And he said to his disciples, Make them sit down by
15 fifties in a company. And they did so, and made them all sit down.
16 Then he took the five loaves and the two fishes, and looking up to heaven,
he blessed them, and brake, and gave to the disciples to set before the
17 multitude. And they [p]did eat, and were all filled: and there was taken
up of fragments that remained to them twelve baskets.
18 And [q]it came to pass, as he was alone praying, his disciples were with
him: and he asked them, saying, Whom say the people that I am?
19 They answering said, [r]John the Baptist; but some *say*, Elias; and others
20 *say*, that one of the old prophets is risen again. He said unto them, But
21 whom say ye that I am? [s]Peter answering said, The Christ of God. And
[t]he straitly charged them, and commanded *them* to tell no man that
22 thing; saying, [u]The Son of man must suffer many things, and be rejected
of the elders and chief priests and scribes, and be slain, and be raised the
third day.
23 And [v]he said to *them* all, If any *man* will come after me, let him deny
24 himself, and take up his cross daily, and follow me. For whosoever will
save his life shall lose it: but whosoever will lose his life for my sake, the
25 same shall save it. For [w]what is a man advantaged, if he gain the whole
26 world, and lose himself, or be cast away? For [x]whosoever shall be
ashamed of me and of my words, of him shall the Son of man be ashamed,
when he shall come in his own glory, and *in his* Father's, and of the holy
27 angels. But [y]I tell you of a truth, there be some standing here, which
shall not taste of death, till they see the kingdom of God.

A. D. 31.

[d] Ps. 37. 3. Matt. 10. 9. Mark 6. 8. ch. 10. 4. ch. 22. 35. 2 Tim. 2. 4.
[e] Matt. 10.11. Mark 6. 10.
[f] Matt. 10. 14.
[g] Acts 13. 51.
[h] Mark 6. 12.
[i] Matt. 14. 1. Mark 6. 14.
[j] ch. 23. 8.
[k] Mark 6. 30.
[l] Matt. 14.13.
[m] Matt. 14.15. Mark 6. 35. John 6. 1,5.
[n] 2 Ki. 4. 42, 43.
[o] Num. 11. 22. Ps. 78. 19, 20.
[p] Ps. 145. 15, 16.
[q] Matt. 16.13. Mark 8. 27.
[r] Matt. 14. 2.
[s] Matt. 16.16. Mark 8. 29. Mark 14. 61. John 1. 41, 49. John 4. 29, 42. John 6. 69. John 7. 41. John 11. 27. John 20. 31. Acts 8. 37. Acts 9. 22. Rom. 10. 9. 1 John 4. 14, 15. 1 John 5. 5.
[t] Matt. 16. 20.
[u] Matt. 16 21. Matt. 17. 22. Matt. 20. 17. Mark 9. 31. ch. 18. 31. ch. 24. 6, 7.
[v] Matt. 10. 38. Matt. 16. 24. Mark 8. 34. ch. 14. 27.
[w] Matt. 16. 26. Mark 8. 36.
[x] Matt. 10. 33. Mark 8. 38. 2 Tim. 2. 12.
[y] Matt. 16. 28. Mark 9. 1.

APOSTLES. (=Matt. x. 1, 5-15; Mark vi. 7-13.) For the exposition, see on Matt. x. 1, 5-15.

7-9.—HEROD THINKS JESUS A RESURRECTION OF THE MURDERED BAPTIST. (= Matt. xiv. 1, 2; Mark vi. 14-16.) For the exposition, see on Mark vi. 14-16.

10-17.—THE TWELVE, ON THEIR RETURN, HAVING REPORTED THE SUCCESS OF THEIR MISSION, JESUS CROSSES THE SEA OF GALILEE WITH THEM, TEACHES THE PEOPLE, AND MIRACULOUSLY FEEDS FIVE THOUSAND. (=Matt. xiv. 13-21; Mark vi. 30-44.) For the exposition, see on Mark vi. 30-44.

18-27.—PETER'S NOBLE CONFESSION OF CHRIST—FIRST EXPLICIT ANNOUNCEMENT OF HIS APPROACHING SUFFERINGS, DEATH, AND RESURRECTION, WITH WARNINGS TO THE TWELVE. (= Matt. xvi. 13-28; Mark viii. 27—ix. 1.) For the exposition, see on Matt. xvi. 13-28.

28-36.—JESUS IS TRANSFIGURED—CONVERSATION ABOUT ELIAS. (= Matt. xvii. 1-13; Mark ix.

28 And 'it came to pass, about an eight days after these [1]sayings, he took
29 Peter and John and James, and went up into a mountain to pray. And
as he prayed, the [a]fashion of his countenance was altered, and his raiment
30 *was* white *and* glistering. And, behold, there talked with him two men,
31 which were Moses and [b]Elias; who appeared in [c]glory, and spake of his
32 decease which he should accomplish at Jerusalem. But Peter and they
that were with him were [d]heavy with sleep: and when they were awake,

A. D. 31.

[*] Matt. 17. 1.
[1] Or, things.
[a] Ex. 34. 29, 35.
[b] 2 Ki. 2. 11.
[c] Phil. 3. 21.
[d] Dan. 8. 18.
  Dan. 10. 9.

2-13.) The time and occasion of this Section, which are of the utmost importance to the right comprehension of it, are most definitely fixed in the opening words of it.

28. And it came to pass, about an eight days after these sayings—meaning, after the first startling announcement of His approaching Sufferings and Death. Matthew and Mark say it was "after six days;" but they *exclude* the day on which "these sayings" were uttered and the Transfiguration-day, while our Evangelist *includes* them. Now, since all the three Evangelists so definitely connect the Transfiguration with this announcement of His Death—so unexpected by the Twelve and so depressing—there can be no doubt that the primary intention of it was to manifest the glory of that Death in the view of Heaven, to irradiate the Redeemer's sufferings, to transfigure the Cross. It will appear, by and by, that the scene took place *at night*. **he took Peter and John and James**—partners before in secular business, now selected, as a kind of sacred triumvirate, to be sole witnesses, first, of the resurrection of Jairus' daughter (Mark v. 37), next, of the Transfiguration, and finally, of the Agony in the garden (Mark xiv. 33), **and went up into a mountain**—probably not mount *Tabor*, according to long tradition, with which the facts scarcely comport, but rather some mountain in the vicinity of the sea of Galilee, **to pray**—for the period He had now reached was a critical and anxious one. But who can adequately express those "strong cryings and tears"? Methinks, as I steal by His side, I hear from Him these plaintive cries, 'Lord, Who hath believed our report? I am come unto mine own, and mine own receive Me not; I am become a stranger unto my brethren, an alien to my mother's children: Consider mine enemies, for they are many, and they hate me with cruel hatred. Arise, O Lord, let not man prevail. Thou that dwellest between the cherubim, shine forth: Show me a token for good: Father, glorify thy name.' These strong cryings and tears pierced the skies: they entered into the ears of the Lord of Sabaoth. **29. And as he prayed, the fashion of his countenance was altered.** Before He cried He was answered, and whilst he was yet speaking He was heard. Blessed interruption to prayer this! **and his raiment was white and glistering.** [ἐξαστράπτων]. Matthew says "His face did shine as the sun, and his raiment was white as the light" (xvii. 2). Mark's description is, as usual, intense and vivid: "His raiment became shining" [στίλβοντα] or 'glittering,' "exceeding white as snow [λευκὰ λίαν ὡς χιών], so as no fuller on earth can white them" (ix. 3). These particulars were doubtless communicated to Mark by Peter, on whom they made such deep impression, that in his second Epistle he refers to them in language of peculiar strength and grandeur (2 Pet. i. 16-18). Putting all the accounts together, it would appear that the light shone, not *upon* Him *from without*, but *out of Him from within*: He was all irradiated: It was one blaze of dazzling, celestial glory; it was Himself glorified. What a contrast now to that "visage more marred than any man, and His form than the sons of men"! (Isa. lii. 14). **30. And, behold, there talked with him two men, which were Moses**

and Elias. Who, exclaims *Bengel*, would not have believed these were *angels* (compare Acts i. 10; Mark xvi. 5), had not their *human* names been subjoined? Moses represented "the law," Elijah "the prophets," and both together the whole testimony of the Old Testament Scriptures and the Old Testament saints, to Christ; now not borne in a *book*, but by *living men*, not to a *coming*, but a *come* Messiah, *visibly*, for they "appeared," and *audibly*, for they "spake." **31. Who appeared in glory, and spake** [ἔλεγον]—rather, 'and were speaking' **of his decease** [τὴν ἔξοδον αὐτοῦ]—'of His exodus;' 'His exit,' or 'His departure.' Beautiful euphemism (or softened expression) for *death*, which Peter, who witnessed the scene, uses in his second Epistle to express his own death, and the use of which single term seems to have recalled the whole scene by a sudden rush of recollection, which he accordingly describes in language of uncommon grandeur (2 Pet. i. 15-18). **which he should accomplish** [ἣν ἔμελλεν πληροῦν]—'which He was going to fulfil' at Jerusalem. Mark the *historical* and *local* character which Christ's death possessed in the eye of these glorified men, as vital as it is charming; and see on ch. ii. 11. What now may be gathered from this statement? First, That a dying Messiah is the great article of the true Jewish Theology. For a long time the Church had fallen clean away from the faith of this article, and even from a preparedness to receive it. But here we have that jewel brought forth from the heap of Jewish traditions, and by the true representatives of the Church of old made the one subject of talk with Christ Himself. Next, The adoring gratitude of glorified men for His undertaking to accomplish such a decease; their felt dependence upon it for the glory in which they appeared; their profound interest in the progress of it; their humble solaces and encouragements to go through with it; and their sense of its peerless and overwhelming glory. 'Go, matchless, adored One, a Lamb to the slaughter! rejected of men, but chosen of God and precious; dishonoured, abhorred, and soon to be slain by men, but worshipped by cherubim, ready to be greeted by all heaven! In virtue of that decease we are here; our all is suspended on it and wrapt up in it. Thine every step is watched by us with ineffable interest; and though it were too high an honour to us to be permitted to drop a word of cheer into that precious but now clouded spirit, yet, as ourselves the first-fruits of harvest, the very joy set before Him, we cannot choose but tell Him that what is the depth of shame to Him is covered with glory in the eyes of heaven, that the Cross to Him is the Crown to us, that that "decease" is all our salvation and all our desire.' And who can doubt that such a scene *did* minister deep cheer to that spirit? 'Tis said they "talked" not to Him, but "*with* Him;" and if they told Him how glorious His decease was, might He not fitly reply, 'I know it all, but your voice, as messengers from heaven come down to tell it me, is music in mine ears.' **32. But Peter and they that were with him were heavy with sleep: and when they were awake** [διαγρηγορήσαντες δὲ]. So certainly most interpreters understand the expres-

33 they saw his glory, and the two men that stood with him. And it came
    to pass, as they departed from him, Peter said unto Jesus, Master, it is
    good for us to be here: and let us make three tabernacles; one for thee,
34 and one for Moses, and one for Elias: not knowing what he said. While
    he thus spake, there came a cloud and overshadowed them: and they
35 feared as they entered into the cloud. And there came a voice out of
36 the cloud, saying, *'*This is my beloved son: hear *ʃ*him. And when the
    voice was past, Jesus was found alone. *ᵍ*And they kept *it* close, and
    told no man in those days any of those things which they had seen.

A. D. 32.
ᵉ Matt. 3. 17.
2 Pet. 1. 16,
17.
ʃ Ex. 23. 21.
Deut.18.15-
18.
Acts 3. 22.
Heb. 2. 3.
Heb. 12. 25.
ᵍ Matt. 17. 9.

sion. But as the word signifies, not 'to awake,' but 'to keep awake,' which agrees much better with the manifest intention of the Evangelist, we should either, with *Meyer* and *Alford*, render the words, 'but having kept awake,' or, better still perhaps, with *Olshausen*, 'having roused themselves up,' or shaken off their drowsiness. From *v.* 37 it would appear that this Transfiguration-scene took place during night, and that the Lord must have passed the whole night on the mountain; for it was "the next day" before He and the three "came down from the hill." This will account for the drowsiness of the disciples. **they saw his glory, and the two men that stood with him.** The emphasis here lies on the word "saw;" so that they were "*eye-witnesses* of His majesty," as one of them long afterwards testifies that they were (2 Pet. i. 16). In like manner, Elijah made it the one condition of Elisha's getting a double portion of his spirit after he went away, that he should see him ascend: "If thou *see me* taken from thee, it shall be so unto thee; but if not, it shall not be so." Accordingly, immediately after the record of Elijah's translation, it is added, "And Elisha *saw it*" (2 Ki. ii. 10, 12). **33. And it came to pass, as they departed from him, Peter said unto Jesus, Master, it is good for us to be here: and let us make three tabernacles; one for thee, and one for Moses, and one for Elias: not knowing what he said.** Peter's speech was so far not amiss. It was indeed good, very good to be there; but for the rest of it, the best that can be said is what our Evangelist says, that he knew not what he said. The poor man's words in such circumstances must not be scrutinized too closely. The next step put an end to the hallucination. The cloud and the voice effectually silenced him. **34. While he thus spake, there came a cloud**—not one of our watery clouds, but the Shechinah-cloud, the pavilion of the manifested presence of God with His people on earth, what Peter calls "the excellent" or "magnificent glory" [τῆς μεγαλοπρεποῦς δόξης], 2 Pet. i. 17. **and overshadowed them: and they feared as they entered into the cloud. 35. And there came a voice out of the cloud**—"*such a voice*," says Peter emphatically [φωνῆς τοιᾶσδε]. "And this voice," he adds, "we heard when we were with him in the holy mount" (2 Pet. i. 17, 18). There must have been something very unearthly and awe-striking in the sound, especially as the articulate vehicle of such a testimony to Christ, to be thus recalled. **saying, This is my beloved Son**—"in whom I am well pleased" (Matt. xvii. 5): **hear him:** Hear Him *reverentially*, hear Him *implicitly* hear Him *alone.* **36. And when the voice was past, Jesus was found alone.** Moses and Elias are gone. Their work is done, and they have disappeared from the scene, feeling no doubt with their fellow-servant the Baptist, "He must increase, but I must decrease." The cloud too is gone, and the naked majestic Christ, braced in spirit, and enshrined in the reverent affection of His disciples, is left—to suffer! Matthew (xvii. 6-8) is more full here: "And when the disciples

heard [the voice], they fell on their face, and were sore afraid (*v.* 6). And Jesus came and touched them, and said, Arise, and be not afraid (*v.* 7.) And when they had lifted up their eyes, they saw no man save Jesus only" (*v.* 8). **And they kept it close, and told no man in those days any of those things which they had seen** — feeling, for once, at least, that such things were unmeet as yet for general disclosure.

Remarks.—1. We know how the first announcement which our Lord made to the Twelve of His approaching Sufferings and Death startled and shocked them. We know, too, with what sternness Peter's entreaty that his Lord would spare Himself was met and put down, (Matt. xvi. 21, &c.) But it is only by studying the recorded connection between these disclosures and the Transfiguration that we gather how protracted had been the depression produced upon the Twelve, and how this probably reacted upon the mind even of our Lord Himself. After the lapse of a week, and during a night of prayer spent on a mountain, that Death, the announcement of which had been so trying to His most select disciples, is suddenly presented in a new and astonishing light, as engaging the wonder and interest of heaven. No doubt, such a view of it was needed. As the Twelve were beyond all doubt reassured by it, so it is not to be doubted that the Redeemer's own spirit was cheered and invigorated by it. 2. We have tried to conceive what might be the strain of those "prayers and supplications, with strong crying and tears" which Jesus poured out on that mountain, ere the glory broke forth from Him. But much must be left unimagined. 'He filled the silent night with His crying,' says *Traill* beautifully, 'and watered the cold earth with His tears, more precious than the dew of Hermon, or any moisture, next unto His own blood, that ever fell on God's earth since the creation.' 3. "As He prayed the fashion of His countenance was altered." Thanks to God, transfiguring manifestations are not quite strangers here. Ofttimes in the deepest depths, out of groanings which cannot be uttered, God's dear children are suddenly transported to a kind of heaven upon earth, and their soul is made as the chariots of Ammi-nadib. Their prayers fetch down such light, strength, holy gladness, as makes their face to shine, putting a kind of celestial radiance upon it. (Compare 2 Cor. iii. 18, with Exod. xxxiv. 29-35.) 4. What a testimony have we here to the *evangelical* scope of the whole ancient economy. Not only is *Christ* the great End of it all, but a *dying* Christ. Nor are we to dissever the *economy* from the *saints* that were reared under it. In heaven, at least, they regard that "Decease" as all their salvation and all their desire, as we see beautifully here. For here, fresh from heaven, and shining with the glory of it, when permitted to talk with Him, they speak not of His miracles, nor of His teaching, nor of the honour which he put upon their Scriptures, nor upon the unreasonable opposition to Him and His patient endurance of it: They speak not of the

37   And [h]it came to pass, that on the next day, when they were come down
38 from the hill, much people met him. And, behold, a man of the company cried out, saying, Master, I beseech thee, look upon my son; for he
39 is mine only child: and, lo, a spirit taketh him, and he suddenly crieth out; and it teareth him that he foameth again, and, bruising him, hardly
40 departeth from him. And I besought thy disciples to cast him out; and
41 they could not. And Jesus answering said, O faithless and [i]perverse generation! how long shall I be with you, and suffer you? Bring thy son
42 hither. And as he was yet a-coming, the devil threw him down, and tare *him.* And Jesus rebuked the unclean spirit, and healed the child, and

A. D. 32.

[h] Matt. 17.14, 21.
Mark 9. 14, 17.
[i] Deut. 32. 5.
Ps. 78. 8.
Matt. 3. 7.
Matt. 12.39, 45.
Matt. 16. 4.
Matt. 23.36.
Acts 2. 40.

glory they were themselves enshrined in, and the glory which He was so soon to reach. Their one subject of talk is "His *decease* which he was going to accomplish at Jerusalem." One fancies he might hear them saying, "Worthy is the Lamb that *is to be* slain!" Those, then, who see no suffering, dying Messiah in the Old Testament read it amiss, if this Transfiguration-scene mean anything at all. 5. In the light of this interview between the two great representatives of the ancient economy and Christ, what are we to think of that theory which some modern advocates of the Personal Reign of Christ on earth during the Millennium contend for—that the saints of the Old Testament are never to be glorified with the Church of the New, but to occupy the lower sphere of a resurrection to some earthly or Adamic condition? The speculation in itself is repulsive enough, and void enough of anything like Scripture support. But in the light of such a scene as this, may we not call it intolerable? 6. What think ye of Christ? Are ye in sympathy with heaven about Him? Doubtless the hymn of the New-Testament Church which best accords with this celestial talk on the mount of Transfiguration is that of the rapt seer in Patmos: "Unto Him that loved us, and washed us from our sins in His own blood, and hath made us kings and priests unto God and His Father, to Him be glory and dominion for ever and ever. Amen" (Rev. i. 5, 6). 7. How cheering is the view here given of the intermediate state between death and the resurrection! No doubt Elijah was translated that He should not see death. But Moses died and was buried. We speak not of those shining bodies, which we know that even angels put on when they came down to talk to the women at the sepulchre of their Lord. But the disembodied saints cannot be conceived to have come down from heaven and talked with Christ as living conscious beings, if the state of the soul between death and the resurrection be one of *unconscious sleep;* no, nor if it be in a state *perfectly passive,* as some good but too speculative divines endeavour to make out. For here is active thought and feeling, aye, and deepest interest in what is passing on earth, particularly what relates to the work, and so, the kingdom of Christ. We presume not to "intrude into those things which we have not seen, vainly puffed up by a fleshly mind." But to the extent we have just expressed, we seem to be on sure Scripture ground. 8. "This is my beloved Son." Is He our Beloved? 9. "Hear Him." Are we doing that? Is His word law to us? Do we like it when it speaks sharp as well as smooth things; when it tells of the worm that dieth not, and the fire that is not quenched, as well as of the many mansions in His Father's house? Does Christ's word carry it over everything that comes into collision with it? And would it not help us just to think, that whatever Christ speaks, the Father is standing over us, as it

enters our ears, and saying, 'Hear that.' Thus, "Except a man be born again, he cannot enter into the kingdom of God"—'*Hear* Him.' "Come unto Me, all ye that labour and are heavy laden, and I will give you rest"—'Hear that.' When dark and crushing events are ready to overwhelm us, "What I do thou knowest not now, but thou shalt know hereafter"—'*Hear* Him.' When walking through the valley of the shadow of death, "I am the Resurrection and the Life: he that believeth in Me, though he were dead, yet shall he live; and he that liveth and believeth in Me shall never die" —'Hear Him!' 10. "It came to pass, as they departed from Him." Ah! Bright manifestations in this vale of tears are always "departing" manifestations. But the time is coming when our sun shall no more go down, and the glory shall never be withdrawn. 11. "Jesus was left alone." And alone He abidingly is and ever will be in the eyes of all heaven, earth, and hell—unique, sole: the Alpha and Omega of all God's purposes, the Church's hopes, and hell's fears! 12. When the three disciples heard the voice from heaven, "they fell on their face, and were sore afraid." But Jesus was not. He was not in the least discomposed. He "came and touched them, and said, Arise, and be not afraid" (Matt. xvii. 6, 7). How was this? Why, it was His proper element. A mere man would, as we say, have had his head turned by such a demonstration in His behalf. At least he would have taken time to recover himself, and get down to his proper level. But Jesus—amidst all this blaze of glory, and celestial talk, and the voice from within the cloud, the voice of God Himself, proclaiming Him His beloved Son, whom all are to hear—is perfectly at home. But indeed it was only a faint anticipation of what He will be when He shall come in His own glory and in the glory of the Father and of the holy angels. 13. Well might Peter, looking back, near the close of his life, to this scene, say, "We have not followed cunningly devised fables, when we made known unto you the power and coming of our Lord Jesus Christ, but were eye-witnesses of His majesty. For He received from God the Father honour and glory, when there came such a voice to Him from the excellent glory [μεγαλοπρεποῦς δόξης], This is my beloved Son, in whom I am well pleased. And this voice which came from heaven, we heard, when we were with Him in the holy mount" (2 Pet. i. 16-18). But, as that chastened disciple delightfully adds, there is something better than even this: "We have also what is firmer, the prophetic word [Καὶ ἔχομεν βεβαιότερον τὸν προφητικὸν λόγον]; whereunto ye do well that ye take heed, as unto a light that shineth in a dark place, until the day dawn, and the day star arise in your hearts" (see on 2 Pet. i. 19). "Until the day break, and the shadows flee away, turn, my Beloved, and be thou like a roe, or a young hart, upon the mountains of Bether" (Song ii. 17).

37-45.—HEALING OF A DEMONIAC BOY—SECON

43 delivered him again to his father. And they were all amazed at the mighty power of God.

But, while they wondered every one at all things which Jesus did, he
44 said unto his disciples, Let these sayings sink down into your ears: for
45 the Son of man shall be delivered into the hands of men. But *j*they understood not this saying, and it was hid from them, that they perceived it not: and they feared to ask him of that saying.

46   Then *k*there arose a reasoning among them, which of them should be
47 greatest. And Jesus, perceiving the thought of their heart, took a child,
48 and set him by him, and said unto them, *l*Whosoever shall receive this child in my name receiveth me; and whosoever shall receive me receiveth him that sent me: *m*for he that is least among you all, the same shall be great.

49   And *n*John answered and said, Master, we saw one casting out devils in thy name; and we forbade him, because he followeth not with us.
50 And Jesus said unto him, Forbid *him* not: for *o*he that is not against us is for us.

51   And it came to pass, when the time was come that *p*he should be
52 received up, he stedfastly set his face to go to Jerusalem, and sent messengers before his face: and they went, and entered into a village of the
53 Samaritans, to make ready for him. And *q*they did not receive him,
54 because his face was as though he would go to Jerusalem. And when his disciples James and John saw *this*, they said, Lord, wilt thou that we command fire to come down from heaven, and consume them, even as

A. D. 32.
j. Matt. 16. 22.
Mark 8. 16.
Mark 9. 32.
ch. 2. 50.
ch. 18. 34.
John 12. 16.
John 14. 5.
2 Cor. 3. 14.
k Matt. 18. 1.
Mark 9. 34.
l Matt. 10. 40.
Matt. 18. 5.
Mark 9. 37.
John 12. 44.
John 13. 20.
1 Thes. 4. 8.
m Matt. 23. 11, 12.
n Mark 9. 38.
Num. 11. 28.
o Matt. 12. 30.
Mark 9 39-41.
ch. 11. 23.
1 Cor. 12. 3.
p 2 Ki. 2. 1.
Mark 16. 19.
John 6. 62.
Acts 1. 2.
Heb. 6. 20.
q John 4. 4. 9.

EXPLICIT ANNOUNCEMENT OF HIS APPROACHING SUFFERINGS. (= Matt. xvii. 14-23; Mark ix. 14-32.) For the exposition, see on Mark ix. 14-32.

46-50. — STRIFE AMONG THE TWELVE WHO SHOULD BE GREATEST, WITH RELATIVE TEACHING — INCIDENTAL REBUKE OF JOHN FOR EXCLUSIVENESS. (= Matt. xviii. 1-5; Mark ix. 33-37.) For the exposition, see on Mark ix. 33-37.

51-56. — THE PERIOD OF HIS ASSUMPTION APPROACHING, CHRIST TAKES HIS LAST LEAVE OF GALILEE — THE SAMARITANS REFUSE TO RECEIVE HIM. (= Matt. xix. 1; Mark x. 1.) It is a remarkable characteristic of this Gospel that the contents of nearly nine chapters of it — beginning with this Section (ch. ix. 51), and going down to ch. xviii. 14 — are, with the exception of two or three short passages, peculiar to itself. As there are scarcely any marks of time and place in all this peculiar portion, it is difficult to fix these with any certainty. But there is reason to believe that the earlier portion of it belongs to the period of our Lord's final journey from Galilee — which was probably a circuitous journey, with the view, perhaps, of ministering in localities not before visited; and that the latter portion of it belongs to the intervals between the Feast of Tabernacles and that of the Dedication, in our Lord's last year (see on John x. 22), and between the Feast of the Dedication and that of His Last Passover — during which intervals our Lord appears to have sojourned chiefly in Peræa, within the jurisdiction of Herod Antipas.

Farewell to Galilee, and Refusal of the Samaritans to Receive Him (51-56). **51. And it came to pass, when the time was come that he should be received up** [ἐν τῷ συμπληροῦσθαι τὰς ἡμέρας τῆς ἀνα ἡμψεως αὐτοῦ] — rather, 'when the days of His assumption were fulfilling,' or 'in course of fulfilment:' meaning not His *death*, as Calvin and some others take it, but His *exaltation* to the Father, as Grotius, Bengel, de Wette, Meyer,

Olshausen, Alford, van Osterzee understand it. It is a sublime expression, taking the sweep of His whole career, as if at one bound He was about to vault into glory. It divides the work of Christ in the flesh into *two great stages;* all that preceded this belonging to the one, and all that follows it to the other. During the one, He formally "came to His own," and "would have gathered them;" during the other, the awful consequences of "His own receiving Him not," rapidly revealed themselves. **he stedfastly set his face to go to Jerusalem** [καὶ αὐτὸς τὸ πρόσωπον αὐτοῦ ἐστήριξε]. The "He" is emphatic here; and the spirit in which He "set (or fixed) his face steadfastly" [= שׂוּם פָּנִים, Jer. xxi. 10; Ezek. vi. 2, which in the LXX. is the same as here] "to go to Jerusalem," is best expressed in His own prophetic language, "I have set my face like a flint" (Isa. l. 7). See on Mark x. 32, and Remark 1 at the close of that Section. Jerusalem was His goal; but the reference here to His final visit must be understood as including two preparatory visits to it, at the feasts of Tabernacles and of Dedication (John vii. 2, 10; and x. 22, 23), with all the intermediate movements and events. **52. And sent messengers before his face: and they went, and entered into a village of the Samaritans, to make ready for him.** He had given no such orders before; but now, instead of avoiding, He seems to court publicity — all now hastening to maturity. **53. And they did not receive him, because his face was as though he would go to Jerusalem.** The Galileans, in going to the festivals at Jerusalem, usually took the Samaritan route (*Joseph.* Antt. xx. 6. 1), and yet seem to have met with no such inhospitality. But if they were asked to prepare quarters *for the Messiah*, in the person of one whose face was as though He would *go to Jerusalem*, their national prejudices would be raised at so marked a slight upon their claims. (See on John iv. 20). **54. And when his disciples James and John saw this, they said, Lord, wilt thou that we command fire to come down from**

55 ʳElias did? But he turned, and rebuked them, and said, Ye know not
56 ˢwhat manner of spirit ye are of. For ᵗthe Son of man is not come to
    destroy men's lives, but to save *them*. And they went to another village.
57 And ᵘit came to pass, that, as they went in the way, a certain *man*
58 said unto him, Lord, I will follow thee whithersoever thou goest. And
    Jesus said unto him, Foxes have holes, and birds of the air *have* nests;
59 but the Son of man hath not where to lay *his* head. And ᵛhe said unto
    another, Follow me. But he said, Lord, suffer me first to go and bury
60 my father. Jesus said unto him, Let the dead bury their dead: but go
61 thou and preach the kingdom of God. And another also said, Lord, ʷI
    will follow thee; but let me first go bid them farewell which are at home
62 at my house. And Jesus said unto him, ˣNo man, having put his hand
    to the plough, and looking back, is fit for the kingdom of God.

10 AFTER these things the Lord appointed other seventy also, and ᵃsent
    them two and two before his face into every city and place, whither
2 he himself would come. Therefore said he unto them,

A. D. 32.

ʳ 2 Ki. 1. 10,
  12.
Acts 4. 29.
30.
Rev. 13. 13.
ˢ Num. 20. 10-
  12.
Job 2. 10.
Job 26. 4.
Rom. 10. 2.
ᵗ John 3. 17.
John 12. 47.
ᵘ Matt. 8. 19.
ᵛ Matt. 8. 21.
ʷ 1 Ki. 19. 20.
ˣ Heb. 6. 4.

CHAP. 10.
ᵃ Matt. 10. 1.
Mark 6. 7.

heaven, and consume them. It was not *Peter* who spoke this, as we should have expected, but those "*sons of thunder*" (Mark iii. 17), who afterwards would have all the highest honours of the Kingdom to themselves, and the younger of whom had been rebuked already for his exclusiveness (*vv.* 49, 50). Yet this was "the disciple whom Jesus loved," while the other willingly drank of His Lord's bitter cup. (See on Mark x. 38-40, and on Acts xii. 2.) And that same fiery zeal, in a mellowed and hallowed form, in the beloved disciple, we find kindling up—in view of deadly error and ecclesiastical presumption—in 2 John 10, and 3 John 10. **even as Elias did?**—a plausible precedent, and the more so, perhaps, as it also occurred in *Samaria* (2 Ki. i. 10-12). **55. But he turned, and rebuked them, and said, Ye know not what manner of spirit ye are of.** 'The thing ye demand, though in keeping with the *legal*, is unsuited to the genius of the *evangelical* dispensation.' The sparks of *unholy* indignation would seize readily enough on this example of Elias; but our Lord's rebuke, as is plain from *v.* 56, is directed to the *principle* involved rather than the animal heat which doubtless prompted the reference. **56. For the Son of man is not come to destroy men's lives, but to save them**—a saying truly divine, of which all His miracles—for salvation, never destruction—were one continued illustration. **And they went to another village**—illustrating His own precept (Matt. x. 23), "When they persecute you in one city, flee ye to another." *Tischendorf* and *Tregelles* greatly curtail the text in this passage, leaving out all that we here inclose in brackets : 54. [Even as Elias.] 55. But he turned and rebuked them, [and said, Ye know not what manner of spirit ye are of. 56. For the Son of man is not come to destroy men's lives, but to save them.] *Lachmann* admits, "Even as Elias," but excludes all the rest. The authority on which this is done, though ancient and weighty, is decidedly inferior, in our judgment, to that in favour of the received text—so far as *vv.* 54, 55, are concerned. For the exclusion of *v.* 56 the authorities are more formidable; and some critics, who abide by the received text up to that verse, think themselves bound to reject it, as probably inserted from Matt. xviii. 11, and Luke xix. 10. But we agree with *Alford* in retaining the whole, on internal as well as external evidence. The saying in Matt. xviii. 11 cannot fairly be identified with this one.

Remarks.—1. How easily may the heat of human anger mingle with zeal for the Lord, and be con-

founded with it, as in the case of James and John here; and how slow are we to learn that "the wrath of man worketh not the righteousness of God" (Jas. i. 20). Confounding the Legal and the Evangelical dispensations, has been the fruitful source, as of woeful corruption of the worship of God, so of hateful persecution in the name of religion. While attempts to graft the spirit of the ancient ritual upon the worship of the Christian Church has led to a monstrous caricature of the temple-service and the Aaronic priesthood in the Church of Rome, the merciless vengeance which was required to be taken, and which sometimes miraculously descended, upon the despisers of Moses' law has been regarded as the model and law of the Christian Church; and Christian magistrates have been hounded on—not by the Church of Rome only, but, alas! by others also—to execute what was called the just judgment of God upon the unbelieving and the heretical. But that great saying of Christ, "The Son of man is not come to destroy men's lives, but to save them," should for ever banish and brand such a mode of treating errorists as contrary to the entire genius of the Gospel. It is a golden saying of *Tillotson*, as *Webster and Wilkinson* remark, that we should never do anything for religion which is against religion.

57-62.—INCIDENTS ILLUSTRATIVE OF DISCIPLE-SHIP. (= Matt. viii. 18-22.) For the exposition, see on Matt. viii. 18-22.

CHAP. X. 1-4.—MISSION OF THE SEVENTY DISCIPLES—THEIR RETURN, AND DISCOURSE OCCASIONED BY THEIR REPORT. As our Lord's end approaches, the preparations for the establishment of the coming Kingdom are quickened and extended.

Mission of the Seventy Disciples (1-16).—**1. After these things**—but how long after does not appear. See introductory remarks on the large portion of this Gospel commencing with ch. ix. 51. **the Lord.** This august appellation is here in the highest degree suitable, the appointment about to be mentioned being, as *Bengel* remarks, truly *lordly*. **appointed other seventy also** [καὶ ἑτέρους, ἑβδομήκοντα]—an unhappy rendering. It should be, as we have pointed the Greek, 'appointed others also, seventy [in number]'—that is, others in addition to the Twelve, to the number of seventy. In all likelihood, as the number Twelve had reference to the number of the tribes of Israel, so the number Seventy had reference to the number of elders on whom the Spirit rested in the wilderness (Num. xi. 24, 25).

[b]The harvest truly *is* great, but the labourers *are* few: [c]pray ye therefore the [d]Lord of the harvest, that he would send forth labourers into his
3 harvest. Go your ways: [e]behold, I send you forth as lambs among wolves.
4 Carry [f]neither purse, nor scrip, nor shoes: and [g]salute no man by the
5 way. And [h]into whatsoever house ye enter, first say, Peace *be* to this
6 house. And if the son of peace be there, your peace shall rest upon it:
7 if not, it shall turn to you again. And [i]in the same house remain, [j]eating and drinking such things as they give: for the [k]labourer is worthy of
8 his hire. Go not [l]from house to house. And into whatsoever city ye
9 enter, and they receive you, eat such things as are set before you: and
[m]heal the sick that are therein; and say unto them, [n]The kingdom of
10 God is come nigh unto you. But into whatsoever city ye enter, and they
receive you not, go your ways out into the streets of the same, and say,
11 Even [o]the very dust of your city, which cleaveth on us, we do wipe off
against you: notwithstanding, be ye sure of this, that the kingdom of
12 God is come nigh unto you. But I say unto you, That [p]it shall be more
13 tolerable in that day for Sodom, than for that city. Woe [q]unto thee,
Chorazin! woe unto thee, Bethsaida! [r]for if the mighty works had been
done in Tyre and Sidon which have been done in you, they had a great
14 while ago [s]repented, sitting in sackcloth and ashes. But it shall be more
15 tolerable for Tyre and Sidon at the judgment, than for you. And [t]thou
Capernaum, which art exalted [u]to heaven, [v]shalt be thrust down to hell.
16 He [w]that heareth you heareth me; and he [x]that despiseth you despiseth
me; [y]and he that despiseth me despiseth him that sent me.
17 And the seventy returned again with joy, saying, Lord, even the devils
18 are subject unto us through thy name. And he said unto them, [z]I
19 beheld Satan as lightning fall from heaven. Behold, [a]I give unto you
power to tread on serpents and scorpions, and over all the power of the

A. D. 32.
[b] Matt. 9. 37, 38. John 4. 35.
[c] 2 Thes. 3.1.
[d] Jer. 3. 15. 1 Cor.12.23.
[e] Matt. 10.16.
[f] Matt. 10. 9, 10. Mark 6. 8. ch. 9. 3.
[g] 2 Ki. 4. 29.
[h] Matt 10.12.
[i] Matt 10.11.
[j] 1 Cor.10.27.
[k] Matt 10.10. 1 Cor. 9. 4.
[l] Eph. 5. 15.
[m] ch. 9. 2.
[n] Isa. 2. 2.
[o] Matt 10.14.
[p] Matt.10.15.
[q] Matt. 11.21.
[r] Ezek. 3. 6.
[s] Jon. 3. 5.
[t] Matt. 11.23.
[u] Gen. 11. 4. Deut. 1. 28.
[v] Ezek. 26.20. Ezek.32.18.
[w] Mark 9. 37. John 13.20.
[x] 1 Thes. 4. 8.
[y] John 5. 23.
[z] John 12. 31.
[a] Mark 16.18.

This appointment, unlike that of the Twelve, was evidently quite *temporary.* All the instructions are in keeping with a brief and hasty *pioneering* mission, intended to supply what of general preparation for coming events the Lord's own visit afterwards to the same "cities and places" (*v.* 1), would not, from want of time, now suffice to accomplish; whereas, the instructions to the Twelve, besides embracing all those given to the Seventy, contemplate *world-wide* and *permanent* effects. Accordingly, after their return from this single missionary tour, we never again read of the Seventy. **and sent them two and two before his face into every city and place, whither he himself would come** [ἔμελλεν αὐτὸς ἔρχεσθαι]—or 'was going to come.' **2. Therefore said he**—or, 'So He said' **unto them, The harvest, &c.** See on Matt. ix. 37, 38, and Remarks 1 and 2 at the close of that Section. **3-12. Go your ways, &c.** See on Matt. x. 7-16. **13-15. Woe unto thee, Chorazin, &c.** See on Matt. xi. 21-24. **16. He that heareth you, &c.** See on Matt. x. 40.

Return of the Seventy, and Discourse occasioned by their Report (17-24). **17. And the seventy returned again**—evidently they had not been long away, **with joy, saying, Lord, even the devils are subject unto us through**—or, 'in' [ἐν] **thy name.** 'Lord, thou hast exceeded thy promise: We had not expected this.' The power to cast out devils, not being expressly in their commission, as it was in that to the Twelve (ch. ix. 1), seems to have filled them with more astonishment and joy than the higher object of their mission. Yet they say, "in Thy name"—taking no credit to themselves, but feeling lifted into a region of unimagined superiority to the powers of evil, simply through their connection with Christ. **18. And he said, I beheld** ['Εθεώρουν] **Satan as**

lightning fall from heaven. As much of the force of this glorious statement depends on the nice shade of sense indicated by the *imperfect tense* in the original, it might have been well to bring it out in the translation:—'I was beholding Satan as lightning falling from heaven:'—*q. d.*, 'I followed you on your mission, and watched its triumphs; while ye were wondering at the subjection to you of devils in My name, a grander spectacle was opening to My view; sudden as the darting of lightning from heaven to earth Satan was beheld by Mine eye falling from heaven!' By that law of association which connects a part with the whole, those feeble triumphs of the Seventy seem to have not only brought vividly before the Redeemer the whole ultimate result of His mission, but compressed it into a moment and quickened it into the rapidity of lightning! We have repeatedly observed that the word rendered "devils" [δαιμόνια] is always used for those spiritual agents employed in *demoniacal possessions*—never for the ordinary agency of Satan in rational men. When, therefore, the Seventy say, "the *demons* are subject to us," and Jesus replies, 'Mine eye was beholding *Satan* falling,' it is plain that He meant to raise their minds not only from the *particular* to the *general,* but from a very *temporary* form of satanic operation to *the entire kingdom of evil.* See John xii. 31, and compare Isa. xiv. 17. **19. Behold, I give unto you**—not with a view to the renewal of their mission, though probably many of them afterwards became ministers of Christ, but simply as disciples. **power to tread on serpents and scorpions**—the latter more venomous than the former. This was to be literally fulfilled at the first starting of the Gospel ministry (Mark xvi. 17, 18; Acts xxviii. 5). But the following words, **and over all the power**

20 enemy: and nothing shall by any means hurt you. Notwithstanding in this rejoice not, that the spirits are subject unto you; but rather rejoice, because [b]your names are written in heaven.

21 In [c]that hour Jesus rejoiced in spirit, and said, I thank thee, O Father, Lord of heaven and earth, that thou hast hid these things from [d]the wise and prudent, and hast revealed them unto babes: even so, Father;

22 for so it seemed good in thy sight. [1]All things [e]are delivered to me of my Father: and [f]no man knoweth who the Son is, but the Father; and who the Father is, but the Son, and *he* to whom the Son will reveal *him.*

23 And he turned him unto *his* disciples, and said privately, [g]Blessed *are*

24 the eyes which see the things that ye see: for I tell you, [h]that many prophets and kings have desired to see those things which ye see, and have not seen *them;* and to hear those things which ye hear, and have not heard *them.*

25 And, behold, a certain lawyer stood up, and tempted him, saying,

26 [i]Master, what shall I do to inherit eternal life? He said unto him,

27 What is written in the law? how readest thou? And he answering said, [j]Thou shalt love the Lord thy God with all thy heart, and with all thy soul, and with all thy strength, and with all thy mind; and [k]thy

28 neighbour as thyself. And he said unto him, Thou hast answered

29 right: this do, and [l]thou shalt live. But he, willing to [m]justify himself, said unto Jesus, And who is my neighbour?

A. D. 32.

[b] Ex. 32. 32.
Ps. 69. 28.
[c] Matt. 11. 25.
[d] 1 Cor. 1. 19.
2 Cor. 2. 6.
[1] Many ancient copies add these words, And turning to his disciples, he said.
[e] Matt. 28. 18.
John 3. 35.
[f] John 1. 18.
John 6. 44.
[g] Matt. 13. 16.
[h] 1 Pet. 1. 10.
[i] Matt. 22. 35.
[j] Deut. 6. 5.
[k] Lev. 19. 18.
[l] Lev. 18. 5.
Neh. 9. 29.
Ezek. 20. 11.
Rom. 10. 5.
[m] ch. 16. 15.

---

of the enemy: and nothing shall by any means hurt you—show that what is meant is the glorious power of faith to "overcome the world" and "quench all the fiery darts of the wicked one," by the communication and maintenance of which to His people He makes them *innocuous* (1 John v. 4; Eph. vi. 16). 20. **Notwithstanding in this rejoice not**—that is, not so much **that the spirits are subject unto you; but rather rejoice, because your names are written in heaven.** So far from forbidding this joy at the expulsion of demons by their instrumentality, He told them the exultation with which He followed it Himself; but since power over demons might unduly elate them, He gives them a higher joy to *balance* it, the joy of having their own names in Heaven's register. (Phil. iv. 3). · **21. In that hour Jesus rejoiced** [ἠγαλλιάσατο]—or 'exulted,' **in spirit**—giving visible expression to His unusual emotions, while the words "in spirit" express the depth of them, **and said, I thank thee** ['Εξομολογοῦμαί σοι]—rather, 'I assent to thee;' but with the idea of full or cordial concurrence, expressed by the preposition. (See on Matt. xi. 25.) **that thou hast hid these things from the wise and prudent, and hast revealed them unto babes: even so, Father; for so it seemed good in thy sight. 22. [And turning to his disciples, he said,]** The words in brackets are in the received text of *Stephens*, though not of the *Elzevirs*, nor in *Beza's* text; and our version, which in some places follows *Beza's* text in preference to the other, omits them here. But the authority for the insertion of them is preponderating. *Tischendorf* inserts them, though *Tregelles* does not. **All things are delivered to me of my Father: and no man knoweth who the Son is, but the Father; and who the Father is, but the Son, and he to whom the Son will reveal him.** This sublime utterance has been regarded by some acute harmonists as but a repetition by Luke of what is recorded in Matt. xi. 25-27, and so, as spoken only once. But besides that the occasions were not the same, the words in the First Gospel merely are, "Jesus answered

and said," whereas here they are, "Jesus exulted in spirit, and said." If this should be thought of less moment, let it be observed that there it is merely said, "At that time," or 'season' [καιρῷ], He spoke thus—with a general reference to the rejection of His Gospel by the self-sufficient; whereas here it is, "*In that hour* Jesus said," with express reference probably to the humble class from which He had had to draw the Seventy, and the similar class that had chiefly welcomed their message. **23, 24. And he turned him unto his disciples, and said privately, Blessed are the eyes that see the things that ye see, &c.** See on Matt. xiii. 16, 17.

For Remarks on the Mission of the Seventy, see those on the analogous Mission of the Twelve, Matt. x.; and for Remarks on the lofty utterance with which this Section closes, see those on the same in Matt. xi. 25-27.

25-37.—QUESTION OF A LAWYER ABOUT THE WAY TO INHERIT ETERNAL LIFE, AND THE PARABLE OF THE GOOD SAMARITAN.

How to Inherit Eternal Life (25-29). **25. And, behold, a certain lawyer stood up, and tempted him**—'tried,' or 'tested Him' [ἐκπειράζων]; in no hostile spirit, yet with no tender anxiety for light on that question of questions, but just to see what insight this great Galilean teacher had. **saying, Master**—'Teacher' [Διδάσκαλε], **what shall I do to inherit eternal life? 26. He said unto him, What is written in the law? how readest thou?**—'an apposite question,' says *Bengel*, 'to a doctor of the law, and putting himself in turn to the test.' **27. And he answering said, Thou shalt love the Lord thy God, &c.**—precisely as Christ Himself had answered another lawyer. See on Mark xii. 29-33. **28. And he said unto him, Thou hast answered right: this do, and thou shalt live.** 'Right: THIS do, and life is thine'—laying such emphasis on "this" as to indicate, without expressing it, *where the real difficulty to a sinner lay*, and thus nonplussing the questioner himself. **29. But he, willing**—or 'wishing' [θέλων], **to justify himself**—to get himself out of the difficulty by throwing upon Jesus the definition of

30   And Jesus answering said, A certain *man* went down from Jerusalem to Jericho, and fell among thieves, which stripped him of his raiment,
31   and wounded *him*, and departed, leaving *him* half dead. And by chance there came down a certain priest that way: and when he saw him, [n]he
32   passed by on the other side. And likewise a Levite, when he was at the
33   place, came and looked *on him*, and passed by on the other side. But a certain [o]Samaritan, as he journeyed, came where he was: and when he
34   saw him, he had compassion *on him*, and went to *him*, and bound up his wounds, pouring in oil and wine, and set him on his own beast, and
35   brought him to an inn, and took care of him. And on the morrow, when he departed, he took out two [p]pence, and gave *them* to the host, and said unto him, Take care of him: and whatsoever thou spendest more, when
36   I come again, I will repay thee. Which now of these three, thinkest
37   thou, was neighbour unto him that fell among the thieves? And he said, He that showed mercy on him. Then said Jesus unto him, [q]Go, and do thou likewise.

A. D. 32.

[n] Job 6.14, 21.
Ps. 38. 11.
Ps. 69. 20.
Pro. 21. 13.
Jas. 2. 13.
1 John 3.16.
[o] Pro. 27. 10.
Jer. 38. 7.
Jer. 39. 16.
John 4. 9.
John 8. 48.
[p] Matt. 20. 2.
[q] ch. 6. 32.
John 13.15.
Rom. 12.20.
1 Pet. 2. 21.
1 John 3.16, 18.
1 John 4.10, 11.

"neighbour," 'which,' as *Alford* remarks, 'the Jews interpreted very narrowly and technically, as excluding Samaritans and Gentiles; **said unto Jesus, And who is my neighbour?**

Parable of the Good Samaritan (30-37). **30. And Jesus answering said, A certain man**—a Jew, as the story shows, **went down from Jerusalem to Jericho**—a distance of eighteen miles northeast, a deep and very fertile hollow, and, as *Trench* says, the *Tempe* of Judea; **and fell among thieves** [λησταῖς]—rather 'robbers.' The road, being rocky and desolate, was a notorious haunt of robbers, then and for ages after, and is even to this day. **which stripped him of his raiment, and wounded him, and departed, leaving him half dead. 31. And by chance there came down a certain priest that way.** Jericho, the second city of Judea, was a city of the priests and Levites, and thousands of them lived there. **and when he saw him**—so it was not *inadvertently* that he acted, **he passed by on the other side**—although the law expressly required the opposite treatment even of the *beast* not only of their *brethren* but of their *enemy* (Deut. xxii. 4; Exod. xxiii. 4, 5; and compare Isa. lviii. 7). **32. And likewise a Levite, when** he was at the place, came and looked on him—a further aggravation, **and passed by on the other side.** If we suppose this priest and Levite to have been returning from their temple duties at Jerusalem, as *Trench* says, it would show that whatever else they had learnt there, they had not learnt what that meaneth, "I will have mercy, and not sacrifice." **33. But a certain Samaritan**—one of a race excommunicated by the Jews; a byword among them, and synonymous with heretic and devil (John viii. 48; and see on ch. xvii. 18); **as he journeyed, came where he was: and when he saw him, he had compassion on him.** Compare what is said of the Lord Himself: "And when the Lord saw her (the widow of Nain), He had compassion on her" (ch. vii. 13). No doubt the priest and Levite had their excuses for passing by their wounded brother.—'Tisn't safe to be lingering here; besides, he's past recovery; and then, mayn't suspicion rest upon ourselves?' So might the Samaritan have reasoned—*but did not*. Nor did he say, 'He would have had no dealings with me (John iv. 9), and why should I with him?' **34. And went to him, and bound up his wounds, pouring in oil and wine**—the remedies used in such cases all over the East (Isa. i. 6), and elsewhere; the *wine* to cleanse the wounds, the *oil* to assuage their smartings. **and set him on his own beast**—himself going on foot, **and brought him to an inn, and**

took care of him. 35. And on the morrow, when he departed, he took out two pence—equal to two days' wages of a labourer, and enough for several days' support, **and gave them to the host, and said unto him, Take care of him: and whatsoever thou spendest more, when I come again, I will repay thee. 36. Which now of these three, thinkest thou, was neighbour unto him that fell among the thieves?**—a most dexterous way of putting the question: first, turning it from the lawyer's form of it, 'Whom am I to love as my neighbour?' to the more pointed question, 'Who is the man that shows that love?' and next, compelling the lawyer to give a reply very different from what he would like—not only condemning his own nation, but those of them who should be the most exemplary; and finally, making him commend one of a deeply-hated race. And he does so, but it is almost extorted. **37. And he said, He that showed mercy on him.** He does not answer, 'The Samaritan'—that would have sounded heterodox, heretical—but "He that showed mercy on him." It comes to the same thing, no doubt, but the circumlocution is significant. **Then said Jesus unto him, Go, and do thou likewise.**

Remark. — O exquisite, matchless teaching! What new fountains of charity has not this opened up in the human spirit—rivers in the wilderness, streams in the desert! what noble Christian Institutions have not such words founded, all undreamed of till that Divine One came to bless this heartless world of ours with His incomparable love—first in words, and then in deeds which have translated His words into flesh and blood, and poured the life of them through that humanity which He made His own! But was this parable designed merely to magnify the law of love, and show who fulfils it and who not? Is not the mind irresistibly directed to Him who, as our Brother Man, "our Neighbour," did this as never man did it? The priests and Levites, says *Trench*, had not strengthened the diseased, nor bound up the broken (Ezek. xxxiv. 4), while He bound up the broken-hearted (Is. lxi. 1), and poured into all wounded spirits the balm of sweetest consolation. All the Church-fathers saw, through the thin veil of this noblest of stories, *the* Story of love, and never wearied of tracing the analogy, though sometimes fancifully enough. 'He hungered'— exclaims *Gregory* of Nazianzum, in the fourth century, in a passage of singular eloquence, in one of his Sermons—'but He fed thousands; He was weary, but He is the Rest of the weary; He is saluted "Samaritan" and "Demoniac," but He *saves him*

38   Now it came to pass, as they went, that he entered into a certain village: and a certain woman named *'Martha received him into her* 39 house. And she had a sister called Mary, which also *'sat at Jesus' feet,* 40 and heard his word. But Martha was *'cumbered about much serving,* and came to him, and said, Lord, dost thou not care that my sister 41 hath left me to serve alone? bid her therefore that she help me. And Jesus answered and said unto her, Martha, Martha, thou art care- 42 ful and troubled about many things: but one thing is needful: and Mary hath chosen that good part, which shall not be taken away from her.

11   AND it came to pass, that, as he was praying in a certain place, when he ceased, one of his disciples said unto him, Lord, *"teach us to* pray, as John also taught his disciples.

A. D. 32.

' John 11. 1.
* Deut. 33. 3.
   Acts 22. 3.
‡ 1 Cor. 7.
   32.

CHAP. 11.
ᵃ Ps. 10. 17.
  Ps. 19. 14.
  Rom. 8. 20,
  27.
  2 Cor. 3. 5.
  Jas. 4. 2,
  3.
  Jude 20.

---

that went down from Jerusalem and fell among thieves,' &c. More of this noble passage will be found on chap. xix. 28-44, Remark 2, at the close of that Section.

38-42.—JESUS IN THE HOUSE OF MARTHA AND MARY. **38. Now it came to pass, as they went, that he entered into a certain village.** The village was Bethany—as to which, see on ch. xix. 29. It will be seen how void of all definite note of time and place are the incidents recorded in this large portion of our Gospel, as noticed on ch. ix. 51. **and a certain woman named Martha received him into her house.** From this way of speaking we gather that the house belonged to her, and from all the notices of her it would seem that she was the elder sister. **39. And she had a sister called Mary, which also**—or 'who for her part,' as *Webster and Wilkinson* put it, as opposed to Martha, **sat**—or 'seated herself' [παρακαθίσασα] **at Jesus' feet.** From the custom of sitting *beneath* an instructor, the phrase 'sitting at one's feet' came to mean being his disciple (Acts xxii. 3). **and heard** [ἤκουε]—or 'kept listening' to **his word. 40. But Martha was cumbered**—or 'distracted' [περιεσπᾶτο] **about much serving, and came to him** [ἐπιστᾶσα] — presenting herself, as from another apartment, in which her sister had *" left* her to serve, or make preparation, *alone,"* **and said, Lord, dost thou not care that my sister hath left me to serve alone?**—'Lord, here am I with everything to do, and this sister will not lay a hand to anything; thus I miss something from Thy lips, and Thou from our hands.' **bid her therefore that she help me.** She presumes not to stop Christ's teaching by calling her sister away, and thus leaving Him without His rapt auditor, nor did she hope perhaps to succeed if she had tried. **41. And Jesus answered and said unto her, Martha, Martha**—emphatically redoubling upon the name, **thou art careful and troubled** [μεριμνᾶς καὶ τυρβάζῃ]. The one word expresses the inward *fretting anxiety* that her preparations should be worthy of her Lord; the other, the outward *bustle* of those preparations. **about many things**—"much serving" (*v.* 40); too elaborate preparation, which so engrossed her attention that she missed her Lord's teaching. **42. But one thing is needful.** The idea of 'Short work and little of it sufficeth for Me' is not so much the lower *sense* of these weighty words, as *implied* in them as the basis of something far loftier than any precept on economy. Underneath that idea is couched another, as to the littleness both of elaborate preparation for the present life and *of that life itself* compared with another. **and Mary hath chosen that**—or 'the' **good part**—not in the general sense of Moses' choice (Heb. xi. 25), and Joshua's (Josh. xxiv. 15), and David's (Ps. cxix. 30); **that is, of**

good in opposition to *bad;* but, of two good ways of serving and pleasing the Lord, choosing *the better.* Wherein, then, was Mary's better than Martha's? What follows supplies the answer: **which shall not be taken away from her.** Martha's choice would be taken from her, for *her services would die with her;* Mary's *never,* being spiritual and eternal. Both were true-hearted disciples, but the one was absorbed in the higher, the other in the lower of two ways of honouring their common Lord. Yet neither would deliberately despise, or willingly neglect, the other's occupation. The one represents the *contemplative,* the other the *active* style of the Christian character.

Remark.—This rebuke of Martha was but for the excess of a valuable quality, which on another occasion appears without that excess. See on Mark xiv. 3, and Remark 1 at the close of that Section. The quality which was commended in Mary has its excesses too. It is true that a predominance of the impulsive activity of the one sister is unfavourable to depth of thought and elevation of feeling; but a predominance of the passive docility of the other sister is apt to generate an unhealthy tone, and lead rather to dreamy speculation or sentiment than to sound knowledge and wisdom. A Church full of Maries would perhaps be as great an evil as a Church full of Marthas. Both are needed, each to be the complement of the other.

CHAP. XI. 1-13.—JESUS TEACHES HIS DISCIPLES TO PRAY, AND GIVES ENCOURAGEMENTS TO IMPORTUNITY AND FAITH IN THE EXERCISE OF IT. **1. And it came to pass, that, as he was praying in a certain place**—where, it is impossible to say; see introductory remarks on ch. ix. 51, **when he ceased, one of his disciples**—struck, no doubt, with both the matter and the manner of our Lord's own prayers, **said unto him, Lord, teach us to pray, as John also taught his disciples.** From this reference to John, it is probable this disciple had not heard the Sermon on the Mount, containing very specific instructions on the subject of Prayer. It is worthy of notice that we have no record of John's teaching on this subject, and that but for this allusion to it we should never have known that he had touched on it. It shows that the Baptist's inner or more private teaching was of a much more detailed nature than we should have supposed; the specimens of it which we have in the Gospels being chiefly what he taught to the general multitude. One would like to have known more of his teaching on the subject of Prayer. But whatever it was, we may be sure he never taught his disciples, when they prayed, to say, "Our Father." That was reserved for a Greater than he.

The Model Prayer (2-4). **2. And he said unto them, When ye pray, say, Our Father,** [*Tischen-*

268

2　And he said unto them, When ye pray, say, *b*Our Father which art in heaven, Hallowed be thy name. *c*Thy kingdom come. Thy will be
3　done, as in heaven, so in earth. Give us *1*day by day our daily bread.
4　And forgive us our sins: for *d*we also forgive every one that is indebted to us. And *e*lead us not into temptation; but deliver us from evil.
5　And he said unto them, Which of you shall have a friend, and shall go unto him at midnight, and say unto him, Friend, lend me three
6　loaves; for a friend of mine *2*in his journey is come to me, and I have
7　nothing to set before him? And he from within shall answer and say, Trouble me not: the door is now shut, and my children are with me in
8　bed; I cannot rise and give thee. I say unto you, *f*Though he will not rise and give him, because he is his friend, yet because of his importunity
9　he will rise and give him as many as he needeth. And *g*I say unto you, Ask, and it shall be given you; seek, and ye shall find; knock, and it
10　shall be opened unto you. For every one that asketh receiveth; and he that seeketh findeth; and to him that knocketh it shall be opened.
11　If *h*a son shall ask bread of any of you that is a father, will he give
12　him a stone? or if *he ask* a fish, will he for a fish give him a serpent? or
13　if he shall ask an egg, will he *3*offer him a scorpion? If ye then, being evil, know how to give good gifts unto your children: how much more shall *your* heavenly Father give the Holy *i*Spirit to them that ask him?

A. D. 32.
b 2 Chr. 20. 6.
Ps. 11. 4.
Isa. 63. 16.
Matt. 5. 16.
Matt. 10. 32.
c Isa. 11. 9.
Dan. 7. 14.
1 Or, for the day.
d Matt. 6. 14, 15.
Eph. 4. 32.
Jas. 2. 13.
e Matt. 6. 13.
ch. 8. 13.
ch. 22. 46.
1 Cor. 10. 13.
Jas. 1. 13.
Rev. 3. 10.
2 Or, out of his way.
f ch. 18. 1.
g 1 John 5. 14.
h Matt. 7. 9.
3 Give.
i Isa. 44. 3
Matt. 7. 11.
John 4. 10.

dorf and *Tregelles*—whom *Alford* follows, and *Meyer* approves—here omit both the word ἡμῶν, "our," and the following words, ὁ ἐν τοῖς οὐρανοῖς, "which art in heaven." But the authority for inserting those words is most decisive, as we judge. *Lachmann* inserts them.] **which art in heaven, Hallowed be thy name.] Thy kingdom come. Thy will be done, as in heaven, so in earth.** [Here again the same critical editors, on the same authority, omit the entire petition—Γενηθήτω τὸ θέλημά σου, ὡς ἐν οὐρανῷ καὶ ἐπὶ τῆς γῆς, "Thy will," &c. But here, also, as we judge, the evidence is clear in favour of the disputed words.] **3. Give us day by day our daily bread.** This is an extension of the petition in Matthew for "*this* day's" supply, to *every* day's necessities. **4. And forgive us our sins, for we also forgive every one that is indebted to us. And lead us not into temptation; but deliver us from evil.** [This last clause is, by the above editors, on the same authority, excluded from the text, but on insufficient warrant, as we judge.] See on Matt. vi. 9-13, with the corresponding Remarks at the close of that Section. There is no closing doxology here. On the question, whether it formed part of the Lord's Prayer in the Sermon on the Mount, see on Matt. vi. 13. Perhaps our Lord purposely left that part *open*; and as the grand Jewish doxologies were ever resounding, and passed, immediately and · naturally, in all their hallowed familiarity into the Christian Church, probably this Prayer was never used in the Christian assemblies but in its present form, as we find it in Matthew, while in Luke it has been allowed to stand as originally uttered.

Encouragements to Importunity and Faith in Prayer (5-13). **5. And he said unto them, Which of you shall have a friend, and shall go unto him at midnight, and say unto him, Friend, lend me three loaves; 6. For a friend of mine in his journey** [ἐξ ὁδοῦ]—the marginal rendering, 'out of his way,' is to be rejected; **is come to me, and I have nothing to set before him.** The heat in warm countries makes evening preferable to day for travelling; but "midnight" is everywhere a most *unseasonable* hour of call, and for that very reason it

is here selected. **7. And he from within shall answer and say, Trouble me not**—the *trouble* making him insensible both to the urgency of the case and the claims of friendship: **the door is now shut, and my children are with me in bed; I cannot rise and give thee**—without such exertion as he was unwilling to make. **8. I say unto you, Though he will not rise and give him, because he is his friend**—or for friendship's sake, **yet because of his importunity** [ἀναίδειαν]. The word is a strong one, signifying 'shamelessness;' expressing his persistency, in the face of all that seemed reasonable, and refusing to take a denial. **he will rise and give him as many as he needeth.** His reluctance once overcome, all the claims of friendship and necessity are felt to the full. The sense is obvious: If the churlish and self-indulgent—deaf both to friendship and necessity—can, after a positive refusal, be won over by sheer persistency to do all that is needed, *how much more* may the same determined perseverance in prayer be expected to prevail with Him whose very nature it is to be "*rich* unto all that call upon Him" (Rom. x. 12). **9-12. And I say unto you, Ask, and it shall be given you . . . If a son shall ask bread of any of you that is a father, &c.** See on Matt. vii. 7-10. **Or if he shall ask an egg, will he offer him a scorpion?**—looking quite like an egg at some distance, but of a deadly nature. **13. If ye then, being evil**—evil though ye be, **know how to give good gifts unto your children: how much more shall your heavenly Father give the Holy Spirit to them that ask him?** In Matt. vii. 11, it is "give *good gifts* to them that ask Him;" here, at a riper stage of His teaching, and to His disciples apart from the multitude, He says "*the Holy Spirit;*" to teach us that this, the Gift of gifts, descending on the Church through Christ, comprehends all "good gifts."

For Remarks on the subjects embraced in this Section, see those on Matt. vi. 2-15, at the close of that Section; and on Matt. vii. 7-11, at the close of that Section.

14-36.—A BLIND AND DUMB DEMONIAC HEALED, AND REPLY TO THE MALIGNANT EXPLANATION PUT UPON THIS—THE REMARK OF A WOMAN IN THE

14   And ^jhe was casting out a devil, and it was dumb. And it came to pass, when the devil was gone out, the dumb spake; and the people

15 wondered. But some of them said, ^kHe casteth out devils through

16 ⁴Beelzebub the chief of the devils. And others, tempting *him*, ^lsought

17 of him a sign from heaven. But ^mhe, knowing their thoughts, said unto them, Every kingdom divided against itself is brought to desolation; and

18 a house *divided* against a house falleth. If Satan also be divided against himself, how shall his kingdom stand? because ye say that I cast out

19 devils through Beelzebub. And if I by Beelzebub cast out devils, by whom do ⁿyour sons cast *them* out? therefore shall they be your judges.

20 But if I ^owith the finger of God cast out devils, no doubt the kingdom of God is come upon you.

21   When ^pa strong man armed keepeth his palace, his goods are in peace:

22 But ^qwhen a stronger than he shall come upon him, and overcome him, he taketh from him all his armour wherein he trusted, and divideth his

23 spoils. He ^rthat is not with me is against me; and he that gathereth not with me scattereth.

24   When ^sthe unclean spirit is gone out of a man, he walketh through dry places, seeking rest; and finding none, he saith, I will return unto

25 my house whence I came out. And when he cometh, he findeth *it* swept

26 and garnished. Then goeth he, and taketh *to him* seven other spirits more wicked than himself; and they enter in, and dwell there: and ^tthe last *state* of that man is worse than the first.

A. D. 33.
j Matt. 9. 32.
Matt.12.22.
k Matt. 9. 34.
Matt.12.24.
4 Beelzebul.
l Matt.12.38.
Matt. 16. 1.
m Matt 12.25.
Mark 3. 24.
John 2. 25.
Rev. 2. 23.
n Mark 9. 38.
ch. 9. 49.
o Ex. 8. 19.
p Matt.12.29.
Mark 3. 27.
Eph. 6. 12.
Eph. 2. 2.
1 Pet. 5. 8.
q Isa. 9. 6.
Isa. 53. 12.
Col. 2. 15.
Heb. 7. 25.
r Matt.12.30.
s Matt.12.43.
t John 5. 14.
Heb. 6. 4.
Heb. 10. 26.
2 Pet. 2. 20.

CROWD, AND THE ANSWER—WARNING ON SEEKING A SIGN. (=Matt. xii. 22-45; Mark iii. 22-30.) See on Matt. xii. 22-28.

Healing of a Demoniac, and Reply to the Malignant Explanation put upon it (14-20). For the exposition of this portion, see on Matt. xii. 22-28.

Parables of the Strong Man and the Unclean Spirit (21-26).

Parable of The Strong Man (21, 22). **21. When a—or 'the,' strong man armed keepeth**—or 'guardeth' [φυλάσση] **his palace** [αὐλήν]. 'This stands for "palace" (says *Olshausen*), a great pile surrounded with fore-courts and halls.' *Meyer* repudiates this sense, contending for the primary meaning of the word, an open 'court.' But though this does not materially affect the statement itself, the secondary meaning is most suitable here, as interpreters generally agree. The palace here meant by our Lord is *man*, whether viewed more largely or in individual souls—men as nations, churches, or individuals: the "strong man" is Satan. His being "armed" points to all the subtle and varied methods by which he wields his dark power over men. **his goods are in peace**—undisturbed, securely in his possession. **22. But when a stronger**—or 'the Stronger' **than he**. Glorious title of the Lord Jesus in relation to Satan! (1 John iii. 8). **shall come upon him, and overcome him**—sublimely expressing the Redeemer's approach, as the Seed of the woman, to bruise the Serpent's head. **he taketh from him all his armour** [τὴν πανοπλίαν αὐτοῦ]—'his panoply,' 'his complete armour.' Vain would be the victory, were not the *means of regaining* his lost power wrested from him. It is this that completes the triumph and ensures the utter overthrow of his kingdom. **23. He that is not with me is against me; and he that gathereth not with me scattereth.** The nature and force of this statement, in relation to the foregoing parable will be best perceived when we have taken up the one that follows.

Parable of The Unclean Spirit (24-26). **24. When the unclean spirit is gone out of a man, he walketh through dry places** [ἀνύδρων]—literally,

'un-watered,' and so desert, uninhabited places; where are no men to possess and destroy; **seeking rest; and finding none**—because out of his element, which is human misery and destruction: **he saith, I will return unto my house whence I came out**: 'It may be I shall find it tired of its new religious ways, and not unwilling to entertain overtures of reconciliation with its old friend.' **25. And when he cometh, he findeth it**—"empty" (Matt. xii. 44); *occupied by no rival*: but further, **swept and garnished**—not only empty, but all ready to receive him; nay, decked out as if to invite his return. **26. Then goeth he, and taketh to him seven other spirits more wicked than himself.** Seven being the number of completeness, a sevenfold diabolic force, the wickedness of each of which exceeds that of the first, is the strongest conceivable expression of a power sufficient to secure them against all disturbance for the future. **and they enter in,** No resistance now. As we say, they walk the course. **and dwell there.** No temporary sojourn or precarious stay do they make now. They *dwell* there as in their own proper and permanent abode. **and the last state of that man is worse than the first.** Matthew adds this important application to the second parable (xii. 45), "Even so shall it be also unto this wicked generation:" implying that the illustration of this parable which that wicked generation was to furnish was but one example of the working of a great general principle. But an awful illustration of it it was which that generation was to furnish. By the ministry of the Baptist their 'heart was turned to the Lord,' to a large extent: then was their opportunity to receive Christ and live; but they did not: so they became worse than at the first, and soon put their very Deliverer to death. These exceedingly vivid parables bear a strong resemblance to each other; but they differ far more widely than they agree. The subject of both is the same —the soul of man changing from the worse to the better. In both the soul is pictured to us as the residence of the Evil One; in the one parable as his "palace," in the other as his "house." In

27   And it came to pass, as he spake these things, a certain woman of the
company lifted up her voice, and said unto him, "Blessed *is* the womb
28 that bare thee, and the paps which thou hast sucked.   But he said, Yea
*v*rather, blessed *are* they that hear the word of God, and keep it.
29   And *w*when the people were gathered thick together, he began to say,
This is an evil generation: they seek a sign; and there shall no sign be
30 given it, but the sign of Jonas the prophet.   For as *x*Jonas was a sign unto
31 the Ninevites, so shall also the Son of man be to this generation.   The
*y*queen of the south shall rise up in the judgment with the men of this
generation, and condemn them: for she came from the utmost parts of
the earth to hear the wisdom of Solomon; and, behold, a *z*greater than
32 Solomon *is* here.   The men of Nineve shall rise up in the judgment
with this generation, and shall condemn it: for *a*they repented at the
preaching of Jonas; and, behold, a greater than Jonas *is* here.
33   No *b*man, when he hath lighted a candle, putteth *it* in a secret place,
neither under a *c*bushel, but on a candlestick, that they which come in
34 may see the light.   The *d*light of the body is the eye: therefore when
thine eye is single, thy whole body also is full of light; but when *thine*
35 *eye* is evil, thy body also *is* full of darkness.   Take heed therefore that
36 the light which is in thee be not darkness.   If thy whole body therefore
be full of light, having no part dark, the whole shall be full of light, as
when [5]the bright shining of a candle doth give thee light.

A. D. 33.
u ch. 1. 28, 48.
v Matt. 7. 21.
Matt. 12. 49.
ch. 8. 21.
Jas. 1. 25.
w Matt. 12. 38, 39.
x Jon. 1. 17.
Jon. 2. 10.
y 1 Ki. 10. 1.
z Isa. 9. 6.
Rom. 9. 5.
Tit. 2. 13.
Phil. 2. 10.
a Jon. 3. 5.
b Matt. 5. 15.
Mark 4. 21.
c Matt. 5. 15.
d Ps. 119. 18.
Matt. 6. 22.
Mark 8. 18.
Acts 26. 18.
Eph. 1. 17, 18.
[5] A candle by its bright shining.

the one parable the *strength* of this mysterious
enemy is the prominent idea; in the other his
uncleanness.   In both parables the soul is delivered
from this mighty and filthy enemy.   But here the
resemblance terminates, and the vast difference
between the two parables comes out.   The unclean
spirit goes out only to come in again; but the strong
man is grappled with and mastered, and the palace
is permanently occupied by the Victor.   The one
is a temporary, if not a voluntary departure; the
other is a total defeat, and an absolute, resistless
expulsion.   In the one case the last state of the
soul is worse than the first; in the other the last
is its best and noblest state.   Both are cases of *conversion;* but in the one case the conversion is partial and abortive; in the other it is thorough and
enduring.   And the cause of this difference is most
strikingly depicted.   Why was it that the unclean
spirit, after going out of the man, entered in again
without a struggle, never more to be dislodged?
Because on his return he found no rival to dispute the ground with him: *the devil was out, but
Christ was not in.*   Precisely the reverse of this
was the reason why, in the other parable, his return was hopeless.   As it was the Stronger than
he that put him out, so *His presence,* as the rightful Occupant of the palace henceforth, *secures it*
against all successful assault for the future.   And
now we are prepared to listen to the great saying
that comes in between the two parables (*v.* 23), and
to apprehend both its import and its weight: "He
that is not with Me is against Me; and he that
gathereth not with Me scattereth."   This last
clause seems to be an allusion to gleaners, whose
labour is lost if they follow not in the wake, or
work not in the company, of their leader.   Thus
are proclaimed these great maxims: ' *Whatever in
religion is disconnected from Christ comes to nothing;*'
' *Neutrality in religion there is none;*' '*The absence of
positive attachment to Christ involves hostility to
Him.*'
   Remark of a Woman in the Crowd, and the Reply
(27-28).   27. And it came to pass, as he spake
these things, a certain woman of the company [ἐκ
τοῦ ὄχλου]—or ' from the crowd,' lifted up her
voice, and said, Blessed is the womb that bare

thee, and the paps which thou hast sucked. 28.
But he said, Yea rather, blessed are they that
hear the word of God, and keep it.   A charming
little incident, and profoundly instructive.   With
true womanly feeling, she envies the mother of
such a wonderful Teacher.   Well, and higher and
better than she had said as much before her, ch. i.
28, 42; and our Lord is far from condemning it.
He only holds up, as " blessed rather," the hearers and keepers of God's word; in other words, *the
humblest real saint of God.*   See on Matt. xii. 49,
50.   How utterly alien is this sentiment from the
teaching of the Church of Rome, which would excommunicate any one of its members that dared to
talk in the spirit of this glorious saying!
   Seeking a Sign (29-36).   29-32. And when the
people—rather, 'the multitudes' [τῶν ὄχλων] were
gathered thick together, he began to say, This is
an evil generation: they seek a sign.   Matthew
tells us (xii. 38) that certain of the scribes and
Pharisees said, "Master, we would see a sign from
thee;" and it was to this that our Lord here replied.   and there shall no sign be given it, but
the sign of Jonas the prophet, &c.   On this and
the three following verses, see on Matt. xii. 38-42.
33-36. No man, when he hath lighted a candle,
putteth it in a secret place, &c.   On this and
the three following verses, see on Matt. v. 14-16;
and on Matt. vi. 22, 23.   But v. 36, here, is peculiarly vivid, expressing what pure, beautiful, broad
perceptions the *clarity of the inward eye* imparts.
   For Remarks on *vv.* 14-20, and 29-32, see those
on the corresponding verses of Matt. xii.: and for
Remarks on *vv.* 33-36, see those on the corresponding verses of Matt. v. and vi. above noted: it
only remains, then, on this Section, that we add
two on the parables here illustrated (*vv.* 21-26), to
bring out more in detail the distinctive features
of the two cases.
   Remarks.—1. In the second parable we have
three successive stages in the history of a soul.
The first is a change for the better: *The unclean
spirit goes out of the man.*   When is this?   Seldom
is it seen in a period of general religious indifference.   Then the strong man hardly needs to guard
his palace; his goods are in undisturbed peace.

37   And as he spake, a certain Pharisee besought him to dine with him:
38 and he went in, and sat down to meat. And ᶜwhen the Pharisee saw *it*,
39 he marvelled that he had not first washed before dinner. And ᶠthe Lord
said unto him, Now do ye Pharisees make clean the outside of the cup

A. D. 33. •

• Mark 7. 3.
John 3. 25.
ᶠ Matt. 23.25.

Gal. 1. 14.

But where a ministry like the Baptist's is attended with great success, and men are stirred to their depths, and many are fleeing from the wrath to come, then may be seen, amongst real conversions, not a few that are but partial, temporary, abortive. For a while, under the terrors of the coming wrath or the joys of the Gospel, all seems changed, and a thorough conversion appears to have taken place—the unclean spirit has gone out of the man. The house has become uncongenial to him. As an unwelcome guest, and out of his element, he takes his leave—"going" rather than "cast out." But there is no real exchange of masters, of services, of felicities; of Christ for Belial, of spiritual principles for carnal, of heavenly for earthly affections. If the old man seems put off, the new man has not been put on; if old things seem to have passed away, all things have not become new. A heap of negatives make up the change: the man has not been born again. Accordingly, when the unclean spirit returns, he finds the house as "empty" as when he left it. But worse—it is now "swept and garnished." This seems to point to such a relapse in the interval as has transformed it out of the unsympathetic state which drove him forth, into a prepared and inviting habitation for him. The soul's lively interest in religion and relish for divine things has cooled down; the standard has been by little and little lowered; carnal interests and affections have returned; the world has re-assumed its faded charms, and sin its enticing forms; devotion, when not intermitted, has dwindled into wretched and hurried generalities. At length sin is tampered with, and the unclean spirit sees his advantage. But he is in no haste to seize his prey. On the contrary, "he goeth and taketh with him seven other spirits more wicked than himself; and they enter in, and dwell there"—never more to go or be put out. And so, "the last state of that man is worse than the first." Not, it may be, in the way of abandoning itself to greater abominations. But it is more utterly hopeless. There are several laws of the moral system which explain this. There is such a thing as God giving men over to a reprobate mind. Nor is the rage of the wicked one to be overlooked in these mysterious escapes from him for a time and subsequent welcomings back. And over and above these, there is the well-known and terrific law, in virtue of which habits and practices, abandoned with difficulty and afterwards taking fresh possession, become more inveterate than ever before—the power of a resisting will being destroyed. Thus is there no medium between the unclean spirit going out of the man, only to come in again, and the effectual expulsion of the strong man by the Stronger than he. There is no safety for the heart of man but in cordial subjection to Christ. 2. In the first parable, see the palace of the soul in secure, but not unguarded, possession of the strong man. This dark master of the soul—"the prince, the god of this world"—is "armed" and "guards" his palace. Some are easily guarded against serious thought and alarm about their eternal state—drowned in fleshly lusts, or engrossing secularities, or scientific pursuits; the cravings of the spirit after peace and fellowship with God, holiness and heaven, either systematically quenched, or never consciously—at least painfully—felt. But when religious convictions and alarms refuse to be lulled, false principles are made

to play about the soul, if possible to seduce it out of its cravings for that relief which only the Gospel of Christ supplies. But when "the Stronger than the strong man" takes the case in hand, this ruler of the darkness of this world must quit his hold. Glorious name of Jesus this—" The Stronger than the Strong One"—to as many as are sighing for emancipation from felt bondage, and not less, but rather more so, to those whom the Son hath made free indeed. Majestic and varied are the manifestations of His superiority to the strong one in this matchless Gospel History. But the secret of His strength to expel this enemy from the soul of man lies in the victory which He achieved over him in His Cross. "*Now*," says He Himself, "*shall the prince of this world be cast out*, and I, *if I be lifted up from the earth*, will draw all men unto me." As it was sin that sold us into the enemy's hands, so when He put away sin by the sacrifice of Himself, He opened the prison-doors and set us free. And now hath He gone up to receive, as His fitting reward, the Gift of the Holy Ghost, by whose agency in the souls of men He grapples with the enemy, and casts Him out, that He may get Him a temple for God, a palace for Himself to dwell in—"When the Stronger than he shall *come upon him.*" Sublime expression this of Christ's approach to the stronghold for a deadly encounter with the strong man. But it may be quick or slow, simple or elaborate in preparation. Now is the "armour" of the strong man put to busy use:—'God is merciful; there have been many worse than thou, with whom, if thou perish, it will go harder still; thou art sorry for sin; thou sighest after holiness; thou hast made some progress; all will yet come right; and there is no such urgent haste.' These whispers of the father of lies lull for a time, but do not last. The urgency of the case is borne in with resistless power by the sinner's mighty Friend, and now the last thrust is given—'Thine is a gone case; it is now all too late.' But this last piece of his infernal "armour" is at length "taken from him;" the soul falls sweetly into the arms of its mighty Friend; the strong man is made to quit his palace, and the Stronger than he, now its real as before its rightful owner, divides the spoil. Fain would the bruised serpent, in his retreat, hiss for rage after the woman's Seed—'What hast Thou gained by the pardon and restoration of this rebel? he hath no taste for Thy company; he is of his father the devil, and the lusts of his father he will continue to do.' But the Stronger than he cries after him, 'I have put my fear in his heart, that he may *not* turn away from Me—Get thee behind Me!'

What, now, is the conclusion of this whole matter? *Freedom from both masters, or entire moral independence, is impossible.* The palace is freed from the usurped dominion of the strong man, only to become the willing recipient of the Stronger than he. But subjection to Christ is no bondage; it is the very law of liberty. "If the Son," then, O my readers, "shall make you free, ye shall be free indeed!"

37-54.—AT THE HOUSE OF A PHARISEE JESUS VEHEMENTLY DENOUNCES THE PHARISEES, WHO ARE EXASPERATED, AND TRY TO ENSNARE HIM. **37. And as he spake, a certain Pharisee besought him to dine with him: and he went in, and sat down to meat. 38. And when the Pharisee saw**

and the platter; but *g*your inward part is full of ravening and wickedness.
40 *Ye* fools, did not he that made that which is without make that which is
41 within also? But *h*rather give alms *6*of such things as ye have; and,
42 behold, all things are clean unto you. But *i*woe unto you, Pharisees!
*j*for ye tithe mint and rue, and all manner of herbs, and pass over judgment and the love of God: these ought ye to have done, and not to leave
43 the other undone. Woe *k*unto you, Pharisees! for ye love the uppermost
44 seats in the synagogues, and greetings in the markets. Woe *l*unto you,
scribes and Pharisees, hypocrites! *m*for ye are as graves which appear not,
and the men that walk over *them* are not aware *of them.*
45   Then answered one of the lawyers, and said unto him, Master, thus
46 saying thou reproachest us also. And he said, Woe unto you also, *ye*
lawyers! *n*for ye lade men with burdens grievous to be borne, and ye
47 yourselves touch not the burdens with one of your fingers. Woe *o*unto
you! for ye build the sepulchres of the prophets, and your fathers killed
48 them. Truly ye bear witness that ye allow the deeds of your fathers:
49 for *p*they indeed killed them, and ye build their sepulchres. Therefore
also said the *q*wisdom of God, *r*I will send them prophets and apostles,
50 and *some* of them they shall slay and persecute: that the blood of all the
prophets, which was shed from the foundation of the world, may be
51 required of this generation; from *s*the blood of Abel, unto the blood of
Zacharias, which perished between the altar and the temple: verily I say
52 unto you, It shall be required of this generation. Woe *t*unto you,
lawyers! for ye have taken away the key of knowledge: ye enter not in
yourselves, and them that were entering in ye *7*hindered.
53   And as he said these things unto them, the scribes and the Pharisees
54 began to urge *him* vehemently, and to provoke him to speak of many
55 things; laying wait for him, and *u*seeking to catch something out of his
mouth, that they might accuse him.
12   IN *a*the mean time, when there were gathered together an innumerable
multitude of people, insomuch that they trode one upon another, he
began to say unto his disciples first of all, *b*Beware ye of the leaven of
2 the Pharisees, which is hypocrisy. For *c*there is nothing covered, that
3 shall not be revealed; neither hid, that shall not be known. Therefore
whatsoever ye have spoken in darkness shall be heard in the light; and

A. D. 33.

g 2 Tim. 3. 5.
Tit. 1. 15.
h Isa. 58. 7.
Dan. 4. 27.
ch. 12. 33.
6 Or. as you
are able.
i Matt.23.23.
j 1Sam.15.22.
Hos. 6. 6.
k Matt. 23. 6.
Mark 12.38,
39.
l Matt. 23.27.
m Ps. 5. 9.
Acts 23. 3.
n Matt. 23. 4.
o Matt. 23.:9.
p Acts 7. 51.
52.
1 Thes.2.15.
Heb. 11. 36-
38.
Jas. 5. 10.
q Pro. 1. 20.
1 Cor. 1. 24.
r Matt. 23.34.
s Gen. 4. 8.
t Matt.23.13
7 Or.
forbade.
u Mark 12.13.

CHAP. 12.
a Matt. 16. 6.
Mark 8. 15.
b Matt. 16.12.
1 Cor. 5. 7.
8.
c Eccl. 12. 14.
Matt.10.26.
Mark 4. 22.
ch. 8. 17.
1 Cor. 4. 5.
Rev. 20. 11,
12.

---

it, he marvelled that he had not first washed before dinner. See on Mark vii. 2-4. 39-52. And the Lord said unto him, Now do ye Pharisees make clean the outside, &c. For the exposition of all these verses, see on Matt., xxiii. 1-36. **53. And as he said these things unto them, the scribes and the Pharisees began to urge him vehemently, and to provoke him to speak of many things; 54. Laying wait for him, and seeking to catch something out of his mouth, that they might accuse him.** How exceedingly vivid and affecting! They were stung to the quick—and can we wonder?—yet had no materials for the charge they were preparing against Him. For Remarks on this Section, see those on Matt. xxiii. 1-39, at the close of that Section.

CHAP. XII. 1-59.—WARNINGS AGAINST HYPO-CRISY, AND AGAINST COVETOUSNESS—WATCHFUL-NESS INCULCATED, AND SUPERIORITY TO EARTHLY ENTANGLEMENTS AT THE CALL OF HIGHER DUTY —DISCERNING THE SIGNS OF THE TIME.
Hypocrisy (1-12). **1. In the mean time**—in close connection, probably, with the foregoing scene. Our Lord had been *speaking out* more plainly than ever before, as matters were coming to a head between Him and His enemies, and this seems to have suggested to His own mind the warning here. He had just Himself illustriously

exemplified His own precepts. **when there were gathered together an innumerable multitude of people, insomuch that they trod one upon another, he began to say unto his disciples first of all**—and afterwards to the multitudes (*v.* 54), **Beware ye of the leaven of the Pharisees, which is hypocrisy.** As leaven is *concealed* within the mass on which it operates, yet works diffusively and masterfully, so is it with hypocrisy. Hypocrisy is of two kinds. *Pretending to be what we are not,* and *concealing what we are.* Though these are so closely allied that the one runs into the other, it is the latter form of it against which our Lord here warns His disciples. When His name could not be confessed but at the risk of reputation, liberty, property, and life itself, the temptation to unworthy concealment of what they were would of course be exceedingly strong; and it is the consequences of such cowardly and traitorous concealment that our Lord is now to point out. Elsewhere He would have us count the cost of *Discipleship* ere we undertake it: Here He would have us count the *cost of hypocrisy*—in the sense of shrinking from the confession of His name before men—ere we resolve on or give way to that fatal step. **2, 3. For there is nothing covered**—from view, **that shall not be revealed; neither hid**—from knowledge, **that shall not be**

that which ye have spoken in the ear in closets shall be proclaimed upon the house-tops.

4 And ^dI say unto you, my friends, Be not afraid of them that kill the
5 body, and after that have no more that they can do. But I will forewarn you whom ye shall fear: Fear him, which after he hath killed hath
6 *power to cast into hell; yea, I say unto you, Fear him. Are not five sparrows sold for two ^ffarthings? and ^gnot one of them is forgotten
7 before God: but even the very hairs of your head are all numbered. Fear not therefore: ye are of more value than many sparrows.
8 Also ^hI say unto you, Whosoever shall confess me before men, him
9 shall the Son of man also confess before the angels of God: but he that
10 denieth me before men shall be denied before the angels of God. And *whosoever shall speak a word against the Son of man, it shall be forgiven him: but unto him that blasphemeth against the Holy Ghost it shall not
11 be forgiven. And ^jwhen they bring you unto the synagogues, and *unto* magistrates, and powers, take ye no thought how or what thing ye shall
12 answer, or what ye shall say: for ^kthe Holy Ghost shall teach you in the same hour what ye ought to say.
13 And one of the company said unto him, Master, speak to my brother,
14 that he divide the inheritance with me. And he said unto him, *Man,
15 who made me a judge or a divider over you? And he said unto them, ^mTake heed, and beware of covetousness: for a man's life consisteth not in the abundance of the things which he possesseth.
16 And he spake a parable unto them, saying, The ground of a certain
17 rich man brought forth plentifully: and he thought within himself, saying, What shall I do, because I have no room where to bestow my
18 fruits? And he said, This will I do: I will pull down my barns, and
19 build greater; and there will I bestow all my fruits and my goods. And

A. D. 33.
d Isa. 8.12,13.
Isa. 51. 7, 8, 12, 13.
Jer. 1. 8.
Matt. 10.28.
Acts 20. 24.
Phil. 1. 28.
1 Pet. 3. 14.
e Ps. 9. 17.
Matt. 10.28.
Matt. 25.41, 46.
2 Pet. 2. 4.
Rev. 1. 18.
f Matt.10.29.
g Acts 15. 18.
h Matt.10.32.
Mark 8. 33.
Rom. 10. 9. 10.
2 Tim. 2.12.
1 John 2.23.
Rev. 2. 13.
i Matt. 12.31, 32.
Mark 3. 28.
1 John 5.16.
j Matt. 10.19.
Mark 13.11.
ch. 21. 14.
k Ex. 4. 12.
1 Pet. 5. 7.
l John 18.36.
m Pro. 23, 16.
1 Tim. 6. 7.
Heb. 13. 5.

known. Therefore whatsoever ye have spoken in darkness, &c. See on Matt x. 26, 27. **4. And I say unto you, my friends.** He calls them "friends" here, not in any loose sense, but, as we think, from the feeling He then had that in this "killing of the body" *He and they* were going to be affectingly one with each other. **Be not afraid of them that kill the body, and after that have no more that they can do**—they *may* go that length, but there their power ends. **5. But I will forewarn you whom ye shall fear: Fear him which after he hath killed**—that is, taken away the life of the body, as at length He does even by natural death, **hath power to cast into hell; yea, I say unto you, Fear him.** How striking the repetition of this word "Fear!" Only the fear of the Greater will effectually expel the fear of the less. **6. Are not five sparrows sold for two farthings?** In Matt. x. 29, it is, "two for one farthing:" so, if one took two farthings' worth, he got one in addition—of such insignificant value were they. **and (yet) not one of them is forgotten before God: 7. But even the very hairs of your head are all numbered. Fear not therefore: ye are of more value than many sparrows.** What incomparable teaching—its simplicity imparting to it a wonderful charm!

8, 9. Also I say unto you, Whosoever shall confess me before men, &c. See on Matt. x. 32, 33. **10. And whosoever shall speak a word against the Son of man . . . but unto him that blasphemeth against the Holy Ghost, &c.** See on Matt. xii. 31, 32. **11, 12. And when they bring you unto the synagogues, &c.** See on Matt. x. 19, 20.

Covetousness (13-34). **13. And one of the company said unto him, Master**—'Teacher' [Διδά-

σκαλε], **speak to my brother, that he divide the inheritance with me:**—*q. d.,* 'Great Preacher of righteousness, help; there is need of Thee in this rapacious world; here am I the victim of injustice, and that from my own brother, who withholds from me my rightful share of the inheritance that has fallen to us.' In this most inopportune intrusion upon the solemnities of our Lord's teaching, there is a mixture of the absurd and the irreverent, the one however occasioning the other. The man had not the least idea that his case was not of as urgent a nature, and as worthy the attention of our Lord, as anything else He could deal with. **14. And he said unto him, Man.** What a contrast is there between this style of address and "*My friends,*" when encouraging His own faithful disciples resolutely to confess Him in the face of all dangers (*v.* 4)! **Who made me a judge or a divider over you?** A remarkable question, coming from such lips, explicitly repudiating an office which Moses assumed (Exod. ii. 14), and afterwards was divinely called to exercise. Not for such a purpose was the Son of God manifested. **15. And he said unto them**—the immense multitude before Him, (*v.* 1), **Take heed, and beware of covetousness**— 'of all covetousness,' or, 'of every kind of covetousness,' is beyond doubt the true reading here. As this was one of the more plausible forms of it, the Lord would strike at once at the root of the evil. **for a man's life consisteth not in the abundance of the things which he possesseth.** A singularly weighty maxim, and not the less so, because its meaning and its truth are equally evident. **16-19. And he spake a parable . . . The ground of a certain rich man brought forth plentifully: And he thought within himself, saying, What shall I do . . . I will pull down my barns, and build greater; and there will I bestow all

I will say to my soul, ⁿSoul, thou hast much goods laid up for many
20 years; take thine ease, eat, drink, *and* be merry. But God said unto him, *Thou* fool, this night ¹thy soul shall be required of thee: then
21 °whose shall those things be which thou hast provided? So *is* he that layeth up treasure for himself, ^pand is not rich toward God.
22   And he said unto his disciples, Therefore I say unto you, ^qTake no thought for your life, what ye shall eat; neither for the body, what ye
23 shall put on. The life is more than meat, and the body *is more* than
24 raiment. Consider the ravens: for they neither sow nor reap; which neither have storehouse nor barn; and ^rGod feedeth them: how much more
25 are ye better than the fowls? And which of you with taking thought can
26 add to his stature one cubit? If ye then be not able to do that thing
27 which is least, why take ye thought for the rest? Consider the lilies how they grow: they toil not, they spin not; and yet I say unto you, that
28 Solomon in all his glory was not arrayed like one of these. If then God so clothe the grass, which is to-day in the field, and to-morrow is cast into the oven; how much more *will he clothe* you, O ye of little faith?
29   And seek not ye what ye shall eat, or what ye shall drink, ²neither be
30 ye of doubtful mind. For all these things do the nations of the world seek after: and your Father knoweth ^sthat ye have need of these things.
31 But ^trather seek ye the kingdom of God; and ^uall these things shall be
32 added unto you. Fear not, little flock; for ^vit is your Father's good
33 pleasure to give you the kingdom. Sell ^wthat ye have, and give alms; provide ^xyourselves bags which wax not old, a treasure in the heavens that faileth not, where no thief approacheth, neither moth corrupteth.
34 For where your treasure is, there will your heart be also.
35,   Let ^yyour loins be girded about, ^zand *your* lights burning; and ye
36 yourselves like unto men that wait for their lord, when he will return

A. D. 33.
ⁿ Pro. 27. 1.
Eccl. 11. 9.
1 Cor.15.32.
Jas. 5. 5
1 Or, do they require thy soul.
Job 20. 22.
Job 21. 13.
Job 27. 8.
Ps. 52. 7.
Dan. 4. 31.
1 Thes. 5. 3.
Jas. 4. 14.
° Ps. 39. 6.
Jer. 17. 11.
^p Matt. 6. 20.
1 Tim. 6.18, 19.
Jas. 2. 5.
^q Matt. 6. 25.
Phil. 4. 6.
^r Job 38. 41.
Ps. 147. 9.
2 Or, live not in careful suspense.
^s 2 Chr. 16.9.
^t Matt. 6. 33.
^u Rom. 8. 31.
^v Matt. 11.25.
^w Matt.19.21.
^x Matt. 6. 20.
^y Eph. 6. 14.
1 Pet. 1. 13.
^z Matt. 25. 1.

my fruits and my goods. And I will say to my soul, Soul, thou hast much goods laid up for many years; take thine ease, eat, drink, and be merry. Why is this man called a "fool"? First, Because he deemed a life of secure and abundant earthly enjoyment the summit of human felicity; and next, because, having acquired the means of realizing this, through prosperity in his calling, he flattered himself that he had a long lease of such enjoyment, and nothing to do but to give himself up to it. *Nothing else is laid to his charge.* 20. But God said unto him, Fool, this night thy soul shall be required of thee. This sudden cutting short of his career is designed to express not only the folly of building securely upon the future, but of throwing one's whole soul into what may at any moment be gone. "His *soul* being required of him" is put in opposition to his own treatment of it—"I will say to my soul, Soul," &c. then whose shall those things be which thou hast provided? Compare Ps. xxxix. 6, "He heapeth up riches, and knoweth not who shall gather them." 21. So is he that layeth up treasure for himself, and is not rich toward God. Here is a picture of present folly, and of its awful issue. Such is the man "who is not rich toward God:" he lives to amass and enjoy such riches only as terminate on *self*, and end with *time;* but as to God's favour which is life (Ps. xxx. 5), and precious faith (2 Pet. i. 1; James ii. 5), and riches in good works (1 Tim. vi. 18), and the wisdom which is better than rubies (Prov. iii. 15), and, in a word, all that the Lord esteems true riches (Rev. ii. 9; iii. 18), he lives and dies *a beggar!*

22-34. And he said unto his disciples, Therefore I say unto you, Take no thought, &c. This and the twelve following verses are but a repetition, with slight verbal difference, of part of the Sermon on the Mount. See on Matt. vi. 25-34. But a word or two of explanation on one or two of the verses may be added here. 25. And which of you with taking thought can add to his stature one cubit? 26. If ye then be not able to do that thing which is least, why take ye thought for the rest? 'Corroding solicitude will not bring you the least of the things ye fret about, though it may double the evil of wanting them. And if not the least, why vex yourselves about things of more consequence?' 29. And seek not ye what ye shall eat, or what ye shall drink, neither be ye of doubtful mind [μὴ μετεωρίζεσθε]—'be not of unsettled mind,' or put off your balance. 32. Fear not, little flock [τὸ μικρὸν ποίμνιον]—a double diminutive, which in German can be expressed, but in English only in colloquial language. The tenderness it is designed to convey is plain enough. for it is your Father's good pleasure [ὅτι εὐδόκησεν ὁ Πατὴρ ὑμῶν]. On this expression, see on Matt. iii. 17. to give you the kingdom. Every word of this little verse is more to be desired than fine gold. How sublime and touching is the contrast between the tender and pitying appellation, "little flock," and the "Good Pleasure" of the Father to give them the Kingdom: the one recalling the insignificance and helplessness of the at that time truly little flock, that literal handful of disciples; the other holding up to their view the eternal love that encircled them, the everlasting arms that were underneath them, and the high inheritance awaiting them! "To give you *the Kingdom:*" Grand word, exclaims *Bengel;* then.why not bread? Well might He say, "Fear not"! 33. Sell that ye have, and give alms, &c. This is but a more vivid expression of Matt. vi. 19, 20.

Watchfulness (35-48). 35. Let your loins be

from the wedding; that, when he cometh and knocketh, they may open
37 unto him immediately. Blessed *[a]are* those servants, whom the lord when he cometh shall find watching: verily I say unto you, that he shall gird himself, and make them to sit down to meat, and will come forth and serve
38 them. And if he shall come in the second watch, or come in the third
39 watch, and find *them* so, blessed are those servants. And *[b]this know*, that if the goodman of the house had known what hour the thief would come, he would have watched, and not have suffered his house to be
40 broken through. Be *[c]ye* therefore ready also: for the Son of man cometh at an hour when ye think not.
41 Then Peter said unto him, Lord, speakest thou this parable unto us,
42 or even to all? And the Lord said, *[d]Who* then is that faithful and wise steward, whom *his* lord shall make ruler over his household, to give *them*
43 *their* portion of meat in due season? Blessed *is* that servant, whom his
44 lord when he cometh shall find so doing. Of a truth I say unto you,
45 *[e]that* he will make him ruler over all that he hath. But and if that servant say in his heart, My lord delayeth his coming; and shall begin to beat the men-servants and maidens, and to eat and drink, and to be
46 drunken; the lord of that servant will come in a day when he looketh

A. D. 33.

[a] Matt. 24. 46.
Matt. 25. 21-23.
2 Tim. 4. 7, 8.
1 Pet. 5. 1-4.
2 Pet. 1. 11.
2 Pet. 3. 14.
Rev. 14. 13.
[b] 1 Thes. 5. 2.
Rev. 16. 15.
[c] Matt 25. 13.
Mark 13. 33.
Rom. 13. 11-14.
2 Pet. 3. 12 14.
[d] Matt. 24. 45, 46.
Matt. 25. 21.
ch. 19. 15-19.
[e] 1 Pet. 5. 4.
Rev. 3. 21.

---

girded about—to fasten up the long outer garment, which was always done before travel and before work (See 2 Ki. iv. 29; Acts xii. 8; and compare, for the sense, Eph. vi. 14; 1 Pet. i. 13.) The meaning is, *Be prepared.* **and your lights burning; 36. And ye yourselves like unto men that wait for their lord, &c.** In the corresponding parable of the Virgins (Matt. xxv. 1, &c.) the preparedness is *for* the wedding; here it is for *return from* the wedding. But in both, the thing intended is *Preparedness for Christ's Coming.* **37. Blessed are those servants, whom the lord when he cometh shall find watching: verily I say unto you, that he shall gird himself, and make them to sit down to meat, and will come forth and serve them.** A promise the most august of all. Thus will the Bridegroom entertain His friends on the solemn Nuptial Day, says *Bengel* sweetly. **38. And if he shall come in the second watch, or come in the third watch, and find them so, blessed are those servants.** To find them ready to receive Him at any hour of day or night, when one might least of all expect Him, is peculiarly blessed. A servant may be truly faithful, even though taken so far unawares that he has not everything in *such* order and readiness for his master's return as he thinks is due to him, and as he both could and would have had if he had had notice of the time of his coming. In this case he would not be willing to open to him "*immediately*," but would fly to preparation, and let his master knock again ere he admit him, and even then *not with full joy*. A too common case this with Christians. But if the servant have himself and all under his charge in such a state that at any hour when his master knocks he can open to him "immediately," and hail his return—what an enviable, "blessed" servant is that! **39. And this know, that if the goodman of the house had known what hour the thief would come, he would have watched, and not have suffered his house to be broken through**—of course; but no credit, no thank to him. **40. Be ye therefore ready also: for the Son of man cometh at an hour when ye think not.** So Matt. xxiv. 42, 44; xxv. 13, &c. How frequently does this recur in the teaching of our Lord; nor less so in that of His apostles! 1 Thess. **v.** 2; 2 Pet. iii. 10, &c. *Is it as frequently heard now?*

41. Then Peter said unto him, Lord, speakest thou this parable unto us, or even to all? He had addressed Himself on this occasion alternately to the Twelve and to the vast assemblage; and Peter, feeling the solemn import of what had just been said coming home to himself, would fain know for which of the two classes it was specially intended. **42. And the Lord said, Who then is.** Our Lord answers the question indirectly by another question, from which they were left to gather what it would be:—'To you certainly, in the first instance, representing the "stewards" of the "household" I am about to collect, but generally to all "servants" in My house.' **that faithful and wise steward** [οἰκονόμος]—'house-steward,' whose it was to distribute to the servants their allotted portion of food. *Fidelity* is the first requisite in a servant; but *wisdom*—discretion and judgment in the exercise of his functions—is the next. **whom his lord shall make**—or will deem fit to be made **ruler over his household, to give them their portion of meat in due season?**—that is, whom his lord will advance to the highest post: The reference is of course to the world to come. (See Matt. xxv. 21, 23.) **43-45. Blessed is that servant, whom his lord when he cometh shall find so doing. Of a truth . . . he will make him ruler over all that he hath. But and if that servant say in his heart, My lord delayeth his coming; and shall begin to beat the men-servants and maidens, and to eat and drink, and to be drunken.** The picture here presented is that of a servant who, in the confidence that his lord's return will not be speedy, throws off the servant and plays the master, maltreating those faithful servants who refuse to join him, seizing on and revelling in the fulness of his master's board; intending, when he has got his fill, to resume the mask of fidelity ere his master appear. **46. The lord of that servant will come in a day when he looketh not for him, and at an hour when he is not aware, and will cut him in sunder** [διχοτομήσει αὐτόν]. *Dichotomy*, or cleaving a person in two, was a punishment not unknown in the East. Compare Heb. xi. 37, "Sawn asunder;" and 1 Sam. xv. 33; Dan. ii. 5. **and will appoint him his portion with the unbelievers** [μετὰ τῶν ἀπίστων]—rather, 'with the unfaithful,' meaning those servants who are found unworthy of trust. In Matt. xxiv. 51 it is, "with

not for *him*, and at an hour when he is not aware, and will [3]cut him in
47 sunder, and will appoint him his portion with the unbelievers. And
*f*that servant, which knew his lord's will, and prepared not *himself*,
48 neither did according to his will, shall be beaten with many *stripes*. But
*g*he that knew not, and did commit things worthy of stripes, shall be
beaten with few *stripes*. For unto whomsoever much is given, of him
shall be much required; and to whom men have committed much, of him
they will ask the more.
49 I am come to send fire on the earth; and what will I, if it be already
50 kindled? But *h*I have a baptism to be baptized with; and how am I
51 [4]straitened till it be accomplished! Suppose *i*ye that I am come to give
52 peace on earth? I tell you, Nay; *j*but rather division: for *k*from henceforth there shall be five in one house divided, three against two, and two
53 against three. The father shall be divided against the son, and the son
against the father; the mother against the daughter, and the daughter
against the mother; the mother-in-law against her daughter-in-law, and
the daughter-in-law against her mother-in-law.
54 And he said also to the people, When *l*ye see a cloud rise out of the
55 west, straightway ye say, There cometh a shower; and so it is. And
when *ye see* *m*the south wind blow, ye say, There will be heat; and it
56 cometh to pass. *Ye* *n*hypocrites, ye can discern the face of the sky and
57 of the earth; but how is it that ye do not discern *o*this time? Yea, and
why even of yourselves judge ye not what is right?

A. D. 33.

[3] Or, cut
him off.
Matt. 24. 51.
f Num.15.30.
Deut. 25. 2.
John 8. 41.
John 15. 22.
Acts 17. 30.
Jas. 4. 17.
g Lev. 5. 17.
1 Tim. 1.
13.
h Matt.20.22.
Mark 10.38.
[4] Or. pained.
i Matt.10.34.
j Mic. 7. 6.
John 7. 43.
John 9. 16.
John 10.19.
k Matt. 10.35.
l Matt. 16. 2.
m Job 37. 17.
n 1 Cor. 1. 19-
27.
o Matt. 16. 3.
ch. 19. 42-
44.
Gal. 4. 4.

---

the hypocrites;" that is, those falsely calling
themselves servants. **47. And that servant,
which knew his lord's will, and prepared not
himself, neither did according to his will, shall
be beaten with many stripes**—his guilt being
aggravated by the extent of his knowledge.
48. But he that knew not—that is, knew it but
partially; for some knowledge is presupposed both
in the name "servant" of Christ, and in his being
liable to punishment at all. **and did commit
things worthy of stripes, shall be beaten with
few stripes.** So that there will be degrees of
future punishment, proportioned to the light enjoyed — the knowledge sinned against. Even
heathens are not without knowledge enough for
future judgment (see on Rom. ii. 12-16); but the
reference here is not to such. It is a solemn truth,
and though *general*, like all other revelations of the
future world, discloses a tangible and momentous
principle in its awards. **For unto whomsoever
much is given, of him shall be much required;
and to whom men have committed much, of
him they will ask the more.** So that when we
are told that men are to be judged according to the
deeds done in the body (Matt. xvi. 27; Rom. ii. 6),
we are to understand not the actions only, but the
principles on which and the whole *circumstances in*
which they were done. Thus equitable will the
Judgment be.
Superiority to Earthly Entanglements (49-53). **49.
I am come to send** [βαλεῖν]—rather, 'to cast' **fire
on the earth.** By "fire" here we are to understand, as *Olshausen* expresses it, the higher spiritual element of life which Jesus came to introduce
into this earth (compare Matt. iii. 11), with reference
to its mighty effects in quickening all that is akin
to it and destroying all that is opposed. To cause
this element of life to take up its abode on earth,
and wholly to pervade human hearts with its
warmth, was the lofty destiny of the Redeemer.
So *Calvin, Stier, Alford,* &c. **and what will I,
if it be already kindled?** [καὶ τί θέλω εἰ ἤδη
ἀνήφθη]—an obscure expression, uttered under
deep and half-smothered emotion. In its general
import all are agreed, but interpreters differ as to
the precise shade of meaning intended. The nearest to the precise meaning seems to be, 'And what
should I have to desire if it were but once kindled?' **50. But I have a baptism to be baptized with**
—clearly His own bloody baptism, which had first
to take place. **and how am I straitened**—not,
'how do I long for its accomplishment,' as many
understand it, thus making it but a repetition of
the former verse; but 'what a pressure of spirit is
upon me' till it be accomplished—completed, over!
Before a promiscuous audience, such obscure language was perhaps fitting on a theme like this;
but O what surges of mysterious emotion in the
view of what was now so near at hand does it
reveal! **51. Suppose ye that I am come to give
peace on earth? I tell you, Nay**—'in the first
instance, the reverse.' **but rather division.**
See on Matt. x. 34-36. **52, 53. For from henceforth there shall be five in one house divided,
three against two, and two against three. The
father . . . against the son, and the son against
the father; the mother . . . the daughter . . .
the mother-in-law, &c.** The connection of all this
with the foregoing warnings about Hypocrisy,
Covetousness, and Watchfulness, is deeply solemn:
'My conflict hastens apace; Mine over, yours
begins; and then, let the servants tread in their
Master's steps, uttering their testimony entire and
fearless, neither loving nor dreading the world,
anticipating awful wrenches of the dearest ties
in life, but looking forward, as I do, to the completion of their testimony, when, after the tempest, reaching the haven, they shall enter into the
joy of their Lord.'
Discerning the Signs of the Time (54-59). **54-56.
And he said also to the people**—rather, 'to the
multitudes' [τοῖς ὄχλοις]: it is a word of special
warning to the thoughtless crowd, before dismissing them. **When ye see a cloud rise out of the
west, straightway ye say, There cometh a shower;
and so it is. And when ye see the south wind
blow, ye say, There will be heat. . . . Hypocrites, ye
can discern the face of the sky and of the earth;
but how is it that ye do not discern this time?**
See on Mark viii. 11. They were wise in their fore-

58 When ^pthou goest with thine adversary to the magistrate, ^q*as thou art* in the way, give diligence that thou mayest be delivered from him; lest he hale thee to the judge, and the judge deliver thee to the officer, 59 and the officer cast thee into prison. I tell thee, thou shalt not depart thence, till thou hast paid the very last ^rmite.

A. D. 33.

^p Pro. 25. 8.
    Matt. 5. 25.
^q Ps. 32. 6.
    Isa. 55. 6.
^r Mark 12.42.

castings as to the things of time, but applied not the same sagacity to things spiritual, and were unable to perceive what a critical, decisive period for the chosen people they had fallen upon. **57. Yea, and why even of yourselves judge ye not what is right?** They might say, To do this requires more knowledge of Scripture and Providence than we possess; but He sends them to their own conscience, as enough to show them who He was, and win them to immediate discipleship. **58. When thou goest with thine adversary to the magistrate, as thou art in the way, give diligence that thou mayest be delivered from him; lest he hale thee to the judge, and the judge deliver thee to the officer, and the officer cast thee into prison.** See on Matt. v. 25, 26. It was the urgency of the case with them, and the necessity of immediate decision for their own safety, that drew forth this repetition of those striking words of the Sermon of the Mount.

Remarks.—1. It will be observed that in dealing with hypocrisy—as indeed with everything else—our Lord passes by all *inferior considerations*, holding forth only its *eternal issues*. It is not that these inferior arguments against hypocrisy and other forms of inconsistency in Christians are of no weight. But since apart from the higher considerations they are powerless against the evil tendencies of the heart, and it is from the higher that the lower derive all their real influence, our Lord will not descend to them in His teaching, but concentrates attention upon the final issues of such conduct. This imparted to His teaching a loftiness and a weight perfectly new to those accustomed only to the drivel of the rabbins. In modern times both kinds of teaching have been exemplified in the Christian Church. In times of spiritual death, or prevailing insensibility to eternal things, preachers of ability have wasted their strength in the pulpit, in analyzing the human faculties and expatiating on the natural operation of the principles and passions of our nature. On such a subject as hypocrisy they would show how unmanly it was to conceal one's sentiments, what a crooked, sneaking, pusillanimous, vacillating disposition it tended to generate, and what general distrust it was apt to beget when it assumed formidable proportions. Such discourses are little else than lectures on practical ethics—very proper in a chair of philosophy, but below the dignity and sanctity of the pulpit. And what has been the effect? Attentive hearers have been *entertained* perhaps; and the preachers have been *complimented* upon their ability. But never have the souls of the people been stirred, and never have the evils so exposed been a whit diminished in consequence. But whenever there is any general awakening from spiritual torpor, and the reality of eternal things comes in any good degree to be felt, the pulpit rises to a higher tone, and our Lord's way of treating spiritual things is adopted; the attention of the people is riveted, their souls are stirred, and the fruits of righteousness more or less appear. On this subject it deserves notice, too, that our Lord knows nothing of that false and mawkish refinement which would represent the *fear of hell* as a selfish and gross motive to present, especially to Christians, to deter them from basely denying or being ashamed of

Him. As the meekness and gentleness of Christ were not compromised by such harsh notes as these, so those servants of Christ who soften down all such language, to please 'ears polite,' have little of their Master's spirit. See on Mark ix. 43-48, and Remark 5 at the close of that Section. 2. The refusal of our Lord to intermeddle with the affairs of this life as a Judge carries with it a great lesson to all religious teachers. Immense indeed is the influence of religious teachers in the external relations of life, but only when it is *indirectly* exercised: whenever they interfere *directly* with secular and political matters, the spell of that influence is broken. If they take a side, as in that case they must do, those on the opposite side cannot help regarding them as adversaries; and this necessarily diminishes, if it does not destroy—with such at least—their professional influence, or the weight they would otherwise carry in their own proper sphere. Whereas, when the ministers of Christ keep themselves aloof from secular disputes and political parties, abiding within their proper sphere, all parties look up to them, and they are often the means of mollifying the bitterest feelings and reconciling the most conflicting interests. Will the servants of Christ weigh this? 3. Though there is a *general* preparedness for Christ's coming which belongs to the character of all who truly love Him, even believers may be more or less taken *by surprise* when He comes. A faithful servant, whose master's return has been delayed long beyond expectation, may cease expecting him at any particular time, and so slacken his preparations for receiving him. When at length he comes and demands admittance, that servant, though not wholly unprepared, may, on hastily glancing over what is under his hand, see many things which *might* have been in better order, and *would*, if he had got but a very little warning. But he must open to his master without delay. He does so, conscious of his general fidelity, and trusting this will appear to his master's kindly eye, yet unable to welcome him with that *full cordiality* which he should have wished to feel. And his master *is* satisfied of his honest fidelity, but fails not to observe, both in the state of his house and the symptoms of confusion which his servant betrays, that He has been taken somewhat by surprise. How different the feeling of that servant who is "always ready," determined that his Master shall *not* take him by surprise! O the gladness of that welcome which Christ's servants are enabled to give Him when always watching and habitually ready! Is not this what is meant by "having an entrance ministered to us abundantly [πλουσίως] into the everlasting kingdom of our Lord and Saviour Jesus Christ?" (2 Pet. i. 11). 4. If Christ's religion be as fire cast into the earth, burning up whatever is opposed to it, admitting of no compromise, and working towards its own unimpeded power over men, it is easy to see why its operation is so slow and small at many periods, and in many places and persons. The fire is too often quenched by the systematic attempt to serve two masters. Jesus will have uncompromising decision, even though it set friends or families at variance—whether rending distant or dearest ties. But if this be trying, it has a natural termination. The more resolute the

13 THERE were present at that season some that told him of [a]the Gali-
2 leans, whose blood Pilate had mingled with their sacrifices. And Jesus
answering said unto them, Suppose [b]ye that these Galileans were sinners
3 above all the Galileans, because they suffered such things. I tell you,
4 Nay: but, except ye repent, ye shall all likewise perish. Or those
eighteen, upon whom the tower in Siloam fell, and slew them, think ye
5 that they were [1]sinners above all men that dwelt in Jerusalem? I tell
you, Nay: but, except [c]ye repent, ye shall all likewise perish.
6 He spake also this parable; [d]A certain *man* had a fig tree planted in
his vineyard; and he came and sought fruit thereon, and found none.
7 Then said he unto the dresser of his vineyard, Behold, these [e]three years
I come seeking fruit on this fig tree, and find none: cut it down; why
8 cumbereth it the ground? And he answering said unto him, Lord, let
9 [f]it alone this year also, till I shall dig about it, and dung *it:* and if it
bear fruit, *well;* and if not, *then* after that thou shalt cut it down.

A. D. 33.

CHAP. 13.
[a] Acts 5. 37.
[b] Job 22. 5-
16.
John 9. 2.
Acts 28. 4.
[1] Or,
debtors.
Matt.18.24.
ch. 11. 4.
[c] Ezek.18.30.
[d] Isa. 5. 2.
Matt.21.19.
[e] Lev. 25. 21.
Rom. 2.4,5.
2 Pet. 3. 9.
[f] Ex. 32. 11.
Joel 2. 17.
Heb. 7. 25.

servants of Christ are, the sooner usually does the opposition to them cease. Besides, active opposition, when seen to be hopeless, is often desisted from, while consistency and strength of character command respect, and are often blessed to the gaining even of the most determined enemies.

CHAP. XIII. 1-9.—THE LESSON 'REPENT OR PERISH,' SUGGESTED BY TWO RECENT INCIDENTS, AND ILLUSTRATED BY THE PARABLE OF THE BARREN FIG TREE.

The Slaughter of certain Galileans (1-3). **1. There were present at that season**—showing that what is here recorded comes, in order of time, immediately after ch. xii. But what the precise season was, cannot certainly be determined. See opening remarks on ch. ix. 51. **some that told him of the Galileans, whose blood Pilate had mingled with their sacrifices.** Possibly these were the followers of Judas of Galilee, who, some twenty years before this, taught that Jews should not pay tribute to the Romans, and of whom we learn, from Acts v. 37, that he drew after him a multitude of followers, who, on his being slain, were all dispersed. About this time that party would be at its height, and if Pilate caused this detachment of them to be waylaid and put to death, as they were offering their sacrifices at oue of the festivals, that would be "mingling their blood with their sacrifices." So *Grotius, Webster and Wilkinson,* but doubted by *de Wette, Meyer, Alford,* &c. News of this—whatever the precise matter referred to may be—having been brought to our Lord, to draw out His views of it, and particularly, whether it was not a judgment of Heaven, He simply points them to the practical view of the matter. **2. And Jesus answering said unto them, Suppose ye that these Galileans were sinners above all the Galileans, because they suffered such things? 3. I tell you, Nay: but, except ye repent, ye shall all likewise perish.** 'These men are not signal examples of divine vengeance, as ye suppose; but every impenitent sinner—*ye yourselves,* except ye repent—shall be like monuments of the judgment of Heaven, and in a more awful sense.' The reference here to the impending destruction of Jerusalem is far from exhausting our Lord's weighty words; they manifestly point to a "perdition" of a more awful kind—*future, personal, remediless.*

The Eighteen on whom the Tower in Siloam Fell (4, 5). **4. Or those eighteen, upon whom the tower in Siloam fell**—probably one of the towers of the city-wall, near the pool of Siloam. Of its fall nothing is known. **and slew them, think ye that they were sinners above all men that**
dwelt in Jerusalem? **5. I tell you, Nay: but, except ye repent, ye shall all likewise perish.**

The Barren Fig Tree (6-9). **6. He spake also this parable; A certain man had a fig tree**—meaning Israel as the visible witness for God in the world; but generally, all within the pale of the visible Church of God: a familiar figure—compare Isa. v. 1-7; John xv. 1-8, &c. **planted in his vineyard**—a spot selected for its fertility, separated from the surrounding fields, and cultivated with special care, with a view solely to fruit. **and he came and sought fruit thereon**—a heart turned to God, the fruits of righteousness. Compare Matt. xxi. 33, 34, and Isa. v. 2. "He *looked* that it should bring forth fruit:" He has a *right* to it, and will *require* it. **and found none. 7. Then said he unto the dresser of his vineyard**—to him whom he employed to take charge of his vineyard, which in this case we know to be Christ. **Behold, these three years**—a long enough trial for a fig tree, and so denoting probably just a *sufficient* period of culture for spiritual fruit. The supposed allusion to the duration of our Lord's ministry is precarious. **I come seeking fruit on this fig tree, and find none: cut it down.** There is a certain indignation in this language. **why cumbereth it the ground?**—not only doing no good, but wasting ground. **8. And he answering said unto him.** This represents Christ as Intercessor, loath to see it cut down so long as there was any hope. (See *v.* 34). **Lord, let it alone this year also, till I shall dig about it, and dung it**—loosen the earth about it and enrich it with manure: pointing to changes of method in the Divine treatment of the impenitent, in order to fresh spiritual culture. **9. And if it bear fruit, [well]**—all then will yet be right; **and if not, then after that thou shalt cut it down**—I will then no longer interpose: all is over.

Remarks.—1. The small incidents recorded at the beginning of this chapter bear irresistible marks of historical truth in the Evangelical Records. Who that had been drawing up an unreal Story would ever have thought of inserting in it such incidents as these? Much less would they ever have occurred to such untutored writers as these Records show their authors to have been. 2. How slow have even Christians been, notwithstanding the explicit teaching of Christ here, to be convinced that extraordinary outward calamities are not necessarily the vengeance of Heaven against unusual criminality! From the days of Job's friends until now the tendency to explain the one of these by the other has been too prevalent. Is it not to this that the prevalent view of Mary Magdalene's character is to be

10, And he was teaching in one of the synagogues on the sabbath. And, 11 behold, there was a woman which had a spirit of infirmity eighteen years, 12 and was bowed together, and could in no wise lift up *herself.* And when Jesus saw her, he called *her to him,* and said unto her, *g*Woman, thou art

A. D. 33.

g Ps. 107. 20.
Isa. 65. 1.
Matt. 8. 16.

traced? (See on ch. viii. 2.) 3. To be within the pale of Revealed Religion and the Church of the living God is a high privilege, and involves a solemn responsibility. The owner of the vineyard, having planted a fig tree in it, "came and sought fruit thereon;" for in the natural course of things fruit, in such a case, was to be expected. But when does God *come,* seeking fruit from men thus privileged? Not at the day of judgment; for though He *will* come and demand it then, the parable represents the tree as still in the ground after the lord of the vineyard has come seeking fruit, and as allowed to remain with a view to further trial. It is *now,* therefore, or during our present state, that God is coming seeking fruit from us. Are we favoured with a Christian education and example? He comes, saying, 'Any fruit?' Have we been placed under a faithful, rousing ministry of the Gospel? He comes, asking, 'What fruit?' Have we been visited with crushing trials, fitted to bring down pride, and soften the heart, and give the lessons of Religion an entrance they never had before? He comes, demanding the fruit. Alas, of multitudes the report must still be—"and found none"! 4. The Lord, we see, notes the length of time that men continue fruitless under the means of spiritual culture. "Behold, *these three years* I come seeking fruit on this fig tree, and find none." Thoughtless men heed this not, but One does. "*How long*, ye simple ones, will ye love simplicity?" is His question. "O Jerusalem, wash thine heart from wickedness, that thou mayest be saved: *how long* shall thy vain thoughts lodge within thee?" "Wilt thou not be made clean? when shall it once be?" "*It is time* to seek the Lord, till He come and rain righteousness upon you," (Prov. i. 22; Jer. iv. 14; xiii. 27; Hos. x. 12). 5. To be cut down is the rich desert of all the fruitless: "Cut it down; why cumbereth it the ground?" As if they were a burden to the earth that bears them, to the place they fill, deforming the beauty and hindering the fruitfulness of God's vineyard. They are borne with, but with a certain impatience and indignation. And even when the fruitless are borne with, it is because of the good offices of an Intercessor, and solely with a view to fresh culture. Were there no one in the kingdom of God answering to this dresser of the vineyard, who pleads, and as is here supposed successfully, for a respite to the tree, we might take this feature of the parable as but a part of its drapery, not to be pressed into the exposition of it. But, with the great facts of mediation before us, it is impossible not to see here something more than drapery. And what is that fresh culture for which He pleads? Why, anything by which truths and lessons hitherto neglected may come with a force upon the heart before unknown, may justly be so regarded. A change of the means of grace; a change of sphere—sometimes in the way of banishing one from all the privileges in which he basked, leading him in a far distant land, when sighing over removal from dear objects and scenes, to reflect upon religious privileges never before valued—the remarkable conversion of some companion; or a religious awakening within the immediate sphere of one's observation: these and a thousand other such things are fitted to give truths and lessons, never heeded before, a new power to impress the heart. And it is with a view to this that many

are in mercy spared after their long-continued impenitence under high religious culture seemed to be but preparing them to be cut down. 7. It is worthy of notice that the respite sought in the parable was not another three years, but just "one year." As in the natural culture, this would be sufficient to determine whether any fruit was to be got out of the tree at all, so in the spiritual husbandry, the thing intended is just *one sufficient trial more.* And surely it is a loud call to immediate repentance when one has any good reason to think that *he* is on his last trial! 8. Genuine repentance, however late, avails to save: "If it bear fruit (well);" and only *if not,* was it to be cut down. The case of the thief on the cross decides this for all time and for every soul. There is not a sinner out of hell—though the most hardened, the furthest gone, the nearest to the flames—but if he only begin to bear fruit, if he do but turn to God with all his heart in the Gospel of His Son, it will deliver him from going down to the pit, it will stay the hand of justice, it will secure his eternal salvation. "Let the wicked forsake his way, and the unrighteous man his thought, and let him return unto the Lord, and He will have mercy upon him, and to our God, and He will abundantly pardon." "As I live, saith the Lord, I have no pleasure in the death of the wicked, but rather that he should turn from his way and live. Turn ye, turn ye, why will ye die, O house of Israel?" 9. The final perdition of such as, after the utmost limits of divine forbearance, are found fruitless, will be pre-eminently and confessedly just: "If not, after that thou shalt cut it down." It is the Intercessor Himself that says this. Mercy herself, who before pleaded for a respite, now acquiesces in, if not demands, the execution. "He that, being often reproved, hardeneth his neck, shall *suddenly* be destroyed, and that *without remedy*" (Prov. xxix. 1). Be wise now, therefore, O ye fruitless; be instructed, ye foolish and unwise: Kiss the Son, lest He be angry, and ye perish from the way, when His wrath is kindled but a little. Blessed are all they that put their trust in Him! Beware lest that come upon you which is spoken of by the prophet, "Because I have purged thee, and thou wast not purged, thou shalt not be purged from thy filthiness any more, till I have caused my fury to rest upon thee" (Ezek. xxiv. 13).

10-17.—A WOMAN OF EIGHTEEN YEARS' INFIRMITY HEALED ON THE SABBATH DAY.

10. And he was teaching in one of the synagogues on the sabbath—time and place left indefinite. (See opening remarks on ch. ix. 51.) **11. And, behold, there was a woman which had a spirit of infirmity eighteen years.** From the expression used in *v.* 16, "whom *Satan* hath bound," it has been conjectured that her protracted infirmity was the effect of some milder form of *possession;* but this is a precarious inference. At all events she was "a daughter of Abraham," in the same gracious sense, no doubt, as Zaccheus after his conversion was "a son of Abraham" (ch. xix. 9). **and was bowed together, and could in no wise lift up herself. 12. And when Jesus saw her, he called her to him, and said unto her, Woman, thou art loosed from thine infirmity. 13. And he laid his hands on her.** The word and the act were simultaneous; **and the effect was instant. and immediately she was made straight, and gloried God.**

280

13 loosed from thine infirmity. And ^hhe laid *his* hands on her: and immediately she was made straight, and glorified God.

14 And the ruler of the synagogue answered ⁱwith indignation, because that Jesus had healed on the sabbath day, and said unto the people, There are six days in which men ought to work: in them therefore come

15 and be healed, and ^jnot on the sabbath day. The Lord then answered him, and said, *Thou* hypocrite, ^kdoth not each one of you on the sabbath loose his ox or *his* ass from the stall, and lead *him* away to watering?

16 And ought not this woman, ^lbeing a daughter of Abraham, whom Satan hath bound, lo, these eighteen years, be loosed from this bond on the

17 sabbath day? And when he had said these things, all his adversaries were ashamed: and all the people rejoiced for all the glorious things that were done by him.

18 Then ^msaid he, Unto what is the kingdom of God like? and whereunto

19 shall I resemble it? It is like a grain of mustard seed, which a man took, and cast into his garden; and it grew, and waxed a great tree; and

20 the fowls of the air lodged in the branches of it. And again he said,

21 Whereunto shall I liken the kingdom of God? It is like leaven, which a woman took and hid in three ⁿmeasures of meal, till the whole was leavened.

22 And ^ohe went through the cities and villages, teaching and journeying toward Jerusalem.

23 Then said one unto him, Lord, are there few that be saved? And he

24 said unto them, ²Strive to enter in at the strait gate: for ^pmany, I say

---

A. D. 33.

h Mark 16.18.
ch 17.14-17.
Acts 9. 17.
i John 5. 15, 16.
Rom. 10. 2.
j Matt.12.10.
Mark 3. 2.
ch. 6. 7.
ch. 14. 3.
k ch 14. 5.
John 7. 21-24.
l ch. 19. 9.
Rom. 4. 12-16.
m Matt.13.31.
Mark 4. 30.
n Matt. 13.33.
o Matt. 9. 35.
Mark 6. 6.
Acts 10. 38.
2 Strive as in agony.
Matt. 7. 13.
p John 7. 34.
John 8. 21.
John 13.33.
Rom. 9. 31.
Rom. 10. 2, 3.

---

14. And the ruler of the synagogue answered with indignation, because that Jesus had healed on the sabbath day, and said unto the people—or 'the multitude' [ὄχλῳ]. 'Not daring,' as *Trench* remarks, 'directly to find fault with the Lord, he seeks circuitously to reach Him through the people, who were more under his influence, and whom he feared less.' There are six days in which men ought to work: in them therefore come and be healed, and not on the sabbath day. From the "hypocrisy" with which the Lord charges him (*v.* 15), we may conclude that zeal for the honour of the Sabbath was only the pretence, and that the glory which this miracle shed upon the Lord Jesus was the real cause of this·ruler's "indignation," as the same writer observes. See Matt. xxi. 15. **15.** The Lord (see on ch. x. 1) then answered him, and said, Hypocrite! How "the faithful and true Witness" tears off the masks which men wear? doth not each one of you on the sabbath loose his ox or his ass from the stall, and lead him away to watering? See on Matt. xii. 10-13. **16.** And ought not this woman, being a daughter of Abraham—that is, not *after the flesh,* or a Jewess, which would be a poor view of His meaning; but *in spirit* (compare ch. xix. 9, and 1 Pet. iii. 6). whom Satan hath bound. Probably there is nothing more intended by this expression than a strong contrast between the exalted character of the woman, and the suffering of which the dark author of all evil had so long made her the victim. lo, these eighteen years. The "behold" here calling attention to the long duration of her malady is not to be overlooked; attesting, as it does, the lively sensibility to human suffering of our great High Priest. be loosed from this bond on the sabbath day? How gloriously the Lord vindicates the superior claims of this woman, in consideration of the sadness and long duration of her suffering, and of her dignity notwithstanding, as an heir of the promise! **17.** And when he had said these things, all his adversaries were ashamed: and all the people—or 'multitude' [ὁ ὄχλος], rejoiced for all the glorious things that were done by him. This remark of the Evangelist attests its own artless truth: the resistless force and pungency of the rebuke not only stung His adversaries, but made them feel themselves thoroughly exposed; while the instantaneous cure of this chronic malady, and more than all, the outburst of divine benevolence which vindicated the act, from its own intrinsic superiority to all acts of mercy towards the lower creation, carried the acclaim of the unsophisticated people.

For remarks on this Section, see on Matt. xii. 9-21, Remarks 1, 2, 4, at the close of that Section.

18-30.—PARABLES OF THE MUSTARD SEED AND THE LEAVEN—REPLY TO THE QUESTION, ARE FEW SAVED?

Parables of the Mustard Seed and the Leaven (18-21). For the exposition of this portion, see on Matt. xiii. 31-33, with Remarks.

Are Few Saved? (22-30). **22.** And he went through the cities and villages, teaching and journeying toward Jerusalem—on His final but circuitous journey from Galilee. See introductory remarks on the portion commencing with ch. ix. 51. **23.** Then said one unto him, Lord, are there few that be saved? This is one of those curious questions which a time of religious inquiry and excitement usually suggests, by taking up their attention with which some flatter themselves that they are religious, but thus only lulling the inward craving after something more substantial. And he said unto them—that is, the multitude; taking no notice of the man or his question, save as furnishing the occasion of a solemn warning not to trifle with so momentous a matter as "salvation." **24.** Strive to enter in [Ἀγωνίζεσθε]. The word signifies to 'contend' as for the mastery, to 'struggle,' expressive of the *difficulty* of being saved, as if one would have to *force his way in* at the strait gate—another figure of the same. See on Matt. vii. 13, 14. for many will seek to enter in, and shall not be able. **25.**

25 unto you, will seek to enter in, and shall not be able. When ^qonce the Master of the house is risen up, and ^rhath shut to the door, and ye begin to stand without, and to knock at the door, saying, ^sLord, Lord, open unto us; and he shall answer and say unto you, ^tI know you not whence

26 ye are: then shall ye begin to say, ^uWe have eaten and drunk in thy

27 presence, and thou hast taught in our streets. But ^vhe shall say, I tell you, I know you not whence ye are: ^wdepart from me, all *ye* workers of

28 iniquity. There ^xshall be weeping and gnashing of teeth, ^ywhen ye shall see Abraham, and Isaac, and Jacob, and all the prophets, in the kingdom

29 of God, and you *yourselves* thrust out. And ^zthey shall come from the east, and *from* the west, and from the north, and *from* the south, and

30 shall sit down in the kingdom of God. And, ^abehold, there are last which shall be first, and there are first which shall be last.

31 The same day there came certain of the Pharisees, saying unto him,

32 Get thee out, and depart hence: for Herod will kill thee. And he said unto them, Go ye, and tell that fox, Behold, I cast out devils, and I do cures to-day and to-morrow, and the third *day* ^bI shall be perfected.

A. D. 33.

q Ps. 32. 6.
Isa. 55. 6.
r Matt. 25.10.
s ch. 6. 46.
t Matt. 7. 23.
u Tit. 1. 16.
v Matt. 7. 23.
Matt. 25.41.
w Ps. 6. 8.
Matt. 25.41.
x Matt. 8. 12.
Matt. 13.42.
Matt 24. 51.
y Matt. 8. 11.
z Gen. 28. 14.
Isa. 60. 3.
a Matt.19.30.
Matt. 20.16.
Mark 10.31.
b Heb. 2. 10.
Heb. 5. 8.

When once the Master of the house is risen up, and hath shut to the door. Awfully sublime and vivid picture! At present He is represented as in a *sitting* posture, as if calmly looking on to see who will "strive," while entrance is practicable. But this is to have an end, by the great Master of the house Himself rising and shutting the door, after which there will be no admittance. **and ye begin to stand without, and to knock at the door, saying, Lord, Lord**—emphatic reduplication, expressive of the earnestness *now* felt, but too late. See on Matt. vii. 21, 22. **open unto us; and he shall answer and say unto you, I know you not whence ye are: 26. Then shall ye begin to say, We have eaten and drunk in thy presence, and thou hast taught in our streets. 27. But he shall say, I tell you, I know you not whence ye are: depart from me, all ye workers of iniquity.** 'What! not know *us*, Lord? Astonishing! Why, we have eaten and drunk in Thy presence. Were we not at that great feast which Matthew the publican made to Thee in his own house? Did we not sit opposite to Thee at his table? Heard we not from Thy lips on that occasion the precious saying, "I came not to call the righteous, but sinners to repentance," a saying which, *in the midst of our sins*, has proved so great a comfort to us?'—'Never knew you, workers of iniquity!' 'But, Lord, in addition to all this, Thou hast taught in our streets. At Capernaum, did we not live next door to Thee, and what glorious teachings of Thine have we not heard there? When the woman with the issue of blood was healed by touching the hem of Thy garment, we were in the crowd that followed Thee through the streets; and when Thou spakest from Peter's boat to the thronging multitudes that lined the shore of the beautiful lake, we stood right opposite to Thee, and could repeat every word of those seven charming parables which were then delivered. Nay, we followed Thee from place to place, from city to city, enchained by Thy matchless teaching: we could repeat most of the Sermon on the Mount, and we heard Thee utter that great word, "Come unto Me, all ye that labour and are heavy laden, and I will give you rest;" and *what a comfort was that to us!* And that glorious word uttered in the streets of Jerusalem on the last, that great day of the feast, we heard, "If any man thirst, let him come unto me and drink." O what scores of such beautiful sayings of Thine did our ears drink in. Never knew *us*, Lord? Impossible!'—"NEVER KNEW YOU, workers of iniquity!" 'But, Lord—' 'Enough: begone!' **28, 29.**

There—in the place of separation from Me, shall **be weeping**—for anguish, **and gnashing of teeth** —for despair, **when ye shall see Abraham, &c. And they shall come from the east, and from the west, &c.** See on ch. vii. 9.

For Remarks on this Section, see on Matt. vii. 13-29, Remarks 3, 4, 5, at the close of that Section. But we may call attention to the two following points here standing out with peculiar vividness:—1. No nearness of external communion with Christ will avail at the Great Day, in place of that "holiness without which no man shall see the Lord." 2. The *style* which Christ announces that He will then assume—that of absolute Disposer of men's eternal destinies—and contrast this with His "despised and rejected" condition when He uttered these words!

31-35.—MESSAGE TO HEROD, AND LAMENTATION OVER JERUSALEM, SUGGESTED BY IT.

Message to Herod (31-33). **31. The same day there came certain of the Pharisees, saying unto him, Get thee out, and depart hence**—'Push on without delay, if thou regardest thine own safety.' **for Herod** (Antipas) **will kill thee** [θέλει σε ἀποκτεῖναι]—'is minded to kill thee.' He was now on His way out of Perea, on the east side of the Jordan, and so out of Herod's dominions, "journeying towards Jerusalem" (*v.* 22). Haunted, probably, by guilty fears, Herod wanted to get rid of Him (see on Mark vi. 14), and seems, from our Lord's answer, to have sent these Pharisees, under pretence of a friendly hint, to persuade Him that the sooner He got beyond Herod's jurisdiction the better it would be for His own safety. Our Lord saw through both of them, and sends the cunning ruler a message couched in dignified and befitting irony. **32. And he said unto them, Go ye, and tell that fox**—that crafty, cruel enemy of God's innocent servants, **Behold, I cast out devils, and I do cures to-day and to-morrow, and the third day I shall be perfected**—or, finish My course, attain completion. 'Plot on and ply thy wiles; I also have My plans; My works of mercy are nearing completion, but some yet remain; I have work for to-day and to-morrow too, and the third day; by that time I shall be where his jurisdiction reaches not; the guilt of My blood shall not lie at his door; that dark deed is reserved for others.' He does not say, as *Bengel* remarks, I preach the Gospel—that would have made little impression upon Herod. In the light of the *merciful* character of Christ's *actions* the *malice* of Herod's *snares* is laid bare. **33. Nevertheless I must walk to-day, and**

33 Nevertheless I must walk to-day, and to-morrow, and the *day* following: for it cannot be that a prophet perish out of Jerusalem.

34 O ᶜJerusalem, Jerusalem, which killest the prophets, and stonest them that are sent unto thee; how often would I have gathered thy children together, as a hen *doth gather* her brood under *her* wings, and ye would

35 not! Behold, ᵈyour house is left unto you desolate: and verily I say unto you, Ye shall ᵉnot see me, until *the time* come when ye shall say, ᶠBlessed *is* he that cometh in the name of the Lord.

14 AND it came to pass, as he went into the house of one of the chief

2 Pharisees to eat bread on the sabbath day, that they watched him. And,

3 behold, there was a certain man before him which had the dropsy. And Jesus answering spake unto the lawyers and Pharisees, saying, ᵃIs it

4 lawful to heal on the sabbath day? And they held their peace. And he

5 took *him,* and healed him, and let him go: and answered them, saying, ᵇWhich of you shall have an ass or an ox fallen into a pit, and will not

6 straightway pull him out on the sabbath day? And they could not answer him again to these things.

7 And he put forth a parable to those which were bidden, when he

8 marked how they chose out the chief rooms; saying unto them, When thou art bidden of any *man* to a wedding, sit not down in the highest

9 room; lest a more honourable man than thou be bidden of him; and he that bade thee and him come and say to thee, Give this man place; and

10 thou begin with shame to take the lowest room. But ᶜwhen thou art

A. D. 33.
ᶜ 2 Chr. 24. 21, 22.
Neh. 9. 26.
Matt. 21. 35, 36.
Matt. 23. 37.
ᵈ Lev. 26. 31, 32.
Ps. 69. 25.
Isa. 1. 7.
Dan. 9. 27.
Mic. 3. 12.
Luke 21. 24.
ᵉ Pro. 1. 24-30.
John 8. 21, 24.
ᶠ Ps. 118. 26.
Matt. 21. 9.
Mark 11. 10.
ch. 19. 38.
John 12. 13.
CHAP. 14.
ᵃ Matt. 12. 10.
ᵇ Ex. 23. 5.
Deut. 22. 4.
ch. 13. 15.
ᶜ Pro. 15. 33.
Pro. 18. 12.
Pro. 25. 6, 7.

to-morrow, and the day following. Remarkable language, expressive of *successive steps* of His work yet remaining, of the calm *deliberateness* with which He meant to go through with them, one after another, to the last, unmoved by Herod's threat, but of the *rapid march* with which they were now hastening to completion! (Compare Luke xxii. 37.) **for it cannot be that a prophet perish out of Jerusalem.** Awful severity of satire this upon 'the bloody city'! 'He seeks to "kill me" does He? Ah! I must be out of Herod's jurisdiction for that: Go tell him I neither fly from him nor fear him, but Jerusalem has ever been, and is once more to become, the prophet's slaughter-house.'

Lamentation over Jerusalem (34-35). **34. O Jerusalem, Jerusalem, which killest the prophets, and stonest them that are sent unto thee; how often would I have gathered thy children together, as a hen doth gather her brood under her wings, and ye would not! 35. Behold, your house is left unto you desolate: and verily I say unto you, Ye shall not see me, until the time come when ye shall say, Blessed is he that cometh in the name of the Lord.** How naturally this melting Lamentation would be wrung from Christ's heart after the words just uttered, let the devout and intelligent reader judge. And yet there are critics of some weight who regard it as but a repetition by the Third Evangelist of the Lamentation uttered considerably later, on His final departure from the Temple, and recorded in its proper place by Matthew (xxiii. 37-39). For the exposition, see on Matt. xxiii. 37-39, with Remarks at the close of that Section.

CHAP. XIV. 1-24.—HEALING OF A DROPSICAL MAN, AND MANIFOLD TEACHINGS AT A SABBATH-FEAST.

Healing of a Dropsical Man on the Sabbath day (1-6). **1. And it came to pass, as he went into the house of one of the chief Pharisees** [τινος τῶν ἀρχόντων τῶν Φαρισαίων]—rather, ' of one of the rulers who belonged to the sect of the Pharisees.' The place and time, as usual in this

portion of the present Gospel, are not indicated. See remarks prefixed to ch. ix. 51. **to eat bread on the sabbath day, that they watched him. 2. And, behold, there was a certain man before him which had the dropsy**—not one of the invited guests probably, but one who presented himself in hope of a cure, though not expressly soliciting it; and it may be that this was all the more readily allowed, to see what He would do. This is confirmed by our Lord "letting Him go" immediately after curing him (*v.* 4). The company, it will be observed, had not yet sat down. **3-6. And Jesus answering spake unto the lawyers and Pharisees, saying, Is it lawful to heal on the sabbath day?** &c. For the exposition of these verses, see on Matt. xii. 10-13, and Remarks 1, 2, at the close of that Section.

Lessons on Humility (7-11). **7. And he put forth a parable to those which were bidden, when he marked how they chose out the chief rooms** [τὰς πρωτοκλισίας]—that is, the couches or seats at the table reserved for the most honoured guests, or the middle parts of the couches which were esteemed the most honourable. His mode of conveying the instruction intended is called a "parable," as teaching something deeper than the outward form of it expressed—because His design was not so much to inculcate mere politeness, or good manners, but, underneath this, universal humility, as appears by *v.* 11. **8. When thou art bidden of any man to a wedding**—'and,' as is implied, 'art taking thy place at the wedding-feast.' Our Lord, as *Bengel* remarks, avoids the appearance of personality by this delicate allusion to a different kind of entertainment from this of His present host. **sit not down in the highest room; lest a more honourable man than thou be bidden of him; 9. And he that bade thee and him come and say to thee, Give this man place; and thou begin with shame to take the lowest room.** To be lowest, says *Bengel,* is only ignominious to him who affects to be highest. **10. But when thou art bidden, go and sit down in the lowest room; that when he that bade thee cometh, he may say unto thee, Friend**—said to the modest guest bidden, go and sit down in the lowest room; that when he that bade thee cometh, he may say unto thee, Friend, go up higher: then shalt thou have worship in the presence of them that sit at meat with thee.

11 For ^dwhosoever exalteth himself shall be abased; and he that humbleth himself shall be exalted.

12 Then said he also to him that bade him, When thou makest a dinner or a supper, call not thy friends, nor thy brethren, neither thy kinsmen, nor *thy* rich neighbours; lest they also bid thee again, and a recompence

13 be made thee. But when thou makest a feast, ^ecall the poor, the maimed,

14 the lame, the blind: and thou shalt be blessed; for they cannot recompense thee: for thou shalt be recompensed at ^fthe resurrection of the just.

15 And when one of them that sat at meat with him heard these things, he said unto him, ^gBlessed *is* he that shall eat bread in the kingdom of

16 God. Then ^hsaid he unto him, A certain man made a great supper, and

17 bade many: and ⁱsent his servant at supper time to say to them that

18 were bidden, Come; for all things are now ready. And they all with one consent began to make excuse. The first said unto him, ^jI have bought a piece of ground, and I must needs go and see it: I pray thee have me

19 excused. And another said, I have bought five yoke of oxen, and I go

20 to prove them: I pray thee have me excused. And another said, I have

Reference column:

A. D. 33.

d Job 22. 29.
Ps. 18. 27.
Pro. 29. 23.
Matt. 23.12.
ch. 18. 14.
Jas. 4. 6.
1 Pet. 5. 5.
e Neh. 8. 10,
12.
Job 31. 14-
20.
Pro. 3 9,
28.
f Dan. 12. 2.
Matt. 25.36.
John 5. 29.
Acts 24. 15.
g Rev. 19. 9.
h Matt. 22. 2.
i Pro. 9. 2, 5.
j Matt. 6. 24
Matt. 13.22.
Luke 8. 14.
John 5. 40.
1 Tim. 6. 9,
10.
2 Tim. 4 10.

---

only, says the same critic, not the proud one (*v.* 9). **then shalt thou have worship** [δόξα]—or 'honour.' The whole of this is but a reproduction of Prov. xxv. 6, 7. But it was reserved for the matchless Teacher to utter articulately, and apply to the regulation of the minutest features of social life, such great laws of the Kingdom of God as the following: **11. For whosoever exalteth himself shall be abased; and he that humbleth himself shall be exalted.** The chaste simplicity and proverbial terseness of this great maxim impart to it a charm only inferior to that of the maxim itself. But see further on ch. xviii. 14.)

Entertaining the Poor (12-14.) **12. Then said he also to him that bade him, When thou makest a dinner or a supper, call not thy friends, nor thy brethren, neither thy kinsmen, nor thy rich neighbours; lest they also bid thee again, and a recompense be made thee**—a fear the world is not afflicted with. Jesus certainly did not mean us to dispense with the duties of ordinary fellowship. But since there was no exercise of *principle* involved in it, save of reciprocity, and selfishness itself would suffice to prompt it, His object was to inculcate, over and above everything of this kind, such attentions to the helpless and provision for them as, from their inability to make any return, would manifest their own disinterestedness, and, like every other exercise of high religious principle, meet with a corresponding gracious recompense. **13. But when thou makest a feast, call the poor, the maimed, the lame, the blind.** Compare this with the classes God himself invites to the great Gospel Feast, *v.* 21. **14. And thou shalt be blessed; for they cannot recompense thee: for thou shalt be recompensed at the resurrection of the just**—as acting from disinterested, God-like compassion for the wretched.

The Great Supper (15-24). **15. And when one of them that sat at meat with him heard these things, he said unto him, Blessed is he that shall eat bread in the kingdom of God.** As our Lord's words seemed to hold forth the future "recompense" under the idea of a great Feast, the thought passes through this man's mind, how blessed they would be who should be honoured to sit down to it. A pious exclamation it seemed to

be; but, from our Lord's reply, it would appear to have sounded in His ears more like Balaam's wish, "Let me die the death of the righteous, and let my last end be like his" (Numb. xxiii. 10)—a wish only to be safe and happy *at last*, while rejecting all *present* invitations to turn to God and live. 'The Great Feast of which you sigh to partake,' says our Lord, 'is prepared already: the invitations are issued, but declined: the Feast, notwithstanding, shall have guests enough, and the table shall be filled: but when its present contemners come to sue for admission to it—as they will yet do—not one of them shall taste of it.' **16. Then said he unto him, A certain man made a great supper.** The blessings of Salvation are in Scripture familiarly set forth as a *Feast*, to signify not merely the rich abundance and variety of them, but their suitableness to our spiritual wants, and the high satisfaction and enjoyment which they yield. Thus, Isa. xxv. 6, "And in this mountain (mount Zion, Heb. xii. 22) shall the Lord of hosts make unto all peoples [לְכָל־הָעַמִּים] a feast of fat things," or rich delicacies, "a feast of wines on the lees," freed from all mixture, "of fat things full of marrow, of wines on the lees well refined." **and bade many.** *Historically*, the Jews are here meant, whom, by taking them into visible covenant, God first invited to partake of salvation; but generally it denotes all within the pale of professed discipleship. **17. And sent his servant at supper time to say to them that were bidden, Come; for all things are now ready**—pointing undoubtedly to the lengthened, but now ripening preparations for the great Gospel call. See on Matt. xxii. 4. **18. And they all with one consent began to make excuse. The first said unto him, I have bought a piece of ground, and I must needs go and see it: I pray thee have me excused. 19. And another said, I have bought five yoke of oxen, and I go to prove them: I pray thee have me excused. 20. And another said, I have married a wife, and therefore I cannot come.** None give a naked refusal. Each has some reason of his own why he ought to be held excused. Three excuses are given as specimens of all the rest; and it will be observed that they answer to the three things which are said to "choke the word" in the parable of the Sower (ch. viii. 14),—

21 married a wife, and therefore I cannot come. So that servant came, and showed his lord these things. Then the master of the house, being angry, said to his servant, Go *ᵏ*out quickly into the streets and lanes of the city, and bring in hither the poor, and the maimed, and the halt, and the 22 blind. And the servant said, Lord, it is done as thou hast commanded, 23 and yet there is room. And the lord said unto the servant, Go out into the highways and hedges, *ˡ*and compel *them* to come in, that my house 24 may be filled. For I say unto you, *ᵐ*That none of those men which were bidden shall taste of my supper.

A. D. 33.

ᵏ Matt. 28.18, 19.
Acts 13. 46.
ⁱ Pro. 1. 20.
2 Cor. 5. 20.
ᵐ Matt. 8. 11, 12.
Matt. 21.43.
Matt. 22. 8.
Acts 13. 46.
Heb. 3 19.

"the care of this world," *v.* 18; "the deceitfulness of riches," *v.* 19; and "the pleasures of this life," *v.* 20. Each differs from the other, and each has its own plausibility; but all arrive at the same result—'We have other things to attend to, more pressing just now.' So far from saying, I decline to come, each represents himself as *only* hindered by something in the way just now: when these are removed, they will be ready. But, notwithstanding these plausibilities, they are held as *refusers;* and when at length they *call,* the Master in turn will *refuse* them. 21. So that servant came, and showed his lord these things. It is the part of ministers, says *Bengel,* to report to the Lord in their prayers the compliance or refusal of their hearers; and certainly, of those first bidden, it could only be said, "Lord, who hath believed our report, and to whom is the arm of the Lord revealed?" (Isa. liii. 1.) Then the master of the house, being angry—at the slight put upon him. At the same time there is *grace* in this anger, showing how sincere he was in issuing his invitation (Ezek. xxxiii. 11). said to his servant, Go out quickly—all now being ready, and waiting, into the streets and lanes of the city. *Historically,* this must mean those within the limits of the city of God (Ps. lxxxvii. 3), but the despised and outcast classes of it—the "publicans and sinners," as *Trench* rightly conceives it; but generally it comprehends all similar classes, usually overlooked in the first provision for supplying the means of grace to a community—half heathen in the midst of revealed light. and in every sense miserable. and bring in hither the poor, and the maimed, and the halt, and the blind. 22. And the servant said, Lord, it is done as thou hast commanded, and yet there is room—implying, first, that these classes *had* embraced the invitation (see Matt. xxi. 32; Mark xii. 37, last clause; John vii. 48, 49); but further, beautifully expressing the longing that should fill the hearts of ministers to see their Master's table filled. 23. And the lord said unto the servant, Go out into the highways and hedges —outside the city altogether. *Historically,* this denotes the heathen, sunk in the lowest depths of spiritual wretchedness, as being beyond the pale of all that is revealed and saving—"without Christ, strangers from the covenant of promise, having no hope, and without God in the world" (Eph. ii. 12): generally, it comprehends all similar classes. Thus, this parable *prophetically* contemplates the extension of the kingdom of God to the whole world; and *spiritually,* directs the Gospel invitations to be carried to the lowest strata, and be brought in contact with the outermost circles, of human society. and compel them to come in. This is not meant to intimate *unwillingness,* as in the first class, but that it would be hard to get them over two difficulties. First, 'We, homeless wretches, that are fain to creep under a "hedge" for shelter, what company are we for such a feast?' Next, 'We who are on the dusty, weary "highway," have no proper dress for such a feast, and are ill in order for such a presence.' How fitly does this represent the difficulties and fears of the *sincere!* Well, and how is this met? 'Take no excuse; beat them out of all their difficulties; dispel all their fears: Tell them you have orders to bring them *just as they are;* make them come without preparation, and without delay.' that my house may be filled— for, as *Bengel* quaintly says, grace as well as nature abhors a vacuum. 24. For I say unto you, That none of those men which were bidden shall taste of my supper. Our Lord here appears to throw off the veil of the parable, and proclaim the Supper *His Own,* intimating that when transferred and transformed into its final glorious form, and the refusers themselves would give all for another opportunity, *He* will not allow one of them to taste of it.

Remarks.—1. Some of the richest of our Lord's teachings were quite *incidental*—drawn forth by casual circumstances occurring in His daily course. Thus, having accepted the invitation of this Pharisee to dine on the Sabbath day, the presence of a dropsical person, whom He resolves to cure, gives occasion to some important teaching on the right observance of that holy day. Then, observing the eagerness of the guests to occupy the places of honour at the table, He instructs them on the subject of Humility. Further, from the quality of the guests—apparently "brethren, kinsmen, rich neighbours"—He takes occasion to inculcate hospitality of a diviner sort, compassionate provision for the wants of those who could make no return, looking to the time when a return of another kind would be made them—when "the merciful should obtain mercy." 'Blessed lot that will be'—exclaims one of the guests, fired for the moment at the thought of a Feast in the kingdom above—'Happy they who shall have the honour of sitting down to it!' Happy indeed, replies the Great Teacher and loving Redeemer; but the present despisers of it shall not be the future partakers of it. Thus did His heavenly wisdom stream forth at every opening, however incidental. "Grace was poured into His lips," and was ready to pour out again whenever it would not be as pearls cast before swine. And should not His disciples strive to copy Him in this? "The lips of the righteous feed many" (Prov. x. 21). There is a certain advantage in *set* discourses, to which the hearers set themselves to listen, expecting something lengthened, formal, solid. But the wisdom that comes out unexpectedly and casually has a freshness and charm peculiar to itself. And it impresses the hearer, far more than all set discoursing, with the conviction that it is the *genuine* and *spontaneous* expression of the speaker's present judgment and feeling. And when it comes as "line upon line, line upon line; precept upon precept, precept upon precept; here a little, and there a little" (Isa. xxviii. 10), its weight is all the greater. (Compare Deut. vi. 7.) 2. The punishment attached to pride, and the reward promised to humility, make themselves good even in the ordinary workings of human society. When a man insists on thrusting himself, as *Lord Bacon*

25　And there went great multitudes with him: and he turned, and said
26　unto them, If ⁿany *man* come to me, ^oand hate not his father, and
　　mother, and wife, and children, and brethren, and sisters, ^pyea, and his
27　own life also, he cannot be my disciple. And ^qwhosoever doth not bear
28　his cross, and come after me, cannot be my disciple. For ^rwhich of you,
　　intending to build a tower, sitteth not down first, and counteth the cost,
29　whether he have *sufficient* to finish *it?* Lest haply, after he hath laid
　　the foundation, and is not able to finish *it*, all that behold *it* begin to
30　mock him, saying, This man began to build, and was not able to finish.

A. D. 33.

ⁿ Deut. 13. 6.
Deut. 33. 9.
Matt.10.37.
^o Rom. 9. 13.
^p Rev. 12. 11.
^q Matt.16.24.
Mark 8. 34.
ch. 9. 23.
^r Pro. 24. 27.
1 Pet. 2. 5.

somewhere expresses it, into the centre of things, there is a kind of social instinct that leads others to resist and take him down; but when one gives place to others, he not only disarms every disposition to take advantage of it, but is usually made to go before his neighbours. Thus, in the ordinary working of the social system, the great principles of the divine administration are revealed; on a small scale, indeed, and often without the smallest reference, on the part of men, to the divine will; but just on that account all the more strikingly manifesting and illustrating a moral government. 3. It is a mistake in religion, alike common and fatal, to regard heaven as a state of simple happiness—mere bliss; higher and more refined than anything conceivable now, but not essentially dependent upon *present character.* If one thing is clearer than another in the Scripture view of the future state, it is that, in point of moral and religious character, it will be but the perfection and development of the present state, both in the righteous and the wicked; and all the conclusions, even of Natural Theology, confirm that view of it. In vain, therefore, do worldlings, living without God and minding only earthly things, exclaim, Blessed is he that shall eat bread in the kingdom of God! Let me die the death of the righteous, and let my last end be like his! The best of heaven's bliss is but getting face to face with Him whom not having seen we love, in whom, though now we see him not, yet believing, we rejoice with joy unspeakable and full of glory. But if we have never felt any of this love to Him and joy in Him, are we capable of heaven? To be "for ever with the Lord," is transport, even in prospect, to such as have tasted that He is gracious, experienced the blessedness of reconciliation, learned to cry, Abba, Father, walk daily in the light of His countenance, and live to please Him. In such as these, it is but a change of sphere, and the new life perfected; it is but the bursting of the flower, the ripening of the fruit. Amidst all its novelties, the children of God will find themselves *at home* in heaven—its company congenial, its services familiar, its bliss not strange. But if so, how is it possible that those who disrelished its language, its exercises, its fellowship here, should have any capacity for it, and, wanting this, be admitted to it? No, "none of those men who were bidden"—but only insulted Him who prepared the feast by slighting His invitation—"shall taste of His Supper." "Be not deceived: God is not mocked; for whatsoever a man soweth, that shall he also reap." 4. How often is it found that while the Gospel is slighted by the classes who enjoy the greatest advantages, who might be expected the most to appreciate it, and whom one would most gladly see brought under its power, it is embraced by those to whom it has last of all been presented, and—judging as we are apt to do—the least likely to value it. Thus it ever is, that there are last which come to be first, and first last. 5. The call addressed to those in the highways and hedges is a glorious

directory to the preachers of the Gospel. If such are invited and expected to come straight to the feast, all *preparation* is out of the question; and all misgivings on their own part, or obstructions on the part of others, on the ground of want of preparation, must be met with one answer—'The invitation found us in that condition, and required immediate compliance.' If this great Gospel truth is not clearly apprehended, and by the preacher himself felt as the sole ground of his own standing in Christ, he cannot urge it upon others, and still less so deal with them as to "compel them to come in." But having got over all his own scruples on that one principle, that the invitations of the Gospel are to sinners *as such*—to sinners *just as they are*—he can and will then effectually meet all difficulties and scruples of earnest, anxious souls; and as he cries to them—

' Come, ye sinners, poor and needy,
　Weak and wounded, sick and sore,
　Jesus ready stands to save you,
　Full of pity, love, and power:
　　He is able,
　He is willing, ask no more'—

he shall hear of one and another falling down before the cross, and saying—

' Just as I am—without one plea,
　But that Thy blood was shed for me,
　And that Thou bidd'st me come to Thee—
　　O Lamb of God! I come.

' Just as I am—and *waiting not*
　To rid my soul of one dark blot,
　To Thee, whose blood can cleanse each spot—
　　O Lamb of God! I come.'

25-35.—ADDRESS ON COUNTING THE COST OF FOLLOWING HIM, DELIVERED BY JESUS TO GREAT MULTITUDES WHO WENT AFTER HIM. **25. And there went great multitudes with him**—on His final journey to Jerusalem. If they were going up to the Passover, moving along, as they were wont to do, in clusters (see on ch. ii. 44), and forming themselves into one mass about the Lord Jesus, this must have occurred after the Feast of Tabernacles and the winter Feast of Dedication, at both of which our Lord was present, after His final departure from Galilee. But the precise time cannot be determined. See remarks prefixed to the portion of this Gospel beginning with ch. ix. 51. **and he turned, and said unto them, 26, 27. If any man come to me, and hate not his father, &c.,** he cannot be my disciple. **And whosoever doth not bear his cross, and come after me, cannot be my disciple.** See on Matt. x. 37, 38. **28. For which of you, intending to build a tower, sitteth not down first, and counteth the cost, whether he have sufficient to finish it? 29. Lest haply, after he hath laid the foundation, and is not able to finish it, all that behold it begin to mock him, 30. Saying, This man began to build, and was not able to finish.** Common sense teaches men not to *begin* any costly work without first seeing that they have wherewithal to *finish* it. And he who does otherwise exposes himself to

286

31 Or what king, going to make war against another king, sitteth not down first, and consulteth whether he be able with ten thousand to meet him

32 that cometh against him with twenty thousand? Or else, while the other is yet a great way off, he sendeth *an ambassage, and desireth

33 conditions of peace. So likewise, whosoever *he be of you that forsaketh not all that he hath, he cannot be my disciple.

34 Salt *is good: but if the salt have lost his savour, wherewith shall it be

35 seasoned? It is neither fit for the land, nor yet for the dunghill; *but* men cast it out. He that hath ears to hear, let him hear.

15 THEN *drew near unto him all the publicans and *sinners for to hear

2 him. And the Pharisees and scribes murmured, saying, This man re-

A. D. 33.

* Job 22. 21.
Matt. 5. 25.
ch. 12. 59.
2 Cor. 6. 2.
* Matt. 19.27, 28.
ch. 18. 22.
* Matt. 5. 13.
Mark 9. 50.

CHAP. 15..
* Matt. 9. 10.
* Ezek. 18.23.
1 Tim. 1.15.

general ridicule. **31. Or what king, going to make war against another king, sitteth not down first, and consulteth whether he be able with ten thousand to meet him that cometh against him with twenty thousand?** No wise potentate will enter on a war with any hostile power without first seeing to it that, despite formidable odds—of "twenty" to "ten thousand," or two to one—he be able to stand his ground. **32. Or else, while the other is yet a great way off, he sendeth an ambassage, and desireth conditions of peace.** If he see that he has no hope of bearing up against such odds, he will feel that nothing remains for him but to make the best terms he can. **33. So likewise, whosoever he be of you that forsaketh not all that he hath, he cannot be my disciple.** 'In the warfare you will each have to wage as My disciples, despise not your enemy's strength, for the odds are all against you; and you had better see to it that, despite every disadvantage, you still have wherewithal to hold out and win the day, or else not begin at all, but make the best you can in such awful circumstances.' In place of this simple and natural sense of the latter parable, *Stier, Alford*, &c., go wide of the mark, making the enemy here meant to be *God*, because of the "conditions of peace" which the parable speaks of. It is the *spirit* of such a case, rather than the mere phraseology, that is to be seized.

34, 35. Salt is good: but if the salt have lost his savour, &c. **He that hath ears to hear, let him hear.** See on Matt. v. 13; and on Mark iv. 9.

Remarks.—1. Better not begin the Christian course, than begin and not finish it. Inconsistency is offensive even to men, and, in the matter of religion, is apt to draw down ridicule and contempt; as is so admirably portrayed in "Pliable" by *Bunyan* in the "Pilgrim's Progress." But to Him whose eyes are as a flame of fire, it is abhorrent. "I would thou wert cold or hot. So then, because thou art lukewarm, and neither cold nor hot, I will spue thee out of my mouth" (Rev. iii. 15, 16). 2. Though the contest for salvation be on our part an awfully unequal one, *the human will*, in the exercise of that "faith which overcometh the world" (1 John v. 4), and nerved by power from above, which "out of weakness makes it strong" (Heb. xi. 34; 1 Pet. i. 5), becomes heroical, and will come off "more than conqueror." But without *absolute surrender of self*, the contest is hopeless.

CHAP. XV. 1-32.—PUBLICANS AND SINNERS WELCOMED BY CHRIST—THREE PARABLES OPENING THE DIVINE PRINCIPLE OF THIS.

1. Then—but when, is not stated and cannot be determined. See remarks prefixed to ch. ix. 51. **drew near** ["Ησαν δε εγγιζοντες]. The phrase implies something *habitual*. See on the same imperfect tense in ch. i. 22, &c. **unto him all the publicans and sinners for to hear him.** Strange

287

auditory for such a Preacher! In fact, among the marvels of this most marvellous History, none is more marvellous than the fact that the most sunken classes of society—we might almost say, its refuse and scum—seem, as by some spell, to have been attracted to the Holy, Harmless, Undefiled One, the Separate from sinners! What could the secret of this be? What but the discovery in *Him* of a compassion for their case against which they had found every other breast steeled. 'Abandoned of men, we had thought ourselves much more so of God: Heaven and earth seemed alike shut against us, and we were ready to conclude that, as outcasts from both, we must live on the wretched life we are living, and then lie down and die without hope. But compassion for the chief of sinners beams in that Eye, and streams forth from those Lips; God is in that Heart, Heaven in that Voice; Never man spake like this Man: As He speaks, God Himself seems to draw near even to us, and say to us in accents of melting love, Return unto Me, and I will return unto you: Who and what He is, we are too ignorant to tell; but we *feel* what He is to us; when *He* is with us, we seem to be in the precincts of heaven.' How far these were the thoughts and feelings of that class, would of course depend on the extent to which they were sick of their evil ways, and prepared to welcome divine encouragement to turn from them and live. But that what drew to Him "all the publicans and sinners for to hear Him" must have something *of this nature*—that of Him and Him alone, if we except His like-minded Forerunner, they saw clearly it could not be said, "No man careth for my soul"—will be evident from the sequel. **2. And the Pharisees and scribes murmured, saying, This man receiveth sinners, and eateth with them.** They were scandalized at His procedure, and insinuated—on the principle that a man is known by the company he keeps—that He must have some secret sympathy with their *character*. But what a truth of unspeakable preciousness do their lips, as on other occasions, unconsciously utter! And Jesus will show them how divine the deed is. Here, accordingly, follow three parables, illustrating the principle on which He drew them to Himself and hailed any symptoms in them of return to God. The three parables, though the same in their general import, present the sinner each of them under a different aspect. The first, as *Bengel* acutely and laconically remarks, represents him, in his *stupidity*, as a silly sheep going astray; the second, like lost property, as '*unconscious of his lost condition*;' the third, as '*knowingly and wilfully estranged from God*.' The first two, as *Trench* well observes, set forth the *seeking* love of God; the last His *receiving* love.

The Parable of THE LOST SHEEP, *with the Moral of it* (3-7). This parable occurs again, and is recorded in Matt. xviii. 12-14; but there it is to show

3 ceiveth sinners, and *c*eateth with them. And he spake this parable unto them, saying,

4 What *d*man of you, having an hundred sheep, if he *e*lose one of them, doth not leave the ninety and nine in the wilderness, and go

5 after that which is lost, until he find it? And when he hath found *it*,

6 he layeth *it* on his shoulders, rejoicing. And when he cometh home, he calleth together *his* friends and neighbours, saying unto them, Rejoice

7 with me; for I have found my sheep *f*which was lost. I say unto you, That likewise joy shall be in heaven over one sinner that repenteth, *g*more than over ninety and nine just persons, which need no repentance.

8 Either what woman, having ten [1]pieces of silver, if she lose one piece, doth not light a candle, and sweep the house, and seek diligently till she

9 find *it?* And when she hath found *it*, she calleth *her* friends and *her* neighbours together, saying, Rejoice with me; for I have found the piece

10 which I had lost. Likewise, I say unto you, There is joy in the presence of the angels of God over one sinner that repenteth.

11, And he said, A certain man had two sons: and the younger of them

12 said to *his* father, Father, give me the portion of goods that falleth *to me*.

A. D. 33.

c Acts 11. 3.
d Matt. 18.12.
e 1 Pet. 2. 25.
f 1 Pet. 2. 10, 25.
g Pro. 30. 12.
[1] Drachma, here translated a piece of silver, is the eighth part of an ounce, which cometh to seven-pence halfpenny, and is equal to the Roman penny.

how precious one of his sheep is to the good Shepherd; here, to show that the shepherd, though it stray never so widely, will seek it out, and when he hath found, will rejoice over it. **3. And he spake this parable unto them, saying, 4. What man of you, having an hundred sheep, if he lose one of them, doth not leave the ninety and nine in the wilderness.** Instead of saying, "Tis but one; let it go; enough remain,' will he not bend all his attention and care, as it were, to the one object of recovering the lost sheep? **and go after that which is lost, until he find it?**—pointing to all the diversified means which God sets in operation for recovering sinners, and the patience and perseverance with which He continues to ply them. **6. And when he cometh home, he calleth together his friends and neighbours, saying unto them, Rejoice with me; for I have found my sheep which was lost.** It is a beautiful principle of our nature, that deep feeling, either of sorrow or of joy, is almost too much for one to bear alone, and that there is a feeling of positive relief in having others to share it. This principle our Lord here proclaims to be in operation even in the divine procedure. **7. I say unto you, That likewise joy shall be in heaven over one sinner that repenteth, more than over ninety and nine just persons, which need no repentance.** It is not *angels* who are meant here as needing no repentance. The angels' place in these parables is very different from this. The class here meant, as needing no repentance, are those represented by *the prodigal's well-behaved brother*, who have "served their Father many years," and not at any time transgressed His commandment—in the outrageous sense of the prodigal. (But see on *v.* 29, 31.) In other words, *such as have grown up from childhood* in the fear of God and as the sheep of His pasture. Our Lord does not say "the Pharisees and scribes" were such; but as there *was* undoubtedly such a class, while "the publicans and sinners" were confessedly the strayed sheep and the prodigal children, He leaves them to fill up the place of the other class, *if they could.*

The Parable of THE LOST COIN, *with the Moral of it* (8-10). **8. Either what woman, having ten pieces of silver, if she lose one piece, doth not light a candle, and sweep the house, and seek diligently till she find it? 9. And when she hath found it, she calleth her friends and her neighbours together, saying, Rejoice with me; for I have found the piece which I had lost. 10. Likewise—**

288

that is, on the same principle, **there is joy in the presence of the angels of God over one sinner that repenteth.** Note carefully the language here employed: it is not, 'joy among' or 'on the part of,' but "joy before" [ἐνώπιον] or "in the presence of the angels of God." True to the idea of the parables, it is the Great Shepherd, the Great Owner Himself, *Whose* properly *the joy is over His own recovered property;* but so vast and exuberant is it (Zeph. iii. 17), that as if He could not keep it to Himself, He "calleth His friends and neighbours together"—His whole celestial family—"saying, Rejoice WITH ME, for I have found MY sheep, I have found MY property, which was lost. In this sublime sense it is "joy," *before* "or in the presence of the angels:" they only 'catch the flying joy,' sharing it *with Him!* The application of this to the reception of those publicans and sinners that stood around our Lord is grand in the extreme: 'Ye turn from these lost ones with disdain, and because I do not, ye murmur at it; but a very different feeling is cherished in heaven: There, the recovery of even one such outcast is watched with interest and hailed with joy; nor are they left to come home of themselves or perish; for, lo! even now the great Shepherd is going after His lost sheep, and the Owner is making diligent search for His lost property; and He is finding it too, and bringing it back with joy, and all heaven is full of it.' Let the reader mark what sublime claims for Himself our Lord covertly puts in here —as if in Him these outcasts beheld, though all unknown to themselves, nothing less than Heaven disclosing itself in the habiliments of earth, the Great Shepherd above, clothed in a garment of flesh, come "to seek and to save that which was lost"!

The Parable of THE PRODIGAL SON, *and the Case of his Elder Brother* (11-32). **11. And he said, A certain man had two sons: 12. And the younger of them**—as the more thoughtless, **said to his father, Father, give me the portion of goods that falleth to me**—weary of restraint, panting for independence, unable longer to abide the check of a father's eye. *This is man*, impatient of divine control, desiring to be independent of God, seeking to be his own master—that sin of sins, as *Trench* well says, in which all subsequent sins are included as in their germ, for they are but the unfolding of this one. **And he divided unto them his living.** Thus God, to use the words of

13 And he divided unto them ᵏ*his* living. And not many days after, the
14 younger son gathered all together, and took his journey into ˡa far
country, and there wasted his substance with riotous living. And when
he had spent all, there arose a mighty famine in that land; and he began
15 to be in want. And he went and joined himself to a citizen of that
16 country; and he sent him into his fields to feed swine. And he would
fain have filled his belly with the husks that the swine did eat: and no
17 man gave unto him. And when he came to himself, he said, How many
hired servants of my father's have bread enough, and to spare, and I
18 perish with hunger! I will ʲarise and go to my father, and will say unto

A. D. 33.

ᵏ Mark 12.44.
ˡ Gen. 6. 5.
Ps. 81. 12.
Jer. 2. 5.
Rom. 1. 21.
Tit. 3. 3.
ʲ 1 Ki. 20. 30.
2 Chr. 33.12,
13.
Lam. 3. 40.
Hos. 14. 3-7.
Jon. 2. 4.

the same penetrating and accurate expositor of the parables, when His service no longer appears a perfect freedom, and man promises himself something far better elsewhere, allows him to make the trial; and he shall discover, if need be by saddest proof, that to depart from Him is not to throw off the yoke, but only to exchange a light yoke for a heavy one, and one gracious Master for a thousand imperious tyrants and lords. 13. **And not many days after**—intoxicated with his new-found resources, and eager for the luxury of using them at will, **he took his journey into a far country**—away from the paternal eye, beyond all danger of rebuke or interference from home, **and there wasted his substance with riotous living** [ἀσώτως] —or 'to the destroying of himself.' His brother's charge against him, that he had "devoured his father's living with harlots," shows what is meant. But ah! this reaches deeper than sensuality. As the whole story is designed to set forth the degradation of our sonship, and the prostitution of our powers to purposes unworthy of our dignity and true destiny, we must understand the language as intended to express all that life of estrangement from God, self-seeking and low desire which are common, in different forms and degrees, to all who live "without God," who "have their portion in this life," who mind "earthly things." So long as his substance lasted, the inward monitor would be silenced, and the prodigal would take his ease, eat, drink, and be merry. At times, he would hear the whisper of expostulation, "Wherefore do ye spend money for that which is not bread, and your labour for that which satisfieth not?" (Isa. lv. 2). But though his means were fast fading, he would say to himself, "The bricks are fallen down, but we will build with hewn stones; the sycamores are cut down, but we will change them into cedars" (Isa. ix. 10). So long as anything remained, he would hold out. "Thou art wearied in the greatness of thy way: yet saidst thou not, There is no hope: thou hast found the life of thine hand: therefore thou wast not grieved" (Isa. lvii. 10). 14. **And when he had spent all, there arose a mighty famine in that land**—a mysterious providence holding back the famine till he was in circumstances to feel it in all its rigour. Thus, like Jonah, whom the storm did not overtake till on the mighty deep at the mercy of the waves, does the sinner feel as if "the stars in their courses were fighting against" him (Jud. v. 20). **and he began to be in want** —the first stage of his bitter experience, and preparation for a change. 15. **And he went and joined himself to a citizen of that country; and he sent him into his fields to feed swine.** His pride, it seems, was not yet humbled; he could not brook the shame of a return. Glad to keep life in any how, behold the son sunk into a swineherd; among the Jews, to whom swine's flesh was prohibited, emphatically vile! He, says *Trench*, who begins by using the world as a ser-

vant, to minister to his pleasure, ends by reversing the relationship. 16. **And he would fain have filled his belly with the husks** [τῶν κερατίων] **that the swine did eat** [καὶ ἐπεθύμει γεμίσαι]— rather, 'was fain to fill,' or ate greedily of the only food he could get. These husks, or pulsepods, were in the East the food of cattle and swine, and in times of distress were the nourishment of the very poorest people, as *Stier* remarks. **and no man gave unto him**—that is, no one minded him, to give him anything better than this. "All thy lovers have forgotten thee; they seek thee not: for I have wounded thee with the wound of an enemy, with the chastisement of a cruel one, for the multitude of thine iniquity; because thy sins were increased" (Jer. xxx. 14). This was his lowest depth: he was perishing unpitied; he was alone in the world; he was ready to disappear from it unmissed. But this is just the blessed turning-point— the midnight before dawn of day. "Thine own wickedness shall correct thee, and thy backslidings shall reprove thee: know therefore and see that it is an evil thing and bitter, that thou hast forsaken the Lord thy God" (Jer. ii. 19). "The Lord brought upon Manasseh's people the captains of the host of the king of Assyria, which took Manasseh among the thorns, and bound him with fetters, and carried him to Babylon. And when he was in affliction, he besought the Lord his God, and humbled himself greatly before the God of his fathers, and prayed unto Him; and He was entreated of him, and heard his supplication, and brought him again to Jerusalem into his kingdom. Then Manasseh knew that the Lord he was God" (2 Chron. xxxiii. 11-13; and see 2 Chr. xii. 7, 8). 17. **And when he came to himself**—as if before he had been "beside himself." How truly does the wise man say, "*Madness* is in the heart of the sons of men while they live, and after that they go to the dead" (Eccl. ix. 3). But in what sense men far from God are beside themselves will presently appear more clearly. **he said, How many hired servants of my father's have bread enough, and to spare, and I perish with hunger!** What a testimony to the *nature* of the home he had left! But did he not know all this ere he departed, and every day of his voluntary exile? He did, and he did not. His heart being wholly estranged from home and steeped in selfish gratifications, his father's house never came within the range of his vision, or but as another name for bondage and gloom. Now empty, desolate, withered, perishing— *home*, with all its peace, plenty, freedom, dignity, starts into view, fills all his vision as a warm and living reality, and breaks his heart. 18. **I WILL ARISE AND GO TO MY FATHER.** The change has come at last, and what a change!—couched in terms of such exquisite simplicity and power as if expressly framed for all heart-broken penitents. **and will say unto him, Father, I have sinned against Heaven, and before thee.** 19. **And am**

19 him, Father, *k*I have sinned against Heaven, and before thee, and am no more worthy to be called thy son: make me as one of thy hired servants.

20 And he arose, and came to his father. But *l*when he was yet a great way off, his father saw him, and had compassion, and ran, and fell on his neck,

21 and kissed him. And the son said unto him, Father, I have sinned against Heaven, *m*and in thy sight, and am no more worthy to be called

22 thy son. But the father said to his servants, Bring forth *n*the best robe, and put *it* on him; and put a ring on his hand, and shoes on *his* feet:

23 and bring hither the fatted calf, and kill *it;* and let us eat, and be

24 merry: for *o*this my son was dead, and is alive again; he was lost, and is found. And they *p*began to be merry.

25 Now his elder son was in the field: and as he came and drew nigh to the

26 house, he heard music and dancing. And he called one of the servants, and

27 asked what these things meant. And he said unto him, Thy brother is come; and thy father hath killed the fatted calf, because he hath received

A. D. 33.

k Lev. 26. 40, 41.
1 Ki. 8. 47, 48.
Job 33. 27, 28.
l Isa. 49. 15.
Acts 2. 39.
Eph. 2. 13, 17.
m Ps. 51. 4.
n Matt. 22.11.
Gal. 3. 27.
Rev. 19. 8.
o Eph. 2. 1.
Eph. 5. 14.
Col. 1. 13.
p Isa. 35. 10.

---

no more worthy to be called thy son: make me as one of thy hired servants. Mark the term, "Father." Though "no more *worthy* to be called his son," the prodigal sinner is taught to claim the *degraded* and *defiled*, but *still existing* relationship, asking, not to be *made* a servant, but *remaining a son* to be made "*as* a servant," willing to take the lowest place and do the meanest work. Ah! and is it come to this? Once it was, 'Any place rather than home.' Now, 'O that home! could I but dare to hope that the door of it would not be closed against me, how gladly should I take any place and do any work, happy only to be there at all!' Well, *that is conversion*—nothing absolutely new, yet all new; old familiar things seen in a new light, and for the first time as realities of overwhelming magnitude and power. By what secret supernatural power upon the heart this change upon the sinner's views and feelings is effected, the parable says not, and could not say, without an incongruous and confusing mixture of the figure and the thing figured—the human story and the spiritual reality couched under it. We have that, however, abundantly elsewhere, (Phil. ii. 13; 1 Cor. xv. 10, &c.) The one object of the parable is to paint the glad WELCOME HOME of the greatest sinners, when—no matter for the present *how*—they "arise and go to their father." 20. **And he arose, and came to his father.** Many a one says, "I will arise," yet sits still. But this is the story of a real conversion, in which purpose is presently turned into practice. **But when he was yet a great way off, his father saw him, and ran.** O yes! when the face is turned homeward, though as yet far, far away, our Father recognizes his own child in us, and bounds to meet us—not saying, 'Let him come to me and sue for pardon first,' but Himself taking the first step. **and fell on his neck, and kissed him.** What! In all his filth? Yes. In all his rags? Yes. In all his haggard, shattered wretchedness? Yes. "Our Father who art in heaven," is this Thy portraiture? It is even so. And because it is so, I wonder not that such incomparable teaching hath made the world new. "Is Ephraim my dear son? Is he a pleasant child? For since I spake against him, I do earnestly remember him still: therefore my bowels are troubled for him; I will surely have mercy upon him, saith the Lord" (Jer. xxxi. 20). 21. **And the son said unto him, Father, I have sinned against Heaven, and in thy sight, and am no more worthy to be called thy son.** This humiliating confession he might have spared, if his object had been mere re-admission to the *advantages* of the parental roof. But the case depicted is one in which such heartless selfishness

290

has no place, and in which such a thought would be abhorred. No, this confession was uttered, as *Trench* well remarks, *after the kiss of reconciliation.* 22. **But the father said.** The son has not said all he purposed, but the explanation of this given by *Trench*, &c., appears to us to miss the mark—that the father's demonstrations had rekindled the filial, and swallowed up all servile feeling. It is, in our judgment, rather because the father's heart is made to appear too full to listen at such a moment to more in this strain. **to his servants.** We know who these represent, in all the three parables spoken on this occasion: they are "the angels of God" (*vv.* 7-10). **Bring forth the best robe, and put it on him.** Compare Zec. iii. 4, 5, "And He answered and spake unto those that stood by, saying, Take away the filthy garments from him. And unto him he said, Behold, I have caused thine iniquity to pass from thee, and I will clothe thee with change of raiment. . . And they clothed him with garments. And the angel of the Lord stood by." See also Isa. lxi. 10; Rev. iii. 18. **and put a ring on his hand.** Compare Gen. xli. 42. **and shoes on his feet.** Slaves went barefoot. Thus have we here a threefold symbol both of *freedom* and of *honour* as the fruit of *perfect reconciliation.* 23. **And bring hither the fatted calf**—kept for festive occasions, **and kill it; and let us eat, and be merry**—denoting the exultation of the whole household: "Likewise, I say unto you, there is joy in the presence of the angels of God over one sinner that repenteth" (*v.* 10). But though the joy ran through the whole household, it was properly the *father's* matter. Accordingly it is added, 24. **For this my son was dead, and is alive again; he was lost, and is found.** Now, twice his son. "He was lost"—both to his Father and to himself, lost to his Father's service and satisfaction, lost to his own dignity, peace, profit. But he "is alive again"—to all these.

But what of the elder brother all this time? That we are now to see.

25. **Now his elder son was in the field**—engaged in his father's business. Compare *v.* 29. "Lo, these many years do I *serve* thee." **and as he came and drew nigh to the house, he heard music and dancing.** 26. **And he called one of the servants.** [The *Stephanic* form of the received text has "his servants;" but our Version properly follows the *Elzevir* form, "the servants," which has decisive weight of external evidence, while the internal evidence is even more decisive.] **and asked what these things meant.** 27. **And he said unto him, Thy brother is come; and thy father hath killed the fatted calf, because he hath received him safe and sound.** 28. **And he was**

28 him safe and sound. And *q* he was angry, and would not go in: therefore
29 came his father out, and entreated him. And he answering said to *his* father,
Lo, these many years do I serve thee, neither transgressed I at any time thy
commandment; and *r* yet thou never gavest me a kid, that I might make
30 merry with my friends: but as soon as this thy son was come, which hath
devoured thy living with harlots, thou hast killed for him the fatted calf.
31 And he said unto him, Son, thou art ever with me, and all that I have
32 is thine. It *s* was meet that we should make merry and be glad: for this
thy brother was dead, and is alive again; and was lost, and is found.

A. D. 33.

q 1Sam. 17. 28.
Isa. 66. 5.
Jon. 4. 1-3.
Acts 11. 2.
r Matt. 20. 11
12.
s Ps. 51. 8.
Isa. 35. 10.
Jon. 4. 10.
Rom. 15. 9-
12.

---

angry, and would not go in: therefore came his father out, and entreated him. As it is the elder brother who now errs, so it is *the same paternal compassion* which had fallen on the neck of the younger that comes forth and pleads with the elder. "Like as a father pitieth his children, so the Lord pitieth them that fear him" (Ps. ciii. 13). 29. **And he answering said to his father, Lo, these many years do I serve thee, neither transgressed I at any time thy commandment.** These last words are not to be pressed beyond their manifest intention — to express the constancy of his own love and service as a son towards his father, in contrast with the conduct of his brother. So Job, when resenting the charge of *hypocrisy*, brought against him by his friends, speaks as if nothing whatever could be laid to his charge: "When he hath tried me, I shall come forth as gold," &c. (Job xxiii. 10-12). And David too (Ps. xviii. 20-24); and the Church, in a time of persecution for righteousness' sake (Ps. xliv. 17-22). And the father in the sequel of this parable (*v.* 31) attests the truth of his son's protestation. **and yet thou never gavest me a kid**—'I say not a *calf*, but not even a *kid*,' that **I might make merry with my friends.** Here lay his misapprehension. It was no entertainment for the gratification of the prodigal: it was a *father's* expression of the joy *he* felt at his recovery. 30. **But as soon as this thy son was come, which hath devoured thy living with harlots, thou hast killed for him the fatted calf.** Mark the unworthy reflection on the common father of both, implied in these expressions—"*thy* son," "*thy* living;" the one brother not only disowning the other, but flinging him back upon his father, as if he should say, 'If such be the emotions which his return awakens, take him, and have joy of him!' 31. **And he said unto him, Son, thou art ever with me, and all that I have is thine.** The father resents not the insult—how could he, after the largeness of heart which had kissed the returning prodigal? He calmly expostulates with him, 'Son, listen to reason. What need for special, exuberant joy over thee? Saidst thou not, "Lo, these many years do I serve thee"? Wherefore then set the whole household a rejoicing over thee? For these is reserved *what is higher still*—the tranquil life-long satisfaction of thy father in thee, as a true-hearted faithful son in thy father's house; nor of the inheritance reserved for thee is aught alienated by this festive and fitting joy over the once foolish but now wise and newly recovered son.' 32. **It was meet that we should make merry and be glad: for this thy brother was dead, and is alive again; and was lost, and is found.** Should he simply take his long-vacant place in the family, without one special sign of wonder and delight at the change? Would that have been *nature?* But *this* being the meaning of the festivity, it would for that very reason be *temporary*. In time, the dutifulness of even the younger son would become the *law* and not the *exception:* he too at length might venture to say,
291

"Lo, these many years do I serve thee;" and of him the father would say, "Son, thou art ever with me." And then it would *not* be "meet that they should make merry and be glad"—as at his first return.

Remarks.—1. The estrangement of the human spirit from God is the deepest and most universal malady of our nature. It may take the form either of impatience of divine authority or of want of sympathy with the things wherein He delighteth. But important as is the distinction between these two forms of estrangement from God, they naturally run into each other, and are inseparable. In placid and amiable natures, what shows itself chiefly is *disrelish of spiritual things*. This may not take any active form, and in that case it is only perceptible in the heart's entire satisfaction *without God*. No fellowship with Him, or even thought of Him, is necessary to such. They get on perfectly well, and even better, when every such thought is away. This is truly a godless life, but it is the life of many of the most attractive and accomplished members of society. In young men it is apt to take the form of dislike of the restraints which divine authority imposes, and a desire to get free from them. But in all, it is the same malady at bottom, with which our fallen nature is smitten. 2. The extent to which men *go from God* varies as much as men themselves; but the freedom they assert in this condition is but bondage under another name. 3. It is not every discovery of the folly and bitterness of departure from God that will move the heart to retrace its steps; often matters go from bad to worse before any decisive change is resolved on; and in most cases it is only when the soul is brought to extremities that it says in earnest, "I will arise and go to my Father." And when, upon so doing, we are welcomed back, and feel the bond that binds us to our Father even firmer and dearer than if we had never departed, we find ours to be just such a case as the sweet Psalmist of Israel sings of: "Such as sit in darkness, and in the shadow of death, being bound in affliction and iron; because they rebelled against the words of God, and contemned the counsel of the Most High: therefore he brought down their heart with labour: they fell down, and there was none to help. Then they cried unto the Lord in their trouble, and he saved them out of their distresses. He brought them out of darkness and the shadow of death, and brake their bands in sunder:—O that men would praise the Lord for his goodness, and for his wonderful works to the children of men!" (Ps. cvii. 10-15.) 4. The pardon of sin is absolutely gratuitous, and reaches down to the lowest depths of estrangement from God and rebellion against his precepts. The one thing required is to "arise and go to our Father." "Go and proclaim these words toward the north, and say, *Return*, thou backsliding Israel, saith the Lord; and I will not cause mine anger to fall upon you: Only acknowledge thine iniquity, and I

16 AND he said also unto his disciples, There was a certain ^arich man which had a steward; and the same was accused unto him that he had
2 wasted his goods. And he called him, and said unto him, How is it that I hear this of thee? give an account ^bof thy stewardship; for thou mayest
3 be no longer steward. Then the steward said within himself, What shall I do? for my lord taketh away from me the stewardship: I cannot dig;
4 to beg I am ashamed. I am resolved what to do, that, when I am put out of the stewardship, they may receive me into their houses.
5 So he called every one of his lord's debtors *unto him*, and said unto the
6 first, How much owest thou unto my lord? And he said, An hundred ¹measures of oil. And he said unto him, Take thy bill, and sit down

A. D. 33.

CHAP. 16.
^a Ps. 24. 1.
^b Matt. 12. 36.
Rom. 14. 12.
1 The word Batus, in the original, containeth nine gallons three quarts.
Ezek. 45. 10, 11, 14.

---

will not cause mine anger to fall upon thee." 5. The sense of reconciliation to God, instead of checking, only deepens the grief of the pardoned believer for the sin that has been forgiven: "That thou mayest remember, and be confounded, and never open thy mouth any more because of thy shame, *when I am pacified toward thee for all that thou hast done*, saith the Lord God." (Ezek. xvi. 63). 'True repentance,' says Dr. Owen, 'waters a free pardon with tears, detests forgiven sin, and aims at the ruin of that which we are assured shall never ruin us.' 6. The deeper sunk and the longer estranged from God any sinner is, the more exuberant is the joy which his recovery occasions. All heaven is represented as ringing with it, while he himself breaks forth into such songs as these—"He brought me up out of a horrible pit, out of the miry clay, and set my feet upon a rock, and established my goings. And He hath put a new song into my mouth, even praise unto our God: Many shall see it, and fear, and trust in the Lord" (Ps. xl. 2, 3). But, 7. This joy over returning prodigals is *not* the portion of those whose whole lives have been spent in the service of their Father in heaven. Yet, instead of grudging the want of this, they should deem it the highest testimony to their life-long fidelity, that something better is reserved for them—the deep, abiding complacency of their Father in heaven. 8. In giving such an interpretation of the parable of the Prodigal Son as, in our judgment, bears consistency with all Scripture truth on its face, we have not adverted to interpretations which seem to us to miss the mark. The notion of not a few, that the younger son represents the *Gentiles*, who early strayed from God, and the elder the *Jews*, who abode true to Him, is rejected by the best expositors; and no wonder, since the publicans and sinners, whose welcome back to God is illustrated by the reception of the prodigal, were Jews and not Gentiles. Clearly this parable has to do, not with nationalities, but with classes or characters. But most interpreters—even such as *Trench*—misapprehend, we think, almost entirely the truth intended to be taught by the conduct of the elder son—who, he thinks, 'represents a form of legal righteousness, not altogether false, but low; who has been kept by the law from gross offences,' &c. Let the reader judge whether this interpretation, or that which we have given is the more consistent and eligible. 9. Was ever teaching like this heard on earth? Did even the Mouth that spake as never man spake utter such words of grace to the vilest—for fulness and melting tenderness of love—on any other recorded occasion? This is the *Gospel within the Gospel*, as it has been well called; and it will stand, while the world lasts, an evidence which no unsophisticated mind can resist, that He who uttered it must have come forth from the very bosom of the Father to declare it, and that him that cometh to Him He will in no wise cast out.

CHAP. XVI. 1-31.—THE PARABLE OF THE UNJUST STEWARD, AND FURTHER TEACHING SUGGESTED BY IT—THE PARABLE OF THE RICH MAN AND LAZARUS. No indication is given of the time and occasion of these two parables—as usual in this portion of our Gospel. (See opening remarks on ch. ix. 51.) But they appear to be in their natural order after the preceding, and a certain distant connection with them has been traced.

The Parable of the Unjust Steward (1-9). This parable has occasioned more discussion and diversity of opinion than all the rest. But judicious interpreters are now pretty much agreed as to its general import. 1. **And he said also unto his disciples**—not the Twelve exclusively, but His followers in the wider sense: **There was a certain rich man**—denoting the Great Lord of all, "the most high God, Possessor of heaven and earth," **which had a steward** [οἰκονόμον]—the manager of his estate; representing all who have gifts divinely committed to their *trust*, and so answering pretty nearly to the "servants" in the parable of the *Talents*, to whom were committed their lord's "goods." **and the same was accused** [διεβλήθη] **unto him that he had wasted his goods** [διασκορπίζων]—rather, 'was wasting his goods.' The word signifies to 'scatter,' and so to 'waste.' Information to this effect was lodged with his master. 2. **And he called him, and said unto him, How is it that I hear this of thee?** And thus does God from time to time—now by startling providences, and now in the secret whispers of conscience—charge home its abuse of gifts, and manifold guilt, very sharply upon the soul. **give an account of thy stewardship**—render up whatever has been entrusted to thee, that I may transfer it to other hands, **for thou mayest be no longer steward.** 3. **Then the steward said within himself, What shall I do? for my lord taketh away from me the stewardship.** His guilt is tacitly admitted, and his one question now is, what is to become of him? **I cannot dig**—brought up as I have been to higher work; **to beg I am ashamed**—his pride could not stand that. What, then, was to be done to prevent starvation? 4. **I am resolved what to do, that, when I am put out of the stewardship, they may receive me into their houses**—'in grateful return for the services I am going to do them.' Thus his one object was, *when cast out of one home to secure another.* This will be found to be the great lesson of the parable.

5. **So he called every one of his lord's debtors unto him, and said unto the first, How much owest thou unto my lord?** 6. **And he said, An hundred measures of oil** [βάτους]. The word indicates a prodigious debt. **And he said unto him, Take thy bill, and sit down quickly**—the business being urgent, **and write fifty**—'write a receipt for only half that quantity: the master, to be sure, will be defrauded, but he will never discover it, and thus half your debt is at once wiped out.' 7. **Then**

7 quickly, and write fifty. Then said he to another, And how much owest thou? And he said, An hundred [2]measures of wheat. And he said unto

8 him, Take thy bill, and write fourscore. And the lord commended the unjust steward, because he had done wisely: for the children of this world are in their generation wiser than [c]the children of light.

9 And I say unto you, [d]Make to yourselves friends of the [3]mammon of unrighteousness; that, when ye fail, they may receive you into everlasting

A. D. 33.

[2] About fourteen bushels and a pottle.

[c] John 12. 36.

[d] ch. 11. 41.

[3] Or. riches.

---

said he to another, And how much owest thou? And he said, An hundred measures [κόρους] of wheat—also a heavy debt. And he said unto him, Take thy bill, and write fourscore—or a fifth less than the actual debt. There is nothing of spiritual significance in these amounts. They represent merely the shrewdness with which the steward dealt with each debtor, with sole reference probably to the greater or less ability of each to render a grateful return to himself when cast upon the world. 8. And the lord—that is, the steward's lord, as he is expressly called in *vv.* 3, 5, **commended the unjust steward**—not the injustice of the steward; for what master would praise his servant for defrauding him? but he commended the man, **because he had done wisely** [φρονίμως]— 'shrewdly,' 'sagaciously,' 'prudently;' with commendable promptitude, foresight, and skilful adaptation of means to end: for "men will praise thee when thou doest well to thyself" (Ps. xlix. 18): **for**—this, now, is the reflection of the glorious Speaker of the parable, **the children of this world are in their generation** [εἰς τὴν γενεὰν τὴν ἑαυτῶν]— rather, 'for their own generation;' that is, for the purposes of their own kind, or sort, or class; their own sphere of interest and action, **wiser** [φρονιμώτεροι]—'shrewder' **than the children of** [the] **light** [τοῦ φωτός]. Let us examine this most weighty saying. It divides all men, according to the all-pervading doctrine of Scripture, into two great classes. The one is called "THE CHILDREN OF THIS WORLD" [τοῦ αἰῶνος τούτου]—(see on Eph. ii. 2), meaning what we call *worldlings.* The Psalmist, after calling this class "men of this world," gives the following striking definition of what he means—"who *have their portion in this life*" (Ps. xvii. 14); and of the same class the apostle says, they "mind" [φρονοῦντες] or 'are taken up with,' "earthly things" (Phil. iii. 19). Their whole ambition, whether their inclinations be grovelling or refined, is bounded by the present sphere, and they have no taste for anything beyond it. The other class are beautifully called "THE CHILDREN OF LIGHT," as being the offspring of supernatural heavenly teaching, for "God, who commanded the light to shine out of darkness, hath shined in our hearts, to give the light of the knowledge of the glory of God in the face of Jesus Christ" (2 Cor. iv. 6). "While ye have the Light [τὸ φῶς], believe in the light, that ye may be the children of light" (John xii. 36). "Ye are all the children of the light and of the day" (1 Thess. v. 5). See also Eph. v. 8. And yet, though the latter class are to the former as superior as light is to darkness, the children of this world have in one point the advantage of the children of light—they excel them in the shrewdness with which they prosecute their proper business. It is not that they are more truly wise; but that in their own sphere they display a sagacity which the children of light may well emulate, and should strive to outdo. Their sphere is indeed a wretched enough one. But let the children of light observe what a definite and firm grasp they take of the objects at which they aim; how shrewdly they adapt their means to their ends, and with what untiring energy, determination,

and perseverance they prosecute their purposes. All these are wasted, to be sure, on perishable objects and in fleeting enjoyments. Spiritual and eternal realities are a region they never penetrate —the new life is an air they never breathe, an undiscovered world, an unborn existence: they know nothing, sympathize with nothing, live for nothing but "their own generation." But why should such excel the children of light *in anything?* This is exactly what our Lord here says they *should not;* and in giving forth this parable He would stir up our jealousy to roll away that reproach— just as on another occasion He sends us for lessons of this same "wisdom" to venomous "serpents" (Matt. x. 16).

Further Teaching suggested by this Parable (9-18). Having laid down the great general principle, that 'it is not enough to have a high and holy *sphere* of action, but there must be such a discreet and determined prosecution of its objects as the children of this world so much excel in'—our Lord now comes to particulars; and, first, to that point of wisdom which the parable most directly illustrates. 9. **And I say unto you, Make to yourselves friends of** [ἐκ] —rather, 'out of' **the mammon of unrighteousness**—that is, by the help of it. The word "mammon" [μαμωνᾶς]—on which see on Matt. vi. 24—stands here just for those *riches* which the children of this world idolize, or live supremely for; and it is called "the mammon of unrighteousness," or "the unrighteous mammon" (*v.* 11), apparently because of the unrighteous abuse of it which so prevails. The injunction, then, is to this effect: 'Turn to your own highest advantage those riches which the unrighteous so shamefully abuse, in the spirit of that forecasting sagacity which this unjust steward displayed.' **that when ye fail** [ὅταν ἐκλίπητε]—that is, in respect of life: a remarkable expression, but suggested here, as we think, from a certain analogy which our departure from this world has to the *breaking up* of the steward's comfortable condition, and his being forced to *quit.* [*Lachmann* and *Tregelles,* retaining the same aoristic tense, adopt the singular ἐκλίπῃ—'when it has failed;' while *Tischendorf* prefers the present tense, ἐκλείπῃ, also in the singular—'when it fails.' *Meyer* and *Alford,* too, decide in favour of the singular, for which the authority is perhaps greater than for the plural of the received text. But even if we should have to adopt this reading, the sense must be held the same; we must still understand our Lord to speak, on that supposition, of the failure of mammon solely by our removal from the present scene.] **they may receive you**—that is, the "friends" ye make by the mammon of unrighteousness, **into everlasting habitations**— into "mansions" more durable than this steward was welcomed into when turned out of doors. But how are these friends to receive us into everlasting habitations? By rising up as witnesses of what we did in their behalf for Jesus' sake. Thus, the only difference between this view of the saints' admission to heaven and that in our Lord's grand description of the Last Judgment (Matt. xxv. 34-40) is, that there Christ Himself as Judge speaks for them, in the character of omniscient

10 habitations. He 'that is faithful in that which is least is faithful also in
11 much; and he that is unjust in the least is unjust also in much. If
    therefore ye have not been faithful in the unrighteous [4] mammon, who will
12 commit to your trust the *f* true *riches?* And if ye have not been faithful
    in that which is another man's, who shall give you that which is your own?
13 No *g* servant can serve two masters: for either he will hate the one, and
    love the other; or else he will hold to the one, and despise the other.
    Ye cannot serve God and mammon.
14   And the Pharisees also, *h* who were covetous, heard all these things:
15 and they derided him. And he said unto them, Ye are they which
    i justify yourselves before men; but God *j* knoweth your hearts: for *k* that
    which is highly esteemed among men is abomination in the sight of
16 God. The *l* Law and the Prophets *were* until John: since that time the
17 kingdom of God is preached, and every man presseth into it. And *m* it
    is easier for heaven and earth to pass, than one tittle of the Law to fail.
18 Whosoever *n* putteth away his wife, and marrieth another, committeth
    adultery: and whosoever marrieth her that is put away from *her* husband
    committeth adultery.

A. D. 33.

e Matt. 25, 21.
ch. 19. 17.
4 Or, riches.
f Eph. 3. 8.
Rev. 3 18.
g Matt. 6. 24.
h Matt. 23. 14.
i ch. 10. 29.
ch. 11. 39, 40.
Jas. 2. 21-
25.
j Ps. 7. 9.
Jer. 17. 10.
Rev. 2. 23.
k 1 Sam. 16. 7.
Jas. 4. 4.
l Matt. 11. 12.
m Ps. 102. 26,
27.
Isa. 40. 8.
Isa. 51. 6.
1 Pet. 1. 25.
n 1 Cor. 7. 10.

Spectator of their acts of beneficence to "His brethren;" while here, these brethren of Jesus are supposed to be the speakers in their behalf. There, Christ says, "I was an hungered, and ye gave Me meat;" for "inasmuch as ye did it unto the least of these my brethren, ye did it unto me." Here, these least of Christ's brethren themselves come forward, one after another, saying, 'I was hungry, and that dear saint gave me bread;' 'and I was naked, and that other saint clothed me;' 'and I was sick, and that saint there paid me such heavenly visits;' 'and I was in prison for Thy name's sake, but that fearless one came unto me, and was not ashamed of my chain.' 'And they did it unto Thee, Lord!' "Come, then," will the King say unto them, "ye blessed of My Father, inherit the kingdom prepared for you from the foundation of the world." 'Thus, like this steward (so teaches Jesus here), when turned out of one home shall ye secure another; but better than he, a heavenly for an earthly, an everlasting for a temporary habitation.' Money is not here made the key to heaven, more than "the deeds done in the body" in general, according to which, as a test of character—not by the merit of which—men are to be judged (2 Cor. v. 10). See on Matt. xxv 31-40, with the corresponding Remarks at the close of that Section. **10. He that is faithful in that which is least is faithful also in much; and he that is unjust in the least is unjust also in much.** A maxim of great pregnancy and value; advancing now from the *prudence* which the steward had, to the *fidelity* which he had not; to that "*harmlessness* of the dove" to which "the serpent," with all his "*wisdom*" or subtilty is a total stranger. But what bearing has this maxim on the subject of our parable? A very close connection. 'As for me (some would say) I have too little of "the unrighteous mammon" to be much interested in this parable.' 'You are wrong,' is the reply: 'That is the speech of the slothful servant, who, because he was entrusted with but one talent by his master, went and hid it in the earth instead of using it. Fidelity depends not on the *amount entrusted*, but on the *sense of responsibility*. He that feels this in little will feel it in much, and conversely.' **11. If therefore ye have not been faithful in the unrighteous mammon**—or, "the mammon of unrighteousness" (*v.* 9), **who will commit to your trust the true riches?**—that which makes one truly rich, the riches of the kingdom above. **12. And if ye have**

not been faithful in that which is another man's —the pecuniary and other earthly means which are but *lent* us, and must be held at best as only *entrusted* to us, **who shall give you that which is your own?** This verse gives an important turn to the subject. Here all we have is *on trust* as stewards, who have an account to render. Hereafter, what the faithful have will be *their own property,* being no longer on probation, but in secure, undisturbed, rightful, everlasting possession and enjoyment of all that is graciously bestowed on us. Thus money is neither to be *idolized* nor *despised:* we must sit loose to it, but use it for God's glory. **No servant can serve**—or, *be entirely at the command of* two masters. This is true even where there is no hostility between them: how much more where they are in deadly opposition! **for either he will hate the one, and love the other; or else he will hold to the one, and despise the other. Ye cannot serve God and mammon.** This shows that the two masters here intended are such as are in uncompromising hostility to each other. (See on the same saying in the Sermon on the Mount, Matt. vi. 24.)

14. And the Pharisees also, who were covetous, heard all these things: and they derided him. [ἐξεμυκτήριζον]—sneered at Him; their master, sin, being too plainly struck at. But it was easier to *ridicule* than to *refute* such teaching. **15. And he said unto them, Ye are they which justify yourselves before men; but God knoweth your hearts: for that which is highly esteemed among men**—who are easily carried away by plausible appearances (see 1 Sam. xvi. 7; and ch. xiv. 11), **is abomination in the sight of God**—who, Himself true, loathes all hypocrisy. **16. The Law and the Prophets were until John: since that time the kingdom of God is preached, and every man presseth into it.** 'While publicans and sinners are eagerly pressing into the kingdom of God, ye, interested adherents of the mere forms of an economy which is passing away, "discerning not the signs of this time," are allowing the tide to go past you, and will be found a stranded monument of blindness and obstinacy.' **17. And it is easier for heaven and earth to pass, than one tittle of the Law to fail.** See on Matt. v. 17, 18. **18. Whosoever putteth away his wife, and marrieth another, committeth adultery: and whosoever marrieth her that is put away from her husband committeth adultery.** See on Matt. xix. 3-9. Far from intend-

19　There was a certain rich man, which was clothed in purple and fine
20　linen, and fared sumptuously every day: and there was a certain beggar
21　named Lazarus, which was laid at his gate, °full of sores, and desiring to
　　　be fed with the crumbs which fell from the rich man's table: moreover
22　the dogs came and licked his sores. And it came to pass, that the
　　　beggar died, and ᴾwas carried by the angels into Abraham's ᑫbosom: the
23　rich man also died, and was buried; and in hell he lifted up his eyes,
　　　being in torments, and seeth Abraham afar off, and Lazarus in his bosom.
24　And he cried and said, Father Abraham, have mercy on me, and send
　　　Lazarus, that he may dip the tip of his finger in water, and ʳcool my
25　tongue; for I ˢam tormented in this flame. But Abraham said, Son,
　　　ᵗremember that thou in thy lifetime receivedst thy good things, and
　　　likewise Lazarus evil things: but now he is comforted, and thou art

A. D. 83.

° Heb. 11. 37.
ᴾ Ps. 34. 7.
　Ps. 91. 10,
　12.
　Ps. 103. 20.
　Heb 1. 14.
　Jas 2. 5.
ᑫ Matt. 8. 11.
ʳ Zec. 14. 12.
ˢ Isa. 66. 24.
　Mark 9. 44.
　Heb. 10. 31.
ᵗ Job 21. 13.
　Ps. 17. 14.
　ch. 6. 24.
　Rom. 8. 7.

---

ing to weaken the force of the law, by these allusions to a new economy, our Lord only sends home, in this unexpected way, its high requirements with a pungency which the Pharisees would not fail to feel.

The Parable of the Rich Man and Lazarus (19-31). This parable, being precisely the converse of the former, was evidently spoken immediately after it, and designed to complete the lesson of *The Right Use of Riches.* As the steward made himself *friends* out of the mammon of unrighteousness, so this rich man made himself, out of the same mammon, an *enemy* — in the person of Lazarus — of a kind to make the ears of every one that heareth it to tingle. As, by acting for eternity, in the spirit of this steward for time, the friends we thus make will on our removal from this scene "receive us into everlasting habitations," so by acting, even while professing to be Christians, in the spirit of this rich man, the enemies we thus make will rise up to shut us out for ever from the mansions of the blest. Such is the striking connection between these two parables. This last one, however, is altogether of a higher order and deeper significance than the former. The thin veil — of exclusion from one earthly home only to be followed by admission into others equally earthly — is thrown off; and the awful bearing of the use we now make of the mammon of unrighteousness upon our eternal state is presented before the eye in the light of the eternal flames, insomuch that the lurid glare of the scene abides with even the most cursory reader.

19. **There was a certain rich man** ["Ανθρωπος δὲ τις]. The connecting particle should not have been omitted here — 'But there was a certain rich man;' in contrast with the man of the former parable: **which was clothed in purple and fine linen** (See Esth. viii. 15; Rev. xviii. 12), **and fared sumptuously every day** — wanting for nothing which appetite craved, and taste fancied, and money could procure. 20. **And there was a certain beggar named Lazarus** — equivalent to the Old Testament *Eleazer.* The naming of this precious saint adds much to the liveliness of the picture; but to conclude from this that the story was founded on fact, is going rather far. Cases of this heartless nature are, alas, but too common everywhere. **which was laid at his gate.** So he had to be carried and laid down at it. **full of sores** — open, running sores, which, as appears from the next verse, had not been closed, nor bound up, nor mollified with ointment (Isa. i. 6). 21. **And desiring to be fed** [ἐπιθυμῶν χορτασθῆναι] **with the crumbs which fell from the rich man's table.** The meaning may either be (as in ch. xv. 16), that 'he was fain to feed' or 'gladly fed,' as *Alford, Webster*

and Wilkinson, &c., take it; or he 'desired to be fed,' but was not: so *Grotius, Bengel, Meyer, Trench,* &c., understand it. The context seems rather to favour this latter view. **moreover the dogs came and licked his sores** — a touching act of brute pity in the absence of human relief. Thus have we here a case of heartless indifference, amidst luxuries of every kind, to one of God's poorest and most afflicted ones, presented daily before the view. 22. **And it came to pass, that the beggar died, and was carried by the angels into Abraham's bosom** — as if he had been seen reclining next to him at the heavenly feast (see on ch. vii. 9). **the rich man also died, and was buried.** The burial of the beggar was too unimportant to mention; but it is said, "the rich man died, and was *buried*" — his carcase borne in pomp to its earthly resting-place. 23. **And in hell he lifted up his eyes** [ἐν τῷ ἅδῃ] — not the final region of the lost, for which another word is used [γέεννα] (Mark ix. 43, 45, 47, &c.), but what we call 'the unseen world.' Yet since the object here is certainly to depict *the whole torment* of the one and *the perfect bliss* of the other, it comes in this case to much the same thing. **being in torments, and seeth Abraham afar off** — quite beyond his reach, yet not beyond his view. **and Lazarus in his bosom.** 24. **And he cried and said, Father Abraham** — a well-founded but unavailing claim of natural descent (see ch. iii. 8; John viii. 37), **have mercy on me** — 'Have mercy on me who never showed any mercy to my fellow-men.' Not daring to cry to God, he applies in his desperation to one who has no power to help him. **and send Lazarus** — the pining victim of his merciless neglect, **that he may** — do what? take him out of that place of torment? No, that he presumes not to ask; but merely, **that he may dip the tip of his finger in water, and cool my tongue; for I am tormented in this flame.** What does this wretched man ask? He asks the *least* conceivable and the *most momentary* abatement of his torment — that is all. But even that is denied him, for two awfully weighty reasons. First, IT IS UNREASONABLE. 25. **But Abraham said, Son** — a stinging acknowledgment this of the *natural* relationship to him which he had claimed: **remember that thou in thy lifetime receivedst thy good things, and likewise Lazarus evil things: but now he is comforted, and thou art tormented.** As it is a great law of God's kingdom that 'the nature of our present desires shall rule that of our future bliss,' so by that law, he whose "good things," craved and enjoyed, were all bounded by time, could look for none after his connection with time had come to an end (see ch. vi. 24). But by the same law, he whose "evil things," all crowded into the present life, drove him to seek, and find, consolation in a

26 tormented. And besides all this, between us and you there is "a great gulf fixed: so that they which would pass from hence to you cannot;
27 neither can they pass to us, that *would come* from thence. Then he said, I pray thee therefore, father, that thou wouldest send him to my father's
28 house: for I have five brethren; that he may testify unto them, lest
29 they also come into this place of torment. Abraham saith unto him,
30 'They have Moses and the Prophets; let them hear them. And he said, Nay, father Abraham: but if one went unto them from the dead, they

A. D. 33.
" 2 Thes. 1. 9.
▾ Isa. 8. 20. Isa. 34. 16.
John 5. 39, 45.
Acts 15. 21.
Acts 17. 11.
2 Tim. 3.15.

---

life beyond the grave, is by death released from all evil and ushered into unmixed and uninterrupted good. See ch. vi. 21. But secondly, IT IS IMPOSSIBLE. 26. **And besides all this**—independently of this consideration, **between us and you there is a great gulf fixed: so that they which would pass from hence to you cannot; neither can they pass to us, that would come from thence.** 'By an irrevocable decree there has been established [ἐστήρικται] a vast impassable abyss between the two states and the occupants of each.' 27. **Then he said**—now abandoning all hope, not only of release but relief for himself, and directing his thoughts to others, **I pray thee therefore, father, that thou wouldest send him to my father's house: 28. For I have five brethren; that he may testify unto them, lest they also come into this place of torment.** There is here no waking up of good in the heart of the lost, but, as *Trench* acutely remarks, bitter reproach against God and the old economy, as not having warned him sufficiently. Abraham's answer rolls back the reproach with calm dignity, as unmerited: '.They *are* sufficiently warned.' 29. **Abraham saith unto him, They have Moses and the Prophets; let them hear them.** Still this does not satisfy. 30. **And he said, Nay, father Abraham**—giving him the lie, **but if one went unto them from the dead, they will repent.** What a reply now is given to this, shutting up the dialogue where it ought to close—when nothing more remains to be said on the one hand, and nothing can be replied on the other. 31. **And he said unto him, If they hear not Moses and the Prophets, neither will they be persuaded though one rose from the dead.** A principle of awful magnitude and importance. The greatest miracle will have no effect on those who are determined not to believe. A *real* Lazarus soon "rose from the dead;" but the sight of him by crowds of people, who were thereby drawn so far towards Christ, only crowned the unbelief and hastened the murderous plots of the Pharisees against the Lord of glory; nor has *His own resurrection,* far more overpowering, yet won over that "crooked and perverse nation."

Remarks.—1. The parable of the Unjust Steward has this in common with the Parable of the *Talents* (Matt. xxv. 14-30), that both represent all we possess as a sacred *Trust* committed to us; for the right use of which we are responsible; and the actual use made of which shall go to determine our eternal state. But in the Parable of the Talents the trust intended comprehends *all endowments* whatsoever that may be turned to the service of Christ; here it is *money* alone, the love of which is the root of all evil (1 Tim. vi. 10), and whose slaves and worshippers were among the audience to which it was addressed (v. 13, 14). There, the talents are to be used for the *Master's* interest; here, the immediate object is to enforce such a use of money as may promote *our own* interest in the highest sense of it. Thus, the same general subject has different aspects, which, though consistent, are not to be confounded. 2. Let us ponder the Lord's weighty saying, that the children of this world are in their generation wiser than the children of light. 'These religious people (methinks I hear some supercilious observer of Christians say—so very impartial as to be "neither cold nor hot") may be all very good, but they have small common sense; their principles are fine—most unexceptionable—but they are wonderfully airy: they somehow want the substance of things earthly; they cannot be grasped; and even those who make so much of them go about them in so unbusinesslike a fashion, and with so little of the shrewdness and energy we are used to in common matters, that one may be excused for not surrendering himself to such notions, and resting contented with those general views which commend themselves to every one, and about which there is no dispute.' This witness is true: spiritual things are all too airy for such persons; they have substance only to faith here, and of that they have none: Theirs is a world of sense; the things which are *seen* are their sphere; and right easily are they grasped, and all congenial to the natural man: in hunting after them they go with the stream—to which the remonstrances of conscience and of Scripture oppose but a feeble barrier. No wonder, then, that shrewdness is stamped upon all that is done in this sphere, and no thanks for it to them and theirs. But ours is a world of faith and hope; and hope that is *seen* is not hope; for what a man seeth, why doth he yet hope for? but if we hope for that we *see not*, then do we with patience wait for it. We know Whom we have believed; we have made our choice, and mean to abide by it, nor will it ever be taken from us. Nevertheless, we stand rebuked. 'Thou hast said too much truth of us, thou cold, supercilious critic of our poor Christianity, but our gracious Master said it before thee. We thank thee not, but we thank Him, and mean, with His help, to wipe away this reproach.' And now, will not my Christian readers try to do it? We know very well it is because the things of this present world are "seen" that they are more vividly apprehended, and so —all "temporal," though they be—more powerfully grasped, than the things which are "not seen," even though they be "eternal." We know full well how keenly we feel the one, and how languidly the other; what sacrifices of time and strength, yea, what risks of life itself men will readily incur, to promote their temporal interests, and how little of all this even the children of God will go through with for those which are eternal. But as our Lord holds this up as a reproach, and here sends us to the worldling for wisdom—even as the sluggard is sent to the ant for activity—let us not rest in *explanations* of the fact, but rather strive to reverse it. What we want from the men of the world is not so much their shrewd management of affairs, as that *vivid apprehension of our own sphere* which shall convert our world ·of *faith* into substance and *sense* to us; then shall we have grasp enough and energy enough; for "this is the victory that overcometh the world, even our faith." Yet along with this—as in

31 will repent. And he said unto him, If they hear not Moses and the Prophets, *w*neither will they be persuaded though one rose from the dead.

A. D. 33.

w John 12. 10.
2 Cor. 4. 3.

temporal things—*habits* of steady vigilance and activity have much to do with success in spiritual things; and this parable will not have produced its proper fruit till the children of light, ashamed of being excelled in anything for eternity by the worldly wisdom of the children of this world, shall bend their efforts to rise above them in all such things, commanding its respect and compelling its admiration for this superiority. "If any of you lack wisdom, let him ask of God, who giveth to all liberally, and upbraideth not; and it shall be given him" (Jas. i. 5). 3. This and similar portions of Scripture have been so sadly abused to support the fatal doctrine of the merit of good works, and especially of charity to the poor and needy, that not a few Christians have been scared away from such scriptures, and are little aware what a test of character at the great day will be the use they make of the pecuniary means with which they are entrusted. Should any say, That can hardly apply to those who have so little of this world's goods as I have, let them consider whether they are not acting the unprofitable servant in the parable of the Talents, who, because his lord had given him but one talent, went and hid it in the earth; and let them remember the pregnant and comprehensive maxim, "He that is faithful in the least is faithful also in much, and he that is unfaithful in the least is unfaithful also in much." 4. How entirely is the divinest teaching thrown away upon those who, like the Pharisaic portion of our Lord's audience, are resolved not to part with the sinful courses which it exposes and condemns! But the "derision" of those "covetous" Pharisees at such teaching as that of this Section was the best evidence of its power. 5. In the parable of the rich man and Lazarus, were the poverty and disease of this dear saint of God so extreme as is here represented, and, to add to all, when laid down at the rich man's gate, in hope of at length moving his compassion, is he represented as dying just as he was? Then, let no one so interpret the promises of divine compassion and provision for the godly poor as to think that they may not be left to live and die as poor and as neglected of men as this Lazarus. But neither let God's providence be maligned on this account, until we know how He deals with the *spirits* of such. Did we know what unseen ministrations of angels He sends them, and with what seasons of nearness to Himself He favours them, in the absence of human consolation, with what light He irradiates their darkness, how out of weakness He makes them strong, and how in patience and hope He makes them to possess their souls—giving them "songs in the night," unknown to the prosperous even of His own children (Rev. xiv. 3)—we should perhaps change our mind, and be almost tempted to envy "Lazarus" with all his miseries. As he looked at the sycophantish visitors who went in and out of the rich man's gate, regardless of him, methinks I hear him saying with the sweet singer of Israel, "There be many that say, Who will show us any good? Lord, lift thou up the light of Thy countenance upon us: Thou hast put gladness in my heart more than in the time when their corn and their wine increased. Deliver my soul from the wicked, from men of the world, which have their portion in this life, and whose belly Thou fillest with Thy hid treasure: As for me, I shall behold Thy face in righteousness; I shall be satisfied, when I wake, with Thy likeness" (Ps. iv. 6, 7;

xvii. 13-15). And see him at last: Those angels are not ashamed of his poverty, nor repelled away by his sores. His wasted skeleton—to men a sightless carcase—is to them beautiful as the shrine of a redeemed spirit; and that spirit is more beautiful still, in its resemblance to God, its likeness to themselves, its meetness for glory. They hover over the beggarly habitation, and surround the mean pallet, and watch the last effort of the spirit to break away from its falling tenement, that at the appointed hour they may convey it in triumph to its celestial home. O that men—that even Christians—would judge less by the outward appearance, and try, like the Lord, to look upon the heart! 6. And how beautiful is the view here given us of the ministrations of angels, especially at the death-bed of the saints. Often do they tell us, they *see* them waiting for them and smiling on them. They are ready to stretch out their arms to them, to signify their readiness at that moment to be taken up by them; and they ask us, sometimes, if *we* do not see them too. Of course we don't, for we live in a world of sense. But they are then leaving it; it has all but closed upon them, and they are getting within the precincts of heaven. Who, then, shall say that they see not what is hid from us; and since what they affirm they see is only what is here represented as a reality, who, with this parable before him, shall say that such sights are but the fruit of a distempered imagination, a picture of the fevered or languid brain? 7. How frequently do the terrors of hell recur, and how terrific are the representations given of it, in the teaching of our Lord! Here, its unutterable and inconceivable horrors are depicted with a vividness altogether astonishing. And the unreasonableness and impossibility of the *slightest* and *briefest* abatement of them, which is here proclaimed as from the other world itself, only completes the representation. And mark how this unreasonableness is grounded wholly on the life and conduct of the lost in the present world—rendering any change in their condition in eternity as hopeless as their being able to undo their past life by living over again and acting otherwise. Need it be asked whether the *perpetuity of hell-torments*, and the *character* of them too—as but the natural development and fitting termination of a life of ungodliness—could be more emphatically taught? 8. Though we are not to press the *language* of the parables unduly, does it not seem a legitimate inference from the whole strain of this Parable, that the lost will, as an aggravation of their torment, in some way or other, either *see* the bliss of the saved in heaven, or have such a vivid knowledge of what it is as will amount to a kind of sight? And are not those other words of Christ confirmatory of this? "Ye shall *see* Abraham, and Isaac, and Jacob, and all the prophets, in the kingdom of God, and you yourselves thrust out"? (ch. xiii. 28). 9. Nowhere is the sufficiency of revealed truth in general, and of the *Old Testament* Scriptures in particular, for all the purposes of *salvation*, so emphatically stated as by our Lord in the closing verses of this chapter, who puts it into the mouth of Abraham from the unseen world. Men are fain to believe that if they had this or that evidence which they have not, they would repent and be converted. And because they are not startled into faith—because their impenitence is not overpowered by resistless occurrences—they think

17 THEN said he unto the disciples, ^aIt is impossible but that offences
2 will come: but ^bwoe *unto him* through whom they come! It were better
    for him that a millstone were hanged about his neck, and he cast into the
3 sea, than that he should offend one of these little ones. Take heed to
    yourselves: ^cIf thy brother trespass against thee, ^drebuke him; and if he
4 repent, ^eforgive him. And if he trespass against thee seven times in a
    day, and seven times in a day turn again to thee, saying, I repent; thou
    shalt forgive him.
5, And the apostles said unto the Lord, Increase our faith. And ^fthe
6 Lord said, If ye had faith as a grain of mustard seed, ye might say unto
    this sycamine tree, Be thou plucked up by the root, and be thou planted
    in the sea; and it should obey you.
7 But which of you, having a servant plowing or feeding cattle, will say
    unto him by and by, when he is come from the field, Go and sit down to
8 meat? And will not rather say unto him, Make ready wherewith I may
    sup, and gird thyself, ^gand serve me, till I have eaten and drunken; and
9 afterward thou shalt eat and drink? Doth he thank that servant because
10 he did the things that were commanded him? I trow not. So likewise
    ye, when ye shall have done all those things which are commanded you,
    say, We are ^hunprofitable servants: we have done that which was our
    duty to do.
11 And it came to pass, ⁱas he went to Jerusalem, that he passed through

A. D. 33.
CHAP. 17.
^a Matt. 18. 6, 7.
Mark 9. 42.
1 Cor 11.19.
^b 2 Thes. 1.6.
^c Matt.18.15.
^d Lev. 19. 17.
Pro. 17. 10.
Jas. 5. 19.
^e 1 Cor. 13. 4.
Col. 3. 12.
^f Matt 17.20.
Matt.21.21.
Mark 9. 23.
Mark 11.23.
^g ch. 12. 37.
^h Job 22. 3.
Job 35. 7.
Ps. 16. 2.
Matt 25.37-40.
Rom. 3. 12.
Rom. 11.35.
1 Cor 9. 16.
Phie. 11.
ⁱ Luke 9. 51.
John 4. 4.

there will be some excuse for them if at last they are found unchanged. But the Lord here shuts us absolutely up to THE REVEALED WORD, as *God's ordained means of all saving effect upon the heart and life.* (See 2 Pet. i. 19; John v. 39, 46, 47; xvii. 17.) And if this be true, need we add, that the *right* and the *duty* of all to "search the Scriptures," and the apostasy from a Scripture foundation of any Church that would prohibit the general searching of them—as the Church of Rome does—follow by necessary consequence?

CHAP. XVII. 1-19.—FURTHER DISCOURSE ON OFFENCES, FAITH, AND HUMILITY.—TEN LEPERS CLEANSED.—Whether this was delivered in continuation of what is recorded in the preceding chapter, it is impossible to say; but probably it came close upon it.

Offences (1-4). **1, 2. Then said he unto the disciples, It is impossible but that offences, &c. It were better for him that a millstone, &c.** See on Mark ix. 42. **3. Take heed to yourselves**—Guard your spirit: **If thy brother trespass against thee, rebuke him; and if he repent, forgive him. 4. And if he trespass against thee seven times in a day, and seven times in a day turn again to thee, saying, I repent; thou shalt forgive him**—that is, 'however often;' seven being the number of completeness. So that this is not a *lower* measure of forgiving love than the "seventy-times seven times" was, enjoined upon Peter; for that was merely because Peter had asked if he was to *stop* at seven times—to which the reply was, ' No, not though it should come to seventy times that number.' See on Matt. xviii. 21, 22.

Faith (5, 6). **5. And the apostles said unto the Lord** (see on Luke xi. 1), **Increase our faith.** What prompted so peculiar a petition? No doubt the felt difficulty of carrying into effect such holy directions—the difficulty first of avoiding offences, and next of forgiving them so divinely. This is the only instance in which *a spiritual operation upon their souls* was solicited of Christ by the Twelve; but a kindred and even higher prayer had been offered to Him before, by one with far

fewer opportunities, which in all likelihood first suggested to them this prayer. See on Mark ix. 24, and Remark 3 at the close of that Section. **6. And the Lord said, If ye had faith as a grain of mustard seed, ye might say unto this sycamine**—or mulberry **tree, Be thou plucked up by the root, and be thou planted in the sea; and it should obey you.** See on Mark xi. 22-24, and Remark 3 at the close of that Section.

Humility (7-10). **7. But which of you, having a servant plowing or feeding cattle, will say unto him by and by**—or 'directly' [εὐθέως]—**when he is come from the field, Go and sit down to meat?** By this way of arranging and pointing the words, the sense is obscured. It would be clearer thus: 'Which of you, having a servant ploughing or feeding cattle, will say unto him, when he is come from the field, Go directly, and sit down to meat.' **8. And will not rather say unto him, Make ready wherewith I may sup, and gird thyself, and serve me, till I have eaten and drunken; and afterward thou shalt eat and drink? 9. Doth he thank that servant because he did the things that were commanded him? I trow not** [οὐ δοκῶ]—or as we say, when much more is meant, 'I presume not,' or 'I should think not.' **10. So likewise ye, when ye shall have done all those things which are commanded you, say, We are unprofitable servants.** The word 'unprofitable' [ἀχρεῖοι], though in modern English denoting the *opposite* of profit, is here used in its proper *negative* sense, 'We have not profited' or 'benefited God at all by our services.' The connection of this with the subject discoursed of may be thus expressed—'But when your faith has been so increased as both to avoid and forgive offences, and do things impossible to all but faith—even then, be not puffed up as though you had laid the Lord under any obligations to you.' (Compare Job xxii. 2, 3; Rom. xi. 35.)

Ten Lepers Cleansed (11-19). **11. And it came to pass, as he went to Jerusalem, that he**—The 'He' is emphatic [καὶ αὐτὸς]—**passed through the midst of Samaria and Galilee** [διὰ μέσου Σαμαρείας]. This may mean, 'between Samaria and Galilee,' that is, on the frontiers of both; but

12 the midst of Samaria and Galilee. And as he entered into a certain village, there met him ten men that were lepers, which ^jstood afar off:

13 and they lifted up *their* voices, and said, Jesus, Master, have mercy on

14 us. And when he saw *them*, he said unto them, ^kGo show yourselves unto the priests. And it came to pass, that, as they went, they were cleansed.

15 And one of them, when he saw that he was healed, turned back, and with

16 a loud voice ^lglorified God, and fell down on *his* face at his feet, giving

17 him thanks: and he was ^ma Samaritan. And Jesus answering said,

18 Were there not ten cleansed? but where *are* the nine? There are not

19 found that returned to give glory to God, save this stranger. And ⁿhe said unto him, Arise, go thy way: thy faith hath made thee whole.

20 And when he was demanded of the Pharisees, when the kingdom of God should come, he answered them and said, The kingdom of God

21 cometh not ¹with observation: neither shall they say, Lo here! or, lo there! for, behold, ^othe kingdom of God is ²within you.

A. D. 33.
j Lev. 13. 46.
k Lev. 13. 2.
Lev. 14. 2.
Matt. 8. 4.
l Ps. 103. 1.
m 2 Ki. 17. 24.
John 8. 48.
n Matt. 9. 22.
Mark 5. 34.
1 Or, with outward show.
John 18. 36.
o Rom. 14.17.
Col. 1. 27.
2 Or, among you.
John 1. 26.
Gal. 6. 15.

without passing through them—as *Meyer, Alford, Webster and Wilkinson,* &c., take it: or, it may mean, "through the midst of Samaria and Galilee," in the sense of passing through those regions —as *de Wette* and *Olshausen* understand it. But in this sense the phrase is scarcely a natural one; nor does it seem to us likely that our Evangelist means his readers to understand that this was a fresh journey through those great divisions of the country. We prefer, therefore, the former sense. But the whole chronology of this large portion of our Gospel is difficult. See remarks prefixed to ch. ix. 51. **12. And as he entered into a certain village, there met him ten men that were lepers, which stood afar off.** See the affecting directions laid down for such in Lev. xiii. 45, 46. That there should be so many as ten in one locality shows how numerous they, as well as possessed persons, must have been in Palestine in our Lord's time—no doubt with a view to the manifestation of His glory in healing them. **13. And they lifted up their voices**—their common misery, as *Trench* remarks, drawing these poor outcasts together (see 2 Ki. vii. 3), nay, causing them to forget the fierce national antipathy which reigned between Jew and Samaritan. **and said, Jesus, Master** [ἐπιστάτα], **have mercy on us.** How quick a teacher is felt misery, even though in some cases (as in all but one here) the teaching may be soon forgotten! **14. And when he saw them, he said unto them, Go show yourselves unto the priests**—that is, as cleansed persons. See on Matt. viii. 4. One of these was a Samaritan; but he too was required to go with the rest, thus teaching him that "Salvation was of the Jews" (John iv. 22). And yet, when ordered to do this, *they had not been cleansed.* A great trial of faith this was. But they obeyed. **And it came to pass, that, as they went, they were cleansed.** In how many different ways were our Lord's cures wrought, and this different from all the rest! Yet it closely resembled the cure of the nobleman's son (John iv. 50-53). **15. And one of them, when he saw that he was healed, turned back, and with a loud voice glorified God.** Forgetting all about the priests, or unable to proceed further, on discovering the change upon him, he returns to His wondrous Benefactor, his emotions finding vent in a loud burst of praise. **16. And fell down on his face at his feet, giving him thanks: and he was a Samaritan.** While he rendered his tribute to Him from whom cometh down every good and perfect gift, he gave thanks at the same time to the mysterious, beneficent Hand by which the cure was wrought. **And as these men**

must have had their faith kindled by the reported wonders of His hand on others like themselves, no doubt they saw in Jesus what the Samaritans of Sychar did—"the Christ, the Saviour of the world" (John iv. 42), however imperfect their conceptions. **17. And Jesus answering said, Were there not ten cleansed?** [οὐχὶ οἱ δέκα ἐκαθαρίσθησαν]—rather, 'Were not the ten cleansed?'—that is, the whole ten. A striking example this of Christ's omniscience, as *Bengel* notices. **but where are the nine?** [οἱ δὲ ἐννέα ποῦ] —'but the nine, where [are they]?' **18. There are not found that returned to give glory to God, save this stranger** [ὁ ἀλλογενὴς οὗτος]—'this alien,' 'this of another race.' The language is that of wonder and admiration, as is expressly said of another exhibition of Gentile faith (Matt. viii. 10). **19. And he said unto him, Arise**—for he was on his face at Jesus' feet, and there, it seems, lay prostrate. **go thy way: thy faith hath made thee whole**—not as the others, merely in body, but in that higher spiritual sense with which His constant language has so familiarized us.

For Remarks on this Section, see those on the Sections referred to in the exposition.

20-37.—THE COMING OF THE KINGDOM OF GOD AND OF THE SON OF MAN. As usual in this portion of our Gospel, we have no notice of time or place. (See opening remarks on ch. ix. 51.) To meet the erroneous views not only of the Pharisees, but of the disciples themselves, our Lord addresses both, announcing the coming of the Kingdom under different aspects. **20. And when he was demanded of the Pharisees, when the kingdom of God should come, he answered them and said, The kingdom of God cometh not with observation** [μετὰ παρατηρήσεως]. The word signifies 'watching' or 'lying in wait for' a person or thing. In this sense, they "watched" our Lord once and again (ch. xiv. 1; xx. 20; Mark iii. 2); and so they "watched" the gates to kill Paul (Acts ix. 24). Here, the precise meaning would seem to be, The kingdom of God cometh not with 'watching' or 'lying in wait for it,' 'straining after it,' as for something outwardly imposing, and at once revealing itself. What follows confirms this. **21. Neither shall they say, Lo here! or, lo there!**—shut up within *this* or *that* sharply defined or visible limit, geographical or ecclesiastical. **for the kingdom of God is within you**—[ἐντὸς ὑμῶν]. This may either mean, 'inside of you;' meaning, that it is of an internal and spiritual character, as opposed to their *outside* views of it: so the best expositors among the Fathers understood it; and so, of the moderns, *Luther, Erasmus, Calvin,*

299

22   And he said unto the disciples, [p]The days will come, when ye shall desire to see one of the days of the Son of man, and ye shall not see
23 *it.* And [q]they shall say to you, See here! or, see there! go [r]not after
24 *them,* nor follow *them.* For as the lightning, that lighteneth out of the one *part* under heaven, shineth unto the other *part* under heaven;
25 so shall also [s]the Son of man be in his day. But [t]first must he
26 suffer many things, and be rejected of this generation. And [u]as it was in the days of Noe, so shall it be also in the days of the Son of
27 man. They did eat, they drank, they married wives, they were given in marriage, until the day that Noe entered into the ark, and the flood
28 came, and destroyed them all. Likewise [v]also as it was in the days of Lot; they did eat, they drank, they bought, they sold, they planted,
29 they builded; but the same day that Lot went out of Sodom it rained
30 fire and brimstone from heaven, and destroyed *them* all. Even thus shall
31 it be in the day when the Son of man [w]is revealed. In that day, he [x]which shall be upon the house-top, and his stuff in the house, let him not come down to take it away: and he that is in the field, let him like-

A. D. 33.

[p] Matt. 9. 15.
    John 17.12.
[q] Matt. 24.23.
    Mark 13.21.
    ch. 21. 8.
[r] 1 John 4. 1.
[s] 1 Tim 6.15.
[t] ch. 9. 22.
[u] Gen. 7. 1.
    Matt. 24.37.
[v] Gen. 19. 1.
[w] Matt. 24. 3,
    27-30.
    Mark 13.26.
    ch. 21. 22,
    27.
    2 Thes. 1. 7.
[x] Job 2. 4.
    Jer 45. 5.
    Mark 6. 25.
    Mark 13.15.

Campbell, Olshausen. Or, it may mean, 'in the midst of you,' or 'amongst you'—as already set up in its beginnings, if they had but eyes to discern it: so *Beza, Grotius, Bengel, Meyer, de Wette, Alford, Webster and Wilkinson.* It seems a weak argument against the former sense, though urged by nearly all who adopt the latter, that the kingdom of God could not be said to be within or in the hearts of the Pharisees, to whom our Lord was addressing himself. For, all that the phrase, in that sense, implies is, that it is 'within men,' as its general character. The question must be decided by the whole scope of the statement; and though others judge this to be in favour of the second sense, we incline, on this ground, to the first. Compare Deut. xxx. 11-14; Rom. xiv. 17.

22. And he said unto the disciples—for they needed light on this subject, as well as the Pharisees, **The days will come** ['Ἐλεύσονται ἡμέραι]—rather, 'There shall come days,' **when ye shall desire to see one of the days of the Son of man, and ye shall not see it**—that is, one day of His own presence amongst them, such as they now had. See Matt. ix. 15. 'So far will the kingdom I speak of be from bringing with it My personal presence, that amidst the approaching calamities and confusion, and the anxiety ye will be in for the infant cause—which will then be felt to lie all upon your own feeble shoulders—ye will be fain to say, O that we had the Master amongst us again but for one day! But ye shall not have Him.' He was to make other and more suitable provision, in the mission of the Comforter, for their fluttering hearts; but of that it was not now the time and place to speak. **23. And they shall say to you, See here! or, see there! go not after them, nor follow them.** A warning, says *Alford*, to all so-called expositors of prophecy and their followers, who cry, Lo there and see here, every time that war breaks out, or revolutions occur. **24. For as the lightning, that lighteneth out of the one part under heaven, shineth unto the other part under heaven; so shall also the Son of man be in his day.** That is, it will be as *manifest* as the lightning. So that the kingdom here spoken of has its *external* and *visible* side too. 'The Lord,' says *Stier* correctly, 'speaks here of His coming and manifestation in a prophetically indefinite manner, and in these preparatory words *blends into one the distinctive epochs.*' When the whole polity of the Jews, civil and ecclesiastical alike, was broken up at once, and its continuance rendered impossible, by the destruction of Jerusalem, it became as manifest to all as

the lightning of heaven that the Kingdom of God had ceased to exist in its old, and had entered on a new and perfectly different, form. So it may be again, ere its final and greatest change at the personal coming of Christ, of which the words in their highest sense are alone true. **25. But first must he suffer many things, and be rejected of this generation.** This shows that the more immediate reference of the previous verse is to an event *soon* to follow the death of Christ. It was designed to withdraw the attention of "His disciples" from the *glare* in which His foregoing words had invested the approaching establishment of His kingdom. **26. And as it was in the days of Noe, so shall it be also in the days of the Son of man. 27. They did eat, . . . drank . . . married . . . were given in marriage, until the day that Noe entered into the ark, and the flood came, and destroyed them all. 28. Likewise also as it was in the days of Lot; they did eat . . . drank, . . . bought . . . sold . . . planted . . . builded; 29. But the same day that Lot went out of Sodom it rained fire and brimstone from heaven, and destroyed them all. 30. Even thus shall it be in the day when the Son of man is revealed.** It will be observed here that what the *flood* and the *flames* found the antediluvians and the Sodomites engaged in were just all the ordinary and innocent occupations and enjoyments of life—eating and drinking, marrying and giving in marriage, in the one case; eating and drinking, buying and selling, planting and building, in the other. Though the antediluvian world and the cities of the plain were awfully wicked, it is not their *wickedness,* but their *worldliness,* their unbelief and indifference to the future, their *unpreparedness,* that is here held up as a warning. Let the reader mark how these great events of Old Testament History—denied, or explained away, now-a-days by not a few who profess to reverence our Lord's authority—are here referred to by Him as facts. The wretched theory of *accommodation* to the popular belief—as if our Lord could lend Himself to this in such cases—is now nearly exploded. **31. In that day, he which shall be upon the house-top, and his stuff in the house, let him not come down to take it away: and he that is in the field, let him likewise not return back.** A warning against that *lingering reluctance to part with present treasures* which induces some to remain in a burning house, in hopes of saving this and that precious article, till consumed and buried in its ruins. The cases here supposed, though

32, wise not return back. Remember [y]Lot's wife. Whosoever [z]shall seek to
33 save his life shall lose it; and whosoever shall lose his life shall preserve
34 it. I [a]tell you, in that night there shall be two *men* in one bed; the one
35 shall be taken, and the other shall be left. Two *women* shall be grinding
36 together; the one shall be taken, and the other left. [3]Two *men* shall be
37 in the field; the one shall be taken, and the other left. And they
answered and said unto him, [b]Where, Lord? And he said unto them,
Wheresoever the body *is*, thither will the eagles be gathered together.

18 AND he spake a parable unto them *to this end*, that men ought
2 [a]always *to* pray, and not to faint; saying, There was [1]in a city a judge,
3 which feared not God, neither regarded man: and there was a widow
in that city; and she came unto him, saying, Avenge me of mine
4 adversary. And he would not for a while: but afterward he said within
5 himself, Though I fear not God, nor regard man; yet [b]because this
widow troubleth me, I will avenge her, lest by her continual coming she
6 weary me. And the Lord said, Hear what the unjust judge saith.
7 And [c]shall not God avenge his own elect, which cry day and night unto

A. D. 33.

[y] Gen. 19. 26.
[z] Matt. 16. 25.
John 12. 25.
[a] 1 Thes. 4. 17.
[3] This verse
is wanting
in many
Greek
copies.
[b] Job 39. 30.

CHAP. 18.
[a] ch. 11. 5.
ch. 21. 36.
Rom. 12. 12.
Eph. 6. 18.
Col. 4. 2.
1 Thes. 5. 17.
[1] In a cer-
tain city.
[b] ch. 11. 8.
[c] 2 Thes. 1. 6.

different, of course, are similar. **32. Remember
Lot's wife**—her "*look back*" and her *doom*. Her
heart was in Sodom still, and that "look" just
said, 'Ah, Sodom! and shall I never enter, never
see thee again? must I bid thee a final adieu?' **33.
Whosoever shall seek to save his life shall lose it;
and whosoever shall lose his life shall preserve it.**
See on Matt. x. 39. **34. I tell you, in that night
there shall be two men in one bed; the one shall
be taken, and the other shall be left. 35. Two
women shall be grinding together** (see on Mark
ix. 42); **the one shall be taken, and the other left.
36. [Two men shall be in the field; the one shall
be taken, and the other left.]** The evidence against
the genuineness of this verse is too strong to admit
of its being printed without brackets, as at least
doubtful, and probably taken from Matt. xxiv. 40.
All the critical editors exclude it from their text,
and nearly all critical expositors concur with
them. *De Wette*, however, inclines to receive it.
The prepared and the unprepared will, says our
Lord, be found mingled in closest intercourse
together in the ordinary walks and fellowships
of life when the moment of severance arrives.
Awful truth! realized before the destruction of
Jerusalem, when the Christians found themselves
forced by their Lord's directions (ch. xxi. 21) at
once and for ever away from their old associates;
but most of all, when the second coming of Christ
shall burst upon a heedless world. **37. And they
answered and said unto him, Where, Lord?**
Where shall this occur? **And he said unto them,
Wheresoever the body is, thither will the
eagles be gathered together.** Though what is
here said of the eagles is true rather of the vul-
tures, yet as both are birds of prey, the former are
named here (and in Matt. xxiv. 28), with an evident
allusion to the *Roman eagles*—the standard of the
Roman army—to signify the vengeance more immediately referred to. 'As birds of prey scent
out the carrion, so wherever is found a mass of
incurable moral and spiritual corruption, there
will be seen alighting the ministers of Divine judgment;' a proverbial saying terrifically verified at
the destruction of Jerusalem, and many times
since, though its most tremendous illustration will
be at the world's final day. For Remarks on this
Section, see those at the close of Mark xiii.

CHAP. XVIII. 1-8.—THE PARABLE OF THE
IMPORTUNATE WIDOW. This delightful parable
was evidently designed to follow up the subject of
the last Section, on the Coming of the Son of man
(v. 8). In so far as the closing verses directed the

thoughts to the Second Personal Appearing of the
Lord Jesus, it was as an event which would occur
when least expected. But lest this should lead—
as it has led—to the inference that it would be very
speedy, or was *quite near at hand*, the more immediate design of this parable was to guard against that
impression, by intimating that it might, on the
contrary, be so long delayed as nearly to extinguish
the expectation of His coming at all. Accordingly,
while the duty of persevering prayer in general is
here enforced, the more direct subject of the parable is unceasing prayer by the widowed and oppressed Church for redress of all its wrongs, for
deliverance out of all its troubles, for transition
from its widowhood to its wedded state, by the
glorious appearing of its heavenly Bridegroom.
**1. And he spake a parable unto them to this end,
that men ought always to pray.** Compare *v.* 7,
"His own elect which cry unto Him day and
night." **and not to faint** [ἐκκακεῖν, or, as the better
supported reading, perhaps, is, ἐγκακεῖν]—'and not
to lose heart,' or 'slacken.' **2. Saying, There was
in a** [certain] **city** [ἔν τινι πόλει] **a judge, which
feared not God, neither regarded man**—regardless
alike of Divine and human judgment; void of all
principle. **3. And there was a widow in that city**
—weak, desolate, defenceless. Compare 1 Tim. v.
5, a verse evidently alluding to what is here said,
"Now she that is a widow indeed, and desolate,
trusteth in God, and continueth in supplications
and prayers night and day." **and she came** [ἤρχετο]
—rather, 'kept coming,' as the imperfect tense
implies. Indeed it was to get rid of this "*continual coming*" that the judge at length gave
her redress. **saying, Avenge me** ['Εκδίκησόν με
ἀπὸ] **of mine adversary**—that is, by a judicial
interposition. **4. And he would not for a while:
but afterward he said within himself, Though I
fear not God, nor regard man; 5. Yet**—I have
some regard to my own comfort: **so because this
widow troubleth me, I will avenge her, lest by
her continual coming** [εἰς τέλος ἐρχομένη]—'her
incessant coming.' In 1 Thess. ii. 16 the same
expression is rendered 'to the uttermost.' **she
weary**—or 'annoy' **me** [ὑπωπιάζῃ με]. **6. And the
Lord**—a name expressive of the authoritative style
in which He now interpreted His own parable,
**said, Hear what the unjust judge saith. 7. And
shall not God**—not like that unprincipled man, but
the infinitely righteous "Judge of all the earth,"
avenge—redeem from oppression, **his own elect**—
who are not like this poor widow in the eye of
that selfish wretch, the objects of indifference and

8 him, though he bear long with them? I tell you ^dthat he will avenge them speedily. Nevertheless when the Son of man cometh, shall he find faith on the earth?

9 And he spake this parable unto certain ^ewhich trusted in themselves

10 ²that they were righteous, and despised others: Two men went up into

11 the temple to pray; the one a Pharisee, and the other a publican. The Pharisee ^fstood and prayed thus with himself, ^gGod, I thank thee, that I am not as other men *are*, extortioners, unjust, adulterers, or even as this

12 publican. I fast twice in the week, I give tithes of all that I possess.

A. D. 33.
^d Heb. 10. 37.
2 Pet. 3. 8, 9.
^e ch. 10. 29.
ch. 16. 15.
² Or, as being righteous.
^f Ps. 135. 2.
^g Isa. 1. 15.
Isa. 58. 2.
Rev. 3. 17.

contempt, but dear to Him as the apple of the eye (Zec. ii. 8). which cry day and night unto him —whose every cry enters into the ears of the Lord of Sabaoth (Jas. v. 4); and how much more their incessant and persevering cries, **though he bear long with them?** [καὶ μακροθυμῶν, or, according to the preferable reading, μακροθυμεῖ ἐπ’ αὐτοῖς]. This rendering is apt to perplex the English reader, to whose ear it fails to convey the obvious sense. The same expression is used in Jas. v. 7— "The husbandman waiteth for the precious fruit of the earth, and *hath long patience for it*" [μακροθυμῶν ἐπ’ αὐτῷ]. So we should render it here, 'though he bear long *for them*,' or 'on their account;' that is, with their oppressors. It is not with His own elect that God has to bear in the case here supposed, but with those that oppress them. And the meaning is, that although He *tolerates* those oppressions for a long time, He will at length interpose in behalf of His own elect. **8. I tell you, he will avenge them speedily** [ἐν τάχει]. As when "His soul was grieved for the misery of Israel" (Judg. x. 16), so "His bowels are troubled" for His own elect, crying to Him day and night from the depths of their oppressions: He is pained, as it were, at the long delay which His wisdom sees necessary, and at the sore trial to which it puts their faith, and is impatient, so to speak, till "the time, the set time," arrive to interpose. **Nevertheless when the Son of man cometh, shall he find faith**—that is, any belief that He will come at all, **on the earth?** 'Yet, ere the Son of man comes to redress the wrongs of His Church, so low will the hope of relief sink, through the length of the delay, that one will be fain to ask, Is there any faith of a coming Avenger, any expectation that the Church's Lord will ever return to her, left on the earth?'

Remarks.—1. Thus the *primary*, the *historical* reference of this parable is to the Church in her widowed, desolate, oppressed, defenceless condition, during the present absence of her Lord in the heavens. And the lessons it teaches, in this view of it, which are two-fold, are most precious. One lesson is, that though we are to be "always ready, not knowing when our Lord may come," we are at the same time not to be surprised though "the Bridegroom should tarry," and tarry so long as to wear out the patience of the most, and almost extinguish the hope of His coming. And the more so, as His coming will be needed, not only because the Bride can never be contented with anything short of the presence of her Beloved, but because in her widowed state she is exposed to all manner of indignities and wrongs, from which her Lord's coming alone will set her completely free. But another lesson is, that in these circumstances prayer is her proper resource, that though He seems to turn a deaf ear to her, she is to "pray always, and not faint," assured that she is dear to her Lord even when He seems to deny her; nay, that her incessant crying to Him is that which will bring Him to her at length; but yet, that the faith of His coming, through the length of the 302

delay, will have reached its lowest ebb, and nearly died out, ere the day dawn and the shadows flee away! It may be added that it would seem a law of the divine administration, that both *judgment* and *mercy*, when long delayed, come at last with a rapidity proportioned to the length of that delay. Of *judgment* it is said, "He that, being often reproved, hardeneth his neck, shall *suddenly* be destroyed, and that without remedy" (Prov. xxix. 1); and so it is said, "Their foot shall *slide* in due time" (Deut. xxxii. 35). Of *mercy* it is here said, When at length it comes, it will come "speedily." But, 2. The application of this delightful parable to *prayer in general* is so obvious as to have nearly hidden from most readers its *more direct* reference; and this general application is so resistless and invaluable that it cannot be allowed to disappear in any public and historical interpretation.

9-14.—THE PARABLE OF THE PHARISEE AND THE PUBLICAN. As the subject of this Section has no connection with the two preceding ones, so the precise time and place of it are, as usual in this portion of our Gospel, left quite indefinite. But the purpose for which it was spoken—the lesson it was intended to convey—is more precisely expressed than in most other cases; for it is expressed both as a preface to it and as the concluding moral of it.

9. And he spake this parable unto certain which trusted in themselves that they were righteous, and despised others: 10. Two men went up into the temple to pray; the one a Pharisee, and the other a publican. On these classes, see on Matt. iii. 1-12, Remark 2, at the close of that Section. **11. The Pharisee stood**—as the Jews did in prayer (Mark xi. 25), **and prayed thus with himself, God, I thank thee, that I am not as other men are, extortioners, unjust, adulterers, or even as this publican.** To have been kept from gross iniquities was undoubtedly a just cause of thankfulness to God; but instead of the devoutly humble, admiring frame which this should inspire, he arrogantly severs himself from the rest of mankind, as quite above them, and with a contemptuous look at the poor publican, thanks God that he has not to stand afar off like him, to hang down his head like a bulrush, and beat his breast like him. But these are only his *moral* excellences. His *religious* merits complete his grounds for self-congratulation. **12. I fast twice in the week, I give tithes**—or the tenth **of all that I possess** [κτῶμαι]—or 'acquire;' 'of all my gains' or 'increase.' Not confining himself to the one divinely prescribed annual fast (Lev. xvi. 29), he was not behind the most rigid, who, as *Lightfoot* says, fasted on the second and fifth days of every week, and gave the tenth not only of what the law laid under tithing, but of "all his gains." Thus, besides doing *all his duty*, he did *works of supererogation;* while sins to confess and spiritual wants to be supplied he seems to have felt none. What a picture of the Pharisaic character and religion! **13. And the publican, standing afar off**

13 And the publican, [h]standing afar off, would not lift up so much as *his* eyes unto heaven, but smote upon his breast, saying, God be merciful to
14 me a sinner. I tell you, this man went down to his house justified *rather* than the other: [i]for every one that exalteth himself shall be abased; and he that humbleth himself shall be exalted.
15 And [j]they brought unto him also infants, that he would touch them:
16 but when *his* disciples saw *it*, they rebuked them. But Jesus called them *unto him*, and said, [k]Suffer little children to come unto me, and

A. D. 33.

[h] Ps. 40. 12.
[i] Job 22. 29.
Job 40.9-13.
Isa. 2.11-17.
Jas. 4. 6.
1 Pet. 5.5,6.
[j] Matt. 19.13.
Mark 10. 13.
[k] Pro. 8. 7.

—as unworthy to draw near; but that was the way to *get* near (Ps. xxxiv. 18; Isa. lvii. 15), **would not lift up so much as his eyes unto heaven**—"blushing and ashamed" to do so (Ezra ix. 6), **but smote [ἔτυπτε]**—rather, 'kept smiting' **upon his breast**—for anguish (ch. xxiii. 48) and self-reproach (Jer. xxxi. 19), **saying, God be merciful [ἱλάσθητι]**—'be propitiated' or 'propitious:' a very unusual word to occur here, and in only one other place used in the New Testament, in the sense of "making reconciliation" by sacrifice (Heb. ii. 17). There *may* therefore be some allusion to this here, though it can hardly be pressed. **to me a sinner** [μοι τῷ ἁμαρτωλῷ]—literally 'to me the sinner;' as if he should say, 'If ever there was a sinner, I am he.' **14.** I tell you—authoritatively, **this man went down to his house justified rather than the other.** The meaning is, 'and not the other.' **for every one that exalteth himself shall be abased; and he that humbleth himself shall be exalted.** This great law of the Kingdom of God is, in the teaching of Christ, inscribed over its entrance-gate as in letters of gold; but how vividly is it here depicted?

Remarks.—1. The grand peculiarity of the Religion of the Bible is *Salvation by Grace;* a Salvation, however, unto holiness—not *by*, but *unto*, good works. It pervades the Old Testament (Ex. xxxiv. 6, 7; Ps. xxv. 7; xxxiv. 18; cxxxviii. 6; cxlvii. 6; Isa. lvii. 15, &c.); though its full disclosure, in connection with the Lamb of God which taketh away the sin of the world, was naturally reserved for the New Testament. And yet, so natural is self-righteousness to the pride of the human heart, that it has found its way even into the doctrinal system of the Church; and by that Apostasy which panders to all the corrupt inclinations of our nature, while preserving the form of evangelical truth, it has been erected into a most subtle scheme which, while apparently ascribing all to *Grace*, is in reality a doctrine of Salvation by *works*. (See the Canons and Decrees of the Council of Trent, Sess. VI. *Decretum de Justificatione;* particularly c. vii. ix. with *Can.* ix. xi. xii. xiii.) Even into Protestant Churches the very same doctrine has found entrance, under different forms of language, and in times of religious indifference and general degeneracy has spread its deadly virus over whole regions once blooming with health; nor is it effectually dislodged in any heart save by Divine teaching. 2. To be self-emptied, or "poor in spirit," is the fundamental and indispensable preparation for welcoming the "grace which bringeth salvation." Wherever this exists, that "mourning" which precedes comfort, that "hungering and thirsting after righteousness" which is rewarded with the "fulness" of it, is invariably found—as in this publican. Such, therefore, and such only, are the truly justified ones. "He hath filled the hungry with good things; and the rich he hath sent empty away" (ch. i. 53).

15-17.—LITTLE CHILDREN BROUGHT TO CHRIST. (= Matt. xix. 13-15; Mark x. 13-16.) *Here at length our Evangelist—after travelling over three*

hundred and fifty-one verses almost alone—gets again upon the line, travelling, as will be seen, in company with the two preceding Evangelists, though each, if one might so speak, on separate rails.

15. And they brought unto him also infants [τὰ βρέφη]. This shows that some, at least, of those called "little" or "young children" in Matt. xix. 13, and Mark x. 13, were literally "babes." **that he would touch them**—or, as more fully given in Matthew, "that He should put his hands on them and *pray*," that is, invoke a blessing on them (Mark x. 16); according to venerable custom (Gen. xlviii. 14, 15). **but when his disciples saw it, they rebuked them.** Repeatedly the disciples thus interposed, to save annoyance and interruption to their Master, but, as the result showed, *always against the mind of Christ.* (Matt. xv. 23, &c.; ch. xviii. 39, 40.) Here, it is plain from our Lord's reply, that they thought the intrusion a useless one, since *infants* were not capable of receiving anything from Him—His ministrations were for *grown people*. **16. But Jesus called them unto him, and said.** In Mark, however, we have a precious addition, "But when Jesus saw it, He was *much displeased*" [ἠγανάκτησε], and said unto them," **SUFFER [THE] LITTLE CHILDREN [τὰ παιδία] TO COME UNTO ME, AND FORBID THEM NOT.** What words are these from the lips of Christ! The price of them is above rubies. But the *reason* assigned, in the words that follow, crowns the statement—**FOR OF SUCH IS THE KINGDOM OF GOD**—or, as in Matt., "OF HEAVEN." **17. Verily I say unto you, Whosoever shall not receive the kingdom of God as a little child shall in no wise enter therein.** See on Mark ix. 36. But the action that followed—omitted by our Evangelist, and only partially given by Matthew, but fully supplied by Mark—is the best of all: "AND HE TOOK THEM UP IN HIS ARMS, PUT HIS HANDS UPON THEM, AND BLESSED THEM" (Mark x. 16). Now, is it to be conceived that all our Lord meant by this was to teach a lesson, not about children at all, but about *grown people;* namely, that they must become childlike if they would be capable of the kingdom of God, and for this reason they should not hinder *infants* from coming to Him, and therefore He took up and blessed *the infants themselves?* Did not the grave mistake of the disciples, which so "much displeased" the Lord Jesus, consist just in this, that they thought infants should not be brought to Christ, *because only grown people could profit by Him?* And though He took the irresistible opportunity of lowering their pride of reason, by informing them that, in order to enter the Kingdom, *instead of the children first becoming like them, they must themselves become like the children*—as a German writer has well expressed it—yet this was but by the way; and returning to the *children themselves,* He took them up in His gracious arms, put His hands upon them, and blessed them, for no conceivable reason but to show that *they were thereby made capable,* AS INFANTS, *of the Kingdom of God.*

17 forbid them not: for *[l]*of such is the kingdom of God. Verily I say unto you, Whosoever shall not receive the kingdom of God as a little child shall in no wise enter therein.

A. D. 33.

[l] 1 Cor. 14. 20.

Remarks.—1. How different the feelings of Jesus from those of His disciples, in this as in so many other cases! They "marvelled that He talked with the woman" of Samaria, while that "talk" was "meat to Him that they knew not of" (John iv. 27, 32): The cries of the Syrophenician woman after Jesus were harsh in their ears, but they were music in His (Matt. xv. 23, 28): And here, they think He has grown people enough to attend to, without being annoyed with untaught children and unconscious babes, who could get no possible good from Him; and so they administer to the expectant parents their damping, miserable "rebuke." But this was not more false in doctrine than the feeling that expressed it was at variance with His. It 'grievously vexed' Him, as the word signifies. His heart yearned after these babes; just as "babes" and "little children;" nor are we capable of knowing the whole heart of Christ towards us if we leave out of it this most touching and beautiful element—the feeling that grievously vexed Him when infants were held back from Him. O what a spectacle was that which presented itself to the eye that was capable (if, indeed, there was one) of seeing into the interior of it—The Only begotten of the Father with an unconscious Babe in His arms; His gentle, yet mighty hands upon it; and His eyes upraised to heaven as the blessing descended upon it! Was not this one of those things which "angels desired to look into?" For He was "seen of angels."

> 'He raised them in His holy arms,
> He blessed them from the world and all its harms:
> Heirs though they were of sin and shame,
> He blessed them in his own and in His Father's name.

> 'Then, as each fond, unconscious child
> *On th' everlasting Parent sweetly smil'd,*
> *Like infants sporting on the shore,*
> *That tremble not at ocean's boundless roar,'* &c.—KEBLE.

3. If Christ was "much displeased" with His disciples for interfering with those who were bringing their infants to Him, surely it is not enough that *we* do not positively *hinder* them. Whatsoever on our part is *fitted* to keep back children from Christ is in effect the same thing, and may be expected to cause the same displeasure. But that is not all. For, as it is an acknowledged rule, that whenever any sin is forbidden, the contrary duty is commanded, so the displeasure of Christ at the attempt to keep back these children from Him carries with it the duty of bringing, or having them brought to Him, and the assurance of His benignant satisfaction with parents that bring them, and every one who does anything to cause them to be brought to Him. Be stirred up, then, and emboldened, believing parents, to bring your babes, even from their first breath, to Jesus; and let the ministers of Christ, and all who would have His gracious complacency resting upon them, as the first and the last step in "feeding His lambs," bring them to Jesus! 4. As the parable of the Good Samaritan has filled Christendom with Institutions for the relief of the wretched, over and above all that individuals have done in private, so this little incident—recorded by three of the Evangelists, yet occupying, even in the most detailed narrative of it, only four brief verses—has, over and above all that it has given birth to in private, filled Christendom with classes for the Christian training of the young; in the earlier ages, in a less systematic and comprehensive form, and chiefly by pastoral superintend-

ence of parental instruction, but in these latter days on a vast scale, and to admirable effect. Nor can we doubt that the eye of Him who, in the days of His flesh, took up little children in His arms, put his hands on them, and blessed them, looks down from the skies in sweet complacency upon such efforts, blesses richly those that in obedience and love to Him engage in them, gathers many a lamb from amongst such flocks, to fold them in His own bosom above, and sends the rest as they grow up into the great world as "a seed to serve Him," a leaven to leaven the lump, that He may not come and smite it with a curse (Mal. iv. 6). 5. Let the intelligent reader note carefully the *standing* which this incident gives to children —even unconscious "infants"—in the Kingdom of God. "Suffer the little children to come unto me, for *of such* is the Kingdom of God." We have given reasons why this cannot mean merely, 'Let little *children* come to me, because *grown people* must be like them if they would enter the Kingdom.' What can be balder than such an interpretation of our Lord's words? But how natural and self-commending is the following sense of them: ' Ye are wrong in thinking that not till these children have grown to manhood can they get any good from Me. They also, even these unconscious babes, have their place, and not the least place, in the Kingdom of Heaven.' But if there could be any doubt whether our Lord was here speaking of the *children themselves,* or only of child-like *men,* surely His putting His hands upon them, and blessing them, ought to set that question at rest. What *could* such actions mean, if not to convey some spiritual blessing, some saving benefit, to the babes themselves? Does any one doubt that children, dying in infancy, are capable of going to heaven? Or, does any Christian think that without the new birth, and the blood that cleanseth from all sin, they will be fit company for heaven's inhabitants, or find themselves in an atmosphere congenial to their nature, or without this will ever see it? But, if infants are capable *of all that saves the soul,* before they are capable of consciously believing in Christ, and even though they die before ever doing so, what follows? "*Can any man forbid water*"—said Peter of the Gentile Cornelius and his company—" *that these should not be baptized, which have received the Holy Ghost as well as we?*" (Acts x. 47). Of course, such application of the baptismal water *to infants* can have no warrant from our incident, save where the infants have been *previously brought to Christ Himself* for his benediction, and only as *the sign and seal* of His promised benediction. But you may say, 'Is not *faith* explicitly and peremptorily required *in order to baptism?*' Yes, and *in order to salvation* too. Nay, "he that believeth not shall be damned." Are those who die in infancy, then, damned— because incapable of believing? 'O no,' it will be said; 'they were not *contemplated* in the demand for faith, in order to salvation.' Just so; and for that reason, since they are capable of the new birth, and forgiveness, and complete salvation—all in infancy and without any faith at all, just as truly as grown people—they are surely capable of the mere outward symbol of it, which brings them within the sacred enclosure, and separates them to a holy service and society, and inheritance amongst the people of God (1 Cor. vii. 14). Within this sacred enclosure, the apostle regards them as "in the Lord," and addresses them as such (Eph. vi. 1), in-

18 And ^{*m*} a certain ruler asked him, saying, Good Master, what shall I do 19 to inherit eternal life? And Jesus said unto him, Why callest thou me

A. D. 33.

^{*m*} Matt. 19. 16.

---

culcating on them obedience to their parents, as "*well pleasing unto the Lord*" (Col. iii. 20). The Christian household is thus to be *a Christian nursery.* Sweet view this of the standing of children that have been from their very birth brought to Christ, and blessed of Him, as believers may not doubt that their children are, and loved as dearly as if He took them up in His very arms, and made the blessing to descend upon them, even life for evermore! For more on this subject, see on ch. xix. 28-44, Remark 5 at the close of that Section.

18-30.—THE RICH YOUNG RULER, AND DISCOURSE SUGGESTED BY HIS CASE. (= Matt. xix. 16-30; Mark x. 17-31.)

The Rich Young Ruler (18-23). **18. And a certain ruler asked him, saying.** Mark says, "And when He was gone forth into the way"—the high road, by this time crowded with travellers on their way to Jerusalem, to keep the Passover—"there came one running, and kneeled to Him, and asked Him," **Good Master, what shall I do**—in Matthew, "What good thing shall I do," **to inherit eternal life? 19. And Jesus said unto him, Why callest thou me good? none is good, save one, that is, God** [Tί με λέγεις ἀγαθόν; οὐδεὶς ἀγαθὸς, εἰ μὴ εἷς ὁ Θεός. So Mark x. 18; and so in the received text of Matt. xix. 17, with trifling variation. But all recent critical editors — *Griesbach, Lachmann, Tischendorf,* and *Tregelles*—give the text of Matt. xix. 17 thus—Tί με ἐρωτᾶς περὶ τοῦ ἀγαθοῦ; εἷς ἐστιν ὁ ἀγαθός: '*Why askest thou me concerning what is Good? One is the Good One:*' *Alford* adopts this into his text; *de Wette* and *Meyer* approve of it; and *Olshausen* thinks it admits of no doubt that this is the genuine reading. In spite of this, we venture to think that nothing but such overwhelming evidence in its behalf as it certainly does not possess would entitle it even to favourable consideration. And this for two reasons: First, It makes our Lord's reply to this sincere and anxious enquirer incredibly inept. The man's question was, "Good Master, what good thing shall I do to inherit eternal life?" Our Lord answers by asking him why he questioned Him regarding what was good—according to this reading. Is it likely our Lord would so answer him? especially as He presently tells him the thing he really wanted to know. But the conclusion of our Lord's reply, according to this reading, crowns its absurdity in our judgment: 'One is the Good One.' If this has any connection at all with what goes before, it must mean that the man had no need to enquire what was the good which men were to do, because One was the Good Being! But if there be no connection here, there is as little in what follows. And looking at this reading of our Lord's reply to a sincere and anxious enquirer after eternal life, nothing could persuade us that our Lord did utter it—in the absence, at least, of overpowering evidence from ancient MSS. and versions. But secondly, Since no one pretends that this is the reading of Mark and Luke, and since *their* account of our Lord's reply, while it gives a clear and pregnant answer to the man's question, differs totally from the sense of this peculiar reading of Matthew, is it not a strong argument against this reading that it yields no proper sense at all, while the received reading gives the clear sense of the other two Gospels? We are well aware of the tendency of early transcribers to assimilate the readings of one Gospel to those of another, especially of two others which agree together; and we could give that consideration some

weight here if the evidence otherwise were in favour of the peculiar reading. Nor do we forget that, *other things being equal,* the more peculiar a reading is the more probably is it the right one. But other things are *not* equal here, but far from it. It only remains, then, that we advert to the external evidence on the subject. Only one MS. of the oldest date—the celebrated *Vatican* (B)— was thought to have this reading; but the recently discovered *Sinaitic* MS. (א), we now know, has it too. Two others (D and L) have it, together with three of the cursive or more recent MSS. Two of the *Syriac* versions, nearly all copies of the *Old Latin* and of the *Vulgate,* and the *Memphitic* or Lower-Egyptian, have it. *Origen,* in the third century, has the first part of it at least; and *Eusebius, Jerome,* and *Augustin* in the fourth. Such is the evidence for this unnatural reading. Now, how stands the evidence on the other side? The only other MS. of oldest date and greatest authority (A) is defective here; but the MSS. with which it usually agrees have the received text. The next weightiest MS. has it—the *Codex Ephraemi rescriptus* (C)—and with it *all other known MSS. of the Gospels,* except those above referred to. An overwhelming number; and in weight, surely counterbalancing those above-mentioned. It is found in the oldest and most venerable of all the *Syriac* versions, the 'Peshito,' and in the text of the most critical one, the 'Philoxenian' or 'Harclean;' though the other reading is inserted in the margin. And it is found in the *Thebaic* or Upper-Egyptian version, which is thought to have claims to great antiquity. Of the Fathers, it is found in *Irenæus,* and substantially in *Justin Martyr,* both of the second century, besides most of the later Fathers. On a review of the whole case, we hesitate not to say, that while the weight of *external* evidence appears to us to be clearly in favour of the received text, the *internal* evidence, arising from the inept character which the other reading gives to our Lord's reply, is decisive against it. We have been the more full in our statement upon this passage, because, while we hold that the true text of the New Testament must in every case be determined by the *whole evidence* which we possess, this passage affords a good example of the tendency of critics to be carried away, in opposition to their own principles, in favour of startling readings, and of the necessity, in such cases—even though one should stand almost alone—of expressing the result of the entire evidence in terms as strong as that evidence warrants. *Scrivener* ("Criticism of the New Testament") vindicates the received text, though with no reference to the inept character which the other one stamps upon our Lord's reply, and admitting too much in favour of the other reading from its *harshness,* and the tendency to *assimilation.* The only able critic who speaks out upon the 'absurdity' of this various reading is *Fritzsche.*]

Our Lord's response consists, first, of a hint by the way, founded on the appellation, "Good Master;" and next, of a direct reply to the enquiry itself. "Why callest thou me good? There is none good but One, [that is], God." Did our Lord mean by this to teach that God only ought to be called "good?" Impossible: for that had been to contradict all Scripture teaching *and His own too.* "A *good* man showeth favour and lendeth" (Ps. cxii. 5); "A *good* man out of the good treasure of his heart, bringeth forth good things" (Matt. xii. 35); "Well done, *good* and faithful servant"

20 good? none *is* good, save one, *that is,* God. Thou knowest the commandments, [n]Do not commit adultery, Do not kill, Do not steal, Do not
21 bear false witness, [o]Honour thy father and thy mother. And he said,
22 All these have I kept from my youth up. Now when Jesus heard these things, he said unto him, Yet lackest thou one thing: sell [p]all that thou hast, and distribute unto the poor, and thou shalt have treasure in
23 heaven: and come, follow me. And when he heard this, he was very sorrowful: for he was very rich.
24 And when Jesus saw that he was very sorrowful, he said, [q]How hardly
25 shall they that have riches enter into the kingdom of God! For it is easier for a camel to go through a needle's eye, than for a rich man to

A. D. 33.

[n] Ex. 20. 12.
Deut. 5. 16.
Rom. 13. 9.
[o] Eph. 6. 2.
Col. 3. 20.
[p] Matt. 6. 19.
Matt. 19. 21.
1 Tim. 6. 19.
[q] Pro. 11. 28.
Pro. 18. 11.
Jer. 5. 5.
1 Tim. 6. 9.
Jas. 2. 5.

(Matt. xxv. 21); "Barnabas was a *good* man, and full of the Holy Ghost" (Acts xi. 24). Unless, therefore, we are to ascribe captiousness to our Lord, He could have had but one object—to teach this youth, on the one hand, that *He declined to be classed along with other "good" people and "good masters;"* and on the other hand, by reminding him that the only *other* sort of goodness, namely, *supreme goodness,* belonged to God alone, to leave him to draw the startling inference—that *that* was the goodness which belonged to Him. Unless this object is seen in the *background* of our Lord's words, nothing worthy of Him can be made out of this first part of His reply. But this hint once given, our Lord at once passes from it to the proper subject of the youth's inquiry. **20. Thou knowest the commandments.** In Matthew (xix. 17, 18) this is more fully given: "But," passing from that point, "if thou wilt enter into life, keep the commandments. He saith unto Him, Which?"—as if He had said, 'Point me out one of them which I have not kept.' "Jesus saith unto him," **Do not commit adultery, Do not kill, Do not steal, Do not bear false witness, Honour thy father and thy mother.** Our Lord purposely confines Himself to the commandments of what is called the *second* table of the law, which he would consider easy to keep, enumerating them all—for in Mark x. 19, "Defraud not" stands for the *tenth* commandment; otherwise the eighth is twice repeated. In Matthew the *sum* of this second table of the law is added, "Thou shalt love thy neighbour as thyself," as if to see if he would venture to say he had kept *that.* **21. And he said, All these have I kept from my youth up:—**"What lack I yet?" (Matt. xix. 20) is an important addition in Matthew, though implied in the shorter answer of the other Evangelists. Ah! this gives us a glimpse of his heart. Doubtless he was perfectly sincere; but something within whispered to him that *his* keeping of the commandments was *too easy* a way of getting to heaven. He felt something beyond this to be necessary; but since after keeping all the commandments he was at a loss to know what that could be, he came to Jesus just upon that point. "Then," says Mark (x. 21), "Jesus, beholding him, loved him," or 'looked lovingly upon him.' His sincerity, frankness, and nearness to the kingdom of God, in themselves most winning qualities, won our Lord's regard even though he turned his back upon Him—a lesson to those who can see nothing loveable save in the regenerate. **22. Now when Jesus heard these things, he said unto him, Yet lackest thou one thing**—but that, alas! was a fundamental, a fatal lack. **sell all that thou hast, and distribute unto the poor, and thou shalt have treasure in heaven: and come, follow me.** As riches were his idol, our Lord, who knew this from the first, lays His great authoritative grasp at once upon it, saying, 'Now give Me up that, and all is right.' No general direction about the disposal of

riches, then, is here given, save that we are to sit loose to them and lay them at the feet of Him who gave them. He who does this with all he has, whether rich or poor, is a true heir of the kingdom of heaven. **23. And when he heard this, he was very sorrowful: for he was very rich.** Matthew, more fully, "he *went away* sorrowful:" Mark, still more fully, "he was sad at that saying, and went away grieved, for he had great possessions." Sorry he was, very sorry, to part with Christ; but to part with his riches would have cost him a pang more. When Riches or Heaven on Christ's terms were the alternatives, the result showed to which side the balance inclined. Thus was he shown to lack the one all-comprehensive requirement of the law—the *absolute subjection of the heart to God,* and this want vitiated all his other obediences. Let us now gather up the favourable points in this man's case, as here presented. First, He was of irreproachable moral character; and this amidst all the temptations of *youth,* for he was a "young man" (Matt. xix. 22), and of *wealth,* for he was "very rich." Secondly, He was restless notwithstanding: his heart craved eternal life. Thirdly, Unlike the "rulers," to whose class he belonged (*v.* 18), he so far believed in Jesus as to be persuaded He could authoritatively direct him on this vital point. And, Fourthly, So earnest was he that he came "running," and even "kneeling" before Him; and that not in any quiet corner, but "when He was gone forth into the *way*"—the open road—undeterred by the virulent opposition of the class to which he belonged, and by the shame he might be expected to feel at broaching such a question in the hearing of so many. How much that is interesting, attractive, loveable, promising, is there here! And yet all was in vain. Eternal life could not be his, for he was not prepared to *give up all* for it. He had not *found* the treasure hid in the field; he had not found the one pearl of great price; for he was not prepared to sell all that he had to possess himself of them (Matt. xiii. 44-46). *Discourse suggested by this case* (24-30). **24. And when Jesus saw that he was very sorrowful**—as he "went away," **he said.** Mark says "He looked round about," as if first He would follow the departing youth with His eye, "and saith unto His disciples," **How hardly shall they that have riches enter into the kingdom of God!** In Mark (x. 24) an explanation of the difficulty is added, "How hard is it for them that *trust* in riches to enter," &c., that is, 'With what difficulty is this idolatrous trust conquered, without which they cannot enter;' and this is introduced by the word, "Children" [Τέκνα]—that sweet diminutive of affection and pity. (See John xxi. 5.) **25. For it is easier for a camel to go through a needle's eye, than for a rich man to enter into the kingdom of God**—a proverbial expression, denoting literally a thing impossible, but figuratively a thing very

26 enter into the kingdom of God. And they that heard *it* said, Who then
27 can be saved? And he said, ᵗThe things which are impossible with men are possible with God.

28, Then ˢPeter said, Lo, we have left all, and followed thee. And he said
29 unto them, Verily I say unto you, ᵗThere is no man that hath left house, or parents, or brethren, or wife, or children, for the kingdom of God's
30 sake, who ᵘshall not receive manifold more in this present time, and ᵛin the world to come life everlasting.

A. D. 33.

ᵗ Jer. 32. 17.
Zec. 8. 6.
Eph. 1. 19,
20.
ˢ Matt.19.27.
ᵗ Deut. 33. 9.
ᵘ Job 42. 10.
ᵛ Rev. 2. 17.
Rev. 3. 21.

difficult. **26. And they that heard it said, Who then can be saved?** 'At that rate, how is any one to be saved? **27. And he said, The things which are impossible with men are possible with God**—'Well, it does pass *human*, but not *divine* power.'

28. Then Peter said—in the simplicity of his heart, as is evident from our Lord's reply, **Lo, we have left all, and followed thee.** He was conscious that the required surrender, which that young ruler had not been able to make, had been made, not only by himself but by his brethren along with him, whom he generously takes in—"*we* have left all." Little, indeed, was Peter's "all." But, as *Bengel* says, the workman's little is as much to him as the prince's much. In Matthew's narrative Peter adds, "What shall we have therefore?" How shall it fare with us? **29, 30. And he said unto them, Verily I say unto you, There is no man that hath left house, or parents, or brethren, or wife, or children, for the kingdom of God's sake, Who shall not receive manifold more in this present time, and in the world to come life everlasting.** In Mark (x. 29, 30) the specification is so full as to take in *every* form of self-sacrifice: "There is no man that hath left house, or brethren, or sisters, or father, or mother, or wife, or children, or lands, for My sake, and the Gospel's, but he shall receive an hundred-fold now in this present time, houses, and brethren, and sisters, and mothers, and children, and lands, with persecutions; and in the world to come eternal life." This glorious promise is worthy of minute study. First, Observe how graciously the Lord Jesus acknowledges at once the completeness and the acceptableness of the surrender, as a thing already made by the attached followers whom He had around Him. 'Yes, Peter, thou and thy fellows have indeed given up all for Me, and it makes you beautiful in Mine eyes; but ye shall lose nothing by this, but gain much.' Next, Observe how our Lord identifies the interests of the kingdom of God with the Gospel's and with His own—saying alternatively, "For the kingdom of God's sake," and "for My sake and the Gospel's." See on Matt. v. 11; and on Luke vi. 22. Further, Observe the very remarkable promise—not of comfort and support, in a mere general sense, under persecution, and ultimate deliverance out of all this into eternal life—but of "an hundred-fold *now in this time;*" and this in the form of a *re-construction of all human relationships and affections, on a Christian basis and amongst Christians, after they have been sacrificed in their natural form, on the altar of love to Christ.* This He calls "manifold more," yea, "an hundred-fold more," than what they sacrificed for His sake. Our Lord was Himself the first to exemplify this in a *new adjustment of His own relationships.* (See on Matt. xii. 49, 50, and Remark 3 at the close of that Section; see also on 2 Cor. vi. 14, 18.) But this, it is added, "with persecutions;" for how could such a transfer take place without the most cruel wrenches to flesh and blood? Nay, the persecution would haply follow them into their new and higher circle,

307

breaking that up too. Well, but "in the world to come life everlasting." And

    'When the shore is won at last,
    Who will count the billows past?'—KEBLE.

The foregoing promises are for *every one* that forsakes his all for Christ—"There is no man," &c. But in Matthew xix. 28, these promises are prefaced by a special promise *to the Twelve:* "And Jesus said unto them, That ye which have followed me, in the regeneration, when the Son of man shall sit in the throne of His glory, ye also shall sit upon twelve thrones, judging the twelve tribes of Israel." The words "in the regeneration" [ἐν τῇ παλιγγενεσίᾳ] may be joined either to what goes *before* or to what follows *after;* and this, of course, materially affects the sense. In the former case it is, "Ye which have followed Me in the regeneration;" the meaning of which is, 'Ye who have followed Me in the new kingdom or economy which I am now erecting—the new life now begun.' Among the few who take this view of it are *Hilary* among the Fathers; *Erasmus* and *Calvin,* among the moderns. But by far the most and best interpreters, with whom we agree, connect the words with what follows: "Ye which have followed Me shall, in the regeneration," &c. But opinions are divided as to what is meant in this case by "the regeneration," and consequently, as to what is meant by the promise that the Twelve should "sit on twelve thrones, judging the twelve tribes of Israel." One class of interpreters, understanding by "the regeneration" the new Gospel kingdom which Christ was erecting, would paraphrase the words thus: 'Ye who have forsaken all and followed Me as no others have done shall, in the new kingdom which I am setting up, and which shall soon become more visible and stable than it now is, give law to and rule the great Christian world' —which is here set forth in Jewish dress, as the Twelve tribes of Israel, to be presided over by the Twelve apostles on Twelve judicial thrones. In this sense certainly the promise has been illustriously fulfilled; and so *Grotius, Lightfoot,* &c., take it. But the majority of interpreters refer it to the yet future glory; and ch. xxii. 28-30 seems to confirm that interpretation. In this case it points to the time of the restitution of all things, when the great apostolic founders of the Christian Church shall be exalted to a distinction corresponding with the services they have rendered. Perhaps there is no need to draw a very sharp line of separation between these two views of the promise here made to the Twelve; and we do better, probably (with *Calvin*), to see in the present *fact,* that the "holy temple" of the Christian Church is "built upon the foundation of the apostles," and those "prophets" that supplemented their labours, "Jesus Christ Himself being the Chief Corner-Stone," the *assurance* that in the future glory their place would correspond with their services in that high office. The reply of our Lord to Peter closes, in Matthew and Mark, with the oft-repeated words, "But many

31 Then ^whe took *unto him* the twelve, and said unto them, Behold, we go up to Jerusalem, and all things ^xthat are written by the prophets
32 concerning the Son of man shall be accomplished. For ^yhe shall be delivered unto the Gentiles, and shall be mocked, and spitefully entreated,
33 and spitted on: and they shall scourge *him,* and put him to death: and
34 the third day he shall rise again. And ^zthey understood none of these things: and this saying was hid from them, neither knew they the things which were spoken.
35 And ^ait came to pass, that, as he was come nigh unto Jericho, a certain

A. D. 33.
^w Matt. 16. 21.
Matt. 17. 22.
^x Ps. 22.
Isa. 53.
^y Matt. 27. 2.
ch. 23. 1.
^z Mark 9. 32.
ch. 2. 50.
^a Matt. 20. 29.
Mark 10. 46.

that are first shall be last, and the last first." See on Matt. xx. 16, and Remark 4 at the close of that Section.

Remarks.—1. Is it not affecting to think how near this rich young ruler came to the kingdom of God without entering it? His irreproachable morals and his religious earnestness, amidst so much that was hostile to both; the ingenuousness with which he looked up to the Lord Jesus as qualified to solve his difficulties and relieve his anxieties on the subject of salvation, though belonging to a class that regarded Him with bitter hostility; and the courage with which he ran to Him, and knelt before Him in the presence of so many, with the eager enquiry, "What shall I do to inherit eternal life?"—when one thinks of all this, and then reads that, after all, "he went away" from Christ, how sad does it make the heart! But we must get to the bottom of this case if we would fully profit by it. What, then, was the defect? One thing only he lacked; but that, as we have said, was fundamental and fatal. "If any man love the world," says the apostle, "the love of the Father is not in him" (1 John ii. 15). Now this was just what this youth did. Others might not have detected it; but He whose eyes were as a flame of fire stood before him. Had anything else been asked of him, he might have stood the test. But the one thing that was demanded of him was the one thing he could not part with—his possessions. He might have kept these and gone to heaven if the Lord had not expressly demanded them. But for this, had he only sat loose to them, and been *prepared* to part with them at the call of duty, that had been quite enough. For while many a one covets the world he does not possess, some sit loose to the world they do possess. The former are idolaters, and "no idolater hath any inheritance in the kingdom of Christ and of God." The latter have, in the eye of Christ, "left all and followed Him, and they shall have treasure in heaven." Thus this youth, instead of keeping, as he thought, all the commandments from his youth up, never kept the first and great commandment, which is to love the Lord our God with all our heart. Had he done so he would not have gone away from Christ. And thus, too, just as in the human body, one may want an eye, or a hand, or a foot, or all of these, and other members too, and yet be a living man, because none of these are *vital;* whereas the heart, being essential to life, cannot be wanted: so the soul may be spiritually alive, and on its way to glory, notwithstanding many imperfections; but there are defects, even one of which is incompatible with life: "Without *faith* it is impossible to please God;" and "If any man have not *the Spirit of Christ,* he is none of His;" and "*Covetousness* is idolatry." 2. While every condition in life has its own snares, the danger of wealth lies in the tendency to idolize it; and it is not unlikely that the apostle had this incident and the reflections that follow it in view when he thus directed Timothy: "Charge them that are rich in

this world, that they be not high-minded, nor *trust* in uncertain riches, but in the living God, who giveth us richly all things to enjoy; that they do good, that they be rich in good works, ready to distribute, willing to communicate; laying up in store for themselves a good foundation against the time to come, that they may lay hold on eternal life" (1 Tim. vi. 17-19). At the same time, this and numberless exhortations to the rich show the folly of taking our Lord's directions to the rich young ruler as a general direction to part with all worldly possessions to the poor in order to get to heaven. In that case such passages as those just quoted would have no meaning at all. Christianity was not designed to obliterate the distinction of ranks and conditions in life, but to teach and beget in the different classes of society the proper feelings towards each other, and towards the common Lord of all. 3. Christians should learn from Christ Himself to appreciate the excellences even of the unconverted, while not blinded by these to what they fundamentally and fatally lack. 4. The Human excellences of the Lord Jesus are not to be regarded as on a level with those of mere men. Though human in their *nature,* they are the excellences of the Only begotten of the Father, which take them quite out of the category of *ordinary* excellences, even though these were faultless. If something of this kind was not underneath our Lord's hint to the young man about there being none good but One, it will be difficult to make any dignified sense out of it at all; but if it was, all is intelligible and worthy of Jesus. And thus *Socinianism,* instead of finding the support here which it is so fain to catch at, is only baffled by it.

31-34.—THIRD EXPLICIT ANNOUNCEMENT OF HIS APPROACHING SUFFERINGS, DEATH, AND RESURRECTION. (= Matt. xx. 17-19; Mark x. 32-34.) For the exposition, see on Mark x. 32-34.

35-43.—A BLIND MAN HEALED. (= Matt. xx. 29-34; "TWO BLIND MEN;" Mark x. 46-52, "BLIND BARTIMEUS.")

35. And it came to pass, that, as he was come nigh unto Jericho—on his way through Peræa to his last Passover, a certain blind man sat by the way-side begging. In Mark the name is given—"blind Bartimæus, the son of Timæus." But there and in Matthew it was "as they departed from," or "went out of Jericho;" and in Matthew it is not one, but "two blind men," beggars, that on this occasion received their sight. Several critics—as *Greswell, Ebrard, Ellicott, Neander, Wieseler,* with some of the Fathers—suppose one to have been healed on *entering,* the other on *leaving* Jericho. Others to whom this seems far-fetched, would leave the facts as recorded to speak independently for themselves. One thing seems clear, that these three narratives must have been written quite apart from each other; and another, that these divergences in the circumstantial details strongly corroborate the historical truth of the facts. Perhaps, *if we knew all the particulars,* we should see no difficulty; but that we have been left so far in the dark, shows that the thing is of

36 blind man sat by the way-side begging: and hearing the multitude pass
37 by, he asked what it meant.   And they told him, that Jesus of Nazareth
38 passeth by.   And he cried, saying, Jesus, *thou* son of David, have mercy
39 on me!   And they which went before rebuked him, that he should hold
his peace: but he cried so much the more, *Thou* son of David, have mercy
40 on me!   And Jesus *b*stood, and commanded him to be brought unto
41 him: and when he was come near, he asked him, saying, What wilt thou
that I shall do unto thee?   And he said, Lord, that I may receive my
42 sight.   And Jesus said unto him, Receive thy sight: *c*thy faith hath
43 saved thee.   And immediately *d*he received his sight, and followed him,
*e*glorifying God: and all the people, when they saw *it*, gave praise unto
God.

A. D. 33.
b Heb. 2. 17.
Heb. 5. 2.
c ch. 17. 19.
d Ps. 33. 9.
Isa. 35. 5.
e Ps. 103. 1.
Isa. 43. 7, 8,
21.
ch. 4. 39.
ch. 5. 26.
ch.17. 15-18.
Acts 4. 21.
Acts 11. 18.
1 Pet. 2. 9.

no moment any way.   Had there been any collusion among the authors of these Gospels, they would certainly have taken care to remove these 'spots on the sun'—as *Chrysostom,* of the Fathers, with *Olshausen, van Osterzee,* and *Alford,* fail not to observe.   **36. And hearing the multitude pass by, he asked what it meant**—a most graphic and natural touch; the *sound* being all he had to tell him what was going on.   **37. And they told him, that Jesus of Nazareth passeth by. 38. And he cried, saying, Jesus, son of David,** in other words, 'Thou promised Messiah.'   That this was the understood sense of the phrase is evident from the acclamation with which the multitude greeted Him on his triumphal entry into Jerusalem (Matt. xxi. 9; see also Matt. xii. 23).   **have mercy on me! 39. And they which went before**—"the multitude" (Matt. xx. 31), **rebuked him, that he should hold his peace**—and not annoy, or impede the progress of Jesus; very much in the spirit of the Twelve themselves but a little before, when infants were brought to Him (see on verse 15, and Remark 1 at the close of that Section), and when the Syrophenician woman "cried after Him" (see on Mark vii. 26).   But O, how differently from them did Jesus feel !   **but he cried so much the more, Son of David, have mercy on me!**   This is that *importunity,* so highly commended and richly rewarded in the Syrophenician woman, and so often enjoined, (ch. xi. 5, &c.; xviii. 1, &c.)   **40. And Jesus stood**—or "stood still," as rendered in Matthew and Mark, **and commanded him to be brought unto him.**   Mark (x. 49-50) has this interesting addition: "And they call the blind man, saying unto him, Be of good comfort: rise, He calleth thee."   It is just as one earnestly desiring an interview with some exalted person, but told by one official after another that it is vain to wait, for he will not succeed—they know it—yet persists in waiting for some answer to his suit, and at length the door opens, and a servant appears, saying, 'You are to be admitted —He has called you.'   No doubt those who thus encouraged the poor man, knew well the cure that would follow.   "And he, casting away his garment, rose, and came to Jesus."   How lively is this touch about the casting away of his garment !   It is evidently the remark of an eye-witness, expressive of the exhilarating hope with which he was immediately filled.   **And when he was come near, he asked him, 41. Saying, What wilt thou that I shall do unto thee?**   It was plain enough to all present what the poor blind man wanted: but Jesus, by this question, would try him; would deepen his present consciousness of need; and would draw out his faith in Him.   See on John v. 6.   **and he said, Lord** [Κύριε].   In Mark the term rendered "Lord" is "*Rabboni*"—an emphatic and confiding exclamation (see on John **xx. 16). that I may receive my sight. 42. And**

Jesus—"had compassion on them, and touched their eyes," says Matthew, "and" **said unto him, Receive thy sight, thy faith hath saved thee. 43. And immediately he received his sight, and**—now as a grateful disciple, **followed him, glorifying God: and all the people, when they saw it, gave praise unto God.**

Remark.—This gracious cure, it will be observed, was quite casual.   Blind Bartimeus sat that day, as usual, by the way-side begging; not dreaming that ere its shadows fell he should see the light of heaven.   But, like other blind people, his ears had doubtless been all the quicker to hear whatever was flying about.   And there can be no doubt that the tidings sent to the imprisoned Baptist—"The blind receive their sight"—had flown to him, with, very possibly, the details of some of the cures.   And just, as in the case of the Syrophenician woman, and in that of the woman with the issue of blood, these tidings had wrought in his heart the conviction that He was the promised Messiah, and such a confidence in His power and grace, that he would say within himself, 'O if He would but pass this way, how should I cry to Him, as "He that cometh in the name of the Lord;" and, poor beggar though I be, the Son of David would not shut His ear against me—*for they tell me He never yet did that to any suppliant.*   And who knows but He will come?   They say he is even now in this region, and if He goes up to Jerusalem to keep the approaching Passover, He likely *will* come this way.   But He may not come when I am here; and yet there is hope:—but what is that stir I hear?   What is it?   "Jesus of Nazareth passeth by!"   O transport!   He comes, He comes!   Now is my time.'   So, ere He comes up, the loud cry is heard, "Jesus, Son of David, have mercy on me!"   In a moving crowd, accompanying some great person on a progress, there are always some who keep ahead of the main body.   These, catching the sound first, officiously try to silence him, that there may be no commotion, no interruption:— 'Stop that dense crowd in order that the case of a beggar may be attended to? why, at that rate He would never get on at all.'   But the earnest suppliant is not to be moved by that.   His opportunity has come, for which he had longed but scarce dared to hope; and he shall not be silenced.   Nay, "so much the more" did he cry, "Son of David, have mercy on me!"   At length the glorious Healer comes up to the spot, and the whole crowd must halt, while He cures this believing beggar.   And first, He commands him to be called.   They hasten through the crowd to the road-side, and bid the poor man be of good cheer, for the Lord has sent for him.   This gives his faith time to ripen.   'I thought it would come to that: Long looked for—come at last: my hopes refused to be damped: they could not silence me; my soul went forth to Him in yet louder cries, and not in

309

19, AND *Jesus* entered and passed through ^aJericho. And, behold, *there*
2 *was* a man named Zaccheus, which was the chief among the publicans,
3 and he was rich. And he sought to see Jesus who he was; and could
4 not for the press, because he was little of stature. And he ran before,
and climbed up into a sycamore tree to see him: for he was to pass that
5 *way*. And when Jesus came to the place, he looked up, and saw him,
and said unto him, Zaccheus, make haste, and come down; ^bfor to-day I
6 must abide at thy house. And he made haste, and came down, and
7 received him joyfully. And when they saw *it*, they all murmured,

A. D. 33.
CHAP. 19.
^a Jos. 6. 26.
1 Ki. 16. 34.
2 Ki. 2. 18-22
Jos. 2. 1.
^b Gen. 18. 3, 5.
Gen. 19. 1, 3.
Ps. 101. 2, 3.
John 14. 23.

vain: I'm to succeed; I shall, I shall!' Thus he comes into the presence of Jesus. "What wilt thou that I shall do unto thee?" As he could not *see* Him, the Lord takes this way of awakening, through his *ears*, the expectation of relief, and gives him an opportunity of presenting in explicit terms the desire of his heart. "Lord," is his ready answer, "that I may receive my sight." It is enough. The Redeemer's heart yearns with compassion; He touches his eyes, and immediately He sees as other men. Like the man out of whom went the legion of devils, he clings to his wondrous Benefactor, pouring out his grateful feelings, in which the wondering people also join. Thus did this man catch his favourable moment, seize his opportunity, and obtain a rich reward. At other times he had cried in vain. And are there no opportunities—no favourable moments still—*analogous* to this, for getting the higher sight, for being healed in the higher sense? Are there not some seasons, rather than others, of which it may be said that "Jesus of Nazareth *passeth by*"? Seasons of affliction are such; but pre-eminently, seasons of religious awakening, of revival, and the effusion of the Spirit. And just as when, after a long, dull calm at sea, the wind gets up, all hands are astir to hoist the sails and catch the breeze, so then, if ever, as Jesus of Nazareth passeth by, should all that feel their need of healing stir up their expectations, and lift up their cries; and though there may be here also officious people who rebuke them, that they should hold their peace, their wisdom will be only to "cry so much the more." Nor can they more readily draw down His compassion and ensure relief, than by refusing to be silenced by such pretended friends.

CHAP. XIX. 1-10.—CONVERSION OF ZACCHEUS THE PUBLICAN. The opening verse shows that this remarkable incident occurred at the same time with the foregoing.

1. And Jesus entered. As the word "Jesus" is not in the original, it should not have been inserted here. The rendering should be, 'And He entered,' showing that the occasion is the same as before. **and passed through** [διήρχετο]—rather, 'was passing through' Jericho—as to which, see on chap. x. 30, 31. **2. And, behold, there was a man named Zaccheus**—the same as *Zacchai*, Ezra ii. 9; Neh. vii. 14. From *v.* 9 it is evident that he was a Jew, and what he says in *v.* 8 would have proved it too. **which was** [καὶ αὐτὸς]—'and the same was' **the chief among the publicans**—a high revenue official, **and he was rich.** Ill-gotten riches some of it certainly was, as we shall see on *v.* 8. For the office and character of the publicans, see on Matt. v. 46, and on ch. xv. 1. **3. And he sought to see Jesus**—not to listen to His teaching, or obtain anything from Him, but merely to see **who he was**—what sort of person this was, about whom there was so much speculation, and after whom such crowds were following. *Curiosity*, then, was his only motive, though his determination not to be baulked was overruled for more than he sought. **and could not for the press, because he was little**

of stature. **4. And he ran before, and climbed up into a sycamore tree**—the Egyptian fig, with leaves like the mulberry—**to see him: for he was to pass that way.** Thus eager to put himself in the way of Jesus, low as his motive was, he was rewarded by what he little dreamt of. **5. And when Jesus came to the place, he looked up**—in the full knowledge of who was in that tree, and preparatory to addressing him, **and saw him, and said unto him, Zaccheus**—whom He had never before seen in the flesh, nor probably heard of by report; but "He calleth His own sheep *by name*, and leadeth them out" (John x. 3). **make haste, and come down; for to-day I must abide at thy house.** Our Lord *invites Himself*, and that in right *royal* style, which waits not for invitations, but—since the honour is done to the subject, not the sovereign—announces the purpose of royalty to partake of the subject's hospitalities. Manifestly our Lord speaks as knowing how the privilege would be appreciated. Accordingly, with an alacrity which in such a person surprises us, he does exactly as bidden. "Make haste;" **6. And he made haste**—"and come down," **and came down**—"for to-day I must abide at thy house," **and received him joyfully.** Whence this so sudden "joy" in the cold bosom of an avaricious publican? The internal revolution was as perfect as it was instantaneous. He who spake to Matthew the publican but those witching words, "Follow me," and "he arose, left all, and followed Him"—He who said to the man with the withered hand, "Stretch forth thine hand," and "he stretched it out, and it was restored whole as the other"—the same said to the *heart* of Zaccheus at one and the same moment as to his ear, "Make haste and come down; for to-day I must abide at thy house." He with whom Zaccheus had to do had but to "speak, and it was done;" though few penetrated to the secret of this as the centurion did, at whose faith Jesus "marvelled" (ch. vii. 7-9). At the same time one can trace the steps of this revolution in the mind of Zaccheus. In the *look* which Christ gave him—"When Jesus came to the place, He looked up," singling him out from all others—he must have seen something of a *purpose* towards himself, which would at once arrest his attention. Then, His addressing him by *name*, as perfectly familiar with him, though He had never seen or heard of him before—this would fill him with amazement, and make the thought instantly flash across his mind, 'This *must* be the Christ He claims to be!' But when the *call* followed, in such wonderful terms—"Make haste, and come down, for to-day I must abide at thy house"— the conscious majesty of it, and the power with which it was spoken, as if sure of instant and glad obedience, doubtless completed the conquest of his mind and heart. But these, though the *avenues* through which Christ found His way into Zaccheus's heart, must not be regarded as the whole explanation of the change upon him. (See on Acts xvi. 14.) **7. And when they saw it, they all murmured.** We have got so

8 saying, ^cThat he was gone to be guest with a man that is a sinner. And Zaccheus stood, and said unto the Lord; Behold, Lord, the half of my goods I give to the poor; and if I have taken any thing from any man
9 by false accusation, I ^drestore *him* four-fold. And Jesus said unto him, This day is salvation come to this house, forsomuch as ^ehe also is a son
10 of Abraham. For ^fthe Son of man is come to seek and to save that which was lost.

A. D. 33.
c Matt. 9. 11, 21, 28, 31, ch. 5. 30.
d Ex. 22. 1.
1 Sam. 12.3.
e ch. 13. 16.
f Matt. 10. 6.
Matt. 15. 24.

accustomed to this in the Gospel History, that we know the classes that must be here referred to— "the Pharisees and scribes" (ch. xv. 2), or their echoes among the multitude. **saying, That he was gone to be guest** [καταλῦσαι]—or, 'take up His lodging,' as the same word is rendered in ch. ix. 12. The word signifies to 'unloose' or 'unyoke,' as travellers do where they are to rest for the night. (See Gen. xxiv. 23, in LXX.) **with a man that is a sinner.** No, captious Pharisees; he *was* a sinner up till a minute ago, but now he is a new creature, as his own lips shall presently make manifest. **8. And Zaccheus stood**—stood forth, openly before all; **and said unto the Lord, Behold, Lord.** Mark how frequently our Evangelist uses this title, especially where lordly *authority*, *dignity, grace,* or *power* is intended. **the half of my goods I give to the poor; and if I have taken any thing from any man by false accusation**—'defrauded,' 'overcharged,' any man, assessing him on a false representation of his means, or of the value of the articles for which he was rated, which was but too common with this class (see ch. iii. 12, 13), **I restore him four-fold.** The "if" here is not meant to express any doubt of the *fact*, but only the difficulty, where there had been so much of this, to fix upon the cases and the extent of the unrighteous exactions. The meaning, then, is, 'in so far as I have done this.' The Roman law required this four-fold restitution; the Jewish law, but the principal, and a fifth more (Num. v. 7). There was no *demand* made for either; but, as if to revenge himself on his hitherto reigning sin (see on John xx. 28), and to testify the change he had experienced, besides surrendering the half of his *fair* gains to the poor, he voluntarily determines to give up all that was ill gotten, quadrupled. And what is worthy of notice, in the presence of all he gratefully addressed this to "the Lord," to whom he owed the wonderful change. **9. And Jesus said unto him**—and this also before all, and for the information of all, **This day is salvation come to this house.** Memorable saying! Salvation has already come, but it is not a day nor an hour old. The word "to this *house*" was probably designed to meet the taunt, 'He is gone to lodge at a sinner's house.' The house, says Jesus, is no longer a sinner's house, polluted and polluting: 'Tis now a saved house, all meet for the reception of Him who came to save.' What a precious idea is *salvation to a house*, expressing the new air that would henceforth breathe in it, and the new impulses from its head which would reach its members. **forsomuch as he also** [καθότι καὶ αὐτὸς]—'inasmuch as even he,' publican though he be, and acting till now in the unprincipled way which even himself has confessed—even he **is a son of Abraham.** He was that by birth, but here it means a partaker of Abraham's *faith*, being mentioned as the sufficient explanation of *salvation* having come to him. (Gal. iii. 26, 29; and for Abraham's faith as evidenced by *works*, as here, see Jas. ii. 22.) **10. For the Son of man is come to seek and to save that which was lost.** A remarkable expression—not '*them*,' but 'that'

which was lost [τὸ ἀπολωλός]; that is, the *mass* of lost sinners. Zaccheus was simply one such; and in saving him, Jesus says He was not going out of His way, but just doing His proper work. He even explains why He waited not for Zaccheus to apply to Him; for, says He, 'My business is to *seek* as well as save such.'

Remarks.—1. Whatever brings souls in contact with Christ is hopeful. When Zaccheus "sought to see Jesus, who He was," nothing probably was further from his mind than becoming His disciple, and a new creature. But that mere *curiosity* of his, and the step he took to gratify it, were the "cords of a man" by which he was drawn into the position for Christ's eye and voice of love and power to reach him. On his part, all was the operation of natural, ordinary, every-day principles of action: on Christ's part, all was supernatural, divine. But *so it is in every conversion.* Hence the importance of bringing those we love, and for whose conversion we long and pray, within the atmosphere of those means, and in contact with those truths, on the wings of which Christ's power and grace are wont to reach the heart. What thousands have thus, all unexpectedly to themselves, been transformed into new creatures! 2. What a testimony to *instantaneous conversion* have we here! Against this there are groundless prejudices even among Christians; which, it is to be feared, arise from want of sufficient familiarity with the laws and activities of the spiritual life. Though the fruit of a sovereign operation of Grace upon their own hearts, Christians are nevertheless in danger of sinking into such a secular spirit, that the *supernatural* character of their Christian life is scarcely felt, and lively spirituality hardly known. No wonder, then, that such should view with suspicion changes like this, which by their instantaneousness reveal a *kind* of divine operation to which they are themselves too great strangers. But what else than *instantaneous* can any conversion be? The *preparation* for it may be very gradual; it may take a hundred or a thousand steps to bring the very means which are to be effectual right up to the heart, and the heart itself into a frame for yielding to them. But once let it come to that, and the transition from death to life *must* be instantaneous—the last surrender of the heart must be so. The result of such words from heaven as "Live"! (Ezek. xvi. 6): "Be thou clean"! (Matt. viii. 3): "Thy sins be forgiven thee"! (Mark xi. 5): "Make haste, and come down; for to-day I must abide at thy house"!—cannot but be instantaneous, as when they issued from the lips of Jesus in the days of His flesh. The "taking away of the stone" *before* Lazarus's resurrection, and "loosing and letting him go" *after* it, as they were human operations, so they took a little time, though not a great deal. But when "the Resurrection and the Life" said, "Lazarus, come forth!" his resuscitation was instantaneous, and could not but be. See on John xi. 39, 44. 3. The best evidence of conversion lies in the undoing or reversal of those things by which our former sinfulness was chiefly marked—the conquest of what

11 And as they heard these things, he added and spake a parable, because he was nigh to Jerusalem, and because *g* they thought that the kingdom
12 of God should immediately appear. He *h* said therefore,

A certain nobleman went into a far country to receive for himself a
13 kingdom, and to return. And he called his ten servants, and delivered
14 them ten ¹pounds, and said unto them, Occupy till I come. But *i* his citizens hated him, and sent a message after him, saying, We will not
15 have this *man* to reign over us. And it came to pass, that, when he was returned, having received the kingdom, then he commanded these servants to be called unto him, to whom he had given the ²money, that he might
16 know how much every man had gained by trading. Then came the first,
17 saying, Lord, thy pound hath gained ten pounds. And he said unto him, Well, thou good servant: because thou hast been *j* faithful in a very

A. D. 33.

g Acts 1. 6.
h Matt. 25.14.
   Mark 13.34.
1 A Pound is twelve ounces and a half; which, at five shillings the ounce, is 3*l*. 2*s*. 6*d*.
i John 1. 11.
2 Silver.
j Matt. 25.21.
   ch. 16. 10.

are called 'besetting sins.' Had Zaccheus lived before chiefly to *hoard up?* Now, "Behold, Lord, the half of my goods I give to the poor." A large proportion of his means this, to part with at once to those who were in want. But further, did Zaccheus become "rich" by appropriating to himself the excess of his exactions "by false accusation"? "If I have taken any thing from any man by false accusation, I restore him four-fold." The frozen heart had melted down, the clenched fist had opened, and—unlike the rich young ruler (ch. xviii. 23)—the idol had been dethroned. This was a change indeed. See on the wise injunctions of the Baptist to the different classes that asked him how they were to manifest their repentance —on ch. iii. 12. 4. When religion comes into the *heart*, it will find its way into the *house*, as into that of Zaccheus. For it is in one's house that one is most *himself*. There, he is on no stiff ceremony; there, if anywhere, he opens out; there he acts as he *is*. Where religion is not, the home is the place to reveal it; where it is, it is the air of home that draws it out, like perfumes which the zephyr wafts to all around. Hence the bold language of the apostle to the jailer of Philippi, "Believe in the Lord Jesus Christ, and thou shalt be saved, and *thy house*" (Acts xvi. 31; and see also *vv.* 14, 15). "The voice of rejoicing and salvation is" not only in the hearts but in the houses, not only in the temples but "in the tabernacles of the righteous" (Ps. cxviii. 15). 5. Till men are converted and become new creatures, they are "*lost*," in the account of Christ—in what sense may be seen in the case of the Prodigal son, who was "*lost*" when a run-away from his father, and "*found*" when he returned and was welcomed back as a penitent. (See on ch. xv. 24.) Accordingly, as being the common condition of all whom Christ came to save, they are represented as "*that* which is lost." But if the worst features of men's fallen state are held forth without disguise in the teaching of Christ, it is only to commend the remedy, and encourage those who have felt it most deeply not to despair. For "the Son of Man is come to seek and to save that which is lost." It was His errand; it is His business; and this glorious case of Zaccheus—He Himself assures us —is but a specimen-case. Multitudes of them there have since been, but there are more to come; and when any are ready to sink under insupportable discoveries of their lost state, we are warranted to tell them that theirs is just a *case* for the Lord Jesus—"for the Son of Man is come to seek and to save that which was lost!"

11-27.—THE PARABLE OF THE POUNDS. That this parable is quite a different one from that of THE TALENTS (in Matt. xxv. 14-30)—although *Calvin, Olshausen, Meyer,* &c., but not *de Wette* and

Neander, identify them—will appear from the following considerations:—First, This parable was spoken "when He was *nigh* to Jerusalem" (*v.* 11); that one, some days after entering it, and from the Mount of Olives. Second, This parable was spoken to the promiscuous crowd; that, to the Twelve alone. Accordingly, Third, Besides the "*servants*" in this parable, who profess subjection to Him, there is a class of "*citizens*" who refuse to own Him, and who are treated differently; whereas in the Talents, spoken to the *former class* alone, this latter class is omitted. Fourth, In the Talents, each *servant* receives a different number of them—five, two, one; in the Pounds, all receive the same one pound (which is but about the sixtieth part of a talent); also, in the Talents, each of the faithful servants shows the *same* fidelity by doubling what he received—the five are made ten, the two four; in the Pounds, each, receiving the same, renders a *different* return—one making his pound ten, another five. Plainly, therefore, the intended lesson is different; the one illustrating *equal fidelity with different degrees of advantage;* the other, *different degrees of improvement of the same opportunities.* And yet, with all this difference, the parables are remarkably similar.

11. And as they heard—or were listening to, **these things, he added and spake** [προσθεὶς εἶπεν] —or 'went on to speak;' which shows that this followed close upon the preceding incident: **a parable, because he was nigh to Jerusalem, and because they thought that the kingdom of God should immediately appear** [ἀναφαίνεσθαι]—or be visibly set up as soon as He reached the capital. So that this was designed more immediately for His own disciples, as is also evident from the nature of the parable itself. **12. He said therefore. A certain nobleman went into a far country** —said to put down the notion that He was just on His way to set up His kingdom, and to inaugurate it by His personal presence. **to receive for himself a kingdom**—to be invested with royalty; as when Herod went to Rome and was there made king: a striking expression of what our Lord went away for and received, "sitting down at the right hand of the majesty on high." **and to return**—at His Second coming. **13. And he called his ten servants, and delivered them ten pounds, and said unto them, Occupy** [Πραγματεύσασθε]—'Negociate,' 'do business,' with the resources entrusted to you. **till I come. 14. But his citizens hated him, and sent a message after him, saying, We will not have this man to reign over us.** It is a great misconception of this parable to confound these "citizens" with the "servants." The one repudiate all subjection to Him; the other, not excepting the unfaithful one, acknowledge Him as Master. By the "citizens"

18 little, have thou authority over ten cities. And the second came, saying,
19 Lord, thy pound hath gained five pounds. And he said likewise to him,
20 Be thou also over five cities. And another came, saying, Lord, behold,
21 *here is* thy pound, which I have kept laid up in a napkin: for *k*I feared
thee, because thou art an austere man: thou takest up that thou layedst
22 not down, and reapest that thou didst not sow. And he saith unto him,
*l*Out of thine own mouth will I judge thee, *thou* wicked servant. *m*Thou
knewest that I was an austere man, taking up that I laid not down, and
23 reaping that I did not sow: wherefore then gavest not thou my money
into the bank, that at my coming I might have required mine own with
24 usury? And he said unto them that stood by, Take from him the pound,
25 and give *it* to him that hath ten pounds. (And they said unto him,
26 Lord, he hath ten pounds.) For I say unto you, *n*That unto every one
which hath shall be given; and from him that hath not, even that he
27 hath shall be taken away from him. But those mine enemies, which
would not that I should reign over them, bring hither, and slay *them*
before me.
28 And when he had thus spoken, *o*he went before, ascending up to
Jerusalem.
29 And *p*it came to pass, when he was come nigh to Bethphage and
Bethany, at the mount called *the mount* of Olives, he sent two of his

A. D. 33.
k Ex. 20. 19,
20.
1Sam.12.20.
Matt.25.24.
2 Tim. 1. 7.
Rom. 8. 15.
Jas. 2. 19.
1John 4.18.
Rev. 21. 8.
l 2 Sam. 1.16.
Job 15. 6.
Matt.12.37.
Tit. 3. 11.
*m*Matt.25.26.
n Matt. 13.12.
Matt. 25.29.
Mark 4. 25.
ch. 8. 18.
o Mark 10.32.
ch. 9. 51.
ch. 12. 50.
John 18.11.
1 Pet. 4. 1.
p Matt. 21.1.
Mark 11. 1.
John 12.12,
16.

historically are here meant the Jews as a nation, who were Christ's "own," as "King of the Jews," but who expressly repudiated Him in this character, saying, "We have no king but Cesar" (John xix. 15.) But *generally*, and in Christendom, this class comprehends all infidel, open rejecters of Christ and Christianity, as distinguished from professed Christians. 15-26. The *reckoning* here is so very similar to that in Matt. xxv. 19-29, that the same exposition will answer for both; if only it be observed that here we have different degrees of future gracious reward, proportioned to the measure of present fidelity. **27. But those mine enemies, which would not that I should reign over them, bring hither, and slay them before me.** Compare 1 Sam. xv. 32, 33. The reference is to the awful destruction of Jerusalem; but it points to the final perdition of all who shall be found in open rebellion against Christ.

For Remarks on this Section, see those on Matt. xxv. 14-30, at the close of that Section.

28-44.—CHRIST'S TRIUMPHAL ENTRY INTO JERUSALEM ON THE FIRST DAY OF THE WEEK—HIS TEARS OVER IT, AND ITS DOOM PRONOUNCED. (=Matt. xxi. 1-11; Mark xi. 1-11; John xii. 12-19.) It will be seen, from the parallels, that we are now coming to those scenes of which we have the concurrent records of all the Four Evangelists. And no wonder, considering how pregnant with the life of the world are those scenes of majesty and meekness, of grace and glory, of patience and power, of death, with elements of unutterable anguish, and life, with issues in its bosom inconceivably glorious. The river, the streams whereof make glad the City of God—but O, with what an awful gladness!—now parts, as befits the river of our Paradise, into its "four heads." **28. And when he had thus spoken, he went before.** See on Mark x. 32, and Remark 1 at the close of that Section; **ascending up to Jerusalem.** Here occurs an important gap, supplied in the Fourth Gospel.

John xii. 1: "Then Jesus, six days before the Passover"—probably after sunset on the *Friday* Evening, or at the commencement of the Jewish *Sabbath*, which preceded the Passover—"came to Bethany, where Lazarus was, which

had been dead, whom He [had] raised from the dead." There, if we are right as to the time of His arrival, He would spend His last Sabbath amongst friends peculiarly dear to Him, and possibly it was on the evening of that Sabbath that "there they made Him a supper, at the house of Simon the leper." See on Mark xiv. 3, &c. At all events, it was on the day following, which was *the First Day of the Week*, that He made this His triumphal Entry into Jerusalem. This corresponded to the *tenth* day of the month *Nisan*, in the Jewish year, the day on which the paschal lamb was separated from the rest of the flock, and *set apart for sacrifice:* it was "*kept up until the fourteenth day*," on which "the whole assembly of the congregation of Israel were to kill it in the evening" [בֵּין הָעַרְבָּיִם] literally, 'between the two evenings' (as in the *margin*); that is, between *three* o'clock—the hour of the evening sacrifice—and six o'clock, or the close of the Jewish day (Exod. xii. 3, 6). Who can believe that this was a mere coincidence? Who that observes how every act in the final scenes was alluded to, arranged and carried out with a calm dignity, as seeing the end from the beginning, can doubt that "Christ *our Passover*" who was to be "*sacrificed for us*," designed, by His solemn entry into the bloody city, yet the appointed place of sacrifice, to hold Himself forth as from this time *set apart for sacrifice?* Accordingly, He never after this properly left Jerusalem—merely sleeping at Bethany, but spending the whole of every day in the city.

The Triumphal Entry into Jerusalem (29-40). **29. And it came to pass, when he was come nigh to Bethphage and Bethany, at the mount called [the mount] of Olives.** Our Evangelist alludes thus generally to Bethany, as if our Lord had merely passed by it, on His way to Jerusalem, because He was not to relate anything about His *stay* there, but only that He took it on His route to the capital. The word "Bethphage" [=בֵּית פַּגֵּי] means '*Fig-house*,' no doubt from the profusion of that fruit which this spot produced. That it lay, as Bethany did, on the eastern side of the mount of Olives, or the side farthest from the capital, is certain: but no

30 disciples, saying, Go ye into the village over against *you;* in the which at your entering ye shall find a colt tied, whereon yet never man sat:
31 loose him, and bring *him hither.* And if any man ask you, Why do ye loose *him?* thus shall ye say unto him, Because ^q the Lord hath need of him.
32 And they that were sent went their way, and found even as he had
33 said unto them. And as they were loosing the colt, the owners thereof
34 said unto them, Why loose ye the colt? And they said, The Lord hath
35 need of him. And they brought him to Jesus: ^r and they cast their garments upon the colt, and they set Jesus thereon.

A. D. 33.
^q Ps. 24. 1.
Ps. 50. 10-
12.
Matt. 21. 2, 3.
Mark 11. 2-
6.
Acts 10. 36.
^r 2 Ki. 9. 13.
Matt. 21. 7.
Mark 11. 7.
John 12. 14.
Gal. 4. 15.

traces of it are now to be found, and whether it was east or west, north or south, of Bethany, is not agreed. The small village of Bethany [בֵּית עֲנָי], meaning '*Date-house,*' yet remains, 'pleasantly situated,' says *Thomson,* 'near the south-eastern base of the mount, and having many fine trees about and above it.' **he sent two of his disciples, 30. Saying, Go ye into the village over against you**—that is, Bethphage; **in the which at your entering ye shall find a colt tied, whereon yet never man sat.** This last remarkable particular is mentioned both by Matthew and Mark. On its significance, see on John xix. 41. **loose him, and bring him hither. 31. And if any man ask you, Why do ye loose him? thus shall ye say unto him, Because the Lord hath need of him**—"and straightway he will send him hither" (Mark xi. 3). Remarkable words! But the glorious Speaker knew all, and had the key of the human heart. (See on verse 5.) It is possible the owner was a disciple; but whether or no, the Lord knew full well what the result would be. A remarkable parallel to it will be found in the case of Samuel (see 1 Sam. x. 2-7); but with this noteworthy difference, that it is impossible to read the narrative of Samuel's directions without observing that he knew himself all the while to be but a *servant* of the Lord, whereas *the Lord Himself* is in every utterance and act of Jesus on this occasion.

32. And they that were sent went their way, and found even as he had said unto them. Mark is so singularly precise here, that it is impossible to doubt that the description is fresh from one of the two disciples sent on this errand; and in that case, who can it be but *Peter,* of whose hand in this Gospel all antiquity testifies and internal evidence is so strong? Probably *John* was the other (compare Mark xiv. 13, with Luke xxii. 8). "And they went their way (says Mark), and found the colt *tied by the door without in a place where two ways met;* and they loose him." Had not the minutest particulars of this grand entry into Jerusalem burned themselves into the memory of those dear disciples that were honoured to take part in the preparations for it, such unimportant details had never been recorded. **33. And as they were loosing the colt, the owners thereof said unto them, Why loose ye the colt? 34. And they said, The Lord hath need of him**—"and (says Mark) they let them go." **35. And they brought him to Jesus.** Matthew here gives an important particular, omitted by the other Evangelists. He says "they brought *the ass and the colt.*" Of course, the unbroken colt would be all the more tractable by having its dam to go along with it. The bearing of this minute particular on the prophecy about to be quoted is very striking. **and they cast their garments upon the colt, and they set Jesus thereon**—He allowing them to act this part of attendants on royalty, as befitting the *state* He was now, for the first and only time, assuming.

Matthew here notes the well-known prophecy which was fulfilled in all this, on which we must pause for a little: "All this was done, that it might be fulfilled which was spoken by the prophet (Zec. ix. 9), saying, Tell ye (or, 'Say ye to') the daughter of Zion"—quoting here another bright Messianic prophecy (Isa. lxii. 11) in place of Zechariah's opening words, "Rejoice greatly, O daughter of Zion; shout, O daughter of Jerusalem: Behold, thy King cometh unto thee." Here the prophet adds, "He is just, and having salvation" or 'helped'—[נוֹשָׁע]; but the Evangelist omits these, passing on to what relates to the *lowly* character of His royalty: "meek, and sitting upon an ass, and a colt, the foal of an ass." It was upon the *foal* that our Lord sat, as Mark and Luke expressly state. While the *horse* was an animal of war, the *ass* was used for purposes of peace. In the times of the Judges, and for a considerable time afterwards, horses were not used at all by the Israelites, and so even distinguished persons rode on asses (Jud. v. 10; x. 4; xii. 14)—but not from any nobleness in that animal, or its being an emblem of royalty, as some say. 'Nor,' to use the words of *Hengstenberg,* 'in all our accounts of the asses of the East, of which we have a great abundance, is there a single example of an ass being ridden by a king, or even a distinguished officer, on any state occasion; whereas here it is expressly in *His royal capacity* that the prophet says Jerusalem's King is to ride upon an ass.' And there are not wanting proofs, adduced by this able critic, that in the East the ass was and is regarded with a measure of *contempt.* And does not the fulfilment of the prophecy which we behold here itself show that *lowliness* was stamped upon the act, royal though it was? 'Into the same city,' adds the critic just quoted, 'which David and Solomon had so frequently entered on mules or horses richly caparisoned, and with a company of proud horsemen as their attendants, the Lord rode on a borrowed ass, which had never been broken in; the wretched clothing of His disciples supplying the place of a saddle-cloth, and His attendants consisting of people whom the world would regard as a mob and rabble.' This critic also, by an examination of the phrase used by the prophet, "the foal of asses," infers that it means an ass still mostly dependent upon its mother, and regards the use of this as a mark of yet greater humiliation in a King. In short, it was the *meekness of majesty* which was thus manifested, entering the city with royal *authority,* yet waiving, during His humbled state, all the external *grandeur* that shall yet accompany that authority. On this remarkable prophecy, so remarkably fulfilled, we notice two other points. First, the familiar and delightful name given to the chosen people, "The daughter of Zion," or, as we might conceive of it, '*the offspring of Zion's ordinances,*' born and nursed amid its sanctities—deriving all their spiritual life from the Religion which had its centre and seat in Zion;

36,   And *as he went, they spread their clothes in the way. And when he

37   was come nigh, even now at the descent of the mount of Olives, the whole multitude of the disciples began to rejoice and praise God with a loud

38   voice for all the mighty works that they had seen, saying, *Blessed be the King that cometh in the name of the Lord: "peace in heaven, and glory in the highest.

39   And some of the Pharisees from among the multitude said unto him,

40   Master, rebuke thy disciples. And he answered and said unto them, I

A. D. 33.

* Matt. 21. 8.
t Ps.72.17,19.
   Ps. 118. 26.
   Zec. 9. 9.
   Matt. 21. 9.
   ch. 13. 35.
   1 Tim. 1.17.
" ch. 2. 14.
   Eph. 2. 14.

next, the prophetic call to the chosen people to "*Rejoice greatly*" at this coming of their King to His own proper city. And the joy with which Jesus was welcomed on this occasion into Jerusalem was all the more striking a fulfilment of this prophecy, that it was far from being that intelligent, deep, and exultant welcome which the prophetic Spirit would have had Zion's daughter to give to her King. For if it was so superficial and fickle a thing as we know that it was, all the more does one wonder that it was so immense in its reach and volume; nor is it possible to account for it save by a wave of feeling—a mysterious impulse—sweeping over the mighty mass from above, in conformity with high arrangements, to give the King of Israel for once a visible, audible, glad welcome to His Own regal City. **36. And as he went**—or proceeded onwards towards the city, **they spread their clothes in the way**—that is, the gathering crowds did so; attracted, probably, in the first instance, by the novelty of the spectacle, but a higher view of it by and by flashing across them. Matthew says, "And a very great multitude"—or 'the immense multitude' [Ὁ δὲ πλεῖστος ὄχλος] "spread their garments in the way; others cut down branches from the trees, and strawed them in the way." This casting of their garments beneath His feet was an ancient Oriental way of expressing the homage of a people towards their sovereign, or one whom they wished to welcome as such—as we see in the case of Jehu (2 Ki. ix. 13). And spreading a gorgeous cloth over the pathway that is to be trodden by a monarch on any great occasion, is our modern way of doing the same thing. **37. And when he was come nigh, even now at the descent of the mount of Olives**—just as He approached the city, **the whole multitude of the disciples**—in the wider sense of that term—"that went before and that followed" (Matt. xxi. 9.)—both the van and the rear of this immense mass, began—or proceeded, **to rejoice and praise God with a loud voice.** The language here is unusually grand, intended to express a burst of admiration far wider and deeper than ever had been witnessed before. **for all the mighty works**—or 'miracles' [δυνάμεων] **that they had seen**—the last and grandest, the resurrection of Lazarus, only crowning a series of unparalleled wonders. **38. Saying,**—"Hosanna" (Matthew, Mark, and John); that is, "*Save now*" [הוֹשִׁיעָה נָּא] Ps. cxviii. 25. **Blessed [be]**—or 'is,' as rendered in Matthew and John. Either way, it is their glad welcome to **the King that cometh in the name of the Lord**—in John (xii. 13), "the King of Israel;" in Matthew (xxi. 9), "the Son of David;" in Mark (xi. 9, 10), after "Blessed is He that cometh in the name of the Lord," another exclamation is added, "Blessed be the Kingdom of our father David, that cometh in the name of the Lord." In all likelihood, the exclamation was variously uttered by the multitude, and the same voices may have varied their acclaim, as they repeated it over and over again, **peace in heaven, and glory in the highest.** The multitude of the *heavenly* host, remarks *Bengel*, said at His birth,

"Peace on *earth*" (ch. ii. 14), this *earthly* multitude say, "Peace in *heaven*." A great truth, indeed, but uttered in ignorance. Christ's entry into Jerusalem now meant peace in both senses; but, alas, they "knew not the things that belonged to their peace." In Matthew and Mark another "Hosanna in the highest" is substituted for this; and, doubtless, it was repeated often enough. In thus uttering the grand Messianic words of Ps. cxviii. 25—which lie embosomed in those rich Evangelical anticipations that formed part of the *Great Hallel*, as it was called, or Passover-Psalms, to be sung by all the people in a few days, and which were understood to refer to the Messiah—they acted, all unconsciously, as the representatives of the true Church welcoming Her King, aye, and of the literal Israel, who will one day hail Him with a transport of joy, but mingled with weeping. (Compare Matt. xxiii. 39, with Zec. xii. 10).

A very important addition is here made in the Fourth Gospel:

John xii. 16-19. "These things understood not His disciples at the first; but when Jesus was glorified, then remembered they (see John xiv. 26) that these things were written of Him"—referring more immediately to the prophecies just quoted from Ps. cxviii. and Zec. ix., but generally to those Messianic portions of the Old Testament which had till then been overlooked—"and that they had done these things unto him." The Spirit, descending on them from the glorified Saviour at Pentecost, opened their eyes suddenly to the true sense of the Old Testament, brought vividly to their recollection this and other Messianic predictions, and to their unspeakable astonishment showed them that they, and all the actors in these scenes, had been unconsciously fulfilling those predictions. "The people therefore that was with Him when He called Lazarus out of His grave, and raised Him from the dead, bare record"—probably telling others in the crowd what they had so recently witnessed, as additional evidence that this *must* be "He that cometh in the name of the Lord." "For this cause the people"—or 'the multitude' [ὁ ὄχλος] "also met Him, for that they heard that He had done this miracle." The crowd was thus largely swelled in consequence of the stir which the resurrection of Lazarus made in and about the city. "The Pharisees therefore said among themselves, Perceive ye"—or 'Ye perceive' [Θεωρεῖτε], "how ye prevail nothing? behold, the world is gone after Him"—a popular way of speaking: 'He is drawing all men after Him;' a saying, as *Bengel* remarks, in which there lay something prophetic, like that of Caiaphas (John xi. 50-52), and that of Pilate (John xix. 19). This was spoken evidently with deep indignation; and was as much as to say, 'We cannot allow this to go any further, steps must be immediately taken to get rid of Him, else all will be lost.'

39. And some of the Pharisees from among the multitude said unto him, Master—'Teacher' —[Διδάσκαλε], **rebuke thy disciples**—a bold throw

315

tell you that, if these should hold their peace, [v]the stones would immediately cry out.

41 And when he was come near, he beheld the city, and [w]wept over it, 42 saying, If thou hadst known, even thou, at least in this thy day, the

this, evidently to try Him, for they could hardly think that it would be done. **40. And he answered and said unto them**—using this Pharisaic interruption as but an opportunity for giving vent to His pent up feelings in the hearing of all around Him, **I tell you that, if these should hold their peace, the stones would immediately cry out** [κεκράξονται, *paulo-post fut.*, This rare tense is better supported here, we think, than the simple future, κράξουσιν, 'will cry out,' adopted by *Tischendorf*, *Tregelles*, and *Alford*, but not *Lachmann*]. In Hab. ii. 11 we have nearly the same saying. But it was proverbial even among the Greeks and Romans, and *Webster and Wilkinson* quote a Greek couplet and a passage from Cicero precisely the same. Hitherto the Lord had discouraged all demonstrations in his favour; latterly He had *begun* an opposite course; on this one occasion He seems to yield His whole soul to the wide and deep acclaim with a mysterious satisfaction, regarding it as *so necessary* a part of the regal dignity in which as Messiah He for this last time entered the city, that if not offered by the vast multitude, it would have *been wrung out of the stones* rather than be withheld!

The Redeemer's Tears over Jerusalem (41, 42). **41. And when he was come near, he beheld the city, and wept over it.** "Mine eye[v]" said the weeping prophet, "affecteth mine heart" (Lam. iii. 51); and the heart in turn fills the eye. Under this sympathetic law of the relation of mind and body, Jesus, in His beautiful, tender humanity, was constituted even as we. What a contrast to the immediately preceding profound joy! But He yielded Himself alike freely to both. **42. Saying, If thou hadst known**—'But, alas! thou hast not.' This "If" is the most emphatic utterance of a *wish* for that which cannot be, or is not likely to be realized. (Compare Jos. vii. 7, in Hebrew, and Job. xvi. 4.) **even thou.** This may be joined to the preceding—'If even thou hadst known' [εἰ ἔγνως καὶ σὺ]. There is deep and affecting emphasis on this "*Thou*:"—'Far as thou art gone, low as thou hast sunk, all but hopeless as thou art, yet if even *thou* hadst known!' **at least in this thy day**—even at this most moving moment. See on ch. xiii. 9. **the things [which belong] unto thy peace!** [τὰ πρὸς εἰρήνην σου]—or, as *Luther* and *Beza* render it, 'which make for thy peace' (*was zu deinem Frieden dienet—quæ ad pacem tuam faciunt*). It has been thought, by *Wetstein* and others since, that there is some allusion here to the original name of the city—"Salem," meaning 'Peace' [שָׁלֵם]. **but now they are hid from thine eyes.** This was among His *last* open efforts to "gather" them, but their eyes were judicially closed. (See on Matt. xiii. 13, 14.)

Jerusalem's Doom Pronounced (43, 44). **43. For the days shall come** ["Οτι ἥξουσιν ἡμέραι]—'For there shall come days' **upon thee, that thine enemies shall cast a trench about thee** [χάρακα]—rather a palisaded 'rampart.' The word signifies any 'pointed stake;' but here it denotes the Roman military *vallum*, a mound or rampart with palisades. In the present case, as we learn from *Josephus*, it was made first of wood; and when this was burnt, a wall of four miles' circuit was built in three days—so determined were the besiegers. This 'cut off all hope of escape,' and consigned the city to unparalleled horrors. (*Joseph.*

Jewish War, v. 6. 2; and xii. 3. 4.) **and compass thee round, and keep thee in on every side, 44. And shall lay thee even with the ground, and thy children within thee; and they shall not leave in thee one stone upon another.** All here predicted was with dreadful literality fulfilled, and the providence which has preserved such a remarkable commentary on it as the record of *Josephus*—an eye-witness from first to last, a Jew of distinguished eminence, an officer of high military capacity in the Jewish army, and when taken prisoner living in the Roman camp, and acting once and again as a negotiator between the contending parties—cannot be too devoutly acknowledged.

Our Evangelist gives no record of the first day's proceedings in Jerusalem, after the triumphal Entry; for what follows (*vv.* 45-48) belongs to the second and subsequent days. Mark disposes of this in a single verse (ch. xi. 11), while in the Fourth Gospel there is nothing on the subject. But in Matt. xxi. 10, 11, 14-16, we have the following precious particulars:

Stir about Him in the City (Matt. xxi. 10, 11). 10. "And when he was come into Jerusalem, all the city was moved"—as the cavalcade advanced—"Saying, Who is this? 11. And the multitude" —rather 'the multitudes' [οἱ ὄχλοι] from the procession itself—"said, This is Jesus, the prophet of," or 'from'—[ὁ ἀπὸ] "Nazareth of Galilee." By this they evidently meant something more than a mere prophet; and from John vi. 14, 15, and this whole scene, it seems plain that they meant by this exclamation that it was the expected Messiah.

Miracles wrought in the Temple (Matt. xxi. 14). 14. "And the blind and the lame came to him in the temple" [ἐν τῷ ἱερῷ]—in the large sense of that word (see on ch. ii. 27), "and He healed them." If these miracles were wrought *after* the cleansing of the temple—as one would gather from Matthew —since they were wrought in the very temple-court from which the money changers had been cleared out—they would set a divine seal on that act of mysterious authority. But as the second Gospel is peculiarly precise as to the order of these events, we incline to follow it, in placing the cleansing of the Temple on the second day. Yet these miracles wrought in the temple on the lame and the blind are most touching, as the *last* recorded miraculous displays of His glory—with the single exception of the majestic Cleansing of the Temple—which He gave in public.

Glorious Vindication of the Children's Testimony (Matt. xxi. 15, 16). 15. "And when the chief priests and scribes saw the wonderful things which he did, and the children crying in the temple, and saying, Hosanna to the Son of David"—which was just the prolonged echo of the popular acclamations on His triumphal entry, but drawn forth anew from these children, on witnessing what doubtless filled their unsophisticated minds with wonder and admiration— "they were sore displeased. 16. And said unto him, Hearest thou what these say?"—stung most of all by this novel testimony to Jesus, as showing to what depths His popularity was reaching down, and from the mysterious effect of *such* voices upon the human spirit. "And Jesus saith unto them, Have ye never read (in Ps. viii. 2) Out of the mouth of babes and sucklings thou hast

things *which belong* unto thy peace! but now they are hid from thine
43 eyes. For the days shall come upon thee, that thine enemies shall ^xcast a trench about thee, and compass thee round, and keep thee in on every

A. D. 33.

^x Isa. 29. 3, 4.
Jer. 6. 3, 6.

perfected praise?" This beautiful psalm is repeatedly referred to as prophetic of Christ, and this is the view of it which a sound interpretation of it will be found to yield. The testimony which it predicts that Messiah would receive from "babes" —a very remarkable feature of this prophetic psalm—was indeed here literally fulfilled, as was that of His being "numbered with the transgressors" (Isa. liii. 12), and "pierced" (Zec. xii. 10); but like those and similar predictions, it reaches deeper than literal babes, even the "babes" to whom are revealed the mysteries of the Gospel. See on Matt. xi. 25.

Thus, it would seem, ended the first memorable day of the Redeemer's last week in Jerusalem. Of the close of it the following is the brief account of the First and Second Gospels, which we combine into one: "And He left them; and when now the eventide was come, He went out of the city into Bethany, with the Twelve, and he lodged there" (Matt. xxi. 17; Mark xi. 11).

Before proceeding to the *Remarks* which this grand scene suggests, let us first retrace it. And here we copy entire the most graphic and beautiful description of it which we have read, by one of the most recent travellers, whose minute and patient accuracy is only equalled by his rare faculty of word-painting. 'From Bethany,' says *Dr. Stanley*, 'we must begin. A wild mountain-hamlet screened by an intervening ridge from the view of the top of Olivet, perched on its broken plateau of rock, the last collection of human habitations before the desert hills which reach to Jericho—this is the modern village of El-Lazarieh, which derives its name from its clustering round the traditional site of the one house and grave which give it an undying interest. High in the distance are the Peræan mountains; the foreground is the deep descent to the Jordan valley. On the further side of that dark abyss Martha and Mary knew that Christ was abiding when they sent their messenger; up that long ascent they had often watched His approach—up that long ascent He came, when, outside the village, Martha and Mary met Him, and the Jews stood round weeping. Up that same ascent He came also at the beginning of the week of His Passion. One night He halted in the village, as of old; the village and the Desert were then all alive,—as they still are once every year at the Greek Easter,—with the crowd of Paschal pilgrims moving to and fro between Bethany and Jerusalem. In the morning He set forth on His journey. Three pathways lead, and probably always led, from Bethany to Jerusalem; one, a steep footpath from the summit of mount Olivet; another, by a long circuit over its northern shoulder, down the valley which parts it from Scopus; the third, the natural continuation of the road by which mounted travellers always approach the city from Jericho, over the southern shoulder, between the summit which contains the Tombs of the Prophets and that called the 'Mount of Offence.' There can be no doubt that this last is the road of the Entry of Christ, not only because, as just stated, it is and must always have been the usual approach for horsemen and for large caravans, such as then were concerned, but also because this is the only one of the three approaches which meets the requirements of the narrative which follows. Two vast streams of people met on that day. The one poured out from the city (John xii. 12); and as they came through the gardens [Dr. S. here

would read, ἐκ τῶν ἀγρῶν, with *Tischendorf* and *Tregelles*—but not *Lachmann*—instead of δένδρων, of the received text], whose clusters of palm rose on the south-eastern corner of Olivet, they cut down the long branches, as was their wont at the Feast of Tabernacles, and moved upwards towards Bethany, with loud shouts of welcome. From Bethany streamed forth the crowds who had assembled there on the previous night, and who came testifying (John xii. 17) to the great event at the sepulchre of Lazarus. The road soon loses sight of Bethany. It is now a rough, but still broad and well-defined mountain track, winding over rock and loose stones; a steep declivity below on the left; the sloping shoulder of Olivet above it on the right; fig-trees below and above, here and there growing out of the rocky soil. Along the road the multitudes threw down the branches which they cut as they went along, or spread out a rude matting formed of the palm-branches they had already cut as they came out. The larger portion—those, perhaps, who escorted Him from Bethany—unwrapped their loose cloaks from their shoulders, and stretched them along the rough path, to form a momentary carpet as He approached. (Matt. xxi. 8; Mark xi. 8.) The two streams met midway. Half of the vast mass, turning round, preceded; the other half followed (Mark xi. 9). Gradually the long procession swept up and over the ridge, where first begins "the descent of the Mount of Olives" towards Jerusalem. At this point the first view is caught of the south-eastern corner of the city. The Temple and the more northern portions are hid by the slope of Olivet on the right; what is seen is only Mount Zion, now for the most part a rough field, crowned with the Mosque of David and the angle of the western walls, but then covered with houses to its base, surmounted by the Castle of Herod, on the supposed site of the palace of David, from which that portion of Jerusalem emphatically the "city of David" derived its name. It was at this precise point, "As He drew near, at the descent of the mount of Olives"—that is, at the point where the road over the mount begins to descend (may it not have been from the sight thus opening upon them?) —that the shout of triumph burst forth from the multitude, "Hosanna to the Son of David! Blessed is He that cometh in the name of the Lord. Blessed is the kingdom that cometh of our father *David*. Hosanna . . . peace . . . glory in the highest." There was a pause as the shout rang through the long defile; and, as the Pharisees who stood by in the crowd (Luke xix. 39) complained, He pointed to the stones which, strewn beneath their feet, would immediately cry out, if "these were to hold their peace." Again the procession advanced. The road descends a slight declivity, and the glimpse of the city is again withdrawn behind the intervening ridge of Olivet. A few moments, and the path mounts again, it climbs a rugged ascent, it reaches a ledge of smooth rock, and in an instant the whole city bursts into view. As now the dome of the Mosque El-Aksa rises like a ghost from the earth before the traveller stands on the ledge, so then must have risen the Temple tower; as now the vast enclosure of the Mussulman sanctuary, so then must have spread the Temple courts; as now the gray town on its broken hills, so then the magnificent city, with its background—long since vanished away—of gardens and suburbs on the

44 side, and ^yshall lay thee even with the ground, and thy children within thee; and they ^zshall not leave in thee one stone upon another; ^abecause thou knewest not the time of thy visitation.

A. D. 33.

y 1 Ki. 9. 7, 8.
z Matt. 24. 2.
a Dan. 9. 24.

western plateau behind. Immediately below was the Valley of the Kedron, here seen in its greatest depth as it joins the Valley of Hinnom, and thus giving full effect to the great peculiarity of Jerusalem, seen only on its eastern side—its situation as of a city rising out of a deep abyss. It is hardly possible to doubt that this rise and turn of the road—this rocky ledge—was the exact point where the multitude paused again, and "He, when He beheld the city, wept over it."' ("Sinai and Palestine," chap. iii.)

Remarks.—1. Often as we have had occasion to observe how unlike the Gospel History is, in almost everything, to an invented Story, it is impossible not to be struck with it in the present Section. That our Lord should at some time or other be made to enter Jerusalem in triumph, would be no surprising invention, considering the claim to be King of the Jews which the whole Narrative makes for Him. But that He should enter it on an ass, and that an unbroken foal attended by its dam; that it should be found by the two who were sent for it precisely "by the door without, in a place where two ways met," and that they should be allowed to carry it away on simply telling the owners that "the Lord had need of it;" that notwithstanding this feeblest of all assumptions of royal state, the small following should grow to the proportions of a vast state-procession, covering His path with their garments as He drew near to the city; and that, aided by the flying reports of Lazarus's resurrection, the multitude should get into such enthusiasm as to hail Him, in terms the most august and sacred which the Jewish Scriptures could furnish, as the long-promised and expected Messiah; that instead of being elated with this, He should at the sight of the city and in the midst of the popular acclamations, dissolve into tears, and that not so much at the prospect of His own approaching sufferings, as at the blindness of the nation to its own true interests; and yet, on the other hand, should feel those acclamations so grateful and befitting, as to tell those irritated ecclesiastics who found fault with them that they *behoved* to be uttered, and if withheld by human lips, the predicted welcome of Jerusalem to its King would be wrung out of the very stones; that the whole of this should be a mystery to the Twelve, at the time of its occurrence, and that not till the resurrection and glorification of Jesus, when the Spirit shed down at Pentecost lighted up all these events, did they comprehend their significance and behold the Grand Unity of this matchless life; that after He had reached Jerusalem, and was amongst the temple-buildings, the echoes of the popular acclaim to Him should be caught up by the children in so marked and emphatic a style as to deepen the ecclesiastic hate, and call forth a demand to Him to stop it, which only rebounded upon themselves by the glorious Scriptural vindication of it which He gave them:—these are circumstances so very different from anything which could be supposed to be an invention, especially when *taken together,* that no unsophisticated mind can believe it possible. And as the first three narratives can be shown to be independent productions, and yet each—while agreeing in the main with all the rest —varies in minute and important details from the others, and only out of all Four can the full account of the whole transaction be obtained, have we not in this the most convincing evidence of the

historic reality of what we read? No wonder that myriads of readers and hearers of these wondrous Narratives over all Christendom—of the educated classes as well as the common people—drink them in as indubitable and living History, without the need of any laboured arguments to prove them true! 2. The blended meekness and majesty of this last entry into Jerusalem is but one of a series of contrasts, studding this matchless History, and attracting the wonder of every devout and intelligent reader. What, indeed, is this whole History but a continued meeting of Lord and Servant, of riches and poverty, of strength and weakness, of glory and shame, of life and death? The early Fathers of the Church delighted to trace these stupendous contrasts in the life of Christ, arising out of the two natures in His mysterious Person—in the one of which He was to humble Himself to the uttermost, while the glory of the other could never be kept from breaking through it. Infested as those early Fathers of the Church were with all manner of heresies on this subject, these facts of the Gospel History formed at once the rich nourishment of their own souls, and the ready armoury whence they drew the weapons of their warfare in defence and illustration of the truth. Hear, for example, how the eloquent Greek, Gregory of Nazianzum (born A.D. 300—died, A.D. 390), regales himself and his audience in one of his discourses, kindling at the assaults to which the Person of his Lord was subjected:—'He was wrapt, indeed, in swaddling clothes; but rising, He burst the wrappings of the tomb. He lay, it is true, in a manger; but He was glorified by angels, and pointed out by a star, and worshipped by Magi. Why do you stumble at the visible [in Him], not regarding the invisible? He had no form nor comeliness to the Jews; but to David He was fairer than the children of men, yea, He glisters on the Mount, with a light above the brightness of the sun, foreshadowing the glory to come. He was baptized, indeed, as man, but He washed away sins as God; not that He needed purification, but that He might sanctify the waters. He was tempted as man, but He overcame as God; nay, He bids us be of good cheer, because He hath overcome the world. He hungered, but He fed thousands; yea, He is Himself the living and Heavenly Bread. He thirsted, but He cried, If any man thirst, let him come unto Me and drink; nay, He promised that those who believe in Him should themselves gush like a well. He was weary, but He is Himself the Rest of the weary and heavy-laden. He was overpowered with sleep; but He is upborne upon the sea, but He rebukes the winds, but He upbears sinking Peter. He pays tribute, but out of a fish; but He is the Prince of dependents. He is saluted "Samaritan," and "Demoniac," but He saves him that went down from Jerusalem and fell among thieves; nay, devils own Him, devils flee before Him, legions of spirits He whelms in the deep, and sees the prince of the devils falling as lightning. He is stoned, but not laid hold of; He prays, but He hears prayer. He weeps, but He puts an end to weeping. He inquires where Lazarus is laid, for He was man, but He raises Lazarus, for He was God. He is sold, and at a contemptible rate, even thirty pieces of silver; but He ransoms the world, and at a great price, even His own blood." After carrying these contrasts down to the Judgment, the eloquent preacher apologizes for the

45　And [b]he went into the temple, and began to cast out them that sold
46 therein, and them that bought; saying unto them, [c]It is written, My
house is the house of prayer: but [d]ye have made it a den of thieves.

A. D. 33.

[b] Matt. 21. 12.
[c] Ps. 93. 5.
[d] Jer. 7. 11.

---

artificial style in which he had indulged, to meet the arts of the adversaries. (Orat. xxxv.) 3. Often as we have had occasion to notice the mysterious *light and shade* which marked the emotions of the Redeemer's soul (as in Matt. xi. 16-30), nowhere are these more vividly revealed than in the present Section. The acclamations of the multitude as He approached Jerusalem were indeed shallow enough, and He was not deceived by them. He had taken their measure, and knew their exact value. But they were the *truth*, and the truth uttered for the first time by a multitude of voices. "Hosanna to the Son of David! Blessed is the King of Israel that cometh in the name of the Lord? Peace in heaven, and glory in the highest!" His soul, from its inmost depths, echoed to the sound. It was to Him as the sound of many waters. When the Pharisees, therefore, bade Him rebuke it—for it was as wormwood to them—He rose to a sublime pitch at the very thought, and, in words which revealed the intense complacency with which He drank in the vast acclaim, "He answered and said unto them, I tell you that if these should hold their peace, the stones would immediately cry out!" Yet, scarcely has this utterance died away from His lips, when, on the City coming into view, He is in tears! What emotions they were which drew the water from those eyes, we shall do better to try to conceive than attempt to express. We do desire to look into them; yet, on such a subject, at least, we say with the poet,—

'But peace—still voice and closed eye
Suit best with hearts beyond the sky.'

Our object in here again alluding to it, is merely to note the impressive fact, that this deep *shade* came over the Redeemer's spirit almost immediately after the *light* with which the acclamations of the multitude seemed to irradiate His soul. 4. If Christ thus felt on *earth* the wilful blindness of men to the things that belong to their peace, shall He feel it less in heaven? The *tears* doubtless are not there; but can that which wrung them from His eyes be absent? The mental *pain* which the spectacle occasioned Him on earth is certainly a stranger to His bosom now; but I, for one, shall never believe that there is nothing at all there which a benevolent heart would feel on earth to see men rushing wilfully on their own destruction. Is it said of the Father, that He "spared not His own Son, but delivered Him up for us all"? (see on Rom. viii. 32). And what is immediately to our point, Does God Himself protest to us, "As I live, saith the Lord God, I have no pleasure in the death of the wicked, *but that the wicked turn* from his way *and live*"? (Ezek. xxxiii. 11). In a word, Is there "joy in the presence," indeed, but not exclusively on the part, "of the angels of God over one sinner that repenteth"—the joy properly of the Shepherd Himself over His recovered sheep, of the Owner Himself over His found property, of the Father Himself over His prodigal son for ever restored to Him? (see on Luke xv.)— and can it be doubted that in the bosom of Him who descended to ransom and went up to gather lost souls, as He watches from His seat in the heavens the treatment which His Gospel receives on earth, while the cordial acceptance of it awakens His deepest joy, the wilful rejection of it, the whole consequences of which He only knows, must go to His heart with equal acute-

ness—though beyond that we may not describe it? And who that reads this can fail to see in it an argument of unspeakable force for immediate flight to Jesus on the part of all who till now have held out? You take such matters easy, perhaps; but Christ did not—nor will you one day. 5. What a beautiful light does Christ's complacency in the Hosannas of the children throw upon His delight in drawing the young to Him! And what Christian parent will not deem himself, or herself, honoured with a rare honour whose children's voices, trained by them to sing Hosannas to the Son of David, send up into the soul of the now glorified Redeemer a wave of delight? See on ch. xviii. 15-17, with the Remarks at the close of that Section.

45-48.—SECOND CLEANSING OF THE TEMPLE, AND SUMMARY OF SUBSEQUENT PROCEEDINGS. (= Matt. xxi. 12, 13; Mark xi. 15-19.) That there was but one cleansing of the temple—either that recorded in the Fourth Gospel, at His first visit to Jerusalem and His first Passover, or that recorded in the other three Gospels, at His last visit to it at the time of the Passover—some critics have endeavoured to make out; but all they have to allege for this is the supposed improbability of two such similar and unusual occurrences, and the fact that while each of the Evangelists records one cleansing, none of them records two. The Evangelists do indeed differ from each other considerably as to the order in which they place certain events; but if a cleansing of the temple occurred at the *outset* of our Lord's ministry—as recorded by John, who ought certainly to know the fact—and if it was never afterwards repeated, it cannot be believed that all the other Evangelists, whose Gospels may be shown to have been written independently of each other, should agree in transferring it to the very *close* of His ministry. Accordingly, most, if not all the Fathers recognized two cleansings of the temple—the one at the outset, the other at the close of our Lord's public life: and with them agree nearly all the best modern critics, *Calvin, Grotius, Lampe, Tholuck, Olshausen, Ebrard, Meyer, Stier, Alford;* compared with whom, those who regard both as one, though acute and learned critics, are, on a question of this nature, of inferior weight, *Wetstein, Pearce, Priestley, Neander, de Wette, Lücke. Lange* once took the latter view, but now contends decidedly for the double cleansing. That our Lord should put forth His *authority* in this remarkable way at His first visit to the city and temple, and so command attention to His claims from the highest authorities at the very outset, was altogether natural and appropriate. And that He should reassert it when He came to the city and temple for the last time, when the echoes of the popular acclaim to Him as the Son of David had scarce died away, but were about to be followed by cries of a very different nature, and His life was to pay the penalty of those claims—that in these circumstances He should vindicate them once more was surely in the highest degree natural. Nor are there wanting in the narratives of the two cleansings, evidences of a *progress* in the state of things from the time of the first to that of the last, which corroborates the fact of the deed being repeated. (See on John ii. 13-22, Remark 1, at the close of that Section.)

Second Cleansing of the Temple (45, 46). **45. And he went into the temple, and began**—or proceeded **to cast out**—but no mention is here made of the "whip of small cords" with which this was done

47 And he taught daily in the temple. But the [e]chief priests and the
48 scribes and the chief of the people sought to destroy him, and could
not find what they might do: for all the people [3]were very attentive to
hear him.

20 AND [a]it came to pass, *that* on one of those days, as he taught the
people in the temple, and preached the Gospel, the chief priests and the
2 scribes came upon *him* with the elders, and spake unto him, saying, Tell
us, by what [b]authority doest thou these things? or who is he that gave
3 thee this authority? And he answered and said unto them, I will also ask
4 you one thing; and answer me: The baptism of John, was it from heaven,
5 or of men? And they reasoned with themselves, saying, If we shall say,
6 From heaven; he will say, Why then believed ye him not? But and if
we **say**, Of men; all the people will stone us: [c]for they be persuaded that
7 John was a prophet. And they answered, That [d]they could not tell
8 whence *it was*. And Jesus said unto them, [e]Neither tell I you by what
authority I do these things.

9 Then began he to speak to the people this parable: [f]A certain man
planted a vineyard, and let it forth to husbandmen, and went into a far
10 country for a long time. And at the season [g]he sent a servant to the
husbandmen, that they should give him of the fruit of the vineyard: but
11 the husbandmen beat him, and sent *him* away empty. And again he
sent another servant: and they beat him also, and entreated *him* shame-
12 fully, and sent *him* away empty. And [h]again he sent a third: and they

A. D. 33.
[e] Mark 11.18.
John 7. 19.
John 8. 37.
[3] Or, hanged
on him.
Acts 16. 14.
CHAP. 20.
[a] Matt. 21.23.
[b] Acts 4. 7.
Acts 7. 27.
[c] Matt. 14. 5.
Matt. 21.26.
ch. 7. 29.
[d] Job 24. 13.
Rom. 1. 18,
21.
2 Cor. 4. 3.
2 Thes. 2. 9,
10.
[e] Job 5.12,13.
[f] Matt. 21.33.
Mark 12. 1.
[g] 2 Ki. 17. 13.
14.
2 Chr. 36.15,
16.
Acts 7. 52.
[h] Neh. 9. 29,
30.

the first time (John ii. 15). It is simply said now, He cast out **them that sold therein, and them that bought**—" and overthrew the tables of the money-changers, and the seats of them that sold doves, and would not suffer that any man should carry any vessel through the temple"—that is, the temple-court. 'There was always,' says *Light-foot*, 'a constant market in the temple, in that place which was called "The Shops," where every day was sold wine, salt, oil, and other requisites to sacrifices; as also oxen and sheep, in the spacious court of the Gentiles.' The "money-changers" were those who, for the convenience of the people, converted the current Greek and Roman money into Jewish coins, in which all temple dues had to be paid. The "doves" being required for sacrifice, as well as young pigeons on several prescribed occasions, could not conveniently be brought from great distances at the annual festivals, and so were naturally provided for them by dealers, as a matter of merchandise (see Deut. xiv. 24-26). Thus the whole of these transactions were, *in themselves*, not only harmless, but nearly indispensable. The one thing about them which kindled the indignation of the Lord of the Temple, now traversing its sacred precincts in the flesh, was the *place* where they were carried on—the *profanation* involved in such things being done within an inclosure sacred to the worship and service of God—and the effect of this in destroying in the minds of the worshippers the sanctity that should attach to everything on which that worship cast its shadow. On His "not suffering any man to carry a vessel through the temple," *Lightfoot* has a striking extract from one of the rabbinical writings, in answer to the question, What is the reverence due to the temple? The reply is, That none go through the court of it with his staff and shoes and purse, and dust upon his feet, and that none make it a common thoroughfare, or let any of his spittle fall upon it. **46. Saying unto them, It is written** (Isa. lvi. 7), **My house is the house of prayer: but ye have made it a den of thieves** [σπήλαιον ληστῶν]—rather, 'of robbers:' of men banded to-

gether for plunder, reckless of principle. So in Matthew and Mark. This also is a quotation, but from Jeremiah (vii. 11)—"Is this house, which is called by my name, become a den of robbers in your eyes? Behold, even I have seen it, saith the Lord." Our Lord uses the very words of the LXX [σπήλαιον ληστῶν]. The milder charge, made on the former occasion—"Ye have made it a house of merchandise"—was now unsuitable. Nor was the authority of the prophet expressly referred to on that occasion, so far at least as recorded, though it was certainly implied in the language of the rebuke. The second Gospel is more exact and full in the quotation from the prophet: "And He taught, saying unto them, Is it not written, My house shall be called of all nations the house of prayer?" (Mark xi. 17). The translation should be, as in the margin, '*for* all nations' [πᾶσι τοῖς ἔθνεσιν], and as in the prophet "for all people," or rather, 'all the nations' [וּלְכָל־הָעַמִּים]. The glimpse here given of the extension of the Church to "every people and tongue and nation," and consequently beyond the ancient economy—which is the burden of the original passage—was not the immediate point for which our Lord referred to it, but the *character* of the house as God's—"*My* house"—and "a house of prayer." And it was the desecration of it *in this light* that our Lord so sternly rebuked.

Summary of Subsequent Proceedings (47, 48). **47. And he taught daily in the temple. But the chief priests and the scribes and the chief of the people sought** [ἐζήτουν]—or 'kept seeking;' that is, from day to day, **to destroy him, 48. And could not find what they might do: for all the people were very attentive to hear him** [ἐξεκρέματο αὐτοῦ ἀκούων]—or 'hung upon His lips.'

For Remarks on this Section, see those on John ii. 13-25, at the close of that Section.

CHAP. XX. 1-19.—THE AUTHORITY OF JESUS QUESTIONED, AND THE REPLY—THE PARABLES OF THE TWO SONS AND OF THE WICKED HUSBANDMEN. (=Matt. xxi. 23-46; Mark xi. 27-xii. 12.) For the exposition, see on Matt. xxi. 23-46.

13 wounded him also, and cast *him* out. Then said the lord of the vineyard, What shall I do? I will send ⁱmy beloved son: it may be they will

14 reverence *him* when they see him. But when the husbandmen saw him, they reasoned among themselves, saying, This is ʲthe heir: come, let us

15 kill him, that the inheritance may be ours. So they cast him out of the vineyard, and ᵏkilled *him*. What therefore shall the lord of the vineyard

16 do unto them? He shall come and destroy these husbandmen, and shall give the vineyard to others. And when they heard *it*, they said, God forbid.

17 And he beheld them, and said, What is this then that is written, ˡThe stone which the builders rejected, the same is become the head of the

18 corner? Whosoever shall fall upon that stone shall be broken; but ᵐon

19 whomsoever it shall fall, it will grind him to powder. And the chief priests and the scribes the same hour sought to lay hands on him; and they feared the people: for they perceived that he had spoken this parable against them.

20 And ⁿthey watched *him*, and sent forth spies, which should feign themselves just men, that they might take hold of his words, that so they might deliver him unto the power and authority of the governor.

21 And they asked him, saying, ᵒMaster, we know that thou sayest and teachest rightly, neither acceptest thou the person *of any*, but teachest

22 the way of God ¹truly: Is it lawful for us to give tribute unto Cesar, or

23 no? But he perceived their craftiness, and said unto them, Why tempt

24 ye me? Show me a ᵖpenny. Whose image and superscription hath it?

25 They answered and said, Cesar's. And he said unto them, Render therefore unto Cesar the things which be Cesar's, and unto God the things

26 which be God's. And they could not take hold of his words before the people: and they marvelled at his answer, and held their peace.

27 Then ᵠcame to *him* certain of the Sadducees, ʳwhich deny that there is

28 any resurrection; and they asked him, saying, Master, ˢMoses wrote unto us, If any man's brother die, having a wife, and he die without children, that his brother should take his wife, and raise up seed unto his brother.

29 There were therefore seven brethren: and the first took a wife, and died

30 without children. And the second took her to wife, and he died child-

31 less. And the third took her; and in like manner the seven also: and

32 they left no children, and died. Last of all the woman died also.

33 Therefore in the resurrection whose wife of them is she? for seven had her to wife.

34 And Jesus answering said unto them, The children of this world marry,

35 and are given in marriage: but they which shall be ᵗaccounted worthy to obtain that world, and the resurrection from the dead, neither marry,

36 nor are given in marriage: neither can they die any more: for they ᵘare equal unto the angels; and are the children of God, ᵛbeing the children

37 of the resurrection. Now, that the dead are raised, ˣeven Moses showed at the bush, when he calleth the Lord the God of Abraham, and the God

38 of Isaac, and the God of Jacob. For ᶻhe is not a God of the dead, but

39 of the living: for ʸall live unto him. Then certain of the scribes

40 answering said, Master, thou hast well said. And after that they durst not ask him any *question at all*.

41 And he said unto them, ᶻHow say they that Christ is David's son?

42 And David himself saith in the book of Psalms, ᵃThe Lᴏʀᴅ said unto my

43 Lord, Sit thou on my right hand, till I make thine enemies thy footstool.

44 David therefore calleth him Lord, how is he then his son?

45 Then, ᵇin the audience of all the people, he said unto his disciples,

A. D. 33.
ⁱ Isa. 7. 14.
John 3. 16.
Rom. 8. 3.
Gal. 4. 4.
ʲ Ps. 2. 6.
Isa. 9. 6.
Col. 1. 15,
16.
Phil.2.9-11.
Heb. 1. 2.
ᵏ John 19.
ˡ Acts 3. 15.
1 Cor. 2. 8.
ˡ Ps. 118. 22.
Matt. 21.42.
1 Pet. 2. 7.
ᵐ Isa. 8. 15.
Dan. 2. 34,
35.
Matt.21.44.
ⁿ Matt. 22.15.
ᵒ Matt. 22.16.
Mark 12.14.
1 Of a truth.
ᵖ Matt. 18.28.
ᵠ Matt. 16. 1,
6, 12.
Matt.22.23.
Mark 12.18.
Acts 4. 1, 2.
Acts 5. 17.
ʳ Acts 23. 6.
ˢ Gen. 38. 8.
Deut. 25. 5.
ᵗ 2 Thes. 1. 5.
Rev. 3. 4.
ᵘ Zec. 3. 7.
Matt.22 30.
Mark 12.25.
1 Cor.15.42,
49, 52.
1 John 3. 2.
Rev. 5. 6-14.
Rev. 7. 9-12.
Rev. 22. 9.
ᵛ Rom. 8. 23.
ᵂ Ex. 3. 6.
Acts 7. 32.
Heb. 11. 9,
35.
ˣ Ps. 16. 5-11.
Ps.73. 23-26.
Ps. 145. 1, 2.
John 11. 25.
Rom. 4. 17.
Col. 3. 3, 4.
Heb. 11. 16.
ʸ Rom. 6. 10,
11.
Rom.14. 7-
9.
2 Cor. 6. 16.
2 Cor. 13. 4.
Col. 3. 3, 4.
ᶻ Matt.22.42.
Mark 12.35.
ᵃ Ps 110. 1.
Acts 2. 34.
1 Cor.15.25.
ᵇ Matt. 23. 1.
Mark 12.38.

20-40.—Eɴᴛᴀɴɢʟɪɴɢ Qᴜᴇsᴛɪᴏɴs ᴀʙᴏᴜᴛ Tʀɪʙᴜᴛᴇ | (=Matt. xxii. 15-33; Mark xii. 13-27.) For the ex-
ᴀɴᴅ ᴛʜᴇ Rᴇsᴜʀʀᴇᴄᴛɪᴏɴ, ᴡɪᴛʜ ᴛʜᴇ Rᴇᴘʟɪᴇs. | position, see on Mark xii. 13-27.
321

46 Beware ᶜof the scribes, which desire to walk in long robes, and ᵈlove greetings in the markets, and the highest seats in the synagogues, and 47 the chief rooms at feasts; which ᵉdevour widows' houses, and for a show make long prayers: ᶠthe same shall receive greater damnation.

21 AND he looked up, ᵃand saw the rich men casting their gifts into the 2 treasury. And he saw also a certain poor widow casting in thither two 3 mites. And he said, Of a truth I say unto you, that ᵇthis poor widow 4 hath cast in more than they all: for all these have of their abundance cast in unto the offerings of God: but she of her penury hath cast in all the living that she had.

A. D. 33.

ᶜ Matt. 23. 5.
ᵈ ch. 11. 43.
ᵉ Matt. 23. 14.
ᶠ Matt. 11. 22, 24.
ch. 10. 10-16.
ch. 12. 47, 48.

CHAP. 21.
ᵃ Mark 12. 41.
ᵇ Pro. 3. 9.
2 Cor. 8. 12.

41-47.—CHRIST BAFFLES THE PHARISEES BY A QUESTION ABOUT DAVID AND MESSIAH, AND DENOUNCES THE SCRIBES. (= Matt. xxii. 41-46, and xxiii. 14; Mark xii. 35-40.) For the exposition, see on Mark xii. 35-40.

CHAP. XXI. 1-4.—THE WIDOW'S TWO MITES. (= Mark xii. 41-44.) Most touching is the connection between the denunciations against those grasping ecclesiastics who "devoured *widows' houses*"—which, according both to Mark and Luke, our Lord had just uttered—and the case of this poor widow, of highest account in the eye of Jesus. The incident occurred, as appears, on that day of profuse teaching—the third day (or the Tuesday) of His last week. In Mark's account of it we read that "Jesus sat," or 'sat down' [καθίσας] "over against the treasury" (Mark xii. 41)—probably to rest; for he had continued long teaching on foot in the temple-court (Mark xi. 27). This explains the opening words of our Evangelist. **1. And he looked up**—from his sitting posture, **and saw**—doubtless as in Zaccheus's case, not quite casually, **the rich men casting their gifts into the treasury** [γαζοφυλάκιον] —a court of the temple where thirteen chests were placed to receive the offerings of the people towards its maintenance (2 Ki. xii. 9; John viii. 20.) These chests were called trumpets, from the trumpet-like shape of the tubes into which the money was dropped, wide at the one end and narrow at the other. Mark (xii. 41) says, "He beheld how the multitude [ὁ ὄχλος] cast money [χαλκὸν] into the treasury" —literally 'brass,' but meaning copper-coin, the offering of the common people—"and many that were rich cast in much" [πολλὰ], literally, 'many [coins]' or 'large [sums].' **2. And he saw a certain poor**—or 'indigent' [πενιχρὰν] **widow casting in two mites** [λῆπτὰ]—"which make a farthing" (Mark xii. 42); that is, the smallest Jewish coin. The term here rendered "farthing" [κοδράντης= quadrans] is the eighth part of the Roman *as;* and thus her whole offering would amount to no more than about the fifth part of our penny. But it was *her all.* "And He called His disciples" (Mark xii. 43) for the purpose of teaching from this case a great general lesson. **3. And he said, Of a truth I say unto you, that this poor widow hath cast in more than they all**—in proportion to her means, which is God's standard of judgment (2 Cor. viii. 12). **4. For all these have of their abundance** [ἐκ τοῦ περισσεύοντος αὐτοῖς]—'of their superfluity;' of what they had *to spare,* beyond what they needed. **cast in unto the offerings**—or 'gifts' [δῶρα] **of God**—the gifts dedicated to the service of God, **but she of her penury** [ὑστερήματος]—'her deficiency;' out of what was *less* than her own wants required, **hath cast in all the living that she had.** In Mark it is "her whole subsistence" [ὅλον τὸν βίον αὐτῆς].

Remarks.—1. Even under the ancient elaborate

and expensive economy, God made systematic provision for drawing out the voluntary liberality of His people for many of the purposes of His worship and service. And here we have a quantity of treasure-chests laid out expressly to receive the free-will offerings of the people; and on this the incident before us turns. Much more is the Christian Church dependent upon the voluntary liberality of its members for the maintenance, efficiency, and extension of its ordinances, at home and abroad. 2. As Jesus "looked up" in the days of His flesh, so He looks down now from the height of His glory, upon "the treasury;" observing who cast in much, and who little, who "of their superfluity," and who "of their penury." 3. Christ's standard of commendable liberality to His cause is not what we give of our abundance, but what we give of our deficiency—not *what will never be missed,* however much that may be, but *what costs us some real sacrifice,* what we give at a pinch; and just in proportion to the relative amount of that sacrifice is the measure of our Christian liberality in His eye. Do the majority of real Christians act upon this principle? Are not those who do so the exceptions rather than the rule? Can it be doubted that if this principle were faithfully carried out by those who love the Lord Jesus Christ, the wants of all our Churches, our schemes of missionary enterprise, and all that pertains to the maintenance and propagation of the Kingdom of Christ, would be abundantly supplied; or if not quite that, supplied to an extent, at least, as yet unknown? The apostle testifies to the Corinthians of "the grace of God bestowed on the churches of Macedonia; how that in a great trial of affliction the abundance of their joy and their deep poverty abounded unto the riches of their liberality. For to their power (he says), yea, and *beyond their power,* they were willing of themselves; (not needing to be asked, but) praying us with much entreaty that we would receive the gift (towards the maintenance of the poor saints at Jerusalem), and their share [τὴν κοινωνίαν] of the ministering to the saints. And this they did, not as we hoped, but (far beyond our expectation) first gave their own selves unto the Lord, and (then) to us by the will of God" (2 Cor. viii. 1-5). Are there many in our day like these Macedonian churches? But it would seem that even then they were the exception; for this same apostle says, even of the bulk of Christians with whom he mixed, that "all sought their own, not the things which were Jesus Christ's" (Phil. ii. 21). In a comparative sense, no doubt, this was meant. But in any sense it was humiliating enough. O will not the touching incident of this Section rouse those who love the Lord Jesus to *raise their standard* of what He claims at their hands? "How much owest thou unto thy Lord?" is a question which, if but heard by each believer within the recesses of his conscience, in the light of what himself hath experienced of the grace of Christ,

5 And [c]as some spake of the temple, how it was adorned with goodly
6 stones and gifts, he said, *As for* these things which ye behold, the days
will come, in the which [d]there shall not be left one stone upon another,
7 that shall not be thrown down. And they asked him, saying, Master, but
when shall these things be? and what sign *will there be* when these things
8 shall come to pass? And he said, [e]Take heed that ye be not deceived:
for many shall come in my name, saying, I am *Christ;* [1]and the time
9 draweth near: go ye not therefore after them. But when ye shall hear
of wars and commotions, be not terrified: for these things must first come
10 to pass; but the end *is* not by and by. Then [f]said he unto them, Nation
11 shall rise against nation, and kingdom against kingdom: and great earthquakes shall be in divers places, and famines, and pestilences; and fearful
sights and great signs shall there be from heaven.
12 But [g]before all these, they shall lay their hands on you, and persecute
you, delivering *you* up to the synagogues, and into [h]prisons, [i]being
13 brought before kings and rulers [j]for my name's sake. And [k]it shall
14 turn to you for a testimony. Settle [l]*it* therefore in your hearts, not to
15 meditate before what ye shall answer: for I will give you a mouth and
wisdom, [m]which all your adversaries shall not be able to gainsay nor resist.
16 And [n]ye shall be betrayed both by parents, and brethren, and kinsfolks,
17 and friends; and [o]*some* of you shall they cause to be put to death. And
18 [p]ye shall be hated of all *men* for my name's sake. But there shall not
19 an hair of your head perish. In your patience possess ye your souls.
20 And [q]when ye shall see Jerusalem compassed with armies, then know
21 that the desolation thereof is nigh. Then let them which are in Judea
flee to the mountains; and let them which are in the midst of it depart
22 out; and let not them that are in the countries enter thereinto. For
these be the days of vengeance, that [r]all things which are written may be
23 fulfilled. But woe unto them that are with child, and to them that give
suck, in those days! for there shall be great distress in the land, and
24 wrath upon this people. And they shall fall by the edge of the sword,
and shall be led away captive into all nations: and Jerusalem shall be
trodden down of the Gentiles, [s]until the times of the Gentiles be fulfilled.
25 And [t]there shall be signs in the sun, and in the moon, and in the
stars; and upon the earth distress of nations, with perplexity; the sea
26 and the waves roaring; men's hearts failing them for fear, and for looking
after those things which are coming on the earth: [u]for the powers of
27 heaven shall be shaken. And then shall they see the Son of man coming
28 [v]in a cloud, with power and great glory. And when these things begin
to come to pass, then look up, and lift up your heads; for your redemption draweth nigh.
29 And [w]he spake to them a parable; Behold the fig tree, and all the
30 trees; when they now shoot forth, ye see and know of your own selves
31 that summer is now nigh at hand. So likewise ye, when ye see these
things come to pass, know ye that the kingdom of God is nigh at hand.

A. D. 33.

[c] Matt. 24. 1.
Mark 13. 1.
[d] 1 Ki. 9. 7-9.
Isa. 64. 10,
11.
Jer. 5. 10.
Jer. 7. 11,14.
Lam. 2. 6-8.
Ezek. 7. 20-
22.
Mic. 3. 12.
Matt. 24. 2.
Mark 13. 2.
ch. 19. 44.
[e] Matt. 24. 4.
Mark 13. 5.
2 Cor. 11.13-
15.
Eph. 5. 6.
2 Thes. 2. 3.
2 Tim. 3.13.
1 John 4. 1.
Rev. 12. 9.
[1] Or, and,
The time.
Matt. 3. 2.
Matt. 4. 17.
[f] Matt. 24. 7.
[g] John 15. 20.
Rev. 2. 10.
[h] Acts 4. 3.
Acts 5. 18.
Acts 12. 4.
Acts 16. 24.
[i] Acts 25. 23.
[j] 1 Pet. 2. 13.
[k] Phil. 1. 28.
2 Thes. 1. 5.
[l] Matt. 10.19.
[m] Acts 6. 10.
[n] Mic. 7. 6.
[o] Acts 7. 59.
Acts 12. 2.
[p] Matt. 10.22.
2 Tim. 3.12.
[q] Matt. 24.15.
[r] Dan. 9. 26,
27.
Zec. 11. 1.
[s] Dan. 9. 27.
Rom. 11.25.
[t] 2 Pet. 3. 10,
12.
[u] Matt. 24.29.
[v] Acts 1. 11.
Rev. 1. 7.
Rev. 14. 14.
[w] Mark 13.28.

might put all his past givings and doings to shame.
What an encouraging word is this of Christ, concerning the poor widow and her two mites, to the
poor of His flock in every age! Let them not hide
their talent in the earth, because it is but one,
but put it out to usury, by "lending it to the
Lord." But, indeed, this class go beyond the rich
in their givings to Christ. Only we would that
each vied with the other in this matter. See, on
this delightful subject, on Mark xiv. 1-11, Remark
6 at the close of that Section. And, perhaps,
much of the fault of the stinted givings of
Christians lies with the ministers of Christ for
not pressing upon them such duties, and such
considerations in support of them, frequently

enough, urgently enough, lovingly enough. That
is a maxim which deserves to be written in letters
of gold (2 Cor. viii. 12): "*If there be first a willing
mind, it is accepted according to what a man hath,
and not according to what he hath not.*" "Ye know
the grace of our Lord Jesus Christ, that though
He was rich, yet for your sakes He became poor,
that ye through His poverty might be rich" (2
Cor. viii. 9).

5-38.—CHRIST'S PROPHECY OF THE DESTRUC-
TION OF JERUSALEM, AND WARNINGS SUGGESTED
BY IT TO PREPARE FOR HIS SECOND COMING—
SUMMARY OF PROCEEDINGS DURING HIS LAST
WEEK. (= Matt. xxiv. 1-51; Mark xiii. 1-37.)
For the exposition, see on Mark xiii. 1-37.

32 Verily I say unto you, This generation shall not pass away till all be
33 fulfilled. Heaven and earth shall pass away; but my words shall not
     pass away.
34   And *take heed to yourselves, lest at any time your hearts be over-
     charged with surfeiting, and drunkenness, and cares of this life, and *so*
35 that day come upon you unawares. For *y*as a snare shall it come on all
36 them that dwell on the face of the whole earth. Watch *z*ye therefore,
     and *a*pray always, that ye may be accounted worthy to escape all these
     things that shall come to pass, and *b*to stand before the Son of man.
37   And *c*in the day-time he was teaching in the temple; and *d*at night he
     went out, and abode in the mount that is called *the mount* of Olives.
38 And all the people came early in the morning to him *e*in the temple, for
     to hear him.

22 NOW *a*the feast of unleavened bread drew nigh, which is called the
2 Passover. And *b*the chief priests and scribes sought how they might
3 kill him; for they feared the people. Then *c*entered Satan into Judas
     surnamed Iscariot, being of the number of the twelve.
4   And he went his way, and communed with the chief priests and
5 captains, how he might betray him unto them. And they were glad,
6 and *d*covenanted to give him money. And he promised, and sought
     opportunity to betray him unto them [1]in the absence of the multitude.
7   Then *e*came the day of unleavened bread, when the passover must be

A. D. 33.

x Rom. 13.13.
     1 Pet. 4. 7.
y 1 Thes. 5. 2.
     2 Pet. 3. 10.
     Rev. 3. 3.
z Matt. 25.13.
     Mark 13.33.
a ch. 18. 1.
b Ps. 1. 5.
     Eph. 6. 13.
     1 John 2.23.
c John 8. 1,2.
d ch. 22. 39.
e Hag. 2, 7.
     Mal. 3. 1.

CHAP. 22.
a Matt. 26. 2.
     Mark 14. 1.
b Ps. 2. 2.
     John 11.47.
c Matt. 26.14.
d Zec. 11. 12.
     1 Tim. 6. 10.
1 Or, without
     tumult.
e Matt. 26.17.
     Mark 14.12.

CHAP. XXII. 1-6.—THE CONSPIRACY OF THE
JEWISH AUTHORITIES TO PUT JESUS TO DEATH—
JUDAS AGREES WITH THE CHIEF PRIESTS TO BE-
TRAY HIS LORD. (= Matt. xxvi. 1-5, 14-16; Mark
xiv. 1, 2, 10, 11.) For the exposition, see on Mark
xiv. 1, 2, 10, 11, with the corresponding Remarks
at the close of that Section.

7-30.—PREPARATION FOR AND LAST CELEBRA-
TION OF THE PASSOVER—INSTITUTION OF THE SUP-
PER — ANNOUNCEMENT OF THE TRAITOR—FRESH
STRIFE WHO SHOULD BE GREATEST. (= Matt.
xxvi. 17-30; Mark xiv. 12-26; John xiii. 10, 11, 18,
19, 21-30.)

Preparation for the Passover (7-13). We have
now arrived, in the progress of the Redeemer's
earthly history, at the fifth day of His last week—
the *Thursday*—on which the preparations now to
be described were made. Here arises a question
of extreme difficulty, a question very early discussed in the Church, a question which has divided,
and to this day divides, the ablest critics: 'Did
our Lord eat the passover with His disciples at
all? and if He did, was it on the same day on which
it was eaten by the rest of the Jews, or was it a
day earlier?' Had we only the testimony of the
first three Evangelists, there could be no doubt
both that He ate the Passover, and that He ate it
on the usual statutory evening—on the fourteenth
day of the month Nisan; for their testimony to
this effect is concurrent and decisive (Mark xiv.
12; Luke xxii. 7; with which the whole of Matt.
xxvi. 17, &c., though less explicit, accords). But,
on the other hand, if we had only the testimony of
the Fourth Evangelist, we should not be perfectly
sure that our Lord ate the paschal supper at all;
or if it should seem clear enough, though not explicitly stated, that the "supper" of John xiii. was
no other than the Passover, one would certainly
have been apt to conclude, from some expressions
in that Gospel, that up to the morning of the *Friday*—when our Lord was before the ecclesiastical
and civil tribunals for judgment—the Jews had
not eaten their Passover, and consequently, that
Jesus and His disciples, if they ate it at all, must
have eaten it a day before the proper time. One
general remark on this question may here be made:

—That from the nature of the case, a mistake on
such a point by all the three first Evangelists,
whose accounts coincide and yet evince themselves
to be independent narratives, was hardly possible;
and as to the Fourth Evangelist—who was himself
so largely concerned in the whole transaction, and
whose Gospel, written after the other three had
been long in circulation, bears evidence of having
been drawn up to supplement the others—it is not
conceivable that there should have been any error
on his part. And as there is not a trace in his
Gospel of any design to correct an error on this
subject in the other three, one is forced to conclude
—apart altogether from the divine authority of the
Gospels—that the first three Evangelists and the
fourth must be at one on this important point. Now
since the testimony of the first three is explicit and
cannot be set aside, while that of the fourth is but
general and presumptive, the conclusion to which
we feel ourselves shut up is, that the Passover was
eaten by our Lord and His apostles on the usual
evening. The expressions in the Fourth Gospel,
which seem to imply the reverse, but which may
all, as we think, be interpreted consistently with
the view we have stated, will be taken up at the
places where they occur.

7. **Then came the day of unleavened bread,
when the passover must be killed.** The day here
alluded to—"the first day of unleavened bread"
(Matt. xxvi. 17)—was the 14th Nisan, when, about
mid-day, labour was intermitted, and all leaven removed from the houses (Exod. xii. 15-17). Then,
"between the two evenings" (Exod. xii. 6, *margin*)
—or between three and six o'clock—the paschal
lamb was killed, and in the evening, when the 15th
Nisan began, was eaten. And though "the days
of unleavened bread" properly began with the 15th,
the preparations for the festival being made on
the 14th, it was popularly called, as here, the
"first" day of unleavened bread—as we learn from
Josephus, whose way of speaking agrees with that
here employed. The two disciples being sent from
Bethany to make the necessary preparations on
the Thursday, our Lord and the other disciples
followed them to the city later in the day, and
probably as evening drew near. 8. **And he sent**

8 killed. And he sent Peter and John, saying, Go and prepare us the passover, that we may eat.
9 And they said unto him, Where wilt thou that
10 we prepare? And he said unto them, Behold, when ye are entered into the city, there shall a man meet you, bearing a pitcher of water; follow
11 him into the house where he entereth in. And ye shall say unto the goodman of the house, The Master saith unto thee, Where is the guest-
12 chamber, where I shall eat the passover with my disciples? And he shall
13 show you a large upper room furnished: there make ready. And they went, and found as he had said unto them: and they made ready the passover.
14 And when the hour was come, he sat down, and the twelve apostles
15 with him. And he said unto them, ² With desire I have desired to eat
16 this passover with you before I suffer: for I say unto you, I will not any
17 more eat thereof, ʲuntil it be fulfilled in the kingdom of God. And he took the cup, and gave thanks, and said, Take this, and divide *it* among
18 yourselves: for ᵍI say unto you, I will not drink of the fruit of the vine, until the kingdom of God shall come.
19 And he took bread, and gave thanks, and brake *it*, and gave unto them, saying, This is my body, which is given for you: this ʰdo in

A. D. 33.
² Or, I have heartily desired.
ʲ ch. 12. 37.
ch. 14. 15.
Acts 10. 41.
John 6. 27, 50.
1 Cor. 5. 7, 8.
Heb. 10. 1-10.
Rev. 10. 9.
ᵍ Jud. 9. 13.
Ps. 104. 15.
Pro. 31. 6, 7.
Isa. 24. 9, 11.
Isa. 25. 6.
Isa. 55. 1.
Zec. 9. 15.
Matt. 26. 29.
Mark 14. 25.
ʰ Ps. 78. 4, 6.
Ps. 111. 4.
1 Cor. 11. 24.

Peter and John, saying, Go and prepare us the passover, that we may eat. 9. And they said unto him, Where? . . . 10. And he said unto them, Behold, when ye are entered into the city, there shall a man meet you, bearing a pitcher of water; follow him into the house where he entereth in. 11. And ye shall say unto the goodman of the house, The Master saith unto thee, Where is the guest-chamber, where I shall eat the passover with my disciples? 12. And he shall show you a large upper room furnished [ἐστρωμένον]—or 'spread;' with tables, and couches, and covering, all ready for supper. Such large apartments were set apart by the inhabitants of the city, for the accommodation of parties from the country. **13. And they went, and found as he had said unto them: and they made ready the passover.** See the similarly minute directions to the two who were sent to procure the ass on which He rode into Jerusalem, ch. xix. 30-32.

Last Celebration of the Passover (14-18). **14. And when the hour was come**—about six o'clock, **he sat down, and the twelve apostles with him**—the whole twelve, Judas included. **15. And he said unto them, With desire I have desired** ['Ἐπιθυμία ἐπεθύμησα]—the strongest expression of intense desire. In Gen. xxxi. 30 the same expression [נִכְסֹף נִכְסַפְתָּה, ἐπιθυμία ἐπεθύμησας] is rendered "thou sore longedst." **to eat this passover with you before I suffer.** The last meal one is to partake of with his family or friends before his departure even for a far distant land, in all probability never to see them again, is a solemn and fond one to any thoughtful and loving person. The last meal of a martyr of Jesus with his friends in the truth, before being led forth to execution, is still more touching. But faint are these illustrations of the emotions with which Jesus now sat down to supper with the Twelve. All the sweetness and all the sadness of His social intercourse with them, from the day that He first chose them to be with Him, were now to be concentrated and heightened to their utmost intensity during the brief hour or two of this their last meal together. But this was no common meal, nor even common passover. It was to be *the point of transition between two divine economies and their respective festivals;* the one to close for ever, the other to run its majestic career through all time, until from a terrestrial form it should dissolve into a form celestial. No wonder,

then, that He said, "With desire I have desired to eat *this* passover with you before I suffer." This, as *Alford* remarks, is the only instance in the Gospels in which the word "suffer" [πάσχω] is used in its absolute sense—as in the Creed, 'He *suffered* under Pontius Pilate.' **16. For I say unto you, I will not any more eat thereof, until it be fulfilled in the kingdom of God**—or, as in Matt. xxvi. 29, "I will not drink henceforth of this fruit of the vine, until that day when I drink it new with you in my Father's kingdom," or "in the kingdom of God" (Mark xiv. 25). The primary application of this, no doubt, is to the *new* Gospel kingdom to be fully erected when the old economy, with its Passover and temple-rites, should disappear. But the best interpreters agree that its only full and proper application is to that celestial kingdom of which He speaks so beautifully in *v.* 30—"that ye may eat and drink at My table in My kingdom," &c.

17. And he took the cup. Several cups of wine were partaken of, or tasted, during the somewhat elaborate rites observed in the celebration of the Passover. This was probably the first one: but it is not to be confounded with the Eucharistic cup mentioned in *v.* 20, and then partaken of for the first time; this *Paschal* cup was now partaken of for the *last* time. **and gave thanks, and said, Take this, and divide it among yourselves.** A false inference has been drawn from this by some expositors—that Christ did not Himself drink of it. The contrary is obvious from His earnest desire to "eat this Passover with them," and of course to drink the Paschal cup; and in what follows He expressly says that He did drink of it. **18. For I say unto you, I will not drink of the fruit of the vine, until the kingdom of God shall come.** See on *v.* 16, of which this is but a repetition, in a form adapted to the cup, as there it was uttered in a form adapted to the paschal lamb and the bread eaten with it.

Institution of the Supper (19, 20). **19. And he took bread, and gave thanks** (see on Mark vi. 41). In Matthew and Mark it is "and blessed it." The one act includes the other. He "gave thanks," not so much here for the literal bread, as for that higher food which was couched under it; and He "blessed" it as the ordained channel of spiritual nourishment. **and brake it, and gave unto them, saying, This is my body, which is**

20 remembrance of me. Likewise also the cup after supper, saying, [i]This cup *is* the new testament in my blood, which is shed for you.

21 But, [j]behold, the hand of him that betrayeth me *is* with me on the

22 table. And truly the Son of man goeth, as [k]it was determined: but

23 woe unto that man by whom he is betrayed! And they began to enquire among themselves, which of them it was that should do this thing.

24 And [l]there was also a strife among them, which of them should be

25 accounted the greatest. And [m]he said unto them, The kings of the Gentiles exercise lordship over them; and they that exercise authority

26 upon them are called benefactors. But [n]ye *shall* not *be* so: [o]but he that is greatest among you, let him be as the younger; and he that is chief, as

A. D. 33.

i 1 Cor.10.16.
j Ps. 41. 9.
  Mark 14.18.
  John 13.21,
  26.
k Acts 2. 23.
  Acts 4. 28.
l Mark 9. 34.
  ch. 9. 46.
m Matt.20.25.
n Jas. 4. 6.
  1 Pet. 5. 3.
o ch. 9. 48.

given for you: this do in remembrance of me. 'The expression, "This is my body,"' says *Alexander* most truly, 'which is common to all the accounts, appears so unambiguous and simple an expression, that it is hard to recognize in it the occasion and the subject of the most protracted and exciting controversy that has rent the Church within the last thousand years. That controversy is so purely theological that it has scarcely any basis in the exposition of the text; the only word upon which it could fasten (the verb *is*) being one which in Aramaic (or Syro-Chaldaic), would not be expressed, and therefore belongs merely to the Greek translation of our Saviour's language. [But this supposes our Lord now spoke in Aramaic—the contrary of which we believe.] Until the strong unguarded figures of the early Fathers had been petrified into a dogma, at first by popular misapprehension, and at last by theological perversion, these words suggested no idea but the one which they still convey to every plain unbiased reader, that our Saviour calls the bread His body in the same sense that He calls Himself a door (John x. 9), a vine (John xv. 1), a root (Rev. xxii. 16), a star, and is described by many other metaphors in Scripture. The bread was an emblem of His flesh, as wounded for the sins of men, and as administered for their spiritual nourishment and growth in grace.' **20. Likewise also the cup after supper**—not after the *Lord's* Supper, as if the taking of the bread and of the cup in it were separated so far as that; but after the *paschal* supper, and consequently immediately after the distribution of the bread. The accounts of Matthew and of Mark would seem to imply that He gave thanks on taking the cup, as well as with the bread; but here, at any rate, and in the most authoritative account, perhaps, which we have, in 1 Cor. xi. 23, &c., that is not said. **saying, This cup is the new testament in my blood, which is shed for you.** In Matthew (xxvi. 28), "This is my blood of the new testament, which is shed for many for the remission of sins." In 1 Cor. (xi. 25) "This cup is the new testament in my blood: this do ye, as oft as ye drink it, in remembrance of me." Most critics now maintain that the word here rendered "testament" [διαθήκη] should be rendered *covenant*, not only here but wherever else it occurs in the New Testament; being used in the Old Testament constantly by the LXX. translators for the well-known Hebrew word signifying 'covenant' [בְּרִית], which never signifies 'testament.' Here, in particular, there is a manifest allusion to Exod. xxiv. 8, "Behold, *the blood of the covenant* [דַּם־הַבְּרִית] which the Lord hath made with you concerning all these words." Now it is beyond doubt that 'covenant' is the fundamental idea, and that in the Old Testament the word is correctly rendered " covenant." But let it be observed, first, that 'testament' or 'will' is the proper classical sense of the Greek word, and

'disposition' or 'covenant' but a secondary sense; and next, that in Heb. ix. 15, &c., the sense of 'testament' appears to be so obviously what the apostle reasons on, that to exclude it there, and restrict the meaning to 'covenant,' can only be made to yield the harshest sense. But the true harmony of both senses of the word, and how, in the case of Christ's death, the one runs into the other, will be seen, not by any criticism on the *word*, but by reflecting on the *thing*. If it be true that by 'covenant,' or eternal divine arrangement, all the blessings of salvation become the rightful possession of believers solely *in virtue of Christ's death*, does not this almost irresistibly suggest to every reflecting mind the idea of a *testator's* death as a most true and exalted conception of the virtue of it? What can be a more natural view of the *principle* on which the fruits of Christ's death become ours than that of a testamentary disposition? Then, observe how near to this idea of His death our Lord Himself came in what He said, when the Greeks sought to "see Jesus" on the eve of His last Passover, "The hour is come when the Son of man should be glorified: Except a corn of wheat fall into the ground and die, it abideth *alone; but if it die, it bringeth forth much fruit"* (John xii. 23, 24). Observe, too, His mode of expression twice over at the Supper-table, "I *appoint* [διατίθεμαι] unto you, as My Father appointed [διέθετο] unto Me, a kingdom" (Luke xxii. 29); "Peace I leave with you; My peace I *give* unto you" (see on John xiv. 27): and it will be seen, we think, how each idea suggests the other. While that of 'covenant' is confessedly the fundamental one, that of '*testament*' is accessory or illustrative only. Yet the one is as real as the other, and presents a phase of the truth exceeding precious. In this view *Bengel* substantially concurs, and *Stier* entirely.

Announcement of the Traitor (21-23). **21-23. But, behold, the hand of him that betrayeth me is with me on the table, &c.** See on John xiii. 21-26.

Fresh Strife Who should be Greatest (24-30). **24. And there was**—rather, here, 'there had been' **a strife among them, which of them should be accounted the greatest.** Some symptoms of the former contention on this subject seem to have reappeared once more; probably just before sitting down to the paschal supper, and perhaps in consequence of seeing the whole paschal arrangements committed to two of the Twelve. (See on Mark ix. 33, &c.) But of all occasions for giving way to such petty ambition and jealousy, this was the worst, and to our Lord must have been the most painful. And if so, who can but wonder at the gentleness with which He here rebukes it? **25. And he said unto them, The kings of the Gentiles exercise lordship over them; and they that exercise authority upon them are called benefactors** [εὐεργέται]—a title which the vanity of princes eagerly coveted.

326

27 he that doth serve. For whether *is* greater, he that sitteth at meat, or
he that serveth? *is* not he that sitteth at meat? but *ᵖ*I am among you as
28 he that serveth. Ye are they which have continued with me in *ᵍ*my
29 temptations. And *ʳ*I appoint unto you a kingdom, as my Father hath
30 appointed unto me; that *ˢ*ye may eat and drink at my table in my
kingdom, *ᵗ*and sit on thrones judging the twelve tribes of Israel.

A. D. 33.	
ᵖ John 13.13.	
Phil. 2. 7.	
ᵍ Heb. 4. 15.	
ʳ ch. 12. 32.	
ˢ ch. 14. 15.	
ᵗ Ps. 49. 14.	

26. But ye shall not be so: but he that is greatest among you, let him be as the younger; and he that is chief, as he that doth serve. Of how little avail has this condemnation of "lordship" and other vain titles been against the vanity of Christian ecclesiastics! **27. For whether is greater, he that sitteth at meat, or he that serveth? is not he that sitteth at meat? but I am among you as he that serveth.** See on Mark x. 42-45, with Remarks 3 and 4 at the close of that Section; also, on John xiii. 6-8, with Remark 2 at the close of that Section. **28. Ye are they which have continued with me in my temptations.** Affecting evidence this, of Christ's tender susceptibility to human sympathy and support! See on *v.* 40; and on John vi. 66, 67; xvi. 32. **29. And I appoint unto you a kingdom, as my Father hath appointed unto me**—or, according to the order of the original text, 'And I appoint unto you, as My Father hath appointed unto Me, a kingdom.' Who is this that dispenses kingdoms, nay, the Kingdom of kingdoms, within an hour or two of His apprehension, and less than a day of His shameful death? These sublime contrasts, however, perpetually meet and entrance us in this matchless History. The 'giving of a given' Kingdom is in our Lord's usual style of speaking, in which He ever holds forth His oneness in counsel with the Father. 'So far from the high claims I advance being an unwarrantable usurpation of divine prerogatives, dishonouring to the Father, it is from Him I have My commission to be here, to do all I do, and dispense all I bestow.' See on Matt. xxviii. 18; and on John v. 19, &c. **30. That ye may eat and drink at my table in my kingdom, and sit on thrones judging the twelve tribes of Israel.** See on ch. xviii. 29.

Remarks.—1. The *feelings of Jesus Himself* have been too much lost sight of in attention to His *work*, in such portions of the History—a somewhat selfish way of reading it, which punishes itself by the dry and not very satisfactory views thence resulting. Blessed Jesus! Do I hear thee, on seating Thyself at the Paschal table, laying open the burden of Thy heart to the Twelve, saying, "With desire I have desired to eat this Passover with you before I suffer," telling them it was the last Passover Thou wouldst eat with them on earth, and the last time Thou wouldst drink with them here below of the fruit of the vine? In this I read, so as I am not able to express it, Thy oneness with us even in our social sympathies. All that makes a last meeting and a last meal with one's family, whole and unbroken, or with friends with whom one has gone in and out for years in joy and sorrow, alike in the commonest and the loftiest intercourse, an occasion of peculiar solemnity and tender interest—all this, it seems, was felt by Thee; and if felt at all, felt surely on this occasion with an intensity unknown to us. For it was more than Thy last meal—it was the last Paschal meal ever to be partaken of even by Thy disciples. Ere another such season came round, the typical Passover was to be exchanged for the commemorative Supper; and even at that very table, the one was sweetly to be transfigured into the other. One can understand, then, the emotion that filled Thy heart, when, surrounded

by the Twelve in that upper room, Thou foundest Thyself arrived at this stage. And yet, how can we enough bless Thee for giving utterance to this; for who else would have ventured to presume it? But there is something else here, which is at least as noteworthy as this. The treason-hatching, the traitor, the plan, the end—and all so near, so very imminent—were full before Thee, blessed Saviour; yea, the traitor himself was sitting at that table: and yet, with what holy calmness Thou reclinest at this meal! One word thou utterest of direct allusion to it—"Before I *suffer*"—just to reveal the spring of surpassing interest Thou didst feel in *that* Passover; but only one. When after this the new Feast was instituted for all that should believe on Thee through their word to the world's end, it was only to explain the deep intent of that Feast that the bloody scene was again alluded to—and so serenely! not at all in the light of the dishonour done to *Thee*, but of the benefit thereby accruing to *them*—not in the light of Thy suffering, but of the expiatory virtue of that blood of Thine to the salvation of a lost world! But here I see another thing, which at once ravishes and melts me. This Feast Thou wouldst have kept up "IN REMEMBRANCE OF THEE"—not Thy death merely, and the benefits thence resulting, but *Thyself*. No one who has a heart at all would like to be forgotten of those he loves; every one would like to be remembered when he is gone. And is it even so with Thee, O Thou whom my soul loveth? Thy love, it seems—like all other love—seeks a response; it will have itself appreciated and reciprocated, and in that Thou hast all Thy desire; thus to see of the travail of Thy soul is Thy satisfaction, Thy reward (Isa. liii. 11). But had sufficient provision not been made for that without this Supper—in that Thy love is shed abroad in Thy people's hearts by the Holy Ghost given unto them—a love *constraining* them to live not unto themselves, but unto Him that died for them and rose again? True, but Thou art not yet contented. Thou wilt be enshrined in the Church's visible services—and that not in the glory of Thy Person, Thy character, Thy teaching, Thy miracles, or all of these together, but of that Decease which was accomplished at Jerusalem, of that dearest act of Self-sacrifice by which Thy people's ransom was paid; Thou wilt be held visibly up as the bruised Messiah, the bleeding Lamb that taketh away the sin of the world. And who shall say what shallow faith has not been deepened, what languishing affections have not been afresh enkindled by this most blessed ordinance, and how much of its spiritual *nourishment* in all time to come the Church of Christ will not owe to this ordinance? O yes, as we sit at that eucharistic table with robes washed and made white in the blood of the Lamb, and as our faith gazes, through its instituted elements of bread and wine, on that bleeding Lamb, now in the midst of the Throne, does not the hymn of redeeming love go up to Him fresher and warmer than ever before, "Unto Him that loved us, and washed us from our sins in His own blood, and hath made us kings and priests unto God and His Father; to Him be glory and dominion for ever and ever, Amen"? 2. In

31 And the Lord said, Simon, Simon, behold, ^uSatan hath desired *to*
32 *have* you, that he may ^vsift *you* as wheat: but ^wI have prayed for thee,
that thy faith fail not: ^xand when thou art converted, strengthen thy

^u 1 Pet. 5. 8.
^v Amos 9. 9.
^w John 17. 9.
^x Ps. 51. 13.

the light of these views, what are we to think of the monstrous abuses of this ordinance, on the one hand by *Unitarians*—who can celebrate it and yet see in it no Atonement, and nothing beyond a memorial banquet in honour of a most heroic Sufferer for virtue—and, on the other hand, by *Romanists*, who bury its precious truths and destroy its quickening efficacy under the detestable abuses of transubstantiation and the mass! On the 'Real Presence' and other eucharistic controversies, see on 1 Cor. xi. 23, &c.

31-39.—THE FALL OF PETER FORETOLD—THE DISCIPLES WARNED OF COMING TRIALS. (= Matt. xxvi. 31-35; Mark xiv. 27-31; John xiii. 36-38.)

Here must be taken in an important particular, omitted by our Evangelist, but supplied in the first two Gospels.

Desertion of Jesus by the Apostles Foretold (Matt. xxvi. 31; Mark xiv. 27, 28). Had we only the first two Gospels, we should have concluded that this was spoken after our Lord had left the upper room, and either reached or was on His way to the Mount of Olives. But from the Third and Fourth Gospels, it would appear to have been spoken while they were yet at the Supper-table. Some suppose that part of it was spoken before they left the supper-room, and the rest during that last and most mournful of all His walks with them, from the city to the Mount of Olives. But we prefer to conceive of that walk as taken *in silence*. Matt. xxvi. 31, "Then saith Jesus unto them, All ye shall be offended because of Me this night" [σκανδαλισθήσεσθε ἐν ἐμοί]—'shall be stumbled in me;' temporarily staggered on seeing their Master apprehended. In the expression, "*All ye*," there may be a reference to the *one* who had just "gone out." Great as was the relief, now for the first time experienced by the Saviour Himself, on the traitor's voluntary separation from a fellowship to which He never in heart belonged (see on John xiii. 31), even in those who remained there was something which burdened the spirit and wounded the heart of the Man of Sorrows. It saddened Him to think that, within one brief hour or two of the time when their hearts had warmed towards Him more than ever at the Paschal and Communion table, they should every one of them be 'stumbled' because of Him: "for it is written (Zec. xiii. 7), I will smite the Shepherd, and the sheep of the flock shall be scattered abroad." 32. "But after I am risen again, I will go before you into Galilee." He falls back upon this striking prophecy, partly to confirm their faith in what they would otherwise hardly think credible; and partly to console Himself with the reflection that it was but one of "the things concerning him" which "would have an end"—that they would be but links in the chain, "doing what God's hand and purpose determined before to be done." The whole of this marvellous prediction, as it stands in the prophet, runs thus: "Awake, O sword, against My Shepherd, and against the Man that is My Fellow [עַל־גֶּבֶר עֲמִיתִי], saith the Lord of hosts: smite the Shepherd, and the sheep shall be scattered; and I will turn mine hand upon the little ones." Here observe, first, that in the prophet, Jehovah calls upon the sword to awake against His Shepherd and smite Him; here, Jesus receives the thrust direct from the Father's own hand: compare John xviii. 11, "The cup which my Father hath given me, shall I not drink it?" Each view of it presents an aspect

of sublime and affecting truth. Next, in the passage, as it stands in Zechariah, two classes are spoken of—"the *sheep*," who are "scattered" on the striking down of their Shepherd (as might be expected, whether literally or figuratively); and "the *little ones*," on whom Jehovah's hand is to be lovingly "turned," to gather or collect them. The former class are the unbelieving nation, who, being staggered and stumbled at a suffering Messiah, turned away from Jesus, and were thereafter nationally scattered or dispersed. The latter are, of course, the little flock of Christ's disciples, who, on the dispersion of the nation, were gathered not only into safety, but to honour and blessedness unspeakable as a redeemed Church. Now mark what turn our Lord here gives to the prophecy. Making no mention, at that solemn moment, of the dispersion of the unbelieving nation, He represents the disciples themselves as both the *dispersed* and the *gathered*. When He their Shepherd, who up to that moment had been their one Bond of dear union, should be smitten—even that night, when the first blow was to be struck at Him by His apprehension—their faith in Him would be momentarily shaken, and "for a small moment" their unbelief would have the same effect as on the nation at large, making them start back and run away, like a flock of sheep when their shepherd is struck down. "But"—now viewing them as "the little ones" on whom Jehovah was to turn His hand—"after I am risen, I will go before you into Galilee;" like a true Shepherd, who, "when He putteth forth His own sheep, *goeth before them*, and *the sheep follow Him*" (John x. 4). The scattered in Gethsemane were to be the gathered in Galilee! How very explicit He is in His announcements now, when on the eve of parting with them till after His resurrection. This manifest allusion to the remainder of the prophecy—"I will turn mine hand upon the little ones"—how beautiful is it! This He only began to do when He went before them into Galilee; for though after His resurrection He had several interviews with them at Jerusalem before this, it was in Galilee that He appears to have collected and rallied them, as the Shepherd of His lately scattered flock, and to have given them some at least of those parting instructions and commissions which may be termed *the initial organization of the Church.* But to return to our Evangelist, whose narrative now is the fullest.

The Fall of Peter Foretold (31-34). **31. And the Lord said, Simon, Simon.** On this reduplication of the name, see on ch. x. 41, and on Matt. xvii. 37. **Satan hath desired to have you** [ἐξητήσατο ὑμᾶς]. The meaning is, 'obtained (by asking) you'—not *thee*, Peter, but *you*, all. **that he may sift you as wheat**—is sifted. "The accuser of the brethren, who accuseth them before God day and night" (Rev. xii. 10), is here represented as accusing these disciples of Christ of hollowness in their attachment to Him; and alleging that if, as in the case of Job (i. 6-12; ii. 1-6), he were only permitted to "sift them," it would soon be seen that there was chaff enough among the wheat, if indeed there would be found, after that sifting, any wheat at all. So he first '*asks* them,' and then he '*obtains* them' (for both ideas are required to complete the sense of the word used) for this sifting purpose. And observe, it is not '*hath* obtained,' but '*obtained*;' that is, it is a transaction *past*, and you are already *given*

33 brethren. And he said unto him, Lord, I am ready to go with thee,
34 both into prison, and to death. And ʸhe said, I tell thee, Peter, the cock shall not crow this day, before that thou shalt thrice deny that thou knowest me.
35 And ᶻhe said unto them, When I sent you without purse, and scrip,
36 and shoes, lacked ye any thing? And they said, Nothing. Then said

A. D. 33.

ʸ Matt. 26. 34.
John 13 38.
ᶻ Matt. 10. 9.
Mark 6. 8,
9.
ch. 9. 3.
ch. 10. 4.

over to him—to the extent of his petition—to be allowed to sift you. **32. But I have prayed for thee, that thy faith fail not** [Ἐγὼ δὲ ἐδεήθην περὶ σοῦ ἵνα μὴ ἐκλείπῃ ἡ πίστις σου]. Here again, it is not, "I *have* prayed for thee," but 'I *prayed* regarding thee.' The "*I*" too is emphatic: *q. d.*, 'While Satan was soliciting and obtaining you all to sift you as wheat, I was engaged in praying regarding thee—as in greater danger than all the rest—that thy faith fail not; and when the transaction between God and SATAN was completed by your being, every one of you, given over for sifting purposes into the enemy's hand, the transaction between God and ME about thee, Peter, was a completed one too—for Me the Father heareth always.' Such is the *import* of these pregnant words of Jesus. But all this was not fully *expressed*. So far from that, it is not improbable that a misapprehension of what our Lord meant by Peter's faith not "*failing*" helped to bolster him up in his false security. What, then, did our Lord mean by this? Not, certainly, that Peter's faith might not give way at all, or to any extent; for in that sense it did fail, and that foully enough. Clearly His prayer was that Peter's faith might not utterly fail—altogether give way—or *perish*. How near it came to that, and how it only stopped short of that, the sequel affectingly showed. See on *v.* 62. **and when thou art converted**—brought back afresh as a penitent disciple, **strengthen thy brethren**—'fortify them against like falls by holding up to them thine own bitter experience.' **33. And he said unto him, Lord, I am ready to go with thee, both into prison, and to death.** In Matthew and Mark it was when our Lord told them they should all be stumbled in Him that night, that Peter said, "Though all men"—or rather, "all," meaning all that sat with him at the table—"shall be offended in Thee, yet will I never be offended" (Matt. xxvi. 33; Mark xiv. 29). But as the answer there given by our Lord is the same as that recorded by our Evangelist, he probably uttered both protestations in his vehemence at one time; his feeling being roused by our Lord singling him out from all the rest. Poor Peter, thou shalt yet pay dear for that unlovely elevation of thyself above the rest of thy brethren, when thy risen Lord shall wring thy heart by asking thee, in presence of these very brethren, "Simon, son of Jonas, lovest thou Me *more than these?*" (see on John xxi. 15-17). Yet no vain-glorious vaunt was this of Peter. It was just the outcoming of conscious attachment: insomuch that all the rest, feeling a cord touched in their own hearts by this protestation, immediately repeated it for themselves. For, add our two first Evangelists, "*Likewise also said all the disciples.*" Dear disciples! Ye spoke out but the feelings of your heart then; your Lord knew that, and doubtless was comforted by it, as a spontaneous utterance of your hearts' affection. But little thought ye how soon it was to be seen—in all of you, but in Peter pre-eminently—that "he that trusteth in his own heart is a fool" (Prov. xxviii. 26). **34. And he said, I tell thee, Peter, the cock shall not crow this day, before that thou shalt thrice deny that thou knowest me.** Most interesting and touching is the fact, that whereas in the first, third, and fourth

Gospels only *one* crowing of the cock is mentioned as sounding the note of Peter's fall, in the second Gospel—which all ancient tradition proclaims, and internal evidence suggests, to have been drawn up under the immediate eye of Peter—it is said that *two* crowings of the cock would sound his fall. And as it is Mark alone who records the fact that the cock did crow twice—the first time after one denial of his Lord, and the second immediately after the last—we have thus an affecting announcement, almost from his own pen, that warning after warning passed unheeded, till the second knell rung in his ears and bitterly revealed how much wiser his Lord was than he.

The fourth Gospel gives all this in a somewhat different and beautiful connection—John xiii. 36-38. Our Lord had been saying (*v.* 33), "Whither I go, ye cannot come. Simon Peter," not prepared for that, "said unto Him, Lord, whither goest Thou? Jesus answered him, Whither I go, thou canst not follow Me now, but thou shalt follow Me afterwards"—meaning to glory through the gate of martyrdom (John xxi. 18, 19). "Peter"—getting a glimpse of His meaning, but only rising to a higher feeling of readiness for anything, "said unto Him, Lord, why cannot I follow Thee now? I will lay down my life for Thy sake. Jesus answered him, Wilt thou lay down thy life for my sake?" What deep though tender irony is in this repetition of his words, which Peter, as he retraced the painful particulars, would feel for many a day after his recovery! "Verily, verily, I say unto thee, the cock shall not crow, till thou hast denied Me thrice."

The Disciples Warned of Coming Trials (35-38). **35. And he said unto them, When I sent you without purse, and scrip, and shoes, lacked ye any thing? And they said, Nothing.** 'Ye see, then, your sufficiency in Me.' **36. Then said he unto them, But now, he that hath a purse, let him take it, and likewise his scrip: and he that hath no sword, let him sell his garment, and buy one.** 'But now that ye are going forth, not as before on a temporary mission, provided for without purse or scrip, but into scenes of continued and severe trial, your *methods* must be different; for purse and scrip will now be needed for support, and the usual means of defence.' **37. For I say unto you, that this that is written** (Isa. liii. 12) **must yet be accomplished in me** [ἔτι]—or, yet remains to be fulfilled, **And he was reckoned among the transgressors.** This is among the very last and most pregnant of that most remarkable series of details which have made the 53rd chapter of Isaiah to read to the Church in every age more like a history, than a prophecy, of the sufferings of Christ and the glories that were to follow them (see on John xix. 18). **for the things concerning me have an end** [τέλος ἔχει]—'are having an end,' or drawing rapidly to a close. **38. And they said, Lord, behold, here are two swords.** Honest souls! They thought He referred to present defence, for which they declare themselves ready, no matter what might be the issue; though they significantly hint that two swords would make sorry enough work. But His answer shows that He meant something else. **And he said unto them, It is enough**—not 'Two will suffice,' but 'Enough of this for the present.'

he unto them, But now, he that hath a purse, let him take *it*, and likewise *his* scrip: and he that hath no sword, let him sell his garment, and
37 buy one. For I say unto you, that this that is written must yet be accomplished in me, And *^a*he was reckoned among the trangressors: for
38 the things concerning me have an end. And they said, Lord, behold, here *are* two swords. And he said unto them, It is enough.

A. D. 33.

^a Isa. 53. 12.
Mark 15. 28,
29.
ch. 23. 32.
2 Cor. 5. 21.
Gal. 3. 13.

The warning had been given, and preparation for coming dangers hinted at; but as His meaning had not been apprehended in the comprehensive sense in which it was meant, He wished to leave the subject.

The Evening in the upper room had now passed into night; for Jesus seemed to linger over that hallowed scene, breathing forth heavenly discourse after the Paschal and Eucharistic services were over, not caring to break up His last and sweetest fellowship with them a moment sooner than the dark work before Him required. But the closing act of that heavenly fellowship is omitted by our Evangelist, though happily supplied in the first two Gospels.

The Closing Hymn (Matt. xxvi. 30; Mark xiv. 26). "And when they had sung an hymn, they went out unto the mount of Olives [ὑμνήσαντες]—literally, 'having hymned;' that is, having chanted, according to the Jewish practice at the close of the Passover, the second part of what the Jews call *The Great Hallel.* It consisted of Ps. cxv., cxvi., cxvii., cxviii.; the first part of it, embracing Ps. cxiii., cxiv., having been sung *during* the Paschal supper. Or, if our Lord and His apostles sang the second part of this immediately after the Passover, and before instituting the Supper, what they closed their hallowed meeting with may have been portions of Ps. cxx.—cxxxvi., which were sometimes sung on that occasion. At any rate, the strain was from a portion of the Psalter eminently Messianic; a portion in which the mystery of redemption is richly conveyed to the spiritual mind. *Bengel* has a remark here, more quaint than correct. 'That Jesus *prayed*,' he says, 'we often read; that He *sang*, never.' But to "sing forth the honour of God's name, and make His praise glorious," is a duty so frequently and peremptorily inculcated on men, that it is inconceivable that "the Man Christ Jesus" should have passed His life without ever so using His voice; and if the saints feel this independently of the command, to be the most exalted and delightful exercise of heart and flesh, and a bright earnest of heaven itself, who shall say that Jesus, amidst the "sorrows" with which He was so familiar, and the "grief" with which He was "acquainted," did not get such "songs in the night," as turned His darkness into light? What a spectacle would that have been—the eleven disciples trying, as best they could, to cheer their sorrowing hearts with those songs of Zion which the Paschal season invariably brought round, and their Lord standing dumb beside them. To me this is inconceivable. But the Hymn is over. The scenes of the upper room have closed, and for the last time the disciples go forth with their blessed Master to the Mount of Olives, in whose garden was now to be transacted the most mysterious of all passages in the Redeemer's History.

Remarks.—1. The heart-breaking reproach which Jesus had already experienced, but which was soon to come down upon Him in its cruelest and most cutting form would seem enough to bear without being aggravated by the desertion of His own disciples. But both these were in the cup which was given him to drink, and both seem to be comprehended in that affecting prophetic complaint. "Reproach hath broken My heart, and I am full of heaviness, and I looked for some to take pity, but there was none; and for comforters, but I found none" (Ps. lxix. 20). See on John xvi. 32. 2. Who can fathom the mingled bitterness and sweetness of the cup which was given to Christ to drink? That there were high ends of righteousness and grace which *demanded* that penal death, who can doubt with those words of Jehovah ringing in his ears, "Awake, O sword, against My Shepherd, and against the Man that is My Fellow, saith the Lord of hosts; smite the Shepherd!" Jesus heard those words, and knew that, summoned by *that call*, the Jewish officers, with Judas at their head, were coming to apprehend Him, and even then making their arrangements. Little did any one then think that Jewish malignity and the awful treachery of covetous Judas were but "doing what God's hand and counsel determined before to be done." But Jesus knew it, and knew that those unconscious instruments of His approaching apprehension, condemnation, and death, were only held back till the Voice should say, Awake now, and smite the Shepherd! Mysterious words, considering Whence they came, and against Whom they were directed! Who, in the view of this, shall say that the death of Christ had not *penal* ingredients, of bitterest taste? But O the sweetness of those words, "My Shepherd—the Man that is My FELLOW!" What inconceivable solace would they carry in their bosom to Him who now referred to them! Accordingly, as if this predicted smiting was hardly present to His mind at all, it is the desertion of Him by those whom most He loved—their being "stumbled in Him" that very night—that seemed so painfully to occupy His thoughts. And yet, with what affecting gentleness and love does He announce it—adding, as if unwilling to leave the wound sticking in them, "But after I am risen, I will go before you into Galilee!" a bright glimpse of the coming fruits of His sufferings which to Himself, who understood it better than they, would be like sunshine from out the cloud. 3. After Peter, let none trust to the conscious strength of his attachment and the warmth of his love to Christ, as any security against the foulest denial of Him in the hour of trial. Of all the Eleven, Peter was foremost in these. Whatever others might afterwards prove themselves to be, none up to that time had stood so high as he. Yet this is the disciple whom His loving yet penetrating and faithful Master singles out and warns as of all the Eleven in the greatest peril; and we know what an affecting commentary on this the result gave. Yet the last to discern such danger as Peter was in are just those who are most exposed to it and least prepared successfully to meet it. 'Me, Lord, me? Why single out me? Once at least have I been singled out from all the rest for clear perception of Thy glory and firm attachment to Thy Person; and am I to be the one man to give way on the approach of danger? Others may, but I never.' This was just the stone at which Peter stumbled. Had he distrusted himself, and betaken himself to his knees, he had there got strength to stand. "The name of the Lord is a strong tower: the righteous runneth into it, and is safe" (Prov. xviii. 10). But what needed Peter this? He was safe enough—

39 And he came out, and went, as he was wont, to the mount of Olives;	A. D. 33.
40 and his disciples also followed him. And *b* when he was at the place, he	*b* Matt 6. 13.
41 said unto them, Pray that ye enter not into temptation. And he was	Mark 14.38.

he knew it. His Master knew better, and bid him "watch and pray, that he enter not into temptation;" but we do not read that he did it. O if believers would but know that the secret of all their strength lies in that consciousness of their own weakness which sends them to the "Strong Tower" to find it, how many such falls would be averted!

39-46.—THE AGONY IN THE GARDEN. (=Matt. xxvi. 36-46; Mark xiv. 32-42; John xviii. 1.)

This is one of those scenes in the Evangelical History which, to have been *written*, must have been *real*. If we could conceive the life of Christ to be but a pious Romance or a mythical Legend, such a scene would have been the last to be thought of, or imagined only to be rejected as a discordant note, a literary blemish. But the existence of such a scene in the Gospel History does more than prove the historic reality of the scene itself: it is a bright testimony to the severe fidelity of the Narrative that contains it. Had the three Evangelists who record this scene, and the fourth who has one remarkably like it (John xii. 27, &c.), been guided in their selection of the materials before them by the desire to glorify their Master in the eyes of their readers, we may be pretty sure they would have omitted what could not fail to repel many well-inclined readers, to stagger for a time even attached disciples, and occasion perplexity and discordance among the most established in the faith. Certain it is that in the age immediately succeeding that of the apostles, some vindication of it was felt to be necessary even for those who were well affected to Christianity (see a remarkable allusion to this scene in the Apocryphal "Gospel of Nicodemus," or "Acts of Pilate," ch. xx.); while its enemies—as *Celsus* at the beginning of the second century, and *Julian* in the fourth—held it up to contempt for the pusillanimity which it displayed, in contrast with the magnanimity of dying Pagans. Some of the vindications of this scene in later times have laid themselves open to the hostile criticism of *Strauss* ("Leben Jesu," iii. 3, § 125, 4th edit.); although his own *mythical* theory cuts a pitiful figure when it has to deal with such unique materials as those of Gethsemane.

The three narratives of this scene, when studied together, will be found to have just that diversity which throws additional light on the whole transaction. That the fourth Evangelist, though himself an eye-witness, has not recorded it, is only in accordance with the plan of his Gospel, which omits the other two scenes of which he was one of three chosen witnesses—the resurrection of Jairus' daughter, and the transfiguration. But just as in place of the one of these—the resurrection of Jairus' daughter—it is the beloved disciple alone who records the grander resurrection of Lazarus; and in place of the other of these—the transfiguration—that beloved disciple records a series of passages in the life, and discourses from the lips, of his Master, which are like a continued transfiguration: so it is he alone who records that mysterious *prelude* to Gethsemane, which the visit of the Greeks to Him, after His last entry into Jerusalem, seems to have occasioned, (John xii. 27, &c.) In the three priceless narratives of this scene, the fulness of the picture is such as to leave nothing to be desired, except what probably could not have been supplied in any narrative; the lines are so vivid and minute and life-like, that we seem ourselves to be eye and ear-witnesses of the whole

transaction; and no one who has had it brought fully before him can ever again have it effaced from his mind.

In this instance, we must deviate somewhat from our usual plan of comment first, and Remarks following. We shall try to sketch the scene, interweaving the triple text, with such slight expository remarks as it requires; and in place of closing Remarks, we shall expatiate at some length upon the successive phases of the scene as they open upon us.

Jesus had passed through every stage of His suffering history except the last, but that last was to be the great and dreadful stage. Nothing now remained but that He should be apprehended, arraigned, condemned, and led forth to Calvary. And how far off was this seizure? Not more probably than *one brief hour*. Like the "silence in heaven for the space of half an hour," between the breaking of the apocalyptic *seals* and the peal of the *trumpets of war*, so was this brief, breathless silence, before the final stage of Christ's career. How, then, was it spent? It was night. Men slept. A profound, Sodom-like security overspread the city that "killed the prophets and stoned them that were sent unto it." But our Shepherd of Israel slept not. "He went forth"—from the upper room and from the city—"over the brook Cedron, where was a garden, into the which he entered, with his (eleven) disciples. And Judas which betrayed him knew the place; for Jesus ofttimes resorted thither with his disciples" (John xviii. 1, 2). With what calm sobriety does the basest of all treacheries begin here to be related! No straining after effect. The traitor knows His favourite resort, and takes it for granted he shall find Him there. Perhaps the family of Bethany were told the night before, in the hearing of the Twelve, that that night the Lord would not be with them. Be this as it may, if Jesus had wished to elude His enemies, nothing would have been easier. But he would not. Already He had said, "No man taketh My life from me; but I lay it down of myself." So He "went as a lamb to the slaughter." The spot selected was well suited to His present purpose. The upper room would not have done; nor would he cloud the hallowed associations of the last Passover, and the first Supper, the heaven-breathing discourse at the supper table and the high-priestly prayer which wound up the whole, by discharging the anguish of His soul *there*. Nor was Bethany so suitable, But the garden was ample enough, while the stillness, and the shady olives, and the endeared recollections of former visits, rendered it congenial to His soul. Here He had space enough to withdraw from His disciples, and yet be within view of them; and the solitude that reigned here would only be broken, at the close of the scene, by the tread of the traitor and his accomplices.

The walk to Gethsemane, we incline to think, was taken in silence. But no sooner was He on the spot, than having said to the whole of them, "Pray that ye enter not into temptation" (Luke xxii. 40), the internal commotion—which may have begun as soon as the "hymn" that closed the proceedings of the upper room died away in silence —would no longer conceal. As soon as He was "at the place," having said to eight out of the eleven, "Sit ye here while I go and pray yonder," He took Peter and James and John aside by themselves, or a little in advance of the rest, and

331

withdrawn from them about a stone's cast, and kneeled down, and prayed,

42 saying, Father, if thou be [3] willing, remove this cup from me: nevertheless

43 [c] not my will, but thine, be done. And there appeared [d] an angel unto

[3] Willing to remove
[e] John 6 38.
[d] Matt. 4. 11.

"saith unto them, My soul is exceeding sorrowful, even unto death: tarry ye here and watch with Me" (Matt. xxvi. 38; Mark xiv. 34). Not, Come and *see* Me, to be My witnesses; but, Come and *watch with Me*, to bear Me company. It did Him good, it seems, to have them by Him. For He had a true humanity, only all the more tender and susceptible than ours, that it was not blunted and dulled by sin. You may say, indeed, if company was what He wanted, He got little of it. True enough. They fell asleep. "I looked for some to take pity, but there was none; and for comforters, but I found none" (Ps. lxix. 20). It *would* have soothed His burdened spirit to have had their sympathy, contracted at its best though it behoved to be. But He did not get it. They were broken reeds. And so He had to tread the wine-press alone. Yet was their presence, even while asleep, not quite in vain. Perhaps the spectacle would only touch His sensibilities the more, and rouse into quickened action His great-hearted compassions. In fact, He did not want even them *too near* Him. For it is said, "He went forward a little;" or, as Luke (xxii. 41), more precisely expresses it, "was withdrawn from them about a stone's cast." Yes, company is good, but there are times when even the best company can hardly be borne.

But now let us reverently draw near and see this great sight, the Son of God in a tempest of mysterious internal commotion—"the bush burning, and the bush not consumed." Every word of the three-fold record is weighty, every line of the picture awfully bright. "Let us put off the shoes from off our feet, for the place whereon we stand is holy ground." "He began," says Matthew, "to be sorrowful and very heavy," or, "to be sorrowful and oppressed" [λυπεῖσθαι καὶ ἀδημονεῖν], Matt. xxvi. 37. Mark uses the last of these words, but places before it one more remarkable: "He began to be sore amazed, and to be very heavy;" or better, perhaps, "to be appalled and to be oppressed" [ἐκθαμβεῖσθαι καὶ ἀδημονεῖν], Mark xiv. 33; and see the former word again in ch. xvi. 5, 6. Although through life He had been "a man of sorrows, and acquainted with grief," there is no ground to think that even the selectest circle of His followers was made privy to them, save on one occasion before this, after His final entry into Jerusalem, when, upon the Greeks "desiring to see Jesus"—which seems to have brought the hour of His "uplifting" overwhelmingly before Him—He exclaimed, "Now is my soul troubled, and what shall I say? Father, save me from this hour? But for this cause came I unto this hour. Father, glorify thy name" (John xii. 27, 28). This was just *Gethsemane anticipated*. But now the tempest rose as never before. "He *began* to be sorrowful," as if till this moment unacquainted with grief. So new to Him, indeed, was the feeling, that Mark, using a singularly bold word, says, He was "appalled" at it; and under the joint action of this "sorrow" and "amazement," He was "very heavy," oppressed, weighed down—so much so, that He was fain to tell it to the three He had taken aside, and most affectingly gave this as His reason for wishing their company: "My soul is exceeding sorrowful, even unto death; tarry ye here and watch with me." 'I feel as if nature were sinking under this load—as if life were ebbing out—as if death were coming before its time—as if I could not survive this.' It is usual to

compare here such passages as that of Jonah, "I do well to be angry *even unto death*" (ch. iv. 9), and even some classical passages of similar import; but these are all too low. In dealing with such scenes as this, one feels as if even the most ordinary phraseology must be interpreted with reference to the unique circumstances of the case. What next? He "kneeled down," says Luke; He "fell on his face," says Matthew; or "fell on the ground," as Mark expresses it (Luke xxii. 41; Matt. xxvi. 39; Mark xiv. 35). Perhaps the kneeling posture was tried for a moment, but quickly became intolerable: and unable to bear up under a pressure of spirit which felt like the ebbing out of life itself, He was fain to seek the dust! And now went up a cry such as never before ascended from this earth; no, not from those lips which dropt as an honeycomb: "O my Father, if it be possible, let this cup pass from me; nevertheless not as I will, but as thou wilt (Matt. xxvi. 39). The variations in Mark (xiv. 36) and Luke (xxii. 42) are worthy of note. Mark's double form of the invocation, "Abba, Father," we may pretty confidently conjecture was the very one our Lord used—the hallowed, endeared form of the mother-tongue "Abba," followed emphatically by the term "Father," that of educated life (Rom. viii. 15). Then Mark breaks up the one expression of Matthew, "If it be possible, let this cup pass," into these two, identical in meaning, "All things are possible unto thee; take away this cup;" while Luke's expression, "If thou be *willing* to remove this cup" (as in the Greek), shows that the "possibility" of the other two Evangelists was understood to be one purely of Divine *will* or arrangement, insomuch that the one word came naturally to be interchanged with the other. (To suppose that our Lord used the identical words of all the three accounts is absurd.) That *tears* accompanied this piercing cry, is not reported by any of the Evangelists—who appear to give rigidly what was *seen* by the three favoured disciples in the clear moonlight, and *heard* by them in the unbroken stillness of the night-air of Gethsemane, ere sleep overpowered their exhausted frames. But those remarkable words in the Epistle to the Hebrews—which, though they seem to express what often took place, have, beyond all doubt, a special reference to this night of nights—leave no doubt of it, as a fact well known in the Christian churches, that on this occasion the tears of the Son of God fell fast upon the earth, while His cries rent the heavens: "Who in the days of His flesh, when He had offered up prayers and supplications, *with strong crying and tears*," &c. (Heb. v. 7). Exquisite here are the words of old Traill, which, though before quoted, are peculiarly appropriate here: "He filled the silent night with His crying, and watered the cold earth with His tears, more precious than the dew of Hermon, or any moisture, next unto His own blood, that ever fell on God's earth since the creation."

But now let us listen to the cry itself. "The cup" to which the Son of God was so averse—"the cup," the very prospect of drinking which so appalled and oppressed Him—"the cup," for the removal of which, if it were possible, He prayed so affectingly—that cup was assuredly no other than the *death* He was about to die. Come, then, thoughtful reader, and let us reason together about this matter. Ye that see nothing in Christ's death but the injustice of it at the hands of men, the excruciating mode of it, and the uncomplaining sub-

44 him from heaven, strengthening him.   And *being in an agony he prayed   more earnestly: and his sweat was as it were great drops of blood falling
45 down to the ground.   And when he rose up from prayer, and was come

A. D. 33.

* John 12. 27.
Heb. 5. 7.

mission to it of the innocent victim — put me through this scene of agonies and cries at the near approach of it. I will not ask you whether you go the length of those pagan enemies of the Gospel, *Celsus* and *Julian*, who could see nothing but cowardice in this Gethsemane-scene, as compared with the last hours of Socrates and other magnanimous pagans; or whether you are prepared to applaud that wretch who, in the days of Henry IV. of France, went to execution jeering at our Lord for the bloody sweat which the prospect of death drew from Him, while he himself was about to die unmoved. But I do ask you, in view of hundreds, if not thousands of the martyrs of Jesus who have gone to the rack or to the flames for His sake, rejoicing that they were counted worthy to suffer for His name, Are you prepared to exalt the servants above their Master, or, if not, can you give any rational account of the amazing difference between them, to the *advantage* of the Master? You cannot, nor on your principles is the thing possible. Yet which of these dear servants of Jesus would not have shuddered at the thought of comparing themselves with their Lord? Is not your system, then, radically at fault? I am not now addressing myself to professed Unitarians, who, with the Atonement, have expunged the Divinity of Christ from their biblical beliefs. If any such would but give me a hearing, I think I have something to say which is not unworthy of their attention. But I address myself more immediately to an increasing class within the pale of orthodox Christianity—a class embracing many cultivated minds—a class who, while clinging sincerely, though vaguely, to the Divinity of Christ, have allowed themselves to let go, as something antiquated and scholastic, the *vicarious* element in the sufferings and death of Christ, and now view them purely in the light of a sublime model of *self-sacrifice*. According to this view, Christ suffered nothing whatever *in the stead* of the guilty, or in order that *they* might *not* suffer, but rather that men might learn from Him how to suffer: Christ simply inaugurated in His own Person a new Humanity, to be "made perfect through sufferings," and hath thus "left us an Example that we should follow His steps." Now, I have no quarrel with this *exemplary* theory of Christ's sufferings. It is too clearly expressed by our Lord Himself, and by His apostles too frequently echoed, for any Christian to have a doubt of it. But my question is, *Will it solve the mystery of Gethsemane?* Will any one venture to say that for a Christian man, who would know how to suffer and die, the best model he can follow is *Christ in Gethsemane*—Christ, in the prospect of His own death, "sore amazed and very heavy, exceeding sorrowful even unto death"—Christ piercing the heavens with that affecting cry, thrice repeated, with His face upon the ground, "O my Father, *if it be possible*, let this cup pass from me" —Christ agonizing till the sweat fell in bloody drops from His face upon the ground: and all this at the mere prospect of the death He was going to die? But He added, you say, "Nevertheless, not my will, but thine be done." I know it well. It is my sheet-anchor. But for this, my faith in the Son of God as the Redeemer of the world would reel to and fro and stagger like a drunken man. But with all this, will you affirm that these feelings of Christ in Gethsemane are those which best befit any other dying man? You

cannot. And if not, does not the hollowness of this view of Christ's sufferings, as an *exhaustive* account of them, or even as the chief feature of them, stand frightfully revealed!

How, then, do *you* explain them? may the reader ask. It is a pertinent question, and I refuse not to meet it. Tell me, then, what means that statement of the apostle Paul, "*He hath made Him to be sin for us, Who knew no sin;* that we might be made the righteousness of God in Him" (2 Cor. v. 21); and that other, "Christ hath redeemed us from the curse of the law, *being made a curse for us*" (Gal. iii. 13). The ablest and most recent rationalizing critics of Germany—*de Wette*, for example—candidly admit that such statements can mean nothing but this, that the absolutely Sinless One was regarded and treated as the Guilty one, in order that the really guilty might in Him be regarded and treated as righteous. If it be asked in what sense and to what extent Christ was regarded and treated as the Guilty One, the second passage replies, "He was "made a curse for us"—language so appallingly strong, that *Bengel* with reason exclaims, as he does also on the other passage, 'Who would have dared to use such language if the apostle had not gone before him?' Says *Meyer*—a critic not over fastidious in his orthodoxy but honest as an interpreter—'The curse of the law would have had to be realized; all who render not complete satisfaction to the law (which no one can do) must experience the infliction of the Divine "wrath;" but that Christ, to rescue them from this outlawry by the curse, is introduced dying *as the Accursed One*, and as *by a purchase-price*, dissolving that curse-relation of the law to them. Compare 1 Cor. vi. 20; vii. 23.'

Now, is this to be regarded as a true representation of the *character* in which Christ suffered and died? With those who sit quite loose to apostolic authority, and regard all such statements as expressing merely Paul's *opinions*, we have here nothing to do. Strange to say, we have now-a-days men high in our schools of learning and in ecclesiastical place, who scruple not to affirm this and many other strange things. But we write for those who regard the statements of the apostle as authoritative, and to them we submit this question: If Christ felt the *penal* character of the sufferings and death which He had to undergo—if, though feeling this more or less throughout all His public life, it was now borne in upon His spirit in unrelieved, unmitigated, total force, during the dread, still hour between the transactions of the upper room and the approach of the traitor—does not this furnish an adequate key to the horror and sinking of spirit which he then experienced? Just try it with this key. In itself, the death He had to die—being in that case not the mere surrender of life in circumstances of pain and shame, but the surrender of it *under the doom of sin*, the surrender of it *to the vengeance of the law*, which regarded Him as the Representative of the guilty (to use again the language even of *de Wette*), could not but be purely revolting. Nor is it possible for us otherwise to realize the horror of His position, as the absolutely Sinless One, now emphatically made sin for us. In this view of it we can understand how He could only brace Himself up to drink the cup because it was the Father's will that He should do it, but that in *that* view of it He was quite

46 to his disciples, he found them sleeping for sorrow, and said unto them, *f* Why sleep ye? rise and pray, lest ye enter into temptation.

A. D. 33.
f Jon. 1. 6.

prepared to do it. And thus have we here no struggle between a *reluctant* and a *compliant* will, nor between a *human* and a *divine* will; but simply between two views of one event: between penal sufferings and death considered in themselves—in other words, being "bruised, put to grief, made an offering for sin"—and all this considered as the Father's will. In the one view, this was, and could not but have been, appalling, oppressing, ineffably *repulsive:* in the other view, it was sublimely *welcome.* When He says, "If it be possible, let this cup pass from Me," He tells me He didn't like it, and couldn't like it; its ingredients were too bitter, too revolting; but when He says, "Nevertheless, not my will, but thine be done," He proclaims in mine ear His absolute obediential subjection to the Father. This view of the cup quite changed its character, and by the expulsive power of a new affection—I will not say, turned its bitterness into sweetness, for I see no signs of sweetness even in that sense, but—absorbed and dissolved His natural repugnance to drink it up. If you still feel the theology of the matter encompassed with difficulty, let it alone. It will take care of itself. You will never get to the bottom of it here. But take it as it stands, in all its wonderful naturalness and awful freshness, and rest assured that just as, if this scene had not actually occurred, it never would nor could have been written down, so on any other view of the Redeemer's extraordinary repugnance to drink the cup than the *penal* ingredient which He found in it, His magnanimity and fortitude, as compared with those of myriads of His adoring followers, must be *given up.*

But to return to the conflict, whose crisis is yet to come. Getting a momentary relief—for the agitation of His spirit seems to have come upon Him by surges—He returns to the three disciples, and finding them sleeping, He chides them, particularly Peter, in terms deeply affecting: "He saith unto Peter, What! could ye not watch with me one hour?" In Mark (which may almost be called Peter's own Gospel) this is particularly affecting, "He saith unto Peter, Simon, sleepest thou? Couldest not thou watch one hour? Watch ye and pray, lest ye enter into temptation. The spirit truly is ready, but the flesh is weak." How considerate and compassionate this allusion to the weakness of the flesh was at that moment, appears by the explanation which Luke gives of the cause of it—an explanation beautifully in accordance with his profession as "the beloved physician" (Col. iv. 14)—"that He found them sleeping *for sorrow*" (Luke xxii. 45). What now? "Again He went away, and prayed, and spake the same words" (Mark xiv. 39). He had nothing more, it seems, and nothing else to say. But now the surges rise higher, beat more tempestuously, and threaten to overwhelm Him. To fortify Him against this, "there appeared an angel unto Him from heaven, strengthening Him:" not to minister to Him *spiritually*, by supplies of heavenly light or comfort—of that He was to have none during this awful scene; nor if it had been otherwise, would it seem competent for an angel to convey it—but simply to sustain and brace up sinking nature for a yet hotter and fiercer struggle. (On this interesting subject, see on John v. 1-47, Remark 1 at the close of that Section.) And now that He *can* stand it, "He is in an agony, and prays more earnestly" [ἐκτενέστερον], 'more in-

tensely or vehemently.' What! Christ pray at one time more earnestly than at another? will some exclaim. O if people would but think less of a systematic or theological Christ, and believe more in the biblical, historical Christ, their faith would be a warmer, aye, and a mightier thing, because it would then be not human but divine. Take it as it stands in the record. Christ's prayer, it teaches you, did at this moment not only admit of more vehemence, but demand it. For "His sweat was as it were great drops," literally, 'clots' [θρόμβοι] "of blood falling down to the ground." [We cannot stay to defend the text here.] What was this? It was just the internal struggle, apparently hushed somewhat before, but now swelling up again, convulsing His whole inner man, and this so affecting His animal nature, that the sweat oozed out from every pore in thick drops of blood, falling to the ground. It was just *shuddering nature* and *indomitable will* struggling together. Now, if death was to Christ only the separation of soul and body in circumstances of shame and torture, I cannot understand this in one whom I am asked to take as my Example, that I should follow His steps. On this view of His death, I cannot but feel that I am asked to copy a model far beneath that of many of His followers. But if death in Christ's case had those elements of *penal vengeance*, which the apostle explicitly affirms that it had—if the Sinless One felt Himself divinely regarded and treated as the Sinful and Accursed One, then I can understand all this scene; and even its most terrific features have to me something sublimely congenial with *such* circumstances, although only its having *really* occurred could explain its being so *written.*

But again there is a lull; and returning to the three, "He found them asleep again (for their eyes were heavy), neither wist they what to answer Him" (Mark xiv. 40), when He chid them, perhaps in nearly the same terms. And now, once more, returning to His solitary spot, He "prayed the third time," saying the same words; but this time slightly varied. It is not now, "O my Father, if it be possible, let this cup pass from me;" but, "O my Father, *if this cup may not pass from me*, except I drink it, thy will be done." Had only one of these two forms of the petition occurred in the same Gospel, we might have thought that they were but verbal differences in the different reports of one and the same petition. But as they both occur in the same Gospel of Matthew, we are warranted in regarding the second as an intentional, and in that case momentous, modification of the first. The worst is over. The bitterness of death is past. He has *anticipated and rehearsed* His final conflict. The victory has now been won on the theatre of an *invincible will*—to "give His life a ransom for many." He shall win it next on the arena of *the Cross*, where it is to become an accomplished fact. "I *will* suffer," is the result of Gethsemane: "It is finished," bursts from the Cross. Without the *deed*, the *will* had been all in vain. But His work was then consummated when into the palpable deed He carried the now manifested will—"*by the which* WILL *we are sanctified* THROUGH THE OFFERING OF THE BODY OF JESUS CHRIST ONCE FOR ALL" (Heb. x. 10).

At the close of the whole scene, returning once more to His three disciples, and finding them still sleeping, worn out with continued sorrow and racking anxiety, He says to them, with an irony of tender but deep emotion, "Sleep on now, and

47   And while he yet spake, behold a multitude, and he that was called
Judas, one of the twelve, went before them, and drew near unto Jesus to
48 kiss him. But Jesus said unto him, Judas, betrayest thou the Son of
49 man with a kiss? When they which were about him saw what would
50 follow, they said unto him, Lord, shall we smite with the sword? And
*g*one of them smote a servant of the high priest, and cut off his right ear.
51 And Jesus answered and said, Suffer ye thus far. And he touched his
52 ear, and healed him. Then Jesus said unto the chief priests, and
captains of the temple, and the elders, which were come to him, Be ye
53 come out, as against a thief, with swords and staves? When I was daily
with you in the temple, ye stretched forth no hands against me: *h*but
54 this is your hour, and the power of darkness. Then *i*took they him,
and led *him*, and brought him into the high priest's house. *j*And Peter
followed afar off.

55   And *k*when they had kindled a fire in the midst of the hall, and
56 were set down together, Peter sat down among them. But a certain
maid beheld him as he sat by the fire, and earnestly looked upon him,
57 and said, This man was also with him. And he denied him, saying,
58 Woman, I know him not. And, *l*after a little while, another saw him,
59 and said, Thou art also of them. And Peter said, Man, I am not. And
about the space of one hour after, another confidently affirmed, saying,
60 Of a truth this *fellow* also was with him; for he is a Galilean. And
Peter said, Man, I know not what thou sayest. And immediately, while
61 he yet spake, the cock crew. And the Lord turned, and looked upon
Peter. *m*And Peter remembered the word of the Lord, how he had said
62 unto him, Before *n*the cock crow, thou shalt deny me thrice. And Peter
went out, and *o*wept bitterly.

63,   And *p*the men that held Jesus mocked him, and smote *him*. And
64 when they had blindfolded him, they struck him on the face, and asked
65 him, saying, Prophesy, who is it that smote thee? And many other
things blasphemously spake they against him.

66   And *q*as soon as it was day, *r*the elders of the people, and the chief
priests, and the scribes, came together, and led him into their council,
67 saying, Art *s*thou the Christ? tell us. And he said unto them, If I tell
68 you, ye will not believe: and if I also ask *you*, ye will not answer me, nor
69 let *me* go. Hereafter *t*shall the Son of man sit on the right hand of the
70 power of God. Then said they all, Art thou then the Son of God? And
71 he said unto them, *u*Ye say that I am. And *v*they said, What need we
any further witness? for we ourselves have heard of his own mouth.

A. D. 33.
g Matt. 26 51.
Mark 14.47.
John 18.10.
Rom 12. 19.
2 Cor. 10. 4.
h Gen. 3. 15.
John 12.27.
Acts 2. 23.
Acts 4. 27.
i Matt. 26. 57.
Acts 8. 32.
j John 18. 15.
k Matt.26.69.
Mark 14.66.
John 18. 17,
18.
l Matt. 26. 71.
Mark 14.69.
John 18 25.
m Matt. 26.75.
Mark 14.72.
n John 13. 38.
o Isa. 66. 2.
Ezek. 7. 16.
2 Cor. 7. 10.
p Ps 69. 1-21.
Isa. 50. 6.
Isa. 52. 14.
Matt.26.67,
68.
Mark 14 65.
q Matt. 27. 1.
r Ps. 2. 1.
Ps. 22. 12,
16.
Acts 4. 26.
Acts 22. 5.
s Matt.26.63.
Mark 14.61.
t Ps. 110. 1.
Dan. 7. 13,
14.
Acts 1. 11.
Acts 3. 21.
1 Thes. 4.16.
Heb. 1.
Heb 8. 1.
u Matt.26 64.
Mark 14.62.
v Matt 26. 65.
Mark 14.63.

take your rest: behold, the hour is at hand, and
the Son of man is betrayed into the hands of sinners. Rise, let us be going: behold, he is at hand
that doth betray me" (Matt. xxvi. 45, 46). While
He yet spake, Judas appeared with his armed band,
and so they proved miserable comforters, broken
reeds. But thus in His whole work He was *alone*,
and "of the people there was none with Him."

Much is said about the *necessity* of an atonement, some stoutly affirming it, while others
accuse the thought of presumption. Of antecedent necessity, on such subjects, I know nothing
at all; and it is possible that some who dispute the
position mean nothing more than this. But one
thing I know, that God under the law did so
educate the conscience that there was seen written, as in letters of fire, over the whole Levitical
economy—
WITHOUT THE SHEDDING OF BLOOD NO REMISSION;
while the great proclamation of the Gospel is--
   PEACE THROUGH THE BLOOD OF THE CROSS.
   And ever as I deal with God on this principle,
I find my whole ethical nature so exalted and puri-

fied—my views and feelings as to sin and holiness
and the sinner's relation to Him with Whom he
has to do, so deepened, enlarged, and sublimed—
while on no other do I find any footing at all—that
I feel I have been *taught* what I am sure I could
never have antecedently *discovered*, the necessity,
in its highest sense—the necessity, that is, in order
to any right relation between God and me—of the
expiatory death of the Lord Jesus; and when,
thus *educated*, I anew approach Gethsemane, that
I may witness the conflict of the Son of God there,
and listen to His "strong crying and tears to Him
that was able to save Him from death," I seem to
myself to have found that key to it all, without
which it is a blot in His life that will not wipe out,
but in the use of which I can open its most difficult wards, and let in light upon its darkest
chambers.

47-54.—BETRAYAL AND APPREHENSION OF JESUS.
(=Matt. xxvi. 47-56; Mark xiv. 43-52; John xviii.
1-12.) For the exposition, see on John xviii. 1-12.
55-71.—JESUS ARRAIGNED BEFORE CAIAPHAS,
CONDEMNED TO DIE, AND SHAMEFULLY EN-

23 AND ^athe whole multitude of them arose, and led him unto Pilate.
2 And they began to accuse him, saying, We found this *fellow* ^bperverting the nation, and ^cforbidding to give tribute to Cesar, saying ^dthat he
3 himself is Christ a king. And ^ePilate asked him, saying, Art thou the King of the Jews? And he answered him and said, Thou sayest *it*.
4 Then said Pilate to the chief priests and *to* the people, ^fI find no fault
5 in this man. And they were the more fierce, saying, He stirreth up the people, teaching throughout all Jewry, beginning from Galilee to this
6 place. When Pilate heard of Galilee, he asked whether the man were a
7 Galilean. And as soon as he knew that he belonged unto ^gHerod's jurisdiction, he sent him to Herod, who himself also was at Jerusalem at that time.
8 And when Herod saw Jesus, he was exceeding glad: for ^hhe was desirous to see him of a long *season*, because ⁱhe had heard many things of him; and he hoped to have seen some miracle done by him.
9 Then he questioned with him in many words; but he answered him
10 nothing. And the chief priests and scribes stood and vehemently accused
11 him. And ^jHerod with his men of war set him at nought, and mocked *him*, and arrayed him in a gorgeous robe, and sent him again to Pilate.
12 And the same day ^kPilate and Herod were made friends together: for before they were at enmity between themselves.
13 And ^lPilate, when he had called together the chief priests and the
14 rulers and the people, said unto them, Ye have brought this man unto me, as one that perverteth the people: and, behold, I, having examined *him* before you, have ^mfound no fault in this man touching those things
15 whereof ye accuse him: no, nor yet Herod: for I sent you to him; and,
16 lo, nothing worthy of death is done unto him. I ⁿwill therefore chastise
17 him, and release *him*. (For ^oof necessity he must release one unto them
18 at the feast.) And ^pthey cried out all at once, saying, Away with this
19 *man*, and release unto us Barabbas: (who for a certain sedition made in
20 the city, and for murder, was cast into prison.) Pilate therefore, willing
21 to release Jesus, spake again to them. But they cried, saying, Crucify
22 *him*, crucify him. And he said unto them the third time, Why, what evil hath he done? I have found no cause of death in him: I will there-
23 fore chastise him, and let *him* go. And they were instant with loud voices, requiring that he might be crucified: and the voices of them and
24 of the chief priests prevailed. And Pilate ¹gave sentence that it should
25 be as they required. And ^qhe released unto them him that for sedition and murder was cast into prison, whom they had desired; but he delivered Jesus to their will.
26 And ^ras they led him away, they laid hold upon one Simon, a Cyrenian, coming out of the country, and on him they laid the cross, that he
27 might bear *it* after Jesus. And there followed him a great company of
28 people, and of women, which also bewailed and lamented him. But Jesus, turning unto them, said, Daughters of Jerusalem, weep not for me,
29 but weep for yourselves, and for your children. For, ^sbehold, the days are coming, in the which they shall say, Blessed *are* the barren, and the
30 wombs that never bare, and the paps which never gave suck. Then ^tshall they begin to say to the mountains, Fall on us; and to the hills, Cover
31 us. For ^uif they do these things in a green tree, what shall be done in the dry?

A. D. 33.

CHAP. 23.
^a Matt. 27. 2.
Mark 15. 1.
John 18.28.
^b 1 Ki. 21. 10-13.
Ps. 35. 11.
Ps. 62. 4.
Ps. 64. 3-6.
Jer. 20. 10.
Jer. 37. 13-15.
Dan. 3. 12.
Acts 17. 7.
Acts 24. 5.
1 Pet. 3. 16-18.
^c Matt. 17.27.
Matt.22. 21.
Mark 12.17.
^d John 19.12.
^e Matt.27.11.
1 Tim. 6. 13.
^f Matt.27.19, 24.
Mark 15.14.
John 18.38.
2 Cor. 5. 21.
1 Pet. 2. 22.
^g ch. 3. 1.
^h ch. 9. 9.
ⁱ Matt. 14. 1.
Mark 6. 14.
^j Isa. 53. 3.
^k Acts 4. 27.
Jas. 4. 4.
^l Matt. 27. 23.
Mark 15 14.
John 18.38.
^m Dan. 6. 4.
ⁿ Matt.27.26.
Mark 15.15.
John 19. 1.
Acts 5. 40, 41.
^o Matt.27.15.
Mark 15. 6.
John 18.39.
^p Acts 3. 14.
1 Or, assented.
Ex. 23. 2.
John 19. 16.
^q Pro. 17. 15.
^r John 19.17.
^s ch. 21. 23.
^t Isa. 2. 19.
Hos. 10. 8.
Rev. 6. 16.
Rev. 9. 6.
^u Pro. 11. 31.
Jer. 25. 29.
Ezek.20.47.
Ezek. 21. 3, 4.
1 Pet. 4. 17.

TREATED—THE FALL OF PETER. (= Matt. xxvi. 57-75; Mark xiv. 53-72; John xviii. 13-27.) For the exposition, see on Mark xiv. 53-72.
CHAP. XXIII. 1-12.—JESUS IS BROUGHT BEFORE PILATE, WHO PRONOUNCES HIM INNOCENT, AND SENDS HIM TO HEROD—FAILING TO DRAW ANYTHING OUT OF HIM, HEROD, WITH HIS MEN OF WAR, SETS HIM AT NOUGHT, AND SENDS HIM BACK TO PILATE. (= Matt. xxvii. 1, 2; Mark xv. 1-5; John xviii. 28-38.) For the exposition, see on John xviii. 28-38.

13-38.—JESUS IS AGAIN BEFORE PILATE, WHO, AFTER AGAIN PROCLAIMING HIS INNOCENCE AND SEEKING TO RELEASE HIM, DELIVERS HIM UP—

32 And ᵛthere were also two others, malefactors, led with him to be put
33 to death. And ʷwhen they were come to the place which is called
²Calvary, there they crucified him, and the malefactors, one on the right
34 hand, and the other on the left. Then said Jesus, Father, ˣforgive them;
for ʸthey know not what they do. And ᶻthey parted his raiment, and
35 cast lots. And ᵃthe people stood beholding. And the rulers also with
them derided *him*, saying, He saved others; let him save himself, if he
36 be Christ, the chosen of God. And the soldiers also mocked him, coming
37 to him, and offering him vinegar, and saying, If thou be the King of the
38 Jews, save thyself. And ᵇa superscription also was written over him in
letters of Greek, and Latin, and Hebrew, THIS IS' THE KING OF
THE JEWS.
39 And ᶜone of the malefactors which were hanged railed on him, saying,
40 If thou be Christ, save thyself and us. But the other answering ᵈrebuked
him, saying, Dost not thou fear God, seeing thou art in the same con-
41 demnation? And we indeed justly; for we receive the due reward of

A. D. 33.	
ᵛ Isa. 53. 12.	
	Matt 27.38.
ʷ Mark 15.22.	
	John 19.17.
² Or, the	
	place of a
	skull.
	Heb. 13. 12.
ᵃ Matt. 5. 44.	
	Acts 7. 60.
	1 Cor. 4.12.
ʸ Acts 3. 17.	
ᶻ Mark 15.24.	
	John 19. 24.
ᵃ Ps. 22. 17.	
	Zec. 12. 10.
ᵇ John 19.19.	
ᶜ Matt. 27.44.	
	Mark 15.32.
ᵈ Eph. 5. 11.	

TOUCHING INCIDENTS ON THE WAY TO CALVARY AND AT THE PLACE OF EXECUTION—THE CRUCIFIXION. (= Matt. xxvii. 31-50; Mark xv. 6-37; John xviii. 38—xix. 30.) For the exposition, see on John xviii. 38—xix. 30.

39-43.—THE TWO THIEVES BETWEEN WHOM JESUS WAS CRUCIFIED. This episode—peculiar to Luke—is one of the grandest in the Gospel History. If only hellish ingenuity could have suggested the expedient of crucifying our Lord between two malefactors, in order to hold Him forth as the worst of the three, only that wisdom which "taketh the wise in their own craftiness" could have made this very expedient irradiate the Redeemer, in His hour of deepest gloom, with a glory as bright to the spiritual eye as it was unexpected.

39. And one of the malefactors (see on John xix. 18) **which were hanged railed on him.** The first two Evangelists say that the *thieves* did so (Matt. xxvii. 44; Mark xv. 32). Now, if we had no more than this general statement, we should naturally conclude that both of them were meant. But after reading what is here recorded—of *one* that did so, and the other that rebuked him for doing it—it is to us astonishing that some sensible commentators should think it necessary to take the statement of the first two Evangelists so strictly as to imply that both of them reviled our Lord; and then to *infer*, without a shadow of ground for it in the text, that some sudden change came over the *penitent* one, which turned him from an unfeeling railer into a trembling petitioner. Is it conceivable that this penitent thief, after first himself reviling the Saviour, should then, on his views of Christ suddenly changing, have turned upon his fellow-sufferer and fellow-reviler, and rebuked him, not only with dignified sharpness, but in the language of *astonishment* that he should be capable of such conduct? Besides, there is a deep calmness in all that he utters, extremely unlike what we should expect from one who had been the subject of a mental revolution so sudden and so total. No, when it is said that "the *thieves* which were crucified with Him cast the same in His teeth," it is merely what grammarians call an 'indeterminate' plural, denoting no more than the unexpected *quarter* or *class* whence, in addition to all others the taunts proceeded. The Evangelists had been telling us that scoffs at the Redeemer proceeded from the *passers by*, from the *ecclesiastics*, and from the *soldiery*; but, as if that had not been enough, they tell us that they proceeded even from *the thieves*—a mode of speaking which no one would think *necessarily* meant both of them. Thus Matthew says, "*They say* unto Him, We have here but five loaves," &c.; whereas we learn from the Fourth Gospel that it was *one* only—Andrew, Simon Peter's brother—that said this (Matt. xiv. 17; John vi. 8). And when Mary poured her precious ointment on her Lord's head, Matthew says that "*His disciples* had indignation at it," and exclaimed against such waste; whereas from the Fourth Gospel we learn that it was *the traitor* that said this. It was but one of the malefactors, then, that, catching up the general derision, "cast the same in His teeth." But *his* taunt had a turn of its own, a sting which the others had not. **saying, If thou be** ('the') **Christ** [ὁ Χριστός], **save thyself and us.** Jesus, "reviled, reviles not again;" but another voice from the cross shall nobly wipe out this dishonour, and turn it to the unspeakable glory of the divine Redeemer. **40. But the other answering rebuked him, saying, Dost not thou fear God** [Οὐδὲ φοβῇ σὺ τὸν Θεὸν]—rather, 'Dost thou too not fear God?' or, 'Dost not even thou fear God?' There is a tacit reference to the godless, reckless spirit which reigned among the bystanders and shot such envenomed shafts at the meek Sufferer that hung between them. In *them* such treatment might be bad enough; but was it indeed coming from one of themselves? 'Let others jeer; but dost *thou?*' "Dost not thou *fear God?*" he asks. 'Hast thou no fear of meeting Him so soon as thy righteous Judge? Thou art within an hour or two of eternity, and dost thou spend it in reckless disregard of coming judgment?' **seeing thou art in the same condemnation?** 'He has been condemned to die, indeed, but is it better with thee? Doth even a common lot kindle no sympathy in thy breast?' But he goes on with his expostulations, and rises higher. **41. And we indeed justly; for we receive the due reward of our deeds.** Owning his crimes, and the justice with which he was paying their awful penalty, he would fain shame his fellow-sufferer into the same feeling, which would have quickly closed his mouth. **but this man hath done nothing amiss** [οὗτος δὲ οὐδὲν ἄτοπον ἔπραξεν]—'this person did nothing amiss;' literally, 'out of place,' and well rendered here "amiss." A very remarkable declaration. He does not acquit Him of all *ordinary crimes*, such as bring men to a judicial death; for with these he knew that our Lord was not charged. The charge of treason had not even a show of truth, as Pilate told His enemies. The one charge against Him was His claim to office and

42 our deeds: but this man hath done nothing amiss. And he said unto
43 Jesus, Lord, remember me when thou comest into *e*thy kingdom. And
Jesus said unto him, Verily I say unto thee, To-day shalt thou be with
me in *f*paradise.

A. D. 33.

e Heb. 1. 3.
Heb. 8. 1.
f Rev. 2. 7.

honours, which in the eyes of His judges amounted to blasphemy. Hear, then, this remarkable testimony in that light: 'He made Himself the promised Messiah, the Son of God—but in this He "*did nothing amiss.*" He ate with publicans and sinners, and bid all the weary and heavy laden come and rest under His wing—but in this He "*did nothing amiss.*" He claimed to be Lord of the Kingdom of God, to shut it at will, but also to open it at pleasure even to such as we are—but in this He "*did nothing amiss!*"' Does his next speech imply *less* than this? Turning now to the Lord Himself, how wonderful is his address! **42. And he said unto Jesus, Lord, remember me when thou comest into thy kingdom** [ἐν τῇ βασιλείᾳ σου] —rather, 'in thy kingdom;' that is, in the glory of it (Matt. xxv. 31; Luke ix. 26). Let us analyze and study this marvellous petition. First, the "Kingdom" he meant could be no *earthly* one, but one *beyond the grave;* for it is inconceivable that he should have expected Him to come down from the cross to erect any *temporal* kingdom. Next, he calls this Christ's own Kingdom—"thy Kingdom." Then, he sees in Christ the absolute right to dispose of that Kingdom to whom He pleased. But further, he does not presume to *ask* a place in that kingdom—though no doubt that is what he means—but with a humility quite affecting, just says, "Lord, *remember me* when," &c. Yet was there mighty faith in that word. If Christ will but "think upon him" (Neh. v. 19), at that august moment when He "cometh in His kingdom," it will do. 'Only assure me that then Thou wilt not forget such a wretch as I, that once hung by Thy side, and I am content.' Now contrast with this bright act of faith the darkness even of the apostles' minds, who could hardly be got to believe that their Master would die at all, who now were almost despairing of Him, and who when dead had almost buried their hopes in His grave. Consider, too, the man's previous *disadvantages* and *bad life.* And then mark how his faith comes out—not in protestations, 'Lord, I cannot doubt—I am firmly persuaded that Thou art Lord of a kingdom—that death cannot disannul Thy title nor impede the assumption of it in due time,' and so on—but as having no shadow of doubt, and rising above it as a question altogether, he just says, "Lord, remember me *when* thou comest," &c.—Was ever faith like this exhibited upon earth? It looks as if the brightest crown had been reserved for the Saviour's head at His darkest moment! **43. And Jesus said unto him.** To the taunt of the other criminal He answered nothing; but a response to this was resistless. The dying Redeemer had not seen so great faith, no not in His nearest and dearest apostles. It was to Him a "song in the night." It ministered cheer to His spirit in the thick midnight gloom that now enwrapt it. **Verily I say unto thee.** 'Since thou speakest as to the King, with kingly authority speak I to thee.' **To-day shalt thou be with me in paradise.** 'Thou art prepared for a long delay ere I come in My Kingdom, but not a day's delay shall there be for thee; thou shalt not be parted from Me even for a moment, but together we shall go, and with Me, ere this day expire, shalt thou be in paradise.' On the meaning of this word "paradise"—employed by the LXX. for the Garden of Eden (Gen. ii. 8, &c.)—it is only

necessary to observe that it was employed by the Jews to express the state of future bliss, both in its lower and higher stages; that, in keeping with this general idea, it is used by the apostle to express "the third heaven" (2 Cor. xii. 2, 4); and that our Lord Himself, in His apocalyptic epistle to the church of Ephesus, manifestly uses it to express the final glory and bliss of the redeemed, under the figure of Paradise Restored: "To him that overcometh will I give to eat of the tree of life, which is in the midst of the paradise of God" (Rev. ii. 7). In our passage, of course, the *immediate* reference is to such bliss as the disembodied spirit is capable of, and experiences, immediately after death; for it was to be on *that very day* that the penitent thief was to be with his dying Lord in paradise. But this is viewed as a thing understood, and so the promise amounts to this, that they were never more to be parted; that he would go with Him into heavenly bliss immediately on his departure; and though the One was to reassume His body in a few days, while the dust of the other would sleep till the resurrection, that their fellowship would never be interrupted!

Remarks.—1. Of all the possible conceptions of a writer of imaginary history, this incident is about the last that would enter the mind even of the most ingenious. While its presence in the Gospel History is to every unsophisticated reader its own evidence of actual occurrence, the glory with which it invests the Cross of Christ is beyond the power of language to express. Verily "He disappointeth the devices of the crafty, so that their hands cannot perform their enterprise: He taketh the wise in their own craftiness, and the counsel of the froward is carried headlong: with Him is strength and wisdom; the deceived and the deceiver are His. He leadeth counsellors away spoiled, and maketh the judges fools" (Job v. 12, 13; xii. 16, 17). 2. How true is that saying of Christ, "One shall be taken and another left!" (ch. xvii. 34-36). It is possible, indeed, that the religious opportunities of the penitent criminal may have been superior to his fellow's. But we have too much evidence, even in this Gospel History, that far better opportunities than he could possibly have enjoyed left the heart all unsoftened. Nor is it the reach of this man's *knowledge* which contrasts so remarkably with the demeanour of the impenitent criminal. It is his ingenuous self-condemnation; his mingled astonishment and horror at the very different temper of his fellow's mind; his anxiety to bring him to a better state of mind, while yet there was hope; and the pain with which he listened to the scoffs of his companion in crime at suffering innocence. Such deep and tender feeling, in contrast with the other's heartlessness on the brink of eternity, is but superficially apprehended until we trace it up to that distinguishing grace which, while it "*left*" one hardened criminal to go to his own place, "*took*" the other as a brand from the fire, lighted up into a blaze of light the few scattered rays of information about Jesus which beamed into his mind, and made him a bright jewel in that crown of glory that encircled the dying Redeemer! 3. How easily can divine grace elevate the rudest and the worst above the best instructed and most devoted servants of Christ! We are such slaves of *average experience* in morals and religion, that we are apt to treat whatever greatly tran-

44 And ^git was about the sixth hour, and there was a darkness over all
45 the ³earth until the ninth hour. And the sun was darkened, and ^hthe
46 veil of the temple was rent in the midst. And when Jesus had cried
with a loud voice, he said, ⁱFather, into thy hands I commend my spirit:
^jand having said thus, he gave up the ghost.
47 Now ^kwhen the centurion saw what was done, he glorified God, saying,

A. D. 33.

g Mark 15 33.
3 Or, land.
h Matt 27.51.
i Ps. 31. 5.
j John 19.30.
k Matt.27.54.

scends it, however well attested, with a measure of scepticism. But however exceptional such cases may seem, the laws of the divine administration in spiritual things—of which our knowledge is but very partial—will be found comprehensive enough to embrace them all. Think how limited must have been the means of knowledge which the Centurion possessed; and, yet, in regard to the power and glory of Christ, what a reach of perception and deep humility did he display, with a faith at which Jesus Himself marvelled! (Luke vii. 6-9). And did not the faith of the Syrophenician woman—heathen though her upbringing had been—draw forth the Redeemer's admiration? (Matt. xv. 28). And what an unwonted spectacle was the woman that washed the Saviour's feet with her tears! (Luke vii. 36, &c.) And who, even of the Twelve, got such a grasp of the Redeemer's power over the subtlest exercises of the human spirit as the man that, without any such opportunities as they enjoyed, exclaimed, "Lord, I believe; help Thou mine unbelief"? And what but a very unusual display of converting grace was that in the case of Zaccheus? (Luke xix). And yet, in some of these cases at least, it is not difficult to see what principles were at work, and how they wrought. As trials are fitted to open the heart, to direct it to the true source of relief, and to make it accessible to divine compassion and grace, so a deep sense of sin and a consciousness of hell-deserving draw the spiritual eye with a quick instinct to Him who came to seek and to save the lost, and rivet it upon Him with reviving and transforming efficacy. While others fasten on features of divine truth of lesser moment, and miss, through prejudice, the right view even of these, such deep-taught souls, with a kind of unerring scent, discover the direction in which relief for them is alone to be found. What to the penitent woman whose tears watered His blessed feet, and what to this poor dying criminal, who felt himself ready to drop into hell, were all the Messianic honours and dignities about which the Twelve kept dreaming and disputing till within an hour or two of their Lord's apprehension? To them one gracious look from that eye of His was more than all such things:

' Poor fragments all of this low earth;
Such as in sleep would hardly soothe
A soul that once had tasted of immortal truth.'—KEBLE.

And thus it was that, divinely taught in *the school of conscious unworthiness and soul-distress,* they shot far ahead of the least instructed but less schooled disciples. And so it still is. Schools of theological and critical training in the knowledge of Scripture are excellent things. But he who trusts in them as his sole key to divine truth and guide to heaven will find them blind guides, while many a one, ignorant of all but his own tongue, and little versed in the literature even of that, has made religious attainments that might put divines and scholars to shame. 4. *Presumption* and *despair,* it has been long ago and well remarked, are equally discountenanced here; the one in the impenitent thief, the other in his penitent fellow. He who flatters himself in his sins, hoping that, as one man was saved in the

agonies of death, another may—and why not he?—should turn to the man who, in the same circumstances and at the same moment, died *unsaved.* But, on the other hand, he who, conscious that he has worse than wasted his life, is sceptical as to both the reality and the value of what are called death-bed repentances, and so is ready to sink into despair, should study the case of this penitent thief. If *real,* the *value* of such death-bed changes is beyond dispute; since Jesus took this man, dying for his crimes, straight with Him to paradise. What, in fact, is wanting to any one's entering into the kingdom of God? Only that he be born again. How instantaneous that change may be, and in fact in every case essentially is, we have already had occasion to observe. See on ch. xix. 1-10, Remark 2 at the close of that Section. And what though there be no time left in one's life to *develop* the change and make it manifest to the world? If it be *real*—and the Searcher of hearts, the Judge of quick and dead, at least knows that —it is enough. And just as we nothing doubt that infants dying ere they attain to the sense of responsibility are capable of heaven, so the undeveloped infancy of the new life in dying penitents has in it a germ which will surely expand in the paradise of God. On the one hand, then, "Be not high-minded, but fear," O sinner, sleeping on a pillow of baseless hope that, after a reckless life, one dying glance at the Saviour will set thee all right. But, on the other hand, fear not, poor despairing sinner, to behold even at the last the Lamb of God that taketh away the sin of the world. For His word is not, "Him that cometh unto me" early, or up to a certain period of life and measure of guilt; but, "*Him that cometh*"—if only he *do come,* and come "UNTO ME, I will in no wise cast out." No limitation at all, either of *time* or *measure of guilt.* It is the 'coming unto Jesus' that secures the sinner against being cast out. 5. How false as well as cheerless, in the light of our Lord's words to this penitent, is the notion of the soul's *sleep,* or total unconsciousness, during the intermediate state between death and the resurrection! "To-day shalt thou be with Me in paradise." Who can take that to mean the mere transference of the soul to some place or state of *safety,* without the consciousness of it, or to the mere certainty of bliss *at the resurrection?* Nor is it that notion only which is rebuked here, but along with it the speculations of not a few who would so cripple the *capacities* of the disembodied spirit as to admit little beyond that 'sleep of the soul' before its re-union with the body. The more our Lord's words here are considered—in the light of such passages as 2 Cor. v. 6-8—the more will it be seen, that the spirits of the just, on their being disengaged from this earthly tabernacle, are immediately ushered into paradise in the bud, and find themselves tasting the bliss of heaven in substance; and thus it is that the language which describes the one merges naturally in that which properly describes only the other. So let us labour that whether present or absent, we may be accepted of Him!

44-56.—THE CRUCIFIXION COMPLETED—SIGNS AND CIRCUMSTANCES FOLLOWING THE DEATH OF THE LORD JESUS—HE IS TAKEN DOWN FROM THE

48 Certainly this was a righteous man. And all the people that came together to that sight, beholding the things which were done, smote their
49 breasts, and returned. And [i]all his acquaintance, and the women that followed him from Galilee, stood afar off, beholding these things.
50 And, [m]behold, *there was* a man named Joseph, a counsellor; *and he*
51 *was* a good man, and a just: (the same [n]had not consented to the counsel and deed of them:) *he was* of Arimathea, a city of the Jews:
52 [o]who also himself waited for the kingdom of God. This *man* went unto
53 Pilate, and begged the body of Jesus. And [p]he took it down, and wrapped it in linen, and laid it in [q]a sepulchre that was hewn in stone,
54 wherein never man before was laid. And that day was the preparation, and the sabbath drew on.
55 And the women also, [r]which came with him from Galilee, followed
56 after, and beheld [s]the sepulchre, and how his body was laid. And they returned, and [t]prepared spices and ointments; and rested the sabbath day, [u]according to the commandment.

24 NOW [a]upon the first *day* of the week, very early in the morning, they came unto the sepulchre, [b]bringing the spices which they had prepared,
2 and certain *others* with them. And they found the stone rolled away
3 from the sepulchre. And [c]they entered in, and found not the body of
4 the Lord Jesus. And it came to pass, as they were much perplexed
5 thereabout, [d]behold, two men stood by them in shining garments: and as they were afraid, and bowed down *their* faces to the earth, they said unto
6 them, Why seek ye [1]the living among the dead? He is not here, but is
7 risen: [e]remember how he spake unto you when he was yet in Galilee, saying, The Son of man must be delivered into the hands of sinful men, and
8 be crucified, and the third day rise again. And [f]they remembered his words,
9 And [g]returned from the sepulchre, and told all these things
10 unto the eleven, and to all the rest. It was Mary Magdalene, and [h]Joanna, and Mary *the mother* of James, and other *women that were*
11 with them, which told these things unto the apostles. And their words seemed to them as idle tales, and they believed them not. Then

A. D. 33.
[i] Ps. 38. 11.
John 19.25.
[m] Matt. 27.57.
Mark 15.42.
John 19.38.
[n] Gen 37. 21, 22.
Gen. 42. 21, 22.
Ex. 23. 2.
1 Tim 5 22.
[o] ch. 2. 25,38.
[p] Matt. 27. 59.
[q] Isa. 53. 9.
[r] ch. 8. 2.
[s] Mark 15.47.
[t] Mark 16. 1.
[u] Ex. 20. 10.
Isa. 56. 2, 6.
Isa. 58. 13.
Jer. 17. 24.

CHAP. 24.
[a] Matt. 28. 1.
Mark 16. 1.
John 20. 1.
[b] ch. 23. 56.
[c] Mark 16. 5.
[d] John 20. 12.
Acts 1. 10.
[1] Or, Him that liveth?
1 Tim. 1.17.
Rev. 1. 18.
[e] Matt. 16.21.
Mark 8. 31.
ch. 9. 22.
[f] John 2. 22.
[g] Matt. 28. 8.
Mark 16.10.
[h] ch. 8. 3.

CROSS AND BURIED—THE WOMEN OBSERVE THE SPOT. (= Matt. xxvii. 51-66; Mark xv. 38-47; John xix. 31-42.) For the exposition, see on Matt. xxvii. 51-66; and on John xix. 31-42.

CHAP. XXIV. 1-12. — ANGELIC ANNOUNCEMENT TO THE WOMEN, ON THE FIRST DAY OF THE WEEK, THAT CHRIST IS RISEN—THEY CARRY THE TRANSPORTING NEWS TO THE ELEVEN, WHO RECEIVE IT INCREDULOUSLY — PETER'S VISIT TO THE EMPTY SEPULCHRE. (=Matt. xxviii. 1-8; Mark xvi. 1-8; John xx. 1-10.)

The Resurrection Announced to the Women (1-8). **1. Now upon the first day of the week, very early in the morning, they came unto the sepulchre, bringing the spices which they had prepared, and certain others with them. 2. And they found the stone rolled away from the sepulchre. 3. And they entered in, and found not the body of the Lord Jesus.** See on Matt. xxviii. 1-4; and on Mark xvi. 1-4. **4. And it came to pass, as they were much perplexed thereabout.** Mark reports their perplexity, before they reached the sepulchre, as to who should roll away the stone that covered the body of their dear Lord; while our Evangelist here, who simply tells us that they found the stone rolled away, records their next and still greater perplexity at finding the sepulchre empty. But as the one vanished as soon as they arrived at the spot, so the other was soon dissipated by the shining ones that appeared to them. **behold, two men stood by them in shining garments** [ἀστραπτ-ούσαις]—garments of dazzling brightness. See

on Mark xvi. 5. **5. And as they were afraid, and bowed down their faces to the earth** (see on ch. i. 12), **they said unto them, Why seek ye the living** [τὸν ζῶντα]—'the Living One,' **among the dead?** Astonishing question! It is not, Why seek ye the *risen* One? but "Why seek ye the Living One among the dead?" See on Rev. i. 18. The surprise expressed in the question implies a certain incongruity in His being there at all; as if, though He might *submit* to it, "it was impossible that He should be *holden* of it" (Acts ii. 24). **6. He is not here, but is risen: remember how he spake unto you when he was yet in Galilee**—to which these women themselves belonged (ch. xxiii. 55.) **7. Saying**—in those explicit announcements, which He made once and again, of His approaching sufferings, death, and resurrection, **The Son of man must be delivered into the hands of sinful men, and be crucified, and the third day rise again.** How remarkable it is to hear angels quoting a whole sentence of Christ's to the disciples, mentioning where it was uttered, and wondering it was not fresh on their memory, as doubtless it was in theirs! See 1 Tim. iii. 16, "Seen of angels;" and 1 Pet. i. 12. **8. And they remembered his words.**

The Incredulity of the Eleven—Peter's Visit to Christ's Sepulchre (9-12). **9. And returned from the sepulchre, and told all these things unto the eleven, and to all the rest. 10. It was Mary Magdalene, and Joanna** (see on ch. viii. 1-3), **and Mary the mother of James, and other** [καὶ αἱ

12 *arose Peter, and ran unto the sepulchre; and stooping down, he beheld the linen clothes laid by themselves, and departed, wondering in himself at that which was come to pass.

13 And, behold, two of them went that same day to a village called
14 Emmaus, which was from Jerusalem *about* threescore furlongs. And
15 they *talked together of all these things which had happened. And it came to pass, that, while they communed *together* and reasoned, *Jesus
16 himself drew near, and went with them. But *their eyes were holden
17 that they should not know him. And he said unto them, What manner of communications *are* these that ye have one to another, as ye walk,
18 and are sad? And the one of them, *whose name was Cleopas, answering said unto him, Art thou only a stranger in Jerusalem, and hast not
19 known the things which are come to pass there in these days? And he said unto them, What things? And they said unto him, Concerning Jesus of Nazareth, *which was a prophet *mighty in deed and word
20 before God and all the people: and *how the chief priests and our rulers
21 delivered him to be condemned to death, and have crucified him. But we trusted *that it had been he which should have redeemed Israel: and besides all this, to-day is the third day since these things were done.
22 Yea, and certain women also of our company made us astonished, which
23 were early at the sepulchre; and when they found not his body, they came, saying, that they had also seen a vision of angels, which said that
24 he was alive. And certain of them which were with us went to the sepulchre, and found *it* even so as the women had said: but him they

A. D. 33.

i John 20. 3, 10.
j Deut. 6. 7.
Mal. 3. 16.
ch. 6. 45.
k Matt. 18. 20.
John 14. 18. 19.
l 2 Ki. 6. 18, 20.
Mark 16. 12.
John 20. 14.
John 21. 4.
m John 19. 25.
n John 3. 2.
John 6. 14.
Acts 2. 22.
o Acts 7. 22.
p Matt. 27. 1, 2, 20.
Mark 15. 1.
ch. 22. 66, 71.
ch. 23. 1, 5.
Acts 3. 13, 15.
Acts 4. 8, 10, 27.
Acts 5. 30, 31.
Acts 13. 27.
q Acts 1. 6.

λοιπαί]—rather, 'and the others,' that were with them, which told these things unto the apostles. See on Mark xvi. 1. **11. And their words seemed to them as idle tales, and they believed them not.** See on *v.* 41, and on Mark xvi. 11. **12. Then arose Peter, &c.** For the details of this, see on John xx. 1, &c.

For Remarks on this Section, see those on the corresponding Section of the First Gospel, Matt. xxviii. 1-15.

13-53.—JESUS APPEARS TO THE TWO GOING TO EMMAUS—THEN TO THE ASSEMBLED DISCIPLES—HIS GLORIOUS ASCENSION, AND RETURN OF THE ELEVEN TO JERUSALEM. (= Mark xvi. 12-19; John xx. 19-23.)

Jesus Appears to The Two Going to Emmaus, &c. (13-35). This most exquisite scene is peculiar to our Evangelist. **13. And, behold, two of them.** For the name of the one, see on *v.* 18. Who the other was is mere conjecture. **went**—or 'were proceeding' [ἦσαν πορευόμενοι] **that same day to a village called Emmaus, which was from Jerusalem about threescore furlongs**—or, about seven and a half miles; but the spot has not been satisfactorily determined. Perhaps they were returning home after the Passover. **14. And they talked together of all these things which had happened. 15. And it came to pass, that, while they communed together and reasoned**—as they exchanged views and feelings, weighing afresh all the facts detailed in *vv.* 18-24, **Jesus himself drew near, and went with them**—coming up behind them, as from Jerusalem (*v.* 18). **16. But their eyes were holden that they should not know him** [τοῦ μὴ ἐπιγνῶναι]—or 'did not recognize Him.' Certainly, as they did not believe that He was alive, His company, as a Fellow-traveller, was the last thing they would expect. But the words, "their eyes were holden," and the express intimation, in another Gospel, that "He appeared to them in another form" (Mark xvi. 12), make it evident that there was a divine operation hindering the recognition of Him until the fitting time. **17. And he**

said unto them, What manner of communications are these that ye have one to another [ἀντιβάλλετε]. The word "have" is too weak. Literally it is, 'that ye cast about' from one to the other, and denotes the earnest discussion that seemed to be going on between them. **as ye walk, and are sad? 18. And the one of them, whose name was Cleopas** (see on Matt. x. 3), **answering said unto him, Art thou only a stranger in Jerusalem, and hast not known the things which are come to pass there in these days?** If he knew not the events of the last few days in Jerusalem, he must be a mere sojourner; if he did, how could he suppose they would be talking of anything else? How artless is all this! **19. And he said unto them, What things?** And they said unto him, **Concerning Jesus of Nazareth, which was a prophet mighty in deed and word before God and all the people: 20. And how the chief priests and our rulers delivered him to be condemned to death**—that is, handed Him over to Pilate, that he might order Him to be put to death. **and have crucified him.** As if feeling it a relief to have some one to unburden his thoughts and feelings to, this disciple goes over the main facts, in his own desponding style, and this was just what our Lord wished. **21. But we trusted that it had been he which should have redeemed Israel** ['Ημεῖς δὲ ἠλπίζομεν ὅτι αὐτός ἐστιν ὁ μέλλων λυτροῦσθαι]—rather, 'But we were hoping that it was He that was to redeem,' &c. The "we" is emphatic:—*q. d.*, 'Others, we know, thought differently; but for our part we,' &c., implying expectations kept up till the recent events so dashed them. They expected, indeed, the promised Deliverance at His hand; but certainly not by His death. **and besides all this, to-day is the third day since these things were done. 22. Yea, and certain women also of our company made us astonished, which were early at the sepulchre; 23. And when they found not his body, they came, saying, that they had also seen a vision of angels, which said that he was alive. 24. And certain of them which were with us went to the sepulchre,**

25 saw not. Then he said unto them, O fools, and slow of heart to believe
26 all that the prophets have spoken! ought ʳnot Christ to have suffered
27 these things, and to enter into his glory? And beginning at ˢMoses and
　　ᵗall the Prophets, he expounded unto them in all the Scriptures the
28 things concerning himself. And they drew nigh unto the village whither
29 they went: and ᵘhe made as though he would have gone farther. But
　　they constrained him, saying, Abide with us; for it is toward evening,
30 and the day is far spent. And he went in to tarry with them. And it
　　came to pass, as he sat at meat with them, he took bread, and blessed *it*,
31 and brake, and gave to them. And their eyes were opened, and they
32 knew him; and he ²vanished out of their sight. And they said one to
　　another, Did not our heart burn within us, while he talked with us by
　　the way, and while he opened to us the Scriptures?
33 　And they rose up the same hour, and returned to Jerusalem, and found
34 the eleven gathered together, and them that were with them, saying, The
35 Lord is risen indeed, and hath ᵛappeared to Simon. And they told what

A. D. 33.

ʳ Acts 17. 3.
Phil 2 6-11.
1 Pet. 1. 11.
ˢ Gen. 3. 15.
Gen. 22. 18.
Gen. 26. 4.
Num. 21. 9.
ᵗ Ps. 16. 9.
Ps. 22.
Jer. 23. 5.
Jer. 33. 14.
Ezek.31.23.
Ezek.37.25.
Dan. 9. 24.
Mic. 7. 20.
ᵘ Gen. 32. 26.
2 Or, ceased
to be seen
of them.
ᵛ 1 Cor. 15. 5.

and found it even so as the women had said; but him they saw not. Not only did His death seem to give the fatal blow to their hopes, but He had been two days dead already, and this was the third. 'It is true,' they add, 'some of our women gave us a surprise, telling us of a vision of angels they had at the empty grave this morning that said He was alive, and some of ourselves who went thither confirmed their statement; but then, Himself they saw not.' A doleful tale truly, and told out of the deepest despondency. **25. Then he said unto them, O fools** [᾽Ω ἀνόητοι]—This is too strong a word. Our Lord never calls His true disciples "fools" [μωροί]. It should be, 'O senseless;' that is, void of discernment. **and slow of heart to believe all that the prophets have spoken!**—or 'spake' [ἐλάλησαν]. **26. Ought not Christ** [ἔδει παθεῖν τὸν Χριστὸν] **to have suffered these things, and to enter into his glory?**—'Behoved it not the Messiah to suffer these things, and to enter into His glory;' that is, Was it not necessary to the fulfilment of the Scriptures that the predicted Messiah should, through the gate of these very sufferings, enter into His glory? It is doubtless to these words that the apostle Peter alludes, when he speaks of the Spirit of Christ who testified in the prophets 'the sufferings that were to light upon Messiah and the following glories' [προμαρτυρόμενον τὰ εἰς Χριστὸν παθήματα καὶ τὰς μετὰ ταῦτα δόξας], 1 Pet. i. 11. 'Ye have had your eye fixed so exclusively on the "glories" (says our Lord), that ye have overlooked the "sufferings" which the prophets told you were to go before and pave the way for them.' **27. And beginning at Moses and all the Prophets, he expounded unto them in all the Scriptures the things concerning himself**—the great Burden of all the Old Testament Scriptures. **28. And they drew nigh unto the village whither they went**—or 'were going' [ἐπορεύοντο]. **and he made as though he would have gone farther**—but only "as though;" for He had no intention of going farther. So when He walked towards them on the sea of Galilee, "He would have passed by them"—but never meant to do it. So Gen. xxxii. 26. (Compare Gen. xviii. 3, 5; xlii. 7.) **29. But they constrained him, saying, Abide with us; for it is toward evening, and the day is far spent. And he went in to tarry with them.** But for this, the whole design of the interview had been lost; but *it was not to be lost*, for He who only wished to be constrained had kindled a longing in the hearts of His travelling companions which was not to be so easily put off. **30. And it came to pass,**

as he sat at meat with them, he took bread, and blessed it, and brake, and gave to them. **31. And their eyes were opened, and they knew** —or 'recognized' [ἐπέγνωσαν] **him; and he vanished out of their sight** [καὶ αὐτὸς ἄφαντος ἐγένετο ἀπ᾽ αὐτῶν]—or 'ceased to be seen of them;' supernaturally disappearing. The stranger first startles them by taking the place of Master at their own table, but on proceeding to that act which reproduced the whole scene of the last Supper, a rush of associations and recollections disclosed their Guest, and He stood confessed before their astonished gaze—THEIR RISEN LORD! They were going to gaze on Him, perhaps embrace Him, but that moment He is gone! It was enough; the end of the whole interview had been gained. **32. And they said one to another, Did not our heart burn within us, while he talked with us by the way, and while he opened to us the Scriptures?** The force of the imperfect tenses here [καιομένη ἦν—ἐλάλει—διήνοιγεν], denoting what they felt *during the whole time* of His walk and talk with them, should if possible be preserved; as thus: 'Was not our heart burning within us whilst He was talking with us on the way, and whilst He was opening to us the Scriptures?' 'Ah! this accounts for it: We could not understand the glow of self-evidencing light, love, glory, that ravished our hearts; but now we do.' They cannot rest — how could they? — they must go straight back and tell the news. They cannot think of sleeping over it. **33. And they rose up the same hour, and returned to Jerusalem, and found the eleven gathered together.** This does not show that the two disciples themselves were not of "the Eleven;" for the expression is used here to denote the *company* or *class*, not the fact of the whole number of them being present on this occasion. **and them that were with them. 34. Saying, The Lord is risen indeed, and hath appeared to Simon.** They think they will bring strange tidings—thrilling intelligence—to their downcast brethren. But ere they have time to tell their tale, their own ears are saluted with tidings not less thrilling: "The Lord is risen indeed [ὄντως], and hath appeared to SIMON." Most touching and precious intelligence this. The only one of the Eleven to whom He appeared *alone* was he, it seems, who had so shamefully denied Him. *What passed at that interview we shall never know here. Probably it was too sacred for disclosure.* See on Mark xvi. 7. **35. And they told what things were done in the way, and how he was known of them in breaking of**

342

things *were done* in the way, and how he was known of them in breaking of bread.

36 And as they thus spake, Jesus himself stood in the midst of them, 37 and saith unto them, Peace *be* unto you. But they were terrified and 38 affrighted, and supposed that they had seen a spirit. And he said unto them, Why are ye troubled? and why do thoughts arise in your hearts? 39 Behold my hands and my feet, that it is I myself: handle me, and see; 40 for a spirit hath not flesh and bones, as ye see me have. And when he 41 had thus spoken, he showed them *his* hands and *his* feet. And while they yet believed not for joy, and wondered, he said unto them, Have ye 42 here any meat? And they gave him a piece of a broiled fish, and of an 43 honey-comb. And *"*he took *it*, and did eat before them.

44 And he said unto them, *"*These *are* the words which I spake unto you, while I was yet with you, that all things must be fulfilled which were written in the law of Moses, and *in* the Prophets, and *in* the Psalms, 45 concerning me. Then *"*opened he their understanding, that they might 46 understand the Scriptures, and said unto them, Thus it is written, and thus it behoved Christ to suffer, and to rise from the dead the third day: 47 and that repentance and *"*remission of sins should be preached in his 48 name among all *"*nations, beginning at Jerusalem. And *"*ye are witnesses 49 of these things. And, *"*behold, I send the promise of my Father upon you: but tarry ye in the city of Jerusalem, until ye be endued with power from on high.

A. D. 33.

" Acts 10. 41.
" Matt. 16.21.
Mark 8. 31,
32.
Mark 9. 31.
ch. 9. 22.
ch. 18. 31,
32.
" Acts 16. 14.
2 Cor. 4. 6.
" Dan. 9. 24.
Acts 13. 38.
1 John 2.12.
" Gen. 12. 3.
Ps. 22. 27.
Isa 49. 6.
Jer. 31. 34.
Hos. 2. 23.
Mic. 4. 2.
Mal. 1. 11.
Gal. 3. 28.
" John 15. 27.
Acts 1. 22.
" Isa. 44. 3.
Joel 2. 28.
John 14. 16,
17.
John 15. 26.
Acts 2. 1.

bread. The two from Emmaus have now their turn, and relate the marvellous manifestation made to them. While thus comparing notes of their Lord's appearances, lo! Himself stands in the midst of them.

Jesus Appears to the Assembled Disciples—Convinces them wondrously of the Reality of His Resurrection—Opens to them the Scriptures on the Subject, and Directs them to Wait for the promised Spirit (36-49). **36. And as they thus spake, Jesus himself stood in the midst of them, and saith unto them, Peace be unto you.** See on John xx. 19-21. **37. But they were terrified and affrighted, and supposed that they had seen a spirit**—the ghost of their dead Lord rather than Himself in the body. (See on Acts xii. 15; and Matt. xiv. 26.) **38. And he said unto them, Why are ye troubled? and why do thoughts arise in your hearts?** [διαλογισμοί]—rather 'reasonings;' that is, whether He were risen or no, and whether this was His very Self. **39. Behold my hands and my feet, that it is I myself: handle me, and see**—lovingly offering them both *ocular* and *tangible* demonstration of the reality of His resurrection. **for a spirit hath not flesh and bones, as ye see me have**—an important statement regarding 'spirits.' He says not "flesh and *blood;*" for the blood is the life of the animal and corruptible body (Gen. ix. 4) which "cannot inherit the kingdom of God" (1 Cor. xv. 50); but "flesh and bones"—implying the *identity*, but *with diversity of laws*, of the resurrection-body. **40. And when he had thus spoken, he shewed them his hands and his feet.** See on John xx. 24-28. **41. And while they yet believed not for joy, and wondered.** They did believe, else, as *Bengel* beautifully remarks, they had not "joyed." But it seemed *too good* to be true. Like the captives from Babylon, "they were as men that dreamed" (Ps. cxxvi. 1, 2). **he said unto them, Have ye here any meat?** **42. And they gave him a piece of a broiled fish, and of an honey-comb**—common, frugal fare, anciently. **43. And he took it, and did eat before them**—that is, so as to let them see Him eating; not for His own necessity, but their conviction.

44. And he said unto them, These are the words **343** which I spake unto you, while I was yet with you. Mark this last expression—"while I was yet with you"—that is, in the days of His flesh. Now, He was as good as removed from them; His life being a new one, the atmosphere He breathed no longer that of this lower world, and His proper home, even for their interests, His Father's house. But 'now ye will understand what I said to you, once and again, to your so great surprise and distress, about the Son of man requiring to be put to death and to rise again. **that all things must be fulfilled which were written in the law of Moses, and in the Prophets, and in the Psalms**—the three current Jewish divisions of the Old Testament Scriptures, **concerning me. 45. Then opened he their understanding, that they might understand the Scriptures.** A statement of unspeakable value: expressing, on the one hand, Christ's *immediate* access to the human spirit and *absolute power over it*, to the adjustment of its vision, and its permanent rectification for spiritual discernment; and, on the other hand, showing that the *apostolic manner of interpreting the Old Testament*, in the Acts and Epistles, *has the direct sanction of Christ Himself.* **46. And said unto them, Thus it is written, and thus it behoved Christ**—or 'the Messiah' [τὸν Χριστὸν], **to suffer, and to rise from the dead the third day**—see on *v.* 26. **47. And that repentance and remission of sins should be preached in his name among all nations, beginning at Jerusalem;** first, because Jerusalem was the metropolitan centre of the then existing kingdom of God (see Rom. i. 16—"to the Jew first;" Acts xiii. 46 ; Isa. ii. 3 ; and see on Matt. x. 6) ; and next, because it was the great laboratory and reservoir of all the sin and all the crime of the nation (ch. xiii. 33), and by beginning *there*, it would be proclaimed for all time that there was mercy in Christ for the chief of sinners (see on Matt. xxiii. 37). **48. And ye are witnesses of these things** (see on Acts i. 8, 22). **49. And, behold, I send** [ἀποστέλλω]—or, 'I am sending,' in the present tense, to intimate its nearness. **the promise of my Father**—that is, what my Father hath promised; or the Holy Ghost, of which Christ is the

50   And he led them out as far as to Bethany; and he lifted up his hands, | A. D. 33.
51 and blessed them. And ^{*d*}it came to pass, while he blessed them, he was | ^{*d*} 2 Ki. 2. 11.
52 parted from them, and carried up into heaven. And they worshipped | Eph. 1. 20.

authoritative Dispenser (John xiv. 7; Rev. iii. 1; v. 6); **but tarry ye in the city of Jerusalem, until ye be endued** [ἐνδύσασθε]—or ' clothed' **with power from on high**—implying (as the parallels show— Rom. xiii. 14; 1 Cor. xv. 53; Gal. iii. 27; Col. iii. 9, 10) their being so penetrated and acted upon by conscious supernatural "power" as to stamp with divine authority the whole exercise of their apostolic office, including, certainly, their *pen* as well as their *mouth.*

Glorious Ascension of the Risen Redeemer (50, 51). **50. And he led them out as far as to Bethany**—not to the village itself, which would be no congenial spot; but "as far as to Bethany"—meaning, probably, to that side of the mount of Olives where the road strikes down to Bethany; for there is every reason to concur in the early tradition that from Mount Olivet our Lord took His flight on high. But how came Jesus and the Eleven to be now together at Bethany, having been last together in Galilee? The feast of Pentecost, now within ten days, would bring the disciples to Jerusalem, and no doubt their Lord appointed to meet them in the neighbourhood of it, probably somewhere on the way to Bethany. **and he lifted up his hands, and blessed them. 51. And it came to pass, while he blessed them, he was parted from them, and carried up into heaven.** Sweet intimation! The Incarnate, Crucified, Risen One, now on the wing for heaven—waiting only for those odorous gales which were to waft Him to the skies --goes away in benedictions, only to continue them, in yet higher style, as the Glorified and Enthroned One, until He come again. And O, if angels were so transported at His birth into this scene of tears and death, what must have been their ecstasy as they welcomed and attended Him up "far above all heavens" into the presence-chamber, and conducted Him to the right hand, of the Majesty on High! Thou hast an everlasting right, O my Saviour, to that august place. The Brightness of the Father's glory, enshrined in our nature, hath won it well, for He poured out His soul unto death. Therefore hath He ascended on high, and led captivity captive, receiving gifts for men, yea for the rebellious, that the Lord God might dwell among them. 'Thou art the King of glory, O Christ.' Lift up your heads, O ye gates, be lifted up, ye everlasting doors, that the King of glory may come in! Even so wilt thou change these vile bodies of ours, that they may be like unto Thine own glorious body; and then, with gladness and rejoicing shall they be brought, they shall enter into the King's palace! For fuller particulars of the Ascension, by the same Evangelist, see on Acts i. 9-11.

Return of the Eleven to Jerusalem (52, 53). **And they worshipped him**—beyond all doubt, in the sense of supreme worship. In the whole Gospel of St. Luke, remarks *Stier*, we have this word to 'worship' [προσκυνεῖν] but in one other place— ch. iv. 7, 8—where it is used of the honour due to God alone; and in the Acts only in the following passages, all in the same sense: ch. [vii. 43]; viii. 27; xxiv. 11; x. 25, 26. In this last passage, though Cornelius meant only subordinate worship, Peter rejected it—as only a *man.* And what was the worship of His bright escort on His way upwards, and of His reception above? (Ps. lxviii. 18, 19). **and returned to Jerusalem**—as instructed to do; but not till, after gazing as if entranced up into the blue vault in which He had disappeared,

they were gently checked by two shining ones, who assured them He would come again to them in the like manner as He had gone into heaven. (See on Acts i. 10, 11.) This made them return, not with disappointment at His removal, but **with great joy: 53. And were continually in the temple**—that is, every day at the regular hours of prayer until the day of Pentecost, **praising and blessing God**—in higher than Jewish strains now, though in the accustomed forms. **Amen.** This "Amen" is excluded from the text by *Tischendorf* and *Tregelles*, in which they are followed by *Alford.* But the authorities in its favour are, in our judgment, decisive. *Lachmann* inserts it. Probably some might less see the import of it *here* than in the other Gospels. But who that has followed our Evangelist, till he leaves his readers with the Eleven, "praising and blessing God" after their Lord's ascension to the Father, could refrain from adding his own "Amen," even though the Evangelist had not written it? It is as though he had said, 'For such wonders, the record of which is here closed, let every reader join with those Eleven continually in praising and blessing God.'

For Remarks on the Resurrection - scene, see those on the corresponding Section of the First Gospel—Matt. xxviii. 1-15. But on the remaining portion of this chapter we add the following—

Remarks.—1. Were we asked to select from the Four Gospels the six verses which bear the most indubitable marks of exact historic reality, we might be at some loss, from the profusion of such that stud the pages of the Evangelical Narrative. But certainly the doleful tale of the two disciples going to Emmaus—of expectations regarding Jesus of Nazareth, raised only to be crushed to the lowest, with the half-trembling, half-hoping allusion to the reports of His resurrection by " certain women of their company," and all this poured into the ear of the risen Saviour Himself, who had overtaken and made up to them as an unknown fellow-traveller (*vv.* 19-24)—this must be held by every competent and candid judge to pass all the powers of human invention. Some, perhaps, will think that the subsequent manifestation in the breaking of bread is stamped with a self-evidencing glory at least equally great. Perhaps it is. Or that scene in the apartment at Jerusalem, where the disciples were met the same evening, when the two who had hastened back from Emmaus entered it to tell their tale of transport, but were anticipated by one equally thrilling, and while they were all unburdening themselves, breathless with joy, the Redeemer made His own appearance in the midst of them! But the difficulty of deciding which is most life-like arises from the multitude of such scenes, whose reality those *photographic* Records have printed indelibly on the minds of all unsophisticated readers in every age and all lands. And what those Records do *not* relate bears higher testimony to them, perhaps, than even their positive statements. Apocryphal Gospels would have been ready enough to tell us what passed between the risen Redeemer and the disciple who thrice denied Him, at their first meeting on the resurrection-morn. But while only one of the Four Evangelists notices the fact at all, even from him all the information we have is contained in the thrilling announcement by the company assembled in the evening to the two from Emmaus, "The Lord is risen indeed, and hath appeared to *Simon!*" Not for the perplexed only do we recur to this subject

53 him, and returned to Jerusalem with great joy: and were continually [e]in the temple, praising and blessing God. Amen.

	A. D. 33.
	[e] Acts 2. 46.

again and again. To look into these things is an exercise as healthy as delightful to those who love the Lord Jesus. For thus do we find ourselves in the midst of them; and the views which such scenes disclose to us of the person of the Lord Jesus, His Work in the flesh, His dying love, His resurrection-power and glory, have such a *historical* form as imparts to them undying life, immortal youth and beauty. 2. How often in hours of darkest despondency are the disciples of the Lord Jesus favoured with His presence, though their eyes for a time are holden that they shall not know Him? For all He does, perhaps, at such seasons is to keep them from sinking, and cheer them with hopes of relief, through the talk, it may be, of some friend who speaks to their case and reminds them of forgotten truths and promises. But this is itself relief enough to be sweet in the meantime; and dimly though Himself may be discerned in all this, the feeling which it begets finds vent in such strains as these,—

> 'Abide with me from morn to eve,
> For without Thee I cannot live:
> Abide with me when night is nigh,
> For without Thee I cannot die.'—KEBLE.

But there are times when the presence of Jesus makes itself almost as manifest as when the eyes of the two at Emmaus were opened and they knew Him. And never, perhaps, more than "in the breaking of bread." It was indeed a common meal which those two prepared for their unknown Guest. But His taking the place of Master at their own table, and His "taking the bread, and blessing, and breaking, and giving to them"—bringing up the whole scene of the Last Supper, and disclosing to them in this Guest their own risen Lord—converted it into a communion in the most exalted sense. And thus sometimes, when we sit down to that table which He hath ordered to be spread, with no higher feeling at the moment than of simple obedience to a commanded duty, He "makes Himself known to us in the breaking of bread" as evidently as if Himself said to us with His own lips, "This is my body which is broken for thee. This cup is the New Testament in my blood shed for many, for the remission of sins; drink thou and all of it." But such vivid disclosures of Jesus to the spirit, like cordials to a sinking frame, are not what we live upon; and just as, when the end was answered, He vanished out of the sight of the two wondering disciples, and, when on the mount of transfiguration the voice was past, Jesus was left alone, the glory gone, and Jesus only, as before, with the three astonished disciples—so are we left to go up through this wilderness leaning on our Beloved through the medium of the *word*, of which Jesus Himself says, "Sanctify them through thy truth: Thy word is truth." 3. What a testimony to the *divine authority* and *evangelical sense* of the Old Testament Scriptures have we in the expositions of them by the Lord Jesus, first to the two going to Emmaus, and afterwards to the company of disciples assembled at Jerusalem on the same evening of the resurrection-day? He who denies, or would explain away, either of these—and both certainly stand or fall together—must settle it with Christ Himself; but with those who, in our day, dispute even His authority, and yet call themselves Christians, this is not the place to dispute —nor, perhaps, would it be of much avail. But, 4. Who that reads with simple faith what is here written of Christ's direct access to the human

spirit, and power to open its faculties to the reception of truth (*v.* 45), can doubt His proper Divinity? It is, indeed, no more than He is said to have done to Lydia (see on Acts xvi. 14); nor is it more than the father of the lunatic boy ascribed to Him with tears (see on Mark ix. 24); and we must get rid of the whole Gospel History ere we can free ourselves of the necessity of believing that Jesus *has* this glorious power over the human heart. But to free ourselves from this obligation we want not. It is our joy that it is written in the Evangelical Narrative as with a sunbeam, and reflected in all the subsequent writings of the New Testament. But for this, who would commit the keeping of his eternal all to Him? But "we know in Whom we have believed, and are persuaded that He is able to keep that which we have committed unto Him against that day" (see on 2 Tim. i. 12). 5. The *identity* of the Risen with the Crucified body of the Lord Jesus is beyond all doubt what our Lord intended to convince His disciples of, by eating before them, and by showing them His hands and His feet, with "the print of the nails." This is a truth of unspeakable importance, and delightful beyond the power of language to express. The varying forms in which He appeared to the disciples, in consequence of which He was not always immediately recognized by them, suggests the high probability that the resurrection bodies of the saints too will possess the same or analogous properties; and the conjecture that a process of progressive glorification during the forty days of His sojourn on earth, and consummated as He "went up where He was before" —though it derives but slender support from the words of John xx. 17, "I am *not yet* ascended"— may possibly have something in it. But one little fact speaks volumes on the perfect identity of the Risen Jesus Himself with Him who in the days of His flesh endeared Himself to the disciples in the familiar intercourses of life—that when His appearance in the garden quite deceived Mary Magdalene, that one word "*Mary!*" fixed His identity to *her* beyond what all other proofs perhaps could have done (see on John xx. 16). And is it beyond the bounds of legitimate inference from this, that *personal recognition*, implying of course the vivid recollection of those scenes of the present life which constitute the ties of dearest fellowship, will be found so to connect the future with the present state—the perfection and glory of the one with the weakness, and wants, and tears, and vanities of the other—as to make it for ever delightfully manifest that with all its glory it is but the efflorescence of the present life of the redeemed? 6. And Thou art gone up to the Father, O Thou whom my soul loveth! It is Thy proper home. Thou hast but ascended up where Thou wast before. And it was expedient for us that Thou shouldst go away. For otherwise the Comforter would not have come. But He *is* come. Thou hast sent Him to us; and He hath glorified Thee as Thou never wast nor, without Him, would have been in the Church. Now, repentance and remission of sins is in course of being preached in Thy name among all nations. Beginning at Jerusalem, bloody Jerusalem, it shall reach in its triumphs the most desperate cases of human guilt. But Thou shalt come again, and receive us to Thyself, that where Thou art we may be also. Even so, come, Lord Jesus! The grace of our Lord Jesus Christ be with all that read these lines. Amen.

THE GOSPEL ACCORDING TO

ST. JOHN.

	CHAP. 1.
1 IN the beginning *was the Word, and the Word was *b* with God, *c* and	*a* Rev. 19. 13
2 the Word was God. The same was in the beginning with God.	*b* Zec. 13. 7.
3 All things were made by him; and without him was not any thing made	*c* Isa. 9. 6. ch. 10. 30.
4 that was made. In him was life; and the life was the light of men.	Phil. 2. 6.

CHAP. I. 1-18.—THE WORD MADE FLESH. As the Fourth Gospel was not written until the other three had become the household words and daily bread of the Church of Christ—thus preparing it, as babes are by milk, for the strong meat of this final Gospel—so, even in this Gospel, the great key-note of it, that " *The Word was made Flesh*," is not sounded until, by thirteen introductory verses, the reader has been raised to the altitude and attempered to the air of so stupendous a truth. **1. In the beginning was the Word, and the Word was with God, and the Word was God.** Three great things are here said of The Word: First, He was "in the beginning" [ἐν ἀρχῇ = בְּרֵאשִׁית, Gen. i. 1]. Thus does our Evangelist commence his Gospel with the opening words of the book of Genesis. Only, as *Meyer* remarks, he raises the historical conception of the phrase, which in Genesis denotes the first moment of *time*, to the absolute idea of *pre-temporality*. That the words "In the beginning" are here meant to signify, 'Before all time' and all created existence, is evident from *v.* 3, where all creation is ascribed to this Word, who Himself, therefore, is regarded as uncreated and eternal. See ch. xvii. 5, 24; Col. i. 17. Second, The Word "was with God" [πρὸς τὸν Θεόν]. This conveys two ideas—that He 'had a conscious personal existence distinct from God,' as one is distinct from the person he is "with;" and that He 'was associated with Him in mutual fellowship.' See on *v.* 18, and observe Zec. xiii. 7, "My Fellow, saith the Lord of hosts" [עֲמִיתִי, '*My Associate*']. Observe, that He who is called "God" here, is in 1 John i. 1, 2, called "THE FATHER:"—"The Word of Life (says this same exalted penman) was with the Father, and was manifested unto us." And such is the familiar language of Scripture, with respect to Him who *absolutely* is "God," but *personally*, and relatively to the Son, is "the Father." Third, The Word "was God" [Θεὸς ἦν ὁ λόγος]. No other translation of this great clause is grammatically possible. Even should the order of the original words be retained (as in *Luther's* German version)—"and God was the Word," the sense will still be the same: 'and God the Word was.' But this is against the genius of the English language. Each of these three pregnant statements is the complement of the other; each successive one correcting any misapprehension to which the others might give rise. Thus: The Word, says the Evangelist, was eternal. Yet this was not the eternity of the Father, nor the eternity of a mere attribute of the Father, but of One who is consciously and personally distinct from, and associated with, the Father. But neither is this the distinctness and fellowship of two different Beings —as if there were a plurality of Gods, but of two subsistences in the one absolute Godhead; in such sort that the absolute Unity of the Godhead—the great principle of all Religion—instead

of being thereby compromised, is only transferred from the region of shadowy abstraction to that of warm personal life and love. But why all these sharp definitions? it may be asked. Not to tell us of certain mysterious internal distinctions in the Godhead, which but for the Incarnation could never, perhaps, have been apprehended at all; but for the purpose of throwing light upon that stupendous assumption of our nature about to be announced, even as that assumption throws light back again upon the eternal distinctions and fellowships of the Godhead. **2. The same was in the beginning with God.** Here the first and second statements are combined into one; emphatically reiterating the eternal distinctness of the Word from God ("the Father"), and His association with Him in the Unity of the Godhead. But now what does this peculiar title "The Word" import? The simplest explanation of it, we think, is this: that what a man's *word* is to *himself*—the index, manifestation, or expression of himself to others— such, in some faint sense, is "The Word" in relation to God; "He hath *declared* Him" (*v.* 18). For the origin and growth of this conception, see Remark 3 at the close of this Section. So much for the *Person* of The Word. Now for His *actings.* **3. All things were made by him**—that is, "all things" in the most absolute sense; as the next clause is intended to make evident; **and without him was not any thing made that was made** [οὐδὲ ἓν ὃ γέγονεν]. The statement is most emphatic— 'without Him was not one thing made that hath been made.' To blunt the force of 'this, it is alleged that the word "by" [διὰ] in "by him" here means no more than 'through,' or 'by means of'—in the sense of subordinate instrumentality, not efficient agency. But this same preposition is once and again used in the New Testament of God's own efficient agency in the production of all things. Thus, Rom. xi. 36, "Of Him" [ἐξ]—as their eternal Source—"and *through* Him" [δι' αὐτοῦ]—by His efficient Agency —"and to Him" [εἰς]—as their last End?—"are all things." And in Col. i. 16 the creation of all things—in the most absolute sense and in the way of efficient agency—is ascribed to Christ: "For by Him [ἐν αὐτῷ] were created all things" [τὰ πάντα] —that is, the entire universality of created things, as the all-comprehensive details that follow are intended to show—"whether they be thrones, or dominions, or principalities, or powers: all things were created *by* Him and for Him" [τὰ πάντα δι' αὐτοῦ καὶ εἰς αὐτὸν ἔκτισται]. See also Heb. i. 10-12, where creation, in the most absolute sense, is ascribed to Christ. **4. In him was life.** From simple *creation*, or calling into existence, the Evangelist now advances to a higher idea—the communication of *life*. But he begins by announcing its essential and original existence in Himself, in virtue of which He became the great *Fontal Principle* of life in all living, but specially in the high-

346

5 And ^dthe light shineth in darkness; and the darkness comprehended it not.

6, There ^ewas a man sent from God, whose name *was* John. The same

7 came for a witness, to bear witness of the Light, that all *men* through

8 him might believe. He ^fwas not that Light, but *was sent* to bear witness of that Light.

9 *That* ^gwas the true Light, which lighteth every man that cometh into

10 the world. He was in the world, and ^hthe world was made by him, and

11 the world knew him not. He ⁱcame unto his own, and his own received

12 him not. But ^jas many as received him, to them gave he ¹power to

d ch. 3. 19.
e Mal. 3. 1.
f Acts 13. 25.
g Isa. 49. 6.
h Ps. 33. 6.
　1 Cor. 8. 6.
i Luke 19.14.
j Isa. 56. 5.
　Rom. 8. 15.
　Gal. 3. 26.
1 Or, the right, or, privilege.

est sense of life. Accordingly, He is styled "The Word of life" (1 John i. 1, 2). **and the life was the light of men.** It is remarkable, as *Bengel* notes, how frequently in Scripture *light* and *life*, on the one hand, and on the other, *darkness* and *death*, are associated: "I am the Light of the world," said Christ: "he that followeth Me shall not walk in darkness, but shall have the *light of life*" (John viii. 12). Contrariwise, "Yea, though I walk," sings the sweet Psalmist, "in the valley of the *shadow of death*, I will fear no evil" (Ps. xxiii. 4). Compare Job x. 21, 22. Even of God, it is said, "Who only hath *immortality*, dwelling in the *light* which no man can approach unto" (1 Tim. vi. 16). Here "the light of men" seems to denote all that distinctive light in men which flows from the life given them—intellectual, moral, spiritual: "For with Thee," says the Psalmist, "is the fountain of *life:* in Thy *light* shall we see light" (Ps. xxxvi. 9). **5. And the light shineth in darkness**—that is, in this dark fallen world; for though the Life was the light of men," they were "sitting in darkness and the shadow of death" when He came of whom our Evangelist is about to speak, with no ability to find the way either of truth or of holiness. In this thick darkness, then—in this obliquity, intellectual and moral, the light of the Living Word "shineth;" that is, by all the rays of natural or revealed teaching with which men were favoured *before* the Incarnation. **and the darkness comprehended it not** [οὐ κατέλαβεν]—'did not take it in.' Compare Rom. i. 28, "They did not like to retain God in their knowledge." Thus does our Evangelist, by hinting at the inefficacy of all the strivings of the *unincarnate* Word, gradually pave the way for the announcement of that final remedy—the Incarnation. Compare 1 Cor. i. 21.

6. There was a man sent from God, whose name was John. In approaching his grand thesis—the historical manifestation of the Word—our Evangelist begins with him who was at once a *herald* to announce Him and a *foil* to set off His surpassing glory. This—by the way—is sufficient to show that the five foregoing verses are not to be understood of the Incarnate Word, or of Christ's life and actions while He was upon the earth; as is alleged, not by Socinians only, but by some sound critics too—over-jealous of anything that seems to savour of the mystical, metaphysical, or transcendental in Scripture. **7. The same came for a witness**—[εἰς μαρτυρίαν]—rather, 'for witness,' **to bear witness of the Light, that all men through him** (John) **might believe. 8. He was not that Light**—rather, 'The Light' [τὸ Φῶς], **but [was sent] to bear witness of that**—or 'The' **Light.** Noble testimony this to John, that it should be necessary, or even pertinent, to explain that *he* was *not* The Light! But John found it necessary himself to make this disavowal (v. 19-21); and certainly none could be more deeply penetrated and affected by the contrast between himself and his blessed Master than he.

(See on Luke iii. 15, 16; and on John iii. 27-34.) From the very first he saw and rejoiced to think that his own night-taper was to wax dim before the Day-spring from on high (ch. iii. 30). **9. That was the true Light, which lighteth every man that cometh into the world.** So certainly this verse may be rendered (with most of the Fathers and the Vulgate; and of the moderns, with *Luther, Erasmus, Calvin, Beza, Bengel, Meyer, van Oosterzee*). But "coming into the world," besides being rather a superfluous, is in Scripture quite an unusual, description of "every man." [It has been observed too—and the remark has great force—that the article τὸν should in that case have been inserted before ἐρχόμενον.] On the other hand, of all our Evangelist's descriptions of Christ, none is more familiar than His "coming into the world." See ch. iii. 19; vi. 14; xii. 46; xviii. 37; and compare 1 John iv. 9; 1 Tim. i. 15, &c. In this view of the words the sense will be, 'That was the true Light which, coming into the world, lighteth every man,' or became "The Light of the World." [So substantially *Lampe, Lücke, de Wette, Tholuck, Olshausen, Luthardt, Ewald, Alford, Webster and Wilkinson.*] If this be the Evangelist's meaning, it beautifully carries on his train of thought in *vv.* 4 and 5: *q. d.*, 'The Life was the Light of men; and though men resisted it when it shone but faintly before the Incarnation, yet when it came into the world (by the Personal assumption of flesh, about to be mentioned), it proved itself the one all-illuminating Light.' **10. He was in the world**—as already hinted, and presently to be more explicitly announced, **and the world was made by him**—for, as has been said, "all things were made by Him," **and the world**—that is, the intelligent world, **knew him not.** The language here is hardly less wonderful than the thought. Observe its compact simplicity and grand sonorousness—"the world" resounding in each successive member of the sentence, and the enigmatic form in which it is couched startling the reader, and setting his ingenuity a-working to solve the vast enigma of 'The world's Maker treading on and yet ignored by the world He made! **11. He came unto his own** [τὰ ἴδια, **and his own** [οἱ ἴδιοι]. It is impossible to give in English the full force of this verse. In the first clause it is 'His own [things]'—meaning 'His own Messianic rights and possessions:' in the second clause, it is 'His own [people];' meaning the peculiar people who were the more immediate subjects of His Messianic kingdom (see on Matt. xxii. 1). **received him not** —that is, as a *people;* for there were some noble exceptions, to whose case the Evangelist comes in the next clause. As for the nation, they said of Him, "This is THE HEIR, come let us kill Him" (Luke xx. 14). **12. But as many as received him** —as many *individuals*, out of the mass of that "disobedient and gainsaying people," as owned and embraced Him in His true character, **to them**

13 become the sons of God, *even* to them that believe on his name: which *[k]*were born, not of blood, nor of the will of the flesh, nor of the will of 14 man, but of God. And *[l]*the Word *[m]*was made *[n]*flesh, and dwelt among us, (and *[o]*we beheld his glory, the glory as of the only begotten of the Father,) *[p]*full of grace and truth.

[k] Deut. 30. 6.
[l] Matt. 1. 20.
[m] Rom. 1. 3.
[n] Heb. 2. 14.
[o] Isa. 40. 5.
[p] Col. 2. 3, 9.

gave he power [ἐξουσίαν]. The word signifies either *authority* ('potestas') or *ability* ('potentia') or both. Here certainly both are included; nor is it easy to say which is the prevailing shade of thought. **to become the sons of God** [τέκνα Θεοῦ] —or rather, 'to become children of God;' not in *name* and *dignity* only, but in *nature* also, as the next verse makes evident. **even to them that believe on his name** [εἰς τὸ ὄνομα αὐτοῦ]. This is a phrase *never used of any creature* in Scripture. To 'believe one' [πιστεύειν τινί] means to 'give credit to a person's testimony.' This is used not only of prophets and apostles, but of Christ Himself, to signify the credit due to His testimony (as ch. iv. 21; v. 46, 47). But to 'believe *upon* one,' or '*on the name* of one,' signifies that *trust* which is proper to be placed on God only; and when applied, as it is here and in so many other places, to the Lord Jesus, it signifies that the persons spoken of placed *supreme faith* in Him. But what kind of sonship is this to which Christ introduces such believers in Him? The next verse tells us. **13. Which were born** [ἐγεννήθησαν]. Observe this word "born," or 'begotten.' It was not a name only, a dignity only, which Christ conferred on them: it was a new *birth*, it was a change of *nature*—the soul being made conscious, in virtue of it, of the vital capacities, perceptions, and emotions of a 'child of God,' to which before it was a total stranger. But now for the Source and Author of that new birth—both negatively and positively. **not of blood**—not of 'superior human descent,' as we judge the meaning to be, **nor of the will of the flesh**—not of 'human generation' at all, **nor of the will of man**—not of man in any of the ways in which his will brings anything about. By this elaborate, three-fold denial of the human and earthly source of this sonship, how emphatic does the following declaration of its real source become! **but of God.** A sonship strictly divine, then, in its source this was which Christ conferred on as many as received Him. Right royal gift, which Whoso confers must be absolutely Divine. For who would not worship Him who can bring him into the family, and evoke within him the life, of the children of God? Now comes the great climax, to introduce and raise us to the altitude of which the foregoing thirteen verses were penned.

14. And the Word was made flesh—or 'made *man*,' or took Human Nature in its present state of frailty and infirmity—in contrast both with what it was before the fall, and with what it will be in the state of Glory—without reference to its sinfulness. So we read, "All flesh is Grass" (1 Pet. i. 24); "I will pour out my Spirit upon all flesh" (Acts ii. 17); "Thou hast given Him power over all flesh" (ch. xvii. 2); "All flesh shall see the salvation of God" (Luke iii. 6). In this sense the word "flesh" is applied to Christ's human nature before His resurrection in Heb. v. 7, "Who in *the days of His flesh*," &c. And this is plainly the meaning of "flesh" here—'The Word was made,' or became Man, in the *present* condition of manhood, apart from its sinfulness in us. The other sense of "flesh" as applied to man in Scripture—'human nature under the law of sin and death,' as in Gen. vi. 3; John iii. 6; Rom. vii. viii.—is wholly inapplicable
348

to Him who was born "the Holy Thing;" who in life was "holy, harmless, undefiled, separate from sinners;" and who in death "offered Himself without spot to God." Thus, by His Incarnation, married to our nature, He is henceforth and for ever personally conscious of all that is strictly human, as truly as of all that is properly divine; and our nature in His Person is redeemed and quickened, ennobled and transfigured. This glorious statement of our Evangelist was probably directed specially against those who alleged that Christ took flesh not really, but only apparently (afterwards called '*Docetæ*', or advocates of 'the *apparent* theory'). Against these this gentle spirit is vehement in his Epistles—1 John iv. 3; 2 John 7, 10, 11. Nor could he be too much so; for with the verity of the Incarnation all that is substantial in Christianity vanishes. **and dwelt among us** [ἐσκήνωσεν ἐν ἡμῖν]. The word strictly signifies 'tabernacled' or 'pitched His tent;' a word peculiar to John, who uses it four times in the Revelation—and in every case in the sense, not of a temporary sojourn, as might be supposed, but of a *permanent stay:* Rev. vii. 15, "Therefore are they before the Throne of God, and serve Him day and night in His temple, and He that sitteth upon the Throne shall *dwell* [σκηνώσει] among them;" and ch. xxi. 3, "And I heard a great voice out of heaven, saying, Behold, the tabernacle of God is with men, and He will *dwell* [σκηνώσει] with them." (So Rev. xii. 12; xiii. 6.) Thus, then, is He wedded for ever to our flesh; He has entered this tabernacle to go no more out. But the specific allusion in this word is doubtless to that tabernacle where dwelt the *Shechinah*, as the Jews called the manifested "glory of the Lord" (see on Matt. xxiii. 38, 39): and this again shadowed forth God's glorious residence, in the person of Christ, in the midst of His redeemed people: Ps. lxviii. 18, "Thou hast ascended on high, Thou hast led captivity captive: Thou hast received gifts for men; yea, for the rebellious also, that the Lord God might dwell [among them]" [לִשְׁכֹּן, τοῦ κατασκηνῶσαι]. See also Lev. xxvi. 11, 12, "And I will set my tabernacle among you, and my soul shall not abhor you. And I will walk among you, and be your God, and ye shall be my people;" and Ps. cxxxii. 13, 14; Ezek. xxxvii. 27. That all this was before the Evangelist's mind, is put almost beyond doubt by what immediately follows. So *Lücke, Olshausen, Meyer, de Wette*—which last critic, rising higher than usual, says that thus were perfected all former partial manifestations of God in *an essentially personal and historically human manifestation.* **(and we beheld his glory.** The word [ἐθεασάμεθα] is more emphatic than the simple "saw" [εἴδομεν]: 'This glory,' the Evangelist would say, 'was revealed to our gaze; yet not to *sense*, which saw in Him only "the carpenter"— no, it was spiritually discerned' (1 Cor. ii. 14). Hence it was that Peter's noble testimony is ascribed, by Him who knew its Source, to Divine teaching (Matt. xvi. 16, 17). **the glory as** [ὡς] **of the only begotten of the Father)**—not a glory 'resembling' or 'like to;' but, according to a well-known sense of the word, a glory 'such as became' or 'was befitting' the Only begotten of the Father. (So *Chrysostom, Calvin, Lücke, Tho-*

15 John bare witness of him, and cried, saying, This was he of whom I
spake, He that cometh after me is preferred before me: [q]for he was
16 before me. And of his [r]fulness have all we received, and grace for grace.
17 For the [s]Law was given by Moses, [t]*but* grace and [u]truth came by Jesus
Christ.

A. D. 30.
[q] Col. 1. 17.
[r] Eph. 1. 6.
[s] Ex. 20. 1.
[t] Rom. 5. 21.
[u] ch. 14. 6.

luck, Olshausen, &c.) On the meaning of the word "Only begotten" [μονογενὴς], see on *v.* 18. But the whole phrase is expressed somewhat peculiarly here: it is 'the Only begotten'—not of [ἐκ], but '[forth] from the Father' [παρὰ Πατρός]; on the sense of which, see on *v.* 18. **full of grace and truth.** Our translators have here followed the grammatical construction of the verse, connecting this last clause with "the Word" [ὁ Λόγος—πλήρης], and thus throwing the intermediate words into a long parenthesis. But if we take it otherwise, and view this last as an independent clause, not unusual in the New Testament, and not requiring to be *grammatically* connected with any of the preceding words—which we prefer—the sense will still be the same. These words "Grace and Truth"—or in Old Testament phraseology, "Mercy and Truth"—are the great key-notes of the Bible. By "GRACE" is meant 'the whole riches of God's redeeming love to sinners of mankind in Christ.' Up to the period of the Incarnation, this was, strictly speaking, only in *promise;* but in the fulness of time it was turned into *performance* or "TRUTH"—that is, fulfilment. The Old Testament word, "Mercy," denotes the rich Messianic promises made to David; while "Truth" stands for God's faithfulness to these promises. Thus, Psalm lxxxix. sings, almost from beginning to end, of these two things, and pleads upon them, as the two great features of one and the same thing: "I will sing of the *mercies* of the Lord for ever: with my mouth will I make known thy *faithfulness* to all generations. For I have said, *Mercy* shall be built up for ever: thy *faithfulness* shalt thou establish in the very heavens. I have found David my servant . . . my *faithfulness* and my *mercy* shall be with Him. My *loving-kindness* will I not utterly take from Him, nor suffer my *faithfulness* to fail. O Lord, where are thy former *loving-kindnesses* which thou swearest unto David in thy *truth?*" And, not to quote more passages, in one great word of the evangelical prophet, and in one of his richest evangelical predictions, we have both ideas combined in that one now familiar expression, "The *Sure Mercies* of David." (Isa. lv. 3; see also Acts xiii. 34; 2 Sam. xxiii. 5.) In Christ's Person all that Grace and Truth which had for long ages been floating in shadowy forms, and darting into the souls of the poor and needy its broken beams, took everlasting possession of human flesh, and filled it full. By this Incarnation of Grace and Truth, the teaching of thousands of years was at once transcended and beggared, and the family of God sprang into manhood.

15. John bare witness of him, and cried—in testimony of the certainty and grandeur of the truth he was proclaiming, and the deep interest of all in it. The strict sense of the words [μαρτυρεῖ καὶ κέκραγεν] is, 'beareth witness and hath cried;' as if the testimony were still continued and the cry still resounding. But such delicate shades of meaning cannot easily be conveyed in any tolerable translation. **saying, This was he of whom I spake, He that cometh after me is preferred before me** [Ὁ ὀπίσω μου ἐρχόμενος ἔμπροσθέν μου γέγονεν] or better, perhaps, 'has got before (that is, 'above') me.' **for he was before me** [πρῶτός μου]. Our translators have here used one English word, "before," to convey the sense of two different Greek words—the one [ἔμπροσθεν] primarily signifying 'before' in respect of *place*, and here of *official rank;* the other [πρῶτος] 'before' in point of *time.* Nor would it be easy to improve the translation without either marring the intentional terseness of the saying by too many words, or departing from the chaste simplicity required in any version of the Scriptures, and so characteristic of ours. Were we to render it, 'My Successor has become my Superior, for He was my Predecessor,' we should, indeed, convey to the mere English reader some idea of the *enigmatic* character and quaint structure of the saying, but we should fail to convey the true sense of the statement; for Christ, though posterior to John, was in no sense his Successor, and though prior to Him was in no proper sense his Predecessor. Doubtless, this enigmatic play upon the different senses of the words "before" and "after" was purposely devised by the Baptist to startle his readers, to set their ingenuity a-working to resolve his riddle, and when found, to rivet the truth conveyed by it upon their mind and memory. It may here be observed, that though it was no part of our Evangelist's plan to relate in detail the calling and ministry of John the Baptist—that having been sufficiently done in the preceding Gospels—he studiously introduces all his weightiest testimonies to his blessed Master; and the one now given seems to have been suggested by what had just been said of the glory of the Only begotten, and designed to confirm it. **16. And of his fulness**—that is, of grace and truth; resuming the thread of *v.* 14, which had only been interrupted for the purpose of inserting that testimony of John. **have all we received, and grace for grace** [χάριν ἀντὶ χάριτος]—that is, as we say, 'grace upon grace;' in successive communications and larger measures, as each was able to take it in. So the best critics understand the clause: other and older interpretations are less natural, and not more accordant with the Greek. The word "truth," it will be observed, is dropt here; and "GRACE" stands alone, as the chosen New Testament word for "all spiritual blessings" with which believers are enriched out of the fulness of Christ. **17. For the Law was given by Moses, but grace and truth came by Jesus Christ.** The law is here placed in opposition both to "grace" and to "truth"—but in different respects, of course. The law is opposed to *grace* only in that sense in which the law contains *no grace.* "The law," says the apostle, "worketh wrath" (Rom. iv. 15), that is, against all who break it; pronouncing a curse upon "every one that continueth not in all things which are written in the book of the law to do them" (Gal. iii. 10). If, then, under Moses, there was any grace for the guilty, it could not issue out of the bosom of the law, as a proclamation of moral duty; for "by the deeds of the law there shall no flesh be justified in His sight, for by the law is the knowledge of sin" (Rom. iii. 20). But the law was not given only to condemn. It "had a shadow of good things to come, though not the very image of the things" (Heb. x. 1); and it was this *shadow* of Gospel-blessings which was given by Moses, while the "truth" or substance of them came by Jesus Christ. The law was but "a figure for the time then present, that could not make the worshippers perfect as

18   No ^{*v*}man hath seen God at any time; the ^{*w*}only begotten Son, which is in the bosom of the Father, he hath declared *him.*

A. D. 30.
v Ex. 33. 20.
w 1 John 4. 9.

pertaining to the conscience; for it was not possible that the blood of bulls and of goats should take away sins" (Heb. ix. 9; x. 4). All the salvation, therefore, that was gotten under Moses was *on the credit* of that one offering for sins which perfects for ever them that are sanctified; and so they without us could not be made perfect (Heb. xi. 40).

18. **No man**—'No one' [οὐδεὶς] **hath seen God at any time**—that is, by immediate gaze; by direct, naked perception. In the light of this emphatic negation of all creature vision of God, how striking is what follows! **the only begotten Son, which is in the bosom of the Father, he hath declared him.** Had such a statement not come from the pen of apostolic authority and inspiration, who could have ventured to write or to utter it? Let us study it a little. [The extraordinary and extremely harsh reading which *Tregelles* here adopts, in deference to three of the oldest MSS., and some other authorities—'the only begotten God'—reading ΟϹ for ΥϹ—is met by such a weight of counter-authority in favour of the received reading, so thoroughly Joannean, that *Tischendorf* abides by it, and all but every critic approves it.] What now is the import of this phrase, "*The Only begotten Son,*" as applied to Christ here by the beloved disciple, and in three other places (ch. iii. 16, 18; 1 John iv. 9), and of "*the Only begotten from the Father,*" in *v.* 14? To say, with the Socinians and some others, that it means no more than "well beloved," is quite unsatisfactory. For when our Lord Himself spoke to the Jews of "*His Father,*" they understood Him to mean that God was His 'proper Father' [πατέρα ἴδιον], and so to claim equality with God; nor did He deny the charge (see on ch. v. 18). And that precious assurance of the Father's love which the apostle derives from His "not sparing His own Son" depends for its whole force on His being His *essential* Son, or partaker of His very nature [τοῦ ἰδίου Υἱοῦ οὐκ ἐφείσατο]; see on Rom. viii. 32. We are shut up, then, to understand the phrase, "Only begotten," as applied to Christ, of the Son's *essential* relation to the Father. The word "begotten," however—like every imaginable term on such a subject—is liable to be misunderstood, and care must be taken not to press it beyond the limits of what is clearly sustained by Scripture. That the Son is essentially and eternally related to the Father, in some real sense, as Father and Son; but that while *distinct* in Person (for "The Word was with God"), He is neither *posterior* to Him in time (for "In the beginning was The Word"), nor *inferior* to Him in nature (for "The Word was God"), nor *separate* from Him in being (for "The same was in the beginning with God"), but *One Godhead* with the Father:—this would seem to come as near to the full testimony of Scripture on this mysterious subject as can be reached by our finite understanding, without darkening counsel by words without knowledge. The peculiar expression in the 14th verse—"The Only begotten Son [forth] from the Father" [παρὰ Πατρὸς], and that equally remarkable one in *v.* 18, "The Only begotten Son which is in (or 'into,' or 'upon') the bosom of the Father" [εἰς τὸν κόλπον τοῦ Πατρὸς] seem to be the complement of each other: the one expressing, as we might say, His relation to the Father's essence—as 'forth from' it; the other, if we might so speak, His non-separation from Him, but this in the form of inconceivable Personal and loving nearness to Him. Thus does our Evangelist positively affirm of Christ, not only what he had just

before denied of all creatures—that He "hath seen God" (see ch. vi. 46)—but that being 'in,' 'into,' or 'on' the bosom of the Father, He had access to His very heart, or, without a figure, that He, and He only, *has absolute knowledge of God.* Well, **he hath declared him** [ἐκεῖνος ἐξηγήσατο]—'He declared him' who only could, as The Word, the Reflection, the Expression of His very Self; He, who, living ever on His bosom, gazes on Him ever, knows Him ever, with an intimate perception, an absolute knowledge peculiar to Himself —He it is whom the Father hath sent to "declare Him." And thus does our Evangelist close this great Introductory Section of his Gospel as he began it, with The Word.

Remarks.—1. Since God so ordered it that the first converts and the infant churches should be thoroughly familiarized with the History of His Son's work in the flesh on the lower platform of the First Three Gospels, ere they were lifted up by this Fourth Gospel to the highest view of it, we may infer, that just as we also have thriven upon the milk of the other Gospels will be our ability to digest and to grow upon the strong meat of this last and crowning Gospel. And might it not be well, in the public exposition of the Gospel History, to advance from the *corporeal* Gospels, as the Fathers of the Church were wont to call them, [τὰ σωματικά], to what by way of eminence they called the *spiritual* Gospel [τὸ πνευματικόν? Nevertheless, even in this Gospel there is an exquisite net-work of concrete outward History, which captivates even the rudest and youngest readers; and it breathes such an atmosphere of love and heaven, that the deep truths which are enshrined in it possess attractions they would not otherwise have had. Thus, each is perfect in its own kind, and all are one pearl of great price. 2. Did our Evangelist, before uttering the keynote of his whole Gospel, pave the way for it by so many introductory verses? What need, then, to put off the shoe from off our feet when we come to tread such holy ground! 3. With respect to the origin and growth of this term, "The Word," in the sense in which it is here used—for it certainly was not used by our Evangelist for the first time-- we find the teaching of the Old Testament from the first tending gradually towards that conception of it which is here presented: "The word of the Lord" is said to have given birth to creation, and to carry into effect all the divine purposes; "wisdom" is spoken of as eternally with God, and rejoicing in the habitable parts of His earth; "The Angel of Jehovah" is identified with Jehovah Himself; men are warned to "kiss the Son, lest He be angry, and they perish from the way;" and the form of that fourth mysterious Person who was seen walking in Nebuchadnezzar's burning fiery furnace, with the three Hebrew youths, was "like the Son of God." These conceptions, combined, would familiarize the thoughtful with something very like what is here said of The Word. Accordingly, the more profound Jewish theologians constantly represented "The Word of the Lord" [*מֵימְרָא דַיָי*] as the Personal Agent by whom all divine operations were performed. In a word, about the time of our Lord the Alexandrian Jews, with *Philo* at their head, engrafting the Platonic philosophy upon their own reading of the Old Testament, had fallen into the familiar use of language closely resembling that employed here; and this phraseology was doubtless current throughout all the region in which our Evangelist

	A. D. 30.
19 And this is the record of John, when the Jews sent priests and Levites	*x* ch. 3. 28.
20 from Jerusalem to ask him, Who art thou? And *x*he confessed, and	Acts 13. 25.
21 denied not; but confessed, I am not the Christ. And they asked him,	*y* Mal. 4. 5.
What then? Art thou *y*Elias? And he saith, *z*I am not. Art thou	*z* Luke 1. 17.

probably wrote his Gospel, and must have been familiar to him. And yet, in two important points, this language of the Jewish Platonists, even where it seems to come the nearest to that of our Evangelist, is vastly removed from it. First, it was so *hazy*, that scholars who have studied their writings the most deeply are not agreed whether by The Word [ὁ Λόγος] they meant a *Person* at all; and next, even if that were certain, this "Word" was never identified by them with the promised *Messiah*. The truth seems to be, that this beloved disciple, having often reflected on such matters in the stillness of his own meditative and lofty spirit, and now, after so long a silence, addressed himself to the task of drawing up one more and final Gospel, did, under the guidance of the Spirit, *advisedly* take up the current phraseology, and not only thread his way through the corrupt elements which had mixed themselves up with the true doctrine of "The Word," but stamp upon that phraseology new conceptions, and enshrine for ever in these eighteen introductory verses of his Gospel the most sublime of all truths regarding the Incarnate Redeemer. 4. Within the limits of this Section all the heresies that have ever been broached regarding the Person of Christ—and they are legion—find the materials of their refutation. Thus, to the *Ebionites* and the *Artemonites* of the second century, to *Noetus* and *Paul of Samosata* of the third, and to *Socinus* and his followers at and since the Reformation—who all affirmed that Christ was a mere man, more or less filled with the Divinity, but having no existence till He was born into our world—our Evangelist here cries, "In the beginning was the Word." To *Arius*, in the fourth century, and to a host of modern followers—who affirmed that Christ, though he existed before all other created beings, was himself but a creature; the first and highest indeed, but still a creature—our Evangelist here cries, "The Word was God:" All things were made by Him, and without Him was not one thing made that was made: In Him was life, and the life was the light of men: as many as received Him to them gave He power to become children of God. The Only begotten Son, who is in the bosom of the Father, He declared Him." To *Sabellius*, in the third century, and not a few speculative moderns—who held that there is but one Person in the Godhead; the Father, Son, and Holy Ghost being but three *modes* in which the one Person has been pleased to manifest Himself for man's salvation—our Evangelist cries, "The Word was in the beginning with God: He is the Only begotten from the Father, and He it is that declared Him." To those afterwards called *Docetæ*—who, as early as the first century, held that Christ took only an apparent, not a real, humanity; and *Apollinaris*, in the fourth century, and some modern followers—who affirmed that Christ, though He took a human body, took no rational human spirit, the Word supplying its place as the only intelligence by which He acted; and the *Nestorians* of the fifth century—who held, or were charged with holding, that that Holy Thing which was born of the virgin was not "the Son of God," but only the son of Mary, to whom the Son of God joined Himself, making two separate persons, though closely united; and finally to the *Eutychians*—who, in the same century, affirmed that the divine and human natures were so blended as to constitute together but one nature,

351

having the properties of both: to one and all of these errorists (in language at least, though there is reason to think not always in actual belief) our Evangelist here cries, in words of majestic simplicity and transparent clearness, "THE WORD WAS MADE FLESH;" using that term "Flesh" in its well-known sense when applied to human nature, and leaving no room for doubt in the unsophisticated reader that He *became Man* in the only sense which those words naturally convey. The Fathers of the Church, who were driven to the accurate study of this subject by all sorts of loose language and floating heresies regarding the person of Christ, did not fail to observe how warily our Evangelist changes his language from "WAS" to "BECAME" [ἦν-ἐγένετο] when he passes from the *pre-existent* to the *incarnate* condition of the Word, saying, "In the beginning *was* the Word—and the Word *was made* flesh." To express this they were wont to say, 'Remaining what He was, He became what He was not.' 5. Did the truth of Christ's Person cost the Church so much study and controversy from age to age against persevering and ever-varying attempts to corrupt it? How dear, then, should it be to us, and how jealously should we guard it, at the risk of being charged with sticking for human refinements, and prolonging fruitless and forgotten controversies! At the same time, 7. The glory of the Only begotten of the Father is best seen and felt, not in the light of mere abstract phraseology—sanctioned though it be by the whole orthodox Church, unexceptionable in form, and in its own place most valuable—but by tracing in this matchless History His footsteps upon earth, as He walked amid all the elements of nature, the diseases of men, and death itself, amidst the secrets of the human heart, and the rulers of the darkness of this world—in all their number, subtlety, and malignity—not only with absolute ease as their conscious Lord, but as if themselves had been conscious of their Master's presence and felt His will to be their resistless law.

19-51.—TESTIMONIES OF THE BAPTIST TO JESUS ADDRESSED TO A JEWISH DEPUTATION AND TO HIS OWN DISCIPLES—JESUS BEGINS TO GATHER DISCIPLES.

Testimony Addressed to a Jewish Deputation (19-28). **19. And this is the record**—or 'testimony,' **of John, when the Jews sent priests and Levites from Jerusalem to ask him, Who art thou?** By "*the Jews*" here, and almost always in this Gospel, is meant—not the Jewish nation, as contrasted with the Gentiles, but—'*the rulers*' of the nation. **20. And he confessed, and denied not; but confessed, I am not the Christ.** In thus disclaiming the Messiahship for himself, he resisted a strong temptation; for many were ready to hail the Baptist as himself the Christ. But as he gave not the least ground for such impressions of him, so neither did he give them a moment's entertainment. **21. And they asked him, What then? Art thou Elias? And he saith, I am not**—that is, not Elijah in his own proper person, whom the Jews expected, and still expect, before the coming of their Messiah. **Art thou that prophet?** [ὁ προφήτης]—rather, 'the prophet;' announced in Deut. xviii. 15, &c., about whom they seem not to have been agreed whether he were the same with the promised Messiah or no. **And he answered, No. 22. Then said they unto him, Who art thou?** that we may give an

22 ²that prophet? And he answered, No. Then said they unto him, Who
art thou? that we may give an answer to them that sent us. What sayest
23 thou of thyself? He said, I *am* the voice of one crying in the wilderness,
24 Make straight the way of the Lord, as ªsaid the prophet Esaias. And
25 they which were sent were of the Pharisees. And they asked him, and
said unto him, Why baptizest thou then, if thou be not that Christ, nor
26 Elias, neither that prophet? John answered them, saying, I baptize with
27 water: ᵇbut there standeth one among you, whom ye know not; he it
is, who coming after me, is preferred before me, whose shoe's latchet I
28 am not worthy to unloose. These things were done in Bethabara beyond
Jordan, where John was baptizing.
29 The next day John seeth Jesus coming unto him, and saith, Behold
30 ᶜthe Lamb of God, ᵈwhich ³taketh away the sin of the world! This is
he of whom I said, After me cometh a man which is preferred before me:
31 for he was before me. And I knew him not: but that he should be
made manifest to Israel, therefore am I come baptizing with water.
32 And John bare record, saying, I saw the Spirit descending from heaven

A. D. 30.

² Or, a
prophet.
ᵃ Isa. 40. 3.
ᵇ Mal. 3. 1.
ᶜ Gen. 22. 7, 8.
Ex. 12. 3.
Num. 28. 3-
10.
Isa. 53. 7.
1 Pet. 1. 19.
Rev. 5. 6.
ᵈ 1 Cor. 15. 3.
Gal. 1. 4.
Heb. 1. 3.
Heb. 2. 17.
Heb. 9. 28.
1 Pet. 2. 24.
1 John 2. 2.
Rev. 1. 5.
³ Or.
beareth.

answer to them that sent us. **What sayest thou
of thyself? 23. He said, I am the voice of one
crying in the wilderness.** His Master was "The
Word;" the herald was but a *voice* crying through
the Judean desert, Make ready for the coming
Lord! See on Matt. iii. 1-3. **24. And they which
were sent were of the Pharisees.** As the Sadducees could hardly be expected to take much
interest in such matters, this explanation is probably intended to do more than tell the reader that
this deputation was of the other sect. It probably
refers to their peculiar jealousy about any innova-
tions on the traditional way of thinking and acting,
and to prepare the reader for their question in the
next verse. **25. And they asked him, and said
unto him, Why baptizest thou then, if thou be not
that — 'the' Christ, nor Elias, neither that —
'the' prophet?** Thinking that he disclaimed
any special connection with the Messiah's kingdom, they very naturally demand his right to
gather disciples by baptism. (See on ch. iii. 28.)
**26. John answered them, saying, I baptize
with water**—with water only; the higher, internal, baptism with the Holy Ghost being the
exclusive prerogative of his Master. (See on
Matt. iii. 11.) **but there standeth one among
you, whom ye know not.** This must have been
spoken after Christ's Baptism, and probably
almost immediately after it. **27. He it is, who
coming after me, is preferred before me**—see on
v. 15. **whose shoe's latchet I am not worthy to
unloose**—see on Matt. iii. 11. **28. These things
were done in Bethabara** [בֵּית עֲבָרָה]—'ferry-house' or
'crossing-place.' But the true reading, as nearly
all the best and most ancient MSS. attest, is
'Bethany:' not, of course, the well-known Bethany, at the foot of mount Olivet, but some
village lying on the east side of the Jordan,
which in the time of *Origen* had disappeared.
beyond Jordan, where John was baptizing.

*Testimony of the Baptist, addressed to his own dis-
ciples* (29-36). **29. The next day**—the crowd, as we
take it, having dispersed, and only his own disciples being present, **John seeth Jesus coming
unto him.** This was probably immediately after
the Temptation, when Jesus, emerging from the
wilderness of Judea on His way to Galilee (*v.* 43),
came up to the Baptist. But it was not to hold
intercourse with him, however congenial that
would have been; for *of this there appears to have
been none at all from the time of His baptism even
till the Baptist's imprisonment and death.* The sole
object of this approach to the Baptist would ap-

pear to have been to receive from him that
wonderful testimony which follows: **and saith**
—immediately catching a sublime inspiration at
the sight of Him approaching: **Behold the Lamb
of God, which taketh away the sin of the world!**
Every word here is emphatic, and precious beyond
all expression. "THE LAMB" here, beyond all
doubt, points to the *death* of Christ, and the
sacrificial character of that death. The offering
of a lamb every morning and evening, and of two
on the morning and evening of every Sabbath day,
throughout all the ages of the Jewish economy,
had furnished such a language on this subject as to
those who heard these words of the Baptist could
need no explanation, however the truth thus expressed might startle them. But in calling Jesus
"*the* Lamb," and "the Lamb *of God*," he held
Him up as the one 'God-ordained, God-gifted,
God-accepted' sacrificial offering. If, however,
there could remain a doubt whether this was what
the words were designed to convey, the explanation which follows would set it at rest—"Which
taketh away the sin of the world." The word
[αἴρων] here used, and the corresponding Hebrew
word [נֹשֵׂא] signify both 'taking up' and 'taking
away.' Applied to sin, they mean to 'be chargeable with the guilt of it' (Exod. xxviii. 38; Lev. v.
1; Ezek. xviii. 20), and to 'bear it away' (as in
many places). In the Levitical victims both ideas
met, as they do in Christ; the people's guilt being
viewed as transferred to them, avenged in their
death, and thus borne away by them (Lev. iv.
15; xvi. 15, 21, 22; and compare Isa. liii. 6-12;
2 Cor. v. 21). "The *sin*," says the Baptist, using
the singular number to denote the collective
burden laid upon the Lamb, and the all-embracing efficacy of the great Sacrifice; and "the sin of
the world"—in contrast with the typical victims
which were offered for Israel exclusively: 'Wherever there shall live a sinner throughout the wide
world, sinking under that burden too heavy for
him to bear, he shall find in this "Lamb of God"
a shoulder equal to the weight.' Thus was the
right note struck at the very outset. And what
balm must it have been to Christ's own spirit to
hear it! Never, indeed, was a more glorious utterance heard on earth; no, nor ever shall be. But it
was uttered, as we think, in the hearing only of
those who were in some measure prepared for it.
**30. This is he of whom I said, After me cometh,
&c.**—recalling the testimony he had borne before,
and recorded in *v.* 15. **31. And I knew him not:
but that he should be made manifest to Israel,**

33 like a dove, and it abode upon him. And I knew him not: but he that sent me to baptize with water, the same said unto me, Upon whom thou shalt see the Spirit descending, and remaining on him, the ^esame is he
34 which baptizeth with the Holy Ghost. And I saw, and bare record that this is the Son of God.
35, Again, the next day after, John stood, and two of his disciples; and
36 looking upon Jesus as he walked, he saith, Behold the Lamb of God!
37 And the two disciples heard him speak, and they followed Jesus.
38 Then Jesus turned, and saw them following, and saith unto them, What seek ye? They said unto him, Rabbi, (which is to say, being
39 interpreted, Master,) where ⁴dwellest thou? He saith unto them, Come and see. They came and saw where he dwelt, and abode with him that
40 day: for it was ⁵about the tenth hour. One of the two which heard John *speak,* and followed him, was Andrew, Simon Peter's brother.

A. D. 30.

* ch. 14. 26.
ch. 20. 22.
Acts 1. 5.
Acts 2. 4.
Acts 4. 8, 31.
Acts 6. 3, 5,
6.
Acts 7. 55.
Acts 9. 17.
Titus 3. 5,6.

4 Or, abidest.
5 That was two hours before night.

---

therefore am I come baptizing with water. 32. And John bare record, saying, I saw [τεθέαμαι] —or 'I have seen' the Spirit descending from heaven like a dove, and it abode upon him. 33. And I knew him not: but he that sent me to baptize with water, the same said unto me, Upon whom thou shalt see the Spirit descending, and remaining on him, the same is he which baptizeth with the Holy Ghost. 34. And I saw —or 'have seen'—[ἑώρακα] that this is the Son of God. There is some appearance of inconsistency between the First and the Fourth Gospels, as to the Baptist's knowledge of his Master before the descent of the Holy Ghost upon Him. Matthew seems to write as if the Baptist had immediately recognized Him, and accordingly recoiled, as a servant, from baptizing his Master: whereas John makes the Baptist himself to say that he "knew Him not," and seem to say that until the Spirit descended upon Him he perceived no difference between Him and the other applicants for baptism that day. But by viewing the transaction in the following light the two statements may be harmonized. Living mostly apart—the One at Nazareth, the other in the Judean desert, to prevent all appearance of collusion—John only knew that at a definite time after his own call his Master would show Himself. As He drew near for baptism one day, the last of all the crowd, the spirit of the Baptist, perhaps, heaving under a divine presentiment that the moment had at length arrived, and an air of unwonted serenity and dignity—not without traits, probably, of the family features—appearing in this Stranger, the Spirit, we may imagine, said to him as to Samuel of his youthful type, "Arise, anoint Him, for this is He!" (1 Sam. xvi. 12). But just then would the incongruity be felt of the servant baptizing the Master, nay, a sinner the Saviour Himself; and then would take place the dialogue, recorded by Matthew, between John and Jesus. Then followed the Baptism, and thereupon the descent of the Spirit. And this visible descent of the Spirit upon Him, as He emerged out of the baptismal water, being the very sign which he was told to expect, he now knew the whole transaction to be divine; and catching up the voice from heaven, "he saw, and bare record that this is the Son of God." So, substantially, the best interpreters.

35. Again, the next day after, John stood [εἱστήκει—or 'was standing;' probably at his accustomed place. The reader will do well to observe that here, and in *v.* 29, we have the beginning of that chronological precision which is so marked a characteristic of this Gospel. and two of his disciples; 36. And looking [ἐμβλέψας]—fixing his eyes with significant gaze upon Jesus as he walked.

353

Observe, it is not said this time that Jesus was coming to John. To have done that once (*v.* 29) was humility enough, as *Bengel* notes. But John saw Him simply "walking" [περιπατοῦντι], as if in solitary meditation; yet evidently designing to bring about that interview with two of John's disciples which was to be properly His first public act. he saith, Behold the Lamb of God! The repetition, in brief, of that wonderful proclamation, in identical terms and without an additional word, was meant both as a gentle hint to go after Him, and to fix the light in which they were to regard Him. And it had the desired effect—as we are now to hear.

The Calling of John and Andrew (37-40). 37. And the two disciples heard him speak, and they followed Jesus. 38. Then Jesus turned, and saw them following [καὶ θεασάμενος αὐτοὺς ἀκολουθοῦντας]—'and looked upon them as they followed' (see on *v.* 36), and saith unto them, What seek ye? Gentle, winning question; remarkable as the Redeemer's *first public utterance.* They said unto him, Rabbi (which is to say, being interpreted, Master,)—an explanation which shows that this Gospel was designed for those who had little or no knowledge of Jewish phraseology or usages. where dwellest thou? As if to say, 'Lord, that is a question not to be answered in a moment; but had we Thy company for a calm hour in private, gladly should we open our burden.' 39. He saith unto them, Come and see— His *second utterance;* more winning still. They came and saw where he dwelt [μένει]—' where He stayed' or 'abode,' and abode—rather 'remained' [ἔμειναν] with him that day: [for]. This word "for" [δὲ] is no part of the original text, as the evidence decisively shows. it was about the tenth hour. According to the Roman reckoning—from midnight to midnight—this would be with us ten o'clock in the morning: according to the Jewish reckoning—from six in the morning to six in the evening—the tenth hour here would be with us four in the afternoon, or within two hours of the close of the day. *Olshausen, Tholuck, Ebrard, Ewald* understand the Evangelist in the former sense; in which case they must have spent with our Lord a far greater length of time than, we think, is at all probable. To us there appears to be no reasonable doubt that the latter reckoning is here meant, which would make their stay about two hours, if they left precisely at the close of the Jewish day, though there is no reason to suppose this. Indeed, the Greeks of Asia Minor and the Romans themselves had latterly begun to reckon time popularly by the *working* day—from six to six. In this sense, *Calvin, Beza, Bengel, Meyer, de Wette, van Osterzee, Alford, Webster*

41 He first findeth his own brother Simon, and saith unto him, We have

42 found the Messias, which is, being interpreted, [6] the Christ. And he brought him to Jesus. And when Jesus beheld him, he said, Thou art Simon the son of Jona: thou shalt be called Cephas, which is, by interpretation, [7]A stone.

43 The day following Jesus would go forth into Galilee, and findeth Philip,

44 and saith unto him, Follow me. Now Philip was of Bethsaida, the city of Andrew and Peter.

45 Philip findeth Nathanael, and saith unto him, We have found him of whom Moses *f*in the Law, and the *g*Prophets, did write, Jesus

46 of Nazareth the son of Joseph. And Nathanael said unto him, Can there any good thing come out of Nazareth? Philip saith unto

47 him, Come and see. Jesus saw Nathanael coming to him, and saith

A. D. 30.
[6] Or, the Anointed.
Ps. 2. 2.
Dan. 9. 25.
[7] Or, Peter.
Matt. 16. 18.
f Gen. 3. 15.
Gen. 22. 18.
Num. 21. 9.
Deut. 18. 18.
g Isa. 9. 6.
Isa. 53.
Mic. 5. 2.
Zec. 6. 12.
Zec. 9. 9.
Mal. 3. 1.

and Wilkinson, understand the Evangelist. **40. One of the two which heard John speak, and followed him, was Andrew, Simon Peter's brother.** It would appear that Andrew was Peter's elder brother. The other was certainly our Evangelist himself—because otherwise there seems no reason why he should not have named him; because, if not, he has not even alluded to his own calling; but chiefly, because it is according to his usual manner to allude to himself while avoiding the express mention of his name, and the narrative here is so graphic and detailed as to leave an irresistible impression on the reader's mind that the writer was himself a party to what he describes. His great sensitiveness, as *Olshausen* says, is touchingly shown in his representation of this first contact with the Lord; the circumstances are present to him in the minutest details; he still remembers the very hour: but he reports no particulars of those discourses of the Lord, by which he was bound to Him for the whole of his life; he allows everything personal to retire.

The Calling of Simon (41, 42). **41. He first findeth his own brother Simon.** Possibly, this may mean 'own brother' in contrast with stepbrothers in the family. But the expression may here be used merely for emphasis. According to the received text [πρῶτος], the meaning is, ' He was the first to find;' but, according to what we think with *Lachmann* and *Tregelles*—but not *Tischendorf*—the better supported reading [πρῶτον], our English version gives the true sense. The meaning probably is, as we familiarly express it, 'the first thing;' that is, immediately on returning home. But the word "findeth" seems to imply that he had to seek for him, and could not rest until he was able to open to him his swelling heart. **and saith unto him, We have found the Messias, which is, being interpreted, the Christ.** See on Matt. i. 16, 21. The previous preparation of their simple hearts, under the Baptist's ministry, made quick work of this blessed conviction, while others kept hesitating till doubt settled into obduracy. And so it is still. **42. And he brought him to Jesus.** Happy brothers, thus knit together by a new tie! If Peter soon outstripped not only Andrew but all the rest, he would still remember that his brother "was in Christ before him," and was the blessed instrument of bringing him to Jesus. **And when Jesus beheld him** (see on 36), **he said, Thou art Simon the son of Jona,** or rather, ["*Jonas*," as rendered in ch. xxi. 17—the full name serving, as *Tholuck* says, to give solemnity to the language (Matt. xvi. 17; John xxi. 17): **thou shalt be called Cephas** [כֵּיפָא], **which is, by interpretation, A stone** [Πέτρος]—'Rock.' See on Matt. xvi. 18.

The Calling of Philip (43, 44). **43. The day following Jesus would go forth** [ἠθέλησεν]—or, 'was minded to go forth' **into Galilee.** From the time when He "came from Nazareth" to be baptized of John, He had lived in Judea until now, when He was on His way back to Galilee. This makes it quite evident that the calling of Simon and Andrew at the sea of Galilee, recorded in Matt. iv. 18, must have been a subsequent transaction. But see on Matt. iv. 18; and on Luke v. 1. **and findeth Philip, and saith unto him, Follow me.** The other three might be said to find Jesus, but Philip was found of Jesus. Yet in every case, "we love Him because He first loved us," and in every case the response on our part must be as cordial as the call on His. **44. Now Philip was of**—rather, 'from' [ἀπὸ] **Bethsaida, the city** [ἐκ τῆς πόλεως]—it should be 'of the city' **of Andrew and Peter**—the city of their *birth* probably; for their place of residence was Capernaum (Mark i. 29). The fact mentioned in this verse throws light on a very small incident in ch. vi. 5 (on which see). That Philip did follow Jesus is not here recorded; but the next two verses more than express this.

The Calling of Nathanael (45-51). **45. Philip findeth Nathanael.** For the evidence that this disciple was no other than "Bartholomew," in the catalogues of the Twelve, see on Matt. x. 3. **and saith unto him, We have found him of whom Moses in the Law**—"for he wrote of Me," says our Lord Himself, ch. v. 46, **and the Prophets**—"who testified beforehand the sufferings of Christ, and the glory that should follow" [τὰς μετὰ ταῦτα δόξας], 1 Pet. i. 11, **did write, Jesus of Nazareth the son of Joseph.** This was the current way of speaking, and *legally* true. See on Matt. i. **46. And Nathanael said unto him, Can there any good thing come out of Nazareth?** Bethlehem, he perhaps remembered, was Messiah's predicted birth-place: Nazareth as a town had no place in prophecy, nor in the Old Testament at all. But its proverbial ill-repute may have been what directly suggested the doubt whether that could possibly be the place, of all places, whence Messiah was to issue. **Philip saith unto him, Come and see.** Noble remedy against pre-conceived opinions! exclaims *Bengel.* Philip, though probably unable to solve the difficulty, could show him where to get rid of it; and Nathanael takes his advice. See on ch. vi. 68. **47. Jesus saw Nathanael coming to him, and saith of him, Behold an Israelite indeed, in whom is no guile!** —not only no hypocrite, but, with a guileless simplicity not always found even in God's own people, ready to follow wherever truth might lead him, saying, Samuel-like, "Speak, Lord, for thy servant heareth." **48. Nathanael saith unto him, Whence knowest thou me?** Conscious that his very heart had been read, and that at this critical moment that which he most deeply felt—a single desire to

48 of him, Behold an Israelite indeed, in whom is no guile! Nathanael saith unto him, Whence knowest thou me? Jesus answered and said unto him, Before that Philip called thee, when thou wast under the fig 49 tree, I saw thee. Nathanael answered and saith unto him, Rabbi, thou 50 art the Son of God; thou art *h*the King of Israel. Jesus answered and said unto him, Because I said unto thee, I saw thee under the fig tree,

A. D. 30.

h Ps. 2. 6.
Ps. 110. 1.
Isa. 9. 7.
Ezek. 37. 21.
Dan. 9. 25.
Hos. 3. 5.

know and embrace the truth—had been expressed. Jesus answered and said unto him, Before that Philip called thee—showing He knew all that had passed at a distance between Philip and him, when thou wast under the fig tree, I saw thee. Of His being there at all the Evangelist says nothing, but tells us that Jesus, to the amazement of Nathanael, saw him there, and what he was there engaged in. What could He be doing? Fortunately we can answer that question with all but certainty. *Lightfoot* and *Wetstein* quote passages from the Jewish rabbins, showing that little knots of earnest students were wont to meet with a teacher early in the morning, and sit and study under a shady fig tree. Thither, probably—hearing that his master's Master had at length appeared, and heaving with mingled eagerness to behold Him and dread of deception—he had retired to pour out his guileless heart for light and guidance. "Good and upright is the Lord," we think we hear him saying; "therefore will He teach sinners in the way: The meek will He guide in judgment, and the meek will He teach His way: The secret of the Lord is with them that fear Him, and He will show them His covenant. My heart is inditing a good matter, I will speak of the things which I have made touching the King, my tongue shall be the pen of a ready writer: Thou art fairer than the children of men, Grace is poured into Thy lips, therefore God hath blessed Thee for ever. O that the salvation of Israel were come out of Zion! Why is His chariot so long in coming? Why tarry the wheels of His chariot? O that Thou wouldest rend the heavens, that Thou wouldest come down, that the mountains might flow down at Thy presence. For from the beginning of the world men have not heard, nor perceived by the ear, neither hath the eye seen, O God, beside Thee, what He hath prepared for him that waiteth for Him. My soul, wait thou only upon God, for my expectation is from Him. Let integrity and uprightness preserve me, for I wait on Thee. Till the day dawn, and the shadows flee away, I will get me to the mountain of myrrh, to the hill of frankincense. Show me a token for good!" (See on Luke ii. 8.) At that moment, of calm yet outstretched expectancy, returning from his fig tree, "Philip"—missing him probably at his house, whither he had gone to seek him, and coming out in search of him—"findeth Nathanael, and saith unto him, We have found Him of whom Moses and the prophets wrote, Jesus of Nazareth, the son of Joseph." 'Of Nazareth? How can that be?' 'I cannot tell, but Come and see, and that will suffice.' He comes; and as he draws near, the first words of Jesus, who breaks the silence, fill him with wonder. 'Would ye see a guileless, true-hearted Israelite, whose one object is to be right with God, to be taught of Him, and be led by Him? this is he!' 'Rabbi, whence knowest thou me?' 'Guileless soul! that fig tree, with all its heaving anxieties, earnest pleadings, and tremulous hopes—without an eye or an ear, as thou thoughtest, upon thee—Mine eye saw it, Mine ear heard it all!' The first words of Jesus had astonished, but this quite overpowered and more than won him. Accordingly, 49. Nathanael an-

swered and saith unto him, Rabbi, thou art the Son of God; thou art the King of Israel—the one denoting His Personal, the other His Official dignity. How much loftier this than anything Philip had said to him! But just as the earth's vital powers, the longer they are frost-bound, take the greater spring when at length set free, so souls, like Nathanael and Thomas (see on ch. xx. 28), the outgoings of whose faith are hindered for a time, take the start of their more easy-going brethren when once loosed and let go. It may, indeed, be asked how Nathanael came so far ahead of the current views of his day as these words of his express. For though "The King of Israel" was a phrase familiar enough to the Jews, in their own sense of it, the phrase "Son of God" was so far from being familiar to them as a title of their promised Messiah, that they never took up stones to stone our Lord till He called Himself, and claimed the prerogatives of, God's own Son. We think there can be no doubt that Nathanael got this from the Baptist's teaching—not his *popular* teaching, recorded in detail, but his *inner* teaching to the circle of his own select disciples, whom he taught to recognize in the Messiah not only "the Lamb of God," but "the Son of God" (see on ch. iii. 27-36). 50. Jesus answered and said unto him, Because I said unto thee, I saw thee under the fig tree, believest thou? 'So quickly convinced, Nathanael, and on this evidence only?'—an expression of admiration. Jesus saw in the quickness and the rapture of this guileless Israelite's faith a noble susceptibility, which He tells him should soon have food enough. And, no doubt, He felt the fragrance to His own spirit of such a testimony. thou shalt see greater things than these. 51. And he saith unto him, Verily, verily, I say unto you, Hereafter. [This phrase "hereafter"—ἀπ' ἄρτι—is excluded from the text by *Lachmann*, *Tregelles*, and *Tischendorf*, in his earlier editions, whom *Alford* follows. But the evidence in its favour is, in our judgment, decisive, and *Tischendorf* has restored it to the text in his last edition. *De Wette*, *Meyer*, and *Olshausen* concur in regarding it as part of the original text.] ye shall see heaven open, and the angels of God ascending and descending upon the Son of man. The key to this great saying is Jacob's vision on his way to Padanaram, (Gen. xxviii. 12, &c.) To show the patriarch that though alone and friendless on earth his interests were busying all heaven, he was made to see "heaven opened, and the angels of God ascending and descending upon a" mystic "*ladder* reaching from heaven to earth." 'By and by,' says Jesus here, 'ye shall see this communication between heaven and earth thrown wide open, and the Son of Man to be the real *Ladder* of this intercourse.' On the meaning of the word "hereafter"—or, as it should rather be, 'henceforth'—see on Mark xiv. 62. Here, for the first time, and at the very opening of His public ministry, our Lord gives Himself that peculiar title—"THE SON OF MAN"—by which He designates Himself almost invariably throughout, even till just before He was adjudged to die, when to the Jewish Sanhedrim He said, "Nevertheless I say unto you, Henceforth [ἀπ' ἄρτι] shall ye see *The Son of Man* sitting at the right hand of

51 believest thou? thou shalt see greater things than these. And he saith unto him, Verily, verily, I say unto you, [i]Hereafter ye shall see heaven open, and the angels of God ascending and descending upon the Son of man.

A. D. 30.

[i] Gen 28. 12.
Matt. 3. 16.
Luke 3. 21.
Acts 7. 56.

power, and coming in the clouds of heaven" (Matt. xxvi. 64). But whilst our Lord hardly ever called Himself by any other name, it is a striking fact that by that name He was never once addressed, and never once spoken of, while He was on earth, and that, with two exceptions, He is never so styled in the succeeding parts of the New Testament. And even these two passages are no proper exceptions. For in the one (see on Acts vii. 56) the martyr Stephen is only recalling our Lord's own words to the Jewish council, as already fulfilled before His own vision in the presence of that same council: in the other passage (see on Rev. i. 13) the beloved disciple—having a vision of Jesus in the symbols of majesty and glory, power and grace, in the midst of the churches, as their living Lord—only recalls the language of Daniel's night vision of "*The Son of Man*," and tells us how he was able to identify this glorious One with Him on whose bosom himself had leaned at every meal when He was on earth, saying that He was "like unto the Son of Man." These peculiar passages, then, instead of contradicting, only confirm the remark, that by this name He was never spoken to, never spoken of, and in the churches never styled, and that it stands alone as His own chosen designation of Himself. Of the seventy-nine times in which it occurs in the Gospels, it is found seldomest in John—only eleven times—being there overshadowed by a still more august name, "The Son of God." Mark uses it but one time more; Luke twenty-six times; but in Matthew it occurs thirty times. This suggests a *Hebraic* origin of the phrase; and indeed there can be no doubt that it is fetched directly from Dan. vii. 13, 14 (on the occasion and scope of which, see on Mark xiii. 26): "I saw in the night visions, and behold [one] like THE SON OF MAN [כְּבַר אֱנָשׁ, ὡς υἱὸς Ἀνθρώπου] came with the clouds of heaven," &c. But what is the import of this peculiar title? It has a two-fold significance, we apprehend. Putting the emphasis on the last word, "The Son of *Man*," or of Humanity, it expresses the great fact that He took flesh of our flesh, that He "was made in the likeness of men," that "as the children were partakers of flesh and blood, He also Himself likewise took part of the same." Accordingly, in several passages it will be found that our Lord designed by this phrase to express emphatically the humiliation to which He had submitted in "being formed in fashion as a man." But when we put the emphasis upon the definite article, "*The* Son of Man," it will be seen that He thereby severs Himself from all other men, or takes Himself out of the category of ordinary humanity. And we believe that He thus holds Himself forth as "The Second Man," in contrast with "the first man, Adam," or, as He is otherwise called, "The Second Adam;" that is, the second Representative Man, in whose Person Humanity stood and was recovered, in opposition to the first Representative man, in whom Humanity fell and was ruined. So much for this peculiar phrase. But what is meant by "the angels of God ascending and descending upon the Son of Man?" Almost all expositors of any depth, from *Origen* to *Calvin*, and from *Calvin* to *Lücke*, and *Olshausen*, and *Tholuck*, and *Stier*, and *Alford*, set aside all reference to miraculous events, and see in it the opening up of a gracious intercourse between heaven

356

and earth through the mediation of the Lord Jesus. If it be asked why, both in Jacob's vision and in our Lord's reference to it here, the angels are not said to "descend and ascend"—as we should expect, from and to their proper abode—but to "ascend and descend," we may give *Lücke's* beautiful suggestion, that they are *left* in their descending office, as if they went up only to come down to us again on yet other errands, and exercise an *abiding* ministry.

Remarks.—1. How sublimely noiseless were the first footsteps of that Ministry whose effects were to be world-wide and for all time—reaching even into eternity! How quietly were those five disciples first called—under one of whom the Christian Church rose first into visible existence, and achieved its earliest triumphs; while another—the youngest of them all, and Peter's companion and coadjutor in all his early sufferings and labours—after surviving them all, contributed to the Canon of Scripture writings which transcend, may we not say, all the rest in the impress which they bear of Christ Himself! See on Matt. xii. 16-21, with Remark 6 at the close of that Section. 2. Every disciple of the Lord Jesus is called in his own way. John and Andrew are drawn to Jesus, after the training they had received from the Baptist, by the sublime strain in which their master directed their attention to Him, and the Saviour's winning encouragement of their own advances. Simon is brought to Jesus by his brother Andrew. Jesus "findeth" Philip, and at once gives him that call to follow Him which needed not to be repeated. But Philip "findeth" Nathanael and fetches him to Jesus. Difficulties exist in that guileless man; but they vanish in a transport of wonder and exultation, on the Saviour revealing him all to himself. Even so it is still. But as He to Whom all come is One, so the grace that worketh in all to bring them is one; and a goodly fellowship it is, whose diversity only enhances the charm of their unity. Even as in the Kingdom of Nature,

'Wisely Thou givest—all around
Thine equal rays are resting found,
Yet varying so on various ground
They pierce and strike
That not two roseate cups are crown'd
With dew alike,'

so in the kingdom of grace. 3. What a glorious note was that to strike at the very outset of the Gospel—ere yet the Lord Jesus had opened His own mouth most sweet'—"Behold the Lamb of God, which taketh away the sin of the world!" and as it was so soon again repeated to the same audience, is it not clear that this was designed to be the great primary proclamation of Christ's servants in every land and in all ages? They are not to think it enough to show to sinners of mankind that there has been given a Lamb of God for the taking away of the sin of the world, and that this is the one all-availing sacrifice for sin; but when they have done this, they are to hold Him forth and bid burdened sinners *behold* Him, and know their burden removed in Him. Never, we may safely say, was any ministry divinely owned and honoured of which this has not been the alpha and the omega; nor has any *such* ministry been without the seals of Heaven's approval. 4. Difficulties in religion are best dealt with by taking a firm

2 AND the third day there was a marriage in Cana of Galilee; and
2 the mother of Jesus was there: and both Jesus was called, and his disci-
3 ples, to the marriage. And when they wanted wine, the mother of Jesus
4 saith unto him, They have no wine. Jesus saith unto her, ^aWoman,

A. D. 30.
^a Matt. 15. 28.
ch. 19. 26.
ch. 20. 13,
15.

grasp of fundamental and undeniable truths. Nathanael's difficulties, though they were those of a sincere enquirer, were certainly not removed before he consented to come to Jesus; nor did Christ Himself remove them as a preliminary to Nathanael's believing on Him. But being furnished with transparent evidence of His claims, that honest heart waited not for more, but uttered forth its convictions at once. Difficulties may be removed, but even if they never be on this side of time, let us not spend our days in doubt and darkness; let us plant our foot upon the rock of manifest truth, and for the rest wait till the day dawn and the shadows flee away. 5. As guile in every form vitiates the religious character and shuts out divine teaching, so to be "without guile" is the beginning of all that is acceptable to God (Ps. xxxii. 2), and carries with it the assurance of Divine guidance in the path of truth and duty. It is one of the great characteristics of the predicted Christ that no deceit should be found in His mouth (Isa. liii. 9); and of a class of Christians distinguished for their fidelity to Him in times of general defection, that in their mouth was found no guile (Rev. xiv. 5); and of the restored remnant of Israel that they shall not speak lies; neither shall a deceitful tongue be found in their mouth (Zeph. iii. 13). All this would seem to imply that entire simplicity and freedom from guile is a character remarkable rather for its rarity even among God's own people. 6. As the joy of discovered truth is in proportion to the ·difficulties experienced in finding it, so when firmness of conviction bursts forth from the heart that has found Christ in a tide of emotion, it is to Him peculiarly grateful, as was that noble exclamation of Nathanael's. 7. If Christ be *Immanuel*, "God with us," we can understand His being the Ladder of mediatorial communication between heaven and earth—uniting in his glorious Person the nature of both, but on no other view of Christ is this explainable; and, in fact, none who dispute the one really believe the other. But 8. What thoughts does this idea of the "Ladder" suggest! Never a groaning that cannot be uttered enters into the ears of the Lord of sabaoth, but it first passes *up* this Ladder—for no man cometh unto the Father but by Him: Never a ray of light, never a breath of love divine, irradiates and cheers the dark and drooping spirit, but it first passes *down* this Ladder; for the Father loveth the Son and hath given all things into his hand, and, if we are "blessed with all spiritual blessings," it is "in Christ." Thus is He not only our "way" to the Father, but the Father's "way" to us. Needest thou, then, poor burdened heart, aught from thy Father, to keep thee from sinking, to bear thee through the trials of life, and to bring thee home at length to thy Father's house in peace? Lie like Jacob at the foot of this glorious Ladder, planted close by thee on this ground but whose top reacheth to heaven, and send up thy petition on this Ladder—make known thy request through Him: then look and listen, and thou shalt see, as Jacob did, "the Lord standing above it, and hear Him speaking down this Ladder into thine own ear the rich assurances of His love and power, His grace and truth, pledged "not to leave thee until He hath done that which He hath spoken to thee of." And with Jacob thou shalt say, "How dread-

357

ful is this place! This is none other than the house of God, and this is the gate of heaven." Well may the angels of God be the winged messengers of such an intercourse; and what a crowded Ladder, and what busy activities, are suggested to us by their thus "ascending and descending" on errands of love to us, the "*descending*" flight of them being the thought with which the curtain of this beautiful scene drops upon us!

CHAP. II. 1-12.—CHRIST'S FIRST MIRACLE, OR THE TURNING OF WATER INTO WINE, AT THE MARRIAGE IN CANA—BRIEF VISIT TO CAPERNAUM. The time of this Section is clearly expressed in the opening verse; and here, again, let the reader note the chronological precision of this Gospel.

Water Turned into Wine (1-11). 1. And the third day there was a marriage in Cana of Galilee. It would take two days to travel from the Judean valley of the Jordan, where He parted with John—never to meet again, so far as we are informed—to Cana; and this marriage-day was the day following, or the third. It is not called Cana in Galilee to distinguish it, as *Eusebius* and *Jerome* thought, from Kaneh in the tribe of Asher (Jos. xix. 28), for that also would be reckoned to Galilee, according to the New Testament division of the country—but merely to note its geographical locality, and to let the reader know that Jesus had now returned to His own region, which He left in order to be baptized of John in Jordan. No remains of the village of Cana now exist; but the most probable site of it was a spot about three hours northward of Nazareth. Nathanael belonged to this village (ch. xxi. 2). and the mother of Jesus was there—whether as a relative or as an intimate acquaintance we have no means of knowing. Our Evangelist, it will be observed, never names the Virgin, but styles her "the mother of Jesus," from that reverence, probably, with which he had learnt to look up to her, especially since he "took her to his own home." 2. And both Jesus was called, and his disciples, to the marriage—by special invitation, probably, at the instance of Jesus' mother. 3. And when they wanted wine [ὑστερήσαντος οἴνου]—' the wine having failed;' perhaps, as *Bengel* suggests, from more being present than had been arranged for, the mother of Jesus saith unto him, They have no wine—evidently expecting some display of His glory, and hinting that now was His time. Not that she had witnessed any displays of His miraculous power before this at home, as *Calvin* thinks. The Evangelist, indeed, by calling this the "beginning of His miracles" (v. 11), seems to say the reverse; nor can we suppose He would make such needless displays before the time. But she had gathered probably enough from Him regarding the miraculous credentials which He was to furnish of His divine commission, to infer that He would on this occasion make a beginning; and with a natural impatience for the revelation to others of what she knew Him to be, and a certain womanly eagerness—mixed possibly with feelings of a less commendable kind—she brings the state of matters before Him. 4. Jesus saith unto her, Woman [γύναι]—no term of disrespect in the language of that day. (See ch. xix. 26; xx. 13.) what have I to do with thee? [Τί ἐμοί καὶ σοί;= מַה־לִּי וָלָךְ]. If such passages as Jos. xxii. 24; Jud. xi. 12; 2 Sam.

5 *b*what have I to do with thee? *c*mine hour is not yet come. His mother
6 saith unto the servants, Whatsoever he saith unto you, do *it*. And there
    were set there six water-pots of stone, *d*after the manner of the puri-
7 fying of the Jews, containing two or three firkins apiece. Jesus saith
    unto them, Fill the water-pots with water. And they filled them up to
8 the brim. And he saith unto them, Draw out now, and bear unto the
9 governor of the feast. And they bear *it*. When the ruler of the feast
    had tasted the *e*water that was made wine, and knew not whence it was,
    (but the servants which drew the water knew,) the governor of the feast
10 called the bridegroom, and saith unto him, Every man at the beginning
    doth set forth good wine; and when men have well drunk, then that
11 which is worse: *but* thou hast kept the good wine until now. This
    beginning of miracles did Jesus in *f*Cana of Galilee, *g*and manifested
    forth his glory; and his disciples believed on him.
12 After this he went down to Capernaum, he, and his mother, and *h*his
    brethren, and his disciples: and they continued there not many days.

A. D. 30.

b 2Sam.16.10.
2Sam.19.22.
Luke 2. 49.
2 Cor. 5. 16.
c Eccl. 3. 1.
ch. 7. 6.
d Mark 7. 3.
Eph. 5. 26.
Heb. 6. 2.
Heb. 9. 10-19.
Heb. 10. 22.
e ch. 4. 46.
f Jos. 19. 28.
g Deut. 5. 24.
Ps. 72. 19.
ch. 1. 14.
ch. 5. 23.
ch. 12. 41.
h Matt.12. 46.

---

xvi. 10, be compared with Matt. viii. 29; Mark i. 24; Luke viii. 28, it will be seen that this, in the current language of the Old and New Testament, is the strongest expression of *no-connection* between the party speaking and the party spoken of. Here, it is an intimation on the part of Jesus to His mother that in thus officiously interfering with Him she was entering a region from which all creatures were excluded. A gentle, yet decided rebuke. (See Acts iv. 19, 20.) **mine hour is not yet come**—a hint that He *would*, nevertheless, do something, but at His own time; and so she understood it, as the next verse shows. 5. **His mother saith unto the servants, Whatsoever he saith unto you, do it.** 6. **And**—or, 'Now' [δὲ] **there were set there six water-pots of stone, after the manner of the purifying of the Jews, containing two or three firkins apiece.** The "firkin" here mentioned [μετρητής], when it stands for the Jewish "bath," is a measure containing about seven and a half gallons; in Attic measure it held nine and a half gallons. Each of these huge water-jars, then, must have held some twenty gallons; designed for "the purifying" of the Jews (see Mark vii. 4). 7. **Jesus saith unto them, Fill the water-pots with water. And they filled them up to the brim.** 8. **And he saith unto them, Draw out now, and bear unto the governor of the feast. And they bare it.** It will be observed that our Lord here *directs* everything, but Himself touches nothing: thus excluding all appearance or suspicion of collusion. Compare Elijah's methods on Carmel, 1 Ki. xviii. 33-35. 9. **When the ruler of the feast had tasted the water that was made wine**—the total quantity being about a hundred gallons! **and knew not whence it was (but the servants which drew the water knew,) the governor**—or, 'the ruler;' it is the same word as before [ἀρχι-τρίκλινος], **of the feast called—or 'calleth'** [φωνεῖ] **the bridegroom, 10. And saith unto him, Every man at the beginning doth set forth**—or 'place,' that is, on his table, ['the'] **good wine; and when men have well drunk** [μεθυσθῶσιν = שָׁכַר], or 'drunk freely,' as Song v. 1. The man is speaking of the general practice. **then that which is worse** —or inferior: **but thou hast kept the good wine until now**—thus testifying, while ignorant of the source of supply, not only that it was real wine, but better than any at the feast. 11. **This beginning of miracles did Jesus in Cana of Galilee, and manifested forth his glory.** Nothing in the least like this is said of the miracles of either prophets or apostles, nor could be said without manifest blasphemy of any mere creature. Being said here,

then, by our Evangelist of the very first miracle of Christ, it is as if he had said, 'This was but the first of a series of such manifestations of the glory of Christ.' **and his disciples believed on him**—that is, were confirmed in the faith which they had reposed in Him before they had any miraculous attestation of what He was.

Brief Visit to Capernaum (12). **12. After this he went down to Capernaum**—said to be "down" because it lay on the shore of the Sea of Galilee. See on Matt. iv. 13. **he, and his mother, and his brethren.** See on Matt. xiii. 55, 56. **and his disciples**—the five so recently gathered, **and they continued there not many days**—for the reason mentioned in the next verse, because the Passover was at hand.

Remarks.—1. All sorts of attempts have been made to reduce this miracle to the level of something natural; some of them too ridiculous to be worth a moment's notice, save to show how desperate are the shifts to which those are driven who are not able to dispute the genuineness of the text; and yet are determined not to bow to the miraculous. Nor is that half-and-half theory of a mere acceleration in the ordinary processes of nature in the vintage—first suggested, in the honesty of his heart, by *Augustin*, and since defended by *Olshausen*—nor *Neander's* theory, that He merely intensified the powers of water so as to produce the same effects as wine, more worthy of acceptance as a satisfactory explanation of the miracle; which stands, and while the world lasts will stand, a glorious monument of the power of the Lord Jesus, and in a form which, as we shall presently see, is pregnant with the richest lessons. 2. In this His first miracle Christ would show what He meant to be throughout His whole ministry—in entire contrast to the ascetic retirement which suited the *legal* position of John. "John came neither eating nor drinking" socially with others: "The Son of Man," says Christ Himself, "came eating and drinking" in that very sense. 3. At a marriage Christ made His first public appearance in any company, and at a marriage He wrought this His first miracle—the noblest sanction that could be given to that divinely appointed institution. 4. As all the miracles of Christ were designed to hold forth the characteristic features of His mission—not only to redeem humanity from the effects of the Fall, but to raise it to a higher platform of existence even than at first—so in the present miracle we see this gloriously set forth. For as the miracle did not make *bad good*, but *good better*, so Christianity only redeems, sanctifies, and

13   And *the Jews' passover was at hand; and Jesus went up to Jerusalem,
14 and ʲfound in the temple those that sold oxen and sheep and doves, and
15 the changers of money sitting: and when he had made a scourge of small
    cords, he drove them all out of the temple, and the sheep, and the oxen;
16 and poured out the changers' money, and overthrew the tables; and said
    unto them that sold doves, Take these things hence; ᵏmake not my
17 Father's house an house of merchandise. And his disciples remembered
    that it was written, ˡThe zeal of thine house hath eaten me up.
18   Then answered the Jews and said unto him, What sign showest thou
19 unto us, seeing that thou doest these things? Jesus answered and said
    unto them, Destroy ᵐthis temple, and in three days I will raise it up.
20 Then said the Jews, Forty and six years was this temple in building,
21 and wilt thou rear it up in three days? But he spake ⁿof the temple of

A. D. 30.
ᶦ Ex. 12. 14.
Num.28.16.
ch. 5. 1.
ʲ Matt. 21. 12.
Mark 11.15.
Luke 19.45.
ᵏ Ps. 93. 5.
1 Tim. 6. 9.
10.
ˡ Ps. 69. 9.
ᵐ Matt. 26.61.
Matt. 27.40.
Mark 14.58.
ⁿ 1 Cor. 3. 16.
1 Cor. 6. 19.
Col. 2. 9.

ennobles the beneficent but abused institution of marriage; and Christ's whole work only turns the water of earth into the wine of heaven. Thus "this beginning of miracles" exhibited the character and "manifested forth the glory" of His entire Mission. 5. As Christ countenanced our seasons of *festivity*, so also that greater *fulness* which befits such; so far was He from encouraging that *asceticism* which has since been so often put for all religion. 6. In what a light does this scene place the Romish views of the blessed Virgin! The doctrine of the 'immaculate conception of the Virgin'—in our day for the first time, even in the Church of Rome, erected into a dogma of the faith —is so outrageous a contradiction of Scriptural truth that none who can take it in are likely to be staggered by the teaching of this or any other portion of Scripture. But even those Romanists who in past times have stopped short of this, as the sober and excellent *Maldonat*, while admitting that there was hardly one of the fathers who did not acknowledge some fault, or error at least, in the Virgin on this occasion, endeavour to explain it away, and refuse to admit that there ever was anything faulty in her, and much less here. But the passage may well be left to speak for itself with all candid readers. 7. Christ's presence is that which turns the water of this and all other social gatherings into wine.

13-22.—CHRIST'S FIRST PUBLIC VISIT TO JERUSALEM AT THE PASSOVER, AND FIRST PURIFYING OF THE TEMPLE.

13. And the Jews' passover—as to which see on Mark xiv. 1, was at hand. Here begins our Evangelist's distinct mention of the successive passovers which occurred during our Lord's public ministry, and which are our only sure materials for determining the duration of it. See more on this subject on ch. v. 1. and Jesus went up to Jerusalem, 14. And found in the temple [ἐν τῷ ἱερῷ]—in the large sense of that word, for which see on Luke ii. 27. Here it probably means the temple-court. those that sold oxen and sheep and doves—for the convenience of those who had to offer them in sacrifice. See Deut. xiv. 24-26. and the changers of money—of Roman into Jewish money, in which the temple dues, &c., had to be paid (see on Matt. xvii. 24). sitting: 15. And when he had made a scourge [φραγέλλιον= *flagellum*] of small cords—likely some of the rushes spread for bedding, and when twisted used to tie up the cattle there collected. 'Not by this slender whip,' says *Grotius* admirably, 'but by divine majesty was the ejection accomplished, the whip being but a sign of the scourge of divine anger.' he drove them all out of the temple, and the sheep, and the oxen [πάντας . . τά τε πρόβατα καὶ τοὺς βόας]—rather, 'drove out all, both the

359

sheep and the oxen.' The men would naturally enough go with them. and poured out the changers' money, and overthrew the tables— expressing the mingled indignation and authority of the impulse. 16. And said unto them that sold doves, Take these things hence; make not my Father's house an house of merchandise. How close is the resemblance of these remarkable words to those in Luke ii. 49, "Wist ye not that I must be about my Father's business!" or 'at my Father's' (see on that passage). Both express the same *consciousness of intrinsic relation to the Temple*, as the seat of His Father's most august worship, and so the symbol of all that is due to Him on earth. Only, when but a Youth *with no authority*, He was simply "a Son IN His own house;" now He was "a Son OVER His own house" (Heb. iii. 6), the proper Representative, and in flesh "the Heir," of His Father's rights. There was nothing wrong in the merchandise; but to bring it, for their own and others' convenience, into that most sacred place, was a high-handed profanation which the eye of Jesus could not endure. 17. And his disciples remembered that it was written (Ps. lxix. 9), The zeal of thine house hath eaten me up—a glorious feature in the predicted character of the suffering Messiah, and rising high even in some not worthy to loose the latchet of His shoes. (See, for example, Exod. xxxii. 19, &c.)

18. Then answered the Jews and said unto him, What sign showest thou unto us, seeing that thou doest these things? Though the act itself, and the words that accompanied it, when taken together, were sign enough, they are not convinced. Yet were they *awed;* insomuch that though at His very next appearance at Jerusalem they "sought to kill him" for speaking of "His Father" just as He did now (ch. v. 18), they, at this early stage, only ask a sign. 19. Jesus answered and said unto them, Destroy this temple—not now the mere *temple-court* [ἱερόν], but the *temple proper* [ναός], and in three days I will raise it up. See on Mark xiv. 58, 59. 20. Then said the Jews, Forty and six years was this temple in building. From the eighteenth year of Herod, from which we are to date this building work of his, until this time, was just a period of forty-six years (*Joseph.* Antt. xv. 11. 1). The word [ᾠκοδομήθη] is rightly rendered 'was in building,' by a peculiar application of the tense—the same tense being similarly used by the LXX. in Ezra v. 16, where the sense is manifestly the same as here. and wilt thou rear it up in three days? 21. But he spake of the temple of his body—in which was enshrined the glory of the eternal Word. (See on ch. i. 14.) By its resurrection the true Temple of God upon earth was reared up, of which the stone temple was

22 his body. When therefore he was risen from the dead, °his disciples remembered that he had said this unto them; and they believed the Scripture, and the word which Jesus had said.

A. D. 30.

° Luke 24. 8, 25, 45.
John 14. 26.

but a shadow; so that the allusion, though to Himself, may be said to take in that temple of which He is the Foundation, and all believers are the "lively stones" (1 Pet. ii. 4, 5). **22. When therefore he was risen from the dead, his disciples remembered that he had said this unto them; and they believed the Scripture**—that is, with an intelligent apprehension of what its testimony on this subject meant, which until then was hid from them. **and the word which Jesus had said.** They believed it before, as they did the Scripture; but their faith in both was another thing after they came to understand it by seeing it verified. *Remarks.*—1. On the question, whether this purification of the temple is one and the same action with that recorded in the first three Gospels (Matt. xxi. 12, 13; Mark xi. 15-19; Luke xix. 45-48), see introductory remarks to Luke xix. 45-48. But the points of difference between the two scenes may here be stated: First, The one took place at the very outset of our Lord's public ministry, and at His first visit to Jerusalem; the other at the very close of it, and at His last visit to Jerusalem. Second, At the former cleansing He used a whip of small cords in clearing the temple-court; at the latter cleansing we read of nothing of this sort. If, then, they were one and the same action, how is it that three Evangelists have recorded it without any mention of this part of it; while the mention of so peculiar a procedure even by one Evangelist can only be explained by its having actually occurred? Third, At the first cleansing all that the Lord said was, "Take these things hence; make not my Father's house an house of merchandise." At the last cleansing His rebuke was withering—"It is written, My house shall be called the house of prayer; but ye have made it a den of robbers" [λῃστῶν]. And it may be added, that on this second occasion He "would not suffer that any man should carry any vessel through the temple," which would hardly have been said, perhaps, of the first cleansing. Fourth, On the first occasion "the Jews," or members of the Sanhedrim (see on ch. i. 19), asked of our Lord a "sign" of His right to do such things; and it was then that He spake that saying about destroying the temple and rearing it up in three days which was adduced, though impotently, as evidence against Him on His trial before the Council; whereas nothing of this is recorded in any of the three accounts of the second cleansing. Indeed, the time for asking of Him signs of His authority was then over. Lastly, At the second cleansing "the chief priests and the scribes, and the chief of the people"—exasperated at His high-handed exposure of their temple-traffic, "sought how they might destroy Him," but could not find what they might do, "for all the people were astonished at His teaching"—all betokening that the crisis of our Lord's public life had arrived; whereas the first cleansing passed away with the simple demand for a sign, and our Lord's reply. However dissatisfied they may have been, the matter appears to have rested there, in the meantime —just as we might presume it would at so early a period in our Lord's ministry, when even many who were sincere enough might be unable to make up their minds, and the prejudices of others had not acquired depth and strength enough for any open opposition. 2. Had this

remarkable clearing of the temple-court not actually occurred, what inventor of a life that never was lived would have thought of such a thing? Or, if the idea itself should not have been so entirely beyond the range of probable conception, who would ever have thought of introducing the idea of the whip of small cords? Of all things, this at least, one should think, must have been *real*, else it could never have been *written*. But if this was real, the whole scene must have been so —the sanctity claimed for the temple-service and the desecration which kindled the jealousy of this Holy One of God, the Son for the honour of His Father's house; the demand for a sign, tacitly owning the actual exercise of resistless authority, with the remarkable reply, too peculiar to have been penned save as having been uttered; and the darkness of the speech even to the disciples themselves until the resurrection of their Lord cleared it all up. No wonder that the bare reading of such a Narrative carries its own evidence in the minds of all the unprejudiced. 3. In Christ's jealousy for the sanctity and honour of His Father's house—both when He came first to it, in His official character, and when He came to it for the last time—what a glorious commentary have we on those words of the last of the prophets: "The Lord, whom ye seek, shall suddenly come to His temple, even the Messenger of the covenant, whom ye delight in: behold, He shall come, saith the Lord of hosts. But who may abide the day of His coming? and who shall stand when He appeareth? for He is like a refiner's fire, and like fuller's soap: And He shall sit as a refiner and purifier of silver: and He shall purify the sons of Levi, and purge them as gold and silver, that they may offer unto the Lord an offering in righteousness" (Mal. iii. 1-3). Thus was He revealed as "a Son over His own House," the Lord of the temple, the Refiner and Purifier of the Church, of all its assemblies, and of each of its worshippers. Compare this: "JEHOVAH is in His holy temple; His eyes behold, His eyelids try, the children of men" (Ps. xi. 4)—with this: "Unto the angel of the church in Thyatira write; These things saith THE SON OF GOD, who hath His eyes as a flame of fire, and His feet are like fine brass; I know thy works . . . and all the churches shall know that I am He which searcheth the reins and hearts: and I will give unto every one of you according to your works" (Rev. ii. 18, 19, 23). This whip of small cords was like the fan in His hand with which He purged His floor;" not "throughly" indeed, but sufficiently to foreshadow His last act towards that faithless people—*sweeping them out of God's house.* The sign which He gives of His authority to do this is a very remarkable one—the announcement, at this the very outset of His ministry, of that coming death by *their* hands and resurrection by *His own*, which were to pave the way for their judicial ejection. This, however, was uttered—as was fitting at so early a period— in language only to be fully understood, even by His disciples, after His resurrection. 4. When Christ says He will Himself rear up the temple of His body, in three days after they had destroyed it, He makes a claim and uses language which would be manifest presumption in any creature— claiming absolute power over His own life. But on this important subject, see more on ch. x. 18.

23—iii. 21.—RESULTS OF CHRIST'S FIRST PUBLIC

23   Now when he was in Jerusalem at the passover, in the feast *day*, many
24 believed in his name, when they saw the miracles which he did. But
25 Jesus did not commit himself unto them, because he knew all *men*, and
needed not that any should testify of man: for *p*he knew what was in
man.

3   THERE was a man of the Pharisees, named Nicodemus, a ruler of the
2 Jews: the same came to Jesus by night, and said unto him, Rabbi, we
know that thou art a teacher come from God: for *a*no man can do these
miracles that thou doest, except *b*God be with him.

3   Jesus answered and said unto him, Verily, verily, I say unto thee,
*c*Except a man be born ¹again, he cannot see the kingdom of God.

A. D. 30.
p 1 Sam. 16. 7.
1 Chr. 28. 9.
Matt. 9. 4.
CHAP. 3.
a ch. 9. 16, 33.
Acts 2. 22.
b Acts 10. 38.
c ch. 1. 13.
2 Cor. 5. 17.
Gal. 6. 15.
Jas. 1. 18.
1 Or, from
above.

VISIT TO JERUSALEM, IN MANY SHALLOW CONVERSIONS AND ONE PRECIOUS ACCESSION. The three last verses of the second chapter, and the first twenty-one verses of the third, form manifestly one subject, in two divisions; the former one brief, because unsatisfactory, the latter of too deep importance in itself and too pregnant with instruction for all, not to be given in full detail.

Unsatisfactory Accessions to Christ at His First Visit to Jerusalem (23-25). **23. Now when he was in Jerusalem at the passover, in the feast [day]** [ἐν τῇ ἑορτῇ]—rather, 'during the feast,' which lasted seven days. What is now to be related is not the result of one day, but of the whole period of this festival. The Cleansing of the Temple, recorded in the preceding verses, occurred probably before the feast began. **many believed in his name** —see on ch. i. 12. These converts, persuaded that His claims were well founded, reposed trust in Him in that sense, and to that extent **when they saw the miracles which he did.** What these were is not here recorded; nor can we get any light from the other Evangelists, as they speak of no public visit to Jerusalem but the last. It is singular that none of these miracles are recorded, since in the very opening of the next chapter Nicodemus refers to the immense force of conviction which they carried (ch. iii. 2), and they are again referred to in ch. iv. 45. **24. But Jesus** [Αὐτὸς δὲ ὁ Ἰησοῦς]—' But Jesus Himself,' or 'Jesus, for His part,' **did not commit**—or 'trust' **himself unto them** [οὐκ ἐπίστευεν αὐτὸν αὐτοῖς]. Though they confided in Him, He did not confide in them, or let Himself down to them familiarly, as He did to His genuine disciples. **because He knew all men.** He saw through them, as He did through all men, and, perceiving the superficial character of the trust they reposed in Him, He reposed none in them. **25. And needed not**—'And because He needed not' [Καὶ ὅτι οὐ χρείαν εἶχεν] **that any should testify of man: for He knew** [αὐτὸς γὰρ]. The language is emphatic, as in the previous verse: 'For Himself knew' **what was in man**—in other words, that all-penetrating perception of what was in man *resided in Himself;* the strongest possible expression of absolute knowledge of *man*, as in ch. i. 18 of *God.*

CHAP. III.—*Night-Interview of Nicodemus with Jesus, issuing in His Accession as a genuine Disciple* (1-21). See introductory remark at the commencement of this Section. **1. There was a man of the Pharisees, named Nicodemus, a ruler of the Jews.** The connecting particle [δὲ] with which the original introduces this scene should not have been omitted, as the Evangelist is now going to show, in continuation of his subject, that *all* the accessions to Christ during this His first public visit to Jerusalem were not like those of whom he had spoken at the close of the preceding chapter. It should have begun thus: 'But (or 'Now') there was a man,' &c.

Nicodemus is a purely Greek name, of frequent occurrence among the later Greeks, whose names were often appropriated by the Jews, especially those of foreign extraction. This Nicodemus, besides being of the stricter sect of the Pharisees, was a "ruler" [ἄρχων], or one of the Sanhedrim. In *v.* 10 he is called a "master," or 'doctor' of the law. It is useless attempting, as *Lightfoot* has done, to identify him with a rabbi of this name who lived at the destruction of Jerusalem. **2. The same came to Jesus.** The true text here clearly is 'to Him' [πρὸς αὐτόν]; this being regarded as but a continuation of the same subject with which the preceding chapter closed. The word "Jesus" no doubt came in first in those Church Lessons which began with ch. iii., and so required it; just as many in the public reading of the Scriptures insert the name of the person instead of "he" or "him," for clearness' sake. So all recent critical editors agree. **by night**—"for fear of the Jews," as is evident from all we read of him: see on ch. vii. 50-52; and on ch. xix. 38, 39. **and said unto him, Rabbi** [= διδάσκαλος], **we know**—meaning, probably, that a general conviction to that effect had been diffusing itself through the thoughtful portion of the worshippers with whom Jerusalem was then crowded, though much yet remained for anxious enquiry regarding His claims, and that as the representative of this class he had now come to solicit an interview with Him. **that thou art a teacher come from God** [ἀπὸ Θεοῦ ἐλήλυθας]— not "sent from God," as is said of the Baptist, ch. i. 6. *Stier* and *Luthardt* call attention to this, as expressing more than a conviction that Jesus was divinely *commissioned*, as were all the prophets. Certain it is that the expression "come from God" is nowhere used of any merely *human messenger*, while this Gospel of ours teems with phraseology of this kind applied to Christ. It is possible, therefore, that Nicodemus *may* have designed to express something indefinite as to Christ's higher claims; though what follows hardly bears that out. **for no man can do these miracles that thou doest, except God be with him.** See on ch. ii. 23. From all these particulars about Nicodemus, we may gather that sincerity and timidity struggled together in his mind. The one impelled him, in spite of his personal and official position, to solicit an interview with Jesus; the other, to choose the "night" time for his visit, that none might know of it. The one led him frankly to tell the Lord Jesus what conviction he had been constrained to come to, and the ground of that conviction; the other, so to measure his language as not to commit himself to more than a bare acknowledgment of a miraculously attested commission from God to men.

3. Jesus answered and said unto him, Verily, verily, I say unto thee, Except a man be born again, he cannot see the kingdom of God. This blunt and curt reply was plainly meant to shake

4   Nicodemus saith unto him, How can a man be born when he is old? can he enter the second time into his mother's womb, and be born?

5   Jesus answered, Verily, verily, I say unto thee, ^dExcept a man be born of water and *of* the Spirit, he cannot enter into the kingdom of God.

6   That which is born of the flesh is flesh; and that which is born of the

7   Spirit is spirit. Marvel not that I said unto thee, Ye must be born

A. D. 30.

^d Isa. 44. 3, 4.
Matt. 3. 11.
Mark 16. 16.
Acts 2. 38.
Titus 3. 5.
1 Pet. 3. 21.

the whole edifice of the man's religion, in order to lay a deeper and more enduring foundation. Nicodemus probably thought he had gone a long way, and expected, perhaps, to be complimented on his candour. Instead of this, he is virtually told that he has raised a question which he is not in a capacity to solve, and that before approaching it, *his spiritual vision required to be rectified by an entire revolution on his inner man.* Had the man been less sincere, this would certainly have repelled him; but with persons in his mixed state of mind—to which Jesus was no stranger (ch. ii. 25) —such methods speed better than more honeyed words and gradual approaches. Let us analyze this great brief saying. "Except a *man*" [τις]—'a person,' or 'one' "be born again," the most universal form of expression. The Jews were accustomed to say of a heathen proselyte, on his public admission into the Jewish faith by baptism, that he was a new-born child. But our Lord here extends the necessity of the new birth to Jew and Gentile alike —to every one. be born again [ἄνωθεν]—or, as the word admits of being rendered, 'from above.' Since both are undoubted truths, the question is, Which is the sense here intended? *Origen* and others of the fathers take the latter view, though *Chrysostom* leaves it undecided; and with them agree *Erasmus, Lightfoot, Bengel, Meyer, de Wette, Lücke, Lange,* and others. But as it is evident that Nicodemus understood our Lord in the sense of a *second* birth, so the scope of our Lord's way of dealing with him was to drive home the conviction of the *nature* rather than the *source* of the change. And accordingly, as the word employed is stronger than "again" [πάλιν] it should be rendered by some such word as 'anew,' 'of new,' 'afresh.' In this sense it is understood, with our translators, by the *Vulgate, Luther, Calvin, Beza, Maldonat, Lampe, Olshausen, Neander, Tholuck, Stier, Luthardt, Campbell, Alford, Webster and Wilkinson.* Considering this to be the undoubted sense of the term, we understand our Lord to say that unless one *begin life anew,* in relation to God—his manner of thinking, and feeling, and acting, in reference to spiritual things, undergoing a *fundamental and permanent revolution,* he cannot see—that is, 'can have no part in'—just as one is said to "see life," "see death," &c. the kingdom of God—whether in its beginnings here or its consummation hereafter. (See on Matt. v. 3; and compare Luke xvi. 16; Matt. xxv. 34; Eph. v. 5.)

4. Nicodemus saith unto him, How can a man be born when he is old? Nicodemus probably referred here to himself. can he enter the second time into his mother's womb, and be born? The figure of the new birth, as we have seen, would have been intelligible enough to Nicodemus if it had been meant only of Gentile proselytes to the Jewish Religion; but that *Jews themselves* should need a new birth was to him incomprehensible.

5. Jesus answered, Verily, verily, I say unto thee, Except a man be born of water and of the Spirit [ἐξ ὕδατος καὶ πνεύματος]—or, more simply, 'of water and the Spirit,' he cannot enter into the kingdom of God. We have here a two-fold explanation of the new birth, so startling to Nicodemus. To a Jewish ecclesiastic, so familiar with the symbolical application of water, in every

variety of way and form of expression, this language was fitted to show that the thing intended was no other than 'a thorough spiritual purification by the operation of the Holy Ghost.' Indeed, this element of *water* and operation of *the Spirit* are brought together in a glorious evangelical prediction of Ezek. xxxvi. 25-27, which Nicodemus might have been reminded of had such spiritualities not been almost lost in the reigning formalism. Already had the symbol of water been embodied in an initiatory ordinance, in the baptism of the Jewish expectants of Messiah by the Baptist, not to speak of the baptism of Gentile proselytes before that; and in the Christian Church it was soon to become the great visible door of entrance into "the kingdom of God," the reality being the sole work of the Holy Ghost. In this way of viewing the two elements—"water" and "the Spirit"—we avoid the unsatisfactory interpretation of the "water," as if our Lord had meant no more than 'Except a man be regenerated by the ordinance of baptism and by the Holy Ghost.' We call this unsatisfactory, because, as the ordinance of baptism was not instituted until Jesus was on the wing for glory, we think it harsh to suppose any direct allusion here to that institution. But neither is it to be reduced, with *Lampe,* &c., to a mere figure for *the truth.* It is undoubtedly the cleansing or purifying property of water which is referred to, in conformity with the familiar ideas of the Jewish ritual and the current language of the Old Testament. But since this was already taking form in an initiatory ordinance, in the ways just mentioned, it would be unreasonable to exclude all reference to baptism; although it would be nearer the truth, perhaps, to say that Baptism itself only embodies in a public ordinance the great general truth here announced—that a cleansing or purifying operation of the Spirit in every one is indispensable to entrance into the kingdom of God. 6. That which is born of the flesh is flesh; and that which is born of the Spirit is spirit. A most weighty general proposition. As *Olshausen* expresses it, 'That which is begotten partakes of the nature of that which begat it.' By "*flesh*" here is meant, not the mere material body, but all that comes into the world by birth—the entire man: yet since "flesh" is here opposed to "spirit," it plainly denotes in this place, not humanity merely, but humanity in its corrupted, depraved condition—humanity in entire subjection to the law of the fall, called in Rom. viii. "the law of sin and death." (See on Rom. viii. 1-9.) So that though a man *could* "enter a second time into his mother's womb, and be born," he would be no nearer this new birth than before. (See Job xiv. 4; Ps. li. 5.) Contrariwise, when it is said, "that which is born of the Spirit is spirit," the meaning is, that the fruit of that operation of the Holy Spirit upon the inner man, which had been pronounced indispensable, is the production of a spiritual nature, of the same moral qualities as His own. 7. Marvel not that I said unto thee, Ye must be born again. If a spiritual nature only can see and enter the kingdom of God, if all we bring into the world with us be the reverse of spiritual, and if this spirituality be solely of the Holy Ghost—no wonder a new birth is indispens-

8 ² again. The *e* wind bloweth where it listeth, and thou hearest the sound thereof, but canst not tell whence it cometh, and whither it goeth: so is every one that is born of the Spirit.

9   Nicodemus answered and said unto him, How *f* can these things be?

10   Jesus answered and said unto him, Art thou a master of Israel, and

11 knowest not these things? Verily, verily, I say unto thee, We speak that we do know, and testify that we have seen: and ye receive not our

12 witness. If I have told you earthly things, and ye believe not, how shall

13 ye believe, if I tell you *of* heavenly things? And *g* no man hath ascended up to heaven, but he that came down from heaven, *even* the Son of man

14 which is in heaven. And *h* as Moses lifted up the serpent in the wilder-

Right margin:

A. D. 30.

² Or, from above.
e Eccl. 11. 5.
1 Cor. 2. 11.
f ch. 6. 52.
g Pro. 30. 4.
ch. 6. 33.
ch. 16. 28.
Acts 2. 34.
1 Cor. 15. 47.
Eph. 4. 9.
h Num. 21. 9.
ch. 8. 28.

---

able. *Bengel*, with his usual acuteness, notices that our Lord here says, not 'we,' but '*ye* must be born again.' And surely after those universal propositions, about what "*a man*" must be, to "enter the kingdom of God," this is remarkable; showing clearly that our Lord meant to hold Himself forth as "*separate from sinners.*" **8. The wind bloweth where it listeth, and thou hearest the sound thereof, but canst not tell whence it cometh, and whither it goeth: so is every one that is born of the Spirit.** The word for wind here is not that usually so rendered [ἄνεμος], which means a gale; but that which signifies the 'breath' of life [πνεῦμα = רוּחַ, *anima*], or the gentle *zephyr*. Hence it is that in the Old Testament, "breath" and "spirit" are constantly interchanged, as analogous (see Job xxvii. 3; xxxiii. 4; Ezek. xxxvii. 9-14). The laws which govern the motion of the *winds* have, indeed, been partially discovered; but the risings, fallings, and change in direction many times in a day, of those *gentle breezes* here referred to, will probably ever be a mystery to us: So of the operation of the Holy Ghost in the new birth.

9. Nicodemus answered and said unto him, How can these things be? Though the subject, says *Luthardt*, still confounds him, the necessity and possibility of the new birth is no longer the point with him, but the nature of it and how it is brought about. From this moment, to use the words of *Stier*, Nicodemus *says nothing more*, but has sunk into a disciple who has found his true teacher. *Therefore* the Saviour now graciously advances in His communications of truth, and once more solemnly brings to the mind of this teacher in Israel, now become a learner, his own not guiltless *ignorance*, that He may then proceed to utter, out of the fulness of His divine knowledge, such further testimonies, both of earthly and heavenly things, as his docile scholar may to his own profit receive. **10. Jesus answered and said unto him, Art thou a master [Σὺ εἶ ὁ διδάσκαλος]**—rather, 'Art thou the teacher.' Perhaps this means only, 'Dost thou occupy the important post of the teacher,' or doctor of the law; not, as some good critics understand it, 'Art thou the well-known,' or 'distinguished teacher,' **of Israel, and knowest not these things?** The question clearly implies that the doctrine of Regeneration was so far disclosed in the Old Testament as to render Nicodemus's ignorance of it culpable. Nor is it merely as something that should be experienced *under the Gospel* that the Old Testament holds it forth—as many distinguished critics allege, denying that there was any such thing as regeneration before Christ. For our Lord's proposition is universal, that no fallen man is or can be spiritual without a regenerating operation of the Holy Ghost; and surely the necessity of a *spiritual obedience*, under whatever name, in opposition to mere mechanical services, which is

proclaimed throughout all the Old Testament, amounts to a proclamation of the necessity of regeneration. **11. Verily, verily, I say unto thee, We speak that we do know, and testify that we have seen**—that is, by *absolute* knowledge and *immediate* vision of God, which "the Only begotten Son in the bosom of the Father" claims as exclusively His own (ch. i. 18). **and ye receive not our witness**—referring to the *class* to which Nicodemus belonged, but from which he was now beginning to be separated. Though our Lord says, "*we* speak" and "*our* testimony," Himself only is intended—probably in emphatic contrast with the opening words of Nicodemus, "Rabbi, *we know*," &c. **12. If I have told you earthly things, [τὰ ἐπίγεια], and ye believe not, how shall ye believe, if I tell you of heavenly things? [τὰ ἐπουράνια]**—rather simply, 'tell you heavenly things.' By the "earthly things" which Christ had just told Nicodemus of is certainly meant *Regeneration*, the one subject of His teaching to him up to this point; and it is so called, it would seem—in contrast with the "heavenly things"—as being a truth even of that more *earthly* economy to which Nicodemus belonged, and as the gate of entrance to the kingdom of God upon *earth*. The "heavenly things" are the things of the new and more heavenly evangelical economy, especially that great truth of salvation by faith in the atoning death of the Son of God, which He was now about to "tell" Nicodemus; though He forewarns him of the probability of people stumbling much more at that than he had done at the former truth—since it had been but dimly unfolded under the *earthly* economy, and was only to be fully understood after the effusion of the Spirit from *heaven* through the exalted Saviour. **13. And no man hath ascended up to heaven, but he that came down from heaven, even the Son of man which is in heaven.** How paradoxical this sounds: 'No one has gone up but He that came down, even He who is at once both up and down.' Doubtless it was intended to startle and constrain his auditor to think that there must be mysterious elements in His Person. The old Socinians, to subvert the doctrine of the pre-existence of Christ, seized upon this passage as teaching that the man Jesus was secretly caught up to heaven to receive his instructions, and then "came down from heaven" to deliver them. But the sense manifestly is this: 'The perfect knowledge of God is not obtained by any man's going up from earth to heaven to receive it—no man hath so ascended; but He whose *proper habitation*, in His essential and eternal nature, is heaven, hath, by taking human flesh, descended as "the Son of Man" to disclose the Father, whom He knows by immediate gaze alike in the flesh as before He assumed it, being essentially and unchangeably " in the bosom of the Father," (ch. i. 18.) Now comes He to tell him the heavenly things. **14. And as**

15 ness, even so must the Son of man be lifted up; that whosoever believeth
16 in him should not perish, but have eternal life. For *i*God so loved the
world, that he gave his only begotten Son, that whosoever believeth in
17 him should not perish, but have everlasting life. For *j*God sent not his
Son into the world to condemn the world; but that the world through
18 him might be saved. He that believeth on him *k*is not condemned: but
he that believeth not is condemned already, because he hath not believed
19 in the name of the only begotten Son of God. And this is the condemna-

A. D. 30.

i Luke 2. 14.
Rom. 5. 8.
Titus 3. 4.
1 John 4. 9.
j Luke 9. 56.
1 John 4.14.
Rom. 5 1.
k Rom. 8. 1.
1 John 5.12.

Moses lifted up the serpent in the wilderness (see Num. xxi. 4-9), **even so must the Son of man be lifted up; 15. That whosoever believeth in him should not perish, but have eternal life.** Since this most heavenly thing, for the reason just mentioned, might be apt to stumble, Jesus holds it forth under a somewhat veiled form, but with sublime precision—calling His death His 'up-lifting' (compare viii. 28; xii. 32, 33); and by comparing it to the up-lifting of the brazen serpent, He still further veiled it. And yet to *us*, who know what it all means, it is, by being cast in this form, unspeakably more lively and pregnant with instruction. But what instruction? Let us see. The venom of the fiery serpents, shooting through the veins of the rebellious Israelites, was spreading death through the camp—lively emblem of the perishing condition of men by reason of sin. In both cases the remedy was divinely provided. In both the way of cure strikingly resembled that of the disease. Stung by serpents, by a serpent they are healed. By "fiery serpents" bitten—serpents, probably, with skin spotted fiery-red—the instrument of cure is a serpent.of brass or copper, having at a distance *the same appearance.* So in redemption, as by man came death, by Man also comes life—Man too, "*in the likeness of sinful flesh*," differing in nothing *outward and apparent* from those who, pervaded by the poison of the serpent, were ready to perish. But as the uplifted serpent had none of the venom of which the serpent-bitten people were dying, so while the whole human family were perishing of the deadly wound inflicted on it by the old serpent, "the Second Man," who arose over humanity with healing in His wings, was without spot or wrinkle or any such thing. In both cases the remedy is *conspicuously displayed:* in the one case on a pole; in the other on the cross, to "draw all men unto Him" (ch. xii. 32). In both cases it is by *directing the eye to the uplifted Remedy* that the cure is effected: in the one case it was the bodily eye, in the other it is the gaze of the soul by "believing in Him," as in that glorious ancient proclamation—"*Look* unto me, and be ye saved, all the ends of the earth," &c. (Is. xlv. 22.) Both methods are stumbling to human reason. What, to any thinking Israelite, could seem more unlikely than that a deadly poison should be dried up in his body by simply looking on a reptile of brass? Such a stumbling-block to the Jews and to the Greeks foolishness was faith in the crucified Nazarene, as a way of deliverance from eternal perdition. Yet was the warrant in both cases to expect a cure equally rational and well-grounded. As the serpent was *God's ordinance* for the cure of every bitten Israelite, so is Christ for the salvation of every perishing sinner; the one however a purely *arbitrary* ordinance, the other divinely *adapted* to man's complicated maladies. In both cases the efficacy is the same. As one simple look at the serpent, however distant and however weak, brought an instantaneous cure; even so, real faith in the Lord Jesus, however tremulous, however distant—be it but *real* faith—brings certain and

instant healing to the perishing soul. In a word, the consequences of disobedience are the same in both. Doubtless many bitten Israelites, galling as their case was, would *reason* rather than *obey*, would *speculate* on the absurdity of expecting the bite of a living serpent to be cured by looking at a piece of dead metal in the shape of one—speculate thus *till they died.* Alas! is not salvation by a crucified Redeemer subjected to like treatment? Has "the offence of the Cross" yet ceased? (compare 2 Ki. v. 12.) 16. **For God so loved the world, that he gave his only begotten Son, that whosoever believeth in him should not perish, but have everlasting life.** Who shall speak or write worthily of such a verse? What proclamation of the Gospel has been so oft on the lips of missionaries and preachers in every age since it was first uttered—what has sent such thrilling sensations through millions of mankind—what has been honoured to bring such multitudes to the feet of Christ—what to kindle in the cold and selfish breasts of mortals the fires of self-sacrificing love to mankind, as these words of transparent simplicity yet overpowering majesty have done? The picture embraces several distinct compartments. First, we have the object of regard, "THE WORLD" [τὸν κόσμον]—in its widest sense, ready to "*perish:*" Next, "THE LOVE OF GOD" to that perishing world —measured by, and only measurable and conceivable by, the gift which it drew forth from Him —He *so* loved the world that He gave," &c.: Then, THE GIFT itself, He so loved the world, that He gave His Only begotten Son; or, in the language of the apostle, He "*spared not* His own Son" (Rom. viii. 32): Further, THE FRUIT of this stupendous gift—negatively, in deliverance from impending perdition, that they "might not perish;" and positively, in the bestowal of "everlasting life:" and finally, THE MODE in which all takes effect—simply by "believing on the Son of God." How would Nicodemus's narrow Judaism become invisible in the blaze of this Sun of righteousness seen rising on "the world" with healing in His wings! 17. **For God sent not his Son into the world to condemn the world; but that the world through him might be saved.** A statement of vast importance. Though "condemnation" is to many the *issue* of Christ's mission (*v.* 19), it is not the *object* of His mission, which is purely a *saving* one. 18. **He that believeth on him is not condemned** [οὐ κρίνεται]—lit., 'is not being judged,' or 'is not coming into judgment.' The meaning is, as the apostle expresses it, that "there is now no condemnation to them which are in Christ Jesus" (Rom. viii. 1). Compare ch. v. 24, "He that heareth my word, and believeth on Him that sent me hath everlasting life, and shall not come into condemnation, but is (or hath) passed from death unto life." **but he that believeth not is condemned already, because he hath not believed in the name of the only begotten Son of God.** Rejecting the one way of deliverance from that condemnation which God gave His Son to *remove*, they thus wilfully *remain* condemned. 19. **And this is the condemnation**—emphatically so;

tion, *l* that light is come into the world, and men loved darkness rather | A. D. 30.
20 than light, because their deeds were evil.   For every one that doeth evil | *l* Isa. 5. 20.
hateth the light, neither cometh to the light, lest his deeds should be | ch. 1. 4.

revealing the condemnation already existing, and *sealing up* under it those who will not be delivered from it. that light [τὸ φῶς]—rather, 'the light' is come into the world—in the Person of Him to whom Nicodemus was listening. and men loved ['the'] darkness [τὸ σκότος] rather than ['the'] light, because their deeds were evil. [On the aorist —ἠγάπησαν—here, see on ch. x. 4.] The deliberate rejection of Himself was doubtless that to which Jesus here referred, as that which would fearfully reveal men's preference for the darkness. 20. For every one that doeth evil hateth the light, neither cometh to the light, lest his deeds should be reproved—by being brought out to the light. 21. But he that doeth ['the'] truth [τὴν ἀλήθειαν]—whose one object in life is to be, and to do what will bear the light, cometh to the light, that his deeds may be made manifest, that they are wrought in God—that all he is and does, being thus thoroughly tested, may be seen to have nothing in it but what is divinely wrought and divinely approved. This is the "Israelite indeed, in whom is no guile."

Remarks.—1. What an air of *naturalness* is there in the first part of this Section, regarding the "many" who believed in Jesus' name when they saw the miracles which He did at His first official visit to Jerusalem, and during the paschal feast. One might have expected that all with whom He came in contact would be divided simply into two classes—those who recognized and those who repudiated His claims; or, if another class should emerge, it would be of the undecided, or the waverers—either unable to make up their minds, or oscillating between the two opposing views of His claims. But here we have a fourth class, or the first class separated into two divisions—the cordial and thorough accessions to Him and the shallow and fickle believers; and of these latter it seems there were "many" who came over on this occasion. Another thing which strikes one—as betokening the absence of everything *artificial* in the drawing up of this narrative—is, that "the miracles" which He did during the feast are not recorded at all; although they were such that not only *they* were won over by them, but the class of which Nicodemus was the most hopeful specimen were convinced by them of our Lord's divine commission. No wonder that unprejudiced readers, even of the highest class, as they bend over these wonderful Records, *feel* them to be true without, perhaps, one conscious reflection on the question, whether they are so or not—guided by that experience and sound judgment which, with the force of an instinct, tells them that *such* a Tale cannot deceive. But 2. If this may be said of the first part of this Section, what shalt be said of the sequel of it—the night interview of Nicodemus with Jesus—a historical picture which, for graphic vividness, interest, and power, surpasses almost everything even in the Gospel History? Two figures only appear on the canvas; but to us it seems that there must have been one other in the scene, whose young and meditative eye scanned, by the night-lamp, the Jewish ruler and Him he had come to talk with, and whose ear drank in every word that fell from both. Our Evangelist himself—was not he there? What pen but that of an eye-and-ear witness could have reported to us a scene whose minute details and life-like touches rivet, and have riveted from the beginning, the very children that read it, never again

to forget it, while the depths and heights of its teaching keep the most mature ever bending over it, and its grandeur, undiminished by time, will stand out to arrest and astonish, to delight and feed the Church so long as a Bible shall be needed by it here below? If this Gospel was written when it probably was, some *sixty* or more years must have elapsed between the occurrence itself and this Record of it for the ages to come. And yet how fresh, how life-like, how new and warm it all is—as if our Evangelist had taken down every word of it that very night, immediately on the departure of Nicodemus. We think we see this anxious ruler—not unaware of his own importance, and the possible consequences of this step to one in his position, yet unable any longer to rest in doubt—stealing along, approaching the humble dwelling where lodged the Lord of glory, and, as he enters, surveying the countenance of this mysterious Person, who courteously receives him and asks him to seat himself. It is Nicodemus who first breaks that silence which was only to be resumed as the last words of the most wonderful announcements ever yet made to any human being fell from the lips of the Son of God, and he who came a trembling enquirer, departed a humble, though secret, disciple. If no other fruit had come of that first visit to Jerusalem, would it not, even by angel-eyes, have been regarded as enough? For, as was said of the precious ointment which Mary purchased to anoint her Lord withal at the supper in Bethany, but in which the Lord Himself saw another and yet dearer purpose—"She is come aforehand to anoint My body to the burying"—so may we say of this Nicodemus, that he was gained, and kept in reserve all the time of Christ's public ministry even till His death, in order that, having purchased an hundred pound weight of myrrh and aloes wherewith to anoint the body, he and Joseph of Arimathea, another secret disciple, might be the honoured instruments of wrapping and laying it in the virgin-sepulchre. Nay, but even if this service had not been rendered by Nicodemus to his dead Lord, that such an 'interview should have taken place between them *in order to its being reproduced here for all time*, was itself alone sufficient fruit of this first visit to Jerusalem; and doubtless the Lord, as He sees of *this* travail of His soul, is satisfied. 3. Nothing is more remarkable in this scene than the varied lights in which the Lord Jesus is exhibited in it. Observe, first of all, how entirely this "Man, Christ Jesus," isolates Himself from all other men, as not within the category of that humanity whose regeneration He pronounces indispensable to entrance into the kingdom of God:—"Except one [τις] be born again." And after giving a reason for this, arising from that kind of human nature which is propagated from parent to child in every descendant of Adam, He adds, "Marvel not that I said unto thee, *Ye* must [Δεῖ ὑμᾶς] be born again." Nor can it be alleged that this is a strain upon the words, which need not be pressed so far as to exclude Himself. For in almost every succeeding verse He continues to speak of Himself as if, though truly man, His connection with humanity were something voluntarily assumed—something superinduced upon His own proper being—that by thus coming into our world He might discharge a great mission of love to the world from His Father in heaven: "We speak that we do *know,*

365

21 ³reproved. But he that doeth truth cometh to the light, that his deeds may be made manifest, that they are wrought in God.

A. D. 30.

³ discovered.

and testify that we have *seen:* No man hath ascended up to heaven but He that *came down from heaven,* even the Son of Man which *is in heaven:* God *sent* His Only begotten Son." Putting all these statements together, how evident is it that our Lord does mean to isolate Himself as Man from that universal humanity which cannot without regeneration enter into the kingdom of God. And, in connection with this, it may be stated that He never once mixes Himself up with other individual men by the use of such pronouns as "we," and "us," and "our"—save where no false inference could possibly be drawn—but always says, "I" and "they," "I" and "you," "Me" and "them," "My" and "your:"—remarkable and most pregnant fact. But next, observe the lofty style into which He rises when speaking of Himself. He could suggest no measure by which to gauge the love of God to a perishing world save the gift of Himself for it: "God *so* loved the world that He *gave* His Only begotten Son." What creature, not lost to all sense of his proper place, would have dared to use such language as this? Then, notice how warily—if we may so express it—our Lord uses the two names by which Himself is designated, "The Son of Man" and "The Son of God." When He would speak of His *uplifting from beneath,* He uses the former—"Even so must the Son of Man be lifted up:" When He would speak of His *descending from above,* as the Father's gift to the world, He uses the latter—"God gave His Only begotten Son." And yet, as if to show that it is One glorious Person who is both these, He uses the one of these—and the lower one too—to express both His higher and His lower natures and His actings in both: "No one [οὐδεὶς] hath *ascended* up to heaven but He that *descended* from heaven, even the Son of man who *is in heaven.*" This was much observed and dwelt on by the Greek Fathers, who called it 'the communication' or 'interchange of properties' [κοινωνία ἰδιωμάτων], in virtue of the Oneness of the Person [διὰ τὴν τῆς ὑποστάσεως ταυτότητα]. But once more, with all this lofty bearing, when speaking of Himself, with what meekness, with what patience, with what spiritual skill, does He deal with this soul, in whom *candour* and *caution* seem to struggle for the mastery—a jealousy, on the one hand, for his own position, and an anxiety, on the other, to get to the bottom of Christ's claims! 4. What a directory for the preachers of the Gospel, and for all who would save souls, have we here! The two great truths, of *Regeneration by the Holy Ghost* and *Reconciliation by the death of Christ,* are here held forth as *the two-fold need* of every sinner who would be saved. Over the portals of the kingdom of God may be seen two inscriptions, as in great letters of fire,—

NO REGENERATION—NO ENTRANCE HERE:
WITHOUT THE SHEDDING OF BLOOD—
NO REMISSION.

Or, to turn it out of the negative into the positive form,—

THE PURE IN HEART SEE GOD:
BELIEVE IN THE LORD JESUS CHRIST AND
BE SAVED.

As the one of these gives us the *capacity* for the kingdom, so the other gives us the *right* to it. The one rectifies our *nature;* the other adjusts our *relation* to God. Without the one *we* cannot see *Him;* without the other *He* will not see *us.* As upon these two pivots saved souls must ever turn, so on these must turn all preaching and teaching that

would be divinely owned. 5. Is it true that the quickening operations of the Holy Ghost are like the gentle breath of heaven—unseen but not unfelt—with laws of movement divinely ordained, yet to us inscrutable; or if to some small extent so to be traced that our expectations may be stimulated, yet as little to be laid down by us as the laws of heaven's breath? Then let the Church at large, let every section of it, and every Christian, beware of *tying down* the Spirit of God to their own notions of the *way* in which, the *measure* in which, the *time* in which, and the *agencies* by which He shall work. There has been far too much of this in all past time, and even until now; and how much the Spirit of the Lord has been thus hindered and restrained, grieved and quenched, who shall tell? He is a "FREE Spirit," but as Himself Divine, is saying, "I will work, and who shall let it?" The one test of His presence is His *effects.* "Every good gift and every perfect is from above." "Do men gather grapes of thorns or figs of thistles?" Since nothing can be done effectually without the Spirit, and Christ Himself without the Spirit is no Saviour at all to *us* (John xvi. 8-15; Rom. viii. 9), our business is to be lying in wait for His blessed breathings, *expecting* them from above (Luke xi. 13), and prepared both to welcome and use them, to hail them wheresoever and in whomsoever we find them, and to put ourselves alongside of those operations of His, giving them our countenance and lending them our agency for carrying them out to their proper ends—just as sailors in a calm watch for the moment when a breeze shall spring up, which they know well may be when they least expect it, and hoist and adjust their sails to it with a speed and a skill at which others wonder, so as to let none of it be lost. 6. Definite, sharp, authoritative, spiritual teaching of divine truth is what alone we may expect will be divinely blessed. It was our Lord's transparent perception of the difference between truth and error, and of what Nicodemus needed, as the *right beginning* of a religious character, that prompted His peculiar manner of dealing with him. But the weighty brevity, the sharpness of those lines of distinction between "perdition" and "salvation," the high authority with which He bore in these great truths upon this enquirer, mingled with such gentle and winning spirituality—it is this that is so remarkable and so pregnant with wisdom for all that would follow Him in dealing with souls. Nor is He in these inimitable. The authority with which *He* uttered these great truths is indeed His own; and of this God says from the excellent glory, "Hear Him." But when *we* utter them, we do it with *His* authority, and have a right to use it, as did the apostolic preachers. Nay, this is our strength. The apologetical tone, or the reasoning tone—if it be the main characteristic of our preaching—will leave no divine impress, no stamp of heaven, upon it. Weak in itself, its effects will be weak too. And do not the facts of the pulpit attest this? "My speech and my preaching was not with enticing words of man's wisdom, but in demonstration of the Spirit and of power; that your faith should not stand in the wisdom of men, but in the power of God."

22-36.—JESUS WITHDRAWS FROM THE CITY TO THE RURAL PARTS OF JUDEA, AND BAPTIZES—THE BAPTIST ALSO, STILL AT LARGE, CONTINUES HIS WORK, AND BEARS HIS LAST AND NOBLEST TESTIMONY TO HIS MASTER.

22. **After these things came Jesus and his**

22   After these things came Jesus and his disciples into the land of Judea;
23 and there he tarried with them, ^mand baptized. And John also was
baptizing in Ænon near to ⁿSalim, because there was much water there:
24 and they came, and were baptized. For ^oJohn was not yet cast into
prison.
25   Then there arose a question between *some* of John's disciples and the
26 Jews about purifying. And they came unto John, and said unto him,
Rabbi, he that was with thee beyond Jordan, ^pto whom thou barest
witness, behold, the same baptizeth, and all *men* come to him.
27   John answered and said, ^qA man can ⁴receive nothing, except it be
28 given him from heaven. Ye yourselves bear me witness, that I said, I
29 am not the Christ, but ^rthat I am sent before him. He ^sthat hath
the bride is the bridegroom: but ^tthe friend of the bridegroom, which
standeth and heareth him, rejoiceth greatly because of the bridegroom's
30 voice. This my joy therefore is fulfilled. He ^umust increase, but ^vI
31 *must* decrease. He ^wthat cometh from above ^xis above all: ^yhe that is
of the earth is earthly, and speaketh of the earth: ^zhe that cometh from

A. D. 30.

^m ch. 4. 2.
ⁿ Gen. 14. 18.
  Gen. 33. 18.
  1 Sam. 9. 4.
^o Matt. 14. 3.
  Luke 3. 19,
  20.
^p ch 1. 34.
^q Heb. 5. 4.
⁴ Or, take
  unto him-
  self.
^r Mal. 3. 1.
^s Matt. 22. 2.
^t Song 5. 1.
^u Isa 9. 7.
^v Phil 3. 8, 9.
^w ch. 8. 23.
^x Matt. 28. 18.
^y 1 Cor. 15. 47.
^z ch. 6. 33.

---

disciples into the land of Judea [εἰς τὴν Ἰουδαίαν γῆν]—not the *province* of Judea, as distinguished from Galilee and Samaria, for the foregoing conversation was held in its capital. But the meaning is, that leaving the city He withdrew to the rural districts, and, it would appear, to some part of the valley-district of the Jordan northward. **and there he tarried with them, and baptized** [ἐβάπτιζεν] or, as we should say, 'kept baptizing;' but only in the sense explained in ch. iv. 2. **23. And** [δὲ]—rather, 'Now,' or 'But,' **John also was baptizing in Ænon** [=יְנ, יְנ]—'an eye,' 'a fountain,' which accords with the Evangelist's explanation at the end of this verse. **near to Salim.** The site of these places cannot now be certainly ascertained. But the scenes of the Master's and the servant's labours could not have been very far apart. **because there was much water there: and they came, and were baptized** [παρεγίνοντο καὶ ἐβαπτίζοντο]—or 'kept coming and getting baptized.' **24. For John was not yet cast into prison.** From the first three Evangelists one would naturally conclude that our Lord's public ministry only began after the Baptist's imprisonment. But here, about six months, probably, after our Lord had entered on His public ministry, we find the Baptist still at his work. How much longer this continued eannot be determined with certainty; but probably not very long. For the great importance of this little verse for the right harmonizing of the Gospels, and determining the probable duration of our Lord's ministry, see on Matt. iv. 12. **25. Then there arose a question between [some of] John's disciples and the Jews** [ἐκ τῶν μαθητῶν Ἰωάννου μετὰ Ἰουδαίων]—rather, 'on the part of John's disciples with the Jews.' But the true reading beyond doubt is, 'with a Jew' [Ἰουδαίου]. The received text has but inferior support. **about purifying**—that is, baptizing; the symbolical meaning of washing with water being put (as in ch. ii. 6) for the act itself. As John and Jesus were the only teachers who baptized *Jews*, discussions might easily arise between the Baptist's disciples and such Jews as declined to submit to that rite. **26. And they came unto John, and said unto him, Rabbi, he that was with thee beyond Jordan.** '*He* was with *thee*,' they say—not 'thou with him.' **to whom thou barest witness** [σὺ μεμαρτύρηκας]—rather, 'to whom thou hast borne witness;' that is, hast been doing it all this time; **behold, the same baptizeth, and all men come to him:**—*q. d.*, 'Master, this man tells us that he to

whom thou barest such generous witness beyond Jordan is requiting thy generosity by drawing all the people away to himself. At this rate, thou shalt soon have no disciples at all.' The reply to this is one of the noblest and most affecting utterances that ever came from the lips of man. **27. John answered and said, A man can receive nothing** [Οὐ δύναται ἄνθρωπος λαμβάνειν οὐδὲν]—rather, as in the *margin*, 'A man can take to himself,' or 'assume nothing;' that is, lawfully, and with any success, **except it be given**—or 'have been given' [ᾖ δεδομένον] him **from heaven:**—*q. d.*, 'Every divinely commissioned person has his own work and sphere assigned him from above.' Even Christ Himself came under this law. See on Heb. v. 4. **28. Ye yourselves bear me witness, that I said, I am not the Christ, but that I am sent before him. 29. He .that hath the bride is the bridegroom: but the friend of the bridegroom, which standeth and heareth him, rejoiceth greatly**—or 'with joy' [χαρᾷ χαίρει] **because of the bridegroom's voice. This my joy therefore is fulfilled. 30. He must increase, but I must decrease:**—*q. d.*, 'I do my heaven-prescribed work, and that is enough for me. Would you have me mount into my Master's place? Said I not unto you, I am not the Christ? The Bride is not mine, why should the people stay with me? Mine it is to point the burdened to the Lamb of God that taketh away the sin of the world, to tell them there is balm in Gilead, and a Physician there. And shall I grudge to see them, in obedience to the call, flying as a cloud, and as doves to their windows? Whose is the Bride but the Bridegroom's? Enough for me to be the Bridegroom's *Friend*, sent by Him to negotiate the match, privileged to bring together the Saviour and those he is come to seek and to save, and rejoicing with joy unspeakable, if I may but "stand and hear the Bridegroom's voice," witnessing the blessed espousals. Say ye, then, they go from me to Him? Ye bring me glad tidings of great joy. He must increase, but I must decrease; this, my joy, therefore, is fulfilled.' **31. He that cometh from above is above all: he that is of the earth is earthly.** As the words in this last clause are precisely the same, they had better have been so rendered:—'He that is of the earth is of the earth;' although the sense is correctly given by our translators, namely, that those sprung of the earth, even though divinely commissioned, bear the stamp of earth in their very work: but, **he that cometh from heaven is above all.** Here, then, is the reason why He must increase, while all human

367

32 heaven is above all. And ^awhat he hath seen and heard, that he testi-
33 fieth; and no man receiveth his testimony. He that hath received his
34 testimony hath ^bset to his seal that God is true. For ^che whom God
   hath sent speaketh the words of God: for God giveth not the Spirit ^dby
35 measure *unto him.* The ^eFather loveth the Son, and hath given all
36 things into his hand. He ^fthat believeth on the Son hath everlasting
   life: and he that believeth not the Son shall not see life; but ^gthe wrath
   of God abideth on him.

A. D. 30.
^a ch. 15. 15.
^b 2 Cor. 1. 22.
^c ch. 7. 16.
^d ch. 1. 16.
Col. 1. 19.
^e Dan. 7. 14.
^f Hab. 2. 4.
^g Gal. 3. 10.
Heb. 10. 29.

teachers must decrease. The Master "cometh from above"—descending from *His proper element,* the region of those "heavenly things" which He came to reveal—and so, although mingling with men and things on the earth, He is not "of the earth," either in Person or Word: The servants, on the contrary, springing of earth, are of the earth, and their testimony, even though divine in authority, partakes necessarily of their own earthiness. So strongly did the Baptist feel this contrast that the last clause just repeats the first. It is impossible for a sharper line of distinction to be drawn between Christ and all human teachers, even when divinely commissioned and speaking by the power of the Holy Ghost. And who does not perceive it? The words of prophets and apostles are undeniable and most precious truth; but in the words of Christ we hear a voice as from the excellent Glory, the Eternal Word making Himself heard in our own flesh. **32. And what he hath seen and heard, that he testifieth.** See on *v.* 11, and on ch. i. 18. **and no man receiveth his testimony.** John's disciples had said, "*All* come to Him" (*v.* 26), Would it were so, says the Baptist, but, alas! they are next to none. Nay, they were far readier to receive himself, insomuch that he was obliged to say, I am not the Christ; and this seems to have pained him. **33. He that hath received his testimony hath set to his seal that God is true**—gives glory to God whose words Christ speaks, not as prophets and apostles, by a partial communication of the Spirit to them. **34. For he whom God hath sent speaketh the words of God: for God giveth not the Spirit by measure [unto him].** Here, again, the sharpest conceivable line of distinction is drawn between Christ and all human inspired teachers: 'They have the Spirit in a *limited* degree; but God giveth not [to him] the Spirit *by measure.*' It means, as *Olshausen* says, the entire fulness of divine life and divine power. The present tense "*giveth*" [διδωσιν] very aptly points out the ever-renewed communication of the Spirit by the Father to the Son, so that a constant flow and re-flow of living power is to be understood (see ch. i. 51). **35. The Father loveth the Son** [ἀγαπᾶ, not φιλεῖ—*diligit,* not *amat*]. The word denotes the love of *character,* as distinguished from the mere love of *person.* But this shade of distinction cannot be expressed in the translation, nor in the present case ought they to be separated. **and hath given all things into his hand.** See on Matt. xi. 27, where we have the same *delivering over* of all things into the hand of the Son, while here, over and above that, we have the deep spring of that august act, in the Father's ineffable *love of the Son.* **36. He that believeth on the Son hath everlasting life**—already hath it. See on *v.* 18; and on ch. v. 24. **and—or rather, 'but' [δὲ] he that believeth not the Son shall not see life.** The contrast here is striking. The one has already a life that will endure for ever: the other not only has it not now, but shall never have it—never see it; **but the wrath of God abideth on him.** It was on Him before, and not being *removed* in the only possible way, by "believing on the Son," it necessarily *remaineth* on him.

Remarks.—1. Here again we have the marriage-relation of Jehovah to the Church—one of the leading Evangelical ideas of the Old Testament—which in Ps. xlv. is transferred to *Messiah,* and is here, **as** in the First Gospel, appropriated by Christ to Himself, who thereby serves Himself Heir to *all* that the Old Testament holds forth of Jehovah's gracious affections, purposes, and relations towards the Church. See on Matt. xxii. 2, and Remark 1 at the close of that Section. 2. What a beautiful and comprehensive idea of the office of the ministry is this, of "Friends of the Bridegroom"—instrumentally bringing the parties together; equally interested in both of them and in their blessed union; rejoicing as they listen to the Bridegroom's voice, with whom the whole originates, by whom all is effected, and from whom flows all the bliss of those united to Him! 3. No test of fidelity in the service of Christ can be more decisive than the spirit here displayed by the Baptist—absorption in his Master's interests, joy at the ingathering of souls to Him, and a willingness to decrease that He may increase, as stars before the rising sun. 4. The difference between Christ and all other, even inspired, teachers is carefully to be observed, and never lost sight of. By this the honour in which the early Church held the Gospels above every other portion of the inspired Scripture is fully justified; nor are the other portions of canonical Scripture thereby disparaged, but rather the contrary, being thus seen in their right place, as all either preparatory to or expository of THE GOSPEL, as the Four Evangelical Records were called — Christ Himself being the chief Corner-stone. 5. When Christ "speaketh the words of God," it is not simply as "The Word made flesh," but (according to the teaching of the Baptist in *v.* 34) as plenarily gifted with the Holy Ghost—that "oil of gladness with which God, even His God, anointed Him above His fellows." As this was prophetically announced in Isa. lxi. 1-3, so it was recognized by Christ Himself (Luke iv. 18). But to guard against the abuse of this truth, as if Christ differed from other teachers only in having the Spirit given Him in larger measure, we shall do well to observe how jealous the fathers of the Church found it necessary to be on this point, when, having to combat such abuses, they decreed in one of their councils, that if any one said that Christ 'spake or wrought miracles by the Spirit of God, as by *a power foreign to Himself,*' he was to be condemned. Thus then—as at His baptism and elsewhere, so here—we have the Father, the Son, and the Holy Ghost, all present, and each in His respective office in the work of redemption. 6. The Son of God is the great Administrator of the kingdom of grace. As this is part of the closing testimony of the Baptist to Him, so does the last book of the New Testament canon conclude with it—"Behold, I come quickly, and *My reward is with Me,* to give to every man according as his work is" (Rev. xxii. 12). But this is not held forth here merely as a great fact. It is to give meaning and weight to what follows (*v.* 36)— that the destinies of all that hear the Gospel, their

4 WHEN therefore the Lord knew how the Pharisees had heard that
2 Jesus made and baptized more disciples than John, (though Jesus himself
3 baptized not, but his disciples,) ^ahe left Judea, and departed again into
Galilee.

A. D. 30.

CHAP. 4.
^a ch. 10. 40.
Matt. 10. 23.
Mark 3. 7.

blissful or blighted eternity, hang upon their reception or rejection of the Son of God. 7. God's attitude towards the unbelieving is that of "wrath" [ὀργή], that is, righteous displeasure, whose judicial expression is called "vengeance" [ἐκδίκησις]. While it repays [ἀποδίδωσι] the unbelieving by excluding them from "seeing life," it does so still more awfully by leaving them under the weight of God's settled, abiding displeasure. And yet, with such teaching sounding in their ears, there are those who confidently teach that there never was, is not, nor can be anything *in God* against sinners, needing to be removed by Christ, but solely *in men* against God. Having formed to themselves certain notions of the *love* and *unchangeableness* of God, which they think incompatible with there being anything in Him against the sinner needing to be removed in order to his salvation, they make the Scripture to bend to these notions, instead of adjusting their own views to its indisputable teaching. This may be consistent enough in those who believe in no authoritative divine Revelation, and regard the Scripture, and Christianity itself, as only designed to quicken and develop the natural religiousness of the human heart. But none who profess to bow to the teaching of Scripture as authoritative and conclusive can, consistently with the concluding words of this chapter, deny that God's view and treatment of the sinner will be that of reconciliation, complacency, and admission to life everlasting, or of abiding wrath or judicial displeasure, and permanent exclusion from life, according as he believes or believes not on the Son; in other words, that we must be not only *internally* but *relatively* right with God, or that He must be gained to us as well as we to Him. That He is willing and waiting to be so is indeed most true, as His whole procedure in the matter of salvation shows; and that neither Christ's death nor our faith in it *make* Him so—as we be slanderously reported and as some affirm that we say—is equally true. But until the sinner meets Him at the Cross, and sets to his own seal to the reconciliation effected by it—until both the Offended and the offending parties embrace each other over the same Sacrifice that taketh away the sin of the world, that love of God which yearns towards the sinner cannot, and will not, reach him. See on Matt. v. 23-26, Remark 7 at the close of that Section. 8. The language of the last six verses of this chapter, regarding Christ, has been thought by not a few critics to go so far beyond the Baptist's point of view, that they cannot persuade themselves that he uttered it as it stands reported here; and they think that the Evangelist himself has, in the exercise of his apostolic illumination and authority, blended the Baptist's fainter and his own clearer views into one full-orbed testimony, as that of the Baptist himself—being his in sense if not in form. We have put this view of *Bengel, Wetstein, Lücke, Olshausen, de Wette, da Costa,* and *Tholuck,* as favourably as we could. But first, if this principle is to be admitted, we can have no confidence that even Christ's own discourses are correctly reported, save that they are too lofty to have been expressed as they are by any human pen; and though this may do very well to authenticate them in the general, there are some statements of our Lord of so peculiar a nature that we should not feel bound to abide by them *as*

they stand, if we could persuade ourselves that they were, *in the form* of them at least, due to the Evangelist himself. Thus is a principle of uncertainty in the testimony of the Gospels introduced, of which no one can see the end, or rather, the end of which has been too sadly seen in the criticism of *Schleiermacher* (on the Gospel of Luke, for example), and after him of *Strauss.* But again, this whole testimony of the Baptist—from *v.* 27—is so homogeneous, as *Meyer* well remarks, so uniform, consistent, and continuous, that one cannot see why the former portion of it should be thought to be strictly his, and the rest betray the Evangelist's own pen. But once more, we have seen already how glorious are the rays of Gospel truth—regarding the Person and the Work of Christ alike—which darted from the lips of His honoured herald (see on ch. i. 29; and on i. 49): and as from Luke xi. 1 it is clear that John's teaching to his disciples took a wider range than anything expressly reported in the Gospels, we have no reason for doubting that this testimony—explicitly related as his, and so entirely in harmony with all his recorded testimonies—was really his, merely because it widens out into something singularly clear and lofty; more especially when we consider that it must have been among the very last testimonies, if not altogether the last, which he was permitted to bear to his blessed Master before his imprisonment.

CHAP. IV. 1-42.—THE RISING JEALOUSY OF THE PHARISEES AT THE SUCCESS OF OUR LORD'S MINISTRY INDUCES HIM TO WITHDRAW FROM JUDEA TO GALILEE—ON THE WAY, HE MEETS WITH AND GAINS THE WOMAN OF SAMARIA, AND THROUGH HER, MANY OF THE SAMARITANS, WITH WHOM HE ABIDES TWO DAYS. (= Matt. iv. 12; Mark i. 14; Luke iv. 14.)

Jesus Leaves Judea for Galilee (1-3). **1. When therefore**—referring back to ch. iii. 22, from which the narrative is now resumed, **the Lord knew how the Pharisees had heard that Jesus made and baptized** [ποιεῖ καὶ βαπτίζει]—or 'was making and baptizing' **more disciples than John.** Word to this effect may have been brought to Him; but, perhaps, by styling Him here "the Lord"—which he does only once again before His resurrection—our Evangelist means that He "knew" it as "knowing all men" (ch. ii. 24, 25). **2. (Though** [Καίτοιγε]—or, 'And yet' **Jesus himself baptized not, but his disciples.)** John, being but a servant, baptized with his own hand: Jesus, as the Master, whose exclusive prerogative it was to baptize with the Holy Ghost, seems to have deemed it fitting that He should administer the outward symbol only through His disciples. Besides, had it been otherwise, undue eminence might have been supposed to attach to the Christ-baptized. **3. He left Judea** —that opposition to Him might not be too soon organized, which at that early stage would have marred His work; **and departed again into Galilee**—by which time John had been cast into prison. Here, then, our Evangelist takes up the thread of the three first Gospels: Matt. iv. 12; Mark i. 14; Luke iv. 14. The period during which our Lord continued in Judea, from the time of His first Passover, appears to have been at least eight months—it being, as we shall see from *v.* 35, now "four months to harvest," which, as usually reckoned, would be late in the month of December; but as this makes the harvest, it would seem, too

4, And he must needs go through Samaria. Then cometh he to a
5 city of Samaria, which is called Sychar, near to the parcel of ground
6 *b*that Jacob gave to his son Joseph. Now Jacob's well was there. Jesus
therefore, being wearied with *his* journey, sat thus on the well: *and* it
was about the sixth hour.
7 There cometh a woman of Samaria to draw water: Jesus saith unto
8 her, Give me to drink. (For his disciples were gone away unto the city
9 to buy meat.) Then saith the woman of Samaria unto him, How is it
that thou, being a Jew, askest drink of me, which am a woman of
Samaria? for *c*the Jews have no dealings with the Samaritans.
10 Jesus answered and said unto her, If thou knewest *d*the gift of God,
and who it is that saith to thee, Give me to drink; thou wouldest have

A. D. 30.
b Gen. 33. 19.
Gen. 48. 22
Jos 24. 32.
c 2 Ki. 17. 24.
Ezra 4. 3.
Neh. 4. 1,2.
Luke 9. 52.
Acts 1. 8.
Acts 10. 28.
d Isa 9. 6.
Isa. 42. 6.
Luke 11 13.
Rom. 8. 32.
1 Cor. 1. 30.
2 Cor. 9. 15.

early, perhaps our Lord did not leave till late in January.

Jesus at Jacob's Well Converses with and Gains the Woman of Samaria (4-26). **4. And** [δὲ]—or, 'Now' **he must needs go through Samaria**—for a geographical reason, no doubt; the nearest way from Judea to Galilee being through the intermediate province of Samaria: but certainly it was not without a higher design—He "needed" to meet with the woman at Jacob's well, and to reap the blessed fruit of that meeting. **5. Then cometh he to a city of Samaria, called Sychar**—the "Shechem" of the Old Testament, about thirty-four miles north of Jerusalem. From the Romans it got the name of "Neapolis," and is now called "Nablous." But see on *v.* 20. In "coming to" this town, however, He came only to its neighbourhood, remaining in the first instance, at Jacob's well, **near to the parcel of ground that Jacob gave to his son Joseph**. This fact, though not expressly stated in the Old Testament, was *inferred* by the Jews from Gen. xxxiii. 19; xlviii. 22 (according to the LXX. translation); Jos. xxiv. 32. **6. Now Jacob's well was there.** 'We enquired of the Samaritans,' says *Dr. Robinson*, 'respecting Jacob's well. They said they acknowledged the tradition, and regarded it as having belonged to the patriarch. It lies at the mouth of the valley (the narrow valley of Nablous) near the south-side. Late as it was, we took a guide and set off for Jacob's well. We were thirty-five minutes in coming to it from the city. The well bears evident marks of antiquity, but was now dry and deserted; it was said usually to contain living water, and not merely to be filled by the rains. A large stone was laid loosely over, or rather in its mouth, and as the hour was now late, we made no attempt to remove the stone and examine the vaulted entrance below. We had also no line with us at the moment, to measure the well; but by dropping in stones, we could perceive that it was *deep* (v. 11). *Maundrell*, who measured the well, found it dug in a firm rock, about three yards in diameter, and thirty-five in depth; five yards being full of water. In 1839, it was found to be only seventy-five feet deep below the vault by which it is covered, with only ten or twelve feet of water; while in 1843, the bottom was found scarcely covered with water.' Various difficulties in the way of this tradition and the identity of the well are satisfactorily disposed of by Dr. Robinson. **Jesus therefore, being wearied with his journey, sat thus** [οὕτως] **on the well** [ἐπὶ τῇ πηγῇ]—rather, 'by the well'—that is, just as one would do in such circumstances, loungingly or at ease; an instance of the graphic style of our Evangelist. In fact, this is perhaps the most *human* of all the scenes of our Lord's earthly history. We seem to be beside Him, overhearing all that is here recorded; nor could any painting of the scene on canvas, however perfect, do other than lower the conception which this exquisite narrative conveys to the devout and intelligent reader. But with all that is *human*, how much also of the *divine* have we here, both blended in one glorious manifestation of the majesty, grace, pity, patience with which "the Lord" imparts light and life to this unlikeliest of strangers, standing midway between Jews and heathens. [and] **it was about the sixth hour**—or *noon-day;* reckoning from six o'clock A.M. From Cant i. 7, we know, as from other sources, that the very flocks "rested at noon." But Jesus, whose maxim was, "I must work the works of Him that sent me while it is day" (ch. ix. 4), seems to have denied Himself that repose, at least on this occasion, probably that He might reach this well when He knew the woman would be there. Once there, however, He accepts the grateful ease of a seat on the patriarchal stone. But, while Himself is resting, what music is that which I hear from His lips, "Come unto Me all ye that labour and are heavy laden, and I will give you *rest?*" (Matt xi. 28). **7. There cometh a woman of Samaria to draw water: Jesus saith unto her, Give me to drink.** For the heat of a noon-day sun had parched His lips. But, while Himself thirsting, "In the last, that great day of the feast, Jesus stood and cried, saying, If any man thirst, let him come unto me and *drink*" (ch. vii. 37). **8. (For his disciples were gone away unto the city to buy meat)** [τροφὰς] —'victuals,' or 'provisions.' This was wisely ordered, that Jesus might be alone with the woman; nor did the disciples return till the dialogue was concluded, and our Lord's object in it entirely gained. **9. Then saith the woman of Samaria unto him, How is it that thou, being a Jew, askest drink of me, which am a woman of Samaria?**—not altogether refusing, yet wondering at so unusual a request from a Jew, as His dress and dialect would at once discover Him to be, to a Samaritan. **for the Jews have no dealings with the Samaritans**—or better without the article, as in the original, 'Jews have no dealings with Samaritans.' Not absolutely none, for the disciples at this very time had gone to buy of the Sycharites, and brought their purchase with them. But the reference is to *friendly* dealings, such as exchange of hospitalities and acts of kindness. It is this national antipathy that gives point to the parable of The Good Samaritan (Luke x. 30, &c.), and to the thankfulness of the Samaritan leper, when he found himself cured by the Lord Jesus (Luke xvii. 16, 18). *Robinson* says the Samaritans 'still maintain their ancient hatred against the Jews, and neither eat, nor drink, nor marry, nor associate with the Jews; but only trade with them.'

10. Jesus answered and said unto her, If thou knewest the gift of God, and who it is that saith

11 asked of him, and he would have given thee *c*living water. The woman saith unto him, Sir, thou hast nothing to draw with, and the well is

12 deep: from whence then hast thou that living water? Art thou greater than our father Jacob, which gave us the well, and drank thereof himself, and his children, and his cattle?

13   Jesus answered and said unto her, Whosoever drinketh of this water

14 shall thirst again: but whosoever drinketh of the water that I shall give him shall never thirst; but the water that I shall give him *f*shall be in

15 him a well of water springing up into everlasting life. The *g*woman saith unto him, Sir, give me this water, that I thirst not, neither come hither to draw.

16,   Jesus saith unto her, Go, call thy husband, and come hither. The

17 woman answered and said, I have no husband.

18   Jesus said unto her, Thou hast well said, I have no husband: for thou hast had five husbands; and he whom thou now hast is not thy husband:

19 in that saidst thou truly. The woman saith unto him, Sir, *h*I perceive

20 that thou art a prophet. Our fathers worshipped in *i*this mountain; and ye say, that in *j*Jerusalem is the place where men ought to worship.

A. D. 30.

c Ex. 17. 6.
Isa. 12. 3.
Isa. 44. 3.
Jer. 2 13.
Zec. 13. 1.
Zec. 14. 8.
Rev. 7. 17.
f ch. 7. 38.
ch 10. 10.
Rom. 5. 21.
2 Cor. 1. 22.
g Rom. 6. 23.
1 John 5.20.
h Luke 7. 16.
Luke 24.19.
ch. 6. 14.
ch. 7. 40.
i Gen. 12. 6.
Jud. 9. 7.
j Deut 12. 5.
2 Chr. 7. 12.
Ps. 78. 68.

---

to thee, Give me to drink; thou wouldest have asked of him, and he would have given thee living water:—*q. d.*, 'In Me thou seest only a petitioner to thee; but if thou knewest Who that Petitioner is, and the gift that God is giving to men, thou wouldst have changed places with Him, gladly suing of Him living water—nor shouldst thou have sued in vain,' gently reflecting on her for not immediately meeting His request. **11. The woman saith unto him, Sir, thou hast nothing to draw with, and the well is deep: from whence then hast thou that living water?** This is the language of one who, though startled by what was said to her, saw that it must have some meaning, and sought by this question to get at the bottom of it. **12. Art thou greater**—already perceiving in this Stranger a claim to some mysterious greatness, **than our father Jacob, which gave us the well, and drank thereof himself, and his children, and his cattle?** For, says *Josephus* (Antt. ix. 14. 3), when it went well with the Jews the Samaritans claimed kindred with them, as being descended from Joseph, but when misfortunes befell the Jews they disowned all connection with them. **13. Jesus answered and said unto her, Whosoever** [Πᾶς ὁ]—rather, 'Every one that' **drinketh of this water shall thirst again: 14. But whosoever drinketh of the water that I shall give him shall never thirst; but the water that I shall give him shall be in him** [γενήσεται ἐν αὐτῷ]—rather, 'shall become in him' **a well of water springing up into everlasting life.** The contrast here is fundamental and all-comprehensive. "This water" plainly means 'this natural water and all satisfactions of a like earthly and perishable nature.' Coming to us from without, and reaching only the superficial parts of our nature, they are soon spent, and need to be anew supplied as much as if we had never experienced them before, while the deeper wants of our being are not reached by them at all; whereas the "water" that Christ gives—*spiritual life*—is struck out of the very depths of our being, making the soul not a *cistern*, for holding water *poured into* it *from without*, but a *fountain* —the word [πηγὴ] had been better so rendered, to distinguish it from the word rendered "well" in *v.* 11 [φρέαρ]—springing, gushing, bubbling up and flowing forth from *within* us, ever fresh, ever living. *The indwelling of the Holy Ghost as the Spirit of Christ* is the secret of this life, with all its enduring energies and satisfactions, as is expressly said (ch. vii. 37-39). ' "Never thirsting," then, just

means that such souls have the supplies *at home.* It is an internal well, "springing up into everlasting life"—by which words our Lord carries the thoughts up from the eternal freshness and vitality of these waters in *us* to the great ocean in which they have their confluence. 'Thither,' says devout *Bengel*, 'may I arrive!' **15. The woman saith unto him, Sir, give me this water, that I thirst not, neither come hither to draw.** This is not obtuseness, for that is giving way: it expresses a wondering desire after she scarce knew what from this mysterious Stranger.

16. Jesus saith unto her, Go call thy husband, and come hither—now proceeding to arouse her slumbering conscience by laying bare the guilty life she was leading, and, by the minute details which that life furnished, not only bringing her sin vividly up before her, but preparing her to receive in His true character that wonderful Stranger to whom her whole life, in its minutest particulars, evidently lay open. **17. The woman answered and said, I have no husband. Jesus said unto her, Thou hast well said, I have no husband: 18. For thou hast had five husbands; and he whom thou now hast is not thy husband: in that saidst thou truly. 19. The woman saith unto him, Sir, I perceive that thou art a prophet. 20. Our fathers worshipped in this mountain**—that is, mount *Gerizim* (Deut. xi. 29; xxvii. 12; Jos. viii. 33; Jud. ix. 7). In the Samaritan Pentateuch, instead of "*Ebal*" (Deut. xxvii. 4)—on which Moses commanded the altar to be erected, with the ten commandments written upon the stones of it (see Deut. xxvii. 1-8)—the word "*Gerizim*" stands; and the Samaritans are tenacious of this reading as their warrant for holding Gerizim to be the divinely-ordained place of public worship, on which they have acted from age to age, and do even to this day. 'There is,' says *Stanley*, 'probably no other locality in which the same worship has been sustained with so little change or interruption for so great a series of years as that of this mountain, from Abraham to the present day. In their humble synagogue, at the foot of the mountain, the Samaritans still worship—the oldest and the smallest sect in the world.' *Robinson* found their whole number scarcely to exceed a hundred and fifty souls. 'Mounts Gerizim and Ebal,' says this last distinguished traveller, 'rise in steep rocky precipices from the valley on each side, apparently some eight hundred feet in height. The sides of both these mountains,

371

21   Jesus saith unto her, Woman, believe me, the hour cometh, [k]when ye
shall neither in this mountain, nor yet at Jerusalem, worship the Father.
22 Ye worship [l]ye know not what: we know what we worship: for [m]salva-
23 tion is of the Jews. But the hour cometh, and now is, when the true
worshippers shall worship the Father in [n]spirit [o]and in truth: for the
24 Father seeketh such to worship him. God [p]*is* a Spirit: and they that
25 worship him must worship *him* in spirit and in truth. The woman saith
unto him, I know that [q]Messias cometh, which is called Christ: when he
26 is come, he will tell us all things. Jesus saith unto her, I that speak
unto thee am *he.*

A. D. 30.

[k] Mal. 1. 11.
Matt. 18. 20.
1 Tim. 2. 8.
[l] 2 Ki. 17. 29.
[m] Isa. 2. 3.
Luke 24. 47.
Rom. 9. 4, 5.
[n] Phil. 3. 3.
[o] ch. 1. 17.
[p] 2 Cor. 3. 17.
[q] Deut. 18. 15.
Dan. 9. 24.

as here seen, were to our eyes equally naked and sterile.' and ye say, that in Jerusalem is the place where men ought to worship. Was this question asked—as *Stier, Alford*, and others think—merely for information on an important religious question? In that case it seems a strange way of meeting our Lord's home-thrust. But if we view it as the question of one who had been stunned by so unexpected a revelation of her sinful life, made to her by one whom she had begun to regard in no common light—all seems clear enough. Though she saw herself all disclosed, she is not yet prepared to break down and ask what hopes there might be for one so guilty. Her convictions have come upon her too suddenly for that. She shifts the question, therefore, from a personal to a public one, though the sequel shows how this revelation of her past life had told upon her. So her reply is not, 'Alas, what a wicked life have I been leading!' but, 'Lo, what a wonderful prophet have I got into conversation with! He will be able to settle that interminable dispute between us and the Jews. Sir, our fathers hold to this mountain,' pointing to *Gerizim*, 'as the divinely consecrated place of worship, but ye Jews say that *Jerusalem* is the proper place: say, which of us is right, thou to whom all such things are doubtless known.' How slowly does the human heart submit to *thorough* humiliation! Compare the prodigal (see on Luke xv. 15). Doubtless our Lord saw through her, and perceived the more immediate object of her question. But how does He meet it? Does He say 'That is not the point just now; but how stands it with thy heart and life? Till that is disposed of theological controversies must be let alone?' The Prince of preachers takes another method: He humours the poor woman, letting her take her own way, allowing her to lead while He follows—but thus only the more effectually gaining His object. He answers her question, pours light into her mind on the *spirituality* of all true worship, even as of its glorious Object, and so brings her insensibly to the point at which He could disclose to her wondering mind Whom she was all the while speaking to.

21. Jesus saith unto her, Woman, believe me, the hour cometh [ἔρχεται ὥρα]—rather, 'there cometh an hour,' **when ye shall neither in this mountain, nor yet at Jerusalem, worship the Father**—that is, shall worship Him at neither place and at no place as an exclusively chosen, consecrated, central place of worship. (See Mal. i. 11; 1 Tim. ii. 8.) Observe how our Lord gently and indirectly raises the woman's views of the great Object of all acceptable worship. She had talked simply of "worship." He says, "The worship of THE FATHER" shall soon be everywhere. 'The point raised will very soon cease to be of any moment, for a total change of dispensation is about to come over the Church:—but now, as to the question itself.' **22. Ye worship ye know not what; we know what we worship [ὃ**

οὐκ οἴδατε—ὃ οἴδαμεν]—rather, 'Ye worship what ye know not: we worship what we know'—*q. d.,* 'Ye worship without any revealed authority, and so, very much in the dark; but in this sense the Jews know what they are about.' **for salvation is of the Jews.** The Samaritans are wrong, not only as to the *place*, but the whole *grounds* and *nature* of their worship; while in all these respects the truth lies with us Jews. For Salvation is not a thing left to be reached by any one who may vaguely desire it of a God of mercy, but something that has been revealed, prepared, deposited with a particular people, and must be sought in connection with, and as issuing from them; and that people "the Jews." Here, and almost here only, our Lord uses the pronoun "we." But observe in what sense. It is not, He and other individual men: It is He and the Jewish nation, "of whom as concerning the flesh, Christ came" (Rom. ix. 5). It is, *We Jews.* In other words, Christ here identifies Himself with others only as touching the family to which as man He belonged; and even that but once or twice. Hence it seems no proper exception to Remark 3 at the close of the Section on Nicodemus (ch. iii. 1-21). **23. But the hour cometh**—or, 'But there cometh an hour,' **and now is**—evidently meaning her to understand that this new economy was in some sense in course of being set up while He was talking to her; a sense which would in a few minutes so far appear, when He told her plainly that He was *the Christ.* **when the true worshippers shall worship the Father in spirit and in truth**—or 'in spirit and truth' [ἐν πνεύματι καὶ ἀληθείᾳ]; **for the Father seeketh such to worship him**—or 'seeketh such to be His worshippers' [τοιούτους ζητεῖ τοὺς προσκυνοῦντας αὐτόν]. **24. God is a spirit: and they that worship him must worship [him] in spirit and [in] truth.** 'As God is a Spirit, so He both invites and demands a spiritual worship, and already all is in preparation for a spiritual economy, more in harmony with the true nature of acceptable service than the ceremonial worship by consecrated *persons, places,* and *times,* which God for a time has seen meet to keep up till the fulness of the time should come.' **25. The woman saith unto him, I know that Messias cometh, which is called Christ: when he is come, he will tell us all things.** If we take our Lord's immediate disclosure of Himself, in answer to these words, as the proper key to their meaning *to His ear,* we can hardly doubt that the woman was already all but prepared for even this startling announcement, which indeed she seems (from *v.* 29) to have already begun to suspect by His revealing her to herself. Thus quickly, under so matchless a Teacher, was she brought up from her sunken condition to a frame of mind and heart capable of receiving the noblest revelations. When she says of the expected Messiah, that He would "tell them all things," this belief was probably founded on Deut.

27　And upon this came his disciples, and marvelled that he talked with
the woman: yet no man said, What seekest thou? or, Why talkest thou
28　with her? The woman then left her water-pot, and went her way into
29　the city, and saith to the men, Come, see a man which told me all things
30　that ever I did: is not this the Christ? Then they went out of the city,
and came unto him.
31　In the meanwhile his disciples prayed him, saying, Master, eat.
32　But he said unto them, *r*I have meat to eat that ye know not of.
33　Therefore said the disciples one to another, Hath any man brought him
34　*ought* to eat? Jesus saith unto them, *s*My meat is to do the will of him

A. D. 30.

r Job 23. 12.
Ps. 63. 5.
Ps. 119. 103.
Pro. 18. 20.
Isa. 53. 11.
Jer. 15. 16.
Acts 20. 35.
s Job 23. 12.
ch. 6. 38.
ch. 17. 4.
ch. 19. 30.

---

xviii. 15. 26. **Jesus saith unto her, I that speak
unto thee am he.** Never did our Lord utter Himself so nakedly to His own people the Jews. He
had magnified them to the woman; but to themselves He was to the last far more reserved than
to her—*proving* to them rather than plainly *telling*
them that He was the Christ. But what would
not have been *safe* among them was safe enough
with her, whose *simplicity* and *docility* at this stage
of the conversation appear from the sequel to have
become perfect. What now will the woman say?
We listen, but all is over. The curtain has dropped. The scene has changed. A new party has
arrived.

*The Disciples Return from Sychar, and the
Woman Returns to it—What passed between Jesus
and the Disciples on this case, and how the Woman
Brought the Sycharites to Jesus* (27-38). **27. And
upon this came his disciples**—who had been to
Sychar to buy provisions (*v.* 8). **and marvelled
that he talked**—or 'was talking' [ἐλάλει] **with the
woman.** Being a Samaritan, they would not expect such a thing. But though our Lord never
went out of His way to *seek* either Samaritans or
Gentiles—ever observing His own direction to the
Twelve when they went forth to preach (see on
Matt. x. 5, 6)—neither did He ever go out of His
way to *avoid* them, when, as in the case of the
Syrophenician Gentile, they came seeking Him
(see on Mark vii. 24, 25), or, as in the case of this
Samaritan woman, Providence threw them in His
way. In this He acted on the great principle
which He Himself laid down in regard to the
Sabbath—that '*Not to do good, when it is in the
power of our hand to do it, is to do evil.*' See on
Matt. xii. 12. Had the disciples seen with the
eyes and felt with the heart of their Master, they
would less have marvelled that He "talked with
the woman"—and many a time have marvelled
that He talked with *themselves.* **yet no man
—'no one' said, What seekest thou?**—'What object hadst Thou? **or, Why talkest thou with
her?**—awed, no doubt, by the spectacle, and
thinking there must be something under it, yet
afraid to meddle with it. **28. The woman then
left her water-pot, and went her way into the
city, and saith to the men, 29. Come** [Δεῦτε],
**see a man which told me all things that ever I
did: is not this the Christ?** [μήτι οὗτός ἐστιν ὁ
Χριστός;] The grammatical form of this question,
which expects a *negative* answer, requires that it
should be rendered, 'Is this'—or rather, 'Can this
be the Christ?' The woman put it thus, as if they
would naturally reply, 'Impossible.' But beneath
that modest way of putting it was the conviction,
that if they would but come and judge for themselves, she would have no need to obtrude upon
them any opinions of hers—which she well knew
would appear unworthy of attention. Thus, by
asking if this could possibly be the Christ—and
so, rather asking to be helped by them than pretending to be their teacher—she in reality drew
their attention to the point, in the least offensive
and yet most effectual way. Observe, too, how
she confines herself to the marvel of His disclosing
to her the particulars of her own life, without
touching on what He had said of Himself. If the
woman's past life was known to the Sycharites—
as who can doubt it was, in so small a place?—
this would at once disarm their prejudices and
add weight to her statement. How exquisitely
natural is all this! Up to our Lord's last words
her attention had been enchained, and her awe
deepened; and certainly the last disclosure was
fitted to hold her faster to the spot than ever.
But the arrival of strangers made her feel that it
was time for her to withdraw; and He who knew
what was in her heart, and what she was going
to the city to do, having said all to her that she
was then able to bear, let her go without exchang-
ing a word with her in the hearing of others.
Their interview was too sacred, and the effect on
the woman too overpowering (not to speak of His
own deep emotion), to allow of its being continued.
But this one artless touch—that she "left her
water-pot"—speaks volumes. The living water
was already beginning to spring up within her;
she found that man doth not live by bread nor
by water only, and that there was a water of
wondrous virtue that raised people above meat
and drink, and the vessels that held them, and
all human things. In short, she was transported,
forgot everything but one, or felt that her water-
pot now would be an encumbrance; and her heart
running over with the tale she had to tell, she
hastens home and pours it out. **30. Then they
went out of the city, and came unto him.** How
different, in this, from the Jews! and richly was
this their openness to conviction rewarded. But
first the Evangelist relates what passed between
Jesus and the disciples after the woman's departure.

31. **In the meanwhile**—during her absence—**his
disciples prayed him, saying, Master, eat.** *Fatigue*
and *thirst* we saw He felt; here is revealed another
of our common infirmities to which the Lord was
subject—*hunger.* **32. But he said unto them, I
have meat to eat that ye know not of.** What
spirituality of mind does this answer breathe!
The pronouns, "*I*" and "*ye*" are emphatically
expressed ['Εγὼ—ὑμεῖς], sharply to mark the contrast between His thoughts and theirs at this time.
'As for Me, I have been eating all this time, and
such food as ye dream not of.' What can that be?
they ask each other; have any supplies been
brought Him in our absence? He knows what
they are saying, though He hears it not. **33.
Therefore said the disciples one to another, Hath
any man brought him [ought] to eat? 34. Jesus
saith unto them, My meat** ['Εμὸν βρῶμα]. Here,
again, the "My" is emphatic, in the same sense. **is
to do**—or rather, ' to be doing' [ἵνα ποιῶ] **the will
of Him that sent me, and to finish his work** [τε-
λειώσω]—changing the tense to that of a *completed*

35 that sent me, and to finish his work. Say not ye, There are yet four months, and *then* cometh harvest? behold, I say unto you, Lift up your
36 eyes, and look on the fields; *t*for they are white already to harvest. And *u*he that reapeth receiveth wages, and gathereth fruit unto life eternal;
37 that both he that soweth and he that reapeth may rejoice together. And
38 herein is that saying true, One soweth, and another reapeth. I sent you to reap that whereon ye bestowed no labour: *v*other men laboured, and ye are entered into their labours.

A. D. 30.

t Matt. 9. 37.
Luke 10. 2.
u Pro. 11. 18.
Dan. 12. 3.
1 Cor. 3. 8.
2 John 8.
Jas. 5. 20.
v Acts 10. 43.
1 Pet. 1. 12.

work. 'A Servant here to fulfil a prescribed work, to *do* and to *finish* that work is "meat" to Me; and of this, while ye were away, I have had my fill.' And of what does He speak thus? Of the condescension, pity, patience, wisdom, He had been laying out upon *one soul*—a very humble woman, and one in some respects repulsive too! But He had gained her, and through her was going to gain more, and lay perhaps the foundation of a great work in the country of Samaria; and this filled His whole soul, and raised Him above the sense of natural hunger. (See on Matt. iv. 4.) **35. Say not ye, There are yet four months, and then cometh harvest?** That this was intended to express the actual interval between the time when our Lord was speaking and the harvest-time that year, we cannot doubt. The arguments against it, by *Alford* and others, as if this were a proverbial speech without any definite reference to the actual time of its utterance—which to us is scarcely intelligible—seem feeble, and the best critics and harmonists regard it here as a note of the actual season of the year at which our Lord spoke—late in December, but more probably January, and, as *Stanley* affirms, from his own observation, even so late as February; though the year he refers to was perhaps an exceptional one, and the month of February seems too late. **behold, I say unto you, Lift up your eyes, and look on the fields; for they are white already to harvest.** 'It wants four months to harvest, ye would say at this season of the natural harvest: but lift up your eyes and look upon those fields in the light of *another* husbandry, for, lo! *in that sense*, it wants not four months nor four days, for they are even now white to harvest, ready for the sickle.' The simple beauty of this language is only surpassed by the glow of holy emotion in the Redeemer's own soul which it expresses. It refers to the *ripeness* of these Sycharites for accession to Him, and the joy of this great Lord of the reapers over the anticipated ingathering. O could we but *so* "lift up our eyes and look" upon many fields abroad and at home, which to dull sense appear unpromising, as *He* beheld those of Samaria, what movements, now scarce in embryo, and accessions to Christ, seemingly far distant, might we not discern as quite near at hand, and thus, amidst difficulties and discouragements too much for nature to sustain, be cheered—*as our Lord Himself was* in circumstances far more overwhelming—with "songs in the night"! [It is surprising that *Tischendorf* should adhere to the punctuation of some certainly ancient MSS. and versions here, in connecting the word "already"—ἤδη—with the following verse; no doubt, because the usual place of that adverb is before, not after, καί. But as this would utterly destroy the sense of our Lord's statements in the two verses, so in the matter of mere punctuation the MSS. and versions are of no authority; and we are as good judges as the ancient transcribers and translators where the punctuation in every case ought to be. Both *Lachmann* and *Tregelles* follow here the punctuation of the received text.] **36. And he that reapeth receiveth wages, and**

gathereth fruit unto life eternal; that both he that soweth and he that reapeth may rejoice together. 37. And herein is that saying true, One soweth, and another reapeth. As our Lord could not mean that the reaper only, and not the sower, received "wages," in the sense of *personal reward* for his work, the "wages" here can be no other than the joy of having such a harvest to gather in—the joy of "gathering fruit unto life eternal." The blessed issue of the whole ingathering is the interest alike of the sower and of the reaper; it is no more the fruit of the last operation than of the first; and just as there can be no reaping without previous sowing, so have those servants of Christ, to whom is assigned the pleasant task of merely reaping the spiritual harvest, no work to do, and no joy to taste, that has not been prepared to their hand by the toilsome and often thankless work of their predecessors in the field. The joy, therefore, of the great harvest festivity will be the common joy of all who have taken any part in the work from the first operation to the last. (See Deut. xvi. 11, 14; Ps. cxxvi. 6; Isa. ix. 3). **38. I sent you** [Ἐγὼ ἀπέστειλα]. The "I" here is emphatic: I, the Lord of the whole harvest. When He says, "I *sent* you," He refers back to their *past* appointment to the apostleship, though it points only to the *future* discharge of it, for they had nothing to do with the present ingathering of the Sycharites. **to reap that whereon ye bestowed no labour**—meaning that much of their future success would arise from the preparation already made for them. **other men laboured**—referring, as we think, to the Old Testament labourers, the Baptist, and *by implication* Himself, though He studiously keeps this in the background, that the line of distinction between Himself and all His servants might not be lost sight of.

The Sycharites, Believing the Woman's Testimony concerning Jesus, are Confirmed in their Faith by personal intercourse with Him—On their invitation Jesus spends two days in Sychar, by which the number of believers in Him is greatly increased (39-42). **39. And many of the Samaritans of that city believed on him for the saying of the woman, which testified, He told me all that ever I did.** What a commentary is this on *v.* 35, "Lift up your eyes, and look on the fields, for they are white already to harvest"! **40. So when the Samaritans were come unto him, they besought him that he would tarry with them: and he abode**—or 'tarried' —it is the same word [ἔμεινεν]—**there two days. 41. And many more believed because of his [own]** word; **42. And said unto the woman, Now we believe, not because of thy saying** [οὐκ ἔτι διὰ τὴν σὴν λαλίάν]—or, 'No longer do we believe because of thy saying;' **for we have heard him ourselves, and know that this is indeed the Christ, the Saviour of the world**—or, according to the order in the original, 'that this is indeed the Saviour of the world, the Christ.' What a marvellous simplicity and docility do these Samaritans display! They first credit the woman's simple testimony, and let her bring them to Jesus; then they are satisfied by one brief interview with Himself that

39 And *"*many of the Samaritans of that city believed on him for the
40 saying of the woman, which testified, He told me all that ever I did. So
*"*when the Samaritans were come unto him, they besought him that he
41 would tarry with them: and he abode there two days. And *"*many more

A. D. 30.
" Gen. 49. 10.
" Gen. 32. 26.
" Isa. 42. 1.
Rom. 15. 8.

He is the Christ, and invite Him to visit them; and when He condescends to do so, His two days' stay not only brings over many more to the same faith in Him, but raises that faith to a conviction—never reached by the Jews, and hardly as yet attained by His own disciples—that as the Christ He was *" the Saviour of the world."* And yet, beyond the supernatural knowledge which He had displayed in His interview with the woman, He does not appear to have wrought any miracle before these Samaritans. Is there anything in the Gospel History more remarkable than this? those were two precious days, surely, to the Redeemer Himself! Unsought, He had come to His own, yet His own received Him not; now those who were not His own had come to Him, been won by Him, and invited Him to their town that others might share with them in the benefit of His wonderful ministry. Here, then, would He solace His already wounded spirit, and have in this outfield village-triumph of His grace a sublime foretaste of the inbringing of the whole Gentile world into the Church. *Olshausen* correctly notes this as 'a rare instance of the Lord's ministry *producing an awakening on a large scale.'*

Remarks.—1. Did He who, when the time to suffer arrived, "set His face like a flint," withdraw from Judea to Galilee when Pharisaic jealousy at Jerusalem would have come too soon to a head, and arrested the work given Him to do? Let His followers learn from Him this wisdom of the serpent while manifesting, with Him, the harmlessness of the dove. Needless exposure is as much to be avoided as a cowardly flight, in times when the truth cannot be confessed without personal danger. 2. In what a light do the condescension, the zeal, the skill, the patience, which Jesus bestowed upon the woman of Samaria place the value of a single soul! Apart from all that followed, what a rescue was effected in that one cause! See a similar care of one soul in the case of the Ethiopian eunuch, with a view to whose illumination Philip the Evangelist was taken out of full and glorious work in the city of Samaria, away to the desert road from Jerusalem to Gaza (Acts viii. 26, &c., on which see). "Brethren," says James, "if any [*one*] of you [τις ἐν ὑμῖν] do err from the truth, and one convert him, let him know that he which converteth a sinner from the error of his way shall save *a soul* from death, and shall hide a multitude of sins" (see on Jas. v. 19, 20). And observe how *casually* this woman of Samaria was gained. Jesus and she were each on their own business at this well; He on His way from Judea to Galilee, and she come from the neighbouring village to draw water. Doubtless such meetings of Jewish men and Samaritan women at that well were customary enough; and had Jesus preserved the usual silence, nothing had come of it. But the opportunity was to Him too precious to be lost. Though the thirst was as real as the weariness, and water as desirable as repose, He certainly disregarded the national antipathies, not so much to mark His superiority to them and disapprobation of them, nor yet merely to slake His thirst, but to draw this woman into a conversation which should not cease till He had gained her soul. O, if such casual opportunities of usefulness were embraced by the followers of Christ as by Christ Himself, how many might be won to Him without ever going out of their way! All that is

wanted is that love of souls which burned in Him, that constant readiness to avail ourselves of openings for Christian usefulness, the present sense of the truth upon the heart, and a spirit of dependence upon Him for that power to open the mind and heart which He possessed and we must get from Him. If we could but say with Him—and just in proportion as we *can* say with Him—"My meat is to be doing the will of Him that sent me, and to finish His work;" if we do but remember that this was said of what He had been doing for one soul, and that of the fruit He was reaping in that one case, He said, "I have meat to eat that ye know not of"—we should need no stimulants to follow Him, and hardly any directions for doing it. But who can tell what may issue out of one conversion? Think of the little maid of Israel (2 Ki. v. 1-14.) See what this once disreputable woman of Samaria did for her fellow-villagers; and who shall say what wide-spread influences, preparing Samaria for the eventual reception of the Gospel, may not have flowed from the precious events of those two days which Jesus spent there? (See on Acts viii. 9-13.) No conversion ought to stand alone. Every disciple of the Lord Jesus should feel himself, like this woman, a missionary for Christ, and every conversion should be like a wave of the sea, begetting another. So that the pains taken on one soul—while of itself, if it issue in conversion, it will be "meat" to any who have the Spirit of Christ—ought to be taken with all the more eagerness and hope, as we have ground to believe that we are thus, in all likelihood, doing good on a large scale. 3. How vividly does the reality of our Lord's human nature—His warm, quivering humanity—His identity with ourselves, not only in all the essential properties but in all the sinless infirmities of our nature, come out here! He is weary with a journey, just as we are; His tongue, like ours, is parched with thirst; He feels, as we do, the cravings of hunger: So He rests Him by Jacob's well, as we should do in like case, and asks, as a thirsty man would do, for a draught of water from the woman of Samaria; and He is provided by His disciples with victuals from Sychar, just as other men. And the life-like, minute lines of detail are so drawn that we feel as if we saw and heard the whole, and the very children that read it feel the same. And yet this is the loftiest and deepest of all the Gospels. Nay, in the dialogue which the Evangelist reports between Jesus and the Woman, these details seem but like the finest net-work of gold in which are set jewels of heavenly lustre and incomparable price—the jewel of unfathomable Dignity, Authority, Grace, Penetration, Patience, in this Petitioner for water; besides all the jewels of spiritual truth never before uttered in such a style. No wonder that this should be regarded as emphatically the Gospel of the Person and Grace of the Lord Jesus, and that our Evangelist should get the surname of "the divine." 4. Mark how Jesus holds Himself forth here as the sovereign Giver, the authoritative Dispenser of the living water; which living water is nothing less than a well-spring of eternal satisfaction opened up in a man's soul, never to dry up. Such a claim on the part of a mere *creature* would not be more offensive than ridiculous. Search the whole Scripture, and see if anything approaching to it was ever taken into the lips of the most emi-

42 believed because of his own word; and said unto the woman, Now we believe, not because of thy saying; for ^zwe have heard *him* ourselves, and know that this is indeed the Christ, ^athe Saviour of the world.

A. D. 30.
^z ch. 17. 8. .
1 John 4.14.
^a 1 John 2. 2.

nent and inspired servants of God. But how majestic, appropriate, and self-evidencing are such claims from the lips of this Speaker! As we read and re-read this dialogue, we feel ourselves in the presence of Grace Incarnate—enshrined, too, not in celestial humanity, but (O wonder of wonders!) in weary, thirsty, hungry flesh, just like our own; sitting down beside us, talking with us, breathing on us its tender love, and laying its warm, fleshly hand upon us, drawing us with cords of a man and bands of love. See on Matt. xi. 28, and Remark 5 at the close of that Section. 5. With what charming simplicity and transparent clearness does one line of this dialogue express the unsatisfactoriness of all earthly satisfactions—"Every one that drinketh of this water shall thirst again." Under the figure of cold waters to a thirsty soul, it covers the whole field of earth's satisfactions, but stamps them as external to us, and coming into us from without; while it represents the soul as the mere reservoir of them, drying up like other cisterns, and needing to be ever replenished. But what a contrast to this immediately follows. Still keeping to the figure of water, Jesus claims it as His prerogative to open in the soul a fountain of living waters that shall never cease to flow, a spring of enduring satisfaction and eternal freshness; thus expressing, with matchless brevity, force, and beauty, the *spirituality*, the *vitality*, the *joy*, the *perpetuity* of that religious change which He effects in all that believe on His name. But now, 6. When we advance to the woman's question about the place where men ought to worship, how wonderful is the breadth and richness of the answer given her. First, our Lord will not dash her by telling· her that her countrymen were in the wrong, until He has first told her how soon the whole question will be at an end. But when He does do so, how definite and positive is the verdict pronounced upon the Samaritan worship. Men talk as if *sincerity* were the only thing of consequence in the worship of God. That the Samaritans were more wanting in this than the Jews there is no· evidence; and the very different reception which our Lord met with from the one than the other would seem to show that they were the more unsophisticated of the two. And yet He says the Samaritans knew not the Object they worshipped, while the Jews did, because Salvation was of the Jews. What can this mean, if it be not that the Samaritans worshipped after ideas and modes of their own, and in doing so were wrong; while the Jews followed divinely communicated ideas and prescribed modes, and therefore theirs was, in that respect, *the only acceptable worship?* But again, when our Lord says that all was right with the Jewish worship, "because *Salvation* is of the Jews," He enunciates the great truth, that in the worship of *sinful* men, as all worshippers on earth are, SALVATION must ever be the key-note —Salvation needed, sought, obtained, extolled; that historically the whole economy of salvation in its preparatory form had been entrusted for conservation to the seed of Abraham; and that so long as they occupied the important position of the ordained depositaries of all Saving Truth, Jerusalem must be regarded as the city of divine solemnities, and its temple as the visible dwelling-place of the Most High. (See Isa. ii. 3.) What a recognition is this of the Old Testament and its Faith, and of the Jews and the Jewish Economy as the living embodiment of it up to

376

that time! But further, mark how explicitly our Lord announces the speedy cessation of all religious distinction between Jew and Gentile, and between one place and another for the worship of God. "There cometh an hour, and now is," when a world-wide worship shall be set up. The rending of the veil of the temple in twain, from the top to the bottom, was the signal-note of that mighty event—the death of Christ—which dissolved for ever these distinctions. From that time forth the middle wall of partition was broken down, and in every place the true incense and a pure offering was free to rise to heaven (Mal. i. 11). How strange it seems (one cannot avoid adding) that notwithstanding these announcements, and the commentaries on them in Gal. iv. and the Epistle to the Hebrews throughout, there should be an influential section of the students of prophecy who contend that the temple-services and the ritual distinctions of Jew and Gentile have *not* been absolutely and finally abolished, and that they will all be re-established during the Millennium! Another thing worthy of especial notice in this comprehensive reply to the woman of Samaria, is the emphatic manner in which the *spirituality* of all acceptable worship is proclaimed, and—what is even of more importance—its being based upon the *Spirituality of God* Himself. This was as true under the Jewish Economy as it has been since its cessation. But since, under an elaborate external and exclusive worship, this neither was nor could be so manifest, nor yet so fully realized by the worshippers themselves, the Lord here speaks as if only now such a spiritual worship was going to be established, because now for the first time since Moses—and in one sense even since the fall itself—to be stripped of sacrificial rites and the observance of time and place. Once more, in this reply, our Lord raises the woman's views of the glorious Object of worship, saying, "*The Father* seeketh such to worship Him." This is the more remarkable, because to the unbelieving Jews He never so speaks of God, and seems studiously to avoid it (ch. viii. 38). In the Sermon on the Mount, addressing His own disciples, He calls Him "your Father," and He teaches them in prayer to say, "Our Father." In His own prayers He says ever, "Father," and once His Agony in the Garden drew from Him the emphatic form, "My Father." From these facts we infer that though this woman was not yet within the circle of those to whom He says, "Your Father," this was so soon to be, that He could with propriety invite her to regard Him as "The Father." So much for the dialogue between our Lord and the woman of Samaria. Turning next to that between Him and the disciples on the woman's departure, we may notice, 7. What rich encouragement it affords to those "fishers of men" who "have toiled all the night" of their official life, and, to human appearance, have "taken nothing." How little might any other than one Eye have seen that the fields of Samaria were white already to harvest; and yet the event proves it to a very remarkable degree, as far as Sychar was concerned. Even so may the desert all unexpectedly rejoice and blossom as the rose; yet never is a harvest reaped that has not first been sown. The sowers may live and die before the harvest-time arrive, and the fruit of their labours be gathered. Yet can the reapers not say to the sowers, We have no need of you. "They that

43 Now after two days he departed thence, and went into Galilee.
44 For *b*Jesus himself testified, that a prophet hath no honour in his
45 own country. Then, when he was come into Galilee, the Galileans
received him, *c*having seen all the things that he did at Jerusalem at
the feast: *d*for they also went unto the feast.
46 So Jesus came again into Cana of Galilee, *e*where he made the water
wine. And there was a certain ¹nobleman, whose son was sick at
Capernaum.
47 When he heard that Jesus was come out of Judea into Galilee, he went
unto him, and besought him that he would come down, and heal his son:
48 for he was at the point of death. Then said Jesus unto him, *f*Except ye

A. D. 30.

b Matt. 13.57.
Mark 6. 4.
Luke 4. 24.
c ch. 2. 23.
ch. 3. 2.
d Deut 16.16.
e ch. 2. 1, 11.
1 Or,
courtier,
or, ruler.
f Matt. 16. 1.
Luke 16. 31.
1 Cor. 1. 22.

---

sow in tears shall reap in joy," though others may do the actual reaping work after they are in their graves. And if the work of the latter is the more joyous, it should bind them sweetly to the sowers to recollect that "*other* men laboured, and they have but *entered into their labours.*" But may not the spiritual eye be trained so as to see what Jesus here saw—the whitening fields, the yellow grain, all invisible to the eye of sense? We have, indeed, much to learn ere we come to this, and the Lord overrules our spiritual obtuseness to try our faith, and then overpower us with the spectacle of nations born in a day. But even then, all *might* probably be seen by the eye of faith. In Tahiti, after nearly twenty years' missionary labour, not one conversion was known to have occurred, and the abandonment of the Mission was all but agreed on. But on the return of the missionaries to the island, after a native war which had driven them from it, they found that two natives, who, unknown to them, had received serious impressions as servants in their families, and had met together for prayer in their absence, had been joined by a number more, and that little remained for the missionaries but to help forward what God Himself had so marvellously begun. Meanwhile, the Directors in London, urged by one or two of their number, who could not endure to see the Mission abandoned had, after a season of special prayer, despatched letters of encouragement to the missionaries. While these were on their way out, a ship was conveying the news to England of the entire overthrow of idolatry in the island.

43-54.—JESUS REACHES GALILEE—HE MAKES A BRIEF STAY AT CANA, AND THERE PERFORMS HIS SECOND GALILEAN MIRACLE, HEALING A NOBLEMAN'S SON LYING DANGEROUSLY ILL AT CAPERNAUM.

43. Now after two days [τὰς δύο ἡμέρας]—it should be, 'after the two days;' that is, of His stay at Sychar (*v.* 40), he **departed thence, and went into Galilee. 44. For Jesus himself testified, that a prophet hath no honour in his own country** [ἐν τῇ ἰδίᾳ πατρίδι]. If "his own country" here meant Galilee, His having no honour in it would seem to be a reason why he should *not* go to it. Hence some of those who think so render the words, He "went into Galilee, *although* He Himself testified," &c. But this is against the sense of the word "for" [γὰρ], and is inadmissible. Others of those who understand "His own country" here to mean Galilee get over the difficulty by connecting the "for" with what follows in the next verse rather than with what goes before, thus: 'The Galileans received Him, not because they appreciated His character and claims—"for" He had grown too common among them for that, according to the proverb—but merely because they had seen His recent miracles at Jerusalem.' This is the view of *Tholuck*, supported by *Lücke* in his 3d Edition, *de Wette*, and *Alford*. But it is

too far-fetched. Hence, some give up Galilee as "His own country," and think *Judea*, or *Bethlehem* as His birth-place, to be meant. So *Origen*, *Maldonat*, *Lücke*, 2d Edition, *Robinson*, *Wieseler*. But our Lord was never either at Bethlehem or in Judea at all from the time of His birth till the commencement of His ministry; and therefore "His own country" can only mean the place of His early life—the scene of such familiar intercourse with others as would tend to make Him grow common amongst them. And what can that be but *Nazareth?*—which is expressly called "His country" [τὴν πατρίδα αὐτοῦ] in Matt. xiii. 54, 57, in precisely the same connection; as also in Mark vi. 4; Luke iv. 24. In this sense all is clear and natural: 'Now after the two days, Jesus, having left the province of Samaria as He had done that of Judea, went into the province of Galilee; but not, as might have been expected, to that part of it where He had been brought up, for Jesus knew that there—in His own country—He would have no honour, according to the proverb: He went, therefore, as the reader shall learn presently, to Cana of Galilee.' So *Calvin, Beza, Grotius, Bengel, Olshausen,* &c. **45. Then, when he was come into Galilee, the Galileans received**—or welcomed him, **having seen all the things that he did at**—'in' [ἐν] Jerusalem **at the feast: for they also went unto the feast** — proud, perhaps, of their countryman's wonderful works at Jerusalem, and possibly won by this circumstance to regard His claims as at least worthy of respectful investigation. Even this our Lord did not despise, for saving conversion often begins in less than this (so Zaccheus, Luke xix. 3).

46. So Jesus came again into Cana of Galilee (see on ch. ii. 1), **where he made the water wine. And there was a certain nobleman** [βασιλικὸς]—'courtier,' or king's servant, one connected with a royal household; such as "Chuza" (Luke viii. 3) or Manaen (Acts xiii. 1). So *Josephus* often uses the word. **whose son was sick at Capernaum. 47. When he heard that Jesus was come out of Judea**—whence the report of His miracles at the paschal feast had doubtless reached him, begetting in Him the hope that He would extend His healing power to his dying son, **into Galilee, he went unto him, and besought him that he would come down**—Capernaum being "down" from Cana on the N.W. shore of the sea of Galilee, **and heal his son: for he was at the point of death. 48. Then said Jesus, Except ye see signs and wonders** [σημεῖα καὶ τέρατα]. The latter word expresses simply the *miraculous* character of an act; the former the *attestation* which it gave of a higher presence and a divine commission. (See on ch. vi. 26.) **ye will not believe.** The poor man did believe, as both his coming and his urgent entreaty show. But how imperfect that faith was, we shall see, and our Lord would

49 see signs and wonders, ye will not believe. The nobleman saith unto him,
50 Sir, come down ere my child die. Jesus saith unto him, *g* Go thy way;
thy son liveth. And the man believed the word that Jesus had spoken
51 unto him, and he went his way. And as he was now going down, his
52 servants met him, and told *him*, saying, Thy son liveth. Then enquired
he of them the hour when he began to amend. And they said unto him,
53 Yesterday at the seventh hour the fever left him. So the father knew
that *it was* at the same hour in the which Jesus said unto him, Thy
54 son liveth; and *h* himself believed, and his whole house. This *is* again
the second miracle *that* Jesus did, when he was come out of Judea into
Galilee.
5 AFTER *a* this there was a feast of the Jews; and Jesus went up to

A. D. 30.

g 1 Ki. 17. 13-15.
Matt. 8. 13.
Mark 7. 29.
Luke 17. 14.
ch. 11. 40.
Acts 14. 9.
h Luke 19. 9.
Acts 2. 39.
Acts 16. 34.

CHAP. 5.
a Lev. 23. 2.
Deut. 16. 1.
ch. 2. 13.

deepen it by such a blunt, and seemingly rough, answer as He made to Nicodemus (ch. iii. 3). **49. The nobleman saith unto him, Sir, come down ere my child die.** 'Ah! while we talk, my child is dying, and if Thou come not instantly, all will be over.' This was faith, but partial, and our Lord would perfect it. The man cannot believe the cure could be wrought without the Physician coming to the patient—the thought of such a thing evidently never occurred to him. But Jesus will in a moment bring him up to this. **50. Jesus saith unto him, Go thy way; thy son liveth. And the man believed the word that Jesus had spoken unto him, and he went his way.** Both effects instantaneously followed: the man believed the word, and the cure shooting quicker than lightning from Cana to Capernaum, was felt by the dying youth. In token of faith, the father takes his leave of Christ—in the circumstances this evidenced full faith. The servants hasten to convey the joyful tidings to the anxious parent, whose faith now only wants one confirmation. **51. And as he was now going down, his servants met him, and told him, saying, Thy son liveth. 52. Then enquired he of them the hour when he began to amend. And they said unto him, Yesterday at the seventh hour the fever left him. 53. So the father knew that it was at the same hour in the which Jesus said unto him, Thy son liveth; and himself believed, and his whole house.** He *had* believed before this—first very imperfectly, then with assured confidence in Christ's word; but now with a faith crowned by "sight." And the wave rolled from the head to the members of his household. "To-day is salvation come to this *house*" (Luke xix. 9); and no mean house this. **54. This is again the second miracle that Jesus did, when he was come out of Judea into Galilee**—that is, not His second miracle after coming out of Judea into Galilee; but 'His second Galilean miracle, and it was wrought after his return from Judea'—as the former was before He went to it.

Remarks.—1. If we are right as to the sense of *vv.* 43, 44—if Jesus, on His return into Galilee, went to Cana, avoiding Nazareth as "His own country," in which He knew that He would have "no honour," according to the proverb which Himself uttered—we have here a strong confirmation of the judgment we have given on the much-disputed question, whether Jesus paid *two visits* to Nazareth after His public ministry commenced, or *only one.* See on Matt. iv. 12, and more fully on Luke iv. 16, &c. As in our view He avoided Nazareth on this occasion, because He had become too *common* among them during His early life, so when He did visit it (Luke iv. 16, &c.), it was only to be upbraided for *never* having yet exhibited to His own town's-people the miraculous powers with the fame of which other places were ringing; and

His reception on that one occasion when He visited Nazareth was quite enough to show that a repetition of His visit would be but "giving that which was holy to the dogs." So He left it, as we believe, never to return. 2. On comparing the faith of the nobleman whose son Jesus healed, with that of the centurion whose servant was restored by the same healing power, we are not to conclude that the believing *disposition* of the one was at all behind that of the other. Did the nobleman "beseech Jesus that He would *come down* and heal his son"—as if the thing could not be done at a distance? The centurion also "sent elders of the Jews, beseeching Him that He would come and heal his servant." It is true that Jesus replied to the nobleman, "Except ye see signs and wonders ye will not believe"—referring to the general unpreparedness even of those who believed in Him to recognize His *unlimited* power—and it is true that the nobleman only proved this by replying, "Sir, come down ere my child die;" while the centurion sent a noble message to Jesus *not* to come to Him, as that would be too great an honour, and besides there was no need, as it could be done equally well by a word uttered at a distance. But we must remember that the nobleman's case occurred almost at the outset of our Lord's ministry, when faith had much less to work upon than when the centurion applied (Luke vii. 2, &c). But what shows that the two cases are as nearly as possible on a par is, that whereas even the centurion's noble message seems to have been an after thought—his faith rising, perhaps, after his first messengers were despatched—the nobleman, as his case became more urgent, reached to the very same faith by another method. For when Jesus answered his entreaty to "come down" by saying, "Go thy way; thy son liveth," "the man believed the word that Jesus had spoken unto him, and he went his way," persuaded the cure could and would be wrought without the great Healer's presence. Thus may two cases, differing in their circumstances and features, be essentially of one character, and thus may a weaker *manifestation* of faith be consistent with an equal *capacity* for faith—the opportunities and advantages of each being different. This might indeed baffle man's power to detect and determine. But it is our comfort to know that it is He with whom both had to do, and from Whom they both experienced such love and grace, who is "ordained to be the Judge of quick and dead."

CHAP. V. 1-47.—THE IMPOTENT MAN HEALED AT THE POOL OF BETHESDA ON THE SABBATH DAY —DISCOURSE OCCASIONED BY THE PERSECUTION ARISING THEREUPON.

The Impotent Man Healed (1-9). The first verse of this chapter raises the most difficult, perhaps, and most controverted, of all questions touching the Harmony of the Gospels and the Duration of

2 Jerusalem. Now there is at Jerusalem, ^bby the sheep ¹*market*, a pool,
3 which is called in the Hebrew tongue ²Bethesda, having five porches. In
these lay a great multitude of impotent folk, of blind, halt, withered,

b Neh. 3. 1.
1 Or, gate.
2 House of mercy.

our Lord's ministry. **1. After this there was a feast of the Jews; and Jesus went up to Jerusalem.** Three Passovers are distinctly mentioned in this Gospel as occurring during our Lord's public ministry: the first in ch. ii. 13, when Jesus paid His first official visit to Jerusalem; another, quite incidentally mentioned in ch. vi. 4; and the last, when Jesus went up to become "our Passover, sacrificed for us" (ch. xii. 2, 12; xiii. 1, 2). If no other Passover occurred than these three, during Christ's public life, then it could not have lasted more than two years and a half: whereas, if the feast mentioned in the first verse of this chapter was a Passover—making four in all—then the Duration of our Lord's public ministry was towards three years and a half. That this feast *was* a Passover, was certainly the most ancient opinion, and it is the opinion of the great majority of critics, (being that of *Irenæus*, as early as the second century, *Eusebius* and *Theodoret*, among the fathers; and of *Luther, Beza, Maldonat, Grotius, Lightfoot, La Clerc, Lampe, Hengstenberg, Greswell, Robinson, Tholuck* in his 6th Edition, and apparently in his 7th and last, *Middleton, Trench, Webster and Wilkinson*, &c.) Those who object to this view all differ among themselves as to what other feast it was, and some of the most acute have given up the hope of determining which it was. (So *Lücke*, at length, *de Wette*, and *Alford*.) That it was a *Pentecost* (as *Cyril* of Alexandria, *Chrysostom* and *Theophylact*, among the fathers; and *Erasmus, Calvin*, and *Bengel* have since thought) is inadmissible, as this Feast—which occurred fifty days after the Passover, or towards the end of May—will appear too late, if we consider that our Lord returned to Galilee in the month of December or January (ch. iv. 35). The Feast of *Tabernacles* (as *Cocceius* and *Ebrard*) is, for the same reason, still more out of the question, as it did not occur till the end of September. All these theories are now given up, by those who object to the Passover, in favour of the Feast of *Purim*, which was observed rather less than a month before the Passover. (So *Keppler*—who first suggested it, but doubtfully—and now *Hug, Olshausen, Wieseler, Meyer, Neander, Tischendorf, Lange*, and *Ellicott*.) But there are very strong objections to this view. First, The Feast of Purim was celebrated over all the country equally with the capital; none went up to Jerusalem to keep it; and the observance of it consisted merely in the reading of the book of Esther in the different synagogues, and spending the two days of it in feasting (Esth. ix. 21, 22): whereas the "multitude" referred to in *v.* 13 seems to imply that it was one of those greater festivals that drew large numbers from the provinces to the capital. It is difficult, indeed, to see why our Lord should have gone up to Jerusalem expressly to keep a feast of this nature, as the words of the first verse clearly imply. For though He was there at the Feast of Dedication (ch. x. 22)—which also was not a principal one—He did not go on purpose to keep it, but was there, or thereabouts, at any rate. But once more the Impotent Man, healed at this feast, was healed on the *Sabbath*—and by comparing *vv.* 9 and 13, one would naturally conclude that this Sabbath was one of the days of the Feast; whereas there is good reason to believe that the Purim was so far from being celebrated on a *Sabbath*, that when it fell on that day, it was put off till after it was over. The only objections to its being a Passover worth noticing are two. First, that our Evangelist, when he means a Passover, expressly names it; whereas here he merely calls it "a feast of the Jews:" and next, that if this be a Passover, it leaves too little time between this one and that of ch. vi. 4, and further, that since Jesus confessedly did not go up to Jerusalem at the next Passover, mentioned in ch. vi. 4—"because the Jews sought to kill Him" (ch. vii. 1)—it would follow that our Lord was about a year and a half absent from Jerusalem—a thing hard to believe. These objections are certainly weighty; but they are not insuperable. We lay no stress upon the fact that the definite article [ἡ ἑορτή], '*the* feast of the Jews' is found in several MSS.—(eight *uncial*, and two of the best *cursive* ones)—supported by the two ancient Egyptian versions; for this reading has not support enough. At the same time it must be observed that all who held to this reading certainly understood the feast intended to be *the* feast, by way of distinction from all the rest, that is, the Passover. But even with the article omitted, it has been shown by *Middleton* (Greek Article I., iii. 1) and *Winer* (xix. 2. *b.*) that its presence is implied, and the sense definite, just in such cases as the present. As to the shortness of the interval between the Passover of ch. v. 1 (supposing it to be one) and that of ch. vi. 4, it does not follow that the interval of *time* was short, because the *events recorded* between them in this Gospel are so few; since it is manifest that our Evangelist, till he comes to the final scenes, confines himself almost wholly to what had been *omitted* by the other Evangelists. To them, therefore, we are to go for the Galilean events which occurred between those Passovers. Finally, as to the long interval of a year and a half between this His second Passover (if so it be), and the Feast of Tabernacles, after the third one, when He next went up to Jerusalem (ch. vii. 2, 10), the reason given for it, in ch. vii. 1, appears sufficient; and as He was to take His final leave of Galilee not very long after, He would have abundant occupation there to fill up the time, while His continuing either in the capital or its neighbourhood nearly all the time between the Feast of Tabernacles and His final Passover—a period of about seven months—would sufficiently compensate for His longer absence from it at an earlier period. On a review of the whole evidence, then, we are decidedly of opinion that the "Feast" here referred to by our Evangelist was THE PASSOVER—and consequently, the *second* of *four* occurring during our Lord's public ministry.

2. Now there is at Jerusalem, by the sheep [market]. The supplement here is an unhappy one, as no such market-place is known. But as the *sheep gate* is mentioned in Neh. iii. 1, 32, and is familiar in the Jewish references to the temple, no doubt the supplement ought to be, as in the *margin*, "by the sheep [gate]," **a pool, which is called in the Hebrew tongue Bethesda** [= בֵּית חִסְדָּא] — that is, 'Mercy-house;' doubtless from the cures wrought there, **having five porches**—for shelter to the patients. That Jerusalem was yet standing when this Gospel was written cannot be inferred, as *Bengel* thought, from the use of the present tense "is." The water here referred to did not necessarily disappear with the overthrow of the city. There are indeed two distinct sites yet to be seen which have been identified with this pool: one, and the more probable site, a ruined reservoir near St. Stephen's gate, which

4 waiting for the moving of the water. For an angel went down at a certain season into the pool, and troubled the water: whosoever then first after the troubling of the water stepped in was made whole of 5 whatsoever disease he had. And a certain man was there, which had 6 an infirmity thirty and eight years. When Jesus saw him lie, and ʰknew that he had been now a long time *in that case*, he saith unto him, ᵈWilt 7 thou be made whole? The impotent man answered him, Sir, I have no man, when the water is troubled, to put me into the pool: but while I 8 am coming, another steppeth down before me. Jesus saith unto him, 9 ᵉRise, take up thy bed, and walk. And immediately the man was made whole, and took up his bed, and walked:

A. D. 30.

ᵇ Ps. 142. 3.
ch. 21. 17.
Heb. 4. 13.
ᵈ Ps. 72. 13.
Ps. 113. 5, 6.
Isa. 55. 1.
Jer. 13. 27.
Luke 18. 41.
ᵉ Matt. 9. 6.
Mark 2. 11.
Luke 5. 24.
Acts 9. 34.

ancient tradition has fixed upon and late investigations strongly confirm ; the other, what is known as the Fountain of the Virgin. But even though all remains of it had disappeared with the destruction of Jerusalem, the Evangelist might have no knowledge of the fact ; nor did he require to know it, as its well-known existence at the time of this incident is all that the word necessarily implies. **3. In these lay a great multitude of impotent folk**—or infirm people, **of blind, halt, withered** [ξηρῶν]—or 'paralyzed' (as Mark iii. 1), **waiting for the moving of the water. 4. For an angel went down at a certain season into the pool, and troubled the water : whosoever then first after the troubling of the water stepped in was made whole of whatsoever disease he had.** The imperfect tense in which these verbs are expressed conveys the idea of use and wont [κατέβαινεν—ἐτάρασσε—ἐγίνετο]—'was wont to descend'—'to trouble the pool'—'to be made whole.' **5. And**—or rather, 'Now' [δὲ] **a certain man was there, which had an infirmity thirty and eight years**—a length of time which to the man himself might seem to render a cure hopeless, and on the principle of a mere *medicinal* virtue in this water, which some even sound critics are too ready to tamper with, undoubtedly would. This, then, was probably the most pitiable of all the patients assembled at the pool, and for that very reason, no doubt, was selected by the Lord for the display of His glory. **6. When Jesus saw him lie, and knew that he had been now a long time in that case.** As He doubtless visited the spot just to perform this cure, so He knew where to find His patient, and the whole previous history of His case (ch. ii. 25). **he saith unto him, Wilt thou be made whole?** Could any one doubt that a sick man would like to be made whole, or that the patients came thither, and this man had returned again and again, just in hope of a cure? But our Lord asked the question, first, to fasten attention upon Himself ; next, by making him detail his case, to deepen in him the feeling of entire helplessness ; and further, by so singular a question, to beget in his desponding heart the hope of a cure. (See on Mark x. 51.) **7. The impotent man answered him, Sir, I have no man, when the water is troubled, to put me into the pool : but while I am coming, another steppeth down before me.** Instead of *saying* he wished to be cured, he just tells with piteous simplicity how fruitless had been all his efforts to obtain it, and how *helpless* and all but *hopeless* he was. Yet not quite. For here he is at the pool, waiting on. It seemed of no use ; nay, only tantalizing—"While I am coming, another steppeth down before me"—the fruit was snatched from His lips. Yet he will not go away. He may get nothing by staying ; he may drop into his grave ere he get into the pool ; but by going from the appointed, divine way of healing, he can get nothing. Wait therefore he will,

wait he does, and when Christ comes to heal him, lo! he is waiting his turn. *What an attitude for a sinner* at Mercy's gate! The man's hopes seemed low enough ere Christ came to him. He might have said, just before "Jesus passed by that way," 'This is no use ; I'll never get in ; let me die at home.' Then all had been lost. But he *held on*, and his perseverance was rewarded with a glorious cure. Probably some rays of hope darted into his heart as he told his tale before those Eyes whose glance measured his whole case. But the word of command consummates his preparation to receive the cure, and instantaneously works it. **8. Jesus saith unto him, Rise, take up thy bed, and walk. 9. And immediately the man was made whole, and took up his bed, and walked.** "He *spake*, and it was *done*." The slinging of his portable couch over his shoulders was designed to show the perfection of the cure.

Such is this glorious miracle. Now let us look at it, as it stands here in the received text ; and next let us examine the *shortened* text presented by most modern Editors of the Greek Testament—which leaves out the last clause of *v.* 3, "waiting for the moving of the waters," and the whole of *v.* 4. The miracle, as it here stands, differs in two points from all other miracles recorded in Scripture : First, It was not one, but a succession of miracles periodically wrought : Next, As it was only wrought "when the waters were troubled," so only upon one patient at a time, and that the patient "who first stepped in after the troubling of the waters." But this only the more undeniably fixed its miraculous character. We have heard of many waters having a medicinal virtue ; but what water was ever known to cure *instantaneously* a single disease? And who ever heard of any water curing all, even the most diverse diseases—"blind, halt, withered"—alike? Above all, who ever heard of such a thing being done only "at a certain season," and most singularly of all, doing it only to the first person who stepped in after the moving of the waters? Any of these peculiarities—much more all taken together—must have proclaimed the supernatural character of the cures wrought. If the text, then, be genuine, there can be no doubt of the miracle, as there were multitudes living when this Gospel was published who, from their own knowledge of Jerusalem, could have exposed the falsehood of the Evangelist, if no such cure had been known there. It only remains, then, that we enquire on what authority the omission of the last clause of *v.* 3, and the whole of *v.* 4, from the text (by *Tischendorf* and *Tregelles*, and approved by *Tholuck, Meyer, Olshausen, Alford,* &c.) is supported. The external evidence against it is certainly very strong. [It is wanting in the newly-discovered *Codex Sinaiticus*, and the *Codex Vaticanus*—א and B—the two earliest known MSS. of the New Testament ; in C, not much later ; in

10   And on *the same day was the sabbath. The Jews therefore said
unto him that was cured, It is the sabbath day: *it is not lawful
11 for thee to carry *thy* bed. He answered them, He that made me
12 whole, the same said unto me, Take up thy bed, and walk. Then
asked they him, What man is that which said unto thee, Take up thy
13 bed, and walk? And he that was healed wist not who it was; for
Jesus had conveyed himself away, ³a multitude being in *that* place.
14 Afterward Jesus findeth him *ʰ*in the temple, and said unto him, Behold,
thou art made whole: *ⁱ*sin no more, lest a worse thing come unto thee.
15 The man departed, and told the Jews that it was Jesus which had made
16 him whole. And therefore did the Jews persecute Jesus, and sought to
slay him, because he had done these things on the sabbath day.

A. D. 30.

* ch. 9. 14.
* Ex. 20. 10.
Neh. 13. 19.
Jer. 17. 21.
Matt. 12. 2.
Mark 2. 24.
Mark 3. 4.
Luke 6. 2.
³ Or, from the multitude that was.
ʰ Ps. 103. 2.
ⁱ Matt. 12.45.

D—which, however, has the disputed clause of *v.* 3; and in three of the cursive or later MSS.; in the ancient version called the Curetonian *Syriac*, and in the two ancient *Egyptian* versions, according to some copies. Besides this, it is fair to add, that there is considerable variety in the words used by the MSS. that have the disputed passage, and that in some MSS. and versions the passage is so marked as to imply that it was not universally received.] But when all the evidence in favour of the disputed passage—external and internal—is combined and well weighed, we think it will appear quite decisive. The external evidence for it is much stronger in fact than in appearance. [It is found — though not in the first, but the second hand — in the *Alexandrian* MS. of date scarcely second to the two oldest, and, in the opinion of some of the best critics, of almost equal authority; in ten other uncial MSS.; in the oldest or Peshito, and indeed all but the Curetonian *Syriac*, and in both the *Old Latin* and *Vulgate* Latin versions — which very rarely agree with the Alexandrian MS. when it differs from the Vatican — showing how very early the disputed words were diffused and recognized: in confirmation of which we have an undoubted reference to the passage by *Tertullian*, in the end of the second and beginning of the third century. Moved by this consideration, no doubt, *Lachmann* inserts the passage.] But the internal evidence is, in our judgment, quite sufficient to outweigh even stronger external evidence against it than there is. First, While the very *strangeness* and, as some venture to say, the legendary air of the miracle may easily account for its *omission*, we cannot see how such a passage could have crept in if it did not belong to the original text. And secondly, The text seems to us to yield no sense, or but an inept sense, without the disputed words. Just try to explain without them this statement of *v.* 7: "Sir, I have no man, when the water is troubled, to put me into the pool: but while I am coming, another steppeth down before me." Who would ever understand how the mere inability of this impotent man to step *first* into the pool should deprive him of its virtue—from whence soever that proceeded—when the water was troubled? Clearly the explanation given in *v.* 4—along with the last clause of *v.* 3—is *necessary* to the understanding of *v.* 7. The two, therefore, must stand or fall together; and as the seventh verse is admitted to be genuine, so, in our judgment, must the rest.

Consequences of this Miracle being wrought on the Sabbath Day (9-16). **9. and on the same day was the sabbath.** Beyond all doubt this was intentional, as in so many other healings, in order that, when opposition arose on this account, men might be compelled to listen to the claims and teaching of the Lord Jesus. **10. The Jews**—that is, those in

381

authority (see on ch. i. 19), **therefore said unto him that was cured, It is not lawful for thee to carry thy bed**—a glorious testimony to the cure, as *instantaneous* and *complete*, from the lips of the most prejudiced! In *ordinary* circumstances the rulers had the law on their side (Neh. xiii. 15; Jer. xvii. 21). But when the man referred them to "Him that had made him whole" as his authority, the argument was resistless. **11. He answered them, He that made me whole, the same said unto me, Take up thy bed, and walk. 12. Then asked they him, What man is that which said unto thee, Take up thy bed, and walk?** They ingeniously parry the man's thrust, asking him, not who had "made him whole"—that would have condemned themselves and defeated their purpose—but who had bidden him "take up his bed, and walk," in other words, who had dared to order a breach of the Sabbath? ''Tis time we were looking after him' —thus hoping to shake the man's faith in his Healer. **13. And** [δὲ]—or rather, '**But**' **he that was healed wist not who it was.** That some one with unparalleled generosity, tenderness, and power had done it, the man knew well enough; but as he had never heard of Him before, so He had disappeared too quickly for any enquiries. **for Jesus had conveyed himself away** [ἐξένευσεν] — had 'slipped out' of the crowd that had gathered, **a multitude being in that place**—to avoid both too hasty popularity and too precipitate hatred (Matt. xii. 14-19; ch. iv. 1, 3). **14. Afterward Jesus findeth him in the temple**—saying, perhaps, "I will go into thy house with burnt offerings; I will pay my vows, which my lips have uttered, and my mouth hath spoken, when I was in trouble" (Ps. lxvi. 13, 14). Jesus, there Himself for His own ends, "findeth him there"—*not all accidentally*, be assured. **and said unto him, Behold, thou art made whole: sin no more, lest a worse thing come unto thee** [ἵνα μὴ χεῖρόν τί σοι γένηται]—or, 'lest some worse thing befal thee—a glimpse this of the reckless life he had probably led *before* his thirty-eight years' infirmity had come upon him, and which not improbably had brought on, in the just judgment of God, his chronic complaint. Fearful illustration this of "the severity of God," but glorious manifestation of our Lord's insight into "what was in man." **15. The man departed, and told the Jews that it was Jesus which had made him whole**—little thinking how unwelcome his grateful and eager testimony would be. "The darkness," as *Olshausen* says, "received not the light which was pouring its rays upon it" (ch. i. 5-11). **16. And therefore did the Jews persecute Jesus, and sought to slay him.** [This last clause —καὶ ἐζήτουν αὐτὸν ἀποκτεῖναι—is excluded from the text by *Tischendorf* and *Tregelles*, on weighty but, as we judge, insufficient authority. *Alford* does the same, and *Lücke, Meyer,* and *de Wette,* approve of the omission, which they regard as a gloss to

17   But Jesus answered them, *[j]*My Father worketh hitherto, and I work.
18   Therefore the Jews *[k]*sought the more to kill him, because he not only had broken the sabbath, but said also that God was his Father, *[l]*making himself equal with God.
19   Then answered Jesus and said unto them, Verily, verily, I say unto you, *[m]*The Son can do nothing of himself, but what he seeth the Father do:
20   for what things soever he doeth, these also doeth the Son likewise. For *[n]*the Father loveth the Son, and showeth him all things that himself doeth: and he will show him greater works than these, that ye may
21   marvel. For as the Father raiseth up the dead, and quickeneth *them;*
22   *[o]*even so the Son quickeneth whom he will. For the Father judgeth no
23   man, but hath *[p]*committed all judgment unto the Son; that all *men*

A. D. 30.	
j ch. 9. 4.	
ch. 14. 10.	
k ch. 7. 19.	
l Zec. 13. 7.	
ch. 10. 30.	
m ch. 8. 23.	
ch. 9. 4.	
n Matt. 3. 17.	
ch. 3. 35.	
o Luke 7. 14.	
Luke 8. 54.	
p Matt.11. 27.	
ch. 3. 35.	
ch. 17. 2.	
Acts 17. 31.	

explain *v.* 18. But the word μᾶλλον—"the more"—which none propose to exclude from the text, presupposes the clause in *v.* 16, and is the strongest argument in favour of it. *Lachmann* retains the clause.] **because he had done these things on the sabbath day.** What to these hypocritical religionists was the doing of the most glorious and beneficent miracles, compared with the atrocity of doing them on the Sabbath day! Having given them this handle, on purpose to raise the first public controversy with them, and thus open a fitting opportunity for laying His claims before them, He rises at once to the whole height of them, in a statement which for grandeur, weight, and terseness exceeds almost anything that ever afterwards fell from Him—at least to His enemies.

Discourse occasioned by the opposition of the rulers to Christ's Working His glorious Miracles on the Sabbath Day (17-47). **17. But Jesus answered them, My Father worketh hitherto, and I work.** The "I" here is emphatic [κἀγώ]—*q. d.,* 'The creative and conservative activity of My Father has known no Sabbath-cessation from the beginning until now, *and that is the law of My working.*' **18. Therefore**—or 'for this cause' [διὰ τοῦτο], **the Jews sought the more to kill him, because he not only had broken the sabbath, but said also that God was his Father** [πατέρα ἴδιον]. This is not strong enough. It should be, 'that God was his own Father;' in the sense of Rom. viii. 32 (see there). **making himself equal with God.** This last clause expresses the sense in which they understood His words. And they were right in gathering this to be His meaning, not from the mere words "My Father," but from His claim of right to act as His Father did, in the like high sphere and by the same law of ceaseless activity in that sphere. And since, instead of instantly disclaiming any such meaning—as He must have done if it was false—He positively sets His seal to it in the following verses, merely explaining how consistent such claim was with the prerogatives of His Father, it is beyond all doubt that we have here an assumption of *peculiar, personal Sonship,* or participation in the Father's essential nature.

19. Then answered Jesus and said unto them, The Son can do nothing of himself [ἀφ' ἑαυτοῦ] —or 'from Himself,' that is, as an originating and independent Actor, *apart from* and *in rivalry of* the Father; which was what they supposed; **but what he seeth the Father do** [ἐὰν μή τι βλέπῃ τὸν πατέρα ποιοῦντα] —'but only what He seeth the Father doing.' The meaning is, 'The Son has and can have no separate interest or action from the Father.' **for what things soever he doeth, these also doeth the Son likewise** [ὁμοίως]—or 'in the like manner:'—*q. d.,* 'On the contrary, whatever the Father doeth, that same doeth the Son, and just as He doeth it.' What claim to absolute

equality with the Father could exceed this—not only to do *whatever* the Father does, but to do it *as* the Father does it? And yet, in perfect conformity with the natural relation of *Father* and *Son,* everything originates with the Former, and is carried out by the Latter. **20. For the Father loveth the Son.** The word here for "loveth" [φιλεῖ] is that which peculiarly denotes *personal* affection, as distinguished from that in the similar statement of the Baptist [ἀγαπᾷ], which peculiarly marks complacency in the *character* of the person loved (see on ch. iii. 35). **and showeth him all things that himself doeth.** As love has no concealments, so it results from the perfect fellowship and mutual endearment of the Father and the Son (see on ch. i. 1, 18,) Whose interests are one, even as Their nature, that the Father communicates to the Son all His counsels; and what has been thus shown to the Son is by Him executed in His mediatorial character. For, as *Alford* properly says, with the Father *doing* is *willing:* it is the Son only who *acts* in *Time.* **and he will show him greater works than these.** The order is more lively in the original—'and greater works than these will He show Him,' **that ye may marvel**—referring to what He goes on to mention (in *vv.* 21-31), and which may be comprised in two great words—"LIFE" and "JUDGMENT"—which *Stier* beautifully calls '*God's Regalia.*' Yet these Christ says the Father and He have, and put forth, in common. **21. For as the Father raiseth up the dead, and quickeneth them**—one act in two stages, the resurrection of the body and the restoration of life to it. This surely is the Father's absolute prerogative, if He have any. **even so the Son quickeneth whom he will**—not only doing the same divine act, but doing it *as the result of His own will,* even as the Father does it. This statement is of immense importance in relation to the miracles of Christ, distinguishing them from similar miracles of prophets and apostles, who as *human instruments* were employed to perform supernatural actions, while Christ did all—as the Father's *commissioned Servant* indeed, but—*in the exercise of His own absolute right of action.* **22. For the Father judgeth no man** [Οὐδὲ γὰρ ὁ πατὴρ κρίνει οὐδένα]—' For neither doth the Father judge any man:' implying that the same thing was meant in the former verse of the "quickening of the dead;" both acts being done, not by the Father *and* the Son, as though twice done, but by the Father *through* the Son as His voluntary Agent. Our Lord has now passed to the second of the "greater works" which He was to show them, to their astonishment (*v.* 20). **but hath committed all judgment unto the Son**—judgment in its most comprehensive sense, or as we should say, all *administration.* **23. That all [men] should honour the Son, even as they honour the Father.** As he who believes that Christ, in the

382

should ^qhonour the Son, even as they honour the Father. He that honoureth not the Son honoureth not the Father which hath sent him.

24 Verily, verily, I say unto you, He that heareth my word, and believeth on him that sent me, hath everlasting life, and shall not come into

25 condemnation; ^rbut is passed from death unto life. Verily, verily, I say unto you, The hour is coming, and now is, when ^sthe dead shall hear the

26 voice of the Son of God: and they that hear shall live. For as the Father hath life in himself, so hath he given to the Son to have life

27 in himself; and ^thath given him authority to execute judgment also,

28 ^ubecause he is the Son of man. Marvel not at this: for the hour is

29 coming, in the which all that are in the graves shall hear his voice, and ^vshall come forth; ^wthey that have done good, unto the resurrection of life; and they that have done evil, unto the resurrection of damnation.

30 I can of mine own self do nothing: as I hear, I judge: and my judgment

A. D. 30.
q Matt. 28.19.
1 John 2.23.
Rev. 5. 8.
r 1 John 3.14.
s Gal. 2. 20.
Eph. 2. 1, 5.
Eph. 5. 14.
Col. 2. 13.
Rev. 3. 1.
t Jer. 10. 10.
Acts 10. 42.
Acts 17. 31.
u Dan. 7. 13.
v 1 Thes.4.16.
1 Cor.15.52.
w Dan. 12. 2.
Matt.25. 32.

foregoing verses, has given a true account of His relation to the Father must of necessity hold Him entitled to the same *honour* as the Father, so He here adds that it was the Father's express intention, in making over all judgment to the Son, that men *should* thus honour Him. **He that honoureth not the Son honoureth not the Father which hath sent Him** [τὸν πέμψαντα αὐτόν]—'which sent Him:' he does not do it in fact, whatever he may imagine, and will be held as not doing it by the Father Himself, who will accept no homage which is not accorded to His own Son. 24. **Verily, verily, I say unto you, He that heareth my word, and believeth on him that sent me**—that is, 'believeth in Him *as having* sent Me,' **hath everlasting life**—hath it immediately on his believing: see on ch. iii. 18; and compare 1 John v. 12, 13; **and shall not come** [ἔρχεται]—rather, 'and cometh not' **into condemnation.** So absolved is he from guilt—so released from the sentence of condemnation, which as a sinner the divine law had fastened upon him—that the life which he enjoys is henceforth and for ever a life of uncondemned, unrebuked right to stand before a holy God on terms of peace and acceptance. **but is passed from** [μεταβέβηκεν ἐκ]—literally, 'hath passed over out of' **death unto life.** What a transition! But though 'freedom from condemnation' is that feature of this new life which our Lord *here* emphatically dwells on, it is quite evident—both from what goes before and what follows after—that it is *life from the dead* in the widest sense which our Lord means us to understand as communicated, of His own inherent will, to all who believe in Him. (Compare 1 John iii. 14.) It is as if He had said, 'I have spoken of the Son's right not only to heal the sick, but to raise from the dead, and quicken whom He will: And now I say unto you, That life-giving operation has already passed upon all who receive my words as the Sent of the Father on the great errand of mercy.' 25. **Verily, verily, I say unto you, The hour is coming** [ἔρχεται ὥρα]—or, 'There cometh an hour;' that is, in its whole fulness it was only "coming," namely, at Pentecost, **and now is**—in its beginnings, **when the dead**—the *spiritually* dead, as is clear from *v.* 28, (see on Luke ix. 60,) **shall hear the voice of the Son of God.** Here our Lord rises from the calmer phrase "hearing *His word*" (*v.* 24) to the grander expression, "hearing *the voice of the Son of God*," to signify that as it finds men in a *dead* condition, so it carries with it a divine *resurrection-power*. **and they that hear shall live**—in the largest sense of the word, as at the close of *v.* 24. 26. **For as the Father hath life in himself, so hath he given** [ἔδωκεν]—or 'gave He' **to the Son to have life in himself.** Does this refer to the essential life of

the Son before all time? (in the sense of ch. i. 4)—as most of the fathers understood it, and *Olshausen, Stier, Alford,* &c., among the moderns understand it; or, does it refer to the purpose of God that this essential life should reside in the Person of the incarnate Son, and be manifested thus to the world?—as *Calvin, Lücke, Luthardt,* &c., view it. The question is as difficult as the subject is high. But as all that Christ says of His *essential* relation to the Father is intended to explain and exalt his *mediatorial* functions, so the one seems in our Lord's own mind and language mainly the starting-point of the other. 27. **And hath given him**—or, as before, 'gave Him' **authority to execute judgment also**—as well as to quicken whom He will (*v.* 21), **because he is the Son of man.** This seems to confirm the last remark, that what Christ had properly in view was the indwelling of the Son's essential life in *humanity* as the great *theatre* and *medium* of divine display, in both the great departments of His work—*life-giving* and *judgment.* The appointment of *a Judge in our own nature* is one of the most august and beautiful arrangements of divine wisdom in Redemption. 28. **Marvel not at this**—this committal of all judgment to the Son of Man, **for the hour is coming**—or, 'there cometh an hour.' But here our Lord adds not, "and now is," as in *v.* 25; because the hour there intended was to arrive almost immediately, and in one sense had already come, whereas the hour here meant was not to arrive till the close of the whole dispensation of mercy. **in the which all that are in the graves shall hear his voice, 29. And shall come forth; they that have done good, unto the resurrection of life**—that is, the resurrection *unto* life everlasting (Matt. xxv. 46), **and they that have done evil, unto the resurrection of damnation** [κρίσεως]—or, 'of judgment,' but in the sense of *condemnation.* It would have been harsh, as *Bengel* remarks, to say, 'the resurrection of death,' though that is meant; for sinners rise only *from death to death.* The resurrection of both classes is an exercise of *sovereign authority;* but in the one case it is an act of *grace,* in the other of *justice.* Compare Dan. xii. 2, from which the language is taken. How awfully grand are these unfoldings of His dignity and authority from the mouth of Christ Himself! And they are all, it will be observed, uttered in the *third* person—as great principles and arrangements from everlasting, independent of the utterance of them on this occasion. Immediately after this, however, He resumes the *first* person. 30. I can of—or 'from' [ἀφ'] mine own self do nothing—apart from, or in rivalry of, the Father, and in any separate interest of My own (see on *v.* 19): **as I hear, I judge: and my**

383

is just; because [x]I seek not mine own will, but the will of the Father
31 which hath sent me. If [y]I bear witness of myself, my witness is not
32 true. There is another that beareth witness of me; and I know that
the witness which he witnesseth of me is true.
33, Ye sent unto John, [z]and he bare witness unto the truth. But I receive
34 not testimony from man: but these things I say, that ye might be saved.
35 He was a burning and [a]a shining light: and [b]ye were willing for a season
36 to rejoice in his light. But [c]I have greater witness than *that* of John:
for [d]the works which the Father hath given me to finish, the same works
37 that I do, bear witness of me, that the Father hath sent me. And the
Father himself, which hath sent me, [e]hath borne witness of me. Ye have
38 neither heard his voice at any time, nor [f]seen his shape. And ye have
not his word abiding in you: for whom he hath sent, him ye believe not.
39 Search [g]the Scriptures; for in them ye think ye have eternal life: and
40 [h]they are they which testify of me. And ye will not come to me, that
41, ye might have life. I [i]receive not honour from men. But I know you,
42, that ye have not the love of God in you. I am come in my Father's

A. D. 30.
[x] Matt. 26. 39.
ch. 4. 34.
ch. 6. 38.
[y] ch. 8. 14.
Rev. 3. 14.
[z] ch. 1. 15.
[a] 2 Pet. 1. 19.
[b] Matt 13. 20.
Matt. 21. 26.
[c] 1 John 5. 9.
[d] ch. 15. 24.
[e] Matt. 3. 17.
Matt. 17. 5.
[f] Deut. 4. 12.
ch. 1. 18.
[g] Isa. 8. 20.
Luke 16.29.
[h] Deut.18.15.
Luke 24.27,
44.
[i] 1 Thes. 2. 6.

Judgment is just; because I seek not mine own will, but the will of the Father which hath sent me:—*q. d.,* 'My judgments are all *anticipated* in the bosom of my Father, to which I have immediate access, and by Me they are only *responded to* and *reflected.* They cannot, therefore, err, since I live for one end only, to carry into effect the will of Him that sent Me.' **31. If I bear witness of myself** [περὶ|—'concerning Myself;' that is, in the sense already explained—standing alone, and setting up a separate interest of my own, **my witness is not true. 32. There is another that beareth witness of me**—meaning, The Father, as is plain from the connection. How brightly the distinction of the Persons shines out here! **and I know that the witness which he witnesseth of me is true.** How affecting is this allusion! Thus did Jesus cheer His own spirit under the cloud of human opposition which was already gathering over His head.

33. Ye sent unto John—referring to the deputation which these same rulers sent to the Baptist (ch. i. 19, &c.), of which, though not present, Jesus was fully cognizant, as of the answer which the Baptist returned. **and he bare witness unto the truth. 34. But I receive not testimony from man** —that is, I depend not on human testimony. That He should have permitted Himself to receive testimony from the Baptist, seemed to the Lord Jesus to need some explanation, lest it should be supposed that He stood in need of it, which therefore He here explicitly says He did not. **but these things I say, that ye might**—or 'may' **be saved.** 'If I refer to John's testimony at all, it is but to aid your faith, in order to your salvation.' **35. He was a burning and a shining light** [ὁ λύχνος ὁ καιόμενος καὶ φαίνων]—literally, 'the burning and shining lamp,' or 'torch:'—*q. d.,* 'the great light of his day.' Christ is never called by the humble word here applied to John—a *light-bearer*—studiously used to distinguish him from his Master, but ever *The Light* [τὸ φῶς] in the most absolute sense. See on ch. i. 6. **and ye were willing for a season**—that is, till they saw that it pointed whither they were not prepared to go, **to rejoice in his light.** There is a play of irony here, referring to the hollow delight with which his testimony excited them. **36. But I have greater witness** [Ἐγὼ δὲ ἔχω τὴν μαρτυρίαν μείζω]—rather, 'The witness which I have is greater' **than that of John: for the works which the Father hath given me to finish, the same works that I do, bear witness of me, that the Father hath sent me**

—not simply as *miracles,* nor even as miracles of *mercy,* but these miracles *as He did them,* with a *will* and a *power,* a *majesty* and a *grace* manifestly *His own.* **37. And the Father himself hath borne witness of me**—not referring, probably, to the voice at His baptism, but, as seems from what follows, to the testimony of the Old Testament Scriptures. (So *Calvin, Lücke, Meyer, Luthardt.*) **Ye have neither heard his voice at any time, nor seen his shape**—never recognized Him in this character. The words, as *Stier* remarks, are designedly mysterious, like many others which our Lord uttered. **38. And ye have not his word abiding in you**—passing now from the *Witness-bearer* to the *testimony* borne by the Father in "the lively oracles:" both were alike strangers to their breasts, as was evidenced by their rejecting Him to whom all that witness was borne. **39. Search the Scriptures** ['Ερευνᾶτε]—or 'Ye search.' As either sense may be adopted consistently with the word itself, we must be guided by what seems to be the strain of our Lord's statement. But on this interpreters are entirely divided, and most are satisfied that theirs is the only tenable sense. The *indicative* sense—'Ye search'—is adopted by *Cyril* among the fathers, and of moderns by *Erasmus, Beza, Lampe, Bengel, Campbell, Olshausen, Meyer, de Wette, Lücke, Tholuck, Webster and Wilkinson.* In the *imperative* sense—'Search'—our translators are supported by *Chrysostom* and *Augustin* among the fathers, and of moderns by *Luther, Calvin, Grotius, Maldonat, Wetstein, Stier, Alford.* Perhaps the former sense—'Ye search'—best accords with what follows. **for in them ye think** [δοκεῖτε] —'deem,' 'consider'; in a good sense, **ye have eternal life: and they are they which testify of me. 40. And ye will not come** [οὐ θέλετε ἐλθεῖν]— rather, 'ye are not willing to come' **to me, that ye might have life:**—*q. d.,* 'With disregarding the Scriptures I charge you not: Ye do indeed busy yourselves about them (He was addressing, it will be remembered, the *rulers*—see on *v.* 16); rightly deeming them your Charter of eternal life: But ye miss the great Burden of them: Of Me it is they testify; and yet to Me ye will not come for that eternal life which ye profess to find there, and of which they proclaim Me the ordained Dispenser.' (See Acts xvii. 11, 12.) Severe though this rebuke was, there is something most touching and gracious in it. **41. I receive not honour** [δόξαν] —'applause,' 'glory,' **from men**—contrasting His own end with theirs, which was to obtain human applause. **42. But I know you, that ye have not**

384

43 name, and ye receive me not: if another shall come in his own name,
44 him ye will receive. How can ye believe, which receive honour one of
45 another, and seek not ʲthe honour that *cometh* from God only? Do not
   think that I will accuse you to the Father: ᵏthere is *one* that accuseth
46 you, *even* Moses, in whom ye trust. For had ye believed Moses, ye
47 would have believed me: ˡfor he wrote of me. But if ᵐye believe not
   his writings, how shall ye believe my words?

A. D. 30.
ʲ Rom. 2. 29.
ᵏ Rom. 2. 12.
ˡ Gen. 3. 15.
Gen. 12. 3.
Gen. 18. 18.
Acts 26. 22.
ᵐ Luke 16.29, 31.

the love of God in you—which would have in-spired you with a single desire to know His mind and will, and yield yourselves to it, in spite of prejudice, and regardless of consequences. **43. I am come in my Father's name, and ye receive me not: if another shall come in his own name, him ye will receive.** How strikingly has this been verified in the history of the Jews. From the time of the true Christ to our time, says *Bengel*, sixty-four false Christs have been reckoned, by whom the Jews have been deceived. **44. How can ye believe, which receive honour one of another, and seek not the honour that cometh from God only.** The "*can*" not here, and the "*will*" not of *v.* 40, are but different aspects of one and the same state of the human heart, under the conscious and entire dominion of corrupt principles and affec-tions—as contrasted with that simplicity and godly sincerity which, as in Nathanael (ch. i. 47), seeks only to know and receive the truth. **45. Do not think that I will accuse you to the Father:**—*q. d.*, 'My errand hither is not to collect evidence to condemn you at God's bar.' **there is one that accuseth you, even Moses, in whom ye trust** [ἠλπίκατε]—or 'hope':—*q. d.*, 'Alas! that will be too well done by another, and him the object of all your religious boastings—Moses;' here put for "*the Law*," the basis of the Old Testament Scrip-tures. **46. For had ye believed Moses, ye would have believed me** [ἐπιστεύετε]—rather, 'If ye be-lieved Moses, ye would believe Me,' **for he wrote of me**—an important testimony, as *Alford* re-marks, to the subject of the whole Pentateuch, "of ME." **47. But if ye believe not his writings** (see on Luke xvi. 31), **how shall ye believe my words?** —a remarkable contrast, not absolutely putting Old Testament Scripture below His own words, but pointing to the office of those venerable docu-ments to *prepare* Christ's way, to the necessity universally felt for *documentary* testimony in re-vealed religion, and perhaps, as *Stier* adds, to the relation which the comparative "*letter*" of the Old Testament holds to the more flowing "words" of "spirit and life" which characterize the New Testament.

Remarks.—1. The light in which the ministry of angels is presented to us in connection with the pool of Bethesda is most interesting and instruc-tive. First, it would appear that one particular angel had charge over the miraculous virtue of this pool. And next, all that he did was to "trouble" the water. That the patient who first stepped in after this owed his cure to *angelical virtue* is not said. The contrary is rather implied, and is in accordance with all else that we read of their ministry. They ministered to the tempted Saviour, but only in the way of bringing Him, as one of them did to Elijah (1 Ki. xix. 5-8), the bodily sustenance for which He had so long confidingly waited (Matt. iv. 11). In the extremity of His agony, there appeared an angel unto Him from heaven, strengthening Him; but for *spiritual* strength there is no reason to suppose that Jesus was indebted to an angel, save in so far as the consciousness of supernatural vigour of body and spirit to sustain the Conflict, certainly imparted by this angel, would tend to reassure Him of His

Father's love and presence with Him in that awful hour. When apprehended, He expressed His con-fidence that He could immediately have, for the asking, more than twelve legions of angels, to free Him—if He desired it—from the hands of men; but that only. In heaven, He tells us, the angels of His dear "little ones" always behold the face of His Father which is in heaven (Matt. xviii. 10)—to receive, we may suppose, His commands con-cerning them. And Lazarus, in the parable, when he died, was carried by angels into Abraham's bosom. But in no case do their ministrations extend beyond what is *outward.* That they have either command or ability to interfere *between the soul and God in things purely spiritual*, or to affect the spiritual life at all save in the way of external ministration, we are bound—with such Scripture statements before us—positively to deny. How different from this is the teaching of the Church of Rome, is known to all. 2. Those who can see in the Discourse which our Lord uttered on this occasion no claim to essential equality with God, and no assertion of the distinct conscious Per-sonality of the Father and the Son, are not likely to see it anywhere else. It is not, in fact, more evidence that such want: it is the right apprecia-tion of the evidence they possess. Nor can there be any doubt that unwillingness—whether con-scious or not—to credit these truths *on any evidence* lies at the bottom of the rejection of them. But those who recognize in this Discourse the Personal distinctions in the Godhead should not overlook these further intimations clearly to be gathered from it—that *unity of action* among the Persons results from *unity of nature;* and that Their one-ness of interest is no unconscious or involuntary thing, but a thing of glorious consciousness, will, and love, of which the Persons themselves are the proper Objects. 3. In the announcement that the *dead* shall *hear* the voice of the Son of God, and hearing shall *live*—first, spiritually at this present time, and then corporeally at the resurrection-day (*vv.* 25, 28, 29)—we have one of those apparent paradoxes which "the wise and prudent" ever stumble at, but to faith are full of glory. See on Matt. xii. 9-21, Remark 3 at the close of that Section. 4. Observe the honour accorded to the Scriptures generally, and the Old Testament Scrip-tures in particular, by the Lord Jesus. Whether we understand Him to bid them "Search the Scriptures," or in the way of commendation to say, "Ye do search the Scriptures," even though this was addressed more immediately to the rulers, the reason assigned for it—that in them they thought they had eternal life—is enough to show that in His view it was alike the *interest* and the *duty* of all to search them. How directly in the teeth of this is the teaching of the Church of Rome, none need to be told. See on Luke xvi. 1-31, Remark 9 at the close of that Section. But 5. In that miserable "searching of the Scriptures" to which the Jewish ecclesiastics certainly ad-dicted themselves—and in which they have been even exceeded by the learned rabbins of later times—we see how possible it is to rest in the mere *Book* without the living *spirit* of it, and above all without the living *Christ* of it—to direct

6 AFTER *a* these things Jesus went over the sea of Galilee, which is *the*
2 *sea* of Tiberias. And a great multitude followed him, because they saw
3 his miracles which he did on them that were diseased. And Jesus went
4 up into a mountain, and there he sat with his disciples. And *b* the pass-
5 over, a feast of the Jews, was nigh. When *c* Jesus then lifted up *his* eyes,
and saw a great company come unto him, he saith unto Philip, Whence
6 shall we buy bread, that these may eat? (And this he said to prove him:
7 for he himself knew what he would do.) Philip answered him, *d* Two
hundred penny-worth of bread is not sufficient for them, that every one
8 of them may take a little. One of his disciples, Andrew, Simon Peter's
9 brother, saith unto him, There is a lad here, which hath five barley
10 loaves, and two small fishes: *e* but what are they among so many? And
Jesus said, Make the men sit down. Now there was much grass in the
11 place. So the men sat down, in number about five thousand. And Jesus
took the loaves; and when he had *f* given thanks, he distributed to the
disciples, and the disciples to them that were set down; and likewise of
12 the fishes as much as they would. When they were filled, he said unto
his disciples, Gather up the fragments that remain, that nothing be lost.
13 Therefore they gathered *them* together, and filled twelve baskets with the
fragments of the five barley loaves, which remained over and above unto
them that had eaten.
14 Then those men, when they had seen the miracle that Jesus did, said,
15 This is of a truth *g* that prophet that should come into the world. When
Jesus therefore perceived that they would come and take him by force, to
make him a king, he departed again into a mountain himself alone.
16 And *h* when even was *now* come, his disciples went down unto the sea,
17 and entered into a ship, and went over the sea toward Capernaum. And
18 it was now dark, and Jesus was not come to them. And the sea arose,
19 by reason of a great wind that blew. So when they had rowed about five
and twenty or thirty furlongs, they see Jesus walking on the sea, and
20 drawing nigh unto the ship: and they were afraid. But he saith unto
21 them, It is I; be not afraid. Then they willingly received him into the
ship: and immediately the ship was at the land whither they went.
22 The day following, when the people which stood on the other side of
the sea saw that there was none other boat there, save that one whereinto
his disciples were entered, and that Jesus went not with his disciples into
23 the boat, but *that* his disciples were gone away alone; (howbeit there
came other boats from Tiberias, nigh unto the place where they did eat

A. D. 32.

CHAP. 6.
a Matt 14. 15.
Mark 6. 35.
Luke 9. 10.
b Ex. 12. 6.
Lev. 23. 5, 7.
Num. 28. 16.
Deut. 16. 1.
ch. 2. 13.
ch. 5. 1.
ch. 11. 55.
ch. 12. 1.
ch 13. 1.
c Matt. 14. 14.
Mark 6. 35.
Luke 9. 12.
d Num. 11. 21,
22.
2 Ki. 7. 2.
Matt. 15. 33.
Mark 6. 37.
Mark 8. 4.
e 2 Ki 4. 43.
Ps. 78. 19, 20.
Matt. 14. 16,
17.
Luke 9. 13.
f Ex. 23. 25.
1 Sam. 9. 13.
Matt. 14. 19.
Matt. 15 36.
Matt. 26. 26.
Luke 24. 30.
1 Tim. 4. 5.
g Gen. 49. 10.
Deut. 18. 15.
18.
Isa. 7. 14.
Isa. 9. 6.
Isa. 35. 5.
Matt. 11. 3.
Matt. 21. 11.
Luke 7. 16.
ch. 1. 21.
ch. 4. 19, 25.
ch. 7. 40.
Acts 7. 37.
h Matt. 14. 23.
Mark 6. 47.

---

the soul to Whom is its main use and chiefest glory.

CHAP. VI. 1-21.—JESUS CROSSES TO THE EASTERN SIDE OF THE SEA OF GALILEE, FOLLOWED BY A GREAT MULTITUDE—HE FEEDS THEM MIRACULOUSLY TO THE NUMBER OF FIVE THOUSAND, AND SENDS HIS DISCIPLES BY SHIP AGAIN TO THE WESTERN SIDE, HIMSELF RETURNING AFTERWARDS WALKING ON THE SEA. (=Matt. xiv. 13-36; Mark vi. 30-56; Luke ix. 10-17.) For the exposition, see on Mark vi. 30-56. But the reader will do well to mark here again the important note of time introduced quite parenthetically at *v.* 4—**And the passover, the feast of the Jews, was nigh.** This, according to our reckoning, was the *third* passover since our Lord entered on His public ministry. See on Mark vi. 34.

22-71.—JESUS, FOLLOWED BY THE MULTITUDES TO CAPERNAUM, DISCOURSES TO THEM, CHIEFLY IN THE SYNAGOGUE, OF THE BREAD OF LIFE—EFFECT OF THIS ON TWO CLASSES OF DISCIPLES.

The Multitudes, finding Jesus gone, cross to the Western Side of the Lake, and find Him at Capernaum (22-25). These verses are a little involved,

from the Evangelist's desire to mention every circumstance, however minute, that might call up the scene as vividly to the reader as it stood before his own view. **22. The day following**—that is, the day after the miracle of the loaves and the stormy night, or the day on which Jesus and His disciples landed at Capernaum, **when the people**—'the multitude' [ὁ ὄχλος], **which stood on the other side of the sea**—not the whole multitude that had been fed, but only such of them as remained over night about the shore, that is, on the *east* side of the lake; for we are supposed to have come, with Jesus and His disciples in the ship, to the *west* side, to Capernaum; **saw that there was none other boat there, save that one whereinto his disciples were entered . . . but that his disciples were gone away alone.** The meaning is, the people had observed that there had been only one boat on the East side where they were, namely, the one in which the disciples had crossed at night to the other, the West side, and they had also observed that Jesus had not gone on board that boat, but His disciples had put off without Him. **23. (How-beit—**adds the Evangelist, in a lively parenthesis,

24 bread, after that the Lord had given thanks:) when the people therefore saw that Jesus was not there, neither his disciples, they also took shipping, and came to Capernaum, seeking for Jesus.

25 And when they had found him on the other side of the sea, they said unto him, Rabbi, when camest thou hither?

26 Jesus answered them and said, Verily, verily, I say unto you, Ye seek me, not because ye saw the miracles, but because ye did eat of the

27 loaves, and were filled. ¹Labour not for the meat which perisheth, but ⁱfor that meat which endureth unto everlasting life, which the Son of

28 man shall give unto you: ʲfor him hath God the Father sealed. Then said they unto him, What shall we do, that we might work the works of

29 God? Jesus answered and said unto them, This ᵏis the work of God,

30 that ye believe on him whom he hath sent. They said therefore unto him, ˡWhat sign showest thou then, that we may see, and believe thee?

Side notes:
A. D. 32.
1 Or, Work not.
ᵉ ch. 4. 14.
Rom. 6. 23.
ʲ Matt. 3. 17.
Matt. 17. 5.
Mark 1. 11.
Mark 9. 7.
Luke 3. 22.
Luke 9. 35.
ch. 1. 33.
ch. 5. 37.
Acts 2. 22.
2 Pet. 1. 17.
ᵏ 1 John 3. 23.
ˡ Mark 8. 11.
1 Cor. 1. 22.

---

there came other boats from Tiberias—which lay near the south-west coast of the lake, whose passengers were part of the multitude that had followed Jesus to the East side, and been miraculously fed: these boats were fastened somewhere, says the Evangelist, **nigh unto the place where they did eat bread, after that the Lord had given thanks)** —thus he refers to the glorious "miracle of the loaves:" and now these boats were put in requisition to convey the people back again to the West side. For, says our Evangelist, **24. When the people—'the multitude,' therefore saw that Jesus was not there, neither his disciples, they also took shipping**—in these boats, **and came to Capernaum, seeking for Jesus. 25. And when they had found him on the other side of the sea**—at Capernaum, probably, as may be gathered perhaps from *vv.* 17-59; although one would infer from the other Gospels that He and the disciples had landed rather somewhere else—it may be in the neighbourhood of it (Matt. xiv. 34, 35; Mark vi. 53).

Jesus, questioned by the Multitudes that had run after Him, about His having got the start of them, changes the Subject, and, from the Loaves they had been filled with, Discourses to them of the Bread of Life (25-59). **25. And when they had found him on the other side of the sea, they said unto him, Rabbi, when camest thou hither?**—astonished at His *being* there, and wondering *how* He could have accomplished it, whether by land or water, and *when* He came; for being quite unaware of His having walked upon the sea and landed with the disciples in the ship, they could not see how, unless He had travelled all night round the head of the lake alone, He could have reached Capernaum, and even then how He could have arrived before themselves. Jesus does not put them through their difficulty, says nothing of His treading on the waves of the sea, nor even notices their question, but takes advantage of the favourable moment for pointing out to them how forward, flippant, and superficial were their spirit and views, and how low their desires.

26. Jesus answered them, Verily, verily, I say unto you, Ye seek me, not because ye saw the miracles [σημεῖα]—literally 'signs;' that is, supernatural tokens of a higher presence and a divine commission, **but because ye did eat of the loaves, and were filled.** From this He proceeds at once to that *other Bread*, just as, with the woman of Samaria, to that *other Water*, (ch. iv.) We should have supposed all that follows to have been delivered by the way-side, or wherever they happened first to meet. But from *v.* 59 we gather that they had probably met about the door of the synagogue—'for that,' says *Light*-

foot, 'was the day in which they assembled in their synagogues'—and that on being asked, at the close of the service, if He had any word of exhortation to the people, He had taken the two breads, the *perishing* and *the living* bread, for the subject of His profound and extraordinary Discourse. **27. Labour** [Ἐργάζεσθε]—or 'work' **not for the meat which perisheth, but for that meat which endureth unto everlasting life, which the Son of man**—taking that title of Himself which denoted His incarnate life, **shall give unto you**—in the sense of *v.* 51: for him hath God the Father **sealed** [τοῦτον γὰρ ὁ πατὴρ ἐσφράγισεν ὁ Θεὸς]—rather, perhaps, 'for Him hath the Father sealed, even God;' that is, marked out and authenticated for that transcendent office, to impart to the world the bread of an everlasting life, and this in the character of "the Son of *Man*." **28. Then said they unto him, What shall we do, that we might work the works of God?**—such works, that is, as God will approve. To this question different answers may be given, according to the *spirit* which prompts the enquiry (see Mic. vi. 6-8; Luke iii. 12-14). Here our Lord, knowing whom He had to deal with, shapes His reply accordingly. **29. Jesus answered and said unto them, This is the work of God, that ye believe on him whom he hath sent** [ἀπέστειλεν]—'Him whom He sent.' This lies at the threshold of all acceptable obedience, being not only the pre-requisite to it but the proper spring of it—in that sense it is the work of works, emphatically "*the* work of God." **30. They said therefore unto him, What sign showest thou then, that we may see, and believe thee? what dost thou work?** But how could they ask "a sign," when many of them scarce a day before had witnessed such a "sign" as had never till then been vouchsafed to men; when after witnessing it they could hardly be restrained from making Him a king; when they followed Him from the one side of the lake to the other; and when, in the opening words of this very Discourse, He had chid them for seeking Him, "not because they *saw the signs*," but for the loaves? The truth seems to be, that they were confounded by the *novel claims* which our Lord had just advanced. In proposing to make Him a king, it was for far other purposes than dispensing to the world the bread of an everlasting life; and when He seemed to raise His claims even higher still, by representing it as the grand "work of God," that they should believe *on Himself* as His Sent One, they saw very clearly that He was making a demand upon them beyond anything they were prepared to accord to Him, and beyond all that man had ever before made. Hence their question, "What dost thou *work?*" **31. Our fathers did eat manna in the desert; as**

31 what dost thou work? Our ^mfathers did eat manna in the desert; as it is written, ⁿHe gave them bread from heaven to eat.

32 Then Jesus said unto them, Verily, verily, I say unto you, Moses gave you not that bread from heaven; but my Father giveth you the true

33 bread from heaven. For the bread of God is he which cometh down from

34 heaven, and giveth life unto the world. Then said they unto him, Lord,

35 evermore give us this bread. And Jesus said unto them, I am the bread of life: ^ohe that cometh to me shall never hunger; and he that believeth

36 on me shall never thirst. But I said unto you, That ye also have seen

37 me, and believe not. All that the Father giveth me shall come to me:

38 and ^phim that cometh to me I will in no wise cast out. For I came down from heaven, ^qnot to do mine own will, ^rbut the will of him that

39 sent me. And this is the Father's will which hath sent me, ^sthat of all which he hath given me I should lose nothing, but should raise it up

40 again at the last day. And this is the will of him that sent me, that ^tevery one which seeth the Son, and believeth on him, may have everlasting life: and I will raise him up at the last day.

A. D. 32.
^m Ex. 16. 15.
Num. 11. 7.
Neh. 9. 15.
1 Cor. 10. 3.
ⁿ Ps. 78. 24.
Neh. 9. 15.
1 Cor. 10. 3.
Rev. 2. 17.
^o Matt. 11. 28.
ch. 7. 37.
Rev. 22. 17.
^p 2 Tim. 2. 19.
1 John 2. 19.
^q Matt. 26. 39.
ch. 5. 30.
^r ch. 4. 34.
^s ch. 10. 28.
ch. 18. 9.
Col. 3. 3.
Jude 1.
^t ch. 4. 14.

---

it is written, He gave them bread from heaven to eat—insinuating the inferiority of Christ's miracle of the loaves to those of Moses:—*q. d.,* 'When Moses claimed the confidence of the fathers, "he gave them bread from heaven to eat"—not for a few thousands, but for millions, and not once only, but daily throughout their wilderness journey.' **32. Then**—or 'therefore' [οὖν] **Jesus said unto them, Verily, verily, I say unto you, Moses gave you not that bread** [δέδωκεν τὸν]—'hath not given you the bread' **from heaven; but my Father giveth you the true bread from heaven.** Every word here is an emphatic contradiction to their statement. 'It was not Moses that gave you the manna, and even it was but from the lower heavens; "but *My Father* giveth you *the true bread,*" and that "*from heaven.*"' **33. For the bread of God is he which cometh down from heaven, and giveth life unto the world.** This verse is perhaps best left in its own transparent grandeur—holding up, as it does, the Bread itself as divine, spiritual, and eternal; its ordained Fountain and essential Substance, Him who came down from heaven to give it, that Eternal Life which was with the Father, and was manifested unto us (1 John i. 2); and its designed objects, "the world." **34. Then**—or 'therefore' **said they unto him, Lord, evermore give us this bread**—speaking now with a certain reverence, as at *v.* 25; the perpetuity of the manna floating perhaps in their minds, and much like the Samaritan woman, when her eyes were but half opened, "Sir, give me this water," &c. (ch. iv. 15). **35. And**—or, 'But' **Jesus said unto them, I am the bread of life.** Henceforth the discourse is all *in the first person*—"I," "Me"—which occurs in one form or other, as *Stier* reckons, thirty-five times. **he that cometh to me**—to obtain what the soul craves, and as the only all-sufficient and ordained Source of supply, **shall never hunger; and he that believeth on me shall never thirst**—shall have conscious and abiding satisfaction. **36. But I said unto you, That ye also have seen me**—rather 'that ye have even seen Me,' **and believe not**—that is, seen Him not in His mere bodily presence, but in all the majesty of His life, His teaching, His works. **37. All that** [which] **the Father giveth me shall come to me: and him that cometh to me I will in no wise cast out. 38. For I came down**—or 'have come down' [καταβέβηκα] **from heaven, not to do mine own will, but the will of him that sent me. 39. And this is the Father's will which hath sent me.** The true reading

beyond doubt here is, 'This is the will of Him that sent Me' [πατρὸς having no sufficient authority], **that of all** [that] **which he hath given me I should lose nothing, but should raise it up again at the last day. 40. And this is the will of him that sent me.** Here the reading of 'the Father which hath sent Me' has much better support than in *v.* 39, though scarcely sufficient, perhaps, to justify its insertion (with *Lachmann, Tischendorf,* and *Tregelles*). **that every one which seeth** [θεωρῶν]—rather, 'beholdeth' **the Son, and believeth on him, may**—or should **have everlasting life: and I will raise him up**—rather, 'and that I should raise him up' **at the last day.** This comprehensive and very grand passage is expressed with a peculiar artistic precision. The opening general statement (*v.* 37) consists of two members: First, "ALL THAT THE FATHER GIVETH ME SHALL COME TO ME:"—*q. d.,* 'Though ye, as I told you, have no faith in Me, My errand into the world shall in no wise be defeated; for all that the Father giveth Me shall infallibly come to Me.' Observe, what is *given* Him by the Father is expressed in the *singular* number and *neuter* gender —literally, 'all [that] which' [πᾶν ὃ]; while those who *come* to Him are put in the *masculine* gender and *singular* number—'him that cometh' [τὸν ἐρχόμενον]. The *whole mass,* so to speak, is gifted by the Father to the Son as a *unity,* which the Son evolves, one by one, in the execution of His trust; so (ch. xvii. 2) "that He should give eternal life to *all that which* thou hast given him" [πᾶν ὃ δέδωκας]. The "*shall* come" of *v.* 37 expresses the glorious *certainty* of it; the Father being pledged to see to it that the gift become a reality. Second, "AND HIM THAT COMETH TO ME I WILL IN NO WISE CAST OUT." As the former was the *divine,* this is just the *human* side of the same thing. True, the "coming" ones of the second clause are just the "given" ones of the first. But had our Lord merely said, '*When those* that have been given me of My Father shall come to Me, I will receive them,'—besides being very flat, the impression conveyed would have been quite different, sounding as if there were *no other laws in operation,* in the movement of sinners towards Christ, but such as are wholly *divine* and *inscrutable* to us; whereas, though He does speak of it as a sublime certainty which men's *refusals* cannot frustrate, He speaks of that certainty as taking effect only by men's *voluntary advances* to Him and acceptance of Him—"Him that cometh to me," "whosoever will"—thus throwing the door wide

41   The Jews then murmured at him, because he said, I am the bread
42 which came down from heaven. And they said, Is not this Jesus, the
Son of Joseph, whose father and mother we know? how is it then that he
43 saith, I came down from heaven? Jesus therefore answered and said
44 unto them, Murmur not among yourselves. No man can come to me,
except the Father which hath sent me draw him: and I will raise him up
45 at the last day. It "is written in the Prophets, And they shall be all
taught of God. Every man therefore that hath heard, and hath learned
46 of the Father, cometh unto me. Not ^{v}that any man hath seen the
47 Father, save ^{w}he which is of God, he hath seen the Father. Verily,
48 verily, I say unto you, ^{x}He that believeth on me hath everlasting life. I
49 am that bread of life. Your fathers did eat manna in the wilderness,
50 and are dead. This is the bread which cometh down from heaven, that

A. D. 32.
^{u} Isa. 54. 13.
Jer. 31. 34.
Mic. 4. 2.
Heb. 8. 10.
Heb. 10. 16.
^{v} ch. 1. 18.
ch. 5. 37.
^{w} Matt. 11. 27.
Luke 10. 22.
ch. 1. 18.
ch 7. 29.
ch. 8. 19.
2 Cor. 4. 6.
^{x} ch. 3. 16, 36.
ch. 5. 24.
1 John 5. 12.

open. Only it is not the simply *willing*, but the actually *coming*, whom He will not cast out. "In no wise" [οὐ μὴ] is an emphatic negative, to meet the fears of the timid—as in Rev. xxi. 27, to meet the presumption of the hardened. These, then, being the emphatic members of the general opening statement, what follows is meant to resume and reiterate them both in another form. But first, we have a parenthetic and emphatic explanation that His mission from heaven to earth had but one object—to carry into effect the Father's purposes: "For I came down from heaven, not to do mine own will"—not to act an independent part—"but," in respect of both the foregoing things, both the *divine* and the *human* side of salvation, to do "the will of Him that sent Me" (*v.* 38). What this two-fold will of Him that sent Him is, we are next sublimely told, *vv.* 39, 40. Thus:

First,   "ALL THAT WHICH THE FATHER GIV- ETH ME SHALL COME TO ME."
This is now emphatically reiterated:
"AND THIS IS THE WILL OF HIM THAT SENT ME, THAT OF ALL THAT WHICH HE HATH GIVEN ME I SHOULD LOSE NOTHING, BUT SHOULD RAISE IT UP AGAIN AT THE LAST DAY."
So much for the *divine* side of man's salvation, whose every stage and movement is inscrutable to us, but infallibly certain.

Secondly, "AND HIM THAT COMETH TO ME I WILL IN NO WISE CAST OUT."
This also is now emphatically reiterated:
"AND THIS IS THE WILL OF THE FATHER WHICH HATH SENT ME, THAT EVERY ONE WHICH SEETH THE SON, AND BELIEVETH ON HIM, MAY HAVE EVER- LASTING LIFE: AND I WILL RAISE HIM UP AT THE LAST DAY."
This is just the *human* side of the same thing. (See on *v.* 54.)

Thus God has a two-fold will about the salvation of men. He wills that those whom He has given in trust to His Son shall be presented faultless before the presence of His glory—redeemed from all iniquity, and their sleeping dust raised incorruptible. But He further wills that if any poor sinner, all ignorant of this secret purpose, but attracted by the grace and glory of His Son, shall believe on Him, he shall have eternal life and be raised up at the last day.
41. The Jews then murmured at him—or 'muttered' [ἐγόγγυζον], not in our Lord's hearing, but He knew it (*v.* 43; ch. ii. 25), **because he said I**
389

am the bread which came down from heaven.
42. And they said, Is not this Jesus, the son of Joseph, whose father and mother we know? how is it then that he—or 'this man' [οὗτος], **saith I came down from heaven?** Missing the sense and glory of this, and having no relish for such sublimities, they harp upon the "Bread from heaven." 'What *can* this mean? Do we not know all about him—where, when, and of whom he was born? And yet he says he came down from heaven?' **43. Jesus therefore answered and said unto them, Murmur not among yourselves. 44. No man can come to me** (in the sense of *v.* 35), **except the Father which hath sent me**—that is, except the Father as the Sender of Me, and to carry out the design of My mission **draw him**— by an internal and efficacious operation; though by all the means of rational conviction, and in a way altogether consonant to their moral nature. (Song i. 4; Jer. xxxi. 3; Hos. xi. 3, 4.) **and I will raise him up at the last day.** See on *v.* 54. Thus this weighty statement amounts to the following: 'Be not either startled or stumbled at these sayings; for it needs divine teaching to understand them, divine drawing to submit to them.' **45. It is written in the Prophets** (in Isa. liv. 13; Jer. xxxi. 33, 34.) Other similar passages may also have been in view. Our Lord thus falls back upon Scripture authority for this seemingly hard saying. **And they shall be all taught of God**—not by *external* revelation merely, but by *internal illumination*, corresponding to the "drawing" of *v.* 44. **Every man therefore that hath heard, and hath learned of the Father**—who hath been thus efficaciously taught of Him, **cometh unto me**—*with absolute certainty*, yet in every case voluntarily, as above explained:—*q. d.,* 'As none can come to Me save as divinely drawn, so none thus drawn shall fail to come.' **46. Not that any man hath seen the Father, save he which is of God** [παρὰ τοῦ Θεοῦ]— or 'from God;' but in the sense of ch. i. 14, "the Only begotten [forth] from the Father." Lest they should confound that "hearing and learning of the Father," to which believers are admitted by divine *teaching*, with His own immediate access to Him, He here throws in a parenthetical explanation; stating, as explicitly as words could do it, how totally different the two cases were, and that only He who is "from God" hath this naked, immediate access to the Father. **47. Verily, verily, I say unto you, He that believeth on me hath everlasting life.** See on ch. iii. 36; and on ch. v. 24. **48. I am that bread of life.** This is repeated from *v.* 35, 'As he that believeth in Me hath everlasting life, so I am Myself the everlasting *Sustenance* of that life.' **49. Your fathers**—of whom ye spake (*v.* 31). Observe, He does not say '*Our* fathers' —by which, as *Bengel* remarks, He would hint

51 a man may eat thereof, and not die. I am the living bread which came down from heaven. If any man eat of this bread, he shall live for ever: and *ᵞ*the bread that I will give is my flesh, which I will give for the life of the world.

52 The Jews therefore *ᶻ*strove among themselves, saying, *ᵃ*How can this **53** man give us *his* flesh to eat? Then Jesus said unto them, Verily, verily, I say unto you, Except *ᵇ*ye eat the flesh of the Son of man, and **54** drink his blood, ye have no life in you. Whoso eateth my flesh, and drinketh my blood, hath eternal life; and I will raise him up at the **55** last day. For my flesh is meat indeed, and my blood is drink indeed. **56** He that eateth my flesh, and drinketh my blood, *ᶜ*dwelleth in me, and I **57** in him. As the living Father hath sent me, and I live by the Father; so

A. D. 32.

ᵛ Heb. 10. 5, 10.
ᶻ ch. 7. 43.
  ch. 9. 16.
  ch. 10. 19.
ᵃ ch. 3. 9.
ᵇ Matt. 26. 26.
ᶜ 1 Cor. 6. 17.
  1 Cor. 12. 27.
  2 Cor. 6. 16.
  Eph. 3. 17.
  Eph. 5. 30.
  1 John 3. 24.
  1 John 4. 15, 16.

that *He* had a higher descent of which they dreamt not. **did eat manna in the wilderness, and are dead**—recurring to their own point about the manna, as one of the noblest of the *ordained* preparatory illustrations of His own office: 'Your fathers, ye say, ate manna in the wilderness, and ye say well, for so they did; *but they are dead*— even they whose carcases fell in the wilderness did eat of that bread: the Bread whereof I speak cometh down from heaven, which the manna never did, that men, eating of it, may *live for ever.*' **50. This, &c. 51. I am the living bread which came down from heaven. If any man eat of this bread, he shall live for ever: and the bread** [καὶ ὁ ἄρτος δὲ]—'aye, and,' or 'yea, and the Bread' **that I will give is my flesh, which I will give for the life of the world.** 'Understand, it is of MYSELF I now speak as the Bread from heaven; of ME if a man eat he shall live for ever; and "THE BREAD WHICH I WILL GIVE IS MY FLESH WHICH I WILL GIVE FOR THE LIFE OF THE WORLD." Here, for the first time in this high discourse, our Lord explicitly introduces His sacrificial *death*—for what impartial student of Scripture can doubt this?— not only as that which constitutes Him the Bread of life to men, but as THAT very element IN HIM WHICH POSSESSES THE LIFE-GIVING VIRTUE. From this time forth, observes *Stier*—and the remark is an important one—we hear no more in this Discourse of "Bread:" that figure is dropped, and the Reality takes its place. The words "I will *give*" may be compared with the words of institution at the Supper, "This is My body which is *given* for you (Luke xxii. 19), and, as the apostle reports it, "*broken* for you" (1 Cor. xi. 24). **52. The Jews therefore strove among themselves**—arguing the point keenly among themselves, **saying, How can this man give us his flesh to eat?**—'Give us his flesh to eat? Absurd.' **53. Then Jesus said unto them, Verily, verily, I say unto you, Except ye eat the flesh of the Son of man, and drink his blood, ye have no life in you.** This is the harshest word He had yet uttered in their ears. They asked how it was *possible* to eat His flesh. He answers with great solemnity, 'It is *indispensable.*' Yet even here a thoughtful hearer might find something to temper the harshness. He says they must not only "eat His *flesh*" but "drink His *blood*," which could not but suggest the idea of His *death*—implied in the separation of one's flesh from his blood. And as He had already hinted that it was to be something very different from a *natural* death, saying, "My flesh I will give for the life of the world" (*v.* 51), it must have been pretty plain to candid hearers that He meant something above the gross idea which the bare terms expressed. And farther, when He added that they "had no *life* in them unless they thus ate and drank," it was impossible they should think He meant that the *temporal* life

they were then living was dependent on their eating and drinking, in this gross sense, His flesh and blood. Yet the whole statement was certainly confounding, and beyond doubt was meant to be so. Our Lord had told them that in spite of all they had "seen" in Him they "did not believe" (*v.* 36). For *their* conviction, therefore, He does not here lay Himself out; but having the ear not only of them but of the more *candid* and *thoughtful* in the crowded synagogue, and the miracle of the loaves having led up to the most exalted of all views of His Person and Office, He takes advantage of their very difficulties and objections to announce, for all time, those most profound truths which are here expressed, regardless of the disgust of the unteachable, and the prejudices even of the most sincere, which His language would seem only designed to deepen. The *truth* really conveyed here is no other than that expressed in *v.* 51, though in more emphatic terms—that Himself, in the virtue of His sacrificial death, is the spiritual and eternal life of men; and that unless men voluntarily appropriate to themselves this death, in its sacrificial virtue, so as to become the very life and nourishment of their inner man, they have no spiritual and eternal life at all. Not as if His death were the *only* thing of value, but it is what gives all else in Christ's Incarnate Person, Life, and Office, their whole value *to us sinners*. **54. Whoso**—or 'He that' **eateth my flesh, and drinketh my blood, hath eternal life.** This is just the positive expression of what in the former verse He had expressed negatively. There it was '*Unless* ye so partake of Me, ye have not life;' here it is, 'Whosoever does so *hath* life everlasting.' **and I will raise him up at the last day.** For the fourth time this is repeated (see *vv.* 39, 40, 44)—showing most clearly that the "eternal life" which such a man "*hath*" cannot be the same with the *future* resurrection-life, from which it is carefully distinguished each time, but a life communicated *here below* immediately on believing (ch. iii. 36; v. 24, 25); but at the same time giving to *the resurrection of the body*, as that which consummates the redemption of *the entire man*, a prominence which, in the current theology, it is to be feared, it has seldom had. (See on Rom. viii. 23; and on 1 Cor. xv. throughout.) **55. For my flesh is meat indeed, and my blood is drink indeed. 56. He that eateth my flesh, and drinketh my blood, dwelleth in me, and I in him.** As our food becomes incorporated with ourselves, so Christ and those who eat His flesh and drink His blood become spiritually *one life*, though *personally* distinct. **57. As the living Father hath sent me** [ἀπέστειλεν] —'sent Me,' to communicate His own life, **and I live by the Father** [διὰ τὸν πατέρα]—not 'through,' but 'by reason of the Father;' My life and His being one life, though Mine is that of *Son*, whose it is to be "*of* the Father" (see ch. i. 18; v. 26).

58 he that eateth me, even he shall live by me. This is that bread which came down from heaven: not as your fathers did eat manna, and are
59 dead: he that eateth of this bread shall live for ever. These things said he in the synagogue, as he taught in Capernaum.
60 Many ^dtherefore of his disciples, when they had heard *this*, said, This
61 is an hard saying; who can hear it? When Jesus knew in himself that his disciples murmured at it, he said unto them, Doth this offend you?
62 What ^eand if ye shall see the Son of man ascend up where he was before?
63 It ^fis the Spirit that quickeneth; the flesh profiteth nothing: the words
64 that I speak unto you, *they* ^gare spirit, and *they* are life. But there are some of you that believe not. For ^hJesus knew from the beginning who
65 they were that believed not, and who should betray him. And he said, Therefore said I unto you, that no man can come unto me, except it were
66 given unto him of my Father. From that *time* many of his disciples went ⁱback, and walked no more with him.
67, Then said Jesus unto the twelve, Will ye also go away? Then

A. D. 32.
^d Matt. 11. 6.
^e ch. 3. 13.
Mark 16.19.
Acts 1. 9.
Eph. 4. 8.
^f 2 Cor. 3. 6.
^g Ps. 119. 50.
Eph. 1. 17.
1 Thes.2.13.
Heb. 4. 12.
^h Matt. 9. 4.
ch. 2. 24.
ch. 13. 11.
ch. 16. 30.
Acts 15. 18.
Rev. 2. 23.
ⁱ Luke 9. 62.
Heb. 6. 4-6.
Heb. 10. 38.
1 John 2 19.

so he that eateth me, even he shall live by me [ὃι ἐμὲ]—not 'through,' but 'by reason of Me.' So that though *one spiritual life* with Him, "the Head of every man is Christ, as the head of Christ is God." (1 Cor. xi. 3; iii. 23.) **58. This is that bread which came down from heaven: not as your fathers did eat manna, and are dead: he that eateth of this bread shall live for ever.** This is a sort of summing up of the whole Discourse, on which let this one further remark suffice—that as our Lord, instead of softening down His figurative sublimities, or even putting them in naked phraseology, leaves the great truths of His Person and Office, and our participation of Him and it, enshrined for all time in those glorious forms of speech, so when we attempt to strip the truth of these figures, figures though they be, it *goes away* from us, like water when the vessel is broken; and hence our wisdom lies in raising our own spirit, and attuning our own ear, to our Lord's chosen modes of expression. It should be added that although this discourse has nothing to do with the Sacrament of the Supper, the Sacrament has everything to do with it, as *the visible embodiment* of these figures, and to the believing partaker giving a *real*, yea the most lively and affecting participation of His flesh and blood, and nourishment thereby of the spiritual and eternal life here below. **59. These things said he in the synagogue, as he taught**—or 'teaching' **in Capernaum.** This would seem to intimate the breaking up of the congregation; rendering it probable that what follows took place after, but probably just after, they had begun to disperse.

The Effect of this Discourse on Two Classes of Hearers: First, *On the prejudiced mass* (60-66). **60. Many therefore of his disciples**—His pretty constant followers, though an outer circle of them, **when they heard this, said, This is an hard saying** —not merely harsh, but insufferable, as the word often means in the Old Testament; **who can hear it?**—or submit to listen to it. **61. When Jesus knew in himself that his disciples murmured at it, he said unto them, Doth this offend you? 62. What and if ye shall see the Son of man ascend up where he was before?** 'If ye are stumbled at what I *have* said, how will ye bear what I *now* say?' Not that His ascension itself would stumble them more than His death, but that after recoiling from the *mention* of the one they would not be in a state of mind to take in the other. **63. It is the Spirit that quickeneth; the flesh profiteth nothing.** Much of His discourse had been about "flesh;" but flesh as such, mere flesh, and all religious

391

notions which originate in the flesh, could profit nothing, much less impart that *life* which the Holy Spirit alone communicates to the soul. **the words that I speak unto you**—rather, 'have spoken' [for λελάληκα is the preferable reading], **they are spirit, and they are life**—the whole burden of this discourse was "*spirit*," not mere flesh, and "*life*" in its highest, not its lower sense; and the words I employed were to be interpreted solely in that sense. **64. But there are some of you that believe not. For Jesus knew from the beginning who they were that believed not, and who should betray him.** As if He had said, 'But it matters little to some of you in what sense I speak, for ye believe not.' This was said, adds the Evangelist, not merely of the outer, but of the inner circle of His disciples; for He knew the traitor, though it was not yet time to expose him. **65. And he said, Therefore said I unto you, that no man can come unto me, except it were given**—or, 'have been given' [ἦ δεδομένον] **unto him of my Father**:—*q. d.*, 'That was why I spoke to you of the necessity of divine teaching, which some of you are strangers to.' This last expression—"except it have been given him of my Father"—plainly shows that by the Father's "drawing" (*v.* 44,) was meant an *internal* and *efficacious* operation; for in recalling the statement here, He says it must be "*given* to a man to come" to Christ. **66. From that time** [ἐκ τούτου]—or 'In consequence of this,' **many of his disciples went back.** Those last words of our Lord seem to have given them the finishing stroke—they could stand it no longer. **and walked no more with him.** Many a journey, it may be, they had taken with Him, but now they gave Him finally up!

Secondly, *On the Twelve* (67-71). **67. Then said Jesus unto the twelve.** This is the first time that they are so called by our Evangelist. **Will ye also go away?** [θέλετε ὑπάγειν]—'Are ye also minded to go away.' The "ye also" [καὶ ὑμεῖς] is specially emphatic, and the appeal is singularly affecting. Evidently Christ *felt* the desertion of Him even by those miserable men who could not abide His statements; and seeing a disturbance even of the *wheat* by the violence of the wind which blew away the *chaff* (not yet visibly showing itself, but open to His eyes of fire), He would nip it at once by this home question. Doubtless there were other hearers besides the Twelve in whose hearts there was some good thing towards the Lord Jesus in spite of their prejudices and difficulties. But matters were too critical with the Twelve at this moment to admit of attention

68 Simon Peter answered him, Lord, to whom shall we go? thou hast
69 the words of eternal life. And *ᵏ*we believe and are sure that thou art
70 that Christ, the Son of the living God. Jesus answered them, Have
71 not I chosen you twelve, and one of you is a devil? He spake of Judas
   Iscariot *the son* of Simon: for he it was that should betray him, being
   one of the twelve.

A. D. 32.

k Mat. 16.16.
Mark 1. 1.
Acts 8. 37.
Rom. 1. 3.
1 John 5. 1.

---

being now given to any others. **68. Then Simon Peter**—whose forwardness in this case was noble, and to the wounded spirit of His Lord doubtless very grateful, **answered him, Lord, to whom shall we go? thou hast the words of eternal life.** 'We cannot deny that *we* have been staggered as well as they, and seeing so many go away who, as we thought, might have been retained by teaching a little less hard to take in, our own endurance has been severely tried, nor have we been able to stop short of the question, Shall *we* follow the rest, and give it up? But when it came to this, our light returned and our hearts were re-assured. For as soon as we thought of going away, there rose upon us that awful question, "To WHOM shall we go?" To the lifeless formalism and wretched traditions of the elders? to the gods many and lords many of the heathen around us? or to blank unbelief? Nay, Lord, we are shut up. *They* have none of that "ETERNAL LIFE" to offer us whereof Thou hast been discoursing, in words rich and ravishing as well as in words staggering to human wisdom. That life we cannot want; that life we have learnt to crave as a necessity of the deeper nature which Thou hast awakened; *"the words* of that eternal life" (the *authority to reveal* it and the *power to confer* it) Thou hast: Therefore will we stay with Thee—we *must*.' **69. And we believe and are sure** [ἡμεῖς πεπιστεύκαμεν καὶ ἐγνώκαμεν]—'And we have believed and know.' The 'we' is emphatic:—'Whatever may be the case with others, *we*' &c. **that thou art that** Christ [ὁ Χριστός]—rather, 'the Christ,' **the Son of the living God.** (See on Matt. xvi. 16.) Peter seems to have added this not merely—probably not so much—as an assurance *to His Lord* of his heart's belief in Him, as for the purpose of fortifying *himself* and his faithful brethren against that recoil from those harsh statements of His which he was probably struggling against with difficulty at that moment. **70. Jesus answered them, Have not I chosen** [ἐξελεξάμην]—'Did I not choose' **you twelve, and one of you is a devil?** 'Well said, Simon Barjonas, but that "we" embraces not so wide a circle as in the simplicity of thine heart thou thinkest; for though I have chosen you but twelve, one even of you twelve is a "devil."' Remarkable expression, at a period comparatively so early, ere yet, probably, the slightest evidence of it had come out to any but His eyes that spake it. It is not "*hath*," but "*is*" a devil; not only the tool, but the temple of Satan [not δαίμων, but διάβολος]. **71. He spake of Judas Iscariot the son of Simon: for he it was that should betray him, being one of the twelve.** These explanatory remarks constitute one of the many striking characteristics of this Gospel—as observed in the Introduction to it.

Remarks.—1. We have seen how, in ch. v., our Lord teaches the essential Unity of the Father and the Son, and yet the Distinction of the Persons, and the Relations of Each to the Other—both in Their own Nature and in the economy of Redemption. Let us now see how the same things are here taught under new aspects. The essential Divinity of the Son is so obviously implied in the following statements, that without it they either are so many turgid nothings, or they are blasphemous

assumptions: "I am the Bread of Life"—"The Bread which I will give is My flesh, which I will give for the life of the world." "If any man eat of this Bread, he shall live for ever"—"He that cometh to Me shall never hunger, and he that believeth on Me shall never thirst"—"Except ye eat the flesh and drink the blood of the Son of man, ye have no life in you"—"Whoso eateth My flesh and drinketh My blood hath eternal life, and I will raise him up at the last day." That His death should be the world's life, and men believing on Him—or drawing from Him thereby the virtue of His death—should never hunger and never thirst, but have in them even now an eternal life, and be by Him raised up at the last day, is what no other man ever ventured to affirm of himself, and no creature could affirm without absurdity. But Christ here affirms and reiterates it in every possible form. Nor, in doing so, does He go beyond what He taught to the woman of Samaria, what He taught afterwards in the streets of Jerusalem, regarding the living water (ch. iv. 10, 13, 14; vii. 37-39), and what He taught in His great proclamation of Rest for the weary (Matt. xi. 28-30). But while asserting these claims to what is essentially divine, how careful is our Lord, in those very statements, to intimate that His consecration, and mission from heaven to earth, to discharge these great functions for the world, was all of God, and that He is but the Father's voluntary Agent in every step of man's salvation: "The Son of man shall give unto you the meat that endureth to everlasting life, for Him hath God the Father sealed"—"My Father giveth you the true bread from heaven"—"This is the Father's will which hath sent Me, that of all which He hath given Me I should lose nothing, but should raise it up again at the last day"—"Every man that hath heard and learned of the Father cometh unto Me." But this introduces a new and still more striking expression both of the proper Divinity of the Son and of the ineffable harmony with which the Father and the Son co-operate in every step of man's salvation. After representing it as the very work of God that men should believe in Him whom He had sent, He says, "No man can come to Me except the Father which hath sent Me draw him." What *creature* could possibly say either of these things—that the work of works which God demands from every man is to believe on *him*, and yet, that this cannot be done by any man without a special divine operation upon his heart? But the glory of Christ's proper Divinity shines, if possible, yet brighter in such statements as these —that it is the express will of His Father, which He came down to do, that of all that which He had given Him He should lose nothing, and that every one that beholdeth the Son and believeth on Him should have everlasting life, and He should raise him up at the last day. Who could possibly credit this of a creature? And what creature, on the faith of it, would come to a creature to get eternal life? Even if he could hope thus to get it, how could he possibly be sure in coming to Him, that Christ would know that he *had* come, or would know *when* he came, so as not to cast him out? And what insufferable presumption would it be in

7 AFTER these things Jesus walked in Galilee: for he would not walk in Jewry, *a*because the Jews sought to kill him.

2, Now *b*the Jews' feast of tabernacles was at hand. His *c*brethren there-
3 fore said unto him, Depart hence, and go into Judea, that thy disciples
4 also may see the works that thou doest. For *there is* no man *that* doeth any thing in secret, and he himself seeketh to be known openly. If thou

A. D. 32.
CHAP. 7.
a ch. 5. 16.
b Lev. 23. 34.
c Matt. 12. 46.
Mark 3. 31.
Acts 1. 14.

any creature to say to any other creature, 'If you come to me for eternal life, I will not cast you out?' In short, He that can say without falsehood and without presumption to the whole world—'If any man come to Me, I will give unto him eternal life, and him that cometh I will in no wise cast out, since all that the Father hath given Me shall come to Me; I have got charge from Him accordingly to receive them, to lose nothing and none of them, but to give them even now eternal life, and to raise every one of them up at the last day'—He must be essentially and properly Divine, personally distinct from, yet in absolute harmony with the Father about the matter of man's salvation in general, and every individual's salvation in particular; nor will, nor can any soul, on the faith of such words, come to Jesus and surrender itself into His hands for salvation accordingly, unless in the perfect assurance that He knows the fact of his doing so—knows when he does it—knows "that He is able to keep that which He has committed unto Him against that day" (see on 2 Tim. i. 12). 2. See here the double view of *faith* ever presented in Scripture—as at once a *duty* comprehensive of all other duties, and a *grace*, of special divine communication. It is the duty of duties; for "This is the work of God, that ye believe in Him whom He hath sent:" and it is a *grace* comprehensive of every other; for though "him that cometh to Me I will in no wise cast out," yet "no man can come to Me except the Father which hath sent Me draw him"— "Every man that hath heard and hath learned of the Father cometh unto Me"—"Therefore said I unto you, that no man can come to Me except it were given unto Him of My Father." Pity that, in the attempts to reconcile these, so much vain and unsavoury controversy has been spent, and that one of them is so often sacrificed to the other; for then they are not what Jesus says they are, but rather a caricature of them. The link of connection between divine and human operation will probably never be reached on earth—if even in heaven. Let us, then, implicitly receive and reverentially hold both; remembering, however, that the *divine* in this case ever precedes, and is the cause of, the *human*— the "drawing" on God's part of the "coming" on ours; while yet our coming is as purely spontaneous, and the result of rational considerations presenting themselves to our minds, as if there were no supernatural operation in the matter at all. 3. What bright marks of truth does the concluding scene of this chapter exhibit! The last thing that would occur to any biographer of a *mythical Christ*—or even filling up from his own fancy a few meagre fragments of real history—would be the entrance of doubts into the innermost circle of those who believed in Him. Or, if even that be conceivable, who would ever have managed such a thought as it is here? The question, "Will *ye also* go away?" is not more the affecting language of wounded feeling—springing from conscious desert of other treatment—than is the reply of Peter the expression of a state of mind too profoundly natural and pregnant ever to have been conceived if it had not been actually uttered. And the answer to this again—to the effect that what Peter expressed

would be all that could be desired if it were the mind and feeling of them all; but that, so far from this, out of only twelve men whom He had chosen one would be found a devil—this has such originality stamped upon it as secures its own reception, as true history, by every intelligent and guileless reader. 4. There are seasons when one's faith is tried to the utmost, particularly by speculative difficulties; the spiritual eye then swims, and all truth seems ready to depart from us. At such seasons, a clear perception, like that of Peter here, that to abandon the faith of Christ is to face blank desolation, ruin, and death; and, on recoiling from this, to be able to fall back, not merely on *first principles* and *immovable foundations*, but on *personal experience of a Living Lord*, in whom all truth is wrapt up and made flesh for us—this is a relief unspeakable. Under that blessed Wing taking shelter, until we are again fit to grapple with the questions that have staggered us, we at length either find our way through them, or attain to a calm satisfaction on the discovery that they lie beyond the limits of present apprehension. 5. The narrowness of the circle of those who rally around the truth, and the unpopularity of their profession, are no security that all of them are true-hearted; for one even of the Twelve was a devil. And the length of time during which Judas remained within the innermost circle of Christ's followers, without discovering to his brethren his real character, or probably being aware of it himself, and the fact that when it did come out, it was drawn forth, as appears, quite casually, and then was matured with such frightful rapidity—do not these things cry aloud to all who name the name of Christ, "Rejoice with trembling!" "Let him that thinketh he standeth, take heed lest he fall"! "Watch and pray, that ye enter not into temptation"!

CHAP. VII. 1-53.—CHRIST AT THE FEAST OF TABERNACLES.

Jesus Declines the Advice of His brethren, to Go Openly to Jerusalem, and Show Himself to the World; but at His own time Goes Quietly up, and about the midst of the feast Stands Forth in the temple Teaching (1-14). **1. After these things**—that is, *all that is recorded after the Discourse of* ch. v. 19-47, **Jesus walked in Galilee**—continuing His labours there, for the reason about to be mentioned; **for he would not walk in Jewry**—or Judea, **because the Jews sought to kill him**—as related in ch. v. 18. This is an exceedingly important piece of information, as we thus learn that our Lord *did not attend the Passover mentioned in* ch. vi. 4—which, according to our reckoning, was the *third* since the opening of His public ministry. **2. Now the Jews' feast of tabernacles was at hand.** This was the last of the three annual festivals, celebrated on the fifteenth of the seventh month—September (see Lev. xxiii. 33, &c.; Deut. xvi. 13, &c.; Neh. viii. 14-18). **3. His brethren therefore** (see on Matt. xiii. 54-56) **said unto him, Depart hence, and go into Judea, that thy disciples also may see**—or 'may behold' [θεωρήσωσιν] **the works that thou doest. 4. For there is no man that doeth any thing in secret, and he himself seeketh to be known openly. If thou do these things, show thyself to the world. 5. For**

393

5 do these things, show thyself to the world. For ^dneither did his brethren
6 believe in him. Then Jesus said unto them, ^eMy time is not yet come:
7 but your time is alway ready. The ^fworld cannot hate you; but me it
8 hateth, ^gbecause I testify of it, that the works thereof are evil. Go ye
     up unto this feast: I go not up yet unto this feast; ^hfor my time is not
9 yet full come. When he had said these words unto them, he abode *still*
10 in Galilee. But when his brethren were gone up, then went he also up
     unto the feast, not openly, but as it were in secret.
11   Then ⁱthe Jews sought him at the feast, and said, Where is he?
12 And ^jthere was much murmuring among the people concerning him: for
     some ^ksaid, He is a good man: others said, Nay; but he deceiveth the
13 people. Howbeit no man spake openly of him for fear of the Jews.
14   Now about the midst of the feast, Jesus went up into the temple,
     and taught.
15   And ^lthe Jews marvelled, saying, How knoweth this man [1]letters,

A. D. 32.
d Mark 3. 21.
e Ps. 102. 13.
Eccl. 3. 1.
ch. 2. 4.
Acts 1. 7.
f ch. 15. 19.
g ch. 3. 19.
h ch. 8. 20.
i ch. 11. 56.
j ch. 9. 16.
ch. 10. 19.
k Matt. 21. 46.
Luke 7. 16.
Luke 18.19.
ch. 6. 14.
l Luke 4. 22.
Acts 2. 7.
[1] Or, learning.

neither did his brethren believe in him. But as we find these "brethren" of the Lord in the "upper room" among the hundred and twenty disciples who waited for the descent of the Spirit after the Lord's ascension (Acts i. 14), they seem to have had their prejudices removed—perhaps after His resurrection. Indeed, here their language is more that of strong prejudice and suspicion—*such as near relatives, even the best, too frequently show in such cases*—than formed unbelief. There was also, probably, a tincture of *vanity* in it. 'Thou hast many disciples in Judea; here in Galilee they are fast dropping off; it is not like one who advances the claims thou dost to linger so long here, away from the city of our solemnities, where surely "the kingdom of our father David" is to be set up: "seeking," as thou dost, "to be known openly," those miracles of thine ought not to be confined to this distant corner, but submitted at headquarters to the inspection of the world.' On hearing such a speech, one might suppose Him going to His Father, and saying, "I am become a stranger unto my brethren, an alien unto my mother's children"! (Ps. lxix. 8). Does not this speech, by the way, tend to confirm the view we have taken of the number of Passovers which occurred during our Lord's public ministry, and which imply His absence from Jerusalem for a time which had appeared unaccountably long? For about a year and a half, according to our reckoning, He had not been there. This seems to many incredibly long. But it would seem as if it had been long enough at least to appear to His "brethren" inconsistent with His claims. **6. Then Jesus said unto them, My time**—for showing Myself to the world—**is not yet come: but your time is alway ready. 7. The world cannot hate you; but me it hateth, because I testify of it, that the works thereof are evil. Go ye up unto this feast**—or, 'the feast,' as, perhaps, is the preferable reading here. **I go not up yet unto this feast; for my time is not yet full come:**—*q. d.*, 'It matters little when ye go up, for ye have no great plans in life, and nothing hangs upon your movements: With Me it is otherwise; on every movement of Mine there hangs what ye know not: The world has no quarrel with you, for ye bear no testimony against it, and so draw down upon yourselves none of its wrath; but I am here to lift up My voice against its hypocrisy, and denounce its abominations; therefore it cannot endure Me, and one false step might precipitate its fury on its Victim's head before the time: Away, therefore, to the feast as soon as it suits you; I follow at the fitting moment, but "My time is not yet full come."' **9. When**—'And

when' he had said these words unto them, he **abode still in Galilee. 10. But when his brethren were gone up, then went he also up unto the feast, not openly, but as it were in secret** [ὡς ἐν κρυπτῷ]—'but in a manner secretly,' not in the caravan-company, as *Meyer* explains it,—see on Luke ii. 44: perhaps by some other route, and at any rate in such a way as not to attract notice. **11. Then the Jews sought him at the feast, and said, Where is he?** "The Jews" here mean the *rulers;* see on ch. i. 19. They sought Him on this occasion certainly for no good end. **12. And there was much murmuring**—or 'muttering' [γογγυσμὸς] **among the people** [ἐν τοῖς ὄχλοις]—'among the multitudes;' the natural expression of a Jewish writer, indicating without design, as *Webster and Wilkinson* remark, the crowded state of Jerusalem at this festival. **concerning him: for some said, He is a good man: others said, Nay; but he deceiveth the people**—or 'the multitude' [τὸν ὄχλον]. These are just the two opposite views of Him and His claims, the one, that He was *honest;* the other, that He was an *impostor.* **13. Howbeit no man spake openly of him**—that is, in His favour—**for fear of the Jews.** As the people who feared the Jews were themselves Jews, this would suffice to show that by "the Jews" in this Gospel we are almost invariably to understand the *rulers* or *leaders* of the people.

14. Now about the midst of the feast ['Ήδη δὲ τῆς ἑορτῆς μεσούσης]—rather, 'Now when it was already the midst of the feast.' It might be the fourth or fifth of the eight days during which it lasted. **Jesus went up into the temple, and taught** [ἐδίδασκεν]. The imperfect tense used implies *continued,* and therefore *formal* teaching, as distinguished from mere casual sayings. In fact, this appears to have been the *first time* that He taught thus openly in Jerusalem. He had kept back till the feast was half through, to let the stir about Him subside; and entering the city unexpectedly, He had begun His "teaching" at the temple, and created a certain awe, before the wrath of the rulers had time to break in upon it.

Amidst many interruptions, Jesus boldly continues His temple-teaching (15-31). **15. And the Jews marvelled, saying, How knoweth this man letters**—or learning, **having never learned**—that is, at any rabbinical school, like Paul under Gamaliel (see Acts xxii. 3; xxvi. 24.) These rulers knew well enough that He had never studied under any human teacher—an important admission, as *Meyer* remarks, against ancient and modern attempts to trace our Lord's wisdom to human sources. Probably His teaching on this occasion was *expository,* manifesting that unrivalled faculty and depth

16 having never learned? Jesus answered them, and said, ^mMy doc-
17 trine is not mine, but his that sent me. If ⁿany man will do his
    will, he shall know of the doctrine, whether it be of God, or *whether* I
18 speak of myself. He ^othat speaketh of himself seeketh his own glory:
    but he that seeketh his glory that sent him, the same is true, and no
19 unrighteousness is in him. Did ^pnot Moses give you the law, and *yet*
20 none of you keepeth the law? ^qWhy go ye about to kill me? The
    people answered and said, ^rThou hast a devil: who goeth about to kill
21 thee? Jesus answered and said unto them, I have done one work, and
22 ye all marvel. Moses ^stherefore gave unto you circumcision; (not because
    it is of Moses, but ^tof the fathers;) and ye on the sabbath day circumcise
23 a man. If a man on the sabbath day receive circumcision, ²that the law
    of Moses should not be broken; are ye angry at me, because I ^uhave
24 made a man every whit whole on the sabbath day? Judge ^vnot accord-
    ing to the appearance, but judge righteous judgment.
25   Then said some of them of Jerusalem, Is not this he whom they seek
26 to kill? But, lo, he speaketh boldly, and they say nothing unto him.
27 Do the rulers know indeed that this is the very Christ? Howbeit we
    know this man whence he is: but when Christ cometh, no man knoweth
    whence he is.

A. D. 32.

^m ch 8. 28.
ch. 12. 49.
ch. 14. 10,
24.
ⁿ Hos. 6. 2, 3.
ch. 8. 43.
^o ch. 5. 41.
ch. 8. 50.
^p Acts 7. 38.
^q Matt. 12. 14.
Mark 3. 6.
ch. 5. 16.
^r ch. 8. 48.
^s Lev. 12. 3.
^t Gen. 17. 10.
² Or,
without
breaking
the law of
Moses.
^u ch. 5. 8.
^v Deut. 1. 16.
Pro. 24. 23.
ch. 8. 15.
Jas. 2. 1.

---

which in the Sermon on the Mount had excited the astonishment of all—though now, no doubt, it would be in a different strain. **16. Jesus**— 'Jesus therefore' (according to the true text) **answered them, and said, My doctrine is not mine**—that is, in the sense repeatedly explained on ch. v. and vi., 'not from Myself,' 'not unauthorized;' 'I am here by divine commission.' **but his that sent me. 17. If any man will do** [θέλῃ] —or better, 'is minded to do' **his will, he shall know of the doctrine, whether it be of God, or whether I speak of myself**—whether it be from above or from beneath, whether it be divine or an imposture of mine own. A principle of immense importance; showing, on the one hand, that singleness of desire to please God is the grand inlet to light on all questions vitally affecting one's eternal interest, and, on the other, that the want of this, whether perceived or not, is the chief cause of infidelity amidst the light of revealed religion. **18. He that speaketh of himself**—not concerning, 'but from himself' [ἀφ' ἑαυτοῦ] **seeketh his own glory: but he that seeketh his glory that sent him, the same is true, and no unrighteousness is in him.** See on ch. v. 41-44. **19. Did not Moses give you** [δέδωκεν]—'Hath not Moses given you' **the law, and yet none of you keepeth the law? Why go ye about**—or 'seek ye' [ζη-τεῖτε] **to kill me?** 'In opposing Me ye pretend zeal for Moses, but to the spirit and end of that law which he gave ye are total strangers, and in going about to kill Me, ye are its greatest enemies.' **20. The people** [ὁ ὄχλος]—'The multitude' **answered and said, Thou hast a devil: who goeth about to kill thee?** The *multitude* who said this had as yet no bad feeling to Jesus, and evidently were not in the secret of the plot now hatching, as our Lord knew, against Him. **21. Jesus answered and said unto them, I have done** —rather, 'I did' [ἐποίησα] **one work, and ye all marvel.** Taking no notice of the popular appeal, as there were those there who knew well enough what He meant, He recalls His cure of the impotent man, and the murderous rage it had kindled (ch. v. 9, 16, 18). It may seem strange that He should refer to an event a year and a half old, as if but newly done; and this is urged as a fatal objection to our Lord's having been so long absent from Jerusalem. But their present attempt "to

kill Him" brought the past scene all fresh up, not only to Him, but without doubt to them too, if indeed they had ever forgotten it; and by this fearless reference to it, exposing their hypocrisy and dark designs, He gave His position great moral strength. **22. Moses therefore gave unto you** —or, 'For this cause hath Moses given you' [δέδω-κεν] **circumcision; (not because it is**—'not that it is' of Moses, but of the fathers;) **and ye on the sabbath day circumcise a man. 23. If a man on the sabbath day receive circumcision, that the law of Moses should not be broken; are ye angry at me, because I have made**—or 'I made' [ἐποί-ησα] **a man every whit whole on the sabbath day?** Though servile work was forbidden on the sabbath, the circumcision of males on that day (which certainly was a servile work) was counted no infringement of the law: How much less ought fault to be found with One who had made a man "every whit whole"—or rather, 'a man's entire body whole' [ὅλον ἄνθρωπον ὑγιῆ]—on the sabbath day? What a testimony to the reality of the miracle, none daring to meet the bold appeal? **24. Judge not according to the appearance, but judge righteous judgment**—'Rise above the *letter* into the *spirit* of the law.'

25. Then said some of them of Jerusalem—'the Jerusalemites;' that is, the citizens—as distinguished from the multitudes from the provinces—and who, knowing the long formed purpose of the rulers to put Jesus to death, wondered they were now letting him teach openly, **Is not this he whom they seek to kill? 26. But, lo**—'And, lo' [Καὶ ἴδε], **he speaketh boldly, and they say nothing unto him. Do the rulers know indeed** [ἔγνωσαν] —'Have the rulers come to know indeed' **that this is the [very] Christ?** [The second ἀληθῶς in this verse is of very doubtful authority.] 'Have they got some new light in favour of His claims?' **27. Howbeit we know this man whence he is: but when** ['the'] **Christ cometh, no man knoweth whence he is.** This seems to refer to some current opinion that Messiah's origin would be mysterious —not *altogether* wrong—from which they concluded that Jesus could not be he, since they knew all about his family at Nazareth.

28. Then—or 'therefore' **cried Jesus**—in a louder tone, and more solemnly witnessing style than usual, **in the temple, as he taught, saying, Ye both**

395

28　Then cried Jesus in the temple, as he taught, saying, *^w*Ye both know me, and ye know whence I am: and *^x*I am not come of myself, but he
29　that sent me *^y*is true, whom *^z*ye know not. But *^a*I know him: for I am
30　from him, and he hath sent me. Then they sought to take him: but no
31　man laid hands on him, because his hour was not yet come. And many of the people believed on him, and said, When Christ cometh, will he do more miracles than these which this *man* hath done?
32　The Pharisees heard that the people murmured such things concerning him; and the Pharisees and the chief priests sent officers to take him.
33　Then said Jesus unto them, *^b*Yet a little while am I with you, and *then* I
34　go unto him that sent me. Ye *^c*shall seek me, and shall not find *me:*
35　and where I am, *thither* ye cannot come. Then said the Jews among themselves, Whither will he go, that we shall not find him? will he go
36　unto *^d*the dispersed among the ³ Gentiles, and teach the Gentiles? What *manner of* saying is this that he said, Ye shall seek me, and shall not find *me:* and where I am, *thither* ye cannot come?
37　In the last day, that great *day* of the feast, Jesus stood and cried,
38　saying, *^e*If any man thirst, let him come unto me, and drink. He *^f*that

A. D. 32.

^w ch. 8. 14.
^x ch. 5. 43.
ch. 8. 42.
^y ch. 5. 32.
ch. 8. 26.
Rom. 3. 4.
^z ch. 1. 18.
ch. 8. 55.
^a Matt.11.27.
ch. 10. 15.
^b ch. 13. 33.
^c Hos. 5. 6.
ch. 8. 21.
ch. 13. 33.
^d Isa. 11. 12.
Jas. 1. 1.
1 Pet. 1. 1.
³ Or, Greeks.
^e Isa. 55. 1.
Rev. 3. 20.
Rev. 22. 17.
^f Deut.18.15.

know me, and ye know whence I am: and I am not come of myself:—*q. d.,* 'True, ye both know myself and my earthly parentage; and *yet* I am not come of myself, &c. **but he that sent me is true** [ἀληθινὸς]—'real;' meaning probably, 'He that sent Me is the only *real* Sender of any one.' **whom ye know not. But I know him: for I am from him, and he hath sent me**—'and He sent me' [ἀπέστειλεν]. **30. Then they sought to take him:** but—rather, 'and yet' [καὶ] **no man laid hands on him**—their *impotence* happily being equal to their *malignity*, **because his hour was not yet come. 31. And many of the people** [δὲ—ὄχλου]—'But many of the multitude' **believed on him, and said, When Christ cometh**—or, 'When the Christ is come' [ὁ Χ.—ἔλθῃ], **will he do more miracles than these which this man hath done?**—*q. d.,* 'If this be not the Christ, what can the Christ do, when he does come—which has not been anticipated and eclipsed by this man?' This was evidently the language of friendly persons, overborne by their spiteful superiors, but unable to keep quite silent.

Officers are sent by the Rulers to Apprehend Jesus; but they, Captivated by His Teaching, Return, confessing their inability to do it (32-46). **32. The Pharisees heard that the people murmured**—or 'heard the multitude muttering [τοῦ ὄχλου γογγύζοντος] such things concerning him.** They heard whispers to this effect going about, and thought it high time to stop Him if He was not to be allowed to carry away the people. **and the Pharisees and the chief priests sent officers to take him**—subordinate officials of their own to seize Him. **33. Then said Jesus [unto them].** The words in brackets [αὐτοῖς] have scarcely any authority. **Yet a little while am I with you, and then I go unto him that sent me. 34. Ye shall seek me, and shall not find me: and where I am, thither ye cannot come**:—*q. d.,* 'Your desire to be rid of Me will be for you all too soon fulfilled: Yet a little while and we part company—for ever; for I go whither ye cannot come, nor, even though ye should at length seek to Him whom now ye despise, shall ye be able to find Him'—referring not to any penitential, but to purely selfish cries in their time of desperation. **35. Then said the Jews**—the *rulers* again, **among themselves, Whither will he**—or 'this man' [οὗτος], **go, that we shall not find him?** They cannot comprehend Him, but seem awed by the solemn grandeur of His warning. **Will he go unto the dispersed** [τὴν διασπορὰν] **among**

the Gentiles, and teach the Gentiles? ['Ελλήνων, "Ελληνας]—'unto the dispersed among the Greeks, and teach the Greeks? Will He go to the Jews of the dispersion—scattered abroad everywhere—and from them extend His teaching even to the Gentiles? (So *Meyer, Lücke, Tholuck,* &c.) By the *Greeks* here are not meant Hellenistic or Greek-speaking Jews, but *Gentiles.* It is well observed by *Neander,* that a presentiment that His teaching was designed to be universal had probably a good deal to do with the irritation which it occasioned. **36. What manner of saying is this that he said, Ye shall seek me, and shall not find me: and where I am, thither ye cannot come?** Thinking this theory of His words too outrageous or contemptible, they are quite baffled as to its meaning, and yet cannot help feeling that something deep lay under it. Jesus, however, takes no notice of their questions; and so for the time the subject dies away. And yet, long after this, Jesus recurs to this warning of His, in discoursing to the Eleven at the Supper table (ch. xiii. 33).

And now we come to one of the grandest of all His utterances.

37. In the last day, that great day of the feast—or 'Now [δὲ] in the last, the great day of the feast;' that is, the eighth day of the feast of Tabernacles (Lev. xxiii. 39). It was a Sabbath, the last feast-day of the year, and distinguished by very remarkable ceremonies. 'The generally joyous character of this feast,' says *Olshausen,* 'broke out on this day into loud jubilation, particularly at the solemn moment when the priest, as was done on every day of this festival, brought forth, in golden vessels, water from the stream of Siloah, which flowed under the temple-mountain, and solemnly poured it upon the altar. Then the words of Isa. xii. 3 were sung, " *With joy shall ye draw water out of the wells of Salvation,*" and thus the symbolical reference of this act, intimated in *v.* 39, was expressed.' 'So ecstatic,' says *Lightfoot,* 'was the joy with which this ceremony was performed—accompanied with sound of trumpets—that it used to be said, Whoever had not witnessed it had never seen rejoicing at all.' On this high occasion, then, He who had already drawn all eyes upon Him by His supernatural power and unrivalled teaching—**Jesus stood**—probably in some elevated position, **and cried**—as if making proclamation in the audience of all the people, **saying, IF ANY MAN THIRST, LET HIM COME UNTO ME, AND DRINK.** What an offer! The deepest cravings of

believeth on me, as the Scripture hath said, ^gout of his belly shall flow
39 rivers of living water. (But ^hthis spake he of the Spirit, which they that
   believe on him should receive: for the Holy Ghost was not yet *given;*
40 because that Jesus was not yet ⁱglorified.) Many of the people therefore,
41 when they heard this saying, said, Of a truth this is ^jthe Prophet. Others
   said, ^kThis is the Christ. But some said, Shall Christ come ^lout of
42 Galilee? Hath ^mnot the Scripture said, That Christ cometh of the seed
43 of David, and out of the town of Bethlehem, ⁿwhere David was? So
44 there was a division among the people because of him. And some of
   them would have taken him; but no man laid hands on him.
45 Then came the officers to the chief priests and Pharisees; and they

A. D. 32.

g Isa. 12. 3.
h Isa. 44. 3.
Joel 2. 28.
ch. 16. 7.
Acts 2. 17.
i ch. 12. 16.
j Deut. 18. 15.
ch. 1. 21.
ch. 6. 14.
k ch. 4. 42.
l ch. 1. 46.
m Ps. 132. 11.
n 1 Sam. 16. 1.

the human spirit are here, as in the Old Testament, expressed by the figure of "*thirst,*" and the external satisfaction of them by "*drinking.*" To the woman of Samaria He had said almost the same thing, and in the same terms (John iv. 13, 14). But what to her was simply affirmed as a *fact* is here turned into a world-wide *proclamation;* and whereas there, the *gift* by Him of the living water is the most prominent idea—in contrast with her hesitation to give Him the perishable water of Jacob's well—here the prominence is given to *Himself* as the Well-spring of all satisfaction. He had in Galilee invited all the WEARY AND HEAVY-LADEN of the human family to come under His wing and they should find REST (Matt. xi. 28), which is just the same deep want, and the same profound relief of it, under another and equally grateful figure. He had in the synagogue of Capernaum (ch. vi.), announced Himself, in every variety of form, as "the BREAD of Life," and as both able and authorized to appease the "HUNGER," and quench the "THIRST," of all that apply to Him. There is, and there can be, nothing beyond that here. But what was on all those occasions uttered in private, or addressed to a provincial audience, is here sounded forth in the streets of the great religious metropolis, and in language of surpassing majesty, simplicity, and grace. It is just Jehovah's ancient proclamation now sounding forth through human flesh, "Ho, EVERY ONE THAT THIRSTETH, COME YE TO THE WATERS, AND HE THAT HATH NO MONEY!" (Isa. lv. 1). In this light, we have but two alternatives; either to say with Caiaphas of Him that uttered such words, "*He is guilty of death,*" or, falling down before Him, to exclaim with Thomas, "MY LORD AND MY GOD!" (Isa. lv.) **38. He that believeth on me, as the Scripture hath said, out of his belly shall flow rivers of living water.** The words, "as the Scripture hath said," refer, of course, to the promise in the latter part of the verse—yet not so much to any particular passage as to the general strain of Messianic prophecy, as Isa. lviii. 11; Joel iii. 18; Zec. xiv. 8; Ezek. xlvii. 1-12; in most of which passages the idea is that of waters issuing from beneath the Temple, to which our Lord compares Himself and those who believe in Him. The expression "out of his belly" means, out of his inner man, his soul, as in Prov. xx. 27. On the "rivers of living water," see on ch. iv. 13, 14. There, however, the figure is "a fountain;" here it is "rivers." It refers primarily to the *copiousness,* but indirectly also to the *diffusiveness,* of this living water to the good of others. **39. (But this spake he of the Spirit**—Who, by His direct Personal Agency, opens up these fountains, these rivers of living water, in the human spirit (ch. iii. 6), and by his indwelling in the renewed soul ensures their unfailing flow. **which they that believe on him should receive**—or 'were about to receive' [ἔμελλον λαμβάνειν]: **for the Holy Ghost was not**

yet [given]. Beyond all doubt the word "given," or some similar word, is the right supplement here, if we are to insert any supplement at all. In ch. xvi. 7 the Holy Ghost is represented not only as *the gift of Christ,* but a Gift the communication of which was *dependent upon His own departure to the Father.* Now, as Christ was not yet gone, so the Holy Ghost was not yet given, **because that Jesus was not yet glorified.)** This is one of those explanatory remarks of our Evangelist himself which constitute a marked feature of this Fourth Gospel. The word "*glorified*" is here used advisedly, to teach the reader not only that the *departure* of Christ to the Father was *indispensable* to the giving of the Spirit, but that this illustrious Gift, direct from the hands of the ascended Saviour, was God's intimation to the world that He whom it had cast out, crucified, and slain, was "His Elect, in whom His soul delighted," and that it was through the smiting of that Rock that the waters of the Spirit—for which the Church was waiting, and with pomp at the feast of Tabernacles proclaiming its expectation—had gushed forth upon a thirsty world. **40. Many of the people**—'the multitude' [ἐκ τοῦ ὄχλου], **when they heard this saying.** The true reading appears to be 'the' or 'His sayings' [τῶν λόγων]; referring not to the last one only, but the whole strain of His discourse, terminating with such a glorious proclamation. **said, Of a truth this is the Prophet.** The only wonder is they did not all say it. "But their minds were blinded." **41. Others said, This is the Christ.** See on ch. i. 21. **But some**—rather, 'others' [ἄλλοι] **said, Shall Christ come out of Galilee?** [Μὴ γὰρ—ὁ Χ. ἔρχεται]—'Doth the Christ then,' or 'What then! Is the Christ to come out of Galilee?' **42. Hath not the Scripture said, That** ['the'] **Christ cometh of the seed of David, and out of the town of Bethlehem, where David was?** We accept this spontaneous testimony to our David-descended, Bethlehem-born Saviour. Had those who gave it made the enquiry which the case demanded, they would have found that Jesus "came out of Galilee" and "out of Bethlehem," both alike in fulfilment of prophecy as in point of fact. (Matt. ii. 23; iv. 13-16.) **43. So there was a division among the people**—'the multitude' [ἐν τῷ ὄχλῳ], **because of him. 44. And some of them**—the more envenomed of those who had taken the adverse side of the question, **would have taken him**—or 'were minded to take Him' [ἤθελον πιάσαι], **but**—or 'yet' [ἀλλὰ], **no man laid hands on him.** See on v. 30.

45. Then came the officers to the chief priests and Pharisees—who had sent them to seize Him (v. 32), and who would appear from the sequel to have been sitting in Council when the officers returned. **and they said unto them, Why have ye not brought him?**—already thirsting for their Victim, and thinking it an easy matter to seize and bring Him. **46. The officers answered, Never**

397

46 said unto them, Why have ye not brought him? The officers answered,
Never man spake like this man.
47, Then answered them the Pharisees, Are ye also deceived? Have [o] any
48, of the rulers or of the Pharisees believed on him? But this people who
49, knoweth not the law are cursed. Nicodemus saith unto them, ([p] he
50, that came [4] to Jesus by night, being one of them,) Doth [q] our law judge
51, *any* man before it hear him and know what he doeth? They answered
52 and said unto him, Art thou also of Galilee? Search, and look: for
53 out [r] of Galilee ariseth no prophet. And every man went unto his own
house.

A. D. 32.
[o] ch. 12. 42. Acts 6. 7. 1 Cor. 1. 20.
[p] ch. 3. 2.
[4] to him.
[q] Deut. 1. 17. Deut. 17. 8.
[r] 1 Ki. 17. 1. 2 Ki. 14. 25. Isa 9. 1, 2. Matt. 4. 15. ch. 1. 46.

---

man spake like this man—Noble testimony of unsophisticated men! Doubtless they were strangers to the profound intent of Christ's teaching, but there was that in it which, by its mysterious grandeur and transparent purity and grace, held them spell-bound. No doubt it was of God that they should so feel, that their arm might be paralyzed, as Christ's "hour was not come;" but even in human teaching there has sometimes been felt such a divine power, that men who came to kill the speaker have confessed to all that they were unmanned.

The Pharisees Break Forth upon the Officers with Rage, but are met with an Unexpected Protestation from Amongst Themselves against their Indecent Haste in Condemning the Untried (47-53). **47. Then answered them the Pharisees, Are ye also deceived?** In their own servants this seemed intolerable. **48. Have any of the rulers or of the Pharisees believed on him?** We are expressly told that "many of them" did, including Nicodemus and Joseph, but not one of these had openly "confessed Him" (ch. xii. 42); and this appeal must have stung such of them as heard it to the quick. **49. But this people** [ὁ ὄχλος οὗτος]—rather, 'this multitude,' this ignorant rabble. Pity these important distinctions between the different classes, so marked in the original of this Gospel, should not be also in our version. **who knoweth not the law**—meaning, by school-learning, which only perverted the law by human additions, **are cursed**—a kind of swearing at them, out of mingled rage and scorn. **50. Nicodemus**—reappearing to us after nearly three years' absence from the history, as a member of the council, then sitting, as would appear, **saith unto them, (he that came to Jesus by night, being one of them,) 51. Doth our law judge any man before it hear him**—rather, 'except it first hear from him' [ἐὰν μὴ ἀκούσῃ παρ' αὐτοῦ πρότερον], **and know what he doeth?**—a very proper but all too tame rejoinder, and evidently more from pressure of conscience than any design to pronounce *positively* in the case. The feebleness of his defence of Jesus, as *Webster and Wilkinson* well remark, presents a strong contrast to the fierceness of the rejoinders of the Pharisees. **52. They answered and said unto him, Art thou also of Galilee?**—in this taunt expressing their scorn of the party. Even a word of caution, or the gentlest proposal to enquire before condemning, was with them equivalent to an espousal of the hated One. **Search, and look: for** [καὶ ἴδε ὅτι]—or better, 'Search and see that' **out of Galilee ariseth no prophet.** Strange! For had not *Jonah*, of Gath-hepher, and even Elijah, so far as appears, arisen out of Galilee? and it may be more, of whom we have no record. But rage is blind, and deep prejudice distorts all facts. Yet it looks as if they were afraid of losing Nicodemus, when they take the trouble to reason the point at all. It was just *because* he had "searched," as they advised him, that he went the length even that he did. **53. And every man went unto his own house**—finding their plot could not at that time be carried into effect. Is your rage thus impotent, O ye chief priests? *N.B.*—On the genuineness of this verse, and of the first eleven verses of the following chapter, we reserve our observations till we come to that chapter.

Remarks.—1. The springs of judgment and of action revealed in the first part of this chapter are so minutely and delicately natural as to defy invention, and to verify the narrative not only as a whole but in all its features. Here are Jesus and "His brethren" according to the flesh: on the principles somewhat largely explained on Luke iv. 24, with Remark 2 at the close of that Section, they have great difficulty in recognizing His claims at all; but His present procedure—so different from all that they presume it ought to be and naturally would be in the great predicted *Messiah*—stumbles them most of all. 'Surely One making such claims should at once and in the most open manner lay them before the public authorities at the capital: but instead of this, Thou hast been absent from Jerusalem for a very unusual time; and now that the last of the yearly festivals is at hand, no symptoms appear of a purpose to attend it: how is this?' The answer to these insinuations is in singular keeping with our Lord's habitual estimate of His own position, and the mingled caution and courage with which He laid and carried out all His plans; while the *indifference* which He stamps upon their movements, and the ground on which He regards them as of no consequence at all—this bears the stamp of entire historical reality. But most of all, perhaps, His going up noiselessly by Himself, after the departure of "His brethren;" and not, as usual, before the commencement of the feast, nor till towards the midst of it; and then—after much speculation what had become of Him, and whether He would venture to appear at all—His proceeding to teach in the temple-court, and that so marvellously as to secure for Himself a footing not to be disturbed, insomuch that even the officers sent to seize Him found themselves unable, through the riveting effect of His teaching, to lay a hand upon Him; and then the rage of the ecclesiastics at this, and—while ascribing it all to a want of learned insight which, if they had been "rulers or Pharisees," they would not have shown—finding, to their mortification, a ruler and a Pharisee of their own number, one sitting beside them, taking the officers' part and rebuking their indecent desire to condemn without a trial: these are details which carry their own truth to the hearts of all readers not blinded by prejudice. 2. When Jesus proclaimed, in such ravishing terms, "If any man thirst, let him come unto Me, and drink," we may well ask, Is there any man who does *not* thirst? *Satisfaction*—if that be the word which covers all the cravings of our nature—is indeed as different as possible in the estimation of different men. With some the

8, JESUS went unto the mount of Olives. And early in the morning he
2 came again into the temple, and all the people came unto him; and he
sat down, and taught them.

3 And the scribes and Pharisees brought unto him a woman taken
4 in adultery; and when they had set her in the midst, they say unto
him, Master, this woman was taken in adultery, in the very act.
5 Now *ᵃ* Moses in the law commanded us, that such should be stoned:
6 but what sayest thou? This they said, tempting him, that they

A. D. 32.

CHAP. 8.
ᵃ Ex. 20. 14.
Lev. 18. 20.
Lev. 20. 10.
Deut. 5. 13.
Deut. 22. 22.
Job 31. 9.
Pro. 6. 29,
32.

gratification of the lusts of the flesh is all the satisfaction desired; others crave domestic and intellectual enjoyment; a third class find the approval of conscience indispensable to their comfort, but, unable to come up to their own standard of character and excellence, are inwardly restless; while a fourth and smaller class groan under felt sinfulness, and—conscious that peace with God and delight in His law after the inward man are the great necessity of their nature and condition, but that these are just what they want and cannot reach—are wretched accordingly. But to one and all of these—embracing every soul of man—Jesus here speaks; though to each His proclamation would be differently understood. The first class He would raise from a sensual to spiritual satisfaction—as from the hollow to the real, from wormwood to honey; the second class He would advance from what is good to what is better, from meat that perisheth—even in its most refined forms —to that which endureth to everlasting life; the third class He would draw upwards from toilsome and fruitless efforts to pacify an uneasy conscience by mere attempted obedience to the law, and when they have come to the fourth stage, of conscious inability to keep the law, and wretchedness for want of peace with God, He would then attract and invite them to *Himself*, as the Well-spring of complete and eternal Satisfaction. *How* He was so He does but partially explain here; but the proclamation of such an astonishing truth was itself enough in the meantime; and those whom its transcendant grace might win over to attach themselves cordially to Him would immediately find in their own experience how true it was, and very soon—on the pentecostal descent of the Spirit—discover the secret of their satisfaction more in detail. But 3. When the Evangelist says that by the "rivers of living water which were to flow out of the belly of them that believed in Him," Jesus meant "*the Spirit,* which believers were about to receive: for the Holy Ghost had not then been given; because Jesus was not yet glorified"—he expresses the great evangelical truth, that it is the Holy Ghost who opens up in the souls of them that believe in Jesus the fountain of a new life, and by His indwelling presence and ever-quickening virtue within them, causes rivers of living water to flow forth from this internal fountain—in other words, makes exuberant and heavenly satisfaction to spring up and flow forth from within their own nature. But whereas He says that this glorious gift of the Spirit was so dependent upon the "*glorification of Jesus,*" that until the one occurred the other could not be looked for—this expresses these further and most precious truths, that *the formal and judicial acceptance of Christ's work* done on earth *by His Father in heaven* behoved to take place ere the Spirit could be permitted to carry it into effect; that the actual descent of the Spirit at Pentecost was the proclamation to the world that His Father had *taken His work off His hands,* so to speak, as a "*finished" work;* and that now the Spirit, in opening up the springs of this new and enduring life in

the souls of them that believed in Jesus, was but carrying into effect *in* men what Christ did on earth *for* men, was but putting them in personal possession and actual experience of the virtue of Christ's work—even as Jesus Himself afterwards said in express terms to the Eleven at the Supper-table, "He shall glorify Me; for He shall receive of Mine, and shall show it"—or 'make it known' [*ἀναγγελεῖ*] "unto you" (see on ch. xvi. 14-16). Thus, as Jesus glorified the Father, so the Spirit glorifies the Son; and by one high, harmonious work of Father, Son, and Holy Ghost, are sinners saved.

CHAP. VIII. 1-11.—THE WOMAN TAKEN IN ADULTERY. The genuineness of this narrative—including the last verse of the foregoing chapter—will be best considered after the exposition. 1. **Jesus**—It should be, 'But Jesus' [Ἰησοῦς δὲ] **went unto the mount of Olives.** This verse should have formed the last verse of ch. vii. The information given will then be, that while "every man went unto his own house," Jesus, who had no home of His own to go to, "went unto the mount of Olives." As "the mount of Olives" nowhere else occurs in this Gospel, and Jesus' spending the night there seems to belong only to the time of His final visit to Jerusalem; this has been thought adverse to the genuineness of the whole Section. The following is *Stier's* explanation of this, with which, however, we are but indifferently satisfied. 'The return of the people to the inert quiet and security of their *dwellings* (ch. vii. 53), at the close of the feast, is designedly contrasted with our Lord's *homeless* way, so to speak, of spending the short night, who is early in the morning on the scene again. One cannot well see why what is recorded in Luke xxi. 37, 38, may not even then thus early have taken place: it might have been the Lord's ordinary custom from the beginning to leave the brilliant misery of the city every night, that so He might compose His sorrowful and interceding heart, and collect His energies for new labours of love; preferring for His resting-place Bethany, and *the Mount of Olives,* the scene thus consecrated by many preparatory prayers for His final humiliation and exaltation.' But see the discussion of this question below. 2. **And early in the morning he came again into the temple, and all the people came unto him; and he sat down, and taught them.**

The Scribes and Pharisees Bring to Jesus a Woman Taken in Adultery for His Decision, and how this Attempt to Entrap Him was foiled (3-11). 3. **And the scribes and Pharisees**—foiled in their yesterday's attempts, and hoping to entrap Him in this new way, **brought unto him a woman taken in adultery; and when they had set her in the midst,** 4. **They say unto him, Master, this woman was taken in adultery, in the very act.** 5. **Now Moses in the law commanded us, that such should be stoned.** The law said merely she should die (Deut. xxii. 22), but in aggravated cases, at least in later times, this was probably by stoning (Ezek. xvi. 40). **but what sayest thou?** [σὺ οὖν τί λέγεις;)—'what now sayest thou?' 6. **This they said, tempting him, that they might**

399

might have to accuse him. But Jesus stooped down, and with *his*
7 finger wrote on the ground, *as though he heard them not.* So when
they continued asking him, he lifted up himself, and said unto them,
*b*He that is without sin among you, let him first cast a stone at her.
8, And again he stooped down, and wrote on the ground. And they
9 which heard it, *c*being convicted by *their own* conscience, went out one
by one, beginning at the eldest, *even* unto the last: and Jesus was left
10 alone, and the woman standing in the midst. When Jesus had lifted
up himself, and saw none but the woman, he said unto her, Woman,
11 where are those thine accusers? hath no man condemned thee? She
said, No man, Lord. And Jesus said unto her, *d*Neither do I condemn
thee: go, and sin no more.

A. D. 32.

b Deut. 17. 7.
Job 5. 12.
Ps. 50. 16-20.
Matt. 7. 1-5.
Rom. 2. 1.
c Gen. 41. 21,
22.
Rom. 2. 23.
1 John 3. 20.
d Luke 9. 56.
Luke 12. 14.
ch. 3. 17.
Rom. 13. 3,
4.

have to accuse him—hoping, whatever He might answer, to put Him in the wrong:—if He said, Stone her, that would seem a stepping out of His province; if He forbade it, that would hold Him up as a relaxer of the public morals. See now how these cunning hypocrites were overmatched. **But Jesus stooped down.** It will be observed He was " *sitting* " when they came to Him (*v.* 2). **and with his finger wrote on the ground.** The words of our translators in Italics—" as though he heard them not"—have hardly improved the sense, for it is scarcely probable He could wish that to be thought. Rather He wished to show them His aversion to enter on the subject. But this did not suit them. They pressed for an answer. **7. So when they continued asking him, he lifted up himself, and said unto them, He that is without sin** —not meaning 'sinless altogether;' nor yet ' guiltless of a literal breach of the Seventh Commandment;' but probably, ' He whose conscience acquits him of *any such* sin,' **let him first cast a stone** [τὸν λίθον]—rather, ' the stone,' referred to in the Mosaic statute, Deut. xvii. 11. **8. And again he stooped down, and wrote on the ground.** The design of this second stooping and writing on the ground was evidently to give her accusers an opportunity to slink away unobserved *by Him,* and so avoid an exposure to His eye which they could ill have stood. Accordingly it is added, **9. And they which heard it**—or, ' But they, when they heard it' [Οἱ δὲ, ἀκούσαντες], **being convicted by their [own] conscience, went out one by one, beginning at the eldest** [ἀπὸ τῶν πρεσβυτέρων]—rather, ' at the elders;' in the official sense, and not the seniors in age. **even unto the last: and Jesus was left alone**—that is, without one of her accusers remaining; for it is added, **and the woman standing in the midst**—in the midst, that is, of the remaining audience. While the trap failed to catch Him for whom it was laid, it caught those who laid it. Stunned by the unexpected home-thrust, they immediately made off—which makes the impudence of those impure hypocrites in dragging such a case before the public eye the more disgusting. **10. When**—'And when' Jesus **had lifted up himself, and saw none but the woman, he said unto her, Woman, where are those thine accusers? hath no man condemned thee? 11. She said, No man, Lord. And Jesus said unto her, Neither do I condemn thee: go, and sin no more.** What inimitable tenderness and grace! Conscious of her own guilt, and till now in the hands of men who had talked of stoning her, wondering at the *skill* with which her accusers had been dispersed and the *grace* of the few words addressed to herself, she would be disposed to listen, with a reverence and teachableness before unknown, to our Lord's admonition. " And Jesus said unto her, Neither do I condemn thee, go and sin no more." He pronounces no

pardon upon the woman—like " Thy sins are forgiven thee;" " Go in peace"—much less does He say that she had done nothing condemnable; He simply leaves the matter where it was. He meddles not with the magistrate's office, nor acts the *Judge* in any sense (ch. xii. 47). But in saying " Go, and sin no more," which had been before said to one who undoubtedly believed (ch. v. 14), more is probably implied than expressed. If brought suddenly to conviction of sin, to admiration of her Deliverer, and to a willingness to be admonished and guided by Him, this call to begin a new life may have carried with it what would ensure and naturally bring about a permanent change.

[The genuineness of this whole Section, including the last verse of ch. vii.—twelve verses—is by far the most perplexing question of textual criticism pertaining to the Gospels. The external evidence against it is immensely strong. It is wanting in the four oldest MSS.—the newly discovered Codex *Sinaiticus* (א), the *Alexandrian* (A), the *Vatican* (B), and the *Ephraem* (C)—and in four other valuable Uncial MSS., although two of these have a blank space, as if something had been left out; it is wanting also in upwards of fifty Cursive MSS.: of ancient versions, it is wanting in the venerable Peshito *Syriac* and its *Philoxenian* revision, in one and probably both the Egyptian versions—the *Thebaic* and *Memphitic*—the *Gothic,* probably the *Armenian,* and two or three copies of the *Old Latin:* several of the fathers take no notice of it—as *Origen, Tertullian, Cyprian, Cyril, Chrysostom:* it is wanting in the most ancient tables of the Sectional contents of the Gospels, though afterwards inserted as an additional Section: the variations in the MSS. which insert it exceed in number and extent those in any other part of the New Testament: and of those MSS. which insert it, four Uncials and upwards of fifty Cursives have an asterisk or other critical mark attached to it, as subject to doubt or requiring investigation. The internal evidence urged against it is, that it unnaturally interrupts the flow of the narrative, whereas if ch. viii. 12 come immediately after ch. vii. 52, all is natural; that the language of this Section is strikingly dissimilar, especially in the particles, to that of John; and that the statement in ch. viii. 1, as to Jesus having gone to the mount of Olives, is one of the strongest grounds of suspicion, since nowhere else in this Gospel is " the mount of Olives" mentioned at all, nor does our Lord's passing the night there agree with this or any stage of His public life except the last. That we have here very strong evidence against the genuineness of this Section, no intelligent and impartial judge will deny. Moved by this evidence, *Lachmann* and *Tischendorf* exclude it from their text; *Tregelles* prints it in small type below the approved text, which *Alford* also does; and hardly any recent critics acknowledge it as

12   Then spake Jesus again unto them, saying, ^e I am the light of the world : he that followeth me shall not walk in darkness, but shall have the light

A. D. 32.

^e Mal. 4. 2.

John's, except *Stier* and *Ebrard*, to whom may be added *Lange* and *Webster and Wilkinson* (though the latter do not, like the former, grapple with the difficulties). But let us look at the other side of the question. Of the four most ancient MSS. which want this Section, the leaves of two at this place have been lost—of A, from ch. vi. 50 to viii. 52; and of C, from ch. vii. 3 to viii. 33. We have, therefore, no certainty whether those MSS. contained it or not. As to the two (L and Δ) whose spaces are not long enough to make it *possible* that they contained this Section, the inference is precarious, since no more may have been intended by those spaces than simply to indicate that there a portion of text was wanting. But it is found in seven Uncial MSS., though the letters in that most remarkable one, the Codex *Bezæ* (D), are said to be very different from the others, while in one of the others but a small number of the verses is given, and in another one verse is wanting; it is found in above three hundred of the Cursive MSS. without any note of question, and above fifty more with an asterisk or other mark of doubt. Of versions, it is found in the *Old Latin*—which may be held to neutralize the fact of its absence in the Peshito Syriac, as the one appears to have been executed for the Western churches about as early as the other for the Eastern; and it is found in the *Vulgate;* while Jerome, to whom we owe that revision of the venerable Old Latin, states that in his time—the fourth century, and we have no MSS. of older date than that—this Section was found 'in many MSS. both Greek and Latin.' Turning now from external to *internal* evidence in favour of this Section, it appears to us to be almost overpowering. Requesting the reader to recall the exposition of it, we confidently ask if historical authenticity is not stamped upon the face of it, and—admitting that *some* such incident as this might not be beyond invention—whether the very peculiar and singularly delicate details of it *could* be other than real. And if the question be, Whether, supposing it genuine, there were stronger motives for its exclusion, or, if spurious, for its insertion? no one who knows anything of the peculiarities of the early Church can well hesitate. The notions of the early Church on such subjects were of the most ascetic description, and to them the whole narrative must have been most confounding. *Augustin* accordingly says, 'Some of slender faith, or rather enemies of the true faith, have removed it from their MSS., fearing, I believe, that an immunity to sin might be thought to be given by it.' Nor was he alone in ascribing the omission of it to this cause. Such a feeling in regard to this Section is sufficient to account for the remarkable fact that it was never publicly read along with the preceding and following context in the early churches, but reserved for some unimportant festivals, and in some of the service-books appears to have been left out altogether. In short, to account for its *omission*, if genuine, seems easy enough; but for its *insertion*, if spurious, next to impossible. Moved by these considerations, a middle course is taken by some. *Meyer* and *Ellicott*, while convinced that it is no part of the Gospel of John, are equally convinced of its historical truth and canonical authority, and observing how closely ch. viii. agrees with Luke xxi. 37, think that to be its proper place. Indeed, it is a singular fact that four of the Cursive MSS. actually place it at the end of Luke xxi. Something very like this is *Alford's* view. This, of course, would quite

explain the mention (in ch. viii. 1) of "the mount of Olives," and our Lord's spending the night there being His last week. But this theory—of a fragment of authentic canonical Gospel History never known to have existed in its proper place (with the exception of four pretty good MSS.), and known only as part of a Gospel to which it did not belong, and with which it was out of keeping—can never, in our judgment, be admitted. *Scrivener*, while impressed with its internal excellence, thinks the evidence against it too strong to be resisted, except on the singular theory that the beloved disciple himself added it in a later edition of his Gospel, and that thus copies having it and copies wanting it ran parallel with each other from the very first—a theory, however, for which there is not the slightest external evidence, and attended, it seems to us, with greater difficulty than that which it is designed to remove. On the whole, though we admit the difficulties with which this question is encompassed, as the narrative itself bears that stamp of originality, truth, purity, and grandeur which accord so well with its place in the Gospel History, so the fact that wherever it is found it is as part of the Fourth Gospel, and among the transactions of the Feast of Tabernacles, is to us the best proof that this is, after all, its true place in the Gospel History; nor does it appear to us to interrupt the flow of the narrative, but entirely to harmonize with it—if we except ch. viii. 1, which must be allowed to remain among the difficulties that we, at least, find it not easy to solve.] But see P.S. p. 486.

Remark.—While a sanctimonious hypocrisy is not unfrequently found among unprincipled professors of religion, a compassionate purity which wins the fallen is one of the most beautiful characteristics of real religion. But till Christ appeared, this feature of religion was but dimly realized, and in the Old Testament but faintly held forth. It was reserved for the Lord Jesus to exhibit it in all its loveliness. In this incident, of the Woman Taken in Adultery, we have it in its perfection, while the spirit of the men that brought her to Jesus, appearing in such vivid contrast to it, acts but as a foil to set it off. See on Luke xv. 1, 2.

12-59.—JESUS CONTINUES HIS DISCOURSE IN THE TEMPLE AMIDST REPEATED INTERRUPTIONS, TILL, ON THEIR PROCEEDING TO STONE HIM, HE PASSES THROUGH THE MIDST OF THEM AND DEPARTS.

Jesus Addresses Himself chiefly to a Hostile Audience, in the way of solemn Testimony, at the climax of which many are won to Him, to whom He Addresses an Encouraging Word (12-32). **12. Then spake Jesus again unto them, saying, I am the light of the world.** As the former references to *water* (ch. iv. 10, 13, 14; and ch. vii. 37, &c.) and to *bread* (ch. vi. 32, &c.) were occasioned by outward occurrences, so possibly may this reference to *light* have been. For, in "the treasury," where it was spoken (see *v.* 20), stood two colossal golden lampstands, on which hung a multitude of lamps, lighted after the evening sacrifice (probably every evening) during the feast of Tabernacles, diffusing their brilliancy, it is said, over all the city. Around these the people danced with great rejoicing. Now, as amidst the festivities of the *water* from Siloam, Jesus cried, saying, "If any man thirst let him come unto me and drink," so now, amidst the blaze and joyousness of this illumination, He proclaims, "I AM THE LIGHT OF THE WORLD"—plainly in the most *absolute* sense. For

13 of life. The Pharisees therefore said unto him, Thou bearest record
14 of thyself; thy record is not true. Jesus answered and said unto them, Though I bear record of myself, *yet* my record is true: for I know whence I came, and whither I go; but *f*ye cannot tell whence I come,
15 and whither I go. Ye *g*judge after the flesh; *h*I judge no man.
16 And yet if I judge, my judgment is true; for *i*I am not alone, but I
17 and the Father that sent me. It *j*is also written in your law, that the
18 testimony of two men is true. I am one that bear witness of myself,
19 and *k*the Father that sent me beareth witness of me. Then said they unto him, Where is thy Father? Jesus answered, *l*Ye neither know me, nor my Father: *m*if ye had known me, ye should have known my Father also.
20 These words spake Jesus in *n*the treasury, as he taught in the temple: and *o*no man laid hands on him; for *p*his hour was not yet come.
21 Then said Jesus again unto them, I go my way, and *q*ye shall seek me,
22 and shall die in your sins: whither I go, ye cannot come. Then said the Jews, Will he kill himself? because he saith, Whither I go, ye cannot
23 come. And he said unto them, *r*Ye are from beneath; I am from above:
24 *s*ye are of this world; I am not of this world. I said therefore unto you, that ye shall die in your sins: *t*for if ye believe not that I am *he*, ye shall
25 die in your sins. Then said they unto him, Who art thou? And Jesus

A. D. 32.
f Ps. 58. 1.
ch. 7. 28.
ch. 9. 29.
g 1 Sam.16. 7.
ch. 7. 24.
h ch. 18. 36.
i ch. 16. 32.
j Deut. 17. 6.
Deut.19.15.
Matt.18.16.
2 Cor. 13. 1.
Heb. 10. 28.
k ch. 5. 37.
2 Pet. 1. 17.
1 John 5. 6-
12.
l ch. 16. 3.
m ch. 14. 7.
n Mark 12.41.
o ch. 7. 30.
p ch. 7. 8.
q ch. 13. 33.
r ch. 3. 31.
s ch. 15. 19.
ch. 17. 16.
1 John 4 5.
t Mark 16.16.

though He gives His disciples the same title (see on ch. v. 14), they are only "light *in the Lord*" (Eph. v. 8); and though He calls the Baptist "the burning and shining light" (or '*lamp*' of his day—see on ch. v. 35), yet "he was *not that Light*, but was sent to bear witness of that Light: That was THE TRUE LIGHT which, coming into the world, *lighteth every man*" (ch. i. 8, 9). Under this magnificent title Messiah was promised of old, Isa. xlii. 6; Mal. iv. 2, &c. he that followeth me—as one does a light going before him, and as the Israelites did the pillar of bright cloud in the wilderness, shall not walk in darkness, but shall have the light of life—the light as of a new world, the light of a newly awakened spiritual and eternal life. 13. The Pharisees therefore said unto him, Thou bearest record of thyself; thy record is not true. How does He meet this specious cavil! Not by disputing the wholesome human maxim that 'self-praise is no praise,' but by affirming that He was *an exception to the rule*, or rather, that *it had no application to Him*. 14. Jesus answered and said unto him, Though I bear record of myself, yet my record is true: for I know whence I came, and whither I go; but ye cannot tell whence I come, and whither I go. See on ch. vii. 28, 29. 15. Ye judge after the flesh—with no spiritual apprehension; I judge no man. 16. And yet if I judge [Καὶ ἐὰν κρίνω δὲ Ἐγὼ]. The "*I*" here is emphatic:—*q. d.*, 'Yet in My case, even if I do judge,' my judgment is true; for I am not alone, but I and the Father that sent me. 17. It is also written in your law, that the testimony of two men is true. 18. I am one that bear witness of myself, and the Father that sent me beareth witness of me:—*q. d.*, 'Ye not only *form* your carnal and warped judgments of Me, but are bent on carrying them into effect; I, though I form and utter My judgment of you, am not here to carry this into execution—that is reserved to a future day; yet the judgment I now pronounce and the witness I now bear is not Mine only, as ye suppose, but His also that sent Me. (See on ch. v. 31, 32.) And these are the two witnesses which your law requires to any fact.' 19. Then said they unto him, Where is thy Father? Jesus answered, Ye neither know me, nor my Father: if

ye had known me, ye should have known my Father also. The same spiritual light and darkness would suffice to reveal to the mind, or to hide from it, at once the Father and the Son, the Sender and the Sent. 20. These words spake Jesus in the treasury—a division, so called, of the fore-court of the temple, part of the court of the women (*Joseph.* Antt. xix. 6. 2, &c.), which may confirm the genuineness of *vv.* 2, 11, as the place where the woman was brought. as he taught in the temple: and no man laid hands on him; for his hour was not yet come. See on ch. vii. 30. In the dialogue that follows, the conflict waxes sharper on both sides. 21. Then said Jesus again unto them, I go my way, and ye shall seek me, and shall die in your sins [ἐν τῇ ἁμαρτίᾳ ὑμῶν]—it should be 'in your sin:' whither I go, ye cannot come. 22. Then said the Jews, Will he kill himself? because he saith, Whither I go, ye cannot come. They evidently saw something more in His words than when He spake thus before (ch. vii. 33-36); but their question now is more malignant and scornful. 23. And he said unto them, Ye are from beneath; I am from above: ye are of this world; I am not of this world. He contrasts Himself here, not as in ch. iii. 31, simply with *earth-born messengers of God*, but with *men sprung from and breathing an opposite element* from His, which rendered it impossible that He and they should have any present fellowship, or dwell eternally together. See again on ch. vii. 34, and on *v.* 44, below. 24. I said therefore unto you, that ye shall die in your sins: for if ye believe not that I am [he] [ὅτι ἐγώ εἰμι], ye shall die in your sins. "That I am [He]." Compare Mark xiii. 6, *Greek*, and Matt. xxiv. 5. They knew well enough what He meant. But He would not, by speaking it out, give them the materials for a charge for which they were watching. At the same time, one is irresistibly reminded by such language, so far transcending what is becoming in *men*, of those ancient declarations of the God of Israel, "I AM HE," &c. (Deut. xxxii. 39; Isa. xliii. 10, 13; xlvi. 4; xlviii. 12.) See on Mark vi. 50. 25. Then said they unto him, Who art thou?—hoping thus to extort an explicit answer; but they are disap-

402

saith unto them, Even *the same* that I said unto you from the beginning.

26 I have many things to say and to judge of you: but [u]he that sent me is true; and I [v]speak to the world those things which I have heard of

27 him. They understood not that he spake to them of the Father.

28 Then said Jesus unto them, When ye have [w]lifted up the Son of man, [x]then shall ye know that I am *he*, and [y]*that* I do nothing of myself;

29 but [z]as my Father hath taught me, I speak these things. And [a]he that sent me is with me: the Father hath not left me alone; [b]for I do always those things that please him.

30, As he spake these words many believed on him. Then said Jesus to

31 those Jews which believed on him, If ye continue in my word, *then*

32 are ye my disciples indeed; and ye shall know the truth, and [c]the truth shall make you free.

33 They answered him, [d]We be Abraham's seed, and were never in bondage to any man: how sayest thou, Ye shall be made free?

34 Jesus answered them, Verily, verily, I say unto you, [e]Whosoever com-

A. D. 32.

[u] ch. 7. 28.
[v] ch. 3. 32.
ch. 15. 15.
[w] ch. 3. 14.
ch. 12. 32.
[x] Rom. 1. 4.
[y] ch. 5. 19, 30.
[z] ch. 3. 11.
[a] ch. 14. 10.
ch. 16. 32.
[b] ch. 4. 34.
ch. 6. 38.
[c] Rom. 6. 14,
18, 22.
Rom. 8. 2.
Jas. 1. 25.
Jas. 2. 12.
[d] Lev. 25. 42.
Matt. 3. 9.
[e] 2 Pet. 2. 19.

pointed. And Jesus saith — 'said' [εἶπεν] unto them, Even the same that I said unto you from the beginning [Τὴν αρχὴν ὅ τι καὶ λαλῶ ὑμῖν]. This clause is in the original somewhat obscure, and has been variously rendered and much discussed. But the sense given in our version seems the true one, and has on the whole the best support. 26. I have many things to say and to judge of you: but he that sent me is true; and I speak to the world those things which I have heard of him:—*q. d.*, 'I could, and at the fitting time will say and judge many things of you (referring perhaps to the work of the Spirit, which is for *judgment* as well as *salvation*, ch. xvi. 8), but what I do say is just the message My Father hath given Me to deliver.' 27. They understood not that he spake to them of the Father.

28. Then said Jesus unto them, When ye have lifted up the Son of man—the plainest intimation He had yet given *in public* of the *manner* and the *authors* of His death. then shall ye know that I am [he], and that I do nothing of myself; but as my Father hath taught me—or, 'as my Father taught Me' [ἐδίδαξεν] I speak these things—that is, they should find out, or have sufficient evidence, how true was all He said, though they would be far from owning it. 29. And he that sent me is with me: the Father hath not left me alone; for I do always those things that please him [τὰ ἀρεστὰ αὐτῷ]—'the things that are pleasing to Him:'—*q. d.*, 'To you, who gnash upon Me with your teeth, and frown down all open appearance for Me, I seem to stand uncountenanced and alone; but I have a sympathy and support transcending all human applause; I came hither to do My Father's will, and in the doing of it have not ceased to please Him; therefore is He ever by Me with His approving smile, His cheering words, His supporting arm.' 30. As he spake these words many believed on him. Instead of wondering at this, the wonder would be if words of such unearthly, surpassing grandeur *could* be uttered without captivating *some* that heard them. And just as "all that sat in the council" to try Stephen "saw his face"—though expecting nothing but death—"as it had been the face of an angel" (Acts vi. 15), so may we suppose that, full of the sweet supporting sense of His Father's presence, amidst the rage and scorn of the rulers, a divine benignity beamed from His countenance, irradiated the words that fell from Him, and won over the candid "many" of His audience. 31. Then said Jesus to those Jews which believed on him, If ye continue in my word,

then are ye my disciples indeed; 32. And ye shall know the truth, and the truth shall make you free. The impression produced by the last words of our Lord may have become visible by some decisive movement, and here He takes advantage of it to press on them "*continuance*" in the faith, since then only were they "His real disciples" (compare ch. xv. 3-8), and then should they *experimentally* "know the truth," and "by the truth be made *spiritually* free."

The Hostile Part of His Audience here Breaking in upon the Words of Encouragement addressed to the Believing Portion, Jesus again addresses Himself to them, and in a yet higher strain of Solemn Testimony (33-53). 33. They answered him, We be Abraham's seed, and were never in bondage to any man: how sayest thou, Ye shall be made free? Who said this? Not surely the very class just spoken of as won over by His divine words, and exhorted to continue in them. Most interpreters seem to think so; but it is hard to ascribe such a petulant speech to newly gained disciples, even in the lowest sense, much less persons *so* gained as they were. It came, probably, from persons mixed up with them in the same part of the crowd, but of a very different spirit. The *pride* of the Jewish nation, even now, after centuries of humiliation, is the most striking feature of their character. 'Talk of freedom to *us?* Pray, when or to whom were we ever in bondage?' This bluster sounds almost ludicrous from such a nation. Had they forgotten their long and bitter bondage in Egypt? their dreary captivity in Babylon? their present bondage to the Roman yoke, and their restless eagerness to throw it off? But probably they saw that our Lord pointed to something else—freedom, perhaps, from the leaders of sects or parties—and were not willing to allow their subjection even to these. Our Lord, therefore, though He knew what slaves they were even in this sense, drives the ploughshare somewhat deeper than this, to a bondage they little dreamt of.

34. Jesus answered them, Verily, verily, I say unto you, Whosoever—or 'Every one that' [πᾶς ὁ] committeth sin—that is to say, 'liveth in the commission of it' (compare 1 John iii. 8; Matt. vii. 23), is the servant of sin—the *bond-servant*, or *slave* of it; for the question is not about free-service, but Who are in *bondage?* (Compare 2 Pet. ii. 19; Rom. vi. 16). The great truth here expressed was not unknown to heathen moralists; but it was applied only to *vice*, for they were total strangers to what in Revealed Religion is called *sin*. But the thought of *slaves* and *freemen* in the house suggests

403

35 mitteth sin is the servant of sin. And *f*the servant abideth not in the
36 house for ever: *but* the Son abideth ever. If *g*the Son therefore shall
   make you free, ye shall be free indeed.
37 I know that ye are Abraham's seed; but ye *h*seek to kill me, be-
38 cause my word hath no place in you. I speak that which I have
   seen with my Father; and ye do that which ye have seen with your
39 father. They answered and said unto him, Abraham *i*is our father.
   Jesus saith unto them, *j*If ye were Abraham's children, ye would do
40 the works of Abraham. But now ye seek to kill me, a man that hath
   told you the truth, which I have heard of God: this did not Abraham.
41 Ye do the deeds of your father. Then said they to him, We be not
42 born of fornication; *k*we have one Father, *even* God. Jesus said
   unto them, *l*If God were your Father, ye would love me: *m*for I proceeded forth and came from God; *n*neither came I of myself, but he
43 sent me. Why *o*do ye not understand my speech? *even* because ye
44 cannot hear my word. Ye *p*are of *your* father the devil, and the
   lusts of your father ye will do. He was a murderer from the beginning,
   and *q*abode not in the truth, because there is no truth in him. When he

A. D. 32.
f Gal. 4. 30.
g Isa. 49. 24.
Rom. 8. 2.
2 Cor. 3. 17.
Gal. 5. 1.
Rev. 1. 5.
Rev. 2. 7, 10.
Rev. 5. 9.
h ch. 7. 19.
i Matt. 3. 9.
j Rom. 2. 28.
Rom. 9. 7.
Gal. 3. 7, 29.
k Isa. 63. 16.
Isa. 64. 8.
Mal. 1. 6.
l 1 John 4. 19.
m ch. 1. 14.
ch. 3. 16.
n ch. 5. 43.
o ch. 7. 17.
p Matt. 13. 38.
q Gen. 3. 1.

to our Lord a wider idea. **35. And the servant—**
or, 'Now the [bond-]servant' abideth not in the
house for ever: [but] the Son abideth ever. **36.
If the Son therefore shall make you free, ye shall
be free indeed.** A very glorious statement, the
sense of which may be thus expressed: 'And if
your connection with the family of God be that of
BOND-SERVANTS, ye have no *natural* tie to the
house; your tie is essentially *uncertain* and *precarious.* But THE SON's relationship to the FATHER
is a *natural* and *essential* one; it is an indefeasible
tie; His abode in it is *perpetual* and *of right:* That
is My relationship, My tie: If, then, ye would have
your connection with God's family made *real,
rightful, permanent,* ye must by the Son be *manumitted* and *adopted* as sons and daughters of the
Lord Almighty.' In this sublime statement there
is no doubt a subordinate allusion to Gen. xxi. 10,
"Cast out this bond-woman and her son, for the
son of this bond-woman shall not be heir with my
son, with Isaac." (Compare Gal. iv. 22-30).

**37. I know that ye are Abraham's seed; but ye
seek to kill me.** He had said this to their face before; He now repeats it, and they do not deny it;
yet are they held back, as by some marvellous spell
—it was the awe which His combined dignity, courage, and benignity struck into them. **because my
word hath no place in you** [οὐ χωρεῖ ἐν ὑμῖν]—
'finds no entrance' or 'room in you.' When did
ever *human prophet* so speak of his words? They
tell us of "the word of the Lord" coming to them.
But here is One who holds up "His word" as that
which ought to find entrance and abiding room for
itself in the souls of all who hear it. **38. I speak
that which I have seen with my Father; and ye
do that which ye have seen with your father.**
See on *v.* 23. **39. They answered and said unto
him, Abraham is our father. Jesus saith unto
them, If ye were Abraham's children, ye would
do the works of Abraham.** He had just said He
"knew they were Abraham's children"—that is,
according to the *flesh;* but the children of his *faith
and holiness* they were not, but the reverse. **40.
But now ye seek to kill me, a man that hath told
you the truth, which I have heard**—or 'which
I heard' [ἤκουσα] **of God: this did not Abraham.**
In so doing ye act in direct opposition to him. **41.
Ye do the deeds of your father. Then said they
to him, We be not born of fornication; we have
one father [even] God.** The meaning is, they
were not an illegitimate race in point of *religion,*
pretending only to be God's people, but were

descended from His own chosen Abraham. **42.
Jesus said unto them, If God were your Father,
ye would love me: for I proceeded forth and
came** — or 'am come' [ἥκω] **from God; neither
came I of myself, but he sent me. 43. Why do ye
not understand my speech? even because ye
cannot hear my word:**—*q. d.,* 'If ye had anything
of His moral image, as children have their father's
likeness, ye would love Me, for I am immediately
of Him and directly from Him. But "My speech"
(meaning His peculiar style of expressing Himself on these subjects) 'is unintelligible to you'
because ye cannot take in the truth which it conveys.'

44. Ye are of your father the devil. This, as
Alford remarks, is one of the most decisive testimonies to the *objective personality* of the devil.
It is quite impossible to suppose an accommodation
to Jewish views, or a metaphorical form of speech,
in so solemn an assertion as this. **and the lusts of
your father**—his impure, malignant, ungodly propensities, inclinations, desires, **ye will do** [θέλετε
ποιεῖν]—or 'are willing to do,' that is, 'willingly
do;" not of any blind necessity of nature, but of
pure natural inclination. **He was a murderer
from the beginning.** The reference here is not to
the murderous spirit which he kindled in Cain
(as *Lücke, de Wette, Tholuck, Alford, Webster and
Wilkinson*), which yields but a tame and very
limited sense, but to that which he did to Man in
the person of *Adam.* So the majority of ancient
and modern interpreters, including *Grotius, Calvin,
Meyer, Luthardt.* The death of the human race,
in its widest sense, is ascribed to the murderous seducer of our race. **and abode not in the
truth.** Since the word [ἔστηκεν] properly means
'*abideth,*' it has been, by *Lücke* and others,
denied that the *fall* of Satan from a former holy
state is here expressed; and some superior interpreters, as *Olshausen,* think this only *implied.* But
though the *form* of the thought is present—not
past—this is to express the important idea, that
his whole character and activity are just *a continual aberration from his own original truth or
rectitude;* and thus his fall is not only the *implied
basis* of the thought, but *part of the statement itself,*
properly interpreted and brought out. **because
there is no truth in him**—because he is void of
all that holy, transparent rectitude which, as
God's creature, he originally possessed. **When he
speaketh a lie, he speaketh of his own** [ἐκ τῶν
ἰδίων]. As the word here is plural, perhaps the

speaketh a lie, he speaketh of his own: for he is a liar, and the
45 father of it. And because I tell *you* the truth, ye believe me not.
46 Which of you convinceth me of sin? And if I say the truth, why do
47 ye not believe me? He 'that is of God heareth God's words: ye therefore
48 hear *them* not, because ye are not of God. Then answered the Jews, and
said unto him, Say we not well that thou art a Samaritan, and hast a
devil?
49 Jesus answered, I have not a devil; but I honour my Father, and ye
50 do dishonour me. And 'I seek not mine own glory: there is one that
51 seeketh and judgeth. Verily, verily, I say unto you, 'If a man keep
52 my saying, he shall never see death. Then said the Jews unto him, Now
we know that thou hast a devil. "Abraham is dead, and the prophets;
and thou sayest, If a man keep my saying, he shall never taste of death.
53 Art thou greater than our father Abraham, which is dead? and the
prophets are dead: whom makest thou thyself?

A. D. 32.

' ch. 1. 12,13.
ch. 6. 45,46,
65.
ch. 10. 26,27.
ch. 17. 6, 8.
1 John 3.10.
1 John 4. 6.
1 John 5. 1.
2 John 9.
3 John 11.
* ch. 3. 15, 16.
ch. 5. 41.
ch. 6. 50.
ch. 7. 18.
ch. 15. 20.
t ch. 5. 24.
ch. 11. 26.
" Zec. 1. 5.
Heb. 11. 13.

meaning is, as *Alford* expresses it, 'of his own resources,' his own treasures (Matt. xii. 35). It means that he has no temptation to it *from without;* it is purely *self-begotten,* springing from a nature which is nothing but obliquity. **for he is a liar, and the father of it**—that is, of lying itself: all the falsehood in the world owes its existence to him. What a verse is this! It holds up the devil, first, as the murderer of the human race; but as this is meant here in the more profound sense of *spiritual* death, it holds him up, next, as the parent of this fallen human family, communicating to his offspring his own evil passions and universal obliquity, and stimulating these into active exercise. But as there is "a Stronger than he," who comes upon him and overcomes him (Luke xi. 21-22), it is only such as "love the darkness" who are addressed as children of the devil (Matt. xiii. 38; 1 John iii. 8-10). **45. And**—or rather, 'But' **because I tell you the truth, ye believe me not**—not *although* He told it them, but *because* He did so, and for the reason given in the former verse. Had He been *less* true, they would have hailed Him the more readily.

46. Which of you convinceth [ἐλέγχει]—rather, 'convicteth' **me of sin?**—or can bring home against Me a charge of sin? **[And] if I say the truth**—the "and" appears not to belong to the genuine text, **why do ye not believe me?** Glorious dilemma! 'Convict me of sin, and reject me: But if ye cannot, why stand ye out against My claims?' Of course they could only be supposed to impeach His *life;* but in one who had already passed through unparalleled complications, and had continually to deal with friends and foes of every sort and degree, such a challenge, thrown wide amongst His bitterest enemies, can amount to nothing short of a claim to *absolute sinlessness.* **47. He that is of God heareth God's words: ye therefore** [διὰ τοῦτο]—or 'for this reason,' **hear them not, because ye are not of God.** How often and how sharply does our Lord in this Discourse draw the line of awful separation between those that *are* and those that *are not* "of God!" The hostile part of His audience were stung to the quick by it. **48. Then answered the Jews, and said unto him, Say we not well that thou art a Samaritan, and hast a devil?** What intense and virulent scorn! (See Heb. xii. 3.) The "say we not well" is a reference to their former charge, "Thou hast a devil," ch. vii. 20. "Samaritan" here means more than 'no Israelite at all:' it means one who *pretended, but had no manner of claim* to connection with Abraham—retorting, perhaps, His denial of their *true* descent from

the father of the faithful. **49. Jesus answered, I have not a devil.** What calm dignity is here! Verily, "when reviled, He reviled not again" (1 Pet. ii. 23). Compare Paul before Festus, "I am not mad, most noble Festus" (Acts xxvi. 25). Our Lord adds not, ' Nor am I a Samaritan,' that He might not even seem to partake of their contempt for a race that had already welcomed Him as the Christ, and begun to be blessed by Him. **but I honour my Father, and ye do dishonour me.** This is the language of *wounded feeling.* But the *interior* of His soul at such moments is only to be seen in such prophetic utterances as these, "For thy sake I have borne reproach: shame hath covered my face: I am become a stranger unto my brethren, an alien unto my mother's children. For the zeal of thine house hath eaten me up, and the reproaches of them that reproached thee are fallen upon me" (Ps. lxix. 7-9). **50. And**—or, 'But' **I seek not mine own glory: there is one that seeketh and judgeth.** There should be a supplement here: 'There is one that seeketh [it]; that is, 'that seeketh My glory and judgeth'—Who requireth "all men to honour the Son even as they honour the Father;" Who will judicially treat him "who honoureth not the Son as honouring not the Father that hath sent Him" (ch. v. 23, and compare Matt. xvii. 5); but Who will yet give to Him (see ch. vi. 37) those who will one day cast their crowns before His throne, in whom He "shall see of the travail of His soul, and be satisfied" (Isa. liii. 11). **51. Verily, verily, I say unto you, If a man keep my saying, he shall never see death:**—thus vindicating His lofty claims, as Lord of the kingdom of life everlasting, and, at the same time, holding out even to His revilers the sceptre of grace. The word "keep" [τηρήσῃ] is in harmony with His former saying to those who believed in Him, "If ye *continue* in my word," expressing the permanency, as a living and paramount principle, of that faith to which He referred. This promise—"he shall never see death"—though expressed before (ch. v. 24; vi. 40, 47, 51), is the strongest and most naked statement yet given of a very glorious truth. In ch. xi. 26 it is repeated in nearly identical terms. **52. Then said the Jews unto him, Now we know that thou hast a devil. Abraham is dead**—or 'died' [ἀπέθανεν], **and the prophets; and thou sayest, If a man keep my saying, he shall never taste of death. 53. Art thou greater than our father Abraham, which is dead?**—or 'died,' and the prophets are dead—or 'died:' **whom makest thou thyself?** 'Thou art now self-convicted; only a demoniac could speak so; the most illustrious of our fathers

54   Jesus answered, If I honour myself, my honour is nothing: [v]it is my
55 Father that honoureth me; of whom ye say, that he is your God: yet
    [w]ye have not known him; but I know him: and if I should say, I know
    him not, I shall be a liar like unto you: but I know him, and keep his
56 saying. Your father Abraham [x]rejoiced to see my day; [y]and he saw *it*,
57 and was glad. Then said the Jews unto him, Thou art not yet fifty
    years old, and hast thou seen Abraham?
58   Jesus said unto them, Verily, verily, I say unto you, Before Abraham
59 was, [z]I am. Then took they up stones to cast at him: but Jesus hid
    himself, and went out of the temple, going through the midst of them,
    and so passed by.

A. D. 32

[v] ch. 16. 14.
    ch. 17. 1.
    Acts 3. 13.
[w] ch. 7. 28.
[x] Gen. 22. 18.
    Luke 10.24.
    Gal. 3. 8,16.
[y] Heb. 11.13.
[z] Ex. 3. 14.
    Isa. 9. 6.
    Isa. 43. 13.
    Mic. 5. 2.
    Col. 1. 17.

are dead, and thou promisest exemption from death to any one who will keep *thy saying!* pray, who art thou?'

The Climax (54-59). **54. Jesus answered, If I honour myself, my honour is nothing: it is my Father that honoureth me; of whom ye say, that he is your God: 55. Yet ye have not known him; but I know him: and if I should say, I know him not, I shall be a liar like unto you: but I know him, and keep his saying** [λόγον] — or 'word.' Our Lord now rises to the summit of holy, naked severity, thereby to draw this long dialogue to a head. **56. Your father Abraham rejoiced to see my day** [ηγαλλιάσατο ἵνα ἴδῃ]—'exulted,' or 'exceedingly rejoiced that he should see;' that is, exulted to see it *by anticipation;* **and he saw it, and was glad** —he *actually* beheld it to his joy. If this mean no more than that he had a prophetic foresight of the Gospel-day—the second clause just repeating the first—how could the Jews understand our Lord to mean that He "had seen Abraham?" And if it mean that Abraham was *then beholding*, in his disembodied spirit, the incarnate Messiah, as *Stier, Tholuck, Alford*, &c., understand it, the words seem very unsuitable to express it. Plainly it speaks of something *past*—he *saw* my day, and *was* glad—that is, surely, while he lived. We understand it therefore to refer to the familiar intercourse which Abraham had with that "Angel of the Lord" who in the History is repeatedly styled "The Lord" or *Jehovah*—the Angel of the covenant, with whom Christ here identifies Himself. On those occasions, says our Lord, Abraham "saw ME." Such is the view of *Olshausen;* but we need not suppose it, with him, to refer to some unrecorded scene. Taking the words in this sense, all that follows will, we think, be quite natural. **57. Then said the Jews unto him, Thou art not yet fifty years old.** No inference, as *Alford* properly says, can be drawn from this as to our Lord's age as man at that time. Fifty years was, with the Jews, the term of ripe manhood, and at that age the Levites ceased to officiate. **and hast thou seen Abraham?** He had not said He saw Abraham, but that Abraham saw *Him*, as being Abraham's peculiar privilege. They, however, give the opposite turn to it—"Hast thou seen Abraham?"—as an honour which it was insufferable for him to pretend to.

58. Jesus said unto them, Verily, verily, I say unto you, Before Abraham was [πρὶν Ἀβραὰμ γενέσθαι]—'Before Abraham came into existence' **I am** [ἐγώ εἰμί]. The difference between the two verbs applied to Abraham and Himself, in this great saying, is to be carefully observed. 'Before Abraham was *brought into being*, I *exist*. The statement, therefore, is not that *Christ came into existence before Abraham did*—as Arians affirm is the meaning: it is that he never *came into* being at all, but *existed* before Abraham had a being; which, of course, was as much as to say that He existed

before all creation, or from eternity, as in ch. i. 1. In that sense, beyond all doubt, the Jews understood Him, as will appear from what follows. **59. Then took they up stones to cast at him**—precisely as they did on a former occasion when they saw that He was making Himself equal with God, ch. v. 18. **but Jesus hid himself, and went out of the temple, [going through the midst of them, and so passed by].** See on Luke iv. 30. [These bracketed words—διελθὼν διὰ μέσου αὐτῶν· καὶ παρῆγεν οὕτως—are excluded from the text, as spurious, by *Lachmann, Tischendorf, Tregelles, Alford;* while *Meyer, de Wette, Ebrard,* and nearly all recent critics, concur in that judgment. *Olshausen* says it is undoubtedly spurious; even *Stier* suspects it; only *Lücke* speaks doubtfully. Yet how stands the evidence? B wants it; but A has it: D wants it; but *all the other* Uncial MSS.—some of them of the greatest value—contain it, as well as the best Cursive MSS. The *Old Latin* and the *Vulgate* want it—early and weighty evidence, no doubt; but evidence about as early and weighty, that of both the principal *Syriac* versions, is in its favour. One of the ancient Egyptian versions, the *Thebaic,* wants it; but the other, the *Memphitic,* has it. With these facts before us, we must regard the unhesitating rejection of this clause as quite unwarrantable; and whereas it is said to be an unauthorized repetition of Luke iv. 30, the words are not quite the same, nor is there anything improbable in our Lord, when precisely the same in circumstances of danger as then, escaping their grasp in the very same way. We certainly think that the clause should be bracketed, as the evidence against it is undoubtedly strong; but more than this, in our judgment, it will not warrant.]

Remarks.—1. What a lurid brightness invests the scene of this long Discourse—the majesty of the one party and the malignity of the other combining to give it this aspect; while the welcome which the words of grace found in the breasts of "many," and the encouraging words addressed to them, threw for the moment a heavenly radiance over the scene, though only to be overcast again! Who could have written this, if it had not been matter of actual occurrence? And who but an eye-witness could have thrown in such details as these? And what eye-witness even could have penned it as it is here penned, save under the ever-present guidance of Him Whom Jesus promised that the Father should send in His name, Who should "teach them all things, and *bring all things to their remembrance* whatsoever He spake unto them?" (ch. xiv. 26). 2. Who can believe that One whose jealousy for His Father's honour even "consumed" Him, should have exposed Himself once and again to the imminent risk of being stoned to death for "making Himself equal with God," *if He was not so,* and *never meant to teach that He was so;* when—either by avoiding those

9 AND as *Jesus* passed by, he saw a man which was blind from *his*
2 birth. And his disciples asked him, saying, Master, who did ^asin, this
3 man, or his parents, that he was born blind? Jesus answered, Neither
hath this man sinned, nor his parents: ^bbut that the works of God should
4 be made manifest in him. I 'must work the works of him that sent me,
5 while it is day: the night cometh, when no man can work. As long as
6 I am in the world, ^dI am the light of the world. When he had thus
spoken, ^ehe spat on the ground, and made clay of the spittle, and he
7 ¹anointed the eyes of the blind man with the clay, and said unto him,
Go, wash ^fin the pool of Siloam, (which is, by interpretation, Sent.) He
went his way therefore, and washed, and came seeing.
8 The neighbours therefore, and they which before had seen him that he
9 was blind, said, Is not this he that sat and begged? Some said, This is

A. D. 32.
CHAP. 9.
^a Matt. 16.14.
Acts 28. 4.
^b ch. 11. 4.
^c ch. 4. 34.
^d ch. 1. 5, 9.
ch. 3. 19.
^e Mark 7. 83.
Mark 8. 23.
1 Or. spread the clay upon the eyes of the blind man.
^f Neh. 3. 15.
Isa. 8. 6.

speeches from which they drew that inference, or by a few words of explanation—He could so easily have avoided such a construction of His words, or explained it away? But as He did neither, but advisedly did the reverse, that Corner-Stone of the Christian religion—the essential Divinity of the Lord Jesus—must be seen to stand firmer than the everlasting hills.

CHAP. IX. 1-41.—JESUS ON THE SABBATH DAY OPENS THE EYES OF A BEGGAR BORN BLIND—WHAT FOLLOWED ON THIS.

Jesus Opens the Eyes of a Beggar Born Blind (1-7). The connection between the close of the preceding chapter and the opening of this one appears so close, that one is apt to conclude that all happened on one day, and that a Sabbath (v. 14). But the violence with which the former chapter closes, and the tranquillity with which this one opens, renders that somewhat doubtful. At all events, the transactions of both chapters could not have been far apart in time. **1. And as Jesus passed by, he saw a man which was blind from his birth**—and who "sat and begged" (v. 8). **2. And his disciples asked him, saying, Master, who did sin, this man, or his parents, that he was born blind?** [ἴνα τυφλὸς γεννηθῇ]—or 'should be born blind.' As the doctrine of the pre-existence of souls, and that of the 'metempsychosis' (the transmission of the soul of one person into the body of another), though held by certain of the more philosophical Jews, was never a current belief of the people, we are not to understand the disciples here to refer to sin committed in a former state of existence; and probably it is but a loose way of concluding that sin *somewhere* had surely been the cause of this calamity. **3. Jesus answered, Neither hath this man sinned, nor his parents: but that the works of God should be made manifest in him:**—*q. d.*, 'The cause was neither in himself nor his parents, but in order to the manifestation of "the works of God" in his cure.' **4. I must work the works of him that sent me, while it is day: the night cometh, when no man can work**—a most interesting statement this, from the mouth of Christ; intimating, first, that He had a precise work to do upon earth, with every particular of it arranged and laid out to Him; next, that all He did upon earth was just "the works of God"—particularly "going about *doing good*," though not exclusively by miracles; further, that each work had its precise *time* and *place* in His programme of instructions, so to speak; hence, again, that as His period for work had a definite termination, so by letting any one service pass by its allotted time, the whole would be disarranged, marred, and driven beyond its destined period for completion; finally, that as man He acted ever under the impulse of these considera-

tions—"the night cometh when *no man* (or no one) can work." **5. As long as I am in the world, I am the light of the world.** Not as if he would cease, after that, to be so; but that He must make full proof of His fidelity, while His earthly career lasted, by displaying His glory. As before the resurrection of Lazarus, says *Alford*, He announces Himself as *the Resurrection and the Life* (ch. xi. 25), so now He holds Himself forth as the Source of that archetypal spiritual *light*, of which the natural, now about to be conferred, is only a derivation and symbol. **6. When he had thus spoken, he spat on the ground, and made clay of the spittle, and he anointed the eyes of the blind man with the clay, 7. And said unto him, Go, wash in the pool of Siloam, (which is, by interpretation, Sent.)** These operations were not so incongruous in their nature as might appear, though it were absurd to imagine that they contributed in the least degree to the effect which followed. (See on Mark vi. 13, and vii. 33, 34.) As the prescribed action was purely symbolical in its design, so in connection with it the Evangelist notices the symbolical name of the pool, as in this case bearing testimony to Him who was *sent* to do what it only *symbolized*. See Isa. viii. 6, where this same pool is used figuratively to denote "the streams that made glad the city of God," and which, humble though they be, betoken *a present God of Israel.* **He went his way therefore, and washed, and came seeing.** See 2 Kings v. 10, 14. But though he "came seeing," it does not appear that he came to Jesus. On the contrary, when he "came seeing," Jesus was not to be seen; nor did they meet at all, it would seem, until, after his expulsion from the synagogue, Jesus "found him" (v. 35).

The Beggar's Neighbours Question him as to the Cure, but, receiving only partial satisfaction, bring him to the Pharisees (8-14). **8. The neighbours therefore, and they which before had seen him that he was blind** [τυφλός]. The true reading here appears plainly to be, 'that he was a beggar' [ὅτι προσαίτης ἦν]—this being what would most immediately identify him, as the following words indeed show. So all recent critical editors, and nearly all critical expositors. **said, Is not this he that sat and begged? 9. Some said, This is he; others said, He is like him: but he said, I am he.** How graphically is the identity of the man thus ascertained; and his own testimony, coming in only to settle the point after it had been raised and occasioned some discussion, acquires thus additional importance. It is a good remark of *Webster and Wilkinson*, that the diversity of opinion is readily accounted for by the great difference in his appearance, which would be made by the removal of the most deforming of blemishes,

407

10 he; others *said*, He is like him: *but* he said, I am *he*. Therefore said
11 they unto him, *g*How were thine eyes opened? He answered and said, A
man that is *h*called Jesus made clay, and anointed mine eyes, and said
unto me, Go to the pool of Siloam, and wash: and I went and washed,
12 and I received sight. Then said they unto him, Where is he? He said,
I know not.
13, They brought to the Pharisees him that aforetime was blind. And it
14 was the sabbath day when Jesus made the clay, and opened his eyes.
15 Then again the Pharisees also asked him how he had received his sight.
He said unto them, He put clay upon mine eyes, and I washed, and do
16 see. Therefore said some of the Pharisees, This man is not of God,
because he keepeth not the sabbath day. Others said, How can a man
that is a sinner do such miracles? And *i*there was a division among
17 them. They say unto the blind man again, What sayest thou of him,
18 that he hath opened thine eyes? He said, *j*He is a prophet. But the
Jews did not believe concerning him, that he had been blind, and received
his sight, until they called the parents of him that had received his sight.
19 And they asked them, saying, Is this your son, who ye say was born
20 blind? how then doth he now see? His parents answered them, and
21 said, We know that this is our son, and that he was born blind: but by
what means he now seeth, we know not; or who hath opened his eyes,
22 we know not: he is of age; ask him: he shall speak for himself. These
words spake his parents, because they *k*feared the Jews: *l*for the Jews

A. D. 32.	
g Eccl. 11. 5.	
Mark 4. 27.	
ch. 3. 9.	
1 Cor.15. 35.	
h Jer. 36. 17, 18.	
Matt. 1. 21-25.	
i Luke 12. 51-53.	
ch. 7. 12, 43.	
ch. 10. 19.	
Acts 14. 4.	
j Deut. 18. 15.	
Luke 24. 19.	
ch. 4. 19.	
ch. 6. 14.	
Acts 2. 22.	
Acts 3. 22, 26.	
Acts 10. 38.	
k ch. 7. 13.	
ch. 12. 42.	
ch. 19. 38.	
Acts 5. 13.	
l Luke 6. 22.	
ch. 16. 2.	
Acts 4. 18.	
Acts 5. 40.	

and the bestowal of the most distinguishing of features. But another remark, of more consequence, might have been made here — that the difficulty which his neighbours had in believing that this was the same man whom they had known as the Blind Beggar, and the need of his own testimony to put the fact beyond all question, is the best evidence of the perfection of the cure. Well, this settled, the next questions naturally are, *How* was it done? and *Who* did it? 10. **Therefore said they unto him, How were thine eyes opened? 11. He answered and said, A man that is called Jesus made clay, and anointed mine eyes, and said unto me, Go to the pool of Siloam, and wash: and I went and washed, and I received sight.** This reply is so fresh and lively that, as *Meyer* says, our Evangelist probably received it from the man himself after he became a believer. **12. Then said they unto him, Where is he? He said—'saith'** [λέγει], **I know not.** No doubt, after the attempt to stone Him, Jesus would not deem it prudent at once to appear in public.

13. They brought to the Pharisees him that aforetime was blind. 14. And—or, 'Now' [δὲ] **it was the sabbath day when Jesus made the clay, and opened his eyes.** The connection between these two verses, and especially what is mentioned in *v.* 16, make it evident that it was our Lord's having wrought this cure on the Sabbath day which induced these people to bring the beggar under the notice of the Pharisees; and so far, therefore, it was done in a spirit of at least suspicion of the glorious Healer. On the systematic performance of such miracles on the Sabbath day, see on ch. v. 9.

The Pharisees Question and Cross-question the Healed Beggar, till, unable to prevail upon him to Repudiate His Blessed Benefactor, or refrain from Testifying to Him, they Excommunicate him (15-34). It is probable that the Pharisees were sitting in council when the following dialogue took place: **15. Then again the Pharisees also asked him how he had received his sight. He said unto them, He put clay upon mine eyes, and I washed, and do see. 16. Therefore said some of** the Pharisees, **This man is not of God, because he keepeth not the sabbath day. Others**—as Nicodemus and Joseph, said, **How can a man that is a sinner do such miracles? And there was a division among them. 17. They say unto the blind man again, What sayest thou of him, that he hath opened thine eyes? He said, He is a prophet**—rightly viewing the miracle as but a "sign" [σημεῖον] of His prophetic commission. **18. But**—'Then,' or 'therefore.' Seeing, if they admitted the truth of the cure, they would likely be shut up to the acknowledgment of His divine commission, *therefore* they took the course of discrediting the fact. **the Jews**—that is, these ruling ecclesiastics (see on ch. i. 19), **did not believe concerning him, that he had been blind, and received his sight, until they called the parents of him that had received his sight. 19. And they asked them, saying, Is this your son, who ye say was born blind? how then doth he now see?** Foiled by the testimony of the young man himself, they hope to throw doubt on the fact by close questioning his parents, who, perceiving the snare laid for them, ingeniously escape it by testifying simply to the identity of their son, and his birth-blindness, leaving it to himself, as a competent witness, to speak to the cure. **20. His parents answered them, and said, We know that this is our son, and that he was born blind: 21. But by what means he now seeth, we know not; or who hath opened his eyes, we know not: he is of age; ask him: he shall speak for himself.** Here, however, they prevaricate, in saying they "knew not who had opened his eyes;" for **"they feared the Jews,"** who had come to an understanding—probably after what is recorded, ch. vii. 50, &c., and by this time pretty well known—that whoever owned Him as the Christ should be put out of the synagogue—*i. e.*, not simply *excluded*, but *excommunicated*. **22. These words spake his parents, because they feared the Jews: for the Jews** had agreed already, that if any man did confess that he was Christ [αὐτὸν ὁμολογήσῃ Χριστὸν]—or 'own Him as Christ,' he should be put out of the synagogue [ἀποσυνάγωγος γένηται]—not only expelled,

408

had agreed already, that if any man did confess that he was Christ, he
23 should be put out of the synagogue. Therefore said his parents, He is of
age; ask him.
24   Then again called they the man that was blind, and said unto him,
25 *ᵐGive God the praise: we know that this man is a sinner. He answered
and said, Whether he be a sinner *or no*, I know not: one thing I know,
26 that, whereas I was blind, now I see. Then said they to him again,
27 What did he to thee? how opened he thine eyes? He answered
them, I have told you already, and ye did not hear: wherefore would
28 ye hear *it* again? will ye also be his disciples? Then they reviled him,
29 and said, Thou art his disciple; but we are Moses' disciples. We know
that God spake unto Moses: *as for* this *fellow*, *ⁿwe know not from
30 whence he is. The man answered and said unto them, Why *ᵒherein is
a marvellous thing, that ye know not from whence he is, and *yet* he hath
31 opened mine eyes. Now we know that *ᵖGod heareth not sinners: but if
any man be a worshipper of God, and doeth his will, him he heareth.
32 Since the world began was it not heard that any man opened the eyes
33 of one that was born blind. If this man were not of God, he could do
34 nothing. They answered and said unto him, Thou wast altogether born
in sins, and dost thou teach us? And they ²cast him out.

A. D. 32.
ᵐ Jos. 7. 19.
1 Sam. 6. 5.
Isa. 66. 5.
ch. 5. 23.
ch. 8. 49.
Rom. 10. 2.
ⁿ ch. 8. 14.
ᵒ ch. 3. 10.
ᵖ Job 27. 9.
Job 35. 12.
Ps. 18. 41.
Ps. 34. 15.
Ps. 66. 18.
Pro. 1. 28.
Pro. 15. 29.
Pro. 28. 9.
Isa. 1. 15.
Jer. 11. 11.
Jer. 14. 12.
Ezek. 8. 18.
Mic. 3. 4.
Zec. 7. 13.
2 Or, excommunicated him.

but 'become' and be held 'unsynagogued,' or, as we say, 'unchurched.' See ch. xii. 42; xvi. 2. **23. Therefore**—or 'for this cause' [Διὰ τοῦτο], **said his parents, He is of age; ask him.** **24. Then again**—'the second time' [ἐκ δευτέρου]—**called they the man that was blind.** Baffled and perplexed, they seem to have put him forth till they should agree among themselves how next to proceed with him, so as to break down the testimony to Jesus which this marvellous cure so plainly furnished, and then to have summoned him back. **and said unto him, Give God the praise**—or, 'Give glory to God' [Δὸς δόξαν τῷ Θεῷ]: we know that this man is a sinner—not wishing him to own, even to the praise of God, that a miracle had been wrought upon him, but to show more regard to the honour of God than ascribe any such act to one who was a sinner. **25. He answered and said, Whether he be a sinner or no, I know not: one thing I know, that, whereas I was blind, now I see.** Not that the man meant to insinuate any doubt in his own mind on the point of His being "a sinner;" but as his *opinion* on such a point would be of no consequence to others, he would speak only to what he *knew* as *fact* in his own case. **26. Then said they**—'They said' to him again, **What did he to thee? how opened he thine eyes?**—hoping by repeated questions to ensnare him; but the youth is more than a match for them. **27. He answered them, I have told you already, and ye did not hear: wherefore would ye hear it again? will ye also be his disciples?** In a vein of keen irony he treats their questions as those of anxious enquirers, almost ready for discipleship! Stung by this, they retort upon *him* as the disciple (and here they plainly were not wrong): for themselves, they fell back upon Moses—about *him* there could be no doubt—but who knew about this upstart? **28. [Then] they reviled him.** [The οὖν of the received text has hardly any authority.] **and said, Thou art his disciple; but we are Moses' disciples. 29. We know that God spake**—or 'hath spoken' [λελάληκεν] **unto Moses: as for this [fellow]**—or simply, 'this [man]:' it is the language of contempt, though probably more affected than real: **we know not from whence he is.** The youth had now no need to say another word; but waxing bolder in defence of his Benefactor, and his views brightening by the

very courage which it demanded, he puts it to them how they could pretend inability to tell whether one who opened the eyes of a man born blind was "of God" or "a sinner"—from above or from beneath—and proceeds to argue the case with remarkable power. **30. The man answered and said unto them, Why herein is a marvellous thing, that ye know not from whence he is, and yet he hath opened mine eyes. 31. Now we know that God heareth not sinners: but if any man be a worshipper of God, and doeth his will, him he heareth. 32. Since the world began was it not heard that any man opened the eyes of one that was born blind. 33. If this man were not of God, he could do nothing.** So irresistible was this argument that their rage burst forth in a speech of the most intense Pharisaism. **34. They answered and said unto him, Thou wast altogether born in sins, and dost thou teach us?**—'Thou, a base-born, uneducated, impudent youth, teach *us*, the trained, constituted, recognized guides of the people in the things of God? Out upon thee!' **and they cast him out**—judicially, no doubt, as we have said (on *v.* 22), as well as in fact. (So *de Wette, Olshausen, Tholuck,* &c.) The allusion to his being "born in sins" seems a tacit admission of his being blind from birth—the very thing they had been so unwilling to own. But rage and enmity to truth are seldom consistent in their outbreaks. The friends of this excommunicated youth, crowding around him with their sympathy, would probably express surprise that one who could work such a cure should be unable to protect his patient from the persecution it had raised against him, or should possess the power without using it. Nor would it be wonderful if such thoughts should arise in the youth's own mind. But if they did, it is certain, from what follows, that they made no lodgment there, conscious as he was that "whereas he was blind, now he saw," and satisfied that if his Benefactor "were not of God, he could do nothing," (*v.* 33). There was a word for him too, which, if whispered in his ear from the oracles of God, would seem expressly designed to describe his case, and prepare him for the coming interview with his gracious Friend. "Hear the word of the Lord, ye that tremble at His word; *Your brethren that hated you, that cast you out for My name's sake,*

35   Jesus heard that they had cast him out; and when he had found him,
36 he said unto him, Dost thou believe on *q*the Son of God? He answered
37 and said, Who is he, Lord, that I might believe on him? And Jesus
    said unto him, Thou hast both seen him, and *r*it is he that talketh
38 with thee. And he said, Lord, I believe. And he worshipped him.
39 And Jesus said, *s*For judgment I am come into this world, *t*that they
    which see not might see, and that they which see might be made blind.
40   And *some* of the Pharisees which were with him heard these words,
41 *u*and said unto him, Are we blind also? Jesus said unto them, *v*If ye
    were blind, ye should have no sin: but now ye say, We see; therefore
    your sin remaineth.

A. D. 32.

q Matt. 14. 33.
Matt. 16. 16.
Mark 1. 1.
ch. 10. 36.
r ch. 4. 26.
s ch. 5. 22.
ch. 3. 17.
ch. 12. 47.
t Matt. 13. 13.
Luke 2. 34.
2 Cor. 2. 16.
u Rom. 2. 19.
v ch. 15. 22.

---

said, Let the Lord be glorified; BUT HE SHALL APPEAR TO YOUR JOY, *and they shall be ashamed"* (Isa. lxvi. 5). But how was *He* engaged to whom such noble testimony had been given, and for whom such persecution had been borne? Uttering, perhaps, in secret, "with strong crying and tears," the words of the prophetic psalm, "Let not them that wait on thee, O Lord God of hosts, be ashamed for My sake; let none that seek thee be confounded for My sake, O God of Israel; because for thy sake I have borne reproach . . . and the reproaches of them that reproached thee are fallen upon Me" (Ps. lxix. 6, 7, 9).

Touching Interview between the Healed Beggar and His Unknown Benefactor—On Recognizing, he Worships Him (35-38). **35. Jesus heard that they had cast him out**—by intelligence brought to Him, **and when he had found him**—shall we say by accident? Not very likely. Sympathy in that breast could not long keep aloof from its object. **he said unto him, Dost thou believe on the Son of God?** A question stretching purposely beyond his present attainments, in order the more quickly to lead him—in his present teachable frame—into the highest truth. **36. He answered and said, Who is he, Lord, that I might**—or rather, 'may' **believe on him?** This is evidently the language of one who *did* believe in Him who had wrought such a marvellous work on him, and who now only yearned to behold and personally to recognize Him. The next two verses show this to be the real state of His mind. **37. And Jesus said unto him, Thou hast both seen him, and it is he that talketh with thee.** The new sense of sight imparted to him had at that moment its highest exercise, in gazing upon "The Light of the world." **38. And he said, Lord, I believe. And he worshipped him**—a *faith* and a *worship*, beyond doubt, meant to express far more than he would think proper to any human "prophet" (*v.* 17); the unstudied, resistless expression, probably, of SUPREME faith and adoration, though without the full understanding of what that implied. **39. And Jesus said**—perhaps at the same time, but after a crowd, including some of the sceptical and scornful rulers, had, on seeing Jesus talking with the healed youth, hastened to the spot. **For judgment I am come**—or *'* came I' [ἦλθον] **that they which see not might see**—rising to that *sight* of which the natural vision communicated to the youth was but the symbol (see on *v.* 5, and compare Luke iv. 18): **and that they which see might be made blind**—judicially incapable of apprehending and receiving the truth, to which they have wilfully shut their eyes. See on Matt. xiii. 12. **40. And some**—rather, 'those' **of the Pharisees which were with him heard these words, and said unto him, Are we blind also?**—we, the constituted, recognized guides of the people in spiritual

things? pride and rage prompting the question. **41. Jesus said unto them, If ye were blind**—If ye wanted light to discern My claims, and only waited to receive it, **ye should have no sin**—none of the guilt of shutting out the light: **but now ye say, We see; therefore your sin remaineth**—Your claim to possess light, while rejecting Me, is that which seals you up in the guilt of unbelief.

Remarks.—1. Although the resurrection of Lazarus was beyond all doubt the greatest of our Lord's miracles, there is one particular in which the miracle of this chapter is even more marvellous. In all our Lord's miracles of healing, and even in the resurrection of the dead, He did but restore what had been already in use by the objects of His power and grace—seeing, hearing, walking, living. But here is one to whom vision is not *restored*, but for the first time *imparted*. And though we are not to suppose that the organ of sight was then *created*—for such "works were finished from the creation of the world"—though the organ was doubtless there from his mother's womb, it had never been capable of action till now, that he was "of age;" and thus, by an act of marvellous power, this man for the first time beheld the light of heaven, and from that time forth saw as other men—insomuch that his neighbours would hardly believe that he was the same man whom they had known as the Blind Beggar, and, as already remarked, it needed his own testimony to put the fact beyond all question. And what is most worthy of notice, it is just in the record of these two greatest of all our Lord's miracles that *the details are the fullest*—so full, and embracing so many minute yet vivid particulars, that it is impossible to doubt that we have them from the very parties concerned; the beloved Evangelist himself being doubtless present wherever his Lord was in the action of this chapter, while for the rest—as already observed—he was indebted, we can hardly doubt, to the newly gained disciple himself, whose eyes the Lord had doubly opened. 2. That all our Lord's beneficent miracles on the bodies of men were designed to illustrate analogous and higher operations on the souls of men, which it was His errand and is His office to perform, has been once and again observed, see on Matt. iv. 12-25, Remark 5, at the close of that Section. But nowhere is this more grandly seen than at the beginning and end of this chapter. Before aught was done to this blind beggar—while the disciples were questioning our Lord as to the cause of the poor man's misfortune, and as soon as He had explained that the primary intention of it was to display in him the works of God which He had come to do, and must do whilst it was day—Jesus said, "As long as I am in the world, I am THE LIGHT OF THE WORLD;" and then it was that, to illustrate that office of His, He miraculously opened this man's eyes. And at the close of the chapter, recurring, in presence of enemies, to the opening of the man's

10 VERILY, verily, I say unto you, [a]He that entereth not by the door into the sheep-fold, but climbeth up some other way, the same is a thief 2 and a robber. But he that entereth in by [b]the door is the shepherd of 3 the sheep. To him [c]the porter openeth; and the sheep hear his voice: 4 and he calleth his own sheep by name, and leadeth them out. And when he putteth forth his own sheep, he goeth before them, and the sheep 5 follow him: for they know his voice. And [d]a stranger will they not follow, but will flee from him: for they know not the voice of strangers. 6 This parable spake Jesus unto them: but they understood not what things they were which he spake unto them.

A. D. 32.

CHAP. 10.
[a] Isa. 56. 10.
Jer. 23. 21.
Heb. 5. 4.
[b] Isa. 61. 1.
Acts 20. 28.
1 Cor. 12. 28.
[c] 1 Pet. 1. 12.
1 Cor. 16. 9.
[d] Pro. 19. 27.
Gal. 1. 8.
Eph. 4. 44.

eyes, He testified, "For judgment came I into this world, that they which see not might see," on the one hand; or—as He afterwards expressed it from His glory in the heavens to Saul of Tarsus, when sending him as a preacher to the Gentiles—"to open their eyes, and turn them from darkness to light, and from the power of Satan unto God" (Acts xxvi. 18): "and," on the other hand, "that they which see might be made blind." Thus, then, let us learn to read in every record of Christ's miracles on the *body* assurances and illustrations of His power and grace in the higher sphere of the *soul.* 3. While in the parents of this youth we have a lively illustration of the terrors of ghostly authority —in inspiring which the priests of the Church of Rome have diabolically improved upon the Jewish ecclesiastics—we have in the youth himself a beautiful illustration of the *courage* which a conscious experience of divine power and grace inspires, of the *strength* which the exercise of that courage in trying circumstances imparts, and of the *wisdom*— above their own—which, in fulfilment of express promise, the Lord has so often from that time to this communicated to His disciples when standing before rulers for His name's sake. See on Matt. x. 19, 20. 4. The accession of this healed man to the ranks of genuine discipleship is one, and not the least instructive, of the many cases of Christ found *without seeking,* referred to on Matt. xiii. 44 46, Remark 1 at the close of that Section. Not like blind Bartimeus did this man cry after Jesus; but, "as Jesus *passed by* (compare Ezek. xvi. 6, 8), He *saw* "this beggar, who had been blind from his birth"—doubtless with that peculiar look with which He *saw* Zaccheus (Luke xix. 5), for His eye affected His heart, and He proceeded to heal him. Not like the other blind man did He first recognize in Jesus "the Son of David;" nor does it appear whether He had even heard of Him before. Certain it is that the first motion was not in the man, or any of his relatives or neighbours, towards Jesus, but in Jesus towards Him. And thus is there a large class, of whom it is said, "I am found of them that sought Me not; I am made manifest unto them that asked not after Me." 5. Was ever virulent determination not to believe on any evidence, and wilful resistance of ocular demonstration, more signally manifested than in those rulers of the Jews, who, after vainly endeavouring to brow-beat this poor unbefriended youth, scornfully expelled him from the synagogue, because he refused to lie before God, and repudiate and malign his unknown Benefactor? But this spirit has not ceased; nor is it to be doubted that, whenever occasions arise for the display of it, the hatred of the world to Christ, in His truth and people, will be found as virulent as it has ever been (ch. xv. 19; Gal. iv. 29).

CHAP. X. 1-42. — Discourse on the Good Shepherd, and Speculation occasioned by it —Discourse at the Feast of Dedication— Jesus takes Refuge from the Fury of His

Enemies beyond Jordan, where many Believe on Him. The discourses and transactions of this chapter, though belonging to two different festivals, between which there was an interval of between two and three months, will be most conveniently embraced in one Section, as the subjects are so much the same that the Remarks which they suggest cannot well be separated. *Discourse on the Good Shepherd* (1-18). This Discourse seems plainly a continuation of the closing verses of the preceding chapter. The figure of a shepherd and his sheep was familiar to the Jewish ear, (see Jer. xxiii.; Ezek. xxxiv.; Zec. xi., &c.) 'This simple creature, the sheep,' says *Luther,* as quoted by *Stier,* 'has this special note among all animals, that it quickly hears the voice of the shepherd, follows no one else, depends entirely on him, and seeks help from him alone, cannot help itself, but is shut up to another's aid.' **1. Verily, verily, I say unto you, He that entereth not by the door**—that is, by the legitimate way; without as yet saying what that was, **into the sheep-fold**—the sacred inclosure of God's true people, **but climbeth up some other way**—not referring to the assumption of ecclesiastical office without an external call—for those Jewish rulers who were specially aimed at had this (see on Matt. xxiii. 2)—but to the want of a true call, a spiritual commission, the seal of heaven going along with the outward authority: it is the assumption of the spiritual guidance of the people *without this* that is meant. **the same is a thief and a robber. 2. But he that entereth in by the door is the shepherd of the sheep**—is a true, divinely recognized shepherd. **3. To him the porter openeth**— 'To him is given right of free access, by order of Him to whom the sheep belong'—for it is better not to give this allusion a more specific interpretation. So *Calvin, Meyer, Luthardt.* **and the sheep hear his voice: and he calleth his own sheep by name, and leadeth them out. 4. And when he putteth forth**—or 'turneth out.' [The *aorist*—ἐκβάλῃ—is here rightly rendered 'putteth forth,' as in Luke i. 51-53; the idea being that of 'a succession of definite acts constituting a habit of so acting.' So probably ἠγάπησαν is to be explained in ch. iii. 19, 'men *love* the darkness,' &c.] **his own sheep, he goeth before them, and the sheep follow him: for they know his voice. 5. And [δὲ]**—rather, 'But' **a stranger will they not follow, but will flee from him: for they know not the voice of strangers. 6. This parable spake Jesus unto them: but they understood not what things they were which he spake unto them.** What is said in these three verses, though admitting of important *application* to every faithful shepherd of God's flock, is in its direct and highest sense true only of "the great Shepherd of the sheep," who in the first five verses seems plainly, under the simple character of a true shepherd, to be drawing His own portrait. So *Lampe, Stier,* &c.

7. Then said Jesus unto them again, Verily,

7 Then said Jesus unto them again, Verily, verily, I say unto you, I am
8 *ᵉ*the door of the sheep. All *ᶠ*that ever came before me are thieves and
9 robbers: but the sheep did not hear them. I am the door: by me if any
   man enter in, he shall be saved, and shall go in and out, and find pasture.
10 The *ᵍ*thief cometh not, but for to steal, and to kill, and to destroy: I
   am come that they might have life, and that they might have *it* more
11 abundantly. I *ʰ*am the good shepherd: the good shepherd giveth his
12 life for the sheep. But he that is an hireling, and not the shepherd,
   whose own the sheep are not, seeth the wolf coming, and *ⁱ*leaveth the
   sheep, and fleeth: and the wolf catcheth them, and scattèreth the sheep.
13 The hireling fleeth, because he is an hireling, and careth not for the
14 sheep. I am the good shepherd, and *ʲ*know my *sheep*, and *ᵏ*am known
15 of mine. As the Father knoweth me, even so know I the Father: and I

A. D. 32.
ᵉ Eph. 2. 18.
Heb. 10. 19.
ᶠ Jer 23. 1.
Jer. 50. 6.
Acts 5. 36, 37.
ᵍ Acts 20. 29.
2 Pet. 2. 1.
ʰ Isa. 40. 11.
Ezek. 34. 23.
Ezek. 37. 24.
ⁱ Zec. 11. 16.
ʲ 2 Tim. 2. 19.
ᵏ Eph. 1. 17.
Phil. 3. 10.
1 John 5. 20.

verily, I say unto you, I am the door of the sheep—that is, *The Way in* to the fold, with all its blessed privileges, alike for the shepherds and the sheep. (Compare ch. xiv. 6; Eph. ii. 18.) **8. All that ever came before me**—the false prophets; not as claiming the prerogatives of Messiah, but as perverters of the people from the way of life leading to Him. So *Olshausen*. **are thieves and robbers: but the sheep did not hear them** —the instinct of their divinely taught hearts preserving them from seducers, and attaching them to the heaven-sent prophets of whom it is said that "the Spirit of Christ was in them" (1 Pet. i. 11). **9. I am the door: by me if any man enter in**—whether shepherd or sheep, **he shall be saved**—the great object of the pastoral office, as of all the divine arrangements towards mankind. **and shall go in and out and find pasture.** He "shall go *in*," as to a place of safety and repose; and he "shall go *out*," as to green pastures and still waters" (Ps. xxiii. 2), for nourishment and refreshing; and all this only transferred to another clime, and enjoyed in another manner, at the close of this earthly scene (Rev. vii. 17). **10. The thief cometh not, but for to steal, and to kill, and to destroy: I am come** — or, "I came' [ἦλθον] that they might have life, and that they might have it more abundantly** [περισσὸν]—or rather, simply, 'have it abundantly.' J came, not to *preserve* a life already possessed, but to *impart* a life before unknown, and to communicate it in rich and unfailing exuberance. What a claim! And yet it is but a repetition, under a new aspect, of what He had taught in the synagogue of Capernaum (ch. vi.); nay, but an echo of all His teaching; and He who uttered these and like words must be either a blasphemer, all worthy of the death He died, or "God with us:" there can be no middle course. **11. I am the good shepherd** — not '*a*,' but emphatically "The Good Shepherd," and, in the sense intended, exclusively so (see Isa. xl. 11; Ezek. xxxiv. 23; xxxvii. 24; Zec. xiii. 7). **the good shepherd giveth** [τίθησιν]—rather, 'layeth down;' as the word is properly rendered in *vv.* 15, 17, **his life for the sheep.** Though this may be said of literal shepherds who, even for their brute flock have, like David, encountered "the lion and the bear" at the risk of their own lives, and still more of faithful pastors, who, like the early bishops of Rome, have been the foremost to brave the fury of their enemies against the flock committed to their care; yet here, beyond doubt, it points to the struggle which was to issue in the willing surrender of the Redeemer's own life, to save His sheep from destruction. **12. But he that is an hireling, and not the shepherd, whose own the sheep are not**—who has no *property* in them. By this He points to His own peculiar relation to the sheep, the same as

His Father's, the great Proprietor and Lord of the flock, who styles Him "My Shepherd, *the Man that is my Fellow*" (Zec. xiii. 7); and though faithful under-shepherds, who are in their Master's interest, feel a measure of His own concern for their charge, the language is strictly applicable only to "the Son over His own house" (Heb. iii. 6). **seeth**—or 'beholdeth' [θεωρεῖ] **the wolf coming.** By this is meant, not (as *Stier*, *Alford*, &c., take it) *the devil* distinctively, but generally, as we judge, whoever comes upon the flock with hostile intent, in whatever form; though the wicked one, no doubt, is *at the bottom* of such movements. So *Lücke*, *Luthardt*. **14. I am the good shepherd.** See on *v.* 11. **and know my [sheep], and am known of mine.** As the word "sheep" is a supplement, it is perhaps better to render the words, 'and know mine, and am known of mine' [γινώσκω τὰ ἐμὰ, καὶ γινώσκομαι ὑπὸ τῶν ἐμῶν]. *Lachmann* and *Tregelles* read, 'and mine know me' [γινώσκουσίν με τὰ ἐμὰ], but, as we judge, on insufficient evidence: *Tischendorf* abides by the received text. **15. As the Father knoweth me, even so know I the Father.** This ought not to have begun a new sentence; for it is properly part of the previous verse. The whole statement will then stand thus: "And I know mine, and am known of mine, even as the Father knoweth Me, and I know the Father." So the *Vulgate*, and *Luther's* version, *Bengel*, *de Wette*, *Lücke*, and nearly every modern critic; and so *Lachmann*, *Tischendorf*, and *Tregelles* print the text. When Christ says He "*knows* His sheep," He means it in the peculiar and endearing sense of 2 Tim. ii. 19; and when He says, "I am known of mine," He alludes to the soul's response to the voice that has inwardly and efficaciously called it; for in this mutual loving acquaintance, ours is the *effect* of His. The Redeemer's knowledge of us, as *Olshausen* finely says, is the *active* element, penetrating us with His power and life; that of believers is the *passive* principle, the reception of His life and light. In this reception, however, an assimilation of the soul to the sublime Object of its knowledge and love takes place; and thus an activity, though a derived one, is unfolded, which shows itself in obedience to His commands. But when our glorious Speaker rises from this mutual knowledge of Himself and His people to another and loftier reciprocity of knowledge—even that of Himself and His Father—and says that the former is *even as* [καθῶς] the latter, He expresses what none but Himself could have dared to utter; though it is only what He had in effect said before (Matt. xi. 27, taken in connection with the preceding and following verses; and Luke x. 21, 22), and what in another and almost higher form He expressed afterwards in His Intercessory

412

16 lay down my life for the sheep. And ‘other sheep I have, which are not
of this fold: them also I must bring, and they shall hear my voice; ᵐand
17 there shall be one fold, *and* one shepherd. Therefore doth my Father
18 love me, ⁿbecause I lay down my life, that I might take it again. No
man taketh it from me, but I lay it down of myself. I have power to
lay it down, and I have power to take it again. This °commandment
have I received of my Father.
19   There was a division therefore again among the Jews for these sayings.
20 And many of them said, He hath a devil, and is mad; why hear ye him?
21 Others said, These are not the words of him that hath a devil. ᵖCan a
devil open the eyes of the blind?
22   And it was at Jerusalem the feast of the dedication, and it was winter.
23 And Jesus walked in the temple, ᑫin Solomon's porch.

A. D. 32.

l Isa. 56. 8.
m Ezek. 37. 22.
Eph. 2. 14.
n Isa. 53. 7.
2 Cor. 5. 15.
Heb. 2. 9.
1 John 3. 16.
o Acts 2. 24.
p Ex. 4. 11.
Ps. 94. 9.
Ps. 146. 8.
Pro. 20. 12.
Isa. 35. 5, 6.
Matt. 11. 5.
q Acts 3. 11.
Acts 5. 12.

Prayer (ch. xvii. 21-23). **and I lay down my life for the sheep.** How sublime is this, following immediately on the lofty claim of the preceding clause! 'Tis just the riches and the poverty of "The Word made flesh;" one glorious Person reaching at once up to the Throne—in absolute knowledge of the Father—and down even to the dust of death, in the voluntary surrender of His life "for the sheep." A candid interpretation of this last clause—"for the sheep"—ought to go far to establish the special relation of the vicarious death of Christ to the Church. **16. And other sheep I have, which are not of this fold** [αὐλῆς]: **them also I must bring.** He means the perishing Gentiles, of whom He speaks as *already* His sheep—in the love of His heart and the purpose of His grace—to "*bring* them" in due time. **and they shall hear my voice.** This is not the language of mere foresight that they would believe, but the expression of a purpose to draw them to Himself by an inward and efficacious call, which would infallibly issue in their spontaneous accession to Him. **and there shall be one fold** [ποίμνη]—rather, ' one flock.' The word for 'fold' in the previous part of the verse, it will be seen, is different. **17. Therefore** [Διὰ τοῦτο] —' For this cause' and 'would be manifest presumption in any mere *creature* to affirm of his own death. It is beyond all doubt the language of One who was conscious that *His life was His own*, which no creature's is, and, therefore, His to surrender or retain *at will.* Here lay the glory of His sacrifice, that it was *purely* voluntary. The claim of "power to take it again" is no less important, as showing that His resurrection, though ascribed to the Father, in the sense we shall presently see, was nevertheless *His own assertion of His own right to life* as soon as the purposes of His voluntary death were accomplished. **This commandment**—that is, to "lay down His life, that He might take it again," **have I received** [ἔλαβον]—rather, ' received I' **of my Father.** So that Christ died at once by "*command*" of His Father, and by such a *voluntary obedience* to that command **doth my Father love me, because I lay down my life.** As the highest act of the Son's love to the Father was the laying down of His life for the sheep at His "commandment," so the Father's love to Him as His *incarnate* Son reached its consummation, and finds its highest justification, in that sublimest and most affecting of all acts. **that I might take it again**—His resurrection-life being indispensable to the accomplishment of the fruit of His death. **18. No man taketh it from me, but I lay it down of myself. I have power to lay it down, and I have power to take it again.** It is impossible for language more plainly and emphatically to express the *absolute voluntariness* of Christ's death, such a voluntariness as it would be

413

as has made Him, so to speak, infinitely dear to the Father. The *necessity* of Christ's death, in the light of these profound sayings, must be manifest to all but the superficial.

Speculation occasioned by this Discourse (19-21). **19. There was a division therefore again among the Jews for**—or 'because of' **these sayings. 20. And many of them said, He hath a devil, and is mad; why hear ye him? 21. Others said, These are not the words of him that hath a devil. Can a devil open the eyes of the blind?** Thus did the light and the darkness reveal themselves with increasing distinctness in the separation of the teachable from the obstinately prejudiced. The one saw in Him only "a devil and a madman;" the other revolted at the thought that such *words* could come from one possessed, and sight be given to the blind by a demoniac; showing clearly that a deeper impression had been made upon them than their words expressed.

Discourse at the Feast of Dedication (22-30). **22. And**—or rather, 'Now,' as beginning a new subject, **it was at Jerusalem the feast of the dedication.** Recent interpreters, with few exceptions, conclude, from the silence of the Evangelist, that our Lord must have remained during the whole interval between the Feast of Tabernacles and this of the Dedication—a period of about two months and a half—either in Jerusalem or its immediate neighbourhood. But the opening words of this section—"Now it was *at Jerusalem*," &c.—imply, we think, the reverse. If our Lord remained so very long at the capital at this time, it was contrary certainly to His invariable practice; and considering how the enmity and exasperation of His enemies were drawing to a head, it does not seem to us very likely. But to suppose, with some harmonists, that our Lord went back during this interval to Galilee, and that a not inconsiderable portion of the matter of the first three Gospels belongs to this period, seems to us against all probability. We therefore take a middle course; and think that our Lord spent the interval between the above festivals partly in Peræa, within the dominions of Herod Antipas (where certainly we find Him at Luke xiii. 31), and partly in Judea, approaching to the suburbs of the capital (where certainly we find Him at Luke x. 38).

This festival of the *Dedication* was celebrated between two and three months after the Feast of Tabernacles. It was instituted by Judas Maccabeus, to commemorate the purification of the temple from the profanations to which it had been subjected by Antiochus Epiphanes (B. C. 165), and kept for eight days, from the 25th Chisleu (about the 20th December)—the day on which Judas began the first joyous celebration of it (1 Macc. iv. 52, 56, 59, and *Joseph.* Antt. xii. 7. 7.) **and it was winter—**

24　Then came the Jews round about him, and said unto him, How long dost thou [1]make us to doubt? If thou be the Christ, tell us plainly.
25　Jesus answered them, I told you, and ye believed not: the works that I
26　do in my Father's name, they bear witness of me.　But [r]ye believe not,
27　because ye are not of my sheep, as I said unto you.　My sheep hear my
28　voice, and I know them, and they follow me: and I give unto them eternal life; and they shall never perish, neither shall any pluck them
29　out of my hand.　My [s]Father, [t]which gave *them* me, is greater than all;
30　and none is able to pluck *them* out of my Father's hand.　I [u]and *my* Father are one.
31,　Then the Jews took up stones again to stone him.　Jesus an-
32　swered them, Many goods works have I showed you from my Father;
33　for which of those works do ye stone me?　The Jews answered him,

A. D. 33.

[1] Or, hold us in suspense.
[r] ch. 8. 47.
1 John 4. 6.
[s] ch. 14. 28.
[t] Ex. 18. 11.
Ps. 145. 3.
Dan. 4. 3.
Mal. 1. 14.
ch. 17. 2, 6.
[u] ch. 17. 11.
1 Cor. 8. 4, 6.
Eph. 3. 9.
1 Tim. 3. 16.
1 John 5. 7.

implying some *inclemency*. Accordingly it is added, **23. And Jesus walked in the temple, in Solomon's porch**—for shelter.　This portico was on the east side of the temple, and *Josephus* says it was part of the original structure of Solomon.　(Antt. xx. 9. 7.)
24. Then came the Jews—that is, as usual in this Gospel, the rulers, as observed on ch. i. 19.　**round about him, and said unto him, How long dost thou make us to doubt?** [τὴν ψυχὴν ἡμῶν αἴρεις]—or better, as in the margin, 'hold us in suspense.'　**If thou be the Christ, tell us plainly.** But when the plainest *evidence* of it was resisted, what weight could a mere *assertion* of it have? nor can it be doubted that they had an ensnaring purpose in the attempt to draw this out of Him.　**25. Jesus answered them, I told you**—that is, in substance (see ch. vii. 37, 38; viii. 35, 36, 58), **and ye believed not: the works that I do in my Father's name, they bear witness of me.　26. But ye** ['Αλλ' ὑμεῖς]. The "ye" is here in emphatic contrast to the "sheep." **believe not, because ye are not of my sheep, as I said unto you.** Our Lord here manifestly refers back to His discourse about the Shepherd and the sheep at the Feast of Tabernacles (*vv.* 1-18).　He did not there *expressly* say what is here mentioned; but the sharp line of demarcation there drawn between the sheep who hear only their own shepherd's voice, and those who are led away by deceivers, implied as much, and what follows shows that His object was, first, to resume that subject, and then to carry it out further and raise it higher than before.　**27. My sheep hear my voice, and I know them, and they follow me.** See on *v.* 8.　**28. And I give unto them eternal life**—not 'I will,' but 'I do give' it them: it is a present gift.　See on ch. iii. 36; v. 24.　**and they shall never perish, neither shall any pluck them out of my hand.** A very grand utterance, couched in the language of majestic, royal, supreme authority.　**29. My Father, which gave**—rather, 'hath given' [δέδωκεν] **them me** (see on ch. vi. 37-39) **is greater than all**—with whom no adverse power can contend (Isa. xxvii. 4); **and none is able to pluck them out of my Father's hand.** The bearing of this statement on what is called by divines *the perseverance of the saints* has not escaped the notice of candid and reverential expositors, even of those churches which repudiate that doctrine. In this view the following remarks of *Olshausen* on these words of our Lord have peculiar value:—'The impossibility of true believers being lost, in the midst of all the temptations which they may encounter, does not consist in their fidelity and decision, but is founded upon the *power of God*.　Here the doctrine of predestination is presented in its sublime and sacred aspect; there is a predestination of the holy, which is taught from

one end of the Scriptures to the other; not, indeed, of such a nature that an "irresistible grace" *compels* the opposing will of man'—of course not—'but so that that will of man which receives and loves the commands of God is *produced* only by God's grace.'　But the statement of *v.* 29 is designed only to introduce that of *v.* 30.　**I and my Father** ['Εγὼ καὶ ὁ Πατήρ]. It should be 'I and the Father' **are one** [ἕν ἐσμεν].　Our language admits not of the precision of the original in this great saying, 'We (two *Persons*) are 'One (*Thing*).' Perhaps '*one interest*' expresses nearly, though not quite, the purport of the saying.　There seemed to be some contradiction between His saying they had been given by His Father into *His own* hands, out of which they could not be plucked, and then saying that none could pluck them out of *His Father's* hands, as if they had not been given *out of* them.　'*Neither they have*,' says He: 'Though He has given them to Me, they are as much in His own almighty hands as ever—they *cannot be*, and when given to Me they *are not*, given away from Himself; for HE AND I HAVE ALL IN COMMON.'　Thus it will be seen, that, though *oneness of essence* is not the precise thing here affirmed, that truth is *the basis of what is affirmed*, without which it would not be true. And Augustin was right in saying the "*We are*" condemns the *Sabellians*, who denied the *distinction of Persons* in the Godhead, while the "*one*" condemns the *Arians*, who denied the unity of their essence.　(*Bengel*, in his terse and pithy way, thus expresses it: Per *sumus* refutatur *Sabellius;* per *unum, Arius.*)
The Ruling Party, having Taken up Stones to Stone Him, our Lord Vindicates what He had said, but on their again Seeking to Seize Him, He Escapes beyond Jordan, where many believe on Him (31-42).　**31. Then the Jews**—the *rulers* again, as in ch. i. 19, **took up stones again to stone him**—and for precisely the same thing as before, the claim of equality with God which they saw He was advancing (ch. v. 18; viii. 58, 59).　**32. Jesus answered them, Many good works** [καλὰ ἔργα]—that is, works of pure benevolence; to which Peter thus alludes (Acts x. 38), "Who went about doing good" [εὐεργετῶν], or as a Benefactor: and see Mark vii. 37.　**from my Father**—not so much by His power, but as directly *commissioned by Him to do them*.　This He says, as *Luthardt* properly remarks, to meet the imputation of unwarrantable assumption of the divine prerogatives—**for which of those works do ye stone me?**—or 'are ye stoning Me;' that is, going to do it.　**33. The Jews answered him, saying, For a good work we stone thee not; but for blasphemy**—whose legal punishment was stoning (Lev. xxiv. 11-16), **and because that thou, being a man**—that is, a man only,

saying, For a good work we stone thee not; but for blasphemy; and
34 because that thou, being a man, makest *v*thyself God. Jesus answered
35 them, *w*Is it not written in your law, I said, Ye are gods? If he called
them gods *x*unto whom the word of God came, and the Scripture cannot
36 be broken; say ye of him, *y*whom the Father hath sanctified, and *z*sent
into the world, Thou blasphemest; because I said, I am *a*the Son of
37 God? If *b*I do not the works of my Father, believe me not. But if I do,
38 though ye believe not me, believe the works; that ye may know and
believe *c*that the Father *is* in me, and I in him.
39 Therefore they sought again to take him: but he escaped out of their
40 hand, and went away again beyond Jordan, into the place *d*where John
41 at first baptized; and there he abode. And many resorted unto him,
and said, John did no miracle: *e*but all things that John spake of this
42 man were true. And *f*many believed on him there.

A. D. 33.
v ch. 5. 18.
w Ps. 82. 6.
x Rom. 13. 1.
y ch. 6. 27.
z ch. 3. 17.
ch. 5. 36.
ch. 8. 42.
a Luke 1. 35.
ch. 9. 35.
b ch. 15. 24.
c ch. 14. 10.
ch. 17. 21.
d ch. 1. 28.
ch. 1. 29.
ch. 3. 30.
f ch. 8. 30.
ch. 11. 45.

makest thyself God. Twice before they understood him to advance the same claim, and both times, as we have seen, they prepared themselves to avenge what they took to be the insulted honour of God, as here, in the way directed by their law. **34.** Jesus answered them, **Is it not written in your law** (Ps. lxxxii. 6)—respecting judges or magistrates, **I said, Ye are gods?**—as being the *official representatives* and *commissioned agents* of God. **35. If he called them gods unto whom the word of God came, and the Scripture cannot be broken; 36. Say ye of him, whom the Father hath sanctified, and sent into the world.** The whole force of this reasoning, which has been but in part seized by the commentators, lies in what is said of the two parties compared. There is both a comparison and a contrast. The *comparison* of Himself with mere men, divinely commissioned, is intended to show, as *Neander* well expresses it, that the idea of a communication of the Divine Majesty to human nature was by no means foreign to the revelations of the Old Testament; but the *contrast* between Himself and all merely human representatives of God—the One, "*sanctified by the Father, and sent into the world,*" the other, "*to whom the word of God*" merely "*came*"—is expressly designed to prevent His being massed up with them as only one of many human officials of God. *It is never said of Christ* that "the word of the Lord came to Him;" whereas this is the well-known formula by which the divine commission- even to the highest of *mere men* is expressed, such as John the Baptist (Luke iii. 2): and the reason is that given by the Baptist himself (see on ch. iii. 31). The contrast is between those "to whom the word of God came"—men of the earth, earthy, who were merely privileged to get a divine *message* to utter, if prophets, or a divine *office* to discharge, if judges—and "Him whom (not being of the earth at all), *the Father sanctified* (or set apart), and *sent into the world*"—an expression *never used of any merely human messenger of God*, and *used only of Himself.* **Thou blasphemest, because I said, I am the Son of God?** Our Lord *had not said*, in so many words, that He was the Son of God, on this occasion. But He had said what beyond doubt amounted to it—namely, that He gave His sheep eternal life, and none could pluck them out of His hand; that He had gotten them from *His Father*, in whose hands, though given to Him, they still remained, and out of whose hand none could pluck them; and that they were *the indefeasible property of Both*, inasmuch as "He and His Father were One." Our Lord considers all this as just saying of Himself, "I am the Son of God"—*One nature*

with Him, yet mysteriously *of Him*. The parenthesis, in *v.* 35—"And the Scripture cannot be broken"—'dissolved' or 'made void' [λυθῆναι]—referring as it does here to the terms used of magistrates in the 82d Psalm, has an important bearing on the *authority* of the living oracles. The Scripture, says *Olshausen*, as the expressed will of the unchangeable God, is itself unchangeable and indissoluble. (Matt. v. 18.) **37. If I do not the works of my Father, believe me not. 38. But if I do, though ye believe not me, believe the works.** There was in Christ's words, independently of any miracles, a self-evidencing truth, majesty, and grace, which those who had any spiritual susceptibility were unable to resist (ch. vii. 46; viii. 30). But, for those who wanted this, "the works" were a mighty help. When these failed, the case was desperate indeed. **that ye may know and believe that the Father is in me, and I in him** —thus reiterating His claim to essential *oneness with the Father,* which He had only *seemed* to soften down, that He might calm their rage and get their ear again for a moment.

39. Therefore they sought again to take him —true to their original understanding of His words, for they saw perfectly well that He *meant* to "make Himself God" throughout all this dialogue, **but he escaped** [ἐξῆλθεν]—'went' or 'passed' **out of their hand**—slipping, as it were, or gliding away out of their grasp, just when they thought themselves sure of having Him. (See on Luke iv. 30; and on ch. viii. 59.) **40. And went away again beyond Jordan, into the place where John at first baptized.** (See on ch. i. 28.) **41. And many resorted unto him**—on whom the Baptist's ministry appears to have left permanent impressions, **and said, John did no miracle: but all things that John spake of this man were true**—what they now heard and saw in Jesus only confirming in their minds the divinity of His forerunner's mission, a mission unaccompanied by any of His Master's miracles. And thus, **many believed on Him there.**

Remark.—As the malignity of His enemies increases, the benignity and grace with which Jesus addresses Himself to His own seem to grow also; as if the sharp drawing off of the one party made Him cling all the more to the other, drew out to them the more of His loving heart, and encouraged a fuller exhibition of the purposes and plans of saving mercy. In proportion, too, as His scornful adversaries seemed bent on depreciating Him, does He Himself seem to rise in the assertion of His own Divine dignity and authority. Thus, after the virulent enmity to Him manifested in the scenes of the former chapter, how lovely is the whole Discourse on the Shepherd and the sheep, extending

11 NOW a certain *man* was sick, *named* Lazarus, of Bethany, the town of
2 ^aMary and her sister Martha. (It ^bwas *that* Mary which anointed the
Lord with ointment, and wiped his feet with her hair, whose brother
3 Lazarus was sick.) Therefore his sisters sent unto him, saying, Lord,
behold, he whom thou lovest is sick.
4 When Jesus heard *that*, he said, This sickness is not unto death, ^cbut
for the glory of God, that the Son of God might be glorified thereby.
5, Now Jesus loved Martha, and her sister, and Lazarus. When he had
6 heard therefore that he was sick, ^dhe abode two days still in the same
7 place where he was. Then after that saith he to *his* disciples, Let us go

A. D. 33.
CHAP. 11.
^a Luke 10.38.
^b Matt. 26. 7.
Mark 14. 3.
Luke 7. 37.
ch. 12. 3.
^c ch. 9. 3.
Phil. 1. 11.
1 Pet. 4. 11, 14.
^d Isa. 55. 8.
ch. 10. 40.

over the first eighteen verses of this chapter! And where shall we find a livelier expression of the relation which Christ sustains both to men and to God, as the only way of access and entrance *for* the one and *to* the Other; of the absolute voluntariness and saving virtue of His death, as the secret of that self-exerting power in the exercise of which He resumed the life which He had of Himself laid down; of the sustenance which He provides for the continuance of the life He imparts, the pasture of His saved sheep; of the Father's love to Him for freely doing all this; and of the mutual knowledge of Himself and His sheep, as bearing no faint resemblance to that of Himself and the Father? But in the Discourse at the Feast of Dedication, we find Him rising if possible, yet higher; speaking of the security that the sheep have, for that eternal life which in the exercise of His royal authority He gives them, in the impossibility of plucking them out of His hand: and lest this should seem to His audience small security, considering how little different from other men He outwardly appeared, He adds that His Father, at least, who gave His sheep to Him, would be admitted even by themselves to be greater than all; and as none could pluck them out of *His* hand, that was all the same as inability to pluck them out of His own hand, for He and the Father were one. This seemed too much, and accordingly they took up stones to stone Him as a blasphemer. But though He addressed to them an argument fitted to soothe and mollify them, He took care, lest it should take down His dignity in their eyes, to close it by reiterating in substance the very statement for which they had attempted to stone Him; and only by divinely eluding their grasp, and retiring to the further side of the Jordan, did they fail to seize before His time the Holy One of God!

CHAP. XI. 1-57.—THE RESURRECTION OF LAZARUS, AND ITS EFFECTS—THE DEATH OF JESUS BEING RESOLVED ON BY THE JEWISH COUNCIL, HE RETIRES OUT OF PUBLIC VIEW—PREPARATIONS FOR THE APPROACHING PASSOVER, AND SPECULATION WHETHER JESUS WILL COME TO IT. It was stated at the close of the former chapter that our Lord, eluding the fury of His Pharisaic adversaries in Jerusalem, "went away again beyond Jordan into the place where John at first baptized, and there abode" (ch. x. 39, 40). The place was probably somewhere about the well-known fords of the Jordan, and not far from Jericho, which was about eighteen miles distant from Jerusalem. Here we now find Him when intelligence reached Him regarding Lazarus.

A Message arriving from Bethany that Lazarus is sick, Jesus, after waiting Two Days, and informing the Disciples that Lazarus had died, Departs thither for the purpose of Raising Him from the Dead (1-16). **1.** Now a certain man was sick, named Lazarus, of—or 'from' [ἀπὸ] Bethany (see on Luke xix. 29), 'of' [ἐκ] the town of Mary

and her sister Martha—thus distinguishing this Bethany from the one "beyond Jordan" above referred to. **2.** (It was that Mary which anointed the Lord with ointment, and wiped his feet with her hair, whose brother Lazarus was sick.) The fact here referred to, though not recorded by our Evangelist till ch. xii. 3, &c., was so well known in the teaching of all the churches, according to our Lord's prediction (see on Mark xiv. 9), that it is here alluded to by anticipation, as the most natural way of identifying her; and Mary is first named, though the younger, as the more distinguished of the two. She "anointed THE LORD," says the Evangelist—led doubtless to the use of this term here, as He was about to exhibit Him illustriously as the *Lord of Life.* **3.** Therefore his sisters sent unto him, saying, Lord, behold, he whom thou lovest is sick. A most womanly appeal to the known affection of her Lord for the patient; yet how reverential! 'Those,' says *Trench*, 'whom Christ loves, are no more exempt than others from their share of earthly trouble and anguish; rather are they bound over to it more surely.' **4.** When—'But when' [δὲ] Jesus heard that, he said, This sickness is not unto death, but for the glory of God, that the Son of God might—or 'may' be glorified thereby [δι' αὐτῆς] —that is, by this "glory of God." Remarkable language this, which from creature lips would have been intolerable. It means that the glory of GOD manifested in the resurrection of the dead Lazarus would be shown to be the glory, personally and immediately, of THE SON. **5.** Now Jesus loved Martha, and her sister, and Lazarus. What a picture! one that in every age has attracted the admiration of the whole Christian Church. No wonder that those sceptics who have so pitifully carped at the ethical system of the Gospel, as not embracing private friendships in the list of its virtues, have been referred to the Saviour's peculiar regard for this family, as a triumphant refutation—if such were needed. **6.** When he had heard—'When he heard' [ἤκουσεν] therefore that he was sick, he abode two days still—rather, 'then [τότε] he abode two days' in the [same] place where he was. Beyond all doubt this was just to let things come to their worst, in order to the display of His glory. But how trying, meantime, to the faith of his friends, and how unlike the way in which love to a dying friend usually shows itself, on which it is plain that Mary reckoned. But the ways of *divine* are not as the ways of *human* love. Often they are the reverse. When His people are sick, in body or spirit, when their case is waxing more and more desperate every day, when all hope of recovery is about to expire—just then and therefore it is that "*He abides two days still in the same place where He is.*" Can they still hope against hope? Often they do not; but "this is their infirmity." For it is His chosen style of acting. We have been well taught it, and should not *now* have the lesson to

8 into Judea again. *His* disciples say unto him, Master, 'the Jews of late
9 sought to stone thee; and goest thou thither again? Jesus answered,
Are there not twelve hours in the day? *f* If any man walk in the day,
10 he stumbleth not, because he seeth the light of this world. But *g* if a man
11 walk in the night, he stumbleth, because there is no light in him. These
things said he: and after that he saith unto them, Our friend Lazarus
12 *h* sleepeth; but I go, that I may awake him out of sleep. Then said his
13 disciples, Lord, if he sleep, he shall do well. Howbeit Jesus spake of his
death: but they thought that he had spoken of taking of rest in sleep.
14, Then said Jesus unto them plainly, Lazarus is dead. And I am glad for
15 your sakes that I was not there, to the intent ye may believe; neverthe-
16 less let us go unto him. Then said Thomas, which is called Didymus,
unto his fellow-disciples, Let us also go, that we may die with him.
17 Then when Jesus came, he found that he had *lain* in the grave four

A. D. 33.

e ch 10. 31.
f Ps. 57. 11.
Ps. 119. 105,
130.
Pro. 4. 18.
Pro. 6. 23.
Pro. 13. 9.
ch. 9. 4.
g Job 12. 24.
Ps 27. 2.
ch. 12. 35.
h Deut. 31. 16.
Dan. 12. 2.
Matt. 9. 24.
Acts 7. 60.
1 Cor. 15. 18,
51.

learn. From the days of Moses was it given sublimely forth as the character of His grandest interpositions, that "the Lord will judge His people, and repent Himself for His servants—*when He seeth that their power is gone*" (Deut. xxxii. 36). 7. Then after that saith he to his disciples, Let us go into Judea again—out of Peræa where He now was. 8. His disciples say unto him, Master, the Jews of late sought [νῦν ἐζήτουν]—rather, 'were but now seeking' to stone thee (see ch. x. 31); and goest thou thither again?—to certain death, as *v.* 16 shows they thought. 9. Jesus answered, Are there not twelve hours in the day? If any man walk in the day, he stumbleth not, because he seeth the light of this world. 10. But if a man walk in the night, he stumbleth, because there is no light in him [τὸ φῶς οὐκ ἔστιν ἐν αὐτῷ]—or 'because the light is not in him.' See on ch. ix. 4. Our Lord's day had now reached its eleventh hour, and having till now "walked in the day," He would not *mis-time* the remaining and more critical part of His work, which would be as fatal, He says, as omitting it altogether; for "if *a man*"—so He speaks, putting Himself under the same great law of duty as all other men—if a man "walk in the night, he stumbleth, because the light is not in him." 11. These things said he: and after that he saith, Our friend Lazarus—illustrious title from such Lips! To Abraham only did the Lord under the Old Testament accord this, and not till hundreds of years after his death (2 Chr. xx. 7; Isa. xli. 8); to which, as something very unusual, our attention is called in the New Testament (Jas. ii. 23). When Jesus came in the flesh, His forerunner applied this name, in a certain official sense, to himself (ch. iii. 29); and into the same fellowship the Lord's chosen disciples are declared to have come (ch. xv. 13-15). *Lampe* well remarks that the phrase here employed—"our friend Lazarus"—means more than "he whom *Thou* lovest" (*v.* 3); for it implies that Christ's affection was *reciprocated* by Lazarus. sleepeth [κεκοίμηται]—or 'has fallen asleep;' but I go, that I may awake him out of sleep. Our Lord had been told only that Lazarus was "sick." But the change which his two days' delay had produced is here tenderly alluded to. Doubtless, His heart was all the while with His dying, and now dead "friend." The symbol of "sleep" for *death* is common to all languages, and familiar to us in the Old Testament. In the New Testament, however, a higher meaning is put into it, in relation to believers in Jesus (see on 1 Thes. iv. 14)—a sense hinted at, and pretty clearly too, in Ps. xvii. 15, as *Luthardt* remarks; and the "awaking out of sleep" acquires a corresponding sense far transcending bare resuscitation. 12. Then said

his disciples, Lord, if he sleep, he shall do well [σωθήσεται]—literally, 'be saved' or 'preserved'—that is, 'shall recover:' and if so, why run the risk of going to Judea? 13. Howbeit Jesus spake of his death: but they thought that he had spoken of taking of rest in sleep. 14. Then said Jesus unto them plainly, Lazarus is dead. 'In the language of heaven,' says *Bengel* beautifully, 'sleep is the death of the saints; but this language the disciples here understood not. Incomparable is the generosity of the divine manner of discoursing; but such is the slowness of men's apprehension that Scripture often has to descend to the more miserable style of human discourse. (See Matt. xvi. 11, &c.)' 15. And I am glad for your sakes that I was not there. This, as is finely remarked by *Luthardt*, certainly implies that if He had been present, Lazarus would not have died; not because He could not have resisted the importunities of the sisters, but because, in presence of the personal Life, death could not have reached His friend. And *Bengel* again makes this exquisite remark, that it is beautifully congruous to the divine decorum that in presence of the Prince of Life no one is ever said to have died. to the intent ye may believe. This is added to explain His "gladness" at not having been present. His friend's death, as such, could not have been to Him "joyous;" the sequel shows it was "grievous;" but "*for them* it was safe" (Phil. iii. 1). 16. Then said Thomas, called Didymus—or 'the twin.' Let us also go, that we may die with him. Lovely spirit, though tinged with some sadness, such as re-appears at ch. xiv. 5, showing the tendency of this disciple to take the *dark* view of things. On a memorable occasion this tendency opened the door to downright, though but momentary, unbelief. (ch. xx. 25.) Here, however, though alleged by many interpreters, there is nothing of the sort. He perceives clearly how this journey to Judea will end, as respects His Master, and not only sees it in peril to themselves, as they all did, but feels as if he could not and cared not to survive His Master's sacrifice to the fury of His enemies. It was that kind of affection which, living only in the light of its Object, cannot contemplate, or has no heart for, life without it.

Martha. Hearing that Jesus was Coming, Goes to Meet Him—Precious Dialogue between These Two (17-27). 17. Then when Jesus came, he found that he had lain in the grave four days. If he died on the day that the tidings came of his illness; if he was, according to the Jewish custom, buried the same day (see on Luke vii. 12; and Acts v. 5, 6, 10); and if Jesus, after two days' farther stay in Peræa, set out on the day following for Bethany

18 days already. Now Bethany was nigh unto Jerusalem, [1]about fifteen
19 furlongs off. And many of the Jews came to Martha and Mary, to
20 comfort them concerning their brother. Then Martha, as soon as she
heard that Jesus was coming, went and met him: but Mary sat *still* in
21 the house. Then said Martha unto Jesus, Lord, if thou hadst been here,
22 my brother had not died. But I know, that even now, [*i*]whatsoever thou
23 wilt ask of God, God will give *it* thee. Jesus saith unto her, Thy brother
24 shall rise [*j*]again. Martha saith unto him, [*k*]I know that he shall rise again
25 in the resurrection at the last day. Jesus said unto her, I am [*l*]the resurrection, and the [*m*]life: he [*n*]that believeth in me, though he were dead,
26 yet shall he live: and whosoever liveth and believeth in me shall never
27 die. Believest thou this? She saith unto him, Yea, Lord: [*o*]I believe
that thou art the Christ, the Son of God, which should come into the
world.
28 And when she had so said, she went her way, and called Mary her
29 sister secretly, saying, The Master is come, and calleth for thee. As
30 soon as she heard *that*, she arose quickly, and came unto him. Now
Jesus was not yet come into the town, but was in that place where
31 Martha met him. The Jews then which were with her in the house, and
comforted her, when they saw Mary, that she rose up hastily and went

A. D. 33.

[1] That is, about two miles.
[*i*] ch. 9. 31.
[*j*] Dan. 12. 2.
1 Thes 4.14.
Phil. 3. 21.
[*k*] Luke 14. 14.
ch. 5. 29.
[*l*] ch. 6. 21.
ch. 6. 39, 40, 44.
Rom. 8 11.
[*m*] ch. 1. 4.
ch. 6. 35.
ch 14. 6.
Col. 3. 4.
1 John 1. 1, 2.
1 John 5. 11.
[*n*] ch. 6. 36
1 John 5. 10.
[*o*] Matt. 16. 16.
ch. 4. 42.
ch. 6. 14, 69.

(some ten hours' journey)—that would make out the four days, the first and last being incomplete. (So *Meyer*.) 18. **Now Bethany was nigh unto Jerusalem, about fifteen furlongs**—rather less than two miles: this is mentioned to explain the visits of sympathy, noticed in the following words, which the proximity of the two places facilitated. 19. **And many of the Jews came** [ἐληλύθεισαν]—rather, 'had come' to Martha and Mary, **to comfort them concerning their brother.** Thus were provided, in a most natural way, so many witnesses of the glorious miracle that was to follow as to put the fact beyond possible question. 20. **Then Martha, as soon as she heard that Jesus was coming, went and met him**—true to the *energy* and *activity* of her character, as seen in the beautiful scene recorded by Luke (x. 38-42—on which see exposition): **but Mary sat [still] in the house** [ἐκαθέζετο]—literally, 'was sitting in the house;' equally true to her *placid, still* character. These undesigned touches charmingly illustrate, not only the minute *historic fidelity* of both narratives, but their *inner harmony.* 21. **Then said Martha unto Jesus, Lord, if thou hadst been here, my brother had not died.** As Mary afterwards said the same thing (*v.* 32), it is plain they had made this very natural remark to each other, perhaps many times during these four sad days, and not without having their confidence in His love at times overclouded. Such trials of faith, however, are not peculiar to them. 22. **But I know, that even now** ['Αλλὰ καὶ νῦν οἶδα]—'Nevertheless, even now, I know' **whatsoever thou wilt**—'shalt' **ask of God.** Energetic characters are usually sanguine, the rainbow of hope peering through the drenching cloud. **God will give it thee**—that is, 'even to the restoration of my dead brother to life,' for that plainly is her meaning, as the sequel shows. 23. **Jesus saith unto her, Thy brother shall rise again**—purposely expressing Himself in general terms, to draw her out. 24. **Martha saith unto him, I know that he shall rise again in the resurrection at the last day**:—*q. d.,* 'But are we never to see him in life till then?' 25. **Jesus said unto her, I am the resurrection, and the life**:—*q. d., 'The who'e power to impart, maintain, and restore life,* resides in Me.' (See on ch. i. 4; v. 21.) What higher claim to supreme Divinity than this grand saying can be conceived? **he that believeth in me, though he**

were dead [κἂν ἀποθάνῃ]—'though he die,' yet **shall he live**:—*q. d.,* 'The believer's death shall be swallowed up in life, and his life shall never sink into death.' As death comes by sin, it is His to dissolve it; and as life flows through His righteousness, it is His to communicate and eternally maintain it. (See on Rom. v. 21.) 26. **And whosoever liveth and believeth in me shall never die.** The temporary separation of soul and body is here regarded as not even interrupting, much less impairing, the new and everlasting life imparted by Jesus to His believing people. **Believest thou this?** Canst thou take this in? 27. **She saith unto him, Yea, Lord: I believe** ['Εγὼ πεπίστευκα]—'I have believed (and do believe).' The "I" is emphatic—'As for me.' **That thou art the Christ, the Son of God, which should come**—or 'that cometh' **into the world**:—*q. d.,* 'And having *such* faith in Thee, I can believe all which that comprehends.' While she had a glimmering perception that Resurrection, in every sense of the word, belonged to the Messianic office and Sonship of Jesus, she means, by this way of expressing herself, to cover much that she felt her ignorance of—as no doubt appertaining of right to Him.

Mary, being sent for, Comes to Jesus Weeping, followed by sympathizing Jews, who weep too. The spirit of Jesus is deeply moved, and He, weeping also, arrives at the Grave (28-38). 28. **And when she had so said, she went her way, and called Mary her sister secretly, saying, The Master is come, and calleth for thee** [πάρεστι καὶ φωνεῖ σε]—'is here, and calleth thee.' The narrative does not give us this charming piece of information, but Martha's words do. 29. **As soon as**—or, 'When' [ὡς] **she heard that, she arose quickly, and came unto him** [ἐγείρεται-ἔρχεται]—rather, 'ariseth,' and 'cometh.' Affection for her Lord, assurance of His sympathy, and hope of his interposition, put a spring into her depressed spirit. 30. **Now Jesus, &c.** 31. **The Jews then which were with her in the house, and comforted**—or 'were comforting' her, **when they saw Mary, that she rose up hastily and went out,** followed her. Thus *casually* were provided witnesses of the glorious miracle that followed, witnesses not prejudiced, certainly, *in favour* of Him who wrought it. **saying, She goeth unto the grave to weep there**—according to Jewish practice for some days after burial. 32. **Then when**

32 out, followed her, saying, She goeth unto the grave to weep there. Then
when Mary was come where Jesus was, and saw him, she fell down at his
feet, saying unto him, Lord, if thou hadst been here, my brother had not
33 died. When Jesus therefore saw her weeping, and the Jews also weeping
34 which came with her, he groaned in the spirit, and [2]was troubled, and
said, Where have ye laid him? They said unto him, Lord, come
35, and see. Jesus [p]wept. Then said the Jews, Behold how he loved
36, him! And some of them said, Could not this man, [q]which opened the
37 eyes of the blind, have caused that even this man should not have died?
38 Jesus therefore, again groaning in himself, cometh to the grave. It was
a cave, and a stone lay upon it.
39 Jesus said, Take ye away the stone. Martha, the sister of him that
was dead, saith unto him, Lord, by this time he stinketh: for he hath

A. D. 33.

[2] he troubled himself.
[p] Gen. 43. 30.
Job 30. 25.
Ps. 35. 13.
Ps. 119. 136.
Isa. 53. 3.
Jer. 9. 1.
Jer. 13. 17.
Luke 19.41.
Rom.12. 16.
Heb. 2. 17, 18.
Heb. 4. 15.
[q] ch. 9. 6.

**Mary was come where Jesus was, and saw him,
she fell down at his feet**—more impassioned than
her sister, though her words were fewer. **saying
unto him, Lord, if thou hadst been here, my
brother had not died.** See on *v.* 21. **33. When
Jesus therefore saw her weeping, and the Jews
also weeping which came with her, he groaned
in the spirit** [ἐνεβριμήσατο]. The word here is not
that usually employed to express groaning. It
denotes any 'strong manifestation of inward emotion;' but here it probably means, 'made a visible
and powerful effort to check His emotion'—to restrain those tears which were ready to gush from
His eyes. **and was troubled** [ἐτάραξεν ἑαυτὸν]—
rather, as in the margin, 'troubled Himself;'
that is, became mentally agitated. The tears of
Mary and her friends acted sympathetically upon
Him, and drew forth His emotions. What a vivid
outcoming of *real* humanity! **34. And said, Where
have ye laid him?** Perhaps it was in order to
retain composure enough to ask this question, and
on receiving the answer to proceed with them to
the spot, that He checked Himself. **They said**—
'say' [λέγουσιν] **unto him, Lord, come and see.**
35. Jesus wept [ἐδάκρυσεν]. This beautifully conveys the sublime brevity of the original word; else
'*shed tears*' might have better conveyed the difference between the word here used and that twice
employed in *v.* 33 [κλαίω], and there properly rendered "weeping"—denoting the loud wail for the
dead, while that of Jesus consisted of *silent tears.*
Is it for nothing that the Evangelist, some *sixty
years* after it occurred, holds up to all ages with
such touching brevity the sublime spectacle of *the
Son of God in tears?* What a seal of His perfect
oneness with us in the most redeeming feature of
our stricken humanity! But was there nothing in
those tears beyond sorrow for human suffering and
death? Could these *effects* move Him without
suggesting the *cause?* Who can doubt that in His
ear every feature of the scene proclaimed that
stern law of the Kingdom, "The wages of *sin* is
death," and that this element in His visible emotion underlay all the rest? See on Mark i. 29-31,
Remark 2 at the close of that Section. **36. Then
said the Jews, Behold how he loved him!** We
thank you, O ye visitors from Jerusalem, for this
spontaneous testimony to the *human softness* of
the Son of God. **37. And** [δὲ]—rather, 'But' **some
of them said, Could not this man, which opened
the eyes of the blind** [τοῦ τυφλοῦ]—not 'of blind
people' generally, but 'of the blind man;' referring to the specific case recorded in the ninth
chapter. **have caused that even** [ἵνα καὶ οὗτος]—
rather, 'have caused also that' **this man should
not have died?** The former exclamation came
from the better-feeling portion of the spectators;
this betokens a measure of suspicion. It hardly

goes the length of attesting the miracle on the
blind man, but—'if, as everybody says, He did
that, why could He not also have kept Lazarus
alive?' As to the restoration of the dead man to
life, they never so much as thought of it. But
this disposition to dictate to Divine power, and
almost to peril our confidence in it upon its doing
our bidding, is not confined to men of no faith.
38. Jesus therefore, again groaning in himself—
in the sense explained on *v.* 33. But whereas
there the rising emotion which He laboured to
check was that of sorrow for suffering and its cause,
here it is of sorrow, or something stronger, at the
suspicious spirit which breathed through this
speech. Yet here, too, the former emotion was
the deeper of the two, now that His eye was about
to rest on the spot where lay, in the still horrors
of death, His *friend.* **cometh to the grave. It**
—'Now it' **was a cave**—the cavity, natural or
artificial, of a rock. This, with the number of
condoling visitors from Jerusalem, and the costly
ointment with which Mary afterwards anointed
Jesus at Bethany, all go to show that the family
were in good circumstances. **and a stone lay upon it**—or 'against it'; for as the Oriental sepulchres of the better classes were hewn out of the
rock, the slab which shut them in might be laid
either horizontally or perpendicularly.
The Act Preparatory to the Resurrection (39-41).
39. Jesus said—'saith' [λέγει], **Take ye away
the stone.** This, remarks *Grotius*, was spoken
to the attendants of Martha and Mary, for it
was a work of no little labour. According to
the Talmudists, says *Lampe*, quoting from *Maimonides*, it was forbidden to open a grave after the
stone was placed upon it. Besides other dangers,
they were apprehensive of legal impurity by contact with the dead. Hence they avoided coming
nearer a grave than four cubits. But He who
touched the leper, and the bier of the widow of
Nain's son, rises here also above these Judaic memorials of evils, every one of which He had come
to roll away. *Observe here what our Lord did
Himself, and what He made others do.* As Elijah
himself repaired the altar on Carmel, arranged the
wood, cut the victim, and placed the pieces on the
fuel, but made the bystanders fill the surrounding
trench with water, that no suspicion might arise
of fire having been secretly applied to the pile
(1 Ki. xviii. 30-35); so our Lord would let the most
sceptical see that, without laying a hand on the
stone that covered His friend, He could recall him
to life. What could be done by human hands He
orders to be done, reserving only to Himself what
transcended the ability of all creatures. **Martha,
the sister of him that was dead**—and as such the
proper guardian of the precious remains; the relationship being *here* mentioned to account for her

419

40 been *dead* four days. Jesus saith unto her, Said I not unto thee, that, if
41 thou wouldest believe, thou shouldest see the glory of God? Then they took away the stone *from the place* where the dead was laid.

And Jesus lifted up *his* eyes, and said, Father, I thank thee
42 that thou hast heard me. And I knew that thou hearest me always: but *r* because of the people which stand by I said *it*, that
43 they may believe that thou hast sent me. And when he thus had
44 spoken, he cried with a loud voice, Lazarus, *come forth. And he that was dead came forth, bound hand and foot with grave-clothes; and *t* his face was bound about with a napkin. Jesus saith unto them, Loose him, and let him go.
45 Then many of the Jews which came to Mary, *u* and had seen the things
46 which Jesus did, believed on him. But some of them went their ways to the Pharisees, and told them what things Jesus had done.
47 Then *v* gathered the chief priests and the Pharisees a council, and said,

A. D. 33.

r ch. 12. 30.
s Deut. 32. 39.
1 Sam. 2. 6.
Ps. 33. 9.
Luke 7. 14.
Luke 8. 54.
Acts 3. 15.
Acts 9. 40.
Rom. 4. 17.
t ch. 20. 7.
u ch. 2. 23.
ch. 10. 42.
ch. 12. 11,
18.
v Ps. 2. 2.
Matt. 26. 3.
Mark 14. 1.
Luke 22. 2.

venturing gently to remonstrate against their exposure, in a state of decomposition, to eyes that had loved him so tenderly in life. **saith unto him, Lord, by this time he stinketh: for he hath been [dead] four days.** (See on *v.* 17.) It is wrong to suppose from this, as *Lampe* and others do, that, like the bystanders, she had not thought of his restoration to life. But certainly the glimmerings of hope which she cherished from the first (*v.* 22), and which had been brightened by what Jesus said to her (*vv.* 23-27), had suffered a momentary eclipse on the proposal to expose the now sightless corpse. *To such fluctuations all real faith is subject in dark hours*—as the example of *Job* makes sufficiently manifest. **40. Jesus saith unto her, Said I not unto thee, that, if thou wouldest believe, thou shouldest see the glory of God?** He had not said those very words; but that was the scope of all that He had uttered to her about His life-giving power (*vv.* 23, 25, 26)—a gentle yet emphatic and most instructive rebuke: 'Why doth the restoration of life, even to a decomposing corpse, seem hopeless in presence of the Resurrection and the Life? Hast thou yet to learn that "if thou canst believe, all things are possible to him that believeth"'? (Mark ix. 23). **41. Then they took away the stone from the place where the dead was laid.**

The Preparatory Prayer (41, 42). **41. And Jesus lifted up his eyes** [ἦρε—ἄνω]. The attitude is somewhat emphatically expressed—'lifted His eyes upward,' marking His calm solemnity (compare ch. xvii. 1). **and said, Father, I thank thee thou hast heard me** [ἤκουσας]—rather, 'heardest me;' referring, as we think, to a specific prayer offered by Him, probably on intelligence of the case reaching Him (*vv.* 3, 4); for His living and loving oneness with the Father was maintained and manifested in the flesh, not merely by the spontaneous and uninterrupted outgoing of Each to Each in spirit, but by specific actings of faith and exercises of prayer about each successive case as it emerged. He prayed, as *Luthardt* well says, 'not for what He wanted, but for the manifestation of what He had;' and having the bright consciousness of the answer in the felt liberty to ask it, and the assurance that it was at hand, He gives thanks for this with a grand simplicity before performing the act. **42. And**—or rather, 'Yet' **I knew that thou hearest me always: but because of the people** [διὰ τὸν ὄχλον]—or 'for the sake of the multitude' which stand by—or 'stand around' [περιεστῶτα], **I said it, that they may believe that thou hast sent me.** Instead of praying now, He simply gives thanks for answer to prayer offered ere He left Peræa, and adds that His

doing even this, in the audience of the people, was not from any doubt of the prevalency of His prayers in any case, but to show the people that *He did nothing without His Father, but all by direct communication with Him.*

The Resurrection-Act (43, 44). **43. And when he thus had spoken, he cried with a loud voice, Lazarus, come forth.** On one other occasion only did He this—on the *Cross*. His last utterance was a "loud cry" (Matt. xxvii. 50). "He shall not *cry*," said the prophet; nor, in His ministry, did He cry. What a sublime contrast is this "loud cry" to the magical "whisperings" and "mutterings" of which we read in Isa. viii. 19, 20. As *Grotius* well remarks, it is second only to the grandeur of that voice which shall raise all the dead (ch. v. 28, 29; 1 Thess. iv. 16). **44. And he that was dead came forth, bound hand and foot with grave-clothes; and his face was bound about with a napkin.**

The Act Disengaging the Risen Man (44). **44. Jesus saith unto them, Loose him, and let him go.** Jesus will no more do this Himself than roll away the stone. As the one was the necessary *preparation* for resurrection, so the other was the necessary *sequel* to it. THE LIFE-GIVING ACT ALONE HE RESERVES TO HIMSELF. Even so in the quickening of the dead to spiritual life, human instrumentality is employed first to *prepare the way*, and then to *turn it to account.*

The Effects of this Miracle on Two Classes (45, 46). **45. Then many**—or, 'Many therefore' **of the Jews which came**—or 'had come' **to Mary**—as sympathizing friends, **and had seen the things which Jesus did, believed on him.** These were of the *candid* class, on whom the effect of so stupendous a miracle, done before their own eyes, could not but be resistless. See on ch. xii. 9-11. **46. But some of them went their ways to the Pharisees, and told them what things Jesus had done.** Those were of the *prejudiced* class, whom no evidence would convince. These two classes continually re-appear in the Gospel History; nor is there ever any great work of God which does not produce both.

The Chief Priests and Pharisees, Alarmed at the Convincing Effect of His Miracles, Resolve in Council to put Jesus to Death (47-53). **47. Then**—or, 'Therefore,' in consequence of the intelligence brought them of this last and grandest of the Lord's miracles, **gathered the chief priests and the Pharisees a council, and said, What do we?** for this man doeth many miracles. **48. If we let him thus alone, all men will believe on him: and the Romans shall come and take away both our place and nation:**—*q. d.*, 'While we trifle, this

48 ⁱ⁰What do we? for this man doeth many miracles. If we let him thus alone, all *men* will believe on him: and ˣthe Romans shall come and take
49 away both our place and nation. And one of them, *named* ʸCaiaphas, being the high priest that same year, said unto them, Ye know nothing
50 at all, nor ᶻconsider that it is expedient for us, that one man should die
51 for the people, and that the whole nation perish not. And this spake he not of himself: but being high priest that year, he prophesied that Jesus
52 should die for that nation; and ᵃnot for that nation only, ᵇbut that also he should gather together in one the children of God that were scattered abroad.
53 Then from that day forth they took counsel together for to put him to
54 death. Jesus ᶜtherefore walked no more openly among the Jews; but went thence unto a country near to the wilderness, into a city called ᵈEphraim, and there continued with his disciples.
55 And ᵉthe Jews' passover was nigh at hand: and many went out of the country up to Jerusalem before the passover, to purify ᶠthemselves.
56 Then ᵍsought they for Jesus, and spake among themselves, as they stood
57 in the temple, What think ye, that he will not come to the feast? Now both the chief priests and the Pharisees had given a commandment, that, if any man knew where he were, he should show *it*, that they might take him.

A. D. 33.

ⁱ⁰ ch. 12. 19.
Acts 4. 16.
ˣ Dan 9. 26.
ʸ Luke 3. 2.
ch. 18. 14.
ᶻ ch. 18. 14.
ch. 19. 12.
ᵃ Isa. 49. 6.
1 John 2. 2.
ᵇ ch. 10. 16.
Acts 13. 47.
Gal. 3. 28.
Eph. 3. 6.
1 Pet. 5. 9.
ᶜ ch. 4. 1. 3.
ᵈ 2 Chr. 13. 19.
ᵉ ch. 2. 13.
ch. 5. 1.
ch. 6. 4.
ᶠ Gen. 35. 2.
Ex. 19. 10.
Num. 9. 6.
1 Sam. 16. 5.
Job 1 5.
Ps. 26. 6.
Acts 24. 18.
ᵍ ch. 7. 11.

man, by his many miracles, will carry all before him; the popular enthusiasm will bring on a revolution, which will precipitate the Romans upon us, and our all will go down in one common ruin.' What a testimony to the reality of our Lord's miracles, and their resistless effect, from His bitterest enemies! But how low the considerations are by which their whole decision is influenced—the fear of a national break-up, which would endanger their own position and interests! **49. And one of them, named Caiaphas, being the high priest that same year, said unto them, Ye know nothing at all, 50. Nor consider that it is expedient for us, that one man should die for the people, and that the whole nation perish not.** He meant nothing more than that there was no use in discussing the matter, since the right course was obvious: the way to prevent the apprehended ruin of the nation was to make a sacrifice of the Disturber of their peace. But in giving utterance to this suggestion of political expediency, he was so guided as to give forth a Divine prediction of deep significance; and God so ordered it that it should come from the lips of the high priest for that memorable year, the recognized head of God's visible people, whose ancient office, symbolized by the Urim and Thummim, was to decide, in the last resort, all vital questions as the oracle of the Divine will. **51. And—or, 'Now' this spake he not of himself: but being high priest that year, he prophesied that Jesus should die for that—**or rather, 'the' nation [τοῦ ἔθνους]; **52. And not for that—**'the' nation only, **but that also he should gather together in one the children of God that were—**or 'are' scattered abroad. This is one of those explanatory remarks of our Evangelist himself, which we have had once and again to notice as one of the characteristics of his Gospel. **53. Then—**or, 'Therefore' from that day forth they took council together for to put him to death.

Jesus, in consequence of this, Goes into comparative Retirement (54). **54. Jesus therefore walked no more openly among the Jews.** How could He, unless He had wished to die before His time? **but went thence unto a—**or rather, 'the' country [τὴν χώραν] near to the wilderness—of Judea, **into a city called Ephraim, and there continued—**or

'tarried' [διέτριβε] with his disciples. What this city of Ephraim was, and where precisely it was, is not agreed. But *Robinson* and *Stanley* identify it with a small village now called *Taijibeh*, about twenty miles north of Jerusalem.

Preparations for the approaching Passover, and Speculation whether Jesus will come to it (55-57). **55. And—**or, 'Now' the Jews' passover was nigh at hand—the *fourth*, according to our reckoning, during our Lord's public ministry; that at which He became "our Passover, sacrificed for us." **and many went out of the country up to Jerusalem before the passover, to purify themselves—**from any legal uncleanness which would have disqualified them from keeping the feast (see Num. ix. 10, &c.; 2 Chr. xxx. 17, &c.) This is mentioned to introduce the graphic statement which follows. **56. Then sought they for Jesus, and spake—**or 'said' [ἔλεγον] among themselves, as they stood in the temple, What think ye, that he will not come to the feast? giving forth their various conjectures and speculations about the probability of His coming or not coming to the feast. **57. Now [both] the chief priests and the Pharisees.** The word "both" [καὶ] should be excluded, as clearly not genuine. **had given a commandment, that, if any man knew where he were, he should show it, that they might take him.** This is mentioned to account for the conjectures whether He would come, in spite of this determination to seize Him.

Remarks.—1. We have already remarked, that as the Resurrection of Lazarus and the opening of the eyes of the Man Born Blind were the most wonderful of all our Lord's miracles, so it is precisely these two miracles which are recorded with the minutest detail, and which stand attested by evidence the most unassailable. One argument only has scepticism been able to urge against the credibility of these miracles—the entire silence of the First Three Evangelists regarding them. But even if we were unable to account for that silence, the positive evidence by which these miracles are attested can in no degree be affected by it. And then this silence of the First Three Evangelists embraces *the whole Judæan ministry* of our Lord, from the very beginning of it down to His Final Entry into Jeru-

12 THEN Jesus, six days before the passover, came to Bethany, ^awhere
2 Lazarus was which had been dead, whom he raised from the dead. There
^bthey made him a supper; and Martha served: but Lazarus was one of
them that sat at the table with him.

3 Then took ^cMary a pound of ointment of spikenard, very costly, and
anointed the feet of Jesus, and wiped his feet with her hair: and the
4 house was filled with the odour of the ointment. Then saith one of his
5 disciples, Judas Iscariot, Simon's *son*, which should betray him, Why was
not this ointment sold for three hundred pence, and given to the poor?
6 This he said, not that he cared for the poor; but because he was a thief,
7 and ^dhad the bag, and bare what was put therein. Then said Jesus, Let
8 her alone: against the day of my burying hath she kept this. For ^ethe
poor always ye have with you; but me ye have not always.

9 Much people of the Jews therefore knew that he was there: and they
came not for Jesus' sake only, but that they might see Lazarus also,
10 whom he had raised from the dead. But ^fthe chief priests consulted that
11 they might put Lazarus also to death; because ^gthat by reason of him
many of the Jews went away, and believed on Jesus.

A. D. 33.
CHAP. 12.
^a ch. 11. 1, 43.
^b Matt. 26. 6.
Mark 14. 3.
^c Song 1. 12.
Song 4. 13.
Luke 10. 38,
39.
ch. 11. 2.
^d Pro. 26. 25.
Pro. 28. 20,
22.
ch. 13. 29.
Eph. 5. 5.
^e Deut 15. 11.
Matt.26. 11.
Mark 14. 7.
^f Pro. 1. 16.
Pro. 4. 16.
Luke 16.31.
^g Mark 15.10.
ch. 11. 45.
Acts 13. 45.

salem. So that if this be any argument against the two miracles in question, it is an argument rather against the entire credibility of the Fourth Gospel—to which we have adverted in the Introduction. **2.** If the resurrections from the dead were the most divine of all the miracles which our Lord performed, this resurrection of Lazarus was certainly the most divine of the three recorded in the Gospel History. On the great lesson which it teaches, even more gloriously than the other two, see on Mark v. 21-43, Remark 5 at the close of that Section. But **3.** The true nature of all these resurrections must be carefully observed. They were none of them a resurrection from the dead to "die no more." They were a mere *re-animation of the mortal body*, until in the course of nature they should die again, to sleep till the Trumpet shall sound, and with all other sleeping believers awake finally to resurrection-life. **4.** Did Jesus suffer the case of Lazarus to reach its lowest and most desperate stage before interposing, and his loving sisters to agonize and weep until their faith in His own power and love, which had done nothing all that time to arrest the hand of death and corruption, had been tried to the uttermost? What is this, but an illustration—the most signal, indeed, yet but one more illustration—of a feature observable in most of His miracles, where *only after all other help was vain* did He Himself step in? In so acting, is it necessary to say that He did but serve Himself Heir, so to speak, to God's own ancient style of procedure towards His people? (See Deut. xxxii. 36; Isa. lix. 16). And will not this help to assure us that "to the upright there ariseth light in the darkness"? (Ps. cxii. 4). **5.** We have seen in Christ's tears over impenitent Jerusalem The Weeping *Saviour:* in Christ's tears over the grave of Lazarus we see The Weeping *Friend.* And just as in the other case, though the tears which bedewed those Cheeks at the sight of impenitence are now no more, He is not even in heaven, at the sight of similar impenitence, insensible to the feeling that drew them forth here below: so when some dear Lazarus has fallen asleep, and his Christian relatives and friends are weeping over his bier and at his grave, we are not to be chilled by the apprehension that Jesus in the heavens merely looks on and drops comfort into the wounded heart—Himself all void of sympathetic emotion—but are warranted to assure ourselves that His heart there is quite as tender

and warm, and quite as quick in its sensibilities, as ever it showed itself to be here; or, in language that will come better home to us, that "we have not an High Priest that cannot," even now, "be touched with the feeling of our infirmities," but was in all points tried like as we are, yet without sin," and this on very purpose to acquire experimentally the capacity to identify Himself to perfection, in feeling as well as in understanding, with the whole circle of our trials. What rivers of divine consolation, O ye suffering disciples of the Lord Jesus, are there here opened up for you! Drink, then, yea, drink abundantly, O beloved! **6.** What a commentary is the determined and virulent resistance even of such evidence, by the ruling Jewish party, on those words of the Parable of the Rich Man and Lazarus—"If they hear not Moses and the prophets, neither will they be persuaded though one rose from the dead!"

CHAP. XII. 1-11.—THE SUPPER AND THE ANOINTING AT BETHANY, SIX DAYS BEFORE THE PASSOVER—THE DEATH OF LAZARUS PLOTTED, TO ARREST THE ACCESSIONS TO CHRIST IN CONSEQUENCE OF HIS RESURRECTION. (= Matt. xxvi. 6-13; Mark xiv. 3-9.)

The Supper and the Anointing at Bethany (1-8). For the exposition of this portion, see on Mark xiv. 3-9, and Remarks 1 to 8 at the close of that Section.

The Death of Lazarus is Plotted, to arrest the Triumphs of Jesus in consequence of his Resurrection (9-11). **9. Much people of the Jews therefore knew that he was there: and they came not for Jesus' sake only, but that they might see Lazarus also, whom he had raised from the dead. 10. But the chief priests consulted that they might put Lazarus also to death; 11. Because that by reason of him many of the Jews went away, and believed on Jesus.** Crowds of the Jews of Jerusalem hastened, it seems, to Bethany (scarce two miles distant), not so much to see Jesus, whom they knew to be there, as to see the dead Lazarus who had been raised to life. This, as was to be expected, issued in immense accessions to Christ (*v.* 19); and, as the necessary means of arresting these triumphs of the hated One, a plot is laid against the life of Lazarus also:—to such a pitch had these ecclesiastics come of diabolical determination not only to shut out the light from their own minds, but to extinguish it from the earth!

For Remarks on these three verses, see those on ch. xi.

12 On ʰthe next day much people that were come to the feast, when they
13 heard that Jesus was coming to Jerusalem, took branches of palm trees,
and went forth to meet him, and cried, ⁱHosanna: Blessed *is* the King of
14 Israel that cometh in the name of the Lord. And Jesus, when he had
15 found a young ass, sat thereon; as it is written, Fear ʲnot, daughter of
16 Sion: behold thy King cometh, sitting on an ass's colt. These things
ᵏunderstood not his disciples at the first: ˡbut when Jesus was glorified,
ᵐthen remembered they that these things were written of him, and *that*
they had done these things unto him.
17 The people therefore that was with him when he called Lazarus out of
18 his grave, and raised him from the dead, bare record. For this cause the
people also met him, for that they heard that he had done this miracle.
19 The Pharisees therefore said among themselves, Perceive ye how ye prevail
nothing? behold, the world is gone after him.
20 And there ⁿwere certain Greeks among them °that came up to worship
21 at the feast: the same came therefore to Philip, which was of Bethsaida
22 of Galilee, and desired him, saying, Sir, we would see Jesus. Philip
cometh and telleth Andrew: and again Andrew and Philip tell Jesus.
23 And Jesus answered them, saying, The ᵖhour is come, that the Son of
24 man should be glorified. Verily, verily, I say unto you, ۹Except a corn
of wheat fall into the ground and die, it abideth alone: but if it die, it
25 bringeth forth much fruit. He ʳthat loveth his life shall lose it; and he
26 that hateth his life in this world shall keep it unto life eternal. If any

A. D. 33
ʰ Luke 19.35.
ⁱ Ps 72. 17-19.
Ps. 118. 25.
Matt. 21. 9, 11.
Matt. 23. 39.
Mark 11. 8, 10.
1 Tim. 1. 17.
ʲ Isa. 62. 11.
Mic. 4. 8.
Zeph 3. 16.
Zec 9. 9.
ᵏ Luke 18.34.
Luke 24.25.
ˡ ch. 7. 39.
Heb. 1. 3.
ᵐ ch. 14. 26.
ⁿ Acts 17. 4.
° 1 Ki. 8. 41.
Acts 8. 27.
ᵖ ch. 13 32.
ch. 17. 1.
۹ 1 Cor.15.36.
Heb. 2 10.
1 John 4.14.
Rev. 5. 9.
ʳ Luke 9. 24.
Luke 17.33.

12-19.—Christ's Triumphal Entry into Jerusalem, on the first day of the week. (= Matt. xxi. 1-9; Mark xi. 1-11; Luke xix. 29-40.) For the exposition, see on Luke xix. 29-40.

20-50.—Jesus is informed that certain Greeks desire to see Him—The exalted Discourse and the Mysterious Scene which followed thereupon—General Results of Christ's Ministry, and Concluding Summary of His Public Teaching.

Jesus, being informed that certain Greeks Desire to See Him, Discourses in an exalted strain on the great truths which that circumstance suggested (20-26). **20. And—**or, 'Now' [δὲ] **there were certain Greeks** ["Ελληνες]—not Grecian Jews ['Ελληνισταί] but Greek or Gentile proselytes to the Jewish faith, who were wont to attend the annual festivals, and particularly this primary one—the Passover. **21. The same came therefore to Philip, which was of—**or 'from' [ἀπὸ] **Bethsaida.** Possibly they came from the same quarter. **and desired—**'requested' or 'prayed' him, **saying, Sir, we would see Jesus**—certainly with far higher objects than Zaccheus (Luke xix. 3). Perhaps our Lord was then in that part of the temple-court to which Gentile proselytes had no access. These men from the *west*, as *Stier* says, represent, at the end of Christ's life what the wise from the *east* represented at the beginning: only these come to the Cross of the King, while those came to His Manger. **22. Philip cometh and telleth Andrew.** As fellow-townsmen of Bethsaida, these two seem to have drawn to each other. **and again Andrew and Philip tell Jesus—**or, according to the reading adopted by *Lachmann, Tischendorf,* and *Tregelles,* 'Andrew and Philip come and tell Jesus,' [ἔρχεται 'A. καὶ Φ. καὶ λέγουσιν 'I.] The minuteness of these details, while they add to the graphic force of the narrative, serve to prepare us for something important to come out of this introduction. **23. And—**or, 'But' [δὲ] **Jesus answered them, saying, The hour is come, that the Son of man should be glorified:**—*q. d.,* 'They would see Jesus, would they? Yet a little moment, and they shall see Him so as now they dream not

of. The middle wall of partition that keeps them out from the commonwealth of Israel is on the eve of breaking down, "and I, if I be lifted up from the earth, shall draw all men unto Me:" I see them "flying as a cloud, and as doves to their cots," and a glorious event for the Son of Man will that be, by which this is to be brought about.' It is His *death* He thus sublimely and delicately alludes to. Lost in the scenes of triumph which this desire of the Greeks to see Him called up before His view, He gives no direct answer to their petition for an interview, but sees that cross which was to bring them in gilded with glory. **24. Verily, verily, I say unto you, Except a corn —**or 'grain' [κόκκος] **of wheat fall into the ground and die, it abideth alone** [αὐτὸς μόνος μένει]—'by itself alone,' **but if it die, it bringeth forth much fruit.** The *necessity* of His death is here brightly expressed, and its proper operation and fruit—*life* springing forth out of death—imaged forth by a beautiful and deeply significant law of the vegetable kingdom. For a double reason, no doubt, this was uttered—to explain what He had said of His death, as the hour of His own glorification, and to sustain His own spirit under the agitation which was mysteriously coming over it in the view of that death. **25. He that loveth his life shall lose it; and he that hateth his life in this world shall keep it unto life eternal.** (See on Matt. xvi. 21-28). Did our Lord mean to exclude Himself from the operation of the great principle here expressed — *self-renunciation the law of self-preservation;* and its converse, *self-preservation the law of self-destruction?* On the contrary, as He became Man to exemplify this fundamental law of the Kingdom of God in its most sublime form, so the very utterance of it on this occasion served to sustain His own spirit in the double prospect to which He had just alluded. **26. If any man serve me, let him follow me; and where I am, there shall also my servant be: If any man serve me, him will my Father honour.** Jesus, it will be observed, here claims the same absolute subjection to Himself, as the law of men's exaltation to honour, as He yielded to the Father.

man serve me, let him follow me; and ᵍwhere I am, there shall also my servant be: if any man serve me, him will *my* Father honour.

27 Now ᵗis my soul troubled; and what shall I say? Father, save me
28 from this hour: ᵘ"but for this cause came I unto this hour. Father, glorify thy name. ᵛThen came there a voice from heaven, *saying,* I
29 have both glorified *it,* and will glorify *it* again. The people therefore that stood by, and heard *it,* said that it thundered: others said, An
30 angel spake to him. Jesus answered and said, ᵂThis voice came not
31 because of me, but for your sakes. Now is the judgment of this world:
32 now shall ˣthe prince of this world be cast out. And I, if I be lifted up
33 from the earth, will draw ʸall *men* unto me. (This he said, signifying what death he should die.)

A. D. 33.

ˢ 1 Thes 4. 17.
ᵗ Luke 12. 50.
   ch. 13. 21.
ᵘ Luke 22.53.
ᵛ 2 Pet. 1. 17.
ʷ ch. 11. 42.
ˣ Luke 10. 18.
   ch. 14. 30.
   ch. 16. 11.
   Acts 26. 18.
   2 Cor. 4. 4.
   Eph. 2. 2.
   Eph. 6. 12.
ʸ Rom. 5. 18.

Mysterious Agitation of Christ's Spirit in prospect of His Death—His Prayer in consequence, and the Answer to it—Jesus Interprets that Answer (27-36). **27. Now is my soul troubled.** He means, at the prospect of His death, just alluded to. Strange view of the Cross this, immediately after representing it as the hour of His glory! (*v.* 23.) But the two views naturally meet, and blend into one. It was the Greeks, one might say, that troubled Him:—'Ah! they shall see Jesus, but *to Him* it shall be a costly sight.' **and what shall I say?** He is in a strait betwixt two. The death of the Cross was, and could not but be, appalling to His soul. But to shrink from absolute subjection to the Father, was worse still. In asking Himself, "What shall I say?" He seems as if thinking aloud, feeling His way between two dread alternatives, looking both of them sternly in the face, measuring, weighing them, in order that the choice actually made might be seen, *and even by Himself be the more vividly felt,* to be a profound, deliberate, spontaneous election. **Father, save me from this hour**—To take this as a question, 'Shall I say, Father, save Me', &c.—as some eminent editors and interpreters do, is unnatural and jejune. It is a real petition, like that in Gethsemane, "Let this cup pass from Me;" only whereas *there* He prefaces the prayer with an "If it be possible," *here* He follows it up with what is tantamount to that—**but for this cause came I unto this hour.** The sentiment conveyed, then, by the prayer, in both cases, is two-fold: First, that only one thing could reconcile Him to the death of the Cross—its being His Father's will that He should endure it—and, next, that in this view of it He yielded Himself freely to it. He recoils, not from subjection to His Father's will, but to show how tremendous a self-sacrifice that obedience involved, He first asks the Father to save Him from it, and then signifies how perfectly He knows that He is there for the very purpose of enduring it. Only by letting these mysterious words speak their full meaning do they become intelligible and consistent. As for those who see *no bitter elements in the death of Christ*—nothing beyond mere dying—what can they make of such a scene? and when they place it over against the feelings with which thousands of His adoring followers have welcomed death for His sake, how can they hold Him up to the admiration of men? **28. Father, glorify thy name** —by some present testimony. **Then came there a voice from heaven, saying, I have both glorified it**—referring specially to the voice from heaven at His *Baptism,* and again at His *Transfiguration,* **and will glorify it again**—that is, in the yet future scenes of His still deeper necessity; although even this very promise was a present and sublime testimony, which would irradiate the clouded spirit of the Son of Man. **29. The people**—'the multitude' [ὄχλος] **therefore that stood by, and heard it, said**

424

that it thundered: others said, An angel spake —'hath spoken' [λελάληκεν] to him—some hearing only a sound; others an articulate, but to them unintelligible, voice. Our Lord now tells them for whom that voice from heaven had come, and then interprets, in a strain even more exalted than before, that "glorification of His name" which the voice announced was yet to take place. **30. Jesus answered, This voice came not because of me, but for your sakes**—[οὐ δι' ἐμὲ, ἀλλὰ δι' ὑμᾶς] —'not for My sake, but for your sakes:' probably to correct, in the first instance, the unfavourable impressions which His momentary agitation and mysterious prayer for deliverance may have produced on the beholders; and then to procure a more reverential ear for those sublime disclosures with which He was now to follow it up—disclosures which seem to have all at once dilated His own soul, for He utters them, it will be seen, in a kind of transport. **31. Now is the judgment of this world**—the world that "crucified the Lord of glory" (1 Cor. ii. 8), considered as a vast and complicated kingdom of Satan, breathing his spirit, doing his work, and involved in his doom, which Christ's death by its hands irrevocably sealed. **Now shall the prince of this world be cast out.** How differently is that fast-approaching "hour" regarded in the kingdoms of darkness and of light! 'The hour of relief from the dread Troubler of our peace—how near it is! Yet a little moment, and the day is ours!' So it was calculated and felt in the one region. "Now shall the prince of this world be cast out," is a somewhat different view of the same event. We know who was right. Though yet under a veil, He sees the triumphs of the Cross in unclouded and transporting light. **32. And I** [Κἀγὼ], **if I be lifted up from the earth, will draw all men unto me.** The "I" here is emphatic: I, in contrast with the world's ejected prince. "If lifted up," means not only *after that I have been lifted up,* but, *through the virtue of that Uplifting.* And does not the death of the Cross in all its significance, revealed in the light, and borne in upon the heart by the power, of the Holy Ghost, possess an attraction over the wide world—to civilized and savage, learned and illiterate alike—which breaks down all opposition, assimilates all to itself, and forms out of the most heterogeneous and discordant materials a kingdom of surpassing glory, whose uniting principle is adoring subjection "to Him that loved them"?—"Will draw all men 'ᴜɴᴛᴏ Mᴇ,'" says He [πρὸς ἐμαυτὸν], or 'to Myself,' as it might more properly be rendered. What lips could presume to utter such a word but His, which "dropt as an honeycomb," whose manner of speaking was evermore in the same spirit of conscious equality with the Father? **33. (This he said, signifying what death** [ποίῳ θανάτῳ]—rather, 'what kind'

34   The people answered him, [2] We have heard out of the law that Christ abideth for ever: and how sayest thou, The Son of man must be lifted up?

35   who is this Son of man? Then Jesus said unto them, Yet a little while [a] is the light with you. [b] Walk while ye have the light, lest darkness come upon you: for [c] he that walketh in darkness knoweth not whither

36 he goeth. While ye have light, believe in the light, that ye may be [d] the children of light. These things spake Jesus, and departed, and did hide himself from them.

37   But though he had done so many miracles before them, yet they

38 believed not on him: that the saying of Esaias the prophet might be fulfilled, which he spake, [e] Lord, who hath believed our report? and to

39 whom hath the arm of the Lord been revealed? Therefore they could

40 not believe, because that Esaias said again, He [f] hath blinded their eyes, and hardened their heart; that they should not see with *their* eyes, nor understand with *their* heart, and be converted, and I should heal them.

41 These things said Esaias, when [g] he saw his glory, and spake of him.

42 Nevertheless among the chief rulers also many believed on him; but because of the Pharisees they did not confess *him*, lest they should be

43 put out of the synagogue: for [h] they loved the praise of men more than the praise of God.

A. D. 33.
[2] 2 Sam 7.13.
Ps. 89. 30.
Ps. 110. 4.
Isa 9. 7.
Isa. 53. 8.
Ezek.37 25.
Dan 2. 44.
Mic. 4. 7.
[a] Isa. 42. 6.
ch. 1. 9.
ch 8. 12.
ch 9. 5.
[b] Jer. 13 16.
Eph. 5. 8.
[c] ch. 11. 10.
1 John 2.11.
[d] Luke 16. 8.
Eph. 5. 8.
1 Thes.5. 5.
[e] Isa. 53. 1.
Rom.10. 16.
[f] Isa 6. 9.
Matt.13.14.
[g] Isa. 6. 1.
[h] ch. 5. 44.

or 'manner of death' he should die)—that is, His being "lifted up from the earth" was meant to signify His being uplifted on the accursed tree (ch. iii. 14; viii. 28). **34. The people**—'The multitude' [ὄχλος] **answered him, We have heard out of the law**—meaning the Scriptures of the Old Testament: referring, no doubt, to such places as Ps. lxxxix. 28, 29; cx. 4; Dan. ii. 44; vii. 13, 14, **that Christ**—'the Christ,' the promised Messiah, **abideth for ever: and how sayest thou, The Son of man must be lifted up? who is this Son of man?** How can that consist with this "uplifting?"ν They saw very well both that He was holding Himself up as *the Christ*, and *a Christ to die a violent death;* and as that ran counter to all their ideas of the Messianic prophecies, they were glad to get this seeming advantage to justify their unyielding attitude. **35. Then**—'Therefore' **Jesus said unto them, Yet a little while is the light with you. Walk while ye have the light, lest darkness come upon you: for**—rather, 'and' [καὶ] **he that walketh in darkness knoweth not whither he goeth. 36. While ye have** ('the') **light, believe in the light, that ye may be the children of light.** Instead of answering their question, He warns them, with mingled majesty and tenderness, against trifling with their last brief opportunity, and entreats them to let in the Light while they had it in the midst of them, that themselves might be "light in the Lord." In this case all the clouds which hung around His Person and Mission would speedily be dispelled, while if they continued to hate the light, bootless were all His answers to their merely speculative or captious questions. (See on Luke xiii. 23.) **These things spake Jesus, and departed, and did hide himself from them.** He who spake as never man spake, and immediately after words fraught with unspeakable dignity and love, had to "hide Himself" from His auditors! What, then, must *they* have been? He retired probably to Bethany. (See Matt. xxi. 17; Luke xxi. 37.)

General Result of Christ's Ministry (37-43). It is the manner of our Evangelist alone, as has been frequently remarked, to record his own reflections on the scenes he describes: but here, having arrived at what was virtually the close of our Lord's public ministry, he casts an affecting glance over the fruitlessness of His whole ministry on the bulk of the now doomed people. **37. But though he had done so many miracles** [σημεῖα] **before them** —which were all but so many glorious "signs" of a Divine Hand in the doing of them, **yet they believed not on him: 38. That the saying of Esaias the prophet might be fulfilled, which he spake** (Isa. liii. 1), **Lord, who hath believed our report? and to whom hath the arm of the Lord been revealed?**—*q. d.*, 'This unbelief did not at all set aside the purposes of God, but, on the contrary, fulfilled them.' **39. Therefore they could not believe, because that Esaias said again** (Isa. vi. 9, 10), **40. He hath blinded their eyes, and hardened their heart; that they should not see with their eyes, nor understand with their heart, and be converted, and I should heal them.** That this expresses *a positive divine act*, by which those who wilfully close their eyes and harden their hearts against the truth are judicially *shut up* in their unbelief and impenitence, is admitted by all candid critics—*Olshausen*, for example—though many of them think it necessary to contend that this is no way inconsistent with the liberty of the human will, which of course it is not. **41. These things said Esaias, when he saw his glory, and spake of him.** A key of immense importance to the opening of Isaiah's vision (Isa. vi.), and all similar Old Testament representations. 'THE SON,' says *Olshausen*, 'is "The King Jehovah" who rules in the Old Testament and appears to the elect, as in the New Testament THE SPIRIT, the invisible Minister of the Son, is the Director of the Church and the Revealer in the sanctuary of the heart.' **42. Nevertheless among the chief rulers also** [καὶ ἐκ τῶν ἀρχόντων]—rather, 'even of the rulers,' such as Nicodemus and Joseph, **many believed on him; but because of the Pharisees**—that is, the *leaders* of this sect; for they were of it themselves **they did not confess** [him]—or 'confess it' [οὐχ ὡμολόγουν], did not make an open confession of their faith in Jesus, **lest they should be put out of the synagogue.** (See on ch. ix. 22, 34.) **43. For they loved the praise of men more than the praise of God.** A severe remark, as *Webster and Wilkinson* justly observe, considering that several at least of these persons afterwards boldly confessed Christ. It indicates the displeasure with which God regarded their con-

	A. D. 33.
44 Jesus cried and said, 'He that believeth on me, believeth not on me,	
45 but on him that sent me. And ʲhe that seeth me seeth him that sent	' Mark 9. 37.
	1 Pet. 1. 21.
46 me. I ᵏam come a light into the world, that whosoever believeth on me	ʲ ch. 14. 9.
47 should not abide in darkness. And if any man hear my words, and	ᵏ ch. 3. 19.
believe not, ˡI judge him not: for ᵐI came not to judge the world, but	ch. 8. 12.
	ch. 9. 5, 39.
48 to save the world. He ⁿthat rejecteth me, and receiveth not my words,	ˡ ch. 5. 45.
hath one that judgeth him: the °word that I have spoken, the same shall	ch. 8. 15.
49 judge him in the last day. For ᵖI have not spoken of myself; but the	ᵐ ch 3. 17.
Father which sent me, he gave me a commandment, what I should say,	ⁿ Luke 10.16.
	° Deut.18.19.
50 and what I should speak. And I know that his commandment is life	Mark 16.16.
everlasting: whatsoever I speak therefore, even as the Father said unto	ᵖ ch 8. 38.
me, so I speak.	ch. 14. 10.

duct at this time, and with which He continues to regard similar conduct.

Concluding Summary of our Lord's Public Teaching (44-50). **44.** Jesus ['I. δὲ]—rather, 'But Jesus' **cried**—expressive of the louder tone and peculiar solemnity with which He was wont to utter such great sayings as these (as ch. vii. 37). **and said.** This and the remaining verses of the chapter seem to be a supplementary record of some weighty proclamations, which, though recorded in substance already, had not been set down in so many words before; and they are introduced here as a sort of *summary and winding up* of His whole testimony. **He that believeth on me, believeth not on me, but on him that sent me. 45. And he that seeth me seeth him that sent me** [θεωρῶν–θεωρεῖ]—or 'beholdeth,' in the emphatic sense of ch. vi. 40. But what a saying is this! Even the Eleven, so late as at the Last Supper, were slow to apprehend the full reality of it (ch. xiv. 7-9). The glory of it they could but partially discern till Pentecostal light irradiated the Person and Mediation of Jesus in the eyes of His apostles. **46. I am come a light into the world, that whosoever believeth on me should not abide in darkness. 47. And if any man hear my words, and believe not** [πιστεύσῃ]. The true reading here, beyond doubt, is, 'and keep them not' [φυλάξῃ], **I judge him not: for I came not to judge the world, but to save the world.** See on ch. iii. 17. **48. He that rejecteth me, and receiveth not my words, hath one that judgeth him: the word that I have spoken, the same shall judge him in the last day.** This in substance will be found said repeatedly before. **49. For I have not spoken**—'spake not' [ἐλάλησα] **of** [ἐξ] **myself; but the Father which sent me, he gave me a commandment, what I should say, and what I should speak. 50. And I know that his commandment is life everlasting: whatsoever I speak therefore, even as the Father said**—or 'hath said' [εἴρηκε] **unto me, so I speak.** See on ch. viii. 28, 38, 47; and similar sayings, emphatically teaching what is here expressed in such terms of majestic dignity.

Remarks.—1. Once and again have we been led to consider what portion of this wonderful History most transcends the powers of human invention. And ever as we seem to have found it, some other portion rises to view and claims the preference. But certainly, of the present Section it may fearlessly be said that, to be *written*, it, at least, must of necessity first have been *real*. For who, sitting down to *frame* such a Life—or what is much the same in relation to powers of invention, to construct it out of a few fragments of fact—would have thought of meeting the desire of those Greeks to see Jesus with such an answer, taking no direct notice of it, but carrying His hearers into the future glorious issues of His death, yet couching even this in such enigmatic terms as to be

scarcely half intelligible to the best instructed of His own disciples? Or, if we are to suppose this possible, who would think of interrupting this strain by a sudden inward agitation of the Speaker arising from no outward cause, but the pure result of what was passing in His own mind; and not only so, but of His *telling* His uninstructed and prejudiced audience that His soul was then agitated, and, amidst conflicting emotions, that He was at a loss what to say; uttering an audible prayer to be saved from His dread approaching "hour," but yet adding that to go through with that hour was just what He had come to it for? Who would have ever put so apparently damaging a thing down in a work which he expected to make way for itself by nothing but *its naked truth?* And then, after the prayer for glorification, with the immediate answer to it, and the explanation of that answer—as if relieved in proportion to the previous sinking—who could have thrown such gleams of exalted, sublime transport into the utterances that follow, and on which only the subsequent history of Christendom has set the seal of full truth? And let it be borne in mind, that if the truth of the History here is thus self-attested, it is the History precisely *as it stands;* not 'the substance' or 'spirit of it'—as some now talk—but this Evangelical Record, just as it here stands; for *entire* it must stand, or fall entire. 2. On the bearing of this agitation of the Redeemer's spirit in the prospect of His "hour," of His prayer for deliverance from it, and yet His submission to it, upon the *penal* character of His sufferings and death, we need but refer the reader to the remarks on that feature of His Agony in the Garden—of which this scene was a kind of momentary anticipation. See on Luke xxii. 39-46. 3. How affecting is the intimation that, just after the utterance of one of the most solemn and compassionate warnings—holding out, almost for the last time, in that spot at least, the sceptre of mercy, but at the same time the danger of closing their eyes upon the Light yet shining on them—He "departed, and did hide himself from them!" What must have been the exasperation of His audience to render that necessary. The Evangelist himself seems saddened at the thought of it, and can find relief under it for himself and his believing readers only in the judicial blindness and hardness which they had been long before taught by prophecy to expect. Nor are those who, in analogous circumstances, have to hold up in vain the glory of Christ, and all day long to stretch out their hands to a disobedient and gainsaying people, precluded from finding the same sad relief; but on the contrary, with their adorable Master, they may confidently say to them that believe not—when conscious that they are pure from the blood of all men, having not shunned

13   NOW before the feast of the passover, when Jesus knew that his hour was come that he should depart out of this world unto the Father, having loved his own which were in the world, he loved them unto the 2 end. And supper being ended, (the *a*devil having now put into the 3 heart of Judas Iscariot, Simon's *son*, to betray him,) Jesus knowing *b*that

A. D. 33.

CHAP. 13.
a Luke 22. 3.
b ch. 3. 35.
ch. 17. 2.
Acts 2. 36.

to declare unto them all the counsel of God — "But I said unto you that ye have even seen Him, and believe not: All that the Father giveth Him *shall* come to Him, and him that cometh to Him He will in no wise cast out." 4. Though a timid policy on the part of real believers is often over-ruled to the getting in of some faint dissent and some feeble protest against extreme measures on the part of those enemies of it to whose society they still adhere—as in the case of Nicodemus and Joseph of Arimathæa—that timid policy itself is highly offensive to God, and injurious to their own spiritual growth, springing as it does from a greater concern to stand well with men than with God. 5. The eternal condition of all who have heard the Gospel, whatever other elements may be found to affect it, will be found essentially to turn on the state of their minds and hearts to-wards Christ—in the way either of cordial subjec-tion to Him or of disobedient rejection of Him. "He that is not with Me is against Me," will be the spirit of the decisions of "That Day" on all that have been brought within the pale of the Gospel.

CHAP. XIII. 1-38.—AT THE LAST SUPPER JESUS WASHES HIS DISCIPLES' FEET—THE DIS-COURSE ARISING THEREUPON, IN THE MIDST OF WHICH THE TRAITOR, BEING INDICATED, LEAVES THE SUPPER-ROOM—THE DISCOURSE RESUMED—PETER'S SELF-CONFIDENCE—HIS FALL PREDICTED. The record of our Lord's public ministry has now been concluded—in the First Three Gospels by a solemn leave-taking of the *Temple,* until then "His Father's House" and the centre of all the Church's solemnities; in this Fourth Gospel by an equally solemn leave-taking of the *People,* in whom until then God's visible kingdom had stood represented. We are now in the Supper-room; the circum-stances preparatory to which our Evangelist pre-sumes his readers to be already familiar with through the other Gospels. What passed in this Supper-room, as recorded in this and the four following chapters, has been felt by the Church in every age to be stamped with a heavenly and divine impress, beyond all else even in this most divine Gospel, if one may so speak, and the glory of which no language can express.

Jesus, at the Supper-Table, Washes His Disciples' Feet (1-11). **1. Now before the feast of the pass-over.** This raises the question whether our Lord ate the passover with His disciples *at all* the night before He suffered; and if so, whether He did so *on the same day* with other Jews or *a day earlier.* To this question we adverted in the Remarks prefixed to the exposition of Luke xxii. 7-13, where we expressed it as our unhesitating convic-tion that He did eat it, and on the same day with others. That the First Three Evangelists expressly state this, admits of no reasonable doubt; and it is only because of certain expressions in the Fourth Gospel that some able critics think them-selves bound to depart from that opinion. So *Greswell* and *Ellicott,* for example; while, among others, *Robinson, Wieseler,* and *Fairbairn* defend the opinion which we have expressed. Now, as this is the first of the passages in the Fourth Gospel which are thought to intimate that the "supper" which our Lord observed, if a pass-over at all, was "before the feast of the pass-

over," as regularly observed, let us see how that is to be met. One way of meeting it is by under-standing "the feast" here to mean, not the Pas-chal supper, but the seven days' "Feast of Un-leavened Bread"—which began on the 15th Nisan, and was ushered in by the eating of the Passover on the 14th. (See Num. xxviii. 16, 17.) So *Robinson.* In this case the difficulty indeed vanishes. But there is no need to resort to that explanation, which seems somewhat unnatural. Understanding the Evangelist to refer to the Pas-chal supper itself, the meaning seems to be, not '*a day* before the passover,' but simply that '*ere* the feast began,' Jesus made solemn preparation for doing at it what is about to be recorded. We know from the other Gospels what precise directions Jesus gave to two of His disciples about getting ready the passover in the large upper room ere He and the other ten left Bethany. (See on Luke xxii. 7-13.) And what deep thoughts on the subject were passing in the mind of our Lord Himself in connection with these arrangements, we are here very sublimely told by our Evangelist (*vv.* 1, 2). See also on Luke xxii. 14-16. The meaning, then, we take it, is simply this, that Jesus, when He proceeded to wash His disciples' feet during the Paschal supper, did so not only with great deliberation, but in conformity with purposes and arrangements "before the feast." So substantially *Stier* and *Fairbairn.* **when Jesus knew that his hour was come that he should depart out of this world unto the Father.** On such beautiful euphemistic allusions to the Redeemer's death, see on Luke ix. 31, 51. **having loved his own which were in the world, he loved them unto the end.** That is, on the edge of His last suf-ferings—when it might have been supposed that His own awful prospects would absorb all His attention—He was so far from forgetting "His own," who were to be left struggling "in the world," after He had "departed out of it to the Father" (ch. xvii. 11), that in His care for them He seemed scarce to think of Himself save in connec-tion with them. Herein is "love," not only endur-ing "to the end," but most affectingly manifested when, judging by a human standard, least to be expected. **2. And supper being ended** [γενομένου]. In this rendering our translators have followed *Luther* and *Beza,* but unfortunately, since from *v.* 26 it seems plain that the supper was not even then ended. The meaning either is, 'And sup-per being prepared,' or 'And supper going on.' So the same word is used, as *Alford* notices, in Matt. xxvi. 6, "While Jesus was in Bethany" [γενομένου], and in ch. xxi. 4, "when it was morning" [πρωΐας γενομένης]. [Of course, this must be the meaning if the reading γινομένου —in the present tense—be adopted, with *Tischen-dorf* and *Tregelles.* But the authority for it is scarcely so strong, we judge, as for the received reading, to which *Lachmann* adheres, and in which *Alford* concurs.]· (the devil having now [ἤδη]—or rather 'already' put into the heart of Judas Iscariot, Simon's son, to betray him)— referring to the compact he had *already* made with the chief priests (see on Mark xiv. 10, 11). **3. Jesus knowing that the Father had given all things into his hands, and that he was come from God, and went to God** [ἐξῆλθεν—ὑπάγει]

tbe Father had given all things into his hands, and that he was come

4 from God, and went to God; he ^criseth from supper, and laid aside his

5 garments; and took a towel, and girded himself. After that he poureth water into a bason, and began to wash the disciples' feet, and to wipe

6 *them* with the towel wherewith he was girded. Then cometh he to Simon Peter: and ¹Peter saith unto him, Lord, ^ddost thou wash my feet?

7 Jesus answered and said unto him, What I do thou knowest not now;

8 but thou shalt know hereafter. Peter saith unto him, Thou shalt never wash my feet. Jesus answered him, ^eIf I wash thee not, thou hast no

9 part with me. Simon Peter saith unto him, Lord, not my feet only, but

10 also *my* hands and *my* head. Jesus saith to him, ^fHe that is washed needeth not save to wash *his* feet, but is clean every whit: and ^gye are

11 clean, but not all. For he knew who should betray him; therefore said he, Ye are not all clean.

A. D. 33.
c Luke 22.27.
Phil. 2, 7, 8.
1 he.
d Matt. 3. 14.
e Ezek. 36.25.
ch. 3. 5.
1 Cor. 6. 11.
Eph. 5. 26.
Titus 3. 5.
Heb. 10. 22.
f Eccl. 7. 20.
Eph. 4. 22- 24.
Eph. 5. 26, 27.
1 Thes.5.23.
g ch. 15. 3.

—or 'came forth from God, and was going to God.' This verse is very sublime, and as a preface to what follows, were we not familiar with it, would fill us with a delightful wonder. An unclouded perception of His essential relation to the Father, the commission He held from Him, and His approaching Return to Him, possessed His soul. **4. He riseth from supper, and laid—** rather, 'layeth' [τίθησι] **aside his garments—** which would have impeded the operation of washing, **and took a towel, and girded himself—** assuming a servant's dress. **5. After that he poureth water into a—'the' bason, and began —or 'proceeded' to wash the disciples' feet.** Three different words are used in Greek to express 'washing,' in three different senses; and all three are used in the New Testament. The *first* [νίπτω—a late form of νίζω] signifies to wash a part of the body,' as the *hands* (Mark vii. 3) and the *feet*. This accordingly is the word used here, and five other times in the verses following, of the washing of the feet. The *second* [λούω, λούεσθαι] signifies to 'wash the whole body,' as in a bath; to *bathe.* This accordingly is the word warily used in *v.* 10, of the washing of the entire person. The *third* [πλύνω] signifies to 'wash *clothes.*' This accordingly is used in Rev. vii. 14— "These are they that washed [ἔπλυναν] their robes;" and in ch. xxii. 14, according to what appears the true reading—" Blessed are they that wash their robes [οἱ πλύνοντες τὰς στολὰς αὐτῶν], &c. The importance of distinguishing the first two will appear when we come to *v.* 10. **and to wipe them with the towel wherewith he was girded.** *Beyond all doubt the feet of Judas were washed,* as of all the rest. **6. Then cometh he to Simon Peter: and Peter saith unto him, Lord, dost thou wash my feet?** Our language cannot bring out the intensely vivid contrast between the "*Thou*" [σὺ] and the "*my*" [μου], which by bringing them together the original expresses. But every word of this question is emphatic. Thus far, and in the question itself, there was nothing but the most profound and beautiful astonishment at a condescension to him quite incomprehensible. Accordingly, though there can be no doubt that already Peter's heart rebelled against it as a thing not to be borne, Jesus ministers no rebuke as yet, but only bids him wait a little, and he should understand it all. **7. Jesus answered and said unto him, What I do thou knowest not now:**—*q. d.,* 'Such condescension *does* need explanation; it *is* fitted to astonish;' **but thou shalt know hereafter** [μετὰ ταῦτα]—lit., 'after these things,' meaning 'presently;' although viewed as a general maxim, applicable to all dark sayings in

God's word, and dark doings in God's providence, these words are full of consolation. **8. Peter saith unto him, Thou shalt never wash—** more emphatically, 'Never shalt thou wash' **my feet:**—*q. d.,* 'That is an incongruity to which I can never submit.' How like the man! **Jesus answered him, If I wash thee not, thou hast no part with me.** What Peter could not submit to was, that the Master should serve His servant. But the whole saving work of Christ was one continued series of such services, only ending with and consummated by the most self-sacrificing and transcendent of all services: "THE SON OF MAN CAME not to be ministered unto, but TO MINISTER, AND TO GIVE HIS LIFE A RANSOM FOR MANY." (See on Mark x. 45.) If Peter, then, could not submit to let his Master go down so low as to wash his feet, *how should he suffer himself to be served*—and so saved—*by Him at all?* This is couched under the one pregnant word "wash," which though applicable to the *lower* operation which Peter resisted, is the familiar scriptural symbol of that *higher* cleansing, which Peter little thought he was at the same time virtually putting from him. It is not humility to refuse what the Lord deigns to do for us, or to deny what He has done, but it is self-willed presumption—not rare, however, in those inner circles of lofty religious profession and traditional spirituality, which are found wherever Christian truth has enjoyed long and undisturbed possession. The truest humility is to receive reverentially, and thankfully to own, the gifts of grace. **9. Simon Peter saith unto him, Lord, not my feet only, but also my hands and my head:**— *q. d.,* 'To be severed from Thee, Lord, is death to me: If that be the meaning of my speech, I tread upon it; and if to be washed of Thee have such significance, then not my feet only, but hands, head, and all, be washed!' This artless expression of clinging, life-and-death attachment to Jesus, and felt dependence upon Him for his whole spiritual well-being, compared with the similar saying in ch. vi. 68, 69 (on which see exposition), furnishes such evidence of *historic verity* as no thoroughly honest mind can resist. **10. Jesus saith to him, He that is washed** [λελουμένος]— not in the *partial* sense denoted by the word used for the washing of the *feet,* but in the complete sense denoted by the word here used, signifying to *wash the entire person; as* if we should render it, 'be that is bathed:' **needeth not**—to be *so* washed any more; needeth no *such* washing a second time. **save to wash** [νίψασθαι] **his feet**—that is, 'needeth to do no more than wash his feet;' the former word being now resumed. **but is clean every whit** [καθαρὸς ὅλος]—'clean as a whole,' or entirely clean. This

12　So after he had washed their feet, and had taken his garments, and was set down again, he said unto them, Know ye what I have done to you? 13, Ye *[h]* call me Master and Lord: and ye say well; for *so* I am.   If *[i]* I then, 14 *your* Lord and Master, have washed your feet, *[j]* ye also ought to wash 15 one another's feet.   For *[k]* I have given you an example, that ye should 16 do as I have done to you.   Verily, *[l]* verily, I say unto you, The servant is not greater than his lord; neither he that is sent greater than he that 17 sent him.   If *[m]* ye know these things, happy are ye if ye do them.

18　I speak not of you all: *[n]* I know whom I have chosen: but, that the scripture may be fulfilled, *[o]* He that eateth bread with me hath lifted 19 up his heel against me.   *[2]* Now I tell you before it come, that, when it 20 is come to pass, ye may believe that I am *he*.   Verily, *[p]* verily, I say unto you, He that receiveth whomsoever I send receiveth me; and he that receiveth me receiveth him that sent me.

21　When *[q]* Jesus had thus said, *[r]* he was troubled in spirit, and testified, and said, Verily, verily, I say unto you, That *[s]* one of you shall betray

A. D. 33.
[h] Luke 6. 46.
1 Cor. 8. 6.
1 Cor. 12. 3.
Phil. 2. 11.
[i] Luke 22.27.
[j] Rom.12. 10.
Gal. 6. 1.
1 Pet. 5. 5.
[k] Phil. 2. 5.
1 Pet. 2. 21.
[l] Luke 6. 40.
[m] Jas. 1. 25.
[n] 2 Tim.2. 19.
[o] Ps 41. 9.
[2] hence-forth.
[p] Luke 10.16.
[q] Luke 22.21.
[r] ch. 12. 27.
[s] Acts 1. 17.

sentence is singularly instructive. Of the *two cleansings*, the one points to that which takes place at the *commencement* of the Christian life, embracing *complete absolution from sin as a guilty state*, and *entire deliverance from it as a polluted life* (Rev. i. 5; 1 Cor. vi. 11)—or, in the language of theology, *Justification* and *Regeneration*. This cleansing is effected *once for all*, and is never repeated. The other cleansing, described as that of "the feet," is such, for example, as one walking from a bath quite cleansed still needs, in consequence of his contact with the earth. (Compare Exod. xxx. 18, 19.) It is the *daily* cleansing which we are taught to seek, when in the spirit of adoption we say, "Our Father which art in heaven—*forgive us our debts;*" and, when burdened with the sense of manifold shortcomings—as what tender heart of a Christian is not?—is it not a relief to be permitted thus to wash our feet after a day's contact with the earth? This is not to call in question the completeness of our past justification. Our Lord, while graciously insisting on washing Peter's feet, refuses to extend the cleansing farther, that the symbolical instruction intended to be conveyed might not be marred. **and ye are clean**—in the first and *whole* sense, **but not all** [ἀλλ' οὐχὶ πάντες]—'yet not all;' **11. For, &c.** A very important statement; as showing that Judas—instead of being at first as true-hearted a disciple as the rest, and merely *falling away* afterwards, as many represent it—*never experienced that cleansing at all which made the others what they were.*

Discourse Explanatory of this Washing (12-17). **12. So after he had washed their feet, and had taken his garments, and was set down again, he said unto them, Know ye what I have done to you?**—that is, 'Know ye the intent of it?' The question, however, was not intended to draw forth an answer, but, like many other of our Lord's questions, to summon their attention to His own answer. **13. Ye call me Master and Lord** [ὁ διδάσκαλος καὶ ὁ Κύριος]—'Teacher and Lord;' *learning* of Him in the one capacity, *obeying* Him in the other: **and ye say well; for so I am.** The conscious dignity with which this claim is made is remarkable, following immediately on His laying aside the towel of service. Yet what is this whole history but a succession of such astonishing contrasts from first to last? **14. If I then, your Lord and Master, have washed your feet**—O ye *servants*, **ye also**—who are but fellow-servants, **ought to wash one another's feet**—not in the narrow sense of a literal washing, profanely caricatured by Popes and Emperors, but by

the very humblest *real* services one to another. **15. For I have given you an example, that ye should do as I have done to you. 16. Verily, verily, I say unto you, The servant is not greater than his lord; neither he that is sent greater than he that sent him.** An oft-repeated saying (see on Matt. x. 24). **17. If ye know these things, happy are ye if ye do them.** A hint that even among real Christians the *doing* of such things would come lamentably short of the *knowing*.

The Traitor is now Indicated (18-27). **18. I speak not of you all**—the "happy *are* ye," of *v*. 17, being on no supposition applicable to Judas. **I know whom I have chosen**—in the *higher* sense: **but, that the scripture may be fulfilled:**—*q. d.*, 'Wonder not that one has been introduced into your number who is none of Mine: it is by no accident: there is no mistake; it is just that he might fulfil his predicted destiny.' **He that eateth bread with me**—"that did eat of *my bread*" (Ps. xli. 9), as one of My family; admitted to the nearest familiarity of discipleship and of social life, **hath lifted up his heel against me**—turned upon Me, adding *insult* to injury. (Compare Heb. x. 29.) In the Psalm the immediate reference is to Ahithophel's treachery against David (2 Sam. xvii.); one of those scenes in which the parallel of his story with that of his great Antitype is exceedingly striking. 'The eating bread,' says *Stier* (with whom, as with others who hold that Judas partook of the Lord's Supper, we agree), derives a fearful meaning from the participation in the sacramental Supper, a meaning which must be applied for ever to all unworthy communicants, as well as to all betrayers of Christ who eat the bread of His Church.' **19. Now** [Ἀπ' ἄρτι]—rather, 'From henceforth' **I tell you before it come** —consider yourselves as from this time forewarned, **that, when it is come to pass**—instead of being staggered, **ye may believe that I am he** —rather, confirmed in your faith: and indeed this did come to pass when they deeply needed such confirmation. **20. Verily, verily, I say unto you, He that receiveth whomsoever I send receiveth me; and he that receiveth me receiveth him that sent me.** See on Matt. x. 40. The connection here seems to be that despite the dishonour done to him by Judas, and similar treatment awaiting themselves, they were to be cheered by the assurance that their office, even as His own, was divine. **21. When Jesus had thus said, he was troubled in spirit, and testified, and said, Verily, verily, I say unto you, That one of you shall betray me.** The

22 me. Then the disciples looked one on another, doubting of whom he
23 spake. Now 'there was leaning on Jesus' bosom one of his disciples,
24 whom Jesus loved. Simon Peter therefore beckoned to him, that he
25 should ask who it should be of whom he spake. He then lying on Jesus'
26 breast saith unto him, Lord, who is it? Jesus answered, He it is to
     whom I shall give a ³sop, when I have dipped *it*. And when he had
27 dipped the sop, he gave *it* to Judas Iscariot, *the son* of Simon. And
     "after the sop Satan entered into him. Then said Jesus unto him, That
28 thou doest, do quickly. Now no man at the table knew for what intent
29 he spake this unto him. For some *of them* thought, ᵛbecause Judas had
     the bag, that Jesus had said unto him, Buy *those things* that we have
     need of against the feast; or, that he should give something to the poor.

A. D. 33.
ᵗ 2 Sam. 12. 3.
ch. 1. 18.
ch. 19. 56.
ch. 20. 2.
ch. 21. 7.
³ Or,
morsel.
Ex. 12. 8.
ᵘ Ps. 109. 6.
Mark 12. 45.
Luke 22. 3.
ch. 6. 70.
Acts 5. 3.
ᵛ ch. 13. 6.

announcement of *v*. 18 seems not to have been plain enough to be quite apprehended, save by the traitor himself. He will therefore speak it out in terms not to be misunderstood. But how much it cost Him to do this, appears from the "trouble" that came over His "spirit"—visible emotion, no doubt—before He got it uttered. What wounded susceptibility does this disclose, and what exquisite delicacy in His social intercourse with the Twelve, to whom He cannot, without an effort, break the subject! **22. Then the disciples looked one on another, doubting**—or 'being in doubt' **of whom he spake.** Further intensely interesting particulars are given in the other Gospels. First, "They were exceeding sorrowful" (Matt. xxvi. 22). Second, "They began to enquire among themselves which of them it was that should do this thing" (Luke xxii. 23). Third, "They began to say unto Him one by one, Is it I? and another, Is it I?" (Mark xiv. 19). Generous, simple hearts! They abhorred the thought, but, instead of putting it on others, each was only anxious to purge *himself*, and know if *he* could be the wretch. Their putting it at once to Jesus Himself, as knowing doubtless who was to do it, was the best, as it certainly was the most spontaneous and artless, evidence of their own innocence. Fourth, Jesus—apparently while this questioning was going on—added, "The Son of Man goeth as it is written of Him: but woe unto that man by whom the Son of Man is betrayed! it had been good for that man if he had not been born" (Matt. xxvi. 24). Fifth, "Judas," *last of all*, "answered and said, *Lord, Is it I?*" evidently feeling that when all were saying this, if he were to hold his peace, that of itself would draw suspicion upon him. To prevent this the question is wrung out of him, but perhaps, amidst the stir and excitement at the table, in a half-suppressed tone—as we are inclined to think the answer also was—"Thou hast said" (Matt. xxvi. 25), or possibly by little more than a sign; for from *v*. 28, below, it is evident that till the moment when he went out he was not openly discovered. **23. Now there was leaning on Jesus' bosom** [ἀνακείμενος]—that is, next Him at the table, and so "on" or 'in His bosom' [ἐν τῷ κόλπῳ] **one of his disciples, whom Jesus loved.** As Jesus certainly loved all the Eleven, this must mean a peculiar, dear love which Jesus had for John. (Compare ch. xi. 3, 4, of Lazarus.) Once and again does our Evangelist thus denote himself. Doubtless it was on account of this love that Jesus placed him next to Himself—in His own bosom—at the table. But it is alluded to here to explain the facility which he had, from his position, of asking his Lord quietly whom He meant. **24. Simon Peter therefore beckoned** 'beckoneth' [νεύει] **to him, that he should ask who it should**—or 'might' **be of whom he spake.** Perhaps Peter reclined at the corresponding place on the other side of Jesus. **25. He**

then lying [ἐπιπεσὼν]—'leaning over' or 'leaning back' **on Jesus' breast, saith unto him**—evidently *in a whisper*, **Lord, who is it? 26. Jesus answered** —'answereth,' clearly also *inaudibly*; the answer being conveyed probably from behind to Peter by John. **He it is to whom I shall give a sop** [τὸ ψωμίον]—rather, 'the sop' **when I have dipped it** —meaning a piece of the bread soaked in the wine or the sauce of the dish; one of the ancient ways of testifying peculiar regard. Compare *v*. 18, "*He that eateth bread with me*." **And when he had dipped the sop, he gave**—or 'giveth' [δίδωσιν] **it to Judas Iscariot, the son of Simon.** Thus the sign of Judas' treachery was an affecting expression, and the last, of the Saviour's wounded love! **27. And after the sop Satan** [τότε]—'then' or 'straightway Satan' **entered into him.** Very solemn are these brief hints of the successive steps by which Judas reached the climax of his guilt. "The devil had already put it into his heart to betray his Lord." Yet who can tell what struggles he went through ere he brought himself to carry that suggestion into effect? Even after this, however, his compunctions were not at an end. With the thirty pieces of silver already in his possession, he seems still to have quailed—and can we wonder? When Jesus stooped to wash his feet, it may be the last struggle was reaching its crisis. But that word of the Psalm, about "one that did eat of His bread who would lift up his heel against Him," probably all but turned the dread scale, and the still more explicit announcement, that one of those sitting with Him at the table should betray Him, would beget the thought, 'I am detected; it is now too late to draw back.' At that moment the sop is given, by which offer of friendship was once more made—and how affectingly! But already "Satan has *entered into him*," and though the Saviour's act might seem enough to recall him even yet, hell is now in his bosom, and he says within himself, 'The die is cast; now let me go through with it; fear, begone!' See on Mark xiv. 1-11, Remark 8 at the close of that Section; also on Luke xi. 24-26. *The Traitor Leaves the Supper-Room* (27-30). **27. Then said**—'saith' [λέγει] **Jesus unto him, That thou doest, do quickly:**—*q. d.*, 'Why linger here? This is not the place for thee; thy presence here is a restraint to us and to thee alike; thy work stands still; thou hast already the wages of iniquity—go work for them.' **28. Now no man at the table knew for what intent he spake this unto him. 29. For some of them thought, because Judas had the bag, that Jesus had said unto him, Buy those things that we have need of against the feast; or, that he should give something to the poor.** A very important statement, showing how carefully Jesus had kept the secret, and Judas his hypocrisy, to the last. **30. He then having received the sop went immediately out—**

30 He then having received the sop went immediately out: and it was night.

31   Therefore, when he was gone out, Jesus said, Now is the Son of man

32 glorified, and [w]God is glorified in him. If [x]God be glorified in him, God shall also glorify him in himself, and shall straightway glorify him.

33 Little children, yet a little while I am with you. Ye shall seek me: and as I said unto the Jews, Whither I go, ye cannot come; so now I

34 say to you. A [y]new commandment I give unto you, That ye love one

35 another; as I have loved you, that ye also love one another. By this shall all *men* know that ye are my disciples, if ye have [z]love one to another.

36   Simon Peter said unto him, Lord, whither goest thou? Jesus answered him, Whither I go, thou canst not follow me now; but [a]thou shalt

37 follow me afterwards. Peter said unto him, Lord, why cannot I follow

A. D. 33.

[w] ch 14. 13.
1 Pet. 4. 11
[x] ch. 17. 1.
[y] Lev. 19. 13.
Gal 6. 2.
Eph. 5. 2.
1 Thes. 4. 9.
Jas. 2. 8.
1 Pet. 1. 22.
1 John 2. 7.
1 John 3. 11.
1 John 4.21.
2 John 5.
[z] Acts 2. 46.
[a] ch 21. 18.
2 Pet. 1. 14.

thus, by his own act and deed, severing himself *for ever* from that holy society with which he never had any spiritual sympathy: **and it was night**—but far blacker night in the soul of Judas than in the sky over his head.

Relieved of the Traitor's Presence, the Discourse is Resumed (31-35). **31. Therefore, when he was gone out, Jesus said**—'saith' [λέγει], **Now is the Son of man glorified.** These remarkable words plainly imply that up to this moment our Lord had spoken *under a painful restraint;* the presence of a traitor within the little circle of His holiest fellowship on earth preventing the free and full outpouring of His heart. This is evident, indeed, from those oft-recurring clauses, "Ye are not all clean," "I speak not of you all," &c. "Now" the restraint is removed, and the embankment which kept in the mighty volume of living waters having broken down, they burst forth in a torrent which only ceases on His leaving the Supper-room and entering on the next stage of His great work—the scene in the Garden. But with what words is the silence first broken on the departure of Judas? By no reflections on the traitor, and, what is still more wonderful, by no reference to the dread character of His own approaching sufferings. He does not even name them, save by announcing, as with a burst of triumph, that the hour of His *glory* has arrived! And what is very remarkable, in five brief clauses He repeats this word "glorify" *five times*, as if to His view a coruscation of glories played at that moment about the Cross. (See on ch. xii. 23.) **and God is glorified in him**—the glory of each reaching its zenith in the death of the Cross! **32. If God be glorified in him, God shall also**—in return and reward of this highest of all services ever rendered to Him, or capable of being rendered, **glorify him in himself, and shall straightway glorify him**—referring now to the Son's Resurrection and Exaltation *after* this service was over, including all the honour and glory then put upon Him, and that will for ever encircle Him as Head of the new creation. **33. Little children** [Τεκνία]. From the height of His own glory He now descends, with sweet pity, to His "little children," *all now His own.* This term of endearment, nowhere else used in the Gospels, and once only employed by Paul (Gal. iv. 19), is appropriated by the beloved disciple himself, who no fewer than seven times employs it in his first Epistle. **yet a little while I am with you. Ye shall seek me**—shall feel the want of Me: **and as I said unto the Jews** (ch. vii. 34; viii. 21). A remarkable word this here—"the Jews." The Eleven were all themselves Jews. But now that He and they were on a higher footing, He leaves the name to those who were *Jews, and nothing but Jews.* **Whither I go, ye cannot come; so now I**

say to you. But, O, in what a different sense! **34. A new commandment I give unto you, That ye love one another; as**—'even as' [καθὼς] I **have loved you, that ye also love one another.** This was the *new* feature of it. Christ's love to His people in giving His life a ransom for them was altogether new, and consequently as a Model and Standard for theirs to one another. It is not, however, something transcending the great moral law, which is "the *old* commandment" (1 John ii. 7; and see on Mark xii. 28-33), but that law *in a new and peculiar form.* Hence it is said to be both *new* and *old* (1 John ii. 7, 8). **35. By this shall all men know that ye are my disciples**—the disciples of Him who laid down His life for those He loved. **if ye have love one to another**—for My sake, and as one in Me; for to *such* love men outside the circle of believers know right well that they are entire strangers. Alas, how little of it there is even within this circle!

Peter, Protesting his Readiness to follow his Master, though it should be to Death, is Forewarned of his shameful Fall (36-38). **36. Simon Peter said**—'saith' [λέγει] **unto him**—seeing plainly, in these directions how to behave themselves, that He was indeed going from them, **Lord, whither goest thou?**—having hardly a glimmering of the real truth. **Jesus answered him, Whither I go, thou canst not follow me now; but thou shalt follow me afterwards.** How different this from what He said to the Jews, "Whither I go, *ye cannot come*" (ch. viii. 21). **37. Peter said**—'saith' unto him, **Why cannot I follow thee now? I will lay down my life for thy sake** [ὑπὲρ σοῦ]—**'for Thee.'** He seems now to see that it was *death* Christ referred to as what would sever Him from them, but is not staggered at following Him thither. Dear soul! It was thy heart's true and conscious affection for thy Master that prompted this speech, rash and presumptuous though it was. **38. Jesus answered him, Wilt thou lay down thy life for my sake?** [ὑπὲρ Ἐμοῦ]—'for Me?' In this repetition of Peter's words there is deep though affectionate irony; and this Peter himself would feel for many a day after his recovery, as he retraced the painful particulars. **Verily, verily, I say unto thee, The cock shall not crow, till thou hast denied me thrice.** See on Luke xxii. 31-34.

Remarks.—1. Among the unique features of this wonderful History, none is more remarkable than the union in the Lord Jesus of a perfect *foresight* of the future, entire preparedness for it, and a calm expectation of it, but yet a certain *freshness* of feeling which unforeseen events awaken in others. He comes into every scene, and holds intercourse with all classes, fully cognizant of every movement for and against Him, and with all hearts open to His gaze. And yet His own movements are so per-

38 thee now? I will *b*lay down my life for thy sake. Jesus answered him, Wilt thou lay down thy life for my sake? Verily, verily, I say unto thee, The cock shall not crow, till thou hast denied me thrice.

A. D. 33.

b Luke 22. :3.
Fro. 16. 18.

fectly natural and manifestly human, that men have difficulty in believing the lofty things which He says of Himself, and all that is said and done in His presence awakens His sensibilities just as if it took Him as much by surprise as it would any other man. Look at this very chapter. With exalted Self-possession He rises from supper, girds Himself with the towel of service, pours water into a basin, and proceeds to wash His disciples' feet—all in the exercise of an eternal and unchanging love, and in furtherance of plans of action laid from the beginning. But see, on the other hand, how naturally each incident and saying at the Supper-table gives rise to another, and the whole susceptibilities of that tender Heart are awakened by the painful disclosures which had to be made, and become keener when the moment arrives for being quite plain. Peter's hesitation first, and then positive refusal, to be washed by his blessed Master had led to a hint how fatal that resolution would be to him in relation to the higher washing. Peter, who had never thought of that, is now all eagerness to be washed in every sense of the word; but he is told that he needs it not, having gotten that already, and so become "clean every whit"—as his fellows at the table with him also were. But the presence of the traitor stifled the word "all," and shaped it into "Ye are clean—but *not all*." Still, as if loath to break it to them too abruptly, and as they evidently failed to catch the precise import of His hint, He proceeds to open up to them His design in washing their feet, holding this up as a high example of that self-denying humility and mutual service by which He expected them to be distinguished before the world. But this again brought up before His mind the dark shadow of the deed about to be done against Him, and the man that was to do it, sitting with Him at the table, and by his presence interrupting, beyond longer endurance, the free flow of His gracious speech during the brief space they were to be together. Now, therefore, He will come nearer to the point and hasten his exit. "I speak not of you all: I know whom I have chosen: but, that the scripture may be fulfilled, He that eateth bread with me hath lifted up his heel against me. Now I tell you before it come, that, when it is come to pass, ye may believe that I am He." And yet, even after He has come this length, He seems to pause; and, as if trying to throw off the unwelcome subject for a moment, He resumes what He had broken off—the lofty mission on which He was sending them forth —"Verily, verily, I say unto you, He that receiveth whomsoever I send receiveth Me; and he that receiveth Me receiveth Him that sent Me." So manifestly is this a resumption of the former subject, that if *vv.* 18, 19 were enclosed in a parenthesis, it would seem not to have been interrupted at all, save by a side hint. But the time for hints is past, and the moment for explicit disclosure has come. No doubt, the last hint— about one eating of His bread who was to lift up his heel against Him—was too plain not to pain the whole Eleven, and almost prevent them listening to anything else. Jesus, therefore, come to a point, will speak to them no more enigmatically. But mark the emotion which precedes the explicit announcement that there is a traitor at the table. "When Jesus had thus said, He was troubled in spirit, and testified, and said"—as if the utterance was almost choked, and the thing would hardly

come out—"Verily, verily, I say unto you, One of you shall betray Me." What we wish to notice here is, that while all is manifestly naked and open beforehand to Him who calmly directed and lovingly presided at this Supper, His quick susceptibilities are kindled, and His heart's deepest emotions are stirred, when He has in naked terms to announce the deed of horror. In short, we have here Divine intelligence and warm Human feeling, so entirely in harmony in one and the same Person, and in every part of one and the same scene, as proclaim their own historic reality beyond all the powers of human invention to imitate. Nor is it the mere facts here presented to us, but the very form and pressure of them, that bear the stamp of manifest truth; so much so, that it is to us inconceivable how, even with the facts before him, they could have been so conveyed by the Evangelist as they are here, save on one explanation—"When the Comforter is come, He shall teach you all things, and bring all things to your remembrance, whatsoever I said unto you" (ch. xiv. 26). To continue this line of remark here were needless. But we cannot refrain from alluding to the *freedom* which Jesus seemed to breathe the moment that the traitor made his exit, and at the same time the sublime transport with which His all-embracing Eye saw in that movement His virtual elevation to glory through the Cross— "Now is the Son of Man glorified, and God is glorified in Him"! On every view of it but one this is inexplicable. That perfect combination of the Divine and the Human in the Subject of this History, which to have been written must have been real —that, and that alone, explains all. 2. How affecting is the contrast between the example here exhibited and the prevailing spirit of Christendom in almost every age of its history! At the most touching period of His intercourse with them—when He was with them for the last time—the Master descends to the position and the offices of a servant to His servants; doing for them the humblest of services: and this in order to exemplify in His own Person what He expected them to be and to do to one another in all succeeding time. To give this the more weight, He holds up the difference between Himself and them. Being themselves but servants, it was no great thing for *them* to serve one another. But if the Master voluntarily went down to that position, much more should they, in whose case to serve was no descent at all below their rightful dignity, but only making full proof of their proper calling. Alas, for the fruit! The pride of the clergy, how early did it blossom, and how proverbial has it become, and, as if to make this all the more noticeable, the language and the forms of humility and service have kept bitter pace with the palpable absence of the reality. How could such ministers teach and beget humility and lovingkindness in the Christian people? Some noble examples, both of ministers and people, are on record; and many, many, doubtless, there have been and are which will never be recorded. But the full and all-impressive manifestation of that humility which minds not high things, but condescends to men of low estate, and that love which lives for others, and thinks no service too mean which ministers to the comfort and well-being of the least of Christ's "brethren," is yet to come—when, "by this shall all men know that we are Christ's disciples, because we have love one to

432

14 LET not your heart be troubled: ye believe in God, believe also in me.

2 In *"my Father's house are many mansions: if *it were* not *so,* I would

3 have told you. *b*I go to prepare a place for you. And if I go and pre-

pare a place for you, I *c*will come again, and receive you unto myself;

that *d*where I am, *there* ye may be also.

4, 5 And whither I go ye know, and the way ye know. Thomas saith

A. D. 33.

CHAP. 14.

a 2 Cor. 5. 1.

Rev. 3. 12,

21.

b ch. 13. 33.

c Acts 1. 11.

d 1 Thes. 4 17.

another." The Lord hasten it in its time! 3. It is of immense consequence to the liberty and strength of Christians to be assured of their standing among the "washed" disciples of the Lord Jesus—the "clean every whit;" instead of having to be ever *trying* to get this length, ever settling that point, and thus all their lifetime subject to bondage. But the opposite error is equally to be eschewed, of supposing that when this point *is* settled, and that standing is attained, we have no more sin needing to be pardoned, no defilement to be washed away. This, we take it, is just what our Evangelist alludes to in his first Epistle, when he says, "If we say that we have no sin"—that is, as we understand it, If we say that being now clean every whit we have quite done with sinning—"we deceive ourselves, and the truth is not in us." On the difference between this statement and the similar one that follows—"If we say that we have not sinned, we make Him a liar, and His word is not in us"—see on 1 John i. 8, 10. On the warning here given to Peter, and the way in which he received it, see on Luke xxii. 31-34, Remark 3 at the end of that Section.

CHAP. XIV. 1-31.—DISCOURSE AT THE TABLE AFTER SUPPER. 'We now come,' says *Olshausen* admirably, 'to that portion of the Evangelical History which we may with propriety call its *Holy of Holies.* Our Evangelist, like a consecrated priest, alone opens up to us the view into this sanctuary. It is the record of the last moments spent by the Lord in the midst of His disciples before His passion, when words full of heavenly thought flowed from His sacred lips. All that His heart, glowing with love, had still to say to His friends, was compressed into this short season. At first the intercourse took the form of conversation; sitting at table, they talked familiarly together. But when the repast was finished, the language of Christ assumed a loftier strain; the disciples, assembled around their Master, listened to the words of life, and seldom spoke a word. At length, in the Redeemer's sublime intercessory prayer, His full soul was poured forth in express petitions to His heavenly Father on behalf of those who were His own. It is a peculiarity of these last chapters, that they treat almost exclusively of the most profound relations—as that of the Son to the Father, and of both to the Spirit; that of Christ to the Church, of the Church to the world, and so forth. Moreover, a considerable portion of these sublime communications surpassed the point of view to which the disciples had at that time attained: hence the Redeemer frequently repeats the same sentiments in order to impress them more deeply upon their minds, and, because of what they still did not understand, points them to the Holy Spirit, who would remind them of all His sayings, and lead them into all truth.'

The Confidence to be reposed in Christ during His Absence, and the loving Design of His Second Coming (1-3). **1. Let not your heart be troubled.** What myriads of souls have not these opening words cheered, in deepest gloom, since first they were uttered! **ye believe in God, believe also in me** [πιστεύετε εἰς τὸν Θεόν, καὶ εἰς ἐμὲ πιστεύετε]. This may with equal correctness be ren-

dered four different ways. 1. As two imperatives —'Believe in God, and believe in Me.' (So *Chrysostom,* and several both Greek and Latin Fathers; *Lampe, Bengel, de Wette, Lücke, Tholuck, Meyer, Stier, Alford.*) But this, though the interpretation of so many, we must regard, with *Webster and Wilkinson,* as somewhat frigid. 2. As two indicatives—'Ye believe in God, and ye believe in Me.' So *Luther,* who gives it this turn—'If ye believe in God, then do ye also believe in Me.' But this is pointless. 3. The first imperative and the second indicative; but to make sense of this, we must give the second clause a future turn— 'Believe in God, and then ye will believe in Me.' To this *Olshausen* half inclines. But how unnatural this is, it is hardly necessary to say. 4. The first indicative and the second imperative, as in our version—'Ye believe in God, believe also in Me.' (So the *Vulgate, Maldonat, Erasmus, Calvin, Beza*—who, however, gives the first clause an interrogatory turn, 'Believe ye in God? Believe also in Me'—*Cranmer's* and the *Geneva* English versions, *Olshausen* prevailingly, *Webster and Wilkinson.*) This alone appears to us to bring out the natural and worthy sense—'Ye believe in God, as do all His true people, and the confidence ye repose in Him is the soul of all your religious exercises, actings and hopes: Well, *repose the same trust in Me.*' What a demand this to make, by one who was sitting familiarly with them at the same Supper-table! But it neither alienates our trust from its proper Object, nor divides it with a creature: it is but *the concentration of our trust in the Unseen and Impalpable One upon His Own Incarnate Son,* by which that trust, instead of the distant, unsteady and too often cold and scarce real thing it otherwise is, acquires a conscious reality, warmth, and power, which makes all things new. *This is Christianity in brief.* 2. **In my Father's house are many mansions**—and so, room for all and a place for each: **if it were not so, I would have told you**—and not have deceived you all this time. **I go**—or, according to what is undoubtedly the true reading, 'because I go' **to prepare a place for you** [ὅτι before πορεύομαι has decisive authority, and is inserted by all critical editors.] The meaning is, 'Doubt not that there is for all of you a place in My Father's house, *for* I am going on purpose to prepare it.' In what sense? First, To establish their right to be there; Second, To take possession of it in their name; Third, To conduct them thither at last. 3. **And if I go and prepare a place for you, I will come again**—strictly, at His Second Personal Appearing; but, in a secondary and comforting sense, to each individually, when he puts off this tabernacle, sleeping in Jesus, but his spirit "present with the Lord." **and receive you unto myself; that where I am, there ye may be also.** Mark here again the extent of the claim which Jesus makes—at His Second Coming to receive His people *to Himself* (see on Eph. v. 27; Col. i. 22; Jude 24), that where *He is,* there they may be also. He thinks it quite enough to re-assure them, to say that where He is, there they shall be.

Christ the Way to the Father, and Himself the Incarnate Revelation of the Father (4-12). **4. And whither I go ye know, and the way ye know.**

unto him, Lord, we know not whither thou goest; and how can we know
6 the way? Jesus saith unto him, I am *e*the way, and *f*the truth, and *g*the
7 life: *h*no man cometh unto the Father, but by me. If *i*ye had known me,
ye should have known my Father also: and from henceforth ye know him,
and have seen him.

8 Philip saith unto him, Lord, show us the Father, and it sufficeth us.
9 Jesus saith unto him, Have I been so long time with you, and yet hast
thou not known me, Philip? *j*he that hath seen me hath seen the
10 Father; and how sayest thou *then*, Show us the Father? Believest thou
not that *k*I am in the Father, and the Father in me? the words that I
speak unto you *l*I speak not of myself: but the Father, that dwelleth in
11 me, he doeth the works. Believe me that I *am* in the Father, and
12 the Father in me: or else believe me for the very works' sake. Verily,
verily, I say unto you, He that believeth on me, the works that I do
shall he do also; and greater *works* than these shall he do; because

A. D. 33.
e Matt. 11. 27.
Rom. 5. 2.
Heb. 9. 8.
f ch. 1. 17.
ch. 8. 32.
g ch. 1. 4.
ch. 6. 35.
h ch. 10. 9.
Rom.15. 16.
2 John 9.
Rev. 5. 8, 9.
i ch. 8. 19.
j Col. 1. 15.
Heb. 1. 3.
k ch. 10. 38.
ch. 17. 21.
1 John 5. 7.
l ch. 6. 19.

5. Thomas saith unto him, Lord, we know not whither thou goest; and how can we know the way? [The reading of this last clause, according to *Lachmann* and *Tregelles*, 'how know we the way?' or with the "and" prefixed by *Tischendorf* —is hardly so well supported as the received text.] It seems strange that when Jesus said they knew both whither He went and the way, Philip should flatly say they did not. But doubtless the Lord meant thus rather to stimulate their enquiries, and then reply to them:—*q. d.*, 'Whither I go ye know —do ye not? and the way too?' Accordingly, verse **6. Jesus saith unto him, I AM THE WAY**—in what sense is explained in the last clause: but He had said it before in these words, "I am the door: *by Me* if any man enter in, he shall be saved" (ch. x. 9). **and THE TRUTH**—the *Incarnate Reality* of all we find in the Father, when through Christ we get to Him; for "in Him dwelleth all the fulness of the Godhead bodily" (Col. i. 19). **and THE LIFE**—the *vitality* of all that shall ever flow into us from the Godhead thus approached and thus manifested in Him: for "this is the true God, and eternal life" (1 John v. 20): **no man cometh unto the Father, but by me.** Of this three-fold statement of what He is, Jesus explains here only the first—His being "the Way;" not as if that were in itself more important than the other two, but because the *Intervention* or *Mediation* of Christ between God and men is the distinctive feature of Christianity. His being the *Truth* and the *Life* gives us what may be called *the Christian aspect of the Godhead*, as the Object of the soul's aspirations and the centre of its eternal bliss: but that God, even as thus viewed, is approachable and enjoyable by men only *through the mediation of Christ*, tells us of that sinful separation of the soul from God, the knowledge and feeling of which constitute the necessary preparative to any and every saving approach to God, and to the believing reception and use of Christ as the Way to Him. Hence it is that our Lord comes back upon this, as in the first instance what needs most to be impressed upon us. **7. If ye had known me, ye should have known my Father also: and from henceforth** [*ἀπ' ἄρτι*]—'from now,' or from this time forth, that I have explained it to you, ye know him, **and have seen him.** Here also our Lord, by what He says, intends rather to gain their ear for further explanation, than to tell them how much they already knew. **8. Philip saith unto him, Lord, show us the Father, and it sufficeth us.** Philip's grossness of conception gives occasion to something more than explanation; but O how winning is even the slight

rebuke! **9. Jesus saith unto him, Have I been so long time with you, and yet hast thou not known me, Philip? he that hath seen me hath seen the Father**—hath seen all of the Father that can or ever will be seen; hath seen the Incarnate Manifestation of the Godhead; **and how sayest thou, Show us the Father?** To strain after expected but impossible discovery can only end in disappointment. Jesus, therefore, shuts up Philip—and with him all who waste their mental energies on such fruitless aims and expectations—to Himself, in whom dwelleth all the fulness of the Godhead bodily. **10. Believest thou not that I am in the Father, and the Father in me? the words that I speak unto you I speak not of**—or 'from' [*ἀπό*] myself: but the Father, that dwelleth in me, he doeth the works. Observe here how, in the expression of this *Mutual Inbeing* of the Father and the Son, our Lord passes insensibly, so to speak, from the *words* He spake to the *works* He did—as the Father's words uttered by His mouth and the Father's works done by His hand. What claim to essential equality with the Father could surpass this? **11. Believe me that I am in the Father, and the Father in me: or else believe me for the very works' sake:**—*q. d.*, 'By all your faith in Me, believe this on My simple *word:* but if so high a claim is more than your feeble faith can yet reach, let the *works* I have done tell their own tale, and it will need no more.' Can anything more clearly show that Christ claimed for His miracles a higher character than those of prophets or apostles? And yet this higher character lay not in the works themselves, but in His manner of doing them. (See on Mark vi. 30-56, Remark 1 at the close of that Section, page 163.) **12. Verily, verily, I say unto you, He that believeth on me, the works that I do shall he do also; and greater works than these shall he do; because I go unto my Father**—rather, 'the Father,' as the true reading appears to be. "The works that I do" and which "they should do also," were those miraculous credentials of their apostolic office which Christ empowered the Eleven to perform. But the "greater works than His" were not any more transcendent *miracles*—for there could be none such, and certainly did none such—but such as He referred to in what He said to Nathanael (ch. i. 51)—that glorious ingathering of souls after His ascension—or "because He went to the Father"—which it was not His own Personal mission to the earth to accomplish. See on the promise, "From henceforth thou shalt catch men," Luke v. 10, and Remark 4 at the close of that Section. The substance, then, of these

13 I go unto my Father. And whatsoever ye shall ask in ^mmy name,
14 that will I do, that the Father may be glorified in the Son. If ye
    shall ask any thing in my name, I will do *it*.
15, If ⁿye love me, keep my commandments. And I will pray the Father,
16 and ^ohe shall give you another Comforter, that he may abide with you
17 for ever; *even* ^pthe Spirit of truth; ^qwhom the world cannot receive,
    because it seeth him not, neither knoweth him: but ye know him; for

A. D. 33.
^m Jas. 1. 5.
1 John 3. 22.
ⁿ 1 John 5. 3.
^o Rom. 8. 15.
^p 1 John 2. 7.
1 John 4. 6.
^q Rom. 8. 7.
1 Cor. 2. 14.

five rich verses (8-12) is this: that the Son is the ordained and perfect manifestation of the Father; that His own word for this ought, to His disciples, to be enough; that if any doubts remained His works ought to remove them; but yet that these works of His were designed merely to aid weak faith, and would be repeated, nay exceeded by His disciples, in virtue of the power He would confer on them after His departure. His miracles, accordingly, apostles wrought, though wholly in His name and by His power; while the "greater" works—not in degree but in kind—were the conversion of thousands in a day, by His Spirit accompanying them.

The Prevalency of Prayer in Christ's Name (13, 14). **13. And whatsoever ye shall ask in my name—as Mediator, that will I do**—as Head and Lord of the Kingdom of God. This comprehensive promise is repeated emphatically in the following verse. **14. If ye shall ask any thing in my name, I will do it.** Observe here, that while they are supposed to ask what they want, not of Him, but of the Father in His name, Jesus says it is He Himself that will "do it" for them. What a claim is this not only to be perfectly cognizant of all that is poured into the Father's ear by His loving disciples on earth, and of all the Father's counsels and plans as to the answers to be given to them, the precise nature and measure of the grace to be given them, and the proper time for it —but to be the authoritative Dispenser of all that these prayers draw down, and in that sense the *Hearer* of prayer! Let any one try to conceive of this statement apart from Christ's essential equality with the Father, and he will find it impossible. The emphatic repetition of this, that if they shall ask anything in His name, He will do it, speaks both the boundless *prevalency* of His name with the Father, and His *unlimited authority* to dispense the answer. But see further on ch. xv. 7.

First great Promise of the Comforter and the blessed Effects of this Gift (15-26). This portion of the Discourse is notable, as containing the first announcement of the Spirit, to supply the personal presence of the absent Saviour. **15. If ye love me, keep my commandments.** Christ's commandments are neither substituted in place of God's commandments in the moral law, nor are they something to be performed over and above that law. But they are that very law of God, laid on His disciples by the Lord Jesus, in the exercise of His proper authority, and to be obeyed as their proper service to Himself as their Lord and Master —from new motives and to new ends; for we are *"not without law to God, but under the law to Christ"* (1 Cor. ix. 21). This demand, on the principles of the two foregoing verses, is intelligible: on any other principles, it were monstrous. **16. And I will, &c.** The connection between this and what goes before is apt to escape observation. But it seems to be this, that as the proper temple for the indwelling Spirit of Jesus is a heart filled with an obediential love to Him—a love to Him which at once yields itself obediently to Him and lives actively for Him—so this was the fitting preparation for the promised gift, and He would accordingly get it for them. But how? **I will pray the**

Father. It is perhaps a pity that the English word "pray" is ever used of Christ's askings of the Father. For of the two words used in the Gospels, that signifying to pray *as we do* —suppliantly, or as an inferior to a superior [αἰτεῖν]—is never used of Christ's askings of the Father, save once by Martha (ch. xi. 22), who knew no better. The word invariably used of Christ's askings by Himself [ἐρωτᾷν] signifies what one asks, not suppliantly, but familiarly, as equals do of each other. *Bengel* notes this, but the subject is fully and beautifully handled by *Trench* ('Synonyms of the New Testament'). **and he shall give you ANOTHER COMFORTER** [ἄλλον παράκλητον]. As this word is used in the New Testament exclusively by John—five times in this Discourse of the Holy Spirit (here; *v.* 26; xv. 26; xvi. 7), and once in his first Epistle, of Christ Himself (ii. 1)—it is important to fix the sense of it. Literally, the word signifies one 'called beside' or 'to' another, to 'aid' him. In this most general sense the Holy Spirit is undoubtedly sent 'to our aid,' and every kind of aid coming within the proper sphere of His operations. But more particularly, the word denotes that kind of aid which an *Advocate* renders to one in a court of justice. So it was used by the Greeks; and so undoubtedly it is used in 1 John ii. 1, "If any man sin, we have an Advocate [παράκλητον] with the Father, Jesus Christ the righteous." But it also denotes that kind of aid which a *Comforter* affords to one who needs such. The question, then, is, Which of these is here intended—the general sense of a Helper; the more definite sense of an Advocate; or the other definite sense of a Comforter? Taking all the four passages in which the Spirit is thus spoken of in this Discourse, that of a Helper certainly lies at the foundation; but that of a *Comforter* seems to us to be the kind of help which suits best with the strain of the Discourse at this place. The comfort of Christ's personal presence with the Eleven had been such, that while they had it they seemed to want for nothing; and the loss of it would seem the loss of everything —utter desolation (*v.* 18). It is to meet this, as we think, that He says He will ask the Father to send them *another* Comforter; and in all these four passages, it is as an all-sufficient, all-satisfying *Substitute for Himself* that He holds forth this promised Gift. But this will open up more and more upon us as we advance in this Discourse. **that he may abide with you for ever**—never to go away from them, as in the body Jesus Himself was about to do. **17. Even the Spirit of truth**— so called for the reason mentioned in ch. xvi. 13; **whom the world cannot receive**—see on 1 Cor. ii. 14; **because it seeth**—or 'beholdeth' him not [θεωρεῖ], **neither knoweth him**—having no spiritual perception and apprehension: **but ye know him; for he dwelleth with you, and shall be in you.** [The reading—ἐστίν—'is with you,' though adopted by *Lachmann* and *Tregelles*, and approved by *Tholuck*, *Stier*, and *Luthardt*, is insufficiently supported. *Tischendorf* abides by the received text, which is approved by *de Wette*, *Meyer*, and *Alford*. *Lücke* is doubtful.] Though the proper fulness of both these was yet future, our Lord, by speaking

435

18 he dwelleth with you, ʳand shall be in you. I will not leave you ¹comfortless:
19 I will come to you. Yet a little while, and the world seeth me
20 no more; but ˢye see me: ᵗbecause I live, ye shall live also. At that day
   ye shall know that ᵘI *am* in my Father, and ye in me, and I in you.
21 He ᵛthat hath my commandments, and keepeth them, he it is that
   loveth me: and he that loveth me shall be loved of my Father, and I
   will love him, and will manifest myself to him.
22 Judas saith unto him, (not Iscariot,) Lord, how is it that thou wilt
23 manifest thyself unto us, and not unto the world? Jesus answered and
   said unto him, If a man love me, he will keep my words: and my
   Father will love him, ʷand we will come unto him, and make our abode
24 with him. He that loveth me not keepeth not my sayings: and ˣthe
   word which ye hear is not mine, but the Father's which sent me.
25 These things have I spoken unto you, being *yet* present with you.
26 But ʸthe Comforter, *which is* the Holy Ghost, whom the Father will send

A. D. 33.

ʳ Matt. 10. 20.
Rom. 8. 10.
1 Cor. 14. 16.
1 John 2. 27.
¹ Or,
  orphans.
ˢ ch. 16. 16.
ᵗ 1 Cor. 15. 20.
ᵘ ch. 10. 38.
  ch. 17. 21.
ᵛ 1 John 2. 5.
  1 John 5. 3.
ʷ Ps 91. 1.
  1 John 2. 24.
ˣ 1 John 4. 16.
  Rev. 3. 20.
  Rev. 21. 3.
ˣ ch. 7. 16.
ʸ Luke 24. 49.

both of present and future time, seems plainly say that they *already* had the substance, though that only, of this great blessing.

18. I will not leave you comfortless [ὀρφανούς] —'orphans,' as in the margin; in a bereaved and desolate condition. **I will come to you** [ἔρχομαι] —rather, 'I am coming to you;' that is, by the Spirit, since it was His presence that was to make Christ's personal departure from them to be no bereavement. **19. Yet a little while, and the world seeth**—'beholdeth' me no more; but ye see—'behold' me. His bodily presence being all the sight of Him which the world was capable of, they were to behold Him no more on His departure to the Father: whereas by the coming of the Spirit the presence of Christ was not only continued to His spiritually enlightened disciples, but rendered far more efficacious and blissful than His bodily presence had been before. **because I live, ye shall live also.** He does not say, 'When I *shall* live, after My resurrection from the dead,' but "Because I do live;" for it is of that inextinguishable Divine life which He was even then living that He is speaking—in reference to which His approaching death and resurrection were but as momentary shadows passing over the sun's glorious disc. See Luke xxiv. 5; Rev. i. 18. And this grand saying Jesus uttered with death immediately in view. What a brightness does this throw over the next clause, **ye shall live also! 20. At**—or 'In' [ἐν] **that day**—of the Spirit's coming, **ye shall know**—or have it made manifest to you **that I am in my Father, and ye in me, and I in you.** See on ch. xvii. 22, 23. **21. He that hath my commandments, and keepeth them, he it is that loveth me.** See on ch. xv. 16. **and he that loveth me shall be loved of my Father, and I will love him, and will manifest myself to him.** Mark the sharp line of distinction here, not only between the Divine Persons, but the actings of love in Each respectively, towards true disciples.

22. Judas saith unto him, (not Iscariot). Delightful parenthesis this! The traitor being no longer present, we needed not to be told that this question came not from *him;* nor even if he had been present would any that knew him have expected any such question from him. But the very name had got an ill savour in the Church ever since that black treason, and the Evangelist seems to take a pleasure in disconnecting from it all that was offensive in the association, when reporting the question of that dear disciple whose misfortune it was to have that name. He is the same with Lebbæus, whose surname was Thaddæus, in Matthew's catalogue of the Twelve. (See on

Matt. x. 3.) **Lord, how is it that thou wilt manifest thyself unto us, and not unto the world?**—a question, as we think, most natural and pertinent, though interpreters (as *Lücke, Stier, Alford*, &c.) think it proceeded from a superficial, outside, Jewish misconception of Christ's kingdom. Surely the loving tone and precious nature of our Lord's reply ought to have suggested a better view of the question itself. **23. Jesus answered and said unto him, If a man love me, he will keep my words** [λόγον]—rather, 'My word:' **and my Father will love him, and we will come unto him, and make our abode with him.** Astonishing disclosure! Observe the links in this golden chain. First, "If a man love Me." Such love is at first the *fruit* of love: "We love Him because He first loved us." Then this love to Christ makes His word dear to us. Accordingly, "If a man love Me, he will keep My word." Further, such is My Father's love to Me, that when any man loves Me, and My word is dear to him, My Father will love that man. Finally, such a man—with heart so prepared and so perfumed—shall become the permanent habitation of both My Father and Me —the seat not of occasional and distant discoveries, but of abiding and intimate manifestations of both My Father and Me, to his unspeakable satisfaction and joy. He shall not have to say with the weeping prophet, "O the Hope of Israel, the Saviour thereof in time of trouble, why shouldest Thou be as a *stranger* in the land, and as a wayfaring man that turneth aside to tarry *for a night?*" but from his own deep and joyous experience shall exclaim, "The Word was made flesh, and *dwelt* among us." He shall feel and know that the Father and the Son have come to make a permanent and eternal stay with him! **24. He that loveth me not keepeth not my sayings.** Hence it follows that all obedience *not* springing from love to Christ is in his eyes no obedience at all. **and the word which ye hear is not mine, but the Father's which sent me.** (See on Matt. x. 40.) It will be observed that when Christ refers back to His Father's authority, it is not in speaking of those who love Him and keep His sayings—in their case it were superfluous—but in speaking of those who love Him not and keep not His sayings, whom He holds up as chargeable with the double guilt of dishonouring the eternal Sender as well as the Sent.

25. These things have I spoken unto you, being yet present [μένων] **with you**—or 'while yet abiding with you.' **26. But the Comforter, which is the Holy Ghost, whom the Father will send in my name, he shall teach you all things**—see

436

in my name, [z]he shall teach you all things, and bring all things to your
27 remembrance, whatsoever I have said unto you. Peace [a]I leave with
you, my peace I give unto you: not as the world giveth, give I unto you.
28 Let not your heart be troubled, neither let it be afraid. Ye have heard
how I said unto you, I go away, and come *again* unto you. If ye loved
me, ye would rejoice, because I said, I go unto the Father: for [b]my

A. D. 33.
[z] 1 John 2. 27.
[a] Phil. 4. 7.
Col. 3. 15.
[b] Isa. 9. 6.
Isa. 42. 1.
Isa. 49. 1-6.
ch. 5. 18.

on *vv.* 16, 17; **and bring all things to your remembrance, whatsoever I have said unto you.**
As the Son came in the Father's name, so the
Father was to send the Spirit in the Son's name,
with like divine authority and power—to do two
great things. First, to "*teach* them all things,"
and second, to "*bring to remembrance* all things
whatsoever Christ had said to them." So imperfectly did the apostles apprehend what Jesus said
to them, that to have recalled it all to them
merely as it fell on their ears from their Master's
lips would have left them the same half-instructed
and bewildered, weak and timid men, as before—
all unfit to evangelize the world either by their
preaching or their writings. But the Spirit was to
teach as well as to *remind* them—to *reproduce the
whole teaching of Christ*, not as they understood
it, but *as He meant it to be understood*. But does
not the promise of the Spirit to "teach them all
things" mean something more than "to bring all
things to their remembrance?" *This* promise at
least does not; for the sense plainly is, "He
shall teach you, and bring to your remembrance
all things whatsoever I have said unto you"—the
teaching and the recalling relating to the same
things, namely, all that Christ had said to them.
Thus have we here a double promise with reference to our Lord's actual teaching—that through
the agency of the Holy Ghost it should stand up
before their minds, when He was gone from them,
in all its *entireness*, as at first *uttered*, and in all
its vast *significance* as by Him *intended*. Before
the close of this same Discourse, our Lord announces an extension even of this great office of
the Spirit. They were not able to take in all that
He had to tell them, and He had accordingly
withheld some things from them. But when the
Spirit should come, on His departure to the
Father, He should "guide them into *all the truth*,"
filling up whatever was wanting to their *complete
apprehension of the mind of Christ*. (See on ch.
xvi. 12-15.) On these great promises rests the
CREDIBILITY, in the highest sense of that term,
OF THE GOSPEL HISTORY, and so, its DIVINE
AUTHORITY.
*Christ's Own Peace, His Legacy and Gift to His
People* (27). **27. Peace I leave with you, my
peace I give unto you.** If the two preceding
verses sounded like a note of preparation for departure, what would they take this to be but a
farewell? But O how different from ordinary
adieus! It *is* a parting word, but of richest import. It is the peace of a parting friend, sublimed
in the sense of it, and made efficacious for all time
by those Lips that "speak and it is done." As
the Prince of peace (Isa. ix. 6) He brought it into
flesh in His own Person; carried it up and down
as His Own—"My peace," as He here calls it;
died to make it ours, through the blood of His
cross; left it as the heritage of His disciples here
below; and from the right hand of the Majesty on
high implants and maintains it by His Spirit in
their hearts. Many a legacy is "left" that is
never "given" to the legatee, many a gift destined
that never reaches its proper object. But Christ
is the Executor of His own Testament; the peace
He "*leaves*" He "*gives*." Thus all is secure.
not as the world giveth, give I unto you.
437

What hollowness is there in many of the world's
givings: but Jesus gives *sincerely*. How superficial, even at their best, are the world's givings:
but Jesus gives *substantially*. How temporary
are all the world's givings: but what Jesus gives
He gives *for ever!* Well, then, might He add,
**Let not your heart be troubled, neither let it be
afraid**—for the entrance of such words into any
honest and good heart necessarily casteth out fear.
*The Gain to Christ Himself of His Departure to
the Father, and the Joy which this should inspire in
His loving People* (28). **28. Ye have heard how I
said unto you, I go away, and come again unto
you. If ye loved me, ye would rejoice, because
I said, I go unto the Father: for my Father is
greater than I.** This is one of the passages which
have in all ages been most confidently appealed to
by those who deny the supreme Divinity of Christ,
in proof that our Lord claimed no proper equality
with the Father: here, they say, He explicitly disclaims it. But let us see whether, on their principles, it would yield any intelligible sense at all.
Were some holy *man* on his deathbed to say as
he beheld his friends in tears at the prospect of
losing him, 'Ye ought rather to rejoice than weep
for me, and if ye loved me ye would'—the speech
would be quite natural, and what many dying
saints *have* said. But should these weeping bystanders ask *why* joy was more suitable than
sorrow, and the dying man reply, "*Because my
Father is greater than I*," would they not start
back with astonishment, if not with horror? Does
not this strange speech, then, from Christ's lips
presuppose such teaching on His part as would
make it hard to believe that He could gain anything by departing to the Father, and render it
needful to say expressly that there was a sense in
which He *could* and *would* do so? Thus this startling saying, when closely looked at, seems *plainly
intended to correct such misapprehensions* as might
arise from the emphatic and reiterated teaching of
His proper equality with the Father—as if joy at
the prospect of heavenly bliss were inapplicable to
Him—as if so Exalted a Person were incapable of
any accession at all, 'by transition from this dismal
scene to a cloudless heaven and the very bosom
of the Father, and, by assuring them that it was
just the reverse, to make them forget their own
sorrow in His approaching joy. The Fathers of the
Church, in repelling the false interpretation put
upon this verse by the Arians, were little more
satisfactory than their opponents; some of them
saying it referred to the *Sonship* of Christ, in
which respect He was inferior to the Father,
others that it referred to His *Human Nature*.
But the human nature of the Son of God is not
less real in heaven than it was upon earth.
Plainly, the inferiority of which Christ here speaks
is not anything which would be the same whether
He went or stayed, but something which would
be removed by His going to the Father—on which
account He says that if they loved Him they
would rather rejoice on His account than sorrow
at His departure. With this key to the sense of
the words, they involve no real difficulty; and in
this view of them all the most judicious interpreters, from Calvin downwards, substantially
concur.

29 Father is greater than I. And now I have told you before it come to pass, that, when it is come to pass, ye might believe.

30 Hereafter I will not talk much with you: 'for the prince of this world

31 cometh, and *d*hath nothing in me. But that the world may know that I love the Father; and *e*as the Father gave me commandment, even so I do. Arise, let us go hence.

A. D. 33.
c ch. 12. 31.
d 2 Cor. 5. 2l.
Heb. 4. 15.
1 Pet. 1. 19.
1 John 3. 5.
e Phil. 2. 8.
Heb. 5. 8.

Jesus about to Die, not because the Prince of this World had anything in Him, but out of Loving Obedience to His Father's Commandment (29-31). **29. And now I have told you before it come to pass**—referring to His departure to the Father, and the gift of the Holy Ghost to follow thereon, **that, when it is come to pass, ye might believe**—or have your faith immoveably established.

30. Hereafter I will not talk much with you:—'I have a little more to say, but My work hastens apace, and the approach of the adversary will cut it short.' **for the prince of this world cometh** (see ch. xii. 31)—cometh with hostile intent, cometh for a last grand attack. Foiled in his first deadly assault, he had "departed"—but "till a season" only (see on Luke iv. 13). That season is now all but come, and his whole energies are to be once more put forth—with what effect the next words sublimely express. **and hath nothing in me**—*nothing of his own* in Me, *nothing of sin* on which to fasten as a righteous cause of condemnation: 'As the Prince of this world he wields his sceptre over willing subjects; but in Me he shall find no sympathy with his objects, no acknowledgment of his sovereignty, no subjection to his demands.' Glorious saying! The truth of it is the life of the world. (Heb. ix. 14; 1 John iii. 5; 2 Cor. v. 21.) **31. But that the world may know that I love the Father; and as the Father gave me commandment, even so I do.** The sense must be completed thus:—'But though the Prince of this world, in plotting My death, hath nothing to fasten on, I am going to yield Myself up a willing Sacrifice, that the world may know that I love the Father, whose commandment it is that I give My life a ransom for many.' **Arise, let us go hence.** Did they then, at this stage of the Discourse, leave the Supper-room, as some able interpreters judge? If so, we cannot but think that our Evangelist would have mentioned it: on the contrary, in ch. xviii. 1, the Evangelist expressly says that not till the concluding prayer was offered did the meeting in the upper-room break up. But if Jesus did not "arise and go hence" when He summoned the Eleven to go with Him, how are we to understand His words? We think they were spoken in the spirit of that earlier saying, "I have a baptism to be baptized with, and how am I straitened till it be accomplished." It was a spontaneous and irrepressible expression of the deep eagerness of His spirit to get into the conflict. If it was responded to somewhat too literally by those who hung on His blessed lips, in the way of a movement to depart, a wave of His hand would be enough to show that He had not *quite* done. Or it may be that those loving disciples were themselves reluctant to move so soon, and signified their not unwelcome wish that He should prolong His Discourse. Be this as it may, that disciple whose pen was dipt in a love to his Master which made His least movement and slightest word during these last hours seem worthy of record, has reported this little hastening of the Lamb to the slaughter with such artless life-like simplicity, that we seem to be of the party ourselves, and to catch the words rather from the Lips that spake than the pen that recorded them.

Remark.—Referring the reader to the general observations, prefixed to this chapter, on the whole of this wonderful portion of the Fourth Gospel, let him recall for a moment the contents of the present chapter. It is complete within itself. For no sooner had the glorious Speaker uttered the last words of it than He proposed to "arise and go." All that follows, therefore, is supplementary. Everything essential is here, and here in what a form! The very fragrance of heaven is in these out-pourings of Incarnate Love. Of every verse of it we may say,

'O, it came o'er my ear like the sweet south,
That breathes upon a bank of violets,
Stealing and giving odour.'—SHAKSPERE.

Look at the varied lights in which Jesus holds forth *Himself* to the confidence and love and obedience of His disciples. To their fluttering hearts —ready to sink at the prospect of His sufferings, His departure from them, and their own desolation without Him, to say nothing of His cause when left in such incompetent hands—His opening words are, "Let not your heart be troubled: ye believe in God, believe also in Me." 'Though clouds and darkness are round about Him, and His judgments are a great deep, yet *ye believe in God*. What time, then, your heart is overwhelmed, *believe in Me*, and darkness shall become light before you, and crooked things straight.' What a claim is this on the part of Jesus—to be in the Kingdom of Grace precisely as God is in that of Nature and Providence, or rather to be the glorious Divine Administrator of all things whatsoever in the interests and for the purposes of Grace; in the shadow of Whose wings, therefore, all who believe in God are to put their implicit trust, for the purposes of salvation! For He is not sent merely to *show* men the way to the Father, no, nor merely to *prepare* that way; but Himself *is* the Way, and the Truth, and the Life. We go not *from* Him, but *in* Him, to the Father. For He is in the Father, and the Father in Him; the words that He spake are the Father's words, and the works that He did are the Father's works; and He that hath seen Him hath seen the Father, for He is the Incarnate manifestation of the Godhead. But there are other views of Himself, equally transcendent, in which Jesus holds Himself forth here. To what a cheerless distance did He seem to be going away, and when and where should His disciples ever find Him again! '"Tis but to My Father's home,' He replies, 'and in due time it is to be yours too.' In that home there will not only be room for all, but a mansion for each. But it is not ready yet, and He is going to prepare it for them. For them He is going thither; for them He is to live there; and, when the last preparations are made, for them He will at length return, to take them to that home of His Father and their Father, that *where He is, there they may be also*. The attraction of heaven to those who love Him is, it seems, to be His Own presence there, and the beatific consciousness that they are *where He is*—language intolerable in a *creature*, but in Him who is the Incarnate, manifested Godhead, supremely worthy, and to His believing people in every age unspeakably reassuring. But again, He had said that in heaven He was to occupy Himself in preparing a place

15, I AM the true vine, and my Father is the husbandman. Every
2 *"*branch in me that beareth not fruit he taketh away; and every *branch*
that beareth fruit he purgeth it, that it may bring forth more fruit.

A. D. 33.

a Matt. 15. 13.
Heb. 6. 8.

for them; so, a little afterwards, He tells them one of the ways in which this was to be done. To "hear prayer" is the exclusive prerogative of Jehovah, and one of the brightest jewels in His crown. But, says Jesus here, "Whatsoever ye shall ask of the Father in My name, THAT WILL I DO"—not as interfering with, or robbing God of His glory, but on the contrary—"that the Father may be glorified in the Son: If ye shall ask anything in My name, I WILL DO IT." Further, He is the *Life* and the *Law* of His people. Much do we owe to Moses; much to Paul: but never did either say to those who looked up to them, "Because I live, ye shall live also; If ye love Me, keep My commandments; If a man love Me, he will keep My word, and My Father will love him, and WE will come unto him, and make OUR abode with him."

Such is Jesus, by His own account; and this is conveyed, not in formal theological statements, but in warm outpourings of the heart, in the immediate prospect of the hour and power of darkness, yet without a trace of that perturbation of spirit which he experienced afterwards in the Garden: as if while the Eleven were around Him at the Supper-table *their* interests had altogether absorbed Him. The tranquillity of heaven reigns throughout this Discourse. The bright splendour of a noon-tide sun is not here, and had been somewhat incongruous at that hour. But the serenity of a matchless sunset is what we find here, which leaves in the devout mind a sublime repose—as if the glorious Speaker had gone from us, saying, "Peace I *leave* with you, *My* peace I *give* unto you: not as the world giveth, give I unto you. Let not your heart be troubled, neither let it be afraid."

CHAP. XV. 1-27.—CONTINUATION OF THE DISCOURSE AT THE SUPPER-TABLE.
The Vine, the Branches, and the Fruit (1-8). By a figure familiar to Jewish ears (Isa. v. 1-7; Ezek. xv.; &c.) Jesus here beautifully sets forth the spiritual Oneness of Himself and His people, and His relation to them as the Source of all their spiritual life and fruitfulness. **1. I am the true vine**—of which the natural vine is no more than a shadow. **and my Father is the husbandman**—the great Proprietor of the Vineyard, the Lord of the spiritual Kingdom. **2. Every branch in me that beareth not fruit he taketh away** [αιρει]; **and every branch that beareth fruit he purgeth it** [καθαιρει], **that it may bring forth more fruit.** There is a verbal play upon the two Greek words for "taketh away" and "purgeth" [*airein—kathairein*], which it is impossible to convey in English. But it explains why so uncommon a word as "purgeth," with reference to a fruit tree, was chosen—the one word no doubt suggesting the other. The sense of both is obvious enough, and the truths conveyed by the whole verse are deeply important. Two classes of Christians are here set forth—both of them *in Christ*, as truly as the branch is in the vine; but while the one class bear fruit, the other bear none. The natural husbandry will sufficiently explain the cause of this difference. A graft may be *mechanically attached* to a fruit tree, and yet take no vital hold of it, and have no *vital connection* with it. In that case, receiving none of the juices of the tree—no vegetable sap from the stem—it can bear no fruit. Such merely mechanical attachment to the True Vine is that of all who believe in the truths of Christianity,

and are in visible membership with the Church of Christ, but, having no living faith in Jesus nor desire for His salvation, open not their souls to the spiritual life of which He is the Source, take no vital hold of Him, and have no living union to Him. All such are incapable of fruit-bearing. They have an external, mechanical connection with Christ, as members of His Church visible; and in that sense they are, not in name only but in reality, branches "in the true Vine." Mixing, as these sometimes do, with living Christians in their most sacred services and spiritual exercises, where Jesus Himself is, according to His promise, they may come into such close contact with Him as those did who "pressed upon Him" in the days of His flesh, when the woman with the issue of blood touched the hem of His garment. But just as the branch that opens not its pores to let in the vital juices of the vine to which it may be most firmly attached has no more vegetable *life*, and is no more capable of bearing *fruit*, than if it were in the fire; so such merely external Christians have no more spiritual life, and are no more capable of spiritual fruitfulness, than if they had never heard of Christ, or were already separated from Him. The reverse of this class are those "in Christ that bear fruit." Their union to Christ is a *vital*, not a mechanical one; they are *one spiritual life* with Him: only in Him it is a Fontal life; in them a derived life, even as the life of the branch is that of the vine with which it is vitally one. Of them Christ can say, "Because I live, ye shall live also:" of Him do they say, "Of His fulness have all we received, and grace for grace." Such are the two classes of Christians of which Jesus here speaks. Observe now the procedure of the great Husbandman towards each. Every fruitless branch He "taketh away." Compare what is said of the barren fig tree, "Cut it down" (see on Luke xiii. 1-9, Remark 5 at the close of that Section). The thing here intended is not the same as "casting it into the fire" (*v*. 6): that is a subsequent process. It is 'the severance of that tie which bound them to Christ' here; so that they shall no longer be fruitless branches *in* the true Vine, no longer unclothed guests at the marriage-feast. That condition of things shall not last always. "The ungodly shall not stand in the judgment, nor sinners in the congregation of the righteous" (Ps. i. 5). But "every branch that beareth fruit"—in virtue of such living connection with Christ and reception of spiritual life from Him as a fruitful branch has from the natural vine—"He purgeth it, that it may bring forth more fruit." Here also the processes of the natural husbandry may help us. Without the pruning knife a tree is apt to go all *to wood*, as the phrase is. This takes place when the sap of the tree goes exclusively to the formation and growth of fresh branches, and none of it to the production of fruit. To prevent this, the tree is *pruned;* that is to say, all superfluous shoots are lopped off, which would have drawn away, to no useful purpose, the sap of the tree, and thus the whole vegetable juices and strength of the tree go towards their proper use—the nourishment of the healthy branches and the production of fruit. But what, it may be asked, is that rankness and luxuriance in living Christians which requires the pruning knife of the great Husbandman? The words of another parable will sufficiently answer that question: "The cares of this world, and the deceitfulness of riches, and the lusts of other things

3 Now *b*ye are clean through the word which I have spoken unto you.
4 Abide *c*in me, and I in you. As the branch cannot bear fruit of itself, except it abide in the vine; no more can ye, except ye abide in me.
5 I am the vine, ye *are* the branches: He that abideth in me, and I in him, the same bringeth forth much *d*fruit: for [1]without me ye can do
6 nothing. If a *e*man abide not in me, he is cast forth as a branch, and is withered; and men gather them, and cast *them* into the fire, and they
7 are burned. If ye abide in me, and my words abide in you, ye shall ask

A. D. 33.
b Eph. 5. 26.
1 Pet. 1. 22.
c Col 1. 23.
1 John 2. 6.
d Hos. 14. 8.
Phil. 4. 13.
1 Or. severed from me.
e Heb 6. 4-6.

entering in, choke the word, and it becometh unfruitful" (see on Mark iv. 19). True, that is said of such hearers of the word as " bring no fruit to perfection" at all. But the very same causes operate to the *hindrance* of fruitfulness in the living branches of the true Vine, and the great Husbandman has to "purge" them of these, that they may bring forth more fruit; lopping off at one time their worldly prosperity, at another time the olive plants that grow around their table, and at yet another time their own health or peace of mind: a process painful enough, but no less needful and no less beneficial in the spiritual than in the natural husbandry. Not one nor all of these operations, it is true, will of themselves increase the fruitfulness of Christians. But He who afflicteth not willingly, but smites to heal—who purgeth the fruitful branches for no other end than that they may bring forth more fruit—makes these "chastenings afterward to yield the peaceable fruit of righteousness" in larger measures than before. **3. Now ye are clean through the word** ["Ηδη ὑμεῖς καθαροί ἐστε διὰ τὸν λόγον]— 'Already are ye clean by reason of the word' **which I have spoken unto you.** He had already said of the Eleven, using another figure, that they were "clean," and "needed only to wash their feet." Here He repeats this, reminding them of the means by which this was brought about— "the word which He had spoken to them." For "as many as received Him, to them gave He power to become the sons of God." He "purified their hearts by faith," and "sanctified them through His truth; His word was the truth." (See on ch. xvii. 17.) Such, then, being their state, what would He have them to do? **4. Abide in me, and I in you.** The latter clause may be taken as a *promise:* ' Abide in Me, and I will abide in you.' (So *Calvin, Beza, Meyer, Lücke, Luthardt* understand it.) But we rather take it as part of one *injunction:* 'See to it that ye abide in Me, and that I abide in you;' the twofold condition of spiritual fruitfulness. (So *Grotius, Bengel, Tholuck, Alford, Webster and Wilkinson* view it.) What follows seems to confirm this. **As the branch cannot bear fruit of itself, except it abide in the vine; no more can ye, except ye abide in me.** Should anything interrupt the free communication of a branch with the tree of which it is a part, so that the sap should not reach it, it could bear no fruit. In order to this it is absolutely necessary that the one abide in the other, in this vital sense of *reception* on the one hand, and *communication* on the other. So with Christ and His people. **5. I am the vine, ye are the branches: He that abideth in me, and I in him, the same bringeth forth much fruit.** This is just the positive form of what had been said negatively in the previous verse. But it is more. Without abiding in Christ we cannot bear any fruit at all; but he that abideth in Christ, and Christ in him, the same bringeth forth—not fruit merely, as we should expect, but—"much fruit:" meaning, that as Christ seeks only a *receptive* soul to be a *communicative* Saviour, so there is no limit to the communication from Him but in the power of reception in us. **for without me**—disconnected from Me, in the sense explained, **ye can do nothing**—nothing spiritually good, nothing which God will regard and accept as good. **6. If a man abide not in me, he is cast forth as a branch, and is withered.** This *withering*, it will be observed, comes before the *burning*, just as the withering is preceded by the *taking away* (v. 2). The thing intended seems to be the decay and disappearance of all that in religion (and in many cases this is not little) which even an external connection with Christ imparts to those who are destitute of vital religion. **and [men] gather them.** Compare what is said in the parable of the Tares: "The Son of Man shall send forth His angels, and they shall *gather* out of His kingdom all things that offend, and them which do iniquity" (Matt. xiii. 41). **and cast them into the fire, and they are burned.** The one proper use of the vine is to bear *fruit.* Failing this, it is useless, save for *fuel.* This is strikingly set forth in the form of a parable in Ezek. xv., to which there is here a manifest allusion: "Son of man, what is the vine tree more than any tree, or than a branch which is among the trees of the forest?"—Why is it planted in a vineyard, and dressed with such care and interest, more than any other tree save only for the *fruit* which it yields?—"Shall wood be taken thereof to do any work? or will a man take a pin of it to hang any vessel thereon?"—Does it admit of being turned to any of the purposes of woodwork, even the most insignificant?—"Behold, it is cast into the fire for fuel"—that is the one use of it, failing fruit;—"the fire devoureth both the ends of it, and the midst of it is burned"—not an inch of it is fit for aught else:—"Is it meet for any work?" **7. If ye abide in me, and my words abide in you.** Mark the change from the inhabitation of *Himself* to that of His *words.* But as we are clean through His word (v. 2), and sanctified through His word (ch. xvii. 17), so He dwells in us through "His words"—those words of His, the believing reception of which alone opens the heart to let Him come in to us. So in the preceding chapter (xiv. 23), "If a man love Me, he will keep My words: and My Father will love him, and we will come unto him, and make our abode with him." And so in the last of His epistles to the churches of Asia, "Behold, I stand at the door and knock: if any man *hear my voice*"—and so my words abide in him, "I will come in to him, and will sup with him, and he with Me" (Rev. iii. 20). **ye shall ask what ye will, and it shall be done unto you.** A startling latitude of asking this seems to be. Is it, then, to be understood with limitations? and if not, would not such boundless license seem to countenance all manner of fanatical extravagance? The one limitation expressly mentioned is all-sufficient to guide the askings so as to ensure the answering. If we but abide in Christ, and Christ's words abide in us, "every thought" is so "brought into captivity to the obedience of Christ," that no desires will rise and no petition be offered but such as are in harmony with the divine

440

8 what ye will, and it shall be done unto you. Herein *ᶠ*is my Father
glorified, that ye bear much fruit; so shall ye be my disciples.

9　As the Father hath loved me, so have I loved you: continue ye in my
10 love. If ye keep my commandments, ye shall abide in my love; even as
I have kept my Father's commandments, and abide in his love.

11　These things have I spoken unto you, that my joy might remain in you,
12 and *ᵍthat* your joy might be full. This *ʰ*is my commandment, That ye
13 love one another, as I have loved you. Greater *ⁱ*love hath no man than
14 this, that a man lay down his life for his friends. Ye are my friends, if
15 ye do whatsoever I command you. Henceforth I call you not servants;
for the servant knoweth not what his lord doeth: but I have called you
friends; *ʲ*for all things that I have heard of my Father I have made
16 known unto you. Ye *ᵏ*have not chosen me, but I have chosen you, and
*ˡ*ordained you, that ye should go and bring forth fruit, and *that* your fruit

A. D. 33.
ᶠ Matt. 5. 16.
Phil 1. 11.
ᵍ ch 16. 24.
1 John 1. 4.
ʰ 1 Thes. 4. 9.
1 Pet. 4. 8.
1 John 3.11.
ⁱ Rom. 5. 7.
Eph. 5. 2.
ʲ Gen. 18. 17-19.
Luke 10.23, 24.
Acts 20. 27.
ᵏ 1 John 4.10.
ˡ Mark 16.15.
Col. 1. 6.

will. The soul, yielding itself implicitly and wholly to Christ, and Christ's words penetrating and moulding it sweetly into conformity with the will of God, its very breathings are of God, and so cannot but meet with a divine response. **8. Herein is my Father glorified** [ἐδοξάσθη — on which peculiar use of the aorist, see on ch. x. 4], **that ye bear much fruit.** As His whole design in providing "the True Vine," and making men living branches in Him, was to obtain *fruit;* and as He purgeth every branch that beareth fruit, that it may bring forth *more fruit;* so herein is He glorified, that we bear *much fruit.* As the husbandman feels that his pains are richly rewarded when the fruit of his vineyard is abundant, so the eternal designs of Grace are seen to come to glorious effect when the vessels of mercy, the redeemed of the Lord, abound in the fruits of righteousness, which are by Jesus Christ unto the glory and praise of God, and then the Father of our Lord Jesus Christ "rests in His love and joys over them with singing." **so shall ye be** [γενή-σεσθε]—or 'become' **my disciples**—that is, so shall ye manifest and evidence your discipleship.

How to Retain Christ's Love and our own Joy (9-11). **9. As the Father hath loved me, so have I loved you.** See on ch. xvii. 22, 26. **continue**—or 'abide' **ye in my love**—not, 'continue ye to love Me,' but 'abide ye in the possession and enjoyment of My love to you;' as is evident from what follows. **10. If ye keep my commandments, ye shall abide in my love**—the obedient spirit of true discipleship attracting and securing the continuance and increase of Christ's loving regard; **even as I have kept my Father's commandments, and abide in his love.** What a wonderful statement is this which Christ makes about Himself. In neither case, it will be observed, is obedience the original and proper ground of the love spoken of. As an earthly father does not *primarily* love his son for his obedience, but because of the filial relation which he bears to him, so the love which Christ's Father bears to Him is not primarily drawn forth by His obedience, but by the Filial relation which He sustains to Him. The Son's Incarnation neither added to nor diminished from this. But it provided a new form and manifestation of that love. As His own Son in our nature, the Father's affection went out to Him as the Son of Man; and just as a human father, on beholding the cordial and constant obedience of his own child, feels his own affection thereby irresistibly drawn out to him, so every beauty of the Son's Incarnate character, and every act of His Human obedience, rendered Him more lovely in the Father's eye, drew down new complacency upon Him, fresh love to Him. Thus, then, it was that by the keeping of His Father's commandments Jesus abode in the possession and enjoyment of His Father's love. And thus, says Jesus, shall it be between you and Me: If ye would retain My love to you, know that the whole secret of it lies in the keeping of My commandments: Never need ye be without the full sunshine of My love on your souls, if ye do but carry yourselves in the same obedient frame towards Me as I do towards My Father. **11. These things have I spoken unto you, that my joy might remain**—'abide' **in you, and that your joy might be full** [πληρωθῇ]—or 'be fulfilled.' We take "these things which Christ had spoken unto them" to mean, not all that Christ uttered on this occasion—as interpreters generally do—but more definitely, the things He had just before said about the true secret of His abiding in His Father's love and of their abiding in His love. In that case, the sense will be this: 'As it is My joy to have My Father's love resting on Me in the keeping of His commandments, so have I told how ye yourselves may have that very joy of Mine abiding in you and filling you full.'

The Love of the Brethren (12-17). **12. This is my commandment, That ye love one another, as I have loved you.** See on ch. xiii. 34, 35. **13. Greater love hath no man than this, that a man lay down his life for his friends.** The emphasis here lies, not on "friends," but on "*laying down his life*" for them:—*q. d.*, 'One can show no greater regard for those dear to him than to give his life for them, and this is the love ye shall find in Me.' **14. Ye are my friends, if ye do whatsoever I command you**—'if ye hold yourselves in absolute subjection to Me.' **15. Henceforth I call you not servants**—that is, in the restricted sense explained in the next words; for servants He still calls them (*v.* 20), and such they delight to call themselves, in the sense of being "under law to Christ" (1 Cor. ix. 21); **for the servant knoweth not what his lord doeth**—knows nothing of his master's *plans* and *reasons*, but simply receives and executes his orders: **but I have called you friends; for all things that I have heard of my Father I have made known unto you**—'I have admitted you to free, unrestrained fellowship, keeping back nothing from you which I have received to communicate.' (See Gen. xviii. 17; Ps. xxv. 14; Isa. l. 4). **16. Ye have not chosen me, but I have chosen you**—a wholesome memento after the lofty things He had just said about their mutual indwelling, and the unreservedness of the friendship to which He had admitted them. **and ordained** [ἔθηκα]—or 'appointed' **you, that ye should go and bring forth fruit**—that is, ye are to give yourselves to this as your proper business. The fruit intended, though embracing

441

should remain; that whatsoever ye shall ask of the Father in my name,
17 he may give it you. These things I command you, that ye love one another.
18   If ^mthe world hate you, ye know that it hated me before *it hated* you.
19 If ⁿye were of the world, the world would love his own: but ^obecause ye are not of the world, but I have chosen you out of the world, therefore
20 the world hateth you. Remember the word that I said unto you, The servant is not greater than his lord. If they have persecuted me, they will also persecute you; ^pif they have kept my saying, they will keep
21 yours also. But all these things will they do unto you for my name's sake, because they know not him that sent me.
22   If ^qI had not come and spoken unto them, they had not had sin: ^rbut
23 now they have no ²cloak for their sin. He ^sthat hateth me hateth my
24 Father also. If I had not done among them the works which none other man did, they had not had sin: but now have they both seen and hated
25 both me and my Father. But *this cometh to pass*, that the word might be fulfilled that is written in their law, ^tThey hated me without a cause.

A. D. 33.

^m Zec. 11. 8.
Matt 5. 11.
Mark 13.13.
Luke 6. 22.
1 John 3. 1.
13.
ⁿ Luke 6. 32,
33.
1 John 4. 5.
^o ch. 17. 14.
^p 1 Sam. 8. 7.
Isa. 53. 1, 3.
Ezek 3. 7.
^q ch. 9. 41.
^r Rom. 1. 20.
Jas. 4. 17.
² Or excuse.
^s 1 John 2.23.
2 John 9.
^t Ps. 35. 19.
Ps. 69. 4.
Ps. 109. 3.

all spiritual fruitfulness, is here specially that particular fruit of "loving one another," which *v.* 17 shows to be still the subject spoken of. **and that your fruit should remain**—showing itself to be an imperishable and ever-growing principle. (See Prov. iv. 18; 2 John 8.) **that whatsoever ye shall ask of the Father in my name, he may give it you.** See on *v.* 7. **17. These things I command you, that ye love one another.** Our Lord repeats here what He had said in *v.* 12, but He recurs to it here in order to give it fresh and affecting point. He is about to forewarn them of the certain hatred and persecution of the world, if they be His indeed. But before doing it, He enjoins on them anew the love of each other. It is as if He had said, 'And ye will have need of all the love ye can receive from one another, for outside your own pale ye have nothing to look for but enmity and opposition.' This, accordingly, is the subject of what follows.

How the World may be Expected to Regard and to Treat Christ's Genuine Disciples (18-21). The substance of these important verses has occurred more than once before. (See on Matt. x. 34-39, and Remark 2 at the close of that Section; and on Luke xii. 49-53, and Remark 4 at the end of that Section.) But the reader will do well to mark the peculiar light in which the subject is here presented. **18. If the world hate you, ye know that it hated me before it hated you. 19. If ye were of the world, the world would love his own: but because ye are not of the world, but I have chosen you out of the world** [ἐξελεξάμην], **therefore the world hateth you.** Here Jesus holds Himself forth as *the* Hated and Persecuted One; and this, not only as going before all His people in that respect, but as being the great Embodied Manifestation of that holiness which the world hates, and the Fountain of that hated state and character to all that believe in Him. From the treatment, therefore, which He met with they were not only to lay their account with the same, but be encouraged to submit to it, and cheered in the endurance of it, by the company they had and the cause in which it lighted upon them. Of course, this implies that if their separation from the world was to bring on them the world's enmity and opposition, then that enmity and opposition would be *just so great* as their separation from the world was, and no greater. Observe again that Christ here ascribes all that severance of His people from the world, which brings upon them its enmity and

opposition, to His own 'choice of them out of it.' This cannot refer to the mere external separation of the Eleven to the apostleship, for Judas was so separated. Besides, this was spoken after Judas had voluntarily separated himself from the rest. It can refer only to such an inward operation upon them as made them entirely different in character and spirit from the world, and so objects of the world's hatred. **20. Remember the word that I said unto you, The servant is not greater than his lord. If they have persecuted me, they will also persecute you; if they have kept my saying, they will keep yours also.** See on Matt. x. 24, 25. **21. But all these things will they do unto you for my name's sake, because they know not him that sent me.** Here again are they cheered with the assurance that all the opposition they would experience from the world as His disciples would arise from its dislike to *Him*, and its estrangement in mind as well as heart from the Father that sent Him. But to impress this the more upon them, our Lord enlarges upon it in what follows.

The Inexcusableness of the World's Hatred of Christ (22-25). **22. If I had not come and spoken unto them, they had not had sin** [οὐκ εἶχον]—rather, 'would not have sin;' that is, of course, *comparatively:* all other sins being light compared with the rejection of the Son of God: **but now they have no cloak** [πρόφασιν]—or 'pretext' for **their sin. 23. He that hateth me hateth my Father also**—so brightly revealed in the incarnate Son that the hatred of the One was just naked enmity to the other. **24. If I had not done among them the works which none other man did** [ἐποίησεν is beyond doubt the true reading: the received text— πεποίηκεν, 'hath done'—has but inferior support]. **they had not had sin**—rather, as before, 'would not have sin,' *comparatively:* **but now have they both seen and hated both me and my Father:** they saw His Father revealed in Him, and in Him they hated both the Father and the Son. In *v.* 22 He places the peculiar aggravation of their guilt in His having "come and spoken to them;" here He makes it consist in their having seen Him do the works which none other man did. See on ch. xiv. 10, 11, where we have the same association of His *works* and His *words*, as either of them sufficient to show that the Father was in Him and He in the Father. **25. But [this cometh to pass], that the word might be fulfilled that is written in their law** (Ps. lxix. 4), **They hated me without a cause.** The New Testa-

26   But "when the Comforter is come, whom I will send unto you from the
Father, *even* the Spirit of truth, which proceedeth from the Father, "he
27   shall testify of me: And "ye also shall bear witness, because "ye have
been with me from the beginning.

A. D. 33.

" Acts 2. 33.
" 1 John 5. 6.
" Acts 1. 8.
" Luke 1. 2.

ment references to this Messianic psalm of suffering are numerous (see ch. ii. 17; Acts i. 20; Rom. xi. 9, 10; xv. 3), and this one, as here used, is very striking.

The Two-fold Witness which Christ was to receive from the Holy Ghost and from His chosen Apostles (26). **26. But when the Comforter is come, whom I will send unto you from the Father, even the Spirit of truth, which proceedeth from the Father.** How brightly are *Father, Son, and Holy Ghost*—in their distinct Personality, brought here before us! While the 'procession' of the Holy Ghost, as it is called, was by the whole ancient Church founded on this statement regarding Him, that He "proceedeth from the Father," the Greek Church inferred from it that, in the internal relations of the Godhead, the Spirit proceedeth *from* the Father only, *through* the Son; while the Latin Church insisted that He proceedeth from the Father *and the Son:* and one short word (*Filioque*) which the latter would exclude and the former insert in the Creed, was the cause of the great schism between the Eastern and the Western Churches. That the *internal* or *essential* procession of the Holy Ghost is the thing here intended, has been the prevailing opinion of the orthodox Churches of the Reformation, and is that of good critics even in our day. But though we seem warranted in affirming—in the technical language of divines—that the *economic* order follows the *essential* in the relations of the Divine Persons—in other words, that in the economy of Redemption the relations sustained by the Divine Persons do but reflect their essential relations—it is very doubtful whether more is expressed here than the *historical* aspect of this mission and procession of the Spirit from the Father by the Agency of the Son. **he shall testify of me** —referring to that glorious Pentecostal attestation of the Messiahship of the Lord Jesus which, in a few days, gave birth to a flourishing Christian Church in the murderous capital itself, and the speedy diffusion of it far and wide. **27. And ye also**—as the other witness required to the validity of testimony among men (Deut. xix. 15) **shall bear witness** [μαρτυρεῖτε]—or 'do bear witness' **because ye have been** [ἐστε]—or 'are' **with me from the beginning.** Our Lord here uses the present tense—"do testify" and "are with Me"—to express the opportunities which they had enjoyed for this office of witness-bearing, from their having been with Him from the outset of His ministry (see on Luke i. 2), and how this observation and experience of Him, being now all but completed, they were already virtually a company of chosen witnesses for His Name.

Remarks.—1. If the strain in which our Lord spoke of Himself in the foregoing chapter was such as befitted only Lips Divine, in no less exalted a tone does He speak throughout all this chapter. For any mere creature, however lofty, to represent himself as *the one Source of all spiritual vitality* in men, would be insufferable. But this our Lord here explicitly and emphatically does, and that at the most solemn hour of His earthly history—on the eve of His death. To abide in Him, he says, is to have spiritual life and fruitfulness; not to abide in Him is to be fit only for the fire—"whose end is to be burned." What prophet or apostle ever ventured to put forth for himself such a claim as this? Yet see how the Father's rights and honours are upheld. My

Father, says Jesus, is the Husbandman of that great Vineyard whose whole spring of life and fruitfulness is in Me; and herein is My Father glorified, that all the branches in the True Vine do bear much fruit. Then, again, such power and prevalency with God does He attach to His people's abiding in Him, and His words abiding in them, that His Father will withhold nothing from such that they shall ask of Him. In a word, so perfect a manifestation of the Father does He declare Himself to be in our nature, that to see Him is to see Both at once, and to hate Him is to be guilty in one and the same act of deadly hostility to Both. 2. When our Lord said, "If ye abide in Me, and *My words* abide in you," He must have contemplated the *preservation of His words in a written Record,* and designed that, over and above the general truth conveyed by His teaching, the precise form in which He couched that truth should be carefully treasured up and cherished by His believing people. Hence the importance of that promise, that the Spirit should "bring all things to their remembrance, whatsoever He had said unto them." (See on ch. xiv. 26.) And hence the danger of those loose views of Inspiration which would abandon all faith even in the words of Christ, as reported in the Gospels, and abide by what is called the spirit or general import of them—as if even this could be depended upon when the form in which it was couched is regarded as uncertain. (See on ch. xvii. 17.) 3. If we would have *Christ Himself* abiding in us, it must be, we see, by "*His words* abiding in us" (*v.* 7). Let the word of Christ, then, dwell in you richly in all wisdom (Col. iii. 16). 4. How small is the confidence reposed in that promise of the Faithful and True Witness, "If ye abide in Me, and My words abide in you, ye shall ask what ye will, and it shall be done unto you"—if we may judge by the formal character and the languid and uncertain tone of the generality of Christian prayers! Surely, if we had full faith in such a promise, it would give to our prayers such a definite character and such a lively assured tone as, while themselves no small part of the true answer, to prepare the petitioner for the divine response to his suit. Such a manner of praying, indeed, is apt to be regarded as presumptuous by some even true Christians, who are too great strangers to the spirit of adoption. But if we abide in our living Head, and His words abide in us, our carriage in this exercise, as in every other, will commend itself. 5. Let Christians learn from their Master's teaching in this chapter whence proceeds much, if not most, of their darkness and uncertainty as to whether they be the gracious objects of God's saving love in Christ Jesus. "If ye keep My commandments," says Jesus, "ye shall abide in My love, even as I have kept My Father's commandments, and abide in His love." Habitual want of conscience as to any one of these will suffice to cloud the mind as to the love of Christ resting upon us. Take, for example, that one commandment which our Lord so emphatically reiterates in this chapter: "This is My commandment, That ye love one another, as I have loved you. These things I command you, that ye love one another." No ordinary love is this. "As I have loved you" is the sublime Model, as it is the only spring of this commanded love of the brethren. How much of this is there among

16 THESE things have I spoken unto you, that ye should not be offended.

2 They shall put you out of the synagogues: yea, the time cometh, "that

3 whosoever killeth you will think that he doeth God service. And *b* these things will they do unto you, because they have not known the Father,

4 nor me. But these things have I told you, that, when the time shall come, ye may remember that I told you of them. And these things I

5 said not unto you at the beginning, because I was with you. But now I go my way to him that sent me; and none of you asketh me, Whither

6 goest thou? But because I have said these things unto you, sorrow hath filled your heart.

7 Nevertheless I tell you the truth; It is expedient for you that I go away: for if I go not away, the Comforter will not come unto you; but

8 *c* if I depart, I will send him unto you. And when he is come, he will ¹re-

A. D. 33.
CHAP. 16.
a Matt.10. 23.
Acts 5. 33.
Acts 8. 1.
Acts 9. 1.
Acts 26. 9.
Rom. 10. 2.
Gal 1. 13.
b Rom. 10. 2.
1 Cor. 2. 8.
1 Tim. 1.13.
c Acts 2. 33.
Eph. 4. 8.
1 Or,
convince.
1 Cor.14. 24.

Christians? To what extent is it characteristic of them—how far is it their notorious undeniable character? (See on ch. xvii. 21.) Alas! whether we look to churches or to individual Christians, the open manifestation of any such feeling is the exception rather than the rule. Or let us try how far the generality of Christians are like their Lord by the world's feeling towards them. We know how it felt towards Jesus Himself. It was what He was that the world hated: it was His fidelity in exposing its evil ways that the world could not endure. Had He been less holy than He was, or been contented to endure the unholiness that reigned around Him without witnessing against it, He had not met with the opposition that He did. "The world cannot hate you," said He to His brethren, "but Me it hateth, because I testify of it, that the works thereof are evil" (ch. vii. 7). And the same treatment, in principle, He here prepares His genuine disciples for, when He should leave them to represent Him in the world—"Remember the word that I said unto you, The servant is not greater than His lord. If ye were of the world, the world would love his own; but because ye are not of the world, but I have chosen you out of the world, therefore the world hateth you." Is it not, then, too much to be feared that the good terms which the generality of Christians are on with the world are owing, not to the near approach of the world to them, but to their so near approach to the world, that the essential and unchangeable difference between them is hardly seen? And if so, need we wonder that those words of Jesus seem too high to be reached at all—"If ye keep My commandments, ye shall abide in My love; even as I have kept My Father's commandments, and abide in His love"? When Christians cease from the vain attempt to serve two masters, and from receiving honour one of another, instead of seeking the honour that cometh from God only; when they count all things but loss, that they may win Christ, and the love of Christ constraineth them to live not unto themselves, but unto Him that died for them and rose again: then will they abide in Christ's love, even as He abode in His Father's love; His joy shall then abide in them; and their joy shall be full.

CHAP. XVI. 1-33.—CONCLUSION OF THE DISCOURSE AT THE SUPPER-TABLE.

Persecution, even unto Death, to be Expected (1-4). **1. These things have I spoken unto you, that ye should not be offended**—or 'scandalized;' referring back both to the warnings and the encouragements He had just given. **2. They shall put you out of the synagogues** [Ἀποσυναγώγους ποιήσουσιν ὑμᾶς]—(see on ch. ix. 22; see also xii. 42): **yea, the time cometh, that whosoever**

killeth you will think that he doeth God service [λατρείαν προσφέρειν]—or 'that he is offering a [religious] service unto God;' as Saul of Tarsus did (Acts xxvi. 9, 10; Gal. i. 9, 10; Phil. iii. 6). **3. And these things will they do unto you, because they have not known the Father, nor me.** See on ch. xv. 21, of which this is nearly a verbal repetition. **4. But these things have I told you, that, when the time** [ὥρα]—or 'the hour' shall **come, ye may remember that I told you of them** —and so be confirmed in your faith and strengthened in courage. **And these things I said not unto you at the beginning, because I was with you.** He *had* said it pretty early (Luke vi. 22), but not so nakedly as in *v.* 2.

His approaching Departure to His Father again Announced, and the Necessity of it in order to the Mission of the Comforter (5-7). **5. But now I go my way to him that sent me.** While He was with them the world's hatred was directed chiefly against Himself; but His departure would bring it down upon them as His representatives. **and none of you asketh me, Whither goest thou?** They *had* done so in a sort, ch. xiii. 36; xiv. 5; but He wished more intelligent and eager enquiry on the subject. **6. But because I have said these things unto you, sorrow hath filled your heart.** And how, it may be asked, could it be otherwise? But this sorrow had too much paralyzed them, and He would rouse their energies. **7. Nevertheless I tell you the truth; It is expedient for you that I go away—**

'My Saviour, can it ever be
That I should gain by losing thee?'—KEBLE.

Yes, **for if I go not away, the Comforter will not come unto you; but if I depart, I will send him unto you.** See on ch. vii. 39, and Remark 3 at the end of that Section; and on ch. xiv. 16.

The Three-fold Office of the Comforter (8-11). This passage, says *Olshausen*, 'is one of the most pregnant with thought in the profound discourses of Christ. With a few great strokes He depicts all and every part of the ministry of the Divine Spirit in the world; His operation with reference to individuals as well as the mass, on believers and unbelievers alike.' It is laid out in three particulars, each of which is again taken up and explained in detail.

8. And when he is come, he will reprove the world of SIN, and of RIGHTEOUSNESS, and of JUDGMENT.

The word rendered 'reprove' [ἐλέγξει] means more than that. *Reproof* is indeed implied, and doubtless the work begins with it. But 'convict,' or, as in the margin, 'convince,' is the thing intended; and as the one word expresses the work of the Spirit on the *unbelieving* portion of man-

444

9 ¹prove the world of sin, and of righteousness, and of judgment: of ᵈsin,
10 because they believe not on me; of ᵉrighteousness, because I go to my
11 Father, and ye see me no more; of ᶠjudgment, because ᵍthe prince of
this world is judged.

A. D. 33.
ᵈ Acts 2. 22.
ᵉ Acts 2. 32.
ᶠ Acts 26. 18.
ᵍ Luke 10.18.

kind, and the other on the *believing*, it is better not to restrict the term to either.

First, 9. **Of SIN, because they believe not on me.** By this is not meant that He shall deal with men about *the sin of unbelief only;* nor yet about that sin as, in comparison with all other sins, *the greatest.* There is no comparison here between the sin of unbelief and other breaches of the moral law, in point of criminality. The key to this important statement will be found in such sayings of our Lord Himself as the following: "He that believeth is not condemned; but he that believeth not is condemned already, because he hath not believed in the name of the Only begotten Son of God: He that heareth My word, and believeth on Him that sent Me, hath everlasting life, and shall not come into condemnation, but is passed from death unto life: He that believeth not the Son shall not see life, but the wrath of God abideth on him" (ch. iii. 18, 36; v. 24). What the Spirit, then, does in the discharge of this first department of His work, is to bear in upon men's consciences the conviction that the one divinely provided way of deliverance from the guilt of *all sin* is believing on the Son of God; that *as soon* as they thus believe, there is no condemnation to them; but that *unless* and *until* they do so, they underlie the guilt of all their sins, with that of this crowning and all-condemning sin superadded. Thus does the Spirit, in fastening this truth upon the conscience, instead of extinguishing, only consummate and intensify the sense of all other sins; causing the convicted sinner to perceive that his complete absolution from guilt, or his remediless condemnation under the weight of all his sins, hangs upon his believing on the Son of God, or his deliberate rejection of Him.

But what, it may be asked, is the sinner to believe regarding Christ, in order to so vast a deliverance? The next department of the Spirit's work will answer that question.

Second, 10. **Of RIGHTEOUSNESS, because I go to my Father, and ye see** [θεωρεῖτε]—or 'behold' —**me no more.** Beyond doubt, it is *Christ's personal righteousness* which the Spirit was to bring home to the sinner's heart. The evidence of this was to lie in the great *historical fact,* that He had "gone to His Father, and was no more visible to men:" for if His claim to be the Son of God, the Saviour of the world, had been a lie, how should the Father, who is "a jealous God," have raised such a blasphemer from the dead, and exalted him to His right hand? But if He was the "Faithful and True Witness," the Father's "Righteous Servant," "His Elect, in whom His soul delighted," then was His departure to the Father, and consequent disappearance from the view of men, but the fitting consummation, the august reward, of all that He did here below, the seal of His mission, the glorification of the testimony which He bore on earth, by the translation of its Bearer to the Father's bosom. This triumphant vindication of Christ's *rectitude* is to us divine evidence, bright as heaven, that He is indeed the Saviour of the world, God's Righteous Servant to justify many, because He bare their iniquities (Is. liii. 11). Thus the Spirit, in this second sphere of His work, is seen convincing men that there is in Christ perfect relief under the sense of *sin,* of which He had before convinced them; and so far from mourning over His absence from us, as an irreparable loss, we learn

to glory in it, as the evidence of His perfect acceptance on our behalf, exclaiming with one who understood this point, "Who shall lay any thing to the charge of God's elect? It is God that justifieth; who is he that condemneth? It is Christ that died, *yea rather, that is risen again, who is even at the right hand of God,*" &c. (Rom. viii. 33, 34). 'But, alas!'—may some say, who have long been "sold under sin," who have too long been willing captives of the prince of this world— 'Of what avail to me is deliverance from any amount of guilt, and investiture even in the righteousness which cannot be challenged, if I am to be left under the power of sin and Satan? for he that committeth sin is of the devil, and to be carnally minded is death.' But you are not to be so left. For there remains one more department of the Spirit's work, which exactly meets, and was intended to meet, your case.

Third, 11. **Of JUDGMENT, because the prince of this world is**—or 'hath been' **judged.** By taking the word "judgment" to refer to the judgment of the great day—as is done even by good interpreters—the point of this glorious assurance is quite missed. Beyond all doubt, when it is said, "The prince of this world hath been *judged*" [κέκριται]—or, in our Lord's usual sense of that term, *condemned*—the meaning is the same as in a former chapter, where, speaking of His *death,* He says, "Now shall the prince of this world be *cast out* [ἐκβληθήσεται ἔξω]; and in both places the meaning clearly is, that the prince of this world is, by the death of Christ, *judicially overthrown,* or *condemned to lose his hold,* and so, "cast out" or *expelled from his usurped dominion* over men who, believing in the Son of God, are made the righteousness of God in Him: so that, looking to Him who spoiled principalities and powers, and made a show of them openly, triumphing over them in His cross, they need henceforth have no fear of his enslaving power. (See Col. ii. 15; Heb. ii. 14; 1 John iii. 8.)

Thus is this three-fold office of the Spirit entirely of one character. It is in all its departments *Evangelical* and *Saving:* bringing home to the conscience the sense of sin, as all consummated and fastened down upon the sinner who rejects Him that came to put away sin by the sacrifice of Himself; the sense of perfect relief in the *righteousness* of the Father's servant, now taken from the earth that spurned Him to that bosom where from everlasting He had dwelt; and the sense of emancipation from the fetters of Satan, whose *judgment* brings to men *liberty to be holy,* and transformation out of servants of the devil into sons and daughters of the Lord Almighty. To one class of men, however, all this will carry *conviction* only; they "will not come to Christ"—revealed though He be to them as the life-giving One—that they may have life. Such, abiding voluntarily under the dominion of the Prince of this world, are *judged in his judgment,* the visible consummation of which will be at the great day. But to another class this blessed teaching will have a different issue—translating them out of the kingdom of darkness into the kingdom of God's dear Son.

The Bearing of the Spirit's Work upon the Work of Christ (12-15). **12. I have yet many things to say unto you, but ye cannot bear them now.**

445

12 I have yet many things to say unto you, but ye cannot bear them
13 now. Howbeit when he, the Spirit of truth, is come, *[h]*he will guide you into all truth: for he shall not speak of himself; but whatsoever he shall
14 hear, *that* shall he speak: and he will *[i]*show you things to come. He shall glorify me; for he shall receive of mine, and shall show *it* unto you.
15 All *[j]*things that the Father hath are mine: therefore said I, that he
16 shall take of mine, and shall show *it* unto you. A little while, and ye shall not see me: and again, a little while, and ye shall see me; because I go to the Father.
17 Then said *some* of his disciples among themselves, What is this that he saith unto us, A little while, and ye shall not see me: and again, a little
18 while, and ye shall see me: and, Because I go to the Father? They said therefore, What is this that he saith, A little while? we cannot tell what
19 he saith. Now Jesus knew that they were desirous to ask him, and said unto them, Do ye enquire among yourselves of that I said, A little while, and ye shall not see me: and again, a little while, and ye shall see me?
20 Verily, verily, I say unto you, That ye shall weep and lament, but the world shall rejoice: and ye shall be sorrowful, but your sorrow shall be
21 turned into joy. A woman when she is in travail hath sorrow, because her hour is come: but as soon as she is delivered of the child, she remembereth no more the anguish, for joy that a man is born into the
22 world. And ye now therefore have sorrow: but I will see you again, and

'A. D. 33.

[h] ch. 14. 26.
1 Cor. 2, 10-13.
Eph. 4. 7.
16.
1 John 2. 20, 27.
[i] Joel 2. 28.
Acts 2. 17, 18.
Acts 11. 28.
Acts 20. 23.
Acts 21. 9, 11.
2 Thes. 2. 3-12.
1 Tim. 4. 1.
2 Tim. 3. 1-5.
2 Pet. 2. 1.
Rev. 1. 1,19.
[j] Matt. 11. 27.
Matt. 28. 18.
Luke 10. 22.
ch. 3. 35.
ch. 17. 10.
Col 1. 19.
Col. 2. 3, 9.

This refers not so much to truths not uttered by Himself at all, as to the full development and complete exposition of truths which at that stage could only be expressed generally or in their germs. **13. Howbeit when he, the Spirit of truth** —so called for the reason mentioned in the next clause, **is come, he will guide you into all truth** [πᾶσαν τὴν ἀλήθειαν]—rather, 'all the truth;' for the reference is not to 'truth in general,' but to 'that whole circle of truth whose burden is Christ and His redeeming work:' **for he shall not speak of himself** [ἀφ' ἑαυτοῦ]. The meaning is not, 'He shall not speak *concerning* Himself,' but 'He shall not speak *from* Himself;' in the sense immediately to be added. **but whatsoever he shall hear**—or receive to communicate, **that shall he speak: and he will show you things to come** [τὰ ἐρχόμενα]— 'the things to come;' referring specially to those revelations which, in the Epistles partially, but most fully in the Apocalypse, open up a vista into the Future of the Kingdom of God, whose horizon is the everlasting hills. **14. He shall glorify me; for he shall receive of mine, and shall show it unto you.** Thus the whole design of the Spirit's office is to glorify Christ—not in His own Person, for this was done by the Father when He exalted Him to His own right hand—but in the view and estimation of men. For this purpose He was to "*receive of Christ*"—that is, all that related to His Person and Work—" and *show it unto them*," or make them, by His inward teaching, to discern it in its own light. The internal or *subjective* nature of the Spirit's teaching—how His office is to discover to the souls of men what Christ is outwardly or *objectively*—is here very clearly expressed; and, at the same time, the vanity of looking for revelations of the Spirit which shall do anything beyond throwing light in the soul upon what Christ Himself is, and taught, and did upon earth. **15. All things that the Father hath are mine: therefore said I, that he shall take** [λήμψεται, as in v. 14]—or, according to what appears the better supported reading, 'receiveth' [λαμβάνει], a lively way of saying 'He is just about to receive' of mine, and shall show it unto you. A plainer expression than this of

absolute community with the Father in all things cannot be conceived, although the "all things" here have reference to the things of the Kingdom of Grace, which the Spirit was to receive that He might show them to us. We have here a wonderful glimpse into the *inner relations* of the Godhead. The design of this explanation seems to be to prevent any mistake as to the relations which He sustained to the Father.

Christ Soon to Go, but Soon to Return, and the Effect of these Movements on those who Loved and those who Hated Him (16-22). **16. A little while, and ye shall not see me** [θεωρεῖτε]—' and ye behold Me not:' and again, a little while, and ye shall see me; because I go to the Father. [The last clause—ὅτι ἐγὼ ὑπάγω πρὸς τὸν πατέρα—is omitted by *Tischendorf* and *Tregelles*, and bracketed by *Lachmann*. But the evidence in its favour is, in our judgment, preponderating; and the question of the disciples in *v.* 17 seems to presuppose it.] **17. Then said some of his disciples among themselves**—afraid, perhaps, to question the Lord Himself on the subject, or unwilling to interrupt Him, **What is this that he saith unto us, A little while, and ye shall not see me**—or, ' and ye behold Me not:' **and again, a little while, and ye shall see me: and, Because I go to the Father? 18. They said therefore, What is this that he saith, A little while?** [τὸ μικρόν]—rather, 'The,' or 'That little while?' **we cannot tell what he saith**—[οὐκ οἴδαμεν τί λαλεῖ]—' We know not what He speaketh of.' **19. Now Jesus knew that they were desirous to ask him**—showing with what tender minuteness He watched how far they apprehended His teaching, what impressions it produced upon them, and what steps it prompted to. **and said unto them, Do ye enquire among yourselves of that I said, A little while,** &c. **20. Verily, verily, I say unto you, That ye shall weep and lament, but the world shall rejoice: and ye shall be sorrowful, but your sorrow shall be turned into joy. 21. A woman when she is in travail hath sorrow,** &c. **22. And ye now therefore have sorrow: but I will see you again, and your heart shall rejoice, and your joy no man taketh from you. The**

446

23 *your heart shall rejoice, and your joy no man taketh from you. And in that day ye shall ask me nothing. *Verily, verily, I say unto you, Whatsoever ye shall ask the Father in my name, he will give *it* you.

24 Hitherto have ye asked nothing in my name: ask, and ye shall receive, that your joy may be full.

25 These things have I spoken unto you in [2]proverbs: but the time cometh, when I shall no more speak unto you in [3]proverbs, but I shall

26 show you plainly of the Father. At that day ye shall ask in my name:

27 and I say not unto you, that I will pray the Father for you; for *the Father himself loveth you, because ye have loved me, and *have believed

28 that I came out from God. I °came forth from the Father, and am come into the world: again, I leave the world, and go to the Father.

29 His disciples said unto him, Lo, now speakest thou plainly, and

30 speakest no [4]proverb. Now are we sure that *thou knowest all things, and needest not that any man should ask thee: by this *we believe that

31 thou camest forth from God. Jesus answered them, Do ye now believe?

A. D. 33.

* Luke 24.41.
ch. 14. 1, 27.
ch. 20. 20.
Acts 2. 46.
Acts 13. 52.
1 Pet. 1. 8.
* ch. 14. 13.
ch. 15. 16.
[2] Or, parables.
[3] Or, parables.
* ch. 14. 21.
* ch. 3. 13.
ch. 17. 8.
° ch. 13. 3.
[4] Or, parable.
* ch. 21. 17.
* ch. 17. 8.

joy of the world at His disappearance seems to show that the thing meant was His removal from them by *death.* In that case, the joy of the disciples at seeing Him again must refer to their transport at His reappearance amongst them on His *resurrection*, when they could no longer doubt His identity. But the words go beyond this: for as His personal stay amongst them after His resurrection was brief, and His actual manifestations but occasional, while the language is that of permanence, we must view His return to them at His resurrection as virtually *uninterrupted by His ascension* to glory (according to His way of speaking in ch. xiv. 18-20). But the words carry us on even to the transport of the widowed Church when her Lord shall come again to receive her to Himself, that where He is, there she may be also.

The Relation of Believers to the absent Saviour and to the Father (23-27). **23. And in that day—** when He should return to them by resurrection, but be in glory, **ye shall ask**—or 'enquire of' **me nothing**—'ye shall not, as ye do now, bring all your enquiries to Me in Person, as one beside you.' **Verily, verily, I say unto you, Whatsoever ye shall ask the Father in my name, he will give it you.** See on ch. xiv. 13, 14; xv. 7. Thus would they be at no real loss for want of Him amongst them, in the way of earthly intercourse, but vastly the better. **24. Hitherto have ye asked nothing in my name.** Ordinary readers are apt to lay the emphasis of this statement on the word "nothing;" as if it meant, 'Hitherto your askings in My name have been next to nothing, but now be encouraged to enlarge your petitions.' Clearly the emphasis is on the words "in My Name," and the statement is absolute: 'hitherto your prayers to the Father have not been offered in My Name;' for, as *Olshausen* correctly says, prayer *in the name of Christ*, as well as prayer *to Christ*, presupposes His *glorification.* **ask**—'When I shall have gone to the Father, ye shall have but to ask in this new, all-prevailing form;' **and ye shall receive, that your joy may be full.** So that the new footing on which they would find themselves with Jesus— no longer beside them to be consulted in every difficulty, but with them, notwithstanding, as an all-prevalent Medium of communication with the Father—would be vastly preferable to the old.

25. These things have I spoken unto you in proverbs—or 'parables;' that is, in obscure language; as opposed to speaking "plainly" in the next clause: **but the time cometh**—'but there cometh an hour,' **when I shall no more speak unto you in proverbs, but I shall show**—or 'tell' **you

plainly of the Father**—that is, by the Spirit's teaching. How "plain" that made all things, compared with anything they took up from Christ's own teaching, will be seen by comparing Peter's addresses after the day of Pentecost with his speeches while his Lord was going out and in with the Twelve. **26. At that day ye shall ask in my name.** He had before *bidden* them do so: here He intimates that this is to be the appropriate, characteristic exercise of the believing Church, in its intercourse with the Father. **and I say not, that I will pray the Father for you**— that is, as if the Father were of Himself *indisposed* to hear them, or as if His own solicitations were needed to incline an *unwilling* Ear. Christ *does* pray the Father for them, but certainly not for this reason. **27. For the Father himself loveth you, because ye have loved me, and have believed that I came out from God.** This love of theirs is that which is called forth by God's eternal love in the gift of his Son, *mirrored* in the hearts of those who believe, and resting on His dear Son.

The Disciples, Re-assured by the greater explicitness of their Master's Statements, are Warned how speedily they will Desert Him (28-32). **28. I came forth from the Father, and am come into the world: again, I leave the world, and go to the Father:**—'Ye have believed that I came out from God, and ye are right; for I came indeed forth from the Father, and am soon to return whence I came.' This echo of the truth alluded to in the preceding verse seems like *thinking aloud*, as if it were grateful to His own spirit on such a subject and at such an hour.

29. His disciples said unto him, Lo, now speakest thou plainly, and speakest no proverb. It was not much plainer than before—the time for perfect plainness was yet to come: but having caught a glimpse of His meaning—for it was little more—they eagerly express their satisfaction, as if glad to make anything of His words. How touchingly does this show both the simplicity of their hearts and the infantile character of their faith! **30. Now are we sure that thou knowest all things**—the very thought of their hearts, in this case, and how to meet it; **and needest not that any man should ask thee: by this we believe that thou camest forth from God.** There was more sincerity in this than enlightened knowledge of the meaning of their own words. But our Lord accepted it so far as it went. **31. Jesus answered them, Do ye now believe?**—'It is well ye do, for that faith is soon to be tested,

32 Behold, the hour cometh, yea, is now come, that ye shall be scattered, every man to [5]his own, and shall leave me alone: and yet I am not
33 alone, because the Father is with me. These things I have spoken unto you, that [r]in me ye might have peace. [s]In the world ye shall have tribulation: but be of good cheer; [t]I have overcome the world.

A. D. 33.
[5] Or, his own home.
[r] Isa. 9. 6.
[s] Acts 14. 22.
[t] Rom. 8. 37.

and in a way ye little expect.' **32. Behold, the hour cometh**—'there cometh an hour,' **that ye shall be scattered, every man to his own** [εἰς τὰ ἴδια]—'his own [home'], as in ch. xix. 27, what he formerly left for My sake, as *Bengel* explains it; **and shall leave me alone: and yet I am not alone.** A deep and awful sense of *wrong* experienced is certainly expressed here, but how lovingly! That He was not to be utterly deserted—that there was One who would not forsake Him—was to Him matter of ineffable support and consolation; but that He should be without all *human* countenance and cheer, who as **M**an was exquisitely sensitive to the law of sympathy, would fill themselves with as much *shame*, when they afterwards recurred to it, as the Redeemer's heart in His hour of need with pungent *sorrow*. "I looked for some to take pity, but there was none; and for comforters, but I found none" (Ps. lxix. 20.) **because the Father is with me**—how near, and with what sustaining power, who can express?

The Intent of this whole Discourse expressed in one comprehensive, closing word (33). **33. These things I have spoken unto you**—not the immediately preceding words, but this whole discourse, of which these were the very last words, and which He thus winds up; **that in me ye might have peace**—in the sublime sense before explained on ch. xiv. 27. **In the world ye shall have tribulation** [ἕξετε]—but this reading has very slender support: the true reading undoubtedly is, 'In the world ye have tribulation' [ἔχετε]; for being already "not of the world, but chosen out of the world," they were already beginning to experience its deadly opposition, and would soon know more of it. So that the "peace" promised was to be far from an unruffled one. **but be of good cheer; I have overcome the world**—not only *before* you, but *for* you, that ye may be not only encouraged, but enabled to do the same. (See 1 John v. 4, 5.) The last and crowning act of His victory, indeed, was yet to come. But it was all but come, and the result was as certain as if all had been already over—the consciousness of which, no doubt, was the chief source of that wonderful calm with which He went through the whole of this solemn scene in the upper room.

Remarks.—1. The language in which the blessed Spirit is spoken of throughout all this last Discourse of Our Lord is quite decisive of His DIVINE PERSONALITY. Nor does *Stier* express himself too strongly when he says that he who can regard all the *personal* expressions applied to the Spirit in these three chapters—"teaching," "reminding," "testifying," "coming," "convincing," "guiding," "speaking," "hearing," "prophesying," "taking"— as being no other than a long-drawn figure, deserves not to be recognized as an interpreter of intelligible words, much less an expositor of Holy Scripture. 2. As there is no subject in Christian Theology on which accurate thinking is of more importance than *the relation of the work of the Spirit to the work of Christ*, so there is no place in which that relation is more precisely defined and amply expressed than in this chapter. For, first, we are expressly told that the Spirit's teaching is limited to that which He receives to communicate (v. 13); **that what He receives is "of that which is**
448

Christ's" [ἐκ τοῦ Ἐμοῦ]—or, in other words, that the Spirit's teaching relates wholly to Christ's Person and Errand into the world; and lest this should seem to narrow undesirably and disadvantageously the range of the Spirit's functions, we are told that Christ's "things" embrace "all the Father's things" (v. 15)—that is to say, all that the Father contemplated and arranged from everlasting for the recovery of men in His Son Christ Jesus. Thus are the Spirit's functions not *narrow*, but only *definite*: they are as wide in their range as the work of Christ and the saving purposes of God in Him; but they are *no wider—no other*. Accordingly, when our Lord lays out in detail the subject-matter of the Spirit's teaching, He makes it all to centre in HIMSELF:—"He shall convince the world of sin, because they believe not on *Me;* of righteousness, because *I* go to My Father, and ye see Me no more; of judgment, because (by *My* "uplifting," ch. xii. 31, 32) the Prince of this world is judged." But secondly, this being so, it clearly follows that the whole design of the Spirit's work is to reveal to men's minds the true nature and glory of Christ's work in the flesh, as attested and crowned by His resurrection and glorification; to plant in men's souls the assurance of its truth; and to bring them to repose on it their whole confidence for acceptance with the Father and everlasting life. Thus, as Christ's work was *objective* and *for* men, the Spirit's work is *subjective* and *in* men. The one is what divines call the *purchase*, the other what they call the *application* of redemption. The one was done outwardly once for all, by Christ on earth; the other is done inwardly in each individual saved soul, by the Spirit from heaven. And thus have we here brought before us the FATHER, the SON, and the HOLY GHOST—one adorable Godhead, distinct in operation even as in Person, yet divinely harmonious and concurrent for the salvation of sinners. 3. How beautifully does Jesus here teach us to travel between the sense of His Personal *absence* and the sense of His spiritual *presence*. He would have us feel the desolating effect of His Personal absence, but not be paralyzed by it, inasmuch as His spiritual presence would be felt to be unspeakably real, sustaining, and consolatory. And by directing them to ask all things of the Father in His name, during the period of His departure, He would teach them to regard His absence for them in heaven to be vastly better for them than His presence with them as they then enjoyed it. At the same time, since even this would be a very inadequate compensation for His Personal Presence, He would have them to rest in nothing short of this, that He was coming again to receive them to Himself, that where He was, there they might be also. 4. In Christ's being "left alone" in His last sufferings, may there not be seen a divine arrangement for bringing out in manifest and affecting fulfilment that typical provision for the great day of atonement: "*And there shall be no man in the tabernacle of the congregation when he* (the high priest) *goeth in to make an atonement in the holy place, until he come out*"? (Lev. xvi. 17). 5. How sweet is the summation of this wonderful Discourse in its closing word—the last that Jesus was to utter to the whole Eleven before He suf-

17 THESE words spake Jesus, and lifted up his eyes to heaven, and said, Father, the hour is come; glorify thy Son, that thy Son also may glorify 2 thee: as ^athou hast given him power over all flesh, that he should give

A. D. 33.

CHAP. 17.

^a Dan. 7. 14.

fered: "These things have I spoken unto you, that IN ME ye might have peace"—not untroubled peace, for "in the world they were to have tribulation;" but the assurance that "He had overcome the world" would make them too more than conquerors.

CHAP. XVII. 1-26.—THE INTERCESSORY PRAYER. For the general character of this portion of the Fourth Gospel, see the opening remarks on ch. xiv. As for this Prayer, had it not been recorded, what reverential reader would not have exclaimed, O to have been within hearing of such a prayer as that must have been, which wound up the whole of His past ministry and formed the point of transition to the dark scenes which immediately followed! But here it is, and with such signature of the Lips that uttered it that we seem rather to hear it from Himself than read it from the pen of His faithful reporter. Were it not almost profane even to advert to it, we might ask the reader to listen to the character given of this Prayer by the first critic, bearing a Christian name, who in modern times has questioned, though he afterwards admitted, the genuineness and authenticity of the Fourth Gospel (*Bretschneider*—with whom, as might be expected, *Strauss* agrees): he calls it 'frigid, dogmatic, metaphysical.' What a commentary on those apostolic words, "The natural man receiveth not the things of the Spirit of God; for they are foolishness unto him: neither can he know them, because they are spiritually discerned" (1 Cor. ii. 14). Happily, the universal instinct of Christendom recoils from such language, and feels itself, while standing within the precincts of this chapter, to be on holy ground, yea, in the very holy of holies. We may add, with *Bengel*, that this chapter is, in the words of it, the most simple, but in sense the most profound in all the Bible; or, as *Luther* said long before, that plain and simple as it sounds, it is so deep, rich, and broad, that no man can fathom it.

The Prayer naturally divides itself into three parts: *First*, What relates to the Son Himself, who offered the prayer (1-5); *secondly*, what had reference more immediately to those Eleven disciples in whose hearing the prayer was uttered (6-19); *thirdly*, what belongs to all who should believe on Him through their word, to the end of the world (20-24); with two concluding verses, simply breathing out His soul in a survey, at once dark and bright, of the whole past results of His mission.

We address ourselves to the exposition of this Prayer, with the warning to Moses sounding in our ears—and let it sound in thine, O reader!— "Put off thy shoes from off thy feet, for the place whereon thou standest is holy ground" (Exod. iii. 5); yet encouraged by the assurance of Him that uttered it, that the Comforter "shall glorify Him—receiving of His, and showing it unto us."

FIRST, *Jesus Prays for Himself* (1-5). **1. These words spake Jesus, and lifted up his eyes to heaven.** 'John,' says *Alford*, 'very seldom depicts the gestures or looks of our Lord, as here. But this was an occasion of which the impression was indelible, and the upward look could not be passed over.' **and said, Father.** Never does Jesus say in prayer, '*Our* Father,' though He directs His disciples to do it; but always "Father," and once, during His Agony, "My Father:" thus severing Himself as Man from all other men, as

the "Separate from sinners," though "Bone of our bone, and Flesh of our flesh." **the hour is come.** But did not the Father, you will say, know that? O yes, and Jesus knew that He knew it. But He had not that narrow and distant and cold view of prayer which some even true Christians have, as if it was designed for nothing else but to express petitions for benefits needed, promised, expected. Prayer is the creature yearning after Him that gave it being, looking up into its Father's face, opening its bosom to the brightness and warmth of His felt presence, drinking in fresh assurances of safety under His wing, fresh inspirations of His love, fresh nobility from the consciousness of its nearness to Him. In prayer believers draw near to God, not merely when necessity drives them, but under the promptings of filial love, and just because "it is good for them to draw near to God." We like to breathe the air of His presence; we love to come to Him, though it were for nothing but to cry, in the spirit of adoption, "Abba, Father." "Walking in the light as He is in the light, we have fellowship One with the other—He with us and we with Him"—uplifting, invigorating, transfiguring fellowship. How much more, then, must Christ's prayers, and this one above all, have been of that character! Hear Him telling His Father here, with sublime simplicity and familiarity, that "the hour was come." What hour? The hour of hours; the hour with a view to which all the purposes of grace from everlasting were fixed; the hour with a view to which all the scaffolding of the ancient economy was erected; the hour with a view to which He had come into the world, and been set apart by Circumcision and Baptism and the Descent of the Spirit; the hour with a view to which He had lived and wrought and taught and prayed; the hour for which Heaven, for the ends of Grace, and Earth and Hell, to defeat those ends, were waiting alike with eager hope: *that* hour was now "come"—virtually come, all but come—'All things,' Father, 'are now ready.' **glorify thy Son**—'Put honour upon Thy Son, by openly *countenancing Him*, when all others desert Him; by *sustaining Him*, when the waters come in unto His soul and He sinks in deep mire where there is no standing; by *carrying Him through* the horrors of that hour, when it shall please the Lord to bruise Him, and make His soul an offering for sin.' **that thy Son [also] may glorify thee**—by a willing and absolute obedience unto death, even the death of the Cross, thus becoming a glorious Channel for the extension to a perishing world of Thine everlasting love. [The καὶ of the received text has insufficient authority, and is excluded by *Lachmann, Tischendorf*, and *Tregelles*.] **2. As thou hast given him** [Καθὼς ἔδωκας]—'According as thou gavest Him' **power over all flesh.** Compare ch. iii. 35, "The Father loveth the Son, and hath given all things into His hand;" Matt. xi. 27, "All things are delivered unto Me of My Father;" xxviii. 18, "All power is given unto Me in heaven and in earth." **that he should give eternal life to as many as thou hast given him.** The phraseology here is very peculiar: 'That *all that* which Thou hast given Him, He should give to *them* eternal life.' On the import of this language and of the whole sentiment expressed by it, see on ch. vi. 37-40, with the corresponding remarks at the close of that Section. **3. And this is life eternal** [ἡ αἰώνιος ζωή], **that they might know thee the**

3 eternal life to as many [b]as thou hast given him. And [c]this is life eternal, that they might know thee [d]the only true God, and Jesus Christ,
4 whom thou hast sent. I have glorified thee on the earth: I have
5 finished the work which thou gavest me to do. And now, O Father, glorify thou me with thine own self with the glory [e]which I had with thee before the world was.
6 I [f]have manifested thy name unto the men which thou gavest me out of the world: thine they were, and thou gavest them me; and they

A. D. 33.

[b] ch. 6. 37.
[c] Isa. 53. 11.
Jer. 9. 24.
[d] 1 Cor. 8. 4.
1 Thes. 1. 9.
[e] ch. 1. 1.
ch. 10. 30.
ch. 14. 9.
[f] Ps. 22. 22.

only true God—the sole Personal, Living God, in glorious contrast with all forms of heathen *polytheism*, mystic *pantheism*, and philosophic *naturalism;* and Jesus Christ, whom thou hast sent. This is the only place where our Lord gives Himself the compound name "JESUS CHRIST," afterwards so current in apostolic preaching and writing. (See on Matt. i. 1.) Here all the words are employed in their strict signification: First, "JESUS," because He "*saves* His people from their sins;" Second, "CHRIST," as *anointed* with the measureless fulness of the Holy Ghost for the exercise of His saving offices (see on Matt. i. 16); Third, "WHOM THOU HAST SENT," in the plenitude of Divine Authority and Power, to save. 'The very juxtaposition here,' as *Alford* properly observes, 'of *Jesus Christ* with *the Father* is a proof, by implication, of our Lord's Godhead. The knowledge of *God and a creature* could not be eternal life, and such an association of the one with the other would be inconceivable.' Thus, then, "the life eternal" of which Jesus here speaks, and which He says it is His proper office to confer, is no merely conscious, unending existence, but a life whose most distinguishing characteristic is acquaintance with the Father of our Lord Jesus Christ, and with Jesus Himself as the Way to the Father, and the Truth and the Life (Job xxii. 21; Matt. xi. 27, &c.) 4. **I have glorified thee on the earth: I have finished the work which thou gavest me to do**—or, keeping to the strict sense of the tenses here employed, 'I glorified Thee on the earth: I finished the work which Thou hast given Me to do' [ἐδόξασα-ἐτελείωσα-δέδωκας]. Observe here, first, the light in which Jesus presents Himself and His work before His Father's view. His whole life here below was, He says, a *glorification of the Father;* but in this He only did, He says, a *prescribed work* — a work "given Him to do." But observe, next, the *retrospective* light in which He speaks of this. He refers to the time when He was "*on the earth*," as a past time: His glorification of the Father was now completed; the "work given Him to do" was a "*finished*" work. Manifestly the work meant was not so much of His work merely as was over at the moment when He now spake; for the great consummating surrender of His life was yet to come. It is *His entire work in the flesh* of which He speaks as now finished. And in the sublime and erect consciousness that He was presenting before the Father's eye a glorification of Him in which He would see no flaw, a finished work in which would be found nothing lacking, He now asks the fitting return: **5. And now**—'the whole purpose I am here for being accomplished,' **O Father, glorify thou me with thine own self** [παρὰ Σεαυτῷ] —or 'beside Thine own Self (*apud Teipsum*, or *Temetipsum*, as the *Vulgate, Calvin*, and *Beza* render it). The nearest, strictest, Personal conjunction is beyond doubt meant, as in ch. i. 1, "The Word was *with* God" [πρὸς τὸν θεόν], and v. 18, The Only begotten Son who is *in*"—'on' or 'into'—"*the bosom* of the Father" [εἰς τὸν κόλπον τοῦ Πατρός]. Compare Zec. xiii. 7, "The Man

that is My Fellow," or 'My Associate' [עֲמִיתִי]. **with the glory which I had with thee** [παρὰ Σοί]— or 'beside Thee,' **before the world was.** That the Son divested Himself of this glory *in some sense* by His incarnation, and continued divested of it during all the days of His flesh, is implied in the words. And that the restoration of this which He here asks was the restoration of what He laid aside—neither more nor less—is equally plain. But what that was is not easily conceived, though more easily conceived than expressed. Abstract theological discussions, as they do nothing whatever to clear this up, so on such a subject they are very unsavoury. But two things seem to meet the facts of the case, and pretty nearly to exhaust all that can safely be said upon the subject. First, In His ordinary intercourse with men here below, He *appeared not to be* what He was, and *appeared to be* what He was not. Instead of its being impossible for any person, at any moment, to doubt that He was the Everlasting Son of the Father in human flesh, it seemed hardly possible to believe it—so entirely like other men was He in His appearance and ordinary movements, and often even more helpless than many other men. Secondly, That this was a *shrouding of His proper glory*, and a continual and sublime exercise of *Self-restraint*, is evident not only from what we know of His proper glory and dignity and freedom, and what He once and again *said* of it, but from the occasional breakings forth of that glory and majesty of His —as if to let men see for a moment Whom they had in the midst of them, and what a carriage He might have assumed if it had been but fitting that His whole glorious Self should be habitually displayed before them. Well, He *submitted* during all the days of His flesh, for the high ends on which He came hither, thus to restrain Himself; and so "the world knew Him not" and "received Him not." But it could not be that He should be contented with this *abnormal* condition; it could not be but that He should desire its cessation and feel it to be such joy as He told His disciples, scarcely a brief half hour before this, they should rejoice in on His account (see on ch. xiv. 28). But the wonder of this restoration of the glory which He had with the Father before all time is, that it was to be *in our nature*. His Divine glory as the Only begotten of the Father was never lost, and could not be parted with; it was inalienable and essential. But during the days of His flesh it was shrouded from human view; it was not externally manifested; in respect of it, He restrained Himself. And what He now asks is, that this veil might be removed from Him as the *Incarnate* One, and that as the risen and ascended Representative of Humanity—the Second Adam—He might be invested and manifested in the glory which He had with the Father before the world was. Transporting thought!

Jesus Prays more immediately for the Eleven (6-19). **6. I have manifested** [Ἐφανέρωσα]—'I manifested' **thy name**—'Thy whole revealed character towards mankind,' **unto the men which**

450

7 have kept thy word. Now they have known that all things whatsoever
8 thou hast given me are of thee. For I have given unto them the
words which thou gavest me; and they have received *them*, and have
known surely that I came out from thee, and they have believed that
9 thou didst send me. I pray for them: *g*I pray not for the world, but
10 for them which thou hast given me; for they are thine. And *h*all
11 mine are thine, and thine are mine; and I am glorified in them. And
now I am no more in the world, but these are in the world, and I come
to thee. Holy Father, *i*keep through thine own name those whom thou
12 hast given me, that they may be one, *j*as we *are*. While I was with
them in the world, I *k*kept them in thy name: those that thou gavest
me I have kept, and *l*none of them is lost, *m*but the son of perdition;
13 *n*that the Scripture might be fulfilled. And now come I to thee; and
these things I speak in the world, that they might have my joy fulfilled
in themselves.

A. D. 33.

g 1 John 5. 19.
h ch. 10. 30.
    ch. 16. 14.
    Rom. 8. 30.
    1 Cor. 3. 21.
    Col. 1. 15.
i 1 Pet. 1. 5.
j ch. 10. 30.
k ch. 6. 39.
    ch. 10. 28.
    Heb. 2. 13.
l Luke 4. 26.
    ch. 18. 9.
    1 John 2. 19.
m ch. 13. 18.
    1 Thes. 2. 3.
n Ps. 109. 8.
    Acts 1. 20.

thou gavest [δέδωκας]—'hast given' me out of the world. He had said to them in the foregoing Discourse, "I have chosen you out of the world" (ch. xv. 19). Here He says the Father had first given them to Him out of the world; and it was in pursuance of that gift from everlasting that He in time made that *choice* of them. **thine they were**—as the sovereign Lord and Proprietor of all flesh (*v.* 2), **and thou gavest them me**—as the Incarnate Son and Saviour, to be themselves separated from the world and saved, in the first instance (according to the principles of ch. vi. 37-40), and then to be separated to the high office of gathering in others; **and they have kept thy word**—*retained* it (Luke viii. 15); not taking it up superficially, as multitudes did, only to abandon it when they saw whither it would lead them, but forsaking all for it. **7. Now they have known that all things whatsoever thou hast given me are of thee. 8. For I have given unto them the words which thou gavest**—'hast given' me; **and they have received them, and have known surely that I came out from thee, and they have believed that thou didst send me** [ἔλαβον—ἔγνωσαν—ἐπίστευσαν]—'they received them, and knew surely that I came out from Thee; and believed that Thou didst send Me;' referring doubtless to their own explicit declaration, but a little before, "Now are we sure"—'Now know we'—"that Thou knowest all things: by this we believe that Thou camest forth from God" (ch. xvi. 30). How benignant is this acknowledgment of the feeble faith of those infantile believers! Yet unless it had been genuine, and He had seen in it the germ of noblest faith afterwards to be displayed, He had not so spoken of it. **9. I pray for them**—not here as *apostles*, but as the following words show, as the representatives of those "chosen out of the world:" **I pray not for the world**—for the things sought for them were totally inapplicable to the world. Not that the *individuals* composing the world were shut out from Christ's compassions (see the last clause of *v.* 21), or ought to be shut out from ours; but they come within the sphere of this prayer only by "being chosen *out of the world.*" **but for them which thou hast given me; for they are thine.** He had just said that the Father "gave them to Him;" but here He says they were the Father's still, for the Father did not give them *out of His own hands* in committing them to the Son's. See on ch. x. 28-30. Accordingly He adds, **10. And all mine are thine, and thine are mine** [τὰ 'Εμὰ Σά ἐστιν, καὶ τὰ Σὰ 'Εμὰ]— 'And all things that are Mine are Thine, and Thy things are Mine.' ABSOLUTE COMMUNITY OF PROPERTY BETWEEN THE FATHER AND THE SON is

here expressed as nakedly as words could do it. **and I am glorified in them. 11. And [now] I am no more in the world, but these are in the world, and I come to thee.** 'Though My struggles are at an end, theirs are not: though I have gotten beyond the scene of strife, I cannot sever Myself in spirit from them, left behind, and only just entering on their great conflict.' **Holy Father**—an expression He nowhere else uses. "*Father*" is His wonted appellation, but "*holy*" is here prefixed, because His appeal was to that perfection of the Father's nature, to "keep" or preserve them from being tainted by the unholy atmosphere of "the world" they were still in. **keep through thine own name** [ἐν τῷ ὀνόματί σου]—rather, in 'Thy name;' in the exercise of that gracious and holy character which, as revealed, is the "name" by which God is known to men. **those whom thou hast given me.** The true reading clearly is 'what thou hast given me' [ᾧ, instead of οὓς]. So *Lachmann, Tischendorf,* and *Tregelles,* with whom the best critics concur. **that they may be one, as we are.** See on *v.* 21. **12. While I was with them in the world, I kept them in thy name**—'I preserved them from defection through the revelation to their souls of that "grace and truth" of Thine which, whenever they were staggered and ready to give way, held them fast.' **those that thou gavest me I have kept**—'Those whom Thou hast given Me I kept' or 'guarded' [δέδωκας—ἐφύλαξα], **and none**—'not one' **of them is lost, but the son of perdition.** If we take the expressions, "children of this world," "child of the devil," "the man of sin," "children of light," "children of Zion," to mean men who have in them the *nature* of the things mentioned as their proper character, then, "the son of perdition" must mean 'he who not only is *doomed* to, but has the materials of perdition already in his character.' So we are to understand the expression "children of wrath" (Eph. ii. 3). **that the Scripture might be fulfilled** (Ps. lxix. 25; cix. 8; Acts i. 16, 20). The phrase 'not one *but* (or 'but only') the son of perdition' [εἰ μὴ] is used in the same sense as in Luke iv. 26, 27 (on which see). 'It is not implied,' as *Webster and Wilkinson* correctly observe, 'that Judas was one of those whom the Father had given to the Son, but rather the contrary. See ch. xiii. 18.' **13. And now** [Νῦν δὲ]—'But now' **come I to thee.** He had just said this before; but He loves to say it again, the yearning of His whole soul after the Father thus finding natural relief. **and these things I speak in the world, that they might have my joy fulfilled in themselves**— 'Such a strain befits rather the upper sanctuary

14 I have given them thy word; °and the world hath hated them,
15 because they are not of the world, even as I am not of the world. I
pray not that thou shouldest take them out of the world, but ᵖthat
16 thou shouldest keep them from the evil. They are not of the world,
17 even as I am not of the world. Sanctify ᑫthem through thy truth: thy
18 word is truth. As thou hast sent me into the world, even so have I
19 also sent them into the world. And ʳfor their sakes I sanctify myself,
that they also might be ¹sanctified through the truth.

A. D. 33.

° 1 John 3.13.
ᵖ Gal. 1. 4.
   2 Thes. 3. 3.
   1 John 5.18.
ᑫ Acts 15. 9.
   Eph. 5. 26.
ʳ 1 Cor. 1. 30.
1 Or, truly
   sanctified.

than the scene of conflict; but I speak so "*in the world,*" that My joy, the joy I experience in knowing that such intercessions are to be made for them by their absent Lord, may be tasted by those who now hear them, and by all who shall hereafter read the record of them.' See on ch. xv. 11; only here the *ground* of that joy seems more comprehensive than there.

14. I have given them thy word; and the world hath hated them [ἐμίσησεν]—'the world hated them,' **because they are not of the world, even as I am not of the world.** See on ch. xv. 18-21. **15. I pray not that thou shouldest take them out of the world**—for that, though it would secure their own safety, would leave the world unblessed by their testimony; **but that thou keep them from the evil** [ἐκ τοῦ πονηροῦ]—or 'from evil;' all evil in and of the world. The translation 'from the evil one' is to be rejected here, as not suiting the comprehensiveness of these petitions. See also, in the Lord's Prayer, on Matt. vi. 13. **16. They are not of the world, even as I am not of the world.** See on *vv.* 6-9; and on ch. xv. 18, 19. This is reiterated here to pave the way for the prayer which follows: **17. Sanctify them through** [ἐν]—or 'in' **thy truth: thy word is truth.** Principles of vast importance are here expressed. Observe, first, the connection between this petition and that of *v.* 15. As that was *negative*—"Keep them"—asking *protection* for them from the poisonous element which surrounded and pressed upon their renewed nature; so this prayer—"*Sanctify* them"—is positive, asking the *advancement and completion* of their begun sanctification. Observe, next, the *medium* or *element* of sanctification. All sanctification is represented as the fruit of *truth*; not truth in general, but what is called distinctively "God's truth," or 'Christ's Father's truth:' in other words, not only *religious* truth—as distinguished from all other truth, physical or metaphysical—but His *revealed truth.* Accordingly, as if to make this more clear—for the sake of those who listened to this prayer, and as many as should have it brought within their reach throughout all time—He defines what He means by "Thy truth," adding that important clause, "*Thy word* is truth." But what, it may be asked, is specifically meant by "Thy word?" This he had already explained in *v.* 14, "I have given them Thy word; and the world hath hated them, because they are not of the world, even as I am not of the world." And in a previous verse (8), "I have given unto them the words which Thou gavest Me, and they have received them," &c. *The whole of His own teaching,* then, as an express communication from the Father, through the Faithful and True Witness, was that "word of truth" through which He prays that they might be sanctified. It had fetched them in already (ch. xv. 3). But they had not done with it when it ceased to drop upon their ear from those Lips into which grace was poured. Nay, it was only when He "went unto His Father, and they saw Him no more," that it was, through the promised teaching of the Spirit, to take its full "sanctifying" effect upon them. For then only was it seen and felt to be but the fulness of all the Old Testament revelations, the perfection of all gracious communications from God to men, "spoken unto us in these last days by His own Son," and the substance of all that was to be unfolded in detail by His apostles in their preaching and by their writings for all time. (Eph. i. 13; Col. i. 5.) Accordingly, just before His ascension, He commissioned these same faithful Eleven, as the representatives of His ministering servants in every succeeding age, to teach the baptized disciples to "observe *all things whatsoever He had commanded them*"—not to the exclusion of all divine truth except that contained in the Gospels, but as comprehensive of all revealed, saving truth. (See on Matt. xxviii. 16-20, Remark 3 at the close of that Section.) But one other thing here must not be passed over. While our Lord holds prominently forth the ordained *medium* or *element* of sanctification—God's word of truth—He ascribes the sanctification which is thereby wrought entirely to God Himself, saying to His Father, "Sanctify *Thou* them." Great principles these in the divine economy of salvation, which cannot be too constantly and vividly present to the minds of believers, and especially of ministers. **18. As thou hast sent**—'sentest' me **into the world, even so have I also sent**—'sent I also' them **into the world.** As their mission was designed for no other end than to carry into effect the purpose of His own mission into the world, so He speaks of the *authority* by which He was sending them into the world as but an extension of the same authority by which Himself was sent of the Father. As He was the Father's Ambassador and Agent, so were they to be His. Nay, He represents them as already sent, just as He represents His own personal work on earth as already at an end; and what His soul is now filled with and looking forward to is the coming fruit of that work, the travail of His soul, and His satisfaction therein. **19. And for their sakes I sanctify myself, that they also might**—or 'may' **be sanctified through the truth** [ἐν ἀληθείᾳ]—'in the truth,' or 'in truth.' As the article is wanting in the original, we may translate, as in the margin, 'that they also may be *truly* sanctified,' in contrast with those *ritual* sanctifications with which as Jews they were so familiar. So *Chrysostom, Luther, Calvin, Beza, Bengel, Meyer.* But since, in 2 John 3, and 3 John 3, 4, the beloved disciple speaks of "walking *in* [the] *truth,*" without the article—meaning certainly not 'walking truly,' but 'walking in the truth of the Gospel'—it is much better to understand our Lord to refer here to that same truth of which he had spoken in *v.* 17 as the element or medium of all sanctification. So *Erasmus, Lücke, Tholuck, Alford, Lange.* 'The only difference,' says *Olshausen* excellently, 'between the application of the same term (sanctify) to Christ and the disciples is that, as applied to Christ, it means *only* to consecrate; whereas in application to the disciples, it means to consecrate with the *additional idea* of previous sanctification,

452

20 Neither pray I for these alone, but for them *also which shall believe
21 on me through their word; that *they all may be one; as *thou,
Father, *art in me, and I in thee, that they also may be one in us: that

since nothing but what is holy can be presented as an offering. The whole self-sacrificing work of the disciples appears here as a mere *result* of the offering of Christ.' But it should be added, in further illustration of the vast difference between the sanctification of the Master and that of the servants, that He does not say, 'I sanctify Myself *through the truth*,' but simply, "I sanctify Myself," that is, 'set Myself apart by Self-consecration;' and while He says of His own sanctification that it was *"for their sakes*," He does not say that they were to be sanctified for others' sakes— though that, in a certain inferior and not unimportant sense, is true enough—but simply, "that they also might be sanctified through the truth." Thus, in language which brings His people into the nearest and most blessed conjunction with Himself—in a common sanctification—does Jesus, by sharpest lines of demarcation, distinguish between Himself and them in that sanctification.

Jesus Prays for all that should ever Believe on Him (20-24). **20. Neither pray I for these alone** [Οὐ περὶ τούτων δὲ ἐρωτῶ μόνον]—'Yet not for these alone do I pray,' **but for them also which shall believe on me.** The true reading here is one we should not have expected—'for them which believe on me' [πιστευόντων—not πιστευσόντων]. But the evidence in its favour is decisive, while the received reading has but feeble support. Of course, the sense is the same; but this reading exhibits the whole company of believers as already before the eye of Jesus in that character—a present multitude already brought in and filling His mighty soul with a Redeemer's "satisfaction." How striking is it, that while all future time is here viewed as *present*, the present is viewed as *past* and gone! **through their word.** The Eleven are now regarded as the carriers of the glad tidings of His salvation "to every creature;" but of course, only as the first of a race of preachers, whose sound was to go into all the earth, and their words unto the ends of the world; whose beautiful feet upon the mountains, as they carried the news of salvation from land to land, were hailed even by the evangelical prophet (Isa. lii. 7). **21. That they all may be one** [ἕν]—'one thing;' **as thou, Father, art in me, and I in thee, that they also may be one** [ἕν]—'one thing' **in us: that the world may believe that thou hast sent**—'sentest' **me.** No language which we at present have can adequately express the full import of these wonderful words, nor can any heart here below completely conceive it. But the three great unities here brought before us may be pointed out. First in order is the Unity of the Father and the Son—"as Thou, Father, art in Me, and I in Thee:" next, the assumption of all believers into that Unity, thus constituting a new Unity—"that they also may be one in Us:" Finally, and as the consequence of this, the Unity of all believers amongst themselves—"that they all may be one," that is, amongst themselves. Had our Lord been here speaking of the absolute or essential unity of the Father and the Son in the Godhead, He could not have prayed that believers might be taken into that Unity. But we have already seen (on ch. x. 30, where the very same remarkable expression is used), what He meant by the Father and Himself being "one thing" [ἕν]. They have *all in common*, They have *one interest*—in the Kingdom of Grace, the salvation of sinners, the recovery of Adam's family. *Oneness of essence* is the manifest

basis of this *community of interest*, as only on that principle would the language be endurable from Human Lips. But the oneness here meant is 'oneness in thought, feeling, purpose, action, interest, property—in the things of salvation.' And it is into *this* Unity that Jesus prays that all believers may be taken up; so as to become one with the Father and the Son *spiritually*, yet really for all the purposes of salvation and glory. This explanation makes it easy to see what is meant by the first petition, that "all believers may be one." It is not *mere* unity—whether in a vast common external organization, or even in internal judgment and feeling about religious matters. It is oneness in the Unity of the Father and the Son—"that they also may be one IN Us"—in the matters of Grace and Salvation. Thus, it is a union *in spiritual life;* a union in *faith* on a common Saviour, in *love* to His blessed name, in *hope* of His glorious appearing: a union brought about by the teaching, quickening, and indwelling of the one Spirit of the Father and the Son in all alike; in virtue of which they have all one common character and interest— in freedom from the bondage of sin and Satan, in separation from this present evil world, in consecration to the service of Christ and the glory of God, in witnessing for truth and righteousness on the earth, in participation of all spiritual blessings in Christ Jesus. But one other thing remains to be noticed in this great prayer—"that the world may believe that Thou didst send Me." This shows clearly that the Unity of believers amongst themselves was meant to be such as would have an outstanding, visible manifestation—such as the vast outlying world might be able to recognize, and should be constrained to own as the work of God. Thus, the grand impression upon the world at large, that the mission of Christ is Divine, is to be produced by the manifested, undeniable *Unity of His disciples* in spiritual life, love, and holiness. It is not a merely formal, mechanical unity of ecclesiastical machinery. For as that may, and to a large extent does, exist in both the Western and Eastern Churches, with little of the Spirit of Christ, yea much, much with which the Spirit of Christ cannot dwell, so, instead of convincing the world *beyond its own pale* of the divinity of the Gospel, it generates infidelity to a large extent within its own bosom. But the Spirit of Christ, illuminating, transforming, and reigning in the hearts of the genuine disciples of Christ, drawing them to each other as members of one family, and prompting them to loving co-operation for the good of the world—this is what, when sufficiently glowing and extended, shall force conviction upon the world that Christianity is divine. Doubtless, the more that differences among Christians disappear —the more they can agree even in minor matters —the impression upon the world may be expected to be greater. But it is not altogether *dependent* upon this; for living and loving oneness in Christ is sometimes more touchingly seen even amidst and in spite of minor differences, than where no such differences exist to try the strength of their deeper unity. Yet till this living brotherhood in Christ shall show itself strong enough to destroy the sectarianism, selfishness, carnality, and apathy that eat out the heart of Christianity in all the visible sections of it, in vain shall we expect the world to be overawed by it. It is when "the Spirit shall be poured upon us from on high," as a Spirit of truth and love, and upon all parts of

22 the world may believe that thou hast sent me. And the glory which thou gavest me I have given them; *"*that they may be one, even as we 23 are one: I in them, and thou in me, *"*that they may be made *ˣ*perfect in one; and that the world may know that thou hast sent me, and hast loved them, as thou hast loved me.

A. D. 33.

" 1 John 1. 3.
1 John 3. 24.
" Col. 3. 14.
ᵃ Heb. 12. 23.

the Christian territory alike, melting down differences and heart-burnings, kindling astonishment and shame at past unfruitfulness, drawing forth longings of catholic affection, and yearnings over a world lying in wickedness, embodying themselves in palpable forms and active measures—it is then that we may expect the effect here announced to be produced, and then it will be irresistible. **22. And the glory which thou gavest—'hast given' me I have given them; that they may be one, even as we are one.** This verse is to be viewed as the proper complement of the former one. Our Lord had prayed that those who believed on Him might be one, and one in the Unity of the Father and the Son. But what *grounds* were there for expecting such a thing, or rather, what *materials* existed for bringing it about? The answer to that question is what we have in the present verse. "In order," says Jesus, "that they *may* be one, even as We are one, I have given unto them the glory which Thou hast given unto Me." The glory, then, here meant is all that which Jesus received from the Father as the *Incarnate Redeemer and Head* of His people—the glory of a Perfect Acceptance as the Spotless Lamb—the glory of Free Access to the Father and Right to be Heard always—the glory of the Spirit's Indwelling and Sanctification—the glory of Divine Support and Victory over sin, death, and hell—the glory of finally inheriting all things. This glory, Jesus says not, 'I *will* give,' but "I *have* given them;" thus teaching us that this glory is the *present* heritage of all that believe, and the divine provision—the heaven-provided furniture—for their attaining even here to that exalted Unity amongst themselves which would stamp the mission of their Lord as Divine even in the eyes of the world. **23. I in them, and thou in me, that they may be made perfect in one [εἰς ἕν]—'into one [thing];' and that the world may know that thou hast sent—'didst send' me, and hast loved them, as thou hast loved me [ἀπέστειλας—ἠγάπησας]—'and lovedst them even as Thou lovedst Me.'** Everything in this verse, save the last clause, had been substantially said before. But while the reiteration adds weight to the wonderful sentiment, the variation in the way of putting it throws additional light on a subject on which all the light afforded us is unspeakably precious. Before, the oneness of believers was said to be simply 'in the Father and the Son.' Here, a certain arrangement of the steps, if we may so speak, is indicated. First in order is the Father's indwelling in the Son, by His Spirit—"Thou in Me;" next, the Son's indwelling in believers by the same Spirit—"I in them:" only "God giveth not His Spirit by measure unto the Son" (ch. iii. 34), but "anointeth Him with the oil of gladness above His fellows" (Ps. xlv. 7), because it is His of right, as the Son and the Righteous One in our nature. Thus is provision made for "their being made perfect into one," or wrought into a glorious Unity, only reflecting the Higher Divine Unity. We have said that the last clause of this verse is the only part of it which had not been expressed before; nor had such an astonishing word been ever uttered before by the Lord Jesus: "that the world may know that thou . . LOVEDST THEM EVEN AS THOU LOVEDST ME."
454

In much that He had before said this was *implied;* but never till now was it actually expressed. Here, again, it is not the essential love of the Son by the Father, in their eternal Divine Personality, that Jesus here speaks of; for with that no creature may intermeddle. It is *the Father's love of His Incarnate Son,* as Head of His redeemed, that is meant—ravishing the Father's eye with the beauty of a divine character, a perfect righteousness, a glorious satisfaction for sin in our nature. This complacency of the Father in the Son passes over to and rests upon all that believe in the Son; or rather it descends from and penetrates through the Head to all the members of that living Unity which is made up of Him and them—"like the precious ointment upon the head, that ran down upon the beard, even Aaron's beard; that went down to the skirts of his garments; as the dew that descended upon the mountains of Zion: for there the Lord commanded the blessing, even life for evermore" (Ps. cxxxiii. 2, 3). But though we should suppose that of all things this was the most *invisible to the world,* yet it seems that even the conviction of this was in some sense to be impressed upon the world: "that the world may know that Thou hast loved them, as Thou hast loved Me." Of course this could only be by its *effects:* nor can even these be expected to convince the world that the Father's love to believers is the same as His love to His own Son, in any but a very general sense, so long as it remains "the world." But it would have a double effect: it would inspire the world, even as such, with a conviction, which they would be unable to resist and could ill conceal, that Christ and Christians are alike of God and owned of God; and that conviction, going deeper down into the hearts of some, would ripen into a surrender of themselves, as willing captives, to that love Divine which sent through the Son salvation to a lost world. **24. Father, I will [θέλω] that they also whom thou hast given me.** [The reading ὅ here, instead of οὓς of the received text—'that that also which Thou hast given Me'—which *Tischendorf* and *Tregelles* have adopted, but not *Lachmann*—is insufficiently supported, as we judge, and to be rejected.] **be with me where I am; that they may behold my glory, which thou hast given me [ἔδωκας]—'gavest Me;'** but the true reading clearly is, 'which Thou hast given Me;' [δέδωκας]: **for thou lovedst me before the foundation of the world.** Here our Lord, having exhausted all His desires for His people which could be fulfilled here below, stretches them, in this *His last petition,* onwards to the eternal state. Let us attend, first, to the *style* of petition *here only* employed by our Lord: "I will." The majesty of this style of speaking is the first thing that strikes the reverential reader. Some good expositors, indeed (as *Beza,* who, instead of the *Volo* of the *Vulgate,* renders it *Velim*), conceive that nothing more is meant by this word than a simple wish, desire, request; and they refer us in proof of this to such passages as Mark x. 35; John xii. 21, (*Gr.*) But such a word from the mouth of a creature cannot determine its sense, when taken up into the lips of the Son of God. Thus, when He said to the leper (Matt. viii. 3), "I will [θέλω], be thou clean!" something more, surely, was meant than a mere

24 Father, [y]I will that they also whom thou hast given me be with me
where I am; that they may behold my glory, which thou hast given me:
25 for thou lovedst me before the foundation of the world. O righteous

wish for his recovery. And such a *will*, we cannot doubt, was meant in this prayer of the Son to the Father, which breathes throughout the spirit of loftiest unity with the glorious Object addressed, and of highest claim to be heard, more particularly occurring as it does in the final petition, a petition manifestly designed to exhaust all that He had to ask in His people's behalf. 'In *vv.* 9, 15, 20,' says *Bengel*, 'He had said, "I pray" [ἐρωτῶ, *rogo*]; now the language rises, and the word is to be rendered "I will;" not by the weak "I desire." Jesus asks in the exercise of a right, and demands with confidence; as Son, not as servant (compare Ps. ii. 8).' To the same effect *de Wette, Meyer, Stier, Alford, Luthardt, Webster and Wilkinson, Lange*. But observe now the two things thus majestically asked. First, "that they also whom Thou hast given Me be with Me where I am." He had before assured His faithful Eleven, as representing all believers, that they should be so; using the same form of expression as here, "I will come again, and receive you unto Myself, that where I am [ὅπου εἰμὶ Ἐγώ], there ye may be also" (see on ch. xiv. 3). In now *asking* what He had before explicitly *promised*, the majestic authority of that "I will" is further revealed. But next, when they have arrived where I am, it is but in order "that they may behold My glory, which Thou hast given Me: for Thou lovedst Me before the foundation of the world." The glory here intended has been already explained. It is not His *essential* glory, the glory of His Divine Personality, but His glory as the Incarnate Head of His people, the Second Adam of a redeemed humanity, in which glory the Father beheld Him with ineffable complacency from everlasting. Jesus regards it as glory enough for us to be admitted to see and gaze for ever upon this *His* glory! This is 'the beatific vision;' but it shall be no mere vision—"we shall be like Him, for we shall see Him as He is" (1 John iii. 2).

Here end the petitions of this wonderful chapter. In the two concluding verses He just breathes forth His reflections into His Father's ear, but doubtless for the benefit of those mortal ears that were privileged to listen to Him, and of all who should read it in this priceless Gospel.

Concluding Breathings forth of the whole past Results of His Mission (25, 26). **25. O righteous Father, the world hath not known thee: but I have known thee, and these have known that thou hast sent me**—or, preserving the strict sense of the tenses, 'the world knew Thee not, but I knew Thee, and these knew that Thou didst send Me;' all this being regarded as *past.* 'The world knew Thee not.' Clearly this refers to its whole treatment of "Him whom He had sent." Accordingly, in a previous chapter, He says, "He that hateth Me hateth My Father also;" "Now have they both seen and hated both Me and My Father;" "All these things will they do unto you for My name's sake, because they know not Him that sent Me" (ch. xv. 23, 24, 21): for, "had they known it," says the apostle, "they would not have crucified the Lord of Glory" (1 Cor. ii. 8). Our Lord, it will be perceived, utters this with a certain tender mournfulness, which is rendered doubly affecting when He falls back, in the next words, upon the very different treatment which the Father had received from Himself—"The world knew Thee not, O righteous Father: *but I knew Thee!*" 'While the world was showing its disregard of Thee in its treatment of Him whom Thou hadst sent, from Me Thou gatest ever the glory due unto Thy name, O Lord, Thou knowest.' But Jesus has another source of consolation in the recognition of His Divine Mission by "THESE" Eleven that were in that upper room with Him, in whom doubtless His eye beheld a multitude that no man could number of kindred spirits to the end of time; just as in "the world" that knew Him not He must have seen the same blinded world in every age:—"I knew Thee, and these knew that Thou didst send Me." Once and again had He said the same thing in this prayer. But here He introduces it for the last time in bright and cheering contrast with the dark and dismal rejection of Him, and of the Father in Him, by the world. One other thing deserves notice in this verse. As before He had said "HOLY Father," when desiring the display of that perfection on His disciples (*v.* 11), so here He styles him "RIGHTEOUS Father," because He is appealing to his righteousness or justice, to make a distinction between those two diametrically opposite classes—"*the world*," on the one hand, which would not know the Father, though brought so nigh to it in the Son of His love, and, on the other, *Himself*, who recognized and owned Him, and along with Him *His disciples*, who owned His mission from the Father. **26. And I have declared** [ἐγνώρισα]—'I declared' or 'made known' **unto them thy name.** He had said this variously before (*vv.* 6, 8, 14, 22); but here He repeats it for the sake of adding what follows: **and will declare it**—or 'make it known' [ἐγνώρισα—γνωρίσω]. As this could not mean that He was to continue His own Personal ministry on earth, it can refer only to the ministry of His apostles after His ascension "with the Holy Ghost sent down from heaven," and of all who should succeed them, as ambassadors of Christ and ministers of reconciliation, to the end of time. This ministry—Jesus here tells His Father—would be but Himself continuing to make known His Father's name to men, or the *prolongation of His own ministry*. How consolatory a truth this to the faithful ministers of Jesus, and under what a responsibility does it lay all who from their lips hear the message of eternal life in Christ Jesus! **that the love wherewith thou hast loved** [ἠγάπησας]—'lovedst' **me may be in them, and I in them.** He had just expressed His desire "that the world may know that Thou lovedst them as Thou lovedst Me" (*v.* 23). Here it is the implantation and preservation of that love in His people's hearts that He speaks of; and the way by which this was to be done, He says, was "the making known to them of the Father's name;" that is, the revelation of it to their souls by the Spirit's efficacious sealing of the Gospel message—as He had explained in ch. xvi. 8-15. This eternal love of the Father, resting first on Christ, is by His Spirit imparted to and takes up its permanent abode in all that believe in Him; and "He abiding in them, and they in Him" (ch. xv. 5), they are "*one Spirit.*" 'With this lofty thought,' says *Olshausen*, 'the Redeemer concludes His prayer for His disciples, and in them for His Church through all ages. He has compressed into the last moments given Him for conversation with His own the most sublime and glorious sentiments ever uttered by mortal lips. But hardly has the sound of the last word died away, when He passes with the disciples over the

Father, *the world hath not known thee: but I have known thee, and 26 these have known that thou hast sent me. And I have declared unto

A. D. 33.
* 1 John 5. 19.

brook Kedron to Gethsemane—and the bitter conflict draws on. The seed of the new world must be sown in Death, that thence Life may spring up.'

Remarks.—1. How strange is the spiritual obtuseness which can imagine it possible that such a Prayer should have been *penned* if it had not first been *prayed* by the glorious One of whom this Gospel is the historic Record! But it is not only the historic reality of this Prayer, in the Life of Jesus, which is self-evidencing. It throws a strong light upon the question of Inspiration also, which in this case at least must be held to attach to the *language* as well as to the *thoughts* which it conveys. In such a case, every intelligent reader must see that apart from the language of this Prayer, we can have no confidence that its thoughts are accurately conveyed to us. But who that has any spiritual discernment, and any of that spiritual taste and delicacy which constant dealing with Scripture in a devout and loving spirit begets, does not feel that the language of this Prayer is all-worthy of the thoughts which it conveys to us—worthy of the Lips that poured forth this Prayer: and what internal testimony to its inspiration could be stronger than this? We are not insensible to the difficulty of explaining all the facts of the Biblical language, considering it as inspired; but let not this despoil us of what is beyond reasonable dispute, as illustrated by the language of this Divine Prayer. Nor need we commit ourselves to the many rash and at least dubious theories, by which it has been sought to explain and reconcile acknowledged difficulties on this subject. Sitting loose to all these, let us nevertheless—planting our foot upon such a Prayer as this—rest perfectly assured that He of Whom the Lord Jesus promised that He should "bring all things to their remembrance, whatsoever He had spoken to them," has so guided the sacred penman in the reproduction of this Prayer that we have it not only in the substance and spirit of it, but in the *form* also in which it was poured forth in the upper room. 2. One feels it almost trifling to ask again whether such a Prayer as this could have been uttered by a creature? But it may not be amiss to call the reader's attention to *the studious care with which Jesus avoids mixing Himself up with His disciples as He associates Himself with the Father.* "Thou in Me," He says, "and I in Thee;" and again, "*I* in *them*, and *they* in Us." This, we think, is one of the most remarkable features in the phraseology of this chapter; and as it has a most important bearing on the subject of the foregoing Remark—the inspiration attaching to the *language*—so it is in singular harmony with our Lord's manner of speaking on other occasions (see on ch. iii. 7, and Remark 3 at the close of that Section; and on ch. xx. 17). 3. Has Christ, in order to give eternal life to as many as the Father hath given Him, obtained from the Father "power over all flesh"? With confidence, then, may we entrust to Him our eternal all, assured "that He is able to keep that which we have committed unto Him against that day" (see on 2 Tim. i. 12). For since His power is not limited to the objects of His saving operations, but extends to "all flesh," He can and assuredly will make "all things to work together for the good of them that love God, of them who are the called according to His purpose." 4. How fixed are the banks within which the waters of "eternal life" flow to men: "This is life eternal, to know Thee the only true

God, and Jesus Christ whom Thou hast sent." Beyond this embankment the water of life may not be sought, and will not be found; and the spurious liberality which would break down this embankment is to be eschewed by all to whom the teaching of the Lord Jesus is sacred and dear. 5. Did Jesus yearn to "ascend up where He was before," and be "glorified beside the Father with the glory which He had along with Him before the world was"? What an affecting light does this throw upon His self-sacrificing love to His Father and to men, in coming hither and staying here during all the period of His work in the flesh—enduring the privations of life, the contradiction of sinners against Himself, the varied assaults of the great Enemy of souls, the slowness of His disciples' apprehension in spiritual things, not to speak of the sight of evil all around Him, and the sense of sin and the curse pressing upon His spirit all throughout, and bringing Him at length to the accursed tree! "Ye know the grace of the Lord Jesus, that though He was rich, yet for your sakes He became poor, that ye through His poverty might be rich." 6. Small indeed was the saving fruit of Christ's personal ministry —few the souls that were thoroughly won to Him; but those few—how dear were they to Him, as the representatives and pledges of a mighty harvest to come! and how does He yearn over those Eleven faithful ones, who represented those that were to gather His redeemed in all time! And will not His faithful servants learn from Him to value and cherish the first fruits of their labours in His service — however few and humble they may be—according to *His* valuation? 7. Hardly anything in this prayer is more remarkable than the *much* that Christ makes in it of the exceedingly small amount of light and faith to which His most advanced disciples had up to that time attained. But He looked doubtless rather to the frame of their hearts towards Him, and the degree of teachableness they had, than to the extent of their actual knowledge—to their *implicit* rather than their *explicit* belief in Him. The servants of Christ have much to learn from Him in this matter. While mere general goodness of heart is of no saving value, a guileless desire to be taught of God, and an honest willingness to follow that teaching wherever it may lead us—which distinguished the Eleven—is, in the sight of God and the estimation of Jesus, of great price. It was precisely this which Jesus commended in Nathanael, and in this respect they were in effect all Nathanaels. Is there not a tendency in some of the servants of Christ, jealous for soundness in the faith, to weigh all religious character in the scales of mere theological orthodoxy? to prefer rounded but cold accuracy of knowledge to the rudimental simplicity of a babe in Christ? to reject an implicit, if it be not an explicit faith? Of course, since the one of these advances surely into the other in the case of all divinely taught believers, even as the shining light shineth more and more unto the perfect day, so those who, under shelter of an implicit faith, advisedly, and after full opportunity, decline an explicit acknowledgment of the distinctive peculiarities of the Gospel, as they are opened up in the writings of the apostles under the full teaching of the Spirit, show clearly that they are void of that childlike faith in which they pretend to rest. But the tender and discerning eye of the true shepherd will look with as much benignity on

them thy name, and will declare *it;* that the love wherewith thou hast loved me may be in them, and ^aI in them.

A. D. 33.

a Eph. x. 17.

the lambs of his flock as on the sheep of his pasture. 8. The whole treatment of believers by the Lord Jesus has three great divisions. The first is the drawing of them, and bringing them to commit their souls to Him for salvation; or in other words, their *conversion:* the second, the preserving of them in this state, and maturing them for heaven; or in other words, their *sanctification:* the third, the bringing of them at length to His Father's house; or in other words, their *glorification.* The first of these stages is, in this prayer, viewed as past. Those for whom He prays have received His word, and are His already. The second being that of which they now stood in need, and all depending upon that, the burden of this prayer is devoted to that sphere of His work: "*Keep* through Thine own name those whom Thou hast given Me;" "I pray not that Thou shouldest take them out of the world, but that Thou shouldest *keep* them from the evil;" "*Sanctify* them through Thy truth, Thy word is truth." One petition only, but that a majestic and all-comprehensive one, is devoted to the third department: "Father, I will that they also whom Thou hast given Me be with Me where I am; that they may behold My glory, which Thou hast given Me: for Thou lovedst me before the foundation of the world." 9. Does Jesus so emphatically pray here for His believing people, first, that His Father would "*keep* them through His own name" (v. 11); and then—dividing this keeping into its negative and positive elements—pray both negatively, that they may be "not taken out of the world, but *kept* from the evil" (v. 15), and positively, "that they may be sanctified through the truth"? (v. 17). What a tender and powerful call is this upon themselves, to keep praying *along with* and *under* their great Intercessor, to His Father and their Father, that He would do for them all that He here asks in their behalf! And is it not an interesting fact, that this "keeping" is the burden of some of the most precious *promises* of God to His ancient people, of many *of their* weightiest prayers, and of some of the chiefest passages of the New Testament; as if it had been designed to provide believers of every age with a Manual on this subject? Thus, "He will *keep* the feet of His saints" (1 Sam. ii. 9); "*Preserve* me, O God: for in Thee do I put my trust" (Ps. xvi. 1); "O that Thou wouldest bless me indeed, and that Thou wouldest *keep me from evil,* that it may not grieve me" (1 Chr. iv. 10); "He that scattered Israel will gather him, and *keep* him as a shepherd doth his flock" (Jer. xxxi. 10). "The Lord is faithful," says the apostle, "who shall stablish you, and *keep you from evil*" (2 Thess. iii. 3); "I know Whom I have believed, and am persuaded that He is able to *keep* that which I have committed unto Him against that day" (2 Tim. i. 12); "Now unto Him that is able to *keep* you from falling (this answers to the negative part of our Lord's petition here) and to *present you faultless* (this is the positive) before the presence of His glory with exceeding joy," &c. (Jude 24). But 10. In thus praying, we not only follow the example, and are encouraged by the model here presented to us, but we utter here below just what our great Intercessor within the veil is continually presenting in our behalf at the right hand of the Majesty on high. Indeed, as this Intercessory Prayer of Christ, though actually presented on earth and before His death, represents His work in the flesh in nearly every verse as

already past—insomuch that He says, "Now I am no more in the world"—we are to regard it, and the Church has always so regarded it, as virtually a Prayer from within the veil, or a kind of specimen of the *things* He is now asking, and the *style* in which He now asks them, at the right hand of God. So that believers should never doubt that whensoever they pour out their hearts for what this Prayer teaches them to ask of the Father in Jesus' name a *double pleading* for the same things enters into the Father's ready ear—theirs on earth and Christ's in heaven; in their case the Spirit making intercession with groanings which often cannot be uttered (see on Rom. viii. 26), and so, as the Spirit who takes of the things of Christ and shows them unto us, making our cries to chime in with the mightier demands of Him who can say, "Father, I WILL". 11. Does Jesus so emphatically represent the Father's "*word*" as the *medium* through which He asks Him to sanctify them, and the very *element* of all true sanctification? How does this rebuke the rationalistic teaching of our day, which systematically depreciates the importance of Biblical truth to men's salvation! Between this view of God's truth, and that of our Lord here, there is all the difference that there is between utter and dismal uncertainty in eternal things, and solid footing and assured confidence founded on that which cannot lie. On the one we cannot live with comfort, nor die with any well-grounded hope; on the other we can rise above the ills of life and triumph over the terrors of death. On nothing less than, "*Thus saith the Lord*," has the soul that repose which it irresistibly yearns for; but on this it enjoys unruffled peace, the peace of God which passeth all understanding. 12. Do believers realize the length and breadth of that saying of Jesus, "*The glory which Thou hast given Me I have given them,* that they may be one even as We are one"? The glory of a perfect *Righteousness;* the glory of a full *Acceptance;* the glory of a free and ready *Access;* the glory of an *indwelling Spirit* of life, and love, and liberty, and universal holiness; the glory of an assured and rightful and abundant *entrance into the everlasting kingdom*—and all this as a presently possessed, and to-be-presently realized glory? And lest this should seem an overstrained exposition of the mind of Christ in v. 22, the words which follow seem almost to go beyond it—"I in them, and thou in Me, that they may be made perfect in one; and that the world may know that Thou hast sent Me, and *hast loved them, as Thou hast loved Me:*" and the Prayer dies away with the expression of the means He had taken and should continue to take, in order "*that the love wherewith Thou hast loved Me* (says He) *may be in them, and I in them.*" It is too much to be feared that few believers rise to this. Yet "this," according to our Lord's intercessory Prayer, "is the heritage of the servants of the Lord, and their righteousness is of Me, saith the Lord" (Isa. liv. 17). A grovelling carnality, a false humility, and an erroneous style of teaching, growing out of both these, seem to be the main causes of the general indisposition to rise to the standing which the Lord here gives to all His believing people. But shall we not strive to shake these off, and "walk in the light as He is in the light"? Then shall we "have fellowship with each other"—He and we—"and the blood of Jesus Christ His Son shall cleanse us from all sin." And then may we sing,—

18 WHEN Jesus had spoken these words, he *^a*went forth with his disciples over the *^b*brook Cedron, where was a garden, into the which he entered,
2 and his disciples. And Judas also, which betrayed him, knew the place;
3 *^c*for Jesus ofttimes resorted thither with his disciples. Judas *^d*then, having received a band *of men* and officers from the chief priests and Pharisees, cometh thither with lanterns and torches and weapons.
4 Jesus therefore, knowing all things that should come upon him, went

A. D. 33.

CHAP. 18.
^a Luke 22. 39.
ch. 14. 20.
Rom. 8. 10.
^b 2 Sam. 15. 23.
^c Luke 21.37.
^d Acts 1. 16.

'So nigh, so very nigh to God,
  I cannot nearer be;
For in the Person of His Son
  I am as near as He.

So dear, so very dear to God,
  More dear I cannot be;
The love wherewith He loves the Son—
  Such is His love to Me.'

CHAP. XVIII. 1-12.—BETRAYAL AND APPRE-HENSION OF JESUS. (= Matt. xxvi. 30, 36, 47-56; Mark xiv. 26, 32, 43-52; Luke xxii. 39, 47-54.) Here all the four Evangelists at length meet again; each of them recording the great historical facts at which we have now arrived—the departure from the upper room and out of the city, the entrance into Gethsemane, the treason of Judas, and the seizure of their Lord. But whereas all the first three Evangelists record the Agony in the Garden, John—holding this, no doubt, as already familiar to his readers—gives us, instead of it, some of the circumstances of the apprehen-sion in more minute detail than had been before recorded.

The Betrayal (1-3). **1. When Jesus had spoken these words, he went forth with his disciples.** With this explicit statement before them, it is surprising that some good critics should hold that the departure took place when Jesus said, "Arise, let us go hence" (ch. xiv. 31), and that all which is recorded in ch. xv. and xvi., including the Prayer of ch. xvii., was uttered in the open air, and on the way to Gethsemane. As to how we are to view the *proposal* to depart so long before it actually took place, see on ch. xiv. 31. **over the brook Cedron** (Kedron)—a deep, dark ravine, to the north-east of Jerusalem, through which flowed this small 'storm-brook' or 'winter-torrent,' and which in summer is dried up. As it is in the *reflective* Gospel only that the circumstance of His crossing the brook Kedron is mentioned, we can hardly doubt that to the Evangelist's own mind there was present the strikingly *analogous* crossing of the same dark streamlet by the royal sufferer (2 Sam. xv. 23); possibly also certain other his-torical associations (see 2 Ki. xxiii. 12): 'Thus surrounded,' says *Stier*, by such memorials and typical allusions, the Lord descends into the dust of humiliation and anguish.' **where was a garden** —at the foot of the mount of Olives, "called Gethsemane" (Matt. xxvi. 30, 36) or 'oil-press' [נגן נל], from the olives with which it was filled, **into the which he entered, and his disciples. 2. And Judas also, which betrayed him, knew the place; for Jesus ofttimes resorted thither with his disciples.** The baseness of this abuse of knowledge in Judas, derived from the privilege he enjoyed of admission to the closest privacies of His Master, is most touchingly conveyed here, though only in the form of simple narrative. Jesus, however, knowing that in this spot Judas would expect to find Him, instead of avoiding it, hies Him thither, as a Lamb to the slaughter. "No man taketh my life from me, but I lay it down of myself" (ch. x. 18). For other reasons why this spot was selected, see on the Agony in the garden (Luke xxii. 39-46), page 331, second column, third para-graph. **3. Judas then** — "He that was called

Judas, one of the Twelve," says Luke (xxii. 47), in language which brands him with peculiar in-famy, as *in* the sacred circle, though in no proper sense *of* it. **having received a band [of men] and officers from the chief priests and Pharisees** [τὴν σπεῖραν, καὶ ἐκ τῶν ἀρχιερέων καὶ Φαρισαίων ὑπη-ρέτας]—rather, 'the band (without the supplement, "of men") and officers' or 'servants of the chief priests and Pharisees.' Two bodies are here men-tioned: "the band," meaning, as *Webster and Wilkinson* express it, the détachment of the Roman cohort on duty at the festival, for the purpose of maintaining order; and the officials of the ecclesi-astical authorities—the captains of the temple and armed Levites. **cometh thither with lan-terns and torches and weapons.** It was full moon, but in case He should have secreted Him-self somewhere in the dark ravine, they bring the means of exploring its hiding-places—little know-ing Whom they had to do with. The other Gos-pels tell us that the time when Judas drew near was "immediately, while Jesus yet spake," that is, while He was saying, after the Agony was over, to the three whom He had found sleeping for sorrow, "Rise, let us be going: behold, he is at hand that doth betray Me" (Matt. xxvi. 46, 47). The next step, as we take it, is the act of Betrayal—not recorded at all, but only alluded to, in our Fourth Gospel; the other Evangelists having given it fully, whom we shall now follow.

"Now he that betrayed Him gave," or had given "them a sign, saying, Whomsoever I shall kiss, that same is he: hold him fast" (Matt. xxvi. 48). The cold-bloodedness of this speech was only exceeded by the deed itself. "And Judas went before them (Luke xxii. 47), and said, Hail, Master! and kissed Him" (Matt. xxvi. 49: see, for illus-tration of the act, 1 Sam. xx. 41; and mark Prov. xxvii. 6.) The impudence of this atrocious deed shows how thoroughly he had by this time mas-tered all his scruples. If the dialogue between our Lord and His captors was *before* this, as some interpreters think it was, the kiss of Judas was purely gratuitous, and probably to make good his right to the money; our Lord having presented Himself unexpectedly before them, and rendered it unnecessary for any one to point him out. But a comparison of the narratives seems to show that our Lord's "coming forth" to the band was *subsequent* to the interview of Judas. "And Jesus said unto him, Friend," ['Εταῖρε]. The dif-ference between the term here studiously em-ployed—which signifies rather 'companion' in mere social intercourse, and which is used on other occasions of remonstrance and rebuke (as Matt. xx. 13; xxii. 12)—and the endearing term properly rendered "friend" (in Luke xii. 4, and John xv. 13-15)—is very striking: "Wherefore art thou come?" (Matt. xxvi. 50). "Betrayest thou the Son of Man with a kiss?" (Luke xxii. 48)— imprinting on the foulest of all acts the mark of tenderest affection? What *wounded feeling* does this express! Of this Jesus showed Him-self on various occasions keenly susceptible—as all generous and beautiful natures are. This brings us back to our own Gospel.

The Apprehension (4-12). **4. Jesus therefore,**

458

5　forth, and said unto them, Whom seek ye? They answered him, Jesus
　of Nazareth. Jesus saith unto them, I am *he.* And Judas also, which
6　betrayed him, stood with them. As soon then as he had said unto
7　them, I am *he,* they went backward, and fell to the ground. Then asked
　he them again, Whom seek ye? And they said, Jesus of Nazareth.
8　Jesus answered, I have told you that I am *he.* If therefore ye seek me,
9　*'*let these go their way: that the saying might be fulfilled which he
　spake, *f*Of them which thou gavest me have I lost none.
10　　Then *g*Simon Peter having a sword drew it, and smote the high
　priest's servant, and cut off his right ear. The servant's name was
11　Malchus. Then said Jesus unto Peter, Put up thy sword into the sheath:
　*h*the cup which my Father hath given me, shall I not drink it?

A. D. 33.

* Ps. 34. 15.
Matt. 6. 26,
34.
1 Pet. 5. 7.
f ch. 6. 39.
ch. 17. 12.
2 Tim. 4. 18.
1 Pet. 1. 5.
Jude 1.
g Matt. 26. 51.
Mark 14. 57.
Luke 22. 49.
h Ps. 75. 8.
Matt. 20. 22.

knowing all things that should come—or 'were coming' upon him, went forth—from the shade of the trees, probably, into open view, indicating His sublime preparedness to meet His captors, and said unto them, Whom seek ye?—partly to prevent a rush of the soldiery upon the disciples, as *Bengel* thinks (see Mark xiv. 51, 52, which may lend some countenance to this), but still more in the exercise of that courage and majesty which so overawed them:—He would not wait to be *taken.* 5. They answered him, Jesus of Nazareth—just the sort of blunt, straightforward reply one expects from military men, simply acting on their instructions. Jesus saith unto them, I am [he]. On this sublime expression, see on Mark vi. 50. And Judas also, which betrayed him, stood with them. No more is recorded here of his part of the scene, but we have found the gap painfully supplied by all the other Evangelists. 6. As soon then as he had said unto them, I am [he], they went backward—recoiled, and fell to the ground—struck down by a power such as that which smote Saul of Tarsus and his companions to the earth (Acts xxvi. 14). It was the glorious effulgence of the majesty of Christ which overpowered them. 'This,' as *Meyer* well remarks, 'occurring before His surrender, would show His *power* over His enemies, and so the *freedom* with which He gave Himself up.' 7. Then asked he them again, Whom seek ye?—giving them a door of escape from the guilt of a deed which *now* they were able in some measure to understand. And they said, Jesus of Nazareth. The stunning effect of His first answer wearing off, they think only of the necessity of executing their orders. 8. Jesus answered, I have told you that I am [he]. If therefore ye seek me, let these go their way—Wonderful self-possession and consideration for others in such circumstances! 9. That the saying might be fulfilled which he spake, Of them which thou gavest—'hast given' me have I lost none. The reference is to such sayings as ch. vi. 39; xvii. 12; showing how conscious the Evangelist was, that in reporting his Lord's former sayings, he was giving them not in *substance* merely, but in *form* also. (See on ch. xvii., Remark 1 at the close of that Section.) Observe, also, how the preservation of the disciples on this occasion is viewed as part of that *deeper preservation* undoubtedly intended in the saying quoted. 10. Then Simon Peter having a sword drew it, and smote the high priest's servant, and cut off his right ear. The servant's name was Malchus. None of the other Evangelists mention the name either of the ardent disciple or of his victim. But John being "known to the high priest" (*v.* 15), the mention of the servant's name by *him* is quite natural, and an interesting mark of truth in a small matter. As to the *right* ear, specified both here and in Luke, the man, as

Webster and Wilkinson remark, 'was likely foremost of those who advanced to seize Jesus, and presented himself in the attitude of a combatant; hence his right side would be exposed to attack. The blow of Peter was evidently aimed vertically at his head.' "And Jesus answered and said, Suffer ye thus far" (Luke xxii. 51). It seems unnatural to understand this as addressed to the captors, as if He had said, 'Suffer My disciples thus far to show their attachment to Me; excuse it to this extent; they shall do nothing more of this kind,' as *Webster and Wilkinson* put it, and *de Wette* and *van Oosterzee* view it. Still less natural does *Alford's* view appear, which takes it as a request to those who were holding and binding Him, to permit Him to heal the wounded ear. It seems plainly to be addressed, as *Meyer* says, to the disciples, bidding them go no further in the way of defending Him; and so the majority of interpreters understand it. "And He touched his ear, and healed him." Luke only records this miracle, which in the apparently helpless circumstances in which our Lord stood, was most signal. But "The Son of Man came not to destroy men's lives, but to save them" (Luke ix. 56), and, even when they were destroying His, to save theirs. 11. Then said Jesus unto Peter, Put up thy sword into the sheath: the cup which my Father hath given me, shall I not drink it? It is remarkable that though the Agony in the Garden is not here recorded, this question expresses with affecting clearness *both* the feelings which during that scene struggled in the breast of Jesus—'*aversion to the cup,* viewed in itself,' and, 'in the light of the Father's will, *perfect preparedness to drink it up.*' (See the exposition of that wonderful scene, on Luke xxii. 39-46.)
In the other Gospels we have some fuller particulars, Matt. xxvi. 52-56: "Put up thy sword into his place: for all they that take the sword shall perish by the sword." 'Those who take the sword must run all the risks of human warfare; but Mine is a warfare whose weapons, as they are not carnal, are attended with no such hazards, but carry certain victory.' "Thinkest thou that I cannot now"—even after things have proceeded so far, "pray to My Father, and He shall presently give Me"—rather, 'place at My disposal' [παραστήσει μοι] "more than twelve legions of angels;" with allusion, possibly, to the one angel who had, in His agony, "appeared to Him from Heaven strengthening Him" (Luke xxii. 43); and in the precise number, alluding to the *twelve* who needed the help, Himself and His eleven disciples. (The full complement of a legion of Roman soldiers was six thousand.) "But how then shall the Scripture be fulfilled that thus it must be?" He could not suffer, according to the Scripture, if He allowed Himself to be delivered from the predicted death.

12 Then the band and the captain and officers of the Jews took Jesus,
13 and bound him, and *ⁱ*led him away to *ʲ*Annas first: for he was father-
14 in-law to Caiaphas, which was the high priest that same year.¹ Now
     *ᵏ*Caiaphas was he which gave counsel to the Jews, that it was expedient
     that one man should die for the people.
15 And Simon Peter followed Jesus, and *so did* another disciple. That
     disciple was known unto the high priest, and went in with Jesus into
16 the palace of the high priest. But Peter stood at the door without.

A. D. 33.
ⁱ Matt. 26. 57.
ʲ Luke 3. 2.
1 And Annas
sent Christ
bound unto
Caiaphas,
the high
priest.
ver. 24.
ᵏ ch. 11. 50.

---

12. Then the band and the captain and ('the') **officers of the Jews took Jesus, and bound him** —but not until He had made them feel that "no man took His life from Him, but that He laid it down of Himself" (ch. x. 18).

In the first three Gospels we have here the following additional particulars: Matt. xxvi. 55, "In that same hour," probably on the way to judgment, when the crowds were pressing upon Him, "said Jesus to the multitudes"—or as in Luke xxii. 52, "unto the chief priests, and captains of the temple, and the elders, which were come to Him"—"Are ye come out as against a thief with swords and staves for to take Me?" He thus keenly yet loftily expresses the indignity which He felt to be done to Him. "I sat daily with you teaching in the temple, and ye laid no hold on Me." "But this is your hour, and the power of darkness" (Luke xxii. 53.) Matthew continues (xxvi. 56) "But all this was done, that the Scriptures of the prophets might be fulfilled."

Here follows, in the first two Gospels, an affecting particular, the mention of which somewhere we should have expected from the sad announcement which Jesus had made at the Supper-table—"All ye shall be offended because of Me this night," &c. (Matt. xxvi. 31; Mark xiv. 27: see opening remarks on Luke xxii. 31-39). It is the same two Evangelists that report this warning who record the too speedy fulfilment.

Desertion and Flight of the Disciples (Matt. xxvi. 56; Mark xiv. 50). "Then all the disciples forsook Him, and fled."

A singular incident is here recorded by Mark alone (xiv. 51, 52): "And there followed Him a certain young man, having a linen cloth cast about his naked body"—they were wont, says *Grotius*, to sleep in linen, and in this condition this youth had started up from his bed: "and the young men laid hold on him"—the attendants of the chief priests, mentioned in John xviii. 3, or some of their junior assistants [but οἱ νεανίσκοι seems not to be genuine]: "And he left the linen cloth, and fled from them naked"—for, as *Bengel* says, in great danger fear conquers shame. The general object for which this was introduced is easily seen. The flight of all the apostles, recorded in the preceding verse, suggested the mention of this other flight, as one of the noticeable incidents of that memorable night, and as showing what terror the scene inspired in all who were attached to Jesus. By most interpreters it is passed over too slightly. One thing is stamped on the face of it—it is the narrative of an *eye-witness* of what is described. The mention of the fate of one individual, and him "a certain young man"—expressively put in the original [εἰς τις νεανίσκος]—of his single piece of dress, and that of "linen," of the precise parties who laid hold of him [though οἱ νεανίσκοι cannot be relied on], and how he managed to make a hair-breadth escape, even though it obliged him to part with all that covered his nakedness—this singular minuteness of detail suggests even more than the pen of an eye-witness. It irresistibly

leads to a further question—Had the writer of this Gospel himself nothing to do with that scene?— '*To me*,' says *Olshausen*, '*it appears most probable that here Mark writes concerning himself.*' So also *Lange.*

Remarks.—1. But once only, from the time that the officers came to take Him till He expired on the cross, did Jesus think fit to show, by any overt act, how *voluntarily* He endured all that was inflicted on Him by the hands of men; and that was immediately before they proceeded to their first act of violence. One such manifestation of His glorious superiority to all the power of earth is what we should perhaps expect; and as it was put forth at the critical moment—when His disciples would be watching with breathless interest to see whether He would endure to be seized, and perhaps His captors were apprehensive of some difficulty in the matter—so it was of such a nature as rendered a second manifestation of it altogether superfluous. From this time forth it must have been seen, by any eye that could read what He had done, that all-unforced, He went as a Lamb to the slaughter. 2. How quickly, when men "sell themselves" to do evil, do their hearts become steeled against all feeling, and capable of whatever blackness of demon-like ingratitude and treachery may be required for the perpetration of the crimes they have resolved on! Think of Judas but a brief hour or two before this, sitting at the Supper-table as one of the apostles of the Lord Jesus, all unsuspected by the rest; think of him but six days before this at the house of Simon the leper, unsuspected in all likelihood even by himself, until his disappointment in the matter of the "three hundred pence" ripened into rage and suggested, apparently for the first time, the foul deed (see on Mark xiv. 1-11, Remark 8 at the close of that Section); and then think of the pitch of wickedness he had now reached. It may be thought that only the continual overawing presence of his Lord kept down the already matured wickedness of his heart. But it should rather be said, it kept the seeds of that wickedness, which undoubtedly were there from the first (ch. vi. 70), from coming to maturity and acquiring their full mastery before the time. Nay, the end which Judas made of himself seems clearly to show how far he was from being a long hardened wretch, what quick work Satan had made of his natural tendencies at the last, and how, when his full criminality stared him in the face, instead of being able to wipe his mouth, as those whose conscience is seared as with a hot iron, he felt it to be insupportable. We make these observations, not to lessen the execration with which the deed and the doer of it are instinctively regarded, but to show that there is nothing in this case of Judas but what may in substance have been done once and again since that time—nothing exceptional to the ordinary working of evil principles in the human heart and life. "Let him," then, "that thinketh he standeth take heed lest he fall!"

13-23. JESUS IS BROUGHT PRIVATELY BEFORE

Then went out that other disciple, which was known unto the high priest, and spake unto her that kept the door, and brought in Peter.

17 Then saith the damsel that kept the door unto Peter, Art not thou

18 also *one* of this man's disciples? He saith, I am not. And the servants and officers stood there, who had made a fire of coals; for it was cold: and they warmed themselves: and Peter stood with them, and warmed himself.

19 The high priest then asked Jesus of his disciples, and of his doctrine.

20 Jesus answered him, *'*I spake openly to the world; I ever taught in the synagogue, and in the temple, whither the Jews always resort; and in

21 secret have I said nothing. Why askest thou me? ask them which heard me, what I have said unto them: behold, they know what I said.

22 And when he had thus spoken, one of the officers which stood by *m*struck Jesus *2*with the palm of his hand, saying, Answerest thou the

23 high priest so? Jesus answered him, *n*If I have spoken evil, bear witness

24 of the evil; but if well, why smitest thou me? Now Annas had sent him bound unto Caiaphas the high priest.

25 And Simon Peter stood and warmed himself. *o*They said therefore unto him, Art not thou also *one* of his disciples? He denied *it*, and

26 said, I am not. One of the servants of the high priest, being *his* kinsman whose ear Peter cut off, saith, Did not I see thee in the garden with

27 him? Peter then denied again: and *p*immediately the cock crew.

28 Then *q*led they Jesus from Caiaphas unto *3*the hall of judgment: and it was early; and *r*they themselves went not into the judgment hall, lest

A. D. 33.
s Luke 4. 15.
ch. 7. 14, 26, 28.
ch. 8. 2.
*m*Isa. 50. 6.
Jer. 20. 2.
Mic. 5. 1.
Acts 23. 2.
2 Or, with a rod.
n Ps. 38. 12-14.
Isa. 53, 7.
Heb. 12. 3.
1 Pet. 2. 23.
o Matt. 26.69, 71.
Mark 14.69.
Luke 22. 58.
p Matt. 26. 74
Mark 14.72.
Luke 22.60.
ch. 13. 38.
q Matt. 27. 2.
Mark 15. 1.
Luke 23. 1.
Acts 3. 13.
3 Or, Pilate's house.
Matt.27.27.
r Acts 10. 28.
Acts 11. 3.

ANNAS FIRST—PETER OBTAINS ACCESS WITHIN THE QUADRANGLE OF THE HIGH PRIEST'S RESIDENCE, AND WARMS HIMSELF AT THE FIRE—THE LORD IS INTERROGATED BY ANNAS—HIS DIGNIFIED REPLY—HE IS TREATED WITH INDIGNITY BY ONE OF THE OFFICIALS—HIS MEEK REBUKE. For the exposition, see on Mark xiv. 53, &c., as far as page 204, second paragraph.

24-27.—JESUS IS LED FROM ANNAS TO CAIAPHAS TO BE JUDGED BY THE SANHEDRIM—THE FALL OF PETER. Our Evangelist, it would seem, had nothing to add to the ample details of the trial and condemnation of the Lord Jesus and the indignities with which He was thereafter treated, and next to nothing on the sad fall of Peter in the midst of these transactions. With all this he holds his readers already familiar, through the records of the three preceding Evangelists. In the first of these four verses, accordingly, he simply tells us that "Annas sent Him bound unto Caiaphas the high priest," without so much as mentioning what this was for, still less giving any particulars of the trial. And though he relates in the briefest terms two of Peter's denials, and the crowing of the cock, this is merely to supply one small but striking particular which had not been noticed in the preceding Gospels—how one of those who charged Peter with being a disciple of Jesus was able to identify him, by his own relationship to the man whose ear Peter had cut off in the garden, and who saw him do it (*v*. 26). For the exposition of all the Evangelical matter embraced by these four verses, see on Mark xiv. 53-72, page 203, second paragraph, and 204, second paragraph to page 211.

28—xix. 16.—JESUS BEFORE PILATE. (=Matt. xxvii. 1, 2, 11-31; Mark xv. 1-20; Luke xxiii. 1-7, 13-25.) As one of the most important details of this varied Section is omitted altogether by our Evangelist, while the rest are given very summarily, we must avail ourselves of the other Gospels in order to have the whole before us for exposition.

From the time of the deposition of Archelaus, and the reduction of Judea to the condition of a Roman province (see on Matt. ii. 22), the power of life and death was taken from the Jewish tribunals. No sentence of death, therefore, which they pronounced could be executed without the sanction of the Roman Governor. Accordingly, as soon as our Lord was condemned by the Sanhedrim to die, and the contemptuous treatment of Him which followed had time to spend itself—it being now early morn—they proceed to bring Him before Pilate that he might authorize His execution.

The Chief Priests, having brought Jesus to the Prætorium, Fail, in the first instance, in Persuading Pilate to Sanction His Execution (28-32). **28. Then led they** ["Αγουσιν]—'Then lead they' **Jesus from Caiaphas unto the hall of judgment** [τὸ πραιτώριον]—rather, 'the *Prætorium*;' that is, the official residence of the Roman Governor. His usual place of residence was at Cæsarea; but during the Passover season it was his duty to be at Jerusalem, on account of the vast influx of strangers, to see that all things were conducted legally and peaceably. **and it was early.** We learn from Mark (xv. 1) that this step was the result of a special consultation: "And straightway in the morning the chief priests held a consultation with the elders and scribes and the whole council" [ὅλον τὸ συνέδριον]—no doubt to arrange their plans and frame their charge, "and bound Jesus, and carried Him away, and delivered Him to Pilate." **and they themselves went not into the judgment hall**—'the Prætorium,' **lest they should be defiled, but that they might eat the passover.** These words have occasioned immense research, and given rise to much controversy and not a few learned treatises. From these words chiefly it has been. argued that the Jews had not eaten the Passover up to the time here referred to, and consequently, as our Lord and His apostles ate it the previous evening, they must have eaten it a day earlier than the proper statutory day. In that case

29 they should be defiled, but that they might eat *the passover. Pilate then went out unto them, and said, What accusation bring ye against
30 this man? They answered and said unto him, If he were not a male-
31 factor, we would not have delivered him up unto thee. Then said Pilate unto them, Take ye him, and judge him according to your law. The Jews therefore said unto him, It *is not lawful for us to put any man to
32 death: That *the saying of Jesus might be fulfilled, which he spake, signifying what death he should die.

A. D. 33.

* Deut. 16, 2.
Matt 27.23.
Acts 23, 28.
* Gen. 49, 10.
Ezek.21.26,
27.
* Matt. 20.19.
ch.12.32,33.

---

there is a manifest discrepancy between the first three Gospels and the fourth, and this on a point not only of considerable importance, but one on which it is difficult to conceive that there should on either side be any mistake. As to this particular passage, it is not easy to see how it helps the theory which it is supposed to establish. For supposing that the proper season for eating the Passover was not to be till *that evening after six o'clock,* and this party that brought Jesus to Pilate *in the morning* had ceremonially defiled themselves by going into the Prætorium, that defilement—as it would only have lasted, according to law, during the one day of twelve hours on which it was contracted—would have passed away of itself before the proper time for eating their Passover. Does not this show that the statement of our Evangelist here has no reference to *the regular time for eating the Passover?* Having already expressed our belief that all the four Gospels are at one on this subject, and that our Lord ate the Passover on the usual day—the 14th of the month Nisan (see opening remarks on the 'Preparation for the Passover,' on Luke xxii. 7-30; and on ch. xiii. 1)—it only remains that we here state what we take to be our Evangelist's meaning in the words before us. We cannot accept the explanation of some good critics—*Robinson,* for example—that by "eating the Passover" the Evangelist means, not the eating of the Paschal lamb, which was the first and principal part of the feast, but keeping the feast of unleavened bread. The passages which are thought to justify this way of speaking are insufficient; it is not, at least, according to the usual language of the Evangelists; and it has a forced appearance. But there is a simpler explanation of the words. If we suppose that the party who were bringing Jesus before the Governor had been so engrossed with the exciting circumstances of His capture and trial and condemnation the previous evening as not to have leisure to eat their Passover *at the proper time;* but that having only deferred it on the ground of unavoidable hindrances, and fully intending to eat it as early *that same day* as this urgent business would allow, they abstained from entering the Prætorium, because by doing so they would have been defiled, and so legally disqualified from eating it till the day was over—we have, in our judgment, a satisfactory explanation of our Evangelist's statement. Nor were similar postponements, and even omissions, of the most solemn observances of their ritual altogether unknown in the Jewish history, as may be seen in *Josephus.* (See an able Essay on this subject in *Fairbairn's* "Hermeneutical Manual.")

29. Pilate then went out unto them—since they would not come in to him, **and said, What accusation bring ye against this man?**—'State your charge.' **30. They answered and said unto him, If he were not a malefactor, we would not have delivered him up unto thee**—a very lame reply. But they were conscious they had *no case* of which Pilate could take cognizance and inferring death, or any punishment at all, according to the Roman law. They therefore simply insin-

uate that the case must have been bad enough before they would have come to him with it, and that having found him worthy of death by their own law, they merely wished him to sanction the execution. **31. Then said Pilate unto them, Take ye him** [λάβετε αὐτὸν ὑμεῖς]—'Take him yourselves,' **and judge him according to your law.** This was not an admission, as some view it, of their independence of him in matters of life and death: for they themselves say the contrary in the very next words, and Pilate surely did not need to learn what his powers were from these Jews. But by this general reply he would throw upon themselves the responsibility of all they should do against this Prisoner: for no doubt he had been informed to some extent of their proceedings. **The Jews therefore said unto him, It is not lawful for us to put any man to death.** See *Josephus* (Antt. xx. 9. 1), who tells us that the high priest was charged with acting illegally for assembling the Sanhedrim that condemned 'James the just' to die, without the consent of the Roman Governor. **32. That the saying of Jesus might be fulfilled, which he spake, signifying what death** [ποίῳ θανάτῳ]—'what kind' or 'manner of death' **he should die**—that is, the death of the *cross,* which Jesus had once and again predicted He should die (Matt. xx. 19; John iii. 14; viii. 28; xii. 32). Had it been left to the Jews to execute their own sentence, it would have been, as their law required in cases of blasphemy, by *stoning.* (Lev. xxiv. 16; 1 Ki. xxi. 10; Acts vi. 13, with vii. 58; and see on ch. x. 32, 33.) But as this would have defeated the divine arrangements, it was so ordered that they should not have this in their power; and the divinely fixed mode of *crucifixion,* being a Roman mode of execution, could only be carried into effect by order of the Roman Governor. Finding it now indispensable to success to get up a criminal charge against their Prisoner, they proceed with shameless audacity to say that they had found Him guilty of what on His trial they seem not so much as to have laid to His charge. This is recorded only in

Luke xxiii. 2: "And they began"—or 'proceeded' "to accuse Him, saying, We have found this [fellow] perverting the nation"—'our nation' the true reading probably is—"and forbidding to give tribute to Cesar, saying that He Himself is Christ a King." In two things this speech was peculiarly base. First, It was a lie that He had ever forbidden to give tribute to Cesar; nay, to some of themselves, not many days before this, in reply to their ensnaring question on this very subject, and with a Roman coin in His hands, He had said, "*Render to Cesar the things which be Cesar's*" (Luke xx. 25). Secondly, Their pretended jealousy for the rights and honours of Cesar was so far from being real, that their restless impatience under the Roman yoke was already creating uneasiness at Rome, and ultimately brought ruin on their whole commonwealth; nor can there be any doubt that if our Lord had given the least indication of a willingness to assume royal honours, in opposition to the Roman power, they would have

33 Then Pilate entered into the judgment hall again, and called Jesus,
34 and said unto him, Art thou the King of the Jews? Jesus answered him,
35 Sayest thou this thing of thyself, or did others tell it thee of me? Pilate
    answered, Am I a Jew? Thine own nation and the chief priests have
36 delivered thee unto me: what hast thou done? Jesus *answered, *My
    kingdom is not of this world. If my kingdom were of this world, then
    would my servants fight, that I should not be delivered to the Jews: but

A. D. 33.

*1 Tim.6. 13.
Rev. 1. 3.
*Isa. 9. 6.
Dan. 2. 44.
Dan. 7. 14.
Luke 12. 14.
ch. 6. 15.
2 Cor. 10. 4.

---

rallied around Him. But how does Pilate treat this charge against the blessed Jesus? It was at least a tangible charge, and whatever suspicion he might have as to the motives of His accusers, it was not to be trifled with. Perhaps rumours of our Lord's regal claims may have reached the Governor's ears; but instead of entering on the subject with the accusers, he resolves to interrogate the Accused Himself, and that alone, in the first instance.

Interview between Pilate and Jesus (33-38). **33. Then Pilate entered into the judgment hall**—'the Prætorium' again, **and called Jesus, and said unto him, Art thou the King of the Jews? 34. Jesus answered him, Sayest thou this thing of thyself, or did others tell it thee of me?**—' Is this question prompted by any evidence which has come to thine ears of treason on My part against the Roman government; or hast thou merely been *put up* to it by those who, having failed to convict Me of aught that is criminal, are yet urging thee to put Me to death?' **35. Pilate answered, Am I a Jew? Thine own nation and the chief priests have delivered thee unto me: what hast thou done?**—*q. d.,* ' Jewish questions I neither understand nor meddle with; but thou art here on a charge which, though it *seems* only Jewish, *may* yet involve treasonable matter. As *they* state it I cannot decide the point; tell me, then, what procedure of thine has brought thee into this position.' In modern phrase, Pilate's object in this question was merely to determine the *relevancy* of the charge, or whether the claims which he was accused of making were of a treasonable nature. If it should be found that they were, the *evidence* of His having actually advanced such claims would still remain to be sifted. **36. Jesus answered, My kingdom is not of this world** ['Η βασιλεία ἡ ἐμή]. The "My" here is emphatic:—*q. d.,* 'This kingdom of Mine.' He does not say it is not '*in*' or '*over*,' but it is not "*of* this world" [ἐκ τοῦ κόσμου τούτου], that is, in its *origin* and *nature;* and so, is no such kingdom as need give thee or thy master the least alarm. **If my kingdom were of this world, then would my servants fight, that I should not be delivered to the Jews**—'a very convincing argument,' as *Webster and Wilkinson* observe; 'for if His servants did not fight to prevent their king from being delivered up to His enemies, much less would they use force for the establishment of His kingdom:' **but now is**—' but the fact is ' **my kingdom not from hence.** Our Lord only says whence His kingdom is *not*—first simply affirming it, next giving proof of it, then re-affirming it. This was all that Pilate had to do with. The *positive* nature of His kingdom He would not obtrude upon one who was as little able to comprehend it as entitled officially to information about it. It is worthy of notice that the "MY," which occurs *four* times in this one verse—*thrice* of His *kingdom* and *once* of His *servants*—is put in the emphatic form. **37. Pilate therefore said unto him, Art thou a king then?** There was no sarcasm or disdain in this question, as *Tholuck, Alford,* &c., allege, else our Lord's answer would have been different. Putting

emphasis upon "*thou,*" his question betrays a mixture of *surprise* and *uneasiness,* partly at the possibility of there being, after all, something dangerous under the claim, and partly from a certain awe which our Lord's demeanour probably struck into him. **Jesus answered, Thou sayest that I am a king** [Σὺ λέγεις ὅτι βασιλεύς εἰμι Ἐγὼ]—or rather, 'Thou sayest [it], for a king I am. **To this end was I**—'have I been' born, **and for this cause came I**—'to this end am I come' **into the world, that I should bear witness unto the truth.** His *birth* expresses His manhood; His *coming into the world,* His existence before assuming humanity: the truth, then, here affirmed, though Pilate would catch little of it, was, that 'His Incarnation was expressly in order to the assumption of Royalty in our nature.' Yet, instead of saying He came to be a king, which is His meaning, He says He came to *testify to the truth.* Why this? Because, in such circumstances, it required a noble courage not to flinch from His royal claims; and our Lord, *conscious that He was putting forth that courage,* gives a turn to His confession expressive of it. It is to this that Paul is commonly understood to allude, in those remarkable words to Timothy: "I charge thee before God, who quickeneth all things, and before Christ Jesus, who before Pontius Pilate witnessed *the good confession*" [τὴν καλὴν ὁμολογίαν] (1 Tim. vi. 13). But we have given our opinion (page 206, first column) that the reference is to the solemn confession which He witnessed before the supreme ecclesiastical council, that He was "THE CHRIST, THE SON OF THE BLESSED," which the apostle would hold up to Timothy as a sublime example of the fidelity and courage which he himself should display. These two confessions, however, are the complements of each other. For, in the beautiful words of *Olshausen,* 'As the Lord owned Himself *the Son of God* before the most exalted theocratic council, so He confessed His *regal dignity* in presence of the representative of the highest political authority on earth.' **Every one that is of the truth heareth my voice.** Our Lord here not only affirms that His word had in it a self-evidencing, self-recommending power, but gently insinuates the *true secret of the growth and grandeur of His kingdom:* it is a KINGDOM OF TRUTH, in its highest sense, into which all souls who have learnt to live and count all things but loss for the truth are, by a most heavenly attraction, drawn as into their proper element; whose KING Jesus is, fetching them in and ruling them by His captivating power over their hearts. **38. Pilate saith unto him, What is truth?**—*q. d.,* 'Thou stirrest the question of questions, which the thoughtful of every age have asked, but never man yet answered.' **And when he had said this**—as if, by putting such a question, he was getting into interminable and unseasonable enquiries, when this business demanded rather prompt action, **he went out again unto the Jews**—thus missing a noble opportunity for himself, and giving utterance to that consciousness of the want of all intellectual and moral certainty, which was the feel-

37 now is my kingdom not from hence. Pilate therefore said unto him, Art thou a king then? Jesus answered, *Thou sayest that I am a king. To this end was I born, and for this cause came I into the world, that I

A. D. 33.
*Luke 23. 3.
1 Tim. 6. 13.

ing of every thoughtful mind at that time. 'The only certainty,' says the elder *Pliny*, quoted by *Olshausen*, 'is that nothing is certain, nor more miserable than man, nor more proud.' 'The fearful laxity of morals,' adds the critic, 'at that time must doubtless be traced in a great degree to this scepticism. The revelation of the eternal truth alone was able to breathe new life into ruined human nature, and that in the apprehension of complete redemption.'

Pilate, again Going Forth to the Jews, Vainly Attempts to Obtain their Consent to the Release of Jesus (38). 38. . . . And when he had said this, he went out again unto the Jews, and saith unto them—in the hearing of our Lord, who had been brought forth to them, I find in him no fault [at all]—that is, no ground of criminal charge, "touching those things whereof ye accuse him" (Luke xxiii. 14). This testimony is all the more important immediately after our Lord's explicit confession that He was a King, and speaking of "His kingdom." But how could Pilate with any truth say else than he did, after the explanation that His kingdom was not of a nature to come into collision at all with Cesar's? Indeed, it is clear that Pilate regarded our Lord as a high-minded Advocate of some mysterious religious principles, more or less connected with the Jewish Faith but at variance with the reigning ecclesiastical system—thoroughly sincere, at the least, but whether more than that he was unable to judge; yet cherishing no treasonable designs and meddling with no political affairs. This conclusion, candidly expressed, so exasperated "the chief priests and elders," who were panting for His death, that afraid of losing their Victim, they pour forth a volley of charges against Him, as if to overbear the Governor by their very vehemence. The precise succession of the incidents and speeches here, as reported by the different Evangelists, it is not quite easy to see, though the general course of them is plain enough.

Matt. xxvii. 12-14 (= Mark xv. 3-5):—"And when He was accused of the chief priests and elders, He answered nothing. Then said Pilate unto Him, Hearest thou not how many things they witness against thee? And He answered him to never a word"—Mark says, "Jesus yet answered nothing," or rather, 'answered nothing more' [οὐκέτι οὐδέν]; that is, nothing more than He *had* answered already to Pilate alone—"insomuch that the governor marvelled greatly." Pilate, fully persuaded of His innocence, seems to have been surprised that He did not refute nor even challenge their charges. But here a very important incident occurred—the transference of Jesus to Herod—which is recorded only in the third Gospel. It is thus introduced:—

Luke xxiii. 4, 5:—"Then said Pilate to the chief priests and to the people, I find no fault in him." (This appears to us clearly to be the same testimony as we found recorded in John, though *Robinson* in his 'Harmony' represents it as a second statement of the same thing.) "And they were the more fierce, saying, He stirreth up the people, teaching throughout all Jewry, beginning from Galilee to this place." They see no hope of getting Pilate's sanction to His death unless they can fasten upon Him some charge of conspiracy against the government; and as *Galilee* was noted for its turbulence (see Luke xiii. 1; Acts v. 37), and our Lord's ministry lay chiefly there, while Pilate might well be ignorant of much disaffection bred

there, beyond his own jurisdiction, they artfully introduce this region as that in which the alleged treason had been hatched, and whence it had at length spread to Judea and the capital. In his perplexity, Pilate, hearing of Galilee, bethinks himself of sending the Prisoner to Herod, in the hope of thereby shaking off all further responsibility in the case. Accordingly we have in the sequel of this third Gospel the following remarkable incident:—

Jesus before Herod Antipas (Luke xxiii. 6-12). 6. "When Pilate heard of Galilee, he asked whether the man were a Galilean. 7. And as soon as he knew that He belonged unto Herod's jurisdiction, he sent Him to Herod, who also was at Jerusalem at that time"—hoping, as we have said, to escape the dilemma of an unjust condemnation or an unpopular release; possibly also in hope of some light being cast upon the case itself. Herod was then at Jerusalem, no doubt to keep the Passover. 8. "And when Herod saw Jesus, he was exceeding glad: for he was desirous to see him of a long season." (See Luke ix. 9.) This is not inconsistent with what is said in Luke xiii. 31; for Herod, though full of curiosity for a considerable time to see Jesus, might not care to have Him wandering about in his own dominions, and too near to the scene of the bloody deed done on his faithful reprover. "Because he had heard many things of Him, and he hoped to have seen some miracle done by him." Fine sport thou expectest, O coarse, crafty, cruel tyrant, as the Philistines with Samson (Jud. xvi. 25). But thou hast been baulked before (see on Luke xiii. 31-33), and shalt be again. 9. "Then he questioned with Him in many words; but He answered him nothing." (See Matt. vii. 6.) 10. "And the chief priests and scribes stood and vehemently accused Him"—no doubt both of *treason*, Herod being a *king*, and of *blasphemy*, for Herod, though of Idumean descent, was by religion a circumcised *Jew*. 11. "And Herod with his men of war" [τοῖς στρατεύμασιν]—or his body guard, "set Him at nought"—stung with disappointment at His refusal either to amuse him with miracles or to answer any of his questions. But a day is coming, O proud Herod, when He who now stands before thee, to outward appearance a helpless prisoner, shall from His great white throne "laugh at thy calamity, and *mock* when thy fear cometh"! —"and arrayed Him in a gorgeous (or 'bright') robe" [ἐσθῆτα λαμπράν]. If this mean, 'of shining white,' as sometimes, it may have been in derision of His claim to be "King of the Jews;" that being the royal colour among the Jews. But if so, he in reality honoured Him, as *Bengel* remarks, just as Pilate did by blazoning His true title on the Cross: "and sent Him again to Pilate" —instead of releasing Him as he ought, having established nothing against Him (vv. 14, 15). Thus, to use again the words of *Bengel*, did Herod implicate himself with Pilate in all the guilt of His condemnation; and accordingly he is classed with him in this deed in Acts iv. 27. 12. "And the same day Pilate and Herod were made friends together: for before they were at enmity between themselves"—perhaps about some point of disputed jurisdiction, which this exchange of the Prisoner might tend to heal.

Pilate, a second and a third time Failing to Obtain the Consent of the Jews to the Release of Jesus, even though Offering to Scourge Him, and Borne

should bear witness unto the truth. Every one that ^yis of the truth
38 heareth my voice. Pilate saith unto him, What is truth?
And when he had said this, he went out again unto the Jews, and

A. D. 33.

y ch. 8. 47.
1 John 3.19.

Down by Clamour, at length, in spite of a Divine Warning, Surrenders Him to their Will (39, 40.) The materials of this portion must be drawn chiefly from the other Gospels.

Luke xxiii. 13-16:—"And Pilate, when he had called together the chief priests and the rulers and the people, said unto them, Ye have brought this man unto me, as one that perverteth the people: and, behold, I, having examined him before you"— from the first three Gospels we should conclude that the whole examination hitherto had been in their presence, while John represents it as private; but in all likelihood the reference here is to what is related in *vv.* 3-5, though too briefly to enable us to see the precise form which the examination took throughout—"have found no fault in this man touching those things whereof ye accuse him: No, nor yet Herod: for I sent you to him; and, lo, nothing worthy of death is done unto Him" [αὐτῷ] —or rather, 'by Him,' as the phrase sometimes means classically, and here must be held to mean. "I will therefore chastise Him, and let Him go" [παιδεύσας—ἀπολύσω]—'When, therefore, I have corrected, I will dismiss Him.' Though the *kind* of correction which he proposed to inflict was not specified by Pilate on this occasion, there can be no doubt that scourging was what he meant, and the event soon proved it. It seems strange to our ideas of justice, that a Roman governor should propose to punish, however lightly, a prisoner whose innocence he had just proclaimed. But it was of the nature of a well meant yet indefensible offer, in hope of saving the prisoner's life.

At this moment, as would appear, two of those strange incidents occurred which throw such a lurid light on these awful transactions. We refer to the *choice of Barabbas* for release at the feast, *in preference to Jesus,* and *the dream of Pilate's wife.*

Matt. xxvii. 15-23:—15. "Now at that feast the governor was wont to release unto the people a prisoner, whom they would." 16. "And they had then a notable (or 'notorious') prisoner called Barabbas"—"which," says Mark (xv. 7), "lay bound with them that had made insurrection with him" [συστασιαστῶν], or 'with his fellow insurgents,' "who (that is, which insurgents) had committed murder in the insurrection." But in Luke (xxiii. 19) the murder is expressly ascribed to this Barabbas, who is also called "a robber." He was evidently the ringleader of this lawless gang; and there we learn that the "sedition" here referred to was "made in the city." "And the multitude," says Mark, "crying aloud, began to desire him to do as he had ever done unto them." This is peculiar to Mark, and enables us vividly to realize the rising of the popular excitement before which Pilate—reluctantly though it was—gave way. But this clamour for the exercise of his usual clemency at the feast suggested another expedient for saving his conscience—the selection of Jesus as the prisoner of his choice for this release; not doubting that between Jesus and such a villain as this Barabbas they would for very shame be forced to prefer the former. But he little knew his men, if he thought that. 17. "Therefore," continues Matthew, "when they were gathered together, Pilate saith unto them, Whom will ye that I release unto you? Barabbas, or Jesus which is called Christ?" 18. "For he knew that for envy they had delivered Him"—that is, out of jealousy at the popularity of Jesus, and fear

of losing their own. This would seem to show that Pilate was not ignorant of the leading facts of this case.

At this stage of the proceedings, or rather just after they had formally begun, the strange message from his wife, recorded only by Matthew, seems to have deepened the anxiety of Pilate to save Jesus, and was probably what induced him to set up Barabbas as the only alternative he would give them for release, if they would not have Jesus. 19. "When he was set down on the judgment seat, his wife sent unto him"—it has been noticed as a striking confirmation of the historical accuracy of this Gospel, that (as *Tacitus* relates, in his Annals, iii. 33, 34) the Governors of provinces had not begun to take their wives with them till the time of Augustus—"saying, Have thou nothing to do with that just man" [μηδὲν σοὶ καὶ τῷ δικαίῳ ἐκείνῳ, see on John ii. 4]: "for I have suffered many things this day in a dream because of Him;" a testimony to the innocence of Jesus, and a warning to Pilate, from the unseen world, which, though finally ineffectual, made doubtless a deep impression upon his mind. 20. "But the chief priests and elders," continues Matthew, "persuaded the multitude that they should ask Barabbas, and destroy Jesus." Possibly they took advantage of the pause in the proceedings, occasioned by the delivering of the message from the Governor's wife. 21. "The governor answered and said unto them, Whether of the twain will ye that I release unto you? They said, Barabbas"—and said it with a vehemence which showed how successful the leaders had been in putting them up to this simultaneous way of clamouring. "And they cried out," says Luke, "all at once, saying, Away with this man, and release unto us Barabbas."

Pilate now makes a last feeble effort to induce them to acquiesce in the release of Jesus. "Pilate therefore," says Luke, "willing to release Jesus, spake again to them;" but what he said is recorded only by the first two Evangelists. 22. "Pilate," says Matthew, "said unto them, What shall I do then with Jesus which is called Christ?"—or, according to the keener form of the question in Mark, "Him whom ye call the King of the Jews?" This was just the thing they could not endure, and Pilate was sharp enough to see it. "But they all cried, Crucify Him, crucify Him" (Luke and Matthew). The shocking cry is redoubled. "And the governor said unto them the third time, Why, what evil hath he done? I have found no cause of death in Him: I will therefore chastise Him, and let Him go" (Luke). Why chastise Him, O Pilate, if thou hast found no fault in Him? But his remonstrances are waxing feebler; this offer of chastisement, already rejected as a compromise, is but another slight effort to stem the torrent, and presently he will give way. They see this, and hasten to bury his scruples in a storm of cries for His crucifixion. What a scene! 23. "But they cried out the more, saying, Let Him be crucified." Luke is more emphatic: "And they were instant with loud voices, requiring that He might be crucified, And the voices of them and of the chief priests prevailed."

A very striking incident is here again related in the first Gospel only.

Matt. xxvii. 24, 25:—24. "When Pilate saw that he could prevail nothing"—his humiliating helplessness was manifest to himself—"but that rather

465

39 saith unto them, I *find in him no fault *at all.* But ye have a custom, that I should release unto you one at the passover: will ye therefore that
40 I release unto you the King of the Jews? Then *a*cried they all again, saying, Not this man, but Barabbas. *b*Now Barabbas was a robber.

19, THEN *a*Pilate therefore took Jesus, and scourged *him.* And the
2 soldiers platted a crown of thorns, and put *it* on his head, and they put
3 on him a purple robe, And said, Hail, King of the Jews! and they smote him with their hands.
4 Pilate therefore went forth again, and saith unto them, Behold, I bring him forth to you, *b*that ye may know that I find no fault
5 in him. Then came Jesus forth, wearing the crown of thorns, and the purple robe. And *Pilate* saith unto them, Behold the man!
6 When *c*the chief priests therefore and officers saw him, they cried out, saying, Crucify *him,* crucify *him.* Pilate saith unto them, Take ye him,

A. D. 33.
*** Matt. 27. 18, 19, 24.
Mark 15. 14.
Luke 23. 4, 14-16.
ch. 19. 4, 6.
*** Acts 3. 14.
b Luke 23.19.

CHAP. 19.
a Isa 50. 6.
Matt. 20. 19.
Matt. 27. 26.
Mark 15. 15.
Luke 18. 33.
b ch. 18. 38.
2 Cor. 5. 21.
c Acts 3. 13.

---

a tumult was made, he took water, and washed his hands before the multitude" (compare, in illustration of this act, Deut. xxi. 6, 7; Ps. xxvi. 6), as a solemn and public protest against the deed, "saying, I am innocent of the blood of this [just] person:" [the words τοῦ δικαίου are omitted by *Tischendorf,* and bracketed by *Lachmann* and *Tregelles.* They appear to be of doubtful authority.] "see ye to it." 'Tis not so easy, O Pilate, to wash out sin, much less the innocent blood of the Holy One of God! But thy testimony to Him, and to the uneasiness of thy conscience in condemning Him, we accept with all thankfulness—to a Higher than thou. 25. "Then answered all the people, and said, His blood be on us, and on our children." O Jerusalem, Jerusalem, how heavy has that word been to thee! And the dregs of that cup of fury, voluntarily called down upon thine own head, are not all drunken yet. "But thou, O Lord, how long?" "And Pilate," says Luke, "gave sentence that it should be as they required. And he released unto them him that for sedition and murder was cast into prison, whom they desired; but he delivered Jesus to their will." There is a heavy reflection conveyed by these words, though they be but the studious repetition of the black facts of the case; for it is not the manner of the first three Evangelists to make reflections on the facts which they record, as the fourth does.

From the fulness of the matter embraced in the foregoing portions of the first three Gospels, it will at once be seen that the beloved disciple, in the two following verses, designed not so much to *record* as merely to *remind* his readers of facts already fully recorded and familiar to all Christians, in order to pave the way for the fuller details of what followed, which he was about to give: **39. But ye have a custom, that I should release unto you one at the passover: will ye therefore that I release unto you the King of the Jews? 40. Then cried they all again, saying, Not this man, but Barabbas. Now Barabbas was a robber.**

CHAP. XIX. 1-16.—*Jesus is Scourged by Pilate —After being Treated with other Severities and Insults, and Two more Efforts to Save Him Failing, He is Delivered Up and Led Away to be Crucified.*

The Scourging and Cruel Mockeries (1-3.) **1. Then Pilate therefore took Jesus, and scourged him.** As a compromise, he had offered before to commit this *less* injustice on the person of the prisoner, in hope of that contenting them. (See page 465, first column, second paragraph, and second column, third paragraph.) But this victim of conflicting emotions is now resigning himself to the fiendish clamours of a Jewish mob, set on by sacerdotal

hypocrites. This scourging, says *Philo Judæus,* was what was inflicted on the worst criminals. The next step was the following, recorded in Matt. xxvii. 27; and Mark xv. 16: "Then the soldiers of the governor took Jesus into the common hall ('the Prætorium'), and gathered unto him the whole band (of soldiers)"—the body of the military cohort stationed there, to take part in the mock-coronation now to be enacted. **2. And the soldiers platted a crown of thorns, and put it on his head** —in mockery of a regal crown, **and they put on him a purple robe**—in mockery of the *imperial purple;* first "stripping Him" of His own outer garment (Matt. xxvii. 28). It is possible that this was the "gorgeous" robe in which Herod arrayed and sent Him back to Pilate (Luke xxiii. 11); but it may have been one of the military cloaks worn by the Roman officers. In Matthew (xxvii. 29) we have the following addition: "they put a reed in his right hand"—in mockery of the regal sceptre —"and they bowed the knee before Him, and mocked Him." **3. And said, Hail, King of the Jews!**—doing Him derisive homage in the form used on approaching the emperors (see also, on the same derisive epithet, page 472). **and they smote him with their hands.** Matthew says "they spit upon Him, and took the reed, and smote Him on the head" (see Mic. v. 1). The best comment on these affecting details is to *cover the face.*

Pilate Again Tries to save the Prisoner (4-13). **4. Pilate therefore went forth again, and saith unto them, Behold, I bring**—or 'am bringing' **him forth to you, that ye may know that I find no fault in him**—' and by scourging and allowing the soldiers to make sport of him, have gone as far to meet your exasperation as can be expected from a judge.' **5. Then came Jesus forth, wearing the crown of thorns, and the purple robe. And Pilate saith unto them, Behold the man!**—There is no reason to think that *contempt* dictated this memorable speech. There was clearly a struggle in the breast of this wretched man. Not only was he reluctant to surrender to mere clamour an innocent person, but a feeling of anxiety about His mysterious claims, as is plain from what follows, was beginning to rack his breast, and the object of his exclamation seems to have been to *move their pity.* But, be *his* meaning what it may, those three words have been eagerly appropriated by all Christendom, and enshrined for ever in its heart, as a sublime expression of its calm, rapt admiration of its suffering Lord. **6. When the chief priests therefore and officers saw him, they cried out, saying, Crucify him, crucify him.** (See page 465, second column, third paragraph.) **Pilate saith unto them, Take ye him, and crucify him: for I find no fault**

7 and crucify *him:* for I find no fault in him. The Jews answered him, ^dWe have a law, and by our law he ought to die, because he 'made himself the Son of God.

8 When Pilate therefore heard that saying, he was the more afraid;

9 and went again into the judgment hall, and saith unto Jesus, Whence

10 art thou? But ^fJesus gave him no answer. Then saith Pilate unto him, Speakest thou not unto me? knowest thou not that I have power to

11 crucify thee, and have power to release thee? Jesus answered, ^gThou couldest have no power *at all* against me, except it were given thee from above: therefore he that delivered me unto thee hath the greater sin.

12 And from thenceforth Pilate sought to release him: but the Jews cried out, saying, ^hIf thou let this man go, thou art not Cesar's friend: ⁱwhoso-

·13 ever maketh himself a king speaketh against Cesar. When Pilate therefore heard that saying, he brought Jesus forth, and sat down in the judgment seat in a place that is called the Pavement, but in the Hebrew, ¹Gabbatha.

A. D. 33.

^d Lev. 24. 16.
* Matt. 26.66.
ch. 5. 18.
ch. 10. 33.
^f Isa. 53. 7.
Matt. 27.12, 14.
^g Gen.45. 7,8.
Ps. 62. 11.
Dan. 4. 17, 25.
Matt. 6. 16.
Luke 22.53.
ch. 7. 30.
Acts 2. 23.
^h Luke 23. 2.
ⁱ Acts 17. 7.
1 That is, elevated.

in him—as if that would relieve *him* of the responsibility, who, by surrendering him to an unrighteous death, incurred it all! **7. The Jews answered him, We have a law, and by our law he ought to die, because he made himself the Son of God.** Their criminal charges having come to nothing, they give that up, and as Pilate was throwing the whole responsibility upon them, they retreat into their own Jewish law, by which, as claiming equality with God (see on ch. v. 18, and viii. 58, 59), He ought to die; insinuating that it was Pilate's duty, even as civil governor, to protect their law from such insult.

8. When Pilate heard that saying, he was the more afraid—the name "SON OF GOD," the lofty sense evidently attached to it by His Jewish accusers, the dialogue he had already held with Him, and the dream of his wife (Matt. xxvii. 19), all working together in the breast of the unhappy man. **9. And went again into the judgment hall—**'the Prætorium,' **and saith unto Jesus, Whence art thou?**—a question relating, beyond all doubt, not to His *mission*, but to His *personal origin.* **But Jesus gave him no answer.** He had said enough; the time for answering such a question was past; the weak and wavering governor is already on the point of giving way. **10. Then saith Pilate unto him, Speakest thou not unto me?** The "me" is the emphatic word in the question. He falls back upon the *pride of office,* which doubtless tended to check the workings of his conscience. **knowest thou not that I have power to crucify thee, and have power to release thee?**—said to work upon the silent Prisoner at once by *fear* and by *hope.* **11. Jesus answered, Thou couldest [οὐκ εἶχες]**—rather, 'Thou shouldest' have no power at all against me—neither to crucify, nor to release, nor to do anything whatever against Me, as *Bengel* expresses it, except it were—'unless it had been' given thee from above.—*q. d.,* 'Thou thinkest too much of thy power, Pilate: against Me that power is none, save what is meted out to thee by special divine appointment, for a special end.' **therefore he that delivered me unto thee**—to wit, Caiaphas; but he only as representing the Jewish authorities as a body, hath the greater sin—as having better opportunities and more knowledge of such matters.

12. And from thenceforth—particularly this speech, which seems to have filled him with awe, and redoubled his anxiety, **Pilate sought to release him**—that is, to gain their *consent* to it: for he could have done it at once on his own authority: **but the Jews cried**—seeing their advantage, and not slow to profit by it, **If thou let this man go,**

thou art not Cesar's friend: whosoever maketh himself a king speaketh against Cesar. 'This,' as *Webster and Wilkinson* observe, 'was equivalent to a threat of *impeachment,* which we know was much dreaded by such officers as the procurators, especially of the character of Pilate or Felix. It also consummates the treachery and disgrace of the Jewish rulers, who were willing, for the purpose of destroying Jesus, to affect a zeal for the supremacy of a foreign prince.' The reader will do well also to observe how they go backwards and forwards in their charges. Failing in obtaining a condemnation on the ground of *treason,* they had just before this fallen back in despair on the charge of *blasphemy.* But as they could not but see how weak that was as an argument with a mere civil governor, they avail themselves of Pilate's manifest embarrassment and vacillation to re-urge the charge of treason, but in the form of a threat against Pilate himself, if he should dismiss the Prisoner. **13. When Pilate heard that saying** —or, according to the preferable reading, 'these sayings,' **he brought Jesus forth, and sat down in** —'upon,' **the judgment seat**—that he might pronounce sentence against the Prisoner, on this charge, the more solemnly, **in a place that is called the Pavement** [λιθόστρωτον], **but in the Hebrew, Gabbatha,** [גבתא]—either from a word signifying to be 'high,' referring to the raised platform on which the judgment seat was placed; or from one signifying the 'back,' from its arched form. As the Greek word denotes, it was a tesselated pavement, much used by the Romans. There is a minute topographical accuracy in the use of this word which a learned defender of the authenticity of the Gospel History has not failed to notice. 'Jesus,' says *Hug,* 'is led out to receive His sentence, and Pilate sat in a place called the *Lithostrōton* to pass judgment (John xix. 13). The transaction is represented as if this place was in front of the Prætor's house, or at least at no great distance from it. And there is, in fact, such a place, which has been formerly overlooked, in the outworks of the Temple. Mention is made of it in an assault which the Romans made upon the Temple, on the side of the tower Antonia (*Joseph.* J. W. vi. 6 and 7). Here is the Lithostroton, and the house of the Prætor must have been opposite to this place. Now he lived, as appears from some incidental passages in *Philo* (compare *Leg. ad Caium* with *Joseph.* Antt. xviii. 4), in Herod's palace, which was certainly in this quarter and neighbourhood, north-west of the tower Antonia and the

467

14   And *ʲ*it was the preparation of the passover, and about the sixth
15 hour: and he saith unto the Jews, Behold your King! But they
cried out, Away with *him*, away with *him*, crucify him. Pilate saith
unto them, Shall I crucify your King? The chief priests answered, *ᵏ*We
16 have no king but Cesar. Then *ˡ*delivered he him therefore unto them to
be crucified.

A. D. 33.

ʲ Matt. 27. 62.
ᵏ Gen. 49. 10.
Ezek. 21. 26,
27.
ˡ Matt. 27. 26,
31.

Temple: so that the proximity of the Lithostroton to the palace, which is implied in John's narrative, is strictly accurate.'

Pilate, After One More fruit'ess Effort to save Him, having finally Yielded the point, Jesus is Delivered Up and Led Away to be Crucified (14-16). **14. And** —or, 'Now' **it was the preparation of the pass-over.** This is another of the passages from which it has been concluded that the regular Passover had not up to that time been kept, and consequently that our Lord, in celebrating it with His disciples the previous evening, had anticipated the proper day for its observance. To this question we have adverted pretty fully—on Luke xxii. 7-30, page 324; on ch. xiii. 1; and on ch. xviii. 28. As to the present passage, there is no evidence that "the preparation of the Passover" means the preparation *for* it. The day before every sabbath was called "the preparation" (Mark xv. 42), from the preparations for its proper observance which were made on the previous day; insomuch that in enumerating the days of the week the Friday would be named 'Preparation' (day). But this was no ordinary 'preparation day.' It was 'the Passover preparation,' as the words of our Evangelist may be rendered; by which we understand that it was not only the Preparation Friday, but the Friday of the Paschal feast. Accordingly, it is called, in *v.* 31, "an high day." **and about the sixth hour.** As it cannot be conceived that our Evangelist meant to say here that it was already *noon*, according to Jewish reckoning—for Mark says (xv. 25), that the crucifixion itself took place at the third hour (nine o'clock, of our reckoning), and that is what we should naturally conclude from the progress of the events—two expedients have been resorted to for clearing up the difficulty, neither of which appears to us quite satisfactory. The one is to adopt the reading "third" instead of "sixth" hour, as *Bengel, Robinson, Webster and Wilkinson* do, and as *Alford* half inclines to do. But the evidence for this reading is so weak that it seems like a tampering with the sacred text to adopt it. The other way of solving the difficulty is to suppose that our Evangelist here adopts the *Roman* method of computation, and means that it was about six o'clock, according to our reckoning. So *Olshausen, Tholuck, Hug,* &c. But as there is no ground to suppose that in other cases our Evangelist adopts the Roman divisions of time, so the hour which that reckoning brings out here can hardly be the right one; for it must have been considerably *later* than six in the morning when that took place which is here related. It remains then to understand the Evangelist to refer to the two broad divisions of the day, so familiar to the Jews, the third and the sixth hours; and to suppose that as the event occurred between the two, the one Evangelist specified the *hither* terminus, while the other takes the *further* one. So *Ellicott* and others. **And he saith unto the Jews, Behold your King!** Having now made up his mind to yield to them, he takes a sort of quiet revenge on them by this irony, which he knew would sting them. This only re-awakens their cry to despatch Him. **15. But they cried out, Away with him, away with him, crucify him. Pilate saith unto them, Shall**

I **crucify your King? The chief priests answered, We have no king but Cesar.** Some of those who thus cried died miserably in rebellion against Cesar forty years afterwards, as *Alford* remarks. But it suited their present purpose. **16. Then delivered he him therefore unto them to be crucified**—against all justice, against his own conscience, against his solemnly and repeatedly pronounced judicial decision that He was innocent whom he now gave up. **And they took Jesus, and led him away.** And so, amidst the conflict of human passions and the advancing tide of crime, the Scripture was fulfilled which said, "He is led as a lamb to the slaughter."

Remarks.—1. If the complicated details of the *ecclesiastical* trial of our Lord bear such indubitable marks of truth as we have seen that they do (see on Mark xiv. 53-72, Remark 9 at the close of that Section, pages 210, 211), surely those of the *political* trial which followed are not less self-evidencing. Think first of the dark consistency with which His accusers held to their point of obtaining a condemnation from Pilate; the facility with which they oscillated between two kinds of charges—of treason against Cesar and treason against God—just as the chances of success by urging the one or the other of these charges seemed to preponderate for the moment; the ingenuity with which they set on the mob to shout for His crucifixion, and the fiendish violence with which, when Pilate wavered at the very last, they bore him down, and by insinuating the disloyalty of sparing the Prisoner, at length extorted compliance. Think, next, of that extraordinary conflict of emotions which agitated the breast of Pilate—such as we may safely say no literary ingenuity could have invented, and so artlessly managed as we have it told in the Evangelical Narratives. Think, finally, of the placid dignity of the Sufferer, in all these scenes—the dignity with which He *speaks*, when alone with Pilate, and what is even more remarkable, the dignity of His *silence* before the multitude and in the presence of Herod. Whether we look at each of these features of the political trial by itself, or at all of them as composing one whole—their originality, their consistency, their wonderful verisimilitude, must strike every intelligent and impartial reader. Can we be surprised that such a History makes way for itself throughout the world without the need of laboured books of evidence, and is rejected or suspected only by perverted ingenuity? Similar remarks are applicable even to the minor details of this Section, such as what is said of *Barabbas;* but the reader can follow this out for himself. 2. As the subjects of Christ's Kingdom are at the same time under the Civil Government of the country in which they reside, and may be helped or hindered by it in their Christian duties according to the procedure of that government towards them, it is plainly both the right and the duty of Christians to procure such civil arrangements as shall be most for the advantage of religion in the land. What these ought to be is a question on which Christians are not agreed, and on which they may reasonably differ; and, indeed, the varying conditions of civil society may render the policy which would be proper or warrantable in one case neither right nor

17   And they took Jesus, and led *him* away. And he bearing his cross | A. D. 33.
^m^went forth into a place called *the place* of a skull, which is called in | ^m^Num.15.36.

---

practicable in another. But since Civil Government never will nor can nor ought to be altogether indifferent to Religion, it is the duty of Christians to endeavour that at least nothing injurious to Religion be enacted and enforced. But the Christian world has grievously erred on this subject. Since the days of Constantine, when the Roman Empire became externally Christian, the desire to turn civil government to the advantage of Christianity has led to the incorporation of such a multitude of civil elements with the government of the Church, that the lines of essential distinction between the political and the religious have been obliterated, not only under Romanism, but even in the constitution of Church and State in the countries of the Reformation; insomuch that the explicit declaration of our Lord to Pilate—"My Kingdom is not of this world"—would scarcely have satisfied the Roman Governor that His master's interests were unaffected by such a kingdom, if explained according to some modern principles of ecclesiastical government. Let Christians but interpret our Lord's explanation of the nature of His kingdom honestly and in all its latitude, and their differences on this subject, if they do not melt away, will become small and unimportant. **3.** If in the sufferings and death of Christ we have the substitution of the Innocent for the guilty, we have a kind of visible exhibition of this in the choice of Barabbas, which was the escape of the guilty in virtue of the condemnation of the Innocent. **4.** Often as we have had occasion to notice in this History the consistency of the divine determinations with the liberty of human actions, nowhere is it more conspicuous than in this Section. Observe how our Lord meets the threat of Pilate, when he asked Him if He knew not that the power of life and death was in his hands. 'No, Pilate, it is not in thine hands, but in Hands which thine only obey; *therefore* is the guilty man who delivered Me unto thee, the more guilty.' But "He taketh the wise in their own craftiness, and the counsel of the froward is carried headlong."

17-30.—CRUCIFIXION AND DEATH OF THE LORD JESUS. (= Matt. xxvii. 32-50; Mark xv. 21-37; Luke xxiii. 26-46.)

No sooner do those envenomed enemies of the Lord Jesus get Him again into their hands, than they renew their mockeries, as we learn from the first two Gospels.

Jesus is Again Subjected to Mockery (Matt. xxvii. 31; Mark xv. 20). "And after they had mocked Him, they took the (purple) robe off from Him, and put His own raiment on Him, and led Him away to be crucified."

The next two steps possess the deepest interest. *Jesus is first Made to Bear His Own Cross, but afterwards they Compel Simon the Cyrenian to Bear it for Him* (17). **And he bearing his cross** went forth—that is, without the city; a most significant circumstance in relation to a provision of the Levitical law. "For," says the apostle, "the bodies of those beasts, whose blood is brought into the sanctuary by the high priest for sin, are burned *without the camp*: Wherefore Jesus also, that He might sanctify the people with His own blood, suffered *without the gate*" (Heb. xiii. 11, 12). None of the Evangelists but John mentions the important fact that Christ was made to bear His own cross; although we might have presumed as much, both from the practice of the Romans, which imposed upon criminals condemned to be crucified

469

the burden of bearing their own cross, as *Plutarch* expressly states, and from our Lord's injunctions to his followers to bear their cross *after Him* (see on Matt. x. 38). But soon, it would appear, it became necessary to lay this burden upon some one else if He was not to sink under it. How this was done our Evangelist does not say, nor that it was done at all. But it had been related by all the three preceding Evangelists.

Matt. xxvii. 32; Mark xv. 21; Luke xxiii. 26:—"And as they came out," says Matthew, "they found a man of Cyrene," in Libya, on the north coast of Africa, "Simon by name," "who passed (or 'was passing') by," says Mark. He was not, then, one of the crowd that had come out of the city to witness the execution; and Mark adds that he was "coming out of the country," probably into the city, all ignorant, perhaps, of what was going on; and was "the father of Alexander and Rufus." This stranger, then, "they compelled to bear His cross." Jesus, it would appear, was *no longer able to bear it.* And when we think of the Agony through which He passed during the previous night, not to speak of other causes of exhaustion, under which the three disciples were unable to keep awake in the garden; if we think of the night He passed with Annas, and the early morn before the Sanhedrim, with all its indignities; of the subsequent scenes before Pilate first, then Herod, and then Pilate again; of the scourging, the crown of thorns, and the other cruelties before He was led forth to execution—can we wonder that it soon appeared necessary, if He was not to sink under this burden, that they should find another to bear it? For we must remember that "He was crucified through weakness" [ἐξ ἀσθενείας], 2 Cor. xiii. 4. (See on the "loud voice" which He emitted on the cross as He expired, page 474.)

It will be observed that this Simon the Cyrenian is said to be "the father of Alexander and Rufus" (Mark xv. 21). From this we naturally conclude that when Mark wrote his Gospel these two persons—Alexander and Rufus—were not only Christians, but well known as such among those by whom he expected his Gospel to be first read. Accordingly, when we turn to Romans xvi. 13, we find these words, "Salute *Rufus,* chosen in the Lord—that is, 'the choice one' or 'precious one in the Lord', and his mother and mine." That this is the same Rufus as Mark supposes his readers would at once recognize, there can hardly be a doubt. And when the apostle calls Rufus' mother 'his own mother,' in grateful acknowledgment of her motherly attentions to himself for the love she bore to his Master, does it not seem that Simon the Cyrenian's conversion dated from that memorable day when, 'passing casually by as he came from the country,' they "compelled him to bear" the Saviour's cross. Sweet compulsion, and noble pay for the enforced service to Jesus then rendered, if the spectacle which his eyes then beheld issued in his *voluntarily* taking up his own cross! Through him it is natural to suppose that his wife would be brought in, and that this believing couple, now "heirs together of the grace of life" (1 Pet. iii. 7), as they told their two sons, Alexander and Rufus, what honour had been put upon their father all unwittingly, at that hour of deepest and dearest interest to all Christians, might be blessed to the fetching in of both those sons. By the time that Paul wrote to the Romans, the elder of the two may have gone to reside in some other place, or de-

18 the Hebrew, Golgotha: where ⁿthey crucified him, and two others with him, on either side one, and Jesus in the midst.

A. D. 33.

ⁿ Isa. 53. 12.

parted to be with Christ, which was far better; and Rufus being left alone with his mother, they only were mentioned by the apostle.

The Spectacle of Christ's Sufferings Draws Tears from the Women that followed Him—His Remarkable Address to Them. For this we are indebted exclusively to the third Gospel.

Luke xxiii. 27-32:—27. "And there followed Him a great company (or 'multitude') of people, and of women, which also"—that is, the women [αἱ]—"bewailed and lamented Him." These women are not to be confounded with those precious Galilean women afterwards expressly mentioned. Our Lord's reply shows that they were merely a miscellaneous collection of females, whose sympathies for the Sufferer—of whom some would know more and some less—drew forth tears and lamentations. "But Jesus turning unto them said, Daughters of Jerusalem, weep not for Me, but weep for yourselves, and for your children." Noble spirit of compassion, rising above His own dread endurances in tender commiseration of sufferings yet in the distance and far lighter, but *without His supports and consolations!* "For, behold the days (or 'days') are coming, in the which they shall say, Blessed are the barren, and the wombs that never bare, and the paps which never gave suck. Then shall they begin to say to the mountains, Fall on us; and to the hills, Cover us." These words, taken from Hos. x. 8, are a lively way of expressing the feelings of persons flying hither and thither despairingly for shelter. The more immediate reference of them is to the sufferings which awaited them during the approaching siege of Jerusalem; but they are a premonition of cries of another and more awful kind (Rev. vi. 16, 17; and compare, for the language, Isa. ii. 10, 19, 21). "For if they do these things in a green tree"—that naturally resists the fire—"what shall be done in the dry," that attracts the flames, being their proper fuel. The proverb plainly means: 'If such sufferings alight upon the innocent One, the very Lamb of God, what must be in store for those who are provoking the flames?'

On Arriving at the Place of Execution, Jesus is Offered Vinegar to drink, but Having Tasted, He Refuses to drink it (17). Our Evangelist only brings us to Calvary. For the rest we are indebted to the first two Gospels. 17. he went forth into a place called the place of a skull—or 'unto the place called Skull-place,' which is called in the Hebrew, Golgotha גֻּלְגָּלְתָּא softened into Γολγοθᾶ]. 'Roll-formed' or 'roll-shaped,' is the idea of the word. But whether this refer to the round shape of the *skulls* of criminals executed there, which has hitherto been the prevailing opinion, or to the shape of the ground—a round hill or knoll there—as others think, is not agreed. That a hill of that form lay to the north of the city seems true enough; but as this would place the spot outside the city, it is at least inconsistent with what is now shown as the place where our Lord suffered, which is within the city, and must have been so then, as *Dr. Robinson* contends—though *Mr. Williams*, who has examined the ground with equal care, endeavours to disprove his positions.

Matt. xxvii. 33, 34; Mark xv. 22, 23:—"And when they were come unto a place called Golgotha, that is to say, A place of a skull, they gave Him vinegar to drink mingled with gall;" using the words of the prophetic Psalm (lxix. 21), "They gave Me also gall for My meat; and in My thirst

they gave Me vinegar to drink." But Mark, no doubt, gives the precise mixture: "They gave Him to drink wine mingled with myrrh." This potion was stupefying, and given to criminals just before execution, to deaden the sense of pain.

'Fill high the bowl, and spice it well, and pour
The dews oblivious: for the Cross is sharp,
The Cross is sharp, and He
Is tenderer than a lamb.'

But *our Lord would die with every faculty clear, and in full sensibility to all His sufferings.*

'Thou wilt feel all, that thou may'st pity all;
And rather would'st Thou wrestle with strong pain,
Than overcloud Thy soul,
So clear in agony,
Or lose one glimpse of heaven before the time.
O most entire and perfect sacrifice,
Renewed in every pulse,' &c.—KEBLE.

The Act of Crucifixion between Two Malefactors (18). 18. Where they crucified him. Four soldiers were employed in this operation, which was done by fastening the body—after being stripped of all clothing save a broad belt round the loins—by nails or bolts driven through the hands to the transverse part of the cross. The feet, though not *always* nailed, but simply bound, to the upright beam, were almost certainly so in this case (Ps. xxii. 16). The body was supported by a piece of wood passing between the legs. The excruciating agony of this kind of death is universally attested, and may easily be supposed. But the shame of it was equal to the torture. and two others with him. In Luke these are called by the general name of "malefactors," or 'evil-doers' [κακούργους]; in Matthew and Mark "thieves," or rather 'robbers' [λῃστάς]: on either side one, and Jesus in the midst—a hellish expedient to hold him up as the worst of the three. But in this, as in many other of their doings, "the Scripture was fulfilled-which saith (Isa. liii. 12), *And He was numbered with the transgressors,*" as it is in Mark xv. 28—though the prophecy reaches deeper than that outside fulfilment. [This entire verse, however (Mark xv. 28), is of extremely doubtful genuineness. *Lachmann* inserts it, no doubt on the strength of the ancient versions; but the MS. evidence against it is very strong, and while *Tregelles* brackets it, *Tischendorf* excludes it altogether. It seems to have come in from Luke xxii. 37, where we have the same words from our Lord's own mouth.]

Jesus now Utters the First of His Seven Sayings on the Cross. Of these Seven *Sayings*—embalmed for ever in the hearts of believers—one is recorded by Matthew, three by Luke, and three by John. This first one is recorded in the third Gospel only.

Luke xxiii. 34: "Then said Jesus,"

First Saying: "FATHER, FORGIVE THEM; FOR THEY KNOW NOT WHAT THEY DO." [*Lachmann* unhappily brackets this most precious verse as of doubtful authority. But the evidence for it, external as well as internal, is most decisive; and both *Tischendorf* and *Tregelles* print it as it stands in the received text.]

The Evangelist seems to intimate that this was said as the executioners were doing, or just as they finished, their dread task. But we must not limit the prayer to them. Beyond doubt, it embraced all who had any hand, directly or indirectly, in the death of Him who offered that prayer—of all of whom, even the most enlightened, the apostle could with truth say, that, "had they known it, they would not have crucified the Lord of glory" (1 Cor. ii. 8: see also Acts iii. 17; xiii.

19   And Pilate wrote a title, and put *it* on the cross. And the writing
20 was, °JESUS OF NAZARETH THE KING OF THE JEWS. This title then read many of the Jews; for the place where Jesus was crucified was nigh to the city: and it was written ᵖin Hebrew, *and* Greek, *and*
21 Latin. Then said the chief priests of the Jews to Pilate, Write not, The
22 King of the Jews; but that he said, I am King of the Jews. Pilate answered, What I have written I have written.
23   Then the soldiers, when they had crucified Jesus, took his garments, and made four parts, to every soldier a part; and also *his* coat: now the coat
24 was without seam, ²woven from the top throughout. They said therefore among themselves, Let us not rend it, but cast lots for it, whose it shall be: that the scripture might be fulfilled, which saith, ᵠThey parted my raiment among them, and for my vesture they did cast lots. These things therefore the soldiers did.

A. D. 33.

° ch. 1. 45, 46, 49.
ch. 18. 33.
ver. 3, 12.
Acts 3. 6.
Acts 26. 9.
ᵖ ch. 5. 2.
ver. 13.
Acts 21. 40.
Acts 22. 2.
Acts 26. 14.
Rev. 16. 16.
² Or, wrought.
ᵠ Ps. 22. 18.
Isa. 10. 7.
Acts 13. 27.

27; and compare 1 Tim. i. 13). ·In a wider and deeper sense still, that prayer fulfilled the great Messianic prediction, "And He made intercession for the transgressors" (Isa. liii. 12)—extending to all whose sins He bore in His own body on the tree. In the Sermon on the Mount our Lord says, "Pray for them which despitefully use you and persecute you" (Matt. v. 44); and here, as in so many other cases, we find Him the first to fulfil His own precept—thus furnishing the right interpretation and the perfect model of the duty enjoined. And how quickly was it seen in "His martyr Stephen," that though He had left the earth in Person, His spirit remained behind, and Himself could, in some of His brightest lineaments, be reproduced in His disciples! (See on Acts vii. 60.) And what does the world in every age owe to these few words, spoken *where* and *as* they were spoken!

In the Title which Pilate Wrote and Put upon the Cross, he proclaims Jesus King of the Jews, and Refuses to Alter it (19-22). **19. And Pilate wrote a title, and put it on the cross. And the writing was, JESUS OF NAZARETH THE KING OF THE JEWS. 20. This title then read many of the Jews; for the place where Jesus was crucified was nigh to the city: and it was written in Hebrew**—that is, Syro-Chaldaic, the language of the country, and **Greek**—the current language, and **Latin**—the official language. These were then the chief languages of the earth, and this secured that all spectators should be able to read it. Stung by this, the Jewish ecclesiastics entreat that it may be so altered as to express, not His regal dignity, but His false claim to it. **21. Then said the chief priests of the Jews to Pilate, Write not, The King of the Jews; but that he said, I am King of the Jews.** But Pilate thought he had yielded quite enough to them; and having intended expressly to spite and insult them by this title, for having got him to act against his own sense of justice, he peremptorily refused them. **22. Pilate answered, What I have written I have written.** And thus, amidst the conflicting passions of men, was proclaimed, in the chief tongues of mankind, from the Cross itself, and in circumstances which threw upon it a lurid yet grand light, the truth which drew the Magi to His manger, and will yet be owned by all the world!

The Garments of Jesus are Parted among the soldiers, and For His Vesture They Cast Lots (23, 24). **23. Then the soldiers, when they had crucified Jesus, took his garments, and made four parts, to every soldier a part**—of the four soldiers who were the executioners, and whose perquisite they were. **and also his coat** [τὸν χιτῶνα]—the Roman tunic, or close-fitting vest: **now the coat was without seam, woven from**

the top throughout. Perhaps, say *Webster and Wilkinson*, denoting considerable skill and labour, as necessary to produce such a garment—the work, probably, of one or more of the women who ministered in such things unto Him (Luke viii. 3). **24. They said therefore among themselves, Let us not rend it, but cast lots for it, whose it shall be: that the scripture might be fulfilled, which saith (Ps. xxii. 18), They parted my raiment among them, and for my vesture they did cast lots. These things therefore the soldiers did.** That a prediction so exceedingly specific—distinguishing one piece of dress from others, and announcing that while *those* should be parted amongst several, *that* should be given by lot to one person—that such a prediction should not only be fulfilled to the letter, but by a party of heathen military, without interference from either the friends or the enemies of the Crucified One, is surely eminently worthy to be ranked among the wonders of this all-wonderful scene. Now come the *mockeries*, which are passed by in silence by our Evangelist, as sufficiently recorded in the first three Gospels. These mockeries came from four distinct quarters.

Jesus is Mocked, first, by the Passers-by. For this particular we are indebted to the first two Gospels.

Matt. xxvii. 39, 40; Mark xv. 29, 30:—"And they that passed by reviled Him, wagging their heads"—in ridicule: see Ps. xxii. 7; cix. 25; and compare Job xvi. 4: Isa. xxxvii. 22; Jer. xviii. 16; Lam. ii. 15—"and saying," "Ah!" [Οὐά] an exclamation here of derision. "Thou that destroyest the temple, and buildest it in three days, save thyself"—" and come down from the cross." If one wonders that in seeking for evidence against our Lord at His trial, His enemies should be obliged to fall back upon a few words uttered by Him at the very outset of his ministry, and after having to distort even these, in order to give them even the appearance of indictable matter, that the charge should break down so completely that the high priest felt he had no pretext for condemning Him unless He could draw something worthy of death from Himself on the spot; much more may one wonder that the same distorted words which had failed at the most solemn moment should now be brought up afresh and cast in the teeth of the blessed One, as He hung upon the cross, even by the passers-by. (See on Mark xiv. 58, 59.) One thing it would seem to show, that the prosecutors in this case had had to send hither and thither for witnesses against our Lord, and collect from all quarters whatever might seem to tell against Him; that in this way the more

471

25 Now there stood by the cross of Jesus his mother, and his mother's
26 sister, Mary the *wife* of [3]Cleophas, and Mary Magdalene. When Jesus
    therefore saw his mother, and [p]the disciple standing by whom he loved,
27 he saith unto his mother, [q]Woman, behold thy son! Then saith he to
    the disciple, Behold thy mother! And from that hour that disciple took
    her [r]unto his own *home*.

A. D. 33.
[3] Or, Clopas.
Luke 24. 18.
[p] ch. 13. 23.
ch. 20. 2.
[q] ch. 2. 4.
[r] Gen. 47. 12.
ch. 1. 11.

it came to be seen that the materials were few and trivial, the more stress would need to be laid upon the little they had to rest on; that thus it had come to be understood that if all failed, this speech at least would suffice to condemn Him; and as the ecclesiastical prosecutors were not likely to proclaim how signally they had failed in making out this charge, and too little time had elapsed between the Trial and the Execution for the proceedings of the Sanhedrim to get abroad, these "passers-by" had cast the saying in our Lord's teeth in their reckless simplicity, taking it for granted that He was now suffering for that speech as for other misdeeds. And yet that memorable speech *in its true sense* was now receiving the first part of its fulfilment —"Destroy ye this Temple;" as in His resurrection it was speedily to be fulfilled in the second part of it—"In three days *I* will raise it up." See John ii. 22.

Jesus is Mocked, secondly, by the Rulers. We have this in the first three Gospels, but most fully —as might be expected—in the first, the peculiarly *Jewish* Gospel.

Matt. xxvii. 41-43; Mark xv. 31, 32; Luke xxiii. 35:—"Likewise also the chief priests, mocking him, with the scribes and elders, said, He saved others; himself he cannot save." In this, as in other taunts (such as Luke xv. 2), there was a deep truth. Both things He could not do; for He had come to give *His* life a ransom for *many*. No doubt this added a sting to the reproach, unknown at that moment save to Himself. But the taunt of the rulers ends not here. "If He be the King of Israel (they add), let Him now come down from the cross, and we will believe Him." *No, they would not;* for those who resisted the evidence from the resurrection of Lazarus, and afterwards resisted the evidence of His own resurrection, were beyond the reach of any amount of merely *external* evidence. But they go on to say, "He trusted in God; let Him deliver Him now, if He will have Him [εἰ θέλει αὐτόν], answering to "seeing He delighted in Him" [יִב יְפֵן, ὅτι θέλει αὐτόν]. These are the words of the Messianic Psalm, xxii. 8. The last words of their taunt are, "for He said, I am the Son of God." We thank you, O ye chief priests, scribes, and elders, for this triple testimony, unconsciously borne by you, to our Christ: first to *His habitual trust in God,* as a feature in His character so marked and palpable that even ye found upon it your impotent taunt; next, *to His identity with the Sufferer of the 22nd Psalm,* whose very words ye unwittingly appropriate, thus *serving yourselves heirs* to the dark office and impotent malignity of Messiah's enemies; and again, to the true sense of that august title which He took to Himself, "THE SON OF GOD," which ye rightly interpreted at the very first (see on ch. v. 18), as a claim to that *oneness of nature* with Him, and *dearness* to Him, which a son has to his father.

Jesus is Mocked, thirdly, by the Soldiers. We have this in the third Gospel only.

Luke xxiii. 36, 37:—"And the soldiers also mocked Him, coming to Him, and offering Him vinegar, and saying, If thou be the King of the Jews, save thyself." They insultingly offer to share with Him their own vinegar, or sour wine,

the usual drink of Roman soldiers, it being about the time of their mid-day meal. In the taunt of the soldiers we have one of those casual touches which so strikingly verify these historical records. While the ecclesiastics deride Him for calling Himself "the *Christ,* the *King of Israel,* the *Chosen,* the *Son of God,*" the soldiers, to whom all such phraseology was mere Jewish jargon, make sport of Him as a pretender to *royalty*—"KING OF the Jews"—an office and dignity which they would think it belonged to them to comprehend.

Jesus Mocked, fourthly, by One of His Fellow-Sufferers—Addresses to the Other, in answer to his penitent, believing Appeal, the Second of His Seven Sayings on the Cross. This is the only one of the four cases of mockery which is recorded by all the first three Evangelists; but the inestimable details are given only by Luke.

Matt. xxvii. 44; Mark xv. 32; Luke xxiii. 39-43:— "The thieves also, which were crucified with Him, cast the same in His teeth." So also Mark. But from Luke—the precision and fulness of whose narrative must rule the sense of the few brief words of the other two—we learn that the taunt came only from *one* of the thieves, whom the *other* in a wonderful style rebuked: "And one of the malefactors which were hanged railed on Him, saying, If thou be Christ, save thyself and us. But the other answering rebuked him, saying, Dost not thou fear God, seeing thou art in the same condemnation? And we indeed justly; for we receive the due reward of our deeds: but this man hath done nothing amiss. And he said unto Jesus, Lord, remember me when thou comest into thy kingdom. And Jesus said unto him"—this is His

Second Saying: "VERILY I SAY UNTO THEE, TO-DAY SHALT THOU BE WITH ME IN PARADISE." For the exposition of this grand episode, see on Luke xxiii. 39-43, pages 337-339.

But we are now at length brought back to our Fourth Gospel.

Jesus, in the Third of His Seven Sayings on the Cross, Commits His Mother to the Beloved Disciple, Who takes Her to His own Home (25-27). **25. Now there stood** [Εἰστήκεισαν]—or 'were standing' **by the cross of Jesus his mother, and his mother's sister, Mary the wife of Cleophas.** This should be read, as in the margin, *Clopas;* the same person, as would seem, with "Alpheus": see on Matt. x. 3. The "Cleopas" of Luke xxiv. 18 was a different person. **and Mary Magdalene.** These dear women clustered around the cross; and where else should one expect them? The male disciples might be consulting for their own safety (though John was not); but those precious women would have died sooner than be absent from this scene. **26. When Jesus therefore saw his mother, and the disciple standing by whom he loved, he saith unto his mother,**

Third Saying: { "WOMAN, BEHOLD THY SON! **27. Then saith he to the disciple,** "BEHOLD THY MOTHER!"

What forgetfulness of self, and what filial love, at such a moment! And what a parting word to both "mother and son"! **And from that hour that ('the') disciple took her to his own [home]**— that is, home with him; for his father, Zebedee,

28   After this, Jesus knowing that ^sall things were now accomplished, ^tthat
29   the Scripture might be fulfilled, saith, I thirst.   Now there was set a
     vessel full of vinegar: and they filled a sponge with vinegar, and put *it*

A. D. 33.
^s Gen. 3. 15.
^t Ps. 69. 21.

---

and his mother, Salome, were both alive, and the latter was here present (Mark xv. 40).

A Supernatural Darkness Overspreads the Sky, about the extremity of which Jesus utters an Awful Cry, being the Fourth of His Seven Sayings on the Cross.

For this deeply significant stage of our Lord's Sufferings on the cross, we have the testimony of the first two Evangelists, and partially of the third. The beloved disciple accordingly passes it by, as sufficiently recorded. Matt. xxvii. 45-49; Mark xv. 33-38; Luke xxiii. 44, 45:—"Now from the sixth hour"—the hour of noon—"there was darkness over all the land unto the ninth hour"—*the hour of the evening sacrifice.* No ordinary eclipse of the sun could have occurred at this time, it being then *full moon*, and this obscuration lasted about *twelve times* the length of any ordinary eclipse. (Compare Exod. x. 21-23.) Beyond doubt, the divine intention of the portent was to invest this darkest of all tragedies with a gloom expressive of its real character. "And about the ninth hour Jesus cried with a loud voice" (Ps. xxii. 1),

Fourth Saying: { "ELI, ELI, LAMA SABACHTHANI? that is to say, MY GOD, MY GOD, WHY HAST THOU FORSAKEN ME?"

There is something deeply instructive in this cry being uttered, not in the tongue which our Lord, we believe, usually employed—the current Greek—but in that of the psalm from which it is quoted; and yet, not as it stands in the *Hebrew* original of that psalm [עֲזַבְתָּנִי], but in the native *Chaldee* [שְׁבַקְתַּנִי], or *Syriac* form ['Ελωΐ, the Syriac form of אֵל]—as if at that awful moment not only would no other words express His mind but those which had been prophetically prepared for that hour, but, as in the Agony in the Garden (see page 332, second column), that the mother-tongue came to Him spontaneously, as most natively and freely giving forth the deep cry. As the darkness commenced at the hour of noon, the second of the Jewish hours of prayer, and continued till the hour of the evening sacrifice, it probably *increased in depth*, and *reached its deepest gloom at the moment of this mysterious cry*—when the flame of the one great "Evening Sacrifice" was burning fiercest. The words, as we have said, were made ready to His hand, being the opening words of that psalm which is most full of the last "Sufferings of Christ and the glories which followed them" [τὰς μετὰ ταῦτα δόξας, 1 Pet. i. 11]. "FATHER," was the cry in the first prayer which He uttered on the cross; for matters had not then come to their worst; "FATHER" was the cry of His last prayer; for matters had then passed their worst. But at this crisis of His sufferings, "Father" does not issue from His lips, for the light of a Father's countenance was then mysteriously eclipsed. He falls back, however, on a title expressive of His *official* relation, which, though more distant in itself, yet when grasped in pure and naked faith, was mighty in its claims, and rich in psalmodic associations—"MY GOD." And what deep earnestness is conveyed by the redoubling of this title! But as for the cry itself, it will never be fully comprehended. An absolute desertion is not indeed to be thought of; but a total eclipse of the *felt* sense of God's presence it certainly expresses. It expresses *surprise*, as

under the experience of something not only *never before known* but *inexplicable* on the footing which had till then subsisted between Him and God. *It is a question which the lost cannot utter.* They are forsaken, *but they know why.* Jesus is forsaken, but *does not know, and asks to know why.* It is thus *the cry of conscious innocence*, but of innocence unavailing to draw down at that moment the least token of approval from the unseen Judge —innocence whose only recognition at that moment lay in the thick surrounding gloom which but reflected the horror of great darkness that invested His own spirit. *There was indeed a cause for it*, and He knew it too—the "why" must not be pressed so far as to exclude this. *He must taste this bitterest of the wages of sin "Who did no sin."* But that is not the point now. In Him there was no cause at all (ch. xiv. 30), and He takes refuge in the glorious fact. When no ray from above shines in upon Him, He strikes a light out of His own breast. If God will not own Him, He shall own Himself. On the rock of His unsullied allegiance to Heaven He will stand, till the light of Heaven return to His spirit. And it is near to come. Whilst He is yet speaking the fierceness of the flame is beginning to abate. One incident and insult more, and the experience of one other predicted element of suffering, and the victory is His. "Some of them that stood there, when they heard that"—the cry just mentioned—"said, This man calleth for Elias" (Matt. xxvii. 47). That in this they simply misunderstood the meaning of His cry—"Eli, Eli"—there can be no reasonable doubt; especially if, as is probable, this remark was made by Hellenistic spectators, or the Greek-speaking Jews from the provinces who had come up to worship at the feast.

Jesus Thirsting, Utters the Fifth of His Seven Sayings on the Cross, and Vinegar being Brought to Him, the Scripture is therein Fulfilled (28, 29).
28. After this, Jesus knowing that all things were now accomplished, that the Scripture might be fulfilled (Ps. lxix. 21), **saith—**
Fifth Saying: "I THIRST."
The meaning is, that perceiving that all prophetic Scripture regarding Him was accomplished, up to the very article of Death, save that one in Ps. lxix. 21, and that the moment had now arrived for the fulfilment of that final one, in consequence of the burning thirst which the fevered state of His frame occasioned (see Ps. xxii. 15)—He uttered this cry in order that of their own accord they might fulfil *their* prophetic destiny in fulfilling *His*. **29. Now there was set a vessel full of vinegar: and they filled a sponge with vinegar, and put it upon hyssop, and put it to his mouth.** The offer of the soldiers' vinegar, on His arriving at Golgotha, might seem to have sufficiently fulfilled the Scripture prediction on this subject already. But our Lord only regards this as properly done when done by "His own," who "received Him not." But in this case it is probable, as in the former, that "when He had tasted thereof, He would not drink it." Though a stalk of hyssop does not exceed eighteen inches in length, it would suffice, as the feet of crucified persons were not raised higher. At this time, some said, "Let alone" ['Αφετε]—that is, probably, 'Stand off,' 'Stop that officious service'—"let us see whether Elias will come to take him down." This was the last cruelty which He was to suffer, and it was one of the most unfeeling.

30 upon hyssop, and put *it* to his mouth. When Jesus therefore had received the vinegar, he said, "It is finished: and he bowed his head, and "gave up the ghost.

A. D. 33.
" Isa 42. 21.
" 1 Thes.5.16.

Jesus Utters the Sixth of His Seven Sayings on the Cross. It is remarkable that while we have this glorious Saying only in the fourth Gospel, we have the *manner* in which it was uttered in the first three, and not in the fourth.

30. When Jesus therefore had received the vinegar, he said—or, as in all the first three Gospels, "He cried with a loud voice"—

Sixth Saying: "It is finished" [Τετέλεσται].

In this one astonishing word believers will find the foundation of all their safety and bliss throughout eternal ages. The "loud voice" does not imply, as some able interpreters contend, that our Lord's strength was so far from being exhausted that He needed not to die then, and surrendered up His life sooner than nature required, merely because it was the appointed time. It was indeed the appointed time, but time that He should be crucified *through weakness* (2 Cor. xiii. 4), and nature was now reaching its utmost exhaustion. But just as even His own dying saints, particularly the martyrs of Jesus, have sometimes had such gleams of coming glory immediately before breathing their last as to impart to them a strength to utter their feelings which has amazed the by-standers, so this *mighty voice* of the expiring Redeemer was nothing else but the exultant spirit of the Dying Victor, perceiving the fruit of His travail just about to be embraced, and nerving the organs of utterance to an ecstatic expression of its sublime feelings in the one word, "*It is finished.*" What is finished? The Law is fulfilled as never before, and never since, in His obedience unto death, even the death of the cross. Messianic prophecy is accomplished; Redemption is completed: "He hath finished the transgression, and made an end of sin, and made reconciliation for iniquity, and brought in everlasting righteousness, and sealed up the vision and prophecy, and anointed a holy of holies." The scaffolding of the ancient economy is taken down: He has inaugurated the kingdom of God, and given birth to a new world.

Jesus, having Uttered the Last of His Seven Sayings on the Cross, Expires.

This Saying is given only by the third Evangelist.

Luke xxiii. 46:—"And when Jesus had cried with a loud voice, He said (Ps. xxxi. 5)—

Seventh Saying: "Father, into thy hands I commend my Spirit."

Yes, the darkness is past, and the true light now shineth. His soul has emerged from its mysterious horrors; "My God" is heard no more, but in unclouded light He yields sublime into His *Father's* hands the infinitely precious spirit—using here also, with His last breath, the words of those Psalms which were ever on His lips. **30. And**—"having said this" (Luke xxiii. 46), **he bowed his head, and gave up the ghost.**

Remarks.—1. When we read that Jesus "bearing His cross, went forth," and thus "suffered without the gate," can we wonder at the apostle's call to his fellow-believers of the house of Israel, "Let us go forth therefore unto Him without the camp"? (Heb. xiii. 13). For what was city, temple, or camp, after the Lord of it had been judicially rejected, contemptuously led forth from it, and without the gate, as one accursed, put to the death of the cross? Behold, their house was left unto them desolate: the Glory was departed: and now, as never before, might be heard by those who still came to tread those

once hallowed courts a Voice saying unto them, "Bring no more vain oblations; incense is an abomination unto me; the new moons and sabbaths, the calling of assemblies, I cannot away with; it is iniquity, even the solemn meeting. Your new moons and your appointed feasts my soul hateth: they are a trouble unto me; I am weary to bear them. And when ye spread forth your hands, I will hide mine eyes from you; yea, when ye make many prayers, I will not hear: your hands are full of blood" (Isa. i. 13-15). Judaism had virtually ceased to exist, and all the grace and glory which it contained—all that "Salvation" which "was of the Jews"—had taken up its abode with the handful of disciples, from whom, as soon as the Holy Ghost should descend upon them at Pentecost, was to emerge the one living Church and Kingdom of God upon earth. Severe, doubtless, would be the wrench to many a Jew which severed him for ever from ecclesiastical connection with that fondly loved, time-honoured temple, and all its beautiful solemnities. One consideration only could reconcile him to it, but that one to the believer would be irresistible: his Lord was not there, and, what was worse, all that he saw there was associated with the dishonour and the death of his Lord; while in the assemblies of the disciples with whom he had now cast in his lot—all mean to the outward eye, and small in numbers, though they might be—Jesus Himself, now in glory, made His presence felt, Whom having not seen, all loved, in Whom, though now they saw Him not, yet believing, they rejoiced with joy unspeakable and full of glory, receiving the end of their faith, even the salvation of their souls. And has not the Lord been judicially cast out and "crucified" afresh "in the street of" another "great city" (Rev. xi. 8), regarding which the word is, "Come out of her, my people"? (Rev. xviii. 4). Trying to flesh and blood once was that wrench too, and others similar which the faithful witnesses for the truth have been called to suffer. But as where Jesus is not, the most gorgeous temples are but splendid desolation to the soul that lives and is ready to die for Him, so the rudest barns are beautiful temples when irradiated with the glory of His presence and perfumed with the incense of His grace. 2. The case of Simon the Cyrenian, won to Jesus by being "compelled" to bear His cross, has had its bright parallels in not a few who have been made to take part in the last sufferings of His martyrs. In one of the Homilies. for example, of the Greek Father, Basil the Great (A.D. 316-379), preached at the anniversary of the erection of the 'church of the Thirty Martyrs' at Cesarea, he tells us that when thirty of the noblest youths of the Roman army were to suffer for confessing Christ, by being condemned to freeze to death standing naked in a cold lake in the depth of winter, and one of them, after mortification had begun, had been tempted by the offer of hot baths to as many of them as would deny their Lord, and had plunged into a bath—only thereby to hasten his death—while the rest were mourning the breach in their number, one of the lictors, won by what he saw and heard from those servants of Jesus, gave away his badge of office, and exclaimed, "I am a Christian," stripped himself naked, and taking his place beside the rest, said, 'Now are your ranks filled up,' and nobly died with them for the name of Jesus. Analogous cases of various kinds will readily occur

31   The Jews therefore, *ʷbecause it was the preparation, *ˣthat the bodies should not remain upon the cross on the sabbath day, (for that sabbath day was *ʸan high day,) besought Pilate that their legs might be broken, 32 and *that* they might be taken away.   Then came the soldiers, and brake the legs of the first, and of the other which was crucified with him. 33 But when they came to Jesus, and saw that he was dead already, they

A. D. 33.
ʷ Mark 15.42;
ˣ Deut 21.23.
ʸ Ex. 12. 16.
Lev. 23. 5-8.
Num.28.17,
18.

to those to whom such victories of the cross are a study; nor is such a bearing in the followers of Christ as Simon the Cyrenian beheld in Him who went as a Lamb to the slaughter perhaps ever in vain. 3. Even natural sympathy, in those who are strangers to what is peculiarly Christian, is beautiful, and to the Christian sufferer grateful. The blessed One was touched by the tears of the daughters of Jerusalem. To the Redeemer's heart they were a grateful contrast to the savage cruelty of the rulers and the rudeness of the unfeeling crowd, and they drew from Him a tender though sad reply. Christians do wrong when they think so exclusively of the absence of grace in any as to overlook or depreciate in them those natural excellences which attracted the love even of the Lord Jesus. (See on Luke xviii. 21, and Remark 3 at the close of that Section.) 4. The *four quarters* whence proceeded the mockeries of Jesus, as He hung on the accursed tree, seem designed to represent the contempt of all the classes into which men can be divided with reference to religion. As the "passers-by" cover the whole region of religious indifference, so "the chief priests, the scribes, and the elders" fitly represent religious hypocrisy: and while in "the soldiers" we recognize the mere underlings of secular authority, whose religion lies all in slavish obedience to their superiors, the "malefactors" represent the notoriously wicked. From all these quarters, in quick succession, the Lord of glory experienced bitter revilings. But "when reviled, He reviled not again." When He did break silence, it was in blessing, and from His Lips salvation flowed. 5. There is something very striking, surely, in the fact that our Lord uttered on the cross precisely *Seven* Sayings—that number which all Scripture teaches us to regard as *sacred* and *complete;* and when we observe that of the Four Evangelists no one reports them all, while each gives some of them, we cannot but look upon them—with *Bengel* —as four voices which together make up one grand Symphony. 'The suffering Lord,' says *Stier* very beautifully, 'hanging upon the cross, broke the silence and opened His lips seven times: these words are to us as the bright lights of heaven shining at intervals through the darkness, or as the loud thunder-tones from above and from within, which *interpret* the cross, and *in which it receives*, so to speak, *another collective superscription.'* Observe now the varied notes of this grand seven-toned Symphony. The *first*, as a prayer for the forgiveness of those who were nailing Him to the tree, proclaims at the very outset the object of His whole mission, the essential character of His work: The *second* opens the kingdom of heaven even to the vilest true penitent that believes in Him: The *third* assures His desolate ones of all needful care and provision here below: The *fourth*, revealing to us the depths of penal darkness to which the Redeemer descended, assures us both that He was made a curse for us and that in our seasons of deepest spiritual darkness we have One who is experimentally acquainted with it, and is able to disperse it: The *fifth*, completing the circle of all previous fulfilments of Scripture in the intense sensation of thirst, and showing thereby that the fevered frame was almost at the extremity of its

475

power of endurance, assures His acutely suffering people of the precious sympathy of Him

         'Who not in vain
     Experienced every human pain:'

The *sixth* is the briefest, brightest, richest proclamation of the glad tidings of great joy for all time, stretching into eternity itself: The *seventh* and last is an exalted Directory for dying believers of every age and in all circumstances—not only providing them with the language of serene assurance in the rendering up of the departing spirit into their Father's hands, but impregnating it with the strength and perfuming it with the odour of "the Firstborn among many brethren." Thus are we "complete in Him."

   31-42.—Circumstances Following the Death of the Lord Jesus—The Burial. (=Matt. xxvii. 57-61; Mark xv. 42-47; Luke xxiii. 50-56.) *The Soldiers, Ordered to Put an End to the Life of the Sufferers, Break the Legs of the Malefactors, but, Perceiving that Jesus was Dead already, they Break Not His Legs, and thus unconsciously Fulfil the Scripture* (31-33). These remarkable circumstances are recorded by our Evangelist alone. **31. The Jews therefore**—meaning, as usual in this Gospel, the *rulers* of the Jews, **because it was the preparation**—that is, "the day before the Sabbath" (Mark xv. 42), or our *Friday*, **that the bodies should not remain upon the cross on the sabbath day**—which, beginning at six in the evening, must have been close at hand. Indeed, Luke (xxiii. 54) says, "the Sabbath *drew on"* [ἐπέφωσκεν] — literally, 'was dawning,' like the morning. There was a remarkable command of the Mosaic law, which required that the body of one hanged on a tree for any sin worthy of death should not remain all night upon the tree, but should in any wise be buried that day; "(for he that is hanged is accursed of God;) that thy land be not defiled" (Deut. xxi. 22, 23). These punctilious rulers were afraid of the land being defiled by the body of the Holy One of God being allowed to remain over night upon the cross; but they had no sense of that deeper defilement which they had already contracted by having His blood upon themselves. **(for that sabbath day was an high day)** [μεγάλη]—or 'a great day;' as being the first Sabbath of the Feast of Unleavened Bread, the most sacred season of the whole Jewish ecclesiastical year. This made those hypocrites the more afraid lest the Sabbath hour should arrive ere the bodies were removed. **besought Pilate that their legs might be broken**—to hasten their death. It was usually done with clubs. **and that they might be taken away**—that is, taken down from the cross and removed. **32. Then came the soldiers, and brake the legs of the first, and of the other which was crucified with him.** Crucifixion being a very lingering death, the life of the malefactors was still in them, and was thus barbarously extinguished. **33. But when they came to Jesus, and saw that he was dead already**—for there were in His case elements of suffering unknown to the malefactors, which would naturally hasten His death, not to speak of His exhaustion from previous care and suffering, all the more telling on the frame now, from its having been en-

34 brake not his legs: but one of the soldiers with a spear pierced his side, and forthwith ^zcame thereout blood and water.

35 And ^ahe that saw *it* bare record, and his record is true: and he knoweth

36 that he saith true, that ye might believe. For these things were done, ^bthat the scripture should be fulfilled, A bone of him shall not be broken.

37 And again another scripture saith, They ^cshall look on him whom they pierced.

38 And ^dafter this, Joseph of Arimathea, being a disciple of Jesus, but

A. D. 33.
^z 1 John 5. 6, 8.
^a ch. 17. 21, 23.
^b Ex. 12. 46. Num. 9. 12.
^c Ps.22. 16,17. Zec. 12. 10.
^d Matt.27. 57. Mark 15.42.

dured in silence. **they brake not his legs**—a fact of vast importance, as showing that the *reality* of His death was visible to those whose business it was to see to it. The *other* divine purpose served by it will appear presently.

To Make Sure that Jesus was Dead, One of the Soldiers with a Spear Pierces His Side—What Flowed from this Wound, and How Another Scripture was thereby Fulfilled (34-37). **34. But one of the soldiers**—to make assurance of the fact doubly sure, **with a spear pierced his side**—making a wound deep and wide, as indeed is plain from ch. xx. 27-29. Had life still remained it must have fled now. **and forthwith came thereout blood and water.** 'It is now well known,' to use the words of *Webster and Wilkinson*, 'that the effect of long-continued and intense agony is frequently to produce a secretion of a colourless lymph within the pericardium (the membrane enveloping the heart), amounting in many cases to a very considerable quantity.'

35. And he that saw it bare—'hath borne' **record, and his record is true: and he knoweth that he saith true, that ye might believe**—'that ye also may believe,' is clearly the true reading [καὶ ὑμεῖς—so *Lachmann, Tischendorf*, and *Tregelles*]; that is, that all who read this Gospel may, along with the writer of it, believe. The use of the third person in this statement, instead of the first, gives solemnity to it, as *Alford* remarks. This solemn way of referring to his own testimony in this matter was at least intended to call attention both to the fulfilment of Scripture in these particulars, and to the undeniable evidence he was thus furnishing of the *reality* of Christ's death, and consequently of His resurrection; perhaps also to meet the growing tendency, in the Asiatic churches, to deny the reality of our Lord's body, or that "Jesus Christ is come in the flesh" (1 John iv. 1-3). But was this all? Some of the ablest critics think so. But if we give due weight to the words of this same beloved disciple in his First Epistle —"This is He that came by water and blood, even Jesus Christ; not by water only, but by water and blood" (1 John v. 6)—it is difficult to avoid thinking that he must have seen in the "blood and water" which flowed from that wounded side a symbolical exhibition of the "blood" of *atonement* and the "water" of *sanctification*, according to ceremonial language, which undoubtedly flow from the pierced Redeemer. Certainly the instincts of the Church have from age to age stamped this sense upon the fact recorded, and when the poet cries—

> 'Rock of Ages! cleft for me,
> Let me hide myself in Thee:
> *Let the water and the blood*
> *From Thy wounded side which flow'd*
> *Be of sin the double cure;*
> *Cleanse me from its guilt and power'*—TOPLADY:

he does but nobly interpret our Evangelist's words to the heart of the living and dying Christian. **36. For these things were done, that the scripture should be fulfilled, A bone of him shall not**

be broken. The Scripture referred to can be no other than the stringent and remarkable ordinance regarding the Paschal Lamb, that *a bone of it should not be broken* (Exod. xii. 46; Num. ix. 12). And if so, we have this apostle, as well as Paul (1 Cor. v. 7), holding forth the Paschal Lamb as a typical foreshadowing of "the Lamb of God." There is indeed in the 34th Psalm a verse which some—regarding it as Messianic—have thought to be the passage referred to by the Evangelist: "He keepeth all his bones; not one of them is broken" (*v.* 20). But that is rather a definite way of expressing the minute care with which God watches over His people in the body; and the right view of its bearing on Christ is to mark how congruous it was that that should be *literally* realized in Him which was designed but *generally* to express the safety of all His saints. But we shall miss one of the most august designs of God in the sufferings of His Son if we rest here. Up to the moment of His death, every imaginable indignity had been permitted to be done to the sacred body of the Lord Jesus—as if, so long as the Sacrifice was incomplete, the Lord, who had laid upon Him the iniquity of us all, would not interpose. But no sooner has He "finished" the work given Him to do than an Unseen Hand is found to have provided against the clubs of the rude soldiers coming in contact with that Temple of the Godhead. Very different from such violence was that *spear-thrust*, for which not only doubting Thomas would thank the soldier, but intelligent believers in every age, to whom the certainty of their Lord's death and resurrection is the life of their whole Christianity. **37. And again another scripture saith** (Zec. xii. 10), **They shall look on him whom they pierced.** This quotation is not taken, as usual, from the Septuagint—the current Greek version—which here is all wrong, but direct from the Hebrew. And there is a remarkable nicety in the choice of the words employed both by the prophet and the evangelist for "piercing." The word in Zechariah [דָּקָרוּ] means to *thrust through* with spear, javelin, sword, or any such weapon. In that sense it is used in all the ten places, besides this, where it is found. How suitable this was to express the action of the Roman soldier is manifest; and our Evangelist uses the exactly corresponding word [ἐξεκέντησαν], while the word used by the LXX. [κατωρχήσαντο] signifies simply to 'insult' or 'triumph over.' There is a quite different word, which also signifies to 'pierce,' used in Ps. xxii. 16, "They *pierced* my hands and my feet" [כָּארִי, in קְרִי]. This word signifies to *bore* as with an awl or hammer—just as was done in fastening our Lord to the cross. How exceedingly striking are these small niceties and precisions!

The Burial (38-42). **38. And after this, Joseph of Arimathea**—a place which cannot now be identified. Matthew (xxvii. 57) says he was "a rich man"—thus fulfilling the prediction that Messiah should be "with the rich in His death" (Isa. liii. 9). Mark (xv. 43) says he was "an honourable counsellor" [εὐσχήμων βουλευτής]—or a member of the Sanhedrim and of superior position—"which secretly *e* for fear of the Jews, besought Pilate that he might take away the body of Jesus: and Pilate gave *him* leave. He came therefore, and 39 took the body of Jesus. And there came also *f* Nicodemus, (which at the first came to Jesus by night,) and brought *g* a mixture of myrrh and 40 aloes, about an hundred pound *weight.* Then took they the body of Jesus, and wound *h* it in linen clothes with the spices, as the manner of 41 the Jews is to bury. Now in the place where he was crucified there was a garden; and in the garden a *i* new sepulchre, wherein was never man

A. D. 33.

e Pro. 29. 25.
ch. 9. 22.
ch. 12. 42.
f ch. 3. 1, 2.
ch. 7. 50.
g 2 Chr. 16.14.
Luke 23.56.
h Acts 5. 6.
i Luke 23.53.

---

also waited for the kingdom of God," or was a devout expectant of Messiah's kingdom. Luke (xxiii. 50, 51) says further of him, " he was a good man and a just; the same had not consented to the counsel and deed of them"—or had not been a consenting party to the condemnation and death of Jesus. Perhaps, however, this does not mean that he openly dissented and protested against the decision and subsequent proceedings of the Council of which he was a member; but simply that he had avoided taking any active part in them, by absenting himself from their meetings. Finally, to complete our knowledge of this important person, for ever dear to the Christian Church for what is about to be related, our Evangelist adds, **being a disciple of Jesus, but secretly for fear of the Jews.** No wonder that he and Nicodemus are classed together. But if before, they were noted for *timid* discipleship, they are now signally one in *courageous* discipleship. Our Evangelist merely says, Joseph **besought Pilate that he might** [be permitted to] **take away the body of Jesus: and Pilate gave him leave.** But Mark, in the following passage, notices the *courage* which this required, and gives some other particulars of the deepest interest.

Mark xv. 43-45:—"Joseph . . . went in boldly" [τολμήσας εἰσῆλθεν]—or 'had the courage to go in,' "and craved the body of Jesus." That act would without doubt identify him *for the first time* with the disciples of Christ. Marvellous it certainly is, that one who while Jesus was yet alive merely refrained from condemning Him—not having the courage to espouse His cause by one positive act— should, now that He was dead, and His cause apparently dead with Him, summon up courage to go in personally to the Roman Governor and ask permission to take down and inter the body. But if this be the first instance, it is not the last, that a seemingly dead Christ has wakened a sympathy which a living one had failed to evoke. The heroism of faith is usually kindled by desperate circumstances, and is not seldom displayed by those who before were the most timid, and scarce known as disciples at all. "And Pilate marvelled if he were already dead" [εἰ ἤδη τέθνηκεν]—or rather, 'wondered that he was dead already'—"and calling the centurion, he asked him whether he had been any while (or 'long') dead." Pilate could hardly credit what Joseph had told him, that He had been dead 'some time,' and before giving up the body to His friends, would learn how the fact stood from the centurion, whose business it was to oversee the execution. "And when he knew it of the centurion," that it was as Joseph had said, "he gave" [ἐδωρήσατο]—or rather, 'made a gift of' "the body to Joseph;" struck, possibly, with the rank of the petitioner and the dignified boldness of the petition, in contrast with the spirit of the other party and the low rank to which he had been led to believe all the followers of Christ belonged. Nor would he be unwilling to show that he was not going to carry this scandalous proceeding any further. But whatever were Pilate's motives, two most blessed objects were thus secured: First, The

reality of our Lord's death was attested by the party of all others most competent to decide on it, and certainly free from all bias—the officer in attendance—in full reliance on whose testimony Pilate surrendered the body. Second, The dead Redeemer, thus delivered out of the hands of His enemies, and committed by the supreme political authority to the care of His friends, was thereby protected from all further indignities; a thing most befitting indeed, now that His work was done, but not to have been expected if His enemies had been at liberty to do with Him as they pleased. How wonderful are even the minutest features of this matchless History! **He came therefore, and took the body of Jesus. 39. And there came also Nicodemus, (which at the first came to Jesus by night).** It is manifestly the Evangelist's design to direct his readers' attention to the *timidity* of both these friends of Jesus in their attachment to Him, when he says that the one was for fear of the Jews only a secret disciple, and reminds us that the visit of the other to Jesus at the outset of His ministry was made by night. **and brought a mixture of myrrh and aloes, about an hundred pound weight**—an immense quantity, betokening the greatness of their love, but part of it probably intended, as *Meyer* says, as a layer for the spot on which the body was to lie. (See 2 Chr. xvi. 14.) **40. Then took they the body of Jesus, and wound it in linen clothes with the spices, as the manner of the Jews is to bury**—the mixed and pulverized myrrh and aloes shaken into the folds, and the entire body, thus swathed, wrapt in an outer covering of "clean linen cloth" (Matt. xxvii. 59). Had the Lord's own friends had the least reason to think that the spark of life was still in Him, would *they* have done this? But even if one could conceive them mistaken, could any one have lain thus enveloped for the period during which He was in the grave, and life still remained? Impossible. When, therefore, He walked forth from the tomb, we can say with the most absolute certainty, "Now is Christ *risen from the dead,* and become the first-fruits of them that slept"! (1 Cor. xv. 20). No wonder that the learned and the barbarians alike were prepared to die for the name of the Lord Jesus; for such evidence was to the unprejudiced resistless. No mention is made of *anointing* in this operation. No doubt it was a hurried proceeding, for fear of interruption, and because it was close on the Sabbath. The women seem to have set the doing of this more perfectly as their proper task "as soon as the Sabbath should be past" (Mark xvi. 1). But as the Lord graciously held it as undesignedly anticipated by Mary at Bethany (Mark xiv. 8), so this was probably all the anointing, in the strict sense of it, which He received. **41. Now in the place where he was crucified there was a garden; and in the garden a new sepulchre, wherein was never man yet laid.** The choice of this tomb was, on *their* part, dictated by the double circumstance that it was so near at hand, and its belonging to a friend of the Lord; and as there was need of haste, even they would

42 yet laid. There ʲlaid they Jesus therefore, because of the Jews' preparation *day;* for the sepulchre was nigh at hand.

20 THE ᵃfirst *day* of the week cometh Mary Magdalene early, when it was yet dark, unto the sepulchre, and seeth the stone taken away from
2 the sepulchre. Then she runneth, and cometh to Simon Peter, and to the ᵇother disciple whom Jesus loved, and saith unto them, They have taken away the Lord out of the sepulchre, and we know not where
3 they have laid him. Peter ᶜtherefore went forth, and that other disciple,
4 and came to the sepulchre. So they ran both together: and the other
5 disciple did outrun Peter, and came first to the sepulchre. And he stooping down, *and looking in,* saw ᵈthe linen clothes lying; yet went he
6 not in. Then cometh Simon Peter following him, and went into the
7 sepulchre, and seeth the linen clothes lie, and ᵉthe napkin, that was about his head, not lying with the linen clothes, but wrapped together in
8 a place by itself. Then went in also that other disciple which came first
9 to the sepulchre, and he saw, and believed. For as yet they knew not
10 the ᶠscripture, that he must rise again from the dead. Then the disciples went away again unto their own home.

A. D. 33.
ʲ Isa. 53. 9.

CHAP. 20.
ᵃ Matt. 28. 1
Mark 16. 1
Luke 24. 1.
ᵇ ch. 13. 23.
ch. 19. 26.
ch. 21. 7, 20, 24.
ᶜ Luke 24.12.
ᵈ ch. 19. 40.
ᵉ ch. 11. 44.
ᶠ Ps. 16. 10.
Isa. 26. 19.
Isa. 53. 10-12.
Hos. 13. 14.
Matt. 16. 21.
Acts 2. 25-32.
Acts 13. 34.
1 Cor. 15. 4.

be struck with the providence which thus supplied it. **42. There laid they Jesus therefore, because of the Jews' preparation day; for the sepulchre was nigh at hand.** There was however one recommendation of it which probably would not strike them; but God had it in view. This was not its being "hewn out of a rock" (Mark xv. 46), accessible only at the entrance, though this doubtless would impress even themselves with its security and suitableness; but its being "a *new* sepulchre" (*v.* 41), "*wherein never man before was laid*" (Luke xxiii. 53); and in Matt. xxvii. 60 it is said that Joseph laid Him "in *his own new tomb,* which he had hewn out in the rock"—doubtless for his own use, and without any other design in it—but the Lord needed it. Thus, as he rode into Jerusalem on an ass "*whereon never man before had sat,*" so now He shall lie in a tomb *wherein never man before had lain,* that from these specimens it might be seen that *in all things* He was "SEPARATE FROM SINNERS."

For remarks on the Burial of Christ, in connection with His Death and Resurrection, see on Matt. xxvii. 51-56, Remarks 4-8 at the close of that Section; and those on ch. xxviii. 1-15, at the close of that Section.

CHAP. XX. 1-31.—ON THE FIRST DAY OF THE WEEK MARY MAGDALENE VISITS THE SEPULCHRE AND RETURNS TO IT WITH PETER AND JOHN—HER RISEN LORD APPEARS TO HER—IN THE EVENING HE APPEARS TO THE ASSEMBLED DISCIPLES, AND AGAIN AFTER EIGHT DAYS—FIRST CLOSE OF THIS GOSPEL.

Mary first Visits the Sepulchre Alone (1). **1.** ['Now'] **The first day of the week cometh Mary Magdalene** (see on Luke viii. 2) **early, when it was yet dark** (see on Matt. xxviii. 1, and on Mark xvi. 2), **unto the sepulchre, and seeth the stone taken away from the sepulchre** (see on Mark xvi. 3, 4).

Mary, Returning to Peter and John, Reports to them that the Sepulchre had been Emptied—They Go to the Grave—The Result of that Visit (2-10). **2. Then she runneth**—her whole soul strung to its utmost tension with trepidation and anxiety, and **cometh to Simon Peter, and to the other disciple whom Jesus loved**—those two who were so soon to be associated in proclaiming the Saviour's resurrection, and **saith unto them, They have taken away the Lord out of the sepulchre, and we know not where they have laid him.** Dear disciple! Thy

dead Lord is to thee "The Lord" still. **3. Peter therefore went forth, and that**—or 'the' **other disciple, and came to the sepulchre**—to see with their own eyes. **4. So they ran both together: and the other disciple**—being the younger of the two, **did outrun Peter**—but love, too, haply supplying swifter wings. How lively is the mention of this little particular, and at such a distance of time! Yet how could the very least particular of such a visit be ever forgotten? **5. And he stooping down, [and looking in].** The supplement here should not be printed in Italics, as the one Greek word [παρακύψας] denotes both the *stooping* and the *looking,* as in *v.* 11, and in 1 Pet. i. 12 ('desire,' or 'stoop down, to look' into): **saw**—rather, 'seeth' [βλέπει] **the linen clothes lying; yet went he not in**—held back probably by a reverential fear. **6. Then cometh Simon Peter following him, and**—being of a bold, resolute character, he at once went into **the sepulchre**—and was rewarded with bright evidence of what had happened: **and seeth the linen clothes lie**—'lying.' **7. And the napkin, that was about his head, not lying with the linen clothes** —loosely, as if hastily thrown down, and indicative of a hurried and disorderly removal, **but wrapped**—or 'folded' **together in a place by itself** —showing with what grand tranquillity "the Living One" had walked forth from "the dead." (See on Luke xxiv. 5.) 'Doubtless,' says *Bengel,* 'the two attendant angels (*v.* 12) did this service for the Rising One; the one disposing of the linen clothes, the other of the napkin.' But perhaps they were the acts of the Risen One Himself, calmly laying aside, as of no further use, the garments of His mortality, and indicating the absence of all haste in issuing from the tomb. **8. Then went in also that**—or 'the' **other disciple which came first to the sepulchre.** The repetition of this, in connection with his not having gone in till after Peter, seems to show that at the moment of penning these words the advantage which each of these loving disciples had of the other was present to his mind. **and he saw and believed.** Probably he means, though he does not say, that He believed in his Lord's resurrection more immediately and certainly than Peter. **9. For as yet they knew**—*i. e.,* understood not the scripture, **that he must rise again from the dead.** In other words, they believed in His resurrection at first, not because they were prepared by Scripture to expect it; but *facts* carried resistless conviction of

	A. D. 33.

11   But *g* Mary stood without at the sepulchre weeping: and as she wept,
12   she stooped down, *and looked* into the sepulchre, and seeth two angels
    in white sitting, the one at the head, and the other at the feet, where the
13   body of Jesus had lain. And they say unto her, Woman, why weepest
    thou? She saith unto them, Because they have taken away my Lord,
14   and I know not where they have laid him. And *h* when she had thus
    said, she turned herself back, and saw Jesus standing, and *i* knew not
15   that it was Jesus. Jesus saith unto her, Woman, why weepest thou?
    whom seekest thou? She, supposing him to be the gardener, saith unto
    him, Sir, if thou have borne him hence, tell me where thou hast laid
16   him, and I will take him away. Jesus saith unto her, Mary! She
    turned herself, and saith unto him, *j* Rabboni! which is to say, Master!
17   Jesus saith unto her, Touch me not; for I am not yet ascended to my
    Father: but go to my *k* brethren, and say unto them, *l* I ascend unto my

g Mark 16. 5.
h Song 3. 3, 4.
Matt. 28. 9.
Mark 16. 9.
i Luke 24.16,
31.
ch. 21. 4.
j Song 2. 8
Matt. 23. 8-
10.
ch. 1. 38, 49.
k Ps. 22. 12.
Matt. 28. 10.
Rom. 8. 29.
Heb. 2. 11.
l ch. 16. 28.
1 Pet 1. 3.

it in the first instance to their minds, and furnished afterwards a key to the Scripture predictions of it. **10. Then the disciples went away again unto their own home.**

Mary, Remaining at the Sepulchre Weeping, is Asked the cause of her tears by Two Angels in White sitting within the Sepulchre—Scarcely has she answered them when Her Risen Lord appears to her, but is not recognized—Transporting Disclosure and Sublime Address of Jesus to her—She goes and tells the tidings to the Disciples (11-18). **11. But Mary stood without at the sepulchre weeping.** Brief had been the stay of Peter and John. But Mary, who may have taken another way to the sepulchre after they left it, lingers at the spot, weeping for her missing Lord, **and as she wept, she stooped down, and looked**—through her tears, **into the sepulchre, 12. And seeth two angels.** There need be no difficulty in reconciling this with the accounts of the angelic appearances at the sepulchre in the other Gospels; since there can be no reasonable doubt, as *Olshausen* suggests, that angels can render themselves visible or invisible as the case may require, and so they may have been seen at one time and soon after unseen—seen also by one party and not by another, one seen by one set of visitants and two by another. 'What wonder,' asks *Alford* pertinently, 'if the heavenly hosts were variously and often visible on this great day, "when the morning stars sang together, and all the sons of God shouted for joy"?' **in white**—as from the world of light (see on Matt. xxviii. 3), **sitting**—as if their proper business had already been finished, but they had been left there to await the arrival of their Lord's friends, and reassure them—**the one at the head, and the other at the feet, where the body of Jesus had lain.** Why this peculiar posture? To proclaim silently, as *Luthardt, Alford,* &c., think, how *entirely* the body of the Lord Jesus was under the guardianship of the Father and his servants. But to us this is not a quite satisfactory explanation of the *posture.* What if it was designed to call mute attention to the narrow space within which the Lord of glory had contracted Himself?—as if they should say, Come, see within what limits, marked off by the space here between us two, THE LORD lay! But she is in tears, and these suit not the scene of so glorious an Exit. They are going to point out to her the incongruity. **13. And they say unto her, Woman, why weepest thou?**—You would think the vision too much for a lone woman. But absorbed in the one Object of her affection and pursuit, she speaks out her grief without fear. **She saith unto them, Because they have taken away my Lord, and I know not where they have laid him**—the very words she had used to Peter

and John (*v.* 2) are here repeated to the bright visitants from the world of light:—*q. d.*, 'Can I choose but weep when thus bereft?' **14. And when she had thus said, she turned herself back, and saw Jesus standing, and knew not that it was Jesus. 15. Jesus saith unto her, Woman, why weepest thou? whom seekest thou?**—questions which, redoubled, so tenderly reveal the yearning desire to disclose Himself to that dear disciple. **She, supposing him to be the gardener.** Clad, therefore, in some such style He must have been. But if any ask, as too curious interpreters do, whence He got those habiliments, we answer, with *Olshausen* and *Luthardt,* where the two angels got theirs. The voice of His first words did not, it seems, reveal Him; for He would *try* her ere He would *tell* her. Accordingly, answering not the stranger's question, but coming straight to her point with him, she **saith unto him, Sir, if thou have borne him hence**—borne *whom?* She says not. She can think only of *One,* and thinks others must understand her. It reminds one of the question of the spouse, "Saw ye him whom my soul loveth?" (Song iii. 3.) **tell me where thou hast laid him, and I will take him away.** Wilt thou, dear fragile woman? But it is the language of sublime affection, that thinks itself fit for anything if once in possession of its Object. It is enough. Like Joseph, He can no longer restrain Himself (Gen. xlv. 1). **16. Jesus saith unto her, Mary!** It is not now the distant, though respectful "Woman." It is the oft-repeated name, uttered, no doubt, with all the wonted manner, and bringing a rush of unutterable and overpowering associations with it. **She turned herself, and saith unto him** [in the Hebrew tongue], **Rabboni! which is to say, Master!** [*Tischendorf* and *Tregelles* introduce into the text what we have placed in brackets—Ἑβραϊστί—on what appears to be preponderating evidence. *Lachmann* brackets it as we have done.] Mary uttered this word in the endeared mother-tongue, and the Evangelist, while perpetuating for all time the very term she used, gives his readers to whom that tongue was unknown the sense of it. But that single word of transported recognition was not enough for woman's full heart. Not knowing the change which had passed upon Him, she hastens to express by her actions what words failed to clothe: but she is checked. **17. Jesus saith unto her, Touch me not; for I am not yet ascended to my Father:**—'Old familiarities must now give place to new and more awful, yet sweeter approaches; but for these the time has not come yet.' This seems the spirit, at least, of these mysterious words, on which much difference of opinion has obtained, and not much that is satisfactory been said. **but go to my brethren.**

479

18 Father, and your Father; and *to* ^mmy God, and your God. Mary ⁿMagdalene came and told the disciples that she had seen the Lord, and *that* he had spoken these things unto her.

19   Then ^othe same day at evening, being the first *day* of the week, when the doors were shut where the disciples were assembled for fear of the Jews, came Jesus and stood in the midst, and saith unto them, Peace *be*

20 unto you. And when he had so said, he ^pshowed unto them *his* hands and his side. ^qThen were the disciples glad when they saw the Lord.

21 Then said Jesus to them again, Peace *be* unto you: ^ras *my* Father hath

22 sent me, even so send I you. And when he had said this, he breathed

23 on *them,* and saith unto them, Receive ye the Holy Ghost: whose ^ssoever sins ye remit, they are remitted unto them; *and* whose soever *sins* ye retain, they are retained.

24   But Thomas, one of the twelve, ^tcalled Didymus, was not with them

A. D. 33.

^m Eph. 1. 17.
ⁿ Matt. 28.10.
   Luke 24.10.
^o Mark 16.14.
   Luke 24.36.
   1 Cor. 15. 5.
^p 1 John 1.1.
^q ch. 16. 22.
^r Isa. 61. 1.
   Isa. 11. 2.
   Matt.28.18.
   ch 17. 18,19.
   Heb. 3. 1.
   2 Tim. 2. 2.
^s Matt.16.19.
   Matt.18.18.
^t ch. 11. 16.

(Compare Matt. xxviii. 10; Heb. ii. 11, 17.) That He had still our Humanity, and therefore "*is not ashamed to call us brethren,*" is indeed grandly evidenced by these words. But it is worthy of most reverential notice, that *we nowhere read of any one who presumed to call Him Brother.* "My brethren?" exclaims devout *Bishop Hall,* 'Blessed Jesus, who are these? Were they not Thy followers? yea, Thy forsakers? . . . How dost Thou raise these titles with Thyself! At first they were Thy *servants;* then *disciples;* a little before Thy death, they were Thy *friends;* now, after Thy resurrection, they were Thy *brethren.* But O, mercy without measure! how wilt Thou, how canst Thou, call *them* brethren whom, in Thy last parting, Thou foundest fugitives? Did they not run from Thee? Did not one of them rather leave his inmost coat behind him than not be quit of Thee? And yet Thou sayest, "Go, tell My brethren!" It is not in the power of the sins of our infirmity to unbrother us.' **and say unto them, I ascend unto my Father, and your Father; and [to] my God, and your God**—words of incomparable glory! Jesus had called God habitually His *Father,* and on one occasion, in His darkest moments, His *God.* But both are here united, expressing that full-orbed relationship which embraces in its vast sweep at once Himself and His redeemed. Yet, note well, He says not, Our Father and our God. All the deepest of the Church Fathers were wont to call attention to this, as expressly designed to distinguish between what God is to Him and what He is to us—*His* Father essentially; *ours* not so: *our* God essentially; *His* not so: *His God* only in connection with us; *our Father* only in connection with Him. **18. Mary Magdalene came and told** [ἔρχεται ἀπαγγέλλουσα]—rather, 'cometh and telleth' **the disciples that she had seen the Lord, and that he had spoken these things unto her.** *To a woman was this honour given, to be the first that saw the risen Redeemer, and that woman was not his mother.*

On the Evening of this First Day of the Week Jesus Appears to the Assembled Disciples (19-23). **19. Then the same day at evening, being the first day of the week, when the doors were shut where the disciples were [assembled], for fear of the Jews.** [The word enclosed in brackets—συνηγμένοι—is probably not genuine.] **came Jesus and stood in the midst.** That this was not an entrance in the ordinary way is manifest not only from the very peculiar manner of expression, but from the corresponding language of Luke xxiv. 36. But there is no need to fancy any *penetrating through the doors,* as several of the Fathers did and some still do: far less reason is there to fear that by holding that He appeared amongst them

without doing so we compromise the *reality* of His resurrection-body. The natural way of viewing it is to conclude that the *laws* of the resurrection-body are different from those of "flesh and blood," and that according to these the risen Saviour, without any miracle, but in the exercise of a power competent to the risen body, presented Himself amongst the assembled disciples. **and saith unto them, Peace be unto you**—not the mere *wish* that even His own exalted peace might be theirs (ch. xiv. 27); but conveying it into their hearts, even as He "opened their understandings to understand the Scriptures" (Luke xxiv. 45). **20. And when he had so said, he showed unto them his hands and his side**—not only as *ocular* and *tangible* evidence of the *reality* of His resurrection (see on Luke xxiv. 37-43), but as through "the *power* of that resurrection" dispensing all His peace to men. **21. Then said Jesus to them again**—now that they were not only calmed, but prepared to listen to Him in a new character. **Peace be unto you.** The reiteration of these precious words shows that this was what He designed to be not only the fundamental but ever-present, ever-conscious possession of His people. **as my Father**—rather, 'the Father' **hath sent me, even so send I you**—or rather, perhaps, 'even so am I sending you,' that is, just about to do it. (See on ch. xvii. 18.) **22. And when he had said this, he breathed on them**—a symbolical and expressive conveyance to them of the Spirit, which in Scripture is so often compared to *breath* (see on ch. iii. 8); **and saith unto them, Receive ye the Holy Ghost**—as an earnest and first-fruits of the more grand and copious Pentecostal effusion, without which it had been vain to send them at all. **23. Whose soever sins ye remit, they are remitted unto them; and whose soever sins ye retain, they are retained.** In any *literal* and *authoritative* sense *this power was never exercised by one of the apostles,* and plainly *was never understood by themselves as possessed by them or conveyed to them.* (See on Matt. xvi. 19.) The power to intrude upon the relation between men and God cannot have been given by Christ to His ministers in any but a *ministerial* or *declarative* sense—as the authorized interpreters of His word—while in the *actings* of His ministers, the real nature of the power committed to them is seen in the exercise of *church discipline.*

After Eight Days Jesus Again Appears to the Assembled Disciples, Giving to Doubting Thomas Affecting Evidence of the Reality of His Resurrection (24-29). **24. But Thomas, one of the twelve, called Didymus, was not with them when Jesus came**—that is, on the evening of the resurrection-day. Why he was absent we know not; but we cannot persuade ourselves, with *Stier, Alford,* and

480

25 when Jesus came. The other disciples therefore said unto him, We have seen the Lord. But he said unto them, Except I shall see in his hands the print of the nails, and put my finger into the print of the nails, and thrust my hand into his side, I will not believe.

26 And after eight days, again his disciples were within, and Thomas with them. *Then* came Jesus, the doors being shut, and stood in the midst,

27 and said, "Peace *be* unto you. Then saith he to Thomas, Reach hither thy finger, and behold my hands; °and reach hither thy hand, and

28 thrust *it* into my side: and be not faithless, but believing. And Thomas

29 answered and said unto him, "My Lord and my God. Jesus saith unto him, "Thomas, because thou hast seen me, thou hast believed: blessed *are* they that have not seen, and *yet* have believed.

30 And *many* other signs truly did Jesus in the presence of his disciples,

31 which are not written in this book: but *these are written, that ye might believe that Jesus is the Christ, the Son of God; and "that believing ye might have life through his name.

A. D. 33.

" Isa. 9. 7.
Mic. 5. 5.
Col. 1. 20.
" Ps. 103. 13, 14.
1 John 1. 1.
" Ps. 73. 25, 26.
Ps. 91. 2.
Ps. 118. 28.
Luke 1. 46, 47.
1 Tim. 1. 17.
" 2 Cor. 5. 7.
1 Pet. 1. 8.
" ch. 21. 25.
" Luke 1. 4.
Rom. 15. 4.
" ch. 3. 15, 16.
ch. 5. 24.
1 Pet. 1. 9.

Luthardt, that it was intentional, from sullen obstinacy. Indeed, the mention here of the fact of his absence seems designed as a loving apology for his slowness of belief. **25. The other disciples therefore said unto him, We have seen the Lord.** This way of speaking of Jesus—as in *v.* 20, and ch. xxi. 7—so suited to His resurrection-state, was soon to become the prevailing style. **But he said unto them, Except I shall see in his hands the print of the nails, and put my finger into the print of the nails, and thrust my hand into his side, I will not believe.** The very form of this speech betokens the strength of his unbelief. For, as *Bengel* says, it is not, '*If I see, I will* believe,' but '*Unless I see,* I will *not* believe;' nor does he think he *will* see, though the rest had told him that they had. How Jesus Himself viewed this state of mind we know from Mark xvi. 14, "He upbraided them with their unbelief and hardness of heart, because they believed not them which had seen Him after He was risen." But whence springs this pertinacity of resistance in such minds? Not certainly from *reluctance* to believe, but as in Nathanael (see on ch. i. 46), from mere dread of mistake in so vital a matter.

26. And after eight days—that is, on the eighth or first day of the following week. They themselves probably met every day during the preceding week, but their Lord designedly reserved His second appearance amongst them till the recurrence of His resurrection-day, that He might thus inaugurate the delightful sanctities of THE LORD'S DAY (Rev. i. 10). **his disciples were within, and Thomas with them. Then came Jesus** [ἔρχεται ὁ Ἰησοῦς] —rather, 'Jesus cometh,' **the doors being shut** (see on *v.* 19), **and stood in the midst**—not 'sat;' for the manifestation was to be, as on the evening of the week preceding, merely to show Himself among them as their risen Lord. **27. Then saith he to Thomas, Reach hither thy finger, and behold my hands; and reach hither thy hand, and thrust it.** This is here rather too strong a word. Probably 'put it'—as the same word [βάλλω] is rendered in ch. x. 4—is the right English word here. **into my side: and be not faithless, but believing.** These words of Jesus, as *Luthardt* remarks, have something rhythmical in them. There are two parallel members, with an exhortation referring to both. And Jesus speaks purposely in the words of Thomas himself, that, as *Lampe* says, he might be covered with shame. But with what condescension and gentleness is this done! **28. [And].** This "And" is evidently no part of the genuine text. **Thomas answered**

and said unto him, My Lord and my God. That Thomas did *not* do what Jesus invited him to do, and what he had made the condition of his believing, seems plain from *v.* 29—"Because thou hast *seen* Me thou hast believed." He is overpowered, and the glory of Christ now breaks upon him in a flood. His exclamation surpasses all that had been yet uttered, nor can it be surpassed by anything that ever will be uttered in earth or heaven. On the striking parallel in Nathanael, see on ch. i. 49. The Socinian evasion of the supreme Divinity of Christ here manifestly taught —as if it were a mere call upon God in a fit of astonishment—is beneath notice, save for the profanity which it charges upon this disciple, and the straits to which it shows themselves reduced. **29. Jesus saith unto him, [Thomas].** The word enclosed in brackets is almost totally destitute of authority. **because thou hast seen me, thou hast believed**—words of measured commendation, but of indirect, and doubtless painfully felt rebuke:—*q. d.,* Thou hast indeed believed; it is well; but it is only on the evidence of thy senses, and after peremptorily refusing all evidence short of that. **blessed are they that have not seen, and yet have believed.** 'Wonderful indeed,' as *Alford* well says, 'and rich in blessing for us who have not seen Him, is this closing word of the Gospel.'

First Close of this Gospel (30, 31). **30. And many other signs**—or 'miracles' **truly did Jesus in the presence of his disciples, which are not written in this book: 31. But these are written** —as sufficient specimens, **that ye might believe that Jesus is the Christ, the Son of God; and that believing ye might have life**—in the sense of ch. vi. 27, &c., **through**—or rather, 'in' His name. Two things about Jesus the Evangelist says his Gospel was written to establish. First, That He was "THE CHRIST," or 'the Messiah,' the great Hope of all heaven-taught souls from the beginning; and next, that this Messiah was "THE SON OF GOD." The one of these titles was the *official* one with which all who were looking for the promised Deliverer were familiar; the other is intended to express His *Personal* dignity and relation to the Father—for claiming which the Jews once and again took up stones to stone Him, and at length put Him to death. Without the Sonship, the Messiahship would be of no avail to sinful men; nor would the Sonship have done aught for us without the Messiahship. But as the two together constitute that "all fulness" which "it hath pleased the Father

481

21 AFTER these things Jesus showed himself again to the disciples at
2 the sea of Tiberias: and on this wise showed he *himself.* There were
together Simon Peter, and Thomas called Didymus, and [a]Nathanael of

A. D. 33.

CHAP. 21.
[a] ch. 1. 45.

should dwell in Him" (Col. i. 19), so in the hallowed phrase, that "*Jesus is the Christ the Son of God,*" we have that full Name which is as ointment poured forth to all that have ever tasted that the Lord is gracious.

Beautiful is the connection between these concluding verses and the last words of the preceding verse, about Thomas:—*q. d.*, 'And indeed, as the Lord pronounced them blessed who not having seen Him have yet believed, so for that one end have the whole contents of this Gospel been recorded, that all who read it may believe on Him, and believing, have life in that blessed Name.'

For Remarks on the Resurrection of Christ, see those on Matt. xxviii. 1-15, at the close of that Section, and on Luke xxiv. 13-53, Remarks 1 and 5 at the close of that Section. But on the distinctive features of the present Section we may add the following

Remarks.—1. Referring to the Remarks already made on Christian womanhood (on Luke viii. 1-3, at the close of that Section), one cannot but notice how exquisitely Woman's position in relation to Christ and His cause come out in this chapter. Indeed, were one internal evidence of the truth of the Bible, and of the divinity of the religion it discloses, to be demanded—one that should be at once decisive and level to ordinary capacity, perhaps *the position which it assigns to Woman* might as safely be fixed upon as any other; for whether we take her destination before the fall, her condition under the fall, or what the religion of the Bible has done to lift her out of it, the finger of God is alike clearly seen. But nowhere in the Bible—nowhere in Christianity—is her place more beautiful than here, in looking, ere others were astir, for the Saviour so dear to her, receiving from the lips that had fed so many His first word as the Risen One—a word, too, of such familiarity and love—and getting a commission from Him to carry the glad tidings to His disconsolate "brethren." O Woman! self-ruined but dearly ransomed, how much owest thou unto thy Lord! The Lord hath need of thee, not only for all thou hast in common with the other sex, but, over and above this, for all that sanctified Woman has to render to Him; and that is much. Some of the services of Woman to Christ are recorded in the New Testament for her encouragement in all time, (see on Mark xiv. 1-11, Remark 2 at the close of that Section; and on Rom. xvi.) But some of the most beautiful specimens of female Christianity will never be heard of till the resurrection-morn.

'Unseen, unfelt their earthly growth,
And self-accused of sin and sloth
They live and die; their names decay,
Their fragrance passes clean away;
Like violets in the freezing blast,
No vernal steam around they cast—
But they shall flourish from the tomb,
The breath of God shall wake them into od'rous bloom.'
KEBLE.

And this should be enough with male or female. 2. As "PEACE" was the *last* word which Jesus spoke to His assembled disciples before He suffered (ch. xvi. 33), so it was His *first* word to them as He presented Himself in the midst of them for the first time on the evening of His resurrection day (v. 19). As this was what His death emphatically *procured* (Eph. ii. 14, 15), so this is what His resurrection emphatically *sealed* (Heb. xiii. 20). Let the peace of God, then, rule in our hearts, to the which also we are called in one body (Col. iii. 15).

3. Did Jesus, when He was announcing to the Eleven His purpose to send them forth on a high mission into the world, even as His Father had sent Him, breathe on them and say, Receive ye the Holy Ghost? How impressively does this proclaim to all who go forth to preach the Gospel, that their speech and their preaching, if it is to be efficacious at all, must not be with enticing words of man's wisdom, but in demonstration of the Spirit and of power! (1 Cor. ii. 4). 4. Is not a Divine seal set upon the faithful exercise of church discipline in *v.* 23? (See on Matt. xviii. 18, and Remark 4 at the close of that Section.) 5. As our Lord, in very emphatic terms, exalts those who have not seen and yet have believed, over those who have believed only on the evidence of their senses, and as the miraculous *introduction* of the Gospel Economy has long ago given place to the noiseless *development* of it under the ordinary laws of the spiritual kingdom, so there is no reason to expect that this will ever on earth be superseded by the re-erection of a supernatural economy and the re-introduction of palpable intercourse between heaven and earth. "Blessed are they that have not seen, and yet have believed," is the fitting description of all who have been or ever shall be drawn to the Lord Jesus from the time of His departure till He come again and receive us to Himself, that where He is, we may be also. Even so, Come, Lord Jesus, come quickly!

CHAP. XXI. 1-25.—SUPPLEMENTARY PARTICULARS—MANIFESTATION OF THE RISEN SAVIOUR TO SEVEN OF THE APOSTLES AT THE SEA OF GALILEE—THE SEQUEL OF THIS—CONCLUSION. That this concluding chapter is an appendix by the Evangelist's own hand was never doubted by Christians till the days of *Grotius.* That *Neander* and *Lücke* should have expressed their opinion that it was written by another hand from *materials* left by John, and so is to be regarded as authentic history but not as the apostle's composition, is to be regretted rather than wondered at, considering their tendencies. We are sorry that *Wieseler* also should have given in to this opinion. But the vast majority of the ablest and most impartial critics are satisfied that there is no ground to doubt its being from the same beloved pen as the rest of this Gospel. It is in almost all the MSS. and Versions. As to the difference of style—of which *Alford,* while admitting it to be John's, makes fully too much—even *Credner,* the most searching investigator of the language of the New Testament, bears the following testimony, which, from him and in the present case, is certainly an impartial one:—'There is not a single external testimony against the 21st chapter; and regarded internally, this chapter displays almost all the peculiarities of John's style.' There is positively no other objection to it except that the Evangelist had already concluded his Gospel at the end of ch. xx. But neither in the Epistles of the New Testament nor in other good authors is it unusual to insert supplementary matter, and so have more than one conclusion.

Of the *ten* manifestations of the Risen Saviour recorded in Scripture, including that in 1 Cor. xv. 6, this in order is the *seventh*—or to His assembled disciples the *third.*

The Miraculous Draught of Fishes (1-12). 1. After these things Jesus showed—or 'manifested' himself again to the disciples at the sea of Tiberias: and on this wise showed he himself.

532

Cana in Galilee, and *b*the *sons* of Zebedee, and two other of his disciples.

3 Simon Peter saith unto them, I go a fishing. They say unto him, We also go with thee. They went forth, and entered into a ship immediately; and that night they caught nothing.

4 But when the morning was now come, Jesus stood on the shore: but
5 the disciples knew *c*not that it was Jesus. Then *d*Jesus saith unto them,
6 ¹Children, have ye any meat? They answered him, No. And he said unto them, *e*Cast the net on the right side of the ship, and ye shall find. They cast therefore; and now they were not able to draw it for
7 the multitude of fishes. Therefore *f*that disciple whom Jesus loved saith unto Peter, It is the Lord. Now when Simon Peter heard that it was the Lord, he girt *his* fisher's coat *unto him*, (for he was naked,) and *g*did
8 cast himself into the sea. And the other disciples came in a little ship; (for they were not far from land, but as it were two hundred cubits,)
9 dragging the net with fishes. As soon then as they were come to land,
10 they saw *h*a fire of coals there, and fish laid thereon, and bread. Jesus
11 saith unto them, Bring of the fish which ye have now caught. Simon Peter went up, and drew the net to land full of great fishes, an hundred and fifty and three: and for all there were so many, yet was not the net broken.

A. D. 33.
b Matt. 4. 21. Luke 24.15, 16, 31.
c ch. 20. 14.
d Ps. 37. 3. Luke 24.41. Phil. 4. 11-13, 19. Heb. 13. 5.
¹ Or, Sirs.
e Matt.17.27. Luke 5. 4, 6, 7.
f Ps. 118. 23. Mark 11. 3. Luke 2. 11. ch. 13. 23. ch. 19. 26. ch. 20. 2.
g Song 8. 7.
h 1 Ki. 19. 6. Matt. 4. 11. Mark 8. 3. Luke 12. 29-31.

This way of speaking shows that after His resurrection He appeared to them but occasionally, unexpectedly, and in a way quite unearthly, though yet really and corporeally. 2. There were **together Simon Peter, and Thomas called Didymus, and Nathanael of**—or 'from' **Cana in Galilee** —as to whose identity with *Bartholomew* the apostle, see on Matt. x. 3; **and the sons of Zebedee.** Here only, as *Stier* observes, does John refer to himself in this manner. **and two other of his disciples**—that is, two other apostles: so there were *seven* in all present. 3. **Simon Peter saith unto them, I go a fishing. They say unto him, We also go**—rather 'come' **with thee. They went forth, and entered into a ship immediately; and that night they caught nothing**—just as at the first miraculous draught; and no doubt it was so ordered that the miracle might strike them the more. The same principle is seen in operation throughout much of Christ's ministry, and is indeed a great law of God's spiritual procedure with His people. (See on Luke v. 1-11, Remark 1 at the close of that Section; and on ch. xi., Remark 4 at the close of that Section.)

4. **But when the morning was now come, Jesus stood on the shore: but the disciples knew not that it was Jesus.** Perhaps there had been some considerable interval since the last manifestation, and having agreed to betake themselves to their secular employment, they would be unprepared to expect Him. 5. **Then Jesus saith unto them, Children.** This term would not necessarily identify Him, being not unusual from any superior; but when they did recognize Him, they would feel it sweetly like Himself. **have ye any meat?** [προσφάγιον]—'any food?' meaning, Have ye caught anything? **They answered him, No.** This was in His wonted style, making them *tell* their case, and so be better prepared for what was coming. 6. **And he said unto them, Cast the net on the right side**—no doubt, by this very specific direction, intending to reveal to them His knowledge of the deep and power over it. 7. **Therefore that disciple whom Jesus loved saith unto Peter, It is the Lord**—again having the advantage of his brother in quickness of recognition (see on ch. xx. 8), to be followed, however, in Peter by an alacrity *all his own.* **Now when Simon Peter heard that it was the Lord, he girt his fisher's coat**

[**unto**]—or 'about' **him, (for he was naked)**—his vest only on, worn next the body, **and did cast himself into the sea**—the shallow part, not more than a hundred yards from the water's edge (*v.* 8); not meaning therefore to swim, but to get sooner to Jesus than in the full boat, which they could hardly draw to shore. 8. **And**—or, 'But' **the other disciples came in a little ship** [τῷ πλοιαρίῳ] —rather, 'in the boat,' **(for they were not far from land, but as it were**—'but about' **two hundred cubits,) dragging the net with** ['the'] **fishes.** 9. **As soon then as they were come to land**—or 'had landed,' **they saw**—'see' a **fire of coals there, and fish laid thereon, and bread.** By comparing this with 1 Ki. xix. 6, and similar passages, the unseen agency by which Jesus made this provision will appear evident. 10. **Jesus saith unto them, Bring of the fish which ye have now caught.** Observe the double supply thus provided—His and theirs. The meaning of this will appear presently. 11. **Simon Peter went up**—went on board, **and drew the net to land full of great fishes, an hundred and fifty and three: and for all there were so many, yet was not the net broken.** The manifest reference here to the former miraculous draught (Luke v. 9) furnishes the key to this scene. There the draught was *symbolical* of the success of their future ministry: While " Peter and all that were with him were astonished at the draught of the fishes which they had taken, Jesus said unto him, Fear not, from henceforth thou shalt catch men." Nay, when first called, in the act of "casting their net into the sea, for they were fishers," the same *symbolic* reference was made to their secular occupation: "Follow me, and I will make you fishers of men" (Matt. iv. 18, 19). Here, then, if but the same symbolic reference be kept in view, the design of the whole scene will, we think, be clear. The *multitude* and the *size* of the fishes they caught symbolically foreshadowed the vast success of their now fast approaching ministry, and this only as a beginning of successive draughts, through the agency of a Christian ministry, till, "as the waters cover the sea, the earth should be full of the knowledge of the Lord." And whereas, at the first miraculous draught, the net "was breaking," through the weight of what it contained —expressive, perhaps, of the difficulty with which,

12 Jesus saith unto them, ⁱCome *and* dine. And none of the disciples
13 durst ask him, Who art thou? knowing that it was the Lord. Jesus then
14 cometh, and taketh bread, and giveth them, and fish likewise. This is
now ^jthe third time that Jesus showed himself to his disciples after
that he was risen from the dead.

15 So when they had dined, Jesus saith to Simon Peter, Simon, *son of*
Jonas, lovest thou me ^kmore than these? He saith unto him, Yea,
Lord; ^lthou knowest that I love thee. He saith unto him, ^mFeed my
16 lambs. He saith to him again the second time, Simon, *son* of Jonas,
lovest thou me? He saith unto him, Yea, Lord; thou knowest that I
17 love thee. He ⁿsaith unto him, Feed my sheep. He saith unto him
^othe third time, Simon, *son* of Jonas, lovest thou me? Peter was grieved
because he said unto him the third time, Lovest thou me? And he
said unto him, Lord, ^pthou knowest all things; thou knowest that I

A. D. 33.
ⁱ Acts 10. 41.
^j ch. 20. 19, 26.
^k Matt. 26. 33.
^l 2 Ki. 20. 3.
^m Acts 20. 28.
Eph. 4. 11.
ⁿ Heb. 13. 20.
1 Pet. 2. 25.
1 Pet. 5. 2, 4.
^o ch. 13. 38.
^p Matt. 9. 4.
Mark 2. 8.
ch. 2. 24, 25.
ch. 16. 30.
Acts 1. 24.
1 Thes. 2. 4.
Rev. 2. 23.

after they had "caught men," they would be able to retain, or keep them from escaping back into the world—while here, "for all they were so many, yet was not the net broken," are we not, as *Luthardt* hints, reminded of such sayings as these (ch. x. 28): "I give unto my sheep eternal life; and they shall never perish, neither shall any pluck them out of my hand"? But it is not through the agency of a Christian ministry that all true disciples are gathered. Jesus Himself, by unseen methods, gathers some, who afterwards are recognized by the constituted fishers of men, and mingle with the fruit of their labours. And are not these symbolized by that portion of our Galilean repast which the fishers found, in some unseen way, made ready to their hand?

The Repast, and the Re-establishment of Peter (12-17). 12. Jesus saith unto them, Come and dine [Δεῦτε, ἀριστήσατε]—sweet familiarity, after such a manifestation of His command over the deep and its living contents! And—or, 'But' none of the disciples durst ask him, Who art thou? knowing that it was the Lord—implying that they *would* have liked Him just to say, "It is I;" but having such convincing *evidence*, they were afraid of being "upbraided for their unbelief and hardness of heart" if they ventured to put the question. 13. Jesus then cometh, and taketh [the] bread, and giveth them, and [the] fish likewise. See on Luke xxiv. 30, 31. 14. This is now the third time that Jesus showed himself [ἐφανερώθη]—rather, 'was manifested' to his disciples—that is, His *assembled* disciples; for if we reckon His appearances to individual disciples, they were certainly more; after that he was risen from the dead.

15. So when they had dined, Jesus saith to Simon Peter. Silence appears to have reigned during the meal; unbroken on *His* part, that by their mute observation of Him they might have their assurance of His identity the more confirmed; and on *theirs*, from reverential shrinking to speak till He did. Simon, son of Jonas, lovest thou me more than these?—referring lovingly to those sad words of Peter, shortly before denying his Lord, "Though *all men* shall be offended because of thee, *yet will I never* be offended" (Matt xxvi. 33), and intending by this allusion to bring the whole scene vividly before his mind and put him to shame. He saith unto him, Yea, Lord; thou knowest that I love thee. He adds not, "more than these," but prefixes a touching appeal to the Saviour's own omniscience for the truth of his protestation, which makes it a totally different kind of speech from his former. Feed my lambs—It is surely wrong to view this term, as some good critics do, as a mere diminutive of affection, and as meaning the same thing as "the sheep." It is much more

according to usage to understand by the "lambs" *young and tender* disciples, whether in age or Christian standing (Isa. xl. 11; 1 John ii. 12, 13), and by the "sheep" the more *mature*. Shall we now say, with many, that Peter was here re-instated in office? Not exactly, since he was not actually excluded from it. But after such conduct as his, the deep wound which the honour of Christ had received, the stain brought on his office, and the damage done to his high standing among his brethren, nay even his own comfort, in prospect of the great work before him, required some such renewal of his call and re-establishment of his position as this. 16. He saith to him again the second time, Simon, son of Jonas, lovest thou me? He saith unto him, Yea, Lord; thou knowest that I love thee. In this repetition of the question, though the wound was meant to be re-opened, the words, "*more than these*" are not repeated; for Christ is a *tender* as well as *skilful* Physician, and Peter's silence on that point was confession enough of his sin and folly. On Peter's repeating his protestation in the same words, our Lord rises higher in the manifestation of His restoring grace. He saith unto him, Feed—or 'Keep' my sheep. It has been observed, particularly by *Trench*, who has some beautiful remarks on this subject in his 'Synonyms of the New Testament,' that the word here is studiously changed from one signifying simply to 'feed' [βόσκω] to one signifying to 'tend' as a shepherd [ποιμαίνω], denoting the *abiding* exercise of the pastoral vocation and its highest functions. 17. He saith unto him the third time, Simon, son of Jonas, lovest thou me? Peter was grieved because he said unto him the third time, Lovest thou me? And he said unto him, Lord, thou knowest all things; thou knowest that I love thee. This was the Physician's deepest incision into the wound, while the patient was yet smarting under the two former probings. Not till now would Peter discern the object of this succession of thrusts. The *third* time reveals it all, bringing up such a rush of dreadful recollections before his view, of his "thrice denying that he knew Him," that he feels it to the quick. It was fitting that he should; it was meant that he should. But this accomplished, the painful dialogue has a delightful conclusion. Jesus saith unto him, Feed my sheep—'My little sheep' [προβάτια] is the reading of *Tischendorf* and *Tregelles*, and approved by *Meyer* and *de Wette*: it has about equal support with that of the received text. If we so read it, we must not understand it to mean "My lambs," as in *v.* 15, but to be used as a varied form, and designed as a sweet diminutive, for "sheep;" just as He calls His disciples, "Little children." It is as if He should say, 'Now, Simon, the last speck of the cloud

18 love thee. Jesus saith unto him, Feed my sheep. Verily, *q* verily, I say unto thee, When thou wast young, thou girdedst thyself, and walkedst whither thou wouldest: but when thou shalt be old, thou shalt stretch forth thy hands, and another shall gird thee, and carry *thee* whither

19 thou wouldest not. This spake he, signifying *r* by what death he should glorify God. And when he had spoken this, he saith unto him, Follow me.

20 Then Peter, turning about, seeth the disciple *s* whom Jesus loved following; which also leaned on his breast at supper, and said, Lord, which is

21 he that betrayeth thee? Peter seeing him saith to Jesus, Lord, and

22 *t* what *shall* this man *do?* Jesus saith unto him, If I will that he tarry

23 *u* till I come, what *v is that* to thee? Follow thou me. Then went this saying abroad among the brethren, that that disciple should not die: yet Jesus said not unto him, He shall not die; but, If I will that he tarry till I come, what *is that* to thee?

24 This is the disciple which testifieth of these things, and wrote these

25 things: *w* and we know that his testimony is true. And there are also many other things which Jesus did, the which, if they should be written

A. D. 33.

q ch. 13. 36.
Acts 12, 3, 4.
r Phil. 1. 20.
1 Pet. 4. 11,
14.
2 Pet. 1. 14.
s ch. 13. 23, 25.
ch. 20. 2.
t Matt. 24. 3,
4.
Luke 13. 23.
Acts 1. 6.
u Matt 16. 27.
Matt. 24. 3.
Matt. 25. 31.
1 Cor. 4, 5.
1 Cor. 11. 26.
Rev. 2. 25.
Rev. 3. 11.
v Deut. 29. 29.
w ch. 7. 17.
ch. 19. 35.
3 John 12.

which overhung thee since that night of nights is dispelled: Henceforth thou art to Me and to My work as if no such scene had ever happened.'

Jesus Forewarns Peter of his Martyr-death, but Declines to Tell him how it should be with the Beloved Disciple—The Misunderstanding of this Corrected (18-23). **18. Verily, verily, I say unto thee, When thou wast young**—embracing the whole period of life to the verge of old age. **thou girdedst thyself, and walkedst whither thou wouldest**—in other words, 'thou wast thine own master:' but **when thou shalt be old**—or 'art grown old' [γηράσης], **thou shalt stretch forth thy hands**—to be bound for execution, though not necessarily meaning *on a cross*. There is no reason, however, to doubt the very early tradition, that Peter's death was by crucifixion. **19. This spake he, signifying by what**—'manner of' **death** [ποίῳ] **he should glorify God**—not, therefore, a mere prediction of the manner of his death, but of the *honour* to be conferred upon him by dying for his Master. And, indeed, beyond doubt, this prediction was intended to follow up his triple restoration:—'Yes, Simon, thou shalt not only feed My lambs, and feed My sheep, but after a long career of such service, shalt be counted worthy to die for the name of the Lord Jesus.' **And when he had spoken this, he saith unto him, Follow me.** By thus connecting the utterance of this prediction with the invitation to follow Him, the Evangelist would indicate the deeper sense in which the call was understood, not merely to go along with Him at that moment, but to come after Him, *taking up his cross.*

20. Then—or, 'But' **Peter, turning about**—showing that he followed immediately as directed. **seeth the disciple whom Jesus loved following; which also leaned on his breast at** [the] **supper, and said, Lord, which is he that betrayeth thee?** The Evangelist makes these allusions to the peculiar familiarity to which he had been admitted on the most memorable of all occasions, perhaps lovingly to account for Peter's somewhat forward question about him to Jesus; which is the rather probable as it was at Peter's suggestion that he had put the question about the traitor which he here recalls (ch. xiii. 24, 25). **Peter seeing him saith to Jesus, Lord, and what** [shall] **this man** [do]?—'What of this man?' or, 'How shall it fare with him?' **22. Jesus saith to him, If I will that he tarry till I come, what is that to thee?** Follow

thou me. From the fact that John alone of the Twelve survived the destruction of Jerusalem, and so witnessed the commencement of that series of events which belong to "the last days," many good interpreters think that this is a virtual prediction of fact, and not a mere supposition. But this is very doubtful, and it seems more natural to consider our Lord as intending to give *no positive indication* of John's fate at all, but to signify that this was a matter which belonged to the Master of both, who would disclose or conceal it as He thought proper, and that Peter's part was to mind his own affairs. Accordingly, in "Follow thou me," the word "*thou*" is emphatic. Observe the absolute disposal of human life which Christ here claims: "IF I WILL that he tarry," &c. **23. Then went this saying abroad among the brethren, that that disciple should not die**—into which they the more easily fell, from the prevalent belief that Christ's Second Coming was then near at hand. **Yet Jesus said not unto him, He shall not die; but, If I will that he tarry till I come, what is that to thee?** The Evangelist is jealous for His Master's honour, which his death might be thought to compromise if such a misunderstanding should not be corrected.

Final Close of This Gospel (24, 25). **24. This is the disciple which testifieth of these things, and wrote these things**—thus identifying the author of the present Gospel, *including this supplementary chapter*, with all that it says of this disciple: **and we know that his testimony is true.** Compare ch. xix. 35. **25. And**—or, 'Moreover' **there are also many other things which Jesus did, the which, if they should be written every one, I suppose** [οἶμαι]—an expression used to show that what follows is not to be pressed too far. **that even the world itself could not contain the books that should be written.** This is to be taken as something more than a mere hyperbolical expression, which would hardly comport with the sublime simplicity of this writer. It is intended to let his reader know that, even now when he had done, he felt his materials so far from being exhausted, that he was still running over, and could multiply 'Gospels' to almost any extent within the strict limits of what "Jesus did." But in the *limitation* of these matchless Histories—in point of length and number alike—there is as much of that Divine wisdom which has presided over and pervades the living oracles, as in their *variety* and *fulness.*

485

every one, ^xI suppose that even the world itself could not contain the
books that should be written.　Amen.

[Amen.] This "Amen" is excluded from the text by *Lachmann, Tischendorf*, and *Tregelles;* and as it seems insufficiently supported, it is probably rather the irresistible addition—shall we say? --of the transcribers, than from the pen of the Evangelist.　See, on the same closing word of the Third Gospel, on Luke xxiv. 53.

Remark.—Thus end these peerless Histories—this Fourfold Gospel.　And who that has walked with us through this Garden of the Lord, these "beds of spices," has not often said, with Peter on the mount of transfiguration, It is good to be here!　Who that has reverentially and lovingly bent over the sacred text has not found himself in the presence of the Word made flesh—has not beheld the glory of the Only begotten of the Father,

full of grace and truth—has not felt His warm, tender hand upon him, and heard that voice saying to himself, as so often to the disciples of old, "Fear not!"　Well, dear reader, "Abide in Him," and let "*His words*"—as here recorded—"abide in thee."　This Fourfold Gospel is the Sun of the Scripture, from which all the rest derives its light. It is, as observed in the Introduction, the serenest spot in the paradise of God; it is the four rivers of the water of life, the streams whereof make glad the City of God.　Into it, as a Reservoir, all the foregoing revelations pour their full tide, and out of it, as a Fountain, flow all subsequent revelations.　Till the day dawn, then, and the shadows flee away, I will get me to this mountain of myrrh, this hill of frankincense! (Song iv. 6.)

P.S.—In discussing the genuineness of the much disputed passage regarding *the woman taken in adultery*, John vii. 53--viii. 11 (pp. 400, 401), we came to the conclusion that it rested on evidence, external and internal, sufficient to satisfy the reasonable enquirer, and that its place—supposing its historical truth and canonical authority admitted—could be no other than that in which it stands in the received text.　But there was one difficulty which we candidly acknowledged we were then unable to remove—as to Jesus having gone, on the evening before, to the mount of Olives (ch. viii. 1). The argument against the passage from this verse is, that 'nowhere else in this Gospel is "the mount of Olives" mentioned at all, nor does our Lord's passing the night there agree with this or any stage of His public life except the last.'　Of this objection we said, at the close of the discussion, that it 'must be allowed to remain among the difficulties that we, at least, find it not easy to solve.'　But since that paragraph was written, it has occurred to us that the following explanation sufficiently meets it.　The first three Gospels record no visit of our Lord to Jerusalem except the last; nor should we have known for certain that He was there at all until He went thither to die, but for the fourth Gospel (see page 21, first column).　It cannot then be proved, from the first three Gospels at least, that His retiring to the mount of Olives,

instead of remaining in the city or going to Bethany, was inconsistent with any earlier stage of His life than the last.　The utmost that could be fairly alleged would be, that the circumstances which led to His going to the mount of Olives at the time of His last visit had no parallel at any earlier stage.　But the contrary of this may be plainly gathered from what is recorded immediately before the disputed passage.　The Pharisees, having sent officers to apprehend Jesus, were galled at their returning not only without Him but with a confession of their impotence to lay hands on so incomparable a Teacher.　Scarcely had they given vent to their rage, when one of themselves hinted at the illegality of condemning a man unheard.　And though this division in their own camp had the effect of paralysing their efforts to arrest the Saviour at that time, it was so critical a juncture that He whose hour was not yet come might well decline to sleep that night in Jerusalem.　In that case, whether He retired to the mount of Olives, only to spend some quiet hours alone, and then retired to sleep at Bethany, or whether He spent the whole night there—as at that season He could safely enough do—is of little moment.　Enough that, either way, the only objection to the genuineness of this passage, from internal evidence, which has any plausibility, admits of sufficient explanation.

PART TWO
ACTS – ROMANS

INTRODUCTION TO THE ACTS OF THE APOSTLES.

THIS Book is the indispensable link of historical connection between the Gospels and the Epistles of the New Testament. Had there been no such record of the events which drew thousands around the standard of the Cross from the memorable day of Pentecost onwards, and of the circumstances out of which churches arose in the principal centres of population and civilization, of intelligence and commerce, Christians would have been driven to construct a history of them out of the incidental allusions to them which abound in the Epistles,—an effort in which the most honest and acute historical critics could have succeeded but indifferently; while the Apocryphal 'Acts of the Apostles,' and other such productions of the second century, are enough to show how little that is worthy of the name of authentic apostolic history would have come down to us from that age. That we should have been thus left, is inconceivable, save on one supposition. Had Christianity been a purely human Religion, the history of its founder and the labours of his immediate followers would have been written just as the inclination and opportunities of writers might chance to prompt them. But if Christianity is a Divine and Supernatural provision for the religious wants of mankind, it is not to be conceived that the history of its Founder—on which all right apprehensions of it depend—and of its Inauguration, as a visible Religious Society among men, should have been left to be written or not written, authentically or the reverse, at the mere caprice of its honest or dishonest, well or ill-informed adherents. Accordingly, while the Gospels are the peerless History of the one, the 'Acts of the Apostles' is the invaluable Record of the other.

I. The AUTHENTICITY AND CANONICAL AUTHORITY of the Acts of the Apostles was never doubted within the Christian Church before the present century—if we except some insignificant heretical sects of the second century, whose dislike to this book seems to have had nothing to do with its authenticity, but to have arisen from the inconsistency of its teaching with their own tenets; in other words, they disparaged it on purely subjective and uncritical grounds. With this exception, it has all ecclesiastical antiquity in its favour.

Though the writings of the Apostolic Fathers had contained no allusions to a historical book like the Acts of the Apostles, it would have been nothing surprising; but even here we find enough to show that they were not unacquainted with it. Thus, in the genuine Epistle of Clement of Rome—whom Paul calls his "fellow-labourer, whose name is in the book of life" (Phil. iv. 3)—there is a clear allusion to those golden words of the Lord Jesus, nowhere else recorded in the New Testament than in Acts xx. 35, "It is more blessed to give than to receive."* Again, *Ignatius*—bishop of Antioch from about the year 69 or 70 till about 107, when he suffered martyrdom under Trajan—in his Epistle to the Ephesians, describes them as 'restored to life by the blood of God'†—an expression which (supposing this Epistle to be genuine) is

---

* *Clem. Rom.* ad Corinth., ii., p. 54. (Patrum Apostolicorum Opera, Ed. 4, *Hefele.* 8vo. Tüb., 1854.) Though Clement may not have taken his allusion to this saying from the Acts, but, as Paul's fellow-labourer in the work of the Gospel, have used it independently, this would only confirm the authenticity of the narrative contained in the Acts.

† *Ignat.*, Ad Eph., p. 152 (ἀναζωπυρήσαντες ἐν αἵματι Θεοῦ).

so peculiar, that it must have been borrowed from those words of Paul to the elders of Ephesus (Acts xx. 28), "the church of God, which he hath purchased with His own blood" (as read in the received text, and certainly found in some early copies). We waive a probable reference to Acts i. 25, in his Epistle to the Magnesians,* and another to Acts x. 41, in his Epistle to the Smyrnæans.† But most certainly in the Acts of the Martyrdom of S. Ignatius—written by the companions of his journey to Rome, and witnesses of his martyrdom there—it is expressly stated that as he neared the city, and Puteoli was pointed out to him, he expressed a desire to track the foot-steps of the apostle Paul; having in view, doubtless, the itinerary of the apostle's route in Acts xxviii. 13, 14.‡ Not long after this (it would appear), *Polycarp*, bishop of Smyrna—appointed probably by the apostle John, and in all likelihood the last of the apostolic bishops—wrote the only one of his Letters which has come down to us, that to the Philippians; in which case it may have been written about the year 108, though it may be a little later. § In this precious Letter there is an unmistakable quota-tion of Acts ii. 24, 'Whom (that is, Christ) God raised up, having loosed the pains of Hades (or of death).' ||

The second century was prolific in Christian literature, orthodox and heretical, sober and romantic, in which (so far as it has come down to us) we find clear references to the Acts of the Apostles. Thus, the work called 'The Shepherd,' by *Hermas*—not that "Hermas" to whom the apostle sends a salutation in Rom. xvi. 14 (as was once maintained by some), but, as is now all but universally believed, another of that name—a brother of Pius I., elected bishop of Rome about the year 144 ¶—this work says there is 'none other name whereby one can be saved but that great and adorable name of His;' alluding pretty plainly to Acts iv. 12.** The works of *Justin Martyr*—who was converted to Christianity about the year 133, and suffered martyrdom under M. Aurelius, about the year 165—were numerous and valuable; and though the greater number of them have perished, those which remain are much to be prized—in one of which, at least, there is a clear reference to Acts vii. 22, as to Moses, as 'not only born among the Egyptians, but counted worthy to be instructed in all the learning of the Egyptians.' †† *Hegesippus*—who was born early in the second century, preceded

* *Ignat.*, Ad Magnes., v., p. 176 (*ut supra*).

† *Ignat.*, Ad Smyrn., iii., p. 225.

‡ Martyr. S. Ignat., v., p. 252; and see *Hefele's* vindication of this document, *Prolegomena*, pp. lxviii.-lxxiii.

§ *Lardner*, Credib., part ii., vol. i., ch. vi., p. 200, 8vo, 1734; and *Burton*, Eccles. Hist. of First Three Centuries, p. 314 (Third Ed. 8vo. Oxford, 1845).

|| *Polycarp*, Ad Philipp., i., p. 256 (*Hefele*). What puts it beyond reasonable doubt that *Polycarp* designedly quotes here from Peter's address in the Acts, not only that the unusual word "pains" (τὰς ὠδῖνας) applied to death, is used by both, but that Polycarp's reading, 'the pains of *Hades*' (ᾅδου)—for which the received text has "the pains of *death*" (τ. θανάτου)—is the actual reading of the Codex Bezæ (D), of the Vulgate (doloribus *inferni*), the Peschito Syriac, and the Memphitic versions, and of *Irenæus* (before the close of the second century). In the touching account of the martyrdom of *Polycarp*—in the reign of M. Aurelius,· and, according to the best authorities, most probably in the year 167—it is related that when his retreat was discovered, and he was urged to seek another hiding-place, he declined, saying, 'The will of God be done,' allud-ing, not improbably, to Acts xxi. 14. But we have no need to rely upon this.

¶ See Hefele (*ut supra*), Prolegg., pp. xciii.-xcvii.; and Burton (*ut supra*), p. 367.

** Herm., Past., lib. i., Visio, iv. 2. In Similit. ix. 28, also, there seems to be a reference to Acts v. 41 ("rejoicing that they were counted worthy to suffer for his name").

†† *Just. Mart.*, Ad Græcos Cohortatio, p. 11., B. (Ed. Bened., fol. Paris. 1742). For the

Eusebius as the first ecclesiastical historian, and died about the year 180—wrote a work in five books, unfortunately lost (with the exception of a Fragment); but Eusebius has preserved so much of what he related as to make it plain that he had before him the Acts of the Apostles.* The inestimable Letters of the Churches of Vienne and Lyons to their brethren in Asia Minor—giving them touching details of the sufferings inflicted on their martyrs during the persecution which raged under M. Aurelius, about the year 177—have been nearly all preserved by Eusebius; and in one of them they state that those heroic martyrs prayed, like Stephen, "Lord, lay not this sin to their charge," quoting the words of Acts vii. 60.† In the Apology for the Christians—addressed by *Athenagoras* (probably) to M. Aurelius, about the year 177 or 178 ‡—there is a probable reference to Acts xvii. 25 ("Neither is worshipped with men's hands, as *though he needed* anything"). §

The foregoing references to the Acts of the Apostles are enough to show that this book was known and prized by the most eminent Christians from the very days of the apostles onwards, till towards the close of the second century ; slight though they are in themselves, and, like most early references to the New Testament, interwoven with the writers' own statements, not given as quotations from any book. But there are three eminent fathers who all flourished towards the close of the second century and into the third, who so explicitly and so repeatedly refer to the Acts by name—and as an undoubted work of Luke, the companion of the apostle Paul—that the most determined opponents of the genuineness and authenticity of this work at once admit that it was known and regarded in their day as the production of Luke. We refer to *Irenæus*, who succeeded the martyr Pothinus, as bishop of Lyons, in 177; *Clement* of Alexandria, who flourished under Severus and Caracalla, from about 193 to 217; and *Tertullian*, presbyter of Carthage, who flourished during the same reigns. From the writings of these three great fathers it is needless to quote, for the reason just given—that it is impossible to doubt, and is not denied, that not only they themselves, but the whole Catholic Church in their day, regarded the Acts of the Apostles as the genuine production of Luke, and entitled to the same confidence as the most undoubted books of the New Testament.

We said that in the early ages the Acts of the Apostles was not received by certain insignificant heretical sects. We referred to the *Ebionites*, or Judaizing Christians, who, shortly after the destruction of Jerusalem, formed themselves into a distinct sect, with Pella, on the eastern side of the Jordan, for their head-quarters; and to the *Marcionites* and *Encratites*, in the latter half of the second century. But the tenets of these sects being in direct collision with the teaching of the Acts, it is easy to see why they rejected it; and there is nothing to show that their hostility to this book was grounded on anything more solid, but clear evidence to the contrary.‖ It was

genuineness of this Treatise, see *Semisch's* Justin Martyr, His Life, Writings, and Opinions. Translated from the German, by *J. E. Ryland.* 2 vols. 12mo. Edinburgh. 1843. (*Clark's* Biblical Cabinet.)

* *Euseb.*, 'H. E.,' ii., 23; iii., 20, 32; iv., 8, 22.

† *Ibid.*, v., 2.

‡ See *Lardner*, Cred., part ii., vol. i., ch. xviii., pp. 400–403 ; *Burton* (*ut supra*), pp. 390, 391, 433 ; *Smith's* Dictionary of Greek and Roman Biography and Mythology, *sub voce*, Athenagoras.

§ προσδεομενος τινος, says the Apostle—ἀπροσδεὴς, says the Apologist.

‖ *Epiphanius*, indeed, says that the Ebionites did not reject the Acts of the Apostles, but alongside of it had an Apocryphal Acts, filled with statements depreciating the apostle Paul. How to reconcile these statements, it is not easy to see, save on the supposition that the

impossible, however, that any body calling themselves Christians could be without some substitute for the Acts, to fill up the gap between the life of Christ and the rise of the first Christian churches. Accordingly, a crop of spurious or apocryphal Acts of the Apostles sprang up in the second century:—the Acts of Paul and Thecla (fathered upon the apostle by an Asiatic presbyter), the Acts of Barnabas (professing to have been written by John Mark), the Acts of Andrew (professing to give an account of his martyrdom), the Acts of Thomas (recognized by the Encratites, &c.), the Acts of Peter and Paul (professing to give an account of their martyrdom), the Acts of Andrew and Matthias, the Acts of Philip, the Acts and Martyrdom of Matthew the apostle, the End of Thomas, the Acts or Martyrdom of Bartholomew, of the apostle Thaddeus, and of the apostle John; together with the two treatises (or modified forms of one treatise) called the 'Clementine Homilies,' and 'Clementine Recognitions'—a manifest fiction. The very titles of these works proclaim their object—to supply that information regarding the life, labours, and death of the apostles, and other eminent preachers in the first age of the Gospel, about which the genuine Acts of the Apostles is silent. That no grains of trustworthy tradition are to be found in these productions, it would be unreasonable to affirm; on the contrary, some incidents and sayings preserved in them have all the appearance of substantial truth. But one has only to place even the best of them, so far as they have-come down to us, side by side with the canonical Acts of the Apostles—comparing their general strain and phraseology—to be convinced that in the one we have, with some grains of not improbable truth, a heap of fiction, dressed up in a coarse style of religious conception and often silly phraseology, totally unlike any book of the New Testament; while in the other we have grave, earnest, solid history, conveyed in simple and easy language, carrying the reader on from stage to stage of the great story of the spread of Christianity and the rise of the first churches, until it leaves him at Rome with the imprisoned apostle.

We have said that not a doubt of the authenticity of this History existed within the Church before the present century; and we have now to add, that such doubts were coincident with the rise of the sceptical or negative criticism of the New Testament in general. In fact, one cannot read any of the recent attacks upon this book, whether in Germany or in our own country, without being convinced that they are the result of a foregone conclusion, and are throughout conducted in the interest of a purely negative Christianity—a Christianity stript of the supernatural, and of everything transcending the sphere of religious morality. The theory of this school of criticism—as matured by the late Dr. Baur of Tübingen, and more or less modified by his disciples, who have found it necessary to abandon some of his positions—is the following:—That this book, so far from being the work of Luke, Paul's companion, had no existence till about the year 120; that the object of the writer or compiler of it being to conciliate Jewish prejudice against the Pauline views of Christianity, as intended equally for Jew and Gentile, he set himself to *construct* the history, rather than to record the actual facts—moulding these apologetically, by omitting this, inserting that, and so shaping the speeches as to make it appear, on the one hand, that Paul

evidence for the canonical Acts was such that they were unable to resist it, but that so much of it as related to the great enemy of their tenets they either kept in the background, or interpreted in the sense and with the explanations of their Apocryphal Acts.

was a stricter observer of the law, and more in harmony with Peter and the Jewish conception of Christianity, than he actually was; and on the other, that Peter and the Church at Jerusalem, intensely Jewish as they were in their conceptions of Christianity, nevertheless recognized the comprehensive principles of the Pauline Christianity, and even took steps to further his special work among the Gentiles.

'Such a notion' (says *Bleek*, whose acuteness and impartiality will be questioned by none, and who concedes, indeed, on some points, more than, we believe, the facts warrant) 'presupposes such deliberate purpose and calculated cunning on the author's part, as must appear altogether unlikely, if we submit without prejudice to the impression which a simple perusal of his work makes upon us. Its advocates are often obliged, in supporting it, to have recourse to utterly unnatural, or decidedly false, combinations, passing over in complete silence much in the book which is quite opposed to their assumptions. We allow at once that, in the first part of his work, Luke has given prominence to whatever in the history of the earlier Christian teachers appeared to be more directly introductory to the labours of the apostle Paul in spreading the Gospel among the Gentiles. This would be of special interest to himself as a Gentile Christian, and to Theophilus. But that in so doing he had the express design of justifying Paul's conduct, cannot be assumed with the least probability, from the way in which events are recorded by him; still less that, as *Baur, Schwegler,* and *Zeller* suppose, he deliberately altered the history to make it fall in with this design. Rather do particular passages show clearly how very far he was, even in the first part of his work, from giving a Pauline hue to everything, in order [as alleged] to establish the glory and apostolical dignity of his leader.'* To this statement we cannot resist adding another, from one who issued it in 1849, but in 1868 has done his utmost elaborately to disprove it—having in the interval gradually abandoned nearly all his old views of the New Testament—now advocating the so-called Tübingen principles of criticism, and appropriating nearly all the particular criticisms, by which Schwegler and Zeller assail the credibility of the Acts of the Apostles. We refer to *Dr. Samuel Davidson's* two Introductions to the New Testament, of the above dates, from the former of which we give the following excellent statement, summing up his argument on this subject:—'In taking leave of this topic, we hesitate not to assert that the idea of the book being fabricated by a later unknown writer, with whatever motive he set about the task, involves the *improbable,* not to say the *impossible,* at every step. The fabricator must have had the Pauline Epistles before him, and studied them with the most minute attention. After becoming intimately familiar with their contents, even to the smallest and apparently the most unimportant particulars, he sat down to write in such a way as to incorporate many notices derived from them with his materials. Here he needed consummate skill, lest the deception should be detected. The art demanded for the work was of the most refined and exquisite nature. *Where did such a man appear in the early times of Christianity?* † It is impossible to point to a phenomenon so marvellous as this. The wakefulness and talents of the person who palmed the history on his own genera-

* Einleitung in das Neue Testament, von FRIEDR. BLEEK. (Edited by his son, *J. F. Bleek.*) Zweite Auflage, Berlin, 1866, § 123, ss. 329, 330.—We have availed ourselves above of the excellent translation of this work by the *Rev. W. Urwick,* vol. i., pp. 353, 354 (Edinburgh, 1869—*Clark's* fourth series), which, though inverting the paragraphs, and combining the large and small type, only improves the sense thereby.

† The Italics in *this,* and a following sentence, are ours—not those in the first sentence.

tion as the authentic production of Paul's companion, must have been extraordinary. *Not so constructed are the forgeries of that period.* They are clumsy and inartificial. They have, therefore, been detected long ago by the test of fair criticism; but the book of Acts has stood the test unshaken. It was reserved for Hegelianism to expose its alleged pretensions—a species of hyper-criticism which would soon reduce the genuine histories of all antiquity to nonentities or forgeries. But we are confident that the credibility of the Acts will be universally acknowledged long after the negative criticism has vanished away, like every temporary extravagance of unbridled reason, or, rather, of unbridled scepticism.'* The attempted *disproof* of all this, which occupies five times as many pages of the new Introduction as were taken up with establishing it in the old one,† we have not been able to read without the deepest pain. Here and there we have adverted, in the following Commentary on the Acts, to some of the more glaring examples of the perverted criticism, and of the worthless reasoning grounded on it, by which *Baur, Schwegler,* and *Zeller,* have tried to destroy the credibility of this book; nor does *Dr. Davidson,* in all his fifty pages on this subject (vol. ii., pp. 307-358), advance almost anything which may not be found in those works of theirs of which the full titles are given in our list of works quoted, &c. ‡ For detailed replies to these attacks and vindication of the credibility of the Acts of the Apostles, we must refer the German reader to *Lekebusch* and *Lechler.*§ Time was when *Dr. Davidson* himself thought—'it need not be stated how the Epistles agree with the Acts in all the particulars on which both speak;' that 'there are no *real* discrepancies, but, on the contrary, such substantial correspondence as might be expected from independent sources, each narrating the same things in his own manner, and with different objects in view;' and that '*Paley* [in his 'Horæ Paulinæ'] has placed this in the clearest light, and thereby vindicated the credibility of the Acts as well as of the Epistles,'—but all this now goes for nothing. ||

It may be thought by some readers that we have dwelt too long on this head; and certainly a few years ago we should have contented ourselves with a more summary statement. But now that the destructive criticism of the German sceptical school is

* Introduction to New Testament, &c., 3 vols. 8vo, London, 1849, vol. ii., pp. 51, 52.—The only thing we have scrupled to give in the above extract is the loose statement about Hegelianism as 'a species of hyper-criticism.' Hegelianism is no species of criticism, but a philosophy. But reducing all known or knowable things, as this philosophy does, to a construction of logical forms, precluding all belief in the strictly supernatural, it obliges its consistent disciples either (with *Strauss*) to reject historical Christianity, as being a professedly supernatural and Divine religion, or (with *Baur,* another of its disciples) to invent 'a species of criticism' by which its historical character may, in sort, be saved, and yet its supernatural features be all eliminated.

† Introduction to the Study of the New Testament, Critical, Exegetical, and Theological, by SAMUEL DAVIDSON, D.D., 2 vols., 8vo, London, 1868, vol. ii., pp. 207-258.

‡ *Baur's* Paulus,—particularly pp. 15-243; *Schwegler's* Nachapostl. Zeitalter,—particularly vol. ii., pp. 75-123; *Zeller's* Apostelgeschichte,—particularly pp. 216-376.

§ See list of works quoted, &c.

|| Professor Jowett has put forth all his strength to show that some of *Paley's* 'Undesigned Coincidences,' between the Acts and the Epistles to the Thessalonians (for example) are not convincing, and in one or two cases with some show of reason. (Epistles of St. Paul, &c., vol. i., pp. 108-130.) But though the form of scepticism which Paley's masterly work was intended to meet has now given place to a more critical and pretentious, though essentially flimsy and captious form—and exception may hence be taken to it as unsuited to our day—it is impossible, we conceive, to read it through with an impartial mind, without finding in it invincible evidence both of the authenticity of the Acts and the genuineness of the Epistles.

coming in upon us like a flood—professing, as it does, to have disproved the authenticity of all the Gospels, the Acts, and a majority of the remaining books of the New Testament,* and when its advocates take upon them to represent all who decline to follow them as *behind the day*—it is time to be a little more explicit.

II. The TITLE of this book—"The Acts of the Apostles" (Πράξεις τῶν ἀποστόλων) —though it could scarcely have been given to it by the author himself, who probably gave it no title at all—must have been very early given and at once adopted, for it is found in the oldest manuscripts; and it has been remarked that the Syriac and Egyptian versions, the former at least dating from the second century (though the word is not otherwise known in those languages) have retained it in the designation of this book. In fact, the quantity of spurious "Acts" to which the second century gave birth leaves no room to doubt that in that century, and probably from the beginning of it, this book was known by no other name. At first sight, however, it seems not particularly appropriate; for, with the exception of Peter and Paul, it records "the Acts" of hardly any of the apostles. But since the Church of Christ started into existence under the instrumentality of apostles; since the door of faith was opened to the Gentiles, under Divine direction, by one apostle; since most of the Gentile churches, of which it records the formation, were indebted for their existence to another of the apostles; and since the Christian Church is said to be "built upon the foundation of the apostles and prophets"—this title was probably fixed on as best fitted to express generally the *apostolic* stamp, which was recognized in all that this book records.

III. With respect to the AUTHORSHIP of this book, all antiquity is agreed in ascribing it to "Luke, the beloved physician," the companion and fellow-labourer of Paul, and the author (according to the unshaken testimony of antiquity) of the Third Gospel. It is addressed to the same "Theophilus" as the Gospel, whose title, "most-excellent" (κράτιστος), being that applied to the Roman governors, Felix and Festus, (Acts xxiii. 26; xxiv. 3; xxvi. 25), seems to imply that he occupied some official position. The author expressly links it on to his Gospel as a sequel to it, calling the one his first discourse, or "former treatise" (ὁ πρῶτος λόγος), and intending this as the 'second' or 'latter' one. The internal evidences of identity of authorship in both books have been traced, with great minuteness of detail, by learned critics, to some of whom we have referred under a former head. The evidences to the contrary, drawn out in detail by the sceptical critics, also referred to, seem to us in no way to disprove identity of authorship, and at most to indicate diversity of written sources employed by the author in such places. Into the discussion of this, however, it would be unsuitable to enter here.

IV. The SOURCES from which the author drew his materials—a perfectly new branch of inquiry in these days of searching criticism, but one of no small interest—have furnished occasion for much diversity of opinion. That written sources were used in relating the transactions of the day of Pentecost, and succeeding days; the appointment of the seven deacons; the preaching, apprehension, defence, and martyrdom of

---

* While *Dr. Baur* acknowledges only *four* books, *Dr. Davidson*, in his new Introduction, recognizes eight more, or *twelve* out of the *twenty-seven* books of the New Testament.

Stephen; the dispersion of the disciples; the labours of Philip in Samaria, and his interview with the Ethiopian eunuch; the accession of Cornelius and the inquiry by the Church at Jerusalem which this occasioned—why should there be any doubt, when we remember the claim which this same author advances, in the Preface to his Gospel, to better information than the "many" who preceded him, inasmuch as he had carefully "traced down all things from the beginning?" (Luke i. 1-4.) While there is sufficient similarity in the style throughout as to show that the work proceeded from one pen, there certainly may be perceived that diversity which, supposing different materials made use of, might naturally be expected. It has been asked how Stephen's long speech before the Sanhedrim could have been in possession of the writer? To this we reply, that Saul doubtless heard that speech; that a man of his acuteness could hardly fail to see that it presented one consistent view of God's dealings with His ancient people, and of their treatment of Him, yet one in the teeth of the reigning system and spirit of his nation; that both, therefore, could not stand; and not being prepared to abandon 'the perfect manner of the law of the Fathers,' he determined to conse-crate all his energies to stamping out Christianity; that after the marvellous change which came over him, having during the three days which he spent without food and sight in Damascus, gone over in thought those passages in Stephen's speech before the Sanhedrim, which had specially irritated him, and now found that truth in them to which he had then been blind, the whole details of the speech, as well as the scene, started up before him one by one, till, on recovering his sight, and beginning to preach Christ, he could commit it to writing nearly as we now have it; and as the Church at Jerusalem would likely have notes of its own, our historian would in all probability be able, by comparison, to present it authentic, as here. We do not say that all this did happen as we have supposed; but if it gives a natural explanation of the fidelity of the speech, as reported in the Acts, it is enough. And it is no small confirmation of this, that as it stands it contains several statements which look so like historical inac-curacies, that all expositors have been perplexed by them, while some set them down as slips of memory, excusable in one ranging over so vast a field of sacred history, and this in circumstances fitted to disturb somewhat his recollection of minute details.

But what are called the "we" passages—where the writer passes from the third person singular or plural ("he" and "they") to the first person plural ("we" did so and so, implying that the writer himself was then one of the party)—these passages have been subjected to elaborate criticism, with the view of showing that the writer of the Acts himself is not there meant. According to some of these critics, Timothy was the writer of the "we" passages, and his document is in those places inserted by the writer of the Acts just as he found it. (So *Bleek** and others.) According to *Schwanbeck*, the author of the passages in question was Silas.† The replies which have been made to these critics by *Davidson* (in his former 'Intro-duction'‡), *Ebrard*,§ *Alford*,|| &c.—to which we must refer for full details, not suitable here—leave no room for reasonable doubt that the passages in question

---

* 'Einleitung,' § 124-125 (Translation, vol. i., pp. 355-561).
† Ueber die Quellen der Apostelgeschichte, Darmstadt, 1847.
‡ Vol. ii., pp. 9-21.
§ 'Gospel History,' § 110 (Translation, pp. 507-512).
|| 'Greek Testament,' &c., vol. ii., Prolegomena, § 1, pp. 1-7.

proceeded from the pen of no other than the author of the book itself. This is the judgment not only of all Christian antiquity, but of all critics up to the present day, save a few who (with the single exception, perhaps, of *Bleek*) belong to the negative school of New Testament criticism.

V. About the PLAN of this History, or the special OBJECT which its author had in view, opinions are divided, but without much reason. As a designed sequel to "the former treatise," the Third Gospel, and expressly intended to be a Digest of "all that Jesus began both to do and teach, until the day in which He was taken up"— it is beyond a doubt that this second Treatise (as we may call it) was prepared and issued as a continuation of the Christian History up to a certain stage of it. How indispensable this sequel was to the Gospel History, we have attempted to express in the opening paragraph of this Introduction. Nor was it less indispensable, theologically (if we may so speak) than historically. To the Gospels it is what the fruit is to the tree that bears it. In the Gospels we see the corn of wheat falling into the ground and dying; in the Acts we see it bringing forth much fruit (John xii. 24). There we see Christ purchasing the Church with His own blood; here we see that purchased Church rising into actual existence—first among the Jews of Palestine, and next among the surrounding Gentiles, until it gains a footing in the great capital of the ancient world—sweeping majestically from Jerusalem to Rome. Nor, as observed at the outset, is this book of less value as an Introduction to the Epistles which follow it, than as a Sequel to the Gospels which precede it. Presupposing, as these Epistles do, the historical circumstances of the parties addressed, and deriving from these circumstances so much of their freshness, point, and force, they would, without this book, in no respect be what they now are, and would in a number of places be scarcely intelligible. And if so, it is scarcely conceivable that this was not one object for which the book was written; or if one may reasonably doubt whether the writer himself had this in view, none who believe that a Divine Hand is to be seen in the preparation of these New Testament books, will readily doubt that it was before the eye of Him who has thus provided so richly for the information and nutriment of the Church in all time—the Wonderful in counsel and excellent in working.

But though the general plan and object of this History seem obvious enough, it is by no means easy to say why, in a narrative covering a space of at least thirty years, some things are related with so much fulness, while others, apparently not less important, are either recorded very summarily, or not at all. In Gal. i. 17, the apostle speaks of a journey into Arabia, which he took shortly after his conversion, and before his first visit to Jerusalem as a Christian; but of this visit we have no mention at all in the Acts. Of his labours from the time of his enforced flight from 'Jerusalem to Tarsus (ch. ix. 30), until Barnabas came for him to labour at Antioch, we have no record; nor of his special labours there (ch. xi. 25, 26). (See Commentary, pp. 62 and 77.) In 1 Cor. xvi. 1, and in Gal. i. 2, we read of "the churches of Galatia" (see also Acts xviii. 23); these, we know, were founded by Paul; but interesting though it must have been to know the particulars of these successful labours, all that relates to this region in the Acts is the following half-sentence (ch. xvi. 6), "Now when they had gone throughout Phrygia and the region of Galatia." (See Commentary, there.) From Acts xviii. 18–23, it is evident that a good deal that might have proved important regarding the close of the apostle's first visit to Corinth, his first brief visit to Ephesus, his progress from Cæsarea to Jerusalem (completing his second missionary tour), and his visit to the Churches of Galatia and Phrygia (at the commencement of his third missionary tour)—is omitted. (On this last particular see Commentary, p. 135.) In Acts xx. 1-3, we have only the briefest record of a section of the apostle's life peculiarly rich in details, happily supplied by the Epistles (of which a summary will be found in Commentary, p. 145). In Rom. xv. 19 the apostle says, "From Jerusalem, and round about unto Illyricum, I have fully preached the gospel of Christ." Probably the confines of this latter region were reached at the time referred to in ch. xx. 1, 2—where, referring to Macedonia, it is said that "when he had *gone over those parts*, and had given them much exhortation, he came into Greece;" but no details whatever are given. (See *Paley's* Horæ Paulinæ, ch. ii., no. iv.) In a word, no one who reads the impassioned relation of his manifold and protracted sufferings and perils in the course of his long missionary life, which the apostle himself gives in 2 Cor. xi. 23-33, can fail to see how little of all this is recorded in the Acts of the Apostles. (See *Paley*, ut supra, ch. iv., no. ix.) Whatever may have been the reason of these abbreviations and omissions, one thing is clear, that to have recorded all this in full would have swelled the book very much beyond its present dimensions, and might not have added to its real utility as a portion of the New Testament.

VI. The DATE AND PLACE OF PUBLICATION cannot be fixed with certainty; but from our remarks in the Commentary on the closing words of the book, it will be seen that we judge it to have been issued not long after the two years of the apostle's imprisonment, without trial, there referred to. And if so, Rome was, almost without doubt, the place of publication.

VII. The CHRONOLOGY of the Acts is involved in great uncertainty; the notes of time which it contains being few, and, except in one or two of them, vague. Happily, the dates of the few events of secular history to which it refers are tolerably well known to us; and by connecting these with the interval specified between some of the occurrences in the lives of the apostles Peter and Paul, here recorded, we can thread our way through the difficulties that surround the apostle's life, and thus approximate to certainty. The secular events we allude to are such as the famine under Claudius Cæsar (ch. xi. 28), the death of Herod Agrippa (ch. xii. 23), the expulsion of the Jews from Rome by the same emperor (ch. xviii. 2), and the entrance of Portius Festus upon the Procuratorship of Judæa (ch. xxiv. 27). Immense research has been brought to bear upon this subject; but the learned are, as might be expected, considerably divided. Every year has been fixed upon as the probable date of the conversion of the apostle Paul, from A. D. 31 (*Bengel*) to A. D. 41 (*Schmid, Wurm*). But the weight of authority is in favour of dates ranging from A. D. 35 to 40—a difference of not more than five years—and the largest number of authorities is in favour of the years 37 or 38. Taking the former of these, to which opinion largely inclines, the following Table of approximate dates may be found useful:—

A. D. 37,	.	. CONVERSION OF SAUL OF TARSUS,	.	.	. Acts ix.
„ 40,	.	. *First* Visit to Jerusalem (after Conversion),	.		„ ix. 26; Gal. i. 18.
„ 42-44, .		. *First* Residence at Antioch,	.	.	. „ xi. 25-30

A.D. 44,	.	.	Second Visit to Jerusalem,	. . .	Acts xi. 30; xii. 25.
„ 45–47,	.		FIRST MISSIONARY JOURNEY,	. . .	„ xiii. 2; xiv. 26.
„ 47–51,	.		Second Residence at Antioch,	. . .	„ xiv. 28.
			Third Visit to Jerusalem,	. . .	{ „ xv. 2–30; Gal. ii. (See Commentary, p. 108.)
			Third Residence at Antioch,	.	„ xv. 35.
„ 51, 53, or 54,			SECOND MISSIONARY JOURNEY,	. . .	„ xv. 36, 40; xviii. 22.
„ 53 or 54,	.		Fourth Visit to Jerusalem,	. . .	„ xviii. 21, 22.
			Fourth Residence at Antioch,	. . .	„ xviii. 22, 23.
„ 54–58,	.		THIRD MISSIONARY JOURNEY,	. . .	„ xviii. 23; xxi. 15.
„ 58,	.		{ Fifth Visit to Jerusalem—Arrest—Imprisonment at Cæsarea, ... }		„ xxi. 15, 27, 30; xxiii. 33, 35.
„ 60 (Aut.), „ 61 (Spring),	}		Voyage to and arrival in Rome,	. . .	„ xxvii.–xxviii. 16.
„ 63,	.	.	Release from Imprisonment, ... At Crete, Colosse, Macedonia, Corinth, Nicopolis, Dalmatia, Troas, ...		„ xxviii. 30. (See Commentary. } 1 and 2 Tim., and Titus.
„ 63, 64, or 65, or possibly so late as 66, 67, or 68,	}		Martyrdom at Rome.		

INTRODUCTION TO THE EPISTLE TO THE ROMANS.

I. THE AUTHENTICITY of this Epistle, as it was universally acknowledged in the early Church—alike by the orthodox Church, who owned the authority of Paul as an apostle of Jesus Christ, and by the heretical sects that disowned him—so it has never been questioned even by the extreme school of sceptical critics, with the exception of an Englishman of the name of *Evanson*, whose forgotten book on the Gospels (1792) most nearly resembles *Strauss's* Life of Jesus, and the extravagant German, *Bruno Bauer*. It is quoted undeniably by *Clement* of Rome, and *Polycarp*, of the Apostolic Fathers; by *Theophilus*, bishop of Antioch, in the Epistle of the Churches of Vienne and Lyons, and by *Irenæus*, in the second century; by *Clement* of Alexandria and *Tertullian*, in the third century; and by all succeeding writers, as canonical Scripture. And so fully does internal evidence attest its genuineness as the production of the apostle Paul, that it is impossible to have any rational doubt of it. The two last chapters, indeed, are regarded as spurious by *Baur* and *Schwegler*, and by *Dr. Davidson*, in his recent Introduction. But it is not denied that external evidence decidedly attests them; and the arguments from internal evidence are 'exceedingly feeble,' as *Davidson* called them in his former Introduction, though now he reproduces them as convincing. *De Wette* and *Meyer*, in the Introduction to their Commentaries on the Epistle, *Bleek*, in his Introduction to the New Testament (§ 154), and others, have vindicated the genuineness of these two chapters, on both external and internal evidence. (On the disputed doxology in ch. xvi. 25–27, see Commentary.)

II. WHEN and WHERE this Epistle was written, we have the means of determining with great precision, from the Epistle itself compared with the Acts of the

Apostles. Up to the date of it the apostle had never been at Rome (ch. i. 11, 13, 15). He was then on the eve of visiting Jerusalem with a pecuniary contribution for its Christian poor from the churches of Macedonia and Achaia, after which his purpose was to pay a visit to Rome, on his way to Spain (ch. xv. 23–28). Now, this contribution we know that he carried with him from Corinth, at the close of his third visit to that city, which lasted three months (Acts xx. 2, 3; xxiv. 17). On this occasion there accompanied him from Corinth certain persons whose names are given by the historian of the Acts (ch. xx. 4); and four of these are expressly mentioned in our Epistle as being with the apostle when he wrote it—Timotheus, Sosipater, Gaius, and Erastus (ch. xvi. 21, 23). Of these four, the third—Gaius—was an inhabitant of Corinth (1 Cor. i. 14), and the fourth—Erastus—was "chamberlain of *the city*" (Rom. xvi. 23), which can hardly be supposed to be other than Corinth. Finally Phœbe—the bearer, as appears, of this Epistle—was a deaconess of the church at Cenchreæ, the eastern port of Corinth (ch. xvi. 1). Putting these facts together, it is impossible to resist the conviction—in which all critics agree—that Corinth was the place from which the Epistle was written, and that it was despatched about the close of the visit above mentioned, probably in the early spring of the year 58.

III. The ORIGIN of the Roman Church is wholly unknown. That it owed its origin to the apostle Peter, and that he was its first bishop—though an ancient tradition, and taught in the Church of Rome as a fact not to be doubted—is refuted by the clearest evidence, and is given up even by candid Romanists. On that supposition, how are we to account for so important a circumstance being passed by in silence by the historian of the Acts, not only in the narrative of Peter's labours, but in that of Paul's approach to the metropolis, of the deputations of Roman "brethren" that came as far as Appii Forum and the Three Taverns to meet him, and of his two years' labours there? And how, consistently with his declared principle—not to build on another man's foundation (ch. xv. 20)—could he express his anxious desire to come to them that he might have some fruit among them also, even as among other Gentiles (ch. i. 13), if all the while he knew that they had the apostle of the circumcision for their spiritual father? And how, if so, is there no salutation to Peter, among the many, in this Epistle—or, if it may be thought that he was known to be elsewhere at that particular time—how does there occur in all the Epistles which our apostle afterwards wrote from Rome not one allusion to such an origin of the Roman Church? The same considerations render it all but certain that this Church owed its origin to no apostle, nor even any prominent Christian labourer, but that among the numerous visitors to that metropolis of the civilized world there would be not a few who, having felt the power of the Gospel, were unable to keep it to themselves, and made it their business, when there, to spread the knowledge of it among their friends and acquaintances. That a large number of Jews and Jewish proselytes resided at this time at Rome, is known to all who are familiar with the classical and Jewish writers of that and the immediately subsequent periods; and that those of them who were at Jerusalem on the day of Pentecost (Acts ii. 10), and formed probably part of the three thousand converts of that day, would, on their return to Rome, carry the glad tidings with them, there can be no doubt. Nor are indications wanting that some of those embraced in the salutations of this Epistle were Christians already of long standing, if not among the earliest converts to the Christian faith. Others of them who had made the apostle's acquaintance elsewhere, and who, if not indebted to him for their first knowledge of Christ, probably owed much to his ministrations, seem to have charged themselves with the duty of cherishing and consolidating the work of the Lord in the capital. And thus it is not improbable that, up to the time of the apostle's arrival, the Christian community at Rome had been dependent upon subordinate agency both for its first beginnings and for the increase of its numbers, aided by occasional visits of stated preachers from the provinces;* and perhaps it may be gathered from the saluta- tions of the last chapter that it was up to that time in a less organized, though far from less flourishing, state than some other churches to whom the apostle had already addressed Epistles.

IV. FOR WHAT CLASS of Christians—Jewish or Gentile—was this Epistle immediately designed? Certain it is that the apostle writes to them expressly as a Gentile Church (ch. i. 13-15; xv. 15, 16); and though it is plain that there were Jewish Christians among them, and the whole argument presupposes an intimate acquaintance on the part of his readers with the leading principles of the Old Testament, this will be sufficiently explained, by supposing that the bulk of them, having, before they knew the Lord, been Gentile proselytes to the Jewish faith, had entered the palo of the Christian Church through the gate of the ancient economy.

V. It remains only to speak briefly of the PLAN and CHARACTER of this Epistle. Of all the undoubted Epistles of our apostle this is the most elaborate, and at the same time the most glowing. It has just as much in common with a theological treatise as is consistent with the freedom and warmth of a real Letter. Referring to the headings which we have prefixed to its successive sections, as best exhibiting the progress of the argument and the connection of its points, we here merely note that its first great topic is what may be termed the *legal relation of man to God*, as a violator of His holy law, whether as merely written on the heart, as in the case of the Heathen; or, as in the case of the Chosen People, as further known by external Revelation—that it next treats of that legal relation as wholly *reversed*, through believ- ing connection with the Lord Jesus Christ; and that its third and last great topic is *the new life* which accompanies this change of relation, embracing at once a blessedness and a consecration to God, which, rudimentally complete already, will open in the future world into the bliss of immediate and stainless fellowship with God. The bearing of these wonderful truths upon the condition and destiny of the Chosen People, to which the apostle next comes, though it seem but the practical application of them to his kinsmen according to the flesh, is in some respects the deepest and most difficult part of the whole Epistle, carrying us directly to the eternal springs of Grace to the guilty in the sovereign love and inscrutable purposes of God; after which, however, we are brought back to the historical platform of the visible Church,

---

* *Irenæus*, in the third book of his Treatise against Heresies (ch. iii.), is quoted by *Olshausen*, as stating that believers from every quarter met there—*in quâ fideles undique conveniunt* (Com- mentary on Romans, p. 71; *Clark's* Translation). But *Irenæus* is entirely misquoted, and his meaning in the passage referred to is one to which many Protestants would demur: *Ad hanc enim* (Romæ) *Ecclesiam, propter potentiorem principalitatem, necesse est omnem convenire Ecclesiam, hoc est, eos, qui sunt undique fideles, in qua semper ab his qui sunt undique conservata est ea quœ est ab apostolis Traditio.*

in the calling of the Gentiles, the preservation of a faithful Israelitish remnant amidst the general unbelief and fall of the nation, and the ultimate recovery of all Israel to constitute, with the Gentiles in the latter day, one Catholic Church of God upon earth. The remainder of the Epistle is devoted to sundry practical topics, winding up with salutations and outpourings of heart delightfully suggestive.

How shall we characterize this wonderful Epistle? Fragmentary answers to this question—or rather some things which may be accepted in lieu of an answer—have once and again forced themselves out in the course of our Exposition, where its depths or its heights would not suffer us to be altogether silent. But we attempt not what cannot but fall below the feeling of every penetrating and reverential student. While all Scripture has stamped its impress indelibly on the Christian world, perhaps it is not too much to say, that for all the precision and the strength which it possesses, and much of the spirituality and the fire which characterize it, the faith of Christendom in its best periods has been more indebted to this Epistle than to any other portion of the Living Oracles. It supplies, to a larger extent than most are aware of, both the bone and the marrow of the Evangelical system, as handed down from the beginning, and as received in the living Church of every name. Its texture is so firm, its every vein so full, its very fibres and ligatures so fine and yet strong, that it requires not only to be again and again surveyed as a whole, and mastered in its primary ideas, but to be dissected in detail, and with unwearying patience studied in its minutest features, before we can be said to have done it justice. Not only every sentence teems with thought, but every clause; while in some places every word may be said either to suggest some weighty thought, or to indicate some deep emotion.

No wonder, then, that this Epistle has employed so many pens, critical, theological, experimental. If, a quarter of a century ago, the learned and laborious *Fritzsche* could say with truth that the interpreters of it were even then almost innumerable,* and all kinds of pens have been employed on it since, it may be thought time now to rest content with what we possess. But the word of the Lord is not so easily exhausted. Almost every interpreter has his own point of view, his own definite object, his own plan and mode of execution, which must necessarily occasion endless variety in the exhibition of one and the same Truth, and by which alone his labours ought to be judged.

Two opposite errors are to be eschewed by the interpreter of this book of the New Testament. If the theological element absorb too much of his attention, he will be in danger of unconsciously forcing its teaching, or at least of substituting for the simplicity and freshness with which it is here given forth, the hardness and dryness of a mere system. But undue jealousy of system, and a morbid determination to make every passage speak for itself, irrespective of its bearings and connections, leads but to laborious trifling; and, springing as it does from a lurking disbelief of the unity of Scripture, it only tends to aggravate that evil. At the same time, nothing is more difficult than, in such an Exposition, to give the due proportion to each of these elements, the Exegetical and the Theological. That he has fully succeeded in doing this, the author of the present work is far from pretending. But if there is one feature of it more than another to which he would venture to claim attention, it is the rigidity with which the Exegetical element is made throughout the basis of its Doctrinal

* Ad Romanos Epist., tom. i., p. 49.

superstructure, and yet the richness and the definiteness of theological teaching which a strict exegesis is seen to yield, and which it is possible to divest to a large extent of its modern technicalities. Such as it is, it is given to the public with unfeigned diffidence, as the fruit of fond and unwearied diggings in an exhaustless mine ; and if it yield to the reader but a small portion of that profit and satisfaction which the study of this matchless Epistle has ministered to the present writer, he will indeed be richly rewarded.

ABERDEEN, *March,* 1870.

CHIEF SOURCES OF AUTHORITY FOR THE TEXT OF THE ACTS OF THE APOSTLES AND THE EPISTLE TO THE ROMANS.—(See Vol. V. pp. xl.-xliii.)

First.—ANCIENT MSS.—*Uncial* and *Cursive.*

I. UNCIAL MSS., Chronologically arranged.

1. Of *the New Testament at large* are the four following:—.

Name.	Probable Date.	Where Deposited.
א—CODEX SINAITICUS, *	4th century,	Imperial Library, St. Petersburg.
B—CODEX VATICANUS, †	4th century,	Vatican Library, Rome.
A—CODEX ALEXANDRINUS, ‡	5th century,	British Museum, London.
C—CODEX EPHRAEMI (*rescriptus*), §	5th century (1st half),	Imperial Library, Paris.

2. Of Uncial MSS. containing *Acts*, are the following:—

D—CODEX BEZÆ (or CANTABRIGIENSIS), ‖	Early in 6th century,	University Library, Cambridge.

* Contains (besides the Old Testament in the LXX. Version) the New Testament *entire.* Published first in splendid fac-simile form, and since in ordinary Greek type, by its distinguished discoverer, with the following title:—'Nov. Test. Sinait. . . . Aen. Fr. Const. *Tischendorf.* Lips. 4to: 1863.' In the following year there was published, in a portable form, a most careful and serviceable collation of this invaluable MS., noting all the corrections found in it, with their probable dates, under the following title:—'A full Collation of the Codex Sinaiticus, with the Received Text of the New Testament; to which is prefixed a Critical Introduction. By *Rev. F. H. Scrivener, M.A.* Cambridge. 12mo. 1864.' Tischendorf judged that four hands had been at work on this MS. as correctors—A (correcting chiefly gross and obvious mistakes, and hardly less ancient than the MS. itself); B (about the end of the sixth century, only in the Gospels, and chiefly the early chapters of Matthew); C (about the seventh century, constituting far the greater number of the changes throughout the whole, and seemingly designed to assimilate the text to that represented by the Received Text); and D (whose hand is not perceptible in the New Testament). Tregelles, however, who spent three whole days in examining the MS., was not convinced that there is evidence of so many hands; and Scrivener (whose impressions from the fac-similes, &c.—for he has not seen the MS. itself—is entitled to weight) inclines to this view.

† Ends, in the first hand, in the middle of Heb. ix. 14. This most valuable MS. has been examined from time to time, and, so far as the jealousy of the Papal authorities would allow, collated. It has at length been published, and republished, with the Papal authority, but with so little critical skill, that au edition by competent hands—carefully distinguishing the *first* from all *subsequent hands,* and noting all its palæographical features—is yet wanting.

‡ Recently published in a more accessible form than that of Woide (1786), under the following title:—'Nov. Test. Græce, ex antiquissimo Codice Alexandriñus.' Edidit *B. H. Cowper.* 8vo, London. 1860.

§ The gaps in this most important MS. are so numerous, that it will be necessary to set down here how much it *contains* of Acts and Romans:—viz., Acts i. 2-iv. 3; v. 35-x. 42; xiii. 1-xvi. 36; xx. 10-xxi. 30; xxii. 21-xxiii. 18; xxiv. 15-xxvi. 19; xxvii. 16-xxviii. 8. Romans i. 1-ii. 5; iii. 21-ix. 6; x. 15-xi. 31; xiii. 10-end.

‖ Published in 1793, by *Kipling,* in letters resembling those of the MS. itself, but not satisfactorily; now re-edited by *Mr. Scrivener,* with such critical care, skill, and accuracy—including a valuable Critical Introduction, and a large body of important annotations—as leaves nothing to be desired, under the following title:—'Bezæ Codex Cantabrigiensis; being an exact copy, in ordinary Greek type, of the celebrated Uncial Græco-Latin MS. of the Four Gospels and Acts of the Apostles, written early in the sixth century, and presented to the University of Cambridge by Theodore Beza in 1581. Edited, with a Critical Introduction, Annotations, and Fac-similes, by *Rev. F. H. Scrivener, M.A.,* Cambridge. 4to. 1864.' The text of this MS., embracing the Gospels and Acts, is of so unexampled a character, that it has occasioned much dissension and diversity of opinion. The results at which Mr. Scrivener has arrived—the grounds of which are stated with such clearness, ability, and fulness, as to entitle them to great weight—are the following:—(1.) That the Greek text must have been copied from a MS., most likely of the *third century at the latest;* that since it resembles so closely and constantly the *Syriac* versions (with which it could hardly have been compared later than the *second century*) and the Old Latin (also of the *second century*), its text, whatever judgment may be formed of its genuineness and purity, must have been widely diffused among both the Eastern and the Western Christians, in the second century. (2.) That the Latin version is, on the whole, an independent translation, made either directly from its own Greek, or from a text almost identical with it;

Name.	Probable Date.	Where Deposited.
E—CODEX LAUDIANUS,*	End of 6th century,	Bodleian Library, Oxford.
G—CODEX PASSIONEI, †	9th century,	Bibliotheca Anglica, Rome.
H—CODEX MUTINENSIS, ‡	9th century,	Ducal Library, Modena.

3. Of Uncial MSS., containing the *Pauline Epistles*, the following are the chief :—

Name.	Probable Date.	Where Deposited.
D—CODEX CLAROMONTANUS, §	6th century,	Imperial Library, Paris.
F—CODEX AUGIENSIS, ‖	9th century,	Trinity College, Cambridge.
G—CODEX BOERNERIANUS, ¶	9th century (towards end of),	Royal Library, Dresden.
J—CODEX PASSIONEI, **	9th century,	Bibliotheca Anglica, Rome.
K—CODEX MOSQUENSIS, ††	9th century,	Library of Holy Synod, Moscow.
E—CODEX SANGERMANENSIS, ‡‡	10th century,	Imperial Library, St. Petersburg.

that the translator often retained in his memory, and perhaps occasionally consulted, both the Old Latin and *Jerome's* revised Vulgate; and that he probably executed his work in Gaul, about the *close of the fifth century*. Of the not a few gaps in both, in the Greek and the Latin of this MS., the following are *wanting in Acts* :—In the *Greek*, ch. viii. 29–x. 14; xxi. 2–10; 15–18. (Some of these, however, being cited by *Wetstein*, in the middle of last century, must have been then extant.) The following are wanting in the *Latin* :—Ch. viii. 20–x. 4; xx. 31–xxi. 2; xxii. 2–10; xxii. 20–end.

* 'A valuable Greek-Latin MS. of the Acts alone, presented, in the seventeenth century, to the University of Oxford by its then Chancellor, Archbishop Laud, from whom it takes its name. It was, doubtless, written in the West of Europe' (*Scrivener*). Its Latin version is peculiar, corresponding closely to its own Greek text, even in its interpolations and rarest various readings. It wants ch. xxvi. 29–xxviii. 26. It was edited by *Thomas Hearne*, in 1636, but requires to be re-edited more critically.

† So called from Cardinal Passione, to whom it formerly belonged. It now belongs to the Anglican library of the Augustinian monks at Rome. It embraces the Acts (beginning in the middle of ch: viii. 10), the Catholic Epistles, and the Pauline Epistles (in the Pauline Ep., under the letter J: it will be described below). It has been carefully collated both by *Tischendorf* and *Tregelles*, but not as yet published.—*Note :* The same letter (G) denotes a MS. of the Pauline Epistles (*Codex Boernerianus*), described below; and care must be taken not to confound them.

‡ This MS. wants, in the first hand, Acts i. 1–v. 28; ix. 39–x. 19; xiii. 36–xiv. 3. It has been carefully collated by *Tischendorf* and *Tregelles*.

§ A Greek-Latin MS., and one of the most important in existence.—*Note :* Care must be taken not to confound this MS. with the *Codex Bezæ* or *Cantabrigiensis*, denoted by the same letter, but containing only the Gospels and Acts—of which this MS. contains none. It contains all the fourteen Pauline Epistles, with a few gaps. In *Romans*, it wants ch. i. 1-7, 27-30, both in the Greek and the Latin, first hand. The Latin version is more independent of, and less altered from, the Greek, than the Latin of the Codex Bezæ and the Codex Laudianus—approaching more nearly to the African type of the Old Latin. Several correctors have been at work on the Greek text of this MS., the chief of which, *Tischendorf*, who published in 1852, thus denotes:—

D**—about the seventh century (a few changes only).
D***—ninth or tenth century (more than 2,000 changes).
Dᵇ—supplied Rom. i. 27 very early.

‖ A Greek-Latin MS., beginning in the middle of Rom. iii. 19; so called from having been brought from the monastery of Augia Dives (or Rich Meadow, Reichenau), on a fertile island in the lower part of Lake Constance, where it may have been written nearly a thousand years ago; bought, in 1718, by Richard Bentley, and preserved in his own (Trinity) College Library. It has been splendidly edited by *Scrivener*, with the accuracy, ability, and fulness afterwards exemplified in the Codex Bezæ, under the following title :—'An Exact Transcript of the Codex Augiensis; a Græco-Latin Manuscript of St. Paul's Epistles, deposited in the Library of Trinity College, Cambridge, and with a Critical Introduction by *Rev. F. H. Scrivener, M.A.*' Royal 8vo. Cambridge, 1859. It abounds, as much as any, with real variations from the common text, and exhibits many corrections —a few by the first hand, some very recent, but by far the greater number in a hand little later than the original writers. The Latin version of this MS. approaches the Vulgate in its best MS.

¶ A Greek-Latin MS.; so called from *Professor Boerner* of Amsterdam, who bought it in 1705. So singular is the resemblance of this MS. to the preceding one (Cod. Augiensis, F), while yet it is plain that the one was not copied from the other, that they must have been both independent copies of the same MS.—probably some centuries older than themselves. (*Scrivener*, 'Plain Introduction,' p. 137; and *Tregelles*—Horne, p. 169.) Though not therefore a distinct authority from P, they form a valuable united testimony to the reading of the ancient and valuable codex from which they must have alike sprung.

** This MS. (described under G of the *Acts*) contains the Pauline Epistles entire.

†† This MS. contains, besides the Pauline Epistles, the Catholic Epistles entire. It wants Rom. x. 18–end.

‡‡ A Greek-Latin MS. of the Pauline Epistles, from the Abbey of St. Germains des Prez, near

in His kingdom then to be revealed. Moreover, there had been a relapse on the part of some into heathen sins against chastity and sobriety (ch. v. 5-7), as also against charity (ch. iv. 3-10; v. 13, 15). There were symptoms in some of want of respectful love and subordination to their ministers; others treated slightingly manifestations of the Spirit in those possessing gifts (ch. v. 19). "Prophesying" was undervalued as compared with other gifts of the Spirit. To give spiritual admonition on these subjects, and at the same time commend what deserved commendation, and to testify his love, was the object of the epistle.

The *Place of Writing* was doubtless Corinth, where Timothy, with Silas, rejoined him (Acts xviii. 5) soon after he arrived (cf. ch. ii. 17), in the autumn of 52 A.D.

The *Time of Writing* was in the early months of St. Paul's one year and a half stay at Corinth (Acts xviii. 11), immediately after having received from Timothy tidings of their state (ch. iii. 6), in the winter of 52 A.D., or early in 53. (Timothy had been sent to enquire, probably from Athens: ch. iii. 1, 2.) For it was written not long after the conversion of the Thessalonians (ch. i. 8, 9), while St. Paul could speak of himself as only *taken from them for a short season* (ch. ii. 17). Thus it was *first in date of all St. Paul's extant epistles:* perhaps the first of Christian records. It is written in the joint names of Paul, Silas, and Timothy, the three founders of the Thessalonian church. The plural "we" is used everywhere, except in ch. ii. 18; iii. 5; v. 27. 'We' is the true reading, ch. iv. 13. The English Version, "I," in ch. iv. 9; v. 1, 23, is not supported by the original (*Edmunds*).

The *Style* is calm and equable, in accordance with the subject, which deals with Christian duties in general, taking for granted the doctrinal truths, which were not as yet disputed. There was no deadly error as yet to call forth vehement bursts of feeling and impassioned argument. The earlier epistles, as we should expect, are practical. It was not until Judaistic and legalizing errors arose at a later period, that he wrote the second group of epistles (five years later—Corinthians, Romans, and Galatians) which unfold the cardinal doctrines of grace and justification by faith. Still later, the epistles from his Roman prison confirm the same. Last of all, the Pastoral Epistles are suited to the Church's developed ecclesiastical constitution, and give directions as to bishops and deacons, and correct abuses and errors of later growth. The style of these earliest letters is more simple, less intense, and less marked by sudden turns of thought. The opening salutation and closing benediction are brief.

The opponents of Paul are *Jews* (ch. ii. 16); whereas in the time of the second group, they are Judaizing Christians. The Gospel preached is that of the coming kingdom of Christ, rather than the cross of Christ; for this best met the Messianic hopes which won Jewish believers to the Christian faith. It also gave the greatest comfort to the infant Church under trials, and in the sacrifice of worldly gains and pleasures. Though ten years elapsed between this epistle and that to the Philippians, yet no two epistles more closely resemble one another. This is due to the healthy condition of the two churches: an honourable feature common to all the churches of Macedonia. In both he drops the official title of apostle in the salutation, and begins with hearty commendations.

Two divisions seem marked by a prayer in the same words at the close of each, "May God Himself," &c. (ch. iii. 11-13: and ch. v. 24).

The prevalence of the Gentile element in this church is shown by the fact, that these two epistles are among the very few of St. Paul's writings in which no quotation occurs from the Old Testament.

(2.) *Codex Fuldensis* is of no less antiquity, and—were it not that in this MS. the Gospels are unfortunately written *in harmony,* instead of separately, we might say—of no less value also. It is so called from the Abbey of Fulda, in Hesse Cassel, where it is deposited. It has been quite recently published, with two fac-similes, under the following title: 'Codex Fuldensis, Novum Testamentum Latic, interprete Hierony mo, Ex MS. to Victoris Capuani, Edidit, Prologomenis introduxit, Commentariis adornaist ERNESTUS RANKE. Accedunt duo Photo-lithographicæ, 8vo. Marb. et Lips., 1868.' It appears that this MS. was written under the instructions of Victor, bishop of Capua, whose episcopate-commenced in the year 541, and was finished in the year 546, at which date it is signed (in the Acts) by Victor himself, who corrected it. There is a remarkable relation between this and the preceding MS. —alike in their errors and peculiar readings; while the differences between them show that the one is no copy of the other, nor both of the same MS., at least throughout. *Ranke* throws out a conjectural explanation of these peculiarities, but judiciously adds, that 'however they are to be explained, we may congratulate ourselves on having, in these two most ancient and approved witnesses, satisfactory evidence of what the New Testament was in its-original condition.'

Third.—CITATIONS FROM ANCIENT ECCLESIASTICAL WRITERS.

As those which are referred to in the various readings in Acts and Romans are specified in the following list of Works quoted or referred to, with the time when the writers flourished, it will be unnecessary to note them here.

The titles of the critical editions of the Greek Testament used in the Gospels will be found in Vol. V., p. xliii. Those used in *Acts* and *Romans* may be more fully enumerated here :—

The beautiful folio edition of Robert Stephens, Paris, 1550, and the two small editions of the Elzevirs of Leyden, 1624 and 1633, represent what is called the Revised Text (*textus receptus*). Where these differ, the Elzevir editions usually follow the last edition of *Theodore Beza* (1598), but sometimes deviate from both. The splendid edition of Dr. John Mill (Oxford, 1707) was not intended as a new and independent text (though it is by many supposed to be such), but was designed simply to be a reprint of Stephens' third or folio edition, with only the *errata* corrected.

The *critical* editions—whose object is, by the help of all the three sources of evidence which we have enumerated, to present the text of the New Testament as nearly as possible in its original form—are the following (*omitting,* however, *those which we have not had occasion to refer to*):—

1 *Novum Testamentum Græce:* Ad fidem Codicum, Versionum et Patrum recensuit, et Lectionis Varietatem adjecit. D. Jo. JAC. GRIESBACH. New Edition. 2 vols. 8vo. London, 1809-10.

2. *Novum Testamentum Græce.* Textum ad fidem Testium Criticorum recensuit J. M. AUG. SCHOLZ. 2 vols. 4to. Lips., 1830-36.

3. *Novum Testamentum Græce et Latine:* CAROLUS LACHMANNUS recensuit. *Philippus Buttmannus* Ph. F. Græcæ Lectionis Auctoritates apposuit. 2 vols. 8vo. Berl., 1842-50.

4. *Novum Testamentum Græce:* Ad Antiquos Testes denuo recensuit, Apparatum Criticum omni studio perfectum apposuit, Commentationem Isagagicam Prætexuit A. F. Const. Tischendorf. Seventh Edition. 8vo, 1859.

5. *The Greek New Testament:* SAM. PRID. TREGELLES, LL.D. 4to. In Parts (unfinished):—
   Part I. Matthew and Mark, 1857.
   —— II. Luke and John, 1860.
   —— III. Acts and Catholic Epistles, 1865.
   —— IV. Romans to 2 Thessalonians, 1869.
   Together with occasional references to the Text of

6. *The Twofold New Testament:* Being a New Translation, accompanying a Newly Formed Text, in parallel columns. By the Rev. THOMAS SHEDDON GREEN, M.A. 4to. London, 1865.

WORKS QUOTED OR REFERRED TO IN ACTS AND ROMANS.

AKERMANN (J. Y.)—Numismatic Illustrations of the New Testament. 8vo. London, 1846.

ALEXANDER (J. A., D.D.)—Commentary on the Prophecies of Isaiah. New Edition, 2 vols. 8vo. Edinburgh, 1865.

———————————— The Acts of the Apostles Explained. 2 vols., crown 8vo. London, 1857.

ALFORD (H., D.D.)—The Greek Testament, with critically revised Text, &c., and Critical and Exegetical Commentary. Vol. ii. Fifth Edition, 8vo. London, 1865.

AMBROSII Opera (Bishop of Milan, A. D. 374–397). Edit. Bened. 2 vols., fol., 1686–90.

AUGUSTINI Opera (Bishop of Hippo, A. D. 395–430). Edit. Bened. 15 vols., fol., 1670–1700, and 1836–39.

BAUMGARTEN (Dr. H. Rostock)—Die Apostelgeschichte, oder der Entwickelungsgang der Kirche von Jerusalem bis Rom. (2nd ed.) Braunschw. 1859. (First Edit. Translated : The Acts of the Apostles, or History of the Church in the Apostolic Age. 3 vols. 8vo. Edinburgh, 1854.)

BAUR (Dr. F. C., Tübingen)—Paulus, der Apostel Jesu Christi. Stüttg., 8vo, 1845.

———————————— das Christenthum u. die Christliche Kirche der drei ersten Jahrhunderte. Tüb. (2nd ed.) 8vo, 1860.

BENGEL (J. A.)—Gnomon Novi Testamenti. Ed. Tert., 8vo, Tom. i., 1835; Tom. ii., 1836.

BEZA (Theod.)—Novum Testamentum Græce; Interpretationes et Annotationes. Ed. Quint. folio, 1598.

BLOOMFIELD (S. T., D.D.)—The Greek Testament, with English Notes, Critical, Philological, and Explanatory. Eighth Edition, 2 vols., 8vo, 1860—Supplementary Vol. Second Edition, 1851.

CALOVIUS (Abr.)—Biblia Illustrata, 4 vols., folio. Dresd., 1719. Vol. iv.

CALVINI (Joan.) in Novum Testamentum Commentarii. Ed. Tholuck, 8vo. Vol. iv., 1833. Vol. v., 1834.

CHRYSOSTOMI (Joan.) Opera (Patriarch of Constantinople, A. D. 398–407), 13 vols., Imp. 8vo. Paris, 1837. Vol. ix.

CONYBEARE (J. W.) and HOWSON (J. S., D.D.)—Life and Epistles of St. Paul. 2 vols. 4to, 1850–52. [Translations and Appendix, by Mr. C.; Historical and Geographical matter chiefly by Dr. H.]

CREDNER (Karl Aug.)—Einleitung in das Neue Testament, 8vo. Halle, 1836.

DELITZSCH (Dr. Franz, Leipzig)—Die Psalmen. New Ed., 2 vols., 8vo. Leipzig, 1867.

DONALDSON (J. W., D.D.)—A Complete Greek Grammar. Second Edition, 8vo. London, 1859.

EBRARD (Dr. J. H. A.)—Wissenschaftliche Kritik der Evangelische Geschichte. 2nd Ed., 8vo. Erlang., 1850. (Translated: The Gospel History, &c.) Edinburgh, 1863.

EDWARDS (Pres. Jonath.)—Works. 6 vols., 8vo. Edinburgh, 1844–47. Vol. ii., 'Original Sin.'

EUSEBII Hist. Eccles. Ed. Vales. 3 vols., fol., 1720. Translated by Cruse, 12mo. London, 1851.

ERASMI Opera. 10 vols. Lugd. Batav., folio. 1703. Vol. vii. (Also, Critici Sacri, 13 vols. folio. 1698–1732. Vol. vii.)

ESTII (Guil.)—In omnes D. Pauli Epistolas Commentarii Mogunt. 3 vols. royal 8vo. Tom. i. 1858.

EWALD (Dr. H. A.)—Die Poetische Bücher des Alten Test., latest edit., 8vo. 1866.

FERME (Ch.)—Logical Analysis of the Epistle of Paul to the Romans. From the Latin. (Wodrow Society vols.) 8vo, 1850.

FRASER (Rev. James, Alness)—The Scripture Doctrine of Sanctification; being a Critical Explication of Romans vi.–viii. 4. 12mo. Edinburgh, 1774.

FRATRUM POLONORUM, qui Unitarii appellantur, Bibliotheca, &c. 7 vols., folio. Irenop., 1856.

FRITZSCHE (D. C. F. A.)—Pauli ad Romanos Epistola. Recensuit et cum Commentariis Perpetuis edidit. 8vo. Hal. Sax., 1836–1843.

GREEN (Rev. T. S., M.A.)—The Twofold New Testament: Being a New Translation, accompanying a Newly Formed Text, 4to. London, 1865.

———————————— Treatise on the Grammar of the New Testament. 8vo. London, 1842; New Edition, 12mo, 1862.

———————————— Critical Notes on the New Testament. 12mo. London. 1867.

GROTIUS (Hug.)—Annotationes in Nov. Test.   Tom. ii., fol.   Paris, 1646.

HACKETT (Professor C. D.)—Commentary on the Original Text of the Acts of the Apostles.   Second Edition.   8vo.   New York, 1858.

HALDANE (R.)—Exposition of the Epistle to the Romans.   Seventh Edition.   2 vols., crown 8vo, 1852.

HIERONYMI Opera (Monk and Presbyter, A. D. c. 370–420).   11 vols., folio, 1734.   Vol. xi.

HITZIG (Dr. Ferd.)—Die Psalmen, historisch krit. Commentar u. Uebersetzung.   New Edit.   8vo, 1863–65.

HODGE (Chas., D.D.)—Commentary on the Epistle to the Romans.   New Edition, 8vo.   Edinburgh, 1864.

HOFMANN (Dr. J. C. K. von)—Schriftbeweis.   8vo.   Nördlingen, 1859, 1860.

HUG (Dr. L.)—Einleitung in die Schriften des Neuen Testaments (4th Ed.), 1847.   (Revised Edition, translated, with Notes, Andover, U.S., 8vo, 1836.)

HUMPHRY (W. G., B.D.)—Commentary on the Acts of the Apostles.   Second Edition, Revised.   Crown 8vo, 1854.

HUPFELD (Dr. H.)—Die Psalmen, übersetzt u. ausgelegt.   8vo.   1855–62.

IRENÆI Opera (Bishop of Lyons, A. D. 177–c. 200), adornavit Stieren.   2 vols. 8vo.   Lips., 1853.

JELF (W. E., B.D.)—Grammar of the Greek Language.   Second Edition, 2 vols. 8vo.   Oxford, 1851.

JOSEPHI Opera.   Edit. Havercamp, 3 vols. 8vo.   Lips., 1782.

JOWETT (Professor B.)—The Epistles of St. Paul to the Thessalonians, Galatians, Romans : with Critical Notes and Dissertations, 2 vols.   London, 8vo, 1855.   Vol. ii.

KÜHNER (Dr. Raph.)—Grammar of the Greek Language.   Translated from the German.   8vo.   London, 1859.

KÖSTER (Dr. D. F. B.)—Die Psalmen, nach ihrer strophischen Anordnung übersetzt, mit Einleitung u. Anmerkungen.   Königsb., 1837.

LANGE (Dr. J. P.)—Geschichte der Kirche dargestellt.   (Apostolic Period.)   8vo.   1853, &c.

——————— Theol. Homil. Bibelwerk : Apostelgeschichte.   Bielef, 1860.   (The same translated : Theological and Homiletical Commentary on the Acts of the Apostles, from the German of Dr. G. V. Lechler and K. Gerok.   2 vols., 8vo.   Edinburgh, 1864.)

LARDNER (Dr. Nath.)—Works.   10 vols., 8vo.   London, 1838.

LECHLER—See LANGE.

——————— (Dr. G. V., Leipzig)—Das Apostolische u. das Nachapostolische Zeitalter, mit Rücksicht auf Unterschied u. Einheit in Lehre. u. Leben dargestellt.   Stüttg., 8vo, 1857.

LIGHTFOOT (Dr. John)—Works.   13 vols., 8vo.   London, 1823.

LOCKE (Jo.)—Paraphrase and Notes on the Epistles of St. Paul to the Galatians, Corinthians, Romans, and Ephesians.   8vo.   London, 1823.

LUTHER (Mart.)—Die Bibel u. s. w. nach der deutschen Uebersetzung Martin Luther's Ed. Menken (2nd), 1826.

MEHRING (H. J. F.)—Brief Pauli an die Römer, übersetzt u. erklärt.   (Part First, ch. i.–v., 8vo.)   Stett., 1859.

MELANCTHONI (Ph.) Opera.   Corpus Reformatorum.   24 vols., 4to.   Edidit C. G. Bretschneider.   Hal. Sax., 1834–56.   Vol. xv. (1848.)

MELVILLE (And.)—Commentarius in Pauli Epistolam ad Romanos.   (Edited for the Wodrow Society, by W. L. Alexander, D.D.)   8vo.   Edinburgh, 1849.

MEYER (Dr. H. A. W.)—Kritisch exegetischer Kommentar über das Neue Testament:—Apostelgeschichte, 8vo (Second Edition): Römer (Second Edition), 1854.

MICHAELIS (J. D.)—Introduction to the New Testament : Translated from the Fourth German Edition, by H. Marsh, D.D.   6 vols., 8vo.   Fourth Edition.   London, 1823.

MIDDLETON (Dr. T. F.)—The Doctrine of the Greek Article applied to the Criticism and Illustration of the New Testament.   With Notes by Rev. H. J. Rose, B.D.   New Edition.   8vo.   London, 1841.

MOSHEIM (J. L.)—De Rebus Christianorum ante Constantinum M. Commentarii.   4to, 1753.

NEANDER (J. Aug. W.)—Geschichte der Pflanzung u. Leitung der Christliche Kirche durch die Apostel. (4th Ed.)   Hamb., 1847.   (The same translated: History of the Planting and Training of the Christian Church by the Apostles.   By J. E. Ryland.   12mo.   London, 1851.)

OECUMENII Opera (10th or 11th century). 2 vols., folio. Paris, 1630–31. Vol. i.

OLSHAUSEN (Dr. H.)—Commentar über sämmtliche Schriften des Neuen Testament. (The same translated, 8vo. Edinburgh. Acts, 1850; Romans, 1849.

ORIGENIS Opera (A. D. 185–253). Ed. Bened. 4 vols. Paris, fol., 1733–59. Vol. iv.

OSIANDER (Luc.)—Enchiridion Controversiarum, &c., cum Calvinianis. Witeb. small 8vo, 1614.

PALEY (W., D.D.)—Works. 4 vols., 8vo, 1838. Vol. ii. Horæ Paulinæ.

PHILIPPI (Dr. F. A.)—Commentar über den Brief Pauli an die Römer. (Second Edition). 8vo. Frankfort, 1856.

PHILONIS (Judæi) Opera. Ed. Mangey. 2 vols., folio. London, 1762.

PUSEY (E. B., D.D.)—Tract XC. By Rev. Dr. Newman (1841), re-edited, with Historical Preface, by Dr. P. 8vo, 1865.

——————————— Eirenicon. Part i. Fourth Thousand. 8vo. Oxford, 1865.

REICHE (J. G.)—Versuch einer Ausführl. Erklärung des Brief Pauli an die Römer mit histor. Einleitungen (2 Parts). 4to. Gött., 1832–34.

——————— Commentarius Criticus in N. T., Rom., &c., 4to. Gott., 1853.

ROBINSON (Dr. E.)—Biblical Researches in Palestine, &c. Second Edition. 3 vols., 8vo. London, 1851.

SCHOLEFIELD (Professor J.)—Hints for an Improved Translation of the New Testament. Third Edition. 12mo, 1850.

SCHWEGLER (Dr. Alb.)—Das Nachapostolische Zeitalter in den Hauptmomenten, Entwickelung. 8vo. Tübingen, 1846.

STIER (Dr. Rud.)—Siebzig ausgewählte Psalmen nach Ordnung u. Zusammenhang ausgelegt. 8vo. Halle, 1834–36.

SMITH (J. Jordanhill)—The Voyage and Shipwreck of St. Paul, &c. Second Edition. Crown 8vo. 1856.

STRAUSS (D. F.)—Leben Jesu (Fourth Edition), 8vo, 1840. (The same translated : The Life of Jesus. 3 vols., 8vo. London, 1846.)

STUART (Professor Moses)—Commentary on the Epistle to the Romans. 8vo. London, 1833.

TERTULLIANI Opera (circ. A. D. 160–220). Ed. Rigalt. folio. Paris, 1695.

THEODORETI Opera (Bishop of Cyrus, in Syria, A. D. 420–57). 10 vols., 8vo. Hal. Sax., 1769–74. Vol. iii., Pars i.

THEOPHYLACTI Opera (Archbishop in Bulgaria, A. D. 1077). 4 vols., fol. Venet., 1754. Vols. ii., iii.

THIERSCH (W. J.)—Die Kirche vom Apostolischen Zeitalter. 8vo, 1852.

THOLUCK (Dr. Aug.)—Uebersetzung u. Auslegung der Psalmen. 8vo. Halle, 1843.

——————— Commentar zum Brief an die Römer. 5th Ed., 8vo. Halle, 1856.

VAUGHAN (C. J., D.D.)—St. Paul's Epistle to the Romans, with Notes. Second Edition. 12mo. London, 1861.

WAKEFIELD (Gilb., B.A.)—Translation of the New Testament, with Improvements. 2 vols., 8vo. London, 1795.

WEBSTER (W., M.A.) AND WILKINSON (W. F., M.A.)—The Greek Testament, with Notes, Grammatical and Exegetical. 2 vols., 8vo. London, 1855-61.

WETTE (Dr. N. M. L., de)—Kurtzgefasstes Exegetisches Handbuch zum Neuen Testament.—Apostelgeschichte (3rd Ed.), 1848. Römer (4th Ed.), 1847.

——————— Die Heilige Schrift des Alten u. Neuen Testaments, übersetzt. Neue Testament. Heidelb. (3rd Ed.) 8vo, 1839.

WETSTEIN (J. J.)—Novum Testamentum Græcum. 2 vols., folio. Amst., 1751-52.

WIESELER (Dr. K.)—Chronologie des Apostolischen Zeitalters. 8vo. Gött., 1848.

WINER (Dr. G. B.)—Grammatik des N. T. Sprachidioms u. s. w. (Sixth Edition.) 1855. (The same translated: Grammar of the New Testament Diction. 8vo, 1859.)

WORDSWORTH (Christoph., D.D.)—The New Testament of our Lord and Saviour Jesus Christ, in the Original Text; with Introductions and Notes. 2 vols., royal 8vo. London, 1862.

ZELLER (Dr. Ed.)—Die Apostelgeschichte nach ihrem Inhalt u. Ursprung kritisch untersucht. 8vo. Stütt., 1854.

THE

ACTS OF THE APOSTLES.

1 THE former treatise have I made, *O Theophilus, of all that Jesus
2 began both to do and teach, until *the day in which he was taken
up, after that he through the Holy Ghost had given commandments unto
3 the apostles whom he had chosen: to *whom also he showed himself

A. D. 33.

CHAP. 1.
* Luke 1. 3.
b 1 Ti. 3. 16.
c 1 Cor. 15. 5.

CHAP. I. Verses 1-11.—INTRODUCTION, WITH
SUPPLEMENTARY PARTICULARS OF THE LAST
DAYS OF OUR LORD UPON EARTH, AND OF HIS
ASCENSION INTO HEAVEN.
Introduction—Last Days of our Lord upon Earth
(1-8). **1. The former treatise**—'The first Account,'
'Narrative,' 'Discourse;' *first* being put for *former* [πρῶτον for πρότερον], as not unfrequently
in most languages. [The apodosis to μὲν, instead
of being expressed by the usual δὲ, is. absorbed
by the subject itself, as *Bengel* notes: *Kühner*,
§ 322, 4; *Donaldson*, § 567.] **have. I made, O
Theophilus** — of whom see on Luke i. 3. This
"former treatise" can be no other than the Third
Gospel, of which the present History was designed
to be the Sequel (see Introduction). **of all
that Jesus began both to do and teach** —
that is, 'of all that Jesus did and taught from
the beginning;' as *Bengel, Humphry,* and. others
rightly understand this expression. It is pressed
too far by *Olshausen,* and after him by several
good critics, who consider the word "began"
here [ἤρξατο] as a hint by the historian, at the
outset, that Christ's whole work on earth is to be
viewed but as a *beginning,* while that in heaven is
but a *continuation* of one and the same work; and
that what is to be related in this book is not so
much the Acts of the Apostles, as the Actings—
through their instrumentality—of the glorified
Redeemer upon earth. Nothing, indeed, can be
more true and delightful than this view of Christ's
present work in the heavens; and when *Lange* says
that 'the reins of Christ's kingdom, of which the
Acts of the Apostles relate the first and fairest part,
are in the pierced hands of our blessed Lord and
Saviour, exalted from the cross to the right hand
of God,' he writes not more beautifully than correctly. But to draw all this from the word
"began" here, is (as *de Wette* and *Meyer* justly
protest) to strain the sense of that word. It is
not, indeed, pleonastic, but means simply (as in a
great many similar cases, where *a course of continuous speech* or *action* is intended) 'proceeded' to
say or to do (Matt. xii. 1; Luke xiii. 25; 2 Cor. iii.
1, and in this same book, ch. ii. 4).

2. Until the day in which he was taken up [ἀνελήμφθη]—whither, our historian says not, it being
too familiarly known to need mention. His being
taken up, or His 'Assumption' [ἀναλήμψις]—
already used by this same writer in his Gospel (ch.
ix. 51), and by Mark (ch. xvi. 19), for which Luke
elsewhere (ch. xxiv. 51) uses the equally expressive word "carried," or 'borne up,' [ἀνεφέρετο]—
was one of those great notabilities among Christians, those dear familiar 'household words,'
which to leave but half expressed by the mouth or
pen was only the more vividly to call them up to
the minds and send them home to the hearts of all
that loved Christ's blessed name. Yet the *Ascension* and the *Assumption* of Christ are not quite
the same. The Ascension [ἀνάβασις] was His own

act (see John vi. 62; xx. 17; Eph. iv. 8): the Assumption was the Father's act, translating Him up
from "the lower parts of the earth," to which He
had descended, far above all heavens, to where
and what He was before—only now in our nature
—in all the mediatorial glory to which His finished work on earth entitled Him (John xvii. 4,
5, 24; Phil. ii. 6-11). **after that he through
the Holy Ghost had given commandments unto**
[ἐντειλάμενος] — or 'had charged'—the apostles
whom he had chosen. This may either mean that
Jesus 'chose the apostles through the Holy
Ghost,' or that the risen Saviour 'through the
Holy Ghost charged the apostles' whom during
His public ministry He had chosen. The former
is the sense given to the expression by the two
chief *Syriac* translators, and by *Augustin, Beza,
Olshausen, de Wette, Green,* probably because nowhere else are such communications of the risen
Redeemer expressly ascribed to the agency of the
Holy Ghost. *Humphry* and *Webster and Wilkinson* incline to apply the statement to both acts—
the choice at the first and the charge at the last—
as both "through the Holy Ghost." But to us it
seems far more natural to take the sense, with our
translators, exclusively in the latter sense—that
is, that it was through the Holy Ghost that
the risen Redeemer gave His final charge to
the apostles whom in the days of His flesh
He had chosen. (So the *Vulgate, Erasmus, Calvin, Bengel, Meyer, Stier, Alford, Hackett, Alexander.*) No doubt Jesus, in the exercise of His
public ministry, did everything "through the
Holy Ghost," and it was for this very end that
God 'gave not the Spirit by measure unto Him'
(John iii. 34). But let it be remembered. that after.
His resurrection—as if to signify the altogether
new relation in which He stood to the Church—
He signalized His first meeting with the assembled disciples by "breathing on them," just after
giving them His "peace," saying, "Receive ye the
Holy Ghost;" thus anticipating the great pentecostal donation of the Spirit from His hands (see
on John xx. 22). And it is on this principle, we
believe, that His parting charges are here said to
have been given "through the Holy Ghost," as if
to mark that He was now all redolent with the
Spirit, and that what had been husbanded during
His suffering work for His own necessary uses was
now set free, was all ready to overflow from Himself to His disciples, and needed but His ascension
and glorification to be formally dispensed and
flow all forth (see on John vii. 39). *Chrysostom*
calls attention to the fact that it was while
charging them in words full of the Spirit that He
was taken up. The charge itself was doubtless
just what is recorded in Mark xvi. 15-18 and
Luke xxiv. 44-49, particularly the great ministerial
commission of Matt. xxviii. 18-20.
3. To whom also he showed himself alive.
As the historian is about to relate how "the

1

alive after his passion by many infallible proofs, being seen of them forty days, and speaking of the things pertaining to the kingdom of God :

4 and, [1] being assembled together with *them*, commanded them that they should not depart from Jerusalem, but wait for the promise of the Father,

5 *d*which, *saith he*, ye have heard of me. For *e*John truly baptized with water; but *f*ye shall be baptized with the Holy Ghost not many days hence.

6 When they therefore were come together, they asked of him, saying,

7 Lord, wilt thou at this time *g*restore again the kingdom to Israel? And

A. D. 33.

1 Or, eating together with them.
Luke 24. 43.
d John 14. 16.
e ch. 11. 16.
f Joel 3. 18.
g Isa. 1. 26.
Dan. 7. 27.
Amos 9. 11.

resurrection of the Lord Jesus" was the great burden of apostolic preaching, so the subject is here fitly introduced by an allusion to the primary evidence on which that great fact rests—His repeated and undeniable manifestations of Himself in the body to the assembled disciples, who, instead of being predisposed to believe it, had to be overpowered by the resistless evidence of their own senses, and were slow to yield even to this (Mark xvi. 14). **after his passion** [μετὰ τὸ παθεῖν αὐτόν] — or, 'after His suffering.' This primary sense of the word "Passion" has nearly fallen into disuse on ordinary subjects; but it is nobly consecrated in the phraseology of the Church to express the Redeemer's final endurances, when He "became obedient unto death, even the death of the cross." **by many infallible proofs.** The one word here used [τεκμηρίοις] is well so rendered, expressing as it does more than mere 'evidences' [σημεῖα], and being used by *Aristotle* to denote 'demonstrative proof.' (*Beza* renders it *certissimis signis*). **being seen of them** [ὀπτανόμενος, an unclassical form, here only used, but twice used by the LXX.] **forty days** [δι' ἡμερῶν τεσσ.]—properly, 'through (a period of) forty days.' (Compare ch. v. 19, *Gr.*) *Chrysostom* rightly takes this expression to mean that the manifestations of the risen Redeemer were not, as in the days of His flesh, continuous, but occasional ; and it is to show *through* what a lengthened period those "infallible proofs" of His resurrection extended that the precise duration of His stay on earth is specified. It is worthy of notice that in the Third Gospel the Resurrection and Ascension of Christ are so connected that we could not have been sure from it alone that they had not both occurred on one day, while here an interval between them of forty days is expressly mentioned. But different objects were in view in the two works. In his Gospel the Ascension of Christ is viewed as the termination of His life on earth, and so is related in more general terms ; in the Acts it is viewed in direct connection with the events which were to follow it—particularly those of the great Pentecostal day and the first gatherings of the Church—and so all the information on the subject which was possessed by the better informed, but is nowhere else recorded, is here communicated. Yet the two statements are regarded as contradictory by *Strauss, Teller,* and even *Meyer ;* while *de Wette* thinks that Luke, while writing his Gospel, may have forgotten the long interval that separated the two events. This is just one of many proofs how insufficient mere critical acumen and learning are to throw light on the sacred writings, if not employed in sympathy with their deeper intent. **and speaking of** (or 'discoursing') **the things pertaining to the kingdom of God.** This reference to "the kingdom of God"—as the burden of Christ's last instructions on earth, as it had been of His very earliest teaching—will be observed with interest by those who, in addition to the truths which Jesus taught, would fain catch even His tones, and who love to cast themselves into the very mould of

His teaching, tracing amidst its enduring elements its gradually advancing forms. When at the very outset He said, as did also His forerunner, "The kingdom of heaven is *at hand*," and when at a further stage He said to the Pharisees, "the kingdom of God hath *reached you*" [ἔφθασεν ἐφ' ὑμᾶς] (Matt. xii. 28), it was only as "a grain of mustard seed"—in its most rudimental germ : now it was all ready to stand out in visible form, as eventually it is to cover the whole earth. **4. And being assembled together with them**—not, as in the margin, 'eating with them,' which is to be disapproved. This appears to have been His very last meeting with them. **commanded** (or 'charged') **them that they should not depart from Jerusalem.** Why? Because it was God's high purpose to *glorify the existing economy*, by causing His Spirit to descend upon the disciples at its ancient seat, and on the occasion of the very first of its annual festivals after the ascension of the Church's Head ; so fulfilling the sure word of prophecy, "Out of Zion shall go forth the law, and the word of the Lord from Jerusalem" (Isa. ii. 3, with which compare Luke xxiv. 49). **but wait for the promise of the Father**—or wait for what the Father had promised, meaning the gift of the Holy Ghost, **which ye have heard of** (or 'from') me. The historian here, in reporting what Jesus said, passes from the indirect to the direct form, in order to give the very words used ; and this would have been sufficiently understood without the supplement, **"saith he,"** of our version. The reference is to something said before that last interview, and so must be to those explicit promises of the Spirit which were made to the disciples at the Supper table the night before He suffered (see John xiv. 16, 26.; xv. 26 ; xvi. 7-11). **5. For John truly baptized with water ; but ye shall be baptized with the Holy Ghost not many days hence.** The number of "days hence" (from the Ascension to the descent of the Spirit) we know to have been exactly *ten ;* for as fifty days had to intervene between Passover and Pentecost (Lev. xxiii. 15, 16), and forty of these had already been spent by our risen Lord upon earth, there remained but ten more till Pentecost, when the Spirit was to descend. But Jesus, instead of telling all this to the disciples, uses the indefinite expression, "not many days hence"—doubtless to keep their expectations awake. **6. When they therefore were come together, they asked of him** [Οἱ μὲν οὖν συνελθόντες ἠρώτων, not ἐπηρ. of the received text]—or, 'They then who had come together, asked Him :' either way the sense is the same, the meeting being not a different and subsequent one, but the same one mentioned before. **saying, Lord, wilt thou** [εἰ = אִם in indirect questions] **at this time restore again the kingdom to Israel?** By this time, no doubt, their gross ideas of "the kingdom" had undergone considerable modification, though to what extent it is impossible to say. At the same time, as their question certainly implies that they looked for *some* restoration of the kingdom to Israel, so they

2

he said unto them, [h] It is not for you to know the times or the seasons, 8 which the Father hath put in his own power. But ye shall receive [2] power, after that the Holy Ghost is come upon you: and ye shall be witnesses unto me both in Jerusalem, and in all Judea, and in Samaria, and unto the uttermost part of the earth.

9 And [i] when he had spoken these things, while they beheld, he was 10 taken up; and a cloud received him out of their sight. And, while they looked stedfastly toward heaven as he went up, behold, two men stood by 11 them [j] in white apparel; which also said, Ye men of Galilee, why stand ye gazing up into heaven? this same Jesus, which is taken up from you into heaven, [k] shall so come in like manner as ye have seen him go into heaven.

A. D. 33.

[h] Deut. 29. 29.
1 Thes. 5. 1.
[2] Or, the power of the Holy Ghost coming upon you.
[i] John 6. 62.
[j] ch. 10. 3.
[k] Dan. 7. 13.
1 Thes. 1. 10.
Rev. 1. 7.

---

are neither rebuked for this nor contradicted. To say, as many expositors do, that our Lord's reply was so intended, is not to listen simply to what He says, but to obtrude upon His words what men think they ought to mean. **7. And he said unto them, It is not for you**—*q. d.*, 'It is no business of yours' to know the times or the seasons [χρόνους ἢ καιροὺς]—rather, 'to know times and seasons;' words by no means synonymous in the usage of the New Testament. By "times" [עִתִּים] are meant periods of some length; and here the reference is to the great epochs of prophecy and the intervals between them: by "seasons" [מוֹעֲדִים] are meant the definite times for the occurrence of the predicted events (see the same terms in 1 Thess. v. 1; Tit. i. 2, 3, *Gr.*) **which the Father hath put in his own power**—[ἔθετο ἐν τῇ ἰδίᾳ ἐξουσίᾳ]. *De Wette, Meyer, Humphry, Webster and Wilkinson, Alexander*, translate, 'which the Father hath established by His own power.' But how should the Father's having arranged and determined all these times and seasons make it inexpedient to disclose them? whereas the Father's having reserved the knowledge of them to Himself was a very sufficient reason why they should not be pried into. Accordingly most interpreters rightly adhere to the sense given by our translators. It is hardly necessary to add that, in ascribing these high arrangements to the Father, our Lord by no means implies His own ignorance of them: it is merely an adherence to the current language and form of Scripture thought, that the eternal decrees for the government of the world and the salvation of the Church emanate from the Father; and the import of the statement simply is, that this was not the time for what they were enquiring about, and that their present business and future work were of so different a nature as to make the question unseasonable and irrelevant. Accordingly He adds: **8. But ye shall receive power** (cf. Luke xxiv. 49), **after that the Holy Ghost is come upon you: and ye shall be witnesses unto me** [μοι]—or rather, according to the true reading, 'witnesses of me,' or, 'my witnesses' [μου is read by א A B C D, μοι only by E; and so *Lachmann* and *Tischendorf*]. **both in Jerusalem, and in all Judea, and in Samaria, and unto the uttermost part of the earth.**

We have here the true key to the plan of the Acts, which records the progress of the Gospel,

FIRST, "*in Jerusalem, and in all Judea*"—this in ch. ii. to ch. viii. 4.

SECONDLY, "*in Samaria*"—this in ch. viii. 5, to v. 25.

THIRDLY, "*unto the uttermost part of the earth*" —of this we have a beautiful *anticipation* in ch. viii. 26 to the end, and the *preparations* for it in ch. ix. to ch. xii.; while the *execution* of it is recorded in ch. xiii. to the end of the book.

The Ascension (9-11). **9. And when he had spoken these things, while they beheld, he was taken up; and a cloud** (as to which see on Luke ix. 34) **received** [ὑπέλαβεν] — 'withdrew' or 'removed' **him out of their sight.** It is not for nothing that the cloud is said to have received him ' "out of their *sight;*" for lest it should be thought that He had simply disappeared while they were looking in some other direction, the historian emphatically says, it was '*while they were looking*,' or 'gazing steadily' [ἀτενίζοντες], that He was taken up, "and a cloud received Him *out of their sight.*" On the same principle, the "double portion" of Elijah's spirit, which Elisha sought from him, was promised on the express condition that he should *see* him ascend: "*If thou see me when I am taken up* from thee, it shall be so unto thee; but if not, it shall not be so." Accordingly, when Elijah went up, it is emphatically said, "And Elisha *saw* it" (2 Ki. ii. 11, 12). See also on Luke ix. 32, where of the transfiguration it is emphatically said that Peter, and James, and John "*saw* His glory, and the two men that stood with Him." **10. And, while they looked stedfastly toward heaven**—following Him with their eager eyes in rapt amazement. This is stated as part of that resistless evidence of their senses on which their whole subsequent testimony was to rest. **behold two men . . . in white apparel** ('white garments') [ἐν ἐσθήσεσιν λευκαῖς, in the plural, is better supported than the singular of the received text, and is adopted by *Lachmann* and *Tischendorf*]. They were angels in human form: see Luke xxiv. 4, where the same phraseology is used of angels. **11. Which also said, Ye men of Galilee, why stand ye gazing up into heaven?**—*q. d.*, 'as if He whom ye love were now lost to you for ever.' **this same Jesus** [Οὖτος ὁ Ἰησοῦς]—'this very Jesus,' who, as the babe of Bethlehem, received at His circumcision the name of "Jesus," who by His friends from that time forward was so known, and even by His enemies was styled "Jesus of Nazareth"—this very Jesus, **which is taken up from you into heaven, shall so come in like manner as ye have seen him go into heaven.** This most delightful assurance is couched in terms so emphatic and expressive as to demand special attention. First, two phrases are employed to express the close analogy which there is to be between the manner of His departure and that of His return: "He shall *so* come" [οὕτως ἐλεύσεται], and "*in like manner* [ὃν τρόπου] as ye have seen Him go"—that is, no doubt, as *personally*, as *visibly*, as *gloriously*. Next, the expression "into heaven" is thrice repeated in this one verse, emphatically announcing that the Return would be just as *corporeal* and as *local* as the Departure before their own eyes had been. By these exhilarating disclosures would these heavenly visitants signify to their wondering auditors that the joyful

12   Then returned they unto Jerusalem from the mount called [l]Olivet, | A. D. 33.
13 which is from Jerusalem a sabbath day's journey. And when they | [l] Zech. 14.4.

expectation of their Lord's return ought to swallow up the sorrow of His departure. And that effect it had immediately; for, as this same Evangelist tells us in his Gospel, "they returned to Jerusalem with great joy," as soon as the angelic messengers left them (Luke xxiv. 52).

Remarks.—1. Often has it been observed that while the Ascension of Christ is seldom referred to in the New Testament, His Resurrection is a theme to which its writers are ever recurring. The reason is obvious. In addressing unbelievers, the Resurrection of Christ was the only palpable attestation of His Messiahship to which an appeal could properly be made; and as to believers, it was the resurrection of Jesus which was the beginning of that new life in our nature—stripped of the curse and indwelt by the Spirit—which He brought in for them by being "made a curse for them;" that resurrection, too, was only in order to His ascension, and was soon followed by it, heaven being the proper element of the new life and the natural home of its glorious Head; and accordingly, wherever the resurrection of Christ is brought up to the view of believers, it is to be viewed as necessarily embracing His ascension to the right hand of the Majesty on·high, as the designed, understood, and fitting sequel to it. 2. On 'restoring again the kingdom to Israel,' two opposite errors are to be carefully avoided. The one is, to understand our Lord's check upon the curiosity of the disciples as amounting to a denial that anything of the kind was ever to be looked for: the other, to hold that He here virtually endorses the Jewish views of "the kingdom," that a visible Jewish theocracy over the whole earth was eventually to be erected—only with Jesus as the King—and that He merely checks their curiosity as to "times and seasons." This latter extreme puts quite as much into it as the former takes out of it. Of the *nature* of the kingdom to be restored to Israel, our Lord here says absolutely nothing. For this we must consult the sure word of prophecy. That "the house of David, and the inhabitants of Jerusalem, when the Spirit of grace and supplication shall be poured upon them," shall yet, *as a nation*, "look upon Him whom they have pierced, and mourn for Him as for an only son, and for a first-born," and, as they come forth from the "fountain opened for them for sin and for uncleanness," shall say, "Blessed is he that cometh in the name of the Lord;" and that "so all Israel shall be saved:"—this much, surely, is plain enough. And if Israel be God's first-born, "the root," of which the Gentiles are but the "branches;" if, when "we are Christ's," we thereby become "Abraham's seed, and heirs according to the promise," while they, when brought to Christ, are but "graffed again into their own olive tree:"—will not this re-adjustment, by which "the Jew first" becomes a living reality, be in no mean sense a 'restoring again' of "the kingdom to Israel?" Yes, even although nothing beyond this be to be looked for now, and eventually realized. But should they, over and above this, come to "dwell in the land which He gave unto Jacob His servant, wherein their fathers dwelt, they and their children, and their children's children for ever" (Ezek. xxxvii. 35)—though in no respect distinguished from other Christian nations, save as being the original stock from which they will gratefully own themselves sprung, as the visible people and kingdom of God—this would be such a still more palpable 'restoration of the kingdom to Israel' as to meet all that Christians seem warranted to expect or desire. Be this latter

opinion, however, well or ill-founded, the one thing which comes manifestly out of our Lord's words here is, that the disciples were to get no light from Him as to the *time* of the kingdom; that they had something else to engross their attention than prying into "times and seasons;" that the Father, whose proper business it was, would see to that; and that their souls, as soon as the baptism of the Holy Ghost came upon them, would be so set on fire, and their hands so full of work, in 'witnessing for Him in Jerusalem, and in all Judea, and in Samaria, and unto the uttermost part of the earth,' that they would willingly allow times and seasons to develop themselves to thoughtful observers in the majestic course of events. Not that *all* enquiry into revealed dates is hereby discouraged, else why should they have been given? "Things which are revealed belong to us, and to our children" (Deut. xxix. 29). But this we may safely say, that on the eve of great and engrossing duties a prying curiosity as to times and seasons is unbecoming and injurious to the spirit; that in no circumstances can such studies be expected to issue in the definite and certain disclosure of what "the Father hath put in His own power;" and that the utmost we are warranted to expect from our most reverential and penetrating enquiries, even into revealed dates, is confirmation of what other scriptures direct us to look for, and a more definite conception of the future stages and arrangements of the Divine kingdom. 3. Would that Christians realized more vividly the delightful and soul-stirring identity between the crucified, risen, ascending, and returning Redeemer—that as that very Jesus who ate and drank, and slept and waked, and wept and groaned, and bled and died here below, is He who rose again from the dead, was seen with men's eyes to go into heaven, and now wields the sceptre of universal dominion; so He will at the time appointed *so* come *in like manner* as He was seen to go into heaven! Would not this put substance in place of the shadows in which our faith of such truths is apt to lose itself; and, connecting earth with heaven in that glorious Person on whom our faith reposes, impart to our Christianity the solidity of the one and the brightness of the other? Nor let the promised presence of the Spirit—precious compensation though that is for the absence of Christ—dim the recollection that our only full consolation under that absence is the assurance of His Personal Return (see on John xvi., Remark 3, at the close of that Section); in prospect of which, instead of looking idly upwards, we learn with joyful alacrity to "occupy till He come." (See also on Luke xxiv. 53.)

12-26.—RETURN OF THE DISCIPLES TO JERUSALEM, AND PROCEEDINGS IN THE UPPER ROOM UNTIL PENTECOST.

Return to Jerusalem—The Upper Room (12-14). **12. Then returned they unto Jerusalem from the mount called Olivet** ['Ελαιῶνος]—a form occurring here only in the New Testament. **which is from Jerusalem a sabbath day's journey**—a distance of two thousand cubits, or between seven and eight furlongs, which tradition had long fixed as the proper limit of a Sabbath-walk. But *Lightfoot's* explanation of this from Josh. iii. 4—as if that established the practice of encamping in the wilderness at the distance of 2,000 cubits from the tabernacle, obliging the worshippers to walk that distance to attend its Sabbath-day's services—is not to be relied on. Here again the Tübingen assailants of this book try (after *de Wette*) to make out a contradiction between this statement and

4

were come in, they went up ^minto an upper room, where abode both
Peter, and James, and John, and Andrew, Philip, and Thomas, Bartholomew, and Matthew, James *the son* of Alpheus, and ⁿSimon Zelotes,
14 and ^oJudas *the brother* of James.   These all continued with one accord
in prayer and supplication, with ^pthe women, and Mary the mother of
Jesus, and with his ^qbrethren.
15   And in those days Peter stood up in the midst of the disciples, and

A. D. 33.

^m Mar. 14. 16.
Lu. 22. 12.
ⁿ Matt. 10. 4.
Lu. 6. 15.
^o Jude 1.
^p Lu. 23. 49.
^q Matt. 13.55.
^r Rev. 3. 4.

that of the Third Gospel, that it was from Bethany
that our Lord ascended (Luke xxiv. 50), fifteen
furlongs from Jerusalem, or double the distance
here given.   But this hardly deserves notice, for
the Third Gospel merely says, "He led them out *as
far as* Bethany" [ἕως εἰς B.] in the direction of it,
and probably to that side of Mount Olivet where
the road strikes down to Bethany (see on Luke
xxiv. 50).   Even *Strauss* (as *Lechler* remarks) sees
nothing in this objection.   *Chrysostom's* conjecture
appears to us objectionable, that the mention here
of a Sabbath-day's journey was suggested to the
historian's mind by our Lord's having ascended on
the Jewish Sabbath.   Still less to support it has
Alford's addition to this conjecture, that it was
intended to take off the offence of our Lord's having led His disciples so long a journey on that
sacred day; for surely the Jews, who frequented
Jerusalem at the festivals, would not need to be
told the distance of Bethany from Jerusalem, and
as for the Gentiles, such an explanation would be
scarcely intelligible. - **13. And when they were come
in** [εἰσῆλθον]—rather, 'when they had entered it,'
that is, the city; not 'the house,' as our translators
seem (with *Beza*) to have understood the expression: **they went up into an upper room** [τὸ
ὑπερῷον]—rather, 'the upper room,' probably no
other than that "large upper room" (Luke xxii.
12) where, as this same writer tells us, their now
glorified Lord had so lately celebrated with them
their last Passover and first Eucharistic Supper.
where abode [ἦσαν καταμένοντες]—not 'had lived,'
but 'had for their stated meeting-place,' both Peter,
and James, and John—'John and James' appears
to be the genuine order of these names here; and
naturally so, as Peter and John are so constantly
together in this History.   As to this catalogue
of the apostles, see on Matt. x. 24, with the
Remarks at the close of that Section.   **14. These
all continued with one accord**—knit by a bond
stronger than death.   The word [ὁμοθυμαδὸν] "with
one accord," is worthy of notice as a characteristic
of Luke's diction, and of this book; being used by
no other New Testament writer, save his own associate Paul, and by him only once (Rom. xv. 6);
but by Luke eleven times, and all in the Acts.   **in
prayer and supplication**—for what?   In the first
place, no doubt, for the descent of the promised
Spirit, and for preparedness to receive the gift;
then for courage to fulfil the high commission they
had received, and for the success of it.   These
topics—about all of which there still hung that
darkness which would only deepen their anxiety
and quicken their cries—would suggest other
topics; and as we can hardly suppose that they
would pray on without interruption from beginning to end of each meeting, it seems reasonable to suppose that the intervals would be
filled up by the free interchange of recollections and reflections on the great scenes of the
life on earth of their now glorified Lord, and
the encouragements thence arising.   The sense
of their own fewness and feebleness, in view of the
great work that lay before them, would exercise a
chastening influence upon their spirits, and drive
them into more entire dependence upon that promised Spirit who was to supply their Lord's place.
5

And thus would the great day of Pentecost, when
at length it arrived, find them far better prepared for its high events than if the Spirit had
descended upon them immediately after their
Lord's departure.

> 'Apostles, Prophets, Pastors, all
> Shall feel the shower of mercy fall,
> And starting at the Almighty's call,
> Give what He gave,
> Till their high deeds the world appal
> And sinners save.'—KEBLE.

with the women—those precious women whose
love to their Lord our historian had himself held
up once and again before the readers of his Gospel
(see on Luke viii. 1-3; xix. 49, 55; xxiv. 10).
and Mary the mother of Jesus—here emphatically
mentioned by herself, instead of her presence
being assumed as one of "the women."   But it is
as one of the worshippers of the now glorified One
that she is here introduced.   *This*, it should be
observed, *is the last mention of her in the New
Testament.*   The Romish fable of her Assumption is (as *Alford* remarks) void of all foundation
even in tradition; still less foundation is there
for the monstrous figment of her Immaculate
Conception, now erected into a doctrine of the
Infallible Church.   **and with his brethren.** These
"brethren" of our Lord, whose names are
given in Matt. xiii. 55, had serious misgivings
as to His Messianic claims up to within a few
months of His death (see on John vii. 2-5); but
as we find them now among the disciples in
the upper room, their difficulties must ere this
time have all vanished.   Probably His resurrection and subsequent manifestations, crowned
by His glorious ascension, dispelled their last
doubts.   On the vexed question, whether James
the son of Alphæus, and James the Lord's brother,
were one and the same person, this verse and the
preceding one have a most important bearing.   It
is difficult to see how they could possibly have
been the same, when we find the apostles here
enumerated, including the son of Alphæus, as one
of the classes that assembled in the upper room;
while the "brethren" of Jesus (including "James
the Lord's brother," we must suppose) are expressly distinguished from them as another class.
We may, indeed, suppose that "His brethren" here
mean only such of them as were not apostles (that
is, however, three of them out of four); but this,
surely, is most unnatural.   Every reader of the
words before us would naturally suppose that the
Lord's "brethren," mentioned immediately after
His mother, included all His family relations properly so called, and that they were a distinct class
from the apostles.

The Vacancy in the Apostleship filled up (15-26).
**15. And in those days Peter stood up in the
midst of the disciples**—'in the midst of the
brethren' [τ. ἀδελφῶν] is the true reading here;
and said—now assuming that leading position
among the apostles to which he had all along
been destined (see on John i. 42, and on Matt.
xvi. 18, 19).   But for the beautiful reconciliation
which took place in the presence of all the rest
(John xxi. 15-17), he could not have ventured
on such a step, nor could the others have deemed

said, (the number "of the names together were about an hundred and,
16 twenty,) Men *and* brethren, this scripture must needs have been fulfilled
 *which the Holy Ghost, by the mouth of David, spake before concerning
17 Judas, 'which was guide to them that took Jesus. For "he was num-
18 bered with us, and had obtained part of "this ministry. Now "this man
purchased a field, with the *reward of iniquity; "and falling headlong, he
19 burst asunder in the midst, and all his bowels gushed out. And it was
known unto all the dwellers at Jerusalem; insomuch as that field is called
20 in their proper tongue, Aceldama, that is to say, The field of blood. For
it is written in the book of Psalms, Let "his habitation be desolate, and
21 let no man dwell therein: and, His ³ bishopric let another take. Wherefore of these men which have companied with us all the time that the
22 Lord Jesus went in and out among us, beginning from the baptism of

A. D. 33.-

* 2 Sa. 23. 2.
Ps. 41. 9.
Heb. 3. 7.
1 Pet. 1. 11.
t John 18. 3.
" Lu. 6. 16.
v ch. 12. 25.
w Mat. 27. 5.
* 2 Pet. 2. 15.
y Ps. 55. 23.
z Ps. 69. 25.
3 Or, office,
or; charge.
Ps. 103. 8.
1 Pet. 5. 2.

it quite seemly. But that scene—and perhaps others unrecorded—would pave the way for what he now did, and for which all in the upper room seem to have been quite prepared. the **number of names**—that is, of persons, as in Rev. iii. 4. **together** [ἐπὶ τὸ αὐτό]—not 'in all,' but 'in the same place,' or 'met together' (as the same phrase means in ch. ii. 1, 44; iii. 1; xiv. 1; Luke xvii. 35). **were about an hundred and twenty.** Many, therefore, of the "five hundred brethren" who saw their risen Lord "at once" in Galilee (1 Cor. xv. 6) must have continued there: the number here mentioned including only as many as were congregated with the eleven in the upper room, awaiting the promised descent of the Spirit. **16. Men and brethren, this scripture** [ταύτην is to be regarded as genuine here, on the ground of *internal* evidence chiefly: see *Tischendorf*] **must needs have been** ('behoved to be') **fulfilled, which the Holy Ghost by the mouth of David spake before concerning Judas, which was guide to them that took Jesus.** (The actual words of this "Scripture" are reserved by the historian until he has recorded the account which Peter gave of that wretched man, after which he brings them in at *v.* 20.) **17. For he was numbered with us, and had obtained part of this ministry** [τὸν κλῆρον τῆς δ.ακονίας ταύτης]—lit., 'the lot of this ministry;' but the word came to be used of anything 'allotted' to a person, in whatever way. **18. Now this man purchased a field with the reward of iniquity.** That this verse, and the following one, make no part of Peter's speech, but are a parenthetical piece of information, inserted by the historian, is the opinion of *Olshausen, Bloomfield, Humphry, Webster and Wilkinson,* &c. But the connecting particles 'and (as *Meyer* remarks) the rhetorical form of the passage seem to forbid this view—in regard to v. 18 at least. Accordingly (with *de Wette, Meyer, Alford, Baumgarten, Lechler,* and *Alexander*) we regard these two verses as part of the apostle's speech; though some of the critics just mentioned take part of *v.* 19 as information furnished by the historian himself—and perhaps justly. It may seem unnatural to suppose that the apostle would tell his hearers what 'every dweller at Jerusalem' knew. But Peter's object in this part of his address seems to have been—first, to call attention to the retributive providence which brought Judas to his miserable end in the very field which was purchased with the reward of his iniquity; and next, to point out the remarkable fulfilment of Scripture in his case. As to the statement itself, it has been selected as an example of manifest contradiction to Matt. xxvii. 7. But if we adopt the *causative* sense of the middle form of the verb here used [ἐκτήσατο], and take the meaning to be, 'was the occasion

of purchasing' (*Kühner*, § 250. 2; *Jelf,* § 362. 6; *Donaldson,* 432. (cc) and (cc₁), the statement is quite consistent with that of Matthew, where the purchase of the field is ascribed to the chief priests, but with Judas's money. This explanation, as might be expected, is flung aside by *de Wette* as suggested by 'harmonistic caprice;' and *Alford*—who is too ready to make concessions of this nature—thinks the two statements, as they stand, and without more information than we possess, irreconcilable. But *Beza, Fritzsche, Meyer, Olshausen, Ebrard, Humphry, Webster* and *Wilkinson, Lechler,* &c., see no difficulty in so understanding the historian's meaning. **and falling headlong**—the rope, probably, on which he hung suspended giving way. **he burst asunder in the midst**—lighting, perhaps, on some sharp rock. **and all his bowels gushed out.** The two accounts of the traitor's end differ only in this, that the details are here given from Peter's lips while they were yet fresh, whereas Matthew, writing long after, records that fact only in general terms. **19. And it was** (or 'became') **known unto all the dwellers at Jerusalem; insomuch as that field is called in their proper tongue**—that is, the Aramaic or Syro-Chaldaic tongue—**Aceldama** ['Ακελδαμά = הֲקַל־דְּמָא] **that is to say, The field of blood.** Matthew (xxvii. 8) says that this name was given to the field from its having been bought with the purchase-money of the blood, not of Judas, but of Jesus. But as the catastrophe here recorded gave it another claim to that dreadful name, some probably would connect the name with the one deed, and some with the other. **20. For it is written in the book of Psalms** (lxix. 25)—now we have at length the actual words of 'this scripture, which behoved to be fulfilled concerning Judas,' **Let his habitation be desolate, and let no man dwell therein: and** (Ps. cix. 8) **his bishopric** [ἐπισκοπήν, 'office' or 'charge'] **let another take** [λαβέτω, not λάβοι, of the received text]. The language of two eminently Messianic Psalms is here combined, with a slight verbal variation in the former member of it, but with none in the latter. In both quotations, however, the plural is converted into the singular, for the purpose of singling out Judas from amongst all the predicted enemies of Messiah. For as the apostle discerned in those psalms a greater than David, so he saw a worse than Ahitophel and his fellow-conspirators against their rightful king. **21. Wherefore of these men which have companied with us all the time that the Lord Jesus went in and out among us**—in the close intimacies of a three years' public life, **22. Beginning from the baptism of John**—by whom our Lord Himself was baptized, and introduced to disciples of His

John, unto that same day that he was taken up from us, must one be ordained *ᵃ*to be a witness with us of his resurrection.

23 And they appointed two, Joseph called Barsabas, who was surnamed

24 Justus, and Matthias. And they prayed, and said, Thou, Lord, which *ᵇ*knowest the hearts of all *men*, show whether of these two thou hast

25 chosen, that he may take part of this ministry and apostleship, from which Judas by transgression fell, that he might go to his own place.

26 And they gave forth their *ᶜ*lots; and the lot fell upon Matthias; and he was numbered with the eleven apostles.

A. D. 33.

ᵃ Matt. 28. 15.
ch. 2. 22.
Heb. 2. 3.
ᵇ John 2. 24.
Heb. 4. 13.
Rev. 2. 23.
ᶜ Lev. 16. 8.
1 Sa. 14. 41,
42.
ch. 13. 19.

---

own, gathered for no other end than to have them prepared 'to welcome Him ; **unto that same day that he was taken up from us, must one be ordained to be a witness with us of his resurrection.** Since twelve men had been solemnly set apart by the Lord of the Church for the work which now lay before them, the apostle deems it indispensable that their ranks, so mournfully broken, should be filled up ere the time should arrive for the commencement of the work. No doubt the correspondence of that number with the number of the tribes of Israel (see on Matt. x. 1-5, Remark 3) had been long before observed by themselves, in which case they would regard the want of one as a serious, if not fatal want. The qualifications for the apostleship here laid down as indispensable are very specific, and should be carefully observed. It was not enough to have seen the Lord Jesus alive after His passion : the candidate behoved to have been His constant follower from the very first to the very last, that from his own personal knowledge he might be qualified to testify to that public *life* which His resurrection glorified, and those *claims* which it conclusively established. **23. And they**—not the eleven only, but the whole meeting, **appointed** [ἔστησαν] — rather, ' presented' (as the same word means in ch. v. 27 and vi. 6) ; that is, put before the apostles as candidates for the vacant office, **two**—nor could many more, probably, be found among these hundred and twenty, having all the qualifications expressly demanded : **Joseph called Barsabas** — that is, 'son of Sabas;' **who was surnamed Justus**—or, ' the just.' It was not unusual at this time for Jews to have Gentile names (see ch. xiii. 9) ; but whether ' the just ' was given, in the present instance, to mark his personal character, cannot be known. (This "Joseph surnamed Barsabas"—of whom we know only what is here stated--is not to be confounded with "Judas surnamed Barsabas," mentioned in ch. xv. 22.) From the mention of these small particulars regarding the candidate who was *not* the object of the Divine choice, *Calvin* ingeniously infers that he had been the apostles' choice; and he and others after him moralize on this selection being Divinely thwarted. But there is no reason to suppose that the mention of these particulars had any other design than to distinguish this Joseph from some other or others of the same name. **and Matthias**—of whom also we know nothing, except that the lot fell upon him in the present case. **24. And they prayed.** If Peter was the speaker here also—as seems probable from the expressions used—the change from the singular to the plural is worthy of notice ("*they* prayed," not 'he prayed') ; showing that, whereas before they were listeners to *him*, this prayer was the act of the whole assembly, only by one mouth. **and said, Thou, Lord,** [Σὺ Κύριε]. 'The word "Lord," placed absolutely, denotes in the New Testament almost universally THE SON" (as *Olshausen* correctly remarks); and the words, "**show whom thou hast chosen**," are decisive.

For the apostles are just Christ's messengers—it is He that sends them, and of Him it is that they bear witness. Here, therefore, we have the first example of a prayer offered to the exalted Redeemer, furnishing indirectly the strongest proof of his Divinity. **which knowest the hearts of all men.** Compare with this the thrice-repeated words of Peter to this same Lord but a few weeks before, John xxi. 15-17 (a confirmation of our conclusion that this prayer was uttered by him) ; also John ii. 24, 25, and Rev. ii. 23 : **show whether of these two thou hast chosen** [ὃν ἐξελέξω ἐκ is the true order]—for though both possessed equally, perhaps, the qualifications demanded, only He who knew the heart could tell which was the worthier to fill so important an office ; **25. That he may take part** [κλῆρον]—or 'take the place' **of this ministry,** [according to what seems the preferable reading—τὸν τόπον διακ. ταύτ.] **from which** [ἀφ' ἧς is the true reading] **Judas by transgression fell, that he might go to his own place**—a terrific contrast (supposing the reading just given to be the true one) between the place which the traitor had filled, all uncongenially, and the place which was to prove not only his destined habitation, but his congenial element, here euphemistically styled "his own place." One of the rabbins (quoted by *Lightfoot*) uses regarding Balaam the very same language. **26. And they gave forth their lots** [ἔδωκαν κλήρους αὐτῶν]—rather, 'lots for them,' according to the true reading [αὐτοῖς]. Of this mode of decision we have some notable examples in Scripture (Josh. vii. 14-18 ; 1 Chr. xxiv. 6 ; Jon. i. 17 ; Luke i. 6). But which of the several ways in which the lot was taken was adopted on the present occasion, is hardly worth enquiring. **and the lot fell upon Matthias; and he was numbered** [συγκατεψηψίσθη]. The word strictly means to ' vote down' or 'condemn ;' but here it evidently means to 'vote in;' **with the eleven apostles**—the whole assembly thus deciding that the broken Twelve had now been Divinely filled up.

Remarks.—1. It surely is not for nothing that we are told here of the "prayer and supplication" with which the disciples filled up the interval between the ascension of their Lord and the descent of the Spirit. Never, probably, has there been any copious effusion of the Spirit on any portion of the Church, or any portion of the Lord's vineyard, which has not been preceded, as here, by a season of special "prayer and supplication," and in most cases (it may be added) by active preparation for it. 2. How touching is Peter's way of speaking of Judas here—as "guide to them that took Jesus;" who "was numbered with the apostles" (as if never of them) ; as "this man," the reward of whose iniquity perpetuated his deed in a field of blood; whose wretched end and vacated office had been held up of old in the prophetic Word—how touching is all this from the lips of one who himself had so foully dishonoured his Lord ! But as Peter was from the first a very dif-

7

2   AND when *the day of Pentecost was fully come, *they were all with
2 one accord in one place. And suddenly there came a sound from heaven,
as of a rushing mighty wind, and it *filled all the house where they were
3 sitting. And there appeared unto them cloven tongues, like as of fire,

A. D. 33.
CHAP. 2.
a Lev. 23. 15.
b ch. 1. 14.
c ch. 4. 31.

ferent character from Judas, so the "look" of Jesus and Peter's own bitter weeping were enough to show that both his sin and his sorrow were those of one truly and tenderly attached to his Lord; the meeting of the risen Lord and his broken-hearted disciple on the morning of the resurrection doubtless sealed their reconciliation and cemented them more closely than ever; and the public manifestation of this in the presence of the other apostles, with the renewing to him of the commission to feed Christ's lambs and sheep, doubtless completed all that remained to be done for his conscious and acknowledged restoration to the position assigned him from the first, as leader of the great work of the kingdom about to be begun. In this character, accordingly, Peter rises in the upper room to lay down what had now to be done; and in the discharge of this duty Judas is spoken of, not as a fallen disciple, but as from the first a dead branch on the Tree of life, a stranger in the Lord's house, an alien from the true commonwealth of Israel, as one never in "his own place," until by his own act and deed he "went to" it. And if there was one such in the selectest of all sacred circles, can it be doubted that in the great day there will be found many who have "eaten and drunk in Christ's presence" to whom He will say, "I never knew you"? 3. How very far from a *priestly* attitude towards his fellow-believers is that of Peter here! He leads, indeed, but associates the brethren with himself—asking *them* to choose one or more candidates for the office of the apostleship; he accepts *their* nomination of two; and before the Lord he lays these two for final decision:—here, also, acting only as their spokesman\ in prayer. And is it not in this humble spirit that we find him acting in all his subsequent recorded procedure?—so little ground is there for the lordly assumptions in his name of those who call themselves his successors, and for that ecclesiastical ambition which has proved the bane and blight of many who repudiate Roman pretensions. (On the extension of the apostolate beyond the limits of the Twelve, and its perpetuation in the Church under the form of a prelatical Episcopate, see on ch. xiv., Remark 8 at the close.)

CHAPTERS II.-VII.—"YE SHALL BE MY WITNESSES IN JERUSALEM" (ch. 1. 8).

CHAP. II. 1-13.—DESCENT OF THE SPIRIT ON THE DAY OF PENTECOST—THE DISCIPLES ALL SPEAK WITH FOREIGN TONGUES, TO THE AMAZEMENT OF THE MULTITUDE.

Descent of the Spirit — The Foreign Tongues (*vv.* 1-4). 1. And when the day of Pentecost—the second of the three annual Jewish festivals, designed to celebrate the ingathering of the wheat-harvest, as the Passover celebrated the barley-harvest. In the Old Testament it is called "the feast of weeks," because observed after the lapse of 'a week of weeks,' or seven full weeks from the morrow after that first Passover-sabbath (Lev. xxiii. 15, 16). It was called "Pentecost" by the Greek-speaking Jews, because observed on the fiftieth day after the time just mentioned. (Both names occur in Tobit ii. 1.) was fully come [ἐν τῷ συμπληροῦσθαι]—more correctly, 'was getting fulfilled,' or 'was getting full;' that is, the preceding evening had passed away—which was reckoned part of the day on which they had entered—and the great Pentecostal day itself had

so far advanced as to be 'getting full.' (Compare the same sense of this word in Luke viii. 23, and see on Mark iv. 37, and on Luke ix. 51.) Our translators, though supported by some of the best critics in their rendering of the word, have certainly put more into it than it strictly expresses and seems here plainly to mean. they were all with one accord [ὁμοθυμαδόν]—see on ch. i. 14; but the true reading here appears to be 'together [ὁμοῦ, *simul*, or *pariter*, as in the Vulgate]: in one place—the solemnity of the day perhaps unconsciously raising in them an expectation of something that would signalize it. The conjecture (of *Olshausen, Baumgarten, Lange,* and others) that the "place" here alluded to was one of the temple-courts is a most improbable one. Besides the unsuitableness of such a place, there is every reason to rely on the ancient tradition, that it was the same "upper-room" (ch. i. 13) where, ever since their return from Mount Olivet, they had daily congregated for prayer and supplication, and where a church was afterwards erected which stood for centuries. 2. And suddenly there came a sound from heaven, as of a rushing mighty wind. 'The whole description (as *Olshausen* remarks) is so picturesque and striking that it could only have come from an eye-witness.' The suddenness, strength, and diffusiveness of the sound strike with deepest awe the whole company, and thus complete their preparation for the heavenly gift. Wind is a familiar emblem of the Spirit (Ezek. xxxvii. 9; John iii. 8; xx. 22). But this was not a rush of actual wind; it was only a sound *as of* it (ὥσπερ). *Neander's* description of this—that 'an earthquake, attended by a whirlwind, suddenly shook the building where they were assembled'—has nothing whatever to support it but his own fancy, labouring to account naturally for the supernatural. Had the historian intended to convey this impression, why did he express himself in terms suggesting something so much more unusual? 3. And there appeared unto them cloven tongues [διαμεριζόμεναι γλῶσσαι]—'disparted' tongues,' or tongue shaped, flame-like appearances, rising from a common centre or root, and not 'streaming through the chamber and floating downwards' (as *Neander* romances), but resting upon each one of that large company: beautiful symbol this of the Spirit's *burning* energy now descending in plentitude upon the Church, and about to pour its full tide through every *tongue,* and over every tribe of men under heaven! Even in the heathen poets (as has been noticed) the appearance of fire playing about the head denotes Divine favour (*Ovid*, 'Fasti' vi. 635; *Virgil*, 'Æneid' ii. 682). But it is to more purpose, perhaps, to call to mind how, under the ancient economy, the descent of fire from heaven upon the sacrifices was the appointed and recognized symbol of the Divine presence and favour (Gen. xv. 17; Lev. ix. 24; 1 Ki. xviii. 38; and cf. Exod. xix. 18). *Neander* would represent this whole scene as purely *internal.* 'The glory (says he) of the inner life then imparted to them might so reflect its splendour on surrounding objects, that by virtue of the internal miracle—the elevation of their inward life and consciousness through the power of the Divine Spirit—the objects of outward perception appeared quite changed. And thus it is not improbable that all which presented itself to them as a perception of the outward

4 and it sat upon each of them. And [d] they were all filled with the Holy Ghost, and [e] began to speak with other tongues, as the Spirit gave them utterance.

5 And there were dwelling [f] at Jerusalem Jews, devout men, out of every
6 nation under heaven. Now [1] when this was noised abroad, the multitude came together, and were [2] confounded, because that every man heard them
7 speak in his own language. And they were all amazed, and marvelled, saying one to another, Behold, are not all these which speak Galileans?
8 And how hear we every man in our own tongue, wherein we were born?
9 Parthians, and Medes, and Elamites, and the dwellers in Mesopotamia,
10 and in Judea, and [g] Cappadocia, in Pontus, and Asia, Phrygia, and Pamphylia, in Egypt, and in the parts of Libya about Cyrene, and

Right margin notes:

A. D. 33.

[d] ch. 1. 5.
[e] Mark 16.17. 1 Cor.12.10, 28, 30.
1 Cor. 13. 1. 1 Cor. 14. 2.
[f] Ex. 23. 17.
[1] when this voice was made.
[2] Or, troubled in mind.
[g] 1 Pet. 1. 1.

---

senses might, in fact, be *only a perception of the predominant inward mental state*—a sensuous objectiveness of what was operating inwardly with Divine power—similar to the ecstatic visions which are elsewhere mentioned in Holy Writ.' Such explanations are not only fitted to shake the credibility of the narrative itself, as a piece of sober history, but encourage a pestilent spirit of scepticism in regard to all that is supernatural in the Bible. **4. And they were all filled with the Holy Ghost, and began to speak with other tongues** —real, living languages, as is quite plain from what follows; **as the Spirit gave** [ἐδίδου]—or 'continued giving' them utterance—implying a prolonged exercise of this strange faculty. The thing uttered—perhaps the same by all—was "the wonderful works of God" (v. 11), possibly in the language of the evangelical Hymns of the Old Testament: at all events, it is clear that the speakers themselves understood nothing of what they uttered.

The Astonishment of the Multitude (5-11). **5. And there were dwelling at Jerusalem** [Ἦσαν δὲ κατοικοῦντες]—not, perhaps, permanently settled there (as some good critics understand the words), but come to stay there during the festival, **Jews, devout men, out of every nation under heaven** —language scarcely hyperbolical; for *Josephus* ('J. W.' ii. 16, 4) testifies to the almost universal dispersion of the Jews long before this. At the same time, only the more religious portion of them would think it incumbent on them to come from great distances to the metropolis to keep the annual festivals. **6. Now when this was noised abroad** [φωνῆς = φημῆς, as often in the LXX., 'the noise'], **the multitude came together, and were confounded, because that every man heard them speak in his own language** —each hearing his own tongue spoken by some one of this strange company. **7. And they were all amazed** [πάντες should not, we think, have been removed from the text by *Lachmann* and *Tischendorf*], **and marvelled, saying** [one to another] [these bracketed words are probably not genuine], **Behold, are not all these which speak Galileans?**—not thereby reflecting on the *sect*, so called (for to these foreigners the disciples of Christ would hardly be thus known), but on the *region*, which was proverbially despised by the pure Palestinian Jews; although its inhabitants were their superiors in general intelligence and liberality, "Galilee of the Gentiles" having freer intercourse with the adjacent populations. **8. And how hear we every man in our own tongue, wherein we were born? 9. Parthians, &c.** In this and the two following verses we have probably the historian's own filling up of the question of the astonished multitude. For it will be observed that the different nationalities, whose tongues were spoken by those rude Galileans, are enumerated in a certain winding geographical

order. Beginning with the Parthians, furthest to the north-east, once the most powerful nation of the East, the list passes to the **Medes**—westward of them; from them it goes to the **Elamites**—here meaning the Persians; after them we have the **dwellers in Mesopotamia**—lying (as its name imports) between the Tigris and the Euphrates. The next class has occasioned some difficulty: **and in Judea.** Since none could be "amazed" at the language of Judea being spoken in Judea itself, and the geographical connection between Judea and the countries mentioned immediately before and after it is not very close, some would read 'in Idumæa,' or 'Lydia,' or 'India.' But as "Judea" is the reading of all the MSS. and versions, conjecture must not be allowed to disturb it. *Bengel's* and *Meyer's* idea, that the Jewish dialect is here referred to as something foreign to these Galileans, is evidently a poor explanation. *Olshausen's* is at least better—that the historian, writing from Rome, had in view the position of his Roman readers, to whom the omission of the tongue of Judea itself would have been unaccountable, since it was his object to show how many different languages were spoken by these unlearned Galileans. **and Cappadocia, in Pontus.** Having in his way south come to Judea, the historian in his list now rises to "Cappadocia," in Asia Minor, and further north to "Pontus," though south-east of the Black Sea. **and Asia**—meaning Proconsular or Roman Asia, that small strip of Asia Minor whose western shore is washed by the Ægean Sea, and nearly corresponding to Ionia, whose capital was Ephesus. **10. Phrygia**—in the centre of Asia Minor; **and Pamphylia**—due south of Phrygia, and washed by the northern shore of the Mediterranean; **in Egypt, and in the parts of Libya about Cyrene.** Libya was that region of northern Africa lying immediately to the west of Egypt, whose northern shore was washed by the Mediterranean. Of its western province—Cyrenaica (or Pentapolis)—the capital was Cyrene, here mentioned (the modern Tripoli); a sea-port and an important Greek city, founded B.C. 630, the birthplace of men celebrated in Greek history. Under the Romans immense numbers of Jews settled here, and enjoyed important privileges. Simon, who bore our Lord's cross, was a Cyrenian (see on John xix. 17-30, p. 469); and the Cyrenians had now a synagogue at Jerusalem (see on ch. vi. 9). Antioch was first evangelized by Christians from Cyprus and Cyrene (ch. xi. 20); and among the prophets and teachers at that flourishing seat of Gentile Christianity was Lucius of Cyrene (ch. xiii. 1). From these southern regions our list again ascends to the **strangers of Rome** [οἱ ἐπιδημοῦντες Ῥωμαῖοι, cf. ch. xvii. 21]—or, 'the Roman sojourners'—that is, the Jews of Rome that were sojourning at Jerusalem, **Jews and proselytes** —both born Jews and Gentiles who had em-

9

11 strangers of Rome, Jews and *h* proselytes, Cretes and Arabians, we do
12 hear them speak in our tongues the wonderful works of God. And they
were all amazed, and were in doubt, saying one to another, What meaneth
13 this? Others *i* mocking said, These men are full of new wine.

A. D. 33.

h Ex. 12. 48.
Isa. 56. 6.
i 1 Cor. 2. 14.

braced the Jewish faith. The list having thus swept windingly from north-east to south-west, and again ascended northwards, closes with the following miscellaneous pair. **11. Cretes and Arabians.** Crete (the modern *Candia*) is that large island of the Mediterranean which stretches across the southern extremity of the Ægean Sea, and celebrated once for its hundred cities. From the time of Alexander the Great large numbers of Jews settled there, which accounts for the mention of them here. Arabia is the well-known country lying immediately to the east of Palestine. An impression of *universality* is evidently designed to be conveyed (as *Baumgarten* remarks) by the wide sweep of this catalogue. **we do hear them speak in our tongues the wonderful works of God.** See on *v.* 4.

How the Multitude regard this Phenomenon (12, 13). Two very different views of it were taken. One class seem to be those foreign Jews who, on hearing the wonderful works of God celebrated in their own tongue by persons totally ignorant of it, were simply confounded, and had no theory on which to explain it: **12. And they were all amazed, and were in doubt** [διηπόρουν, or—οῦντο]—were quite at a loss (cf. ch. v. 24; Luke ix. 7; xxiv. 4), **saying one to another, What meaneth this?** [Τί ἂν θέλοι τοῦτο εἶναι;]—'What may this mean?' The other class appear to have been the native Jews, to whom the foreign tongues were unintelligible; and that they were of the hostile party appears but too clearly from the contempt with which they regarded the whole scene: **13. Others mocking** [διαχλευάζ., the strengthened form of the verb, is the true reading] **said, These men are full of new wine** [γλεύκους]—rather, 'sweet wine;' that is, not "new wine," but wine preserved in its original state (which was done by various processes), and which was very intoxicating.

Remarks.—1. The relation which the work of the Spirit bears to that of Christ has already been explained (see on John xvi. 14, and Remark 2 at the close of that Section, p. 448); more particularly its bearing on the glorification of Christ at the Father's right hand (see on John vii. 39, and Remark 3, at the close of that Section, p. 339). But there is another aspect of the Spirit's work of scarcely less importance—the contrast between the new and the old economies, or between the period before and after the descent of the Spirit on the day of Pentecost. On this point there are two extremes to be avoided. The one is, that until the day of Pentecost, the souls of believers were total strangers to the operations of the Spirit, and consequently, however devout and religious men might be under the ancient economy—however God-fearing and righteous—they could not, in strict propriety be called *regenerate* and *spiritual.* Some good critics and otherwise orthodox divines hold this; founding chiefly upon the statement, that the Holy Ghost "was not yet given, because that Jesus was not yet glorified" (John vii. 39). But besides that this is opposed alike to the letter of some passages of Scripture and to the spirit of it all, the general analogy of Divine truth —which proclaims that only the pure in heart shall see God, and which ascribes all sanctification to the operations of the blessed Spirit—points assuredly in a very different direction. Let any one try to enter into some of the breathings of Old Testament saints, even in patriarchal times (see,

for example, Gen. xlix. 18), and especially those of the sweet Psalmist of Israel, and then say if he can find anything, even in the New Testament— however superior in its *point of view*—more characteristic of a renewed nature and of true spirituality. But the other extreme—which would reduce the superiority of the one economy to the other, in respect of the Spirit's work, to one merely of greater *copiousness* and *extension*—is not less to be avoided. The day of Pentecost lifted the Church out of infancy into manhood; out of darkness, about the whole work and kingdom of Christ, into marvellous light; out of the externality of the law into the spirituality of the Gospel; out of the distance and dread of servants into the nearness and confidence of dear children; out of the bondage of sinners into the conscious liberty of the children of God. And though this was not all developed at once, the change dates fundamentally from the day of Pentecost; its peculiar features began immediately to appear in the disciples of the Lord Jesus; and in the apostolic Epistles we find its principles and details unfolded in all their breadth, riches, and glory. 2. The Pentecostal "tongues" have occasioned much learned discussion, most of it as worthless as it is wearisome. The laborious and learned efforts to disprove the miraculous character of these utterances, mostly by German critics, scarcely deserve notice—such as that they were no articulate languages at all, but incoherent shouting sounds, uttered in a state of religious enthusiasm; or, that though a real language, it was their own and mother tongue, only spoken on this occasion in so excited a way as to seem to others like foreign languages. Such explanations, in themselves almost ridiculous, so flatly contradict the statements of the historian which they profess to clear up, that one has only to read the narrative itself, with an intelligent attention to its phraseology, to be convinced of their baselessness. That it was in real articulate languages that the disciples spake "the wonderful works of God;" that these tongues were unknown to those who used them; but that they were recognized by the different nationalities then present to be their own:—this, which is stated in naked terms by the historian, is the only view of the subject which his words can without force be made to express. The difficulties which devout and believing critics have felt in the subject have arisen partly from their finding no evidence of the use of these languages in the subsequent preaching of the Gospel in foreign lands—which they imagine must have been the chief intention of such a gift—and partly from certain things about "the gift of tongues" in the Corinthian Church, (1 Cor. xiv.) But there is no ground for thinking that the Pentecostal utterances were *a permanent gift of speaking in foreign languages,* or that they were intended for any but the immediate purpose which they most completely served—to arrest the attention of multitudes of Jews from every land (compare 1 Cor. xiv. 22, "Wherefore tongues are for a *sign*"), and to afford them irresistible evidence that the predicted effusion of the Spirit "in the last days" had now taken place; that, by settling down on the disciples of the crucified Nazarene, God was in this august way glorifying His Son Jesus; that if they would experience the promised blessings of Messiah's kingdom, they must flock under the wing of this risen and glorified Nazarene; and

14   But Peter, standing up with the eleven, lifted up his voice, and said
unto them, Ye men of Judea, and all *ye* that dwell at Jerusalem, be this
15   known unto you, and hearken to my words: for these are not drunken,
16   as ye suppose, seeing it is *but* the third hour of the day.   But this is that
17   which was spoken by the prophet Joel; And *j* it shall come to pass in the
last days, saith God, *k* I will pour out of my Spirit upon all flesh: and
your sons and your *l* daughters shall prophesy, and your young men shall
18   see visions, and your old men shall dream dreams: and on my servants
and on my handmaidens I will pour out in those days of my Spirit;
19   *m* and they shall prophesy: and *n* I will show wonders in heaven above,
and signs in the earth beneath; blood, and fire, and vapour of smoke:
20   the *o* sun shall be turned into darkness, and the moon into blood, before
21   that great and notable day of the Lord come: and it shall come to pass,
that *p* whosoever shall call on the name of the Lord shall be saved.

A. D. 33.
j Isa. 44. 3.
Eze. 11. 19.
Eze. 36. 27.
Joel 2. 23.
Zech. 12.10.
k Ps. 72. 6.
Pro. 1. 23.
Is. 32. 15,16.
ch. 10. 45.
l ch. 21. 9.
m ch. 21. 4.
1 Cor.12 10.
28.
1 Cor. 14. 1.
n Joel 2. 30.
o Matt.24.29.
p Rom. 10.13.

(though this indirectly) that soon the spectacle now beheld in the streets of Jerusalem would be seen in every land, when, in all the "tongues" of men, the unsearchable riches of Christ should be proclaimed. As to the "gift of tongues" at Corinth, though in some respects it undoubtedly resembled what took place on the day of Pentecost, it differed from it so considerably that we only confuse both by mixing them up the one with the other: each is best explained by itself; and not until we have viewed each independently shall we be able to perceive at what points they meet and part.

14-47.—PETER NOW STANDING FORTH FOR THE FIRST TIME PREACHES CHRIST—THE WONDERFUL FRUIT—BEAUTIFUL BEGINNINGS OF THE CHRISTIAN CHURCH.

Peter Preaches Christ to the Assembled Multitude (14-36). **14.** But Peter, standing up (along) with the eleven—by which they held themselves forth at once as the responsible representatives of the new Faith, lifted up his voice, and said [ἀπεφθέγξατο]—'spake forth,' implying the formality and solemnity of it; unto them, Ye men of Judea, and all ye that dwell at Jerusalem, be this known unto you, and hearken to my words [ἐνωτίσασθε, only here and Gen. iv. 23, LXX.]—an exordium befitting this high occasion: **15.** For these—these disciples, pointing doubtless to the whole inspired company, are not drunken, as ye suppose, seeing it is but the third hour of the day—nine o'clock in the morning (see Eccl. x. 16; Isa. v. 11; 1 Thess. v. 7). This was the first of the three hours of prayer into which the Jewish day was divided, the hour of the morning sacrifice in the temple; and no Jew was allowed to taste anything till he had offered his morning prayer. **16.** But this is that which was spoken by the prophet Joel (ch. ii. 28-32). [*Tischendorf* omits the word "Joel" from his text, but against the strongest authorities.] **17.** And it shall come to pass in the last days, saith God. In the Hebrew and the LXX the expression is more indefinite—'And it shall come to pass afterward,' or 'in the futurity' [וְהָיָה אֲחֲרֵי כֵן, Καὶ ἔσται μετὰ ταῦτα]; but the meaning is the same, as is evident from Isa. ii. 2, and Mic. iv. 1, where "the last days" denote the time of the Messiah. And they are so called as closing up the ancient economy, terminating all preparatory arrangements, and constituting the final dispensation of God's kingdom upon earth. (Compare Heb. i. 1, "God hath in *these last days* spoken unto us by his Son;" ch. ix. 26, "Now once in *the end of the world* hath he appeared;" 1 Cor. x. 11, "They are written for our admonition, on whom *the ends of the world* are come.") I will pour out of my Spirit upon all flesh. As the *copiousness* of this gift is denoted by the 'pouring out' (cf. Prov. i. 23; Zech. xii. 10),

so its *universality* is expressed by its being for "all flesh;" the one in contrast with the mere drops of all preceding time, and the other in contrast with the restriction of the Spirit to certain privileged persons or classes under the ancient economy. Accordingly, the prediction goes on to interpret itself in detail. *First*, there is to be no distinction of *sex:* **and your sons and your daughters shall prophesy**—that is, shall speak by Divine inspiration and with Divine authority. (The foretelling of future events is not necessarily included in the prophetic gift, as meant in Scripture.) This indiscriminate employment of both sexes, with which the prediction begins, would strike the devout part of the audience as remarkably fulfilled in the hundred and twenty inspired disciples, among whom, there can be no doubt, that women would form an observable portion. *Next*, there is to be no distinction of *age:* **and your young men shall see visions, and your old men shall dream dreams.** This is expressed in accommodation to the mode in which the Spirit operated under the old economy, but need not be held to announce a continuance under the Gospel of precisely the same kind of communication. In the New Testament, at least, we find visions and dreams to be rather the exception than the rule. *Finally*, there is to be no distinction of *rank:* **18. And on my servants and on my handmaidens I will pour out in those days of my Spirit; and they shall prophesy.** This also appears to have been strikingly fulfilled in some of the gifted servants of the Church, both male and female. **19. And I will show wonders in heaven above, and signs in the earth beneath; blood, and fire, and vapour of smoke: 20. The sun shall be turned into darkness, and the moon into blood, before that great and notable day of the Lord come.** Great political and ecclesiastical revolutions, issuing in the entire overthrow of ancient and dominant systems, are symbolically expressed in the Old Testament by the derangement and obscuration of the heavenly bodies (as Isa. xiii. 6-13; xxxiv. 4, 5; Ezek. xxxii. 7, 8; Joel ii. 10, 11). This well-known prophetic language was employed by our Lord in his prophecy of the destruction of Jerusalem (see on Mark xiii. 24, 25); and to this the prediction quoted by Peter beyond doubt refers, when he seeks to fix the attention of his audience upon "the great and notable day of the Lord"—the day that closed their day of grace as a nation; the day when, "the judgment being set, and the books opened," they were adjudged to lose their standing as God's visible witness upon earth, and to have their whole civil and ecclesiastical polity swept away. **21. And it shall come to pass, that whosoever shall call on the name of the**

11

22 Ye men of Israel, hear these words; Jesus of Nazareth, a man approved
of God among you [q] by miracles and wonders and signs, which God did
23 by him in the midst of you, as ye yourselves also know: him, [r] being
delivered by the determinate counsel and foreknowledge of God, ye have
24 taken, and by wicked hands have crucified and slain: whom [s] God hath
raised up, having loosed the pains of death: because it was not possible
25 that he should be holden of it. For David speaketh concerning him, [t] I
foresaw the Lord always before my face; for he is on my right hand, that
26 I should not be moved: therefore did my heart rejoice, and my tongue
27 was glad; moreover also my flesh shall rest in hope: because thou wilt
not leave my soul in hell, neither wilt thou suffer thine [u] Holy One to see

A. D. 33.
[q] Heb. 2. 4.
[r] Luke 24.44. ch. 4. 28.
[s] ch. 3. 15. ch. 4. 10. ch. 10. 40. ch. 13. 30. ch. 17. 31. Rom. 4. 24. Rom. 8. 11.
[t] Ps. 16. 8.
[u] Dan. 9. 24. Luke 1. 35.

Lord shall be saved. This prophetically announces the permanent establishment of the Economy of Salvation, to follow on the dissolution of the Jewish State—when salvation, no longer confined to a peculiar people, should be world-wide, embracing "whosoever should call upon the name of the Lord," that is, should believingly invocate that Name at which every knee must bow (Phil. ii. 9-11: see on Rom. x. 11-13, and on 1 Cor. i. 2).

22. Ye men of Israel, hear these words; Jesus of Nazareth, a man approved of God [ἄνδρα ἀπὸ τοῦ Θεοῦ ἀποδεδειγμένον, or ἀποδ. ἀπὸ τ. Θ.]—rather, 'proved to be from God,' **among you by miracles and wonders and signs, which God did by him in the midst of you, as ye yourselves [also] know.** (The "also" here [καὶ] is evidently not of the genuine text.) The apostle's object is to show that Jesus of Nazareth, whom they deemed guilty of a blasphemous assumption of Divine claims, was indeed Divinely sent, and had, in a variety of ways, been Divinely attested to be all that He claimed to be. **23. Him, being delivered by the determinate counsel and foreknowledge of God**—that is, delivered both by God's fixed *purpose* and by His perfect *foresight* of all the steps which that involved, **ye have [taken, and] by wicked hands have crucified and slain**—rather, 'ye, by the hand of lawless persons, crucified and slew.' (The word rendered "ye have taken and" [λαβόντες] is wanting in authority, and the singular, 'hand,' is better supported than "hands.") The 'hand,' however, or agency by which the apostle here charges the Jews with crucifying the Lord of glory is not *their own*, but that of the Roman soldiers, under Pilate's directions (as nearly all good interpreters agree). These are called 'lawless persons' [ἀνόμων]—as in 1 Cor. ix. 21, and 1 Cor. vi. 1, they are called "the unjust" [ἄδικοι]. Three things are remarkable in this statement of the apostle: *First*, the courage which could charge upon an immense miscellaneous street-audience—in the calmest attitude, and in the most naked terms—the death of the Christ of God; and the man that did this had himself, but a few weeks before, quailed at the word of a maid in the high priest's palace. *Second*, the tenderness which tempered this awful charge with the announcement of an eternal purpose of God in that very death, and so paved the way for the exhibition of this crucified Messiah as their now exalted Lord and Saviour. *Third*, the dread harmony with which one and the same event is presented as at once a deed of unparalleled criminality on men's part, and of fixed eternal decree on the part of God. **24. Whom God hath raised up**—thus augustly reversing their sentence of condemnation upon Him; **having loosed the pains of death.** The word rendered "pains" [ὠδῖνας], which signifies 'travail-pangs,' is used here to express 'the throes of death,' which in this case gave birth to a new life; and, as the apostle doubtless had in his eye such passages as Ps. xviii. 4, and cxvi. 3, and the word there used is rendered by the LXX. "sorrows," but in some other places "cords" or "bands," it is probable that the apostle has here combined both ideas, representing, by an unusual figure, this agonizing death of the Son of God—bitter, yet brief, like the pains of labour, and issuing like them in a new life—as "cords" or "bands" vainly binding Him, since God so speedily dissolved them. **because it was not possible that he should be holden of it.** Glorious saying! It was impossible, indeed, that "the Living One" should remain among the dead (see on Luke xxiv. 5); but here the impossibility refers (as appears from what follows) to the prophetic assurance that in point of fact He should not see corruption. **25. For David speaketh concerning him** [εἰς αὐτὸν]—or 'with reference to Him,' (see Eph. v. 23, *Gr.*) The quotation consists of four verses—Ps. xvi. 8-11—which are given exactly as in the LXX. **I foresaw** [προωρώμην, *Dep.*, in Att. = ἑωρώμην πρό]—or, 'saw before [me]' **the Lord always before my face**—kept Him ever before mine eye, in a spirit of believing confidence; **for he is on my right hand**—to succour and uphold me, **that I should not be moved: 26. Therefore did my heart rejoice, and my tongue was glad.** In the Psalm the word is "my glory" [כְּבוֹדִי], which the LXX. render not unfitly, 'my tongue,' whose power of articulation is the distinguishing *glory* of man above the lower animals. **moreover also my flesh**—my body, as distinguished from the soul, just before mentioned. **shall rest**—rest in the grave, as appears from what follows, **in hope**—in the confident hope of a blessed resurrection, as the next words show to be meant: **27 Because thou wilt not leave my soul in hell**—[εἰς ᾅδην, according to the much better supported reading, and as in the LXX.; not ᾅδου, as in the received text]. Though the old English word "hell" did not necessarily denote the 'place of future torment'—the word for which in the New Testament is quite different [γέεννα]—it irresistibly suggests that to the modern reader; and as this is certainly not meant here, the original and now pretty familiar word, 'Hades' [=שְׁאוֹל] should have been retained, which means simply 'the unseen world,' or the state or place into which the disembodied spirit enters after death. (See on Luke xvi. 23.) But is the translation '*in* Hades' a correct rendering of the original words, or should they not be rendered, '*unto* Hades?' They certainly were understood to mean 'in Hades' by, probably, all the fathers; and they are so rendered in the Vulgate, and by *Erasmus*, *Luther*, *Calvin*, and *Beza* (*apud inferos*). For the speaker in the Psalm was understood to say, not that he should not be left to *go into* Hades (or to die by the hands of his enemies), but that he should not

28 corruption. Thou hast made known to me the ways of life; thou shalt make me full of joy with thy countenance.

29 Men *and* brethren, ³ let me freely speak unto you ᵛ of the patriarch David, that he is both dead and buried, and his sepulchre is with us unto

30 this day. Therefore being a prophet, ʷ and knowing that God had sworn with an oath to him, that of the fruit of his loins, according to the flesh,

31 he would raise up Christ to sit on his throne; he, seeing this before, spake of the resurrection of Christ, ˣ that his soul was not left in hell, neither

32 his flesh did see corruption. This Jesus hath God raised up, ʸ whereof we

A. D. 33.

³ Or, I may.
ᵛ ch. 13. 36.
ʷ 2 Sa. Y. 13.
Luke 1. 32.
Rom. 1. 3.
2 Tim. 2. 8.
ˣ Ps. 16. 10.
ch. 13. 35.
ʸ ch. 1. 8.
ch. 3. 15.

be left to *remain in* it—on the contrary, that he should be shown the path of resurrection-life *out of* it; and *Bengel* tries to justify this rendering from three passages in which the same verb and preposition are used in the sense of 'leaving in' (Lev. xix. 10; Ps. xlix. 11; Job xxxix. 14). But since only the last of these passages is to the purpose, and even in it the stricter sense of 'leaving *unto*' would suit equally well, this argument is of no value; and if 'in Hades' is to be defended at all, it must be because the *sense* demands it. But it does not. For precisely the same sense comes out of the stricter sense—'*unto*:' thus, 'Thou wilt not leave my soul unto Hades'—to *remain* there as its rightful prey; **neither wilt thou suffer thine Holy One**—[τὸν ὅσιόν σου = חֲסִידְךָ in קרי]. The usual word for "holy" [ἅγιος, קָֹדֶשׁ] denotes *separation* from a common to a sacred use, which is the most generic and comprehensive feature of a holy character. But the much less usual word here employed expresses *benignity* or *mercy*; one characteristic feature of a holy character being put for the whole. But since in the Psalm itself, according to the present *text*, this word is in the *plural* number—'thine holy ones' [חֲסִידֶיךָ], but in the *margin* is *singular* [חֲסִידְךָ in קרי], the question is, Did the apostle quote the Psalm exactly as it stood in the text *then* used, or did he himself alter it from the plural to the singular, in order to fix its application to Christ? Different critics decide differently; but for ourselves, we cannot doubt that in the text as Peter found it the word was in the *singular* number. For first, though the majority of the existing Hebrew MSS. have the plural reading, a very great number have the singular—no fewer than 180 of *Kennicott's* and *de Rossi's* MSS. Next, the Septuagint version has the singular, in the identical terms of the apostle's quotation, and all the other ancient versions accord with it. Then the apostle Paul, in a precisely similar argument from this Psalm, quotes the word in question in the singular (ch. xiii. 35-37). Lastly, the singular number alone suits the strain of the Psalm; the speaker is one throughout; and the singular number is used from the first verse to the last: how improbable, then, is it that the plural number should have been used in this one word only! **to see corruption.** The word here used [שַׁחַת] might certainly as well be rendered 'the pit,' and more properly, as some think—having regard to the right etymology [שׁוּחַ]. But, since the Septuagint gives it the sense of "corruption," not only here but in several other places [as if from שָׁחַת], it had not improbably a double etymology (like one or two other words). The apostle, at least, must have understood the word in the sense of "corruption;" and if all but rationalistic interpreters are right in holding that the Psalmist's expectation stretched beyond temporal deliverances to triumph over death and the grave, we can hardly make the apostle's argument consist with this at all, save in the sense of exemp-

tion from such a power of the grave as to involve corruption in it. But it will be necessary to recur to this important verse in the Remarks at the close of this Section. 28. **Thou hast made known to me the ways of life—of resurrection-life; thou shalt make me full of joy with thy countenance** —when I shall have sat down at the right hand of the Majesty on high, as the following words more fully express: "In thy presence is fulness of joy; at thy right hand are pleasures for evermore."

29. **Men and brethren**, let me [ἐξὸν = ἔστω, imperat., as in Vulgate, *liceat*; or (more probably), indic., ἐστί = ἔξεστι, *licet*, as in 2 Cor. xii. 4] **freely speak unto you**—make a frank appeal to yourselves, **of the patriarch David—so** called as the founder of the royal line, as Jacob's sons are called "the twelve patriarchs" (ch. vii. 8), as the founders of the Israelitish race; **that he is both dead and buried, and his sepulchre is with us unto this day**—containing all that remains of his mortal-dust. The apostle expresses himself in softened terms (as *Bengel* says), his only object being to show that he who in this psalm was to see no corruption could not be David himself. 30. **Therefore being a prophet**—and. so penning this psalm "in the Spirit," **and knowing**—from the explicit promises made to him regarding his *seed* and *throne* (2 Sam. vii.), which from thenceforward became materials for these psalmodic outpourings, in which he was carried quite beyond himself and his own times into the glorious future of the kingdom of God, (as in Ps. lxxxix. and cxxxii.) **that God had sworn with an oath to him, that of the fruit of his loins, [according to the flesh, he would raise up Christ] to sit on his throne.** The words here bracketed [τὸ κατὰ σάρκα ἀναστήσειν τὸν Χριστόν] are certainly not genuine. [They are wanting in ℵ A B C D, &c., the Vulgate, and nearly all ancient versions and fathers: *Lachmann* and *Tischendorf* reject them, and nearly all critics decide against them. They doubtless crept in from an explanatory gloss in the margin. ἐπὶ τὸν θρ. αὐτ. also is the true reading at the end of the verse.] Leaving out this clause, the whole verse will read thus: 'Therefore being a prophet, and knowing that God had sworn with an oath to him, that of the fruit of his loins He would set [One] upon his throne.' 31. He, seeing this before, **spake of the resurrection of Christ**—not that Peter means to say that David was conscious of not speaking in this psalm of Christ's resurrection and not his own; but that *the prophetic spirit* in David, knowing all that was to come to pass, so directed the thoughts and shaped the language of David, that in point of fact he "spake of the resurrection of Christ," **that his soul was not left** [not κατελείφθη, as in the received text, which has next to no support, but ἐγκατ. and οὔτε-οὔτε] **in hell** (or the disembodied state), **neither his flesh did see corruption** (in the grave). 32. **This Jesus** [Τοῦτον τὸν Ἰ.]—'This very Jesus' (as in ch. i. 11, and *v.* 36 below), **hath God raised up, whereof we all are witnesses.** Thus explicitly and cour-

13

33 all are witnesses. Therefore *z*being by the right hand of God exalted, and *a*having received of the Father the promise of the Holy Ghost, he
34 hath *b*shed forth this, which ye now see and hear. For David is. not ascended into the heavens: but he saith himself, *c*The LORD said unto
35 my Lord, Sit thou on my right hand, until I make thy foes thy footstool.
36- Therefore let all the house of Israel know assuredly, that God *d*hath made that same Jesus, whom ye have crucified, both Lord and Christ.
37   Now when they heard *this*,. *e*they were pricked in their heart, and said unto Peter and to the rest of the apostles, Men *and* brethren, what shall we do ?
38   Then Peter said unto them, *f*Repent, and be baptized every one of you in the name of Jesus Christ for the remission of sins, and ye shall receive
39 the gift of the Holy Ghost. For the *g*promise is unto you, and *h*to your

A. D: 33.
z Phil. 2. 9.
Heb. 10. 12.
a John 15.26.
ch. 1. 4.
b Eph. 4. 8.
c Ps. 110. 1.
Matt. 22.44.
1 Cor. 15.25.
Eph. 1. 20.
Heb. 1. 13.
d ch. 5. 31.
e Zech. 12.10.
ch. 9. 6.
f Luke 24. 47.
g Rom. 9. 8.
h Joel 2. 28.

ageously does the apostle interpret this prediction of that resurrection of Jesus of Nazareth which the whole company then standing before them, filled with the Holy Ghost, were ready to attest on the evidence of their own senses. **33. Therefore being by the right hand of God exalted** [Τῇ δεξιᾷ]—not '*to* the right hand of God' (as *Olshausen, de Wette, Hackett, Webster and Wilkinson*, render the words, against good Greek usage), but "*by* the right hand of God" (as in our version, with the Vulgate, *Luther, Calvin, Beza, Meyer, &c.*)—that is, by a glorious forth-putting of Divine power. This sense suits best with the whole scope of the argument, which was to prove that God had reversed and undone their treatment of Jesus—raising Him whom they slew, and exalting to supreme power and glory Him whom they had brought so low. **and having received of the Father the promise of the Holy Ghost**—that is, the promised Spirit, **he hath shed forth this, which** (in its *effects*) **ye** [now] **see and hear.** (The "now" is an addition to the genuine text.) **34. For David is not ascended into the heavens**—that is, *in the body;* indeed, he had already appealed to themselves whether all that remained of David in the body was not still in the midst of them. Of the *separate spirit* of David the apostle is not here speaking, and therefore no conclusion regarding the state of the disembodied spirit can legitimately be drawn from these words. **but he saith himself, The Lord said unto my Lord, Sit thou on my right hand, 35. Until I make thy foes thy footstool.** 'David himself (argues the apostle) cannot possibly be the subject of this prophetic psalm of his, for he calls the person intended 'his Lord;' and David's sepulchre, with all that remains of his mortal body, is still in the midst of us. But one there was who claimed to be at once David's Son and David's Lord: Him God raised from the dead without seeing corruption, whereof we all are witnesses; Him, too, hath God exalted to his right hand, in proof of which He hath shed forth that promised Spirit whose operations have startled this whole assembly.' **36. Therefore**—to sum up all in one brief word, **let all the house of Israel**—to whom, as the then existing people of God, the proclamation behoved to be first formally made, **know assuredly**—know by indisputable facts, know by fulfilled predictions, know by the seal of the Holy Ghost set upon both, **that God hath made**—for it was Peter's special object to show that these novel and startling events, instead of crossing the purposes and arrangements of the God of Israel, were just His own majestic steps; **that same Jesus** [τοῦτον τὸν I.]—'this very Jesus' (as in *v.* 32, and ch. i. 11), **whom ye have crucified.** 'The sting (says *Bengel*) is at the close:' very true; but he who thus

smites hastens in the very next words to heal: **both Lord and Christ.** (Our version rightly retains the word "both" [και], omitted in the *Elzevir*, though retained in the *Stephanic* form of the received text. The evidence for it is decisive.) Not the "Christ" merely, for that was scarcely enough to bring about the desired impression; but the "Lord" also, whom David in spirit adored, and to whom every knee must bow in subjection—this was fitted to make them "look upon Him whom they had pierced and mourn for Him.'

Glorious Fruit of this first Preaching of Christ, in the Conversion and Baptism of about three thousand souls—Beautiful Beginnings of the Christian Church (37-47). **37. Now when they heard this, they were pricked in their heart.** The word here used [κατενύγησαν]—not classical, but several times occurring in the LXX.—signifies to be 'distressed' (as Gen. xxxiv. 7) and to 'have compunctious visitings' (as 1 Ki. xxi. 28). This, beyond doubt, was the begun fulfilment of one of the brightest Messianic predictions (Zech. xii. 10), whose full accomplishment is reserved for the day when "all Israel shall be saved" (see on Rom. xi., particularly *v.* 26). **and said unto Peter, and to the rest of the apostles**—the convinced now probably crowding about the apostles, and each asking of the one nearest to him, **Men and brethren, what shall we do?** This is that beautiful spirit of genuine compunction which begets tender and eager docility, and which, on discovering the whole past life to have been one frightful and fatal mistake, seeks only to be set right for the future, no matter what this may involve of change and of sacrifice. Of this the most illustrious case on record is that of Saul of Tarsus (see on ch. ix. 6).

38. Then Peter said unto them, Repent. For the meaning of this word, see on Matt. iii. 2. Here it certainly includes the reception of the Gospel, as the proper issue of that inner revolution which they were then undergoing. **and be baptized every one of you.** There is something nobly expansive and exhaustive in this invitation, to every one of that vast audience, henceforth to regard Him whom they had so recently put to death in quite a new light, and, with grief for that dreadful act, to enrol themselves amongst His declared and devoted disciples. **in the name of Jesus Christ for the remission of sins**—baptism being the visible seal of that remission; **and ye shall receive the gift of the Holy Ghost**—the gift of the indwelling Spirit, of which tongues and other supernatural gifts were but the external *attestations.* **39. For the promise** —of the Holy Ghost, the grand blessing of the new covenant (Joel ii. 28, 29) which was to descend upon the Church from the risen and glorified Saviour (see on John vii. 37-39), **is unto you, and to your children—of the seed of Abraham; and—**

40 children, and ¹to all that are afar off, *even* as many as the Lord our God shall call. And with many other words did he testify and exhort, saying, Save yourselves from this untoward generation.

41 Then they that gladly received his word were baptized : and the same

42 day there were added *unto them* about three thousand souls. And ʲthey continued stedfastly in the apostles' doctrine and fellowship, and in

43 breaking of bread, and in prayers. And fear came upon every soul :

44 ᵏand many wonders and signs were done by the apostles. And all that

45 believed were together, and had ˡall things common ; and sold their possessions and goods, and ᵐparted them to all *men,* as every man had

46 need. And they, continuing daily with one accord ⁿin the temple, and °breaking bread ⁴from house to house, did eat their meat with gladness

A. D. 33.
ⁱ Eph. 2. 13.
ʲ Rom. 13.12.
Eph. 6. 18.
Col. 4. 2.
ʲ 2 Tim. 1. 13.
Heb. 10. 25.
ᵏ Mark 16.17.
ch. 4. 33.
ˡ ch. 4. 32.
ᵐ Isa. 58. 7.
ⁿ Luke 24.53.
° ch. 20. 7.
⁴ Or, at home.

next after you (for the rule was, "to the Jew first"), to all that are afar off—meaning the Gentiles, who are expressly so described in Isa. lvii. 19 (quoted in Eph. ii. 13, 17). *Meyer* and others object to this view of the "far off," because Peter did not till long after this come to see the right of the Gentiles to admission to the Church. But this is to mistake the fact ; for Peter had no difficulty about the admission of *circumcised* Gentiles, but only about their admissibility, simply as believers, without circumcision. *Meyer's* own interpretation of the "far off," as meaning the foreign Jews, is to be rejected on this additional ground, that a large number of that very class were among the persons addressed. even as many as the Lord our God shall call [προσκαλέσηται]—'shall call to Himself,' or bring to hear the joyful sound. 40. And with many other words did he testify and exhort. This shows that we have here not the whole of what Peter addressed to the multitude, though what *is* given is doubtless reported as he uttered it ; and, from the following clause, it would seem pretty clear that only the more practical parts of the discourse—only the home appeals with which the discourse was wound up—are omitted, the burden of them, as given in the words immediately following, being deemed enough. saying, Save yourselves from this untoward generation—as if Peter, already foreseeing the hopeless impenitence of the nation at large, would have his hearers press in immediately for themselves, and so secure their own salvation. 41. Then they that [gladly] received his word. [The bracketed word—ἀσμένως—is insufficiently supported.] were baptized [Οἱ μὲν οὖν ἀποδεξάμενοι τ. λόγον αὐτοῦ ἐβαπτίσθησαν]—rather, 'They then, having received his word, were baptized.' and the same day there were added [unto them] about three thousand souls. Fitting inauguration this of the new kingdom, as emphatically an economy of the Spirit ! And was not this first draught of "men" before Thine eye, O blessed Saviour—to whom the whole future of Thy kingdom lay open from the first—when Thou saidst to this same trembling apostle, as he lay crouching at Thy feet in his own boat, overwhelmed by the miraculous draught of fishes, "Fear not, Simon ; from henceforth thou shalt catch men"? As to the baptism of this vast multitude, 'it is difficult (remarks *Olshausen*) to say how three thousand could be baptized in one day, according to the old practice of complete submersion ; and the more so as in Jerusalem there is no water at hand, except Kedron and a few pools. The difficulty can only be removed by supposing that they already employed sprinkling, or baptized in houses in large vessels. Formal submersion in rivers, or larger quantities of water, probably took place only where the locality conveniently allowed of it.' 42. And they continued

stedfastly in the apostles' doctrine and fellowship ['Ἦσαν δὲ προσκαρτεροῦντες τῇ διδαχῇ τ. ἀποστ. καὶ τ. κοινωνίᾳ]—better, 'And they attended constantly upon the apostles' teaching, and on fellowship'—that is, they yielded themselves readily to those instructions which, in their raw state, would be indispensable to the consolidation and establishment of that immense multitude suddenly admitted to visible discipleship, and were found regularly at the stated meetings of the believers for Christian fellowship and mutual edification. This last appears to us the most natural sense of the word "fellowship" here, which (with the article) must be viewed as something on which the baptized disciples attended regularly, *besides* "the apostles' teaching :" to interpret it, however, (as *Olshausen, Alford, Hackett,* and *Baumgarten* do) of 'community of goods' is surely harsh ; for how could they be said to 'attend constantly upon' that? Still less suitable is it to understand the word of 'sacramental fellowship,' which seems clearly intended by what follows : and in breaking of bread. From ch. xx. 7, 11, and 1 Cor. x. 16, it seems pretty certain that partaking of the Lord's Supper is what is here meant. But just as when the Lord's Supper was first instituted it was preceded by the full paschal meal, so a frugal repast seems for a considerable time to have preceded the Eucharistic feast. and in prayers—social prayers, and probably stated seasons for it. 43. And fear came upon every soul—a deep awe rested on the whole outside community (so *Bengel, Olshausen, Meyer, de Wette,* &c.): compare ch. v. 5; Luke i. 65. It seems a mistake to apply this (as *Chrysostom* and *Humphry* do) to the believers themselves. and many wonders and signs were done by the apostles. The word "wonders" [τέρατα] represents the miracles in the light of their *supernatural character,* while the word "signs" [σημεῖα] expresses the visible evidence which this gave of a *Divine presence* with the workers. 44. And all that believed were together [ἐπὶ τὸ αὐτό]—or 'at one place' statedly assembled ; and had all things common. How they carried this out is expressed in the next verse. 45. And sold their possessions and goods, and parted them to all men, as every man had need. See on ch. iv. 34-37. 46. And they, continuing daily with one accord in the temple—observing the stated forms of Jewish worship. and breaking bread from house to house [κατ᾽ οἶκον]—rather (as in *margin*) 'at home,' or, better still, in 'private houses,' or 'privately;' in contrast with the publicity of the Jewish services, yet no doubt at some stated place or places of meeting. did eat their meat with gladness [ἐν ἀγαλλιάσει]—'with an exultant feeling.' and singleness of heart—their new views of Jesus, and of God in Him, opening up springs of thought and feeling which absorbed every other : compare

15

47 and singleness of heart, praising God, and ^phaving favour with all the people. And ^qthe Lord added to the church daily such as should be saved.

A. D. 33.

P Rom. 14.1.,
q Rom. 8. 30.

Eccl. ix. 7, "Go thy way, eat thy bread with joy, and drink thy wine with a merry heart; for God now accepteth thy works." See also on ch: viii. 39. 47. Praising God, and having favour with all the people—their lovely demeanour attracting the admiration of all who observed them. And the Lord—the Lord Jesus, as the glorified Head and Ruler of the Church. So *Bengel, Meyer,* and *Alexander* rightly understand the term here. The transition from "God," in the first clause of this verse, to "the Lord" in this clause, confirms this sense. added [προσετίθει]—'kept adding' [to the church]—that is, the visible fellowship of believers; and as it was the exalted Lord that did this, the statement implies, that both their inward conversion and the courage which made this issue in their outward accession to the company of the believing was of the Lord's gracious operation upon their hearts. daily such as should be saved. This can hardly be the sense [which would require σωθησομένους]. The strict sense of the words is, 'those who were being (or getting) saved;' a form of expression suggested probably to the historian by what he had just said was the burden of Peter's entreaties—"*Save yourselves* from this untoward generation." 'And the Lord (adds the historian) sent this word so powerfully to the hearts of the people that there were daily accessions to the ranks of such as thus saved themselves.' It will be observed that we have bracketed the words "to the Church" [τῇ ἐκκλησίᾳ] as being certainly of doubtful authority. [They are wanting in א A B C, &c., and in the Vulgate and most ancient versions; but they are found in D E, &c., and supported by both Syriac versions. *Lachmann* rejects them, but *Tischendorf* inserts them. If not genuine, they were probably inserted first on the margin as an explanation of the sense, and thence crept into the text of those MSS. that contain them.] Strong as is the external evidence against them, internal evidence pleads strongly for them: first, because we can assign a good reason for their dropping out of the genuine text—from the want of them in the corresponding verse, 41; and next, because of the abruptness with which the whole account of this Pentecostal transaction would terminate without them. So much so that all, or nearly all who reject the words "to the Church" make the first three words of ch. iii. to be the closing words of this chapter—"together" [ἐπὶ τὸ αὐτό]—as does the Vulgate. But this makes very doubtful sense and questionable Greek.

Remarks.—1. The reader will do well to observe, at the very outset, the strictly *Jewish point of view* from which the apostle of the circumcision here addresses his Jewish auditors. The same feature is observable in all his subsequent addresses. , Nor is there any reason to suppose that this was done merely in accommodation to his hearers. *The relation of the new to the old economy* was naturally the first point to be settled by every devout Jew; and to the intelligent Jewish believer in Jesus the exposition of this feature of the Gospel would be invested with intense interest. The apostle's own mind was evidently filled with it, and probably it was to him the one all-engrossing aspect of it, until the vision which he had at Joppa and his subsequent visit to Cornelius enlarged the field of his vision. 2. If under the Gospel "whosoever shall call on the name of the Lord shall be saved,"

surely the perdition that shall avenge a despised and rejected Saviour is fitly bound up with the gracious offer. As "that great and notable day of the Lord," which swept impenitent Israel off the stage of the visible Church, avenged the crucifixion of the Incarnate, and the contemptuous rejection of the risen, glorified, and Heaven-attested Redeemer, so "the acceptable year of the Lord" will, to those who welcome it not, be turned into "the day of vengeance of our God." Jesus is to them that believe a chief corner-stone, elect, precious; but unto them that be disobedient, He is a stone of stumbling and a rock of offence. He that believeth shall be saved; he that believeth not shall be damned. 3. When will Christians cease to regard the decrees of God as at variance with the liberty of the human will? If it be possible to make anything of human language, the 23rd verse of this chapter holds forth the death of Christ as the result equally of both. It is the difficulty of seeing the principle of reconciliation that causes any hesitation about receiving one or other of these, and holding both equally. But let us once begin to reserve our faith in the clear testimony of Scripture, until we are able to reconcile it with some known truth with which it seems at variance, and there is an end to *faith,* as such, in the naked testimony of Scripture, and the rationalistic principle of interpretation takes possession of the mind. Never in the present life will the harmony of the Divine decrees and the freedom of the human will be demonstrated, or even clearly discerned. Whether even in the future state this will come within the range of finite vision admits of great doubt. But even though it should yet be cleared up in the present state, our faith in these truths is not to be suspended until then, nor even then yielded to either or both of them as a homage to *demonstrated,* but simply to *revealed* truth. 4. The Messianic character of the 16th Psalm, with the apostle's argument from it, has occasioned much diversity of opinion among critics. (1.) The rationalistic school—whose criticism goes to the exclusion of all that is strictly supernatural and prophetic in the Old Testament—see in this Psalm only the poetic outpouring of a pious Israelite, who, towards the close of it, is confident he shall not be left to die by his enemies' hand, but be D'vinely protected and abundantly blessed. So *Hitzig, Köster,* and *Ewald,* who make no allusion at all to the apostle's view of the psalm; while *Hupfeld* protests against being bound to follow the apostolic exegesis of the Old Testament (and perhaps he would have said the same of our Lord's too). *Grotius*—whose tendencies were in the same direction, though not developed to this extent—takes the same view of the psalm, but admits a secondary application of it to Christ, as 'not remaining long under the power of death.' How the same language can be supposed to express one person's hope of *not dying,* and another's hope of not remaining *long dead,* it is not easy to see. (2.) *Calvin,* who is followed by some of the best modern critics—such as *Hengstenberg* and *Tholuck,* to whom may be added *Alexander*—views the entire psalm as meant of David himself, but regards the words of the 10th and 11th verses as expressing his assurance of safety, not from any temporal danger, but from the dominion of death and the grave—an assurance of eternal life and blessedness with God; and since this would have been a baseless expectation but for Christ's resurrection,

3 NOW Peter and John went up together into the temple at the ^{*a*} hour
2 of prayer, *being* the ninth *hour*. And a certain man lame from his

Peter, according to them, only seizes on the deeper import of the psalm in viewing it as a prophecy of Christ's resurrection. But however this may be thought to bring out the Messianic character of the psalm, it does not, at least, seem to be the apostle's way of viewing it. If words have any meaning, he lays down the following positions:—That the speaker, in the verses under consideration, expected to rise from the grave without seeing corruption; that this was not true of David himself; and that, as it had been realized in one person, and one only—Jesus of Nazareth—the verses in question must have been intended by the prophetic Spirit to express *His* assurance of resurrection from the grave without seeing corruption. In view of this, *Delitzsch*—whose view of this psalm accords in the main with that of Calvin—contends (in language, however, not very intelligible) that 'David's hope has found in Christ its full objective truth, while for David himself it has in Him also a subjective truth, so that the truth of its lyrical subjectivity has its foundation in the truth of its prophetic objectivity.' The following, after much reflection, is the view which we have been led to take of the whole subject:—That Messiah is the proper subject of the hope here expressed; and since the speaker is one and the same throughout, that Messiah is the primary subject of the whole psalm. This was the view of probably all the fathers, and of most of the elder orthodox interpreters, as it is of *Stier* in our own time. But it is not necessary to suppose, with most of the foregoing expositors, that David, in penning this psalm, thought of any one beyond himself. Nor is there anything in it, until near the close, which might not have proceeded from any saint under the ancient economy. But on advancing to his hope of eternal life and blessedness with God, he expresses himself, under the power of that prophetic Spirit by which he "spake," in terms applicable only to his future Seed. In so doing the Psalmist does not pass *out of himself into Christ*, but only says of himself, and of all saints with him, what, being strictly true only of *One Saint*, becomes true of himself and of them only in its most comprehensive sense and at their own time. Or, to be more explicit, since the resurrection of David's Seed without seeing corruption is the foundation on which rests all assurance of ultimate redemption from the power of death and the grave, we may, in this sense, legitimately see both these truths expressed in the psalm. And whereas we have said that we regard Christ Himself as the primary subject of the whole psalm—since there is no evidence of one speaker in it giving place to another—we mean by this merely that Christ, who, in the days of His flesh, undoubtedly used the 'Psalter' as His manual of devotion, while entering into the earlier part of this psalm like any other saint, would of course find expressed in the latter part of it an assurance of resurrection exclusively His own. Nor does this in the least militate against the use of the entire psalm, in the sense already explained, by David himself, and all the saints of the old covenant, as it can now be employed, with a fuller apprehension of its meaning, by the whole Church of God. *Stier* throws out here a beautiful conjecture, which we cannot help thinking is well grounded; and if so, it throws an important light on the apostolic applications of Old Testament Scripture to Christ. It is this, that as, on His way to Emmaus, the risen Saviour, "beginning at Moses, and all the

prophets, expounded unto them (the two that accompanied Him) in all the Scriptures, the things concerning Himself;" and as the same evening He said to the assembled disciples, "These are the words which I spake unto you while I was yet with you, that all things must be fulfilled which were written in the law of Moses, and in the Prophets, *and in the Psalms*, concerning me;" and then opened their understandings, that they should understand the Scriptures" (Luke xxiv. 27, 44, 45)—they were from that time furnished, not only with the true key to the Messianic interpretation of the Old Testament in general, but with some of the choicest illustrations of it, and this very passage as one of them. And if so, we cannot wonder that Peter, filled with the Holy Ghost, on the day of Pentecost, should, in this his first public address to his nation—and Paul afterwards—fasten and comment so confidently upon so striking a prophetic expression of the resurrection of Christ. 5. Those who hold that Christ has not yet taken possession of David's throne, nor will until the millennium —when He will set it up at its seat in Jerusalem, reigning there in visible glory over the restored tribes of Israel, and through them over the whole earth—seem to us to contradict the plain statement of the apostle here, that the resurrection and exaltation of Jesus to the right hand of God, as both Lord and Christ, until His enemies be made His footstool, is the Divine fulfilment of that prediction. No other interpretation of the apostle's language seems to us possible without violence. 6. What a lively picture have we in the concluding verses of this chapter of primitive Christianity! Bound together by the common tie of a newborn faith in the crucified One as the Christ of God, and the joyful consciousness of life through His name—their faith strengthened, their views enlarged, and their souls fed from day to day through the apostles' teaching and their fellowship in the Supper and in prayer—their very meals were eaten with hearts running over with joy and love; while all— feeling that they were now one family, having one interest — threw their substance into a common stock for behoof of all. What should specially fix our attention here is not the particular steps which this new feeling prompted them to take, and which, in similar circumstances, might quite fitly be taken again. These met the great, the immediate necessities of the infant Church of Christ, but they are manifestly unsuited to an advanced stage of Christianity; nor even in the early Church do they seem to have been long acted upon. But what is so worthy of notice is the all-absorbing character, and the great strength, of religious conviction and spiritual feeling which could make such sacrifices possible. And since the Spirit of the Lord is not straitened, nor has ever been withdrawn from the Church, should we not unceasingly pray and confidently expect that these primitive days may be restored to us, when the Christian community shall be as joyous as in a new-formed world—as loving, as self-sacrificing as at the first; though manifesting it in forms more adapted to the maturity of the Church and of the world?

CHAP. III. 1-26.—PETER HEALS A LAME MAN AT THE TEMPLE - GATE—HIS ADDRESS TO THE WONDERING MULTITUDE.

The Lame Man Healed (1-8). How long after Pentecost the following incident occurred it is impossible to say, but probably not long. **1. Now**

mother's womb was carried, whom they laid daily at the gate of the temple which is called Beautiful, *b* to ask alms of them that entered into
3 the temple; who seeing Peter and John about to go into the temple
4 asked an alms. And Peter, fastening his eyes upon him with John, said,
5 Look on us. And he gave heed unto them, expecting to receive some-
6 thing of them. Then Peter said, *c* Silver and gold have I none; but such as I have give I thee: *d* In the name of Jesus Christ of Nazareth rise
7 up and walk. And he took him by the right hand, and lifted *him* up;.
8 and immediately his feet and ancle bones received strength. And he *e* leaping up stood, and walked, and entered with them into the temple,
9 walking, and leaping, and praising God. And *f* all the people saw him
10 walking and praising God: and they knew that it was he which sat for alms at the Beautiful gate of the temple: and they were filled with wonder and amazement at that which had happened unto him.
11 And as the lame man which was healed held Peter and John, all the people ran together unto them in the porch *g* that is called Solomon's,

A. D 33.

CHAP. 3.
b Luke 18. 35.
John 9. 8.
c Matt. 10. 9.
1 Cor. 4. 11.
2 Cor. 6. 10.
2 Cor 8. 9.
Jas. 2. 5.
1 Pet. 4. 10.
d Matt 7. 22.
Mark 16 17.
ch. 4. 10.
e Isa. 35. 6.
Luke 6. 23.
John 5. 8,
9, 14
f Mark 2, 11.
ch. 4. 21.
g John 10. 23.
ch. 5. 12.

Peter and John. These two are found first associated together by their Master, along with James, as a sacred triumvirate (Mark v. 37; ix. 2; xiv. 33); then by themselves (Luke xxii. 8, and see John xiii. 23, 24; xxi. 20, 21). Now we find them constantly together; but John, as being yet young, only as a silent actor, though unflinching witness for his Master, by the side of Peter (see on ch. iv. 13). **went** (or 'were going') **up together**—were on their way up **to the temple** [τὸ ἱερόν]—in what sense, see on Luke ii. 27; **at the hour of prayer,** [being] **the ninth hour.** The hours of public prayer at the Jewish temple were 9 A.M.; 12 noon; and 3 P.M. This last was "the ninth hour," reckoning, as the Jews did, from six in the morning; and it was the hour of "the evening sacrifice," when a large number were wont to congregate at the temple (Luke i. 10). **2. And a certain man lame from his mother's womb**—and now "above forty years old." (ch. iv. 22). As the Lord Jesus had signalized His power by opening the eyes of a man born blind (John ix.), so the "virtue" that had now "gone out of Him" as the glorified Redeemer, and that now rested upon His apostolic witnesses endued with the Spirit, displays itself in this first recorded miracle by the healing of a man lame from his birth. **was carried** [ἐβαστά-ζετο]—either 'was wont to be carried,' or 'was in the act of being carried' just at that time: the latter sense is probably meant here. **whom they laid daily at the gate of the temple which is called Beautiful.** Thus would his lameness be familiar to all the frequenters of the temple. The gate alluded to was probably a two-leaved gate described by *Josephus*, though not under that name, as the most massive and gorgeous of all the gates, made largely of Corinthian brass, and plated over with gold and silver, fifty cubits high by forty broad ('J. W.' v. 5, 3; and 'Antt.' xv. 11, 3). **to ask alms of them that entered into the temple; 3. Who seeing Peter and John about to go into the temple asked an alms. 4. And Peter, fastening his eyes upon him with John, said, Look on us**—that through the eye faith might be aided in its birth. "On *us*," says Peter, assuming no superiority to himself over his silent and younger companion in the apostleship. **5. And he gave heed unto them, expecting to receive something of them. 6. Then** (or 'But') **Peter said, Silver and gold have I none.** Though all the proceeds of the houses and lands sold by the disciples were 'laid at the apostles' feet,' they touched none of it for themselves, and were personally as poor as before. **but such as I have**

give I thee—"as poor, yet making many rich; as having nothing, and yet possessing all things" (2 Cor. vi. 10). **In the name of Jesus Christ of Nazareth**—'by the virtue that resides in that blessed One whom I invoke,' **rise up and walk**—that the immediateness and thoroughness of this cure might be seen by all. What a lofty superiority breathes in these words! Uttered with supernatural power, they doubtless begat in this poor man the faith which sent healing virtue through his diseased members. **7. And he took him by the right hand, and lifted him up.** Such actions of the apostle were so strikingly like those of his Lord in the performance of several of his miracles (Matt. viii. 15; ix. 27; xiv. 31; xx. 34; Mark viii. 25; Luke vii. 14) that he would seem to have been conscious that his now glorified Lord was now only repeating through him His wonderful works upon earth. **and immediately his feet and ancle bones received strength.** This specification of the *soles* [βάσεις] and *ancles* [σφυρά] comes fitly from "the beloved *physician*," and is one of several internal confirmations of his being the author of this History. **8. And he leaping up stood, and walked, and entered with them into the temple, walking, and leaping, and praising God.** Every word here is emphatic, expressing both the perfectness and the instantaneousness of the cure.

The gathering Multitude filled with wonder (9-11). **9. And all the people saw him**—as they assembled in the temple courts at the hour of prayer, **walking and praising God**—so that the miracle had the utmost publicity, while the man's grateful thanksgivings in the temple would call attention to the Divine source of the cure, and to the Christian instrument of it. **10. And they knew that it was he which sat for alms at the Beautiful gate of the temple**—and so could both identify the man and have ocular demonstration for themselves of the cure; **and they were filled with wonder and amazement at that which had happened unto him.**

11. And as the lame man which was healed held Peter and John. (The true reading here is evidently the more simple one, 'And as he held Peter and John.' If this was the commencement of a Church Lession, it is easy to see how the additional words would be introduced for connection's sake.) How exquisitely natural is this! And what a touching proclamation of the instrumental source of the cure would this clinging of the healed man to his benefactors be! **all the people ran together unto them in the porch that**

12 greatly wondering. And when Peter saw *it*, he answered unto the
people, Ye men of Israel, why marvel ye at this? or why look ye so
earnestly on us, as though by our own [h]power or holiness we had made
13 this man to walk? The [i]God of Abraham, and of Isaac, and of Jacob,
the God of our fathers, [j]hath glorified his Son Jesus; whom ye delivered
up, and denied him in the presence of Pilate, when he was determined to
14 let *him* go. But ye denied [k]the Holy One [l]and the Just, and desired a
15 murderer to be granted unto you; and killed the [1]Prince of life, whom

A. D. 33.

[h] 2 Cor. 3. 5.
[i] ch. 5. 30.
[j] John 7. 39.
[k] Ps. 13. 10.
     Mark 1. 24.
[l] ch. 7. 52.
1 Or,
   Author.
Heb. 2. 10.

is called Solomon's (see on John x. 23) greatly
wondering. How vividly do these graphic details
bring the whole scene before us! And thus was
Peter again furnished with a vast audience,
whose wonder at the spectacle of the healed
beggar clinging to his benefactor prepared them
to hearken to his words.

Peter again addresses the astonished multitude
(12-26). **12. And when Peter saw it, he answered
unto the people, Ye men of Israel, why marvel
ye at this?** Miracles are marvels only in relation
to the limited powers of man and the laws by
which nature is habitually governed. In relation
to the power and will of Him who made nature
and its laws what they are—should He change
them, either less or more, in order to proclaim to
men His immediate presence, and summon their
attention to a message from Himself—they are no
marvel at all. **as though by our own power or
holiness we had made this man to walk?**—*q. d.*,
'Neither the might nor the merit of this cure are
due to us, who are but the agents of Him we now
preach unto you.' **13. The God of Abraham, and
of Isaac, and of Jacob, the God of our fathers,
hath glorified his Son Jesus**—*q. d.*, 'Think not
that we bring you any new religion when we
preach to you Jesus of Nazareth; His claims are
in no wise hostile to the God of our fathers; nay,
it is just the God of Abraham, Isaac, and Jacob
that hath glorified Him whom ye despised and
rejected; the new covenant lay all along in the
bosom of the old, and Jesus of Nazareth is the
life of both; in Him all the revelations of God
from the beginning have their object and end.'
The word here rendered "Son" [παῖς] signifies
any youth, whether son or servant. In the sense
of 'servant' it is used of *Israel* (Luke i. 54), of
David (Luke i. 69), and even of *Christ* (Matt. xii.
18) by our translators themselves. That "Son"
is the real sense here is not at all likely—both
because the usual and proper word for that [υἱός]
is not that here used, and also because the apostle
seems studiously to avoid the use of that word,
keeping himself strictly to the *Jewish point of view*
and the familiar phraseology of the Old Testament.
Now, in the latter half of Isaiah's prophecies,
containing the sublimest Messianic strains, the
name by which the Messiah is most frequently
held forth is 'THE SERVANT OF THE LORD' [עֶבֶד
יְהוָה], who should fulfil all His pleasure; and this
word "Servant" the LXX., in every case but
one, render by the word here used [παῖς]. Thus,
in Isa. xlii. 1, "Behold my *Servant* [עַבְדִּי, ὁ παῖς
μου], whom I uphold; mine Elect, in whom my
soul delighteth," &c.—quoted of Jesus in Matt.
xii. 18; ch. xlix. 6, "It is a light thing that thou
shouldest be my *servant* [עֶבֶד לִי, παῖδα μου], to raise
up the tribes of Jacob . . . I will also give thee for
a Light to the Gentiles, that thou shouldest be my
Salvation unto the ends of the earth;" ch. lii. 13,
"Behold, my servant [עַבְדִּי, ὁ παῖς μου] shall deal
prudently, He shall be exalted and extolled, and
be very high;" ch. liii. 11, "By His knowledge

shall my righteous servant [צַדִּיק עַבְדִּי, to which the
LXX. does not correspond] justify many." Compare Zech. iii. 8, "Behold, I will bring forth my
servant" [עַבְדִּי, in this one case rendered by the
LXX. τὸν δοῦλον μου]; and Phil. ii. 7, 8, "Took
upon Him the form of a *servant* . . . and became
obedient (as a servant) unto death;" John xvii. 4,
"I have glorified thee on the earth, I have finished *the work which thou gavest me to do*. In this
high sense of the term, then, the word [παῖς]
should here, without doubt, be rendered, 'hath
glorified His servant Jesus'—with reference to His
mediatorial *work*, while "Son" [υἱός] is used with
reference to His *Personal relation* to the Father;
and so all the best critics now view the former
phrase. **whom ye delivered up, and denied him in
the presence of Pilate.** The denial here referred to
seems to be that scandalous answer which they gave
to Pilate's question—"Shall I crucify *your King?*"
—"We have no king but Cæsar" (John xix. 15);
thus repudiating all that constituted the hope and
glory of the chosen nation. This conduct of theirs
towards Jesus was the more aggravated, says the
apostle, as it was displayed before Pilate, **when
he was determined to let him go** [κρίναντος ἐκείνου
ἀπολύειν]—or when he had decided to dismiss Him.
14. But ye ['Υμεῖς δὲ]—"Ye," in emphatic contrast
to Pilate, **denied the Holy One and the Just** [τὸν
ἅγιον καὶ δίκαιον]—rather, 'the Holy and Just One.'
The language emphatically holds up One Person,
to whom those two epithets exclusively apply; at
the same time, it implies that the audience themselves either were or should be familiar with it,
as characteristic of the predicted Messiah (Ps. xvi.
10; Isa. liii. 9, 11; Luke iv. 34: cf. John viii. 46;
x. 36). **and desired a murderer to be granted
unto you**—demanding not only the sacrifice of the
pre-eminently innocent, but the acquittal of the
atrociously guilty. **15. And killed the Prince of
life.** With what heroic courage does Peter here
charge his audience with the heaviest of all conceivable crimes, and with what terrific strength
of language, rising into a climax of astonishing
power, are these charges clothed! The word
which in this verse, and in ch. v. 31, is rendered
"Prince" [ἀρχηγός] is in Heb. ii. 10 rendered
"Captain," and Heb. xii. 2, "Author." This last
is evidently the sense here, but with the idea of
'Leader,' as having, by His resurrection, not only
brought in life from the dead to His believing
people, but Himself become 'the first that should
rise from the dead.' There is a manifest contrast
between *them* as the *destroyers* and *Him* as the
Giver of life. But that this Giver of life to men
should Himself be capable of dying, and be slain
by men—this is the wonder of wonders. Glorious, yet awful paradox truly this is—Ye "killed
the Prince of life"! **whom God hath raised from
the dead; whereof we are witnesses. 16. And
his name through** (or, 'on account of') **faith** [ἐπὶ
τῇ πίστει: cf. ch. iv. 21] **in his name hath made
this man strong, whom ye see and know: yea,
the faith which is by him hath given him the
perfect soundness in the presence of you all.**

16 God hath raised from the dead; whereof we are witnesses. And ^mhis name through faith in his name hath made this man strong, whom ye see and know; yea, the faith which is by him hath given him this perfect soundness in the presence of you all.

17 And now, brethren, I wot that through ignorance ⁿye did *it*, as *did*
18 also your rulers. But those things, which God before had showed ^oby the mouth of all his prophets, that Christ should suffer, he hath so
19 fulfilled. Repent ye therefore, and be converted, that your sins may be blotted out, when the times of refreshing shall come from the presence of
20 the Lord; and he shall send Jesus Christ, which before was preached
21 unto you: whom ^pthe heaven must receive until the times of ^qrestitution of all things, which God hath spoken by the mouth of all his holy prophets since the world began.

	A. D. 33.
	^m Matt. 9. 22.
	ch. 4. 10.
	ch. 14. 9.
	1 Pet. 1. 21.
	ⁿ Luke 23. 34.
	John 16. 3.
	ch. 13. 27.
	1 Cor. 2. 8.
	1 Tim. 1.13.
	^o Ps. 22.
	Isa. 50. 6.
	Dan. 9. 26.
	^p ch. 1. 11.
	Heb. 8. 1.
	^q Matt. 17. 11.

With what skill does the apostle use the miracle both to glorify his ascended Lord and to bring the guilt of His blood more resistlessly home to his audience! Three things (as *Alexander* remarks) are here brought prominently forward to enhance the proof of Divine agency in this cure: first, the notoriousness of the man's previous condition,—"whom ye *see* and *know*;" next, the completeness of his restoration,—"this *perfect soundness*;" third, its publicity,—"*in the presence of you all.*" But, it should be added, the emphatic and reiterated connection between *faith in the name of Jesus* and this instantaneous and perfect cure (not the lame man's, but Peter's own faith)was designed to show that this was no mere interposition of Divine power, but an act of the slain, risen, and glorified Nazarene through him, His apostolic witness. But our preacher, like his Master, "will not break the bruised reed." His heaviest charges are prompted by love, which now hastens to assuage the wounds it was necessary to inflict.

17. And now, brethren, I wot (or 'know') that through ignorance ye did it, as did also your rulers. (See Luke xxiii. 34; John xvi. 3; ch. xiii. 27; 1 Cor. ii. 8; 1 Tim. i. 13.) 18. But those things, which God before had showed by the mouth of all his prophets, that Christ [τὸν χριστὸν]—rather, 'the Christ;' but the true reading evidently is, 'that His Christ' [adding αὐτοῦ] should suffer, he hath so fulfilled. The doctrine of a SUFFERING MESSIAH was totally at variance with the current views of the Jewish Church, and hard to digest even by the Twelve, up to the day of their Lord's resurrection. Our preacher himself revolted at it and protested against it, when first nakedly announced, for which he received a terrible rebuke. Here he affirms it to be the fundamental truth of ancient prophecy, realized unwittingly by the Jews themselves, yet this by a glorious Divine ordination. How great a change had the Pentecostal illumination wrought upon his views ! 19. Repent ye therefore, and be converted [ἐπιστρέψατε]—or, 'turn ye,' that your sins may be blotted out, when the times of refreshing shall come from the presence of the Lord [ὅπως ἂν ἔλθωσιν καιροὶ ἀναψύξεως]. It should be 'in order that seasons of refreshing may come from the presence of the Lord;' as nearly every good interpreter admits, and as our translators themselves render this very phrase in Luke ii. 35. The rendering "when" has been borrowed from the Vulgate ('ut cum') and *Beza* ('postquam'); but *Beza's* examples and those of *Scholefield* (who alone now defends it) are not in point; and that rendering is certainly inaccurate. The 'seasons of refreshing' here meant are, as we think, that definite and, to the Jewish mind, familiar period of lengthened repose, prosperity, and joy, which all the prophets hold forth to the distracted Church and a miserable world, as eventually to come, and which is here, as it is in all the prophets, made to turn upon the national conversion of Israel. 20. And he shall send Jesus Christ [Καὶ ἀποστείλῃ]—rather, 'And that He may send Jesus Christ' [the verb being under the influence of ὅπως ἂν of the previous verse], which before was preached unto you [τὸν προκεκηρυγμένον ὑμῖν I. X.]. This reading has hardly any support, (only a few cursive MSS.) The true reading, as all the best and most ancient MSS. (א A B C D E and a host of others, with *Chrysostom,* though the Vulgate and *Origen* have the received reading), and all critical editors agree, is, 'He shall send you the fore-ordained' or 'predestined Messiah, Jesus' [τὸν προκεχειρισμένον ὑμῖν Χριστὸν Ἰ.ησοῦν]. 21. Whom [the] heaven must receive until the times of restitution of all things [ἄχρι χρόνων ἀποκαταστάσεως πάντων]. This far-reaching expression is probably meant to comprehend the rectification of all the disorders of the fall, and the interval "until" that consummation embraces (as *Bengel* remarks) the whole period between the Ascension of Christ and His Second Coming in glory. which [ὧν, by *attr.* for οὓς, sc. χρόνους] God hath spoken by the mouth of [all] his holy prophets since the world began—a loose expression for a chain of harmonious prophetic testimony from the earliest period (as in Luke i. 70). The word "all," enclosed in brackets, is evidently an addition to the genuine text. Here arises a question of some importance : Does the apostle intend thus to intimate that both those two events—the 'seasons of refreshing' to come upon the Jewish nation on its 'repentance and conversion,' and the 'sending of Jesus Christ when "the times of restitution of all things" shall arrive—are to be contemporaneous ? or are they to be regarded as marking two successive periods ? Undoubtedly both are here presented *at one view,* and both are alike suspended upon the nation's repentance and conversion, with the view of shutting them up to that saving change as the one hope of national recovery and the proper preparative for both events. But as that will hold equally true whether those events are to be contemporaneous or successive, it seems clear that the question cannot be decided out of this passage; and interpreters will probably incline to the one view of it or the other, according to their views of the predicted events themselves, and their general conception of the future of Christ's kingdom. To us it appears that the apostle's design in referring here to these 'seasons' and "times" at all was to meet the difficulty which his Jewish hearers would have in understanding why Jesus, if He was indeed the promised Messiah, should, instead of staying on earth to set up His kingdom, have gone away into heaven. His absence, the

20

22 For Moses truly said unto the fathers, A ʳ Prophet shall the Lord your
God raise up unto you of your brethren, ˢ like unto me; him shall ye
23 hear in all things whatsoever he shall say unto you.   And it shall
come to pass, *that* ᵗ every soul, which will not hear that Prophet, shall
24 be destroyed from among the people.   Yea, and all the prophets from
Samuel and those that follow after, as many as have spoken, have like-
25 wise foretold of these days.   Ye ᵘ are the children of the prophets, and
of the covenant which God made with our fathers, saying unto Abraham,
26 ᵛ And in thy seed shall all the kindreds of the earth be blessed.   Unto
ʷ you first God, having raised up his Son Jesus, sent him to bless you,
ˣ in turning away every one of you from his iniquities.

A. D. 33.
ʳ Deut.18.15.
ch. 7, 37.
ˢ Heb. 3. 2-5.
ᵗ Heb. 2. 2,3.
Heb. 10. 29.
Heb. 12. 25.
ᵘ ch 2. 39.
Rom. 9.4,8.
Rom. 15. 8.
ᵛ Gen. 12. 3.
Gal 3. 8.
ʷ Luke 21.47.
ˣ Matt. 1. 21.

apostle tells them, is a necessary part of the Divine purpose; but that fully accomplished, He will as certainly come again from heaven as He has gone to it—"Heaven *must* receive Him;" but only "*until* the times of restitution of all things," &c.

22. [For] Moses truly said (Deut. xviii. 15)—here quoted almost *verbatim*—[**unto the fathers**]. The bracketed words [γὰρ and πρὸς τ. πατέρας] are clearly not genuine, being attested only by a few cursive MSS.; but they are an ancient addition. **A prophet shall the Lord your God raise up unto you of your brethren, like unto me** (*i. e.*, Moses)—particularly in 'intimacy of communication with God,' and 'as the mediatorial Head of a new order of things.' (See.Heb. iii. 2-6.) The apostle takes it for granted that, in the light of all he had just said, it would be seen at once that One only had any claim to be that Prophet. **him shall ye hear in all things whatsoever he shall say unto you. 23. And it shall come to pass, that every soul, which will not hear that prophet, shall be destroyed from among the people.** This part of the prediction is emphatically added, in order to shut up the audience to the obedience of faith, on pain of being finally 'cut off' from the congregation of the righteous (Ps. *i.* 5). **24. Yea, and all the prophets from Samuel and those that follow after, as many as have spoken, have likewise foretold** [προκατήγγειλαν, but the simple κατήγγειλαν is perhaps the better supported reading] **of these days**—the days of Messiah; all of them pointing, with more or less distinctness, to "the time of reformation" (Heb. ix. 10). **25. Ye are the children of the prophets, and of the covenant —and so the natural heirs of all its provisions and blessings, which God made with our fathers, saying unto Abraham** (Gen. xii. 3; xxii. 18), **And in thy seed** (see on Gal. iii. 16) **shall all the kindreds of the earth be blessed. Unto you first God, having raised up**—not (as we think) 'raised up from the dead,' but 'provided, prepared, and gifted,' **his Son [Jesus]** [τὸν παῖδα αὐτοῦ Ἰησοῦν]—rather, 'His servant [Jesus]' (see on *v.* 13). *Lachmann* and *Tischendorf* exclude from their text the bracketed word "Jesus"—perhaps with reason; though the evidence for it is considerable (A B and some other MSS., as against C D E and most versions as well as fathers). **sent him to bless you** [εὐλυγοῦντα]—*lit.*, 'sent Him blessing you;' as it were laden with that blessing of blessings, the forgiveness of sins, as the apostle immediately adds, **in turning away every one of you from his iniquities**—*q. d.*, 'Hitherto we have been looking too much for a Messiah who should shed outward blessings upon the nation generally, and through it upon the world. But we have learned other things, and now announce to you that the great blessing with which Messiah has come laden is

'the turning away of every one of you from his iniquities.'

Remarks.—1. The fact that the first Christians, under apostolic direction, observed the Jewish hours of prayer at the temple as well as their own hours of social worship, from the day of Pentecost onwards, is worthy of special notice. They probably were unaware for some time of the precise relation in which these stood to each other, and would at first be apt to suppose that both services were to go on harmoniously, Christianity being regarded as but a fully developed Judaism. 'Christianity immediately and originally (says *Baumgarten* justly) was nothing else than the fulfilment and completion of Judaism.' Those who believed in Jesus, so far from ceasing to be Jews, only then began to be called and to be Jews in the true and proper sense of the term (see Rev. ii. 9; Phil. iii. 3). Consequently, it was both natural and necessary that the apostles and first Christians should simply follow all the rules of life which prevailed among their countrymen. The temple of Israel is also their sanctuary (see ch. ii. 46; v. 12). The hours of prayer for Israel are also their hours of prayer (ch. ii. 42; iii. 1), &c. But even though the apostles had seen clearly from the first that the one mode of Divine worship was intended to give place to the other, it is not at all certain that they would have ventured of their own accord to discontinue the old services; and it is very certain that if they had, they would have arrested the progress of the Gospel among the timid multitude, and precipitated upon themselves the violence of the ecclesiastics. By degrees only would the waning character of Judaism, after the glory had departed from it, dawn upon their minds; and the more enlightened would be ready to say, even while joining in the temple services, "That which decayeth and waxeth old is ready to vanish away" (Heb. viii. 13). Thus the two services seem to have gone on sweetly together until the question was practically settled by the fall of the temple and the entire dissolution of the Jewish state. And, if we mistake not, analogous cases will be found in the history of the Christian Church, in which the reward of patience and caution has been similarly reaped. When Luther, in 1522, was shut up in the castle of Wartburg, Carlstadt was endangering all that had been gained by insisting, at Wittemberg, on the laity partaking of the cup in the Eucharist ere yet they had light as to their warrant to do so. Hearing of this, the reformer stole away from his retreat, and, re-appearing at Wittemberg, at the risk of his life, allowed the people to receive the sacrament in the form most edifying to themselves. This restored the broken peace, and soon the half-instructed people themselves demanded and received the cup. In the following year Zwingli, at Zürich, acted upon the same principle, when, though he had opened the eyes of the Council and

21

4 AND as they spake unto the people, the priests, and the [1]captain of
2 the temple, and the Sadducees, came upon them, being [a]grieved that
they taught the people, and preached through Jesus the resurrection from
3 the dead. And they laid hands on them, and put *them* in hold unto
4 the next day: for it was now eventide. Howbeit many of them which
heard the word believed; and the number of the men was about five
thousand.
5 And it came to pass on the morrow, that their rulers, and elders, and
6 scribes, and [b] Annas the high priest, and Caiaphas, and John, and Alex-

A. D. 33.

CHAP. 4.
1 Or, ruler,
Luke 22. 4.
ch. 5. 24.
[a] Neh 2. 10.
Job 5. 2.
Eccl. 4. 4.
[b] Luke 3. 2.
John 11. 49.
John 18. 13.

the more intelligent classes to the unscriptural character of certain popish usages, he yet would not give his consent to the public abolition of them until the people generally should be prepared to go along with them; and he was soon rewarded by a popular demand for what, had it been done before, would have had to be forced upon them. Let the wise consider this. 2. The intelligent reader will again observe how exclusively the apostle confines himself to *the Jewish point of view* in preaching the Gospel—insisting that it was the God of their fathers who had sent Jesus, and who, when they slew Him, raised Him from the dead and gave Him glory; that all this was but the fulfilment of the prophetic testimony from the beginning; and therefore, that while in now receiving Jesus they would only be repairing the error which in ignorance they had already committed, and would thus experience the blessedness promised to their nation, they would, by rejecting Him, consummate their guilt and seal their national doom. This was the one view of Christ's claims which the Jewish mind was then capable of taking in, and probably all that then occupied the mind even of the apostle himself; and as it brings out the true relation between the old and the new economies, and the harmony of Scripture, it is never to be lost sight of, even under the more comprehensive views of Christianity and the Church which the accession of the Gentiles has introduced. (See on ch. ii. 14-47, Remark 1, at the close of that Section.) 3. When the apostle says that "heaven must receive" the ascended Saviour "*until the times of restitution of all things*" (whatever that may definitely mean), it seems impossible to doubt that he meant to announce a *protracted absence*—an absence of uncertain length, no doubt, but yet of extended duration. When, therefore, we find our Lord enjoining watchfulness in the prospect of His coming, and preparedness for an unexpected return, and His apostles, in the same strain, telling us that He will come as a thief in the night, and so forth, we must take care that we frame no theories of His Second Coming that will not admit of both views of it; and, tried by this test, some theories, now engrossing the attention of many warm-hearted Christians, will, as we think, be found wanting. 4. With what skill and power does the apostle, seeing himself surrounded and gazed on by a wondering multitude, seize his opportunity, and, founding on resistless facts, drive home to the conscience of his auditors their guilt in crucifying the Lord of Glory; then soothe their awakened minds by assurances of forgiveness on turning to the Lord, and a glorious future as soon as this shall come to pass—to terminate with the Personal Return of Christ from the heavens whither He has ascended—ending all with warnings, from their own Scriptures, to submit to Him if they would not perish, and with calls to receive from Him the blessings of salvation.

CHAP. IV. 1-37.—PETER AND JOHN BEFORE

THE SANHEDRIM—THEIR DISMISSAL AND RETURN TO THE ASSEMBLED DISCIPLES, WHO, ON HEARING THEIR REPORT, COMMIT THEIR CAUSE TO THE LORD IN PRAYER—THE ASTONISHING ANSWER, AND ITS RESULTS.
Peter and John arrested—Prodigious increase of disciples (1-4). 1. And as they spake unto the people, the priests, and the captain of the temple [ὁ στρατηγὸς τοῦ ἱεροῦ]—the commanding officer of the Levitical guard in charge of the temple, annoyed at the disturbance created around it, and the Sadducees—"who say that there is no resurrection" (ch. xxiii. 8), irritated at the apostles for preaching the resurrection of Jesus, which, if true, demolished the Sadducean doctrine, came upon them, 2. Being grieved that they taught the people, and preached through Jesus the resurrection from the dead [ἐν τῷ I.]—rather, 'preached in Jesus the resurrection from the dead.' It was not the resurrection from the dead as a *doctrine* which they insisted on, but the *fact* that Jesus had risen from the dead; but as the doctrine followed irresistibly from the fact, the enmity of this sect against the preachers was immediately aroused. *Alexander* properly calls attention to the emphatic form here employed [τὴν ἀνάστασιν τὴν ἐκ νεκρῶν: cf. Luke xx. 35]—'the resurrection, that from the dead,' as expressing a rising very different from anything which the Gentile readers of this book would ever dream of. 3. And they laid hands on them, and put them in hold unto the next day: for it was now eventide—the miracle having been wrought so late as three o'clock P.M. (ch. iii. 1). 4. Howbeit many of them which heard the word believed. For illustration of this delightful statement, *Calvin* refers to 2 Tim. ii. 9 (where, by the way, a play upon the words *bound* and *bonds* will be observed), "Wherein I suffer trouble, even unto bonds [δεσμῶν], but the word of God is not bound" [δέδεται]: and the number of the men [τ. ἀνδρῶν]—meaning probably the males, exclusive of women; though the word sometimes includes both, was [ἐγενήθη]—'became,' or 'came to be' in all about five thousand. And this in Jerusalem, where the means of detecting the imposture or crushing the fanaticism—if such it had been—were within every one's reach, and where there was every inducement to sift it to the bottom. [*Tischendorf* excludes ὡσεὶ from his text. *Lachmann* brackets it in the form of ὡς; *Alford* is doubtful about it. But the evidence for it rather preponderates, and the historian would probably not give the number so definitely.]
Peter, questioned about the Miracle, courageously testifies to Jesus (5-12). 5. And it came to pass on the morrow, that their rulers, and elders, and scribes. This was a regular meeting of the Sanhedrim (see on Matt. ii. 4). 6. And Annas the high priest, and Caiaphas. See on Luke iii. 2 (in opening Remarks on Matt. iii.) and on John xviii. 13 (in exposition of Mark xiv. 53-72, pp. 202, 203). and John, and Alexander—of whom nothing is known, and as many as were of the kindred of

ander, and as many as were of the kindred of the high priest, were
7 gathered together at Jerusalem. And when they had set them in the
midst, they asked, *c* By what power, or by what name, have ye done this?
8 Then *d* Peter, filled with the Holy Ghost, said unto them, Ye rulers of
9 the people, and elders of Israel, if we this day be examined of the good
10 deed done to the impotent man, by what means he is made whole; be it
known unto you all, and to all the people of Israel, *e* that by the name of
Jesus Christ of Nazareth, whom ye crucified, whom God raised from the
11 dead, *even* by him doth this man stand here before you whole. This
f is the stone which was set at nought of you builders, which is become
12 the head of the corner. Neither *g* is there salvation in any other: for
there is none other name under heaven given among men whereby we
must be saved.
13. Now when they saw the boldness of Peter and John, and *h* perceived
that they were unlearned and ignorant men, they marvelled; and they
14 took knowledge of them, that they had been with Jesus. And beholding
the man which was healed standing with them, they could say nothing
15 against it. But, when they had commanded them to go aside out of
16 the council, they conferred among themselves, saying, *i* What shall we
do to these men? for that indeed a notable miracle hath been done by

A. D. 33.

c Ex. 2. 14.
Matt. 21.23.
ch. 7. 27.
d Matt. 10 19.
Mark 13.11.
Luke 12. 11,
12.
Luke 21. 14,
15.
e ch. 3. 6.
f Ps. 118. 22.
Isa. 28. 16.
Matt. 21.42.
Rom. 9. 33.
g Matt. 1. 21.
ch. 10. 43.
Rom. 3. 24.
6.
1 Tim. 2. 5,
6.
Heb 2. 3.
h Matt. 11.25.
1 Cor. 1. 27.
i John 11. 47.
John 12 19.

the high priest. The public influence which Annas had acquired may be judged of by this, that though the Romans made a practice of setting up and displacing the high priests at pleasure, for their own political ends, the office was filled by Caiaphas and five of his sons in succession. **were gathered together at Jerusalem** [εἰς I., the received reading, has scarcely any support: ἐν is evidently the genuine text]. The true sense, according to the arrangement of the words, is, 'their rulers in Jerusalem were gathered together;' that is, as many of them as were in the city at that time. **7. And when they had set them in the midst**—the council sitting in a semicircle (as *Maimonides*, quoted by *Lightfoot*, says), **they asked, By what power, or by what name, have ye done this?**—thus admitting the reality of the miracle, which, indeed, afterwards they confess themselves unable to deny (v. 16). **8. Then Peter, filled with the Holy Ghost**—according to the Lord's own promise (Mark xiii. 11; Luke xxi. 15), **said unto them, Ye rulers of the people, and elders of Israel, 9. If we this day be examined of the good deed done to the impotent man, by what means he is made whole** [ἐν τίνι—or rather, 'by whom he is made whole:' both the question itself and the answer to it in the next verse seem to favour this latter sense. **10. Be it known unto you all, and to all the people of Israel**—as if emitting a formal judicial testimony to the entire nation through its rulers, now solemnly convened, **that by the name of Jesus Christ of Nazareth, whom ye crucified, whom God raised from the dead** (see on ch. iii. 13, &c., and Remark 2 at the close of that Section), **even by him doth this man stand here before you whole**—for it appears from v. 14 that the healed man was at that moment before their eyes. **11. This is the stone which was set at nought of you builders, which is become the head of the corner.** This application of Ps. cxviii. 22, already made by our Lord Himself before some of the same "builders" (Matt. xxi. 42), is here repeated with peculiar propriety after the deed of rejection had been consummated, and the rejected One had, by His exaltation to the right hand of the Majesty on high, become "the head of the corner." **12. Neither is there salvation in any other: for there is none other name under heaven given among men whereby we**

must be saved. How sublimely does the apostle, in these closing words, shut up these rulers of Israel to Jesus for salvation, and in what universal and emphatic terms does he hold up his Lord as the one Hope of men! It is not 'may,' but *"must be saved,"* if saved at all, in this only way. *How the Council Feel and Act* (13-22). **13. Now when they saw the boldness of Peter and John, and perceived that they were unlearned and ignorant men.** By the one word [ἀγράμματοι] they mean 'men uninstructed in the learning of the Jewish schools;' and by the other [ἰδιῶται], 'men of the common sort,' from whom such intelligence and such a bearing were not to be looked for. **they took knowledge of them** [ἐπεγίνωσκον]—or 're-cognized them,' **that they had been with Jesus**—or identified them as persons whom they had seen before in company with Jesus; their wonder sharpening their recollection. So *Meyer, Alford, Baumgarten, Hackett, Lechler,* &c., understand this remarkable statement; and perhaps they are right. But the historian's remark may mean rather, that in the whole demeanour of these men the Council observed what irresistibly brought Jesus Himself before their view, as He had stood before them but a few weeks before, and convinced them that their intercourse with Him was what had stamped upon them this calm, lofty heroism :—'We thought we had got rid of Him; but, lo! He re-appears in these men, and all that troubled us in the Nazarene Himself has yet to be put down in these His disciples.' What a testimony to these primitive witnesses! Would that the same could be said of their successors! **14. And beholding** [τὲ is the true particle here: δὲ has hardly any support]; **'Beholding also' the man which was healed standing with them**—no longer "laid at the gate" (ch. iii. 2), **they could say nothing against it. 15. But, when they had commanded them to go aside out of the council, they conferred**—or 'proceeded to confer' [συνέβαλλον is better supported than συνέβαλον of the received text] **among themselves, 16. Saying, &c.** Though the apostles were not present at these consultations, others who afterwards became "obedient to the faith" may have been; not to speak of Saul of Tarsus: from them our historian might easily learn what is related in this verse and the next. **What shall we do to these men? for that indeed**

23

them *is* manifest *j* to all them that dwell in Jerusalem; and we cannot
17 deny *it.* But that it spread no further among the people, let us straitly
18 threaten them, that they speak henceforth to no man in this name. And
they called them, and commanded them not to speak at all nor teach in
the name of Jesus.

19 But Peter and John answered and said unto them, *k*Whether it be
right in the sight of God to hearken unto you more than unto God, judge
20 ye. For *l*we cannot but speak the things which *m*we have seen and
21 heard. So, when they had further threatened them, they let them go,
finding nothing how they might punish them, because *n*of the people:
22 for all *men* glorified God for that *o*which was done. For the man was
above forty years old on whom this miracle of healing was showed.

23 And being let go, *p*they went to their own company, and reported all
24 that the chief priests and elders had said unto them. And when they
heard that, *q*they lifted up their voice to God with one accord, and said,
Lord, *r*thou *art* God, which hast made heaven, and earth, and the sea,
25 and all that in them is: who by the mouth of thy servant David hast
said, *s*Why did the heathen rage, and the people imagine vain things?
26 The kings of the earth stood up, and the rulers were gathered together

	A. D. 33.

j ch. 3. 9, 10.
k ch. 5. 29.
Gal. 1. 10.
l ch. 1. 8.
ch. 2. 32.
m ch. 22. 15.
1 John 1. 1,
3.
n Matt. 14. 5.
Matt. 21. 26.
Luke 20. 6,
19.
Luke 22. 2.
ch. 5. 26.
ch. 3. 7, 8.
p ch. 12. 12.
q Ps. 103. 1.
Ps. 107. 1, 2.
r Ex. 20. 11.
2 Ki. 19. 15.
Isa. 44. 6.
Jer. 10. 10.
Jer. 32. 17.
s Ps. 2. 1.

a notable miracle [γνωστὸν σημεῖον]—'a notorious miracle' hath been done by them is manifest to all them that dwell in Jerusalem; and we cannot deny it. And why should ye wish to deny it, O ye rulers, but that ye hate the light, and will not come to the light, lest your deeds should be reproved? 17. But that it spread no further among the people, let us straitly (or 'strictly') threaten them, that they speak henceforth to no man in this name. Impotent device! Little knew they the fire that was burning in the bones of those heroic disciples. 18. And they called them, and commanded [them] not to speak at all nor teach in the name of Jesus—[αὐτοῖς has next to no MS. authority.]

19. But Peter and John answered and said unto them, Whether it be right in the sight of God to hearken unto you more than unto God, judge ye. 20. For we cannot but speak the things which we have seen and heard. Who can fail to observe here a rare union of sober, respectful appeal to the better reason of their judges, and of calm, deep determination to abide the consequences of a testimony that could not be withheld—betokening a power above their own resting upon them, according to their Master's promise. That promise extended both to "*how* and *what* they should speak" (Matt. x. 19, πῶς ἢ τί)—both to *the thing to be said* and *the manner of saying it;* and it would be difficult to decide whether in the one or the other of these, Peter's reply on this occasion was the more remarkable. 21. So, when they had further threatened them,—or, added a threat to the prohibition recorded in *v.* 18, they let them go, finding nothing how they might punish them, [μηδὲν εὑρίσκοντες τὸ πῶς]—rather, 'no means of punishing them' (not, no *cause* for doing so), because of the people—for fear of a riot: for all men glorified God for that which was done. They were at no loss for a pretext to punish them, but knew not how to do so without a popular tumult, knowing the deep and general impression that so manifest a miracle had produced. 22. For the man was above forty years old on whom this miracle of healing was showed. But what availed the most resistless evidence to men determined beforehand not to receive any?

Peter and John, let go, report these proceedings to the assembled disciples, who thereupon in a sublime Prayer commit their now critical cause to the Lord

(23-30). 23. And being let go, they went to their own [company]. How sweet is the contrast here presented, between the dismissers and the dismissed, and the two companies they represented: in the one of which the two apostles felt themselves as sheep among wolves, in the other breathing the air of home among their own, in the common faith and love of Jesus! and reported all that the chief priests and elders had said unto them. 24. And when they heard that, they—that is, the assembled disciples, lifted up their voice to God with one accord [ὁμοθυμαδὸν]—one voice leading, but the breasts of all heaving sympathetically and echoing every word of this brief, comprehensive, mighty prayer; and said, Lord [Δέσποτα]. This word, rarely used in the New Testament, and never but with intentional emphasis, signifies the 'absolute master' of another, whether really or in the speaker's feeling. Here it is used to express that in God which this small and feeble company feel themselves thrown back upon, and which it was their privilege to invoke (see on Luke ii. 29). thou art [God]. The bracketed word [ὁ Θεὸs] is of doubtful authority [it is wanting in ℵ A B, Vulgate and Memphitic versions, and some principal fathers; and it is struck out of the text by *Lachmann* and *Tischendorf*]. But though the external authority for it is weaker, the internal evidence in its favour is considerable. [It seems easier to account for its omission, though genuine, than for its insertion if spurious, since as ὁ occurs twice with only Θ. intervening, a transcriber might easily pass from the first one to πρήσας, omitting the two intervening words.] Accordingly, *de Wette, Meyer,* and *Alford* decide in favour of these bracketed words. But if left out, the sense will be, 'Thou art He which' &c., which hast made heaven, and earth, and the sea, and all that in them is:—'against Whom, therefore, all creatures are powerless,' 25. Who by the mouth of thy servant David hast said—in Ps. ii. 1-2; a Psalm which, though anonymous, was ascribed to David by the Jews themselves, and internal evidence is in favour of this: Why did the heathen rage, and the people imagine vain things? 26. The kings of the earth stood up, and the rulers were gathered together against the Lord, and against his Christ [מְשִׁיחוֹ]—'His Anointed One,' or 'His Messiah.' David in spirit sees with astonishment "the heathen," 'the peoples,' "the

27 against the Lord, and against his Christ. For of a truth against *t* thy holy child Jesus, *u* whom thou hast anointed, both Herod and Pontius Pilate, with the Gentiles, and the people of Israel, were gathered together,
28 for *v* to do whatsoever thy hand and thy counsel determined before to be
29 done. And now, Lord, behold their threatenings: and grant unto thy
30 servants, *w* that with all boldness they may speak thy word, by stretching forth thine hand to heal; and *x* that signs and wonders may be done by *y* the name of thy holy child Jesus.
31 And when they had prayed, *z* the place was shaken where they were assembled together; and they were all filled with the Holy Ghost, and they spake the word of God with boldness.
32 And the multitude of them that believed *a* were of one heart and of, one soul: neither *b* said any *of them* that ought of the things which he
33 possessed was his own; but they had all things common. And with *c* great power gave the apostle's *d* witness of the resurrection of the Lord
34 Jesus: and *e* great grace was upon them all. Neither *f* was there any among them that lacked: *g* for as many as were possessors of lands or houses sold them, and brought the prices of the things that were sold,
35 and laid *them* down at the apostles' feet: *h* and distribution was made
36 unto every man according as he had need. And Joses, who by the apostles was surnamed Barnabas, (which is, being interpreted, The son of

A. D. 33.
t Heb. 7. 26.
u Isa. 61. 1. John 10.36.
v ch. 2. 23.
w Isa. 58. 1. Eze. 2. 6. ch. 19. 8. Eph. 6. 19. 2 Thes. 3. 1.
x ch. 5. 12.
y ch. 3. 6, 16.
z ch. 2. 2, 4. ch. 16. 26.
a ch. 5. 12. Rom. 15. 6. Phil. 1. 27.
b Phil. 2. 2. ch 2. 44.
c 1 Thes. 1. 6.
d ch. 1. 22.
e ch. 2. 47.
f Jas. 1. 27. 1 John 3. 17.
g ch. 2. 45.
h ch. 6. 1.

kings of the earth," and "the rulers," in deadly combination against the sway of Jehovah and His Anointed One, and asks "why" this is. This godless, Christless confederacy our praying disciples behold, at that moment, in full and fierce operation. **27.** **For of a truth [in this city].** The words here inserted in brackets [ἐν τῇ πόλει ταύτῃ] are most evidently part of the original text (being in ℵ A B D E, many cursives, and nearly all versions), and were probably intended to answer to the words "upon my holy hill of Zion," in the Psalm. **against thy holy child Jesus**—rather 'Servant Jesus;' see on ch. iii. 13. **whom thou hast anointed**—not as David was, by a human prophet pouring oil on his head, but by the Father Himself with the immeasurable anointing of the Holy Ghost; **both Herod and Pontius Pilate, with the Gentiles, and the people of Israel**—not only the supreme Roman and Jewish authorities, but the people of both, all combined, **were gathered together, 28. For to do whatsoever thy hand and thy counsel determined before to be done**—meaning, 'to do what His counsel determined to be done by His hand,' a well-understood colloquialism, like that of ch. xiv. 17. On the mysterious concurrence, here so distinctly expressed, of a voluntary combination of human parties against the Lord Jesus, and the purpose of God from eternity in that death, see on ch. ii. 23, and Remark 2, at the close of that Section. **29. And now, Lord, behold their threatenings.** Looking upon the threatenings of the Sanhedrim as a declaration of war by the combined powers of the world against their infant cause, they seek not, in a spirit of heated enthusiasm, to hide from themselves its critical position, but calmly ask the Lord of heaven and earth to 'look upon their threatenings.' **and grant unto thy servants, that with all boldness they may speak thy word, 30. By stretching forth thine hand to heal; and that signs and wonders may be done by the name of thy holy child**—rather, as before, 'Servant' Jesus. Rising above self, they ask only fearless courage to testify for their Master, and Divine attestation of their testimony by miracles of healing, &c. being done by their instrumentality through the name of Jesus, as the Father's Anointed Servant.

The Answer and its Results (31-37). **31. And when they had prayed, the place was shaken where they were assembled together.** Manifestly this was no ordinary earthquake, extending to the city generally, or any portion of it beyond the "place" where they were assembled. The concussion was evidently quite local, filling all present, doubtless, with awe, and giving glorious token of the commotion which the Gospel, sounding forth from their lips, was speedily to create (see ch. xvii. 6, and compare ch. xvi. 26), and of the overthrow of all opposing powers in which this was to issue! **and they were all filled with the Holy Ghost, and they spake the word of God with boldness.** **32. And the multitude of them that believed were of one heart and of one soul: neither said any of them that aught of the things which he possessed was his own; but they had all things common.** The Spirit rested upon the entire community, first, in the very way they had asked, so that they "spake the word with boldness" (*v.* 29-31); next, in melting down all selfishness, and absorbing even the feeling of individuality in an intense and glowing realization of Christian unity. The community of goods was but an outward expression of this, and, in such circumstances, it was altogether natural and touching. **33. And with great power**—great effect on men's minds, **gave the apostles witness of the resurrection of the Lord Jesus**—the one burden of their testimony, which, to all who intelligently received it, carried in its bosom salvation and life everlasting; **and great grace was upon them all**—the grace of God rested copiously and manifestly on the whole infant community. **34. Neither was there any among them that lacked: for as many as were possessors of lands or houses sold them, and brought the prices of the things that were sold, 35. And laid them down at the apostles' feet**—as. they sat, it may be, in the meetings above the rest; but the expression may be meant here figuratively, from the practice of disciples to sit literally beneath their masters. **36. And Joses.** This reading is in no uncial MS. The true reading is evidently 'Joseph:' **who by the apostles was surnamed Barnabas, (which is, being interpreted,**

25

37 consolation,) a Levite, *and* of the country of Cyprus, having land, ⁵sold *it,* and brought the money, and laid *it* at the apostles' feet.

The son of consolation,) [παρακλήσεως], or, perhaps, 'exhortation,' as the word more directly signifies, and more usually means in the New Testament (perhaps answering to בַּר נְבוּאָה, 'son of prophecy,' as *Grotius* suggests). If this be the thing intended, the name may have been intended to denote his warm, loving, and successful preaching—as to which, see on ch. xi. 22-24. Still the element of "consolation" seems to have been in the view of those who gave Barnabas this name (see on ch. ix. 27). **a Levite**—of whom, as of the priests, very few embraced the faith of Jesus: **of the country of Cyprus**—of which island, in the Mediterranean, in connection with the Gospel, we shall by and by hear more (ch. xi. 19-20, &c.), 37. **Having land.** The Levites, though, as a *tribe,* they had no inheritance, might, and did acquire property as *individuals* (see Deut. xviii. 8). **sold it, and brought the money, and laid it at the apostles' feet.** This is specified, not merely as a signal example of that spirit of generous self-sacrifice which pervaded all, but to introduce to us—in connection with this his first offering to the Lord Jesus—a name which the sequel of this history has rendered dear to every Christian.

Remarks.—1. The weakness of the recent attempts to shake the credit of this book, considered as authentic history, is strikingly seen in the light of such a chapter as this. Look at the bearing of the two parties. Awed by the signal miracle so openly wrought, yet determined to resist the evidence which it bore to Him whom they had put to death, the ecclesiastics, in full conclave, question the humble apostles on the subject, hoping to terrify them either into a disavowal of the act itself, or into silence regarding it as a testimony to their crucified and risen Lord. But the heroism of those simple men, and the grandeur of their testimony before that grave assembly, startle and confound them. And not knowing which of the two alternatives they were shut up to was the worst—to deny the miracle, while the evidence of its truth was in the midst of them, or to admit the resurrection of the Lord Jesus, which it manifestly attested, and fall down and worship Him—they order the court to be cleared, that they might consult among themselves. The resolution come to is simply to silence the preachers, in the confident expectation that a peremptory mandate only was needed. To their consternation, the men decline to obey; not defiantly, but by a calm appeal to themselves whether it would be right to obey them rather than God, and by a respectful expression of their inability to refrain from proclaiming what their own eyes and ears had to tell of their blessed Master. This would doubtless have been visited with summary punishment, had the Council been sure that they had the people with them. But knowing as they did that the whole city was ringing with the miracle—the beneficence of which was not less signal than the power by which it was done—they were obliged to dismiss them with an impotent repetition of their threats. Unruffled, they hie them to "their own"—their fellow-disciples—assembled together in deep anxiety, no doubt, to learn the fate of their trusty leaders. From the report they gave in, the critical condition of the infant cause flashes at once upon the meeting—with the authorities, on the one hand, determined to silence their testimony, and the apostles, on the other, giving notice that they shall not be silenced. What is to be done? With one accord they lift up their voice to God, sublimely asking

Him to look at this state of matters, and come to the rescue—not of them, but of His anointed cause—by giving them the needful courage to testify to Jesus in face of all danger, and by so sealing their testimony from heaven as to ensure its triumph. Whilst they are yet speaking, the place shakes at the presence of the Lord; the Holy Ghost fills the souls of all that were there, and that boldness to speak the word which they had sought is at once felt and exemplified: their hearts are knit together, and the disinterested emotion of 'none for himself,' but each for all,' takes possession of the whole multitude of the disciples, expressing itself in a way and to an extent before unheard of. What unprejudiced reader does not see artless narrative, life-like, self-attesting historic truth stamped upon all this! 2. The strictly *Jewish point of view,* from which the apostle addresses the Sanhedrim and the disciples pour out their hearts in prayer, must again be observed, throughout this chapter. (See on ch. ii. 14-47, Remark 1, at the close of that section.) 3. When one reads that most explicit and peremptory statement of the apostle here, "Neither is there salvation in any other; for there is none other name under heaven given among men whereby we must be saved," what is to be thought of the growing tendency of what are called liberal theologians to disconnect salvation, not only from all faith in Jesus, but from all biblical beliefs—from everything, in short, but the state of the heart—a thing so indefinite and flexible that every one will put his own meaning on it? When men's liberality in religion comes so low down as this, they will not long retain their belief in salvation itself, considered as an eternal deliverance from a lost state, and all religion will eventually evaporate into mere sentiment. Nor will any alternative be found by the intelligent and awakened mind, but in the surrender of the heart to Jesus as the one revealed Way of a sinner's salvation, or in the abandonment of all certainty about eternal things. 4. As the bearing of Peter and John brought up before the Jewish Council the recollection of Jesus Himself, so that Image lives still in the minds even of the enemies of His Gospel, and will be recognized by them in those who live for Him and breathe the atmosphere of His presence. And is it not worthy of a Christian's highest ambition to extort such a testimony, even from those who cannot bear his ways, that he has "been with Jesus"? 5. The whole history of the opposition which our Lord and His apostles met with illustrates this humbling truth, that there is an unbelief which no amount of mere evidence for the Gospel will cure, and which only becomes the more virulent the clearer the evidence for the truth becomes. In the present case the evidence of an instantaneous and marvellous miracle of healing was before the eyes of the Jewish rulers; and, that this miracle was wrought in the name of Him whom they had crucified, but whom the apostles testified that God had raised from the dead and exalted to His right hand, was not disputed, and could not possibly be denied; yet all this failed to dislodge the unbelief of these ecclesiastics, who, being determined beforehand not to be convinced, became only the more exasperated in proportion as the light shone more brightly around them. And is it not so still? Let us cease, then, to wonder when the clearest evidence proves unavailing; and feeling how powerless we are to carry the heart by mere demonstration, let us cast the case upon Him who

5   BUT a certain man named Ananias, with Sapphira his wife, sold a
2 possession, and *"kept back *part* of the price, his wife also being privy *to*
3 *it*, and brought a certain part, and laid *it* at the apostles' feet. But
   b Peter said, Ananias, why hath Satan *c* filled thine heart [1]to lie to the
4 Holy Ghost, and to keep back *part* of the price of the land? Whiles it
   remained, was it not thine own? and after it was sold, was it not in thine

A. D. 33.

CHAP. 15.
a Josh. 7. 1.
b Num. 30. 2.
c Luke 22. 3.
[1] Or, to deceive.

---

turned a "Saul of Tarsus" into "Paul an apostle of. Jesus Christ." 6. When the apostles said, "We cannot but speak the things which we have seen and heard," they gave utterance to a great Christian principle. 'On many things which our eyes and ears have attested to us (to use the words of *Calvin*) we both may and ought to keep silence, when the preservation of peace is the matter in hand; for to make a noise about things not necessary is the part of an inhuman and unworthy obstinacy. But it is otherwise when the Gospel of Christ is concerned, involving, as that does, the glory of God and the salvation of men. To suppress this by human interdicts, which God has ordered to be proclaimed, is a base and sacrilegious iniquity, especially when it is uttered by those whose mouths God has manifestly opened as chosen witnesses and preachers of Christ. Whoso commands silence in this case does his best to abolish the grace of God and the salvation of men.' 7. But, for the encouragement of Christ's faithful witnesses in such circumstances, let it be observed, that a courageous testimony for the truth has often proved, as it did in this case, the best security against suffering for it; while timid submission to the enemies of the truth, instead of mollifying, has often emboldened them to proceed further than but for this they would have dared to go. 8. How sweetly are Christ's suffering witnesses, in times of persecution, drawn and knit together; and when, on being unexpectedly released from impending danger, they return to the society of "their own," how entirely at home with each other do they feel, beyond anything that mere human relationship could beget! Pity that in times of peace this feeling among Christians is so very weak. 9. Let the reader ponder the prayer which this assembly of primitive disciples sent up to heaven on hearing the report of Peter and John. Even the fact that it was the disciples themselves, and not apostles, that gave it utterance is worthy of notice. For though the spokesman *may* have been an apostle, the mere fact that this is not said, while it is expressly said that it was the assembled disciples that lifted up their voice in prayer, seems clearly to show that it was simply as a Christian mouthpiece of Christian men and women that the spokesman—whoever he was—offered this prayer. But it is the matter, and strain, and form of this prayer to which we now call attention. Directing their eye up to Him whose word had called everything into being, they remind Him that His own prophetic word had foretold and pictured forth the very hostility they were now encountering; and this done, they simply ask Him to look at this state of things, to embolden them to speak for Jesus, and to attest from heaven the word which they should give forth. While they yet spake, the answer came, and as gloriously as speedily. But it is the simplicity and directness of the prayer to which we would bespeak attention. Knowing that He to whom they spake was near to them, and pledged in their behalf, they come at once to the point—telling Him that they are *shut up to Him*, and that they *rely on Him*. With this they have done. And oh what power is there in such prayer—with its childlike confidence,

reverential dignity, sublime brevity! 10. If the "love of money is the root of all evil" (1 Tim. vi. 10), surely that state of the infant Church in which "none said that aught that he possessed was his own" must be deemed the highest spiritual condition of the Church of Christ upon earth; and as this was the result of a copious effusion of the Holy Ghost upon them—when, feeling themselves shut up to Divine preservation against a hostile world, which they were nevertheless prepared to encounter, they cast themselves upon Him who made heaven and earth, and whom no events could take by surprise—so there seems nothing wanting to the attainment of the same spiritual elevation but the same childlike faith, the same dependence on the Lord of all, the same all-absorbing devotedness to Jesus, the same love unto all the saints, as having one precious interest to uphold against a hostile world.

CHAP. V. 1-21.—ANANIAS AND SAPPHIRA—TRIUMPHS OF THE GOSPEL—ARREST AND MIRACULOUS DELIVERANCE OF PETER AND JOHN—RESUMPTION OF THEIR PUBLIC TEACHING.

Ananias and Sapphira (1-11).—1. But a certain man named Ananias, with Sapphira his wife, sold a possession, 2. And kept back part of the price, his wife also being privy to it, and brought a certain part—pretending it to be the whole proceeds of the sale. We have here (as *Olshausen* says) 'the first trace of a shade upon the pure, bright form of the young Church. Probably among the new Christians a kind of holy rivalry had sprung up, every one eager to place his means at the disposal of the apostles.' Thus might the new-born zeal of some outrun their abiding principle, while others might be tempted to seek credit for a liberality which was not in their character. The coolness with which this couple planned the deception aggravated the guilt of it. 3. But Peter said, Ananias, why hath Satan filled thine heart —that is, Why hast thou *suffered* him to do it? implying that Satan is powerless over the hearts of men until they give him encouragement. Compare *v.* 4, "Why hast thou conceived this thing in thine heart?" and see on Mark xiv. 1-11, Remark 8, at the close of that Section; and on John xiii. 27. ·to lie to (or 'deceive') the Holy Ghost—that is, to lie to men so manifestly under His immediate illumination and direction that it was not so much the human instrument as the Divine indwelling Spirit that he attempted to deceive. It is astonishing that *Neander* should speak of·it as doubtful whether Peter detected the dissimulation and hypocrisy of this couple 'by a glance into the secret recesses of their hearts, imparted by the immediate influence of God's Spirit, or by *a natural sagacity* derived from .the same source.' Nothing can be clearer than that the historian represents Peter as conscious of supernatural illumination and direction, and wishing the culprits and the whole assembly to recognize this as his sole warrant for proceeding in the matter as he did. and to keep back part of the price of the land? [*Tischendorf*, contrary to his own principal authorities, inserts σε after νοσφισασθαι. *Lachmann* adheres to the received text, which wants it.] 4. Whiles it remained, was it

27

own power? why hast thou conceived this thing in thine heart? thou
5 hast not lied unto men, but unto God. And Ananias hearing these
words *d*fell down, and gave up the Ghost: and great fear came on all
6 them that heard these things. And the young men arose, *e*wound him
up, and carried *him* out, and buried *him.*
7   And it was about the space of three hours after, when his wife, not
8 knowing what was done, came in. And Peter answered unto her, Tell
me whether ye sold the land for so much? And she said, Yea, for so
9 much. Then Peter said unto her, How is it that ye have agreed together
*f*to tempt the Spirit of the Lord? Behold, the feet of them which have
10 buried thy husband *are* at the door, and shall carry thee out. Then fell
she down straightway at his feet, and yielded up the ghost: and the
young men came in, and found her dead, and, carrying *her* forth, buried
11 *her* by her husband. And great fear came upon all the church, and upon
as many as heard these things.

A. D. 33.

d Num.14.37.
2 Ki 1. 10-
14.
2 Ki. 2. 24.
Jer. 5. 14,
1 Cor. 4. 21.
2 Cor. 10. 2,
6.
2 Cor. 13. 2,
10.
e Lev. 10. 4.6.
Deut.21.23.
2 Sa. 18, 17.
John 19. 40.
f Ex. 17. 2.
Num.14.22
Matt. 4. 7.
1 Cor.10.29.

not thine own? and after it was sold, was it
not in thine own power? A striking appeal to
themselves, in presence of the whole Christian
assembly, whether all the sacrifices which had
been made for the support of the new community
had not been purely voluntary—the sales first,
and then the surrender of the proceeds. why
hast thou conceived this thing in thine heart?
It was this conception of the thing in his own
heart which opened the door of it for Satan first
to enter in, and then to fill it with this shocking
plan. thou hast not lied unto men, but unto
God—in the sense explained on *v.* 3; and compare
Ps. li. 4. Nothing could more clearly imply both
the distinct Personality and the proper Divinity
of the Holy Ghost. 5. And Ananias hearing these
words fell down, and gave up the ghost: and
great fear came on all them that heard [these
things]—that is, on those *without* the Christian
circle, who, instead of disparaging the followers of
the Lord Jesus, as they might otherwise have
done on the discovery of such hypocrisy, were
awed at the manifest presence of Divinity amongst
them, and the mysterious power of throwing off
such corrupt matter which rested upon the young
Church. [The ταῦτα at the end of this verse,
though implied, is evidently an addition to the
genuine text.] 6. And the young men [οἱ νεώ-
τεροι] arose, wound him up, and carried him
out—*i. e.,* out of the city (compare Luke vii. 12;
John xi. 31), and buried him. It is a great mistake to suppose (with *Mosheim, Olshausen, Meyer,*
and others) that these were an inferior order of
ministers. They were merely some of the younger
and more active members of the Church, not in
the capacity of office-bearers, nor coming forward
now for the first time, but who probably had
already volunteered their services in making
subordinate arrangements. In every thriving
Christian community such warm young volunteers may be expected, and will be found eminently useful.
7. And it was about the space of three hours
after. As the Jewish hours of prayer were at
intervals of three hours from each other (see ch.
ii. 15; iii. 1; ix. 9), it has been remarked, as not
improbable, that the meetings of the Christians
were so also, and that Sapphira must have been
now coming in, as her husband before had done, to
attend one of the stated public assemblies of the
Christians. when his wife, not knowing what
was done, came in. 8. And Peter answered unto
her, Tell me whether ye sold the land for so
much?—naming the sum. And she said, Yea, for
so much. Thus was coolly carried out this coolly-
concerted plan, which was divinely permitted

to be gone through with, that the whole guilt
of it might be laid bare and brought home before
all the assembly to this wretched woman, ere the
vengeance of Heaven descended upon her. 9.
Then Peter said unto her, How is it that ye have
agreed together (see on *v.* 2) to tempt the Spirit
of the Lord?—of the Lord Jesus, as the usual style
of this book would incline us to understand "the
Lord" here. They thus virtually agreed to tempt
or try the Spirit of the Lord whether they could
not escape detection by that Omniscient Spirit,
of whose supernatural presence with the apostles
they had had such abundant evidence. behold,
the feet of them which have buried thy husband
are at the door, and shall carry thee out. How
awfully graphic is this! 10. Then fell she down
straightway at his feet, and yielded up the ghost:
and the young men [οἱ νεανίσκοι]—in the sense before explained, though the term is slightly varied,
came in, and found her dead, and, carrying her
forth, buried her by her husband. The later Jews
buried before sunset of the day of death. Here
again the reader should be on his guard against
the tendency to weaken the miraculous character
of the judgment that befell this couple; as when
Neander would represent it, in the case of
Ananias, as the result of the astonishment and
terror, produced on him by the detection of his
sin and the holy denunciations of a man speaking
to his conscience with such divine confidence;
and in the case of Sapphira, by the impression of
her husband's fate in addition to all this. Even
Olshausen would admit that the death might be
a natural event, though, *in the circumstances,* it
may be regarded as miraculous. Such comments
cannot fail to shake one's confidence in the narrative itself, if he gives any heed to them. No
doubt astonishment, terror, and burning shame
would be in them like fuel to the flame of Divine
vengeance; but this is a very different statement
from *Neander's.* 11. And great fear came upon all
the church. No doubt this effect on the Christian
community itself was the chief design of so startling a judgment, which had its counterpart, as
the sin itself had, in *Achan* (Josh. vii.), while
the period at which it occurred—the commencement of a new era—was also similar. '*It is
worthy of remark* (says *Lechler*), *that here the
word* "church" [ἐκκλησία] *occurs for the first
time in the Acts.* Hitherto it is "the disciples"
(ch. i. 15); "all that believed" (ch. ii. 44); "the
multitude of them that believed" (ch. iv. 32).
Luke here names "the whole Church" as a collection. It is not to be viewed as accidental that
this collective idea of the Church is first brought
forward in connection with that event which

28

12 And *by the hands of the apostles were many signs and wonders wrought among the people; (and *they were all with one accord in Solo-
13 mon's porch. And *of the rest durst no man join himself to them: *but
14 the people magnified them. And believers were the more added to the
15 Lord, multitudes both of men and women;) insomuch that they brought forth the sick ² into the streets, and laid *them* on beds and couches, *that at the least the shadow of Peter passing by might overshadow some of
16 them. There came also a multitude *out* of the cities round about unto Jerusalem, bringing *sick folks, and them which were vexed with unclean spirits: and they were healed every one.
17 Then *the high priest rose up, and all they that were with him, (which
18 is the sect of the Sadducees,) and were filled with ³ indignation, and "laid
19 their hands on the apostles, and put them in the common prison. But °the angel of the Lord by night opened the prison doors, and brought
20 them forth, and said, Go, stand and speak in the temple to the people
21 *all the words of this life. And when they heard *that*, they entered into the temple early in the morning, and taught. *But the high priest

A. D. 33.

g Heb. 2. 4.
h ch. 3. 11.
i John 9. 22.
    John 12. 42.
    John 19. 38.
j ch 2. 47.
² Or, in every str:et.
k Matt. 9. 21.
    Matt. 14.36.
l Ma:k 16.17.
m ch. 4. 1, 2.
³ Or, euvy.
n Luke 21.12.
o Ps. 34. 7.
    ch. 16. 23.
    Heb. 1. 14.
p John 6. 68.
    John 17. 3.
q ch. 4. 5, 6.

appears as an imposing act of "Divine church-discipline"' (as *Thiersch* expresses it). **and upon as many as heard these things.**
Triumphs of the Gospel (12-16).—12. **And by the hands of the apostles were many signs and wonders wrought among the people; and they were all with one accord (or by common consent) in Solomon's porch**—(see on ch. iii. 11.)' 13. **And of the rest durst no man join** (or 'attach') **himself to them**—(see the Greek of Luke x. 11; xv. 15; chs. v. 36; ix. 26.) Of the outside, unconverted, though impressed class, none ventured, after what had taken place, to profess discipleship. This is the only sense of the statement; and in this sense it is taken by nearly every good interpreter, ancient and modern. *Alford's* interpretation, that none of the Christians presumed to put themselves on an equality with the apostles, hardly deserves mention. **but the people** [ὁ λαός]—the common people, **magnified them.** Awed as were all who were unprepared to yield themselves to the truth, the populace—having fewer prejudices and interests at stake than others—were unable to restrain their admiration of the apostles and of the infant community. 14. **And believers** —visible converts, **were the more added to the Lord, multitudes both of men and women.** The parenthesis within which this verse and the preceding one, with the latter clause of *v.* 12, are placed in the authorized version, is both unnecessary and injurious to the sense, as it connects what follows the parenthesis with the first part of *v.* 12; whereas it is meant as a result also of all that comes after it. 'The childhood of the Church at this period (says *Humphry*, not incorrectly) may be compared with that of its Divine Founder, who increased in wisdom and stature, and in favour with God and man.' 15. **Insomuch that they brought forth the sick into the streets** [κατὰ τὰς πλατείας]—'by streets,' or from street to street, **and laid them on beds** [κλινῶν, or κλιναρίων, which is a much better supported reading]—the softer cushions of the rich, **and couches** [κραββάτων]—the coarser pallets of the poor; all classes thus flocking to these wonder-working men, **that at the least** [ἵνα κἂν]—'that if but' **the shadow of Peter passing by**—as he went from his own abode to the place of meeting in Solomon's porch, **might overshadow some of them.** That this was no more than a superstitious expectation of miraculous virtue from Peter's shadow is certainly not the impression which the passage naturally conveys; nor, with ch. xix. 12 before us, can we well

doubt that on certain occasions miraculous virtue did flow forth with such exuberance as to justify expectations of this nature on the part of the people. (See on Luke vi. 19; and compare 2 Ki. xiii. 21). 16. **There came also a multitude out of the cities round about** [τὸ πλῆθος τῶν πέριξ πόλεων]—rather, 'the population of the surrounding towns,' **unto Jerusalem, bringing sick folks, and them which were vexed with unclean spirits: and they were healed every one.** *Now did the predicted greatness of Peter*, as the directing spirit of the earliest Church (Matt. xvi. 18), *rise to its height.*
Arrest and Miraculous Deliverance of the Apostles—Resumption, by Divine Command, of their Public Teaching (17-21).—17. **Then the high priest rose up, and all they that were with him**—that is, his more immediate friends and supporters, **which is the sect of the Sadducees,**—exasperated beyond others, for the reason already mentioned (see on ch. iv. 2), **and were filled with indignation,** 18. **And laid** [their] **hands on the apostles** [αὐτῶν is an ill-supported addition to the text], **and put them in the common prison.** 19. **But the** (or 'an') **angel of the Lord by night** [not διὰ τῆς νυκτός, as in the received text, but simply νυκτός, according to the best authorities]—that is, in the course of the same night, **opened the prison doors, and brought them forth, and said,** 20. **Go, stand and speak in the temple to the people all the words of this life.** Beautiful expression of that *life in the Risen One* which was the burden of all their preaching! 21. **And when they heard that, they entered into the temple early in the morning, and taught.** How self-possessed!—the indwelling Spirit making the glory of their testimony so to irradiate their own souls, and their wonderful liberation so to confirm it, as to lift them above fear.
Remarks.—1. The severe fidelity with which our historian—immediately after picturing the beautiful disinterestedness of the young Christian community—proceeds to relate a foul case of covetousness and duplicity in two of its members, with the terrible punishment that so speedily overtook it, without any explanation or reflection of his own, cannot but strike the thoughtful reader as an indubitable mark of authenticity in the narrative itself. As for the occurrence itself, though no one, perhaps, would have expected it in such a state of the infant Church as the close of the preceding chapter describes, it is, nevertheless, in thorough consonance with **all that we**

29

came, and they that were with him, and called the council together, and all the ʳsenate of the children of Israel, and sent to the prison to have

A. D. 33.

ʳ Ps. 105. 23.

know of the workings of the human heart in a state of high religious excitement. In such circumstances as those before depicted, characters like Ananias and Sapphira may be expected to appear—so powerfully wrought upon by the truth, and by the manifest seal of Heaven upon it, as to join themselves to so Divinely-owned a society without thorough heart-sympathy with them and entire surrender to the Lord. So powerful, however, is the sympathy which they do feel, that, once sucked into the atmosphere of Christians, and henceforth mingling constantly with them, they catch their impulses, and are ready, for a considerable time and to a large extent, to go along with them. At length their real character comes out, which, indeed, only waited for some adequate occasion to call it forth. That occasion, in the case of Ananias and Sapphira, was the sale of their property. In resolving to dispose of it for behoof of the Church they were probably quite sincere. While every one was surrendering his all, they could not think of being behind. Besides, it would be noticed by those who knew their means, and would be regarded in an ill light. So they go away, perhaps from some meeting at which they had seen other brethren offering princely gifts, to vie with them in self-sacrifice. They dispose of their property, and have the proceeds in hand ready for surrender at the apostles' feet, when, lo! at the sight of such a sum, the thought occurs to them whether, after all, it was quite right, fitting, or necessary that they should part with the whole. Perhaps their first proposal to one another was to state openly that what they contributed was but part of what they had realized by the sale. But this, on reflection, would seem fitted to raise remarks on the selfishness of reserving a part. Still clinging to the money, yet loath to want the credit of disinterestedness, their next thought, perhaps, was, whether by laying down at the apostles' feet what they agreed to surrender as the price of the land, they might not leave it to be concluded, without expressly saying so, that it was the whole proceeds; and they might flatter themselves that by this way of putting it there would be no lie in the matter. One almost fancies this to be implied in Peter's question to Sapphira—as if he had designed to bring out of her, more explicitly than had been expressed by the donors, the real truth. Be this as it may, they played with the temptation until they made up their minds to practise a deception in the matter upon the apostles and the brethren. The apostle treats Sapphira differently from Ananias. To her he opens a way of escape, by the admission—if she would have made it—that the sum gifted was but part of the price. On him he brings down at once, and before all, the charge of falsehood in its most aggravated form, expostulating with him on the absence of all temptation to such a deed, provided they were right-hearted. But the history of religious movements in all time proves that the desire to establish a religious reputation beyond the actual attainments of the parties cherishing it is with some a very strong principle of action; and when this works on a covetous nature, and in connection with money, we may expect manifestations of it not very unlike to that here recorded. With respect to the severity of the punishment, let these following things be observed:—*First,* Peter did not call down the vengeance of Heaven, nor (so far as appears) even announce what would happen in the case of Ananias, insomuch that some have

thought it took the apostle as much by surprise as others in the assembly—a view we cannot concur in. *Second,* The deception—deliberately planned, and in the absence of all temptation—was openly practised amidst blazing evidences of a Divine presence in the Christian assemblies, and daily manifestations of transparent simplicity and overflowing liberality on the part of others. *Third,* Had such a high-handed sin, which could not long have remained hid, been allowed to pass, or been only exposed and censured, the unparalleled love and liberality of the infant Church would have come under just suspicion; the wonder and admiration which it was attracting would have been converted into a very different feeling, and the credit of the young community would have been speedily destroyed. As it was, the effect produced was of the deepest character, and eminently salutary. But one such example in the Church was quite enough, proclaiming for all time that He who walketh among the golden candlesticks hath His eyes as a flame of fire, and will give unto every one according to his works. 2. The personality of Satan, and his subtlety and skill in turning even the highest religious movements to his own purposes; but, at the same time, that there is a "Stronger than he," who is able to outwit him, and make his wrath to praise Him—these truths stand out on the very surface of this narrative very strikingly. 3. The entire freedom of the human will, even when most under the dominion of the wicked one, is strikingly seen in the apostle's expostulations on the subject with Ananias and Sapphira (*vv.* 3, 4). 4. Two things are to be equally valued in the Gospel—that *life from the dead* in the Risen Saviour which it proclaims, and "the *words* of this life," or the Divine testimony regarding it, or (as it is called in Isa. liii. 1) "our *report*" as ambassadors for Christ. (See Rom. x. 14-16.) True, "the words of this life" are but the casket which contains the pearl of great price—the vessel in which the waters of life are held. But when the vessel is shattered, what becomes of the water it contained? Even so will the life everlasting evaporate as soon as the Divine message, authoritatively conveying it to the acceptance of men, is thrown away. 5. 'There is (says a German writer, quoted by *Gerok*) a Divine " but" which often puts all human plans to shame. Men are prepared with their human designs, when this "but" steps in. Joseph says to his brethren, "Ye thought evil against me, *but* God meant it for good." David complains that "the kings of the earth set themselves, and the rulers take counsel together, against the Lord and His Anointed; *but* He that sitteth in the heavens laugheth at them, the Lord hath them in derision," (Ps. ii.)' 6. How delightfully is the ministry of angels in behalf of the cause, as well as "the heirs, of salvation," displayed in such interpositions as that here recorded (*v.* 19).

21-42.—THE TWO APOSTLES BROUGHT BEFORE THE SANHEDRIM AND INTERROGATED—PETER'S NOBLE REPLY—BY GAMALIEL'S ADVICE THEY ARE DISMISSED, BUT SCOURGED, AND COMMANDED TO BE SILENT—THEY DEPART REJOICING, AND CONTINUE THEIR TEACHING.

Hearing that the Apostles are at large and publicly Teaching, the Sanhedrim send for them and question them (21-28). — **21.** But the high priest came, and they that were with him, and called the council together, and all the senate [γερουσίαν, the word used by the LXX. to denote the assembled elders] of the children of Israel. This

22 them brought. But when the officers came, and found them not in the
23 prison, they returned, and told, saying, The prison truly found we shut with all safety, and the keepers standing without before the doors: but
24 when we had opened, we found no man within. Now when the high priest ⁵and the captain of the temple and the chief priests heard these
25 things, they doubted of them whereunto this would grow. Then came one and told them, saying, Behold, the men whom ye put in prison are standing in the temple, and teaching the people.
26 Then went the captain with the officers, and brought them without violence: ᵗfor they feared the people, lest they should have been stoned.
27 And when they had brought them, they set *them* before the council:
28 and the high priest asked them, saying, ᵘDid not we straitly command you, that ye should not teach in this name? and, behold, ye have filled Jerusalem with your doctrine, and ᵛintend to bring this man's blood ʷupon us.
29 Then Peter and the *other* apostles answered and said, ˣWe ought to
30 obey God rather than men. The God of our fathers raised up Jesus,
31 whom ye slew and ʸhanged on a tree. Him ᶻhath God exalted with his

A. D. 33.
ˢ Luke 12. 4.
ch. 4. 1.
ᵗ Matt. 14. 5.
Matt. 21. 26.
Matt. 26. 5.
Luke 20. 6, 19.
Luke 22. 2.
ᵘ ch. 4. 18.
ᵛ 1 Ki. 18. 17 18.
1 Ki. 21. 20,
ch. 2. 23.
ch. 3. 15.
ch. 7. 52.
ʷ Matt. 23. 35.
Matt. 27. 25.
ˣ Gal. 1. 10.
ʸ Gal. 3. 13.
1 Pet. 2. 24.
ᶻ Phil. 2. 9.
Heb. 2. 10.
Heb. 12. 2.

was evidently an unusually general convention of the authorities, hastily summoned. **and sent to the prison to have them brought. 22. But when the officers came, and found them not in the prison, they returned, and told, 23. Saying, The prison [truly] found we shut with all safety,** and the keepers standing [without] before the doors—rather, 'at the doors' [ἐπὶ here being preferable to πρό]. The bracketed words [μὲν and ἔξω] want authority: but **when we had opened, we found no man within.** This miracle, it will be observed, was precisely the converse of that recorded in ch. xvi. 26, where, though all the prison doors were thrown open, none of the prisoners sought to escape: here, while all the doors were fast shut, the imprisoned apostles were found at large without. **24. Now when the high priest** [ἱερεὺς, not ἀρχ.; but the context shows that the officiating high priest is what is meant] **and the captain of the temple and the chief priests**—in the wider sense of that term, **heard these things, they doubted of them** (or 'were in perplexity about them') **whereunto this would grow**—and what wonder, since they were fighting against God? **25. Then came one and told them.** The Sanhedrim sat in a chamber at the south side of the temple, while Solomon's porch, where Peter appears to have 'spoken unto the people all the words of this life,' was in another direction. **[saying.]** This bracketed word is an addition to the true text. **Behold, the men whom ye put in prison are standing in the temple, and teaching the people.**
26. Then went the captain with the officers, and brought them without violence: for they feared the people, lest they should have been stoned. How great must have been the popular enthusiasm in favour of the apostles — whose beneficent miracles no doubt won the admiration even of those who held aloof from them, while their own miraculous liberation from prison would inspire the general community with awe—when even the officers of the Sanhedrim were afraid of becoming the victims of popular violence if they laid a rough hand upon them! But in what a hateful light does this exhibit those hypocritical, hardened ecclesiastics! They are astonished, they are dismayed; but they have all unawed by the miraculous tokens of God's presence with the apostles, and have only the fear of the mob before their eyes! **27. And when they had brought them, they set them before the**

council: **and the high priest asked them, 28. Saying, Did not we straitly** (or strictly) **command you.** The true text here would seem to be not in the form of a question, but of an affirmation:—'We strictly commanded you' [omitting Οὐ, which crept naturally in after ἐπηρώτησεν of v. 27], **that ye should not teach in this name? and, behold, ye have filled Jerusalem with your doctrine.** Noble witness this, both to the success of their preaching, and (for the reason mentioned in ch. iv. 4) to the truth of their testimony, from reluctant lips! **and intend to bring this man's blood upon us.** They avoid (as *Bengel* remarks) naming Him whom the apostle gloried in holding up before them. In speaking thus, of bringing His blood upon them, they seem haunted by disagreeable recollections of their own recent imprecation, "His blood be on us and on our children" (Matt. xxvii. 25), and perhaps of the traitor's words as he threw down their money, "I have sinned, in that I have betrayed the innocent blood" (Matt. xxvii. 4).
Peter's Noble Reply (29-32). **29. Then Peter and the [other] apostles answered and said, We ought to obey God rather than men.** This is the expression not of defiant rebellion, even in the best of causes, but of a constraint which they cannot but believe will have an echo in the breasts of their judges themselves, and an indirect protestation that nothing but the overpowering command of God Himself would have warranted or induced them to disobey the command of men placed lawfully in authority over them. (See on ch. iv. 19, 20.) **30. The God of our fathers raised up Jesus.** This is understood to mean 'raised Him from the dead,' by *Chrysostom, Erasmus, Meyer,* and *Alexander.* But (as *de Wette* says) it suits better the progress of the thought to take it in the sense of 'raised up of the seed of David,' as in ch. xiii. 23: see also ch. iii. 22, and the same word in Luke i. 69. So *Calvin, Bengel,* and *Lechler.* **whom ye slew and hanged on a tree** [διεχειρίσασθε κρεμάσαντες]—rather, 'hanged and slew,' or 'slew by hanging,' as also in ch. x. 39. This naked and bold reference to the ignominy attached to that mode of death was evidently intended to bring out more vividly the contrast between their treatment of Him and God's, to be expressed in the next verse. (See on ch. ii. 22; iii. 10, 11.) **31. Him hath God exalted with his right hand to be a Prince and a Saviour** [ἀρχηγὸν καὶ σωτῆρα]—the one word expressing that *Royalty*

right hand *to be* ᵃa Prince and ᵇa Saviour, ᶜfor to give repentance to
32 Israel, and forgiveness of sins. And ᵈwe are his witnesses of these things;
and *so is* also the Holy Ghost, whom God hath given to them that
obey him.
33   When they heard *that*, they were cut *to the heart*, and took counsel to
34 slay them. Then stood there up one in the council, a Pharisee, named
ᵉGamaliel, a doctor of the law, had in reputation among all the people,
35 and commanded to put the apostles forth a little space; and said unto
them, Ye men of Israel, take heed to yourselves what ye intend to do as
36 touching these men. For before these days rose up Theudas, boasting
himself to be somebody; to whom a number of.men, about four hundred,
joined themselves: who was slain; and all, as many as ⁴obeyed him,
37 were scattered, and brought to nought. After this man rose up Judas
of Galilee in the days ᶠof the taxing, and drew away much people after
him: he also perished; and all, *even* as many as obeyed him, were dis-
38 persed. And now I say unto you, Refrain from these men, and let them

A. D. 33.

ᵃ Ps. 2. 6.
Iss. 9. 6.
Eze. 4. 21.
Eze. 37. 45.
Dan. 9. 25.
Dan. 10. 21.
ch. 3. 15.
ᵇ Matt. 1. 21.
ᶜ Eph. 1. 7.
Col. 1. 14.
ᵈ Luke 24. 47,
48.
John 15. 26,
27.
2 Cor. 13. 1.
ᵉ ch. 22. 3.
⁴ Or,
believed.
ᶠ Luke 2. 1.
Luke 13. 1.

which all Israel looked for in Messiah, the other the *Saving* character of it which they had utterly lost sight of. Each of these features in our Lord's work enters into the other, and both make one glorious whole. (See on ch. iii. 15; Heb. ii. 10.) **for to give repentance to Israel, and forgiveness of sins.** "Israel," it will be observed, is here represented as the immediate object of the whole Divine purpose of mercy in Christ, as being the direct children of the promise. Hence, the rule of preaching was ever "to the Jew first." In fact, at this earliest stage of the Christian Church the accession of the Gentiles as all was probably not before the apostle's mind, and any express allusion to it would have needlessly grated on the ears of a hostile Sanhedrim. (See on ch. ii. 14-47, Remark 1, at the close of that Section.) But it is of more importance to observe the two august titles here given to Jesus, and the sense in which they are used. While Jesus dispenses His gifts as a *"Prince,"* the gifts themselves are those of a *"Saviour"* — "repentance and the remission of sins." (Compare Zech. vi. 13; and see ch. iv. 12.) On the relation of the one of these to the other, see on ch. xx. 21. **32. And we are his witnesses of these things** [τῶν ῥημάτων τούτων]—'of these matters,' meaning here matters of fact, of which Peter affirms himself and his fellow-apostles to be competent witnesses; **and [so is] also the Holy Ghost**—attesting these facts by undeniable miracles. **whom God hath given to them that obey him** [τοῖς πειθαρχοῦσιν αὐτῷ]—that is, that render to Him the obedience of *faith* in His Son (cf. ch. vi. 7; Rom. xvi. 26).

The deadly Rage of the Sanhedrim at this Testimony is calmed by Gamaliel (33-39). **33. When they heard that, they were cut to the heart.** The word used here and in ch. vii. 54 [διεπρίοντο] signifies 'were cut through,' but the sense is rightly given in our version: **and took counsel to slay them.** How different this feeling, and the effect of it, from that 'pricking of the heart' which drew from the first converts on the day of Pentecost the cry, "Men and brethren, what shall we do?" The words used in the two places are strikingly different. (See ch. ii. 37.) **34. Then stood there up one in the council, a Pharisee, named Gamaliel** [= גַּמְלִיאֵל, Num. i. 10], **a doctor of the law, had in reputation among all the people.** In all probability he was one of that name celebrated in the Jewish writings for his wisdom, the son of Simeon—possibly the same Simeon who took the infant Saviour in his arms (Luke ii. 25, &c.), and grandson of the celebrated rabbi Hillel. He died eighteen years before the destruction of Jerusalem. (So *Lightfoot*, who is, however, a little too positive.) **and commanded to put the apostles forth**—or, 'the men forth,' according to what is probably the true reading [attested by אAB and the Vulgate, Memphitic, and Armenian versions. The received reading is supported by many more MSS., and by the Syriac versions and others, and some fathers. But internal evidence, as we think, is in favour of τ. ἀνθρώπους, and this is the reading of *Lachmann* and *Tischendorf*, and approved by *Meyer*, but not by *de Wette* and *Alford*]—a [little] **space.** [The τι after βραχὺ is unauthorized.] If Gamaliel was now (as *Lightfoot* thinks) president of the assembly, it was his business to give this order; but in that case the historian would scarcely have called him simply "one in the council." **35. And said unto them, Ye men of Israel, take heed to yourselves what ye intend to do as touching these men. 36. For before these days rose up Theudas, boasting himself to be somebody; to whom a number of men, about four hundred, joined themselves: who was slain; and all, as many as obeyed him, were scattered, and brought to nought.** *Josephus* (Antt. xx. 5, 1) speaks of a deceiver of the name of Theudas, who headed an insurrection some twelve years after this; and as the circumstances appear to agree with what is here said, *de Wette*, *Meyer, Neander, Lechler*, and others take them to be the same person, in which case our historian is held to have fallen into a chronological error. But the error of our historian in this case (as *Olshausen* says) is double: he has not only named before Judas a man who lived long after him, but he has made Gamaliel name a man who lived after himself. This should be a little too much even for the laxest interpreters to palm upon such a historian as Luke. It is surely far more natural (with some of the best interpreters) to suppose that among the many raisers of insurrection against the Roman authority who appeared among the Jews, by the testimony of *Josephus*, this was one, in the days of Augustus, of whom he makes no mention. (See on Luke xiii. 1-3.) **37. After this man rose up Judas of Galilee in the days of the taxing** [τῆς ἀπογραφῆς] (see on Luke ii. 2), **and drew away much people after him: he also perished; and all, even as many as obeyed him were dispersed.** (See *Josephus*, Antt. xviii. 1, 1.) **38. And now I say unto you, Refrain from these men, and let them alone: for if this counsel or this work be of men, it will come to**

alone: for *ᵍ*if this counsel or this work be of men, it will come to nought:

39 but *ʰ*if it be of God, ye cannot overthrow it; lest haply ye be found even *ⁱ*to fight against God.

40 And to him they agreed: and when they had called the apostles, and *ʲ*beaten *them*, they commanded that they should not speak in the name

41 of Jesus, and let them go. And they departed from the presence of the council, *ᵏ*rejoicing that they were counted worthy to suffer shame for his

42 name. And daily in the temple, and in every house, they ceased not to teach and preach Jesus Christ.

6 AND in those days, *ᵃ*when the number of the disciples was multiplied,

A. D. 33.

ᵍ Prov.21..0.
  Isa. 8. 10.
ʰ Matt.16.18.
  1 Cor. 1. 25.
ⁱ ch. 9. 5.
  Mark 13. 9.
ʲ Luke 20.10.
ᵏ Matt. 5. 12.
  Rom. 5. 3.

CHAP. 6.
ᵃ Ps. 72. 16.

nought: 39. But if it be of God, ye cannot overthrow it—rather, 'ye shall not be able to overthrow it,' [the future, δυνήσεσθε, being better supported than δύνασθε], **lest haply ye be found even** [καὶ]—rather, 'also,' **to fight against God**—as well as against these disciples of Jesus. This neutral policy, in the exasperated and murderous temper of the council at that time, was true wisdom; although personal neutrality is hostility to Christ, as Himself teaches (Luke xi. 23).

The Council, having ordered the Apostles to be Scourged, and to cease from Speaking in the name of Jesus, Dismiss them—They depart rejoicing, and cease not to Teach and Preach Jesus (40-42). **40. And to him they agreed: and when they had called the apostles, and beaten** (or 'scourged') **them** [δείραντες]—for disobeying their orders; possibly also as a compromise with the more violent portion of the Council—too like what Pilate in the case of our Lord, even when pronouncing Him innocent, offered to these same Jewish authorities, and carried into effect (Luke xxiii. 16; John xix. 1). **41. And they departed from the presence of the council, rejoicing that they were counted worthy to suffer shame for his name.** The true reading, beyond doubt, is 'for the Name;' the pronoun "His" [αὐτοῦ] having hardly any MS. support. In this case, of course, "*the* Name" which is above every name, is sweetly emphatic (as in 3 John 7 in the Greek), and is at once intelligible. They rejoiced (as *Humphry* well puts it) that they were thought worthy by God to be dishonoured by man. (See Matt. v. 12; 1 Pet. iv. 14, 16.) *This was their first taste of persecution*, and it felt sweet for His sake on account of whom they suffered it. **42. And daily in the temple, and in every house** [κατ' οἶκον]—rather, 'and privately' (see on ch. ii. 46), **they ceased not to teach and preach Jesus Christ**—Jesus as the Messiah.

Remarks.—1. How refreshing is the contrast here presented between the impotent rage and embarrassment of these Jewish ecclesiastics—intent only on preserving their own status, with all their traditional prejudices, and steeled against whatever evidence was fitted to overthrow it—and that lofty heroism which in those simple men gave such grand utterance to unwelcome truth, and which, without aught of unseemly defiance, calmly announced their inability to refrain from testifying to their Lord! But "this is the victory which overcometh the world, even our faith" (1 John v. 4). This faith—bright and burning in Peter's breast, through the power of the Holy Ghost resting upon him—made him at once victorious and calm. Nor has it lost aught of its power through lapse of time. Yet, though the highest of all the forces by which humanity is or ever shall be moved, it lives only in those who receive "all the *words* of this life;" and what goes under its name—in the language of that transcendental, intuitional, unbiblical Christianity, with which some are now intoxicated—is but an impotent caricature of it.

The apostle's way of representing the glorified Saviour's occupation in heaven confirms the view given of it in our comments upon the opening words of this book—namely, that His work in heaven is but the continuance of His work upon earth, and that all which is done by the instrumentality of men in gathering sinners under His wing, and planting, upholding, and extending His Church throughout the world, is strictly *His own doing*, to whom, for this intent, is given all power in heaven and in earth, and who, for this end also, hath the residue of the Spirit. The express design for which God hath exalted Him, says the apostle, is to "*give* repentance to Israel and the remission of sins;" not only to open the way for these, and invite men to them, but Himself to *dispense* them; for nothing short of this is a satisfactory sense of the apostle's language. 'We have already (says *Olshausen*) found this "repentance" in conjunction with the "remission of sins," as the great object of the preaching of the Gospel.' But here there is a more precise intimation in the word "to *give*"—namely, that this "repentance" is not a thing which can be produced by the will of man, but must be effected by grace. All Pelagian modes of conception, therefore, stand in most decided opposition to this passage. But that repentance as well as remission is strictly a work Divine and gracious, though it be clearly conveyed in this passage, is not the precise truth of which we now speak. It is that Jesus, as the glorified Administrator of the new covenant, is not merely the Channel but the *Dispenser* of all spiritual blessings. "The Father loveth the Son, and hath given all things into His hand." This is the proper *Regal Activity* of Jesus, and will be until all things are put under His feet, and the ends of the Mediatorial Economy have been fully accomplished. 3. The mode in which Gamaliel proposed that the new Faith should be dealt with is based upon a stable principle of the Divine government—that falsehood in religion, as in everything else, is destined to come to nought, despite of all attempts to prop it up; while truth, however resolutely and perseveringly opposed, will eventually triumph. Religious persecution, if we look to its permanent results, is a mistake no less than a crime. As a means of extinguishing error it is superfluous, and against truth it is vain. 4. The joy with which the apostles tasted their first sufferings for Jesus' sake is intelligible only to those to whom His name is dear. But such have in every age felt the love of Christ constraining them, as a principle of all-subduing power—bracing them up in times of persecution to heroic endurance; in times of peace prompting them to self-sacrificing efforts to spread His name, and habitually impelling them to walk worthy of Him, and adorn His doctrine.

CHAP. VI. 1-15.—FIRST ELECTION AND ORDINATION OF DEACONS—CONTINUED TRIUMPHS OF THE GOSPEL—STEPHEN IS ARRESTED, AND CHARGED BEFORE THE SANHEDRIM WITH HOSTILITY TO MOSES,

there arose a murmuring of the Grecians ^bagainst the Hebrews, because
2 their widows were neglected ^cin the daily ministration. Then the twelve
called the multitude of the disciples *unto them*, and said, ^dIt is not reason
3 that we should leave the word of God, and serve tables. Wherefore,
brethren, ^elook ye out among you seven men of honest report, full of the
4 Holy Ghost and wisdom, whom we may appoint over this business. But
we ^fwill give ourselves continually to prayer, and to the ministry of the
5 word. And the saying pleased the whole multitude: and they chose
Stephen, a ^gman full of faith and of the Holy Ghost, ^hand Philip, and
Prochorus, and Nicanor, and Timon, and Parmenas, and Nicolas a prose-
6 lyte of Antioch: whom they set before the apostles: and when ⁱthey
had prayed, ^jthey laid *their* hands on them.
7 And ^kthe word of God increased; and the number of the disciples
multiplied in Jerusalem greatly; and a great company ^lof the priests
were obedient to the faith.

A. D. 33.

^b ch 9. 29.
ch. 11. 20.
^c ch. 4. 35.
^d Ex. 18. 17.
2 Tim. 2. 4.
^e Deut. 1. 13.
^f ch. 2. 42.
^g ch. 11. 24.
^h ch. 8. 5.
ch. 21. 8.
ⁱ ch. 1. 24.
^j ch. 8. 17.
ch. 9. 17.
ch. 13. 3.
1 Tim. 4.14.
^k Col. 1. 6.
2 Tim. 3. 1.
^l John 12. 42.

First Election and Ordination of Deacons (1-6). **1. And in those days, when the number of the disciples was multiplied** [πληθυνόντων]—'when the disciples were growing numerous.' As this took place not long before Stephen's death, at which Saul of Tarsus was present (ch. vii. 58; viii. 1), it could hardly have occurred earlier than two or three years after the great day of Pentecost. **there arose a murmuring of the Grecians** ['Ελληνιστῶν]—not Greeks, but Greek-speaking Jews, who for the most part were born in foreign countries; **against the Hebrews** — those Jews, born in Palestine, whose mother-tongue was Hebrew (more strictly Syro-Chaldaic or Aramaic), and who regarded the "Grecians" as an inferior class of Jews; **because their widows were neglected** [παρεθεωροῦντο] — or 'overlooked.' The imperfect tense conveys the idea of 'getting overlooked,' by those whom the apostles employed to distribute the liberality of the Christian community, and who, it would appear, were of the 'Hebrew' class, as being probably the most numerous. The complaint was, in all likelihood, well founded, though we cannot suspect the distributors of intentional partiality. It was really (as *Olshausen* remarks) just an emulation of love, each party wishing to have their own poor cared for in the best manner. **in the daily ministration**—the daily distribution either of alms or of food; probably the latter (see on *v.* 2). **2. Then the twelve called** [προσκαλεσάμενοι] —or 'convened' **the multitude** [τὸ πλῆθος]—the general body of the disciples unto them, and said, It is not reason [Οὐκ ἀρεστόν ἐστιν]—It is not agreeable or 'satisfactory.' A feeling of dislike is implied—'We must not be made to submit longer to this.' **that we should leave the word of God**—have our time and attention drawn off from the preaching of the Word. It thus appears that they regarded this as their primary work, and that whatever hindered them, to any extent, from prosecuting this, however important in its own place, was to be shaken off as soon as provision could be made for having it otherwise attended to. **and serve tables** [διακονεῖν τραπέζαις]—not 'money-tables,' or 'counters' for distributing alms (for the word "serve," 'minister to,' or 'supply,' is scarcely applicable to that), but 'provision-tables.' So the sense seems to be, 'that we should occupy ourselves in overseeing the distribution of provisions.' **3. Wherefore, brethren, look ye out**—ye, the multitude: the election was to be strictly popular. **among you**—of your own number, **seven men of honest report** —*lit.*, 'men testified to;' that is, bearing a good reputation (so ch. x. 22; and more explicitly 1 Tim.

iii. 7). **full of the [Holy] Ghost**—or 'full of the Spirit,' according to another reading; not full of miraculous gifts (which, for the duties required, would have been no qualification) but men *spiritually gifted*; although on two of the men chosen on this occasion miraculous power did rest. [We have bracketed the word "Holy," as of doubtful authority. *Tischendorf* rejects it, but *Lachmann* does better in simply bracketing it, as the evidence for and against ἁγίου—both external and internal—is nearly equal.] **and wisdom**—here meaning 'discretion,' aptitude for practical affairs. **whom we** (the apostles) **may appoint over this business** [χρείας]—or 'duty.' Thus we see that while the *election* was vested in the Christian people, the *appointment* lay with the apostles, as spiritual rulers. **4. But we will give ourselves continually**—that is, more exclusively than had been possible while they had to attend to the daily distribution of provisions. **to prayer**—that is, probably, not private prayer, but the 'public worship' in the assemblies of the Church, **and to the ministry of the word**—the other great division of apostolic work. [Observe the contrast between διακονία τ. λόγου and διακονεῖν τραπέζαις.] **5. And the saying pleased the whole multitude: and they chose Stephen, a man full of faith and of the Holy Ghost, and Philip, and Prochorus, and Nicanor, and Timon, and Parmenas, and Nicolas a proselyte of Antioch.** As these names are all Greek, it is not unlikely that the first six were all of the Grecian class, with whom the "proselyte" Nicolas would be supposed to sympathize. If this was so, it would effectually restore mutual confidence. We cannot, however, be quite certain of it, as the Jews at this time often took Greek names. There is no ground whatever for the tradition that this Nicolas was the founder of the heretical sect of the "Nicolaitanes" (Rev. ii. 15). **6. Whom they set before the apostles: and when they** (the apostles) **had prayed, they laid their hands on them**—the one act proclaiming that all official gifts flowed from the Church's glorified Head, the other symbolizing the communication of these to the chosen office-bearers through the recognized channels.

Continued Triumphs of the Gospel—Stephen distinguishes himself, both by his Preaching and his Miracles (7-10). **7. And the word of God increased; and the number of the disciples multiplied in Jerusalem greatly**—prosperity crowning the beautiful spirit which reigned in this mother-community of Christians. **and a great company of the priests were obedient to the faith**—a phrase implying that the believing reception of the Gospel is an act of obedience, and if so, surely

8 And Stephen, full of faith and power, did great wonders and miracles
9 among the people. Then there arose certain of the synagogue, which is
called *the synagogue* of the Libertines, and Cyrenians, and Alexandrians,
10 and of them of Cilicia and of Asia, disputing with Stephen. And ^mthey
were not able to resist the wisdom and the spirit by which he spake.
11 Then ⁿthey suborned men, which said, We have heard him speak blas-
12 phemous words against Moses, and *against* God. And they stirred up
the people, and the elders, and the scribes, and came upon *him*, and
13 caught him, and brought *him* to the council, and set up false witnesses,
which said, This man ceaseth not to speak blasphemous words against
14 this holy place, and the law: for ^owe have heard him say, that this Jesus
of Nazareth shall ^pdestroy this place, and shall change the ¹customs

A. D 33.
^m Ex. 4. 12.
Isa. 54. 17.
Luke 21.15.
ⁿ 1 Ki. 21.10.
Matt.26.59.
John 16. 3.
^o ch. 25. 8.
^p Dan. 9. 20.
Mic 3. 12.
Zech 11. 1.
1 Or, rites.
Heb. 8. 13.
Heb. 9.
Heb. 10.

it is the highest. (See John. vi. 29: compare Rom. i. 5; xvi. 20; and see on Rom. ii. 8.) This accession of a great multitude of the priests was the crowning triumph of the Gospel, whose peaceful prosperity was now at its greatest height. For, after Stephen's teaching and trial made it clear that the sacerdotal interests could not stand with the Gospel, such priestly accessions became rare indeed.

8. And Stephen, &c. The foregoing narrative of the first election and ordination of deacons might probably not have been given at all, but that it seemed necessary to the understanding of what follows regarding the martyr Stephen, that the reader should know what first brought him into public notice. **full of faith**—but the true reading here certainly is, 'full of grace' [χάριτος—with אA B D, and more than twenty MSS.; the Vulgate, and most ancient versions, and many fathers. It is adopted by *Lachmann* and *Tischendorf*, and approved by all critical commentators. The received reading, πίστεως, has but inferior support, and those MSS. which have it probably repeated it from *v.* 5.] **and power**—here meaning supernatural power, as is evident from what follows, **did great wonders and miracles among the people. 9. Then there arose certain of the synagogue, which is called the synagogue of the Libertines**—*Libertini;* Jewish 'freedmen.' Pompey, after overrunning Judea, in the year B. C. 63, carried an immense number of Jews as prisoners of war to Rome, where they were sold as slaves. They were afterwards manumitted, with liberty to adhere to their own religion; but Tiberius, as *Tacitus* informs us (Ann. ii. 85), expelled them or their children, to the number of four thousand, from Italy on account of their religion. Of these many would no doubt settle in Palestine, and reside in Jerusalem. **and Cyrenians**—Jews of Cyrene (see on ch. ii. 10), **and Alexandrians**—Jews of Alexandria. The form of the expression [τῶν ἐκ τῆς συναγωγῆς τῆς λεγομένης Λιβερτίνων, καὶ Κυρηναίων καὶ Ἀλεξανδρέων] would seem to imply that these three classes of foreign Jews had one synagogue; while the next two classes seem distinguished from these [καὶ τῶν ἀπὸ Κιλικίας ·καὶ Ἀσίας]: nevertheless, as the rabbins say that there were no fewer than 480 synagogues in Jerusalem, and all nationalities had their own, it is possible that the five different classes here named had each their own synagogue—arranged, however, in two groups (as *Lechler* remarks)—those of Roman and African descent, and those of Asia Minor. **and of them of Cilicia**—amongst whom may have been Saul of Tarsus (ch. vii. 58; xxi. 39), **and of Asia**—(see on ch. xvi. 6.) *Lachmann* excludes this last clause from his text, but the evidence for it is decisive: *Tischendorf* retains it. These five classes of foreign Jews combined in **disputing with Stephen**—as the enemy of their

common religion. **10. And they were not able to resist the wisdom and the spirit by which he spake**—what he spake, and the power with which he spake it, being alike resistless.

Foiled in argument, his opponents raise an insurrection against Stephen, and have him arrested, brought before the Sanhedrim, and charged with hostility to the National Religion—His beautiful serenity before the Council (11-15). **11. Then they suborned** [ὑπέβαλον]. This is the proper sense of the word, with reference to witnesses or informers, **men, which said, We have heard him speak blasphemous words against Moses**—referring, doubtless, to what he had said of the impending disappearance of the whole Mosaic system (see *v.* 14): **and against God**—referring probably to the supreme dignity and authority which he would claim for Christ as the Head of that new economy that was speedily to supersede the old (compare ch. vii. 56, 59, 60). **12. And they stirred up the people, and the elders, and the scribes, and came upon him, and caught him, and brought him to the council, 13. And set up false witnesses, which said, This man ceaseth not**—a testimony to his unflagging zeal and activity, **to speak [blasphemous] words against this holy place, and the law.** The true reading here seems to be 'to speak words against the holy place and the law [Βλάσφημα and τούτου being insufficiently attested]. **14. For we have heard him say, that this Jesus of Nazareth shall destroy this place, and shall change the customs which Moses delivered us.** It is surely catching at a straw for the Tübingen critics (*Baur* and *Zeller*), in their eagerness to disprove the authenticity of this book, to charge its author with falsehood, in calling these men "false witnesses" (*v.* 13), since Stephen's own speech in the next chapter proves that he must have said the very things which those witnesses testified against him. The falsehood of their charges against Stephen (as of those against our Lord Himself) lay not in the statements they charged Stephen with, but in the *turn* they gave to them, and especially in the *hostility to the religion of their fathers*, which they insinuated that he had displayed. What Stephen certainly announced was the approaching change in the Divine economy; and as a Jew of foreign extraction (which he appears to have been), he was a peculiarly fitting preacher of this to his foreign brethren of the synagogue above mentioned. But, as the result showed, he was too far in advance of them. **15. And all that sat in the council, looking stedfastly on him, saw his face as it had been the face of an angel** —a play of heavenly radiance attesting to all who beheld his countenance the divine calm of the spirit within—the fruit of the felt presence of his glorified Lord. This shining countenance (says *Chrysostom*) was the glory of Moses too; **and** *Humphry* well observes that, as if in refutation

15 which Moses delivered us. And all that sat in the council, looking stedfastly on him, saw his face as it had been the face of ^qan angel.

A. D. 33.

^q Matt. 23. 3.

of the charge of hostility to Moses, he receives the same mark of Divine favour which had been vouchsafed to Moses (Exod. xxxiv. 30)—"And when Aaron and all the children of Israel, saw Moses, behold, the skin of his face shone; and they were afraid to come nigh him."

Remarks.—1. 'How prominently (we here adopt the excellent remark of *Lechler*) does the truth here stand before us, that the Word of God, and that only, is the means of salvation in the Church of Christ! The apostles firmly resisted the temptation to lose themselves in a Martha-service —"caring about many things," and to become engrossed therein, with a view to put a stop to the discontent. On the contrary, they make for themselves only freer hands and more ample leisure for the ministry of the Word. This is the apostolic calling. This is their chief business— "the ministry of reconciliation." The apostolic Church approves itself as the Church of the Word; and every Church which will be truly apostolical must also be a Church of the Word. The more the Word of God steps behind the word of man—behind ceremonies, behind human rules and ordinances of the Church, behind affairs of government and mechanical service—the more is it removed from what it should be.' 2. How easily may misunderstandings arise amongst the most loving and devoted followers of the Lord Jesus; but yet how quickly and effectually may these be healed where honest intentions, love, and wisdom reign? In the present case the multitude of converts, all pouring in the proceeds of their sold property into a common stock at the apostles' feet, and their raw and but half-consolidated state for some time, would seem imperatively to demand the personal superintendence of the apostles at the daily distribution of what the necessitous required. But as this could hardly have gone beyond a general oversight, and the work would no doubt be got through as speedily as possible, it is easy to see how, with the best intentions, irregularities might occur, and apparent partialities be shown. Nor is there any good reason to doubt that a preference for the native poor— representing the majority of the needy—over those of foreign extraction may have been half-unconsciously shown. But what a beautiful model for imitation in all similar cases does the choice of this assembly furnish! Though we have reason to think that the majority of them belonged to the class complained of, they choose (as would seem) the whole of the new distributors from among the complaining minority. By this, whether the complaint was well or ill-founded, they effectually put an end to it, and restored confidence and harmony to the whole body. 3. How superior to the lust of power do the apostles here show themselves to be, in not only divesting themselves of the immediate superintendence of temporal affairs in the Christian community (though the responsibility for its general well-being they could not shake off), but giving the choice of those who were to be entrusted with this temporal oversight to the disciples at large! 4. How little of formal organization did the apostles give to the Church at first, and when an emergency arose which demanded something more, how entirely was the remedy suggested by the reason of the thing! Had the life and prosperity of the Church depended upon hierarchical orders, ritual observances, and mechanical arrangements, how differently would the apostles have acted! But if it depended, as we have seen that it did (Remark 1), on the *Word*—

preached and received in the power of the Spirit —then did the apostles act, in relation to all external matters, just as might have been expected —providing for them as the occasion demanded, and only as the necessities of each case required. 5. Though the new office-bearers are not expressly called *Deacons* here, it is universally admitted that this was the first institution of that order in the Church; the success of the expedient securing its permanency, and the qualifications for "the office of a deacon" being laid down in one of the apostolic epistles immediately after that of "a bishop" (1 Tim. iii. 8-13). For a considerable time they appear to have been known only as "the seven," from their original number (ch. xxi. 8); and it must have been only as the need of such church officers came to be felt elsewhere, and the number seven was not adhered to, that the name "deacon" became their fixed official designation, either given or acquiesced in by the apostles. 6. Though the equitable distribution of the means of temporal support to the needy was the sole object of the first institution of deacons in the Church, the standard of qualification laid down for this office is notably high. *First*, they were to be of "honest report"—of good reputation. It was not enough that they should *be* good; they must have a *character* for goodness among their fellows. Without this the whole influence, even of real excellence, upon others is neutralized. And if this be true of private, it is more so of official life. In the present-case, the *confidence* entertained by the needy themselves in those set apart to supply their wants was plainly the principal secret of their satisfaction with the change, and the general harmony that resulted. And if a good reputation is requisite in an office so humble as that of a deacon of the Church, much more surely in "pastors and teachers." But *next*, they were required to be "full of the Holy Ghost," which can mean nothing less than eminent for spiritual gifts — such as faith, love, zeal, humility. Nor is the need for such qualities in those who go in and out before the people as bearers of office, however humble, a whit less now than it was then. *Lastly*, they were to be men of "wisdom," without which neither a name for worth, nor the highest spirituality, are sufficient qualifications for ecclesiastical office. In the distribution of alms in any form, sound judgment is indispensable; and the apostles showed their own judgment in demanding this of those who were to relieve them of the burden they had till then to bear. But the higher the official position which any one occupies in the Church, so much the more important is this qualification of "wisdom." For want of it, how much energy and zeal are misdirected, and what a fruitless expenditure of heavy labour and precious resources is seen from time to time in the Church of Christ! 7. The whole conduct of Stephen's opponents—in first trying to silence him by argument, and when this failed, raising against him a storm of popular indignation, suborning men to swear against him false charges of hostility to the faith Divinely committed to their fathers—is so entirely in keeping with the procedure of the same class towards our Lord before, and towards His apostles and others afterwards, and with the spirit which the nation has evinced towards Christ ever since, that this most life-like part of the narrative will at once be seen to attest its own historical accuracy. But the sequel of this history will furnish even more striking illustrations of this remark. 8. How easily can

7, THEN said the high priest, Are ^athese things so? And he said, Men, | A. D. 33.
2 brethren, and fathers, hearken; The God of glory appeared unto our | ^a Matt. 26.61.

unscrupulous malignity pervert the truth, even when professing, with the utmost plausibility, only to express it! Just as the charge brought against our Lord, at His trial before the Sanhedrim, regarding the destruction of the temple, would, to a superficial hearer, have a considerable appearance of truth, and yet was so false that even the high priest would not condemn Him upon it; so the charge against Stephen, of hostility to Moses and the religion of his fathers, while it had apparent ground in the principal scope of his preaching, was thoroughly false, and by himself afterwards proved to be so. *Calvin*, in a fine comment upon *v.* 14 of this chapter, warns those who were associated with him in the work of Reformation not to think it unreasonable that those wounds which Satan was permitted to inflict even upon the Son of God should reach to them also. 'When,' says he, 'we teach that men are so depraved as to be the captives of sin and evil lusts, straightway our enemies raise the calumny that we deny men to be voluntary sinners, and hold them to be so impelled to evil as to be free of blame, and extinguish in ourselves all motive to well-doing. Because we deny to the good works of the saints all strictly meritorious worth, inasmuch as they have always some defect in them, we are charged with destroying the distinction between good and bad works. Because we say that the righteousness of man is founded on the grace of God alone, and that the souls of the godly can rest only on the death of Christ, they charge us with giving loose reins to the flesh, and making the law of no more use. Hard indeed it is (he adds) to lie under such charges; but we must not be scared away by them from the defence of the good cause. For precious to God is His own truth; and it should be to us, although to them that perish it be the savour of death unto death (2 Cor. ii. 16).'

CHAP. VII. 1-60.—STEPHEN'S DEFENCE BEFORE THE SANHEDRIM—HIS MARTYRDOM.

1. Then said the high priest, Are these things so?

Stephen defends himself by a Historical Sketch of God's procedure towards Israel, and of Israel's conduct in return.

Part First: *From the call of Abraham to the settlement of Jacob and his family in Egypt* (1-16). **2. And he said, Men, brethren, and fathers, hearken.** In this long defence Stephen takes a much wider range, and answers the charges brought against him less directly, than we should have expected. But when we find his accusers stung to the quick by what seems a mere recital of historical facts—especially as the drift of them is expressed in the concluding summary — we may be sure that they were selected and presented with no ordinary skill. What was the precise object aimed at has occasioned much discussion and division of opinion. But it seems clearly to have been twofold: *first*, by an induction of facts, to show that the national platform which they now idolized, though Divinely erected, had been of slow growth, and that the then existing state of things, which was no older than Solomon, had been expressly declared by the Lord Himself to be but external and shadowy, pointing to something else which was spiritual and far better; *second*, by a similar induction of facts, to show that the whole history of the nation, from the earliest period down to the latest, had, on their part, been little else than one continued *misapprehension* of God's high designs towards fallen

man through them, as His covenant people, and *rebellion* against these gracious purposes; while on God's part it was the triumphant establishment of His own plans, in spite of them, and even by means of them. In their murderous treatment of the Lord Jesus, then, and their present opposition to His witnesses, Stephen would have them to know that they were but filling up their fathers' iniquity; while God was, in spite of them and by means of them, laying the foundations of the kingdom that was never to be moved. Incidentally, this long historical sketch would serve another purpose—to clear himself of the charge of hostility to Moses, and the Divinely-instituted religion of the nation; every sentence showing not merely such familiarity with even its minute details as devout and habitual study only could impart, but that reverence for all parts of the Divine procedure, and the very words in which they are expressed and explained and vindicated, as only a profound faith in the God of Israel and His living oracles could have inspired. But this with Stephen was but a secondary object, or rather no object at all; his soul being filled with one purpose, to seize the opportunity now afforded him of vindicating before the highest tribunal of the nation the truth of God which in his person was on its trial. That Stephen delivered this speech, not in the mother-tongue, but in Greek, is next to certain, from the conformity of its style to that of the Septuagint, and from the conformity of some of its details to that translation where it diverges from the Hebrew text; and if he was a Hellenistic or Greek-speaking Jew, as there is every reason to think he was, this would be to him the more natural language. In this case we have here no mere translation of the speech (as in the case of Paul's address on the castle stairs, ch. xxii.), but the original. But how, in this case (one may ask) could the speech have been preserved? That the whole is the composition of a later period is only what the Tübingen critics might have been expected to affirm, though on that supposition probably none but themselves would suppose it likely to be constructed as it is; and *Hackett* only expresses what every intelligent reader of it must feel, that 'its peculiar character impresses upon it a seal of authenticity; for no one would think of framing a discourse of this kind for such an occasion. Had it been composed ideally, or after some vague tradition, it would have been thrown into a different form, and its relevancy to the charge which called it forth would have been made more obvious.' That Saul of Tarsus, as a member of the Sanhedrim, wrote it down and afterwards communicated it to our historian, his companion in travel, is certainly unlikely. But that notes of it were taken by several who were present is scarcely to be doubted, arrested as they would be by the angelic expression of his countenance (ch. vi. 15), and expecting that in such circumstances something worth hearing would surely be spoken. And if they once began, they were not likely to stop in recording so uncommon an address. And violent as was the rage of the Council at the closing words of the speech, it is not to be doubted that it made a deep impression on some at least, through whose notes of it the Christians might obtain it; and after Saul's conversion—whose part in the execution of Stephen (*v.* 58) indelibly impressed the whole scene upon his memory (see ch. xxii. 20)—it is not impossible that when its echoes were once wakened up, he may have been able to fill in some points in the narrative, or

father Abraham, when he was in Mesopotamia, before he dwelt in Charran, 3 and said unto him, *b*Get thee out of thy country, and from thy kindred, 4 and come into the land which I shall show thee. Then *c*came he out of the land of the Chaldeans, and dwelt in Charran: and from thence, when his father was dead, he removed him into this land, wherein ye now dwell. 5 And he gave him none inheritance in it, no, not *so much as* to set his foot on: yet he *d*promised that he would give it to him for a possession, 6 and to his seed after him, when *as yet* he had no child. And God spake

A. D. 33.
b Gen. 12. 1.
c Gen. 11. 31.
Gen. 12. 4.
Heb. 11. 8.
d Gen. 12. 7.
Gen. 13. 15.
Gen. 17. 8.
Gen. 26. 3.
Ex. 6. 7, 8.

some features in the closing description of the effect produced, of which our historian has availed himself.

The God of glory—magnificent appellation! (as *Bengel* well calls it,) fitted at the very outset to rivet the devout attention of his audience. It denotes here not so much that visible glory (called the Shechinah) which attended so many of the Divine manifestations (as *de Wette, Meyer, Alford,* and *Hackett*), as the glory of those manifestations themselves—of which every Jew regarded this manifestation to Abraham as the fundamental one. It is the glory of that free grace towards sinners of mankind, which, when it proceeded to concentrate itself in one family, did in pure sovereignty select Abraham to be the parent, and, through his seed, the depositary of that grace which in the fulness of time was to flow forth to all nations. appeared unto our father Abraham, when he was in Mesopotamia, before he dwelt in Charran — or 'Haran' · חָרָן; LXX., Χάρραν—in Greek writers, Κάρραι; Latin, *Carræ,* where Crassus fell, ignominiously defeated by the Parthians]. It lies about fifty miles from Ur. Though this first call of Abraham is not recorded in Genesis, it is clearly implied in Gen. xv. 7, "I am the Lord that brought thee out of Ur of the Chaldees;" and the same statement is repeated in Neh. ix. 7. The Jewish commentator *Philo,* and the historian *Josephus* (both nearly contemporary with Stephen), concur in representing the first call of Abraham as given when he was in Ur. 3. And said unto him, Get thee out of thy country, and from thy kindred, and come into the land which I shall show thee. 4. Then came he out of the land of the Chaldeans, and dwelt in Charran: and from thence, when his father was dead, he removed him into this land, wherein ye now dwell. This last statement seems to contradict the account given in Gen. xi. 26, 32; and xii. 4, from which one would certainly conclude that Abraham's father, instead of being dead when he migrated to Canaan, lived sixty years after that. (Thus, "Terah lived *sixty years* and begat Abram, Nahor, and Haran;" "And the days of Terah were *two hundred and five years,* and Terah died in Haran;" "And Abram was *seventy and five years* old when he departed out of Haran." Adding, then, to Terah's seventy years, when Abram was born—and supposing him to be the eldest of the family—the seventy-five years of Abram's age, when he removed to Canaan, we have Terah only one hundred and forty-five years old at that date, leaving sixty years more of his life to run after that). This difficulty has occasioned much discussion and diversity of opinion. *Grotius, de Wette,* and *Meyer* have an easy way of disposing of the matter by alleging a chronological error on the part of Stephen. But as *Philo* has represented the matter very much as Stephen does, *Lechler* and others prefer to say that he simply followed the current tradition; and *Alford* endeavours to account for the Jews having fallen into this mistake. But let us see how others solve the difficulty. *Olshausen* and *Stier,* follow-

ing the rabbins, have adopted a most unnatural interpretation—namely, that when Abraham's removal to Canaan is said to have been 'after his father's death,' it means not his natural but his *spiritual* death, or his apostasy to idolatry (Josh. xxiv. 2). A more natural solution is, that when it is said "Terah was seventy years old, and begat Abram, Nahor, and Haran" (Gen. xi. 26), the meaning is that he was seventy when the eldest of his three sons was born, and that Abraham, though mentioned before Nahor and Haran, as being the most important of the three, was probably the youngest. 'This (says *Alexander,* who takes this view) would enable us to fix the birth of Abraham at such a distance from that of his elder brother or brothers as would bring his seventy-fifth year after the natural death of his father.' 'But this (says *Olshausen,* and with reason, we suspect) will not fill up sixty years.' Better than this, in our judgment, is *Bengel's* view (though pronounced by *Lechler* 'purely fanciful,' and by *Alford* 'lamentable'), that though Abraham came to Canaan while his father was alive, it was only as a stranger—his settled abode being then with his father at Haran —and that it was only on his father's demise that Abraham permanently settled in Canaan. This would account for the Jewish tradition on the subject, and quite well explain Stephen's statement. But it hardly accord's with the natural sense of the account given in Genesis. It only remains to state the view taken by *Baumgarten,* which seems best to meet the difficulty—that in Genesis the historian relates at once, in the eleventh chapter, all he has to say of the ancestry and nearest relations of Abraham, ending with the death of his father, in order that when he came to open in the next chapter the more peculiar history of the father of the faithful, he might be able to relate his call and migration to Canaan as the proper starting-point of the covenant transactions, unembarrassed by any reference to his fleshly connections, and that Stephen, reading the history in this light (as, indeed, *Philo* seems to have done, and so, probably, others also), holds forth the calling of Abraham as being after his father's death. If this be the case, instead of this being properly a chronological error, it is simply the light in which the original account, as it stands in Genesis, naturally presents itself to the devout mind. The reader, however, having thus before him all the different views of the matter, can judge for himself. 5. And he gave him none inheritance in it, no, not so much as to set his foot on—for, though he got by purchase the cave of Machpelah for a burial-place, his having to buy it only confirms Stephen's statement, that God gave him, as a gift of heaven, none inheritance in it. yet he promised that he would give it to him for a possession, and to his seed after him, when as yet he had no child. Both the land and the seed to inherit it were thus, at the first, matter of pure promise—to be apprehended by mere faith on Abraham's part. 6. And God spake on this wise. That his seed should sojourn in a strange

on this wise, 'That his seed should sojourn in a strange land; and that they should bring them into bondage, and entreat *them* ᶠevil four hundred

7 years. And the nation to whom they shall be in bondage will I judge, said God: and after that shall they come forth, and ᵍserve me in this

8 place. And ʰhe gave him the covenant of circumcision: ⁱand so *Abraham* begat Isaac, and circumcised him the eighth day; ʲand Isaac *begat* Jacob; and Jacob ᵏ*begat* the twelve patriarchs.

9 And ˡthe patriarchs, moved with envy, sold Joseph into Egypt: ᵐbut

10 God was with him, and delivered him out of all his afflictions, ⁿand gave him favour and wisdom in the sight of Pharaoh king of Egypt; and he

11 made him governor over Egypt and all his house. Now there came a dearth over all the land of Egypt and Chanaan, and great affliction: and

12 our fathers found no sustenance. But when Jacob heard that there was

13 corn in Egypt, he sent out our fathers first. And at the second *time* Joseph was made known to his brethren; and Joseph's kindred was made

14 known unto Pharaoh. Then ᵒsent Joseph, and called his father Jacob to

15 *him*, and all his kindred, threescore and ᵖfifteen souls. So Jacob went

16 down into Egypt, ᵠand died, he, and our fathers, and ʳwere carried over into Sychem, and laid in ˢthe sepulchre that Abraham bought for a sum of money of the sons of Emmor *the father* of Sychem.

A. D. 33.
ᵉ Gen. 15. 13.
  1 Pet. 2. 11.
ᶠ Ex. 12. 40.
  Gal. 3. 17.
ᵍ Ex. 3. 12.
ʰ Gen. 17. 9.
ⁱ Gen. 21. 2.
  1 Chr. 1. 34.
  Matt. 1. 2.
ʲ Gen. 25. 26.
ᵏ Gen. 29. 31.
  Gen. 35. 18.
ˡ Gen. 37. 4.
ᵐ Gen. 39.2,3.
ⁿ Gen. 42. 6.
ᵒ Gen. 45. 9.
ᵖ Gen. 46. 27.
  Deut. 10.22.
  Including the wives of his brethren.
ᵠ Gen. 49. 33.
ʳ Ex. 13. 19.
ˢ Gen. 23. 16.

---

land; and that they should bring them into bondage, and entreat them evil four hundred years—that is, speaking in round numbers, as in Gen. xv. 13, 16. The exact period was four hundred and thirty years (Exod. xii. 40; Gal. iii. 17). (Though the structure of the sentence seems to imply that they were not only 'brought into bondage,' but 'evil entreated' four hundred years, it is to the former only that the four hundred years are intended to apply.) **7. And the nation to whom they shall be in bondage will I judge, said God**—that is, visit with avenging judgments; **and after that shall they come forth, and serve me in this place.** Stephen, it will be observed, combines here two promises into one—that to Abraham (Gen. xv. 16), and that to Moses (Exod. iii. 12)—his object being merely to give a rapid summary of the leading facts. **8. And he gave him the covenant of circumcision**—that is, the covenant of which circumcision was the visible, sacramental token: **and so**—that is, according to the arrangements of this covenant, **Abraham begat Isaac, and circumcised him the eighth day; and Isaac begat Jacob; and Jacob begat the twelve patriarchs**—so called as being the founders of the twelve tribes of Israel.

9. And the patriarchs, moved with envy, sold Joseph into Egypt: but God was with him. Here Stephen brings forward his first example of *Israel's misapprehension of God's purposes and opposition to them, in spite of which, and by means of which, those purposes were accomplished.* **10. And delivered him out of all his afflictions, and gave him favour and wisdom in the sight of Pharaoh king of Egypt; and he made him governor over Egypt and all his house.** *Thus again was the stone which the builders rejected made the head of the corner.* **11. Now there came a dearth over all the land of Egypt and Chanaan, and great affliction: and our fathers found no sustenance.** [*Lachmann*, on good external authority, leaves out γῆν, reading 'all Egypt.' But there is nearly equal authority for retaining it; probability is in favour of it; and *Tischendorf* inserts it.] **12. But when Jacob heard that there was corn in Egypt** [εἰς Αἴγυπτον is manifestly the true reading here, not ἐν Ἀ—ῳ, as in the received text], **he sent out our fathers first. 13. And at the second time Joseph was made known to his brethren; and Joseph's kindred was made**

known unto Pharaoh. *And so were the enemies of God's chosen one, who were his own brethren, made to bow in submission to him.* The bearing of these features of the narrative on all that Stephen was arraigned for preaching must strike every thoughtful reader; but we have thought it well to put the main positions in Italics, to call attention to them. **14. Then sent Joseph, and called his father Jacob to him, and all his kindred, threescore and fifteen souls.** This is strictly according to Gen. xlvi. 27 and Exod. i. 5, as rendered in the LXX, which Stephen follows. The Hebrew text of both passages makes the number "seventy." Probably five are included in the one reckoning which are excluded in the latter; though which five is not quite agreed on. **15. So Jacob went down into Egypt.** [*Tischendorf*, on insufficient authority, strikes out εἰς Αἴγ., and *Alford* brackets it; *Lachmann* retains it.] **and died, he, and our fathers. 16. And were carried over into Sychem, and laid in the sepulchre that** [ᾧ is clearly the true reading here—by *attr.* for ὁ, into which it has been corrected in the received text] **Abraham bought for a sum of money of the sons of Emmor**—or "Hamor" (Gen. xxxix. 19), the father **of Sychem**—or "Shechem:" in John iv. 5. (on which see note) it is called "Sychar." Three difficulties occur in this verse. (1.) It seems to say that both Jacob and his sons were buried at Shechem; whereas in Gen. l. 13 it is said that Jacob's sons buried their father, not at Shechem, but in the cave of the field of Machpelah or Hebron, according to his own dying charge (ch. xlix. 29, 30). (2.) It says that Jacob's sons were buried at Shechem, of which no mention is made in Old Testament history. (3.) It says that the sepulchre at Shechem was bought by Abraham; whereas Gen. xxxiii. 18,19, ascribes the purchase to Jacob. As to Jacob's own burial-place, it is not very likely that Stephen fell into a mistake in a matter so notorious—confounding Hebron with Shechem; nor is it necessary to suppose that Stephen, in saying they "were carried over into Sychem, and laid in the sepulchre," &c., meant that both "he and our fathers" were both so carried. If we suppose "he and our fathers" to apply only to the party last mentioned—namely, Jacob's sons, not himself—that difficulty disappears. Then, as to the burial of Jacob's sons at Shechem, there is

17 But when *the time of the promise drew nigh, which God had sworn
18 to Abraham, the people grew and multiplied in Egypt, till another king
19 arose, which knew not Joseph. The same dealt subtilly with our kindred,
and evil-entreated our fathers, so that they cast out their young children,
to the end they might not live.
20 In "which time Moses was born, and was ¹exceeding fair, and nourished
21 up in his father's house three months: and when he was cast out,
Pharaoh's daughter took him up, and nourished him for her own son.
22 And Moses was ⁿlearned in all the wisdom of the Egyptians, and ʷwas

A. D. 33.
ᵗ Gen. 15. 13, 16.
2 Pet. 3,8,9.
ᵘ Ex. 2. 2.
¹ Or, fair to God.
Heb. 11. 2ᵗ.
ᵛ 1 Ki. 4. 29.
2 Chr. 9. 22.
ʷ Luke 24.19.

nothing in the Old Testament to contradict it, though it is not expressly recorded. In this speech several other things are referred to as known facts, of which we have no record in the Old Testament. But it is expressly stated that Joseph was buried there (Josh. xxiv. 32); and *Jerome*, in the fourth century of the Christian era, says (Epp. 686) that the sepulchre of the twelve patriarchs was then to be seen at Sichem. As to the remaining difficulty, it is surely hasty to conclude that Stephen has here confounded the purchase of the field of Machpelah or Hebron by Abraham with the purchase of Shechem by Jacob. Is it unnatural to suppose that after a very long time from the period when Abraham bought this field, the original possessor having retaken it, Jacob finally secured it to himself by repurchasing it? Certain it is that Jacob had an altercation with these Amorites, or sons of Emmor, about some property, and that "with his sword and with his bow" he wrenched what on his deathbed he bequeathed to Joseph (Gen. xlviii. 22). But what, it may be asked, would have been the use to Abraham of two burying places—one at Hebron and another at Shechem? It may as well be asked why Jacob should have purchased a burying-place at Shechem, or anywhere else, when that at Hebron would naturally descend to him—that sepulchre where rested the ashes of his grand-parents, Abraham and Sarah; the ashes of both his own parents, Isaac and Rebekah; the ashes also of his wife Leah; and where he charged his sons to lay himself (Gen. xlix. 30, 31). We only add that, by the most recent accounts, it would appear that Hebron is not regarded in the country itself as the resting-place of Joseph's brethren. (See 'The Sepulchre in Sychem," in *Journal of Sacred Literature* for April, 1864; and 'The Mosque of Hebron,' in *Stanley's Sermons in the East*). The solutions we have given of the difficulties of this verse, though only submitted for the reader's consideration, are at least preferable to the short and easy way of charging an error on the speaker.

The Defence continued—Part Second: *From the Settlement in Egypt to the Exodus* (17-36). 17. But when [Καθὼς δὲ]—rather, 'But as' the time of the promise (that is, for its fulfilment) drew nigh, which God had sworn to Abraham [ὤμοσεν]—or, according to the best attested reading (adopted by *Lachmann* and *Tischendorf*,) 'which God had agreed to Abraham' [ὡμολόγησεν] the people grew and multiplied in Egypt. For more than 200 years they amounted to no more than seventy-five souls. How prodigious, then, must have been their multiplication in the following centuries, when 600,000 men fit for war, besides women and children, came up out of Egypt! Indeed, it has been pronounced an impossibility, and on this among other grounds the historical character of the Pentateuch has been attacked, not only by professed infidels, but by some high in ecclesiastical rank, who are weak enough to think that they can retain the Christian Faith

while rejecting, as unhistorical, those fundamental books of the Old Testament to the veracity of which the great Author and Subject of the Christian Faith attaches His most solemn seal. But the statistics and laws of population, when applied to the whole circumstances of the Hebrew people in Egypt, have been shown to be at least so far in accordance with this prodigious increase as to prove that there is nothing incredible in it; and beyond this we are not concerned to go. 18. Till another king arose [ἕτερος, not ἄλλος]—*q. d.*, 'a king of a different sort,' pointing to another dynasty (as *Lechler* notes), which knew not Joseph. After the lapse of centuries, and in a new dynasty, this might seem not surprising. But "knew not Joseph" is intended to convey more than mere want of knowledge. The memory of great events in the history of nations is not readily lost. Written records, and even popular traditions, preserve them fresh for centuries; and the organic changes which took place in Egypt during Joseph's administration would make it impossible that the memory of the country's obligations to him should perish within the period here referred to. *Ingratitude* is evidently meant to be stamped upon the royal procedure towards the descendants and countrymen of one to whom Egypt owed its preservation. 19. The same dealt subtilly (or cunningly) with our kindred, and evil-entreated our fathers, so that they cast out their young children [τὰ βρέφη αὐτῶν]—'their babes,' but the males only are meant: to the end they might not live—(see Exod. i. 22.) The martyrdom of these 'innocents' of Israel has been compared to that of the babes of Bethlehem.

20. In which time—of deepest depression and urgent need, Moses was born—the destined deliverer; their extremity being God's opportunity (see Deut. xxxii. 36; Isa. lix. 15, 16). and was exceeding fair [ἀστεῖος τῷ Θεῷ]—'fair to God' (as in *margin*), or, perhaps, 'divinely fair.' (See on Heb. xi. 23). and nourished up in his father's house three months—at the peril of his parents' lives; but "through faith . . . they were not afraid of the king's commandment" (Heb. xi. 23). 21. And when he was cast out ['Εκτεθέντα]—or 'exposed;' for his mother "could not longer hide him" (Exod. ii. 3). [ἐκτεθέντος, adopted by *Lachmann*, though supported by א A B C D, &c., is probably a grammatical correction. *Tischendorf* abides by the received text, which is approved by *Meyer*, *de Wette*, and *Alford*.] Pharaoh's daughter took him up, and nourished him for her own son—a most wonderful providence, which secured not only his preservation from certain death at that time, but the highest training thereafter which the most advanced kingdom then existing could supply. Nor, as we shall immediately see, was he a dull learner. 22. And Moses was learned in all the wisdom of the Egyptians [ἐπαιδεύθη ἐν πάσῃ σοφίᾳ—the preposition being better attested than the want of it in the received text]. The statement contained in this verse is nowhere

23 mighty in words and in deeds. And ˣwhen he was full forty years old,
24 it came into his heart to visit his brethren the children of Israel. And
seeing one *of them* suffer wrong, he defended *him*, and avenged him
25 that was oppressed, and smote the Egyptian : ²for he supposed his
brethren would have understood how that God by his hand would
26 deliver them: but they understood not. And the next day he showed
himself unto them as they strove, and would have set them at one again,
27 saying, Sirs, ye are brethren; why do ye wrong one to another? But he
that did his neighbour wrong thrust him away, saying, ʸWho made thee
28 a ruler and a judge over us? wilt thou kill me, as thou didst the Egyptian
29 yesterday? Then ᶻfled Moses at this saying, and was a stranger in the
land of Madian, where he ᵃbegat two sons.

A. D. 33.

ˣ Ex. 2. 11,
12.
Heb. 11. 24,
26.
² Or, now.
ʸ Matt. 21.27.
Luke 12. 14.
John 18, 36
37.
John 19. 12-
15.
ᶻ Ex. 2. 15.
Ex. 4. 19, 20.
ᵃ Num. 12. 1

to be found in the Old Testament — another proof of the rashness of concluding that because Stephen's statements cannot be all verified from the Old Testament, their accuracy is to be suspected. "The wisdom of the Egyptians"—proverbial five centuries after this, in Solomon's time, and apparently famed even in Moses' time—was all communicated to this apt pupil. *Philo* (the Jewish commentator on Moses) represents him as having had tutors from the most celebrated foreign schools, and accomplished in geometry, music, and philosophy; and though we need not take this too literally, there can be no doubt that he took intelligently in whatever he was taught. **and was** (as the fruit of this training) **mighty in** [his] **words and in deeds.** (The word 'his' [αὐτοῦ] is certainly part of the genuine text.) Compare with this what is said of the "Prophet like unto Moses" in Luke xxiv. 19. It may seem strange that one who, by his own account, was "slow of speech and of a slow tongue"—probably defective in utterance (Exod. iv. 10)—should be held forth as "mighty in his words." But his recorded speeches—not to speak of his wonderful writings — are in a high degree worthy of the epithet "mighty." In what "deeds" he was mighty we read not, unless it refer to the skill with which he led Israel out of Egypt, and through the wilderness to the borders of the promised land. But the reference, perhaps, is to some unrecorded circumstances in his early life. What *Josephus* says of his military exploits is hardly to be depended on; but when he tells us that his ability was acknowledged ere he left Egypt, there is no reason to question his accuracy. **23. And when he was full forty years old.** Here, and in *vv.* 30 and 36, the life of Moses is represented as embracing three periods of forty years each. The Jewish writers affirm the same; and though in the Old Testament this is not expressly stated, it says he was one hundred and twenty years old when he died (Deut. xxxiv. 7), which exactly tallies with this. **it came into his heart to visit his brethren the children of Israel.** By this time he had, in the exercise of faith, deliberately "refused to be called the son of Pharaoh's daughter; choosing rather to suffer affliction with the people of God, than to enjoy the pleasures of sin for a season; esteeming the reproach of Christ greater riches than the treasures in Egypt: for he had respect unto the recompense of the reward" (Heb. xi 24-26). His heart, now yearning with love to his people as God's chosen family, and heaving, no doubt, with the consciousness of a Divine vocation to set them free, he goes forth to look them in the face, and see if some occasion will not present itself for coming to some understanding with them on this subject. **24. And seeing one of them suffer wrong, he defended him, and avenged him that was oppressed, and**

smote the Egyptian—in the heat of his indignation going further, probably, than he intended. *Humphry* quotes from *Diodorus Siculus* (i. 77) an Egyptian law requiring the subjects to rescue any one whom they should see ready to be slain, or suffering violence at the hands of another; and if that could not be done, to kill the oppressor. **25. For** [δὲ]—'But' or 'Now,' explaining the view under which he acted, **he supposed his brethren would have understood how that God by his hand would deliver them.** Though this is Stephen's own comment, it is one naturally suggested by the narrative in Exodus. He probably imagined this a suitable occasion for rousing and rallying them under him as their leader; thus anticipating his work, and so running unsent. *Calvin* thinks Moses was Divinely directed not only in interfering in the quarrel, but in slaying the Egyptian. But as the narrative certainly does not say this, so to us—especially when viewed in the light of the forty years' exile in Midian—it seems to imply the reverse. **but they understood not.** Reckoning on a spirit in them congenial with his own, he had the mortification to find it far otherwise. This furnishes to Stephen another example of *Israel's slowness to apprehend and fall in with the Divine purposes of love.* **26. And the next day he showed himself unto them** [ὤφθη αὐτοῖς]. This mode of expression (with which compare Exod. ii. 13) confirms the view given by Stephen, and implied in the narrative, that Moses expressly intended by these two visits to his people to present himself to them as their destined deliverer, in the hope of being recognized by them in this character. **as they strove, and would have set them at one again** [συνήλαςεν αὐτοὺς εἰς εἰρήνην]—'urged them to peace' comes nearest to the sense. An air of authority is implied. **saying, Sirs, ye are brethren**—[the emphatic ὑμεῖς after ἀδελφοί ἐστε is of more than doubtful authority.] Here it is not an Israelite and an Egyptian, but two Israelites, or parties of Israelites, in collision with each other. Moses, grieved at the spectacle, interposes as a mediator; but his interference, as unauthorized, is resented by the party in the wrong, *whom Stephen identifies with the mass of the nation* (see *v.* 35), just as Messiah's own interposition had been spurned by Stephen's present hearers. **27. But he that did his neighbour wrong thrust him away, saying, Who made thee a ruler and a judge over us?** Compare the similar treatment of Christ Himself (Matt. xxi. 23), "By what authority doest thou these things? and who gave thee this authority?" **28. Wilt thou kill me, as thou didst the Egyptian yesterday?** Moses had thought the deed unseen (Exod. ii. 12), but, to his surprise and alarm, he now finds himself mistaken. **29. Then fled Moses at this saying**—for "when Pharaoh heard this thing he sought to slay Moses" (Exod. ii. 15). No doubt

30 And when forty years were expired, there appeared to him in the wilderness of mount Sinai an *b* Angel of the Lord in a flame of fire in a
31 bush. When Moses saw *it*, he wondered at the sight: and as he drew
32 near to behold *it*, the voice of the Lord came unto him, *saying*, *c* I *am* the God of thy fathers, the God of Abraham, and the God of Isaac, and
33 the God of Jacob. Then Moses trembled, and durst not behold. Then *d* said the Lord to him, Put off thy shoes from thy feet: for the place
34 where thou standest is holy ground. I have seen, I have seen the affliction of my people which is in Egypt, and I have heard their groaning, and am come down to deliver them. And now come, I will send thee into Egypt.
35 This Moses whom they refused, saying, Who made thee a ruler and a judge? the same did God send *to be* a ruler and a deliverer *e* by the hand
36 of the Angel which appeared to him in the bush. He *f* brought them out, after that he had showed wonders and signs in the land of Egypt,
37 and in the Red sea, *g* and in the wilderness forty years. This is that

A. D. 38.
b Gen. 48. 16.
Ex. 3. 2.
Deut. 33. 16.
Isa. 63. 9.
Zech. 13. 7.
John 1. 14.
Titus 2. 13.
c Gen. 50. 24.
Ex. 3. 6, 15.
Matt. 22. 32.
ch. 3. 15.
Heb. 11. 16.
d Ex. 3. 5.
Josh. 5. 15.
e Ex. 14. 19.
Num. 20. 16.
f Ex. 13. 41.
Deut. 6. 21.
g Ex. 16. 1.
Num. 9. 15.

he had before this become an object of jealousy in Pharaoh's court, as a too aspiring and dangerous foreigner; and the courtiers, thinking the time had now come for getting rid of him, would with eager haste carry tidings to the king of the deed done, and work upon his fears until he gave orders to despatch him. **and was a stranger in the land of Madian**—or 'Midian,' in Arabia [מִדְיָן; μαδιάμ in LXX.], not the locality of the great body of the Midianites, which was certainly far to the eastward of this region, but a tract of land near to the desert of Sinai, as the sequel of this narrative shows, inhabited by a portion of that people who had migrated thither for pastoral purposes: **where he begat two sons.**

30. And when forty years were expired—(see on *v.* 23), **there appeared to him in the wilderness of mount Sina**—the wilderness or desert of that mountain-range which went, it would appear, under the general name of *Horeb*, but is here called (from the individual mountain whence the law was given) *Sinai*: **an Angel of the Lord.** The better attested reading is simply 'an,' or 'the angel.' Whichever way we render it, 'the Angel of the covenant' is clearly meant, since He immediately calls Himself JEHOVAH (compare *v.* 38), **in a flame of fire in** (or 'of') **a bush** [βάτου]. This bush—burning, yet not consumed—was no doubt designed to hold forth the two chief characters by which the Church of God has been in every age distinguished—persecuted, but not forsaken; cast down, but not destroyed; chastened, but not killed; dying, but behold it lives (2 Cor. iv. 9; vi. 9). **31. When Moses saw it, he wondered at the sight** [ἐθαύμασεν. Tischendorf reads —άζεν, 'kept wondering.' The authorities are about equal]: **and as he drew near to behold** [κατανοῆσαι]—or to 'contemplate' it, **the voice of the Lord came unto him, 32. [Saying], I am the God of thy fathers, the God of Abraham, and [the God of]** Isaac, **and [the God of]** Jacob. (The bracketed words are insufficiently attested.) In this sublime announcement the glorious Speaker identifies Himself with all the Divine manifestations, covenant-transactions, and rich promises made to the father of the faithful, and transmitted to the heirs of promise through Isaac and Jacob. **Then Moses trembled**—(compare Heb. xii. 21: Gen. xxviii. 17; Ps. xcix. 1; cxix. 120; Hab. iii. 16) **and durst not behold.** The history says, "Then Moses hid his face, for he was afraid to look upon God" (Exod. iii. 6). **33. Then said the Lord to him, Put off thy shoes from thy feet.** Stephen may seem to have reversed here the order in

which the Divine command was given—which was *before*, not *after*, proclaiming who it was that spake to him from the bush (Exod. iii. 5, 6). The words of Stephen, however, simply are, 'But the Lord said to him [Εἶπεν δὲ αὐτῷ ὁ K.], Put off,' &c. Moses recoiled from the spectacle as too awful in glory for him to gaze on; and when the Lord bade him not draw nigh, the meaning simply was, 'with covered feet,' implying a positive wish for his approach with shoes off. **for the place where thou standest** [ἐφ' ᾧ is preferable to ἐν ᾧ] **is holy ground.** The Oriental custom of uncovering the feet in token of reverence, whether in approaching royalty or in a temple drawing near to God, is well known, and prevails to this day. The priests ministered in the tabernacle (say the Rabbins) with uncovered feet. **34. I have seen, I have seen** [Ἰδὼν εἶδον, as in the LXX. = רָאֹה רָאִיתִי, Exod. iii. 7—which our version renders, "I have surely seen"] **the affliction of my people which is in Egypt, and I have heard their groaning, and am come down to deliver them. And now come, I will send thee into Egypt** [ἀποστείλω, aorist subjunctive, is much better attested than —ελῶ of the received text, and rightly adopted by *Lachmann* and *Tischendorf*].

35. This Moses whom they refused, saying, Who made thee a ruler and a judge? [ἄρχοντα καὶ δικαστήν]. By "judge" here is plainly meant 'avenger,' answering to 'deliverer,' or 're-deemer,' in the next clause: **the same did God send** [the imperfect, ἀπέσταλκεν, is better attested than the aorist, ἀπέστειλεν, of the received text] **to be a ruler and a deliverer** ἄρχοντα καὶ λυτρωτήν]. Stephen, it will be observed, purposely selects such terms in characterizing Moses as would make the intended parallel between him and Christ—*rejected by the nation, but chosen of God*—unmistakeable. **by the hand** [ἐν χειρί]—rather, 'with the hand' [σὺν being the better attested reading] **of the Angel which appeared to him in the bush.** Here again "the stone which the builders refused was made the head of the corner." **36. He brought them out after that he had showed** [ποιήσας]—rather, 'He brought them out, having (that is, *after* bringing them out) showed' wonders and signs in the land of Egypt, and in the Red sea, and in the wilderness forty years.

The Defence continued—Part Third: *From the Exodus to the Erection of Solomon's Temple* (37-50). **37. This is that Moses which said unto the children of Israel** (Deut. xviii. 15), **A Prophet shall**

42

Moses which said unto the children of Israel, [h]A Prophet shall the Lord your God raise up unto you of your brethren, [3]like unto me; him [i]shall
38 ye hear. This [j]is he that was in the church in the wilderness with [k]the Angel which spake to him in the mount Sina, and *with* our fathers: [l]who
39 received the [m]lively oracles to give unto us: to whom our fathers would not obey, but thrust *him* from them, and in their hearts turned back again
40 into Egypt, saying [n]unto Aaon, Make us gods to go before us: for *as for* this Moses, which brought us out of the land of Egypt, we wot not
41 what is become of him. And they made a calf in those days, and offered sacrifice unto the idol, and rejoiced in the works of their own hands.

A. D. 33.
[h] Deut. 13. 15.
[3] Or, as myself.
[i] Matt 17. 5.
[j] Ex. 19. 3.
[k] Isa. 63. 9.
Gal. 3. 19.
Heb. 2 2.
[l] Ex. 21. 1.
John 1. 17.
[m] Rom 3. 2.
[n] Ex. 32 1.

[the Lord your] **God raise up unto you.** The authority for the bracketed words is rather weak. Probably they were added from the passage in Deuteronomy. **of your brethren, like unto me; [him shall ye hear.]** (Compare the words of Peter, ch. iii. 22.) These last words also, enclosed in brackets, are of doubtful genuineness. They may have been added from the Old Testament passage. *Lechler* calls attention to the rhetorical emphasis unmistakably lying in the repeated and forcible way in which the person of Moses is here referred to—the 35th, 36th, 37th, and 38th verses all beginning with his person—thus: "This Moses" (35); "He" [Οὗτος], or 'He it was that' (36); "This is that Moses" (37); "This is he" (38). The obvious design of this emphasis was to hold forth more vividly the *contrast between God's choice of him and the nation's rejection of him,* as a mirror in which might be seen their recent treatment of the Greater than Moses, followed up, as it now was, by their refusal of His messengers. In the 37th verse Stephen reminds his hearers that, blindly as they now set up Moses as the great object of a devout Israelite's regard, Moses himself, in his grand testimony, had held himself forth, not as the last and great prophet of Israel, but only as a humble precursor and small model of Him to whom absolute submission was due by all. **38. This is he that was in the church** [ἐν τῇ ἐκκλησίᾳ]—the collective body of God's chosen people viewed as 'assembled' from time to time for public religious purposes: hence it has come to denote the whole body of the faithful under the Gospel, or particular sections of them. **in the wilderness with the Angel which spake to him in the mount Sina, and with our fathers.** As to this "Angel," see on *v.* 30: **who received the lively oracles** [λόγια ζῶντα]—or 'living oracles;' not meaning in the first instance, 'life-giving oracles,' but 'living' in opposition whether to the pretended oracles of the heathen or to a mere dead letter; hence, 'efficacious,' 'vitalizing,' **to give unto us.** Here Stephen represents Moses as alike near *to the angel,* from whom he received all the institutions of the ancient economy, and *to the people,* to whom he faithfully reported the living oracles as he received them, and among whom he as faithfully set up the Divine institutions. The reader will observe how, in bearing this high testimony to Moses, Stephen incidentally rebuts the main charge for which he was now on trial—that of disparaging Moses and the law; although, as already observed, he so rises above himself throughout, that to vindicate the ways of God against those who had all along misunderstood and sought to thwart them, appears to be his one object. **39. To whom our fathers would not obey, but thrust him from them.** Here Stephen shows that *the deepest dishonour ever done to Moses came from the nation that now professed the greatest jealousy for his honour:* **and in their hearts turned back again into Egypt**—not mean-

ing by this expression that they wished to return literally to Egypt, but that their hearts (as appears by what follows) still clung to the idolatry of Egypt, into which we are expressly told that they had sunk when they dwelt there, (Ezek. xx. 7). *In this Stephen would have his hearers read the downward career on which they themselves were now entering.* **40. Saying unto Aaron, Make us gods to go before us.** In using the word "gods" in the plural number, Stephen only follows the LXX. translation of the Hebrew word [אֱלֹהִים], which our translators also do in the Old Testament passage referred to: "Up, make us *gods* which shall go before us," &c.; and when Aaron made the golden calf, "they said (according to our version), These be thy *gods,* O Israel, which brought thee up out of the land of Egypt" (Exod. xxxii. 1, 4). And yet there is no reason to suppose that they desired a plurality of visible representations of God, and still less that they believed in a plurality of gods. Certainly as Aaron made them only one representation, so it was of that *one* that they said, this was what brought them up—meaning such a representation of Him who did so, as the Egyptian idolaters had familiarized them with: **for [as for] this Moses** [ὁ γὰρ Μ. οὗτος]—an expression of contempt for his authority over them, even while owning him as their deliverer from Egypt, **which brought us out of the land of Egypt, we wot not what has become of him.** Thus does Stephen continue to hold up the nation as *all along acting in proud rebellion against God in the treatment of His highest servants and His most sublime revelations through them.* **41. And they made a calf in those days**—in imitation of the ox and bull in Egypt, and indeed generally in the East; as appears by the Nineveh sculptures. The ox, as the symbol of agriculture, and so of all that supports human life, was naturally selected for special honour in the idolatry of symbols. As one of the cherubic forms in the holy of holies, it was employed in the tabernacle and temple service, not as an object of worship, but to convey symbolic instruction, and so exalt the conceptions of the worshippers. It is worthy of notice, that whereas the Old Testament historian ascribes the making of this image to Aaron, Stephen ascribes it to the people; and indeed no one can read the history without perceiving that Aaron merely yielded to the clamour of a people maddened at that moment with idolatrous inclinations, to the dishonour alike of Him who had brought them out of Egyptian bondage, and of Moses, His instrument in this great deliverance. **and offered sacrifice unto the idol** [τῷ εἰδώλῳ]. In the strictest sense it was not an idol, but intended as a visible representation of Jehovah; but it was regarded as nothing less than idolatry by Him who, in the second commandment, had condemned not only the *worshipping* but even the *making* for purposes of worship, of any graven

43

42 Then °God turned, and gave them up to worship the ᵖhost of heaven; as it is written in the book of the Prophets, ᑫO ye house of Israel, have ye offered to me slain beasts and sacrifices *by the space of* forty years in
43 the wilderness? Yea, ye took up the tabernacle of Moloch, and the star of your god Remphan, figures which ye made to worship them: and I will carry you away beyond Babylon.
44 Our fathers had the tabernacle of witness in the wilderness, as he had appointed, ⁴speaking unto Moses, that ʳhe should make it according to
45 the fashion that he had seen: which ˢalso our fathers ⁵that came after brought in with ⁶Jesus into the possession of the Gentiles, whom God
46 drave out before the face of our fathers, unto the days of David; who ᵗfound favour before God, and desired ᵘto find a tabernacle for the God
47, of Jacob. But Solomon built him an house. Howbeit ᵛthe Most High

A. D. 33.
° Eze. 20 25.
Rom. 1. 24.
2 Thes.2.11.
ᵖ Deut. 17. 3.
ᑫ Amos 5. 25.
⁴ Or, who spake.
ʳ Heb. 8. 5.
ˢ Josh. 3. 14.
⁵ Or, having received.
⁶ That is, Joshua.
ᵗ 1 Sam. 16.1.
ᵘ 1 Ki. 8. 17.
ᵛ 2 Chr. 2. 6.

image, and had told them how jealous He was on this subject. And no wonder, for all worship by the aid of, or through the medium of, visible representations of created objects has sooner or later degenerated into the worship of the objects themselves; and even where it does not reach to naked idolatry, it tends to materialize and debase the worship of Him who is a spirit. **and rejoiced in the works of their own hands.** Thus does Stephen hold forth the deep degradation into which the nation had sunk, when, after all that the Lord had done for them, they became intoxicated with idolatrous joy in a thing of their own handiwork. **42. Then God turned**—changing His method with them: as they had turned from Him, so now He turned from them, **and gave them up**—judicially abandoned them (see on Rom. i. 24) **to worship the host of heaven**—to star-worship, a fact which, though not expressly mentioned in the Pentateuch, is implied in those forms of idolatry to which we know that they were addicted, such as the worship of Moloch, presently to be mentioned. **as it is written in the book of the prophets**—the twelve minor prophets, regarded as one book (the words are from Amos v. 25-27) **O ye house of Israel, have ye offered to me slain beasts and sacrifices by the space of forty years in the wilderness?** **43. Yea**—rather, 'And' [Καὶ] **ye took up the tabernacle of Moloch,** [τὴν σκηνήν]. This was probably a small portable shrine, containing the image of the horrid deity. The meaning of these two verses, which is a little obscure, seems to be, 'Did ye offer to Me the sacrifices which I required?' and yet ye bore about at the same time the shrine of Moloch!' The form of the question in v. 42 [with μὴ] supposes the proper answer to be in the negative; and what is added is designed to show that, since the two actions were in direct contradiction to each other, it could be only a hypocritical and abhorred worship which, with such idolatrous hearts and hands, they offered to the living God. **and the star of your god** [not 'the god,' according to *Lachmann* and *Tischendorf*, the evidence for the received text being stronger] **Remphan,** or 'Rephan.' The word is variously spelt in the MSS. **figures**—[τύπους] —or 'images,' **which ye made to worship them.** Two kinds of idolatry are here charged upon the Israelites: that of the golden calf, and that of the heavenly bodies—Moloch and Remphan being deities representing apparently the Divine powers ascribed to nature under different aspects. Remphan (or, as in the LXX, Rephan) is put for "Chiun" in Amos v. 26, which Stephen is quoting, and is supposed to answer to *Saturn.* But as the object was rather to fasten on the nation the charge of foul and varied idolatry, than to specify the particular forms of it, there is the less necessity

for going here into the learned speculations to which these words have given rise. **and I will carry you away beyond Babylon.** The word used by the prophet is not Babylon, but "Damascus" (Amos v. 27), whither the ten tribes were carried captive. But Stephen seems purposely to have changed this into "Babylon," the well-known region of the captivity of Judah, with which his hearers would have most sympathy. And as both captivities were equally the fulfilment of the ancient threatening, that they should be dispersed among the nations for their departure from the Lord (Lev. xxvi. 33), the substitution of the one captivity for the other, in Stephen's quotation, was in the strict line of the prophecy. **44. Our fathers had** [ἐν before τοῖς πατράσιν has but weak support] **the tabernacle of witness in the wilderness, as he had appointed**—that is, they were Divinely entrusted with the custody of it; and this is mentioned to show how aggravated was the guilt of that idolatry in which they indulged, having such tokens of the Divine presence constantly in the midst of them: **speaking unto Moses, that he should make it according to the fashion that he had seen.** Here again Stephen, by his way of alluding to such Divine arrangements, indirectly shows how far he was from disparaging Moses and the ancient economy. **45. Which also our fathers that came after** [διαδεξάμενοι]—rather, 'Which also our fathers having received it (that is, the custody of the tabernacle) by succession' from their ancestors, **brought in with Jesus** (that is, Joshua) **into the possession of the Gentiles** [ἐν τῇ κατάσχεσει]. So the *Vulgate,* and after it *Calvin, Grotius, Humphry,* and *Hackett* [taking ἐν as = εἰς]. Another rendering has been adopted by *de Wette, Meyer, Alford, Webster and Wilkinson,* and *Alexander*—'brought in with Joshua at the taking possession of (the territory of) the Gentiles.' (This would be preferable if the active sense of the word rendered 'possession' were sufficiently proved, which however it scarcely is). **whom God drave out before the face of our fathers, unto the days of David**—for till then Jerusalem continued in the hands of the Jebusites. But Stephen's object in mentioning David is to hasten from the tabernacle which he set up, to the temple which his son built, in Jerusalem; and this only to show, from their own Scriptures (Isa. lxvi. 1, 2), that *even that temple,* magnificent though it was, *was not the proper resting-place of Jehovah upon earth*—as His audience and the nation had all along been prone to imagine. **46. Who found favour before God, and desired** [ἠτήσατο]—or, 'asked for himself' **to find a tabernacle** [σκήνωμα]—a more permanent dwelling than the usual one [σκηνή], **for the God of Jacob. 47. But Solomon built him an house. 48. Howbeit**

44

48, dwelleth not in temples made with hands; as saith the prophet, heaven
49 *[w]is* my throne, and earth *is* my footstool : what house will ye build me?
50 saith the Lord; or what *is* the place of my rest? Hath not my hand made all these things?
51 Ye *[x]stiff-necked and [y]uncircumcised* in heart and ears, ye do always
52 resist the Holy Ghost: as your fathers *did*, so *do* ye. *[z]Which* of the prophets have not your fathers persecuted? and they have slain them which showed before of the coming of *[a]the Just One*; of whom ye have
53 been now the betrayers and murderers: who *[b]have* received the law by the disposition of angels, and have not kept *it*.

A. D. 33.
[w] Isa. 66. 1, 2.
Matt. 5. 34.
Matt. 23. 22.
[x] Isa. 48. 4.
[y] Eze. 44. 9.
[z] 2 Chr. 36. 16.
Matt. 23. 34.
1 Thes. 2. 15.
[a] ch. 3. 14.
[b] Ex. 20. 1.
Gal. 3. 19.
Heb. 2. 2.

the Most High dwelleth not in [temples] made with hands. The word "temples," though in the received text, is evidently not genuine. The idea is thus quite general—'dwelleth not in man-made buildings.' Solomon himself sublimely expresses this in his prayer at the consecration of the temple (2 Chr. vi. 18): "But will God in very deed dwell with men on the earth? behold, heaven and the heaven of heavens cannot contain thee; how much less this house which I have built!" **as saith the prophet** (Isa. lxvi. 1, 2)—that is, the Lord by the prophet. **49. Heaven is my throne, and earth is my footstool: what house will ye build me? saith the Lord; or what is the place of my rest? 50. Hath not my hand made all these things?** The prophet goes on to say that the chosen and proper resting-place of Jehovah is the "contrite heart that trembleth at His word," and that the time was coming when those who clung to the temple and its ritual would be objects of Divine abhorrence, as great as the rankest idolaters; while the true spiritual worshippers, though but a despised and excommunicated remnant, would find the Lord upon their side, and interposing gloriously in their behalf (*vv.* 2-5). From this it will be seen how singularly apposite to Stephen's case was this reference. He contents himself, however, with quoting the first verse and part of the second, condemning that idolatrous attachment to the material temple and its external services which was the cause of all their rage at his preaching, and of his now standing at their bar on a charge of impiety. The attempt made by the Tübingen critics (*Baur* and *Zeller*) to make out that Stephen meant here to condemn the temple and its services *in themselves*, or out and out—and so stood self-convicted of the charge brought against him—affords a good specimen of the wretched character of their criticism. The same style of reasoning would prove Isaiah and most of the ancient prophets to have been opposed to the whole external services of the economy under which they lived—an opinion which some of themselves have not scrupled to express.

The Defence concluded, in a brief and pungent statement of the Nation's Treatment of the Lord's Designs and Messengers from first to last (51-53). **51. Ye stiff-necked and uncircumcised in heart and ears.** [*Lachmann* adopts the plural καρδίαις, for which the external evidence is rather better than for καρδίᾳ of the received text. The internal evidence, however, is not so good. *Tischendorf* adheres to the received text.] **ye do always resist the Holy Ghost: as your fathers did, so do ye.** On this verse *Olshausen, Humphry, Webster and Wilkinson* fall in too readily with the notion of some of the older critics, that symptoms of impatience and irritation in the audience here induced Stephen not only to cut short his historical sketch, but to pass abruptly from calm narrative to sharp invective. But since little further light could have been thrown upon Israel's perversity from subsequent periods of the national history, as recorded in their own Scriptures, it is more natural to view this and the two following verses as a vivid summing up—the concentrated expression and brief import—of the whole Israelitish history, in the form of a charge, and certainly the heaviest conceivable, of *grossness of heart and continuous resistance of the Holy Ghost* in all the Divine procedure towards them, from the beginning down to that very moment. (So *Meyer, Alford, Baumgarten, Hackett, Alexander*, and *Lechler*.) In using the familiar Old Testament phrases, "stiff-necked and uncircumcised in heart and ears," Stephen doubtless meant to serve his auditors heirs to their fathers' incorrigible perversity and heathenish carnality. **52. Which of the prophets have not your fathers persecuted? and they have slain them which showed before of the coming of the Just One; of whom ye have been** [γεγένησθε]—rather, 'ye were' [ἐγένεσθε] being the better supported reading, **now the betrayers and murderers.** In these most withering words the still darker features of the national character are boldly held up—*deadly hostility to the messengers of God*, whose highest mission was to announce the coming of "THE RIGHTEOUS ONE," that well-known prophetic title of Messiah (Isa. liii. 11; Jer. xxiii. 6; &c.), and *this crime, consummated by the betrayal and murder of Messiah Himself by their own hands.* One word more is added. **53. Who have received** [Οἵτινες ἐλάβετε]—rather, 'Who [are the parties that] received the law;' thus identifying those who had just killed the Prince of life with those who had at the beginning of their economy received the law at mount Sinai, as one corporate personality—one in privilege, responsibility, and guilt. **by the disposition of angels** [εἰς διαταγὰς ἀγγέλων]. This expression is peculiar, and has occasioned some discussion. Literally, it is 'at the arrangements of angels,' which, no doubt, means 'through their instrumentality.' [For this sense of εἰς, compare Matt. xii. 41, and see *Winer*, xxxii. 4 *b*, and xlix. *a*, c.] This interesting fact, that the ministration of angels was employed in the sublime scenes of the giving of the law at mount Sinai is not expressly recorded in the Old Testament; but it is certainly implied in Ps. lxviii. 17, "The chariots of God are twenty thousand, even thousands of angels: the Lord is among them [as in] Sinai, in the holy place" (compare also Deut. xxxii. 2, in the LXX.): it is explicitly stated (as if it had been a known fact) in Gal. iii. 19, and Heb. ii. 2); the general doctrine of Scripture regarding the ministry of angels, especially in all the higher operations of providence and grace, is quite in accordance with it; and *Josephus* and *Philo* both speak of it as a recognized fact. **and have not kept it.** This closing word may seem to sum up their guilt somewhat weakly, after the awful charge brought against them in the foregoing verse, of being the betrayers and murderers of the Lord of glory. But as he was there, not to bring home a charge of guilt against

54 When they heard these things, they were cut to the heart, and they
55 gnashed on him with *their* teeth. But he, being full of the Holy Ghost,
looked up stedfastly into heaven, and saw the glory of God, and Jesus
56 standing on the right hand of God, and said, Behold, ^cI see the heavens
57 opened, and the ^dSon of man standing on the right hand of God. Then
they cried out with a loud voice, and stopped their ears, and ran upon
58 him with one accord, and ^ecast *him* out of the city, ^fand stoned *him :*
and ^gthe witnesses laid down their clothes at a young man's feet, whose
59 name was Saul. And they stoned Stephen, calling upon *God*, and

A. D 33.
^c Eze. 1. 1.
Matt. 3. 16.
Mark 1. 10.
Luke 3. 21.
Rev. 4. 1.
^d Dan. 7. 13.
Heb. 9. 24.
^e Heb. 13. 12.
^f Lev. 24. 16.
^g Deut. 13. 9.
Deut.. 17. 7.

them, but to rebut their charge against himself — of dishonouring the law — he shows, rather, consummate wisdom in rolling that charge back upon themselves, by first reminding them that the law had been committed to them as a sacred trust by Jehovah Himself, amidst august angelic ministrations at Sinai, and then, in a word (as the result of his long historic induction of facts) protesting that, throughout their entire history, they 'had not kept it.'

Martyrdom of Stephen (54-60). **54. When they heard these things, they were cut to the heart, and they gnashed on him with their teeth.** If they could have answered him, how different would have been their temper of mind! **55. But he, being full of the Holy Ghost, looked up stedfastly into heaven, and saw the glory of God**—that is, such a visible manifestation as was vouchsafed so frequently of old; **and Jesus standing on the right hand of God**—the place of co-equal power and honour. Ye who can transfer to canvass such scenes as these, in which the rage of hell grins horrible from men, as they sit condemned by a frail prisoner of their own, and see heaven beaming from his countenance and opening full upon his view, I envy you, for I find no words to paint what, in the majesty of the Divine text, is here so simply told. 'But how could Stephen in the council chamber see heaven at all?' I suppose this question never occurred but to critics of narrow soul, one of whom (*Meyer*) conjectures that he saw it through the window! and another, of better mould (*Alford*), that the scene lay in one of the courts of the temple. As the sight was witnessed by Stephen alone, the opened heavens are to be viewed as revealed only to his bright beaming spirit. But why was Jesus seen *standing* on this occasion, and not *sitting?*—the posture which the glorified Saviour is elsewhere invariably represented as occupying (Ps. cx. 1; Matt. xxvi. 64; Mark xvi. 19; Eph. i. 20; Col. iii. 1; Heb. i. 3; viii. 1; x. 12; xii. 2). *Augustin* replies, that Christ *sits* as a *Judge*, but on this occasion *stood* as an *Advocate*. This *Calvin* thinks somewhat far-fetched, giving it as his own opinion that the sitting and the standing postures both mean the same thing, since neither can be literally understood. But this decides nothing. For, granting that these postures are to be understood figuratively, the question will still remain, Do they both mean the same thing? And as it seems impossible to doubt that in Ps. cx. 1, and especially in the use made of it in Heb. x. 12, 13, the idea of *rest* after the completion of a work, and calm *expectation* of the fruit of that work, so, for our part, we cannot doubt that the *standing* posture here exceptionally ascribed to Christ, at the right hand of God, is intended to express the eager interest with which He watched from the skies the scene in that council-chamber, and the full tide of His Spirit, which He was at that moment engaged in pouring into the heart of His heroical witness, till it beamed in radiance from his very countenance. **56. And said, Behold, I see the heavens opened, and the Son of man standing on the right hand of God.** This (to use the words of *Alford*) is the only time that our Lord is by human lips called THE SON OF MAN after his ascension. (Rev. i. 13, and xiv. 14, are not instances.) And why here? Stephen, full of the Holy Ghost, speaking now not of himself at all (*v.* 55), but entirely by the Spirit, is led to repeat the very words in which Jesus Himself, *before this same council*, had foretold His glorification (Matt. xxvi. 64), assuring them that that exaltation of THE SON OF MAN, which they should hereafter witness, to their dismay, was already begun and actual. **57. Then they cried out with a loud voice, and stopped their ears, and ran upon him with one accord.** Compare the remarkably similar scene at the trial and condemnation of our Lord (Matt. xxvi. 64). To men of their mould and in their temper, Stephen's last seraphic words could only bring matters to extremities ; but this served to reveal the diabolical spirit which they breathed. **58. And cast him out of the city**—as the law required to be done in cases of blasphemy (Lev. xxiv. 14; Num. xv. 35; 1 Ki. xxi. 13 : and see Heb. xiii. 12), **and stoned him** [ἐλιθοβόλουν]—rather, 'proceeded to stone him ;' for the actual stoning is recorded in the next verse. **and the witnesses**—those whose hands were required by the law to be first upon the criminal. Such a provision was probably intended to meet the reluctance to be the first to inflict so painful a capital punishment. **laid down their clothes** [ἱμάτια]—their loose outer garments, to be taken charge of while they did their murderous work, **at a young man's feet, whose name was Saul.** Such is our historian's calm, purely historical, yet thrilling way of introducing his readers to one to whom Christianity—whether as unfolded in the New Testament or as established in the world, and wrought into the religious thinking and phraseology of Christendom—owes more, perhaps, than to all the other apostles together. Here he is, already in all likelihood having a seat in the Sanhedrim, about thirty years of age, an eager participator in the murder of one of the most distinguished witnesses for Christ. See on ch. viii. 1, and his own affecting confession of this to Jesus Himself, ch. xxii. 20. But was this a legal proceeding? Looking at John xviii. 31 (see there), one should say not. Yet nothing seems wanting to it but the actual sentence of condemnation, which may have been pronounced, though not here recorded. Certainly the subsequent proceedings against the Christians, to imprisonment and even to death, with the letters of authorization issued by the high priest to such as Saul of Tarsus, with the view of arresting all who called on the name of Jesus, imply a large amount of power over the *lives* and *liberties* of the Jews on the part of their ecclesiastical superiors—either independent of the civil governor, or, which is more probable, by a tacit understanding that he should not interfere. **59. And they stoned Stephen** [ἐλιθοβόλουν]—the imperfect tense here denoting the continuance and

46

60 saying, Lord Jesus, receive [h] my spirit. And he kneeled down, and cried with a loud voice, Lord, lay not this sin to their charge. And when he

A. D. 33.

[h] Ps. 31. 5.

protracting of the operation till it ended in death. **calling upon [God], and saying, Lord Jesus, receive my spirit.** A most unhappy supplement of our translators is this word "God" here—as if, while addressing the Son, he was really calling not upon Him, but upon the Father. The sense is perfectly clear without any supplement at all [ἐπικαλούμενον καὶ λέγοντα]—'invoking and saying' (as the *Vulgate, Calvin*, and *Beza* render it), **Lord Jesus** —He being the Person intended, and addressed by name (compare ch. ix. 14). Even *Grotius, de Wette*, and *Meyer* so understand the words, the two latter adding several examples of direct prayer to Christ from the New Testament. *Pliny*, in his well-known letter to the Emperor Trajan (A. D. 110 or 111), says it was part of the regular Christian service to address, in alternate strains, a hymn to Christ as God. *In presenting to Jesus the identical prayer which Himself had on the cross offered to His Father, Stephen renders to his glorified Lord absolute Divine worship, in the most sublime form, and at the most critical moment of his life.* And in this committal of his spirit to Jesus, Paul afterwards followed the footsteps of the first martyr, with a calm and exultant confidence that with Him it was safe for eternity: "I know Whom I have believed, and am persuaded that He is able to keep that which I have committed unto Him against that day" (2 Tim. i. 12). For more on this subject see on 1 Cor. i. 2. **60. And he kneeled down, and cried with a loud voice**—with something of the gathered energy of his dying Lord (see on John xix. 30), **Lord**—that is, beyond all doubt, 'Lord JESUS,' whom, as Lord, he had just before invoked. **lay not this sin to their charge.** Comparing this with the prayer of his dying Lord, who can fail to see how very richly this martyr of Jesus had drunk into his Master's spirit, and that in its loftiest, divinest form? **And when he had said this, he fell asleep.** *This is never said of the death of Christ*—partly, no doubt, because the New Testament writers would not, by using such a term, even *seem* to teach that the death of Christ was not a real death; but partly, too, to indicate the bitter ingredients in the death of the Head, as contrasted with the stingless placidity of that of His members. (See on 1 Thess. iv. 14.)

Remarks—1. How different was Stephen's reading of the Old Testament from that of the learned ecclesiastics before whom he pleaded! They read them merely as the story of their own separation from among the nations of the earth to be the Lord's peculiar people, and of the establishment and preservation of those peculiar laws and institutions, which constituted a wall of separation between them and all other nations, and which were their boasts. Stephen read them as the Record of God's high designs of grace and glory, which were eventually to reach the whole human family through the seed of Abraham, as the Divinely-appointed channel, as a light shining in a dark place, until the day should dawn and the Sun of Righteousness should arise with healing in His wings. They read in their Scriptures only God's favour for themselves as His chosen people; he read in them only Israel's incurable misapprehension from age to age of God's purposes and plans of mercy, and their obstinate resistance of them. And are there no parallels to this in later ages? Or, rather, does not all Church History proclaim that there are two ways of reading the lively oracles and the providence of God—the *carnal* and the *spiritual*; that the great mass of

professing Christians—including worldly ecclesiastics of every name—belong to the former class, while a far less proportion of both belong to the latter; and that these two classes differ in nothing essential from the assembled judges who sat to try Stephen, and the friendless prisoner at their bar, whose address was too high for their grovelling apprehensions to reach, and yet too stinging for their self-complacency to pardon? 2. What a study for those who feel in themselves a vocation to serve the Lord in some special sphere is the history of Moses! Who can wonder at his mistaking the pulsations of this feeling, when roused by the ill treatment of a countryman at the hand of an Egyptian, for a call to begin the work of deliverance then and there? The event taught him, to his cost, that he had anticipated his time by forty years. And, what is remarkable, when his time at length came, the difficulty then was to persuade him to stir at all, or that it would be of any avail to do so. How differently did He act of whom Moses wrote! (See on Luke iii. 41-50, Remark 6, at the close of that Section.) 3. When men 'do not like to retain God in their knowledge, God gives them over to a reprobate mind,' and they sink from higher to lower, from more refined to grosser forms of religious and moral degeneracy. Stephen traces this in his address, from the rejection of Moses in Egypt to the golden calf in the wilderness, and from that to the abominations and cruelties of Moloch-worship in Palestine; and Paul traces it in the heathen world, in the dark picture of their idolatries and abominations which he draws in the opening chapter of his Epistle to the Romans; nor are illustrations of this principle wanting in Christendom. (See on Rom. i. 18-32, Remarks 3, 5, 6, at the close of that Section.) 4. In the earliest stages of the struggle between the Gospel and its Jewish enemies, since the apostles could not be spared, we have seen them shielded— partly by the heroic courage imparted to them, and partly by miraculous interpositions in their behalf —from the violence which was ready to crush them. But, that men might see from the first how believers could die for the name of the Lord Jesus, the most distinguished disciple who was not in the number of the twelve was Divinely surrendered to the popular fury. And the death of this first martyr of Jesus has for ever consecrated martyrdom in times of persecution. And what bright encouragement to the persecuted and martyred servants of Jesus lies in the glorious manifestation of Himself which He vouchsafed to Stephen just before the fury of his enemies burst forth upon him! Nor is it at all certain that it went beyond what has been experienced, times without number, by those that have since suffered for His name, if any reliance is to be placed upon human testimony—testimony borne in circumstances the least open to the charge either of imposition or enthusiasm. 5. What a sublime contrast is presented by that bruised and mangled *body*, from whose pale lips there issued in the agonies of death the placid petition, "Lord Jesus, receive my spirit," and the *soul* which at such a moment sent it up! No dying shriek for mercy is this—such as is extorted at times from the worst of men in their dying moments. It is the unruffled language of one who, just before, had given bread for stones— breathing out a prayer for the forgiveness of his murderers; it is the gentle utterance of one expecting next moment to drop into the arms of his present Lord. 6. As invoking the name of Jesus seems to have been a characteristic and

8 had said this, he fell ⁱasleep.   AND ᵃSaul was consenting unto his death.

And at that time there was a great persecution against the church which was at Jerusalem: and they ᵇwere all scattered abroad through-
2 out the regions of Judea and Samaria, except the apostles.   And devout men carried Stephen *to his burial*, and ᶜmade great lamentation
3 over him.   As for Saul, ᵈhe made havoc of the church, entering into every house, and haling men and women, committed *them* to prison.
4 Therefore ᵉthey that were scattered abroad went every where preaching the word.

A. D. 33.

ⁱ 1 Thes. 4. 13.

CHAP. 8.
ᵃ ch. 7. 58.
ᵇ ch. 11. 19.
ᶜ 2 Sam. 3. 31.
ᵈ 1 Cor, 15. 9.
Gal. 1. 13.
Phil. 3. 6.
ᵉ Matt. 10. 23.
ch. 11. 19.
1 Cor. 14. 31.

familiar mark of the early Christians, so to do this just as the spirit is passing out of time into eternity, and in these solemn circumstances to commit to Jesus that most precious of all deposits —one's own spirit—asking Him to receive it on its flight from the body, is such an act of *supreme worship* as no devout dying believer can be conceived to have offered to one whom he believed to be no more than *a creature*, or to be other than "God over all blessed for ever;" and if the great apostle did not habitually do this very thing which Stephen did with his last breath, what meaning can be put upon the words already quoted, penned by him when about to seal his testimony with his blood, "I know Whom I have believed, and am persuaded that he is able to keep that which I have committed unto Him against that day"? (2 Tim. i. 12.)   7. What a Religion is that which teaches men to pray for their murderers, in the very spirit as well as the words of Him who was the First to exemplify His own precept, "Love your enemies, bless them that curse you, do good to them that hate you, and pray for them which despitefully use you, and persecute you" (Matt. v. 44); and what a harvest of such has the Church of Christ produced—from the days of Stephen down to the martyrs of Madagascar in our own day—showing that Jesus lives in His people still, returning in His suffering servants blessing for cursing!

CHAP. VIII.—XII. "YE SHALL BE WITNESSES . . . IN ALL JUDEA, AND IN SAMARIA" (ch. i. 8).

CHAP. VIII. 1-25.—PERSECUTION OF THE CHURCH AT JERUSALEM, PARTICULARLY BY SAUL—HOW OVERRULED—TRIUMPHS OF THE GOSPEL IN SAMARIA—THE CASE OF SIMON MAGUS.

Persecution of the Church at Jerusalem, particularly by Saul (1-3).   **1. And Saul was consenting unto his death** [ἦν συνευδοκῶν τῇ ἀναιρέσει αὐτοῦ] —was heartily approving of his execution. The word conveys more than mere 'consent' (as will be seen from Luke xi. 48; Rom. i. 32; 1 Cor. vii. 12, 13).   How much more there was in this case his own confession long afterwards reveal to us, ch. xxii. 20; xxvi. 9-11; and see below, *v.* 3.   **And at that time** [ἐν ἐκείνῃ τῇ ἡμέρᾳ]—literally, 'on that day.'   In this literal sense it is understood by the *Vulgate, Calvin, Beza, Bengel, de Wette, Meyer, Hackett,* and *Lechler,* most of whom urge that the tide of the persecution which had swept away Stephen is here said to have rolled on from that hour.   But there is no need to take it quite so literally, and what follows hardly accords with that.   The phrase is employed in the same indefinite sense of "at that time" (in which our translators take it here) in John xiv. 20; xvi. 23-26; and Mark ii. 20 (according to the true reading).   But, no doubt it was the facility with which the enemies of the Gospel had got rid of Stephen that stimulated them to proceed against the whole party of Christians at Jerusalem; for

the persecuting passion, like every other passion, is fed by exercise, and they might think it wise to strike while the iron was hot.   **and they were all scattered abroad throughout the regions of Judea and Samaria, except the apostles.**   This statement is not to be taken too literally.   Probably it means only that all the more prominent disciples were fain to flee, agreeably to their Lord's directions (Matt. x. 23).   At all events not a few of them must have soon returned, as is evident from ch. ix. 26-30.   The apostles remained, not certainly as being less exposed to the heat of persecution, but to watch over the infant cause, at whatever risk, where it was most needful to cherish it, and probably under the impression that Jerusalem being the centre of the whole Christian movement, they were not warranted to abandon it without express authority.   **2. And devout men** [ἄνδρες εὐλαβεῖς]—pious Jews, impressed probably with admiration for Stephen, and secretly inclined to Christianity, though not yet prepared, especially while the persecution raged, openly to declare themselves.   **carried Stephen to his burial.**   The words "to his burial" should not have been put in Italics, as the word which our translators render "carried" [συνεκόμισαν] implies as much.   **3. As for Saul, he made havoc of the church, entering into every house**—like an Inquisitor (as *Bengel* says), **and haling men and women, committed them to prison.**   'As he could not (says *Baumgarten*) discover any public meetings, he goes about entering into every house where he suspects there are Christians dwelling, and casts them into prison.   It was perhaps at this time that for the purpose of detecting the confession of Jesus under the outward guise of Judaism, he had recourse to the dreadful means which he himself speaks of in ch. xxvi. 11, "compelling them to blaspheme."'   Indeed, the best commentary on the historian's description of his procedure here will be found in his own affecting confessions, many years after this, which are once and again repeated in varied forms: see ch. xxii. 4; xxvi. 9-11; 1 Cor. xv. 9; Gal. i. 13; Phil. iii. 6; 1 Tim. 1. 13.

How this was Overruled to the furtherance of the Gospel, particularly in Samaria (4-8).   **4. Therefore they that were scattered abroad went every where** [διῆλθον]—'went up and down' or 'in all directions,' **preaching the word.**   The least that this can mean is that they went through the principal parts of Palestine; Samaria being particularized only because a detailed account of what took place there was to be subjoined.   Accordingly, after Saul's conversion, it is said, "Then had the churches (or, according to the genuine reading, 'the Church') *rest throughout all Judea and Galilee*" (see on ch. ix. to 31); which implies that before this the Gospel had obtained a footing in all those parts.   Also, when Peter "passed throughout all quarters" (that is, of Palestine), he found "saints at Lydda," and there seems hardly to have been a spot in which there were not disciples (ch.

	A. D. 34.
5 Then *ʲ*Philip went down to the city of Samaria, and preached Christ	*ʲ* ch. 6. 5.
6 unto them. And the people with one accord gave heed unto those	*ᵍ* Matt. 10. 1.
things which Philip spake, hearing and seeing the miracles which he did.	Mark 9. 26.
7 For *ᵍ*unclean spirits, crying with loud voice, came out of many that were	Mark 16.17.
possessed *with them:* and many taken with palsies, and that were lame,	Luke 10.17.
8 were healed. And there was great joy in that city.	John 14.12.
	Heb. 2. 4.
9 But there was a certain man called Simon, which beforetime in the	*ʰ* ch. 13. 6.
same city used *ʰ*sorcery, and bewitched the people of Samaria, *ⁱ*giving	*ⁱ* ch. 5. 36.
10 out that himself was some great one: to whom *ʲ*they all gave heed,	*ʲ* Rom. 1. 23.
from the least to the greatest, saying, This man is the great power of	Eph. 4. 14.
	Rev. 13. 3.

ix. 32-43). Thus faithfully and successfully, when at length driven out of Jerusalem, was the Master's injunction carried out, "Ye shall be witnesses unto me in all Judea." But this was not all; for in a subsequent chapter we read that "they which were scattered abroad upon the persecution that arose about Stephen travelled as far as Phenice, and Cyprus, and Antioch, preaching the word to none but unto the Jews only," and that some of these zealous preachers, bursting the fetters that bound their fellow-preachers to the Jews exclusively, preached at Antioch to the Gentiles also, and with immense success. (See on ch. xi. 19-21.) From these intensely interesting facts being reserved by the historian until after the conversion of Cornelius, the general reader is apt to think that they occurred subsequently to that in point of time. But they plainly belong to the period immediately following the dispersion of the Christians from Jerusalem on the death of Stephen.

5. Then Philip—not the apostle of that name (as some of the fathers supposed), for in that case (as *Grotius* observes) the apostles would have had no need to send some of themselves to lay their hands on the newly-baptized disciples (*vv.* 14-17). It was the deacon of that name, who in the list of the seven stands next to Stephen, likely as being the next most prominent. Probably (as *Meyer* supposes) the persecution was especially directed against Stephen's colleagues. **went down to the city of Samaria** [εἰς πόλιν Σαμαρείας]. *Lachmann* inserts the article before πόλιν, the transcribers, doubtless, understanding the capital to be meant, and deeming the article necessary to express this. But the authorities are decisive against it, and *Tischendorf* properly adheres to the received text]. Our translators, by rendering the phrase "*the* city of Samaria," evidently understood the capital to be meant; and so *Erasmus, Calvin, Beza, Grotius, Hackett,* &c., take it. But the very same phrase is used in John iv. 5—"*a* city of Samaria"—where Sychar is expressly named as the city meant. If this be the sense of the phrase here, Samaria means the region or country; and so *Lightfoot, Bengel, de Wette, Meyer, Olshausen, Neander, Humphry, Alford, Webster and Wilkinson,* and *Lechler,* understand it. Probably Sychar is meant—a place at this time of growing importance. Both the religious excitement which Simon Magus caused, and the subsequent triumphs of the Gospel in that place accord well with what we read of Sychar in the Gospel of John (ch. iv.)—as a place over which a great religious change had come some years before—a change whose good effects still remained; whose imperfect character laid them open to the impostures of Simon Magus, in the first instance, but whose reality and strength enabled them to see through the cheat when exposed to the light of the glorious Gospel which Philip brought them. Perhaps we should mark the providence which sent a Grecian, or Hellenistic, Jew to a people who, from national antipathy, might

have been less disposed (as *Webster and Wilkinson* remark) to a native of Judea. **7. For unclean spirits, crying with loud voice, came out of many that were possessed with them: and many taken with palsies, and that were lame, were healed.** *Lechler,* while calling attention to *Bengel's* acute remark on this verse—that Luke in the Acts never uses the word 'demons' [δαιμόνια] when speaking of the possessed, while in his Gospel he uses it oftener than the other evangelists—demurs very properly to *Bengel's* inference from this—namely, that the power of possession had waxed weaker since the death of Christ. *Lechler's* own observation is worth noticing—how remarkable it is that in the Acts possession does not occur among the Israelites, but only in heathen territories—as in Ephesus (ch. xix. 12)—or in the boundary between Judaism and heathenism, as in the country of Samaria. Perhaps the reason of this was, that as the rage of Satan was in this particular form naturally roused first in the Jewish territory, where Christ came to disturb his reign, and the triumphs of Christ over him were already sufficiently displayed there, so now, when the Gospel was marching into his heathen territories, it was natural that his rage should be transferred thither, and a fitting thing that its signal triumphs over him there also should in this history be recorded. **8. And there was great joy in that city**—joy over the change wrought by the Gospel in it, and over the varied cures by which its Divine character was attested. This joy of the converted Samaritans was like that of the Jewish Christians at Pentecost (ch. ii. 46, 47). *Simon Magus believes and is baptized* (9-13). **9. But there was** [προϋπῆρχεν]—'was there before;' preceding Philip in operating on the people, **a certain man, called Simon, which beforetime in the same city used sorcery** [μαγεύων]—using magical arts, **and bewitched** ('astounded' or 'startled') **the people of Samaria, giving out that himself was some great one: 10. To whom they all gave heed, from the least to the greatest.** [*Lachmann* and *Tischendorf* leave out πάντες, but all the leading MSS. have it; and instead of being inserted to 'fill up the sense,' as *Alford* says, it was far more likely to be left out just because the sense was filled up by what follows.] **saying, This man is the great power of God**—or, according to the reading which has far the greatest authority [of א A B C D E, &c., the Vulgate, and other ancient versions], 'This is that power of God which is called great' [Οὗτός ἐστιν ἡ δύναμις τ. Θ. ἡ καλουμένη μεγάλη]; that power which is by all of us acknowledged to be pre-eminent—a sort of incarnation of Divinity. The learned efforts to identify this impostor, and to collect the particulars of his life and opinions, have issued in little that is satisfactory. All that probably can be depended on is, what *Justin Martyr* (himself a native of this region) attests, that he was a Samaritan. That after his exposure and rejection by the apostles he attempted to combine a corrupt form of Christianity

11 God. And to him they had regard, because that of long time he had
12 bewitched them with sorceries. But when they believed Philip preaching
the things *k* concerning the kingdom of God, and the name of Jesus
13 Christ, they were baptized, both men and women. Then Simon himself
l believed also: and when he was baptized, he continued with Philip, and
wondered, beholding the ¹miracles and signs which were done.
14 Now when the apostles which were at Jerusalem heard that Samaria
15 had received the word of God, they sent unto them Peter and John: who,
when they were come down, prayed for them, *m* that they might receive
16 the Holy Ghost. (For *n* as yet he was fallen upon none of them: only
17 *o* they were baptized in *p* the name of the Lord Jesus.) Then *q* laid they
their hands on them, and they received the Holy Ghost.
18 And when Simon saw that through laying on of the apostles' hands the
19 Holy Ghost was given, he offered them money, saying, Give me also this
power, that on whomsoever I lay hands, he may receive the Holy Ghost.

A. D. 34.
k ch. 1. 3.
l Luke 8. 13.
Jas. 2. 19.
1 signs and
great.
miracles.
m Matt. 18. 19.
John 14. 13,
14.
John 16. 23,
24.
ch. 2. 33.
Phil. 2. 19.
n ch. 19. 2.
o Matt. 28 1¹.
ch. 2. 38.
p ch. 10. 48.
q ch. 6. 6.
Heb. 6. 2.

with Oriental or Grecian philosophy (*Irenæus*, in the second century, calls him the master and progenitor of all heretics)—is simply not improbable, in which case he may be considered as heralding other and more systematic efforts in the same direction afterwards. The Tübingen critics, as might be expected, take advantage of the legendary character of some of these traditions, and the uncertainty attaching to all of them, to impugn the historical credibility of this whole narrative—a method of criticism which would destroy the credit of much in ancient history that rests on the surest evidence. 11. And to him they had regard, because that of long time he had bewitched them [διὰ τὸ ἱκανῷ χρόνῳ . . . ἐξεστακέναι]—'because that for a considerable time they had been bewitched' the perfect tense having an intransitive sense), with sorceries. This, coupled with the rapidity with which they attached themselves to Philip, strikingly shows both how ripe the people of this region were for some religious change, and how much they lacked fundamental training. If our Lord's stay among them was the cause of the one, the shortness of that stay, and their imperfect knowledge of Old Testament truth, is a sufficient explanation of the other. 12. But when they believed Philip preaching [the things] concerning the kingdom of God, and the name of Jesus Christ, they were baptized, both men and women. (The bracketed article [τὰ] is wanting in authority, and unnecessary to the sense.) The detection of Simon's frauds would help to extend and deepen the effects of Philip's preaching. 13. Then Simon himself believed also. Left without followers, he thinks it best to join the man who had fairly outstripped him, not without a touch of real conviction. and when he was baptized. What a light does this throw on what is called *Baptismal Regeneration!* he continued with [ἦν προσκαρτερῶν]—'was in constant attendance upon' Philip, and wondered, beholding the miracles and signs which were done. Our translators have here departed from the received text, which reads as in the *margin*, 'the signs and great wonders which were done.' *Tischendorf* omits the word 'great' [μεγάλους], as our translators do; but *Lachmann*, on greatly preponderating authority, as we judge, retains it. The historian's remark here throws a strong light on Simon's true character—astonishment at the miracle, rather than joy in the Gospel, being the predominant element in the feelings of this new convert.

The Apostolic Visit to the New Converts—Peter's Interview with Simon Magus (14-25). 14. Now when the apostles which were at Jerusalem

heard that Samaria had received the word of God, they sent unto them Peter and John—showing that Peter was regarded only as their own equal. At the same time, by selecting the two most prominent of their number, they show the importance they attached to this first accession of a city to Christ. 15. Who, when they were come down, prayed for them, that they might receive the Holy Ghost. 16. (For as yet he was fallen upon none of them: only they were baptized in the name of the Lord Jesus) 17. Then laid they their hands on them, and they received the Holy Ghost. While the prayer seems to have been one act [the verb is in the aorist, προσηύξαντο], the imposition of hands and the descent of the Spirit, was a succession of acts in each case or in clusters [as the imperfects, ἐπετίθουν and ἐλάμβανον, imply]. That the reference here is to the supernatural gifts of the Spirit, or such a communication of the Spirit as made itself visibly or audibly manifest, there cannot be a reasonable doubt. The baptism of adult believers and the renewing of the Holy Ghost went together (1 Cor. xii. 13; Tit. iii. 5-7). What is here recorded, therefore, of the communication of the Holy Ghost by the laying on of the apostles' hands, sometime after the parties had been baptized, must have been a superadded thing; and as it was but occasional, so it was invariably attended by miraculous manifestations. See ch. x. 44, where it followed Peter's preaching; and ch. xix. 1-7, where, as here, it followed the imposition of apostolic hands. This being the first accession and baptism of a large body of disciples, through the instrumentality of one who was not himself an apostle, it was fitting that the new-born church of this city should be taught the proper position and authority of those Divinely-appointed founders of the Church; and this visit to them of a deputation from the mother-church at Jerusalem, consisting of the two most prominent members of the apostolic body, was just the thing to produce that effect. Beautiful certainly was the spectacle here first exhibited, of Jew and Samaritan one in Christ. 18. And when Simon saw [θεασάμενος is the received reading, but Ἰδὼν is better supported] that through laying on of the apostles' hands the Holy Ghost was given, he offered them money. Hence the term *Simony*, to denote trafficking in sacred things, but chiefly the purchase of ecclesiastical offices. 19. Saying, Give me also this power, that on whomsoever I lay hands, he may receive the Holy Ghost. This was evidently a plan for recovering, through the new Faith, that influence over the people as a wonder-worker which their

20 But Peter said unto him, Thy money perish with thee, because thou 'hast thought that 'the gift of God may be purchased with money.
21 Thou hast neither part nor lot in this matter: for thy 'heart is not right
22 in the sight of God. Repent therefore of this thy wickedness, and pray
23 God, "if perhaps the thought of thine heart may be forgiven thee. For I perceive that thou art in the gall 'of bitterness, and *in* the bond of
24 iniquity. Then answered Simon, and said, Pray ye "to the Lord for me, that none of these things which ye have spoken come upon me.
25 And they, when they had testified and preached the word of the Lord, returned to Jerusalem, and preached the Gospel in many villages of the Samaritans.

A. D. 34.
r 2 Ki. 5. 16.
Matt. 10. 8.
s ch. 2. 38.
ch. 11. 17.
t Jer. 17. 9.
2 Tim. 3. 5.
u Isa. 55. 7.
Dan. 4. 27.
v Heb. 12. 15.
w Gen. 20. 7.
Ex. 8. 8.
Num. 21. 7.
Job 42. 8.

conversion to Christ had quite destroyed; revealing not only how entirely his conversion, such as it was, had failed to check his spiritual ambition, but how ignorant he was of the first principles of that Gospel which he had embraced. **20. But Peter said unto him, Thy money perish with thee.** This is the language of mingled horror and indignation, reminding us of our Lord's rebuke of Peter himself (Matt. xvi. 23), **because thou hast thought that the gift of God may be purchased with money.** [κτᾶσθαι]—rather, 'hast thought to acquire the gift,' &c. **21. Thou hast neither part nor lot in this matter.** It is a needless refinement of *Bengel* to distinguish between these two words in such a phrase, which plainly is but an emphatic expression for 'no share at all' (cf. in LXX., Deut. xviii. 1; Ps. xvi. 5; Isa. lvii. 6): **for thy heart is not right in the sight of God.** This is the fidelity of a true minister to one awfully self-deceived. **22. Repent therefore of this thy wickedness, and pray God**—'pray the Lord' is evidently the true reading here [κυρίου, with א A B C D E, &c.; the Peshito Syriac; some MSS. of the Vulgate and other versions—not τ. Θεοῦ, and so *Lachmann* and *Tischendorf*], **if perhaps the thought of thine heart may be forgiven thee**—this expression of doubt as to his forgiveness being designed to impress on him the greatness of his sin, and awaken alarm in his mind. **23. For I perceive that thou art in the gall of bitterness** —*lit.*, 'into' it [εἰς], as if steeped in it, **and in the bond of iniquity**—as if chained to it. **24. Then answered Simon, and said, Pray ye to the Lord for me.** The "ye" here [ὑμεῖς] is emphatic—'Your prayer will be more efficacious than mine' (as *Webster and Wilkinson* well put it). Peter had urged him to pray for himself: he asks these wonder-working men to do it for him; having no confidence in the prayer of faith, but thinking that such men as these must possess some peculiar interest with Heaven. **that none of these things which ye have spoken come upon me**—not that the thought of his heart might be forgiven him (as Peter entreated him to seek), but only that the evils threatened might be averted from him. While this confirms Peter's view of his melancholy case, it shows that Christianity, as something divine, still retained its hold on him. Tradition (as already observed)—though not much to be relied on—represents this miserable man as turning out a great heresiarch, mingling Oriental and Grecian philosophy with some Christian elements. **25. And they** (Peter and John), **when they had testified and preached the word of the Lord**—that is, both in the city where Philip's labours had been so richly blessed and in the surrounding parts, as the word implies [διαμαρτυράμενοι]. **returned to Jerusalem, and preached the gospel in many villages of the Samaritans**—embracing the opportunity of their journey back to Jerusalem to fulfil their Lord's commission (ch. i. 8) to the

whole region of Samaria. [Agreeably to this, the imperfects—ὑπέστρεφον and εὐαγγελίζοντο—are better supported than the aorists, ὑπέστρεψαν and εὐαγγελίσαντο, of the received text.]

Remarks.—1. The infant Church having no visible existence up to this time, save at Jerusalem, was at its lowest point of depression when, after the slaughter of so eminent a witness for Christ as Stephen, the public meetings of the Christians appear to have ceased, and that bloody persecutor, Saul of Tarsus, went from street to street, and house to house, searching for disciples, sparing neither age nor sex—intent upon stamping out the last embers of that fire from heaven which had been kindled on the day of Pentecost. But just then it was that the Gospel took a first start; not only breaking loose from its dependence on the capital, to which the ancient economy was entirely linked, but trying for the first time those wings on which it was to fly to the uttermost parts of the earth. It was just that attempt to crush the Gospel which was the immediate occasion of this signal dispersion of it. As the disciples fled from Jerusalem, and were scattered abroad without the apostles, like shepherdless sheep, we might fancy them trembling for the ark of God, and anticipating the worst. But

'Know, the darkest part of night
Is before the dawn of light.'

New circumstances presented all things to them in a new light. Instead of having their hopes dashed and their energies crushed, they found their field of vision and of action only enlarged and brightened. As their hold on Jerusalem, with all its ancient associations and endearments, got loosened, it was only to disclose to them something of the more extended career on which the Church was about to enter. And so it has ever been, that just at evening time it has been light. 2. Were these dispersed preachers, then, ordained and official ministers of Christ? Certainly not; and all the best and most recent critics not only recognize, but call special attention to the fact. 'The dispersed (says *Lechler* excellently) were not apostles, for the apostles remained behind in Jerusalem. At the most, a few of them belonged to the elected Seven (ch. vi.), and even these were not directly called as authorized ministers of the Word. But the great majority of the dispersed Christians held no ecclesiastical office whatever. Yet they preached wherever they came, without being called to do so by official duty and express commission, but entirely from the internal pressure of faith, which cannot but speak that which affects the heart, from the impulse of the Spirit by which they were anointed, and from love to the Saviour, to whom they were indebted for the forgiveness of their sins and for their blessed hopes. Thus this spread of the Gospel without the holy city, this planting of the Church of

26   And ^xthe angel of the Lord spake unto Philip, saying, Arise, and go toward the south, unto the way that goeth down from Jerusalem unto

Christ in the regions of Palestine—indeed, even beyond those regions—was effected not by the apostles, but chiefly by other Christians who held no office, in virtue of the universal priesthood of believers. According to human ideas of Church government and office, it ought not to have taken place. But the Lord of the Church does not so confine Himself even to the apostolate established by Himself, as that everything must take place entirely through it in order to be lawful, pleasing to God, blessed, and full of promise. Christ thus shows that no man, and no finite office is indispensable.' (Similar sentiments are expressed by *Baumgarten*.) Official functionaries of the Church are often slow to recognize such truths, and so are found not seldom resisting movements and calling in question results, as irregular and disorderly, which are manifestly of God. But, 3. Though private Christians are at full liberty to work for Christ, according to their opportunities and gifts, and their evangelistic labours should be owned and encouraged, they are not to regard themselves as an independent agency, and much less to ignore or attempt to supersede the regular channel of the Christian ministry. In the visit of the apostolic deputation to the Samaritan converts, the welcome given to it, and the Divine seal set upon its authority, we have a beautiful illustration of the harmony that should reign amongst all the diversified agencies of the Church for the promotion of the common cause. 4. The religious history of Samaria (as we find it in the Fourth Gospel and in the Acts) holds forth encouragement regarding places in which the truth, richly sown, has borne little fruit. For the labour bestowed on them may prove to have been but the preparation of the ground for other labourers and other appliances, that were to perfect what was lacking at the first. Thus was it with Samaria, sown first by the great Sower Himself, and only afterwards reaped by Philip and others. (See on John iv. 1-42, Remark 7 at the close of that Section.) 5. Religious imposture—as probably in Simon Magus—usually begins in an honest but unenlightened enthusiasm for some religious views, guided by vanity and the lust of power. When this is successful in creating a party, and bringing considerable numbers under its influence—kept together with difficulty where solid truth and exalted motives of action are wanting—unscrupulous measures are almost invariably resorted to, to preserve what has been acquired; and honest enthusiasm, then giving place to secretiveness and cunning, gradually ripens into willful imposture. Thus is realized what might seem impossible, a combination of religious feeling and of conscious fraud—the latter by degrees absorbing the former. Mere sincerity, then, in the maintenance of religious opinions, and self-sacrificing absorption in the propagation of them, as they are no evidence of the truth of them, so they are not to be relied on even for its own continuance, and in the case of errorists often degenerate into what was never dreamt of at the first, and discover a strange mixture of the deceived and the deceiver in one and the same person, according to the apostle's striking saying, "Evil men and seducers will wax worse and worse, *deceiving and being deceived*" (2 Tim. iii. 13). Illustrations of this in our own time may be seen in Mormonism and Agapemonism. 6. Contrast Simon's request, "Give me this *power*" with our Lord's words to the Twelve, when they reported to Him how "even the spirits had been subject to them through

His name"—"Notwithstanding in this rejoice not, that the spirits are subject unto you; but rather rejoice because your names are written in heaven" (Luke x. 17, 20). These two opposite feelings—that of Simon, on the one hand, and that here expressed by our Lord—are the characteristics of two opposite sorts of ecclesiastics. 7. Though fickleness in religion, as in everything else, is fatal to solid progress, we are not to confound with this that unsteadiness which is almost characteristic of children in the Christian as well as in the natural life, and which with time and training disappear. The readiness of the Samaritans to fall in with Simon's impostures, though the result of their defective training, showed the spiritual thirst which had been awakened in them; and the joy with which they forsook him, on Philip's bringing the Gospel to their hearts, and health to their homes, with the subsequent establishment of a Christian community among them—sealed by apostolic hands with the gift of the Holy Ghost—is an evidence that they had passed out of religious instability—all the more solid in the faith, probably, from their previous experience of "the depths of Satan." And so should we judge of similar cases, as they still arise. Unawakened, stupid souls, immersed in the world, or steeped in literary and scientific pursuits —who fall in with the current religious systems, or are indifferent to all religion—such are never imposed upon by plausible religionists, nor run any risk of being sucked into a current of religious fanaticism. But then they are equally inaccessible to the truth itself, and right and wrong feelings on religion are alike strangers to their breasts. Whereas those whose souls have been touched with a sense of their wretchedness without God, though, in their thirst for satisfaction, they may be imposed upon by religious plausibilities, and carried away from the true resting-place of the heart, will, on discovering their mistake and finding the truth, lay faster hold of it, and become all the more enlightened and stable Christians for the humbling experience they have come through. At the same time it is not to be doubted that 'growing in grace, and in the knowledge of our Lord and Saviour Jesus Christ,' is the only sure preservative against 'falling from our own stedfastness' (2 Pet. iii. 17, 18). Accordingly, in a very striking passage on the subject of religious delusions, not unlike this of Simon Magus, the apostle intimates that the Christian ministry was the gift of the Church's glorified Head, on the one hand for maturing and bringing it to eventual perfection, and on the other for curing childish instability—"That ye be no longer children, tossed to and fro, and carried about by every wind of doctrine, by the sleight of men and cunning craftiness, whereby they lie in wait to deceive," &c. (Eph. iv. 14.) 8. Indignant feeling and sharp rebuke are not inconsistent with tenderness and pity in the treatment of those who make a gain of godliness, even though to some extent self-deceived. Nor can we expect to do them any good until their self-complacency has been thus dashed to the ground. Compare what is said of Christ Himself, "When he had looked round about on them with *anger*, being *grieved* for the hardness of their heart," &c. (Mark iii. 5.)

26-40.—*The Ethiopian Eunuch.* 'With the foregoing narrative (says *Olshausen*) of the progress of the Gospel among the Samaritans is connected another, which points to the diffusion of the doctrine of the Cross among the remotest nations.

52

27 Gaza, which is desert. And he arose and went: and, behold, a ^yman of
Ethiopia, an eunuch of great authority under Candace queen of the
Ethiopians, who had the charge of all her treasure, and ^zhad come to
28 Jerusalem for to worship, was returning, and sitting in his chariot read
29 Esaias the prophet. Then the Spirit said unto Philip, Go near, and join
30 thyself to this chariot. And Philip ran thither to *him*, and heard him
read the prophet Esaias, and said, Understandest thou what thou read-
31 est? And he said, How can I, except some man should guide me? And

A. D. 34.

y Ps. 68. 31.
Ps. 87. 4.
Isa. 43. 6.
Jer .13. 23.
Zeph. 3. 10.
z 1 Ki. 8. 41.
Ps. 68. 29.
Isa. 56. 3-8.
John 12. 20.

The simplicity of the chamberlain of Meroe forms a remarkable contrast with the craft of the magician just described.' **26. And the** (or 'an') **angel of the Lord spake unto Philip, saying, Arise, and go toward the south unto the way** (that is, so as to get into the way) **that goeth down from Jerusalem into Gaza, which** [αὔτη]—that is, not Gaza itself, but the way, **is desert.** Gaza was the southernmost city of Palestine, situated at the border of the desert leading to Egypt. It is mentioned as early as Gen. x. 19; it was allotted to the tribe of Judah; but it was seized and held by the Philistines, and became one of their five principal cities. There was such a road to it, across mount Hebron, which Philip might take without requiring to go first to Jerusalem (as *Von Raumer's* 'Palestine' shows). Indeed, there were, and still are, two such roads at least (*Robinson's* 'Palestine,' ii. p. 321). The next clause, therefore, "which is desert"—a tract of country without villages or fixed habitations—was probably intended to define the one which Philip was to take, so as not to miss the returning eunuch. (So *Bengel, Alford, Baumgarten, Hackett, Lechler.*) Others take Gaza itself as what was "desert;" some of these referring it to the ancient Gaza, which was then a ruin, though rebuilt with the same name (as *Olshausen, Humphry,* &c.), while others apply it even to the rebuilt Gaza, which was destroyed by the Romans, (so *Hug,* &c.) But as that destruction did not take place till after this book must have been published, this interpretation must be set aside. Nor does any application of the phrase, "which is desert," to the town give point to the direction to Philip, as the word Gaza would be enough to guide him to the spot, whether old or new, standing or ruined. Little better is it to suppose this (as several critics do) to be a parenthetical explanation of the historian himself, to enable his readers to identify the spot. By far the simplest explanation of the clause, then, is to refer it to the way or road which the angel would have Philip take, to compass his object. **27. And he arose and went.** To leave a city where his hands were full of his Master's work, to go far away on a desert road, and to be kept in ignorance of the object of the journey—was fitted to stagger the faith of our zealous evangelist. But, like Paul, he "was not disobedient to the heavenly vision;" and, like Abraham, "he went out, not knowing whither he went." **and, behold, a man of Ethiopia** —the name anciently given to Upper or Southern Egypt, of which Meroe—a rich island formed by two branches of the Nile—was the capital. **an eunuch of great authority.** Eunuchs were generally employed for confidential offices in the East, as to some extent they are still; and although, from their being so much employed about royal persons, this name was sometimes given to those who were not literally eunuchs, there is no sufficient reason to doubt that it is here used in its literal sense—not (as some take it) in the general sense of 'a grandee.' The prohibition of the Mosaic law against the

admission of such to the congregation (Deut. xxiii. 1) has been pleaded against this. But the approach there intended seems not to relate to any but born Israelites, and so would have excluded all proselytes; and even though it did not, from the case of Ebed-melech (Jer. xxxviii. 7-13, and xxxix. 16-18)—of whom we can scarcely doubt that he had a place in the congregation—there is reason to think that this law was not so rigidly enforced as to prove a bar to the recognition of one in the high position of this Ethiopian, even though a literal eunuch. **under Candace queen of the Ethiopians.** We learn from *Pliny* ('H. N.' vi. 29), who flourished during the reign of Vespasian, that this had for many years been the family name of the queens of Upper Egypt—like *Abimelech, Pharaoh, Cæsar,* &c., and *Eusebius* ('E. H.' ii. 10) says that as in Sheba (South Arabia), so here, females were allowed to reign. **who had the charge of all her treasure** [γάζης]—a peculiar Persian word for the royal treasure, (*Quint. Curt.* iii. 13. 5); **and had come to Jerusalem for to worship**—to keep the recent feast of Pentecost, as a Gentile proselyte to the Jewish Faith. See the glorious promise to such, Isa. lvi. 3-8. **28. Was returning.** Having come so far, he not only stayed out the days of the festival, but prolonged his stay till now. It says much for his fidelity and value to his royal mistress that he had such liberty. But the faith in Jehovah and love of His worship and Word, with which he was imbued, sufficiently explain this. **and sitting in his chariot read Esaias the prophet**—no doubt, in the Greek translation, called the LXX. *Olshausen,* taking it for granted that he was reading in the original Hebrew, concludes from this that he was a born Jew. But besides that the historian says nothing as to the language of the copy he used, the whole description conveys the impression that he was an Ethiopian heathen by birth. Not contented with the statutory services in which he had joined, he beguiles the tedium of the journey homeward by reading the Scriptures. But this is not all; for as Philip "heard him read the prophet Esaias," he must have been reading aloud; and though it was customary, as it still is, in the East to read aloud, since he was audible even to Philip, the probability is that he was reading not for his own benefit only, but for that of his charioteer also. **29. Then the Spirit said unto Philip**—by an unmistakable voice within, as in ch. x. 19; xvi. 6, 7, **Go near, and join thyself to this chariot.** This would reveal to Philip the hitherto unknown object of his journey, and encourage him to expect some fruit of his interview with this stranger. **30. And Philip ran thither to him, and heard him read the prophet Esaias, and said, Understandest thou what thou readest?** [Ἄρα γε.] The particles here used imply that a negative, rather than an affirmative, answer was expected. To one so engaged this would be deemed no rude question, while the eager appearance of the speaker, and the question itself, would indicate a readiness to supply any want of insight that might be felt.

53

32 he desired Philip that he would come up and sit with him. The place of
the Scripture which he read was this, [a]"He was led as a sheep to the
slaughter; and like a lamb dumb before his shearer, so opened he not his
33 mouth: in his humiliation his judgment was taken away: and who shall
34 declare his generation? for his life is taken from the earth. And the
eunuch answered Philip, and said, I pray thee, of whom speaketh the
35 prophet this? of himself, or of some other man? Then Philip opened
his mouth, and began [b]at the same scripture, and preached unto him
Jesus.
36   And as they went on *their* way, they came unto a certain water: and
the eunuch said, See, *here is* water; what [c]doth hinder me to be bap-
37 tized? And Philip said, [d]If thou believest with all thine heart, thou
mayest. And he answered and said, I [e]believe that Jesus Christ is the
38 Son of God. And he commanded the chariot to stand still: and they
went down both into the water, both Philip and the eunuch; and he
39 baptized him. And when they were come up out of the water, [f]the
Spirit of the Lord caught away Philip, that the eunuch saw him no

A. D. 34.
[a] Isa. 53. 7.
Phil. 2. 7, 8.
[b] Luke 24. 27.
ch. 18. 28.
2 Cor. 1. 20.
Col. 2. 17.
1 Pet. 1. 11-
13.
[c] ch. 10. 47.
[d] Matt. 28. 19.
Mark 16. 16.
[e] Matt. 16. 16.
John 6. 69.
John 9. 35.
John 11. 27.
Rom. 10. 10.
[f] 1 Ki. 18. 12.
2 Ki. 2. 16.
Eze. 3. 12.
2 Cor. 12. 2-
4.

---

31. And he said, How can I [Πῶς γὰρ ἂν δυναίμην]—'Why, how should I,' **except some man should guide me?** Beautiful expression at once of humility and docility; the invitation to Philip which immediately followed, **And he desired Philip that he would come up and sit with him,** being but the natural expression of this. **32. The place** [περιοχή] —the 'portion,' or 'section;' not 'contents' (as most modern critics render the word (from 1 Pet. ii. 6, where the verb certainly has this sense) **of the scripture which he read was this.** What follows is from Isa. liii. 7, 8, almost *verbatim* as in the LXX., **He was led as a sheep to the slaughter; and like a lamb dumb before his shearer, so opened he not his mouth: 33. In his humiliation his judgment was taken away: and who shall declare his generation? for his life is taken from the earth.** The proper exposition of the several clauses of this prediction belongs rather to a commentary on the evangelical prophet than to this place; and since Philip would dwell rather on the brightly Messianic character of this whole chapter than on the precise sense of the verses here quoted, it will not be necessary to stay on them here. Rather let us wonder that this, of all predictions of Messiah's sufferings in the Old Testament the most striking, should have been that which the eunuch was reading before Philip joined him. He could hardly miss to have heard at Jerusalem of the sufferings and death of Jesus, and of the existence of a continually increasing party who acknowledged him to be the Messiah. But his question to Philip, whether the prophet in this passage meant himself or some other man, clearly shows that he had not the least idea of any connection between this prediction and those facts. **34. And the eunuch answered Philip, and said, I pray thee, of whom speaketh the prophet this? of himself, or of some other man?** The respect with which he here addresses Philip was prompted by his reverence for one whom he perceived to be his superior in divine things, his own worldly position sinking before this. **35. Then Philip opened his mouth** (see on Matt. v. 2), **and began at the same scripture**—founding on it as his text, **and preached unto him Jesus**—showing Him to be the glorious Burden of this wonderful prediction, and interpreting it in the light of the facts of His history.

36. And as they went on their way, they came unto a certain water: and the eunuch said, See, here is water ['Ιδοὺ ὕδωρ]—'Behold water,' as if already, his mind filled with light and his soul set free, he was eagerly looking out for the first water in which he might seal his reception of the truth, and be enrolled among the visible disciples of the Lord Jesus. **what doth hinder me to be baptized?** Philip had probably told him that this was the ordained sign and seal of discipleship, but the eunuch's question was likely the first proposal of its application to himself. **37. [And Philip said, If thou believest with all thine heart, thou mayest. And he answered and said, I believe that Jesus Christ is the Son of God.]** This entire verse is wanting in the oldest and best MSS.—אABCGH, &c.; in the best MS. of the Vulgate (the *Codex Amiatinus* of the first hand), in the Peshito Syriac, and in both the Egyptian versions; in *Chrysostom* also. It must be regarded, therefore, as an interpolation: but certainly it is a very early one; for we find it both in the Greek of *Irenæus* and in the Latin version of it, in the second century. We may conclude, therefore, that as the transition from the eunuch's question to the act of baptizing him seemed too abrupt, this verse was added on the margin of the few MSS. which contain it, and afterwards introduced into the text, to express what *would have been demanded* of the eunuch, as a confession of his faith, at the time when this addition was made. **38. And he commanded the chariot to stand still: and they went down both into the water** [εἰς τὸ ὕδωρ]. This may be rendered 'unto the water,' meaning the valley where the water was (so *Webster and Wilkinson*, after *Robinson*). But this seems plainly to be short of the sense intended; for (as *Hackett* observes) the next verse tells that they came "out of the water" [ἐκ τοῦ ὕδατος]. Clearly, the meaning is, as our version renders it, "into the water," both standing in it; **both Philip and the eunuch; and he baptized him**—probably laving the water upon him; but the precise form, and whether it was uniform or (as is more likely) variable, is not perfectly certain, nor yet of much consequence. **39. And when they were come up out of the water, the Spirit of the Lord caught away Philip.** To deny the supernatural character of this removal of Philip (as *Olshausen*, *Meyer*, *Bloomfield*, *Hackett*, and others do) is vain. It stands out on the face of the expressions, "caught away" [ἥρπασε], "saw him no more" [εἶδεν αὐτὸν οὐκέτι], "was found" [εὑρέθη]. In fact, on comparing what is here said of the eunuch with what we read of Elijah (1 Ki. xviii. 12; 2 Ki. ii. 16), it will be seen to be but a repetition of the Lord's

54

40 more: and he went on his way rejoicing. But Philip was found at ^gAzotus: and passing through he preached in all the cities, till he came to Cesarea.

A. D. 34.
^g Josh. 15.46.
Zech. 9. 6.

method with the ancient prophets on important occasions. (So *Bengel, Alford, Lechler,* and the great majority of interpreters.) The word, to "catch away" [ἁρπάζω], is used (as *Bengel* notes) to express a similarly supernatural removal, in 2 Cor. xii. 2, and 1 Thess. iv. 17. **and he went on his way rejoicing.** He had found Christ, and the key to the Scriptures; his soul was set free, and his discipleship sealed; he had lost his teacher, but gained what was infinitely better; he felt himself a new man, and "his joy was full." Tradition says he was the first preacher of the Gospel in Ethiopia; and how, indeed, could he choose but "tell what the Lord had done for his soul"? Yet there is no certainty as to any historical connection between his labours and the introduction of Christianity into that country. **40. But Philip was found at** [εὑρέθη εἰς, *q. d.,* 'was found brought to:' see *Winer,* 50. 4, *b,* and 65. 8]. The idea is that of 'made his appearance,' or 'was next heard of at;' an expression confirming the miraculous manner of his transportation: **Azotus**—the ancient "Ashdod," (1 Sam. v. 1, &c.) **and passing through he preached in all the cities**—lying along the coast, proceeding northwards—Lydda, Joppa, &c. **till he came to Cesarea**—fifty-five miles north-west of Jerusalem, on the Mediterranean, just south of mount Carmel; and so named by Herod, who rebuilt it, in honour of Cæsar Augustus. At the time when this was written Cæsarea was the place where the Roman Procurators resided. Henceforth we lose sight of zealous and honoured Philip, with the exception of a momentary re-appearance when Paul visited him at Cæsarea, where he resided (ch. xxi. 8)—as by and by we shall lose sight even of Peter. As the chariot of the Gospel rolls on, other agents are raised up, each suited to his work. But "he that soweth and he that reapeth shall rejoice together" (see on John iv. 37).

Remarks. — I. The bearing of this beautiful episode on the commission given forth by the risen Saviour to His apostles, "Ye shall be My witnesses both in Jerusalem and in Samaria, and in all Judea, and unto the uttermost parts of the earth," is worthy of notice. So fully had they executed the first part of this commission, that, even their enemies themselves being judges, they had "filled Jerusalem with their doctrine" (ch. v. 28). When persecution drove them from Jerusalem, the brethren then went to "Samaria and all Judea," preaching the Word. The time for the formal opening of the door of faith unto the Gentiles had not yet quite come; but doors for reaching them being meantime providentially opened, it was doubly anticipated—on the one hand by the simple impulses of Christian love in the dispersed disciples (see on *v.* 4), constraining them to declare even to the Gentiles what they had seen and heard, and here, by express Divine direction to Philip, taking him out of the midst of blessed work in Samaria, to fetch in a distinguished Gentile proselyte then on his way home to Upper Egypt from Jerusalem. And not only so, but whereas it was to the apostles that the commission was given, we see this witness borne "in all Judea and in Samaria, and (initially) to the uttermost part of the earth," not by the apostles themselves, who remained in Jerusalem, but by the dispersed disciples, apparently without any special call; nor was Philip Divinely directed to carry the Gospel to the eunuch until he had been richly

blessed in voluntary work at Samaria. What does all this proclaim? Surely, that while provision is Divinely made for the work of the Church being formally and officially done, it is the privilege of all that love the Lord Jesus to embrace whatever openings the providence of God may present for extending or building up the kingdom of Christ, according to their gifts; and wherever the joy of God's salvation is strong in any community of Christians, there will such breakings forth of voluntary effort be sure to occur; and when they have the seal of Heaven set upon them—often even more visibly than upon the stated work of the ministry—it will be the part of wise ministers of Christ to recognize and hail such efforts, regulating and comprehending them within the sphere of their own labours, as so much additional gain for their Master. 2. Philip, though called away from a sphere of labour in which he was Divinely owned, to go on a desert track, and without any further information, "was not disobedient unto the heavenly vision." One soul thereby gained to Christ was his reward: many others, it may be, were gathered in through him; but of this no trace remains in history. Yet, doubtless, in the eye of Heaven that service was of more importance than any which he might have rendered to the cause of Christ by remaining in Samaria. And since the good that the servants of Christ are to do depends not so much on the largeness of the field, or its apparently promising character, as on the Master's countenance in their work, they will do well to ensure this first, by studying to know His will in all their movements, following simply the manifest leadings of His providence and the guidance of His Spirit. 3. The preparation of the eunuch for receiving the Gospel was as remarkable as that of the instrument for bringing it to him. His conversion first to the Jewish Faith; his strong desire to mingle in its religious services, leading him, though occupying a high and responsible post, to take a journey to Jerusalem to keep the festival of Pentecost; his remaining there for some time after it was over, evidently from the interest which he felt in all that related to his new Religion; his not only having a copy of the Scriptures in his possession (no doubt the Greek Septuagint), but reading it aloud on his way home; still more, "the place of the scripture which he read"—of all others the richest in the Old Testament in Evangelical matter; then Philip's coming up just as he had come to the meek submission of the slaughtered Lamb, in a somewhat obscure part of the chapter; the eagerness with which the traveller, coming up to him, asked if he understood it; his frank confession that he needed a guide, and his invitation to the traveller to come up and sit with him; and, beyond all, the alacrity with which he drank in Philip's exposition of the work of Christ from that text, his eager desire to be baptized at the first place where water was found, and the joy with which he went on his way alone after this—all these majestic steps in this case show a Divine preparation for the result, as instructive as it is remarkable. Another such series of preparatory steps we shall by and by find in the case of Cornelius (ch. x.)—just the reverse of the case of Saul of Tarsus (ch. ix.); and there can be no doubt that similar preparations in providence are made in every age and every land for most of the more important

55

9   AND ^aSaul, yet breathing out threatenings and slaughter against the
2 disciples of the Lord, went unto the high priest, and desired of him letters

A. D. 35.
^a ch. 8. 3.

accessions to Christ, whether of individuals or of territories. In the view of this, should not the servants of Christ be on the watch, and lie in wait to be employed on such errands as this of Philip? and if they did, perhaps they would have more of them than otherwise falls to their lot. 4. Are we, or are we not, to regard Philip's views of the 53rd chapter of Isaiah, and the change on the eunuch's views in consequence, as indicating the true interpretation of that chapter? That after being Divinely directed to meet this distinguished convert to the Jewish Faith, and bring him to the reception of the Gospel, Philip should have been permitted to do this by an erroneous (even though honest) application of that celebrated prophecy to Christ, and that the eunuch, yielding to this false view of the connection between the Faith he had before embraced and that now propounded to him, was baptized and departed rejoicing in what was, to a large extent, a mistake—is not for a moment to be thought of. Nor let it be said that though Philip took "this scripture" as his start-ing-point, it was the historical sketch which he would doubtless give him of the life, death, resur-rection, and ascension of Jesus, with the subsequent descent of the Spirit, and the beginnings of the Church, that he would lay the chief stress upon, and that would constitute the ground of the eunuch's faith and joy, and not the sense put upon that prophetic chapter. On the contrary, the natural impression certainly is, that Philip's express design was to show, and that he succeeded in showing, to this enquiring eunuch that "this scripture" which he had been reading had its Divinely intended and proper fulfilment in the sufferings and death of "Jesus"—the history and the prophecy being just the complement of each other. If this be correct, it refutes some modern theories of the interpretation of prophecy. We speak not here of those which are based on the denial of all that is supernatural in the Old Testa-ment, but of such as that of the late Dr. Arnold—that prophecy is not intended to predict historical events at all, and has to do only with *principles*, holding forth the conflict of good and evil, and the ultimate issues of both. But even such theories as that of the late Dr. J. A. Alexander, in his 'Commentary on Isaiah'—that not Christ person-ally, but Christ and His Church together, as one complex, mystical Person, is the proper subject of all the Messianic prophecies—must be regarded, we think, in the light of this narrative, as an inadequate key to the interpretation of that chapter. Though there is an important truth at the bottom of that theory, we cannot but think that, as a key for the interpretation of this chapter, it would have been positively in Philip's way, if it had been before his mind at all; and that the facility and directness with which he got from "this scripture" to "Jesus," whom he preached from it, and the readiness with which the eunuch fell in with the view given him of the chapter and the tidings brought him of Jesus, speak much for the old and all but una-nimous opinion of the Church, that the personal sufferings of Christ, and the glories to follow them, are the direct and proper burden of this prophetic chapter. 5. The joy with which the eunuch embraced Christ crucified, and went on his way after his baptism admits of no satisfactory explan-ation save that of the expiatory character of Christ's death. We have the old Socinian theory of it now dressed up in new forms and more plaus-ible phraseology, by a school of divines professing

orthodoxy, but fond of inveighing against all tradi-tional conceptions of biblical truth. Such hold forth Christ's sufferings and death simply as a historical event, but one by which God intended that a transcendent example should be given to the world of self-sacrifice in His service, by drink-ing into the spirit of which we are to be made partakers of the glory in which He now reigns. Who can possibly suppose that this, or anything like this, was what made the eunuch go on his way rejoicing? But if, as Peter told Cornelius and his company, "the word which God sent unto the children of Israel" was a word "*preaching peace by Jesus Christ*" (ch. x. 36); if, as Paul told the Jews in the synagogue of Antioch, "*through this man was preached unto them the forgiveness of sins*, and *by Him all that believe are justified from all things*" (ch. xiii. 38, 39); if, in short, he taught the eunuch, in terms of the prophetic chapter which he was reading, that "the Lord laid on Him the iniquity of us all"—then is the joy of the eunuch easily understood. For it is the joy of a purged conscience, the joy of peace with God through the blood of the cross, the joy of having found the God with whom He had become acquainted through the Old Testament a recon-ciled Father—a joy which every pardoned child of God understands from his own experience—a joy which would send him home lightened of his chiefest burden, to serve his mistress in a new character and to higher ends than ever before.

CHAP. IX. 1-43.—THE CONVERSION, BAPTISM, PREACHING, AND FIRST PERILS OF SAUL OF TARSUS AT DAMASCUS AND JERUSALEM—THE PEACE AND PROSPERITY OF THE CHURCH IN PALESTINE—PETER AT LYDDA HEALS ÆNEAS OF THE PALSY, AND RAISES DORCAS TO LIFE AT JOPPA.

Conversion of Saul (1-9). **1. And Saul, yet breathing out** [ἐμπνέων]—*lit.*, 'inwardly breath-ing,' that is, 'heaving with' **threatenings and slaughter**—'menace and murder.' The emphatic "yet" [ἔτι] is intended to note the remarkable fact, that up to this moment his blind persecuting rage against the disciples of the Lord burned as fiercely as ever. In the teeth of this, *Neander* and *Olshausen* picture him 'deeply impressed with Stephen's joyful faith, remembering passages of the Old Testament confirmatory of the Messiah-ship of Jesus, and experiencing such a violent struggle as would inwardly prepare the way for the designs of God towards him.' And *Stanley*, in his 'Sermons in the East,' and in 'St. Paul on his Way to Damascus,' (No. VIII.) says, 'He had doubtless had better feelings stirring within him from what he had seen of the death of Stephen and of the good deeds of the early Christians. In this way his conversion, sudden as it seemed at last, had been long prepared. His conscience had been ill at ease with itself; and in this perplexity and doubt it needed only that one blessed inter-position of his merciful Lord to recall him to a sense of his better self.' That such a man could have heard such an address as Stephen's without deep thoughts and feelings being stirred within him, was, indeed, hardly possible. But that it stag-gered or softened him, that it inclined him to think favourably of the Christian faith, that it produced anything but a more resolute determination to root it out as a pestilent heresy, his whole conduct, from that time up to the moment when the manifestation of Jesus Himself to him took place, conclusively disproves. *Bengel's* note on the word "yet" briefly expresses the true state of the case,—'Thus,

to Damascus to the synagogues, that if he found any [1]of this way, whether they were men or women, he might bring them bound unto
3 Jerusalem. And [b]as he journeyed, he came near Damascus: and sud-
4 denly there shined round about him a light from heaven: and he fell to the earth, and heard a voice saying unto him, Saul, Saul, why persecutest
5 thou [c]me? And he said, [d]Who art thou, Lord? And the Lord said, I am Jesus whom thou persecutest. [e]*It is* hard for thee to kick against
6 the pricks. And he, trembling and astonished, said, Lord, [f]what wilt thou have me to do? And the Lord *said* unto him, Arise, and go into

A. D. 35.
1 of the way.
ch. 19. 9.
b oh. 22. 6.
ch. 26. 12.
c Matt. 25.40.
1 Cor 12 12.
d 1 Tim. 1.1½.
e ch. 5. 39.
f Luke 3. 10.
ch. 2. 37.

in the utmost fervour of sinning, was he laid hold of and converted.' Nor are such sudden conversions from bitter enmity to burning love at all inconsistent with known laws, or without example in the history of the human mind. The "slaughter," which the historian says that Saul yet breathed, points to cruelties the particulars of which are supplied by himself nearly thirty years afterwards: "And I persecuted this way *unto the death*" (ch. xxii. 4); "and when they were *put to death*, I gave my voice ('or vote') against them. And I punished them oft in every synagogue, and compelled them to (or 'did my utmost to make them') blaspheme; and being exceedingly mad against them, I persecuted them even unto strange (that is, 'foreign') cities" (ch. xxvi. 10, 11). All this, be it observed, was *before* his present journey. **went unto the high priest, 2. And desired of him letters**—of authorization; showing that, under the Roman power at this time, the Sanhedrim at Jerusalem had jurisdiction over Jews resident in foreign parts. **to Damascus**—the capital of Syria, and the great highway between eastern and western Asia, about 130 miles N.E. of Jerusalem; the most ancient city, perhaps, in the world, and 'lying in the centre of a verdant and inexhaustible paradise.' It abounded, as appears from *Josephus* ('Jewish Wars,' ii. 20, § 2), both with Jews—and accordingly this verse speaks of more synagogues than one in it—and with Gentile proselytes to the Jewish faith. Thither the Gospel had penetrated; and Saul, flushed with past successes, undertakes to crush it out. **that if he found**—as the grammatical form of the expression [ἐὰν εὕρῃ] implies, was to be expected. **any of this way** [τῆς ὁδοῦ]—*lit.,* 'any of the way;' a remarkable abbreviation to express the Christian Faith, one which evidently had its rise among the Christians themselves, and probably the very earliest—occuring only in this book, but there four times (here, and in ch. xix. 9, 23; xxiv. 22). It seems intended to denote that what to the earliest Christians was felt to be most characteristic in the Gospel, was not so much the *object* to which it conducted those that embraced it, as the *way* of reaching it, through a crucified Saviour. **whether they were men or women.** Thrice are women specified as objects of Saul's cruelty, and as an aggravated feature of it (ch. viii. 3; xxii. 4; and here). **he might bring them bound unto Jerusalem.** It may be that some who where won to Christ during the first triumphs of the Gospel left Jerusalem thereafter, and, going as far as Damascus, felt constrained to "speak the things which they had seen and heard." Be this as it may, there is every reason to believe that some of those "who were scattered abroad upon the persecution that arose about Stephen," travelled as far as Damascus, and doubtless there "preached the word," not without success. **3. And as he journeyed, he came near Damascus.** So ch. xxii. 6. Tradition points to a bridge near the city as the spot referred to. Events which are the turning points in one's history so imprint themselves upon the memory,

that circumstances the most trifling in themselves acquire, by connection with them, something of their importance, and are recalled with inexpressible interest. **and suddenly**—at what time of day, is not said; for artless simplicity reigns here; but he himself emphatically states, in one of his narratives of it, that it was "*about noon*" (ch. xxii. 6), and in the other, "*at mid-day*" (ch. xxvi. 13), when there could be no deception. **there shined round about him a light from heaven** [ἐκ, which *Lachmann* and *Tischendorf* adopt, is better supported than ἀπὸ of the received text]. In his defence before the people he calls this "a great light" (ch. xxii. 6), and to Agrippa he describes it as "above the brightness of the sun" (ch. xxvi. 13)—which then was shining at its full strength. This light enwrapt not only Saul himself, but "them which journeyed with him" (ch. xxvi. 13); and in his address to the people he says, "they which were with me saw the light" (ch. xxii. 9)—minute particulars, evincing the objective reality of this heavenly manifestation. **4. And he fell to the earth**—and his companions fell with him (ch. xxvi. 14), **and heard a voice saying unto him**—"in the Hebrew tongue" (ch. xxvi. 14), **Saul, Saul**—a reduplication (says *de Wette*) full of tenderness. Accordingly, though his name was soon changed into "Paul," we find in both his own narratives of the scene, after the lapse of many years, the original form retained, even in the Greek, just as here; neither he nor the historian (who doubtless often heard him describe the scene) daring to alter, in the smallest tittle, the overpowering words addressed to him. **why persecutest thou me?** No language can express the affecting character of this question, addressed from the right hand of the Majesty on high to a poor, infuriated, persecuting mortal. **5. And he said, Who art thou, Lord?** The word "Lord" here is an indefinite term of respect for some unknown but exalted speaker. That Saul *saw*, as well as *heard*, this glorious Speaker, is expressly said by Ananias (*v.* 17, and ch. xxii. 14), by Barnabas (ch. ix. 27), and by himself (ch. xxvi. 16); and in claiming apostleship, he explicitly states that he had "*seen* the Lord" (1 Cor. ix. 1; xv. 8), which can refer only to this scene. **And the Lord said.** The true reading probably is, 'And He said,' I am Jesus whom thou persecutest. The pronouns "I" and "THOU" are both emphatically and touchingly expressed here ['Εγώ—σύ], while the term "JESUS" is purposely chosen, to convey to him the thrilling information, that the hated Name which he sought to hunt down—"*the Nazarene*," as it is in ch. xxii. 8—was now speaking to him from the skies, "crowned with glory and honour" (see ch. xxvi. 9). [It is hard for thee to kick against the pricks. 6. And he, trembling and astonished, said, Lord, what wilt thou have me to do? And the Lord said unto him.] The last clause of *v.* 5, and the first half of *v.* 6, which we have enclosed within brackets, are found in no Greek MS. either uncial or cursive; and though it is in the authorized Vulgate,

7 the city, and it shall be told thee what thou must do. And *g* the men which journeyed with him stood speechless, hearing a voice, but seeing
8 no man. And Saul arose from the earth; and when his eyes were opened, he saw no man: but they led him by the hand, and brought
9 *him* into Damascus. And he was three days without sight, and neither did eat nor drink.

A. D. 35.
g Dan. 10. 7.
Matt. 24.40,
41.
ch. 22. 9.
ch. 26. 13,
14.

the best copies of that version want them. But as the entire passage occurs in the apostle's own accounts of his conversion, it has thus doubtless crept into this place. And it will be convenient to take in the exposition of them here. (In the genuine text the words that follow the interpolation begin thus: 'But [ἀλλὰ] rise and go into the city,' &c.) The metaphor of an ox, only driving the goad deeper by kicking against it, is a classic one, and here forcibly expresses not only the vanity of all his measures for crushing the Gospel, but the deeper wound which every such effort inflicted upon himself. The question, 'What shall I do, Lord?' or "Lord, what wilt thou have me to do?" indicates a state of mind singularly interesting (see on ch. ii. 37). Its elements seem to be these: first, resistless conviction that "Jesus whom he persecuted"—now speaking to him—was "Christ the Lord" (see on Gal. i. 15, 16); next, as a consequence of this, that not only all his religious views, but his whole religious character, had been an entire mistake—that he was up to that moment fundamentally and wholly wrong; further, that though his whole future was now a blank, he had absolute confidence in Him who had so tenderly arrested him in his blind career, and was ready both to take in all His teaching, and to carry out all His directions. **Arise, and go into the city, and it shall be told thee what thou must do.** See on the similar direction given to Philip, ch. viii. 26. **7. And the men which journeyed with him stood speechless** [ἐννεοί, or, as the best MSS. write it, ἐνεοί]. If the word "stood" here is to be taken literally for the standing posture, it seems inconsistent with the apostle's own account in ch. xxvi. 14, where he says they all "fell to the earth." One explanation of this is, that while all fell, Saul remained prostrate, while the rest quickly arose. (So *Bengel* and *Baumgarten*). Another is, that they first stood transfixed with wonder, and then sank down (so *Grotius*); while *de Wette, Meyer, Olshausen,* and *Humphry* see no need to reconcile the two statements, looking upon such trifling discrepancies in different reports of a most exciting scene, as just what might be expected. But perhaps a simpler and more natural explanation is to understand the statement—"they *stood* speechless"—to mean no more than that 'they remained speechless,' according to a sense of the word "stood" in Greek, and indeed in most languages. In this case, the statement tells us nothing about their posture, but merely reports their *silence.* (So *Hackett, Webster and Wilkinson,* and *Lechler.*) **hearing a voice** [τῆς φωνῆς]—rather, 'the voice,' **but seeing no man.** This (as *Humphry* remarks) explains the reason of their remaining speechless: though they heard the voice, they saw not the speaker. But how, then, does Paul say afterwards, they "heard *not* the voice of Him that spake to him"? (ch. xxii. 9.) No doubt the explanation is, that they heard the *sound,* but not the *articulate words;* just as "the people that stood by" when the Greeks came up to worship at the feast are expressly said to have heard the *voice* "which came from heaven" to Jesus, yet heard it so inarticulately that some thought it mere thunder, while others who heard better thought "an angel spake to Him" (John xii. 28, 29). Apparent discrepancies like these, in the different narratives of the same scene in one and the same book of Acts, furnish the strongest confirmation both of the facts themselves and of the book which records them. **8. And Saul arose from the earth; and when his eyes were opened, he saw no man—** 'seeing nothing' [οὐδὲν, in place of οὐδένα] is the slightly preferable reading. After beholding the glory of the Lord, since he "could not see for the glory of that light" (ch. xxii. 11), he would involuntarily close his eyes to protect them from the glare, and on opening them again he found his vision gone. That the apostle never recovered entirely from this supernatural blindness; that the "thorn in the flesh, the messenger of Satan sent to buffet him" (2 Cor. xii. 7), was just this weakness of the eyes; and that it is to it that he refers when he reminds the Galatians that they would if possible have plucked out their own eyes and given them to them (Gal. iv. 15) is a supposition which *Humphry* and others conceive to be not without reason; but to us such suppositions only show on what strange collocations of passages conclusions the most surprising can be drawn. But see on *v.* 18. **9. And he was three days without sight, and neither did eat nor drink—**that is, according to the Hebrew mode of computation, he took no food during the remainder of that day, the entire day following, and so much of the subsequent day as elapsed before the visit of Ananias. Such a period of entire abstinence from food, in that state of mental absorption and revolution into which he had been so suddenly thrown, is in perfect harmony with known laws and numerous facts. But what three days must those have been! 'Only one other space of three days' duration can be mentioned of equal importance in the history of the world' *(as Howson* well observes). Since Jesus had been revealed not only to his *eyes,* but to his *soul* (see on Gal. i. 15, 16), the double conviction must have immediately flashed upon him, that his whole reading of the Old Testament hitherto had been wrong, and that the system of legal righteousness in which he had, up to that moment, rested and prided himself was false and fatal. What materials these for spiritual exercise during those three days of total darkness, fasting, and solitude! On the one hand, what self-condemnation, what anguish, what death of legal hope, what difficulty in believing that in such a case there could be hope at all; on the other hand, what heart-breaking admiration of the grace that had "pulled him out of the fire," what resistless conviction that there must be a purpose of love in it, and what tender expectation of being yet honoured, as a chosen vessel, to declare what the Lord had done for his soul, and spread abroad the savour of that Name which he had so wickedly, though ignorantly, sought to destroy—must have struggled in his breast during those memorable days! Is it too much to say that all that profound insight into the Old Testament, that comprehensive grasp of the principles of the Divine economy, that penetrating spirituality, that vivid apprehension of man's lost state, and those glowing views of the perfection and glory of

58

10 And there was a certain disciple at Damascus, named Ananias; and to
him said the Lord in a vision, Ananias. And he said, Behold, I *am here*,
11 Lord. And the Lord *said* unto him, Arise, and go into the street which
is called Straight, and enquire in the house of Judas for *one* called Saul,
12 of [h]Tarsus: for, behold, he prayeth, and hath seen in a vision a man
named Ananias coming in, and putting *his* hand on him, that he might
13 receive his sight. Then Ananias answered, Lord, I have heard by many
of this man, how much evil he hath done to thy saints at Jerusalem:
14 and here he hath authority from the chief priests to bind all [i]that call
15 on thy name. But the Lord said unto him, Go thy way: for [j]he is
a chosen vessel unto me, to bear my name before [k]the Gentiles, and
16 [l]kings, and the children of Israel: for [m]I will show him how great things
he must suffer for my name's sake.

A. D. 35.

h ch. 21. 39.
i ch. 7. 59.
ch. 22. 16.
.1 Cor. 1. 2.
j ch. 13. 2.
ch. 22. 21.
ch. 23. 17.
Rom. 1. 1.
1 Cor. 15.10.
k Rom. 1. 5.
Rom. 11.13.
Gal. 2. 7, 8.
l ch. 25. 22.
ch. 26. 1.
m ch. 20. 23.
ch. 21. 13.

---

the Divine remedy; that beautiful ideal of the loftiness and the lowliness of the Christian character, that large philanthropy and burning zeal to spend and be spent, through all his future life, for Christ, which distinguish the writings of this chiefest of the apostles and greatest of men—were all quickened into life during those three successive days! [The Greek reader will observe in the phrase μὴ βλέπων, the subjective μὴ expressive of the vain effort to see; while in the following phrase, οὐκ ἔφαγεν, the objective οὐκ expresses the simple fact that he took no food. See *Jelf*, 739; *Winer*, 55. 5.]

Through the instrumentality of Ananias, Saul's sight is restored—He is Baptized, and is filled with the Holy Ghost—After continuing with the disciples at Damascus for some time, he begins to preach, to the astonishment of all (10-21). **10. And there was a certain disciple at Damascus, named Ananias; and to him said the Lord**—that is, the Lord Jesus, as is evident from all that follows, **in a vision, Ananias.** Of this man Paul himself afterwards bears this testimony, in his address to the people, that he was "a devout man according to the law, having a good report of all the Jews which dwelt there" (ch. xxii. 12), to show that the national religion could be in no way hostile to anything taught by him, since he had been taken by the hand by one of such strict Jewish orthodoxy and high repute. **And he said, Behold, I am here, Lord. 11. And the Lord said unto him, Arise, and go into the street which is called Straight.** There is still (says *Maundrell*) a street of this name in Damascus, about half a mile in length, running from east to west through the city. **and enquire in the house of Judas for one called Saul.** In the minuteness of these directions—even to the very name of the street—by the glorified Jesus to this Jewish disciple, there is something noteworthy. Compare the angel's direction to Cornelius—that Peter would be found "lodging with one Simon a tanner, whose house was by the sea side" (ch. x. 6). But are not all things which we call great or small, trivial or important, measured by another geometry in heaven from what they are on earth—by their bearing on the Divine purposes and the progress of the kingdom of grace among men? **of Tarsus**—(see on ch. xxi. 39.) **for, behold, he prayeth**—"breathing" no longer "threatenings and slaughter," but only struggling desires after light and life in the Persecuted One. Beautiful note of encouragement this as to the frame in which Ananias would find the persecutor! **12. And hath seen in a vision a man named Ananias.** [*Lachmann* and *Tischendorf* exclude from their text the clause ἐν ὁράματι, but on insufficient authority, as it appears to us.] Thus, as in the case of Cornelius and Peter afterwards, there was a mutual preparation of

each for each. But what is remarkable here, we have from the historian's pen no account of the vision which Saul had of Ananias coming in to him and putting his hands upon him for the restoration of his sight: we only know it from this interesting allusion to it in the vision which he tells us that Ananias himself had. **13. Then Ananias answered, Lord, I have heard by many of this man.** Instead of the perfect tense, "I have heard" [ἀκήκοα], the aorist [ἤκουσα], "I heard," appears to us to have decidedly the best support. This gives definiteness to the reports which Ananias had "heard by many" of this dread inquisitor, the terror of whose name had, it seems, gone before him to Damascus. **how much evil he hath done to thy saints at Jerusalem.** This relation of the disciples to Christ, as "His saints," is noticed by *Bengel* as evidence of His proper Divinity; and certainly, in connection with Ananias' familiar yet reverential way of addressing the glorified Redeemer, and his authoritative style in directing Ananias, this cannot be deemed a strained inference. Accordingly, in the next verse, Ananias describes the disciples as those "that called on Christ's name." See on ch. vii. 59, 60; and compare 1 Cor. i. 2. 'If Christ (says *Lechler*) has "His saints"—an expression which in the Old Covenant could only refer to Jehovah—then by this expression divine honour is ascribed to Him.' **14. And here he hath authority from the chief priests to bind all that call on thy name.** Thus it would seem that not only the terror of his name, but the news of this dread commission, had travelled before him from the capital to the doomed spot. But, indeed, the three days that had already passed since Jesus appeared to him in the way, and the news of what had happened—which could not but be immediately spread through Damascus—would naturally lead to enquiries of Paul's companions as to the object of their visit; and to this, in all likelihood, Ananias refers in this last clause. **15. But the Lord said unto him, Go thy way**—*q. d.*, 'Do as thou art bidden, without gainsaying; his days of hostility to Me are at an end.' **for he is a chosen vessel unto me** [σκεῦος ἐκλογῆς]. This word "vessel" (as *Alford* observes) is afterwards used once and again by the apostle himself in illustrating the sovereignty of God's electing grace (Rom. ix. 21-23; 2 Cor. iv. 7; 2 Tim. ii. 20, 21; Zech. iii. 2). **to bear my name before the Gentiles.** This great characteristic of his ministry, as distinguished from that of Peter, is here appropriately placed first; and it had that place in his own estimation ever afterwards (Gal. ii. 7, 8). **and kings**—as Herod Agrippa and Nero, **and the children of Israel**—to whom he invariably presented the Gospel first. **16. For I will show him** [ὑποδείξω]. The word signifies to 'indicate' or 'hint,' rather than to manifest plainly (as in Matt.

59

17 And ⁿAnanias went his way, and entered into the house; and putting his hands on him, said, Brother Saul, the Lord, *even* Jesus, that appeared unto thee in the way as thou camest, hath sent me, that thou mightest

18 receive thy sight, and ^obe filled with the Holy Ghost. And immediately there fell from his eyes as it had been scales: and he received sight forth-

19 with, and arose, and was baptized. And when he had received meat, he was strengthened.

^pThen was Saul certain days with the disciples which were at Damascus.

20 And straightway he preached Christ in the synagogues, ^qthat he is the

A. D. 35.
ⁿ ch. 22. 12, 13.
^o ch. 2. 4.
ch. 4. 31.
ch. 8. 17.
ch. 13. 52.
^p ch. 26. 20.
1 Sa. 10. 10
Gal. 1. 17.
^q ch. 8. 37.

iii. 7). Accordingly, it is evident, from the subsequent history, that though the apostle was prepared by successive hints given him from above, for the worst that could happen to him, he had no knowledge of the precise form in which his sufferings were to come upon him at any stage of his Christian history until he found himself in the midst of them. See ch. xx. 22, 23; xxi. 11-13. **how great things he must suffer for my name's sake**—*q. d.*, 'Much he has done against that Name; but now, when I show him what great things he must suffer for it, he shall count it his honour and privilege, feeling in himself, by a retribution that will be sweet to him, what he so cruelly made others to feel.' The Redeemer and Ananias converse with each other as Friend with friend; yet neither forgets that it is Master and servant that are talking together. **17. And Ananias went his way, and entered into the house; and putting his hands on him, said, Brother Saul.** How beautifully child-like are the faith and the obedience of Ananias here to the heavenly vision! No longer beholds he in Saul the dreaded persecutor: now he is "brother Saul," and his style of address is that of brother to brother in Jesus. **the Lord hath sent me, [even] Jesus that appeared unto thee in the way as thou camest.** This is the order of the words as they stand in the original; and it would have been better to retain it, as showing clearly that "*the Lord*" in this whole transaction—as indeed almost invariably throughout this book, and for the most part in the Epistles too—means the risen and glorified One, JESUS, the Lord of the Church, invested with all power in heaven and in earth for its behoof, and with it alway, even unto the end of the world. Such knowledge on the part of Ananias, of the appearance of Jesus to him on his way to Damascus, would convince Saul at once that this was the man whom Jesus had already in vision prepared him to expect. That the two men were total strangers to each other up to this moment is evident on the face of the narrative; and yet the rationalistic critics would have us believe that they were intimate acquaintances! **that thou mightest receive thy sight, and be filled with the Holy Ghost.** Ananias, it will be observed, does not tell Saul what the glorified Redeemer had communicated to himself about his future career. 'It was not for Saul (says *Bengel* well) to know of how great account he already was.' As the actual descent of the Holy Ghost upon Saul, through the instrumentality of Ananias, and in fulfilment of the expressed purpose of this heaven-directed visit, is not recorded, we cannot be quite certain whether it took place before or after his baptism, nor are expositors agreed upon this point. While it usually *followed* baptism, it *preceded* the baptism of Cornelius and his company (ch. x. 44-48). But what is of much more importance to observe is, that this gift of the Holy Ghost came through one who was not an apostle, nor (so far as we are informed) occupying any official position whatever. Looking, however, at ch. xxii. 12, it is likely that

he was a Christian of note at Damascus; and as no organized church had probably been formed there as yet, he probably took a leading part in the private meetings of the disciples for "reading, exhortation, and prayer" (1 Tim. iv. 13). **18. And immediately there fell from his eyes as it had been scales** [ὡσεὶ λεπίδες]—not actual scales, but something *resembling* the falling of such from the eyes; just as on the day of Pentecost there sat on the disciples "cloven tongues (not of fire, but) *like as* of fire" [ὡσεὶ πύρος] (ch. ii. 3). 'This shows (as *Webster and Wilkinson* pertinently remark) that the blindness as well as the cure was supernatural. Substances like scales would not form naturally in so short a time.' The *medical* precision of the beloved physician's language here is worthy of note. **and he received sight [forthwith].** This bracketed word [παραχρῆμα], though one of which our historian is fond, both in his Gospel and in the Acts, is wanting in authority here. On the purely fanciful style of criticism by which Humphry infers that this cure was never complete, see on *v.* 8. As this restoration of sight is recorded in the same simple style in which the *complete* and *instantaneous* cures of our Lord are recorded in the Gospels (cf. Matt. xx. 34; Mark x. 52; &c.), and those of the apostles in this same book (cf. chs. iii. 7; x. 34; xiv. 10; &c.), it seems almost ludicrous to suppose, from Gal. iv. 15, that the Galatians proposed to supply the apostle's lack of vision by a gift of their own. As to the thorn in the flesh, it had better be left in its obscurity. **and arose, and was baptized**—in compliance with the call of Ananias, not here recorded, but reported long afterwards by himself in his address to the people of Jerusalem (ch. xxii. 16), "And now why tarriest thou? arise, and be baptized, and wash away thy sins, calling on the name of the Lord." No doubt the baptism was performed by the hands of Ananias himself. For further particulars of this interview, see on ch. xxii. 12-21. **19. And when he had received meat, he was strengthened**—for the bodily exhaustion occasioned by his three days' fast would be not the less real, though unfelt during his mental struggles; and now that these were over, the sensation of hunger (as in the case of our Lord after His forty days' fast) would come upon him in all its keenness (see on Matt. iv. 2). **Then was Saul certain days with the disciples which were at Damascus**—making their acquaintance in another way than either he or they had anticipated, and regaining his tone by the fellowship of the saints; but not certainly in order to learn from them what he was to teach, which he expressly disavows (Gal. xii. 16). **20. And straightway**—that is, after the "certain days" spent in private with the disciples (*v.* 19), **he preached Christ.** The true reading here unquestionably is, 'he preached Jesus' [with ℵ A B C E, &c., and most versions]—in favour of which the internal evidence from *v.* 22 is nearly as strong as the external: **in the synagogues.** The plurality of synagogues at Damascus, here noted, shows that there must have been a large body of Jews there;

21 Son of God. But all that heard *him* were amazed, and said, ʳ Is not this he that destroyed them which called on this name in Jerusalem, and came hither for that intent, that he might bring them bound unto the 22 chief priests? But Saul increased the more in strength, and ˢ confounded the Jews which dwelt at Damascus, proving that this is very Christ. 23 And after that many days were fulfilled, ᵗ the Jews took counsel to kill 24 him: but their laying await was known of Saul. And they watched the 25 gates day and night to kill him. Then the disciples took him by night, and ᵘ let *him* down by the wall in a basket.	A. D. 35. ʳ Matt. 13. 54. 55. ch. 8. 3. Gal. 1. 13. ˢ ch. 18. 28. ᵗ ch. 23. 12. ch. 25. 3. ᵘ Josh. 2. 15. 1 Sam. 19. 12.

and *Josephus* (as *Olshausen* remarks) mentions that no fewer than ten thousand of them perished there in the reign of Nero (J. W., i. 2, 25). **that he is the Son of God. 21. But all that heard him were amazed, and said, Is not this he that destroyed them which called on this name in Jerusalem, and came hither for that intent, that he might bring them bound unto the chief priests?** This, it will be observed, was not the language of the *Christians*—whose astonishment no doubt found full vent before this, and to whom all would be fully explained in private—but of his Jewish auditors in the synagogues, to whom his previous persecuting career, and the object of his present visit, were, it seems, by this time well known.

The Jews of Damascus, exasperated at Saul's preaching, seek to kill him—His narrow escape (22-25). **22. But Saul increased the more in strength, and confounded the Jews which dwelt at Damascus, proving that this is very Christ** [ὁ X.]—or more simply, 'that this is the Christ.' Had we only this record to guide us, we should certainly have supposed that Saul never left Damascus from the time that he entered it, blinded by the glory of the heavenly manifestation, until he came to Jerusalem (*v.* 26). But we learn from the apostle himself (Gal. i. 17, 18) that, before going up to Jerusalem after his conversion, he "went into Arabia, and returned again unto Damascus," and that "then, after three years (from the time of his conversion) he went up to Jerusalem." That no allusion to this should be made in the Acts is not more remarkable than that this same Luke, in his Gospel, should write as if the Holy Family went straight from Jerusalem to Nazareth, immediately after the presentation of the infant Saviour in the temple; omitting all allusion to the flight into Egypt, the stay there, and the return thence, which constituted so important a feature in the early history of our Lord upon earth, and for which we are indebted to Matthew's Gospel. The main difficulty is where, in the verses before us, this visit of Saul to Arabia should come in—whether *before* the Jews of Damascus sought to kill him (that is, between *vv.* 21 and 22), or *after* it (between *vv.* 25 and 26). The latter is the view of *Bengel, Olshausen,* and *Baumgarten:* the former that of *Beza, Neander, Meyer, Humphry, Alford, Hackett, Webster and Wilkinson.* That the apostle did not leave Damascus till he was driven from it for his life, might seem the most natural supposition; but that after this flight he should have again imperiled his life by returning to it, even after the lapse of some two years, is, though not impossible, scarcely probable; nor can one see any important object to be gained by his returning to it at all again. But if we suppose that it was after his first preaching of Christ in the synagogues that he withdrew for a lengthened period into Arabia, and that he "returned again unto Damascus" (Gal. i. 17)—that city, in the vicinity of which he had been so marvellously brought to Christ, and in which the first opening of his mouth as a preacher had produced such a sensation—we can readily conceive that his now matured ability to plead for Christ would, with his Master's presence, be attended with powerful results, so powerful as to bear down all opposing argument, 'confounding the Jews which dwelt at Damascus, by his proofs that Jesus was Christ;' but that, failing to convince, he only exasperated them, and soon found that his very success must cut short his stay there. This seems to us to be the most natural way of filling up the gap in our narrative, and may explain the peculiar form of expression used in *v.* 23. **And after that many days were fulfilled.** The expression is studiously indefinite [ἐπληροῦντο ἡμέραι ἱκαναί]—*lit.*, 'but as a considerable number of days were getting fulfilled,' **the Jews took counsel to kill him: 24. But their laying await** [ἐπιβουλή]—'their plot' was known **of Saul. And they watched the gates day and night to kill him. 25. Then the disciples.** *Lachmann* and *Tischendorf* have 'his disciples' [αὐτοῦ for —ον—with A B C E, and the cod. Amiat. of the Vulgate]. But strong as is the external evidence in its favour, that for the received reading is not inconsiderable [E G H, and both Syriac versions, both the Egyptian, &c.], while the internal evidence appears to us strongly to favour the received text. **took him by night, and let him down by the wall in a basket.** The full extent of his danger appears only from his own account of it long after, in recounting to the Corinthians the perils he had come through for Christ's sake: "In Damascus the governor, under Aretas the king, kept the city of the Damascenes with a garrison, desirous to apprehend me"—the exasperated Jews having obtained from the governor a military force, the more surely to compass his destruction; "and through a window in a basket was I let down by the wall, and escaped his hands" (2 Cor. xi. 32, 33). The "window" was probably one of those overhanging windows in the walls of eastern cities which were then common, and are to be seen in Damascus to this day. The "basket" [σπυρίς] in which he was lowered, as described by Luke, was one of the same kind as that employed in gathering up the fragments of the seven loaves with which our Lord fed the four thousand (Mark viii. 8). The word used by the apostle himself [σαργάνη] denotes only the wickerwork of which it was made. Before taking our leave of Damascus, as the scene of the apostle's labours, it is delightful to observe that there were "disciples" there, numerous enough and courageous enough to effect, at their own risk, the great preacher's escape from the hands both of his blood-thirsty enemies and of the military force by which he was guarded; and though there can be no doubt that some of these had, like Ananias, been brought to Christ before Saul's own conversion—for it was in pursuit of them that he came to Damascus—it is reasonable to suppose that their number was not a little increased, as well as their faith strengthened, by his labours; and thus, even there, were they not in vain in the Lord.

26 And [v]when Saul was come to Jerusalem, he assayed to join himself to the disciples: but they were all afraid of him, and believed not that he was 27 a disciple. But [w]Barnabas took him, and brought *him* to the apostles, and declared unto them how he had seen the Lord in the way, and that he had spoken to him, and how he had preached boldly at Damascus in 28 the name of Jesus. And he was with them coming in and going out at 29 Jerusalem. And he spake [x]boldly in the name of the Lord Jesus, and disputed against the [y]Grecians: [z]but they went about to slay him. 30 *Which* when the brethren knew, they brought him down to Cesarea, and 31 sent him forth to Tarsus. Then [a]had the churches rest throughout

A. D. 37.

[v] ch. 12. 17.
Gal. 1. 17.
[w] ch. 4. 36.
ch. 11. 22-25.
ch. 13. 2.
[x] Eph. 6. 19.
[y] ch. 6. 1.
ch. 11. 20.
[z] 2 Cor. 11. 26.
[a] Ps. 119. 165.

Saul, coming to Jerusalem, is introduced by Barnabas to the disciples—To escape assassination at the hand of the Jews, exasperated at his preaching, he is brought down to Cæsarea, and sent to Tarsus—The Church in Palestine has rest and prospers (26-31)). **26. And when Saul**—or 'when he' [omitting ὁ Σ. as *Lachman* and *Tischendorf* do, though on scarcely preponderating authority], **was come to Jerusalem** [εἰς and ἐν have nearly equal support]. The special object of this his first visit to Jerusalem after his conversion was—as he himself tells the Galatians (Gal. i. 18)—to "see Peter;" not to learn anything from him (for this he is very careful to repudiate, Gal. i. 11, 12, 16-20), but to inform him, as the leading apostle, of his conversion and calling, but more particularly the specific sphere to which his labours were to be directed—namely, to the Gentiles pre-eminently; and to confer with him in brotherly fellowship on the things of the kingdom. **he assayed to join himself to the disciples**—simply as one of them, leaving his high commission to manifest itself. **but they were all afraid of him, and believed not that he was a disciple**—knowing him only as a persecutor of the Faith; the rumour of his conversion, if it ever was cordially believed, passing away during his long absence in Arabia, and the news of his subsequent labours in Damascus perhaps not having reached them. **27. But Barnabas took him, and brought him to the apostles**—that is, to Peter and James; for "other of the apostles saw I none," says he to the Galatians (Gal. i. 18, 19). Probably none of the other apostles were there at that time. 'Barnabas (says *Howson*) being of Cyprus, which was within a few hours' sail of Cilicia, and annexed to it as a Roman province, and Saul and he being Hellenistic Jews, and eminent in their respective localities, they may very well have been acquainted with each other before this.' However this may be, what is here said of Barnabas is in fine consistency with the character given of him in ch. xi. 24, as "a good man, and full of the Holy Ghost and of faith," and with the name given to him by the apostles, "The son of 'exhortation' or consolation" (ch. iv. 36). After Peter and James were satisfied, the disciples generally would at once receive the new convert. **and declared unto them how he had seen the Lord in the way, and that he** (the Lord) **had spoken to him**—that is, how he had received his commission direct from their glorified Lord Himself. It is not impossible that Barnabas may have been at Damascus, and brought these particulars of Saul's conversion with him; but this is mere conjecture. **28. And he was with them coming in and going out at Jerusalem**—for fifteen days lodging with Peter, as we learn from himself in Gal. i. 18 [εἰς Ἱερ. is decidedly better than ἐν here]. **29. And he spake boldly in the name of the Lord Jesus, and disputed against the Grecians**—the Hellenistic or Greek-speaking Jews (see on ch. vi. 1). He seems to have specially directed his addresses to this class as being himself one of them, and, in the days of his ignorance, notorious for his virulence against the new Faith. **but they went about to slay him.** Thus was he made to feel, throughout his whole Christian course, what he himself had made others so cruelly to feel—the cost of discipleship. **30. Which when the brethren knew** [ἐπιγνόντες]—or 'came to the knowledge of,' **they brought him down to Cesarea**—on the coast (see on ch. viii. 40); accompanying him thus far. But Paul left Jerusalem thus abruptly for another reason than the danger to which his life was, for the second time, exposed. He received express instructions to that effect from his glorified Lord: "It came to pass (says he, in his defence before the people), that, when I was come again to Jerusalem, even while I prayed in the temple, I was in a trance; and saw Him (the glorified One) saying unto me, Make haste, and get thee quickly out of Jerusalem, for they will not receive thy testimony concerning me. And I said, Lord, they know that I imprisoned and beat in every synagogue them that believed on thee: and when the blood of thy martyr Stephen was shed, I also was standing by, and consenting unto his death, and kept the raiment of them that slew him:"—*q. d.,* 'Can it be, Lord, that they will resist the testimony of one whom they knew to be the bitterest of all the persecutors of Thy name, whom only resistless evidence could have overpowered and won to Thee?' "And he said unto me, Depart: for I will send thee far hence unto the Gentiles:"—*q. d.,* 'Enough; Jerusalem is steeled against all evidence; the Gentiles afar off are to be thy peculiar sphere' (ch. xxii. 17-21). Under these solemn impressions—communicated probably to the brethren, who would be glad of this confirmation of their own urgent entreaties to him to hasten away—he would yield himself to their affectionate solicitations; and so they brought him to Cæsarea, **and sent him forth to Tarsus.** The natural conclusion from this would be that he went by sea, direct to Tarsus, sailing due north from Cæsarea, and landing at the mouth of the river Cydnus, the harbour for Tarsus. But since he himself tells us that, after this departure from Jerusalem, he "came into the regions of Syria and Cilicia" (Gal. i. 21), the probability is that he landed at Seleucia (see on ch. xiii. 4), proceeded thence by land to Antioch, and from this penetrated northward into Cilicia, ending his journey at Tarsus. For some interesting particulars regarding Tarsus, see on ch. xxi. 39. As this (says *Howson*) was his first visit to his native city since his conversion, so it is not certain that he ever was there again (see on ch. xi. 25, 26). Now it probably was that he became the instrument of gathering into the fold of Christ those "kinsmen," that "sister," and perhaps her "son," of whom mention is made in Rom. xvi. 7, 11, 21; and in ch. xxiii. 16, &c. **31. Then had the churches.** But the true reading here seems to be 'the Church' [ἡ ἐκκλησία, with A B C, &c., and most versions], which *Lachmann* and *Tischendorf* adopt (and *de Wette,*

62

all Judea and Galilee and Samaria, and were edified; and walking in the fear of the Lord, and in the comfort of the Holy Ghost, were multiplied.

32 And it came to pass, as Peter passed throughout [b]all *quarters,* he came
33 down also to the saints which dwelt at Lydda. And there he found a certain man named Eneas, which had kept his bed eight years, and was
34 sick of the palsy. And Peter said unto him, Eneas, [c]Jesus Christ maketh thee whole: arise, and make thy bed. And he arose imme-

A. D 37.
[b] ch. 1. 8.
ch. 8. 14.
[c] Matt. 8. 3.
Matt. 9 6.
23. 30.
John 2. 11.
John 5. 8.
ch 3. 6.
ch. 4. 10.

Alford, and *Lechler* approve, though not *Meyer).* Indeed, it is hardly conceivable that 'churches,' in any proper sense of the term, should have been formed thus early "throughout all Judea and Galilee and Samaria." rest [εἰρήνην]—or 'peace.' This rest or peace, however, was not so much owing to Saul's conversion as probably to the Jews themselves having other things to attend to. For at that very time (as *Lardner* notices) they were filled with alarm at the Emperor Caligula's persistent determination to have an image of himself set up in the temple of Jerusalem; to prevent which they sent an influential deputation to remonstrate with him; and when this failed, and Petronius, governor of Syria, was ordered to make war on the Jews, in order to force on them this obnoxious measure, thousands of them hastened to implore him not to do this, or, if he was resolved on it, to take their lives rather than oblige them to yield. It was delayed, however, only on the intercession of Herod Agrippa, whose influence with the emperor at that time was great; and but for Caligula's death, the measure would probably have been carried out, (*Josephus,* Antt. viii. 8. 1-8; *Lardner,* I. ch. ii. and viii.) This was sufficient to withdraw for some time the attention of the Jews from the Christians, and give them rest. **throughout all Judea and Galilee and Samaria.** This incidental notice of the extent to which Christianity had spread and converts been made in all the great scenes of our Lord's ministry, where the facts proclaimed by the heralds of the Cross could be best attested, is extremely interesting (see on ch. viii. 4). **and were edified; and walking in the fear of the Lord, and in the comfort of the Holy Ghost, were multiplied.** The structure of the sentence [εἶχον εἰρήνην, οἰκοδομουμένη καὶ πορευομένη τῷ φόβῳ τ. κυρίου, καὶ τῇ παρακλήσει .τ. ἁγίου πνεύματος ἐπληθύνετο] will hardly bear this sense —which our translators have adopted from *Beza,* in opposition to the Vulgate, *Luther, Calvin,* and the best modern critics. The true sense appears to be this: 'Then had the Church rest throughout all Judea, and Samaria, and Galilee, being built up and walking in the fear of the Lord, and was replenished with the comfort of the Holy Ghost.' It is objected to this rendering of the last clause (by *Alford* and *Alexander*) that the word πληθύνω, though classically it signifies to 'make full' or 'be full,' is never so used in Hellenistic Greek, but always in the sense of to 'multiply.' So (with *Meyer, Webster and Wilkinson,* and *Hackett*) they render this clause, 'was multiplied by the exhortation (or 'consolation,' or 'aid,' or 'encouragement') of the Holy Ghost.' But this is a most unusual idea in the New Testament; and though to 'multiply' seems the sense of the word elsewhere in the New Testament, the two ideas of 'multiply' and 'fill' are so cognate that the word is in the LXX. used in the sense of 'fill,' often enough to show that it is as good Hellenistic as classical Greek (*ex. gr.,* Gen. xviii. 20; Deut. xxviii. 2; Ps. iv. 7; lxv. 13; xcii. 14). We therefore have no hesitation in translating, 'were replenished with the Holy Ghost' (with the Vul-

gate, *Luther, Calvin, de Wette,* and *Baumgarten*). The outward peace which the Church enjoyed was improved (says the sacred historian) to its internal consolidation and advancement; their walk before men in the fear of the Lord, and their inward consolation through the power of the Holy Ghost, going sweetly together. The way has now been prepared by the narrative of Saul's conversion and early labours, for relating those wonderful events in his missionary life which were to occupy the principal part of this book. But as the sacred historian had still to relate some particulars of the doings and sufferings of that "apostle of the circumcision," with which hitherto we have been chiefly occupied—and most of all, the last great honour conferred upon him, of "opening the door of faith to the Gentiles"—he now returns to him, leaving him finally when he has to take up the career of a still greater apostle, (ch. xiii.)

Peter at Lydda heals Æneas of the palsy, and raises Dorcas to life at Joppa (32-43). **32. And it came to pass, as Peter passed throughout all [quarters].** Our translators seem here to have inserted a wrong supplement, as what follows makes it pretty clear that not places, but persons, are meant. The historian's object is to inform us that the apostle made a tour of inspection or visitation amongst all the disciples throughout the country. The supplement, therefore, if any were needed, should be, 'as Peter passed through all' (the disciples), **he came down also to the saints which dwelt at Lydda.** But no supplement is required, "as Peter passed through all" [διὰ πάντων] being rendered quite intelligible by the next clause. (So the Vulgate, *Calvin, Beza,* and nearly every modern interpreter.) Lydda is (says *Robinson*) some ten or twelve miles south-east of Joppa—the same as the Hebrew *Lod* (Ezra ii. 33; Neh. vii. 37); and the Greek *Diospolis.* **33. And there he found a certain man named Eneas**—probably, from his Greek name, a Hellenistic Jew. As he is simply called 'a man' of such a name, *Bengel, Humphry,* and *Lechler* conclude he was not then a believer, though he must have heard of the cures which Jesus wrought. *Meyer, Alford,* and *Alexander* are doubtful. But since the historian tells us that a general conversion of the district resulted from the cure of this man, is it likely that he would have said nothing of Æneas's own conversion if he had not been a believer before? Accordingly (with *Hackett* and *Webster and Wilkinson*), we judge that he was himself one of "the saints which dwelt at Lydda." **which had kept his bed** (or 'pallet:' see on ch. v. 15) **eight years, and was sick of the palsy** (or 'paralyzed'). **34. And Peter said unto him, Eneas, Jesus Christ maketh thee whole.** The immediate presence and power of the glorified Redeemer, eclipsing and almost absorbing the instrument by whom He wrought, is strikingly expressed in these words. See on ch. iii. 6. **arise, and make thy bed** [στρωσόν σεαυτῷ, sc., κράββατον]—not, "take up thy bed," as once and again our Lord said to the bedridden (Mark ii. 11, &c.), to evince the complete-

35 diately. And all that dwelt in Lydda and *d*Saron saw him, and *e*turned to the Lord.

36 Now there was at Joppa a certain disciple named Tabitha, which by interpretation is called ²Dorcas: this woman was full *f*of good works

37 and alms-deeds which she did. And it came to pass in those days, that she was sick, and died: whom when they had washed, they laid *her* in

38 *g*an upper chamber. And forasmuch as Lydda was nigh to Joppa, and the disciples had heard that Peter was there, they sent unto him two men, desiring *him* that he would not ³delay to come to them.

39 Then Peter arose and went with them. When he was come, they brought him into the upper chamber: and all the widows stood by him weeping, and showing the coats and garments which Dorcas made while

40 she was with them. But Peter *h*put them all forth, and kneeled *i*down, and prayed; and turning *him* to the body *j*said, Tabitha, arise. And

41 she opened her eyes: and when she saw Peter, she sat up. And he gave her *his* hand, and lifted her up; and when he had called the saints and

42 widows, he presented her alive. And it was known throughout all Joppa;

A. D. 37.
d 1 Chr. 5. 16.
e ch. 11. 21.
2 Or, Doe, or, Roe.
f Ro. 31. 31.
1 Tim. 2.10.
1 Tim. 5.10.
Tit. 3. 8.
Jas. 1. 27.
g ch. 1. 13.
3 Or, be grieved.
h Matt. 9. 25.
i 1 Ki. 17. 19-23.
2 Ki. 4. 32-36.
ch. 7. 60.
ch. 20. 36.
j Mark 5. 41.
John 11.43.

ness of the cure (see on John v. 8); but 'spread' or 'sort thy bed'—an operation which would quite as effectually show the perfectness of his cure. **And he arose immediately.** 35. **And all that dwelt in Lydda and Saron** [τὸν Σαρωνᾶν; or, according to the best MSS., Σάρωνα]—the Sharon of the Old Testament [הַשָּׁרוֹן]; not any town or village, but (as the article shows) the rich flat coast district which stretches southward from Cæsarea to Joppa. **saw him, and turned to the Lord**—that is (according to the accustomed phraseology of this book) the Lord Jesus. As to the bearing of this statement on Æneas's own discipleship, see on *v.* 33. The "all" here need not be taken with strict literality. All that is meant seems to be, that this event resulted in a general conversion throughout the district.

36. **Now there was at Joppa**—the modern *Jaffa*, the ancient sea-port of Palestine, and still the sea-port of Jerusalem, from which it lies distant forty-five miles to the north-west. **a certain disciple named Tabitha, which by interpretation is called Dorcas**—the one the Syro-Chaldaic, the other the Greek name for an *antelope* or *gazelle*, which, from the grace of its motions and the beauty of its eyes, was frequently employed as a proper name for women. The interpretation of the name is given by the historian, to signify that it expressed the character which she bore among the Christians of the place. **this woman was full of good works and alms-deeds which she did**—eminent for the active generosities of the Christian character. 37. **And it came to pass in those days, that she was sick, and died: whom when they had washed**—according to the custom of all civilized nations towards the dead. Though the washing of the corpse was in this case, of course, a female operation, the participle is in the masculine gender [λούσαντες], as the writer's object was not to express *by whom* the thing was done, but simply to state what *was* done by those whose business it was (*Winer*, xxvii. 6). **they laid in an** (or 'the') **upper chamber**—of the house where she was (compare 1 Ki. xvii. 19). 38. **And forasmuch as Lydda was nigh to Joppa** (see on *v.* 32), **and the disciples had heard that Peter was there, they sent unto him two men, desiring him that he would not delay to come to them.** The direct form, 'Delay not to come to us' [ὀκνήσης . . . ἡμῶν], is decidedly better supported. This request shows that miraculous gifts were not possessed by the disciples generally (as *Bengel* notes).

39. **Then Peter arose and went with them.**

When he was come, they brought him into the upper chamber: and all the widows—whom she had clad or fed, stood by him weeping, and showing the coats and garments which Dorcas made [ἐποίει]—that is (as the tense implies), 'had been in the habit of making.' **while she was with them.** 40. **But Peter put them all forth, and kneeled down, and prayed**—the one in imitation of His Master's way (Luke viii. 54, and compare 2 Ki. iv. 33); the other in striking contrast with it. The *kneeling* befitted the lowly servant, but not the Lord Himself—*of whom it is never once recorded that He knelt in the performance of a miracle:* and this although, during His mysterious soul-agony in the garden, one of the three evangelists who record that scene, states expressly that He "*kneeled down*," and the two others, that He "fell on His face," and "upon the ground." **and turning him to the body said, Tabitha, arise. And she opened her eyes: and when she saw Peter, she sat up.** This graphic minuteness of detail imparts to the narrative an air of charming reality. 41. **And he gave her his hand, and lifted her up**—precisely as His Lord had done to his own mother-in-law (Mark i. 31). **and when he had called the saints**—whose fellow-disciple she was, **and widows**—whose benefactress she had been, **presented her alive.** 42. **And it was known throughout all Joppa; and many believed in the Lord**—the Lord Jesus; unable to resist the living evidence of the Divine power put forth in His name upon one known to all in the place. 43. **And it came to pass, that he tarried many days in Joppa** —no doubt taking advantage of the opening for His Master's work which the miracle on Dorcas created, as well as imparting further instruction to the disciples. **with one Simon a tanner**—a trade regarded by the Jews as half unclean, and consequently disreputable, from the contact with dead animals and blood which was connected with it. For this reason, even by other nations, it was usually carried on at some distance from towns; accordingly, Simon's house was "by the sea side" (ch. x. 6). Peter's lodging there shows him already to some extent above Jewish prejudice.

Remarks.—1. It is greatly to be regretted that some able critics, even among the orthodox and believing—with the view, apparently, of conciliating the sceptical, and themselves perhaps suffering from a reigning scepticism—have shown a disposition to explain all the cases of conversion recorded in the New Testament by the one law of a gradual development of religious convictions

43 *k* and many believed in the Lord. And it came to pass, that he tarried many days in Joppa with one Simon a tanner.

A. D. 37.

k John 11. 45.

and impressions, aided by outward events, and only Divinely directed. Least of all can this case of Saul of Tarsus be so explained. No doubt his rare natural abilities and previous training at the feet of Gamaliel would go to rich account in his subsequent career; nor have we any reason to doubt that his views would undergo a progressive enlargement, and his personal Christianity ripen as he advanced. But the great turning-point was the manifestation of Christ to him on his way to Damascus. Up to that moment his feeling towards Jesus of Nazareth was that of un-mixed hatred, and the express errand on which he journeyed to Damascus was to extirpate the faith of Him in that city. But as soon as he knew that the voice which addressed him from the heavens was that of Jesus Himself, he yielded himself up in trembling but absolute subjection to His authority as the Christ of God. Now, he was His servant as heartily and wholly as till that moment he had been His enemy. As yet, indeed, he had no intelligent apprehension of the work of Christ —that, perhaps, was reserved for Ananias to im-part to him—but the change then wrought on him was as total, as instantaneous, as little the result of any previous thoughts and feelings, as any mental change can be conceived to be. In another place (on Matt. xiii. 44-46, Remark 1) we have adverted to the important difference between two great classes of conversion : the one illustrating that Divine saying, "I am found of them that sought me not, I am made manifest unto them that asked not after me" (Isa. lxv. 1 ; Rom. x. 20)—and if ever there was such a case, surely this of Saul of Tarsus was it—the other fulfilling the promise, "Ye shall seek me, and find me, when ye shall search for me with all your heart" (Jer. xxix. 13) ; and such was the case of Cornelius, in the next chapter. 2. The identity of the risen and glorified Jesus with Him who was nailed to the accursed tree, receives delightful illustration from this scene on the way to Damascus. As it was for believing in the resurrection and glorifica-tion of the crucified Nazarene that Saul perse-cuted the Christians, so the vision of Him now in actual glory, and His own proclamation, that He was the Object against whom he was rushing, carried irresistible conviction to him that the Christians were in the right. Ever afterwards did he refer to that vision as evidence that he " had seen Jesus Christ our Lord," and so had that indispensable qualification for the apostleship. If, then, all this was not an illusion, it follows that that same Jesus whom the Jews nailed to the cross is now, in His risen body, in the heavens. 3. What unutterable consolation is in the bosom of that expostulation, "Saul, Saul, why persecutest thou Me?" Even on the well-known principle, that the dearer any one is to another the more he identifies himself with him in feeling—accounting himself injured by the injuries done to his friend —this question shows that the strength of Christ's attachment to His disciples on earth had suffered no abatement by His removal to heaven, and by the new sphere of life on which He had now entered. But further, since few, if any, of those in whom He considered Himself persecuted by Saul were among the number of His disciples when on earth, it must have been their disciple-ship simply—no matter when or how brought about—that formed the strong bond of attach-ment to them on Christ's part, in virtue of which every injury inflicted upon them was, to His feeling, a violence done to Himself. But there

is more in it than this. His own explicit testi-mony, and that of His apostles, is, that whoso-ever believeth in Him is *one life* with Him—even as the head and members of one and the same body ; for "we are members of His body, of His flesh, and of His bones" (Eph. v. 30). On this principle, as a wound inflicted on the extremities thrills upwards to the head, Jesus would have Saul to know that his persecuting arm beneath was felt by Himself above. And should not those who love their ascended Saviour take the full comfort of this wonderful truth? To believe the fact that Christ in heaven *recognizes* and *realizes* His oneness with believers on earth, is not enough. It is that He *feels* it; for so much is certainly implied in His most tender expostula-tion with this ruthless persecutor. And as there is nothing which Christians less vividly apprehend than this, so there is nothing more fitted to help them to it than to let this expostu-lation from the heavens with Saul of Tarsus sink deep into their hearts. 4. That the men who jour-neyed with Saul to Damascus were themselves drawn partially within the blaze of this scene, and were employed to lead the converted persecutor blind into the city—while yet total strangers to the internal revolution which it effected in him— was befitting the wisdom that reigned in this wonderful dispensation. For thus were provided unexceptionable witnesses to the reality of the outward facts, and all the more so from their entire ignorance of the change which they had wrought on the man whom they attended. But a deeper wisdom reigned in the subsequent steps. Since the conversion of Saul, at the very moment of it, amounted to nothing more than the absolute subjugation of his spirit to Jesus as the very Christ of God and the Lord of glory—without any explicit knowledge of the Gospel—and the teaching, if any, which he received from Ananias before his baptism would be brief and elementary, those memorable three days were permitted to intervene, during which he "was without sight, and neither did eat nor drink." We have already indicated the prob-able character and direction of the exercises which during those three days were to him in-stead of bodily sustenance—exercises which would stamp their impress on his whole future ministry, and perhaps his writings too (see exposition of *v.* 9). But their influence in so quickly ripening him into a powerful preacher of the Faith which he was on his way to Damascus to destroy, can hardly escape any thoughtful reader. Scarcely less remarkable were the steps which followed, by which this rare convert was to be prepared for his great work. The Lord had said to him, as he lay prostrate before Him, "Arise, and go into the city, and it shall be told thee what thou must do." But the three days are drawing to a close, and no director has appeared. At length one named Ananias, in vision, enters his chamber and puts his hand on him, that he may receive his sight; while Ananias himself, by another vision, is directed to go to Saul of Tarsus, whom he will find in such a street, at the house of such a man—and find, too, in the act of prayer—who also has seen in vision that very man, Ananias by name, who is to lay his hand on him for the recovery of his sight! At the sound of that dread name—Saul of Tarsus— Ananias is startled, for it is terror to all Chris-tians; and the very errand on which he has now come has travelled to Damascus before him. But the Lord hushes his fears, assuring him that he is no longer the bloody persecutor, but to Him a

10 THERE was a certain man in Cesarea called Cornelius, a centurion of | A. D. 41.
2 the band called the Italian *band, a* ^adevout *man,* and one that feared | ^a ch. 22. 12.

chosen vessel for eminent service in the Gospel, for which he is to be as great a sufferer as he himself had made others to be. Not disobedient unto the heavenly vision, Ananias goes boldly to the man with the dreaded name, and delivers his commission. Immediately the film drops from the eyes of the new convert, he is baptized, receives sustenance, remains some days in private fellowship with the disciples, and straightway preaches Christ in the synagogues of Damascus, waxing mightier from day to day, and bearing down all opposition. Could it be that out of such unparalleled preparations there should not come forth a witness for Christ of signal power? 5. That Ananias occupied no official position among the Christians of Damascus (as noted in the exposition of *v.* 17) we may with tolerable certainty conclude, from his being described simply as "a certain disciple." Yet this was the man whom the great Head of the Church Himself sent to baptize the chiefest of the apostles and the most distinguished of all preachers, to be the instrument through whom his vision should return to him, and through whom the Holy Ghost should descend on him; nor were any other human hands laid upon him after those of this "certain disciple." Are we then to infer that any Christian may at any time baptize another on his profession of faith, and that no forms of human ordination should have place in the Church? That certainly would be in the teeth of our apostle's own instructions in his Pastoral Epistles, and in opposition to what appears to have been the regular practice in the apostolic churches; but thus much may safely be inferred from the case of Saul, that where no constituted Church of Christ exists, and official instrumentality is not to be had, the essential ordinances of the visible Church may be performed by those whom the providence or secret direction of God may point out as fittest for doing it, and the work of the ministry discharged by those whom the gifts of the Holy Ghost have qualified for the exercise of it. 6. What was Saul's object in withdrawing to Arabia, in the midst (as we judge) of his first labours at Damascus as a preacher of Christ, and in returning to it, after a lapse of probably more than two years, to continue his preaching labours? Not to enter on a new sphere of evangelistic labour—as some think. For why, if he was to return to Damascus, should he have left it at all, at a time when his work was telling so powerfully there upon the Jewish mind? and why, if preaching had been his object, does he make no allusion to it to the Galatians, when, in mentioning to them his visit to Arabia, it would certainly have been to his purpose to tell them that he had gone thither after leaving Damascus, preaching his own Gospel, without any communication with the other apostles? Instead of this, he simply says he went into Arabia and returned to Damascus (Gal. i. 17). That he never preached in Arabia none will say; but the object of this lengthened visit appears to us to have been the enjoyment of a period of retirement and repose. Perhaps the excitement attending the change in his character and occupation demanded this, and his contendings with the Jews as to the sense of the Old Testament required deeper study and more prayerful reflection than he could possibly have given it since the light of heaven had broken in upon his darkened understanding. And if the prophets, after giving forth their Messianic predictions, had themselves to "search what, or what manner of time, the Spirit of Christ which was in them did signify,

when it testified beforehand the sufferings of Christ and the glories which were to follow them" (1 Pet. i. 11)—we may well conceive how it should be indispensable to the maturing of this great apostle's gift for opening the Messianic sense of the Old Testament Scriptures, that he should have to spend a lengthened period in searching them, "comparing spiritual things with spiritual," as he expressly tells us that he did (1 Cor. ii. 13). Certain it is, that in such researches, as in everything else, "the soul of the diligent shall be made fat" (Prov. xiii. 4). 7. What internal evidence of truth does the account of Saul's first visit to Jerusalem, after his conversion, bear to the unsophisticated reader. His object was (as himself afterwards writes to the Galatians, i. 18) to see Peter. But he obtrudes not himself and his commission direct upon that apostle; he simply "assays to join himself to the disciples," as one of their number. But the sight of him awakens their fears, and their recollection of his dreadful proceedings in time past begets the suspicion that he may only be putting on the cloak of discipleship for the purpose of identifying and seizing them. Here it is that Barnabas steps in, and in beautiful consistency with that "goodness" elsewhere ascribed to him (ch. xi. 24), and which shone through all his proceedings, he brings him not to the disciples at large, but to the apostles—whose satisfaction would speedily dispel the fears of the rest—informing them of the circumstances of his conversion, and of his subsequent labours at Damascus in the cause of the Gospel. This was enough for the apostles, and through them for all; and now he is constantly with them, coming in and going out testifying boldly of Christ, particularly to the Hellenistic class of Jews to which himself belonged, until his life was in danger from them, and then his friends hurried him off to Cæsarea and thence to his native Tarsus. Are these the marks of an artfully dressed-up narrative, as the critics of the Tübingen school allege?—pretending to a historical insight of which, in its deeper and only worthy sense, they are signally destitute. 8. The rest or peace which the Church at this time had from Jewish persecution (the hands of the Jews being then full enough of their own endangered interests), and the consequent increase of the disciples and prosperity of the Christian cause, has had its parallels once and again in later times. How often, for example, did it happen at the time of the great Reformation, that when the cause of Protestantism was in imminent danger from the Popish princes of the empire—and from the emperor himself, who was ever ready to league with the Pope to crush it—the danger that all were in, of being overwhelmed by the victorious and ever-advancing Turks, procured the reformers and reforming princes a blessed breathing time, during which their cause acquired both growth and consolidation. And thus it is that oftentimes the Lord, not by holding their enemies' hands, but by simply giving them other work to do, effectually interposes in behalf of His people—thus exemplifying, as in numberless other ways, that ancient law of His kingdom—"The Lord will judge His people, and repent Himself for His servants, when he seeth that their strength is gone" (Deut. xxxii. 36).

CHAP. X. 1-48.—ACCESSION AND BAPTISM OF CORNELIUS AND HIS PARTY, OR, THE FIRST-FRUITS OF THE GENTILES. We here enter on an entirely new phase of the Christian Church, the "opening

God with all his house, which gave much alms to the people, and prayed
3 to God alway. He [b]saw in a vision evidently, about the ninth hour of
the day, [c]an angel of God coming in to him, and saying unto him,
4 Cornelius. And when he looked on him, he was afraid, and said, What
is it, Lord? And he said unto him, Thy prayers and thine alms are
5 come up for [d]a memorial before God. And now send men to Joppa, and
6 call for *one* Simon, whose surname is Peter. He lodgeth with one [e]Simon
a tanner, whose house is by the sea-side: he [f]shall tell thee what thou
7 oughtest to do. And when the angel which spake unto Cornelius was
departed, he called two of his household servants, and a devout soldier
8 of them that waited on him continually; and when he had declared all
these things unto them, he sent them to Joppa.
9 On the morrow, as they went on their journey, and drew nigh unto

A. D. 41.

[b] ch. 11. 13.
[e] Ps. 34. 7.
Ps. 91. 11.
ch. 5. 19.
Heb. 1. 14.
[d] Ps. 141. 2.
Phil. 4. 18.
Heb. 13. 16.
Jas. 5. 16.
1 Pet. 3. 12.
Rev. 5. 8.
Rev. 8. 3.
[e] ch 9. 43.
[f] John 7. 17.
ch. 9. 6.
ch. 11. 14.

of the door of faith to the Gentiles;" in other words, the recognition of Gentile, on terms of perfect equality with Jewish, discipleship, without the necessity of circumcision. Some beginnings had been already made in this direction (see on ch. xi. 20, 21); and Saul probably acted on this principle from the first, both in Arabia—if he preached there—and in Syria and Cilicia. But had *he* been the prime mover in the admission of uncircumcised Gentiles into the Church, the Jewish party, who were never friendly to him, would probably have acquired such strength as to bring the Church to the verge of a disastrous schism. But it was wisely ordered that on Peter—"the apostle (specially) of the circumcision"—should be conferred the honour of initiating this great movement, as before of the first admission of Jewish believers (see on Matt. xvi. 19). After this, however, one who had already come upon the stage was to eclipse this "chiefest of the apostles."

Cornelius, by Divine direction, sends for Peter (1-8). **1. There was a certain man** | Ἦν of the received text is wanting in all the MSS. except one cursive, the verb being reserved to *v.* 3—εἶδεν. It has come in from the versions. Accordingly the translation should be, 'A certain man . . . saw,' &c.] **in Cesarea** (see on ch. viii. 40) **called Cornelius, a centurion** [ἑκατοντάρχης, the termination in ος is rather more frequent in the New Testament, though the other is more prevalent (says *Winer*, viii. 1) in later Greek] **of the Italian** [band]—a cohort of Italians, as distinguished from native soldiers. That such Italian cohorts served in Syria is proved by an ancient coin, of which a copy will be found in *Akerman's* 'Numismatic Illustrations of the New Testament;' and one of these might very naturally be stationed at Cæsarea, as a body-guard to the Roman procurator who resided there. **2. A devout man**—an uncircumcised convert to the Jewish faith, of whom at this time there were a very great number, **and one that feared God with all his house.** Not contented with regulating his own life by religious principle, he had brought his whole household under the influence of Revealed Religion. **which gave much alms to the people**—that is, the Jewish people; and did so, no doubt, on the same principle which actuated another centurion before him (Luke vii. 5), thinking it no "great thing" that they who had 'sown unto him spiritual things should reap his carnal things' (1 Cor. ix. 11), **and prayed to God alway**—that is, at every stated season (see on next verse). **3. He saw in a vision evidently** (or 'distinctly'), about [ὡσεί. So *Tischendorf*, with the received text. But *Lachmann* adds περί, which has preponderating authority. The sense is the same.] **the ninth hour of the day** (3 P.M.; see on ch. iii. 1)—the hour of the evening sacrifice and of evening prayer,

according to the Jewish ritual. From *v.* 30 it would appear that he had been fasting "until" this hour; beginning, possibly, from the previous season of prayer, the sixth hour, or noon (*v.* 9). **an angel of God coming in to him, and saying unto him, Cornelius. 4. And when he looked on him, he was afraid, and said, What is it, Lord?**—language which, though half tremulously uttered, betokened childlike reverence and humility. **And he said unto him, Thy prayers and thine alms**—by the one his soul going out to God, and his hand by the other to men, **are come up for a memorial before God**—that is, an offering bringing thee into acceptable remembrance, an odour unto God of a sweet smell (see Lev. ii. 2 and Rev. viii. 1). **5. And now send men to Joppa, and call for one Simon.** The word "one," printed in italics in the authorized version, belongs to the genuine text [Σ. τινα. The word apparently dropped out, from its occurring in the next verse. *Lachmann* and *Tischendorf* properly insert it]. **whose surname is Peter**—both his names being given, for greater precision. **6. He lodgeth with one Simon a tanner, whose house is by the sea-side** (see on ch. ix. 11, 43): [he shall tell thee what thou oughest to do]. These bracketed words are totally destitute of authority here, being wanting in all the MSS. of any value, and all the most ancient versions. They seem to be made up out of *v.* 32, and ch. ix. 6. **7. And when the angel which spake unto Cornelius was departed, he called**—immediately doing as directed, and thus showing the simplicity of his faith. In all probability he despatched the messengers the same evening: **two of his household servants.** *Lechler* thinks the word here used [οἰκετῶν] intended to denote persons above the rank of household servants [δούλων]; but though sometimes so used (as by *Herodotus*), New Testament usage seems against any such distinction (see Luke xvi. 13; Rom. xiv. 4; 1 Pet. ii. 18). **and a devout soldier of them that waited on him continually**—not merely one of the "soldiers under him" as a centurion (Matt. viii. 9), but one of a select number of them in personal attendance upon him, to whom, doubtless—though beneath himself in rank—the centurion was peculiarly drawn by the tie of their common piety. Now-a-days (says *Bengel* pertinently) he who is deemed the successor of Peter receives more splendid legations. Who this "devout soldier" was, cannot with any probability be conjectured; for *da Costa's* reasons for identifying him with the writer of the second Gospel, though ingenious and beautiful, are nothing more. **8. And when he had declared all these things unto them**—a pious familiarity (says *Bengel*) towards domestics, **he sent them to Joppa.**

Peter's Vision (9-16). **9. On the morrow, as they went on their journey, and drew nigh unto the**

the city, Peter went up upon the house-top to pray about the *g*sixth
10 hour: and he became very hungry, and would have eaten: but while
11 they made ready, he fell into a trance, and *h*saw heaven opened, and a
certain vessel descending unto him, as it had been a great sheet knit
12 at the four corners, and let down to the earth: wherein were all manner
of four-footed beasts of the earth, and wild beasts, and creeping things,
13 and fowls of the air. And there came a voice to him, Rise, Peter; kill,
14 and eat. But Peter said, Not so, Lord; for *i*I have never eaten any
15 thing that is common or unclean. And the voice *spake* unto him
again the second time, *j*What God hath cleansed, *that* call not thou
16 common. This was done thrice: and the vessel was received up again
into heaven.
17 Now, while Peter doubted in himself what this vision which he had
seen should mean, behold, the men which were sent from Cornelius had
18 made enquiry for Simon's house, and stood before the gate, and called,
and asked whether Simon, which was surnamed Peter, were lodged there.
19 While Peter thought on the vision, the Spirit *k*said unto him, Behold,
20 three men seek thee. Arise *l*therefore, and get thee down, and go with
21 them, doubting nothing: for I have sent them. Then Peter went down
to the men which were sent unto him from Cornelius, and said, Behold,

A. D. 41.

g Ps. 55. 17.
ch. 11. 5.
h Eze. 1. 1.
Matt. 3. 16.
ch. 7. 56.
Rev. 19. 11.
i Lev. 11. 4.
Lev. 20. 25.
Deut. 14. 3.
Eze. 4. 14.
Rom. 10. 2.
j Matt. 15.11.
Rom. 14.14.
17, 20.
1 Cor. 10.
25.
1 Tim. 4. 4.
Tit. 1. 15.
k John 16. 13.
ch. 11. 12.
ch. 16. 6.
ch. 21. 4.
l Matt. 28.19.
Mark 16.15.
ch. 15. 7.

---

city, Peter went up upon the house-top—or flat roof; the chosen place in the East, even to this day, for cool retirement, **to pray about the sixth hour** (noon): **10. And he became very hungry, and would have eaten** [ἤθελεν γεύσασθαι]—rather, 'wished to eat.' It was meal-time, indeed; but his being "very hungry" [πρόσπεινος] was no doubt a special preparation for what was to follow. **but while they made ready** [αὐτῶν, not ἐκείνων—as in the received text—is the true reading; and so *Lachmann* and *Tischendorf*], **he fell into a trance** [ἐγένετο is preferable to ἐπέπεσεν, of the received text.] In a state of "trance," the ordinary consciousness, and the perceptions of the external world, seem to have been in abeyance; things which, in ordinary circumstances would be invisible, being exclusively seen. In the state of 'vision,' this cessation of the ordinary laws of sense and perception probably did not exist, or took place but partially. **11. And saw heaven opened, and a certain vessel descending** [unto him]. These bracketed words [ἐπ' αὐτὸν] are evidently not genuine. **as it had been a great sheet, knit at the four corners** [ἀρχαῖς]—'extremities,' or 'ends.' So all the elder interpreters. *Bishop Middleton's* rendering (after *Wakefield*)—to which *Humphry*, *Alford, Webster and Wilkinson* adhere—'fastened to the ends of four ropes'—is without warrant (see *Bloomfield's* good note). *Meyer's* rendering—'bound to four corners,' as meaning the four quarters of the heavens—though approved by *Neander*, is unnatural. **and let down to the earth: 12. Wherein were all manner of four-footed beasts** [πάντα τὰ τετράποδα τ. γ.](properly, 'all the four-footed beasts') **of the earth**—the visional representation being that of *all* such animals, **and wild beasts, and creeping things, and fowls of the air**—the *clean* and the *unclean* all mixed together. (In the genuine text the words "of the earth" come after "creeping things.") **13. And there came a voice to him, Rise, Peter; kill, and eat. 14. But Peter said, Not so** [μηδαμῶς]—'By no means,' 'Not at all,' Lord; **for I have never eaten any thing that is common or unclean**—or (according to a well-supported reading [καὶ for ἤ], 'common and unclean;' that is, not separated (or divinely sanctified to holy uses) for food, and so, unclean. **15. And the voice spake unto him again the second**

time, What God hath cleansed, that call not (or 'make not') **thou common** [σὺ μὴ κοίνου]: *q. d.*, 'Ceremonial distinctions are now at an end, and Gentiles, heretofore debarred from access to God through the instituted ordinances of His Church, are now admissible on terms of entire equality with His ancient people.' **16. This was done thrice** [ἐπὶ τρίς] (see Gen. xli. 32): and **the vessel was received up again**—rather, 'immediately' [εὐθὺς having much better support than πάλιν] into heaven.

Arrival of the Messengers—Peter, Divinely directed to go down to them, obeys—They tell their errand, are invited in, and lodged (17-23). **17. Now, while Peter doubted in himself what this vision which he had seen should mean.** Of course, the trance was by this time at an end. The reply to his difficulty about eating what was unclean could not fail to convince him that some great principle of action was embodied in this vision, and what that might be he was anxiously considering, when, **behold, the men which were sent from Cornelius had made enquiry for Simon's house, and stood before the gate, 18. And called, and asked** [ἐπυνθάνοντο]—'were [in the act of] enquiring;' that is, were doing so at the very time when the Spirit was supernaturally informing Peter of the fact, **whether Simon, which was surnamed Peter, were lodged there. 19. While Peter thought**—*lit.*, 'cast about in his mind' [ἐνθυμουμένου; but this has hardly any support] **on the vision, the Spirit said** unto him, Behold, **three men seek thee.** *Tischendorf* reads, 'Men seek thee' [leaving out τρεῖς] but on insufficient evidence; *Lachmann* rightly retains the word. **20. Arise therefore, and get thee down, and go with them, doubting nothing** [μηδὲν διακρινόμενος]—'making no scruple:' **for I have sent them** [ἐγὼ ἀπέσταλκα.] The "I" here is gloriously emphatic: 'I, with Whom thou hast been holding entranced intercourse—I it is that have sent them.' **21. Then Peter went down to the men** [which were sent unto him from Cornelius.] These bracketed words [τ. ἀπεσταλμένους ἀπὸ τ. Κορν.] are wanting, and properly left out by *Lachmann* and *Tischendorf*. They were probably added to introduce a new sectional church lesson. **and said, Behold, I am he whom ye seek: what is the cause wherefore ye are come?** This ques-

22 I am he whom ye seek: what *is* the cause wherefore ye are come? And they said, Cornelius the centurion, a just man, and one that feareth God, and of *m* good report among all the nation of the Jews, was warned from God by an holy angel to send for thee into his house, and to hear words
23 of thee. Then called he them in, and lodged *them*.
And on the morrow Peter went away with them, and certain brethren
24 from Joppa accompanied him. And the morrow after they entered into Cesarea. And Cornelius waited for them, and had called together his
25 kinsmen and near friends. And as Peter was coming·in, Cornelius met
26 him, and fell down at his feet, and worshipped *him*. But Peter took him
27 up, saying, *n* Stand up; I myself also am a man. And as he talked with him, he went in, and found many that were come together.
28 And he said unto them, Ye know how that *o* it is an unlawful thing for a man that is a Jew to keep company, or come unto one of another nation; but *p* God hath showed me that I should not call any man
29 common or unclean. Therefore came I *unto you* without gainsaying, as *q* soon as I was sent for: I ask therefore for what intent ye have sent for
30 me? And Cornelius said, Four days ago I was fasting until this hour;

A. D. 41.

m ch. 22. 12.
n Ex. 34. 14.
Deut.11.16.
2 Ki. 17. 36.
Ps. 81. 9.
Matt. 4. 10.
Luke 4. 8.
ch. 14. 14.
15.
Col. 2. 18.
Rev. 14. 7.
Rev. 19. 10.
Rev. 22. 9.
o John 4. 9.
John 18. 28.
ch. 11. 3.
Gal. 2. 12.
14.
p ch. 15. 8,
9.
Eph. 3. 6.
q Gal. 1. 16.

tion seems to have been asked by Peter without any communication made to him regarding either the men or their errand, and purely in obedience to the Spirit's direction. **22. And they said, Cornelius the centurion, a just man, and one that feareth God**—fine testimony this from his own servants; **and of good report among all the nation of the Jews**; this was added, doubtless, to conciliate the favourable regard of the Jewish apostle: **was warned from God by an holy angel to send for thee into his house, and to hear words of thee.** See on ch. xi. 14. **23. Then called he them in, and lodged them**—thus anticipating to some extent that fellowship with the Gentiles which he was so soon formally to inaugurate, after it should be Divinely sealed.
Peter's departure with the Messengers to Cornelius —The Meeting of Peter and Cornelius (23-27). **23. And on the morrow Peter.** It should be 'he,' the name being a later addition, perhaps as a connecting word. **went away with them, and certain brethren from Joppa accompanied him.** These were six in number, as we learn from himself (ch. xi. 12), and they were taken in order to witness what Peter was now prepared to believe would be pregnant with great consequences. **24. And the morrow after they entered**—or, 'he entered,' according to what is presumably the true reading [though εἰσῆλθον and —εν have about equal support]. **into Cesarea. And Cornelius waited** (or 'was waiting') **for them, and had called together his kinsmen and near friends.** From this it would seem that he had been long enough at Cæsarea to form relationships there, and at least that there he had intimate friends, whose presence he was not ashamed to invite to a religious meeting of the most solemn nature, and likely to affect his whole future. **25. And as Peter was coming in, Cornelius met him**—a mark of highest respect, **and fell down at his feet, and worshipped him. 26. But Peter took him up, saying, Stand up: I myself also am a man.** In the East this way of showing respect was customary not only to kings but to others of superior station; but among the Greeks and Romans (as *Grotius* says) it was reserved for the gods. Not that we have the smallest reason to suppose that Cornelius meant to pay divine honours to Peter by this attitude; but the apostle regarded it as an act of religious homage, which his own insignificance as a mere mortal instrument, Divinely chosen to open the door of faith to this centurion,

would not endure. *Alford* justly remarks, that 'those who claim to have succeeded Peter have not imitated this part of his conduct.' But this only verifies 2 Thess. ii. 4 (compare Rev. xix. 10; xxii. 9). **27. And as he talked** ('talked familiarly') **with him** [συνομιλῶν] in emphatic contrast with the abject position towards Peter which Cornelius had just before assumed. **he went in, and found many that were come together**—a noble opportunity for the apostle, of which he was not slow to avail himself.
Peter, introduced to the assembled company, asks formally what he is sent for—The Reply of Cornelius (28-33). **28. And he said unto them, Ye know how that it is an unlawful thing for a man that is a Jew to keep company, or come unto one of another nation.** There was no express prohibition to this effect, and intercourse to a certain extent was undoubtedly kept up, as is evident from the Gospel History; but intimate social fellowship was not practised, as being contrary to the spirit of the law, and (as is usual in such cases) the law was strained injuriously in this direction (see John xviii. 28). **but God hath showed me that I should not call any man common or unclean**—from which it is evident that the apostle had already caught the import of the vision, and was prepared at once to carry it out. **29. Therefore came I unto you without gainsaying, as soon as I was sent for: I ask therefore for what intent ye have sent for me?** The whole speech is full of dignity, the apostle beholding in the company before him a new brotherhood, into whose devout and enquiring minds he is ready, as Divinely directed, to pour the light of new and surprising truth. **30. And Cornelius said, Four days ago.** If the messengers were despatched on the *first* day, and on the *second* reached Joppa, started for Cæsarea on the *third*, and on the *fourth* arrived, this would make out the four days. **I was fasting until this hour.** *Lachmann* reads thus: 'Four days ago I was praying in my house at the ninth hour' [leaving out νηστεύων, καί]. His external authorities are weighty, perhaps of equal strength with those for the received text, but internal evidence is against him; for while it is easy to account for the dropping out of this short clause from many MSS.—no mention of fasting being made in *v.* 3—its insertion, if spurious, can hardly be accounted for. *Tischendorf* abides by the received text. **and at the ninth [hour].** The bracketed word [ὥραν] is an unauthorized addition to the

and at the ninth hour I prayed in my house, and, behold, ^r a man stood
31 before ^s me in bright clothing, and said, Cornelius, ^t thy prayer is heard,
32 ^u and thine alms are had in remembrance in the sight of God. Send
therefore to Joppa, and call hither Simon, whose surname is Peter; he is
lodged in the house of *one* Simon a tanner by the sea-side: who, when
33 he cometh, shall speak unto thee. Immediately therefore I sent to thee;
and thou hast well done that thou art come. Now therefore are we all
here present before God, to hear all things that are commanded thee of
God.
34 Then Peter opened *his* mouth, and said, ^v Of a truth I perceive that
35 God is no respecter of persons: but ^w in every nation he that feareth him,
36 and worketh righteousness, is accepted with him. The word which *God*
sent unto the children of Israel, ^x preaching peace by Jesus Christ: (^y he is
37 Lord of all :) that word, *I say*, ye know, which was published throughout

A. D. 41.
^r ch. 1. 10.
^s Luke 24. 4.
^t Dan. 10. 12.
^u Heb. 6. 10.
^v Deut.10.17.
2 Chr. 19. 7.
Job 34. 19.
^w Rom. 2. 13.
Rom. 3. 22.
1 Cor.12.13.
^x Isa. 57. 19.
Eph. 2. 17.
Col. 1. 20.
^y Rom. 10.12.
1 Cor. 15.27.
Eph. 1. 20.
1 Pet. 3. 22.

text. **I prayed in my house, and behold, a man
stood before me in bright clothing** (see on Matt.
xxviii. 3). **31. And said, Cornelius, thy prayer is
heard, and thine alms are had in remembrance
in the sight of God. 32. Send therefore to Joppa,
and call hither Simon, whose surname is Peter;
he is lodged in the house of one Simon a tanner by
the sea-side: who, when he cometh, shall speak
unto thee.** Here again *Lachmann* shortens the
text, omitting all the last clause [ὃς παραγενόμενος
λαλήσει σοι]; but the evidence for it is preponderating, and *Tischendorf* inserts it. **33. Immediately
therefore I sent to thee; and thou hast well
done that thou art come. Now therefore are we
all here present before God, to hear all things
that are commanded thee of God**—rather, 'of
the Lord,' according to the better attested reading
[ἀπὸ τ. K. —ἀπό, as being less natural, is preferable to ὑπό of the received text, though both are
about equally attested. So *Lachmann and Tischendorf*]. Beautiful expression this of preparedness to receive the expected communication from
this heaven-commissioned teacher, and delightful
encouragement to Peter to give free utterance to
what was no doubt already on his lips!
  *Peter now preaches Christ to Cornelius and his
party* (34-43). **34. Then Peter opened his mouth
and said, Of a truth I perceive**
—'The events of these days past, and the scene
I now behold, have made it evident to me,' **that
God is no respecter of persons**—not, 'I see that
there is no capricious favouritism with God,' for
Peter would never imagine such a thing; but (as
the next clause plainly shows to be the meaning)
'I see that God has respect only to personal
character in His acceptance of men, and that
national and ecclesiastical distinctions are of no
account with Him.' **35. But in every nation**—not,
'in every *religion*,' according to a common distortion of these words. **he that feareth him, and
worketh righteousness, is accepted with him.** As
the two-fold description here given of the Divinely-
accepted man is just the well-known Old Testament description of him who, within the pale of
Revealed Religion, was regarded as truly godly, it
cannot be alleged that Peter meant it to denote a
merely *virtuous* character in the heathen sense;
and as the apostle had learnt enough from the
messengers of Cornelius, and from his own lips, to
convince him that the whole religious character
of this Roman officer had been cast in the mould
of the Jewish Faith, there can be no doubt that
the apostle meant to describe exactly such saintship, in its internal spirituality and external fruitfulness, as God had already pronounced to be
genuine and approved; and since to such "He
giveth more grace," according to the law of His

kingdom (Jas. iv. 6; Matt. xxv. 29), He now sends
Peter, not to be the instrument of his *conversion*—
as is very frequently said—but simply to show
him the way of God more fully, as before to
the Ethiopian eunuch. **36. The word which God
sent unto the children of Israel.** The apostle,
though addressing a company of Gentiles, and
about to proclaim Christ and salvation to them,
will have them distinctly to know that to the
Jews first the word of salvation was sent, even as
the facts of it took place on the special theatre of
the ancient economy. **preaching peace by Jesus
Christ.** This is the sum of all Gospel truth
(see Isa. lii. 7; lvii. 19; Eph. ii. 17; Col. i. 20), and
standing as it does at the outset of all that the
apostle was to say about Christ and His errand
into the world, it clearly shows what it was that
he thought it most important that men so new to
the glad tidings should first of all lay hold of. (**he
is Lord of all**)—Gentiles as well as Jews; *q. d.*, 'I
have said that the glad tidings were first sent
unto the children of Israel; but not for them only
was the word of this salvation designed, for this
Jesus hath God exalted to embrace under the
canopy of His peace the Gentile and the Jew alike,
whom the blood of His cross hath cemented into
one reconciled and accepted family' (Eph. ii. 13-18).
37. That word, &c. [ῥῆμα—not λόγον, as in *v.* 36]—
rather, 'matter.' The grammatical structure of this
whole passage is somewhat perplexed, and various
ways of pointing the text and bringing out the sense
have been adopted. *Tischendorf* so points the text
as to bring out the following sense, given substantially by *Bengel* and *de Wette* (in which *Olshausen,
Baumgarten*, and *Alford* concur): 'Of a truth, I
perceive that God is no respecter of persons, &c.,
[even] the word which God sent to the children
of Israel; He is Lord of all. Ye know what took
place throughout all Judea,' &c. But this is very
forced. We must regard the statement about the
acceptance of all who fear God and work righteousness, which the apostle says he now perceived
(*vv.* 34, 35), as complete within itself; and all that
follows must, as we think, be rendered thus (with
Scholefield): 'The word which He sent unto the
children of Israel, preaching peace by Jesus Christ
(He is Lord of all), ye know; [even] the matter
which took place throughout all Judea, beginning
from Galilee,after the baptism which John preached,
[concerning] Jesus of Nazareth, how God anointed
Him,' &c. [The only difference between this rendering and that of the authorized version, is in
making οἴδατε, at the opening of *v.* 37, the governing verb, not to ῥῆμα, which comes after it, but to
τὸν λόγον, with which the preceding verse opens;
and in taking ῥῆμα, not as equivalent to λόγον
in the verse before, but as denoting the subject-

all Judea, and began from Galilee, after the baptism which John
38 preached; how ᶻGod anointed Jesus of Nazareth with the Holy Ghost
and with power: who went about doing good, and healing all that were
39 oppressed of the devil: for ᵃGod was with him. And we are witnesses
of all things which he did both in the land of the Jews, and in Jerusalem;
40 whom they slew and hanged on a tree: him God raised up the third day,
41 and showed him openly; not ᵇto all the people, but unto witnesses chosen
before of God, *even* to us, who ᶜdid eat and drink with him after he rose
42 from the dead. And ᵈhe commanded us to preach unto the people,
and to testify ᵉthat it is he which was ordained of God *to be* the Judge
43 of ᶠquick and dead. To ᵍhim give all the prophets witness, that
through his name whosoever believeth in him shall receive remission
of sins.
44 While Peter yet spake these words, the Holy Ghost fell on all them

A. D. 41.

ᶻ Luke 4. 18.
  Heb. 1. 9.
ᵃ Col. 2. 9.
ᵇ John 14.17.
ᶜ John 21. 13.
ᵈ Matt. 28, 19.
ᵉ John 5. 22.
ᶠ Rom. 14. 9.
2 Cor. 5. 10.
2 Tim. 4. 1.
1 Pet. 4. 5.
ᵍ Isa. 63. 11.
Jer. 31. 34.
Dan. 9. 21.
Mic. 7. 18.
Zech. 13. 1.
Mal. 4. 2.

matter of the "word," = דָּבָר, and so rendering γενόμενον, not "published," which it cannot properly
mean, but 'took place,' 'happened,' 'occurred.']
ye know. The facts, it seems, were too notorious
and extraordinary to be unknown to those who
mixed so much with Jews, and took so tender an
interest in all Jewish matters, as they did;
though, like the eunuch, they knew not the significance of them. **which was published** [τὸ
γενόμενον ῥῆμα]—'the matter which took place,'
throughout all Judea, and began [ἀρξάμενον,
not —ος, though the MSS. favour it. The construction is against it] **from Galilee**—(Luke iv.
14, 37, 44; vii. 37; ix. 6; xxiii. 5). **after the
baptism which John preached**—(see on ch. i. 22.)
38. How God anointed Jesus of Nazareth ['Ιησ. τ.
Ν., ὡς ἔχρισεν αὐτὸν ὁ Θ.]—['Concerning'] Jesus
of Nazareth, how God anointed Him **with the
Holy Ghost**—that is, at His baptism; thus visibly
and audibly proclaiming Him Messiah, "The
Lord's Christ." For it is not His unction for
personal holiness at His incarnation that is here
referred to—as many of the fathers and some
moderns take it, who view this and similar statements more theologically than exegetically—but
His solemn investiture with the gifts for His
Messianic office, in which he presented Himself
after His baptism to the acceptance of the people.
(See on Matt. iii. 13-17, Remark 2, p. 15.) **and
with power**—the fruit of that glorious Anointing, **who went about doing good** [εὐεργετῶν]—
diffusing beneficence; referring to the beneficent
character of His mission in general, and all the
features of it, but particularly (as appears by the
next clause) to the beneficent character of all His
miracles, which was their predicted character
(Isa. xxxv. 5, 6). **healing all that were oppressed**
[καταδυναστευομένους]—or 'tyrannized over.' **of
the devil**—whether in the form of demoniacal
possession, or more indirectly, as in her "whom
Satan had bound with a spirit of infirmity eighteen
years" (Luke xiii. 16); thus showing Himself the
promised Redeemer from all evil. **for God was
with him.** Thus gently does the apostle rise to
the supreme dignity of Christ, with which he
closes, accommodating himself to the imperfect
capacity of his audience to apprehend the things
of the kingdom. **39. And we [are] witnesses** [ἐσμεν
is not genuine]—no objects of superstitious reverence, but simply *witnesses;* yet eye and ear-witnesses to the great historical facts on which the
Gospel is based. **of all things which he did both
in the land of the Jews**—including Galilee, of
course; for the apostle, addressing Gentiles,
speaks in general terms. **and in Jerusalem**—the
metropolis not only of their nationality, but of
their whole Religion. **whom** [ὃν καὶ]—'whom also'

they slew and hanged on a tree [ἀνεῖλον
κρεμάσαντες]—rather, 'hanged on a tree and slew;'
or 'slew by hanging' (as in ch. v. 30). See on
Gal. iii. 13. **40. Him God raised up the third
day, and showed him openly** [ἔδωκεν αὐτὸν ἐμφανῆ
γενέσθαι]—literally, 'gave Him to become manifest;' that is, so exposed Him in His resurrection-body to the senses of men, that they were
qualified to attest the fact of His being raised
from the dead. **41. Not to all the people**—for
it was not fitting that He should subject Himself,
in His risen condition, to a second rejection in
Person. **but unto witnesses chosen before of
God** [προκεχειροτονημένοις]. The word signifies to
'choose by show of hands,' and then to 'choose'
in any way. **even to us, who did eat and drink
with him after he rose from the dead.** Not the
less certain, therefore, was the fact of His resurrection, though withholding Himself from general
gaze in his risen body. **42. And he commanded
us to preach unto the people**—the Jewish people,
and to testify that it is he which—'He it is'
[αὐτός. *Lechler* properly says here, that though the
external authorities are in favour of οὗτος—which
Lachmann adopts—it is probably a correction, in
consequence of the frequency and regularity with
which οὗτος occurs in this address. *Tischendorf*
abides by αὐτός]. **was ordained of God to be the
Judge of quick and dead.** He had before proclaimed
Him "Lord of all," for the dispensing of "*peace*"
to all alike: now he announces Him Lord for
the exercise of *judgment* upon all alike. On this
grand ordination, see John v. 22, 23, 27; and ch.
xvii. 31. Thus have we here all Gospel truth in
brief. But *Forgiveness through this exalted One* is
the closing note of Peter's beautifully simple
discourse. **43. To him give all the prophets
witness**—*i. e.*, 'This is the burden, generally, of
the prophetic testimony.' It was fitter thus to
give the spirit of their testimony than to quote
them in detail on such an occasion. But let this
apostolic statement of the evangelical import of the
Old Testament writings be devoutly weighed by
those who are disposed to rationalize away this
element in that part of Scripture. **that through
his name**—by virtue of what He is and what He
hath done (compare 1 Cor. vi. 11). **whosoever
believeth in him**—'Ye Gentiles whom I now
address, as well as we of Abraham's seed.' **shall
receive remission of sins**—a noble practical conclusion to the whole discourse.

*The Holy Ghost descends on the whole Gentile
audience, who thereupon speak with tongues and
magnify God, to the astonishment of the Jewish
converts present — They are baptized by Peter's
direction* (44-88). **44. While Peter yet spake these
words**—and probably as the last words were drop-

45 which heard the word. And they of the circumcision which believed
were astonished, as many as came with Peter, [h] because that on the Gen-
46 tiles also was poured out the gift of the Holy Ghost. For they heard
47 them speak with tongues, and magnify God. Then answered Peter, Can
any man forbid water, that these should not be baptized, which have
48 received the Holy Ghost [i] as well as we? [j] And he commanded them to
be baptized [k] in the name of the Lord. Then prayed they him to tarry
certain days.

A. D. 41.
h ch. 11. 18.
Gal. 3. 14.
i ch. 11. 17.
ch. 15. 8.
9.
Rom. 10.12.
j 1 Cor. 1. 17.
k ch. 2. 38.
ch. 8. 16.

ping from his lips, **the Holy Ghost fell**—by sensible manifestation; all speaking with foreign tongues (*v.* 46)—**on all them which heard the word.** **45. And they of the circumcision which believed** [πιστοί = —εύοντες] **were astonished, as many as came with Peter**—the six Jewish brethren 'that accompanied Peter from Joppa' (ch. xi. 12, and ch. x. 23), **because that on the Gentiles also was poured out the gift of the Holy Ghost.** Their wonder arose not from the descent of the Spirit upon men of Gentile birth, but from His descending on them whilst yet uncircumcised. **46. For they heard them speak with tongues, and magnify God.** The tongues used on this occasion were clearly not intended for the preaching of the Gospel, but merely as incontestable evidence that the Holy Ghost was resting on them (see on 1 Cor. xiv. 22, "Wherefore tongues are for a *sign*"). The "For" at the beginning of the verse makes this evident. It was the same with the tongues spoken on the day of Pentecost. But just as the miracle then consisted not in the mere employment of foreign tongues, but in proclaiming in those tongues, to them unknown, "the wonderful works of God;" so here this company of Cornelius are heard "magnifying God" in foreign languages. Nor is there any reason why these Gentile converts, speaking as the Spirit gave them utterance, may not have magnified God in similar strains of Old Testament inspiration, as we supposed it probable that the Jewish converts on the day of Pentecost did (see on ch. ii. 11); in which case the company of Peter that listened to them would the more marvel. **Then answered Peter, 47. Can any man forbid water, that these should not be baptized.** This is a sort of challenge thrown out to his own six Jewish brethren, who might be supposed to object to the recognition of their Gentile brethren without circumcision. A great principle is here expressed. He does not say, 'Having received the Spirit, what need have they of water?' But, 'Having received the supernatural seal of real discipleship, who can refuse them the visible token of it?' **which have received** [οἵτινες ἔλαβον]—*i. e.,* 'since they have received' **the Holy Ghost as well as we?**—which has put them on a level with ourselves in all that is saving. **48. And he commanded them to be baptized.** As "Jesus himself baptized not, but His disciples" (John iv. 2), His apostolic representatives seem to have acted on the same principle, save on rare occasions (see on 1 Cor. i. 14, 17). **In the name of the Lord.** *Lachmann's* reading, 'in the name of Jesus Christ,' is perhaps best attested; but this (as *Meyer* says) is probably an alteration, to mark the *Christian* character of the act. *Tischendorf* abides by the received text. **Then prayed they him to tarry certain days**—golden days (as *Bengel* says); spent in refreshing fellowship, and in imparting and receiving fuller teaching on the great topics of the apostle's discourse.
Remarks.—1. We have adverted to the fact that the Gospel was preached with success to uncircumcised Gentiles before Peter was sent to Cornelius (see on ch. viii. 4, and Remark 1, at the close

of that Section). The strong feelings of the dispersed believers, who, after Stephen's martyrdom, went everywhere preaching the word, would not suffer them, it appears, to confine themselves to their brethren of the circumcision. Meeting with Gentiles, equally needing and equally capable of salvation by the Gospel, they felt themselves impelled to proclaim the glad tidings to them also; and they did it not in vain. But since this was so new a feature in the Divine economy, and the prejudices of the Jews against any breaking down of the distinction were so intense and general, that even after they believed, they could hardly shake it off, it seemed meet to the wisdom of God to give the extension of the Gospel to uncircumcised Gentiles a more august and formal sanction, once for all, than any success vouchsafed to the spontaneous labours of warm-hearted believers would have lent to it. And this is what we have in the present chapter. And the steps in this case were as notable as in the conversion and preparation of Saul of Tarsus to be a preacher of Christ, because in both cases the issues to the cause of the Gospel were to be so vast. Yet how different the two cases! Saul, nursed under Divine Revelation, and of 'the straitest' sect of his Religion, was up to the moment of his conversion a bitter enemy of Christ: Cornelius, born a heathen, but learning in Judea (where, as a military man, he had been quartered) that 'salvation was of the Jews,' had surrendered his heart to the God of Abraham, was regulating his life and household by the Faith which he had embraced, and had at least one of his soldiers, like-minded with himself in spiritual things, on a more intimate footing with him than the rest. Thus adorning his religious profession, the eye of God rested on him with complacency as an accepted worshipper; and as, like the Ethiopian eunuch before Philip was sent to him, he wanted only the knowledge of Jesus, the Lord brings this about in a way worthy of Him who is wonderful in counsel and excellent in working. That apostle, through whose instrumentality the first ingathering of Jewish believers took place on the day of Pentecost, is now honoured to open the door of faith unto the Gentiles, in the persons of Cornelius and his company. With this view Cornelius is directed in vision to send for Peter, while Peter, on the other hand, taught by a vision that the Gentiles are no longer unclean, is by the Spirit informed that messengers are waiting for him, whom he is to accompany, as men Divinely sent to him. Cornelius, in full expectation of Peter's arrival, prepares to receive and cordially welcomes him; each having his respective party with him—the representatives of the two great sections of mankind, Jew and Gentile, coming together for the first time, with the formal recognition of heaven, on a footing of perfect religious equality. The expectations of both parties are wound up, doubtless, to a high pitch; and silence having been broken—by each party explaining how, on his part, this strange meeting had come about—Peter delivers his Gospel message. Whilst he is yet speaking the Holy Ghost descends upon the whole

72

11 AND the apostles and brethren that were in Judea heard that the

2 Gentiles ^ahad also received the word of God. And when Peter was come up to Jerusalem, ^bthey that were of the circumcision contended with him,

3 saying, ^cThou wentest in to men uncircumcised, and didst eat with them.

4 But Peter rehearsed *the matter* from the beginning, and expounded *it* ^dby order unto them, saying,

5 I ^ewas in the city of Joppa praying: and in a trance I saw a vision, A

₀A. D. 41.

^a Gen. 49. 10.
Amos 9. 11, 12.
Zech. 2. 11.
^b Gal. 2. 12.
^c ch. 10. 28.
^d Luke 1. 3.
^e ch. 10. 9.

Gentile portion of the audience—evidencing His presence, as on the day of Pentecost, by their magnifying God in foreign tongues; the Jewish portion of the audience is filled with wonder, and Peter, after challenging objection, orders them—all uncircumcised as they were—to be visibly admitted into the fellowship of believers by the rite of baptism. At their invitation Peter stays some days with these new Gentile brethren — eating and drinking with them freely, no doubt, in disregard now of all his old prejudices. Thus grandly was the admission of the Gentiles to be fellow-citizens with the saints, and of the household of God, established Divinely for all time. 2. The honour in this case put upon *prayer*—as before in the case of Saul of Tarsus—ought not to pass unnoticed. Just as some other sign of the change that had come over Saul might have been given to Ananias; but that which was fixed upon (the last, by the way, that would have been thought of by any but a simple relator of facts), as it was that in the convert's exercise which was the most befitting his new circumstances, so it shows what the eye of God beheld in him with the greatest satisfaction: even so here, it was "about the ninth hour"—the hour of evening Jewish prayer, and doubtless while himself in the act of prayer—that the angel of God appeared in vision to Cornelius. Perhaps he was praying for more light; and as the centurion in the Gospel—being quartered in Capernaum, and enjoying the advantage of familiarity with His mighty works and wondrous words—had outstripped his Jewish teachers, and passed from Judaism to Jesus; so this man, after having got all out of Judaism which he could extract without Christ, feeling still that his soul was not satisfied, was crying to God, "If I wash myself with snow water, and make my hands never so clean; yet shalt thou plunge me in the ditch, and mine own clothes shall abhor me. For He is not a man, as I am, that I should answer Him, and we should come together in judgment. Neither is there any daysman betwixt us, that might lay his hand upon us both." "Oh that thou wouldest rend the heavens, that thou wouldest come down, that the mountains might flow down at thy presence. For since the beginning of the world men have not heard, nor perceived by the ear, neither hath the eye seen, O God, besides thee, what He hath prepared for Him that waiteth for Him." "Show me a token for good" (Job ix. 30-33; Isa. lxiv. 1, 4; Ps. lxxxvi. 17). If anything like this was the burden of Cornelius' prayer, how seasonable was the Divine response to it! But at any rate, it was, beyond doubt, while he was praying that the promise of new light was sent him, and it was "his prayers" first that the angel told him had "come up as a memorial before God." Nor was it otherwise with Peter; for it was while on the house-top, whither he had gone up "to pray," and about the noon-tide hour of Jewish prayer, that he had the trance which prepared him for the messengers of Cornelius, and the Spirit's direction to go with them.

'The saint beside the ocean pray'd,
The soldier in his chosen bower,
Where all his eye survey'd
Seem'd sacred in that hour.

'To each unknown his brother's prayer,
Yet brethren true in dearest love
Were they—and now they share
Fraternal joys above.

'There daily through Christ's open gate
They see the Gentile spirits press,
Brightening their high estate
With dearer happiness.'
KEBLE.

And does not the experience of the Church, and of individual believers in every age, attest, quite as decisively, the value which the Lord sets upon prayer? When has any remarkable revival of religion taken place, or light in darkness broken in upon struggling believers, which has not been preceded by much prayer? (Compare the example of Jesus Himself, Mark i. 35; Luke vi. 12; ix. 28, and Remarks there.) 3. The principle, that where the Holy Ghost has been already conferred, the visible sign of entrance into the fellowship of the Church cannot reasonably be withheld, is plainly one of more extensive application than the particular case here recorded. One application of it, to infants brought to Jesus, has been noticed on Luke xviii. 15-17, Remark 5; and *Calvin* makes this application of it too. But it admits of very varied application.

CHAP. XI. 1-18.—PETER VINDICATES HIM-SELF BEFORE THE CHURCH AT JERUSALEM FOR HIS PROCEDURE TOWARDS THE GENTILES—THE OBJECTORS ARE SATISFIED, AND GLORIFY GOD.

1. And the apostles and brethren that were in Judea [κατὰ τὴν I.]—rather, 'throughout Judea' (see on ch. 'xv. 23), **heard that the Gentiles had also received the word of God**—and heard it, doubtless, with unmingled satisfaction. The only thing which some heard with displeasure was Peter's recognition of them, as on a perfect equality with the Jewish brethren, without circumcision. This novelty, and the sensation which it produced, would cause the news to fly swiftly through the country. **2. And when Peter was come up to Jerusalem**—probably hastening his return thither, in order to report the great revolution which God had wrought in his views about the Gentiles, and to meet any difficulties which might be felt on the subject. **they that were of the circumcision** — the circumcised believers; but here probably referring to the zealots for circumcision, including, not improbably, apostles as well as others. **contended with him**, 3. **Saying, Thou wentest in to men uncircumcised, and didst eat with them**—(see on ch. x. 28.) These objectors, it will be observed, scruple not to demand of Peter—though the first among the apostles, and up to this time the prime mover in the Church —an explanation of his conduct; nor does Peter, in his reply, insinuate that in this they had been wanting in proper deference to his authority—a manifest proof that such authority was unknown alike to them and to him. **4. But Peter rehearsed the matter from the beginning, and expounded it by order** ['Αρξάμενος, ἐξετίθετο] — rather, 'But Peter beginning, laid it out,' or 'set it forth in order' unto them, saying,

5-11. I was in the city of Joppa praying: and in a trance I saw a vision, A certain vessel descend,

certain vessel descend, as it had been a great sheet, let down from heaven
6 by four corners; and it came even to me: upon the which when I had fastened mine eyes, I considered, and saw four-footed beasts of the earth,
7 and wild beasts, and creeping things, and fowls of the air. And I heard
8 a voice saying unto me, Arise, Peter; slay, and eat. But I said, *f* Not so, Lord: for nothing common or unclean hath at any time entered into
9 my mouth. But the voice answered me again from heaven, What God
10 hath cleansed, *that* call not thou common. And this was done three
11 times: and all were drawn up again into heaven. And, behold, immediately there were three men already come unto the house where I was,
12 sent from Cesarea unto me. And *g* the Spirit bade me go with them, nothing doubting. Moreover these *h* six brethren accompanied me, and
13 we entered into the man's house: and *i* he showed us how he had seen an angel in his house, which stood and said unto him, Send men to Joppa,
14 and call for Simon, whose surname is Peter; who shall tell thee words,
15 whereby thou and all thy house shall be saved. And as I began to speak,
16 the Holy Ghost fell on them, *j* as on us at the beginning. Then remembered I the word of the Lord, how that he said, *k* John indeed baptized
17 with water; but *l* ye shall be baptized with the Holy Ghost. Forasmuch *m* then as God gave them the like gift as *he did* unto us, who believed on
18 the Lord Jesus Christ, what *n* was I, that I could withstand God? When

A. D. 41.

f Eze. 4. 14.
g John 16. 13.
ch. 8. 29.
ch. 10. 19,
20.
ch. 15. 7.
h ch. 10. 23.
i ch. 10. 30.
ch. 12. 11.
Heb. 1. 14.
j ch. 2. 4.
ch. 4. 31.
k Matt. 3. 11.
Mark 1. 8.
Luke 3. 16.
John 1. 26.
ch. 1. 5.
l Isa. 44. 3.
Joel 2. 28.
Joel 3. 18.
m Matt. 20. 14,
15.
ch. 15. 8, 9.
n Job 9. 12-
14.
Dan. 4. 35.
ch. 10. 47.

as it had been a great sheet, let down from heaven by four corners; and it came even to me. The historian himself only says it was "let down to the earth" (ch. x. 11). This additional particular from the apostle's own lips gives vividness to the scene. **6. Upon the which when I had fastened mine eyes, I considered.** This emphatic language (also not in the historian's narrative, ch. x. 12) is designed to express the eager gaze with which he looked upon it. **and saw four-footed beasts of the earth, and wild beasts, and creeping things, and fowls of the air.** Here the narratives are for several verses almost identical. [In *v.* 8—"nothing common," &c.—πᾶν is clearly not genuine; it should therefore be, 'for a common or unclean thing' (or 'anything common or unclean') 'hath never entered into my mouth']. **12. And the Spirit bade me go with them, [nothing doubting].** We have bracketed the last two words, as of doubtful authority: they may have been copied from ch. x. 23; but internal evidence is rather favourable to them here also. **Moreover these six brethren accompanied me.** This important specification we have only from Peter himself, the historian being more general (ch. x. 23). It is doubtless mentioned to show how careful he had been to provide a sufficiency of competent witnesses of so great a transaction. **and we entered into the man's house.** No mention is here made of the name of Cornelius, much less of his high position. as if that were of any weight in deciding the question. To the charge, "Thou wentest in to *men* uncircumcised," he simply says, he entered into the uncircumcised *man's* house, to whom he had been Divinely directed. **13. And he showed us how he had seen an angel** [τὸν ἄγγελον]—rather, 'the angel,' of whom the rumour may have spoken, or (if not so definite as this) to whom the historian himself had several times referred (ch. x. 3, 22, 30). **in his house, which stood and said unto him, Send men to Joppa**—better, 'Send to Joppa' [ἄνδρας being probably not genuine], **and call for Simon, whose surname is Peter; 14. Who shall tell thee words, whereby** [ἐν οἷς]—or 'wherein,' *i. e.,* in the 'reception of which,' **thou and all thy house shall be saved.** The historian's own statement of

this (ch. x. 6) is much more general than what he here puts into the mouth of Peter. So also the report of it by the deputies of Cornelius (ch. x. 22), and by Cornelius himself (ch. x. 32). But as Peter tarried with Cornelius certain days, during which they doubtless talked over this wonderful scene, perhaps this fuller and richer form of what the angel said to Cornelius was communicated to Peter; or Peter may have *expressed* what certainly the angel *designed* in bidding him send for Peter. *Let the reader observe here, that 'salvation' is made to hang upon 'words'*—that is, *the Gospel message concerning Christ.* The "house" or 'household' of Cornelius is here associated with himself in the promised salvation, because he feared God "with all his house" (*v.* 2). But see on Luke xix. 9, and Remark 4 at the end of that Section. **15. And as I began to speak**—in point of fact, it was not till he was closing his address; but the apostle's design was to intimate how quickly, as cause and effect, the one was followed by the other. **the Holy Ghost fell on them, as on us at the beginning**—meaning the day of Pentecost; the attestation of this effusion of the Spirit, as well as the effusion itself, being the same as then. **16. Then remembered I the word of the Lord** (ch. i. 5), **how that he said, John indeed baptized with water; but ye shall be baptized with the Holy Ghost.** The contrast between water-baptism and that of the Spirit—as the special gift of the glorified Christ, and the highest object of believing aspiration—rushed upon his mind and decided the question with him. **17. Forasmuch then as God gave them the like gift as he did unto us, who believed on the Lord Jesus Christ.** The sense would be more clear thus: 'Forasmuch, then, as God gave to them who believed on the Lord Jesus Christ (that is, upon their believing in Him) the like gift as He did unto us,' and that the highest gift which the ascended Lord of all has to bestow even upon us—the baptism of the Holy Ghost, **what was I, that I could withstand God?**—'Was I to be found withstanding God by refusing them the outward rite of entrance into the visible fellowship of the saints, and so standing apart from them as if they were still unclean?' **18. When they heard these things, they held**

they heard these things, they held their peace, and glorified God, saying, Then ° hath God also to the Gentiles granted repentance unto life.

19 Now ᵖ they which were scattered abroad upon the persecution that arose about Stephen travelled as far as Phenice, and Cyprus, and Antioch,

A. D. 41.

° Rom. 10. 12.
Rom. 15. 9.
Gal. 3. 26.
ᵖ ch. 8. 1.

their peace, and glorified God [ἐδόξαζον]—the imperfect tense, implying more than a momentary burst of praise: their mouths, shut to find fault, were immediately opened to glorify God, **saying, Then** [Ἄραγε] . . . **granted**—rather, 'So, then, God hath granted to the Gentiles also' **repentance unto life**—a very different spirit this from what the same party afterwards showed when Paul adduced equally resistless evidence in favour of the same line of procedure followed by him. The expression, "repentance unto life," means 'repentance, whose proper issue is life.' Compare 2 Cor. vii. 10, "repentance unto salvation." To 'grant' this is something more than what *Grotius* makes it, to be willing to grant pardon upon repentance. The case of Cornelius was so manifestly one of grace reigning in every stage of his religious history, that we can hardly doubt that this very thing was meant to be conveyed here; and this is just the grace that reigns in every real conversion.

For *Remarks* on this Section, see those on ch. x. 19-30.—RISE OF GENTILE CHRISTIANITY AT ANTIOCH—THE LABOURS THERE OF BARNABAS AND SAUL—THEIR MISSION TO JERUSALEM WITH A CONTRIBUTION FROM ANTIOCH FOR THE FAMINE-STRICKEN DISCIPLES THERE.

Immediately after the martyrdom of Stephen, we were told that there was a great persecution against the church which was at Jerusalem; "that the disciples were all scattered abroad except the apostles;" and that "they that were scattered abroad went," not only "throughout the regions of Judea and Samaria," but "everywhere preaching the word" (ch. viii. 1, 4). To what distant localities some of these dispersed disciples carried the word, our historian would seem to a cursory reader not to state. But he only reserves it till he has recorded the triumphs of the Gospel in Samaria, and the accession of the Ethiopian eunuch (ch. viii.); the conversion, and first evangelistic labours and perils of Saul of Tarsus, followed by some notices of the progress of the Gospel in Palestine (ch. ix.); the introduction of Cornelius and his Gentile friends into the Christian Church through the instrumentality of Peter (ch. x.); and the happy meeting on this subject which took place at Jerusalem (ch. xi. 1-18). These matters disposed of, our historian returns back to the point from which he started—the travels and labours of the dispersed disciples immediately after the martyrdom of Stephen.

Evangelistic travels of the scattered disciples—At Antioch the Gospel is preached for the first time to the Gentiles, and with signal success (19-21). **19. Now they which were scattered abroad upon the persecution that arose about Stephen** [ἐπὶ Στεφάνῳ]—not "about Stephen" in the sense of 'concerning' [περὶ], nor about (the time of) Stephen (which would require the genitive), but 'over,' 'after,' or 'resulting from (what happened to) Stephen,' **travelled as far as Phenice, and Cyprus, and Antioch, preaching the word to none but unto the Jews only.** *Phenicia* was that strip of Mediterranean coast which, commencing a little to the north of Cæsarea, stretches northward for upwards of a hundred miles, half way to Antioch. *Cyprus* is that rich and productive island of the Mediterranean lying to the south-west of Seleucia, from whose eastern promontory it may be seen on a clear day. Between Phenicia and Cyprus an

active commercial intercourse subsisted. That the preaching of these scattered disciples bore fruit in Phenicia, we may safely conclude from the incidental mention of "disciples" at *Tyre*, at *Ptolemais* (now St. Jean d'Acre), and at *Sidon*—all in Phenicia—whom Paul visited long after this (ch. xxi. 3-7; xxvii. 3). Nor is it likely that their labours were fruitless in *Cyprus*, into which the Gospel had penetrated before—for Barnabas was a Cypriot (ch. iv. 36), and Mnason (ch. xxi. 16), and even some of the dispersed themselves (*v.* 20). As for *Antioch*—which stands out as prominently in the history of the earliest GENTILE Christianity as Jerusalem of its JEWISH division—some account of it may fitly be given here.

A little to the north of Damascus there rises from the mountain range of Anti-Libanus the ancient river Orontes, which, after flowing due north for more than two hundred miles, has its course bent westwards by the mountain-chain of Amanus, whence, after a south-westerly course of less than twenty miles, it empties itself into the Mediterranean. At the bend of this noble river, on its left bank, and at the foot of an abrupt hill called Silphius, Seleucus Nicator—one of Alexander's greatest generals and successors, and the founder of the Seleucidæ, or Greek kings of Syria—built the city of ANTIOCH in the year 300 B. C., as the capital of his Syrian kingdom. Following out the policy of his illustrious master, to *Hellenize* his Asiatic dominions, he founded Greek colonies in most of his provinces, whose capital cities should become centres of Western civilization; and amongst these, Antioch —enjoying unequalled advantages, natural and geographical—rose to the rank of Queen of the East. By its harbour at Seleucia it commanded the Mediterranean trade of the West, while through the open country lying to the east of the Lebanon range the whole East lay open to it. It was the policy of Seleucus and his successors to encourage the Jews to settle in these Greek cities. With this view, equal rights and privileges with those enjoyed by the Greeks were accorded to them by Seleucus (*Josephus*, Antt. xii. 3. 1). Attracted by these advantages, and the nearness, amplitude, and beauty of the city, immense numbers of Jews settled there; and though Antiochus Epiphanes oppressed them, his successors hastened to undo his acts, and not only did they celebrate their worship there in peace, and even with some splendour, but large numbers of proselytes from among the Greeks came over to them from time to time (*Josephus*, J. W. vii. 3. 3). Under the Romans Antioch was regarded as second only to Rome and Alexandria, while its Christian history has secured for it a veneration second only to Jerusalem itself. As a Greek colony, the language and literature of Greece predominated, without eclipsing the native Oriental element, while a strong Jewish element also held its ground. With this mixture of nationalities, blending their respective characteristics, it need not surprise us that a metropolis situated geographically as Antioch was, and embracing a population of above half a million of souls, should have become the Rome of the East. The learning of every sort which flourished in it, and the great extent of its population, is attested by Cicero [*Locus nobilis celebris quondam urbs et copiosa, atque eruditissimis hominibus liberalissimisque studiis affluens.*—Pro. Archiâ, 3]; and

20 preaching the word to none but unto the Jews only. And some of them
    were men of Cyprus and Cyrene, which, when they were come to Antioch,
21 spake ^qunto the Grecians, preaching ^rthe Lord Jesus. And ^sthe hand
    of the Lord was with them: and a great number believed, and turned
22 ^tunto the Lord. Then tidings of these things came unto the ears of the
    church which was in Jerusalem: and they sent forth ^uBarnabas, that he
23 should go as far as Antioch. Who, when he came, and had seen the
    grace of God, was glad, and ^vexhorted them all, that with purpose of

A. D. 41.

q ch. 6. 1.
r Eph. 3. 8.
s Luke 1. 66.
t ch. 9. 35.
ch. 26. 18.
u ch. 9. 27.
v ch. 13. 43.
ch. 14. 22.
Jude 3, 20.

for nearly a thousand years it continued to be one of the most populous and wealthy cities of the world. It is now a poor miserable place of eighteen thousand inhabitants, of whom only a small proportion are—what the disciples were first called at Antioch—Christians. Of the first introduction of Christianity into this once celebrated city, and its earliest Christian activities, we are now to hear.

20. And some of them were men of Cyprus and Cyrene. Cyrene lay on the southern shore of the Mediterranean, between Carthage and Egypt, where Jews were settled in large numbers (see on ch ii. 10; and compare ch. vi. 9). **which, when they were come to Antioch** [ἐλθόντες]—not 'come in,' or 'had entered' [εἰσελθ.—as in the received text, the *Vulgate* and *Beza*, on very slight authority], **spake unto the Grecians** [ἑλληνιστὰς]—or 'Greek-speaking Jews,' **preaching the Lord Jesus.** But this cannot be what the historian means; for not only had the Gospel been from the first preached to this class of Jews, but these preachers of Cyprus and Cyrene themselves belonged to it; and we had just been told that the word had been preached in Phenice and Cyprus and Antioch to Jews only. Can we suppose, then, that the historian would repeat this statement, with reference to the Greek-speaking Jews of Antioch, as something new and singular; and that he would tell us, besides, that when tidings of the accession of this class to Christ reached Jerusalem, it was deemed so surprising as to demand a special deputation to the spot to examine into it; and that it was to the honour of Barnabas, the deputy despatched to Antioch, that he recognized in these converts a real work of Divine grace? Still, the true reading must be determined, not presumptively, but on evidence. And certainly the weight of external evidence is on the side of the received reading. But that in favour of another reading—'Greeks' [ἕλληνας]—is undoubtedly good; and even if it were less weighty than it is, the internal evidence for it, which is overwhelming, ought to decide the point in its favour. [The external evidence stands thus: ἑλληνιστας is read by א* D** E G, and most others; ἕλληνας is read by א^c A D. The Vulgate and some other versions seem not to distinguish between the two terms, in point of meaning; and while in some of the Greek fathers (as *Chrysostom*) the *text* has the received reading, the *commentary* takes the sense to be not "Grecians," but 'Greeks.'] Accordingly, nearly all the best critics, from *Grotius* downwards, have understood the historian to mean, that these Cypriotic and Cyrenian disciples did a thing never done before—preached the word for the first time to the *uncircumcised Gentiles* of Antioch; and so *Griesbach*, *Lachmann*, and *Tischendorf* have transferred into their text what is manifestly the true reading—'*Greeks.*' But what, it may be asked, moved these preachers to break ground so new? If the question had been put to themselves, probably they would have found no other answer than this,—"We cannot but speak the things which we have seen and heard." And it was enough. What had proved light and life to themselves they

felt certain would prove an equal boon to the great Gentile world. But probably they did not reason the matter at all. The fire burning in their own bosoms would not be pent up. "That which we have seen and heard declare we unto you, that ye may also have fellowship with us, and truly our fellowship is with the Father and with his Son Jesus Christ" (1 John i. 3). What now was their success in this novel field? **21. And the hand of the Lord** [יַד יְהוָה]—His converting power, put forth by His Spirit, was with them: **and a great number believed, and turned unto the Lord**—or [according to the reading of *Lachmann* and *Tischendorf*—πολύς τε ἀριθμὸς ὁ πιστεύσας], 'a great number, who believed, turned to the Lord;' though the evidence for both readings is pretty equal. *These conversions*, be it remembered, *took place* BEFORE *the accession of Cornelius and his party*. Nay, whereas we read of no direct influence which the accession of Cornelius and his house had on the further progress of the Gospel among the Gentiles, there here open upon us operations upon the Gentiles from quite a different quarter, and attended with ever-growing success. In fact, the only great object served by the case of Cornelius was *the formal recognition of the principle, which that case ever afterwards secured*, (see on ch. xv.)

Tidings of these surprising accessions having reached Jerusalem, Barnabas is deputed to examine into them on the spot—The delightful result (22-24). **—22. Then tidings of these things came unto the ears** [Ἠκούσθη εἰς τὰ ὦτα, a peculiar Hebraistic phrase, though not elsewhere occurring in this peculiar form: cf. Isa. v. 9 (LXX.); Matt. x. 27; Luke i. 44; Jas. v. 4] **of the church which was in Jerusalem: and they sent forth Barnabas, that he should go as far as Antioch.** Two notable facts are to be observed here. It was not one of the Twelve who was sent on this delicate mission of enquiry, but—as yet, at least—simply a 'teacher,' of influence at Jerusalem; nor was he sent by the apostles, but by "the church which was in Jerusalem," the apostles at the most presiding and going cordially along with the appointment. Perhaps his being himself a Cypriot might recommend him for an investigation into the proceedings of Cypriot and Cyrenian disciples; but no doubt his personal standing and character at Jerusalem was the main ground of choice; and certainly the result, as given in the following terms, amply justified the selection: **23. Who, when he came, and had seen the grace of God, was glad** [ἐχάρη]—or 'rejoiced,' **and exhorted them all** [παρεκάλει]—an allusion, perhaps, to the name, 'son of exhortation,' given him by the apostles, **that with purpose of heart** (as opposed to a hasty and fickle discipleship) **they would cleave unto the Lord.** Each party seems to have acted towards the other in a beautiful spirit. As for the new converts, instead of regarding Barnabas with prejudice and suspicion, as an intruder on the labours of their own teachers, they, and their teachers themselves, seem to have hailed his visit, and to have put

24 heart they would *ʷ*cleave unto the Lord. For he was a good man, and full of the Holy Ghost and of faith: *ˣ*and much people was added unto the Lord.

25, Then departed Barnabas to *ʸ*Tarsus, for to seek Saul: and when he
26 had found him, he brought him unto Antioch. And it came to pass, that a whole year they assembled themselves ¹with the church, and

A. D. 41.

ʷ Deut. 10. 20.
1 Cor. 15. 58.
Gal. 2. 20.
ˣ ch. 5. 14.
ʸ ch. 9. 30.
1 Or, in the church.

themselves cordially under him as an honoured deputy from the mother Church, who would confirm and advance them in the Faith, the rudiments of which only they had as yet received. But no less admirable was the spirit of Barnabas. Unlike some ecclesiastics of subsequent times—jealous for their own position, and looking with unfriendly eye on the evangelistic labours of simple Christians as irregular and disorderly—this disinterested and noble-minded teacher no sooner saw the grace of God in these uncircumcised converts than he owned it as divine, and rejoiced in it; nor could he find aught at first to do among them, save to exhort them all that (guarding against fickleness) with purpose of heart they would cleave unto the Lord. The question of circumcision seems never to have come up. The reality first, and then the permanence of the grace given to them, seem to have been his whole care; and the historian evidently wishes his readers to regard this as the result of rare spirituality and large-heartedness on the part of Barnabas—adding, as he does, this significant remark, 24. **For he was a good man, and full of the Holy Ghost and of faith.** The sense of "good" here is evidently 'large-hearted' (cf. Rom. v. 7), 'liberal-minded,' rising above narrow Jewish sectarianism; while in virtue of the fulness of the Holy Ghost he clearly discerned and had entire sympathy with the grace of God in these Gentile converts, and in the exercise of his "fulness of faith," he shook himself free from those traditional trammels which might have warped his judgment and blunted his courage. **and much people was added unto the Lord**—such an increase of disciples at that important capital being a Divine seal set upon the beautiful spirit displayed by both parties. Did Barnabas now return to Jerusalem, leaving the work at Antioch in the hands that began it, and just as he found it; or—as Paul afterwards left Titus among the converts at Crete, to "set in order the things that were wanting, and ordain elders in every city" (Tit. i. 5)—did he organize them, and hand over the spiritual care of them to elders ordained from among themselves for that purpose? He did neither of these things. They seem not to have been sufficiently advanced for the *former* plan; and probably Antioch was deemed too important a capital, and the kind of fruit which it had yielded to Christ was of too novel a character, for the *latter* method. Accordingly, Barnabas judged it fit to remain at Antioch, to build up with his hand and extend the work so auspiciously begun. That in doing so he set aside the original preachers, is not for a moment to be supposed; and, as we shall by and by find one of them at least occupying an important post in this church at Antioch, we are safe in concluding that, with the same large-heartedness which actuated him from the first, he associated them with him in his labours. Such at any rate was the vigorous growth of the work, that he was fain to leave it for a time, in order to fetch as an associate the man who, of all others in the Church, was the most fitted to aid him in such a sphere of labour.

Barnabas, finding the work at Antioch too much for him, goes to Tarsus for Saul, with whom he

labours *there for a whole year with much success, and this first of all the Gentile churches is honoured to be the birthplace of the term* CHRISTIANS (25, 26). **25. Then departed Barnabas** — or, 'departed he,' according to the better reading, **to Tarsus**— a short run by sea from Seleucia, which he would probably prefer to the more tedious land-route, which would have obliged him to thread the defiles of the Amanus range of mountains as one rounds the north - east head of the Mediterranean, at the Gulf of Issus. **for to seek Saul**—entrusting the church at Antioch meantime, beyond all doubt, to the honoured brethren to whose instrumentality it had owed its existence. Barnabas had been the first at Jerusalem to recognize the genuineness of Saul's conversion, and, on the first visit of the great convert to Jerusalem after the change, to convince the brethren there that in the dread persecutor they had not an enemy in disguise, but a true brother, and already a mighty preacher of the Faith which once he destroyed (ch. ix. 26, 27). That visit lasted but fifteen days (Gal. i. 18); for such was the boldness of his preaching in the capital, that, to prevent his assassination, the brethren had to hurry him off to Cæsarea, and thence to Tarsus. Probably Barnabas alone discerned, at this early stage of his ministry, those peculiar endowments in the new convert in virtue of which he was to eclipse all others. How he spent his time at Tarsus—at this his first visit to his native city since his conversion, and probably his last—we can but conjecture from incidental notices; but the words that follow, **26. And when he had found him**, may imply that he had been on some evangelistic tour. (For on his way from Cæsarea to Tarsus he appears to have taken the land-route through Syria and Cilicia (see on ch. ix. 30; and cf. Gal. i. 21); and as he was afterwards sent with Judas, Silas, and Barnabas, with the letter of the council at Jerusalem "unto the brethren which were of the Gentiles in Antioch and Syria and Cilicia" (ch. xv. 23), we may not unnaturally conjecture, that having been instrumental in gathering out "brethren" all along Syria and Cilicia, as he passed through them, he was engaged in visiting some of them when Barnabas "found him.") Be this as it may, Saul at once embraces the call, **and he brought him unto Antioch**—the two going lovingly together to the Syrian capital. That Barnabas did not err in his expectations from his young coadjutor, we are now to learn. **And it came to pass, that a whole year they assembled themselves with** [εν]—rather 'in' **the church**, that is, in its meetings, **and taught much people**—they met the believers in all their stated assemblies, taking the lead, no doubt, in their public devotions—though that is not said—but occupying themselves chiefly in "teaching them to observe all things whatsoever Jesus had commanded them." For the teaching committed by the ascending Lord of the Church to His servants (Matt. xxviii. 19, 20) was of two kinds, for which two different words are used—first, "*making disciples*" [μαθητεύειν], and next, *instructing* the disciples so made [διδάσκειν]. And since it is the latter of these departments of ministerial work

taught much people. And the disciples were called Christians first in Antioch.

27 And in these days came [z]prophets from Jerusalem unto Antioch.
28 And there stood up one of them named Agabus, [a]and signified by the Spirit that there should be great dearth throughout all the world: which
29 came to pass in the days of Claudius Cesar. Then the disciples, every man according to his ability, determined to send [b]relief unto the brethren
30 which dwelt in Judea: which also they did, and sent it to the [c]elders by the hands of Barnabas and Saul.

A. D. 43.
[z] ch. 2. 17.
ch. 13. 1.
1 Cor. 12.28.
[a] ch. 21. 10.
Eph. 4. 11.
[b] Rom. 15.26.
1 Cor. 16. 1.
2 Cor. 9. 1.
Gal. 2. 10.
1 Pet. 4. 11.
[c] 1 Pet. 5. 1.

which is here intended, it is the second of the two words which is here employed [διδάξαι]. At the same time, it is clear, from the sequel of this history, that they were no less successful in adding to the church at Antioch than in building it up. And thus in that great and many-sided community there stood forth a church which, for solidity of organization and warm impulsive Christian life, became the first contributor to the necessities of the Jewish brethren, and the great missionary centre for diffusing Christianity among the heathen; and the Gospel there achieved for itself a name which —with whatever intention originally given—will live and be gloried in as long as the world lasts, as the symbol of all that is most precious to the fallen family of man. **And the disciples were called** [χρηματίσαι]—or 'got the name of' **CHRISTIANS first in Antioch.** That this name originated *outside* the Church itself, we may be pretty sure; for we never find the disciples so calling themselves; on the contrary, the apostle Peter refers to it in his first Epistle apparently as a term of reproach ("If any man suffer as a *Christian*, let him not be *ashamed*," 1 Pet. iv. 16); and Agrippa's way of using the term when Paul made his defence before him (ch. xxvi. 28) seems to imply as much. But neither is it likely to have originated with the *Jewish* enemies of the Gospel; for besides that "Nazarene" was the term of contempt used by them (ch. xxiv. 5), as it still is, the name of "Christian" would seem to Jewish ears to imply that these disciples of Jesus were followers of the Messiah—which we may be sure that no unbelieving Jew would even seem to admit. The term, therefore, must have originated with the *heathen* portion of the community, and with the *Latins*, rather than the Greeks of Antioch—as the termination of the word seems to imply (like *Pompeiani, Cæsariani, Herodiani*, as *de Wette*, after *Wetstein*, remarks). But whatever the origin of the term, its import is of more consequence; and doubtless it was intended to express *that* about the Christian Faith which the preachers of it and the disciples of it were perpetually speaking of, and dwelling upon, as their all-in-all—CHRIST. In this view of it— whether owing its origin to Jew or Gentile, Greek or Roman, friend or foe—who can wonder that, once given to them, it was felt to be too appropriate, too beautiful, too dear, to be ever allowed to die?

One other incident only in the history of this beautiful Church of uncircumcised Gentiles at Antioch remains to be noticed, before the historian (after a parenthetical chapter) is prepared to come to its principal characteristic—its missionary character and doings.

Barnabas and Saul are sent to Jerusalem with a contribution from Antioch for the famine-stricken brethren of the circumcision there (27-30). **27. And in these days came prophets**—that is, 'inspired teachers, or persons speaking with supernatural authority;' a class with which we shall frequently meet in the sequel, who sometimes (as on this occasion) foretold future events, though that is not

at all necessarily implied in the use of the term. In the lists of the Divinely instituted Church-offices (1 Cor. xii. 28; Eph. iv. 11) they stand in rank next to the apostles, in virtue of their inspiration, as revealers of the Divine mind, and are associated with them as constituting the Divine authority by which the Church was to be ordered. **from Jerusalem unto Antioch.** This was virtually a Divine recognition of the Gentile Christianity of Antioch, and of the importance of that first of Gentile churches. **28. And there stood up one of them named Agabus, and signified by the Spirit**—by Divine inspiration, **that there should be great dearth** [μεγάλην . . . ἦτις, which is better supported than μέγαν . . . ὅστις of the received text] **throughout all the world** [ὅλην τὴν οἰκουμένην]—the whole Roman empire (see on Luke ii. 1): **which came to pass in the days of Claudius [Cesar].** The word "Cæsar" here is an explanatory gloss, not belonging to the original text (as MSS. and versions make quite clear). 'It appears (says *Humphry*) that the world was much afflicted with scarcity in the reign of Claudius. Four local famines are mentioned: (1.) In his first and second years (A. D. 41), at Rome (*Dio. Cass.* ix. p. 949); (2.) in his fourth year, in Judea (*Joseph.* Antt. xx. 2. 5; *Euseb.* H. E., ii. 8); (3.) in his ninth year, in Greece (*Euseb.* Chron. i. 79); (4.) in his eleventh year, at Rome (*Sueton.* Vit. Claud. xvii. ; *Tacit.* Ann. xii. 42). History does not indeed inform us of an universal famine in the reign of Claudius, any more than it speaks of an universal census under Augustus Cæsar (Luke ii. 1). But universal taxing might be decreed, though but partially carried into effect; and the whole world might suffer dearth in the reign of Claudius, though the famine was intense only at particular times and places.' The one here referred to appears to be the second of the four above enumerated, which took place A. D. 41—*an important date this for tracing out the chronology of the Acts.* (See Introduction.) **29. Then the disciples, every man according to his ability, determined to send relief unto the brethren which dwelt in Judea.** The manner of expression here seems clearly to imply that this spirited proposal originated, not with Barnabas and Saul, but with the disciples themselves, in the spontaneous exercise of Christian love to their suffering brethren of the circumcision—a grace which seems to have shone the brightest in the earliest days of the churches, as it still does in every new community of believers. **30. Which also they did, and sent it to the elders.** Here, for the first time in the Acts, the term "elders" (or 'presbyters') is used to denote an office in the Christian Church. And as no definition is given of its nature and functions, these must be gathered from a comparison of the various passages where it occurs. That it was borrowed from the *synagogue*, and that the Christian churches were constituted after its model, and not that of the *temple*, is beyond reasonable dispute. **by the hands** [χειρός]—rather, 'by the hand' **of Barnabas and Saul**—regarded jointly as one custodier. This

12   NOW about that time Herod the king ¹stretched forth *his* hands to 2 vex certain of the church. And he killed James the brother of John with the sword.

A. D. 44.

CHAP. 12
¹ Or, began.

—the reader should observe—was Saul's *second visit to Jerusalem* after his conversion.

Remarks.—1. We must advert here again to the relation which the Divine recognition of the uncircumcised Gentile believers of Antioch bears to that of Cornelius and his party. This, at Antioch, was the spontaneous outgoing of zeal for Christ and love to the souls of men: that (as *Lechler* well expresses it) was 'the legitimizing of this extra-official activity' by the Lord of the Church. 'God, in Cornelius, and in the apostle Peter (he adds), *sanctioned the principle* of the conversion of the Gentiles; but the first successful inroad into the territory of heathenism—the founding of the metropolis of Gentile Christianity in the Church at Antioch—was effected, not by Peter nor by any other apostle, but by simple members of the Church.' Nor should we overlook the fact, already noted, that when a deputy was sent from Jerusalem to investigate this new state of things, it was not one of the Twelve, but an esteemed and influential "teacher," that was sent; nor did the apostles send him, but "the church which was at Jerusalem," the apostles probably just presiding and going cordially along with the measure. 2. How beautiful is the large-hearted and loving liberality with which both parties treated each other—the Gentile Christians at Antioch, in welcoming a Jewish Christian who might have been supposed to come on an errand not altogether welcome, an errand wearing the appearance at least of distrust; and Barnabas, on his part, in not regarding with suspicion the spontaneous labours of those simple disciples of Cyprus and Cyrene, but, when he "saw the grace of God" in their Gentile converts (as if that had been the one thing to which he looked), recognizing it with joy, and finding at first nothing to do among them but to "exhort them all that with purpose of heart they would cleave unto the Lord." The question of circumcision seems never to come up: he troubles them not on that subject, but simply counsels them to stedfast adherence to the Lord Jesus. And since the historian expressly ascribes this to his rare spirituality and benignant liberality, we cannot fail to draw the inference that characters such as his will be quicker to discern the grace of God in others—in however unusual a way it meets them—than small points of difference between them. 3. What a spectacle does this church at Antioch present at the period to which the close of this chapter brings us! It grows so on the hands of Barnabas that he has to leave it—to the care, no doubt, of those to whom it owed its existence—to fetch Saul from Tarsus as his fellow-labourer; and in the hands of these eminent men it so advances, that, out of ground broken from the hard heathen rock, it becomes a garden of the Lord, a church which, for vigour and enterprise, was fast outstripping that at Jerusalem, and which became the first contributor to the necessities of the saints there, and the originator of missions to the heathen. Indeed, in Jerusalem and throughout Judea, Christianity was regarded as an offshoot from Judaism—a heretical and impious form of it by its enemies, and by its friends as Judaism perfected; and so it would certainly have been regarded at Antioch had the converts there been exclusively Jews or Jewish proselytes. But the novelty of a church consisting of Gentile disciples of a crucified Jew could not fail to attract general

attention; and the name which their fellow-citizens gave them (no matter from what motive) —not Nazarenes, as they were called by the Jews, but CHRISTIANS—marks a memorable era in the development of the great purpose of God, that among the Gentiles was now to be preached the unsearchable riches of Christ.

CHAP. XII. 1-25. — PERSECUTION OF THE CHURCH BY HEROD AGRIPPA I.—MARTYRDOM OF JAMES, AND MIRACULOUS DELIVERANCE OF PETER—MISERABLE END OF HEROD, AND PROGRESS OF THE GOSPEL—BARNABAS AND SAUL RETURN, WITH JOHN MARK, TO ANTIOCH.

Herod persecutes the Church, and puts James, the brother of John, to death (1, 2). **1. Now about that time**—about the time referred to at the close of the preceding chapter. Whether Barnabas and Saul returned to their post at Antioch immediately after executing their commission, or remained throughout the trying period to which this chaper refers, cannot with certainty be determined. But see on *v.* 25. The exact date can only be approximated (see Introduction). **Herod the king.** This was Herod Agrippa I., before whose son—Herod Agrippa II.—Paul made his celebrated defence, (ch. xxvi.) This one was grandson to Herod the Great, being the son of Aristobulus and Berenice (of the Maccabean or Hasmonean line). He was brought up at Rome with Caligula and Claudius. On the accession of Caligula to the empire he obtained from him the dominions of his uncles, Philip and Herod Antipas—Batanæa, Trachonitis, and Auranitis (after the death of Philip); Galilee and Peræa (on the banishment of Antipas to Gaul); and Abilene (of which Lysanias had been tetrarch)— with the title of king. On the accession of Claudius he was further invested with the sovereignty of Samaria and Judea; thus having at length all the dominions over which his grandfather had reigned, and from which he derived an immense revenue. The accuracy of the sacred writer (says *Paley*), in the expressions which he uses here, is remarkable. There was no portion of time for thirty years before, nor ever afterwards, in which there was a king at Jerusalem, or one exercising that authority in Judea and to whom that title could be applied, save this Herod during the last three years of life, within which period the transaction here recorded took place (for his son, though a king, did not reign over Judea). From *Josephus* we learn that his characteristics were, not the cruelty of Herod the Great, nor the licentiousness of his uncle Herod Antipas, but rigidity in his observance of Jewish rites, gentleness, beneficence, and love of popularity. Plainly it was this last characteristic, combined with the first, which prompted the persecuting acts recorded in the first part of the chapter, while the vain-glorious exhibition related in the latter part of it is easily explained by the last characteristic. As we learn from the same Jewish historian that he resided for the most part at Jerusalem, we can easily see how ready he would be to listen to the complaints of the irritated Jewish rulers regarding the progress which the Gospel was making even in the capital, and to their urgent solicitations for his royal interposition to put a stop to it. **stretched forth his hands to vex certain of the church** [ἐπέβαλεν τ. χεῖρας κακῶσαί τινας τῶν ἀπὸ τ. ἐκκλ.]—laid hands on certain of those who were of the Church, to 'vex or injure them.' The peculiar expression, 'certain of those who were of the Church,' cannot justly be

3 And because he saw it pleased the Jews, he proceeded further to take
4 Peter also. (Then were *a* the days of unleavened bread.) And *b* when he had apprehended him, he put *him* in prison, and delivered *him* to four quaternions of soldiers to keep him; intending after Easter to bring him
5 forth to the people. Peter therefore was kept in prison: but ² prayer was made without ceasing of the church unto God for him.
6 And when Herod would have brought him forth, the same night Peter was sleeping between two soldiers, bound with two chains: and the

A. D. 44.

a Ex. 12. 14.
b John 21. 18.
2 Or. instant and earnest prayer was made.
2 Cor. 1. 11.
Eph. 6. 18.

---

taken to mean those who held office in it (as *Webster and Wilkinson*, referring to some ancient versions which so render it). It seems, as in ch. vi. 9, to mean merely 'certain persons belonging to the Church.' Herod did not think of setting on foot, in the first instance, any general persecution against the Christian body; but if an example were made of its most distinguished leaders, he probably supposed that this would suffice to disperse, if not extinguish it. 2. *And he killed James the brother of John with the sword*—in all likelihood by beheading, which (as *Lightfoot* shows) was regarded by the Jews as the extreme of ignominy. Of this elder James we know nothing, except what we read in the Gospels and here—that he was one of the three who, of all the Twelve, were alone privileged to witness the transfiguration, the resurrection of Jairus' daughter, and the agony in the garden; that he and his younger brother John were called by their Master 'sons of thunder;' that through their mother they applied for the right and left-hand posts of honour in the expected kingdom; and that, when asked if they were able to drink of their Master's cup and be baptized with His baptism, and replying that they were, Jesus told them they should indeed have that to do, but that what they sought was under other arrangement: finally, we have James here, as a martyr of Jesus, indeed drinking of his Master's cup and with his bloody baptism at length baptized. One wonders that we have no account of his apostolic labours, and that while Stephen's death is so circumstantially recorded, that of James is disposed of in one brief verse. Of this latter circumstance several explanations have been given. But as the Baptist was privately and summarily despatched, and his death recorded in a few brief words (Mark vi. 27), the probability is, that the slaughter of James was equally summary, and embraced no particulars of interest. As to his apostolic labours—since of "the first three" of the apostles, *Peter*, engrossed with the public work of his Master, could take no oversight of the Church at Jerusalem, and *John*, the other member of this triumvirate, always accompanied Peter—the principal charge of the church in Jerusalem would devolve on this elder *James;* and though his labour in this capacity would be too quiet to yield historical materials worthy of preservation in this book, his fervid character, now mellowed, with his position among the Twelve, would gain him the esteem and love of the Church, and make his value to the Christian cause in Jerusalem so well known to those who sought its destruction, that they would give Herod no rest until he consented to rid them of this obnoxious head of the Christian interest at the capital.

Herod apprehends Peter, to slay him also—His miraculous deliverance and departure from Jerusalem (3-19). He could spring only upon one more prized victim; and, flushed with their first success, they prevail upon Herod to seize him too. 3. *And because he saw it pleased the Jews*—popularity being his ruling passion, *he proceeded further to take Peter also*—whose loss, at this stage of the

Church, though not so irreparable as it would have been at an earlier stage, would, besides other great evils, have deprived us of his inestimable First Epistle, not to speak of the Second. *Then were the days of unleavened bread* [αἰ before ἡμέραι, though not required, is well attested]. See on Mark xiv. 1. This is here mentioned to prepare the reader for the delay of his execution, and what grew out of this, about to be related. 4. *And when he had apprehended him, he put him in prison, and delivered him to four quaternions of soldiers to keep him*—that is, to four parties of four each, corresponding to the four Roman watches; two watching in prison and two at the gates, and each party being on duty for the space of one watch. *intending after Easter* [μετὰ τὸ πάσχα]—it should be, 'after the passover;' that is, after the conclusion of the festival. (The word employed in our authorized version being an ecclesiastical term of later date, is improperly used here.) *to bring him forth* [ἀναγαγεῖν]—or, 'bring him up,' to the people—but scarcely for trial: it probably means 'to bring him up' aloft to the view of the people in his execution; for the people were getting as virulent in their opposition to Christians as the rulers. And as the more private and summary execution of James may have been complained of as not having effect enough, Herod determines to gratify both rulers and people with the public spectacle of the slaughter of Peter. But because there was a prejudice against trying or putting any one to death during the currency of a religious festival, 5. *Peter therefore was kept in prison*—till the festival should close; little thinking that his own end was nearer than Peter's (as *Hackett* well remarks). *but prayer was made without ceasing* [ἦν ἐκτενὴς γινομένη]—'instant,' 'earnest,' 'urgent prayer continued to be made' *of the church*—not in public assembly, for it was evidently not safe to meet thus, but in little groups in private houses, one of which was Mary's (v. 12). And this was kept up during all the seven days of unleavened bread. *unto God for him*—[περὶ is fully better attested, and more probable than ὑπὲρ of the received text.] No doubt it was for his deliverance that they prayed.

6. *And when Herod would have brought him forth* [ἔμελλεν . . . προάγειν]—'was going to bring him forth,' *the same night*—but a few hours, therefore, before his intended execution. Thus long were the disciples kept waiting—their prayers apparently unavailing, and their faith, as would seem from the sequel, waxing feeble. Such, however, is the *law* of God's procedure (Deut. xxxii. 36; and see on Luke v. 1-11, Remark 1; on John xi., Remark 4; and on John xxi. 3). *Peter was sleeping between two soldiers, bound with two chains: and the keepers before the door kept the prison.* Roman prisoners had a chain fastened at one end to the wrist of their right hand, and at the other to the wrist of a soldier's left hand, leaving the right arm of the keeper free, in case of any attempt to escape. For greater security, the prisoner was sometimes,

7 keepers before the door kept the prison. And, behold, *c*the angel of the Lord came upon *him*, and a light shined in the prison: and he smote Peter on the side, and raised him up, saying, Arise up quickly. And his

8 chains fell off from *his* hands. And the angel said unto him, Gird thyself, and bind on thy sandals. And so he did. And he saith unto him,

9 Cast thy garment about thee, and follow me. And he went out, and followed him; and *d*wist not that it was true which was done by the

10 angel; but thought he *e*saw a vision. When they were past the first and the second ward, they came unto the iron gate that leadeth unto the city; which *f*opened to them of his own accord: and they went out, and passed on through one street; and forthwith the angel departed from him.

11 And when Peter was come to himself, he said, Now I know of a surety, that *g*the Lord hath sent his angel, and *h*hath delivered me out of the hand of Herod, and *from* all the expectation of the people of the Jews.

12 And when he had considered *the thing*, he *i*came to the house of Mary the mother of *j*John, whose surname was Mark; where many were

13 gathered together praying. And as Peter knocked at the door of the

14 gate, a damsel came *3*to hearken, named Rhoda. And when she knew

A. D. 44.
c Ps. 34. 7.
Isa. 37. 36.
Dan. 6. 22.
ch. 5. 19.
Heb 1. 14.
d Ps. 126. 1.
e ch. 10. 3.
Heb. 1. 14.
f ch. 16. 26.
g Ps. 34. 7.
Dan. 3. 27.
Dan. 6. 22.
h Job 5. 19.
Ps. 33. 18.
Ps. 41. 2.
Ps. 97. 10.
2 Cor. 1. 8-10.
2 Pet. 2. 9.
i ch. 4. 23.
j ch. 15. 37.
3 Or, to ask who was there.

---

as here, chained to two soldiers, one on each side. (See ch. xxi. 33.) Ye think your prey secure, bloodthirsty priests, and thou obsequious tyrant, who to "please the Jews," hast shut in this most eminent of the servants of Christ within double gates, guarded by double sentinels, while double keepers and double chains seem to defy all rescue! So thought the chief priests, who "made the sepulchre of the Lord sure, sealing the stone and setting a watch." But "He that sitteth in the heavens shall laugh at you." Meanwhile, Peter is "sleeping!" In a few hours he expects a stingless death; "neither counts he his life dear unto him, so that he may finish his course with joy, and the ministry which he has received of the Lord Jesus." In this frame of spirit he has dropt asleep, and lies the picture of peace. **7. And, behold, the angel** (rather, ' an angel ') **of the Lord came upon him**—expressive of the suddenness and unexpectedness of the visit (compare Luke ii. 9, and ch. xxiii. 11). **and a light shined in the prison** [ἐν τῷ οἰκήματι]—' in the chamber;' not the prison-house at large, but the cell in which Peter lay. **and he smote Peter on the side, and raised him up, saying, Arise up quickly. And his chains fell off from his hands. 8. And the angel said unto him, Gird thyself** [Ζῶσαι is better than περίζ.— of the received text; and so *Lachmann* and *Tischendorf*], **and bind on thy sandals. And so he did. And he saith unto him, Cast thy garment about thee** [τὸ ἱμάτιον]—his tunic, which he had thrown off for the night, **and follow me.** In such graphic minuteness of detail we have a charming mark of reality; while the rapidity and curtness of the orders, and the promptitude with which they were obeyed, betoken the despatch which, in the circumstances, was necessary. **9. And he went out, and followed [him]** [αὐτῷ is probably not genuine, though, of course, understood]; **and wist not that it was true which was done by the angel; but thought he saw a vision**—so little did the apostle look for deliverance! **10. When they were past the first and the second ward** [Διελθόντες δὲ πρώτην φυλακὴν κ. τ. λ.]—' When they had passed through the first and second guard.' The English reader is apt to think that it is places of confinement that are here meant, whereas it is guards of soldiers *through* whom they had to pass. **they came unto the iron gate that leadeth unto the city.** We can only conjecture the details here

alluded to, not knowing the plan and position of the prison. **and they went out, and passed on through one street; and forthwith the angel departed from him**—that is, as soon as he had placed him beyond pursuit. Thus, "He disappointeth the devices of the crafty, so that their hands cannot perform their enterprise" (Job v. 12). **11. And when Peter was come to himself**—when he had recovered from his bewilderment, and had time to look back upon all the steps that had followed each other in such rapid succession, **he said, Now I know of a surety, that the Lord hath sent his angel, and hath delivered me out of the hand of Herod, and from all the expectation of the people of the Jews**—another evidence that Peter expected nothing on this occasion but to seal his testimony with his blood.

12. And when he had considered the thing, he came to the house of Mary the mother of John, whose surname was Mark—who was so called to distinguish him from the apostle of that name, as Mary is so described here to distinguish her from the other Maries. That this Mark was the writer of the second Gospel, though generally supposed, we have given our grounds for questioning. (Introduction to that Gospel, p. xxxiii.) This Mary 'must (as *Webster and Wilkinson* remark) have had a house of some pretensions to receive a large number; and, accordingly, we read that her brother Barnabas (Col. iv. 10) was a person of substance (ch. iv. 37). She must also have been distinguished for faith and courage, to allow such a meeting in the face of persecution.' To such a house it was natural that Peter should come. **where many were gathered together praying**—doubtless for Peter's deliverance, and continuing, no doubt, on this the last of the days of unleavened bread, which was their last hope, all night in prayer to God. **13. And as Peter**—rather, 'as he' (according to the better reading) **knocked at the door of the gate, a damsel came to hearken**—not to open (for neither was this a time, nor an hour of the night, for that) but to listen who was there. The word [ὑπακούω] signifies to answer a knock at the door. **named Rhoda.** With a charming simplicity the name of this girl is recorded—familiar, probably, at the time among the disciples at Jerusalem as the person who played so important a part in this scene, and here preserved for all time to her honour. **14. And when she knew Peter's voice. He had** before (says *Humphry*) been so recognized (Matt.

81

Peter's voice, she opened not the gate for gladness, but ran in, and told
15 how Peter stood before the gate. And they said unto her, Thou art mad. But she constantly·affirmed that it was even so. Then said they, It *k* is
16 his angel. But Peter continued knocking: and when they had opened
17 *the door*, and saw him, they were astonished. But he, beckoning unto them with the hand to hold their peace, declared unto them how the Lord had brought him out of the prison. And he said, Go show these things unto James, and to the brethren. And he departed, and went into another place.
18 Now as soon as it was day, there was no small stir among the soldiers,
19 what was become of Peter. And when Herod had sought for him, and found him not, he examined the keepers, and commanded that *they* should be put to death. And he went down from Judea to Cesarea, and *there* abode.
20 And Herod [4] was highly displeased with them of Tyre and Sidon: but they came with one accord to him, and, having made Blastus [5] the king's chamberlain their friend, desired peace; because *l* their country was
21 nourished by the king's *country*. And upon a set day Herod, arrayed in royal apparel, sat upon his throne, and made an oration unto them.

A. D. 44.

k Gen. 48. 16.
Matt. 18.10.
Luke 24.37, 38.
[4] Or, bare an hostile mind, intending war.
[5] that was over the king's bedchamber.
l 1 Ki. 5. 9.
2 Chr. 2. 10, 15.
Ezra 3. 7.
Eze. 27. 17.
Hos. 2. 8, 9.
Amos 4. 6, 9.
Hag. 1. 8-11.
Hag. 2. 16.

xxvi. 73). **she opened not the gate for gladness, but ran in, and told how Peter stood before the gate.** How exquisitely natural is this part of the narrative! **15. And they said unto her, Thou art mad**—one of those exclamations which onê can harldly resist on hearing what seems far 'too good to be true.' **But she constantly affirmed** [δϊσχυρί-ζετο]—'persisted in affirming' **that it was even so. Then said they, It is his angel**—his disembodied spirit, his ghost; anything, in fact, rather than himself. Strange, that though this had been the burden of their fervent prayers, during all the days of unleavened bread, they dispute themselves out of it as a thing incredible. Still, it is but like the unbelief of the disciples who ." believed not *for joy* and wondered " at the tidings of their Lord's resurrection. **16. But Peter continued knocking**—delay being dangerous : **and when they had opened the door, and saw him, they were astonished. 17. But he, beckoning unto them with the hand to hold their peace.** A lively touch this. In the hubbub of joyful and wondering interrogatories there might mingle reflections, thrown out by one against another, for holding out so long against the testimony of Rhoda; while the emotion of the apostle's own spirit would be too deep and solemn to take part in such demonstrations, or to utter a word till, with his hand, he had signified his wish for perfect silence. **declared unto them how the Lord had brought him out of the prison. And he said, Go show these things unto James, and to the brethren.** Whether this was James the Less, the son of Alphæus, or "James the Lord's brother," or whether these were the same or two different persons—the latter an extremely difficult question—see on ch. xv. 13. However these questions be answered, the James here meant must have been singled out as being then at the head of the Church in Jerusalem, which we find him to be both in ch. xv. 13 and in ch. xxi. 18. **And he departed, and went into another place**—according to his Lord's express command (Matt. x. 23). When told, on a former miraculous liberation from prison, to go and speak unto the people (ch. v. 20), he did it; but in this case, to present himself in public would have been to tempt God by rushing upon certain destruction. To what place the apostle retired is quite uncertain. Romish critics conjecture (as might be supposed) that he went to Rome—an exceedingly improbable con-

jecture. *Bengel's* is much more likely, that it was some place that lay at no great distance. But, be this as it may, it is to be observed that here *all history of the apostle Peter terminates in the Acts.* He re-appears at ch. xv. as a principal speaker in the council at Jerusalem ; but of his apostolic proceedings no further account is given. Another has come upon the stage, whose proceedings it is our historian's chief object to relate. **18. Now as soon as it was day.** His deliverance must have been during the fourth and last watch of the night—from three to six A.M., else he must have been missed by the keepers at the change of the watch (as *Wieseler* remarks). **there was no small stir among the soldiers, what was become of Peter. 19. And when Herod had sought for him, and found him not, he examined** [ἀνακρίνας]—sat in judgment upon the keepers—who, either like the keepers of our Lord's sepulchre, had "shaken, and become as dead men" (Matt. xxviii. 4), or had slept on their watch and been divinely kept from awaking, **and commanded that they should be put to death.** Impotent vengeance! **And he** (Herod) **went down from Judea to Cesarea** —to preside (as we shall see from *Josephus* presently) at the games there celebrated in honour of his friend and patron Claudius, **and there abode.**

Herod's miserable end—Progress of the Gospel (20-24). **20. And Herod was highly displeased** with [θνμωμαχῶν]—'bore a hostile grudge' at (as in the *margin*), **them of Tyre and Sidon**—for some reason unknown ; but the effect of this on their commercial relations made the latter glad to sue for peace. **but they came with one accord to him, and, having made Blastus the king's chamberlain their friend, desired peace; because their country was nourished by the king's country**—as of old. Thus (Ezek. xxvii. 17) "Judah and the land of Israel, they were thy merchants [O Tyre!], they traded in thy market wheat," &c. Solomon and Zerubbabel got the Tyrians to send them cedars from Lebanon for the building of the first and second temples, for which they paid in grain (1 Ki. v. 9; Ezra iii. 7). Perhaps the famine (ch. xi. 28) had some effect in bringing about the reconciliation. **21. And upon a set day Herod, arrayed in royal apparel, sat upon his throne** [βήματος]—'his tribunal,' erected (if we

22 And the people gave a shout, *saying, It* [m] *is* the voice of a god, and not
23 of a man. And immediately the angel of the Lord [n] smote him, because
[o] he gave not God the glory: and he was eaten of worms, and gave up the
ghost.
24, But [p] the word of God grew and multiplied. And Barnabas and Saul

A. D. 44.

[m] Jude 16.
[n] 1 Sam. 25. 38.
[o] Ps. 115. 1.
[p] Isa. 55. 11.

suppose *Josephus* to be correct in this detail) in the theatre, and made an oration unto them—to the Tyrian and Sidonian deputies, but in presence of the people. **22. And the people gave a shout, saying, It is the voice of a god, and not of a man. 23. And immediately the (or 'an') angel of the Lord smote him, because [ἀνθ' ὦν] he gave not God the glory: and he was eaten of worms, and gave up the ghost.** The medical precision of the phrase here employed to describe Herod's disease [γενόμενος σκωληκόβρωτος] — in which it has the advantage of *Josephus's*—has been often remarked on, as coming naturally from "the beloved physician." It is remarkable that this Herod's grandfather, Herod the Great, died of the same horrible disease. *Josephus's* account of Herod's death (Antt. xix. 8. 2) strikingly confirms that of our historian. According to him, Herod was at Cæsarea (as Luke represents him to be), presiding over the games in honour of Cæsar. On the second day of the games, the theatre being filled to the ceiling, Agrippa entered at daybreak, clothed in a robe all inwrought with silver, on which the rays of the morning sun alighting, he appeared as if all irradiated with glory: voices here and there saluted him as a god; and on his making an oration to them, they shouted, We have taken thee for a man, but henceforth we recognize in thee a god! The king rebuked them not, nor showed any displeasure at this impiety; but after awhile, looking up, he saw an owl perched on a rope over his head, and immediately, taking this for an ill omen, he was filled with remorse, and seized with violent pain in his bowels, exclaiming to his friends, Your god is already come to his life's end, and he whom you saluted immortal is going away to die. To such a height did the pain rise, that he had to be carried hastily into the palace, where, after five days' torture, he expired in his fifty-fourth year. The slight difference between this account and Luke's tends only to confirm the accuracy of it.

24. But the word of God grew and multiplied —*q. d.*, 'Not only was the royal persecutor ignominiously swept from the stage, while his intended victim was spared to the Church, but the cause which he and his Jewish instigators sought to crush was only furthered and glorified.'

Return of Barnabas and Saul, with John Mark, to Antioch. **25. And Barnabas and Saul returned from Jerusalem.** It is impossible to determine with certainty whether they came to Jerusalem before, during, or after Herod's proceedings against James and Peter. Critics are divided between the first and last suppositions. But the natural inference from the language of the historian is that they arrived before it, in which case it must have been just before it; and as their mission would be soon fulfilled, they probably kept themselves quiet, and left as soon as Herod departed for Cæsarea. **when they had fulfilled their ministry** [τ. διακονίαν] or 'service;' referring to the contribution from Antioch for the distressed brethren at Jerusalem, which they went thither to deliver (ch. xi. 29, 30). **and took with them John, whose surname was Mark.** Being nephew to Barnabas (Col. i. 10), the proposal to take him was probably in consequence both of his own application and of the opinion which

his uncle had formed of him (see on ch. xv. 37-39).

Remarks.—1. The artless simplicity with which the minute details of this remarkable chapter are related attests their historical accuracy. At the same time (to use the words of *Humphry*) 'it is highly dramatic, resembling the plot of an ancient tragedy; the principal incidents being—the death of one apostle, the deliverance of another, the recognition of Peter by Rhoda, his restoration to the anxious disciples, the chagrin of the baffled persecutor, his exaltation, speedily followed by the catastrophe of his death, with the triumphant close, "but the word of God grew and multiplied."' But the subsidiary incidents are no less stirring—the delay of the Divine interposition in behalf of Peter, up to the last watch of the last night of the last of the days of unleavened bread; the keeping up of the prayers of the Church for him to the very last; the arrival of Peter at the door of the house where many, at the last hour of the night, were in the act of prayer for him, and yet the difficulty of convincing them that it was he; the angelic ministration by which this deliverance was wrought in every step of it, and the celestial ease with which, at a touch, chains fell off, guards were passed, and iron gates flew open of themselves; the shifting of the scene to Cæsarea, and of the reader's interest, from the persecuted Christians to the persecuting king; his successful negotiation with the deputies from Tyre and Sidon, his elation, his pompous appearance, his royal apparel, and his oration to them from his tribunal before the people; their acclamation to him as a god, the immediateness of the Divine vengeance taken upon him for his impiety, the loathsomeness of the disease with which he was smitten, and the rapidity with which he came to his miserable end. While these diversified incidents have all the stirring interest of a deep-laid tragedy, they carry with them such an air of quiet naturalness and entire simplicity, that the unsophisticated reader is unable to doubt that he has before him a piece of authentic history. 2. As this book records the extension of the Gospel by distinct steps from Jerusalem to Judea and Samaria, and from thence to the uttermost part of the earth, so it exhibits the hostility to the Gospel—first, of the Jewish ecclesiastics (ch. iii.-v.); next, of them and the people combined (ch. vi.-viii. 3); and finally, of both these and the king at their head. The chief priests and elders and scribes stirred up the people, and the king pandered to the malignant passions of both, for his own ends. But He who "stayeth His rough wind in the day of the east wind" (Isa. xxvii. 8) vouchsafed, in pity to His infant cause, a breathing time between each of these hostile assaults. After the first dismissal of the apostles from the Jewish council, and the fresh descent of the Spirit upon the assembled believers, in answer to prayer, their numbers greatly multiplied, their love and liberality flowed forth, the presence of the Lord in the midst of them was manifested with terrible vividness, an awe of them seemed to rest upon the whole community, and the astounding miracles of the apostles upon the sick of the surrounding towns could not fail to spread the name and fame of their cause far and wide, (ch. iv., v.) The subsequent miraculous liberation of the apostles from

25 returned from Jerusalem, when they had fulfilled *their* [6] ministry, and took with them John, whose surname was Mark.

prison and their growing boldness in proclaiming the Gospel, the election of deacons (by which the different interests of the believers were adjusted and their love preserved), and finally, the power and success of a new witness for the truth in the person of Stephen, so strengthened the Church that, when the people joined with their rulers in putting Stephen to death, and Saul proceeded by terrible measures to extirpate them, root and branch, even this, so far from succeeding, only scattered the seed; nor did their numbers even in Jerusalem seem to diminish. Believers were soon found in plenty, not only in Samaria and throughout Judea, but in Africa and along the Mediterranean coast, in Phenicia and Antioch; and at Antioch the first church of the Gentiles was planted, whence went forth the Gospel, by successive missionary deputations, to Gentiles far and wide. And the dread inquisitor, Saul of Tarsus, was himself converted; and by his preaching, even at the hazard of his life, gave glorious earnest of what he was yet to achieve for the Gospel of Christ. Cornelius also, and his party, being solemnly and formally admitted into the Church without circumcision, preparation was then made for Jesus becoming, on the widest scale, a light to lighten the Gentiles as well as the glory of His people Israel. Thus was the Church prepared to abide the third and, apparently, most formidable onslaught upon it—by priests, people, and king combined. And how unscathed did it come forth from this furnace! James, the brother of John, was indeed 'chased up to heaven' by it; but as for his murderer, "the angel of the Lord chased him, and destruction came upon him at unawares." "This is the portion of a wicked man with God, and the heritage of oppressors, which they shall receive of the Almighty" (Ps. xxxv. 5, 8; Job xxvii. 13). 3. One cannot but be struck with the close resemblance which the martyrdom of James by one Herod bears to that of the Baptist by another. Both fell a sacrifice to their fidelity to the cause to which they had consecrated their lives; both were distinguished by peculiar marks of their Master's regard; and yet no interposition was made by Him in behalf of either, and both were slaughtered ruthlessly—the one certainly, and the other probably, in private—and no details of the death of either have been left on record. It is indeed recorded by *Eusebius* (E. H. ii. 9), on the testimony of Clement of Alexandria, who gives it as a credible tradition, that the officer who led him forth to be tried, struck with his testimony, confessed himself a Christian, and was led away with him to execution, asked his forgiveness, got from him the kiss of peace, and along with him sealed his testimony with his blood. It may be so, and certainly such things did happen more than once at a later period; but it cannot be implicitly relied on. At all events, such dark passages in the Divine administration are not few in number. "Thy way is in the sea, and thy path in the great waters, and thy footsteps are not known" (Ps. lxxvii. 19); but "as for God, His way is perfect: the word of the Lord is tried: He is a buckler to all those that trust in him" (Ps. xviii. 30). See on Mark vi. 14-29, Remark 4, p. 158. 4. If the permitted slaughter of James, after that of Stephen, had any effect in shaking the faith of the disciples at Jerusalem, the marvellous interposition in behalf of Peter would at least convince them that his death was owing neither to want of power to deliver him, nor to want of interest on high in their struggling cause. And as

they reflected on the position occupied by the two apostles, they would probably persuade themselves that the work of James on earth was perhaps done, that his place could be more easily supplied than that of Peter, and that this great instrument had been spared a little longer because "the Lord had need of him." And so they might sing—alike of the death *permitted* in the one case and in the other *averted*—"Precious in the sight of the Lord is the death of his saints" (Ps. cxvi. 15). 5. The efficacy of prayer receives singularly vivid illustration from this deliverance of Peter. The prayers of a few parties of persecuted Christians meeting in private houses—of which this of Mary's, though probably the principal, was but one—entering into the ears of the Lord of sabaoth, sent down the angel, whose touch snapped the chains of Peter, eluded the vigilance of four quaternions of soldiers, enabled him to thread the guards, threw open the iron gate, and set the apostle in safety. But the delay of this answer to their prayers to the very last moment is quite as instructive as the glorious response given to it at the last. Of course, this was to try their faith and patience in prayer; and it did so try them, that though they kept on praying, and the night before the expected execution continued all night in prayer to God, their reception of the report that Peter was at the door showed how low their hopes of his deliverance' had come. Indeed, we often pray for what we can hardly credit the bestowment of, when it comes in answer to our prayers. Yet this argues not so much downright unbelief as that kind of it incident to the best, in this land of shadows, which perceives not so clearly as it might how very near heaven and earth—the Lord and His praying people—are to each other. Truly, the lesson of that parable of Jesus, to the end "that men ought always to pray, and *not to faint*," is hard to learn; insomuch that "when the Son of man cometh, shall He find faith on the earth" (any belief that He is coming at all)? See on Luke xviii. 1-8, and Remarks on that Section. 6. How beautiful is the picture of Peter—the night before his expected execution, and up to the moment when deliverance came to him from heaven—sleeping between two soldiers bound with two chains, while the keepers before the door kept the prison! The slaves of a scepticism that is blind to the glory of everything supernatural obtrude upon us their pitiful theories of a flash of lightning loosing Peter's chains, or of the jailor, false to his charge, setting him free; while a later school of them, tired of such trifling with common sense, do violence to all ancient historical testimony, and all true internal evidence, by endeavouring to disprove the genuineness and credibility of the record itself. And these are the writers who lay claim to the exclusive possession of 'critical feeling!' But the time is coming when such criticism will be consigned to oblivion; nor would it be noticed here but for the wave of rationalistic scepticism which, sweeping across from Germany to England, has, by a variety of circumstances, had the effect of unsettling the faith of some able and earnest men. 6. How strikingly and variedly is the ministry of angels brought out in this chapter. 'It suffices not the angel (says *Lechler*, quoting from another author) to rescue the person of the apostle: he faithfully and carefully condescends to every want of the sleeping Peter. First, he awakens him, then he speaks to him as a mother who dresses her sleepy child; girdle, shoes, cloak—things which to an angel might be trifling—he hands to him (as it were) and

13 NOW there were *^a* in the church that was at Antioch certain prophets and teachers; as *^b* Barnabas, and Simeon that was called Niger, and Lucius of Cyrene, and Manaen, which had been brought up

A. D. 45.

CHAP. 13.
a ch. 14. 26.
b ch. 11. 22

helps him to put on. Nothing of his effects should be left behind, that his departure may not be like the flight of a criminal.' Turning from Peter to Herod, and from Jerusalem to Cæsarea, we find angels engaged in another kind of ministration—smiting the vain-glorious tyrant with a loathsome disease at the moment of his greatest elevation, and hurrying him to his grave. "The angel of the Lord encampeth round about them that fear him, and delivereth them. O taste and see that the Lord is good: blessed is the man that trusteth in him" (Ps. xxxiv. 7, 8); whereas "He taketh the wise in their own craftiness; and the counsel of the froward is carried headlong" (Job v. 13).

CHAP. XIII.-XXVIII.—("**YE SHALL BE MY WITNESSES . . . UNTO THE UTTERMOST PART OF THE EARTH,**" Ch. i. 8.)

CHAP. XIII. 1-4.—THE CHURCH AT ANTIOCH —BARNABAS AND SAUL, CALLED OF THE HOLY GHOST TO LABOUR AMONG THE GENTILES, ARE BY THAT CHURCH SET APART AND SENT FORTH. 'The first seven chapters of this book (says *Baumgarten*) might be entitled, The Church *among the Jews;* the next five (viii.-xii.), The Church *in Transition from Jews to Gentiles;* and the last sixteen (xiii.-xxviii.), The Church *among the Gentiles.*' Though Christianity had already spread beyond the limits of Palestine, still the Church (to use the words of *Olshausen*) continued a stranger to *formal* missionary effort. Casual occurrences, particularly the persecution at Jerusalem (ch. viii. 2), had hitherto brought about the diffusion of the Gospel. It was from Antioch that teachers were first sent forth with the definite purpose of spreading Christianity, and organizing churches with regular institutions (ch. xiv. 23).

State of the church at Antioch—Call, ordination, and dismission of Barnabas and Saul as missionaries to the heathen (1-4). **1. Now there were in the church that was at Antioch certain prophets and teachers; as Barnabas, and Simeon that was called Niger, and Lucius of Cyrene, and Manaen, which had been brought up with Herod the tetrarch, and Saul.** This whole verse should read thus: 'Now there were at Antioch, in the church that was there [Ἦσαν δὲ τινες ἐν Ἀντιοχείᾳ κατὰ τ. οὖσαν ἐκκλησίαν], prophets and teachers; both Barnabas and Simeon called Niger, and Lucius the Cyrenæan [ὁ Κυρηναῖος], and Manaen, foster-brother of Herod the tetrarch, and Saul.' The word "certain" [τινες] is with reason excluded from the text by *Lachmann and Tischendorf.* It is at least unnecessary. Our version, by prefixing "as" to the five names given in this verse, conveys to the English reader the impression that there were more prophets and teachers at Antioch than these five; whereas the historian's phrase [ὅ τε] is intended to express the reverse of this—namely, that these five were the whole number: just as in ch. i. 13, where the same phrase is rendered "both" (though in modern English we apply "both" only to two). The word we have rendered 'foster-brother' [σύντροφος], though sometimes used in the wide sense of 'a comrade in youth,' ordinarily denotes 'one suckled at the same breast;' and the best critics so understand it here. These five names deserve notice. *Barnabas* is named first, no doubt as occupying the chief place at that time in the church of Antioch, while *Saul*—as having come last on this field, and possibly also as the youngest of the five—is last named. Of the three

intermediate names, just enough is said to enable us with tolerable certainty to identify them. To begin with the middle one—" *Lucius,*" the same probably to whom Paul sends a salutation in his Epistle to the Romans (ch. xvi. 21), here called "the Cyrenæan," as if by that name he would be at once recognized—this man must have been one of those "Cypriots and Cyrenæans," by whom the Gospel was first brought to Antioch (ch. xi. 20). Though but a simple "disciple," when persecution drove him from Jerusalem, he had given evidence, when associated with Barnabas and Saul in the care of the church at Antioch, of capacity for the higher departments of the Christian ministry, and having "purchased to himself a good degree," had been at length endowed from on high with the prophetical gift. Coming next to "*Simeon*" (of whom we know nothing beyond what is here stated), if he was called "Niger" from his tawny complexion, may we not conclude that he also was from the warm south, and one of those to whom Antioch first owed the Gospel? In connection with the remaining name, "*Manaen,*" the same as "Menahem," one of the kings of Israel (2 Ki. xv. 14), a singular fact is added. One wonders to find that among the prophets and teachers of a Christian church at Antioch was the 'foster-brother' of so licentious and cruel a character as Herod the tetrarch. But is it much more surprising than to find among the blessed women who accompanied the Lord Jesus Himself, in one of His preaching tours through Galilee, and ministered to Him of their substance, "Joanna, the wife of Chuza, *Herod's steward?*" (See on Luke viii. 1-3.) If this Manaen was attracted to Peræa after his foster-brother's accession to power, he might have heard the Gospel from the lips of Christ Himself when He sojourned there, or from one of His disciples; and if he came to Jerusalem among the multitudes who flocked to it at Pentecost, and was one of the thousands of converts during those first days of the Gospel, remaining with them till driven thence by persecution, he may just as well have joined the small party who found their way to Antioch as have gone anywhere else, and may have been honoured, along with them, to plant the standard of the Cross there. And if so, then *in the five men here named we have just the original founders of the church at Antioch* (three of them at least), with Barnabas, to whom all would look up, and Saul, who was soon to eclipse even him. How differently did these two foster-brothers turn out—the one, abandoned to a licentious life and stained with the blood of the most distinguished of God's prophets, though not without his fits of reformation and seasons of remorse; the other, a devoted disciple of the Lord Jesus, and prophet of the Church at Antioch! But this is only what may be seen in every age: "Even so, Father, for so it seemeth good in thy sight." With respect to the two offices here mentioned, the "prophets" of the New Testament, as we have seen (on ch. xi. 27), did not necessarily predict future events, though they often did so. They were simply inspired persons, immediately revealing by the Spirit the mind of the great Head of the Church. Hence, in the lists of the New Testament offices, they stand always next to the apostles, as along with them giving law to the Christian Church—"First, apostles; secondarily, prophets" (1 Cor. xii. 28): "Built upon the foundation of the apostles and pro-

2 with Herod the tetrarch, and Saul. As they ministered to the
Lord, and fasted, the Holy Ghost said, Separate *c* me Barnabas and
3 Saul for the work *d* whereunto I have called them. And when they

A. D. 45.

c Num. 8. 14.
d Matt. 9. 38.

phets" (Eph. ii. 20): "And he gave some, apostles, and some, prophets" (Eph. iv. 11). Compare also Rev. xviii. 20. (The reader must be careful not to confound the "prophets" in these passages with those of the Old Testament, to whom there is no reference.) The "teachers," as the name imports, addicted themselves to the second great department of the Christian ministry—"teaching them" (as Christ gave it forth on mount Olivet just before His ascension), "to observe all things whatsoever I have commanded you" (Matt. xxviii. 20). While the prophets seem to have acted as teachers also, it does not appear that the teachers were necessarily prophets. To which of the two offices the five here named are to be respectively assigned, we cannot be certain; but if, as we can hardly doubt, Barnabas and Saul were the distinguished "teachers," we cannot be far wrong in presuming that the other three, while acting as their assistants in the teaching department, were endued with the prophetic gift also; a presumption confirmed by the fact that the prophetic call, to which we are next to come—"Separate me Barnabas and Saul"—must have proceeded from others than themselves; and if so, surely from one or other of the remaining three.

We now come to the memorable incident which gave birth to by far the most important movement in the Christian Church, next to its first formation on the day of Pentecost.

2. As they ministered to the Lord [Λειτουργούν-των]. This word, though in classical Greek signifying to perform any public duties, is used in the Septuagint to denote the exercise of the *priestly* functions (compare Heb. x. 11, *Gr.*), and in the New Testament expresses the corresponding functions in the Christian Church. **and fasted, the Holy Ghost said**—said how? speaking, no doubt, through one of the "prophets" named in *v.* 1. **Separate me** ['Αφορίσατε μοι]. It is worthy of notice that the apostle himself uses the same word to express two Divine acts (the one of *providence*, the other of *grace*) towards himself, designed to prepare him for the great work to which he was called—the one at his *birth*, the other at his *conversion* to Christ: "When it pleased God (says he), who separated me [ἀφορίσας] from my mother's womb, and called me by His grace, to reveal His Son in me," &c. (Gal. i. 15, 16); and again, "Paul, a servant of Jesus Christ, called to be an apostle, separated [ἀφορισμένος] unto the Gospel of God," &c. (Rom. i. 1). Those who deny the *Personality* of the Holy Ghost must find it hard to make any tolerable sense of the command which He is here said to have issued; while His supreme and proper *Divinity* is evident on the face of it; for who could suppose a mere creature saying, "Separate *unto Me* Barnabas and Saul for the work whereunto I have summoned them?" The authenticity of this history may be called in question; but if that be admitted, it speaks for itself as to the faith of the early Church regarding the Holy Spirit. **Barnabas and Saul for the work whereunto I have called them** [προσκέκλημαι, here used in a middle sense]—rather 'summoned them;' probably by some explicit communication made through one of the "prophets" named in *v.* 1. This is the more probable, as it will be observed that the express purpose of this summons is not at all mentioned in the terms of it; and yet the whole church at Antioch, as if quite understanding that the purpose of it was to carry the Gospel to the

heathen, immediately proceeded to set them apart to that work. And since *fasting* was an exercise observed on occasions of unusual solemnity, is it not altogether probable that the church at Antioch had assembled on this occasion for special prayer with fasting, on the subject of its duty towards the great heathen world, in the hope that some definite intimation of the Divine will in this matter might be vouchsafed to them? Certain it is that the conversion of the Gentiles had been laid upon Saul as his peculiar vocation from the very time of his conversion (ch. xxvi. 16-18; ix. 15); nor would his capacious spirit deem any field that had yet opened to him sufficiently wide to meet such a destination; and since frequent communications on this subject could hardly fail to pass between him and Barnabas, in the course of their work at Antioch, we may be very sure that Barnabas, whom the Lord himself had destined to be his companion, would cordially enter into the desire for some wider field, and offer to accompany his young coadjutor as soon as the mind of their common Lord should be made known to them. Probably, as the Lord's time for sending them forth drew near, the subject would be borne in upon the minds of both with increasing force, and, spreading from them to the other "prophets and teachers" at Antioch, would go from them to the brethren at large, to whose Gentile nationality and enterprising spirit the proposal to go on a mission to the heathen would present lively attractions. Such, or something very like this, we may well suppose, would be the object of that meeting which we are now considering, at which the Lord, by one of those prophets, said, "Separate unto me Barnabas and Saul for the work whereunto I have summoned them." Nor was the church at Antioch "disobedient unto the heavenly vision;" for, adds the historian, **3. And when they had fasted and prayed.** As they were ministering to the Lord and fasting when this supernatural direction came to them, so now, in fulfilling it, they engage in the same exercises. **and laid their hands on them** (see on ch. vi. 6)—"recommending them (as we afterwards learn that they did, ch. xiv. 26) to the grace of God for the work which they had to fulfil." **they sent them away**—that is, this church itself did so. And thus did they go forth with a double call: they were summoned forth to this work by the Holy Ghost, and by the church at Antioch they were 'sent away.' Accordingly the historian adds—

4. So they, being sent forth by the Holy Ghost, departed.

Remarks.—1. How little mere critical acumen, especially when tainted by unhappy rationalistic prejudice, suffices to throw light on such a history as this—or rather, how it often darkens what is perfectly clear—appears strikingly in the argument of *Schleirmacher* against the historical accuracy of this book, drawn from the order in which the five persons are named in *v.* 1. He thinks it incredible that, in any authentic narrative of these events, the last place should have been assigned to Saul. Even *Bengel* and *Baumgarten*, who set this down to the apostle's modesty and humility, have not taken such a natural view of the passage as they might have done. In the light of the simple explanation we have given, we venture to think that the historian has arranged the names just as the circumstances of the case at the time would naturally suggest. Be this, however, as it may,

had fasted and prayed, and laid *their* hands on them, ^ethey sent *them* away.

4   So they, being sent forth by the Holy Ghost, departed unto Seleucia;

A. D. 45.
^e ch. 14. 26.
ch. 15. 40.

can anything more painfully show how critical sagacity can distort what it seeks to illustrate, than this petty cavil of the great German? 2. The distinction between what is *official* and what is purely *spontaneous* in the work of the Church, comes instructively out in this short Section. Not to speak of the labours of Stephen at Jerusalem and of Philip at Samaria—though holding no official position, that we know of, beyond that of deacons for the distribution of temporal provisions—it was surely good substantial missionary work which was done, all spontaneously, by those persecuted disciples who found their way to Antioch; and a rare seal it was which the Lord put upon it, when out of it He made to stand forth that new thing in Christianity—a church of the uncircumcised, and one which so won the admiration of Barnabas that he was constrained to throw himself into it as a congenial field of labour, and found it rich beyond his unaided power of cultivation. But when something more systematic, more continuous, more difficult was required in the missionary field, and Barnabas and Saul were to be honoured to undertake it, an express order of the Spirit comes through prophetic men to "Separate unto Him" those two men for the missionary work whereunto He had summoned them. Yet this being done by the laying on of hands, with prayer and fasting, they are said to have been "sent forth," not by the church that set them apart, but "by the Holy Ghost." It is impossible not to see in this an evidence that *there was designed to be in the Church a work of ministry of a higher and more formal character than the spontaneous evangelistic efforts of private Christians*, which the Church should nevertheless develop and encourage, and on which the Lord will assuredly smile. And further, from this incident it will be seen to be the will of the great Head of the Church that those whom He has called to such official work should not go forth to it of themselves, but should by the Church, through its recognized organs, be taken by the hand and solemnly set apart to it. These two spheres of Christian labour—the official and the non-official—agree well together, and each is fitted to strengthen the other. On the one hand, those private Christians whose gifts and impulses for evangelistic labour will not suffer them to keep silence, but constrain them to speak the things which they have seen and heard, should be content to occupy their own sphere, and be satisfied with the success —sometimes astonishing—which attends their casual, scattered, miscellaneous efforts, without intruding into the higher spheres of the Christian ministry; which when they do, they make it painfully evident to all discerning persons that they are out of their proper walk. But those, on the other hand, who have been solemnly set apart to official service in the Church, should beware of frowning down the work of such as have received no formal 'separation' to it, and viewing its results with suspicion, as irregular and disorderly. In times of spiritual lethargy there will be few such efforts to put down. But when the dry bones of an apathetic Christian community begin to be shaken, and the breath of the Spirit of God enters into a multitude of souls in different places, then it is that quickened Christians, rejoicing in a felt salvation, speak, because they believe, wherever they have an open door; and while in general confining themselves to very limited spheres and quiet

modes of operation, some discover themselves to possess rare preaching gifts, whose fervid addresses are listened to by gathering thousands, and hundreds are turned through them from darkness to light, as they move about from place to place. Such work it will be the wisdom of the true ministers of Christ to recognize and to hail. The solid fruit of it, when the workmen have departed to another place, remains for them to gather, in the accession to their flocks of souls added to the Lord, to be by them built up on their most holy Faith, in a deepened earnestness, diffusing itself perhaps over the entire worshipping community, and in a quickened tone imparted to their own ministry. It is only when such zealous labourers, lifted off their feet by the success they have had, begin to think of settling down in some one place, and setting up for themselves as pastors of a flock, that they are to be blamed. But neither in this case need the ministers of Christ disturb themselves; for the most effectual way of dealing with such persons is to leave them to themselves, until their folly becomes manifest to all men, and they themselves are fain to leave a field which the result has proved their incapacity to cultivate. 3. The strength and activity into which this Antiochene church appears to have risen so rapidly may furnish materials for thought as to how the energies of young Christian communities may be developed. The peculiar way in which the Gospel first reached them, and the novelty at that time of a church composed, as theirs was, of the uncircumcised, tended no doubt to stamp upon it a certain freedom from traditional trammels, and a simplicity and freshness of character all its own. But even when Barnabas came to them from Jerusalem, and remained to labour amongst them, aided afterwards by Saul from Tarsus, no jarring seems to have occurred between what may be called the official and the non-official elements, but both seem to have worked harmoniously, and the Gospel to have made steady progress. Then, when the predicted famine brought distress upon their Jewish brethren in Palestine, they raised a contribution for them, thinking probably that if the Jews had sown unto them spiritual things, it was no great thing if they in turn should reap of their carnal things (1 Cor. ix. 11). And as this act appears to have been self-prompted on the part of the Gentile Christians at Antioch, rather than done in compliance with the suggestions of Barnabas and Saul, we are disposed to think that the very absence of apostles and apostolic men, at the first formation of this church, tended to develop a spirit of self-reliance and spontaneous activity, which rose into vigour when they were more fully organized. Certain it is that, in proportion as the people in Christian churches are overlaid by ecclesiastical machinery, and are accustomed to have all things done for them by men officially set apart for such purposes, their own energies either lie dormant or are greatly cramped; whereas, when they are taught and encouraged from the first to show practically what they owe to the Lord who bought them, to their fellow-believers scattered abroad, and to the vast outlying world, they are not slow to learn the lesson. What beautiful illustrations of this are afforded by the religious activities of young Christian communities that have sprung up within our own time in various parts of the world—in the South Seas, in the revived Nestorian Church, and in some parts of

5 and from thence they sailed to *f* Cyprus.　And when they were at Salamis, they preached the word of God in the synagogues of the Jews: and they
6 had also John *g* to *their* minister.　And when they had gone through the

India!　4. The peculiar fitness of the two men selected by the Spirit to inaugurate the grand Missionary Enterprise must strike every intelligent reader.　Barnabas, as a Levite, a man of substance and a Cypriot, already of mature years, would carry a certain weight with him; his largeness of heart (ch. xi. 24), and persuasiveness of address (ch. iv. 36), would find him ready audience for his Master's message; while that fulness of the Spirit and of faith by which he was distinguished would raise him above hardships and dangers, draw forth his compassion for perishing souls, and enable him to hold up to them the sovereign remedy with unction and power.　It may surprise us that we have no such specimens of his preaching as of Saul's, nor indeed any express mention of his having ever addressed the people whom they visited; but, perhaps, that is owing to the particular department of the work which he selected.　If we put together all that we read of him, we shall probably not err in supposing that while Saul undertook the more public proclamation of the Gospel, and disputed with those who opposed themselves, the less prominent but scarcely less important department of private intercourse —answering enquiries, filling up the outlines and enlarging on the topics rapidly touched by his companion—fell to the lot of 'the son of exhortation.'　As for Saul, his wonderful power of adapting himself equally to Jewish and Gentile audiences, to the refined Greeks of Athens and the rude barbarians of Lycaonia, to crowds in the streets of Jerusalem and to a few women assembled for prayer on the green bank of a river at Philippi, to a sanhedrim of Jewish ecclesiastics, and to the civil tribunal before Agrippa and Festus, has impressed every thoughtful reader of his history; while his heroic devotedness to Him whose Gospel he had once hoped to root out from the earth, and that rare combination of intellectual power, energy of purpose, and womanly tenderness, which make his addresses go to the stoutest heart, stamp him as a man of an age.　We speak not here of his writings, but of his qualities by nature and his gifts by grace as a missionary preacher and teacher of Christianity, in which he stands forth confessedly unmatched.　But if each of these men was richly endowed for the work entrusted to them, their adaptation to each other is not less observable.　The service which Barnabas rendered to Saul on his first visit to Jerusalem after his conversion, in removing the scruples of the apostles as to his real character, would never be forgotten; and his going to Tarsus for him, and the harmony and success with which they laboured together at Antioch, went together to Jerusalem with a contribution for their necessitous brethren, and together returned to renew their labours, until they received the Divine call to go forth on this great mission—all go to show them well matched, probably by nature, and certainly by long association in the work of the Lord.　Finally, it ought not to escape notice that those who were Divinely selected to begin the great missionary enterprise were not novices—however gifted, however devoted—but men already inured to work of that very kind, both in the Jewish field and in the Gentile; while the younger of them, who was to eclipse not only his senior but all others in the service of Christ, had already endured no little hardship as a good soldier of Jesus Christ, his life having more than once been in imminent peril

from the enemies of the Gospel.　Is there no lesson here to the churches of our own day, as to the choice of men for the missionary work?　We may, indeed, be glad to take what materials we have, rather than neglect the great duty of making disciples of all nations until men of high capacity and Christian attainments volunteer their services. But if there is one truth which more clearly than another stands out on the face of this narrative, it is this, that the Lord of the Church deems the missionary work a field for the highest endowments both of nature and of grace; and that as those who possess them should be prepared to consecrate them to this work, when the Divine will to that effect is sufficiently indicated, so the Church should count it an honour and privilege to give away to this service the best of its sons.

FIRST MISSIONARY JOURNEY (Ch. xiii. 4— xiv. 26).

4-52.—BARNABAS AND SAUL AT SALAMIS AND PAPHOS IN CYPRUS, AT PERGA IN PAMPHYLIA, AND AT ANTIOCH IN PISIDIA.

Sailing to Cyprus, they preach in the synagogues of Salamis—At Paphos Elymas is struck blind, and the Proconsul is converted (4-12).　4. **So they, being sent forth by the Holy Ghost, departed unto Seleucia; and from thence they sailed to Cyprus** —in order to take ship there (see the account of Antioch and Cyprus on ch. xi. 19).　'The two apostles (says *Baumgarten* beautifully) are now standing on the shore of that great sea which washes the islands and the coasts on which are situated the central interests of the nations and languages of the earth.　Shall they then at once set off for the ultimate object of their labours, or only attempt gradually to draw near to that their highest but remotest aim?　To their spiritual eye, piercing into the remote distance, the great island of Cyprus is the first object that presents itself.　It was the birthplace of Barnabas, and the native country of all those who had especially contributed to the formation of the first church of the Gentiles in Antioch.　How could they ever pass this island, which possessed so many ties and attractions to them?　Such considerations induced them to make Cyprus their first landing-place, and the first scene of their labours.'　5. **And when they were at Salamis**—the Grecian capital of the island, situated on its eastern side, and not many hours' sail from Seleucia, **they preached the word of God in the synagogues of the Jews.**　At this busy mercantile port immense numbers of Jews were settled; which accounts for its being here said that they had more than one synagogue, in which Barnabas and Saul preached, while other cities had one only.　*Zeller* (of the Tübingen school of critics) makes a miserable attack on the authenticity of this book, grounded on their being sent forth to preach to the Gentiles while yet they are represented as beginning their mission by doing just the reverse—preaching to the Jews and neglecting the Gentiles.　But who knows not that that the apostles in this matter acted throughout on a principle?—"To the Jew first, and also to the Greek" (Rom. i. 16).　See on *vv.* 46, 47.　**and they had also John** (John Mark, ch. xii. 25) **to their minister** [ὑπηρέτην]—or, 'as their officer.'　With regard to the official so called in the Jewish synagogue, see on Luke iv. 20.　But Mark, no doubt, was their 'assistant' in a more general sense, performing all the subordinate services of the mission. With what fruit they now preached is not said;

88

isle unto Paphos, they found a ^{h} certain sorcerer, a false prophet, a Jew,
7 whose name *was* Bar-jesus: which was with the deputy of the country, Sergius Paulus, a prudent man; who called for Barnabas and Saul, and
8 desired to hear the word of God. But ^{i} Elymas the sorcerer (for so is his name by interpretation) withstood them, seeking to turn away the deputy
9 from the faith. Then Saul, (who also *is called* Paul,) filled with the
10 Holy Ghost, set his eyes on him, and said, O full of all subtilty and all mischief, ^{j} *thou* child of the devil, *thou* enemy of all righteousness, wilt

A. D. 45.
^{h} Ex. 22. 18.
Lev. 20. 6
Deut. 18.10.
^{i} Ex. 7. 11.
2 Tim. 3. 8.
^{j} Gen. 3. 15.
Matt. 13.38.
John 8. 44.
1 John 3. 8.

and as success is always noticed in this book, its silence here is ominous. **6. And when they had gone through the isle**—'the whole isle,' according to what is clearly the true reading. [א A B C D E, &c., and most ancient versions, have ὅλην before τ νῆσον; and so *Lachmann* and *Tischendorf*.] **unto Paphos**—on the opposite or west side of the island, a distance of a hundred miles along its southern shore; the Roman capital of the island, where the proconsul resided. **they found a certain sorcerer**—'a certain man, a sorcerer' or 'magian,' is the true reading [ἄνδρα τινὰ μάγον], **a false prophet, a Jew** (better, 'a Jewish false prophet'), **whose name was Bar-jesus** [= בַּר יֵשׁוּ] —*i. e.,* 'son of Jesus' or 'Joshua.' This was one of a numerous class of impostors who at this time of general unbelief were patronized even by cultivated Romans. But the aggravation of this man's case was his being one of God's chosen family, who, by giving himself over to this miserable occupation, virtually proclaimed himself an apostate from the Faith of his fathers; and his nationality is noted here, no doubt, as a brand upon him. By calling him "a false prophet," the historian probably means that he was actuated by a lying spirit, which gives peculiar significance to the expression afterwards applied to him—'son of the devil.' And the Arabic name which he took (see on *v.* 8) seems to show, that while wishing to sink his Jewish nationality, he sought that kind of disguise which would give him weight with his dupes. **7. Which was with the deputy of the country** [σὺν τ. ἀνθυπάτῳ]. It should have been rendered, 'with the proconsul,' or (retaining the original word) 'with the *Anthupatos;*' for this name was reserved for the governors of settled provinces, that were placed under the Roman Senate, and is never given in the New Testament to Pilate, Festus, or Felix, who were but *procurators,* or subordinate administrators of unsettled, imperial, military provinces. Now, since Augustus had reserved Cyprus for himself, its governor would in that case have been not a proconsul, but simply a procurator, had not the emperor afterwards restored it to the senate—as a Roman historian (*Dio Cassius,* liii. 12; liv. 4) expressly states. 'That the title which Dion Cassius employed as well as St. Luke, really did belong to the Roman governors of Cyprus, appears from an inscription on a Greek coin belonging to Cyprus itself, and struck in the very age in which Sergius Paulus was governor of that island. It was struck in the reign of Claudius Cæsar, whose head and name are on the face of it; and in the reign of Claudius Cæsar St. Paul visited Cyprus. On this coin the same title [ἀνθύπατος] is given to Cominius Proclus which is given by St. Luke; and the coincidence which it shows is of that description that it is sufficient of itself to establish the authenticity of the work in which the coincidence is found' (*Bishop Marsh's* 'Lectures on the Authenticity of the New Testament,' quoted by *Akerman* in 'Numismatic Illustrations of the Narrative Portions of the New Testament'). *Grotius* and *Bengel,* not aware of these facts, have missed the

mark here. **Sergius Paulus, a prudent man** [ἄνδρι συνετῷ]—'an intelligent man;' **who called for Barnabas and Saul, and desired** [ἐπιζήτησεν]—'earnestly desired' **to hear the word of God.** *Baumgarten* supposes, from the manner in which this verse is expressed, that 'the apostles had fallen in with this Jew in Paphos, and informed him of their object and the message they were charged with,' and that he had 'subsequently reported this to the proconsul as a remarkable piece of news.' But this is neither required by the historian's language nor probable in itself. As an impostor like this was not likely to carry to the proconsul tidings of the arrival of other teachers at all, much less of such teachers, so the public position of the proconsul would ensure *his* hearing soon enough of the arrival of such men, the more especially if his thirst for truth was known to those about him; and that thirst—evinced by the eagerness with which he drank in the testimony of our missionaries—would naturally induce him to send for them. **8. But Elymas the sorcerer**—or 'the wise' **(for so is his name by interpretation).** It is an Arabic word, signifying 'wise.' **withstood them**—perceiving probably with what avidity the proconsul was drinking in the word, and fearing a dismissal of himself in consequence, **seeking to turn away the deputy from the faith. 9. Then Saul, (who also is [called] Paul)**—and henceforward Paul only. The practice of giving second names, which sometimes absorbed the first, is of old standing. Many explanations have been given of the change in this case from Saul to Paul. *Jerome's* one (adopted by *Augustin* and several modern critics)—that it was designed to commemorate the conversion of the proconsul, whose surname was Paulus—seems to us a poor one; nor does the historian mention the change in connection with this, but rather with the withering address to Elymas. That it was intended (as *Bengel* and others think) as an allusion to his insignificance of stature and appearance (2 Cor. x. 1)—the word signifying 'little'—is, in our judgment, not probable. The most natural explanation seems to be, that by this slight change in the first letter of the name, it was not only converted from a Hebrew to a Roman name, and a quite common one, but rendered smoother—though the *coincidence* between the sense of the word and his personal appearance would occur to most people. **filled with the Holy Ghost**—the spirit of inspiration coming mightily upon him, **set his eyes on him.** (Our English version properly omits the 'and' before this clause, which is not well attested.) It has been remarked that our historian, both in his Gospel and in the Acts, is given to noticing the *attitude* in which anything of striking interest was said or done. **10. And said.** Henceforward Barnabas sinks into the background, and Paul is the great figure on the historic canvass. His whole soul, now drawn out as never before, shoots by the lightning-gaze of his eye, through the dark and tortuous spirit of the sorcerer. What a picture! **O full of all subtilty and all mischief** [ῥαδιουργίας.] The word signifies 'readiness for anything.'

11 thou not cease to pervert the right ways of the Lord? And now, behold, *k* the hand of the Lord *is* upon thee, and thou shalt be blind, not seeing the sun for a season. And immediately there fell on him a mist and a darkness; and he went about seeking some to lead him by the hand.

12 Then the deputy, when he saw what was done, believed, being astonished at the doctrine of the Lord.

13 Now when Paul and his company loosed from Paphos, they came to Perga in Pamphylia: and *l* John departing from them returned to Jerusalem.

14 But when they departed from Perga, they came to Antioch in Pisidia,

15 and went into the synagogue on the sabbath day, and sat down. And *m* after the reading of the Law and the Prophets, the rulers of the synagogue sent unto them, saying, Ye men *and* brethren, if ye *n* have any word of exhortation for the people, say on.

A. D. 45.
k Ex. 9. 3.
2 Ki. 6. 18.
Job 19. 21.
Ps. 32. 4.
1 Sam. 5. 6, 9, 11.
Ps. 38. 2.
Ps. 39. 10, 11.
l ch. 15. 38.
Col. 4. 10.
2 Tim. 4.14.
m Luke 4. 16.
n ch. 2. 40.
ch. 20. 2.
Rom. 12.18.
Heb. 13. 22.

knavish dexterity. child [υἱὲ] ('son') of the devil, thou enemy of all righteousness. These words were not (as *Chrysostom* well says) words of passion; for immediately before uttering them it is said he was "filled with the Holy Ghost." wilt thou not cease to pervert the right (or 'straight') ways of the Lord?—so called in contrast with his own, which were both perverse and perverting, and pointing to his having up to that hour made a trade of leading his fellow-creatures astray. 11. And now, behold, the hand of the Lord is upon thee, and thou shalt be blind, not seeing [μὴ βλέπων: see on ch. ix. 9] the sun for a season—the temporary character of the judgment being mercifully designed to lead him to repentance. But the tradition that it did so is hardly to be depended on. And immediately there fell on him a mist (as the consequence of this) and a darkness; and he went about seeking some to lead him by the hand—a graphic way of representing the reality of the miracle and his helplessness in consequence. There is a medical precision here which comports well with the profession of our historian. 12. Then the deputy, when he saw what was done, believed, being astonished at the doctrine of the Lord—thus so marvellously attested. Compare Mark i. 27. What fruit, if any, followed this remarkable conversion, or how long after it the missionaries remained at Paphos, we have no means of knowing.

At Perga John Mark deserts them, and returns to Jerusalem (13). 13. Now when Paul and his company loosed ['Ἀναχθέντες]—'had set sail' from Paphos. Observe the mode of expression here, showing clearly that henceforward our historian has to do chiefly with Paul. Barnabas is already in the background. they came to Perga in Pamphylia. The distance, in a north-westerly direction, from Paphos, on the west side of the island of Cyprus, to Attaleia, on the Gulf of Pamphylia (see on ch. xiv. 25) is not much greater than from Seleucia to Salamis, on the east side of the island. What induced our missionaries now to proceed thither, we can only conjecture. But we may naturally suppose that Barnabas having persuaded Paul to begin at Cyprus, with which he was so well acquainted, Paul, in turn, might plead for their trying next the regions lying westward of his own Cilicia, as he himself had already broken ground to the east of it. At all events, the issues of this movement abundantly justified it. Perga was the metropolis of the region of Pamphylia, situated on the river Cestrus, about seven miles due north from Attaleia. and John departing from them returned to Jerusalem. Since Paul afterwards peremptorily refused to take Mark with him on his second missionary journey, because he

had departed (or 'fallen off') from them from Pamphylia, and had not gone with them to the work (ch. xv. 38), we must infer that he had either wearied of it, or been deterred by the difficulties and dangers which he anticipated in it. This unhappy affair was the occasion of the separation of Paul and Barnabas when they resolved on a second missionary journey. (See on ch. xv. 37-40.)

At Antioch, in Pisidia, Paul preaches in the synagogue—His discourse (14-41). 14. But when they departed from Perga—apparently without making any stay, or doing anything evangelistic there. So, at least, we naturally infer from the silence of the historian in this place, and his expressly stating that on their way back "they preached the word in Perga" (ch. xiv. 25). There must have been a reason for this; and the probable one (as given by *Howson*) will appear immediately. they came to Antioch in Pisidia (or 'of Pisidia') —almost due north from Perga, and so called to distinguish it from the Syrian Antioch, from which they had set out. It was a long and rugged journey; and lying as it did almost through entirely rugged mountain-passes, while 'rivers burst out at the bases of huge cliffs, or dash down wildly through narrow ravines,' it must have been a perilous one. The whole region was, and to this day is, infested by robbers, as ancient history and modern travels abundantly attest; and there can be little doubt that to this very journey Paul many years after alludes, when he speaks amidst his "journeyings often," of his *perils of rivers* (as the word is), and his *perils of robbers* (2 Cor. xi. 26). If this journey were taken in May—and much earlier than that the passes would have been blocked up with snow—it would account for their not staying at Perga, whose hot streets are then deserted— 'men, women, and children (to use the words of *Howson*, to whom we are indebted for these remarks), flocks, herds, camels, and asses, all ascending at the beginning of the hot season from the plains to the cool basin-like hollows on the mountains, moving in the same direction with our missionaries.' and went into the synagogue on the sabbath day, and sat down. 15. And after the reading of the law and the prophets—a current phrase from the Old Testament Scriptures, which it was the invariable practice (as it still is) to read at public worship. the rulers of the synagogue sent unto them, saying, Ye men and brethren, if ye have any word of exhortation for the people, say on. [The received text omits the "any" here; but the τις of our version is well supported.] The missionaries had either taken their places where the rabbins usually sat, on purpose to be invited to address the assembly,

16 Then Paul stood up, and beckoning with *his* hand, said, Men of Israel,
17 and ye that fear God, give audience. The God of this people of Israel
chose our fathers, and exalted the people when they dwelt as strangers in
the land of Egypt, and with an high arm brought he them out of it.
18 And about the time of forty years [1]suffered he their manners in the
19 wilderness. And when he had destroyed seven nations in the land of
20 Chanaan, he divided their land to them by lot. And after that he gave
unto them judges about the space of four hundred and fifty years, until
21 Samuel the prophet. And afterward they desired a king: and God gave
unto them Saul the son of Cis, a man of the tribe of Benjamin, by the
22 space of forty years. And [o]when he had removed him, he raised up
unto them David to be their king; to whom also he gave testimony, and
said, I have found David the *son* of Jesse, a man after mine own heart,
23 which shall fulfil all my will. Of [p] this man's seed hath God, according
24 to *his* promise, raised unto Israel a Saviour, Jesus: when John had

A. D. 45.

[1] etropo-
phoresen,
perhaps
for etro-
phopho-
resen,
bore, or,
fed them,
as a nurse
beareth,
or, feedeth
her child,
according
to the
LXX., and
so Chry-
sostom.
[o] Hos. 13. 11.
[p] Rom. 1 3.

or their arrival as teachers had become known, and that would be enough.

16. Then Paul stood up, and beckoning with his hand—as his manner was (ch. xxi. 40; xxvi. 1). **said, Men of Israel, and ye that fear God**—meaning by the latter expression such religious proselytes as were present. These were in the habit of uniting with the Jews in all acts of ordinary worship. [The article before φοβούμ. shows that a different class from Ἄνδες Ἰσραηλ. is intended.] **give audience. 17. The God of this people of Israel chose our fathers, and exalted the people when they dwelt as strangers in the land of Egypt**—by marvellous interpositions in their behalf, when in their deepest depressions; **and with an high arm**—by a signal exercise of His power, **brought he them out of it. 18. And about the time of forty years suffered he their manners in the wilderness** [ἐτροποφόρησεν]. This reading has indeed excellent support, [אBC²DGH, &c.; the Vulgate; the Peshito Syriac (*marg.*); and of the fathers, *Chrysostom, Theophylact*, &c.] But the other reading—given in the margin of our English Bible, and differing from the former by only one letter [ἐτροφοφόρησεν], which means 'carried,' 'tended,' or 'cherished' them (as a nurse the infant in her bosom)—has nearly equal external evidence [ACE, a number of cursives, and both Syriac versions], while the internal evidence in its favour seems conclusive. For the apostle is not here setting forth (as was Stephen's great object) the ingratitude and rebellion of Israel in the wilderness, but making it his object in every verse to point out how much God had done for them. Besides, in Deut. i. 31—where Moses says, "thou hast seen how that the Lord thy God *bare* thee, as a man doth bear his son"—the word used by the Septuagint is the very one here employed by the apostle, according to the corrected text (compare Num. xi. 12). We confidently conclude, therefore, with nearly all good critics, that this is the true reading. **19. And when he had destroyed seven nations in the land of Chanaan**—namely, the Hittites, the Girgashites, the Amorites, the Canaanites, the Perizzites, the Hivites, and the Jebusites" (Deut. vii. 1). **he ivided their land to them by lot** [κεκληροδό-τησεν; but the true rendering clearly is —ονό-μησεν, used actively, as in Num. xxxiv. 18, and 1 Ki. ii. 8: the sense is the same]. **20. And after that he gave unto them judges about the space of four hundred and fifty years.** As this appears to contradict 1 Ki. vi. 1, various solutions have been proposed. Taking the words as they stand in the Greek—thus, 'after that, by the space of four hundred and fifty years, he gave

judges'—the meaning may be, that about 450 years elapsed from the time of the covenant with Abraham *until* the period of the judges; which is historically correct, the word "about" showing that chronological exactness was not aimed at. But taking the sense to be as in our version—that it was the period of the judges itself which lasted about 450 years—this statement also will appear historically correct, if we include in it the interval of subjection to foreign powers which occurred during the period of the judges, and understand it to describe the whole period from the settlement of the tribes in Canaan to the establishment of royalty. Thus, from the exodus to the building of the temple, were 592 years (*Josephus*, Antt. viii. 31): from this period deduct 40 years in the wilderness, 25 years of Joshua's rule (*Josephus*, Antt. v. 1. 29), 40 years of Saul's reign (*v.* 21), 40 of David's, and the first four years of Solomon's reign (1 Ki. vi. 1); and there will remain just 443 years; or, in round numbers, "about 450 years" **until Samuel the prophet. 21. And afterward they desired a king: and God gave unto them Saul the son of Cis, a man of the tribe of Benjamin**—a casual coincidence in the name and in the tribe to which the speaker himself belonged, which would probably flash across his mind while speaking; **by the space of forty years.** With this duration of Saul's reign (not mentioned in the Old Testament) *Josephus* coincides (Antt. vi. 14. 9). **22. And when he had removed him, he raised up unto them David to be their king; to whom also he gave testimony, and said, I have found David the son of Jesse, a man after mine own heart, which shall fulfil all my will.** The apostle gives in a few words the substance of Ps. lxxxix. 20; 1 Sam. xiii. 14; and (perhaps also of) Ps. lxxviii. 70-72; for he is hastening rapidly from David to Christ. **23. Of this man's seed hath God, according to his promise, raised** [ἤγειρεν]—or, according to the preferable reading, 'brought forth' [ἤγαγεν] **unto Israel a Saviour, Jesus.** This reading [that of אABEGH, &c., both Egyptian versions, and several fathers] gives the very word (as *Alford* observes) which is employed by the Septuagint in Zech. iii. 8, "behold, I will bring forth [ἄγω, מְבִיא] my Servant the Branch." The emphasis of the statement lies, first, in the *seed* from which Christ sprang—that of David—and the *promise* that He should do so, which was thus fulfilled; and next, in the *character*—that of a SAVIOUR—in which this promised Messiah was at length given, His personal name JESUS being added just to express this saving character (see on Matt. i. 21). **24. When John had first preached before his**

91

first preached before his coming the baptism of repentance to all the people of Israel.

25 And as John fulfilled his course, he said, Whom think ye that I am? I am not *he*. But, behold, there cometh one after me, whose shoes of *his*

26 feet I am not worthy to loose. Men *and* brethren, children of the stock of Abraham, and whosoever among you feareth God, to you is the word

27 of this salvation sent. For they that dwell at Jerusalem, and their rulers, ⁹ because they knew him not, nor yet the voices of the Prophets which are read every sabbath day, they have fulfilled *them* in condemning

28 *him*. And though they found no cause of death *in him*, yet desired they

29 Pilate that he should be slain. And when they had 'fulfilled all that was written of him, they took *him* down from the tree, and laid *him* in a

30, sepulchre. But ʳ God raised him from the dead: and ˢ he was seen many

31 days of them which came up with him from Galilee to Jerusalem, who

32 are his witnesses unto the people. And we declare unto you glad tidings,

33 how that the ᵗ promise which was made unto the fathers, God hath fulfilled the same unto us their children, in that he hath raised up Jesus again; as it is also written in the second psalm, ᵘ Thou art my Son, this

A. D. 45.

⁹ ch. 3. 17.
Luke 22.34.
John 8. 28.
John 15. 21.
John 16. 3.
Rom. 11.8,
10, 25.
1 Cor. 2. 8.
ʳ Matt. 28. 6.
ch. 2. 24,
32.
Heb. 13. 20.
ˢ Matt. 28.16.
ch. 1. 3.
1 Cor. 15. 5.
ʈ Gen. 3. 15.
ʂ Gen. 12. 3.
Gen. 12. 3.
Gen. 22. 18,
Rom. 4. 13.
Gal. 3. 16.
ᵘ Ps. 2. 7.
Heb. 5. 5.

---

coming [πρὸ προσώπου = לִפְנֵי τῆς εἰσόδου αὐτοῦ]—rather, 'before His entrance' or introduction to public life, **the baptism of repentance to all the people of Israel.**

25. And as John fulfilled his course, he said, Whom think ye that I am? I am not he. But, behold, there cometh one after me, whose shoes of his feet I am not worthy to loose. 26. Men and brethren, children of the stock of Abraham, and whosoever among you feareth God—both Israelites and proselytes to the Israelitish Faith (see on *v.* 16). **to you**—of both classes, **is the word of this salvation sent**—or, 'sent forth' [the compound ἐξαπεστάλη is manifestly the true reading]. **27. For they that dwell at Jerusalem, and their rulers, because they knew him not, nor yet the voices of the Prophets which are read every sabbath day, they have fulfilled them in condemning him.** The structure of this sentence is a little obscure. What our translators have rendered "knew Him not" [τοῦτον] seems plainly to mean 'knew it not,' meaning "the word of this salvation," spoken of in the preceding verse. In this case the sense will run thus: 'For they that dwell at Jerusalem, and their rulers, being ignorant of this [word], and the voices of the prophets which are read every sabbath day, have fulfilled [them] by condemning Him.' The apostle here speaks as if the more immediate guilt of Christ's death lay with the rulers and people of the metropolis, to which he foudly hoped that those residing at such a distance as Antioch would not set their seal. **28. And though they found no cause of death in him**—anxiously as they sought it (Matt. xxvi. 59, 60), **yet desired they Pilate that he should be slain. 29. And when they had fulfilled all that was written of him, they took him down from the tree, and laid him in a sepulchre.** Though the burial of Christ was an act of honour and love to Him by the disciples to whom the body was committed, yet, since his enemies looked after it, and obtained a guard of soldiers to keep watch over it, as the remains of their own victim, the apostle regards this as the last manifestation on their part of enmity to the Saviour, that his hearers might see how God had laughed their precautions to scorn by undoing their act—as about to be mentioned. **30. But God raised him from the dead: 31. And he was seen many days of them which came up with him from Galilee to**

Jerusalem—that is, by those who, having gone out and in with Him in closest intimacy during all His public ministry, which lay chiefly in Galilee, and having accompanied Him on his last journey to Jerusalem, could not possibly be mistaken as to the identity of the risen One. **who** (therefore) **are his** (unexceptionable and sufficient) **witnesses unto the people.** The word 'now' [νῦν after οἵτινες], 'who are now His witnesses,' seems on the whole the true reading. **32. And we declare unto you glad tidings, how that the promise which was made unto the fathers, 33. God hath fulfilled** [ἐκπεπλήρωκεν]—rather, 'completely fulfilled,' **the same unto us their children, in that he hath raised up Jesus again** [ἀναστήσας]—rather, "in that He hath raised up Jesus;" though our translators have rightly (as we think) taken this to mean, from the dead. The word has not indeed that sense, unless when associated with some word or words fixing it to that meaning (as at ch. ii. 26); and so some good critics take the meaning here to be, 'in that he sent' or 'brought forward Jesus.' So *Calvin* [excitato Jesu], *Beza* [suscitato], *Grotius* [exhibens], *Bengel* [quum suscitavit]; also *Olshausen, Humphry, Alexander, Lechler.* But the two following verses seem to fix the meaning here to resurrection from the dead. So the Vulgate [resuscitatus], and *Luther* auferwecket hat]; also *Meyer, de Wette, Alford, Hackett, Webster and Wilkinson.* **as it is also written in the second psalm**—or, according to another reading, 'the first psalm;' that psalm being regarded as a general introduction to the whole Psalter, in which view the one that followed would be reckoned the first, as indeed it is numbered in several Hebrew MSS. Still the evidence in favour of the received reading immensely preponderates. [In favour of πρώτῳ are D only of extant MSS., though *Origen* and other early fathers must have so read it: in favour of δευτέρῳ are ℵ A B C E G H, &c.; the Vulgate and most ancient versions; with *Chrysostom* and other fathers. The only argument in favour of πρώτῳ is, that it might more naturally have been corrected into δευτέρῳ than the reverse. Accordingly, *Lachmann* and *Tischendorf* adopt it; and it is preferred by *Erasmus, Meyer, Olshausen, Alford, Lechler.* But this consideration is hardly sufficient to outweigh the preponderating evidence in favour of δευτέρῳ]. **Thou art my Son, this day have I begotten thee.** *Augustin*, with some moderns, apply this to Christ's eternal generation from the

34 day have I begotten thee. And as concerning that he raised him up from the dead, *now* no more to return to corruption, he said on this wise,

35 I will give you the sure mercies of David. Wherefore he saith also in another *psalm*, *ᵛ*Thou shalt not suffer thine Holy One to see corruption.

36 For David, *²*after he had served his own generation by the will of God,

37 fell on sleep, and was laid unto his fathers, and saw corruption: but he, whom God raised again, saw no corruption.

38 Be it known unto you therefore, men *and* brethren, that *ʷ*through this

39 man is preached unto you the forgiveness of sins: and *ˣ*by him all that believe are justified from all things, from which ye could not be justified

A. D. 45.

ᵛ Ps. 16. 10.
² Or, after he had in his own age served the will of God.
Ps. 78. 72.
ʷ Jer. 31. 34. Dan. 9. 24.
ˣ Isa. 53. 11. Gal. 2. 16.

Father. 'The expression (says *Alexander*) "I have begotten thee" means, I am thy Father: "To-day" refers to the date of the decree itself: but this, as a Divine act, was eternal, and so must be the Sonship it affirms.' This, however, is a forced way of interpreting the words, and not at all consistent with the context, which clearly connects the Sonship with the resurrection of Christ. Does the apostle, then, mean to say that Christ *became* God's Son—for the first time, and in the only sense in which He was the Son of God —by His resurrection from the dead? That cannot be; for, besides that it would contradict the whole strain of the New Testament regarding Christ's relation to the Father, it is in direct contradiction to the apostle's own statements in Rom. viii. 32, where he reasons on the Sonship of Christ as one of eternal essence; and even still more in Rom. i. 4, where he says of the resurrection of Christ, that he was thereby only "*declared*" (defined or determined) to be the Son of God with power"—in other words, the resurrection of Christ was merely the *manifestation* of a Sonship which existed before, but was only then "declared with power." Are we not warranted, then, on the apostle's own authority, in understanding his meaning here to be the same—"To-day," meaning that memorable day of His resurrection from the dead, when God, by an act not to be misunderstood, proclaimed that He whom men slew, by hanging Him on a tree, was none other than His own Son. As *Meyer* happily expresses it, 'it was the Divine legitimation of His Sonship.' Such *declarative* meaning of the verb 'to be' is familiar to every reader of the Bible (see, for example, John x. 15; ch. xv. 8); and in this sense nearly all good interpreters agree that this verse is to be understood. **34. And as concerning that he raised him up from the dead, now no more to return to corruption**—that is, to the grave, where death reigns: compare Rom. vi. 9, "Christ being raised from the dead, dieth no more; death hath no more dominion over him." Christ went to the *place*, but not the *state* of corruption (*v*. 37). **he said on this wise** (or 'thus')—namely in Isa. lv. 3, **I will give you the sure mercies of David** [τὰ ὅσια Δ. = חַסְדֵי דָוִד, τὰ πιστά]—literally, 'the sure sanctities of David.' The word, however, is sometimes used in the sense of "mercies" in the Old Testament. The whole riches of the everlasting covenant—its varied "*grace*" or "*mercies*" —are here meant; and they are characterized in the prophecy, first, as 'sanctities,' to signify that, as they quite transcend the sphere of things seen and temporal, so they separate to a holy character all such as receive them; but they are further characterized as "sure," to denote the certainty with which they would at length, through David's Seed, be all substantiated (see more on this subject on John i. 14, p. 349). But how do these words prove the resurrection of Christ? 'They presuppose it (as *Olshausen* says); for since an eternal kingdom was promised to David, the Ruler of this kingdom could not remain under the power of death. But to strengthen the indefinite prediction by one more definite, the apostle adduces Ps. xvi. 10, of which Peter had given the same explanation (see on ch. ii. 27, 30, 31); both apostles denying the possibility of its proper reference to David.' **36. For David, after he had served his own generation by the will of God** [ἰδίᾳ γενεᾷ ὑπηρετήσας τῇ τ. Θεοῦ βουλῇ]—rather, 'served for his own generation the counsel' or 'purpose of God' (so the Vulgate, *Luther, Beza, Grotius, Bengel, Olshausen, de Wette, Meyer, Bloomfield, Alford, Webster and Wilkinson, Lechler*). The rendering of our authorized version, however, has good support (as *Erasmus, Calvin, Hackett*). The meaning (as we understand it) is, that this "man after God's own heart" yielded himself an instrument for the accomplishment of God's high designs, contributing 'for his own generation' that portion of the preparations for the kingdom of His Son which was assigned him, which, when he had completed, he **fell on sleep** [ἐκοιμήθη]—or simply, 'fell asleep,' **and was laid unto his fathers** —rather, 'was added unto his fathers' [προσετέθη πρὸς = וַיֵּאָסֶף אֶל־אֲבוֹתָיו, Judg. ii. 10; see also Gen. xxv. 8, 17]. It is not without reason that *Bengel, Olshausen*, and others, see in this expression a dim recognition by the saints of the Old Testament, even from the earliest times, of the distinct existence of the soul after death. **and saw corruption**. David, therefore—argues this apostle, as Peter had done before (ch. ii. 24-36)—could not have been the proper subject of these sayings of his, which had their proper fulfilment in that Son of his, of whom alone it could *not* be said with truth that He "fell on sleep, and was gathered to his fathers, and saw corruption." Accordingly he adds, **37. But he, whom God raised again, saw no corruption**.

38. Be it known unto you therefore, men and brethren, that through this man is preached unto you the forgiveness of sins. As this is the first necessity of the sinner, so it is the first experienced blessing of the Gospel. The expression "through this Person" [διὰ τούτου] is of course to be connected with "forgiveness" (not the 'preaching' of it), and the meaning is, 'forgiveness through this Person is preached unto you.' **39. And by him all that believe are justified from all things, from which** [ὧν = ἀφ᾽ ὧν, by *attr.*] **ye could not be justified by the law of Moses**. The sense of this verse requires a pause to be made after "all things," and the next clause is to be viewed not as an *exceptional* clause, but as *explanatory* of the former one— thus: 'By Him the believer is justified from all things (all the charges of the broken law); a thing which the law of Moses is so far from being able to do, that it justifies from nothing.' It is a mere perversion of this great announcement to make it mean, 'The law, though it

93

40 by the law of Moses. Beware therefore, lest that come upon you which
41 is spoken of in *ʸ* the Prophets; Behold, ye despisers, and wonder, and perish: for I work a work in your days, a work which ye shall in no wise believe, though a man declare it unto you.
42 And when the Jews were gone out of the synagogue, the Gentiles besought that these words might be preached to them the ³ next
43 sabbath. Now when the congregation was broken up, many of the Jews and religious proselytes followed Paul and Barnabas: who, speaking to
44 them, persuaded them to continue in *ᶻ* the grace of God. And the next sabbath day came almost the whole city together to hear the word of God.
45 But when the Jews saw the multitudes, they were filled with envy, and *ᵃ* spake against those things which were spoken by Paul, contradicting
46 and blaspheming. Then Paul and Barnabas waxed bold, and said, *ᵇ* It was necessary that the word of God should first have been spoken to you: but *ᶜ* seeing ye put it from you, and judge yourselves unworthy of ever-

A. D. 45.

ʸ Hab. 1. 5.
³ in the week between,
or, in the sabbath between.
ᶻ Tit. 2. 11.
Heb. 12. 15.
1 Pet. 5. 12.
ᵃ ch. 18. 6.
1 Pet. 4. 4.
Jude 10.
ᵇ ch. 3. 26.
Rom. 1. 16.
ᶜ Ex. 32. 10.
Deut. 32.21.
Isa. 55. 5.
Matt. 21.43.
Rom. 10.19.

met most cases, had no provision for the pardon of some sins; but it is otherwise under Christianity.' It will be observed that the deeper sense of justification—its *positive* side—is reserved for the Epistles, addressed to the justified themselves; also, whereas it is the *resurrection* of Christ which is chiefly dwelt upon here and throughout the Acts —because the first thing in order to bring peace to the guilty through Christ was to establish His Messiahship by the fact of His resurrection from the dead—in the Epistles, it is His *death*, as the way of reconciliation, which is chiefly unfolded. **40. Beware therefore, lest that come upon you which is spoken of in the Prophets.** Though the following quotation is from Hab. i. 5 (and nearly as in the LXX.), this is held forth as the general strain of all "the prophets." **41. Behold, ye despisers, and wonder, and perish: for I work a work in your days, a work which ye shall in no wise believe, though a man declare it unto you**—that is, 'even though announced on unexceptionable testimony.' The words, as originally uttered, were a merciful but fruitless warning against the approaching destruction of Jerusalem by the Chaldeans and the Babylonish captivity. As such, nothing could more fitly describe the more awful calamity impending over the generation which the apostle addressed.

The congregation solicit another hearing of such truths; and many of them, following Paul and Barnabas, being already won to the truth, are now counselled to persevere (42, 43). **42. And when the Jews were gone out of the synagogue, the Gentiles besought that these words might be preached to them the next sabbath**—[Ἐξιόντων δὲ ἐκ τ. συναγωγῆς τ. Ἰουδαίων, παρεκάλουν τὰ ἔθνη κ. τ. λ.] The received text here cannot be correct, and is almost void of any authority. [It has no MS. support at all, except some cursives; though G has τὰ ἔθνη, and one or two others.] It suggests the staggering question, How came these Gentiles to be in the synagogue? for they were not religious proselytes; this class being expressly named in the following verse. The genuine text, beyond all doubt [being supported by ℵ A B C D E, &c., the Vulgate and most ancient versions, *Chrysostom* and other fathers, and adopted by *Lachmann* and *Tischendorf*] is this: 'Now when they (the apostles) were going out (of the synagogue), they (the congregation) besought that these words might be spoken to them the next sabbath' [Ἐξιόντων δὲ αὐτῶν παρεκάλουν εἰς τὸ μεταξὺ σάββατον λαληθῆναι αὐτοῖς τὰ ῥήματα ταῦτα]. The *marginal* rendering of the last words 'in the week between,' or 'in the sabbath between,' though according to the classical sense of the original

phrase, is less agreeable to our historian's manner than that of our authorized version, which is that of *Josephus* also, and is confirmed by v. 44, where "the next sabbath" [τῷ ἐχομένῳ σαββ. or ἐρχομ., as in the received text] evidently means the day referred to in the previous verse. **43. Now when the congregation was broken up, many of the Jews and religious proselytes—won to the Gospel, and clinging to their spiritual benefactors, followed Paul and Barnabas—these names being now and henceforward, with one exception, inverted (see on ch. xiv. 14); who, speaking to them**—following up the discourse in the synagogue by some further words of counsel and encouragement, **persuaded** [ἔπειθον]—or 'urged' them (as in ch. xix. 8, and xxviii. 23) **to continue in the grace of God**—not in 'the Gospel' (objectively), as the fruit of God's undeserved favour (as *Hackett* takes it), but 'in the (experienced) grace of God,' which through the Gospel had taken possession of them (subjectively—as *Calvin* and *Bengel* view it).

Next sabbath nearly all the city flock to hear the word of God—Enraged at this, the Jews oppose and malign the truth—whereupon Paul and Barnabas, with solemn protestation turn to the Gentiles, and with such success that the rage of their Jewish enemies causes their expulsion—They shake off the dust of their feet against them, while the new converts are filled with joy and with the Holy Ghost (44-52). **44. And the next sabbath day came almost the whole city together to hear the word of God**—or 'of the Lord,' according to another reading; but the evidence for both is pretty equal. The intervening days had evidently been spent in further enquiry on the part of the congregation, and further instruction in private to such as sought it; and the excitement communicating itself to the Gentiles, they now for the first time crowded along with the stated worshippers into the synagogue. **45. But when the Jews**—meaning the zealots for exclusive Judaism, **saw the multitudes, they were filled with envy** [ζήλου]—rather, 'with indignation,' **and spake against those things which were spoken by Paul, contradicting and blaspheming.** There is nothing more awful, even to this day, than Jewish fury and execration of the name of Jesus of Nazareth, when thoroughly roused. **46. Then Paul and Barnabas waxed bold, and**—rising into the highest style of a last and lofty protestation, **said, It was necessary that the word of God should first have been spoken to you**—necessary, both because of the position which the Jews occupied in the immediate terms of the promise, and in obedience to the express injunctions of their Master (Luke xxiv. 47: see on *v.* 5). **but seeing**

47 lasting life, lo, we turn to the Gentiles. For so hath the Lord commanded us, *saying,* ᵈ I have set thee to be a light of the Gentiles, that thou shouldest be for salvation unto the ends of the earth.

48 And when the Gentiles heard this, they were glad, and glorified the word of the Lord: ᵉ and as many as were ordained to eternal life believed.

49 And the word of the Lord was published throughout all the region.

50 But the Jews stirred up the devout and honourable women, and the chief men of the city, and ᶠ raised persecution against Paul and Barnabas, and

51 expelled them out of their coasts. But ᵍ they shook off the dust of their

52 feet against them, and came unto Iconium. And the disciples ʰ were filled with joy, and with the Holy Ghost.

A. D. 45.

ᵈ Isa. 42. 6.
Isa. 49. 6.
Luke 2. 32.
ᵉ ch. 2. 47.
2 Tim. 2. 19.
ᶠ 1 Thes. 2.
14-16.
2 Tim. 3. 11.
ᵍ Luke 9. 5.
ʰ Matt. 5. 12.
John 16. 22.
ch. 2. 46.
1 Pet. 1. 8.

---

ye put it from you, and judge yourselves unworthy of everlasting life—' passing sentence, as it were, upon yourselves of exclusion from eternal life '—a mode of expression not so uncommon as *Hackett* represents, and intelligible to every one. " All they that hate me (says Wisdom, Prov. viii. 36) love death." lo, we turn to the Gentiles—not as if they were never again to preach to the Jews, but to signify that their message was only in the first instance to them, and that their rejection of it but opened the way for its being carried to the Gentiles. **47. For so hath the Lord commanded us, saying** (Isa. xlix. 6), **I have set thee** (the Messiah) **to be a light of the Gentiles, that thou shouldest be for salvation unto the ends of the earth.** From this Paul inferred that he was but following out this destination of his Lord, in transferring to the Gentiles those unsearchable riches which were now by the Jews rejected and despised. These and other predictions must have been long before this brought vividly home to Paul's mind in connection with his special vocation to the Gentiles. **48. And when the Gentiles heard this, they were glad**—glad to perceive that their accession to Christ was matter of Divine arrangement as well as apostolic effort, **and glorified the word of the Lord** (Jesus)—by a cordial reception of it, giving to it the obedience of faith. Compare John iii. 33, "He that hath received his testimony hath set to his seal that God is true;" and 2 Thess. iii. 1, " Finally, brethren, pray for us, that *the word of the Lord may* have free course, and *be glorified.*" **and as many as were ordained** [τεταγμένοι]—or 'appointed,' **to eternal life believed.** A very remarkable statement, which cannot, without force, be interpreted of anything lower than this—that *a Divine ordination to eternal life is the cause,* not the effect, *of any man's believing.* Grotius (and after him many others, as *Humphry*) plead ingeniously for a middle sense of the verb, and translate thus : ' As many as disposed (or 'addicted') themselves to eternal life '—referring to 1 Cor. xvi. 15. But this, besides having very much of a strained appearance, is vapid, and almost tautological. In favour of the authorized version are such critics as *Bengel, Olshausen, Meyer, de Wette, Winer, Alford, Hackett, Webster and Wilkinson.* 'In the words, "as many as were ordained to eternal life," we must reckon (says *Olshausen,* himself a Lutheran) the idea which pervades the whole Scriptures of a predestination of saints. The attempts which have been made to evade it are in the highest degree forced.' **49. And the word of the Lord was published throughout all the region**—implying some stay in Antioch and missionary activity in its vicinity, if this was done by Paul and Barnabas ; but it may have been owing to the missionary zeal of the new converts (*v.* 52) that the Gospel penetrated to the surrounding parts. **50. But the Jews stirred**

up the devout [and] honourable women. The bracketed word "and" is an addition to the genuine text. The class meant is one—the female proselytes of distinction, unhappily jaundiced against the new preachers by those Jewish ecclesiastics to whom they had learned to look up as the interpreters of the lively oracles in which they had found the only true repose. The potent influence of the female character, both for and against the truth, may be seen in the Church history of every age. **and the chief men of the city, and raised persecution against Paul and Barnabas, and expelled them out of their coasts** —an easier thing than to refute them. **51. But** (as a solemn protest against this treatment, and repudiation of all responsibility for the consequences) **they shook off the dust of their feet against them**—as directed by the Lord Himself (see on Matt. x. 14), **and came unto Iconium**— a populous city about forty-five miles south-east from Pisidian Antioch, at the foot of mount Taurus, on the borders of Lycaonia, Phrygia, and Pisidia, and in later times largely contributing to the consolidation of the Turkish empire. **52. And the disciples**—who, though not themselves expelled, had to endure sufferings for the Gospel, as we learn from ch. xiv. 22. **were filled with joy, and with the Holy Ghost**—Who not only raised them above shame and fear, as professed disciples of the Lord Jesus, but filled them with joy in His salvation. 'St. Luke on several occasions (says *Humphry,* pertinently), after mentioning events which might be thought disheartening, notices the joy and elevation of spirit by which they were followed. So it was after Herod's persecution (ch. xii. 24), after the scourging in presence of the Sanhedrim (ch. v. 41), and after the Ascension (Luke xxiv. 52).'

Remarks. — 1. The scene at Paphos bears a striking analogy (as *Baumgarten* remarks) to that of the magicians, Jannes and Jambres, withstanding Moses when he stood before Pharaoh in Egypt. Their conduct is described by Paul himself in terms very similar to those here employed: "Now as Jannes and Jambres withstood Moses, so do these also resist the truth" (2 Tim. iii. 8). But the analogy only serves to awaken our attention to the great difference between the two periods. The magicians were Egyptians and heathens: Elymas was a Jew, his real name being Par-Jesus. Further, Pharaoh, the king of Egypt, surrenders himself to the unholy influence of his sorcerers, and allows himself to be taken captive by it. Sergius Paulus, the Roman lord of the island of Cyprus, is so far from allowing himself to be ruled by his sorcerer Elymas, that he defies all his powers of resistance, and gives his fullest confidence to the messengers of God. The fact which has already forced itself on our notice in its different elements—namely, the turning of the Jews from God and the turning of the Gentiles to Him—is here brought before us

14 AND it came to pass in Iconium, that they went both together into the synagogue of the Jews, and so spake, that a great *a*multitude both of **2** the Jews and also of the Greeks believed. But the unbelieving Jews stirred up the Gentiles, and made their minds evil affected against the **3** brethren. Long time therefore abode they speaking boldly in the Lord, *b*which gave testimony unto the word of his grace, and granted signs and **4** wonders to be done by their hands. But the multitude of the city was **5** divided: and part held with the Jews, and part with the apostles. And when there was an assault made both of the Gentiles, and also of the

A. D. 45.

CHAP. 14.
a Isa. 11. 11.
ch. 11. 24.
ch. 13.43,46.
ch. 17. 4.
ch. 18. 8.
b Mark 16.20.
Rom. 15.19.
1 Cor. 2. 4.
Heb. 2. 4.

in a highly significant manner, and comprised in a single instance. 2. As the blindness inflicted on Elymas was the first miracle of Paul (it is at least the first recorded one)—wrought, too, upon a Jew when the apostle was just beginning his work among the Gentiles, and followed by the conversion of a Gentile in high official position, the first-fruits of a harvest to follow; as the historian's language implies that the soul of the apostle was drawn out on this occasion as never before; and as it is at this stage of the history that the new name of 'Paul' is first given to him, to be thenceforward the name by which he was ever to be known—we can hardly doubt that his actual call to be an *apostle* of Jesus Christ was now for the first time sealed, and his great gifts for the apostolic service of Christ for the first time revealed to his own consciousness; and since Barnabas never once comes forward as a public speaker in the record of this missionary tour, we may take it for granted that he also now perceived, and (as might be expected) generously acquiesced in the manifest design of the great Lord of both, that the prominent position should henceforth be taken by his gifted colleague, while he aided the work in other ways, hardly less important in their own place. 3. On comparing Paul's address to the Jews at Antioch, and his other recorded addresses in Jewish synagogues, with those of Peter at Jerusalem, it will appear that he was at least quite as well qualified to deal with his own countrymen as "the apostle of the circumcision" himself. But how different the bearing of these two honoured apostles towards the Gentiles! We have but one recorded address of Peter to a Gentile audience—that to Cornelius and his friends. And what is its character and complexion? He begins it apologetically; he cannot open his proper subject until he has first explained how he comes to occupy so novel a position as that of a preacher to the Gentiles: even when he has done this, he still seems to feel himself on new ground; nor, in holding forth Christ to these Gentiles, does he ever stretch beyond the Jewish point of view, exhibiting Him, even to them, simply as the great Burden of prophetic testimony to the children of Israel, though designed for all. True, Cornelius, as a devout proselyte to the Jewish Faith, must have been well prepared for this way of preaching Christ. Still, it is impossible not to perceive, both in the speaker himself and in his discourse, the *Jew* throughout. Now, compare this with Paul's way of addressing both the barbarians of Lycaonia and the Greeks of Athens, and it will at once be seen that the speaker addresses Gentiles on Gentile ground—Jewish associations and Jewish phraseology being studiously, yet quite naturally and easily, avoided. In short, while quite as much at home with his own countrymen as if his whole ideas had been exclusively Jewish, he is to Gentile audiences as Gentile, in the point of view from which he presents the Gospel, as if he had been a converted Pagan. This flexibility of mind in dealing with men—this power of presenting the grandest truths in forms adapted to all classes, constitutes one chief feature of his superiority to all the other apostles; a feature which—as one conscious of possessing it, and determined to turn it to the best account for the Gospel—he has himself described in language the most impressive: "Unto the Jews I became as a Jew, that I might gain the Jews; to them that are under the law, as under the law, that I might gain them that are under the law; to them that are without law, as without law, (being not without law to God, but under the law to Christ,) that I might gain them that are without law. To the weak became I as weak, that I might gain the weak: I am made all things to all men, that I might by all means save some" (1 Cor. ix. 20-22).

CHAP. XIV. 1-28.—PROCEEDINGS AT ICONIUM, LYSTRA, AND DERBE—RETRACING THEIR STEPS, PAUL AND BARNABAS RETURN TO ANTIOCH IN SYRIA, AND REPORT TO THE CHURCH THE EVENTS OF THEIR FIRST MISSIONARY JOURNEY.

At Iconium, meeting with similar success and similar opposition as at Antioch in Pisidia, Paul and Barnabas flee for their lives to Lystra, and preach there (1-7). **1. And it came to pass in Iconium** (as to which, see on ch. xiii. 51), **that they went both together into the synagogue of the Jews** (see on ch. xiii. 46), **and so spake, that a great multitude both of the Jews and also of the Greeks believed**—meaning, no doubt, the religious proselytes, as distinguished from the heathen population of the city, now to be mentioned. As this discourse would be in substance the same as at Antioch in Pisidia, the historian records only the fruit of it; and *this method he follows in all the subsequent history*, when he comes to the apostle's address to his countrymen from the castle stairs, which was too important in itself, and too different from all his preceding discourses, not to be given in full. **2. But the unbelieving Jews** [ἀπειθήσαντες is preferable to—θοῦντες of the received text]—rather, ' the disbelieving Jews;' for the word means, to 'disbelieve,' 'refuse compliance,' or 'be disobedient' (and by this last word is often rendered in our version). It expresses positive disbelief of the Gospel. **stirred up the Gentiles** [τ. ἐθνῶν]—' the heathen,' and **made their minds evil affected**—or 'embittered them' **against the brethren**—the converts as well as the preachers. **3. Long time therefore abode they**—because, in spite of the opposition, their success was so great; **speaking boldly in the Lord** [ἐπὶ τ. Κυρίῳ: cf. Luke iv. 4, ἐπ' ἄρτῳ]—meaning, 'in dependence' or 'in reliance on the Lord;' that is, the Lord Jesus, **which gave testimony unto the word of his grace**—a notable definition this of the Gospel (as *Bengel* remarks), whose whole burden is GRACE, **and granted** ('granting') **signs and wonders**—that is, gave miraculous attestation to it **to be done by their hands.** [The καὶ before διδόντι, in the received text, is evidently not genuine.] **4. But the multitude of the city was divided: and part held with the Jews, and part with the apostles. 5. And when there was an assault made.** The word [ὁρμὴ] properly signifies

Jews with their rulers, ^cto use *them* despitefully, and to stone them,
6 they were ware of *it*, and ^dfled unto Lystra and Derbe, cities of Lycaonia,
7 and unto the region that lieth round about: and there they preached
   the Gospel.
8 And ^ethere sat a certain man at Lystra, impotent in his feet, being a
9 cripple from his mother's womb, who never had walked: the same heard
   Paul speak: who stedfastly beholding him, and ^fperceiving that he had
10 faith to be healed, said with a loud voice, ^gStand upright on thy feet.
11 And he leaped and walked. And when the people saw what Paul had
   done, they lifted up their voices, saying in the speech of Lycaonia, ^hThe
12 gods are come down to us in the likeness of men. And they called Barnabas, Jupiter; and Paul, Mercurius, because he was the chief speaker.
13 Then the priest of Jupiter, which was before their city, brought oxen and
   garlands unto the gates, ⁱand would have done sacrifice with the people.
14 *Which* when the apostles, Barnabas and Paul, heard *of*, ^jthey rent their
15 clothes, and ran in among the people, crying out, and saying, Sirs, why
   do ye these things? ^kWe also are men of like passions with you, and

(marginal references)
A. D. 46.
^c 1 Thes. 2.
   14-16.
   2 Tim. 3.11.
^d Matt. 10.23.
   ch. 16. 1, 2.
   2 Tim. 3.11.
^e John 5. 5.
   ch. 3. 2.
^f Matt. 8. 10.
   Matt. 9. 28.
   Matt. 13.58.
   Mark 10.52-
^g Isa. 35. 6.
   Luke 7. 14
   Luke 13.11-
   13.
^h ch. 28. 6.
ⁱ Dan. 2. 46.
^j Matt. 26.65.
^k Jas. 5. 17.
   Rev. 19. 10.

'a rush,' 'onset,' or any impetuous movement. But here it can scarcely mean so much, since they had time to consider what to do, and actually escaped it. Probably it denotes some organized movement with a view to set upon them. **both of the Gentiles, and also of the Jews with their rulers, to use them despitefully** (or 'insult', **and to stone them**—on which, see *Paley's* observation in Remark 4, at the close of this Section. 6. **They were ware of it** [Συνιδόντες]—rather, 'they reflected on,' or 'considered it' (as in ch. xii. 12); that is, considered whether it were wiser to brave or to bend to this gathering storm; **and fled** (according to the direction, Matt. x. 23) **unto Lystra and Derbe**—the one some twenty miles to the south, the other about sixty miles to the east of Iconium, somewhere about the bases of what is called the Black Mountain and the roots of Mount Taurus; but their exact position has not yet been discovered. **cities of Lycaonia**—a wide district of Asia Minor, lying between Phrygia, Cilicia, and Cappadocia, **and unto the region that lieth round about: 7. And there they preached the gospel.**

At Lystra, Paul having healed a born cripple, the people are scarce restrained from sacrificing to them as gods (8-18). 8. **And there sat a certain man at Lystra, impotent in his feet, being a cripple from his mother's womb** [ὑπάρχων, after μητρὸς αὐτοῦ, is evidently not genuine], **who never had walked**—[περιεπατήκει, preferable to *Tischendorf's* aorist,—περιεπάτησεν.] As such, this cripple would naturally be regarded as an incurable. 9. **The same heard Paul speak.** There being no mention of a synagogue, probably the Jews here were too few to have one. The apostle, therefore, seeing this cripple seated—and possibly having a presentiment that the power of the Lord would be present to heal him by his instrumentality, and thus make way for the truth into the people's hearts—may have gathered a knot around this spot and addressed them. **who stedfastly beholding him, and perceiving that he had faith to be healed.** In all likelihood the apostle, looking to this born cripple, would dwell on the Saviour's miracles of healing, and the grant of the same power to His chosen witnesses, as evinced by Peter's healing the lame man at the beautiful gate of the temple (ch. iii. 1-8), and possibly also of Æneas (ch. ix. 33). And perceiving from the eagerness with which the helpless man drank in his words, that he was prepared to put his own case into the Redeemer's hands, the Spirit of the

glorified Healer came upon him, and he 10. **Said with a loud voice, Stand upright on thy feet.** The effect was instantaneous and the cure perfect. **And he leaped** (or 'sprang up') **and walked.** [The *spring*, being one act, is put in the aorist—ἥλατο, not ἥλλετο, as in the received text; whereas the *walk*, being continuous, is in the imperfect, περιεπάτει.] 11. **And when the people saw what Paul had done, they lifted up their voices, saying in the speech of Lycaonia**—which, whether a corruption of the Greek tongue, well understood in this region, or a Semitic dialect, or the remains of some aboriginal tongue, is not known. **The gods are come down to us in the likeness of men**—just such an exclamation as we should expect from a rude and unsophisticated people. But (as *Webster and Wilkinson* justly say) 'that which was a superstition in Lycaonia, and for which the whole creation groaned, became a reality at Bethlehem.' 12. **And they called Barnabas, Jupiter**—the father of the gods, (as *Chrysostom* thinks) from his commanding mien: **and Paul, Mercurius**—the messenger and attendant of Jupiter, and the spokesman of the gods. This latter character was that which suggested the application of this name to Paul, **because he was the chief speaker. 13. Then the priest of** [the image of] **Jupiter, which was** [erected] **before their city**—or 'the city' (according to the better reading); that is, at the gates and in front of the city, as its tutelary deity, **brought oxen and garlands unto the gates**—not oxen adorned with garlands (as *de Wette* and others), but oxen for sacrifice, and garlands to decorate probably the altar, the temple, and those engaged in the service. **and would have done sacrifice** (along) **with the people** [τ. ὄχλοις]—'the crowds.' 14. **[Which] when the apostles, Barnabas and Paul, heard of.** Here the name of Barnabas, for once since the scene before the proconsul of Cyprus, is put first—evidently because the historian had just before stated that the Lycaonians had given to him the name of Jupiter, who, as compared with Mercurius (the name given to Paul), behoved to take the precedence. On the *apostleship* of Barnabas, see Remark 8, at the close of this Section. **they rent their clothes**—the ancient Oriental way of expressing intense grief, **and ran in among the people** [εἰσεπήδησαν]—but the true reading evidently is, 'ran out' or 'burst forth [ἐξέπ.] into the crowd,' **crying out, and saying, 15. And saying, Sirs, why do ye these things?** This was something more than that abhorrence of idolatry which took

preach unto you that ye should turn from [l]these vanities [m]unto the living God, [n]which made heaven, and earth, and the sea, and all things
16 that are therein: who [o]in times past suffered all nations to walk in their
17 own ways. Nevertheless [p]he left not himself without witness, in that he did good, and [q]gave us rain from heaven, and fruitful seasons, filling our
18 hearts with food and gladness. And with these sayings scarce restrained they the people, that they had not done sacrifice unto them.
19 And [r]there came thither *certain* Jews from Antioch and Iconium, who persuaded the people, [s]and, having stoned Paul, drew *him* out of the
20 city, supposing [t]he had been dead. Howbeit, as the disciples stood round about him, he rose up, and came into the city.

A. D. 46.
[l] 1 Sam. 12. 21.
Jer. 14. 22.
[m] 1 Thes. 1. 9.
[n] Rev. 14. 7.
[o] Ps. 81. 12.
1 Pet. 4. 3.
[p] Rom. 1. 20.
[q] Lev. 26. 4.
Job 5. 10.
[r] ch. 13. 45.
[s] 2 Cor. 11. 25.
[t] 2 Cor. 1. 8.

---

possession of the Jews as a nation from the time of the Babylonish captivity: it was that delicate sensibility to everything which affects the honour of God, which Christianity—giving us in God a reconciled Father—alone can produce; making the Christian instinctively feel himself to be wounded in all dishonour done to God, and filling him with mingled horror and grief when such gross insults as this are offered to Him. **We also are men of like passions with you** [ὁμοιοπαθεῖς ὑμῖν ἄνθρωποι] —'men of like nature (or similarly constituted) with yourselves.' (The phrase, "like passions," is correct enough, if understood in a physical sense—as implying like infirmities—but not in the moral sense.) How unlike either imposture or enthusiasm is this, and how high above all self-seeking do these men of Christ show themselves to be! **and preach unto you that ye should turn from these vanities**—the familiar and most expressive name in the Old Testament for idols of every sort. **unto the living God**—[ἐπὶ Θεὸν ζῶντα is better supported than the emphatic form of the received text, τ. Θεὸν τ. ζ.] This is the most glorious and distinctive of all the names of God; expressive of that which separates Him infinitely not only from all dead idols, but from all pantheistic conceptions of Him, which confound and identify Him with the works of His hands—His "having life in Himself," as the great Fontal Principle of life in His creatures—life conscious and personal—life essential, independent, eternal, changeless,—in virtue of which we, who are a faint shadow of Himself, as living persons, are able to hold rational and intelligent fellowship with Him, spirit with Spirit. These are the household words of Bible truth; but to all beyond its pale they are an unknown tongue: and not more so to the rude barbarian than to the cultivated and refined philosopher. Compare 1 Thess. i. 9. **which made heaven, and earth, and the sea, and all things that are therein.** This idea of *creation*, utterly unknown alike to rude and to cultivated heathenism, would not only define what was meant by "the living God," but open up a new world, on after reflection, to the more thoughtful part of the audience. **16. Who in times past suffered all nations to walk in their own ways**—that is, interfered not with their own unaided search after truth and happiness, by extending to them the Revelation which He had vouchsafed to the seed of Abraham (see on ch. xvii. 30; and 1 Cor. i. 21). And yet, not without guilt on their part was this privation (see on Rom. i. 20), nor were they left so absolutely to themselves as not to have the means of "feeling after Him," as we are now to hear. **17. Nevertheless** [Καίτοιγε]—'Although indeed.' **he left not himself without witness.** Though the heinousness of idolatry is represented as so much less in the heathen, by how much they were outside the pale of Revealed Religion, the apostle takes care to add, that the heathen have divine

"witness" enough to leave them "without excuse." **in that he did good** [ἀγαθουργῶν is preferable to —ποιῶν]—scattering His beneficence everywhere and in a thousand forms. **and gave us rain from heaven, and fruitful seasons**—on which human subsistence and all human enjoyment depend. In Lycaonia, where rain is peculiarly scarce, as ancient writers attest, this allusion would have all the greater effect. **filling our hearts**—or 'your hearts,' according to another reading. **with food and gladness**—a natural colloquialism, the heart being gladdened by the food supplied to the body. **18. And with these sayings scarce restrained they the people, that they had not done sacrifice unto them.** In spite of this, and of the apostle Peter's repudiation of all such undue honours (see on ch. x. 26), how soon did idolatrous tendencies begin to show themselves in the Christian Church, at length to be systematized and enjoined in the Church of Rome!

The minds of the Lycaonians being poisoned by Jews from Antioch and Iconium, a popular tumult is excited, and Paul, being stoned and drawn out of the city, is left for dead. Recovering, however, he withdraws with Barnabas to Derbe (19-21). **19. And** —rather, 'But' [δὲ]. **there came thither certain Jews from Antioch and Iconium.** Furious zeal that must have been which would travel so far to counteract the missionaries of the Cross, and how bitter and determined it was may be seen by the result. **who persuaded the people**—'gained over the crowds,' 'the populace,' or 'the mob' [πείσαντες τ. ὄχλους]. **and, having stoned Paul.** "Once (writes he to the Corinthians) was I stoned" (1 Cor. xi. 25); and the allusion must be to this scene at Lystra, for that at Iconium (v. 5) was not an accomplished fact. The mob seem to have let Barnabas alone, Paul, as the prominent actor and speaker, being the object of all their rage. The words seem to imply that it was the Jews who did this; and no doubt they took the lead (v. 19); but it was the act of the instigated and fickle mob along with them. **drew him out of the city.** By comparing this with ch. vii. 58, it will be seen that the Jews must have been the chief actors in this scene. **supposing he had been dead**— [νομίζοντες is slightly preferable to νομίσαντες, and τεθνηκέναι to τεθνάναι.] **20. Howbeit, as the disciples stood round about him**—'having surrounded or encircled him.' So his labours here had not been in vain: "disciples," we see, had been gained, who now rallied around the bleeding body; and we shall afterwards see ground to conclude that among these must have been that most valued of all his future companions and fellow-labourers—TIMOTHEUS (see on ch. xvi. 1-3). **he rose up.** It is just possible that this recovery was natural; the insensibility occasioned by such treatment as he had received, sometimes passing away of itself, and leaving the patient less hurt

21   And the next day he departed with Barnabas to Derbe. And when they had preached the Gospel to that city, and [1]had taught many,
22 they returned again to Lystra, and *to* Iconium, and Antioch, confirming the souls of the disciples, *and* exhorting them to continue in the faith, and that [u]we must through much tribulation enter into the king-
23 dom of God. And when they had [v]ordained them elders in every church,

A. D. 46.

[1] had made many disciples.
[u] Matt. 10 38.
Matt. 16. 24.
Rom. 8. 17.
[v] Tit. 1. 5.

than appears. But certainly the impression naturally left on the mind by the words is, that the restoration was miraculous; and so the best interpreters understand the words. This is confirmed by what follows. **and came into the city**—out of which he had been dragged as a corpse. Noble intrepidity! Yet he did not again venture to present himself as a preacher after such treatment. **and the next day he departed with Barnabas to Derbe** (see on *v.* 6)—a journey for which he would hardly have been fit if his recovery had been quite natural.
Retracing their steps, they return to Antioch, whence they started, and report their proceedings (21-23). **21. And when they had preached the gospel to that city, and had taught many**—rather, 'had made disciples of a considerable number' [μαθητεύσαντες ἱκανούς]. It is a pity that our version (following the Vulgate) has not observed the important distinction between the two words used in Matt. xxviii. 19, 20,—the one for 'making disciples,' the other for "teaching" the disciples so made. That distinction is carefully observed in this book. The former word is used here; nor could the other have properly been used where the Gospel was now for the first time preached, and there was no time for any after "teaching:" but the latter is used in ch. xi. 26, where, the disciples having been already made, the thing aimed at was their establishment in the faith and growth in grace. **they returned again.** They appear to have experienced no persecution here, since the apostle, long after this, when reminding Timothy of what he endured for the Gospel "at Antioch, at Iconium, at Lystra," seems studiously to omit Derbe (2 Tim. iii. 11). Beyond this our missionaries did not see fit for the present to prosecute their journey. Not that they were hurried home by urgent business—else they might have gone by a considerably shorter route than they took —taking a south-easterly direction from Derbe to Tarsus, and thence to Antioch. And one would imagine that, when so near the home of his youth, the great apostle, whose human affections were so keen, would prefer that route. But he had reasons for returning by the way he came, which with him were of paramount weight. 'At Derbe (says *Howson* admirably) Paul was not far from the well known pass which leads down from the central table-land to Cilicia and Tarsus. But his thoughts did not centre in an earthly home. He revisted the places where he had been reviled and persecuted, but where he◆had left, as sheep in the desert, the disciples whom his Master had enabled him to gather. They needed building up and strengthening in the Faith, comforting in the midst of their inevitable suffering, and fencing round by permanent institutions. Undaunted, therefore, by the dangers that awaited them, our missionaries return to them, using words of encouragement which none but the founders of a true Religion would have ventured to address to their earliest converts, that "we can only enter into the kingdom of God by passing through much tribulation." **to Lystra, and to Iconium, and Antioch**—taking these places now, of course, in the reverse order from the former visit. **22. Confirming the souls of the disciples.** Whatever

may be pleaded in favour of Episcopal *Confirmation* of the young, it would be absurd to take the term here employed in any such technical sense : 'Establishing' in the Faith is clearly the sense; as appears, indeed, from what follows. **exhorting them to continue in the faith.** The "and" of our authorized version prefixed to this clause injures the sense; for the historian does not say that they 'confirmed their souls *and* exhorted them,' but "confirmed their souls (*by*) exhorting them to continue in the Faith" which they had before embraced, **and** (warning them) **that we must through much tribulation** [διὰ πολλῶν θλίψεων]—or 'through many troubles,' **enter into the kingdom of God. 23. And when they had ordained them elders** [Χειροτονήσαντες δὲ αὐτοῖς πρεσβυτέρους]—literally, 'Having chosen them elders by show of hands'—that is, having superintended such choice on the part of the disciples ; and there is the best reason to conclude that this is the sense intended by the historian, and not "ordained" (as our version, following in this case the Vulgate and *Luther*, rather than *Beza*, have rendered the term). There is no evidence in the New Testament that, in apostolic times, the word had lost its proper meaning: this is beyond doubt its meaning in 2 Cor. viii. 19; and there is indisputable evidence that the concurrence of the people was required in all elections to sacred office in the earliest ages of the Church. The expression used (says *Lechler*) leads to the idea that the apostles appointed and conducted a congregational election; and to this also points the precedent (in ch. vi.) of the election of the seven deacons in Jerusalem, conducted by the apostles. 'And, indeed (adds the same writer, with much judgment), it consisted with the nature of the transaction that the apostles should give the most decided weight to the public opinion and confidence of the members of the church. The distance of these Asiatic churches from Antioch in Syria, which was the mother church, taken in connection with the circumstances of time and place—by reason of which they, being at the commencement detached from the synagogue, were in want of a social footing, and were obliged to find such footing in themselves; and also, opposed as they were to the hostile Jewish multitude, they were necessarily obliged to exist compact and united among themselves—all this made an independent church-government, and therefore overseers, indispensably necessary.' **in every church** [κατ᾽ ἐκκλησίαν]. Comparing this expression with the similar one in ch. ii. 46 [κατ᾽ οἶκον], which our version renders "from house to house," but which probably means simply, 'in private houses' (see on that verse), it may mean that they caused elders to be chosen for these churches, not in the sense of some for each of them, but of several for all of them; and what is said (in ch. xvi. 2) of Timothy, who appears to have belonged to Lystra, that he "was well reported of by the brethren that were at Lystra *and Iconium*," might imply that he acted in this capacity in both places. But the former sense is preferable, since there is no evidence that in the apostolic churches the elders were placed over different churches; nor would it be deemed necessary to copy so literally the model

and had prayed with fasting, they commended them to the Lord, on whom
24 they believed. And after they had passed throughout ^wPisidia, they came
25 to Pamphylia. And when they had preached the word in Perga, they
26 went down into Attaleia; and thence sailed to ^xAntioch, from whence
   ^ythey had been recommended to the grace of God for the work which
   they fulfilled.
27 And when they were come, and had gathered the church together,
   they rehearsed all that God had done with them, and how he had

A. D. 46.

^w ch. 13. 13,
14.
ch. 15. 38.
^x ch. 11. 19,
25.
ch. 13. 1.
ch. 15. 12,
30.
^y ch. 13. 1, 3.

of the Jewish synagogues. **and had prayed with
fasting**—lit., 'fastings.' Compare ch. xiii. 3, from
which it appears that our missionaries set these
elders apart to their sacred work, just as they had
been themselves, except that no mention is here
made of the "laying on of hands." One thing,
at least, seems clear, that if this last clause refers
to the *ordination* of these elders, the former clause
cannot be meant to express the same thing, but
must refer to the *choice* of them. **they commended** [παρέθεντό]—or 'committed' them—all
these churches, **to the Lord**—that is, the Lord
Jesus, **on whom they** ('had') **believed** [πεπιστεύ-
κεισαν]. 24. **And after they had passed throughout
Pisidia, they came to Pamphylia. 25. And when
they had preached** (or 'spoken') **the word in
Perga**—now doing what for some reason they appear not to have done on their former visit,
though probably without visible fruit. **they went
down into Attaleia**—the sea-port, on the Gulf of
Pamphylia, which drew to itself the commerce
both of Egypt and Syria. **26. And thence sailed
to Antioch** (touching first at Seleucia), **from
whence they had been recommended to the
grace of God** (ch. xiii. 3) **for the work which they
fulfilled.**
  **27. And when they were come, and had gathered
the church together, they rehearsed** [ἀνήγγελλον
is preferable to ἀνήγγειλαν of the received text]
all that God had done with them [μετ' αὐτῶν]—
considering themselves but as His instruments.
and (in particular) **how he had opened the** (or
rather, and 'a') **door of faith unto the Gentiles**—to
such as had not been even proselytes before. The
"door of faith unto the Gentiles," which God
opened to our missionaries, appears to mean, not
only the outward openings which He gave them
for reaching the ears of the Gentiles, but that
entrance for the Gospel among them which secured
its believing reception. Compare ch. xvi. 14,
"whose heart the Lord opened;" 1 Cor. xvi. 9,
"For a great door and *effectual* is opened unto
me;" 2 Cor. ii. 12, "Furthermore, when I came
to Troas to preach Christ's gospel, and a door was
opened unto me of the Lord;" Col. iv. 3, "Withal
praying also for us, that God would open unto us
a door of utterance." As their call and mission
had been solemn and formal in the presence of the
church, and by the church of Antioch as well as
by the Holy Ghost, it was a fitting thing that to
that church they should hasten to give in the
report of the mission just concluded. And O with
what eager joy would they tell their chequered
tale and its wonderful results, and with what
transport would the true-hearted members of that
vigorous church drink in their story! **28. And
[there] they abode.** [The bracketed word has but
slender authority]. **long time** [χρόνον οὐκ ὀλίγου]
—'no little time' **with the disciples**—how long
cannot be certainly determined; but since, from
the commencement of the mission till they left
Antioch to go up to attend the council at Jerusalem, some four or five years elapsed, and since
the missionary journey would occupy less than
two years, the difference would be the period

of their stay at Antioch. (But see Chronological
Table.)
  Remarks.—1. The carping character of the objections made by the Tübingen school of critics to
the historical credibility of this book is nowhere
more contemptible than in this chapter. The
remarks of *Baur*, of *Zeller*, and of *Schwegler* on
the sameness of the incidents in different places—
on the suspicious resemblance of the cure of this
Lystran cripple to those of Peter; on the speech
of Lycaonia, as a clumsy invention of the writer;
on the legendary character of the worship offered
to the missionaries; and on the Jewish character of
the expostulation addressed to the rude heathens:
these objections have so little even of the semblance of force, that instead of its being necessary
to refute them, the difficulty is to conceive how
acute critics should waste their time in hunting
for them and holding them up. Such arguments
—though here and there we are compelled to
notice them—we cannot disfigure our pages by
refuting in detail. But it may not be out of place
to warn young students against being carried away
by that show of acute and learned criticism with
which these laborious triflers contrive to conceal
the shallowness of their argumentation. 2. At
the very opening of this precious History it was
observed that it is not so much a Record of
"the Acts of the Apostles," as of the actings of the
glorified Redeemer Himself, who, as Lord of the
Church which He hath purchased with His own
blood, employed His apostles and others to gather,
to organize, and to feed that Church. Such is
the view of the Church on earth which this chapter presents to our view. Thus, at Iconium,
"long time abode Paul and Barnabas there, speaking boldly in reliance on the Lord (Jesus), who
gave testimony to the word of His grace, granting
signs and wonders to be done by their hands." On
their way home from this missionary tour they
committed all the churches they had formed at
their first visit—at Lystra, Iconium, and Antioch
—"to the Lord (Jesus) on whom they had believed;" and in reporting at Antioch all their proceedings, they did but "rehearse all that God had
done with them" (as His instruments), and "how
He had opened to the Gentiles a door of faith."
If this view of the present relation of Christ in
heaven to the Church on earth be steadily borne
in mind, it will not only throw a glory around this
Book of the Church in its earliest stage, but transfigure the true history of the Church of Christ in
every age. 3. The exclamation of the Lycaonians
as to Barnabas and Paul, that "the gods had
come down to them in the likeness of men," shows
what a yearning there is in the hearts even of the
most unenlightened tribes after the Incarnation of
the invisible Godhead; even as the glad reception
of it, with the deep spiritual repose and the elevation of humanity itself which the true Incarnation has imparted, is evidence enough that this is
the consummation of the eternal purposes of love
to men. 4. What a contrast does the horror of
Barnabas and Paul at the attempted worship of
them by the simple Lycaonians present to the

28 °opened the door of faith unto the Gentiles.   And there they abode long time with the disciples.

A. D. 46.

° 1 Cor. 16. 9.

self-satisfaction which the idolatrous adulation of the people gave to Herod Agrippa, when they shouted, "It is the voice of a god, and not of a man," and for which the angel of the Lord smote him with the horrible disease of which he died! (ch. xii. 21-23.) But in the light of this horror of our missionaries, what are we to think of that clerical ambition which, once indulged, craved its continuance and growth until nothing would content it short of claims nakedly idolatrous. 'And what would these apostles have done (say *Leonhard and Spiegel*, quoted by *Lechler*) if they had seen the adoration of their pretended bones, the worship of their images, and the idolatry which is now practised with them?' And is the spirit which loves to be so regarded quite dead in some Protestant Churches? 5. In *Paley's* incomparable 'Horæ Paulinæ'—the object of which is to demonstrate the truth of the apostolic Church History from a great number of 'Undesigned Coincidences' between the Epistles of Paul and the Acts of the Apostles—an argument is built on the *stoning* of Paul at Lystra, recorded in this chapter, which is too beautiful not to be here extracted. '"*Once* (saith Paul) was I stoned" (2 Cor. xi. 25). Does the history relate that St. Paul, prior to the writing of this epistle, had been stoned more than once? The history mentions distinctly one occasion upon which St. Paul was stoned—viz., at Lystra in Lycaonia. "There came thither certain Jews from Antioch and Iconium, who persuaded the people, and, having stoned Paul, drew him out of the city, supposing he had been dead" (ch. xiv. 19). And it mentions also another occasion in which "an assault was made both of the Gentiles, and also of the Jews with their rulers, to use them despitefully, and to stone them;" but "they were ware of it (the history proceeds to tell us) and fled unto Lystra and Derbe." This happened at Iconium prior to the date of this [second] epistle [to the Corinthians]. Now had the assault been completed—had the history related that a stone was thrown, as it relates that preparations were made both by Jews and Gentiles to stone Paul and his companions; or even had the account of this transaction stopped, without going on to inform us that Paul and his companions "were aware of their danger and fled"—a contradiction between the history and the epistle would have ensued. Truth is necessarily consistent; but it is scarcely possible that independent accounts, not having truth to guide them, should thus advance to the very brink of contradiction without falling into it.' 6. The three-fold procedure of Paul and Barnabas, in revisiting the young churches gathered out by them at their former visit, forms a noble model for that of the Christian churches in our own day whose missionaries are engaged in similar work to that here recorded. *First*, they "confirm the souls of the disciples, exhorting them to continue in the Faith" which they had embraced, and forewarning them of the trials through which they must pass to glory. This was the *ministration of the word*, which must lie at the foundation of all establishment in the faith and growth in grace. *Next*, they proceed to *organize* them, so that they might have within themselves the means of their own consolidation, nurture, and extension. Nor did they do this for them: they simply presided over and directed their own choice of elders from amongst themselves. 'And yet (as *Lechler* says) these were youthful communities, in which as yet no long Christian experience, no stedfastness of Christian character, no deep in-

sight, could be sought.' To this it may not be amiss to add the observations of *Baumgarten*,—'It has been a question whether in this organization of their body the Christians were permitted to co-operate, or whether the apostles in these regulations acted as possessing fulness of power, and of themselves nominated and appointed these presbyters. From all that we have hitherto discovered in the work before us, of the relation subsisting between the apostles and the believers, we find it antecedently impossible to suppose this. It is true, these believers are but recent converts; but still they are unhesitatingly spoken of as believers in the Lord (*v.* 23), and as such they are partakers of the same Spirit which fills the apostles. Now, it is inconceivable that such communion of the Spirit should not have been duly recognized in a matter like this, which most immediately concerned the believers. And, inasmuch as the mode of proceeding in the election of the seven deacons stands forth as a model at all times for the initiatory organization of churches, it is impossible to suppose that in the times immediately succeeding the apostles, the concurrence of the laity in the nomination of bishops should have been held to be so essential as was undeniably the case (see *Guericke*, 'Christliche Archæologie,' English translation, pp. 37, 38, and *Augusti*, 'Denkwürdigkeiten,' xi. 259, &c.), unless this had been the practice from the very beginning of the Gentile Church, at whose threshold we are now standing. On this supposition, the custom of the apostolical missionaries to leave the several bands of Christian converts for a while, to follow a purely internal development becomes easily explicable; for in this period it was the apostle's object that the several characters and capacities which the Holy Spirit had called into being should manifest and distinguish themselves, in order to their attaining to their appropriate position and employment in the Church, by the judgment of the whole body and the ratification of the apostles.' But *lastly*, our apostolic missionaries spent with each of these young Christian churches a season of prayer with fasting, that they might solemnly "commit them to the Lord on Whom they had believed." What paternal wisdom and grace did this three-fold treatment of these young churches display! 7. Though the Gentile church at Antioch would to a large extent be prepared for the tidings brought them by Paul and Barnabas, of considerable accessions to Christ from among the heathen of other places, the extent to which Gentile Christianity had spread, could not fail to astonish them; and taking this in connection with the systematic, persevering, and deadly opposition of the heads of the Jewish community, and most of all when the Gentiles were addressed and appeared ready to flock under the wing of Christ, the impression would grow upon them that the Gospel, spurned away by the Jews, was now to find its home among the Gentiles, and that their own Antioch —honoured to be the birthplace of Gentile Christianity—ought now to consecrate its chief strength to the extension of the Faith and Church of Christ over the wide heathen world, at least to the extent of not grudging its great teachers to that work whenever the providence of God and their own missionary impulses should call for the surrender of them, as in course of time we shall find was the case. 8. The 14th verse of this chapter raises some important questions which may fitly be noticed here. *First*, Were there more apostles, in the strict sense of that term, than the

15 And ^acertain men which came down from Judea taught the brethren, *and said,* Except ye be circumcised after the manner of Moses, ye

A. D. 52.

^a Gal. 2. 12.

original Twelve; including Matthias, whose appointment in the room of Judas came as near as possible, in the manner of it, to that in which the Twelve were selected and set apart? *Second,* Since Paul was confessedly on a level, in point of apostolic authority, with these Twelve, are we to regard his case as *exceptional;* or was he but one of *an extended apostolate,* which included Barnabas and others in the apostolic age? *Third,* Even supposing the apostleship of Paul to have been exceptional, must we not still admit that there existed in the apostolic age—outside this circle—a more extended though perhaps lower apostleship, in which are to be reckoned Barnabas and others? *Fourth,* Should this be granted, was such an apostolate designed to continue in the Church of Christ; and are its permanent possessors the prelatical bishops of those churches which are constituted on the hierarchical principle?—What were the qualifications for the apostleship, in the strictly official sense of that term? (1.) The ability to attest the resurrection of Christ, from having seen Him after He rose from the dead (ch. i. 21, 22; xxii. 14, 15; 1 Cor. ix. 1; xv. 8). (2.) An immediate Divine call (Rom. i. 1; 1 Cor. i. 1; Gal. i. 1; Eph. i. 1; Col. i. 1; 1 Tim. i. 1; 2 Tim. i. 1). (3.) The possession of miraculous gifts (2 Cor. xii. 12; Rom. xv. 18, 19). (4.) The consciousness of infallible guidance (ch. xv. 28) and of Divine authority for the government of the Church (2 Cor. x. 8). Now, were these qualifications transmitted, or in their nature transmissible, beyond the apostolic age? With the first age of the Church they of necessity expired; and certainly the whole procedure in the upper room, in the matter of a successor to Judas, supposes the office to be *peculiar* and *intransmissible.* In this case the apostleship of Paul must needs have been exceptional. So he himself represents it in 1 Cor. xv. 8-10; and while every other allusion which he makes to it is of the same tenor, there is nothing anywhere said of Barnabas which clearly ascribes to him the above qualifications. But neither must we, on the other hand, overlook certain facts, which seem to imply that in *some* sense the term *apostle* was applied to others besides Paul and the Eleven. Thus, in the verse which has given occasion to these remarks, "the *apostles* Barnabas and Paul:" compare also *v.* 4, "Part held with the Jews, and part with the *apostles*"—meaning Paul and Barnabas. In confirmation of this we are referred to 1 Cor. ix. 5, 6, where Paul claims the rights of the apostleship for Barnabas as well as himself, as being engaged in the same apostolic work; also Gal. ii. 9, where both are spoken of as engaged in the apostleship of the Gentiles. Again, the risen Saviour "was seen (says Paul) of Cephas, *then of the Twelve,* after that of above five hundred brethren at once . . . after that of James, *then of all the apostles*" (1 Cor. xv. 5-7)—as if there were many such *in addition* to "the Twelve." Then, to the Galatians (i. 19) Paul says, "Other of the apostles saw I none, save James, the Lord's brother"—who certainly was *not* one of the Twelve, and yet seems here to be called an apostle. Further, we read of "false teachers, deceitful workers, transforming themselves into the apostles of Christ" (2 Cor. xi. 13); and the great Head of all the churches commends Ephesus for having "tried them which said they were apostles, and were not, and had found them liars" (Rev. ii. 2)—as if the number of the apostles had not been so restricted as to preclude deceitful workers from transform-

ing themselves into such, and with such plausible pretensions as to require to be tried ere the cheat could be detected. In a word, we are referred to Rom. xvi. 7—"Salute Andronicus and Junia (if the name be that of a woman, or 'Junias,' if a man be intended) . . . who are *of note among the apostles*"—which, it is alleged, most naturally means, 'who are *noted apostles.*' Of these arguments some appear to have hardly any force. Thus, in the last passage, if the person named along with Andronicus is properly rendered *Junia,* and denotes a *woman,* few will think that a female apostle is here meant, or that there were any such; and as to the allegation that 'noted apostles' is the natural sense of the words, it is enough to say that a majority of the best critics hold the reverse (see our comment on that verse), and take them in the same sense as our translators. Then, the argument drawn from 1 Cor. xv. 5-7—"seen of Cephas, then of *the Twelve* . . . after that of above five hundred brethren at once . . . then of *all the apostles*"—would seem to prove too much; not only implying that the apostolate was extended far beyond the limits of the Twelve even before Christ left the earth—which who can readily believe?—but giving to this additional company of apostles a place (after the "five hundred brethren") very unlike what one would expect of such a body. On Gal. i. 19—"Other of the apostles saw I none save James, the Lord's brother"—it is unsafe to rely, as the statement is so ambiguous on this particular point that some think it proof positive that this James is here named as one of the Twelve; while others think that the apostle means here to ascribe no apostleship to this James at all, and that the meaning simply is, 'Other of the apostles saw I none—but James, the Lord's brother, I did see.' (See on that verse.) The argument from the pretensions to apostleship which some false teachers advanced (2 Cor. xi. 13), and whom the Ephesian church is commended for having tried and detected (Rev. ii. 2), is much more plausible; since it seems hard to conceive how, if the apostolate was limited to the original number—only Paul being exceptionally added—such pretensions could be advanced at all, or need to be tried. But why should it be presumed that the limitation of the apostolate, and the exceptional character of Paul's apostleship, must have been so well known to all the churches that no false teacher could have the face to pretend that his claim to the apostleship was as valid as Paul's, or if he did, that the imposture would so immediately discover itself to all real Christians as to supersede the necessity of trying him? Surely this is too much to presume, and our own impression is quite the reverse. One argument, then, alone remains, which to us appears to have real force—the way in which Barnabas is spoken of in connection with Paul. *Supposing* Barnabas to have been an apostle, in all respects officially equal with Paul, the language employed in speaking of him is certainly quite suitable; and had we no reasons for coming to a different conclusion, that sense would be quite natural. The only question then is, Do they admit naturally of a sense which would *exclude* Barnabas from official equality with Paul, or from the apostleship in any strict sense? Two of them surely do. In 1 Cor. ix. 5, 6, Paul is merely asserting his right to temporal maintenance and the ordinary comforts of domestic life, against those who insinuated that indulgences of this nature were not consistent in those who advanced the

2 cannot be saved. When therefore Paul and Barnabas had no small dissension and disputation with them, they determined that [b] Paul and Barnabas, and certain other of them, [c] should go up to Jerusalem unto the

A. D. 12.
[b] Gal. 2. 1.
[c] 1 Sam. 8. 7.

high claims which Paul did ; and in self-defence he asks whether that was unlawful in him which was permitted to the other apostles, to the brethren of the Lord, and to Cephas, and whether he and Barnabas, who were fellow-workers in all the same fields of labour, were to be singled out as alone, of all these, unworthy of such rights. But does not the apostle expressly say, "we as well as other apostles" (*v.* 5)? True ; but, besides that he has himself chiefly in view in that "we," every one must see that he is writing (or dictating) with no regard to rigid accuracy of arrangement ; for after saying "we as well as other apostles, and as the brethren of the Lord," he adds, "and Cephas"—as if Cephas had not himself been one of those other apostles. The other passage (Gal. ii. 9) seems less decisive, as it merely affirms that in the dispute about circumcision, when "James, Cephas, and John"—who seemed to be "pillars" of the Jewish party—perceived the grace that was given to Paul, they gave the right hand of fellowship to him and his companion, Barnabas, who together represented and stood for Gentile liberty, and came to the understanding that the two parties should divide the field between them ; the one taking charge of the Jewish, the other of the Gentile department. This, therefore, proves nothing. It only remains, then, to explain our own verse—Acts xiv. 14—"the apostles Barnabas and Paul." That the historian does here (and in *v.* 4) class both under one denomination—"apostles"—is plain enough. But in what sense? Not merely as Paul's companion, but in their *missionary* character. In no other character had Paul as yet stood forth among his brethren. His distinctively official apostolic authority had as yet no scope for its exercise. And since in the missionary character of his apostleship there was no perceptible, and hardly any real difference—if any at all—between him and Barnabas, why might not our historian, with propriety enough, style them both "apostles," without implying that there was not, and never would be, any difference between the two as apostles ? If this be correct, it is easy to see how a certain laxity in the use of the term "apostle" —even by Paul himself, whenever he had not to maintain his own strict apostleship—and so by our historian, might obtain currency, and get into the phraseology of the early Church, without implying that an extended apostolate, to be perpetuated in the Church's *bishops*, was from the first understood to exist. Such, accordingly, we find to be the fact. The name of 'apostles' was given even to the Seventy disciples by Irenæus and Tertullian (towards the close of the second and beginning of the third century), and several other fathers write as if there were many apostles. Yet these same writers carefully distinguish between such and the original apostles, strictly so called. As to the figment of an episcopal succession of such apostles, heirs to the original office, there is about as little to support it in solid patristic evidence as there is warrant for it in Scripture.

CHAP. XV. 1-35.—COUNCIL AT JERUSALEM ON THE QUESTION OF CIRCUMCISION—ITS PROCEEDINGS AND RESULTS—HOW CARRIED OUT.

The brethren at Antioch being troubled about circumcision by Judaizing zealots from Jerusalem, Paul and Barnabas, with certain others, are sent up to Jerusalem on the subject—The brethren of Phenice and Samaria rejoice to hear from them of

the conversion of the Gentiles (1-3). **1. And certain men which came down from Judea taught the brethren, and said, Except ye be circumcised** [περιτέμνησθε of the received text, and —τμηθῆτε, of *Lachmann* and *Tischendorf*, have about equal support] **after the manner of Moses, ye cannot be saved.** It may seem strange, after Peter had satisfied the brethren at Jerusalem, that the admission of Cornelius and his Gentile friends, as uncircumcised believers, to the fellowship of the Church, was according to the will of God (ch. xi. 18), that the question should be raised afresh. But inveterate prejudices, especially in religion, die hard ; and "that the Gentiles should be fellow-heirs, and of the same body, and partakers of His promise in Christ by the Gospel," without passing through the gateway of circumcision, was a truth so novel at that time, that nothing could reconcile even sincere believers to it but the Divine seal set upon it in the case of Cornelius, while to the mere adherents of an ancestral creed, with its traditional usages, it would seem revolutionary and destructive. If such zealots for exclusive Judaism might be expected to have their stronghold anywhere, it would be at Jerusalem, the metropolitan seat of the ancient Religion. And since at Antioch the uncircumcised believers had not only been recognized as a true Church of Christ, but become the parent of a Gentile Christianity which threatened to eclipse that of the mother church of Jerusalem and its little daughters, we can hardly wonder at those Jewish zealots making a stand now as for life or death. The question, indeed, was much larger and more fundamental than might seem. For though the immediate point in dispute was only whether 'circumcision after the manner of Moses was necessary to salvation,' it was 'to the whole law' that they wished to bind the Gentiles (as is evident from *v.* 5) ; and, says the apostle to the Galatians (*v.* 3), "I testify to every man that is circumcised, that he is a debtor to do the whole law." On the same principle (as *Humphry* observes) 'the baptism of John stands for his whole ministry (ch. i. 22 ; Luke xx. 4). **2. When therefore Paul and Barnabas had no small dissension and disputation with them** [ζητήσεως, not συζ.— of the received text, which has no Uncial support.] That Paul and Barnabas should take the lead in this debate was natural, not only as being themselves Jews, but as having taught at Antioch the opposite doctrine. But the zealots (whom the apostle afterwards scrupled not to call "false brethren," Gal. ii. 4) were not to be put down by argument ; and as they appear to have succeeded so far as to create an uneasy feeling among the Gentile converts (*v.* 24, and Gal. ii. 11-13), alleging probably that the brethren at Jerusalem were on their side, **they** (the brethren at Antioch) **determined** [ἔταξαν]—or 'arranged,' **that Paul and Barnabas, and certain other of them.** We know the name of only one of these "other" deputies—"Titus ;" but as the apostle says of him, that being "a Greek" he would not compel him to be circumcised—in order that the liberty of the Gentile converts might be vindicated in his person (Gal. ii. 4-6)—we may conclude that the other deputies were of the uncircumcised as well as he, and were sent expressly to represent that interest at Jerusalem. (On the time of this visit, see Introduction.) **should go up to Jerusalem unto the apostles and**

3 apostles and elders about this question. And *ᵈbeing brought on their way by the church, they passed through Phenice and Samaria, *ᵉdeclaring the conversion of the Gentiles: and they caused great joy unto all the
4 brethren. And when they were come to Jerusalem, they were received of the church, and *of* the apostles and elders, and they declared all things
5 that God had done with them. But there ¹rose up certain of the sect of the Pharisees which believed, saying, That it was needful to circumcise them, and to command *them* to keep the law of Moses.
6 And the apostles and elders came together for to consider of this
7 matter. And when there had been much disputing, Peter rose up, and said unto them, Men *and* brethren, ye know how that a good while ago God made choice among us, that the Gentiles by my mouth should hear
8 the word of the Gospel, and believe. And God, *ᶠwhich knoweth the hearts, bare them witness, *ᵍgiving them the Holy Ghost, even as *he did*

A. D. 52.

ᵈ Rom. 15.24.
1 Cor. 16. 6.
3 John 6. 8.
ᵉ ch. 14. 27.
¹ Or, rose up, said they, certain.
ᶠ 1 Chr. 28. 9.
1 Chr.29.17.
Jer. 11. 20.
Jer. 17. 10.
Jer. 20. 12.
ch. 1. 24.
Heb. 4. 13.
Rev. 2. 23.
ᵍ ch. 10. 44.
ch. 11. 15.

elders about this question. In Gal. ii. 2, the apostle says he "went up by revelation;" but this is not inconsistent (as is by some alleged) with its being the present journey. As before he was sent forth both by the Holy Ghost and by the church at Antioch (ch. xiii. 3, 4), so now, though going to Jerusalem with a commission from the church at Antioch, he might at the same time be Divinely directed to comply with that call. **3. And being brought on their way** (or 'escorted') **by the church**—in token of respect, and to mark the importance attached to this journey, **they passed through Phenice and Samaria**—along the great Roman road which followed the coast line from north to south, a road even yet not quite obliterated; **declaring** (to the Christians of those parts) **the conversion of the Gentiles.** We have seen that some of the scattered disciples "travelled as far as Phenice and Cyprus, preaching to none but unto the Jews only" (see on ch. xi. 19). Here we have the fruits of their labour in those parts. Those in Phenicia would seem to have belonged, chiefly at least, to Tyre (ch. xxi. 3-6) and Sidon (ch. xxvii. 3). **and they caused great joy unto all the brethren.** If these converts were from among "the Jews only," they must have had more enlarged views of Christianity than the zealots of Judea; but perhaps a Gentile element may have helped to liberalize them.

On reaching Jerusalem, the Antiochene deputies are received by the whole church, and Paul and Barnabas relate their missionary proceedings—The zealots having insisted that the Gentile converts should be circumcised, the apostles and elders hold a Council to decide the question (4-6). **4. And when they were come to Jerusalem.** This was the apostle's *third* visit to Jerusalem after his conversion; and it was on this occasion that the circumstances related in Gal. ii. 1-10 took place (see there). **they were received**—'received cordially,' or 'welcomed' [παρεδέχθησαν, as the rarer form, is perhaps preferable to ἀπεδ.—of the received text.] **of the church**—here evidently meaning the members of the church at Jerusalem generally, as distinguished from its office-bearers, who are next mentioned. **and of the apostles and elders**—at a convention of all the Christians at Jerusalem, as a mark of respect to the deputies of so distinguished a body of Christians as that of Antioch; in the expectation, too, of hearing from them exciting tidings of the work among the Gentiles; and hoping that the ferment amongst themselves on the subject of circumcision might thus receive a check: **and they declared all things that God had done with them**—(see on ch. xiv. 27.) **5. But there rose up certain of the sect of the Pharisees which believed**—'of the

believing Pharisees;' just the quarter from which such zealots might be expected to arise: **saying, That it was needful to circumcise them**—that is, the whole Gentile converts of Antioch, whose accession to Christianity the deputies had just "declared." **and to command them to keep the law of Moses.** They did not question the reality of their conversion, nor the propriety of recognizing them as believers, but contended that their right to the blessings of the Abrahamic covenant and their standing in the church was incomplete without circumcision.

6. And the apostles and elders came together—not, however, without "the church," as appears from vv. 12, 22, 23. **for to consider of this matter.** It will be observed that when they had simply to *hear* from the deputies what God had wrought among the Gentiles through them, they were received not only by "the apostles and elders," but by "the church" (v. 4); but when it became necessary *to deliberate* and *decide* on the vital question of circumcising those Gentile converts, it is said, "the apostles and elders came together to consider of this matter." It will be seen, however, from the sequel of this narrative that the apostles and elders did not, like most hierarchical councils in later times, sit 'with closed doors.'

The debate—The address of Peter—The report of the Missionaries—The summing-up and proposal of James (vv. 7-21). **7. And when there had been much disputing**—*the apostles*, meanwhile, *sitting silent*, Peter rose up—the paramount position which he had all along occupied at Jerusalem, and the part assigned him in receiving Cornelius and his Gentile party into the Church, giving him a peculiar claim to be heard on this question; **and said unto them.** It has been remarked that this is the last mention of Peter in the Acts of the Apostles; and in this view it is delightful to find him here pronouncing in favour of those enlarged views of the Church, to the establishment of which the life-labours of Paul were devoted. **Men and brethren, ye know how that a good while ago**—many years before this; as if to intimate that long before this they ought to have held the question to be settled by the facts which he was about to mention: **God made choice among us**—or 'among you,' according to the preferable reading. **that the Gentiles by my mouth should hear the word of the gospel, and believe**—(ch. x.) **8. And God, which knoweth the hearts**—implying that the state of the heart before God is the real test of one's rightful standing in the visible Church; and though this cannot be certainly known to men, no principle can be sound which goes in the face of it: **bare them witness, giving them the Holy Ghost, even as he did**

9 unto us; and [h]put no difference between us and them, [i]purifying their
10 hearts by faith. Now therefore why tempt ye God, to put [j]a yoke upon
the neck of the disciples, which neither our fathers nor we were able to
11 bear? But [k]we believe that through the grace of the Lord Jesus Christ
we shall be saved, even as they.
12   Then all the multitude kept silence, and gave audience to Barnabas
and Paul, declaring what miracles and wonders God had wrought among
the Gentiles by them.
13   And after they had held their peace, James [l]answered, saying, Men
14 *and* brethren, hearken unto me: Simeon hath declared how God at the
first did visit the Gentiles, to take out of them a people for his name.
15, And to this agree the words [m]of the prophets; as it is written, After
16 [n]this I will return, and will build again the tabernacle of David, which
is fallen down; and I will build again the ruins thereof, and I will set it
17 up; that the residue of men might seek after the Lord, and all the Gentiles, upon whom my name is called, saith the Lord, who doeth all these
18 things. Known unto God are all his works from the beginning of the

A. D. 52.

[h] Rom. 3. 9,
22, 29, 30.
Rom. 10.11.
Col. 3. 11.
[i] ch. 10.43.
Rom. 8. 1.
34.
1 Cor. 1. 2.
Col. 1. 14.
1 Pet. 1. 22.
[j] Matt. 23. 4.
Gal. 5. 1.
[k] Rom. 3. 24,
Eph. 1. 7.
Eph. 2. 8.
Heb. 9. 12-
14.
[l] ch. 12. 17.
[m] Isa. 11. 10.
[n] Isa 54. 1-5.
Amos 9. 11.

---

unto us—(ch. x. 44.) **9. And put no difference
between us and them, purifying their hearts
by faith.** Whereas "the uncircumcision of the
flesh" of those Gentile converts was regarded by
the zealots as rendering them 'unclean,' Peter
says, that God, in "purifying their *hearts* by
faith," had abolished that outward distinction
between Jew and Gentile, making both one in
Christ. **10. Now therefore why tempt** (or 'try')
ye God—standing in the way of His demonstrated
purpose, **to put a yoke upon the neck of the
disciples, which neither our fathers nor we
were able to bear?** This, as has been already
remarked, was not the yoke of mere burdensome
ceremonies, but of an obligation to fulfil "the
whole law," to which every one became "debtor"
who was circumcised (Gal. v. 1-3); a yoke which,
just in proportion as one became more earnest and
spiritual, he would feel himself the more unable
to bear. **11. But we believe that through the
grace of the Lord Jesus [Christ]** (this bracketed
word is of very doubtful authority) **we shall
be saved, even as** (that is, no otherwise than)
they—circumcision being to the Jew no advantage, and the want of it to the Gentile no loss,
in the matter of salvation; for the grace of the
Lord Jesus must do all for both, and the same for
each. **12. Then all the multitude** [πᾶν τὸ πλῆθος]
kept silence ['Εσίγησεν]. As the same word in
the next verse is used to signify that Barnabas
and Paul 'ceased speaking,' it is not improbable
that Peter's address gave rise to fresh discussion—
in which case, as it was "the multitude" that
ceased, we must infer that others besides "the
apostles and elders" had been allowed to take
part in the discussion. Be this as it may, the
rising of Paul and Barnabas put an end to it.
and gave audience to Barnabas and Paul. Barnabas is here *once more* named first, as being much
longer and better known in Jerusalem than the
young apostle of the Gentiles. **declaring what
miracles (or 'signs') and wonders God had
wrought among the Gentiles by them.** This
narrative, coming in immediately after Peter's
account of the introduction of Cornelius and his
party into the Church without circumcision, was
plainly designed to show that God had acted on
the same principle with them, throughout all their
missionary labours, as he had done with Peter;
the signs and wonders wrought among the Gentiles through them having set the same Divine seal
on their proceedings, as the descent of the Spirit

upon Cornelius and his friends had done upon
those of Peter.
**13. And after they had held their peace, James
answered.** Whether this was James the son of
Alphæus, or James "the Lord's brother," or
whether these were one and the same person—see
on ch. xxi. 18. At any rate, he occupied the
leading position in Jerusalem (ch. xii. 17; xxi. 18);
and in that capacity presiding in this assembly, he
here sums up and indicates the judgment which
he deemed it fitting that the assembly should pronounce, and the course proper to be taken for carrying it out. His decision, though given as his own
judgment only, could not but have great weight
with the opposing party, from his known conservative reverence for all Jewish usages within
the circle of Israelitish Christianity. **saying, Men
and brethren, hearken unto me: 14. Simeon**—a
Hebrew variation of "Simon" (as in 2 Pet. i. 1,
Gr.), the Jewish and family name of Peter, here
perhaps used at the outset of his address (as
a Hebrew addressing Hebrews) to propitiate the
Jewish zealots; **hath declared how God at the
first**—answering to Peter's "good while ago" (*v.* 7),
did visit the Gentiles, to take out of them—in
the exercise of His adorable sovereignty, **a people
for** (the honour of) **his name**—or to show forth
His praise. **15. And to this agree the words of
the prophets**—the prophets generally; but particularly, **as it is written** (in Amos ix. 11, 12—
here given nearly as in the Septuagint): **16. After
this I will return**—or revisit in mercy the covenant people, **and will build again the (fallen)
tabernacle of David**—that is, will restore its
decayed splendour; **and I will build again the
ruins thereof, and I will set it up**—not again in
outward magnificence—for that had passed for ever
away—but in spiritual glory, under David's Son
and Lord. **17. That the residue of men**—those
outside the pale of the Jewish economy, **might
seek after the Lord, and all the Gentiles, upon
whom my name is** (or 'has been') **called** [ἐπικέ-
κληται]—all the Gentiles who, on their believing,
should have His name called on them, or, as being
now "fellow-citizens with the saints" should be
called by his name, **saith the Lord, who doeth [all]
these things.** The word "all" here seems clearly
a late addition to the text. **18. Known unto God
are all his works from the beginning of the world.**
This is the reading of the majority of MSS.; though
a very ancient reading (adopted by *Tischendorf* and
most critics after him, except *Lachmann*) closes
(*v.* 17) thus: 'saith the Lord who doeth these things.

19 world. Wherefore my sentence is, that we trouble not them which from
20 among the Gentiles °are turned to God: but that we write unto them,
that they abstain *P*from pollutions of idols, and *from* *q*fornication, and
21 *from* things strangled, *r* and *from* blood. For Moses of old time hath in
every city them that preach him, being *s*read in the synagogues every
sabbath day.
22   Then pleased it the apostles and elders, with the whole church, to
send chosen men of their own company to Antioch with Paul and Barnabas; *namely,* Judas surnamed *t*Barsabas, and Silas, chief men among the
23 brethren: and they wrote *letters* by them after this manner; The apostles

A. D. 52.

° 1 Thes. 1. 9.
P Gen. 25. 2.
   Ex. 20. 3.
   Eze. 20. 50.
   1 Cor. 6. 1.
q 1 Cor. 6. 9.
   Col. 3. 5.
   1 Pet. 4. 3.
r Gen. 9. 4.
   Lev. 3. 17.
s ch. 13. 15.
t ch. 1. 23.

known from the beginning of the world,' or, 'from of old'—omitting the rest of *v.* 18 [γιωστὰ ἀπ' αἰῶνος]. The sense is the same; and the point of the statement is, that as it had been all along the purpose of God to reconstruct the decayed Jewish Church on a wider basis than before—embracing all believing Gentiles—so He had given abundant notice of this in the writings of the prophets; and since Himself was to be the sole Doer of these things, He was only now doing what it was from the first in His mind to do, and thus it was no novelty. 19. **Wherefore my sentence**—rather, 'judgment' [ἐγὼ κρίνω]—**is, that we trouble not** (with needless Jewish burdens) **them which from among the Gentiles are turned** [ἐπεστρέφουσιν]—rather, 'are turning,' **to God.** This great work is regarded as in progress, and indeed was rapidly advancing; and since insisting on the circumcision of all Gentile converts would undoubtedly check that progress, his judgment was decidedly against this. 20. **But that we write unto them, that they abstain from pollutions**—from all that was polluting either in itself or in the estimation of their Jewish brethren. Four such things are now specified: First, **of idols**—that is, things polluted as having been offered in sacrifice to idols. The heathen were accustomed to give away or sell portions of such animals. From such food James would enjoin the Gentile converts to abstain, lest it should seem to the Jews that they were not entirely weaned from idolatry. (See Rom. xiv. 15; 1 Cor. viii. 10, 11.) Next, **and from fornication.** It may seem strange that a thing in itself sinful should be here mixed up with things indifferent, and only to be avoided as offensive to the Jews. So strange has it appeared to some critics, that they have tried to give another sense to the word and another turn to the suggestion regarding it. But the only satisfactory sense of the word here is its natural and proper sense. Let it be remembered that this was the characteristic sin of heathendom, and unblushingly practised by all ranks and classes. Were the Gentile converts, therefore, to give way to this sin—of which they might well be thought in danger—it would proclaim them to the Jews, whose Scriptures branded it as a heathen abomination, to be still joined to their old idols. Thirdly, **and from things strangled**—that is, from all flesh having the blood still in it. Lastly, blood itself: **and from blood**—in whatever form, as having been peremptorily forbidden to the Jews, and the eating of which, therefore, by the Gentile converts, could not but shock their prejudices (see on *vv.* 28, 29). 21. **For Moses of old time hath in every city them that preach him, being read in the synagogues every sabbath day**—thus keeping alive in every Jew those feelings which such practices would shock, and which, therefore, the Gentile converts must carefully respect, if the oneness of both classes in Christ was to be practically preserved. This seems to us the most natural sense of the allusion

to Moses here, (that of *Calvin, Olshausen, de Wette, Meyer, Humphry, Hackett, Alford,* &c.) Another view of it (that of *Erasmus, Grotius, Thiersch,* and *Lechler*)—that the authority of Moses was in no danger of being lowered by the admission of uncircumcised Gentiles into the Church, seeing that he was "read in the synagogues every sabbath day"—seems to us a much less probable one. Be this as it may, the course suggested by James seems to have immediately commended itself to all present; for it is added, 22. **Then pleased it the apostles and elders, with the whole church.** There is no reason for supposing that as "the apostles and elders" *represented* the church-members as a body, their decision was simply *regarded* as that of the people. The natural sense of the words suggests some *positive assent* on the part of "the whole church," so far as they were present, to the decision of the apostles and elders; and all the more if they took part in the discussion (see on *v.* 12). To us it would seem that the active and open procedure of the meeting, after James had ceased speaking, was conducted by "the apostles and elders," but that on their unanimous decision being announced, and the church members generally being appealed to for their consent, they signified it in such a way that in recording the final decision the historian might naturally say, "it pleased the whole church," as well as "the apostles and elders," to do what follows: **to send chosen men of their own company**—or, 'having chosen men from among themselves, to send them, **to Antioch with Paul and Barnabas;** [namely] **Judas surnamed Barsabas**—not to be confounded with the apostle "Judas the brother of James" (ch. i. 13), surnamed Thaddeus (Matt. x. 3); nor is there any evidence that he was a brother of "Joseph called Barsabas" (ch. i. 23). Nothing is known of him beyond what is here said. **and Silas**—the same as 'Silvanus,' in the Epistles. He became Paul's companion on his second missionary journey (*v.* 40); and the affection which the apostle cherished towards him seems to have been **as** constant as it was warm. **chief** (or 'leading') **men among the brethren**— and as such purposely selected, in order to express the esteem in which they held the church at Antioch and their deputies now present; and—since the matter affected all Gentile converts—to give weight to the decision of this important assembly. We are told (in *v.* 32) that they were "prophets;" and it was in this capacity probably that their eminence in the church at Jerusalem had been attained. 23. **And they wrote letters by them.** This is the earliest mention of *writing* as an element in the development of Christianity; for though it occurs in John xx. 30, 31, and xxi. 24, 25, that Gospel was not published till long after this book. And the combination here of written and oral transmission of an important decision reminds us of the first occasion of writing mentioned in the Old Testament, where a similar combination occurs (Exod. xvii. 14).

and elders and brethren *send* greeting unto the brethren which are of the

24 Gentiles in Antioch and Syria and Silicia: Forasmuch as we have heard, that certain "which went out from us have troubled you with words, subverting your souls, saying, *Ye must* be circumcised, and keep

25 the law; to whom we gave no *such* commandment: it seémed good unto us, being assembled with one accord, to send chosen men unto you with

26 our beloved Barnabas and Paul, men "that have hazarded their lives for

27 the name of our Lord Jesus Christ. We have sent therefore Judas and

28 Silas, who shall also tell *you* the same things by ²mouth. For it seemed good to "the Holy Ghost, and to us, to lay upon you no greater burden

29 than these necessary things; that "ye abstain from meats offered to idols, and ʸfrom blood, and from things strangled, and from fornication: from which if ye keep yourselves, ye shall do well. Fare ye well.

A. D. 52.

" Gal. 2. 4.
Gal. 5. 12.
Tit. 1 10.
1 John 2.19.
ʸ ch. 13. 50.
ch. 14. 19.
1 Cor. 15.30.
2 Cor. 11.23,
26.
² word.
ʷ John 16. 13.
1 Cor. 7. 25,
40.
ᶻ ch. 21. 25.
Rev. 2. 14.
ʸ Lev 17. 14.

Only, whereas *there* it is the deep *difference* between Israel and the Gentiles which is proclaimed, *here* (as *Baumgarten* excellently remarks) it is the *obliteration* of that difference through faith in the Lord Jesus. after, this manner; **The apostles and elders and brethren.** The true reading of this clause is of some consequence, from its bearing on the question, whether "the brethren"—the Christian people at large—had any voice in this assembly along with "the apostles and elders." The one reading is, 'The apostles and the elders, brethren.' This is the reading of the five chief MSS. of the New Testament (א A B C D), of the Vulgate, and of one or two other (though inferior) versions, and even of *Irenæus* (in the Latin). Accordingly, it is adopted by *Lachmann,* and approved by *Neander* and *Alford.* But the received reading is supported by most of the other Uncial MSS., by both the Syriac and other ancient versions, and by *Chrysostom, Theophylact* and other fathers, who might be expected to prefer the other reading. There is therefore a fair case for calling in internal evidence; and believing (with *Meyer, de Wette,* and *Lechler*) that it is far more probable that the received reading should be rejected, as favouring the co-operation of "the brethren" with "the apostles and elders," and that that reading would be preferred which represented "the apostles and elders" as themselves "the brethren" who wrote the letter—we hesitate not (with *Tischendorf*) to prefer the received reading. Besides, it seems to us that the word "brethren" is not a very natural addition to "the apostles and elders," by way of describing them, and certainly is unusual. And if we are correct in supposing that "the whole church" (mentioned in the previous verse) were permitted to give a positive assent to the decision of "the apostles and elders," what more natural than that the Letter which all thus resolved to send should run in the name of all the parties? [send] greeting. As this word (χαίρειν) —so familiar in Greek epistles—occurs only in one other place of the New Testament (if we except the letter of the Greek general, Claudius Lysias, ch. xxiii. 26), namely, in the Epistle of this same James (i. 1), it seems to show that both Letters were drawn up by one hand—that of James—and thus to authenticate the document here given (as *Bengel* acutely observes). unto the brethren which are of the Gentiles in Antioch and Syria and Cilicia—showing that Christian communities existed not only in Syria but in Cilicia, which owed their existence in all likelihood to the labours of the great apostle, in the interval between his flight to Tarsus from Jerusalem (ch. ix. 29, 30) and his departure in company with Barnabas for Antioch (see on ch. xi. 25, 26). 24. Forasmuch as we have heard, that certain which went out from us— without the authority or even the knowledge of

the church at Jerusalem, though they belonged to it, and probably pretended to represent its views, subverting (or 'unsettling') your souls [ἀνασκευά-ζοντες]. Such strong language is evidently designed to express indignation at this attempt, by an unauthorized party, to bring the whole Christian Church under Judaical and legal bondage. [saying, Ye must be circumcised, and keep the law]: to whom we gave no [such] commandment. The bracketed words are of very doubtful authority, and probably taken from *vv.* 1 and 5. *Lachmann* and *Tischendorf* exclude them. If we omit them, the genuine words, 'to whom we gave no charge,' will mean simply that they were wholly unauthorized by the church at Jerusalem. 25. It seemed good unto us being assembled with one accord (see on ch. ii. 1), to send chosen men—or 'to choose out men, and send them unto you,' with our beloved Barnabas and Paul (named as before; see on *v.* 12): 26. Men that have hazarded [παραδε-δωκόσιν]—*lit.,* 'rendered up,' as in *will* they did, their lives for the name of our Lord Jesus Christ. Noble testimony to those beloved men! It was doubtless prompted more immediately by the thrilling narrative to which they had just listened from their own lips (*v.* 12); but such a reference to the sacrifices they had made for Christ was judiciously inserted in this Letter, in order to give them, along with their own deputies, the highest weight with those to whom they wrote. 27. We have sent therefore Judas and Silas, who shall also tell you the same things by mouth [διὰ λόγου]— or 'by word' (word of mouth). They had thus a double expression of the mind of the council: As in *writing* it would be more explicit, less liable to be misunderstood or perverted, and more easy of transmission to different places; so when the contents of the Letter were communicated and enlarged on *verbally* by the deputies from Jerusalem, the impression would naturally be much deepened. Besides, it was considerate and tender to send men who would be able to say of Barnabas and Paul what could not be expected to come from themselves, but what, though the Christians of Antioch knew it long before, would come with double weight as a testimony borne to them from Jerusalem. 28. For it seemed good to the Holy Ghost, and to us—the One inwardly guiding the other; as if it had been said (as *Olshausen* expresses it), 'It seemed good to the Holy Ghost in' or 'by us.' They acted throughout this whole business under the consciousness of Divine guidance, the glorified Lord of the Church directing them by His Spirit, to lay upon you no greater burden than these necessary things; 29. That ye abstain from meats offered to idols, and from blood, and from things strangled, and from fornication: from which if ye keep yourselves, ye shall do well. Fare ye well. The

30 So when they were dismissed, they came to Antioch: and when they
31 had gathered the multitude together, they delivered the epistle: *which*
32 when they had read, they rejoiced for the ³ consolation. And Judas and
Silas, being ²prophets also themselves, ᵃexhorted the brethren with many
33 words, and confirmed *them*. And after they had tarried *there* a space,
34 they were let ᵇgo in peace from the brethren unto the apostles. Notwith-
35 standing it pleased Silas to abide there still. Paul ᶜalso and Barnabas
continued in Antioch, teaching and preaching the word of the Lord, with
many others also.

A. D. 52.

³ Or, ex-
hortation.
² ch. 2. 17,18.
ch. 11. 27.
1 Cor.12.23.
ᵃ ch. 14. 22.
ch. 18. 23.
ᵇ 1 Cor. 16.11.
Heb. 11. 31.
ᶜ ch. 13. 1.

whole strain of these prohibitions, and of *vv.* 20,
21, implies that they were designed as concessions to Jewish feelings on the part of the Gentile
converts, and not as things which were all of unchanging obligation. The only cause for hesitation
arises from " fornication " being mixed up with
the other three things; which has led many to
regard all of them as permanently prohibited.
But the remarks on *v.* 20 may clear this. The
then state of heathen society in respect of all
the four things seems the reason for so mixing
them up.

**30. So when they were dismissed, they came
to Antioch: and when they had gathered the
multitude together, they delivered the epistle:
31. Which when they had read, they rejoiced for
the consolation** [τ. παρακλήσει]. As the same
word is in the next verse properly rendered
"exhorted," the meaning is thought by some (as
Beza, Meyer, Humphry, Webster and Wilkinson)
to be ' they rejoiced for the exhortation ' or ' advice,' (as in *marg.*) But since the prevalent feeling
which this Letter would produce at Antioch was
that of *relief* at the liberty from Jewish bondage
which the zealots would fain have imposed upon
them, and since ' exhortation ' or ' advice ' is not
the burden of the Letter—not at least what they
naturally would "rejoice for"—we are inclined
to prefer the sense of " consolation," as in our
version (in which *Luther, Calvin, Grotius, Beza,
de Wette, Alford*, and *Lechler* concur). **32. And
Judas and Silas, being prophets also themselves**
—as well as Paul and Barnabas—that is, inspired
teachers (see on ch. xi. 27, and xiii. 1), **exhorted
the brethren with many words** [διὰ λόγου πολλοῦ]
—rather, ' with much discourse,' **and confirmed
them**—opening up, no doubt, the great principle
involved in the controversy now settled, namely,
gratuitous salvation, or the purification of the heart
by faith alone (as expressed by Peter, *vv.* 9, 11),
and dwelling on the necessity of harmony in principle and affection between the Gentile disciples
and their Jewish brethren. **33. And after they
had tarried there a space** [χρόνον], or ' some
time ;' but how long cannot with certainty be
determined, **they were let go in peace** [μετ'
εἰρήνης]—' with peace,' the customary parting salutation, though in this case at least it would be
no formality, **from the brethren unto the apostles**
—or (as appears to be the true reading), ' to
those that had sent them' [πρὸς τ. ἀποστεί-
λαντες]. **34. [Notwithstanding it pleased Silas
to abide there still.]** The evidence against the
genuineness of this verse is decisive [it is wanting
in א A B E G H, and in about fifty cursives; in
the Syriac, the Vulgate, and other versions, and
in the two most critical of the later fathers—
Chrysostom and *Theophylact* only C and D have
it—the latter of scarce any authority in additions;
and the printed Vulgate, on the authority of
one inferior MS., inserts it]. No doubt this late
addition to the text was suggested by the apparent
inconsistency of *v.* 33 with *v.* 40 ; and in point of
fact, it is by no means improbable that Silas had

returned to Antioch before the second missionary
journey was proposed. **teaching and preaching
the word of the Lord**—the "teaching" being
directed to the disciples, and the " preaching " to
those who were without. **with many others**
(many other labourers) **also.** How rich must
Antioch have been at this time in the ministrations of the Gospel ! *To this period we must refer
the painful scene between Paul and Peter, described
in* Gal. ii. 11-14. 'The inconsistency,' says *Professor Lightfoot*, ' which St. Peter thus appears
to have shown so soon after his championship of
Gentile liberty at the congress, is rather in favour
of than against this view ; for the point of St.
Paul's rebuke is his inconsistency. But in fact
there is no alternative. An earlier residence at
Antioch (Acts xiii. 1-3) is out of the question; for
St. Paul is plainly narrating events in chronological order. Neither, again, can a later occasion
(Acts xviii. 23) be meant, for it does not appear
that Barnabas was with him then.' (See also
Howson's full and able statement, as against *Paley*
and *Wieseler*, vol. ii., pp. 244-250.)

Remarks.—1. When we find with what extreme
difficulty Jewish Christians—to whom circumcision had been for ages the Divine signature of
the covenant-people—could bring themselves to
recognize in uncircumcised Gentiles their brethren
in the Faith, even after this had been clearly
shown to be the will of God, should not Christians
strive to shake themselves free from the prejudices
which traditional teaching and ancestral usage
tend to beget, so as to be ready to enter cordially
into the work of God, wherever it clearly discovers itself to be His, even though in forms and
modes very different from those to which they
have been accustomed? At the same time, remembering how the same apostle who so earnestly
inculcated and so uniformly acted on this principle,
enjoins upon the strong in such things that they
should bear with the infirmities of the weak
(Rom. xiv., xv.), it will be the wisdom of those
who have surmounted prejudice themselves to
treat with forbearance and love their weaker
brethren, who, while equally conscientious with
themselves, are not able to act with the same
freedom as they are. 2. This famous Council of
Jerusalem—the first that was ever held in the
Christian Church—unquestionably involves a principle of Church action for all time. But since the
most unwarrantable assumptions have been built
on this as a precedent, not only by the Church of
Rome, but by other hierarchical Churches, care
must be taken—before any precedent be drawn
from this council in justification of the procedure
of subsequent councils in the Christian Church—in
the first place, to see that the *composition* of the two
bodies be substantially the same—and particularly,
that they be *not* composed exclusively of what
are called the clergy ; and next, since the supernatural illumination and the Divine authority
flowing from it, which resided in the apostles,
have most certainly been withdrawn (for the signs
of its presence, which the apostles exhibited,

36　And some days after, Paul said unto Barnabas, Let us go again and
visit our brethren ^din every city where we have preached the word of the
37　Lord, *and see* how they do.　And Barnabas determined to take with them
38　^eJohn, whose surname was Mark.　But Paul thought not good to take
him with them, ^fwho departed from them from Pamphylia, and went not

A. D. 52.
^d ch. 14. 1.
^e ch. 12. 12.
ch. 13. 5.
Col. 4. 10.
^f ch. 13. 13.

---

cannot be produced by any existing body of Christians, *that no such illumination and authority be claimed* by any modern council or synod of the Church; but that—trusting in the gracious guidance of Him who walketh in the midst of the golden candlesticks, and who hath said, "If ye abide in Me, and my words abide in you, ye shall ask what ye will, and it shall be done unto you"—the decisions of all modern councils, synods, or assemblies of the Church should be given forth to such as are in church-fellowship with them, to be by them observed simply as the condition of their continued unity. 3. It has been observed by *Lechler*, that 'not the whole resolution of the assembly is referred to the Holy Ghost, but only the weighty decision'—not to impose on the Gentiles a yoke which would have destroyed the freedom of the Gospel (*v.* 28); whereas the resolution to send deputies to the Christians of Antioch is introduced merely with the words, "It seemed good *unto us,* being assembled with one accord" (*v.* 25). We are not sure that any such distinction was intended by the different phraseology of the two verses. Nay, rather, when, in the latter of the two verses, it is said, "It seemed good to the Holy Ghost, *and to us,*" it would seem that the whole result of these solemn deliberations is referred at once to a Divine and a human source; the Holy Ghost being regarded as the animating and guiding Spirit of the assembly, and the members of it, who either gave utterance to their judgment or assented to that judgment as expressed by others, doing so in the full conviction of a Higher presence and direction throughout. 4. In every age there have been *purists* in the Church, who insist on right principles being gone through with in all circumstances, without regard to the views and feelings of those who want light to approve of them. Let such study the beautiful action of this council. Beyond all reasonable doubt, abstinence from "things strangled, and from blood," was enjoined on the Gentile Christians merely out of tenderness to the views and feelings of their weaker brethren of the circumcision. And when the thing to be avoided is merely the denying of ourselves in what we can perfectly well do without, who that loves his brother in the Lord would not do so, when by an opposite course he has reason to believe that he will wound a brother's conscience and probably endanger a brother's soul? Such voluntary sacrifices, however, are not to be confounded with cowardly compromises—such as that of the great apostle of the circumcision on one occasion, for which he was rebuked by the greater apostle of the Gentiles (Gal. ii. 11-13).　Nor is it necessary to give in to every weak prejudice, on the plea of not hurting the conscience of others. Such intolerable bondage is no real benefit to the weak, who should learn to grow into strength and liberty in Christ Jesus.

36-40.—PAUL PROPOSES TO BARNABAS TO REVISIT THE SCENES OF THEIR FORMER MISSION—A KEEN DISSENSION ARISING BETWEEN THEM REGARDING THE PROPRIETY OF AGAIN TAKING JOHN MARK WITH THEM, THEY PART COMPANY TO PROSECUTE SEPARATE MISSIONARY TOURS.

The Proposal (36). **36. And some days after**—that is, after the return of Judas and Silas to Jerusalem. How long after, is left undetermined; but as Antioch seems now to have been rich in Christian agency (*v.* 35), if this suggested to Paul the thought that he and his coadjutor could well be spared for a time, and kindled the desire to set out afresh on missionary work, perhaps the interval was not long. **Paul said unto Barnabas, Let us go again and visit our brethren in every city where we have preached the word of the Lord, and see how they do.** Not, then—in the first instance at least—to break new ground did he propose to go, but to visit the converts already made, to see whether they were holding fast, whether advancing or declining, &c.—a pattern this for successful missionaries in every age, whether in the home or in the foreign field. 'Reader (asks holy *Bengel*), how stands it with thee?' Yet we agree with *Baumgarten,* that a still further diffusion of the Gospel must have been contemplated by the apostle in this journey. first, because the extension of the Gospel among the Gentiles had been so laid upon him, in his original call, as the great work of his apostolic life, that he could scarcely have planned such a journey without having that in view; next, because the proceedings of the council at Jerusalem, which Paul and Silas carried with them to communicate to the Gentile churches already formed, were evidently designed to meet a much wider diffusion of the Gospel among the Gentiles than had then taken place; and lastly, because the very first step which the apostle took on his arrival at Lystra—namely, to add Timotheus to his party, but not until he had circumcised him—plainly shows that, instead of confining himself to the mere visitation of churches already founded, he was laying himself out on this journey for pushing the kingdom of Christ alike among Jews and Gentiles wherever he could find an open door. Still, his more immediate object must have been to "visit the brethren in every city where they had preached the word of the Lord, and see how they did." 'We notice here (as *Howson* remarks), for the first time, a trace of that tender solicitude for his converts, that earnest longing to see their faces, which appears in the letters which he wrote afterwards, as one of the most remarkable and attractive features of his character. He thought, doubtless, of the Pisidians and Lycaonians, as he thought afterwards at Athens and Corinth of the Thessalonians, from whom he had been lately "taken in presence, not in heart, night and day praying exceedingly that he might see their face, and perfect that which was lacking in their faith."' **37. And Barnabas determined**—rather, 'counselled,' or 'was minded.' [The received reading, ἐβουλεύσατο, is rightly preferred by *Tischendorf,* though on less MS. authority than ἐβούλετο—*volebat*—which *Lachmann* adopts, but which seems a correction, to suit the supposed sense]. **to take with them John, whose surname was Mark.** They were uncle and nephew, as we learn from Col. iv. 10. **38. But Paul thought not good to take him with them, who departed from them** [τὸν ἀποστάντα ἀπ' αὐτῶν]—rather, 'who had fallen away from them.' **from Pamphylia, and went not with them to the work.** The painful circumstance here referred to is recorded in

39 with them to the work. And *^g*the contention was so sharp between them, that they departed asunder one from the other: and so Barnabas took
40 Mark, and sailed unto Cyprus; and Paul chose Silas, and departed, being recommended by the brethren unto the grace of God.

A. D. 52.	
g ch. 6. 1.	
Ps. 105. 33.	
Ps. 119. 91.	
Eccl. 7. 10.	

ch. xiii. 13 (on which see). **39. And the contention was so sharp between them.** The single word here rendered 'sharp contention' [παροξυσμὸς] is a strong one, expressing 'irritation,' 'exacerbation.' **that they departed asunder one from the other.** Said they not truly to the Lystrians (ch. xiv. 15) that they were men of like passions with themselves? But which of these two servants of Christ was to blame in this case? *First,* that John Mark had either tired of the work, or shrunk from the dangers and fatigues that yet lay before them, was undeniable; and Paul concluded that what he *had* done he might, and probably would, do again. Was he wrong in this? See Prov. xxv. 19. But, *secondly,* to this Barnabas might reply that no rule was without exception; that one failure, in a young Christian, was not enough to condemn him for life; that if near relationship might be thought to warp his judgment, it also gave him opportunities of knowing the man better than others; and that as he was himself anxious to be allowed another trial—and the result makes this next to certain—in order that he might wipe out the effect of his former failure, and show what "hardness he could now endure as a good soldier of Jesus Christ," his petition ought not to be rejected. Now, since John Mark *did* retrieve his character in these respects, and a reconciliation took place between Paul and him—a reconciliation so cordial that the apostle expresses more than once the confidence he had in him, and the value he set upon his services (Col. iv. 10, 11; 2 Tim. iv. 11)—it may seem that events showed Barnabas to be in the right, and Paul too harsh and hasty in his judgment. But, in behalf of Paul, it may well be answered, that, not being able to see into the future, he had only the unfavourable past to judge by; that the gentleness of Barnabas (ch. iv. 36; xi. 24) had already laid him open to imposition (see on Gal. ii. 13), to which near relationship would in this case make him more liable; and that, in refusing to take John Mark on this missionary journey, Paul was not judging his Christian character or pronouncing on his fitness for future service, but merely providing in the meantime against being again put to serious inconvenience, and having their hands weakened by a possible second desertion. On the whole, then, it seems clear that each of these great servants of Christ had something to say for himself in defence of the position which they respectively took up; that while Barnabas was quite able to appreciate the grounds on which Paul proceeded, Paul was not so competent to judge of the considerations which Barnabas probably urged; that while Paul had but one object in view—to see that the companion of their arduous work was one of thoroughly congenial spirit and sufficient nerve—Barnabas, over and above the same desire, might not unreasonably be afraid for the soul of his nephew, lest the refusal to allow him to accompany them on their journey might injure his Christian character, and deprive the Church of a true servant of Jesus Christ; and that while both sought only the glory of their common Master, each looked at the question at issue to some extent through the medium of his own temperament, which grace sanctifies and refines, but does not destroy—*Paul,* through the medium of absolute devotion to the Cause and Kingdom of Christ, which, warm and

womanly as his affections were, gave a tinge of lofty sternness to his resolves where that seemed to be affected; *Barnabas,* through the medium of the same singleness of heart in Christ's service, though probably not in equal strength (Gal. ii. 13), but also of a certain natural gentleness which, where a Christian relative was concerned, led him to attach more weight to what seemed for his spiritual good than Paul could be supposed to do. In these circumstances, it seems quite possible that they might have amicably 'agreed to differ,' each taking his own companion, as they actually did. But the 'paroxysm' (as the word is)—the 'exacerbation,' which is expressly given as the cause of their parting—shows but too plainly that human infirmity at length sundered those who had sweetly and lovingly borne together the heat and burden of the day during a protracted tour in the service of Christ. "Therefore let no man glory in men" (1 Cor. iii. 21). As for John Mark, although, through his uncle's warm advocacy of his cause, he was put in a condition to dissipate the cloud that hung over him, how bitter to him must have ever afterwards been the reflection that it was his culpable conduct which gave occasion to whatever was sinful in the strife between Paul and Barnabas, and to a separation in action, though no doubt with mutual Christian regard, between those who had till then wrought nobly together!

But this sore evil was overruled to the furtherance of the cause that was dear to both, in a way and to an extent which in all aftertime would fill themselves with wonder. Two missionary journeys come out of this dispute, instead of one; and whatever route Barnabas may have taken after going to Cyprus, and whatever the result of his tour, Paul—instead of his course being limited, as at first intended, to the places where he had before preached the word of the Lord—was Divinely led into Europe, to break new and far more important ground than before. **and so Barnabas took Mark, and sailed unto Cyprus; 40. And Paul chose Silas** (Silvanus)— going two and two, just as the Twelve and the Seventy were sent forth (Mark vi. 7; Luke x. 1). Whether Silas had returned to Antioch, or had to be sent for to Jerusalem, we cannot tell. But doubtless they had discovered themselves, while labouring together at Antioch, to be of kindred spirit; and when Barnabas failed him, the apostle would at once turn to Silas, who, from what the apostle says of him elsewhere, would rejoice to be associated with him in such work, and proved himself worthy of the apostle's choice. **being recommended by the brethren unto the grace of God**—or 'the grace of the Lord' (according to a slightly preferable reading), that is, of the Lord *Jesus,* the glorified Head of the Church, and Director of all its movements. This 'recommendation' of the missionaries to 'the grace of the Lord by the brethren' of Antioch, was no doubt by some solemn service (see ch. xiii. 3; xiv. 26), and, as would appear, by "the brethren" in the most general sense of the term—probably by a prayer-meeting of the whole body of believers. It does not follow from the historian's silence that Barnabas was not so recommended too; for this is the last mention of Barnabas in the History, whose whole object now is to relate the proceedings of Paul. Nor does it seem quite fair (with

110

41 And he went through Syria and Cilicia, confirming the churches.
16 Then came he to *[a]*Derbe and Lystra: and, behold, a certain disciple was
2 there, *[b]*named Timotheus, (the son of a certain woman, which was a
3 Jewess, and believed; but his father *was* a Greek:) which *[c]*was well
reported of by the brethren that were at Lystra and Iconium. Him
would Paul have to go forth with him; and *[d]*took and circumcised him

A. D. 52.

CHAP. 16.
[a] ch. 14. 6.
[b] ch. 19. 22.
[c] ch. 6. 3.

2 Tim. 3.15.
[d] 1 Cor. 9. 20.

de Wette, Meyer, Howson, Alford, Hackett, Webster and Wilkinson) to infer from this that the church at Antioch took that marked way of showing their sympathy with Paul in opposition to Barnabas.

Remarks.—1. How careful should Christians, and especially Christian ministers and missionaries, be to guard against rash judgment and hot temper towards each other, especially where on both sides the glory of Christ is the ground of difference! How possible is it that in such cases both parties may, on the question at issue, be more or less in the right! How difficult is it for the most faithful and devoted servants of Christ, even under the commanding influence of grace—differing as they do in their natural temperament—to see even important questions precisely in the same light! And if, with every disposition to yield what is unimportant, they still feel it a duty each to stand to his own point, how careful should they be to do it lovingly, each pursuing his own course without disparagement of his Christian brother! 2. How affectingly does the Lord overrule such difference of judgment, and such manifestations of human infirmity, by making them "turn out rather unto the furtherance of the Gospel!" In this case it was eminently seen, not only in setting free from each other minds which —though capable of harmonious action—seem to have been fully better fitted, both by nature and by grace, for serving the common cause as directors of others than by labouring permanently together; but also in providing two missionary parties in place of one, who, instead of travelling over the same ground, and carrying their dispute over all the regions where before they had laboured so lovingly together, took quite different routes, and thus at once consolidated and extended the kingdom of Christ!

SECOND MISSIONARY JOURNEY (Ch. xv. 41—xviii. 22.)

41—xvi. 3.—VISITATION OF THE CHURCHES FORMERLY ESTABLISHED—AT LYSTRA TIMOTHEUS IS ADDED TO THE MISSIONARY PARTY.

Progress through Syria and Cilicia (41). **41. And he went through Syria and Cilicia, confirming the churches** (see on *v.* 23)—taking probably the same route as when he was despatched in haste from Jerusalem to Tarsus, when we have reason to think that he went by land (see on ch. ix. 30). It is very likely (says *Howson*) that Paul and Barnabas made a deliberate and amicable arrangement to divide the region of their first mission between them—Paul taking the *continental*, and Barnabas the *insular*, part of the proposed visitation. If Barnabas visited Salamis and Paphos, and if Paul (travelling westward), after passing through Derbe, Lystra, and Iconium, went as far as Antioch in Pisidia, the whole circuit of the proposed visitation was actually accomplished; for it does not appear that any converts had been made at Perga and Attaleia.

CHAP. XVI. 1-3.—*At Lystra Timotheus is taken into the Missionary party.* **1. Then came he to Derbe and Lystra: and, behold, a certain disciple was there**—that is, at Lystra, not at Derbe (as some conclude from ch. xx. 4). See on *v.* 2. **named**

111

Timotheus. As Paul styles this youth his "own son in the faith" (1 Tim. i. 2), and as he had attained to some standing among the Christians of that region before the apostle's second visit, it must have been at his first missionary visit that he was gained to Christ, and in all likelihood in those critical moments and trying circumstances related in ch. xiv. 19, 20. His would be one of 'the souls of the disciples confirmed' by the apostle on his return home by the same route, 'exhorted to continue in the faith,' and warned "that we must through much tribulation enter into the kingdom of God " (ch. xiv. 21, 22). **the son of a certain woman, which was a Jewess, and believed.** 'The unfeigned faith which dwelt first in his grandmother Lois' descended from her to 'his mother Eunice;' thence it passed to this dear youth (2 Tim. i. 5), who 'from a child knew the Holy Scriptures' (2 Tim. iii. 15). His gifts and destination to the ministry seem to have been supernaturally attested before this (1 Tim. i. 18), or at least at the time of his ordination (1 Tim. iv. 18). **but his father was a Greek.** Such mixed marriages (as *Howson* observes), though seldom occurring in Palestine, and disliked by the stricter Jews (being forbidden by the Mosaic law, Deut. vii. 3), must have been very frequent among the Jews of the dispersion, especially in remote districts, where but few of the scattered people were settled. **2. Which was well reported of by the brethren that were at Lystra and Iconium.** The mention of Lystra here, and not of Derbe, favours the belief that Timothy belonged to Lystra. As the apostle speaks of him some ten years after this as still young (1 Tim. iv. 12), he must have been a mere youth at the time here spoken of. Yet had he already gained a reputation (as we here learn) among all the Christians, not only of his own place, but of Iconium, where his spiritual father had met with the like ill-treatment. **3. Him would Paul have to go forth with him.** Though Silas took the place of Barnabas, it is consistent with all that we know of the great apostle that he should set his heart upon the society and services of a youth like Timothy, on whose love and devotedness, as his son in the Gospel, he could thoroughly and always reckon; whose character and gifts had been already proved; and whom he could employ on errands which he might not feel warranted in imposing upon Silas. And a treasure to him he proved to be—the most attached and serviceable of all his associates. (See Phil. ii. 19-23; 1 Cor. iv. 17; xvi. 10, 11; 1 Thess. iii. 1-6.) His double connection—with the Jews by the mother's side, and by the father's with the Gentiles—would strike the apostle as a peculiar qualification for his own sphere of labour. *Wieseler* remarks that 'Timothy, so far as appears, is the first Gentile who after his conversion comes before us as a regular missionary; for what is said of Titus, in Gal. ii. 3, refers to a later period.' Though we differ from that distinguished chronologer, when he ascribes the visit which Titus paid to Jerusalem in company with Paul to a later period than this, his remark about Timothy is nevertheless correct, as we think; for we have no evidence that Titus was 'a regular missionary' at the time of that visit. **and took and circum-**

because of the Jews which were in those quarters: for they knew all that
4 his father was a Greek. And as they went through the cities 'they

cised him. This act—which any Israelite might perform—seems to have been done by Paul himself. **because of the Jews which were in those quarters: for they knew all that his father was a Greek.** From this one would infer that his father (who perhaps was now dead) had never become a proselyte to Judaism; for against the wishes of a Gentile father (as the Jews themselves say) no Jewish mother was permitted to circumcise her son. And this will explain why all the religion of Timothy is traced (2 Tim. i. 5) to the female side of the family. The circumcision of Timothy, before being taken into this missionary party, was an indispensable step. For if the mere report that Paul at a later period had brought a Greek into the temple occasioned an uproar in Jerusalem, and endangered the apostle's life (ch. xxi. 27-31), how could he expect to make any progress in this missionary tour to preach Christ—"to the Jew first," and only after that to the Gentiles—if his principal assistant and constant companion had not been a circumcised person? On the one hand, in refusing to compel Titus to be circumcised, at the mere bidding of Judaizing Christians, as necessary to salvation (Gal. ii. 3), he only vindicated "the truth of the Gospel" (Gal. ii. 5): in circumcising Timothy, on the other hand, "to the Jews he became as a Jew, that he might gain the Jews." It is probable that the ordination of Timothy (1 Tim. iv. 14; 2 Tim. i. 6) took place now; and as it was done "before many witnesses" (1 Tim. vi. 12), it was probably a solemn service, and attracted a considerable concourse.

Remarks.—1. The stability of the first Christian missions, as well as their rapid progress, must be ascribed in a large degree to the wise union of the *conservative* with the *aggressive* principle on which the apostle conducted them. The first Gentile converts must have been extremely rude in knowledge, and all inexperienced in the management of a Christian congregation, even of the smallest dimensions. But besides the instructions which they would receive at their first reception of the Gospel, it will be remembered that they were revisited on the apostle's return, confirmed in the faith, exhorted to stedfastness, and faithfully warned of the cost of discipleship; that elders were ordained over every cluster of believers; and that on parting with them they were solemnly commended to the Lord with prayer and fasting (ch. xiv. 21-23). Then, after a long interval, during which the hearts of the missionaries yearned after them, a fresh journey was projected and carried out, for the express purpose of revisiting their converts; and doubtless this visit would contribute largely to the consolidation and growth of those young churches. In like manner, the churches which were afterwards gathered out of Corinth, Ephesus, &c., were revisited once and again, and to them were addressed those Epistles which, though they have become the heritage of all the churches of Christ, were designed in the first instance for the instruction and direction of the churches whose names they bear. Thus anxiously did the first great missionaries of the Cross watch over and cherish the work of their hands, "lest in any way the tempter should have tempted them, and their labour have been in vain" (1 Thess. iii. 5); and if one would see into the very heart of those model missionaries, as they "travailed in birth again" for their converts, let him read the second and third chapters of the First Epistle to the Thessalonians. And should not the churches of our day—with all their mis-

sionary agents abroad, and missionary directors or committees at home—study to imbibe the same spirit, and act upon the same principle in the case of their converts? 2. The account here given of the circumcision of Timothy, in contrast with the non-circumcision of Titus, has furnished the Tubingen school (*Baur, Zeller, Schwegler*) with a fitting occasion for the display of their peculiar criticism. It suits their views to contend for the genuineness of the Epistle to the Galatians; but it does not suit their views—or rather it is fatal to them—to admit the genuineness of the Acts of the Apostles. Accordingly, as Paul tells us in the Galatians (ii. 3), that he would not compel Titus to be circumcised, because he was a Greek, while in the Acts he is represented as taking and circumcising Timothy, "because of the Jews of those quarters" where he was going, though every one "knew that his father was a Greek"—this is made out to be a flat and clumsy contradiction, such as shows the book that contains it to be no genuine production. According to this style of criticism, why have they not discovered the Epistle to the Galatians itself to be spurious, since it makes the apostle to say in one chapter, "Behold, I Paul say unto you, that if ye be circumcised Christ shall profit you nothing" (Gal. v. 2); and in the very next chapter (vi. 15), "In Christ Jesus neither circumcision availeth any thing, nor uncircumcision, but a new creature"? Men who cannot see, or will not admit, that a change of circumstances may warrant and even demand a change of procedure, are not fit to be critics of the New Testament or of any sensible writings. That the circumstances *were* different in the cases of Titus and of Timothy here—sufficiently so to justify, if not to require, a different line of action—is so plain, that after what we have said on *v.* 3, it is not necessary to add a word. To a thorough critic, who penetrates beneath the surface of the facts, the apparent contradiction, so far from being staggering, is just what would corroborate the genuineness of both the productions in which the two statements are contained. 3. The 'undesigned coincidence' between the account given of Timothy in this narrative of his accession to the missionary party, and that of the apostle himself in his Second Epistle to Timothy (ch. i. 5), is a striking confirmation of the truth of both works. (See *Paley's* 'Horæ Paulinæ,' xii., No. ii.) In the Epistle all the religion of this admirable Christian is traced to the female side. The "unfeigned faith" which dwelt first in his grandmother Lois passed down (as we have seen) from her to his mother Eunice; and thence, like the precious ointment upon the head of Aaron, that ran down upon the beard, and went down to the skirts of his garments (Ps. cxxxiii. 2), it descended to the youth who proved such a treasure to the apostle, both in his travels, when he was preaching Christ with burning zeal amid difficulties and hardships, and afterwards when he became a prisoner of Jesus Christ—from his first association with him to the very close of his career in martyrdom for Christ. Here, in the History, the impression one naturally forms of his Greek father is, that he had not been a proselyte to the Jewish Faith, else he would probably have had Timothy circumcised in infancy; and from its being said that Paul now "took and circumcised him," the probability is that his Greek father was either dead by this time, or that he had deserted his wife—as was not uncommon in the case of such unequal marriages. At all events, while the *Epistle* traces all the religion of

delivered them the decrees for to keep, that *f* were ordained of the apostles
5 and elders which were at Jerusalem. And *g* so were the churches established in the faith, and increased in number daily.
6 Now when they had gone throughout Phrygia and the region of
Galatia, and were forbidden of the Holy Ghost to preach the word in

A. D. 53.
f ch. 15. 28.
g ch. 15. 41.
Col. 1. 23.
Col. 2. 2.
Jude 20, 21.

Timothy to the mother's side, the *History* traces none of it to the father's. But this suggests another remark: 4. The strength and preciousness of the maternal influence in the religious training of the young is seen all the more in this case from the disadvantages on the father's side under which Timothy laboured. If the mother's piety was decided before she formed a matrimonial connection with an unconverted Gentile, it was a step which cannot be justified, and one that must have cost her many a trial. But if her religious training had not taken decisive hold of her heart up to the time of her marriage, that step—especially in a region where Jewish families were few—was not so unnatural, nor would it be so injurious to conscience. At the same time, as she certainly was a woman of "unfeigned faith," and was honoured to transmit the same to this child of hers, she must have had to struggle into it through adverse influences and deadening intercourse with an irreligious husband. Perhaps the contrast between her mother's hallowed house and the withering secularity of her husband's, drove her to the God of her fathers, and disclosed to her spiritual necessities which she had never felt under the parental roof. And if this was the means of deciding for the first time her choice of "the good part," all her early training would then come back upon her, and turn to more precious account than it had ever done before. So, at any rate, it has often been in the experience of Christian mothers. And how did all this tell upon Timothy? Had he been a raw convert at the time of his first reception of the Gospel—like the other disciples who stood round about the apparently lifeless body of Paul at Lystra (ch. xiv. 20)—he had not so quickly risen to reputation among the brethren at Lystra and Iconium (ch. xvi. 2); nor would he have had in him probably those qualities which drew him to the greatest of the apostles, and which, when matured, made him the greatest treasure of his apostolic life. All this must be traced instrumentally to the training he had received, the example he had witnessed, and the prayers and tears which doubtless watered both, under the parental roof. Probably the mixture of Gentile blood was an advantage to him intellectually; but to his mother we certainly owe all that hallowed and directed his natural endowments. And what Christian mother or guardian of the young may not well be encouraged amid all her struggles, and stimulated to put forth her best energies, to train up her children "in the nurture and admonition of the Lord," by the blessed result in this case of Timothy!

4-15.—AFTER REVISITING THE CHURCHES AND DELIVERING THE DECREES OF THE COUNCIL, PAUL AND SILAS BREAK NEW GROUND IN PHRYGIA AND GALATIA, BUT ARE DIVINELY CONSTRAINED TO TURN WESTWARD TO MACEDONIA, OUR HISTORIAN JOINING THE MISSIONARY PARTY AT TROAS—AT PHILIPPI, LYDIA IS CONVERTED AND BAPTIZED, WITH HER HOUSEHOLD.

Progress through the cities—Entrance into Phrygia and Galatia—The mysterious double arrest, and the journey to Troas (4-8). **4. And as they went through the cities they delivered them the decrees for to keep, that were ordained of the apostles and elders which were at Jerusalem. 5. And so were the churches established in the faith,**

and increased in number (that is, the number of their members) daily. If the views of these young Gentile churches were enlarged and their love warmed by the written evidence laid before them of the triumph of Christian liberty at Jerusalem, and the wise measures there taken to preserve the unity of the Jewish and Gentile converts, this would naturally tend to inflame their zeal to gather in others; for any increase of spiritual life, whether in an individual or in a church, begets missionary zeal. Thus would the 'establishing of the churches in the faith' lead to the "daily increase of their numbers," as cause and effect.

6. Now when they had gone throughout Phrygia—proceeding in a north-westerly direction, across mount Taurus, and entering Asia Minor, **and the region of Galatia**—lying to the north of Phrygia. At this time must have been formed "the churches of Galatia" (Gal. i. 2; 1 Cor. xvi. 1), which were founded by our apostle, as he tells us himself in his Epistle to them some years afterwards (particularly ch. iv. 19), and which were already in existence when he was on his *third* missionary journey—as we learn from ch. xviii. 23, where it appears that he was no less successful in Phrygia. Why these proceedings—so interesting, we should think—are not here detailed, it is not easy to say. The reasons which critics have suggested do not appear to us very satisfactory: such as that the historian had not joined the party (so *Alford*), for he is minute enough on many things which occurred long before he joined the party; that the main stream of the Church's development was from Jerusalem to Rome, and the apostle's labours in Phrygia and Galatia lay quite out of the line of that direction (so *Baumgarten*), for his labours in regions quite as much out of it on his former journey are minutely detailed; and that the historian was now in haste to bring the apostle to Europe (so *Olshausen*). This last reason probably comes the nearest to the true cause of the historian's brevity here. But even this is not quite satisfactory; since long after the principal European churches had been established, when relating the proceedings of the apostle's third and last missionary journey, he begins his narrative with these few words, "And after he had spent some time there (at Antioch), he departed (for the third and last time), and went over all the country of Galatia and Phrygia in order, confirming the churches" (ch. xviii. 23)—not only implying that churches had been formed in those regions of which he neither before nor there gives any detailed account, but omitting all particulars of this visit and of those important movements of the Judaizers to which reference is made in the Epistle to the Galatians. We must then just conclude, that as some things behoved to be omitted to bring this book within the required limits, the particulars of the formation of churches in Phrygia and Galatia (possibly communicated to the historian with less fulness) were designedly passed over. **and were forbidden of the Holy Ghost**—speaking unmistakeably by some prophet (see on ch. xi. 27). **to preach the word in Asia**—not the great Asiatic continent, of course, nor even the rich peninsula now called Asia Minor (for they had already laboured and had much fruit there), but only that strip of its western coast which

113

7 Asia, after they were come to Mysia, they assayed to go into Bithynia:
8 but the Spirit suffered them not.   And they passing by Mysia ^h came
9 down to Troas.   And a ⁱ vision appeared to Paul in the night: There
   stood a man of Macedonia, and prayed him, saying, Come over into
10 Macedonia, and help us.   And after he had seen the vision, immediately
   we endeavoured to ^j go into Macedonia, assuredly gathering that the Lord
   had called us for to preach the Gospel unto them.
11 Therefore loosing from Troas, we came with a straight course to

A. D. 53.

^h 2 Cor. 2. 12.
  2 Tim. 4.13.
ⁱ Num. 12. 6.
  ch. 2. 17.
  ch. 10. 30.
^j Ps. 119. 160.
  Eccl. 9. 10.
  Rom. 12.11.
  2 Cor. 2. 13.

constituted the Roman province of Asia, usually termed Proconsular Asia. Nor were they excluded from this region save for the time; for we shall find the apostle afterwards labouring here with much success. (See on ch. xviii. 19, &c.) **7. After they were come to Mysia**—lying north-westward of Phrygia, but where, as being part of Roman Asia, they had been forbidden to labour, **they assayed** (or 'attempted') **to go into Bithynia** [not κατὰ τὴν B., as in the received text, with G H, &c., but εἰς τ. B., with ℵ A B C D E, &c., and most of the Greek fathers: so *Lachmann* and *Tischendorf*]. The meaning seems to be, that they made their arrangements with the view of entering this province, lying to the north-east of Mysia, on the southern shore of the Black Sea. **but the Spirit** —'the Spirit of Jesus' would seem to be the true reading here [so ℵ A B C * * D E, &c., the Vulgate, both Syriac versions, &c., and several of the fathers. So *Lachmann* and *Tischendorf*]. This reading, however, is so peculiar that one cannot but stand in doubt of it. Yet compare the last words of *v.* 10. **suffered them not**— speaking authoritatively by some prophet. But why, it may be asked, did the Spirit not suffer them to preach the Gospel in those regions? Probably, *first*, because Europe was ripe for the labours of our missionary party; and, *secondly*, because other instruments were to have the honour of establishing the Gospel in the eastern regions of Asia Minor—especially the apostle Peter, if we may gather so much from 1 Pet. i. 1. By the end of the first century, as we learn from the celebrated Epistle of Pliny the Roman Governor to the Emperor Trajan, Bithynia was filled with Christians. There seems much force in the following remarks of *Baumgarten*:—'This is the first time that the Holy Ghost is expressly spoken of as determining the course they were to follow in their efforts to evangelize the nations, and it was evidently designed to show that whereas hitherto the diffusion of the Gospel had been carried on in unbroken course, connected by natural points of junction, it was now to take a leap to which it could not be impelled but by an immediate and independent operation of the Spirit; and though primarily this intimation of the Spirit was only negative, and referred but to the immediate neighbourhood, we may certainly conclude that Paul took it for a sign that a new epoch was now to commence in his apostolic labours.' **8. And they passing by Mysia** [Παρελθόντες]—or 'going through' it without stopping, **came down to Troas**—a city on the north-east coast of the Ægean Sea, the boundary of Asia Minor on the west, on the theatre of the great Trojan war. Why did they come thither? Because (we doubt not) the successive prohibitions to labour any longer in the East had led the capacious spirit of the great apostle to feel that some entirely new field was now to be opened for him; and by coming to the nearest port from which he might take shipping, he would there be in readiness to go wherever he might be ordered.

Divinely directed, they proceed westward to Macedonia, accompanied by our historian himself, and

reach Philippi—Conversion and baptism of Lydia and her household (9-15). **9. And a vision appeared to Paul in the night**—but while awake; otherwise it would have been called a dream. **There stood a man of Macedonia, and prayed him, saying, Come over into Macedonia, and help us.** Stretching his eye across the Ægean Sea from Troas, on the north-east, to the Macedonian Hills, visible on the north-west, the apostle could hardly fail to think this the destined scene of his future labours; and if he retired to rest with this thought, he would be thoroughly prepared for the remarkable intimation of the Divine will now to be given him. This visional Macedonian discovered himself in part, it may be, by his dress, but certainly by what he said. And yet it was a cry, not of conscious *desire* for the Gospel, but of deep *need* of it, and unconscious *preparedness* to receive it, not only in that region, but, we may well say, throughout all that western empire, which Macedonia might be said to represent. Yes! The literature and the arts of Greece, and the all-subduing and nobly-ruling power of Rome have failed to reach the deadly maladies of our fallen nature; and all Heathendom, in the person of this Macedonian, is crying for its only effectual cure, which these missionaries of the Cross possess and are only waiting for this call to administer. **10. And after he had seen the vision, immediately we endeavoured** [ἐζητήσαμεν]—'we sought;' that is, probably, made the necessary enquiries how and when they could set sail for Europe. **to go into Macedonia.** The "WE," here first introduced into this History, is a modest intimation that the historian himself had now joined the missionary party—thus making four in number. The modern objections to this ancient and natural application of the change to the first person plural (" We "), are frivolous; and the attempts of *de Wette* and others, after *Schleiermacher*, to show that Timotheus is the person meant—and of some, that Silas is intended—are very weak. Whether (as *Wieseler* conjectures) Paul's broken health had anything to do with this arrangement for having "the beloved physician" with him, can never be known with certainty; but that he would deem himself honoured in taking care of so precious a life, there can be no doubt. **assuredly gathering that the Lord** — the Lord Jesus, who, by His Spirit, was the glorious Director of all their movements, and specially in the present case: compare the peculiar reading of *v.* 7; "but the Spirit *of Jesus* suffered them not."

11. Therefore loosing from Troas, we came with a straight course [εὐθυδρομήσαμεν] — *lit.,* 'we ran straight;' that is, in nautical phrase, 'ran before the wind,' **to Samothracia**—a lofty island in the Ægean sea, north-westward from Troas, and about midway between this and Neapolis. *Howson* observes that the wind must have set in strong from the south or SSE., to bring them there so soon, as the current is strong in the opposite direction; and they afterwards took five days to what they now did in two (ch. xx. 6). **and the next day to Neapolis**—on the Macedonian, or rather Thracian, coast, about

12 Samothracia, and the next *day* to Neapolis; and from thence to *ᵏ* Philippi, which is ¹ the chief city of that part of Macedonia, *and* a colony: and we
13 were in that city abiding certain days. And on the ²sabbath we went out of the city by a river-side, where prayer was wont to be made; and we sat
14 down, and spake unto the women which resorted *thither.* And a certain woman named Lydia, a seller of purple, of the city of *ˡ*Thyatira, which worshipped God, heard *us:* whose heart *ᵐ* the Lord opened, that she
15 attended unto the things which were spoken of Paul. And when she was baptized, and her household, she besought *us,* saying, If ye have judged

A. D. 52.

ᵏ Phil. 1. 1.
¹ Or, the first.
² sabbath day.
ch. 13. 42.
ch. 18. 4.
ˡ Rev. 2. 18.
ᵐ Luke 24. 45.
Eph. 1. 17.

---

sixty-five miles from Samothracia. **12. And from thence to Philippi**—about ten miles inland, to the westward, and so called after Philip of Macedon, the father of Alexander the Great, who built and fortified it. **which is the chief city of that part of Macedonia** [ἥτις ἐστίν πρώτη τῆς μερίδος τ. Μακηδονίας πόλις]—or, 'which is the first' or 'a chief city of the district of Macedonia.' In the former sense—'the first city' (as in the margin) —the meaning will be, the first city one comes to in Macedonia, proceeding from Neapolis. (So *Bengel, Winer, Olshausen, Alford, Lechler.*) But there seem decisive objections to this. If 'a chief city' (*urbs primaria*) be the meaning, it is to tell us that it had the distinction which that word, attached to certain places, conferred. (So *de Wette, Humphry, Hackett,* &c.) The former sense at one time seemed to us the preferable; but we now incline rather to the latter, which the next clause seems to favour: **and a** (Roman) **colony**—that is, possessing all the privileges of Roman citizenship, and, as such, both exempted from scourging and (in ordinary cases) from arrest, and entitled to appeal from the local magistrate to the emperor. Since the Pisidian *Antioch* and *Troas* were also 'colonies,' and yet are not so called by our historian, the fact is probably mentioned here of Philippi on account of the frequent references to Roman privileges and duties in the sequel of the chapter. **and we were in that city abiding certain days**—reconnoitring the ground and waiting until the Sabbath should come round. As their rule was to begin with the Jews and religious proselytes, they would have nothing probably to do until the time when they knew that they would convene for public worship.
At Philippi, Lydia is gained, and, with her household, baptized (13-15). **13. And on the sabbath**—the first after their arrival, as the words imply, **we went out of the city**—or, according to what is clearly the true reading, 'outside the (city) gate' [πόλεως is the received reading, according to E G H, &c. But א A B C D, and the Vulgate, and other versions, have πύλης]. **by a river-side**—not the *Strymon,* as some good critics think, for this was too far away, but one of the small streams which gave name to the place ere the city was founded. The *Gangas* is that which recent travellers judge most likely to be the one intended. **where prayer was wont to be made**—not, 'where was wont to be a place of prayer' (as *Neander, de Wette, Meyer, Humphry, Hackett, Lechler*); for what sense is there in this, as applied either to a building or to a place of any kind? but 'where a prayer-meeting was wont to be held.' It is plain there was no synagogue at Philippi (contrast ch. xvii. 1), the number of the Jews being small. The meeting appears to have consisted wholly of women, and these not all Jewish by birth. The neighbourhood of streams was preferred, on account of the ceremonial washings used on such occasions. **and we sat down, and spake unto the women which resorted**

thither—a humble congregation, and a simple manner of preaching. *But here and thus were gathered the first fruits of Europe unto Christ, and they were of the female sex,* of whose accession and services honourable mention will again and again be made. **14. And a certain woman named Lydia**—a common name among the Greeks and Romans, **a seller of purple**—purple dyes or fabrics, **of the city of Thyatira**—on the confines of Lydia and Phrygia. The Lydians, and particularly the inhabitants of Thyatira, were celebrated for their dyeing, in which they inherited the reputation of the Tyrians. Inscriptions to this effect, yet remaining, confirm the accuracy of our historian. This woman appears to have been in good circumstances, having an establishment at Philippi large enough to accommodate the missionary party (*v.* 15), and receiving her goods from her native town. **which worshipped God**—a familiar expression for proselytes from among the Gentiles, the outward evidence of which was their uniting in the public worship of the Jews. As such, this woman was one of this small congregation of worshippers. **heard us: whose heart the Lord opened** [διήνοιξεν]—'thoroughly opened.' It is the Lord *Jesus* who is here meant: see *v.* 15, and compare Luke xxiv. 45; Matt. xi. 27. **that she attended** [πρόσεχειν]—or 'gave heed,' **unto the things which were spoken of Paul**—'showing (says *Olshausen*) that *the inclination of the heart towards the truth originates not in the will of man.* The first disposition to turn to the Gospel is a 'work of grace.' Observe the place here assigned to 'giving heed' to the truth—that kind of attention which consists in having the whole mind engrossed with it, and in apprehending and drinking it in, in its vital and saving character. **15. And when she was baptized, and her household**—probably without much delay. The mention of baptism here (for the first time in connection with the labours of Paul, though it was doubtless performed on all his former converts) indicates a special importance in this first European baptism. Here also is the first mention of a Christian *household.* Whether it included children—also in that case baptized—is not explicitly stated; but the presumption, as in other cases of households baptized, certainly is that it did. Yet the question of Infant Baptism must be determined on other grounds; and such incidental allusions form only part of the historical materials for ascertaining the practice of the Church. **she besought us, saying, If ye have judged me to be faithful to the Lord** —that is, if ye deem me a genuine believer in the Lord Jesus (as her baptism implied that they did). There is a beautiful modesty in this plea, but there was a constraining force in it: **come into my house, and abide there. And she constrained us** [παρεβιάσατο]. The word (as in Luke xiv. 29) implies that she would take no denial.
Remarks.—1. What regions should be selected at any given time for missionary operations, and by whom they should be undertaken, is a question involving such mysterious elements, that the most

115

me to be faithful [n] to the Lord, come into my house, and abide *there*. And she constrained us.

A. D. 53.
[n] Gal. 6. 10.

honest solution of it may sometimes prove to be wrong. But even then, "unto the upright there ariseth light in the darkness;" and "the meek will He judge in judgment, the meek will He teach His way" (Ps. cxii. 4; xxv. 9). Paul and Silas doubtless exercised their best judgment, and probably cherished high hopes of success, after their fruitful progress "throughout Phrygia and the region of Galatia," in moving westward towards Proconsular "Asia;" and yet they "were forbidden of the Holy Ghost to preach the word in Asia." No reason appears to have been assigned, nor any other field for their labours as yet pointed out. So, again thrown on their own judgment, they deem it advisable to proceed northward to Bithynia; but "the Spirit (again interposing) suffered them not." What now is to be done? The East seems decisively shut out from them: can it be that they are now to cross the sea and penetrate into Europe? Perhaps that word in his original call—"*far* hence unto the Gentiles" (ch. xxii. 21)—was borne in emphatically upon the great apostle; and the East being now tolerably dotted with the Gospel, the question perhaps arose, What if the great Western seats of civilization, literature, art, and power, should now be our destination? Certainly, if this was his actual thought, the course which the missionary party now took was just what they would naturally adopt; for by "going through Mysia," without stopping to labour in it, and "coming down to Troas," they would put themselves in readiness to take shipping in whatever direction they might there be Divinely instructed to proceed. And is there not here encouragement for missionary churches and missionary servants of the Lord Jesus, as to the choice of their fields of foreign labour? Divine light and guidance are not to supersede the exercise of our own prayerful judgment, but may be expected just as we are faithful in the use of it, and simple in all the steps we take for the furtherance of our Master's cause. 2. If we could but pierce deep enough into the spiritual necessities of this fallen world, what Macedonian cries for help might we not hear from all quarters night and day—enough to rouse all the churches of Christendom, and call forth missionaries in clouds to say, Here am I, send me! Never, certainly, does the Church rightly engage in the missionary enterprise, nor any of its agents go forth aright, save in response to this Macedonian cry—in which the human heart sets its unconscious seal to the last command of the Risen Saviour, to make disciples of all nations. 3. How noiseless was the first triumph of the Gospel in Europe, as brought to it by the great apostle! Though there was no synagogue of the Jews at Philippi, he would conclude there must be Jews there, who would meet for worship somewhere on the Sabbath day; and finding on enquiry that there was a spot by a river-side where some Jewish women were wont to meet for prayer on that day, he would "assuredly gather" that there he would be able to feel his way to the work which the Lord had for him to do. Accordingly, on the arrival of the hallowed day, he is found, with his missionary companions, in the midst of this humble gathering of devout females. What passed between them at their first meeting—whether, as being Jews themselves, they were requested, or volunteered, to conduct the devotions usual in such circumstances—we know not. All we know is, that instead of standing up formally before them and discoursing to them, as in a

synagogue, they simply "sat down"—probably on the slope of the river's bank—"and spake (or talked) unto the women which resorted thither." Such were the circumstances—the least formal that can well be conceived—in which the first soul was won to Christ on European soil by the instrumentality of Paul. And wherever an open door can be got—whether on the hill-side or in the city, where pours the busy crowd; in temple, synagogue, cathedral, meeting-house, or on the slope of a river's bank; to thousands, hundreds, tens (as here), or to one (as when Philip was sent to the Ethiopian eunuch)—there are the time and the circumstances for preaching the unsearchable riches of Christ; and miserable is the system of thought which would restrict this to certain consecrated times and places, to the loss of opportunities never to be recalled of reaching the souls of men! "Preach the word *in season*," says Paul to Timothy (2 Tim. iv. 2), but "*out of season*" too—as his blessed Master had done before him. (See on Matt. iv. 12-25, Remark 3, at the close of that Section, p. 23). 4. By what trivial circumstances are one's whole life, character, and destiny, even for eternity, affected and determined! Had Lydia's business as a purple-seller not brought her in contact with Jewesses—to whom she would expose her wares, and the more zealous of whom would draw her into religious conversation—she had never, perhaps, embraced the Jewish Faith; and had she not been led, in prosecution of her evidently thriving business, to set up house at Philippi, and been among the Jewish worshippers on this Sabbath day by the river-side, she had not had her "heart opened to attend to the things which were spoken by Paul." Thus were the very conditions of her conversion furnished by circumstances in her history quite unconnected with religion. So was it with the Centurion at Capernaum (see on Luke vii. 1-10; Remark 1, at the close of that Section, p. 248); and so in numberless other cases from age to age. And if so much for all eternity depends on so little in time—and that little often so trivial, and but very partially under our own control—what need in every step to commit our way to Him "of Whom, and through Whom, and to Whom are all things!" 5. To "give heed" to the preaching of the Gospel seems a very simple thing; and none who enter our modern places of worship can doubt that multitudes do listen with thoughtful and reverent attention to the discourses which are delivered there, without any Divine operation opening their hearts to do so. Thus probably listened all the women to whom Paul spake by the river-side. But since Lydia's "attention" is expressly ascribed to an operation of the Lord Himself, opening her heart to give heed to the things which Paul spake, it must have been something very different from the interest with which the other women heard what the apostle had to say, and with which the generality even of attentive hearers still listen to their preachers. Of this the results are the best proof. That any of the other women were drawn to Christ, we have no evidence; but on the mind of Lydia was wrought an entire revolution. She rested not till she was baptized, and her household; she insisted on the missionaries—if they judged her a genuine disciple of the Lord Jesus—taking up their abode in her house; the voice of rejoicing and salvation was heard in that house forthwith (Ps. cxviii. 15), and it was sanctified by the word of God and prayer; on the liberation of Paul and Silas from prison, they bent their steps to this

16 And it came to pass, as we went to prayer, a certain damsel [o]possessed
with a spirit [3]of divination met us, which brought her masters [p]much
17 gain by soothsaying: the same followed Paul and us, and cried, saying,
These men are the servants of the most high God, which show unto us the
18 way of salvation. And this did she many days. But Paul, being [q]grieved,
turned and said to the spirit, I command thee in the name of Jesus Christ
to come out of her. [r]And he came out the same hour.
19 And [s]when her masters saw that the hope of their gains was gone, [t]they
caught Paul and Silas, [u]and drew *them* into the [4]market place unto the
20 rulers, and brought them to the magistrates, saying, These men, being
21 Jews, do [v]exceedingly trouble our city, and teach customs, which are not
22 lawful for us to receive, neither to observe, being Romans. And the

A. D. 53.

[o] 1 Sam. 28. 7.
[3] Or, of Python.
[p] ch. 19. 24.
[q] Mark 1. 25, 34.
[r] Mark 16. 17.
[s] ch. 19. 25. Phil. 3. 19.
[t] 2 Cor. 6. 5.
[u] Matt. 10. 18.
[4] Or, court.
[v] 1 Ki. 18. 17. ch. 17. 6.

Christian house as their natural home so long as they remained at Philippi; and on their departure, Timothy and Luke appear to have made her house their head-quarters, staying to form what proved the thriving Philippian church. Such were the blessed fruits of the opening of one woman's heart to "give heed to" the words of eternal life, spoken to others as well as her by a river-side. And so it still is, that one is taken and another left: Even so, Father, for so it seemeth good in thy sight. Come from the four winds, O Breath, and breathe upon the slain, that they may live! 6. 'Baptism (says *Lechler*) occurs twice in this chapter, and both times a whole family is baptized (*vv.* 15, 33). For the first time since Luke records the missionary acts of Paul does he mention the baptism of the converted; and it is significant that in both instances here all belonging to the parties concerned are baptized along with them. Both passages (*vv.* 15 and 33) have been quoted in favour of Infant Baptism, as an apostolic custom, on the supposition that the family certainly numbered little children, (as *Bengel* asks, Quis credat, in tot familiis nullum fuisse *infantem?*—'Who can believe that in so many families there was not one infant?') But this cannot be so surely maintained as that an argument can be founded on it. The chief importance of the transaction rests not on whether there were children in the family, and how young they may have been, but on the indisputable fact, that in both cases the whole house—all belonging to the families—were baptized along with the head of the house. This at once suggests the idea of *a Christian family—a Christian household.* Personal decision is a great matter, but *the mere salvation of isolated individuals is not biblical teaching.* The unity of the family in Christ, *the consecration of the household by grace*—all belonging to one Lord—is here represented to us as something well-pleasing to God. And it is a remarkable fact, that this side of salvation in the apostolic history is first prominently brought before us on European ground.' This extract, though it may not convey the whole truth on this important subject, expresses what we conceive to be a great principle—the *domestic* character which these transactions stamp upon the earliest Christianity.

16-40.—Paul and Silas, having expelled a Soothsaying Spirit from a Slave Girl, are, at the instigation of her Masters, seized, scourged, imprisoned and manacled, but miraculously set free—The Jailor is converted and baptized, with all his Household—Paul and Silas, asserting their outraged Liberties as Roman Citizens, make the Magistrates conduct them forth from the Prison and solicit their Departure.

A Soothsaying Spirit, striving to mar their work, is expelled by Paul and Silas, in consequence of which they are seized, scourged, imprisoned, and manacled (16-24). **16. And it came to pass, as we went to prayer** [πορευομένων ἡμῶν εἰς προσευχήν.] It was not as they were proceeding to pray in Lydia's house, but (as the words imply), as they were on their way to the usual prayer-place—probably by the same river-side—that this took place; therefore not on the same day with what had just occurred. **a certain damsel**—'a female servant,' and in this case (as appears by *v.* 19) a slave: **possessed with a spirit of divination** [πνεῦμα Πύθωνος, but Πύθωνα is the preferable reading]—that is, a spirit supposed to be inspired by the Pythian Apollo, or of the same nature. The reality of this demoniacal possession is as undeniable as that of any in the Gospel history. **met us, which brought her masters much gain by soothsaying: 17. The same followed Paul and us, and cried, saying, These men are the servants of the most high God, which show unto us the way of salvation.** Glorious testimony this, but given for a hellish end: see on Mark iv. 24. **18. And this did she many days**—that is, on many successive occasions when on their way to their usual place of meeting, or when engaged in religious services. **But Paul being grieved**—for the poor victim; grieved to see such power possessed by the enemy of man's salvation, and grieved to observe the malignant design with which this high testimony was borne to Christ.

19. And when her masters saw that the hope of their gains was gone, they caught Paul and Silas—as the leading men of the party, **and drew them into the market place** [εἰς τ. ἀγορὰν]—the place of public assembly, the Forum, where the courts were held, **unto the rulers** (in general), **20. And brought them to the magistrates** [στρατηγοῖς]—the *Duumviri*, who in the colonies went by the name of the *Prætors;* **saying, &c.** We have here a full and independent confirmation of the reality of this supernatural cure, since on any other supposition such conduct would be senseless. **These men, being Jews**—objects of dislike, contempt, and suspicion by the Romans, and at this time of more than usual prejudice; **do exceedingly trouble our city.** See similar charges, ch. xvii. 6; xxiv. 5; 1 Ki. xviii. 17. There is some colour of truth in all such accusations, in so far as the Gospel—and generally the fear of God as a reigning principle of human action—is in a godless world a thoroughly *revolutionary* principle. How far external commotion and change will in any case attend the triumph of this principle depends on the breadth and obstinacy of the resistance it meets with. **21. And teach customs, which are not lawful for us to receive, neither to observe, being Romans.** Here also there was a measure of truth, as the introduction of new gods was forbidden by the laws, and this might be thought to apply to any change of re-

multitude rose up together against them: and the magistrates rent off
23 their clothes, *w*and commanded to beat *them*. And *x*when they had laid
many stripes upon them, they cast *them* into prison, charging the jailor to
24 keep them safely: who, having received such a charge, thrust them into
the inner prison, and made their feet fast in the *y*stocks.
25   And at midnight Paul and Silas prayed, and *z*sang praises unto
26 God: and the prisoners heard them. And *a*suddenly there was a great
earthquake, so that the foundations of the prison were shaken: and
immediately *b*all the doors were opened, and every one's bands were
27 loosed. And the keeper of the prison awaking out of his sleep, and seeing
the prison doors open, he drew out his sword, and would have killed
28 himself, supposing that the prisoners had been fled. But Paul cried
with a loud voice, saying, *c*Do thyself no harm; for we are all here.

A. D. 53.

w 2 Cor. 6. 5.
2 Cor.11.23.
x Luke 21. 12.
Eph. 3. 1,
13.
Rev. 2. 10.
y Jer. 20. 2.
Matt. 5. 10.
ch. 5. 41.
Col 1. 24.
2 Tim. 1. 8.
a ch. 4. 31.
b ch. 5. 19.
ch. 12. 7, 10.
c Ex. 20. 13.
1 John 3.15.

ligion. But the whole charge was pure hypocrisy; for as these men would have let the missionaries preach what Religion they pleased, if they had not dried up the source of their gains, so they conceal the real cause of their rage under colour of a zeal for religion, and law, and good order: so ch. xvii. 6, 7; xix. 25, 27. 22. **And the multitude rose up together against them.** So ch. xix. 28, 34; xxi. 30; Luke xxiii. 18. **and the magistrates rent off their clothes** (that is, Paul and Silas's clothes); ordering the lictors or rod-bearers to tear them off, so as to expose their naked bodies (see on *v.* 37). The word [περιρρή-ξαντες] expresses the roughness with which this was done to prisoners, preparatory to whipping. **and commanded to beat them**—without any trial (*v.* 37), to appease the popular rage. Thrice, it seems, Paul endured this indignity (2 Cor. xi. 25). **23. And when they had laid many stripes upon them**—the bleeding wounds from which were not washed off till it was done by the converted jailor (*v.* 33), **they cast them into prison, charging the jailor to keep them safely: 24. Who, having received such a charge, thrust them into the inner prison** — pestilential cells (to use the words of *Howson*), damp and cold, from which the light was excluded, and where the chains rusted on the prisoners. One such place may be seen to this day on the slope of the Capitol at Rome. **and made their feet fast in the stocks** [εἰς τὸ ξύλον]—'to the wood;' an instrument of torture as well as confinement, made of wood bound with iron, with holes for the feet, which were stretched more or less apart, according to the severity intended. (*Origen*, at a later period, besides having his neck thrust into an iron collar, lay extended for many days with his feet four holes on the rack.) Though jailors were proverbially unfeeling, the manner in which the order was given in this case would seem to warrant all that was done.

Paul and Silas are miraculously set free, and the Jailor, with all his household, converted and baptized (25-34). **25. And at midnight Paul and Silas prayed, and sang praises unto God** [προσευχόμενοι ὕμνουν τ. Θεόν]—'as they prayed,' or 'kept singing praises unto God;' that is, while engaged in pouring out their hearts in prayer, had broken forth into singing, and were hymning loud their joy. As the word here employed [ὕμνουν] is that used to denote the Paschal hymn sung by our Lord and His disciples after their last passover (Matt. xxvi. 30), and which we know to have consisted of Ps. cxiii.-cxviii., which was chanted at that festival, it may have been portions of the psalms—so rich in such matter—which our joyous sufferers chanted forth. Nor could any be more seasonable and inspiring to them than those very six psalms, which every devout Jew would no doubt have by

heart. *"He giveth songs in the night"* (Job xxxv. 10). Though their bodies were still bleeding and tortured in the stocks, their spirits, under 'the expulsive power of a new affection,' rose above suffering, and made the prison walls resound with their song. 'In these midnight hymns (says *Neander*), by the imprisoned witnesses for Jesus Christ, the whole might of Roman injustice and violence against the Church is not only set at nought, but converted into a foil to set forth more completely the majesty and spiritual power of the Church, which as yet the world knew nothing of. And if the sufferings of these two witnesses for Christ are the beginning and the type of numberless martyrdoms which were to flow upon the Church from the same source, in like manner the unparalleled triumph of the spirit over suffering was the beginning and the pledge of a spiritual power which we afterwards see shining forth so triumphantly and irresistibly in the many martyrs of Christ who were given up as a prey to that same imperial might of Rome.' **and the prisoners heard them** [ἐπηκρο-ῶντο]—'kept listening to them,' so that the prisoners, instead of being asleep, were wide awake, and, no doubt, rapt in wonder at what they heard in such circumstances. **26. And suddenly there was a great earthquake**—in answer, doubtless, to the prayers and expectations of the sufferers, that, for the truth's sake and the honour of their Lord, some interposition might take place. **so that the foundations of the prison were shaken: and immediately all the doors were opened, and every one's bands** (the bands of all the prisoners) **were loosed**—not, of course, by the earthquake, but by a miraculous energy accompanying it. By this and the joyous strains which they had heard from the sufferers—not to speak of the change wrought on the jailor—these prisoners could hardly fail to have their hearts in some measure opened to the truth; and this part of the narrative seems the result of information afterwards communicated by one or more of these men. **27. And the keeper of the prison awaking out of his sleep, and seeing the prison doors open, he drew out his sword, and would have killed himself, supposing that the prisoners had been fled**—knowing that his life was a forfeited one in that case (see ch. xii. 19; xxvii. 42). **28. But Paul cried with a loud voice**—the better to arrest the fatal deed, **Do thyself no harm; for we are all here.** What divine calmness and self-possession! No elation at their miraculous liberation, or haste to take advantage of it: but one thought filled the apostle's mind at that moment—anxiety to save a fellow creature from sending himself into eternity, ignorant of the only way of life; and his presence of mind appears in the assurance which he so

29 Then he called for a light, and sprang in, and came trembling, and fell
30 down before Paul and Silas, and brought them out, and said, Sirs,
31 what [d] must I do to be saved? And they said, 'Believe on the Lord
32 Jesus Christ, and thou shalt be saved, and thy house. And they spake
33 unto him the word of the Lord, and to all that were in his house. And
he took them the same hour of the night, and washed *their* stripes; and
34 was baptized, he and all his, straightway. And when he had brought

A. D. 53.

[d] Luke 3. 10.
John 6. 27-
29.
ch. 2. 37.
ch. 9. 6.
* Isa. 45. 22.
John 3. 16,
36.

promptly gives to the desperate man, that his prisoners had none of them fled, as he feared. But how, it has been asked by recent sceptical critics, could Paul in his inner prison know what the jailor was about to do? In many conceivable ways, without supposing any supernatural communication. Thus, if the jailor slept at the door of "the inner prison," which suddenly flew open when the earthquake shook the foundations of the building; if, too, as may easily be conceived, he uttered some cry of despair on seeing the doors open; and if the clash of the steel, as the affrighted man drew it hastily from the scabbard, was audible but a few yards off, in the dead midnight stillness —increased by the awe inspired in the prisoners by the miracle—what difficulty is there in supposing that Paul, perceiving in a moment how matters stood, after crying out, stepped hastily to him, uttering the noble entreaty here recorded? Not less flat is the question, why the other liberated prisoners did not make their escape;—as if there were the smallest difficulty in understanding how, under the resistless conviction that there must be something supernatural in their instantaneous liberation without human hand, such wonder and awe should possess them as to take away for the time not only all desire of escape, but even all thought on the subject. **29. Then he called for a light, and sprang in, and came trembling, and fell down before Paul and Silas, 30. And brought them out, and said.** How graphic this rapid succession of minute details, evidently from the parties themselves—the prisoners and the jailor— who would talk over every feature of the scene once and again, in which the hand of the Lord had been so marvellously seen! **Sirs, what must I do to be saved?** If this question should seem in advance of any light which the jailor could be supposed to possess, let it be considered, *first,* that the "trembling" which came over him could not have arisen from any fear for the safety of his prisoners, for they were all there; and if it had, he would rather have proceeded to secure them again, than leave them and fall down before Paul and Silas. For the same reason, it is plain that his trembling had nothing to do with any account he would have to render to the magistrates. Only one explanation of it can be given —that he had become all at once alarmed about his spiritual state, and that though, a moment before, he was ready to plunge into eternity with the guilt of self-murder on his head—without a thought of the sin he was committing and its awful consequences—his unfitness to appear before God and his need of salvation now flashed full upon his soul, and drew from the depths of his spirit the cry here recorded. If still it be asked how it could take such definite shape, let it be considered, *secondly,* that the jailor could hardly be ignorant of the nature of the charges on which these men had been imprisoned, seeing they had been publicly whipped by order of the magistrates, which would fill the whole town with the facts of the case, including that strange cry of the demoniac from day to day—" These men are the servants of the most high God, which *show unto us the way of salvation*"—words proclaiming not only the

Divine commission of the preachers, but the news of salvation they were sent to tell, the miraculous expulsion of the demon, and the rage of her masters. All this, indeed, would go for nothing with such a man, until roused by the mighty earthquake which made the building to rock; despair then seizing him at the sight of the open doors, the sword of self-destruction was suddenly arrested by words from one of those prisoners such as he would never imagine could be spoken in their circumstances—words evidencing something divine about them. Then would flash across him the light of a new discovery: 'That was a true cry which the Pythoness uttered, "These men are the servants of the most high God, which show unto us the way of salvation!" This I now must know, and from them—as Divinely sent to me—must I learn that "way of salvation!"' **31. And they said, Believe on the Lord Jesus Christ.** [*Lachmann* and *Tischendorf omit* χριστὸν from their texts, with א A B, &c. But the majority of MSS. have it; and internal evidence, we think, favours it, as the apostle would probably give the saving name in its fullest form in such circumstances.] **and thou shalt be saved.** The brevity, simplicity, and directness of this reply are, in the circumstances, singularly beautiful. Enough at that moment to have his faith directed simply to the Saviour, with the assurance that this would bring to his soul the needed and sought salvation —the *how* being a matter for after teaching. **and thy house.** See on Luke xix. 9; and Remark 4, at the close of that Section. **32. And they spake unto him the word of the Lord**—unfolding now, doubtless, more fully what "the Lord Jesus Christ" was, to whom they had pointed his faith, and what the 'salvation' was which this would bring him. **and to** (or 'with,' according to another reading) **all that were in his house**— who from their own dwelling (under the same roof no doubt with the prison) had crowded round the apostles, aroused first by the earthquake. From their addressing the Gospel message "to all that were in the house," it is not necessary to infer that it contained no children, but merely that as it contained adults besides the jailor himself, so to all of these—as alone of course fit to be addressed—they preached the word. **33. And he took them** [Ἀναγαγών]; the word implies removal to another place: **the same hour of the night, and washed their stripes**—' in the well (says *Howson*) or fountain, which was within or near the precincts of the prison.' The mention of "the same hour of the night" seems to imply that they had to go forth into the open air, and that, unseasonable as the hour was, they did so. These bleeding wounds had never been thought of by the indifferent jailor. But now, when his whole heart was opened to his spiritual benefactors, he cannot rest until he has done all in his power for their bodily relief. **and was baptized, he and all his, straightway**—probably at the same fountain, since it took place "straightway," the one washing on his part being immediately succeeded by the other on theirs. **34. And when he had brought them into his house,** he set meat before them [παρέθηκεν τράπεζαν]—

119

them into his house, *f*he set meat before them, *g*and rejoiced, believing in God with all his house.

35 And when it was day, the magistrates sent the serjeants, saying, Let
36 those men go. And the keeper of the prison told this saying to Paul, The magistrates have sent to let you go: now therefore depart, and go in
37 peace. But Paul said unto them, They have beaten us openly uncondemned, *h*being Romans, and have cast *us* into prison; and now do they thrust us out privily? nay verily; *i*but let them come themselves and
38 fetch us out. And the serjeants told these words unto the magistrates:
39 and they feared, when they heard that they were Romans. And they came and besought them, and brought *them* out, and *j*desired *them* to
40 depart out of the city. And they went out of the prison, and entered into *the house of* Lydia: and when they had seen the brethren, they *k*comforted them, and departed.

A. D. 57.

f Luke 5. 29.
Luke 19. 6.
g Ps. 5. 11.
Rom. 5. 2.
Heb. 3. 6.
1 Pet. 1. 6, 8.
h ch. 22. 25.
i Ps. 37. 6.
Mic. 7. 9, 10.
Matt. 10. 16.
j Matt. 8. 34.
k 1 Thes. 3. 2, 3.
1 Thes. 4. 18.
1 Thes. 5. 11, 14.

lit., 'prepared (or 'set out') a table; a familiar classical expression, used also in Hebrew, Ps. xxiii. **5. and rejoiced, believing**—*lit.,* 'exulted, having believed;' that is, was full of joy in the consciousness of his new state as a believer; **believing in God**—as a converted heathen; for (as *Alford* correctly notes) the faith of a Jew would not be so expressed. **with all his house**—the wondrous change on himself and the whole house filling his soul with joy. It is a good remark of *Baumgarten,* that 'this is the second house which in the Roman city of Philippi was consecrated by faith in Jesus, and of which the inmates, by hospitable entertainment of the Gospel witnesses, were sanctified to a new beginning of domestic life, pleasing and acceptable to God. The first result came to pass in consequence simply of the preaching of the Gospel; the second was the fruit of a testimony sealed and ennobled by suffering.'

Next morning the magistrates order their release —Paul and Silas, standing upon their violated rights as Roman citizens, decline to be thus dismissed, and oblige the affrighted magistrates to come personally to conduct them forth out of the prison, and solicit their departure from the city— They then comply, go to Lydia's house, and having seen and comforted the brethren, depart (35-40). **35. And when it was day, the magistrates sent the serjeants** [τ. ῥαβδούχους]—'rod-bearers;' 'lictors' was their technical name: **saying, Let those men go.** The cause of this change can only be conjectured. When the commotion ceased, reflection would soon convince them of the injustice they had done, even supposing the prisoners had been entitled to no special privileges; and if rumour reached them that the prisoners were somehow under supernatural protection, they might be the more awed into a desire to get rid of them. **36. And the keeper**—overjoyed to have such orders to execute, **told this saying to Paul, The magistrates have sent to let you go: now therefore depart, and go in peace.** Very differently does Paul receive these orders: **37. But Paul said unto them**—to the serjeants, who had entered the prison with the jailor, that they might be able to report that the men had departed. **They have beaten us openly** [Δείραντες ἡμᾶς δημοσίᾳ]—'have scourged us in public' (in designed contrast to the proposed dismissal of them "*privily*"). The *publicity* of the injury done to them, exposing their naked and bleeding bodies to the rude populace, was evidently the most stinging feature of it to the apostle's delicate feelings, and to this accordingly he alludes to the Thessalonians—probably a year after—"even after that we had suffered before, and *were shamefully entreated,*' or 'insulted' [ὑβρισθέντες], "as ye know, at Philippi" (1 Thess. ii. 2). 120

uncondemned—that is, without being put on trial and convicted, **being Romans**—in whose case both the scourging and the imprisonment without trial were illegal. From this it would appear that Silas was a Roman citizen as well as Paul. **and now do they thrust us out privily** [ἐκβάλλουσιν]? Something more than 'hurrying out' this word expresses: it is 'driving out.' **nay verily** ('no indeed'); **but let them come themselves and fetch us out**—by an open and formal act, which would be equivalent to a public declaration of their innocence. **38. And the serjeants told these words unto the magistrates: and they feared, when they heard that they were Romans. 39. And they came** in person, not now sending the lictors, **and besought them**—to forgive the wrong done to them, and not to inform upon them. What a contrast this suppliant attitude of the prætors of Philippi to their tyrannical conduct the day before. See Isa. lx. 15; Rev. iii. 9. **and brought them out** [ἐξαγαγόντες]—'conducted them forth' from the prison into the open street, which the missionaries had demanded, **and desired** [ἠρώτων]—or 'requested' **them to depart out of the city**—perhaps fearing, lest their longer stay should afresh excite the populace. **40. And they went out of the prison.** Having attained their object—to vindicate their civil rights, by the infraction of which in this case the Gospel in their persons had been illegally affronted—they had no mind to carry the matter further. Their citizenship was valuable to them only as a shield against unnecessary injuries to their Master's cause. What a beautiful mixture of *dignity* and *meekness* is this! **and entered into the house of Lydia**—as if to show by this leisurely proceeding that they had not been made to leave, but were at full liberty to consult their own convenience; **and when they had seen the brethren**—not only her family and the jailor's, but *probably others now gained to the Gospel,* **they comforted them** [παρεκάλεσαν]—rather, perhaps, 'exhorted' them, which would include comfort, **and departed**—but not all; for two of the party appear to have remained behind at Philippi (see on ch. xvii. 14):—*Timotheus,* 'of whom (to use the words of *Howson*) the Philippians learned the proof, "that he honestly cared for their state, and was truly like-minded with St. Paul, serving with him in the Gospel as a son with his father" (Phil. ii. 19-23); and *Luke,* "whose praise is in the Gospel," though he never praises himself or relates his own labours, and though we only trace his movements in connection with St. Paul, by the change of a pronoun or the unconscious variation of his style.' Here, accordingly, and onwards, the narrative is again in the *third*

17 NOW when they had passed through Amphipolis and Apollonia, they
2 came to Thessalonica, where was a synagogue of the Jews: and Paul, as

person, nor is the pronoun changed to the *second* till we come to ch. xx. 5. 'The modesty with which St. Luke leaves out all mention of his own labours need hardly be pointed out. We shall trace him again when he rejoins St. Paul in the same neighbourhood. His vocation as a physician may have brought him into connection with these contiguous coasts of Asia and Europe; and he may (as *Mr. Smith* suggests, 'Shipwreck,' &c.) have been in the habit of exercising his professional skill as a surgeon at sea.'

Remarks.—1. Christianity is essentially revolutionary, bringing into captivity every thought to the obedience of Christ. It casts out devils, exposes every religious cheat, and tolerates no compromise of truth and error, good and evil. No wonder, then, that it is felt by all the powers of evil, both in hell and on earth, as an enemy to be put down by whatever means—whether by pretended friendship (as in the testimony borne by this soothsaying spirit to Paul and Silas) or by false charges of hostility to the peace of society, as a plea for putting it down by force—charges which have just enough of truth in them to give them plausibility—as when Paul and Silas were charged by the enraged masters of that wretched slave girl with turning everything upside down. But the quarrel of Christianity is only with what is ungodly and evil, and it is revolutionary only as it is in deadly hostility to all that is so. It expels only the poison from humanity, and infuses into it only what is healthful and ennobling. Even this it does by an internal and noiseless operation. And thus is it the only true and divine Panacea for the ills under which our nature languishes. 2. How different is the carriage of Paul and Silas in the dungeon of Philippi from that stoical endurance of agony unmoved, which is all that heroism without religion can rise to! How deeply they felt the violation of their rights, and the insult, shame, and pain of a public exposure of their naked backs to the scourge, we know well; for their complaint of it made the magistrates to tremble, and the touching allusion to it long after to the Thessalonian Church, showed how the apostle still felt it (1 Thess. ii. 2). Nor would the torture of the stocks, and the smarting of their bleeding backs on the earthen floor of that dismal hole go less acutely through their sensitive frames. And doubtless this was what the authorities of Philippi intended. But just in these circumstances—to the flesh of extreme wretchedness—and at the season of deepest darkness (the midnight hour), while they were pouring out their souls in prayer to God, the light of heaven irradiates their darkness, they pass irresistibly from the minor into the major tone, breaking forth into songs of praise so loud that the other prisoners 'kept listening to them,' in rapt astonishment (we may be sure) at sounds so unusual issuing from a dungeon. This is not impassive stoicism; it is the transport of the soul triumphing over both shame and pain; it is the sense of God's presence deadening the sense of everything else—'the expulsive power of a new affection,' in the noblest sense of the phrase. 3. As the question of the trembling jailor—"Sirs, what must I do to be saved?"—is substantially the cry of every awakened sinner, though the degree of light and the depth of anxiety which it expresses will vary in every case; so the reply to it—"Believe in the Lord Jesus Christ, and thou shalt be saved, and thy house"—is to all alike the one true and all-satisfying answer. 'They place the Person of

Christ,' says *Lechler*, 'in whom alone is salvation, directly and without circumlocution, before the enquiring soul. They demand faith in Him—nothing more, but also nothing less. *Fide solā*—By faith only—is the motto of the apostle Paul, as it was of the Reformers after his example. They do not require of the jailor—ready and willing to do anything—various performances and works, but simply *faith*, that is, cordial acceptance and appropriation of the personal Saviour, along with absolute confidence. But the faith to which the jailor attained constrained him also to all possible services and works of love and gratitude,' &c. 4. How beautifully are the deadened affections quickened into life, so soon as the Gospel of a present salvation through faith in a crucified Saviour takes possession of the heart. As Lydia, so soon as the Lord opened her heart to the grace of the Gospel and she had been received into the fellowship of believers by baptism, would have Paul and Silas to take up their abode in her house; so the jailor, as soon as his heart was won to the Saviour, took the liberated apostles "the same hour of the night, and washed their stripes, and (after being baptized) brought them into his house, set meat before them, and rejoiced, believing in God with all his house." 5. The carriage of Paul and Silas towards the magistrates of Philippi affords a noble example for all ages. They submitted meekly to the shameful violation of their rights as Roman citizens, by those whose duty it was to see them respected. But when an astounding interposition of Heaven in their behalf, inspired their persecutors with dread of them, and caused them to give an order for their liberation and departure; then came the time for those injured servants of Christ to assert their rights. With calmness and dignity, declining to be thus ordered out stealthily, they require the magistrates who had wronged them to come in person, and opening the prison doors, themselves to conduct them forth. Galling as this must have been, they have nothing for it but to comply. So coming in person, they beg the forgiveness of the injured missionaries, and conducting them forth request their departure. And this being all that those servants of Christ desired, they at once comply. Nothing secular, social, or political, which may be turned to the account of the Gospel, is by these men of sober faith disregarded; but in any other view nothing of that nature is set any store by.

CHAP. XVII. 1-34.—AT THESSALONICA THE SUCCESS OF PAUL'S PREACHING ENDANGERING HIS LIFE, HE IS DESPATCHED BY NIGHT TO BEREA, WHERE HIS MESSAGE MEETS WITH ENLIGHTENED ACCEPTANCE—A HOSTILE MOVEMENT FROM THESSALONICA OCCASIONS HIS SUDDEN DEPARTURE FROM BEREA—HE ARRIVES AT ATHENS—PROCEEDINGS THERE.

Arrival at Thessalonica—Success there among the Jews and Gentile Proselytes (1-4). **1. Now when they had passed** (or 'travelled') **through** [Διοδεύσαντες]. **Amphipolis**—thirty-three miles southwest of Philippi, on the river Strymon, and on the north coast of the Ægean Sea; **and Apollonia**—thirty miles south-west of Amphipolis, but the exact site is not known; **they came to Thessalonica**—thirty-seven miles due west of Apollonia, at the head of the Thermaic (or Thessalonian) Gulf, at the north-west extremity of the Ægean Sea—the principal and most populous city in Macedonia. 'We see at once (says *Howson*, excellently) how appropriate a place it was for one of the starting-points of the Gospel in Europe, and

his manner was, went *a* in unto them, and three sabbath days reasoned
3 with them out of the scriptures; opening and alleging *b* that Christ must
needs have suffered, and risen again from the dead; and that this Jesus,
4 ¹whom I preach unto you, is Christ. And *c* some of them believed, and
consorted with Paul and *d* Silas; and of the devout Greeks a great multitude, and of the chief women not a few.
5 But the Jews which believed not, moved with envy, took unto them
certain lewd fellows of the baser sort, and gathered a company, and set
all the city on an uproar, and assaulted the house of *e* Jason, and sought
6 to bring them out to the people. And when they found them not, they
drew Jason and certain brethren unto the rulers of the city, crying,
These *f* that have turned the world upside down are come hither also;
7 whom Jason hath received: and these all *g* do contrary to the decrees of

A. D. 53.
a Luke 4. 16.
ch. 9. 20.
ch. 13. 5, 14.
b Luke 24. 26,
46.
Gal. 3. 1.
¹ Or, whom,
said he, I
preach.
c ch. 28. 24.
d ch. 15. 22,
27, 32, 40.
e Rom. 16.21.
f 1 Ki. 18. 17.
g Ezra 4. 12.
Dan. 3. 12.

can appreciate the force of what Paul said to the Thessalonians within a few months of his departure from them; "From you, the word of the Lord sounded forth like a trumpet, not only in Macedonia and Achaia, but in every place" (1 Thess. i. 8). **where was a** (rather, 'the') **synagogue of the Jews**—implying that (as at Philippi) there was no synagogue at Amphipolis and Apollonia, and that here were the headquarters of the Jews in northern Macedonia. **2. And Paul, as his manner was** (always to begin with the Jews), **went in unto them.** That this was an act which, after the shameful treatment they had received at Philippi, required some coorage and superiority to indignity for the Gospel's sake, the apostle himself tells the Thessalonians, when writing to the converts three some months after this: "We were bold in our God to speak unto you," &c. (1 Thess. ii. 2). **and three sabbath days reasoned with them** [διελέγετο αὐτοῖς]—or, 'continued to discourse to them' **out of the scriptures. 3. Opening and alleging** [παρατιθέμενος]—'putting before' or 'representing' to them this great truth, as the sum of all the Scriptures quoted and commented on, **that Christ must needs have suffered, and risen again from the dead** [τὸν Χριστὸν ἔδει παθεῖν καὶ ἀναστῆναι]—'that it behoved the Christ (the promised Messiah) to suffer and rise from the dead.' **and that this Jesus, whom I preach unto you, is Christ**—or, 'that this is the Christ, (even) Jesus whom I preach unto you.' His preaching, it seems, was chiefly expository, and designed to establish from the Old Testament Scriptures, *first*, that the predicted Messiah was to be a suffering and dying, and therefore a rising Messiah; and *next*, that this Messiah was none other than Jesus of Nazareth. **4. And some of them believed, and consorted** [προσεκληρώθησαν] —or, 'cast in their lot' **with Paul and Silas; and of the devout Greeks**—Gentile proselytes, and as such, stated worshippers with the Jews (see on ch. xvi. 14), **a great multitude, and of the chief women**—female proselytes of distinction, **not a few.** But besides this multitude of Gentile proselytes, male and female, who were won to the Gospel in the Jewish synagogue, it would appear —from the remarkable passage in 1 Thess. i. 9, 10 —that not a few had been gained to Christ fresh from idolatry. It is possible that the same parties are referred to in both places; or it may be that the missionaries remained somewhat longer than the three sabbaths of their labour in the synagogue. During their stay, however, the apostle tells the Thessalonians that he had laboured for his own support "night and day, that he might not be chargeable to any of them" (1 Thess. ii. 9). of which he again reminds them in his second Epistle (iii. 7-9). In both places he

speaks of the "toil and trouble" which this involved; but he received considerate supplies once and again from the converts of Philippi, of which he fails not to make honourable acknowledgment in his letter to that church (Phil. iv. 15, 16).

The unbelieving Jews, enraged at the success of the Gospel, having raised a tumult, in the midst of which they sought the lives of the missionaries, the brethren despatch them by night to Berœa (5-10). **5. But the Jews which believed not, moved with envy** (or 'jealousy')—seeing their influence likely to be destroyed [*Tischendorf* omits all these words; but though the MSS. vary considerably, the three oldest—א A B with E &c.—have the principal part of the clause, and the reasons for its exclusion seem scarcely sufficient]—**took unto them certain lewd fellows of the baser sort** [τῶν ἀγοραίων τινὰς ἄνδρας πονηροὺς]—better, 'certain worthless idlers;' *lit.,* 'worthless market people' (=*subrostrani*)—that is, idle loungers about the place of public resort, such as are to be found in all large towns, particularly those of the East, and usually of indifferent character, ready for any excitement: **and gathered a company** [ὀχλοποιήσαντες]—'raised a mob.' **and assaulted the house of Jason**—with whom Paul and Silas lodged (*v.* 7). He appears to be the same as Paul's kinsman of that name, to whom, in his Epistle to the Romans (xvi. 21), he sends a salutation; and as that name (as *Grotius* remarks) was sometimes used as a Greek form of the word *Joshua*, he was probably a Hellenistic Jew. At all events, he must have been among the converts of Thessalonica. **and sought to bring them** (Jason's lodgers) **out to the people**—or expose them to the turbulent rabble. **6. And when they found them not**—no doubt because they had been warned to keep out of the way, **they drew Jason and certain brethren unto the rulers of the city** [ἐπὶ τ. πολιτάρχας]—'to the *politarchs*' (*lit.,* 'city-rulers'). It is remarkable that the word, in this form, occurs nowhere else as a title of civic office; but it occurs (as *Howson* notes) in an inscription on a marble arch still existing in Thessalonica, on which are the names of the seven *politarchs* of the city at the time when that archway was erected, the masonry of which consists of blocks of marble six feet thick—so minute is the accuracy of our sacred Historian. **crying, These that have turned the world upside down.** What a testimony to the success of the Gospel, even from its enemies! See on ch. xvi. 20, 21, and Remark 1 at the close of that Section. **are come hither also; 7. Whom Jason hath received**—or 'harboured.' **and these all do contrary to the decrees of Cesar, saying**—that is, by saying, for no illegal act was charged against them. All that their enemies pretended was that

8 Cesar, saying [h] that there is another king, *one* Jesus. And they troubled the people and the rulers of the city, when they heard these things.

9 And when they had taken security of Jason, and of the other, they let them go.

10 And [i] the brethren immediately sent away Paul and Silas by night unto

11 Berea: who coming *thither* went into the synagogue of the Jews. These were more noble than those in Thessalonica, in that they received the word with all readiness of mind, and searched [j] the scriptures daily,

12 whether those things were so. Therefore many of them believed; also of

13 honourable women which were Greeks, and of men, not a few. But when the Jews of Thessalonica had knowledge that the word of God was preached of Paul at Berea, [k] they came thither also, and stirred up the

14 people. And [l] then immediately the brethren sent away Paul, to go

A. D. 53.

[h] Luke 23. 2.
John 19. 12.
1 Pet. 2. 15.
[i] ch. 9. 25.
ch. 23. 23,
24.
Josh. 2. 15,
16.
1 Sam. 19.
13, 17.
[j] Isa. 34. 16.
Luke 10. 20.
John 5. 39.
[k] Luke 11. 52.
1 Thes. 2. 15.
[l] Matt. 10. 23.

they were *constructive* traitors, for the reason next mentioned. **that there is another king, [one] Jesus.** As the mention of "Him that was born king of the Jews" alarmed Herod (Matt. ii. 2, 3), so the regal claims of our Lord alarmed Pilate; and though His explanation of the sense in which He claimed royalty set the mind of Pilate at rest upon that point (John xviii. 33-38), the reiterated assertions of His enemies, that the claim did involve treason against Cesar, worked so successfully upon Pilate's fears that he was induced by that consideration alone to surrender Him. It is possible that these Jews of Thessalonica really imagined that the "Gospel of the kingdom" involved some political doctrine; but it is more likely that from the very first this had become a *stock* argument with the unbelieving Jews against the Gospel when every other failed, and that in this factious sense it was now put before the heathen magistrates, in hopes of working on their loyalty. In this, as will now appear, they were but too successful. **9. And when they had taken security** (or 'bail') **of Jason, and of the other** [τ. λαιπῶν]—rather, 'of the rest;' that is, of such others as were charged with countenancing and encouraging this disloyal teaching, **they let them go.**

10. And the brethren immediately sent away Paul and Silas by night—for it would have been as useless as rash to attempt any further preaching at that time, and the conviction of this probably made his friends the more willing to pledge themselves against any present continuance of missionary effort. It would appear, however, from the First Epistle to the Thessalonians, that the apostle both earnestly desired and confidently expected soon to return—indeed, that he made several efforts towards a return, 'but Satan hindered him' (1 Thess. ii. 17, 18). The cause of this intense anxiety to revisit them was a fear lest the hot persecution to which they were exposed for the Gospel's sake should shake their constancy in the Faith; and such was the pressure of this apprehension upon his spirit, that when he could neither go to them himself, nor abide longer without tidings from them, he sent Timotheus (of whose motions since he was left at Philippi, see on v. 14) "to know their faith, lest by any means the tempter should have tempted them, and his labour have been in vain. But when Timotheus came from them to him, and brought him good tidings of their faith and love, and that they had good remembrance of him, always, longing to see him, as he also to see them, he was comforted over them in all his affliction and distress by their faith," &c. (1 Thess. iii. 5-7.) **unto Berea**—upwards of fifty miles south-west of Thessalonica; a town even still of considerable population and importance.

At Berœa their message meets with enlightened acceptance—A hostile movement, instigated by the unbelieving Jews of Thessalonica, occasions the sudden departure of Paul—He arrives at Athens (10-15). **10. who coming thither went into the synagogue of the Jews**—the first thing after their arrival, as the words imply; an act which, in their circumstances, showed unabated courage and confidence in their message. **11. These were more noble than those in Thessalonica.** The comparison is only between *the Jews* of the two places, for in Thessalonica the triumphs of the Gospel among the Gentiles were at least as great as at Berœa. At all events, a flourishing and permanent church was established at Thessalonica, which was not the case—so far as we know—at Berœa. **in that they received the word with all readiness of mind**—heard it not only without prejudice, but with eager interest, "in an honest and good heart" (Luke viii. 15), with sincere desire to be taught aright (see John vii. 17). Mark the "nobility" ascribed to this state of mind. **and searched the Scriptures daily whether these things were so**—whether the *Christian* interpretation which the apostle put upon the Old Testament Scriptures were the true one. **12. Therefore many of them believed**—convinced that Jesus of Nazareth, whom Paul preached, was indeed the great Promise and Burden of the Old Testament Scriptures; **also of honourable women**—women, that is, of what we call the better or upper class, **which were Greeks, and of men**—that is, men which were Greeks, **not a few.** The upper classes in these European Greek and Romanized towns (as *Webster and Wilkinson* remark) were probably better educated than those of Asia Minor. **13. But when the Jews of Thessalonica had knowledge that the word of God was preached of Paul at Berea** [καὶ ἐν τ. B.]—'in Berœa too,' they came thither also, and stirred up the people—their blind zeal prompting them to travel above fifty miles to have the missionaries of Christ hunted out of Berœa, as they had been out of their own city. Thus had they of Iconium done, when they followed Paul and Barnabas to Lystra. But O what memories would this bring back to Paul of the time when he verily thought with himself that he ought to do many things contrary to the name of Jesus of Nazareth, and did them too! (ch. xxvi. 9, 10.) **14. And then immediately the brethren**—the converts gathered at Berœa. **sent away Paul**—as had been done before from Jerusalem (ch. ix. 30), and from Thessalonica (v. 10). How long he stayed at Berœa we know not; but as we know that he longed and expected soon to return to the Thessalonians (1 Thess. ii. 17), it is probable he remained some weeks at least, and only abandoned his intention of revisiting Thessalonica at that time when the viru!ence

15 as it were to the sea: but Silas and Timotheus abode there still. And
they that conducted Paul brought him unto Athens: and ^mreceiving
a commandment unto Silas and Timotheus for to come to him with all
speed, they departed.

16 Now while Paul waited for them at Athens, ⁿhis spirit was stirred in
17 him, when he saw the city ²wholly given to idolatry. Therefore disputed
he in the synagogue with the Jews, and with the devout persons, and in
18 the market daily with them that met with him. Then certain philosophers of the Epicureans, and of the Stoics, encountered him. And some
said, What will this ³ babbler say? other some, He seemeth to be a setter

A D 53.

^m ch. 18. 5.
ⁿ Ex. 32. 19, 20.
Ps. 119. 158.
Jer. 20. 9.
Mic. 3. 8.
Mark 3. 5.
2 Pet. 2. 8.
² Or, full of idols.
³ Or, base fellow.

of his enemies there, stimulated by his success at
Berœa, brought them down thither to counterwork
him. **to go as it were to the sea** [ὡς ἐπὶ τ.
θάλασσαν]. The precise idea intended to be conveyed by this phrase is not very clear. That it
was only a feint (as some critics think) can hardly
be the meaning. But whether it means that he
was sent only *in the direction of the sea,* with the
view of skirting along the coast by a land journey
(as others think), or that he did proceed to Athens
by sea (as most understand the phrase) must
be left in some doubt. The land journey was
certainly a long one (not less than 250 miles),
while with a fair wind they might reach Athens
in three days. Perhaps it had not been determined, until he should reach the coast, what
direction he should next take; and it may have
been the mere providence of God, presenting to
him a vessel bound for Athens, that fixed him to
proceed thither. It is in favour of this view that
it was not till his arrival at that capital that the
convoy of Berœan brethren, who had accompanied
him thus far, were sent back to Berœa to bid
Silas and Timotheus follow him thither. **but
Silas and Timotheus abode there still**—to encourage the converts, and cherish, as at Philippi,
the work accomplished. But how came Timotheus
to be here at all? We left him at Philippi with
Luke, when Paul took his departure (see on ch.
xvi. 40). We have seen (on *v.* 4) that during the
apostle's stay at Thessalonica, brief though it was,
the Philippians "sent once and again to his
necessity" (Phil. iv. 16). Their first contribution
was probably despatched by Timothy soon after
the apostle left them, and merely as a love-token;
taking the advantage of Timothy's departure to
rejoin his great coadjutor. But on finding that
the very success of the apostle at Thessalonica
had so abridged his time for working at his craft,
that though he laboured hard he would earn little,
it is likely that Timothy returned to Philippi,
partly to tell the good news, and partly to represent
the temporal circumstances of their father in the
Faith; and if they sent him back with a fresh
contribution, that would both explain his statement in Phil. iv. 16, and show how Timothy came
to be at Thessalonica. Whether he went with
Paul and Silas to Berœa, or followed them
thither, is not said. But here he was left with
Silas when Paul went to Athens. **15. And they
that conducted Paul brought him unto Athens:
and receiving a commandment unto Silas and
Timotheus for to come to him with all speed,
they departed.** The apostle probably wished their
company and aid in addressing himself to so new
and great a sphere as Athens. Accordingly it is
added that he "waited for them" there, as if
unwilling to do anything till they came. That
they did come, there is no good reason to doubt
(as some excellent critics do). For though Paul
himself says to the Thessalonians that he "thought
it good to be left at Athens alone" (1 Thess. iii. 1),
he immediately adds that he "sent Timotheus to

establish and comfort them" (*v.* 2); meaning, surely,
that he despatched him from Athens back to
Thessalonica. He had indeed sent for him to
Athens; but when it appeared that little fruit
was to be reaped there, while Thessalonica was
in too interesting a state to be left uncherished,
he seems to have thought it better to send him
back again. The other explanations which have
been suggested seem less satisfactory. Timotheus
rejoined the apostle at Corinth (ch. xviii. 5).
   Disputations at Athens (16-21). **16. Now while
Paul waited for them at Athens, his spirit was
stirred** [παρωξύνετο]—or 'roused' **in him, when
he saw** [θεωροῦντι, or rather —τος]—'while beholding' **the city wholly given to idolatry** [κατεί-
δωλον]—'covered with idols;' referring to the
city, not the citizens. *Petronius,* a contemporary
writer at Nero's court, says satirically, that it
was easier to find a god at Athens than a man.
The sight of this, in his solitary walks through
the city, roused his spirit. **17. Therefore disputed**
(or 'discussed') **he in the synagogue with the
Jews, and with the devout persons.** The second
"with" here should be omitted; for the Jews and
the devout persons assembling together in the
synagogue, the discussion was with both at once.
The sense is not that he went to the Jews
because the Gentile Athenians were steeped in
idolatry; but, 'Therefore set he himself to lift up
his voice to the idol-city, but, as his manner was,
he began with the Jews,' and, perhaps, while congratulating them on their purer Faith, he would
upbraid them with their want of zeal in allowing,
unrebuked, such idolatry around them. **and in
the market**—or 'market-place,' as the place of
public resort, **daily with them that met with
him** [τ. παρατυγχάνοντας]—who chanced to be
there, or came in his way. **18. Then certain
philosophers of the Epicureans**—the followers of
Epicurus; a well-known school of *atheistic materialists,* who maintained that the universe is the
product of chance, and that pleasure was the chief
end of human existence—a principle which the
more sober disciples of this school interpreted in a
refined sense, while the sensual explained it in its
coarser meaning: **and of the Stoics**—the followers
of Zeno, an equally celebrated but opposite school
of philosophy, essentially *pantheistic,* whose principle was that the universe was under the law of
an iron necessity, the spirit of which was what is
called the Deity; and that a passionless conformity
of the human will to this law, unmoved by all
external circumstances and changes, is the perfection of virtue. While therefore the Stoical was
in itself superior to the Epicurean system, both
were alike hostile to the Gospel. **And some said,
What will this babbler say?** [σπερμολόγος.] This
word, which means 'a picker-up of seeds'—bird-
like—is applied to a gatherer and retailer of scraps
of knowledge, a prater; a general term of contempt for any pretended teacher. **other some** (or
'others'), **He seemeth to be a setter forth** [κατ-
αγγελεὺς] **of strange gods** [ξένων δαιμονίων]—'of

forth of strange gods: because he preached unto them Jesus, and the
19 resurrection. And they took him, and brought him unto [4] Areopagus,
saying, May we know what this new doctrine, whereof thou speakest, *is?*
20 For thou bringest certain strange things to our ears: we would know
21 therefore what these things mean. (For all the Athenians and strangers
which were there spent their time in nothing else, but either to tell, or to
hear some new thing.)
22 Then Paul stood in the midst of [5] Mars' hill, and said, *Ye* men of
23 Athens, I perceive that in all things ye are °too superstitious. For as I
passed by and beheld your [6]devotions, I found an altar with this inscription, TO THE UNKNOWN GOD. Whom therefore ye ignorantly
24 worship, him declare I unto you. God that made the world and all

Marginal notes:

A. D. 54.

[4] Or. Mars' hill. It was the highest court in Athens.

[5] Or. the court of the Areopagites.

° Jer. 50. 38.

[6] Or. gods that ye worship.

---

foreign divinities.' The word 'demons' is here used, not in the Jewish, but in the Greek sense, of 'objects of worship.' In his speech on the Areopagus we shall find the apostle taking up the very term here employed, as the starting-point of his address to the Athenians (see *v.* 24). **because he preached unto them Jesus, and the resurrection**—not that they took "Jesus" and "the resurrection" as the foreign divinities preached by Paul (as *Chrysostom* formerly, and some good critics still maintain). The divinities they meant were *Jehovah,* as the God of Revealed Religion, and *Jesus* as the risen Saviour and Judge of mankind. This resurrection from the dead would to them be a startling novelty. **19. And they took him, and brought him unto Areopagus**—that is, 'Mars' hill;' an eminence over against the Acropolis, on the west side of that citadel rock. 'On this hill (as *Howson* says) had sat the most awful court of judicature from time immemorial, to pass sentence on the greatest criminals, and to decide on the most solemn questions connected with religion. No place in Athens was so suitable for a discourse on the mysteries of religion.' The apostle, however, was not here on his *trial* (as some formerly thought, and the Tübingen school still allege), as is evident on the face of the narrative. There is nothing of religious fanaticism or intolerance on the part of his questioners. Curiosity, not without a mixture of contempt, alone prompts their enquiries. They merely desired a fuller exposition of what this novel teacher had in broken conversations thrown out in the Agora (or market-place). **saying, May we know** [Δυνάμεθα γνῶναι] — extremely polite, yet half ironical; the questioners, in their Greek pride, being quite satisfied (as *Lechler* remarks) that they knew all things already, and better than this barbarian Jew could tell them. **what this new doctrine** (or 'teaching'), **whereof thou speakest, is?** **20. For thou bringest certain strange things** [ξενίζοντα τινα] — 'certain foreign-sounding things'] **to our ears: we would know therefore what these things mean. 21. For all the Athenians and strangers which were there spent their time in nothing else, but either to tell or to hear some new thing** [καινότερον] — *lit.,* 'newer thing;' as if what was new (says *Bengel*) 'becoming presently stale, they craved something newer still.' This lively description of the Athenian character is abundantly attested by their own writers.

Paul on Mars' Hill (22-31). **22. Then Paul stood in the midst of Mars' hill, and said**—'taking his stand in the midst of Mars' hill (or 'Areopagus'), said.' This prefatory allusion to the position he occupied shows (says *Baumgarten*) the writer's wish to bring the situation vividly before us. **Ye men of Athens, I perceive that in all things ye are too superstitious** [ὡς δεισιδαιμονεστέρους]—rather

(with nearly all modern as well as ancient Greek interpreters), 'extremely devout,' 'very god-fearing,' 'much given to religious worship;' a conciliatory and commendatory introduction, founded on his own observation of the symbols of devotion with which their city was covered, and from which all Greek writers, as well as the apostle, inferred the exemplary religiousness of the Athenians. The authorized translation (though it only follows the Vulgate, *Erasmus,* and *Luther*) is here extremely unfortunate; inasmuch as it not only implies that only *too much* superstition was blameable, but represents the apostle as repelling his hearers in the very first sentence: whereas the whole discourse is studiously courteous. It is true that the word, in classical usage, is capable of either a favourable or an unfavourable sense; but just for that reason ought the nature of the case to decide in favour of the former. **23. For as I passed by, and beheld your devotions** [τὰ σεβάσματα ὑμ.] — rather, 'the objects of your devotion,' or 'your sacred things;' referring, as is plain from the next words, to their works of art consecrated to religion. **I found an altar with this inscription, TO THE UNKNOWN GOD** [Ἀγνώστῳ Θεῷ]—or, 'To an Unknown God;' erected, probably, to commemorate some divine interposition which they were unable to ascribe to any known deity. That there were such altars, Greek writers attest; and on this the apostle skilfully fastens at the outset, as the text of his discourse, taking it as evidence of that dimness of religious conception which, in virtue of his better light, he was prepared to dissipate. **Whom therefore ye ignorantly worship** [ἀγνοοῦντες εὐσεβεῖτε]. "Ignorantly" is too harsh a rendering. It should be, 'Ye worship, *not knowing* Him' (alluding to the inscription just mentioned). **him declare I unto you** [καταγγέλλω]—'Him set I forth unto you;' taking up their own word regarding him (see on *v.* 18). [*Lachmann's* and *Tischendorf's* reading—ὅ —τοῦτο—'*What* therefore ye worship . . . *that* set I forth,' which is that of good MSS., and of the Vulgate, would seem to have internal evidence in its favour, though the received text is well supported.] How very unlike this is to all his previous discourses—if we except that to the idolaters of Lycaonia! (ch. xiv. 15-17.) But the reason is obvious. His subject was not, as in the synagogues, the Messiahship of Jesus; but THE LIVING GOD, in opposition to the materialistic and pantheistic polytheism of Greece, which subverted all true Religion. Nor does he come with *speculation* on this profound subject—of which they had had more than enough from others—but with an authoritative 'announcement' of Him after whom they were groping; not giving Him any name, however, nor even naming the Saviour Himself, but unfolding the true character of both as they were able to receive it. **24. God that made the world and all things**

things therein, seeing that he is ᵖLord of heaven and earth, ᑫdwelleth not
25 in temples made with hands; neither is worshipped with men's hands,
' as though he needed any thing, seeing ˢhe giveth to all life, and breath,
26 and all things; and hath made of one blood all nations of men for to
dwell on all the face of the earth, and ᵗhath determined the times before
27 appointed, and ᵘthe bounds of their habitation; that ᵛthey should seek
the Lord, if haply they might feel after him, and find him, ʷthough he
28 be not far from every one of us: for ˣin him we live, and move, and have
our being; ʸas certain also of your own poets have said, For we are also
29 his offspring. Forasmuch then as we are the offspring of God, ᶻwe ought
not to think that the Godhead is like unto gold, or silver, or stone, graven

A. D. 51.

ᵖ Matt.11.25.
ᑫ ch. 7. 48.
ʳ Ps. 50. 8.
ˢ Num.16.22.
Isa. 42. 5.
ᵗ Deut 30.20.
ᵘ Deut. 32. 8.
ʷ Rom. 1. 20.
ʷ 1 Ki. 8. 27.
ˣ Col. 1. 17.
Heb. 1. 3.
ʸ Tit. 1. 12.
ᶻ Isa. 40. 18.

therein. The most profound philosophers of Greece were unable to conceive any fundamental distinction between God and the universe. Thick darkness, therefore, behoved to rest on all their religious conceptions. To dissipate this, the apostle sets out with a sharp statement of the fact of *creation*, as the central principle of all true religion. **seeing that he is Lord of heaven and earth**—holding in free and absolute subjection all the works of His hands; presiding in august Royalty over them, as well as pervading them all as the Principle of their being. How different this from the blind Force or Fate to which all creatures were regarded as in bondage! **dwelleth not in temples made with hands.** This thought—so familiar to Jewish ears (see 1 Ki. viii. 27; Isa. lxvi. 1, 2; and ch. vii. 48), and so elementary to Christians—would serve only more sharply to define to his heathen audience the spirituality of that living, personal God whom he 'announced' to them. **25. Neither is worshipped with men's hands**—or 'ministered to by human hands' [θεραπεύεται ὑπὸ χειρῶν ἀνθρωπίνων (which is better than ἀνθρώπων)], **as though he needed any thing.** No less familiar as this thought also is to us, even from the earliest times of the Old Testament (Job xxxv. 6-8; Ps. xvi. 2, 3; l. 12-14; Isa. xl. 14-18), it would pour a flood of quite new light upon any candid heathen mind that was able to take it in. It will be observed that these two statements—the one referring to the *buildings* erected for the worship of their divinities ("dwelleth not in temples made with hands"), and the other to the *priests* that served in them ("neither is ministered to by human hands")—together make up one grand position, that the Maker of the world and all that is in it cannot stand in need either of the one or the other of these. **seeing he giveth** [αὐτὸς διδους]—better, 'since it is Himself that giveth' **to all life, and breath, and all things.** The Giver of all cannot surely be dependent for aught upon the receivers of all (1 Chr. xxix. 14). This is the culminating point of a pure Theism. **26. And hath made of one blood all nations** [πᾶν ἔθνος]—' every nation' **of men for to dwell on all the face of the earth.** Holding, with the Old Testament teaching, that in the blood is the life (Gen. ix. 4; Lev. xvii. 11; Deut xii. 23), the apostle (says *Baumgarten*) sees this life-stream of the whole human race to be one, flowing from one source. [The shortened reading—"hath made of one" (ἐξ ἑνός, leaving out the important word "*blood*")—which is the reading of א A B, and a few other MSS., and of the Vulgate, and one or two other versions, is adopted by *Lachmann* (who usually follows the Vulgate); but not by *Tischendorf*, though he usually follows the above MSS. The great majority of MSS. and versions, with most of the Greek fathers, have the word "blood" as in the received text; and as it is not likely

to have been inserted if not genuine, we cannot doubt it is the true reading.] **and hath determined the times [before] appointed, and the bounds of their habitation.** But the true reading beyond doubt is, 'fixed the set times, and the bounds of their habitation' [προστεταγμένος is the only reading of authority: προετετ. of the received text has next to none]. The apostle here opposes both Stoical Fate and Epicurean Chance, ascribing the *periods* and *localities* in which men and nations flourish to the sovereign will and pre-arrangements of a living God. **27. That they should seek the Lord**—('seek God' is the much better supported reading.) That is the high end of all these arrangements of Divine Power, Wisdom, and Love. **if haply they might feel after him**—as men groping their way in the dark, **and find him**—a lively picture of the murky atmosphere of Natural Religion. **though he be not far from every one of us.** The difficulty of finding God outside the pale of Revealed Religion lies not in His distance from us, but in our distance from Him, through the blinding effect of sin. **28. For in him we live, and move, and have our being** [καὶ ἐσμὲν]—more simply, 'live, and move, and exist.' This means, not merely (as *Meyer* explains it), 'Without Him we have no *life*, nor that *motion* which every inanimate nature displays, nor even *existence* itself:' it means that God is the living immanent Principle of all these in men. It will be observed that the words, "in Him we live, and move, and exist," constitute in themselves a *descending* series; but viewed in relation to the speaker's purpose, they have (as *Lechler* notices) all the force of an *ascending* climax. Life, it is true, is more than motion, and motion more than bare being; but the apostle's thought is, 'Without God—isolated and apart from God—we should have no *life;* consequently, no *motion;* and so, no *existence.*' **as certain also of your own poets have said, For we are also his offspring.** This is the first half of the fifth line, word for word, of an astronomical poem of *Aratus*, a Greek countryman of the apostle's, and his predecessor by about three centuries. It is found also (nearly as here) in a religious hymn of *Cleanthes* of Troas, a contemporary of *Aratus*. But, as our speaker hints, the same sentiment is to be found in other Greek poets. They meant it, doubtless, in a *pantheistic* sense; but the truth which it expresses the apostle turns to his own purpose—to teach a pure, personal, spiritual Theism. Probably during his quiet retreat at Tarsus (ch. ix. 30), revolving his special vocation to the Gentiles, he gave himself to the study of so much Greek literature as might be turned to Christian account in his future work. Hence this and his other quotations from the Greek poets (1 Cor. xv. 33; Tit. i. 12). **29. Forasmuch then as we are the offspring of God, we ought not to think** (*the courtesy of this language is worthy of notice*) **that the Godhead is**

30 by art and man's device. And ^athe times of this ignorance God winked
31 at; but ^bnow commandeth all men every where to repent: because he
   hath appointed a day, in the which ^che will judge the world in righteousness by *that* man whom he hath ordained; *whereof* he hath ⁷given assurance unto all *men*, in that he hath raised him from the dead.
32 And when they heard of the resurrection of the dead, some mocked:

A. D. 54.
^a Rom. 3. 25.
^b Luke 24.47.
^c Rom. 2. 16.
2 Tim. 4. 1.
⁷ Or. offered faith
1 Cor. 15.

like unto gold, or silver, or stone, graven by art and man's device—rather, 'graven by the art or device of man.' One can hardly doubt that the apostle would here point to those matchless monuments of the plastic art in gold, and silver, and costliest stone, which lay so profusely beneath and around him. The more intelligent Pagan Greeks no more pretended that these sculptured gods and goddesses were real deities, or even their actual likenesses, than Romanist Christians do their images; and Paul doubtless knew this: yet here we find him condemning all such efforts to represent visibly the invisible God. How shamefully inexcusable, then, are the Greek and Roman Churches in paganizing the worship of the Christian Church by the encouragement of pictures and images in religious service. In the eighth century the second Council of Nicœa decreed that the image of God was as proper an object of worship as God Himself. 30. **And the times of this ignorance God winked at** [ὑπεριδὼν]—*lit.*, and better, 'overlooked;' that is, bore with, without interposing to punish it otherwise than by suffering the debasing tendency of such worship to develop itself. Compare ch. xiv. 16, "Who in times past suffered all nations to walk in their own ways;" and see on Rom. i. 24, &c. **but now**— now that a new light has risen upon the world, **commandeth**: *q. d.* 'That duty—all along lying upon man, estranged from his Creator, but hitherto only silently recommending itself and little felt— is now peremptory.' **all men every where**—(compare Col. i. 6, 23; Tit. ii. 11). There is here a tacit allusion to the narrow precincts of favoured Judaism, within which immediate and entire repentance was ever urged. The word 'repentance' is here used (as in Luke xiii. 3, 5; xv. 10) in its most comprehensive sense of 'repentance unto life.' 31. **Because** [Καθότι is better supported than Διότι of the received text] he **hath appointed a day, in the which he will judge.** 'Aptly (says *Bengel*) is this uttered on the Areopagus, the seat of judgment.' But how different, in every feature of it, from any heathen conception of Divine judgment is that here announced! **the world in righteousness by that man whom he hath ordained**—compare John v. 22, 23, 27; and ch. x. 42. **whereof he hath given assurance** (that is, ground of assurance) **unto all men, in that he hath raised him from the dead**— the most patent evidence to mankind at large of the judicial authority with which the Risen One is clothed.

The Result (32-34). 32. **And when they heard of the resurrection of the dead, some mocked.** As the Greek religion was but the glorification of the present life, by the worship of all its most beauteous forms, the Resurrection—which presupposes the vanity of the present life, and is nothing but life out of the death of all that sin has blighted—could have no charms for the true Greek. It gave the death-blow to his fundamental and most cherished ideas; nor, until these were seen to be false and fatal, could the Resurrection, and the Gospel of which it was a primary doctrine, seem otherwise than ridiculous. **and others said, We will hear thee again of this matter. 33. So Paul departed from among them.** Whether he

would have opened, to any extent, the Gospel scheme in this address, if he had not been interrupted, or whether he reserved this for exposition afterwards to earnest enquirers, we cannot tell: only the speech is not to be judged of as quite complete. 34. **Howbeit certain men clave (or** 'attached themselves') **unto him, and believed.** Instead of mocking or politely waiving the subject, having listened eagerly, they joined themselves to the apostle for further instruction, the consequence of which was that they "believed." **among the which was Dionysius** [καὶ Δ.]—even Dionysius, **the Areopagite,** a member of that august tribunal. Ancient tradition says he was placed by the apostle over the little flock at Athens. Certainly (as *Olshausen* says) the number of converts there, and of men fit for office in the church, was not so great that there could be much choice. **and a woman named Damaris**—not certainly one of the apostle's audience on the Areopagus, but won to the Faith either before or after. Nothing else is known of her. Of any further labours of the apostle at Athens, and how long he stayed, we are not informed. Certainly he was not driven away. But (as *Howson* admirably says) 'it is a serious and instructive fact that the mercantile population of Thessalonica and Corinth received the message of God with greater readiness than the highly educated and polished Athenians. Two letters to the Thessalonians, and two to the Corinthians, remain to attest the flourishing state of those churches. But we possess no letter written by St. Paul to the Athenians; and we do not read that he was ever in Athens again.'

Remarks.—1. What wonderful powers of adaptation to different classes of minds does the apostle show in his proceedings at Thessalonica and Berœa, on the one hand, and on the other at Athens! At Thessalonica, having common ground with the Jews and with the Gentile proselytes, in the Scriptures of the Old Testament, he takes these as his starting-point, establishing the great position that the predicted Messiah was to be a suffering and glorified, a dying and rising Redeemer, and that Jesus of Nazareth, whom he came to proclaim to them—since He alone answered to this character—must be the Christ of God. Having for three successive sabbaths discoursed in this strain, he carried conviction not only to some of his Jewish hearers, who at once attached themselves to the missionaries, but to a great multitude of proselyte Greeks, including not a few women of superior station—not to speak of conquests beyond this circle (1 Thess. i. 9). At Berœa the same course was pursued, and with the like success, the audience there daily searching the Old Testament Scriptures, to see whether the sense put upon them, and the positions founded on them, were correct. Even at Athens, 'in the synagogue of the Jews, he disputed,' probably much as he had done at the two former places. But in the Agora (or market-place) and on the Areopagus, how different his line of procedure! How he dealt with the comers and goers in the place of public concourse we only know from the remarks of his motley hearers: some of them calling him a "babbler," or contemptible teacher, while others thought he was holding forth the

127

33 and otuers said, We will hear thee again of this *matter.* So Paul de-
34 parted from among them. Howbeit certain men clave unto him, and

A. D. 54.
ch. 20. 1.

merits and claims of some new deities. But from this we may gather that he had confined himself to a simple proclamation of the great *facts* of Christ's life, death, and resurrection. Entirely different from both these methods was the line of discourse on the Areopagus, where he had to deal with speculative thinkers, who " by wisdom knew not God ;" having speculated themselves out of the first principles of all religious truth, and been for ages wandering in endless mazes of error and uncertainty. In dealing with such minds he first lays down, in a few great strokes, the fundamental truths of all Theism :—the personality of God; the relation of the universe to Him as the work of His hands, and every moment upheld, beautified, and blessed by Him; His consequent independence of His creatures, but their absolute dependence upon Him; their need of Him, and obligation to feel after Him as their chief good—with the folly and wickedness of attempting to represent this glorious Being in a visible form by statuary of any kind wrought by the hands of men. Having done this in a strain of studied courtesy and calm sublimity, he goes on to say that as God had borne with such unworthy treatment only because of the darkness that till then had brooded over men's minds, so the time for such endurance had come to an end, with the new light that had at length burst upon the world by the mission and work, the death and resurrection, of Jesus Christ, and the appointment of Him to be the Righteous Judge of the world. Now that these stupendous events have taken place—leaving men without excuse—God will endure their estrangement from Him no longer, but requires all men, on hearing these glad tidings, to repent and turn unto Him from whom they have wandered so far astray, and who, by that Man whom He hath ordained, will at length bring them into righteous judgment. Not an allusion is there here to the Old Testament Scriptures, on which he had based all his reasonings and appeals to the Thessalonians and Bereans of the Synagogue; nor does the apostle feed the Athenian pride by indulging in speculative reasoning and rhetorical appeal, which would but have left them where they were. A simple and positive statement of the great fundamental truths of all religion, a brief outline of the facts of the Gospel, and a respectful intimation of the urgency of the matter and the awful responsibility of all who heard such truths, is the substance of this memorable discourse. And who can fail to observe the versatility of the apostle's mind—his rare power of adapting the same truths to every variety of audience he had to address. And yet one common principle reigns in all his addresses. Though the difference between the Jewish and the Greek point of view, in approaching religious truth, was extreme, *the supernatural and authoritative character* of the Gospel provision for man's spiritual recovery is that feature of it which to both is made most prominent. Self-commending as the truths of the Gospel are, reasonable in itself as is the service which it requires, soul-satisfying and ennobling as all have found it to be who have made trial of it, it is not on these grounds alone—nor primarily— that the apostle presses the Gospel of Christ upon either Jew or Gentile. It is as the story of a Person Divinely gifted to the world, and supernaturally accredited; it is as a series of indisputable *facts*, supernaturally attested ; it is as God's gracious interposition in behalf of a world perishing through estrangement from Himself ; it is as His message

from heaven, inviting us back to Himself by Jesus Christ. Wonderful, indeed, is the suitableness of the Gospel to our felt necessities, and never does the soul close with it but in the view of this. But as it would be no cure at all for our spiritual maladies, were it not seen to be *direct from God Himself*, so it is as a message from heaven that the soul in every case embraces it; and in this light did Paul ever hold it forth both to the sign-seeking Jews and the wisdom-loving Greeks. 2. It will be observed that at Thessalonica the proportion of " Jews " who were won over to the Gospel was much smaller than of " the devout Greeks," and that the riot which brought the new converts before the magistrates, and obliged them to despatch Paul and Silas by night to Berœa, was instigated by Jews, out of hatred to the Gospel. To this the apostle alludes in his First Epistle to the Thessalonians (ii. 14-16) in a tone of melancholy, which, while it gives remarkable confirmation to the history (to which *Paley* adverts, Horæ Paulinæ, ix. 5), shows that he regarded it as a premonitory symptom of "the wrath that was coming on them to the uttermost." But the point here specially calling for notice is the contrast between bodies of men who have proved unfaithful to high privileges and those who, with little light, have begun to value and improve what they have. The Jews first manifested the degeneracy into which they had long been sinking by the rejection and crucifixion of their promised Messiah ; and from that time their character as a nation rapidly declined—their fanatical adherence to the most distorted conceptions of their own Religion begetting in them intense hatred of spiritual and evangelical truth, and stimulating them to acts of turbulence, which at length brought upon them national destruction. Those few of them who in almost every place embraced the Gospel—the " remnant according to the election of grace"—were but the exceptions which prove the rule. How different was it with the Gentiles ! Those of them who had already taken the important step of embracing the light of the Jewish Faith were the readier to recognize and rejoice in the still brighter light of the Gospel ; and so the majority of the earliest disciples of the Lord Jesus (after the first few years of the Gospel) consisted probably of those who had before been proselytes to the Religion of the Old Testament. And the same principle will be found in operation still ; and nations, churches, families, and individuals will find that "to him that hath shall be given, but from him that hath not shall be taken away even that which he seemeth to have." 3. From what is said of the mode in which the Berœans tested the preaching of Paul, three things undeniably follow : *First,* That the people at large, as well as the ministers of the Church, are both entitled and bound to search the Scriptures— implying both the careful and continuous reading of them, and the exercise of a discriminating judgment as to the sense of them ; *Secondly,* That they are both entitled and bound to try the teaching which they receive from the ministers of the Church, whether and how far it accords with the Word of God ; *Thirdly,* That no faith but such as results from personal conviction that what is taught is truth, according to the Word of God, ought to be demanded, or is of any avail. Tried by these three tests, what is the Church of Rome but a gigantic Apostasy from the apostolic Faith ; withholding, as it does systematically, the Scriptures from the common people, demanding from them,

128

[9] believed: among the which *was* Dionysius the Areopagite, and a woman named Damaris, and others with them.

A. D. 54.

[9] ch. 18. 8.

instead, implicit faith in its own teaching, and anathematizing—not to say punishing, even to imprisonment and death, when it can—all who persist in reading the Scriptures for themselves, and trying even its teaching by that standard? 4. The record of Paul's proceedings at Athens, here given, bears on its face the clearest marks of historic truth, not only in outline, but in detail. Who that knows anything of the Athens of that time is not struck with the lively description of his first impressions of the idolatrous city, of his disputations in the Agora, and of the eagerness of that novelty-hunting people to get a speech from him on the Areopagus? Above all, is not the discourse itself stamped with a Pauline courtesy and frankness; a characteristic breadth, depth, and grasp; a lining off of the dispensation of forbearance, by reason of the darkness in which men had to grope their way to truth, and of the dispensation of peremptory demand for universal and immediate repentance, by reason of the light which has now burst upon the world—all bespeaking the mind and mouth of that one man whose image and superscription are so familiar to the intelligent readers of the New Testament? Yes, the authenticity of the facts, and the truth of this record of them as they stand, carry their own vouchers here. 5. The impressions produced upon a thoughtful mind by such a scene as that which presented itself to the eye of Paul in Athens and on the Areopagus, are the very best test of its predominant tone and character. That one of such intelligence should be able to survey such a scene without admiration, and to discourse on it without complimenting—without even alluding to—the high culture and exquisite genius stamped upon its architectural forms, and the life that breathed in its statuary—will seem to those who look at such things only *in themselves* to be evidence of a hard mind, a dull soul, a want of aesthetic culture and poetic sentiment, a want, in short, of all refinement; evidence of a one-sidedness which can see nothing good in anything beyond its own narrow range of vision. But what it proves is simply this, that the perversion of genius, even by the most exquisite creations of art designed to minister to the dishonour of God, so weighed down the apostle's spirit and distressed his soul, that it left neither room nor heart for admiration of the prostituted gifts that gave birth to such productions. 'The apostle Paul (says *Lechler* admirably), whilst he views the works of art in Athens, cannot separate the artistic designs from the thoughts which are expressed by them, and the purposes for which they were made. The beautiful temples, the glorious statues, &c., are essentially the creations of the heathen spirit and the instruments of polytheistic worship; the city adorned with works of art is a "city wholly covered with idols." And therefore the sight of this world of art awakens in him a moral indignation at the error and sin against the living God which is contained therein. The Spirit of God never permits a judgment entirely apart from religion and morality.' Yes, 'the one-sidedness' is not Paul's—the 'narrow range of vision' is not his; but it is that of those who look at such things from a sublunary point of view. As objects which appear great when one is close by them dwindle into insignificance when seen from a great height, and in their relation to other objects before unperceived, so those works of art which, when viewed purely as human productions, bespeak transcendent genius and fill the mind with

129

only a feeling of admiration, are, when seen in the light of the dishonour to God to which they were designed to minister, regarded only as evidences of moral obliquity, and produce only an all-absorbing feeling of pain. When David sang,

"One thing have I desired of the Lord,
  That will I seek after:
That I may dwell in the house of the Lord
  All the days of my life," &c.,

he might be called one-sided—some would say, narrow-minded—but only in that highest and noblest sense which puts every object and every pursuit into its right place and keeps it there, bringing all that is subordinate and fleeting into captivity to that which is primary and enduring. When Mary is commended for "choosing the good part which shall not be taken from her," it was just this all-absorbing, all-consuming "desire of one thing" which is held up to her praise, and He who so commended her made it evident how He would have regarded the polytheistic creations of Athenian genius; nor will any whose minds and hearts have been steeped, as Paul's was, in the spirit of Christ, think and feel otherwise than in entire unison with the great apostle on this occasion. 6. It can never be too deeply impressed upon the students of classical literature and ancient philosophy that the idea of *Creation* is nowhere to be found in it, and was utterly unknown alike to the heathen people and the profoundest thinkers of antiquity. (See *Ritter's* 'History of Philosophy,' *Hävernick's* 'Introduction to Pentateuch,' and similar works.) With the absence of all idea of Creation—the confusion of nature and of God—there must of course have been the absence of all proper conception of Divine rule and human duty, of sin, and of future retribution; nor could the unity of the human family and the history of the world be properly conceived. What a flood of light, then, must have been thrown upon any heathen mind, earnest enough to follow it, and capable of taking it in, by this brief discourse of the great apostle; and how much does the world owe to that "day-spring from on high" which hath visited it, giving light to them that sat in darkness and in the shadow of death, to guide their feet into the way of peace! And, as if to show how entirely we are dependent on Revelation for all the Religious Truth which we possess, it is worthy of notice how prone men are, as soon as they depart from Revealed Truth as their standard of faith, to sink—even under the Gospel—into the very errors of Heathenism. Do we not find the Church of Rome, on the one hand, setting up an elaborate system of image-worship—thus paganizing that which abolished Paganism—whilst, on the other hand, a subtle Pantheism among metaphysicians, and a gross Materialism among the students of physical science, are undermining in many the sense of a LIVING GOD: a God, that is, having consciousness and personality, the Creator and Lord of heaven and earth, and in the exercise of His rectoral authority at once inviting and demanding the subjection and love of all his reasonable creatures. 7. What thoughts are suggested to the thoughtful mind by that inscription, "to the unknown God!" Multitudes have gods many and lords many, which they "know" well enough, and on whose altars they worship their favourite pursuit—to which they sacrifice time, strength, thought, affection—all that constitutes their proper selves. But what heart is there of all these that has not another altar to

18 AFTER these things Paul departed from Athens, and came to Corinth; **2** and found a certain Jew ^anamed Aquila, born in Pontus, lately come from Italy, with his wife Priscilla; (because that Claudius had com-

A. D. 54.

CHAP. 18.
^a Rom. 16. 3.

Him whose their breath is and whose are all their ways—Whom their conscience craves, though in vain—Who is yearning after them, but finds no response—to Whom they look not as a Friend, and Whom they know not as a Father—Whom they never take into their plans of life, and with Whom they would rather have nothing to do—the "Unknown" God! But far though they are from Him, how near is He to them, "for in Him they live, and move, and exist." He is as near to thee (says a German preacher, quoted by *Lechler*) as the law of the Holy One in thy conscience, as the longing after salvation in thy soul, as the involuntary cry for help and the ceaseless sighing after peace in thy heart and mouth. 8. What is called *The General Judgment*, or a judgment of all mankind at one and the same time, stands out so clearly in this discourse on the Areopagus that one should think it impossible for any Christian to gainsay it. And yet a considerable class of intelligent and warmhearted Christians of our day contend against it, because it will not harmonize with their view of the relation of Christ's Second Coming to the Millennium—in other words, with their view of the purposes for which Christ is to come the second time. Controversy with such devoted friends of the Gospel is unpleasant, and here, at least, would be out of place. But to fix the proper sense of the text of Scripture is the business of a Commentator on it; and in discharge of that duty, let us invite the reader's attention, first, to the *objects* of this judgment—the world—that is, as the word denotes, '*the inhabited world*' [τ. οἰκουμένην], which only prejudice can deny to mean, 'the world of mankind at large;' and next, to the *time* of this judgment—"He hath appointed *a day*" for doing it. To reply that a day in Scripture does not necessarily mean a day of twenty-four hours, is to miss the point of the argument for a general judgment from the phrase in question. Nobody thinks of a day of twenty-four hours when he reads this verse, nor ever naturally inquires *what length of time it will take* to complete this great transaction. What every one understands by "a day" here is just 'a certain definite time,' on the arrival of which this judgment will begin, and from and after which it will continue uninterruptedly to its close. '*One continuous uninterrupted transaction*' is what the words naturally express, and '*the judgment of the whole inhabited world*' is that continuous uninterrupted transaction. How consonant this is to the general tenor of Scripture, to the instincts of our spiritual nature, and to all that is august in the Divine procedure, let the reader judge. 9. It is impossible not to be struck with the little fruit which the Gospel had in the metropolis of Greek culture, as compared with commercial communities and rural populations. And as if to invite us to enquire whether there be not a principle in this, history tells us that some of the most sublime writers of the Neo-Platonic school—who wrote hymns in praise of the Godhead, or the great principle of motion, life, and love in the universe, though they lived in the midst of Christians, and had every facility for studying Christianity—never yielded themselves to it, and lived and died outside its pale. The truth is, that where speculation is prosecuted for its own sake—the intellect restlessly active, but the heart and life all neglected—pride only is engendered, and in this state the sharp, definite realities and dread certainties of revealed truth are neither intellectually apprehended nor

morally appreciated. On the other hand, the men of action and enterprise, and those of simple purpose, more naturally sympathize with the earnest character and practical aim of Gospel truth. In short, the reception of the Gospel is the grand test of the simplicity of the heart. It is hid from the wise and prudent, and revealed unto babes. We preach Christ crucified, to the Jews a stumbling-block, and to the Greeks foolishness; but unto them who are called, both Jews and Greeks, Christ the power of God, and the wisdom of God (1 Cor. i. 23, 24).

CHAP. XVIII. 1-22. — PAUL REACHES AND LABOURS AT CORINTH, WHERE HE IS REJOINED BY SILAS AND TIMOTHY, AND, UNDER DIVINE ENCOURAGEMENT, MAKES A LONG STAY — AT LENGTH, RETRACING HIS STEPS, BY EPHESUS, CÆSAREA, AND JERUSALEM, HE RETURNS, FOR THE LAST TIME, TO ANTIOCH, THUS COMPLETING HIS SECOND MISSIONARY JOURNEY.

Paul, arriving at Corinth, takes up his abode with Aquila (1-3). **1. After these things Paul**—or 'And he' (the authorities for both are about equal) **departed from Athens, and came to Corinth.** This city, celebrated alike in classic and in the earliest Church history, was of the highest antiquity, reaching back to the earliest authentic Grecian history. It was situated on the isthmus between the Ægean and Ionian Seas, having right in front of it (on the south side) a natural citadel of rock rising 2,000 feet sheer up above the level of the sea, called the *Acrocorinthus*. It was a place of great military strength until, in its struggles with Rome, it was so ruined that it became as proverbial for its poverty as before for its wealth and magnificence. Julius Cæsar, however, appreciating its great natural strength in a military point of view, and its advantages as an emporium of commerce, made it a Roman colony; and by the encouragement given to population, commerce, and art, it soon rose to even more than its former splendour. It became the capital of the Roman province of Achaia, and was the residence of the proconsul. It was this re-built Corinth that Paul now came to—the centre of commerce alike for east and west, having a considerable Jewish population, and larger probably at this time than usual, owing to the banishment of the Jews from Rome by Claudius Cæsar (*v.* 2). Such a city was a noble field for the Gospel, which, once established there, would naturally diffuse itself far and wide. Yet Christianity had formidable enemies to overcome ere it could secure for itself a footing in Corinth. It had to struggle equally against the *speculative tendencies* of the more intellectual class and the *refined sensuality* for which Corinth became a proverb even in Greece — a sensuality which was even clothed with a sacred character and employed in the services of religion. **2. And found a certain Jew named Aquila, born in Pontus**—the most easterly province of Asia Minor, stretching along the southern shore of the Black Sea. From this province there were Jews at Jerusalem on the great Pentecostal day (ch. ii. 9), and the Christians of it are included among 'the strangers of the dispersion,' to whom Peter addressed his First Epistle (1 Pet. i. 1). **lately come from Italy, with his wife Priscilla**—or 'Prisca,' as the word is abbreviated in 2 Tim. iv. 19, and (according to the true reading) in Rom. xvi. 3. From these Latin names one would conclude that they had resided so long in Rome as to sink their

3 manded all Jews to depart from Rome:) and came unto them. And
because he was of the same craft, he abode with them, *b*and wrought:
4 for by their occupation they were tent-makers. And he reasoned in the
5 synagogue every sabbath, and persuaded the Jews and the Greeks. And
*c*when Silas and Timotheus were come from Macedonia, Paul was pressed
in *d*the spirit, and testified to the Jews *that* Jesus *1was* Christ.

A. D. 54.

b 1 Cor. 4. 12.
1 Thes. 2. 9.
c ch. 17. 14.
d Job 32. 18.
1 Or, is the
Christ.

Jewish family names. **because that Claudius had commanded all Jews to depart from Rome.** This decree is thus alluded to by *Suetonius*, in his Life of Claudius Cæsar (c. 25): 'The Jews, as they were continually raising disturbances, at the instigation of Christ, he expelled from Rome' [Judæos impulsore Chresto assidue tumultuantes Romæ expulit]. (Chrestus for Christus, says *Humphry*, was a common mistake, according to Tertullian, Apol. 3.) But the inference which some have drawn from this loose statement of *Suetonius*—in which he appears to mix up events belonging to different times and occasions—namely, that these dissensions arose from disputes about Christianity between some zealous Jewish Christians already settled at Rome and their unbelieving opponents, is very precarious. Though there is reason to believe that Christian Jews were already settled in Rome, it is hardly conceivable that their numbers and influence were such as to produce commotions, provoking the emperor to banish the whole race from the city. **and came unto them. 3. And because he was of the same craft, he abode with them.** Whether this couple were converted before Paul made their acquaintance, or were won over to Christ through intercourse with him, is a question on which commentators are pretty equally divided. In favour of their previous conversion is—(l.) That no mention is made of their conversion by the apostle's instrumentality, which, in the case of persons occupying from this time forward so important a place in the apostolic history, we might have expected; (2.) That all we read of them suggests the idea of *ripe* Christians, rather than of new converts. (So *Olshausen, Wieseler, Hackett, Lange.*) Against their previous conversion *Meyer* urges the following arguments (which are held conclusive by *Baumgarten, Alford, Lechler,* &c.): (1.) That, judging by this historian's manner, if Aquila had been a Christian before, he would have said, he found, not "a certain *Jew,*" but 'a certain *disciple;*' and, (2.) The sole reason given for his coming to live with him was his being of "the same craft;" and as the banishment of "all Jews" from Rome is said to have brought Aquila from Italy, we are to look upon him as up to this time simply a tent-making Jew. But it has been answered to this, that the reason why he is called "a certain *Jew*" (rather than a *disciple*), is, that the writer is going to state what brought him from Rome to Italy, namely, the imperial decree which banished "*all Jews*" from Rome. To us this appears quite satisfactory. Indeed, this identical phrase, "*a certain Jew,*" is applied to the Christian Apollos, *v.* 24; and though the reason why the apostle went to stay with this couple was certainly not the man's Christianity, but his trade, we cannot deem this any evidence that he was not then a Christian. The reply to the first argument in favour of his previous conversion—that the writer wished to keep to the more important fruits of Paul's labour at Corinth—does not appear satisfactory; and the second argument is not answered at all—the improbability of this couple occupying so prominent a place in the subsequent history, if they were new converts at Corinth. The rapid progress which Paul made immediately after his

conversion is a rare case. On the whole, **we** incline to the prior conversion of this couple. Be this as it may, they appear to have been in good circumstances, and after travelling much to have eventually settled at Ephesus. The Christian friendship now first formed continued warm and unbroken, and the highest testimony is once and again borne to them by the apostle. **and wrought.** Every Jewish youth, whatever the pecuniary circumstances of his parents, was taught some trade (see on Luke ii. 42); and Paul made it a point of conscience to work at that which he had probably been bred to, partly that he might not be burdensome to the churches, and partly that his motives as a minister of Christ might not be liable to misconstruction. To both these he makes frequent and sometimes touching reference in his Epistles. **for by their occupation they were tent-makers.** 'If the father of the young Cilician (says *Howson*) sought to make choice of a trade which might fortify his son against idleness, or against adversity, none would occur to him more naturally than the profitable occupation of the making of tents, the material of which was haircloth, supplied by the goats of his native province, and sold in the markets of the Levant by the well-known name of *cilicium.*' *He labours with little success and much opposition in the synagogue, but afterwards for a year and a half with great success in a private house* (4-11). **4. And he reasoned** (or 'discoursed') **in the synagogue every sabbath, and persuaded** [ἔπειθε]—'sought to persuade' **the Jews and the Greeks** [τε 'Ι. καὶ "Ε.]—'both Jews and Greeks;' that is, proselyte Gentiles, who attended the synagogue. **5. And when Silas and Timotheus were come from Macedonia**—that is, from Thessalonica, whither Silas had probably accompanied Timothy when sent back from Athens (see on ch. xvii. 15), **Paul was pressed in the spirit** —but the true reading is, 'pressed by the word.' [τ. λόγῳ is supported by most MSS., and these the oldest; ℵ A B D E, &c., with the Vulgate, and all the best versions: τ. πνεύματι, only by H. and some others, and by indifferent version authority.] This, as the more difficult reading and so powerfully supported, is undoubtedly to be preferred; expressing not so much the apostle's zeal and assiduity in preaching it, as some inward *pressure* which at this time he experienced in the work (to convey which more clearly was probably the origin of the common reading). What that pressure was we happen to know, with singular minuteness and vividness of description, from the apostle himself, in his First Epistles to the Corinthians and Thessalonians (1 Cor. ii. 1-5; 1 Thess. iii. 1-10). He had come away from Athens, as he remained there, in a depressed and anxious state of mind, having there met, for the first time, with unwilling Gentile ears. He continued, apparently for some time, labouring alone in the synagogue of Corinth, full of deep and anxious solicitude for his Thessalonian converts. His early ministry at Corinth was coloured by these feelings. Self deeply abased, his power as a preacher was more than ever felt to lie in demonstration of the Spirit. At length Silas and Timotheus arrived with exhilarating tidings of

6   And *when they opposed themselves, and blasphemed, *he shook *his* raiment, and said unto them, Your *blood *be* upon your own heads; I
7   *am clean: *from henceforth I will go unto the Gentiles.   And he departed thence, and entered into a certain *man's* house, named Justus, *one* that worshipped God, whose house joined hard to the synagogue.
8   And *Crispus, the chief ruler of the synagogue, believed on the Lord with all his house: and many of the Corinthians hearing believed, and
9   were baptized.   Then *spake the Lord to Paul in the night by a vision,
10   Be not afraid, but speak, and hold not thy peace: for *I am with thee, and no man shall set on thee to hurt thee: *for I have much people in
11   this city.   And he ²continued *there* a year and six months, teaching the word of God among them.
12   And when Gallio was the deputy of Achaia, the Jews made insurrection with one accord against Paul, and brought him to the judgment seat,
13   saying, This *fellow* persuadeth men to worship God contrary to the law.
14   And when Paul was now about to open *his* mouth, Gallio said unto the Jews, *If it were a matter of wrong or wicked lewdness, O *ye* Jews, reason
15   would that I should bear with you: but if it be a question of words

A. D. 66.

e 1 Pet. 4. 4.
f Neh. 5. 13.
Matt. 10. 14.
Luke 9. 5.
ch. 13. 51.
g Lev. 20. 9.
2 Sam. 1. 16.
Eze. 18. 13.
Eze. 33. 4.
h Eze. 3. 18.
Eze. 33. 9.
i ch. 23. 23.
j 1 Cor. 1. 14.
k Isa. 58. 21.
l Isa. 41. 10.
Jer. 1. 18.
Matt. 23. 20.
Rom. 8. 31.
m 2 Tim. 2. 19.
2 sat there.
n ch. 23. 29.
ch. 25. 11.

the faith and love of his Thessalonian children, and of their earnest longings again to see their father in Christ; bringing with them also, in token of their love and duty, a pecuniary contribution for the supply of his wants. This seems to have so lifted him as to put new life and vigour into his ministry. *He now wrote his* FIRST EPISTLE TO THE THESSALONIANS, in which the "pressure" which resulted from all this strikingly appears. (See Introduction to 1 Thess.) Such emotions are known only to the ministers of Christ, and, even of them, only to such as "travail in birth until Christ be formed in" their hearers. (It is the same word as is used in the well-known passage, "The love of Christ *constraineth* us," 2 Cor. v. 14.) **and testified to the Jews that Jesus was Christ** —or, 'that the Christ was Jesus' (as the grammatical form of the clause more strictly is).

6. And when they opposed themselves, and blasphemed, he shook his raiment (see Neh. v. 13), **and said unto them, Your blood be** (or 'is,' or 'shall be') **upon your own heads** (see Ezek. xxxiii. 4-9; Matt. xxvii. 24, 25): **from henceforth I will go unto the Gentiles**—'the heathen;' just as he protested at Antioch in Pisidia (ch. xiii. 46). **7. And he departed thence, and entered into a certain man's house, named Justus**—not changing his lodging, as if Aquila and Priscilla up to this time had been with the opponents of the apostle (as *Calvin* and *Alford* understand the expression), but merely ceasing any more to testify in the synagogue, and henceforth carrying on his labours in this house of Justus, which, 'joining hard to the synagogue,' would be easily accessible to such of its worshippers as were still open to light. Justus, too, being probably a proselyte, would more easily draw a mixed audience than the synagogue. From this time forth conversions rapidly increased. **8. And Crispus, the chief ruler of the synagogue, believed on the Lord with all his house**—an event (to use the words of *Howson*) 'felt to be so important that the apostle deviated from his usual practice (1 Cor. i. 14-16), and baptized him, as well as Caius (Gaius), and the household of Stephanas, with his own hand.' **and many of the Corinthians hearing believed, and were baptized.** These were the beginning of the church of Corinth. **9. Then spake the Lord to Paul in the night by a vision, Be not afraid, but speak, and hold not thy peace 10. For I am with thee, and no man shall set on thee to hurt thee.** From this it would seem that these signal successes were

stirring up the wrath of the unbelieving Jews, and probably the apostle feared being driven by violence, as before, from the scene of such promising labour. He is re-assured, however, from above. **for I have much people in this city**—'whom (as *Baumgarten* correctly observes), in virtue of their election to eternal life, he already designates as His' (cf. ch. xiii. 48). **11. And he continued there a year and six months, teaching the word of God among them.** This is meant to embrace the whole period of this his first visit to Corinth, and not merely of so much of it as has already been treated of. *During some part of this period he wrote his* SECOND EPISTLE TO THE THESSALONIANS. (See Introduction to 2 Thess.)

At the instigation of the Jews, Paul is arraigned before the Proconsul, who, after hearing the case, dismisses it with contempt, and the head of the accusing party is assaulted with impunity before the Proconsul (12-17). **12. And when Gallio was the deputy of Achaia** [ἀνθυπατεύοντος]—'the proconsul' (see on ch. xiii. 7). The use of this term here is another striking confirmation of the historical accuracy of this book, since Tiberius had changed this province from a senatorial to an imperial one, and accordingly sent thither a *Procurator* (as *Tacitus* states, Ann. i. 76); but Claudius having restored its senatorial character (as we learn from *Suetonius*, Claud. 25), its proper governor would be, as here stated, a *Proconsul* (see on ch. xiii. 7). This Gallio was brother to the celebrated philosopher Seneca, Nero's tutor, who afterwards passed sentence of death upon both of them. **the Jews made insurrection with one accord against Paul, and brought him to the judgment-seat, 13. Saying, This [fellow]**—rather, 'This man' **persuadeth men to worship God contrary to the law**—meaning the *Jewish* law: "your law," as Gallio, correcting them, somewhat contemptuously calls it (v. 15). The charge probably refers to his not requiring his Gentile converts to be circumcised; and certainly it is a testimony to his success among them. **14. And when Paul was now about to open his mouth, Gallio said unto the Jews, If it were a matter of wrong or wicked lewdness**—'had it been any wrong or villany,' that is, any offence punishable by the magistrate, **reason would that I should bear**—'I should in reason have borne' **with you. 15. But if it be a question**—or, rather 'questions' (according to what is evidently the true reading) **of words and names, and of your law** [περὶ λόγου καὶ ὀνομάτων καὶ νόμου τοῦ καθ'

and names; and *of* your law, [o] look ye *to it;* for I will be no judge of
16, such *matters.* And he [p] drave them from the judgment seat. Then all
17 the Greeks took [q] Sosthenes, the chief ruler of the synagogue, and beat
him before the judgment seat. And Gallio cared for none of those
things.
18 And Paul *after this* tarried *there* yet a good while, and then took his
leave of the brethren, and sailed thence into Syria, and with him Priscilla
and Aquila; having shorn [r] *his* head in [s] Cenchrea: for he had a vow.

A. D. 56.

[o] Matt. 27. 4, 24.
[p] Rom. 13. 3, 4.
[q] 1 Cor. 1. 1.
[r] Num. 6. 18. ch. 21. 24. 1 Cor. 9. 20.
[s] Rom. 16. 1.

ὑμᾶς]—'of language and terms, and your own law.' **look ye to it; [for] I will be no judge of such matters.** (The "for" wants authority, and the clause is more spirited without it.) In this Gallio only laid down the proper limits of his office. **16. And he drave them from the judgment seat**—'chased them from the tribunal,' or contemptuously ordered them out of court, annoyed at such a case. **17. Then all [the Greeks].** The bracketed words, though they are in a majority of MSS., are wanting in the three oldest [א A B], and in the Vulgate version; and the probability is, that this being the obvious sense of the statement, the words were inserted as a marginal gloss, and afterwards found entrance into the text. (*Lachm.*, *Tisch.*, and *Treg.* exclude them.) The parties who made the assault could be no other than Greeks, whose admission, uncircumcised, into the fellowship of believing Jews had enraged the *unbelieving* party of them and occasioned the prosecution. **took Sosthenes, the chief ruler of the synagogue**—who probably succeeded Crispus on his conversion to the Christian Faith, though he may have been his associate in the same office: for, from ch. xiii. 15, it would appear that some synagogues had more than one ruler. He certainly had allowed his blind zeal to carry him so far as to head the Jewish mob that dragged Paul before the proconsul, and so might be said to deserve the rough handling which he now got. **and beat him before the judgment seat**—that is, under the very eye of the judge. It is an interesting question whether this was the same Sosthenes as Paul associates with himself in his First Epistle to the Corinthians, calling him "Sosthenes our brother" (1 Cor. i. 1), or quite another person. *Meyer*, *Baumgarten*, *Alford*, and *Lechler* think it in the last degree improbable that they were the same person; while *de Wette* and *Howson*, though concurring, write more cautiously. With them we once agreed; but considering that the only place in which "Sosthenes our brother" is mentioned at all is in an Epistle to these very Corinthians, and that there he speaks of him as one who would be quite well-known to them, we now think that *Theodoret*, among the Greek fathers, and after him *Calvin*, *Bengel*, *Humphry*, and *Webster and Wilkinson*, have reason on their side in pronouncing it every way probable that they were the same person. It is sometimes the most violent opposers of the truth who, when their eyes are once opened, are the readiest to yield themselves to it; perhaps the example of Crispus before him had weight; and to the once persecuting Saul such a convert, not to speak of the influence he would thence have, would be peculiarly dear. **and Gallio cared for none of those things**—willing enough, perhaps, to see these turbulent Jews, for whom probably he felt contempt, themselves getting what they hoped to inflict on another, and indifferent to whatever was beyond the range of his office and disturbed his ease. His brother eulogises his loving and loveable manners, saying, among other things, that no man could be more beloved by any one than he was by every one. Religious indifference, under the influence of an easy and amiable temper, reappears from age to age.

Leaving Corinth, Paul retraces his steps, by Ephesus, Cæsarea, and Jerusalem—Arriving at Antioch, he completes his Second Missionary Journey (18-22). **18. And Paul after this tarried there yet a good while.** But during this long residence at Corinth it would appear that he took missionary excursions into the interior of the province, and not without fruit; for whether the expression at the opening of his Second Epistle to the Corinthians (ch. i. 1)—"with all the saints which are in all Achaia"—refer to little churches, or only to individual believers scattered through the province, it certainly implies that they were not few in number. **and then took his leave of the brethren, and sailed thence into Syria** [εἰς τ. Σ.]—rather 'for Syria;' that is, for Antioch, its capital, and the starting-point of this mission to the Gentiles which he feels to be for the present concluded. **and with him Priscilla and Aquila.** The order in which these names are here placed—the wife first—is the more remarkable, as it seems to be henceforward invariable (see on *v.* 26; Rom. xvi. 3; 2 Tim. iv. 19. No doubt, the reason of it is to be found in her greater prominence and helpfulness to the Gospel. Silas and Timotheus accompanied him too, as also Caius (Gaius) and Aristarchus, as appears from ch. xix. 22, 29. Of Silas, as Paul's companion, we read no more. Probably (as *Webster and Wilkinson* conclude) he accompanied him as far as Jerusalem (from which he had come at first to Antioch, as one of the deputies of the council), and there remained. He appears to have after that put himself in connection with Peter, and the churches of Asia Minor, being mentioned by him for the last time in his First Epistle v. 12). **having shorn his head.** This may, according to the construction of the sentence, apply either to Paul or to Aquila. The Vulgate, *Theophylact*, *Grotius*, *Meyer*, and *Howson*, apply it to Aquila, partly as being the person immediately before mentioned, and partly regarding the act as too Jewish for Paul to have observed. But nearly every other critic and expositor regards it as obviously meant of Paul, the prominent person in this whole passage; and with them we agree. **in Cenchrea**—it should be 'Cenchreæ,' which was the eastern harbour of Corinth, about ten miles distant, where (as appears from Rom. xvi. 1) a church had been formed. **for he had a vow.** That this was not the Nazarite vow (Num. vi.; and see on Luke i. 15) is next to certain. It was probably one made in one of his seasons of difficulty or danger. The shaving of the hair was no part of the ceremony of taking the vow, but a token of release from it after its objects were accomplished. And if, to complete the ceremony, he designed to offer the usual sacrifice within the prescribed thirty days (see *Josephus*, J. W. ii. 15. 1), that would explain the haste with which he left Ephesus (*v.* 21), and—if he failed to reach it in time—explain also the subsequent observance of a similar

19 And he came to Ephesus, and left them there: but he himself entered
20 into the synagogue, and reasoned with the Jews. When they desired
21 *him* to tarry longer time with them, he consented not; but bade them
farewell, saying, 'I must by all means keep this feast that cometh in
Jerusalem: but I will return again unto you, " if God will. And he
22 sailed from Ephesus. And when he had landed at Cesarea, and gone up,
23 and saluted the church, he went down to Antioch. And after he had

A. D. 56.

t Deut. 16. 1.
ch. 19. 21.
u 1 Cor. 4. 19.
Heb. 6. 3.
Jas. 4. 15.
Matt. 26.39.
Rom. 1. 10.
Rom. 15.52.

vow at Jerusalem, on the recommendation of the brethren (ch. xxi. 24). The present one at Corinth was voluntary, and shows that even in heathen countries he systematically studied the prejudices of his Jewish brethren. 19. **And he came to Ephesus**—the celebrated capital of Ionia, and at this time of Proconsular Asia. It was a place of great commercial importance, and became the metropolis of the churches of Asia Minor. It was a sail right across, from the west to the east side of the Ægean Sea, of some eight or ten days with a fair wind. **and left them** (that is, Aquila and Priscilla) **there.** For the reason why this is specially mentioned here, see on v. 26. **but he himself entered into the synagogue**—not to continue labouring there, but, taking advantage of the brief opportunity of the vessel's putting in there, to lift up his voice for Christ: **and reasoned** [διελέχθη]—or 'discoursed' **with the Jews.** The word is not (as in ch. xvii. 2 and xviii. 4) in the *imperfect* tense, denoting continuous action, but in the *aorist*, expressing a transient act, for the reason just mentioned. He had been forbidden of the Holy Ghost to preach the word in "Asia" (ch. xvi. 6); but he would not consider that as precluding this passing exercise of his ministry when Providence brought him to its capital; nor did it follow that the prohibition was still in force. 20. **When they desired him to tarry longer time with them.** The Jews seldom rose against the Gospel till the successful preaching of it stirred their enmity; but there was no time for that here. **he consented not;** 21. **But bade them farewell, saying, I must by all means keep this feast**—probably Pentecost (*Wieseler*), **that cometh in Jerusalem: but I will return again unto you, if God will.** The fulfilment of this promise is recorded in ch. xix. 1. **And he sailed from Ephesus.** 22. **And when he had landed at Cesarea**—leaving the vessel there, **and gone up**—that is, to Jerusalem, **and saluted the church.** In these few words does the historian despatch the apostle's FOURTH VISIT TO JERUSALEM after his conversion. The expression 'going *up*' is invariably used of a journey to the metropolis; and thence, naturally, **he went down to Antioch.** Perhaps the vessel reached too late for the feast, as he seems to have done nothing in Jerusalem beyond 'saluting the church,' and privately offering the sacrifice with which his vow (v. 18) would conclude. It is left to be understood, as on his arrival from his first missionary tour, that ' *when he was come, and had gathered the church together, he rehearsed all that God had done with him* ' (ch. xiv. 27) on this his SECOND MISSIONARY JOURNEY.

Remarks.—1. The language of the apostle, in taking leave of the synagogue of Corinth—" Your blood be (or is) upon your own heads; I am clean; from henceforth I will go unto the Gentiles "—is so strong, that one is apt to conclude that, having opened a place of meeting of his own at the house of Justus, he never thereafter entered the synagogue, but commenced a purely Christian service, and perhaps at the regular hours of Jewish worship. But though we have no certainty on the point there are the strongest grounds for questioning this. (1.) It would have certainly soon come to be known among the Jews, far and near, that he had entirely broken with them, and this would have shut him out from all access to them; and as it was to prevent this that he circumcised Timothy before taking him with him on this journey, it is not likely that he would so soon act upon a policy the very opposite. (2.) As the mention of Justus's house being situated "hard by the synagogue" is immediately followed by the statement that "Crispus, the ruler of the synagogue, believed on the Lord with all his house," it is hardly credible that the worship of the two places went on at the same time, or even that they stood in an entirely hostile attitude to each other; nor is it easy to believe that the new meeting would have been allowed to continue for such a length of time undisturbed as it appears to have done, with its members continually increasing. But if we suppose that all the apostle meant to intimate in the synagogue was, that from that time forth he would dispute no more with them there; if we understand him to have continued his attendance at the synagogue, though only as a simple worshipper, and held his own meeting, perhaps, at the close of the synagogue services—thus enabling, and indeed enticing as many of the worshippers as still desired to hear him, to drop out of the one place into the other; and finally, if he made it understood that he was no enemy of "Moses and the prophets," but only their faithful interpreter, in preaching Him who came not to destroy, but to fulfil, and was the true "Hope of Israel:"—all becomes intelligible. We can then understand how Crispus, though the ruler of the synagogue, might think it no inconsistent thing, when his services at the synagogue were over, to listen to the expositions of Paul at his own meeting, until, unable to resist the conviction that Jesus was the Christ, he yielded himself to baptism. And as the apostle would thus be free from at least captious opposition, and be at liberty to expatiate in his own mighty way on the unsearchable riches of Christ, the number of the believers would thus be steadily increased, until, with large accessions of Gentiles, the unbelieving party could no longer stand it, but took their usual course of raising a commotion, and dragging the apostle before the magistrate as a disturber of the peace. This, too, would account for his having the same access to the Jews of other places as before, notwithstanding his apparent secession at Corinth. Perhaps others might learn from this not to be too precipitate in severing themselves entirely even from corrupt systems with which they have been long connected, and to try first the effect of faithful testimony for the truth, and next, the effect of initiatory measures of separation, when no hope of general reformation appears to remain. 2. If the apostle came home to Antioch, after his *first* missionary tour, brimful of intelligence which could not fail to thrill his hearers, as he "rehearsed all that God had done with them, and (particularly) how he had opened the door of faith unto the Gentiles," what must have been the feelings of his auditors as he related to them the details of his *second* journey, now concluded! Doubtless, there was now no such novelty in the accession of the

134

spent some time *there*, he departed, and went over *all* the country of ^vGalatia and Phrygia in order, strengthening ^wall the disciples.

24 And ^xa certain Jew named Apollos, born at Alexandria, an eloquent man, 25 *and* mighty in the Scriptures, came to Ephesus. This man was instructed

A. D. 56.

^v Gal. 1. 2.
^w Isa. 35. 3.
^x 1 Cor. 1. 12.
Tit. 3. 13.

Gentiles as had given such interest to the former mission. But this mission had a novelty of its own, perhaps hardly less thrilling—the plantation of the Gospel in Europe; and that not in obscure and uninfluential places, but in the important capital of eastern Macedonia (Philippi), in the populous and stirring capital of its western division (Thessalonica), and in the great capital of Achaia, the seat of so much Greek culture and refined sensuality—Corinth. Those who heard the narrative of these great triumphs of the Gospel must have seen in them the evidence of a power which nothing could withstand, and have beheld in spirit the mystic Warrior on his white horse, with the crown that was given him, going forth conquering and to conquer (Rev. vi. 2). And with such feelings, what enlargement and elevation of soul must have been imparted to the brethren at Antioch, and how ready would they be to encourage still further the great missionary work! And is it not thus that the two great departments of the Church's work act and re-act upon each other—spiritual life within begetting the irrepressible desire to impart itself to those that. are without, and the tidings of success in the ingathering of those that are afar off warming the affections, quickening the energies, and enlarging the whole character of the Church at home?

THIRD AND LAST MISSIONARY JOURNEY (23— xxi. 16).

23.–xix. 7. FIRST PART OF THIS JOURNEY, EMBRACING THE CENTRAL PARTS OF ASIA MINOR— EPISODE REGARDING APOLLOS, THE ARRIVAL AT EPHESUS, AND THE CASE OF CERTAIN DISCIPLES OF JOHN THE BAPTIST.

Visit to the Churches of Galatia and Phrygia (23). **23. And after he had spent some time there —but probably not long, he departed** — little thinking he was never more to return, **and went over (or 'through') [all] the country of Galatia and Phrygia.** Galatia, being the region that would first be come to—proceeding in a north-westerly direction from Antioch—is here mentioned before Phrygia; whereas in ch. xvi. 6, as Phrygia would be first entered, the order is the reverse. **In order**—meaning, probably, in the order in which the churches lay [καθεξῆς = cl. ἐφεξῆς, an exclusively *Lucan* word, being used by no other New Testament writer, but by Luke five times—Luke i. 3; viii. 1; Acts iii. 24; xi. 4—and here]. These places were now visited, as would seem, for the fourth time. From the Epistle to the Galatians we may gather that proceedings, some of them painful, must have taken place in connection with certain of these churches. On the omission of all details of the visitation of these churches of Asia Minor, see on ch. xvi. 6. One thing lay near the apostle's heart on this journey—the raising of a contribution for the poor saints of Palestine from all the Gentile churches, to be by him carried to Jerusalem and presented to the church there, as an offering of love and token of oneness with their Jewish brethren. An understanding that something of this kind should be done had been come to even at the council of Jerusalem, as a means of cementing the two great sections of believers; and the apostles tells the Galatians that this was a scheme into which he eagerly entered (Gal. ii. 9, 10). Accordingly, we find him referring to it both in his First Epistle to the Corinthians (xvi.

1-4) and in his Second (viii., ix.), and in his Epistle to the Romans (xv. 25, 26): see also ch. xxiv. 17. It was in immediate connection with this interesting object, and with the view of having their contributions ready on his arrival, that he now directed all the churches of Galatia and that of Corinth to establish a regular collection on the first day of every week (1 Cor. xvi. 1, 2); which has ever since that time probably been converted into a public usage throughout all Christendom—though it cannot be shown that the *public* weekly offering is quite the same as the " laying *by himself* in store " [παρ ἑαυτῷ] which the apostle enjoins. (See on I Cor. xvi. 1, 2.) Timotheus and Erastus, Gaius and Aristarchus, appear to have accompanied him on his journey (ch. xix. 22, 29; 2 Cor. i. 1), and, from 2 Cor. we may presume, Titus also.

Episode concerning Apollos at Ephesus and Corinth (24-28). This is one of the most interesting and suggestive incidental narratives in this precious History. It is introduced here, apparently, as occurring about the time at which the historian has arrived. **24. And a certain Jew named Apollos**—a contraction from Apollonius (in which form the Cambridge MS. writes it), as Silas from Silvanus, &c. **born at Alexandria**—the celebrated capital of lower Egypt, on the south-eastern shore of the Mediterranean; and called after its founder, Alexander the Great, who, three centuries before Christ, planned it out to be the metropolis of his western dominions. As a site for such a purpose it was magnificent; and such were its resources, that by degrees it rose to immense population and wealth. As might be expected, its population was a very mixed one. The Greek element predominated; but Jews were there in great numbers —*Philo*, who lived there near about this time, reckons them then at a million; native Egyptians also formed, of course, part of the population; and in addition to these there were representatives of almost every other nation. Nowhere was there such a fusion of Greek, Jewish, and Oriental peculiarities; and an intelligent Jew, educated in that city, could hardly fail to manifest all these elements in his mental character. **an eloquent man**—turning his Alexandrian culture to high account as a speaker, **and mighty in the scriptures**—his eloquence enabling him to express clearly, and enforce skilfully what, as a Jew, he had gathered from a diligent study of the Old Testament Scriptures. *Lechler* thinks it probable that, as an Alexandrian, he was indebted to the school of Philo both for his method of Scriptural interpretation and for his eloquence. But the Platonic character of Philo's school of Old Testament interpretation was so alien from anything which would have led to a humble reception of Christian truth, that we rather wonder at that excellent man and able critic making such a concession to the modern enemies of the truth; nor can we imagine Apollos to have had almost anything in common with that school, except its rooted faith in the supernatural foundation of the Jewish Religion and in the inspiration of the Scriptures, and a love of biblical interpretation. **came to Ephesus**—on what errand is not known; but probably to exercise his gifts in opening to his Jewish brethren the truths which he had received; perhaps, also, to enquire into the truth and character of those events which had given

in the way of the Lord; and being [y]fervent in the spirit, he spake and
taught diligently the things of the Lord, knowing [z]only the baptism of
26 John. And he began to speak boldly in the synagogue: whom when
Aquila and Priscilla had heard, they took him unto *them*, and ex-
27 pounded unto him the way of God more perfectly. And when he was
disposed to pass into Achaia, the brethren wrote, exhorting the disciples
to receive him: who, when he was come, [a]helped them much which had

A. D. 54.

[y] Rom. 12.11.
[z] ch. 19. 3.
[a] John 1. 12,
13.
1 Cor. 3. 6.
2 Cor. 1. 24.
2 Cor. 10.14.
1 Pet. 5. 2, 3.

so new a complexion to the doctrine of Christ since he received it, and of which he could hardly fail to have heard at least something. **25. This man was instructed in the way of the Lord**—that is, the Lord *Jesus* (according to the usual phraseology of this book), not God the Father, as *Lechler* understands it, as if Apollos had known little more than God's design to send a Redeemer to Israel; **and being fervent in the spirit.** Having a warm heart, and conscious, probably, of his gifts and attainments, he burned to impart to others the truth he had himself received. **he spake and taught** [ἐλάλει καὶ ἐδίδασκεν]—the tense here used implying *continuousness* from meeting to meeting. This took place at Ephesus, whither Apollos had come. And as the Jews of Ephesus had only got as much of the Gospel from Paul on his late visit as he could impart to them while his vessel lay at that port, and which served only to whet their appetite for more (*vv.* 19-21), they would the more readily listen to the expository eloquence and fervour of Apollos, in the same direction, so far, as the teaching of Paul. **diligently** [ἀκριβῶς]—rather 'accurately,' or 'soundly.' (It is the same word as is rendered 'perfectly,' in *v.* 26.) Of course this means only 'accurately' so far as his knowledge went, as is evident from what follows: **the things of the Lord**—but the true reading is, **'the things of Jesus.'** [This is the reading of א A B D E, &c., of the Vulgate, of both Syriac versions, and most others; and so *Lachm., Tisch.,* and *Treg.* The received reading has but inferior support.] **knowing only the baptism of John.** He was instructed, probably, by some disciple of the Baptist, in the whole circle of John's teaching concerning Jesus, but no more: he had yet to learn the new light which the outpouring of the Spirit at Pentecost had thrown upon the Redeemer's Death and Resurrection, as appears from ch. xix. 2, 3. **26. And he began to speak boldly** (or 'with freedom') **in the synagogue.** This seems to imply that the 'speaking and teaching' of the previous verse had been at more private meetings, and that having thus cautiously felt his way, he afterwards began to discourse in the synagogue. **whom when Aquila and Priscilla had heard.** The proper order here, we think, is, 'Priscilla and Aquila' (see on *v.* 18). [The majority of MSS., it is true, concur with the received text; but א A B E have Priscilla first, with the Vulgate, &c. So *Lachm.* and *Treg.*, though *Tischendorf* abides by the received order. *Meyer* and *Lechler* think the reversed order was transferred to this verse from *v.* 18; but internal evidence—founded on the usage of other undoubted passages, and seeming to point to some superiority in Priscilla—appear to us to turn the scale in favour of her name being first here also.] **they took him unto them** (privately)—that is, to their own house; joying to observe the extent of Scriptural knowledge and evangelical truth which he displayed, and the fervency, courage, and eloquence with which he gave it forth. **and expounded unto him the way of God more perfectly**—opening up those truths, to him as yet unknown, on which the Spirit had shed such glorious light. One cannot but ob-

serve how providential it was that this couple should have been left at Ephesus when Paul sailed thence for Syria; and no doubt it was chiefly to pave the way for the better understanding of this episode that the fact is expressly mentioned by the historian in *v.* 19. Nor can one help admiring the humility and teachableness of so gifted a teacher in sitting at the feet of a Christian woman and her husband. **27. And when he was disposed to pass into Achaia**—of which Corinth, on the opposite coast (see on *v.* 1) was the capital; there to proclaim that Gospel which he now more fully comprehended. If it be asked why he wished to go into Achaia, *Lechler* replies, that 'a delicate reserve might prevent him, after being fully instructed, from again coming forward in Ephesus, where he had already appeared with such unripe and defective knowledge. But since "the brethren" of Ephesus wrote to the disciples of Achaia, "exhorting them to receive him," as is stated in the very next clause, we can hardly doubt that they were quite cognizant of the enlargement of his views, and, so far from thinking less of him for it, joyfully furthered his desire to go to a field more suited to his gifts. The probability rather is, that Aquila and Priscilla, knowing fully the nature of the Corinthian field, convinced him that it opened up a richer sphere for the peculiar style of his teaching than Ephesus, where the ground had as yet been scarcely broken, and that the handful of believers there, concurring with them, joined them in this letter of recommendation. **the brethren.** We had not before heard of such, gathered at Ephesus; but the desire of the Jews there to whom Paul preached to retain him amongst them for some time (*v.* 20), and his promise to return to them (*v.* 21), seem to indicate some drawing towards the Gospel, which, no doubt, the zealous private labours of Priscilla and Aquila would ripen into discipleship. **wrote, exhorting the disciples to receive him**—a beautiful specimen of 'letters of recommendation' (as ch. xv. 23, 25-27; and see 2 Cor. iii. 1), by which, as well as by interchange of deputations, &c., the early churches maintained active Christian fellowship with each other: who, when he was come, **helped them much**—was a great acquisition to the Achaian brethren, **which had believed through grace.** If this is the right way of rendering the words, it is one of those incidental expressions which show that *faith's being a production of God's grace in the heart* was so current and recognized a truth that it was taken for granted, as a necessary consequence of the general system of grace, rather than expressly insisted on. In this sense the words have certainly been understood by the majority of interpreters. But *Grotius, Bengel, Olshausen, Meyer, Webster and Wilkinson,* and *Lechler,* connect the words "through grace" with Apollos, not with the Corinthian converts—translating thus: 'who, when he was come, helped much through grace who had believed;' and though once disinclined to this, we now judge it to be the true sense of the statement. For what the historian tells us is not that Apollos helped the believers at Corinth, by operating successfully *on themselves*—to the enlargement of their knowledge, the fur-

28 believed through grace: for he mightily convinced the Jews, *and that* publicly, *b* showing by the Scriptures that Jesus [3] was Christ.

19 AND it came to pass, that, while Apollos was *a* at Corinth, Paul having passed through the upper coasts came to Ephesus: and finding certain

2 disciples, he said unto them, Have ye received the Holy Ghost since ye believed? And they said unto him, *b* We have not so much as heard

3 whether there be any Holy Ghost. And he said unto them, Unto what

4 then were ye baptized? And they said, Unto John's *c* baptism. Then said Paul, *d* John verily baptized with the baptism of repentance, saying unto the people, that they should believe on him which should come after

A. D. 52.
b ch. 9. 22.
[3] Or, is the Christ.
CHAP. 19.
a 1 Cor. 1. 12.
b ch. 8. 16.
1 Sam. 3. 7.
c ch. 18. 25.
d ch. 1. 5.
ch. 11. 16.
ch. 13. 24.

therance of their faith, their growth in grace: in that case it might have been quite natural to tell us that it was those whom the grace of God had first brought into subjection to Christ who were thus furthered in the divine life by Apollos. But the whole service which the historian says Apollos rendered to the Corinthian believers, "when he was come"—or, on his first arrival—consisted in his *adding to their numbers from without,* or at least bearing down all opposition from their Jewish adversaries. And since the whole stress of the statement is laid upon the success of Apollos's labours among the unbelieving Jews, it seems more natural to understand the historian to mean that it was "through grace" that Apollos carried all before him in his discussions *with them,* than that he should have meant to tell us that those who were believers long before he arrived had "believed through grace." **28. For he mightily convinced the Jews** [εὐτόνως διακατηλέγχετο]—'stoutly bore down,' 'foiled' or 'confuted' them: the expression is very emphatic. **and [that] publicly** [δημοσίᾳ]—not in the synagogue merely, for in that case it would have likely been named (as in ch. xvii. 1, 2, 10; and *vv.* 4, 19, 26), but in some other public place; **showing by the scriptures that Jesus was Christ**—or (according to strict grammatical form), 'that the Christ was Jesus,' which, when compared with *v.* 25, seems to imply a richer testimony than with his partial knowledge he was at first able to bear; and the power with which he bore down all opposition in argument is that which made him such an acquisition to the brethren. Thus his ministry would be as good as another visitation to the Achaian churches by the apostle himself (see 1 Cor. iii. 6); and the more as, in so far as he was indebted for it to Priscilla and Aquila, his ministrations would have a decidedly *Pauline* cast. But though "when he came," or on his first arrival, he seems to have laid himself out almost exclusively for those that were *without*—'helping them which had believed' chiefly in this way—we can hardly suppose that this would last very long; and as the apostle expressly reminds the Corinthians that Apollos "watered" what he himself had "planted," we thus gather that after awhile this distinguished teacher applied his peculiar gifts to the building up of the work of God *within* the Church, taking it up where Paul had left it.

CHAP. XIX. 1-7.—*Paul arrives at Ephesus, and meets with certain disciples of the Baptist, who, on receiving from him fuller light, are baptized, receive the Holy Ghost, and speak with tongues.* **1. And it came to pass, that, while Apollos was at Corinth**—where his ministry was so powerful that a formidable party in the church of that city gloried afterwards in his type of preaching in preference to Paul's (1 Cor. i. 12; iii. 4), no doubt from the marked infusion of Greek philosophic culture which distinguished it, and which seemed to be the very thing which the apostle studiously avoided (1 Cor.

ii. 1-5): **Paul having passed through the upper coasts** (or 'parts')—meaning the interior parts of Asia Minor, travelling westwards towards Ephesus; with reference to which (as lying on the sea-coast) all from Galatia and Phrygia was elevated, and partly mountainous. **came to Ephesus** (see on ch. xviii. 19)—thus making good his conditional promise (ch. xviii. 21): **and finding certain disciples, 2. He said unto them** [εὑρών-Εἶπε, or, according to, perhaps, the true reading, εὑρεῖν-Εἶπε τε, 'found, And said'], **Have ye received the Holy Ghost since ye believed?** ['Ελάβετε πιστεύσαντες]—rather, 'Did ye receive the Holy Ghost on believing?' from which it is natural to infer that the one did not of necessity carry the other along with it (see on ch. viii. 14-17). Why this question was asked, we cannot tell; but it was probably in consequence of something that passed between them from which the apostle was led to suspect the imperfection of their light. They were probably at the same stage of Christian knowledge as Apollos when he came to Corinth, and, having newly arrived, had no communication with any Christians at Ephesus. **And they said unto him, We have not so much as heard whether there be any Holy Ghost.** This cannot be the meaning, since the personality and office of the Holy Ghost, in connection with Christ, formed an especial subject of the Baptist's teaching. Literally, 'We did not even hear whether the Holy Ghost was [given],' that is, at the time of their baptism. That the word 'given' is the right supplement, seems plain from the nature of the case; and it is the same in John vii. 39, on the same subject. **3. And he said [unto them]** (the bracketed words are probably not genuine), **Unto** (or 'Into') **what then were ye baptized? And they said, Unto** (or 'Into') **John's baptism. 4. Then said Paul, John verily baptized with the baptism** (or 'baptized the baptism') **of repentance, saying unto the people, that they should believe on him which should come after him, that is,** on [Christ] Jesus. (The word "Christ" is clearly not genuine.) The point of contrast is between two stages in the development of the same Gospel truth—a rudimental and a ripe Gospel; the former represented by John's baptism, in which Christ and His salvation was rather expected than actually come. This state of things, strictly speaking, terminated not with the commencement of Christ's public ministry, but with the descent of the Holy Ghost at Pentecost; as is evident from John's own statement: "I indeed baptize you with water unto repentance, but there cometh the Mightier than I after me, He shall baptize you with the Holy Ghost"—which He certainly did not do until after His ascension. Nor is this affected by the fact that Jesus Himself "made and baptized (through others) more disciples than John;" for as the kingdom was represented as still only in prospect, so "the Holy Ghost was not then given, because Jesus was not yet glorified" (John vii. 39). It was this baptism of the Spirit, from the hands

5 him, that is, on Christ Jesus. When they heard *this*, they were baptized
6 ᵉin the name of the Lord Jesus. And when Paul had laid *his* hands

A. D. 56.

ᵉ Gal. 3 27.

of John's risen Master, unto a new life—which made the whole life and work of Christ another thing from what it was conceived to be before that grand event—that these simple disciples were uninformed about, and that Paul communicated to them (the bare subject of which is given in *v.* 4). 5. **When they heard this, they were baptized**—not, however, by Paul himself (see 1 Cor. i. 14), in (or 'into') **the name of the Lord Jesus**—into the whole fulness of the new economy, as now opened up to their believing and teachable minds. (To the double baptism of these disciples we shall advert in the Remarks at the close of this Section.) 6. **And when Paul had laid his hands upon them, the Holy Ghost came on them; and they spake with tongues, and prophesied**—(see on ch. x. 44-46.) 7. **And all the men were about twelve**—and, from the mode of expression used, probably all men.

Remarks.—1. The episode about Apollos from Alexandria, and the account of the twelve disciples whom Paul found at Ephesus—both apparently at the same imperfect stage of Christian knowledge denoted by "the Baptism of John"—bear such internal marks of truth as not only to speak for themselves, but to a large degree to inspire confidence in the whole strain of the History in which they lie embosomed. Observe the particulars of Apollos's Christian history up to the time when Aquila and Priscilla took him aside; their perception of the imperfect ground on which he stood, and their confidence that, though occupying a position inferior to his, they could impart to him what he knew not, but would dearly value; the humility and teachableness with which he drank in what they opened up to him, and the readiness with which he set out for a sphere more suited to his peculiar gifts, of which Aquila and Priscilla would doubtless give him full particulars; in a word, the Ephesian letter of recommendation to the Achaian brethren, and the success with which he laboured in Corinth (the capital of Achaia):—these are incidents which form one consistent and uncommon whole; which, whether we look at them as a unity or in their component parts, were not in the least likely to occur either to a pure fabricator or a wilful distorter of history. Much of the same thing may be said of the account of the twelve Joannean disciples. *Paley* (in his 'Horæ Paulinæ,' ch. iii. No. v.) compares this account of Apollos in the Acts with what is said of him in the First Epistle to the Corinthians, as one of the many 'Undesigned Coincidences' between the Acts and the Epistles, confirming the authenticity of both. What he dwells on is the evidence which the Epistle incidentally furnishes, that Apollos must have been at Corinth after Paul's departure from it, and before that Epistle was written; which *Paley* shows to be just what we gather from the historical statements of the Acts. On this his reasoning is quite conclusive. But something may perhaps be added to it, not less interesting. From the Epistle we gather that the spirit of party had got into the Corinthian church, its members crying up their favourite teachers to the disparagement of the rest. Paul was the favourite of one class, Apollos the oracle of another, while a third took to Cephas (or Peter). Now, we know so much of the peculiarities of Paul and Peter that we can easily understand what should attract some to the one and some to the other; whereas, but for this one historical notice of Apollos we should have known nothing of him at all. Here, however, we find the very charac-

teristics which were fitted to attract a considerable party at Corinth, who would dislike, or at least not take to the method of Paul. We know that the Corinthians had all the Greek love of wisdom—a wisdom, however, which, for the most part, sacrificed the substance to the form. This wisdom the apostle studiously eschewed—calling it "the wisdom of words"—and this "lest the cross of Christ should be made of none effect." Now, there can be no doubt that Apollos's teaching would wear the aspect of that very "wisdom of words" which Paul repudiated. For being "a Jew of Alexandria," and "an eloquent man," he would be familiar, not only with the school of his great countryman, Philo, who taught and wrote there, but with the rhetoric of the other schools of Alexandria. That he came to Alexandria a disciple of Philo, or of any Alexandrian school, there is not the least reason to believe. On the contrary, he was of the Baptist's school, whose lowliness and Christian standing, so far as it went, were the reverse of what he would learn either from the Platonic Philo, or the Pagan rhetoricians; and being "mighty in the Scriptures," his teaching would likely be of a *Biblical* character, on which his "fervour of spirit" would kindle: in short, he would be a thoroughly believing man, whose gifts were consecrated to the illustration and enforcement of Divine truth, so far as he knew it. Then, again, the humility and teachableness with which he sat at the feet of Aquila and Priscilla, who certainly were Paul's scholars, the enlargement of his views which followed on this, and the zeal with which he went to Corinth to give forth what he had learnt—all go to show that his teaching at Corinth could not have differed from that of Paul in the substance and scope of it, nor in anything whatever save in *method;* nor even in this, in any such sense as to affect the saving efficacy of it. Indeed, we have Paul's own testimony that Apollos only "watered" what he himself had "planted." Nevertheless—allowing his Alexandrian culture to have been sanctified to the utmost, and laid at the feet of Jesus—we can hardly doubt that it would shine through his teaching, nor hesitate to believe that, on the apostle's own principle of "becoming all things to all men, that by any means he might gain some," he would feel himself justified, if not called upon, to deal with those wisdom-loving Greeks as one who knew and could wield to saving purposes their own weapon. And if so, then here was a field for one-sided admiration of Apollos, to the disparagement of Paul. It is needless to prosecute this subject further. Enough that we have shown how well the historical account of Apollos in the Acts and the allusions to his influence at Corinth agree together. 2. The question, Why were the twelve disciples who had been previously baptized with the baptism of John, after being instructed by Paul, baptized again into the name of the Lord Jesus? has given rise to considerable difference of opinion. The Anabaptists of the Reformation-period and the Church of Rome agreed in regarding the Joannean and the Christian baptisms as essentially different, while the Protestants generally held them essentially the same. But since there is a sense in which both may be held to be right—the substance of what John taught being beyond doubt identical with Christianity, while in respect of development they certainly differed widely—we must be governed entirely by the *practice* of Christ Himself and of the apostolic church. What, then, was that?

138

upon them, the Holy Ghost came on them; and they ⌠spake with
7 tongues, and prophesied.   And all the men were about twelve.

A. D. 54.
⌠ ch. 2. 4.

First, there is no evidence to show that our Lord caused those disciples of John who came over to Him to be re-baptized; and from John iv. 1, 2, we naturally conclude that they were not. Indeed, had those who first followed Jesus from among the Baptist's disciples required to be re-baptized, the Saviour must have performed the ceremony Himself, and such a thing could not fail to be recorded; whereas the reverse is intimated in the passage just quoted. Next, though it is said that all who entered the Church on the day of Pentecost, to the number of three thousand, were baptized, it is evident from the whole narrative that these were all new converts, and did not include any of the hundred and twenty who issued forth from the upper room filled with the Holy Ghost, nor any who had been disciples of Christ before. Lastly, while all the baptisms of which we read in the sequel of the New Testament are of fresh converts and their households, with the exception of these twelve disciples whom Paul instructed at Ephesus, the remarkable and somewhat perplexing fact is that *Apollos*, though at precisely the same stage of Christian development with these re-baptized disciples, *was not re-baptized* (so far as we read; and the details in his case are so minutely given, that this fact would certainly not have been passed over if it had taken place). From all the facts the conclusion appears irresistible, that those who had been baptized with the baptism of John were not held to need any further water-baptism on their becoming followers of Christ, either during His own stay on earth, or after the Pentecostal effusion of the Spirit; in other words, that their first initiation by baptism into Christ—all rudimental though it was —was regarded as carrying their total subjection to Him, and participation of all that He had to bestow. And if it still be asked, In what light, then, are we to regard the single case of re-baptization recorded of these twelve disciples? The answer may perhaps be found by comparing their case with that of Apollos. They both "knew only the baptism of John." But in all likelihood the twelve disciples had newly arrived at Ephesus when Paul "found" them, and had come from one of those many quarters where knots of half-instructed disciples were in the habit of meeting together for religious exercises. Amongst these they had been baptized, and evidently were sincere believers, as far as their light went. But Paul, finding their knowledge of Christian truth very imperfect, instructed them fully in the way of the Lord; and their views and feelings having now undergone a great change, they would probably regard themselves as new converts, and be as desirous of being "baptized into the name of the Lord Jesus" as Paul could be that they should. Of all this we cannot be certain, but something like it seems extremely probable on reading the narrative; whereas the natural impression on reading what is said of Apollos is just the reverse. *He* comes to Ephesus already "instructed in the way of the Lord, fervent in the spirit, and mighty in the Scriptures," though yet only on the Joannean platform; and what Priscilla and Aquila did for him seems to have been simply to impart to him those facts of the new economy with which he was unacquainted. And just as those disciples who passed from the ranks of the Baptist to those of Christ needed and received no new baptism, so this already distinguished Christian teacher, having merely received a riper view of those great evangelical truths which he already believed and taught,

neither needed nor received re-baptization. 3. The most accomplished theologian may learn from the humblest private Christian what is of more value than all his learning. The pity is, that as there are few such who would, like Apollos, sit at the feet of a Priscilla and Aquila, so there are not many who, like that couple, would venture to put any such to the test. Nevertheless, humility and teachableness are the unfailing characteristics of sanctified learning; and those Christian teachers who are prepared to learn from *any one*, are pretty sure to be rewarded with what their books have failed to teach them, from some who have studied in a higher school. And if so, then private Christians, male and female, conscious of the possession of truth to which their teachers have not attained, have a duty to discharge to them from which they do not well entirely to shrink. 'It is instructive (says *Lechler*) that a man so important and influential in the apostolic age as Apollos, should have been indebted to a plain married couple for his peculiar preparation for the ministry, and for his introduction into positive Christian truth. These were the persons who first took notice of him and his promising gifts, but who also perceived what was defective in him; these were they who initiated him —certainly more highly gifted and more learned than themselves—more thoroughly in the Christian truth; these were they who assisted his coming to Corinth, and did their best to place the right man in the right place. Here, accordingly, simple laity—and especially a woman of a pious disposition and of solid Christian knowledge—have performed what, according to our ideas, is the business of theological institutions and ecclesiastical boards —a proof of the universal priesthood of the apostolic times.' Of course, there is a self-conceit which may easily crop out in such, the discouragement of which, on the part of teachers, they will interpret into unteachable pride. "But wisdom is justified of her children." The teachable will be humble, and the modest will not presume, while faith and love will overpower the infirmities of both in the common salvation and the one living Head. 4. Every natural gift and acquirement, when laid at the feet of Jesus and sanctified to His service, is to be used to the uttermost, instead of being suppressed. As Aquila and Priscilla, from their long residence at Corinth, must have known the love there cherished for Greek wisdom, from which the Christians would not be quite weaned, there can hardly be a doubt that they perceived in Apollos the very gifts which were fitted to attract and edify that church; and that Paul having "planted" the truth there, on the principle of eschewing that wisdom which the Corinthians were apt to idolize, Apollos might now "water" it even more effectually than the apostle himself, by showing them that the same truth admitted of diversified illustration, and presenting to them in his own teaching an 'eloquence' akin to what they had been wont to idolize, yet wholly consecrated to the service of Christ. Be this as it may, as Aquila and Priscilla seem to have been the principal Christians as yet at Ephesus, no doubt the suggestion that Apollos should go to Corinth originated with them; the letter of the brethren 'exhorting the disciples' of that church 'to receive him,' must have been prompted, if not dictated, by them; and, availing himself of the information which they would give him as to the state of Corinth, he seems to have found immediate entrance, and in overpowering the Jews in argument, and so 'helping much the believing,'

8   And ⁹ he went into the synagogue, and spake boldly for the space of
three months, disputing and persuading the things ʰ concerning the king-
9   dom of God.   But ⁱ when divers were hardened, and believed not, but
spake evil ʲ of that way before the multitude, he departed from them, and
separated the disciples, disputing daily in the school of one Tyrannus.
10 And ᵏ this continued by the space of two years; so that all they which
dwelt in Asia heard the word of the Lord Jesus, both Jews and Greeks.
11, And ˡ God wrought special miracles by the hands of Paul: so ᵐ that
12 from his body were brought unto the sick handkerchiefs or aprons,
and the diseases departed from them, and the evil spirits went out
of them.
13   Then ⁿ certain of the vagabond Jews, exorcists, ᵒ took upon them to
call over them which had evil spirits the name of the Lord Jesus,
14 saying, We adjure you by Jesus whom Paul preacheth.   And there were

A. D. 57.

⁹ ch. 17. 2.
ʰ ch. 1. 3.
  ch. 28. 23.
ⁱ 2 Ki. 17. 14.
  2 Chr. 30. 8.
  Neh. 9. 16,
  17,
  2 Tim. 1.15.
  2 Pet. 2. 2.
  Jude 10.
ʲ ch. 9. 2.
ᵏ ch. 20. 31.
ˡ Mark 16.20.
  2 Ki. 4. 29.
ᵐ
ⁿ Matt. 13.27.
ᵒ Mark 9. 38.
  Luke 9. 49.

there can be no doubt that his peculiar gifts went
to rich account.   It will be the wisdom of the
Church, then, to develop every natural gift, and
avail itself of every natural acquirement in its
teachers, turning all into the channel of Christ's
service.

8-41. — GLORIOUS FRUITS OF THE APOSTLE'S
LABOURS AT EPHESUS.

*After three months' labour in the synagogue,
finding himself resisted and the work retarded by
the unbelieving, he withdraws, as at Corinth, with
the converts to the lecture-room of Tyrannus, which
for two years became a centre of evangelization for
all Proconsular Asia, and the scene of glorious
Gospel triumphs* (8-20).   **8. And he went into the
synagogue, and spake boldly** [ἐπαρρησιάζετο]—
'spake with freedom,' **for the space of three
months,** disputing and persuading **the things
concerning the kingdom of God.   9. But when
divers** (or 'certain') **were hardened, and believed
not**—implying, however, that others, and probably
a considerable number, believed, **but spake evil
of that way** [κακολογοῦντες τὴν ὁδὸν]—' calumniating' or 'speaking ill of the way' (see on ch. ix. 2),
before the multitude, he departed from them—
just as he had done at Corinth (ch. xviii. 7), **and
separated the disciples**—withdrawing to a separate
place of meeting, for the sake both of the converts
already made, that he might be able to confirm
and build them up, and of the unprejudiced multitude, that they might no longer be poisoned by a
systematic and determined opposition to the truth:
disputing (or 'discoursing') **daily in the school** (or
'lecture-room') **of** [one] **Tyrannus.**   (The word
"one"—omitted by *Lachmann, Tischendorf,* and
Tregelles—is probably not genuine.)   The attempt
made by *Meyer* to make it probable that this
Tyrannus was a Jew, and his school of a rabbinical character, is not successful.   The almost universal opinion, that (whether converted or not) he
was one of those Greek teachers of rhetoric or
philosophy, who opened schools in all the principal
cities of Greece and Roman Asia, has everything
to confirm it.   **10. And this continued by the
space of two years**—in addition to the former
three months.   See on ch. xx. 31.   But during
some part of this period he must have paid
a second unrecorded visit to Corinth, since the one
next recorded (see on ch. xx. 2, 3) is twice called
his *third* visit (2 Cor. xii. 14; xiii. 1).   See on 2
Cor. i. 15, 16, which might seem inconsistent with
this.   The passage across was quite a short one
(see on ch. xviii. 19).   Towards the close of this long
stay at Ephesus, as we learn from 1 Cor. xvi. 8,
he wrote his FIRST EPISTLE TO THE CORINTHIANS;
also (though on this opinions are divided), the
EPISTLE TO THE GALATIANS.   (See Introductions

to those Epistles.)   And just as at Corinth his
greatest success was after his withdrawal to a
separate place of meeting (ch. xviii. 7-10), so was it
at Ephesus.   **so that all they which dwelt in** (Proconsular or Roman) **Asia heard the word of the
Lord** [Jesus].   (The bracketed word "Jesus" here
has scarcely any authority, and is evidently not
genuine.)   **both Jews and Greeks.**   This is that
"great door and effectual" which was "opened
unto him" while resident at Ephesus, as he tells
his Corinthian converts (1 Cor. xvi. 8, 9), and
which induced him to make it his head quarters
for so long a period.   The unwearied and varied
character of his labours here are best seen in his
own subsequent address to the Elders of Ephesus,
(ch. xx. 17, &c.)   And thus (as *Baumgarten* says)
Ephesus became the 'ecclesiastical centre for the
entire region, as indeed it remained for a very long
period.'   Churches arose eastward, at Colosse,
Laodicea, and Hierapolis, either through his own
labours or those of his faithful helpers whom he
sent out in different directions—Epaphras, Archippus, Philemon (Col. i. 7; iv. 12-17; Philem. 23).
11. And God wrought special miracles [Δυνάμεις
οὐ τὰς τυχούσας]—'no ordinary miracles.'   **by the
hands of Paul: 12. So that from** ('even from')
his body were brought—'brought away' is the
preferable reading [ἀποφέρεσθαι]—**unto the sick
handkerchiefs or aprons.**   The meaning is, that
both were brought, and that the cures were wrought
whether the one *or* the other were used.   See on ch.
v. 15.   **and the diseases departed from them, and
the evil spirits went out of them.**   How different
were these miracles from the magical arts practised at Ephesus! (*vv.* 18, 19.)   "*God*" wrought
these "miracles" merely "*by the hands of Paul;*"
and the very exorcists (*v.* 13) observing that the
name of Jesus was the secret of all his miracles,
hoped, by aping him in this, to be equally successful; while the result of all, in the "magnifying of
the Lord Jesus" (*v.* 17), showed that in working
them the apostle took care to hold up Him whom
he *preached* as the source of all the miracles which
he *wrought.*
13. Then certain of the vagabond Jews [περιερ-
χομένων Ἰουδ.]—simply, 'wandering' or 'travelling'
Jews, who went from place to place practising
exorcism, or the art of conjuring evil spirits to
depart out of the possessed.   That such a power
did exist, for some time at least, seems implied in
Matt. xii. 27.   But, no doubt, this would breed
imposture; and the present case is very different
from that referred to in Luke ix. 49, 50.   **took
upon them to call over them which had evil
spirits the name of the Lord Jesus, saying, We
adjure you**—rather, 'I adjure you' (according to
what is beyond doubt the true reading) **by Jesus**

seven sons of *one* Sceva, a Jew, *and* chief of the priests, which did so.
15 And the evil spirit answered and said, Jesus ^pI know, and Paul I know;
16 but who are ye? And the man in whom the evil spirit was leaped on
   them, and overcame them, and prevailed against them, so that they fled
17 out of that house naked and wounded. And this was known to all the
   Jews and Greeks also dwelling at Ephesus; and fear ^qfell on them all,
18 and the name of the Lord Jesus was magnified. And many that
19 believed came, ^rand confessed, and showed their deeds. Many of them
   also which ^sused curious arts brought their books together, and burned
   them before all *men :* and they counted the price of them, and found *it*
20 fifty thousand *pieces* of silver. So ^tmightily grew the word of God and
   prevailed.
21   After ^uthese things were ended, Paul purposed ^vin the spirit, when he
   had passed through Macedonia and Achaia, to go to Jerusalem, saying,
22 After I have been there, ^wI must also see Rome. So he sent into
   Macedonia two of them ^xthat ministered unto him, Timotheus and
   ^yErastus; but he himself stayed in Asia for a season.
23   And ^zthe same time there arose no small stir about ^athat way.

A. D. 58.

p Matt. 8. 29.
Mark 1. 24.
Mark 5. 7.
q Luke 1. 65.
Luke 7. 16.
ch. 2. 43.
ch. 5. 5,
11.
r Jer. 3. 13.
Matt. 3. 6.
s Isa. 30. 22.
Dan. 2. 2.
t Col. 1. 6.
u Rom. 15.25.
Gal. 2. 1.
v ch. 20. 22.
w Rom. 15.21.
x ch. 13. 5.
y Rom. 16.21.
2 Tim. 4.20.
z Cor. 1. 8.
a ch. 9. 2.

---

whom Paul preacheth—a striking testimony to the power of Christ's name in Paul's mouth. **14. And there were seven sons of one Sceva, a Jew, and chief of the priests**—head, probably, of one of the twenty-four courses of the priests, **which did so.** It will appear from *v.* 16 that only two of the seven did so on this occasion. **15. And the evil spirit answered and said, Jesus I know, and Paul I know** [γινώσκω—ἐπίσταμαι]—'Jesus I know, and Paul I am acquainted with.' Probably the latter word (though somewhat stronger) was not intended to express any greater knowledge of Paul than of Jesus, but merely to vary the expression (see Mark i. 24, 34). **but who are ye?**—an expression of unmeasured contempt for which they were evidently quite unprepared. But worse still: **16. And the man in whom the evil spirit was.** Mark the clear line of demarcation here between "*the evil spirit* which answered and said," and "*the man in whom the evil spirit was.*" The reality of such possessions could not be more clearly expressed. **leaped on them, and overcame** [κατακυριεύσας ἀμφοτέρῳ]—rather, 'mastered them both' (for this reading is not only better attested externally [ἀμφοτέρων than αὐτῶν of the received text], but has internal evidence in its favour; for it never would have crept into the text if not genuine.) **and prevailed against** (or 'overpowered') **them, so that they fled out of that house naked and wounded. 17. And this was known to all the Jews and Greeks also dwelling at Ephesus; and fear fell on them.** And who can wonder that so appalling a testimony, at once against those profane impostors, and in favour of Paul and the Master whom he preached, should spread far and wide, and fill with fear all that heard it? nor is what follows more to be wondered at: **and the name of the Lord Jesus was magnified. 18. And many that believed came, and confessed, and shewed their deeds. 19. Many** ('a considerable number') **of them also which used curious arts** [τὰ περίεργα πραξάντων]—'who had practised the magic arts.' The word signifies 'things overdone,' and is here significantly applied to arts in which laborious but senseless incantations were practised. **brought their books together** (containing the mystic formularies), **and burned them before all**—the *imperfect tense* graphically expressing the progress and continuance of the conflagration. These miserable dupes of magicians, and other pretended traffickers with in-

visible powers, having got their eyes opened, now come forward openly acknowledging how shamefully they had been deluded, and how deeply they had allowed themselves to be implicated in such practices. **and they counted the price of them, and found it fifty thousand pieces of silver**—about £2,000, supposing it to be the *drachma*, the current coin of the Levant, the value of which was about tenpence sterling. From their nature, those books would be costly; and books in general then bore a higher value than now.

Whilst Paul is preparing to leave for Macedonia and Achaia, the idol-makers of Ephesus, whose craft was suffering through the success of the Gospel, raise a tumult in the city, which is with difficulty quelled by the civil authorities (21-41). **21. After these things were ended** (or 'completed')—implying something like a natural finish to his long period of labour at Ephesus; **Paul purposed in the spirit** [ἐν τ. πνεύματι]—'in his spirit,' **when he had passed through Macedonia and Achaia, to go to Jerusalem, saying, After I have been there, I must also see Rome.** Mark here the vastness of the apostle's missionary plans, which seem only to have expanded the more ground he overtook and the more victorious his course. 'No Alexander (says *Bengel*), no Cæsar, no other hero approaches the large-mindedness of this *little* Benjamite (a play upon the word *Paulus*). The truth of Christ, faith in and love to Christ, made his heart wide as the ocean.' The plans here expressed were all of them fulfilled, although he 'saw Rome' only as a prisoner of Jesus Christ. **22. So he sent into Macedonia two of them that ministered unto him, Timotheus and Erastus**—as his pioneers, in order (as he tells the Corinthians) to "bring them in remembrance of his ways which were in Christ" (1 Cor. iv. 17), or, in other words, to communicate his mind to them on various matters. (Compare also 1 Cor. xvi. 10.) After a brief stay, he wished Timothy to return to him (1 Cor. xvi. 11). That this Erastus was the same who is called (in Rom. xvi. 23) "the chamberlain of the city" (of Corinth) is very doubtful. He is again mentioned in 2 Tim. iv. 20. **but he himself stayed in** (Roman) **Asia for a season**—meaning, in the province (in contrast with "Macedonia," in the previous clause), and at Ephesus, its capital city.

23. And the same time—of Paul's proposed departure, **there arose no small stir about that**

24 For a certain *man* named Demetrius, a silversmith, which made silver
25 shrines for Diana, brought *b*no small gain unto the craftsmen; whom he called together with the workmen of like occupation, and said, Sirs, ye
26 know that by this craft *c*we have our wealth. Moreover ye see and hear, that not alone at Ephesus, but almost throughout all Asia, this Paul hath persuaded and turned away much people, saying that they *d*be
27 no gods which are made with hands: so that not only this our craft is in danger to be set at nought; but also that the temple of the great goddess Diana should be despised, and her magnificence should be destroyed, whom all Asia and the world worshippeth.
28 And when they heard *these sayings*, they were full of wrath, and cried

A. D. 59.

b ch. 16. 16, 19.
c Pro. 15. 2*s*.
1 Tim. 6. 10.
Rev. 18. 16.
d Ps. 115. 4.
Isa. 41. 24.
Isa. 44. 10-20.
Isa. 46. 7.
Jer. 10. 3.
ch. 17. 29.
1 Cor. 8. 4.

(rather, 'the') **way**—(see on ch. ix. 2.) **24. For a certain man named Demetrius, a silversmith, which made silver shrines for** (rather, ' of ') **Diana**—or 'Artemis' (the one the Latin, the other the Greek name of the goddess); the tutelary goddess of the Ephesians. But the great divinity of the Greeks, who was so called, differed in some important respects from the Ephesian Artemis, who was more allied—in her supposed properties—to Astarte and other Oriental divinities of the female sex. These "shrines" or 'temples' were small models of the Ephesian temple and of the shrine or chapel of the goddess—or of the shrine **and statue alone**—which were purchased by visitors as memorials of what they had seen, and were carried about and deposited in houses as a charm. The models of the chapel of *our Lady of Loretto*, and such like, which the Church of Rome systematically encourages, are such a palpable imitation of this heathen practice, that it is no wonder it should be regarded by impartial judges as *Christianity Paganized*, or *Baptized Paganism*. **brought no small gain unto the craftsmen**—the master-artificers. **25. Whom he called together with the workmen of like occupation**—rather, ' with the workmen in that line;' that is, the artizans who worked for masters, including all who manufactured for sale any sort of memorial of the temple or its service: and said, **Sirs, ye know that by this craft we have our wealth. 26. Moreover ye see and hear.** The evidences of this state of things were, it seems, to be seen, and the report of it was in everybody's mouth. **that not alone at Ephesus, but almost throughout all** (Proconsular) **Asia, this Paul hath persuaded and turned away much people** [ἱκανὸν ὄχλον]—' a considerable multitude.' Noble testimony this, from an enemy's mouth, to the vast extent to which idolatry had suffered through Paul's labours, even though we allow for some exaggeration, with the view of exciting the auditors. **saying that they be no gods which are made with hands.** The universal belief of *the people* was that they were gods, though the more intelligent regarded them only as habitations of Deity, and some, probably, as mere aids to devotion. It is exactly so in the Church of Rome. **27. So that not only this our craft** [μέρος]—*lit.*, ' our share' (of the business), **is in danger to be set at nought; but, &c.**—*q.d.*, 'that indeed is a small matter; but there is something far worse.' So the masters of the poor Pythoness put forward the *religious revolution* which Paul was attempting to effect at Philippi, as the sole cause of their zealous alarm, to cloak the self-interest which they felt to be touched by his success (ch. xvi. 19-21). In both cases religious zeal was the hypocritical pretext; self-interest the real moving cause of the opposition made. **but also that the temple of the great goddess Diana should be despised** (' counted as nought '), **and her magnificence should be destroyed, whom**

all Asia and the world worshippeth. (For full particulars on this subject the reader is referred to *Howson*, and to a recent work, entitled, 'Ephesus and the Temple of Diana,' by *E. Falkener*, 1862, from which we give the following summary, and of the former of which we avail ourselves in the sequel of the exposition.) The antiquity of Ephesus is amazing, and its history long, varied, and splendid. Its ruins, if excavated, would, no doubt, richly reward the pains, if even the site of the temple were ascertained. It is still, however, an unexplored mine. The ruins, though principally Grecian, are some of them of older date. The city seems to have been geometrically planned. It contained vast public buildings besides the temple. The Agora was probably above 300 feet square, with a vestibule of at least 400 more. The Gymnasia were probably five in number—one of them not less than 450 by 377 feet in area, while the largest was 925 by 685, occupying 15 acres of ground, or twice the enclosure of the British Museum. The Theatre (*v.* 29) was the largest ever erected, being 660 feet in diameter (40 feet more than the major axis of the Coliseum). Allowing 15 feet to each, it would accommodate 56,700 spectators (whereas Drury Lane Theatre, in London, holds only 3,200, and Covent Garden 2,800). It contained also innumerable temples. But all is now a desert. It is with the temple, however, and its worship that we have here chiefly to do. It was reckoned one of the wonders of the world. It was built about 550 B.C., of pure white marble, and though burned by a fanatic on the night of the birth of Alexander the Great, B.C. 356, was rebuilt with more splendour than before. It was 425 feet long by 220 broad, and the columns, 127 in number, were 60 feet in height, each of them the gift of a king, and thirty-six of them enriched with ornament and colour. It was what the Bank of England is in the modern world, the larger portion of the wealth of Western Asia being stored up in it. It was continually receiving new decorations and additional buildings, statues, and pictures by the most celebrated artists, and kindled unparalleled admiration, enthusiasm, and superstition. *Its very site is now a matter of uncertainty.* The little wooden image of Diana was as primitive and rude as its shrine was sumptuous; not like the *Greek* Diana, in the form of an imposing huntress, but quite Asiatic, in the form of a many-breasted female (emblematic of the manifold ministrations of nature to man), terminating in a shapeless block. Like some other far-famed idols, it was believed to have fallen from heaven (*v.* 35); and models of it were not only sold in immense numbers to private persons, but set up for worship in other cities. What power must have attended the preaching of that one man by whom the death-blow was felt to be given to so gigantic and witching a superstition !

28. And when they heard these sayings, they

142

29 out, saying, ᵉ Great *is* Diana of the Ephesians.   And the whole city was
filled with confusion: and having caught ᶠGaius ᵍ and Aristarchus, men
of Macedonia, Paul's companions in travel, they rushed with one accord
30 into the theatre.   And when Paul would have entered in unto the people,
31 the disciples suffered him not.   And certain of the chief of ʰ Asia, which
were his friends, sent unto him, desiring *him* that he would not adventure
32 himself into the theatre.   Some therefore cried one thing, and some
another: for the assembly was confused; and the more part knew not
33 wherefore they were come together.   And they drew Alexander out of
the multitude, the Jews putting him forward.   And ⁱ Alexander beckoned
34 with the hand, and would have made his defence unto the people.   But
when they knew that he was a Jew, all with one voice about the space of
two hours cried out, Great *is* Diana of the Ephesians.
35   And when the town-clerk had appeased the people, he said, *Ye* men of
Ephesus, what man is there that knoweth not how that the city of the
Ephesians is ¹ a worshipper of the great goddess Diana, and of the *image*
36 which fell down from Jupiter?   Seeing then that these things cannot be

A. D. 59.

ᵉ Jer. 50. 28.
  Hab. 2. 18.
  19.
  Rev. 13. 4.
ᶠ Rom. 16.2?.
  ᵉ Cor. 1. 1ᶜ
ᵍ ch. 20. 4.
  ch 27. 2.
  Col. 4. 10.
  Phile. 24.
ʰ Pro. 16. 7.
  ch. 16. 6.
  1 Pet. 1. 1.
  Rev. 1. 11.
ⁱ ch 12. 17.
  ch. 13. 16.
  ch. 21. 20.
  1 Tim. 1. 20.
  2 Tim. 4. 14.
1 the temple
  keeper.

were full of wrath, and cried out, saying, Great is
Diana of the Ephesians.   This was the civic cry of
a populace so proud of their temple that (as *Strabo*
says) they refused to inscribe on it the name of
Alexander the Great, though he offered them the
whole spoil of his eastern campaign if they would
do it.   29. And the [whole] city (probably "whole"
is not genuine) was filled with confusion: and
having caught Gaius and Aristarchus, men of
Macedonia, Paul's companions in travel—being
disappointed of Paul himself; just as at Thessalonica they laid hands on Jason (ch. xvii. 5, 6).
The fellow-travellers of the apostle here named
are also mentioned in ch. xx. 4; xxvii. 2; Rom.
xvi. 23; 1 Cor. i. 14; and probably in 3 John 1.
If it was in the house of Aquila and Priscilla
(whom Paul left at Ephesus on his first incidental
visit to it, ch. xviii. 19) that the apostle now found
an asylum from the fury of the Ephesian mob,
that would explain what he says of them in Rom.
xvi. 3, 4, that "for his life they laid down their
own necks." they rushed with one accord into
the theatre—a vast pile (see p. 142) whose ruins are
even now a wreck of immense grandeur.   30. And
when Paul would have entered (or 'wished to
enter') in unto the people—'the *demos*;' that is,
the people met in public assembly; with noble forgetfulness of self.   the disciples suffered him not
[οὐκ εἴων]—the *tense* implying, perhaps, that they
had to use some effort, and with difficulty prevented him.   31. And certain of the chief of Asia,
which were his friends [τ. 'Ασιαρχῶν]—'And some
even of the Asiarchs, who were friendly to him.'
These Asiarchs were wealthy and distinguished
citizens of the principal towns of the Asian province, chosen annually, and ten of whom were
selected by the Proconsul to preside over the
games celebrated in the month of May (the same
month which Romanism dedicates to *the Virgin*).
It was an office of the highest honour, and greatly
coveted.   Certain of these, it seems, were favourably inclined to the Gospel—at least were Paul's
"friends"—and knowing the passions of an Ephesian mob, excited during the festivals, sent unto
him, desiring ('beseeching') him that he would
not adventure himself into the theatre.   32.
Some therefore cried one thing, and some
another: for the assembly was confused; and
the more part knew not wherefore they were
come together.   33. And they drew Alexander
out of the multitude, the Jews putting him
forward—rather, 'And some of the multitude
urged forward Alexander, the Jews thrusting him
143

forward.'   As the blame of such a tumult would
naturally be thrown upon the Jews, who were
regarded by the Romans as the authors of all
religious disturbances, they seem to have put
forward this man to clear themselves of all responsibility for the riot.   (*Bengel's* conjecture, that this
was Alexander the coppersmith, 2 Tim. iv. 14, has
little to support it.)   And Alexander beckoned
with the hand (cf. ch. xiii. 16; xxi. 40), and would
have made his defence—'wished to speak in
defence,' unto the people.   34. But when they
knew ['Επιγνόντες δὲ]—' But when they came to
know' that he was a Jew, all with one voice
about the space of two hours cried out—'one
shout arose from them all, for about two hours,
crying out,' Great is Diana of the Ephesians.
The very appearance of a Jew had the opposite
effect to that intended.   To prevent him obtaining
a hearing, they drowned his voice in one tumultuous shout in honour of their goddess, which rose
to such frantic enthusiasm as took two hours to
exhaust itself.

35. And when the town-clerk [ὁ γραμματεὺς]
—the keeper of the public archives, and a magistrate of great authority, had appeased the
people—' calmed,' or 'stilled the multitude,'
which the very presence of such an officer would
go far to do, he said, Ye men of Ephesus, what
man is there that knoweth not how that the
city of the Ephesians is a worshipper [νεωκόρον]—
lit., 'the *neocoros*,' or 'warden.'   The word means
'temple-sweeper,' then 'temple-guardian.'   Thirteen cities of Asia had an interest in the temple;
but Ephesus was honoured with the charge of it.
(In like manner, as *Webster and Wilkinson* remark,
various cities have claimed this title with reference to the *Virgin*, or certain saints.)   of the
great goddess Diana, and of the image which fell
down from Jupiter [Διοπετοῦς]—'of the Jove-dropt,'
or 'sky-dropt' [image].   See on *v.* 27.   'Scarcely less
veneration (says *Humphry*) is paid at the present
day to the clay miracle-working images of the Virgin at Einsiedeln in Switzerland, Mariazell in
Styria, &c.—the works, probably, of early Byzantine
or Oriental artists.   (*Raoul-Rochette*, in *Lord
Lyndsay* on Christian Art, i. 78.)   A still closer
analogy to the image falling from Jupiter may
perhaps be found in the traditional likenesses of
Christ, which, as were pretended, were "not made
with hands" [ἀχειροποίηται], and by means of
which the Christian Church was first reconciled
to the reception and veneration of images.   (See
Gibbon, ch. xlix., and *Gretser's* treatise in defence

37 spoken against, ye ought to be quiet, and to do nothing rashly. For ye have brought hither these men, which are neither robbers of churches,
38 nor yet blasphemers of your goddess. Wherefore if Demetrius, and the craftsmen which are with him, have a matter against any man, [2] the law
39 is open, and there are deputies: let them implead one another. But if ye enquire any thing concerning other matters, it shall be determined in
40 a [3] lawful assembly. For we are in danger to be called in question for this day's *j* uproar, there being no cause whereby we may give an account
41 of this concourse. And *k* when he had thus spoken, he *l* dismissed the assembly.

A. D. 59.

[2] Or, the court days are kept.

[3] Or, ordinary.

j 1 Ki. 1. 41.
Matt. 26. 5.

k Pro. 15. 1.
Eccl. 9. 17.

i Ps. 65. 7.
2 Cor. 1. 8,
10.

of them, entitled, "De Imaginibus non Manufactis," 1625.)' **36. Seeing then that these things cannot be spoken against, ye ought to be quiet, and to do nothing rashly.** Standing on purely legal ground, he urges that such was notoriously the constitution and fixed character of the city, with which its very existence was all but bound up; 'And did they suppose that all this was going to be overturned by a set of itinerant orators? Ridiculous! What did they mean, then, by raising such a stir?' **37. For ye have brought hither these men, which are neither robbers of churches** [ἱεροσύλους]—rather, 'temple-plunderers;' that is, sacrilegious persons (or 'revilers'), **nor yet blasphemers of your goddess.** This is a remarkable testimony, showing that the apostle had, in preaching against idolatry, studiously avoided (as at Athens) insulting the feelings of those whom he addressed—a lesson this to missionaries and ministers in general. **38. Wherefore if Demetrius, and the craftsmen which are with him, have a matter** (of complaint) **against any man, the law is open, and there are deputies** [ἀγοραῖοι ἄγονται καὶ ἀνθύπατοι εἰσὶν]—rather, 'court-days are being holden, and there are proconsuls' (see on ch. xiii. 7); meaning, probably, not that there were more than one proconsul there, but that he was there, with his council, as a court of appeal. **let them implead one another.** 39. **But if ye enquire** [ἐπιζητεῖτε]—'are in pursuit of' **anything concerning other matters** [τι περὶ ἑτέρων]—but probably the true reading is, 'if ye are seeking anything further,' [τι περαιτέρω—which, though supported only by B and about fifteen cursives, with one MS. of the Vulgate (*ulterius*), has internal evidence decidedly in its favour, and is adopted by *Lachm.*, *Tisch.*, and *Treg.*]; **it shall be determined in a** ('in the') **lawful assembly. 40. For we** (the public authorities) **are in danger to be called in question**—'of being impeached' by our superiors **for** ('about') **this day's uproar, there being no cause whereby** ('no ground on which') **we may give an account of this concourse. 41. And when he had thus spoken, he dismissed the assembly.**

Remarks.—1. As the necessity under which Paul felt himself to transfer his labours from the synagogue to a separate place of meeting, first at Corinth and next at Ephesus, was one of the steps by which his own mind and those of his Jewish coadjutors were gradually loosened from the exclusiveness of the ancient economy, so unforeseen and resistless events in Providence have from age to age been more effectual than all arguments would have been without them, in setting the faithful servants of Christ free from ancestral prejudices; enabling them to discover, and emboldening them to avail themselves of the liberty wherewith Christ hath made them free. Had the disciples who hung about Jerusalem not been all scattered abroad, with the exception of the apostles, by the persecution which arose after the martyrdom of Stephen, they had probably never preached even to their Jewish brethren; still less would those

who found themselves in the midst of heathens at Antioch have preached to such the unsearchable riches of Christ, and reared up there a beautiful church of uncircumcised Gentiles. *Events* forced upon them a course of action which, though at first they might go into with some hesitation, they would afterwards feel to have been their privilege from the first. So at the time of the glorious Reformation, almost every step was rather forced on than deliberately chosen; so it has been in some events of our own day; and so, we doubt not, it will yet be, in the ecclesiastical struggles which wise men see to be approaching. Thus it is that men are gradually prepared for occupying positions and discharging duties from which they would shrink, and for which they might prove unqualified, were they called to them all at once, and by the mere force of argument. 2. 'In the silversmith, Demetrius, and his companions (says *Gerok*) we recognize—*first*, The abject slaves of business, who, in the pursuit of temporal gain, have lost all regard for eternity; *next*, the blind adherents of established customs, who, from every fresh movement of the Spirit, fear the disturbance of their ease, and, indeed, the destruction of the world; *thirdly*, the self-satisfied priests of the Beautiful, who, in idolatrous veneration for nature and art, *acknowledge no consciousness of sin, and no need of grace.* Compare *Goethe's* poem, 'Great is Diana of the Ephesians,' and his confession in his correspondence with Jacobi— 'I am even now one of the Ephesian silversmiths, who has spent his whole life in the contemplation and admiration and adoration of the wonderful temple of the goddess (Nature), and in imitation of her mysterious forms; and in whom it cannot possibly stir up an agreeable feeling, if any apostle will obtrude another and a formless God' [that is, a living and invisible Author of Nature]; *fourthly,* the hypocritical zealots for the Church and Religion, who, with their apparent zeal for God's house, have only their own interest in view.' 3. The cry, "Great is Diana of the Ephesians," suggests also to *Gerok* the following striking practical thoughts :—'(1.) Great and glorious is the kingdom of nature; but we find our true home and our right place only in the Kingdom of Grace. (2.) Great and beautiful are the works of the human mind in art and science; but without the discipline of the Divine Spirit and the light of the Christian Revelation, art and science fall into the grossest error. (3.) Great and strong is the power of the human will; but with the best will, we can render to the holy God no pure service and build no worthy temple, if His Spirit cleanse not our hearts into His sanctuary and perfect His strength in our weakness. (4.) Great and remarkable are the histories of earthly kingdoms (as Greece and Rome); but the Cross-kingdom of Jesus Christ triumphs over all. Ephesus lies in ruins, and the temple of Diana in ashes; but the gates of hell shall not prevail against the Church of Christ.' 4. When we think with what difficulty

20 AND after the uproar was ceased, Paul called unto *him* the disciples,
2 and embraced *them*, and ^adeparted for to go into Macedonia. And when
   he had gone over those parts, and had given them much exhortation, he
3 came into Greece, and *there* abode three months. And when ^bthe Jews

A. D. 59.
CHAP. 20.
a 1 Cor. 16. 5.
  2 Cor. 7. 5.
b 2 Cor.11.26.

complicated systems of religious fraud and superstition, which have for ages held peoples in abject bondage and fear, are made to lose their hold, one cannot but wonder at the rapid success of the Gospel in the hands of Paul at Ephesus, not only in the explosion of the 'curious arts' there practised, but even in shaking to its centre the magnificent worship of the witching temple, which it afterwards entirely extinguished. And if this Gospel is still the power of God unto salvation to every one that believeth, and the Holy Ghost, at Pentecost sent down from heaven, is not withdrawn, should not the Church of God—in now sending forth men of God in the spirit of Paul, not to blaspheme, but to assail the gigantic and hoary superstitions which still hold sway over millions of our race—expect the like results? 5. What discerning mind can fail to see in the *principles* which lie at the foundation of Romish superstition the same idolatrous and irrational character which distinguished the worship of the Ephesian temple; and opposed as these are fundamentally to those of the New Testament, who does not perceive that the growth of this system is the growth of all that is antichristian, that its existence is the blot of Christendom, and that its overthrow—root and branch—is essential to the triumph of the kingdom of God?

CHAP. XX. 1-17. PAUL FULFILS HIS PURPOSE OF PROCEEDING AGAIN TO MACEDONIA AND GREECE —RETURNING THENCE, ON HIS ROUTE FOR JERUSALEM, HE REVISITS PHILIPPI AND TROAS, AND MEETS THE ELDERS OF EPHESUS AT MILETUS. *Leaving Ephesus, the apostle proceeds through Macedonia and Greece, staying three months at Corinth—Being prevented by plots against his life from proceeding by sea to Syria, on his route for Jerusalem, he returns, as he came, through Greece and Macedonia, taking ship from Philippi to Troas* (1-5). This section of the apostle's life, though peculiarly rich in matter, is related with great brevity in the History. Its details must be culled from his own Epistles. 1. **And after the uproar was ceased, Paul called unto him the disciples, and embraced them, and departed**—not driven out, but of deliberate purpose, and (as would appear from 1 Cor. xvi. 8) not till after Pentecost; **for to go into Macedonia**—in pursuance of the *first* part of his plan, as laid down in ch. xix. 21. From his Epistles we gather the following most interesting particulars:—*First,* That, as might be expected from its position on the coast (see on ch. xvi. 8), he revisited Troas; and whereas on his former visit he appears to have done no missionary work there, he now went there expressly "to preach Christ's Gospel," and found 'a door opened unto him of the Lord' (Jesus) (2 Cor. ii. 12), which he entered so effectually as to lay the foundation of a church there (as appears from *vv.* 6, 7, below). *Secondly,* That he would have remained longer there, but for his uneasiness at the non-arrival of Titus, whom he had despatched to Corinth to finish the collection for the poor saints at Jerusalem, which Paul wished to take with him (1 Cor. xvi. 1, 2; 2 Cor. viii. 6); but still more, that he might bring him word what effect his first Epistle to that church had produced. *Thirdly,* That in this state of mind, afraid of something wrong, he "took leave" of the brethren at Troas, and went from thence into Macedonia. No doubt it was the city of PHILIPPI that he came to—landing at

Neapolis, its seaport (see on ch. xvi. 11, 12)—as appears by comparing 2 Cor. xi. 9, where "Macedonia" is named, with Phil. iv. 15, where it appears that Philippi is meant. Here he found the brethren, whom he had left on his former visit in circumstances of such deep interest, a consolidated and thriving church, generous and warmly attached to their father in Christ, under the superintendence, probably, of our historian, "the beloved physician" (see on ch. xvi. 40). All that is said by our historian of this Macedonian visit is contained in the second verse of this chapter,—that he "went over those parts, and gave them much exhortation." *Fourthly,* Titus not having reached Philippi so soon as the apostle, "his flesh had no rest, but he was troubled on every side: without were fightings, and within were fears" (2 Cor. vii. 5). *Fifthly,* At length Titus arrived, to the joy of the apostle, the bearer of better tidings from Corinth than he had dared to expect (2 Cor. vii. 6, 13), but chequered by painful intelligence of the efforts of a hostile party to undermine his apostolic reputation there (2 Cor. xi. &c.) *Sixthly,* Under the mixed feelings which this produced, he wrote (from Macedonia, and probably Philippi) his SECOND EPISTLE TO THE CORINTHIANS (see Introduction to that Epistle), despatching Titus with it, and along with him two other unnamed deputies, expressly chosen to take up and bring their collection for the poor saints at Jerusalem, and to whom he bears the beautiful testimony, that they were "the glory of Christ" (2 Cor. viii. 22, 23). *Seventhly,* It must have been at this time that he penetrated as far as to the confines of "Illyricum," lying along the shores of the Adriatic (Rom. xv. 19). He would naturally wish that his second Letter to the Corinthians should have some time to produce its proper effect ere he revisited them, and this would appear a convenient opportunity for a north-western circuit, which would enable him to pay a passing visit to the churches at Thessalonica and Bercœ, though of this we have no record. On his way southward to Greece, he would preach the Gospel in the intermediate regions of Epirus, Thessaly, and Bœotia (see Rom. xv. 19), though of this we have no record. (For the collection and arrangement of these particulars we are chiefly indebted to *Howson*.) 2. **And when he had gone over those parts, and had given them much exhortation, he came into Greece**—meaning Greece at large. This fulfilled the *second* part of the apostle's plan, as laid down in ch. xix. 21, where "Achaia," which he "purposed to pass through," means the same as "Greece" here; the latter word being the old name, and the former the then official name of the whole country. 3. **And there abode three months.** Though the province only is mentioned, it is evidently the city of CORINTH that is meant, just as in *v.* 1 the province of "Macedonia" meant the city of Philippi. Some rough work he anticipated on his arrival at Corinth (2 Cor. x. 1-8, 11; xiii. 1-10), though he had reason to expect satisfaction on the whole; and as we know there were other churches in Achaia besides that at Corinth (2 Cor. i. 1; xi. 10), he would have time enough to pay them all a brief visit during the three months of his stay there. This period was rendered further memorable by the despatch of the EPISTLE TO THE ROMANS, written during his stay at Corinth, and sent by "Phœbe, a servant (or 'deaconess') of the

145

laid wait for him, as he was about to sail into Syria, he purposed to
4 return through Macedonia. And there accompanied him into Asia,
Sopater of Berea; and of the Thessalonians, *c*Aristarchus and Secundus;
*d*and Gaius of Derbe, *e*and Timotheus; and of Asia, *f*Tychicus and
5, *g*Trophimus. These going before tarried for us at Troas. And we sailed
6 away from Philippi after the *h*days of unleavened bread, and came unto
them *i*to Troas in five days; where we abode seven days.
7 And upon *j*the first *day* of the week, when the disciples came together
*k*to break bread, Paul preached unto them, ready to depart on the

A. D. 60.

c ch. 27. 2.
d ch. 19. 29.
e ch. 16. 1.
f Eph. 6. 21.
g ch. 21. 29.
2 Tim. 4.20.
h Ex. 12. 14.
i ch. 16. 8.
j John 20. 1.
k ch. 2. 42.

church at Cenchreæ (see on ch. xviii. 3), a lady apparently of some standing and substance, who was going thither on private business, (see on Rom. xvi. 1, and Introduction to Epistle to Rom.) **And when the Jews laid wait for him, as he was about to sail into Syria.** He had intended to embark—probably at Cenchreæ, the eastern harbour of Corinth—for Palestine, on his route to Jerusalem; thus making out the *third* part of his plan, as laid down in ch. xix. 21; but having detected some conspiracy against his life by his unrelenting Jewish adversaries—as at Damascus (ch. ix. 22-25), and at Jerusalem (ch. ix. 29, 30)—he changed his plan, and so **he purposed** (or 'resolved') **to return** (as he had come) **through Macedonia.** As he was never more to return to Corinth, this route would bring him, for the last time, face to face with the attached disciples of *Berœa, Thessalonica,* and *Philippi.* But this land journey consumed so much more time than the voyage originally contemplated, that the apostle had to hasten at last in order to reach Jerusalem at the desired time (*v.* 16). **4. And there accompanied him into Asia** [ἄχρι τ. 'Α.]—'as far as Asia.' The natural inference from this expression would be, that some, at least, of the seven persons about to be named went no further than the Asian province; but since we know that some of them went with him all the way to Jerusalem, the probability is that they all did so, as representatives to the mother-church at Jerusalem of uncircumcised believers, gathered from the chief regions of the apostle's missionary labours among the heathen, and bearers of the collection from all the Gentile churches to the poor saints of the circumcision. **Sopater of Berea.** The true reading appears to be 'Sopater, son of Pyrrhus' (so *Lachm., Tisch.,* and *Treg.*) There is no sufficient reason for supposing that this person's father is here mentioned to distinguish him from Sosipater (in ch. xvi. 21), which is but a fuller form of the same word. It seems quite as probable that they were the same person. **and of the Thessalonians, Aristarchus** —(see on ch. xix. 29.) His name re-appears in ch. xxvii. 2; Col. iv. 10; Philem. 24. **and Secundus** —of whom nothing else is known; **and Gaius of Derbe.** (This is merely the Latin name 'Caius,' written in the Greek form.) Since we read of a Gaius of Macedonia (ch. xix. 29), and here of a Gaius of Derbe, of a Gaius of Corinth, who was the apostle's "host" there (Rom. xvi. 23), and of a Gaius to whom the beloved disciple addressed his Third Epistle—in which he calls him "his well-beloved Gaius, whom he loved in the truth" (3 John 1)—it is a question of some interest whether we have any means of reasonable conjecture as to the identity or difference of some or all of these persons. We have only internal evidence to guide us; and considering the different regions in which the residence in each case is fixed, and the extreme commonness of the name 'Caius,' it seems better (though at one time we judged otherwise) to conclude that more than one such at least is meant in the four places referred to; and this is
146

the general opinion. **and Timotheus.** The phrase "of Derbe," in the previous clause, is evidently meant of Gaius alone, and not intended to include Timotheus—whose designation was not here required after what had been said of him in ch. xvi. **and of** (the province of) **Asia, Tychicus, and Trophimus.** As Trophimus is expressly said to have been an Ephesian (ch. xxi. 29), the probability is that Tychicus was so also. They seem to have put themselves from this time forward at the apostle's disposal, and to have been to the very last a great comfort to him (see Eph. vi. 21, 22; Col. iv. 7; ch. xxi. 29; 2 Tim. iv. 12, 20). We have here enumerated seven companions of the apostle in his final journey to Jerusalem. All of them were Gentile believers. Three were Europeans—Sopater, Aristarchus, and Secundus; and four were Asiatics—Gaius, Timotheus, Tychicus, and Trophimus. No doubt they were deputed by their respective churches, with all who were associated with them, to carry their contributions for the poor Jewish disciples of Palestine. From the next verse we learn that our historian was now of the party; and, although he is not named (probably as having originally come from Jerusalem, to which the others were strangers), Silas must have been of it too, as Paul's companion on this third missionary journey. **5. These going before** (perhaps to announce and prepare for the apostle's coming) **tarried for us at Troas.** It will be observed, from the resumption of the first person plural "us," that our historian had now rejoined the apostle, and his presence is indicated by a minuter specification of time and other particulars. Having been left at Philippi (see on ch. xvi. 40), he would now bring on the collection of that church. **6. And we sailed away from Philippi after the days of unleavened bread**—(that is, after the Passover.) Comparing this with 1 Cor. xvi. 8, we gather that the "three months" spent at Corinth (*v.* 3) were the winter months. **and came unto them to Troas in five days**—(see, for the time now taken, on ch. xvi. 11.) This was the apostle's third and last visit to Troas. **where we abode seven days** —that is, arriving on a Monday, they stayed over the next Jewish Sabbath and the Lord's day following; occupying themselves, doubtless, in refreshing and strengthening fellowship with the brethren during the interval. The vivid style of one who was himself present will here be observed. No doubt our historian kept a journal, more or less full, of which he now availed himself.
Meeting with the disciples at Troas—Paul's preaching protracted till midnight—Eutychus restored to life—The communion, the repast, and the parting at break of day (7-12). **7. And upon the first day of the week, when the disciples came together** —rather, 'when we had come together,' according to the much better supported reading [ἡμῶν, for τ. μαθητων], **to break bread.** This, when compared with 1 Cor. xvi. 2, and other similar allusions, plainly indicates that the Christian observance of the first day of the week—afterwards emphatically termed 'The Lord's Day'—was already a fixed

8 morrow; and continued his speech until midnight. And there were
many lights *l* in the upper chamber, where they were gathered together.
9 And there sat in a window a certain young man named Eutychus, being
fallen into a deep sleep: and as Paul was long preaching he sunk down
with sleep, and fell down from the third loft, and was taken up dead.
10 And Paul went down, and *m* fell on him, and embracing *him* said,
11 *n* Trouble not yourselves; for his life is in him. When he therefore was
come up again, and had broken bread, and eaten, and talked a long
12 while, even till break of day, so he departed. And they brought the
young man alive, and *o* were not a little comforted.
13 And we went before to ship, and sailed unto Assos, there intending to
take in Paul: for so had he appointed, *p* minding himself to go afoot.
14 And when he met with us at Assos, we took him in, and came to Mity-
15 lene. And we sailed thence, and came the next *day* over against Chios;
and the next *day* we arrived at Samos, and tarried at Trogyllium; and

A. D. 60.

l Luke 22 12.
ch. 1. 13.
m 1 Ki. 17. 21.
2 Ki. 4. 34.
n Matt. 9. 24.
Mark 5. 39.
Luke 7. 13.
John 11. 40.
ch. 9. 40.
o Isa. 40. 1.
Eph. 6. 22.
1 Thes. 3. 2.
1 Thes. 4. 18.
1 Thes. 5. 11, 14.
2 Thes. 2. 16.
p Mark 1. 35.

practice of the churches. **Paul preached** [διελέ-γετο]—or 'discoursed,' the *tense* implying continued action; 'kept discoursing' **unto them, ready to depart on the morrow; and continued his speech until midnight. 8. And there were many lights in the upper chamber.** This is not to be regarded as a mere piece of graphic detail by an eye-witness (as *Howson* and *Hackett* regard it), but rather as increasing the heat and contributing to drowsiness (as suggested by *Webster and Wilkinson*); and the next clause seems to confirm this: **where they were gathered together**—but the true reading beyond doubt is, 'where we were gathered together' [ἦσαν of the received text is supported only by some cursives and later writers; all the Uncials have ἦμεν]. **9. And there sat in a window** [ἐπὶ τῆς θυρίδος]—rather, 'the window;' that is, the window-seat or recess (cf. 2 Cor. xi. 33)—**a certain young man named Eutychus, being fallen into a deep sleep: and as Paul was long preaching he sunk down with sleep, and fell down from the third loft** (or 'storey'). The window projected (according to the side of the room where it was situated) either over the street or over the interior court; so that in either case he fell on the hard earth or pavement below. **and was taken up dead.** That *de Wette* should take this to mean, 'taken up for dead,' or 'apparently dead,' and appeal to the words of *v.* 10, "Trouble not yourselves, *for his life is in him*"—as if that meant, 'his life is still in him,' or 'he is but apparently dead'—need surprise no one; but that *Olshausen* should so understand the words, is indeed surprising. The whole narrative, read in its natural sense, conveys the impression that the youth was taken up literally "dead." **10. And Paul went down, and fell on him**—just as Elijah did upon the dead son of the woman of Sarepta (1 Ki. xvii. 21), and Elisha upon the dead son of the Shunammite (2 Ki. iv. 34)—a strong confirmation of the natural sense of the statement that Eutychus was taken up quite dead. **and embracing him said, Trouble not yourselves; for his life is in him**—not, 'is still in him,' as if never out; but in the same sense in which our Lord said of Jairus' dead daughter, "Why make ye this ado, and weep? the damsel is not dead, but sleepeth" (Mark v. 39) It was in him when Paul spoke, as having been restored to him, like the lives of the Zarephite's and Shunammite's sons—no otherwise. (But see further on *v.* 12.) **11. When he therefore was come up again, and had broken bread, and eaten**—*lit.*, 'and had broken the bread [τὸν ἄρτον appears to be the true reading] and tasted' [γευσάμενος]. The former expression seems plainly to denote the

celebration of the Lord's Supper; their intention to do so being expressed in *v.* 7, but their actually doing it nowhere if not here. The latter expression, 'and had tasted,' is nowhere used of the celebration of the Supper, whereas in ch. x. 10 (*Gr.*) it is applied to taking a common meal; and since only the apostle himself is here said to have tasted, it must be meant to denote his taking some refreshment before setting out on his long foot-journey, which, as he had spent the whole night preaching and talking, would be indispensable to him. **and talked a long while, even till break of day, so he departed.** How life-like is this record of dear Christian fellowship—as free and gladsome as, in such circumstances, it must have been peculiarly solemn! See Eccl. ix. 7. **12. And they brought the young man alive.** There is a manifestly designed contrast between the statement 'taken up dead' (*v.* 9) and 'brought alive' here, which leaves no reasonable ground to doubt that it was an extinct life which had been restored. and **were not a little comforted** [παρεκλήθησαν]—including the addditional idea of 'confirmed in the faith.'

Continuing his route to Jerusalem, he reaches Miletus, whence he sends for the elders of Ephesus (13-17). **13. And we went before to ship, and sailed unto Assos, there intending to take in Paul: for so had he appointed, minding himself to go afoot** [πεζεύειν]—to go by land (see on Mark vi. 33). In sailing southward from Troas to Assos, one has to round Cape Lectum, and keeping due east, to run along the northern shore of the Gulf of Adramyttium, on which it lies. This is a sail of nearly forty miles; whereas by land, cutting right across in a south-easterly direction, from sea to sea, by that excellent Roman road which then existed, the distance was scarcely more than half. The one way Paul wished his companions to take, while he himself—longing perhaps to enjoy a period of solitude—took the other, joining the ship by appointment at Assos. **14. And when he met with us at Assos, we took him in, and came to Mitylene**—the capital of the beautiful and classical island of Lesbos, which lies opposite the eastern shore of the Ægean Sea, about thirty miles south of Assos, in whose harbour they seem to have lain for the night. **15. And we sailed thence, and came the next day over against Chios**—now Scio: one of the most beautiful of those islands between which and the coast the sail is so charming. They appear not to have touched at it. **and the next day we arrived at** [παρεβάλομεν εἰς]—rather (as *Humphry* renders it) 'pushed across' **Samos**—another island coming quite close to the mainland, and about as far south of Chios

147

16 the next *day* we came to Miletus. For Paul had determined to sail by Ephesus, because he would not spend the time in Asia: for ^qhe hasted, if it were possible for him, ^rto be at Jerusalem ^sthe day of Pentecost.

17 And from Miletus he sent to Ephesus, and called the ^telders of the

18 church. And when they were come to him, he said unto them, Ye know, ^ufrom the first day that I came into Asia, after what manner I have been

19 with you at all seasons, serving the Lord with all humility of mind, and

A. D. 60.

^q ch. 18. 21.
ch. 19. 21.
ch. 21. 4,
12.
^r ch. 24. 17.
^s ch. 2. 1.
1 Cor. 16. 8.
^t 1 Tim 4.14
^u ch. 18. 19.

as it is south of Lesbos ; **and tarried at Trogyllium**—an anchorage on the projecting mainland, not more than a mile from the southern extremity of the island of Samos. **and the next day we came to Miletus**—on the mainland, the ancient capital of Ionia, near the mouth of the Mæander. **16. For Paul had determined to sail by** [παραπλεῦσαι τὴν Ἐφ.]—'to sail past' **Ephesus.** He was right opposite to it when approaching Chios. **because, &c.** 'It appears (as *Humphry* remarks) from this, and from *v.* 13, that in the voyage from Philippi to Patara (ch. xxi. 1), St. Paul was able to direct his own course, having perhaps hired a small coasting vessel :' at Patara he meets with a merchant-ship, in which he is conveyed across the sea to Tyre ; **because he would not spend the time** [ὅπως μὴ γένηται αὐτῷ χρονοτριβῆσαι]— 'that he might not have to spend time,' **in Asia**—the Asian province, of which Ephesus was the chief city: **for he hasted, if it were possible for him, to be at Jerusalem the day of Pentecost**—as a suitable season for giving in the great collection from all the Western churches, for keeping the feast, and for clearing his apostolic position with the church, then represented in large number at Jerusalem. The words imply that there was considerable ground to doubt if he would attain this object—for more than three of the seven weeks from Passover to Pentecost had already expired—and they are inserted evidently to explain why he did not once more visit Ephesus.

17. And from Miletus he sent to Ephesus, and called the elders of the church. As he was now some forty miles south of Ephesus, we might think that more time would be lost by sending thus far for the elders to come to him, than by going at once to Ephesus itself, when so near it. But if unfavourable winds and stormy weather had overtaken them, his object could not have been attained, and perhaps he was unwilling to run the risk of detention at Ephesus by the state of the church and other causes. It will be observed that those here called "elders" or 'presbyters' [πρεσβύτεροι] are in' *v.* 28 called "overseers" or 'bishops;' but see the note there.

Remarks.—1. In the light of the particulars enumerated by us at the outset of this Section, how intense appears the apostle's activity in the diffusion of the Gospel, and how tremulous his anxiety lest the converts gained, and the churches formed by him should from any cause be hindered in their Christian progress, or poisoned by the enemies of the truth ! No wonder that he stamped his noble impress so deeply upon the early churches, as his writings have done permanently upon all Christendom. 2. It is a theory of the Tübingen school of criticism, and of some other too liberal critics, that what are called the "We" passages in the Acts—that is, all the portions of that book in which the writer uses the first person plural, " we " and " us "—were written by *Timothy.* Among other proofs of the untenableness of this position, this has been noticed as one, that after Timothy had been mentioned by the historian as one of seven companions who accompanied the apostle from Macedonia (*v.* 4), he says, "These (seven, including Timotheus) going before tarried for *us* at Troas " (*v.* 5); clearly showing that Timotheus could not have been one of the party tarried for, and could not have been the penman of this statement. 3. The first explicit intimation that the apostles taught the Christians to observe the first day of the week, as a day for the celebration of public worship and the participation of the Lord's Supper, is in this Section, where it is expressly said that having stayed "seven days" at Troas, the apostle and his party met the Christians "on the first day of the week;" clearly implying that they awaited the return of that as the sacred day for this purpose. 'And with this (says *Lechler*) the circumstance strikingly agrees, that the observance of the Sunday is first mentioned in a congregation of *Gentile* Christians, since, from the nature of the case, the custom would be introduced earlier and more easily among Gentile than among Jewish Christian congregations.' We are very far, however, from agreeing with *Lechler* as to the light in which this institution is to be regarded by the Church. 4. The length of the apostle's discourse on this occasion, and the protracting of the meeting until break of day, while they are no excuse for lengthened services and protracted night-meetings *as a rule*, do justify both—if justification were needed—in peculiar circumstances ; and those who condemn indiscriminately all religious services,which deviate greatly from the usual length, the usual seasons, and the usual modes —though occasioned by purely temporary circumstances, conducted in other respects unexceptionably, distinguished by nothing so much as the exaltation of Christ, and resulting in manifest and remarkable blessing—show that they set more store by the means than the end, and have little of the spirit of the great apostle, who himself acted on the maxim which he prescribed to Timothy, "in season, *out of season* " (2 Tim. iv. 2). See on Matt. iv. 12-23, Remark 3, p. 23.

18-38.—PAUL'S ADDRESS TO THE ELDERS OF EPHESUS—THE AFFECTING PARTING. 'The evidence furnished by this speech (says *Alford* excellently), as to the literal report in the Acts of the words spoken by Paul, is most important. It is a treasure-house of words, idioms, and sentiments peculiarly belonging to the apostle himself.' But this hinders not *Baur* and his Tübingen followers from insisting that it bears every mark of having been composed by the writer. The address consists of three parts : a retrospect of the past, *vv.* 18-21; a glance into the future, *vv.* 22-27; and counsels to the Ephesian presbyters, 28-35.

1. *Retrospect of the past* (18-21). **18 And when they were come to him, he said unto them, Ye know, from the first day that I came into Asia, after what manner I have been with you at all seasons**—appealing to themselves as witnesses of the Christian integrity and fidelity of his whole official intercourse with them. **19. Serving the Lord,** [δουλεύων τῷ K.] The word here used (as *Alford* notes) is employed six times by our

with many tears, and temptations, which befell me by the lying in wait
20 of the Jews: *and* how I kept back nothing that was profitable *unto you*,
but have showed you, and have taught you publicly, and from house to
21 house, testifying °both to the Jews, and also to the Greeks, °repentance
22 toward God, and faith toward our Lord Jesus Christ. And now, behold,
°I go bound in the spirit unto Jerusalem, not knowing the things
23 that shall befall me there: save that °the Holy Ghost witnesseth in
24 every city, saying that bonds and afflictions ¹abide me. But °none of
these things move me, neither count I my life dear unto myself, so °that
I might finish my course with joy, and °the ministry which °I have re-
25 ceived of the Lord Jesus, to testify the gospel of the grace of God. And

A. D. 60
° ch. 18. 6.
° Mark 1. 15.
ch. 2. 38.
° ch. 19. 21.
° ch. 21. 4, 11.
1 Thes. 3. 3.
1 Or, wait
for me.
° Rom. 8. 35.
2 Cor. 4. 16.
° 2 Tim. 4. 7.
° ch. 1. 17.
° Gal. 1. 1.

apostle, but by no other New Testament writer (though twice it occurs in our Lord's expression, "Ye cannot serve God and mammon," Matt. vi. 24; Luke xvi. 13). **with all humility of mind, and with [many] tears.** The bracketed word "many" [πολλῶν] is evidently a later addition [אABDE wanting it, with the Vulgate, &c., while those which have it are, with the exception of C, and the *Peshito Syriac*, of inferior weight]. **and temptations** (or 'trials"), **which befell me by the lying in wait**' (or 'the plots') **of the Jews.** Self-exaltation was unknown to him; and ease of mind: He "sowed in tears," from anxieties both on account of the converts for whom he "travailed in birth," and of the Jews, whose bitter hostility was perpetually plotting against him, interrupting his work, and endangering his life. **20. And how I kept back** (timidly withheld from fear of consequences) **nothing that was profitable [unto you**—edification only dictating what he should communicate and what withhold; **but have showed you, and have taught you publicly, and from house to house.** 'Did an *apostle* (asks *Bengel* whose functions were of so wide a range not feel satisfied without private as well as public ministrations — how then should *pastors* act?' **21. Testifying** [Διαμαρτυρόμενος]—the compound word implying the 'thorough,' complete character of the testimony, **both to the Jews, and also to the Greeks**—better, 'both to Jews and Greeks,' who, lying under a common malady, are recoverable only by a common treatment, **repentance toward God, and faith toward our Lord Jesus Christ.** *Bengel* and some other critics would restrict the word "repentance" here to the change "toward God," which the *Gentiles* were required to undergo, and "faith toward our Lord Jesus Christ," to the change in their view of Him required of the *Jews.* But the majority of the best critics understand both terms—and with justice—to describe the two-fold change which passes upon every one who comes under the saving power of the Gospel, whether Jew or Gentile. In this view of the words, "REPENTANCE" denotes that state of the soul which arises from a discovery of its contrariety to the righteous demands of the Divine law. This is said to be "*toward God*," because seeing Him to be the Party dishonoured by sin, it feels all its acknowledgments and compunctions to be properly due to Him as the Great Lawgiver, and directs them to Him accordingly; condemning, humbling itself, and grieving before Him, looking also to Him as its only Hope of deliverance. "FAITH" is said to be "*toward our Lord Jesus Christ*," because, in the frame of mind just described it eagerly credits the testimony of relief Divinely provided in Christ, gladly embraces the overtures of reconciliation in Him, and directs all its expectations of salvation, from its first stage to its last, to Him as the one appointed Medium of all grace from God to a sinful world.

Thus we have here a brief summary of all Gospel preaching. And it is easy to see why Repentance is here put before Faith; for the former must of necessity precede the latter. There *is*, indeed, a repentance subsequent to faith, the fruit of felt pardon and restoration—that which drew the tears with which the Saviour's feet were once so copiously moistened (see Luke vii. 37, 38, 47; and Ezek. xvi. 63). But that is not the light in which it is here presented.

Glance into the future (22-25). **22. And now, behold, I go.** The "I" is emphatic:—*q. d.*, 'As for me, I go' **bound in the spirit unto Jerusalem.** This does not mean (as *Erasmus, Grotius,* and *Bengel* interpret it), 'knowing by the prophetic spirit that I am to be bound, and so feeling myself already bound, as a prisoner of Jesus Christ'—with which the following words do not all accord. Nor yet are we to take "the spirit" here to mean the Holy Ghost, as the Greek fathers and others generally understood it. The usual phraseology of the apostle leads us to take the expression in the simple sense of an 'internal pressure,' the result of that higher guidance which shaped all his movements, and which in the present case, while all-powerful in itself, left him in the dark as to what was to happen to him at Jerusalem, as expressed in the next clause. **not knowing the things that shall befall me there: 23. Save that the Holy Ghost witnesseth**—'witnesseth to me,' is undoubtedly the true reading; **in every city**—probably, by prophetic utterances on the subject, from city to city; as in ch. xxi. 10, 11. Analogous premonitions of coming events—especially to distinguished servants of Christ, and in critical circumstances —are not unknown to the general methods of God's providence; and those here alluded to could not fail to season and brace the apostle's spirit for whatever might occur. **saying that bonds and afflictions abide** (or 'await') **me. 24. But none of these things move me, neither count I my life dear unto myself, so that I might finish my course.** *Alford* notes this as a similitude peculiarly Pauline (see ch. xiii. 25; 2 Tim. iv. 7; 1 Cor. ix. 24-27; Phil. iii. 14). Another very ancient reading is, 'But I count my life of no account, nor is it so precious to myself as to finish,' &c.; but the text of this reading is somewhat confused, and the sense is pretty much the same. **with joy, and the ministry which I have received of the Lord Jesus, to testify** [διαμαρτύρασθαι]—'to testify thoroughly' (see for this word on *v.* 21). **the gospel of the grace of God.** In this noble expression of entire devotion to the service of Christ, and preparedness for the worst that could befall him in such a cause, note, first, his jealousy for the peculiar character of his mission, as *immediately from Christ Himself*, on which all the charges against him turned; next, the Burden of that Gospel which he preached—GRACE: it was "the Gospel of the Grace of God." **25. And now, be-**

149

now, behold, [d]I know that ye all, among whom I have gone preaching the
26 kingdom of God, shall see my face no more. Wherefore I take you to
27 record this day, that I *am* [e]pure from the blood of all *men.* For I have
28 not shunned to declare unto you all [f]the counsel of God. Take [g]heed
therefore unto yourselves, and to all the flock over the which the Holy
Ghost [h]hath made you overseers, to feed the church of God, [i]which he

A. D. 60.

[d] Rom.15.23.
[e] 2 Cor. 7. 2.
[f] Luke 7. 30.
[g] 1 Tim. 4.16.
[h] 1 Cor. 12.28.
[i] Eph. 1. 7.

hold, **I know that ye all, among whom I have gone preaching the kingdom [of God].** (The bracketed words are of very doubtful authority.) **shall see my face no more.** As he had just said that he was going to Jerusalem, not knowing what was to befall him there (*v.* 22), we are not to regard this as a prophetic utterance of an undoubted fact, but as what the apostle in his peculiar circumstances fully expected. Whether, therefore, he ever did see them again must be decided purely on its own evidence. That he did again visit that region, after a first imprisonment, there is reason to think; but even if he did, we may very well believe that he never saw again the very persons now addressed. **26. Wherefore I take you to record this day, that I am pure from the blood of all men**—a deeply solemn way of expressing conscious freedom from guilt, in respect both of the subjects brought before them and the faithfulness with which these were pressed upon them. (See ch. xviii. 6; and compare 1 Sam. xii. 3, 5; Ezek. iii. 17-21; xxxiii. 8, 9. **27. For I have not shunned to declare unto you all the counsel** (or 'purpose') **of God**—God's gracious design of saving souls by His Son Jesus Christ, and erecting a kingdom of such saved souls on the earth (cf. Luke vii. 30).

Counsels to the Ephesian Presbyters (28-35). **28. Take heed therefore unto yourselves**—a caution reminding us of the apostle's warning style to Timothy (2 Tim., *passim*). **and to all the flock.** Observe here how the *personal* is put before the *pastoral* care. **over the which the Holy Ghost hath made you.** 'We are not informed (to use the words of *Lechler*) how the elders at Ephesus were ordained to the ministry; but from analogy (ch. vi. 2-6; xiv. 23) it is to be supposed that they were chosen under the apostle's direction, and not without the church's co-operation, and were set apart by prayer and the imposition of hands. This was the human and visible side of the transaction; but the apostle draws attention to the invisible and Divine side. It was the Holy Ghost who acted. He properly appointed and commissioned the persons; they were bound and responsible to Him. . . . And if He works and decides, so must He dwell in the members of the Church who act; accordingly, the appointment of elders to the pastoral office by the Holy Ghost rests on the universal priesthood of believers as a presupposition, instead of being, as it might at first sight appear, a hierarchical idea.' **overseers** [ἐπισκό-πους]—or 'bishops.' This word—which occurs five times in the New Testament (here, and Phil. i. 1; 1 Tim. iii. 2; Tit. i. 7; 1 Pet. ii. 25)—is in every other place rendered by our translators 'bishops:' here only they have rendered it "overseers." Why? Beyond doubt to avoid the obvious inference that the same persons are here called "elders" (*v.* 17) and "bishops." So early did the hierarchical views of the clergy find this passage to be in their way, that *Irenæus* (in the second century) says that Paul on this occasion 'convened the bishops *and* presbyters;' and since only one class is mentioned in the text, *Irenæus* adds, 'who were from Ephesus and from the other neighbouring towns' (*Adv. Hær.* ii. 14. 2). 'Here (says *Alford* candidly) we see, first, the two distinguished—

bishops and presbyters—as if both were sent for, in order that the titles might not seem to belong to the same persons; and, second, other neighbouring churches brought in, in order that there may not seem to be "bishops" in one church only. That neither of these was the case is clearly shown by the plain words of this verse, "he sent *to Ephesus* and summoned *the elders of the church.*" So early did interested and disingenuous interpretations begin to cloud the light which Scripture might have thrown on ecclesiastical questions. The English version has hardly dealt fairly in this case with the sacred text, in rendering, by the word "overseers," what is rendered in all other places (and ought to have been here) "bishops," that the fact of elders and bishops having been originally and apostolically synonymous might be apparent to the ordinary English reader, which now it is not.' To the same effect speak all other candid writers. Whether, consistently with these admissions, an episcopal superiority of one presbyter over several others can be shown to have apostolic sanction, this is not the place to enquire. Enough it is here to insist that not a vestige of it is to be found in this place, and that the plain sense of Scripture shall not be tampered with to meet the requirements of any system, either of doctrine or of ecclesiastical polity. **to feed** [ποιμαίνειν]—a word denoting the whole pastoral care (see on Matt. ii. 6, and on John xxi. 16), **the church of God**—or, 'the Church of the Lord.'

Which of these two very important readings [τοῦ Θεοῦ, or τοῦ Κυρίου] is the true one, is a question of great difficulty, which has long divided, and still divides, the best critics. The *external* evidence in favour of both readings is pretty nearly equal, though perhaps slightly preponderating in favour of 'the Church of the Lord,' [א and B, with about twenty cursive MSS., have τ. Θεοῦ, supported by the Vulgate, in all its undoubted copies, the Peshito Syriac, and the Philoxenian Syriac in the *text.* Of Patristic authorities, *Ignatius,* about A.D. 107 (if we can depend on the genuineness of the Epistle) uses the phrase, 'the blood of God,' and several of the fathers must have so read. On the other hand, A C (of the first hand) D E, and fourteen or fifteen cursives have τ. Κυρίου, supported by the *margin* of the Philoxenian Syriac, the two Egyptian versions (the Memphitic and Thebaic), and some later versions. Of the fathers, *Athanasius,* the great champion of the proper Divinity of Christ in the fourth century (if the reading hitherto acquiesced in be the true one), says that the Scriptures, as we have them, have by no means transmitted the expression, 'the blood of God' (*contra Apollinar.*); and even though another reading of these words of Athanasius should neutralize it as a testimony against the received reading of our text, it is hardly credible that that father could have read as we do, 'the blood of God,' without using it in controversy with the Arians, or rather (as the Arians themselves would very likely urge it as in favour of their views) repelling the argument against the supreme Divinity of Christ which it might seem to furnish. In *Chrysostom* the readings fluctuate; nor is the genuineness of the commentary on Acts by any

29 hath purchased [j]with his own blood. For I know this, that after my
departing [k]shall grievous wolves enter in among you, not sparing the
30 flock. Also [l]of your own selves shall men arise, speaking perverse things,
31 to draw away disciples after them. Therefore watch, and remember,
that by [m]the space of three years I ceased not to warn every one night

A. D. 60.

[j] Heb. 9. 14.
[k] Matt. 7. 15.
[l] 1 John 2.
　　19.
[m] ch. 19. 10.

---

means beyond doubt.] Since, then, the external evidence is so nearly balanced, the decision must rest on the *internal* evidence. And how does that stand? In favour of 'the Church of God' it is pleaded, *first,* that Paul never uses the phrase 'Church of the Lord,' but ten times the phrase "Church of God;" and *next,* that "the Church of *God,*" which He purchased with His own blood," is an idea so startling that it was much more likely to be afterwards softened into 'Church of the Lord,' than this smooth expression to be thrust out of the text (supposing it genuine), in favour of the much more harsh one of our received text. There is certainly great force in these considerations. But, on the other hand, it is argued, that the very frequency with which the apostle uses the phrase, "Church of God," was just the thing which would lead transcribers to conclude, if they found 'Church of *the Lord*' in this one place, that it must be a copyist's mistake, and so to change it into the familiar one, "Church *of God.*" So that if it is alleged that the 'purchase of the Church with the blood of *God*' was so very unusual an expression that it was not likely ever to get into the text if not genuine, it may just as well be affirmed that 'the Church of *the Lord*' was with Paul so unusual a phrase that it was not likely to get into the text here if not genuine. Thus the *internal* evidence seems to us to be about as equally balanced as the *external;* at all events, we can see no ground for the dogmatic confidence with which *Scrivener* pronounces in favour of the one, and *Lechler* for the other. (*Lachm.* and *Treg.*, who usually follow the Vulgate, decide in this case against it, and in favour of 'Church of the Lord,' and so does *Tischendorf*. *Griesbach* approves of a reading evidently made up of both—'the Church of the Lord and God'—which, though the later external authority for it is tolerable, has no pretensions to equality with the one or the other of the two naked terms. And though *Scrivener* thinks that all the copies which have this double reading are testimonies in favour of the *received* one, we may just as well argue that they are testimonies in behalf of the *other* reading. *Bengel*[G] decides in favour of "Church of God;" and so *Alford* now, though formerly his view was the reverse. *Scrivener* says the received reading, though different from that of the majority of copies, 'is pretty sure to be correct;' and after fairly stating the whole evidence, he concludes by saying that when all is weighed, 'there will remain little room for hesitation.' *Lechler*, on the other hand, considers 'Church of the Lord' to be 'certainly the true reading;' as do *Olshausen, Meyer,* and *de Wette,* who consider 'the blood of God' an expression quite foreign to the New Testament. No doubt it is, if this passage be excepted; but to conclude against it here on that ground would oblige us to stand in doubt of whatever happens to be but once expressed. On the whole, though we slightly incline to 'the Church *of the Lord*' as the true reading, we find it extremely difficult to decide in favour of either of the two against the other, and should prefer to see them both printed in the text as alternative readings: thus training the general reader to know that in certain cases it is almost impossible to decide with certainty which of two readings was the original one. The bearing

151

of each of them on the Person and Work of Christ will be seen presently.
which he hath purchased [περιποιήσατο]. The word (in the middle voice) signifies, not strictly to *buy* [= ἀγοράζεσθαι, 1 Cor. vi. 20; 2 Pet. ii. 1; Rev. v. 9], but anyhow to 'acquire for one's-self,' to 'gain possession of,' as one's own. **with his own blood**. "His own" is emphatic; but it is even more so in the true reading [not διὰ τ. ἰδίου αἵματος, but διὰ τ. αἵματος τοῦ ἰδίου, which is read by ℵ A B C D E, &c.]—*q. d.,* 'That glorified Lord who from the right hand of power in the heavens is gathering and ruling the Church, and by His Spirit, through human agency, hath set you over it, cannot be indifferent to its welfare in your hands, seeing He hath given for it His own most precious blood, thus making it His own by the dearest of all ties.' The transcendent sacredness of the Church of Christ is thus made to rest on the *dignity of its Lord* and the consequent *preciousness of that blood which He shed for it.* And as the sacrificial, atoning character of Christ's death is here plainly *expressed*, so His supreme dignity is *implied* as clearly by the second reading as it is expressed by the first. What a motive to *pastoral fidelity* is here furnished! **29. For I know this**—or, more simply (according to another good reading) 'I know.' **that after my departing shall grievous wolves enter in among you, not sparing the flock. 30. Also of your own selves shall men arise, speaking perverse** (or 'crooked') **things.** 'As a member of the body may be strained (says *Lechler*), and by violent bending put into a distorted position, so also truths may be perverted, placed in false relations to each other, distorted by exaggeration, changed into caricatures of that which they originally represented. And this is the nature of all false doctrine. Error is only a misrepresentation of truth; every false doctrine has some truth at bottom, which is misrepresented by the fault of men.' **to draw away disciples**—rather, 'the disciples' [τοὺς μαθ.] **after them.** Two classes of coming enemies are here announced: the one more external to themselves, the other bred in the bosom of their own community: both were to be teachers; but the one class are styled "grievous wolves," not sparing, that is, making a prey of, the flock; the other, simply sectarian 'perverters' of the truth, with the view of drawing a party after them. Perhaps the one pointed to that subtle poison of Oriental Gnosticism which we know to have very early infected the Asiatic churches; the other to such Judaizing tendencies as we know to have troubled nearly all the early churches. (See the Epistles to the *Ephesians, Colossians,* and *Timothy;* also those to the seven churches of Asia, Rev. ii. and iii.) The remedy against this, and *all* that tends to injure and corrupt the Church, now follows. **31. Therefore watch.** This great duty of pastors applies to every age of the Church. **and remember**—keep in view, as a model which ye will do well to copy, how **that by the space of three years**—speaking in round numbers, it being more than two years, **I ceased not to warn**—[νουθετῶν, a word, as *Alford* notes, used in the New Testament only by our apostle, and by him seven times besides this.] **every one night and day with tears.** What an appeal to be able to make; and if (as *Bengel* says) this was

32 and day with tears. And now, brethren, I commend you to God, and ⁿto the word of his grace, which is able ^oto build you up, and to give
33 you an ^pinheritance among all them which are sanctified. I ^qhave
34 coveted no man's silver, or gold, or apparel. Yea, ye yourselves know, ^rthat these hands have ministered unto my necessities, and to them that
35 were with me. I have showed you all things, how that ^sso labouring ye ought to support the weak, and to remember the words of the Lord Jesus, how he said, ^tIt is more blessed to give than to receive.
36 And when he had thus spoken, he kneeled down, and prayed with
37 them all. And they all wept sore, and ^ufell on Paul's neck, and kissed
38 him, sorrowing most of all for the words which he spake, that they should see his face no more. And they accompanied him unto the ship.

A. D. 60.
ⁿ Heb. 13. 9.
^o John 17.17.
ch. 9. 31.
^p Eph. 1. 18.
Col. 3. 24.
^q 1 Sam. 12.3.
1 Cor. 9. 12.
2 Cor. 7. 2.
^r 1 Cor. 4. 12.
^s Rom. 15. 1.
Eph. 4. 28.
^t Matt. 10. 8.
1 Cor. 9. 12.
2 Cor. 11. 9.
^u Gen. 45. 14.

an apostle's part, how much more a pastor's! **32. And now, [brethren]** (this bracketed word has hardly sufficient authority), **I commend you to God** —as the Almighty Conservator of His people, **and to the word of his grace** (see on *v.* 24), **which** ('who') **is able to build you up** [the simple verb οἰκ. is preferable to the compound ἐποικ., which *Tischendorf* inconsistently approves), **and to give you an inheritance.** Observe how salvation—not only in its *initial stages* of pardon and regeneration, but in all its *subsequent stages* of 'up-building,' even to its *consummation* in the final inheritance—is here ascribed to the 'ability' of God to bestow it, as in Rom. xvi. 25; Eph. iii. 20; particularly Jude 24: and compare 2 Tim. i. 12, where *the same thing is ascribed to Christ.* **among all them which are sanctified.** It is remarkable that the only other place where this precise phrase is used is in the speech of our apostle before Agrippa (ch. xxvi. 18), confirming the impression which this whole address conveys to the reader, that it is here recorded as delivered. And if it should be said (as the Tübingen school scruple not to do) that this only proves that both speeches proceeded from one pen—not that they were the words of Paul—then another coincidence, quite as striking, will tend to fix the Pauline authorship of both addresses:—in one only of our apostle's Epistles does a phrase precisely like this occur, and that is just in his Epistle to these same Ephesians (ch. i. 18), "That ye may know what is . . . the riches of the glory of His *inheritance among the saints*" (ἐν τοῖς ἁγίοις). It will be observed that sanctification is here viewed as the final character and condition of the heirs of glory, considered as one saved company. **33. I have coveted no man's silver, or gold, or apparel.** Compare 2 Cor. xii. 14, "I seek not yours, but you." **34. Yea, ye yourselves know, that these hands**—doubtless, holding them up before them, as he afterwards did before Agrippa —though the force of the act there consisted in their being in chains (ch. xxvi. 29); **have ministered unto my necessities, and to them that were with me.** See ch. xviii. 3; and 1 Cor. iv. 12; ix. 6 (written from Ephesus); also 1 Thess. ii. 9. **35. I have showed you all things, how that so labouring**—that labouring, as I myself have done, for others as well as myself, **ye ought to support the weak** (cf. 1 Thess. v. 14), **and to remember the words of the Lord Jesus, how he** [ὅτι αὐτὸς]— ('how Himself') **said, It is more blessed to give than to receive.** This golden saying, snatched from oblivion, and here added to the Church's abiding treasures, is apt to beget the wish that more of what issued from those lips which "dropped as an honeycomb," had been preserved to us. But see on John xxi. 25.

The Parting (36-38). **36. And when he had thus spoken, he kneeled down, and prayed with them**
152

all. 37. And they all wept sore, and fell on Paul's neck, and kissed him, 38. Sorrowing most of all for the words which he spake, that they should see his face no more. And they accompanied him unto the ship. Nothing can be more touching than these three concluding verses, leaving an indelible impression of rare ministerial fidelity and affection on the apostle's part, and of warm admiration and attachment on the part of these Ephesian presbyters. Would to God that such scenes were more frequent in the Church!

Remarks.—1. We have had occasion before to remark in the great apostle a combination of qualities rarely found in the same person, but where found in any strength constituting a principal element of true greatness. In this address, for example, what a breadth of view, combined with the minutest attention to the ordinary interests of life, is observable; the one so far from begetting indifference to the other, that each seemed the complement and strength of the other. Observe, too, the tenacity with which, in 'all humility of mind, and tears, and trials, through the plots of the Jews,' he maintained his ministerial fidelity; keeping back from the Ephesian church nothing which was profitable, teaching publicly and from house to house, and, in this thoroughgoing way of indoctrinating them in the truth, making it his great object to establish them in the two cardinal principles of Repentance towards God, and Faith towards our Lord Jesus Christ. See next, his fearless determination to go to the Jewish capital, as Divinely directed, regardless of predicted and expected bonds and imprisonment; and—if he could but finish his course with joy, and his testimony to the grace of the Gospel—ready to yield up even his life in the cause of his adorable Lord Jesus. And what a protestation to be able to make to these presbyters, after so lengthened a sojourn among them and incessant ministrations to them, that he was "pure from the blood of all" among them, inasmuch as he "had not shunned to declare to them the whole counsel of God." No claim, of course, is here advanced to faultless perfection in the discharge of his ministerial duties; but he does claim to be free from conscious and wilful unfaithfulness to any soul in the course of this long ministry. Notice further, his holy jealousy for the prosperity of this Ephesian community of believers after his departure, and in particular—anticipating both the entrance of grievous wolves in sheep's clothing from without, and the upspringing from within themselves of schismatic, sectarian, selfish, and sinister persons, who would seek to alienate the disciples from their fellowship, and so break up their beautiful church—anticipating these sore evils, see how he enjoins the presbyters to take heed first to themselves and then to the flock—at once purchased by the blood of God's own Son and placed by the

21 AND it came to pass, that after we were gotten from them, and had launched, we came with a straight course unto Coos, and the *day* follow-

A. D. 60.

CHAP. 21.

Holy Ghost under their care—to keep watch, and to do as he had done who, for three years, had not ceased to warn every one night and day with tears. Finally, how touching, and even sublime, is the appeal which he was able to make to the unselfishness with which he had from first to last gone in and out among them; how, instead of coveting any man's silver, or gold, or apparel, those hands of his had wrought—no doubt over night, when his ministerial labours might rather have called for rest—to support not himself only, but his companions; and how he had taught them that, labouring in the same spirit, they also should support the weak, and act ever upon the golden maxim of their common Lord, "It is more blessed to give (not money·only, but whatever one has to give to them that need) than to receive." And, as if to crown all, what a picture is presented to us in his kneeling down with them all on the sea shore, and pouring out his heart in prayer with them, in the sore weeping of all of them, the falling of each on his neck and kissing him—showing the tender familiarity of their affection—and that word which completed the pungency of their sorrow at parting with him, "that they should see his face no more"! Where shall we find in all the Church's records such a combination of greatness and tenderness of soul—such a union of ministerial humility, fidelity, purity, and self-sacrifice—such unwearied prosecution, amid tears, of one object, the grandest that man can undertake, relieved only by manual labour for the support of himself and his companions? O ye servants of Christ, study this model; on your knees drink in the spirit of it, and enter into its every detail: so shall its impress be stamped upon you as ye are able to take it on, and then shall it not have been here presented to us in vain. 2. If there be one characteristic of the theology of Paul which is more *Pauline* than another, it is his doctrine of GRACE, as the spring of all the Divine procedure towards fallen man from everlasting, the principle of the whole scheme of salvation, the secret of every step in the believer's recovery from sin and all its effects, and in his eventual experience of life eternal. In this address that characteristic is strikingly brought out, both when he describes himself as set "to testify the glad tidings of THE GRACE OF GOD" (*v.* 24), and when he "commends" the Ephesian presbyters "to God and to THE WORD OF HIS GRACE" (*v.* 32)—as if that "word" had but one burden—the *Grace* of God. By this the soundness of all preaching should be tested. Occasional *concessions* to this doctrine are no evidence of conformity to the preaching of Paul. That preaching only is Pauline the soul of which is the doctrine of Grace, considered as the prime element in all salvation. 3. If the received reading of *v.* 28 be the genuine one, what a view does it give of "the Church of God" as "purchased with *His own blood.*" Nor need such language repel us as altogether incongruous. For analogous expressions are certainly found elsewhere in the New Testament, particularly in the writings of this apostle. Thus, when he says that God "*spared not* His own Son, but *delivered him up* for us all" (Rom. viii. 32)—alluding beyond all doubt to Abraham's sacrifice of paternal feeling in being prepared to surrender to death "his son, his only son Isaac, whom he loved"—he certainly means to ascribe to God in the *surrender of His Son to death* a sacrifice of Paternal feeling, which, however transcending all that man experiences in such an act, the apostle was unable to express save in language derived from what

men experience in such cases. Compare, too, Rom. v. 7, 8, "Scarcely for a righteous man will one die; yet peradventure for a good man some would even dare to die. But *God* commendeth *His* love toward us, in that, while we were yet sinners, Christ died for us." Besides, if the humanity of the Lord Jesus was that of God's own Son, "the blood of Jesus," which the beloved disciple calls "the blood of God's own Son" (1 John i. 7), was the blood of "the Word made flesh," of Him who "was with God" and "was God" (John i. 1, 14). There is thus strict doctrinal truth in such language; and though expressed in this strong form nowhere else—from which we may well infer that such phraseology should not become too familiar—the sweeping condemnation of it as intolerable, may reasonably be suspected to spring from secret dislike to the truth which it expresses, that the blood shed for the Church had a strictly DIVINE VALUE, arising from the transcendent Dignity of the Victim. If, on the other hand, the true reading of this verse be, 'the Church of *the Lord*, which He hath purchased with His own blood," in what a light does it hold forth *the Lord Jesus*, by the shedding of whose blood on the cross God is here expressly said to have made the Church His own property! Of a mere man, however highly endowed—of any creature, however exalted—is it conceivable that such a statement should have been made? And thus, whichever reading of this verse is preferred, the supreme Dignity of Him whose blood it speaks of stands out in the strongest light. 4. The efficacy of Christ's death, as expressed in this verse, should not be overlooked. While in the language of the sacrificial economy it is constantly represented as *expiatory;* with reference to lawful captivity, as a *ransom-price;* in the light of an inheritance, as the *testator's death*, securing all to the legatee; and of alienated property, as a purchase-price: here, without any allusion to the previous condition of the Church—whether as alienated, or lost, or aught else—God is said to have gained rightful possession of the Church, or made it His own, by the blood of Jesus Christ. Explain this as we may—when all the representations of it are put together, and all that is peculiar to each is combined into one general idea—what is that idea but (in the language of our apostle himself) that God "made peace" with the guilty "through the blood of the cross," and that Christ is "a propitiation through faith in His blood, to declare God's righteousness for the remission of sins, that He might be just and the Justifier of him that believeth in Jesus." In times like these—when this the most characteristic element of the death of Christ is refined away, and nothing is held up to the sin-sick soul but the self-abnegation of Christ in enduring so patiently the ill treatment of men, and God's love in sending Him to exhibit such a character—it is of vital importance to show how inadequate such representations are to convey the import of passages like this before us, and to cling to the substitution of Christ, "the Just for the unjust," as that which alone can meet the crushing sense of our own deserts as sinners before God.

CHAP. XXI. 1-40.—SAILING FROM EPHESUS, THEY LAND AT TYRE, AND THENCE, SAILING TO PTOLEMAIS, THEY PROCEED BY LAND TO CÆSAREA AND JERUSALEM—MEETING WITH JAMES AND THE BRETHREN THERE—THE UPROAR AND SEIZURE OF PAUL—THE CHIEF CAPTAIN'S TREATMENT OF

2 ing unto Rhodes, and from thence unto Patara: and finding a ship
3 sailing over unto Phenicia, we went aboard, and set forth. Now when
we had discovered Cyprus, we left it on the left hand, and sailed into
Syria, ^aand landed at Tyre: for there the ship was to unlade her burden.
4 And finding disciples, we tarried there seven days: ^bwho said to Paul
5 through the Spirit, that he should not go up to Jerusalem. And when
we had accomplished those days, we departed and went our way; and
they all brought us on our way, with wives and children, till *we were* out
6 of the city: and ^cwe kneeled down on the shore, and prayed. And when
we had taken our leave one of another, we took ship; and they returned
home again.
7 And when we had finished *our* course from Tyre, we came to
Ptolemais, and saluted the brethren, and abode with them one day.
8 And the next *day* we that were of Paul's company departed, and came
unto Cesarea: and we entered into the house of Philip the ^devangelist,

A. D. 60.

^a Judg. 10. 6.
2 Sam. 8. 6.
Isa. 7. 2.
Matt. 4. 24.
Luke 2. 2.
ch. 15. 21,
41.
ch. 18. 18.
ch. 20. 23.
^b ch. 20. 23.
^c 1 Ki. 8. 54.
Ps. 95. 6.
Mark 1. 40.
ch. 7. 60.
ch. 9. 40.
ch. 20. 36.
^d ch. 8. 40.
Eph. 4. 11.
2 Tim. 4. 5.

HIM—PERMISSION GIVEN HIM TO ADDRESS THE PEOPLE FROM THE CASTLE STAIRS.

Departure from Ephesus and landing at Tyre—The seven days' stay there—Departure, and landing at Ptolemais (1-7). **1. And it came to pass, that after we were gotten from them** [ἀποσπασθέντες ἀπ᾽ αὐτῶν]—or 'torn from them.' This word being used in Luke xxii. 41 in the sense of simply 'withdraw,' *de Wette* and *Humphry* would take it here in the same sense; but the majority of critics, with *Chrysostom,* take it to convey here the idea of 'tearing away,' expressive of the difficulty and pain with which they let their dear father in the Faith away: **and had launched, we came with a straight course** [εὐθυδρομήσαντες]—running before the wind, as the nautical phrase is, **unto Coos** [Κῶν, but the true reading clearly is Κῶ]—'unto Cōs,' as the proper spelling is ; an island about forty miles due south from Miletus, and coming close to the mainland. Here they passed the night. **and the day following unto Rhodes**—another and much larger island, lying some fifty miles to the south-east, of brilliant classic memory and beauty; **and from thence unto Patara**—a town on the magnificent mainland of Lycia, almost due east from Rhodes. It was devoted to the worship of Apollo, and was the seat of an oracle (called 'Apollo Pataræus.') **2. And finding a ship**—their former one either going no further, or being bound for a port which would not suit them, **sailing over** [διαπερῶν], or 'crossing' **unto Phœnicia** (see on ch. xi. 19), **we went aboard, and set forth.** One would almost take this to be an extract from a passenger's journal, so graphic are its details. **3. Now when we had discovered** ['Ἀναφανέντες—passive for active; not ἀναφάναντες, which has next to no support]—the nautical phrase is, 'having sighted' **Cyprus, we left it on the left hand**—that is, steered south-east of it, leaving it on the north-west, **and sailed into Syria** [εἰς Συρ.]—rather, 'for Syria.' The term "Syria" is here used in its Roman acceptation, as the province to which Phœnicia and Palestine belonged. **and landed at Tyre**—the celebrated ancient seat of maritime commerce for both east and west. It might be reached from Patara in about two days. **for there the ship was to unlade her burden**—to discharge her cargo: it was this that gave the apostle time for what follows. **4. And finding disciples** [ἀνευρόντες τοὺς μαθητάς]. The proper rendering is, 'And finding up,' or, as we say, 'finding out the disciples.' For, from what is recorded in ch. xi. 19 (on which see), they probably expected to find such ; and the word implies some search. Probably they were not many, but we shall see that

they included some gifted persons. **we tarried there seven days**—no doubt for the same reason as at ch. xx. 6, 7 (see there); but of course the ship's movements not only admitted of this stay, but necessitated it. And thus did outward providences minister to what was far higher—as in so many other cases. **who said to Paul through the Spirit** (that is, through prophetic utterance on the part of some of these "disciples"), **that he should not go up to Jerusalem**—(see on ch. xx. 23, and on vv. 11-14.) The prophetic gift in this case (says *Chrysostom*) was the gift of knowledge, not the gift of wisdom ; for while the knowledge of sad things to befall the apostle at Jerusalem was of the Spirit, the entreaty not to go thither was of themselves. **5. And when we had accomplished those days**—completed the time of their stay allowed by the ship's company, **we departed and went our way; and they all brought us on our way**—or 'escorted us,' **with wives and children, till we were out of the city : and we kneeled down on the shore, and prayed**—(see on ch. xx. 36.) Observe here, that the *children* of these Tyrian disciples not only were taken along with their parents, but must have joined in this act of solemn worship. (See on Eph. vi. 1.) **6. And when we had taken our leave one of another, we took ship** ('embarked'); **and they returned home again. 7. And when we had finished our course** ('And having completed the passage') **from Tyre, we came to Ptolemais**—so called from one of the Ptolemies, when it belonged to Egypt ; anciently called *Accho* (Judg. i. 31), now *Acca,* and by Europeans, *St. Jean d'Acre,* or *Acre,* the principal seaport town of Syria, lying about thirty miles south of Tyre. Its military importance has made it a coveted prize from age to age. **and saluted the brethren**—disciples probably gathered, as at Tyre, on the occasion mentioned in ch. xi. 19; **and abode with them one day.**

Land journey to Cæsarea—Stay with Philip the Evangelist—Picture of his family—Arrival of Agabus, and his prediction regarding Paul—The unsuccessful attempt to dissuade him from going to Jerusalem (8-14). **8. And the next day we [that were of Paul's company] departed.** (These bracketed words are wanting in the oldest and best MSS., and seem to have got into the text as the connecting words at the head of some Church Lesson.) **and came unto Cæsarea**—a distance by land, skirting southwards along the coast, of about thirty miles. **and we entered into the house of Philip the evangelist**—a term (as *Howson* observes) answering, perhaps, very much to our *missionary.* This is he by whose ministry such joy had been diffused over Samaria, (ch. viii.)

9 which was *one* of the seven; and abode with him. And the same man
10 had four daughters, virgins, *which did prophesy. And as we tarried
there many days, there came down from Judea a certain prophet, named
11 *Agabus. And when he was come unto us, he took Paul's girdle, and
bound his own hands and feet, and said, Thus saith the Holy Ghost, *So
shall the Jews at Jerusalem bind the man that owneth this girdle, and
12 shall deliver *him* into the hands of the Gentiles. And when we heard
these things, both we, and they of that place, besought him not to go up
13 to Jerusalem. Then Paul answered, *What mean ye to weep and to
break mine heart? for *I am ready not to be bound only, but also to die
14 at Jerusalem for the name of the Lord Jesus. And when he would not
be persuaded, we ceased, saying, *The will of the Lord be done.
15 And after those days we took up our carriages, and went up to Jeru-
16 salem. There went with us also *certain* of the disciples of Cesarea,
and brought with them one Mnason of Cyprus, an old disciple, with
whom we should lodge.

A. D. 60.
*ch. 6. 5.
ch. 8. 28.
f Joel 2. 28.
ch. 2. 17.
*ch. 11. 28.
*Eph. 3. 1.
Eph. 6. 20.
Phil. 1. 7.
2 Tim. 2. 9.
*ch. 20. 24.
*Rom. 8. 35.
1 Cor. 4. 9.
2 Cor. 4. 10.
Phil. 1. 20.
Col. 1. 24.
2 Tim. 4. 6.
*Gen. 43. 14.
1 Sam. 3.18.
Matt. 26.42.
Luke 22. 42.

which was one of the seven—the second named of the seven deacons (ch. vi. 5), who would seem to have 'purchased to himself a good degree' (1 Tim. iii. 13). He and Paul now meet for the first time, a full quarter of a century from that time. 9. And the same man had four daughters, virgins, which did prophesy—in fulfilment of Joel ii. 28 (see on ch. ii. 18). This fact seems to be mentioned here solely as a high distinction, which it was deemed fitting that the reader should know had been conferred on so devoted a servant of the Lord Jesus; and we may fairly regard it as indicating the high tone of religion in his family. 10. And as we tarried there many days ['Επιμενόντων δὲ ἡμῶν ἡμέρας πλείους]—'And while we were staying some days more,' that is, 'prolonging our stay.' Finding himself in good time for Pentecost at Jerusalem, he would feel it a refreshing thing to his spirit to hold Christian communion for a few days with such a family. there came down from Judea—the news of Paul's arrival having spread, a certain prophet, named Agabus—no doubt the prophet of that name with whom we met in ch. xi. 28. It may seem strange that the historian should here introduce him as if for the first time. *Lechler's* supposition, that 'here that earlier passage was lost sight of' (or that the historian had forgotten his having mentioned him so particularly and so shortly before), is derogatory even to any good historian. *Meyer's* alternative supposition, which *Alford* approves, seems the most probable, that different sources of information may have been drawn upon in the two cases. 11. And when he was come unto us, he took Paul's girdle, and bound his own hands and feet, and said, Thus saith the Holy Ghost, so shall the Jews at Jerusalem bind the man that owneth this girdle—for though it was the Romans that did this, it was at the Jews' instigation (compare v. 33 with ch. xxviii. 17); and shall deliver him into the hands of the Gentiles. Such dramatic methods of announcing important future events would bring the old prophets to remembrance (compare Isa. xx. 2, &c.; Jer. xiii. 1; Ezek. vi. 1). This prediction and that at Tyre (v. 4) were intended not to prohibit him from going, but to put his courage to the test, and, when he stood the test, to deepen and mature it. 12. And when we heard these things, both we, and they of that place (the Cæsarean Christians) besought him not to go up to Jerusalem. 13. Then Paul answered, What mean ye to weep and to break mine heart? Beautiful union of manly resoluteness and womanly tenderness, alike removed from mawkishness and stoicism! for I am ready not to be bound only—

q. d., 'If that is all, let it come.' but also to die at Jerusalem for the name of the Lord Jesus. It was well he could add this, for he had that also to do at Rome. Those who are familiar with the history of the great Reformation of the sixteenth century will be reminded here of the heroic answer of Luther, when warned not to go to the Diet of Worms, in 1521—'Though there were as many devils in Worms as there are tiles on the house-tops, I will go.' 14. And when he would not be persuaded, we ceased, saying, The will of the Lord be done—making up their minds to the worst.

Arrival at Jerusalem, and glad reception by the brethren—At a meeting next day with James and all the elders, Paul details the work of God among the Gentiles by his ministry—The satisfaction created by these tidings, and the advice given for the purpose of conciliating the sticklers for Jewish usages among the converts of the metropolis (15-25). 15. And after those days we took up our carriages [ἀποσκευασάμενοι]—'we put up our baggage,' and went up to Jerusalem—for the *fifth* time since his conversion; thus concluding his *third* and *last* missionary tour (so far as recorded); for though he accomplished the fourth and last part of the plan sketched out in ch. xix. 21—"after I have been at Jerusalem I must also see Rome"—it was as "a prisoner of Jesus Christ" that he entered it. The apostle was full of anxiety about this visit to Jerusalem, from the numerous prophetic intimations of danger awaiting him, and from having reason to expect the presence at this feast of the very parties from whose virulent rage he had once and again narrowly escaped with his life. Hence we find him asking the Roman Christians to wrestle with him in prayer, "for the Lord Jesus Christ's sake, and for the love of the Spirit, *that he might be delivered from them that believed not in Judea,*" as well as "that his service which he had for Jerusalem (the great collection for the poor saints there) might be accepted of the saints" (Rom. xv. 30, 31). 16. There went with us also certain of the disciples of Cesarea, and brought with them [ἄγοντες—Μνάσωνι]—(rather, 'and conducted us to') one Mnason of Cyprus, an old disciple—not an *aged* disciple, but 'a disciple of old standing;' perhaps one of the three thousand converted on the day of Pentecost, if not drawn by the Saviour Himself during His earthly ministry. He had come probably with the Cypriots (ch. xi. 20), "preaching the Lord Jesus unto the Greeks," and now he appears settled at Jerusalem, and is honoured to be the host of the missionary party; for it is added, with whom we should (or 'were to') lodge.

155

17 And 'when we were come to Jerusalem, the brethren received us
18 gladly. And the *day* following Paul went in with us unto ᵐJames; and
19 all the elders were present. And when he had saluted them, he declared
ⁿparticularly what things God had wrought among the Gentiles by ᵒhis
20 ministry. And when they heard *it*, they glorified the Lord, and said
unto him,
Thou seest, brother, how many thousands of Jews there are which
21 believe; and they are all ᵖzealous of the law: and they are informed of
thee, that thou ᵠteachest all the Jews which are among the Gentiles to
forsake Moses, saying that they ought not to circumcise *their* children,
22 neither to walk after the customs. What is it therefore? the multitude
23 must needs come together: for they will hear that thou art come. Do

A. D. 60.

ᶦ ch. 15. 4.
ᵐ ch. 15. 13.
Gal. 1. 19.
Gal. 2. 9.
Jas. 1. 1.
ⁿ Rom. 15.18.
1 Cor. 3.5-9.
ᵒ ch. 1. 17.
ch. 20. 24.
ᵖ ch. 22. 3.
Rom. 10. 2.
Gal. 1. 14.
ᵠ ch. 6. 11.
Gal. 5. 1.

17. And when we were come to Jerusalem, the brethren—the disciples generally; as distinguished from the officials, James and all the elders, with whom he met next day (*v.* 18), **received us gladly** [ἀπεδέξαντο]. This compound verb, which Luke alone uses in the New Testament, and he seven times besides this place, is here also much better supported than the simple verb [ἐδεξ.] of the received text. **18. And the day following Paul went in with us unto James; and all the elders were present** — to report himself formally to the acknowledged head of the church at Jerusalem, with his associates in office (see on ch. xv. 13), and probably to deliver over the great collection from all the Gentile churches. Had any other apostle been at Jerusalem on this occasion, it could hardly have failed to be noted.

But who was this James?—a question which *Neander* pronounces (and not without reason) one of the most difficult in the apostolic history. Plainly, he was the same James to whom Peter desired the news of his miraculous release from prison to be conveyed (ch. xii. 17), and the same who presided at the great council on Circumcision, (ch. xv. 13, &c.) That he was the same with him whom Paul calls "James the Lord's brother" (Gal. i. 19, see Mark vi. 3), is equally evident. Was he, then, the same with the apostle "James, the son of Alphæus" (Mark iii. 18, &c.)—commonly called James the Less, to distinguish him from James the son of Zebedee, and brother of John? So thought *Jerome*, and after him than many modern critics. But there are, in our opinion, insuperable difficulties in this view—which we have pointed out on the words, "and with His brethren" (ch. i. 14). It follows, then, that this James was not one of the Twelve, nor is he anywhere called an apostle. Why, then, did he occupy so prominent a position among the Christians at Jerusalem, being their acknowledged head? The most obvious answer to this would be, his near relationship to our Lord. He was "the Lord's brother," in the opinion of not a few, as being His *cousin*—by a common mode of speech: but this appears to us improbable. The other view is, that he was our Lord's *half-brother;* and if so, he must either have been Joseph's son by a former marriage (this is the opinion of many, both in early times and more recently), or else the son of Joseph and Mary, after the birth of our Lord of the Virgin. To this opinion—which is that of some of the ablest critics—we incline. But however this question is decided, since there were other "brethren of the Lord's" besides James (Mark vi. 3), there must have been some other reason for his prominence and authority in Jerusalem; and beyond doubt the esteem in which he was held by all his fellow-citizens and countrymen in general, as well as by the Christian portion of them, and the remarkable wisdom which he displayed in mediating between the Gentile and Jewish sections of the Church, which

made him equally trusted by both—were the secret of that influence which, coupled with his near relationship to the common Lord of all, according to the flesh, raised him to the position which we find him occupying in the Acts. *Josephus* (Antt. xx. 9. 1—though the passage has been questioned) bears testimony to the estimation in which he was held by the Jews, whose chief men deplored the murder of him by fanatical enemies of his Christian testimony; and *Hegesippus*, a Christian writer who flourished not long after the death of the Apostle John—whose writings are unfortunately lost, but from which, on this subject, *Eusebius* (H. E. ii. 23) extracts an interesting account of his martyrdom—says he was surnamed by all "James the Just." (See, in addition, Remark 3, at the close of this Section.)

19. And when he had saluted them, he declared particularly [καθ᾽ ἓν ἕκαστον]—related in detail, **what things God had wrought among the Gentiles by his ministry**—taking it up probably where he had left off his narrative at the great convention (cf. ch. xv.; *v.* 15), and in that case relating the particulars of both his Second and his Third missionary tours (cf. ch. xiv. 27). In this narrative he would doubtless refer to the persevering efforts of the Judaizing party to shrivel up the Church of Christ into a Jewish sect, which he had had from time to time to meet and counterwork. **20. And when they heard it, they glorified the Lord**—'glorified God' is the much better attested reading. They were constrained to own the hand of God in his procedure, and justify his principles and his actings, notwithstanding the strong Jewish complexion of the church at Jerusalem. **and said unto him, Thou seest, brother, how many thousands** [πόσαι μυριάδες]—'how many myriads;' a hyperbolical expression for an immense number, if meant of the converts of Jerusalem only, though if intended for those of Judea at large it was scarcely an exaggeration: **of Jews**—'among the Jews' [ἐν τ. Ἰουδαίοις] is the true reading; **there are which believe; and they are all zealous of** (or 'zealots for') **the law: 21. And they are informed of thee** [Κατηχήθησαν δὲ περὶ σοῦ]—'But they have been taught to believe about thee;' it had been studiously impressed upon them, **that thou teachest all the Jews which are among the Gentiles**—that is, all the Jews residing in foreign countries, **to forsake Moses** [ἀποστασίαν ἀπὸ Μ.]—'apostasy from Moses,' **saying that they ought not to circumcise their children, neither to walk after the customs.** This calumny of the unbelieving Jews would find easy credence among the Christian zealots for Judaism in the metropolis. **22. What is it therefore? the** (rather, 'a') **multitude must needs come together: for they will hear that thou art come. 23. Do therefore this that we say to thee-**

therefore this that we say to thee: We have four men which have a vow
24 on them; them take, and purify thyself with them, and be at charges
with them, that they may *shave *their* heads: and all may know that
those things, whereof they were informed concerning thee, are nothing;
25 but *that* thou thyself also walkest orderly, and *keepest the law. As
touching the Gentiles which believe, we *have written *and* concluded that
they observe no such thing, save only that they keep themselves from
things offered to idols, and from blood, and from strangled, and from
fornication.
26 Then Paul took the men, and the next day purifying himself with
them entered into "the temple, *to signify the accomplishment of the
days of purification, until that an offering should be offered for every one
of them.
27 And when the seven days were almost ended, the Jews which were of
Asia, when they saw him in the temple, stirred up all the people, and laid
28 "hands on him, crying out, Men of Israel, help: this is the man *that
teacheth all *men* every where against the people, and the law, and this
place: and further brought Greeks also into the temple, and hath pol-
29 luted this holy place. (For they had seen before with him in the city
*Trophimus an Ephesian, whom they supposed that Paul had brought
30 into the temple.) And all the city was moved, and the people ran
together: and they took Paul, and drew him out of the temple: and forthwith the doors were shut.
31 And as they went about to kill him, tidings came unto the chief cap-

A. D. 60.

' Num. 6. 2,
13, 18.
ch. 18. 18.
' 1 Cor. 9. 20.
' Gen. 9. 4.
Lev. 17. 14.
1 Cor. 5. 1.
9, 11.
1 Cor. 8.
1 Cor. 10.
2 Thes. 4. 3.
Heb. 13. 4.
" ch. 24. 18.
* Num. 6. 13.
" Mark 10. 30.
Luke 21. 12.
ch. 4. 3.
ch. 5. 18.
ch. 26. 21.
* that
Rom. 8. 35.
2 Cor. 4. 9.
2 Cor. 12. 10.
1 Thes. 2.
14, 16.
2 Tim. 3. 1?.
* Matt. 5. 11.
ch. 24. 5, 6.
1 Cor. 4. 12.
1 Pet. 2. 12.
* ch. 20. 4.
2 Tim. 4. 20.

We have four men—Christian Jews, no doubt, which have a vow on them—the Nazarite vow apparently, (Num. vi. 1, &c.) Perhaps they had been kept ready on purpose. 24. Them take, and purify thyself with them. It will not follow from this (as some critics have too hastily concluded) that Paul himself was asked, and consented to take on him, the Nazarite vow. From the nature of that vow, which plainly contemplated some lengthened duration, it seems to us extremely unlikely that it would be thought of in the present case. All that seems meant here is, that Paul should so 'purify himself' ceremonially, as to be able to present himself as a cleansed man in the temple on the completion of these four men's vow. and be at charges with them [δαπάνηδον ἐπ' αὐτοῖς]—'pay expenses for them,' or defray the cost of the sacrifices legally required of them, along with his own; which was deemed a mark of Jewish generosity: that they may shave their heads (Num. vi. 9): and all may know that those things, whereof they were informed concerning thee, are nothing; but that thou thyself also walkest orderly, and keepest the law—not despising its ceremonial usages, but ready to comply with them. 25. As touching the Gentiles which believe, we [ἡμεῖς]—'we ourselves,' have written and concluded that they observe no such thing, save only that they keep themselves from things offered to idols, and from blood, and from strangled, and from fornication. This shows that, with all their conciliation to Jewish prejudice, the Church of Jerusalem was taught to adhere to the decision of the famous council held there, (ch. xv.) 26. Then Paul—at once falling in with this conciliatory and brotherly suggestion, for "to the Jews he became as a Jew, that he might gain the Jews" (1 Cor. ix. 20), took the men, and the next day purifying himself with them entered into the temple, to signify—'signifying,' that is, announcing to the attendant priest, the accomplishment of the days of purification, until that an offering should be

offered for every one of them—(see Num. v. 13-21.)
Uproar and seizure of Paul, who is only rescued from assassination by the commander of the garrison (27-32). 27. And when the seven days were almost ended, the Jews which were of Asia. The Jews here mentioned were in all likelihood Ephesian Jews, since they recognized the Ephesian Trophimus; and if so, we may well suppose that, bearing Paul a grudge ever since the events recorded in ch. xix. 9, &c., they would be the first to instigate a tumult against him. when they saw him in the temple, stirred up all the people, and laid hands on him, 28. Crying out, Men of Israel, help: This is the man that teacheth all men every where against the people, and the law, and this place: and further brought Greeks also into the temple, and hath polluted this holy place. As the foulest charges have usually some foundation in fact, the historian here deems it necessary to explain what that was in this case. 29. (For they had seen before with him in the city Trophimus an Ephesian [τὸν 'Εφέσ.]—it should be 'the Ephesian;' for he had been mentioned before as accompanying the apostle from Ephesus (ch. xx. 4): whom they supposed that Paul had brought into the temple.) It is a good exclamation of *Lechler* here, 'How narrowly are the servants of God watched, and what great reason have they to take heed to their steps! The world gives heed to those we walk with, and judges preachers by their company.' 30. And all the city was moved, and the people ran together: and they took Paul, and drew him out of the temple: and forthwith the doors were shut—probably that the murder they meant to perpetrate might not pollute that holy place. 31. And as they went about ('sought') to kill him, tidings came [ἀνέβη]—'came up,' a graphic allusion to the elevated position of the castle, which was built by Herod the Great on a high rock at the north-west corner of the great temple area, and called, after Mark Antony, the castle or

157

32 tain of the band, that all Jerusalem was in an uproar: who ²immediately took soldiers and centurions, and ran down unto them: and when they
33 saw the chief captain and the soldiers, they left beating of Paul. Then the chief captain came near, and took him, and *ᵃ*commanded *him* to be bound with two chains; and demanded who he was, and what he had
34 done. And some cried one thing, some another, among the multitude: and when he could not know the certainty for the tumult, he com-
35 manded him to be carried into the castle. And when he came upon the stairs, so it was, that he was borne of the soldiers for the violence of
36 the people. For the multitude of the people followed after, crying, *ᵇ*Away with him.
37 And as Paul was to be led into the castle, he said unto the chief captain, May I speak unto thee? Who said, Canst thou speak Greek?
38 Art not thou that ¹Egyptian, which before these days madest an uproar, and leddest out into the wilderness four thousand men that were mur-
39 derers? But Paul said, *ᶜ*I am a man *which am* a Jew of Tarsus, *a city* in Cilicia, a citizen of no mean city: and, I beseech thee, *ᵈ*suffer me to
40 speak unto the people. And when he had given him licence, Paul stood on the stairs, and beckoned with the hand unto the people. And when

A. D. 60.
* ch. 23, 27.
ᵃ Judg.15.13.
ch. 12, 6.
ch. 20, 23.
ch. 22, 25–
2².
ch. 28, 20.
ᵇ Luke 23.18.
John 19, 15.
ch. 22, 22.
1 This Egyp-
tian rose
A.D. 55.
* ch. 9, 11.
ch. 22, 3.
ch. 23, 34.
2 Cor. 11.
22.
Phil. 3, 5.
Col. 4, 3.
2 Tim. 2, 9.
Heb. 11, 36.
ᵈ 1 Pet. 3, 15.
1 Pet. 4, 16.

fortress of Antonia; **unto the chief captain of the band** [τ. χιλιάρχῳ τ. σπείρας]—properly, 'the prefect' or 'tribune of the cohort;' the commander of the garrison quartered in the castle, Claudius Lysias (ch. xxiii. 26). The full number of the cohort was 1000 men: *Josephus* informs us (Jewish War, v. 5, 8) that the garrison were ordered to remain under arms during the festivals in case of any outbreak. **that all Jerusalem was in an uproar.** This part of the narrative is particularly graphic. **32. Who immediately took soldiers and centurions, and ran down unto them: and when they saw the chief captain and the soldiers, they left beating of Paul.**

The tribune orders Paul to be bound with handchains and had to the barracks, taking him for a noted desperado; but on learning who he is, he gives him permission to address the people from the castle stairs (33-40). **33. Then the chief captain came near, and took him, and commanded him to be bound with two chains** (see on ch. xii. 6); and demanded **who he was** [τίς ἂν εἴη]—'who he might be,' and **what he had done.** **34. And some cried one thing, some another, among the multitude.** The difficulty would be so to state his alleged crimes as to justify their proceedings to a Roman officer. **and when he could not know the certainty for the tumult, he commanded him to be carried into the castle** [ἄγεσθαι εἰς τ. παρεμβολήν]—' to be brought into the barracks,' or that part of the castle which was allotted to the soldiers. **35. And when he came upon the stairs, so it was, that he was borne of the soldiers for the violence of the people. 36. For the multitude of the people followed after, crying, Away with him**—as before of his Lord (Luke xxiii. 18; John xix. 15). **37. And as Paul was to be led into the castle ('the barracks'), he said unto the chief captain, May I speak unto thee? Who said, Canst thou speak Greek? 38. Art not thou that Egyptian** [Οὐκ ἄρα σὺ εἶ]. As the grammatical form of the question implies that a negative answer is expected (and in this case, to the surprise of the officer), the strict rendering of it should be, 'Thou art not then that Egyptian,' &c.—Is it possible that thou art not?—**which before these days madest an uproar** ('an insurrection'), **and leddest out into the wilderness four thousand men that were murderers?** [τ. σικαρίων]—'of the *sicarii,*' or

'assassins.' *Josephus* twice over gives an account of this impostor and false prophet in his 'Antiquities' (xx. 8. 6), and in his 'Wars' (ii. 13, 5). Both these accounts agree with what is said here, save that instead of 4000 Sicarii, Josephus, in the latter passage, says he collected about 30,000 men, whom he lured to his cause. But if we suppose that of this large force 4000 were desperadoes, the two statements are not at all inconsistent. **39. But Paul said, I am a man which am a Jew of Tarsus, a city in Cilicia, a citizen of no mean city**—better, 'I am a Jew of Tarsus, a citizen of no mean city, of Cilicia.' 'The answer of the apostle (remarks *Humphry*) to the two questions of the Roman captain is such as to show at once that he could speak Greek with elegance, and that he was entitled to respectful treatment. The word rendered "citizen" [πολίτης] (he adds), implying the possession of civil rights, is emphatic and appropriate; for Tarsus was a free city, having received its liberty from Mark Antony (*Appian*, Bell. Civ. v. 7). It was "no mean city," for it enjoyed the title of *metropolis* of Cilicia, which, together with other privileges, was conferred on it by Augustus (*Dio Chrys.* Orat. xxxiv. p. 415). *Strabo,* in his interesting account of Tarsus (Lib. xiv. 674), says it surpassed even Athens and Alexandria in its zeal for philosophy, differing from those great schools in one respect—that its students were all natives, and it was not resorted to by foreigners. The natives, however, were not content with a home education, but went abroad to complete their studies, like St. Paul (ch. xxii. 3), and often did not return. Rome was full of them. Tarsus derived its civilization, and indeed its origin, from Greece, having been founded, as its mythology shows, by an Argine colony.' and, **I beseech thee, suffer me to speak unto the people. 40. And when he had given him licence, Paul stood on the stairs, and beckoned with the hand unto the people.** 'What nobler spectacle (exclaims *Chrysostom,* or some other in his name, quoted by *Hackett*) than that of Paul at this moment! There he stood, bound with two chains, ready to make his defence to the people. The Roman commander sits by, to enforce order by his presence. An enraged populace look up to him from below. Yet in the midst of so many dangers, how self-possessed is he, how tranquil!' And when

there was made a great silence, he spake unto *them* in the Hebrew tongue, saying,

22 MEN, [a]brethren, and fathers, hear ye my defence *which I make* now 2 unto you. (And when they heard that he spake in the Hebrew tongue 3 to them, they kept the more silence: and he saith,) I [b]am verily a man *which am* a Jew, born in Tarsus, *a city* in Cilicia, yet brought up in this city [c]at the feet of [d]Gamaliel, *and* taught [e]according to the perfect manner of

A. D. 60.
CHAP. 22.
[a] ch. 7. 2.
[b] ch. 9. 30.
2 Cor. 11.22.
Phil. 3. 5.
[c] Deut. 33. 3.
[d] ch. 5. 34.
[e] ch. 26. 5.

there was made a great silence—the people awed at the permission given him by the commandant, and seeing him sitting as a listener, **he spake unto them in the Hebrew tongue**—the Syro-Chaldaic, the vernacular tongue of the Palestine Jews since the captivity.

Remarks.—1. It will be observed that the predictions of impending suffering, in connection with this visit of the apostle to Jerusalem, became not only more frequent but more and more clear the nearer the time for their fulfilment came to be. So was it with the Old Testament predictions of the first appearing of our Lord in the flesh, and His own predictions of His last sufferings. And like foreshadowings of suffering for the truth, waxing clearer and more unmistakeable as the time approaches, prepare the faithful servants of Christ for meeting calmly, and enduring triumphantly, what in earlier stages of their testimony they might probably have shrunk from. 2. 'To find disciples (says *Lechler* finely) was an important event in the journal of the travelling apostles. If the learned, the naturalists, the judges of the fine arts, inquire in their travels after the curiosities of science, nature, and art, a servant of Jesus, on the contrary, directs his eye to the rarities in the kingdom of Jesus; and his most delightful discovery is to meet with the children of God.' 3. In what passed between Paul and the official brethren at Jerusalem, with James at their head, we have a beautiful example—deeply worthy of study and imitation—of firm adherence to essential principles on the one hand, and, on the other, of forbearance and concession in things subordinate. As James had in the famous council (ch. xv.) maintained the freedom of the Gentile believers from the bondage of Jewish ordinances, so he and the elders associated with him glorify God on this occasion for the conversion of so many Gentiles through Paul's instrumentality, never proposing that any ceremonial yoke should be imposed upon them. In one who appears to have had an intensely conservative reverence for all the observances of the ancient economy—insomuch that *Josephus* testifies to the reverence in which he was held by the whole Jewish community (by whom he was known as JAMES THE JUST)—this joy at the accession to Christ of uncircumcised Gentiles, and firmness in resisting the imposition of the ceremonial yoke upon the Gentile converts, was very admirable. But, on the other hand, representing, as James and the elders did, the church of the metropolis of Judaism, whose members, entirely Jewish, were strongly tinctured with Jewish prejudice, and jealous of whatever tended to loosen the hold of Jewish peculiarities on the minds of the chosen people, they deemed it highly expedient that Paul, who had been industriously represented as "teaching all the Jews which were among the Gentiles to forsake Moses," should give some public evidence that this was a calumny. And James having suggested a way by which this could be at once done, our apostle immediately falls in with it and carries it into effect. It may, indeed, be said that this proved a fatal step, since it was by entering into the temple, to announce to the priest the com-

pletion of the days of his ceremonial purification that he was supposed to have "brought Greeks with him into the temple, and so to have polluted that holy place." But this was only the immediate occasion of a charge which his Jewish enemies were evidently waiting for some opportunity of fastening upon him—of being an enemy to Moses; and from their temper and treatment of him on this occasion there can be little doubt that, failing this, they would speedily have found some other plea for setting upon him. As the advice was in the circumstances a wise one, so the ready compliance with it on the part of Paul showed his entire freedom from narrowness and fanaticism in the advocacy even of great truths. (See on ch. iii., Remark 1, and on ch. xv. 1-35, Remark 4, at the close of those Sections.) 2. What zeal for Christ was that which, when seized, hustled, and ready to be assassinated by an infuriated Jewish mob; when wrested out of their hands with difficulty by order of the tribune, who knew nothing of the circumstances, and only sought to preserve the peace; when bound with hand-chains, and in this condition—ascending the castle stairs on his way to the barracks, from whence he beheld the masses of the people that thronged the declivity below him—hurried to address them; and—when permission to do so was asked in excellent Greek, to the astonishment of the tribune, and granted at once—prompted him to tell the story of his conversion, as the most convincing way of bringing the glory of the crucified Redeemer before them; a story whose narrative form and unvarnished, unimpassioned character only showed how sober was his present enthusiasm, how reasonable and resistless his surrender to Christ, and how entire was his devotion to His cause!

CHAP. XXII. 1-30. — PAUL'S DEFENCE FROM THE STAIRS OF THE FORTRESS—THE RAGE OF THE AUDIENCE BURSTING FORTH, THE COMMANDANT HAS HIM BROUGHT INTO THE FORT TO BE EXAMINED BY SCOURGING, BUT LEARNING THAT HE IS A ROMAN, HE ORDERS HIS RELEASE, AND COMMANDS THE SANHEDRIM TO TRY HIM.

The Defence (1-21). **1. Men, brethren, and fathers**—more simply, 'Brethren and fathers,' **hear ye my defence which I make now unto you.** 2. **(And when they heard that he spake in the Hebrew tongue** (see on ch. xxi. 40) **to them, they kept the more silence.** They could have understood him in Greek, and doubtless fully expected the renegade to address them in that language; but the sound of their holy mother-tongue awed them into deeper silence. **and he saith).** This sketch of his life having been already made use of, in illustration of the remarkable account given of his conversion, by the historian in ch. ix., a few supplementary notes are all that seem requisite here. 3. **I am verily a man which am a Jew** ('I am a Jew'), **born in Tarsus** (see on ch. xxi. 39), **[a city] in Cilicia, yet brought up in this city at the feet** (see on Luke x. 39) **of Gamaliel** (see on ch. v. 34) —a fact of great importance in the apostle's history, standing in the same relation to his future career as Moses' education in the Egyptian court to the work for which he was destined; **and taught according to the perfect manner of the**

159

the law of the fathers, and *f* was zealous toward God, *g* as ye all are this
4 day. And *h* I persecuted this way unto the death, binding and delivering
5 into prisons both men and women. As also the high priest doth bear me
witness, and *i* all the estate of the elders: from *j* whom also I received
letters unto the *k* brethren, and went to Damascus, to bring them which
6 were there bound unto Jerusalem, for to be punished. And *l* it came to
pass, that, as I made my journey, and was come nigh unto Damascus
about noon, suddenly there shone from heaven a great light round about
7 me. And I fell unto the ground, and heard a voice saying unto me,
8 Saul, Saul, why persecutest thou me? And I answered, Who art thou,
Lord? And he said unto me, I am Jesus of Nazareth, whom thou per-
9 secutest. And *m* they that were with me saw indeed the light, and were
10 afraid; but they heard not the voice of him that spake to me. And I
said, What shall I do, Lord? And the Lord said unto me, Arise, and
go into Damascus: and there it shall be told thee of all things which are
11 appointed for thee to do. And when I could not see for the glory of
that light, being led by the hand of them that were with me, I came into
12 Damascus. And *n* one Ananias, a devout man according to the law,
13 *o* having a good report of all the *p* Jews which dwelt *there*, came unto me,
and stood, and said unto me, Brother Saul, receive thy sight. And
14 the same hour I looked up upon him. And he said, *q* The God of
our fathers hath *r* chosen thee, that thou shouldest know his will,
and *s* see that *t* Just One, and *u* shouldest hear the voice of his mouth.
15 For *v* thou shalt be his witness unto all men of *w* what thou hast seen and
16 heard. And now why tarriest thou? arise, and be baptized, and *x* wash
17 away thy sins, calling *y* on the name of the Lord. And *z* it came to pass,
that, when I was come again to Jerusalem, even while I prayed in the
18 temple, I was in a trance; and saw him saying unto me, Make haste,

A. D. 60
f Gal. I. 14.
g Rom. 10. 2.
h ch. 8. 3.
Phil. 3. 6.
1 Tim. 1.13.
i Luke 22. 66.
ch. 4. 5.
j ch. 9. 2.
k Rom. 9. 3.
l ch. 26. 12.
m Dan. 10. 7.
n ch. 9. 17.
o ch. 10. 22.
p 1 Tim. 3. 7.
q ch. 3. 13.
ch. 5. 30.
r ch. 26. 16.
Rom. 1. 1.
Gal. 1. 1.
Tit. 1. 1.
s 1 Cor. 9. 1.
1 Cor. 15. 8.
t ch. 3. 14.
ch. 7. 52.
Heb. 7. 21.
1 John 1. 1.
u 1 Cor. 11.23.
Gal. 1. 12.
v ch. 23.11.
w ch. 4. 20.
ch. 26. 16.
x ch. 2. 38.
Heb. 10. 22.
y ch. 9. 14.
Rom. 10.13.
z 2 Cor. 12. 2.

law of the fathers—'according to the rigidity of the ancestral law,' the strictest form of traditional Judaism; and **was zealous** (or 'a zealot') **toward God, as ye all are this day**—his own murderous zeal against the disciples of the Lord Jesus being merely reflected in their present treatment of himself. **4. And I persecuted this** ('the') **way unto the death, binding and delivering into prisons, &c. 5. As also the high priest** (still alive, it seems) **doth bear me witness, and all the estate of the elders**—the whole Sanhedrim (cf. Luke xxii. 66, *Gr.*); a powerful appeal this: **from whom also I received letters unto the brethren** (in the Jewish Faith), **and went to Damascus, to bring them which were there bound unto Jerusalem, for to be punished. 6, 7. And it came to pass, &c. 8. And I answered, Who art thou, Lord? And he said unto me, I am Jesus of Nazareth**—'Jesus the Nazarene,' **whom thou persecutest. 9. And they that were with me saw indeed the light, and were afraid.** The external evidence against this last clause is strong, but besides that there is nearly equal authority for it, internal evidence bespeaks it genuine; it being a favourite phrase of Luke, as *Tischendorf* notes—being used by him four times elsewhere, and only once by any other New Testament writer. Accordingly *Tischendorf*, who had excluded it in a former edition, restores it in his last one; and though *Lachm.* and *Treg.* reject it, *Meyer, de Wette, Lechler,* and *Alford* pronounce in favour of it. **but they heard not the voice of him that spake to me. 10, 11. And I said, &c. . . . I came into Damascus. 12. And one Ananias, a devout man according to the law, having a good report of all the Jews which dwelt there.** One would not know from this description of Ananias that he was

a Christian at all, the apostle's object being to hold him up as unexceptionable even to the most rigid Jews. **13. Came unto me, and stood, and said unto me, Brother Saul, receive thy sight. And the same hour I** [Κἀγὼ αὐτῇ τ. ὥρα]—'And I the self-same hour,' **looked up upon him. 14. And he said, The God of our fathers hath chosen thee**—studiously linking the new economy upon the old, as but the sequel of it, both having one glorious Author; **that thou shouldest know his will, and see that** ('the') **Just One** (cf. ch. iii. 14; vii. 52), **and shouldest hear the voice of his mouth**—in order to place him on a level with the other apostles who had "seen the (Risen) Lord." **15. For thou shalt be his witness unto all men of what thou hast seen and heard. 16. And now why tarriest thou? arise, and be baptized, and wash away thy sins** [βάπτισαι καὶ ἀπόλουσαι: cf. 1 Cor. vi. 11, *Gr.*]—*lit.*, 'have thyself baptized and thy sins washed away.' Remission of sins is obtained solely through faith in the Lord Jesus, (ch. x. 43, &c.); but baptism being the visible seal of this, it is here and elsewhere naturally transferred from the inward act of faith to that which publicly and formally proclaims it. **calling on** [ἐπικαλη-σάμενος]—'having (that is, *after* having) called on,' referring to the confession of Christ which *preceded* baptism, **the name of the Lord**—'on His name' is the true reading (the received text having but inferior support). **17. And it came to pass, that, when I was come again to Jerusalem**—for the first time after his conversion; see on ch. ix. 30: even (rather 'and') **while I prayed in the temple**—thus calling their attention to the fact, that after his conversion he kept up his connection with the temple as before, **I was in a trance; 18. And saw him saying unto me, Make**

^aand get thee quickly out of Jerusalem: for they will not receive thy
19 testimony concerning me. And I said, Lord, ^bthey know that I im-
20 prisoned and ^cbeat in every synagogue them that believed on thee: and
^dwhen the blood of thy martyr Stephen was shed, I also was standing
by, and ^econsenting unto his death, and kept the raiment of them that
21 slew him. And he said unto me, Depart: for ^fI will send thee far hence
unto the Gentiles.
22 And they gave him audience unto this word, and *then* lifted up their
voices, and said, ^gAway with such a *fellow* from the earth; for it is not
23 fit that ^hhe should live. And as they cried out, and cast off *their* clothes,
24 and threw dust into the air, the chief captain commanded him to be
brought into the castle, and bade that he should be examined by scourg-
25 ing; that he might know wherefore they cried so against him. And as
they bound him with thongs, Paul said unto the centurion that stood
by, ⁱIs it lawful for you to scourge a man that is a Roman, and uncon-
26 demned? When the centurion heard *that*, he went and told the chief
captain, saying, Take heed what thou doest: for this man is a Roman.
27 Then the chief captain came, and said unto him, Tell me, art thou a
28 Roman? He said, Yea. And the chief captain answered, With a great
sum obtained I this freedom. And Paul said, But I was *free*-born.
29 Then straightway they departed from him which should have ¹examined
him: and the chief captain also was afraid, after he knew that he was a
Roman, and because he had bound him.
30 On the morrow, because he would have known the certainty wherefore

A. D. 60.

^a Matt.10.14.
^b ch. 8. 3.
^c Matt. 10.
17.
1 Cor. 15. 9.
Phil. 3. 6.
1 Tim. 1.13.
^d ch. 7. 58.
^e Luke 11.48.
ch. 8. 1.
Rom. 1. 32.
^f ch. 13. 2.
ch. 18. 6.
ch. 26. 17.
Rom. 1. 5.
Rom. 11.13.
Rom. 15.16.
Gal. 1. 15.
Gal. 2. 7.
8.
Eph. 3. 7,
8.
1 Tim. 2. 7.
2 Tim. 1.
11.
^g ch. 21. 36.
^h ch. 25. 24.
ⁱ ch. 16. 37.
1 Or,
tortured
him.

---

haste, and get thee quickly out of Jerusalem: for
they will not receive thy testimony concerning
me. 19. And I said, Lord, they know that I imprisoned and beat in every synagogue them that
believed on thee: 20. And when the blood of thy
martyr Stephen was shed, I also was standing by, and consenting [unto his death]. (The
bracketed words are too weakly supported, and
have probably got in here from ch. viii. 1.) and
kept the raiment of them that slew him. 21.
And he said unto me, Depart: for I will send thee
far hence [μακρὰν]—'far away' unto the Gentiles.
On this thrilling dialogue between the Redeemer
and His chosen vessel—nowhere else related—see
on ch. ix. 30.

*The concluding words of this Defence having
raised an uproar among the crowd, the Tribune,
ignorant of the cause, orders him to be removed
to the castle and examined by scourging, but is
restrained and alarmed on learning that he is a
Roman citizen—Next day, having had him released, he orders him to be tried by the Sanhedrim*
(22-30). 22. And they gave him audience unto
this word, and then lifted up their voices, and
said, Away with such a fellow from the earth;
for it is not fit [καθῆκεν, in the imperfect—'was
not fit,' has decisive authority; καθῆκεν has hardly
any: it is a mixture of the direct and indirect way
of reporting a speech ; but it is needless to follow
this in the translation] that he should live.
Their national prejudices lashed into fury at the
mention of a mission to the Gentiles, they would
speedily have done to him as they did to Stephen,
but for the presence and protection of the Roman
officer. The profanation of the temple by the presence of Gentiles seemed nothing to Gentiles being
deliberately placed on a level in religious privileges with the covenant-people. 23. And as they
cried out, and cast off their clothes—'tossed their
garments' (their cloaks), and threw dust into the
air—in token of rage. 24. The chief captain commanded him to be brought into the castle, and
bade that he should be examined by scourging—

according to the Roman practice; that he might
know wherefore they cried so against him. Paul's
speech being to him in an unknown tongue, he
concluded, from the horror which it kindled in the
vast audience, that he must have been guilty of
some crime. 25. And as they bound him with
thongs [προέτειναν, or—ον αὐτὸν τοῖς ἱμᾶσιν]—
'were stretching him out (or "putting him on the
stretch") with thongs'; that is, fixing him in this
way for receiving the keen strokes of the scourgers.
[The received text—' he bound him' (προέτεινεν)—
is here properly departed from by our translators,
with *Beza*: it has next to no support.] Paul
said unto the centurion that stood by—to superintend the torture, and receive the confession
expected to be wrung from him, Is it lawful for
you to scourge a man that is a Roman, and uncondemned? See on ch. xvi. 37. 26. When the
centurion heard that, he went and told the chief
captain, saying, Take heed what thou doest—the
true reading clearly is, 'What doest thou?' ["Οσα
being insufficiently attested]. for this man is a
Roman. 27. Then the chief captain came, and
said unto him, Tell me, art thou a Roman?—
showing that his being of Tarsus, which he had
told him before (ch. xxi. 39), did not necessarily
imply, at least in his estimation, that he was
a Roman citizen. He said, Yea. 28. And the
chief captain answered, With a great sum obtained I this freedom. Roman citizenship was
bought and sold in the reign of Claudius, we know,
at a high price: at a subsequent date, for next to
nothing. But to put in a false claim to this privilege was a capital crime. And Paul said, But I
was [free] born [γεγέννημαι]—'born to it;' either
by purchase or in reward of services, on the part
of his father or some ancestor. 29. Then straightway they departed from him which should have
examined him: and the chief captain also was
afraid, after he knew that he was a Roman, and
because he had bound him. See on ch. xvi. 38.
30. On the morrow, because he would have
known the certainty wherefore he was accused

he was accused of the Jews, he loosed him from *his* bands, and [j]commanded the chief priests and all their council to appear, and brought Paul down, and set him before them.

23 AND Paul, earnestly beholding the council, said, Men *and* brethren, I
2 [a]have lived in all good conscience before God until this day. And the high priest Ananias commanded them that stood by him [b]to smite him
3 on the mouth. Then said Paul unto him, God shall smite thee, *thou* whited wall: for sittest thou to judge me after the law, and [c]commandest
4 me to be smitten contrary to the law? And they that stood by said,
5 Revilest thou God's high priest? Then said Paul, [d]I wist not, brethren,

A. D. 60.

[j] Matt. 10.17.
Luke 21. 12.

CHAP. 23.
[a] 1 Cor. 4. 4.
2 Cor. 1. 12.
2 Tim. 1. 3.
[b] 1 Ki. 22. 24.
Jer. 20. 2.
[c] Lev. 19. 35.
Deut. 25. 1.
John 7. 51.
[d] ch. 24. 17.

of the Jews, he loosed him from his bands, and commanded the chief priests and all their council to appear [ὅλον τὸ συνέδριον]—'the entire Sanhedrim to assemble,' and brought Paul down, and set him before them. Note here the power to order a Sanhedrim to try this case, assumed by the Roman officers and acquiesced in on their part.

Remarks.—Here again one cannot but mark that rare combination of great qualities which made Paul that man of ten thousand which he was. We have seen on ch. xxi. (Remark 2, at the close of that Section) how, immediately after being rescued with some difficulty from assassination by the military tribune, and standing manacled on the castle stairs, on his way to the barracks, he pleaded for and obtained permission to address the multitude that stood thick beneath him; and we have now seen what a calm and sublime account he could give in such circumstances of his miraculous conversion to the Lord Jesus on his way to Damascus, and of the vision which he had thereafter of his Lord in the temple, warning him that his efforts to gain his countrymen in the metropolis would be fruitless —that he must escape from it without delay, and that, instead of making his countrymen his chief care, he was to be sent far away to the Gentiles. That word, however, "unto *the Gentiles*," rousing their national prejudices to the uttermost, lashed the mob into a mad fury, which, but for the presence of the tribune, would quickly have produced fatal results. The commanding officer—helpless from his ignorance of the language in which Paul had delivered his address, and concluding that he must be some desperado, and probably an Egyptian, who before that had made insurrection at the head of a formidable band of assassins—has him tightened with thongs, as already his hands had been bound with chains, to prepare him for the lash by which he thought to extort from him a confession of his crimes. In these critical circumstances, Paul, rising to the dignity of a Roman citizen, calmly demands of the attendant centurion whether such procedure towards a Roman was legal. This leads to an interview with the tribune himself, who, knowing that if the prisoner were indeed a Roman, he had acted illegally, anxiously questions him on the subject. In this interview, the dignity, calmness, and perfect presence of mind with which the apostle carried himself contrasts finely with the conscious inferiority of the tribune, in point of civil position, to the man whom he had so dishonoured. Accordingly, while the commanding officer is glad to have him loosed from his bonds and handed over to the Sanhedrim for trial, as the proper tribunal, the apostle is just as ready to stand before these ecclesiastics as before he had been to meet face to face the military authority.

CHAP. XXIII. 1-35.—PAUL BEFORE THE SANHEDRIM, BY PROCLAIMING HIMSELF A PHARISEE ON THE SUBJECT OF THE RESURRECTION, DIVIDES

THE RIVAL FACTIONS, FROM WHOSE VIOLENCE THE TRIBUNE HAS HIM REMOVED INTO THE BARRACKS, WHERE HE IS CHEERED BY A NIGHT-VISION OF HIS GLORIFIED LORD—AN INFAMOUS CONSPIRACY TO ASSASSINATE HIM BEING PROVIDENTIALLY DEFEATED, HE IS DESPATCHED BY NIGHT TO CÆSAREA, WITH A LETTER FROM THE TRIBUNE TO FELIX, BY WHOM ARRANGEMENTS ARE MADE FOR A HEARING OF HIS CAUSE.

Paul before the Sanhedrim (1-5). 1. And Paul, earnestly beholding the council—with a look of conscious integrity and unfaltering courage, perhaps also recognizing some of his early fellow-pupils, said, Men and brethren, I have lived in all good conscience before God until this day. The phrase here rendered "lived before (or 'to') God" [πεπολίτευμαι τ. Θεῷ] is understood by *Meyer*, *Lechler*, and others to assert no more than the conscientious discharge of his office. But as the word has a primary reference to 'polity,' or 'citizenship,' there is good reason to think that the apostle here intended to affirm that he had ever been, and since his conversion to Christ, was as much as ever an honest, God-fearing member of "the commonwealth of Israel;" and (as *Humphry* says) it was probably the boldness of this assertion which called forth the outrage described in the next verse. 2. And the high priest Ananias commanded them that stood by him to smite him on the mouth—a method of silencing a speaker common in the East (says *Hackett*) to this day; and our Lord was treated with the same indignity (John xviii. 22). But for a judge thus to treat a prisoner on his trial, for merely prefacing his defence by a protestation of his integrity, was infamous. 3. Then said Paul unto him, God shall smite thee—as indeed He did; for he was killed by an assassin during the Jewish war (*Josephus*, J. W. ii. 17. 9), thou whited wall—that is, hypocrite! (See Matt. xxiii. 27.) This epithet, however, though correctly describing the man, must not be defended as addressed to a judge; although the remonstrance which follows, for sittest thou to judge me after the law, and commandest me to be smitten contrary to the law? ought to have put him to shame. 4. And they that stood by said, Revilest thou God's high priest? 5. Then said Paul, I wist not, brethren, that he was the high priest. All sorts of explanations of this have been given. The high priesthood was in a state of great confusion and constant change at this time (as appears from *Josephus*), and the apostle's long absence from Jerusalem, and perhaps the manner in which he was habited, or the seat he occupied, with other circumstances to us unknown, may account for such a speech. But if he was thrown off his guard by an insult which touched him to the quick, 'what (says *Hackett*) can surpass the grace with which he recovered his self-possession, and the frankness with which he acknowledged his error? If his conduct in yielding to the momentary impulse was not that of Christ himself under a similar provo-

that he was the high priest: for it is written, Thou [e]shalt not speak evil
of the ruler of thy people.
6 But when Paul perceived that the one part were Sadducees, and the
other Pharisees, he cried out in the council, Men *and* brethren, [f]I am a
Pharisee, the son of a Pharisee: [g]of the hope and resurrection of the
7 dead I am called in question. And when he had so said, there arose a
dissension between the Pharisees and the Sadducees: and the multitude
8 was divided. For [h]the Sadducees say that there is no resurrection,
9 neither angel, nor spirit; but the Pharisees confess both. And there
arose a great cry: and the scribes *that were* of the Pharisees' part arose,
and strove, saying, [i]We find no evil in this man: but [j]if a spirit or an
10 angel hath spoken to him, let [k]us not fight against God. And when
there arose a great dissension, the chief captain, fearing lest Paul should
have been pulled in pieces of them, commanded the soldiers to go down,
and to take him by force from among them, and to bring *him* into the
11 castle. And [l]the night following, the Lord stood by him, and said,
Be of good cheer, Paul: for as thou hast testified of me in Jerusalem, so
must thou bear witness also at Rome.

A. D. 60.

e Ex. 22. 28. Jude 8.
f Phil. 3. 5.
g ch. 28. 20.
h Matt. 22. 23. Mark 12. 18. Luke 20. 27.
i Pro. 16. 7. Luke 23. 4.
j ch. 22. 7.
k ch. 5. 39. ch. 9. 4, 5. ch. 11. 17.
l Ps. 46. 1. Ps. 109. 31. Isa. 41. 10. Isa. 43. 2. Jer. 15. 19-21. ch. 2. 25. ch. 18. 9. ch. 27. 23.

cation (John xviii. 22, 23), certainly the manner in which he atoned for his fault was *Christ-like*.' **for it is written** (Exod. xxii. 28), **Thou shalt not speak evil of the ruler of thy people.** Excellent is *Humphry's* remark at the close of his note on this verse, that 'More edification may be derived from observing how speedily and gracefully he recovered his equanimity, than from contending, against the plain meaning of the words, that he was altogether exempt from human weakness.'

Observing how the parties in the council were balanced, Paul takes advantage of it by proclaiming his agreement with the Pharisees on the subject of the Resurrection, and thus obtains the protection of that party against the Sadducees (6-9). **6. But when Paul perceived**—from the discussion which plainly had by this time arisen between the parties, **that the one part were Sadducees, and the other Pharisees, he cried out**—raising his voice above both parties, **I am a Pharisee, the son of a Pharisee**—'a son of Pharisees' is the best attested reading; in which case the meaning is, belonging to a family who from father to son had long been such: **of the hope and resurrection of the dead**—that is (as good critics take it), 'of the hope of a resurrection of the dead;' or (with others), 'of the Messianic hope in general, as ch. xxviii. 20. The former suits the apostle's object better, as the resurrection was the one point to which he sought to direct attention. **I am called in question.** This was not the vague hope of immortality—the utmost to which the heathen could rise—but the definite hope of a resurrection-state. By this adroit stroke Paul engages the whole Pharisaic section of the council in his favour; the doctrine of a resurrection being common to both, though they would totally differ in their *application* of it. This was of course quite warrantable, and the more so as it was already evident that no impartiality in trying his cause was to be looked for from such an assembly. **7. And when he had so said, there arose a dissension between the Pharisees and the Sadducees: and the multitude was divided. 8. For the Sadducees say that there is no resurrection, neither angel, nor spirit** (see on Luke xx. 37); **but the Pharisees confess both**—that is, both the resurrection of the body and the existence of spiritual beings. **9. And there arose a great cry: and the scribes**—the true reading appears to be, 'scribes' (without the article); **that were of the Pharisees' part arose, and strove, saying, We find no evil in this man: but**—as to those startling things which he brings to our ears, **if a spirit or an angel hath spoken to him**—referring, perhaps, to his trance in the temple, of which he had told them (ch. xxii. 17). They put this favourable construction upon his proceedings for no other reason than that they had found him one of their own party; they cared not to enquire into the *truth* of what he alleged, over and above their opinions, but only to explain it away as something not worth raising a noise about. **[let us not fight against God].** (This bracketed clause is clearly an addition to the genuine text.) [It is wanting in א A B C E, &c., the Vulgate, &c., and is supported chiefly by two late Uncials, G H.] The sense, then, will be, 'but what if a spirit or angel hath spoken to him?' The clause, "let us not fight against God," seems clearly taken from the similar expression of Gamaliel (ch. v. 39), in circumstances not dissimilar to those here, in order to complete the sentence. But it is possible that the conclusion of the sentence was drowned in the hubbub, which the next verse shows to have been intense.

The tribune fearing, from the hubbub in the council, that the prisoner's life is in danger, has him removed by force into the barracks, where he is cheered by a night-vision of his Lord, assuring him he should yet testify for Him at Rome, even as he had done at Jerusalem (10, 11). **10. And when there arose a great dissension** [στάσεως]—'uproar' (cf. ch. xix. 49, *Gr.*), **the chief captain, fearing lest Paul should have been pulled in pieces of them, commanded the soldiers to go down, and to take him by force from among them, and to bring him into the castle** ('the barracks'). This shows that the tribune had not been himself present, and further, that instead of the Sanhedrim trying the cause, the proceedings quickly consisted in the one party attempting to seize the prisoner, and the other to protect him. **11. And the night following**—his heart perhaps sinking in the solitude of his barrack-ward, and thinking, perhaps, that all the predictions of danger at Jerusalem were now to be fulfilled in his death there, **the Lord**—THE LORD JESUS, his glorified but ever-present Master, **stood by him, and said, Be of good cheer, [Paul].** (This bracketed word is clearly not genuine.) **for as thou hast testified of me** [διεμαρτύρω τὰ περὶ Ἐμοῦ]—'as thou hast thoroughly testified the things concerning Me.' In this emphatic sense of 'thorough testimony,' the **same**

12 And when it was day, ^m certain of the Jews banded together, and bound themselves under a curse, saying that they would neither eat
13 nor drink till they had killed Paul. And they were more than forty
14 which had made this conspiracy. And they came to the chief priests and elders, and said, We have bound ourselves under a great curse, that we
15 will eat nothing until we have slain Paul. Now therefore ye with the council signify to the chief captain that he bring him down unto you to-morrow, as though ye would enquire something more perfectly concerning him: and we, or ever he come near, are ready to kill him.
16 And ⁿ when Paul's sister's son heard of their lying in wait, he went
17 and entered into the castle, and told Paul. Then ^o Paul called one of the centurions unto *him*, and said, Bring this young man unto the chief
18 captain; for he hath a certain thing to tell him. So he took him, and brought *him* to the chief captain, and said, Paul the prisoner called me unto *him*, and prayed me to bring this young man unto thee, who hath
19 something to say unto thee. Then the chief captain took him by the hand, and went *with him* aside privately, and asked *him*, What is that
20 thou hast to tell me? And he said, ^p The Jews have agreed to desire thee that thou wouldest bring down Paul to-morrow into the council, as
21 though they would enquire somewhat of him more perfectly. But do not thou yield unto them; for there ^q lie in wait for him of them more than forty men, which have bound themselves with an oath, that they will neither eat nor drink till they have killed him: and now are they ready,

A. D. 60.

^m Isa. 8. 9,
10.
ch. 25. 3.
Rom. 8. 31.
¹ Or, with
an oath of
execra-
tion.
1 Sam. 3. 17.
1 Sam. 20.
13.
1 Sam. 25.
22.
2 Sam. 3. 9.
1 Ki. 2. 23.
1 Ki. 19. 2.
Matt. 26. 74.
ⁿ Job 5. 13.
Pro. 21. 30.
^o Matt. 10. 16.
Eph. 5. 15.
^p ch. 20. 3.
ch. 25. 3.
^q Ps. 10. 9.
Ps. 37. 12,
32.
Pro. 1. 16.
Pro. 4. 16.
Isa. 59. 7.

compound word is used in ch. xx. 21, 24 (on which see). **in Jerusalem, so must thou bear witness also at Rome**—*q. d.*, 'Thy work in Jerusalem is done, faithfully and well; but thou art not to die here; thy purpose, next to "see ‚Rome" (ch. xix. 21), shall not be disappointed, and there also must thou bear witness of Me. As this vision was not unneeded now, so we shall find it cheering and upholding him throughout all that befell him up to his arrival there.

A conspiracy to assassinate Paul is providentially discovered, and made known to the tribune (12-21). **12. And when it was day, [certain of] the Jews**—"the Jews" is manifestly the true reading. It was the great body of his enemies who combined, though only a formidable band of them volunteered to act. **banded together, and bound themselves under a curse**—*lit.*, 'anathematized themselves,' or solemnly wished themselves accursed (or damned, if they did not do what they proposed. (See 1 Sam. xiv. 24; 2 Sam. iii. 35.) This was what poor Peter did when he denied his Lord (see on Mark xiv. 71, p. 207). **saying that they would neither eat nor drink till they had killed Paul. 13. And they were more than forty which had made this conspiracy. 14. And they came to the chief priests and elders, and said, We have bound ourselves under a great curse**—the words are very emphatic, **that we will eat** ('taste') **nothing until we have slain Paul. 15. Now therefore ye with the council signify to the chief captain that he bring him down unto you [to-morrow,** (the bracketed word is clearly not genuine.) **as though ye would enquire something more perfectly concerning him.** That these high ecclesiastics fell in readily with this infamous plot is clear; indeed, what will not unscrupulous and hypocritical religionists do under the mask of religion? The narrative bears unmistakeable internal marks of truth. **and we, or ever he come near, are ready to kill him.** Their plan was to assassinate him on his way down from the barracks to the council. The case was critical; but He who had pledged His word to him, that he should testify for Him at Rome, provided unexpected means of defeating this well-laid scheme. **16. And when Paul's sister's son** (see on ch. ix. 30) **heard of their lying in wait, he went and entered into the castle, and told Paul.** If this lad was then residing at Jerusalem for his education, like Paul himself, he may have got at the schools those hints of the conspiracy on which he so promptly acted. **17. Then Paul called one of the centurions unto him, and said, Bring this young man unto the chief captain; for he hath a certain thing to tell him.** Observe here, how although Divinely assured of safety, Paul never allows this to interfere with the duty he owed to his own life and the work he had yet to do. (See on ch. xxvii. 22-25, 27.) **18. So he took him, and brought him to the chief captain, and said, Paul the prisoner called me unto him, and prayed me to bring this young man unto thee, who hath something to say unto thee. 19. Then the chief captain took him by the hand.** A little lad, then, quite in his boyhood, he must have been, and this small incident throws a pleasing light on the kind-hearted impartiality of this officer. **and went with him aside privately, and asked him, What is that thou hast to tell me? 20. And he said, The Jews have agreed to desire thee that thou wouldest bring down Paul to-morrow into the council, as though they would enquire**—'as if thou wert going to enquire' seems the true reading [μέλλων], **somewhat of him more perfectly. 21. But do not thou yield unto them; for there lie in wait for him of them more than forty men, which have bound themselves with an oath, that they will neither eat nor drink till they have killed him: and now are they ready, looking for a promise from thee.** Thus, as is often the case with God's people, not till the last moment, when the plot was all prepared, did deliverance come.

On hearing of this conspiracy, the tribune, enjoining silence on his informer, despatches Paul by night to Cæsarea, under a strong escort, with a letter stating the circumstances to Felix the Procurator, that, as civil governor of the province, he might bring him

22 looking for a promise from thee.　So the chief captain *then* let the young
man depart, and charged *him, See thou* tell no man that thou hast showed
these things to me.

23　And he called unto *him* two centurions, saying, Make ready two hundred soldiers to go to Cesarea, and horsemen threescore and ten, and
24 ² spearmen two hundred, at the third hour of the night; and provide
them beasts, that they may set Paul on, and bring *him* safe unto Felix
25, the governor.　And he wrote a letter after this manner: Claudius Lysias
26, unto the most excellent governor Felix *sendeth* greeting.　This ʳman was
27 taken of the Jews, and should have been killed of them: then came I
with an army, and rescued him, having understood that he was a Roman.
28 And *ˢ*when I would have known the cause wherefore they accused him,
29 I brought him forth into their council : whom I perceived to be
accused of questions *ᵗ*of their law, *ᵘ*but to have nothing laid to his
30 charge worthy of death or of bonds.　And when it was told me how
that the Jews laid wait for the man, I sent straightway to thee, and
*ᵛ*gave commandment to his accusers also to say before thee what *they had*
against him.　Farewell.

31　Then the soldiers, as it was commanded them, took Paul, and brought
32 *him* by night to Antipatris.　On the morrow they left thè horsemen to
33 go with him, and returned to the castle: who, when they came to
*ᵂ*Cesarea, and delivered the epistle to the governor, presented Paul also
34 before him.　And when the governor had read *the letter*, he asked of
what province he was.　And when he understood that *he was ˣ*of Cilicia;
35 I *ʸ*will hear thee, said he, when thine accusers are also come.　And he
commanded him to be kept *ᶻ*in Herod's judgment-hall.

A. D. 60.
² Or,
archers,
or, javelin
casters.
ʳ ch. 12. 6.
ch. 20. 23.
ch. 21. 33.
ch. 22. 25-
29.
ch. 23. 10.
ch. 24. 7.
ch. 28. 20.
ˢ ch. 22. 30.
ᵗ ch. 18. 15.
ch. 24. 5, 6.
ch. 25. 19.
ᵘ Ps. 27. 12.
Ps. 35. 11.
Matt. 5. 11,
12.
Mark 15. 3.
ᵛ ch. 24. 8.
ᵂ ch. 8. 40.
A city on
the north-
west of
Canaan.
ˣ ch. 6. 9.
ch. 21, 39,
ʸ ch. 24. 1.
ch. 25. 16.
ᶻ Matt.27.27.

*to trial—Arrangements for this are accordingly
made* (22-35).　22. **So the chief captain then let
the young man depart, and charged him, See thou
tell no man that thou hast showed these things
to me.**　23. **And he called unto him two centurions, saying, Make ready two hundred soldiers
to go to Cæsarea, and horsemen threescore and
ten, and spearmen** [δεξιολάβους]—a peculiar word,
the sense of which seems well expressed here, **two
hundred**—in all, four hundred and seventy men,
consisting of heavy-armed and light-armed troops,
with a body of cavalry; a formidable guard for
such an occasion; but Roman officials felt their
honour concerned in the preservation of the public
peace, and the danger of an attempted rescue
would seem to require it : the depot at Jerusalem
was large enough to spare this convoy.　**at the
third hour of the night** (nine o'clock).　24. **And
provide them beasts, that they may set Paul on**
—as relays, and to carry baggage; **and bring him
safe unto Felix the governor** (or 'Procurator').
See on ch. xxiv. 2, 25.　25. **And he wrote a letter
after this manner: 26. Claudius Lysias**—the former was the Roman name he would take on purchasing his citizenship, the latter his Greek family
name, **unto the most excellent governor Felix**—an
honorary title of office, **sendeth greeting.　27. This
man was taken of the Jews, and should have been
killed of them: then came I with an army** [σὺν τ.
στρατεύματι]—'with the military' or 'soldiery,' **and
rescued him, having understood that he was a
Roman.　28. And when I would have known the
cause wherefore they accused him, I brought him
forth into their council: 29. Whom I perceived
to be accused of questions of their law, but to
have nothing laid to his charge worthy of death
or of bonds.** Amidst all his difficulty in getting
at the charges laid against Paul, enough, no doubt,
came out to satisfy him that the whole was a question of religion, and that there was no case for a
civil tribunal.　30. **And when it was told me how
that the Jews laid wait**—or 'that they laid wait'
[ὑπὸ τ. Ἰουδ. being probably not genuine], **for the
man, I sent straightway to thee, and gave commandment to his accusers also to say before
thee [what they had against him.　Farewell].**
As these bracketed words [τὰ πρὸς αὐτόν. Ἔρ-
ρωσο] are of very doubtful authority, if we reject
them, the close of the letter will run thus : '1
sent [him] straightway to thee, and gave commandment to his accusers also, to tell their own
tale before thee.'　Though this was not done when
he wrote, it would be done ere the letter reached.
31. **Then the soldiers, as it was commanded
them, took Paul, and brought him by night to
Antipatris**—a town but recently identified; formerly supposed to be about forty-two miles from Jerusalem, on the way to Cæsarea, leaving twenty-six
miles further to go to their destination : in that case
they would have difficulty in reaching Jerusalem
again the following day (as they did, *v.* 32); but
a much shorter Roman road has been discovered,
which entirely removes the difficulty.　The town
was so named by Herod the Great, in honour of
his father, Antipater.　32. **On the morrow they
(the foot soldiers) left the horsemen to go with
him, and (they themselves being no longer needed
as a guard) returned to the castle** ('the barracks'):
33. **Who, when they came to Cæsarea, and delivered the epistle to the governor, presented
Paul also before him.　34. And when the governor**—or, 'when he' [ὁ ἡγεμὼν being insufficiently
attested] **had read the letter, he asked of what
province he was** — the letter having described
him simply as a Roman citizen.　**And when he
understood that he was of Cilicia; 35. I will hear
thee**—the compound word [Διακούσομαι] implies
'a thorough hearing,' **said he, when thine accusers are also come.　And he commanded him**
[κελεῦσαι is preferable to ἐκέλευσεν of the received
text] **to be kept in Herod's judgment-hall**—'the
prætorium;' that is the palace built at Cæsarea

24 AND after *a* five days *b* Ananias the high priest descended with the
elders, and *with* a certain orator *named* Tertullus, who informed the
2 governor against Paul. And when he was called forth, Tertullus began
to accuse *him*, saying, Seeing *c* that by thee we enjoy great quietness, and
3 that very worthy deeds are done unto this nation by thy providence, we
accept *it* always, and in all places, most noble Felix, with all thankful-
4 ness. Notwithstanding, that I be not further tedious unto thee, I pray
5 thee that thou wouldest hear us of thy clemency a few words. For *d* we
have found this man ¹ a pestilent *fellow*, and a mover of sedition among
all the Jews throughout the world, and a ringleader of the sect of the
6 Nazarenes: who *e* also hath gone about to profane the temple: whom we
7 took, and would have *f* judged according to our law. But *g* the chief
captain Lysias came *upon us*, and with great violence took *him* away out
8 of our hands, commanding *h* his accusers to come unto thee: by examining of whom thyself mayest take knowledge of all these things whereof
9 we accuse him. And the Jews also assented, saying that these things
were so.
10 Then Paul, after that the governor had beckoned unto him to speak,

A. D. 60.

CHAP. 24.
a ch. 21. 27.
b ch. 23. 2, 30, 35.
ch. 25. 2.
c Ps. 12. 2.
Ps. 55. 21.
Jude 16.
d Luke 23. 2.
ch. 6. 13.
ch. 16. 20.
ch. 17. 6.
ch. 21. 28.
1 Cor. 4. 12, 13.
1 Pet. 2. 12.
¹ a p ague.
e ch. 21. 28.
f John 18. 31.
g ch. 21. 33.
h ch. 23. 30.
ch. 25. 5, 6.

by Herod, and now occupied by the Roman pro-curators, in one of the buildings attached to which Paul was ordered to be kept.

Remark.—Though Paul, when insulted before the Sanhedrim by the high priest, appears not free from human infirmity, his calm and fearless bear-ing as a witness for Christ, conscious of his inno-cence and superior to all personal and party considerations, stands out only to more advantage. And as the cheering visit which his glorified Lord vouchsafed to him that very night was evidence enough of the estimation in which he was held and the value put on his services by Him to whom they were so cheerfully rendered, so the remark-able discovery and defeat of the plot against his life, and the powerful protection provided for him on his way from Jerusalem to Cæsarea, by one who knew nothing of the case, and who intended only the preservation of the peace and the securing of the ends of justice, showed that he and his cause were under a higher guardianship than man's; nor could he well fail to say within himself, as he travelled by night under an escort of nearly five hundred troops, to protect him against forty assassins—"The angel of the Lord encampeth round about them that fear him, and delivereth them."

CHAP. XXIV. 1-27. PAUL, ACCUSED BY A PROFESSIONAL PLEADER BEFORE FELIX, MAKES HIS DEFENCE, AND IS REMANDED FOR A FURTHER HEARING—AT A PRIVATE INTERVIEW FELIX TREMBLES UNDER PAUL'S PREACHING, BUT KEEPS HIM PRISONER FOR TWO YEARS, WHEN HE IS SUCCEEDED BY FESTUS.

A Deputation from the Sanhedrim, employing a professional pleader, formally accuse Paul before Felix the Procurator (1-9). **1. And after five days** —or, on the fifth day after their departure from Jerusalem, **Ananias the high priest descended with the elders**—or, 'certain elders' [πρεσβ. τινῶν, though regarded as a gloss by a number of critics, is better attested, and is adopted by *Lachmann* and *Tregelles. Tischendorf* in this case, contrary to his usual authorities, adheres to the received text, τῶν πρεσβ.] These were a deputation from the Sanhedrim. **and with a certain orator named Tertullus**—one of those Roman advocates who trained themselves for the higher practice of the metropolis by practising in the provinces, where the Latin language, employed in the courts, was but imperfectly understood, and Roman forms were not familiar; **who informed**—or 'laid information

before,' **the governor** (or 'put in the charges') against Paul. The name Tertullus (a diminutive from *Tertius*), which was common among the Romans, shows his Latin descent. **2. And when he was called forth, Tertullus began to accuse him, saying, Seeing that by thee we enjoy great quietness, and that very worthy deeds are done unto this nation by thy providence**—or 'excel-lent results flow from thy care.' This very word "providence" was a common one, even on the coinage, to express the imperial care for the right administration of the country. **3. We accept it always, and in all places, most noble Felix, with all thankfulness.** In this flattery there was a measure of truth, for Felix did act with some vigour and success in suppressing lawless violence; as is attested both by *Josephus* (Antt. xx. 8. 4), and by *Tacitus* (Ann. xii. 54). **4. Notwithstanding,** ('But') **that I be not further tedious unto thee, I pray thee that thou wouldest hear us of thy clemency a few words. 5. For we have found this man a pestilent fellow** [λοιμὸν]—'a plague,' 'a pest,' **and a mover of sedition among all the Jews**— exciting disturbances among them, **throughout the world** [οἰκουμένην, as in Luke ii. 1]. This was a *first* charge, and it was true only in the sense explained on ch. xvi. 20. **and a ringleader of the sect of the Nazarenes**—a *second* charge, and true enough. **6. Who also hath gone about** ('who even attempted') **to profane the temple.** This was a *third* charge, and it was wholly false. **whom we took** ('whom we also seized'), [and would have judged according to our law. **7. But the chief captain Lysias came upon us, and with great violence took him away out of our hands, 8. Commanding his accusers to come unto thee.**] This long bracketed passage has hardly any support, while all the principal MSS. want it. If genuine, this is very hard to account for, while their insertion (at first in the margin) may have been designed to bring before the reader—out of ch. xxi., xxiii.—the facts here omitted. But it is hardly to be supposed that this obsequious pleader would make so false and calum-nious a charge against a public officer as that in *v.* 7. **by examining of whom thyself mayest take knowledge of all these things whereof we accuse him**—as if the matter were quite safe in Felix's hands. **9. And the Jews also assented, saying that these things were so.**

Paul's Defence (10-21). **10. Then Paul, after that the governor had beckoned unto him to**

answered, Forasmuch as I know that thou hast been of many years [2] a judge unto this nation, I do the more cheerfully answer for myself:
11 because that thou mayest understand, that there are yet but twelve days
12 since I went up to Jerusalem for [i] to worship. And [j] they neither found me in the temple disputing with any man, neither raising up the
13 people, neither in the synagogues, nor in the city: neither can they prove
14 the things whereof they now accuse me. But this I confess unto thee, that after the [k] way which they call heresy, so worship I the [l] God of my fathers, believing all things which are written in [m] the Law and in the
15 Prophets: and [n] have hope toward God, which they themselves also allow, that [o] there shall be a resurrection of the dead, both of the just and
16 unjust. And [p] herein do I exercise myself, to have always a conscience
17 void of offence toward God, and *toward* men. Now after many years [q] I
18 came to bring alms to my nation, and offerings. Whereupon [r] certain Jews from Asia found me purified in the temple, neither with multitude,
19 nor with tumult. Who [s] ought to have been here before thee, and object,
20 if they had ought against me. Or else let these same *here* say, if they have found any evil doing in me, while I stood before the council,

A. D. 60.
[2] Felix was made procurator over Judea.
A. D. 63.
i ch. 21. 26.
j ch. 25. 8.
ch. 28. 17.
k Ps. 119. 46.
Amos 8. 14.
l 2 Tim. 1. 3.
m ch. 26. 22.
2 Cor. 1. 20.
n ch. 23. 6.
o Dan. 12. 2.
Matt. 22.31.
p ch. 23. 1.
q ch. 11. 29.
ch. 20. 16.
r ch. 21. 26.
s ch. 23. 30.

speak, answered, Forasmuch as I know that thou hast been of many years a judge unto this nation. He had been in this province for six or seven years, and in Galilee for a longer period. I do [the more] **cheerfully answer for myself**—[εὐθύμως is far better attested than —μότερον of the received text.] Paul uses no flattery, but simply expresses his satisfaction at having to plead before one whose long official experience of Jewish matters would enable him the better to understand and appreciate what he had to say. **11. Because that thou mayest understand** (canst easily learn), **that there are yet but twelve days since I went up to Jerusalem**—viz., *first,* the day of his arrival in Jerusalem (ch. xxi. 15-17); *second,* that of the interview with James (ch. xxi. 18, &c.); *third,* that of the vow (ch. xxi. 26); *fourth, fifth, sixth,* and *seventh,* days of the vow, ending in the arrest (ch. xxi. 27, &c.); *eighth,* that of his appearance before the Sanhedrim (ch. xxii. 30; xxiii. 1-10); *ninth,* that of the conspiracy and its defeat (ch. xxiii. 12); *tenth,* the despatch of Paul from Jerusalem on the evening of the same day (ch. xxiii. 23, 31); and the remaining period referred to in ch. xxiii. 33; xxiv. 1. This short period is mentioned to show how unlikely it was that he should have had time to do what was charged against him. **for to worship**—a very different purpose from that imputed to him. **12. And they neither found me in the temple disputing with any man, neither raising up the people, neither in the synagogues, nor in the city: 13. Neither can they prove** [παραστῆσαι is the true reading: the received *Stephanic* text (but not the *Elzevir*) adds με, which makes nonsense] **the things whereof they now accuse me.** Having specified several particulars, he challenges proof of any one of the charges brought against him. So much for the charge of *sedition.* **14. But this I confess unto thee**—in which Felix, however, would see no crime, **that after the way which they call heresy** [αἵρεσιν—*lit.,* and better, 'a sect.' **so worship I the God of my fathers** [τῷ πατρῴῳ Θεῷ]—'the ancestral' or 'father God.' There are two arguments in this statement. *First,* Our nation is divided into what they call '*sects*'—the sect of the Pharisees and that of the Sadducees; and all the difference between them and me is, that I belong to neither of these, but to another sect, or religious section of the nation, which, from its Head, they call *Nazarenes:*—for that reason, and that alone, am I hated. *Second,* The Roman law allows every nation to worship its own deities; I claim protection under that law, worshipping the God of my ancestors, even as they do, only of a different sect of the common Religion. **believing all things which are written in the Law and in the Prophets.** Here, disowning all opinions at variance with the Old Testament Scriptures, he challenges for the Gospel which he preached the authority of the God of their fathers. So much for the charge of *heresy.* **15. And have hope toward God, which they themselves also allow, that there shall be a resurrection [of the dead], both of the just and unjust.** The bracketed word [νεκρῶν] seems clearly not genuine. This appeal to the Faith of his accusers shows that they were chiefly of the *Pharisees,* from which it would appear that the favour of that party—to which he owed in some measure his safety at the recent council (ch. xxiii. 6-9)—had been quite momentary. **16. And herein** ['Εν τούτῳ]—rather, 'on this ground,' 'accordingly,' or, in view of that awful day just referred to (2 Cor. v. 10), **do I exercise myself.** The "I" here is emphatic [αὐτὸς]:—*q. d.,* 'whatever they do, this is my study,' **to have always a conscience void of offence toward God, and toward men.** (Compare ch. xxiii. 1; 2 Cor. i. 12; ii. 17):—*q. d.,* 'These are the great principles of my life, and how different from turbulence and sectarianism!' **17. Now after many** ('several') **years**—years' absence from Jerusalem. **I came to bring alms to my nation**—referring to the collection from the churches of Macedonia and Greece, which he had taken such pains to gather. This only allusion in the Acts to what is dwelt upon so frequently in his own Epistles (Rom. xv. 25, 26; 1 Cor. xvi. 1-4; 2 Cor. viii. 1-4) throws a beautiful light on the truth of this History. (See *Paley's* Horæ Paulinæ, ch. ii. 1.) **and offerings**—connected with his Jewish vow (see next verse). **18. Whereupon certain Jews from Asia found me purified in the temple, neither with multitude, nor with tumult**—not polluting it by my own presence, and neither gathering a crowd nor raising a stir. **19. Who ought to have been here before thee, and object, if they had ought against me.** If these Asiatic Jews had any charge to bring against him, in justification of their arrest of him, why were they not there to substantiate it? **20. Or else** (passing all that preceded my trial before the Jewish Sanhedrim) **let these same here say, if they have found** ('if they found') **any evil doing in me,**

21 except it be for this one voice, that I cried standing among them, *^t*Touching the resurrection of the dead I am called in question by you this day.

22 And when Felix heard these things, having more perfect knowledge of *that* way, he deferred them, and said, When Lysias the chief captain

23 shall come down, I will know the uttermost of your matter. And he commanded a centurion to keep Paul, and to let *him* have liberty, and *^u*that he should forbid none of his acquaintance to minister or come unto him.

24 And after certain days, when Felix came with his wife Drusilla, which was a Jewess, he sent for Paul, and heard him concerning the faith in

25 Christ. And as he reasoned of righteousness, temperance, and judgment to come, Felix trembled, and answered, Go thy way for this time; when

26 I have a convenient season I will call for thee. He hoped also that *^v*money should have been given him of Paul, that he might loose him:

A. D. 60.

t ch. 23. 6.
ch. 26. 6, 8.
ch. 28. 20.
u ch. 27. 3.
ch. 28. 16.
v Ex. 23. 8.
Deut. 16. 19.
1 Sam. 8. 3.
1 Sam. 12. 3.
2 Chr. 19. 7.
Job 15. 34.
Ps. 26. 10.
Pro. 17. 3,
23.
Pro. 19. 6.
Pro. 29. 4.
1 Tim. 6.
10.

while I stood before the council. No doubt his hasty speech to the high priest might occur to them, but the provocation to it on his part was more than they would be willing to recall. **21. Except it be for this one voice, that I cried standing among them, Touching the resurrection of the dead I am called in question by you this day.** This would recall to the Pharisees present their own inconsistency in befriending him then, and now accusing him.

Decision deferred, and Paul kept prisoner, though not a close one (22, 23). **22. And when Felix heard these things, having more perfect knowledge of that way**—'the way' (see on ch. ix. 2), **he deferred them, and said, When Lysias the chief captain** ('the chiliarch' or 'tribune') **shall come down, I will know the uttermost of your matter.** Felix might have dismissed the case as a tissue of unsupported charges. But if, from his interest 'in the matter, he really wished to have the presence of Lysias and of others concerned, a brief delay was not unworthy of him as a judge. Certainly, so far as recorded, neither Lysias nor any other parties appeared again in the case. It would seem, however, from *v.* 23, that *at that time* his prepossessions in favour of Paul were strong. The probability is, that while unable to condemn—being convinced of the futility of the charges against him—yet unwilling to enrage the Jews by an acquittal, he made his desire to confer with Lysias a pretext for delaying judgment. **23. And he commanded a centurion** ('the centurion') **to keep Paul, and to let him have liberty, and that he should forbid none of his acquaintance to minister or come unto him.**

Felix, having invited Paul to explain before himself and Drusilla the Faith of Christ, trembles under his preaching, but dismisses him to a more convenient season—After keeping him prisoner for two years, Felix is succeeded by Porcius Festus, the apostle being left bound (24-27). **24. And after certain days, when Felix came with his wife Drusilla, which was a Jewess.** This beautiful but infamous woman was the third daughter of Herod Agrippa I., who was eaten of worms (see on ch. xii. 1), and a sister of Agrippa II., before whom Paul pleaded, ch. xxvi. She was (says *Josephus*) 'given in marriage to Azizus, king of the Emessenes, who had consented to be circumcised for the sake of the alliance. But this marriage was soon dissolved, after the following manner: When Festus was procurator of Judea, he saw her, and being captivated with her beauty, persuaded her to desert her husband, transgress the laws of her country, and marry himself' (Antt. xx. 7. 1, 2). Such was this "wife" of Felix. **he sent for Paul, and heard**

him concerning the faith in Christ. Perceiving, from what he had heard on the trial, that the new sect which was creating such a stir was represented by its own advocates as but a particular development of the Jewish Faith, he probably wished to gratify the curiosity of his Jewish wife as well as his own, by a more particular account of it from this distinguished champion. And no doubt Paul would so far humour this desire as to present to them the great leading features of the Gospel. But from *v.* 25 it is evident that his discourse took an entirely practical turn, suited to the life which his two auditors were notoriously leading. **25. And as he reasoned** [Διαλεγομένου] ('discoursed') **of righteousness, temperance** [ἐγκρατείας]—'sobriety,' 'self-control,' and ('the') **judgment to come.** He discoursed of "righteousness," with reference to the *public* character of Felix; of "temperance," with reference to his *private* immorality; and of "the judgment to come," when he should be called to an awful account for both. **Felix trembled** [ἔμφοβος γενόμενος]—'became afraid;' and no wonder. For he ruled, says *Tacitus* ('Ann.,' *v.* 9; xii. 54), with a mixture of cruelty, lust, and servility; and relying on the influence of his brother Pallas at court, he thought himself at liberty to commit every sort of crime with impunity. How noble the fidelity and courage which dared to treat of such topics in such a presence, and what withering power must have been in those appeals which made even a Felix to tremble! **and answered, Go thy way for this time; when I have a convenient season I will call for thee.** Alas for Felix! This was his golden opportunity, but—*like multitudes still*—he missed it. Convenient seasons in abundance he found to call for Paul, but never again to "hear him concerning the Faith in Christ," and writhe under the terrors of the wrath to come. Even in these moments of terror he had no thought of submission to the Cross or a change of life. The word discerned the thoughts and intents of his heart, but that heart even then clung to its idols; even as Herod, who "did many things, and heard John gladly," but even in his best moments was enslaved to his lusts. **26. He hoped also that money should have been given him**—'at the same time also hoping that money would be given him' **of Paul** [that he might loose him]. (This bracketed clause is evidently an explanatory gloss without authority.) Bribery in a judge was punishable by the Roman law, but the spirit of a slave (to use the words of *Tacitus*) was in all his acts, and his "communing with Paul"—as if he cared for either him or his message—simply added hypocrisy to meanness. The position in life of Paul's Christian

168

27 wherefore he sent for him the oftener, and communed with him. But after two years Porcius Festus came into Felix' room: and Felix, *w*willing to show the Jews a pleasure, left Paul bound.

25 NOW when Festus was come into the province, after three days he

A. D. 62.

w Ex. 23. 2.
Pro. 29. 25.
ch. 12. 3.
ch. 25. 9.

visitors might beget the hope of extracting something from them for the release of their champion; but the apostle would rather lie in prison than stoop to this! wherefore he sent for him the **oftener, and communed with him**—under pretext of 'anxious enquiry' after salvation, perhaps, and very possibly curious to know more of this new Religion and the prisoner's connection with it; but secretly hoping to weary him out, or his friends, and thus extract from them a bribe to set him at liberty: thus rendering any real benefit by all these interviews hopeless. 27. **But after two years.** What a trial to this burning missionary of Christ to suffer such a tedious period of inaction! How mysterious it would seem! But this repose would be medicine to his spirit: he would not and could not be entirely inactive, so long as he was able by pen and message to communicate with the churches; and he would doubtless learn the salutary truth that even he was not essential to his Master's cause. That Luke wrote his Gospel during this period, under the apostle's superintendence, is the not unlikely conjecture of able critics. **Porcius Festus**—of whom little is known. He died, as we learn from *Josephus* (Antt. xx. 8. 9, to 9. 1), a few years after this. **came into Felix' room.** Poor Felix was recalled on accusations against him by the Jews of Cæsarea, and only acquitted through the intercession of his brother at court (see *Josephus,* Antt. xx. 8. 10). **and Felix, willing to show the Jews a pleasure**—'to earn the thanks of the Jews' (which, however, he did not), **left Paul bound.** He does not appear to have been bound from the time when Lysias set him free (ch. xxii. 30) until Felix, on being superseded, had him again manacled, for the mean purpose of ingratiating himself with the Jews; and in this condition he was afterwards brought forth before Herod Agrippa (ch. xxvi. 29).

Remarks.—1. The skill with which our apostle adapted his addresses to his audience, and to the occasion, has been before remarked. Here we have a striking illustration of it. In his reply to Tertullus, it was easy to rebut the charge of sedition. He had but to challenge proof of it, and ask why the witnesses of it were not there to substantiate the charge. But the charge of being "the ringleader of the Nazarene sect" he meets with studious and noteworthy precision: admitting that in the way which they called "a sect" he discharged his religious duties; but protesting that he did this only to "the God of his fathers," and that his Faith, instead of being a deviation from the ancestral creed, was but the submission of his heart to "all things which were written in the law and the prophets;" in particular, that he held, with his accusers themselves, the hope of a Resurrection, "both of the just and of the unjust;" that he was at pains to have at all times an uncondemning conscience towards both God and men; that his errand to Jerusalem, at the time when he was charged with breach of law, was a purely religious one—to bring alms to his nation and present offerings to God; that he was found in the temple in the quiet and orderly discharge of religious duty; that he was ready to meet any witness who had aught to lay to his charge; and that what had raised all the hubbub, which had issued in his being sent down to Cæsarea for trial, was nothing but an exclamation in the Jewish

Sanhedrim about his faith in the Resurrection, which had set the Pharisees who held it and the Sadducees who denied it to quarrelling with each other about him, thus bringing the tribune down to preserve the peace. In this line of defence, with the exception of what he says on the charge of sedition, the apostle confines himself rigidly to the charge of apostasy from the ancestral Faith—not giving even an outline of the facts of the Gospel, as being unsuitable on such an occasion. But observe how entirely he changes his ground when standing before Felix and Drusilla at a private interview, that they might "hear him concerning the faith in Christ." That he would omit all mention of that "Faith," is not for a moment to be supposed. But brief appears to have been all that was said on that subject. The couple before whom he stood were living an infamous life, not to speak of Felix as a governor. The opportunity, therefore, of dealing faithfully with them being too precious to be lost, the apostle comes right up to their consciences, discoursing to them of "righteousness, temperance, and the judgment to come," with such sharp, down-bearing power, that Felix trembled under it. After what had happened to the Baptist for this kind of fidelity, a less disinterested servant of Christ would have chosen topics less unpalatable, for which sufficient excuse might have been found in the object for which the interview was arranged—to "hear him (not on such topics, but) concerning the faith in Christ." But Paul was his Master's servant, not his own, and "exercised himself to have always a conscience void of offence," *first,*" towards God," and then only (and in the highest sense) "towards men."—A noble model! 2. It is not said that Drusilla trembled under Paul's preaching; and there is not the least ground to think that she did. Though a Jewess, and as such likely to understand better and be more alive to what Paul was saying, just for that reason was she the less likely—after having so shamelessly overridden all her early convictions—to be staggered by anything that Paul preached. Felix certainly was the less hardened of the two; and, as has been seen ever since the days of Jezebel, bad women are doubly bad. 3. In spiritual things, as in things temporal, the pregnant words of the poet are true—'There is a tide in the affairs of men.' 4. The strong probability at which we have hinted (on *v.* 27), that the two years' imprisonment of Paul were turned to blessed account, will bring to the recollection of many the cases of such as *John* in the isle of Patmos, of *Luther* in the castle of Wartburg, of *Bunyan* in the jail at Bedford, and of *Rutherford* in the prison at Aberdeen:—for which the Church of God, as long as it exists upon earth, will have cause to be thankful. Thus "maketh He the wrath of man to praise Him."

CHAP. XXV. 1-27.—FESTUS AT JERUSALEM REFUSES TO TRY PAUL THERE, BUT GIVES THE PARTIES A HEARING AT CÆSAREA — ON HIS OFFERING TO PAUL ANOTHER HEARING AT JERUSALEM, HE IS CONSTRAINED TO APPEAL TO THE EMPEROR—HEROD AGRIPPA II., ON A VISIT TO FESTUS, AND CONSULTED ABOUT THIS CASE, DESIRES TO HEAR THE APOSTLE, WHO IS ACCORDINGLY BROUGHT FORTH.

Festus, coming to Jerusalem, is urged to have Paul tried there—He declines, but promises the parties a hearing at Cæsarea (1-5). 1. Now when

2 ascended from Cesarea to Jerusalem. Then ^athe high priest and the
3 chief of the Jews informed him against Paul, and besought him, and
desired favour against him, that he would send for him to Jeru-
4 salem, laying wait ^bin the way to kill him. But Festus answered,
that Paul should be kept at Cesarea, and that he himself would depart
5 shortly *thither*. Let them therefore, said he, which among you are
able, go down with *me*, and accuse this man, ^cif there be any wickedness
in him.
6   And when he had tarried among them ¹more than ten days, he went
down unto Cesarea; and the next day, sitting on the judgment seat,
7 commanded Paul to be brought. And when he was come, the Jews
which came down from Jerusalem stood round about, ^dand laid many
and grievous complaints against Paul, which they could not prove.
8 While he answered for himself, Neither against ^ethe law of the Jews,
neither against the temple, nor yet against Cesar, have I offended any
9 thing at all. But Festus, ^fwilling to do the Jews a pleasure, answered
Paul, and said, Wilt thou go up to Jerusalem, and there be judged of
10 these things before me? Then said Paul, I stand at Cesar's judgment
seat, where I ought to be judged : to the Jews have I done no wrong, as
11 thou very well knowest. For ^gif I be an offender, or have committed
any thing worthy of death, I refuse not to die : but if there be none of
these things whereof these accuse me, no man may deliver me unto them.
12 ^hI appeal unto Cesar. Then Festus, when he had conferred with the

A. D. 62.
CHAP. 25.
^a ch. 24. 1.
^b ch. 33. 12.
^c ch. 18. 14.
1 Or, as some copies read, no more than eight or ten days.
^d Esth. 3. 8. Ps. 27. 12. Ps. 35. 1. Mark 15. 3.
^e ch. 6. 13.
^f Deut. 27.19. 2 Chr. 19. 6. Pro. 29. 25. ch. 12. 3. ch. 24. 27. ch. 25. 9, 14
^g ch. 18. 14.
^h Pro. 14. 8. Pro. 21. 22. Eccl. 9. 18. Matt. 10.18. ch. 26. 32. Eph. 5. 15.

Festus was come into the province [ἐπαρχία].
Judea belonged to the Roman province of Syria,
which was under the imperial rule, and administered by a *Procurator* [ἐπίτροπος]. See on ch. xiii. 7.
**after three days he ascended from Cesarea to
Jerusalem**—to make himself acquainted with the
great central city of his government without delay.
2. Then the high priest—'the chief priests' is
clearly the true reading [οἱ ἀρχιερεῖς]. **and the
chief of the Jews**—Festus calls them afterwards
'the whole multitude of the Jews' (v. 24), **informed him** ('laid information before him') **against
Paul, and besought him, 3. And desired favour**—
entreating it as a boon, **against him**. If we take
the word "favour" here in the sense of "judgment" against him (as in v. 15), it amounted to
asking him for condemnation without even a trial;
and v. 16 would seem to confirm this. **that he
would send for him to Jerusalem, laying wait
in the way to kill him.** How deep must have
been their hostility when, two years after the
defeat of their former attempt, they thirst as
keenly as ever for his blood! Their plea for
having the case tried at Jerusalem, where the
alleged offence took place, was plausible enough ;
but from v. 10 it would seem that Festus had been
made acquainted with their causeless malice, and
that in some way which Paul was privy to. **4.
But Festus answered, that Paul should be kept**
('in custody') **at Cesarea, and that he himself
would depart shortly thither. 5. Let them
therefore, said he, which among you are able**
[Οἱ δυνατοὶ]—'the men of power,' 'weight,' 'influence,' **go down with me, and accuse this man,
if there be any wickedness in him.**

*The Hearing at Cæsarea before Festus—Being
asked if he would abide a judgment at Jerusalem,
the apostle declines, and appeals to the Emperor,
to which Festus assents (6-12).* **6. And when he
had tarried among them more than ten days.**
Instead of this reading, the weight of authority
is plainly in favour of 'not more than eight or
ten days' [ἡμέρας οὐ πλείους ὀκτὼ ἢ δέκα]. **he
went down unto Cesarea; and the next day,
sitting on the judgment seat, commanded Paul**

to be brought. **7. And when he was come, the
Jews which came down from Jerusalem stood
round about, and laid many and grievous complaints against Paul** [καταφέροντες, not φέρ. of
the received text, which has next to no evi-
dence], **which they could not prove.** From his
reply, and Festus' statement of the case before
Agrippa, these charges seem to have been a jumble
of political and religious matter which they were
unable to substantiate, and vociferous cries that
he was unfit to live. **8. While he answered for
himself, Neither against the law of the Jews,
neither against the temple, nor yet against
Cesar, have I offended any thing at all.** This
reply, not given in full, was probably little more
than a challenge to prove any of their charges,
whether political or religious. **9. But Festus,
willing to do the Jews a pleasure**—to ingratiate
himself with the Jews, **answered Paul, and said,
Wilt thou go up to Jerusalem, and there be
judged of these things before me?** If this was
meant in earnest, it was temporizing and vacillating. But, possibly, anticipating Saul's refusal, he
wished merely to avoid the odium of refusing to
remove the trial to Jerusalem. **10. Then said
Paul, I stand at Cesar's judgment seat**—*i. e.*, I
am already before the proper tribunal. This
seems to imply that he understood Festus to
propose handing him over to the Sanhedrim for
judgment (and see on v. 11), with a mere promise of
protection from himself. But from going to Jerusalem at all he was too well justified in shrinking,
for there assassination had been quite recently
planned against him. **to the Jews have I done no
wrong, as thou very well knowest** [κάλλιον]—*lit.*,
'knowest better;' better than to press such a
proposal ; or, 'full well.' **11. For if**—'if then,'
according to the true reading [Εἰ μέν οὖν], **I be an
offender, or have committed any thing worthy
of death, I refuse not to die: but if there be
none of these things whereof these accuse me,
no man may deliver me unto them** [αὐτοῖς
χαρίσασθαι]—'may surrender me to their pleasure.'
I appeal unto Cesar—right of appeal to the
supreme power, in cases of life and death, was

council, answered, Hast thou appealed unto Cesar? unto Cesar shalt thou go.

13 And after certain days king Agrippa and Bernice came unto Cesarea
14 to salute ⁱFestus. And when they had been there many days, Festus declared Paul's cause unto the king, saying, ʲThere is a certain man left
15 in bonds by Felix: about whom, when I was at Jerusalem, the chief priests and the elders of the Jews informed *me*, desiring *to have* judgment
16 against him. To whom I answered, It is not the manner of the Romans to deliver any man to die, before that he which is accused have the accusers face to face, and have ᵏlicence to answer for himself concerning
17 the crime laid against him. Therefore, when they were come hither, without any delay on the morrow I sat on the judgment seat, and com-
18 manded the man to be brought forth. Against whom, when the accusers stood up, they brought none accusation of such things as I supposed:
19 but ˡhad certain questions against him of their own superstition, and of
20 one Jesus, which was dead, whom Paul affirmed to be alive. And be-cause ²I doubted of such manner of questions, I asked *him* whether he
21 would go to Jerusalem, and there be judged of these matters. But when Paul had appealed to be reserved unto the ³hearing of Augustus, I com-
22 manded him to be kept till I might send him to Cesar. Then ᵐAgrippa

A.D. 62.
ⁱ 1 Sam. 13. 10.
1 Sam. 25. 14.
2 Sam. 8. 10.
2 Ki. 10. 13.
Mark 15. 18.
ʲ ch. 24. 27.
ᵏ Deut. 17. 4.
Deut. 19. 17, 18.
Pro. 18. 13.
ch. 26. 1.
ˡ ch. 18. 15.
ch. 23. 29.
1 Cor. 1. 18.
1 Cor. 2. 14.
² Or, I was doubtful how to enquire hereof.
³ Or, judgment.
ᵐ ch. 9. 15.

---

secured by an ancient law to every Roman citizen, and continued under the empire. Had Festus shown any disposition to pronounce final judgment, Paul, strong in the consciousness of his innocence and the justice of a Roman tribunal, would not have made this appeal; but when the only other alternative offered him was to give his own consent to be transferred to the great hotbed of plots against his life, and to a tribunal of unscrupulous and bloodthirsty ecclesiastics whose vociferous cries for his death had scarcely subsided, no other course was open to him. **12. Then Festus** —little expecting such an appeal, but bound to respect it, **when he had conferred with the council**—his assessors in judgment, as to the admissibility of the appeal, answered, Hast thou appealed unto Cesar? unto Cesar shalt thou go—as if he would add, 'and see if thou fare better.'

Herod Agrippa II., being on a visit to Festus, and consulted on this case, desires to hear the Apostle— He is accordingly brought forth, the king and his sister Bernice, in pompous form and with a distinguished retinue, taking their places in the audience-hall (13-23). **13. And after certain days king Agrippa**—great grandson of Herod the Great, and Drusilla's brother (see on ch. xxiv. 24). On his father's awful death (ch. xii. 23), being thought too young to succeed (only seventeen), Judea was attached to the province of Syria. Four years after, on the death of his uncle Herod, he was made king of the northern principalities of Chalcis, and afterwards got Batanea, Iturea, Trachonitis, Abilene, Galilee, and Perea, with the title of king. He died A.D. 100, after reigning fifty-one years. **and Bernice**— his sister. She was married to her uncle Herod, king of Chalcis, on whose death she lived with her brother Agrippa—not without suspicion of incestuous intercourse, which her subsequent licentious life tended to confirm. **came unto Cesarea to salute Festus**—to pay his respects to him on his accession to the procuratorship. **14. And when they had been there many days** [πλείους] —'several days,' **Festus declared Paul's cause** [ἀνέθετο—later Greek in this sense: cf. Gal. ii. 2, *Gr.*]—'laid Paul's cause before the king'— taking advantage of the presence of one who might be presumed to know such matters better than himself; though the lapse of 'several days'

ere the subject was touched on shows that it gave Festus little trouble. **saying, There is a certain man left in bonds by Felix; 15. About whom, when I was at Jerusalem, the chief priests and the elders of the Jews informed me, desiring to have judgment against him. 16. To whom I answered, It is not the manner of the Romans to deliver** ('surrender') **any man** [to die]. (The bracketed words [εἰς ἀπώλειαν] are insufficiently supported, and seem an explanatory gloss.) **before that he which is accused have the accusers face to face, and have licence** [τόπον—later Greek in this sense] **to answer for himself concerning the crime laid against him. 17. Therefore, when they were come hither, without any delay on the morrow I sat on the judgment seat, and commanded the man to be brought forth. 18. Against** ('around') **whom, when the accusers stood up, they brought none accusation of such things as I supposed**—such crimes as I naturally concluded he would be charged with, punishable by the civil law. **19. But had certain questions against him of their own superstition** —rather, 'religion.' See on the same word [δεισιδαιμονία] in ch. xvii. 22. It cannot be supposed that Festus, in addressing his Jewish royal guest, would use such a word in any discourteous sense. **and of one Jesus.** 'Thus (says *Bengel*) speaks this miserable Festus of Him to whom every knee shall bow.' **which was dead, whom Paul affirmed to be alive**—showing that the resurrection of the Crucified One had been the burden, as usual, of Paul's preaching. The insignificance of the whole affair in the eyes of Festus is manifest. **20. And because I doubted of such manner of questions** —the "I" is emphatic—'I, as a Roman judge, who could not be expected to understand such matters, and so was at a loss how to deal with them; **I asked him, whether he would go to Jerusalem, and there be judged of these matters. 21. But when Paul had appealed to be reserved unto the hearing of Augustus**—the imperial title, first conferred by the Roman senate on Octavius, and for sometime cautiously accepted, but at length boldly assumed. **I commanded him to be kept till I might send him to Cesar. 22. Then Agrippa said unto Festus, I would also hear** ('should like to hear') **the man myself.** No doubt Paul was right when he said, "The king knoweth of these

said unto Festus, I would also hear the man myself. To-morrow, said he, thou shalt hear him.

23 And on the morrow, when Agrippa was come, and Bernice, with ⁿ great pomp, and was entered into the place of hearing, with the chief captains and principal men of the city, at Festus' commandment Paul was brought

24 forth. And Festus said, King Agrippa, and all men which are here present with us, ye see this man, about whom all the multitude of the Jews have dealt with me, both at Jerusalem, and *also* here, crying that

25 he ought not °to live any longer. But when I found that ᴾ he had committed nothing worthy of death, and that he himself hath appealed

26 to Augustus, I have determined to send him. Of whom I have no certain thing to write unto my lord. Wherefore I have brought him forth before you, and specially before thee, O king Agrippa, that, after

27 examination had, I might have somewhat to write. For it seemeth to me unreasonable to send a prisoner, and not withal to signify the crimes *laid* against him.

26 THEN Agrippa said unto Paul, Thou ᵃart permitted to speak for

A. D. 62.

ⁿ Ex. 3. 19.
Ps. 39. 5,
6.
Ps. 62. 9,
10.
Ps. 144. 4.
Eccl. 1. 2.
Isa. 5. 14.
Isa. 14. 11.
Rom. 8. 20.
Jas. 1. 11.
1 Pet. 1. 24.
° ch. 22. 22.
ᴾ Luke 23. 4.
ch. 23. 9,
29.
ch. 26. 31.
John 18. 38.

CHAP. 26.
ᵃ ch. 25. 16.
Pro. 18. 13.

things . . . for I am persuaded that none of these things are hidden from him; for this thing was not done in a corner" (ch. xxvi. 26). Hence his curiosity to see and hear the man who had raised such commotion, and was remodelling to such an extent the old Jewish life.

23. And on the morrow, when Agrippa was come, and Bernice, with great pomp [φαντασίας, 'display'—later Greek in this sense]—in the same city (as *Wetstein* notes) in which their father, on account of his pride, had perished, eaten of worms, **and was entered into the place of hearing, with the chief captains**—'the chiliarchs' or 'tribunes' (see on ch. xxi. 32). *Josephus* (J. W. iii. 4. 2) says that five cohorts—whose full complement was 1000 men each—were stationed at Cæsarea. **and principal men of the city**—both Jews and Romans. 'This (as *Webster and Wilkinson* observes) was the most dignified and influential audience Paul had yet addressed; and the prediction, ch. ix. 15, was now fulfilled, though afterwards still more remarkably at Rome (ch. xxvii. 24; 2 Tim. iv. 16, 17): **at Festus' commandment Paul was brought forth.**

Festus opens the proceedings with a statement of the case (24-27). **24. And Festus said, King Agrippa, and all men which are here present with us, ye see this man, about whom all the multitude of the Jews have dealt with me, both at Jerusalem, and also here, crying that he ought not to live any longer. 25. But when I found that he had committed nothing worthy of death, and that he himself hath appealed to Augustus, I have determined** ('I determined') **to send him. 26. Of whom I have no certain thing**—meaning, 'nothing definite,' nothing that could be fastened on as a charge, **to write unto my lord** [τ. κυρίῳ]—'to the lord' or 'sovereign;' meaning Nero. 'The writer's accuracy (says *Hackett*) should be remarked here. It would have been a mistake to apply this term ("lord") to the emperor a few years earlier. Neither Augustus nor Tiberius would allow himself to be called *dominus* ("lord"), because it implied the relation of master and slave. The appellation had now come (rather, was now coming) into use as one of the imperial titles.' **Wherefore I have brought him forth before you, and specially before thee, O king Agrippa, that, after examination had, I might have somewhat to write. 27. For it seemeth to me unreasonable to send a prisoner, and not withal to signify the crimes laid against him**

[μὴ καὶ τὰς κατ' αὐτοῦ αἰτίας σημᾶναι]—'without also stating the charges against him.'

Remark.—If Felix cuts a sorry figure in the preceding chapter, Festus in this one shows not much better. No doubt he was perplexed in consequence of his ignorance of the Jewish Religion, the parties it created, and the questions which it raised. So that though he at first declined to try the cause of Paul at Jerusalem, and intimated his intention to take it up at Cæsarea, he might, without inconsistency, have been anxious to transfer it to Jerusalem, on finding that the means of getting to the bottom of it could best be had there. But when the charges brought against the prisoner by Tertullus at Cæsarea, and assented to by his Jewish accusers, so completely broke down—since of crime against the State there was none, and even their charges of sacrilege in religious matters proved baseless—it was the duty of an upright judge at once to acquit the prisoner. If there had existed evidence against him, his accusers ought to have had it ready when formally summoned to appear in the cause at Cæsarea. Failing that, there was no pretext for delay in the acquittal of the prisoner; and it was a cruel alternative to shut him up to—either to have his cause transferred to Jerusalem, where his life, already attempted, would be at the mercy of his enemies, or to make his appeal to the emperor. The keen sense of this wrong appears in the apostle's reply to the proposal of Festus that he should go to Jerusalem; and for all the injustice, and hardship, and danger involved in that proposal Festus was alone to blame. Nor did he commit this wrong under any misapprehension. The explanation given of it by the historian—that he was "willing to do the Jews a pleasure"—is one that would naturally suggest itself even though it had not been expressed; and it leaves a foul blot upon his administration. But "it was of the Lord," that He might fulfil the word which He spake in the night season to His servant, when shut up in the castle at Jerusalem from the fury of his enemies, "Be of good cheer, for as thou hast testified of Me in Jerusalem, so must thou bear witness also at *Rome*" (ch. xxiii. 11).

CHAP. XXVI. 1-32.—PAUL'S DEFENCE OF HIMSELF BEFORE AGRIPPA, WHO PRONOUNCES HIM INNOCENT, BUT CONCLUDES THAT THE APPEAL TO CÆSAR MUST BE CARRIED OUT.

The Defence, interrupted by Festus, but only the more impressively continued and triumphantly concluded (1-29). This speech, though in substance

thyself. Then Paul stretched forth the hand, and answered for
himself:

2   I think myself happy, king Agrippa, because I shall answer for myself
this day before thee touching all the things whereof I am accused of the

3 Jews: especially *because I know* thee to be [1] expert in all customs and
questions which are among the Jews: wherefore I beseech thee to hear

4 me patiently. My manner of life from my youth, which was at the first

5 among mine own nation at Jerusalem, know all the Jews; which knew
me from the beginning, if they would testify, that [b] after the most straitest

6 sect of our religion I lived a Pharisee. And now I stand and am judged

7 for the hope of [c] the promise made of God unto our fathers: unto which
promise [d] our twelve tribes, instantly serving *God* [2] day and night, hope
[e] to come. For which hope's sake, king Agrippa, I am accused of the

8 Jews. Why should it be thought a thing incredible with you, that God

9 should raise [f] the dead? I [g] verily thought with myself, that I ought to

10 do many things contrary to the name of Jesus of Nazareth. Which
[h] thing I also did in Jerusalem: and many of the saints did I shut up in
prison, having received authority [i] from the chief priests; and when they

A. D. 62.

CHAP. 26.
[1] a knower.
Deut. 17.
14-20.
ch. 25. 26.
[b] ch. 22. 3.
Gal. 1. 13.
Phil. 3. 5.
[c] Gen. 3. 15.
Gen. 22. 18.
Gen. 49. 10.
Deut. 18.15.
Mal. 3. 1.
Mal. 4. 2.
[d] Jas. 1. 1.
[2] night and
day.
Luke 2. 37.
[e] Phil. 3. 11.
[f] Dan. 12. 2.
[g] John 16. 2.
[h] ch. 8. 3.
[i] ch. 22. 5.

the same as that from the fortress-stairs of Jerusalem (ch. xxii.), differs from it in so far as it is less directed to meet the charge of apostasy from the Jewish Faith, and gives more enlarged views of his remarkable change and apostolic commission, and of the Divine support under which he was enabled to brave the hostility of his countrymen. At the same time, as its details, together with those of ch. xxii., have been considered in the exposition of ch. ix., it will be enough to refer the reader to that exposition, and the Remarks at its close; a few running remarks only being added here on particular verses. **1. Then Agrippa said unto Paul, Thou art permitted to speak for thyself**—'of, or about, thyself,' according to what seems the true reading [περὶ in place of ὑπέρ]. **Then Paul stretched forth the hand.** It is a peculiarity of this historian to notice postures, gestures, &c. (see Luke i. 22, 41; iv. 16, 39; ch. ix. 39, 41; xx. 9, 37: particularly in introducing speeches, as ch. i. 15; ii. 14; iii. 4; v. 17; x. 34; xii. 17; xiii. 9, 16; xiv. 9; xvii. 22. **and answered for himself** [ἀπελογεῖτο]—'made his defence.'

2. I think myself happy, king Agrippa, because I shall answer for myself ('because I am to make my defence') **this day before thee touching all the things whereof I am accused of the Jews: 3. Especially because I know thee to be expert in all customs and questions which are among the Jews.** His father was zealous for the law, and himself, as *Josephus* states (Antt. xx. 1. 3), held the office of president of the temple and its treasures, and had the appointment of the high priest, which he received from Claudius. **wherefore I beseech thee to hear me patiently.** The idea of 'indulgently' is also conveyed by the word [μακροθύμως]. **4. My manner of life from my youth, which was at the first among mine own nation at Jerusalem, know all the Jews; 5. Which knew me from the beginning**—plainly showing that he received his education, even from early youth, at Jerusalem. See on ch. xxii. 3. **if they would testify** [ἐὰν θέλωσιν]—'if they were willing to testify;' but this they were not, it being too strong a point in his favour: **that after the most straitest** ('the strictest') **sect of our religion I lived a Pharisee**—the Pharisees were confessedly the strictest of the sects, and he refers to this in order to meet the charge, that as a Hellenistic Jew he had contracted among the Heathen lax ideas of Jewish peculiarities. **6. And now I stand**

and am judged for the hope of the promise made of God unto our fathers—that is, for believing that the promise of Messiah, the Hope of Israel (ch. xiii. 32; xxviii. 10), had been fulfilled in Jesus of Nazareth risen from the dead, and glorified at the right hand of power. **7. Unto which promise our twelve tribes** (Jas. i. 1, and see on Luke ii. 36), **instantly** [ἐν ἐκτενείᾳ]—or, 'intently' (cf. ch. xii. 5, *Gr.*) **serving God** [λατρεῦον]—'offering worship' (see on the word "ministered," ch. xiii. 2) **day and night** ('night and day'), **hope to come.** The apostle rises into language as catholic as the thought which he expresses—representing his despised nation, all scattered though it now was, as twelve great branches of one ancient stem, in all places of their dispersion offering to the God of their fathers one unbroken worship, reposing on one great "promise" made of old unto their fathers, and sustained by one "hope" of "coming" to its fulfilment; the single point of difference between him and his countrymen, and the one cause of all their virulence against him, being, that his hope had found rest in One already come, while theirs still pointed to the future. **For which hope's sake, king Agrippa, I am accused of the Jews**—or (without the article), 'of Jews;' of all quarters the most surprising for such a charge to come from. The charge of *sedition* is not so much as alluded to throughout this speech; it was indeed a mere pretext. **8. Why should it be thought a thing incredible with you, that God should raise the dead?**—rather, 'Why is it judged a thing incredible with you if God raises the dead?' the case being viewed as an accomplished fact. No one dared to call in question the overwhelming evidence of the resurrection of Jesus, which proclaimed Him to be the Christ, the Son of God; the only way of getting rid of it, therefore, was to pronounce it incredible. But *why*, asks the apostle. *is it so judged?* Leaving this pregnant question to find its answer in the breasts of his audience, he now passes to his personal history. **9. I verily thought with myself, that I ought to do many things contrary to the name of Jesus of Nazareth. 10. Which thing I also did in Jerusalem: and many of the saints did I shut up in prison** ('in prisons'), **having received authority from the chief priests; and when they were put to death, I gave my voice** [ψῆφον]—*ltt.*, 'my vote,' but generally a 'verdict' or 'voice' of assent, against

173

11 were put to death, I gave my voice against *them.* And [j]I punished them
oft in every synagogue, and compelled *them* to blaspheme; and, being
exceedingly mad against them, I persecuted *them* even unto strange cities.
12 Whereupon, [k]as I went to Damascus with authority and commission from
13 the chief priests, at mid-day, O king, I saw in the way a light from
heaven, above the brightness of the sun, shining round about me and
14 them which journeyed with me. And when we were all fallen to the
earth, I heard a voice speaking unto me, and saying in the Hebrew
tongue, Saul, Saul, why persecutest thou me? *It is* hard for thee to
15 kick against the pricks. And I said, Who art thou, Lord? And he
16 said, I am Jesus, whom thou persecutest. But rise, and stand upon thy
feet: for I have appeared unto thee for this purpose, to [l]make thee a
minister and a witness both of these things which thou hast seen, and of
17 those things in the which I will appear unto thee; delivering thee from
18 the people, and *from* the Gentiles, [m]unto whom now I send thee, to [n]open
their eyes, *and* [o]to turn *them* from darkness to light, and [p]*from* the power
of Satan unto God, that [q]they may receive forgiveness of sins, and [r]inheritance among them which are [s]sanctified by faith that is in me.
19 Whereupon, O king Agrippa, I was not disobedient unto the heavenly
20 vision: but [t]showed first unto them of Damascus, and at Jerusalem, and
throughout all the coasts of Judea, and *then* to the Gentiles, that they
21 should repent and turn to God, and do [u]works meet for repentance. For
these causes [v]the Jews caught me in the temple, and went about to

A. D. 62.

[j] ch. 22. 19.
[k] ch. 9. 3. ch. 22. 6.
[l] 1 Tim. 1. 12.
[m] ch. 22. 21. Rom. 1. 5.
[n] Isa. 35. 5. Isa. 42. 7. Luke 1. 79. John 8. 12.
[o] 2 Cor. 6. 14. Eph. 4. 18. Eph. 5. 8. Col. 1. 13. 1 Pet. 2. 9.
[p] 1 John 3. 5.
[q] Luke 1. 77.
[r] Eph. 1. 11.
[s] ch. 20. 32.
[t] ch. 9. 20.
[u] Isa. 55. 7. Matt. 3. 8. Luke 3. 8-14. Luke 19. 8, 9. Eph. 5. 1-25.
[v] ch. 21. 30.

them. 11. And I punished them oft in every synagogue ('in all the synagogues'), **and compelled them to blaspheme** [ἠνάγκαζον]—that is, 'put force upon them' for that purpose (cf. Gal. vi. 12, *Gr.*); **and, being exceedingly mad against them, I persecuted them even unto strange** (or, 'foreign') **cities. 12. Whereupon** [Ἐν οἷς]—that is, In prosecution of which objects, **as I went to Damascus,** &c. **13. At mid-day, O king, I saw in the way a light from heaven, above the brightness of the sun, shining** ('flashing') **round about me and them which journeyed with me. 14. And,** &c. **15. And I said, Who art thou, Lord? And he said, I am Jesus, whom thou persecutest. 16. But rise, and stand upon thy feet: for I have appeared unto thee for this purpose.** Here (as *Alford* justly remarks) the apostle appears to condense into one statement various sayings of his Lord to him in visions at different times, in order to present at one view the grandeur of the commission with which his Master had clothed him. **to make thee a minister** [ὑπηρέτην] **and a witness both of these things which thou hast seen**—thus putting him on a level with those "eye-witnesses and ministers [ὑπηρέται] of the word" mentioned in Luke i. 2, **and of those things in the which I will appear unto thee**—referring to visions which he was hereafter to be favoured with (as ch. xviii. 9, 10; xxii. 17-21; xxiii. 11; 2 Cor. xii.: and see Gal. i. 12). **17. Delivering thee from the people** (of the Jews), **and from the Gentiles.** He was all along the object of Jewish malignity, and was at that moment in the hands of the Gentiles; yet he calmly reposes on his Master's assurances of deliverance from both, at the same time taking all precautions for safety and vindicating all his legal rights. **unto whom now I send thee.** The emphatic "I" (says *Bengel*) denotes the authority of the Sender. **18. To open their eyes.** This and what follows—though needed in another sense by the Jews also—as is evident from *v.* 23—is specially meant here of the Gentiles, last mentioned. **[and] to turn [them].** As the "and" and "them" here are a supplement by our translators, the meaning and the better rendering probably is, 'To open their eyes, that they may turn' (as in *v.* 20); the latter as the consequence of the former. **from darkness to light.** The whole passage leans on Isa. lxi. 1, quoted by our Lord, with reference to His own ministry, in the synagogue of Nazareth (Luke iv. 18); **and from the power of Satan unto God.** Observe here the connection between being "turned from darkness" and "turned from the power of Satan," whose whole power over men lies in keeping them *in the dark.* Hence the expression, "the rulers of the darkness of this world" (Eph. vi. 12). See on 2 Cor. iv. 4. **that they may receive forgiveness of sins, and inheritance among them which are sanctified by faith that is in me.** It will be observed that *Faith* is here made the instrument of salvation at once in its first stage, "forgiveness of sins," and in its last, admission to the home of the sanctified; and that the faith which introduces the soul to all this is emphatically declared by the glorified Redeemer to be a faith resting upon Himself—"Faith, even that which is on Me" [πίστει τῇ εἰς ἐμέ]. And who that believes this can refrain from casting his crown before Him, and offering Him supreme worship? **19. Whereupon, O king Agrippa, I was not disobedient unto the heavenly vision.** This musical and elevated strain—which carries the reader along with it, as it doubtless did the hearers—bespeaks the lofty region of thought and feeling to which the apostle had risen while rehearsing his Master's communications to him from heaven. **20. But showed first unto them of Damascus, and at Jerusalem, and throughout all the coasts of Judea, and then to the Gentiles.** His visit to Arabia is here omitted, because, beginning with the Jews, his object was to mention first the places where his former hatred of the name of Christ was best known: the mention of the Gentiles, so unpalatable to his Jewish audience, is reserved to the last. **that they should repent and turn to God, and do works meet for** ('worthy of') **repentance**—a brief description of repentance and its befitting fruits, suggested probably by the Baptist's teaching (Luke iii. 7, 8). **21. For these causes the Jews caught me in the**

22 kill *me*. Having therefore obtained help of God, I continue unto this day, witnessing both to small and great, saying none other things than
23 those which ʷthe Prophets and ˣMoses did say should come; that ʸChrist should suffer, *and* that he ᶻshould be the first that should rise from the dead, and should ᵃshow light unto the people, and to the Gentiles.
24 And as he thus spake for himself, Festus said with a loud voice, Paul,
25 ᵇthou art beside thyself; much learning doth make thee mad. But he said, I am not mad, most noble Festus; but speak forth the words of
26 truth and soberness. For the king knoweth of these things, before whom also I speak freely: for I am persuaded that none of these things are
27 hidden from him; for this thing was not done in a corner. King Agrippa, believest thou the Prophets? I know that thou believest.
28 Then Agrippa said unto Paul, ᶜAlmost thou persuadest me to be a
29 Christian. And Paul said, ᵈI would to God, that not only thou, but also all that hear me this day, were both almost, and altogether such as I am, except these bonds.

A. D. 62.

ʷ Rom. 3. 21.
ˣ John 5. 46.
ʸ Ps. 22.
   Isa. 53.
   Zech. 12.10.
   Luke 18.31-33.
   Luke 24.26.
ᶻ Matt. 27.53.
   1 Cor.15.20.
   Col. 1. 18.
   Rev. 1. 5.
ᵃ Isa. 42. 6.
   Isa. 60. 1.
ᵇ 2 Ki. 9.11.
   John10. 20.
   1 Cor. 1. 23.
   1 Cor. 2. 13.
ᶜ Mark 6. 20.
ᵈ 1 Cor. 7. 7.

temple, and went about to kill me. **22. Having therefore obtained help of God** [ἐπικουρίας τῆς παρὰ τ. Θεοῦ]—'succour, even that which cometh from God.' **I continue** [ἔστηκα]—'I stand;' that is, hold my ground unto this day, **witnessing**—*q. d.*, 'Since this life of mine, so marvellously preserved, in spite of all plots against it, is upheld for the Gospel's sake, I regard myself as living only to bear testimony' both **to small and great.** But in doing this, I am **saying none other things than those which the Prophets and Moses did say should come; 23. That Christ** ('the Christ,' or 'Messiah') **should suffer, and that he should be the first that should rise from the dead, and should show light unto the people, and to the Gentiles.** The sense is, that in testifying that the predicted Messiah was to be a suffering one, and that rising from the dead He should show light both to the Jews and to the Gentiles, he had only said what their own Scriptures had foreshown. The statement that the Christ "should be the *first* that should rise from the dead," was thus reached: Since it was to be in the character of a suffering and risen Messiah that He was to erect His kingdom and shed all its blessings on the world (Ps. xxii.; lxix.; Isa. lii. 14, 15; liii., particularly *vv.* 10-12); and the subjects of this kingdom of illuminated believers were to be taken from amongst mortal men, Messiah Himself would of necessity be "the *first* that should rise from the dead."

24. And as he thus spake for himself—'was thus making his defence,' **Festus said**—'saith' [φησίν, not ἔφη, is the true reading] **with a loud voice**—'surprised and bewildered,' Paul, **thou art beside thyself; much learning doth make thee mad**—is turning thy head. The union of flowing Greek, deep acquaintance with the sacred writings of his nation, reference to a resurrection, and other doctrines—to a Roman utterly unintelligible —and, above all, lofty religious earnestness, so strange to the cultivated, cold-hearted sceptics of that day, may account for this sudden exclamation. **25. But he said, I am not mad, most noble Festus; but speak forth the words** ('speak forth words') **of truth and soberness.** Can anything surpass this reply for readiness, self-possession, and calm dignity? Every word of it refuted the governor's rude charge, though Festus probably did not intend to hurt the prisoner's. feelings. **26. For the king knoweth of these things** (see on *vv.* 1-3), **before whom also I speak freely: for I am persuaded that none of these things are hidden from him; for this thing was not done in a corner. 27. King Agrippa, believest**

thou **the Prophets? I know that thou believest.** The courage and confidence here shown proceeded from a vivid persuasion of Agrippa's knowledge of the *facts* and his faith in the *predictions* which they verified; and the king's reply is the highest testimony to the correctness of these presumptions and the immense power of such bold yet courteous appeals to conscience. **28. Then Agrippa said unto Paul, Almost thou persuadest me to be a Christian** [Ἐν ὀλίγῳ με πείθεις]. There is certainly some difficulty in this translation, there being no other clear instance of this meaning of the phrase. Some of the best critics think the only true sense of the words to be, 'With a little persuadest thou me,' which they understand as an ironical response to the apostolic question—to this effect, 'Ah, Paul, thou art for making me a Christian rather too summarily—I am not to be so easily turned.' But the apostle's reply seems clearly to show that *he* at least did not so understand the king; and it is not likely that he misunderstood him. Others, who also object to the rendering of our version, think the sense of the phrase to be, 'In little [time] thou wilt persuade me to be a Christian'—*q. d.*, 'At this rate you will soon have me over to your opinions;' which they take to have been meant seriously, though not very deeply. But though the words will bear the sense of 'In little [time],' the tense used—not the future, 'thou wilt persuade me;' but the present, "thou persuadest me," suits ill with such a rendering of the words; and the apostle's reply seems to us quite fatal to it. One other sense of the words, different from that of our version, remains, 'In a little [measure] thou art persuading me to be a Christian'—*q. d.*, 'You are really making some impression upon me;' 'I feel myself *a little* drawn over to your opinions.' Not that Agrippa is to be supposed, in saying this, to mean anything more than a high compliment to the persuasiveness of the speaker; though it may well be supposed that there was more in it than he would let his manner show. But the chief, and to us all-sufficient recommendation of this view of the words—which is that of *Tyndale* and *Cranmer*, and defended by *Alexander*—is, that it is the only one which the apostle's response perfectly meets. **29. And Paul** [**said**] (This bracketed word should be printed in italics, as required in the translation, but not in the original, according to the best authorities), **I would to God, that not only thou, but also all that hear me this day, were both almost, and altogether such as I am** [καὶ ἐν ὀλίγῳ

30 And when he had thus spoken, the king rose up, and the governor, and
31 Bernice, and they that sat with them. And when they were gone aside,
they talked between themselves, saying, *ʰ*This man doeth nothing worthy
32 of death or of bonds. Then said Agrippa unto Festus, This man might
have been set at liberty, *ᶦ*if he had not appealed unto Cesar.

A. D. 62.
ʰ ch. 23, 9.
ch. 25, 25.
1 Pet. 3, 16.
1 Pet. 4, 14.
ᶦ ch. 25, 11.

καὶ ἐν πολλῷ]—*lit.*, 'both in little and in much such
as I am;' or, according to the reading best supported (and adopted by *Lachmann, Tischendorf,*
and *Tregelles*), 'both in little and in great' [με-
γάλῳ, excellently rendered in the Vulgate, *et in
modico et in magno*]. Whichever of these readings we adopt, the sense is the same, that whereas
Agrippa had gone so far as to say (with how
much sincerity, the apostle would not choose
to enquire) that he was a *little* drawn to the
apostle's views, that magnanimous servant of
Christ, seizing upon the admission, and repeating
the very words of it, wishes to God that not
Agrippa only, but the whole audience, were not
only *in little*, but *in much* (or *in great*), such as he
was; that is, not *somewhat* a Christian, but *out-
and-out* a Christian. In this view of the words it
will at once be seen that they express only in
another form, both what the authorized version
conveys, and what the other rendering does not
—'In a little [time] thou wilt persuade me to be a
Christian;' while it avoids the objections we have
mentioned against this latter translation, and what
seems a want of strict grammatical warrant for
the authorized rendering. The only one of the
proposed translations which it does not agree with
is the ironical one, which, though so powerfully
contended for, appears to us to be wholly out of
place. The objection taken to the authorized
version (and equally applicable to ours) by the
advocates of the ironical sense—that the word
"Christian" was at that time only a term of
contempt, and therefore not likely to have been
used seriously by Agrippa—has no force except on
the other side; for, taking it seriously, the sense,
according to the authorized version is, 'Thou wilt
soon have me over'—or, according to our proposed
version, 'I feel myself beginning to come over to
that despised sect.' except these bonds—doubtless holding up his two chained hands (see on
ch. xii. 6), which, in closing such a noble utterance,
must have had an electrical effect.

30. And [when he had thus spoken], the king
rose up (the bracketed words are certainly an
addition to the true text). He was not over easy,
we may be sure. and the governor, and Bernice,
and they that sat with them. 31. And when
they were gone aside, they talked between themselves, saying, This man doeth nothing worthy
of death or of bonds—an important, though an
almost superfluous testimony. 32. Then said
Agrippa unto Festus, This man might have been
set at liberty, if he had not appealed unto
Cesar. But what object could the apostle have in
making this appeal, save to prevent his being
taken for trial where he knew he had no justice
to expect, unless Festus should at Jerusalem
show a-courage which Pontius Pilate wanted in
a better cause, and which his predecessor Felix
had shown himself destitute of in this very case?
King Agrippa had but to pronounce in favour of
the immediate liberation of this innocent man,
and Festus would no doubt have at once given the
warrant. But possibly they thought themselves
precluded from taking any action after that appeal
had transferred the case to a higher tribunal.

Remarks.—1. Letting alone spiritual discernment, who that has any nice perception of the
workings of human feeling under different cir-

cumstances—such as might be supposed to actuate
Paul and Festus and Agrippa respectively on this
occasion—and of what would be a natural expression of these as they came out in this assembly, as
distinguished from literary invention or embellish-
ment, can fail to see in this chapter unadorned
though vigorous and noble history; and what but
a sceptical spirit, a low moral tone, and perverted
scholarship, directed to the establishment of a
preconceived theory, could find in it—as the
Tübingen critics do (*Zeller,* for example)—only one
of a series of unhistorical addresses, drawn up
apologetically long after the events, in the interest
of a Pauline, or more catholic party in the Church,
and with the view of supplanting the Petrine
or more Jewish views? One would be ashamed
to have to refer to such literature, were it not
that the learning and ingenuity which it displays,
after having wrought much mischief in the land
of its birth, have at length begun to make some
impression even in our own country, and that the
sceptical tendency which has recently set in
amongst us is fed by such wretched speculations.
But its effects will assuredly die away, not so
much through the force of any replies that may
be made to it, as under the power of the naked
text upon the devout and candid students of it,
while 'evil men and seducers will wax worse and
worse, deceiving and being deceived.' 2. The
commission from the glorified Redeemer to His
once bitter enemy is so grandly expressed in this
address before King Agrippa, that we may here
pause upon it for a moment. Three things in it
may be noticed. First, *The position which Christ
occupies.* As the commission issues authoritatively
from Him—"*I* send thee"—so all the effects which
the commission contemplates, since they could only
be instrumentally wrought by any creature, must
be effected, if at all, by Him from whom the
commission flows. And what are those effects?
"I send thee to the (chosen) people, and to the
Gentiles, to open their eyes, that they may turn
from darkness to light, and from the power of
Satan unto God." Plainly, He who sends men
to do such things must either have the power
and intention to do them Himself, through their
instrumentality, or must be mocking them when
He thus sends them forth. But, further, while it
is He who, by opening blind eyes, makes them
turn from darkness to light, and from the power
of Satan unto God, their standing before God
as His pardoned and reconciled people, and
their final inheritance among the sanctified, is
represented as due solely to their *faith in Him.*
It makes no difference to these conclusions,
whether we regard the words of this commission
as literally so addressed to him at any one time,
or as the apostle's own concentrated summary of
all that had been expressed to him by his glorified
Lord on many successive occasions. In this latter
view, which seems the correct one, it is even
more striking, as holding forth what we may style
The Pauline Theology, with respect to Christ's
position in the Divine economy—which we may
expect to find, and which we do find, running
through all his Epistles to the churches. Secondly,
*The relation to each other of spiritual illumination,
conversion, and faith.* As the reason why men are
content to remain in darkness and in bondage to

27 AND when ^ait was determined that we should sail into Italy, they delivered Paul and certain other prisoners unto *one* named Julius, a

A. D. 62.
^a ch. 25. 12.

the enemy of God is, that they are blind to their true condition, so, as soon as their eyes are Divinely opened to see clearly what and where they are, they turn from this discovered darkness to the "marvellous light" of "the glory of God in the face of Jesus Christ," and, at the same time and in the same act, from the dominion of Satan to subjection to God. But wonderful as is this transformation of nature and exchange of services, it is not this which effects their reconciliation to God, and entitles them to ultimate admission among the sanctified above. It is by *faith* in the Lord Jesus alone—"faith that is in ME"—that men "obtain forgiveness of sins and inheritance among them that are sanctified." For this alone rectifies their position, and adjusts their relationship to God; giving them right of approach to Him immediately as His pardoned and reconciled children, and right of admission to see Him face to face in the kingdom prepared "for them from the foundation of the world." Thirdly, *The superhuman power of the Gospel ministry.* That it does possess such power —opening blind eyes, and so causing men to turn from darkness to light, and from the power of Satan unto God—is the distinguishing characteristic of it as here held forth. But as that power lies not at all in the commissioned ambassadors of Christ, but wholly in Him that sends them, so they have here at once the materials of deepest humility and of highest encouragement, in the discharge of that commission, knowing that they "can do all things," though only "through Christ that strengtheneth them," and that of their converts they can say, "In Christ Jesus I have begotten you through the Gospel." 3. The view which Festus expressed of Paul's state of mind ("Thou art beside thyself"), and the exalted calmness of the reply ("I am not mad, most noble Felix, but do speak forth words of truth and soberness") remind us of the apostle's remarkable words to the Corinthians: "Whether we be beside ourselves, it is to God; or whether we be sober, it is for your cause: for the love of Christ constraineth us" (2 Cor. v. 13, 14). No doubt he spoke in an elevated tone; and when he came to the glowing words at which Festus interrupted him, he probably seemed as one carried quite beyond himself, while expatiating on the vast purpose of grace which his risen Lord had commissioned him to carry out. To one who knew nothing of those things, and cared as little, this holy enthusiasm would seem like the outpourings of one not quite himself—of one whose head had been turned by too much study; but the reply—especially when followed up by that appeal to the king which drew from him so remarkable a testimony to the power with which he pleaded for Christ; and, above all, when this was followed up by the wish to God that he and all present were in everything like himself with one thrilling exception— the chains upon those uplifted hands of his—this reply, we say, so followed up, while it nobly refuted the charge of Festus, revealed the true secret of the enthusiasm which had suggested it, and indeed was itself but a varied display of that very enthusiasm. 'No, most noble Festus, I am not beside myself; but the love of Christ constraineth me: and what wonder? For who could undergo such a change, and receive such a commission, and for simply fulfilling it have to stand here charged with hostility both to law and religion, and relate the amazing facts of such a case with the apathy of a sceptic? No: "If I be beside myself, it is to God"—in sight of whom the wonder would

be if I were not what I seem to thee—"or if I be sober," speaking forth the words of truth and soberness, "it is for your cause" who hear me this day, "if by any means I may save some." And is not this still the fitting attitude for those who plead for Christ, either in defending the truth or while praying them in Christ's stead to be reconciled to God? And those who go forth in this attitude, when they rise above the fear or favour of men, and realize the invisible and eternal issues of their pleading, may lay their account with seeming to the indifferent to be beside themselves; or if, to remove this impression, they "be sober"—presenting the awful truths which they handle in the light of sober but resistless realities, it will be but "for their cause." In either case, and in both at once, the secret of their procedure will be that of the apostle—"The love of Christ constraineth us." 4. On the whole, viewing this as the last public occasion on which the great apostle was to be "brought before kings and governors for Jesus' sake, for a testimony unto them," one cannot but be struck with the crowning character of it, and feel how well, during his last imprisonment and in the near prospect of sealing his testimony with his blood, he could say with respect to these public appearances for his Lord, as well as his whole career from the date of his conversion, "I have fought a good fight" (2 Tim. iv. 7).

CHAP. XXVII. 1—XXVIII. 16.—THE VOYAGE TO ITALY—THE SHIPWRECK AND SAFE LANDING AT MALTA—THE WINTERING, AND NOTABLE OCCURRENCES THERE—PROSECUTION OF THE VOYAGE AS FAR AS PUTEOLI, AND LAND JOURNEY THENCE TO ROME.

'It may be safely asserted (says *Humphry*, most truly) that no historical description of a long voyage and shipwreck has come down to us from ancient times so circumstantial, accurate, and natural in its details, as that which is contained in this chapter. The *transactions* of the narrative require our close attention; and the *style* is not less deserving of careful notice, inasmuch as it shows a great familiarity not only with the technical terms in use among the Greek sailors, but with the metaphorical and poetical language peculiar to a sea-faring life.' Of all the helps to a right exposition and felicitous illustration of this most difficult chapter, none is equal to 'The Voyage and Shipwreck of St. Paul (with Dissertations on the Life and Writings of St. Luke and the Ships and Navigation of the Ancients),' by JAMES SMITH, ESQ. of Jordanhill (2nd edit. 1856). The author's early and long familiarity with yachting, the industry and skill with which he applied his classical knowledge to the study of ancient navigation, his leisurely voyaging over the track of St. Paul, and minute personal inspection of all the places mentioned in this chapter, even his geological attainments—in connection with the elevation or depression of land—in so far as it might affect our inferences from present to past appearances; all these have given this accomplished gentleman qualifications for elucidating this chapter possessed, perhaps, by no other —qualifications which he has employed with the highest success. Of this work every expositor, since its publication, has largely and properly availed himself. From a careful study of the style of this chapter, Mr. Smith has arrived at the conclusion that, 'though accurate, it is unprofessional. No sailor (says he) would have written in a style so little like a sailor; no man not a sailor would

2 centurion of Augustus' band. And entering into a ship of Adramyttium, we launched, meaning to sail by the coasts of Asia; *one* [b] Aristarchus, a
3 Macedonian of Thessalonica, being with us. And the next *day* we touched at Sidon. And Julius [c] courteously entreated Paul, and gave
4 *him* liberty to go unto his friends to refresh himself. And when we had launched from thence, we sailed under Cyprus, because the winds were
5 contrary. And when we had sailed over the sea of Cilicia and Pamphylia, we came to Myra, *a city* of Lycia.
6 And there the centurion found a ship of Alexandria sailing into Italy;
7 and he put us therein. And when we had sailed slowly many days, and scarce were come over against Cnidus, the wind not suffering us, we sailed

A. D. 62.
CHAP. 27.
[b] Eze. 33. 31.
Matt. 10. 18.
Mark 10. 17-22.
ch. 19. 29.
ch. 20. 4.
Col. 4. 10.
Jas. 1. 23.
[c] 2 Sam. 18. 33.
ch. 28. 16.
1 Cor. 4. 8.

have written a narrative of a sea-voyage so consistent in all its parts, unless from actual observation. This peculiarity of style is to me, in itself, a demonstration that the narrative of the voyage is an account of real events, written by an eyewitness. A similar remark may be made on the geographical details. They must have been taken from actual observation, for the geographic knowledge of the age was not such as to enable a writer to be so minutely accurate in any other way.' *Dr. Howson's* illustrations of this chapter constitute one of the best portions of his masterly work.

From Cæsarea to Myra, in Lycia (1-5). **1. And when it was determined that we should sail into** (or 'for') **Italy**—that is, that they should go to Rome by sea. The "*we*" here re-introduces the Historian as one of the company. Not that he had left the apostle from the time when he last included himself (ch. xxi. 18), but by his arrest and imprisonment they were parted until now, when they met in the ship. **they delivered Paul and certain other prisoners** — state-prisoners going to be tried at Rome; of which several instances are on record: **unto one named Julius**—who treats the apostle throughout with such marked courtesy (*vv.* 3, 43; ch. xxviii. 16), that it has been conjectured (by *Bengel,* for example) that he had been present when Paul made his defence before Agrippa (see ch. xxv. 23), and was impressed with his lofty bearing. **a centurion of Augustus' band** [σπεῖρης Σεβαστῆς] —'the Augustan cohort,' an honorary title given to more than one legion of the Roman army, implying, perhaps, that they acted as a body-guard to the emperor or procurator, as occasion required. **2. And entering into** (or 'embarking in') **a ship of Adramyttium**—a seaport of Mysia, which constituted part of the Roman province of Asia. Probably they found no ship at Cæsarea bound for Italy, and availed themselves of a small coasting vessel belonging to Adramyttium, on her return voyage, not doubting that somewhere, on their westward course, they would meet with a ship bound for Italy that would take them in. This accordingly they did at Myra. **we launched** ('set sail'), **meaning to sail by the coasts of Asia**—but (according to the true reading) the meaning is, 'And embarking in a ship of Adramyttium, going to sail along the coasts of Asia;' that is, to coast along the southern shores of Proconsular Asia [μέλλοντι, not μέλλοντες, is the true reading; agreeing with πλοίω]. **[one] Aristarchus, a Macedonian of Thessalonica, being with us.** It is a pity our translators have inserted such a supplement as 'one' here, as if this Aristarchus had now been introduced to the reader for the first time. For in the uproar at Ephesus the historian had told us that the mob laid hold of " Gaius and *Aristarchus,* men of *Macedonia* " (ch. xix. 29). And he is again named (ch. xx. 4) as one of the seven who accompanied Paul, and said to be of *Thessalonica,* as

here. See also Col. iv. 10 and Philem. 24, where the apostle styles him his fellow-prisoner. The statement of the historian here is simply this : 'Aristarchus, the Macedonian of Thessalonica, being with us.' (The very absence of the article before "Macedonian," in Greek, arises from the fact that he was already familiar to the reader. **3. And the next day we touched** ('landed') **at Sidon.** To reach this ancient and celebrated Mediterranean port—about seventy miles north of Cæsarea—in one day, they must have had a good wind. **And Julius courteously entreated Paul** (see on *v.* 1), **and gave him liberty to go unto his friends**—no doubt disciples, gained probably all along the Phœnician coast, from the time when first the ground was broken there (see on ch. xi. 19 and xxi. 4). **to refresh himself**—which after his long confinement would not be unnecessary. Such small details are in this case extremely interesting. **4. And when we had launched** ('set sail') **from thence, we sailed under Cyprus, because the winds were contrary.** The wind blowing from the westward, probably with a touch of the north, which was adverse, they sailed *under the lee* of Cyprus, keeping it on their *left,* and steering between it and the mainland of Phœnicia. **5. And when we had sailed over** [διαπλεύσαντες]—'sailed through' **the sea of Cilicia and Pamphylia** (see on ch. xiii. 13) —coasts with which Paul had been long familiar ; the one, perhaps, from boyhood, the other from the time of his first missionary tour, **we came to Myra, a city of Lycia**—a port a little east of Patara (see on ch. xxi. 1).

Embarking in a merchant ship, bound for Italy, they set sail from Myra, but, in consequence of adverse winds, have great difficulty in reaching Fair Havens, in Crete (6-8). **6. And there the centurion found a ship of Alexandria sailing into Italy ; and he put us therein.** As Egypt was the granary of Italy, and this vessel was laden with wheat (*v.* 35), we need not wonder it was large enough to carry 276 souls, passengers and crew together (*v.* 37). Besides, the Egyptian merchantmen—among the largest in the Mediterranean—were equal to the largest merchantmen in our day. It may seem strange that, on their passage from Alexandria to Italy, they should be found at a Lycian port. But even still it is not unusual to stand to the north towards Asia Minor, for the sake of the current. **7. And when we had sailed slowly many days**—owing to contrary winds, **and scarce** [μόλις]—'with difficulty,' **were come over against Cnidus**—a town on the promontory of the peninsula of that name, having the island of Cös (see on ch. xxi. 1) to the west of it. Had the wind been as favourable as it was adverse, they might have made the distance from Myra to Cnidus—130 miles—in little more than a day. They would naturally have put in at Cnidus, whose large harbour was inviting ; but as the strong westerly current prevented them from making it, **we sailed under (the lee of) Crete**

8 under [1]Crete, over against Salmone; and, hardly passing it, came unto a place which is called the Fair Havens; nigh whereunto was the city *of* Lasea.

9   Now when much time was spent, and when sailing was now dangerous,

10 [2]because the fast was now already past, Paul admonished *them*, and said unto them, Sirs, I perceive that this voyage will be with [3]hurt and much damage, not only of the lading and ship, but also of our lives.

11 Nevertheless the centurion believed the master and the owner of the ship,

12 more than those things which were spoken by Paul. And because the haven was not commodious to winter in, the more part advised to depart thence also, if by any means they might attain [d] to Phenice, *and there* to winter; *which is* an haven of Crete, and lieth toward the south-west and north-west.

A. D. 62.

[1] Or, Candy, a large island in the Mediterranean. Tit. 1. 5, 12.

[2] The Fast was on the tenth day of the seventh month. Lev. 23. 27. Num. 29. 7.

[3] Or, injury.

[d] ch. 11. 19.

—for a particular account of which island, see Introduction to Epistle to Titus, **over against** (or 'in the direction of ') **Salmone**—the cape at the eastern extremity of the island. **8. And, hardly passing it** [Μόλις παραλεγόμενοι αὐτὴν]— 'with difficulty coasting along it,' owing to the westerly currents and head-winds, **came unto a place which is called the Fair Havens**—or, as being the name of a harbour (and the article not being prefixed), 'Fair Havens;' an anchorage near the middle of the south coast, and a little east of Cape Matala, which is the southernmost point of the island. A charming account of a visit to this anchorage is given by Mr. Smith in Appendix No. iii., entitled, 'Extract from the Journal of the Yacht "St. Ursula," Hugh Tennent, Esq. of Wellpark, Glasgow, dated *Calolimounias* (that is, "Fair Havens"), 16th January, 1856, by the *Rev. George Brown*.' **nigh whereunto was the city of Lasea.** No other writer mentions this town; and its ruins have been but recently observed and identified by the gentlemen of the party who visited the coast in the yacht 'St. Ursula'—*Hugh Tennent, Esq.*, the owner of the yacht, and his near relative, the *Rev. George Brown*—in 1856. When at Fair Havens, on asking where 'Lasea' was, the answer of their guide was—Two hours' walk to the eastward, close to Cape Leonda; but it is now a desert place. So, getting under weigh, they ran along the coast five miles to this cape. Here two white pillars having been observed by one of the ladies, standing on an eminence near the shore, the vessel hove to, and two of the gentlemen landed. Presently the remains of a city, with the ruins of two temples, were discovered. On asking the name of the place of some peasants, they at once answered, *Lasæa*. 'So (says Mr. Brown) there could be no doubt.' *Contrary to the advice of Paul, they again put to sea, hoping to reach Phœnicia, and there to winter— But being caught in a violent storm, they drift far westward, and are ready to give up all for lost* (9-20). **9. Now when much time was spent**— since leaving Cæsarea. But for unforeseen delays they might have reached the Italian coast before the stormy season. **and when sailing**—that is, the navigation of the open sea, **was now dangerous, because the fast was now already past**—the fast, that is, of the day of Atonement; answering to the end of September and beginning of October, or the autumnal equinox. About this time writers of authority pronounce the navigation of that sea unsafe, and for more than three months thereafter. Since, therefore, all hope of completing the voyage during that season was abandoned, the question next was, whether they should winter at Fair Havens, or move to Port Phœnicé, a harbour about forty miles to the westward. On this question our apostle gave his opinion, strongly urging that

they should winter where they were. **Paul admonished them, 10. And said unto them, Sirs, I perceive that this voyage will be with hurt and much damage** [ὕβρεως–ζημίας, see on *v.* 21], **not only of the lading and ship, but also of our lives.** There is no reason to suppose that this apprehension, and the advice founded on it, were prompted by any Divine communication; for when, at a later stage, he did speak from Divine authority, he openly says so. Here we have simply the exercise of his own good judgment, aided by some experience. Mr. Smith thought that 'a bay open to nearly one-half of the compass could not have been a good winter harbour.' But, in a note to his second edition he states that, from the observations and survey of the Rev. George Brown, it appears that Fair Havens is so well protected by islands and reefs, that it must be a very tolerable harbour to winter in; and that, considering the suddenness, frequency, and violence with which the gales of northerly winds spring up, and the certainty that if such a gale sprang up in the passage from Fair Havens to Lutro, the ship must be driven off to sea, the prudence of the master and owner was extremely questionable, and that the advice given by St. Paul may probably be supported even on nautical grounds. The event certainly justified his decision. **11. Nevertheless the centurion believed the master and the owner of the ship, more than those things which were spoken by Paul.** He would naturally think them best able to judge. **12. And because the haven was not commodious to winter in, the more part advised to depart thence [also].** The "also" here, though a natural *supplement*, is in the *text* quite insufficiently attested. [*Tischendorf* retains it—κἀκεῖθεν; but *Lachm.* and *Treg.* have ἐκεῖθεν]. **if by any means they might attain to Phenice** [φοίνικα]—rather 'Phœnix,' which Mr. Smith identifies with the modern *Lutro;* and Mr. Brown is satisfied that he is right, as is *Alford* also. But *Hackett*, for reasons presently to be mentioned, opposes this view. **and there to winter; which is an haven of Crete, and lieth toward the south-west and north-west** [βλέποντα κατὰ λίβα καὶ κατὰ χῶρον]. *Hackett*—from the usual sense of this phrase—understands it of the direction in which *the two coasts of the haven* lay, which of course would mean just the opposite direction to what the expression would denote, if (as Mr. Smith contends) it is designed to express the direction in which *the winds were blowing.* If *Hackett* is right (and *Humphry* and *Lechler* take the same view), it is the modern *Phineka*, a harbour quite near to Lutro, but facing the west. Certainly this allows of the phrase being rendered, as most naturally in our version, "looking towards." But since no anchorage which opened to the *west* would be good for this vessel, Mr. Smith thinks the meaning

13 And when the south wind blew softly, supposing that they had ob-
14 tained *their* purpose, loosing *thence*, they sailed close by Crete. But not
long after there [4]arose against it a tempestuous wind, called [5]Euroclydon.
15 And when the ship was caught, and could not bear up into the wind, we
16 let *her* drive. And running under a certain island which is called Clauda,
17 we had much work to come by the boat: which when they had taken up,
they used helps, undergirding the ship; and, fearing lest they should fall
18 into the quicksands, strake sail, and so were driven. And we being exceedingly tossed with a tempest, [c]the next *day* they lightened the ship;
19 and the third *day* [f]we cast out with our own hands the tackling of the
20 ship. And when neither sun nor stars in many days appeared, and no
small tempest lay on *us*, all hope that we should be saved was then
taken away.

A. D. 62.
[4] Or. beat.
[5] A north-east wind.
Ps. 107. 25-27.
[c] Matt. 16.26.
Luke 16. 8.
Phil. 3. 7. 8.
Heb. 12. 1.
[f] Job 2. 4.
Jon. 1. 5.
Mark 8. 35, 37.
Luke 9. 24, 25.

must be that a westerly wind would lead into it, or that 'it lay in an *easterly* direction from such a wind;' and the next verse would seem to confirm this.

13. And when the south wind blew softly, supposing that they had obtained their purpose —for with such a wind they had every prospect of reaching their destined winter quarters in a few hours, **loosing** thence, **they sailed close by** (or 'coasted close along') **Crete**. [The adverb, ἆσσον, is printed in the Vulgate, and from it in the received text, as the name of a Cretan city ('Ασσος); and *Erasmus* and *Luther* so take it. But it is plainly the comparative of ἄγχι—'nearer;' meaning that they 'hugged the shore.'] **14. But not long after there arose against it** [κατ᾽ αὐτῆς]—that is, not over against the ship [πλοῖον], but 'down from' the island [νήσου]; meaning down from the high ground along the south coast, **a tempestuous wind** [ἄνεμος τυφωνικός]—'a typhonic wind;' like a typhoon or tornado, causing a whirling of the clouds, owing to the meeting of opposite currents of air: **called Euroclydon** [Εὐροκλύδων]. This word occurs nowhere else; and there can hardly be a doubt that the much better supported reading—'Euro-Aquilo,' meaning a 'north-east' wind—is the true one. [Εὐρακύλων is the reading of ℵ A B*, and of the Vulgate, Memphitic, and Thebaic versions. The received reading has only G H, and later MSS., though supported by the Peshito Syriac. Still *Tischendorf* retains the received reading, but not *Lachmann* and *Tregelles*.] **15. And when the ship was caught, and could not bear up into the wind** [ἀντοφθαλμεῖν]—lit., 'face the wind,' **we let her drive** [ἐπιδόντες ἐφερόμεθα]—'giving in, we let ourselves drive' before the gale. **16. And running under** (the lee of) **a certain island** [Νησίον]—'islet,' **which is called Clauda**—lying between twenty and thirty miles south-west of Crete. It is called *Gozzo* in the charts; but Mr. Brown found that on the spot it still retains its ancient name, *Chlauda*. **we had much work to come by the boat**—'were with difficulty able to secure the boat.' But why so? If the ship was to live out the storm, they would first hoist the boat on board. It had, as usual, been towed behind; but now that the gale had sprung up, and a violent storm was raging, it could hardly fail, after more than twenty miles' dragging after the gale, to be filled with water, and so would with difficulty be secured, even though under the lee of this islet the water would be comparatively smooth, and so most favourable for the operation. **17. Which when they had taken up, they used helps** (or 'stays'), **undergirding the ship**—that is, passing four or five turns of a cable-laid rope round the hull or frame of the ship, to enable her to resist the violence of the seas, an operation rarely resorted to in modern seamanship: **and, fearing**

lest they should fall into the quicksands. 'The word (as *Humphry* says) was sometimes used in that general sense; but with the article [εἰς τὴν Σύρτιν] it must be restricted (at least here) to the place properly so called—the *Syrtis Major*—on the coast of Africa, a gulf dangerous from its shoals, lying south-west of Crete.' It should then be, 'fearing lest they should drift on the Syrtis.' **strake** (or, 'struck') **sail** [χαλάσαντες τὸ σκεῦος]. This cannot be the meaning; for 'it would be equivalent (to use the words of *Mr. Smith*) to saying that, fearing a certain danger, they deprived themselves of the only possible means of avoiding it, and let themselves be driven directly towards the Syrtis.' The sense must be, 'they lowered the gear,' or, 'let down the tackling;' here, perhaps, referring to the heavy mainyard with the sail attached to it, and hoisting a small storm-sail instead. **and so were driven**—or 'borne along,' on the starboard tack (as *Mr. Smith* says); the only course by which she could avoid falling into the Syrtis. With this notice concludes the first eventful day. **18. And we being exceedingly tossed with a tempest, the next day they lightened the ship** [ἐκβολὴν ἐποιοῦντο]—lit., 'made an out-throw;' a nautical phrase for throwing the cargo overboard to lighten the ship (compare Jon. i. 5). **19. And the third day we** (passengers and crew together) **cast out with our own hands the tackling of the ship**—whatever they could do without, that carried weight: this further effort to lighten the ship seems to show that it was now in a *leaking* condition, as will presently appear more evident. **20. And when neither sun nor stars in many** (or, 'several') **days appeared**—probably most of the fourteen days mentioned (*v.* 27). This continued thickness of the atmosphere prevented their making the necessary observations of the heavenly bodies by day or by night; so that they could not tell where they were, **and no small tempest lay on us, all hope that we should be saved was then taken away.** 'Their exertions (says *Mr. Smith*) to subdue the leak had been unavailing; they could not tell which way to make for the nearest land, in order to run their ship ashore—the only resource for a sinking ship; but unless they did make the land, they must founder at sea. Their apprehensions, therefore, were not so much caused by the fury of the tempest as by the state of the ship.' From the inferiority of ancient to modern naval architecture, leaks were sprung much more easily, and the means of repairing them were fewer than now. Hence the far greater number of shipwrecks from this cause.

Paul addresses those on board on the misfortune that had overtaken them by going against his advice, but assures them, on the authority of a Divine revelation, of eventual deliverance for all of them, at the same time warning them that they must lose the

21   But after long abstinence Paul stood forth in the midst of them, and
said, Sirs, ye should have hearkened unto me, and not have loosed from
22 Crete, and to have gained this harm and loss." And now I exhort you to
be of good cheer: for there shall be no loss of *any man's* life among you,
23 but of the ship.   For *ᵍ*there stood by me this night the angel of God,
24 whose I am, and whom *ʰ*I serve, saying, *ⁱ*Fear not, Paul; thou must be
brought *ʲ* before Cesar: and, lo, God hath given *ᵏ*thee all them that sail
25 with thee.   Wherefore, sirs, be of good cheer: for I *ˡ*believe God, that it
26 shall be even as it was told me.   Howbeit *ᵐ*we must be cast upon a certain island.
27   But when the fourteenth night was come, as we were driven up and
down in Adria, about midnight the shipmen deemed that they drew near
28 to some country; and sounded, and found *it* twenty fathoms: and when
they had gone a little farther, they sounded again, and found *it* fifteen
29 fathoms.   Then fearing lest we should have fallen upon rocks, they cast
four anchors out of the stern, and wished for the day.

A. D. 62.

ᵍ Ps. 25. 14.
Amos 3. 7.
ch. 23. 11.
ʰ Dan. 6. 16.
Rom. 1. 9.
2 Tim. 1.3.
ⁱ Isa. 41. 10,
14.
Isa. 43. 1, 2.
ʲ ch. 19. 21.
ch. 23. 11.
ch. 25. 11.
ᵏ Gen. 39. 5,
23.
Job 22. 29,
30.
Job 42. 8.
Isa. 6. 13.
ˡ Luke 1. 45.
ᵐ ch. 28. 1.

ship and be cast on some island (21-26).   **21. But
after long abstinence.** A large ship loaded with
wheat could not have been in want of provisions
during such a voyage, even for such a number as
it had on board.   But the impossibility of cook-
ing, and the constant occupation and engrossment
of all hands, would put regular meals out of
thought.   'The hardships (says *Mr. Smith*) which
the crew endured during a gale of such continuance, and their exhaustion from labouring at the
pumps, and hunger, may be imagined, but are not
described.' **Paul stood forth in the midst of
them, and said, Sirs, ye should have hearkened
unto me**—not meaning by this to reflect on them
for the past, but only to claim their confidence for
the future; **and not have loosed from Crete, and
to have gained this harm and loss**—'and so have
been spared this turmoil and damage.'   To 'gain
a loss' is, in Greek and Latin, to avoid it (as
Humphry says).   The word "harm" here [ὕβρις]
seems to refer, not to actual injuries done either
to the persons or the ship, but to the tear and
wear of mind and body occasioned by the violence of the storm; while "loss" [ζημία] points
to the damage and loss which the ship and its
cargo had sustained.   **22. And now I exhort
you to be of good cheer: for there shall be no
loss of any man's life among you, but of the
ship** [πλὴν for ἀλλά, as ἀλλὰ for πλὴν in Mark
ix. 8, says *Humphry;* but this is colloquial in
almost every language, which interchanges "save"
and "but"].   **23. For there stood by me this
night the** ('an') **angel of God**—as ch. xvi. 9, and
xxiii. 11; **whose I am** (see on Rom. i. 1), **and
whom I serve** [λατρεύω]—in the sense of religious
worship (see on ch. xiii. 2) and total religious consecration,   **24. Saying, Fear not, Paul; thou must
be brought before Cesar**: and, lo, God hath given
thee all them that sail with thee.   **25. Wherefore, sirs, be of good cheer: for I believe God,
that it shall be even as it was told me.** While
the crew were toiling at the pumps, Paul was
wrestling in prayer, not for himself only and
the cause in which he was going a prisoner to
Rome, but, with true magnanimity of soul, for all
his shipmates; and God heard him, "giving him"
(remarkable expression!) all that sailed with him.
On the morning after receiving this Divine communication, gathering all around him, he reports it,
adding, with a noble simplicity, "*for I believe God*,
that it shall be even as it was told me," and encouraging all on board to "be of good cheer" in
the same confidence.   What a contrast to this (as
Humphry well remarks) is the speech of Cæsar, in

181

similar circumstances, to his pilot, bidding him (as
Plutarch reports) keep up his spirit, because he
carried Cæsar and Cæsar's Fortune.   The Roman
general knew no better name for the Divine Providence, by which he had been so often preserved,
than *Cæsar's Fortune*.   **26. Howbeit we must be
cast upon a certain island**—'on some island.'
From the explicit particulars—that the ship would
be lost, but not one that sailed in it, and that
they 'must be cast on some island'—one would
conclude that he had had a visional representation of a total wreck, of a mass of human beings
struggling with the angry elements, and of one
and all of those whose figure and countenance had
daily met his eye on deck standing on some unknown island-shore.   From what follows, it would
seem that Paul from this time was regarded with
a deference akin to awe.
   The wreck and safe landing on Malta (27-44).
27. But when the fourteenth night—that is, from
the time when they left Fair Havens, was come, as
we were driven up and down in Adria—or, ' were
drifting about in Adria.'   By this term is not
meant here the modern *Adriatic* (which has been
one great source of the mistake in regard to the
island on which the wrecked party were thrown),
but that sea which lies between Greece, Italy, and
Africa.   **about midnight the shipmen deemed
that they drew near to some country** [προσά-
γειν τινὰ αὐτοῖς χώραν]—'that some land was
nearing them;' no doubt, from the peculiar sound
of the breakers, as on a rocky coast.   What
a graphic character does this nautical language
give to the narrative!   **28. And sounded, and
found it twenty fathoms**—implying that they
were rapidly drifting on some shore.   **29. Then
fearing lest we should have fallen upon rocks,
they cast four anchors out of the stern.** 'The
ordinary way (says *Mr. Smith*) was to cast the
anchor, as now, from the *bow;* but ancient ships,
built with both ends alike, were fitted with hawse-
holes in the stern, so that in case of need they could
anchor either way.   And when the fear was, as
here, that they might fall on the rocks *to leeward*,
and the intention was to run the ship ashore as
soon as daylight enabled them to fix upon a safe
spot—the very best thing they could do was to
anchor by the stern.   In stormy weather two
anchors were used, and we have instances of four
being employed, as here.'   and **wished** ('anxiously,'
or 'devoutly wished') **for the day**—the remark this
of one present, and, with all his shipmates, alive
to the horrors of their condition.   'The ship (says
Mr. Smith) might go down at her anchors, or the

And as the shipmen were about to flee out of the ship, when they had let down the boat into the sea, under colour as though they would have
31 cast anchors out of the foreship, Paul said to the centurion and to the
32 soldiers, [a]Except these abide in the ship, ye cannot be saved. Then the soldiers cut off the ropes of the boat, and let her fall off.
33 And while the day was coming on, Paul besought *them* all to take meat, saying, This day is the fourteenth day that ye have tarried and
34 continued fasting, having taken nothing. Wherefore I pray you to take *some* meat; for this is for your health: for [o]there shall not an hair fall
35 from the head of any of you. And when he had thus spoken, he took bread, and [p]gave thanks to God in presence of them all: and when he
36 had broken *it*, he began to eat. Then were they all of good cheer, and
37 they also took *some* meat. And we were in all in the ship two hundred
38 threescore and [q]sixteen souls. And when they had eaten enough, they lightened the ship, and cast out the wheat into the sea.
39 And when it was day, they knew not the land: but they discovered a certain creek with a shore, into the which they were minded, if it were
40 possible, to thrust in the ship. And when they had [6]taken up the

A. D. 62.

[a] Isa. 38. 21.
Matt. 4. 7.
[o] 1 Ki. 1. 52.
Matt. 10. 30.
Luke 12. 7.
Luke 21. 18.
[p] 1 Sam. 9. 13.
Matt. 15. 36.
Mark 8. 6.
John 6. 11.
1 Tim. 4. 3, 4.
[q] ch. 2. 41.
ch. 7. 14.
Rom. 13. 1.
1 Pet. 3. 20.
[6] Or, cut the anchors, they left them in the sea, etc.

coast to leeward might be iron-bound, affording no beach on which they could land with safety. Hence their anxious longing for day, and the ungenerous but natural attempt—not peculiar to ancient times—of the seamen to save their own lives by taking to the boat.'

30. And as the shipmen ('sailors') **were about to flee out of the ship**—under cover of night, **when they had let down the boat into the sea, under colour as though they would have cast** [ἐκτείνειν]—rather, 'carried out,' that is, by the boat, **anchors out of the foreship** (or 'bow.'). 'It is to be observed (says *Mr. Smith*) that casting anchors out of the foreship could have been of no possible advantage in the circumstances, and that as the pretext could not deceive a seaman, we must infer that the officers of the ship were parties to the unworthy attempt, which was, perhaps, detected by the nautical skill of St. Luke, and communicated by him to St. Paul.' **31. Paul said to the centurion and to the soldiers**—the only parties now to be trusted, and whose own safety was now imperilled, **Except these abide in the ship, ye cannot be saved.** The soldiers and passengers could not be expected to possess the necessary seamanship in so very critical a case; the flight of the crew, therefore, might well be regarded as certain destruction to all who remained. Though fully assured, in virtue of a Divine pledge, of ultimate safety to all on board, Paul speaks and acts throughout this whole scene in the exercise of a sound judgment on the indispensable *human* conditions of safety; and as there is no trace of any feeling of inconsistency between these two things in his mind, so even the centurion, under whose orders the soldiers acted on Paul's views, seems never to have felt perplexed by the two-fold aspect—Divine and human—in which the same thing presented itself to the mind of Paul. **32. Then the soldiers cut off the ropes of the boat**—it had been already lowered, **and let her fall off**—let the boat drift away.

33. And while the day was coming on—that is, in the interval between the cutting off of the boat and the approach of the anxiously wished for daybreak, **Paul**—now looked up to by all the passengers as the man to direct them, **besought them all to take meat**—to partake of a meal, **saying, This day is the fourteenth day that ye have tarried** [προσδοκῶντες]—or 'awaited' some breathing time, **having taken nothing**—or, taken

no regular meal (see on *v.* 21). **34. Wherefore I pray you to take some meat; for this is for your health: for there shall not an hair fall** ('perish' or 'be lost') **from the head of any of you**—[ἀπολεῖται, not πεσεῖται of the received text, is the true reading.] Beautiful union this of confidence in the Divine pledge, and of care for the whole ship's health and safety! **35. And when he had thus spoken, he took bread**—'a loaf,' assuming the lead, **and gave thanks to God in presence of [them] all**—an impressive act in such circumstances, fitted to plant a testimony for the God he served in the breasts of all, **he began to eat.** This would certainly not be regarded by the Christians in the ship in the light either of a celebration of the Lord's Supper or of a love-feast —as some strangely imagine—but purely as a meal to recruit exhausted nature, which Paul shows them, by his own example, how a Christian partakes of. **36. Then were they all of good cheer, and they also took some meat**—'took food;' the first full meal since the commencement of the gale. Such courage in desperate circumstances as Paul here showed is wonderfully infectious. **37. And we were in all in the ship two hundred threescore and sixteen souls. 38. And when they had eaten enough, they lightened the ship, and cast out the wheat into the sea.** With fresh strength after the meal, they make a third and last effort to lighten the ship, not only by pumping, as before, but by throwing the whole cargo of wheat into the sea (see on *v.* 6).

39. And when it was day, they knew not the land. This has been thought surprising in sailors accustomed to that sea. But the scene of the wreck is remote from the great harbour (as *Mr. Smith* says), and possesses no marked features by which it could be recognized, even by a native, if he came unexpectedly upon it; not to speak of the rain pouring in torrents (ch. xxviii. 2), which would throw a haze over the coast even after day broke. Immediately on landing they knew where they were (ch. xxviii. 1). **but they discovered a certain creek with a shore**—or level beach. Every creek of course must have a shore; but the meaning is, a *practicable* shore, in a nautical sense—*i. e.*, one with a smooth beach, in contradistinction to a rocky coast (as *v.* 41 shows). **into the which they were minded, if it were possible, to thrust in the ship.** This was their one chance of safety. **40. And when they had taken up the anchors.**

anchors, they committed *themselves* unto the sea, and loosed the rudder-bands, and hoised up the mainsail to the wind, and made toward shore.

41 And falling into a place where two seas met, ʳthey ran the ship aground: and the fore part stuck fast, and remained unmoveable, but the hinder

42 part was broken with the violence of the waves. And the soldiers' counsel was ˢto kill the prisoners, lest any of them should swim out, and escape.

43 But the centurion, ᵗwilling to save Paul, kept them from *their* purpose; and commanded that they which could swim should cast *themselves* first

44 *into the sea*, and get to land: and the rest, some on boards, and some on *broken pieces* of the ship. And so it came to pass, that they escaped ᵘall safe to land.

28 AND when they were escaped, then they knew that the island was

2 called ᵃMelita. And the barbarous people ᵇshowed us no little kindness: for they kindled a fire, and received us every one, because of the present rain, and because of the cold.

3 And when Paul had gathered a bundle of sticks, and laid *them* on the

A. D. 62.
ʳ 2 Cor. 11.25.
ˢ Pro. 12. 10.
Eccl. 9. 3.
Isa. 59. 7.
Rom. 3. 15.
ᵗ Pro. 16. 7.
Jer. 38. 10.
ch. 23. 10.
ᵘ Ps. 107. 30.
Amos 9. 9.

CHAP. 28.
ᵃ Or, Malta.
ch. 27. 26.
ᵇ ch. 27. 3.
Rom. 1. 14.
1 Cor. 14 11.
Col. 3. 11.
Heb. 13. 1,
2.

---

they committed themselves unto the sea [τὰς ἀγκύρας περιελόντες εἴων εἰς τ. θάλασσαν]. The marginal rendering here evidently is the right one, ' And having cut the anchors, they left them in the sea.' **and loosed the rudder-bands.** Ancient ships (says *Mr. Smith*) were steered by two large paddles, one on each quarter. When anchored by the stern in a gale, it would be necessary to lift them out of the water, and secure them by lashings or rudder-bands, and to loose these when the ship was again got under weigh, **and hoised up the mainsail** [ἀρτέμονα]. The 'artemon' was certainly (says *Mr. Smith*) the foresail, not the mainsail; and a sailor will at once see that this was the best possible sail that could be set in the circumstances. How necessary must the crew have been to execute all these movements, and how obvious the foresight which made their stay indispensable to the safety of all on board (see on *v.* 31). **to the wind** [τ. π. ιεούσῃ, sc. αὔρᾳ], **and made toward shore**—or, 'bore down on the beach.' **And falling into a place where two seas met** [τόπον διθάλασσον]—*lit.*, 'a place of two seas;' a place 'which had sea on both sides.' The word is used both for an isthmus and a strait. *Mr. Smith* thinks that here it refers to the channel (not more than a hundred yards broad) which separates the small island of Salmone from Malta, forming a communication between the sea inside the bay and that outside. **they ran the ship aground** ('ashore'): **and the fore part stuck fast, and remained unmoveable, but the hinder part was broken** [ἐλύετο]—rather, ' was breaking;' that is, was fast going to pieces, **with the violence of the waves.** [*Lachmann* and *Tischendorf* leave out τ. κυμάτων, ending the verse with ὑπο τ. βίας. For this there is the authority of א A B. But all other MSS. and all the versions have the received text; and *Meyer* is probably right in conjecturing that the omission most likely arose from the transcriber's eye having passed from the τῶν before κυμάτων to the τῶν which begins the next verse.] 'The rocks of Malta (says *Mr. Smith*) disintegrate into extremely minute particles of sand and clay, which, when acted upon by the currents or surface agitation, form a deposit of tenacious clay; but in still waters, where these causes do not act, mud is formed; but it is only in creeks, where there are no currents, and at such a depth as to be undisturbed by the waves, that the mud occurs. A ship, therefore, impelled by the force of a gale into a creek with such a bottom, would strike a bottom of mud graduating into tenacious clay, into which the fore part would fix itself and be held fast, while the stern was exposed to the force

of the waves.' 42. **And the soldiers' counsel was to kill the prisoners, lest any of them should swim out, and escape.** Roman cruelty, which made the keepers answerable with their own lives for the safety of their prisoners, is here reflected in this heartless proposal. 43. **But the centurion, willing** ('wishing') **to save Paul, kept them from their purpose.** Great must have been the influence of Paul over the centurion's mind to produce such an effect. **and commanded that they which could swim should cast themselves first into the sea, and get to land:** 44. **And the rest, some on boards, and some on [broken pieces] of the ship** [ἐπί τινων τῶν ἀπὸ τ. πλοίου]—' on some of the things from the ship,' such as planks or articles of furniture flung out for the purpose. **And so it came to pass, that they escaped all safe to land.** All followed the swimmers in committing themselves to the deep; and according to the Divine pledge, and Paul's confident assurance given them, every soul got safe to land—yet without miracle.

CHAP. XXVIII. 1-10.—*Notable Occurrences at Malta.* 1. **And when they were escaped, then they knew**—'then we knew' is evidently the true reading [ἐπέγνωμεν]. **that the island was called Melita** (see on ch. xxvii. 39). The opinion that this island was not Malta to the south of Sicily, but Meleda in the Gulf of Venice—which till lately had respectable support among competent judges—is now all but, if not entirely, exploded; recent examination of all the places on the spot, and of all writings and principles bearing on the question, by gentlemen of the highest qualifications—particularly *Mr. Smith*—having set the question, it may now be affirmed, at rest. 2. **And the barbarous people**—so called, merely as speaking neither the Greek nor the Latin language. (Compare Rom. i. 14; 1 Cor. xiv. 11; Col. iii. 11.) They were originally Phœnician colonists (see *Diod. Sic.*, v. 12, quoted by *Humphry*). Their dialect was probably the Punic (or Carthaginian dialect of the Phœnician language). **showed us no little** (' no ordinary') **kindness: for they kindled a fire, and received us every one, because of the present rain**—'the rain that was (then) on us;' not now falling for the first time, but then falling heavily, **and because of the cold.**' They welcomed them all, drenched and shivering, to these most seasonable marks of friendship. In this these 'barbarians' contrast favourably with many since, bearing the Christian name. The life-like style of the narrative here and in the following verses gives it a great charm. 3. **And when Paul had gathered a bundle of**

4 fire, there came a viper out of the heat, and fastened on his hand. And when the barbarians saw the *venomous* beast hang on his hand, they said among themselves, *c* No doubt this man is a murderer, whom, though he

5 hath escaped the sea, yet vengeance suffereth not to live. And he shook

6 off the beast into the fire, and *d* felt no harm. Howbeit they looked when he should have swollen, or fallen down dead suddenly: but after they had looked a great while, and saw no harm come to him, they changed their minds, and *e* said that he was a god.

7 In the same quarters were possessions of the chief man of the island, whose name was Publius; who received us, and lodged us three days

8 courteously. And it came to pass, that the father of Publius lay sick of a fever and of a bloody flux: to whom Paul entered in, and *f* prayed, and

9 *g* laid his hands on him, and healed him. So when this was done, others

10 also, which had diseases in the island, came, and were healed: who also honoured us with *h* many honours; and when we departed, they laded *us* with such things as were necessary.

11 And after three months we departed in a ship of Alexandria, which

A. D. 62.

c Luke 13. 2.
John 9. 2.
d Ps. 91. 13.
Mark 16.18.
Luke 10.19.
e ch. 8. 10.
ch. 10. 25.
ch. 14. 11.
Rev. 22. 8,
9.
f 1 Ki. 17. 20-
22.
Jas. 5. 14.
g Matt. 9. 18.
Mark 6. 5.
Mark 7. 32.
Mark 16.18·
Luke 4. 40.
h Matt. 15. 6.
1 Tim. 5.
17.

sticks ('a quantity of dry sticks'), **and laid them on the fire.** The vigorous activity of Paul's character is observable in this comparatively trifling action (as *Webster and Wilkinson* remark). **there came a viper out of the heat** [ἀπὸ τ. θέρμης is the only authorized reading: ἐκ of the received text has next to no support, and διεξελθοῦσα is better than ἐξ.]—'a viper darted out from the heat.' Having laid itself up among the sticks on the approach of the cold winter season, and thus lain torpid, it had suddenly recovered from its torpor by the heat. **and fastened (its fangs) on his hand.** Vipers dart at their enemies sometimes several feet at a bound. They have now disappeared from Malta, owing to the change which cultivation has produced. **4. And when the barbarians saw the venomous beast hang on** ('hanging from') **his hand, they said among themselves, No doubt this man is a murderer**—an impression which might be strengthened by seeing the chains on his hands ; **whom, though he hath escaped the sea, yet vengeance suffereth not to live.** Thus it appears *they believed in a supreme, resistless, avenging Eye and Hand*—vague though doubtless their notions were of *where* it resided. **5. And he shook off the beast into the fire, and felt no harm.** (See Mark xvi. 18.) **6. Howbeit they looked** ('kept looking') **when he should have swollen, or fallen down dead suddenly**—being no doubt familiar with the effect of such bites: **but after they had looked a great while, and saw no harm come to him, they changed their minds, and said that he was a god.** From "a murderer" to "a god ;" just as the Lycaonians, from "sacrificing to" Paul and Silas, fell to "stoning them" (ch. xiv. 13, 19).

7. In the same quarters ('the neighbourhood of that place') **were possessions of the chief man** [τ. πρώτῳ] (or, 'the First man') **of the island, whose name was Publius.** As this man's father was still alive (*v.* 8), he himself would hardly be so styled if this distinction was that of the *family.* It must, therefore, have been his *official* title. Accordingly, two inscriptions have been discovered in the island—the one in Greek, the other in Latin —containing the same words here employed, and proving that this was the proper official title of the Maltese representative of the Roman Prætor of Sicily, to whose province Malta belonged. **who received** ('welcomed') **us, and lodged** (or 'entertained') **us**—not only Paul's company, but the 'courteous' centurion, **three days courteously**— till proper winter accommodation could be ob-
184

tained for them. **8. And it came to pass, that the father of Publius lay sick of a fever**—*lit.,* 'fevers ;' meaning that which was intermittent. **and of a bloody flux** [δυσεντερία]—'dysentery.' 'This (as *Hackett* says) is one of those expressions in Luke's writings that have been supposed to indicate his professional training as a physician. (See ch. xii. 23; xiii. 11; Luke xxii. 44.) It is correct to attach to them that significancy. No other writer of the New Testament exhibits this sort of technical precision in speaking of diseases.' **to whom Paul entered in, and prayed**—thus precluding the supposition that any charm resided in himself, **and laid his hands on him, and healed him.** Thus, as our Lord rewarded Peter for the use of his boat (Luke v. 3, &c.), so Paul richly repays Publius for his hospitality. And as before we observed the fulfilment of one prediction of the ascending Redeemer, "They shall take up serpents," so here we have another, "they shall lay hands on the sick, and they shall recover" (Mark xvi. 18). **9. So when this was done, others** ('the rest') **also, which had diseases in the island, came, and were healed** ('kept coming and getting healed') : **10. Who also honoured us with many honours** [τιμαῖς]—'presents,' tokens of gratitude and regard; **and when we departed, they laded us with such things as were necessary.** This was not taking hire for the miracles wrought among them (Matt. x. 8), but merely accepting such grateful expressions of feeling—particularly in providing what would minister to their comfort during the voyage—as showed the value they set upon the presence and labours of the apostle amongst them, and which it would have hurt their feelings to refuse. Whether any permanent effects of this three months' stay of the greatest of the apostles were left at Malta, we cannot certainly say. But though little dependence is to be placed upon the tradition that Publius became bishop of Malta, and afterwards of Athens, we may well believe the accredited tradition, that the beginnings of the Christian Church at Malta sprang out of this memorable visit.

Departure from Malta—Prosecution of the voyage as far as Puteoli, and land-journey thence to Rome (11-15). **11. And after three months we departed in a ship of Alexandria** (see on ch. xxvii. 6), **which had wintered in the isle**—no doubt driven in by the same storm which had wrecked on its shores the apostle's vessel—an incidental mark of consistency in the narrative; **whose sign** —or figure-head; the figure, carved or painted

12 had wintered in the isle, whose sign was Castor and Pollux.　And landing
13 at Syracuse, we tarried *there* three days.　And from thence we fetched a
　　compass, and came to Rhegium: and after one day the south wind blew,
14 and we came the next day to Puteoli: where we found *brethren, and
　　were *desired to tarry with them seven days: and so we went toward
15 Rome.　And from thence, when the brethren heard of us, they came to
　　meet us as far as Appii Forum, and the Three Taverns: whom when Paul
　　saw, he thanked God, and took courage.

A. D. 63.
Ps. 119. 63.
Matt. 10.11.
ch. 9. 42, 43.
ch. 19. 1.
ch. 21. 4. 7,
8.
Gen. 7. 4.
Gen. 8. 10.
ch. 20. 6.

on the bow, which gave name to the vessel. Such figure-heads were anciently as common as now. **was Castor and Pollux** [Διοσκούροι]—'the Dioscuri;' that is, Castor and Pollux, the tutelar gods of mariners, to whom all their good fortune was ascribed. 'St. Anthony is substituted for them (remark *Webster and Wilkinson*) in the modern superstitions of Mediterranean sailors. They carry his image in their boats and ships. It is highly improbable that two ships of Alexandria should have been casually found, of which the owners were able and willing to receive on board such a number of passengers. We may then reasonably conceive that it was compulsory on the owners to convey soldiers and state-travellers' (ch. xxvii. 6). **12. And landing at Syracuse**—the ancient and celebrated capital of Sicily, on its eastern coast; about eighty miles, or a day's sail, north from Malta: **we tarried there three days**—probably from the state of the wind. Doubtless, Paul would wish to go ashore, to find out and break ground amongst the Jews and proselytes whom such a mercantile centre would attract to it; and if this was allowed at the outset of the voyage (ch. xxvii. 3), much more readily would it be now, when he had gained the reverence and confidence of all classes with whom he came in contact. At any rate, we cannot wonder that he should be regarded by the Sicilians as the founder of the church of that island. **13. And from thence we fetched a compass** [περιελθόντες]—*lit.*, 'went round;' that is, proceeded circuitously, or (in nautical phrase) *tacked*, working probably to windward (as *Mr. Smith* thinks), and availing themselves of the sinuosities of the coast, the wind not being favourable. What follows confirms this. **and came to Rhegium**—now *Reggio*, a seaport on the south-west point of the Italian coast, opposite the north-east point of Sicily, and at the entrance of the narrow straits of Messina. **and after one day the south wind blew**—'a south wind sprang up;' and so they were now favoured with a fair wind, the want of which probably kept them three days at Syracuse, and then obliged them to tack, and put in for a day at Rhegium. **and we came the next day to Puteoli**—now *Pozzuoli*, situated on the northern part of the magnificent bay of Naples, about 180 miles north of Rhegium, a distance which they might make, running before their "south wind," in about twenty-six hours. The Alexandrian corn ships (says *Howson*, whose authority is the philosopher Seneca) enjoyed a privilege peculiar to themselves, of not being obliged to strike their topsail on landing. By this they were easily recognized, as they hove in sight, by the crowds that we find gathered on the shore on such occasions. **14. Where we found brethren**—implying, probably, that it was an agreeable surprise to them to find such, and **were desired** ('requested') **to tarry with them seven days**. That they did so stay seems implied; and as they had now parted with their ship, it is probable that Julius would find the delay as convenient for himself as for Paul and his company, as he would thus have time to transmit

185

intelligence to Rome, and receive instructions for the reception of his charge. However this may be, the apostle had thus an opportunity of spending the day of rest with the Christians of the place —all the more refreshing from his long privation in this respect, and as a seasoning for the unknown future that lay before him at the metropolis. **and so** (at the close of these seven days) **we went toward Rome** [εἰς τ. P. ἤλθομεν]—'came to Rome.' Our translators, observing that in the very next verse something is recorded which occurred before their arrival at Rome, have rendered this 'to' by "toward." But there was no need for this. For they started from Puteoli for Rome; and as they were only stopped on the way by the unexpected arrival of two parties of brethren from the capital to meet them—the one at Appii Forum, the other at Three Taverns—the fact of their arrival at Rome is first mentioned, and then this incident which occurred by the way. **15. And from thence** (that is, from Rome), **when the brethren heard of us** [τὰ περὶ ἡμῶν]—'heard of our circumstances' or 'matters;' probably by letter from Puteoli, which would be conveyed by the bearer of the centurion's despatches to the capital. As this is the first mention of Christians already at Rome, we naturally ask how Christianity was first introduced there. Now it is one of the most remarkable facts in the history of the first planting of Christianity, that while we have in the New Testament explicit and lively accounts of its first introduction into Asia Minor, Proconsular Asia, Macedonia, and Achaia, neither in the New Testament nor in the genuine writings of the early Church, subsequent to the close of the Canon of Scripture, have we any available accounts of the first introduction of Christianity into the great metropolis of the ancient world. That the apostle Peter was there, we have no reasonable ground to doubt; but that he was not there before the last year of his life, is equally beyond reasonable doubt. We have, in fact, no evidence that the first beginnings of the Church of Rome were owing to the labours of any eminent teacher; and from all that can be gathered from the silence of the New Testament—in connection with the small but extremely interesting salutations in the closing chapter of the Epistle to the Romans, and from the confused and contradictory traditions of the fathers, we are shut up to the belief that Christianity was first brought to Rome, and first took root there, through the visits paid to it by private Christians from the provinces, from the great Pentecostal season (see ch. ii. 10) onwards. (But see Introduction to Epistle to Romans). **they came to meet us as far as Appii Forum**—a town forty-one miles south-east from Rome, **and the Three Taverns**—'and Three Taverns' (without the article, as the name of a place: see on ch. xxviii. 8). This place was thirty miles from Rome. It would thus appear that they came from Rome in two parties—one stopping short at the nearer, the other going on to the more distant place. **whom when Paul saw, he thanked God**—for such a welcome. How sensitive he was to such Christian

16 And when we came to Rome, the centurion delivered the prisoners to the captain of the guard: but *k* Paul was suffered to dwell by himself with

A. D. 63.
k ch. 24. 23.

affection, all his Epistles show, (Rom. i. 9-12, &c.) and took courage—his long-cherished purpose to "see Rome" (ch. xix. 21), there to proclaim the unsearchable riches of Christ, and the Divine pledge that in this he should be gratified (ch. xxiii. 11), being now about to be auspiciously realized.

Remarks.—Probably there never was any detailed account of a disastrous voyage, ending in the total wreck of the vessel and the safe landing of every soul on board—amounting to nearly four hundred—which bore more unequivocal marks of historic truth; and yet even this portion of the Acts of the Apostles, including the subsequent account of what passed at Malta, has not escaped the attacks of the destructive school of criticism. It is admitted, for example, by *Zeller* that the substance of these two chapters belongs indubitably to the oldest materials of the book; but he contends that spurious matter has crept into it throughout. The examples which he gives of this are such as are either utterly frivolous, or admit of easy enough explanation; and this whole style of criticism—based on foregone conclusions, and designed to support a theory both of the book and of Pauline Christianity which would scarcely be worthy of refutation but for the ingenuity, acuteness, and learning with which it is supported—might be made to shake the credit of most historical records; in which there are nearly always some circumstances which at first appear improbable, and some which seem contradictory, while the language is often such as to afford to sceptical minds materials of suspicion. The whole history of the Tübingen school of criticism affords one of the most striking illustrations of the extent to which the acutest and most learned men may allow themselves to be committed in support of a theory once taken up and confidently advocated, especially when that theory has the charm of being perfectly novel, of being a reconstruction of all Christianity, and of furnishing to those who sit uneasy under the authority of the New Testament and the supernatural character of the events which it records an imposing body of evidence in proof of its unhistorical and unreliable character. Time will no doubt dissolve this whole fabric of hostile criticism, which has already lost much of its ground in the land of its birth. But as its withering effects have, to some extent, been felt in this country, so even when these pass away, the same spirit of unsanctified criticism may be expected to give birth to other forms of assault on the canonical books and on the truths which they proclaim, and must be sedulously guarded against, especially by those who are apt to set too much store by mere learned criticism. 2. The distinguishing features of our apostle's character, and of his religious principles, come out nowhere more nobly than in this narrative. There was something about him which, from the first, seems to have commanded the deep respect of the centurion Julius; and his whole procedure throughout the voyage showed such loftiness of character, and yet soundness of judgment—such confidence in the Divine communications made to him, yet healthy attention to the means of safety and of bodily strength—such anxious solicitation for the welfare of all, yet cheerfulness of spirit and desire to diffuse it over all—that nowhere in this book does he show to more advantage; and one sees in him the saviour of a vast multitude of human beings, hardly more in fulfilment of a Divine promise to himself, than in the exercise of his large and ready wisdom (see Eccl. ix. 13-18). But his re-

ligious principles come out quite as strikingly here. Divine agency and human instrumentality—the one controlling all the circumstances so as to secure a most unlikely issue, the other providing the indispensable conditions of that issue—are here not only recognized by the apostle, as perfectly consistent with each other, but acted on as a matter of course, as if in his own mind they created no difficulty at all, and were not so much as thought of in the light of conflicting principles. He who acted on such principles throughout this voyage may surely be expected, in his writings, whenever he has occasion to touch upon and expound them (as in his Epistle to the Romans, ch. ix.), to hold forth and plead for what his own conduct here exemplified; and those who so interpret those writings as to set aside the one of these principles as inconsistent with the other would do well to study a little more deeply the apostle's procedure during this voyage. 3. "And so we came to Rome," says the historian (*v.* 14), as the goal of all that both he and the great apostle had been so anxiously looking forward to. 'How would the heart of the apostle and his companions beat (says *Lechler*) in anxious expectation, when the imperial city of heathendom, with its cupolas and battlements, lay before their eyes! But how also would the heart of the Roman Cæsar have beat in his palace had he had a presentiment that at this moment, in the form of a Jewish prisoner, there entered by the gates a power before which the Roman empire and the whole heathen world would crumble into dust! This was even a more decisive moment than when formerly it was said, *Hannibal ante portas* (Hannibal is at the gates).'

16-31.—PAUL AT ROME—CONCLUSION.

The measure of liberty accorded to him—His first interview with the Jews of Rome (16-23). **16. And when we came to Rome**—or, 'had entered Rome' [εἰσῆλθ. seems the true reading]. Thus is our apostle at length brought to the renowned capital of the ancient world—situated on the banks of the Tiber, about sixteen miles from its mouth, and at that time containing about two millions of inhabitants. **[the centurion delivered the prisoners to the captain of the guard]**. Though the evidence against this clause is decisive [ὁ ἑκατόνταρχος παρέδωκεν τ. δεσμίους τ. στρατοπεδάρχῳ—wanting in א A B, and all the most ancient MSS. and versions, and found apparently but in a few of the later MSS. and a number of cursives: it is easy to account for its getting in, though not genuine, as probably stating a fact; but if genuine, very difficult to explain its dropping out], there is no good reason for doubting what it states. This "captain of the guard" then was the 'Prætorian Prefect,' to whose custody, as commander of the Prætorian guard (the highest military authority in the city), were committed all who were to come up for judgment before the emperor. Ordinarily, there were two such prefects; but from A.D. 51 to 62 one distinguished general—*Burrus Afranius,* who had been Nero's tutor—held that office; and as this bracketed clause speaks of "*the* captain," as if there were but one, *Wieseler* is led to fix the apostle's arrival at Rome to be not later than the year 62. But even though there had been two when Paul arrived, he would be committed only to one of them, who would be *the* captain of the guard to him. At most, therefore, this argument—supposing the clause it is built on to be genuine—could furnish only confirmation of such chronological conclusions as can be other-

17 a soldier that kept him. And it came to pass, that after three days Paul called the chief of the Jews together: and when they were come together, he said unto them, Men *and* brethren, though [l]I have committed nothing against the people or customs of our fathers, yet was [m]I delivered prisoner
18 from Jerusalem into the hands of the Romans. Who, [n]when they had examined me, would have let *me* go, because there was no cause of death
19 in me. But when the Jews spake against *it*, I [o]was constrained to
20 appeal unto Cesar; not that I had ought to accuse my nation of. For this cause therefore have I called for you, to see *you*, and to speak with *you :* because that [p]for the hope of Israel I am bound with this
21 [q]chain. And they said unto him, We neither received letters out of Judea concerning thee, neither any of the brethren that came showed or
22 spake any harm of thee. But we desire to hear of thee what thou thinkest: for as concerning this sect, we know that every where [r]it is spoken against.

A. D. 68.
l ch. 24. 12.
ch. 25. 8.
m ch. 21. 33.
n ch. 22. 24.
ch. 24. 10.
ch. 25. 8.
ch. 26. 31.
o ch. 25. 11.
p ch. 26. 6, 7.
q ch. 26. 29.
Eph. 3. 1.
Eph. 4. 1.
Eph. 6. 20.
2 Tim. 1.
16.
r Luke 2. 34.
ch. 24. 5.
1 Pet. 2. 12.

wise established. But since no dependence can be placed upon the clause, no chronological inferences should be based on it. **but Paul was suffered to dwell.** Leaving out the preceding clause, this "but," of course, goes with it [ἐπετράπη τ. Παύλῳ is the genuine text]. **by himself**—or in quarters of his own, **with a soldier** ('the soldier') **that kept** (or 'guarded') **him.** See on ch. xii. 6. This privilege was allowed in the case of the better class of prisoners, not accused of any flagrant offence, on finding security—which in Paul's case would not be difficult among the Christians. The extension of this privilege to the apostle may have been due to the terms in which Festus wrote about him; but far more probably it was owing to the high terms in which Julius spoke of him, and his express intercession in his behalf. It was overruled, however, for giving the fullest scope to the labours of the apostle compatible with confinement at all. As the soldiers who kept him were relieved periodically, he would thus make the personal acquaintance of a great number of the Prætorian guard; and if he had to appear before the Prefect from time to time, the truth might thus penetrate to those who surrounded the emperor, as we learn from Phil. i. 12, 13 that it did. **17. And it came to pass, that after three days Paul**—'that he' (according to the true reading) **called the chief of the Jews together**—meaning the rulers of the synagogues and others of position and influence. These he 'called together,' being of course now precluded from going to them, as he otherwise would have done. Ever since Pompey settled the Jewish captives, whom he brought with him from the East (B.C. 61), in that part of Rome called now the 'Trastevere,' on the further side of the river—manumitting many of them—the number of Jewish residents at the capital continued to increase; and as they were active and enterprising, they grew wealthy and influential, and from time to time sent considerable sums to Palestine for the service of the temple, and other religious purposes. At length, being suspected of encouraging the treasonable designs of their countrymen in the East, and being themselves of a restless spirit, they began to be treated rigorously, and Claudius (as we have seen, ch. xviii. 2) banished them the city. But, long before the time here referred to, they were permitted to return, and at this time—which was early in the reign of Nero—they enjoyed full toleration, all was quiet with them, and they were both numerous and prosperous. (Their place of residence still is where it then was—in what is now called 'The Ghetto.') To call "the chief of the Jews together," and state his case to them in

the first instance, was according to his uniform custom of going—"to the Jew first." **and when they were come together, he said unto them, Men and brethren, though I have committed nothing against the people or customs of our fathers, yet was I delivered prisoner from Jerusalem into the hands of the Romans**—that is, the Roman authorities, Felix and Festus. **18. Who, when they had examined me, would have let me go, because there was no cause of death in me**—no capital crime. So ch. xiii. 28. **19. But when the Jews spake against it, I was constrained to appeal unto Cesar; not that I had ought to accuse my nation of**—q. d., 'I am here not as their accuser, but as my own defender, and this not of choice but necessity.' His object, in alluding thus gently to the treatment he had received from the Jews, was plainly to avoid whatever might irritate his visitors at the first, especially as he was not aware whether any or what information against him had reached their community. **20. For this cause therefore have I called for you, to see you, and to speak with you** ('have I requested to see and speak with you'): **because that for the hope of Israel** (see on ch. xxvi. 6, 7) **I am bound with** (or 'wear') **this chain**—q. d., 'This cause is not so much mine as yours; it is the nation's cause; all that is dear to the heart and hope of Israel is bound up with this case of mine.' From the touching allusions which the apostle makes to his chains—before Agrippa first, and here before the leading members of the Jewish community at Rome, at his first interview with them—one cannot but gather that his great soul felt keenly his being in such a condition; and it is to this keenness of feeling, under the control of Christian principle, that we owe the noble use which he made of it in these two cases. **21. And they said unto him, We neither received letters out of Judea concerning thee, neither any of the brethren that came showed or spake any harm of thee. 22. But we desire** [Ἀξιοῦμεν]—'we deem it proper,' or 'due,' **to hear of thee what thou thinkest: for as concerning this sect, we know that everywhere it is spoken against.** This statement has been pronounced incredible; and believing critics (as *Tholuck*) have thought that these Jews here dishonestly concealed the truth, while rationalistic critics make it a handle against the authenticity of the history itself. But the distinction which they make between Paul himself, against whom they had heard nothing, and his "sect," as everywhere spoken against, is a presumption in favour of their sincerity; and, as *Meyer* well says, until the apostle appealed to Cæsar, the Jews of Palestine would have no

23   And when they had appointed him a day, there came many to him
into *his* lodging; *to whom he expounded and testified the kingdom of
God, persuading them concerning Jesus, t both out of the law of Moses,
24 and *out of* the Prophets, from morning till evening. And u some believed
25 the things which were spoken, and some believed not. And when they
agreed not among themselves, they departed, after that Paul had spoken
one word, Well spake the Holy Ghost by Esaias the prophet unto our
26 fathers, saying, v Go unto this people, and say, Hearing ye shall hear, and
27 shall not understand; and seeing ye shall see, and not perceive: for w the
heart of this people is waxed gross, and their ears are dull of hearing, and
their eyes have they closed; lest they should see with *their* eyes, and hear
with *their* ears, and understand with *their* heart, and should be converted,
28 and I should heal them. Be it known therefore unto you, that the sal-
29 vation of God is x sent unto the Gentiles, and *that* they will hear it. And
when he had said these words, the Jews departed, and had great reasoning
among themselves.

A. D. 63.
* Luke 24. 27.
ch. 17. 2, 3.
ch. 26. 22,
23.
t ch. 26. 6.
u ch. 14. 4.
ch. 18. 6-8.
Rom. 3. 3.
v Isa. 6. 9.
Jer. 5. 21.
Eze. 12. 2.
Matt. 13. 14.
Mark 4. 12.
Luke 8. 19.
John 12. 40.
Rom. 11. 8.
w Isa. 44. 18.
x Matt. 21. 41.
ch. 26. 17.
Rom. 11. 11.

occasion to send information to Rome against him,
while the unexpected turn which the case took by
his appeal to Cæsar occurred so late, that no
information on the subject would travel from
Jerusalem to Rome in advance of the apostle
himself. The apparent freedom from prejudice
here expressed is best explained by reference to
the danger which the Jews of Rome felt themselves
to be in of fresh persecution, should any disturbances break out amongst themselves—which a keen
collision between them and the Christians would
be sure to provoke. It was this, probably, that
induced the Jewish community of Rome, as a
body, to ignore the Christianity which was springing up in the capital around them; and the same
motive would now induce them to express themselves with such prudent reserve as they do here.
(So *Humphry, Philippi, Hackett*, and substantially
Lechler.)

*Second Interview with the Jews of Rome—His expo-
sition of the Christian Faith to them continued from day
to day—The two-fold issue of this, and the apostle's
final testimony to his countrymen* (23-29). **23. And
when they had appointed him a day, there came
many to him into his lodging** [ξενίαν] : the word
denotes one's place of stay as a *guest* (Philem. 22).
It was probably not "his own hired house" (*v.* 30),
but that of some Christian friend, possibly Aquila's
and Priscilla's (for they had returned to Rome, as
we find from Rom. xvi. 3), who would deem it a
privilege to receive him; though he would soon
find himself more at liberty in a house of his
own. **to whom he expounded and testified the
kingdom of God**—opening up the great spiritual
principles of that kingdom, in opposition to the
contracted and secular views of it entertained by
the Jews; **persuading them concerning Jesus**—
as the ordained and predicted Head of that kingdom, **both out of the law of Moses, and out of
the Prophets**—drawing his materials and arguments from a source mutually acknowledged,
from morning till evening. 'Who would not
wish to have been present?' exclaims *Bengel;* but
virtually we *are* present while listening to those
Epistles which he dictated from his prison at
Rome, and to his other Epistolary expositions of
Christian truth against the Jews. **24. And some
believed the things which were spoken, and some
believed not**. What simplicity and candour are
in this record of a result, repeated from age to age,
where the Gospel is presented to a promiscuous
assemblage of sincere and earnest enquirers after
truth, of frivolous worldlings, and of prejudiced
bigots! **25. And when they (the Jews) agreed not
among themselves**—the discussion having passed

into a debate between the two parties into which
the visitors were now divided, respecting the arguments and conclusions of the apostle, **they departed**—the materials of discussion being felt by
both parties to be exhausted; **after that Paul had
spoken one word**—uttered one solemn parting testimony, from those Scriptures regarded by both
alike as "the Holy Ghost speaking" to Israel,
**Well spake the Holy Ghost by Esaias the pro-
phet unto our fathers**—or, 'your fathers' (according to the better reading), **26. Saying, Go unto
this people, and say, Hearing ye shall hear, and
shall not understand, &c. 27. For . . . their
eyes have they closed; lest they . . . should
be converted** [ἐπιστρέψωσιν]—or, 'and return,'
and I should heal them. See on Matt. xiii.
13-15, and John xii. 38-40. With what pain
would this stern word be wrung from him whose
"heart's desire and prayer to God for Israel was
that they might be saved," and who "had great
heaviness and continual sorrow in his heart" on
their account! (Rom. ix. 2; x. 1.) **28. Be it known
therefore unto you, that the salvation of God is
sent unto the Gentiles, and that they will hear
it**. See on ch. xiii. 44-48. 'This "departure to
the Gentiles" (says *Bengel*) he had intimated to
the perverse Jews at *Antioch* (ch. xiii. 46), and at
Corinth (ch. xviii. 6); now at *Rome:*—thus in
Asia, Greece, and *Italy*.' 29. [**And when he had
said these words, the Jews departed, and had
great reasoning among themselves.**] This verse
we formerly regarded (with *Olshausen*) as genuine;
but as it is wanting in some of the principal
authorities [א A B E, with many cursives; in the
text of the *Vulgate*, and apparently in that of the
Peshito *Syriac*], and is found only in some later
MSS. [as G H]—while internal evidence seems
pretty equal on both sides—we must view it as at
least doubtful.

Conclusion (30, 31). **30. And Paul dwelt two
whole years in his own hired house** (see on *v.* 23)
—yet in custody; for it is added, **and received all
that came in unto him**—while it is not said that he
went to the synagogue or anywhere else, enjoying,
in the uninterrupted exercise of his ministry, all
the liberty of a *guarded* man. **31. Preaching the
kingdom of God, and teaching those things which
concern the Lord Jesus Christ, with all confidence, no man forbidding him.**

Thus closes this most precious monument of the
beginnings of the Christian Church, in its march
from East to West, among the Jews first, whose
centre was *Jerusalem;* next among the Gentiles,
with *Antioch* for its head-quarters; finally, its ban-

30   And Paul dwelt two whole years in his own hired house, and received | A. D. 63.
31   all that came in unto him, preaching ^y the kingdom of God, and teaching | ^y ch. 4. 31.

ner is seen waving over imperial *Rome*, foretokening its universal triumphs. That distinguished apostle whose conversion, labours, and sufferings for "the faith which once he destroyed" occupy more than half of this History, it leaves a prisoner unheard, so far as appears, for two years. His accusers, whose presence was indispensable, would have to await the return of spring before starting for the capital, and might not reach it for many months; nor, even when there, would they be so sanguine of success—after Felix, Festus, and Agrippa had all pronounced him innocent—as to be impatient of delay. And if witnesses were required to prove the charge advanced by Tertullus, that he was "a mover of sedition among all the Jews throughout the (Roman) world" (ch. xxiv. 5), they must have seen that, unless considerable time were allowed them, the case would certainly break down. If to this be added the capricious delays which the emperor himself might interpose, and the practice of Nero to hear but one charge at a time, it will not seem strange that the Historian should have no proceedings in the case to record for two years. Having begun this history of his, probably, before the apostle's arrival, its progress at Rome under his own eye would furnish exalted employment, and beguile many a tedious hour of his two years' imprisonment. Had the case come on for hearing during this period, much more if it had been disposed of, it is hardly conceivable that the History should have closed as it does. But if, at the end of this period, the Narrative only wanted the decision of the case, while hope deferred was making the heart sick (Prov. xiii. 12); and if, under the guidance of that Spirit whose seal was on it all, it seemed of more consequence to put the Church at once in possession of this History, than to keep it back indefinitely for the sake of what might come to be otherwise known—we cannot wonder that it should be wound up as it is in its two concluding verses. All that we know of the apostle's proceedings and history beyond this must be gathered from *the Epistles of the Imprisonment*—those to the Ephesians, to the Philippians, to the Colossians, and to Philemon—written during this period; and from the *Pastoral Epistles*—those to Timothy and that to Titus—which in our judgment are of subsequent date. From the former class of Epistles we learn the following particulars:—*First*, That the trying restraint laid upon the apostle's labours by his imprisonment had only turned his influence into a new channel, the Gospel having in consequence penetrated even into the palace, and pervaded the city, while the preachers of Christ were emboldened; and though the Judaizing portion of them, observing his success among the Gentiles, had been led to inculcate with fresh zeal their own narrower gospel, even this had done much good by extending the truth common to both. (See on Phil. i. 12-18; iv. 22). *Secondly*, That as, in addition to all his other labours, "the care of all the churches came upon him from day to day" (2 Cor. xi. 28), so with these churches he kept up an active correspondence by means of letters and messages, and on such errands he wanted not faithful and beloved brethren enough, ready to be employed—*Luke, Timotheus, Tychicus,* (John) *Mark, Demas, Aristarchus, Epaphras, Onesimus, Jesus,* called Justus, and, for a short time, *Epaphroditus.* (See on Col. iv. 7, 9-12, 14; Philem. 23, 24; and Introd. to Eph., Phil., and Philem.) That the apostle suffered martyrdom under Nero at Rome has never been doubted. But whether this

took place at the close of this present imprisonment, or whether he was acquitted and set at liberty on this occasion, resumed his apostolic labours, and after some years more was again apprehended, condemned, and executed—is a question which has latterly given rise to much discussion. In the absence of explicit testimony in the New Testament, the burden of proof lies certainly with the advocates of a second imprisonment. Accordingly, they appeal, *first*, to the Pastoral Epistles, as referring to movements of the apostle himself and of Timothy, which cannot, without straining, be made to fit into any period prior to the appeal which brought the apostle to Rome; which bear marks throughout of a more advanced state of the Church, and more matured forms of error, than can well have existed when he came first to Rome; and which are couched in a manifestly riper style than any of his former Epistles. And they appeal, *secondly*, to the testimony of the fathers—*Clement* of Rome, *Eusebius*, and *Jerome*—as at least confirming these conclusions. On the other hand, it is contended by several modern critics (*de Wette, Winer, Wieseler, Davidson, Schaff,* not to mention *Petavius* and *Lardner* formerly), that no mention is made in the New Testament of any liberation and second imprisonment; that no earlier writer than *Eusebius*, in the fourth century, expressly states it as a fact, and he apparently on no good authority, while *Jerome* and others appear to have simply followed *Eusebius;* and that as to the evidence from the Pastoral Epistles in favour of this theory, it is more apparent than real. To discuss these arguments would be unsuitable here: they belong rather to an Introduction to the Pastoral Epistles; but they have been handled with great ability by the advocates of a double imprisonment (*Michaelis, Hug, Gieseler, Neander, Credner, Lange,* &c., besides earlier critics), whose arguments appear to us as convincing, as their number is far greater than that of their opponents.

Remarks.—If ever that great characteristic of genuine love—"that it beareth all things, believeth all things, hopeth all things, endureth all things"—was pre-eminently exemplified, it was by him who penned that description of it, in his treatment of his brethren after the flesh, from the very beginning of his labours among them as a preacher of Christ up to the last interview with them recorded in this chapter. And there are special features of this character in him which, the more they are studied, will the more raise him in our estimation, as, next to his Great Master, perhaps the noblest model for imitation by Christian ministers in general, by converted Jews in particular, as missionaries to their brethren according to the flesh, and by those priests of the Church of Rome whose eyes have been opened to see its errors, and whose services thenceforward have been consecrated to the trying work of preaching Christ to their former co-religionists. Alas! how little do we see of that combination of burning zeal with large wisdom, of that union of firmness and flexibility, of that high-minded sensitiveness to what was due to himself, and yet readiness to put up with affronts and return good for evil, which constitute such marked features in the great apostle's character, such potent elements in his success as a servant of Christ, and so much of the secret of his surpassing and enduring influence on Christendom. To Peter, it is true, was assigned distinctively "the gospel of the circumcision," while that "of the uncircumcision was committed" to Paul (Gal.

189

those things which concern the Lord Jesus Christ, with all *confidence, no man forbidding him.

A. D. 63.

* Acts 4. 13.

ii. 7); but while out of his Jewish sphere Peter was nothing, Paul, besides his incomparable services in the Gentile field, was the most powerful of all labourers among his own countrymen also. There is not one recorded instance of the conversion of Gentiles through Peter's sole instrumentality—the case of Cornelius and his party being that of one Divinely brought to him (if we may so say), and of whom it was told him that he was all ready to receive the truth from his lips; and as Peter needed a vision from heaven to convince him that Gentiles were, under the Gospel, on the same footing before God as the Jews, so when he did open the Gospel to this proselyte and prepared Gentile, he did it in a way peculiarly Jewish, such as we should expect from one cast (so to speak) in the mould of the ancient economy. On the other hand, while the appropriate sphere of our great apostle was undoubtedly among the Gentiles, and the Church of Christ

has taken its stamp of universality from him pre-eminently, how powerful were his reasonings, and how noble his appeals to his own countrymen in the synagogues, in the streets of Jerusalem, and before the legal tribunals, not to speak of the wonderful light which he throws upon the Old Testament Scriptures in his Epistles! To this we have adverted once and again in the course of our Exposition of this precious record of the first triumphs of the Gospel; but the scenes with which it closes constrain us to leave our readers with this commanding figure before their eye—yet not without writing beneath it two mottoes from his own pen :—

" By the grace of God I am what I am,"

AND

"God forbid that I should glory, save in the cross of our Lord Jesus Christ, whereby the world is crucified unto me, and I unto the world"!

ROMANS.

1 PAUL, a servant of Jesus Christ, called *to be* an apostle, separated
2 unto the gospel of God, (which he had promised afore by his prophets in

TITLE.—In the most ancient MSS. the Pauline Epistles, being placed by themselves under the general heading, 'Epistles of Paul' [ΕΠΙΣΤΟΛΑΙ ΠΑΥΛΟΥ], have no separate titles, save a simple announcement of the party addressed: Thus,—'To the Romans' [ΠΡΟΣ ΡΩΜΑΙΟΥΣ], 'To the Galatians,' 'To Titus.'

CHAP. I. 1-17.—SALUTATION AND INTRODUCTION—THE THEME OF THE EPISTLE ANNOUNCED. *The Salutation* (1-7). Instead of the "greeting" [χαίρειν] familiar to us in the epistolary compositions of the Greeks, and once used in the New Testament (Jas. i. 1), the Pauline Epistles begin with a benediction on those addressed, as do also the second of John and that to Jude. Peculiar, however, to the salutation of the present Epistle is the addition here of doctrinal statements (as *Olshausen* observes), by means of which it is converted into a small self-contained whole. In the Epistles to the Galatians and to Titus a similar peculiarity may be observed, but in a less degree. So rich and exuberant is the Salutation here, that it will conduce to clearness to subdivide it into its several parts.

Being a comparative stranger to those whom he is about to address, the Epistle opens with an account of himself.

(1.) *The writer's three-fold account of himself.*
1. Paul (on this name, see on Acts xiii. 9), a servant of Jesus Christ ['Ιησ. Χου—not Χου 'Ιησ., with *Tisch.* and *Treg.*, on the sole authority of B and the Old Latin Vulgate, with *Augustin* and *Ambrose* (who doubtless followed their own Latin version); while the received text is supported by all the other Uncials, many cursives, several ancient versions, and Greek and Latin fathers : *Lachmann* abides by the received text.] In the New Testament several words are used for "servant," all of which, except one, convey the idea of *free service* [θεράπων, ὑπηρέτης, οἰκέτης, διάκονος, παῖς—this last word being used with the same latitude as *garçon* in French]. The one denoting *bond-service*, is that here used [δοῦλος]—see Gal. iii. 28; 1 Tim. vi. 1; Rev. vi. 15, *Gr.* It is a word of more frequent occurrence than all the rest, and properly means 'slave.' Accordingly, *Luther* renders it by the word which denotes menial service ('Knecht'), *Conybeare*, 'a bondsman;' *Green*, 'a bond-servant.' But since the repulsive ideas which servility suggests to our minds is apt to cling unpleasantly to such terms, it is perhaps better to avoid them in translating—always bearing in mind, however, that in expressing the relation of Christ's servants to Himself, this term invariably means, 'one who is *the property of another*,' and so is 'subject to his *will, and wholly at his disposal.*' Among the earliest Christians, indeed, so great was felt to be the honour and privilege of standing in such a relation to Christ, that it absorbed every repulsive association attaching to the word that expressed it, insomuch that in the Apocalypse it is employed to express the standing even of the glorified saints to God and the Lamb; while their services in that capacity are expressed by the term denoting *religious* service—"His *servants* [δοῦλοι] shall *serve*

Him" [λατρεύσουσιν] (Rev. xxii. 3). In this sense, then—that of entire subjection and devotion to another—it is applied in the New Testament to the disciples of Christ at large (ch. vi. 22; xiv. 4; 1 Cor. vii. 21-23; Rev. xix. 2, 5), as in the Old Testament it had been applied to all the people of God (Ps. cxxxv. 1; Isa. lxv. 13; Dan. iii. 26). But over and above this, as the prophets and kings of Israel had in an *official* sense been styled "the servants of Jehovah" [עבדי] (Deut. xxxiv. 5; Josh. i. 1), so do the apostles of the Lord Jesus style themselves "the servants of Christ," expressing thereby such subjection and devotion to Him as they would never have yielded to a mere creature. In the same spirit the Baptist spoke of himself as unworthy to do for his Master, Christ, the meanest office of a slave (Mark i. 7). In this absolute sense, then, does the writer here call himself "a servant of Jesus Christ."

But next he describes himself as **called [to be] an apostle** [κλητὸς ἀπόστολος]. Some render this 'a called apostle;' but as that would seem to imply that there might be apostles who were not called, we think the rendering of our version is to be preferred. The calling here referred to is that glorious manifestation of Christ which placed him on a level with the original Twelve (1 Cor. xv. 7, 8; Acts xxvi. 16-18).

Finally, he describes himself as **separated unto the gospel**. At three distinct stages of his life he was Divinely "separated;" and the same word is used to express them all. First, at his birth, "When it pleased God, who separated me [ἀφορίσας] from my mother's womb" (Gal. i. 15)—so ordering all the circumstances of it, and all the events succeeding it, up to the time of his conversion, as to train him for his great work as a servant of Christ. Next, when called at once to the faith and the apostleship of Christ, he was officially "separated [ἀφωρισμένος] unto the Gospel," as here expressed. Lastly, in the church at Antioch, immediately before his designation to the missionary vocation, "the Holy Ghost said, Separate me ['Αφορίσατε] Barnabas and Saul for the work whereunto I have called them" (Acts xiii. 2). **the gospel of God**—meaning, not the Gospel 'about God' (as *Chrysostom* takes it), but the Gospel of which God is the glorious Author (as ch. xv. 16; 2 Cor. xi. 7; 1 Thess. ii. 8, 9; 1 Pet. iv. 17). He calls it "the Gospel of God" here, because in the next two verses he was going to speak more immediately of what *God* had to do with it.

(2.) *This Gospel no novelty, but only the fulfilment of ancient prophecy.*
2. Which he had promised afore by his prophets in the holy scriptures. Though the Roman church was Gentile by nation (see on *v.* 13), yet, as most of them had been proselytes to the Jewish Faith, they are here reminded that in embracing the Gospel they had not cast off Moses and the prophets, but only yielded themselves the more intelligently and profoundly to the testimony of God in that earlier Revelation (Acts xiii. 32, 33).

191

3 the holy Scriptures,) concerning his Son Jesus Christ our Lord, which was
4 made of the seed of David according to the flesh; and ¹declared *to be*
  the Son of God with power, according to the Spirit of holiness, by the

A. D. 60.

¹ determined.

(3.) *Christ*—as THE SEED OF DAVID and THE SON OF GOD—*the grand burden of the Gospel.*

3. Concerning, &c. It would have been better if the order in which the words of this and the following verse stand in the original had been followed in our version, as they are in nearly every other—thus : 'Concerning His Son, which was made of the seed of David according to the flesh, and declared to be the Son of God with power, according to the Spirit of holiness, by the resurrection from the dead, [even] Jesus Christ our Lord.'

Concerning his Son. Does this mean that the *Gospel itself,* or that the *promise* of it in the Old Testament, was "Concerning his Son?" Most critics, probably, say the latter ; but (with *Calvin, Bengel, Olshausen, Lange,* &c.) we think the former the more natural—that the grand Burden of the Gospel of God is His own Son, whose glorious Person the apostle now proceeds to unfold.

which was made of the seed of David. As that was the predicted Messianic line (2 Sam. vii. 12, &c.; Ps. lxxxix. *passim;* Isa. ix. 6, 7 ; xi. 1 ; lv. 3; Jer. xxiii. 5), Jesus of Nazareth behoved to come of it, if He was to have any just claim to be "the Christ of God" (see Matt. xxii. 42; John vii. 42). Accordingly this is grandly dwelt on in the angelic annunciation of His birth by the angel to the blessed Virgin (Luke i. 32), while the descent of His legal father also from David was emphatically recognized to himself by the same angel (Matt. i. 20; see Luke i. 27); and His birth at the royal city was announced to the shepherds as one of the most notable circumstances of this great event (Luke ii. 11). The apostles were at pains to bring this claim of Jesus of Nazareth to be their predicted Messiah under the notice of their countrymen, in their earliest pleadings with them (Acts ii. 30-32 ; xiii. 22, 23 ; 2 Tim. ii. 8).

according to the flesh—that is (beyond all reasonable doubt), 'according to His *human nature:* compare John i. 14, "The Word was *made flesh*" (or ' became man '); ch. ix. 5, "of whom, *as concerning the flesh*" [κατὰ σάρκα], or ' in respect of His human nature,' 'Christ came;" 1 John iv. 2, 3, "Every spirit that confesseth that Jesus Christ is come in the flesh" (or 'in true humanity'). But this sense will more clearly appear to be the only true one by what follows.

4. And declared to be the Son of God [ὁρισθέντος]—'marked off,' ' pointed out,' and so ' declared,' or 'evinced'—as the best critics, ancient and modern, take the sense to be. [The Old Latin—apparently confounding ὁρισθέντος with προορισθ.—rendered it *prædestinatus,* which Jerome unhappily retained in the Vulgate ; and though *Estius* apologizes for it, he admits it to be a forced interpretation. *Erasmus* has some excellent remarks on this word.] It cannot escape the attentive observer of these words how warily the apostle changes his language here. "He was *made* (he says) of the seed of David according to the flesh ;" but he does not say, 'He was made the Son of God ;' on the contrary, he says, He was only " *declared* (or 'manifested') to be the Son of God"—precisely as in John i. 1, 14, "In the beginning *was* the Word . . . And the Word *was made* flesh ;" and Isa. ix. 6, "Unto us a *Child* is born, unto us a *Son is given.*" Thus is the Sonship of Christ held forth, not as a thing of time and of human birth, but as an essential and uncreated Sonship ; the Son of God being by His Incarnation

192

only enshrined in our nature, and thus efflorescing into public manifestation. But not until His resurrection from the dead could even His most penetrating disciples say, in the fullest sense, "We beheld His glory." Then only, and thus, was He "manifested to be the Son of God"—

with power. If we connect this with the preceding words—"the Son of God with power"—the meaning is, that that power which He all along possessed, but which was veiled from human view until then, shone brightly forth when He arose from the dead. (So the Vulgate, *Chrysostom, Melancthon, Calvin, Philippi, Lange,* &c., understand it, as we ourselves did formerly.) But it seems better to connect these words with "declared ;" and then the sense is, He was ' with power declared,' or gloriously evinced to be the Son of God by His resurrection. (So *Luther, Beza, Bengel, Fritzsche, Meyer, Tholuck,* &c.)

according to the Spirit of holiness [κατὰ πνεῦμα ἁγιωσύνης]—an uncommon and somewhat difficult phrase, the sense of which depends on whether we have here a *climax* or a *contrast*. Those who would set aside the testimony here borne to the Divinity of Christ hold that the apostle is not contrasting the lower and the higher *natures* of Christ, but describing the transition of Christ from a lower to a higher *condition of existence,* or out of his humbled state, from birth to death, into the exalted state of resurrection and glory. In this case, "the Spirit of holiness" is understood to mean either the Holy Ghost or that ' spiritual energy' which dwelt in him beyond other men, and manifested itself pre-eminently at his resurrection. Those who acknowledge nothing in Christ higher than mere Humanity, of course take this view ; but some of the orthodox interpret this passage substantially in the same way. But since beyond all doubt "the flesh," in such passages, means 'human nature' in its frailty and mortality (see on John i. 14, p. 348), and consequently Christ's being made of the seed of David "according to the flesh" must mean His being descended from David 'in respect of His human *nature,*' it follows that His being "declared to be the Son of God with power, *according to the Spirit of holiness,*" must mean that He was manifested to be such according to His other and higher *nature,* which we have seen to be that of the uncreated, essential "Son of God." But why should the apostle call this "the *Spirit ?*" Doubtless because he had spoken of His human nature under the name of "the *flesh;*" and "flesh" and "spirit" are the usual contrasts to each other. In 2 Cor. iii. 17 (says *Tholuck*)—"*Now the Lord is the Spirit*"—the substance or element that constitutes the higher Personality of Christ is called *Spirit.* And if "God is a Spirit" (John iv. 24), why should not this incarnate God be entitled to the name of "*Spirit*" in an absolute sense ? *Clement* of Rome (Ep. 2, c. 9) [or whoever wrote that epistle] has these words, 'Christ the Lord, being first Spirit, became flesh' [Χριστὸς ὁ κύριος, ὢν μὲν πνεῦμα, ἐγένετο σάρξ]. In the same sense are we to understand that expresssion in Heb. ix. 14, "the eternal Spirit;" and in 1 Tim. iii. 16 we have the same contrast between " flesh" and "spirit" as here.' But one question more occurs, Why is this Higher Nature of Christ termed "the Spirit *of holiness?*" In all probability, because if he had said "according to the Holy Spirit," his readers would certainly have understood him to be

5 resurrection from the dead: by whom "we have received grace and
apostleship, ²for obedience to the faith among all nations, ᵇfor his name:
6, among whom are ye also the called of Jesus Christ: to all that be in
7 Rome, beloved of God, called *to be* saints: Grace to you and peace from
God our Father, and the Lord Jesus Christ.
8 First, ᶜI thank my God through Jesus Christ for you all, that your

A. D. 60.

ᵃ Eph. 3. 8.
² Or. to the
obedience
of faith.
ᵇ Acts 9. 15.
ᶜ Phil. 1. 8.

---

speaking about *the Holy Ghost;* and it was to
avoid this that we think he used the uncommon
phrase, "according to the Spirit of holiness" [*q.d.*,
'quoad spiritum sacrosanctum.' It may here be
observed that ἁγιωσύνη, as distinguished from
ἁγιότης, may be presumed from its *form* to denote
'the subjective condition,' as distinguished from
'the objective quality.']

by the resurrection from the dead [ἐξ ἀναστά-
σεως νεκρῶν]—*lit.*, 'by the resurrection of the
dead;' the risen Head being here regarded as but
the First-fruits of them that sleep. [*Luther* wrongly renders ἐξ here, 'since,' or 'after'—misled probably by the Vulgate's *ex*, which, though capable
of this sense, was in all likelihood intended to
convey the idea of 'by' or 'through.'

(4.) *From this glorious Person flowed the writer's
grace and apostleship—The world-wide scope of his
message—Its efficacy at Rome.*

5. By whom we have received [ἐλάβομεν]—'we
received;' that is, at the period of his conversion.
In the plural "we" there is no reference to any
other than himself. In epistolary compositions (as
Tholuck remarks) the plural is largely used, and the
New Testament writers, as *Cicero* sometimes does,
alternate between the plural and the singular in
the same breath (see 2 Cor. v. 11; Col. iv. 3;
2 Pet. i. 15, 16). **grace and apostleship**—not
exactly 'the grace of apostleship' (by what grammarians call *hendiadys*, as *Chrysostom, Beza,
Philippi*, &c., take it). The "grace" is what he
had in common with all believers; the "apostleship" was peculiar to the selected few. But since
grace made him at one and the same time a
believer and an apostle, we can hardly doubt
that the former is here referred to only as his
Divine preparation for the latter: cf. Eph. iii. 8,
"To me who am less than the least of all saints
is this *grace* given that I should *preach*," &c.;
and 1 Tim. i. 12-14, "I thank Christ Jesus, who
hath enabled me . . . *putting me into the ministry,*
who was before a blasphemer. . . . And the *grace*
of our Lord was exceeding abundant," &c. **for obedience to the faith** [εἰς ὑπακοὴν πίστεως]—rather,
'for the obedience of faith;' or in order that men
might yield to the Gospel the highest of all
homage, which is to believe it (John vi. 28, 29;
1 John iii. 23). hence the phrase to "*obey* the
Gospel" (ch. x. 16; 2 Thess i. 8: cf. ch. xvi. 26;
Acts vi. 7). **among all nations, for** (or 'in behalf
of') **his name**—that is, for spreading abroad the
savour of it, manifesting His work, character,
and glory (Phil. ii. 10). "The *name* of the Lord"
is a phrase of such frequent occurrence in the
Old Testament, that it became a household word
for all that is most precious in His revealed
character. Yet that very phrase, and in exactly
the same sense, is appropriated to Christ by all
the New Testament writers. And so studiously
is this done, that no impartial reader can doubt
that they regarded Jesus of Nazareth as having
rightfully *served Himself heir both to all the perfections of the God of Israel and to all the relations
in which He stood to His people.* (See on Matt.
xxii. 1, 2, and Remark 1 at the close of that
Section, p. 107.)

6. Among whom are ye also—but only along
with others; for the apostle ascribes nothing

special to the church of Rome (as *Bengel* observes,
referring to 1 Cor. xiv. 36). **the called of Jesus
Christ**—not 'the called by Him' (as *Luther*, &c.,
though that is a truth), but 'Christ's called ones,'
or the called who belong to Him (so *Erasmus,
Meyer, Lange*, &c.)—being called, not as all that
hear the Gospel are (Matt. xx. 16), but internally
and efficaciously. And now at length comes—

(5.) *The Salutation itself.*

7. To all (such called ones) **that be in Rome,
beloved of God** (cf. Deut. xxxiii. 12; Col. iii. 12),
called [to be] saints—called internally and efficaciously "to be holy and without blame before
Him in love" (Eph. i. 4): see on "called to be an
apostle," *v.* 1. **Grace to you**—that most precious
of New Testament words, expressing the whole
riches of God's everlasting love to sinners of mankind in Christ Jesus (see on this word in John
i. 14, p. 349; and on ch. v. 20, 21). **and peace**—
through the blood of the cross (Eph. ii. 13-17;
Col. i. 20), in virtue of which He who cannot look
upon sin is styled "The God of peace" (Heb. xiii.
20; 1 Thess. v. 23; ch. xvi. 20); which peace,
when reflected into the believing bosom, "passeth
all understanding" (Phil. iv. 7). To this peace all
believers are called "in one body" (Col. iii. 15);
and thus, when set down in a world full of strife,
they are among them as "peacemakers," and as
such "the children of God." **from God our
Father, and the Lord Jesus Christ.** 'Nothing
(says *Olshausen*) speaks more decisively for the
Divinity of Christ than these juxtapositions of
Christ with the eternal God which run through
the whole language of Scripture, and the derivation of purely Divine influences from Him also.
The name of no man can be placed by the side of
the Almighty. He only in whom the Word of
the Father, who is Himself God, became flesh,
may be named beside Him; for men are commanded to honour Him even as they honour the
Father' (John v. 23).

Introduction (8-16). **First** [Πρῶτον μὲν]—not
intending any 'second,' but merely using this
word as an opening for his brimful heart. [*Bengel*
finds an apodosis to μὲν in the δὲ of *v.* 13:—*q.d.*,
'Already, *indeed,* are ye beloved of God, called to
be saints, *but* I long to impart to you something
more.' This, however, seems forced.] **I thank
my God** [εὐχαριστῶ. This term of later Greek is
a favourite one with our apostle, being used by
him about twenty-five times, while by no other
New Testament writer is it used above three or
four times.] **through Jesus Christ** (see Heb.
xiii. 15) **for you all**—'regarding you all' is the
true reading [περί, not ὑπέρ], **that your faith is
spoken of throughout the whole world.** The
fact of a Christian church springing up in the
metropolis without any apostolic, or even noted,
instrumentality, could not but cause lively astonishment and joy to the Christians of other places,
to whom the news would quickly spread, through
the frequent visits paid to the capital from all the
provinces; nor could it fail to attract the notice
of many who were not Christians. The same is
said of the faith of the Thessalonian Christians,
whose bright walk and missionary zeal compelled
general and wide spread attention to the change
wrought on them, and of course to that which

9 faith is spoken of throughout the whole world. For God is my witness, whom I serve [3]with my spirit in the gospel of his Son, that without

10 ceasing I make mention of you always in my prayers; making request (if by any means now at length I might have a prosperous journey [a]by the

11 will of God) to come unto you. For I long to see you, that [e]I may impart unto you some spiritual gift, to the end ye may be established;

12 that is, that I may be comforted together [4]with you by the mutual faith both of you and me.

13 Now I would not have you ignorant, brethren, that [f]oftentimes I purposed to come unto you, (but [g]was let hitherto,) that I might have some

14 fruit [5]among you also, even as among other Gentiles. I [h]am debtor both to the Greeks and to the Barbarians, both to the wise and to the unwise.

15 So, as much as in me is, I am ready to preach the Gospel to you that are at Rome also.

16 For [i]I am not ashamed of the gospel of Christ: for [j]it is the power of

A. D. 60.

[3] Or. in my spirit.
[d] Jas. 4. 15.
[e] ch. 15. 29.
[4] Or. in you.
[f] ch. 15. 23.
[g] Acts 16. 7.
1 Thes. 2. 18.
[5] Or. in you.
[h] Ps 40. 9.
Mark 8. 38.
1 Cor. 9. 16.
[i] 2 Tim. 1. 8.
1 Pet. 4. 16.
[j] Ps. 110. 2.
1 Cor. 1. 18.
2 Cor. 10. 4.

produced it (1 Thess. i. 8-10). **9. For God is my witness, whom I serve** [λατρεύω]—'in the sense of religious service' (as this word always signifies in the LXX, and in the New Testament), **with my spirit**—or 'inmost soul' (cf. Luke i. 47; Matt. v. 3; Mark viii. 12; John xi. 33; xiii. 21; Acts xvii. 16; 1 Thess. v. 23), **in the gospel of his Son**—to which his whole religious life and official activities were consecrated, **that without ceasing I make mention of you always in my prayers; 10. Making request,** &c. According to what is probably the most ancient division of these verses—adopted in nearly every version but our own, and by every critic—they should read thus: 9. 'For God is my witness . . . how unceasingly I make mention (or remembrance) of you; 10. Always in my prayers making request,' &c. When one puts alongside of this the similar language used to the Ephesians (ch. i. 15, 16), the Philippians (ch. i. 3, 4), the Colossians (ch. i. 3, 4), and the Thessalonians (1 Thess. i. 2, 3)—what catholic love, what all-absorbing spirituality, what impassioned devotion to the glory of Christ, what incessant transaction with Heaven about the minutest affairs of the kingdom of Christ upon earth, are thus seen to meet in this wonderful man! **(if by any means now at length I might have a prosperous journey** [εὐοδωθήσομαι]—rather, 'I may have a way opened,' **by the will of God) to come unto you.** Though long anxious to visit the capital, he met with a number of providential hindrances (*v.* 13; ch. xxv. 22; Acts xix. 21; xxiii. 11; xxviii. 15); insomuch that *nearly a quarter of a century* elapsed, after his conversion, ere his desire was accomplished, and that only as "a prisoner of Jesus Christ." Thus taught that his whole future was in the hands of God, he makes it his continual prayer that at length the obstacles to a happy and prosperous meeting might be removed. **11. For I long to see you, that I may impart unto you some spiritual gift** —not any supernatural gift (as *Bengel*, &c.), but some purely spiritual gift, the character of which the next verse specifies (see 1 Cor. i. 7). **to the end ye may be established; 12. That is, that I may be comforted together with you** [συμπαρακληθῆναι ἐν ὑμῖν]—strictly, 'that we may have mutual comfort in you;' **by the mutual faith both of you and me**—that is, that by my witnessing your spiritual prosperity there may arise consolation to both of us. 'Not wishing (as *Jowett* happily expresses it) to "lord it over their faith," but rather to be a "helper of their joy," the apostle corrects his former expressions: My desire is to instruct you and do you good, that is, for us to instruct and do one another good: in giving I

shall also receive.' 'Nor (says *Calvin*) is he insincere in so speaking, for there is none so poor in the Church of Christ who may not impart to us something of value: it is only our malignity and pride that hinder us from gathering such fruit from every quarter.' 'How widely different (exclaims *Bengel*) is the apostolic style from that of the court of Papal Rome!'

13. Now I would not have you ignorant, brethren, that oftentimes I purposed to come unto you, but was let ('hindered') **hitherto**—chiefly by his desire to go first to places where Christ was not known (see ch. xv. 20-24), **that I might have some fruit** (of my ministry) **among you also, even as among other Gentiles.** The GENTILE origin of the Roman Church is here so explicitly stated, that those who conclude, merely from the Jewish strain of the argument, that they must have been mostly Israelites, decide in opposition to the apostle himself. (But see *Introduction* to this Epistle.) **14. I am debtor both to the** (cultivated) **Greeks**—amongst whom might be classed the educated Romans, who prided themselves on their Greek culture (see *Cic.* de fin. ii. 15—*non solum Græcia et Italia sed etiam omnis Barbaria*), **and to the** (rude) **Barbarians, both to the wise and to the unwise**—to all alike, without distinction of race or of culture. From this it has been argued that "the gift of *tongues*" must have been designed to facilitate the preaching of the Gospel in foreign countries. (So several of the fathers, and in modern times those who lean much on the fathers—*Wordsworth*, for example, quotes in support of it 1 Cor. xiv. 18). But if such a continued miracle had been wrought wherever our apostle preached beyond the region of Greek culture, and during all the intercourse which he kept up in those places, how is it that neither *he* nor *his* biographer has anywhere dropped a hint of it? To us this notion appears as improbable in itself as it is void of all evidence as matter of fact. **15. So, as much as in me is, I am ready** [τὸ κατ' ἐμὲ πρόθυμον—probably =ἐστι ἡ προθυμία] **to preach the gospel to you that are at Rome also.** An all-subduing sense of obligation to carry the Gospel to men of every class, from the rudest to the most refined, drew him with a yearning desire to the great capital.

16. For I am not ashamed of the gospel [of Christ]. These bracketed words are clearly an addition to the genuine text, as nearly all critics agree. [They are found only in K L D*** (a corrector so late as the ninth or tenth century), several cursives, and some late versions; but wanting in א A B C D* E G, a number of cursives, some of the principal copies of the Old Latin, the Vulgate, and

194

God unto salvation to every one that believeth; to the Jew first, and also | A. D. 60.
17 to the Greek.   For *k* therein is the righteousness of God revealed from | *k* ch. 3. 21.
faith to faith: as it is written, *l* The just shall live by faith. | *l* Hab. 2. 4.

---

both Syriac versions, and the principal fathers.] The language implies that it required some courage to bring to 'the mistress of the world' what "to the Jews was a stumbling-block, and to the Greeks foolishness." But its intrinsic glory, as God's life-giving message to a dying world, so filled his soul, that like his blessed Master he "despised the shame." FOR IT IS THE POWER OF GOD UNTO SALVATION TO EVERY ONE THAT BELIEVETH; to the Jew first, and also to the Greek. [There is no sufficient reason for bracketing πρῶτον, as *Lachmann* does; for the evidence of its genuineness is decisive.] Here, and in *v.* 17, the apostle announces the grand theme of his ensuing argument, the substance of which is, SALVATION (the one overwhelming necessity of perishing men) EMBODIED IN A MESSAGE FROM GOD TO MEN (that every hearer of it may be assured that in it he hears God's message to himself), WHICH WHOSOEVER CREDITS SHALL FIND TO BE THE POWER OF GOD TO HIS OWN SALVATION: —*the Jew* first (to whom, in virtue of his ancient standing, the message is first to be carried), and *the Greek* as well. 17. For therein is THE RIGHTEOUSNESS OF GOD revealed.

Though the sense of this great word, "THE RIGHTEOUSNESS OF GOD," will open upon us as we advance in the argument of this Epistle, it may be well to state here at the outset what we understand by it. *First*, then, it does not mean God's 'rectitude' or 'clemency,' as an attribute of His nature, or a feature of His moral government (as *Origen* and *Chrysostom* among the fathers, and, with a certain modification, *Osiander* the reformer; and in our own day *Hofmann*, in his 'Schrift-beweis'). Everything said of this "righteousness" in the progress of the apostle's argument disproves such a notion. It must therefore mean that righteousness which God *provides* for men, or which He *bestows* upon men, or which He *approves* in men. These ideas, though distinct in themselves, do in the present case run into and presuppose one another. The predominant shade of thought, however, is perhaps not so much 'the Divinely provided and Divinely bestowed righteousness' (as *Beza* and others take it) as 'the Divinely approved and Divinely accepted righteousness,' (so *Luther, Calvin, Fritzsche, Tholuck*, &c.) See, for example, ch. iii. 20 ("justified *in his sight*"); Gal. iii. 11 ("justified in the sight of God"); ch. ii. 13 ("just *before God*"); and 2 Cor. v. 21 ("He was made sin for us who knew no sin, that we might be made the righteousness of God in him"). *Secondly*, It does not mean 'an implanted and inherent righteousness wrought in men by Divine grace.' This is what the Church of Rome teaches (*Canon. et Decret. Conc. Trid.*: Decr. 'De Justificatione,' vi. 7), though *Estius* expresses a very different doctrine, on ch. ii. 12, *Tertio*; it is what *Grotius* and the Remonstrant (or Semi-pelagian) party in the Dutch Church held; and it is what in the present day a party in the Church of England, headed by *Dr. Pusey*, contend for as being the doctrine of their own Church as well as that of Rome; while some otherwise sound Protestants, going along with them in this, are thus surrendering the citadel of Protestantism. In direct opposition to all these views is the teaching of this great Epistle throughout—that "the righteousness of God" is a righteousness 'reckoned' or 'imputed to us,' founded on the entire work of Christ in the

flesh, or "His obedience unto death, even the death of the cross," in our behalf. The verse above quoted—"He was made sin for us who knew no sin, that we might be made the righteousness of God IN HIM" (2 Cor. v. 21)—can mean nothing else than that it is the sinless One's being made sin for us, that gives us who believe our righteous standing before God. And since the "sin" which Christ was "made" for us, was certainly not any *personal sin of His*, nor *sin infused into Him*, but simply *sin reckoned to Him*, even so "the righteousness of God," which the believer is "made in him," can be neither any personal righteousness of his own, nor any righteousness infused into or wrought in him, but a righteousness simply reckoned or imputed to Him. Nay, even as reckoned to us, it is still IN HIM that we are thus constituted righteous. True—and the truth is a fundamental one—the union between the believer and Christ being a real and vital one, constituting them *one spirit* (1 Cor. vi. 17), it is impossible that the justified believer, from the moment of this union, should be other than personally and inherently righteous, or truly holy. But this does not constitute his justifying righteousness—it is *not* this that makes him "the righteousness of God." But all this will unfold itself as we proceed with the apostle's argument.

Such, then, is "the righteousness of God" which is to constitute the chief theme of this Epistle. But, next, it is revealed—from faith to faith [ἐκ πίστεως εἰς πίστιν]. Some of the many senses put upon this rather difficult clause (which *Estius* carefully enumerates) may be dismissed at once as unworthy of notice:—such as that it means, 'from the faith of the Law to the faith of the Gospel;' or, 'from the faith of the Old Testament to the faith of the New;' 'from a general faith in the Gospel to an appropriating faith in it to one's self;' 'from the faith of the preacher to the faith of the hearer;' 'from the faith of the promising God to the faith of the believing man.' But there are three other interpretations which claim more attention. *First*, 'From one degree of faith to another—from a weaker to a stronger—from a lower to a higher.' (So several of the fathers; and of the moderns, *Erasmus, Luther, Melancthon, Calvin, Beza, Grotius, Estius, Meyer*, &c.) But it is fatal to this view, as we think, that it introduces a foreign element into the apostle's argument—an argument which has nothing to do with progressive *stages* or *degrees* of faith, but solely with *faith itself*, as the appointed way of receiving the righteousness of God. *Second*, 'As it begins in faith, so in faith it ends—in other words, it is all of faith.' (So *Œcumenius* of the fathers; and of the moderns, *Bengel, Alford, Hodge, Wordsworth*.) But this makes one statement of what the apostle seems studiously to make two, and connects the words "righteousness" and "faith," while the apostle appears studiously to disjoin them. *Third*, and this we without hesitation adopt: Let it be observed that the words here rendered "from faith" [ἐκ πίστεως], *wherever else they occur in this Epistle*, mean 'by,' or 'through faith;' and they are so rendered by our translators themselves even in the sequel of this same verse—"as it is written, The just shall live *by* faith." Precisely so in ch. iii. 30; iv. 16 ("of" or "by faith"); v. 1; ix. 30, 32 ("of faith"—"by faith"); x. 16. This is to us decisive in favour of rendering the clause thus:

195

18 For ^mthe wrath of God is revealed from heaven against all ungodliness and unrighteousness of men, who hold the truth in unrighteousness.

A. D. 60.

^m Acts 17. 30.

'The righteousness of God is revealed [to be] of' or 'by faith, unto faith.' But what does 'unto faith' mean? It may mean either 'unto those who believe' [= εἰς τοὺς πιστεύοντας], as *Tholuck, Conybeare, Philippi;* or (which we much prefer) 'in order to faith' [εἰς τὸ πιστευθῆναι, or πιστεύσαι ἡμᾶς], as the same preposition is rendered in *v.* 5 of this chapter, and in ch. vi. 16, 19; viii. 15; x. 10; xiii. 14. So *de Wette, Olshausen, Fritzsche* (whose remarks are worthy of special notice), *Stuart, Scholefield, Bloomfield, Jowett.* If this have less point (says the last-named critic, it is more in accordance with the style of St. Paul than the preceding explanations, and may be defended by the quotation from Habakkuk, which shows that the real stress of the passage is not on "to faith," but "from," or "by faith," as it is written (in Hab. ii. 4), **The just shall live by faith.** This is precisely as in the Hebrew, except that there it is, 'by *his* faith' [וְצַדִּיק בֶּאֱמוּנָתוֹ יִחְיֶה]. The LXX. translate, 'shall live by *my* faith'—meaning, probably, by 'faith in Me'—[reading, no doubt, 'for ו]. The prophet's words mean either, 'The just (or the justified) by faith shall live;' or 'The just shall live (or 'have life') by faith.' This latter seems clearly what both the prophet and the apostle, in quoting him, mean to say. Indeed, according to the argument and the phraseology of this Epistle, to say that 'the justified by faith shall live,' is rather a truism: since to "be justified," and to "live," are not, in the apostle's sense, cause and effect, but just two aspects of one and the same 'life of justification.' It may be added, that this golden maxim of Old Testament theology is thrice quoted in the New Testament, namely, here; in Gal. iii. 11; and in Heb. x. 38)—showing that the Gospel way of 'LIFE BY FAITH,' so far from subverting or disturbing, only takes up and develops the ancient method.

Remarks.—1. What manner of persons ought the ministers of Christ to be, according to the pattern here set up:—absolutely subject and officially dedicated to the Lord Jesus; separated unto that Gospel of God which contemplates the subjugation of all nations to the faith of Christ; debtors to all classes—the refined and the rude—to bring the Gospel to them all alike, all shame in the presence of the one, as well as pride before the other, sinking before the glory which they feel to be in their message; yearning over all faithful churches, not lording it over them, but rejoicing in their prosperity, and finding refreshment and strength in their fellowship! 2. The peculiar features of the Gospel, here brought prominently forward, should be the devout study of all who preach it, and guide the views and the taste of all who are privileged statedly to hear it:—namely, that it is "the Gospel of God," as a message from heaven, yet not absolutely new, but, on the contrary, only the fulfilment of Old Testament promise; that not only is Christ the great theme of it, but Christ in the very nature of God, as His own Son, and in the nature of men, as partaker of their flesh—Christ, whose resurrection from the dead not only wiped away the reproach of the cross, but gloriously vindicated His claim to be the Son of God, even in His veiled condition, Christ, as now the Dispenser of all grace to men and of all gifts for the establishment and edification of the Church, Christ the Righteousness provided of God for the justification of all that believe in His name; in a word, that in this glori-

ous Gospel, when thus preached, there resides the very power of God to save Jew and Gentile alike who embrace it. 3. While Christ is to be regarded as the ordained *Channel* of all grace from God to men, let none imagine that His proper Divinity is in any respect compromised by this arrangement, since He is here expressly associated with "God the Father," in the prayer that is offered for "grace and peace"—which include all spiritual blessings—to rest upon this Roman church. 4. While this Epistle teaches, in conformity with the teaching of our Lord Himself, that all salvation is suspended upon *faith*, this is but half a truth, and will certainly minister to self-righteousness, if dissociated from another feature of the same truth, here explicitly taught, that this faith is *God's own gift*—for which accordingly, in the case of the Roman believers, he "thanks his God through Jesus Christ." 5. Christian fellowship, as indeed all real fellowship, is a mutual benefit; and as it is not possible for the most eminent saints and servants of Christ to impart any refreshment and profit to the meanest of their brethren without experiencing a rich return into their own bosoms, so just in proportion to their humility and love will they feel their need of it and rejoice in it.

18-22. THIS GRATUITOUS JUSTIFICATION NEEDED BY ALL ALIKE, SINCE THE WRATH OF GOD OVERHANGS ALL ALIKE, AS SINNERS—AND FIRST, THE HEATHEN WORLD—ITS STATE DEPICTED.

Great general Proposition: *The wrath of God is revealed against all iniquity* (18). **18. For the wrath of God** [ὀργὴ θεοῦ]—His holy displeasure and rectoral vengeance against sin. However distasteful such language may be to some ears, it is amongst the household words of the New Testament as well as of the Old (for example, Matt. iii. 7; John iii. 36; ch. ii. 5, 8; v. 1; ix. 22; Eph. ii. 3; v. 6; Col. iii. 6; 1 Thess. i. 10; ii. 16; Heb. iii. 11; iv. 3; Rev. vi. 16; xiv. 10; xix. 10), **is revealed heaven.** But where revealed? and how? 'In the Gospel message itself,' say some (as *Beza, Grotius, Estius, Stuart, Wordsworth*). But besides that this sounds harsh, why, it has been well asked, did not the apostle in that case say, as in the previous verse, "For *therein* [ἐν αὐτῷ] is the wrath of God revealed"? Others understand here, not any existing manifestations of Divine wrath against sin, but what is to burst forth at the day of judgment—"the wrath to come." (So *Chrysostom, Jowett*, &c.) But this surely is against the natural sense of the words. What the apostle refers to is, in our judgment, 'the whole visible procedure of God in the moral government of the world,' by which He 'reveals,' or palpably displays, His holy displeasure against sin (as *Olshausen*), and particularly His making sin its own punishment, as described so awfully in the sequel of this chapter (so *Fritzsche*, and some of the best interpreters). This wrath of God is said to be "revealed from heaven," to signify the lofty jealousy of that Eye, as a flame of fire, that looketh upon all the inhabitants of the earth, and the might of that unseen Hand that is upon every form of iniquity under the whole heaven, to take vengeance on it. **against all ungodliness** [ἀσέβειαν]—or, 'impiety;' meaning all the *irreligiousness* of men, or their living (no matter how virtuously, yet) without any conscious reference to God, and without any proper feelings towards Him: **and unrighteousness of men** [ἀδικίαν]—that is, men's whole *deviations from moral rectitude,*

19 Because that which may be known of God is manifest ⁶in them; for
20 God hath showed *it* unto them. For the invisible things of him from
     the creation of the world are clearly seen, being understood by the things
     that are made, *even* his eternal power and Godhead; so ⁷that they are

A. D. 60.

⁶ Or, to them.
⁷ Or, that
    they may
    be.

whether in heart, speech, or behaviour. Either of these terms, standing alone, may and usually does carry the sense of the other; but when both are used together, they must be distinguished, and the distinction can only be what we have given. Now, as no human being can plead guiltless of "all un-godliness" and "all unrighteousness," it follows that every child of Adam in his sins is the object of Heaven's deserved and impending wrath. Thus all-comprehensive is the apostle's statement, em-bracing Jew and Gentile alike in its dread sweep. But as this was too general to suit his purpose, of shutting up all alike to gratuitous justification in the Lord Jesus, he now proceeds to details, bring-ing the charge of guilt first against *the heathen world*, and next against *the chosen people*. And first, *The progressive degeneracy* (18-23), *the retributive punishment* (24-27), *and the consummated penal debasement* (28-32) *of the whole heathen world*. The value of the following picture is immensely en-hanced by its containing a historical sketch, rather than a mere description, of heathen degeneracy, traced down from its earliest stage after the fall.

The progressive degeneracy of the heathen world (18-23). **18. who hold the truth in unrighteousness** [τ. ἀληθείαν ἐν ἀδικίᾳ κατεχόντων]—*lit.*, 'who hold down' or 'stifle the truth in (or 'by') unrighteous-ness.' (Compare the use of the same word in Luke iv. 40—"stayed him," or 'held him back'—also in 2 Thess. ii. 6, 7, "what *withholdeth*," "he who now *letteth*," or 'hindereth.') So all critics under-stand the word here, and so all the ancient and nearly all modern versions but our own render it—'detain' the truth—or, as *Calvin* explains it, 'sup-press' or 'obscure' it. But when he and *Beza* and *Reiche* render the words "in unrighteous-ness" by 'unjustly,' with a view (as he says) to perspicuity, they miss an important truth which nearly every other critic justly dwells on—namely, that the "unrighteousness" of the heathen world, or their depraved passions and practices, were the very element in which, and by means of which, the truth which they possessed was stifled—the light they enjoyed darkened. Thus are the heathen represented as having light, or possessing truth, even when left to themselves, without that revela-tion which the chosen people enjoyed; and yet as holding it down, suppressing or stifling it, by and in their unrighteousness. Compare Matt. vi. 22, 23, "The light of the body is the eye: if, therefore, thine eye be single, thy whole body shall be full of light. But if thine eye be evil, thy whole body shall be full of darkness. If, therefore, the light that is in thee be darkness, how great is that darkness!" And the action of this principle on the heathen mind is expressed in Ephesians iv. 17, 18, "That ye henceforth walk not as other Gentiles walk, in the vanity of their mind, having the understand-ing darkened, being alienated from the life of God through the ignorance that is in them, because of the blindness ('hardness') of their heart." **19. Because that which may be known of God** [τὸ γνωστόν]. Three senses have been put upon this expression: (1.) the *known* of God (so the *Old Latin* and *Vulgate, de Wette*, &c.); (2.) the *knowable* of God (so *Erasmus, Calvin, Beza, Grotius, Tholuck, Stuart, Conybeare, Mehring, Green*); (3.) the *know-ledge* of God (as the *Syriac, Chrysostom, Luther, Fritzsche*). The first and last of these senses, in the only sense of them which has much to recommend

them, almost resolve themselves into the middle one—that of our own version, which we think de-cidedly the preferable. It is objected to this sense, that though in the classics it is the usual sense, yet the LXX. and the New Testament use it in the sense, not of what *may be*, but of what *is* known. But besides that this is but partially true [see *v.* 20, ἀναπολογήτους, and ch. ii. 1, ἀναπολόγητος], as the word is not very common anywhere, and the senses run into each other, we must be guided in each case solely by the context. It is further objected, that all which may be known of God is *not* "manifest" to the heathen; and therefore the sense cannot be 'that which *may be*,' but 'that which *is* known is manifest in them.' But the apostle does not say '*all* that may be known,' but only "*that* which may be known;" and to show that he did not mean 'all,' he expressly specifies in the next verse what of God it was that they did know—namely, "his eternal power and Godhead." This, then, is what **is manifest in them** [ἐν αὐτοῖς]—not 'among them' (as *Erasmus, Grotius, Fritzsche*), meaning what the heathen philosophers attained to by reflection, amidst the brutish ignor-ance of the mass of the people, but (as all the best interpreters take it) 'within them,' in the sense which the next verse will more fully explain. **for God hath showed it unto them** [ἐφανέρωσεν]—'for God showed it unto them,' in the constitution stamped upon man's nature in his creation, in which the conviction of a God is deeply rooted, and through the perception of Him in the works of His hand resulting from this. **20. For the invisible things of him from the creation of the world** [ἀπὸ κτίσ. κόσμ.]—not 'by means of,' but 'since the time of' the world's creation [=ἀπὸ καταβολῆς κόσμ., Luke xi. 50] **are clearly seen**—[ἀόρατα—καθορᾶται. See *Fritzsche's* note in de-fence of the intensive import of κατά here, denied by *Alford*]. There is here an incomparable *oxy-moron* (says *Bengel*), or a bold, paradoxical play of words; the *unseen* things of God are *clearly seen*, and surely (he adds), if anywhere, it is in creation that these invisibilities of God become visible to human intelligence. *Aristotle* (de mundo, 6) has a remarkable statement, identical with this—'In every mortal by nature the invisible God becomes by those very works visible.' **being understood by the things that are made**—[νοούμενα, 'perceived,' 'apprehended' by the νοῦς.] The apostle, then, does not say that without *reflection* even "the things that are made" will discover God to men. He says exactly the reverse. And thus is to be explained the brutish ignorance of God that reigns among the more debased and unreflecting heathen, the atheistic speculations in modern times of some subtle metaphysicians, and the negation of all Theism on the part of many enthusiastic students of the mere facts and laws of the material uni-verse; while to the calm, unprejudiced exercise of thought upon the *mind* which is seen to reign in every department of "the things that are made," God is brightly beheld. **even his eternal power and Godhead** [θειότης]. This word signifies not 'The Godhead' [which is θεότης], but that pro-perty of *Divineness* which belongs to Him who called this creation into being. Two things are thus said to be clearly discovered to the reflecting intelligence by the things which are made—*First*, That *there is an Eternal Power*; and, *Secondly*, That this is neither a blind physical '*Force*' nor a pantheistic

21 without excuse: because that, when they knew God, they glorified *him* not as God, ⁿneither were thankful; but ^obecame vain in their imagina-
22 tions, and their foolish heart was darkened. Professing ^pthemselves to be
23 wise, they became fools, and changed the glory of the uncorruptible ^qGod into an image made like to corruptible man, and to birds, and four-footed beasts, and creeping things.
24 Wherefore ^rGod also gave them up to uncleanness through the lusts of their own hearts, ^sto dishonour their own bodies between ^tthemselves:
25 who changed ^uthe truth of God into a ^vlie, and worshipped and served the creature ⁸more than the Creator, who is blessed for ever. Amen.

A. D. 60.

ⁿ Ps. 106. 13.
^o 2 Ki. 17. 15.
^p Jer. 10. 14.
^q Isa. 40. 18.
^r Ps. 81. 12.
   Acts 7. 42.
^s 1 Cor. 6. 18.
^t Lev. 18. 22.
^u 1 Thes. 1. 9.
^v Isa. 44. 20.
   Amos 2. 4.
⁸ Or, rather.

'spirit of nature,' but a living, conscious *Divine Person,* whose outgoing energy is beheld in the external universe. And, what is eminently worthy of notice, the outward creation is here represented, not as the *parent,* but only as the *interpreter,* of our faith in God. That faith has its primary sources within our own breast (*v.* 19); but it becomes an *intelligent and articulate conviction* only through what we observe around us (*v.* 20). And thus are the inner and outer revelation of God just the complement of each other, making up between them one universal and immoveable conviction *that God is.* With this most striking apostolic statement agree the latest conclusions of the most profound speculative students of Theism. **so that they are without excuse** [εἰς τὸ εἶναι]—or, '**so** that they might be without excuse' (in the event of their failure). Though the latter shade of meaning is more conformable to the words used, the former is what one would more naturally expect; but each presupposes the other. **21. Because that, when they knew** God (in the sense of *v.* 19)—even while still retaining some real knowledge of God, and ere they sank down into the state next to be described, **they glorified him not as God, neither were thankful**—neither yielding Him the *adoration* due to Himself, nor rendering the *gratitude* which His beneficence demanded, **but became vain in their imaginations** [ἐν τ. διαλογισμοῖς]—'in their reasonings,' 'thoughts,' 'speculations' about God. The word rendered, "became vain" [ἐματαιώθησαν], and the corresponding word, 'vanity' [ματαιότης], almost always refer to the *idolatrous* tendencies and practices of men (Jer. ii. 5; 2 Ki. xvii. 15; Acts xiv. 15). The word rendered "imaginations" is mostly used in a bad sense, and here refers to men's proud and restless dissatisfaction with the simple verities regarding God, which are "manifest in them," their cravings after something more satisfactory, and the thoughts, reasonings, or speculations to which these gave rise. **and their foolish heart** [ἀσύνετος] — '**their senseless,**' '**stupid** heart;' meaning their whole inner man, **was darkened.** How instructively is the downward progress of the human soul here traced! When once darkness is suffered to overspread the mind, an impotent stupidity of all the active powers of the soul is the result; and thus the truth which God left with and in men, instead of having free scope to acquire strength and develop itself, came by degrees to be lost, and the still, small voice of conscience, first disregarded, was next thwarted, and at length systematically disregarded. **22. Professing themselves to be** [Φάσκοντες εἶναι]— '**boasting that they were**' **wise, they became fools, 23. And changed the glory of the uncorruptible God into an image made like to corruptible man**—that is, they exchanged the one for the other. The expression is taken from Ps. cvi. 20, (and in the words of the LXX.) They exchanged *God* for *man*—the *incorruptible* for the *corruptible;* nay, Him who is the essence and fountain of all

that is glorious, for a mere inanimate *image,* fashioned after the likeness of perishable man. The allusion here is doubtless to the *Greek* worship, and the apostle may have had in his eye those exquisite chisellings of the human form which lay so profusely beneath and around him as he stood on Mars' hill, and "beheld their devotions," or 'the objects of their worship' (see on Acts xvii. 29). But, as if that had not been a deep enough degradation of the living God, there was found 'a lower deep' still. **and to birds, and four-footed beasts, and creeping things**—referring now to the *Egyptian* and *Oriental* worship. In the face of these plain declarations of the *descent* of man's religious belief from loftier to ever lower and more debasing conceptions of the Supreme Being, there are expositors of this very Epistle (as *Reiche* and *Jowett*) who, believing neither in any Fall from primeval innocence, nor in the noble traces of that innocence which lingered even after the fall, and were only by degrees obliterated by wilful violence to the dictates of conscience, maintain that man's religious history has been all along a struggle to *rise,* from the lowest forms of nature-worship, suited to the childhood of our race, into that which is more rational and spiritual.

The retributive punishment. **24. Wherefore God also** — in righteous retribution, **gave them up** [παρέδωκεν]. This Divine abandonment of men is here strikingly traced in three successive stages, at each of which the same word is used (*vv.* 24, 26, and 28, where the word is rendered "gave over"). **to uncleanness through** [ἐν]—rather, '**in**' **the lusts of their own hearts, to dishonour their own bodies between themselves** [ἐν ἑαυτοῖς]—or, according to the preferable reading [ἐν αὐτοῖς], 'with each other;' but the sense is the same. 'As they deserted God (says *Grotius*), God in turn deserted them—not giving them Divine (*i.e.,* supernatural) laws, and suffering them to corrupt those which were human; not sending them prophets, and allowing the philosophers to run into absurdities. He let them do what they pleased, even what was in the last degree vile, that those who had not honoured God might dishonour themselves.' **25. Who changed** [Οἵτινες μετήλλ.= *Quippe qui*]—'Inasmuch as they changed,' or, 'Being such as changed' (the pronoun here used assigning the reason for what went before). **the truth of God into a lie**—or 'into the lie;' that is, the *true* God into the *false* (the abstract is here put for the concrete), the Living into the lying. In the Old Testament the idols of the heathen are constantly represented as 'vanity,' and 'a lie.' **and worshipped** [ἐσεβάσθησαν, here only] **and served** [ἐλάτρευσεν]—in their *hearts* paying homage, and in their religious exercises worshipping by outward *acts,* **the creature more than** (or 'rather than') **the Creator** [παρὰ τὸν κτίσαντα. παρά, with *accusative,* 'along by,' 'beyond,' *præter, contra*). Professing merely to worship the Creator *by means of* the creature, they soon came to lose

26 For this cause God gave them up unto vile *w* affections: for even their women did change the natural use into that which is against nature: **27** and likewise also the men, leaving the natural use of the woman, burned in their lust one toward another; men with men working that which is unseemly, and receiving in themselves that recompense of their error **28** which was meet. And even as they did not like 9 to retain God in *their* knowledge, God gave them over to 10 a reprobate mind, to do those things **29** *x* which are not convenient: being filled with all unrighteousness, forni-

A. D. 60.

w Gen. 19. 5. Jude 10.

9 Or, to acknowledge.

10 Or, a mind void of judgment.

x Eph. 5. 4.

sight of the Creator *in* the creature. How aggravated is the guilt of the Church of Rome, which, under the same flimsy pretext, does shamelessly what the heathen are here condemned for doing, and with light which the heathen never had! **who is blessed for ever. Amen.** By this doxology the apostle instinctively relieves the horror which the penning of such things excited within his breast: an example to such as are called still to expose like dishonour done to the blessed God. **26. For this cause God gave them up** (see on *v.* 24) **unto vile affections** [πάθη ἀτιμίας]—'shameless passions.' The expression is very strong, but not so strong as the monstrousness of the thing intended would have warranted. **for even their women**—that sex whose priceless jewel and fairest ornament is modesty, and which, when that is once lost, not only becomes more shameless than the other sex, but lives henceforth only to drag the other sex down to its own level, **did change the natural use into that which is against nature: 27. And likewise also the men, leaving the natural use of the woman, burned in their lust one toward another; men with men working that which is unseemly.** The practices here referred to, though too abundantly attested by classic authors, cannot be described and illustrated from them without trenching on things 'which ought not to be even named among us as becometh saints.' 'At the period when the apostle wrote, unnatural lusts broke out (says *Tholuck*) to the most revolting extent, not at Rome only, but over the whole empire. He who is unacquainted with the historical monuments of that age—especially *Petronius, Suetonius, Martial,* and *Juvenal*—can scarcely figure to himself the frightfulness of these excesses.' (See also *Grotius, Wetstein, Fritzsche.*) *Reiche*, indeed, throws doubt upon the apostle's accuracy, alleging that the Christian world has been at various times no better in these respects than the heathen. No doubt passages can be produced from ecclesiastical writers, at different periods, in which charges quite as strong as anything in this chapter are, with too much justice, laid at the door of the Christian Church. (See, for example, one from *Salvian,* in the fifth century, which *Tholuck* quotes.) But besides that (as *Tholuck* observes) the very heathen writers themselves (*Seneca,* for example, *de brev. vit.,* c. 16) expressly blame the vicious character of the heathen deities for much of the immorality which reigned among the people, whereas all vice is utterly alien to Christianity, the worst vices of humanity have since the glorious Reformation (which was but true Christianity restored, and raised to its legitimate ascendancy) almost disappeared from European society. To return, then, to the state of the heathen world, we may add (with *Bloomfield*) that the disclosures lately made by the disinterment of Herculaneum and Pompeii (Roman towns near Naples, overwhelmed by the terrible eruption of Mount Vesuvius, A.D. 79—first discovered in 1713, and now gradually undergoing disentombment) are such as too fully bear out and illustrate all that the apostle says or hints on the tremendous abominations of even the most civil-

ized nations of the ancient world. Indeed, it was just the most civilized that were plunged the deepest in the mire of pollution, the barbarians being (as will appear from the 'Germania' of *Tacitus*) comparatively virtuous. Observe how, in the retributive judgment of God, vice is here seen consuming and exhausting itself. When the passions, scourged by violent and continued indulgence in *natural* vices, became impotent to yield the craved enjoyment, resort was had to artificial stimulants by the practice of *unnatural* and monstrous vices. How early these were in full career, in the history of the world, the case of Sodom affectingly shows; and because of such abominations, centuries after that, the land of Canaan 'spued out' its old inhabitants. Long before this chapter was penned, the Lesbians and others throughout refined Greece had been luxuriating in such debasements; and as for the Romans, *Tacitus,* speaking of the emperor Tiberius, tells us that new words had then to be coined to express the newly invented stimulants to jaded passions. No wonder that, thus sick and dying as was this poor Humanity of ours under the highest earthly culture, its many-voiced cry for the balm in Gilead and the Physician there—"Come over and help us"—pierced the hearts of the missionaries of the Cross, and made them "not ashamed of the Gospel of Christ!" **and receiving in themselves that recompense of their error which was meet**—alluding to the many physical and moral ways in which, under the righteous government of God, vice was made self-avenging.

The consummated penal debasement of the heathen world. **28. And even as they did not like** [οὐκ ἐδοκίμασαν = ἀπεδοκίμασαν]—or 'disliked,' though the negative form of the expression is intended to convey its own shade of thought, **to retain God in their knowledge** [ἔχειν ἐν ἐπιγνώσει]—'to have God in recognition,' **God gave them over** (or 'up,' see on *v.* 24) **to a reprobate mind** [εἰς ἀδόκιμον νοῦν]. The word signifies 'disapproved' on trial (as metals, when they are assayed and found worthless), 'reprobate;' and, next, as the result of this, 'rejected,' 'cast away.' But it is very difficult to convey in any English translation the play upon words which has been long observed in the two terms here employed. [The Vulgate and *Calvin* have tried it in Latin—Et sicut non.*probaverunt* . . . tradidit Deus in *reprobum* sensum (*reprobam* mentem—*Calvin*). *Conybeare's* version is not good English—'As they thought fit to *cast out* the acknowledgment of God, God gave them over to an *outcast* mind.' *De Wette's* version comes pretty near it—'Und so wie sie die Kenntnisz Gottes *verwarfen,* so gab sie Gott einem *verworfenen* Sinnepreis.' Were we, at some sacrifice of smooth English, to retain this alliteration, perhaps it might not be too harsh to translate thus: 'And even as they *reprobated* retaining God in their knowledge, God gave them over to a *reprobate* mind.' **to do those things which are not convenient** [τὰ μὴ καθήκοντα]—in the old sense of that word, that is, 'not becoming,' 'indecorous.' **29. Being filled with all unrighteousness** [Πεπληρωμένους πάσῃ ἀδικίᾳ. The dative

cation, wickedness, covetousness, maliciousness ; full of envy, murder,
30 debate, deceit, malignity; whisperers, backbiters, ʸhaters of God, despiteful, proud, boasters, inventors of evil things, disobedient to parents,
31 without understanding, covenant-breakers, ¹¹without natural affection,
32 implacable, unmerciful: who knowing the judgment of God, that they

A. D. co.
ʸ Num.10. 5. Deut. 7. 10. Ps. 81. 15.
¹¹ Or. unsociable.

in place of the genitive (as *Green* remarks) in this and the following nouns may here be regarded as used designedly to convey, by the entire expression, the idea of an engrossing process, as distinguished from that of mere fulness. See 2 Cor. vii. 4 for a similar idea]. On comparing this, the longest, with some of the other lists of vices which occur in the Pauline Epistles (1 Cor. vi. 9, 10; Gal. v. 19-21; 1 Tim. i. 9, 10; 2 Tim. iii. 2-4), it will be evident that the order in which they are placed follows associations sometimes of *sound* (as *Jowett* says) and sometimes of *sense*. Not without reason, therefore, does *Fritzsche* recommend the student of the sacred text not to spend his time and ingenuity in arranging into distinct classes words whose meaning, and vices whose characteristics, differ only by a slight shade from each other. A word or two in explanation of the probable sense of some of the terms will suffice. The first word, then, 'unrighteousness' [ἀδικία] is a general term, purposely used, perhaps, at the outset. [**Fornication**]. This bracketed word [πορνεία, immediately preceding πονηρία] must be regarded as an addition to the genuine text. It is supported only by one Uncial MS., L, and several cursives, the Syriac version, and one or two later Greek fathers; but is wanting in אABC (D is here defective), and K, some cursives, and many fathers. Its resemblance to the next word [πονηρία] may have occasioned its introduction; and the circumstance of this vice not being included in such a list, may have seemed so incredible as to give rise to the interpolation. The critical editors reject it, and critics generally pronounce against it. **wickedness** [πονηρια] — perhaps 'villany;' **covetousness** — invariably classed in the New Testament with some of the worst vices (Jer. xxii. 17; Hab. ii. 19; Mark vii. 22; Eph. v. 3; Col. iii. 5; 2 Pet. ii. 3), and pointing probably to outrageous manifestations of it. It is not used in the sense of 'lust' [=ἐπιθυμία], as *Jowett* thinks. **maliciousness** [κακία] — 'wickedness,' 'badness,' in a passive sense, as vice is distinguished from 'villany.' **full** [μεστούς]. The change of word here (of precisely the same import as that used at the beginning of the verse) is evidently adopted merely to vary the construction of the profusion of nouns following from the preceding ones [and the *accusative* here, as in the opening word, is—as *Erasmus* and others have remarked—under the influence of ποιεῖν, at the close of the preceding verse]. **of envy, murder** [φθόνου, φόνου]. The alliteration here shows that the sound of the one word suggested the other. **debate** (or 'strife'), **deceit, malignity** [κακοηθείας]—'rancour,' 'ill-nature;' **whisperers** [ψιθυριστάς]. The 30th verse should have begun with this word, as the form of the original shows a change in the construction of the words that follow from that of the preceding ones. Accordingly, most critics so arrange the verses. **30. Backbiters** [καταλάλους] —rather, 'slanderers.' The former word refers to *secret*, this to *open* slander. **haters of God** [θεοστυγεῖς]—'God-hated,' being the classical sense of this not very common word, is that which some superior critics give it here; understanding by it 'abhorred of the Lord,' as denoting the detestableness of their character in His sight (cf. Prov. xxii. 14; Ps. lxxiii. 20). But the active sense of the word, adopted in our version, and by the majority of expositors, though rarer, agrees perhaps better

with the context, whose object is, by a series of examples, to set forth the evil principles, feelings, and practices which reigned in the heathen world. **despiteful** [ὑβριστὰς]—'insolent,' or 'insulters' (cf. Matt. xxii. 6, "entreated them spitefully;" Luke xviii. 32; Acts xiv. 5; 1 Thess. ii. 2); **proud, boasters, inventors of evil things, disobedient to parents, 31. Without understanding, covenant - breakers** [ἀσυνέτους, ἀσυνθέτους] — another alliteration (see on *v.* 29), **without natural affection, [implacable].** The evidence against this bracketed word is decisive. (It is found only in CKL with D***—a late corrector—with several cursives and versions; whereas it is wanting in אABD*EG, the Old Latin and Vulgate, and the Memphitic version. *Lachm., Tisch., and Treg.* omit it.) **unmerciful.** *Green* translates this verse with ingenious terseness and uniformity, though the improvement is questionable: 'Senseless, faithless, heartless, pitiless.' **32. Who** [Οἵτινες]—'Such as,' knowing [ἐπιγνόντες]—'knowing well' the [righteous] judgment of God [τὸ δικαίωμα—see on ch. v. 16]—the stern law of Divine procedure, to which every man's conscience bears witness, **that they which commit such things are worthy of death.** The word "death" is here used in its widest known sense—namely, the uttermost of Divine vengeance against sin. What that is will be variously conceived according to the light enjoyed. The mythic representations of *Tartarus* sufficiently show how the heathen conscience in classic lands pictured to itself the horrors of the future "death." **not only do the same**—which, under the pressure of temptation and in the heat of passion, they might do, even while abhorring it, and abhorring themselves for doing it, **but have pleasure in** (or 'consent to') **them that do them** [συνευδοκοῦσιν]. The word conveys the idea of positive satisfaction in a person or thing (see on Acts viii. 1). The charge here brought against the heathen world is, that they deliberately set their seal to such actions by encouraging and applauding the doing of them in others. This is the climax of our apostle's charges against the heathen; and certainly, if the things are in themselves as black as possible, this settled and unblushing satisfaction at the practice of them, apart from all the blinding effects of present passion, must be regarded as the darkest feature of human depravity.

Remarks.—1. "The wrath of God" against sin has all the dread reality of a "revelation from heaven" sounding in the consciences of men, in the self-inflicted miseries of the wicked, and in the vengeance which God's moral government, sooner or later, takes upon all who outrage it. Nor is this "wrath of God" confined to high-handed crimes, or the grosser manifestations of human depravity, but is "revealed" against all violations of Divine law of whatever nature—" against all ungodliness," as well as "unrighteousness of men," against all disregard of God in the conduct of life, as well as against all deviations from moral rectitude; and therefore, since no child of Adam can plead guiltless either of "ungodliness" or of "unrighteousness," to a greater or less extent it follows that every human being is involved in the awful sweep of this "wrath of God." There is a tendency among some critics to explain away all such language, as purely anthropathic, or as merely

which commit such things are worthy *of death, not only do the same, but have pleasure in them that do them.

A. D. co
* Deut. 17. 6.

accommodated from human feeling to the Divine nature; and some of the soundest divines think that they exhaust its legitimate application to God when they say it expresses 'the punitive justice of God,' or 'the calm, undeviating *purpose* of the Divine mind, which secures the connection between sin and misery.' (So *Hodge*). But "*wrath*"—whatever be meant by it in relation to God—is a *feeling*, not a *purpose;* nor can it, in any fair sense of the word, be identified with *justice.* Of *passion*, indeed—in the human sense of the term—there can be none in the Divine nature. But are we to strip the Divine nature of all that we mean by the word 'feeling?' Is there no such thing *essentially* as *love* in Him of whom it is said, "God is love?" Those who say so—alleging that all such language must be understood metaphorically, not metaphysically, and that all such ideas are regulative, rather than real in God—divest the Godhead of all that is fitted to awaken the affection of love in reasonable creatures. Straining after metaphysical accuracy, they dry up the springs of all that the Bible enjoins, and the human heart feels to be its own proper emotions, towards God. If God loves no object and no quality, nor is capable of dislike or displeasure against aught that is unlike Himself, how can He be capable even of approving or disapproving? And if not that, what *Personality*, that is worth the name, remains to the Godhead? 2. The apostle places the terrible truth, that the wrath of God is revealed from heaven against all ungodliness and unrighteousness of men, in the forefront of his argument on Justification by faith, in order that upon the basis of *universal condemnation* he may rear the edifice of a free, world-wide Salvation; nor can the Gospel be scripturally preached or embraced, save as the good news of salvation to those who are all equally "lost." 3. We must not magnify the supernatural Revelation which God has been pleased to make of Himself, through Abraham's family to the human race, at the expense of that elder and, in itself, lustrous Revelation which He has made to the whole family of man through the medium of their own nature and the creation around them. Without the latter, the former would have been impossible; and those who have not been favoured with the former will be without excuse, if they are deaf to the voice and blind to the glory of the latter. 4. Wilful resistance of light has a retributive tendency to blind the moral perceptions and weaken the capacity to apprehend and approve of truth and goodness; and thus is the soul prepared to surrender itself, to an indefinite extent, to error and sin. 5. Pride of wisdom, as it is a convincing evidence of the want of it, so it makes the attainment of it impossible (*v.* 22 ; and cf. Matt. xi. 25 ; 1 Cor. xiii. 18-20). 6. As idolatry, even in its most plausible forms, is the fruit of unwerthy views of the Godhead, so its natural effect is to vitiate and debase still further the religious conceptions; nor is there any depth of degradation too low and too revolting for men's ideas of the Godhead .to sink to, if only their natural temperament and the circumstances they are placed in be favourable to their unrestrained development. The apostle had Greece and Egypt in his eye when he penned verses 23-25. But the whole Paganisms of the East at this day attest its accuracy, from the more elaborate idolatry of India and the simpler and more stupid idolatry of China, down to the childish rudiments of nature-worship prevalent among the savage tribes. Alas! Christendom itself

furnishes a melancholy illustration of this truth ; the constant use of material images in the Church of Rome, and the materialistic and sensuous character of its entire service (to say nothing of the less offensive but stupider service of the Greek Church) debasing the religious ideas of millions of nominal Christians, and lowering the whole character and tone of Christianity as represented within their immense pale. 7. Moral corruption invariably follows religious debasement. The grossness of Pagan idolatry is only equalled by the revolting character and frightful extent of the immoralities which it fostered and consecrated. And so strikingly is this to be seen in all its essential features in the East at this day, that missionaries have frequently been accused by the natives of having forged the whole of the latter part of this chapter, as they could not believe that so accurate a description of themselves could have been written eighteen centuries ago. The kingdoms of Israel and Judah furnish a striking illustration of the inseparable connection between religion and morals. As the great sin of the kingdom of *Israel* lay in corrupting and debasing the worship of Jehovah, so the sins with which they were charged were mostly of the grosser kind—intemperance and sensuality: *Judah*, on the other hand, remaining faithful to the pure worship, were for a long time charged mostly with formality and hypocrisy; and only as they fell into the idolatries of the heathen around them did they sink into their vices. And may not a like distinction be observed between the two great divisions of Christendom—the Popish and the Protestant? To test this, we must not look to Popery, surrounded with, and more or less influenced by, the presence and power of Protestantism; nor to Protestantism under every sort of disadvantage, internal and external. But look at Romanism where it has unrestrained liberty to develop its true character, and see whether impurity does not there taint society to its core, pervading alike the highest and the lowest classes; and then look at Protestantism where it enjoys the same advantages, and see whether it be not marked by a comparatively high standard of social virtue. 8. To take pleasure in what is sinful and vicious for its own sake, and knowing it to be such, is the last and lowest stage of human recklessness. 'The innate principle of self-love (says *South*, in a sermon on the last verse of this chapter —we take the passage from *Wordsworth*), that very easily and often blinds a man as to any impartial reflection upon himself, yet for the most part leaves his eyes open enough to judge truly of the same thing *in his neighbour*, and to hate that *in others* which he allows and cherishes *in himself.* And, therefore, when it shall come to this, that he approves, embraces, and delights in sin as he observes it even in the person and practice of *other men*, this shows that the man is wholly transformed from the creature that God first made him; nay, that he has consumed those poor remainders of good that the sin of Adam left him; that he has worn off the very remote dispositions and possibilities to virtue; and, in a word, has turned grace first, and afterwards nature itself, out of doors.' Yet, 9. This knowledge can never be wholly extinguished in the breast of man. So long as reason remains to them, there is a still, small voice in the worst of men, protesting, in the name of the Power that implanted it, "that they which do such things are worthy of death."

2 THEREFORE thou art inexcusable, O man, whosoever thou art that
judgest: for wherein thou judgest another, thou condemnest thyself; for
2 thou that judgest doest the same things. But we are sure that the
judgment of God is according ^ato truth against them which commit such
3 things. And ^bthinkest thou this, O man, that judgest them which do
such things, and doest the same, that thou shalt escape the judgment of
4 God? Or despisest thou ^cthe riches of his goodness and forbearance
^dand long-suffering; ^enot knowing that the goodness of God leadeth thee
5 to repentance? But after thy hardness and impenitent heart ^ftreasurest
up unto thyself wrath against the day of wrath and revelation of the
6 righteous judgment of God; who ^gwill render to every man according
7 to his deeds: to ^hthem who by patient continuance in well-doing seek
8 for glory and honour and immortality, eternal life; but ⁱunto them that

A. D 60.
CHAP. z.
^a Isa. 25. 19.
21.
2 Thes. 4.6.
^b Pro. 11. 21.
^c Eph. 1. 7.
^d Ex. 34. 6.
^e 2 Pet. 3. 9
^f Jas. 5. 3.
^g Matt. 16.27.
^h 2 Cor. 4. 17.
Jude 21.
Rev. 2. 7.
ⁱ Isa. 3. 11.
2 Thes. 2.
12.

CHAP. II.—1-29. THE JEW UNDER CONDEMNA-
TION NO LESS THAN THE GENTILE. From those
without, the apostle now turns to those *within*,
the pale of Revealed Religion—the self-righteous
Jews, who looked down upon the uncovenanted
heathen as beyond the pale of God's mercies—
deeming themselves, as the chosen people, secure,
however inconsistent their life might be. Alas!
what multitudes wrap themselves up in like fatal
confidence who occupy the corresponding position
in the Christian Church.

*Expostulation with the Jew for condemning and
contemning the Gentiles—The final judgment will
turn on character alone, there being no respect of
persons with God* (1-11). 1. **Therefore** [Διό]. The
connection is not with the immediately preceding
verse (as *Grotius, Tholuck, Hodge,* &c.), but with
the whole preceding argument, and particularly
the sweeping statement of ch. i. 18—*q. d.,* 'If the
wrath of God is revealed from heaven against all
ungodliness and unrighteousness of men, the Jew
has no more any righteous standing before God
than the Gentile, on whom, therefore, it ill becomes
him to look down with contempt.' (So *Meyer,* &c.)
**thou art inexcusable, O man, whosoever thou art
that judgest.** It is quite unnatural to suppose
that the apostle is here still treating of the Gentiles
—inveighing against the better class of them for
condemning the more vicious (as *Calvin*), or against
their magistrates (as *Grotius*)—and equally so to
suppose that he has neither the Jew nor the
Gentile particularly in view, but self-righteous
condemners and despisers of others in general (as
Beza). Nothing can well be more evident than
that, having finished his description of the "ungodliness and unrighteousness" of the Gentiles—
against which he had said that "the wrath of
God is revealed from heaven" (ch. i. 18)—he is
now proceeding to deal with the other great division of mankind—the Jews. (So *Bengel, Fritzsche,*
and all the best expositors.) And it has been
well observed, as justifying this view of a complete change in the party addressed, that whereas in describing the character of the Gentiles
the apostle uses the third person plural (" they "),
he uses throughout all this chapter (save in
the digression of *vv.* 12-16), the second person
singular (" thou ") in dealing with those who
looked down upon the Gentiles. **for wherein** [ἐν
ᾧ]. This may either mean simply, 'in that' [ἐν
τούτῳ ὅτι], 'inasmuch as' (so *Erasmus, Beza,
Mehring,* &c.), or, as in our version, 'in that
wherein,' as in ch. xiv. 22. (So the Vulgate and
Calvin [in quo], *Luther,* and other good interpreters.) Probably the former is the right
shade of signification, since the Jews are not
charged with precisely the same sins as the Gentiles, but with being condemners of others, whilst
themselves stood chargeable with sins equally

offensive to God. **thou judgest another** [τὸν
ἕτερον]—'the other;' meaning, the other party referred to, the Gentiles, **thou condemnest thyself;
for thou that judgest doest the same things.**
Beyond doubt the apostle, in penning this verse,
had our Lord's precept in view, "Judge not, that
ye be not judged . . . And why beholdest thou
the mote," &c. (Matt. vii. 1-3). 2. **But we are
sure** [Οἴδαμεν δὲ]—'But we know;' it is a recognized principle of all true religion, **that the judgment of God is according to truth against them
which commit such things** — whether they be
Jews or Gentiles. 3. **And thinkest** [Λογίζῃ]—
'reckonest' thou this, **O man, that judgest them
which do such things, and doest the same, that
thou shalt escape the judgment of God?** Cf. Matt.
iii. 9, "And think not to say within yourselves,
We have Abraham to our father," &c. 4. **Or
despisest thou the riches of his goodness and**
('his') **forbearance and** ('his') **long-suffering;
not knowing that the goodness of God leadeth**
(or 'is leading') **thee to repentance**—is designed,
as it is adapted, to do so. It is a sad mark of
depravity when all that is designed and fitted to
melt, only hardens the heart (cf. 2 Pet. iii. 9; Eccl.
viii. 11). 5. **But after thy hardness and impenitent
heart treasurest up.** Several critics follow *Lachmann's* punctuation here, making this to be but a
continuation of the preceding sentence—thus,
'not knowing that the goodness of God is leading
thee to repentance, and that after thy hardness
and impenitent heart thou art treasuring up,' &c.
But this seems to us no improvement. **unto thyself wrath against** [ἐν]—rather, 'in,' **the day of
wrath**—*i. e.,* 'to come on thee in the day of wrath.'
and ('of the') **revelation of the righteous judgment of God.** The awful idea here expressed is,
that the sinner is amassing, like hoarded treasure,
an ever-accumulating stock of Divine wrath, to
burst upon him in the day of the revelation of
the righteous judgment of God. And of whom is
this said? Not of monstrous sinners, but of those
who boasted of their purity of faith and life. 6.
**Who will render to every man according to his
deeds.** This great truth (taken from Prov. xxiv.
12, as in the LXX.), which is the key to the whole
reasoning of this chapter, is in the next four verses
applied to the two classes into which all mankind
will at the great day be found to have ranged themselves, showing that the final judgment will turn
upon *character* alone. 7. **To them who by patient continuance in** (or 'patience in') **well-doing**
—referring to the *enduring* character of a truly
holy life: cf. Luke viii. 15, "That on the good
ground are they which in an honest and good heart,
having heard the word of God, keep it, and bring
forth fruit *with patience.*" **seek for glory and
honour and immortality** [ἀφθαρσίαν]—'incorruption.' **eternal life; 8. But unto them that are con-

are contentious, and do not obey the truth, but obey unrighteousness,
9 indignation and wrath, tribulation and anguish, upon every soul of man
10 that doeth evil, of the ʲ Jew first, and also of the ¹ Gentile; but ᵏ glory,
honour, and peace, to every man that worketh good, to the Jew first, and
also to the ²Gentile.
11, For there is ˡ no respect of persons with God. For as many as have
12 sinned without law shall also perish without law; and as many as have
13 sinned in the law shall be judged by the law, for ᵐ not the hearers of the
14 law *are* just before God, but the doers of the law shall be justified. For
when the Gentiles, which have not the law, do by nature the things contained in the law, these, having not the law, are a law unto themselves:
15 which show the work of the law written in their hearts, ³ their conscience
also bearing witness, and *their* thoughts ⁴ the mean while accusing or else
16 excusing one another, in ⁿ the day when God shall judge the secrets of
men ° by Jesus Christ according to my gospel.
17 Behold, ᵖ thou art called a Jew, and restest �q in the law, ʳ and makest

A. D. 60.
ʲ 1 Pet. 4. 17.
¹ Greek.
ᵏ 1 Pet. 1. 7.
² Greek.
ˡ Job 34. 19.
Luke 20. 21.
ᵐ Jas. 1. 22.
³ Or, the conscience witnessing with them.
⁴ Or. between themselves.
ⁿ Rev. 20. 12.
° John 5. 22.
ᵖ ch. 9. 6.
q Mic. 3. 11.
ʳ John 8. 41.

tentious [Τοῖς δὲ ἐξ ἐριθείας]—'But to the men of strife,' or 'contention' (compare John xviii. 37, "Every one *that is of* the truth, heareth my voice.") The reference is to the *acrimony* with which the Gospel had been resisted by the ruling party among the Jews, and this as springing from a deep-rooted enmity to the truth; of which the apostle could speak from bitter experience (see Acts xiii. 44-46; xvii. 5, 13; xviii. 6, 12; and cf. 1 Thess. ii. 15, 16). **and do not obey the truth, but obey unrighteousness** [ἀπειθοῦσιν μὲν τ. ἀληθείᾳ, πειθομένοις δὲ τ. ἀδικίᾳ]. The grammatical form of these two clauses shows that they are but the negative and positive sides of one statement—'But to the men of strife, and who, instead of obeying the truth, obey unrighteousness;' **indignation and wrath.** The right order of these two words is beyond doubt the reverse of this, 'wrath and indignation' [θυμὸς καὶ ὀργή, is only in D***—a corrector of the ninth or tenth century—K L, and several cursives, in the Peshito Syriac, and in *Chrysostom* and *Theodoret.* But ὀργ. καὶ θυμ. in אA B (C is defective here) D*E G, and some cursives; several versions, and most fathers—*Lachm., Tisch.,* and *Treg.* rightly adopt this latter reading]. **9. Tribulation and anguish.** The first of these pairs, 'wrath and indignation,' are in the bosom of a sin-avenging God—the former expressing God's 'settled displeasure' against evil-doers, the latter, the uprising of this; the next pair, "Tribulation and anguish," are the effects of those awful affections of the Divine Mind on and in the sinner himself. **upon every soul of man that doeth evil, of the Jew first**—first in perdition, if unfaithful; but, if obedient to the truth, first in salvation; as in the next verse is expressed. **10. But glory, honour, and peace, to every man that worketh good, to the Jew first, and also to the Gentile. 11. For there is no respect of persons with God.**

But how, might the Jew ask, can Jew and Gentile be judged by the same standard of *character* alone, when the one has a written Revelation of duty, and the other wants it? The following digression is intended to meet this.

Jew and Gentile will be judged by the standard of duty which they respectively possess (12-16). **12. For as many as have sinned** [ἥμαρτον]—'For as many as sinned' here below; not 'that sinned at all,' but 'that are *found in sin*' (as *Bengel* rightly notes) at the judgment of the great day. That this is the sense, the whole context clearly shows. **without law**—that is, without the advantage of a positive Revelation; **shall also perish without**
203

law—exempt from the charge of rejecting or disregarding it. Their character will meet with its appropriate award, and on nothing else will the judgment of such turn. **and as many as have sinned** ('as sinned') **in the law**—within the pale of a positive, written Revelation, **shall be judged by the law**—tried and treated by the higher standard of that written Revelation. **13. For not the hearers of the law**—that is, the mere possessors of it, **are just before God, but the doers of the law shall be justified. 14. For when the Gentiles, &c.**—*q. d.,* 'As touching the Jews, in whose ears the written law is continually resounding, the condemnation of as many of them as are found sinners at the last involves no difficulty; but even as respects the heathen, when they **which have not the law**—who are strangers to the law in its positive and written form, **do by nature the things contained in the law**—abstaining from some of the things which are condemned, and practising some of the things enjoined by universal morality, **these, having not the law, are a law unto themselves: 15. Which show the work of the law written in their hearts**—deeply engraven on their moral nature, **their conscience also bearing witness** [συμμαρτυρούσης αὐτῶν τ. συνειδήσεως]—'their conscience blending its witness,' *i. e.,* with the law, **and their thoughts the mean while** [μεταξὺ ἀλλήλων: cf. Acts xv. 9]—rather, 'and their thoughts between themselves' (as in *marg.*), or, 'one with another,' **accusing or else excusing** ('them'). Since there is a voice within the breasts even of the heathen which witnesses for righteousness and against iniquity, condemning or commending them by turns, according as they violate or obey its stern dictates, their final condemnation for all the sin in which they live and die will carry its dreadful echo in their own breasts. **16. In the day when** [the received reading, ὅτε, is better than ᾗ, which *Lachmann* adopts] **God shall judge the secrets of men** (cf. Eccl. xii. 14; 1 Cor. iv. 5); here specially referring to the unfathomed depths of hypocrisy in the self-righteous, whom the apostle had to deal with: **by Jesus Christ according to my gospel**—my teaching as a preacher of the Gospel (cf. Acts xvii. 31). This whole verse seems clearly to be the conclusion of the unfinished statement of *v.* 12.

Expostulation with the Jew resumed and concluded (17-29). **17. Behold** ['Ἴδε]—but the true reading is beyond doubt, 'But if,' [Εἰ δὲ. Such *Itacisms* are common in ancient MSS.] **thou art called a Jew, and restest in the law, and makest**

18 thy boast of God, and *'knowest *his* will, and ⁵approvest the things that
19 are more excellent, being instructed out of the law; and art confident
    that thou thyself art a guide of the blind, a light of them which are in
20 darkness, an instructor of the foolish, a teacher of babes, ᶠwhich hast
21 the form of knowledge and of the truth in the law. Thou *therefore
    which teachest another, teachest thou not thyself? thou that preachest a
22 man should not steal, dost thou steal? thou that sayest a man should
    not commit adultery, dost thou commit adultery? thou that abhorrest
23 idols, *dost thou commit sacrilege? thou that makest thy boast of the
24 law, through breaking the law dishonourest thou God? For the name
    of God is blasphemed among the Gentiles through you, as it *is
    written.
25   For *circumcision verily profiteth, if thou keep the law: but if thou
    be a breaker of the law, thy circumcision is made uncircumcision.
26 Therefore ʸif the uncircumcision keep the righteousness of the law, shall
27 not his uncircumcision be counted for circumcision? And shall not

A. D. 60.
ᶜ Deut. 4. 8. Neh. 9. 13, 14. Ps. 147. 19, 20. Luke 12.47. John 13. 17. 1 Cor. 8.1,2.
⁵ Or, triest the things that differ.
ᵗ 2 Tim. 3. 5. ᵘ Matt. 23. 3. ᵛ Mal. 3. 8. ʷ 2 Sam. 12. 14. Isa. 52. 5. Eze. 36. 20.
ˣ Gal. 5. 3.
ʸ Acts 10. 34.

thy boast of God, 18. And knowest his will, and
approvest the things that are more excellent
[δοκιμάζεις τὰ διαφέροντα]—or (as in *marg.*), 'triest
the things that differ,' (see Phil. i. 10, and *marg.*)
But as the former is the natural result of the
latter action, it probably is the thought intended.
being instructed out of the law; 19. And art
confident that thou thyself art a guide of the
blind, a light of them which are in darkness,
20. An instructor of the foolish, a teacher of
babes, which hast the form [τ. μόοφωσιν]—or,
'shaping out,' of knowledge and of the truth in
the law—not being left, like the heathen, to vague
conjecture of Divine things, but favoured with
definite and precise information from heaven. 21.
Thou therefore which teachest another, teachest
thou not thyself? thou that preachest a man
should not steal, dost thou steal? 22. Thou that
sayest a man should not commit adultery, dost
thou commit adultery? thou that abhorrest idols
—as the Jews certainly did, even after their captivity, though bent on them before, dost thou
commit sacrilege? [ἱεροσυλεῖς]—not, as some excellent interpreters, 'dost thou rob idol temples?'
(which the word would naturally mean in Pagan
usage,) but 'dost thou profane sacred things?'
The other the Jews did not, but this they too
frequently committed (see Neh. xiii. 10-12; Mal. i.
13, 14; iii. 8, 9; Matt. xxi. 12, 13). 23. Thou that
makest thy boast of the law, through breaking
the law dishonourest thou God? 24. For the
name of God is blasphemed among the Gentiles
through you, as it is written—in your own Scriptures. (See 2 Sam. xii. 14; Isa. lii. 5; Ezek. xxxvi.
20, 23.)
    25. For circumcision verily profiteth. To be a
circumcised Jew, born within the pale of revealed
Religion, overshadowed from infancy by Divine
ordinances, and daily familiarized with the most
quickening, elevating, and sanctifying truths—this
is an advantage not to be overestimated (ch. iii.
1, 2; ix. 4, 5). if thou keep the law—if thou yield
thyself to these gracious influences, and the light
that shines around thee be reflected in thy character and walk: but if thou be a breaker of the
law—if thy Judaism be all outside, thy circumcision is made uncircumcision—in that case
thou art in the sight of God an uncircumcised
heathen. 26. Therefore if the uncircumcision
keep the righteousness of the law [τὰ δικαιώ-
ματα (see on ch. v. 16)]—'the righteous precepts
of the law.' shall not his uncircumcision be
counted for circumcision? The general principle here expressed is clear enough, that as circumcision will not protect the unrighteous from

the consequences of their bad life, so the want of
it will not invalidate the claims of true righteousness. But whether the apostle is here putting a real
or only a hypothetical case, is a question of some
difficulty, on which critics are not agreed. Those
who take the apostle to mean such a keeping of
the law as justifies before God—a complete and
perfect obedience to the requirements of the moral
law—pronounce the case here supposed a purely
hypothetical one. (So *Alford, Hodge*, &c.) But
as that impossibility was just as true of Jews as
of Gentiles, it seems wide of the mark. To us it
appears that it is *reality* in personal religion which
the apostle has here in view; and that what he
affirms is, that as circumcision—considered as the
mere external badge of the true Religion—will not
compensate for the want of subjection in heart
and life to the law of God, so neither will the
absence of circumcision invalidate the standing
before God of the man whose heart and life are
in conformity with the spirit of His law. But
this suggests another question. Is such conformity
in heart and life to the law of God—or such
personal religion as He will recognize—possible
without the pale of Revealed Religion? Now,
though the apostle probably had no one class of
mankind in view while penning this verse, it is
scarcely natural to suppose that he was putting a
case which he knew could never be realized.
What *sort* of case, then, would sufficiently meet his
statement? That he was thinking of heathen men
who 'act up to the light of nature,' as people
speak—and as *Grotius, Olshausen,* and others suppose here—we cannot think; for this is plainly
inconsistent with the apostle's own teaching.
But just as in the days of Melchizedek and Job
men were found beyond the pale of the Abrahamic
covenant, yet not without a measure of revealed
light, so might there occur innumerable cases of
heathens—especially after the Babylonish captivity—benefiting so far by the dispersed Jews as
to attain, though but in rude outline, to right
views of God and of His service, even though
not open proselytes to the Jewish Religion. Such
cases—without referring to that of *Cornelius* (Acts
x.), who, outside the external pale of God's covenant, had come to the knowledge of the truths
contained in it, manifested the grace of the
covenant without the seal of it, and exemplified
the character and walk of Abraham's children,
though not called by the name of Abraham—such
cases seem sufficient to warrant and explain all
that the apostle here says, without resorting to
the supposition of a purely hypothetical case.
27. And shall [not] uncircumcision which is by

204

uncircumcision which is by nature, if it fulfil the law, judge ^zthee, who
28 by the letter and circumcision dost transgress the law? For ^ahe is not a
Jew which is one outwardly; neither *is that* circumcision which is out-
29 ward in the flesh: but he *is* a Jew ^bwhich is one inwardly; and ^ccircum-
cision *is that* of the heart, ^din the spirit, *and* not in the letter; whose
praise *is* not of men, but of God.

3 WHAT advantage then hath the Jew? or what profit *is there* of
2 circumcision? Much every way: chiefly, because that unto ^athem were
3 committed the oracles of God. For what if ^bsome did not believe? shall
4 their ^cunbelief make the faith of God without effect? God ^dforbid: yea,
let ^eGod be true, but every ^fman a liar; as it is written, ^gThat thou
mightest be justified in thy sayings, and mightest overcome when thou
art judged.

	A. D. 60.
z	Matt. 12. 41.
a	Matt. 3. 9.
	John 8. 39.
	Gal. 6. 15.
b	John 1. 47.
c	Col. 2. 11.
d	ch. 7. 6.

	CHAP. 3.
a	Deut. 4. 7.
b	Heb. 4. 2.
c	Num. 23. 19.
d	Job 40. 8.
e	John 3. 33.
f	Ps. 62. 9.
g	Ps. 51. 4.

nature—or, 'the natural uncircumcision,' **if it fulfil the law, judge thee.** If this verse is but a continuation of the question in the preceding verse (which the Greek most naturally suggests, and which several good critics prefer), the whole question will run thus:—'shall not his uncircumcision be counted for circumcision, and the natural uncircumcision, fulfilling the law, judge thee,' &c. But it is fully more agreeable to New Testament usage to regard them (with our version) as two distinct questions, of which the latter is certainly an advance upon the former. **who by** (or 'through') **the letter and circumcision dost transgress the law**—that is, in spite of those two fences, "the letter" of Revelation, "and circumcision," the badge of it, dost break 'through' both, and live inconsistently. **28. For he is not a Jew which is one outwardly; neither is that circumcision which is outward in the flesh: 29. But he is a Jew which is one inwardly; and circumcision is that of the heart, in the spirit, and not in the letter; whose praise is not of men, but of God.** The name of "Jew," and the rite of "circumcision," were designed as outward symbols of a separation from the irreligious and ungodly world unto holy devotedness. in heart and life to the God of salvation. Where this is realized, the signs are full of significance; but where it is not, they are worse than useless.

Remarks.—1. Amidst all the inequalities of religious opportunity measured out to men, and the mysterious bearing of this upon their character and destiny for eternity, the same great principles of judgment, in a form suited to their respective discipline, will be applied to all, and perfect equity will be seen to reign throughout every stage of the Divine administration. 2. Of the three deep foundations on which all Revealed Religion reposes, we had two in the first chapter of this Epistle —the *Physics* and the *Metaphysics* of Natural Theology (ch. i. 19, 20). Here we have the third—the *Ethics* of Natural Theology. The testimony of these two passages is to the theologian invaluable, while in the breast of every teachable Christian it wakens such deep echoes as are inexpressibly solemn and precious. 3. High religious professions are a fearful aggravation of the inconsistencies of such as make them; and the instinctive disgust which they beget in those who flatter themselves that because they make no religious profession they cannot at least be charged with hypocrisy—though that affords no excuse for shameless irreligion—is but an echo of the Divine abhorrence of those who "have a form of godliness, but deny the power thereof." 4. As no external privileges or badges of discipleship will shield the unholy from the wrath of God, so neither will the want of them shut out from the kingdom of heaven such as have experienced

without them that change of heart which the seals of God's covenant were designed to mark. In the sight of the great Searcher of hearts, the Judge of quick and dead, the renovation of the character in heart and life is all in all. In view of this, have not all baptized, sacramented disciples of the Lord Jesus, who "profess that they know God, but in works deny Him," need to tremble—who, under the guise of friends, are "the enemies of the cross of Christ?"

CHAP. III. 1-20.—JEWISH OBJECTIONS ANSWERED—THE JEW, ACCORDING TO HIS OWN SCRIPTURES, UNDER LIKE CONDEMNATION WITH THE GENTILE.

Jewish objections answered (1-8).—First Objection: 1. **What advantage then hath the Jew? or what profit is there of circumcision?** 'If the final judgment will turn solely on the state of the heart, and this may be as good in the Gentile *without* as in the Jew *within* the sacred enclosure of God's covenant, what better are we Jews for all our advantages?' *Answer:* 2. **Much every way: chiefly, because** [πρῶτον μὲν γὰρ—see *Donaldson*, 618—ὅτι] —rather, 'First, that.' Our version here (following *Beza*) departs from this the proper meaning of the word, rendering it "chiefly," no doubt, because no 'second' and 'third' advantages of the Jew follow. But there was no need. It suited the apostle's argument to dwell on this particular advantage of the Jew, and the rest could easily be imagined. **that unto them were committed** (or, 'they were entrusted with') **the oracles of God** [τὰ λόγια τ. Θεοῦ]. This remarkable expression (which the LXX. use in Num. xxiv. 4, 16; Ps. xii. 6; xviii. 30), denoting 'Divine communications' in general [θεόσφατα], is transferred to the sacred Scriptures, to express their oracular, divinely authoritative character. In this sense Stephen, in his address before the Sanhedrim, calls them "the lively (or 'living') oracles" [λόγια ζῶντα] (Acts vii. 38). 3. **For what if some did not believe** —or 'proved unfaithful.' It is the unbelief of the great body of the nation which the apostle points at; but as it sufficed for his argument to put the supposition thus gently, he uses this word "some" to soften prejudice. **shall their unbelief make the faith of God without effect?**—'invalidate,' or 'nullify, the faithfulness of God?' 4. **God forbid** [μὴ γένοιτο]—'Let it not be:' *q. d.*, 'Away with such a thought:' an expression not unknown to later Greek, and in the LXX. used in Gen. xliv. 17; Josh. xxii. 29 [=וְחָלִלָה], a favourite expression of our apostle, when he would not only repudiate a supposed consequence of his doctrine, but express his abhorrence of it. **yea, let God be true, but every man a liar; as it is written** (Ps. li. 4), **That thou mightest be justified in thy sayings, and mightest overcome when thou art judged.**

5   But if our unrighteousness commend the righteousness of God, what
shall we say? *Is* God unrighteous who taketh vengeance? (I [h] speak as
6, a man) God forbid : for then [i] how shall God judge the world? For if
7 the truth of God hath more abounded through my lie unto his glory;
8 why yet am I also judged as a sinner? and not *rather*, (as we be slanderously reported, and as some affirm that we say,) Let [j] us do evil, that good
may come? whose damnation is just.
9   What then? are we better *than they?* No, in no wise: for we have
before [1] proved both Jews and Gentiles, that [k] they are all under sin;
10, as it is written, [l] There is none righteous, no, not one: there is none that
11, understandeth, there is none that seeketh after God. They are all gone
12 out of the way, they are together become unprofitable; there is none that
13 doeth good, no, not one. Their [m] throat *is* an open sepulchre: with their
14, tongues they have used deceit: the [n] poison of asps *is* under their lips:
15, whose [o] mouth *is* full of cursing and bitterness: their [p] feet *are* swift to
16, shed blood: destruction and misery *are* in their ways; and the way
17, of peace have they not known: there [q] is no fear of God before
18, their eyes.

A. D. 60.
[h] 1 Cor. 9. 8. Gal. 3. 15.
[i] Gen. 18. 25. Job 34. 17. Ps. 9. 8.
[j] ch. 5. 20. ch. 6. 1, 15. Jude 4.
[1] charged. ch. 1. 28.
[k] Gal. 3. 22.
[l] Ps. 14. 1
[m] Ps. 5. 9. Jer. 5. 16. Matt. 23. 27, 28.
[n] Ps. 140. 3.
[o] Ps. 10. 7.
[p] Pro. 1. 16.
[q] Gen. 20. 11. Ps. 36. 1. Luke 23. 40.

The apostle here follows the LXX. in place of the Hebrew and our own version of the Psalm—"when thou judgest." But the general sentiment is the same in both—that we are to vindicate the righteousness of God at whatever expense to ourselves.

Second Objection: **5. But if our unrighteousness commend** [συνίστησιν] — 'establisheth,' or 'maketh manifest' (as in ch. v. 8), **the righteousness of God, what shall we say? Is God unrighteous who taketh vengeance?** [ὁ ἐπιφερων τ. ὀργήν]—'who inflicteth,' or 'is to inflict wrath;' *i. e.*, who is the destined Judge. **I speak as a man**: *q. d.*, 'At this rate the more faithless we are, so much the more illustrious will the fidelity of God appear; and in that case, for Him to take vengeance on us for our unfaithfulness would be (to speak as men profanely do) unrighteousness in God.' *Answer:* **6. God forbid: for then how shall God judge the world?**—*q. d.*, 'Far from us be such a thought; for that would strike down all future judgment.' **7. For if the truth of God hath more abounded through my lie**—*i. e.*, If His faithfulness is rendered all the more conspicuous by my want of it. **unto his glory; why yet am I also judged as a sinner? 8. And** [why should we] **not** [rather say], (as we be **slanderously reported, and as some affirm that we say,) Let us do evil, that good may come? whose damnation** (or 'condemnation') **is just**—a further illustration of the same sentiment: *q. d.,* 'Such reasoning amounts to this —which, indeed, we who preach salvation by free grace are slanderously accused of teaching—that the more evil we do, the more glory will redound to God: a damnable principle.' Thus the apostle, instead of refuting this principle, thinks it enough to hold it up to execration, as one that shocks the moral sense.

That the Jew is under like condemnation with the Gentile, proved from his own Scriptures (9-19). **9. What then? are we better** [than they?]—'Have we the pre-eminence?' 'Do we excel?' [προεχόμεθα, *præcellimus*—the middle used like the active]. **No, in no wise** [οὐ πάντως=οὐδαμῶς, for πάντως οὐ] (1 Cor. xvi. 12, *Winer,* § 61). They had, indeed, that vast advantage over the heathen, that they had the oracles of God to teach them better; but since this was not effectual, it only aggravated their guilt. **for we have before proved** [προαιτιασάμεθα]. This word is rendered 'arraigned' by the Vulgate [præcausati sumus], *Beza* [criminati sumus], *Calvin* [constituimus], &c. But the pre-

ferable sense seems to be, 'brought home the charge,' or (as in our version) 'proved;' referring to the reasoning of ch. i. and ii. So *Erasmus* [ante causis redditis ostendimus], *Luther* [erwiesen], *Bengel* [convicimus], &c. **both Jews and Gentiles, that they are all under sin; 10. As it is written,** &c. The passages which here follow—from the Psalms, the Proverbs, and Isaiah—were indeed suggested by particular manifestations of human depravity occurring under his own eye; but as this only showed what man, when unrestrained, is in his present condition, they were quite pertinent to the apostle's purpose. The passages are given in substance rather than to the letter. **There is none righteous, no, not one: 11. There is none that understandeth, there is none that seeketh after God. 12. They are all gone out of the way, they are together become unprofitable; there is none that doeth good, no, not one** (Ps. xiv. 1-3; liii. 1-3). From generals the apostle now comes to particulars, culling from different parts of Scripture passages which speak of depravity as it affects *the different members of the body;* as if to show more affectingly how, "from the sole of the foot even to the head, there is no soundness" in us. **13. Their throat is an open sepulchre** (Ps. v. 9): *q. d.,* 'What proceeds out of their heart, and finds vent in speech and action through the throat, is like the pestilential breath of an open grave;' **with their tongues they have used deceit** (Ps. v. 9)—*q. d.,* 'That tongue which is man's glory (Ps. xvi. 9; lvii. 8) is prostituted to the purposes of deception;' **the poison of asps is under their lips** (Ps. cxl. 3)—*q. d.,* 'Those lips which should "drop as an honeycomb," and "feed many," and "give thanks unto His name" (Song iv. 11; Prov. x. 21; Heb. xiii. 15), are employed to secrete deadly poison :' **14. Whose mouth is full of cursing and bitterness** (Ps. x. 7)—*q. d.,* 'That mouth which should be "most sweet" (Song v. 16), being "set on fire of hell" (Jas. iii. 6), is filled with burning wrath against those whom it should only bless:' **15. Their feet are swift to shed blood** (Prov. i. 16; Isa. lix. 7)—*q. d.,* 'Those feet which should "run the way of God's commandments" (Ps. cxix. 32) are employed to conduct men to deeds of darkest crime:' **16. Destruction and misery are in their ways; 17. And the way of peace have they not known** (Isa. lix. 7, 8). These two last clauses are a supplementary statement about men's *ways,* suggested by what had been said about the "feet," and they express the

19 Now we know that what things soever the law saith, it saith to them who are under the law; that ʳevery mouth may be stopped, and ˢall the 20 world may become ²guilty before God. Therefore ᵗby the deeds of the law there shall no flesh be justified in his sight: for ᵘby the law *is* the knowledge of sin.
21 But now ᵛthe righteousness of God without the law is manifested, 22 being witnessed by the Law and the Prophets; even the righteousness of God *which is* by faith of Jesus Christ unto all and upon all them that

A. D. 60.

ʳ Eze. 16. 63.
ˢ ch. 2. 2.
² Or, subject to the judgment of God
ᵗ Ps. 143. 2.
ᵘ ch. 7. 7.
ᵛ Heb. 11. 4.

mischief and misery which men scatter in their path, instead of that peace which, as strangers to it themselves, they cannot diffuse. There is no fear of God before their eyes (Ps. xxxvi. 1)— *q. d.,* 'Did the eyes but "see Him who is invisible" (Heb. xi. 27), a reverential awe of Him with whom we have to do would chasten every joy and lift the soul out of its deepest depressions; but to all this the natural man is a stranger.' How graphic is this picture of human depravity finding its way through each several organ of the body into the life; and yet how small a part of the "desperate wickedness" that is *within* (Jer. xvii. 9) "proceedeth *out of* the heart of man!" (Mark vii. 21-23; Ps. xix. 12.)

19. Now we know that what things soever the law (that is, the Scripture, regarded as a law of duty: cf. John x. 34) **saith, it saith to them who are under the law** (and of course, therefore, to the Jews); **that every mouth** (that would open itself in self-justification) **may be stopped, and all the world may become guilty before God** [ὑπόδικος γένηται]—'come under the judgment of God,' or stand condemned at His bar.
The grand Inference from all the foregoing reasonings now stated (20). **20. Therefore by the deeds of the law**—by compliance with its requirements, **there shall no flesh be justified**—that is, 'be held and treated as righteous,' as is plain from the whole scope and strain of the argument, **in his sight**—at His bar (Ps. cxliii. 2): **for by the law is the knowledge of sin.** (See on ch. iv. 15; vii. 7; 1 John iii. 4.)
Rémarks.—1. The place here assigned to the Scriptures is worthy of special notice. In answer to the question, "What advantage hath the Jew? or, What profit is there of circumcision?" modern ritualists of every description would have pointed to the priesthood and the temple, with all its imposing ritual, as the glory of the ancient Economy. But in the apostle's esteem, "the Oracles of God" were the jewel of the ancient Church, from the knowledge of which springs all enlightened and acceptable worship of God. 2. God's Eternal Purposes and man's Free Agency, as also the doctrine of Salvation by Grace and that of the unchanging Obligations of God's Law, have in every age been subjected to the charge of inconsistency by those who will bow to no truth which their own reason cannot fathom. But amidst all the clouds and darkness which in this present state envelop the Divine administration and many of the truths of the Bible, such broad and deep principles as are here laid down, and which shine in their own lustre, will be found the sheet-anchor of our faith. "Let God be true, and every man a liar;" and as for such advocates of Salvation by grace as say, "Let us do evil, that good may come"—"their damnation is just." 3. How broad and deep does the apostle in this Section lay the foundations of his great doctrine of Justification by Free Grace—in the disorder of man's whole nature, the consequent universality of human guilt, the condemnation of the whole world, by reason of the breach of Divine law, and the im-

possibility of justification before God by obedience to that violated law! Only when these humiliating conclusions are accepted and felt, are we in a condition to appreciate and embrace the Grace of the Gospel, next to be opened up.

21-31.—GOD'S JUSTIFYING RIGHTEOUSNESS, THE GRAND DIVINE REMEDY—SOME OF ITS PROPERTIES—INFERENCES FROM THE DOCTRINE, AND AN OBJECTION ANSWERED.
First: *God's Justifying Righteousness is alike new and old* (21). **21. But now**—[Νυνὶ δὲ]. We may view this either as a particle of *transition* to a new stage of the argument (as *Fritzsche, Meyer, de Wette,* and *Alford* take it) or as a particle of *time,* to mark the bright contrast between the dim perception of this truth under the Law and the full manifestation of it "*now*" under the Gospel (as *Grotius, Bengel, Tholuck, Philippi,* and *Hodge* understand it). But these two ideas, though quite different, are both so very natural, that whichever of them came up first would almost certainly suggest the other. **the righteousness of God** (see on ch. i. 17) **without the law**—that righteousness to which our obedience to the law contributes nothing whatever (v. 28; Gal. ii. 16), **is manifested** [πεφανέρωται]—'hath been manifested,' **being witnessed by the Law and the Prophets** — being attested by the Old Testament Scriptures themselves. Thus this justifying righteousness is at once *new,* as only now fully disclosed, and *old,* as predicted and foreshadowed in the ancient Scriptures.

Second: *This Righteousness is absolutely gratuitous, and for all believers* (22-24). **22. Even the righteousness of God [which is] by faith of Jesus Christ**—that is, by faith *in* Him (the genitive of the Object of faith), **unto all and upon all them that believe** [εἰς π. ἐπὶ καὶ πάντας—the three last of these words are wanting in א, though supplied by the corrector C, about the seventh contury, and in B and C, in the Thebaic and some other of the versions; and they are omitted by one or two Greek fathers; but they are found in all the other Uncial MSS., in the Vulgate and both the Syriac versions, and in most Greek fathers; and as they were far more likely to be omitted from the genuine text, as superfluous, than to be foisted in where they had no place, there can hardly be any doubt of their genuineness. *Lachmann* and *Tregelles* exclude them; but nearly all good critics pronounce in favour of them]. It is far-fetched to understand 'unto all of the Jews' and 'upon all of the Gentiles'—as some of the fathers did, whom *Bengel* follows. Yet it is hardly satisfactory to regard the two statements as but an emphatic reiteration of the same thing—as *Tholuck* and others do. The shade of difference between them seems to be this, that the righteousness which is by faith of Jesus Christ is *extended* "unto all," and *rests* "upon all them that believe," whether Jews or Gentiles. Thus emphatically does the apostle proclaim the great truth, that all believers, without distinction or exception, are put in possession of this gratuitous justification, purely by faith in

23 believe; for ^wthere is no difference: for ^xall have sinned, and come short
24 of the glory of God; being justified freely ^yby his grace through the
25 redemption that is in Christ Jesus: whom God hath ³set forth to ^zbe a
propitiation through faith in his blood, to declare his righteousness for
26 the ⁴remission of sins that are past, through the forbearance of God; to
declare, *I say*, at this time his righteousness: that he might be just, and
the justifier of him which believeth in Jesus.
27 Where ^a*is* boasting then? It is excluded. By what law? of works?
28 Nay; but by the law of faith. Therefore we conclude ^bthat a man is

A. D. 60.	
^w Col. 3. 11.	
^x Gal. 3. 22.	
^y Eph. 2. 8.	
³ Or. fore-ordained.	
^z Lev. 16. 15.	
⁴ Or. passing over.	
^a 1 Cor. 1. 29.	
^b Gal. 2. 16.	

Christ Jesus. for there is no difference: 23. For all have sinned—'For all sinned' [ἥμαρτον]. The aorist is here used, as the thing affirmed is regarded, in respect of the whole race, as already an accomplished fact]. and [do] come short of the glory of God—that is, 'of the praise' or 'approval' of God: as the same word [δόξα] is used in John xii. 43, &c., and as the best interpreters take it here. Though men differ greatly in the *nature* and *extent* of their sinfulness, there is absolutely no difference between the best and the worst of men, in the *fact*, that "all have sinned," and so underlie the wrath of God. 24. Being justified freely [δωρεὰν]—without anything done on our part to deserve it (compare 2 Thess. iii. 8, where the same word is rendered "for nought") by his grace—gratuitously, in the sole exercise of His spontaneous love.

Third: *God is just in thus justifying believers* (24-26). through the redemption that is in Christ Jesus. A vastly important clause this, teaching us that though justification is quite gratuitous, it is not a mere *fiat* of the Divine will, but based on a "Redemption"—that is, 'the payment of a Ransom,' in Christ's death. It is true that the word [ἀπολύτρωσις], though properly meaning 'redemption on payment of a ransom,' is used also for redemption or deliverance of any sort, without reference to a ransom-price. But here, and almost universally in the New Testament, it is used, beyond all reasonable doubt, of redemption in the strict sense of the term; since in almost every place it is expressly said to be "through the blood of Christ." 25. Whom God hath set forth ('God set forth') [to be] a propitiation [ἱλαστήριον = כַּפֹּֽרֶת]. In the only other place where this word occurs in the New Testament (Heb. ix. 5) it refers to the 'propitiatory' or "mercy-seat" in the Holy of holies of the Jewish tabernacle; and the LXX. use the word in this sense. Hence several of the fathers, and after them *Luther, Calvin, Olshausen, Philippi*, &c., translate here, 'Whom God hath set forth for a propitiatory' or 'mercy-seat.' But probably the LXX. missed the strict sense of the Hebrew word which they so render; and as Christ is nowhere else so represented, the true sense of the term appears to be given by our own translators (following the Vulgate and *Beza*)—'a propitiation,' or 'propitiatory sacrifice.' (In this sense *Fritzsche, Meyer, de Wette, Alford,* and *Hodge* concur.) through faith in his blood [διὰ πίστεως ἐν τῷ αὐτοῦ αἵματι]. Some of the best interpreters, observing that 'faith *upon*' is the usual phrase in Greek, not "faith *in*" Christ, would place a comma after "faith," and understand the words as if written thus, 'to be a propitiation, in His blood, through faith.' But the same apostle writes, "Ye are all the children of God by *faith in Christ Jesus*" (Gal. iii. 26); and again, "Wherefore I also, after I heard of your *faith in the Lord Jesus* (Eph. i. 15)—where this identical phrase is used. Why, then, should he not have written here, 'faith in His blood?' (*Fritzsche* defends this

sense at length; and *Olshausen* strenuously contends for it.) Besides, the order of the two clauses —if we make two of them—is just the reverse of what we should expect in that case; whereas if, with our version, and most others, we take them as one, all is natural. to declare his righteousness for the remission of sins that are past, through the forbearance of God. This is rather an unhappy rendering of the original words [εἰς ἔνδειξιν τ. δικαιοσύνης αὐτοῦ διὰ τ. πάρεσιν τ. προγεγονότων ἁμαρτημάτων ἐν τ. ἀνοχῇ τ. Θ.] Properly, the words mean, 'for the manifestation of his righteousness, on account of the passing by of the sins that went before, in the forbearance of God.' 'The sins' which are here referred to are not those of the believer before he embraces Christ, but those committed *under the ancient economy*, before Christ came to "put away sin by the sacrifice of Himself." Hence the apostle, instead of using the common word which signifies "*remission*" [ἄφεσις], studiously uses a very different word, nowhere else employed, signifying 'pretermission' or 'passing by;' and hence also this 'passing by' is ascribed to "the *forbearance* of God," who is viewed as not so much *remitting* as *bearing with them* until an adequate atonement for them should be made. In thus not imputing them, God *was* righteous; but He was not *seen* to be so: there was no "manifestation of His righteousness" in doing so under the ancient economy. But now that God can "set forth" Christ as a "propitiation through faith in His blood," the righteousness of His procedure, in passing by the sins of believers before, and in now remitting them, is "manifested," declared, brought fully out to the view of the whole world. 26. To declare, [I say], at this time his righteousness—'For the showing forth of His righteousness at this present time' (meaning the present Gospel time), that he might ('may') be just, and the justifier of him which believeth in Jesus—'of him which is of the faith of Jesus.' Glorious paradox! 'Just in punishing,' and 'merciful in pardoning,' men can understand; but 'just in justifying' the guilty startles them. But the propitiation through faith in Christ's blood resolves the paradox, and harmonizes the seemingly discordant elements. For in that "God hath made Him to be sin for us who knew no sin," *justice* has full satisfaction; and in that "we are made the righteousness of God in Him," *mercy* has all her desire. [The word 'Ιησοῦ, at the close of this verse, is capriciously rejected in *Tischendorf's* text, though wanting only in FG, one cursive, and three copies of the Old Latin; while it is found in א ABCK, several cursives, the two principal MSS. of the Vulgate, the Peshito Syriac, and several Greek fathers. *Lachmann* and *Tregelles* retain it.]

Inferences from this doctrine of gratuitous justification by faith—An objection answered (27-31).
Inference First: *Boasting is excluded only by this way of justification.* 27. Where is boasting then? It is excluded. By what law?—'On what principle?' of works? Nay; but by the law (or, on the

208

29 justified by faith without the deeds of the law. *Is he* the God of the
  Jews only? *is he* not also of the Gentiles? Yes, of the Gentiles also:
30 seeing *it is* one God which shall justify the circumcision by faith, and
31 uncircumcision through faith. Do we ^c then make void the law through
  faith? God forbid: yea, we establish the law.

A. D. 60.
^c ch. 4. 14.
Ps. 119. 126.
Jer. 8. 8, 9.
Matt. 5. 17.
Matt. 15. 6.

principle) **of faith. 28. Therefore we conclude that a man is justified by faith without the deeds of the law.** There is weighty evidence in favour of 'For' here, in place of "Therefore;" and most critics regard it as the true reading—though we think incorrectly. [Οὖν is found in B C D *** —a corrector of about the ninth or tenth centuries —K L, and many cursives, both Syriac versions, and most Greek fathers; but γάρ is found in א A D E F G, and some cursives, some copies of the Old Latin, and the Vulgate. This is strong testimony; but internal evidence (by which we mean here the connection of the train of thought) seems to us to pronounce for the received reading. *Tischendorf* adheres to the received text: *Griesbach, Lachmann,* and *Tregelles* adopt γάρ.] The following view of the train of thought will show why we deem the received reading, "Therefore," more suitable:—'It is the unavoidable tendency of dependence upon our own works, less or more, for acceptance with God, to beget a spirit of "boasting." But that God should encourage such a spirit in sinners, by any procedure of His, is incredible. This, therefore, stamps falsehood upon every form of justification by works, whereas the doctrine that—

> Our faith *receives* a righteousness
> That makes the sinner just—

manifestly and entirely excludes "boasting;" and this is the best evidence of its truth.'

Inference Second: *This way of salvation, and no other, is adapted alike to Jew and Gentile* (29, 30). **29. Is he the God of the Jews only? is he not also of the Gentiles? Yes, of the Gentiles also.** The way of salvation must be one equally suited to the whole family of fallen man; but the doctrine of justification by faith is the only one that lays the basis of a Universal Religion; this, therefore, is another mark of its truth. **30. Seeing [it is] one God which shall**—or, 'one is the God who shall' **justify the circumcision by faith** [ἐκ πίστ.] **and uncircumcision through faith** [διὰ τ. πίστ.] The future—"shall justify"—is used here to denote the fixed purpose of God to act on this principle in all time. *Origen*, and after him *Bengel*, considered that it is the justification of the Jew which is here said to be '*of* faith,' as being the born heirs of the promise; while that of the Gentiles, as being previously "strangers to the covenants of promise," is said to be only "*through* faith," as admitting them into a new family. But, besides that this is too far-fetched, it seems to be contradicted by Gal. iii. 8, where the same phrase—'*of* faith'—which is here said to be used of the Jews, is applied to the justification of the Gentiles. With most critics, we regard it as but a varied statement of the same truth, but with a slight shade of difference in the sense; the first expression—'of faith'—denoting the ordained *method* of justification; the second, "through faith," the instrument or channel through which it comes to us. Similar examples of two nearly equivalent statements will be found in *v.* 22, and in Gal. iii. 22 (compare 23).

Objection (31). **31. Do we then make void the law through faith?** 'Does this doctrine of justification by faith, then, dissolve the obligation of the law? If so, it cannot be of God; but away with such a thought, for it does just the reverse.' **God**

forbid: yea, we establish the law. The reader should carefully observe, that, important as was this objection, and opening up as it did so noble a field for the illustration of the peculiar glory of the Gospel, the apostle does no more here than indignantly repel it, intending at a subsequent stage of his argument (ch. vi.) to resume and discuss it at length.

Remarks.—1. It cannot be too much insisted on, that according to the doctrine of this Epistle throughout, and particularly of the present chapter, one way of a sinner's justification is taught as well in the Old Testament as in the New—though more dimly, of course, in the twilight of Revelation, and only now in unclouded light. 2. As there is no difference in the *need*, so is there none in the *liberty to appropriate* the provided Salvation. The best need to be saved by faith in Jesus Christ; and the worst only need that. On this common ground all saved sinners meet in the Church below, and will stand for ever. (See on Luke vii. 36-50, p. 255.) 3. The love of God and His grace to the guilty, apart from the sacrifice of Christ, would yield no solid relief to the convinced and trembling sinner. It is on the atoning sacrifice of Christ as the one propitiatory and all-sufficient sacrifice, which God in unspeakable love hath set forth to the eye of the guilty, that his faith fastens for deliverance from wrath; and though he knows that he is "justified *freely* by God's *grace*," it is only because it is "*through the redemption* that is in Christ Jesus" that he is able to find peace and rest even in this. 4. The strictly accurate view of believers under the Old Testament is not that of a company of *pardoned* men, but of men whose sins, *put up with and passed by* in the mean time, awaited a *future expiation* in the fulness of time; or, to express it otherwise, of men pardoned *on the credit* of an atonement which all the sacrifices of their own economy did not yield, and only rendered to Justice when, "in the end of the world, Christ appeared to put away sin by the sacrifice of Himself" (see on Luke ix. 31; and on Heb. ix. 15, and xi. 39, 40). 5. It is a fundamental requisite of all true religion, that it tend to humble the sinner and exalt God; and every system which breeds self-righteousness, or cherishes boasting, bears falsehood on its face. 6. The fitness of the Gospel to be a universal religion, beneath which the guilty of every name and degree are invited and warranted to take shelter and repose, is a glorious evidence of its truth. 7. The glory of God's law, in its eternal and immutable obligations, is then only fully apprehended by the sinner, and then only felt in the depths of his soul, when, believing that "He was made sin for him who knew no sin," he sees himself "made the righteousness of God in Him." Thus we do not make void the law through faith; yea, we establish the law. 8. This chapter, and particularly the latter part of it, which *Olshausen* calls 'the Acropolis of the Christian Faith'—is (and here we use the words of *Philippi*) the proper seat of the Pauline doctrine of Justification, and the grand proof-passage of the Protestant doctrine of the Imputation of Christ's righteousness and of Justification, not on account of, but through faith alone.' To make good this doctrine, and reseat it in the faith and affection of the Church, was worth all the bloody struggles that it cost our fathers; and it will be the wisdom

4   WHAT shall we then say that Abraham our father, as pertaining to the flesh, hath found?

2   For if Abraham were justified by works, he hath *whereof* to glory; but

3   not before God.   For what saith the Scripture?   Abraham believed

4   ^aGod, and it was counted unto him for righteousness.   Now to ^bhim

5   that worketh is the reward not reckoned of grace, but of debt.   But to him that worketh not, but believeth on him that justifieth the ^cungodly, his faith is counted for righteousness.

6   Even as David also describeth the blessedness of the man, unto whom

7   God ^dimputeth righteousness without works, *saying*, ^eBlessed *are* they

8   whose iniquities are forgiven, and whose sins are covered.   Blessed *is* the man to whom the Lord will not impute sin.

A. D. 60.

CHAP. 4.
^a Gen. 15 6.
Gal. 3. 6.
Jas. 2. 23.
^b ch. 11. 6.
^c Josh. 24. 2.
Acts 13. 39.
Gal. 2. 16.
^d Jer. 23. 6.
1 Cor. 1. : 0.
2 Cor. 5. 19.
21.
Rev. 5. 9.
^e Ps. 32. 1, 2.

and safety, the life and vigour of the churches, to "stand fast in this liberty wherewith Christ hath made them free, and not be again entangled," in the very least degree, "with the yoke of bondage."

CHAP. IV. 1-25.—THE FOREGOING DOCTRINE OF JUSTIFICATION BY FAITH ILLUSTRATED FROM THE OLD TESTAMENT.

The apostle has been all along careful to guard his readers against the supposition that he was teaching them any absolutely new doctrine. New, it might indeed be called, in respect of the flood of new light which had been thrown upon it by the work of Christ in the flesh. But it was of the utmost importance to show that God's way of justifying the ungodly had been from the first the same that it now is; not only that it had been *predicted* and *foreshadowed* under the ancient economy (ch. i. 2; iii. 21), but that it had been *in operation* from the first. That accordingly is what the apostle now proceeds to do. And as *Abraham*, "the father of the faithful," and *David*, the "man after God's own heart," were regarded as the very pillars of the ancient economy (see Matt. i. 1), he first adduces the Scripture testimony regarding the one, and then confirms this by the testimony of the other.

First: *Abraham was justified by faith* (1-5). **1. What shall we then say that Abraham our father, as pertaining to the flesh, hath found?** —or, rather, 'hath found as pertaining to the flesh;' meaning 'by all his natural efforts or legal obedience.' [*Lachm.* and *Trey.* put εὑρ. immediately before 'Αβρααμ, on the weighty evidence of אACDEFG, several cursives, four MSS. of the Old Latin, the Vulgate, and some Greek fathers; while *Tischendor.* abides by the received order of the words—on the authority of BKL, most cursives, both Syriac versions, Chrysostom, and one or two other fathers. Perhaps internal evidence should decide in favour of the received order, as being the more difficult.] **2 For if Abraham were justified by works, he hath whereof to glory; but not before God—** *q.d.*, 'If works were the ground of Abraham's justification, he would have matter for boasting; but as it is perfectly certain that he has none in the sight of God, it follows that Abraham could not have been justified by works.' So *Calvin* and the best expositors. And to this agree the words of Scripture. **3. For what saith the Scripture? Abraham believed God, and it (that is, his believing) was counted unto him for righteousness** (Gen. xv. 6). Romish expositors and Arminian Protestants make this to mean that God accepted Abraham's act of believing as a substitute for complete obedience. But this is at variance with the whole spirit and letter of the apostle's teaching. Throughout this whole argument, *faith* is set in direct opposition to *works*, in the matter of justification, and even in the next two verses. The

meaning, therefore, cannot possibly be that the mere act of believing—which is as much a work as any other piece of commanded duty (John vi. 29; 1 John iii. 23)—was counted to Abraham for all obedience. The case of Abraham here adduced (as *Meyer* justly observes) is not that of a man simply trusting or having confidence in God, but of one confiding in a promise which pointed to *Christ.* What makes Abraham the father of all believers is something far more than the subjective state of heart implied in the general state of trust in God: it is the essential oneness of the Object of Abraham's faith with that of all Christians— *implicitly* apprehended and embraced by him, and *explicitly* by them—it is this (as *Meyer, Tholuck, Philippi*, and others remark) that makes the faith of Abraham, in the view of our apostle, the grand pattern case of justification by faith. Faith, in his case as in ours, is but the instrument that puts us in possession of the blessing gratuitously bestowed. Even *Jowett* says, 'The faith of Abraham, though not the same with a faith in Christ, was analogous to it: (1) as it was a faith in unseen things (Heb. xi. 17-19); (2) as it was prior to, and independent of, the law (Gal. iii. 17-19); and (3) as it related to the promised seed in whom Christ was dimly seen' (Gal. iii. 8). **4. Now to him that worketh** (as a servant for wages) **is the reward not reckoned of grace**—as z. matter of favour, **but of debt**—as a thing of right. **5. But to him that worketh not, but believeth on him that justifieth the ungodly, his faith is counted for righteousness.** The apostle in this verse expresses himself in language the most naked and emphatic, as if to preclude the possibility of either misapprehending or perverting his meaning. The faith, he says, which is counted for righteousness is the faith of " him who *worketh not.*" But as if even this would not make it sufficiently evident that God, in justifying the believer, has no respect to any personal merit of his, He explains further what He means, by adding the words, "but believeth on Him who *justifieth the ungodly;*" those who have no personal merit on which the eye of God, if it required such, could fasten as a recommendation to His favour. *This*, says the apostle, *is the faith which is counted for righteousness.* So much for the case of Abraham.

Second: *David sings of the same gratuitous justification* (6-8). **6. Even as David also describeth [λέγει]—**'speaketh,' 'pronounceth,' **the blessedness of the man, unto whom God imputeth righteousness without works**—whom, though void of all good works, He nevertheless regards and treats as righteous. **7. [Saying], Blessed are they whose iniquities are forgiven, and whose sins are covered. 8. Blessed is the man to whom the Lord will not impute sin.** These two first verses of Ps. xxxii. (which are taken *verbatim* from the LXX., and exactly correspond to the Hebrew) speak

9   *Cometh* this blessedness then upon the circumcision *only*, or upon the uncircumcision also? for we say that faith was reckoned to Abraham for righteousness.

10   How was it then reckoned? when he was in circumcision, or in uncir-
11 cumcision? Not in circumcision, but in uncircumcision. And *ʃ* he received the sign of circumcision, a seal of the righteousness of the faith which *he had yet* being uncircumcised: that *ᵍ* he might be the father of all them that believe, though they be not circumcised; that righteousness
12 might be imputed unto them also: and the father of circumcision to them who are not of the circumcision only, but who also walk in the steps of that faith of our father Abraham, which *he had* being *yet* uncircumcised.

13   For the promise, that he should be the *ʰ* heir of the world, *was* not to Abraham, or to his seed, through the law, but through the righteousness
14 of faith. For *ⁱ* if they which are of the law *be* heirs, faith is made void,
15 and the promise made of none effect: because the law worketh wrath:
16 for where no law is, *there is* no transgression. Therefore *it is* of faith, that *it might be* *ʲ* by grace; to the end the promise might be sure to all the seed; not to that only which is of the law, but to that also which is of

A. D. 60.

ʃ Gen. 17. 10.
Ex. 12. 13.
Ex. 31. 13.
17.
Eze. 20. 12, 20.
ch. 9. 6.
ᵍ Matt. 8. 11.
Luke 19. 9.
John 8. 39.
Gal. 3. 7.
. 29.
Gal. 6. 16.
ʰ Gen. 12. 3.
Gen. 17. 4.
5, 16.
Gen. 22. 17.
Gen. 28. 14.
Gen. 49. 10.
Ps. 2. 8.
Gal. 3. 29.
ⁱ Gal. 3. 18.
ʲ ch. 3. 24.
Col. 3. 11.

---

in express terms only of 'transgression forgiven, sin covered, iniquity not imputed;' but as the negative blessing necessarily includes the positive, the passage is strictly in point. And here we have another proof that the "righteousness" here, and throughout this whole argument, intended by the apostle is used in a *strictly judicial* sense, since it is put in opposition to the *imputation of sin.* In any other sense the apostle's argument would be inept.

The case of Abraham further illustrated (9-22). **9. Cometh this blessedness then upon the cir-cumcision only, &c., for we say that faith was reckoned to Abraham for righteousness. 10. How was it then reckoned? ... Not in circumcision, but in uncircumcision. 11. And he received the sign of circumcision, a seal of the righteousness of the faith which he had yet being uncircumcised: that he might be the father of all them that believe, though they be not circumcised** [δι' ἀκρο-βυσ-ίας]. The mode of expression here changes, [from ἐν ἀκροβ.] The precise idea intended seems to be that of 'piercing,' or 'breaking *through,*' in order to get into a certain state;' and being used of the Gentiles, expresses their attaining to a justified state through faith, *in spite* of the seeming barrier of their "uncircumcision." **that righteous-ness might be imputed unto them also.** The import of these three verses may be thus ex-pressed: 'Say not, All the blessedness of which David sings is spoken of the *circumcised*, and is therefore no evidence of God's *general* way of justifying men; for Abraham's justification took place long before he was circumcised, and so could have no dependence upon that rite: nay, the "sign of circumcision" was given to Abraham as "a seal" (or token) of the (justifying) righteous-ness which he had *before* he was circumcised; in order that he might stand forth to every age as *the parent believer*—the model man of justification by faith—after whose type, as the first public example of it, all were to be moulded, whether Jew or Gentile, who should hereafter believe to life everlasting.' **12. And the father of circum-cision to them who are not of the circumcision only.** Here the same sentiment is expressed, but in a somewhat unexpected form—namely, that Abraham is the father of circumcision to all uncircumcised believers. This cannot refer to the distinctive peculiarities of the circumcised, in which uncircumcised Gentiles could of course have no share: it simply means that all that was of essential and permanent value in the standing before God of the circumcised—all that circum-cision chiefly set its seal on—is shared in by the believing children of Abraham who are strangers to the circumcision of the flesh.

What had just been said of *circumcision* is now, in the next five verses, applied to the *law.* **13. For the promise, that he should be the heir of the world.** To understand this in any *local* or *terri-torial* sense—of the land of Canaan, as a type of heaven (with *Calvin*) or of the millennial reign over the earth (with *Alford*)—is surely away from the apostle's purpose. Nor does it seem to meet the case to view it (with *Hodge*) as just a general promise of blessedness. The allusion seems clearly to be to the promise, "In thee shall all the families of the earth be blessed." In this case Abraham is "the heir of the world" *religiously* rather than locally. *By his Religion he may be said to rule the world.* As the parent of that race from whom the world has received "the lively oracles," of whom it is said that "Salvation is of the Jews," and " of whom as concerning the flesh Christ came, who is over all, God blessed for ever "—in this sublime sense is Abraham "the heir of the world." (So, substantially, *Beza, Olshausen, Webster and Wilkinson,* &c.) This promise, then, reasons the apostle here, **was not to Abraham, or to his seed, through the law**—was not given to them under the Mosaic covenant, or in virtue of their obedience to the law, **but through the righteous-ness of faith**—in virtue simply of his faith in the Divine promise. **14. For if they which are of the law be heirs**—If the blessing is to be earned by obedience to the law, **faith is made void**—the whole Divine method is subverted. **15. Because the law worketh wrath**—has nothing to give to those who break it but condemnation and ven-geance: **for where no law is, there is no transgression.** It is just the law that makes transgression, in the case of those who break it; nor can the one exist without the other. **16. Therefore it is of faith, that it might be by grace; to the end the promise might be sure to all the seed; not to that only which is of the law, but to that also which is of the faith of Abraham; who is the father of us all.** We have here a general summary of the foregoing

211

17 the faith of Abraham; *k*who is the father of us all, (as it is written, I have made thee a father of many nations,) ¹before him whom he believed, *even* God, who *l*quickeneth the dead, and calleth those *m*things which be not as though they were.

18 Who against hope believed in hope, that he might become the father of many nations, according to that which was spoken, *n*So shall thy seed

19 be. And being not weak in faith, *o*he considered not his own body now dead, when he was about an hundred years old, neither yet the deadness

20 of Sara's womb: he staggered not at the promise of God through unbelief;

21 but was strong in faith, giving glory to God; and being fully persuaded

22 that what he had promised he was able also to perform. And therefore it was imputed to him for righteousness.

23, Now *p*it was not written for his sake alone, that it was imputed to

24 him; but for us also, to whom it shall be imputed, if we believe *q*on him

25 that raised up Jesus our Lord from the dead; who *r*was delivered for our offences, and *s*was raised again for our justification.

A. D. 60.
k ch 9. 8.
1 Or, like unto him.
l Eph. 2. 1.
1 Tim. 6.13.
m 1 Cor. 1. 28.
1 Pet. 2. 10.
n Gen. 15. 5.
o Heb. 11. 11.
p 1 Cor. 10.11.
2 Tim. 3.16.
q Acts 13. 30.
1 Pet. 1. 21.
r Isa. 53. 5.
Dan. 9. 24.
Heb. 9. 28.
1 Pet. 3. 15.
1 John 1. 7.
1 Cor 15.17.
1 Pet. 1. 21.

reasoning:—*q. d.*, 'Thus justification is by *faith*, in order that its purely *gracious* character may be seen, and that all who follow in the steps of Abraham's faith—whether of his natural seed or no—may be assured of the like justification with the parent-believer.' **17. (As it is written** (Gen. xvii. 5), **I have made thee a father of many nations,**) **before him whom he believed** [κατέναντι οὗ ἐπίστευσεν Θεοῦ]. This difficult construction may be resolved in two ways:—either as in our version—"before God, whom he believed"' [οὗ being by *attr.* for ᾧ ἐπίστευσεν], or 'before God, before whom he believed' [κατέναντι Θεοῦ, κατέναντι οὗ ἐπίστευσεν, in which case there is no attraction.] This latter construction (which *Winer, Meyer, Alford,* and *Philippi* prefer) makes perhaps the best Greek. But though critics are divided between these two views of the grammatical form, the sense is the same in both:—'Abraham is the father of us all, even of those who were not in existence in his day, in the eye of that God whom his faith apprehended.' [even] **God, who quickeneth the dead, and calleth those things which be not as though they were.** To give life to the dead, and existence to the non-existent, is the glorious prerogative of Him on whom Abraham's faith reposed. What he was required to believe being above nature, his faith had to fasten upon God's power to surmount physical incapacity, and call into being what did not then exist. But God having made the promise, Abraham believed Him in spite of those obstacles. This is still further illustrated in what follows.

18. Who against hope (when no ground for hope appeared) **believed in hope**—cherished the believing expectation [παρ' ἐλπίδα ἐπ' ἐλπίδι. παρά, with *acc.*, 'to beside;' hence, *præter: ἐπὶ* with *dat.*, denotes actual 'superposition;' hence the actual 'basis,' ethical 'occasion,' or 'moving principle'], **that he might become the father of many nations** [εἰς τὸ γενέσθαι, not as the matter or immediate object of his faith—for Paul never uses the verb πιστεύειν with εἰς followed by an infinitive for the object of faith—but either '*in order* to his becoming,' or, better, 'with the *result* of his becoming,' the father of many nations]: **according to that which was spoken, So** (that is, 'Such as the stars of heaven,' Gen. xv. 5) **shall thy seed be. 19. And being not weak in faith, he considered not** [οὐ κατενόησεν]—reflected not on, paid no attention to, those physical obstacles, both in himself and in Sarah, which might seem to render the fulfilment hopeless, **when he was about an hundred years old**—he was then ninety-nine;

neither yet the deadness of Sara's womb: 20. He staggered ('hesitated') **not** [διεκρίθη. In the New Testament, διακρίνω, in middle, signifies 'to doubt,' 'hesitate,' and the same sense attaches, as here, to 1 aor. pass.] **at the promise of God through unbelief; but was strong** [ἐνδυναμώθη, 'was strengthened,' 'showed himself strong'] **in faith, giving glory to God**—as able to make good His word against all obstacles; **21. And being fully persuaded** [πληροφορηθεὶς, of *persons*, 'fully assured;' of *things*, 'fully,' or 'on sure grounds, believed,' as in Luke i. 1] **that what he had promised he was able also to perform.** The glory which Abraham's faith gave to God consisted in this, that, firm in the persuasion of God's ability to fulfil His promise, no difficulties shook him. **22. And therefore it was imputed to him for righteousness**—*q. d.*, 'Let all then take notice that this was not because of anything meritorious in Abraham, but merely because he so *believed*.'

The application of this whole argument about Abraham (23-25). **23. Now it was not written for his sake alone, that it was imputed to him**—'These things were not recorded as mere historical facts, but as illustrations for all time of God's method of justification by faith.' **24. But for us also, to whom it shall be imputed, if we believe on him that raised up Jesus our Lord from the dead.** The only difference between the two cases is, that our faith rests on the act of God in raising up Jesus our Lord from the dead as an accomplished *fact*, while Abraham's faith reposed on a *promise* that God would raise him up a seed in whom all nations should be blessed. **25. Who was delivered for our offences** [διὰ τὰ παραπτώματα ἡμῶν]—'on account of our offences;' that is, in order to expiate them by His blood, **and was raised again for our justification** [διὰ τὴν δικαίωσιν ἡμῶν]—'on account of,' 'for the sake of our justification;' that is, 'in order to our being justified.' Since the resurrection of Christ was the Divine assurance that He had "put away sin by the sacrifice of Himself"—but for which men could never have been brought to credit it—our justification is fitly made to rest on that glorious Divine act.

Remarks.—**1.** The doctrine of justification by works, as it generates self-exaltation, is contrary to the first principles of all true Religion (see on ch. iii. 21-31; Remark 5, at the close of that Section. **2.** The way of a sinner's justification has been the same in all time, and the testimony of the Old Testament on this subject is one with that of the New (see on ch. iii. 21-31, Remark 1).

5 THEREFORE being justified by faith, we have [a]peace with God | A. D. 60.
2 through our Lord Jesus Christ: by whom also we have access by faith | [a] Isa 32. 17.

3. Faith and works, in the matter of justification, are opposite and irreconcileable, even as grace and debt (see on ch. xi. 6). If God "justifies the ungodly," works cannot be, in any sense or to any degree, the ground of justification. For the same reason, the first requisite, in order to justification, must be (under the conviction that we are "ungodly") to despair of it by works; and the next, to "believe in Him that justifieth the ungodly"— that hath a justifying righteousness to bestow, and is ready to bestow it, upon those who deserve none, and to embrace it accordingly. 4. The sacraments of the Church were never intended, and are not adapted, to *confer* grace, or the blessings of salvation, upon men. Their proper use is to set a Divine *seal* upon *a state already existing*, and so they *presuppose*, and do not *create* it. As circumcision merely "sealed" Abraham's already existing acceptance with God, so is it with the sacraments of the New Testament. 5. As Abraham is "the heir of the world"—all nations being through his Seed Christ Jesus "blessed in him"— so the transmission of the true Religion, and all the salvation which the world will ever experience, shall yet be traced back with wonder, gratitude, and joy, to that morning dawn when "the God of glory appeared unto our father Abraham, when he was in Mesopotamia, before he dwelt in Charran" (Acts vii. 2). 6. Nothing gives more glory to God than simple faith in His word, especially when all things seem to render the fulfilment of it hopeless. 7. All the Scripture examples of faith were recorded on purpose to beget and encourage the like faith in every succeeding age (see ch. xv. 4). 8. *Justification*, in this argument, cannot be taken—as Romanists and other errorists insist—to mean a change upon men's *character;* for besides that this is to confound it with *Sanctification*, which has its appropriate place in this Epistle, the whole argument of the present chapter—and nearly all its more important clauses, expressions, and words—would in that case be unsuitable, and fitted only to mislead. Beyond all doubt it means exclusively a change upon men's *state* or *relation to God;* or, in scientific language, it is an *objective*, not a *subjective* change—a change from guilt and condemnation to acquittal and acceptance. And the best evidence that this is the key to the whole argument is, that it opens all the wards of the many-chambered lock through which we are introduced to the riches of this Epistle.

CHAP. V.–VIII.—The Fruits of Justification in Privilege and in Life.

CHAP. V. 1-11. — THE PRIVILEGES OF THE JUSTIFIED.

The First great head of his subject—the *proof* and *illustration* of the Doctrine of Justification by Faith—being now concluded, the apostle here enters on the Second great division, the *fruits* of justification. These are of two kinds—those of *Privilege* and those of *Life*. The former of these is the subject of the present Section, while in the eighth the two following chapters, and sublimely treated together. Of the Privileges of the Justified, four are enumerated and dwelt on in this Section— First: *Peace with God* (1, 2). **1. Therefore being** ('having been') **justified by faith, we have peace with God through our Lord Jesus Christ.** There is another reading of this verse for which the external evidence is so strong, that, until lately, we thought ourselves bound to regard it as the true one. It differs only by a single letter from

213

that of the received text; but it converts the indicative into the subjunctive mood, or the declaratory form of the statement—"*we have* peace"—into the hortatory form, "*let us have* peace." [In favour of ἔχομεν, of the received text, we have only B** (about eighth century) F G, and several cursives, the Peshito Syriac, and one or two Greek fathers; but for ἔχωμεν we have א A B* C D K L, and about 30 cursives; 4 copies of the Old Latin and the Vulgate ("habeamus"); the Memphitic, the Philox. Syriac, and the Æthiopic; *Chrysostom*, *Augustin*, and other Greek and Latin fathers]. Should we be obliged to regard this very strong evidence as decisive (as do *Scholz*, *Fritzsche*, *Tregelles*, and *Green*), it would still bring out the same sense as the received text, though not so directly. For since, if *required* to have peace with God, we must be *entitled* to have it, the hortatory form of the statement—'Let us have peace with God'— amounts just to this, that as peace with God is the native consequence of a justified state, believers should realize it, or have the joyful consciousness of it as their own. Nor let it be said (as *Olshausen*, *Alford*, and *Philippi*, do) that it is incongruous to bid us have what it is God's prerogative to bestow; for we are elsewhere exhorted to "have grace" (Heb. xii. 28), which surely is not less the pure gift of God than the peace which flows from justification. But though the sense, according to both readings, is substantially the same, there are three internal evidences in favour of the received text—or the indicative form of the statement ("we have peace")—to which, on mature reflection, we feel constrained to yield. (1.) The sense is beyond question indicative or declaratory throughout all this Section, specifying as matter of fact the various privileges of the justified believer; and if so, it certainly is more natural that the first one should be put in the indicative mood, "we *have* peace," than subjunctively—'*let us have peace*'—while all the others are specified as matter of fact in the indicative form. (2.) The testimony of the fathers in favour of the subjunctive form is of very little weight, and is fitted rather to create a suspicion against it, from their known tendency to give an ethical and hortatory form to simple doctrinal statements. *Chrysostom*, for example, though one of the most accurate of the Greek expositors, entirely misses the sense of this verse, not only throwing it into the hortatory form, but regarding it as an exhortation to cease from sinning. His words are, 'Let us have peace with God—that is, let us no longer sin' [τουτέστι μηκέτι ἁμαρτάνομεν]; and *Origen*, *Theodoret*, and other Greek fathers go equally far astray in interpreting this verse. But above all (3.) The interchange of o long and o short—which is the whole difference between the two readings in the present case, and is technically called *Itacism*—is so common in ancient Greek MSS. that the question whether more of them have the one form than the other ought not of itself to decide the question in which form the word came from the apostle himself. And as this is the one ground on which the subjunctive reading has any claim to be received, it ought to give way before the very strong internal evidence in favour of the indicative or declaratory form of the statement. (Accordingly, *Lachmann* and *Tischendorf* abide by the received text, of which *de Wette*, *Meyer*, *Philippi*, and *Alford* approve.)

The next thing is to fix the precise sense of the words, "we have peace with God through our

into this grace *b* wherein we stand, *c* and rejoice in hope of the glory of God.

3 And not only *so*, but *d* we glory in tribulations also: knowing that
4 tribulation worketh patience; and patience, experience; and experience,
5 hope:- and *e* hope maketh not ashamed; because *f* the love of God

A. D. 60.

b 1 Cor. 15. 1.
c Heb. 3. 6.
d Matt. 5. 11.
e Phil. 1. 20.
f 2 Cor. 1. 22.

Lord Jesus Christ" [πρὸς τ. Θεόν—the preposition denoting 'ethical relation' (*Donaldson*, 486), as in Acts ii. 47; xxiv. 16]. *Calvin* and others take this peace to mean 'peace of conscience,' or that tranquillity of soul which springs from a sense of our reconciliation to God. But this is rather a consequence of the peace here meant than the peace itself. "Peace with God" here is clearly *God's being at peace with us*, or the cessation of His wrath, the removal of His righteous displeasure against us because of sin now put away "through our Lord Jesus Christ" (so *Melville, Alford, Philippi, Hodge*). It is true that the knowledge that God is now at peace with us cannot but quell all guilty fears and tranquillize the conscience; but the great truth here expressed is that the justified believer is no longer the object of God's displeasure. The knowledge of this blessed truth must ever be beyond the reach of those who rest their hopes of acceptance, whether more or less, on their own imperfect conformity to the laws of God.

2. By whom also we have access [τὴν προσαγωγὴν ἐσχήκαμεν]. Our translators, following the Vulgate and *Luther*, have gone wrong here. The true sense, as given by *Beza*, is, 'By whom we have had the access,' or 'our access.' by faith into this grace wherein we stand. [*Tischendorf* omits τῇ πίστει, and *Lachm.* and *Treg.* bracket them, on the authority of B D E (apparently) F G, four copies of the Old Latin, and later witnesses. But they are sufficiently attested, we think, by א A (which has ἐν τῇ πίστει), and many cursives, the Vulgate ('fide,' 'in fide,' 'per fidem,' in different copies), the Syriac, the Æthiopic, and many Greek and Latin fathers. That the words might more easily slide out of the genuine text, as superfluous, than creep in as an interpolation, will surely be admitted.] The question here is, Have we in this clause a second privilege of the justified (as *Beza, Tholuck*, and others think), or only a thought suggested by the first one? The latter we regard (with *Meyer, Philippi, Mehring, Hodge*) as the right answer; and in that case the whole statement may be thus conveyed, 'Not only do we owe to our Lord Jesus Christ this first and greatest blessing of a justified state—"peace with God"—but to Him we are indebted even for our "access into this grace" of gratuitous justification, "wherein we stand," and which is the ground of that peace.' We must not (with *Tholuck*) press the word "access," or 'introduction,' so far as to suppose that it alludes to the usage in Eastern courts of strangers being conducted into the king's presence by an official Introducer [προσαγωγεύς], Jesus Christ acting this part for us with God (as in Eph. ii. 18; iii. 12—the only other places in the New Testament where that word is used). The word signifies access or approach to any object—whether a thing, a state, or a person, though more commonly the last. What is meant here is the permanent 'standing' of a justified state, which we owe (says the apostle) to "our Lord Jesus Christ."

Second : *Exultant hope of the glory of God.* and [we] rejoice in hope of the glory of God. The word here rendered "rejoice" [καυχώμεθα] properly denotes that swell of emotion which leads to loud speaking—either in the way of 'vaunting'—

'bragging'—without any warrantable ground—or of legitimate 'exultation' or 'triumph.' This last is the thing here intended; and as the same word is thrice used in this Section, it had been better if it had been rendered by the same English word, instead of three different ones—"rejoice" (v. 2), "glory" (v. 3), and "joy" (v. 11). The meaning is, that as our gratuitous justification gives to us who believe *present* peace with God, so it secures our *future* glory, the assured prospect of which begets as triumphant a spirit as if it were a present possession. (See more on "hope," *v.* 4).

Third : *Triumph in tribulation* (v. 3). 3. And not only [so], but we glory in tribulations also—not, surely, for their own sake, for as such they are "not joyous but grievous;" but knowing that tribulation worketh patience. To 'work' anything, in the sense of 'producing' it, is a favourite Pauline word—used by Peter but once, and by James only twice, but by Paul twenty-one times, eleven of which are in this Epistle. The "patience" which tribulation worketh is the quiet endurance of what we cannot but wish removed, whether it be the withholding of promised good (as ch. viii. 25), or the continued experience of positive ill (as here). There is, indeed, a patience of unrenewed nature which has something noble in it, though in many cases it is the offspring of pride, if not of something lower. Men have been known to endure every form of privation, torture, and death, without a murmur, and without even visible emotion, merely because they deemed it unworthy of them to sink under unavoidable ill. But this proud, stoical hardihood has nothing in common with the *grace* of patience—which is either the meek endurance of ill, because it is of God (Job i. 21, 22; ii. 10), or the calm waiting for promised good till His time to dispense it come (Heb. x. 36); in the full persuasion that such trials are Divinely appointed, are but for a definite period, and are not sent without abundant promises of "songs in the night." If such be the "patience" which "tribulation worketh," no wonder it is added. 4. And patience [worketh] experience [δοκιμὴν]—rather 'proof,' as the same word is rendered in 2 Cor. ii. 9; xiii. 3; Phil. ii. 22—that is, experimental *evidence* that we have 'believed through grace' [Vulgate and *Calvin*, 'probatio'], and experience (or 'proof') hope—"of the glory of God." Thus have we hope in two distinct ways, and at two successive stages of the Christian life —*First*, Immediately on believing, along with the sense of "peace with God" (v. 1); *Next*, After the reality of this faith has been 'proved,' particularly by the patient endurance of trials sent to test it. We first get it by looking *away from ourselves* to the Lamb of God; next, by looking *into* or *upon ourselves* as transformed by that "looking unto Jesus." In the one case, the mind acts (as they say) *objectively;* in the other, *subjectively.* The one is (in the language of some divines) the *assurance of faith;* the other, the *assurance of sense*. The next six verses, instead of going on to some new fruit of justification, are but one lengthened and noble illustration of the solid character of this "hope of the glory of God." 5. And hope maketh not ashamed—putteth not to shame, as empty

is shed abroad in our hearts by the Holy Ghost, which is given unto us.

6 For when we were yet without strength, [1] in due time Christ died for the 7 ungodly. For scarcely for a righteous man will one die: yet peradven-

A. D. 60.

1 Or, according to the time.
Heb. 9. 26.

hopes do, or, is not of a character to disappoint those in whose bosoms it springs up as the proper consequence of perceived justification (cf. ch. ix. 33; x. 11). **because the love of God** [ἡ ἀγάπη τοῦ Θ.]—not our love to God (as *Theodoret, Augustin,* and of moderns, as *Webster and Wilkinson,* view it), but God's love to us, as is clear from *v.* 8, and, indeed, from the whole strain of these six verses. So it is understood by nearly every good interpreter. **is shed abroad** [ἐκκέχυται]—or 'poured out;' a lively and familiar figure for a 'rich' or 'copious communication' (see the same word in Mark ii. 22, of wine; and of the Holy Spirit, in Acts ii. 17, 33; x. 45; Tit. iii. 6). **in our hearts**—which are, as it were, bedewed with it, **by the Holy Ghost, which is** ('was') **given unto us**—given either at the great Pentecostal effusion, viewed as the formal donation of the Spirit to the Church of God for all time, or on each one's own accession to Christ (John vii. 38, 39). It should be observed that *here we have the first mention in this Epistle of the Holy Ghost,* whose work in believers is so fully treated in chapter viii. The argument of the apostle is to the following effect: 'That assured hope of glory which the perception of our justification begets will never disappoint us; for how can it, when we feel our hearts, by the Holy Ghost given unto us, drenched in sweet, all-subduing sensations of God's wondrous love to us in Christ Jesus!' This leads the apostle to expatiate on the amazing character of that love.

6. For when we were yet without strength, in due time Christ died for the ungodly. [Ἔτι γὰρ Χριστὸς ὄντων ἡμῶν ἀσθενῶν κατὰ καιρὸν ὑπὲρ ἀσεβῶν ἀπέθανεν. The unusual separation here of ἔτι from ἀσθενῶν, to which it belongs (as in *v.* 8, ἔτι ἁμαρτωλῶν), seems to have perplexed the transcribers of MSS., occasioning various readings; none of which, however, are sufficiently supported to deserve notice here—save the repetition of ἔτι before κατὰ καιρὸν, which *Lachm.* and *Treg.* adopt, on the weighty external testimony of אABCD*FG, two cursives, four copies of the Old Latin (but not the Vulgate, as *Tischendorf* incorrectly says), both the Syriac versions, the Memphitic, and several fathers. But this second ἔτι, which perplexes the sense, is rightly rejected by *Tischendorf* as a transcriber's addition, suggested by the unusual separation of the first one from its proper adjective. Nor is this separation so very unusual: it occurs not only in other places of the New Testament, but in *Achilles Tatius, Euripides,* and *Plato.* —See *Fritzsche* and *Meyer,* also *Winer,* § 61. 4. The worst explanation is that of *Tholuck,* who thinks that 'Paul, having forgotten the ἔτι at the commencement, may have put down the second by an oversight'—which *Fritzsche* justly pronounces 'ridiculous.' Three notable properties of God's love to us in Christ are here specified—answering the questions, For whom? In what circumstances? and When? FIRST, For whom? "Christ (replies the apostle) died for the *ungodly.*" In the preceding chapter the apostle, with the view of expressing in the most emphatic and unmistakeable form the absolutely gratuitous character of our justification, had said that God "justifieth the *ungodly*" (ch. iv. 5). Here, to convey, in the strongest terms, the absolutely unmerited character of God's love to us in the gift of His Son, He says that "Christ died for the *ungodly*"—for those

whose character and state were repugnant to His nature and offensive to the eyes of His glory. The preposition here rendered "for" [ὑπὲρ] does not mean 'instead,' or ' in the place of' [which is ἀντί], but simply 'for the benefit of.' *How* Christ's death benefits us, therefore, must be determined, not by the use of this word, but by the nature of the case, and the context in each place where the word is used. In the case of Christ's death—which is expressly styled by our Lord Himself (Matt. xx. 28), "a *Ransom* in the stead of many" [ἀντὶ πολλῶν], and a Propitiatory Sacrifice (ch. iii. 25)—there can be no doubt that the substitutionary character of it is meant to be understood, and consequently, that in the *nature of the thing,* though not in the precise *meaning of the words,* the one preposition [ὑπέρ] involves, in a great many passages (such as 2 Cor. v. 15, 20, 21; Gal. iii. 13; 1 Pet. iii. 18), the idea of the other [ἀντί]. Indeed, the best classical writers (as *Euripides, Plato, Demosthenes*) use the one preposition freely in the sense of the other, wherever the idea of both is implied. SECOND, In what circumstances? "When we were without strength" (replies the apostle). But in what sense? Not (we think) in the sense of impotence to obey the law of God (according to most critics)—that is not the point here—but impotence to do what he says God sent His Son to accomplish, namely, to "justify" us (*v.* 9), or "reconcile us to God" (*v.* 10). The meaning here, then, of our being "without strength," is, that we were in a state of *passive helplessness* to deliver ourselves out of our perishing condition as sinners—'helpless [in our sins],' as *Conybeare* expresses it. THIRD, When was this done? "In due time," is the reply [κατὰ καιρόν]—rather, 'at the [appointed] season;' when the *necessity* for it was affectingly brought to light (1 Cor. i. 21), and when the august *preparations* for it were all completed (Gal. iv. 4; Heb. i. 2; ix. 26). On the first of these three properties of God's love to us, in the gift of His Son, the apostle now proceeds to enlarge. **7. For scarcely for a righteous man** [ὑπὲρ δικαίου] **will one die: yet peradventure for a good man some would even dare to die** [ὑπὲρ γὰρ τοῦ ἀγαθοῦ τάχα τὶς καὶ τολμᾷ ἀποθανεῖν]—'for, for the good man one perhaps does dare to die.' On the precise sense of this verse there has been much and (as we think) needless diversity of opinion. Everything depends on the sense in which the words "righteous" and "good" are to be taken. *Luther* and *Erasmus,* taking them in a neuter sense—not of persons, but of abstract qualities—make the apostle to mean, 'Scarcely will one die for that which is right and good.' But this is at variance with the whole strain of the passage; and the notion of dying for an abstract idea is entirely foreign (as *Jowett* well observes) to the language both of the New Testament and of the age in which it was written. Again, *Meyer* (observing that the article, which is wanting before "righteous," is placed before "good") understands the former clause of a righteous *man,* but takes the latter clause in a neuter sense, of *that* which is good. But besides that this is unnatural, it is liable to the same objection as before, of making the apostle speak of dying for an idea. Finally, *Calvin, Beza, Fritzsche,* &c., take both words as used synonymously—in this sense: 'To die even for a worthy character is a thing scarcely known

215

8 ture for a good man some would even dare to die. But *⁹* God commendeth his love toward us, in that, while we were yet sinners, Christ died for
9 us. Much more then, being now justified by *ʰ* his blood, we shall be
10 saved *ⁱ* from wrath through him. For if, when we were enemies, *ʲ* we were reconciled to God by the death of his Son, much more, being reconciled, we shall be saved *ᵏ* by his life.

A. D. 60.

⁹ John 15. 13.
1 Pet. 3. 18.
ʰ 1 John 1. 7.
ⁱ 1 Thes. 1.
10.
ʲ 2 Cor. 5. 18.
ᵏ John 14. 19.

among men, though such a case perhaps *may* occur.' But if this is what the apostle meant, it could surely have been expressed less baldly than by repeating the same thing in two successive clauses; not to say that the idea itself seems somewhat flat. It remains, then, that with the majority of good interpreters we take the sense to be as in our own version, as far the simplest and most natural. In this case, "a *righteous* man" is one simply of unexceptionable character, while "the *good* man" (emphatically so called) is one who, besides being unexceptionable, is distinguished for goodness, a benefactor to society. This distinction is familiar in classic literature; and as it cannot but have existed in fact among the Jews, there is no need to search for any definite expressions of it in the Old Testament. It only remains to notice the repetition of the "for" at the beginning of both clauses, which is to be explained thus: 'For scarcely is an instance to be found among men of one dying even for a righteous character; [I say, scarcely] *for* in behalf of a benefactor to society one does, perhaps, meet with such a case.' (So *Bengel, Olshausen, Tholuck, Alford, Philippi, Hodge.*) Beyond this, then, men's love for men, even in the rarest cases, will not go. Behold, now, the contrast between this and God's love to us in the gift of His Son. 8. **But God commendeth** [συνίστησιν]—'setteth forth,' 'displayeth' (see the same word in ch. iii. 5; xvi. 1; 2 Cor. iii. 1), **his** (own) **love toward us** [τ. ἑαυτοῦ ἀγάπην] **in that, while we were**—far from being positively "good," or even negatively "righteous," while we were yet (or 'still') **sinners**—a state which His soul hateth, **Christ died for us.** This is not exactly how we should have expected the argument to run. 'Men (he had been saying) will hardly die for men even when "righteous," though for one emphatically "good" one might be found doing so in some rare case; but *God* commendeth His love to us in that, while we were yet sinners'—what? '*He Himself* died for us' would seem the natural conclusion of the argument. But as this would hardly have been congruous, he puts it thus, "God commendeth His love to us, in that, while we were yet sinners, *Christ* died for us." Who can fail to see what a light this throws upon the Person of Christ? Had the apostle regarded Christ as a mere creature, however exalted—had he held Him to be in no proper sense of the essence of the Godhead—the comparison he has drawn between what men will do for one another and what God has done for us in Christ, is surely a halting one. For thus it would run: 'Hardly will any man die even for the best of men; but God so loved us that an exalted *creature* died for us.' Now what force is there in this? But if Christ is *so* of the essence of the Godhead as to be God manifested in the flesh, sent of God to give His life a Ransom for many—if He is *so* of the essence of the Godhead, that in all that He was and all that He did God was *in Him* of a truth, then His dying for us was as really a Personal sacrifice on the part of God as the glorious perfection of His nature will permit us to conceive and express. This makes the parallel a strict one, and the contrast sublime. Now comes the overpowering contrast, emphatically redoubled.

9. **Much more then, being** ('having been') **now justified by his blood, we shall be saved from wrath through him. 10. For if, when we were enemies** [ἐχθροὶ ὄντες]—not in the *active* sense of the word, as meaning 'persons cherishing enmity towards God' (so *Grotius*), but obviously in the *passive* sense, 'objects of God's enmity,' or 'righteous hatred,' in respect of our sinful character, as all the best interpreters agree (as *Calvin, Fritzsche, Meyer, de Wette, Alford, Hodge*); **we were reconciled to God**—here also not in the active sense, of a restoration of our good feeling towards God, but obviously of His towards us. [See *Fritzsche* on διαλάσσειν and καταλλάσσειν, notes, pp. 276-280.] **by the death of his Son, much more, being** ('having been') **reconciled, we shall be saved by his life.** Here let the reader observe that the whole Mediatorial work of Christ is divided into two grand stages—the one already completed on earth, the other now in course of completion in heaven. The first of these is called "Justification by His blood," in the one verse, and in the other, "Reconciliation to God by the death of His Son:" the second is called "Salvation from wrath through Him," in the one verse, and in the other "Salvation by His life." What the one of these imports is plain enough; but the other—"Salvation from wrath through Him"—may require a word of explanation. It denotes here the whole work of Christ towards believers, from the moment of justification, when the wrath of God is turned away from them, till the Judge on the great white Throne shall discharge that wrath upon them that "obey not the Gospel of our Lord Jesus Christ;" and that work may all be summed up in "keeping them from falling, and presenting them faultless before the presence of His glory, with exceeding joy" (Jude 24): thus are they "saved from wrath through Him." Now the apostle's argument is, that if the one *has been* already done, much more may we assure ourselves that the other *will be* done. The ground of this argument (à *majore ad minus*) is the irresistible fact that the thing which *has been done* was at once inconceivably *difficult* and *repulsive*, whereas what *has to be done* is in all respects the reverse. For our "justification" cost Him "His blood," and He has already shed it—our "reconciliation to God" was the reconciliation of '*enemies*,' and by the *death* of His Son; yet even this has been gone through and completed; whereas our "salvation from wrath through Him," as it costs Him no suffering, so it is for friends, whom it is sweet to serve. Thus, the whole statement amounts to this: 'If that part of the Saviour's work which cost Him His blood, and which had to be wrought for persons incapable of the least sympathy either with His love or His labours in their behalf—even our "justification," our "reconciliation"—is already completed; how much more will He do all that remains to be done, since He has it to do, not by death-agonies any more, but in untroubled "life," and no longer for enemies, but for friends—from whom, at every stage of it, He receives the grateful response of redeemed and adoring souls!'

With one other privilege of the justified the apostle closes this Section.

216

11   And not only *so*, but we also joy in God through our Lord Jesus Christ, | A. D. 60.
by whom we have now received the *l*atonement. | *l* 2 Cor. 5. 19.

Fourth: *Triumph in God Himself* (11). **11. And not only so, but we also joy** [καυχώμενοι, *scil.*, ἐσμέν. So most word good interpreters. *Alford* and *Green* retain the participial idea, as continuing καταλλαγέντες of *v.* 10; but this is unnatural]. **In God through our Lord Jesus Christ, by whom we have now received the atonement** [τ. καταλλαγήν]—more strictly (as in the *margin*), 'the reconciliation.' So the same word, as a verb, is properly rendered in *v.* 10, and the noun itself is so rendered in 2 Cor. v. 18, 19. In fact, the earlier meaning of the English word "atonement" (as *Trench* shows) was 'the *reconciliation* of two estranged parties'—that is, bringing them to be again 'at-one;' whereas now, "atonement" means that which constitutes the procuring cause of reconciliation. The three preceding fruits of justification were all of kindred nature—benefits to ourselves, calling for gratitude; this fourth and last one may be termed a purely disinterested one. Our first feeling towards God, after we have obtained peace with Him, is that of clinging gratitude for so costly a salvation; but no sooner have we learned to cry, Abba, Father, under the sweet sense of reconciliation, than 'gloriation' in Him takes the place of dread of Him, and now He appears to us "altogether lovely!"

Remarks.—1. How gloriously does the Gospel evince its Divine origin, by its laying the foundations of the Christian life in the restoration of the sinner to a righteous standing, and consequent peace with God, gratuitously bestowed on him through faith in the Lord Jesus, instead of leaving him vainly to strive after and struggle into it by his own efforts at obedience. 2. As only believers possess the true secret of patience under trials, so when trials Divinely sent afford them the opportunity of evidencing the reality and strength of their faith by the grace of patience under them, though in themselves "not joyous, but grievous" (Heb. xii. 17), they may well "count it all joy when they fall into them, knowing that the trying of their faith worketh patience" (Jas. i. 2, 3). 3. Hope, in the New Testament sense of the term, is not a lower degree of faith or assurance (as many now say, 'I *hope* for heaven, but am not *sure* of it'), but invariably means 'the confident expectation of future good.' It presupposes faith; and what faith *assures* us will be ours, hope accordingly *expects.* In the nourishment of this hope, the soul's look *outward* to Christ for the ground of it, and *inward* upon ourselves for evidence of its reality, must act and re-act upon each other. 4. It is the proper office of the Holy Ghost to beget in the soul the full conviction and joyful sense of the love of God in Christ Jesus to sinners of mankind, and to ourselves in particular; and where this exists, it carries with it such an assurance of final salvation as cannot deceive. 5. The death of Christ for sinners and enemies, as an act of Self-sacrificing love for others, stands out absolutely unique and alone. It admits of *illustration*, indeed, from the annals of self-sacrifice for country, kindred, friend, among men; but every such comparison is at the same time a contrast, and acts only as a foil to set off the peerless character of the love of God to men in the death of His Son. 6. Though the justification of believers is sometimes ascribed to the "*blood*" of Christ (as in *v.* 9), and sometimes to His "*obedience*" (as in *v.* 19), or—combining both into one—to His "*righteousness*" (as in *v.* 18); the same thing is everywhere meant—namely, the vicarious mediatorial work of Christ, considered as one whole. It is true that the ex-

piatory element of that work lay in His blood—His death. But still, when any one feature of that work is specified, it will always be found that this is owing merely to some point in the argument suggesting the mention of that feature, and not to any intrinsic efficacy towards justification in that, to the exclusion of the other parts of Christ's mediatorial work. Thus, in *vv.* 9 and 10, the apostle having occasion to dwell on what Christ did for men in the light of an incomparable self-sacrifice, naturally speaks of His "*blood*" as that which "justifies" us—His "*death*," as "reconciling" us to God. Whereas in *vv.* 18 and 19, his object being to contrast with the effects of Adam's *transgression*, in placing his seed in the condition of sinners, what Christ has done for us, he naturally fastens on the obediential character of Christ's work, saying, "even so by the *obedience* of One shall the many be made righteous." By overlooking this, some German divines of the Reformation-period attached undue importance to the passive sufferings and death of Christ, as constituting the whole meritorious ground of the believer's justification, while others were disposed to assign the same place to His active obedience. And we have in our own day, schools of theology of nearly the same character as these. The true corrective for all such narrow views of the work of Christ is to regard it in its *entireness* as God's gracious provision for our complete recovery out of our fallen condition, and only to dwell, as our apostle does, on its several features or stages, as the exigencies of our argument or discourse may call for it. 7. Gratitude to God for redeeming love, if it could exist without delight in God Himself, would be a selfish and worthless feeling; but when the one rises into the other—the transporting sense of eternal "reconciliation" passing into 'gloriation in God' Himself—then the lower is sanctified and sustained by the higher, and each feeling is perfective of the other.

12-21.—COMPARISON AND CONTRAST BETWEEN ADAM AND CHRIST IN THEIR RELATION TO THE HUMAN FAMILY.

This profound and most weighty Section has occasioned an immense deal of critical and theological discussion, in which every point, every clause, almost every word, has been contested. It will require, therefore, a pretty minute examination; and it may conduce to clearness of apprehension to state, in the form of a heading at the outset, the scope and import of each successive division of it.

But before proceeding to the exposition in detail, the reader should observe the terms employed in this great Section to express that deed of *Adam*, on the one hand, which has involved all his posterity in its penal consequences; and on the other hand, what we receive through *Christ*, the Second Adam. Four different terms are employed to express the one, and three to denote the other. The four terms, with reference to the Fall, are, First, "The *sin*" [ἁμαρτία]—*vv.* 12, 20, 21; Second, "The *transgression*" [παράβασις]—*v.* 14; Third, "The *offence*," or rather '*trespass*' [παράπτωμα]—*vv.* 15 (twice), 16, 18, 20; Fourth, "The *disobedience*" [παρακοή]—*v.* 19. The first word, "sin"—from the verb [ἁμαρτάνειν] 'to miss the mark,' and hence, 'to err,' or 'deviate'—is the most general, in Bible usage, and of far the most frequent occurrence; being used nearly two hundred times, and in the LXX. more than double that number. Hence, as the most comprehensive term,

217

12 Wherefore, as by one man sin entered into the world, and death by
13 sin; and so death passed upon all men, ²for that all have sinned: (for

it is both the *first* and the *last* used in this Section; being selected (in *v.* 12) to start the comparison, and again (in *v.* 21) to wind it up. The second term, "transgression" (literally, 'going over' or 'beyond' the proper point, place, or path), and the third term, 'trespass'—from the verb [παρα-πίπτειν], 'to fall beside' or 'aside,' and hence to 'deviate'—scarcely differ at all, as will be seen, in their shades of meaning; and here they are both obviously used for mere variety, to denote that one first 'deflection' or 'deviation' from rectitude in which all mankind have become involved. The fourth and only remaining term, "disobedience," needs no explanation—expressing clearly enough that feature of Adam's sin in the light of which the *obediential* character of Christ's righteousness is most brightly seen. The three equally expressive terms employed to denote what we owe to Christ are, First, What is here rendered "the free gift" [χάρισμα], or rather, '*the gift of grace.*'—*vv.* 15, 16; Second, What is rendered 'the gift' [ἡ δωρεά], but better rendered, '*the free gift*'—*vv.* 15, 17; and, Third, What is also rendered "the gift" [τὸ δώρημα] —but better, '*the bestowal*' or '*the boon*'—*v.* 16. These words speak for themselves, expressing the absolutely gratuitous character of the whole fruits of redemption by the Second Adam. We are now prepared to take the verses of this Section in detail.

First: *Adam's first sin was the sin, and procuring cause of the death, of all mankind* (12). **12.** **Wherefore** [Διὰ τοῦτο]—that is, 'Things being so;' so as they have been shown to be in the whole previous argument of this Epistle. To suppose (as most interpreters do) that the reference is merely to what immediately precedes, is not at all natural; for (as *Fritzsche* says) the immediate statements are quite incidental, whereas what follows is primary, fundamental, all-comprehensive—a grand summation of the whole state of our case, viewed as ruined on the one hand in Adam, and on the other as recovered in Christ. **as by one man** (Adam) **sin entered into the world** [εἰς τ. κόσμον εἰσῆλθεν. There is nothing emphatic in the repetition of the εἰς here; for verbs compounded with εἰς, whenever followed by a noun, invariably repeat the preposition before the noun. In the New Testament this same word is used with a noun following it about 130 times, and never without the εἰς repeated].

By the word "sin" here many good interpreters understand 'the principle of sin,' or, in other words, 'human depravity;' others, 'the commission of sin,' or what is termed 'actual sin.' And certainly the word "entered" might seem to suggest something *active.* But what follows shows, we think, conclusively that in neither of these senses of the term does the apostle here use it. For when he adds, **and death by sin,** it seems quite plain that he intends that sin which was the procuring cause of the death of all mankind; which certainly is neither the sinful principle inherited from Adam nor yet the actual sin of each individual. What, then, can this be but *the first sin*—otherwise called "the transgression," "the trespass," "the disobedience," throughout this Section. But how could an act past and done be said to "enter into the world." Not as an *act*, but as a *state* of guilt or criminality, attaching to the whole human family—as what follows more fully expresses. (So in substance *Bengel, Hodge, Philippi, Wordsworth.*)

and so death passed upon [διῆλθεν]—or, 'went

218

through' all men—pervaded or came to attach to the whole race. [The words ὁ θάνατος are omitted before διῆλθεν by D E F G.; one cursive, some copies of the Old Latin, and one MS. of the Vulgate; and several times by *Augustin.* On this certainly inferior evidence *Tischendorf* excludes it from his text. But the following authorities appear to us decisive in favour of retaining them: א A B C K L, many cursives, the Vulgate (except Cod. Fuld.)—'mors pertransiit'—and other versions, also most of the fathers, including *Augustin* himself. *Lachm.* and *Treg.* retain it.] **for that**— not 'in whom,' as several of the fathers—after the Old Latin and the Vulgate—with *Beza* and others understood the words [ἐφ' ᾧ=*in quo*] rather unnaturally, but as *Calvin* and all the best interpreters who take the words as our version does, 'inasmuch as' **all have sinned** [ἥμαρτον]—'all sinned;' that is, in that one first sin.

The reader will do well to pause here, and after reading the whole verse afresh, to consider how inadequately—we do not say the poor *Pelagian* explanation comes up to the language of it, namely, that Adam's bad *example* has infected all his posterity; but .even that more respectable and far better supported interpretation of it, that the *corrupt nature* inherited from Adam drags all his posterity into sin. Let it be repeated, that the apostle is speaking only of that sin of which death is the righteous penalty; and consequently, when he adds, that "so death passed upon all men, for that all sinned," he can only mean, 'for that all are held to have themselves sinned in that first sin.' But how is this to be understood? Not certainly in the sense of some inexplicable *oneness of personality* (physical or otherwise) in Adam and all his race; for no one's sin can in any intelligible sense be the personal sin of any but himself. All must be resolved into a Divine arrangement, by which Adam was constituted in such sense the head and representative of his race that his sin and fall were held as theirs, and visited penally accordingly. Should the justice of this be questioned, it may be enough to reply that men do, in point of fact, suffer death and many other evils on account of Adam's sin—so, at least, all who believe in a Fall at all will admit—and this involves as much difficulty as the imputation of the guilt which procured it. But should the justice of both be disputed, the only consistent refuge will be found in a denial of all moral government of the world. The only satisfactory key to the manifold sufferings, moral impotence, and death of all mankind, will be found in a *moral* connection between Adam and his race. And when we find a corresponding arrangement for the *recovery* of men through a Second Adam— though we shall never be able to solve the mystery of such moral relations—the one will be found to throw such a steady and beautiful light upon the other, that we shall be forced, as we "look into these things," to exclaim, "O the depth of the riches both of the wisdom and knowledge of God! How unsearchable are His judgments, and His ways past finding out!" (See *Hodge's* masterly statement on the words "all sinned.")

One little word in this verse has given rise to so much troublesome discussion and diversity of interpretation—the word "*as*" [ὥσπερ] with which the verse starts ("Wherefore, *as* by one **man**," &c.)—that it will be necessary to advert to the different views taken of it ere we can fix satisfactorily its precise import here. Is this, then, meant to denote the first member of a comparison (what

until the law sin was in the world: but ^m sin is not imputed when there
14 is no law.   Nevertheless death reigned from Adam to Moses, even over
them that had not sinned after the similitude of Adam's transgression,

grammarians call a *protasis*)? If so, where is the second member (the *apodosis*, as grammarians say)? (1.) Some (as *de Wette*, and after him *Conybeare*) see none, and so regard this as no member of any comparison. Accordingly they translate the clause thus: ' Wherefore [it is] like as by one man,' &c. (so *de Wette*); or thus: 'This therefore is like the case when,' &c. (so *Conybeare*, who refers to the Greek of Matt. xxv. 14 for a parallel case). But it is fatal to this interpretation, that it makes the sin and death of mankind in Adam to be the apostle's principal topic in this Section; whereas it is here introduced only to illustrate by contrast what we owe to Christ. (2.) Others, admitting that the "as" of this verse *is* the first member of a comparison, find the second in the sequel of this same verse; while some find it in the word "so" [οὕτως]; translating "even so" instead of "and so." But this makes bad Greek [for καὶ οὕτως is not = οὕτω καί]. Others (as *Erasmus* and *Beza*) find it in the word "and" ("and death by sin"), translating ' so death by sin.' But besides that this makes a very weak comparison, it compares the wrong parties—namely, Adam and his posterity—whereas it is Adam and Christ whom this Section throughout compares and contrasts. (3.) *Tholuck* thinks that the apostle *has* announced a comparison with the word "as" in *v.* 12, and has virtually completed it in the sequel; but that having started off, before doing so, to develop his first statement, he forgot the precise form in which he began it, and so completes it in substance rather than in form. This, however, is rather loosing the knot than cutting it. Yet *Calvin's* view comes to much the same thing in more guarded language. He finds the second member of the comparison in *v.* 15; but as it certainly is not there in logical form, he thinks that the apostle, engaged with something far higher than verbal accuracy, fills up what he had at *v.* 12 left incomplete, without regard to the precise form of the opening sentence. (4.) Others still, and these the majority of interpreters, find the second member of the comparison—begun in *v.* 12—no nearer than *vv.* 18, 19, each of which begins with a resumption of the first member of the comparison, nearly as in *v.* 12, and ends with a full and formal completion of it: "Therefore, *as* [ὡς] by the offence of one, &c., *even so* [οὕτω καί] by the righteousness of one," &c.—"For as [ὥσπερ] by one man's disobedience, &c., *so* [οὕτω καί] by the obedience of one," &c.

To us there appears to be no real difference between any of the views which recognize in *v.* 12 only the first member of a comparison between Adam and Christ. All admit that the second member of the comparison, regarding Christ, is what the apostle's mind was full of; that all that he says in the development and illustration of the first, regarding Adam, is only introduced with the view of enhancing the second; and that this second, *so far from being held in suspense* or entirely postponed *till the 18th verse*, crops out in one form or other from the 15th verse—where, having mentioned Adam, the apostle adds, "who is the figure of Him that was to come"—onwards from verse to verse until, at *vv.* 18 and 19, it only *culminates* in a redoubled statement, which, for clearness and comprehensiveness, leaves nothing to be desired. If, then, it be granted on the one hand that the formal summation of the whole statement is re-

served to the end, it surely need not be denied, on the other, that the apostle is less careful about the verbal balance of the two members of the comparison than about a distinct and vigorous expression of his meaning in regard to the two great Heads of the human family.

Having thus disposed of the points which have been raised on this opening verse, the remaining ones need not detain us so long.

Second: *The reign of death from Adam to Moses proves the imputation of sin during all that period; and consequently the existence of a law, other than that of Moses, of which sin is the breach* (13, 14). **13. For until the law** [ἄχρι νόμου]—not 'until (the *cessation*) of the law,' or till the time of Christ; as *Chrysostom* and *Augustin*, with other fathers, and *Erasmus*, strangely understood the expression. Clearly, the meaning is, as expressed in *v.* 14, "from Adam to Moses," or until the *giving* of the law, **sin was in the world**—the same "sin," obviously, as that meant in *v.* 12; which we have seen is, not 'actual sin' (with *Stuart* and others), nor (with more and better interpreters) 'the principle of sin' inherited from Adam, but that sin whose penalty was death—the first sin, considered in its *criminality*, exposing all mankind penally to death. **but sin is not imputed when there is no law.** This is nothing else than a general principle, identical with that expressed in ch. iv. 15—" where no law is, there is no transgression"—and much the same as in 1 John iii. 4, " sin is the transgression of the law." It is surprising that so sagacious an interpreter as *Calvin* should have followed *Luther* here (as he himself has been followed by *Beza, Tholuck, Stuart*, &c.) in taking the 'imputation' of sin here to mean the *sense* or feeling of sin by men themselves. For this, besides putting an unwarranted sense on the word 'imputation,' confuses and obscures the apostle's statement, which plainly is, that God's treatment of men, from Adam to Moses, shows them to have been ' reckoned' sinners, and consequently violators of some Divine law other than that of Moses. *Alford*, while admitting the proper sense of 'imputation' here, yet gives it a turn even worse than the above—making the meaning to be, ' sin is not *fully* imputed where there is no law.' The view we have given, as it is the simplest, so it is the only one, as we think, that suits the purposes of the apostle's argument; as will appear from what follows. **14. Nevertheless**—*q. d.*, ' Yet, though according to this sound principle it might have been supposed that mankind, from Adam to Moses, being under no law expressly and outwardly revealed, could not be held liable to death as breakers of law—even then,' **death reigned** [ἐβασίλευσεν]—that is, 'held unresisted and universal sway,' **from Adam to Moses, even over them that had not sinned after the similitude of Adam's transgression.**

But who are they? *Infants* (say some) who, being guiltless of actual sin, yet subject to death, must be sinners in a very different sense from Adam. (So *Origen, Augustin, Melancthon, Beza, Edwards, Haldane,* and others. But why should Infants be specially connected with the period "from Adam to Moses," since they die alike in every period? And if the apostle meant to express here the death of infants, why has he done it so enigmatically? Besides, the death of infants is comprehended in the universal mortality, on account of the first sin, so emphati-

15 who is the figure of him that was to come. But not as the offence, so also *is* the free gift. For if through the offence of one many be dead, much more the grace of God, and the gift by grace, *which is* by one man, 16 Jesus Christ, hath abounded ⁿunto many. And not as *it was* by one that sinned, *so is* the gift: for the judgment *was* by one to condemna-

A. D. 60.
ⁿ Isa. 53. 11.
Matt. 20. 28.
Matt. 26. 28.
Heb. 9. 2?.
1 John 2. 1.

cally expressed in *v.* 12 : what need, then, to specify it here? and why, if not necessary, should we presume it to be meant here, unless the language unmistakeably point to it—which it certainly does not? The meaning, then, must be, that ‘death reigned from Adam to Moses, even over those that had not, like Adam, transgressed against a positive commandment, threatening death to the disobedient.’ (So most interpreters.) In this case, the particle “even,” instead of specifying one particular class of those who lived “from Adam to Moses” (as the other view supposes), merely explains what it was that made the case of those who died from Adam to Moses worthy of special notice—namely, that ‘though unlike Adam, and all since Moses, those who lived between the two had no positive threatening of death for transgression, “nevertheless, death reigned *even over them*.” **who is the figure** [τύπος] (or ‘type’) **of him [that was] to come** [τοῦ μέλλοντος]—‘of the future one,’ Christ. The phrase is taken in a neuter sense—‘the type of *that which* was to be,’ or ‘of the then future state of things’—by *Erasmus, Bengel, Green*, &c. But the mention twice in this same verse of *Adam* by name, and the thoroughly Pauline idea of a “second Adam ” (as *Meyer* remarks) puts it beyond reasonable doubt that our version gives the true sense of the phrase here—“*Him* that was to come.” The clause itself is inserted (as *Alford* says) on the first mention of the name “Adam,” as the *one man* of whom he is speaking, to recall the purpose for which he is treating of him—as *the figure of Christ*. The point of analogy intended here is plainly the *public character* which both sustained, neither of the two being regarded in the Divine procedure towards mankind as mere *individual* men, but both alike as *representative* men. Some take the proper supplement here to be, ‘Him [that is] to come,’ understanding the apostle to speak from his own time, and to refer to Christ’s Second Coming. (So *Fritzsche, de Wette, Alford*.) But this is unnatural, since the whole analogy here contemplated between the Second Adam and the First has been in full development ever since “ God exalted Him to be a Prince and a Saviour,” and it will only remain to be consummated at His Second Coming. The simple meaning is—as nearly all interpreters agree—that Adam is a type of Him who was to come after him in the same public character, and so to be “the Second Adam.”

Third : *The cases of Adam and Christ present points of contrast as well as of resemblance* (15-17). **15. But** (‘Howbeit’) **not as the offence** [παράπτωμα]—‘the trespass,’ **so also is the free gift** [τὸ χάρισμα]—‘the gift of grace,’ or ‘gracious gift:’ in other words, ‘The two cases present points of contrast as well as resemblance.’

First point of contrast : *If God permitted the sin of the one Head of humanity to blight the many, much more may we rest assured, that through the merit of the other Head the many will be blessed*. **For if through the offence of one many be dead, much more the grace of God, and the gift by grace, which is by one man, Jesus Christ, hath abounded unto many.** Pity ,it is that our translators omitted the articles in this verse, as they throw so much light on the precise parties and things contrasted. Literally the verse runs thus, ‘For if

through the trespass of the one the many died (in that one man’s first sin), much more did the grace of God, and the free gift by grace [ἡ χάρις τ. Θεοῦ καὶ ἡ δωρεὰ ἐν χάριτι], even that of the one man Jesus Christ [τῇ τοῦ ἑνὸς ἀνθρώπου ’I. X.], abound unto the many.’ By ‘the many,’ in both members of this comparison, is meant the *mass* of mankind, represented respectively by Adam and Christ ; and the opposition of these “many” is neither to *few* men, nor to *all* men, but to ‘*the one man*’ who represented them respectively. It is of great importance to the right understanding of the whole argument to observe this. By ‘the gift of grace,’ or “ the free gift,” is meant—as in *v.* 17—the glorious gift of *justifying righteousness*. This is expressly distinguished from “ the *grace* of God,” from which that gift is here said to flow, as the *effect* from the *cause*; and both are said to ‘‘ abound ” towards us in Christ, in what sense will appear in the next two verses. Finally, The “ much more,” of the one case than the other, does not mean that we get much more of good by Christ than of evil by Adam (for it is not a case of quantity at all), but that we have much more reason to expect—or it is much more agreeable to our ideas of God—that the many should be benefited by the merit of one, than that they should suffer for the sin of one ; and if the latter has happened, *much more* may we assure ourselves of the former. [*Fritzsche* and *Meyer* connect ἐν χάριτι, not with what goes before, but with what follows—thus, ‘much more did the grace of God and the free gift abound through grace,’ or ‘richly abound ;’ but this is unnatural. It has been observed that by the use of the *dative* (τῷ τοῦ ἑνὸς παραπτώματι—instead of διὰ with the genitive, the causal sin of Adam is conceived of as identified with the agent himself, and invested with a sort of living energy, taking deadly effect on all his race. Perhaps this is to press the grammatical form a little too far ; but there can be no doubt that it expresses the very idea intended by the apostle.]

Second point of contrast : *The condemnation was for one sin, but the justification covers many offences*. **16. And not as [it was] by one that sinned.** [Instead of δι’ ἑνὸς ἁμαρτήσαντος, *Griesbach* reads ἁμαρτήματος, but on inferior authority; it bears marks, as *Fritzsche* says, of being a correction of the received reading: it is rejected by *Lachm., Tisch*., and *Treg*.] **so [is the] gift** [τὸ δώρημα]—‘the bestowal,’ ‘the boon.’ This is but a varied expression of what was said at the opening of the preceding verse—*q.d.*, ‘Now for another point of contrast,’ **for the judgment was by one to condemnation.** Our translators have rendered two different prepositions in this verse by the same word “ *by* ”—thus : ‘And not as it was *by* one that sinned [δι’ ἑνός] . . . for the judgment was *by* one to condemnation’ [ἐξ ἑνός]. From this we may infer that they understood both statements to refer to ‘ one *person*’—namely, Adam (as several of the fathers, *Fritzsche, de Wette, Meyer, Alford, Philippi, Lange*). But since the contrast in this verse is plainly not between the two *persons* at all—Adam and Christ—but between the one *offence* which brought condemnation and the “*many offences*” which are covered in justification, it seems to us quite clear that the true rendering of the verse—as the two different pre-

17 tion, but the free gift *is* of many offences unto justification. For if [3] by one man's offence death reigned by one; much more they which receive abundance of grace and of the gift of righteousness shall reign in life by 18 one, Jesus Christ.) Therefore as [4] by the offence of one *judgment came* upon all men to condemnation; even so, [5] by the righteousness of one *the* 19 *free gift came* upon all men unto justification of life. For as by one

A. D. CO.
[3] Or, by one offence.
[4] Or, by one offence.
[5] Or, by one righteousness.

positions employed seem indeed to indicate—is as follows : 'And not as it was *by* one that sinned [δι' ἑνός], so is the boon ; for the judgment was *of* one [offence or .'trespass'] to condemnation [ἐξ ἑνός], but,' &c. (So the majority of interpreters.) The "of" in this case denotes the criminal source or procuring cause of the condemnation of the human race to death.

but the free gift [τὸ χάρισμα]—'the gift of grace,' or 'the gracious gift.' **is of many offences** ('trespasses') **unto justification** [ἐκ πολλῶν ἁμαρτημάτων εἰς δικαίωμα. This form of the word "justification". [δικαίωμα] signifies, 'what is ordained' or 'decreed,' the 'sentence pronounced;' thus differing from the more usual form [δικαιωσύνη], which signifies the state, habit, or quality of him who is 'just' [δίκαιος]. Here it is used in its strict sense, to denote the righteous acquittal pronounced upon those on whom the 'gift of grace' [χάρισμα] has been conferred. The expression 'of many trespasses'—evidently suggested by the foregoing one 'of one trespass'—presents the trespasses covered in justification in a peculiar light, as in some sense the procuring cause of the glorious remedy ; as if the cry of these countless offences had gone up to heaven, but instead of drawing down vengeance, had wakened the Divine compassions, and given birth to the wondrous provision of grace in Christ Jesus. The whole statement, then, amounts to this: 'The condemnation by Adam was for *one sin;* but the justification by Christ is an absolution not only from the guilt of that first offence, mysteriously attaching to every individual of the race, but from the *countless offences* into which, as a germ lodged in the bosom of every child of Adam, it unfolds itself in his life.' This is the meaning of what the next verse tells us of, 'grace *abounding* towards us in the *abundance of the gift* of righteousness.' It is a grace not only rich in its *character*, but rich in *detail;* a "righteousness" not only rich in *a complete justification* of the guilty, condemned sinner, but rich in the *amplitude of the ground* which it covers, leaving no one sin of any of the justified uncancelled, but making him, though loaded with the guilt of myriads of offences, "the righteousness of God in Christ ! "

17. For if by one man's offence. (This reading is preferable to *Tischendorf's*—'by one offence' [ἐν ἑνὶ παραπτώματι]—which is supported by A D E F G, two copies of the Old Latin, and no other authorities ; whereas the received reading is supported by א B C K L, many cursives, two copies of the Old Latin, the Vulgate —*in unius delicto* — both Syriac versions, and the Memphitic, and most of the fathers. *Lachm.* and *Treg.* retain it, and most critics prefer it.) **death reigned by** ('the') **one; much more they which receive** ('the') **abundance of grace and of the gift of righteousness**—that is, 'justifying righteousness,' **shall reign in life by one** ('through the one'), **Jesus Christ.** We have here the two ideas of *vv.* 15 and 16 sublimely combined into one, as if the subject had grown upon the apostle as he advanced in his comparison of the two cases. Here, for the first time in this Section, does he speak of that LIFE which springs out of justifica-

tion, in contrast with the death which springs from sin and follows condemnation. The proper idea, therefore, of the word "life" here is, 'Right to live'—'Righteous life'—life possessed and enjoyed with the good will, and in conformity with the eternal law, of "Him that sitteth on the Throne ;" life, therefore, in its widest sense—life in the whole man and throughout the whole duration of human existence, the life of blissful and loving relationship to God in soul and body for ever and ever. It is worthy of note, too, that while he says death "reigned *over*" us through Adam, he does not say Life 'reigns over us' through Christ; lest he should seem to invest this new life with the very attribute of the death—that of fell and malignant tyranny—of which we were the hapless victims. Nor does he say Life reigns *in* us, which would have been a Scriptural enough idea ; but, which is much more pregnant, " *We* shall reign in life." While *freedom* and *might* are implied in the figure of 'reigning,' 'life' is represented as the glorious territory or atmosphere of that reign. And by recurring to the idea of *v.* 16—as to the "many offences" whose complete pardon shows "the abundance of grace and of the gift of righteousness"—the whole statement amounts to this: 'If one man's one offence let loose against us the tyrant power of Death, to hold us as its victims in helpless bondage, "much more," when we stand forth enriched with God's "abounding grace," and in the beauty of a complete absolution from countless offences, shall we expatiate in a life Divinely owned and legally secured, "reigning" in exultant freedom and unchallenged might, through that other matchless " One," Jesus Christ!' (On the import of the *future* tense in this last clause, see on *v.* 19 and ch. vi. 5.)

Fourth: *To sum up all in one word—To TWO MEN Humanity owes its ruin and its recovery: condemnation to the one, justification to the other; death to the one, life to the other* (18, 19). **18. Therefore** ["Αρα οὖν—or, 'Now then;' the matter standing as we have thus at length shown [*rebus ita comparatis:* ἄρα has respect rather to the internal, οὖν more to the external cause (says *Klotz* ad Devar, quoted by *Meyer*)]. Thus the apostle explicitly resumes the unfinished comparison of *v.* 12, in order to give *formally* the concluding member of it, which had been done once and again *substantially* in the intermediate verses. **as by the offence** (or 'trespass') **of one [judgment came]**—or rather, 'it came,' **upon all men to condemnation; even so by the righteousness [δικαιώματος] of one [the free gift came]**—rather, 'it came,' **upon all men unto justification [δικαίωσιν] of life** or, 'it resulted in' this.

But the marginal rendering of this verse is equally admissible: 'as by one trespass . . . so by one righteousness' [δι' ἑνός παραπτώματος—δι' ἑνός δικαιώματος]. The argument in favour of this sense is the absence of the article in both clauses before "one," and the similar expression in *v.* 16, "the judgment was of one [offence] to condemnation"—as we have explained that clause. Accordingly many interpreters pronounce for it (as *Beza, Grotius, Ferme, Locke, de Wette, Meyer, Conybeare, Alford, Mehring, Webster and Wilkinson*, the Revised Version, *Jowett, Wordsworth,*

man's disobedience many were made sinners; so by the obedience of one shall many be made righteous.

20   Moreover °the law entered, that the offence might abound. But where

A. D. 60.
° John 15, 22.
Gal. 3. 19.

Green). But the objections to it are—(1.) That the comparison *here* is between the *persons*, not the *acts* —between the many's condemnation for the one's offence and the many's justification through the one's righteousness; (2.) That though "one righteousness" may fitly enough—perhaps even sublimely—express the oneness of Christ's whole work, or the Divine acceptance of it [δικαίωμα] as the meritorious ground of justification, it is an expression nowhere else used, and scarcely in conformity with the strain of the reasoning in this Section; (3.) That after the abundant recurrence of the word "one" in a masculine sense, to denote the *persons* respectively of Adam and Christ, the absence of the article in this case need not require us to take the word in a neuter sense, if otherwise there is ground to think that the reference is to Adam and Christ. In view of all this, though formerly inclined to the sense of 'one offence' and 'one righteousness,' we now rather prefer the sense of our own version (in favour of which are the Vulgate, *Erasmus, Luther, Calvin, Bengel, Fritzsche, Tholuck, Philippi, Hodge, Lange*). It may be added that some (as *Alford*, and the authors of the Revised Version) take the form here translated "righteousness" [δικαίωμα—hero apparently suggested by the previous παράπτωμα] to mean 'one righteous act;' and *Green* renders it 'one achievement of righteousness.' But the idea of a 'decree' or 'sentence'—which this form certainly conveys—is sufficiently preserved if we understand "the righteousness of one" here to mean the whole work of Christ considered as *judicially pronounced upon and Divinely accepted*. Finally, the lofty expression "justification of life" is just a vivid combination of two distinct ideas already expatiated upon, and means 'justification entitling to, and issuing in, the rightful possession and enjoyment of life' [εἰς δικαίωσιν ζωῆς—the 'genitive of destination:' δικαίωσις is here distinguished from δικαίωμα, as the *act* of justifying is from the *result*].

19. For as by ['the'] one man's disobedience ['the'] many were made [κατεστάθησαν]—'constituted,' or 'held to be,' sinners; so by the obedience of ['the'] one shall ['the'] many be made [κατασταθήσονται] righteous [παρακοή—ὑπακοή. The latter word doubtless here suggested the use of the former—here only in this Section—to contrast with it.] On this great verse observe, *first*, that by the "obedience" of Christ here is plainly meant more than what divines calls His *active* obedience, as distinguished from His sufferings and death; it is the entire work of Christ in its *obediential* character. Our Lord Himself represents even His death as His great act of obedience to the Father: "This commandment (*i. e.*, to lay down and resume His life) have I received of my Father" (John x. 18). *Second*, The significant word [καθίστημι] twice here rendered "made," does not signify to ' *work a change upon* ' a person or thing, but to '*establish*,' '*constitute*,' or '*ordain*,' as will be seen from all the places where it is used. Here, accordingly, it is intended to express that *judicial act* which holds men, in virtue of their connection with Adam, as sinners; and in connection with Christ, as righteous. *Third*, The change of *tense* from the past to the future—'as through Adam we *were* made sinners, so through Christ we *shall be* made righteous'—delightfully expresses the *enduring* character of the act, and of the economy to which such acts belong, in contrast

with the ruin, for ever past, of believers in Adam. (See on ch. vi. 5.) *Fourth*, The "all men" of *v.* 18, and the "many" of *v.* 19, are the same party, though under a slightly different aspect. In the latter case the contrast is between the *one* representative (Adam—Christ) and the *many* whom he represented; in the former case, it is between the one *head* (Adam—Christ) and the *race*, affected for death and life respectively by the actings of that one. Only in this latter case (as *Meyer* here clearly recognizes) it is the redeemed family of man that is alone in view; it is *Humanity* as actually lost, but also as actually saved—as ruined and recovered. Such as refuse to fall in with the high purpose of God to constitute His Son a 'second Adam,' the Head of a new race—and so, as impenitent and unbelieving, finally perish—have no place in this Section of the Epistle, whose sole object is to show how God repairs in the Second Adam the evil done by the First. Thus the doctrine of *universal restoration* has no place here. Thus, too, the forced interpretation (of a great many expositors, as *Alford*) by which the 'justification of all' is made to mean a justification merely in *possibility* and *offer* to all, and the 'justification of the many' to mean the *actual* justification of as many as believe, is completely avoided. And thus, finally, the harshness of comparing a *whole* fallen family with a recovered *part* is got rid of. However true it be in *fact* that part of mankind are not saved, this is not the *aspect* in which the subject is here presented. It is *totals* that are compared and contrasted; and it is the *same total* in two successive conditions—namely, *the human race* as ruined in Adam and recovered in Christ.

Fifth : *But if the whole purposes of God towards men centre in Adam and Christ, where does the Law come in, and what was its use?* It was given to *reveal more fully the Ruin that came by the one and the Recovery brought in by the other* (20, 21). **20.** Moreover the law entered [παρεισῆλθεν]—'entered incidentally' or 'parenthetically.' It is important to preserve this shade of meaning, which the compound word certainly conveys, and which—though not always intended to be pressed—was here, we think, plainly designed to be conveyed. Several of the Greek fathers advert to it; the Vulgate expresses it [subintravit]; and *Calvin* [intervenit]. *Beza*, whom our version has done ill here in following, sinks it [introiit]; but it is recognized by nearly every modern critic, from *Erasmus* downwards. *Bengel*, with his usual acuteness, notices that this compound verb—'the law entered *subordinately*'—is designed as the antithesis to the simple one, "sin *entered*," in *v.* 12; adding, 'Sin is older than the law.' In Gal. ii. 4 the same word is by our translators properly rendered, "came in privily." The meaning, then, here is, that *the promulgation of the law at Sinai was no primary or essential feature of the Divine plan*, but it was "added" (Gal. iii. 19) for a subordinate purpose— the more fully to reveal the evil occasioned by Adam, and the need and glory of the remedy by Christ. that the offence ('the trespass')—meaning, as throughout all this Section, 'the one first transgression of Adam,' might abound [πλεονάσῃ]— literally, 'might be more,' or 'be multiplied.' The immediate reference is not to the *recognition* and *sense* of sin by men themselves, although that is the natural *result* [for, as *Philippi* says, the apostle does not write ἵνα πλεονάσῃ ἡ ἐπίγνωσις τ. ἁμαρ-

222

21 sin abounded, grace did ^pmuch more abound : that as sin hath reigned unto death, even so might grace reign through righteousness unto eternal life by Jesus Christ our Lord.

A. D. co.

P Luke 7. 47.
1 Tim. 1. 14.

τίας]. God intended, says the apostle, by the giving of the law to make it appear that the multiplied breaches of it which would certainly ensue were but the varied activity of that first transgression, and so to show what a fearful thing that first sin was—as not only "entering into the world," but becoming the active principle and constitutive character of the whole race. It is as if the apostle had said, 'All our multitudinous breaches of the law are nothing but *that one first offence*, lodged mysteriously in the bosom of every child of Adam as an *offending principle*, and *multiplying itself* into myriads of particular offences in the life of each.' What was one *act* of disobedience in the head has been converted into a vital and virulent *principle* of disobedience in all the members of the human family, whose every act of wilful rebellion proclaims itself the child of the original transgression. But where sin abounded ('was multiplied'), grace did much more abound [ὑπερεπερίσσευσεν]—rather, 'did exceedingly abound,' or 'superabound.' The comparison here is between the multiplication of one offence into countless transgressions, and such an overflow of grace as more than meets that appalling case. 21. That as sin hath reigned—'That as sin reigned' [ἐβασίλευσεν]. Observe here the marked change in the term employed to express the great original transgression. It is no longer "the offence" or 'trespass'—that view of the matter has been sufficiently illustrated—but, as better befitted this comprehensive and sublime summation of the whole matter, the great general term *SIN*, with which this Section opened, is here resumed. unto death. Our version has here followed *Luther's* and *Beza's* translation ; though the words [ἐν τῷ θανάτῳ] signify 'in death.' But even those who render the words thus rightly seem for the most part to understand it as meaning '*through death*' (and so *Calvin* translates it), as opposed to the Grace which in the next clause is said to reign "*through* righteousness." But as the prepositions are not the same, so this makes quite a wrong antithesis, and brings out at the best a very dubious sentiment. The true sense seems clear on the face of the words—'that as Sin reached its uttermost end "in death," and thus revelled (so to speak) in the complete destruction of its victims,' even so might grace reign. In *v.* 14 we had the reign of *death* of the fallen in Adam, and in *v.* 17 the reign in *life* of the justified in Christ. Here we have the reign of the mighty *causes* of both these—of SIN, which clothes Death as a Sovereign with venomous *power* (1 Cor. xv. 56) and with awful *authority* (ch. vi. 23), and of GRACE, the grace which originated the scheme of salvation, the grace which "sent the Son to be the Saviour of the world," the grace which "made Him to be sin for us who knew no sin," the grace which "makes us to be the righteousness of God in Him ;" so that "we who receive *the abundance of grace* and of the gift of righteousness do reign in life by One, Jesus Christ !" through righteousness—not *ours* certainly ('the obedience of Christians,' to use the wretched language of *Grotius*); nor yet exactly 'justification' (as *Stuart*, &c.), but rather, 'the justifying righteousness of Christ' (as *Beza*, *Alford*, *Philippi*, and, in substance, *Olshausen*, *Meyer*); the same which in *v.* 19 is called His "obedience," meaning His whole mediatorial work in the flesh. This is here represented as the *righteous medium* through which Grace reaches its objects and attains all its ends, the stable throne from which Grace as a Sovereign dispenses its saving benefits to as many as are brought under its benign sway. unto eternal life—which is Salvation in its highest form and fullest development for ever, by Jesus Christ our Lord. Thus, on that "Name which is above every name" the echoes of this hymn to the glory of "Grace" die away, and "Jesus is left alone."

The profound and inestimable teaching of this golden Section of our Epistle has been somewhat obscured, we fear, by the unusual quantity of nice verbal criticism which it seemed to require, and the necessity of distinguishing some theological ideas in it which are apt to be confounded. It may not be superfluous, therefore, to bring it out more fully by the following

Remarks.—1. If this Section do not teach that the whole race of Adam, standing in him as their federal head, 'sinned in him and fell with him in his first transgression,' we may despair of any intelligible exposition of it. The apostle, after saying that Adam's sin introduced death into the world, does not say "and so death passed upon all men, for that" *Adam* "sinned," but "for that *all sinned*." Thus, according to the teaching of the apostle, 'the death of all is for the sin of all ;' and as this cannot mean the personal sins of each individual, but some sin with which unconscious infants are charged equally with adults, it can mean nothing but the one 'first transgression' of their common head, regarded as *the sin of each* of his race, and punished, as such, with death. It is vain to start back from this imputation to all of the guilt of Adam's first sin, as wearing the appearance of *injustice*. For not only are all other theories liable to the same objection in some other form—besides being inconsistent with the text—but the actual *facts of human nature*, which none dispute, and which cannot be explained away, involve essentially the same difficulties as the great *principle* on which the apostle here explains them. Whereas, if we admit this principle, on the authority of our apostle, a flood of light is at once thrown upon certain features of the Divine procedure, and certain portions of the Divine oracles, which otherwise are involved in much darkness ; and if the principle itself seem hard to digest, it is not harder than the *existence of evil*, which as a fact admits of no dispute, but as a feature in the Divine administration admits of no explanation in the present state. 2. What is commonly called *original sin*—or that depraved tendency to evil with which every child of Adam comes into the world—is not formally treated of in this Section ; and even in the seventh chapter it is rather its *nature* and *operations* than its *connection with the first sin* which is handled. But indirectly, this Section bears indubitably testimony to it, representing the one original offence—unlike every other—as having an *enduring vitality* in the bosom of every child of Adam, as a principle of disobedience, whose origin and virulence have gotten it the familiar name of 'original sin.' 3. In what sense is the word "*death*" used throughout this Section? Not certainly as mere *temporal* death, as Arminian and, in general, all shallow commentators affirm. For as Christ came to undo what Adam did—and that is all comprehended in the word "death"—it would hence follow that Christ has merely dissolved the sentence by which soul and body are parted in death ; in other words, merely procured the resurrection of the body.

6   WHAT shall we say then? Shall we continue in sin, that grace may abound?

2   God forbid. How shall we, that are dead [a]to sin, live any longer
3   therein? Know ye not, that [b]so many of us as [1]were baptized into Jesus

A. D. 60.

CHAP. 6.
[a] Gal. 6. 14.
[b] Col. 3. 3.
[1] Or, are.

But the New Testament throughout teaches that the Salvation of Christ is from a vastly more comprehensive "death" than that. Yet neither is death here used merely in the sense of *penal evil* —that is, 'any evil inflicted in punishment of sin and for the support of law' (according to *Hodge*). This seems to us a great deal too indefinite, making death a mere figure of speech to denote 'penal evil' in general—an idea foreign, as we think, to the simplicity of Scripture—or at least making death, strictly so called, only one part of the thing meant by it, which ought not to be resorted to if a more simple and natural explanation can be found. By "death," then, in this Section, we understand the sinner's *destruction* in the only sense in which he is capable of it. Even temporal death is called "destruction" (Deut. vii. 23; 1 Sam. v. 11, &c.), as extinguishing all that men regard as life. But a destruction extending to the *soul* as well as the body, and *into the future world*, is clearly expressed in such passages as Matt. vii. 13; 2 Thess. i. 9; 2 Pet. iii. 16. This is the penal "death" of our Section; and in this all-comprehensive view of it we retain its proper sense. Life—as a state of enjoyment of the favour of God, of pure fellowship with Him, and voluntary subjection to Him—is a blighted thing from the moment that sin is found in the creature's skirts: in that sense the threatening, "In the day that thou eatest thereof thou shalt surely die," was carried into immediate effect in the case of Adam when he fell, who was thenceforward "dead while he lived." Such are all his posterity from their birth. The separation of soul and body in temporal death carries the "sinner's destruction" a stage further; dissolving his connection with that world out of which he extracted a pleasurable, though unblest, existence, and ushering him into the presence of his Judge—first as a disembodied spirit, but ultimately in the body, too, in an enduring condition—"to be punished (and this is the final state) with *everlasting destruction* from the presence of the Lord, and from the glory of His power." This final extinction in soul and body of all that constitutes life, but yet eternal consciousness of a blighted existence—this, in its amplest and most awful sense, is "DEATH!" Not that Adam understood all that. It is enough that he understood "the day" of his disobedience to be the terminating period of his blissful "life." In that simple idea was wrapt up all the rest. That he should comprehend its *details* was not necessary. Nor is it necessary to suppose all that to be intended in every passage of Scripture where the word occurs. Enough that all we have described is in the bosom of the *thing*, and will be realized in as many as are not the happy subjects of the Reign of Grace. Beyond doubt, the whole of this is intended in such sublime and comprehensive passages as this: "God ... gave His ... Son, that whosoever believeth in Him *might not* PERISH, *but have everlasting* LIFE" (John iii. 16). And should not the untold horrors of that "DEATH"—already "reigning over" all that are not in Christ, and hastening to its consummation —quicken our flight into "the Second Adam," that having "received the abundance of grace and of the gift of righteousness we may reign in LIFE by the One, Jesus Christ"?

CHAP. VI. 1-23.—THE FRUITS OF JUSTIFICATION IN THE NEW LIFE.

In the opening remarks on the foregoing chapter it was stated that the second great Head of the apostle's subject, the Fruits of Justification in Privilege and in Life, extended over three chapters—the sixth, seventh, and eighth. In the first eleven verses of the preceding chapter the *Privileges* of the Justified are handled, the remaining verses being a digression. The new *Life* of the believer falls now to be opened up. To this fruitful topic the apostle devotes two whole chapters; in the present chapter treating of the *Union of believers to Christ* as the source of the new life, and in the following one continuing this subject, but following it up with some profound considerations on *the great principles of sin and holiness* in fallen men, both under law and under grace.

The general bearing of Gratuitous Justification on a Holy Life (1, 2). **1. What shall we say then?** This, it will be observed, is a marked characteristic of our apostle's style in this Epistle—to mark sudden transitions to a new branch of his subject, as a mode of putting and answering questions, or a way of calling attention to some important statement (cf. ch. iii. 5; iv. 1; vii. 7; viii. 31; ix. 14, 30). **Shall we continue in sin** [ἐπιμενοῦμεν]. But this reading, in the *future* tense, has hardly any support [and has been occasioned, no doubt, as *Fritzsche* and *Meyer* suggest, by the immediately preceding future, ἐροῦμεν—ἐπιμενοῦμεν]. The only well-supported reading is in the *subjunctive* mood [ἐπιμένωμεν]—'May we,' or, more idiomatically, 'Are we to continue in sin?' (On this *deliberative subjunctive*, as grammarians call it, see *Kühner*, § 259, 1. b.) **that grace may abound?**—acting on the detestable principle, 'The more sin, the more scope for grace to pardon it.' This objection, with the very phraseology in which it is couched, was plainly suggested by the closing verses of the foregoing chapter, about 'grace superabounding over the abundance of sin.' It is thus indisputable that the doctrine which the apostle has been all along teaching and elaborately proving in this Epistle is that of a purely *gratuitous justification*. For had his doctrine been that salvation depends *in any degree* upon our good works, no such objection to it could have been raised; whereas against the doctrine of a purely gratuitous justification the objection is plausible, nor has there ever been an age in which it has not been urged. That it *was* brought against the apostles, we know from ch. iii. 8; and we gather from Gal. v. 13, 1 Pet. ii. 16, and Jude 4, that some did give occasion to the charge; but that it was a total perversion of the doctrine of Grace the apostle here proceeds to show.

2. God forbid [Μὴ γένοιτο]—'That be far from us;' the instincts of the new creature revolting at the thought. **How shall we, that are dead to sin, live any longer therein?**—lit., and more forcibly, 'We who died to sin (in the way presently to be explained), How shall we live any longer therein' [οἵτινες ἀπεθάνομεν, 'such who have,' *quippe qui*—more expressive than οἱ ἀπεθ. So ch. iv. 1. 25, 32; ii. 15. See *Jelf*, § 816. 5]. 'It is not (says *Grotius*, very well here) the entire impossibility, but rather the shamefulness of it which is thus expressed, as in Matt. vi. 28, and Gal. iv. 9. For shameful, sure it is, after we have been washed, to roll again into the mire.'

How union to Christ effects the believer's death to

4 ᶜChrist were baptized into his death? Therefore we are ᵈburied with him by baptism into death; that like as Christ was raised up from the dead by the glory of the Father, even so we also should walk in newness

A. D. 60.
ᶜ 1 Cor. 15. 29.
ᵈ Col. 2. 12.

sin and resurrection to new life (3-11). **3. Know ye not, that so many of us as were baptized into Jesus Christ**—'Christ Jesus' it should be; for that is the reading not only of *all* the MSS., but even of the received text, and yet our version (as printed, at least) has "Jesus Christ." The meaning is, "baptized," not into the *acknowledgment* of Christ only, but 'into the *participation* of all that He is for sinners' (cf. Matt. xxviii. 19; 1 Cor. x. 2; Gal. iii. 27), sealed with the seal of heaven, and formally entered and articled (so to speak) as to all the *benefits*, so also to all the *obligations* of Christian discipleship in general; but more particularly, **were baptized into his death?**—as the hinge of His whole work. That it is so, must be manifest on the surface of the New Testament to every impartial reader. But the growing tendency to regard the death of Christ as but the completion of a life of self-devotion—which men have simply to copy—may render it fit that we should here set down a few of the more emphatic expressions of its sacrificial and life-giving virtue:—Matt. i. 22; xx. 28; Luke xxii. 19, 20; John i. 29; iii. 14-16; vi. 51, 53-56; x. 15, 17, 18; xii. 32; Acts xx. 28; (and passing over our own Epistle) 1 Cor. i. 23, 24; v. 7; xv. 3; 2 Cor. v. 14, 21; Gal. ii. 20; iii. 13; iv. 4, 5; Eph. i. 7; ii. 13, 16; v. 25; Col. i. 20-22; Tit. ii. 14; Heb. ix. 14; x. 10, 12, 14, 19; xiii. 12, 20; 1 Pet. i. 18, 19; ii. 24; 1 John i. 7; ii. 2; Rev. i. 5, v. 9; vii. 14. Since, then, He was "made sin," yea "a curse for us," "bearing our sins in His own body on the tree," and "rising again for our justification," our whole sinful case and condition, thus taken up into His person, has been brought to an end in His death. Whoso, then, has been baptized into Christ's death has formally surrendered the whole state and life of sin, as in Christ a dead thing. He has sealed himself to be not only "the righteousness of God in Him," but "a new creature;" and as he cannot be in Christ to the one effect and not to the other—for they are one and inseparable—he has bidden farewell, by baptism into Christ's death, to his entire connection with sin. "How," then, "can he live any longer therein?" The two things are as contradictory in the fact as they are in the terms. Of all this the apostle says, 'Know ye it not?'—as if it were among the household truths of the Christian Faith, lying as it does at the foundation of our standing as believers before God. Not that *as put in this Epistle* they had ever been brought before these Roman Christians, probably, until they read them here; nor is it likely, indeed, that any of the churches save those who were favoured with Pauline teaching were much better off. But they were of that nature that they only needed to be presented to intelligent and teachable believers to be recognized and acquiesced in as the very truths in which they had been rudimentally instructed from the first. Compare the similar saying of our Lord to His disciples at the Supper-table, John xiv. 5 (on which see *Commentary*, p. 434).

4. Therefore we are buried with him [συνετάφημεν]—rather, 'we were buried with Him;' for the thing is viewed as a past act, done and completed at once on their reception of the Gospel, and baptismally sealed on their profession of it, by baptism into death. It is thus that this and the preceding clauses must be separated, to make the sense clear. It is not,

'by baptism we are buried with Him into death,' which makes no sense at all; but 'by *baptism with Him into death* we are buried with Him;' in other words, 'by the same baptism which publicly enters us into His *death*, we are made partakers of His *burial* also.' To leave a dead body unburied is represented, alike in heathen authors as in Scripture, as the greatest indignity (Rev. xi. 8, 9). It was fitting, therefore, that Christ, after "dying for our sins according to the Scriptures," should "descend into the lower parts of the earth" (Eph. iv. 9). As this was the last and lowest step of His humiliation, so it was the honourable dissolution of His last link of connection with that life which He laid down for us; and we, in being 'buried with Him by our baptism into His death,' have by this public act severed our last link of connection with that whole sinful condition and life which Christ brought to an end in His death. **that like as Christ was raised up from the dead by the glory of the Father**—or, by such a forth-putting of the Father's *power* as made that act to be the effulgence of the Father's whole glory. Compare 1 Cor. vi. 14; 2 Cor. xiii. 4; Eph. i. 19, &c. So nearly all good critics. (*Beza* erroneously renders διὰ τῆς δόξης, 'into, the glory of the Father.' See *Grotius, Fritzsche*, and *Meyer*, on this use of the word.) The resurrection of Christ is here, as generally in the New Testament, ascribed to the Father, who therein proclaimed His judicial satisfaction with and acceptance of His whole work in the flesh. **even so we also should walk in newness of life.** The parallel here is not (as the apostle's language might seem to say) between Christ's resurrection and our *walking* in newness of life, but between Christ's resurrection and *our resurrection* to newness of life—henceforth to *walk* in it. Believers, immediately on their union to the risen Saviour, rise to a new resurrection-life—the life, in fact, of their risen Lord—as is once and again emphatically expressed in the sequel. Here, taking this for granted, the apostle advances to the practical development of this new life, saying, in effect, 'That like as Christ was raised from the dead by the glory of the Father, even so we also, *risen with Him*, should, as new creatures, walk conformably.' But what is that "newness?" Surely if our *old* life, now dead, and buried with Christ, was wholly sinful, the *new*, to which we rise with the risen Saviour, must be altogether a holy life; so that every time we go back to "those things whereof we are now ashamed" (*v.* 21), we belie our resurrection with Christ to newness of life, and "forget that we have been purged from our old sins" (2 Pet. i. 9). Whether the mode of baptism by immersion be alluded to in this verse, as a kind of symbolical burial and resurrection, does not seem to us of much consequence. Many interpreters think it is; and it may be so. But as it is not clear that baptism in apostolic times was exclusively by immersion (see Acts ii. 41), so *sprinkling* and *washing* are indifferently used in the New Testament to express the cleansing efficacy of the blood of Jesus. And just as the woman with the issue of blood got virtue out of Christ by simply *touching* Him, so the essence of baptism seems to lie in the simple *contact* of the element with the body, symbolizing living contact with Christ crucified; the mode and extent of suffusion being indifferent and variable with climate and circumstances.

5 of life. For *if we have been planted together in the likeness of his
6 death, we shall be also *in the likeness* of *his* resurrection: knowing this,
  that *our old man is crucified with *him*, that *the body of sin might be
7 destroyed, that henceforth we should not serve sin. For he that is dead
8 is ²freed from sin. Now *if we be dead with Christ, we believe that we
9 shall also live with him: knowing that *Christ being raised from the
10 dead dieth no more; death hath no more dominion over him. For in

A. D. 60.

* Phil. 3. 10.
ƒ Gal. 2. 20.
ᵍ Col. 2. 11.
2 justified.
ʰ 2 Cor. 5. 1.
1 Tim. 2. 11.
John 14. 19.
ᶦ Rev. 1. 18.

**5. For if we have been planted together
in the likeness of his death** (*i. e.*, with Him in
the likeness of His death, [σύμφυτοι γεγόναμεν
τῷ ὁμοιώματι]—'if we have become born' or
'formed together.' The word here rendered
'planted together' (used here only) is not derived
from the word which signifies to 'plant' [φυτεύω],
as our version takes it (following the Vulgate and
Syriac versions, with *Chrysostom, Erasmus, Luther,
Calvin,* and *Beza,* but from the word [φύω], which
signifies, in the passive, to 'be begotten,' 'be
formed,' or 'be by nature' (such and such). See
Fritzsche on this word. Nevertheless, the intended
idea comes out the same on either etymology—
namely, *oneness with Christ in* the true import and
intent of *His death.* **we shall be also in the likeness
of his resurrection**—*q. d.,* 'Since Christ's death and
resurrection are inseparable in their efficacy, union
with Him in the one carries with it· participation
in the other, for privilege and for duty alike.'
The *future* tense is used of participation in His
resurrection, not as if the principal reference were
to the future glory—for the resurrection of believers with Christ is expressly said (in *v.* 11) to be
a present reality—but because this is but partially
realized in the present state. (See on ch. v. 19.)
6, 7. Knowing this, &c. The apostle now grows
more definite and vivid in expressing the sin-
destroying efficacy of our union with the crucified
Saviour: **that our old man is** ('was') **crucified
with him.** The important phrase, "our old man,"
is not (as *Grotius,* and such as he, conceive of it)
'our old manner of living' (*vivendi ratio*); that is
rather the practical outcome of the thing intended: it is just 'our old selves' (morally and
spiritually), that is to say, *all that we were in* our
old unregenerate condition, before union with
Christ (cf. Col. iii. 9, 10; Eph. i. 22-24; Gal. ii.
20; v. 24; vi. 14; also John iii. 3; Tit. iii. 5; and
see *Beza* and *Meyer*). **that** ('in order that') **the
body of sin might be destroyed** (in Christ's death)
[καταργηθῇ]—or 'annulled,' or 'abolished;' that
is, reduced virtually to the condition of death by
crucifixion. This is a favourite word with our
apostle, used only once by any other of the
New Testament writers, and that his own companion Luke (xiii. 7), but twenty-five times in
the confessedly Pauline Epistles, besides once in
Hebrews (ii. 14). [to the end] **that henceforth
we should not serve sin** [τοῦ μηκέτι δουλεύειν]—
or 'be in bondage to sin.' It is of no small importance to fix the precise sense of "the body of
sin" here [τὸ σῶμα τῆς ἁμαρτίας]. A great many
critics take it figuratively, for 'the mass of sin.'
(So *Chrysostom* and other fathers, Greek and
Latin; *Erasmus, Calvin, Grotius, Philippi, Hodge,*
&c.) But the marked allusions to the actual body
which we find in nearly all the corresponding
passages forbid our expounding it in this loose
way. Thus, a few verses below, "Let not sin
therefore reign in *your mortal body*," &c. (*v.* 12);
"Neither yield ye *your members* as instruments of
unrighteousness," &c. (*v.* 13); "As ye have yielded
your members servants to uncleanness," &c. In
ch. vii. 23 "the law of sin" is said to be "in the
members": and in ch. viii. 13, "living after the

226

flesh" is spoken of as doing "the deeds of the
body." These passages put it, we think, beyond
doubt that by "the *body* of sin," some connection
of sin with our corporeal nature is intended. But
neither must we go to the opposite extreme, of
concluding that the *body* is here spoken of as *the
proper seat* or *principle of sin.* As *de Wette* correctly
says, and *Alford* after him, this is not true, for the
seat of sin, as such, does not lie in the body but in
the will. *Vaughan* goes the length of explaining
it of 'the material body, with its proneness to sensual and other evil;' and, much akin, *Webster* and
Wilkinson, of 'the corrupt nature regarded in its
physical acts and affections.' When all the passages in which such phraseology is used are
weighed together, we think it will appear clearly
that whatever may be the reason for the *body*
being so expressly named, *the whole principle of
sin* in our fallen nature is here meant—its most
intellectual and spiritual, equally with its lower
and more corporeal, features. It only remains to
enquire why this is called the body of sin. The more
immediate occasion of it was undoubtedly (as *Beza*
says) the mention of *Christ's* crucifixion and burial;
and as the crucifixion and burial of our old man
with him (the nailing of us, so to say, as the doomed
children of Adam, to the accursed tree, and thereafter laying us in His grave) was to be emphatically
put before the reader, nothing could be more
natural than to represent this as bringing to an
end "the *body* of sin." Taking it in this sense,
the expression denotes (to use the words of *Beza*)
'man as he is born, in whom sin itself dwells;' or
more comprehensively, 'sin as it dwells in us in
our present *embodied* condition, under the law of
the fall.' This sense will be seen to come out
clearly in *v.* 12, and in ch. xii. 1.

7. For he that is dead is freed from sin ["Ο
γὰρ ἀποθανὼν δε δικαίωται ἀπὸ τῆς ἁμαρτίας]—
'For he that hath died hath been set free
from sin;' *lit.,* 'hath been justified,' 'absolved,'
'acquitted,' 'got his discharge from sin.' As
death dissolves all claims, so the whole claim
of sin, not only to "reign unto death," but to
keep its victims in sinful bondage, has been
discharged once for all, by the believer's penal
death in the death of Christ; so that he is no
longer a "*debtor* to the flesh, to live after the
flesh" (ch. viii. 12). **8. Now if we be dead** ('if we
died') **with Christ, we believe that we shall also
live with**—'the future (to use the words of
Hodge) referring not to what is to happen hereafter, but to what is the certain consequence of
our union with Christ.' The apostle here recalls
the sentiment of *v.* 5, in order to continue that
train of thought (see on *v.* 5). **9. Knowing
that Christ being raised from the dead dieth
no more; death hath no more dominion over
him.** Though Christ's death was in the most
absolute sense a voluntary act (John x. 17, 18;
Acts ii. 24), that voluntary surrender gave death
a rightful "dominion over *Him.*" But this
once past, "death hath," even in that sense,
"dominion over Him no more." **10. For in that
he died** ["Ο γὰρ ἀπέθανεν]. The strict rendering
(as *Fritzsche* shows) is, 'The death which He

that he died, he died unto sin once: but in that he liveth, he liveth unto
11 God. Likewise reckon ye also yourselves to be dead indeed unto sin, but
j alive unto God through Jesus Christ our Lord.
12 Let *k* not sin therefore reign in your mortal body, that ye should obey
13 it in the lusts thereof. Neither yield ye your members *as* ³ instruments
of unrighteousness unto sin: but yield yourselves unto God, as those that
are alive from the dead, and your members *as* instruments of righteous-
14 ness unto God. For *l* sin shall not have dominion over you: for ye are
not under the law, but under grace.

A. D. 60.

j 1 Cor. 6. 20.
Gal. 2. 19.
Col. 3. 3.
k Eph. 4. 22.
³ arms, or.
weapons.
l ic. 7. 19.
Gal. 5. 18.
Tit. 2. 14.
Matt. 1. 21.

died.' **he died unto** (that is, in obedience to the claims of) **sin once** [ἐφάπαξ] — 'once for all;' as Heb. vii. 27; ix. 12; x. 10: **but in that he liveth, he liveth unto** (in obedience to the claims of) **God.** There never, indeed, was a time when Christ did not 'live unto God.' But in the days of His flesh He did so, under the continual burden of sin "laid on Him" (Isa. liii. 6; 2 Cor. v. 21); whereas, now that He has "put away sin by the sacrifice of Himself," He "liveth unto God," the acquitted and accepted Surety, unchallenged and unclouded by the claims of sin. **11. Likewise reckon ye also yourselves** (even as your Lord) **to be dead indeed** [μὲν]—not 'dead in very deed,' or 'truly' [ἀληθῶς], as the English reader is apt to suppose, but 'dead on the one hand;' though the particle scarcely admits of being weakly enough rendered in English. **unto sin, but alive unto God through Jesus Christ our Lord.** The true reading appears to be, 'in Christ Jesus,' omitting the words "our Lord." [So A B D E F G, some cursives, and a majority of the versions, including the Vulgate; and so *Lachm., Tisch.,* and *Treg.* The received text is supported by C K L (א has τῷ κυρίῳ ἡμῶν alone), and by some cursives and versions. The fathers vary.]

Believers reminded of the incentives to holiness which arise out of this death to sin and life to God through union to the crucified and risen Saviour (12-21). Not content with showing that his doctrine has no tendency to relax the obligations to a holy life, the apostle now calls upon believers to manifest the sanctifying tendency of their new standing in the dead and Risen Christ.

N.B.—*As in this and the following verses the words* "Sin," "God," "Obedience," "Righteousness," "Uncleanness," and "Iniquity," *are figuratively used to represent a* MASTER, we shall print them in capitals, to make this manifest to the eye, and so save explanations.

12. Let not SIN **therefore** (as though it were still your Master) **reign in your mortal body, that ye should obey it** (Sin) **in the lusts thereof**—i. e., the lusts of the body, as the Greek makes evident [εἰς τὸ ὑπακούειν αὐτῇ ἐν ταῖς ἐπιθυμίαις αὐτοῦ]. But another reading has rather the better support, and is probably the correct one—'that ye should obey the lusts thereof,' [omitting αὐτῦ ἐν. It is found in א A B C*, and some few cursives, in the Vulgate, the Peshito Syriac, the two Egyptian, and some other versions, with several fathers, adopted by *Lachmann, Tischendorf,* and *Tregelles,* and approved by *de Wette, Meyer,* &c. The received reading is supported by C*** (a corrector of about the ninth century), K L, several cursives, the Philoxenian Syriac, and one or two later versions, and most of the Greek fathers. There is some, though inferior authority, for omitting τ. ἐπιθυμίαις, and some, though less still, for stopping at ὑπακούειν—omitting αὐτῦ.] The sense, however, is the same. The "**body**" is here viewed as the instrument by which all the sins of the heart become facts of the outward life, and as itself the seat of the lower appetites; and it is called "our *mortal body*"—not so much to cheer us with the thought of how soon we shall have done with it (as some), still less to warn us how short-lived are the pleasures of sin (as others), but—probably to remind us how unsuitable is the reign of sin in those who are "alive from the dead." But the reign here meant is the unchecked dominion of sin *within* us. Its *outward acts* are next referred to. **13. Neither yield** [παριστάνετε]—or 'present' **ye your members as instruments of unrighteousness unto** SIN: **but yield** ('present') **yourselves.** Observe how grandly the thought rises here. Not only does it rise from a negative exhortation in the first clause to a positive in the second, but it rises from the *members* in the one clause to our whole renewed *selves* in the other. Being alive now unto God from the dead, he bids us, instead of yielding the members of such to the obedience of their old Master, first yield our whole new selves **unto** GOD (as our new and rightful Master), **as [those that are] alive from the dead**—Do this *in the capacity of* men risen with Christ, and (as the natural fruit of this) **your members** (till now prostituted to sin) **[as] instruments** (for the practice) **of righteousness unto God.** A significant transition also has been noticed here from one tense to another. In the first clause—"Neither yield ye your members instruments of unrighteousness"—the *present* tense is used [παριστάνετε], denoting the *habitual* practice of men in their old unregenerate state; in the next clause, "but yield yourselves unto God," it is the *aorist* [παριστήσατε]—suggesting the *one act for all,* of self-surrender, which the renewed believer performs immediately on his passing from death to life, and to which he only sets his continuous seal in all his after-life.

But what if indwelling sin should prove too strong for us? The reply of the next verse is, But it will not. **14. For** SIN **shall not have dominion over you** (as the slaves of a tyrant lord): **for ye are not under the law, but under grace**—[ὑπὸ νόμον — ὑπὸ χάριν. ὑπὸ with *accus.* denotes 'motion to underneath'—figuratively, 'moral subjection.'] The sense and force of this profound and precious assurance all depends on what is meant by being "under the law" and being "under grace." Mere philological criticism will do nothing to help us here. We must go to the heart of all Pauline teaching to discover this. To be "UNDER THE LAW," then, is, first, to be 'under its claim to entire obedience on pain of death;' and so, secondly, to underlie the curse of the law as having violated its righteous demands (Gal. iii. 10). And since any power to fulfil the law can reach the sinner only through Grace—of which the law knows nothing—it follows, lastly, that to be "under the law" is to be shut up under an *inability to keep it,* and consequently to be the *helpless slave of sin.* On the other hand, to be "UNDER GRACE," is to be under the glorious canopy and saving effects of that "Grace which bringeth salvation" and reigns

15　What then? shall we sin, [m]because we are not under the law, but under grace?

16　God forbid.　Know ye not, that to whom ye yield yourselves servants to obey, his servants ye are to whom ye obey; whether of sin unto death, or

17　of obedience unto righteousness?　But God be thanked, that ye were the servants of sin, but ye have obeyed from the heart that form of doctrine

18　[4]which was delivered you.　Being then [n]made free from sin, ye became

19　the servants of righteousness.　I speak after the manner of men because of the infirmity of your flesh: for as ye have yielded your members servants to uncleanness and to iniquity unto iniquity; even so now yield

20　your members servants to righteousness unto holiness.　For when ye

21　were the servants of sin, ye were free [5]from righteousness.　What fruit had ye then in those things whereof ye are now ashamed? for the end of

A. D. 60.

[m] 1 Cor. 9. 21.
2 Cor. 7. 1.
Gal. 2. 17,
18.
Eph 2. 8,
10.
[4] whereto
ye were
delivered.
[n] Luke 1. 74,
75.
1 Cor. 7. 22.
Gal. 5. 1.
1 Pet 2. 16.
[5] to right-
eousness.

'through righteousness unto eternal life by Jesus Christ our Lord' (see on ch. v. 20, 21). The curse of the law has been completely lifted from off them; they are made "the righteousness of God in Him," and they are "alive unto God through Jesus Christ." So that, as when they were "under the law," Sin *could not but* have dominion over them, so now that they are "under grace," Sin *cannot but* be subdued under them. If before, Sin resistlessly triumphed, Grace will now be more than conqueror. (See the excellent remarks of *Calvin* here.)

15. What then? shall we sin [ἁμαρτήσομεν]. But this *future* tense, as in *v.* 1, has hardly a vestige of support. The only authorized form here is the *subjunctive* [—ωμεν]—'May we sin,' or (more idiomatically), 'Are we to sin' (see on *v.* 1), **because we are not under the law, but under grace? God forbid.** The apostle here resumes the statement of *v.* 1 under a somewhat new form, with the view of pressing home on believers the inconsistency and ingratitude of so acting, and in fact the certainty that they will not. **16. Know ye not**—Does not every one know that dictate of common sense (John viii. 34), **that to whom ye yield yourselves servants to obey** ('unto obedience'), **his servants ye are to whom ye obey**—to whom ye yield that obedience, **whether of SIN unto death**—that is, 'issuing in death' (in the awful sense explained on ch. v. 12-21, Remark 3, at the close of that Section), **or of OBEDIENCE unto righteousness**—that is, resulting in a righteous character as the enduring and eternal condition of the servant of new Obedience (see 1 John ii. 27; John viii. 34; 2 Pet. ii. 19; Matt. vi. 24). **17. But God be thanked, that ye were the servants of SIN, but**—a peculiar, though intelligible enough and not quite unexampled, mode of expression. The emphasis lies on the word "*were.*" It is equivalent to 'God be thanked that *though* ye were, *yet*,' &c.—'Praised be God, that is a state of things now past and gone!' (See *Fritzsche*, and cf. 1 Cor. vi. 11; Eph. v. 8. *Winer's* objection—§ lxvi. 7—has no force. **ye have obeyed** [ὑπηκούσατε]—rather, 'ye obeyed;' meaning, in their reception of the Gospel, **that form of doctrine which was delivered you** [ὑπηκούσατε εἰς ὃν παρεδόθητε τύπον διδαχῆς, by *attr.* for ὑπηκ. τῷ τύπῳ εἰς ὅν—]. The marginal rendering is the only right one, 'that form ('mould' or 'pattern') into which ye were delivered;' as melted wax or metal is poured into the mould. (Nearly all good critics agree in this.) The idea is, that the teaching to which they had heartily yielded themselves had stamped its own impress upon them.

18. Being then—it should be, 'And being;' for we have here but the continuation and conclusion of the preceding sentence—not a new one: **made free from SIN, ye became the servants of** ('ser-

228

vants to') **RIGHTEOUSNESS** [ἐδουλώθητε τῇ δικαιωσύνῃ]—*lit.*, 'ye became enslaved to Righteousness;' but in the sense explained on ch. i. 1, where the apostle styles himself 'a bond-servant of Jesus Christ.' The case is one of emancipation from entire servitude to one Master, only to entire servitude to another, whose property we are (see on ch. i. 1). There is no middle state of personal independence: for that we were never made, and to that we have no claim. When we would not that God should reign over us, we were in righteous judgment "sold under Sin:" now, being through grace "made free from sin," it is only to become "servants to Righteousness"—which is our true freedom. **19. I speak after the manner of men**—descending, for illustration, to the level of common affairs, **because of the infirmity of your flesh**—the weakness of your spiritual apprehension: **for as ye have yielded**—'as ye yielded,' the thing being viewed as now past, **your members servants to UNCLEANNESS and to INIQUITY** unto (the practice of) **iniquity; even so now yield your members servants to RIGHTEOUSNESS unto holiness** [εἰς ἁγιασμὸν]—rather, 'unto (the attainment of) sanctification;' as the word in this form is rendered in 2 Thess. ii. 13; 1 Cor. i. 30; 1 Pet. i. 2. The sense is this: 'Looking back upon the *heartiness* with which ye served Sin, and the *lengths* ye went to, be stimulated now to like zeal and like exuberance in the service of a better Master.' **20. For when ye were the servants** ('were servants') **of SIN, ye were free from** (rather, '*in respect of*) **RIGHTEOUSNESS**—[ἐλεύθεροι ἦτε τῇ δικαιωσύνῃ—the 'dative of reference to;' 'free with reference to.'] Difficulties have been made about this clause where none exist. The import of it appears clearly to be this:—'Since no servant can serve two masters, much less where their interests come into deadly collision, and each demands the whole man, so, while ye were in the service of Sin, ye were in no proper sense the servants of Righteousness, and never did it one act of real service; whatever might be your conviction of the claims of Righteousness, your real services were all and always given to Sin: Thus had ye full proof of the nature and advantages of Sin's service.' The searching question with which this is followed up shows that this is the meaning.

21. What fruit had ye then [τότε]—or 'at that time,' [in those things] **whereof ye are now ashamed?** The Syriac version gives a different punctuation of this verse, which gives a different turn to the sense, as follows: 'What fruit had ye then? [things] whereof ye are now ashamed,' &c. In that case the "fruit" does not mean the *profit* of sin, but the *actings* of sin. This punctuation has been followed by *Clement* of Alexandria, and one or two other

22 those things *is* death. **But** now being made free from sin, and become
servants to God, ye have your fruit unto holiness, and the end everlasting
23 life. For °the wages of sin *is* death; but the *P*gift of God *is* eternal life
through Jesus Christ our Lord.

A. D. 60

° Gen. 2. 17.
P John 3. 14.
1 Pet. 1. 3.
Tit. 1. 2.

Greek fathers; by *Erasmus, Luther,* and *Melanc-thon;* by *Tholuck, de Wette, Olshausen, Philippi, Alford, Webster and Wilkinson, and Green;* with *Lachmann* and *Tischendorf,* but not *Tregelles.* With *Beza,* we think this is forced. It is, indeed, contended (by *Reiche, Olshausen, de Wette,* and *Alford*) that "fruit" in the New Testament is used, not of 'advantage' or ' benefit,' but of ' actings.' But it has been well replied that it is not the word "fruit" alone which we have here, but the phrase "having fruit," which may well express something different; and in ch. i. 13 the same phrase of " having fruit" is certainly not used of acts done, but of benefit expected. Taking this view of the sense, the punctuation of our own version has the support of at least as many and as good critics as the other (such as *Chrysostom, Calvin, Beza, Grotius, Estius, Wetstein, Bengel, Fritsche, Meyer, Hodge*). The whole verse down to "ashamed" seems clearly to be (as *Meyer* says) one connected question :—' What fruit had ye in those things whereof ye are now ashamed?' **for the end of those things is death.** In the light of their own dreadful experience in the past of Sin's service, what permanent *advantage,* and what abiding *satisfaction,* have those things yielded? The apostle answers his own question:—' Abiding *satisfaction,* did I ask? They have left only a sense of "shame." Permanent *advantage?* " The end of them is *death.*'" By saying they were "*now* ashamed," he makes it plain that he is not referring to that disgust at themselves and remorse of conscience by which those who are the most helplessly "sold under sin" are often stung to the quick; but that ingenuous feeling of self-reproach which pierces and weighs down the children of God as they think of the dishonour which their past life did to His name, the ingratitude it displayed, the violence it did to their own conscience, its deadening and degrading effects, and the death—"the second death"—to which it was dragging them down, when mere Grace arrested them. On the sense of "death" here, see on ch. v. 12-21, note 3, and on *v.* 16 of this chapter: see also Rev. xxi. 8.

22. But now—as if to get away from such a subject were unspeakable relief, **being made free from SIN, and become servants to GOD**—in the absolute sense intended throughout all this passage. **ye have**—not ' ought to have,' but do ' have,' in point of fact, **your fruit unto holiness** [εἰς ἁγιασμὸν]—'unto sanctification,' as in *v.* 19; meaning that *permanently holy state and character* which is built up out of the whole " fruits of righteousness " which believers successively bring forth. They "have their fruit" *unto* this—*i.e.,* all *going towards* this blessed result. **and the end everlasting life**—as the final state of the justified believer; the beatific experience not only of complete exemption from the fall with all its effects, but of the perfect life of acceptance with God and conformity to His likeness, of unveiled access to Him, and ineffable fellowship with Him through all duration. **23. For the wages** [ὀψώνια]. The word signifies military supplies, 'pay' in kind rather than money [the plural usage is late]. **of sin is death; but the gift of GOD is eternal life through** ('in') **Jesus Christ our Lord.** This concluding verse—as pointed as it is brief—contains the marrow, the most fine gold, of the Gospel. As the labourer is worthy of his hire,

and feels it to be his due—his own of right—so is death the due of sin, the wages the sinner has well wrought for—his own. But "eternal life" is in no sense or degree the wages of our righteousness; we do nothing whatever to earn or become entitled to it, and never can: it is therefore, in the most absolute sense, "THE GIFT OF GOD." Grace reigns in the bestowal of it in every case, and that "in Jesus Christ our Lord," as the righteous Channel of it. In view of this, who that hath tasted that the Lord is gracious can refrain from saying, "Unto Him that loved us, and washed us from our sins in his own blood, and hath made us kings and priests unto God and His Father; to Him be glory and dominion for ever and ever" (Rev. i. 5, 6).

Remarks.—1. Antinomianism (as *Hodge* says) is not only an error, it is a falsehood and a slander, when represented as the natural tendency of the Gospel doctrine of Gratuitous Justification. That "we should continue in sin, that grace may abound," not only is never the deliberate sentiment of any real believer in the doctrine of Grace, but is abhorrent to every Christian mind, as a monstrous abuse of the most glorious of all truths. 2. As the death of Christ is not only the expiation of guilt, but the death of sin itself in all who are vitally united to Him, so the resurrection of Christ is the resurrection of believers, not only to acceptance with God, but to newness of life; and by these principles should all who name the name of Christ examine themselves whether they be in the faith. 3. As the most effectual refutation of the oft-repeated calumny, that the doctrine of Salvation by grace encourages to continue in sin, is the holy life of those who profess it, let such ever feel that the highest service they can render to that Grace which is all their hope, is to "yield themselves unto God, as those that are alive from the dead, and their members instruments of righteousness unto God" (*vv.* 12, 13). By so doing they will "put to silence the ignorance of foolish men," secure their own peace, carry out the end of their calling, and give substantial glory to Him that loved them. 4. The fundamental principle of Gospel-obedience is as original as it is divinely rational: that ' we are set free from the law in order to keep it, and are brought graciously under servitude to the law in order to be free.' So long as we know no principle of obedience but the terrors of the law, which condemns all the breakers of it, and knows nothing whatever of grace either to pardon the guilty or to purify the stained, we are shut up under a moral impossibility of genuine and acceptable obedience; whereas when Grace lifts us out of this state, and through union to a righteous Surety, brings us into a state of conscious reconciliation and loving surrender of heart to a God of salvation, we immediately feel the glorious *liberty to be holy;* and the assurance that " Sin shall not have dominion over us" is as sweet to our renewed tastes and aspirations as the ground of it is felt to be firm, " because we are not under the Law, but under Grace." 5. As this most momentous of all transitions in the history of a man is wholly of God's free grace, the change should never be thought, spoken, or written of, but with lively thanksgiving to Him who so loved us, as in *v.* 17. 6. Christians in the service of God should emulate their former selves in the zeal and steadiness with which they served Sin,

7 KNOW ye not, brethren, (for I speak to them that know the law,) how
2 that the law hath dominion over a man as long as he liveth? For *a* the
woman which hath an husband is bound by the law to *her* husband so
long as he liveth; but if the husband be dead, she is loosed from the law
3 of *her* husband. So then *b* if, while *her* husband liveth, she be married
to another man, she shall be called an adulteress: but if her husband be
dead, she is free from that law; so that she is no adulteress, though she
be married to another man.
4 Wherefore, my brethren, ye also are become *c* dead to the law by the
body of Christ; that ye should *d* be married to another, *even* to him who
5 is raised from the dead, that we should bring forth fruit unto God. For

A. D. 60.

CHAP. 7.
a 1 Cor. 7. 39.
b Matt. 5. 32.
Mark 10. 12.
Luke 16. 18.
Heb. 13. 4.
c Gal. 2. 19.
Gal. 5. 18.
Eph. 2. 15.
Col. 2. 14.
1 Pet. 2. 24.
d Hos. 2. 19.
2 Cor. 11. 2.

and the length to which they went in it. To stimulate this holy rivalry, let us often "look back to the rock whence we were hewn, the hole of the pit whence we were digged," in search of the enduring advantages and permanent satisfactions which the service of Sin yielded; and when we find to our "shame" only gall and wormwood, let us follow a godless life to its proper "end," until, finding ourselves in the territories of "death," we are fain to hasten back to survey the service of Righteousness—that new Master of all believers—and find Him leading us sweetly into abiding "holiness," and landing us at length in "everlasting life." 7. Death and life are before all men who hear the Gospel: the one, the natural issue and proper reward of sin; the other, the absolutely free "GIFT OF GOD" to sinners, "in Jesus Christ our Lord." And as the one is the *conscious* sense of the hopeless loss of all blissful existence, so the other is the conscious possession and enjoyment of all that constitutes a rational creature's highest "life" for evermore (*v.* 23). Ye that read or hear these words, "I call heaven and earth to record this day against you, that I have set before you life and death, blessing and cursing: therefore choose life, that both thou and thy seed may live!" (Deut. xxx. 19.)

CHAP. VII. 1-25.—SAME SUBJECT CONTINUED. Here the apostle prosecutes his argument on the New Life of the justified believer through Union to Christ; presenting the subject in some beautiful lights, and going to the depths of action in our spiritual nature both before and after conversion.

The believer's severance from the law through union to Christ illustrated from the law of marriage (1-6). In the preceding chapter the apostle had given his believing readers the cheering assurance that 'SIN should not have dominion over them, because they were not *under the law,* but under grace.' But *how* they came to be no longer under the law, he had not particularly shown. Generally, it had been made clear enough throughout the whole preceding argument; but here the apostle goes into the profound principles involved in the change.

1. Know ye not, brethren, for I speak to them that know the law. The law of Moses is particularly in view—with which, though not themselves Jews (see on ch. i. 13), these Roman Christians were sufficiently acquainted; but the thing here stated is true of any good marriage law, being founded in nature: how that the law **hath dominion over a man as long as he liveth?** —that is, so long, and no longer. Most of those who think that the apostle is here teaching the *death of the law,* suppose the law to be here meant, and not the married person; and they translate accordingly, 'so long as it (the law) liveth.' But this is plainly wrong; for as the apostle is stating a well-known fact regarding the marriage law, it

would have been absurd to say that it has dominion so long as it lives or has dominion. Clearly the thing meant is, that the law's dominion over a man ceases with the *man's* life. 2. For the woman which hath an husband is bound by the law to her husband so long as he liveth; but if the husband be dead ('if he die'), she is loosed from the law of her husband. 3. So then if, while her husband liveth, she be married to another man, she shall be called an adulteress: but if her husband be dead ('die'), she is free from that law; so that she is no adulteress, though she be married ('joined') to another man.

4. Wherefore, my brethren, ye also are become dead [ἐθανατώθητε]—'were put to death,' or 'became dead,' to the law by the body of Christ—through union to that "body broken for them," that ye should be married ('joined') to another, [even] to him who is ('that was') raised from the dead, [to the intent] that we should bring forth fruit unto God. It has been thought by a number of excellent critics that the apostle has here expressed the opposite of what his argument required—has said that *we* died to the law; whereas his *argument is,* that the *law* died to *us*—and that he purposely inverted the figure to avoid the harshness to Jewish ears of such an idea as *the death of the law.* (So *Origen, Chrysostom, Calvin, Tholuck, de Wette*—who ascribes the inversion of the figure to confusion in the apostle's mind—*Hodge, Webster and Wilkinson, Vaughan.*) But if this idea would sound harsh to Jewish ears, it would not be softened by insinuating without expressing it, much less by saying just the reverse of what was meant. But they mistake the apostle's design in employing this figure, which was merely to illustrate the general principle, that '*death dissolves legal obligation.*' It was essential to his argument that *we,* not the law, should be the dying party, since it is we that are "crucified with Christ," and not the law. This death dissolves our marriage-obligation to the law, leaving us at liberty to contract a new relation—to be joined to the Risen One, in order to spiritual fruitfulness, to the glory of God. (So *Beza, Fritzsche, Olshausen, Alford,* &c.) The confusion, then, is in the expositors, not the text; and it has arisen from not observing that, *like Jesus Himself, believers are here viewed as having a double life*—the old sin-condemned life, which they lay down with Christ, and the new life of acceptance and holiness to which they rise with their Surety and Head; and all the issues of this new life, in Christian obedience, are regarded as the "fruit" of this blessed marriage-union to the Risen One.

But another thing must be observed in this profound verse. It seems to ascribe to the believer not only a double marriage (first to the law and then to Christ), but a double marriage to Christ Himself—first to the cruci-

when we were in the flesh, the [1] motions of sins, which were by the law,
6 did work in our members [e] to bring forth fruit unto death. But now
we are delivered from the law, [2] that being dead wherein we were held;
that we should serve [f] in newness of spirit, and not *in* the oldness of
the letter.
7 What shall we say then? *Is* the law sin?
God forbid. Nay, [g] I had not known sin but by the law: for I had

A. D. 60.	
1 passions.	
e Jas. 1. 15.	
2 Or, being dead to that.	
f John 4. 23. Gal. 5. 22.	
g ch. 3. 20.	

fied and then to the risen Christ. But this is only apparent. The spiritual reality, rightly apprehended, dissipates the seeming incongruity. When the apostle says that we become dead to the law by the body of Christ (or, that our marriage-relation to the law ceased with our union to the Crucified One), and then adds that this was in order to our being united to the Risen One, the meaning is not that the union to *Christ crucified* was dissolved, in order to our union to *Christ* risen. It is the necessities of the figure that occasioned this manner of speech. And what is meant is plainly this, that the expiatory death of Christ, to whom they have been united by faith, as thoroughly dissolved the claims of the law on believers as the husband's death sets his wife at liberty; and now that Christ is risen from the dead, that same union to Him is in reality their new marriage to the Living One—in virtue of which the *requirements* of the law are so far from being disregarded, or more feebly met, than when we were in bondage to it, that the "fruit" of our marriage-union to the Risen One is an obedience to God such as we never did nor could yield before. See John xv. 8, where the "fruit" of union to Christ is quite similarly set forth—only there under the figure of a *vegetable*, as here of a *conjugal* union.

How such holy fruitfulness was impossible while we were under the law, and before our union to Christ, is now declared. **5. For when we were in the flesh.** Here, for the first time in this Epistle, is introduced that remarkable and expressive phraseology of which so much use is made in the next chapter and in the Epistle to the Galatians, which all Christendom (earnest and enlightened Christendom, at least) has ever since regarded as a precious inheritance, has incorporated into its vocabulary and used as household words, and will never consent to dispense with in expressing some of the deepest truths and principles of spiritual religion. What is meant by "the flesh" in such statements we have endeavoured to explain on John iii. 6 (Commentary, p. 362), where we have the proper *matrix*—the rudimentary germ—of such phraseology; though it pervades the ethical portions of the Old Testament. It means our fallen nature, all that we bring into the world by birth, humanity under the entire law of the fall, the law of sin and death, our nature as corrupted, depraved, and under the curse. To "*be in* the flesh," then, must mean to be in our unregenerate state, under the unbroken, unsubdued dominion of our corrupt principles and affections. But the full import of this pregnant expression will open upon us as we advance in the exposition of this chapter and the following one. **the motions of sins** [τὰ παθήματα]—'the affections,' 'passions,' or 'feelings (prompting to the commission) of sins,' **which were by the law**—or, by occasion of it, as it forbade those sins, and by doing so only the more fretted or irritated our corruptions towards the commission of them (as will more fully appear on *vv.* 7-9), **did work in our members**—the members of the body, considered as the instruments by which these inward stirrings find vent in action, and become facts of the life (see on ch. vi.

6), **to bring forth fruit unto death**—death in the sense of ch. vi. 21. Thus hopeless is all holy fruit before union to Christ.

6. But now (see on the same expression in ch. vi. 22) **we are delivered from the law** [κατηργήθημεν ἀπὸ τ. νόμ.]—'loosed,' 'set free' (see on this word in ch. vi. 6), **that being dead wherein we were held** [ἀποθανόντος]. But this reading has absolutely *no authority*, and is inconsistent with the whole strain of the argument. (It is not even the reading of the received text, as printed by R. Stephens in 1550; and it found its way into the Elzevir text, probably through a mistake of *Beza's*, whose text it there followed—as *Mill, Bengel,* &c., state.) It is now universally agreed that the true reading (that of *Stephens*' received text) is, '*we being dead* [to that] wherein we were held' [ἀποθανόντες]. For the death spoken of is not *the law's*, but *our's* who believe, through union to the crucified Saviour. **that we should serve** [ὥστε δουλεύειν]—'so that we serve;' for it is the actual *result*, not the *intention*, which the apostle intends to express (as the present tense shows). **in** ('the') **newness of** ('the') **spirit, and not in the oldness of the letter**—not in our old way of literal, mechanical obedience to the Divine law, as a set of external rules of conduct, and without any reference to the state of our hearts; but in that new way of spiritual obedience which, through union to the risen Saviour, we have learned to render (cf. ch. ii. 29; 2 Cor. iii. 6).

The believer's helplessness while under the law is no fault of the law itself (7-13). **7. What shall we say then?** See on this phraseology in ch. vi. 1. **Is the law sin? God forbid**—*q. d.,* 'I have said that when we were in the flesh the law stirred our inward corruption, and was thus the occasion of deadly fruit: But is the law *to blame* for this? Far from us be such a thought.' Nay [ἀλλά]— 'On the contrary' (as the same conjunction means in ch. viii. 37 and 1 Cor. xii. 22), **I had not known sin but by the law.** *From these words downwards, through the whole chapter, the apostle speaks*—no longer in the first and second persons plural, but—wholly *in the first person singular*: not thus personating either *the Jewish nation* or *mankind in general* (as some of the fathers, and several modern critics quite erroneously conceive), but depicting his own views and feelings, his own state and character, at different periods of his religious history. But another thing, of even more importance, will be observed. From *v.* 7 to the end of *v.* 13 the apostle speaks entirely in the *past tense;* whereas from *v.* 14 to the end of the chapter he speaks exclusively in the *present tense.* And as the words of *v.* 9, 'I was alive without the law *at one time'* [ποτὲ], clearly refer to his unconverted state, so we shall see, when we come to expound them, that all from *v.* 14 to the end of the chapter is a description of his converted state, and can only be thus properly understood.

When the apostle here says, "I had not known sin but by the law," it is important to fix precisely what he means by the word "sin." It certainly is not sin in *act* (as *Fritzsche* views it—who says, 'he who sins knows sin,' that is, by experience)— for this will not at all suit what follows. Nor is

8 not known lust, ³except the law had said, ʰThou shalt not covet. But ⁱsin, taking occasion by the commandment, wrought in me all manner of
9 concupiscence. For ʲwithout the law sin *was* dead. For I was alive without the law once: but when the commandment came, sin revived,
10 and I died. And the commandment, ᵏwhich *was ordained* to life, I found
11 *to be* unto death. For sin, taking occasion by the commandment, deceived
12 me, and by it slew *me*. Wherefore ˡthe law *is* holy, and the commandment holy, and just, and good.
13 Was then that which is good made death unto me? God forbid. But sin, that it might appear sin, working death in me by that which is good; that sin by the commandment might become

A. D. 60.

³ Or, concupiscence.
ʰ Ex. 20. 17.
Deut. 5 2'.
Josh. 7. 21.
Mic. 2. 2.
ⁱ ch. 4. 15.
ʲ 1 Cor. 15.56.
ᵏ Lev. 18. 5.
Eze. 20. 13.
2 Cor. 3. 7.
ˡ Ps. 19. 8.
1 Tim. 1. 8.

it sin in general—I had not known 'such a thing as sin,' to use the words of *Alford*, who seems to take this view; for though it is true that this is learned from the law, such a sense will not suit what is said of it in the following verses, where the meaning is the same as here. The only meaning which suits all that is said of it in this place is 'the *principle* of sin *in the heart* of fallen man.' The sense, then, is this: 'It was by means of the law that I came to know what a virulence and strength of sinful propensity I had within me.' The *existence* of this it did not need the law to reveal to him; for even the heathens recognized and wrote of it: but the dreadful nature and desperate power of it the law alone discovered—in the way now to be described. **for I had not known lust** [ἐπιθυμίαν], **except the law had said, Thou shalt not covet** [ἐπιθυμήσεις]. **8. But sin** (*i. e.*, my indwelling corruption), **taking occasion by the commandment, wrought in me all manner of concupiscence** [ἐπιθυμίαν]. Here the same Greek word is unfortunately rendered by three different English ones—"lust," "covet," "concupiscence"—which obscures the meaning. By using the word "lust" only—in the wide sense of all 'irregular desire,' or every out-going of the heart towards anything forbidden—the sense will best be brought out thus: 'For I had not known lust, except the law had said, Thou shalt not lust. But sin, taking occasion by the commandment (that commandment which expressly forbids it) wrought in me all manner of lusting.' See Prov. ix. 17, "Stolen waters are sweet, and bread eaten in secret is pleasant." Compare also the well-known saying of *Horace*, *Nitimur in vetitum nefas, cupimusque negata*. This gives a deeper view of the tenth commandment than the mere words suggest. The apostle saw in it the prohibition not only of desire after *certain things there specified*, but of 'desire after *everything Divinely forbidden;*' in other words, all 'lusting' or 'irregular desire.' It was this which "he had not known but by the law." The law forbidding all such desire so stirred his corruption that it wrought in him "all manner of lusting"—desire of every sort after what was forbidden. **For without the law**—*i. e.*, Before its extensive demands and prohibitions come to operate upon our corrupt nature, **sin [was]** (rather, 'is') **dead**—*i. e.*, the sinful principle of our nature lies so dormant, so torpid, that its virulence and power are unknown, and to our feeling it is as good as "dead." **9. For I was alive without the law once** [ποτὲ]—'at one time,' or 'formerly'—*q. d.*, 'In the days of my ignorance, when, in this sense, a stranger to the law, I deemed myself a righteous man, and, as such, entitled to life at the hand of God.' **but when the commandment came**—forbidding all irregular desire, for the apostle sees in this *the spirit of the whole law*, **sin revived**—'came to life;' in its malignity and strength it

unexpectedly revealed itself, as if sprung from the dead: **and I died**—'saw myself, in the eye of a law never kept and not to be kept, a dead man.' **10. And (thus) the commandment, which was [ordained] to life**—more simply, 'which was for life;' that is, designed to give life through the keeping of it, I found [αὕτη]—'this I found' **to be unto death**—through the breaking of it. **11. For sin** (that is, my sinful nature), **taking occasion by the commandment, deceived me**—drew me aside into the very thing which the commandment forbade, **and by it slew me**—discovered me to myself to be a condemned and gone man (cf. *v.* 9, "I *died*"). **12. Wherefore** ['Ωστε]—'So that,' 'Thus, then,' **the law is holy, and the commandment**—that one in particular, so often referred to, which forbids all lusting, and on which some reflection might seem to have been cast in the preceding verses—even that commandment is holy, and just, and good.

13. Was then that which is good made [γέγονεν] —'Has then that which is good become.' But the true reading evidently is, 'Did then that which is good become' [ἐγένετο] **death unto me? God forbid**—*q. d.*, 'Does the blame of my death, then, lie with the good law? Away with such a thought.' **But sin** (became death unto me) **to the end, that it might appear sin**—a rare and pregnant expression, meaning, 'that it might be seen in its true light,' in all its naked deformity, **working death in** (rather, 'to') **me by that which is good; that sin by the commandment might become exceeding sinful** [καθ' ὑπερβολὴν ἁμαρτωλὸς]—'that its enormous turpitude might stand out to view, through its turning God's holy, just, and good law into a provocative to the very thing which it forbids.'

So much for *the law in relation to the unregenerate*, of whom the apostle takes himself as the example —*first*, in his ignorant, self-satisfied condition; *next*, under humbling discoveries of his inability to keep the law, through inward contrariety to it; *finally*, as self-condemned, and already, in law, a dead man. Some enquire to what period of his recorded history these circumstances relate. But there is no reason to think they were wrought into such conscious and explicit discovery at any period of his history before he "saw the Lord in the way;" and though, "amidst the multitude of his thoughts within him" during his memorable three days' blindness immediately after that, such views of the law and of himself would doubtless be tossed up and down till they *took shape* much as they are here described (see Acts ix. 9), we regard this whole description of his inward struggles and progress rather as the *finished result* of all his past recollections and subsequent reflections on his unregenerate state—which he throws into historical form only for greater vividness.

As indwelling sin was too powerful for the law to control while we were under it, so our subjection to the law even in our regenerate state is due, not to the

14 exceeding sinful. For we know that the law is spiritual: but I am
15 carnal, ᵐsold under sin. For that which I do I ⁴allow not: for what ⁿI
16 would, that do I not; but what I hate, that do I. If then I do that
17 which I would not, I consent unto the law that *it is* good. Now then it
18 is no more I that do it, but sin that dwelleth in me. For I know
that °in me (that is, in my flesh,) dwelleth no good thing: for to will is
present with me; but *how* to perform that which is good I find not.
19 For the good that I would I do not: but the evil which I would not, that

A. D. 60.

ᵐGen. 37. 27. 36.
Gen. 40. 15.
1 Ki. 21. 20, 25.
Matt. 28.25.
⁴ know.
ⁿ Gal. 5. 17.
° Gen. 8. 21.

law itself, but wholly to the gracious renovation of our inner man (14-25).

We have observed that while the apostle speaks *in his own person* from v. 7 to the end of the chapter, he speaks *in the past tense* down to the end of *v.* 13, and thereafter, from *v.* 14 to the end of the chapter, *in the present tense.* We believe that this forms the key to the true sense of those two much controverted divisions of the chapter respectively; *vv.* 7-13 depicting his *unregenerate* state and experience, while in *vv.* 14 to end we have a vivid picture of what he felt and how he acted in his *renewed* character. The best evidence of this will be found, not in any single verse or isolated statement in this portion, but in the whole strain of it, to which we request very careful attention.

14. For we know—that is, it is a recognized principle. But this manner of speaking is sometimes employed to express, not what is actually and consciously recognized, but what cannot be denied, and will commend itself on reflection to every thoughtful reader. **that the law is spiritual** [πνευματικὸs] —in its nature and demands. Just as a "spiritual man" is a man transformed—animated and led by the Holy Spirit, so the law—which is "holy, just, and good" (*v.* 12), embodying the demands of Him who is a Spirit—cannot but breathe spirituality in its nature and intent. **but I am carnal** [σαρκινός. The true reading—if external evidence alone is to decide—is beyond all doubt σαρκινός. But this properly signifies '*fleshy*,' and denotes the material of which a thing is made—which is not at all suitable here—while σαρκικός (which hardly occurs in classical Greek, and then, as would appear, only in *Plutarch*, who is late), judging from the termination, has reference to *character*. Either, therefore, the two forms were used interchangeably by the New Testament writers or copyists, or, if we must distinguish them, σαρκινός certainly is an error, and σαρκικός, however ill-attested by external authority, is, without doubt; the true reading. [See *Fritzsche's* note on the word, and *Winer*, § 16. 3. γ.] The apostle's meaning is made perfectly plain, first, by the opposition of "carnal" to "spiritual"—*q. d.,* 'The law, being spiritual, demands spiritual obedience; but that is just what I, being carnal, am incapable of yielding.' But the meaning is rendered still more evident by the explanatory clause which follows: **sold under sin**—enslaved to it as my tyrant-master. The "I" here is of course not the regenerate man, of whom this is certainly not true; but (as will presently appear) neither is it the unregenerate man—from whose case the apostle has passed away. It remains, then, that it is *the sinful principle in the renewed man,* as is expressly stated in *v.* 18. **15. For that which I do I allow not** [γινώσκω]—literally (as in *marg.*), 'I know not;' I recognize it not, approve it not: cf. Ps. i. 6, "The Lord *knoweth* the way of the righteous." 'In obeying the impulses of my carnal nature I act rather as the slave of another will than my own as a renewed man.' **for what I would, that do I not**—better, 'for not what I would ('what I wish' or 'desire')

that I do' [the τοῦτο here is omitted by *Tischendorf* on quite inferior evidence, but retained by *Lachmann* and *Tregelles*]. **but what I hate, that do I. 16. If then I do that which I would not**—'If what I would not, that I do,' **I consent unto the law that it is good**—the judgment of my inner man going along with the law. **17. Now then it is no more I** (*my renewed self*) **that do it** ('that work it'), **but sin that dwelleth in me**—that principle of sin that still has its abode in me. To explain this and the following statements, as many do (even *Bengel* and *Tholuck*), of the sins of unrenewed men against their better convictions, is to do painful violence to the apostle's language, and to affirm of the unregenerate what is untrue. That co-existence and mutual hostility of "flesh" and "spirit" in the same renewed man, which is so clearly taught in ch. viii. 4, &c., and Gal. v. 16, &c., is the true and only key to the language of this and the following verses. It is hardly necessary to say that the apostle means not to disown the blame of yielding to his corruptions, by saying, 'It is not he that does it, but sin that dwelleth in him.' Early heretics thus abused his language; but the whole strain of the passage shows that his sole object in thus expressing himself was to bring more vividly before his readers *the conflict of two opposite principles,* and how entirely, as a new man—honouring from his inmost soul the law of God—he condemned and renounced his corrupt nature, with its affections and lusts, its stirrings and its outgoings, root and branch. 'The acts of a slave (says *Hodge*, excellently) are indeed his own acts; but not being performed with the full assent and consent of his soul, they are not fair tests of the real state of his feelings.' **18. For I know that in me** (**that is, in my flesh,**) **dwelleth no good thing**—or better, 'For I know that there dwelleth not in me, that is, in my flesh, any good.' **for to will** (or 'desire') **is present with me; but** [how] **to perform that;** **which is good** (the supplement "how," in our version, weakens the statement) **I find not**—or (according to what appears to have most evidence) simply, 'not so' [οὔ]. Here, again, we have the *double self* of the renewed man: *q. d.,* 'In me dwelleth no good; but this corrupt self is not my true self; it is but sin dwelling in my real self, as a renewed man.' **19. For the good that I would I do not: but the evil which I would not, that I do.** Nothing, as a comment on this verse, can be better than the following remarks of *Hodge:* 'The numerous passages quoted by commentators in illustration of this and the preceding verses (see *Grotius* and *Wetstein*), though they may throw light upon the *language,* are expressive of *feelings* very different from those of the apostle. When an impenitent man says he is sorry for his sins, he may express the real state of his feelings; and yet the import of this language is very different from what it is in the mouth of a man truly contrite. The word *sorrow* expresses a multitude of very different feelings. Thus, also, when wicked men say they approve the good, while they pursue the wrong, their approbation is something very different from

20 I do. Now if I do that I would not, it is no more I that do it, but sin
21 that dwelleth in me. I find then a law, that, when I would do good,
22 evil is present with me. For I ^p delight in the law of God after the
23 ^q inward man: but I see another law in my members, warring against the
    law of my mind, and bringing me into captivity to the law of sin which
24 is in my members. O wretched man that I am! who shall deliver me
25 from ⁵ the body of this death? I thank God through Jesus Christ our

A. D. 60.

^p Ps. 1. 2.
Ps. 119. 16
24, 35.
Isa. 51. 7.
^q 2 Cor. 4. 16.
⁵ Cr. this
body of
death.

Paul's approbation of the law of God. And when *Seneca* calls the gods to witness, "that what he wills he does not will" (*quod volo me nolle*), he, too, expresses something far short of what the language of the apostle conveys. This must be so, if there is any such thing as experimental or evangelical religion—that is, if there is any difference between the sorrow for sin and desire of good in the mind of a true Christian, and in the unrenewed and willing votaries of sin, in whom conscience is not entirely obliterated.' **20. Now if I do that I would not, it is no more I that do it, but sin that dwelleth in me**—in the sense, however, explained on *v.* 17. **21. I find then a law** [τὸν νόμον]—rather, 'this law,' **that, when I would do good, evil is present with me.** The conflict here graphically described, between a self that 'desires' to do good and a self that in spite of this does evil, cannot be the struggles between conscience and passion in the *unregenerate*, because the description given of this "desire to do good," in the verse immediately following, is such as cannot be ascribed, with the least show of truth, to any but the *renewed.* **22. For I delight in the law of God after the inward man**—*q. d.*, 'from the bottom of my heart.' The word [συνήδομαι] used here only, and well rendered " delight," expresses, especially in connection with the words "after the inward man," the deep joy of the whole spiritual and emotional nature in the law of God, and conveys (as does the weaker word of *v.* 16, rendered "consent") a state of mind and heart to which the unregenerate man is beyond all doubt a stranger. **23. But I see another law** [ἕτερον, not ἄλλον]—rather, 'a different law' **in my members** (see on *v.* 5), **warring against the law of my mind, and bringing me into captivity to the law of sin which is in my members.** In this most pregnant verse, three things are to be observed : *First,* That the word "law" means *an inward principle of action, good or evil, operating with the fixedness and regularity of a law.* The apostle found two such laws within him: the one, "the law of sin in his members," called (in Gal. v. 17, 24) "the flesh which lusteth against the spirit," "the flesh with the affections and lusts"—*i. e.,* the sinful principle in the regenerate; the other, "the law of the mind," or the holy principle of the renewed nature. *Second,* When the apostle says he "sees" the one of these principles " warring against" the other, and " bringing him into captivity" to itself, *he is not referring to any actual rebellion going on within him while he was writing, or to any captivity to his own lusts then existing.* He is simply describing the two conflicting principles, and pointing out what it was the inherent property of each to aim at bringing about. It is "THE LAW OF THE MIND" —renewed by grace—to set its seal to God's law, approving of it and delighting in it, sighing to reflect it, and rejoicing in every step of its progress towards the complete embodiment of it : It is "THE LAW OF SIN in the members" to dislike and seduce us out of all spirituality, to carnalize the entire man, to enslave us wholly to our own corruptions. Such is the unchanging character of these two principles in all believers; but the relative strength of each is different in different

Christians. While some come so low, through "iniquities prevailing against them" (Ps. lxv. 3), that "the law of the mind" can at times be scarce felt at all, and they "forget that they have been purged from their old sins" (2 Pet. i. 9); others, habitually "walking in the Spirit," so "crucify the flesh, with the affections and lusts," that "the law of sin" is practically dead. But it is with *the unchanging character of the two principles—not the varying strength of them—*that this verse has to do. *Third,* When the apostle describes himself as "*brought into captivity*" by the triumph of the sinful principle of his nature, he clearly speaks in the person of a *renewed* man. Men do not feel themselves to be in captivity in the territories of their own sovereign and associated with their own friends—while breathing a congenial atmosphere, and acting quite spontaneously. But here the apostle describes himself when drawn under the power of his sinful nature, as forcibly seized and reluctantly dragged to his enemy's camp, from which he would gladly make his escape. This ought to settle the question, whether he is here speaking as a regenerate man or the reverse. **24. O wretched man that I am! who shall deliver me from the body of this death?** The apostle speaks of the "body" here with reference to "the law of sin" which he had said was "in his members," but merely as the instrument by which the sin of the heart finds vent in action, and as itself the seat of the lower appetites (see on ch. vi. 6, and on *v.* 5 of this chapter); and he calls it "the body of *this* death," as feeling, at the moment when he wrote, the horrors of that death into which it dragged him down (ch. vi. 21, and again on *v.* 5 of this chapter). But the language is not that of a sinner newly awakened to the sight of his lost state: it is the cry of a living but agonized believer, weighed down under a burden which, though not his renewed self, is yet so dreadfully himself—as being responsible for it—that he cannot choose but long to shake it off from his renewed self. Nor does the question imply ignorance of the way of relief at the time referred to. It was designed only to prepare the way for that outburst of thankfulness for the Divinely provided remedy which immediately follows. **25. I thank God** [Εὐχαριστῶ]—or (according to the rather preferable and livelier reading) [χάρις], 'Thanks to God,' the glorious Source, **through Jesus Christ**—the blessed Channel of deliverance. **So then** (to sum up the whole matter) **with the mind I myself serve the law of God, but with the flesh the law of sin**—*q. d.,* 'Such then is the unchanging character of these two principles within me : God's holy law is dear to my renewed mind, and has the willing service of my new man, although that corrupt nature which still remains in me listens to the dictates of sin.'

It is hoped that the foregoing exposition of this profound and much controverted Section will commend itself to the thoughtful, exercised reader. Every other view of it will be found equally at variance with the apostle's language, when taken as a whole, and with Christian experience. Certain it is that those who have most successfully sounded the depths of the heart, both under sin

Lord. ⁷ So then with the mind I myself serve the law of God, but with the flesh the law of sin.

and under grace, are the least able to conceive how any Christian can understand it of the unregenerate, and instinctively perceive in it a precious expression of their own experience as the struggling children of God. The great *Augustin* found no rest but in this view of it; and he was followed by those noble reformers, *Luther* and *Melancthon, Calvin* and *Beza.* Of the moderns, *Olshausen* and *Philippi, Hodge* and *Alford*, take the same view, though it is to be regretted that weighty names are ranged on the other side. See a fine treatise on this whole subject, full of acute though modest criticism and Christian experience, by Fraser of Pitcalzian, minister of Alness, edited after his death by Dr. John Erskine (1774), under the title of 'The Scripture Doctrine of Sanctification, being a Critical Explication and Paraphrase of Romans vi.-viii. 4, against the false Interpretations of *Grotius, Hammond, Locke, Whitby, Taylor*,' &c.

Remarks.—1. This whole chapter was of essential service to the Reformers in their contendings with the Church of Rome. When the divines of that corrupt Church, in a Pelagian spirit, denied that the sinful principle in our fallen nature—which they called 'Concupiscence,' and which is commonly called 'Original Sin'—had the nature of *sin* at all, they were triumphantly answered from this chapter, where—both in the first part of it, which speaks of it in the unregenerate, and in the second, which treats of its presence and actings in believers—it is explicitly, emphatically, and repeatedly called "*sin.*" As such, they held it to be *damnable.* (See the 'Confessions' both of the Lutheran and Reformed Churches.) In the following century, the orthodox in Holland had the same controversy to wage with 'the Remonstrants' (the followers of Arminius), and they waged it on the field of this chapter. 2. 'In the language of the New Testament (we use here the judicious words of *Hodge*), "the spiritual" are those who are under the control of the Spirit of God; and "the carnal" are those who are under the control of their own nature. As, however, even in the renewed, this control of the Spirit is never perfect —as the flesh even in them retains much of its original power—they are forced to acknowledge that they too are carnal. There is no believer, however advanced in holiness, who cannot adopt the language here used by the apostle. In 1 Cor. iii. 3, in addressing believers, he says, "Are ye not carnal?" In the imperfection of human language the same word must be taken in different senses. Sometimes *carnal* means entirely or exclusively under the control of the flesh. At other times it has a modified sense, and is applicable to those who, although under the dominion of the Spirit, are still polluted and influenced by the flesh. It is the same with all similar words. When we speak of "saints and sinners," we do not mean that saints, such as they are in this world, are not sinners. And thus when the Scriptures classify men as *spiritual* and *carnal*, they do not mean to teach that the spiritual are not carnal. It is therefore only by giving the words here used their extreme sense—a sense inconsistent with the context—that they can be regarded as inapplicable to the regenerated. The mystical writers, such as *Olshausen*—in accordance with the theory which so many of them adopt, that man consists of three subjects or substances, body, soul, and spirit [σῶμα, ψυχή, and πνεῦμα]—say that by "flesh" [σάρξ], in such connections, we are to understand the entire psychical life [*das ganze*

seelische Leben], which only is in man the seat of sin, and not the spirit [πνεῦμα] or higher element of our nature. In angels, on the contrary, the "spirit" [πνεῦμα] is itself the seat of sin; and they, therefore, are incapable of redemption. And in man, when sin invades the "spirit" [πνεῦμα], then comes the sin against the Holy Ghost, and redemption becomes impossible. This is only a refined or mystical rationalism, as "spirit" [πνεῦμα] is only another name for *reason;* and the conflict in man is reduced to the struggle between sense and reason, and redemption consists in giving the higher powers of our nature ascendancy over the lower. According to the Scriptures, the whole of our fallen nature is the seat of sin, and our subjective redemption from its power is effected, not by making reason predominant, but by the indwelling of the Holy Ghost. The conflicting elements are not sense and reason [the *anima* and *animus*], but the flesh and spirit, the human and Divine—what we derive from Adam and what we obtain through Christ. "That which is born of the flesh is flesh, and that which is born of the Spirit is spirit" (John iii. 6).' 3. Here we see how perfectly consistent moral *Inability* is with moral *Responsibility* (see *v.* 18; Gal. v. 17). To use again the language of the same powerful writer, 'As the Scriptures constantly recognize the truth of these two things, so are they constantly united in Christian experience. Every one feels that he cannot do the things that he would, yet is sensible that he is guilty for not doing them. Let any man test his power by the requisition to love God perfectly at all times. Alas! how entire our inability! Yet how deep our self-loathing and self-condemnation!' 4. If the first sight of the Cross by the eye of faith kindles feelings never to be forgotten, and in one sense never to be repeated —like the first view of an enchanting landscape— the experimental discovery, in the later stages of the Christian life, of its power to beat down and mortify inveterate corruption, to cleanse and heal from long-continued backslidings and frightful inconsistencies, and so to triumph over all that threatens to destroy those for whom Christ died, as to bring them safe over the tempestuous seas of this life into the haven of eternal rest—this experimental discovery is attended with yet more heart-affecting wonder, draws forth deeper thankfulness, and issues in more exalted adoration of Him whose work Salvation is from first to last. 5. It is sad when such topics as these are handled as mere questions of Biblical interpretation or of systematic theology. Our great apostle could not treat of them apart from personal experience, of which the facts of his own life and the feelings of his own soul furnished him with illustrations as lively as they were apposite. When one is unable to go far into the investigation of indwelling sin, without breaking out into an "O wretched man that I am!" and cannot enter on the way of relief without exclaiming, "I thank God through Jesus Christ our Lord," he will find his meditations rich in fruit to his own soul, and may expect, through Him who presides in all such matters, to kindle in his readers or hearers the like blessed emotions. And shall it not be so even now, with our humble attempts to open up and carry home these profound and moving statements of Thy lively oracles, O Lord?

CHAP. VIII.—Conclusion of the whole argument — The glorious completeness of them that are in Christ Jesus.

8 *THERE is* therefore now no condemnation to them which are in **2** Christ Jesus, who [a]walk not after the flesh, but after the Spirit. For the law of the Spirit of life in Christ Jesus hath made me free from the

A. D. 60.

CHAP. 7.
a Gal. 5. 16.

In this surpassing chapter the several streams of the preceding arguments meet and flow in one "river of the water of life, clear as crystal, proceeding out of the throne of God and of the Lamb," until it seems to lose itself in the ocean of a blissful eternity.

1-13. THE TRIUMPH OF THE JUSTIFIED, RENEWED, AND STRUGGLING BELIEVER OVER INDWELLING CORRUPTION, AND AT LENGTH OVER DEATH ITSELF, SECURED THROUGH THE INDWELLING OF THE SPIRIT OF LIFE IN CHRIST JESUS. **1. There is therefore now no condemnation to them which are in Christ Jesus.** It is a question among interpreters whether this is an inference from the immediately preceding context (as most commentators hold), or (as *Fraser, Tholuck,* and *Hodge*) from the whole preceding argument. The truth expressed—that there is no condemnation to them that are in Christ Jesus—is certainly no inference from the latter part, at least, of the preceding chapter, nor is it natural to suppose it drawn even from the first part of it. Beyond all doubt it is taken from the first branch of the argument (ch. iii. 5.), and is here regarded as an established truth which may now be assumed. At the same time, what is said in *v.* 2 of "the law of sin and death"—the subject which had been so fully treated in the latter part of ch. vii.—shows that that same subject is still in the apostle's thoughts, and is what gave occasion to the inferential words, "Now therefore," or, 'In these circumstances, then.' And we regard the whole statement as amounting to this : 'Dire and deadly as is the struggle we have depicted between the law of the renewed mind and the law in the members, it is the struggle, after all, of those who cannot fail in it—of those who are in Christ Jesus, and as such have the very standing before God of Christ Himself. But this is no mere legal *arrangement*—it is a union in *life;* believers, through the indwelling of Christ's Spirit in them, having one life with Him, as truly as the head and the members of the same body have one life. **[who walk not after the flesh, but after the Spirit.]** The evidence against the genuineness of this bracketed clause is so strong, that on all the laws of textual evidence it must be held to be no part of the original text—in which case the probability is that it crept in from *v.* 4, where it occurs precisely as here, and that it was introduced in order to make the transition from the statement of *v.* 1 to that of the 2d and following verses more easy.

[The external evidence stands thus : The *whole* clause—μὴ κατὰ σάρκα περιπατοῦσιν, ἀλλὰ κατὰ πνεῦμα—is wanting in א (though supplied by C, a corrector of about the seventh century) BCD*FG, some cursives, d* (the Latin of C), g (about the ninth century), the Egyptian and the Ethiopic versions, several Greek fathers, and Augustin of the Latin (in whose writings, however, the absence of such a clause is no sufficient proof of its non-recognition). On the other hand, the *whole* clause is found only in D*** (a corrector of about the ninth or tenth century) E K L, most cursives, d *** (a corrector of the Latin of D, about the same date) the Arabic and Slavonic versions (both late), *Theodoret, Theophylact, Œcumenius.* The *first* member of the clause—μὴ κατὰ σάρκα περιπατοῦσιν—AD**b(a corrector of D, about the seventh century), one cursive d* * (corrector of Latin of D, also about the seventh century), f (Latin of Cod. Augiens., about the ninth century), the Vulgate

(*'qui non secundum carnem ambulant'*), the Peshito Syriac, Gothic, and later versions, *Chrysostom* (more than once), and many Latin fathers. Such is the external evidence. Is there any *internal* evidence to outweigh this testimony against the clause? Since there is fair evidence for the first half of it, is that part of it *by itself* likely to be genuine? Surely not. We think it will be generally admitted either that the whole clause, or that no part of it, stood originally in the text. Which, then, is mostly likely? If genuine, how came it to pass that the whole clause fell out of so many of the most trustworthy authorities for the text, and that only one-half of it should be found in even a fair number of them? For this no good reason, we think, can be assigned. On the other hand, there seems a natural tendency to insert some such clause, to make the transition from the subject of the first verse to that of the second more easy than it is without it. Even internal evidence, then, so far as there is any, seems rather against than for the clause.]

2. For the law of the Spirit of life in Christ Jesus hath made me free [ἐλευθέρωσεν]—'freed me,' referring to the time of his conversion. As the sense of this verse must rule that of the profound verse which follows it, and two very different senses of it have been contended for, it must be examined with some care. By "the law of the Spirit of life in Christ Jesus," some of the elder German divines (as *Calovius*), followed by *Witsius, Bengel, Reiche,* and in our own day by *Haldane* and *Hodge,* understand *the Gospel.* In accordance with this, they naturally take "the law of sin and death" to mean the law of God. *Hodge's* six reasons for this are briefly these: (1.) This verse is intended to explain why there is no condemnation to believers; now, if it means (as most critics hold) that the regenerating power of the Spirit frees believers from the power of their inward corruption, it will follow that our regeneration is the cause of our justification, which is totally opposed to the apostle's teaching. But if this verse is understood to express the believer's deliverance from the condemning law of God through the Gospel, it gives an adequate explanation of the statement of *v.* 1. (2.) The deliverance here spoken of is represented as one already accomplished : this is true of the believer's deliverance from the law through the Gospel, but is not true of his deliverance from indwelling corruption, which is a gradual process. The former, therefore, must give the true sense, the latter not. (3.) The Gospel may justly be called "the law of the Spirit," as (in 2 Cor. iii. 8) "the ministration of the Spirit;" He being its author—while the law of God may be termed "the law of sin and death," as being productive of both, as the apostle himself says, ch. vii. 5, 13, &c. If this is correct, the subject of this and the immediately following verses will be seen to be not sanctification (as most critics suppose), but justification. These reasons, however, appear to us quite insufficient to justify so unnatural an interpretation. (1.) The most plausible argument is that *v.* 2 is intended to explain why there is no condemnation to believers; but (so far as we understand it) the sense which *Hodge* gives to *v.* 2 makes it no explanation, but a mere reiteration of the statement of *v.* 1, only in another form. (2.) The believer's deliverance from the dominion of indwelling sin through union to

3 law of sin and death. For *b* what the law could not do, in that it was | A. D. 60.
weak through the flesh, God, sending his own Son in the likeness of sinful | *b* Heb..7. 18.

Christ (which, as we take it, is meant in *v.* 2), is an accomplished fact, as much as his justification; and the gradual mortification of it in daily life, through the growing strength of the renewed principle, is quite consistent with this. (3.) To make "the law of the Spirit of life in Christ Jesus," mean simply *the Gospel*, is to put (as it appears to us) a strained, not to say a shallow, sense on so rich an expression; while to suppose that the apostle calls the holy law of God "the law of sin and death," is something repulsive. To use the words of *Fraser* (who, without knowing it, almost echoed the words of *Chrysostom* against some who before him had taken the same view of this verse (the passage will be found in 'Philippi,' p. 280), 'It were not consistent with the reverence due to the law of God, nor with the truth, to call it "the law of sin and death." Yea, it could not be so called but in plain contradiction to the vindication the apostle had made of it (ch. vii. 7), "Is the law *sin?* God forbid;" and *v.* 13, "Was that which is good made death to me? God forbid."' No, it is the Holy Ghost who is here meant. And before we notice the import of the statement itself, it is important for the student of this Epistle to observe that *only once before has THE HOLY GHOST been expressly named in this Epistle* (in ch. v. 5), and that *only now and here does His Personal Agency in believers begin to be treated.* Little space, indeed, does the subject occupy. The formal treatment of it is limited to *the first twenty-six verses of this chapter.* But within this space some of the richest matter, dear to Christian experience, is compressed; and as almost every verse in this portion opens up some fresh view of the Spirit's work, the light which it throws upon this vital department of the work of redemption is out of all proportion to the space which it fills.

Let us now observe the import of this pregnant phrase, "the Spirit of life in Christ Jesus." He is called "the Spirit of *life*," as opening up in the souls of believers a fountain of spiritual life (see John vii. 38, 39); just as he is called "the Spirit of truth," as "guiding them into all truth" (John xvi. 13), and "the Spirit of counsel and might, the Spirit of knowledge and of the fear of the Lord" (Isa. xi. 2), as the Inspirer of these qualities. And He is called "the Spirit of life *in Christ Jesus*," because it is as members of Christ that He takes up His abode in believers, who in consequence of this have one life with their Head. And as the word "*law*" here has, beyond all reasonable doubt, the same meaning as in ch. vii. 23—namely, 'an inward principle of action, operating with the fixedness and regularity of a law,' it thus appears that "*the law of the Spirit of life in Christ Jesus*" here means, 'that new principle of action which the Spirit of Christ has opened up within us—the law of our new being.' This "*sets us free,*" as soon as it takes possession of our inner man, "from the law of sin and death,"—*i. e.,* from the enslaving power of that corrupt principle which carries death in its bosom. The "strong man armed" is overpowered by the "Stronger than he;" the weaker principle is dethroned and expelled by the more powerful; the principle of spiritual life prevails against and brings into captivity the principle of spiritual death—"leading captivity captive." If this now be the apostle's meaning, the "For," with which the verse opens, does not assign the *reason*, but supplies the *evidence* of what goes before (as in Luke vii. 47, and other places); in other words, the meaning is not,

'There is no condemnation to believers, *because* they have got the better of their inward corruption' (very different doctrine this certainly from the apostle's); but 'The triumph of believers over their inward corruption, through the power of Christ's Spirit in them, *proves* them to be in Christ Jesus, and as such absolved from condemnation.' This completely meets the only objection to our view of the verse which we think has any weight. But this is now to be explained more fully.

3. For what the law could not do, &c. 'Few texts (says *Fraser* truly) have been more teased with the criticisms of the learned, which do often tend rather to darken than to give light to it, or to the subject of it;' and *Fritzsche* refers to the exceeding difference that obtains among interpreters, both as to the structure of the verse and the explanation of its meaning. But this is hardly to be wondered at, considering the very unusual structure of the clause, and the equally unusual language of the entire statement. Let us examine it, clause by clause. What, then, was it that "the law could not do, in that it was weak through the flesh?" 'It could not *justify* the breakers of it,' say those who think that Justification is the subject of these verses, (as *Hodge*, &c.) But it cannot be said with propriety that the reason why the law could not justify the guilty was that it was "weak through the flesh," or by reason of our corruption. It is clearly, we think, the law's inability to *free us from the dominion of* sin that the apostle has in view; as has partly appeared already (see on *v.* 2), and will more fully appear presently. The law could irritate our sinful nature into more virulent action, as we have seen in ch. vii. 5; but it could not secure its own fulfilment. How that is accomplished comes now to be shown. **In that it was weak through the flesh**—not '*because of* the flesh' [διὰ τὴν σάρκα], as the English reader would suppose, but '*through the medium of* the flesh' [διὰ τῆς σάρκος]; *i. e.,* having to address itself to us through a corrupt nature, too strong to be influenced by mere commands and threatenings. **God, &c.** The sentence is somewhat imperfect in its structure, which occasions a certain obscurity. It has been proposed to fill it up thus: 'What the law could not do . . . God [did by] sending,' &c. But it is as well to leave it without any supplement, understanding it to mean, that *whereas* the law was powerless to secure its own fulfilment—for the reason given—God took the method now to be described for attaining that end. **sending** ('having sent') **his own Son** [τὸν ἑαυτοῦ υἱόν]. This and similar expressions most plainly imply (as *Meyer* properly notices) that Christ was God's "OWN SON" *before* He was sent—that is, in His own proper Person, and independently of His mission and appearance in the flesh (see on ch. viii. 32; Gal. iv. 4); and if so, He not only has the *very nature* of God, even as a son has his father's nature, but is essentially OF the Father, though in a sense too mysterious for any language of ours properly to define (see on ch. i. 4). But why is this peculiar relationship put forward here? To *enhance the greatness* and *define the nature* of the relief provided as coming *from beyond the precincts of sinful humanity altogether,* yea, *immediately from the Godhead itself.* **in the likeness of sinful flesh** [ἐν ὁμοιώματι σάρκος ἁμαρτίας]—*lit.,* 'in the likeness of the flesh of sin.' a very remarkable and pregnant expression. 'It is not in the likeness of *flesh*—for truly He "was made flesh" (John xi. 14)—but 'in the likeness ol

4 flesh, and [1] for sin, condemned sin in the flesh: that the righteousness of
  the law might be fulfilled in us, who walk not after the flesh, but after
5 the Spirit. For they that are after the flesh do mind the things of the

A. D. CO.
[1] Or, by a sacrifice for sin.

the flesh of *sin;*' in other words, He was made in the *reality* of our flesh, but only in the *likeness* of its sinful condition. (See the excellent observations of *de Wette.*) [*Similitudo*—says *Tertullian*, quoted by *Meyer*—ad *titulum* peccati *pertinebit non ad substantiæ mendacium;* referring to the Docetic heresy of our Lord's having assumed only an apparent Humanity.] He took our nature, not as Adam received it from his Maker's hand, but as it is in us—compassed with infirmities—with nothing to distinguish Him as man from sinful men, save that He was without sin. Nor does this mean that Christ took every property of Humanity save sin; for sin is *no property of Humanity at all*, but only the disordered state of our own souls, as the fallen family of Adam—a disorder affecting and overspreading our whole nature, indeed, but still purely *our own.* **and for sin** [καὶ περὶ ἁμαρτίας]—*lit.*, 'and about sin.' Had this been a quite unusual expression, it might have meant simply, 'on the business of sin' (*de peccato*), as the Vulgate renders it [though not the *Codex Amiatinus*, which has *propter peccatum*]; and this at one time we took to be the thing intended. But since this very phrase is profusely employed in the LXX. to denote the Levitical 'offerings for sin' (nearly sixty times in the one book of Leviticus), and since in that sense it is twice used in the Epistle to the Hebrews (x. 6, 8)—in a quotation from Ps. xl. [= חֲטָאָה]—we cannot reasonably doubt that this (which is the marginal reading of our own version) was the sense intended by the apostle, and that it would be so understood by all his readers who were familiar with the Greek of the Old Testament. The meaning, then, in this view of it, is that God accomplished what the law could not, by the mission of His own Son in the likeness of sinful flesh; yet not by His mere Incarnation, but by sending Him *in the character of a sin offering* (compare, for the language, 2 Cor. v. 21—"He hath *made Him to be sin* for us"). Still, the question returns, What was it that God did by the mission of His Son as a sin offering in our nature, "when the law could not do it." The apostle's answer is, He **condemned sin in the flesh**—not in order to the *pardon* of it (as *Calvin, Hodge*, &c.); for justification, as we have seen, is not the thing here intended, but 'inflicted on it judicial vengeance in the flesh of Christ,' and so *condemned it to lose its hold over men*—at once to let go its iron grasp, and ultimately to be driven clean away from the domain of human nature in the redeemed. (So *Beza, Fraser, Meyer, Tholuck, Alford, Philippi.*) In this glorious sense our Lord says of His approaching death (John xii. 31)—"Now is the *judgment* of this world; now shall the prince of this world be *cast out;*" and again (John xvi. 11), "When He (the Spirit) shall come, He shall convince the world of . . . judgment, because the prince of this world is *judged*"—*i. e.*, condemned to let go his hold of men, who, through the Cross shall be emancipated into *the liberty and power to be holy.* (See Commentary on that verse.)

We may add to these expository remarks, that *Luther*—who seldom goes far wrong—has entirely missed the sense of the expression, "and for sin." Connecting it, not with the 'sending' of Christ, but with His 'condemning sin' when sent, he translates thus: He 'condemned sin in the flesh *through sin,*' which, if it be sense at all, yields only a bad sense. And *Bengel*, unlike himself,

distorts the proper order of the words even more (thus : 'condemned sin' in Christ's flesh 'for sin' in ours).

4. That ('In order that') **the righteousness of the law** [not δικαιοσύνη, but δικαίωμα]—'the righteous demand of the law;' the practical obedience which it calls for (see on this form of the word in ch. v. 16), **might be fulfilled in us**—or, as we should express it, be 'realized' in us. *Calvin, Fritzsche, Hodge*, and *Philippi* take this to mean, 'that the *justifying* righteousness of the law might be *imputed* to us; partly (in the case of some of them) because they take justification still to be the subject discoursed of; partly because they hold it untrue that the righteousness of the law is any otherwise fulfilled in us; and partly because they think that if our own *personal* obedience were meant, the second clause of the verse would be but a repetition of the first. But is it not unnatural to suppose that the apostle is still dwelling on justification, of which he had already treated so largely? And what is it that this verse conveys which had not been over and over again expressed, and, according to their own interpretation, once or twice said even in the preceding verses? Nor is it a wholesome thing, as we think, to be so very jealous of any expression that sounds like an assertion that believers fulfil the requirements of the law? For, do they not do so? And is it not the express object of ch. vi., in the first part of it, to *show* that they do, and in the second to bid believers accordingly *see* that they do? That their obedience is not *perfect* is no more a truth than that it is a *real* and *acceptable* obedience through Christ. (As to the use of the passive voice here, "might be fulfilled" in us, it seems far-fetched to infer—as *de Wette, Olshausen*, and *Alford* do—that it is used 'to show that the work is not our's, but God's by His grace.') **who walk.** This is the most ancient of all expressions to denote 'the bent of one's life,' whether in the direction of good or of evil (see Gen. v. 24; vi. 9; xlviii. 15; Ps. i. 1; Isa. ii. 5; Mic. iv. 5; Mal. ii. 6; Luke i. 6; Eph. iv. 17; 1 John i. 6, 7). **not after** (according to the dictates of) **the flesh, but after the Spirit.** In this and the following verses it is difficult to say whether by "the Spirit" as opposed to "the flesh," the apostle means *the Holy Spirit*, as the indwelling principle of the new life in believers, or *the renewed mind* itself, under the operation of that indwelling Spirit. Both are in active operation in every spiritual feeling and act. While the whole gracious frame and activity of the soul is due to *the Holy Ghost* as the indwelling Source of it—"the Spirit of life in Christ Jesus" (*v.* 2)—the thing wrought is not wrought passively, mechanically, involuntarily in us, but is the spontaneous life and frame, emotions and actings, of *the renewed mind.* But from *v.* 9, it would seem that what is more immediately intended by "the spirit" is *our own mind*, as renewed and actuated by the Holy Ghost. (See *Philippi*, pp. 288, 289.)

5. For they that are after ('according to') **the flesh**—under the dominating influence of the fleshly principle, **do mind** [φρονοῦσιν] **the things of the flesh**—*i. e.*, give their engrossing attention to them : cf. Phil. iii. 19, "who *mind* [φρονοῦντες] earthly things," and Matt. xvi. 23 (Gr.) Men must be under the predominating influence of one or other of these two principles, and, according as the one or the other has the

238

6 flesh; but they that are after the Spirit ᶜ the things of the Spirit. For
²to be carnally minded *is* death; but ³to be spiritually minded *is* life
7 and peace. Because ⁴ the carnal mind *is* enmity against God : for it is
8 not subject to the law of God, neither indeed can be. So then they that
are in the flesh cannot please God.
9   But ye are not in the flesh, but in the Spirit, if so be that ᵈ the Spirit
of God dwell in you. Now if any man have not the ᵉSpirit of Christ, he
10 is none of his. And if Christ *be* in you, the body *is* dead because of sin;
11 but the Spirit *is* life because of righteousness. But if the Spirit of him
that raised up Jesus from the dead dwell in you, he that raised up Christ

A. D. 60.

ᶜ Gal. 5. 22.
² the mind-ing of the flesh.
³ the mind-ing of the Spirit.
⁴ the mind-ing of the flesh.
ᵈ 1 Cor. 3. 16.
ᵉ John 3. 34.

mastery, will be the complexion of their life, the character of their actions. 'The bent of the thoughts, affections, and pursuits (as *Hodge* says) is the only decisive test of character.' **6. For.** This is scarcely to be taken as a mere particle of transition here, like 'But' or 'Now;' but neither is it intended to assign a reason for the statement of *v.* 5. The mind of the apostle is running upon "the law of sin and death;" which occupied the closing portion of ch. vii., and of which mention is again made now in *v.* 5; and intending to go a little deeper into it, he starts that subject afresh with this connecting particle. **to be carnally minded** [Τὸ φρόνημα τῆς σάρκος]—'the mind,' or (as *marg.*), 'the minding of the flesh;' that is, the pursuit of fleshly ends, **is death**—not only *ends in* death (as *Alford*) but even now "*is*" death; that is, it carries death in its bosom, so that all such are "dead while they live" (1 Tim. v. 6; Eph. ii. 1, 5)—as the best critics agree. **but to be spiritually minded**—'the mind,' or (*marg.*), 'the minding of the spirit;' that is, the pursuit of spiritual objects, **is life and peace**—not "life" only, in contrast with the "death" that is in the other pursuit, but "peace" also: it is the very element of the soul's deepest repose and true bliss. **7. Because the carnal mind is enmity against God.** The desire and pursuit of carnal ends is a state of enmity to God wholly incompatible with true life, and peace in the soul. **for it is not subject** ('doth not submit itself') **to the law of God, neither indeed can be**—'neither indeed can it;' *i. e.*, in such a state of mind there neither is nor can be the least subjection to the law of God. Many things may be done which the law requires, but nothing either is or can be done *because* God's law requires it, or purely to please God. **8. So then**—'And so;' **they that are in** (and, therefore, under the government of) **the flesh cannot please God**—having no obediential principle, no capacity, no desire to please Him.
9. But ye are not in the flesh, but in the Spirit, if so be [εἴπερ]—not 'seeing that' (as *Chrysostom* and other Greek fathers, also *Beza* and *Olshausen*); for this is at least a very doubtful, if not inadmissible sense of the word (though it seems to occur in this sense in 2 Thess. i. 6), and *Meyer*, though defending this sense of the word, admits that it is unsuitable here. **that the Spirit of God dwell in you.** This does not mean, 'if the *disposition* or *mind* of God dwell in you; but if *the Holy Ghost* dwell in you,' (see 1 Cor. vi. 11, 19; iii. 16, &c.) It thus appears that to be "in the spirit" means here, not to be under the power of God's Spirit, but to be under the dominion of *our own renewed mind;* for the indwelling of God's Spirit is given as the *evidence* that we are "in the spirit." Now ('But') **if any man have not the Spirit of Christ.** Again, this does not mean 'If any man have not the *disposition* or *mind* of Christ,' but 'If any man have not the

Holy Spirit, here called "the Spirit of Christ," just as he is called "the Spirit of life in Christ Jesus" (see on *v.* 2). It is as "the Spirit of Christ" that the Holy Ghost takes possession of believers, introducing into them all the gracious dove-like dispositions which dwelt in Him (Matt. iii. 16; John iii. 34). Now if any man's heart be void, not of such dispositions, but of the blessed Author of them, "the Spirit of Christ," **he is none of his**—though intellectually convinced of the truth of Christianity, and even in a general sense influenced by its spirit. Sharp, solemn teaching this!
10. And if Christ be in you—by His indwelling Spirit, in virtue of which we have one life with Him. Who can fail to see, from this way of speaking of the Holy Ghost—called indiscriminately "the Spirit of God," "the Spirit of Christ," and "Christ" Himself (as an indwelling life in believers)—that it admits of but one consistent explanation, namely, that the Father, the Son, and the Holy Ghost are *Essentially One*, yet *Personally distinct*, in the One adorable Godhead? *Bengel*, who, as usual, notices this, refers his readers to the following passages, containing similarly striking collocations of the Persons of the Godhead, and of their respective offices: ch. v. 5, 8; xiv. 17, 18; xv. 16, 30; Mark xii. 36; John xv. 26; Acts ii. 33; 1 Cor. vi. 11; *vv.* 13, 19; 2 Cor. iii. 3; Gal. iv. 6; Eph. i. 17; ii. 18, 22; Heb. ii. 3, 4; 1 Pet. i. 2 (see also Commentary on Matt. iii. 16, 17, Remark 3, at the close of that Section, p. 15). **the body** [τὸ μὲν σῶμα]—'the body indeed' **is dead because of** ('by reason of') **sin; but the Spirit is life because** (or, 'by reason of') **of righteousness.** As the apostle does not mean to say that the body is dead as a consequence of Christ's being in us, it would have been well if the word 'indeed' [μὲν] had been retained in the translation, which would have left no doubt as to the sense, which amounts to this : 'If Christ be in you, the body, it is true, is dead because of sin; *but,*' &c. Expositors are not agreed as to the precise import of this verse; but the following verse seems to fix the sense to the *mortality of the bodies* of believers—*q. d.*, 'If Christ be in you by His indwelling Spirit, though your "bodies" have to pass through the stage of "death," in consequence of the first Adam's "sin," your spirit is instinct with new and undying "life," brought in by the "righteousness" of the second Adam.' (So the best interpreters, but most fully *Hodge*.)
11. But ('And') **if the Spirit of him that raised up Jesus from the dead dwell in you** —*i. e.*, 'If He dwell in you as the Spirit of the Christ-raising One,' or 'in all the *resurrection-power* which He put forth in raising Jesus,' **he that raised up Christ from the dead.** Observe here (what *Bengel* notes, and after him *Meyer*, *Alford* and *Philippi*) the significant change of name from JESUS, as the historical Individual

239

from the dead shall also quicken your mortal bodies [5] by his Spirit that dwelleth in you.

12   Therefore, brethren, we are debtors, not to the flesh, to live after the
13 flesh.   For [f] if ye live after the flesh, ye shall die: but if ye through the
14 Spirit do mortify the deeds of the body, ye shall live.   For as many
15 as are led by the Spirit of God, they are the sons of God.   For [g] ye

A. D. 60.

5 Or, because of his Spirit.

f ch. 1. 4-6. Gal. 6. 8.

g Heb. 2. 15.

whom God raised from the dead, to CHRIST, the same Individual, considered as the Lord and Head of all His members, or of redeemed Humanity. '*Jesus* (says *Bengel*) points to Himself; *Christ* to us: the one, as His proper name, relates to His Person; the other, as an appellative, to His office.' **shall also quicken your mortal bodies**—rather, 'shall quicken even your mortal bodies by His Spirit that dwelleth in you [διὰ τοῦ ἐνοικοῦντος αὐτοῦ πνεύματος]. Our version has here followed *Beza's* text (which *Elzevir* also does), deviating from the received text (of *Stephens*), which has 'by reason of His Spirit that dwelleth in you' [διὰ τὸ ἐνοικοῦν αὐτοῦ πνεῦμα]. The *external* evidence for both readings is good; but it certainly preponderates in favour of the latter reading—'by reason of;' and *internal* evidence is decidedly on the same side, since it would be much more natural for a copyist to write "by His Spirit," even though wrong, than the more unusual phrase, '*by reason of* His Spirit,' though right [διὰ with *acc.* is supported by B D E F G K L, and far the most of the cursives; by the old Latin and Vulgate, ('propter'), the Peshito and Thebaic versions; by *Origen*, *Chrysostom* (in this text and the comment on it), and of the Latin fathers, *Irenæus* (in the Latin), *Tertullian*, *Hilary*, *Augustin*, and others— διὰ with *gen.* is in א A C, about 15 cursives, the Philox. Syriac, Memphitic, and both Æthiopic versions; with several Greek fathers. See an interesting dispute, as to which was the most ancient reading, in Athanas., quoted by *Reiche* and *Tischendorf*. *Lachmann* and *Tischendorf* both adopted *Beza's* reading (with *gen.*) in their earlier and smaller editions, and both in their later and larger have abandoned it for the *acc.* reading, adopted by *Tregelles*]. The sense may be thus conveyed: 'Your bodies indeed are not exempt from the death which sin brought in, but your spirits even now have in them an undying life; and if the Spirit of Him that raised up Jesus from the dead dwell in you, even these bodies of yours, though they yield to the last enemy and the dust of them return to the dust as it was, shall yet experience the same resurrection as that of their living Head, in virtue of the indwelling of the same Spirit in you that quickened Him.'

12. Therefore, brethren, we are debtors, not to the flesh, to live after the flesh—*q. d.*, 'Once we were sold under Sin (ch. vii. 14); but now that we have been set free from that hard master, and become servants to Righteousness (ch. vi. 22), we owe nothing to the flesh, we disown its unrighteous claims, and are deaf to its imperious demands.' Glorious sentiment! **13. For if ye live after the flesh, ye shall die**—in the sense of ch. vi. 21; **but if ye through the Spirit do mortify the deeds of the body** (see on ch. vii. 23), **ye shall live**—in the sense of ch. vi. 22. [The two futures here are not the same: "Ye shall die" is μέλλετε ἀποθνήσκειν—"Ye shall live," ζήσεσθε. μέλλω, as distinguished from the simple future, denotes an action already begun, or at least in preparation, rather than wholly future: see on Matt. ii. 13, p. 7. If that shade of meaning was intended, it would express the sad truth that a life of carnality is not only the sure

prelude to endless death, but fuel for the final flame. But the converse is equally true of a life of spirituality, to express which, however, only a simple future is employed. And as the usage of μέλλω is so various, perhaps nothing more was meant by the use of it in the first clause than to vary the futures.] As to the sentiment itself, the apostle is not satisfied with assuring them that they are under no *obligations* to the flesh, to hearken to its suggestions, without reminding them where it will end if they do; and he uses the word "mortify" (put to death) as a kind of play upon the word "die" just before—*q. d.*, 'If ye do not kill sin, *it* will kill you.' But he tempers this by the bright alternative, that if they do, through the Spirit, mortify the deeds of the body, such a course will infallibly terminate in "life" everlasting. This leads the apostle into a new line of thought, opening into his final subject—the "glory" awaiting the justified believer.

Remarks.—1. 'There can (says *Hodge*, with as much neatness as truth) be no safety, no holiness, no happiness, to those who are out of Christ—no *safety*, because all such are under the condemnation of the law (*v.* 1); no *holiness*, because such only as are united to Christ have the Spirit of Christ (*v.* 9); no *happiness*, because to be "carnally minded is death" (*v.* 6).' 2. The sanctification of believers, as it has its whole foundation in the atoning death, so it has its living spring in the indwelling of the Spirit of Christ (*vv.* 2-4). 3. No human refinement of the carnal mind will make it spiritual, or compensate for the absence of spirituality. "Flesh" and "spirit" are essentially and unchangeably opposed (not *substantially*, however—as some dream—but *morally*); nor can the carnal mind, as such, be brought into real subjection to the law of God. Hence, 4. The estrangement between God and the sinner is mutual. For as the sinner's state of mind is "enmity against God" (*v.* 7), so in this state he "cannot please God" (*v.* 8). 5. While the consciousness of spiritual life in our renewed souls is a glorious assurance of resurrection-life in the body also—in virtue of the same quickening Spirit whose inhabitation we already enjoy (*v.* 11)—yet whatever professions of spiritual life men may make, it remains eternally true that "if we live after the flesh we shall die," and only "if we through the Spirit do mortify the deeds of the body, we shall live" (compare with *v.* 13, Gal. vi. 7, 8; Eph. v. 6; Phil. iii. 18, 19; 1 John iii. 7, 8).

14-27.—THE SONSHIP OF BELIEVERS — THEIR FUTURE INHERITANCE—THE SPIRIT'S INTERCESSION FOR THEM.

The sonship of believers (14-16). **14. For as many as are led by the Spirit of God, they are the sons of God**—'these are sons of God.' The reader will observe the new light in which the Spirit is here held forth. In the preceding verses He was spoken of simply as a *power* or *energy*, in virtue of which believers mortify sin; now the apostle holds Him forth in His personal character, as a gracious, loving GUIDE, whose "leading"—enjoyed by all in whom is the Spirit of God's own dear Son—proves them also to be "sons

have not received the spirit of bondage again [h] to fear; but ye have
16 received the Spirit [i] of adoption, whereby we cry, Abba, Father. The
[j] Spirit itself beareth witness with our spirit, that we are the children
17 of God: and if children, then heirs; [k] heirs of God, and joint-heirs
with Christ; if so be that we suffer with *him*, that we may be also
glorified together.
18 For I reckon that [l] the sufferings of this present time *are* not worthy
19 *to be compared* with the glory which shall be revealed in us. For [m] the
earnest expectation of the creature waiteth for the [n] manifestation of the

A. D. 60.

[h] 2 Tim. 1. 7.
1 John 4.
  · 18.
[i] Isa. 56. 5.
[j] 2 Cor. 1. 22.
Eph. 1. 13.
[k] Acts 26. 18.
[l] 2 Cor. 4. 17.
[m] 2 Pet. 3. 13.
[n] 1 John 3. 2.

of God." **15. For ye have not received**—rather,
'For ye received not;' that is, when ye believed
through grace, **the spirit of bondage.** The
meaning is, The spirit ye then received **was** not a
spirit of bondage, **again** [gendering] **to fear** [πάλιν
εἰς φόβον]—as when ye were under the law which
"worketh wrath "—*q. d.*, 'That was your condition before ye believed—living in legal bondage,
haunted with incessant forebodings under a sense
of unpardoned sin—it was not to perpetuate
that wretched state that ye received the Spirit:'
but ye have received ('ye received') **the Spirit of
adoption, whereby we cry** [ἐν ᾧ κράζομεν]—rather,
'wherein we cry.' The word "cry" is emphatic,
expressing the spontaneousness, the strength, and
the exuberance of the filial emotions. In Gal. iv.
6 this cry is said to proceed from *the Spirit* in us,
drawing forth the filial exclamation in our hearts
—here it is said to proceed from *our own hearts*
under the vitalizing energy of the Spirit, as the
very element of the new life in believers (see on
v. 4; and cf. Matt. x. 19, 20). But why does the
apostle write both these synonymous words, *Abba*
and *Father!* "Abba" is the Aramaic or Syro-
Chaldaic word for "Father;" and the Greek word
for this is added, not surely to tell his readers
that both mean the same thing, but for the same
reason which drew both words from the lips of
Christ Himself during His Agony in the Garden
(Mark xiv. 36—see Commentary on this, p. 332,
second column). He doubtless loved to utter His
Father's name in both the accustomed forms,
beginning with His cherished mother-tongue,
and adding that of the learned. So the High-
landers of Scotland, accustomed equally to Gaelic
and English, might in their devotions pass naturally from the language of their childhood to that
in which all their education had been received.
In this view the use of both words here has a
charming simplicity and warmth. **16. The Spirit
itself** [Αὐτὸ τὸ πνεῦμα]—it should be 'Himself.'
It is unfortunate that our English version here
and elsewhere follows the Greek construction,
which requires the *pronoun* to be in the *neuter*
gender, to agree with the noun which in that
language is *neuter.* Even in the Greek original of
John xvi. 13—where it was of special importance
to mark that what was meant by this neuter noun
was *a living Person*—there, even in the Greek,
the masculine pronoun, "HE," is used [ἐκεῖνος τὸ
πνεῦμα]. This is our warrant for using the English
'He' and 'Himself' in every place where it is
clear, as it is here (and even more so in *vv.* 26, 27),
that the Holy Ghost as a living Divine Person is
meant. **beareth witness with our spirit, that we
are the children**—rather, 'that we are children'
of God. The testimony of our own spirit is borne
in that cry of *conscious sonship,* "Abba, Father;"
but it seems we are not therein alone, for the Holy
Ghost within us—yea, even in that very cry which
it is His to draw forth—sets His own distinct seal
to ours; and thus, "in the mouth of *two witnesses*"
the thing is established.

It is interesting to observe that, whereas in *v.*

14 the apostle called us "*sons* of God" [υἱοὶ Θεοῦ],
referring to our *adoption,* here the word changes
to "*children*" [τέκνα], referring to our new birth.
The one expresses the *dignity* to which we are
admitted; the other the *new life* which we *receive.*
The latter is more suitable here, because a son by
adoption might not be heir of the property, whereas
a son by *birth* certainly is; and this is what the
apostle is now coming to.

The inheritance of the sons of God (17-25). **17.
And if children, then heirs** [καὶ κληρονόμοι]—
'heirs also.' **heirs of God**—of our Father's kingdom
(compare Gal. iv. 7, "and if a *son*, then an heir
of God through Christ"), and **joint-heirs** [συγκλη-
ρονόμοι] **with Christ**—as "the First-born among
many brethren" (*v.* 29), and as "Heir of all things"
(Heb. i. 2: compare Rev. iii. 21, "To Him that
overcometh will I grant to *sit with Me in My
throne;*" **if so be that we suffer with him** [συμπά-
σχομεν], **that we may be also glorified together**
[συνδοξασθῶμεν]—'that we may be glorified with
Him.' This necessity of conformity to Christ in
suffering, in order to participation in His glory,
is taught alike by Christ Himself and by His
apostles (John xii. 24-26; Matt. xvi. 24, 25; 2 Tim.
ii. 12).

18. For I reckon [Λογίζομαι]—as in ch. iii. 28,
expressive not of doubt (as *Jowett*), but of reflection—*q. d.*, 'For when I speak of our present
sufferings and our future glory, I consider that
there is no comparison between them:' **that the
sufferings of this present time** [τοῦ νῦν καιροῦ]—
'of the present season' or 'period;' this word
being chosen, rather than the more indefinite
'time' [χρόνου], to remind the Christian reader of
its definite and transitory character, in contrast
with the eternity of the future glory; **are not
worthy to be compared with** [οὐκ ἄξια πρός—of
this construction, see examples in *Wetstein.*] **the
glory which shall be revealed in us** [εἰς ἡμᾶς].
So *Beza,* after the Vulgate; but it should be
'unto,' 'toward,' or 'for us' (as *Luther, Calvin,
Bengel,* and most good critics). For the glory here
meant is not so much the glorified condition of
believers themselves as that which shall *break
upon them* in the celestial state. The spirit of
the whole statement may be thus conveyed:
'True, we must suffer with Christ, if we would
partake of His glory; but what of that? For if
such sufferings are set over against the coming
glory, they sink into insignificance.'

19. For, &c. 'The apostle (says *Hodge*), fired
at the thought of the future glory of the saints,
pours forth this splendid passage (to the end
of *v.* 22), in which he represents the whole creation groaning under its present degradation, and
looking and longing for the revelation of this
glory as the end and consummation of its existence.' **the earnest expectation of the creature**—
rather, 'the creation,' **waiteth for** ('is waiting
for') &c. The words here used are exceedingly
strong. That one rightly rendered "earnest expectation" [ἀποκαραδοκία]—used elsewhere only in
Phil. i. 20—denotes a 'continuous watching,' or

20 sons of God. For °the creature was made subject to vanity, not willingly,
21 but by reason of him who hath subjected *the same* in hope; because the creature itself also shall be delivered from the bondage of corruption into
22 the glorious liberty of the children of God. For we know that ⁶the whole
23 creation groaneth ᵖ and travaileth in pain together until now. And not only *they*, but ourselves also, which have ᵠthe first-fruits of the Spirit, even we ourselves groan within ourselves, waiting ʳfor the adoption, *to*
24 *wit*, the redemption of our body. For we are saved by hope : but hope

A. D. 60.
° Gen. 3. 19.
Gen. 5. 29.
Gen. 6. 13.
⁶ Or, every creature.
ᵖ Jer. 12. 11.
ᵠ 2 Cor. 5. 5.
Eph. 1. 14.
ʳ Luke 20 36.

'pursuing as with outstretched head ;' while the word too feebly rendered "waiteth" [ἀπεκδέχεται] denotes 'awaiting with eagerness' (see *vv.* 23, 25 ; 1 Cor. i. 7 ; Phil. iii. 20 ; Heb. ix. 28—where the same word is used of the same events), (**the manifestation** (or 'revelation') **of the sons of God**—meaning ' the redemption' of their bodies from the grave (as expressed in *v.* 23), which will reveal their sonship now hidden. (See on Luke xx. 36, *Commentary*, p. 186 ; and on Rev. xxi. 7.) **20. For the creature** ('the creation') **was made subject to vanity, not willingly** — *i. e.*, through no natural principle of decay. The apostle, personifying creation, represents it as only submitting to the vanity with which it was smitten, on man's account, in obedience to that superior power which had mysteriously linked its destinies with man's. And so he adds, **but by reason of him who hath subjected the same in hope; 21. Because** [διὰ τὸν ὑποτάξαντα ἐπ' ἐλπίδι, ὅτι]—or, ' by reason of Him who subjected it in hope, That.' As the words will bear either sense, interpreters are divided as to which shade of thought was intended. (The latter is preferred by *Beza, Fritzsche, de Wette, Meyer, Tholuck, Philippi, Jowett, Webster and Wilkinson.*) We prefer that of our own version (with the Vulgate, *Luther, Calvin, Grotius, Bengel, Olshausen, Alford*) : compare the same phrase ("in hope," put absolutely), Acts ii. 26 ; and see it (in another form) in *v.* 24. **the creature itself also**—rather, 'even the creation itself,' **shall be delivered from the bondage of corruption**—that is, from its bondage to the principle of decay, **into the glorious liberty** [εἰς τ. ἐλευθερίαν τ. δόξης]—rather, 'into the liberty of the glory' **of the children of God**—meaning, into something of the same liberty which shall characterize the glorified state of the children of God themselves ; in other words, the creation itself shall, in a glorious sense, be delivered into that same freedom from blight and debility, corruptibility and decay, in which the children of God, when raised up in glory, shall expatiate. **22. For we know that the whole creation groaneth and travaileth in pain together until now. 23. And not only [they] but ourselves also** [Οὐ μόνον δὲ, ἀλλὰ καὶ αὐτοί]—rather, 'And not only so, but even we ourselves ;' that is, besides the inanimate creation, **which have the first-fruits of the Spirit**—meaning, not 'the Spirit's first-fruits,' but ' the Spirit as the first-fruits' of our full redemption (compare 2 Cor. i. 22 ; Eph. i. 13 ; iv. 30—where the meaning is not "*by* which ye are sealed," as if the Spirit were the Author of the sealing, but "*with* which " the Spirit being Himself the seal). The Spirit, given to believers as "the first-fruits" of what awaits them in glory, moulds the heart to a heavenly frame, and attempers it to its future element : **even we ourselves**—notwithstanding that we have the first-fruits of heaven already within us, **groan within ourselves**—both under that "body of sin and death " which we carry about with us, and under the manifold "vanity and vexation of spirit" that are written upon every object and

every pursuit and every enjoyment under the sun ; **waiting for** [ἀπεκδεχόμενοι, see on *v.* 19] **the adoption**—meaning the revelation or manifestation of the adoption, [**to wit,**] **the redemption of our body**—from the grave ; for (as *Bengel* notes) that is not called liberty by which we are delivered from the body, but by which the body itself is liberated from death.

Such seems to us the simplest and most natural interpretation of this noble passage. But it has been much controverted. No one passage, indeed, has given rise to more controversy, and whole treatises have been written to discuss and expound it. Though the interpretations put upon it have been many, they are all reducible to three : First, that "the whole creation" here means 'the whole created universe.' Such is the strange view of *Olshausen*, who views it, however, in a mystical sense, as the yearning of all creature-life after its destined perfection. But unless it be maintained that the whole created universe was "made subject to vanity" through the sin of man, which would be absurd, this interpretation must be rejected as a mere dream. Next, that "the creation" here means, 'the rational creation,' or 'mankind in general.' So *Augustin, Locke, Stuart, Webster and Wilkinson.* But how could it be said that mankind in general were 'unwillingly subjected to vanity,' since in this very Epistle the sin that brought this vanity upon them is represented as *their own* (ch. v. 12) ; and how could it be said that the rational creation, or mankind in general, were 'subjected to vanity, in hope of being delivered from the bondage of corruption into the liberty of the glory of the children of God,' or, finally, that they are now "groaning and travailing in pain together, waiting for the adoption"? &c. It remains, then, lastly, since "the creation" here cannot mean *Christians*—for in *v.* 23 they and it are expressly distinguished from each other—that it must mean, ' *that creation which forms part of one system with man, yet exclusive of man himself.*' So (although with considerable diversity in minor particulars) the great majority of interpreters—as *Irenæus* and *Chrysostom* of the fathers ; *Erasmus, Luther, Melancthon, Calvin* and *Beza, Melville* and *Ferme, Grotius, Estius, Bengel, Cocceius, Reiche, Fritzsche, Neander, Tholuck, Meyer, de Wette, Philippi, Alford, Hodge, Wordsworth.* If for man's sake alone the earth was cursed, it cannot surprise us that it should share in his recovery. And if so, to represent it as sympathizing with man's miseries, and as looking forward to his complete redemption as the period of its own emancipation from its present sin-blighted condition, is a beautiful thought, and in harmony with the general teaching of Scripture on the subject. (See 2 Pet. iii. 13.)

24. For we are saved by hope [Τῇ γὰρ ἐλπίδι ἐσώθημεν]. This sense of the words makes hope the instrument of salvation, which it can only be if we view hope as nothing else (to use the words of *Alford*) than 'faith in its prospective attitude.' Still hope is *not* faith, but is that which begets it ; and in the New Testament they are carefully distin-

242

that *is seen is not hope: for what a man seeth, why doth he yet hope
25 for? But if we hope for that we see not, *then* do we with patience
wait for *it*.

26 Likewise the Spirit also helpeth our infirmities: for *we know not
what we should pray for as we ought: but "the Spirit itself maketh
27 intercession for us with groanings which cannot be uttered. And *he
that searcheth the hearts knoweth what *is* the mind of the Spirit,
⁷because he maketh intercession for the saints "according to *the will
of* God.

A. D. 60.

* 2 Cor. 4. 18.
Heb. 11. 1.
ᶠ Matt. 20.22.
ᵘ Zech. 12.10.
Matt. 10.20.
Gal. 4. 6.
Eph. 6. 18.
ᵛ 1 Thes. 2. 4.
⁷ Or, that.
ʷ 1 John 5.14.

guished. The true sense, as the great majority of good critics admit, is, 'For in hope we are saved;' that is, our salvation—in that sense of it which the preceding verses refer to—is in the present state rather in hope than in actual possession. **but hope that is seen is not hope**—for the very meaning of hope is the expectation that some good now *future* will become *present: for* **what a man seeth, why doth he yet hope for ?**—since the latter ends when the other comes. **25. But if we hope for that we see not, [then do] we with patience wait for it**—*i. e.*, then, patient waiting for it is our fitting attitude.

The Spirit's Intercession for the Saints (26, 27). **26. Likewise the Spirit also, &c.**—*q. d.*, 'I have already shown you the varied offices of the blessed Spirit towards believers—how He descends into their souls as the Spirit of life in Christ Jesus, making them members of Christ, and one life with their glorious Head; how in the power of this new life they are freed from the law of sin and death, walking henceforth not after the flesh but after the Spirit, minding supremely the things of the Spirit, and through the Spirit mortifying the deeds of the body; how He dwells in them as the Guide of the sons of God, as the Spirit of adoption teaches them to cry, "Abba, Father," witnesses with their spirit that they are children of God, and is in them as the first-fruits of their full redemption: but this is not all, for—"*Likewise also* the Spirit" **helpeth** ['Ωσαύτως δὲ καί]—rather, 'But after the like manner doth the Spirit also help' **our infirmities**. The true reading, beyond doubt, is in the singular number — 'our infirmity.' The infirmity meant is not merely the one infirmity regarding prayer here specified, but *the general weakness of the spiritual life*—of which one example is here given, **for we know not what we should pray for as we ought**. It is not the proper *matter* of prayer that believers are at so much loss about, for the fullest directions are given them on this head; but to ask for the right things "as they ought" is the difficulty. This arises partly from the dimness of our spiritual vision in the present veiled state, while we have to "walk by faith, not by sight" (1 Cor. xiii. 9; 2 Cor. v. 7), and the large admixture of the ideas and feelings which spring from the fleeting objects of sense that there is in the very best views and affections of our renewed nature; partly also from the necessary imperfection of all human language as a vehicle for expressing the subtle spiritual feelings of the heart. In these circumstances, how can it be but that much uncertainty should surround all our spiritual exercises, and that in our nearest approaches, and in the freest outpourings of our hearts to our Father in heaven, doubts should spring up within us whether our *frame* of mind in such exercises is altogether befitting and well-pleasing to God? Nor do these anxieties subside, but rather deepen, with the depth and ripeness of our spiritual experience. **but the Spirit itself**—rather, 'Himself.' See, on the *personal* sense of the pronoun in such places, on *v.* 16. **maketh in-**

tercession [for us]. The bracketed words are omitted by *Lachmann, Tischendorf,* and *Tregelles,* on good authority; but of course they are *implied,* and hence their tendency to get into the text. **with groanings which cannot be uttered** [ἀλα-λήτοις]—that is, which cannot be expressed in articulate language. What sublime and affecting ideas are these, for which we are indebted to this passage alone !—*q. d.,* 'As we struggle to express in articulate language the desires of our hearts, and find that our deepest emotions are the most inexpressible, we "groan" under this felt inability. But not in vain are these groanings. For "the Spirit Himself" is in them, giving to the emotions which Himself has kindled the only language of which they are capable; so that though on our part they are the fruit of impotence to utter what we feel, they are at the same time the intercession of the Spirit Himself in our behalf.' **27. And**—rather, 'But' (all inarticulate though these groanings be) **he that searcheth the hearts knoweth what is the mind of the Spirit, because he**—that is, the Spirit. Here our translators have properly departed from the *neuter* sense of the word "Spirit," when meant of the Holy Ghost; rendering it "He." The pity is that they did not carry out the same principle in the preceding verse, and in *v.* 16. **maketh intercession for the saints according to [the will of] God**. It had been as well, perhaps, that the words had been allowed to stand without any supplement—"according to God." But if a supplement was to be introduced, 'according to [the mind of] God' would have been better, as corresponding to "the mind of the Spirit" in the preceding clause. As the Searcher of hearts, He watches the surging emotions of them in prayer, and knows perfectly what the Spirit means by the groanings which He draws forth within us, because that blessed Intercessor pleads by them only for what God Himself designs to bestow. 'The assurance which we have (says *Alford* well) that God the Heart-Searcher interprets the inarticulate sighings of the Spirit in us is not, strictly speaking, His Omniscience, but the fact that the very Spirit who thus pleads does it in pursuance of the Divine purposes, and in conformity with God's good pleasure.' Some render the words thus: 'knoweth the mind of the Spirit, *that* He maketh intercession,' &c. (So *Calvin, Meyer,* &c.) But though the Greek will admit of this, the other sense suits the apostle's strain of thought better, as well as brings out a better sense. It is accordingly that which most adopt.

Remarks.—1. Are believers "led by the Spirit of God"? (*v.* 14.) How careful, then, should they be not to "grieve the Holy Spirit of God" ! (Eph. iv. 30.) Cf. Ps. xxxii. 8, 9, "I will . . . *guide* thee with mine eye. *Be not* (then) *as the horse, or as the mule,*" &c. 2. "The spirit of bondage" to which many Protestants are "all their lifetime subject," and the 'doubtsome faith' which the Popish Church systematically inculcates, are both rebuked here, being in direct and painful contrast

28   And we know that *^x* all things work together for good to them that
29 love God, to them who are the called according to *his* purpose. For

A. D. 60.
^x Gen. 50. 20.

to that "spirit of adoption," and that witness of the Spirit, along with our own spirit, to the fact of our sonship, which it is here said the children of God, as such, enjoy (*vv.* 15, 16). *Philippi*, noticing this, refers to the great Protestant divines who noticed it also. And *Olshausen* only echoes the statements of the 'Westminster Confession,' *John Owen, Halyburton,* &c., when he says that 'On the foundation of this immediate testimony of the Holy Spirit, all the regenerate man's conviction finally rests. For the faith in the Scripture itself [in the supreme sense of the word "faith"] has its basis in this experience of the principle which it promises, and which flows into the believer while he is occupied with it.' The same profound writer notices also the important testimony borne by this verse against the *pantheistic* confusion of the Divine and the human spirit. 3. As suffering with Christ is the ordained preparation for participating in this glory, so the insignificance of the one, as compared with the other, cannot fail to lighten the sense of it, however bitter and protracted (*vv.* 17, 18). 4. It cannot but swell the heart of every intelligent Christian to think that if external nature has been mysteriously affected for evil by the fall of man, it only awaits his completed recovery, at the resurrection, to experience a corresponding emancipation from its blighted condition into undecaying life and unfading beauty (*vv.* 19-23). 5. It is not when believers, through sinful 'quenching of the Spirit,' have the fewest and faintest glimpses of heaven that they sigh most fervently to be there; but, on the contrary, when, through the unobstructed working of the Spirit in their hearts, "the first-fruits" of the glory to be revealed are most largely and frequently tasted, then, and just for that reason, is it that they "groan within themselves" for full redemption (*v.* 23). For thus they reason: If such be the drops, what will the ocean be? If thus "to see through a glass darkly" be so very sweet, what will it be to "see face to face"? If when "my Beloved stands behind our wall, looking forth at the windows, showing Himself through the lattice" (Song ii. 9) —that thin, transparent veil which hides the unseen from mortal view—if, even thus, He is to me "Fairer than the children of men," what shall He be when He stands confessed before my undazzled vision the Only-begotten of the Father in my own nature, and I shall be like Him, seeing Him as He is? 6. "The patience of hope" (1 Thess. i. 3) is the fitting attitude for those who with the joyful consciousness that they are already "*saved*" (2 Tim. i. 9; Tit. iii. 5), have yet the painful consciousness that they are saved but *in part;* or, that, "being justified by His grace, they are made (in the present state) heirs according to the hope (only) of eternal life" (Tit. iii. 7). 7. As prayer is the breath of the spiritual life, and the believer's only effectual relief under the "infirmity" which attaches to his whole condition here below, how cheering is it to be assured that the blessed Spirit, cognizant of it all, comes in aid of it all; and in particular, that when believers— unable to articulate their case before God—can at times do nothing but lie "groaning" before the Lord, these inarticulate groanings are the Spirit's own vehicle for conveying into "the ears of the Lord of Sabaoth" their whole case; that they come up before the Hearer of prayer as the Spirit's own intercession in their behalf; and that they are recognized by Him that sitteth on the Throne as embodying only what, in His own 'mind,' He had

determined before to bestow upon them! 8. What a view do those two verses (26, 27) give of the relations subsisting between the Divine Persons in the economy of redemption and the harmony of their respective operations in the case of each of the redeemed!

28-39.—Triumphant Summary of the whole Argument.

In this incomparable Section the apostle expatiates over the whole field of his preceding argument, his spirit swelling and soaring with his vast and lofty theme, and carrying his readers along with him, out of all the trials and tears and uncertainties of things present, into the region of cloudless and eternal day. To subdivide this Section would be intolerable; for after the first verse or two the thoughts rush along like a cataract, and refuse to be arrested by any artificial breaks.

28. And—rather, 'Moreover,' 'Now,' or some other such word, to mark, better than the ordinary copulative "And," what this verse clearly is—a transition to a new train of thought : **we know,** &c. The order in the original, which is more striking, is this : 'We know' that to them **that love God, all things work together for good,** to them who are the called according to his purpose—his eternal purpose. Two characteristics of believers are here given—one descriptive of *their* feeling towards God, the other of *His* feeling towards them; and each of these is selected with the evident view of suggesting the true explanation of the delightful assurance here conveyed, that all things are, and cannot but be, co-operating for good to such. Let us look at each of them, for it will be found that there is a glorious consistency between the eternal purposes of God and the free agency of men, though the link of connection is beyond human—probably even created —apprehension. First, 'To them that love God all things are working together for good.' Because such souls, persuaded that He who gave His own Son for them cannot but mean them well in all His procedure, fall naturally and sweetly in with it; and thus learning to take in good part whatever He sends to them, however trying to flesh and blood, they render it impossible—so to speak —that it should do other than minister to their good. But, again, "To them who are the called according to his purpose all things are"—in the same intelligible way—"working together for good." Because, believing that there *is* such an eternal purpose, within the cloud of whose glory the humblest believer is enrapt, they see "His chariot paved with love" (Song iii. 10); and knowing that it is in pursuance of this purpose of love that they have been "called into the fellowship of his Son Jesus Christ" (1 Cor. i. 9), they naturally say within themselves, 'It cannot be that He "of Whom, and through Whom, and to Whom are all things," should suffer that purpose to be thwarted by anything really adverse to us, or that he should not make all things—dark as well as light, crooked as well as straight—to co-operate to the furtherance and final completion of His high design. Glorious assurance! And of this the apostle says, "We know" it. It was a household word with the household of faith : not that, *as here exhibited,* it had perhaps ever before struck one of his readers; but, as already observed, with the teaching they had already received and the Christian experience which was common to all who had tasted that the Lord was gracious, it had but to be put before them to be at once recognized as an undoubted and precious truth.

whom *ʸ* he did foreknow, *ᶻ* he also did predestinate *"to be* conformed to the image of his Son, *ᵇ* that he might be the first-born among many 30 brethren. Moreover whom he did predestinate, them he also *ᶜ* called; and whom he called, them he also *ᵈ* justified; and whom he justified, them he also glorified.

31   What shall we then say to these things? If God *be* for us, who *can be* 32 against us? He that spared not his own Son, but delivered him up for

A. D. 60.
ʸ Ex. 33. 12.
ᶻ Ps. 1. 6.
Jer. 1. 5.
ˢ Eph. 1. 5.
ᵃ John 17. 22.
ᵇ Col. 1. 18.
ᶜ 1 Cor. 1. 24.
ᵈ 1 Cor. 6. 11.

29. For—as touching this "calling according to His purpose," **whom he did foreknow, he also did predestinate**—or 'fore-ordain.' In what sense are we to take the word "foreknow" here? 'Those who He foreknew would repent and believe,' say *Pelagians* of every age and every hue. But this is to thrust into the text what is contrary to the whole spirit, and even letter, of the apostle's teaching, as will appear from the following chapter; see also 2 Tim. i. 9. In ch. xi. 2 and Ps. i. 6 God's "knowledge" of His people cannot be restricted to a mere foresight of future events, or acquaintance with what is passing here below. Does "whom He did foreknow," then, mean 'whom He fore-ordained?' That can hardly be, since both words are here used, and the thing meant by the one is spoken of as the *cause* of what is intended by the other. It is difficult, indeed, for our limited minds to distinguish them as states of the Divine Mind towards men, especially since in Acts ii. 23, "the counsel" is put *before* "the foreknowledge of God," while in 1 Pet. i. 2, "election" is said to be "*according to* the foreknowledge of God." But probably God's "foreknowledge" of His own people means His *peculiar, gracious complacency in them,* while His "predestinating" or "fore-ordaining" them signifies His fixed *purpose,* flowing from this, to "save them and call them with an holy calling" (2 Tim. i. 9). 'According to Pauline doctrine (says *Olshausen*—and the testimony is remarkable from a Lutheran) there is a *predestination of saints,* in the proper sense of the words: that is, not that God knows beforehand that they will by their own decision be holy, but that he creates this very decision in them.' [**to be**] **conformed to the image of his Son** [συμμόρφους]—or, 'be counterparts of His Son's image;' to be sons, that is, after the pattern or model of *His* Sonship in our nature, **that he might be the first-born among many brethren**—the First-born being the Son by nature; His "many brethren" sons by adoption: He, in the Humanity of the Only-begotten of the Father, bearing our sins on the accursed tree; they in that of mere men ready to perish by reason of sin, but redeemed by His blood from condemnation and wrath, and transformed into his likeness: He "the First-born from the dead;" they "that sleep in Jesus," to be in due time "brought with Him:" "The First-born," already "crowned with glory and honour;" His "many brethren," "when He shall appear, to be like Him, for they shall see Him as he is." **30. Moreover**—rather, 'And' or 'Now;' for the same train of thought is still in course of development, **whom he did predestinate, them he also called**—*q. d.,* 'In "predestinating us to be conformed to the image of His Son," He settled all the successive steps of it; the "*predestination*" of them from everlasting being followed up by the "*calling*" of them in time. The word "called" (as *Hodge* and others truly observe) is never *in* the Epistles of the New Testament applied to those who have only the *outward invitation* of the Gospel (as in Matt. xx. 16; xxii. 14). It always means 'internally, *effectually, savingly* called;' denoting the *first great step* in personal salvation, and answering to "conversion."

Only, whereas the word *conversion* expresses the *change of character* which then takes place, this 'calling' expresses the *Divine authorship* of the change, and the *sovereign power* by which we are summoned—Matthew-like, Zaccheus-like—out of our old, wretched, perishing condition, into a new, safe, blessed life. **and whom he** (thus) **called, them he also justified**—brought into the definite state of reconciliation, acceptance, and righteous standing already so fully described; **and whom he justified, them he also glorified**—brought to final glory (see *vv.* 17, 18). Noble climax, and how rhythmically expressed! And all this is viewed as past; because, starting from the past decree of "predestination to be conformed to the image of God's Son," of which the other steps are but the successive unfoldings, all is beheld as one entire, eternally completed salvation.

31. What shall we then say to these things? As *Bengel* says, with his own unrivalled terseness, 'We can no further go, think, wish.' This whole passage, in fact—on to *v.* 34, and even to the end of the chapter—strikes all thoughtful interpreters and readers as transcending almost everything in language; while *Olshausen* notices the 'profound and colossal' character of the thought. **If God** [be] **for us, who** [can be] **against us?**—If God be *resolved* and *engaged* to bring us through, all *our* enemies must be *His;* and "Who would set the briers and thorns against Him in battle? He would go through them, He would burn them together" (Isa. xxvii. 4). What strong consolation is here! Nay, but the great pledge of all has already been given. For, **32. He** ['Ος γε]—rather, 'He, surely.' It is a pity to lose the emphatic particle of the original, when it can be expressed idiomatically (as it cannot always be) in our own language. [See *Kühner,* § 317. 2, and *Jelf,* § 735, 6.] *Bengel* notices that full sweetness of exultation which this little particle here conveys. **that spared not his own Son** [τοῦ ἰδίου υἱοῦ οὐκ ἐφείσατο]—'withheld not,' or 'kept not back His own (proper) Son.' Both of these most expressive phrases, as well as the entire thought, were suggested by Gen. xxii. 22 (as in the LXX.), where Jehovah's touching commendation of Abraham's conduct is designed to furnish something like a glimpse into the spirit of His own act in *surrendering* His own son. "Take now (said the Lord to Abraham) thy *son,* thine *only, whom thou lovest,* and . . . offer him for a burnt offering" (Gen. xxii. 2); and only when Abraham had all but performed that loftiest act of self-sacrifice, did the Lord interpose, saying, "Now I know that thou fearest God, seeing thou HAST NOT WITHHELD THY SON, THINE ONLY SON, from me." In the light of this incident, then, and of this language, our apostle can mean to convey nothing less than this, that in "not sparing His own Son, but delivering Him up," or surrendering Him, God exercised, in His *Paternal* character, a mysterious act of *Self-sacrifice,* which, though involving none of the *pain* and none of the *loss* which are inseparable from the very idea of self-sacrifice on our part, was not less real but, on the contrary, as far transcended any such acts of ours as His nature is above the creature's. But this is

33 us all, how shall he not with him also freely give us all things? Who
shall lay any thing to the charge of God's elect? *It is* God that justi-
34 fieth; who *is* he that condemneth? *It is* Christ that died, yea rather,
that is risen again, who is even at the right hand of God, *f* who also
35 maketh intercession for us. Who shall separate us from the love of
Christ? *shall* tribulation, or distress, or persecution, or famine, or naked-
36 ness, or peril, or sword? As it is written, *g* For thy sake we are killed

A. D. 60.

e Isa. 50. 8.
Gal. 3. 8.
f Isa. 53. 12.
Heb. 7. 25.
1 John 2. 1,
2.
g Ps. 44. 22.
John 16. 2.

inconceivable if Christ be not God's "own (or 'proper') Son," partaker of His very nature, as really as Isaac was of his father Abraham's. It was in that sense, undoubtedly, that the Jews charged our Lord with making Himself "equal with God" (John v. 18)—a charge which He in reply forthwith proceeded, not to disown, but to illustrate and confirm. Understand Christ's Sonship thus, and the language of Scripture regarding it is intelligible and harmonious; but take it to be an *artificial* relationship, ascribed to Him in virtue either of His miraculous birth or His resurrection from the dead, or the grandeur of His works, or all of these together, and the passages which speak of it neither explain of themselves nor harmonize with each other. **but delivered him up**—not to *death* merely (as many take it), for that is too narrow an idea here, but 'surrendered Him,' in the most comprehensive sense: cf. John iii. 16, "God so loved the world that He GAVE His only begotten Son." **for us all**—*i. e.*, for all believers alike; as nearly every good interpreter admits must be the meaning here. **how shall he not**—how can we conceive that He should not, **with him also**—that is, along with Him, **freely give us all things?**—all other gifts being not only immeasurably *less* than this gift of gifts, but virtually *included* in it. 33. **Who shall lay any thing to the charge of** [ἐγκαλέσει]—or, 'bring a charge against' **God's elect.** Here, for the first time in this Epistle, believers are styled the "*elect.*" In what sense this is meant will appear in next chapter. [It is] **God that justifieth**; 34. **Who is he that condemneth?** It is **Christ that died.** A number of expositors (after *Ambrose* and *Augustin*) read this as a question: "God that justifieth?" (Will *He* bring a charge against His own elect?) "Who is he that condemneth? Christ that died?" (Will *He* condemn them?) So *Erasmus, Locke, de Wette, Olshausen, Alford, Jowett, Webster and Wilkinson, Green;* and so *Lachmann* prints his text. But besides that this 'creates (as *Tholuck* remarks) an unnatural accumulation of questions, it is (to use the not too strong language of *Fritzsche*) intolerable; for God is thus represented as the judge; but it is the part of a judge not to accuse, but either to acquit or condemn the accused.' We may add (with *Meyer*) that such an idea is against all Scripture analogy, and could never come into the apostle's mind—that after he had spoken of God's being so for us that none can be against us, and His giving such a Gift as secures every other, and having on the ground of this challenged *any* to criminate God's elect—he should turn round and ask, if "God that justified" would at the same time criminate them, or "Christ that died" for them would at the same time "condemn" them. Plainly, it is to *creatures* only that he throws down the challenge, asking which of *them* would dare to bring a charge against those whom God has justified—would condemn those for whom Christ died. **yea, rather, that is risen again**—to make good the purposes of His death. Here, as in some other cases, the apostle delightfully corrects himself (see on ch. i. 12, and Gal. iv. 9), not meaning that

the resurrection of Christ was of more saving value than His death, but that "having put away sin by the sacrifice of Himself"—which, however precious to us, was to Him of unmingled bitterness—it was incomparably more delightful to think that He was again *alive*, and living to see to the efficacy of His death in our behalf. **who is even** (rather, 'who is also') **at the right hand of God.** The right hand of the king was anciently the seat of honour (1 Sam. xx. 25; 1 Ki. ii. 19; Ps. xlv. 9), and denoted participation in the royal power and glory (Matt. xx. 21). The classical writings have familiarized us with the same idea. Accordingly, Christ's sitting at the right hand of God—predicted in Ps. cx. 1, and historically referred to in Mark xvi. 19; Acts ii. 33; vii. 56; Eph. i. 20; Col. iii. 1; 1 Pet. iii. 22; Rev. iii. 21—signifies the *glory* of the exalted Son of man, and the *power* in the government of the world in which He participates. Hence it is called "sitting on the right hand of *Power*" (Matt. xxvi. 64), and "sitting on the right hand of the *Majesty* on high" (Heb. i. 3). **who also maketh intercession for us**—using all His boundless *interest* with God in our behalf. 'His session (says *Bengel*) denotes His *power* to save us; His intercession, His *will* to do it.' But how are we to conceive of this intercession? Not as of one pleading 'on bended knees and with outstretched arms,' to use the expressive language of *Calvin*. But yet, neither is it merely a figurative intimation that the power of Christ's redemption is continually operative (as *Fritzsche* and *Tholuck* represent it); nor (with *Chrysostom*) merely to show the fervour and vehemence of His love for us. It cannot be taken to mean less than this, that the glorified Redeemer, conscious of His claims, expressly *signifies His will* that the efficacy of His death should be made good to the uttermost, and signifies it in some such royal style as we find Him employing in that wonderful Intercessory Prayer which He spoke *as from within the veil* (see John xvii. 11, 12): "Father, I WILL that they also whom thou hast given me be with me where I am" (see on *v.* 24 of that chapter). But *in what form* this will is expressed is as undiscoverable as it is unimportant. 35. **Who shall separate us from the love of Christ?** This does not mean 'our love to Christ;' as if one should say, Who shall hinder us from loving Christ?—but 'Christ's love to us,' as is clear from the closing words of the chapter, which refer to the same subject. Nor would the other sense harmonize with the scope of the chapter, which is to exhibit the ample ground that there is for the believer's confidence in Christ. 'It is no ground of confidence (as *Hodge* observes) to assert, or even to feel, that we will never forsake Christ; but it is the strongest ground of assurance to be convinced that his love will never change.' **shall tribulation, or distress, or persecution, or famine, or·nakedness, or peril, or sword?**—*q. d.*, 'None of these, nor all of them together, how terrible soever to the flesh, are tokens of God's wrath, or the least ground for doubt of His love.' And from whom could such a question come better than from one who had himself for Christ's sake endured so much? (See 2 Cor. xi. 21-33; 1

246

37 all the day long; we are accounted as sheep for the slaughter. Nay, [h] in
all these things we are more than conquerors, through him that loved us.
38 For I am persuaded, that neither death, nor life, nor angels, nor [i] princi-
39 palities, nor powers, nor things present, nor things to come, nor height,
nor depth, nor any other creature, shall [j] be able to separate us from the
love of God, which is in Christ Jesus our Lord.

A. D. 60.

[h] 2 Chr. 20, 25.
1 John 5. 4.
[i] Col. 1. 16.
1 Pet. 3. 22.
[j] John 10, 28.
Col. 3. 3.

Cor. iv. 10-13). *Calvin* (says *Tholuck*) makes the noble reflection, that the apostle says not 'What,' but "Who"—just as if all creatures, and all afflictions, were so many gladiators taking arms against the Christians. **36. As it is written** (Ps. xliv. 22), **For thy sake we are killed all the day long; we are accounted as sheep for the slaughter.** This is quoted as descriptive of what God's faithful people may expect from their enemies *at any period* when their hatred of righteousness is roused, and there is nothing to restrain it (see Gal. iv. 29). **37. Nay, in all these things we are more than conquerors** [ὑπερνικῶμεν] **through him that loved us**—not (as *Hodge* takes it) 'We are so far from being conquered by all these things, that they do us, on the contrary, much good;' for though this is true enough, the word means simply, 'We are pre-eminently conquerors' (see on ch. v. 20). So far are they from 'separating us from Christ's love, that it is just "through Him that loved us" that we are victorious over them.' **38. For I am persuaded, that neither death, nor life, nor angels, nor principalities, nor powers** [οὔτε δυνάμεις]. This last clause ("nor powers")—if we are to be guided by *external* authorities alone—ought certainly to stand, not here, but at the close of the verse, which will then read thus: "nor angels, nor principalities, nor things present, nor things to come, nor powers." [Thus read אABCDEFG, six cursives, four copies of the Old Latin, and the Vulgate (not the Clementine edition). So *Lachmann, Tischendorf*, and *Tregelles;* also most recent critics, while the received order is supported only by K L, most cursives, the Syriac, and some later versions, with (apparently) most of the Greek fathers.] But who can bring himself to believe that the apostle so wrote—that one of the harshest and baldest collocations of the conceivable enemies of believers was placed there by one who has here drawn up a catalogue otherwise perfect? How to account for this arrangement having found its way into so many MSS. may be very difficult to say; but in the meantime we must hold the received order of the clauses as that of the apostle himself. **nor things present, nor things to come**—no condition of the present life, and none of the unknown possibilities of the life to come; **39. Nor height, nor depth, nor any other creature**—rather, 'created thing,' any other thing in the whole created universe of God, **shall be able to separate us.** 'All the terms here (as *Olshausen* says) are to be taken in their most general sense, and need no closer definition. The indefinite expressions are meant to denote all that can be thought of, and are only a rhetorical paraphrase of the conception of *allness.*' **from the love of God, which is in Christ Jesus our Lord.** Thus does this wonderful chapter, with which the argument of the Epistle properly closes, leave us who are "justified by faith," in the arms of everlasting Love, whence no hostile power or conceivable event can ever tear us. "Behold what manner of 'love is this!" And "what manner of persons ought we to be," who are thus "blessed with all spiritual blessings in Christ!"

Remarks.—1. How ennobling is the thought that the complicated movements of the Divine govern-

ment of the world are all arranged in express furtherance of the "good" of God's chosen! (*v.* 28.) 2. To whatever conformity to the Son of God in dignity and glory believers are or shall hereafter be raised, it will be the joy of every one of them—as it is most fitting—"that in all things He should have the pre-eminence" (Col. i. 18), and be recognized as "the First-born among many brethren" (*v.* 29). 3. As there is a beautiful harmony and necessary connection between the several doctrines of grace, so (to use the words of *Hodge*) must there be a like harmony in the character of the Christian. He cannot experience the joy and confidence flowing from his election without the humility which the consideration of its being gratuitous must produce; nor can he have the peace of one who is justified without the holiness of one who is called. 4. However difficult it may be for finite minds to comprehend the emotions of the Divine Mind, let us never for a moment doubt that, in "not sparing His own Son, but delivering Him up for us all," God made a real sacrifice of all that was dearest to His heart, and that in so doing He meant for ever to assure His people that all other things which they need—inasmuch as they are nothing to this stupendous gift, and indeed but the necessary sequel of it—will in due time be forthcoming. In return for such a sacrifice on God's part, what can be considered too great on ours? 5. If there could be any doubt as to the meaning of the all-important word "JUSTIFICATION," in this Epistle—whether, as the Church of Rome teaches, and many others affirm, it means '*infusing* righteousness into the unholy, so as to *make* them righteous,' or, according to Protestant teaching, '*absolving, acquitting*, or *pronouncing righteous* the guilty'—*v.* 33 ought to set such doubt entirely at rest. For the apostle's question in this verse is, 'Who shall *bring a charge against* God's elect?'—in other words, 'Who shall *pronounce*' or '*hold them guilty?*' seeing that "God *justifies*" them: showing, beyond all doubt, that to "justify" was intended to express precisely the opposite of 'holding guilty;' and consequently (as *Calvin* triumphantly argues) that it means '*to absolve from the charge of guilt.*' 6. After the same unanswerable mode of reasoning, we are entitled to argue, that if there could be any reasonable doubt in what light the *death* of Christ is to be regarded in this Epistle, *v.* 34 ought to set that doubt entirely at rest. For there the apostle's question is, Who shall "*condemn*" God's elect, since "Christ *died*" for them: showing beyond all doubt (as *Philippi* justly argues) that it was the *expiatory* character of that death which the apostle had in view. 7. What an affecting view of the love of Christ does it give us to learn that His greatest *nearness* to God and most powerful *interest* with Him—as being 'seated on His right hand' —is employed in behalf of His people here below! 8. What everlasting consolation and good hope through grace arise from the fact, as variously as it is grandly expressed in this Section, that all that *can* help us is on the side of those who are Christ's, and all that *can* hurt us is a conquered foe! 9. Are we who "have tasted that the Lord is gracious" both "kept by the *power* of God through faith unto salvation" (1 Pet. i. 5), and

247

9 I SAY the truth in Christ, I lie not, my conscience also bearing me
2 witness in the Holy Ghost, that I have great heaviness and continual
3 sorrow in my heart. For [a] I could wish that myself were [1] accursed from
4 Christ for my brethren, my kinsmen according to the flesh: who [b] are
Israelites; to whom *pertaineth* the adoption, and the glory, and the

A. D. 60.

CHAP. 9.
[a] Ex. 32. 32.
[1] Or,
separated.
[b] Deut. 7. 6.

---

embraced in the arms of Invincible *Love?* Then
surely, while "building ourselves up on our most
holy faith," and "praying in the Holy Ghost,"
only the more should we feel constrained to "*keep
ourselves in the love of God*, looking for the mercy
of our Lord Jesus Christ unto eternal life" (Jude
20, 21).

CHAP. IX.-XI.—THE BEARING OF THE FORE-
GOING TRUTHS UPON THE CONDITION AND DES-
TINY OF THE CHOSEN PEOPLE, ON THE DOCTRINE
OF ELECTION, AND ON THE CALLING OF THE
GENTILES.
In opening up so thoroughly the way of Salvation by Grace—alike for Jew and Gentile—through
Faith alone in the Lord Jesus, the far-reaching
mind of our apostle could not fail to perceive
that he was raising questions of a profound and
delicate nature, as to God's elect nation, which
had rejected Christ, as to the promises made to
them, and what was to become of them; also,
whether all distinction of Jew and Gentile was
now at an end, and if not, what might be its
precise nature and future development. In preaching, or in less elaborate Epistles, a glance at the
principles involved in these questions might be
sufficient. But this great Epistle afforded just the
appropriate occasion for handling them thoroughly
and once for all; which, accordingly, he now
proceeds to do in three chapters, as remarkable
for profundity and reach as any of the preceding
ones.

CHAP. IX. 1-33.—THE TRUE ISRAEL HAS NOT
BEEN REJECTED—HOW ISRAEL AFTER THE FLESH
HAS FALLEN—AND HOW, IN THE CASE OF BOTH,
AND IN THE CALLING OF THE GENTILES, THE WORD
OF GOD HAS TAKEN EFFECT.
Introduction to this topic (1-5). Too well aware
that he was regarded as a traitor to the dearest
interests of his people (Acts xxi. 33; xxii. 22;
xxv. 24), the apostle opens this division of his
subject by giving vent to his real feelings with
extraordinary vehemence of protestation. **1. I
say the truth in Christ**—as if steeped in the spirit
of Him who wept over impenitent and doomed
Jerusalem (cf. ch. i. 9; 2 Cor. xii. 19; Phil. i. 8), **I
lie not, my conscience also bearing me witness
in the Holy Ghost**—*q. d.*, 'my conscience as
quickened, illuminated, and even now under the
direct operation of the Holy Ghost.' Doubtless
the apostle could speak thus as no uninspired
Christian can. At the same time, it should not
be forgotten that to speak and act "in Christ,"
with a conscience not only illuminated, but under
the present operation of the Holy Ghost, is not
peculiar to the supernaturally inspired, but is the
privilege, and ought to be the aim, of every believer. **2. That I have great heaviness and
continual sorrow**—'great grief and unceasing
anguish' **in my heart**—the bitter hostility of his
nation to the glorious Gospel, and the awful consequences of their unbelief, weighing heavily and
incessantly upon his spirit. The grace which
revolutionized the apostle's religious views and
feelings did not (we see) destroy, but only intensified and elevated his natural feelings; and Christians should study to show that the same is true
of them also. **3. For I could wish that myself
were accursed from Christ** [Ἠχόμην γὰρ αὐτὸς

248

ἐγὼ ἀνάθεμα εἶναι ἀπὸ τοῦ Χριστοῦ—or better,
ἀνάθ. εἶναι αὐτὸς ἐγὼ, κ. τ. λ.] for ('in behalf of')
my brethren, my kinsmen according to the flesh.
In proportion as he felt himself spiritually severed
from his nation, he seems to have realized all the
more vividly his natural relationship to them.
Some interpreters, deeming such a wish as is
here expressed to be too strong for any Christian
to utter, or even conceive, have rendered the
opening words, 'I did (once) wish;' understanding
it of his former unconverted state. The Old Latin
version and the Vulgate revision of it led the way
in this wrong direction (*optabam*), and *Pelagius*
followed. Even *Luther* fell into this mistake (*Ich
habe gewünscht*). But what sense or force does
this interpretation yield? No doubt, when a
virulent persecutor of Christians, the apostle had
no desire for any connection with Christ, and
wished the very name of Christ to perish. But can
that be all that is here meant? or even if it were,
would the apostle have expressed it in the terms
here employed—that he wished, not Christ and
Christians accursed, but himself accursed from
Christ, and this not for the truth's sake, but for
his brethren's sake? It is true that the verb is
in the past (the imperfect) tense. But according
to the Greek idiom, the strict meaning of the
phrase is, 'I was going to wish, and should have
wished, had that been lawful, or could it have
done any good (or, according to the English idiom)
'I could have wished.' [See *Winer*, § 41. *a;
Donaldson*, § 426. *ff; Hermann*, de part. ἄν.; also
Fritzsche and *de Wette*, on this place; and compare
the analogous use of the imperfect in Acts xxv.
22, and Gal. iv. 20.] Much also has been written
on the word "accursed," to soften its apparent
harshness, and represent it as meant only in a modified sense. But if we view the entire sentiment
as a vehement or passionate expression of *the
absorption of his whole being* in the salvation of his
people, the difficulty will vanish; and instead of
applying to this burst of emotion the cold criticism which would be applicable to definite ideas,
we shall rather be reminded of the nearly identical
wish so nobly expressed by Moses, Exod. xxxii.
32, "Yet now, if thou wilt forgive their sin . . .
and *if not*, blot me, I pray thee, out of thy book
which thou hast written." This is what *Bacon*
(quoted by *Wordsworth*) calls 'an ecstasy of
charity and infinite feeling of communion' ('Advancement of Learning').

4. Who are Israelites, &c. [Οἵτινες, *quippe qui*]
—that is, 'Inasmuch as they are.' So ch. i. 25, 32;
ii. 15; vi. 2. The connection is this: 'And
well may I feel thus towards a people so illustrious for all that can ennoble a people—in
their origin, their calling, the exalted trusts committed to them, and that Debt of all debts
which the world shall for ever owe them, the
Birth of its Redeemer from them. "Who are
Israelites"—the descendants of him who "had
power with God and prevailed," and whose family
name "Jacob" was changed into "Israel" (or
'Prince of God'), to hand down through all time this
pre-eminent feature in his character (Gen. xxxii.
28). What store the apostle set by this title, as one
which he could and did claim, as well as any of
those from whom he was now separated in faith,
may be seen from ch. xi. 1; 2 Cor. xi. 22; Phil.

²covenants, and the giving of the law, and the service *of God*, and the
5 promises; whose *are* the fathers, and of whom as concerning the flesh,
Christ *came*, who is over all, God blessed for ever. Amen.

A. D. 60.

² Or. testaments.

iii. 5. **to whom pertaineth** (more simply, 'whose is') **the adoption.** This is not to be confounded with the internal, spiritual, vital 'adoption' which flows from union to God's own Son, and which is the counterpart of regeneration. It was a purely external and theocratic, *yet real*, adoption, separating them by a sovereign act of grace from the surrounding heathenism, and constituting them a *Family of God.* (See Exod. iv. 22; Deut. xiv. 1; xxxii. 6; Isa. i. 2; Jer. iii. 4; xxxi. 9; Hos. xi. 1; Mal. i. 6.) The higher adoption in Christ Jesus is (as *Meyer* says) but the antitype and completion of this. To belong to the visible Church of God, and enjoy its high and holy distinctions, is of the sovereign mercy of God, and should be regarded with devout thankfulness; and yet the rich enumeration of these, as attaching to a nation at that very time excluding themselves by unbelief from the spiritual and eternal significance of them all, should warn us that the most sacred external distinctions and privileges will avail nothing to salvation without the heart's submission to the righteousness of God (*vv.* 31-33). **and the glory.** This is not to be taken in the loose sense which many interpreters give it—the *glorious* height of privilege, &c., to which they were raised (so *Origen, Chrysostom, Bengel, Fritzsche*); nor yet (as *Calvin, Beza, Grotius*) 'the ark of the covenant,' whose capture by the Philistines was felt by the dying wife of Phineas to be "the departure of the glory" (1 Sam. iv. 21). With the great majority of good interpreters, we take it to mean that 'glory of the Lord,' or 'visible token of the Divine presence in the midst of them,' which rested on the ark and filled the tabernacle during all their wanderings in the wilderness; which in Jerusalem continued to be seen in the tabernacle and temple, and which only disappeared when, at the Captivity, the temple was demolished, and the sun of the ancient economy began to go down. The later Jews gave to this glory the now familiar name of the '*Shechinah*' [שְׁכִינָה, from שָׁכַן, 'to let one's self down,' and hence to 'dwell']. (See on John i. 14, Commentary, p. 348; also on Acts. vii. 1; 2 Cor. iii. 7, where "the *glory* of his (Moses') countenance" means the visible radiance which his *nearness* to God in the mount left upon his face; and Heb. ix. 5, where "the cherubim of *glory* shadowing the mercy-seat" are so called, to express the radiance which overspread the blood-sprinkled mercy-seat, symbolical of the mutual *nearness of God and His people* through the efficacy of an atoning sacrifice. It was the distinguishing honour of the Israelites that to them only was the whole method of Redemption, and the result of it in "the Lord God dwelling among them" (Ps. lxviiii. 18), disclosed in type; and thus to them pertained "the glory:" **and the covenants.** The word is here used in the plural number, not to denote 'the old and the new covenants' (as *Augustin, Jerome,* and some of the elder German divines), for all the things here enumerated belong to the ancient economy; nor 'the tables of the covenant' (as *Beza, Grotius,* &c.), for that would be to make it the same with the next particular, "the giving of the law;" but the *one covenant* with Abraham *in its successive renewals*, to which the Gentiles were "strangers," and which is called (also in the plural) "the covenants of promise" (Eph. ii. 12). See also Gal. iii. 16, 17. [*Lachmann* adopts the singular form

249

of this word (ἡ διαθήκη) on the rather weighty authority of B D E F G; the Vulgate (but not cod. Amiat.); and several of the Greek fathers. The received text is found in א C K, and apparently all the cursives; several copies of the Old Latin, the best MS. of the Vulgate (Amiatinus), both the Syriac and other versions, and the same Greek fathers as are relied on for the singular. And as it would be quite natural to write the word in the singular (though plural in the original), since the thing meant is singular—but certainly not the reverse—*Tischendorf* and *Tregelles* rightly adhere to the plural of the received text, as nearly all good critics do.] **and the giving of the law** — from mount Sinai, and entrusting that precious treasure to their safe keeping, which the Jews justly regarded as their peculiar honour (ch. ii. 17; Deut. xxvi. 18, 19; Ps. cxlvii. 19, 20). **and the service [of God]**—rather, 'the service [of the sanctuary'], or better, without any supplement, simply, 'the service' [ἡ λατρεία]; meaning the whole Divinely instituted religious service, in the celebration of which they were brought so nigh to God. **and the promises**—the great Abrahamic promises, successively unfolded, and which had their fulfilment only in Christ (see Heb. vii. 6; Gal. iii. 16, 21; Acts xxvi. 6, 7). **5. Whose are the fathers**—here probably the three great fathers of the covenant—Abraham, Isaac, and Jacob—by whom God condescended to name Himself (Exod. iii. 6, 13; Luke xx. 37). **and** (most exalted privilege of all, and as such, reserved to the last) **of whom as concerning the flesh** (see on ch. i. 3), **Christ [came]** [ἐξ ὧν ὁ Χριστός]—or 'of whom is Christ, as concerning the flesh.' **who is over all, God**—rather, 'God over all,' **blessed for ever. Amen** [ὁ ὢν ἐπὶ πάντων Θεὸς εὐλογητὸς εἰς τ. αἰῶνας]. To get rid of the bright testimony here borne to the supreme Divinity of Christ, various expedients have been adopted.

(1.) *Erasmus* suggested that a period might be placed after 'of whom is Christ as concerning the flesh;' in which case what follows is a doxology to the Father for such a gift—'He who is over all, God, be blessed for ever.' This suggestion was approved by the Polish (Socinian) commentator, *Enjedin,* and it has been followed by *Wetstein, Fritzsche, Reiche, Meyer, Jowett.* But there are two objections to this: *First,* That everywhere in Scripture (both in the Hebrew of the Old Testament, and in the Greek of the New) the word "blessed" *precedes* the name of God, on whom the blessing is pronounced—thus, "Blessed be the Lord, the God of Israel" (Ps. lxxii. 18, and Luke i. 68), "Blessed be God, even the Father of our Lord Jesus Christ" (2 Cor. i. 3, and Eph. i. 3). Even *Socinus* admitted this to be a valid objection, and it seems to us fatal. But further, when the apostle here says of Christ that He came of the Israelites "*as concerning the flesh,*" we naturally expect, according to his usual style of thought, that the next clause will make some reference to His higher nature. This accordingly he does sublimely, according to the received punctuation of this verse, and the almost universal way of translating and understanding it; but if we adopt the above suggestion of *Erasmus* —putting a period after 'of whom is Christ according to the flesh'—the statement ends with an abruptness and the thought is broken in a way not usual, certainly, with the apostle. *Fritzsche* and *Meyer* see no force in this, thinking that a

6   Not as though the word of God hath taken none effect. For ^cthey
7 *are* not all Israel which are of Israel : neither, ^dbecause they are the seed
of Abraham, *are they* all children: but, in ^eIsaac shall thy seed be called.
8 That is, They which are the children of the flesh, these *are* not the

A. D. 60.
^c Gal. 6. 16.
^d Gal. 4. 23.
^e Gen. 21. 12.
Heb. 11. 18.

statement of Christ's fleshly descent did not require to be followed up by any allusion to a higher nature. But *de Wette* admits the force of it. It is further argued (by *Stuart, Alford,* and others) that the supposed doxology would be out of place, the sad subject on which he was entering suggesting anything but a doxology, even in connection with Christ's Incarnation. But this need not be pressed. Unhappily, both *Lachmann* and *Tischendorf* lend their countenance to this interpretation, by placing a period in their texts after the word "flesh" [σάρκα]—the latter giving as his reason that Christian antiquity did not connect the words "God over all" with Christ, but with the Father. But the passages quoted by him (after *Wetstein*) to prove this were merely intended to maintain the supremacy of the Father in the one Godhead (against those who confounded the Persons); and the best proof that they were not meant in the sense they are quoted for is, that some of those same fathers build an argument for the Divinity of Christ on this very passage.

(2.) Another expedient, also suggested by *Erasmus,* was to place a period after the words "over all" (of whom as concerning the flesh Christ came, who is "over all"). In this case these words are indeed made to refer to Christ, but only in this sense, that Christ is "over all" that came before him ; and what follows is a doxology, as before, to God the Father—'God be blessed for ever.' This was adopted by *Locke,* and has been followed by *de Wette* in his translation. But though this does yield a sort of contrast in Christ to His descent from Israel "according to the flesh," it is surely a poor one ; the doxology which it yields is (as *Meyer* truly says) miserably abrupt ; and it has the same fatal objection as the former—the wrong placing of the word "blessed." It is a valid objection also to this punctuation, that in that case the word "God" would have required the article [ὁ Θεός]. See *Middleton's* note on this verse.

(3.) Failing these two expedients, a conjectural change of the text has been resorted to. *Schlicting,* another of the Polish (Socinian) commentators, suggested that the Greek words [ὁ ὤν] should be transposed, and both the accent and breathing of the latter word changed [into ὧν ὁ], making the sense to be 'whose is the Supreme God'—that is, not only does Christ, as concerning the flesh, belong to the Israelites, but theirs also is the God over all. This desperate shift was approved by *Crellius* (an acute critic of the same Polish school), by *Whiston* and *Taylor* of Norwich (well-known Arians of last century), and by *Whitby* (who sank into Arianism in his later days). But besides the worthlessness of the conjecture itself, conjectural emendations of the text—in the face of all manuscript authority—are now justly banished from the domain of sound criticism.

It remains, then, that we have here no doxology at all, but a naked statement of fact—that while Christ is "of" the Israelitish nation, "*as concerning the flesh,*" He is *in another respect* "God over all, blessed for ever." (In 2 Cor. xi. 31 the very Greek phrase which is here rendered "who is," is used in the same sense; and cf. ch. i. 25, *Gr.*) In this view of the passage—as a testimony to the supreme Divinity of Christ—besides all the orthodox fathers, all the ablest modern critics, with the exception of those above named, concur. 'I, for

250

my part,' says *Michaelis* (quoted by *Middleton*)—a critic not overscrupulous in such matters—'sincerely believe that Paul here delivers the same doctrine of the Divinity of Christ which is elsewhere unquestionably maintained in the New Testament.' (See also *Bengel's* and *Philippi's* unusually long notes on this passage.)

Though Israel after the flesh has fallen, the Elect Israel has not failed (6-13). Lest his readers should conclude, from the melancholy strain of the preceding verses, that that Israel which he had represented as so dear to God, and the object of so many promises, had quite failed, the apostle now proceeds to open up an entirely new feature of his subject, which, though implied in all he had written and indirectly hinted at once and again, had not before been formally expounded—the distinction between the *nominal* and the *real,* the carnal and the *spiritual* Israel. **6. Not as though the word of God hath taken none effect** [ἐκπέπτωκεν] —or 'failed' (as the simple verb is rendered, Luke xvi. 17). **For they are not all Israel which are of Israel**—better, 'For not all they which are of Israel are Israel'—*q. d.,* 'Think not that I mourn over the total loss of Israel, for that would involve the failure of God's word to Abraham ; but not all that belong to the natural seed, and go under the name of " Israel," are *the* Israel of God's irrevocable choice.' The difficulties which encompass this profound subject of ELECTION lie not in the apostle's teaching, which is plain enough, but in the truths themselves, the evidence for which, taken by themselves, is overwhelming, but whose perfect harmony is beyond human, perhaps even finite, comprehension. The great source of error here lies, as we humbly conceive, in hastily inferring, as too many critics do—from the apostle's taking up, at the close of this chapter, the calling of the Gentiles in connection with the rejection of Israel, and continuing this subject through the two next chapters—that the Election treated of in the body of this chapter is *national,* not *personal* Election, and consequently is Election merely to *religious advantages,* not to *eternal salvation.* In that case the argument of *v.* 6, with which the subject of Election opens, would be this : 'The choice of Abraham and his seed has not failed ; because though Israel has been rejected, *the Gentiles* have taken their place ; and God has a right to choose what nation He will to the privileges of His visible kingdom.' But so far from this, the Gentiles are not so much as mentioned at all till towards the close of the chapter; and the argument of this verse is, that '*all of Israel itself* is not rejected, but *only a portion of it,* the remainder being *the* "Israel" whom God has chosen in the exercise of His sovereign right.' And that this is a choice not to mere external privileges, but to eternal salvation, will abundantly appear from what follows.

7. Neither, because they are the seed of Abraham, are they all children:—*q. d.,* 'Not in the line of mere fleshly descent from Abraham does the election run; else Ishmael, Hagar's child, and even Keturah's children, would be included, which they were not.' **but—as the promise runs, in Isaac shall thy seed be called** (Gen. xxi. 12). 'On this principle, the true Election consists of such of Abraham's seed as God hath unconditionally chosen.' **8. That is, They which are the children of the flesh, these are not the children of God:**

children of God: but the children of the promise are counted for the

9 seed. For this *is* the word of promise, *ᶠ*At this time will I come, and

10 Sara shall have a son. And not only *this;* but when *ᵍ*Rebecca also had

11 conceived by one, *even* by our father Isaac, (for *the children* being *ʰ* not yet born, neither having done any good or evil, that the purpose of God according to election might stand, not of works, but of him that calleth,)

12 it was said unto her, The ³elder shall serve the ⁴younger. As it is written,

13 *ⁱ*Jacob have I loved, but Esau have I hated.

14 What shall we say then? *ʲIs there* unrighteousness with God? God

15 forbid. For he saith to Moses, *ᵏ*I will have mercy on whom I will have mercy, and I will have compassion on whom I will have compassion.

16 So *ˡ*then *it is* not of him that willeth, nor of him that runneth, but of

A. D. 60.
ᶠ Gen. 18. 10.
Gen. 21. 2.
ᵍ Gen. 25. 21.
ʰ Eph. 1. 4.
³ Or, greater.
⁴ Or, lesser.
ⁱ Deut. 21.15.
Luke 14. 26.
ʲ Deut. 32. 4.
2 Chr. 19.7.
ch. 2. 1.
ᵏ Ex. 33. 19.
ˡ Ps. 115. 3.

but the children of the promise are counted for the seed. 9. For this is the word of promise, &c. 10. And not only [this], or [so]; but when Rebecca also had conceived by one, even by our father Isaac. 11. (For the children being not yet born, neither having done any good or evil, that the purpose of God according to election might stand, not of works, but of him that calleth, 12. It was said unto her, The elder shall serve the younger. 13. As it is written (Mal. i. 2, 3), Jacob have I loved, but Esau have I hated. It might be thought that there was a natural reason for preferring the child of Sarah, as being Abraham's true and first wife, both to the child of Hagar, Sarah's maid, and to the children of Keturah, his second wife. But there could be no such reason in the case of Rebecca, Isaac's only wife; for the choice of her son Jacob was the choice of one of two sons by the same mother, and of the younger in preference to the elder, and before either of them was born, and consequently before either had done good or evil to be a ground of preference; and all to show that the sole ground of distinction lay in the unconditional choice of God—"*not of works, but of Him that calleth.*" These last words show conclusively the erroneousness of the theory by which some get rid of the doctrine of *personal* Election in this chapter—namely, that the apostle is treating of the choice, neither of persons nor of nations, but merely of the terms or conditions on which He will save men, and which he has a sovereign right to fix. For in that case the apostle would have said here, 'That the purpose of God according to election might stand, not of works—*but by faith.*' But instead of this, he says, "Not of works (of any merit on our part), but of Him that calleth"— *i. e.,* purely of His own will to call whom He pleaseth. 'It is doing great violence to the meaning (says *Olshausen*) to refer the 'purpose according to election—which did not depend upon the works that were not in existence, but rested upon the holy will alone of Him who calleth whom He will, Jacob only and not Esau—to refer this purpose (with *Beck*) simply to the right of primogeniture, or (with *Tholuck*) to the occupation of the theocratic land.' Though the predictions respecting Jacob and Esau had reference to their *posterity,* and were fulfilled in them, it is the unconditional choice of the one *individual,* rather than the other, on which the apostle reasons. 'The word "serve" (*v.* 12) need not be understood (adds *Olshausen*) of political servitude, but must be referred to a state of spiritual dependence into which Esau was brought by throwing away his birthright, while the stream of grace flowed away to Jacob. All the assurances that to "hate" here does not mean to hate, but only to "love less," or bestow a less advantage, will not satisfy the conscientious expositor, since he cannot overlook the fact that St. Paul has selected from the passage of Scripture

251

which he quotes a very strong and offensive expression. Nor does it signify that in that passage (Mal. i. 2, 3) the immediate question is of *outward circumstances,* since these also [in the case of such symbolical persons] are to be viewed as expressions of the wrath of God.' Compare a subsequent verse of the same chapter, "The people against whom the Lord hath indignation for ever" (Mal. i. 4).

The righteousness of this sovereign procedure (14-24). This topic is handled in the form of answers to two objections, which are so far from being merely hypothetical, that they have been in every age, and are to this day, the grand, indeed the only plausible, objections to the doctrine of *personal Election.*

First Objection. — 'The doctrine — that God chooses one and rejects another, not on account of their works, but purely in the exercise of His own good pleasure—is *inconsistent with the justice of God.*' The answer to this objection extends to *v.* 19, where we have a second objection. 14. **What shall we say then?** (see on ch. vi. 1) **Is there unrighteousness with God? God forbid.** Here we again quote from *Olshausen,* whose statement is all the more remarkable from his *Lutheran* point of view. 'It is only (says that profound and candid critic) in this severe manner of interpretation (understanding the argument to be of *personal election to eternal salvation*) that the question, "Is there unrighteousness with God?" has any meaning, and that the thrilling answer of *v.* 15 is at all suitable. The mitigated view of *vv.* 6-13 (supposing them to treat only of *national election to external advantages*) affords no occasion for such thoughts at all, and therefore the interpreter can in no way evade the stringent connection of thought.' (To the same effect *Hodge* argues very forcibly.) 15. **For he saith to Moses** (Exod. xxxiii. 19), **I will have mercy on whom I will have mercy** [ἐλεῶ]—'on whom I have mercy,' **and I will have compassion on whom I will have compassion** [οἰκτείρω]—' on whom I have compassion;' *q. d.,* 'There *can* be no unrighteousness in God's choosing whom He will, for to Moses He expressly claims a right to do so.' Yet it is worthy of notice that this is expressed in the positive rather than the negative form: It is not, 'I will have mercy on *none but* on whom I will;' but 'I will have mercy on *whomsoever* I will.' The reader ought not to overlook the principle on which the apostle here argues the question with his readers. 'As when God *says* a thing it must be true, so when God *does* a thing it must be right. But God does say He chooses whom He will; therefore it is both true that He does so, and doing it, it cannot but be right.' 16. **So then it is not of him that willeth** (or hath the inward *intention*), **nor of him that runneth** (maketh the active *exertion*): see, for illustration of this phrase,

17 God that showeth mercy. For the Scripture saith unto Pharaoh, Even
  ᵐfor this same purpose have I raised thee up, that I might show my
  power in thee, and that my name might be declared throughout all the
18 earth. Therefore hath he mercy on whom he will *have mercy*, and whom
  he will he hardeneth.
19   Thou wilt say then unto me, Why doth he yet find fault? for ⁿwho
20 hath resisted his will? Nay but, O man, who art thou that ⁵repliest
  against God? °Shall the thing formed say to him that formed *it*, Why
21 hast thou made me thus? Hath not the ᵖpotter power over the clay, of
  the same lump to make �q one vessel unto honour, and another unto dis-
22 honour? *What* if God, willing to show *his* wrath, and to make his
  power known, endured with much long-suffering the ʳvessels of wrath
23 ⁶fitted to destruction; and that he might make known the riches of his

A. D. 60.

ᵐ Ex. 9. 16.
Pro. 16. 4.
ⁿ Job 9. 12.
⁵ Or, an-
swerest
again, or,
disputest
with God?
° Isa. 29. 16.
Isa. 45. 9.
Isa. 64. 8.
ᵖ Jer. 18. 6.
q 2 Tim. 2.20.
ʳ 1 Thes. 5. 9.
⁶ Or, made
up.

1 Cor. ix. 24, 26; Phil. ii. 16; iii. 14. Both the 'willing' and the 'running' are indispensable to salvation; yet salvation is owing to neither, but (is purely) **of God that showeth mercy.** This is strikingly expressed in Phil. ii. 12, 13: "Work out your own salvation with fear and trembling: for it is God which, *out of His own good pleasure*, worketh in you both to *will* and to *do*." 17. **For the Scripture saith unto Pharaoh** (Exod. ix. 16). Observe here the light in which the Scripture is viewed by the apostle. **Even for this same purpose have I raised thee up** [εἰς αὐτὸ τοῦτο ἐξήγειρά σε]—rather, 'saith to Pharaoh, For this very purpose did I raise thee up.' The apostle had shown that God claims the right to *choose* whom He will; here he shows by an example that God *punishes* whom He will. But (as *Hodge* says) 'God did not make Pharaoh wicked; He only forebore to make him good, by the exercise of special and altogether unmerited grace.' **that I might show my power in thee, and that my name might be declared throughout all the earth.** It was not that Pharaoh was worse than others, that he was so dealt with, but that his *character* and *position* combined rendered him a fit subject for the display, as on a great theatre, of God's righteous displeasure against the despisers of His authority, for all time. 18. **Therefore hath he** (or, 'So then He hath')—the result is that He hath **mercy on whom he will [have mercy]**—rather, 'on whom He will,' without any supplement, **and whom he will he hardeneth**—by judicially abandoning them to the hardening influence of sin itself (ch. i. 24, 26, 28; Ps. lxxxi. 11, 12; Heb. iii. 3, 8, 13), and of the surrounding incentives to it (Matt. xxiv. 12; 1 Cor. xv. 38; 2 Thess. ii. 17). So much for the first objection to the doctrine of Divine Sovereignty.

Second Objection. — 'This doctrine is *incompatible with human responsibility*.' 19. **Thou wilt say then unto me, Why** [Τί], or (according to another reading) 'Why, then' [μοι οὖν, Τί οὖν] **doth he yet find fault? for who hath resisted his will?** [ἀνθέστηκεν]—'who resisteth his will' (for the perfect of this verb has the sense of a present):—*q. d.*, 'If God chooses and rejects, pardons and punishes, whom He pleases, why are those blamed who, if rejected by Him, cannot help sinning and 'perishing?' This objection shows, quite as conclusively as the former one, the real nature of the doctrine objected to—that it is Election and Non-election to eternal salvation, *prior to any difference of personal character:* this is the only doctrine that could suggest the objection here stated, and to this doctrine the objection *is* plausible. What now is the apostle's answer? It is two-fold: *First,* 'It is irreverence and presumption in the creature to arraign the Creator.' 20. **Nay but** [Μενοῦνγε. This compound adverb (mostly of late

Macedonian usage) occurs in ch. x. 18; Luke xi. 28; and Phil. iii. 8. *Wetstein,* on Luke xi. 28, gives classical examples of its use]. **O man, who art thou that repliest against God? Shall the thing formed say to him that formed it, Why hast thou made me** ('why didst thou make me') **thus?** (see Isa. xlv. 9.) 21. **Hath not the potter power over the clay, of the same lump to make one vessel unto honour, and another unto dishonour?** The objection (as *Hodge* says) is founded on ignorance or misapprehension of the relation between God and His sinful creatures. It supposes that He is under obligation to extend His grace to all, whereas He is under obligation to none. All are sinners, and have forfeited every claim to His mercy; it is therefore perfectly competent to God to spare one and not another, to make one vessel to honour and another to dishonour. He, as a sovereign Creator, has the same right over them that a potter has over the clay. But it is to be borne in mind that Paul does not here speak of God's right over His creatures *as creatures,* but *as sinful creatures;* as He himself clearly intimates in the next verses. It is the cavil of a sinful creature against his Creator that he is answering, and he does so by showing that God is under no obligation to give His grace to any, but is as sovereign as in fashioning the clay.' But, *Second,* 'There is nothing unjust in such sovereignty.' 22. **What if God, willing to show** ('designing to manifest') **his wrath**—His holy displeasure against sin, **and to make his power** (to punish it) **known, endured with much long-suffering the vessels of wrath**—that is, 'destined to wrath,' just as "vessels of mercy," in the next verse, mean 'vessels destined to mercy:' compare Eph. ii. 3, "children of wrath." **fitted to destruction.** It is well remarked by *Stuart,* that the 'difficulties which such statements involve are not to be got rid of by softening the language of one text, while so many others meet us which are of the same tenor; and even if we give up the Bible itself, so long as we acknowledge an omnipotent and omniscient God, we cannot abate in the least degree from any of the difficulties which such texts make.' Be it observed, however, that if God, as the apostle teaches, expressly 'designed to manifest His wrath, and to make His power (in the way of wrath) known,' it could only be by punishing some, while He pardons others; and if the choice between the two classes was not to be founded, as our apostle also teaches, on their own doings, but on God's good pleasure, the decision behoved ultimately to rest with God. Yet, even in the necessary punishment of the wicked (as *Hodge* again observes), so far from proceeding with undue severity, the apostle would have it remarked that God "endures with much long-suffering" those objects of His righteous displeasure. **23.**

252

glory on the vessels of mercy, which he had afore prepared unto glory,
24 even us, whom he hath called, not of the Jews only, but also of the Gentiles?
25   As he saith also in Osee, [s]I will call them my people, which were not
26 my people; and her beloved, which was not beloved. And [t]it shall come
to pass, *that* in the place where it was said unto them, Ye *are* not my
27 people; there shall they be called the children of the living God. Esaias
also crieth concerning Israel, Though [u]the number of the children of
28 Israel be as the sand of the sea, a remnant shall be saved: for he will
finish [7]the work, and cut *it* short in righteousness: [v]because a short work
29 will the Lord make upon the earth. And as Esaias said before, [w]Except
the Lord of Sabaoth had left us a seed; we [x]had been as Sodoma, and
been made like unto Gomorrha.

A. D. 60

[s] Hos. 2. 23.
1 Pet. 2. 10.
[t] Hos. 1. 10.
[u] Isa. 10. 22,
23.
[7] Or. the account.
[v] Isa. 23. 22.
Isa. 30. 12,
14.
Dan. 9. 26,
27.
Matt 21.21.
[w] Isa 1. 9.
Lam. 3. 22.
[x] Isa. 13. 19.

And that he might make known the riches of his glory on the vessels of mercy. The word "glory" seems to be used here in the same peculiar sense as in ch. vi. 4; in which case the whole expression denotes that 'glorious exuberance of Divine mercy' which was manifested in choosing and eternally arranging for the salvation of sinners. **which he had afore prepared unto glory, 24. Even us, whom he hath called** [Οὓς καὶ ἐκάλεσεν ἡμᾶς]—rather, 'Whom he also called, even us;' that is, that He might make known the riches of His glory in not only 'afore preparing,' but in 'due time effectually *calling* us.'

The Calling of the Gentiles, and the preservation of only a Remnant of Israel, both Divinely foretold —The true secret of both events (24-33).

Here, for the first time in this chapter, the calling of the Gentiles is introduced; all before having respect, not to the substitution of the called Gentiles for the rejected Jews, but to the choice of one portion and the rejection of another of the same Israel. Had Israel's rejection been total, God's promise to Abraham would *not* have been fulfilled by the substitution of the Gentiles in their room; but Israel's rejection being only partial, the preservation of "a remnant," in which the promise was made good, was but "according to the election of grace." And now, for the first time, the apostle tells us that along with this elect remnant of *Israel* it was God's purpose to "take out of the *Gentiles* a people for His name" (Acts xv. 14), and that this had been sufficiently announced in the Old Testament Scriptures. Into this new subject the apostle—according to his usual way—slides almost imperceptibly, in the middle of the present verse; so that without careful notice the transition is apt to be overlooked. **not of the Jews only, but also of the Gentiles?** ('not from among Jews only, but also from among Gentiles.')

25. **As he saith also in Osee** ('Hosea')—observe here again our apostle's way of viewing the Old Testament Scriptures: **I will call them my people, which were not my people; and her beloved, which was not beloved** ('I will call the no-people, my people, and her that was not beloved, beloved'). This is quoted (though not quite to the letter) from Hos. ii. 23, a passage relating immediately, not to the heathen, but to the kingdom of the ten tribes; but since they had sunk to the level of the heathen, who were 'not God's people,' and in that sense "not beloved," the apostle legitimately applies it to the heathen, as "aliens from the commonwealth of Israel, and strangers to the covenants of promise." (So 1 Pet. ii. 10.) 26. **And** (another quotation from Hos. i. 10) **it shall come to pass, that in the place where it was said unto them, Ye are not my people; there shall they be called the children** ('called sons') **of the living God.** The expression, "in the place where

... there," must not be taken too strictly, as referring to some particular locality, as Palestine, 'where (to use the words of *Fritzsche*, who takes this view) it was long questioned whether the Gentiles were admissible to Christian fellowship.' It seems designed only to give greater emphasis to the gracious change here announced, from Divine exclusion to Divine admission to the privileges of the people of God. 27. **Esaias also**—'But Esaias' **crieth** [κράζει]—an expression denoting a solemn testimony openly borne. (See John i. 15; vii. 28, 37; xii. 44; Acts xxiii. 24, 41.) **concerning Israel, Though the number of the children** ('sons') **of Israel be as the sand of the sea, a remnant** [τὸ κατάλειμμα]—rather, 'the remnant;' meaning the elect remnant *only*, **shall be saved: 28. For he will finish the work, and cut it short** [Λόγον γὰρ συντελῶν καὶ συντέμνων]—rather, 'For He is finishing the matter and cutting it short' **in righteousness: because a short work** ('matter') **will the Lord make upon the earth.** [*Lachmann* and *Tregelles* omit ἐν δικαιοσύνῃ ὅτι λόγον συντετμημενον, with א A B, three cursives, and the Syriac; but *Tischendorf* rightly retains them, with D E F G K L, and nearly all cursives, the old Latin and Vulgate, the Philox. Syriac, and later versions, and most of the fathers; for it is far easier to account for their omission, though genuine, than for their insertion if not.] The passage is taken from Isa. x. 22, 23, as in the LXX. The sense given to it by the apostle may seem to differ from that intended by the prophet. But the aptness of the quotation for the apostle's purpose, and the sameness of sentiment in both places will at once appear, if we understand those words of the prophet which are rendered "the consumption decreed shall overflow with righteousness" to mean, that while a remnant of Israel should be graciously spared to return from captivity, "the decreed consumption" of the impenitent majority should be "replete with righteousness" or illustriously display God's righteous vengeance against sin. The "short reckoning" seems to mean the speedy completing of His word, both in cutting off the one portion and saving the other. 29. **And as Esaias said** ('hath said') **before**—meaning probably in an earlier part of his book, namely, ch. i. 9. **Except the Lord of Sabaoth**—i. e., 'the Lord of Hosts:' the word is Hebrew, but occurs so in the Epistle of James (ch. v. 4), and has thence become naturalized in our Christian phraseology. **had left us a seed**—meaning 'a remnant,' small at first, but in due time to be a seed of plenty (cf Ps. xxii. 30, 31; Isa. vi. 12, 13), **we had been** ('become') **as Sodoma, and been made like unto Gomorrha.** But for this precious seed, the chosen people would have resembled the cities of the plain, both in degeneracy of character and in merited doom.

30 What shall we say then? That the Gentiles, which followed not after righteousness, have attained to righteousness, even the righteousness
31 which is of faith; but Israel, which followed after the law of righteous-
32 ness, [y]hath not attained to the law of righteousness. Wherefore? Because *they sought it* not by faith, but as it were by the works of the law:
33 for [z]they stumbled at that stumblingstone; as it is written, [a]Behold, I lay in Sion a stumblingstone and rock of offence: and whosoever believeth on him shall not be [8]ashamed.
10 BRETHREN, my heart's desire and prayer to God for Israel is, that

A. D. 60.

[y] Gal. 5 4.
[z] Luke 2. 34.
1 Cor. 1. 23.
[a] Ps. 118. 22.
Isa. 8. 14.
Isa. 28. 16.
Matt. 21. 42.
1 Pet. 2. 6, 8.
[8] Or, confounded.

---

30. What shall we say then? (see on ch. vi. 1)—'What now is the result of the whole?' The result is this—very different from what one would have expected, **That the Gentiles, which followed not after righteousness, have attained to righteousness, even the righteousness which is of faith.** As we have seen that "the righteousness of faith" is the righteousness which *justifies* (see on ch. iii. 22, &c.), this verse must mean that 'the Gentiles, who, while strangers to Christ, were quite indifferent about acceptance with God, having embraced the Gospel as soon as it was preached to them, experienced the blessedness of a justified state. **31. But Israel, which followed** ('following') **after the law of righteousness, hath not attained** ('attained not') **to the law of righteousness.** [Here again *Lachm.* and *Treg.* omit the second δικαιοσύνης—in which case the meaning will be 'attained not to the law'—with א A B D E G, three cursives, three copies of the old Latin, and one or two fathers. But *Tischendorf* rightly inserts it, though on the far less external authority of F K L, nearly all cursives, two copies of the old Latin (though a late corrector only of the one), the Vulgate, both the later Syriac and other later versions, with several fathers. Manifestly this reading was occasioned by a misunderstanding of the sense, and the recurrence of the same word.] The difficulty of this verse is to fix the precise sense in which the word "law" is used. That "the law of righteousness" means (by Hypallage, as grammarians say) 'the righteousness of the law' (so *Chrysostom, Calvin, Beza, Bengel,* and others) is not to be endured. The view of *Meyer* and others—that it means *ideally* 'the justifying law,' is (as *de Wette* says) artificial. Nor must we take the word "law," as some do, to be superfluous, merely because the verse will explain without it. The word "law" is used here, plainly in the same sense as in ch. vii. 23, to denote 'a principle of action:'—q. d., 'Israel, though sincerely and steadily seeking after the true principle of acceptance with God, nevertheless missed it.' (So, in effect, *de Wette,* and several other interpreters.) **32. Wherefore? Because [they sought it] not by faith, but as it were** (rather simply, 'as') **by the works of the law**—as being thus attainable, which justification is not. Since, therefore, it is attainable only by faith, they missed it. **for** (it is more than doubtful whether this "for" stood originally in the text; but it was very natural to insert it) **they stumbled at that stumblingstone** [λίθον προσκόμματος] — better, 'against the stone of stumbling, meaning *Christ*. But in this they only did, **33. As it is written** (Isa. viii. 14; xxviii. 16), **Behold, I lay in Sion a stumblingstone and rock of offence: and whosoever believeth on him**—or, less definitely, 'believeth thereon,' **shall not be ashamed.** (On the rendering of this last word, see on ch. x. 11.) Two Messianic predictions are here combined, as is not unusual in quotations from the Old Testament. Thus combined, the prediction brings together both the classes of whom the apostle is treating—those to whom

Messiah should be only a Stone of stumbling, and those who were to regard Him as the Corner-Stone of all their hopes.

Thus expounded, this chapter presents no serious difficulties—none, in fact, which do not arise out of the subject itself, whose depths are unfathomable; whereas on every other view of it the difficulty of giving it any consistent and worthy interpretation is in our judgment insuperable.

Remarks.—1. On all subjects which from their very nature lie beyond human comprehension, it will be our wisdom to set down what God says in His Word, and has actually done in his procedure towards men, as indisputable, even though it contradict the results at which, in the best exercise of our limited judgment, we may have arrived. To do otherwise—demanding the removal of all difficulties in the Divine procedure, as the indispensable condition of our subjection to it—is as unwise as it is impious, driving the inquisitive spirit out of one truth after another, until not a shred even of Natural Religion remains. 2. What manner of persons ought "God's elect" to be—in *humility*—when they remember that He "hath saved them and called them, not according to their works, but according to His own purpose and grace, given them in Christ Jesus before the world began (2 Tim. i. 9); in *thankfulness,* for "Who maketh thee to differ, and what hast thou that thou didst not receive?" (1 Cor. iv. 7;) in *godly jealousy* over themselves, remembering that "God is not mocked," but "whatsoever a man soweth that shall he also reap" (Gal. vi. 7); in "*diligence* to make our calling and election sure" (2 Pet. i. 10); and yet in calm *confidence,* that "whom God predestinates, and calls, and justifies, them (in due time) He also glorifies" (ch. viii. 30). 3. Sincerity in religion, or a general desire to be saved, with assiduous efforts to do right, will prove fatal as a ground of confidence before God, if unaccompanied by implicit submission to His revealed method of salvation (*vv.* 31-33). 4. In the rejection of the great mass of the chosen people, and the inbringing of multitudes of estranged Gentiles, God would have men to see a law of His procedure which the judgment of the great day will more vividly reveal—that "the last shall be first, and the first last" (Matt. xx. 16).

CHAP. X. 1-21.—SAME SUBJECT CONTINUED. *The yearning of the apostle's heart after Israel's salvation all the greater by reason of their religious zeal* (1, 2). **1. Brethren, my heart's** ('my own,' or 'my very heart's') **desire** [εὐδοκία τῆς ἐμῆς καρδίας]. The word here rendered "desire" expresses 'entire complacency' (see on Matt. xi. 26)—that in which the heart would experience full satisfaction. **and prayer to God for Israel**—'for them,' is beyond doubt the true reading: the subject being continued from the close of the preceding chapter. At the commencement of a Church Lesson it would be natural to insert the catch-word "for Israel," and thus it

2 they might be saved. For I bear them record ^athat they have a zeal
3 of God, but not according to knowledge. For they being ignorant of
^bGod's righteousness, and going about to establish their own ^cright-
eousness, have ^dnot submitted themselves unto the righteousness of
4 God. For ^eChrist *is* the end of the law for righteousness to every one
that believeth.
5 For Moses describeth the righteousness which is of the law. ^fThat the
6 man which doeth those things shall live by them. But the righteousness
which is of faith speaketh on this wise, ^gSay not in thine heart, Who
shall ascend into heaven? (that is, to ^hbring Christ down *from above;*)
7 or, Who shall descend into the deep? (that is, to ⁱbring up Christ again
8 from the dead.) But what saith it? The word is nigh thee, *even* in thy
mouth, and in thy heart: that is, the word of faith, which we preach;
9 that if thou shalt confess with thy mouth the Lord Jesus, and shalt

A. D. 60.
CHAP. 10.
^a John 16. 2.
Phil. 3. 6.
^b ch. 1. 17.
ch. 3. 22, 26.
2 Pet. 1. 1.
^c Phil. 3. 9.
^d Heb. 10. 20.
^e Matt. 5. 17.
Gal. 3. 24.
^f Lev. 18. 5.
Luke 10.27.
^g Deut. 30.12.
^h Heb. 8. 1.
ⁱ 1 Cor. 15. 3, 4.

would creep into the text. **that they might be saved** [εἰς σωτηρίαν]—'for [their] salvation! Having before poured forth the anguish of his soul at the general unbelief of his nation and its dreadful consequences (ch. ix. 1-3), he here expresses in the most emphatic terms his desire and prayer for their salvation. **2. For I bear them record** (or, 'witness')—as well he could from his own sad experience, **that they have a zeal of** ('for') **God, but not according to knowledge** (cf. Acts xxii. 3; xxvi. 9-11; Gal. i. 13, 14). He alludes to this well-meaning of his people, notwithstanding their spiritual blindness, not certainly to excuse their rejection of Christ and rage against His saints, but as some ground of hope regarding them (see 1 Tim. i. 13).

Self-righteousness the fatal rock on which Israel split—Christ the Divinely-provided, Divinely-predicted, only, and all-sufficient righteousness of the sinner, whether Jew or Gentile, that believeth (3-13). **3. For they being ignorant of God's righteousness**—i. e., that righteousness which God *approves* and *provides* for the justification of the guilty (see on ch. i. 17). **and going about** ('seeking') **to establish their own righteousness, have not submitted themselves** [ὑπετάγησαν]—'submitted themselves not' **unto the righteousness of God.** The apostle views the general rejection of Christ by the nation as one act. **4. For Christ is the end** (the object or aim) **of the law for** (justifying) **righteousness to every one that believeth**—i. e., contains within Himself all that the law demands for the justification of such as embrace Him, whether Jew or Gentile (Gal. iii. 24); *bestowing* that righteousness and life which the law *holds forth* but *cannot give.* 'The law (says *Bengel*, naively) hounds a man till he betake himself to Christ; then it says to him, Thou hast found an asylum, I pursue thee no more; thou art wise, thou art safe.'

5. For Moses describeth the righteousness which is of the law, That the man which doeth [ποιήσας] **those things** (which the law enjoins) **shall live by them**—(Lev. xviii. 5; &c.) *Lachm.* and *Treg.* have ἐν αὐτῇ—'shall live in (or 'by') it,' meaning, 'the righteousness of the law,'—for which there are א A B, three cursives, two copies of the Old Latin (one a late corrector only), the Vulgate (*in ea*), Gothic, and later versions. But this is insufficient evidence; and *Tischendorf* (with the best critics) prefers the received text.] This is the one way of justification and life which the law recognizes, the only "righteousness which is of (or by our own obedience to) the law." **6. But the** (justifying) **righteousness which is of** (that is, which is obtained by) **faith speaketh on this wise** [οὕτως]—'speaketh thus;' its language or import is to this effect (quoting in substance Deut. xxx.

13, 14, and with a running comment on the words quoted, to bring out their Christian reading). **Say not in thine heart, Who shall ascend into heaven? that is** (in effect), **to bring Christ down [from above]**—*q. d.*, 'Ye have not to sigh over the impossibility of attaining to justification; as if one should say, Ah! if I could but get some one to mount up to heaven and fetch me down Christ, there might be some hope; but since that cannot be, mine is a desperate case.' **7. Or, Who shall descend into the deep? that is** (in effect), **to bring up Christ [again] from the dead.** This is another case of impossibility suggested by Prov. xxx. 4, and perhaps also Amos ix. 2. These were probably proverbial expressions of impossibility, (cf. Ps. cxxxix. 7-10; Prov. xxiv. 7, &c.) **8. But what saith it?** [It saith] —continuing the quotation from Deut. xxx. 14, **The word is nigh thee**—easily accessible, **even in thy mouth**—when thou confessest Him, **and in thine heart**—when thou believest on Him. The thoughtful student of this passage will observe, that though it is of *the law* that Moses is speaking in the place quoted from, yet it is of the law as Israel shall be brought to look upon it when the Lord their God shall circumcise their heart "to love the Lord their God with all their heart," &c. (*v.* 6); and thus, in applying it, the apostle (as *Olshausen* truly observes) is not merely appropriating the language of Moses, but keeping in the line of his deeper thought. **that is, the word of faith, which we preach**—i. e., the word which men have to believe for salvation (compare, for the phrase, 1 Tim. iv. 6). **9. That if thou shalt confess** ["Ὅτι ἐὰν ὁμολογήσῃς]—or 'For (or 'Because) if thou shalt confess.' The words will bear either sense. If the latter rendering is adopted (as most versions and the majority of critics do), we have in this verse the apostle's own remarks, confirming the foregoing statements as to the simplicity of the Gospel method of salvation. But (with *Calvin, Beza, Fritzsche, Ferme, Locke, Conybeare,* and *Jowett*) we prefer the sense given by our own version. In this case the apostle is here expressing in full what he holds to be the true Christian reading of the words of Moses in the passage quoted; in other words, the sense which those words of Moses yield to the intelligent Christian reader of them, with the blaze of Gospel light illuminating those ancient oracles of God—namely, "That if thou shalt confess" **with thy mouth the Lord Jesus** [κύριον Ἰησοῦν]—meaning either, 'If thou shalt confess with thy mouth Jesus as [the] Lord' (so *de Wette* and *Green* translate the words); in which case, compare 1 Cor. xii. 3; Rom. xiv. 9; Phil. ii. 11; or the meaning may be more general—'If thou shalt confess the Lord Jesus with thy mouth;' the

believe in thine heart that God hath raised him from the dead, thou
10 shalt be saved. For with the heart man believeth unto righteousness;
11 and with the mouth confession is made unto salvation. For the Scripture saith, *ʲ*Whosoever believeth on him shall not be ashamed.
12 For *ᵏ*there is no difference between the Jew and the Greek; for the
13 *ˡ*same Lord over all *ᵐ*is rich unto all that call upon him. For *ⁿ*whosoever shall call upon the name of the Lord shall be saved.
14 How then shall they call on him in whom they have not believed?
and how shall they believe in him of whom they have not heard? and how
15 shall they hear without *ᵒ*a preacher? and how shall they preach except
they be sent? as it is written, *ᵖ*How beautiful are the feet of them that
16 preach the gospel of peace, and bring glad tidings of good things! But
*�q*they have not all obeyed the Gospel. For Esaias saith, *ʳ*Lord, who
17 hath believed [1] our [2] report? So then faith *cometh* by hearing, and

A. D. 60.

ʲ Isa. 28. 16.
Jer 17. 7.
ᵏ Acts 15. 9.
ˡ Acts 10. 36.
ᵐ Eph. 1. 7.
Eph. 2. 4, 7.
ⁿ Joel 2. 32.
Ac s 2. 21.
ᵒ Tit. 1. 3.
ᵖ Isa. 52. 7.
�q Heb. 4. 2.
ʳ John 12. 38.
1 the hearing of us.
2 Or. preaching.

emphasis in this case being on the open confession of Christ (Matt. x. 32; 1 John iv. 15), and "the Lord Jesus" being but a wonted form of that name which is above every name. We used to take the words in the former sense; but this latter (that of our own version) is probably the correct sense. At the same time, the confession of "the Lord Jesus" can only be genuine in the cordial recognition of Him as "the Lord," as well as "Jesus." **and shalt believe in thine heart that God hath raised him** ('that God raised Him') **from the dead** (see on ch. iv. 25), **thou shalt be saved.** The confession of the mouth, of course, comes, in point of time, after the belief of the heart; but it is put first here to correspond with the foregoing quotation from Deut. xxx. 14—"in thy mouth and in thy heart" (*v.* 8). In 2 Pet. i. 10 also, the "calling" of believers is put before their "election," as that which is first 'made sure,' although in point of time it comes after it. In the next verse, however, the two things are placed in their natural order. **10. For with the heart man believeth unto righteousness**—the righteousness of justification, **and with the mouth confession is made unto salvation.** This confession of Christ's name, especially in times of persecution, and whenever obloquy is attached to the Christian profession, is an indispensable test of discipleship. In Rev. xxi. 8 those who have not the courage to make such confession are meant by the "fearful." **11. For the Scripture saith**—in Isa. xxviii. 16, a glorious Messianic passage, **Whosoever believeth on him shall not be ashamed.** Here, as in ch. ix. 33, the quotation is from the LXX. In the original Hebrew it is, 'shall not make haste' [ישׁיחׁ]—meaning (as we understand it), 'shall not fly for escape, as from apprehended danger.' The LXX. rendering [καταισχυνθήσεται] here made use of is but another phase of the same idea. In the former case, the 'security' which the believer has is viewed as a *felt* security, producing 'calm continuance;' in the latter case, it is an *intrinsically solid* security—never putting to shame. **12. For there is no difference between the Jew and the Greek; for the same Lord over all** [ὁ γὰρ αὐτὸς Κύριος πάντων πλουτῶν]—'the same Lord of all [is] rich;' or, 'The same [is] Lord of all, rich.' Perhaps this last is the thing intended. But the reference, we take it, is not to *God the Father* (as *Calvin, Grotius, Olshausen, Hodge*), but to *Christ*, as may be seen by comparing *vv.* 9, 12, 13, and observing the apostle's usual style on such subjects. (So *Origen, Chrysostom, Melville, Bengel, Fritzsche, Meyer, de Wette, Tholuck, Stuart, Alford, Philippi*). The word 'rich' is a favourite Pauline term to express the

exuberance of that saving grace which is in Christ Jesus, **unto all that call upon him.** This confirms the application of the preceding words to *Christ;* since to call upon the name of the Lord Jesus is a customary New Testament phrase. (See Acts vii. 59, 60; ix. 14, 21; xxii. 16; 1 Cor. i. 2; 2 Tim. ii. 22: and compare Acts x. 36; Phil. ii. 11. **13. For** (as the Scripture saith): **whosoever** [πᾶς γὰρ ὅς]. The phrase is emphatic—'Every one whosoever,' or, 'Whosoever he be that' **shall call upon the name of the Lord shall be saved.** These words are from Joel ii. 32; and they are quoted also by Peter in his great Pentecostal sermon (Acts ii. 21) with evident application to Christ. Indeed, this is but one of many Old Testament passages of which *Jehovah* is the Subject, and which in the New Testament are applied to *Christ*—an irrefragable proof of His proper Divinity. But on this most significant phrase the reader will find more on 1 Cor. i. 2. (Even *de Wette* on this passage notices that, in Eph. iii. 8, our apostle speaks of "the unsearchable *riches* of Christ.")

But this Universality of the Gospel call supposes the universal proclamation of it, obnoxious though that be to the Jews (14, 15). **14. How then shall they call on him in whom they have not believed? and . . . believe in him of whom they have not heard? and . . . hear without a preacher? 15. And . . . preach except sent?**—*q. d.,* 'True, the same Lord over all is rich unto all alike that call upon Him; but this calling implies believing, and believing hearing, and hearing preaching, and preaching *a mission to preach.* Why, then, take ye it so ill, O children of Abraham, that in obedience to our heavenly mission (Acts xxvi. 16-18) we preach among *the Gentiles* the unsearchable riches of Christ?' **as it is written** (Isa. lii. 7), **How beautiful are the feet of them that preach the gospel of peace, and bring glad tidings of good things!** The whole chapter of Isaiah from which this is taken, and the three that follow, are so richly Messianic, that there can be no doubt "the glad tidings" there spoken of announce a more glorious release than that of Judah from the Babylonish captivity, and the very feet of its preachers are called "beautiful" for the sake of their message. What a call and what encouragement is here to missionary activity in the Church!

All this was foretold in their own Scriptures, together with the rejection of the message by the Jews, and its reception by the Gentiles (16-21). **16. But they have not all obeyed the gospel**—the Scripture has prepared us to expect the general rejection of the Gospel message. **For Esaias saith** (liii. 1), **Lord, who hath believed our report?**—*q. d.,* 'Where shall one find a believer?' The prophet speaks as if next to

18 hearing by the word of God. But I say, Have they not heard? Yes
verily, 'their sound went into all the earth, and their words unto the
19 ends of the world. But I say, Did not Israel know? First Moses saith,
t I will provoke you to jealousy by *them that are* no people, *and* by a
20 *u* foolish nation I will anger you. But Esaias is very bold, and saith,
v I was found of them that sought me not; I was made manifest
21 unto them that asked not after me. But to Israel he saith, All day
long I have stretched forth my hands unto a disobedient and gainsaying people.

A. D. 60.

s Ps. 19. 4.
Matt. 24. 14.
Matt. 26. 13.
Matt. 28. 19.
Mark 6. 15.
Col. 1. 6, 23.
t Deut. 32. 21.
u Tit. 3. 3.
v Isa. 65. 1.
ch. 9. 30.

none would believe. The apostle softens this into "They have *not all* believed." 17. So then faith cometh by hearing, and hearing by the word of God—*q. d.*, 'Thus have we a Scripture confirmation of the truth that faith supposes the hearing of the Word, and this a commission to preach it.' 18. But I say, Have they not heard? ('Did they not hear?')—Can Israel, through any region of his dispersion, plead ignorance of these glad tidings, or of God's intention that they should be everywhere proclaimed? Yes verily [μενοῦνγε] —see on ch. ix. 20—'Nay verily,' their sound went into all the earth, and their words unto the ends of the world. These beautiful words are from Ps. xix. 4. Whether the apostle quoted them as in their primary intention applicable to his subject (as *Olshausen*, *Alford*, &c.), or only 'used Scriptural language (as *Hodge* says) to express his own ideas, as is done involuntarily almost by every preacher in every sermon' (so *Calvin* and many critics), expositors are not agreed. But though the latter may seem the more natural —since 'the rising of the Sun of righteousness upon the world' (Mal. iv. 2), 'the day-spring from on high visiting us, giving light to them that sat in darkness, and guiding our feet into the way of peace' (Luke i. 78, 79), must have been familiar and delightful to the apostle's ear—we cannot doubt that the irradiation of the world with the beams of a better sun, by the universal diffusion of the Gospel of Christ, must have been a mode of speaking quite natural, and to him scarcely figurative; not to say that in that very Psalm (as *Alford* and others justly observe) the glory of God in His *Word* is represented as transcending and eclipsing that of His *works* in nature, of which this verse more immediately speaks. 19. But I say, Did not Israel know?—that is, from their own Scriptures, of God's intention to bring in the Gentiles? First, Moses saith—or, 'was the first (in the prophetic line) to say,' I will provoke you to jealousy by [them that are] no people [ἐπ' οὐκ ἔθνει]—not *against*' (as the Vulgate), nor 'by' (as *Beza* and our version), but '*on account of* a no-nation' [see *Fritzsche* on the force of ἐπί here]. [and] by a foolish nation—'on account of a nation without understanding,' will I anger you. The words are from Deut. xxxii. 21, (almost entirely as in the LXX.) In that chapter Moses prophetically sings the future destinies of his people; and in this verse God warns His ancient people that, because they had moved Him (that is, because in after-times they would move Him) to jealousy with their "no gods," and provoked Him to anger with their vanities, He, in requital, would move them to jealousy by receiving into His favour a no-nation, and provoke them to anger by adopting a nation void of understanding. 20. But Esaias is very bold, and saith—*i. e.*, is still plainer, and goes even the length of saying, I was found of them that sought me not—that is, until *I* sought *them;* I was made ('became') manifest unto them that asked not after me—that is, until the invitation from Me came to them. That

the calling of the Gentiles was meant by these words of the prophet (Isa. lxv. 1), is manifest from what immediately follows: "I said, Behold me, behold me, unto a nation that was not called by my name." 21. But to [Πρὸς δὲ]—rather, 'But with regard to' Israel he saith, All day ('All the day') long I have stretched out ('did I stretch forth') my hands—the attitude of gracious entreaty — unto a disobedient and gainsaying people. These words, which immediately follow the announcement just quoted of the calling of the Gentiles, were enough to forewarn the Jews both of God's purpose to eject them from their privileges, in favour of the Gentiles, and of the cause of it on their own part.

Remarks.—1. Mere sincerity, and even earnestness in religion—though it may be some ground of hope for a merciful recovery from error (see 1 Tim. i. 13)—is no excuse, and will not compensate, for the deliberate rejection of saving truth, when in the providence of God presented for acceptance, (*vv.* 1-3; and see Remark 3, at the close of ch. ix.) 2. The true cause of such rejection of saving truth, by the otherwise sincere, is the prepossession of the mind by some false notions of its own. So long as the Jews "sought to establish their own righteousness," it was in the nature of things impossible that they should "submit themselves to the righteousness of God;" the one of these two methods of acceptance being in the teeth of the other. 3. Is there one soul sighing for salvation, but saying within itself, 'Ah! Salvation is beyond *my* reach: others may be able to lay hold of it; but for me, who have so long and so perseveringly set at nought all His counsel and despised all His reproof, Christ seems so far off that I may as well think to mount up to heaven and pluck Him down, or descend into the deep to bring Him up from thence?' How gloriously does the apostle here teach us to deal with such a case. 'The word (says he) is nigh thee, in thy mouth and in thy heart—the word of faith which we preach: Christ is *in the heart* of every one who believeth on Him, *in the mouth* of whoso confesseth Him; and whosoever will, let him take the water of life freely.' 4. How will the remembrance of the simplicity, reasonableness, and absolute freeness of God's plan of salvation overwhelm those that perish from under the sound of it? (*vv.* 4-13.) 5. How piercingly and perpetually should that question—"How SHALL THEY HEAR WITHOUT A PREACHER?"—sound in the ears of all the churches, as but the apostolic echo of their Lord's parting injunction, "PREACH THE GOSPEL TO EVERY CREATURE" (Mark xvi. 15); and how far below the proper standard of love, zeal, and self-sacrifice, must the churches as yet be, when with so plenteous a harvest the labourers are yet so few (Matt. ix. 37, 38), and that cry from the lips of pardoned, gifted, consecrated men—"Here am I, send me" (Isa. vi. 8)—is not heard everywhere! (*vv.* 14, 15.) 6. The blessing of a covenant-relation to God is the irrevocable privilege of no people and no church: it can be preserved only by fidelity, on

11 I SAY then, ^aHath God cast away his people? God forbid. For ^bI also am an Israelite, of the seed of Abraham, *of* the tribe of Benjamin.
2 God hath not cast away his people which he ^cforeknew. Wot ye not what the Scripture saith ¹of Elias? how he maketh intercession to God
3 against Israel, saying, Lord, ^dthey have killed thy prophets, and digged
4 down thine altars; and I am left alone, and they seek my life. But what saith the answer of God unto him? I have reserved to myself seven thousand men, who have not bowed the knee to *the image of* Baal.
5 Even ^eso then at this present time also there is a remnant according
6 to the election of grace. And ^fif by grace, then *is it* no more of works; otherwise grace is no more grace. But if *it be* of works, then is it no more grace; otherwise work is no more work.
7 What then? ^gIsrael hath not obtained that which he seeketh for;
8 but the ^helection hath obtained it, and the rest were ²blinded (according

A. D. 60.
CHAP. 11.
^a 1 Sam. 12. 22.
Jer. 31. 37.
^b 2 Cor. 11.2ₐ Phil. 3. 5.
^c ch. 8. 29.
1 in Elias?
^d 1 Ki. 19. 10.
^e ch. 9. 27.
^f Deut. 9. 4, 5.
^g ch. 10. 3.
^h John 10. 28. 2 Tim. 2.19.
2 Or, hardened.

our part, to the covenant itself (*v.* 19). **7.** God is often found by those who apparently are the farthest from Him, while He remains undiscovered by those who think themselves the nearest (*vv.* 20, 21; and see Matt. viii. 11, 12; xix. 30). **8.** How affectingly is the attitude of God towards the ungrateful and persevering rejecters of His love here presented to us—all the day long extending the arms of His mercy even to the disobedient and gainsaying. This tenderness and compassion of God, in His dealings even with reprobate sinners, will be felt and acknowledged at last by all who perish, to the glory of God's forbearance and to their own confusion, imparting to their misery its bitterest ingredient.

CHAP. XI. 1-36.—SAME SUBJECT CONTINUED AND CONCLUDED—THE ULTIMATE INBRINGING OF ALL ISRAEL, TO BE, WITH THE GENTILES, ONE KINGDOM OF GOD ON THE EARTH.

The scope of this chapter is to explain the present condition, and open up the future prospects of Israel; and the sum of it is, that although God might seem to have cast off His covenant-people, this rejection was neither *total* nor *final:* —not total, for even now there is a chosen remnant, that have believed through grace; not final, for a time is coming when all Israel shall be saved.

First: *Even now, Israel is not* WHOLLY *rejected* (1-10). **1.** I **say then, Hath** ('Did') **God cast away his people?** God **forbid.** Our Lord did indeed announce that 'the kingdom of God should be *taken from* Israel' (Matt. xxi. 41); and when asked by the Eleven, after His resurrection, if He would at that time "*restore* the kingdom to Israel," His reply is a virtual admission that Israel was in some sense already out of covenant (Acts i. 9). Yet here the apostle teaches that, in two respects, Israel was *not* "cast away." *First*, Israel is not *wholly* cast away. **For I also am an Israelite** (see Phil. iii. 5)—and so a living witness to the contrary; **of the seed of Abraham**—of pure descent from the father of the faithful; **of the tribe of Benjamin** (Phil. iii. 5)—that tribe which, on the revolt of the ten tribes, constituted, with Judah, the one faithful kingdom of God (1 Ki. xii. 21), and after the captivity was, along with Judah, the kernel of the Jewish nation (Ezra iv. 1; x. 9). **2.** God hath ('did') **not cast away his people** (i. e., *wholly*) **which he foreknew.** On the word "foreknew," see on ch. viii. 29. **Wot** (i. e., Know) **ye not what the Scripture saith of Elias?**—*lit.*, 'in Elias;' meaning, 'in the Section about Elias,' **how he maketh intercession** (or 'pleadeth') **against Israel,** [saying,] 3. Lord, **they have killed thy prophets,** [and] **digged down thine altars.** The two bracketed words—"saying" (*v.* 2) and "and" (*v.* 3)—are clearly not genuine; and *v.* 3

should read, 'They have killed thy prophets, they have digged down thine altars,' and **I am left alone** ('I only am left'), and **they seek my life. 4. But what saith the answer of God unto him?** [ὁ χρηματισμὸς]. The noun here rendered "answer of God" is nowhere else used in the New Testament, though the verb is used seven times in that sense—a sense derived from the LXX. It means a 'Divine communication,' in whatever way received. The words now to be quoted are from 1 Ki. xix. 18, almost *verbatim.* **I have reserved to myself seven thousand men, who have not bowed the knee to [the image of]** Baal. There is no need of the supplementary words of our version. To 'bow the knee to Baal' is surely intelligible enough. **5. Even so then at this present time** [ἐν τῷ νῦν καιρῷ]—'in this present season;' meaning, this period of Israel's rejection, there is [γέγονεν]—'there obtains' **a remnant according to the election of grace**—*q. d.,* 'As in Elijah's time the apostasy of Israel was not so universal as it seemed to be, and as he in his despondency concluded it to be, so now, the rejection of Christ by Israel is not so appalling in extent as one would be apt to think: There is now, as there was then, a faithful remnant; not, however, of persons naturally better than the unbelieving mass, but of persons graciously chosen to salvation.' (See 1 Cor. iv. 7; 2 Thess. ii. 13.) This establishes our view of the argument on Election in ch. ix., as not being an Election of Gentiles in the room of Jews, and merely to religious advantages, but a sovereign choice of some of Israel itself, from amongst others, to believe and be saved. (See on ch. ix. 6.) **6. And** ('Now') **if** (it be) **by grace**—that is, the Election, [then] **is it no more of works; otherwise grace** ('becomes') **is no more grace. But if it be of works, then is it no more grace; otherwise work is no more work.** (The latter of these statements, beginning with "But," has very weighty external evidence against it; but, with *Tischendorf*, we retain it for the reasons stated by him. (See also *Fritzsche's* long and able note. Such seeming redundancies are not unusual with our apostle.) The general position here laid down is fundamental, and of unspeakable importance. It may be thus expressed: There are but two possible sources of salvation—men's works and God's grace; and these are so essentially distinct and opposite, that salvation cannot be of any combination or mixture of both; it must be wholly either of the one or of the other. (See Remark 3, at the close of ch. iv.)

7. What then?—How stands the case? **Israel hath not obtained that which he seeketh for; but the election hath obtained it, and the rest were blinded** [ἐπωρώθησαν]—better thus: 'What

258

as it is written, [i] God hath given them the spirit of [3] slumber, [j] eyes that they should not see, and ears that they should not hear;) unto this day.

9 And David saith, [k] Let their table be made a snare, and a trap, and a
10 stumblingblock, and a recompence unto them: let their eyes be darkened, that they may not see, and bow down their back alway.

11   I say then, Have they stumbled that they [l] should fall? God forbid: but *rather* through [m] their fall salvation *is come* unto the Gentiles, for to
12 provoke them to jealousy. Now if the fall of them *be* the riches of the world, and the [4] diminishing of them the riches of the Gentiles; how
13 much more their [n] fulness! For I speak to you Gentiles, inasmuch as
14 [o] I am the apostle of the Gentiles, I magnify mine office; if by any means I may provoke to emulation *them which are* my flesh, and
15 [p] might save some of them. For if the casting away of them *be* the reconciling of the world, what *shall* the receiving *of them be*, but life from the dead?

16   For [q] if the first-fruit *be* holy, the lump *is* also *holy;* and if the root *be*

A. D. 60.

[i] Isa. 29. 10.
[3] Or, remorse.
[j] Deut. 29. 4.
Isa. 6. 9.
Jer. 5. 21.
Eze. 12. 2.
[k] Ps 69. 22.
[l] Eze. 18. 23.
Eze. 33. 11.
[m] Acts 13. 46.
[4] Or, decay, or, loss.
[n] Jer. 30. 4.
Mic. 5. 7.
Zech. 2. 11.
[o] Acts 9. 15.
[p] 1 Cor. 7. 16.
Jas. 5. 20.
[q] Lev. 23. 10.

Israel is in search of (meaning justification, or acceptance with God—see on ch. ix. 31), this he found not [τούτου of the received text has next to no authority: τοῦτο is the true reading]: but the election found it (that is, the elect remnant of Israel), and the rest were hardened' (or judicially given over to the hardness of their own hearts). **8. (According as it is written** (in Isa. xxix. 10, and Deut. xxix. 4), **God hath given them the spirit of slumber** [κατανύξεως]—not 'remorse' (as in *marg.*, and as the derivation of the word might suggest), but 'stupor' or 'torpor' [see *Fritzsche's* 'Excursus' on this word, pp. 549-563]. **eyes that they should not see, and ears that they should not hear; unto this** ('this present') **day. 9. And David saith**—in Ps. lxix. 22, 23, which, in such a Messianic Psalm, must be meant of the rejecters of Christ, **Let their table be made a snare, and a trap, and a stumblingblock, and a recompence unto them**—*q. d.,* 'Let their very blessings prove a curse to them, and their enjoyments only sting and take vengeance on them.' **10. Let their eyes be darkened, that they may not see, and bow down their back alway**—'and ever bow thou down their back;' expressive either of the *decrepitude* or of the *servile condition* to come on the nation through the just judgment of God. The apostle's object in making these quotations is to show that what he had been compelled to say of the then condition and prospects of his nation was more than borne out by their own Scriptures. But now,

Secondly: *Israel, even as a nation, is not* FINALLY *rejected, but is destined to a glorious recovery* (11-31). **11. I say then, Have they stumbled** ('Did they stumble') **that they should fall? God forbid: but [rather].** This supplementary "rather" is superfluous. **through their fall** [παραπτώματι]— *lit.,* 'trespass;' probably 'lapse' is best: **salvation is come unto the Gentiles, for to provoke them to jealousy.** Here, as in ch. x. 19 (quoted from Deut. xxxii. 21), we see the principle of emulation Divinely called into exercise as a stimulus to what is good. **12. Now if the fall of them** ('their lapse') **be the riches of the** (Gentile) **world**—as being the occasion of their accession to Christ, **and the diminishing of them**—that is, the reduction of the *true* Israel to so small a remnant; **the riches of the Gentiles; how much more their fulness!**—their full recovery (see on *v.* 26): *q. d.,* 'If an event so untoward as Israel's fall was the occasion of such unspeakable good to the Gentile world, of how much greater good may we expect an event so blessed as their full recovery to

be productive?' **13. I speak** ('I am speaking') **to you Gentiles**—another proof that this Epistle was addressed not to Jewish but to *Gentile* believers (see on ch. i. 13), **inasmuch as I am the apostle of the Gentiles, I magnify** ('glorify') **mine office.** The clause beginning with "inasmuch" should be read as a parenthesis. **14. If by any means I may provoke to emulation** [them which are] **my flesh** (see on *v.* 11: cf. Isa. lviii. 7), **and might** ('may') **save some of them. 15. For if the casting away of them.** The apostle had denied that they were cast away (*v.* 1), and here he affirms it; but both are true. They *were* cast away, though neither totally nor finally; and it is of this partial and temporary rejection that the apostle is speaking: **be the reconciling of the** (Gentile) **world, what shall the receiving of them be, but life from the dead?** It is surely very strained to explain this of the literal resurrection, as most modern critics, following some of the fathers, do; but to take it as a mere proverbial expression for the highest felicity (as *Grotius,* &c.) is far too loose. The meaning seems to be, that the reception of the whole family of Israel, scattered as they are among all nations under heaven, and the most inveterate enemies of the Lord Jesus, will be such a stupendous manifestation of the power of God upon the spirits of men, and of His glorious presence with the heralds of the Cross, as will not only kindle devout astonishment far and wide, but so change the dominant mode of thinking and feeling on all spiritual things as to seem like a *resurrection from the dead.*

16. For ('But') **if the first-fruit be holy, the lump is also** [holy]; **and if the root be holy, so** [are] **the branches.** The Israelites were required to offer to God the first-fruits of the earth—both in their raw state, in a sheaf of newly reaped grain (Lev. xxiii. 10, 11), and in their prepared state, made into cakes of dough (Num. xv. 19-21), by which the whole produce for that season was regarded as *hallowed.* It is probably the latter of these offerings that is here intended, as to it the word "lump" best applies; and the argument of the apostle is, that as the separation unto God of Abraham, Isaac, and Jacob, from the rest of mankind, to be the parent stem of their race, was as real an offering of first-fruits as that which hallowed the produce of the earth, so, in the Divine estimation, it was as real a separation of the mass or "lump" of that nation in all time to God. The figure of the "root" and its "branches" is of like import—the consecration of the one of them extending to the other. **17.**

17 holy, so *are* the branches. And if *r* some of the branches be broken off, *s* and thou, being a wild olive tree, wert graffed in *5* among them, and with
18 them partakest of the root and fatness of the olive tree; boast *t* not against the branches. But if thou boast, thou bearest not the root,
19 but the root thee. Thou wilt say then, The branches were broken off,
20 that I might be graffed in. Well; because of unbelief they were broken off, and thou standest by faith. Be *u* not high-minded, *v* but
21 fear: for if God spared not the natural branches, *take heed* lest he also spare not thee.
22 Behold therefore the goodness and severity of God: on them which fell, severity; but toward thee, goodness, if *w* thou continue in *his* good-
23 ness: otherwise *x* thou also shalt be cut off. And they also, *y* if they abide not still in unbelief, shall be graffed in: for God is able to graff them in
24 again. For if thou wert cut out of the olive tree, which is wild by nature, and wert graffed contrary to nature into a good olive tree; how much more shall these, which be the natural *branches*, be graffed into their own olive tree!
25 For I would not, brethren, that ye should be ignorant of this mystery,

A. D. 60.
r Jer. 11. 16.
Ps. 50. 11, 16.
Isa. 6. 13.
Isa. 27. 1f.
Eze. 15. 6, 8.
Matt. 8. 11, 12.
s Eph. 2. 12.
5 Or, for them.
t 1 Cor. 10. 12.
u ch. 12. 16.
v Phil 2. 12.
w 1 Cor. 15. 2.
Heb. 3. 6
x John 15. 2.
y Zech. 12. 10.
Matt. 23. 39.
2 Cor. 3. 16.

And if—rather, 'But if'—*q. d.*, 'If, notwithstanding this consecration of Abraham's race to God,' **some of the branches.** The mass of the unbelieving and rejected Israelites are here called "some," not, as before, to meet Jewish prejudice (see on ch. iii. 3, and on "not all," in ch. x. 16), but with the opposite view of checking Gentile pride. **and thou, being a wild olive tree,** ('wast') **graffed in among them.** Though it is more usual to graft the superior cutting upon the inferior stem, the opposite method, which is intended here, is not without example: **and with them partakest** ('wast made partaker'—along with the branches left, the believing remnant) **of the root and fatness of the olive tree** (the rich grace secured by covenant to the true seed of Abraham): 18. **Boast not against the** (rejected) **branches. But if thou** (do) **boast** (remember that), **thou bearest not** ('it is not thou that bearest') **the root, but the root thee**—*q. d.*, 'If the branches may not boast over the root that bears them, then may not the Gentile boast over the seed of Abraham; for what is thy standing, O Gentile, in relation to Israel, but that of a branch in relation to the root? From Israel hath come all that thou art and hast in the family of God; for "salvation is of the Jews"' (John iv. 22). 19. **Thou wilt say then** (as a plea for boasting), **The branches were broken off, that I might be graffed in.** 20. **Well** —*q. d.*, 'Be it so, but remember that,' **because of unbelief they were broken off, and thou standest** (not as a Gentile, but solely) **by faith.** But as faith cannot live in those "whose soul is lifted up" (Hab. ii. 4), **Be not high-minded, but fear** (Prov. xxviii. 14; Phil. ii. 12). 21. **For if God spared not the natural branches** (sprung from the parent stem), **take heed lest he also spare not thee** (a mere wild graft). The former might, beforehand, have been thought very improbable; but, after that, no one can wonder at the latter. 22. **Behold therefore the goodness and severity of God: on them which fell, severity**—in rejecting the chosen seed [ἀποτομία appears to be the true reading, not —ίαν], **but toward thee, goodness**—'the goodness of God' (according to the reading best supported). The goodness referred to is God's sovereign goodness in admitting to a covenant-standing those who before were "strangers to the covenants of promise" (Eph. ii. 12·20). **If thou continue in his goodness**—in believing dependence on that pure goodness which made thee what thou art: **otherwise thou also shalt be cut**

off. 23. **And they also** ('Yea, and they'), **if they abide not still in unbelief, shall be graffed in: for God is able to graff them in again.** This appeal to the *power* of God to effect the recovery of His ancient people implies the vast difficulty of it—which all who have ever laboured for the conversion of the Jews are made depressingly to feel. That intelligent expositors should think that this was meant of *individual* Jews, re-introduced from time to time into the family of God on their believing on the Lord Jesus, is surprising; and yet those who deny the *national* recovery of Israel must and do so interpret the apostle. But this is to confound the two things which the apostle carefully distinguishes. Individual Jews have been at all times admissible, and have been actually admitted, to the Church through the gate of faith in the Lord Jesus. This is the "remnant, *even at this present time*, according to the election of grace," of which the apostle, in the first part of the chapter, had cited himself as one. But here he manifestly speaks of something *not* then existing, but to be looked forward to as a great future event in the Divine economy—the re-ingrafting of *the nation as such*, when they "abide not in unbelief." And though this is here spoken of merely as a supposition (*if* their unbelief shall cease)—in order to set it over against the other supposition, of what will happen to the Gentiles if they shall not abide in the faith—the supposition is turned into an explicit prediction in the verses following. 24. **For if thou wert cut** ('wert cut off') **out of the olive tree, which is wild by nature, and wert graffed contrary to nature into a good olive tree: how much more shall these, which be the natural branches, be graffed into their own olive tree?** This is just the converse of what is said in *v.* 21: 'As the excision of the merely *engrafted* Gentiles through unbelief is a thing much more to be expected than was the excision of the *natural* Israel, before it happened, so the restoration of Israel, when they shall be brought to believe in Jesus, is a thing far more in the line of what we should expect than the admission of the Gentiles to a standing which they never before enjoyed.' 25. **For I would not, brethren, that ye should be ignorant of this mystery.** The word "mystery," so often used by our apostle, does not mean, as with us, something incomprehensible, but 'something before kept secret, either wholly or for the most part, and now only fully disclosed,' (cf. ch. xvi. 25; 1 Cor. ii. 7·10; Eph. i. 9, 10; iii.

lest ye should be wise in your own conceits, that [6] blindness in part is
26 happened to Israel, until [2] the fulness of the Gentiles be come in. And
　so [a] all Israel shall be saved: as it is written, [b] There shall come out of
27 Sion the Deliverer, and shall turn away ungodliness from Jacob: for
28 [c] this *is* my covenant unto them, when I shall take away their sins. As
　concerning the Gospel, *they are* enemies for your sakes: but as touching
29 the election, *they are* [d] beloved for the fathers' sakes. For the gifts and
30 calling of God *are* without [e] repentance. For as ye in times past have

A. D. 60.

[6] hardness.
[2] Luke 21. 24.
[a] Isa. 60. 15.
[b] Ps. 14. 7.
Isa. 59. 20.
[c] Jer. 31. 31.
Heb. 10. 16.
[d] Deut. 9. 5.
[e] Num. 23.19.

3-6, 9, 10, &c.) **lest ye should be wise in your
own conceits**—as if ye alone were now and
in all time coming to be the family of God.
that blindness ('hardness') **in part** [ἀπὸ μέρους
= κατὰ μ.] **is happened to** ('hath come upon')
Israel—*i. e.*, hath come partially, or upon a portion
of Israel (so *Beza, Grotius, Fritzsche,* &c.); not 'to
some extent' (as *Calvin,* &c.), for the blindness or
hardness was *total* on those on whom it fell at all;
but (says the apostle) it fell only on a *part* of the
chosen race. **until the fulness of the Gentiles
be** ('have') **come in**—*i. e.*, not the general conversion of the world to Christ, as many take it;
for this would seem to contradict the latter part
of this chapter, and throw the national recovery
of Israel too far into the future; besides, in *v.* 15
the apostle seems to speak of the receiving of
Israel, not as following, but as contributing largely
to bring about the general conversion of the
world: clearly it means, 'until the Gentiles have
had their *full* time of the visible Church all to
themselves, while the Jews are out, which the
Jews had till the Gentiles were brought in.' See
on Luke xxi. 24 (in Commentary on Mark xiii. 20,
p. 193). **26. And so all Israel shall be saved**—
not 'all the *spiritual* Israel,' Jew and Gentile (as
one or two of the fathers, and *Luther, Calvin,* &c.),
for throughout all this chapter, the apostle by
"Israel" means exclusively the *natural* seed of
Abraham, whom he sharply distinguishes from
the Gentiles; nor the whole believing *remnant* of
the natural Israel, (as *Bengel, Olshausen,* &c.)
Clearly the meaning here is, *The Israelitish nation
at large.* To understand this great statement, as
some still do, merely of such a gradual inbringing
of *individual* Jews, that there shall at length
remain none in unbelief, is to do manifest violence
both to it and to the whole context. It can only
mean the ultimate, ingathering of Israel as a
nation, in contrast with the present "remnant."
(So most of the fathers—*Beza, Fritzsche, Tholuck,
Reiche, Meyer, de Wette, Alford, Philippi, Hodge,
Lange.*) Some of these critics would seem to
advocate the inbringing of every individual Israelite; others, only of 'the mass' or 'majority;' but
if they mean simply 'the nation at large,' as
opposed to 'a remnant,' they have brought out, as
it appears to us, the precise idea of the apostle.

Three confirmations of this cheering announcement now follow: two from the prophets, and
a third from the Abrahamic covenant itself.
First confirmation—from the prophets. **as it
is written, There shall come out of Sion
the Deliverer, and shall turn away**—'He shall
turn away' (without the "and") is the true
reading, **ungodliness from Jacob.** The apostle,
having drawn his illustrations of man's *sinfulness*
chiefly from Ps. xiv. and Isa. lix., now seems (as
Bengel observes) to combine the language of the
same two places regarding Israel's *salvation* from
it. In the one place the psalmist longs to see
"the salvation of Israel coming *out of Zion*" (Ps.
xiv. 7); in the other, the prophet announces that
"the Redeemer (or, "Deliverer") shall come to
(or, for) Zion" (Isa. lix. 20). But as all the

glorious manifestations of Israel's God were regarded as issuing out of Zion, as the seat of His
manifested glory (Ps. xx. 2; cx. 2; Isa. xxxi. 9),
the turn which the apostle gives to the words
merely adds to them that familiar idea. And
whereas the prophet announces that He "shall
come *to* (or, '*for*') them that turn from transgression in Jacob," while the apostle makes him
say that He shall come "to turn away ungodliness *from* Jacob," this is taken from the LXX.
version, and seems to indicate a different reading
of the original text. The sense, however, is
substantially the same in both. *Second confirmation*—from the prophets. **27. For this** [Καὶ]
—rather, 'And (again),' introducing a new quotation: **is my covenant unto them** [αὕτη αὐτοῖς ἡ
παρ ἐμοῦ διαθ.]—'this is the covenant from me unto
them,' **when I shall take away their sins.** This,
we believe, is rather a brief summary of Jer. xxxi.
31-34, than the express words of any prediction.
Those who believe that there are no predictions
regarding the literal Israel in the Old Testament
that stretch beyond the end of the Jewish economy,
are obliged to view these quotations by the apostle
as mere adaptations of Old Testament language
to express his own predictions (*Alexander* on
Isaiah, for example). But how forced this is, we
shall presently see. *Third confirmation*—from the
Abrahamic covenant itself. **28. As concerning the
Gospel, they are enemies for your sakes**—that
is, they are regarded and treated as enemies (in
a state of exclusion, through unbelief, from the
family of God) for the benefit of you Gentiles; in
the sense of *vv.* 11, 15. **but as touching the
election** (of Abraham and his seed), **they are
beloved**—even in their *state of exclusion,* **for the
fathers' sakes. 29. For the gifts and calling**
—'For the gifts and the calling' **of God are
without repentance** ['Αμεταμέλητα]—'are not to
be,' or 'cannot be, repented of.' By the "*calling*
of God," in this case, is meant that sovereign act
by which God, in the exercise of His free choice,
"called" Abraham to be the father of a peculiar
people; while "the *gifts* of God" here denote the
articles of the covenant which God made with
Abraham, and which constituted the real distinction between his and all other families of the
earth. Both these, says the apostle, are irrevocable; and as the point for which he refers to this
at all is the *final destiny* of the Israelitish nation,
it is clear that *the perpetuity through all time of the
Abrahamic covenant* is the thing here affirmed.
And lest any should say that though Israel, *as a
nation,* has no destiny at all under the Gospel, but
as a people disappeared from the stage when the
middle wall of partition was broken down, yet the
Abrahamic covenant still endures in the *spiritual*
seed of Abraham, made up of Jews and Gentiles
in one undistinguished mass of redeemed men
under the Gospel—as if to preclude that supposition, the apostle expressly states that the very
Israel who, as concerning the Gospel, are regarded
as "enemies for the Gentiles' sakes," are "*beloved
for the fathers' sakes;*" and it is in proof of this
that he adds, "For the gifts and the calling of

not [7] believed God, yet have now obtained mercy through their unbelief;

31 even so have these also now not [8] believed, that through your mercy they

32 also may obtain mercy. For God hath [9] concluded them all in unbelief, that he might have mercy upon all.

33 O the depth of the riches both of the wisdom and knowledge of God! how unsearchable *are* his judgments, and his ways past finding out!

34 For [f] who hath known the mind of the Lord? or who hath been his

35 counsellor? or [g] who hath first given to him, and it shall be recompensed

36 unto him again? For [h] of him, and through him, and to him, *are* all things: to [10] whom *be* glory for ever. Amen.

A. D. 60.

[7] Or, obeyed.
[8] Or, obeyed.
[9] Or, shut them all up to gether.
[f] Isa. 40. 13.
[g] Job 35. 7.
[h] 1 Cor. 8. 6. Col. 1. 16.
[10] him.
Rev. 1. 6.

God are without repentance." But in what sense are the now unbelieving and excluded children of Israel "beloved for the fathers' sakes?" Not merely from ancestral *recollections*, as one looks with fond interest on the child of a dear friend for that friend's sake—a beautiful thought of the late *Dr. Arnold*, and not foreign to Scripture in this very case (see 2 Chr. xx. 7; Isa. xli. 8); but it is from ancestral *connections* and *obligations*, or their lineal descent from and oneness in covenant with the fathers with whom God originally established it. In other words, the natural Israel—not "the *remnant* of them according to the election of grace," but THE NATION, sprung from Abraham according to the flesh—are still an elect people, and as such, "beloved." The very same love which chose the fathers, and rested on the fathers as a parent stem of the nation, still rests on their descendants at large, and will yet recover them from unbelief, and reinstate them in the family of God. **30. For as ye in times past have not believed** (or, 'obeyed') **God**—that is, yielded not to God "the obedience of faith," while strangers to Christ, **yet have now obtained mercy through** (by occasion of) **their unbelief** (see on *vv.* 11, 15, 28); **31. Even so have these** (the Jews) **now not believed** (or, 'now been disobedient'), **that through your mercy** (the mercy shown to you) **they also may obtain mercy.** Here is an entirely new idea. The apostle has hitherto dwelt upon the unbelief of the Jews as making way for the faith of the Gentiles—the exclusion of the one occasioning the reception of the other; a truth which could yield to generous, believing Gentiles but mingled satisfaction. Now, opening a more cheering prospect, he speaks of the mercy shown to the Gentiles as a means of Israel's recovery, which seems to mean that it will be by the instrumentality of believing Gentiles that Israel as a nation is at length to "look on Him whom they have pierced, and mourn for Him," and so to "obtain mercy." (See 2 Cor. iii. 15, 16.) **32. For God hath concluded them all in unbelief** [Συνέκλεισεν τοὺς πάντας εἰς ἀπείθειαν]— 'hath shut up all into unbelief' or 'disobedience:' our version, by rendering it "*them* all," leaves the impression (as *Scholefield* observes) that it is of *Jews* only that this is said; whereas the argument requires it to be understood of both the great divisions of mankind that are treated of in this chapter—hath shut up all (both Jew and Gentile) into unbelief. **that he might have mercy upon all**—the same "all" of whom he had been discoursing; that is, the Gentiles first, and after them the Jews (so *Fritzsche, Tholuck, Olshausen, de Wette, Philippi, Stuart, Hodge*). Certainly it is not 'all men without limitation' (as *Meyer* and *Alford*); for the apostle is not here dealing with individuals, but with those great divisions of mankind, Jew and Gentile. And what he here says is, that God's purpose was to shut up each of these divisions of men to the experience, first, of an unhumbled, condemned state, without Christ, and then to the experience of His mercy in Christ.

The adorableness of this plan of Divine mercy (33-36). In these concluding verses the apostle yields himself up to the admiring contemplation of the grandeur of that Divine plan which he had sketched out. **33. O the depth of the riches both of the wisdom and knowledge of God!** Many able expositors render this, 'of the riches and wisdom and knowledge of God.' (So *Erasmus, Grotius, Bengel, Fritzsche, Tholuck, Olshausen, Alford, Philippi, Lange*.) The words will certainly bear this sense; and then we have three distinct things drawing forth the apostle's admiration: first, 'the depth of God's riches'—a term which, when the apostle uses it alone (ch. x. 12; Eph. iii. 8; Phil. iv. 19), seems to mean the riches of His *grace* (which accordingly *de Wette* renders it here [*Gnadenreichthums*]—contrary to his usual strict literality); next, the depth of His "wisdom;" and lastly, the depth of His "knowledge." But (with *Luther, Calvin, Beza*, and *Hodge*) we prefer our own version; partly because "the riches of God" is a much rarer expression with our apostle than the riches of this or that perfection of God; but still more because the words immediately following limit our attention to the unsearchableness of God's "*judgments*," by which are probably meant His decrees or plans (Ps. cxix. 75), and of "his *ways*," or the method by which He carries these into effect. And all that follows to the end of the chapter seems to show that while the *Grace* of God to guilty men in Christ Jesus is presupposed to be the whole theme of this chapter, that which called forth the special admiration of the apostle, after sketching at some length the Divine purposes and methods in the bestowment of this Grace, was 'the depth of the riches of God's *wisdom* and *knowledge*' in these purposes and methods. The "knowledge," then, points probably to the vast sweep of Divine comprehension herein displayed; the "wisdom" to that fitness to accomplish the ends intended which is stamped on all this procedure. **34. For who hath known the mind of the Lord?** (see Job xv. 8; Jer. xxiii. 18) **or who hath been his counsellor?** (see Isa. xl. 13, 14). **35. Or who hath first given to him, and it shall be recompensed unto him again?** —'and shall have recompense made to him again?' (see Job xxxv. 7; xli. 11.) These questions, it will thus be seen, are just quotations from the Old Testament, as if to show how familiar to God's ancient people was the great truth which the apostle himself had just uttered—that God's plans and methods in the dispensation of His Grace have a reach of comprehension and wisdom stamped upon them which finite mortals cannot fathom, much less could ever have imagined before they were disclosed. **36. For of him** [ἐξ αὐτοῦ]—as their *Eternal Source*, as 1 Cor. viii. 6, and (though of a more limited sphere) 1 Cor. xi. 12, **and through him** [δί αὐτοῦ]—as the sole *Efficient Agent* in the production and conservation of them. [On this application of διά with the

12 I BESEECH you therefore, brethren, by the mercies of God, that *ª*ye present your bodies a living sacrifice, holy, acceptable unto God, *which* **2** *is* your reasonable service. And be not conformed to this world; but

A. D. 60.

CHAP. 12.
ª 1 Cor. 6. 13.

genitive to the primary agent of anything, see *Winer*, 8. 47. i; and *Fritzsche*, on Rom. i. 5, p. 15.] **and to him** [εἰς αὐτὸν]—as their *Last End*, **are all things**—the manifestation of the glory of His own perfections being the ultimate, because the highest possible, design of all His procedure from first to last : **to whom** ('to Him') **be glory for ever. Amen.**

In this three-fold view of God many of the fathers saw a covert reference to the three Persons of the Godhead (and they are followed by *Estius, Olshausen*, and *Tholuck*); but here, at least, that cannot be admitted, as '*to* Him' can have no reference to any known property or work of *the Spirit*. Thus grandly, and with a brevity and rhythm worthy of the sublimity of the thoughts, does the apostle sum up, not only this profound and comprehensive chapter, but the whole doctrinal portion of this Epistle.

Remarks.—1. It is an unspeakable consolation to know that in times of deepest religious declension and most extensive defection from the truth the lamp of God has never been permitted to go out, and that a faithful remnant has ever existed—a remnant larger than their own drooping spirits could easily believe. 2. The preservation of this remnant, even as their separation at the first, is all of mere grace. 3. When individuals and communities, after many fruitless warnings, are abandoned of God, they go from bad to worse (*vv.* 7-10). 4. God has so ordered His dealings with the great divisions of mankind, "that no flesh should glory in his presence." Gentile and Jew have each in turn been "shut up to unbelief," that each in turn may experience the "mercy" which saves the chief of sinners. 5. As we are "justified by faith," so are we "kept by the power of God through faith"—faith alone—unto salvation (*vv.* 20-32). 6. God's covenant with Abraham and his natural seed is a perpetual covenant, in equal force under the Gospel as before it. Therefore it is that the Jews as a nation still survive, in spite of all the laws which, in similar circumstances, have either extinguished, or destroyed the identity of, other nations. And therefore it is that the Jews as a nation will yet be restored to the family of God, through the subjection of their proud hearts to Him whom they have pierced. And as believing Gentiles will be honoured to be the instruments of this stupendous change, so shall the vast Gentile world reap such benefit from it that it shall be like the communication of life to them from the dead. 7. Thus has the Christian Church the highest motive to the establishment and vigorous prosecution of *Missions to the Jews:* God having not only promised that there shall be a remnant of them gathered in every age, but pledged Himself to the final ingathering of the whole nation, assigned the honour of that ingathering to the Gentile Church, and assured them that the event, when it does arrive, shall have a life-giving effect upon the whole world. 8. Those who think that in all the evangelical prophecies of the Old Testament the terms "Jacob," "Israel," &c., are to be understood solely of *the Christian Church*, would appear to read the Old Testament differently from the apostle, who, from the use of those very terms in Old Testament prophecy, draws arguments to prove that God has mercy in store for *the natural Israel.* 9. Mere intellectual investigations into Divine truth in general, and the sense of the living oracles in particular, as they have a

hardening effect, so they are a great contrast to the spirit of our apostle, whose lengthened sketch of God's majestic procedure towards men in Christ Jesus ends here in a burst of *admiration*, which loses itself in the still loftier frame of *adoration.*

CHAP. XII. 1-21.—THE CHRISTIAN LIFE—ITS GENERAL CHARACTER AND SPECIFIC DUTIES.

The strictly Doctrinal teaching of this great Epistle being now concluded, the apostle, as a wise master-builder, follows it up in this and the remaining chapters by impressing on believers the holy obligations which their new standing and life in Christ imposed upon them. In doing this he first puts clearly before them, in a couple of verses, the general character of all Christian service, and then goes at some length into a variety of details.

The general character of all Christian service— SELF-CONSECRATION, *in our whole spirit and soul and body, to Him who hath called us into the fellowship of His Son Jesus Christ* (1, 2). **1. I beseech you therefore, brethren**—in view of all that has been advanced in the foregoing part of this Epistle, **by the mercies of God** [διὰ = πρὸς τῶν οἰκτιρμῶν = רַחֲמִים]—those mercies whose free and unmerited nature, glorious channel, and saving fruits have been opened up at such length, **that ye present** [παραστῆσαι]—see on ch. vi. 13, where (as also in *vv.* 16, 19) the same word is used, and there rendered "yield:" **your bodies**—that is, 'yourselves in the body,' considered as the organ of the inner life (see on ch. vi. 12). As it is through the body that all the evil that is in the unrenewed heart comes forth into palpable manifestation and action, so it is through the body that all the gracious principles and affections of believers reveal themselves in the outward life. The Christian must never forget that as corruption extends to the whole man, so does sanctification (see 1 Thess. v. 23, 24). **a living sacrifice**—a glorious contrast to the legal sacrifices, which, save as they were *slain*, were no sacrifices at all. The death of the one 'Lamb of God, taking away the sin of the world,' has swept all dead victims from off the altar of God, to make room for the redeemed themselves, as 'living sacrifices' to Him who made "Him to be sin for us;" while every outgoing of their grateful hearts in praise, and every act prompted by the love of Christ, is itself a sacrifice to God of a sweet-smelling savour (Heb. xiii. 15, 16). **holy.** As the Levitical victims, when offered without blemish to God, were regarded as holy, so believers, 'yielding themselves to God as those that are alive from the dead, and their members as instruments of righteousness unto God,' are, in His estimation, not ritually but really "holy," and so **acceptable** [εὐάρεστον]—'well pleasing **unto God**—not as the Levitical offerings were pleasing to God, merely as appointed symbols of spiritual ideas, but which, when offered by those who were void of the character which they represented, were hateful to God, (Isa. i. 13-15; lxvi. 3; &c.): believers in their renewed character and endeared relationship to God through His Son Jesus Christ are objects of Divine complacency intrinsically, when presenting to Him their bodies a living and holy sacrifice. **[which is] your reasonable service** [τὴν λογικὴν λατρείαν ὑμῶν]—rather, 'your rational worship ;' not as opposed to a superstitious worship (as *Calvin*), or to the senselessness of idol-worship

b be ye transformed by the renewing of your mind, that ye may prove *c* what *is* that good, and acceptable, and perfect will of God.

3   For I say, through the grace given unto me, to every man that is among you, not to think *of himself* more highly than he ought to think; but to think ¹soberly, according as God hath dealt *d* to every man the

A. D. 60.
b Eph. 1. 18.
Col. 3. 10.
c 1 Thes. 4. 3.
1 to sobr ety.
d 1 Ccr. 12. 7.

(as others), but in contrast with the ceremonial character of the Levitical worship (as most interpreters agree) : cf. 1 Pet. ii. 2, the only other place where the same word [λογικὸς] is used to express "the milk of *the word*," or ' the rational milk,' in contrast with the material substance on which babes are nourished. This presentation of ourselves as living monuments of redeeming mercy, and as Divine property in the highest sense, is here called ' worship' [λατρεία]. "Service," indeed, it is, as our version renders it ; yet not that of a ' servant' [διακονία], but of a ' priest.' For as all believers are "priests unto God" (Rev. i. 6), so their whole Christian life is just a continuous exercise of this exalted priesthood—' their rational worship,' So 1 Pet. ii. 5, "Ye are . . . a royal priesthood, to offer up spiritual sacrifices, acceptable to God through Jesus Christ" (compare John iv. 24).

In the next verse the same great worship of *self-consecration* is inculcated under another aspect. The apostle had bidden us present our *bodies* a living sacrifice to God. But since it is by our bodies that we move about, and mix in society, and come in contact with all the various phases of life, how are we to carry out our Christianity in the evil and bewitching world around us? The next verse gives both a negative and positive answer to this question. **2. And be not conformed to this world** [μὴ συσχηματίζεσθε τῷ αἰῶνι τούτῳ. With *Tischendorf* and *Tregelles*, the imperative of this verb, and the following one, is, for the reasons given by him, to be preferred to the infinitive—συσχηματίζεσθαι and μεταμορφοῦσθαι—which, on very weighty external evidence certainly, *Lachmann* adopts]—' fashion not yourselves according to [the pattern of] this world ;' **but be ye transformed.** See Matt. xvii. 2, where this word is rendered "transfigured;" and in 2 Cor. iii. 18, "changed :" **by the renewing of your mind**—[ὑμῶν is probably not genuine; nor is it needed, for without it the sense is the same.] The thing enjoined is not a mere outward disconformity to the ungodly world, many of whose actions in themselves may be virtuous and praiseworthy, but such an inward spiritual transformation as makes the whole life new—new in its motives and ends, even where the actions differ in nothing from those of the world—new, considered as a whole, and in such a sense as to be wholly unattainable save through the constraining power of the love of Christ. **that ye may prove**—that is, prove experimentally, or learn by proof (see on the word "experience," in ch. v. 4), **what is that good, and acceptable**—'the good and well-pleasing,' **and perfect will of God.** Most modern critics render the words thus : 'that ye may prove (or 'discern ') the will of God [even], what is good, 'and acceptable, and perfect.' (So *Erasmus, Tholuck, Fritzsche, Meyer, de Wette, Alford, Philippi, Hodge, Lange*, &c.) But we think it yields but doubtful sense to say 'that ye may prove what is the will of God, even what is acceptable;' for who could doubt that what is the will of God is acceptable to Him? The rendering of our own version, which we think decidedly preferable, is that of the Vulgate, *Luther, Calvin, Beza, Estius, Reiche*, &c. In this view the "will of God," which believers are experimentally to prove, is said to have three characteristics to

recommend it : It is "*good*," as it demands only what is essentially and unchangeably good (see ch. vii. 10); it is '*well-pleasing*,' in contrast with all that is arbitrary, as demanding only what God has eternal complacency in (compare Mic. vi. 8 with Jer. ix. 24); and it is "*perfect*," as it requires nothing else than the perfection of God's reasonable creature, who, in proportion as he attains to it, reflects God's own perfection. But what, it may be asked, is that 'conformity to the world' which Christians are to avoid? Not, surely, its expressly sinful practices ; for when these are meant, they are branded with their own names. Clearly the thing meant is, that general course or way of life which characterizes "the children of this world," who "mind earthly things." Not being spiritual themselves, they can have no sympathy with anything spiritual—their ambitions, interests, and affections are all bounded by and centred in "the world," which "passeth away, and the lust thereof." The "children of light," on the contrary, "being risen with Christ," have a life of their own—the life of pardoned and reconciled believers : renewed in the spirit of their mind, they breathe a new air, they have new interests and affections, and their sympathies are all spiritual and heavenly. Since, then, these two classes of mankind are, religiously, so contrary the one to the other, what real fellowship can either have with the other? As the former cannot possibly have conformity in spirit with the latter, so the latter cannot cultivate conformity with the former, without grieving the Holy Spirit of God, wherewith they have been sealed unto the day of redemption, blunting badly the edge of their spirituality, and at length "forgetting that they were purged from their old sins." (See on ' the thorny ground,' in the Parable of the Sower, p. 146.) But after all, the true preservative of believers against ' conformity to the world' is to 'be renewed in the spirit of their mind.' It is the lively presence and ruling power of the positive element that will alone effectually keep out of the heart the negative one. Such, then, is the great general work of the Christian life—the comprehensive business of the redeemed. But to rest in generalities, however precious, is not our apostle's way in writing to the churches. He hastens, as usual, to the details of Christian duty; those specified being almost exclusively

Relative duties—A modest estimate and loving exercise of our own gifts, relatively to those of other believers (3-8). **3. For I say**—with Divine authority, **through the grace given unto me**—as an apostle of Jesus Christ ; thus exemplifying his own precept by modestly falling back on that office which both warranted and required such plainness towards all classes : **to every man that is among you, not to think of himself more highly than he ought to think; but to think soberly** [μὴ ὑπερφρονεῖν παρ ὃ δεῖ φρονεῖν ἀλλὰ φρονεῖν εἰς τὸ σωφρονεῖν]. It is impossible to convey in good English the emphatic play which each word here has upon another,—' not to be high minded above what he ought to be minded, but so to be minded as to be sober-minded.' To be ' high-minded above what he ought to be minded' is merely a strong way of characterizing all undue self-elevation. **according as God hath dealt to every man the**

4 measure of faith. For as we have many members in one body, and all
5 members have not the same office; so *°we, being* many, are one body in
6 Christ, and every one members one of another. Having *ƒ* then gifts
differing according to the grace that is given to us, whether prophecy,
7 *ᵍlet us prophesy* according to the proportion of faith; or ministry, *let us*
8 *wait* on *our* ministering; or *ʰ*he that teacheth, on teaching; or *ⁱ*he
that exhorteth, on exhortation: he that ²giveth, *let him do it* ³with
simplicity; *ʲ*he that ruleth, with diligence; he that showeth mercy, with
cheerfulness.
9   *Let* love be without dissimulation. Abhor that *ᵏ*which is evil; cleave
10 to that which is good. *Be* kindly affectioned one to another ⁴with
11 brotherly love; in honour preferring one another; not slothful in busi-

A. D. 60.

° Eph. 1. 23.
ƒ 1 Pet. 4. 10.
ᵍ 1 Cor. 12. 10.
ʰ Gal. 6. 6.
ⁱ Acts 15. 32.
² Cr.
  imparteth.
³ Or.
  liberally.
ʲ Acts 20. 28.
ᵏ Amos 5. 15.
⁴ Or, in the
  love of the
  brethren.

measure of faith. Faith is here viewed as the inlet to, or seed-bed of, all the other graces, and so as the receptive faculty of the renewed soul—*q. d.,* 'As God hath given to each his particular capacity to take in the gifts and graces which He designs for the general good.' **4. For as we have many members in one body, and all members have not the same office; 5. So we, being many, are one body in Christ, and every one**—[ὁ δὲ καθ' εἶς, a solecism of later Greek for καθ' ἕνα. *Lachmann* and *Tregelles* have τὸ δὲ κ. τ. λ.; so *Tischendorf* before; but the evidence is undoubtedly for the received text; and *Tischendorf* in his last edition returns to it, considering τὸ δὲ more like a correction than the other.] **members one of another.** The same diversity in unity obtains in the body of Christ, whereof all believers are the several members, as in the natural body. **6. Having then gifts differing according to the grace that is given to us.** Observe here how all the gifts of believers alike are viewed as communications of mere "*grace.*" **whether** (we have the gift of) **prophecy**—that is, of inspired teaching (as in Acts xv. 32). Any one speaking with Divine authority—whether with reference to the past, the present, or the future—was termed a prophet, (Exod. vii. 1, &c.) **[let us prophesy] according to the proportion of faith** [κατὰ τ. ἀναλογίαν τ. πίστεως]—rather, 'the proportion of our faith.' Many Romish expositors, and some Protestant (as *Calvin, Bengel, Hodge,* and, though hesitatingly, *Beza*), render this 'the analogy of faith,' understanding by it 'the general tenor' or 'rule of faith,' divinely delivered to men for their guidance. But this is against the context, whose object is to show that, as all the gifts of believers are according to their respective capacity for them, they are not to be puffed up on account of them, but to use them purely for their proper ends. **7. Or ministry, [let us wait]** on (or 'be occupied with') **our ministering** [διακονίᾳ]. The familiar word here used imports any kind of service from the dispensing of the word of life (Acts vi. 4) to the administering of the temporal affairs of the Church (Acts vi. 1-3). The latter seems intended here, being distinguished from 'prophesying,' 'teaching,' and 'exhorting.' **he that teacheth.** Teachers are expressly distinguished in the New Testament from prophets, and put after them, as exercising a lower function (Acts xiii. 1; 1 Cor. xii. 28, 29). Probably it consisted mainly in opening up the evangelical bearings of Old Testament Scripture; and it was in this department apparently that Apollos showed his power and eloquence (Acts xvii. 24). **8. Or he that exhorteth.** Since all preaching — whether by apostles, prophets, or teachers—was followed up by exhortation (Acts xi. 23; xiv. 22; xv. 32, &c.), many think that no specific class is here in view.

But if liberty was given to others to exercise themselves occasionally in exhorting either the brethren generally or small parties of the less instructed, the reference may be to them. **he that giveth**—in the exercise of private benevolence, probably, rather than in the discharge of diaconal duty. **[let him do it] with simplicity** [ἀπλότητι]. So the word probably means. But, as simplicity seems enjoined in the next clause but one of this same verse, perhaps the meaning here is, 'with liberality,' as the same word is rendered in 2 Cor. viii. 2; ix. 11. **he that ruleth** [προιστάμενος] — whether in the Church or his own household (see 1 Tim. iii. 4, 5), where the same word is applied to both, **with diligence** [ἐν σπουδῇ]—with earnest purpose; **he that showeth mercy, with cheerfulness** — not only without grudging either trouble or pecuniary relief, but feeling it to be "more blessed to give than to receive," and to help than be helped.

Sundry other modes of manifesting love to the brethren (9, 10). **9. [Let] love be without dissimulation**—'Let your love be unfeigned' (as in 2 Cor. vi. 6; 1 Pet. ii. 22; and see 1 John iii. 18). **Abhor that which is evil; cleave to that which is good.** What a lofty tone of moral principle and feeling is here inculcated! It is not, Abstain from the one, and do the other; nor, Turn away from the one, and draw to the other; but, Abhor the one, and cling, with deepest sympathy, to the other. Probably *Calvin* and others are right in thinking that, as this precept both follows and precedes an injunction to pure affection, the "evil" to be abhorred here specially refers to whatever is unkind or injurious to a brother, and that the "good" to be clung to points to the reverse of this. **10. Be, &c.**—better, 'In brotherly love be affectionate one to another; in [giving or showing] honour outdoing each other.' The word rendered 'prefer' [προηγούμενοι] means, rather, 'to go before,' 'take the lead'—*i. e.,* 'show an example.' How opposite is this to the reigning morality of the heathen world; and though Christianity has so changed the spirit of society that a certain beautiful disinterestedness and self-sacrifice shines in the character of not a few who are but partially, if at all, under the transforming power of the Gospel, it is only those whom "the love of Christ constrains to live not unto themselves," who are capable of habitually acting in the spirit of this precept.

Personal Duties (11, 12). As all the duties inculcated in this chapter, from *v.* 3 to the end, are *relative,* one can hardly suppose that the six *personal* duties (as they are usually termed) were intended as a formal statement of all belonging to that class. They seem, therefore, to have been suggested to the apostle's mind rather as a necessary *balance* to the relative duties which he had just been inculcating. They are laid down in the form

265

12 ness; *ˡ* fervent in spirit; serving the Lord; rejoicing *ᵐ*in hope; *ⁿ*patient
13 in tribulation; continuing instant in prayer; distributing *ᵒ*to the neces-
14 sity of saints; given *ᵖ*to hospitality. Bless them which persecute you:
15 bless, and curse not. Rejoice with them that do rejoice, and weep with
16 them that weep. *Be* of the same mind one toward another. Mind not

A. D. 60.

ˡ Rev. 3. 15.
ᵐ Heb. 3. 6.
ⁿ Heb. 10. 36.
ᵒ Heb. 6. 10.
ᵖ Heb. 13, 2.

of two triplets—one in each of the two verses. **11.** (Be) **Not slothful in business** [Τῇ σπουδῇ]. The word here rendered "business" means 'zeal,' 'diligence,' 'purpose;' denoting energy of action : **fervent** (or 'burning') **in spirit.** This is precisely what is said of Apollos, Acts xviii. 25, that he was "fervent in spirit" (the same phrase as here); of evil times to come on the Christian world our Lord predicted, that "because iniquity should abound, the love of many would wax cold" (Matt. xxiv. 12); the glorified Head of all the churches had this against the church of Ephesus, that they had "left their first love" (Lev. ii. 4); and of the Laodicean Church He says, "I would thou wert cold nor hot. So then, because thou art neither cold nor hot, I will spue thee out of my mouth" (Rev. iii. 15, 16). As the zeal of God's house consumed Himself, the Lord Jesus cannot abide a lukewarm spirit. A "fervent" or burning "spirit" is what He must seek in all who would be like Him. **serving the Lord**—that is, the Lord *Jesus* : cf. Eph. vi. 5-8. (It is one of the strangest facts in the textual criticism of the New Testament, that 'serving the time,' 'occasion,' 'opportunity'—a reading which, in the ancient MSS., would hardly differ, if at all, from the reading of our version [contracted thus : K͞Ω or KP͞Ω, which might be intended either for κυρίῳ or καιρῷ] —should have found its way into the received text, in the *Stephanic* form of it, though not the *Elzevir* text, and been adopted in *Luther's* version. There is, indeed, respectable MS. authority for it. [*Scrivener*, in his collation of ℵ, says that κω is for καιρω, and that it is found in D*FG, two copies of the Old Latin, and copies of it mentioned by *Jerome* and *Rufinus.*] But the external evidence for the reading adopted in our version is decisive [ABD** and ***—two correctors of D, of the seventh and of the ninth or tenth centuries—EL, and nearly all the cursives; three copies of the Old Latin, the Vulgate, and nearly all versions; of the Greek fathers, *Athanasius* and *Chrysostom*]. It may be difficult to account for the introduction of the ungenuine reading; but since both words, in their contracted form, were written alike, some transcribers, or those who dictated to them, might think that this was what the apostle meant to express. Nor need we wonder at this, when we find *Fritzsche, Olshausen, Meyer,* and *Lange* still defending it. But the sense which this reading yields, if defensible at all, seems exceedingly flat in such a triplet as that of this verse; and the ground on which it is defended shows a misapprehension of the apostle's object in this clause. It is said that to exhort Christians to serve the Lord—the most general of all Christian duties—in the midst of a set of specific details, is not what the apostle would likely do. But the sense of serving the Lord here is itself specific and restricted, intended to qualify the '*diligence*' and the '*fervency*' of the preceding clause, requiring that "*serving*" or '*pleasing*' *the Lord* should ever be present and uppermost as the ruling spirit of all else that they did as Christians—the atmosphere they were to breathe, whatever they were about. Nearly all critics agree in this; and *de Wette's* remark is not amiss, that the other reading savours more of worldly shrewdness than of Christian morality; adding, that while the Christian may and should

avail himself of time and opportunity (Eph. v. 16), he may not *serve* it. **12. Rejoicing,** &c. In this second triplet; it is more lively to retain the order and the verbs of the original: 'In hope, rejoicing; in tribulation, enduring; in prayer, persevering.' Each of these exercises helps the other. If our "hope" of glory is so assured that it is a rejoicing hope, we shall find the spirit of 'endurance in tribulation' natural and easy; but since it is "prayer" which strengthens the faith that begets hope, and lifts it up into an assured and joyful expectancy, and since our patience in tribulation is fed by this, it will be seen that all depends on our 'perseverance in prayer.' The apostle now returns to the other class of duties, the enumeration of which had but for a moment been interrupted in order to inculcate the personal ones just specified.

Relative Duties resumed (13-21). **13. Distributing** ('imparting') **to the necessity of saints; given to hospitality** [φιλοξενίαν]—that is, the entertainment of strangers. 'During times of persecution (as *Hodge* remarks), and before the general institution of houses of entertainment, there was peculiar necessity for Christians to entertain strangers. As such houses are still rarely to be met with in the East, this duty continues to be there regarded as one of the most sacred character. [A corrupt and absurd reading —μνείαις for χρείαις, 'imparting to the *memories* of the saints'—is actually found in D*FG, in one copy of the Old Latin (but that the best, the Codex Amiat.), and some of the fathers. It is even defended by *Mill.* But, as *Meyer* says, it no doubt owes its existence to the reverence into which the martyrs had grown at the time when those MSS. were written. The authority of all other MSS. and versions is against it—and common sense.] **14. Bless**—that is, Wish and call down by prayer a blessing on them **which persecute you : bless, and curse not.** This precept is taken from the Sermon on the Mount, which, from the numerous allusions to it, more or less direct, in different parts of the New Testament, seems to have been the storehouse of Christian morality among the churches. **15. Rejoice with them that rejoice, [and] weep with them that weep** [Χαίρειν —κλαίειν. On the infinitive as imperative, see *Kühner*, § 306, Rem. 11; and *Donaldson*, § 526. For other examples of the same usage, see Luke ix. 3; Phil. iii. 16]. The copulative "and" is probably not genuine. What a beautiful spirit of sympathy with the joys and sorrows of others is here inculcated! But it is only one charming phase of the unselfish character which belongs to all living Christianity. What a world will ours be when this shall become its reigning spirit! Of the two, however, it is more easy to sympathize with another's sorrows than his joys, because in the one case he *needs* us; in the other not. But just for this reason the latter is the more disinterested, and so the nobler. **16. Be of the same mind one toward another**—*lit.,* 'Being of the same mind.' But this is not to be understood merely as part of the preceding sentence: it is merely a resumption of the participial construction of most of these exhortations (as *vv.* 12, 13), and is to be regarded as a distinct and independent counsel to cherish and manifest a lively feeling of

high things, but [5]condescend to men of low estate.　Be not wise in your own conceits.

17　Recompense to no man evil for evil.　Provide things honest in the
18　sight of all men.　If it be possible, as much as lieth in you, live peace-
19　ably with all men.　Dearly beloved, avenge not yourselves, but *rather* give place unto wrath: for it is written, [q]Vengeance *is* mine; I will
20　repay, saith the Lord.　Therefore [r]if thine enemy hunger, feed him; if he thirst, give him drink: for in so doing thou shalt heap coals
21　of fire on his head.　Be [s]not overcome of evil, but overcome evil with good.

A.D. 60.

[5] Or, be contented with mean things.

[q] Deut. 32,35.
Ps. 94. 1.
Heb. 10. 30.

[r] Pro. 25. 21.
Matt. 5. 44.

[s] Matt. 18.21, 22.
1 Pet. 2. 21.

the common bond which binds all Christians to each other, whatever diversity of station, cultivation, temperament, or gifts may obtain among them.　This is finely enlarged on in the two following clauses: **Mind** ('Minding') **not high things** —Cherish not ambitious or aspiring purposes and desires, which, as they spring from selfish severance of our own interests and objects from those of our brethren, are quite incompatible with the spirit inculcated in the preceding clause: **but condescend** ('condescending') **to men of low estate** [τοῖς ταπεινοῖς συναπαγόμενοι].　As the noun here may be either masculine or neuter, some critics prefer the neuter, thinking it forms a more natural contrast to the preceding clause, thus: 'Minding not high things, but inclining unto the things that be lowly' (so *Calvin, Fritzsche, de Wette, Meyer,* and *Philippi*).　But the verb—which signifies to 'be drawn away along with,' and is used sometimes in a bad sense (as Gal. ii. 13 and 2 Pet. iii. 17)— agrees best with the *masculine* sense of our own version.　(In this sense it is taken here generally by the Greek fathers, and by *Erasmus, Beza, Grotius, Estius, Bengel, Tholuck, Alford*).　**Be not wise in your own conceits.**　This is just the application of the caution against high-mindedness to the estimate we form of our own mental character.

17. **Recompense** ('Recompensing') **to no man evil for evil** (see on *v.* 14).　**Provide** ('Providing') **things honest** [καλά]—that is, 'honourable,' **in the sight of all men.**　The idea here—taken from Prov. iii. 4—is the care which Christians should take so to demean themselves as to command the respect of all men.　18. **If it be possible** (*i.e.,* If others will let you), **as much as lieth in you** [τὸ ἐξ ὑμῶν]—'on your part,' or, 'so far as dependeth on you,' **live peaceably** [εἰρηνεύοντες]—or 'keep peace' **with all men.**　The impossibility of this in some cases is hinted at, to keep up the hearts of those who, having done their utmost unsuccessfully to live in peace, might be tempted to think the failure was *necessarily* owing to themselves.　But how emphatically expressed is the injunction to let nothing on our part prevent it!　Would that Christians were guiltless in this respect!　The next precept is evidently suggested by this one.　Peace *is* broken, in spite of all that the Christian has done to preserve it, and wrong *will be* inflicted on him, which he will find it hard to bear.　What then?　19. **Dearly beloved, avenge not yourselves** (see on *v.* 14), **but** [rather] **give place unto wrath** [δότε τόπον τ. ὀργῇ].　Ordinary readers take this to mean, 'give room,' or 'space to wrath' to spend itself; and our translators must have so understood the precept.　But besides that the phrase "give place" suggests rather the sense of 'give scope to' the exercise of, and might seem to imply the stimulating of an enemy's wrath, the following context clearly shows that the "wrath" referred to is *God's* avenging wrath, which, instead of taking into our own hands, we are here enjoined to give room for or await.　So nearly every inter-

preter, ancient and modern, explains the injunction.　20. **Therefore**—or, 'But' (according to a well-supported reading) **if thine enemy hunger, feed him; if he thirst, give him drink.**　This is taken from Prov. xxv. 21, 22, which, without doubt, supplied the basis of those lofty precepts on that subject which form the culminating point of the Sermon on the Mount.　**for in so doing thou shalt heap coals of fire on his head.**　The sense of this clause is much disputed.　In *Jerome's* time, and by the Greek interpreters, it was generally understood in the unfavourable sense of aggravating our enemy's guilt—*q. d.,* 'That will be the most effectual vengeance, as effectual as if you heaped coals of fire on his head.'　And so, among modern interpreters, *Beza, Estius, Grotius, Tholuck, Alford.*　But *Jerome, Augustin,* and other Latin fathers, *Erasmus, Luther, Bengel, Reiche, Tholuck, Meyer, de Wette, Olshausen, Fritzsche, Philippi, Lange, Hodge* (last edition), take the expression in the good sense, in which now it is almost universally quoted—namely, that by returning good for our enemy's evil we may expect at length to subdue and overpower him—as burning coals consume all that is inflammable—into shame and repentance.　And though we formerly judged otherwise, we are now constrained to regard this as the true sense.　The next verse would seem to confirm this.　21. **Be not overcome of evil**—for then you are the conquered party, **but overcome evil with good**—and then the victory is yours; you have subdued your enemy in the noblest sense.

Remarks.—1. Let it never be forgotten that the redeeming mercy of God in Christ is, in the souls of believers, the living spring of all holy obedience (*v.* 1).　2. As redemption under the Gospel is not by the sacrifice of irrational victims, as under the law—when redemption was only in promise, and could only be held forth in type—but "by the precious blood of Christ," by which now "once in the end of the world" sin hath been put completely and for ever away (1 Pet. i. 18, 19; Heb. ix. 26), so all the sacrifices which believers are now called to offer are "living sacrifices;" and summed up, as they all are, in *self-consecration* to the service of God, they are "holy," they are "acceptable unto God," and they together make up 'our rational service.'　In this light, what are we to think of the so-called '*unbloody sacrifice of the mass, continually offered to God as a propitiation for the sins both of the living and the dead,*' which the adherents of Rome's corrupt faith have for ages been taught to believe is the highest and holiest act of Christian worship?　The least that can be said of it is, that it is in flat contradiction to the teaching of this Epistle to the first Christians of Rome.　3. There is no snare against which Christians have more need to be on their guard than that of supposing that they are at liberty to be conformed to the world to any extent short of what is positively sinful.　If nothing else will convince them of this, the gradual sapping

13 LET every soul ^a be subject unto the higher powers. For ^b there is no
2 power but of God: the powers that be are ¹ ordained of God. Whosoever therefore resisteth the power, resisteth the ordinance of God: and
3 they that resist shall receive to themselves damnation. For ^c rulers are
not a terror to good works, but to the evil. Wilt thou then not be
afraid of the power? Do ^d that which is good, and thou shalt have
4 praise of the same: for he is the minister of God to thee for good. But
if thou do that which is evil, be afraid; for he beareth not the sword in
vain: for he is the minister of God, a revenger to *execute* wrath upon
5 him that doeth evil. Wherefore ^e *ye* must needs be subject, not only for
6 wrath, but also for conscience' sake. For, for this cause pay ye tribute

A. D. 60.

CHAP. 13.
^a 1 Cor. 7. 21.
Tit. 3. 1.
^b Pro. 8. 15.
Dan. 2. 21.
Dan. 4. 32.
John 19. 11.
¹ Or,
ordered.
^c 2 Sam. 23. 3.
Ps. 94. 20.
^d 1 Pet. 3. 13.
^e Ec. 1. 8. 2.

and mining of their own spirituality, which inevitably results from such a course, to all who
have ever tasted that the Lord is gracious, cannot
fail to inspire them with the suspicion that all is
not right; and if any tenderness is left to them,
they must sooner or later come to see that, in their
vain attempt to serve two masters, they are reaping the fruit of neither service—laying up for
themselves a store of varied disappointment, and
strewing the pathway of return to their first Husband with thorns and briers. As it is by "the
washing of regeneration and renewing of the Holy
Ghost" that we first come to apprehend, in all its
reality, breadth, and grandeur, "what is the good
and acceptable and perfect will of God," so it is
only by "living in the Spirit," and "walking in the
Spirit"—and so ever afresh "transformed by the
renewing of our mind"—that we are able to discern clearly what is the proper carriage before
the world which Christians should maintain, and
thus steer safely between the extremes of *ascetic
seclusion from it* and *sinful conformity to it.*
4. Self-sufficiency and lust of power are peculiarly
unlovely in the vessels of mercy, whose respective
graces and gifts are all a Divine trust for behoof of
the common body, and of mankind at large. As
forgetfulness of this has been the source of innumerable and unspeakable evils in the Church of
Christ, so the faithful exercise by every Christian
of his own peculiar office and gifts, and the loving
recognition of those of his brethren as all of equal
importance in their own place, would put a new
face upon the visible Church, to the vast benefit
and comfort of Christians themselves, and to the
admiration of the world around them. 5. What
would the world be if it were filled with Christians
having but one object in life, high above every
other—to "serve the Lord"—and throwing into
this service 'alacrity' in the discharge of all
duties, and abiding 'warmth of spirit!' (*v.* 11.)
6. Oh how far is even the living Church from exhibiting the whole character and spirit so beautifully portrayed in the latter verses of this chapter!
(*vv.* 12-21.) What need of a fresh baptism of the
Spirit in order to this! And how "fair as the
moon, clear as the sun, and terrible as an army
with banners," will the Church become, when at
length instinct with this Spirit! The Lord hasten
it in its time!

CHAP. XIII. 1-14.—SAME SUBJECT CONTINUED
—POLITICAL AND SOCIAL RELATIONS—MOTIVES.

In such a state of things as existed at Rome
when the apostle wrote, the Christians there
must often have been perplexed as to the estimate
they were to form, and the duties they owed, to
"the power" that so tyrannically and degradingly
ruled there; especially as the whole fabric of
Roman society heaved with the elements of
insubordination and insurrection, and as the
Jews in particular had, in the days of Claudius,
been banished the capital for their restless and

insurrectionary tendencies (Acts xviii. 2). It
was natural, therefore, to pass from the social to
the political duties of believers; and this accordingly occupies the chief portion of the present
chapter.

*The relation and duties of the Christian to the civil
magistrate* (1-6). 1. Let every man (every man of
you) **be subject unto the higher powers** [ἐξουσίαις
ὑπερεχούσαις] — rather, 'submit himself to the
authorities that are over him.' **For there is no
power** ('authority') **but of God: the powers that
be**—'the existing authorities,' whatever they are,
are ('have been') **ordained of God**—[ἐξουσίαι seems
not genuine. In this case the translation is
'those that be have been ordained,' &c.] 2. **Whosoever therefore resisteth the power**—'So that
he who setteth himself against the authority'
**resisteth the ordinance of God: and they that
resist shall receive to themselves damnation**—
or 'condemnation' (according to the old sense of
the word); that is, not from the magistrate, but
from God, whose authority in the magistrates is
resisted. 3. **For rulers**—according to the true
intent of their office, **are not a terror to good
works, but to the evil**—'to the good work, but
to the evil,' is plainly the true reading [τ. ἀγαθῷ
ἔργῳ—κακῷ]. **Wilt thou then** (have cause to) **not
be afraid of the power?** ('authority.') **Do that
which is good, and thou shalt** ('wilt') **have
praise of the same.** Doubtless, this was written
before Nero had stretched forth his hands against
the Christians; for though, as *Alford* remarks,
this would not have affected the general principles
here taught, it could hardly have failed to modify
the phraseology. 4. **For he is the minister of
God to thee for good. But if thou do that
which is evil, be afraid; for he beareth not the
sword**—the official symbol of the authority to
punish which is inherent in the magistrate's office,
in vain: for he is the minister of God, a revenger
('avenger') **to [execute] wrath upon him that
doeth evil.** 5. **Wherefore ye must needs be
subject** ('submit yourselves'), **not only for** ('because of the') **wrath**—or, for fear of the magistrate's vengeance, **but also for conscience' sake**—
out of conscientious reverence for God's authority.
It is hardly necessary to say that it is of *Magistracy in general*, considered as a Divine ordinance,
that this is spoken: and the statement applies
equally to all forms of government, from an
unchecked despotism—such as flourished when
this was written, under the Emperor Nero—to
a pure democracy. The inalienable right of all
subjects to endeavour to alter or improve the
form of government under which they live is left
untouched here. But since Christians were constantly charged with turning the world upside
down, and since there certainly were elements
enough in Christianity of moral and social revolution to give plausibility to the charge, and
tempt noble spirits, crushed under misgovern-

also: for they are God's ministers, attending continually upon this very
7 thing. Render *ʲ*therefore to all their dues: tribute to whom tribute *is due;* custom to whom custom; *ᵍ*fear to whom fear; honour to whom honour.

8 Owe no man any thing, but to love one another: *ʰ*for he that loveth
9 another hath fulfilled the law. For this, Thou shalt not commit adultery, Thou shalt not kill, Thou shalt not steal, Thou shalt not bear false witness, Thou shalt not covet; and if *there be* any other commandment, it is briefly comprehended in this saying, namely, *ⁱ*Thou shalt love thy
10 neighbour as thyself. Love worketh no ill to his neighbour: therefore love *is* the fulfilling of the law.

11 And that, knowing the time, that now *it is* high time *ʲ*to awake out
12 of sleep: for now *is* our salvation nearer than when we believed. The night is far spent, the day is at hand: let us therefore cast off the works
13 of darkness, and *ᵏ*let us put on the armour of light. Let *ˡ*us walk ²honestly, as in the day; not in rioting and drunkenness, not in cham-
14 bering and wantonness, not *ᵐ*in strife and envying: but *ⁿ*put ye on the

A. D. 60.	
ʲ Luke 20. 25.	
ᵍ Lev. 19. 3.	
1 Sam. 12.	
13.	
Pro. 24. 21.	
Eph. 5. 33.	
Eph. 6. 5.	
ʰ Matt. 7. 12.	
ⁱ Lev. 19. 18.	
Matt 22.39.	
Luke 10. 27.	
Gal. 5. 14.	
ʲ 1 Cor 15.34.	
ᵏ Eph. 6. 13.	
ˡ Phil. 4. 8.	
2 Or.	
decently.	
ᵐ Gal. 5. 15,	
21, 26.	
Jas. 3. 14.	
ⁿ Gal. 3. 27.	

ment, to take redress into their own hands, it was of special importance that the pacific, submissive, loyal spirit of those Christians who resided at the great seat of political power should furnish a visible refutation of this charge. **6. For, for this** cause **ye pay tribute also**—or, 'ye pay.' Critics differ as to whether this is a counsel to pay, or a statement of the fact that they did pay:—*q. d.*, 'This is the reason why ye pay the contributions requisite for maintaining the civil government,' **for they are God's ministers, attending continually upon** (or 'to') **this very thing.**

From magistrates the apostle now comes to other officials, and from them to men related to us by whatever tie.

Civil duties in general (7). **7. Render therefore to all their dues: tribute** [τ. φόρον = κῆνσον]—the poll-tax and land-tax (see on Matt. xvii. 25), **to whom tribute is due; custom** [τὸ τέλος]—export and import duty, **to whom custom; fear**—reverence for superiors, **to whom fear; honour**—the respect due to persons of distinction, **to whom honour.**

The all-comprehensive relative duty—love (8-10). **8. Owe no man any thing, but to love one another.** Love is the only debt which can never be paid off, for it is always due: **for he that loveth another** [τὸν ἕτερον—*lit.*, 'the other,' in relation to himself; his "neighbour" (as *v.* 9; Luke x. 29, 36), **hath fulfilled the law**—for the law itself is nothing but an injunction to manifest love in all relationships and all circumstances. **9. For this** (commandment), **Thou shalt not commit adultery, (and this) Thou shalt not kill, (and this) Thou shalt not steal, (and this) [Thou shalt not bear false witness].** This clause—to complete the supposed intention of the apostle to quote the four last precepts of the Decalogue—has but slight external support [but one uncial—א—; numerous cursives; the printed Vulgate, but not the best MSS. of it; the Philox. Syriac and Memphitic versions: on the other hand, it is wanting in A B (C is defective here) D E F G (K is defective here) L; several cursives; the Old Latin and best copies of the Vulgate, the Peshito Syriac, and the Hebrew versions, with several Greek fathers. As to internal evidence, it was much more likely to be added to the genuine text than to be lost out of it], **(and this) Thou shalt not covet; and if there be any other commandment**—which is equivalent to saying, 'And whatever other commandment

there is;' for the apostle did not mean to express any doubt of there being other commandments, but to excuse himself from quoting any more, for the reason about to be given. **it is briefly comprehended** ('it is headed up') **in this saying,** namely, **Thou shalt love thy neighbour as thyself.** The apostle here confines himself to the second table of the law, because it is relative duties he is treating of. **10. Love worketh no ill to his (or 'one's') neighbour: therefore love is the fulfilling of the law.** As love, from its very nature, studies and delights to please its object, its very existence is an effectual security against our wilfully injuring him. Now follow some

General motives to the faithful discharge of all these duties (11-14). **11. And that** [Καὶ τοῦτο]—rather, 'And this' [do], **knowing the time** ('season')—"these last days" (Heb. i. 2), "the end of the world" (Heb. ix. 26); that is, the final economy of grace, before the second coming of Christ, **that now it is high time** [ὥρα ἤδη]—'that now is the hour' for us **to awake out of sleep**—of stupid, fatal indifference to eternal things: **for now is our salvation**—'the salvation,' or simply 'salvation' (in the sense of ch. v. 9, 10; viii. 24). **nearer than when we (first) believed.** This is in the line of all our Lord's teaching, which represents the decisive day of Christ's second appearing as at hand, to keep believers ever in the attitude of wakeful expectancy, but without reference to the *chronological* nearness or distance of that event. **12. The night (of evil) is far spent, the day** (of consummated triumph over it) **is at hand: let us therefore cast off (as a** worn-out dress) **the works of darkness**—all works holding of the kingdom and period of darkness, with which, as followers of the risen Saviour, our connection has been dissolved, **and let us put on the armour of light**—the armour which befits "the children of the light," described at large in Eph. vi. 11-18: see also 1 Thess. v. 8. **13. Let us walk honestly** [εὐσχημόνως]—'becomingly,' 'decorously,' **as in the day**—*q. d.*, 'Men choose the night for their revels, but our night is past, for we are all the children of the light and of the day (1 Thess. v. 5): let us therefore only do what is fit to be exposed to the light of such a day.' **not in rioting and drunkenness**—varied forms of intemperance; denoting revels in general, usually ending in intoxication; **not in chambering and wantonness**—varied forms of impurity; the one pointing to definite acts, the other more general; **not in strife and envying**

Lord Jesus Christ, and °make not provision for the flesh, to *fulfil* the lusts *thereof.*

14 HIM that ^ais weak in the faith receive ye, *but* ¹not to doubtful dis-
2 putations. For one believeth that he ^bmay eat all things: another, who
3 is weak, eateth herbs. Let not him that eateth despise him that eateth
not; and ^clet not him which eateth not judge him that eateth: for God
4 hath received him. Who ^dart thou that judgest another man's servant?
to his own master he standeth or falleth. Yea, he shall be holden up;
for God is able to make him stand.
5 One ^eman esteemeth one day above another: another esteemeth every
6 day *alike.* Let every man be ²fully persuaded in his own mind. He
that ³regardeth the day, regardeth *it* unto the Lord; and he that
regardeth not the day, to the Lord he doth not regard *it.* He that
eateth, eateth to the Lord, for ^fhe giveth God thanks; and he that

A. D. 60.
° Gal. 5. 16.
CHAP. 14.
^a 1 Cor. 8. 9.
1 Or, not to judge his doubtful thoughts.
^b 1 Cor.10.25.
^c Col. 2. 16.
^d Jas. 4. 12.
^e Gal. 4. 10.
2 Or, fully assured.
³ Or, observeth.
^f 1 Cor. 10.31.
1 Tim. 4. 3.

—varied forms of that venomous feeling between man and man which reverses the law of love. **14. But**—to sum up all in one word, **put ye on the Lord Jesus Christ**—in such wise that Christ only may be seen in you (see 2 Cor. iii. 3; Gal. iii. 27; Eph. iv. 24; **and make not provision** [προνοιαν μὴ ποιεῖσθε]—'take not forethought,' **to [fulfil] the lusts** [thereof]:— *q. d.,* 'Direct none of your attention to the cravings of your corrupt nature, how you may provide for their gratification.'

Remarks.—1. How gloriously adapted is Christianity for human society in all conditions! As it makes war directly against no specific forms of government, so it directly recommends none. While its holy and benign principles secure the ultimate abolition of all iniquitous government, the reverence which it teaches for magistracy, under whatever form, as a Divine institution, secures the loyalty and peaceableness of its disciples amid all the turbulence and distractions of civil society, and makes it the highest interest of all States to welcome it within their pale, as in this, as well as every other sense, 'the salt of the earth, the light of the world.' 2. Christianity is the grand specific for the purification and elevation of all the social relations—inspiring a readiness to discharge all obligations, and, most of all, implanting in its disciples that love which secures all men against injury from them, inasmuch as it is the fulfilling of the law. 3. How should the rapid march of the kingdom of God, the advanced stage of it at which we have arrived, and the ever-nearing approach of the perfect day—nearer to every believer the longer he lives — quicken all the children of light to redeem the time, and, seeing that they look for such things, to be diligent that they may be found of Him in peace, without spot, and blameless! (2 Pet. iii. 14.) 4. In virtue of 'the expulsive power of a new and more powerful affection,' the great secret of persevering holiness in all manner of conversation will be found to be "Christ IN US, the hope of glory" (Col. 1. 27), and Christ ON US, as the character in which alone we shall be able to shine before men (2 Cor. iii. 3).

CHAP. XIV. 1-23.—SAME SUBJECT CONTINUED —CHRISTIAN FORBEARANCE.

The subject here—and on to ch. xv. 13—*is the consideration due from stronger Christians to their weaker brethren* (with special reference to the Jewish peculiarities), which is but the great law of love (treated of in ch. xiii.) in one particular form.

1. Him that is weak in the faith—rather, 'in **faith**;' that is, not 'Him that is weak in the truth believed' (as *Calvin, Beza, Alford, Webster*

and Wilkinson), but 'Him whose faith wants that firmness and breadth which would raise him above small scruples.' (So *Erasmus, Grotius, Estius, Fritzsche, Meyer, de Wette, Tholuck,* &c.) **receive ye**—to cordial Christian fellowship, [but] **not to doubtful disputations** [εἰς διακρίσεις διαλογισμῶν]—rather, perhaps, 'not to the deciding of doubts, or scruples;' *i. e.,* not for the purpose of arguing him out of them, which indeed usually does the reverse; whereas to receive him to full brotherly confidence and cordial interchange of Christian affection is the most effectual way of drawing them off. Two examples of such scruples are here specified, touching Jewish *meats* and *days.* 'The strong,' it will be observed, are those who held these to be abolished under the Gospel; 'the weak' are those who had scruples on this point.

Meats (2-4). **2. [For]** (this supplement is superfluous) **one believeth that he may eat all things** —having learned the lesson taught to Peter (Acts x. 9-16, 28). **another, who is weak, eateth herbs** —restricting himself probably to a vegetable diet, for fear of eating what might have been offered to idols, and so would be unclean, (see 1 Cor. viii.) **3. Let not him that eateth despise him that eateth not; and let not him which eateth not judge** (sit censoriously in judgment upon) **him that eateth: for God hath received him**—as one of His dear children, who in this matter acts not from laxity, but religious principle. **4. Who art thou that judgest another man's** (rather, 'another's') **servant?**—*i. e.,* CHRIST'S, as the whole context shows, especially *vv.* 8, 9. **to his own master he standeth or falleth. Yea, he shall be holden up** [σταθήσεται δὲ]—'But stand he shall,' **for God**—or 'the Lord' (according to what is probably the true reading), that is, his Master, Christ, **is able to make him stand**—able to make good his standing; meaning, not at the day of judgment (of which the apostle comes to treat in *v.* 10), but here, in the true fellowship of the Church, in spite of thy censures.

Days (5). **5. One man esteemeth one day above another: another esteemeth every day.** The supplement "alike" here injures the sense. **Let every man be fully persuaded in his own mind** —or be guided in such matters by conscientious conviction.

The principle to be regarded in both cases (6). **6. He that regardeth the day, regardeth it unto the Lord**—the Lord CHRIST, as before; **and he that regardeth not the day, to the Lord he doth not regard it**—each doing what he believes to be his Lord's will. **He that eateth, eateth to the Lord, for he giveth God thanks; and he that**

7 eateth not, to the Lord he eateth not, and giveth God thanks. For
8 [g]none of us liveth to himself, and no man dieth to himself. For whether we live, we live unto the Lord; and whether we die, we die unto the Lord: whether we live therefore, or die, we are the Lord's.
9 For [h] to this end Christ both died, and rose, and revived, that he might be [i] Lord both of the dead and living.
10   But why dost thou judge thy brother? or why dost thou set at nought thy brother? for [j] we shall all stand before the judgment seat of Christ.
11 For it is written, [k] *As* I live, saith the Lord, every knee shall bow to me,
12 and every tongue shall confess to God. So then [l] every one of us shall give account of himself to God.

A. D. 60.

[g] 1 Cor. 6. 19,
Gal. 2. 20,
[h] Isa. 53. 10-
·12.
Luke 21.26,
2 Cor. 5. 15.
[i] Acts 10. 36,
Phil. 2. 10,
11.
[j] Matt. 25.31,
Jude 14, 15,
[k] Isa. 45. 23,
[l] Matt. 12.36.

eateth not, to the Lord he eateth not, and giveth God thanks. The one gave thanks to God for the flesh which the other scrupled to use—the other did the same for the herbs to which, for conscience' sake, he restricted himself. (The bearing of these statements upon the *perpetuity of the Sabbath* we reserve for the *Remarks* at the close of this chapter.)

The general principles—Individual responsibility to Christ (7-12). **7. For none of us liveth to himself** (see on 2 Cor. v. 14, 15)—to dispose of himself or shape his conduct after his own ideas and inclinations; **and no man** ('no one' of us Christians) **dieth to himself. 8. For whether we live, we live unto the Lord**—the Lord Christ; see next verse; **and whether we die, we die unto the Lord: whether we live therefore, or die, we are the Lord's.** Nothing but the most vapid explanation of these remarkable words could make them endurable to any Christian ear, if Christ were *a mere creature.* For Christ is here—in the most emphatic terms, and yet in the most unimpassioned tone—held up as the supreme Object of the Christian's life, and of his death too; and that by the man whose horror of creature-worship was such, that when the poor Lycaonians would have worshipped himself, he rushed forth to arrest the deed, directing them to "the living God" as the only legitimate Object of worship (Acts xiv. 15). Nor does Paul *teach* this here, but rather *appeals* to it as a known and recognized fact of which he had only to remind his readers. And since the apostle, when he wrote these words, had never been at Rome, he could only know that the Roman Christians would assent to this view of Christ, because it was *the common teaching of all the accredited preachers of Christianity, and the common faith of all Christians.* **9. For to this end Christ [both] died, [and rose], and revived**—'and lived;' that is, lived again (according to the bettér reading). The bracketed word "both" [και], and the clause,"and revived" [και ἀνέστη], are certainly an addition to the genuine text [και is found only in C*** (a corrector of about the ninth century), D (about the seventh), L, several cursives, the Vulgate (cod. Amiat.), the Philoxenian Syriac and some Greek fathers; but is wanting in א A B C * D * (and ***), E F G, numerous cursives, two copies of the Old Latin, and the Vulgate (except cod. Amiat.), and several Greek fathers. και ἀνέστη is found in no Uncial MS., and only in some cursives.] **that he might be Lord both of the dead and** ('of the') **living.** The grand object of His death was to *acquire* this absolute Lordship over His redeemed, both in their living and in their dying, as His of right. But why this novel idea here of Christ being *Lord over the dead?* Does it not seem to contradict what our Lord says, that God is *not* the God *of the dead,* but of the living? (Matt. xxii. 32.) And even if not, what here suggested it to the

apostle's mind? The true answer to these questions is finely given by *Bengel* in the following passage:—'The living and reviving triumph with the living Goel. The living God is God of the living (Matt. xxii. 32). The revived Christ is Lord of the reviving. In *vv.* 7. 8 Paul places this "life" *before* "death;" and as he advances in *v.* 9, places that "life" *after* "death," as in ch. viii. 38 (cf. *v.* 34). "Christ," says he, "died that He might acquire dominion over the dead;" "Christ revived, that He might acquire dominion over the living." Christ "has died;" therefore "death" (the act, or rather the passive experience of dying, and the state of death) shall not tear us from Him. Christ "is risen;" therefore "life" (in the world to come) shall not tear us from Him. The dominion of Christ over the dead (the author adds) refutes the *psycho-pannychia* (or *the sleep of the soul* between death and the resurrection), against which, indeed, the appearance of Moses and Elias (Matt. xvii. 3), the resurrection of the saints (Matt. xxvii. 52, &c.), and the hope of Paul, &c. (Phil. i. 23; 2 Cor. v. 8; Heb. xii.23), constitute solid arguments'—and so on.

10. But why, &c. The original here is more lively: 'But thou (the weaker believer), why judgest thou thy brother? And thou again (the stronger), why despisest thou thy brother?' **for we shall all** (the strong and the weak together) **stand before the judgment seat of Christ**—'the judgment seat of God' is beyond all doubt the true reading here. It would have been more natural to have written (as in 2 Cor. v. 10), the judgment seat of *Christ,* as the whole preceding context shows that this was what was in the apostle's mind (and hence, doubtless, the reading of the received text). Why, then, did he *not* so write? Evidently to accommodate his statement to the quotation which was to follow, and the inference which he was to draw from it in the following verse: **11. For it is written** (Isa. xlv. 23), **As I live, saith the Lord** (*Hebrew,* JEHOVAH), **every knee shall bow to me, and every tongue shall confess to God.** The passage, as it stands in the prophet, has no immediate reference to any 'day of judgment,' but is a prediction of the ultimate subjugation to the true God (in Christ) of every soul of man; but this of course implies that they shall bow to the award of God upon their character and actions. **12. So then** (infers the apostle) **every one of us shall give account of himself to God.** Now, if it be remembered that all this is adduced quite incidentally, to show that CHRIST is the absolute Master of all Christians, to rule their judgments and feelings towards each other while "living," and to dispose of them 'dying,' the testimony which it bears to the absolute Divinity of Christ will appear remarkable. On any other view, the quotation to show that we shall all stand before the judgment seat of *God* would be a strange proof that Christians are all amenable to *Christ.*

13 Let us not therefore judge one another any more: but judge this
rather, that ^mno man put a stumblingblock, or an occasion to fall, in *his*
14 brother's way. I know, and am persuaded by the Lord Jesus, ⁿthat
there is nothing ⁴unclean of itself: but ^oto him that esteemeth any thing
15 to be ⁵unclean, to him *it is* unclean. But if thy brother be grieved with
thy meat, now walkest thou not ⁶charitably. Destroy not him with thy
16 meat for whom Christ died. Let ^pnot then your good be evil spoken of:
17 For ^qthe kingdom of God is not meat and drink; but righteousness, and
peace, and joy in the Holy Ghost.
18 For he that in these things serveth Christ ^ris acceptable to God, and
19 approved of men. Let ^sus therefore follow after the things which make
20 for peace, and things wherewith ^tone may edify another. For meat
destroy not the work of God. All ^uthings indeed *are* pure; but *it is*
21 evil for that man who eateth with offence. *It is* good neither to eat
flesh, nor to drink wine, nor *any thing* whereby thy brother stumbleth,

A. D. 60.
^m1 Cor. 8. 9.
1 Cor. 10.23,
24.
ⁿ Acts 10. 14
15.
Tit. i. 15.
⁴ common.
^o 1 Cor. 8. 7.
⁵ common
⁶ according
to charity.
^p ch. 12. 17.
^q 1 Cor. 8. 8.
^r 2 Cor. 8. 21.
^s Ps. 34. 14.
ch. 12. 18.
^t 1 Cor. 14.12.
^u Acts 10. 15.

Subject of Christian forbearance resumed (13-23).
13. Let us not therefore judge ('assume the office
of judge over') **one another any more: but judge
this rather, that no man put a stumblingblock,
or an occasion to fall, in his brother's way**—a
beautiful sort of play upon the word 'judge,'
meaning, 'But let this be your judgment, not to
put a stumblingblock,' &c. **14. I know, and am
persuaded by** (or rather, 'in') **the Lord Jesus**—
as "having the mind of Christ" (1 Cor. ii. 16),
that there is nothing unclean of itself. Hence
it is that he calls those "the strong" who believed
in the abolition of all ritual distinctions under
the Gospel (see Acts x. 15): **but [εἰ μή]**—'save
that' to him that esteemeth any thing to be
unclean, to him it is unclean:—*q. d.,* 'and therefore, though *you* can eat of it without sin, he
cannot.' **15. But if thy brother be grieved** (has
his weak conscience hurt) **with [thy] meat [διὰ
βρῶμα]**—rather, 'because of meat.' The word
"meat" is purposely selected as something contemptible, in contrast with the tremendous risk
run for its sake. Accordingly, in the next clause,
that idea is brought out with great strength:
**Destroy not him with (' by') thy meat for whom
Christ died.** The worth (as *Olshausen* says) of
even the poorest and weakest brother cannot be
more emphatically expressed than by the words,
"for whom Christ died." The same sentiment
is expressed with equal sharpness in 1 Cor. viii. 11.
*Whatever tends to make any one violate his conscience
tends to the destruction of his soul; and he who
helps, whether wittingly or no, to bring about the one
is guilty of aiding to accomplish the other.* **16. Let
not then your good**—*i. e.,* this liberty of yours as
to Jewish meats and days, well founded though
it be, **be evil spoken of**—by reason of the
evil it does to others. **17. For the kingdom
of God**—or, as we should say, Religion; *i. e.,*
the proper business and blessedness for which
Christians are formed into a community of
renewed men in thorough subjection to God (cf.
1 Cor. iv. 20), **is not meat and drink [βρῶσις
καὶ πόσις]**—'eating and drinking,' **but righteousness, and peace, and joy in the Holy Ghost**—
a beautiful and comprehensive division of living
Christianity. The first—"righteousness"—has
respect to *God*, denoting here 'rectitude,' in its
widest sense (as in Matt. vi. 33); the second—
"peace"—has respect to *our neighbours*, denoting
'concord' among brethren (as is plain from *v.* 19:
cf. Eph. iv. 3; Col. 14, 15); the third—"joy in
the Holy Ghost"—has respect to *ourselves.* This
phrase, "joy in the Holy Ghost," represents
Christians as so thinking and feeling, under the
workings of the Holy Ghost, that their joy may
be viewed rather as that of the blessed Agent
who inspires it than their own. (See on ch. viii.
15; on Gal. v. 25; and on Jude 20.)
18. For he that in these things—'in this' is
the true reading; meaning, in this threefold life,
serveth Christ. Observe here again how, though
we do these three things as a "kingdom of *God*,"
yet it is "*Christ*" that we serve in so doing;
the apostle passing here from God to Christ as
naturally as before from Christ to God—in a way
inconceivable, if Christ had been viewed as a
mere creature (cf. 2 Cor. viii. 21). **is acceptable
to God, and approved of men**—for these are
the things which God delights in, and men are
constrained to approve (compare Prov. iii. 4;
Luke ii. 52; Acts ii. 47; xix. 20). **19. Let us
therefore follow after the things which make
for peace, and things wherewith one may edify
another**—more simply, 'the things of peace, and
the things of mutual edification.' **20. For** (' For
the sake of') **meat destroy not the work of God**
—see on *v.* 15. The apostle sees in whatever tends
to violate a brother's conscience the *incipient*
destruction of God's work (for every converted
man is such)—on the same principle as "he that
hateth his brother is a murderer" (1 John iii. 15).
All things indeed are pure—'clean;' the ritual
distinctions being at an end; **but it is evil for
that man** (there is criminality in the man) **who
eateth with offence** — *i. e.,* so as to stumble a
weak brother. **21 It is good neither to eat flesh,
nor to drink wine, nor [any thing]** ('nor to do any
thing') **whereby** (' wherein') **thy brother stumbleth, or is offended, or is made weak**—rather,
'is weak.' These three words, it has been remarked, are each intentionally weaker than the
other:—*q. d.,* 'Which may cause a brother to
stumble, or even be obstructed in his Christian
course; nay—though neither of these may follow
—wherein he continues weak; unable wholly to
disregard the example, and yet unprepared to
follow it.' But this injunction to abstain from
flesh, from *wine,* and from *whatsoever* may hurt
the conscience of a brother, must be properly
understood. Manifestly, the apostle is treating
of the regulation of the Christian's conduct with
reference simply to the prejudices of the weak in
faith; and his directions are to be considered not
as *prescriptions for one's entire life-time,* even to
promote the good of men on a large scale, but
simply as cautions against the too free use of
Christian liberty in matters where other Christians,
through weakness, are not persuaded that such
liberty is Divinely allowed. How far the *principle*
involved in this may be legitimately extended, we
do not inquire here; but ere we consider that ques-

22 or is offended, or is made weak.　Hast thou faith? have *it* to thyself
before God.　Happy *is* he that condemneth not himself in that thing
23 which he alloweth.　And he that [7]doubteth is damned if he eat, because
he eateth not of faith: for whatsoever [v]*is* not of faith is sin.

A. D. 60.

[7] Or,
staggers.
ch. 4. 20.
[v] Tit. 1. 15.

tion, it is of great importance to fix how far it is here actually expressed, and what is the precise nature of the illustrations given of it.　**22. Hast thou faith?**—on such matters: **have it to thyself** (within thine own breast) **before God**—a most important clause.　It is not mere *sincerity*, or a private *opinion*, of which the apostle speaks: it is conviction as to what is the truth and will of God.　If thou hast formed this conviction in the sight of God, keep thyself in this frame before Him.　Of course, this is not to be over-pressed, as if it were wrong to discuss such points at all with our weaker brethren.　All that is here condemned is such a zeal for small points as endangers Christian love.　**Happy is he that condemneth not himself in that thing which he alloweth**—allows himself to do nothing, about the lawfulness of which he has scruples; does only what he neither knows nor fears to be sinful.　**23. And** (rather, 'But') **he that doubteth is damned** (see on the word "damnation," ch. xiii. .2) **if he eat, because** [he eateth] **not** of faith (on the meaning of "faith" here, see on *v.* 22): **for whatsoever is not of faith is sin**—a maxim of unspeakable importance in the Christian life.

Remarks.—1. Whatever rigid sticklers for the necessity of orthodoxy on every truth of the Bible and every point of the Christian Faith may say, nothing can be clearer from this chapter than that some points in Christianity are unessential to Christian fellowship; so that, though one may be in error upon them, he is not on that account to be excluded either from the communion of the Church or from the full confidence of those who have more light.　Those, therefore, who—affecting more than ordinary zeal for the honour and truth of God—deny the validity of this distinction between essential and non-essential truths must settle the question, not with us, but with the apostle.　2. Acceptance with God is the only proper criterion of right to Christian fellowship.　Whom God receives, men cannot lawfully reject (*vv.* 3, 4).　3. As there is much self-pleasing in setting up narrow standards of Christian fellowship, so one of the best preservatives against the temptation to do this will be found in the continual remembrance that CHRIST is the one Object for whom all Christians live, and to whom all Christians die: this will be such a living and exalted bond of union between the strong and the weak as will overshadow all their lesser differences and gradually absorb them (*vv.* 7-9).　4. From what is said in *v.* 5 about the observance of days, *Alford* judges it impossible that sabbatical obligation to keep any day, whether seventh or first, was recognized in apostolic times.　But this is precarious ground.　Were it not as legitimate to argue that our Lord could never have said, "The sabbath was made for *man*, and not man for the sabbath," and that "The Son of Man is Lord even of the sabbath day" (Mark ii. 27, 28: see on Matt. xii. 1-8, p. 70), if it was so speedily to vanish away, as if His lordship over it consisted only in His right to abolish it.　Neither of these ways of settling the question of 'the perpetuity of a day of holy rest' will satisfy the thorough inquirer, who will think it his duty to look at *all* sides of the subject; and whoever considers how inadequate any considerations of mere expediency must prove—when once the belief in its essential sacredness is destroyed—to uphold that observance of the

Lord's Day which all devout minds regard as essential to the best interests of religion and morality, will be slow to think that the apostle meant the Sabbath to be ranked by his readers amongst those vanished Jewish festival days which only "weakness" could imagine to be still in force—a weakness which those who had more light ought, out of love merely, to bear with.　5. The consideration of the common Judgment seat at which the strong and the weak shall stand together will be found another preservative against the unlovely disposition to sit in judgment one on another (*vv.* 10-12).　6. How brightly does the supreme Divinity of Christ shine out in this chapter!　The exposition itself supersedes further illustration here.　7. Though forbearance is a great Christian duty, indifference to the distinction between truth and error is not thereby encouraged.　The former is, by the lax, made an excuse for the latter.　But our apostle, while teaching 'the strong' to bear with the "weak," repeatedly intimates in this chapter where the truth really lay on the points in question, and takes care to call those who took the wrong side the "weak."　8. With what holy jealousy ought the purity of the conscience to be guarded, since every deliberate violation of it is incipient perdition! (*vv.* 15, 20.)　Some, who seem to be more jealous for the honour of certain doctrines than for the souls of men, enervate this terrific truth by asking how it bears upon the 'Perseverance of the saints;' the advocates of that doctrine thinking it necessary to explain away what is meant by "destroying the work of God" (*v.* 20), and by "destroying him for whom Christ died" (*v.* 15), for fear of the doctrinal consequences of taking it nakedly; while the opponents of that doctrine are ready to ask, How could the apostle have used such language if he had believed that such a catastrophe was impossible?　The true answer to both lies in dismissing the question as impertinent.　The apostle is enunciating a great and eternal principle in Christian ethics—that *the wilful violation of conscience contains within itself a seed of destruction;* or, to express it otherwise, that the total destruction of the work of God in the renewed soul, and, consequently, the loss of that soul for eternity, needs only the carrying out to its full effect of such violation of the conscience.　Whether such effects *do* take place, in point of fact, the apostle gives not the most distant hint here; and therefore that point must be settled elsewhere.　But, beyond all doubt, as the position we have laid down is emphatically expressed by the apostle, so the interests of all who call themselves Christians require it to be proclaimed and pressed on every suitable occasion.　9. Zeal for comparatively small points of truth in a poor substitute for the substantial and catholic and abiding realities of the Christian life (*vv.* 17, 18).　10. "Peace" amongst the followers of Christ is a blessing too precious to themselves, and, as a testimony to them that are without, too important to be ruptured for trifles, even though some lesser truths be involved in these (*vv.* 19, 20).　Nor are those truths themselves disparaged or endangered thereby, but the reverse.　11. Many things which are lawful are not expedient.　In the use of any liberty, therefore, our question should be, not simply, Is this lawful? but even if so, Can it be used with safety to a brother's conscience?

15 WE [a] then that are strong ought to bear the [b]infirmities of the weak,
2 and not to please ourselves. Let [c] every one of us please *his* neighbour
3 for *his* good [d] to edification. For even Christ pleased not himself; but,
as it is written, [e] The reproaches of them that reproached thee fell on me.
4 For [f] whatsoever things were written aforetime were written for our
learning; that we through patience and comfort of the Scriptures might
5 have hope. Now [g] the God of patience and consolation grant you to be
6 like minded one toward another [1] according to Christ Jesus; that ye may
with one mind *and* one mouth glorify God, even the Father of our Lord
Jesus Christ.
7 Wherefore receive ye one another, [h] as Christ also received us, to the
8 glory of God. Now I say that [i] Jesus Christ was a minister of the circumcision for the truth of God, [j] to confirm the promises *made* unto the
9 fathers: and [k] that the Gentiles might glorify God for *his* mercy; as it is
written, [l] For this cause I will confess to thee among the Gentiles, and
10 sing unto thy name. And again he saith, [m] Rejoice, ye Gentiles, with

A. D. 60.

CHAP. 15.
a Gal. 6. 1.
b ch. 14. 1.
c 1 Cor. 9. 19.
Phil. 2. 4. 5.
d ch. 14. 19.
e Ps. 69. 9.
f 2 Tim. 3.16.
g 1 Cor. 1. 10.
1 Pet. 3. 2).
1 Or. after
the ex-
ample of.
h ch. 5. 2.
i Matt. 15.2l.
John 1. 11.
j 2 Cor. 1. 20.
k John 10. 16.
l Ps. 18. 49.
m Deut.32.43.

How will it affect my brother's soul? (*v.* 21.) It is permitted to no Christian to say, with Cain, "Am I my brother's keeper?" (Gen. iv. 9.) 12. Whenever we are in doubt as to a point of duty—where abstinence is manifestly sinless, but compliance not clearly lawful—the safe course is ever to be preferred, for to do otherwise is itself sinful. 13. How exalted and beautiful is the Ethics of Christianity—by a few great principles teaching us how to steer our course amidst practical difficulties, with equal regard to Christian liberty, love, and confidence!

CHAP. XV. 1-13.—SAME SUBJECT CONTINUED AND CONCLUDED.

1. We then that are strong—on such points as have been discussed, the abolition of the Jewish distinction of meats and days under the Gospel (see on ch. xiv. 14, 20), **ought to bear the infirmities of the weak, and not to please ourselves** —ought to think less of what we may lawfully do, than of how our conduct will affect others. **2.** Let every one of us. [The γὰρ of the received text after Ἕκαστος has hardly any support, is quite out of place, and is properly disregarded in our version.] please—that is, lay himself out to please, his neighbour (not indeed for his mere gratification, but) for his good (with a view) to (his) edification. **3.** For even Christ pleased not (lived not to please) himself; but, as it is written (Ps. lxix. 9), The reproaches of them that reproached thee fell on me—(see on Mark x. 42-45, p. 181.) **4.** For whatsoever things were written aforetime were written for our learning ('instruction'); that we through patience and comfort of the Scriptures ('through the comfort and the patience of the Scriptures'), might have hope:—*q. d.*, 'Think not that because such portions of Scripture relate immediately to Christ, they are inapplicable to you; for though Christ's sufferings, as a Saviour, were exclusively His own, the *motives* that prompted them, the *spirit* in which they were endured, and the *general principle* involved in His whole work—self-sacrifice for the good of others—furnish our most perfect and beautiful model; and so all Scripture relating to these is for our instruction. And since the duty of *forbearance*, the strong with the weak, requires "patience," and this again needs "comfort," all those Scriptures which tell of *patience* and *consolation*, particularly of the patience of Christ, and of the consolation which sustained Him under it, are our appointed and appropriate nutriment, ministering to us "*hope*" of that blessed day when these shall no more be needed.' (See on ch. iv., Remark 7, at the close.) For

the same connection between "patience" and "hope," see on ch. xii. 12, and on 1 Thess. i. 3. **5.** Now the God of patience and consolation. Such beautiful names of God are taken from the graces which He inspires: as "the God of hope" (*v.* 13), "the God of peace" (*v.* 33), &c. grant you to be like minded [τὸ αὐτὸ φρονεῖν]—'of the same mind,' according to Christ Jesus. It is not mere unanimity which the apostle seeks for them; for unanimity may be in evil, which is to be deprecated. But it is "*according to Christ Jesus*"—after the sublimest model of Him whose all-absorbing desire was to do, 'not His own will, but the will of Him that sent Him' (John vi. 38). **6.** That ye may with one mind and one mouth glorify God, even the Father of our Lord Jesus Christ—rather, 'that with one accord ye may with one mouth glorify the God and Father of our Lord Jesus Christ,' the mind and the mouth of all giving harmonious glory to His name. What a prayer! And shall this never be realized on earth?

7. Wherefore—Returning to the point, **receive ye one another, as Christ also received us**— 'received you' is clearly the true reading, **to the glory of God.** If Christ received us, and bears with all our weaknesses, well may we receive and compassionate one another; and by so doing God will be glorified. **8.** Now—'For' is certainly the true reading: the apostle is merely assigning an additional motive to Christian forbearance: **I say that Jesus Christ was** [γεγενῆσθαι]—'has become,' **a minister of the circumcision**—a remarkable expression, meaning 'the Father's Servant for the salvation of the circumcision (or, of Israel)' **for the truth of God**—to make good the veracity of God towards His ancient people; **to confirm the** (Messianic) **promises made unto the fathers.** In order to cheer the Jewish believers, whom he might seem to have been disparaging, and to keep down Gentile pride, the apostle holds up Israel's salvation as the primary end of Christ's mission. But next, after this, Christ was sent to the Gentiles. **9. And that the Gentiles might glorify God for his mercy.** A number of quotations from the Old Testament here follow, to show that God's plan of mercy embraced, from the first, the Gentiles along with the Jews. **as it is written** (Ps. xviii. 49), **For this cause I will confess to thee among the Gentiles, and sing unto thy name. 10. And again he saith**—or 'it saith' (Deut. xxxii. 43), **Rejoice, ye Gentiles,** (along) **with his people** (Israel). This is according to the LXX. (The absence of "with" in the Hebrew might suggest another sense, but the context confirms that here

11 his people. And again, [n] Praise the Lord, all ye Gentiles; and laud
12 him, all ye people. And again, Esaias saith, [o] There shall be a root
of Jesse, and he that shall rise to reign over the Gentiles; in him
13 shall the Gentiles trust. Now the God of hope fill you with all joy
and peace in believing, that ye may abound in hope, through the power
of the Holy Ghost.
14 And [p] I myself also am persuaded of you, my brethren, that ye also
are full of goodness, [q] filled with all knowledge, able also to admonish one
15 another. Nevertheless, brethren, I have written the more boldly unto
you in some sort, as putting you in mind, because [r] of the grace that is
16 given to me of God, that [s] I should be the minister of Jesus Christ to the

A. D. 60.

[n] Ps. 117. 1.
[o] Isa. 9. 6, 7.
Isa. 11. 1.
Rev. 5. 5.
Rev. 22. 16.
[p] 2 Pet. 1. 12.
1 John 2.
21.
[q] 1 Cor. 8. 1.
[r] Gal. 1. 15.
[s] Gal. 2. 7,
9.
1 Tim. 2. 7.

given. **11. And again** (Ps. cxvii. 1), **Praise the Lord, all ye Gentiles; and laud him, all ye people** [כָּל־הָאֻמִּים]—'all the peoples;' that is, the various nations outside the pale of Judaism. **12. And again, Esaias saith** (ch. xi. 10), **There shall be a root** [ἡ ῥίζα]—'the root' **of Jesse** —meaning, not 'the root from which Jesse sprang,' but 'the root that is sprung from Jesse' (that is, from Jesse's son, David: see Rev. xxii. 16). **and he that shall rise to reign over the Gentiles; in him shall the Gentiles trust.** So the LXX. (in substantial, though not verbal, agreement with the original). **13. Now, &c.** This seems a closing prayer, suggested not so much by the immediately preceding context, as by the whole subject-matter of the Epistle thus far. **the God of hope** (see on *v.* 5) **fill you with all joy and peace in believing, that ye may abound in hope.** As *peace* and *joy* are the native fruits of *faith* (ch. v. 1, 2, 11; Gal. v. 22), so *hope* of the glory of God necessarily accompanies or flows from all three, especially faith, the root of the whole. Hence, the degree in which one of these is possessed will be the measure in which all are experienced. When 'the God of hope *fills* us with *all* joy and peace in believing,' we cannot but "*abound* in hope," **through the power of the Holy Ghost**—to whom, in the economy of redemption, it belongs to inspire believers with all gracious affections.

Remarks—1. No Christian is at liberty to regard himself as an isolated disciple of the Lord Jesus, having to decide questions of duty and liberty solely with reference to himself. As Christians are one body in Christ, so the great law of love binds them to act in all things with tenderness and consideration for their brethren in 'the common salvation.' 2. Of this unselfishness CHRIST is the perfect Model of all Christians. 3. Holy Scripture is the Divine storehouse of all furniture for the Christian life, even in its most trying and delicate features (*v.* 4). 4. The harmonious glorification of the God and Father of our Lord Jesus Christ by the whole body of the redeemed, as it is the most exalted fruit of the scheme of redemption, so it is the last end of God in it (*vv.* 5-7). 5. The prayer of *v.* 13 sheds an interesting light on the relation of "hope" to "faith," in the usage of the New Testament. As *hope* does not terminate on the *past* work of Christ, so none of its fruits in us are ascribed to hope. We are never said to hope for pardon, peace, reconciliation, union to Christ, access to God, or the indwelling of the Spirit. The apostle does indeed say in one place (Gal. v. 5), "We through the Spirit wait for the hope of righteousness (or justification) by faith." But this is said, not experimentally, but doctrinally; and the import of it is, 'Be not moved away by false teachers from the hope of the Gospel, as ye were taught it by me: They would persuade you that faith in Christ is not enough for you Gentiles, and that except ye be circumcised and keep the law of Moses, ye cannot be saved; but we who are taught "by the Spirit," whether we be Jews or Gentiles, hope for no righteousness but by faith alone.' Here, then, "hope" refers merely to the ground on which the apostle rested all his own expectations of anything whatever of a saving nature, and is not at all put in contrast with "faith." And if this is the only passage in which "justification" even seems to be the object of *hope*, we are safe in affirming that hope, as distinct from faith, is in the New Testament always represented as fastening on what is *future* in the work of Christ, and *subsequent* to the believer's justification; such as His glorious appearing the second time, without sin, unto the salvation of them that look for Him, the believer's preservation from falling, and being at length presented before the presence of His glory with exceeding joy, and being thenceforward for ever with the Lord. If these, then, are the appropriate objects of "hope," while "faith" appropriates the cross and crown of Christ as the ground of our righteous standing before God, and new life in our risen Head, the prayer of *v.* 13 becomes not only more intelligible, but rich in import. There can be no "hope"—that prayer implies—till first there be "faith," and the "joy and peace" that spring from "believing;" but as this faith necessarily begets "hope," and a hope only measured by the strength of our faith, the apostle, desiring his Roman Christians to have large hope, prays that "the God of hope" might *fill* them with *all* joy and peace in believing, in the confident persuasion that then they would "*abound in hope*, through the power of the Holy Ghost."

14-33.—CONCLUSION: IN WHICH THE APOSTLE APOLOGIZES FOR THUS WRITING TO THE ROMAN CHRISTIANS, EXPLAINS WHY HE HAD NOT YET VISITED THEM, ANNOUNCES HIS FUTURE PLANS, AND ASKS THEIR PRAYERS FOR THE COMPLETION OF THEM.

14. And I myself also am persuaded of you, my brethren. 'Now I am persuaded, my brethren, even I myself, concerning you,' **that ye also are full of goodness**—of inclination to all I have been enjoining on you, **filled with all knowledge** (of the truth expounded), **able also** (without my intervention) **to admonish one another. 15. Nevertheless, brethren, I have written the more boldly unto you in some sort** ('measure'), **as putting you in mind, because of the grace that is given to me of God**—as an apostle of Jesus Christ, **16. That I should be the minister** [λειτουργὸν] — 'a minister' (in the sense of 'ministering to the Lord,' explained on Acts xiii. 2) **of Jesus Christ** ('Christ Jesus,' according to the true reading) **to the Gentiles**—a further proof that this Epistle was meant in the first

Gentiles, ministering the gospel of God, that the ²offering up of the
17 Gentiles might be acceptable, being sanctified by the Holy Ghost. I
have therefore whereof I may glory through Jesus Christ *in those things
18 which pertain to God. For I will not dare to speak of any of those
things *which Christ hath not wrought by me, ⁿto make the Gentiles
19 obedient, by word and deed, through ᵂmighty signs and wonders, by the
power of the Spirit of God; so that from Jerusalem, and round about
20 unto Illyricum, I have fully preached the gospel of Christ. Yea, so have
I strived to preach the Gospel, not where Christ was named, ˣlest I
21 should build upon another man's foundation: but as it is written, ʸTo
whom he was not spoken of, they shall see; and they that have not heard
shall understand.
22 For which cause also ᶻI have been ³much hindered from coming to
23 you. But now having no more place in these parts, and ᵃhaving a great
24 desire these many years to come unto you; whensoever I take my journey
into Spain, I will come to you: for I trust to see you in my journey,
ᵇand to be brought on my way thitherward by you, if first I be some-
25 what filled ⁴with your *company*. But now ᶜI go unto Jerusalem to
26 minister unto the saints. For ᵈit hath pleased them of Macedonia and
Achaia to make a certain contribution for the poor saints which are at

A. D. 60.
³ Or, sacri-
ficing.
Isa. 66. 20.
Phil. 2. 17.
ᵗ Heb. 5. 1.
ᵘ Acts 21. 19.
1 Cor. 3. 6-
9.
ᵛ ch. 1. 5.
ᵂ Acts 19. 11.
ˣ 2 Cor. 10.
13.
ʸ Isa. 52. 15.
ᶻ ch. 1. 13.
³ Or, many
ways, or,
often-
times.
ᵃ Acts 19. 21.
ᵇ Acts 15. 3.
⁴ with you.
ᶜ Acts 24. 17.
ᵈ 1 Cor. 16. 1.
2 Cor. 8. 1.
2 Cor. 9. 2.

instance for a *Gentile* Church (see on ch. i. 13),
ministering [ἱερογοῦντα] — 'ministering [as a
priest' in] the gospel of God, that the offering
up of the Gentiles—as an oblation to God in their
converted character, might be acceptable, being
sanctified by the Holy Ghost—the end to which
the ancient offerings typically looked. 17. I
have therefore whereof I may glory—or with
the article (which seems the true reading), 'I
have my glorying' through ('in') Jesus Christ—
'Christ Jesus,' as the reading even of the received
text is here, in those things which pertain to God
—in the things of the ministry committed to me
of God. 18. For I will not dare to speak of any
(or 'aught') of those things which Christ hath
not wrought by me—a modest though somewhat
obscure form of expression, meaning, 'I will not
dare to go beyond what Christ *hath* wrought by
me;' in which form, accordingly, the rest of the
sentence proceeds. Observe here how all that
Paul achieved as a minister of Christ, he says
that 'Christ wrought by him'—the living Redeemer only working in and by him. by word
and deed—by preaching and working. What this
working was he explains in the next clause.
19. Through mighty signs—'in the power of
signs' and wonders—*i. e.*, glorious miracles, by
the power of the Spirit of God—'of the Holy
Ghost' (as the true reading would seem to be).
This seems intended to account for the efficacy of
the word preached, as well as for the working of
the miracles which attested it. so that from Jerusalem, and round about unto (or 'as far as')
Illyricum—lying to the extreme north-western
boundary of Greece, and corresponding to the
modern Croatia and Dalmatia (2 Tim. iv. 10).
See *Paley's* 'Horæ Paulinæ,' ch. ii., No. iv.; and
Acts xx. 1, 2. I have fully preached the gospel
of Christ. 20. Yea, so have I strived [Οὕτως δὲ
φιλοτιμούμενον]—or, 'Yet (in doing) so, ambitious'
(see 2 Cor. v. 9; 1 Thess. iv. 11, *Gr.*) to preach
the gospel, not where Christ was (already) named,
lest I should (or 'that I might not') build upon
another man's foundation: 21. But (might act)
as it is written (Isa. lii. 15), To whom he was not
spoken of (or 'To whom no tidings of Him came'),
they shall see; and they that have not heard
shall understand.
22. For which cause also—Being so long occupied

in breaking fresh ground, I have been much [τὰ
πολλὰ]—or, 'these many times,' hindered from
coming to you (see on ch. i. 9-11). 23. But now
having no more place in these parts [μηκέτι
τόπον ἔχων ἐν τοῖς κλίμασι τούτοις]—'no longer
having place (or "room") in these quarters;' that
is, no unbroken ground, no spots where Christ
had not been preached. and having a great desire
[ἐπιποθίαν]—'having a longing,' these many years
to come unto you (ch. i. 9-11); 24. Whensoever
I take my journey into Spain. Those who think
our apostle was never at large after his first imprisonment at Rome will of course hold that this never
was; while those who believe, as we do, that he
underwent a second imprisonment, prior to which
he was at large for a considerable time after his
first, incline naturally to the other opinion. [I will
come to you.] The external evidence against the
genuineness of this bracketed clause is exceedingly
strong [ℵ A B C D E F G, the Old Latin Vulgate,
Peshito Syriac, and other versions, a number of
the fathers, all wanting it], while that for it is very
slight [only L, with nearly all cursives, the Philox.
Syriac and later versions, with two or three
Greek fathers, having it]. Naturally, therefore,
we should pronounce against them; but since it
was extensively believed that this purpose of the
apostle was never fulfilled, there is strong reason
to suspect that the clause was omitted from a
false regard for the apostle's credit. And though
we cannot go the length of *Tischendorf*, who believes that the words were struck out advisedly,
we nevertheless incline to regard them, with him,
as part of the genuine text, though *Lachmann*
and *Tregelles* omit them. Anyhow, since it
cannot be doubted that the apostle here looks
forward to a visit to Rome, on the occasion of a
proposed visit to Spain, this clause, or one of
similar import, must be understood. for I trust
to see you in my journey—or 'as I pass through,'
and to be brought on my way thitherward by you,
if first I be somewhat filled with your company
—*q. d.*, 'I should indeed like to stay longer with
you than I can hope to do, but I must, to some
extent at least, have my fill of your company.'
25. But now I go unto Jerusalem to minister
('ministering') unto the saints—in the sense immediately to be explained. 26. For, &c.—better,
'For Macedonia and Achaia have thought good to

27 Jerusalem. It hath pleased them verily; and their debtors they are. For if the Gentiles have been made partakers of their spiritual things,
28 *their duty is also to minister unto them in carnal things. When therefore I have performed this, and have sealed to them *this fruit,
29 I will come by you into Spain. And *I am sure that, when I come unto you, I shall come in *the fulness of the blessing of the gospel of Christ.
30 Now I beseech you, brethren, for the Lord Jesus Christ's sake, and *for the love of the Spirit, *that ye strive together with me in *your*
31 prayers to God for me; that *I may be delivered from them that [5]do not believe in Judea; and that my service which *I have* for Jerusalem may
32 be accepted of the saints; that I may come unto you with joy by *the
33 will of God, and may with you *be refreshed. Now the God of peace *be* with you all. Amen.

A. D. 60.
* 1 Cor. 9. 11.
Gal. 6. 6.
f Phil. 4. 17.
g oh. 1. 11.
h Eph. 3. 8.
i Phil. 2. 1.
j 2 Cor. 1. 11.
Col. 4. 12.
k 2 Thes. 3. 2.
5 Or, are disobedient.
l Jas. 4. 15.
m 2 Cor. 7. 13.
2 Tim. 1. 16.
Phile. 7.

make a certain contribution for the poor of the saints which are at Jerusalem.' (See Acts xxiv. 17.) 27. It hath pleased them verily; and their debtors they are—'They have thought it good; and their debtors verily they are;' *q. d.*, 'And well they may, considering what the Gentile believers owe to their Jewish brethren.' For if the Gentiles have been made partakers of their spiritual things, their duty is also ('they owe it also') to minister [λειτουργῆσαι]—as a *religious* service (see on *v.* 16) unto them in carnal things. Compare 1 Cor. ix. 11; Gal. vi. 6; and see Luke vii. 4, and Acts x. 2. 28. When therefore I have performed this, and have sealed (*i. e.*, 'delivered over safely') to them this fruit (of the faith and love of the Gentile converts), I will come ('proceed') by you into Spain (see on *v.* 24). 29. And I am sure ('I know') that, when I come unto you, I shall come in the fulness of the blessing of [the gospel of] Christ. 'The blessing of Christ' (without the bracketed words) is, beyond doubt, the true reading. [They are wanting in every Uncial MS. but L, and several cursives; and though they are in the *printed* Vulgate and both Syriac versions, they are wanting in the best copies of the Vulgate, in some other versions, and in many Latin fathers. As to internal evidence, the addition of them to the genuine text is easily accounted for; but not their dropping out of it.] The apostle was not disappointed in the confidence he here expresses, though his visit to Rome was in very different circumstances from what he expected (Acts xxviii. 16, to the end).

30. Now I beseech you, brethren, for the Lord Jesus Christ's sake, and for the love of the Spirit [διὰ τ. Κυρίου ἡμῶν . . . καὶ διὰ τ. ἀγάπης κ.τ.λ—see *Winer*, § 47. *d.*]—'by our Lord Jesus Christ, and by the love of the Spirit;' not the love which the Spirit bears to us, but that love which he kindles in the hearts of believers towards each other:—*q. d.*, 'By that Saviour whose name is alike dear to all of us, and whose unsearchable riches I delight to proclaim, and by that love one to another which the blessed Spirit diffuses through all the brotherhood, making the labours of Christ's servants a matter of common interest to all, I beseech you' that ye strive together with me in your prayers to God for me—implying that he had his grounds for anxious fear in this matter. 31. That I may be delivered from them that do not believe [τ. ἀπειθούντων]—or, 'that do not obey;' that refuse to the Gospel the obedience of faith, as in ch. ii. 8. in Judea. He saw the storm that was gathering over him in Judea, which, if at all, would certainly burst upon his head when he reached the capital; and the event too clearly showed the correctness of these apprehensions:

and that my service which I have for Jerusalem (see on *vv.* 25-28) may be accepted of ('prove acceptable to') the saints. Nor was he without apprehension lest the opposition he had made to the narrow jealousy of the Jewish converts against the free reception of their Gentile brethren should make this gift of theirs to the poor saints at Jerusalem less welcome than it ought to be. He would have the Romans, therefore, to join him in wrestling with God that this gift might be gratefully received, and prove a cement between the two parties. But further, strive with me in prayer, 32. That I may come unto you with ('in') joy by the will of God (Acts xviii. 21; 1 Cor. iv. 19; xvi. 7; Heb. vi. 3; Jas. iv. 15), and may with you be refreshed—or, 'find refreshment,' after all his labours and anxieties, and so be refitted for future service. 33. Now the God of peace be with you all. Amen. The peace here sought is to be taken in its widest sense: the peace of reconciliation to God, first, "through the blood of the everlasting covenant" (Heb. xiii. 20; 1 Thess. v. 23; 2 Thess. iii. 16; Phil. iv. 9); then, the peace which that reconciliation diffuses among all the partakers of it (1 Cor. xiv. 33; 2 Cor. xiii. 11: and see on ch. xvi. 20); more widely still, that peace which the children of God, in beautiful imitation of their Father in heaven, are called and privileged to diffuse far and wide through this sin-distracted and divided world (ch. xii. 18; Matt. v. 9; Jas. iii. 18; Heb. xii. 14).

Remarks.—1. Did "the chiefest of the apostles" apologize for writing to a Christian church which he had never seen, and a church that he was persuaded was above the need of it, save to "stir up their pure minds by way of remembrance" (2 Pet. i. 13; iii. 1); and did he put even this upon the sole plea of apostolic responsibility? (*vv.* 14-16). What a contrast is thus presented to hierarchical pride, and in particular to the affected humility of the bishop of this very Rome! How close the bond which the one spirit draws between ministers and people—how wide the separation produced by the other! 2. There is in the Christian Church no real priesthood, and none but figurative sacrifices. Had it been otherwise, it is inconceivable that the 16th verse of this chapter should have been expressed as it is. Paul's only priesthood and sacrificial offerings lay, first, in ministering to them, as "the apostle of the Gentiles," not the sacrament, with the 'Real Presence' of Christ in it, or the sacrifice of the mass, but "the Gospel of God," and then, when gathered under the wing of Christ, presenting them to God as a grateful offering, "being sanctified (not by sacrificial gifts, but) by the Holy Ghost" (see Heb. xiii. 9-16). 3. Though the debt we owe to those by whom we

16 I COMMEND unto you Phebe our sister, which is a servant of the
2 church which is at *a*Cenchrea: that *b*ye receive her in the Lord, as
becometh saints, and that ye assist her in whatsoever business she hath
need of you: for she hath been a succourer of many, and of myself also.
3, Greet *c*Priscilla and Aquila my helpers in Christ Jesus: who have for
4 my life laid down their own necks: unto whom not only I give thanks,
5 but also all the churches of the Gentiles. Likewise *greet* *d*the church
that is in their house. Salute my well beloved Epenetus, who is *e*the
6 first-fruits of Achaia unto Christ. Greet Mary, who *f*bestowed much

A. D. 60.

a Acts 18. 18.
b Phil. 2. 29.
  3 John 5, 6.
c Acts 18. 2.
  2 Tim. 4.19.
d 1 Cor. 16.
  19.
  Col. 4. 15.
  Phile. 2.
e 1 Cor. 16.15.
f 1 Tim. 5.10.

have been brought to Christ can never be discharged, we should feel it a privilege, when we
have it in our power, to render them any lower
benefit in return (*vv.* 26, 27). 4. Formidable designs against the truth and the servants of Christ
should, above all other ways of counteracting them,
be met by combined prayer to Him who rules all
hearts and controls all events; and the darker the
cloud, the more resolutely should all to whom
Christ's cause is dear "strive together in their
prayers to God" for the removal of it (*vv.* 30, 31).
5. Christian fellowship is so precious that the
most eminent servants of Christ, amidst the toils
and trials of their work, find it refreshing and
invigorating; and it is no good sign of any ecclesiastic that he deems it beneath him to seek and
enjoy it even amongst the humblest saints in the
Church of Christ (*vv.* 24, 32).

CHAP. XVI. 1-27.—CONCLUSION, EMBRACING
SUNDRY SALUTATIONS, CAUTIONS, AN ENCOURAGE-
MENT, A BENEDICTION, AND A CONCLUDING DOXO-
LOGY.

Recommendation of Phœbe to the Roman church
(1, 2). 1. I commend unto you Phebe our sister,
which is a servant [διάκονον]—or, 'deaconess,'
of the church which is at Cenchrea. The word
is "Cenchreæ," the eastern port of Corinth (see
on Acts xviii. 18). That in the earliest churches
there were deaconesses, to attend to the wants of
the female members, there is no good reason to
doubt. So early at least as the reign of Trajan,
we learn from Pliny's celebrated letter to that
Emperor—A.D. 110 or 111—that they existed in
the eastern churches. Indeed, from the relation
in which the sexes then stood to each other, something of this sort would seem to have been a
necessity. Modern attempts, however, to revive
this office have seldom found favour; either from
the altered state of society or the abuse of the
office, or both. Yet in Protestant Prussia, and in
the Lutheran missions of the East, they seem to
be a real success. 2. That ye receive her in the
Lord—that is, as a genuine disciple of the Lord
Jesus, as ('so as') becometh saints—so as saints
should receive saints, and that ye assist her
in whatsoever business she hath ('may have')
need of you—some private business of her
own: for she hath been a succourer of many,
and of myself also (see Ps. xli. 1-3; 2 Tim. i.
16-18).

Sundry salutations (3-16). 3. Greet (or, 'Salute')
Priscilla. The true reading here, beyond all
doubt, is 'Prisca;' but this is only a contracted
form of "Priscilla" (as in 2 Tim. iv. 19), as "Silas"
of "Silvanus:" and Aquila. It will be observed
that the wife is here named before the husband,
as also in Acts xviii. 18 (and *v.* 26, according to
what we take to be the true reading). From this
we may infer that she was the more energetic of
the two, of superior mind, and more helpful to
the Church. 4. Who have for my life laid down—
'Who did for my life lay down' their own necks
—that is, risked their own lives to save that of
the apostle. The occasion referred to was either

278

that of his first visit to Corinth (Acts xviii.
6, 9, 10), or more probably what took place at
Ephesus, as recorded in Acts xix. 30, 31; and
cf. 1 Cor. xv. 32). They must by this time have
returned from Ephesus—where we last find
them in the History of the Acts—to Rome,
whence the edict of Claudius had banished
them (Acts xviii. 2); and if they were not the
leading members of that Christian community,
they were at least the most endeared to our
apostle. **unto whom not only I give thanks,
but also all the churches of the Gentiles**
—whose special apostle this dear couple had
rescued so heroically from imminent danger. **5.
Likewise greet the church that is in their house**
—no doubt, the Christian assembly that statedly
met there for worship. And it is natural to
suppose, from his occupation as a tent-maker
(Acts xviii. 3), that his premises would accommodate larger gatherings than those of most others.
Probably this devoted couple had written to the
apostle such an account of the stated meetings
at their house as made him feel at home with
them, and include them in this salutation, which
doubtless would be read at their meeting with
peculiar interest. **Salute my [well] beloved
Epenetus, who is the first-fruits** (*i.e.*, the first
convert) **of Achaia unto Christ.** But as this
was not the fact, so neither is it what the apostle
says. The true reading, beyond all question, is,
'the first-fruits of Asia unto Christ'—that is,
Proconsular Asia. (See on Acts xvi. 6.) ['Aχαίας
is found in only one Uncial MS., L, and in the
two correctors of D. Every other MS., and nearly
all versions, have 'Aσίας]. In 1 Cor. xvi. 15 it is
said that "the household of Stephanas was the
first-fruits of Achaia." And though, if Epænetus
was a member of that family, the two statements
might be reconciled, according to the received
text, there is no need to resort to that supposition,
as we have seen that the true reading is otherwise. This Epænetus, as the first believer in
Roman Asia, was dear to the apostle (see Hos. ix.
10; and Mic. vii. 1).

None of the names mentioned from *vv.* 5-15 are
otherwise known. One wonders at the number
of them, considering that the writer had never
been at Rome. But as Rome was then the centre
of the civilized world, to and from which journeys
were continually taken to the remotest parts,
there is no great difficulty in supposing that so
active a travelling missionary as Paul would, in
course of time, make the acquaintance of a
considerable number of the Christians then residing at the capital.

6. Greet Mary, who bestowed much labour on us
—labour, no doubt, of a womanly kind. [*Lachm.*
and *Treg.* have ὑμᾶς—' who bestowed much labour
on *you*'—with א A B C *, and several cursives,
the Peshito Syriac, and other versions: then the
similar reading, ἐν ὑμῖν, is found in D E F G, the
Old Latin, and Vulgate: while ἡμᾶς is only in L,
and a corrector of C, the great majority of cursives,
and the Philox. Syriac. But, with *Tischendorf,*

7 labour on us. Salute Andronicus and Junia, my kinsmen, and my
fellow-prisoners, who are of note among the apostles, who also *g* were in
8, Christ before me. Greet Amplias my beloved in the Lord. Salute
9, Urbane our helper in Christ, and Stachys my beloved. Salute Apelles
10 approved in Christ. Salute them which are of Aristobulus' *1 household.*
11 Salute Herodion my kinsman. Greet them that be of the *2 household*
12 of Narcissus, which are in the Lord. Salute Tryphena and Tryphosa,
who labour in the Lord. Salute the beloved Persis, which laboured
13 much in the Lord. Salute Rufus *h* chosen in the Lord, and his mother
14 and mine. Salute Asyncritus, Phlegon, Hermas, Patrobas, Hermes,

A. D. 60.

g 2 Cor. 5. 17.
2 Cor. 12. 2.
Gal. 1. 22.
1 Or,
friends.
2 Or,
friends.
h John 13. 18.
John 15. 16.
Eph. 1. 4.
1 Pet. 1. 2.
2 John 1.

we hold that not even this weighty external authority could justify the adoption of so entirely inappropriate a reading as '*you*' here. The received reading here *must* be right.] 7. **Salute Andronicus and Junia**—or, as it might be, '**Junias**,' a contracted form of '**Junianus**:' in this case, it is a man's name. But if, as is more probable, the word be, as in our version, "**Junia**," the person meant was no doubt either the wife or the sister of Andronicus. **my kinsmen**—or, '**relatives**,' **and my fellow-prisoners**—on what occasion, it is impossible to say, as the apostle elsewhere tells us that he was "in prisons more frequent" (2 Cor. xi. 23); **who are of note** (or '**distinguished**') **among the apostles** [ἐπίσημοι ἐν τοῖς ἀποστόλοις]. Those who think the word "apostle" is used in an extended sense in the Acts and Epistles take this to mean, 'noted apostles,' and of course read *Junias*, as a man's name. (So *Chrysostom*—though he inconsistently reads 'Junia,' regarding it as a *woman's* name—*Luther, Calvin, Estius, Bengel, Olshausen, Tholuck, Alford, Jowett*). Those, on the other hand, who are not clear that the word "apostle" is applied, in the strictly official sense, beyond the circle of the twelve, and others besides these, understand, by the expression here used, 'persons esteemed among,' or 'by the apostles.' (So *Beza, Grotius, de Wette, Fritzsche, Meyer, Stuart, Philippi, Hodge, Lange.*) Of course, if "Junia," as a woman's name, is what the apostle wrote, this latter must be the meaning; and the use of the article— "among *the* apostles"—which would probably have been omitted if the former sense was meant, seems to us to decide in favour of the latter. **who also were in Christ before me.** The apostle writes as if he envied them this priority in the faith. And, indeed, if to be "in Christ" be the most enviable human condition, the earlier the date of this blessed translation the greater the grace of it. This latter statement about Andronicus and Junia seems to throw some light on the preceding one. Very possibly they may have been among the first-fruits of Peter's labours, gained to Christ either on the day of Pentecost or on some of the succeeding days. In that case they may have attracted the special esteem of those apostles who for some time resided chiefly at Jerusalem and its neighbourhood.; and our apostle, though he came late in contact with the other apostles, if he was aware of this fact, would have pleasure in alluding to it. 8. **Greet Amplias** —a contracted form of '**Ampliatus**;' **my beloved in the Lord**—an expression of dear Christian affection. 9. **Salute Urbane** [Οὐρβανὸν]—rather, '**Urbanus**:' it is a man's name. **our helper** [συνεργὸν]—'fellow-labourer,' **in Christ.** 10. **Salute Apelles approved** [τόν δόκιμον]—'the approved one,' **in Christ**—or, as we should say, 'that tried Christian'—a noble commendation. **Salute them which are of Aristobulus' [household].** It would seem, from what is said of Narcissus in the fol-

lowing verse, that this Aristobulus himself had not been a Christian, but that the Christians of his household simply were meant; very possibly some of his slaves. 11. **Salute Herodion my kinsman**—(see on *v.* 7.) **Greet them that be of [the household of] Narcissus, which are in the Lord**—which implies that others in his house, including probably himself, were not Christians. 12. **Salute Tryphena and Tryphosa, who labour in the Lord**—two active females. **Salute the beloved Persis** (another female), **which laboured much in the Lord**—referring, probably, not to official services, such as would fall to the deaconesses, but to such higher Christian labours— yet within the sphere competent to woman—as Priscilla bestowed on Apollos and others (Acts xviii. 18). 13. **Salute Rufus chosen** ('the chosen') **in the Lord**—meaning, not 'who is one of the elect,' as every believer is, but 'the choice,' or 'precious one,' in the Lord. (See 1 Pet. ii. 4; 2 John 13.) We read in Mark xv. 21 that Simon of Cyrene, whom they compelled to bear our Lord's cross, was "the father of Alexander and Rufus." From this we naturally conclude that when Mark wrote his Gospel Alexander and Rufus must have been well known as Christians among those by whom he expected his Gospel to be first read; and, in all likelihood, this was that very "Rufus;" in which case our interest is deepened by what immediately follows about his mother. **and** (salute) **his mother and mine.** The apostle calls her 'his own mother,' not so much as our Lord calls every elderly female believer His mother (Matt. xii. 49, 50), but in grateful acknowledgment of her motherly attentions to himself, bestowed no doubt for his Master's sake, and the love she bore to his honoured servants. To us it seems altogether likely that the conversion of Simon the Cyrenian dated from that memorable day when "passing (casually) by, as he came from the country" (Mark xv. 21: for commentary on which, see p. 469), "they compelled him to bear the" Saviour's cross. Sweet compulsion, if what he thus beheld issued in his *voluntarily* taking up his own cross! Through him it is natural to suppose that his wife would be brought in, and that this believing couple, now "heirs together of the grace of life" (1 Pet. iii. 7), as they told their two sons Alexander and Rufus, what honour had unwittingly been put upon their father at that hour of deepest and dearest moment to all Christians, might be blessed to the inbringing of both of them to Christ. In this case, supposing the elder of the two to have departed to be with Christ ere this letter was written, or to have been residing in some other place, and Rufus left alone with his mother, how instructive and beautiful is the testimony here borne to her!

14. **Salute Asyncritus, Phlegon, Hermas, Patrobas, Hermes**—'Hermes, Patrobas, Hermas' is, beyond doubt, the right order of these names: **and**

15 and the brethren which are with them. Salute Philologus, and Julia, | A. D. 60.
Nereus, and his sister, and Olympas, and all the saints which are with
16 them. Salute *i* one another with an holy kiss. The churches of Christ
salute you.
17 Now I beseech you, brethren, mark them *j* which cause divisions and
offences contrary to the doctrine which ye have learned; and *k* avoid
18 them. For they that are such serve not our Lord Jesus Christ, but *l* their
own belly; and *m* by good words and fair speeches deceive the hearts of
19 the simple. For your obedience is come abroad unto all *men*. I am
glad therefore on your behalf: but yet I would have you wise *n* unto
20 that which is good, and *3* simple concerning evil. And the God of peace
shall *4* bruise Satan under your feet shortly. The grace of our Lord Jesus
Christ *be* with you. Amen.

A. D. 60.
i 1 Pet. 5. 14.
j Acts 15.
1 Tim. 6. 3.
k 1 Cor. 5. 9.
2 Thes. 3. 6.
2 Tim. 3 5.
Tit. 3. 10.
2 John 10.
l Phil. 3. 19.
m Col. 2. 4.
2 Pet. 2. 3.
n Matt.10.16.
3 Or, harmless.
4 Or, tread.
Gen. 3. 15.

the brethren which are with them. **15. Salute Philologus, and Julia, Nereus, and his sister, and Olympas, and all the saints which are with them.** These have been thought to be the names of ten less notable Christians than those already named. But this will hardly be supposed if it be observed that they are divided into two pairs of five each, and that after the first of these pairs it is added, "and the brethren which are with them," while after the second pair we have the words, "and all the saints which are with them." This, perhaps, hardly means that each of the five in both pairs had 'a church at his house,' else probably this would have been more expressly said. But at least it would seem to indicate that they were each a centre of some few Christians who met at his house—it may be for further instruction, for prayer, for missionary purposes, or for some other Christian objects. These little peeps into the rudimental forms which Christian fellowship first took in the great cities, though too indistinct for more than conjecture, are singularly interesting. Our apostle would seem to have been kept minutely informed as to the state of the Roman church, both as to its membership and its varied activities, probably by Priscilla and Aquila. **16. Salute one another with an holy kiss.** (So 1 Cor. xvi. 20; 1 Thess. v. 26; 1 Pet. v. 14.) The custom prevailed among the Jews, and doubtless came from the East, where it still obtains. Its adoption into the Christian churches, as the symbol of a higher fellowship than it had ever expressed before, was probably as immediate as it was natural. In this case the apostle's desire seems to be, that on receipt of his epistle, with its greetings, they should in this manner expressly testify their Christian affection. It afterwards came to have a fixed place in the Church service, immediately after the celebration of the Supper, and continued long in use. In such matters, however, the state of society and the peculiarities of different places require to be studied. **The churches of Christ salute you.** 'All the churches' is the reading of every Uncial MS.; the word "all" gradually falling out, as seeming probably to express more than the apostle would venture to affirm. But no more seems meant than to assure the Romans in what affectionate esteem they were held by the churches generally; all that knew he was writing to Rome having expressly asked their own salutations to be sent to them. (See *v.* 19.)

Cautions (17-19). **17. Now I beseech you, brethren, mark them which cause divisions and offences contrary to the doctrine which ye have learned**—'which ye learned;' and **avoid them.** The fomenters of "divisions" who are here meant are probably those who were unfriendly to the truths

280

taught in this epistle; while those who caused "offences" were probably those referred to in ch. xiv. 15, as haughtily disregarding the prejudices of the weak. The direction as to both is, first, to "mark" such, lest the evil should be done ere it was fully discovered; and next, to "avoid" them (cf. 2 Thess. iii. 6, 14), so as neither to bear any responsibility for their procedure nor seem to give them the least countenance. **18. For they that are such serve not our Lord [Jesus] Christ**—'our Lord Christ' appears to be the true reading. **but their own belly**—not in the grosser sense, but in the sense of 'living for low ends of their own' (compare Phil iii. 19); **and by good words and fair speeches** [διὰ εὐλογίας]. These words are wanting in D* E F G, several cursives, and the Old Latin. But besides the good evidence in their favour, the omission of them is easily accounted for, as *Meyer* says, by Homœoteleuton — εὐλογίας — καρδίας.] **deceive the hearts of the simple**—the unwary, the unsuspecting (see Prov. xiv. 15). **19. For your obedience**—your tractableness, or readiness to be led (as the close of the verse seems to show is the meaning here), **is come abroad unto all.** (The supplement "men" had better have been left out.) **I am glad therefore on your behalf: but yet I would have you wise unto that which is good, and simple**—'harmless,' as in Matt x. 16, from which the warning is taken, **concerning evil** [εἰς]—rather, 'unto evil' (as in the former clause): — *q. d.,* 'Your reputation among the churches for subjection to the teaching ye have received is to me sufficient ground of confidence in you; but ye need the serpent's wisdom to discriminate between transparent truth and plausible error, with that guileless simplicity which instinctively cleaves to the one and rejects the other.'

Encouragement and benediction (20). **20. And the God of peace shall bruise Satan under your feet shortly.** The apostle encourages the Romans to persevere in resisting the wiles of the devil, with the assurance that, as good soldiers of Jesus Christ, they are "shortly" to receive their discharge, and have the satisfaction of 'putting their feet upon the neck' of that formidable Enemy—a symbol familiar, probably in all languages, to express not only the completeness of the defeat, but the abject humiliation of the conquered foe (see Josh. x. 24; 2 Sam xxii. 41; Ezek. xxi. 29; Ps. xci. 13). Though the apostle here styles Him who is thus to bruise Satan, "the God of peace," with special reference to the "divisions" (*v.* 17) by which the Roman Church was in danger of being disturbed, this sublime appellation of God has here a wider sense, pointing to the whole 'purpose for which the Son of God was manifested, to

21   Timotheus °my work-fellow, ᵖand Lucius, and ᵠJason, and ʳSosipater, 22 my kinsmen, salute you. I Tertius, who wrote *this* epistle, salute you 23 in the Lord. Gaius ˢmine host, and of the whole church, saluteth you. ᵗErastus the chamberlain of the city saluteth you, and Quartus a 24 brother. The ᵘgrace of our Lord Jesus Christ *be* with you all. Amen. 25   Now to him that is of power to stablish you ᵛaccording to my gospel, and the preaching of Jesus Christ, according ʷto the revelation of the 26 mystery, ˣwhich was kept secret since the world began, but ʸnow is made manifest, and by the scriptures of the prophets, according to the commandment of the everlasting God, made known to all nations for the

A. D. 60

° Acts 16. 1.
ᵖ Acts 13. 1.
ᵠ Acts 17.˙5.
ʳ Acts 20. 4.
ˢ 1 Cor. 1. 14.
ᵗ Acts 19. 24.
ᵘ 1 Thes. 5. 28.
ᵛ ch. 2. 16.
ʷ Col. 1. 27.
ˣ 1 Cor. 2. 7.
ʸ 2 Tim. 1.10.

---

destroy the works of the devil' (1 John iii. 8); and indeed this assurance is but a reproduction of the first great promise, that the Seed of the woman should bruise the Serpent's head (Gen. iii. 15). **The grace of our Lord Jesus Christ be with you. [Amen.]** The "Amen" here has no MS. authority. What comes after this, where one would have expected the epistle to close, has its parallel in Phil. iv. 20, &c., and, being in fact common in epistolatory writings, is simply a mark of genuineness.

The salutations of the apostle's friends at Corinth (21-23). **21. Timotheus my work-fellow** — 'my fellow-labourer' (see Acts xvi. 1-5). The apostle (as *Bengel* says) mentions him here rather than in the opening address to this church, as he had not been at Rome. **and Lucius**—not Luke; for the fuller form of 'Lucas' is not "Lucius," but 'Lucanus.' The person meant seems to be "Lucius of Cyrene," who was among the "prophets and teachers" at Antioch with our apostle before he was summoned into the missionary field (Acts xiii. 1). **and Jason** (see Acts xvii. 5). He had probably accompanied or followed the apostle from Thessalonica to Corinth ; **and Sosipater** (see Acts xx. 4) **my kinsmen, salute you**—[ἀσπάζεται is much better supported than —ονται, of the received text.] **22. I Tertius, who wrote this** ('the') **epistle**—as the apostle's amanuensis or penman, **salute you in the Lord.** So usual was it with the apostle to dictate instead of writing his epistles, that he calls the attention of the Galatians to the fact that to them he wrote with his own hand (Gal. vi. 11). But this Tertius would have the Romans to know that, far from being a mere scribe, his heart went out to them in Christian affection ; and the apostle, by giving his salutation a place here, would show what sort of assistants he employed. **23. Gaius mine host, and** (the host) **of the whole church, saluteth you**—(see Acts xx. 4.) It would appear that this Gaius was one of only two persons whom Paul baptized with his own hand (cf. 3 John 1). His Christian hospitality appears to have been something uncommon. **Erastus the chamberlain** (or, 'treasurer') **of the city**—doubtless the city of Corinth (see Acts xix. 22; 2 Tim. iv. 20), **saluteth you, and Quartus a brother** [ὁ ἀδελφ]—'the,' or 'our brother,' as Sosthenes and Timothy are called, 1 Cor. i. 1; 2 Cor. i. 1 (*Greek*). Nothing more is known of this Quartus.

Benediction repeated (24). **24. The grace of our Lord Jesus Christ be with you all. Amen**—a repetition of the benediction precisely as in v. 20, save that it is here invoked on them "all," and that the "Amen" here is undoubted.

Concluding Doxology (25-27). The genuineness of this whole Doxology has been questioned, but on wholly insufficient grounds. [It is *omitted* only in F G and its Latin version ; but even in each of these *a blank space is left after v. 24*, implying that something was wanting; but it is found in all

other extant MSS., Uncial and cursive. It is *misplaced*, however, in a number of MSS. and several versions, which introduce it at the close of ch. xiv.—for which some not unnatural reasons may be assigned ; but this is manifestly the right place for it]. **25. Now to him that is of power** [δυναμένῳ]—or, as in Jude 24, "Now unto Him that is able" **to stablish**—confirm or uphold **you according to my gospel, and the preaching of Jesus Christ**—in conformity with the truths of that Gospel which I preach, and not I only, but all to whom has been committed "the preaching of Jesus Christ," **according to the revelation of the mystery** (see on ch. xi. 25), **which was kept secret since the world began**—*lit.*, 'which had been kept in silence during eternal ages.' **26. But now is made manifest.** The reference here is to that peculiar feature of the Gospel economy which Paul himself was specially employed to carry into practical effect, and to unfold by his teaching— the introduction of the Gentile believers to an equality with their Jewish brethren, and the new, and, to the Jews, quite unexpected form which this gave to the whole Kingdom of God, (cf. Eph. iii. 1-10, &c.) This the apostle calls here a mystery hitherto undisclosed (in what sense the next verse will show), but now fully unfolded; and his prayer for the Roman Christians, in the form of a doxology to Him who was able to do what he asked, is that they might be established in the truth of the Gospel, not only in its essential character, but specially in that feature of it which gave themselves, as Gentile believers, their whole standing among the people of God. **and by the scriptures of the prophets, according to the commandment of the everlasting God, made known to all nations for** (in order to) **the obedience of faith.** Lest they should think, from what he had just said, that God had brought in upon his people so vast a change on their condition without giving them any previous notice, the apostle here adds that, on the contrary, "the scriptures of the prophets" contain all that he and other preachers of the Gospel had to declare on these topics, and, indeed, that the same "everlasting God" who "from eternal ages" had kept these things hid had given "commandment" that they should now, according to the tenor of those prophetic Scriptures, be imparted to every nation for their believing acceptance. **27. To God only wise, [be] glory**—'to the only wise God.' **through Jesus Christ**—'to whom [be]'—*q. d.*, 'To Him, I say, be the glory' **for ever. Amen.** At the outset of this doxology, it will be observed that it is an ascription of glory to the *power* that could do all this. At its close it ascribes glory to the *wisdom* that planned and that presides over the gathering of a redeemed people out of all nations. The apostle adds his devout "Amen," which the reader —if he has followed him with the astonishment and delight of him who pens these words—will fervently echo.

27 obedience of faith: to ᶻ God only wise, *be* glory through Jesus Christ for ever. Amen.

Written to the Romans from Corinthus, *and sent* by Phebe, servant of the church at Cenchrea.

A. D. 60.

ᶻ 1 Tim. 1. 17.
Jude 25.

Remarks.—1. In the minute and delicate manifestations of Christian feeling, and lively interest in the smallest movements of Christian life, love, and zeal, which are here exemplified, combined with the grasp of thought and elevation of soul which this whole epistle displays, as indeed all the writings of our apostle, we have the secret of much of that grandeur of character which has made the name of Paul stand on an elevation of its own in the estimation of enlightened Christendom in every age, and of that influence which, under God, beyond all the other apostles, he has already exercised, and is yet destined to exert, over the religious thinking and feeling of men. Nor can any approach him in these peculiarities without exercising corresponding influence on all with whom they come in contact. 2. "The wisdom of the serpent and the harmlessness of the dove"—in enjoining which our apostle here only echoes the teaching of his Lord (Matt. x. 16)—is a combination of properties the rarity of which among Christians is only equalled by its vast importance. In every age of the Church there have been real Christians whose excessive study of the serpent's wisdom has so sadly trenched upon their guileless simplicity, as at times to excite the distressing apprehension that they were no better than wolves in sheep's clothing: nor is it to be denied, on the other hand, that, either from inaptitude or indisposition to judge with manly discrimination of character and of measures, many eminently simple, spiritual, devoted Christians, have throughout life exercised little or no influence on any section of society around them. Let the apostle's counsel on this head (*v.* 19) be taken as a study, especially by young Christians, whose character has yet to be formed, and whose permanent sphere in life is but partially fixed;

and let them prayerfully set themselves to the combined exercise of both those qualities. So will their Christian character acquire solidity and elevation, and their influence for good be proportionably extended. 3. Christians should cheer their own and each other's hearts amidst the toils and trials of their protracted warfare, with the assurance that it will have a speedy and glorious end. They should accustom themselves to regard all opposition to the progress and prosperity of Christ's cause—whether in their own souls, in the churches with which they are connected, or in the world at large—as just "Satan" in conflict, as ever, with Christ their Lord; and they should never allow themselves to doubt that "the God of peace" will "shortly" give them the neck of their Enemy, and make them to bruise the Serpent's head (*v.* 20). 4. As Christians are held up and carried through solely by Divine power, working through the glorious Gospel, so to that power, and to the wisdom that brought that Gospel nigh to them, they should ascribe all the glory of their stability now, as they certainly will of their victory at last. 5. Has "the everlasting God" "commanded" that the Gospel "mystery," so long kept hid, but now fully disclosed, shall be "made known to all nations for the obedience of faith"? (*v.* 26.) Then, what "necessity is laid upon" all the churches, and every Christian, to send the Gospel "to every creature!" And we may rest well assured that the prosperity or decline of churches, and of individual Christians, will have not a little to do with their faithfulness or indifference to this imperative duty.

The ancient Subscription at the end of this epistle—though of course of no authority—appears to be in this case quite correct.

282

PART THREE
I CORINTHIANS — REVELATION

PREFACE.

In giving to the public the concluding volume of this Commentary, I have to call attention to the principle on which I have given preference in the notes to other readings than those of the English Authorized Version. The commonly "Received Text" was formed in an age when the value of old authorities was not so well understood as it is in our own. My aim, therefore, has been generally to mention those readings alone which are supported by the agreeing testimony of the oldest witnesses—viz., *first*, uncial MSS. (*i. e.*, written in *capital letters*, a proof of antiquity), ranging from the fourth to the eighth century; *secondly*, the oldest versions; *thirdly*, the earliest Fathers. The versions referred to are all of a date as early as the first five centuries, and some as far back as the second; and reflect the ancient Greek texts, which they severally translated, so accurately as to retain the very *order* of the words. It confirms the testimony of the few oldest MSS. we have extant, as compared with the numerous modern cursive MSS. (*i. e.*, written in small letters), on which the Received Text rests, that the more nearly we approach the genuine text of the versions (as in the Vulgate by the Amiatine codex, and the Syriac by the Curetonian MSS.), the more their text agrees with their oldest MSS., and diverges from the modern MSS. Though some older readings than those of the oldest extant MSS. *may be* preserved in modern MSS., yet, as we have no means of testing which are such, whereas we have the mainly concurring testimony of three classes of independent witnesses in behalf of many readings against those of the Received Text, it is better to rest content with reproducing, on the strongest evidence, the text as it stood, at latest, in the fourth century, and probably much earlier, than to *conjecture* what was the text of the autographs themselves. The Fathers of the first four centuries (especially *Origen*) quote nearly all the Greek text, as they *then* had it; and in some disputed readings their testimony is the more trustworthy, as the force of their argument rests on the *verbal* accuracy of their quotation. The old MSS., it is true, differ often among themselves; but this very discrepancy makes their witness, in passages when they concur, the more weighty against the Received; for it shows they did not copy from one another, but are independent witnesses. The agreement among the numerous modern MSS. creates a suspicion that they copy one another, and so present the uniform text found in the Constantinopolitan MSS.

The following are the abbreviations:—A. Alexandrine MS.: the Old and New Testaments: given by Cyril Lucas, patriarch of Constantinople, to Charles I.: now in the British Museum: written in the fifth century. א. The Sinaitic MS. of the whole New Testament, and part of the Old Testament: of the fourth century: found by *Tischendorf* in the St. Catherine's Convent, Mount Sinai: now in St. Petersburg. B. Vatican MS.: Old and New Testaments: the fourth century: deficient from Heb. ix. 14 to the end of Hebrews; also, it wants Epistles to Timothy, Titus, Philemon, Apocalypse. C. The Palimpsest or Rescript MS. of Ephrem the Syrian: his writings were on the parchment, the ancient text, fragments of the Old and New Testaments, having been removed with a sponge—a common practice when writing materials were scarce: Hase, by a chemical process, restored the latter: of the fifth century: in Paris. D. The Cambridge MS. of Beza: of the sixth century: the Gospels and Acts. Δ. The Clermont MS. of Beza: in Paris: all St. Paul's Epistles, except a few verses: of the sixth century. F. Augian MS. of St. Paul's Epistles: in Cambridge. G. The Boernerian MS. of Paul's Epistles: resembling closely F: both of the ninth century, and wanting Hebrews. H. The Coislin MS. at Paris: fragments of St. Paul's Epistles: the sixth century, but in text agreeing with the oldest: the transcriber has a note,—'This copy was collated [anteblethe] with a copy in Cæsarea, belonging to the library of St. Pamphilus, and written with his own hand.' B. The Basilian MS. (not THE B Vaticanus): in the Vatican: of the beginning of the eighth century.

The versions quoted were made from Greek MSS. of the earliest times. There was originally one Latin version (*vetus Itala*), from which the various ante-Jerome Latin versions vary slightly: from their agreement with citations of African Fathers, *Tertullian*, &c., *Wiseman* thinks Africa was the original home of their archetypal text: in the second century, as this Latin version was known to *Irenæus's* translator. They follow an older Greek text than that of *Origen's* time, akin to the singular one of D, and not to the Alexandrine, *f* accompanying Δ, *g* accompanying G, *h*, *Primasius* on the Apocalypse, *d* accompanying, but not translated from, D (3 John).

Jerome's Vulgate (*Vulg.*) was written 383 A.D., correcting from *old* Greek MSS. only such passages of the previous Latin version as affected the sense. Thus the Vulgate represents the reading of Greek MSS., considered by so great a scholar as *old in the fourth century*. Sixtus V. revised it in 1590, and Clement VIII., in spite of his predecessor's anathema against any corrector, made 2,000 corrections. Unfortunately for the infallibility of both, the Amiatine MS., of 541 A.D. proves that both differ widely from *Jerome's* true text.

The Coptic, or Memphitic version (*Copt.*), is of Lower Egypt: in the third century. The Thebaic, or Sahidic, is of Upper Egypt. The Syriac (*Syr.*) is that restored to the ancient text by Syrian MSS. from the Natrian Monastery: now in British Museum: published by *Cureton*. The Peshito (*pure*) Syriac version was made in the second century.

Irenæus, Origen, Cyprian, Hilary, and *Lucifer*, are valuable witnesses for the old readings of the text, from the second to the fourth century.

I take this opportunity of acknowledging my great obligations to the Rev. A. Moody Stuart, which, through desire of brevity, were insufficiently recognized in vol. iii., Commentary on the Song of Solomon. The five main divisions, the three notes of time, quotations from Greek Fathers, and from old black-letter English Bibles, were derived from his valuable work on that difficult book of Holy Writ. In so comprehensive a work as the present, the commentator can only in a small degree be original in his researches for each sacred book, and must in the main gather from the Commentaries of others:—

'―――― apis Matinæ more modoque
Grata carpentis thyma per laborem.'

May the fruit so gathered be unto the eternal life of many, "that both he that soweth, and he that reapeth, may rejoice together."

ANDREW ROBERT FAUSSET, M.A.

HEWORTH, YORK, *November*, 1869.

INTRODUCTION.

FIRST CORINTHIANS.

THE authenticity of this epistle is attested by *Clement* of Rome ('Ep. to Corinth.,' c. 47), *Polycarp* ('Ep. to Philipp.,' c. 11), *Ignatius* ('Ad Eph.,' 2), and *Irenæus* ('Adversus Hæreses,' iv., 27, 3). The city to which it was sent was famed for its commerce, chiefly due to its situation between the Ionian and Ægean seas, on the isthmus connecting the Peloponnese with Greece. In St. Paul's time it was capital of Achaia, and seat of the Roman proconsul (Acts xviii. 12). The state of morals in it was notorious, even in the heathen world; so much so, that 'to Corinthianize' was proverbial for 'to play the wanton;' hence arose dangers to the purity of the church at Corinth. That church was founded by St. Paul on his first visit (Acts xviii. 1-17), in his second missionary journey.

Occasion and Subject.—He had been the instrument of converting many Gentiles (ch. xii. 2) and some Jews (Acts xviii. 8), notwithstanding the vehement opposition of his countrymen (Acts xviii. 5), during the year and a half of his sojourn there. The converts were chiefly of the humbler classes, (ch. i. 26, &c.) Crispus (ch. i. 14; Acts xviii. 8), Erastus, and Gaius (Caius) were, however, men of rank (Rom. xvi. 23). A variety of classes is implied in ch. xi. 22. The risk of contamination by contact with surrounding corruptions, and the temptation to crave for Greek philosophy and rhetoric (which Apollos's eloquent style rather fostered, Acts xviii. 24, &c.), in contrast to Paul's simple preaching of Christ crucified (ch. ii. 1, &c.), as well as the opposition of certain teachers, naturally caused him anxiety. Emissaries from the Judaizers of Palestine boasted of 'letters of commendation' from Jerusalem, the metropolis of the faith. They did not, it is true, insist on circumcision in refined Corinth, where the attempt would have been hopeless, as they did among the simpler people of Galatia; but they attacked the apostolic authority of Paul (ch. ix. 1, 2; 2 Cor. x. 1, 7, 8), some declaring themselves followers of Cephas, the chief apostle; others boasting that they belonged to Christ Himself (ch. i. 12; 2 Cor. x. 7), whilst they haughtily repudiated all subordinate teaching. They gave out themselves for apostles (2 Cor. xi. 5, 13). The ground taken was, that Paul was not one of the twelve, nor an eye-witness of the Gospel facts, and durst not prove his apostleship by claiming sustenance from the Church. Another section avowed themselves followers of Paul; but did so in a party spirit, exalting the minister rather than Christ. The followers of Apollos, again, unduly prized his Alexandrian eloquence, to the disparagement of the apostle, who studiously avoided any deviation from Christian simplicity (ch. ii. 1-5). In this last party there may have arisen an Antinomian tendency, in order to defend their own immorality: hence their denial of the resurrection, and their adoption of the Epicurean motto, prevalent in heathen Corinth, "Let us eat and drink, for to-morrow we die" (ch. xv. 32). Hence, perhaps, arose their connivance at the incestuous intercourse kept up by one of them with his stepmother. The household of Chloe informed St. Paul of other evils: contentions, divisions, and lawsuits brought against brethren in heathen law courts by professing Christians (ch. vi. 1); the abuse of spiritual gifts into occasions of display and fanaticism (ch. xiv.); the interruption of public worship by simultaneous ministrations; and decorum violated by women speaking unveiled (contrary to Oriental usage), and so usurping the office of men; and even the holy communion desecrated by revellings. These evils induced him to send Timothy (ch. iv. 17) to them, after his journey to Macedonia. Other messengers, also, came from Corinth, consulting him on (1.) meats offered to idols; (2.) celibacy and marriage; (3.) the due exercise of spiritual gifts in public worship; (4.) the collection for the saints at Jerusalem, (ch. xvi. 1, &c.)

St. Paul's Visits and Letters to Corinth.—Ch. v. 9, "I wrote unto you in an epistle not to company with fornicators," implies that St. Paul had written a previous letter to the Corinthians. Probably in it he had enjoined a contribution for the poor saints at Jerusalem; whereupon they asked directions as to the mode; to which he now replies (ch. xvi. 2). It also announced his intention of visiting them on his way to Macedonia; and again, on his return from Macedonia; which purpose he changed, on hearing the unfavourable report from Chloe's household (ch. xvi. 5-7), for which he was charged with fickleness (2 Cor. i. 15, 16, 17). In the first epistle which we have, the fornication is alluded to only in a summary way, as if he were rather replying to an excuse set up after his rebuke, than introducing it for the first time (*Alford*). Preceding this former letter, he seems to have paid a *second* visit: for in 2 Cor. xii. 14; xiii. 1, he speaks of his intention of paying them a *third* visit, implying he had already *twice* visited them. See also notes on 2 Cor. ii. 1; xiii. 2; also i. 15, 16. It is hardly likely that during his three years' sojourn at Ephesus (Acts xix. 10; xx. 31) he would have failed to revisit his Corinthian converts, which he could so readily do by sea, there being constant maritime intercourse between the two cities. This second visit was probably short (cf. ch. xvi. 7), and attended with pain (2 Cor. ii. 1), occasioned by the scandalous conduct of so many of his converts. His milder censures having then failed to produce reformation, he wrote briefly, directing them "not to company with fornicators." On their misapprehending this injunction, he explained it fully in the first of the two extant epistles (ch. v. 9-12). That the *second* visit is not mentioned in Acts is no objection to its having really taken place, as that book is fragmentary, and omits other leading incidents in St. Paul's life—*e. g.*, his visit to Arabia (Gal. i. 17-21).

The *Place of Writing* is fixed to be Ephesus (ch. xvi. 8). The subscription in the English version, "From Philippi," has no authority, and probably arose from a mistaken translation of ch. xvi. 5, 'for *I am passing through* Macedonia.' At the time of writing, St. Paul implies (ch. xvi. 8) that he intended to leave Ephesus after Pentecost *of that year.* He really did leave it about Pentecost, (57 A. D.) Cf. Acts xix. 21. The Passover imagery (ch. v. 7) makes it likely that the season was about Easter. Thus the date of the epistle is fixed with tolerable accuracy, about Easter, certainly before Pentecost, in the third year of his residence at Ephesus, 57 A. D. For other arguments, see *Conybeare* and *Howson's* 'Life and Epistles of St. Paul.'

The epistle is written in the name of Sosthenes "(our) brother." Perhaps he is the same as the Sosthenes, Acts xviii. 17, and was converted subsequently. He bears no part in the epistle itself, the apostle in the next verse (*v.* 4, &c.) using the first person: so Timothy, 2 Cor. i. 1. The bearers of the epistle were probably Stephanas, Fortunatus, and Achaicus (see the subscription), whom he mentions (ch. xvi. 17, 18) as with him then, but as about to return to Corinth; he therefore commends them to the regard of the Corinthians.

SECOND CORINTHIANS.

THE following reasons seem to have induced St. Paul to write this second epistle:—(1.) That he might explain the reasons for his having deferred to pay his promised visit, by taking Corinth as his way to Macedonia (1 Cor. iv. 19; ch. i. 15, 16; cf. 1 Cor. xvi. 5); and so that he might set forth his apostolic walk in general (ch. i. 12, 24; vi. 3-13; vii. 2). (2.) That he might commend their obedience to the directions in his first epistle, and at the same time direct them to forgive the offender, as having been punished sufficiently (ch. ii. 1-11; vii. 6-16). (3.) That he might urge them to collect for the poor saints at Jerusalem (ch. viii. 1-9, 15). (4.) That he might maintain his apostolic authority and reprove gainsayers.

The external testimonies for *its genuineness* are—*Irenæus* ('Hæreses,' iii., 7, 1), *Athenagoras* ('De Resurrectione Mortuorum'), *Clement* of Alexandria ('Stromata,' iii., sec. 94; iv., sec. 101), *Tertullian*, ('De Pudicitia,' ch. xiii.)

The *Time of Writing* was after Pentecost, A.D. 57, when St. Paul left Ephesus for Troas. Having stayed in the latter place for some time, preaching the Gospel with effect (ch. ii. 12), he went on to Macedonia, being eager to meet Titus there, having been disappointed in his not coming to Troas, as had been agreed on between them. Having heard from him the tidings he so much desired, of the good effect produced on the Corinthians by his first epistle, and having tested the liberality of the Macedonian churches (ch. viii. 1), he wrote this second epistle, and then went on to Greece, where he abode three months; then, after travelling by land, reached Philippi on his return at Passover or Easter, 58 A.D. (Acts xx. 1-6.) So that this epistle must have been written about autumn, 57 A.D.

Macedonia was the *Place* from which it was written (ch. ix. 2, where the present, 'I am boasting,' implies his presence *then* in Macedonia). In Asia (Lydian) he had undergone some great peril (ch. i. 8, 9), whether the reference be (*Paley*) to the tumult at Ephesus (Acts xix. 23-41), or (*Alford*) to a dangerous illness in which he despaired of life. Thence he passed by Troas to Philippi, the first city which would meet him in entering Macedonia. The importance of the Philippian church would induce him to stay there some time: as also his desire to collect from the Macedonian churches for the poor saints at Jerusalem. His anxiety is recorded (ch. vii. 5) as occurring *when he came into Macedonia*, and therefore must have been at *Philippi*, which was the first city of Macedonia in coming from Troas; here, too, from ch. vii. 6, compared with *v.* 5, must have been the scene of his receiving the comforting tidings from Titus. "Macedonia" is used for *Philippi* in ch. xi. 9, as is proved by comparison with Phil. iv. 15, 16. *Alford* argues, from ch. viii. 1, where he speaks of the "grace . . . bestowed on the *churches* (plural) of Macedonia," that Paul must have visited *other* churches in Macedonia, besides Philippi, when he wrote—*e.g.*, Thessalonica, Berea, &c.—and that Philippi, the *first* on his route, is less likely to have been the scene of writing than the *last* on his route, whichever it was; perhaps Thessalonica. But Philippi, being the chief town of the province, was probably the place to which all the collections of the churches were sent. Ancient tradition, too (as appears from the subscription), favours the view that Philippi was the place from which this epistle was sent by the hands of Titus, who received, besides, a charge to prosecute at Corinth the collection which he had begun at his first visit (ch. viii. 6). The Vatican MS. and old Syriac version state "Philippi."

The *Style* is varied, and passes rapidly from one phase of feeling to another : now joyous and consolatory, again severe and full of reproof; at one time gentle and affectionate, at another, sternly rebuking opponents, and upholding his apostolic dignity. This variety accords with the warm character of the apostle, which nowhere is manifested more beautifully than in this epistle. His bodily frailty, and the chronic malady under which he suffered, and which is often alluded to (ch. iv. 7; v. 1-4; xii. 7-9 : cf. note, i. 8), must have been especially trying to his ardent temperament. Besides this, was the pressing anxiety of the "care of all the churches." At Corinth, as elsewhere, Judaizing emissaries wished to bind legal fetters of letter and form (cf. ch. iii. 3-18) on the freedom and catholicity of the Church. On the other hand, there were freethinkers, who defended their immorality by infidel theories (1 Cor. xv. 12, 32-36). These were the 'fightings without' and 'fears within' (ch. vii. 5, 6) which agitated the apostle's mind, until Titus brought him comforting tidings from Corinth. Even then, whilst the majority at Corinth had testified their repentance, and, as St. Paul had desired, excommunicated the incestuous person, and contributed for the poor Christians of Judea, there was still a minority who contemptuously resisted the apostle. These accused him of crafty motives, as if he had personal gain in view in the collection; and this, notwithstanding his scrupulous care to be above possibility of reasonable suspicion, by having others besides himself to take charge of the money. This insinuation was palpably inconsistent with their other charge, that he could be no true apostle, as he did not claim maintenance from the churches which he founded. Another accusation they brought of cowardly weakness; that he was always threatening severe measures without daring to execute them (ch. x. 8-16; xiii. 2); and that he was vacillating in his teaching and practice; circumcising Timothy, yet withholding circumcision from Titus; a Jew among the Jews, a Greek among the Greeks. That most of these opponents were of the Judaizing party, appears from ch. xi. 22. They seem to have been headed by an emissary from Judea ("he that cometh," ch. xi. 4), who had brought "letters of condemnation" (ch. iii. 1) from members of the church at Jerusalem, and who boasted of his pure Hebrew descent, and his close connection with Christ Himself (ch. xi. 13, 23). His partizans contrasted his high pretensions with the timid humility of St. Paul (1 Cor. ii. 3), and his rhetoric with the apostle's unadorned style (ch. xi. 6; x. 10, 13). It was this state of things at Corinth, reported by Titus, that caused St. Paul to send him back forthwith thither with this second epistle, addressed, not to Corinth only (1 Cor. i. 2), but to all the churches also "in all Achaia" (ch. i. 1), which had in some degree been affected by the same causes. The widely different tone in different parts of the epistle is due to the diversity which existed at Corinth between the penitent majority and the refractory minority. The former he addresses with the warmest affection; the latter with menace and warning. Two deputies, chosen by the churches to take charge of the contribution to be collected at Corinth, accompanied Titus (ch. viii. 18, 19, 22).

GALATIANS.

THE internal and external evidence for St. Paul's *Authorship* is conclusive. The *Style* is characteristically Pauline. The superscription, and allusions to the apostle of the Gentiles in the first person throughout, establish the fact (ch. i. 1, 13-24; ii. 1-14). His authorship is also upheld by the unanimous testimony of the ancient Church : cf. *Irenæus*

('Adversus Hæreses,' iii., 7, 2) (Gal. iii. 19); *Polycarp* (' Philipp.,' iii.) quotes Gal. iv. 26, and vi. 7 ; *Justin Martyr*, or whoever wrote the 'Oratio ad Græcos,' alludes to Gal. iv. 12, and v. 20 : cf. *Tertullian*, (' De Præscriptione,' ch. lx.)

The epistle was written "*to the churches of Galatia*" (ch. i. 2), a district of Asia Minor, bordering on Phrygia, Pontus, Bithynia, Cappadocia, and Paphlagonia. The inhabitants (Gallo-Græci, contracted into Galati, another form of 'Kelts') were Gauls in origin, the latter having overrun Asia Minor, after they had pillaged Delphi, about B. C. 280, and at last permanently settled in the central parts, thence called Gallogræcia or Galatia. Their character, as shown in this epistle, is in entire consonance with that ascribed to the Gallic race by all writers. *Cæsar* (' B. G.,' iv., 5), 'The infirmity of the Gauls is, that they are fickle in their resolves, fond of change, and not to be trusted.' So *Thierry* (quoted by *Alford*), 'Frank, impetuous, impressible, eminently intelligent, at the same time extremely changeable, inconstant, fond of show, perpetually quarrelling, the fruit of excessive vanity.' They received St. Paul at first with all joy and kindness; but soon wavered in their allegiance to the Gospel, and hearkened as eagerly now to Judaizing teachers as they had before to him (ch. iv. 14-16). The apostle himself had been the first preacher among them (Acts xvi. 6; Gal. i. 8; iv. 13 [see note; '*on account of* infirmity of flesh I preached unto you at the first:' implying that sickness detained him among them], 19); and had then probably founded churches, which at his subsequent visit he "strengthened" in the faith (Acts xviii. 23). His first visit was about A. D. 51, during his second missionary journey. *Josephus* (' Antiquities,' xvi., 62) testifies that many Jews resided in Ancyra in Galatia. Among these, doubtless, as elsewhere, he began his preaching. And though subsequently the majority in the Galatian churches were Gentiles (ch. iv. 8, 9), yet these were soon infected by Judaizing teachers, and almost suffered themselves to be persuaded to undergo circumcision (ch. i. 6; iii. 1, 3; v. 2, 3; vi. 12, 13). Accustomed as the Galatians had been, when heathen, to the mystic worship of Cybele (prevalent in the neighbouring Phrygia), and the theosophistic doctrines connected with it, they were the more readily led to believe that the full privileges of Christianity could only be attained through an elaborate system of ceremonial symbolism (ch. iv. 9-11; v. 7-12). They even gave ear to the insinuation that Paul himself observed the law among the Jews, though he persuaded the Gentiles to renounce it, and that his motive was to keep his converts in a subordinate state, excluded from the full privileges of Christianity, which were enjoyed by the circumcised alone (ch. iv. 16; v. 11 : cf. with ch. ii. 17); and that in "becoming all things to all men," he was an interesting flatterer (ch. i. 10), aiming at forming a party for himself : moreover, that he falsely represented himself as an apostle divinely commissioned by Christ, whereas he was but a messenger sent by the Twelve and the church at Jerusalem, and that his teaching was now at variance with that of St. Peter and James, "pillars" of the Church, and therefore ought not to be accepted.

His *Purpose*, then, in writing was—(1.) To defend his apostolic authority (ch. i. 11-19; ii. 1-14). (2.) To counteract the evil influence of the Judaizers (chs. iii. and iv.), and to show that their doctrine destroyed the very *essence of* Christianity, by lowering its spirituality to an outward ceremonial. (3.) To give exhortation for strengthening Galatian believers in faith towards Christ, and in the fruits of the Spirit, (chs. v. and vi.) He had already, face to face, testified against the Judaizing teachers (Acts xviii. 23; ch. i. 9; iv. 16); and now that he has heard of the continued and increasing prevalence of the evil, he writes *with his own hand* (ch. vi. 11 : a labour which he usually delegated to an amanuensis) to oppose it. The sketch he gives of his apostolic career confirms the account in Acts, and shows his independence of human authority, however exalted. His protest against Peter, in ch. ii. 14-21, disproves the figment, not merely of *papal*, but even of *that apostle's* supremacy; and shows that Peter, save when specially inspired, was fallible like other men.

There is much in common between this epistle and that to the Romans, on the subject of justification by faith only, and not by the law. But the epistle to the Romans handles the subject in a didactic and logical mode, without any special reference; this epistle, controversially, and with special reference to the Judaizers.

The *Style* combines the two extremes, sternness (ch. i.; iii. 1-5) and tenderness (ch. vi. 19, 20), both characteristic of a man of strong emotions, and alike well suited for acting on an impressible people, such as the Galatians. The beginning is abrupt, as suited the urgency of the question and the greatness of the danger. A tone of sadness, too, is apparent, such as might be expected in a warm-hearted teacher who had just learned, that those whom he loved were forsaking his teachings for those of perverters of the truth, as well as giving ear to calumnies against himself.

The *Time of Writing* was *after* the visit to Jerusalem recorded in Acts xv. 1, &c.— *i. e.*, A. D. 50—if that visit be, as seems probable, identical with that in ch. ii. 1, &c. Further, as chs. i. 9 ("as we said *before*") and iv. 16 ('Have (*Alford*) I *become* your enemy?"—viz., at my second visit, whereas I was welcomed by you at my first visit), refer to his second visit, this epistle must have been written after the date of that visit (the autumn of A. D. 54). Acts xviii. 23 implies that, at his second visit, the Galatians were well established in the faith, which made their speedy declension the stranger. Ch. iv. 13, "Ye know how . . . I preached . . . at the first" (Greek, 'at the former time'), implies that Paul, at the time of writing, had been *twice* in Galatia; and ch. i. 6, "I marvel that ye are *so soon* removed," implies that he wrote not long after having left Galatia the second time; probably in the early part of *his residence at Ephesus* (Acts xviii. 23; xix. 1, &c., from A. D. 54, the autumn, to A. D. 57, Pentecost) (*Alford*). *Conybeare* and *Howson*, from the similarity in argument between this epistle and that to the Romans, think it was *not written till his stay at Corinth* (Acts xx. 2, 3), during the winter of 57-58, whence he wrote his epistle to the Romans; certainly, in the theory of the earlier writing of it from Ephesus, it does seem unlikely that the two epistles to the Corinthians, so dissimilar, should intervene between those so similar as the epistles to the Galatians and Romans; or that the epistle to the Galatians should intervene between the second to the Thessalonians and the first to the Corinthians. The decision between the two theories rests on the words, "so soon." If these be not considered inconsistent with three years having elapsed since his second visit to Galatia, the argument, from the similarity to the epistle to the Romans, seems to me conclusive. Three years would be "soon," seeing they had shown no signs of apostasy at his second visit (Acts xviii. 23). This epistle seems written on the spur of the exigency—tidings having reached him *at Corinth*, from Ephesus, of the Judaizing of many of his Galatian converts—in an admonitory and controversial tone, to maintain the great principles of Christian liberty and justification by faith only; that to the Romans is a more deliberate and systematic exposition of the same central truths, subsequently, to a church with which he was personally unacquainted. See note, ch. i. 6, for *Birks's* view. *Paley* ('Horæ Paulinæ') remarks how perfectly adapted the argument is to the historical circumstances under which the epistle was written. Thus, that to the Galatians, a church which Paul had founded, he puts mainly upon *authority;* that to the Romans, to whom he was not personally known, entirely upon *argument.* The tone is that of reproof, not praise or thanksgiving.

Divisions.—There are two controversial portions, and a concluding *hortatory* one. The *first* (chs. i. and ii.) defends his apostolical authority and his independency of the Twelve. The *second,* the *polemical* portion (chs. iii. and iv.), by argument (ch. iii.), appeal (ch. iv. 12-20), and illustration (ch. iv. 1-7, 21-30), establishes justification by faith, and not by the deeds of the law. The *third* portion (chs. v. and vi.) warns (ch. iv. 31; v. 6), illustrates a real fulfilment of the law (ch. v. 13-26), practically instructs and recapitulates (ch. vi.) (*Ellicott*).

EPHESIANS.

THE heading (ch. i. 1), and ch. iii. 1, show that this epistle claims to be that of St. Paul. This claim is confirmed by the testimonies of *Irenæus* ('Hæreses,' v., 2, 3; and i., 8, 5), *Clemens* ('Alexandrinus Stromata,' iv., sec. 65; and 'Paed.,' i., sec. 8), *Origen* ('Adv. Cels.,' iv., 211). It is quoted by *Valentinus* (120 A. D.), *viz.*, iii., 14-18, as we know from *Hippolytus* ('Refutation of Hæres.,' p. 193). *Polycarp* ('Ep. Philipp.,' ch. xii.) testifies to its canonicity. So *Tertullian* ('Adv. Marcion,' v., 17). *Ignatius* ('Eph.,' xii.) alludes to the frequent and affectionate mention made by St. Paul of the Christian state, privileges, and persons of the Ephesians, in his epistle.

Two theories, besides the ordinary one, have been held on the question, *to whom* the epistle is addressed. *Grotius,* after *Marcion,* maintains that it was addressed to the church at Laodicea, and that *it* is the epistle to which St. Paul refers, Col. iv. 16. But the epistle to the Colossians was probably written *before* that to the Ephesians, as appears from the parallel passages in Ephesians bearing marks of being expanded from those in Colossians; and *Marcion* seems to have drawn his notion, as to our epistle, from misinterpreting St. Paul's allusion (Col. iv. 16). *Origen,* and *Clement* of Alexandria, and even *Tertullian,* who refers to *Marcion,* give no sanction to his notion. No single MS. contains the heading, "to the saints that are at Laodicea." The very resemblance of our epistle to that to the Colossians is against the theory; for if the former were really the one addressed to Laodicea, St. Paul would not have deemed it necessary that the churches of Colosse and Laodicea should interchange epistles. The greetings, moreover (Col. iv. 15), which he sends *through the Colossians to the Laodiceans,* are quite incompatible with the idea that Paul wrote an epistle *to the Laodiceans* at the same time, and by the same bearer, Tychicus (the bearer of our epistle, as well as of that to Colosse); for who, under such circumstances, but would send the greetings *directly* in the letter to the party saluted? The letter to Laodicea was evidently written some time *before* that to Colosse. *Archbishop Usher* has advanced the second theory: That it was an *encyclical* letter, headed, as in MSS. B and א, "to the saints that are . . . and to the faithful," the name of each church being inserted in the copy sent to it; and that its *being sent to Ephesus first,* occasioned its being entitled, as now, the Epistle to the Ephesians. *Alford* objects to this :—(1.) It is at variance with the spirit of the epistle, which is addressed to one set of persons throughout, co-existing in one place, and as one body, and under the same circumstances. (2.) The improbability that the apostle, who in two of his epistles (2 Cor. and Gal.) has so plainly specified their encyclical character, should have here omitted such specification.   (3.) The still greater improbability that he should have written a circular epistle to a district, of which Ephesus was the commercial capital, addressed to various churches, yet from its very contents (as by the opponents' hypothesis) not admitting of special application to the church of that metropolis, in which he had spent so long a time, and to which he was so affectionately bound.   (4.) The inconsistency of this hypothesis with the address of the epistle, and the universal testimony of the ancient Church.   The absence of personal greetings is not an argument for either of the two theories; for similarly there are none in Gal., Phil., 1 and 2 Thess., 1 Tim.   The better he knows the parties addressed, and the more general and solemn the subject, the less he seems to give of individual notices.   Writing, as he does, on the constitution and prospects of Christ's universal Church, he refers the Ephesians, as to personal matters, to the bearer of the epistle, Tychicus (ch. vi. 21, 22).   As to the omission of "which are at Ephesus" (ch. i. 1), in MSS. B ℵ, and *Origen*, so "in Rome" (Rom. i. 7) is omitted in some old MSS.: it was probably done by churches *among whom it was read*, in order to generalize the reference of its contents, and especially where the subject is catholic.   The words are found in the margin of B, from a first hand; and are found in A C Δ G *f g*, Vulgate.   If the omission be not due to the neighbouring churches, it must have been designed with a view to making it general in character when read to them, though primarily designed for the Ephesian church.

St. Paul's first visit to Ephesus (on the sea coast of Lydia, near the river Cayster) is related in Acts xviii. 19-21.   The work, begun by his disputations with the Jews in his short visit, was carried on by Apollos (Acts xviii. 24-26), and Aquila, and Priscilla.   At his second visit, after his journey to Jerusalem, and thence to the east regions of Asia Minor, he remained at Ephesus "three years" (Acts xix. 10, the "two years" in which verse are only *part* of the time, and Acts xx. 31); so that the founding and rearing of this church occupied an unusually large portion of his time and care; whence his language shows a warmth of feeling, a free outpouring of thought, and a union in spiritual privileges and hope between him and them (ch. i. 3, &c.), such as are natural from one so long and so intimately associated with those whom he addresses.   On his last journey to Jerusalem, he sailed by Ephesus, and summoned the elders of the Ephesian church to him at Miletus, where he delivered his farewell charge (Acts xx. 18-35).

Our epistle was addressed to the Ephesians during the early part of his imprisonment at Rome, immediately after that to the Colossians, to which it bears a close resemblance,— the apostle having in his mind generally the same great truths.   It is an undesigned proof of genuineness that the two epistles, written about the same date, and under the same circumstances, bear a closer mutual resemblance than those written at distant dates, and on different occasions.   (Cf. ch. i. 7, with Col. i. 14; ch. i. 10, with Col. i. 20; ch. iii. 2, with Col. i. 25; ch. v. 19, with Col. iii. 16; ch. vi. 22, with Col. iv. 8; ch. i. 19, ii. 5, with Col. ii. 12, 13; ch. iv. 2-4, with Col. iii. 12-15; ch. iv. 16, with Col. ii. 19; ch. iv. 32, with Col. iii. 13; ch. iv. 22-24, with Col. iii. 9, 10; ch. v. 6-8, with Col. iii. 6-8; ch. v. 15, 16, with Col. iv. 5; ch. vi. 19, 20, with Col. iv. 3, 4; ch. v. 22-33, vi. 1-9, with Col. iii. 18; ch. iv. 24-25, with Col. iii. 9; ch. v. 20-22, with Col. iii. 17, 18.)   Tychicus and Onesimus were being sent to Colosse; the former bearing the two epistles to the two churches respectively, the latter furnished with a letter of recommendation to Philemon, his former master, residing at Colosse.   The date was probably four years after parting with the Ephesian elders at Miletus (Acts xx.), about 62 A. D., before his imprisonment had become of the severe kind, which appears in his epistle to the Philippians.   From ch. vi. 19, 20, it is plain he had at the time, though a prisoner, some degree of freedom in preaching, which accords with Acts xxviii. 23, 30, 31, where he is represented as receiving at his lodgings all inquirers. His imprisonment began in February, 61 A. D., and lasted "two whole years" at least.

The church of Ephesus was made up of converts, partly Jews and partly Gentiles (Acts xix. 8-10). The epistle addresses a church so constituted (ch. ii. 14-22). Ephesus was famed for its idol temple of Artemis, or Diana, which, after having been burnt down by Herostratus, on the night that Alexander the Great was born (B. C. 355), was rebuilt at enormous cost, and was one of the wonders of the world. Hence, perhaps, have arisen his images drawn from a beautiful temple,—the Church being in true inner beauty that which the temple of the idol tried to realize in outward show (ch. ii. 19-22). The epistle (ch. iv. 17; v. 1-13) implies the profligacy for which the Ephesian heathen were notorious. Many of the same expressions occur in the epistle, as in St. Paul's address to the Ephesian elders. Cf. ch. i. 6, 7, and ch. ii. 7, as to "grace," with Acts xx. 24, 32: this may well be called 'the epistle of the grace of God' (*Alford*). Also, as to his "bonds," ch. iii. 1, and ch. iv. 1, with Acts xx. 22, 23; also ch. i. 11, as to "the counsel of God," with Acts xx. 27; also ch. i. 14, as to "the redemption of the purchased possession," with Acts xx. 28; also ch. i. 14, 18, ch. ii. 20, and ch. v. 5, as to "building up" the "inheritance," with Acts xx. 32.

The object of the epistle is 'to set forth the ground, the course, and the end of *the Church of the Faithful in Christ.* He speaks to the Ephesians as a sample of the Church universal' (*Alford*). Hence, "the Church" throughout the epistle is spoken of in the singular, not the plural. The Church's foundation, its course, and its end, are his theme alike in the larger and smaller divisions. 'Everywhere the foundation of the Church is in *the will of the Father;* the course of the Church is by *the satisfaction of the Son;* the end of the Church is the *life in the Holy Spirit*' (*Alford*). Cf. respectively ch. i. 11; ii. 5; iii. 16. This having been laid down as a matter of doctrine (this part closing with a sublime doxology, ch. iii. 14-21), is then made the ground of practical exhortations. In these latter, also (from ch. iv. 1, onward), the same threefold division prevails; for the Church is represented as founded on the counsel of 'God the Father, who is above all, through all, and in all,' reared by the "one Lord," Jesus Christ, through the "one Spirit" (ch. iv. 4-6, &c.), who give their respective graces to the several members. These last are therefore to exercise all these graces in the several relations of life, as husbands, wives, servants, children, &c. The conclusion is, that we must put on "the whole armour of God" (ch. vi. 13).

The sublimity of the *Style* corresponds to the sublimity of the subjects, and exceeds almost that of any of his epistles. It is appropriate that those to whom he so wrote were Christians long grounded in the faith. The very sublimity is the cause of the difficulty of style, and of the presence of peculiar expressions.

PHILIPPIANS.

THE *Internal Evidence* for its authenticity is strong. The style, manner of thought, and doctrine, accord with St. Paul's. The incidental allusions establish his authorship. *Paley* ('Horæ Paulinæ,' ch. vii.) instances the mention of the object of Epaphroditus' journey to Rome, the Philippian contribution to St. Paul's wants, Epaphroditus' sickness (ch. i. 7; ii. 25-30; iv. 10-18), the fact that Timothy had been long with St. Paul at Philippi (ch. i. 1; ii. 19), the reference to his being a prisoner at Rome now for a long time (ch. i. 12-14; ii. 17-28), his willingness to die (cf. ch. i. 23, with 2 Cor. v. 8), the reference to the Philippians having seen his maltreatment at Philippi (ch. i. 29, 30; ii. 1, 2).

External Evidence is equally decisive. *Polycarp*, 'Ad Philippenses,' sects. 3 and 11, A. D. 107: so that Philippians who had witnessed Epaphroditus' return, and the first reading of Paul's epistle, may have been living when *Polycarp* wrote. *Marcion*, in *Tertullian* (140 A. D.), recognizes its authenticity. So the 'Muratorian Fragment.' *Irenæus* ('Adversus Hæreses,' iv., 18, sec. 4); *Clement* of Alexandria ('Pædagogus,' l., i., p. 107); the epistle of the churches of Lyons and Vienne (177 A. D.), in *Eusebius's* 'Ecclesiastical History,' v., 2; *Tertullian* ('Resurrectione Carnis,' c. xxiii.); *Origen* ('Celsus, l., iii., p. 122); *Cyprian* ('Testimonie sagainst the Jews,' iii. 39).

Philippi was *the first* (*i. e.*, farthest from Rome, and *first which met Paul in entering Macedonia*) *city of the district*, called *Macedonia Prima* (as lying *farthest eastward*). The Greek (Acts xvi. 12) should not be translated "the *chief* city," as English version (*Alford*). Not it, but Thessalonica, was the *chief* city of the province, and Amphipolis, of the district called Macedonia Prima. It was a *Roman* 'colony' (Acts xvi. 12), made so by Augustus, to commemorate his victory over Brutus and Cassius. A *colony* was a portion of Rome itself transplanted to the provinces, and a portrait of the mother city (*Aulius Gellius*, xvi., 13). Its inhabitants were Roman citizens, having the right of voting in the Roman tribes, governed by their own senate and magistrates, and not by the governor of the province, with the Roman law, and Latin language.

Paul, with Silas and Timothy, planted the Gospel there (Acts xvi. 12, &c.) in his second missionary journey, A. D. 51. Doubtless he visited it again on his journey from Ephesus into Macedonia (Acts xx. 1); and Acts xx. 3, 6, expressly mentions his third visit, on his return from Greece (Corinth) to Syria, by way of Macedonia. His sufferings at Philippi (Acts xvi. 19, &c.) strengthened the Christian bond between him and his Philippian converts, who also were exposed to trials for the Gospel's sake (1 Thess. ii. 2). They alone sent supplies for his temporal wants—*twice* shortly after he had left them (ch. iv. 15, 16), and again, a third time, shortly before writing this epistle (2 Cor. xi. 9; ch. iv. 10, 18). This fervent attachment was, perhaps, in part due to the fact that few Jews were in Philippi, as in other scenes of his labours, to sow the seeds of distrust. There was no synagogue, but merely a Jewish Proseucha, or oratory, by the river side. So that there only do we read of his meeting no opposition from Jews, but only from the masters of the divining damsel, whose gains had been put an end to by her being dispossessed. The trial of his patience by the check to his zeal, when he was forbidden by the Spirit to enter Asia, Bithynia, and Assyria, and the hopes kindled by the vision inviting him to Macedonia, then the success of his preaching at Philippi, after the temporary check and the miraculous zeal set to it in the conversion of the gaoler, and the affection of his converts, all endeared Philippi especially to him.

Though the Philippian church was as yet free from Judaizing influence, yet it needed to be forewarned of that danger which might at any time assail it from without (ch. iii. 2); even as such evil influences had crept into the Galatian churches. In ch. iv. 2, 3, we find a trace of the fact recorded in the history (Acts xvi. 13, 14), that *female* converts were among the first to receive the Gospel.

As to the state of the church, we gather from 2 Cor. viii. 1, 2, that its members were *poor*, yet most *liberal*; and from ch. i. 28-30, that they were undergoing persecution. Their only blemish was, on the part of some members, a tendency to dissension. Hence arise his admonitions against disputings (ch. i. 27; ii. 1-4, 12, 14; iv. 2).

The *Object* is general: not only to thank the Philippians for their contribution sent by Epaphroditus, who was now, in returning, to take back the apostle's letter, but to express his Christian sympathy, and to exhort them to a life consonant with that of Christ, and to warn them against existing dissensions, and future possible assaults of Judaizers. It is remarkable in this epistle alone, amidst many commendations, there are no express censures of those addressed. No doctrinal error or schism had as yet sprung up; the only blemish hinted at is, that some of the Philippian church were wanting in lowliness, whence resulted disputation. Two women, Euodias and Syntyche, are mentioned as having so erred. The epistle may be divided into *three* parts :—(1.) Affectionate address; reference to his own state as a prisoner at Rome, and to theirs, and to his mission of Epaphroditus to them, (chs. i. and ii.) Epaphroditus probably held a leading office in the Philippian church—perhaps as a presbyter. After Tychicus and Onesimus had departed (A. D. 62), carrying the epistles to the Ephesians, Colossians, and Philemon, St. Paul was cheered in his imprisonment by the arrival of Epaphroditus with the Philippian contribution. That faithful "brother, companion in labour, and fellow-soldier," had brought on himself, by the fatigues of the journey, a dangerous sickness (ch. ii. 25, 26, 30). But now that he was recovered, he "longed" to return to his Philippian flock, and in person to relieve their anxiety on his behalf; and the apostle gladly availed himself of the opportunity of writing a letter of grateful acknowledgments and Christian exhortations. (2.) Caution against Judaizing teachers, supported by reference to his former and present feeling towards Jewish legalism, (ch. iii.) (3.) Admonitions to individuals, and to the Church, thanks for their seasonable aid, and concluding benedictions.

This epistle was written from Rome during the imprisonment, the beginning of which is related in Acts xxviii. 16, 20, 30, 31. The reference to "Cæsar's household" (ch. iv. 22), and to the "palace" (ch. i. 13 ['*Prætorium*']; probably *the barrack of the Prætorian body-guard*, attached to "the palace" of Nero), confirms this. During his first imprisonment at Rome, he was in custody of the Prætorian Prefect, with which agrees the specification of the 'Prætorium,' ch. i. 13; and his situation in ch. i. 12-14, agrees with his situation in the first two years of his imprisonment (Acts xxviii. 30, 31). The following reasons show that it was written towards *the close* of that imprisonment :—(1.) He expresses his expectation of the immediate decision of his cause (ch. ii. 23). (2.) Enough time had elapsed for the Philippians to hear of his imprisonment, to send Epaphroditus to him, to hear of Epaphroditus' arrival and sickness, and send back word to Rome of their distress (ch. ii. 26). (3.) It must have been written after the three other epistles from Rome—viz., Colossians, Ephesians, and Philemon; for Luke is no longer with him (ch. ii. 20), otherwise he would have been specified as saluting them, having formerly laboured among them, whereas he is mentioned as with him in Col. iv. 14; Phile. 24. Again, in Eph. vi. 19, 20, his freedom to preach is implied; but in ch. i. 13-18, his bondage is dwelt on: *not himself*, but *others*, preached, and made his imprisonment known. Again, in Phile. 22, he anticipates his release, which contrasts with the more depressed anticipations of this epistle. (4.) A considerable time had elapsed since the beginning of his imprisonment, for 'his bonds' to have become so widely known, and to have produced such good effects for the Gospel (ch. i. 13).   (5.) There is evidently an increase in the rigour of his imprisonment now, as compared with the early stage, as described in Acts xxviii. (cf. ch. i. 29, 30; ii. 27).   History furnishes a probable clue to account for this increase of rigour.   In the second year of St. Paul's imprisonment (A. D. 62), Burrus, the Prætorian Prefect, to whose custody he had been committed (Acts xxviii. 16, "the captain of the guard"), died; and Nero, the emperor, having divorced Octavia, and married Poppæa, a Jewish proselytess (who then caused her rival, Octavia, to be murdered, and gloated over the head of her victim), exalted Tigellinus, the chief promoter of the marriage, a monster of wickedness, to the Prætorian Prefecture.   It was then he seems to have been removed from his own house into the Prætorium, or barrack of the Prætorian guards, attached to the palace, for stricter custody; hence he writes less hopefully as to the result of his trial (ch. ii. 17; iii. 11).   Some of the Prætorian guards who had the custody of him before would then naturally make known his "bonds," in accordance with ch. i. 13; from the smaller Prætorian body-guard at the palace, the report would spread to the general permanent Prætorian camp, which Tiberius had established north of the city, outside of the walls.   He had arrived in Rome, February, 61; the 'two whole years (Acts xxviii. 30) in his own hired house' ended February, 63; so that the date of this epistle, written shortly after, evidently whilst the danger was imminent, would be about spring or summer, 63.   The providence of God averted the danger.   He probably was thought beneath the notice of Tigellinus, who was more intent on court intrigues.   The death of Nero's favourite, Pallas, the brother of Felix, this same year, also took out of the way another source of danger.

The *Style* is abrupt and discontinuous, his fervour leading him to pass rapidly from one theme to another (ch. ii. 18, 19-24, 25-30; iii. 1-15).   In no epistle does he use so warm expressions of love.   He lays aside his official tone, and does not give his title, "apostle," that he may make them feel he regards them as friends and equals.   Like his midnight song of praise in the Philippian prison, this epistle from his Roman confinement is singularly joyous.   In ch. iv. 1, he seems at a loss for words sufficient to express all the ardour of his affection for the Philippians: "My brethren dearly beloved and longed for, my joy and crown, so stand fast in the Lord, my dearly beloved."   The mention of bishops and deacons, in ch. i. 1, is due to the late date, at a time when the church had begun to assume that order which is laid down in the pastoral epistles, and which continued prevalent in the first and purest age of the Church.   In 107 A. D. Philippi was visited by *Ignatius*, on his way to martyrdom at Rome.   Immediately afterwards *Polycarp*, of Smyrna, wrote to the Philippians, sending, at their request, a copy of all the letters of *Ignatius* which were in the possession of the church at Smyrna.   The same faith and sympathy with sufferers for Christ distinguished them in this later time as in St. Paul's days.   Their religion was practical and emotional, rather than speculative; whence there is but little of doctrine and quotation from the Old Testament.   Their gold mines, whilst furnishing the means of their early liberality, occasioned the need of warnings against covetousness, which are found in *Polycarp's* 'Epistle.'   On the whole, we cannot doubt that the graces which distinguished them in the succeeding generation, after Paul, were due in part to this epistle, as well as his oral teaching.

COLOSSIANS.

ITS *Genuineness* is attested by *Justin Martyr* ('Contra Tryphonen,' p. 311, b.), who quotes "the first-born of every creature," in reference to Christ, from ch. i. 15. *Theophilus* of Antioch, 'To Autolychus,' ii., p. 100. *Irenæus* (ch. iii., 14, 1) quotes expressly from this epistle to the Colossians (ch. iv. 14). *Clement* of Alexandria ('Stromata,' i., p. 325) quotes ch. i. 28; elsewhere he quotes ch. i. 9-11, 28; ii. 2, &c.; ii. 8; iii. 12, 14; iv. 2, 3, &c. *Tertullian* ('De Præscriptione Hæreticorum,' ch. vii.) quotes ch. ii. 8; 'De Resurrectione Carnis,' ch. xxiii., he quotes ch. ii. 12, 20, and ch. iii. 1, 3. *Origen* ('Contra Celsus,' v., 8) quotes ch. ii. 18, 19.

Colosse (or, as in B, 'Colassæ') was a city of Phrygia, on the river Lycus, a branch of the Meander. Supposed to have occupied the site of the modern Chonos. The church there was mainly composed of Gentiles (cf. ch. i. 21; ii. 13). *Alford* infers, from ch. ii. 1, that Paul had not seen its members, and therefore could not have been its founder, as *Theodoret* thought. Ch. i. 7, 8, suggests the probability that Epaphras was the first founder. The date of its foundation must have been subsequent to Paul's visitation, "strengthening in order" all the churches of Galatia and Phrygia (Acts xviii. 24); for otherwise he must have visited the Colossians, which ch. ii. 1 implies he had not. Had Paul been their father in the faith, he would have alluded to it, as in 1 Cor. iii. 6, 10; iv. 15; 1 Thess. i. 5; ii. 1. It is only in the epistles to the Romans and Ephesians, and this, such allusions are wanting: in that to the Romans, because, as in Colosse, he had not been the instrument of their conversion; in that to the Ephesians, owing to the general nature of the epistle. Probably, during Paul's "two years'" stay at Ephesus, when "*all which dwelt in Asia* heard the word of the Lord Jesus" (Acts xix. 10, 26), Epaphras, Philemon, Archippus, Apphia (Phile. 2, 13, 19), and other natives of Colosse, becoming converted at Ephesus, were subsequently the first preachers in their own city. This will account for their personal acquaintance with, and attachment to, Paul and his fellow-ministers, and for his loving language as to them, and their salutations to him. So also with respect to "them at Laodicea" (ch. ii. 1).

The *Object* is to counteract Jewish false teaching (of which Paul may have heard through Onesimus and Epaphras, ch. iv. 12; Phile. 23), by setting before the Colossians their standing in Christ alone (exclusive of other heavenly beings), the majesty of His person (ch. i. 15), and the completeness of the redemption wrought by Him; hence they ought to be conformed to their risen Lord (ch. iii. 1-5), and to exhibit that conformity in all relations of ordinary life. Ch. ii. 16, 18, "new moon . . . sabbath days," shows that the false teaching opposed is that of *Judaizing* Christians, mixed up with Oriental theosophy (ch. ii. 8, 9, 16-23), angel worship, and the asceticism of certain Jewish sects, especially the Essenes (cf. *Josephus*, 'Bell. Jud.,' ii., viii., 2-13). These theosophists professed a deeper insight into the world of spirits, and a nearer approach to heavenly purity and intelligence, than the simple Gospel affords. *Conybeare* and *Howson* think that some Alexandrian Jew had appeared at Colosse, imbued with *Philo's* Greek philosophy, combining with it the rabbinical theosophy and angelology afterwards embodied in the Cabbala. *Josephus* ('Antiquities,' xii., 3, 4) informs us that Alexander the Great had garrisoned Lydia and *Phrygia* with 2,000 Mesopotamian and Babylonian *Jews* in the time of a threatened revolt. The Phrygians themselves had a mystic tendency in their worship of Cybele, whence they would receive more readily the incipient Gnosticism of

Judaizers, which afterwards developed itself into the strangest heresies. In the pastoral epistles, the evil had reached a more deadly phase (1 Tim. iv. 1-3; vi. 5), whereas he brings no charge of immorality in this epistle : a proof of its being much earlier.

The *Place of Writing* seems to have been Rome, during his first imprisonment, (Acts xxviii.) In Introduction to the epistle to the Ephesians, it was shown that the three epistles—Ephesians, Colossians, and Philemon—were sent at the same time, viz., during the freer portion of his imprisonment, before the death of Burrus. Ch. iv. 3, 4, 8, 9; Eph. vi. 19, 20, imply greater freedom than he had whilst writing to the Philippians, after the promotion of Tigellinus to be Prætorian Prefect. See Introduction to Philippians.

This epistle, though *carried* by the same bearer, Tychicus, who bore that to the *Ephesians*, was *written* previously to that epistle, probably early in 62 A. D.; for many phrases similar in both appear more expanded in the epistle to the Ephesians (cf. also note, Eph. vi. 21). The *epistle to the Laodiceans* (ch. iv. 16) was *written* before that to the Colossians.

The *Style* is peculiar: many Greek phrases occur, found nowhere else. [Cf. ch. ii. 8, *ho sulagōgōn*, "*spoil* you;" *edeigmatisen en parrhesia*, 'making a show of them openly' (ch. ii. 15); *katabrabeueto*, 'beguile of your reward,' and *embateuōn*, "intruding" (*v.* 18); *ethelothreskeia*, "will-worship," *plesmone*, "satisfying" (*v.* 23); *aischrologia*, "filthy communication" (ch. iii. 8); *brabeueto*, "rule" (*v.* 15); *paragoria*, "comfort" (ch. iv. 11).] The loftiness and artificial elaboration correspond to the nature of his theme—the majesty of Christ's person and office—in contrast to the beggarly system of the Judaizers, the discussion of which was forced on him by the controversy. Hence arises his use of unusual phraseology. On the other hand, in the epistle to the Ephesians, subsequently written, in which he was not so hampered by the exigencies of controversy, he dilates on the same truths, so congenial to him, more at large, and uncontroversially, in the fuller outpouring of his spirit, with less of the elaborate and antithetical language of system, such as was needed in cautioning the Colossians against the particular errors threatening them. Hence arises the similarity of phrases in the two epistles written to two cities which, from vicinity, were sure to need much the same counsel, about the same time, and generally in the same vein of spiritual thought; whilst the peculiar phrases of the epistle to the Colossians are such as are natural, considering its controversial purpose.

FIRST THESSALONIANS.

THE *Authenticity* of this epistle is attested by *Irenæus* ('Adversus Hæreses,' v., 6, 1), quoting ch. v. 23; *Clement* of Alexandria ('Pædagogus,' i., 88), quoting ch. ii. 7; *Tertullian* ('De Resurrectione Carnis,' sec. 24), quoting ch. v. 1; *Caius* in *Eusebius* ('Ecclesiastical History,' vi., 20); *Origen*, ('Contra Celsus,' iii.)

Object.—Thessalonica was at this time capital of the Roman second district of Macedonia (*Livy*, 45, 29). It lay on the Bay of Therme, and was always, as now, under its modern name Saloniki, a place of considerable commerce. After his imprisonment and scourging at Philippi, St. Paul (ch. ii. 2) passed on to Thessalonica; and in company with Silas (Acts xvii. 1-9) and Timotheus (Acts xvi. 3; xvii. 14: cf. with ch. i. 1; iii. 1-6; 2 Thess. i. 1) founded the church there. The Jews, as a body, rejected the Gospel when.

preached for three successive Sabbaths (Acts xvii. 2); some few "believed and consorted with Paul and Silas; and of the devout (*i. e.*, proselytes to Judaism) Greeks a great multitude, and of the chief women not a few." The believers received the word joyfully, notwithstanding trials (ch. i. 6; ii. 13) from their own countrymen and from the Jews (ch. ii. 14-16). His stay at Thessalonica was doubtless not limited to the three weeks specified in Acts xvii. 2; for his labouring there with his hands for support (ch. ii. 9; 2 Thess. iii. 8), his receiving supplies there more than once from Philippi (Phil. iv. 16), his making many converts from the Gentiles (ch. i. 9; and as A D [but not so א B E] read, Acts xvii. 4, 'of the devout *and* of the Greeks a great multitude'), and his appointing ministers,—all imply a longer residence. Probably as at Pisidian Antioch (Acts xiii. 46), at Corinth (Acts xviii. 6, 7), and at Ephesus (Acts xix. 8, 9), having preached the Gospel to the Jews, when they rejected it, he turned to the Gentiles. He probably thenceforth held the Christian meetings in the house of Jason (Acts xvii. 5), perhaps 'the kinsman' of Paul, mentioned in Rom. xvi. 21. His subject of teaching seems to have been the coming and kingdom of Christ, as we may infer from ch. i. 10; ii. 12, 19; iii. 13; iv. 13-18; v. 1-11, 23, 24; and that they should walk worthy of it (ch. iv. 1). It is an undesigned coincidence between the two epistles and Acts xvii. 5-9, that the very charge which the assailants of Jason's house brought against him and other brethren was, "These do contrary to the decrees of Cesar, saying that there is another *king*, one Jesus." As in the case of the Lord Jesus (John xviii. 33-37; xix. 12: cf. Matt. xxvi. 64), they perverted the doctrine of Christ's coming kingdom into a ground for the charge of treason against Cesar. The result was, Paul and Silas had to flee under cover of night to Berea. But the church had been planted, and ministers appointed; nay, they virtually became missionaries themselves, for which they possessed facilities in the extensive commerce of their city, and both by word and example were extending the Gospel in Macedonia, Achaia, and elsewhere (ch. i. 7, 8). From Berea also, Paul, after having planted a Scripture-loving church, was obliged to flee, by the Thessalonian Jews who followed him thither. Timothy (who seems to have come to Berea separately from Paul and Silas: cf. Acts xvii. 10, with 14) and Silas remained there still, when Paul proceeded by sea to Athens. Whilst there, he more than once longed to visit the Thessalonians again, and see personally their spiritual state, and "perfect that which was lacking in their faith" (ch. iii. 10); but "Satan (probably using the Thessalonian Jews as his instruments, John xiii. 27) hindered" him (ch. ii. 18: cf. Acts xvii. 13). He therefore sent Timotheus, who seems to have followed him to Athens from Berea (Acts xvii. 15), immediately on his arrival, to Thessalonica (ch. iii. 1): glad as he would have been of Timothy's help in the midst of Athenian opponents, he felt he must forego it for the sake of the Thessalonian church. Silas does not seem to have come to Paul *at Athens* at all, though Paul had desired him and Timothy to "come to him with all speed" (Acts xvii. 15); but with Timothy (who from Thessalonica called for him at Berea) joined Paul *at Corinth* first: cf. Acts xviii. 1, 5, "When Silas and Timothy were come *from Macedonia*." The epistle makes no mention of Silas *at Athens*, as it does of Timothy (ch. iii. 1).

Timothy's account of the Thessalonian church was highly favourable. They abounded in faith and charity, and reciprocated his desire to see them (ch. iii. 6-10). Still, as nothing human on earth is perfect, there were some defects. Some had too exclusively dwelt on Christ's coming kingdom, so as to neglect the sober-minded discharge of present duties (ch. iv. 11, 12). Some who had lost relatives needed comfort, in their doubts as to whether they who died before Christ's coming would have a share with those found alive,

II. Cursive MSS. of the Greek Testament.

Of these, upwards of 1,200 are known to exist—all enumerated and briefly described by *Mr. Scrivener* ('Plain Introduction to the Criticism of the New Testament,' pp. 142–210): viz., 601 of the Gospels; of the Acts and Catholic Epistles, 229; 283 of the Pauline Epistles; and of the Apocalypse, 102—deducting several duplicates, &c., of each class. But of all these MSS. scarcely 100 have been satisfactorily examined—in the Gospels, between thirty and forty; about the same number in the Acts and Catholic Epistles; rather more in the Pauline Epistles; and in the Apocalypse, twelve or thirteen. Their testimony, therefore, as a whole, can be but partially ascertained as yet, and as we refer to them in Acts and Romans only in general terms, it does not seem desirable to specify and describe any of them here.

Second.—Ancient Versions.

In addition to the statements on this head in Vol. V., pp. xlii.–xliii., the following particulars regarding the two Latin versions may be here noticed:—

1. The *Old Latin* Version—of the *second century*—of which about thirty MSS. exist, was published at Rome, in 3 vols. folio (1743–9), by D. P. Sabatier, and that portion of it containing the Four Gospels was issued in a superior style, in 2 vols. folio, also at Rome (1749), by Jos. Blanchini. But it is only within the last forty years that the peculiar style of it, as indicative of the country in which it originated, has been subjected to critical investigation. *Eichhorn*, indeed, early in the present century, with whom others concurred, had indicated his opinion that it was executed in *North Africa;* but the late *Cardinal Wiseman* was the first to furnish all but conclusive evidence of this origin, from a comparison of its style with that of extant North African writers, ecclesiastical and profane. ('Two Letters on some parts of the Controversy' concerning the genuineness of 1 John v. 7, first published in the 'Catholic Magazine,' 1832–3; republished at Rome, with additions, 1835; and again issued in 'Essays on Various Subjects,' 3 vols., 1853, vol. i., pp. 1–70.) This decision has been accepted by nearly all critics since. But within the last few months a contribution has been made to the evidence in favour of this conclusion, so important, that the question ought now to be held as set at rest. By a most elaborate analysis of the vocabulary, grammar, and other linguistic peculiarities of this Version, as compared with some forty other works of nearly the same date, it is put beyond all dispute, that the style of this Version represents simply the *popular Roman style,* as distinguished from that of the polished literature, especially as found in the provinces, and particularly in the Roman Colony of North Africa. (The work to which we refer is entitled, 'Itala und Vulgata. Das Sprachidiom der Urchristlichen Itala und der Katholischen Vulgata unter Berücksichtigen der Römischen Volkssprache durch Beispiele erläutert von Hermann Rönsch.' 8vo. Marburg u. Leipzig, 1869.)

2. *Jerome's Revision* of this venerable Version—issued in successive parts, from the year 384 to about 405, and commonly called *the Vulgate*—exists in a far from correct form in the Sixtine and Clementine Vulgate, alone recognized in the Church of Rome. Happily, three or four MSS. of this Revision, besides MSS. containing portions of it, are still extant, of which two are beyond price.

(1.) *Codex Amiatinus;* so called from the Cistercian Monastery of Monte Amiatino, whence it was brought to the Laurentian Library at Florence, where it now lies. It embraces the whole Bible, almost entire, and was written about the year 541, by the Abbot Servandus. It was badly edited in 1840, by *Fleck,* but far better by *Tischendorf,* in 1850, and re-issued in 1854. *Tregelles* also prints it in the inside column of his critical Greek Testament. It is the best MS. of the Vulgate. But

---

Paris, whence, on the burning of the abbey during the first French Revolution, it found its way to its present place of deposit. Being, however, a mere transcript of D (*Claromontanus*), it has no independent value, though sometimes cited, and merely attests the condition of D when this transcript was taken. It wants Rom. viii. 21–33; xi. 15–25.

SECOND THESSALONIANS.

ITS *Genuineness* is attested by *Polycarp* ('Epistola ad Philippenses,' sec. 11), who alludes to ch. iii. 15. *Justin Martyr* ('Dialogue with Trypho,' p. 193, 32) alludes to ch. ii. 3. *Irenæus* (vol. iii., ch. vii., sec. 2) quotes ch. ii. 8. *Clement* of Alexandria quotes ch. iii. 2, as Paul's words ('Stromata' 1., 5, p. 554; 'Pædagogus,' i., 17). *Tertullian* ('De Resurrectione Carnis,' ch. xxiv.) quotes ch. ii. 1, 2, as part of Paul's epistle.

Design.—The accounts from Thessalonica, after Paul's sending the first epistle, represented the faith and love of the Christians there as on the increase, and their constancy amidst persecutions unshaken. One error, however, resulting in practical evil, had sprung up. The apostle's description of Christ's sudden second coming (1 Thess. iv. 13, &c., and v. 2), and the *possibility* of its being at any time, led them to believe it *actually* at hand. Some professed to know by "the Spirit" (ch. ii. 2) it was so; others alleged that Paul had said so when with them. A letter, too, purporting to be from the apostle to that effect, seems to have been circulated among them. (That ch. ii. 2 refers to such a spurious letter, rather than to St. Paul's first epistle, appears likely from the statement, ch. iii. 17, as to his autograph salutation being the mark whereby his genuine letters might be known.) Hence some neglected their daily business, and threw themselves on the charity of others, as if their sole duty was to wait for the coming of the Lord. This error, which needed rectifying, forms a leading topic. He tells them (ch. ii.) that before the Lord shall come there must first be a great *apostasy*, and *the Man of Sin* be revealed; and that the Lord's sudden coming is no ground for neglecting daily business; that to do so would only bring scandal on the Church, and was contrary to his own practice among them (ch. iii. 7-9), and that the faithful must withdraw themselves from such disorderly professors (ch. iii. 6, 10-15). Thus, there are *three* divisions:—(1.) Ch. i. 1-12, Commendations of the Thessalonians' faith, love, and patience, amidst persecutions. (2.) Ch. ii. 1-17, The error as to Christ's immediate coming corrected, and the previous rise and downfal of the Man of Sin foretold. (3.) Ch. iii. 1-16, Exhortations to orderly conduct, with prayers for them to the God of peace, followed by his autograph salutation and benediction.

Date.—As the epistle is written in the joint names of Timothy and Silas, as well as his own, and as these were with him at Corinth, and not with him for a long time subsequently to his having left that city (cf. Acts xviii. 18, with xix. 22; indeed, as to Silas, it is doubtful whether he was ever subsequently with Paul), it follows, the *place* of writing must have been Corinth, and the *date*, during the one 'year and six months' of his stay there, Acts xviii. 11 (viz., beginning with the autumn, A. D. 52, and ending with the spring, A. D. 54), say about six months after his first epistle, in A. D. 53.

Style.—The style is not different from that of Paul's other writings, except in the prophetic portion (ch. ii. 1-12). As is usual, in more solemn passages (for instance, in the denunciatory and prophetic portions, e. g., cf. Col. ii. 8, 16, with *v.* 3; 1 Cor. xv. 24-28, with *vv.* 8, 9; Rom. i. 18, with *vv.* 8, 10) his diction is lofty, abrupt, and elliptical. As the former epistle dwells on the second advent, in its aspect of glory to the sleeping and the living saints (1 Thess. iv. and v.), so this epistle dwells on its aspect of everlasting destruction to the wicked, and him who shall be the final consummation of wickedness, the Man of Sin. So far was Paul from labouring under an erroneous impression (which rationalists impute to him), as to Christ's speedy coming, when he wrote his first epistle.

that he had distinctly told them, when with them, the same truths as to the precursory apostasy, which he now insists upon in this second epistle (ch. ii. 5). Several coincidences occur between the two epistles, confirming the genuineness of the latter. Thus, cf. ch. iii. 2, with 1 Thess. ii. 15, 16 : cf. Acts xvii. 6; again, ch. ii. 9, the Man of Sin ' coming after the working of Satan,' with 1 Thess. ii. 18; iii. 5, where Satan's incipient work, as the *hinderer* of the Gospel, and *the tempter*, appears; again, *warning* is enjoined, 1 Thess. v. 14; but, in his second epistle, when the evil had grown worse, stricter discipline (ch. iii. 6, 14): ' withdraw from' the "company" of such.

Paul probably visited Thessalonica on his way to Asia subsequently (Acts xx. 4), and took with him thence Aristarchus and Secundus, Thessalonians : the former became his "companion in travel," and shared with him his perils at Ephesus, also his shipwreck, and was his "fellow-prisoner" at Rome (Acts xxvii. 2; Col. iv. 10; Phile. 24). According to tradition, he became bishop of Apamea.

PASTORAL EPISTLES.

FIRST TIMOTHY.

Genuineness.—The ancient Church never doubted their being canonical and written by St. Paul. They are in the Peshito Syriac version of the second century. *Muratori's* 'Fragment on the Canon of Scripture,' at the close of the second century, acknowledges them. *Irenæus* ('Adversus Hæreses,' I. and III., iii., 3; IV., xvi., 3; II., xiv., 8; III., xi., 1; I., xvi., 3) quotes ch. i. 4, 9; vi. 20; 2 Tim. iv. 9-11; Titus iii. 10. *Clement* of Alexandria ('Stromata,' ii., 457; iii., 534, 536; i., 350) quotes ch. iv. 1, 20; 2 Tim., as to *deaconesses;* Titus i. 12. *Tertullian* ('De Præscriptione Hæreticorum,' xxv. and vi.) quotes ch. vi. 20; 2 Tim. i. 14; ch. i. 18; vi. 13, &c.; 2 Tim. ii. 2; Titus iii. 10, 11; and 'Adversus *Marcion.*' *Eusebius* includes the three in the 'universally acknowledged' Scriptures. Also, *Theophilus* of Antioch ('Ad Autolycum,' iii., 14) quotes ch. ii. 1, 2; Titus iii. 1; and *Caius* (in *Eusebius*, 'Ecclesiastical History,' vi., 20) recognizes their authenticity. *Clement* of Rome, in the end of the first century (in his first 'Epistle to Corinthians,' ch. xxix.), quotes ch. ii. 8. *Ignatius*, in the beginning of the second century (in 'Epistle to Polycarp,' sec. 6), alludes to 2 Tim. ii. 4. *Polycarp*, in the beginning of the second century ('Epistle to Philippians,' ch. iv.), alludes to 2 Tim. ii. 4; and (in ch. ix.) to 2 Tim. iv. 10. *Hegesippus*, in the end of the second century (in *Eusebius*, 'Ecclesiastical History,' iii., 32), alludes to ch. vi. 3, 20. *Athenagoras*, in the end of the second century, alludes to ch. vi. 16. *Justin Martyr*, in the middle of the second century ('Dialogue, contra Tryphonem,' 47), alludes to Titus iii. 4. The Gnostic *Marcion* alone rejected these epistles.

The *Heresies Opposed* form the transition from Judaism, in its ascetic form, to Gnosticism, as subsequently developed. The references to legalism are clear (ch. i. 7; Titus i. 10, 14; iii. 9). Traces of beginning Gnosticism are also unequivocal (ch. i. 4). The Gnostic theory of a two-fold principle from the beginning, evil as well as good, appears in germ in ch. iv. 3, &c. In ch. vi. 20, the term *Gnosis* (' science ') itself occurs. Another Gnostic error—viz. that 'the resurrection is past'—is alluded to in 2 Tim.

ii. 17, 18: cf. 1 Cor. xv. 12, 32, 33. The Judaism is not that which is opposed in the earlier epistles, and which tried to join the law with faith in Christ for justification. It first passed into that phase which appears in the epistle to the Colossians, whereby will-worship and angel-worship were superadded to Judaizing opinions. A further stage appears in the epistle to the Philippians, iii. 2, 18, 19, whereby *immoral practice* accompanied false doctrine as to the resurrection. This descent from legality to superstition, and from superstition to godlessness, appears more matured in the references in these pastoral epistles. The false teachers know not the true use of *the law* (ch. i. 7, 8), and have *put away good conscience*, as well as *the faith* (ch. i. 19; iv. 2); *speak lies in hypocrisy*, are *corrupt in mind*, and regard *godliness as a means of earthly gain* (ch. vi. 5; Titus i. 11); *overthrow the faith* by heresies *eating as a canker, saying* the *resurrection is past, leading captive silly women, ever learning yet never knowing the truth, reprobate as Jannes and Jambres* (2 Tim. iii. 6-8), *defiled, unbelieving, professing to know God, but in works denying Him, abominable, disobedient, reprobate* (Titus i. 15, 16). This description accords with the catholic epistles of St. John and St. Peter, and the epistle to the Hebrews. This fact proves the later date of these pastoral epistles, as compared with Paul's earlier epistles. The Judaism reprobated is not that of an earlier date, so scrupulous as to the law: it was now tending to immorality. On the other hand, the Gnosticism opposed is not the *anti-Judaic* Gnosticism of a later date, which arose upon the overthrow of Judaism by the destruction of Jerusalem and the temple, but the intermediate phase between Judaism and Gnosticism, in which Oriental and Greek elements were amalgamated with Judaism, just prior to the overthrow of Jerusalem.

The *Directions as to Church Governors*, "bishop-elders, and deacons," are such as were natural for the apostle to give to Timothy, the president of the church at Ephesus, and to Titus, holding the same office in Crete, for securing the due administration of the Church when he should be soon no more, and at a time when heresies were rapidly springing up. Cf. his similar anxiety in his address to the Ephesian elders (Acts xx. 21-30). The Presbyterate (elders: *priest* is a contraction from presbyter) and Diaconate had existed from the earliest times (Acts vi. 3; xi. 30; xiv. 23). Timothy and Titus, as overseers (so *bishop* subsequently meant), were to exercise the same power in ordaining elders *at Ephesus*, which the apostle had exercised in his *general* supervision of all the Gentile churches.

The *Peculiar Modes of Thought and Expression* are such as the *difference of subject and circumstances of those addressed* and *those spoken of* in these epistles, as compared with the other epistles, would lead us to expect. Some of these phrases occur in Galatians, in which, as in the pastoral epistles, he, with characteristic fervour, attacks the false teachers. Cf. ch. ii. 6; Titus ii. 14, "gave Himself for us," with Gal. i. 4: ch. i. 17; 2 Tim. iv. 18, "for ever and ever," with Gal. i. 5: "before God," ch. v. 21; vi. 13; 2 Tim. ii. 14; iv. 1, with Gal. i. 20: "a pillar," ch. iii. 15, with Gal. ii. 9· "Mediator," ch. ii. 5, with Gal. iii. 20: "in due season," Gal. vi. 9, with ch. ii. 6; vi. 15; Titus i. 3. [Fifty such words, peculiar to these epistles, have been noticed: *e. g.*, "faithful is the saying" (ch. i. 15); *hugiainousa*, "sound;" *kekausteriasmenōn*, "seared" (ch. iv. 2, 7); "old wives' fables," *graodeis muthous;* "slow bellies," *gasteres argai* (Titus i. 12).] Paul's having written these letters with his own hand, as those to the Galatians and Philemon, accounts for the greater conciseness, abruptness, and forcible phrases, than in those dictated to an amanuensis.

Time and Place of Writing.—The FIRST EPISTLE TO TIMOTHY was written not long after Paul had left Ephesus for Macedon (ch. i. 3). Now, as Timothy was in Macedon with Paul (2 Cor. i. 1), on the occasion of Paul's having passed from Ephesus into that country (Acts xix. 22; xx. 1), whereas the first epistle of Timothy contemplates a longer stay of Timothy in Ephesus, *Mosheim* supposes that Paul was nine *months* (of the "three years'" stay, mostly at Ephesus, Acts xx. 31) in Macedonia and elsewhere [perhaps Crete] (the mention of only "three months" and "two years," Acts xix. 8, 10, favours this, the remaining nine months being spent elsewhere), and that during these nine months Timothy, in Paul's absence, superintended the church of Ephesus. It is not likely that Ephesus and the neighbouring churches should have been left long without church officers and organization, rules respecting which are given in this epistle. Moreover, Timothy was still "a youth" (ch. iv. 12), which he could hardly be called *after* Paul's first imprisonment, when he must have been at least thirty-four years of age. Lastly, in Acts xx. 25, St. Paul asserts his *knowledge* that *the Ephesians should not all see his face again;* so that ch. i. 3 will thus refer to his sojourn at Ephesus, recorded in Acts xix. 10, whence he passed into Macedonia. But the difficulty is to account for the false teachers having sprung up almost immediately (according to this theory) after the foundation of the church. However, his visit (Acts xix.) was not his first. The beginning of the church at Ephesus was probably made at his visit a year before (Acts xviii. 19-21). Apollos, Aquila, and Priscilla, carried on the work (Acts xviii. 24-26). Thus, as to the sudden growth of false teachers, there was time enough for their springing up; moreover, the first converts at Ephesus were under the, at first, imperfect Christian teachings of Apollos, imbued with the tenets of *Philo* of Alexandria, Apollos's native town, combined with John the Baptist's Old Testament teachings. Besides, Ephesus, from its position in Asia, its notorious voluptuousness and sorcery (Acts xix. 18, 19), and its lewd worship of Diana (answering to the Phœnician Ashtoreth), was likely soon to tinge Christianity in some of its converts with Oriental speculations and Asiatic licentiousness. Thus the phase of error presented in this epistle, being *intermediate between Judaism and later Gnosticism* (see above), would be such as might occur at an *early* period in the *Ephesian* church, as well as later, when we know it had open "apostles" of error (Rev. ii. 2, 6), and Nicolaitanes infamous in practice. As to the close connection between this first epistle and the second (which must have been written at the close of Paul's life), on which *Alford* relies for making the first also written at the close of St. Paul's life, the similarity of circumstances, the person addressed being the same, and either in Ephesus at the time, or at least connected with Ephesus as its church-overseer, and having heretics to contend with, of the same stamp as in the first epistle, would account for the connection. There is not so great identity of tone as to compel us to adopt the theory that some years *could not* have elapsed between the two epistles.

However, all these arguments against the later date may be answered. This first epistle may refer, not to the *first* organization of the church under bishops, or elders and deacons, but to the *moral qualifications* laid down at a later period for those officers, when scandals rendered such directions needful. Indeed, the object for which he left Timothy at Ephesus he states (ch. i. 3) to be, not to organize the church for the first time, but to restrain the false teachers. The directions as to the choice of fit elders and deacons refers to the filling up of vacancies, not to their first appointment. The institution for church-widows implies an established organization. As to Timothy's "youth," it may be said of one *young* compared with Paul, now "the aged" (Phile. 9), and to some of the Ephesian elders, senior to Timothy, *their overseer.* As to Acts xx. 25, doubtless "all" of the elders of Ephesus called to Miletus 'never saw Paul's face' afterwards, as he 'knew' (by inspiration) would be the case, which obviates the need of *Alford's* lax view, that Paul was wrong in this his inspired anticipation (for such it was, not a mere boding surmise). Thus he probably visited Ephesus again (ch. i. 3; 2 Tim. i. 18; iv. 20 : he would hardly have been *at Miletum*, so near Ephesus, without visiting Ephesus), after his first imprisonment in Rome, though *all* the Ephesian elders whom he had addressed formerly at Miletus did not again see him. The similarity of subject and style, and of the *state of the* church between the two epistles, favours the view that they were near one another in date. Against the early date is the difficulty of defining when, during Paul's two or three years' stay at Ephesus, we can insert an absence of Paul from Ephesus long enough for the requirements of the case, which imply a lengthened stay and superintendence of Timothy at Ephesus (see, however, ch. iii. 14, on the other side), after having been "left" by Paul there. Timothy did not stay there when Paul left Ephesus (Acts xix. 22; xx. 1; 2 Cor. i. 1). In ch. iii. 14, Paul says, "I write, hoping to come unto thee *shortly;*" but on the earlier occasion of his passing from Ephesus to Macedon he had no such expectation, but had planned to spend the summer in Macedon and the winter in Corinth (1 Cor. xvi. 6). The expression, "*Till* I come," &c. (ch. iv. 13), implies that Timothy was not to leave his post till Paul should arrive. This and the former objection, however, do not hold good against *Mosheim's* theory. Moreover, Paul, in his farewell address to the Ephesian elders, *prophetically anticipates* the rise of false teachers *hereafter* of their own selves; therefore this first epistle, which speaks of their *actual* presence at Ephesus, would naturally be not prior, but subsequent, to the address—*i. e.,* would belong to the later date. In the epistle to the Ephesians the Judæo-Gnostic errors are not noticed, which seems against their having been then in existence; however, they are alluded to in the contemporaneous sister-epistle to Colossians, (Col. ii.)

Whatever doubt may remain as to the date of the first epistle, there can be hardly any as to that of the second. In 2 Tim. iv. 13, Paul directs Timothy to bring the books and cloak which the apostle had left at Troas. Assuming that the visit to Troas referred to is the one mentioned in Acts xx. 5-7, it will follow that the cloak and parchments lay for about seven years at Troas, that being the time that elapsed between the visit and Paul's first imprisonment at Rome—a very unlikely supposition. Again, when, during his first imprisonment, he wrote to the Colossians (Col. iv. 14) and Philemon (Phile. 24), Demas was with him; but when he was writing (2 Tim. iv. 10), Demas had forsaken him, from love of this world, and gone to Thessalonica. He is generally deserted now (2 Tim. i. 15); but neither before the first imprisonment (Acts xxviii. 30), nor during it, when he writes other epistles, is he so. Again, when he wrote to the Ephesians, Colossians, Philippians, and Philemon, he had good hopes of a speedy liberation; but in 2 Tim. iv. 6-8, 16, he anticipates immediate death, having been at least once already tried. Again, he is in this epistle represented as in closer confinement than when writing those former epistles in his first imprisonment—even in Philippians, which represents him in greater uncertainty as to his life, he cherished the hope of soon being delivered (Phil. ii. 24: contrast 2 Tim. i. 16-18; ii. 9; iv. 6-8, 18). Again (2 Tim. iv. 20), he speaks of having left Trophimus sick at Miletum. This could not have been on the occasion, Acts xx. 15; for Trophimus was with Paul at Jerusalem shortly afterwards (Acts xxi. 29). Besides, he would thus be made to speak of an event six or seven years after its occurrence as a recent event; moreover, Timothy was, on that occasion of the apostle being at Miletum, with Paul, and therefore needed not to be informed of Trophimus's sickness

there (Acts xx. 4-17). Also, the statement (ch. iv. 20), "Erastus abode at Corinth,"
implies that St. Paul had shortly before been at Corinth, and left Erastus there; but
Paul had not been at Corinth for several years before his first imprisonment, and in the
interval Timothy had been with him; so that he did not need to write subsequently
about that visit. He must therefore have been liberated after his first imprisonment
(indeed, Heb. xiii. 23, 24, expressly proves that the writer was *in Italy* and *at liberty*),
and resumed his apostolic journeyings, and been imprisoned at Rome again, whence,
shortly before his death, he wrote 2 Timothy.

Eusebius ('Chronicles,' anno 2083, beginning October, A. D. 67) says, 'Nero, to his
other crimes, added the persecution of Christians : under him the apostles Peter and
Paul consummated their martyrdom at Rome.' So *Jerome* ('Catalogus Scriptorum
Ecclesiasticorum'), 'In the fourteenth year of Nero, Paul was beheaded at Rome for
Christ's sake, on the same day as Peter, and was buried on the Ostian Road, in the
thirty-seventh year after the death of our Lord.' *Alford* conjectures the pastoral epistles
were written near this date. The interval was possibly filled up (so *Clement* of Rome
states that Paul preached as far as 'to the extremity of the west') by a journey to Spain
(Rom. xv. 24, 28), according to his original intention. *Muratori's* 'Fragment on the
Canon' (about 170 A. D.) also alleges Paul's journey into Spain. So *Eusebius, Chrysostom,*
and *Jerome.* Be that as it may, he seems, shortly before his second imprisonment, to
have visited Ephesus, where new elders governed the church (Acts xx. 25), say in the
latter end of 66 A. D., or beginning of 67. Supposing him thirty at his conversion, he
would now be upwards of sixty, and older in constitution than in years, through hardships—even four years before, he called himself "Paul the aged" (Phile. 9).

From Ephesus he went into Macedonia (ch. i. 3). He may have written the first
epistle to Timothy from that country. But his use of "went," not 'came'—"When
I went into Macedonia"—implies he was not there when writing. Wherever he was, he
writes uncertain how long he may be detained from coming to Timothy (ch. iii. 14, 15).
Birks' shows the probability that he wrote from Corinth, between which city and Ephesus
the communication was easy. His course, as on both former occasions, was from Macedon to Corinth. There is a coincidence between ch. ii. 11-14 and 1 Cor. xiv. 34, as to
women being silent in church; and ch. v. 17, 18, and 1 Cor. ix. 8-10, as to the maintenance of ministers, on the same principle as the Mosaic law, that the ox should not be
muzzled that treadeth out the corn; and ch. v. 19, 20, and 2 Cor. xiii. 1-4, as to charges
against elders. It would be natural for the apostle, *in the very place where these directions
had been enforced,* to reproduce them in his letter.

The date of the epistle to Titus must depend on that assigned to 1 Timothy, with
which it is connected in subject, phraseology, and tone. There is no difficulty in the
epistle to Titus, *viewed by itself,* in assigning it to the earlier date—viz., before Paul's first
imprisonment. In Acts xviii. 18, 19, Paul, in journeying from Corinth to Palestine, for
some cause or other landed at Ephesus. Now, we find (Titus iii. 13) that Apollos, in going
from Ephesus to Corinth, was to touch *at Crete* (which seems to coincide with Apollos's
journey from Ephesus to Corinth, recorded Acts xviii. 24, 27; xix. 1); therefore it is
not unlikely that Paul may have taken Crete similarly on his way between Corinth and
Ephesus, or been driven out of his course to it in one of his three shipwrecks, spoken of
in 2 Cor. xi. 25, 26 : this will account for his taking Ephesus on his way from Corinth
to Palestine. At Ephesus, Paul may have written the epistle to Titus (*Hug*): there he
would meet Apollos, and give the epistle to Titus to his charge, before Apollos's departure

for Corinth by way of Crete, and before the apostle's departure for Jerusalem (Acts xviii. 19-21, 24). Moreover, on Paul's way back from Jerusalem and Antioch, he travelled some time in Upper Asia (Acts xix. 1); it was then, probably, that his intention to 'winter at Nicopolis' was realized, there being a town of that name between Antioch and Tarsus, lying on Paul's route to Galatia (Titus iii. 12). Thus, 1 Timothy will be placed two and a half years later (Acts xx. 1 : cf. ch. i. 3).

Alford's classing the epistle to Titus with 1 Timothy, as written after Paul's first Roman imprisonment, stands or falls with his argument for assigning 1 Timothy to that date. Indeed, *Hug's* unobjectionable argument for the earlier date of the epistle to Titus, favours the early date assigned to 1 Timothy, which is so much akin to it, if other arguments do not counterbalance this. The church of Crete had been just founded (Titus i. 5), yet the same heresies are censured in it as in Ephesus, which shows that no argument, such as *Alford* alleges against the earlier date of 1 Timothy, can be drawn from them (Titus i. 10, 11, 15, 16 ; iii. 9, 11). But *vice versâ*, if, as seems likely, the first epistle to Timothy be assigned to the later date, the epistle to Titus must, from similarity of style, belong to the same period. *Alford* traces Paul's last journey *before his second imprisonment*, thus:—To Crete (Titus i. 5), Miletus (2 Tim. iv. 20), Colosse (fulfilling his intention, Phile. 22), Ephesus (ch. i. 3; 2 Tim. i. 18), from which neighbourhood he wrote the epistle to Titus, Troas, Macedonia, Corinth (2 Tim. iv. 20), Nicopolis (Titus iii. 12) *in Epirus*, where he had intended to winter:· a place in which, being a Roman colony, he would be free from tumultuary violence, and yet be open to a direct attack from foes in the metropolis. Being known in Rome as leader of the Christians, he was probably (*Alford*) arrested as implicated in causing the fire in 64 A. D., attributed by Nero to them, and was sent to Rome by the Duumvirs of Nicopolis. There he was imprisoned as a common malefactor (2 Tim. ii. 9); his Asiatic friends deserted him, except Onesiphorus (2 Tim. i. 16). Demas, Crescens, and Titus left him. Tychicus he had sent to Ephesus. Luke alone remained with him (2 Tim. iv. 10-12). Under these circumstances, he writes the second epistle to Timothy, whilst Timothy was at Ephesus (2 Tim. i. 18 ; ii. 17: cf. ch. i. 20), begging him to come before winter, and anticipating his own execution soon (2 Tim. iv. 6, 13, 21). Tychicus was perhaps the bearer of the second epistle (2 Tim. iv. 12). His defence was not made before the emperor in person, for the latter was then in Greece (2 Tim. iv. 16, 17). Tradition represents that he was executed by the sword—his Roman citizenship would exempt him from torture—probably late in 67 A. D., or 68 A. D., the last year of Nero.

Timothy is first mentioned (Acts xvi. 1) as dwelling in Lystra (not Derbe : cf. Acts xx. 4; 2 Tim. iii. 11). His mother was a Jewess, named Eunice (2 Tim. i. 5); his father, "a Greek" (*i. e.*, a Gentile). The absence of mention of the father subsequently, implies he died during Timothy's infancy. As Timothy is mentioned as "a disciple" in Acts xvi. 1, he must have been converted before, and this by St. Paul (ch. i. 2), probably at his former visit to Lystra (Acts xiv. 6): at the same time, probably, that his Scripture-loving mother, Eunice, and grandmother, Lois, were converted to Christ from Judaism (2 Tim. iii. 14, 15). From that time he was probably under the superintendence of the elders (Acts xiv. 21-23). Not only the good report given of him by the brethren of Lystra, but also his origin, partly Jewish, partly Gentile, adapted him specially for being St. Paul's assistant in missionary work, labouring as the apostle did in each place—firstly, among the Jews, then among the Gentiles. The combination of the churches of Lystra and Iconium, in testifying to his character (Acts xvi. 2), implies that already he was employed in some such office as afterwards was his life-work—viz, as 'messenger of the churches.' His tried fitness determined St. Paul's selection. In order to obviate Jewish prejudices, concerning one of half-Israelite parentage remaining uncircumcised, he first circumcised him. This was not inconsistent with his carrying about the Jerusalem decree, the charter of Gentile liberty in Christ. He accompanied Paul in his tour through Macedonia; but when the apostle went forward to Athens, Timothy and Silas remained in Berea. Having been sent back by Paul to visit the Thessalonian church, he brought his report to the apostle at Corinth (Acts xviii. 1, 5; 1 Thess. iii. 2, 6). Hence we find his name with St. Paul's in the addresses of both epistles to Thessalonians, written at Corinth. We again find him 'ministering to' St. Paul during the lengthened stay at Ephesus (Acts xix. 22). Thence he was sent before Paul into Macedonia and to Corinth (1 Cor. iv. 17; xvi. 10). He was with Paul when he wrote the second epistle to Corinthians (2 Cor. i. 1); and the following winter in Corinth, when Paul sent from thence his epistle to Romans (Rom. xvi. 21). On Paul's return to Asia, through Macedonia, he went forward and waited for the apostle at Troas (Acts xx. 3-5). Next we find him with Paul during his imprisonment at Rome, when the apostle wrote the epistles to Colossians (Col. i. 1), Philemon (Phile. 1), and Philippians (Phil. i. 1). He was imprisoned and set at liberty about the same time as the writer of the Hebrews (Heb. xiii. 23). In the pastoral epistles we find him mentioned as left by the apostle at Ephesus, to superintend the church there (ch. i. 3), as a vicar apostolic, rather than a bishop. The last notice of him is in the request which Paul makes to him (2 Tim. iv. 21), to "come before winter"—i. e., about 67 A. D. (*Alford*). *Eusebius* ('Ecclesiastical History,' iii., 42) reports that he was first bishop of Ephesus; and *Nicephorus* ('Ecclesiastical History,' iii., 11) represents that he died by martyrdom, being clubbed to death at the great feast of Artemis, the licentiousness of which he denounced. If, then, St. John resided and died in that city, it must have been *at a later period*. *Calmet* thinks he was "the angel of the church at Ephesus," and that the praise and the censure accord with the character of Timothy as represented in the Acts and the epistles. The Lord's promise of the tree of life to him that overcometh, Rev. ii. 7, accords with 2 Tim. ii. 4-6. Paul himself ordained him evangelist (2 Tim. iv. 5), with laying on of his own hands, and those of the presbytery, in accordance with Paul's own inclination (Acts xvi. 3), and prophetic intimations given respecting him by prophets (ch. i. 18; iv. 14; 2 Tim. i. 6: cf. Paul's own case, Acts xiii. 1, 2). His self-denying character is shown by his leaving home at once to accompany the apostle, and submitting to circumcision for the Gospel's sake; also by his abstemiousness (noticed in ch. v. 23), notwithstanding his bodily infirmities, which would have warranted a generous diet. Diffidence and want of boldness in dealing with the difficulties of his position, and morbid dislike of responsibility, seem to have been a defect in his otherwise beautiful character (1 Cor. xvi. 10; ch. iv. 12; v. 20, 21; 2 Tim. i. 7). His education under females, his infirmity of constitution, his sensitiveness even to tears, and a temperament easily moved by softer emotions, made necessary several of St. Paul's monitions (ch. v. 2; 2 Tim. i. 4; ii. 22).

The *Design* of the first epistle was—(1.) To direct Timothy to charge the false teachers against continuing to teach other doctrine than the Gospel (ch. i. 3, 20: cf. Rev. ii. 1-6). (2.) To give him instructions as to the orderly conducting of worship, the qualifications of bishops and deacons, and the selection of widows who should, in return for church charity, do appointed service (chs. ii. to vi. 2). (3.) To warn against covetousness, a sin prevalent at Ephesus, and to urge to good works (ch. vi. 3-19).

SECOND TIMOTHY.

THE *Place of Writing.*—St. Paul, in the interval between his first and second imprisonment, after having written the first epistle to Timothy from Macedonia or Corinth (*Birks*)
(if we are to adopt the opinion that 1 Timothy was written after his first imprisonment),
returned to Ephesus, as he intended, by way of *Troas*, where he left the books, &c. (mentioned, ch. iv. 13), with Carpus.   From Ephesus he went to Crete for a short visit, and
returned, and then wrote to Titus.   Next, he went by *Miletus* to Corinth (ch. iv. 20),
thence to Nicopolis (Titus iii. 12), whence he proceeded to Rome.   From his prison there
he wrote the second epistle to Timothy, shortly before his martyrdom.   It is not certain
where Timothy was at the time.   Some of the internal evidences favour his having been
then at Ephesus : thus the salutation of Priscilla and Aquila, who generally resided
there (ch. iv. 19); also that of the household of Onesiphorus, who is stated in ch. i.
16-18, to have ministered to Paul *at Ephesus*, implying Onesiphorus's residence there.
Also, the Hymeneus of ch. ii. 17 seems to be the same as the Hymeneus at Ephesus
(1 Tim. i. 20); and probably "Alexander the coppersmith" (ch. iv. 14) is the same as the
Alexander joined with Hymeneus, and possibly the same as the Alexander put forward
by the Jews to clear themselves, not to befriend Paul, at the riot *in Ephesus* (Acts xix.
33, 34).   The difficulty is, on this supposition, how to account for ch. iv. 12, 20.   (But
see the notes there.)   If Timothy was at Ephesus, why did he need to be told that *Paul
had sent Tychicus to Ephesus*, or that *Paul had left Trophimus himself in Ephesus* (Acts
xxi. 29), *sick at Miletus*, which was only thirty miles from Ephesus?   Troas lay on the
road to Rome from either Ephesus or Pontus; so that ch. iv. 13 will accord with the
theory of either Ephesus or any other place, in the north-west of Asia Minor, being
Timothy's place of sojourn.   Probably he had the general superintendence of the Pauline
churches in Asia Minor, combining the office of *evangelist*, or *itinerant missionary*, with
that of *presiding overseer*.   Ephesus was probably his head-quarters.

   Time of Writing.—(1.) Paul's first imprisonment (described, Acts xxviii.) was much
milder than that alluded to in 2 Timothy.   In the former, he had liberty to lodge
in his own hired house, and to receive all comers, guarded only by a single soldier; in
the latter, he was so closely confined that Onesiphorus with difficulty found him: he was
chained, his friends had forsaken him, and he had narrowly escaped execution from the
Roman emperor.   Mediæval legends represent the Mamertine prison, or Tullianum, as
the scene of his incarceration with Peter.   But this is irreconcilable with the fact of
Onesiphorus, Linus, Pudens, &c., having access to him.   He was probably under military
custody, as in his former imprisonment, though of a severer kind (ch. i. 16-18; ii. 9; iv.
6-8, 16, 17).   (2.) The visit to Troas (ch. iv. 13) can hardly have been that mentioned,
Acts xx. 5-7—the last before his first imprisonment; for, if it were, the interval between
that visit and the first imprisonment would be seven or eight years—a period unlikely
for him to have allowed to pass without sending for his cloak and parchments, when they
might have been of service to him in the interim.   (3.) Paul's leaving Trophimus sick at
Miletus could not have been on the occasion mentioned, Acts xx. 15; for subsequently
Trophimus was with Paul in Jerusalem (Acts xxi. 29).   (4.) The words (ch. iv. 20),
"Erastus abode at Corinth," imply that St. Paul had shortly before been at Corinth, where
he left Erastus.   But before his first imprisonment, Paul had not been at Corinth for
several years: in the interval Timothy had been with him; so that Timothy did not need

at a later period to be told about that visit (Acts xx. 2, 4). For all these reasons, the imprisonment during which he wrote 2 Timothy is shown to be his second. Moreover, Heb. xiii. 23, 24, represents the writer (probably Paul) as *in Italy*, and *at liberty*. So *Clement* of Rome (b. i., 5), the disciple of Paul, explicitly states, ' In the east and west, Paul, as a preacher, instructed *the whole world* (*i. e.*, the Roman empire) in righteousness; and having gone to the *extremity of the west*, and having borne witness before the rulers (of Rome), he so was removed from the world.' This implies that he fulfilled his design (Rom. xv. 24-28) of a missionary journey *into Spain. Muratori's* ' Canon of the New Testament' (about 170 A. D.) mentions 'the journey of Paul from Rome to Spain.' See *Routh* (' Reliq. Sacr.,' vol. iv., pp. 1-12).

His martyrdom is universally assigned to Nero's reign (*Eusebius*, 'Ecclesiastical History,' ii., 21; *Jerome*, 'Catalogus Scriptorum,' ch. v., p. 35). Five years thus elapsed between the first imprisonment, 63 A. D. (Acts xxviii.), and his martyrdom, June, 68 A. D.—the last year of Nero's reign. He was probably arrested by the magistrates in Nicopolis (Titus iii. 12), in Epirus, in the winter, on a double charge: first, of having conspired with the Christians, as Nero's partizans alleged, to set fire to Rome, A. D. 64; secondly, of introducing a novel and unlawful religion. His friends all left him, except Luke: Demas, from ' love of this present world;' the others, from various causes (ch. iv. 10, 11). On the first charge he was acquitted. His liberation from his first imprisonment took place in 63 A. D., the year before the great fire at Rome, which Nero made the pretext for persecuting the Christians. Every cruelty was heaped on them: some were crucified, some arrayed in the skins of wild beasts, and hunted to death by dogs; some, wrapped in pitch robes, were set on fire by night to illuminate the circus of the Vatican and gardens of Nero, whilst that monster mixed among the spectators in the garb of a charioteer. But now (67 or 68 A. D.) some years had elapsed since that first excitement. Hence Paul, being a Roman citizen, was treated in his trial with a greater respect for forms of law, and was acquitted (ch. iv. 17) on the first charge, of having instigated the Christians to their supposed incendiarism before his last departure from Rome. Alexander the coppersmith seems to have been a witness against him (ch. iv. 14). Had he been condemned on the first charge, he would probably have been burnt alive, as the preceding martyrs were, for *arson*. His judge was the city Præfect. *Clemens Romanus* specifies that his trial was (not before the emperor, but) 'before the rulers.' No advocate ventured to plead his cause, no patron appeared for him, such as, under ordinary circumstances, might have aided him; for instance, one of the powerful Æmilian house, under which his family possibly enjoyed clientship (ch. iv. 16, 17), whence he may have taken his name Paul. The place of trial was possibly one of the great basilicas in the Forum, two of which were called the Pauline Basilicas, from L. Æmilius Paulus, who had built one and restored the other. He was remanded for the second stage of his trial. He did not expect this to come on till the following "winter" (ch. iv. 21); whereas it took place about midsummer—if in Nero's reign, not later than June. In the interim, Luke was his only constant companion; but one friend from Asia, Onesiphorus, had diligently sought and visited him in prison, undeterred by danger. Linus, too, the future bishop of Rome, Pudens, the son of a senator, and Claudia, his bride, perhaps the daughter of a British king (note, ch. iv. 21), were among his visitors; and Tychicus, before he was sent by Paul to Ephesus (ch. iv. 12), perhaps bearing this epistle.

Object.—He was anxious to see his disciple Timothy before his death, and that Timothy should bring Mark with him (ch. i. 4; iv. 9, 11, 21). But feeling how uncertain it was whether Timothy should arrive in time, he felt it necessary, also, to give him by letter a last warning as to the heresies, the germs of which were then being scattered. Hence he writes exhortations to faithfulness, zeal for sound doctrine, and patience amidst trials—a charge which Timothy's constitutional timidity needed, if we are to judge from the apostle's earnestness in urging him to boldness in Christ's cause (1 Tim. v. 22, 23 ; ch. ii. 2-8 ; iv. 1-5).

St. Paul's Death.—*Dionysius*, bishop of Corinth (quoted in *Eusebius*, ' Ecclesiastical History,' ii., 25), about A. D. 170, is the earliest authority for the tradition that Peter suffered martyrdom at Rome, 'about the same time' as Paul, after having laboured for some time there. He calls Peter and Paul 'the founders of the Corinthian and Roman churches.' The Roman presbyter, *Caius* (about A. D. 200), mentions the tradition that Peter suffered martyrdom in the Vatican. But (1.) Peter's work was *among the Jews* (Gal. ii. 9), whereas Rome was a Gentile church (Rom. i. 13). Moreover (2.) the first epistle of Peter (i. 1; v. 13) represents him as labouring *in Babylon*, in Mesopotamia. (3.) The silence of St. Paul's epistles written at Rome, negatives the tradition of Peter's having founded, or laboured long at Rome ; though it is possible he may have endured martyrdom there. His martyrdom, certainly, was not, as *Jerome* says, ' on the same day' with that of Paul, else Paul would have mentioned Peter's being at Rome in ch. iv. 11. Paul, according to *Caius* (quoted in *Eusebius*, 'Ecclesiastical History,' ii., 25), suffered martyrdom *on the Ostian way.* So also *Jerome*, who gives the date—the fourteenth year of Nero. It was common to send prisoners, whose death might attract too much notice at Rome, to some distance, under a military escort, for execution; hence the soldier's *sword*, not the executioner's *axe*, was the instrument of his decapitation (*Orosius*, ' History,' vii., 7). Paul appears, from Phil. i., to have had his partizans even in the palace, and certainly must have exercised such an influence as would excite sympathy in his behalf ; to avoid which, the execution was ordered outside the city. Cf. *Tacitus* (' History,' iv., 11). The Basilica of St. Paul, first built by Constantine, now stands outside Rome, on the road to Ostia. Before the Reformation, it was under the protection of the kings of England, and the emblem of the order of the Garter is still to be seen among its decorations. The traditional spot of the martyrdom is the *tre fontane*, not far from the Basilica (*Conybeare* and *Howson*).

TITUS.

Its *Genuineness.*—*Clement* of Rome quotes it (' Epistola ad Corinthios,' c. ii.); *Irenæus* (i., 16, 3) refers to it as Paul's; *Theophilus* ('Ad Autolycus,' iii., sec. 14) quotes it as Scripture. Cf. *Clement* of Alexandria ('Stromata,' i., 350); *Tertullian* (' Præscriptione Hæreticorum,' vi.); *Justin Martyr*, (' Dial. with Trypho,' xlvii.)

Time and Place of Writing.—This epistle seems to have been written subsequently to his first imprisonment, when Paul was on his way to Nicopolis (ch. iii. 12) in Epirus, where he purposed passing the winter, and where he was apprehended, shortly before his martyrdom, A. D. 67. *Birks* thinks, from the similarity of the epistle to Titus and 1 Timothy, that both were written from the same place, Corinth, at dates not widely apart: 1 Timothy shortly after coming to Corinth, before he planned a journey to Epirus; the epistle to Titus afterwards. The journey to Crete and Ephesus for the bearers of his letters would be easy from Corinth, and he could himself thence easily pass into Epirus. He had shortly before visited Crete, wherein a church existed (though without due organization), the first foundation of which he may have partly laid at his former visit (Acts xxvii. 7, &c.), when on his way to his first imprisonment at Rome. *Ellicott* thinks he wrote from Ephesus, before going to Nicopolis, by way of Miletus and Corinth. That he returned to the East after his first imprisonment appears probable, from Phil. ii. 24; Phile. 22. However, there may have been seeds of Christianity sown in Crete, even before his first visit, by the Cretians who heard Peter's preaching on Pentecost (Acts ii. 11).

Occasion of Writing.—Corrupt elements soon showed themselves in the Cretian church, similar to those noticed in the epistles to Timothy as existing in the Ephesian church—Judaism, false pretensions to science, and practical ungodliness. Paul, on his late visit, had left Titus in Crete to establish church government, and ordain *presbyters* (*deacons* are not mentioned). Titus had been several times employed by Paul on a mission to the Corinthian churches, and had probably thence visited Crete, which was within easy reach of Corinth. Hence the suitableness of his selection by the apostle for superintending the Cretian church. Paul now follows up, with instructions by letter, those he had already given to Titus in person on the qualifications of elders, and the graces becoming the old, the young, and females, and warns him against the unprofitable speculations so rife in Crete. The national character of the Cretians was low in the extreme, as Epimenides, quoted in ch. i. 12, paints it. *Livy*, xliv., 45, stigmatizes their *avarice; Polybius*, vi., 46, 9, their *ferocity* and *fraud;* and vi., 47, 5, their *mendacity;* so much so, that 'to Cretanise' is another name for *to lie:* they were included in the proverbial three infamous initials K or C, 'Cappadocia, Crete, Cilicia.'

Notices of Titus.—It is strange that he is never mentioned in Acts; and there seems none of those mentioned in that book who exactly answers to him. He was a Greek, and therefore a Gentile (Gal. ii. 1, 3), and converted by Paul (ch. i. 4). He accompanied the apostle on the deputation sent from the church of Antioch to Jerusalem, to consult the apostles respecting the circumcision of Gentile converts (Acts xv. 2); and, agreeably to the decree of the council there, was not circumcised. He was with Paul at Ephesus, whence he was sent to Corinth to commence the collection for the Jerusalem saints, and to ascertain the effect of the first epistle on the Corinthians (2 Cor. vii. 6-9; viii. 6; xii. 18), and there showed an unmercenary spirit. He next proceeded to Macedon, where he rejoined Paul, who had been already eagerly expecting him at Troas (2 Cor. ii. 12, 13, "Titus my brother;" vii. 6). He was then employed by the apostle in preparing the collection for the poor saints in Judea, and became the bearer of the second epistle to the Corinthians (2 Cor. viii. 16, 17, 23). Paul in it calls him "my partner and fellow helper concerning you." His being located in Crete (ch. i. 5) was subsequent to Paul's first imprisonment, and shortly before the second, about 67 A. D., ten years subsequent to the last notice of him in 2 Corinthians, 57 A. D. He probably met Paul, as the apostle desired, at Nicopolis; for his subsequent journey into Dalmatia thence (or else from Rome, whither he may have accompanied Paul) would be more likely than from the distant Crete (2 Tim. iv. 10, written *subsequently to the epistle to Titus*). In the unsettled state of things then, Titus's episcopal commission in Crete was to be but temporary, Paul requiring the presence of Titus with himself, whenever Artemas or Tychicus should arrive in Crete and set him free from his duties there (ch. iii. 12).

Tradition represents him to have died peaceably in Crete, as archbishop of Gortyna, at an advanced age.

PHILEMON.

THE *Testimonies to its Authenticity.*—*Origen* (' Homily xix. on Jeremiah,' vol. i., p. 185, ed. Huet.) cites it as the letter of Paul to Philemon concerning Onesimus ; *Tertullian* ('Against Marcion,' v., 21), ' The brevity of this epistle is the sole cause of its escaping the falsifying hands of Marcion ;' *Eusebius* (' Ecclesiastical History,' iii., 25) mentions it among ' the universally acknowledged [*homologoumena*] epistles of the canon ;' *Jerome* (' Proæmium in Philemonem,' iv., 442) argues for it against those who objected to its canonicity, as if its subject were beneath an apostle ; *Ignatius* (' Eph. ii.' and ' Magnes. xii.') alludes to Phile. 20. Cf. epistle to *Polycarp*, (chs. i. and vi.) Its brevity is the cause of its not being often quoted by the Fathers. *Paley* (' Horæ Paulinæ') has shown striking proofs of its authenticity in the undesigned coincidences between it and the epistle to the Colossians.

Place and Time of Writing.—This epistle is closely linked with that to the Colossians. Both were carried by the same bearer, Onesimus (with whom Tychicus is joined in the epistle to the Colossians: Col. iv. 7-9). The persons sending salutations are the same, except one, Jesus, called *Justus* (Col. iv. 11). In both, Archippus is addressed (*v.* 2 ; Col. iv. 17). Paul and Timothy stand in the headings of both. In both, Paul appears as a prisoner (*v.* 9 ; Col. iv. 18). It was therefore written at the same time and place as the epistle to the Colossians (just before that to the Ephesians)—viz., at Rome, during Paul's first imprisonment, A. D. 62, in the freer portion of it : for *v.* 22 implies his expectation of a speedy release.

Object.—Onesimus, of Colosse ("one of you," Col. iv. 9), slave of Philemon, had fled from his master to Rome, after having probably defrauded him (*v.* 18). He there was converted to Christianity by St. Paul ; being induced by him to return, he was furnished with this epistle, recommending him to Philemon's favourable reception, as now no longer a mere servant, but also a brother in Christ. Paul ends by requesting Philemon to prepare him a lodging, as he trusted soon to be set free, and visit Colosse. This epistle is addressed also to Apphia, supposed, from its domestic subject, to have been Philemon's wife, and Archippus (a minister of the Colossian church, Col. iv. 17), for the same reason, supposed to be a near relative and inmate.

Onesimus, in the Apostolical Canons (lxxiii.), is said to have been emancipated by his master. The Apostolical Constitutions (vii., 46) state that he was consecrated by Paul, bishop of Berea, in Macedonia, and that he was martyred at Rome. *Ignatius* (' Epistola ad Ephesum,' i.) speaks of him as bishop of the Ephesians.

Style.—It has been happily termed, from its graceful delicacy, ' the polite epistle.' Yet there is nothing of insincere compliment, miscalled politeness. It is manly and straightforward, without misrepresentation or suppression of facts ; at the same time captivatingly persuasive. *Alford* quotes *Luther's* description : ' This epistle showeth a right, noble, lovely example of Christian love. Here we see how St. Paul layeth himself out for poor Onesimus, and with all his means pleadeth his cause with his master, and so setteth himself as if he were Onesimus, and had himself done wrong to Philemon.

Yet all this doeth he, not with force, as if he had right thereto, but he strippeth himself of his right, and thus enforceth Philemon to forego his right also. Even as Christ did for us with God the Father, thus also doth St. Paul for Onesimus with Philemon : for Christ also stripped Himself of His right, and by love and humility enforced (?) the Father to lay aside His wrath and power, and to take us to His grace for the sake of Christ, who lovingly pleadeth our cause, and with all His heart layeth Himself out for us : for we are all His Onesimi, to my thinking.' *Hackett*, in *Smith's* 'Dictionary of the Bible,' observes, 'St. Paul was the common friend of the parties at variance. He must conciliate a man who had good reason to be offended. He must commend the offender, and yet neither deny nor aggravate the fault. He must assert the new ideas of Christian equality in the face of a system which hardly recognized the humanity of the enslaved. He could have placed the question on the ground of his own personal rights, and yet must waive them, in order to secure an act of spontaneous kindness. His success must be a triumph of love, and nothing be demanded for the sake of the justice which could have claimed everything. He limits his request to a forgiveness of the wrong and a restoration to favour, and yet so guards his words as to leave scope for all the generosity which benevolence might prompt towards one whose condition admitted of so much alleviation. These are contrarieties not easy to harmonize ; but St. Paul has shown a tact in dealing with them which, in being equal to the occasion, could hardly be greater.' Cf. the letter of the younger *Pliny* ('Ep.,' ix., 21), interceding for a runaway slave. Our epistle, independently of its inspiration, is vastly superior.

HEBREWS.

Its *Canonicity and Authorship.*—*Clement* of Rome (end of the first century, A. D.) refers to it more frequently than to any other canonical book, adopting its words just as those of the other books of the New Testament ; not, indeed, giving to either the term "Scripture," which he reserves for the Old Testament (the canon of the New Testament not yet having been formally established), but certainly not ranking it below the other New Testament acknowledged epistles. As the writer of our epistle claims *authority*, *Clement's* adoption of extracts is virtually sanctioning its authority, and this in the apostolic age. It seems 'transfused into *Clement's* mind,' (*Westcott*, 'Canon,' xxii.) *Justin Martyr* quotes it as establishing the titles "Apostle" and "Angel," as applied to the Son of God. *Clement* of Alexandria refers it expressly to Paul, on the authority of *Pantænus*, chief of the Catechetical school in Alexandria (middle of the second century), saying, that as Jesus is termed the "Apostle" sent to the Hebrews, Paul, through humility, does not in it call himself apostle of the Hebrews, being apostle to the Gentiles. *Clement* also says that Paul, as the Hebrews were prejudiced against him, prudently omitted his name in the beginning : that it was originally written in *Hebrew* for the Hebrews, and that Luke translated it into *Greek* for the Greeks ; whence the style is similar to that of Acts. He, however, quotes frequently the existing Greek epistle as St. Paul's. *Origen* quotes it as St. Paul's epistle. However, in his 'Homilies' he regards the style as 'more Grecian' than St. Paul's, but the thoughts as the apostle's ; adding, that the 'ancients who handed down the tradition of its Pauline authorship must have had good reason for doing so, though God alone knows the certainty who was the actual writer' (*i. e.*, 'transcriber,' or else *interpreter*, of the apostle's thoughts). The Peshito version contains it. In the African church, in the beginning of the third century, *Tertullian* ascribes it to Barnabas. *Irenæus*, bishop of Lyons, is mentioned in *Eusebius* as quoting from it, though without expressly referring it to Paul. About the same period, *Caius*, the presbyter in Rome, mentions only *thirteen* epistles of Paul; whereas, if the epistle to the Hebrews were included, there would be *fourteen*. The canon fragment of the end of the second century, or beginning of the third, published by *Muratori*, apparently omits it. The Latin church did not recognize it as Paul's for a considerable time after the beginning of the third century. So *Novatian*, of Rome, *Cyprian*, of Carthage, and *Victorinus*, of the Latin church. But in the fourth century, *Hilary*, of Poitiers (A. D. 368), *Lucifer*, of Cagliari (A. D. 371), *Ambrose*, of Milan (A. D. 397), and other Latins, quote it as Paul's; and the fifth Council of Carthage (A. D. 419) formally reckons it among his fourteen epistles.

Style.—As to the *similarity* of *style to that of St. Luke*, this is due to his having been so long the companion of Paul. *Chrysostom* says, 'Each imitated his teacher: Luke imitated Paul, flowing along with more than river-fulness; but Mark imitated Peter, who studied brevity of style.' Besides, there is a greater predominance of Jewish feeling and familiarity with the peculiarities of their schools apparent in this epistle than in St. Luke's writings. There is no clear *evidence* for attributing the authorship to *him*, or to *Apollos* (*Alford's* theory). The grounds alleged for the latter are its supposed Alexandrian phraseology. But this is such as any Palestinian Jew might have used. Paul, from his Hebræo-Hellenistic education at Jerusalem and Tarsus, was familiar with *Philo's* modes of thought, which are not necessarily all derived from his Alexandrian, but also from his Jewish education. There was an Alexandrian synagogue at Jerusalem (Acts vi. 9). It would be unlikely that the Alexandrian church should have so undoubtingly asserted the Pauline authorship, if Apollos, *their own countryman*, had really been the author. The oratorical style—a characteristic of Apollos at Corinth, whereas Paul there spoke in words unadorned by man's wisdom—is designedly adapted to those whom St. Paul addresses. To the Greek Corinthians, who were in danger of idolizing human eloquence, he writes in an unadorned style, in order to fix their attention more on the Gospel itself. But the Hebrews were in no such danger. His Hebræo-Grecian education would enable him to write in a style attractive to the Hebrews at Alexandria, where Greek philosophy had been blended with Judaism. The Septuagint, framed at Alexandria, formed a connecting link between the latter and the former; and it is remarkable that all the quotations from the Old Testament, excepting two (ch. x. 30; xiii. 5), are from the LXX. Since the peculiarities of the LXX. are interwoven into the argument, the Greek epistle must be an original, not a translation. Had the original been Hebrew, the quotations would have been from the Hebrew Old Testament. The same follows from the play on similarly-sounding words in the Greek, alliterations, and rhythmically-constructed periods. *Calvin* observes, If the epistle had been written in Hebrew, ch. ix. 15-17 would lose all its point, which rests upon the double meaning of the Greek *diathece*, a 'covenant,' or a 'testament;' whereas the Hebrew *berith* means only 'covenant.'

Internal Evidence favours the Pauline authorship. Thus the topic so fully handled, that Christianity is superior to Judaism, inasmuch as the reality exceeds the type which gives place to it, is a favourite one with St. Paul (cf. 2 Cor. iii. 6-18; Gal. iii. 23-25; iv. 1-9, 21-31, wherein allegorical interpretation appears in its divinely-sanctioned application—a mode pushed to an unwarrantable excess in the Alexandrian school). So the

Divine Son appears in ch. i. 3, &c., as in other epistles of Paul (Phil. ii. 6; Col. i. 15-20), as *the Image*, or manifestation, *of the Deity*. His lowering Himself for man's sake similarly (cf. ch. ii. 9, with 2 Cor. viii. 9; Phil. ii. 7, 8). Also His final exaltation (cf. ch. ii. 8; x. 13; xii. 2, with 1 Cor. xv. 25-27). "Mediator" is peculiar to Paul (cf. ch. viii. 6, with Gal. iii. 19, 20). Christ's death is represented as the sacrifice for sin prefigured by the Jewish sacrifices, (cf. Rom. iii. 22-26; 1 Cor. v. 7, with chs. vii.-x.) The phrase, "God of peace," is peculiar to St. Paul (cf. Rom. xv. 33; 1 Thess. v. 23; ch. xiii. 20. Also cf. 1 Cor. xii. 4; ch. ii. 4, margin). Justification, or 'righteousness by faith,' appears in ch. xi. 7; x. 38, with the same quotation (Hab. ii. 4) as in Rom. i. 17; iv. 22; v. 1; Gal. iii. 11; Phil. iii. 9. The Word of God is the "sword of the Spirit" (cf. ch. iv. 12, with Eph. vi. 17). Inexperienced Christians are *children* needing *milk—i. e.*, instruction in the *elements;* whereas riper Christians, as *full-grown men*, require *strong meat* (cf. ch. v. 12, 13; vi. 1, with 1 Cor. iii. 1, 2; xiv. 20; Gal. iv. 9; Eph. iv. 13). Salvation is represented as *boldness of access to God by Christ* (cf. ch. x. 19, with Rom. v. 2; Eph. ii. 18; iii. 12). Afflictions are a *fight* (ch. x. 32 : cf. Phil. i. 30; Col. ii. 1). The Christian life is a *race* (ch. xii. 1 : cf. 1 Cor. ix. 24; Phil. iii. 12-14). The Jewish ritual is a *service* (Rom. ix. 4 : cf. ch. ix. 1-6). Cf. "subject to bondage," ch. ii. 15, with Gal. v 1. Other characteristics of Paul's style appear—viz., a propensity ' to go off at a word,' and enter on a long parenthesis suggested by it; a fondness for play upon words of similar sound, and for repeating some favourite word. Frequent appeals to the Old Testament, and quotations linked by "and again" (cf. ch. i. 5; ii. 12, 13, with Rom. xv. 9-12). Also quotations in a peculiar application (cf. ch. ii. 8, with 1 Cor. xv. 27; Eph. i. 22). Also passages quoted, not as the LXX., and with the addition "saith the Lord," not in the *Hebrew*, in Rom. xii. 19 , ch. x. 30.

Alexandrianisms.—The supposed Alexandrian (which are rather Philon-like) characteristics of the epistle are probably due to the fact that the Hebrews were generally then imbued with Alexandrian conceptions of *Philo*, &c. Paul, without colouring Gospel truth, 'to the Jews became (in style) as a Jew, that he might win the Jews' (1 Cor. ix. 20). This accounts for its being unanimously recognized as St. Paul's epistle in the Alexandrian and Jerusalem churches; and it was probably to the Hebrews in those churches that it was addressed. Not one Greek Father ascribes the epistle to any but Paul; whereas in the Western and Latin churches, which it did not reach for some time, it was for long doubted, owing to its anonymous form, and generally less distinctively Pauline style. Their reason for not accepting it as Paul's, or, indeed, as canonical, for the first three centuries, was *negative*—insufficient evidence for it; not positive evidence against it. The positive evidence is generally for its Pauline origin. To the Gentile churches of North Africa and Rome, in the second century, this epistle was an anonymous document (see 1 John), not opening as other epistles, though closing like them ; peculiar in style, and Jewish in argument. So they went beyond the Alexandrian church (*Origen*), who only doubted its *authorship*, not its *authority*. The destruction of Jerusalem, previous to the full growth of Christianity in North Africa, curtailed intercourse with those Jews to whom the epistle to the Hebrews was addressed. In the Latin churches, owing to their distance from the Hebrews addressed, there was no generally-received tradition on the subject. The epistle was, in fact, but little known ; whence we find it not mentioned at all in the canon of *Muratori*. When at last, in the fourth century, the Latins found that it was received as Pauline and canonical, on good grounds, in the Greek churches, they universally acknowledged it.

Place of Writing.—*The personal notices* all favour its Pauline authorship—viz., his intention to visit those addressed shortly, along with Timothy, styled "our brother" (ch. xiii. 23); his being then in prison (ch. xiii. 3, 19); his formerly having been imprisoned in Palestine, according to English version reading, and Codex Sinaiticus, ℵ (ch. x. 34); the salutation transmitted from believers of Italy, which implies that *Rome* was the place of writing (ch. xiii. 24). A reason for not prefixing the name may be the rhetorical character of the epistle, which led the author to waive the usual epistolary address.

Design.—He shows the superiority of Christianity over Judaism, in that it was introduced by One far higher than the angels or Moses, through whom the Jews received the law; its priesthood and sacrifices are far less perfecting, as to salvation, than those of Christ; He is the substance of which the former are but the shadow, and the type necessarily gives place to the antitype; now we no longer are kept at a comparative distance, as under the law, but have access through the opened veil—*i. e.*, Christ's flesh: hence he infers the danger of apostasy, to which Jewish converts were tempted when they saw Christians persecuted, while Judaism was tolerated by the Roman authorities; also the obligation to a life of faith, of which, even in the less perfect Old Testament dispensation, the Jewish history contained bright examples. He concludes in the usual Pauline mode, with practical exhortations and pious prayers for them.

His Mode of Address is hortatory, rather than commanding, as we might have expected from St. Paul addressing the Jews. He does not write to the *rulers* of the Jewish Christians, for in fact there was no exclusively Jewish church; his epistle, though primarily addressed to the Palestinian Jews, was intended to include the Hebrews of adjoining churches. He inculcates obedience to church rulers (ch. xiii. 7, 17, 24): a tacit obviating of the objection that he was, by writing this epistle, interfering with the prerogative of Peter the apostle of the circumcision, and James the bishop of Jerusalem. Hence arises his delicate dealing with them (Heb. xiii. 22). So far from being surprised at discrepancy of style between an epistle to Hebrews and epistles to Gentile Christians, it is just what we should expect. The Holy Spirit guided him to choose means best suited to his end. *Wordsworth* notices a peculiar Pauline construction, Rom. xii. 9 [*He agape anupokritos, apostugountes*], 'Let your love be without dissimulation, ye abhorring . . . evil:' found nowhere else save Heb. xiii. 5 [*Aphilarguros ho tropos, arkoumenoi*], 'Let your conversation be without covetousness, ye being content with,' &c. (a noun singular nominative absolute, suddenly passing into a participle nominative plural absolute). So, in quoting Old Testament Scripture, the writer quotes it as *a Jew* writing to Jews, 'God *spoke* to our fathers,' not 'it is *written.*' So ch. xiii. 18, "we trust we have a good conscience," is altogether Pauline (Acts xxiii. 1; xxiv. 16; 2 Cor. i. 12; iv. 2; 2 Tim. i. 3). Though he has not prefixed his name, he has given at the close his apostolic salutation, "Grace be with you all." This 'salutation with his own hand' he declared (2 Thess. iii. 17, 18) his "token (of identification) in every epistle." So 1 Cor. xvi. 21, 23; Col. iv. 18. The same prayer of greeting closes *every one* of his epistles, and is not found in any epistle of the other apostles in St. Paul's lifetime; but is found, after St. Paul's death, in the last book of the New Testament Revelation, and subsequently in the epistle of *Clement* of Rome. This proves that, by whomsoever the body of the epistle was committed to writing (whether a mere amanuensis, or a companion of Paul by the Spirit's gift of *interpreting tongues*, 1 Cor. xii. 10, transfusing Paul's Spirit-taught sentiments into his own Spirit-guided diction), Paul at the close sets his seal of sanction to the whole, as *really his*. The Alexandrian church theory (*Origen, Clement*), that the thoughts are St. Paul's, the composition St. Luke's or *Clement's* of Rome, is probably due to *criticism* on the diversity of style; and led to the transfer of the epistle from the tenth place to the fourteenth at the end of St. Paul's epistles, in the Greek canon. If any interpreted, as composer of this epistle, St. Paul's thoughts, St. Luke, his companion and the recorder of his speeches in Acts, is the probable one. St. Luke has caught much of St. Paul's style in his own acknowledged writings.

Reception in the East before the West.—The churches of the East, and Jerusalem, their centre, *to which quarter it was first sent*, received it as St. Paul's, from the earliest times, according to *Cyril*, bishop of Jerusalem (A. D. 349). *Jerome*, though bringing with him from Rome the prejudices of the Latins against the epistle to the Hebrews, aggravated, doubtless, by its seeming sanction of the Novatian heresy (ch. vi. 4-6), was constrained by facts to receive it as Paul's, on the almost unanimous testimony of all Greek Christians from the earliest times; and was probably the main instrument in correcting the past error of Rome in rejecting it. *St. Augustine* also held it canonical. The testimony of the Alexandrian church is peculiarly valuable, for it was founded by Mark, who was with Paul at Rome in his first confinement, when this epistle seems to have been written (Col. iv. 10), and who possibly was the bearer of this epistle, at the same time visiting Colosse on the way to Jerusalem (where Mark's mother lived), and thence to Alexandria.

St. Peter's Testimony.—Moreover, 2 Pet. iii. 15, 16, shortly before Peter's death, and like his first epistle written by 'the apostle of the circumcision,' to the *Hebrew* Christians dispersed in the East, saith, "As our beloved brother Paul . . . hath written *unto you*"— *i. e.*, to the *Hebrews;* also the words added, "as also in *all* his epistles," distinguished the *epistle to the Hebrews* from the rest: then he further speaks of it as on a level with "*other* Scriptures," thus asserting at once its Pauline authorship and Divine inspiration: an interesting illustration of the power of Christian faith and love. St. Peter, who had been openly rebuked by Paul (Gal. ii. 7-14), fully adopted what St. Paul wrote : there was no difference in the Gospel of the apostle of the circumcision and that of the apostle of the uncircumcision. It strikingly shows God's sovereignty, that He chose, as the instrument to confirm the *Hebrews*, Paul, *the apostle of the Gentiles;* and, on the other hand, Peter, to open the Gospel door to the *Gentiles* (Acts x. 1, &c.), though being *the apostle of the Jews:* thus perfect unity reigns amidst the diversity of agencies.

Rome's Error.—Rome, in the person of *Clement* of Rome, originally received this epistle. Then followed a period in which it ceased to do so. In the fourth century, Rome retracted her error : *a plain proof she is not unchangeable or infallible.* As far as Rome is concerned, the epistle to the Hebrews was not only lost for three centuries, but never would have been recovered, but for the Eastern churches ; it is therefore a happy thing for Christendom that *Rome is not the Catholic church.*

Date: Persons Addressed.—It plainly was written before the destruction of Jerusalem ; for that event would have been mentioned had it gone before (cf. ch. xiii. 10). The whole argument (cf. ch. viii. 4, 5 ; ix. 6, 7) implies the temple service was then going on. Probably, to churches in which the Jewish members were the more numerous, as those in Jerusalem and Judea, and perhaps Alexandria. In the latter city were the greatest number of resident Jews, next to Jerusalem. In Leontopolis, in Egypt, was another temple, with the arrangements of which *Wieseler* thinks the notices in this epistle more nearly corresponded than with those in Jerusalem. It was from Alexandria that the epistle appears first to have come to the knowledge of Christendom. Moreover, 'the epistle to the Alexandrians,' mentioned in the 'Canon' of *Muratori*, may be this epistle to the Hebrews. He addresses the Jews as "the people of God" (ch. ii. 17; iv. 9; xiii. 12), "the seed of Abraham"—*i. e,* the primary stock on which Gentile believers are grafted, to which Rom. xi. 16-24 corresponds; but he urges them to come out of the carnal earthly Jerusalem, and to realize their spiritual union to "the heavenly Jerusalem" (ch. xii. 18-23; xiii. 13). The Hebrews addressed are supposed familiar with the temple services, accustomed to discuss Scripture interpretation, and acquainted with the Alexandrian philosophy. Thirty-two quotations of the Old Testament occur, of which sixteen are from the Psalms. Certain of those addressed had goods, with which they relieved the distressed (ch. vi. 10; x. 34: cf. Rom. xv. 26; Acts ii. 45; iv. 34). These notes accord with *Jerusalem* being the church primarily addressed. Anticipations of Jerusalem's coming doom occur in ch. vi. 8; viii. 13; x. 25, 37; xii. 27. A reference to St. James's martyrdom probably occurs (A. D. 62), ch. xiii. 7: St. Paul's first imprisonment at Rome was 61-63 A. D. So the date of this epistle was probably A. D. 63, shortly before St. Paul's release.

Language.—The use of Greek, rather than Hebrew, is due to the epistle being intended, not merely for the Hebrew, but for *Hellenistic* Jew converts, not only in Palestine, but elsewhere: a view confirmed by the use of the LXX. *Bengel* thinks (cf. 2 Pet. iii. 15, 16, explained above) the Jews primarily, though not exclusively, addressed, were those who had left Jerusalem on account of the war, and were settled in Asia Minor.

Interlinking of Homologoumena and Antilegomena Scriptures.—The notion of its having been originally in Hebrew arose probably from its Hebrew tone, method, and topics. It is reckoned among the epistles, *not at first generally acknowledged,* along with James, 2 Peter, 2 and 3 John, Jude, and Revelation. A beautiful link exists between these and *the universally-acknowledged* epistles. Hebrews unites the ordinances of Leviticus with their antitypical fulfilment. St. James is the link between the doctrines of Christianity and the universal law of moral duty—a commentary on the sermon on the mount—harmonizing the decalogue law of Moses, and the revelation to Job and Elias, with the Christian law of liberty. 2 Peter links the teaching of Peter with that of Paul. Jude links the earliest unwritten (Enoch's prophecy) to the latest written revelation. The two shorter epistles of John, like Philemon, apply Christianity to the details of Christian life, showing that Christianity can sanctify all earthly relations.

Effect.—This epistle meets the spiritual needs of the Hebrew Christians, persecuted by their Jewish brethren, and cast down at the prospect of soon losing the distinctive glories of the nation, by showing that in Christ they have a better leader and mediator than Moses, a better Sabbath than the Judaical, a better atonement than the sacrifices, and a better city than the earthly Jerusalem. The result was, they did not apostatize. Migrating to Pella beforehand, they escaped the fate of the inhabitants of the doomed city.

Division.—See note (*Delitzch*), ch. x. 19.

JAMES.

CALLED by *Eusebius* ('Ecclesiastical History,' ii., 23, about A. D. 330) first of the Catholic epistles—*i. e.*, those addressed to the Church in general, as distinguished from St. Paul's epistles, addressed to particular churches or individuals. In the oldest MSS. (except ℵ, or Codex Sinaiticus) extant, they stand *before* the epistles of St. Paul. Of them, two only are mentioned by *Eusebius* as *universally acknowledged* ('Homologoumena')—viz, the first epistle of St. Peter, and the first epistle of St. John. *All* are found in every existing MS. of the whole New Testament.

Canonicity.—It is not to be wondered at that epistles not addressed to particular churches (particularly that of St. James, to the Israelite believers scattered abroad) should be for a time less known. The first mention of St. James's epistle by name occurs early in the third century, in *Origen*, ('Commentary' on John i. 19, 4, 306; born about 185; died 254 A. D.) *Clemens Romanus* (first epistle to the Corinthians, ch. x.: cf. Jas. ii. 21, 23; ch. xi.: cf. Heb. xi. 31; Jas. ii. 25) quotes it. So also the *Shepherd of Hermas* quotes ch. iv. 7. *Irenæus* ('Hæreses,' iv., 16, 2) is thought to refer to ch. ii. 23. *Clemens Alexandrinus* commented on it, according to *Cassiodorus*. *Ephrem Syrus* ('Opp. Graec.,' iii., 51) quotes ch. v. 1. A strong proof of its authenticity is afforded by its being in the old *Syriac* version, which contains no other of *the disputed books* ('Antilegomena,' *Eusebius*, iii., 25), except the epistle to the Hebrews. *Eusebius* terms *the disputed books* 'acknowledged by the majority' [*Gnorima homōs tois pollois*]. He says St. James's epistle was publicly read then in most churches as genuine. No Latin Father before the fourth century quotes it; but soon after the council of Nice it was admitted as canonical, both by the East and West, and specified as such in the councils of Hippo and Carthage (A. D. 397). This is just what we might expect: a writing known only partially at first, when subsequently it obtained a wider circulation, and the proofs were better known of its having been recognized in apostolic churches, which had *men endowed with the discernment of spirits*, qualifying them for discriminating between inspired and uninspired writings, was universally accepted (1 Cor. xiv. 37). Though *doubted* for a time, at last the disputed books (St. James, 2 and 3 John, Jude, and Revelation) were universally accepted; so that no argument for the Old Testament Apocrypha can be drawn from their case : as to *it*, the Jewish church had *no doubt;* it was *known not* to be inspired.

Objections.—*Luther's* objection ('an epistle of straw, and destitute of evangelic character') was due to his mistaken idea, that ch. ii. opposes justification by faith, not by works, taught by St. Paul. But the two apostles, whilst looking at justification from distinct standpoints, harmonize and mutually complement the definitions of one another. Faith precedes love and the works of love; without them it is dead. St. Paul regards faith in the justification of the sinner *before God;* St. James, in the justification of the believer *evidently before men.* The error which James meets was the Jewish notion, that their possession and knowledge of the law of God would justify, even though they disobeyed it —an error not wholly unnoticed by St. Paul (cf. ch. i. 22, with Rom. ii. 17-25). Ch. i. 3, and iv. 1, 12, seem plainly to allude to Rom. v. 3; vi. 13; vii. 23; xiv. 4. Also, the tenor of ch. ii., on 'justification,' complements St. Paul's teaching, so as to correct the Jewish notions, that descent from Abraham was enough, and that belief, apart from godliness, would save.

Personal History.—St. Paul (Gal. ii. 9) arranges "James, Cephas, John," in the order in which their epistles stand. The St. James who wrote this epistle (according to most ancient writers) is called (Gal. i. 19) "the Lord's brother." He was son of Alpheus, or Cleopas (Luke xxiv. 13-18), and Mary, sister of the Virgin Mary. Cf. Mark xv. 40, with John xix. 25, which identifies the mother of James the less with the wife of Cleopas, not with the Virgin Mary, Cleopas's wife's sister. Cleopas is the Hebrew, Alpheus the Greek, mode of writing the name. Many, as *Hegesippus* (*Eusebius*, 'Ecclesiastical History'), distinguish "the Lord's brother" from the son of Alpheus. But the Gospel according to the Hebrews, quoted by *Jerome*, represents James, *the Lord's brother*, as present at the institution of the Eucharist, and therefore identical with the *apostle*. So the apocryphal Gospel of James. In Acts, James, who is put foremost in Jerusalem after the death of James, son of Zebedee, is not distinguished from James, the son of Alpheus. He is not mentioned as one of the Lord's brethren in Acts i. 14, but as one of the "apostles" (Gal. i. 19). He is called "the less" (lit., *the little*, Mark xv. 40) to distinguish him from James, the son of Zebedee. *Alford* considers James, the brother of the Lord, the author of the epistle, to have been the eldest of the sons of Joseph and Mary after Jesus (cf. Matt. xiii. 55), and that James, the son of Alpheus, is distinguished from him by *the latter* being called "the less"—*i. e.*, junior. His arguments against the Lord's brother, the bishop of Jerusalem, being the apostle, are—(1.) The Lord's brethren did not believe on Jesus at a time when the apostles had been already called (John vii. 3, 5) ; therefore none of the Lord's brethren could be among the apostles (but it does not follow from John vii. 3 that *no one* of them believed); (2.) The apostles' commission was to preach the Gospel *everywhere*, not to be bishops in a particular locality (but it is unlikely that one not an apostle should be bishop of Jerusalem, to whom even apostles yield deference : Acts xv. 13, 19; Gal. i. 19; ii. 9, 12). The Saviour's last command to the apostles collectively, to *preach the Gospel everywhere*, is not inconsistent with each having a particular sphere of labour in which he should be a missionary bishop, as Peter is said to have been at Antioch.

Coincidence with the Sermon on the Mount.—He was surnamed "the just." It needed peculiar wisdom so to preach the Gospel as not to disparage the law. As bishop of Jerusalem, writing to the twelve tribes, he sets forth the Gospel in its relation to the law, which the Jews so reverenced. As St. Paul's epistles are a commentary on the doctrines flowing from the death and resurrection of Christ, so St. James's epistle has a close connection with His teaching during His life, especially His sermon on the mount. In both, the law is represented as fulfilled in love : the language is palpably similar (cf. ch. i. 2, with Matt. v. 12 ; ch. i. 4, with Matt. v. 48 ; ch. i. 5 ; v. 15, with Matt. vii. 7-11 ; ch. ii. 13, with Matt. v. 7, and vi. 14, 15 ; ch. ii. 10, with Matt. v. 19 ; ch. iv. 4, with Matt. vi. 24 ; ch. iv. 11, with Matt. vii. 1, 2 ; ch. v. 2, with Matt. vi. 19). The whole spirit breathes the same Gospel-*righteousness* which the sermon on the mount inculcates as the highest realization of the law. St. James's own character, as "the just," or *legally righteous*, disposed him to this coincidence (cf. ch. i. 20 ; ii. 10 ; iii. 18, with Matt. v. 20). It also fitted him for presiding over a church zealous for the law (Acts xxi. 18-24 ; Gal. ii. 12). If any could win the Jews to the Gospel, he was most likely who presented a pattern of Old Testament righteousness, combined with evangelical faith (cf. also ch. ii. 8, with Matt. v. 44, 48). Practice, not profession, is the test of obedience (cf. ch. ii. 17 ; iv. 17, with Matt. vii. 21-23). Sins of tongue, however lightly regarded by the world, are an offence against the law of love (cf. ch. i. 26 ; iii. 2-18, with Matt. v. 22 : also any swearing, ch. v. 12 : cf. Matt. v. 33-37).

Object: Persons Addressed.—The absence of the apostolic benediction is probably due to its being addressed, not merely to the believing, but also, indirectly, to unbelieving Israelites. To the former he commends humility, patience, and prayer; to the latter he addresses awful warnings (ch. v. 7-11; iv. 9; v. 1-6). The object of the epistle is twofold. (1.) To warn against the prevalent Jewish sins: *formalism* as contrasted with true religious *service* [*threskeia*] (ch. i. 27); *fanaticism*, which, under the cloak of religious zeal, was rending Jerusalem (ch. i. 20); *fatalism* (ch. i. 13); *mean crouching* to the rich (ch. ii. 2); *evil speaking* (ch. iii. 3-12; iv. 11); *partizanship* (ch. iii. 14); *boasting* (ch. ii. 5; iv. 16); *oppression* (ch. v. 4). (2.) To teach Christians *patience* in trial (ch. i. 2), in good works (ch. i. 22-25), under provocation (ch. iii. 17), under oppression (ch. v. 7), under persecution (ch. v. 10). The ground of patience is the Lord's speedy coming to right all wrong (ch. v. 8) (*Meyrick* in *Smith,* 'Dictionary ').

Date and Martyrdom.—St. James was martyred at the Passover. The epistle was probably written just before. The destruction of Jerusalem, foretold ch. v. 1, &c., ensued a year after his martyrdom, (69 A. D.) *Hegesippus* (quoted in *Eusebius,* ii., 23) narrates that he was set on a pinnacle of the temple by the scribes and Pharisees, who begged him to restrain the people, who were in large numbers embracing Christianity. 'Tell us,' said they in the presence of the people gathered at the feast, 'which is the door of Jesus?' St. James replied, with a loud voice, 'Why ask ye me concerning Jesus, the Son of man? He sitteth at the right hand of power, and will come again on the clouds of heaven.' Many thereupon cried, 'Hosanna to the Son of David!' But St. James was cast down headlong by the Pharisees, and praying, "Father, forgive them, for they know not what they do," he was stoned and beaten to death with a fuller's club. The Jews, exasperated at St. Paul's rescue from their hands, therefore wreaked their vengeance on St. James. The publication of his epistle to the dispersed Israelites, to whom it was probably carried by those who came up to the periodical feasts, made him obnoxious, especially to the higher classes, because it foretold the woes soon about to fall on them and their country. Their taunting question, 'Which is the door of Jesus?' (*i. e.,* By what door will he come when he returns?) alludes to his prophecy, "the coming of the Lord draweth nigh . . . behold, the Judge standeth before the *door*" (Matt. xxiv. 33; ch. v. 8, 9). Heb. xiii. 7 probably refers to the martyrdom of James, who had been so long bishop over the Jewish Christians at Jerusalem: "Remember them which have (rather, 'had') the rule (spiritually) over you, who have spoken unto you the word of God: whose faith follow, considering *the end* of their conversation."

Inspiration.—His inspiration as an apostle is referred to in Acts xv. 19, 28, "*My sentence* is," &c.; "It seemed good to *the Holy Ghost and to us,*" &c. His episcopal authority is implied in the deference paid to him by St. Peter and St. Paul (Acts xii. 17; xxi. 18; Gal. i. 19; ii. 9). The Lord had appeared specially to him after the resurrection (1 Cor. xv. 7). St. Peter, in his first epistle (universally received as canonical), tacitly confirms the inspiration of St. James's epistle, by incorporating with his own inspired writings no less than ten passages from St. James. The 'apostle of the circumcision,' St. Peter, and the first bishop of Jerusalem, would naturally have much in common. Cf. ch. i. 1, with 1 Pet. i. 1; ch. i. 2, with 1 Pet. i. 6; iv. 12, 13; ch. i. 11, with 1 Pet. i. 24; ch. i. 18, with 1 Pet. i. 3; ch. ii. 7, with 1 Pet. iv. 14; ch. iii. 13, with 1 Pet. ii. 12; ch. iv. 1, with 1 Pet. ii. 11; ch. iv. 6, with 1 Pet. v. 5, 6; ch. iv. 7, with 1 Pet. v. 6, 9; ch. iv. 10, with 1 Pet. v. 6; ch. v. 20, with 1 Pet. iv. 8. Its being written in the purest Greek shows it was intended, not only for the Jews at Jerusalem, but also for the Hellenistic—*i. e.*, Greek-speaking—Jews.

The *Style* is curt and sententious, gnome following after gnome. A Hebraic character prevails, as appears in the poetic parallelisms (ch. iii. 1-12). Cf. ch. ii. 2, "assembly;" margin, *synagogue*. The images are analogical arguments, combining at once logic and poetry. Eloquence and persuasiveness are prominent.

The similarity to Matthew, the most Hebrew of the gospels, is what we might expect from the bishop of Jerusalem writing to Israelites. In it the higher spirit of Christianity is seen putting the Jewish law in its proper place. The law is enforced in its everlasting spirit, not in the letter, for which the Jews were so zealous. The doctrines of grace—the distinguishing features of St. Paul's teaching to the Hellenists and Gentiles—are less prominent, having been already taught by that apostle. St. James shows to the Jewish Christians, who still kept the legal ordinances down to the fall of Jerusalem, the spiritual principle of the law—viz., love manifested in obedience. To sketch 'the perfect man,' *continuing* in the Gospel *law of liberty*, is his theme.

FIRST PETER.

ITS *Genuineness* is attested by 2 Pet. iii. 1 (see Introduction); also by *Polycarp* (in *Eusebius*, iv., 14), who, in writing to the Philippians, quotes many passages: in ch. ii. he quotes 1 Pet. i. 13, 21, and iii. 9; in ch. v., 1 Pet. ii. 11. *Eusebius* says of *Papias* ('Ecclesiastical History,' iii., 39), that he, too, quotes Peter's first epistles. *Irenæus* ('Hæreses,' iv., 9, 2) expressly mentions it; and in book iv., 16, 5, ch. ii. 16. *Clement* of Alexandria ('Stromata,' i., 3, p. 544) quotes ch. ii. 11, 12, 15, 16; and p. 562, ch. i. 21, 22; and book iv., p. 584, ch. iii. 14-17; and p. 585, ch. iv. 12-14. *Origen* (in *Eusebius*, 'Ecclesiastical History,' vi., 25) mentions it; in 'Homily vii.,' on Joshua, vol. ii., p. 63, he mentions *both* epistles; and 'Commentary' on Psalms, and on John, he mentions ch. iii. 18-21. *Tertullian* ('Scorp.,' ch. xii.) quotes 1 Pet. ii. 20, 21; and ch. xiv., 1 Pet. ii. 13, 17. *Eusebius* states it as the opinion of those before him, that this was among *the universally acknowledged* epistles. The Peshito Syriac Version contains it. The fragment of the canon called *Muratori's* omits it. Excepting the Paulician heretics, who reject it, all ancient testimony is on its side. The *internal evidence* is equally strong. The author calls himself the apostle Peter (ch. i. 1), and "a witness of Christ's sufferings," and an "elder" (ch. v. 1). The energy of style harmonizes with the warmth of Peter's character; and, as *Erasmus* says, this epistle is full of apostolical dignity and authority, worthy of the leader among the apostles.

Personal History.—Simon, or Simeon, was a native of Bethsaida, on the sea of Galilee, son of Jonas, or John. With his father and his brother Andrew, he carried on trade as a fisherman at Capernaum, his subsequent abode. He was married; and tradition represents his wife's name as *Concordia* or *Perpetua*. *Clemens Alexandrinus* says she suffered martyrdom, her husband encouraging her to be faithful unto death: 'Remember, dear, our Lord.' His wife's mother was restored from a fever by Christ. He was brought to Jesus by his brother Andrew, who had been a disciple of John the Baptist, but was pointed to the Saviour as "the Lamb of God" by his master. Jesus, on first beholding him, gave him the name by which chiefly he is known, indicative of his subsequent character and work in the Church, "Peter" (Greek), or "Cephas" (Aramaic), *a stone*. He did not join our Lord finally until a subsequent period. The leading incidents in his apostolic life are :—His walking on the troubled waters to meet Jesus, but sinking through doubting ; his bold acknowledgment of the Divine person and office of Jesus, not-withstanding the difficulties in the way of such belief, whence he was then also designated as *the stone*, or *rock;* his rebuke by his Lord, when announcing what was so unpalatable to carnal prejudices, Christ's coming death; his passing from one extreme to the opposite, on Christ's offering to wash his feet; his self-confident assertion that *he* would never forsake his Lord, whatever others might do, followed by his base denial of Christ thrice with curses ; his deep penitence; Christ's full forgiveness and prophecy of his faithfulness unto death, after his profession of "love" as often repeated as his previous denial. These incidents illustrate his character as zealous, pious, and ardently attached to the Lord, at the same time impulsive, rather than calmly and continuously stedfast. Prompt in action, and ready to avow his convictions boldly, he was hasty in judgment, precipitate, and too self-confident ; the result was that, though he abounded in animal courage, his moral courage was too easily overcome by fear of man's opinion. A wonderful change was wrought in him by his restoration after his fall, through the grace of his risen Lord. His ardour became sanctified, being chastened by a spirit of unaffected humility. His love to the Lord was increased, whilst his mode of manifesting it now was in doing and suffering for His name, rather than in loud protestations. Thus, when imprisoned and tried before the Sanhedrim, for preaching Christ, he boldly avowed his deter-mination to continue to do so. He is well called ' the mouth of the apostles.' His faithfulness led to his apprehension by Herod Agrippa, with a view to his execution; from which, however, he was delivered by the angel of the Lord, in answer to the Church's prayers.

After the ascension he took the lead in the Church ; and on the descent of the Holy Spirit at Pentecost, he exercised the designed power of ' the keys' of Christ's kingdom, by opening the door of the Church, in preaching, for the admission of thousands of Israelites ; still more so in opening (in obedience to a special revelation) an entrance to the "*devout*" (*i. e.*, Jewish proselyte from heathendom) *Gentile* Cornelius: the forerunner of the harvest gathered in from *idolatrous* Gentiles at Antioch. This explains in what sense Christ said, "Upon this rock I will build my Church"—viz., on Peter's preaching of Christ, the true "Rock," by connection with whom only he was given the designation : a title shared in common by the rest of the apostles, as the first founders of the Church on Christ, "the chief corner-stone." A name is often given in Hebrew, not that the person is actually the thing itself, but has some special relation to it, as Elijah means *Mighty Jehovah:* so Simon is called Peter 'the rock;' not that he is so save by connection with Jesus, the only true Rock (Isa. xxviii. 16 ; 1 Cor. iii. 11). As subsequently he identified himself with "Satan," and is therefore *called so*, in the same way, by his clear confession of Christ the Rock, he became identified with Him, and is accordingly so called. There is no instance of Peter's having ever claimed or exercised supremacy ; on the contrary, he is represented as *sent* by the apostles at Jerusalem to confirm the Samaritans baptized by Philip the deacon: again, at the council of Jerusalem, not he, but James the president, or leading bishop in that city, pronounced the authoritative decision, Acts viii. 14 ; xv. 19, "My *sentence* is," &c. A kind of primacy (though certainly not supremacy) was given him on the ground of his age, and prominent boldness on impor-tant occasions. Hence he is called "first" in enumerating the apostles. Hence arise the phrases, "Peter and the eleven," "Peter and the rest of the apostles ;" and Paul, in going up to Jerusalem after his conversion, went to see Peter in particular.

Once only he again betrayed the same vacillation through fear of man's reproach, which had caused his denial of his Lord. Though at the Jerusalem council he advocated the exemption of Gentile converts from ceremonial observances, yet he, after having associated in closest intercourse with the Gentiles at Antioch, withdrew from them, through dread of the prejudices of his Jewish brethren who came from James, and timidly dissembled his conviction of the religious equality of Jew and Gentile; for this, Paul openly withstood (Gal. ii. 11-14) him: a plain refutation of his alleged *supremacy* and *infallibility* (except where specially inspired, as in writing his epistles). In all other cases he showed himself to be, indeed, as Paul calls him, "a pillar." Subsequently we find him in "Babylon," whence he wrote this first epistle to the Israelite believers of the dispersion, and the Gentile Christians united in Christ, in Pontus, Galatia, Cappadocia, Asia, and Bithynia.

Jerome ('De Scriptorum Ecclesiasticorum,' i.) states that 'Peter, having been bishop of Antioch, and having preached to believers of the circumcision in Pontus, &c. (plainly from ch. i. 1), in the second year of Claudius, went to Rome to refute Simon Magus, and for twenty-five years there held the episcopal chair, down to the last year of Nero, *i. e.*, the 14th, by whom he was crucified with his head downwards, declaring himself unworthy to be crucified as his Lord, and was buried in the Vatican, near the triumphal way.' *Eusebius* ('Chron. Ann.,' iii.) also asserts his episcopate at Antioch: his assertion, that Peter founded that church, contradicts Acts xi. 19-22. His journey to Rome to oppose Simon Magus, arose from *Justin's* story of the statue found at Rome (really the statue of the Sabine god, *Semo Sancus*, or Hercules, mistaken as if Simon Magus were worshipped by that name, 'Simoni Deo Sancto:' found in the Tiber in 1574, or on an island in the Tiber in 1662), combined with Acts viii. 9-24. The twenty-five years' bishopric is chronologically impossible, as it would make Peter, at the interview with Paul at Antioch, to have been then for some years bishop of Rome! His crucifixion is certain, from Christ's prophecy, John xxi. 18, 19. *Dionysius* of Corinth (in *Eusebius*, 'Ecclesiastical History,' ii., 25) asserted, in an epistle to the Romans, that Paul and Peter planted both the Roman and Corinthian churches, and endured martyrdom in Italy at the same time. So *Tertullian* ('Contra Marcion,' iv., 5; and 'Præscriptio Hæreticorum,' c. xxxvi., 38). Also *Caius*, the presbyter of Rome (in *Eusebius*, 'Ecclesiastical History,' ii., 25), asserts that some memorials of their martyrdom were to be seen at Rome on the road to Ostia. So *Eusebius* ('Ecclesiastical History,' ii., 25; and 'Demonstratio Evangelicæ,' iii., 116). So *Lactantius*, ('De Mortibus Persecutorum,' c. ii.) Many of the details are palpably false: whether the *whole* be so or not is dubious, considering the tendency to concentrate at Rome events of interest (*Alford*). What is certain is, that Peter was not there before the epistle to the Romans (58 A. D.), otherwise he must have been mentioned in it; nor during Paul's first imprisonment at Rome, otherwise he would have been mentioned in some one of Paul's many other epistles written from Rome; nor during Paul's second imprisonment, at least when he was writing the second epistle to Timothy, just before his martyrdom. He *may* have gone to Rome after Paul's death, and, as tradition represents, been imprisoned in the Mamertine dungeon, and crucified on the Janiculum, on the eminence of St. Pietro in Montorio, and his remains deposited under the great altar in the centre of the famous basilica of St. Peter. *Ambrose* ('Ep.,' xxxiii., ed. Paris, 1586, p. 1,022) relates that St. Peter, not long before his death, being overcome by the solicitations of his fellow-Christians to save himself, was fleeing from Rome at early dawn, when he met our Lord, and falling at His feet, on asking, 'Lord, whither goest thou?' received the answer, 'I go to be crucified afresh.' On this he returned, and joyfully went to martyrdom. The church called 'Domine quo vadis,' on the Appian way, commemorates the legend. It is not unlikely that the whole tradition is built on the connection which existed between Paul and Peter. As Paul, 'the apostle of the uncircumcision,' wrote epistles to Galatia, Ephesus, and Colosse, and to Philemon at Colosse, making the Gentile Christians the persons prominently addressed, and the Jewish Christians subordinately so, so, *vice versâ*, Peter, 'the apostle of the circumcision,' addressed the same churches—the Jewish Christians in them primarily, and the Gentile Christians also secondarily.

Whom he Addresses.—The heading (ch. i. 1), 'to the elect strangers (spiritually, *pilgrims*) *of the dispersion*,' marks Christians of the *Jewish* dispersion as prominently addressed; still including also *Gentile* Christians as grafted into the Christian Jewish stock by adoption, and so being part of the true Israel. Ch. i. 14; ii. 9, 10; and iv. 3, prove this. Thus he, the apostle of the circumcision, sought to unite in one Christ Jew and Gentile, promoting the same work as Paul, the apostle of the uncircumcision. The provinces are named by Peter in the order proceeding from north-east to south and west. Pontus was the country of the Christian Jew Aquila. To Galatia Paul paid two visits, founding and confirming churches. Crescens, his companion, went there about the time of Paul's last imprisonment, just before his martyrdom. Ancyra was subsequently its ecclesiastical metropolis. Men of Cappadocia, as well as of "Pontus" and "Asia," were among the hearers of Peter's effective sermon on Pentecost when the Spirit descended on the Church; these brought home to their native land the first tidings of the Gospel. Proconsular "Asia" included Mysia, Lydia, Caria, Phrygia, Pisidia, and Lycaonia. In Lycaonia were the churches of Iconium, founded by Paul and Barnabas; of Lystra, Timothy's birth-place, where Paul was stoned at the instigation of the Jews; and of Derbe, the birth-place of Gaius, or Caius. In Pisidia was Antioch, where Paul was the instrument of converting many, but was driven out by the Jews. In Caria was Miletus, containing doubtless a Christian church. In Phrygia, Paul preached both times when visiting Galatia in its neighbourhood: in it were the churches of Laodicea, Hierapolis, and Colosse, of which last Philemon and Onesimus were members, and Archippus and Epaphras leaders. In Lydia was the Philadelphian church, favourably noticed, Rev. iii. 7, &c.; that of Sardis—the capital, and of Thyatira, and of Ephesus, founded by Paul, and a scene of the labours of Aquila, Priscilla, and Apollos, and subsequently of more than two whole years' labour of Paul again—censured, for falling from its first love, in Rev. ii. 4. Smyrna of Ionia was in the same quarter; and, as one of the seven churches, receives unqualified praise. In Mysia was Pergamos. Troas, too, is known as the scene of Paul's preaching and raising Euty-chus to life, and of his subsequently staying for a time with Carpus. Of "Bithynia," no church is expressly named in Scripture elsewhere. When Paul at an earlier period 'assayed to go into Bithynia,' the Spirit suffered him not. But afterwards, we infer from ch. i. 1, the Spirit did impart the Gospel to that country, possibly by Peter's ministry. In government, these several churches, it appears from ch. v. 1, 2, "feed," &c., were much in the same state as when Paul addressed the Ephesian "elders" at Miletus (Acts xx. 17, 28, "feed") in similar language: elders or presbyter-bishops ruled, whilst the apostle exercised the general superintendence. They were exposed to persecutions, apparently not systematic; rather annoyances and reproach, arising from their not joining heathen neighbours in riotous living, into which, however, some were in danger of falling. The evils among themselves, which are reproved, were ambition and lucre-seeking on the part of the presbyters (ch. v. 2, 3), evil thoughts and words among the members, and a want of sympathy towards one another.

His Object seems, by the prospect of their heavenly portion, and by Christ's example, to afford consolation to the persecuted, and prepare them for a greater approaching ordeal; and to exhort all—husbands, wives, servants, presbyters, and people—to a due discharge of relative duties, so as to give no handle to the enemy to reproach Christianity, but rather to win them to it, and so establish them in "the true grace of God wherein they stand" (ch. v. 12). See, however, note, there. *Alford* rightly argues, that "exhorting and testifying," there, refer to Peter's *exhortations* throughout the epistle, grounded on *testimony* which he bears to *the Gospel truth already well known to his readers by the teaching of Paul in those churches.* They were already introduced *into* (so the Greek, ch. v. 12) this *grace of God* as their safe *standing ground* (cf. 1 Cor. xv. 1). Therefore he does not set forth a complete statement of Gospel grace, but falls back on it, as already known (cf. ch. i. 8, 18; iii. 15; 2 Pet. iii. 1). Not that Peter servilely copies the style and teaching of Paul, but as an independent witness, in his own style, attests the same truths. We may divide the epistle into—(I.) The inscription (ch. i. 1, 2). (II.) The stirring up of a pure feeling in believers as born again of God. By the motive of *hope* to which God has regenerated us (*vv.* 3-12); bringing forth the fruit of *faith*, considering the costly price paid for our redemption from sin (*vv.* 14-21). Being purified by the Spirit unto *love* of the brethren as begotten of God's eternal Word, as spiritual priest-kings, to whom alone Christ is precious (*v.* 22—ch. ii. 10); after Christ's example in suffering, maintaining a good *conversation* in every relation (*v.* 10—ch. iii. 14), and a good *profession* of faith, as having in view Christ's once offered sacrifice, and His future coming to judgment (*v.* 15—ch. iv. 11); and exhibiting *patience in adversity*, as looking for future glorification with Christ—(1.) in general as Christians, *vv.* 12-19; (2.) each in his own sphere, ch. v. 1-11. 'The title "beloved" marks the separation of the second part from the first (ch. ii. 11); and of the third part from the second (ch. iv. 12)' (*Bengel*). (III.) The conclusion.

Time and Place of Writing.—It was plainly before the open and *systematic* persecution of Nero's later years. That this epistle was written after Paul's epistles, during his imprisonment at Rome, ending A. D. 63, appears from the acquaintance which Peter in this epistle shows he has with them. Cf. ch. ii. 13, with 1 Tim. ii. 2-4; ch. ii. 18, with Eph. vi. 5; ch. i. 2, with Eph. i. 4-7; ch. i. 3, with Eph. i. 3; ch. i. 14, with Rom. xii. 2; ch. ii. 6-10, with Rom. ix. 32, 33; ch. ii. 13, with Rom. xiii. 1-4; ch. ii. 16, with Gal. v. 13; ch. ii. 18, with Eph. vi. 5; ch. iii. 1, with Eph. v. 22; ch. iii. 9, with Rom. xii. 17; ch. iv. 9, with Rom. xii. 13; Phil. ii. 14; Heb. xiii. 2; ch. iv. 10, with Rom. xii. 6-8; ch. v. 1, with Rom. viii. 18; ch. v. 5, with Eph. v. 21; Phil. ii. 3, 5-8; ch. v. 8, with 1 Thess. v. 6; ch. v. 14, with 1 Cor. xvi. 20. Moreover, in ch. v. 13, Mark is mentioned as with Peter in Babylon. This must have been after Col. iv. 10 (A. D. 61-63), when Mark was with Paul at Rome, but intending to go to Asia Minor. Again, in 2 Tim. iv. 11 (A. D. 67 or 68), Mark was in or near Ephesus, in Asia Minor; and Timothy is told to bring him to Rome. It is likely it was after this—viz., after Paul's martyrdom—that Mark joined Peter, and, consequently, that this epistle was written. It is not likely that Peter would have intrenched on Paul's field of labour—the churches of Asia Minor—*during Paul's lifetime.* The death of the apostle of the uncircumcision, and the consequent need of some one to follow up his teachings, gave to the occasion testimony given by Peter to the same churches, collectively, in behalf of

the same truth.   The relation in which the Pauline Gentile churches stood towards the
apostles at Jerusalem favours this view.   Even the Gentile Christians would naturally
look to the spiritual fathers of the church at Jerusalem—the centre whence the Gospel
had emanated—for counsel, wherewith to meet Judaizing Christians and heretics ; and
Peter, always prominent among the apostles in Jerusalem, would, even when elsewhere,
feel a deep interest in them, especially when they were by death bereft of Paul's guidance.   *Birks* ('Horæ Evangelicæ') suggests that false teachers may have appealed from
Paul's doctrine to that of James and Peter.   Peter then would naturally write to confirm
the doctrines of grace, and tacitly show there was no difference between his teaching and
Paul's.   *Birks* prefers dating the epistle A. D. 58, after Paul's second visit to Galatia,
when Silvanus was with him, and so could not have been with Peter (A. D. 54), and before
his imprisonment at Rome, when Mark was with him, and so could not have been with
Peter (A. D. 62) ; perhaps when Paul was detained at Cæsarea, and so debarred from personal intercourse with those churches.   I prefer the view previously stated.   This sets
aside the tradition that Paul and Peter suffered martyrdom together at Rome.   *Origen*
and *Eusebius's* statement, that Peter visited the churches of Asia in person, seems very
probable.

The *Place of Writing* was Babylon, on the Euphrates (ch. v. 13).   It is improbable
that, in the midst of matter-of-fact communications and salutations, in a remarkably plain
epistle, the symbolical language of prophecy (viz., "Babylon" for *Rome*) should be used.
Josephus ('Antiquities,' xv., 2, 2 ; 3, 1) states that there was a *great multitude of Jews*
in the Chaldean Babylon; it is therefore likely that 'the apostle of the circumcision'
would at some time visit them.   Some maintain that the Babylon meant was in Egypt,
for that Mark preached in and around Alexandria after Peter's death, and therefore it is
likely he did so along with that apostle in the same region previously.   But no mention
elsewhere *in Scripture* is made of this Egyptian Babylon, but only of the Chaldean one.
And though, towards the close of Caligula's reign, a persecution drove the Jews thence
to Seleucia, and a plague five years after still further thinned their numbers, yet this does
not preclude their return and multiplication during the twenty years between the plague
and the writing of the epistle.   Moreover, the order in which the countries are enumerated—from north-east to south and west—is such as would be adopted by one writing
from the Oriental Babylon on the Euphrates, not from Egypt or Rome.   Indeed, *Cosmas
Indicopleustes*, in the sixth century, understood the Babylon meant to be *outside* the
Roman empire.   Silvanus, Paul's companion, became subsequently Peter's, and was the
carrier of this epistle.

Style.—Fervour and practical truth, rather than logical reasoning, are characteristic
of this epistle, as of its energetic, warm-hearted writer.   His familiarity with Paul's
epistles, shown in the language, accords with what we should expect from Paul's having
'communicated the Gospel which he preached among the Gentiles' (as revealed specially
to him) to Peter, among others "of reputation" (Gal. ii. 2).   Individualities occur, such
as baptism ; "the answer of a good conscience toward God" (ch. iii. 21) ; 'consciousness
of God' (Greek, ch. ii. 19), as a motive for enduring sufferings ; 'living hope' (ch. i. 3) ;
"an inheritance incorruptible, undefiled, and that fadeth not away" (ch. i. 4) ; "kiss of
charity" (ch. v. 14).   Christ is viewed less in relation to His past sufferings than as at
present exalted, and hereafter to be manifested in all His majesty.   *Glory* and *hope* are
prominent in this epistle (ch. i. 8) ; so that *Weiss* entitles him 'the apostle of hope.'
The realization of future bliss as near, causes him to regard believers as but "strangers"

and "sojourners" here. Chastened fervour, deep humility, and ardent love appear, as we should expect from one who had been so graciously restored after his grievous fall. 'Being converted,' he truly does 'strengthen his brethren' (Luke xxii. 32). His fervour shows itself in often repeating the same thought.

In some passages he shows familiarity with the epistle of James—the apostle of especial weight with the Jewish legalizing party—whose inspiration he thus confirms (cf. ch. i. 6, 7, with Jas. i. 2, 3; ch. i. 24, with Jas. i. 10; ch. ii. 1, with Jas. i. 21; ch. iv. 8, with Jas. v. 20, quoting Prov. x. 12; ch. v. 5, with Jas. iv. 6, quoting Prov. iii. 34). In most cases, Old Testament quotations are the common ground of both. 'Strongly susceptible to outward impressions, liveliness of feeling, dexterity in handling subjects, dispose natures like that of Peter to repeat the thoughts of others' (*Steiger*).

The diction of this epistle and of his speeches in Acts is very similar: an undesigned coincidence, as a mark of genuineness (cf. ch. ii. 7, with Acts iv. 11; ch. i. 12, with Acts v. 32; ch. ii. 24, with Acts v. 30; x. 39; ch. v. 1, with Acts ii. 32; iii. 15; ch. i. 10, with Acts iii. 18; x. 43; ch. i. 21, with Acts iii. 15; x. 40; ch. iv. 5, with Acts x. 42; ch. ii. 24, with Acts iii. 19, 26).

There is, too, a recurrence to the language of the Lord at the last interview after His resurrection, recorded in John xxi. Cf. "the Shepherd . . . of . . . souls" (ch. ii. 25); "Feed the flock of God," "the chief Shepherd" (ch. v. 2, 4, with John xxi. 15-17); also, "Whom . . . ye *love*" (ch. i. 8; ii. 7, with John xxi. 15-17: and 2 Pet. i. 14, with John xxi. 18, 19). *Wiesinger*, 'He who, in loving impatience, cast himself into the sea to meet the Lord, is also the man who most earnestly testifies to the hope of His return: he who dated his own faith from the sufferings of his Master, is never weary in holding up the suffering form of the Lord before his readers, to stimulate them: he before whom the death of a martyr is in assured expectation, is the man who, in the greatest variety of aspects, sets forth the duty, as well as the consolation, of suffering for Christ: as a rock of the Church, he grounds his readers against the storm of present tribulation on the true Rock of Ages.'

SECOND PETER.

Its *Authenticity and Genuineness.*—If not a gross imposture, *its internal witness* is unequivocal. It has *Peter's* apostleship in its heading: not only his surname, but his original name, *Simon*, or *Simeon*—he thus, at the close of life, reminding his readers who he originally was before his call. Again, in ch. i. 16-18, he mentions *his presence at the transfiguration*, and *Christ's prophecy of his death;* and in ch. iii. 15, *his brotherhood with Paul.* Again, in ch. iii. 1, the author speaks of himself as author of the former epistle. It is, moreover, addressed so as to *include* (but not to be restricted to) the same persons as the first, whom he presupposes to be acquainted with the writings of Paul, by that time recognized as "Scripture" (ch. iii. 15, "the longsuffering of God:" cf. Rom. ii. 4). This implies *a late date*, when Paul's epistles (including Romans) already had become generally diffused, and accepted as Scripture. The Church of the fourth century had, besides the testimony we have of the *doubts* of earlier Christians, other external evidence which we have not, and which, doubtless, under God's overruling Spirit, decided them on accepting it. It is hard to understand how a book palpably false (as it would be, if Peter be not the author) could have been accepted in the canon established in the councils of

Laodicea, 360 A.D. (if the fifty-ninth article be genuine), Hippo, and Carthage in the fourth century (393 and 397). The whole tone of the epistle disproves its being an imposture. He writes as not speaking of himself, but *moved by the Holy Ghost* (ch. i. 21). Such a fraud in the first ages would have brought only shame and suffering, alike from Christians and heathen, on the perpetrator; there was then *no temptation to pious frauds*, as in later times. That it must have been written in the earliest age is plain, from the *wide gulf in style* which separates it and the other New Testament Scriptures from even the earliest and best of the post-apostolic period. *Daillé* well says, ' God has allowed a fosse to be drawn by human weakness around the sacred canon, to protect it from all invasion.'

Traces of acquaintance with it appear in the earliest Fathers. *Hermas* (' Similies,' vi., 4 : cf. ch. ii. 13), '*Luxury* in the day . . . luxuriating with their own deceivings ;' and *Shepherd* (' Vision,' iii., 7), 'They have left their true way ' (cf. ch. ii. 15); and (' Vision,' iv., 3), ' Thou hast escaped this world' (cf. ch. ii. 20). *Clement* of Rome (' Ad Corinthios,' c. vii., ix., and x., as to *Noah's preaching* and *Lot's* deliverances), ' *The Lord* making it *known* that He does not abandon those that trust in Him, but appoints those otherwise inclined to *judgment*' (cf. ch. ii. 5-7, 9). *Irenæus*, A. D. 178 (' the day of the Lord is as a thousand years '), and *Justin Martyr*, allude to ch. iii. 8. *Hippolytus* (' De Antichristo') refers to ch. i. 21, ' *The prophets spake not of their own private* ability and *will*, but what was (revealed) to them alone by God.' The difficulty is, neither *Tertullian, Cyprian, Clement* of Alexandria, nor the oldest Syriac (Peshito) version (the *later* Syriac has it), nor the fragment, *Muratori's* ' Canon,' mention it. The first writer who expressly named it is *Origen*, in the third century (' Homily' on Joshua; also fourth ' Homily' on Leviticus, and thirteenth on Numbers), who names it ' Scripture,' quoting ch. i. 4 ; ii. 16. However (in *Eusebius*, ' Ecclesiastical History,' vi., 25), he mentions that the second epistle was doubted by some. *Firmilian*, bishop of Cappadocia (in 'Epistle ad Cyprian '), speaks of Peter's *epistles* as warning us to avoid heretics (a monition which occurs in the *second*, not the *first* epistle). Now, *Cappadocia* is one of the countries (cf. 1 Pet. i. 1, with ch. iii. 1) addressed ; and it is striking, that from Cappadocia we get the earliest decisive testimony. ' Internally it claims to be written by Peter; and this claim is confirmed by the Christians of that very region in whose custody it *ought* to have been found' (*Tregelles*).

The books disputed (*Antilegomena*), as distinguished from those universally recognized (*Homologoumena*), are :—Epistles, 2 Peter, James, 2 and 3 John, Jude the Apocalypse, epistle to Hebrews (cf. *Eusebius*, ' Ecclesiastical History,' iii., 3, 25). The *Antilegomena* stand in quite a different class from *the Spurious:* of these there was no *dispute; they were* universally rejected—*e. g., the Shepherd of Hermas, the Revelation of Peter, the Epistle of Barnabas. Cyril* of Jerusalem (A. D. 348) enumerates *seven* Catholic epistles, including 2 Peter: so also *Gregory* of Nazianzum (389 A. D.), and *Epiphanius*, A. D. 367. The oldest Greek MSS. extant (of the fourth century) contain the *Antilegomena. Jerome* (' De Viris Illustribus') conjectured, from a supposed difference of style, that Peter, being unable to write Greek, employed a different translator of his Hebrew dictation in the *second* epistle; not the same as translated the *first* into Greek. Mark is said to have been his translator of the Gospel according to St. Mark : all gratuitous conjecture.

The same views pervade both epistles. In both he looks for the Lord's coming suddenly, and the end of the world (cf. ch. iii. 8-10, with 1 Pet. iv. 5); the inspiration of the prophets (cf. 1 Pet. i. 10-12, with ch. i. 19-21; iii. 2); the new birth by the Divine

Word a motive to abstinence from worldly lusts (1 Pet. i. 22; ii. 2: cf. ch. i. 4; also 1 Pet. ii. 9, margin, with ch. i. 3, both containing in the Greek the rare word 'virtue;' also 1 Pet. iv. 17, with ch. ii. 3).

It is not strange that *distinctive peculiarities of Style* should mark each epistle, the design not being the same. Thus, the *sufferings* of Christ are more prominent in the first epistle, its object being to encourage Christian sufferers; the *glory* of the exalted Lord in the second, its object being to communicate fuller "knowledge" of Him as the antidote to the false teaching against which Peter warns his readers. Hence His title of redemption, "Christ," is employed in the first epistle; but in the second, "the Lord." *Hope* is characteristic of the first epistle; *full knowledge*, of the second. In the first he puts his *apostolic authority* less prominently forward than in the second, wherein his design is to warn against false teachers. The same difference is observable in Paul's epistles. Contrast Phil. i. 1; 1 Thess. i. 1; 2 Thess. i. 1, with 1 Cor. i. 1; Gal. i. 1. The reference to Paul's writings, as already existing in numbers, and as a recognized part of *Scripture*, implies that this epistle was written at a late date, just before Peter's death.

Striking verbal coincidences occur: cf. 1 Pet. i. 19, end, with ch. iii. 14, end; ch. i. 3, 'His own' [*idia*]; ii. 16; iii. 17, with 1 Pet. iii. 1, 5. The omission of the Greek article, 1 Pet. ii. 13, with ch. i. 21; ii. 4, 5, 7. Moreover, two words occur, ch. i. 13, "tabernacle," *i. e.*, the body, and *v.* 15, "decease," which at once remind us of the transfiguration narrative in the gospel (Luke ix. 31 [*exodos*], 33). Both epistles refer to the deluge, and to Noah as the *eighth* saved. Though the first epistle abounds in *quotations* of the Old Testament, whereas the second contains none, yet *references* to the Old Testament occur often (ch. i. 21; ii. 5-8, 15; iii. 5, 6, 10, 13). Cf. [*apothesis*] 1 Pet. iii. 21, "putting away," with ch. i. 14; 1 Pet. i. 17 [*anastraphete*], "*pass* the time," with ch. ii. 18; 1 Pet. iv. 3 [*peporeumenous*], "walked in," with ch. ii. 10; iii. 3; "called you," 1 Pet. i. 15; ii. 9; v. 10, with ch. i. 3.

Moreover, more verbal coincidences with the speeches of Peter in Acts occur in this *second*, than in the *first*, epistle. Cf. [*lachousi*] "obtained," ch. i. 1, with Acts i. 17; ch. i. 6, "godliness," with Acts iii. 12 [the only passage where *eusebeia* occurs, except in the pastoral epistles]; and ch. ii. 9, with Acts x. 2, 7; ch. ii. 9, "punished," with Acts iv. 21 [the only places where *kolazomai* occurs]; ch. iii. 2, the double genitive, with Acts v. 32; "the day of the Lord," ch. iii. 10, with Acts ii. 20, where only it occurs, except 1 Thess. v. 2.

Jude 17, 18, testifies for its genuineness and inspiration, by adopting its very words, and by referring to it as received by the churches to which he wrote, "Remember ye the words which were spoken before of the *apostles* of our Lord Jesus Christ; how that they told you *there should be mockers in the last time, who should walk after their own ungodly lusts.*" Jude, therefore, must have written *after* 2 Peter, to which he plainly refers: not before, as *Alford* thinks. No less than eleven passages of Jude rest on similar statements of 2 Peter:—Jude 2, cf. ch. i. 2; Jude 4, cf. ch. ii. 1; Jude 6, cf. ch. ii. 4; Jude 7, cf. ch. ii. 6; Jude 8, cf. ch. ii. 10; Jude 9, cf. ch. ii. 11; Jude 11, cf. ch. ii. 15; Jude 12, cf. ch. ii. 17; Jude 16, cf. ch. ii. 18; Jude 18, cf. ch. ii. 1, and iii. 3. In the same way Isaiah (iv. 1-4) leans on the somewhat earlier prophecy of Micah, whose inspiration he thereby confirms. *Alford* reasons that, because Jude, in many of the passages akin, is fuller than 2 Peter, he must be prior. This by no means follows. It is at least as likely, if not more so, that the briefer is the earlier, rather than the fuller. The dignity and energy of the style are quite consonant to what we should expect from the prompt, ardent foreman of the apostles. The difference of style between 1 and 2 Peter accords with the distinctness of the subjects.

The *Date* would be about 68 or 69 A. D., about a year after the first, shortly before the destruction of Jerusalem, the typical precursor of the world's end, to which ch. iii. so solemnly calls attention, after Paul's ministry had closed (cf. aorist, 'wrote,' past time, ch. iii. 15), just before Peter's own death. It was written to *include* the same persons, perhaps in or about the same place, as the first. Being without salutations of individuals, and entrusted to the care of no one church, or particular churches, as the first is, but directed generally "to them that have obtained like precious faith with us," it took a longer time in being recognized as canonical. Had Rome been the place of its composition or publication, it could hardly have failed to have had an early acceptance—an incidental argument against the tradition of Peter's martyrdom *at Rome*. The remote scene of its composition, Babylon, or else some of the contiguous regions beyond the Roman empire, and of its circulation, Cappadocia, Pontus, &c., will additionally account for its tardy, but at last universal, acceptance in the Catholic Church. The former epistle, through *its more definite address*, was earlier in its general acceptance.

Object.—In ch. iii. 17, 18, the twofold design is set forth—viz., to guard his readers against "the error" of false teachers, and to exhort them to grow in experimental "knowledge of our Lord and Saviour." The ground on which this *knowledge* rests is stated, ch. i. 12-21—viz., the inspired testimony of apostles and prophets. The danger now, as of old, was about to arise from false teachers, who soon were to come, as Paul also (to whom reference is made, ch. iii. 15, 16) testified in the same region. The grand antidote is 'the *full knowledge* of our Lord and Saviour,' through which we know God the Father, partake of His nature, escape from the world's pollutions, and have entrance into Christ's kingdom. The aspect of Christ presented is not so much that of past *suffering*, as of future *reigning*—His present *power*, and future kingdom. This aspect is best fitted to counteract the *theories of* false teachers who 'deny' His *Lordship* and His *coming* again— the two very points which, as an *apostle and eye witness*, Peter attests (His "power" and His "coming"); also, to counteract *their evil example in practice*, blaspheming the way of truth, despising governments, slaves to covetousness and filthy lusts of the flesh, whilst boasting of Christian freedom, and, worst of all, apostates from the truth. The *knowledge of Christ*, as the knowledge of "the way of righteousness," "the right way," is the antidote. Hence "the preacher of righteousness," Noah, and 'righteous Lot,' are instanced as escaping the destruction which overtook the 'unrighteous;' and Balaam, as exemplifying the awful result of "unrighteousness" such as characterized the false teachers. Thus the epistle forms one connected whole, the parts being bound together by mutual relation, and the end corresponding with the beginning. Cf. ch. iii. 14, 18, with ch. i. 2, in both "grace" and "peace" being connected with "the knowledge" of our Saviour: cf. also, ch. iii. 17, with ch. i. 4, 10, 12; and ch. iii. 18, "grow in grace and knowledge," with the fuller ch. i. 5-8; and ch. ii. 21, and ch. iii. 13, "righteousness," with ch. i. 1; and oh. iii. 1, with ch. i. 13; and ch. iii. 2, with ch. i. 19.

The *germs* of Carpocratian and Gnostic heresies already existed; but the actual manifestation of them is spoken of as *future* (ch. ii. 1, 2, &c.): another proof that this epistle was written in the apostolic age, before the *development* of the Gnostic heresies in the end of the first and beginning of the second centuries. The description is too general to identify the heresies with any particular subsequent heresy, but applies generally to them all.

Though distinct in aim from the first epistle, a connection may be traced. The neglect of the warnings to circumspection in the walk led to the evils foretold in the second epistle. Cf. the warning against abuse of Christian *freedom*, 1 Pet. ii. 16, with ch. ii. 19, "While they promise them *liberty*, they themselves are the *servants of corruption;*" also the caution against *pride*, 1 Pet. v. 5, 6, with ch. ii. 18, "they speak great swelling words of vanity."

FIRST JOHN.

ITS *Authorship.*—*Polycarp*, the disciple of John ('Ad Philippenses,' c. vii.), quotes ch. iv. 3. *Eusebius* ('Ecclesiastical History,' iii., 39) says of *Papias*, a hearer of John, and friend of *Polycarp*, 'He used testimonies from the first epistle of John.' *Irenæus*, according to *Eusebius* ('Ecclesiastical History,' v., 8), often quoted this epistle. So, in his work *against heresies* (iii., 15, 5, 8), he quotes from John by name, ch. ii. 18, &c.; and in iii. 16, 7, he quotes ch. iv. 1-3; v. 1; and 2 John vii. 8. *Clement* of Alexandria ('Stromata,' ii., 66, p. 464) refers to ch. v. 16, as in John's *larger epistle*. See other quotations ('Stromata,' iii., 32, 42; iv., 102). *Tertullian* ('Adversus Marcion,' v., 16) refers to ch. iv. 1, &c.; 'Adversus Praxean,' xv., to ch. i. 1. See his other quotations, xxviii.; and 'Contra Gnosticos,' xii. *Cyprian* ('Epistle,' xxviii., 24) quotes, as John's, ch. ii. 3, 4; and 'De Oratione Domini,' v., quotes ch. ii. 15-17; and 'De Opere and Eleemos,' ch. i. 8; and 'De Bono Patientiæ,' ii., quotes ch. ii. 6. *Muratori's* 'Fragment' on the canon states, 'There are two of John (the gospel and epistle?) esteemed catholic,' and quotes ch. i. 3. The Peshito Syriac contains it. *Origen* (in *Eusebius*, vi., 25) speaks of the first epistle as genuine, and 'probably the second and third, though all do not recognize the latter two:' 'On the Gospel of John,' tom. xiii., vol. ii., he quotes ch. i. 5. *Dionysius* of Alexandria, *Origen's* scholar, cites the words of this epistle as those of the evangelist John. *Eusebius* ('Ecclesiastical History,' iii., 24) says, John's first epistle and gospel are *acknowledged without question* by those of the present day, as well as by the ancients. So also *Jerome* (in 'Catalogus Ecclesiasticorum Scriptorum'). The opposition of *Cosmas Indicopleustes*, in the sixth century, and that of *Marcion*, because our epistle was inconsistent with his views, are of no weight against such irrefragable testimony.

The internal evidence is equally strong. Neither the gospel, nor our epistle, can be pronounced an imitation; yet both, in style and modes of thought, are evidently of the same mind. The *individual* notices are not so numerous or obvious as in Paul's writings, as was to be expected in a *catholic* epistle; but such as there are, accord with John's position. He implies his apostleship, perhaps alludes to his gospel, and the affectionate tie which bound him as an *aged* pastor to his spiritual "children," in ch. ii. 18, 19; in ch. iv. 1-3, he alludes to the false teachers as known to his readers; and in ch. v. 21, warns them against the idols of the surrounding world. It is no objection against its authenticity, that the doctrine of the *Word*, or Divine second person, existing from everlasting, in due time made flesh, appears in it, as also in the gospel, as opposed to the heresy of the Docetæ *in the second century*, who denied that our Lord *is come in the flesh*, and maintained He came only in outward *semblance;* for the same doctrine appears in Col. i. 15-18; 1 Tim. iii. 16; Heb. i. 1-3. The germs of Docetism, though not fully developed till the second century, were in existence in the first. The

Spirit, presciently through John, puts the Church beforehand on its guard against the coming heresy.

To whom Addressed.—Augustine ('Quæst. Evang.,' ii., 39) says this epistle was written *to the Parthians.* *Bede,* in a prologue to the seven Catholic epistles, says that *Athanasius* attests the same. By the *Parthians* may be meant the Christians living beyond the Euphrates, in the Parthian territory, outside the Roman empire, 'the church at Babylon elected together with' the churches in the Ephesian region, the quarter to which Peter addressed his epistles. As Peter addressed the flock which John subsequently tended (and in which Paul formerly ministered), so John, Peter's close companion after the ascension, addresses the flock among whom Peter had been when he wrote. Thus "the elect lady" answers to 'the church elected together.' See further confirmation of this view, Introduction to 2 John. It is not necessarily an objection, that John never is known to have personally ministered in the Parthian territory. For neither did Peter personally minister to the churches in Pontus, Galatia, Cappadocia, Asia, Bithynia, though he wrote his epistles to them. Moreover, in John's prolonged life, we cannot dogmatically assert that he did not visit the Parthian Christians, after Peter's ministry had ceased, on the mere ground of absence of extant testimony. This is as probable a view as *Alford's*, &c., that in the passage of Augustine, 'to the Parthians,' is to be altered by conjecture, and that the epistle is addressed to the churches at and around Ephesus, on the ground of the fatherly, affectionate address in it, implying his personal ministry among his readers. But his position, as probably the only surviving apostle, accords very well with his addressing, in a Catholic epistle, a cycle of churches which he may not have specially ministered to in person, with fatherly counsel, by virtue of his apostolic superintendence of all the churches.

Time and Place of Writing.—This epistle seems to have been written subsequently to his gospel, as it assumes the readers' acquaintance with the gospel facts and Christ's speeches; also with the special aspect of the incarnate *Word,* as God *manifest in the flesh,* set forth more fully in his gospel. The tone of address, as a father addressing his "*little children*" (the continually recurring term), accords with the view that this epistle was written in John's old age, perhaps about 90 A.D. In ch. ii. 18, "it is the last time," probably does not refer to any particular event, as the destruction of Jerusalem, which was now many years past, but refers to the nearness of the Lord's coming, as proved by the rise of *antichristian teachers,* the mark of *the last time.* It was the Spirit's purpose to keep the Church always expecting Christ as ready to come at any moment. The whole Christian age is *the last time,* in the sense that no other dispensation is to arise till Christ comes. Cf. "these last days," Heb. i. 2. Ephesus may be conjectured to be the place whence it was written. The allusions to the germs of Gnostic heresy accord with Asia Minor being the *place,* and the last part of the apostolic age the *time,* of writing.

Contents.—The leading subject is, *fellowship with the Father* and *the Son* (ch. i. 3). Two principal divisions may be noted:—(1.) Ch. i. 5; ii. 28: the theme of this portion is stated at the outset, "*God is light, and in Him is no darkness at all;*" consequently, in order to have fellowship with Him, we must *walk in light;* connected with which is the *confession* and subsequent *forgiveness of* our *sins* through *Christ's propitiation* and *advocacy,* without which forgiveness there could be no light or fellowship with God: a further step in thus walking in the light is, positively *keeping God's commandments,* the sum of which is *love,* as opposed to *hatred,* the acmé of disobedience to God's word: negatively, he exhorts them according to their several stages of spiritual growth, *children, fathers, young men,* in consonance with their privileges as *forgiven, knowing the Father,* and *having over-come the wicked one, not to love the world,* which is incompatible with the indwelling of *the love of the Father;* and to be on their guard against the *antichristian* teachers already in the world, who were not of the Church, but of the world; against whom the true defence is, that his believing readers, who have the *anointing* of God, should *continue to abide in the Son and in the Father.* (2.) The second division (ch. ii. 29; v. 5) discusses the theme with which it opens, *"He is righteous;"* consequently (as in the first division), *"every one that doeth righteousness is born of Him."* *Sonship* in us involves our purifying ourselves as He is pure, even as we *hope to see, and therefore to be made like our Lord, when He shall appear:* in this second, as in the first division, both a positive and a negative side are presented of 'doing righteousness as He is righteous;' involving a contrast between the children of God and the children of the devil. *Hatred* marks the latter; *love,* the former: this love gives assurance of acceptance with God for ourselves and our prayers, accompanied as they are (ch. iii. 23) with obedience to His great commandment, to 'believe on Jesus, and love one another:' the seal (*v.* 24) of His dwelling in us and assuring our hearts, is the Spirit which He hath given us. In contrast to this (as in the first division), he warns against false spirits, the notes of which are, *denial of Christ,* and *adherence to the world.* *Sonship,* or birth of God, is then more fully described: its essential feature is unslavish free *love to God, because God first loved us,* and *gave His Son to die for us,* and consequent *love to the brethren,* grounded on their being sons of God like ourselves, and so *victory over the world:* this victory being gained only by the man who *believes in Jesus as the Son of God.* (3.) *The conclusion* establishes this last central truth, on which rests our fellowship with God, *Christ's having come by the water* of baptism, *the blood* of atonement, and *the witnessing Spirit,* which *is truth.* As in the opening he rested this cardinal truth on the apostles' witness of the eye, the ear, and the touch, so now at the close he rests it on *God's witness,* which is accepted by the believer, in contrast with the unbeliever, who *makes God a liar.* Then follows his closing statement of his *reason for writing* (ch. v. 13: cf. the corresponding ch. i. 4, at the beginning)—namely, that *believers in Christ the Son of God may know that they have* (now already) *eternal life* (the source of "joy," ch. i. 4: cf. similarly his object in writing the gospel, John xx. 31), and so have confidence as to their prayers being answered (corresponding to ch. iii. 22, in the second part); for instance, their intercessions for a *sinning brother* (unless his sin be a *sin unto death*). He closes with a brief summing up of the epistle, the dignity, sanctity, and safety from evil of the children of God, in contrast to the sinful world, and a warning against *idolatry,* literal and spiritual: "Keep yourselves from idols." John is 'the apostle of love,' but a *love* which presupposes *faith,* and exhibits itself in *obedience.*

Though the epistle is not directly polemical, the *occasion* which suggested writing was probably the rise of antichristian teachers; *because* he knew the spiritual character of the several classes whom he addresses—*children, youths, fathers*—he feels it necessary to confirm them in the faith and joyful fellowship of the Father and Son, and to assure them of the reality of the things they believe, that so they may have the *full* privileges of believing.

Style.—His peculiarity is fondness for aphorism and repetition. His tendency to repeat his own phrases arises partly from the affectionate, hortatory character of the epistle; partly, also, from its Hebraistic form, abounding in parallel clauses, as distinguished from the Grecian, logical style of Paul; also, from his child-like simplicity of spirit, which, full of one grand theme, repeats, and dwells on it with fond enthusiasm. Moreover, as *Alford* well says, the appearance of uniformity is often produced by want of deep enough exegesis to discover the real differences in passages which seem to express the same. Contemplative, rather than argumentative, he dwells more on the general than on the particular—on the inner, than on the outer Christian life. Certain fundamental truths he recurs again and again to,—at one time enlarging on, and applying them, at another time repeating them in their condensed simplicity. The thoughts do not march onward by successive steps, as in Paul, but rather in circles drawn round one central thought, which he reiterates, ever reverting to it, and viewing it, now under its positive, now under its negative aspect. Many terms which in the gospel are given as Christ's, in the epistle appear as the favourite expressions of John, naturally adopted from the Lord. Thus the contrasted "flesh" and "spirit," "light" and "darkness," "life" and "death," "abide in Him:" "fellowship with the Father and Son, and with one another," is a favourite phrase, not found in the gospel, but in Acts, and Paul's epistles. In him appears the harmonious union of opposites, adapting him for his high functions in the kingdom of God—contemplative repose of character, at the same time ardent zeal, combined with all-absorbing love: less adapted for outward work, such as Paul's, than for spiritual service. He handles Christian verities, not as abstract dogmas, but as living realities, personally enjoyed in fellowship with God in Christ, and with the brethren. Simple, at the same time profound, his writing is in consonance with his spirit, unrhetorical, and undialectic, gentle, consolatory, and loving: the reflexion of the Spirit of Him in whose breast he lay at the Last Supper, and whose beloved disciple he was. *Ewald* in *Alford*, speaking of the 'unruffled and heavenly repose' which characterizes this epistle, says, 'It appears to be the tone, not so much of a father talking with his beloved children, as of a glorified saint addressing mankind from a higher world. Never in any writing has the doctrine of heavenly love—a love working in stillness, ever unwearied, never exhausted—so thoroughly approved itself as in this epistle.'

John's Place in the Building up of the Church.—As Peter founded, and Paul propagated, so John completed the spiritual building. As the Old Testament puts prominently forward the *fear of God*, so John, the last writer of the New Testament, gives prominence to the *love of God*. Yet, as the Old Testament is not all limited to presenting the fear of God, but sets forth also His *love*, so John, as a representative of the New Testament, whilst breathing the spirit of love, gives also the plainest and most awful warnings against sin, in accordance with his original character as Boanerges, 'son of thunder.' His mother was Salome, mother of the sons of Zebedee, probably sister to Jesus' mother (cf. John xix. 25, "his mother's sister," with Matt. xxvii. 56): so that he was cousin of our Lord. To his mother, under God, he may have owed his first serious impressions. Expecting, as she did, the Messianic kingdom in glory, as appears from her petition, Matt. xx. 20-23, she doubtless tried to fill his young and ardent mind with the same hope. *Neander* distinguishes three leading developments of the Christian doctrine—the Pauline, the Jacobean (between which the Petrine forms an intermediate link), and the Johannean. John, in common with James, was less disposed to the intellectual, dialectic cast of thought which distinguishes Paul. He had not, like the apostle of the Gentiles, been brought to faith and peace through severe conflict; but, like James, had reached his Christian individuality through a quiet development. James, however, had passed through a moulding in Judaism previously, which, under the Spirit, caused him to present Christian truth in connection with the law, in so far as the latter in its spirit, though not letter, is permanent, and not abolished, but established under the Gospel. But John, from the first, had drawn his whole spiritual development from *the personal view of Christ*, the model man, and from intercourse with Him. Hence, in his writings, everything turns on one simple contrast: divine *life* in communion with Christ, death in separation from Him, as appears from his characteristic phrases, '*life, light, truth; death, darkness, lie.*' 'As James and Peter mark the gradual transition from spiritualized Judaism to the independent development of Christianity, and as Paul represents independent Christianity in opposition to the Jewish stand-point, so the *contemplative* element of John reconciles the two, and forms the closing point in the training of the apostolic Church' (*Neander*). John is the *Philo-Jesus*, as Peter is the *Philo-Christos*. His *thunder-like* ardour, whence he and James were called Boanerges, hardly agrees with the popular view of him as soft and feminine. John, in running to the tomb, is the more impetuous; Peter, the least restrained by awe, first enters (John xx. 4-6). Peter's anxiety to know as to John's end marks the affection between the two (John xxi. 21). They are ever together after the Lord's ascension (Acts iii. 1; iv. 13). John, who had called for fire upon the Samaritans, accompanies Peter to confirm the first converts among them.

SECOND AND THIRD JOHN.

THEIR *Authenticity.*—That these two epistles were written by the same author, appears from their similarity of tone, style, and sentiments. That John, the beloved disciple, was the author (as of the first epistle), appears from *Irenæus* ('Adversus Hæreses,' i., 16, 3), who quotes 2 John 10, 11; and 2 John 7 in iii., 16, 8, mistaking it, however, as if occurring in 1 John. *Clement* of Alexandria (A. D. 192, 'Stromata,' ii., 66), implies his knowledge of other epistles besides the first, which he calls the *larger;* and in fragments of his 'Adumbrations' (p. 1,011), he says, 'John's second epistle, which was written to the virgins [Greek, *parthenous:* perhaps *parthos* is what was meant], is the simplest; but it was written to a certain Babylonian, named *the Elect lady.*' *Dionysius* of Alexandria (in *Eusebius*, 'Ecclesiastical History,' vii., 25) observes that John never names himself in his epistles, 'not even in the second and third, although they are short, but simply calls himself the presbyter:' a confutation of those who think John *the apostle* distinct from John *the presbyter*. *Alexander* of Alexandria cites 2 John 10, 11, as John's (*Socrates*, 'Historia Ecclesiastica,' i., 6). *Cyprian* ('De Hæreticis Baptizandis'), in referring to the bishops at the council of Carthage, says, 'John the apostle, in his epistle, said, If any come to you' (2 John 10): so that this epistle, and therefore its twin sister, 3 John, was recognized as apostolic in the North African church. The *Muratori* 'Fragment' is ambiguous. The second and third epistles were not in the Peshito or old Syriac version. *Cosmas Indicopleustes*, in the sixth century, says, that in his time the Syriac church only acknowledged three out of the Catholic epistles—1 Peter, 1 John, and James. But *Ephrem Syrus* quotes the second epistle of John. *Eusebius* ('Ecclesiastical History') reckons both epistles among the *Antilegomena*, or *controverted* Scriptures, as distinguished from the *Homologoumena*, or *universally acknowledged* from the first. Still, his own opinion was, that the two minor epistles were genuine, remarking as he does (in 'Demonstratio Evangelica,' iii., 5), that in John's '*epistles*' he does not mention his own name, nor calls himself an apostle or evangelist, but an "elder" (2 John 1; 3 John 1). *Origen* (in *Eusebius*, 'Ecclesiastical History,' vi., 25) mentions the second and third epistles; but adds, '*not all* admit (implying that *most* do) their genuineness.' *Jerome* ('De Viris Illustribus,' ix.) mentions the two latter epistles as attributed to John the presbyter, whose sepulchre was shown among the Ephesians in his day. But the designation, "elder," was used of the apostles by others (*e. g.*, *Papias* in *Eusebius*, 'Ecclesiastical History,' iii., 39), and by St. Peter, an apostle, of himself (1 Pet. v. 1). Why, then, should not John also use this designation, in consonance with the humility which leads him not to name himself or his apostleship in the first epistle? The 'Antilegomena' were generally recognized as canonical soon after the Council of Nice (A. D. 325). Thus *Cyril* of Jerusalem, A. D. 349, enumerates fourteen epistles of Paul, and seven Catholic epistles. So *Gregory* of Nazianzum, in A. D. 389. The councils of Hippo, 393, and Carthage, 397, adopted a catalogue of New Testament books exactly agreeing with our canon. So our oldest extant Greek MSS. Of the thirteen verses in 2 John, eight are found in 1 John. A forger would never have termed him 'John *the elder*.' The second and third epistles of John, from their brevity (which *Origen* notices), and the private nature of their contents, were less read in the earliest Christian assemblies, and less quoted by the Fathers; hence arose their non-universal recognition at the first. Their private nature makes them the less likely to be spurious, for there seems no purpose in their forgery. The style and colouring, too, accord with that of the first epistle.

To whom Addressed.—The third epistle is directed to Gaius or Caius. Whether Gaius of Macedonia (Acts xix. 29), or Gaius of Corinth (Rom. xvi. 23; 1 Cor. i. 14), or Gaius of Derbe (Acts xx. 4), it is hard to decide. *Mill* believes Gaius, bishop of Pergamos ('Apostolic Constitutions,' vii., 40), a convert of John, and a man of wealth, is implied, *vv.* 4, 5. Gaius of Corinth was a 'host of the church.'

The address of the second epistle is more disputed. It opens, "The elder unto the *elect lady*." And it closes, "The children of thy *elect* sister greet thee." Now, 1 Pet. i. 1, 2, addresses the *elect* in Asia, &c., and closes (1 Pet. v. 13), "The church that is *at* Babylon, *elected* together with you, saluteth you." Putting together these facts, with the quotations (above) from *Clement* of Alexandria, and the fact that the word "church" comes from the Greek [*kyriake*] cognate to the Greek for "lady" [*kyria*, belonging to the Lord, *kyrios*], *Wordsworth's* view is probable. As Peter in Babylon had sent salutations of *the elect Church* in the then *Parthian* (see above on *Clement* of Alexandria) *Babylon* to her *elect sister* in Asia, so John, the metropolitan president of the elect church in Asia, writes to *the elect lady*—*i. e.*, church—in Babylon. *Neander*, &c., think the Greek [*kyria*] not to mean "lady," but her *proper name;* and that she had a 'sister, a Christian matron,' then with John.

Date and Place of Writing.—*Eusebius* ('Ecclesiastical History,' iii., 25) relates that John, after the death of Domitian, returned from his exile in Patmos to Ephesus, and went on missionary tours into the heathen regions around, and also made visitations of the neighbouring churches, and ordained bishops and clergy. Such journeys are mentioned, 2 John 12; 3 John 10, 14. If *Eusebius* be right, both epistles must have been written after the Apocalypse, in his old age, which harmonizes with their tone, and in or near Ephesus. It was on one of his visitation tours that he designed to rebuke Diotrephes (3 John 9, 10).

JUDE.

Its *Author.*—He calls himself in the address, "servant of Jesus Christ, and brother of James." See Introduction to epistle of James, in proof of James the *apostle*, and James *the Lord's brother* (he does not call himself so, both in humility, and because he was not *strictly* Jesus' brother), bishop of Jerusalem, being the same. Gal. i. 19, alone, proves this. Similarly, Jude the brother of our Lord, and Jude the apostle, seem the same. *Jerome* ('Contra Helvidium') rightly maintains that by the Lord's brethren are meant his cousins, children of Mary and Cleophas (Alphæus). From 1 Cor. ix. 5 (as "brethren of the Lord" stands between "other apostles" and "Cephas"), it seems natural to think that the *brethren of the Lord* are distinguished from the apostles only because *all* his brethren were not apostles—only James and Jude. Jude's reason for calling himself "brother of James," was that James, as bishop of Jerusalem, was better known than himself. Had he been, strictly, *brother of our Lord*, he would have so entitled himself. His not mentioning his *apostleship* is no proof that he was not one; for so James omits it in his heading; and Paul, in the epistles to the Philippians, Thessalonians, and Philemon. Had the writer counterfeited the apostle Jude, he would have called himself an 'apostle.' He was also called Lebbæus and Thaddæus, probably to distinguish him from Judas Iscariot, the traitor. Lebbæus [from Hebrew, *leeb*, 'heart'] means *courageous.* Thaddæus is the same as Theudas [from *thad*, the 'breast.' Rather, as it appears in Syriac, under the form 'Adai,' from *hodah*, 'to praise']. Luke and John, writing later than Matthew, when there would be no confusion between him and Judas Iscariot, give his name Judas. The only circumstances concerning him in the gospels occur, John xiv. 22, "Judas saith unto him, not Iscariot, Lord, how is it that thou wilt manifest thyself unto us, and not unto the world?" &c. *Jerome* ('Annotationes in Matthæum') says, that he was sent to Edessa, to Abgarus, king of Osroene, or Edesea, and that he preached in Syria, Arabia, Mesopotamia, and Persia, where he suffered martyrdom. The story is told on *Eusebius's* authority, that Abgarus, on his sick-bed, having heard of Jesus' power to heal, sent to beg Him to come and cure him; to which the Lord replied, praising his faith, that though he had not seen the Saviour, he yet believed; adding, 'As for what thou hast written, that I should come to thee, it is necessary that all those things for which I was sent should be fulfilled by me in this place, and that having fulfilled them, I should be received up to Him that sent me. When, therefore, I shall be received into heaven, I will send unto thee some one of my disciples, who shall both heal thy distemper and give life to thee and those with thee.' Thomas is accordingly said to have been inspired to send Thaddæus for the cure and baptism of Abgarus. The letters are said to have been shown Thaddæus among the archives of Edessa. It is possible such a message was verbally sent, and its substance registered in writing afterwards (cf. 2 Ki. v., and Matt. xv. 22). *Hegesippus* (in *Eusebius,* 'Ecclesiastical History,' iii., 20) states, that when Domitian inquired after David's posterity, some grandsons of Jude, called the Lord's brother, were brought into his presence. Being asked as to their possessions, they said that they had thirty-nine acres, of the value of 9,000 denarii, out of which they paid him taxes, and lived by labour, a proof of which they gave by showing the hardness of their hands. Being interrogated as to Christ and His kingdom, they replied, that it was not of this world, but heavenly; and that it would be manifested at the end, when He would come in glory to judge the living and the dead.

Authenticity.—*Eusebius* ('Ecclesiastical History,' iii., 25) reckons it among the *Anti-legomena* or *controverted* Scriptures, 'though recognized by the majority.' The reference to the contest of Michael, the archangel, with the devil, for the body of Moses, not mentioned elsewhere in the Old Testament, but found in the *apocryphal* Book of Enoch, probably raised doubts as to its authenticity, as *Jerome* ('Catalogus Scriptorum Ecclesiasticorum,' iv.) says. Moreover, its not being addressed to one particular church or individual, caused it not to be so immediately recognized as canonical. A counterfeiter would have avoided using what did not occur in the Old Testament, and which might be regarded as apocryphal.

As to the Book of Enoch, if quoted by Jude, his quotation gives an inspired sanction only to *the truth of that passage*, not to the whole book; just as Paul, by inspiration, sanctions particular sentiments from *Aratus, Epimenides,* and *Menander,* but not all their writings. Rather, as there is some variation between Jude's statement and that of the Book of Enoch, Jude, though probably not ignorant of the Book of Enoch, stamps with inspired sanction the *current* TRADITION *of the Jews* (as 'Enoch prophesied, *saying*,' favours) as to Enoch's prophecies; just as Paul mentions the names of the Egyptian magicians, "Jannes and Jambres," not in the Old Testament. At all events, the prophecy ascribed to Enoch by Jude was really his, being sanctioned as such by this inspired writer. He was directed by the Spirit to take the one inspired gem out of the mass of earth that surrounded it, and set it in the gold of the inspired volume. So the tradition (cf. Deut. xxxiv. 6) as to the archangel Michael's dispute with Satan concerning Moses' body, is by Jude's inspired authority (*v.* 9) declared true. The Book of Enoch is quoted by *Justin Martyr, Irenæus, Clement* of Alexandria, &c. Bruce, the Abyssinian traveller, brought home three copies in Ethiopic from Alexandria, of which Archbishop Lawrence, in 1821, gave an English translation. The Ethiopic was a version from the Greek, and the Greek a version from the Hebrew, as the names of the angels in it show. The Apostolic Constitutions, *Origen* ('Contra Celsum'), *Jerome,* and *Augustine,* pronounced it not canonical. Yet it is edifying, vindicating God's government of the world, natural and spiritual, and contradicting no Scripture statement. The name *Jesus* never occurs, though "Son of man," so often given to Messiah in the gospels, is frequent, and terms are used expressive of His dignity, character, and acts, exceeding the views of Messiah in any other Jewish book. The writer seems to have been a Jew, thoroughly imbued with Daniel's sacred writings. Though many coincidences occur between its sentiments and the New Testament, the Messianic portions are not distinct enough to prove that the writer knew the New Testament. Rather, he seems to have immediately preceded Christ's coming, about the time of Herod the Great, and so gives a most interesting view of believing Jews' opinions before our Lord's advent. The Trinity is recognized, ch. lx. 13, 14. Messiah is 'the Elect One' existing from eternity, ch. xlviii. 2, 3, 5; 'all kings shall fall down before, worship, and fix their hopes on this Son of man,' ch. lxi. 10-13; xlviii. 3, 4; He is the supreme Judge, ch. lx. 10, 11; lxviii. 38, 39. There shall be a future retribution, ch. xciii. 8, 9; xciv. 2, 4; xcv.; xcvi.; xcix.; ciii. The eternity of future punishment, ch. ciii. 5. It is quoted in the Book of Zohar, before Christ's time. But it is doubtful whether our extant Book of Enoch be the same as that quoted in Zohar. It contains much that professes to be Noah's prophecies, besides Enoch's. *Volkmar,* in *Alford,* thinks the book was written at the time of the sedition of Barchochebas (A. D. 132), by a follower of Rabbi Akiba, the upholder of that impostor. This would make the book antichristian in its origin. If this date be correct, doubt less it copied some things from Jude, giving them the Jewish, not the Christian, colouring.

Eusebius ('Demonstratio Evangelica,' iii., 5) remarks, it accords with John's humility that, in 2 and 3 John, he calls himself "the elder." For the same reason James and Jude call themselves "servants of Jesus Christ." *Clemens Alexandrinus* ('Adumbrations, in Ep. Jud.,' p. 1,007) says, 'Jude, through reverential awe, did not call himself *brother*, but *servant*, of Jesus Christ, and brother of James.'

Tertullian ('De Cultu Fœminarum,' c. iii.) cites the epistle as that of the apostle James. *Clemens Alexandrinus* quotes it (*vv.* 8, 17) as Scripture ('Stromata,' iii., 2, 11; and (*v.* 5) in 'Pædagogus,' iii., 8, 44). The *Muratori* 'Fragment' (170 A. D.) asserts its canonicity (*Routh,* 'Reliquiæ Sacræ,' i., 306). *Origen* ('Commentary' on Matt. xiii. 55) says, 'Jude wrote an epistle of few lines, but one filled full of the strong words of heavenly grace.' Also, in 'Commentary' on Matt. xxii. 23, he quotes *v.* 6; and on Matt. xviii. 10, he quotes *v.* 1. He calls the writer 'Jude the apostle,' in the Latin remains of his works (cf. *Davidson,* 'Introduction,' iii., 498). *Jerome* ('Catalogus Scriptorum Ecclesiasticorum,' iv.) reckons it among the Scriptures. Though the oldest MSS. of the Peshito omit it, *Ephrem Syrus* recognizes it. *Wordsworth* reasons: St. Jude, we know, died before St. John—*i. e.*, before the beginning of the second century. Now, *Eusebius* ('Ecclesiastical History,' iii., 32) tells us that St. James was succeeded in the bishopric of Jerusalem by Symeon his brother; and also that Symeon sat in that see till A. D. 107, when, as a martyr, he was crucified, in his 120th year. We find that the epistle to Jude was known in the East and West in the second century; it was therefore circulated in Symeon's lifetime. It never would have received currency such as it had, nor would Symeon have permitted a letter bearing the name of an apostle, his own brother Jude, brother of his own apostolical predecessor, St. James, to have been circulated, if it were not really St. Jude's.

To whom Addressed.—The references to Old Testament history, *vv.* 5, 7, and to Jewish tradition, *v.* 14, &c., make it likely that *Jewish* Christians are the readers to whom Jude mainly (though including *all* Christians, *v.* 1) writes, just as the kindred epistle, 2 Peter, is addressed primarily to the same: cf. Introductions to 1 and 2 Peter. The persons stigmatized were not merely *libertines* (*Alford*), though that was one of their prominent characteristics, but heretics in *doctrine,* "denying the only Lord God, and our Saviour Jesus Christ." Hence he urges believers "earnestly to contend for *the faith* once delivered unto the saints." Insubordination, self-seeking, and licentiousness, the fruit of Antinomian teachings, were the evils against which Jude warns his readers; reminding them that, to build themselves in their most holy faith, and to pray in the Holy Ghost, are the only safeguards. The same evils, along with mocking scepticism, shall characterize the last days before the final judgment, even as in the days when Enoch warned the ungodly of the coming flood. As Peter was in Babylon in writing 1 Pet. v. 13, probably also in writing 2 Peter (cf. Introductions to 1 and 2 Peter), it seems not unlikely that Jude addressed his epistle primarily to *the Jewish Christians in and about Mesopotamian Babylon* (a place of great resort to the Jews in that day), or else to *the Christian Jews dispersed in Pontus, Galatia, Cappadocia, Asia, and Bithynia*, the persons addressed by Peter. For Jude is expressly said to have preached in *Mesopotamia* (*Jerome,* 'Annotationes in Matthæum'), and his epistle, consisting of only twenty-five verses, contains no less than eleven passages from 2 Peter, (see the list, Introduction to 2 Peter). Probably *v.* 4 witnesses to the fulfilment of Peter's prophecy, "There *are* certain men *crept in unawares,* who were before of old ordained [Greek, 'forewritten'—*i. e.*, announced *beforehand*—by the apostle Peter's *written* prophecy] to this *condemnation*, ungodly men, *denying* the only Lord God, and our Lord Jesus Christ." Cf. 2 Pet. ii. 1, "There *shall be* false teachers among you who *privily shall* bring in *damnable* heresies, even *denying the Lord* that bought them, and bring upon themselves swift *destruction.*" Also, *vv.* 17, 18 refer to *the very words* of 2 Pet. iii. 3, 'Remember the words which were spoken before of the *apostles* of our Lord Jesus; how they told you there should be *mockers in the last time,* who should *walk after their own* ungodly *lusts.*' This proves, in opposition to *Alford,* that Jude's epistle is later than Peter's (whose inspiration he thus confirms, as Peter confirms Paul's, 2 Pet. iii. 15, 16), not *vice versâ.* Jude depicts adversaries of Christianity in general; St. Peter, heretical *teachers* in particular.

Time and Place of Writing.—*Alford* thinks that, considering St. Jude was writing to Jews, and citing signal instances of Divine vengeance, it is very unlikely he would have omitted to allude to the destruction of Jerusalem, if he had written after that event, which uprooted the Jewish polity. He conjectures from the tone and references, that the writer lived in Palestine. The title "brother of James" would be best understood in the region where James as bishop was well known. But as to the former, negative evidence is doubtful; for neither does John allude in his epistles, written after the destruction of Jerusalem, to that event. *Mill* fixes on A. D. 90, after the death of all the apostles, save John. I incline to think, from *vv.* 17, 18, that some time had elapsed since the second epistle of Peter (written probably about A. D. 68 or 69), and, therefore, that the epistle of Jude was written *after* the destruction of Jerusalem.

REVELATION.

ITS *Authenticity.*—The author calls himself *John* (ch. i. 1, 4, 9 ; xxii. 8). *Justin Martyr* ('Dialogue,' p. 308, A. D. 139-161) quotes from it as *John the apostle's work,* the prophecy of the millennium of the saints, to be followed by the general resurrection and judgment. This testimony of *Justin* is referred to also by *Eusebius* ('Ecclesiastical History,' iv., 18). *Justin,* early in the second century, held his controversy with *Trypho,* a learned Jew, at *Ephesus,* where John had been living thirty or thirty-five years before. He says that 'the Revelation had been given to John, one of the twelve apostles of Christ.' *Melito,* bishop of Sardis (about 171 A. D.), *one of the seven churches addressed,* a successor, therefore, of one of the seven angels, is said by *Eusebius* ('Ecclesiastical History,' iv., 26) to have written treatises on the Apocalypse *of John.* The testimony of the bishop of Sardis is the more impartial, as Sardis is one of the churches severely reproved (ch. iii. 1). So *Theophilus* of Antioch (about 180 A. D.), according to *Eusebius* (iv. 26), quoted testimonies from the Apocalypse of John. *Eusebius* says the same of *Apollonius,* who lived in Asia Minor in the end of the second century. *Irenæus* (about 195 A.D.), a hearer of *Polycarp,* the disciple of John, supposed by *Archbishop Usher* to be the *angel of the church of Smyrna,* is decided, again and again, in quoting the Apocalypse as the work of the apostle John ('Hæreses,' iv., 20, 11; iv., 21, 3 ; iv., 30, 4 ; v., 26, 1; v., 30, 3 ; v., 35, 2). In v., 30, 1, he cites the mystical number of the beast, 666 (ch. xiii. 18), as in all old copies, and confirmed orally to him by those who had seen St. John; and adds, 'We do not hazard a confident theory as to the name of Antichrist ; for if it had been necessary that his name should be proclaimed openly at the present time, it would have been declared by him who saw the apocalyptic vision ; *for it was seen at no long time back, but almost in our generation, towards the end of Domitian's reign.*' In his work *against heresies*, ten years after *Polycarp's* martyrdom, he quotes the Apocalypse twenty times, and makes long extracts from it, as inspired Scripture. These testimonies of persons contemporary with John's immediate successors, and more or less connected with the region of the seven churches to which Revelation is addressed, are most convincing. *Tertullian*, of North Africa, about 220 A.D. ('Adversus Marcion,' iii., 14), quotes the apostle John's description, in the Apocalypse, of the sword proceeding out of the Lord's mouth (ch. xix. 15), and (in 24) the heavenly city, (ch. xxi.) Cf. ' De Resurrectione,' xxvii. ; ' De Anima,' viii., 9, &c. ; ' De Præscriptione Hæreticorum,' xxxiii. The *Muratori* ' Fragment on the Canon' (about A.D. 170) refers to John, 'the predecessor of Paul'—viz., in the apostleship —as writing to the seven churches. *Hippolytus*, bishop of Ostia, near Rome, about 240 A.D. ('De Antichristo,' p. 67), quotes ch. xvii. 1-18, as the writing of John the apostle. Among *Hippolytus's* works, there is specified in the catalogue on his statue, a treatise ' On the Apocalypse and Gospel according to John.' *Clement* of Alexandria, about 200 A.D. ('Stromata,' vi., 13), alludes to the twenty-four seats on which the elders sit, as mentioned by John in the Apocalypse (ch. iv. 5); also (in ' Quis Dives Salvus,' sect. 42), he mentions John's return from Patmos to Ephesus, on the death of the Roman tyrant. *Origen* (about 233 A.D., ' Commentary on Matthew,' in *Eusebius*, ' Ecclesiastical History,' vi., 25) mentions John as author of the Apocalypse, without any doubts as to its authenticity ; also (in 'Commentary on Matthew,' tom. xvi., 6), he quotes ch. i. 9, and says, ' John seems to have beheld the Apocalypse in the island of Patmos.' *Victorinus*, bishop of Petau, in Pannonia, who suffered martyrdom under Diocletian, in 303 A.D., wrote the earliest extant commentary on the Apocalypse. Though the *Old Syriac Peshito* version does not contain the Apocalypse, yet *Ephrem Syrus* (about 378 A.D.) quotes it as canonical, and ascribes it to John.

Its *Canonicity* and inspiration (according to a scholium of *Andreas* of Cappadocia) are attested by *Papias*, a hearer of John and associate of *Polycarp*. *Papias* was bishop of Hieropolis, near Laodicea, one of the seven churches. *Wordsworth* conjectures that the rebukes of Laodicea in Revelation influenced the council of Laodicea to omit Revelation from its list of books to be *read publicly* (?). The epistle of the churches of Lyons and Vienne to the churches of Asia and Phrygia (in *Eusebius*, 'Ecclesiastical History,' v., 1-3), in the persecution under M. Aurelius, A.D. 177, quotes ch. i. 5 ; iii. 14 ; xiv. 4, and xxii. 11, as Scripture. *Cyprian*, about 250 A.D., also (in ' Ep.,' xiii.) quotes ch. ii. 5 as Scripture ; and (in ' Ep.,' xxv.) he quotes ch. iii. 21, as of the same authority as the gospel. (See *Alford's* ' Prolegomena,' from whom mainly this summary of evidence has been derived.) *Athanasius* (in his ' Festival Epistle') enumerates the Apocalypse among the *canonical* Scriptures, to which none must add, and from which none must take away. *Jerome* (in ' Epistola ad Paulinum ') includes in the canon the Apocalypse, adding, ' It has as many mysteries as words. All praise falls short of its merits. In each of its words lie hid manifold senses.' Thus an unbroken chain of testimony, down from the apostolic period, confirms its canonicity and authenticity.

St. John's Authorship.—The *Alogi* ('Epiphanius Hæreses,' xxxi.) and *Caius*, the Roman presbyter (*Eusebius*, iii., 28), towards the end of the second, and beginning of the third century, rejected St. John's Apocalypse on captious grounds. *Caius*, according to *Jerome* ('De Viris Illustribus,' about 210 A.D.), attributed it to *Cerinthus*. *Dionysius* of Alexandria mentions many before his time who rejected it, because of its obscurity, and because it seemed to support *Cerinthus's* dogma of an earthly carnal kingdom; whence they attributed it to *Cerinthus*. *Dionysius*, scholar of *Origen*, and bishop of Alexandria (A. D. 247), admits its inspiration (in *Eusebius*, 'Ecclesiastical History,' vii., 10), but attributes it to some John distinct from the apostle, on the ground of its difference of style from that of St. John's gospel and epistle; also because the name John is several times mentioned in the Apocalypse, but is always kept back in both gospel and epistle; moreover, neither does the epistle make allusion to the Apocalypse, nor the Apocalypse to the epistle; and the style is not pure Greek, but abounds in solecisms.

Eusebius wavers in opinion ('Ecclesiastical History,' xxiv., 39) as to whether it is, or is not, to be ranked among the undoubtedly canonical Scriptures. His antipathy to the millennial doctrine would give an unconscious bias to his judgment. *Cyril* of Jerusalem (about A. D. 386, 'Catechesis,' iv., 35, 36) omits the Apocalypse in enumerating the New Testament Scriptures to be read privately, as well as publicly. 'Whatever is not read in the churches, that do not even read by thyself: the apostles and ancient bishops of the Church, who transmitted them to us, were far wiser than thou art.' Hence, we see that, in his day, the Apocalypse was not read in the churches. Yet (in 'Catechesis,' i., 4) he quotes ch. ii. 7, 17; and (in 'Catechesis,' i., 16, 13) he draws the prophetical statement from ch. xvii. 11, that the king who is to humble the three kings (Dan. vii. 8, 20) is the *eighth king*. In chs. xv. and xxvii., he similarly quotes from ch. xii. 3, 4. *Alford* conjectures *Cyril* at some time changed his opinion; and these references to the Apocalypse were slips of memory, whereby he retained phraseology which belonged to his former, not his subsequent, views. The sixtieth canon (if genuine) of the Laodicean council, in the fourth century, omits the Apocalypse from the canonical books. But the council of Carthage has it in the canon, (397 A. D.) The Eastern church in part doubted—the Western church, after the fifth century, universally recognized—the Apocalypse. *Cyril* of Alexandria ('De Adoratione,' 146), though implying that some doubted its genuineness, himself undoubtingly accepts it as the work of St. John. *Andreas* of Cesarea, in Cappadocia, recognized as genuine and canonical, and wrote the first *connected* commentary on, the Apocalypse. The sources of doubt were :—(1.) The antagonism of many to the millennium in it; (2.) Its obscurity and symbolism caused it not to be read in the churches, or taught to the young. But *the most primitive* tradition is unequivocal in its favour. In a word, the objective evidence is decidedly for it; the only arguments against it were subjective.

The writer's addresses to the churches of Proconsular Asia (ch. ii. 1) accord with the concurrent tradition, that after John's return from his exile in Patmos, at the death of Domitian, under Nerva, he resided for long, and died at last, in Ephesus, in the time of Trajan (*Eusebius*, 'Ecclesiastical History,' iii., 20, 23). If the Apocalypse were not the inspired work of John, purporting, as it does, to be an address from their superior to the seven churches of Proconsular Asia, it would have assuredly been rejected *in that region*, whereas the earliest testimonies *in those churches* are all in its favour. One person alone was entitled to use language of authority, such as is addressed to the seven angels of the churches—namely, John, the last surviving apostle and superintendent of all the churches. Also, it accords with John's manner to assert the accuracy of his testimony, both at the beginning and end of his book (cf. ch. i. 2, 3, and xxii. 8, with John i. 14; xix. 35; xxi. 24; 1 John i. 1, 2). Again, it accords with the view of the writer being *an inspired apostle*, that he addresses the angels, or presidents, of the several churches, as a *superior* addressing inferiors. Also, he commends the church of Ephesus for trying and convicting "them which *say they are apostles*, and are not;" by which he implies his own claim to apostolic inspiration (ch. ii. 2), as declaring in the seven epistles Christ's will revealed through him. None but St. John could, without a design to deceive, have assumed the simple title "John," without addition. One alone—namely, the *apostle*—would be understood by the designation at that time, and in Asia. Also, 'the fellow-servant of angels, and brother of prophets' (ch. xxii. 9) is more likely to be the celebrated apostle John than any less known person bearing the name.

As to the difference of style, as compared with the gospel and epistle, *the difference of subject* in part accounts for it—the visions of the seer, transported above the region of sense, appropriately taking a form of expression abrupt, and unbound by the grammatical laws which governed his calmer and more deliberate writings. Moreover, being a Galilean Hebrew, John, in writing a Revelation akin to the Old Testament prophecies, naturally reverted to their Hebraistic style. *Alford* notices features of resemblance between the styles of the Apocalypse and John's gospel and epistle:—(1.) The characteristic appellation of our Lord, peculiar to John exclusively, "the Word of God" (ch. xix. 13: cf. John i. 1; 1 John i. 1). (2.) The phrase, "he that overcometh" (ch. ii. 7, 11, 17; iii. 5, 12, 21; xii. 11; xv. 2; xvii. 14; xxi. 7: cf. John xvi. 33; 1 John ii. 13, 14; iv. 4; v. 4, 5). (3.) The Greek [*alethinos*], "true," as opposed to that which is shadowy and unreal. This term, found only once in St. Luke (Luke xvi. 11), four times in St. Paul (1 Thess. i. 9; Heb. viii. 2; ix. 24; x. 22), is found nine times in St. John's gospel (John i. 9; iv. 23, 37; vi. 32; vii. 28; viii. 16; xv. 1; xvii. 3; xix. 35), four times in John's first epistle (1 John ii. 8; v. 20), and ten times in Revelation (ch. iii. 7, 14; vi. 10; xv. 3; xvi. 7; xix. 2, 9, 11; xxi. 5; xxii. 6). (4.) The diminutive for "Lamb" [*arnion*, 'lambkin'] occurs twenty-nine times in the Apocalypse. The only other place where it occurs is John xxi. 15. In John's writings alone is Christ called *directly* "the Lamb" (John i. 29, 36). In 1 Pet. i. 19, He is called "as a lamb without blemish," in allusion to Isa. liii. 7. So "witness," or "testimony" (ch. i. 2, 9; vi. 9; xi. 7, &c.: cf. John i. 7, 8, 15, 19, 32; 1 John i. 2; iv. 14; v. 6-11). "Keep the word," or "commandments" (ch. iii. 8, 10; xii. 17, &c.: cf. John viii. 51, 55; xiv. 15). The assertion of the same thing positively and negatively (ch. ii. 2, 6, 8, 13; iii. 8, 17, 18: cf. John i. 3, 6, 7, 20; 1 John ii. 27, 28). Cf. also 1 John ii. 20, 27, with ch. iii. 18, as to the spiritual *anointing*. The seeming solecisms are attributable to that inspired elevation which is above mere grammatical rules, and arrest attention by the peculiarity of phrase, so as to pause and search into some deep truth beneath. The vivid earnestness of the inspired writer, handling a subject so transcending all others, raises him above ordinary rules; so that he abruptly passes from one grammatical construction to another, as he graphically sets the thing described before the eye. This is not due to ignorance of grammar, for he 'has displayed a knowledge of grammatical rules in other more difficult constructions' (*Winer*). *The connection of thought* is more attended to than grammatical connection. Another consideration to be taken into account is, that two-fifths of the whole being the recorded language of others, he moulds his style accordingly. Cf. *Tregelles's* 'Introduction to Revelation from Ancient Authorities.'

Tregelles well says (' New Testament Historic Evidence'), 'There is no book of the New Testament for which we have such clear, ample, and numerous testimonies in the second century, as we have for the Apocalypse The more closely the witnesses were connected with the apostle John (as was *Irenæus*), the more explicit is their testimony. That doubts should prevail in after ages, must have originated either in ignorance of the earlier testimony, or else from some supposed intuition of what an apostle *ought* to have written. The objections on the ground of internal *style* can weigh nothing against the actual evidence. It is in vain to argue *à priori*, that St. John *could* not have written this book, when we have the evidence of several competent witnesses that he *did* write it.'

Relation of the Apocalypse to the rest of the Canon.—*Gregory* of Nyssa (tom. iii., p. 601) calls Revelation 'the last book of grace.' It completes the volume of inspiration; so that we are to look for no further revelation till Christ Himself shall come. Appropriately the last book completing the canon was written by John, the last survivor of the apostles. The New Testament is composed of the historical books, the gospels and Acts, the doctrinal epistles, and the one prophetical book, Revelation. The same apostle wrote the last of the gospels, and probably the last of the epistles, and the only prophetical book of the New Testament. All the books of the New Testament had been written, and were read in the church assemblies, some years before John's death. His life was providentially prolonged, that he might give Scripture its final attestation. About 100 A. D., the bishops of Asia (angels of the seven churches) came to John at Ephesus, bringing him copies of the three gospels—Matthew, Mark, and Luke—and desired of him a statement of his apostolical judgment concerning them; whereupon he pronounced them authentic, genuine, and inspired, and at their request added his own gospel, to complete the fourfold aspect of the gospel of Christ (cf. *Muratori's* 'Canon,' *Eusebius*, iii., 24; *Jerome*, 'Procemium in Matthæum;' *Victorinus*, 'On the Apocalypse;' *Theodoret*, 'Mopsuestia'). A Greek divine, quoted in 'Allatius,' calls Revelation 'the Seal of the whole Bible.' The canon would be incomplete without Revelation. Scripture is a complete whole, its component books, written in a period ranging over 1,500 years, being mutually connected. Unity of aim and spirit pervades the entire, so that the end is the necessary sequence of the middle, and the middle of the beginning. Genesis presents man and his bride in innocence and blessedness, followed by man's fall through Satan's subtlety, and man's consequent misery, his exclusion from Paradise, and its tree of life and delightful rivers. Revelation presents, in reverse order, man first liable to sin and death, but afterwards made conqueror through the blood of the Lamb; the first Adam and Eve, represented by the second Adam, Christ, and the Church, His spotless bride, in Paradise, with free access to the tree of life and the crystal water of life that flows from the throne of God. As Genesis foretold the bruising of the serpent's head by the woman's seed, so Revelation declares the final accomplishment of that prediction, (chs. xix., xx.)

Place and Time of Writing.—The best authorities among the Fathers state that John was exiled under Domitian (*Irenæus*, v., 30; *Clement* of Alexandria; *Eusebius*, 'Ecclesiastical History,' iii., 20). *Victorinus* says that he had to labour in the mines of Patmos. At Domitian's death, 95 A. D., he returned to Ephesus under the emperor Nerva. Some think it was immediately after his return that he wrote the account of the visions vouchsafed to him in Patmos (ch. i. 2, 9). But ch. x. 4 seems to imply that he wrote the visions immediately after seeing them. Patmos is one of the Sporades, in circumference about thirty miles. 'It was fitting that when forbidden to go beyond certain bounds of the earth, he was permitted to penetrate the secrets of heaven,' (*Bede*, 'Explan. Apocalypse,' on ch i.) *Irenæus* says, 'Revelation was seen no long time ago, almost in our own generation, at the close of Domitian's reign.' Revelation has several coincidences of phrase and thought with the preceding epistles of Saints Paul and Peter. Heb. x. 37, cf. ch. i. 4, 8; xxii. 12: Heb. xi. 10, cf. ch. xxi. 14 : Heb. xii. 22, 23, cf. ch. xiv. 1: Heb. viii. 1, 2, cf. ch. xi. 19; xv. 5; xxi. 3 : Heb. iv. 12, cf. ch. i. 16; ii. 12, 16; xix. 13, 15 : Heb. iv. 9, cf. ch. xx. : also 1 Pet. i. 7, 13; iv. 13, with ch. i. 1 : 1 Pet. ii. 9, with ch. v. 10 : 2 Tim. iv. 8, with ch. ii. 26, 27 ; iii. 21 ; xi. 18: Eph. vi. 12, with ch. xii. 7-12 : Phil. iv. 3, with ch. iii. 5 ; xiii. 8 ; xvii. 8; xx. 12, 15'; Col. i. 18, with ch. i. 5 : 1 Cor. xv. 52, with ch. x. 7; xi. 15-18. The Pauline benediction (ch. i. 4) implies it was written after Paul's death, which was under Nero; for, during St. Paul's life, St. John would have avoided the characteristic greeting of St. Paul.

To what Readers Addressed.—The inscription states that it is addressed to the seven churches of Asia—*i. e.*, Proconsular Asia. St. John's reason for fixing on *seven* (for there were more than seven churches in the region meant by "Asia"—for instance, Magnesia and Tralles), was doubtless because *seven* is the sacred number, implying totality and universality : so it is implied that John, through the seven churches, addresses in the Spirit the Church of all places and ages. The Church in its various states of spiritual life or deadness is represented by the seven churches, and is addressed with consolation or warning accordingly. Smyrna and Philadelphia alone of the seven are honoured with unmixed praise, as faithful in tribulation, and rich in good works. Heresies of a decided kind had by this time arisen in the churches of Asia, and the love of many waxed cold; whilst others advanced to greater zeal, and one had sealed his testimony with his blood.

Object.—It begins with admonitory addresses to the seven churches from the Divine Son of man, whom John saw in vision, after a brief introduction, setting forth the main subject—viz., to "show unto His servants things which must shortly come to pass," (chs. i.-iii.) Ch. i. 5-9 is the foundation of the whole book, Christ's person, offices as our Redeemer, second coming, and the intermediate tribulation of those who in patient per-severance wait for His kingdom. From ch. iv. to the end is mainly prophecy, with exhortations and consolations interspersed, similar to those addressed to the seven churches (the representatives of the universal Church of every age), and so connecting the body of the book with its beginning, which forms its appropriate introduction.

Three schools of interpretation exist :—(1.) The Preterists, who hold that almost the whole has been fulfilled. (2.) The Historical Interpreters, who hold that it comprises the history of the Church from St. John's time to the end of the world, the seals being *chronologically* succeeded by the trumpets, and the trumpets by the vials. Against this scheme it is objected that the prophecies, if they be, as alleged, fulfilled, ought to supply an argument against infidelity; but its advocates differ widely among themselves as to the fulfilments, so that no such argument is derivable from them for the faith. (3.) The Futurists, who consider almost the whole as yet future, to be fulfilled immediately before Christ's second coming. The first theory was not held by any of the earliest Fathers, and is only held by Rationalists, who limit John's vision to things within his own horizon— Pagan Rome's persecutions of Christians, and its consequently anticipated destruction. The Futurist school is open to this great objection: it would leave the Church of Christ unprovided with prophetical guidance under her fiery trials for 1,700 or 1,800 years. Now, God has said, "Surely He will do nothing, but He revealeth His secret unto His servants the prophets." The Jews had a succession of prophets who guided them with the light of prophecy; what their prophets were to them, that the apocalyptic Scriptures have been, and are, to us. Moreover, ch. i. 3; xxii. 6, 7, 12, 20, the beginning and the end, assert a speedy fulfilment. Also, a strictly literal interpretation of Babylon, &c., is improbable.

Alford, following *Isaac Williams,* draws attention to the parallel connection between the Apocalypse and Christ's discourse on the Mount of Olives, Matt. xxiv. The seals plainly bring us down to the second coming of Christ, just as the trumpets also do (cf. ch. vi. 12-17; viii. 1, &c.; xi. 15), and as the vials also do (ch. xvi. 17): all three run parallel, and end in the same point. Certain 'catchwords' (*Wordsworth*) connect the three series of symbols together. They do not succeed in historical and chronological sequence, but move side by side, the subsequent series filling up in detail the same picture which the preceding had drawn in outline. So *Victorinus* (on ch vii. 2), the earliest commentator on the Apocalypse, says, 'The order of the things said is not to be regarded, since often the Holy Spirit, when He has run to the end of the last time, again returns to the same time and supplies what He has less fully expressed.' And *Primasius* ('Ad Apocalypsin in Fine'), 'In the trumpets he gives a description by a pleasing *repetition,* as is his custom.'

At the very beginning, St. John hastens, by anticipation (as was the tendency of all the prophets), to the grand consummation. Ch. i. 7, "Behold, He cometh with clouds," &c.; *vv.* 8, 17, "I am the beginning and *the ending*—the first and *the last.*" The seven epistles exhibit the same anticipation of the end. Ch. iii. 12, 'He that overcometh, I will write upon him the name of the city of my God, which is new Jerusalem, which cometh down out of heaven:' cf., at the close, ch. xxi. 2. So also ch. ii. 28, "I will give him the morning star:" cf. at the close, ch. xxii. 16, "I am the bright and morning star."

Again, the *earthquake* that ensues on the opening of the sixth seal, is one of the *catchwords*—*i. e.,* a link connecting chronologically this sixth seal with the sixth trumpet (ch. ix. 13; xi. 13): cf. also the seventh vial, ch. xvi. 17, 18. The concomitants of the opening of the sixth seal, in no full and exhaustive sense, apply to any event, save the terrors which shall overwhelm the ungodly just before the coming of the Judge.

Again, *the beast out of the bottomless pit,* between the sixth and seventh trumpets (ch. xi. 7), connects this series with the section, chs. xii., xiii., xiv., concerning the Church and her adversaries.

Again, the sealing of the 144,000 under the sixth seal (ch. vii.), connects this seal with the section, chs. xii.-xiv.

Again, the loosing of the four winds by the four angels standing on the four corners of the earth, under the sixth seal, ch. vii. 1, answers to the loosing of the *four* angels at the Euphrates, under the sixth trumpet, ch. ix. 14.

Moreover, links occur in the Apocalypse connecting it with the Old Testament. For instance, the "mouth speaking great things" (ch. xiii. 5), connects the *beast that blasphemes against God, and makes war against the saints,* with *the little horn,* or last king, who, arising after the ten kings, shall *speak against the Most High, and wear out the saints;* also, cf. the 'forty-two months' (ch. xiii. 5), or "a thousand two hundred and threescore days," with the 'time, times, and the dividing of time,' of Daniel vii. 8, 11, 25. Moreover, the 'forty-two months,' ch. xi. 2, answering to ch. xii. 6, and xiii. 5, link together the period under the sixth trumpet, to the section, chs. xii., xiii., xiv.

Auberlen observes, 'The history of salvation is mysteriously governed by holy numbers. They are the scaffolding of the organic edifice. They are not merely outward indications of time, but indications of nature and essence. Not only nature, but history, is based in numbers. Scripture and antiquity put numbers as the fundamental forms of things, where we put ideas.' As number is the regulator of the relations and proportions of the natural world, so does it enter most frequently into the revelations of the Apocalypse, which sets forth the harmonies of the supernatural, the immediately divine. Thus the most supernatural revelation leads us the farthest into the natural, as was to be expected, seeing the God of nature and of revelation is one. *Seven* is the number for perfection (cf. ch. i. 4; iv. 5, the *seven* Spirits before the throne; also, ch. v. 6, the Lamb's *seven* horns and *seven* eyes). Thus *the seven churches* represent the Church Catholic in its totality. *The seven seals—trumpets—vials*, are each a complete series, fulfilling perfectly the Divine course of judgments. *Three and a half* is opposed to the divine (seven), but is broken in itself, and, in the moment of its highest triumph, is overwhelmed by judgment. *Four* is the number of the world's extension; *seven* is that of God's revelation in the world. In the *four* beasts of Daniel there is a recognition of some power above them, whilst there is a mimicry of the *four* cherubs of Ezekiel, the heavenly symbols of all creation in its due subjection to God (ch. iv. 6-8). So the four corners of the earth, the four winds, the four angels loosed from the Euphrates, and Jerusalem lying "four-square," represent world-wide extension. The sevenfoldness of the Spirits on the part of God corresponds to the fourfold cherubim on the part of the created. John, seeing more deeply into the essentially God-opposed character of the world, presents to us, not the *four* beasts of Daniel, but the *seven* heads of the beast, whereby it arrogates to itself the *seven*fold perfection of *the Spirits of God;* at the same time that, with characteristic self-contradiction, it has *ten* horns, the number peculiar to the world-power. Its unjust usurpation of the sacred *seven* is marked by the addition of an *eighth* to the *seven* heads; also by the beast's own number, 666, which in units, tens, and hundreds, verges upon, but falls short of, *seven*. The judgments on the world are complete in *six:* after the sixth seal, and the sixth trumpet, there is a pause. When *seven* comes, there comes "the kingdom of our Lord and His Christ." Six is the number of the world given to judgment. Moreover, *six* is half of *twelve*, as *three and a half* is half of *seven*. *Twelve* is the number of the Church: cf. the *twelve* tribes of Israel, the *twelve* stars on the woman's head (ch. xii. 1), the *twelve* gates of new Jerusalem (ch. xxi. 12-16). *Six* symbolizes the world broken, and without solid foundation. Twice twelve is the number of the heavenly elders; twelve times twelve thousand, the number of the sealed elect: the tree of life yields twelve manner of fruits (ch. xxii. 2). Doubtless, besides this symbolic force, there is a chronological meaning in the numbers; but as yet, though a *commanded* subject of investigation, they have received no solution which we can be *sure* of. They are intended to stimulate reverent enquiry, not to gratify speculative curiosity; when the event shall have been fulfilled, they will show the Divine wisdom of God, who ordered all things in minutely harmonious relations, and left neither the times nor the ways to haphazard.

The arguments for the year-day theory are as follows:—Dan. ix. 24, "Seventy weeks are determined upon," where the Hebrew may be *seventy sevens;* but *Mede* observes, the Hebrew word means always seven of *days*, and never seven of *years* (Lev. xii. 5; Deut. xvi. 9, 10, 16). Again, the number of *years'* wandering of the Israelites was made to correspond to the number of *days* in which the spies searched the land—viz., *forty:* cf. "each day for a year," Num. xiv. 33, 34. So in Ezek. iv. 5, 6, "I have laid upon thee the *years* of their iniquity, according to the number of the *days*, three hundred and ninety days . . . forty days: I have appointed thee *each day for a year*." St. John, in Revelation itself, uses *days* in a sense which can hardly be literal. Ch. ii. 10, "Ye shall have tribulation *ten days:*" the persecution of *ten years,* recorded by *Eusebius,* seems to correspond to it. In the year-day theory there is still quite enough of obscurity to exercise the patience and probation of faith; for we cannot say precisely *when* the 1,260 years *begin:* so that this theory is quite compatible with Christ's words, " Of that day and hour knoweth no man," &c. However, it is a difficulty in this theory that "a thousand years," in ch. xx. 6, 7, can hardly mean 1,000 by 360 days—*i. e.,* 360,000 years. The first resurrection there must be literal, even as *v. 5* must be taken literally, "*the rest of the dead* lived not again until the thousand years were finished." To interpret the former spiritually, would entail the need of interpreting the latter so, which would be most improbable; for it would imply that *the rest of the* (spiritually) *dead lived not* spiritually until the end of the thousand years, and then, that they did come spiritually to life. 1 Cor. xv. 23, "they that are Christ's at His coming," confirms the literal view. The Fathers between the apostolic age and that of Constantine held the Chiliastic (pre-millennial) view. From the first, Rome was connected with antichrist. Under Constantine, Christianity being established, Christians began looking at its existing temporal prosperity as fulfilling the prophecy, and ceased to look for Christ's promised reign on earth.

A lower or primary historical fulfilment of the symbols is likely, typical of the ultimate and exhaustive fulfilment at last, which shall vindicate God's *grand* scheme as a whole before the universe. Hence language is often used which only in part is fulfilled in the primary event, and awaits its fullest realization in the consummation.

LIST OF
AUTHORS CONSULTED, AND ABBREVIATIONS.

I CORINTHIANS—REVELATION.

For the Letters and Abbreviations designating the *Ancient Manuscripts* and *Versions* referred to in this portion of the Volume, the reader will consult the INTRODUCTION.

ALF................Alford's Greek Testament.
AUB...............Auberlen on Daniel and Revelation : Clark's Foreign Library.
BILR..............Bilroth's Commentary on the Epistle to the Corinthians.
BENG.............Bengel's Gnomon Novi Testamenti.
BIRKS............Birk's Horæ Apostolicæ.
CALV..............Calvin's Commentaries.
CHRYS...........Chrysostom's Homilies.
CON. & HOWS....Conybeare and Howson's Life and Epistles of St. Paul.
DE BURGH........De Burgh's Exposition of Revelation.
EDM...............Edmunds' Commentary on 1st and 2nd Thessalonians.
ELLICOTT.........Bishop Ellicott's Commentaries on the Epistles.
EST...............Estius in Poli Synopsis.
GLASS.............Glassius in Poli Synopsis.
GREEN...........Green's Grammar of the New Testament Dialect.
GROT.............Grotius in Poli Synopsis.
HAMM............Hammond in Poli Synopsis.
HEND.............Henderson on Inspiration.
HINDS.............Bishop Hinds', The Three Temples; also, History of the Rise of Christianity.
JUN...............Junius in Poli Synopsis.
KELLY...........W. Kelly's Translation of the Revelation : Williams and Norgate.
L. DE DIEU.......L. de Dieu in Poli Synopsis.
LUCKE...........Lücke's Commentary on St. John's Epistles.
MAGEE...........Archbishop Magee on the Atonement.
MENOCHIUS......Menochius in Poli Synopsis.
MIDDLETON.......Bishop Middleton on the Greek Article.
OLSH..............Olshausen's Commentaries : Clark.
PAL...............Paley's Horæ Paulinæ.
PEARS............Bishop Pearson on the Creed.
PI.................Piscator in Poli Synopsis.
ROSENM..........Rosenmüller Scholia on the New Testament.
SMITH.............Smith's Dictionary of the Bible.

STEIG...............Steiger's Commentary on St. Peter's Epistles.

THEOPHYL........Theophylact.

THOL ....Tholuck's Commentary on the Epistle to the Hebrews.

TI....................Tirinus in Poli Synopsis.

TITTM.............Tittmann's Greek Synonyms of the New Testament.

TREG...............Tregelles' Printed Text of the Greek Testament, and The Revelation
                   from Ancient Authorities.

TRENCH...........Archbishop Trench's Greek Synonyms of the New Testament.

TRENCH...........Commentary on the Epistles to the Seven Churches of Asia Minor.

VATABLUS.........Vatablus in Poli Synopsis.

VITRINGA.........Synagogue and Temple, translated by Bernard : London, Fellowes.

WAHL.............Wahl Clavis Novi Testameni.

WHATELY.........Archbishop Whateley : MS. Criticisms furnished by himself to the
                   Commentator; Cautions for the Times.

WORDSWS.........Bishop Wordsworth on the Apocalypse; also on the Canon of
                   Scripture.

TRANSL...........Translate, Translation.

N. S. E. W.......North, South, East, West.

GR..................Greek.

HEB.................Hebrew.

LIT.................Literally.

FIG.................Figuratively.

SING...............Singular.

PLUR...............Plural.

E. V.................English Version.

LXX................The Septuagint Greek Version of the Old Testament, translated from
                   the Hebrew at Alexandria, for the use of the Hellenistic Jews.

VULG..............The Latin Vulgate Version of Jerome.

For other Versions. see Introduction.

CORINTHIANS.

1 PAUL, called *to be* an apostle of Jesus Christ through the will of God,
2 ^aand Sosthenes *our* brother, unto the church of God which is at
Corinth, to them that ^bare sanctified in Christ Jesus, ^ccalled *to be* saints,
with all that in every place call upon the name of Jesus Christ our
3 ^dLord, ^eboth theirs and ours: Grace *be* unto you, and peace, from God
our Father, and *from* the Lord Jesus Christ.
4 I thank my God always on your behalf, for the grace of God which is
5 given you by Jesus Christ; that in every thing ye are enriched by him,
6 ^fin all utterance, and *in* all knowledge; even as ^gthe testimony of Christ
7 was confirmed in you: so that ye come behind in no gift; waiting for

A. D. 59.

CHAP. 1.
a Acts 18. 17.
b John 17. 19.
ch. 6. 9-11.
c Rom. 1. 7.
2 Tim. 1. 9.
d ch. 8. 6.
e Rom. 3. 22.
f 2 Cor. 8. 7.
g Acts 20. 28.
2 Tim. 1. 8.
Rev. 1. 2.

CHAP. I. 1-31.—INSCRIPTION—THANKSGIVING
FOR THEIR SPIRITUAL STATE—REPROOF OF DIVI-
SIONS—HIS PREACHING CHRIST ALONE.

1. called to be—[found in א B G *g v*, not in A Δ *f*,
of the oldest MSS. Possibly inserted from Rom.
i. 1; but as likely to be genuine.] Translate, 'a
called apostle.' Though vindicating his apostleship, he ranks himself with all the "called" (*v*. 2).
through the will of God—not through my own
merit. St. Paul's call as 'an apostle by the will
of God,' whilst constituting the ground of the
authority he claims (cf. Gal. i. 1), is a reason for
humility on his part (ch. xv. 8, 10). In assuming
the ministerial office, a man should do so, not of
his own impulse, but by the will of God (Jer. xxiii.
21). Paul, if left to his own will, would never
have been an apostle (Rom. ix. 16). **Sosthenes**—
see 'Introduction.' Gallio had driven the Jews
who accused Paul from the judgment seat. The
Greek mob, who disliked the Jews, took the
opportunity then of beating Sosthenes, the ruler
of the Jewish synagogue, whilst Gallio looked on
and refused to interfere, being secretly pleased
that the mob should second his own contempt for
the Jews. Paul probably at this time had showed
sympathy for an adversary in distress, which
issued in the conversion of the latter. So Crispus
also, the previous chief ruler of the synagogue,
had been converted. Saul the persecutor turned
into Paul the apostle, and Sosthenes the leader in
persecution against that apostle, were two trophies
of grace that, side by side, would appeal with
double power to the church at Corinth. **2. the
church of God.** He calls it so notwithstanding
its many blots. Sectaries vainly anticipate the
final sifting (Matt. xiii. 27-30). 'It is a dangerous
temptation to think there is no church where there
is not apparent perfect purity. It was enough for
Paul, in recognizing the Corinthians as a church,
that he saw among them evangelical doctrine,
baptism, and the Lord's supper.' It was the
Church *of God*, not of this or of that favourite
leader. **at Corinth**—a church at dissolute Corinth
—a paradox of grace! **sanctified**—*consecrated, set
apart as holy to God* **in** (by union with) **Christ
Jesus.** There is no Greek for "to them that are;"
translate simply, 'men sanctified,' &c. **called to
be saints**—rather, 'called saints,' saints by calling,
all professing members of the church. As "sanctified in Christ" implies the fountain of holiness,
the believer's original sanctification in Christ (ch.
vi. 11; Heb. x. 10, 14; 1 Pet. i. 2) in the purposes
of God's grace; so 'called saints' refers to their
actual *call* (Rom. viii. 30), and the end of that call,

that they should be holy (1 Pet. i. 15). **with all
that in every place call upon . . . Christ**—the
true Catholic Church (a term first used by *Ignatius*,
'ad Smyrnæôs,' c. 8); not those who call themselves from Paul, Cephas, &c. (*v*. 12), but all,
wherever they be, who call on their Saviour in
sincerity (cf. Eph. iii. 15; 2 Tim. ii. 22). Being
one in this essential, they ought not to mar the
church's unity by divisions (ch. xi. 16; xiv. 33).
The life of faith is a life of prayer. To *call upon
Jesus* is to call upon God (Acts vii. 59; ix. 14).
both theirs and ours—'in every place which is
their home . . . and our home also,'—the Christians
throughout Achaia, not residing in Corinth, the
capital (2 Cor. i. 1). St. Paul feels the home of
his converts to be also his own (Rom. xvi. 13).
"Ours" refers to Paul and Sosthenes' and the
Corinthians' home (*Alford*). Rather, 'both their
Lord and our Lord (ch. viii. 6; Eph. iv. 5)—a
virtual reproof of the divisions of the Corinthians,
as if Christ were divided (*v*. 13). 'If places divide
Christians, yet their common Lord unites them'
(*Chrysostom*). **3. peace**—peculiarly needed in the
Corinthian church (Rom. i. 7).

4. He puts foremost the causes for praise and
hope among them, not to discourage them by the
succeeding reproof, and in order to appeal to their
better selves. **my God** (Rom. i. 8)—*mine*, as
honouring me by having blessed the building of
which *I* laid the foundation (ch. iii. 6-10). **always**—
(cf. Phil. i. 3, 4.) **the grace . . . given you**—(cf.
v. 7.) **by . . . Christ**—lit., IN *Christ;* given you
as members in Christ. **5. utterance.** *Billroth*
translates, *doctrine*. Ye are rich in *preaching of
the Word*, and in *knowledge* of it. The English version, as in 2 Cor. viii. 7, is better; for St. Paul,
purposing presently to dwell on the *abuse* of the
two gifts on which the Corinthians prided themselves—*utterance* (speech) and *knowledge* (chs. i.
20; iii. 18; iv. 19; xiii., xiv.)—previously gains
their goodwill by congratulating them on *having*
those gifts. **6.** According as the testimony of (of
and concerning) Christ (who is both the object and
author of this testimony) (ch. ii. 1; 1 Tim. ii. 6;
2 Tim. i. 8) was confirmed *among* you—i.e., by
God, through my preaching, and through the
miracles accompanying it (ch. xii. 4; Heb. ii. 4).
Or better, as the English version, God *confirmed*
(cf. Heb. ii. 3), or gave effect to, the Gospel *in* the
Corinthians, *by their accepting it*, and setting their
seal to its truth, through the inward power of His
Spirit, and the outward miracles accompanying it.
7. ye come behind—are inferior to other Christians
elsewhere. **in no gift**—not that all had all gifts,

8 the [1] coming of our Lord Jesus Christ : who [h] shall also confirm you unto the end, *[i] that ye may be* blameless in the day of our Lord Jesus Christ.

9 God [j] *is* faithful, by whom ye were called unto [k] the fellowship of his Son Jesus Christ our Lord.

10 Now I beseech you, brethren, by the name of our Lord Jesus Christ, that ye all speak the same thing, and *that* there be no [2] divisions among you; but *that* ye be perfectly joined together in the same mind

11 and in the same judgment. For it hath been declared unto me of you, my brethren, by them *which are of the house* of Chloe, that there

12 are contentions among you. Now this I say, [l] that every one of you saith, I am of Paul; and I [m] of Apollos; and I of [n] Cephas; and I of Christ.

13 Is [o] Christ divided ? was Paul crucified for you ? or were ye baptized

A. D. 59.

1 revelation.
Col. 3. 4.
[h] 2 Thes. 3. 3.
[i] 1 Thes. 5.
    23.
[j] Isa. 49. 7.
Heb. 10. 23.
[k] John 15. 4.
1 John 4. 13.
2 schisms.
ch. 11. 18.
[l] ch. 3. 4.
[m] Acts 18. 24.
[n] John 1. 42.
[o] 2 Cor. 11. 4.
Eph. 4. 5.

---

but different persons among them had different gifts, (ch. xii. 4, &c.). **waiting for the coming of . . . Christ**—the crowning proof of their 'coming behind in no gift.' Christ's future coming exercises *faith, hope,* and *love* (cf. 2 Tim. iv. 8; Titus ii. 13). 'Leave to others their *memento mori,* do thou cherish this joyous expectation of the Lord's coming' (*Bengel*). The Greek [ἀπεκδεχο- μένους] implies, 'to expect constantly to the end, till the event comes to pass' (Rom. viii. 19). 8. **Who**—God (*v.* 4), not Jesus Christ (*v.* 7), in which case it would be, 'in *His* day.' **unto the end**—viz. 'the coming of Christ.' **blameless in the day of . . . Christ** (1 Thess. v. 23). After that day there is no danger (Eph. iv. 30.) Now is our day to work, and the day of our enemies to try us; then will be the day of Christ, and of His glory in the saints. 9. **faithful**—to His promises (Phil. i. 6; 1 Thess. v. 24). **called**—according to His purpose (Rom. viii. 28). **unto the fellowship of . . . Jesus**—to be fellow-heirs with Christ (Rom. viii. 17-30), being like Him, sons of God (2 Thess. ii. 14; 1 Pet. iv. 13; 1 John i. 3). *Chrysostom* remarks, that the name of Christ is oftener mentioned in this than in any other epistle, the apostle designing thereby to draw them away from their party admiration of particular teachers to Christ alone.

10. Now—Greek [δέ], *But.* Ye already have *knowledge, utterance,* and *hope; but* maintain also *love.* **brethren.** The very title is an argument for *love.* **by the name of . . . Christ**—whom St. Paul wishes to be all in all, instead of their naming themselves from their party leaders. **speak the same thing**—not different things, as ye do (*v.* 12), in variance. **divisions**—lit., *splits, schisms.* **but**—*but rather.* **perfectly joined together** [κα- τηρτισμένοι]—the opposite to "divisions;" applied to *healing a wound,* or *making whole a rent.* **mind . . . judgment** [νοῖ—γνώμῃ]—the view taken by the *understanding,* and the *practical decision* as to things to be done; *notional belief* and *sentiment.* When we are not knit together in charity, we may hold the same *notions,* and yet differ in *sentiment* (*Theophylact*). **11.** (Ch. xi. 18.) **by them . . . of the house of Chloe**—a matron resident at Corinth. The Corinthians "wrote" to the apostle (ch. vii. 1), consulting him concerning marriage, the eating of things offered to idols, the decorum to be observed by women in religious assemblies; but they said not a syllable about the disorders that had crept in. *That* information reached Paul by other quarters. Hence his language is, "It hath been declared unto me," &c.; "it is reported" (ch. v. 1, 2). All this he says *before* he notices their *letter,* which shows that it did not give him any intimation of those evils. An undesigned proof of genuineness (*Paley*). Observe his prudence. He names the family, to let it be seen that he

made his allegation not without authority. He does not name the individuals, not to excite odium against them. He tacitly implies that the information ought rather to have come to him directly from their presbyters, as they had consulted him about matters of less moment. **contentions**—not so severe a word as "divisions," or *schisms* (*margin, v.* 10). **12. this I say**—this is what *I mean* in saying "contentions". **every one of you saith**—ye say severally, 'glorying in men' (*v.* 31; ch. iii. 21, 22), one, I am of Paul; another, I am of Apollos, &c. Not that they formed *de- finite* parties, but they individually betrayed the *spirit* of party in contentions about different favourite teachers. St. Paul will not allow himself to be flattered even by those who made his name their party cry, so as to connive at the dishonour thereby done to Christ. These, probably, were converted under his ministry. Those alleging the name of Apollos, Paul's successor at Corinth (Acts xviii. 24, &c.), were attracted by his rhetorical style, probably acquired in Alexandria (ch. iii. 6), as contrasted with the 'weak bodily presence' and 'contemptible speech' of the apostle (ch. ii. 1, 4; 2 Cor. x. 10). Apollos did not willingly foster this spirit of undue preference (ch. iv. 6); nay, to discourage it, he would not repeat his visit just then (ch. xvi. 12). **I of Cephas**—Judaizers who sheltered themselves under the name of St. Peter, the apostle of the circumcision, (*Cephas* is the Hebrew, *Peter* the Greek name: John i. 42; Gal. ii. 11, &c.) The subjects in chs. vii.-ix. were probably suggested as matters of doubt by them. The church there began from the Jewish synagogue, Crispus the chief ruler, and Sosthenes, his successor, being converts. Hence Jewish leaven, though not so much as elsewhere, is traceable (2 Cor. xi. 22). *Petrism* afterwards sprang up rankly at Rome. If it be wrong to boast, 'I am of Peter,' how much more to boast, 'I am of the Pope' (*Bengel*). **I of Christ**—a fair pretext to slight the ministry of Paul (ch. iv. 8; 2 Cor. x. 7-11).

13. Is Christ divided ?—into various parts, so that He hath sharers in His power, and so some of you call yourselves after Him; others after this and that leader ? Surely not (*Theodoret*). But since the Greek particle, requiring the negative answer, does not occur in this clause, as it does in the next, I prefer (as Vulgate), 'Christ (*i. e.,* the body of Christ: cf. Rom. xvi. 7) *is divided*' by your divisions. 'To glory in Christ's name amid discords is to rend Him in pieces. Then only doth He reign in us when He is to us the bond of sacred unity' (*Calvin*). The unity of His body is not to be cut in pieces, as if all did not belong to Him, the One Head. **was Paul crucified for you ?** The Greek interrogation [μή;] implies that a negative answer is expected :—'Was it Paul

234

14 in the name of Paul? I thank God that I baptized none of you but
15 [p] Crispus and [q] Gaius; lest any should say that I had baptized in mine
16 own name. And I baptized also the household [r] of Stephanas: besides,
I know not whether I baptized any other.
17 For [s] Christ sent me not to baptize, but to preach the Gospel: not with
wisdom of [3] words, lest the cross of Christ should be made of none effect.
18 For the preaching of the cross is to them [t] that perish [u] foolishness; but
19 unto us which are saved it is [v] the power of God. For it is written, [w] I
will destroy the wisdom of the wise, and will bring to nothing the under-
20 standing of the prudent. Where [x] *is* the wise? where *is* the scribe?
where *is* the disputer of this world? hath [y] not God made foolish the
21 wisdom of this world? For [z] after that in the wisdom of God the world

A. D. 59.

[p] Acts 18. 8.
[q] Rom. 16. 23.
[r] ch. 16. 15.
[s] Acts 26. 17.
[3] Or, speech.
[t] 2 Cor. 2. 15.
[u] Acts 17. 18.
[v] Rom. 1. 16.
[w] Isa. 29. 14.
[x] Isa. 33. 18.
[y] Job 12. 17. Isa. 44. 25. Rom. 1. 22.
[z] Luke 10. 21.

(*surely you will not say so*) that was crucified for you?' In the former question the majesty of "CHRIST," the Anointed One of God, implies the impossibility of His being "divided." In the latter, '*Paul's*' insignificance implies the impossibility of *his* being the head of redemption—"crucified for" them, and giving his name to the redeemed. This, which is true of Paul, the *founder* of the church of Corinth, holds equally good of Cephas and Apollos, who had not such a claim as Paul there. **crucified . . . baptized.** The cross claims us for Christ as redeemed by Him, baptism as dedicated to Him. **in the name**—rather [εἰς τὸ ὄνομα], '*into* the name' (Gal. iii. 27), implying the *incorporation* involved in the idea of baptism. **14.** I thank God's providence now, who so ordered it that I baptized none of you but Crispus (the former ruler of the synagogue, Acts xviii. 8), and Gaius (written by the Romans *Caius*—the host of Paul at Corinth, and of the church, Rom. xvi. 23; a person, therefore, in good circumstances). Baptizing was the office of the deacons (Acts x. 48); the apostles' office was to establish and superintend generally the churches. The deacons had more time for giving the necessary *instruction preparatory to baptism.* Crispus and Gaius, &c., being among the first converts, were baptized by Paul himself, who founded the church. **15. Lest any should say**—'[I adduce this] lest any say,' &c. **that I had baptized.** So Δ G *f g*; but ℵ A B C *v* read, '*ye were baptized* [ἐβαπτίσθητε] into my name.' **16. household of Stephanas**—"the first-fruits of Achaia;" *i.e.*, among the first converted there (ch. xvi. 15, 17). It is likely that such 'households' included infants (Acts xvi. 33). Infant baptism was the Church's usage from the earliest ages.

17. St. Paul says this not to depreciate baptism, for he exalts it most highly (Rom. vi. 3). He baptized some, and would have baptized more, but that his and the apostles' peculiar work was to preach the Gospel—to found, by their autoptic testimony, particular churches, and then to superintend the churches in general. **sent me** [ἀπέστειλεν]—lit., *as an apostle.* **not to baptize**—even in Christ's name, much less in my own. **not with wisdom of words**—Greek, *word; speech; philosophical reasoning* in *oratorical language,* which the Corinthians so unduly valued in Apollos, and the want of which in St. Paul they were dissatisfied with (2 Cor. x. 10). **cross of Christ**—the sum and substance of the Gospel (*v.* 23; ch. ii. 2). **be made of none effect**—viz., by men thinking more of the human eloquence in which the Gospel was set forth than of the Gospel itself, of Christ crucified, the sinner's only remedy. **18. preaching, &c.**—lit., *the word,* as to the cross, in contrast to the 'wisdom of *word,*' so-called, *v.* 17. **them that perish**—rather, *them that are perishing* [τοῖς ἀπολλυμένοις], viz., by preferring human 'wisdom of word' to the "cross of Christ" (John iii. 18). It is not their final state that is referred to. So also in 2 Cor. ii. 15, 16. **us which are saved.** In the Greek the collocation is more modest—'to them that are being saved (that are in the way of salvation), "us"'—*i. e.*, with whom we venture to class ourselves. **power of God**—including "the wisdom of God" (*v.* 24); the opposite of "foolishness" (Rom. i. 16; xv. 13). What seems to the world "weakness" in God's plan (*v.* 25), and in its mode of delivery by His apostle (ch. ii. 3), is really "power" *for* them, and *in* them, unto salvation. What seems "foolishness," because wanting man's 'wisdom of word' (*v.* 17), is really the highest "wisdom of God" (*v.* 24). **19. I will destroy**—slightly altered from the LXX., Isa. xxix. 14. The Hebrew is, 'The wisdom of the wise shall perish, and the understanding of their prudent men shall be hid.' St. Paul, by inspiration, gives the sense of the Spirit, by making God the cause of their *wisdom perishing,* &c., "*I* will destroy," &c. **understanding of the prudent**—lit., *of the understanding ones.* **20. Where? &c.**—Nowhere; for God 'brings them to nought' (*v.* 19). **the wise**—the Greek philosopher. **the scribe**—Jewish (cf. the Jew and Greek of this world contrasted with the godly wise, *vv.* 22, 23). **the disputer**—whether Jew or Greek. Jewish speculative disputers were called *Darshan,* and mystical expositions of Scripture *Midrashim* (cf. 'Questions;' Acts xxvi. 3; Titus iii. 9). St. Paul applies Isa. xxxiii. 18 here in a higher sense: there the primary reference was to temporal deliverance, here to eternal. *V.* 22, which is in threefold opposition to *v.* 18 there, sanctions this higher application—the Lord, in the threefold character of "Judge," "Lawgiver," and "King," being the sole ground of glorying to His people (*v.* 31). **of this world**—rather, 'dispensation (or *age*) . . . world.' The Greek words [αἰῶνος—κόσμου] are distinct. The former is *this world-course,* in a moral point of view, as opposed to the Christian order of things; the latter is the *world* viewed externally. **made foolish**—shown the world's philosophy to be folly, because it lacks faith in Christ crucified: has treated it as folly, and not used its help in converting and saving men (*vv.* 26, 27). **21. after that**—rather, *whereas.* **in the wisdom of God.** (1.) '*In the sphere of* God's wisdom' the world's wisdom *has no place;* for by it the world was not enabled to know God. This interpretation suits well the previous "*Where?*" (2.) 'The world by its wisdom knew not God *in God's wisdom*' (i. e., *in the Gospel*) (*v.* 24; ch. ii. 6, 7). (3.) 'The heathen world knew not God in the wisdom of God,' which they might have gleaned from His works (Rom. i. 20, 21). The general principle (1.) comprises both God's wisdom in nature and in grace, and leaves no scope for glorying in man, which there would be if the world by its wisdom could know God (*v.* 29). **world by**

by wisdom knew not God, it pleased God by the foolishness of preaching
22 to save them that believe. For the [a]Jews require a sign, and the Greeks
23 seek after wisdom: but we preach Christ crucified, unto the [b]Jews a
24 stumblingblock, and unto the Greeks foolishness; but unto them which
are called, both Jews and Greeks, Christ [c]the power of God, and [d]the
25 wisdom of God. Because [e]the foolishness of God is wiser than men; and
the weakness of God is stronger than men.
26 For ye see your calling, brethren, how that [f]not many wise men after
27 the flesh, not many mighty, not many noble, *are called:* but [g]God hath
chosen the foolish things of the world to confound the wise; and God
hath chosen the weak things of the world to confound the things which
28 are mighty; and base things of the world, and things which are despised, hath God chosen, *yea,* and [h]things which are not, [i]to bring to
29 nought things that are: that no flesh should glory in his presence.

A D. 59.

[a] Matt. 12.38.
Luke 11.16.
[b] Isa. 8. 14.
[c] Matt. 11. 6.
[c] Rom. 1. 4.
[d] Col. 2. 3.
[e] 2 Cor. 4. 7.
[f] John 4. 46-
53.
John 7. 48.
Acts 13. 7.
12.
Jas. 7. 11-
13.
[g] Ps. 8. 2.
[h] Rom. 4. 17.
[i] ch. 2. 6.

wisdom—rather, 'by *its* [τῆς] wisdom,' or *its philo-sophy* (John i. 10; Rom. i. 28). **knew not God**—whatever other knowledge it attained (Acts xvii. 23, 27). The deistic theory, that man can by the light of nature discover his duty to God, is dis-proved by the fact that man *has* never discovered it without revelation. All the stars and moon cannot make day; that is the prerogative of the sun. Nor can nature's highest gifts make the moral day arise; that is the office of Christ. **it pleased God**—referring to Jesus' words (Luke x. 21). **by the foolishness of preaching**—by that preaching (*the preached Gospel*) which the world (unbelieving Jews and Gentiles alike) deem *fool-ishness.* **22. For**—lit., *Whereas.* A B C Δ, Vul-gate, add '*also,*' taking up the "whereas" of *v.* 21, and *additionally* illustrating that 'the world knew not God.' **a sign.** אA B C Δ G, Vulgate, read 'signs.' The *singular* was a correction from Matt. xii. 38; xvi. 1; John ii. 18. The signs the Jews craved were not mere miracles, but direct tokens from heaven that Jesus was Messiah (Luke xi. 16). **Greeks seek . . . wisdom**—viz., a philo-sophic demonstration of Christianity. Christ, in-stead of *demonstrative* proof, demands *faith* on the ground of *His word,* and of reasonable evidence that the alleged revelation is His word. Chris-tianity begins not with solving intellectual diffi-culties, but with satisfying the heart that longs for forgiveness. Hence, not the refined Greeks, but the theocratic Jews, were the chosen organ for propagating revelation. Again, intellectual Athens (Acts xvii. 18-21) received the Gospel less readily than commercial Corinth. **23. we**— Paul and Apollos. **Christ crucified.** The Greek expresses not the mere fact of His crucifixion, but the *per-manent character* acquired by it, whereby He is now a Saviour (Gal. iii. 1). A Messiah crucified was the stone on which the Jews stumbled (Matt. xxi. 44). A religion so seemingly contemptible in its origin could not have succeeded, if it had not been divine. **unto the Greeks.** אA B C Δ G *f g,* Vulgate, *Origen, Cyprian,* read 'unto the *Gen-tiles.*' **24. called** (cf. *v.* 26)—"us which are (being) saved" (*v.* 18): the elect called effectually (Rom. viii. 28-30). **Christ.** "Crucified" is not here added, because when the offence of the Cross is overcome, "Christ" is received, not only in His Cross, but in His life and His future kingdom. **power**—so meeting the requirements of the Jews who sought "a sign." Jesus Himself is the greatest sign. The Cross (the death of a slave), which to the Jews (looking for a temporal Mes-siah) was a "stumblingblock," is really "the power of God" to the salvation of all who believe. These are incontrovertible "signs." **wisdom of God**—so really exhibiting in the highest degree

that which the Greeks sought after—*wisdom* (Col. ii. 3). **25. the foolishness of God**—*i. e.,* God's plan of salvation, which men deem "foolishness" (*v.* 21). **weakness of God** — Christ "crucified through weakness" (2 Cor. xiii. 4, the *stumbling-block* of the Jews), yet "living by the *power* of God." So He *perfects strength* out of His servants' weakness (ch. ii. 3; 2 Cor. xii. 9). **is wiser . . . stronger than men**—is not only wiser than men's wisdom, and stronger than men's strength, but is wiser and stronger *than men themselves,* whatever they have or are (Rom. v. 6). It effects revolu-tions in the individual, and will do so in the whole world, such as man never could. **26. ye see**—rather, from the prominence of the verb in the Greek, "see" (imperative) (Vulgate). **your calling**—God's way in calling you; or *your external condition* (ch. vii. 20). **not many wise . . . are called.** *Anselm* supplies, 'were your callers.' What St. Paul is dwelling on (cf. *vv.* 27, 28) is the weakness of the instrumentality employed to convert the world. The English version accords with *v.* 24. 'The whole history of the Church is a progressive victory of the ignorant over the learned, the lowly over the lofty, until the emperor himself laid down his crown before the cross of Christ' (*Olshausen*). **wise . . . after the flesh**—the wisdom of this world acquired by human study without the Spirit (contrast Matt. xvi. 17). **27. the foolish things**—a general phrase for *all persons and things foolish.* Even *things* (and those, too, accounted by "the world" *foolish things*) are chosen by God to confound *persons* (and those, too, persons *wise*). This is the force of the change from neuter to masculine, **to confound.** The Greek is stronger—'*in order that* He might put to shame,' &c. God confounds the wise by effecting through His in-struments, without human wisdom, what the worldly wise, with it, cannot effect—viz., to save men. **chosen . . . chosen.** The repetition indi-cates the gracious deliberateness of God's purpose (Jas. ii. 5). **28. yea, and things which are not.** "Yea" is not in the Greek. A C Δ G *f g* omit "and." Thus the clause, "things which are not" (are regarded as nought), is in apposition with "foolish . . . weak . . . base (*i. e.,* low-born) and despised things." God has chosen all four (as the only realities), though regarded as *things that are not* (nonentities) to bring to nought things that are. אB, Vulgate, read 'and.' **29. no flesh should glory.** For they who *glory* (boast) because of human greatness and wisdom are "put to shame" (*v.* 27; Isa. xl. 6). **in his presence.** So Vulgate, אA B C Δ G *f g,* read 'in *God's* presence.' Glory not *before* Him, but in Him (*Bengel*). Here Paul turns to his aim, to warn them that the

30 But of him are ye in Christ Jesus, who of God is made unto us wisdom,
31 and righteousness, and sanctification, and redemption : that, according
    as it is written, *ʲ* He that glorieth, let him glory in the Lord.

2   AND I, brethren, when I came to you, came *ᵃ*not with excellency of
2 speech or of wisdom, declaring unto you the testimony of God. For I
   determined not to know any thing among you, *ᵇ* save Jesus Christ, and
3 him crucified. And *ᶜ* I was with you *ᵈ* in weakness, and in fear, and in
4 much trembling. And my speech and my preaching *ᵉ was* not with
   ¹ enticing words of man's wisdom, but in demonstration of the Spirit and
5 of power: that your faith should not ²stand in the wisdom of men, but
   ᶠ in the power of God.
6 Howbeit we speak wisdom among them that *ᵍ* are perfect : yet not the

A. D. 59.

ʲ Jer. 9. 23.

CHAP. 2.
ᵃ ch. 1. 17.
    2 Cor. 11. 6.
ᵇ Gal. 6. 14.
    Phil. 3. 8.
ᶜ Acts 18. 1.
ᵈ 2 Cor. 10. 1.
ᵉ 2 Pet. 1. 16.
1 Or, per-
    suasible.
2 be.
ᶠ 2 Cor. 4. 7.
ᵍ Eph. 4. 13.

preachers in whom they gloried had no ground for glorying in themselves; so the hearers ought to glory not in them, but in the Lord (chs. iii. 21; iv. 6). **30. But . . . ye**—in contrast to them that "glory" in worldly wisdom. **of him are**—not of yourselves (Eph. ii. 8), but of Him (Rom. xi. 36), having become His children in Christ. *From Him ye are* (*i. e.,* have spiritual existence, who once were spiritually among the "things which are not," (*v.* 28). **in Christ**—by living union with Him. Not 'in the flesh' (*vv.* 26-29). **of God**—*from* God: emanating *from* and sent by Him. **is made unto us**—*was* once for all (Aorist) *made* to us, to our eternal gain. **wisdom**—unattainable by the worldly mode of seeking it (*vv.* 19, 20: contrast Col. ii. 3; Prov. viii.; Isa. ix. 6). As Christ is God's gift to believers, all that is Christ's is made over to them—*wisdom* in its essence and perfection, &c., to be gradually developed in our union with Him. By it we become "wise unto salvation," and "walk not as fools, but as wise" (Eph. v. 15 ; 2 Tim. iii. 15). **righteousness**—our justification (Jer. xxiii. 5, 6 ; Rom. iv. 25 ; 2 Cor. v. 21 ; Isa. xlii. 21 ; xlv. 24). **sanctification**—by His Spirit (1 Pet. i. 2). His sanctification or consecration to God is the source of our sanctification (*v.* 2), which is perfect in Him, but gradually developed in us (John xvii. 19). Hereafter our righteousness and sanctification shall be both perfect and inherent. Now the righteousness wherewith we are *justified* is perfect, but not inherent; that wherewith we are *sanctified* is inherent, but not perfect (*Hooker*). "Righteousness" and "sanctification" are joined in the Greek (by τε καί between them) as essentially *but one* thing, as distinguished from the "wisdom" in *devising* the plan for us (Eph. i. 8), and "re-demption," the *final completion* of it in the deliverance of the body (the position of "redemption" last shows that this is the sense) (Luke xxi. 28 ; Rom. viii. 23 ; Eph. i. 14 ; iv. 30). **31. glory in the Lord** (Jer. ix. 23, 24)—not in the flesh, nor in the world (*v.* 29). In contrast to morbid slavish self-abasement, St. Paul joins with humility the elevating consciousness of our dignity in Christ. God strips us of self-glory, that we may be clothed with true glory in Him.

CHAP. II. 1-16.—ST. PAUL'S SUBJECT OF PREACHING CHRIST CRUCIFIED, NOT IN WORLDLY, BUT HEAVENLY WISDOM.

1. And I—*So I, I also,* as one of the 'foolish, weak, and despised' instruments employed by God: 'glorying in the Lord,' not in man's wisdom (ch. i. 27-31). My mode of speaking and acting accords with God's plan. **when I came** (Acts xviii. 1, &c.) Paul might, had he pleased, have used an ornate style, having studied at Tarsus of Cilicia, famed for learning: here he read the *Cilician* Aratus' poems (which he quotes, Acts xvii. 28), and Epimenides (Titus i. 12), and Men-ander (1 Cor. xv. 33). Grecian intellect prepared

the way for the Gospel, but failed to regenerate the world; for this a superhuman power is needed. *Hellenistic* (Grecizing) Judaism at Tarsus and Alexandria was the connecting link between the schools of Athens and those of the Rabbis. No more fitting birthplace could there have been for the apostle of the Gentiles than Tarsus. He had the *Roman citizenship,* which protected him from sudden violence. He was reared in the *Hebrew divine law* at Jerusalem. Thus, as the three elements, Greek cultivation, Roman polity (Luke ii. 1), and the Jewish divine law, combined at Christ's time to prepare the world for the Gospel, so the same three met in the apostle to the Gentiles. **testimony of God**—"the testimony *of Christ*' (ch. i. 6): therefore Christ is God. So B D G *f g,* Vulgate. But א A C read 'the *mystery* of Christ' (cf. *v.* 7). The one thing that I determined to know among you was Jesus Christ (His person) and Him crucified (His office). Christ's crucifixion was not to be kept in the background, to avoid offending learned heathens and Jews. Nay, Paul *judged* it to be the central truth to know savingly, so as to speak effectively, every-where (Phil. iii. 10). Christ's *person* and Christ's *office* are the sum of the Gospel. **3. I**—the *preacher:* as *v.* 2 describes the *subject,* and *v.* 4 the *mode* of preaching. **weakness**—personal and bodily (2 Cor. x. 10 ; xii. 7, 9 ; Gal. iv. 13). **trembling**—(cf. Phil. ii. 12.) Not cowardly *fear,* but *trembling anxiety to perform duty;* anxious conscientious-ness in contrast to "eye service" (Eph. vi. 5 ; 2 Cor. vii. 15 ; Phil. ii. 12). His very weakness, as that of Christ crucified, his theme, was made the power of God (ch. i. 27). **4. my speech**—in private. **preaching**—in public (Matt. x. 27). Or, *discourse* on doctrines; *preaching,* lit., *heralding,* of facts. **enticing**—Greek, *persuasive.* **man's wisdom**—"man's" is omitted in B Δ G *ʲ g*: retained in א A C. **demonstration of the Spirit,** &c. *Persuasion* is man's means of moving his fellow-man. Ministers should rather seek God's, which is *demonstration,* inspiring implicit faith by the power of the Spirit (then exhibited outwardly by miracles, and in-wardly by working on the heart, now in the latter only, the more important way) (Matt. vii. 29; Acts vi. 10 ; Rom. xv. 19). **5 stand in the wisdom of men**—rest on, owe its origin and continuance to, it.

6, 7. Yet the Gospel, so far from being at vari-ance with "wisdom," is a wisdom infinitely higher than that of the world. **we speak**—resuming "we" (preachers, I, Apollos, &c.) from ch. i. 23, only that here, "we speak," refers to something less public (cf. *v.* 7) than 'we preach.' For "wis-dom" here denotes, not the whole Christian doctrine, but its deeper principles. **perfect**—*among the matured in Christian experience,* who alone can appreciate the Christian wisdom: dis-tinguished not only from *worldly* men, but also

wisdom of this world, nor of the princes of this world, that come to
7 nought: but we speak the wisdom of God in a mystery, *even* the hidden
8 *wisdom,* [h] which God ordained before the world unto our glory: which
[i] none of the princes of this world knew: for had they known *it,* they
9 would not have crucified the Lord of glory. But as it is written, [j] Eye
hath not seen, nor ear heard, neither have entered into the heart of man,
10 the things which God hath prepared for them that love him. But [k] God
hath revealed *them* unto us by his Spirit: for the Spirit searcheth all
11 things, yea, the deep things of God. For what man knoweth the things
of a man, [l] save the spirit of man which is in him? [m] even so the things

A. D. 59.

[h] Rom 16.25.
2 Tim. 1. 9.
[i] Acts 13. 27.
[j] Isa. 64. 4.
[k] Matt. 16.17.
Luke 2. 26.
Eph. 3. 3, 5.
1 Pet. 1. 12.
1 John 2.27.
Rev. 1. 1.
[l] Jer. 17. 9.
[m] Rom. 11.33.

from *babes* (1 John ii. 12-14), who, though "in Christ," retain much that is "carnal" (ch. iii. 1, 2), and cannot therefore understand the deeper truths (ch. xiv. 20: *margin,* Heb. v. 14); or, "*those sincere in the faith*" (Phil. iii. 15) (*Theodoret*). "Mystery," or "hidden wisdom" (*v.* 7), is not some *hidden tradition besides the Gospel* (like the Church of Rome's 'disciplina arcani' and doctrine of reserve), but the *unfolding* of the treasures of knowledge once hidden in God's counsels, but *now* announced to all, and intelligently comprehended in proportion as the hearers' inner life became perfectly renewed. (Cf. instances of such 'mysteries,' ch. xv. 51; Rom. xi. 25; Eph. iii. 3, 5, 6.) "God" (*v.* 7) is opposed to "this world," the apostles to "the princes" (philosophers, rhetoricians, and rulers) (*v.* 8: cf. ch. i. 20). **come to nought** (ch. i. 28). They are transient; therefore their wisdom is not real. Translate, '*are being brought* to nought'—viz., by God's choosing the "things which are not (the *weak and despised things of the Gospel*), to bring to nought [the same verb, καταργεῖν] things that are" (ch. i. 28). **7. wisdom of God**—contrasted with the wisdom *of men* and *of this world* (*vv.* 5, 6). **in a mystery.** We speak God's wisdom, dealing with a mystery—*i. e.,* not *to be kept hidden,* but heretofore so, and *now revealed* (Col. i. 26; Eph. iii. 5, 6; Rom. xvi. 25, 26). The Pagan mysteries were revealed only to a few; the Gospel mysteries to all who would obey the truth (2 Cor. iv. 3). Ordinarily "mystery" refers to those from whom the knowledge is *withheld.* In the epistles it refers to those to whom it is *revealed.* It is hidden in God till brought forward; and when brought forward, it still remains hidden to the carnal. **ordained**—lit., *foreordained* (cf. *v.* 9), *foredestined* [προώρισεν]. **before the world**—Greek, '*before the ages*' (of time); *i. e.,* from eternity. This infinitely antedates worldly wisdom: before not only the world's wisdom, but eternally before the world itself and its ages. **unto our glory**—ours both now and hereafter, from "the Lord of *glory*" (*v.* 8). Elsewhere, "to *His* glory," for He is glorified in our being so through Him (Eph. i. 6; John xvii. 10, 24). **8. Which**—wisdom: the strongest proof of the natural man's destitution of heavenly wisdom. **the princes of this world.** Herod, Pilate, Annas, and Caiaphas represent the worldly great in church and state, philosophers and rhetoricians. **crucified the Lord of glory**—implying the inseparable connection of Christ's humanity and His divinity. "The Lord of glory" (which He had in His own right before the world was, John xvii. 4, 24) was "crucified." The Son has the Father's title, comprehending all the fulness of the Godhead (Acts vii. 2; Eph. i. 17; Ps. xxiv. 7, *Melek hakkabod*). **9. But** [ἀλλά]—in strong contrast to "which none of the princes of this world knew." Paul says, "*But* God hath revealed them unto us." Instead of using his own words he quotes God's. **as it is written, Eye hath not seen, &c.** The Greek is,

'We speak (supplied from *v.* 8) things which eye saw not (heretofore), &c., things which [A B read "as many things soever as:" ὅσα. Δ G *fg*, Vulgate, read as the English version] God prepared, &c. But' [δέ, not so strong an adversative as the former "but," which contrasts the two main opposites. This latter "but" puts a slight contrast between the two subordinate clauses, "God hath *prepared*" from everlasting, but now "hath *revealed* the things to us."] The quotation is not verbatim, but an inspired *exposition* of the "wisdom" (*v.* 6) from Isa. lxiv. 4 (cf. lii. 15; lxv. 17). The exceptive words, "O God, *beside* (i. e., except) thee," are not quoted directly, but virtually expressed in the exposition (*v.* 10). "None *but thou,* O God, sees these mysteries: *God hath revealed them to us by His spirit. God's seeing the mysteries ensures His revealing them to His people.* **entered**—lit., *come up into* the heart: '*alah 'al leeb : the rising of an earnest desire in the heart.* A Hebraism (cf. *margin,* Jer. iii. 16). In Isa. lxiv. it is, "Prepared (*lit.,* 'will do') for him that *waiteth for* him;" here, "for them that *love* Him." For Isaiah spake to them who *waited for* Messiah as future; St. Paul, to them who *love Him* as having appeared (1 John iv. 19: cf. *v.* 12, end). 'Love conducts to a far richer world of knowledge than earthly means could open to the conception' (*Olshausen*). **10. revealed . . . by . . . Spirit.** Inspiration of thoughts (so far as truth essential to salvation is concerned) makes the *Christian* (chs. iii. 16; xii. 3; Matt. xvi. 17; John xvi. 13; 1 John ii. 20, 27); that of *words,* the PROPHET (*v.* 13; 2 Sam. xxiii. 1, 2; 1 Ki. xiii. 1, 5; 2 Pet. i. 21). The secrets of revelation remain secret, not because God will not reveal them (for the very notion of *revelation* implies an unveiling of what was veiled), but because natural men have not the will or power to comprehend them. The Spirit-taught alone know these secrets (Ps. xxv. 14; John vii. 17; xv. 15). **unto us—the** "perfect" believers (*v.* 6). Intelligent men may understand the outline of doctrines; but without the Holy Spirit's revelation these will be to them a mere skeleton, correct, but wanting life (Luke x. 21). **the Spirit searcheth**—working in us and with our spirits (cf. Rom. viii. 16, 26, 27). The Old Testament shows us God (the Father) for us; the gospels, God (the Son) with us; the Acts and epistles, God (the Holy Ghost) in us (ch. iii. 16). **deep things of God** (Ps. xcii. 5)—His divine Being, attributes, and counsels. The Spirit delights to explore the infinite depths of the Divine mind, and then reveal them to us as far as is for our profit (Deut. xxix. 29). This proves the personality and the Godhead of the Holy Ghost. "Searcheth" indicates not ignorance, but accurate knowledge, and delight in the contemplation (Rev. ii. 23). Contrast "the depths of Satan" (Rev. ii. 24). He who has Christ revealed to him, has all things revealed in Him (ch. iii. 22). **11. what man, &c.**—lit., *who of* MEN knoweth *the things of a* MAN, *save the spirit of*

12 of God knoweth no man, but the Spirit of God. Now we have received, not the spirit of the world, but *the spirit which is of God; that we
13 might know the things that are freely given to us of God. Which °things also we speak, not in the words which man's wisdom teacheth, but which the Holy Ghost teacheth; comparing spiritual things with
14 spiritual. But ᵖthe natural man receiveth not the things of the Spirit of God: for they are foolishness unto him: neither ᵠcan he know *them*,
15 because they are spiritually discerned. But ʳhe that is spiritual ³judg-
16 eth all things, yet he himself is ⁴judged of no man. For ˢwho hath known the mind of the Lord, that he ⁵may instruct him? But ᵗwe have the mind of Christ.

A. D. 59.

ⁿ Rom. 8. 15.
° 2 Pet. 1. 16.
ᵖ Matt.16.23.
ᵠ Rom. 8. 5.
Jude 19.
ʳ Pro. 28. 5.
3 Or, dis-
cerneth.
4 Or, dis-
cerned.
ˢ Job 15. 8.
5 shall.
ᵗ Ps 25. 14.

that man? **things of God knoweth no man—**rather, '*none* knoweth,' not angel or man. **but the Spirit of God.** Supply, *and he to whom the Spirit of God reveals them* (so Matt. xi. 27, end). Even in the case of man, so infinitely inferior to God, none of his fellow-men, but his own spirit alone, knows (whether that knowledge be great or small) what is within him. Man's spirit is the organ wherewith he receives God's Spirit, through Whom alone he can know God. **12. we have received, not the spirit of the world**—the "spirit that now worketh in the children of disobedience" (Eph. ii. 2). This spirit is natural in the unregenerate, and needs not to be *received* (Ezek. xiii. 3; 1 John iv. 4). **spirit which is of [ἐκ] God**—*i. e.*, which comes FROM God. We have received it only by the *gift* of God, whose Spirit it is (v. 11). **that we might know**—experimentally. **things that are freely given to us of God**—God's gift of salvation in Christ, now preached without admixture of worldly wisdom (v. 4), and the "things which God hath prepared for them that love Him" (v. 9). **13. also**—we not only *know* by the Holy Ghost, but *we also speak* the "things freely given to us of God" (v. 12). **the Holy Ghost.** So ℵ: but A B C G, Vulgate, read 'the Spirit' simply, without "Holy." **comparing spiritual things with spiritual**—expounding the Spirit-inspired Old Testament, by comparison with the Gospel revealed by the same Spirit; conversely illustrating the Gospel mysteries by comparing them with the Old Testament types. So the Greek [συγκρίνειν], "comparing" (2 Cor. x. 12). *Wahl* translates '*explaining* (as the Greek for Hebrew *potheer*, Gen. xl. 8, LXX.) to spiritual (*i. e.*, Spirit-taught) men, spiritual things (the things which we ourselves are taught by the Spirit).' Spirit-taught men alone can comprehend spiritual truths (vv. 6, 9, 10, 14, 15; ch. iii. 1). The preacher speaks to the unspiritual (ch. iii. 1), in trust that the Spirit may by the Word make them spiritual. *Vorstius* translates 'combining spirituals with spirituals,'—*i. e.*, spiritual things with spiritual words, which we should not do were we to use words of worldly wisdom to expound spiritual things (so vv. 1, 4; 1 Pet. iv. 11). Perhaps the generality of the neuters comprehends these several notions. Combining spirituals with spirituals: implying both that spiritual things are only suited to spiritual persons (so "things" comprehended *persons*, ch. i. 27), and also that spiritual truths can only be combined with spiritual (not worldly-wise) words; and lastly, spirituals of the Old and New Testaments can only be understood by mutual comparison, not by combination with worldly or natural "wisdom" (chs. i. 21, 22; ii. 1, 4-9: cf. Ps. cxix. 18). **14. natural man** [ψυχικός]. As contrasted with the *spiritual* man, he is one in whom *the animal soul* [*psyche*] overbears his *spirit*, which latter is without the Spirit of God (Jude 19). So the *animal* (English version, "natural") body, or body led by the lower nature (including

289

both man's fallen *reason* and *heart*), is contrasted with the Spirit-quickened body (ch. xv. 44-46). The *carnal* man is one led by unregenerate appetites, or by a self-seeking mind, not necessarily one of low sensuality, but estranged from the divine life. [ψυχικός regards the natural man in the *intellectual*, σαρκικός, in the *ethical*, point of view.] 'Carnality' is the *practical* manifestation of the "natural" or 'animal mind;' "devilish," or 'demon-like,' 'led by an evil spirit,' is the worst type (Jas. iii. 15). **receiveth not**—*accepts not*, though offered to him, and 'worthy of being *received* by all men' (1 Tim. i. 15). **foolishness unto him**—whereas he seeks "wisdom" (ch. i. 22). **neither can he**—not only *does* he not, but he *cannot* know, and therefore has no wish to 'receive' them (Rom. viii. 7). **15. he that is spiritual**—lit., 'the spiritual (man).' In v. 14 the Greek is '*A*' (not "*the*") natural man. *The spiritual* is *the* man distinguished as he in whom the Spirit rules. In the unregenerate the spirit, the organ of the Holy Spirit, is overridden by the animal soul, and is in abeyance, so that such a one is never called "spiritual." **judgeth all things**—and persons by their true standard (cf. chs. vi. 2-4; xiv. 24; 1 John iv. 1), in so far as he is spiritual. '*Discerneth* . . . *is discerned*,' better accord with the translation, v. 14. Otherwise, for "discerned," in v. 14, translate 'judged of,' to accord with "judgeth . . . is judged," in this 15th verse. He has a practical insight into Gospel verities, though not infallible or impeccable (Matt. xxviii. 20; John xvi. 13). As the believer and the Church have the Spirit, and are yet not therefore impeccable, so he and the Church have the Spirit, and yet are not infallible or impeccable. Both are infallible and impeccable only in the *degree* in which they are led by the Spirit. The Spirit leads into all truth and holiness; but His influence on believers and the Church is as yet partial. Jesus alone, who had the Spirit without measure (John iii. 34), is both infallible and impeccable. Scripture, because written by men who, whilst writing, were infallibly inspired, is unmixed truth (Prov. xxx. 5; Ps. xii. 6). **himself is judged of no man** —that is not spiritual; and even by them only partially (ch. iv. 3). **16. For**—proof that the spiritual man "is judged of no man." In order to judge him, the natural man must 'know the mind of the Lord.' But who of natural men 'knows' that? **that he may instruct him**—*i.e.*, so as to set Him right as His counsellor (Isa. xl. 13, 14, LXX. [συμβιβάσει].) Natural men, in judging spiritual men, who 'have the mind of the Lord,' are virtually wishing, as counsellors, to set to right their KING. **we have the mind of Christ.** So A C ℵ *i*, Vulgate. But B Δ G *g*, 'of the Lord'—in our degree of capability to apprehend it. Isa. xl. refers to JEHOVAH; therefore, as it is applied here to *Christ*, He is Jehovah.

CHAP. III. 1-23.—ST. PAUL COULD NOT SPEAK TO THEM OF DEEP SPIRITUAL TRUTHS, AS THEY

3 AND I, brethren, could not speak unto you as unto spiritual, but as
2 unto carnal, *even* as unto babes in Christ. I have fed you with [a]milk, and not with meat: for hitherto ye were not able *to bear it*, neither yet
3 now are ye able. For ye are yet carnal: for whereas *there is* among you envying, and strife, and [1]divisions, are ye not carnal, and walk [2]as men?
4 For while one saith, I am of Paul; and another, I *am* of Apollos; are ye not carnal?
5 Who then is Paul, and who *is* Apollos, but ministers by whom ye
6 believed, even [b]as the Lord gave to every man? I [c]have planted,
7 [d]Apollos watered; but God [e]gave the increase. So then neither is he that planteth any thing, neither he that watereth; but God that giveth
8 the increase. Now he that planteth and he that watereth are one: [f]and every man shall receive his own reward, according to his own labour.
9 For [g]we are labourers together with God: ye are God's [3]husbandry, *ye are* God's [h]building.

A. D. 59

CHAP. 3.
a Heb. 5. 13.
1 Pet. 2. 2.
1 Or, factions.
2 according to man.
b Rom. 12. 3.
c Acts 18. 4.
d Acts 19. 1.
e Isa. 55. 10.
f Ps. 62. 12.
Rom. 2. 6.
Rev. 2. 23.
g Acts. 15. 4.
3 Or, tillage.
h Eph. 2. 20.
Col 2. 7.
Heb. 3. 3, 4.

WERE CARNAL, CONTENDING FOR THEIR TEACHERS: THESE ARE BUT WORKERS FOR GOD, TO WHOM THEY MUST GIVE ACCOUNT. THE HEARERS ARE GOD'S TEMPLE, WHICH THEY MUST NOT DEFILE BY CONTENTIONS FOR TEACHERS, WHO, AS ALL THINGS, ARE THEIRS, BEING CHRIST'S.

1. And I—*i. e.*, as the natural (animal) man cannot receive, so *I also could not (was not able—* viz., at my second visit—to) *speak unto you* deep things of God, since spiritual things can be made intelligible only *to the spiritual* (ch. ii. 13); *but I* was compelled to speak to you *as* I would *to* MEN OF FLESH. א A B C Δ G *f g*, Vulgate, read this for "carnal." *Fleshy* [σαρκίνοις] implies men wholly *of flesh*. Carnal, or *fleshly*, implies not that they were *wholly* unregenerate (ch. ii. 14), but that they had a *carnal tendency* [v. 3, σαρκικόι] (for instance, their divisions), notwithstanding their conversion (ch. i. 4-9). **babes**—neophytes; contrasted with the *perfect* (fully matured) *in Christ* (Col. i. 28: cf. Heb. v. 13, 14). They had life in Christ, but it was weak. He blames them for being still in a degree (not *altogether;* therefore he says "*as*") *babes* in Christ, when by this time they ought to have "come unto a perfect man, unto the measure of the stature of the fulness of Christ" (Eph. iv. 13). In Rom. vii. 14, also the oldest MSS., read, 'I am a man *of flesh*,' which goes towards proving that Paul there describes his *regenerate* but imperfect state. **2. milk**—the elementary "principles of the doctrine of Christ" (Heb. vi. 1). The profounder doctrines in this epistle were for the more mature believers among them. **3. envying**—jealousy, *rivalry*. This refers to their *feelings;* "strife," to their *words;* "divisions," to their *actions*. An ascending climax: *envying* produced *strife*, and strife *divisions* (factious parties) [διχοστασίαι is supported by א Δ G *f g*; but A B C, Vulgate, omit it]. His language becomes severer as he proceeds: in ch. i. 11 he had only said "contentions;" he now multiplies words (cf. the stronger term, ch. iv. 6, than in ch. iii. 21). **carnal**—"strife" is a "work of the flesh" (Gal. v. 20). The "flesh" includes all feelings that aim not at the glory of God and the good of our neighbour, but at gratifying self: not merely the lower appetites. **walk as men**—as unregenerate men (cf. Matt. xvi. 23). "After the flesh, not after the Spirit," as becomes those regenerate by the Spirit (Rom. viii. 4; Gal. v. 25, 26). **4. (Ch. i. 12.) are ye not carnal?** א A B C Δ G *f g*, Vulgate, read 'Are ye not *men?*' —*i. e.*, 'walking as men' unregenerate (v. 3). **5. Paul . . . Apollos.** א A B C Δ G *f g*, Vulgate, read in the reverse order, *Apollos . . . Paul.* He puts Apollos before himself, in humility. **who then**—seeing that ye severally strive so for your

favourite teachers, "Who is (of what intrinsic power is) Paul?" If so great an apostle reasons so of himself, how much more does humility, rather than self-seeking, become ordinary ministers. **but ministers, &c.** So א. A B C Δ G *f g*, Vulgate, have no "but." "Who is Apollos . . . Paul? (mere) ministers (a lowly word appropriate here, *servants*) by whom (not "*in* whom;" *by whose ministrations*) ye believed." **as the Lord gave to every man** —*i. e.*, to the several ministers (Rom. xii. 6, 7). **6. I . . . planted, Apollos watered** (Acts xviii. 1; xix. 1). Apollos was born in the learned city Alexandria: he originally "knew only the baptism of John;" but subsequently, being taught in the Gospel by Aquila and Priscilla at Ephesus, he, at his own desire, was sent by the brethren to Corinth, and there followed up the work which St. Paul had begun. Eloquent and mighty in the Scripture, "he mightily convinced the Jews . . . publicly, showing by the scriptures that Jesus was Christ." Paul's *forte* was in *planting* new churches. **God gave the increase**—i. e., *the growth* (v. 10; Acts xviii. 27). "He helped them much which had believed through *grace*." Ministers are nothing, and God is all in all; yet God works by instruments, and promises the Spirit in the faithful use of means. This is the dispensation of the Spirit: ours is the ministry of the Spirit. **7. neither is he that . . . any thing . . . but God**—viz., is all in all. "God" is emphatically last in the Greek, 'He that giveth the increase (namely), GOD.' Here follows a parenthesis, from *v.* 8 to *v.* 21, where, "Let no man glory in MEN" stands in antithetic contrast to GOD here. **8. one**—one in standing before God; able to do nothing without God. It is only their relative *faithfulness with their gifts* which will place them higher or lower (Matt. xxv. 14-30); therefore they ought not to be made by you the occasion of party divisions. **and every man**— rather, '*but* (δέ) every man.' Though in service they are essentially "one," yet every minister is separately responsible, and "shall receive *his own* (emphatically repeated) reward, according to *his own* labour." The *reward* is something over and above personal salvation (*vv.* 14, 15; 2 John 8). He shall be rewarded according to, not the amount of work done, but "according to his own labour." It shall be said to him, "Well done, thou good and (not *successful*, but) *faithful* servant, enter thou," &c. **9. Translate, as the Greek collocation, and the emphasis on "God" thrice repeated, requires,** 'For (in proof that "each shall receive reward according to his own labour," from God) it is of God that we are fellow-workers (labouring *with*, through His marvellous condescension, but

10 According to the grace of God which is given unto me, as a wise master-builder, I have laid *i* the foundation, and another buildeth thereon. But *j* let every man take heed how he buildeth thereupon.
11 For other foundation can no man lay than *k* that is laid, *l* which is Jesus
12 Christ. Now if any man build upon this foundation gold, silver, pre-
13 cious stones, wood, hay, stubble; every man's work shall be made manifest: for the day *m* shall declare it, because it *4* shall be revealed by fire;
14 and the fire shall try every man's work of what sort it is. If any man's
15 work abide which he hath built thereupon, he shall receive a reward. If any man's work shall be burnt, he shall suffer loss: but he himself shall be saved; *n* yet so as by fire.
16 Know *o* ye not that ye are the temple of God, and *that* the Spirit of

A. D. 59.

i Rom. 15.20.
Rev. 21. 14.
j 1 Pet. 4. 11.
k Isa. 28. 16.
Matt. 16.18.
2 Cor. 11. 4.
Gal. 1. 7.
l Eph. 2. 20.
m 1 Pet. 1. 7.
4 is revealed.
Luke 2. 35.
n Jude 23.
o 2 Cor. 6. 16.

under, belonging to, and *drawing all our grace from* Him as His servant, ch. xv. 10; 2 Cor. iii. 5; v. 20; vi. 1: cf. Acts, xv. 4; *Note,* 1 Thess. iii. 2) of God, that ye are the field (agriculture), of God that ye are the building.' "Building" is a new image, suited better than husbandry to set forth the different kinds of teaching and their results, which he is now about to discuss. 'To edify' or 'build up' the Church is similarly used, Eph. ii. 21, 22; iv. 29.

10. grace . . . given unto me (*v.* 5). St. Paul puts this first, to guard against usurping a particle of the Divine glory in pronouncing himself "a WISE master-builder." **wise**—i. e., *skilful.* His *skill* is shown in *laying the foundation* (ch. ii. 2). The unskilful builder lays none (Luke vi. 49). Christ is the foundation (*v.* 11). **another**—whoever comes after me. He does not name *Apollos,* for he speaks generally of *all successors.* His warning, "Let every man (especially, though not exclusively, every *teacher*) take heed how," &c., refers to other successors than Apollos, who doubtless did not build wood, hay, &c., on the foundation (cf. ch. iv. 15). Believers, too, have to take heed what superstructural doctrine they build upon Christ in themselves and in those whom they influence. **how**—with what material: how far *wisely,* and in builder-like style (1 Pet. iv. 11). **buildeth thereupon.** Here the *superstructure* raised *on* Christ is not, as in Eph. ii. 20, 21, of believers, the "lively stones" of the Church (1 Pet. ii. 5), but *the doctrinal and practical teaching* which succeeding teachers superadded to Paul's first teaching; not that they taught what was false, but their teaching was subtle and speculative, rather than solid and simple. **11.** (Isa. xxviii. 16; Acts iv. 12; Eph. ii. 20.) **For.** My warning (*v.* 10) is as to the superstructure, not as to *the foundation:* "For other *foundation* can no man lay than [παρά, *besides*] that laid (by God)." **Jesus Christ**—the person as well as the doctrine; *Jesus,* GOD-SAVIOUR; *Christ,* MESSIAH or ANOINTED. **can no man lay**—since the only one recognized by God is already laid. **12. Now** [δέ] "But." The "gold, silver, precious stones," which all can bear fire (Rev. iii. 18; xxi. 18, 19; Isa. liv. 11), are *teachings* that will stand the test of judgment: "wood, hay, stubble," are those which cannot,—not positive heresy, for that would destroy the *foundation* (which all admitted is Christ), but teaching mixed up with human philosophy and Judaism—curious rather than useful. Besides the *teachings,* the superstructure represents also the *persons* cemented to the Church, the reality of whose conversion, through the teachers' instrumentality, will be tested at the last day. Where there is the least grain of real faith, it shall never be lost (1 Pet. i. 7; iv. 12): the straw only feeds the fire (Matt. v. 19). **13. Every man's work** — each superstructure on the foundation. **the day**—of

the Lord (ch. i. 8; Heb. x. 25). "*The* day"—i. e., the day of days, the long-expected day. **declare it**—old English for 'make it clear' (ch. iv. 5). **it shall be revealed by fire**—it, i. e., "every man's work." '*He,*' the Lord, whose day it is (2 Thess. i. 7, 8). Lit., '*is being revealed* (the present implies the *certainty* and *nearness* of the event, Rev. xxii. 10, 20) *in* tire' (Mal. iii. 2, 3; iv. 1). The *fire* (figurative here, as the *gold, hay,* &c.) is not *purgatory* (as Rome teaches, i. e., *purificatory* and *punitive*), but *probatory;* not restricted to those dying in 'venial sin'—the supposed *intermediate class* between those entering heaven at once, and those dying in mortal sin, who go to hell—but *universal,* testing the godly and ungodly alike (2 Cor. v. 10: cf. Mark ix. 49). This fire is not till the *last* day; the supposed fire of purgatory begins *at death.* The fire of St. Paul is to try the *works,* the fire of purgatory the *persons,* of men. St. Paul's fire causes "loss" to the sufferers; Rome's purgatory, great gain—viz., heaven at last to those purged by it, if only it were true. It was not this doctrine that gave rise to prayers for the dead, but the practice of praying for the dead (which crept in from the mistaken solicitude of survivors), that gave rise to the doctrine. **14. abide**—the testing fire (Matt. iii. 11, 12). **which he hath built thereupon** —*on the foundation.* **reward**—*wages,* as a builder. Converts built on Christ, the foundation, through his faithfulness, shall be his "crown of rejoicing" (2 Cor. i. 14; 1 Thess. ii. 19). **15. If . . . be burnt** —If any man's work consist of such materials as the fire will destroy. **suffer loss**—i. e., forfeit the special "reward;" not that he shall lose salvation (which is a *free gift,* not a "reward," or wages), for he remains on the foundation (*v.* 12; 2 John 8). **saved; yet so as by fire**—rather, 'so as if *through* fire' (Zech. iii. 2; Amos iv. 11; Jude 23). The 'as if' shows the phrase to be figurative: having *a narrow escape* (Ps. lxvi. 12; Isa. xliii. 2). The 'Lord suddenly coming to His temple' in flaming "fire," all parts of the building which will not stand that fire will be consumed; the builders will escape with personal salvation, but with the loss of their work. Again, we may regard the superstructure as representing less essential matters superadded to the essentials: a man may err as to the former, and have the mortification of seeing much of his labour lost, and yet be saved; but not so as to the latter (cf. Phil. iii. 15).

16. Know ye not—It is no new thing I tell you, in calling you "God's building;" ye are the noblest of buildings, "the temple of God." **ye**—Christians form together one vast temple. Not, 'ye are *temples,*' but "ye are *the temple*" collectively, and "lively stones" (1 Pet. ii. 5) individually. **God . . . Spirit**—God's indwelling, and that of the Holy Spirit, are one; and therefore the Holy Spirit is God. No literal "temple" is recognized in the Christian Church. The only one is the

17 God dwelleth in you? If any man [5]defile the temple of God, him shall
18 God destroy: for [p]the temple of God is holy, which *temple* ye are. Let
 [q]no man deceive himself. If any man among you seemeth to be wise in
19 this world, let him become a fool, that he may be wise. For the wisdom
 of this world is foolishness with God. For it is written, [r]He taketh
20 the wise in their own craftiness. And again [s]The Lord knoweth the
 thoughts of the wise, that they are vain.
21, Therefore let no man glory in men. For [t]all things are yours; whether
22 Paul, or Apollos, or Cephas, or the world, or life, or death, or things
23 present, or things to come; all are yours; and [u]ye are Christ's; and
 [v]Christ *is* God's.
4 LET a man so account of us as of the ministers of Christ, [a]and stewards

A. D. 59.

[6] Or,
  destroy.
[p] Heb. 3. 1.
[q] 1 ro. 3. 7.
  Isa. 5. 21.
[r] Job 5. 13.
[s] Ps. 94. 11.
[t] 2 Cor 4. 5.
[u] Rom. 14. 8.
  Gal. 3. 29.
[v] ch. 8. 6.
  Heb. 1. 3.

CHAP. 4.
[a] Luke 12.42.

spiritual temple, the wh ole body of believing wor shippers which the Holy Spirit dwells in (ch. vi. 19; John iv. 23, 24). The *synagogue* was the model of the Christian house of worship. The temple was the *house of sacrifice,* rather than of prayer. Prayers in the temple were silent and individual (Luke i. 10; xviii. 10-13), not joint and public, nor with reading of Scripture, as in the synagogue. The temple (as ναός means, from a root 'to dwell') was the earthly *dwelling-place of God,* where alone He put His name. The synagogue (*i. e.,* an *assembly*) was the place for assembling. God now has His earthly temple, not of wood and stone, but the congregation of believers, the 'living stones' in the 'spiritual house.' Believers are all spiritual priests in it. Jesus, our High Priest, has the only literal priesthood (Mal. i. 11; Matt. xviii. 20; 1 Pet. ii. 5). 17. If any . . . defile . . . destroy —rather, as the *Greek is* the same in both, '*destroy* . . . destroy;' or [φθείρει, φθερεῖ], 'If any *corrupt,* God will give him to *corruption.*' God repays in kind by righteous retaliation. The *destroyer* shall be destroyed. The *destroyers* are distinct from the *unwise builders* (vv. 12, 15); these hold fast the "foundation" (u. 11); therefore, though they lose their superstructure and the special reward, yet they are themselves saved, though by a narrow escape: those, on the contrary, assailed with *corrupt* teaching the foundation, and so the temple itself, and shall therefore be destroyed. All, whether teachers or laymen by profession, are "priests unto God" (Exod. xix. 6; 1 Pet. ii. 9; Rev. i. 6). As the Aaronic priests were doomed to die if they violated the old temple (Exod. xxviii. 43; Lev. xvi. 2), so any Christian who violates the spiritual temple shall perish eternally (Heb. x. 26). All who build hay, &c., as a superstructure, are herein warned; for though, if they retain "the foundation," they shall be saved, however narrowly, yet they are in danger of *corrupting* this, which would entail their own *destruction. Theophylact,* from the parallelism between *v.* 15 and *v.* 17, takes *v.* 15, 'he shall be reserved (not annihilated as his work) so as to be burned in the fire' eternally; answering to 'him God shall destroy' (Mark ix. 44). But this Greek of "saved" is not so used in the New Testament. *V.* 17 seems rather a further and more deadly stage of error. holy—*inviolable* (Hab. ii. 20). which temple ye are—or 'the which [δῑτινες] (*i. e.,* holy) are ye;' therefore, to tamper with the *foundation* being a violation of the temple's inviolability entails ruin. 18. seemeth—i.e., *is, and is regarded* by himself and others. wise in this world—wise in mere worldly wisdom (ch. i. 20). let him become a fool—by receiving the Gospel in its unworldly simplicity, and so abjuring worldly wisdom, that he may seek the true wisdom from God, the obedience of faith (Gal. vi. 7). 19. with God—*in the judgment of* God. it is written—in Job v. 13.

This formula of quoting Scripture establishes the canonicity of Job. He taketh the wise in their own craftiness—proving the "foolishness" of the world's wisdom, since God makes it the very snare to catch those who think themselves so wise. Lit., *He who taketh* [δρασσόμενος], *graspeth with his hand,* &c., the whole sentence not being quoted, but only the part which suited St. Paul's purpose. 20. From Ps. xciv. 11, LXX. There it is *of men;* here it is "of the wise." St. Paul by inspiration states the class whose "thoughts" [διαλογισμούς; Hebrew, *Machsheboth*] (rather, "reasonings," as suits the context) the Spirit designated in the psalm, "vanity"—viz., the "proud" (*v.* 2) and worldly wise, whom God in *v.* 8 calls "fools," though they "boast themselves" of their *wisdom* in pushing their interests (*v.* 4). 21. let no man glory in men—as the sphere *in* which he glories; resuming *v.* 4: cf. ch. i. 12, 31, where the true object of glorying is stated: "THE LORD." Also ch. iv. 6. For all things—not only *all men.* For you to glory in men is lowering yourselves from your high position as heirs of *all things.* All (including your teachers) belong to Christ, and therefore to you, by your union with Him: He makes them and all things work together for your good (Rom. viii. 28). Ye are not for the sake of them, but they for you (2 Cor. iv. 5, 15). They belong to you, not you to them. 22. Enumeration of the "all things." The teachers in whom they gloried he puts first (ch. i. 12). He omits after "Cephas," *or Christ,*to whom exclusively some (ch. i. 12) professed to belong; for he stands infinitely above the category, Paul, Apollos, &c.; since only through Him they are what they are; but substitutes "ye are Christ's" (*v.* 23). world, or life, or death, or things present (until Christ's coming and kingdom) . . . things to come (after it). Not only shall they not "separate you from the love of God in Christ" (Rom. viii. 38, 39), but they "all are yours" (Mark x. 29, 30), as they belong to Christ your head (Heb. i. 2). 23. ye are Christ's—not Paul's or Apollos's, &c. (Matt. xxiii. 8-10; Rom. xiv. 8). Not merely a section, but ye *all* are Christ's (ch. i. 12). Christ is God's (ch. xi. 3). God is the ultimate end of all, even of Christ, His co-equal Son (ch. xv. 28; Phil. ii. 6-11).

CHAP. IV. 1-2L—TRUE VIEW OF MINISTERS —THE JUDGMENT IS NOT TO BE FORESTALLED— MEANWHILE THE APOSTLES' LOW STATE CONTRASTS WITH THE CORINTHIANS' PARTY PRIDE; NOT THAT ST. PAUL WOULD SHAME THEM, BUT AS A FATHER WARN THEM; FOR WHICH END HE SENT TIMOTHY, AND WILL SOON COME HIMSELF.

1. a man—every man. account of us—Paul and Apollos, and all duly-called teachers. ministers of Christ—not heads of the Church in whom we are to glory: the headship belongs to Christ alone; we are but His *servants* ministering to you (ch. i. 12,

2 of the mysteries of God. Moreover it is required in stewards, that a man
3 be found faithful. But with me it is a very small thing that I should
be judged of you, or of man's ¹judgment: yea, I judge not mine own
4 self. For I know nothing by myself; yet am I not hereby justified:
5 but he that judgeth me is the Lord. Therefore ᵇjudge nothing before
the time, until the Lord come, who both will bring to light the hidden
things of darkness, and will make manifest the counsels of the hearts:
and ᶜthen shall every man have praise of God.
6 And these things, brethren, I have in a figure transferred to myself
and *to* Apollos for your sakes; ᵈthat ye might learn in us not to think
of men above that which is written, that no one of you be puffed up for
7 one against another. For who ²maketh thee to differ *from another?*
and ᵉwhat hast thou that thou didst not receive? now if thou didst
receive *it*, why dost thou glory, as if thou hadst not received *it?*
8 Now ye are full, ᶠnow ye are rich, ye have reigned as kings without

A. D. 59.

1 day.
ch, 3. 13.
ᵇ Matt. 7. 1.
Luke 6. 87.
Rom. 2. 1.
Rom. 14. 4.
Jas. 4. 11.
Rev 20. 12.
ᶜ Rom. 2. 2).
2 Cor 5. 10.
ᵈ Rom. 12. 3.
2 distin-
guisheth
thee.
ᵉ John 3. 27.
1 Pet. 4. 10.
ᶠ Rom. 12. 3,
Gal 6. 3.
Rev. 3. 17.

13; iii. 5, 22). **stewards** (Luke xii. 42; 1 Pet. iv. 10)—not the depositaries, but dispensers of the grace given us ("rightly dividing," or *dispensing it*) to others. The Chazan, or *overseer*, in the synagogue answered to the *bishop* or "angel" of the church. He called seven of the synagogue to read the law every Sabbath, and *oversaw* them. The Parnasin of the synagogue, like the ancient 'deacon' of the church, took care of the poor (Acts vi.), and subsequently preached in subordination to the presbyter or bishop, as Stephen did. The Church is not the appendage to the priesthood; but the minister is God's steward to the Church. Man shrinks from close contact with God: hence he puts a priesthood between, and serves God by deputy. The minister's office is to "preach" (lit., *proclaim as a herald*, Matt. x. 27) "the mysteries of God," so far as they have been revealed, if his hearers will receive them. *Josephus* says the Jewish religion made known to all the people the mysteries of their religion, whilst the Pagans concealed theirs from all but the 'initiated' few. **2. Moreover.** אABCΔG, Vulgate, read [ὧδε λοιπόν] 'Moreover HERE' (*i. e.*, on earth): or the 'here' may be put at the close of the previous sentence, and 'moreover' at the beginning of the next (*Lachmann*)—'stewards of the mysteries of God here.' Moreover, *in the case of stewards, enquiry is made, that one may be found faithful,*—another argument against the Corinthian preferences of teachers for their *gifts;* whereas what is required in stewards is *faithfulness* (*margin*, 1 Sam. iii. 20; Heb. iii. 5). But even as to this, God's stewards await not man's judgment to test them, but the testing which shall be in the day of the Lord. **3. it is a very small thing**—*lit.*, 'it amounts to a very small matter;' not that I despise *your* judgment, but as compared with God's it almost comes to nothing. **judged . . . of man's judgment**—*lit.*, 'man's day' (here personified) contrasted with *the day* (ch. iii. 13) *of the Lord* (v. 5). All days previous to that day *are man's days.* The thrice-recurring Greek for *judged . . . judge . . . judgeth* (v. 4), is *judicially discerned . . . discern . . . discerneth*, as in ch. ii. 14, 15 [ἀνακρίνω, decide in judgment upon one]. **4. by myself.** Translate, 'I am conscious to myself of no (ministerial) unfaithfulness.' **yet am I not hereby justified**—therefore conscience is not an infallible guide. St. Paul did not consider his so. He had a good conscience (2 Cor. i. 12); but God might see unfaithfulness in him which his own conscience could not yet accurately detect. Much of his labour might prove "stubble" in the testing day. "Justified" here refers to *sanctifying righteousness.* Of his justification he has no doubt (Rom. v. 1); but of *the degree of his sanctifying*

righteousness he cannot be infallibly sure till the judgment day, when he will gain or lose reward accordingly (ch. iii. 14, 15). **5.** Disproving the judicial power claimed by the Romish priesthood in the confessional. **Therefore**—as the Lord is the sole Decider. **judge** [Κρίνετε]—not the same Greek as in *v.* 3, 4, where the meaning is to *decide on* the merits of one's case. Here *judgments* in general are forbidden, which presumptuously forestall God's prerogative. **Lord**—Jesus Christ, whose "ministers" we are (v. 1), and who is to be the Judge (John v. 22, 27; Acts x. 42; xvii. 31). **manifest . . . hearts**—our judgments now (as those of the Corinthians respecting their teachers) are necessarily defective: we only see the outward *act;* we cannot see the *motives.* 'Faithfulness' (v. 2) will be estimated, and the "Lord" will 'justify' men's work, or the reverse (v. 4), according to "the counsels of the *hearts*." **then shall every man have praise** (ch. iii. 8; 1 Sam. xxvi. 23; Matt. xxv. 21, 23, 28)—rather, '*his due* praise,' not exaggerated, such as the Corinthians heaped on favourite teachers; '**THE PRAISE**' (so the Greek) due for acts estimated by the motives. "Then," not 'before;' therefore wait till *then* (Jas. v. 7).

6. And [δέ]—'But' my remarks do not apply to myself and Apollos alone. **in a figure transferred to myself**—*i. e.*, I have represented under the persons of Apollos and myself (whose names have been made a party cry) what holds good of *all* teachers, making us two a *figure* or *type* of all the others [μετεσχημάτισα]: under our names I mean others to be understood whom I do not name, in order not to shame you. **not to think**, &c. So אC read. But ABΔG*fg*, Vulgate, omit 'think.' 'That in us (as your example) ye might learn (this) not (to go) beyond what is written.' ΔG*g* read singular, 'beyond *that which* is written.' אABC read plural, '*the things* which are written;' perhaps referring to what he had himself written in this epistle. Revere the *silence* of holy writ as much as its *declarations:* so you will less dogmatize on what is not revealed (Deut. xxix. 29). **puffed up for one**—viz., 'for one (favourite minister) against another.' The Greek indicative [φυσιοῦσθε] implies, 'that ye be not puffed up **AS YE ARE.**' **7.** Translate [διακρίνει], 'Who distinguisheth thee (above another)? not thyself, but God. **and** [Greek, δέ]—'*but.*' If, '*however*,' thou appealest to thy pre-eminent gifts, 'what hast thou that thou didst not receive?' **glory, as if thou hadst not received it**—as if it was to thyself, not to God, thou owest it. **8.** Irony. Translate [ἤδη κεκορεσμένοι], '*Already* ye are filled full (with spiritual food),

us: and I would to God ye did reign, that we also might reign with you.

9 For I think that God hath set forth us [3] the apostles last, [g] as it were appointed to death: for [h] we are made a [4] spectacle unto the world, and

10 to angels, and to men. We *are* [i] fools for Christ's sake, but ye *are* wise in Christ: [j] we *are* weak, but ye *are* strong: ye *are* honourable, but we

11 *are* despised. Even·unto this present hour we both hunger, and thirst, and are naked, and are [k] buffeted, and have no certain dwelling-place;

12 and [l] labour, working with our own hands: [m] being reviled, we bless;

13 being persecuted, we suffer it; being defamed, we entreat: we are made as the filth of the world, *and are* the offscouring of all things unto this day.

14 I write not these things to shame you, but, as my beloved sons, I warn

15 *you.* For though ye have ten thousand instructors in Christ, yet *have*

A. D. 59.

[3] Or, us the last apostles, *as.*

[g] Ps. 44. 22. 2 Cor. 4. 11.
[h] Eph. 6. 12. Heb. 10. 33.
[4] theatre.
[i] Acts 26. 24.
[j] 2 Cor. 13. 9.
[k] Acts 23. 2.
[l] Acts 18. 3. 1 Tim. 4. 10.
[m] Matt. 5. 44. 1 Pet. 2. 23.

already ye are rich, ye have made yourselves kings, without us.' Ye act as if ye needed no more to "hunger after righteousness," as though already ye had reached the "kingdom" for which Christians have to strive and suffer. Ye are so puffed up with your favourite teachers, and your own fancied attainments in knowledge through them, that ye feel like those 'filled full' at a feast, or as a "rich" man glorying in his riches; so ye feel ye can now do "without us," your first spiritual fathers (*v.* 15). But before the "kingdom" and the "*fulness* of joy," at the marriage feast of the Lamb, must come the cross, to every true believer (2 Tim. ii. 5, 11, 12): so the self-complacent Laodiceans (Rev. iii. 17: cf. Hos. xii. 8). *Temporal* riches *tended* at Corinth to generate this spiritual self-sufficiency: the contrast to the apostle's literal "hunger and thirst" (*v.* 11) proves this. I would . . . ye did reign—'I would *indeed*' [γε] that your kingdom had begun. **that we also might reign with you.** Your spiritual prosperity would redound to us, your fathers in Christ (ch. ix. 23). When you reach the kingdom, you shall be our "crown of rejoicing, in the presence of our Lord Jesus" (1 Thess. ii. 19). **For.** We may well desire that the time of 'reigning' were come, to relieve us from our present trials; "for," &c. **I think.** The Corinthians (Greek, ch. iii. 18) '*thought*' themselves "wise in this world." St. Paul, in contrast, 'thinks' that God has set forth him and his fellow-ministers "last"—*i. e.,* lowest. The apostles fared worse .than even the prophets, who, though sometimes afflicted, were often honoured (2 Ki. v. 9; viii. 9). **us the apostles.** St. Paul includes Apollos with the apostles, in the broader sense. So Rom. xvi. 7; 2 Cor. viii. 23. (Greek for 'messengers,' *apostles.*) **appointed to death**—as criminals condemned. **a spectacle** —*theatron: a theatrical spectacle.* So Heb. x. 33, "made *a gazingstock* by afflictions." Criminals "appointed to death" in St. Paul's time were exhibited as a gazingstock to amuse the populace in the amphitheatre, and "set forth last" in the show, to fight with wild beasts, (cf. *Tertullian,* 'De Pudicitia,' xiv.) **unto the world**—to the whole world, "the whole family in heaven and earth" (Eph. iii. 15). As Jesus was "seen of angels" (1 Tim. iii. 16), so His followers are a spectacle to angels, who take a deep interest in the progressive steps of redemption. St. Paul tacitly implies that, though "last" in the world's judgment, Christ's servants are deemed by angels a spectacle worthy of their intense regard. However, since "the world" is comprehensive, and is applied in this epistle to the evil especially (ch. i. 27, 23), and since spectators (in the image from the amphitheatre) gaze at the show with savage delight, rather than sympathy for the sufferers, *bad*

angels are included, besides *good.* The generality of the term "angels," and its frequent use in a good sense, as well as Eph. iii. 10; 1 Pet. i. 12, imply *good* as well as *bad* angels, though, for the reasons above, the bad be principally meant. **10.** Irony. How much your lot (*supposing it to be real*) is to be envied, and ours to be pitied! **fools** (chs. i. 21; iii. 18: cf. Acts xvii. 18; xxvi. 24) **for Christ's sake . . . in Christ**—our union with Christ only entails on us, "FOR THE SAKE OF" Him, reproach as "fools;" yours gives you full fellowship IN Him as "wise" (i. e., *supposing you really are all you seem,* ch. iii. 18). **we are weak, but ye are strong** (ch. ii. 3; 2 Cor. xiii. 9)—in a worldly point of view (*v.* 9); but contrast 2 Cor. xii. 9, 10; Rev. iii. 17, 18. **we are despised** (2 Cor. x. 10)—because of our "weakness," and our not using worldly philosophy and rhetoric, while ye Corinthians and your teachers are (seemingly) so "honourable." Contrast with "despised," Gal. iv. 14. **11.** (2 Cor. xi. 23-27.) **naked**—*i. e.,* insufficiently clad (Rom. viii. 35; 2 Tim. iv. 13). **buffeted** —as a *slave* (1 Pet. ii. 20), the reverse of the state of the Corinthians, 'reigning as *kings*' (Acts xxiii. 2). Paul's master was "buffeted" when about to die a slave's death (Matt. xxvi. 67). **have no certain dwelling**—like Jesus (Matt. viii. 20). **12. working with our own hands**—"even unto this present hour" (*v.* 11): so continuous are my hardships. This is not stated in the *narrative* of St. Paul's proceedings *at Ephesus,* whence he wrote this epistle (though it is expressly stated of him *at Corinth,* (cf. Acts xviii. 3, &c., and xix.) But in his *address* to the Ephesian elders at Miletus (Acts xx. 34), he says, "Ye yourselves know that these hands have ministered unto my necessities," &c. The undesignedness of the coincidence thus indirectly brought out is incompatible with forgery. **13.** All this we bear in the opposite to the self-assertive spirit of the world (Matt. v. 39): a tacit reproof to the self-sufficiency of the Corinthians (*v.* 8). **defamed, we entreat**—viz., God for our defamers, as Christ enjoined (Matt. v. 10, 44). Or, we reply submissively and deprecatingly. **filth**— the *sweepings* of a cleaning. Or *persons sacrificed for the public good* in a national calamity. Christ is the true *Katharma,* or *cleansing expiation,* **of all things**—not of the "world" only. **14. I write not these things to shame you**— for not relieving my needs (ch. ix. 15). **warn**— rather, 'admonish' as a father uses 'admonition' to 'beloved sons,' not provoking them to wrath (Eph. vi. 4). The Corinthians might well be 'ashamed' at the disparity between the father, St. Paul, and his spiritual children, themselves. **15. For**—I say, 'my sons,' **though ye have ten thousand**—implying that the Corinthians had more "instructors" than was desirable. **instruc-**

ye not many fathers: for " in Christ Jesus I have begotten you through

16 the Gospel. Wherefore I beseech you, ° be ye followers of me.

17   For this cause have I sent unto you Timotheus, ᴾ who is my beloved son, and faithful in the Lord, who shall bring you into remembrance of my ways which be in Christ, as I teach every where in every church.

18, Now some are puffed up, as though I would not come to you. But ᵠI

19 will come to you shortly, if the Lord will, and will know, not the speech

20 of them which are puffed up, but the power. For ʳ the kingdom of God

21 *is* not in word, but in power. What will ye? shall I come unto you with a rod, or in love, and *in* the spirit of meekness?

5   IT is reported commonly *that there is* fornication among you, and such fornication as is not so much as named ª among the Gentiles, ᵇ that one

2 should have his father's ᶜ wife. And ye are puffed up, and have not

A. D. 59.

" Rom. 15.20
Acts 18. 4.
Gal. 4. 19.
Tit. 1. 4.
Jas. 1. 18.
° ch. 11. 1.
ᴾ Acts 19. 22
2 Tim. 1. 2.
ᵠ Acts 19. 21.
2 Cor. 1. 15
ʳ 1 Thes. 1. 5

CHAP. 5.
ª Eph. 5. 3.
ᵇ Deut. 27.20
ᶜ 2 Cor. 7. 12.

---

tors—*tutors* [παιδαγωγούς] who had the care of rearing, but not the rights or affection of the father, who alone had begotten them spiritually. **in Christ.** St. Paul admits that these "instructors" were not mere legalists, but *evangelical* teachers. He uses a stronger phrase of himself in begetting them spiritually "in Christ Jesus," implying both the saviour's *office and person.* As Paul was the means of *regenerating* them, and yet 'baptized none of them save Crispus, Gaius, and the household of Stephanas,' regeneration cannot be inseparably *in* and *by* baptism (ch. i. 14-17). **16. be ye followers of me**—lit., *imitators;* viz., in my ways, which be in Christ (*v.* 17; ch. xi. 1); not in my crosses (*vv.* 8-13; Acts xxvi. 29; Gal. iv. 12).

17. For this cause—that ye may the better "be followers of me" (*v.* 16), through his admonitions. **sent unto you Timotheus** (ch. xvi. 10 ; Acts xix. 21, 22). 'Paul purposed in the spirit, when he had passed through Macedonia and *Achaia,* to go to Jerusalem. So he sent to Macedonia Timotheus and Erastus.' Here it is not expressly said, he sent Timothy into Achaia (of which Corinth was the capital), but it is *implied,* for he sent him with Erastus *before him.* As he therefore purposed to go into Achaia, the probability is they were to go thither also. They are said only to have been sent into *Macedonia,* because it was the country to which they went immediately from Ephesus. The undesignedness of the coincidence establishes the genuineness of both the epistle and the history. In both, Timothy's journey is closely connected with St. Paul's own (cf. *v.* 19). Erastus is not specified in the epistle, probably because it was Timothy who was charged with St. Paul's orders. The seeming discrepancy shows that the passages were not taken from one another (*Paley*). **son**— *i. e.*, converted by me (cf. *vv.* 14, 15 ; Acts xiv. 6, 7, with xvi. 1, 2 ; 1 Tim. i. 2, 18 ; 2 Tim. i. 2). Translate, ' My son, beloved and faithful in the Lord.' **bring you into remembrance.** He does not say, 'shall *teach* you,' lest they should be hurt at being taught by a youth like Timothy. Timothy, from his spiritual connection with St. Paul, was best suited to *remind* them of the apostle's "ways in Christ"—*i. e.*, walk and teaching (2 Tim. iii. 10), which they in part, not altogether (ch. xi. 2), had forgotten. **as I teach every where in every church.** What the Spirit directed Paul to teach "everywhere" else must be necessary at Corinth (ch. vii. 17). A *form* of teaching is implied: from it other teachers had departed. **18. Now**—Greek, 'But' [δέ]. I have sent Timothy; BUT not because I do not intend to come myself, as some are puffed up to fancy as if I dared not come. A *puffed-up* spirit was the Corinthians' besetting sin (ch. v. 2). **19.** An emphatical negation of their supposition

(*v.* 18). **shortly**—after Pentecost (ch. xvi. 8). **if the Lord will**—a wise proviso (Jas. iv. 15). He does not seem to have been able to go as soon as he intended. **and will know**—take cognizance of. **but the power.** I care not for their high sounding "speech;" what I desire to know is, whether they be really *powerful* in the Spirit, or not. A predominant feature of Grecian character was a love for power of *discourse,* rather than of godliness. **20. kingdom of God**—*i. e.*, living fellowship in the Gospel (Luke xvii. 21 ; Rom. xiv. 17). **is not in word.** Translate, as in *v.* 19, "speech." Not empty 'speeches;' but the manifest "power" of the Spirit attests "the kingdom of God" (the *reign of the Gospel* spiritually) in a church or in an individual (cf. ch. ii. 1, 4 ; 1 Thess. i. 5). **21. with a rod, or in love.** The Greek "in" is in both clauses: Is it IN the character of one using the *rod* that I am to come, or IN love and the spirit of meekness? (Isa. xi. 4 ; 2 Cor. xiii. 3.) Nothing but the consciousness of superhuman power could have prompted a poor tentmaker to utter such bold words.

CHAP. V. 1-13.—THE INCESTUOUS PERSON— THE CORINTHIANS REPROVED FOR CONNIVANCE, AND WARNED TO PURGE OUT THE LEAVEN— QUALIFICATION OF HIS FORMER COMMAND AS TO ASSOCIATION WITH SINNERS.

As a *puffed-up spirit* caused their strifes, St. Paul humbles them by convicting them of sin. The best community may have an individual offender; but its duty is to punish such a one. In this the Corinthians had failed. **1. commonly** [ὅλως]—rather, ' with all your self-satisfaction, it is *actually,* or *after all,* reported,' &c. The Greek word is adversative to a negative sentence understood or expressed. 'There ought to be no fornication at all; but *nevertheless,* it *absolutely* is reported.' So I must come invested "with a rod" (ch. iii. 21). **It is reported.** The Corinthians, though they "wrote" (ch. vii. 1) on other points, gave St. Paul no information on those which bore against themselves. These matters reached the apostle indirectly (ch. i. 11). **so much as named.** So א. But A B Δ G *fg*, Vulgate, Lucifer, omit "named." ' Fornication so gross as (escapes reprobation) not even among the heathen, so that one (of you) hath (in concubinage; not *marriage,* as *Alford* thinks) his father's wife'—*i. e.*, his stepmother, whilst his father is still alive (as Reuben, Gen. xxxv. 22; Lev. xviii. 8). She was a heathen, for which reason he does not direct his rebuke against her (cf. *v.* 12, 13). Neither Christian nor Gentile *law* would have sanctioned such a *marriage,* however Corinth's profligacy might wink at the concubinage. **2. puffed up**—with your own wisdom and the eloquence of your favourite teachers, when ye ought to be ' mourning' at the

rather mourned, that he that hath done this deed might be taken away
3 from among you. For [d]I verily, as absent in body, but present in spirit,
have [1]judged already, as though I were present, *concerning* him that
4 hath so done this deed, in the name of our Lord Jesus Christ, when ye
are gathered together, and my spirit, [e]with the power of our Lord Jesus
5 Christ, to [f]deliver such an one unto Satan for the destruction of the
flesh, that the spirit may be saved in the day of the Lord Jesus.
6   Your glorying *is* not good. Know ye not that [g]a little leaven leaven-
7 eth the whole lump? Purge out therefore the old leaven, that ye may
be a new lump, as ye are unleavened. For [h]even Christ [i]our passover
8 [2]is sacrificed for us: therefore [j]let us keep [3]the feast, not with [k]old

A. D. 59.

[d] Col. 2. 5.
[1] Or, determined.
[e] Matt. 18.18.
[f] Job 2. 6.
[g] Gal. 5. 9.
[h] Isa. 53. 7.
[i] John 19. 14.
[2] Or, is slain.
[j] Ex. 12. 15.
[3] Or, holy day.
[k] Deut 16. 3.

scandal to religion by the incest. Paul *mourned* because they did not mourn and repent, but were "puffed up" (ch. iv. 19; Jer. xiii. 17; 2 Cor. ii. 4; xii. 21). **that**—ye have not so mourned as to lead to the result *that,* &c. **taken away from among you**—by excommunication. The incestuous person was brought to repentance, in the interval between the first and second epistles (2 Cor. ii. 5-10). Excommunication in the Church corresponded to that in the Synagogue, there being a lighter and heavier form—the latter an utter separation from church-fellowship, the former exclusion from the Lord's supper only, but not from church. **3. For I Are ye** not grieved? for *I* for my part have decided. **as absent.** So ℵ G *fg.* But A B C Δ, Vulgate, read [']being absent.' **present in spirit** (2 Ki. v. 26; Col. ii. 5). **so done**—rather, 'perpetrated,' as the Greek [κατεργασάμενον] is stronger than that for "done" in *v.* 2. "So"—*i. e.,* so scandalously, whilst called a brother. **4. In the name of our Lord Jesus Christ**—*i. e.,* invested with His authority, as His earthly representative (2 Cor. ii. 10, end). Join this with 'when ye have been gathered together, and my spirit' (wherewith I am "present" as president of your synod, though "absent in body," *v.* 3). Paul, speaking of himself, says, "spirit;" of Christ, "power." Christ's presence is promised to His Church "gathered together in His name" (Matt. xviii. 18 - 20). Christ's "power" will ratify their sentence (John xx. 23; Matt. xviii. 18): so join "with the power of our Lord Jesus Christ, to deliver such an one unto Satan." Their decree was passed according to St. Paul's *judgment* (*v.* 3) as presiding in spirit (2 Cor. xiii. 3-10). Infallible judgment was limited to the apostles: for they alone could work miracles as credentials to attest it. Their successors, to establish their claim to it, must produce miracles (2 Cor. xii. 12). Even the apostles in ordinary cases, where not specially inspired, were fallible (Acts viii. 13, 23; Gal. ii. 11-14). Three degrees of excommunication are mentioned in the Talmud,— *niddui* (exclusion from eating with others, &c., for thirty days), *cheerem* (anathema for ninety days), *shammatta* (perpetual exclusion). **5.** Besides excommunication (which the Corinthians had the power of), St. Paul delegates here to them *his* power as an inspired apostle, of *inflicting corporeal disease or death* in punishment for sin [" to deliver [παραδοῦναι, temporarily; not *ἐκδοῦναι*, to give up utterly] unto Satan such an one" —i. e., *so heinous* a sinner]. See instances, Acts v. 1-11; xiii. 11; 1 Tim. i. 20. As Satan receives power to try the godly, as Job (Job ii. 4-7), Paul (2 Cor. xii. 7), and Peter (Luke xxii. 31), much more the ungodly. Satan, the "accuser of the brethren" (Rev. xii. 10), the "adversary" (1 Pet. v. 8), demands the sinner's punishment for sin (Zech. iii. 1; Luke xiii. 16). God lets Satan have his way at times (cf. Ps. cix. 6). Here it is not finally, but for the affliction of the body (ch. xi.

30, 32), so as to *destroy fleshly lust* (Matt. v. 29). He does not say, 'for the destruction of the *body*,' for *it* shall share in redemption (Rom. viii. 23); but of the corrupt "flesh," which "cannot inherit the kingdom of God," and the lusts of which prompted this offender to incest (Rom. vii. 5; viii. 9, 10, 13). The "destruction of the flesh" answers to "*mortify* the deeds of the *body*," only that this is done by one's self, that by chastisement from God (cf. 1 Pet. iv. 1, 2, 6). **the spirit may be saved**—the spiritual part, in the believer the organ of the Holy Spirit, involving the salvation of the body too. Temporary affliction often leads to permanent salvation (Ps. lxxxiii. 16). Satan in God's hand becomes, in spite of himself, an instructor of believers.

6. Your glorying in your attachments and your teachers (ch. iii. 21), whilst all the while ye connive at such a scandal, is quite unseemly. **a little leaven leaveneth the whole lump** (Gal. v. 9) —one bad member infects the whole church. Little thieves let in greater ones. With *present* complicity in the guilt, and danger of future contagion (ch. xv. 33; 2 Tim. ii. 17). **7. old leaven**—the remnant of the "old" (Eph. iv. 22-24) heathenish and natural corruption. The Jews used extreme care in searching their houses, and 'purging out' every particle of leaven at the passover (Deut. xvi. 3, 4). So Christians are continually to search and purify their hearts (Ps. cxxxix. 23, 24). **as ye are unleavened**—in relation to your Christian calling, free from the leaven of sin (ch. vi. 11). St. Paul often grounds exhortations on the assumption of Christian professors realizing their high calling (Rom. vi. 3, 4). Regarding the Church as the passover 'unleavened lump,' he entreats them to correspond in fact with the Christian normal state. 'For Christ our passover (Exod. xii.; John i. 29) *was* once for all (Aorist: English version, "is") sacrificed.' The feast of unleavened bread followed the slaying of the lamb: so Christ *having been once for all sacrificed*, the feast is now going on, in which let there be no leaven of evil left unpurged from among you, the 'unleavened lump.' He alludes to the passover two or three weeks before kept by the Jewish Christians (ch. xvi. 8). The Jewish passover naturally gave place to our Christian Easter. The time, however, of *keeping feast* (of which the Lord's supper is representative)—i. e., *leading the Christian life of joy* in Christ's finished work (cf. Prov. xv. 15)—is not limited, as the passover, to one season, but is ALL our time: for the benefits of the once-for-all completed sacrifice of *our* Lamb extends through all this Christian dispensation: in no part of our time is the leaven of evil to be admitted. **for us.** So ℵ. But A B Δ G *fg*, Vulgate, omit. **8. not . . . old leaven**—of our unconverted state. **malice**—the opposite of "sincerity," which allows no leaven of evil to be mixed up with good (Matt. xvi. 6). **wickedness**—the opposite of "truth," which al-

296

leaven, neither with the leaven of malice and wickedness; but with the unleavened *bread* of sincerity and truth.

9, I wrote unto you in an epistle *‘*not to company with fornicators: yet
10 not altogether with the fornicators of this world, or with the covetous, or extortioners, or with idolaters; for then must ye needs go out *ᵐ* of
11 the world. But now I have written unto you not to keep company, *ⁿ*if any man that is called a brother be a fornicator, or covetous, or an idolater, or a railer, or a drunkard, or an extortioner; with such an one
12 no *°*not to eat. For what have I to do to judge them also *ᵖ*that are
13 without? do not ye judge them that are within? But them that are without *ᑫ*God judgeth. Therefore put away from among yourselves that wicked person.

6 DARE any of you, having a matter against another, go to law before
2 the unjust, and not before the saints? Do ye not know that *ᵃ*the saints shall judge the world? and if the world shall be judged by you,

A. D. 59.

l 2 Cor. 6. 14.
m John 17. 15.
n Matt. 18. 17.
Rom. 16. 17.
2 John 10.
o Gal. 2. 12.
p Mark 4. 11.
Col. 4. 5.
1 Tim. 3. 7.
q Eccl. 12. 14.
Heb. 13. 4.

CHAP. 6.
a Ps. 49. 14.
Ps. 149. 5-9.
Dan. 7. 22.
Luke 22. 30.
Rev. 2. 26.
Rev. 20. 4.

lows not evil to be mistaken for good. "Malice" [κακία] means the evil *habit* of mind; "wickedness" [πονηρία] its *outcoming* in word and deed. "Sincerity" [εἰλικρίνεια] expresses literally a thing which, examined *by sunlight,* is found unadulterated.

9. I wrote unto you in an epistle—Greek, 'in THE epistle:' a former one not now extant. That St. Paul does not refer to the *present* letter is clear, as no direction 'not to company with fornicators' occurs in the previous part; also the words, 'in *the* epistle,' could not have been added if he meant, 'I have just written' (2 Cor. x. 10). '*His letters*' (plural) confirm this. 2 Cor. vii. 8 uses the same phrase, in referring to our *first* epistle, as here is used in referring to a *former* one. It probably was a brief reply to enquiries of the Corinthians: *our* first epistle, as it enters more fully into the same subject, has superseded the former, which the Holy Spirit did not design for the Church in general. See my 'Introduction.' **10.** Limitation of the prohibition alluded to in *v.* 9. As in dissolute Corinth to 'company with no fornicators,' &c., would be almost to company with none in the (unbelieving) world, ye need not 'altogether' forego intercourse (cf. ch. x. 27). As "fornicators" sin against themselves, so "extortioners" against their neighbours, and "idolaters" against God. The attempt to get "out of the world," in violation of God's will (John xvii. 15), led to monasticism and its evils. **11. But now I have written**—"now," not *time;* but, '*the case being so*'—viz., that 'to avoid fornicators,' &c., *of the world,* you would have to leave it altogether. So "now," Heb. xi. 16. Thus we avoid making the apostle *now* retract what he had before commanded. **I have written**—*i. e.,* my meaning in what I wrote was, &c. **a brother**—contrasted with a 'fornicator, &c., *of the world*' (*v.* 10). There is less danger in associating with open worldlings than with carnal professors. Here, as in Eph. v. 3, 5, "covetousness" is joined with "fornication," the common fount of both being 'the fierce longing of the creature, which has turned from God, to fill itself with inferior objects of sense' (*Trench*). Hence idolatry and lust go together; and the covetous man is termed an "idolater" (Num. xxv. 1, 2). The Corinthians were not open idolaters, but ate things offered to idols, making a compromise with the heathen; so they connived at fornication, (ch. viii. 4, &c.) Cf., similarly, fornication combined with idolatrous compromise, after the pattern of Israel (Rev. ii. 14). **no not to eat**—at the same table; whether at the love feasts (Agapæ) or in private, much more at the Lord's table. Too often the guests 'are not

as children in one family, but like a heterogeneous crowd at an inn' (*Bengel*) (cf. 2 John x. 11). **12. For.** 'Ye might have known my meaning so; FOR,' &c. **what have I to do.** My concern is not with unbelievers *outside,* I referred to those *within* the Church. **also.** *Those within* give me enough to do without those outside also. **do not ye,** &c.—ought ye not to judge them that are within? *God* shall judge them that are without. By your judging them within, as I do, you will save them from His condemning judgment. **13. God judgeth.**—*g,* Vulgate, read 'will judge.' God is the Judge of the heathen, not we (Rom. ii. 12-16). St. Paul prepares the way for the censure of their going to law with saints before heathen tribunals, instead of judging such cases themselves (ch. vi. 1-8). **Therefore.** So א. But A B C Δ G *fg,* Vulgate, omit it. **put away . . . that wicked**—sentence of excommunication, from Deut. xxiv. 7.

CHAP. VI. 1-11.—LITIGATION OF CHRISTIANS IN HEATHEN COURTS CENSURED—ITS EXISTENCE BETRAYS A WRONG SPIRIT—BETTER TO BEAR WRONG NOW; HEREAFTER THE DOERS OF WRONG SHALL BE SHUT OUT OF HEAVEN. **1. Dare**—implying treason against Christian brotherhood. **before the unjust.** Gentile judges are so termed by an epithet appropriate to the subject, which concerns *justice.* Though all Gentiles are not towards men *unjust,* yet in the highest view of justice which has regard to God, the Supreme Judge, they are so: Christians, regarding God as the only Fountain of justice, should not expect justice from them. **before the saints.** The Jews abroad were permitted to refer disputes to Jewish *arbitrators.* So the Christians were allowed to have Christian arbitrators. The bishops had jurisdiction in civil cases: criminal cases went to ordinary tribunals (*Eusebius,* 'Vit. Constant.' iv. 27; 'Rescript of Arcadius and Honorius, Cod. Justin.,' I. 4, 7). **2. Do ye not know**—a truth universally recognized by Christians. Notwithstanding all your glorying in your "knowledge," ye are acting contrary to it (ch. i. 5; viii. 1). א A B C Δ G, Vulgate, *fg,* have 'Or' before 'know ye not'—*i. e.,* 'What! (expressing surprise) know ye not,' &c. **saints shall judge**—i. e., *rule,* including *judgment:* as assessors of Christ (Matt. xix. 28; Luke xxii. 29, 30; Isa. xi. 4: cf. Ps. xlix. 14; Dan. vii. 22, 27; Rev. ii. 26; iii. 21; xx. 4). The distinction between the saints who *rule* and the world which is ruled is the same as between the elected (Matt. xx. 23) twelve apostles, who sit on thrones judging, and Israel's twelve tribes, judged by them. To *reign,* and to be *saved,* are not necessarily synonymous. As Jehovah employed angels to ordain the law when on Sinai He

3 are ye unworthy to judge the smallest matters? Know ye not that we shall ^bjudge angels? how much more things that pertain to this life!
4 If then ye have judgments of things pertaining to this life, set them to
5 judge who are least esteemed in the church. I speak to your shame. Is it so, that there is not a wise man among you? no, not one that shall be
6 able to judge between his brethren? But brother goeth to law with
7 brother, and that before the unbelievers. Now therefore there is utterly a fault among you, because ye go to law one with another. ^cWhy do ye not rather take wrong? why do ye not rather *suffer yourselves* to be
8 defrauded? Nay, ye do wrong, and defraud, and that ^d*your* brethren.
9 Know ye not that ^ethe unrighteous shall not inherit the kingdom of God?

Be not deceived: neither fornicators, nor idolaters, nor adulterers, nor
10 effeminate, nor abusers of themselves with mankind, nor thieves, nor covetous, nor drunkards, nor revilers, nor extortioners, shall inherit the
11 kingdom of God. And such were some of you; ^fbut ye are washed, but ye are sanctified, but ye are justified in the name of the Lord Jesus, and by the Spirit of our God.

A. D 59.
b Matt. 25.41.
2 Pet. 2, 4.
Jude 6.
c Pro. 20. 22.
Matt. 5. 39, 41.
Luke 6. 29.
Rom. 12.17.
1 Thes. 5.15.
1 Pet. 2. 19, 23.
1 Pet. 3. 9.
d 1 Thes. 4. 6.
e Ex. 23. 1.
Isa. 3. 11.
Zech. 5. 3.
Acts 24. 25.
1 Tim. 1. 9.
f John 13.10.
Acts 22. 16.
Eph. 5. 26.
Heb. 10. 22.
1 Pet. 3. 21.

established His throne in Israel, so at His coming the saints with transfigured bodies shall administer the kingdom for and under Him. The nations of the earth and Israel, the foremost in the flesh, shall be the *subjects* of the Lord and His saints. The mistake of the Chiliasts was, they restricted the kingdom to the terrestrial part. Besides this earthly glory, there shall be the heavenly glory of the saints reigning above, and holding such intercourse with mortals as Christ, Moses, and Elias, in glory, had with Peter, James, and John, in the flesh, at the transfiguration (2 Tim. 2, 12; 2 Pet. i. 16, 18). Here the "world" includes *both* those to be condemned with the bad angels (ch. xi. 32), and those to be brought into obedience to Christ ruling with His saints. Cf. Matt. xxv. 32, 40, "all nations," "these my brethren," on the thrones with Him. **judged by** [*ἐν*] **you**—*lit.*, 'IN' your persons as the judges. So the Greek 'in' means *by means of, in the person of* (English version, "by"; Acts xvii. 31, "He will judge the world BY that man whom He hath ordained." **smallest matters**—the weightiest earthly question is infinitely *small* compared with those to be decided on the judgment day. **3. judge angels.** We who are now "a spectacle to angels" shall then, *by Christ in us*, "judge (bad) angels." What Christ is and does, the Church is and does (2 Pet. i. 4; 1 John iv. 17, end). The saints shall join in pronouncing the sentence of the Judge (Jude 6; Rev. xx. 4). Believers shall, as administrators of the kingdom under Jesus, put down all rule hostile to God. **4. judgments**—i. e., *cases for judgment.* **least esteemed**—lit., *those of no esteem.* Any, however low in the church, rather than the heathen. Earthly questions, being secondary in the eyes of Christians, are delegated to those in a secondary position. **5. your shame.** He checks their *puffed-up* spirit (ch. v. 2). To shame you out of your present unworthy course, I have said (*v.* 4), 'Set the least esteemed to judge.' **Is it so?**—Are you so helpless that, &c.? **not a wise man**—though ye admire "wisdom" so much (ch. i. 22). The title 'Cacham,' or *wise man*, was applied to each Rabbi in Jewish councils. **no, not one**—not even one, amidst so many reputed for wisdom (ch. iii. 18). **shall be able**—when applied to. **brethren**—lit., *brother*; i. e., judge between brother and brother. Such a wise person as had the gift of church government. **6. But**—emphatically answering *v.* 5. Translate, 'Nay,' &c. **7. utterly a fault**

[*ἥττημα*]—lit., *a shortcoming* (not so strong as *sin*). Your going to law at all is a falling short of your high privileges: your doing so *before unbelievers* aggravates it. **rather take wrong** (Prov. xx. 22; Matt. v. 39, 40). **8. ye**—emphatic. *Ye*, whom your Lord commanded to return good for evil, *on the contrary*, "do wrong (by taking) and defraud" (by retaining what is intrusted to you). Contrast the Church's first love (Acts iv. 32). **9. unrighteous.** Translate, 'doers of wrong:' referring to *v.* 8 (Gal. v. 21). **kingdom of God**—which is a kingdom of *righteousness* (Rom. xiv. 17).

fornicators—alluding to ch. v.; also below, *v.* 13-18. **effeminate** — self-polluters, of unnatural lusts. **11. ye are washed**—the Greek middle voice, 'ye have had yourselves washed.' This implies admission to the *benefits of salvation* generally; of which the parts are (1.) *Sanctification,* the setting apart from the world, and numbering among the "saints" (Rom. i. 7: so ch. vii. 14; John xvii. 19). In 1 Pet. i. 2 it means the *setting apart* of one as *consecrated by the Spirit in the eternal purpose of God.* (2.) *Justification* from condemnation, through the righteousness of God in Christ by faith (Rom. i. 17). The order, *sanctification* before *justification,* shows that *consecration* is here meant, not *progressive* sanctification. "Washed" precedes both, and refers to the putting away of sins in repentance, of which water baptism is the sacramental seal (Acts xxii. 16). The Spirit, as the seed of new life, is the agent of the being "sanctified," or consecrated to God (John iii. 5; Eph. v. 26; Titus iii. 5; Heb. x. 22). St. Paul, in charity and faith in God's promises, presumes that baptism realizes its design, and that those outwardly baptized inwardly enter into communion with Christ (Gal. iii. 27). He presents the grand ideal which those alone realize in whom the inward and the outward baptism coalesce. At the same time, he recognizes that this, in many cases, does not hold good (*v.* 8-10), leaving it to God to decide who are really "washed." He warns all that, being "washed," they return not to their *filth;* that being "sanctified," they *profane* not themselves again; that being "justified," they incur no fresh *guilt.* **in the name of . . . Jesus, and by the Spirit**—Greek, 'IN the Spirit'; *i. e.*, by His *in*-dwelling. Both clauses belong to the three—"washed, sanctified, justified." **our God**—"our" reminds them that amidst all his reproofs God is still the common God of himself and them.

12   All *ᵍ* things are lawful unto me, but all things are not ¹ expedient: all things are lawful for me, but I will not be brought under the power of
13   any.   Meats for the belly, and the belly for meats: but God shall destroy both it and them.   Now the body *is* not for fornication, but *ʰ* for
14   the Lord, and *ⁱ* the Lord for the body.   And *ʲ* God hath both raised up
15   the Lord, and will also raise up us *ᵏ* by his own power.   Know ye not that your bodies are the members of Christ? shall I then take the members of Christ, and make *them* the members of an harlot?   God forbid.
16   What! know ye not that he which is joined to an harlot is one body?
17   *ˡ* for two, saith he, shall be one flesh.   But *ᵐ* he that is joined unto the
18   Lord is one spirit.   Flee fornication.   Every sin that a man doeth is without the body: but he that committeth fornication sinneth *ⁿ* against
19   his own body.   What! *ᵒ* know ye not that your body is the temple of the

A. D. 59.	
ᵍ ch. 10. 23.	
³ Or,	
profitable.	
ʰ Rom 7. 4.	
1 Thess. 4. 3.	
ⁱ Eph. 5. 23.	
ʲ Rom. 6. 5.	
ᵏ Eph. 1. 19.	
ˡ Gen. 2. 24.	
Matt 19. 5.	
ᵐ John 17. 21.	
Eph. 4. 40.	
Eph. 5. 30.	
ⁿ Rom. 1. 24.	
1 Thess. 4. 4.	
ᵒ 2 Cor. 6. 16.	

12-20.—Refutation of the Antinomian Plea that Fornication is Lawful because Meats are so.
12. All things are lawful unto me. St. Paul's own words on some former occasion (cf. ch. x. 23) were made a pretext for excusing the eating of meats offered to idols, and so of what was generally connected with it (Acts xv. 29), "fornication" (perhaps in the letter of the Corinthians to St. Paul, ch. vii. 1). St. Paul had referred only to things *indifferent*, and things within the sphere of Christian *liberty* (John viii. 34-36). They wished to treat fornication as such, as though the existence of bodily appetites proved the *lawfulness* of their gratification. **me.** St. Paul makes himself a sample of Christians in general. **but I—** whatever others do. **lawful . . . brought under the power.** There is a play on similar sounds [ἔξεστιν —ἐξουσιασθήσομαι]. All things are *in my power*, but I will not be *brought under the power of any* (of the "all things"). He who commits "fornication" forfeits his legitimate power, and is "brought under the power" of an harlot) (*v.* 15: cf. ch. vii. 4). The "power" ought to be in the hands of the *believer*, not in the *things which he uses*, else his liberty is forfeited—he ceases to be his own master (John viii. 34-36; Gal. v. 13; 1 Pet. ii. 16; 2 Pet. ii. 19). Unlawful things ruin thousands; "lawful" things (unlawfully used), ten thousands. **13.** The argument from the indifference of meats (ch. viii. 8; Rom. xiv. 14, 17: cf. Mark vii. 18; Col. ii. 20-22) to that of fornication does not hold good. Meats doubtless are indifferent (with, however, the qualification discussed, ch. x. 23, &c.), since both they and the "belly," for which they are created, are to be "destroyed" at Christ's coming to change believers' natural bodies into spiritual bodies (ch. xv. 44, 52). But 'the body is not (created) for fornication, but for the Lord, and the Lord for the body' (as its Redeemer, who hath Himself assumed and united Himself to the body): "And God hath raised up the Lord, and will also raise up us" (*i.e.*, our bodies) to eternal existence; therefore the "body" is not, like the "belly," after having served a temporary use, to be destroyed. Now "he that committeth fornication sinneth against his own body" (*v.* 18). Therefore fornication is not indifferent. Here is the germ of the three subjects handled in subsequent sections: (1.) The relation between the sexes. (2.) The question of meats offered to idols. (3.) The resurrection of the body. A real essence underlies the superficial phenomena of the present organization of the body: this germ, when all the particles are scattered, involves the resurrection of the body incorruptible. **14.** (Rom. viii. 11.) **raised up**—rather, "raised" (a simple verb), to distinguish it from

"will also raise *up* us" [ἐξεγερεῖ, א C, Vulgate. But A Δ *f*, ἐξεγείρει, *raiseth* up], a compound. Believers shall be raised up *out of* the rest of the dead (*note*, Phil. iii. 11); the first resurrection (Rev. xx. 5). **us.** Here he speaks of his being possibly in the grave when Christ comes; elsewhere, of his being possibly alive (1 Thess. iv. 17). In either event, the Lord's coming, rather than death, is the Christian's expectation (Rom. viii. 19). **15.** Resuming *v.* 13, "the body is . . . for the Lord" (ch. xii. 27; Eph. iv. 12, 15, 16; v. 30, 31). **shall I then take?** (Hebrew, *laquach*)—*deliberately* alienating them from Christ. For they cannot be at once "the members of an harlot" and "of Christ." Moral and spiritual ruin is caused by such sins, which human wisdom held to be actions as blameless as eating. **16.** Fornicators are "members of an harlot" (*v.* 15). **joined**—by carnal intercourse; lit., cemented to [κολλώμενος] (Num. xxv. 3). **one body**—with her. **saith he**—God speaking by Adam (Gen. ii. 24; Matt. xix. 5). **two . . . shall be one flesh.** Eve was taken out of Adam, "flesh of his flesh," to be rejoined to him as "one flesh." **17. one spirit**—with Him . In union with a harlot, the fornicator becomes one "body" with her, not one "spirit;" for the spirit—the normal organ of the Holy Spirit in man—is in the carnal so overlaid with what is sensual that it is in abeyance. The believer not only has his body sanctified by union with Christ's body, but also becomes "one spirit" with Him (John xv. 1-7; xvii. 21; 2 Pet. i. 4: cf. John iii. 6). **18. Flee.** Our safety in such temptations is *flight* (Gen. xxxix. 12; Job xxxi. 1). **Every sin that**—Greek, ' *Whatsoever* a man doeth.' Every *other* sin—even gluttony, drunkenness, and self-murder—are comparatively *external to* the body (Mark vii. 18; Prov. vi. 30-32). This sinner injures, but does not alienate the body: he rather sins against the body's temporary organization, and against the soul, than against the body's permanent essence, designed "for the Lord." "But" the fornicator alienates that body which is the Lord's, and makes it one with a harlot's body, and so "sinneth (commits sacrilege, *v.* 19) against his own body." **19.** Proof of *v.* 18. **your body**—not 'bodies.' As in ch. iii. 17 he represented the whole company of believers, the Church, as "the temple of God" the Spirit; so here, the *body* of each individual is viewed as the "temple of the Holy Ghost." So John xiv. 23. Still, though many, the several members form one temple, the whole collectively being that which each is in miniature individually. As the Jews had one temple only, so in the full sense all Christian churches and individual believers form one temple only. "Your (*plural*) body" is distinguished here from "his own (*particular, individual*) [ἴδιον] body" (*v.* 18). In sinning against "his own

Holy Ghost *which is* in you, which ye have of God, and ^p ye are not your
20 own? For ^q ye are bought with a price: therefore ^r glorify God in your
body, and in your spirit, which are God's.

7 NOW concerning the things whereof ye wrote unto me: *It is* good for
2 a man not to touch a woman. Nevertheless, ^a *to avoid* fornication, let
every man have his own wife, and let every woman have her own hus-
3 band. Let ^b the husband render unto the wife due benevolence: and
4 likewise also the wife unto the husband. The wife hath not power of
her own body, but the husband: and likewise also the husband hath not
5 power of his own body, but the wife. Defraud ye not one the other, except
it be with consent for a time, that ye may give yourselves to fasting and
prayer; and come together again, that ^c Satan tempt you not for your
6 incontinency. But I speak this by permission, ^d *and* not of command-
7 ment. For ^e I would that all men were even as ^f I myself. But ^g every
man hath his proper gift of God, one after this manner, and another after
8 that. I say therefore to the unmarried and widows, ^h it is good for them
9 if they abide even as I. But ⁱ if they cannot contain, let them marry: for
10 it is better to marry than to burn. And unto the married I command,

A. D. 59.

^p Rom. 14. 7.
2 Cor. 5. 15.
Tit. 2. 14.
^q Gal. 3. 13.
Heb. 9. 12.
1 Pet. 1. 18.
Rev. 5. 9.
^r Matt. 5. 16.
2 Cor. 7. 1.

CHAP. 7.
^a Pro. 5. 19.
^b Ex. 21. 10.
1 Pet. 3. 7.
^c 1 Thes. 3. 5.
^d 2 Cor. 8. 8.
2 Cor. 11.17.
^e Acts 26. 29.
^f ch. 9. 5.
^g Matt. 19.12.
ch 12. 11.
^h ver. 26.
ⁱ 1 Tim. 5.14.

---

body," the fornicator sins against "your body,"
that of "Christ," whose 'members your bodies'
are (*v.* 15). Fornication is a sacrilegious desecration
of God's temple to profane uses. The unseen, but
more efficient, Spirit of God in the spiritual temple
now takes the place of the visible Shekinah in the
material temple. The whole man is the temple,
the soul the inmost shrine, the understanding and
heart the holy place, the body the porch and exterior. Chastity is the guardian of the temple, to
prevent anything unclean entering which might
provoke the indwelling God to abandon it as defiled (*Tertullian*, ' De Cultu Fœminarum '). None
but God can claim a temple: here the Holy Ghost
is assigned one; therefore the Holy Ghost is God.
not your own (*v.* 18: cf. *v.* 20). We have no
right to alienate our body, which is the Lord's.
In ancient servitude the slave's person was wholly
his master's property, not his own. *Purchase* was
one way of acquiring a slave. Man has *sold himself* to sin (1 Ki. xxi. 20; Rom. vii. 14). Christ
buys him to Himself, to serve Him (Rom. vi.
16-22). **20. bought with a** [*great*] **price** — therefore Christ's blood is strictly a ransom paid to
God's justice, by the love of God in Christ, for our
redemption (Matt. xx. 28; Acts xx. 28; Gal. iii.
13; Heb. ix. 12; 1 Pet. i. 18, 19; 2 Pet. ii. 1; Rev.
v. 9). Whilst He thus took off our obligation to
punishment, He laid upon us an obligation to
obedience (ch. vii. 22, 23; Rom. xiv. 9). If we
accept Him as our Prophet to reveal God to us,
and our Priest to atone for us, we must also accept
Him as our King to rule over us as wholly His
(Isa. xxvi. 13). **in your body**—as "in" a temple
(cf. John xiii. 32; Rom. xii. 1; Phil. i. 20). **and
in your spirit** [so ℵ], **which are God's**—not in
A B C Δ G *fg*, Vulgate. Not needed, as the context refers *mainly* to the "body" (*vv.* 16, 18, 19).
The "spirit" is *incidentally* mentioned, *v.* 17, which
gave rise to the interpolation.

CHAP. VII. 1-40.—REPLY TO THEIR ENQUIRIES
AS TO MARRIAGE—THE GENERAL PRINCIPLE IN
ALL THINGS IS, ABIDE IN YOUR STATION, FOR THE
TIME IS SHORT.
1. The Corinthians in their letter had asked
questions tending to disparage marriage, and implied that it was better to break off marriage with
an unbeliever. **good**—i. e., *expedient*, because of
"the present distress;" *i. e.*, the unsettled state of
the world, and the likelihood of persecutions tearing asunder marriage-ties. Heb. xiii. 4 opposes

Romish notions of superior *sanctity* in celibacy.
Another reason why celibacy may be a matter of
Christian *expediency* is (*vv.* 34, 35), 'that ye may
attend upon the Lord without distraction.' But
these are exceptional cases, and in exceptional
times. **2.** The general rule—**to avoid fornication**—
lit., '*on account of the fornications*' [διὰ τὰσ πορ-
νείασ] to which, as prevalent at Corinth, and not
counted sins among the heathen, the unmarried
might be tempted. The *plural* marks irregular
lusts, as contrasted with the *unity* of marriage.
let every man have—a positive command to the
great majority of the world who have not con-
tinency (*v.* 5). The dignity of marriage (Eph. v.
25-32) lies in the fact that it signifies the mystical
union between Christ and the Church. **3, 4.** *Duty
of cohabitation between the married.* **due benevolence.** ℵ A B C Δ G *fg*, Vulgate, read simply [ὀφει-
λήν], 'Let due'—*i. e.*, conjugal cohabitation, *due*
by marriage **contract** (cf. *v.* 4). **4.** A paradox.
She *hath not power over* her body; yet it is *her
own*. The *oneness of body* in which marriage places
husband and wife explains this. One complements the other. Neither without the other realizes the perfect ideal of man. **5. Defraud ye not**
—viz., of the conjugal "due" (*v.* 3: cf LXX.,
Exod. xxi. 10). **give yourselves**—lit., *be at leisure
for;* be *free from interruptions for;* on some *special
'season'* [καιρόν]; as before Easter (Exod. xix. 15;
Joel ii. 16; Zech. vii. 3). **fasting and prayer.**
A B Δ G *fg*, Vulgate, omit "fasting and;" ℵ C support the words. Interpolated by ascetics. **come
together.** ℵ A B C Δ G read 'be together,' viz., in the
regular married state. **Satan**—who thrusts in his
temptations to unholy thoughts amidst the holiest
exercises. **for your incontinency**—*because of* your
inability to "contain" (*v.* 9) natural propensities,
which Satan takes advantage of. **6. by permission** ... **not of commandment**—not, *by God's
permission to me to say it;* but, 'by way of permission to you, not as a commandment;' not what you
must, but what you *may* do. "This" refers to the
directions, *vv.* 2-5. **7. even as I**—having the gift
of continence (Matt. xix. 11, 12). This wish does
not hold good absolutely, else the extension of
mankind and of the Church would cease; but
relatively to "the present distress" (*v.* 26). **8. to
the unmarried**—in general, of both sexes (*vv.* 10,
11). **and widows**—in particular. **even as I**—unmarried (ch. ix. 5). **9. if they cannot contain**
(*v.* 5). **burn**—with the flame of lust, which con-

11 *yet* not I, but the Lord, ⱼ Let not the wife depart from *her* husband: but
and if she depart, let her remain unmarried, or be reconciled to *her* husband: and let not the husband put away *his* wife.

12 But to the rest speak I, not the Lord: If any brother hath a wife that
believeth not, and she be pleased to dwell with him, let him not put her

13 away. And the woman which hath an husband that believeth not, and

14 if he be pleased to dwell with her, let her not leave him. For the unbelieving husband is sanctified by the wife, and the unbelieving wife is
sanctified by the husband: else ᵏ were your children unclean; but now

15 are they holy. But if the unbelieving depart, let him depart. A brother
or a sister is not under bondage in such *cases:* but God hath called us

ⱼ Jer. 3. 20.
Mal. 2. 14,
16.
Matt. 5. 32.
Matt. 19. 6-
9.
Mark 10.11,
12.
Luke 16.18.
ᵏ Mal. 2. 15,
16.
Ezra 6. 2.
Isa. 52 1.
Acts 10. 27.
Rom. 11.16.

sumes the whole inner man. The dew of God's grace must stifle the flame, or it will thrust men into hell-fire. **10. not I, but the Lord**—(cf. *vv.* 12, 25, 40.) Ordinarily he writes on *inspired apostolic authority* (ch. xiv. 37); here on the *direct* authority of the *Lord Himself* (Mark x. 11, 12). In both cases the things written are inspired by the Spirit of God; but not all for all times, nor all on essentials. The wisdom of Scripture is shown no less in what they leave open questions, than in what they *positively* decide. **Let not the wife depart**—'separate herself,' or 'be separated from.' **11. But and if she depart**—'But if even she be separated.' If the sin of separation has been committed, whether owing to her or him, that of a new marriage is not to be added. **be reconciled**—by appeasing her husband's displeasure, and recovering his good will. **let not the husband put away his wife.** In Matt. v. 32 the only exception allowed is, 'saving for fornication,' which constitutes divorce itself.

12. to the rest (besides "the married," *v.* 10, where both husband and wife are believers)—the Corinthians had enquired about believers married to unbelievers. **not the Lord**—by any former direct command. **she be pleased** [συνευδοκεῖ]—'consents:' implying his wish firstly, with which hers *concurs.* So despised was Christianity that wives often left their husbands who embraced it. **13. the woman**—a believer. **let her not leave him.** אABCΔGƒ*g*,Vulgate, read 'her husband,' for "him." The Greek [ἀφιέτω] for "leave" is the same as *v.* 12, "put away." Translate, 'let her not *put away* her husband.' The wife had the power of divorce by Greek and Roman law. **14. sanctified.** Those connected with the people of God are *hallowed* thereby, so that the latter may retain the connection without impairing their own sanctity (cf. 1 Tim. iv. 5); nay, rather imparting to the former some of their own hallowed character, so, *through the believer's holy influence,* preparing the way for the unbeliever becoming **sanctified** inwardly by faith. Contrast legal uncleanness (Hagg. ii. 12, 13). Heathenism, brought face to face with Christianity, must succumb, not *vice versâ.* **by the wife, and the unbelieving wife is sanctified by**—rather, 'in . . . in;' in the person of; in virtue of the marriage-tie between them. **by the husband.** So C. But ABΔG אƒ*g*, read 'in the brother.' It is the fact of the husband being a 'brother'—i. e., *a Christian,* though the wife is not so, that sanctifies the union. **else were your children unclean**—i. e., *beyond the sanctified pale of God's people.* **but now** (as it is) **are they holy**—*within that pale:* relatively *hallowed,* in Providential destination, and by a pious parent's influence. The Jews regarded heathens as "unclean," and all of the elect nation as "holy"—i. e., partakers of the holy covenant. Children were included in it, as God made it not only with Abraham, but with his "seed after" him (Gen. xvii. 7). So the faith of one Christian

parent gives to the children a relationship to the Church, just as if both were Christians (cf. Rom. xi. 16). Timothy, the bearer of this epistle, is an instance (Acts xvi. 1; 2 Tim. i. 5). St. Paul appeals to the recognized principle, that the infants of heathen parents would not be admissible to Christian baptism, because there is no faith in the parents; but where one is a believer, the children are not aliens from, but admissible into, the Christian covenant: for the Church presumes that the believing parent will rear the child in Christianity. Lydia's and the gaoler's households were baptized along with the believing heads of the houses. The faith of the head was regarded as consecrating the family, so that its members, whether children or adults, if interposing no obstacle, were fit recipients of baptism (Acts xvi. 4). The covenant with Abraham was sealed in infants by a sacrament: why should not Christians also seal it in their children? (*Calvin,* 'Inst.,' b. iv. c. xvi. 6.) Infant baptism tacitly superseded infant circumcision, just as the Christian Lord's day superseded the Jewish Sabbath, without our having express command for, or record of, the transference. The setting aside of circumcision and of Sabbaths in the case of the Gentiles was indeed expressly commanded by the apostles; but the substitution of infant baptism and of the Lord's day was tacitly adopted, not expressly enacted. No explicit mention of it occurs till *Irenæus* (b. ii. c. 22) and *Justin Martyr* (2 'Apolog.'), in the second century; but no Christians disputed its propriety till 1500 years after Christ. Anabaptists would defer baptism till maturity, as the child cannot understand the nature of it. But a child may be heir of an estate, though incapable of using or comprehending its advantage: he is not hereafter to *acquire the title* to it: he will hereafter understand his claim, and be capable of employing his wealth: he will then, moreover, become responsible for the use he makes of it. Relative consecration does not dispense with personal regeneration. **15. if the unbelieving depart, let him depart.** Translate, 'separateth himself:' offended with her Christianity, and refusing to live with her unless she renounce it. **brother or a sister is not under bondage**—is not bound to renounce the faith for the sake of retaining her husband. (So Deut. xiii. 6; Matt. x. 35-37; Luke xiv. 26.) The believer has not the same obligation in a union with an unbeliever, as in one with a believer. In the former case he is not bound, if the unbeliever wish to separate, to force such a one to stay in continual discord; in the latter, nothing but "fornication" justifies separation. **but God hath called us to peace.** Our Christian calling tends to "peace" (Rom. xii. 18), not quarrelling—therefore the believer should not ordinarily depart from the unbelieving consort (*vv.* 12-14). Better still it would be not to enter such unequal alliances at all (*v.* 40; 2 Cor. vi. 14).

16 ¹to peace. For what knowest thou, O wife, whether thou shalt save *ᵗthy* husband? Or ²how knowest thou, O man, whether thou shalt

17 save *thy* wife? But as God hath distributed to every man, as the Lord hath called every one, so let him walk. And *ᵐ*so ordain I in all churches.

18 Is any man called being circumcised? let him not become uncircumcised. Is any called in uncircumcision? let *ⁿ*him not be circumcised.

19 Circumcision *°*is nothing, and uncircumcision is nothing, but *ᵖ*the keep-

20 ing of the commandments of God. Let *q*every man abide in the same

21 calling wherein he was called. Art *r*thou called *being* a servant? care

22 not for it: but if thou mayest be *ˢ*made free, use *it* rather. For he that is called in the Lord, *being* a servant, is the Lord's ³freeman: likewise

23 also he that is called, *being* free, is *ᵗ*Christ's servant. Ye *ᵘ*are bought

24 with a price; be not ye the servants of men. Brethren, let every man, wherein he is called, therein abide with God.

25 Now concerning virgins *ᵛ*I have no commandment of the Lord: yet I give my judgment, as one *ʷ*that hath obtained mercy of the Lord *ˣ*to be

A. D. 59.

1 in peace.
Rom. 12.18.
ᵗ 1 Pet. 3. 1.
2 what.
ᵐ 2 Cor. 11.23.
ⁿ Acts 15.
Gal. 5. 2.
° Gal. 6. 15.
Col. 3. 11.
ᵖ John 15.14.
1 John 2. 3.
q Eph. 4. 1.
r Gal. 3: 28.
³ Isa. 58. 6.
³ made free.
John 8. 36.
ᵗ Gal. 5. 13.
ᵘ Lev. 25. 42.
ᵛ 2 Cor. 8. 8.
ʷ 1 Tim. 1.16.
ˣ 1 Tim. 1.12.

16. By staying with thy unbelieving partner thou mayest save him or her. Enforcing "peace" with the unbelieving consort (*v.* 15, end). So Ruth the Moabitess became a convert to her husband's faith: Joseph and Moses probably gained over their wives. Conversely, the unbelieving husband may be won by the believing wife (1 Pet. iii. 1). *Alford* explains *v.* 15, 'If thy unbelieving consort wishes to depart, let him go, that thou mayest live "in peace:" for *thou canst not be sure of converting him*, so as to make it obligatory on thee at all costs to keep him against his will.' **save**—be the instrument of saving (Jas. v. 20). **17.** But—Greek [εἰ μή], '*If not.*' 'Only.' The "But" favours the former view. *But if* there be *no* hope of gaining over the unbeliever, still the general principle holds good, 'As *the Lord* hath allotted to each, as *God* hath called each, so let him walk' (so א A B C Δ G *f g*, Vulgate, transpose "Lord" and "God"); *i. e.*, let him walk in the calling allotted to him. The heavenly calling does not set aside our earthly callings, as the marriage relation. Christianity can maintain itself in all outward relations, without requiring us to forsake them. **so ordain I in all churches**—ye also therefore should obey.
18. not become uncircumcised — by surgical operation (1 Macc. i. 15). Such were called *meshukim*; *recutiti.* Some, in excess of anti-Jewish feeling, might be tempted to this. **let him not be circumcised** — as the Judaizing Christians would have him (Acts xv; Gal. v. 2).
19. Circumcision is nothing . . . but the keeping of the commandments of God—viz., *is all in all.* Gal. v. 6 defines the Gospel commandment, "faith which worketh by love;" and Gal. vi. 15, "a new creature" (cf. 1 John iii. 26). Circumcision was a commandment of God; but not for ever, as "love." **20. the same calling**—*i. e.*, the *condition* from which he is called—a Jew, a Greek, a slave, or a freeman. **21. care not for it**—let it not be a trouble to thee that thou art a slave. **use it rather.** Either, (1.) Continue rather in thy state as a servant (*v.* 20; Gal. iii. 28; 1 Tim. vi. 2). The Greek, 'But if *even* thou mayest be made free, rather *use* it,' and the context (*vv.* 20, 22), are cited for this view. What is advised thus is not slavery, but contentment under one's existing condition (*v.* 24), though an undesirable one, since in union with Christ all outward disparities are compensated (*v.* 22). Be not unduly impatient to cast off '*even*' thy condition as a slave *by unlawful means* (1 Pet. ii. 13-18), as Onesimus did by fleeing (Phile. 10-18). The precept (*v.* 23), 'Become

not [γίνεσθε] the servants of men,' implies that slavery is abnormal (cf. Lev. xxv. 42). "Menstealers," or slave-dealers, are classed in 1 Tim. i. 10 with "murderers." Or, (2.) 'If called, being a slave, to Christianity, be content; but yet, if *also* (besides *spiritual* freedom) thou canst be free (*bodily;* a still *additional* good, which if thou canst not attain, be satisfied without; but which, if offered, despise not), *use the opportunity of becoming free, rather than* remain a slave.' This view more accords with the Gospel, and is fully justified by the Greek; and (*v.* 23) "use *it*" refers plainly to the words just before, "*be made free*" (2 Pet. ii. 19). **22. For**—being spiritually free, one ought to be só bodily also. **the Lord's freeman** (Phile. 16)—rather, "freedman," spiritually *made free* by the Lord: from sin, John viii. 36; from the law, Rom. viii. 2; from "circumcision," *v.* 19; Gal. v. 1. **Christ's servant** (ch. ix. 21)—deprived of the false liberty of self-indulgence. Love makes Christ's service perfect freedom (Matt. xi. 29, 30; Gal. v. 13; 1 Pet. ii. 16). **23.** be (become) **not ye.** St. Paul changes from "thou" (*v.* 21) to "ye." YE ALL are "bought" with the costly blood of Christ to be free men (ch. vi. 20)—'become not servants to men,' either externally or spiritually. Christian freemen should not be servile adherents to party leaders (ch. iii. 21, 22; Matt. xxiii. 8-10; 2 Cor. xi. 20). The external and internal conditions, as far as attainable, should correspond, and the former be subservient to the latter (cf. *v.* 21, 32-35). **24.** abide with God—chiefly careful of his standing towards God, rather than towards men. This clause, "with God," limits the precept (*v.* 20). A man may cease to "abide in his calling," and yet not violate the precept here. If a man's calling be not favourable to his "abiding with God" (in holy fellowship with Him), he may use lawful means to change it (cf. *Note, v.* 21).
25. Now (Greek, 'But') . . . **no commandment of the Lord: yet . . . my judgment**—I have no authoritative *commandment* from the Lord as to their abiding in their state (*v.* 20), but I give my *opinion* (cf. *v.* 40; ch. xiv. 37; 1 Thess. iv. 15). The Lord inspires me to give you only a *recommendation*, which you are free to adopt or reject (*vv.* 10, 11). It was a positive command, for the Lord had already made known His will (Mal. ii. 14, 15; Matt. v. 31, 32). In *v.* 12 the Old Testament commandment of God to put away strange wives (Ezra x. 3), St. Paul by the Spirit revokes. **mercy of the Lord** (1 Tim. i. 13). He attributes his gifts (in-

26 faithful. I suppose therefore that this is good for the present [4] distress;
27 *I say,*that *it is* good for a man so to be. Art thou bound unto a wife? seek not to be loosed. Art thou loosed from a wife? seek not a wife.
28 But and if thou marry, thou hast not sinned; and if a virgin marry, she hath not sinned. Nevertheless such shall have trouble in the flesh: but I spare you.
29 But [y]this I say, brethren, the time *is* short: it remaineth, that both
30 they that have wives be as though they had none; and they that weep, as though they wept not; and they that rejoice, as though they rejoiced
31 not; and they that buy, as though they possessed not; and they that use this world, as [z]not abusing *it:* for [a]the fashion of this world passeth
32 away. But I would have you without carefulness. [b]He that is unmarried careth for the things [5]that belong to the Lord, how he may please
33 the Lord: but he that is married careth for the things that are of the
34 world, how he may please *his* wife. There is difference *also* between a wife and a virgin. [c]The unmarried woman careth for the things of the Lord, that she may be holy both in body and in spirit: but she that is married careth for the things of the world, how she may please *her* hus-
35 band. And this I speak for your own profit; not that I may cast a snare upon you, but for that which is comely, and that ye may attend upon the Lord without distraction.

A. D. 59.

4 Or, necesssity.
y Job 14. 1, 2.
Ps. 39. 4, 7.
Ps. 90. 5,
10.
Ps. 103. 15,
16.
Eccl. 6. 12.
Eccl. 9. 10.
Rom. 13.11,
12.
1 Pet 4. 7.
2 Pet. 3. 8,
9.
1 John.2.17.
z ch. 9. 18.
a Ps. 39. 6.
Jas. 4. 14.
1 John 2.
17.
b 1 Tim. 5. 5.
5 of the Lord.
c Luke 10. 40.

cluding inspiration) to God's grace alone. **faithful** —*trustworthy* in dispensing the inspired directions received by me from the Lord. **26. I suppose**— 'I consider.' **this**—viz., "for a man so to be," in the same state in which he is (*v.* 27). **for** [διά]— by reason of. **the present distress**—to which believers were then beginning to be subjected, making the married state less desirable, and which should prevail throughout the world before the destruction of Jerusalem, according to Christ's prophecy (Matt. xxiv. 8-21: cf. Acts xi. 28). **27.** Illustrating *v.* 26. Neither the married (those "bound to a wife") nor the unmarried (those "loosed from a wife") are to "seek" a change of state (cf. *v.* 20, 24). **28. trouble in the flesh**—in their outward state, by reason of the present distress; not *sin,* which is the trouble of the *spirit,* **but I spare you.** The emphasis (Greek) is on "I." *My* motive in advising you so is, to "spare *you*" such trouble. Augustine explains, 'I spare you further details of the inconveniences' of matrimony, lest the incontinent may at the peril of lust be deterred from it. The "But" then follows naturally in *v.* 29. My motive in the concession (*v.* 28) is, because 'I have regard to your infirmity:' "But" I qualify this concession by saying, "the time," &c.

29 this I say—a summing up the practical inference from what precedes (ch. xv. 50). **the time**— the *season* [ὁ καιρός] of this present dispensation up to the Lord's coming (Rom. xiii. 11). He uses the Greek which the Lord used in Luke xxi. 8; Mark xiii. 33. **short**—lit., *contracted.* **it remaineth.** A B Δ א read 'the season is shortened in order that *henceforth* both they,' &c.—*i. e.*, the effect which the shortening of the time ought to have is, 'that for the remaining time both they,' &c. G, Cyprian, and Vulgate support the English version. **as though they had none**—in real or permanent possession; not making idols of them. **30. they that weep . . . wept not** (cf. 2 Cor. vi. 10)—not letting grief gain uncontrolled mastery. **they that buy . . . possessed not**—(cf. Isa. xxiv. 1, 2.) Christ specifies as the condemning sin of Sodom not merely open profligacy, but that "they bought, they sold," &c., as men whose all was in this world (Luke xvii. 28). "Possessed" [κατέ-

χοντες] implies a *holding fast of a possession:* this the Christian will not do, for his "enduring substance" is elsewhere (Heb. x. 34). **31. not abusing it**—by *overmuch using* of it. "Abusing" here is not so much *perverting,* as *using it to the full,* as our chief portion (cf. Luke x. 40-42). As the planets, turning on their own axis, yet revolve round the sun, so, whilst we act in our worldly sphere, God is to be the centre of our desires. **fashion**—the present fleeting *form* [σχῆμα], not the essence, perisheth (Rev. xx. and xxi.: cf. Ps. xxxix. 6, "vain show;" Ps. lxxiii. 20, "a dream;" Jas. iv. 14, "a vapour"). **passeth away**—not merely *shall pass,* but *is* now actually *passing away.* The image is from a *shifting* scene in a play on the stage (1 John ii. 17). St. Paul inculcates not so much outward denial of earthly things, as the inward spirit, whereby the married and the rich, as well as the unmarried and the poor, would be ready to sacrifice all for Christ. **32. But.** Connect with *v.* 31. 'The world's fashion passeth,' and so entails anxious care on its votaries; "*but* I would have you," &c. **without carefulness**—not merely 'without trouble,' but without 'distracting cares' [ἀμερίμνους]. **careth** —if he uses aright the advantages of his condition. **33. married careth for . . . world.** When marriage ties are made paramount, instead of subordinate to His service (Luke xvii. 27), not when marriage is what God designed (Heb. xiii. 4). **34. difference also**—not merely the unmarried and the married *man* differ in respective duties, but *also* the *wife* and the *virgin.* A woman undergoes a greater change than a man in contracting marriage. So G *f g.* But א A B Δ read [καὶ μεμέρισ-ται] (*vv.* 33, 34) 'He that is married careth for the world, AND is divided (in heart, Matt. vi. 24). Also the woman that is unmarried, and the virgin that is unmarried, careth for the things of the Lord.' **35. for your own profit**—not to display *my* apostolic authority. **not . . . cast a snare upon you**—upon your conscience. Not that, by hard injunctions, I may entangle you with scruples, where there is no sin. **comely**—*becoming* under present circumstances. **attend upon** [εὐπά-ρεδρον]—*lit.,* 'assiduously wait on:' *sitting down* to the duty (cf. Luke x. 39, Mary; Luke ii. 37, Anna;

36 But if any man think that he behaveth himself uncomely toward his virgin, if she pass the flower of *her* age, and need so require, let him do
87 what he will, he sinneth not: let them marry. Nevertheless he that standeth stedfast in his heart, having no necessity, but hath power over his own will, and hath so decreed in his heart that he will keep his virgin,
38 doeth well. So *d* then he that giveth *her* in marriage doeth well; but he that giveth *her* not in marriage doeth better.
39 The *e* wife is bound by the law as long as her husband liveth; but if her husband be dead, she is at liberty to be married to whom she will;
40 *f* only in the Lord. But she is happier if she so abide, after my judgment: and I think also that I have the Spirit of God.

8 NOW *a* as touching things offered unto idols, we know that we all
2 have *b* knowledge. Knowledge puffeth up, but charity edifieth. And *c* if any man think that he knoweth any thing, he knoweth nothing yet as
3 he ought to know. But if any man love God, *d* the same is known of
4 him. As concerning therefore the eating of those things that are offered in sacrifice unto idols, we know that *e* an idol *is* nothing in the world,
5 *f* and that *there is* none other God but one. For though there be that *g* are called gods, whether in heaven or in earth, (as there be gods many,

A. D. 59.	
d Heb. 13. 4.	
e Rom. 7. 2.	
f 2 Cor. 6. 14.	
Deut. 17. 3.	
CHAP. 8.	
a Acts 15. 20.	
b Rom. 14. 14.	
c Gal. 6. 3.	
1 Tim. 6. 4.	
d Ex. 33. 12.	
Nah. 1. 7.	
Matt. 7. 21.	
Gal. 4. 9.	
2 Tim. 2. 19.	
e Isa. 41. 24.	
f Deut. 4. 39.	
Deut. 6. 4.	
Deut 32. 9	
Isa. 37. 16.	
Isa. 44. 8.	
Isa. 45. 5.	
Jer. 10. 10.	
g John 10. 34.	

1 Tim. v. 5). **distraction**—the same [Greek, ἀ-περισπάστως] as "cumbered" (Luke x. 40, Martha). **36. behaveth ... uncomely**—is *not* treating his daughter *becomingly*, in leaving her unmarried beyond the flower of her age, and debarring her from lawful gratification as a marriageable woman. **need so require**—if regard to the feelings and welfare of his daughter require it. Opposed to "having no necessity" (*v.* 37). **let them marry**—the daughter and her suitor. **37. stedfast**—not to be turned from his purpose by obloquy. **having no necessity**—arising from the natural inclinations of the daughter. **power over his own will** —when, owing to his daughter's will not opposing him, he has power to effect his will. **decreed** —determined. **38. her.** א A B Δ *f*, Vulgate, have 'his own virgin daughter.' **but.** A B Δ G א *f g*, Vulgate, have 'and.'

39. bound by the law. So א G C. But A B Δ *f* omit "by the law." **only in the Lord**—let her marry *only a Christian* (2 Cor. vi. 14), and *in the fear of the Lord.* **40. happier** (*vv.* 1, 28, 34, 35). **I think also**—'I also;' just as you Corinthians *think* much of your opinions, *so I also give* mine by inspiration: so in *v.* 25. *Think* does not imply doubt, but often well-grounded assurance (John v. 39).

CHAP. VIII. 1-13.—ON PARTAKING OF MEATS OFFERED TO IDOLS.

1. Though to those knowing that an idol has no existence, the question of eating idol-meats (referred to in the letter of the Corinthians, cf. ch. vii. 1) might seem unimportant, it is not so with some; and their infirmities should be respected. The portions of victims not offered on the altars belonged partly to the priests, partly to the offerers; and were eaten at feasts in the temples and in private houses, and were often sold in the markets; so that Christians were constantly tempted to receive them, which was forbidden (Num. xxv. 2; Ps. cvi. 28). The apostles forbade it in their decree (Acts xv., and xxi, xxv.); but St. Paul here rests his precepts rather on his own independent apostolic authority. **we know that we all have knowledge.** The Corinthians had referred to their "knowledge" (viz., of the indifference of meats, as in themselves having no sanctity or pollution). He replies, 'We are aware that we all have (speaking *generally*, and so far as Christian *theory* goes: for in *v.* 7 he speaks of

304

some who *practically* have *not*) this knowledge.' **Knowledge puffeth up**—when without "love." Here a parenthesis begins: the main subject is resumed in the same words *v.* 4. "As concerning (touching) the eating," &c. 'Puffing up' pleases self. 'Edifying' benefits one's neighbour. Knowledge says, All things are lawful for me: Love adds, But all things do not edify (ch. x. 23; Rom. xiv. 15). **edifieth**—builds *up* the spiritual temple (chs. iii. 9; vi. 19). **2. And.** Greek, 'But;' so א Δ G *f g*; but A B, Vulgate, omit it. The absence of the connecting particle gives an emphatical sententiousness suitable to the subject. The first step to knowledge is to know our ignorance. Without love there is only the *appearance* [δοκεῖ] of knowledge. **that he knoweth** [εἰδέναι]. So Vulgate. But א A B Δ G *f* read [ἐγνωκέναι] *hath personal experimental acquaintance*, not merely *knowledge of a fact*, which the Greek of the received text, and of "we know," or *are aware*, (*v.* 1) means. **as he ought to know**—experimentally, in the way of "love." **3. love God**—the source of love to our neighbour (1 John iv. 11, 12, 20; v. 2). **the same**—lit., *this man;* he who loves, not he who 'thinks that he knows,' without "charity" or love (*vv.* 1, 2). **is known of him**—is known with approval; is acknowledged by God as His (Ps. i. 6; 2 Tim. ii. 19: contrast Matt. vii. 23). Or, 'is known of God, so that *he knows God*' (the antithesis and *v.* 2 require this sense). To love is to know God: he who thus knows God has been first known by God (cf. ch. xiii. 12; Gal. iv. 9). **4. As concerning, &c.**—resuming *v.* 1, "As touching," &c. **idol is nothing**—has no true being in nature. This does not contradict ch. x. 20; for here it is the GODS *believed to be represented by the idols*, which are denied to have any existence; not the *devils* which really under the idols delude the worshippers. **none other God.** So א C. But A B Δ G *f g*, Vulgate, omit [ἕτερος] "other." Cf. the first commandment. **5.** 'For even supposing (which is not really the case) there exist gods so called (2 Thess. ii. 4), whether in heaven (as the sun, moon, &c., Deut. iv. 19) or in earth (as deified kings, &c.), as there be (a recognized fact, Deut. x. 17; Ps. cxxxv. 5; cxxxvi. 2) gods many and lords many.' Angels and human rulers are termed *gods*, as exercising a divinely-delegated power (cf. Exod. xxii. 9 with *v.* 28; Ps. lxxxii. 1, 6; John x. 34, 35). Heathen

6 and lords many,) but *ʰ* to us *there is but* one God, the Father, *ⁱ* of whom *are* all things, and we ¹ in him; and *ʲ* one Lord Jesus Christ, *ᵏ* by whom
7 *are* all things, and we by him. Howbeit *there is* not in every man that knowledge: for some with conscience of the idol unto this hour eat *it* as a thing offered unto an idol; and their conscience being weak is defiled.
8 But meat commendeth us not to God: for neither, if we eat, ² are we the
9 better; neither, if we eat not, ³ are we the worse. But take heed, lest by any means this ⁴ liberty of yours become a stumblingblock to
10 them that are weak. For if any man see thee which hast knowledge sit at meat in the idol's temple, shall not the conscience of him which is
11 weak be ⁵ emboldened to eat those things which are offered to idols; and through thy knowledge shall the weak brother perish, for whom Christ
12 died? But *ˡ* when ye sin so against the brethren, and wound their weak
13 conscience, ye sin against Christ. Wherefore, if meat make my brother

A. D. 59.

ʰ Mal. 2. 10.
Eph 4. 6.
ⁱ Acts 17. 24.
Rom 11.36.
¹ Or. for him.
ʲ Acts 2. 36.
ᵏ John 1. 3.
² Or. have we the more.
³ Or. have we the less.
⁴ Or. power.
⁵ edified.
ˡ Matt. 25.40.
Acts 9. 4.

"gods" are but *supposed gods :* yet *real powers of evil* suggest them, and gain ascendancy over man through them. **6. to us**—believers. **of whom**—from whom, as the First Cause and Source. Creation is His exclusive prerogative. **we in him**—rather, 'we *for* Him,' or '*unto* [εἰς] Him.' God the FATHER is the end *for* whose glory believers live. In Col. i. 16 all things are said to be created "*by*" Christ, and also "*for* Him" (CHRIST). *So entirely are the Father and Son one* (cf. Rom. xi. 36; Heb. ii. 10). The Holy Ghost, who brings all to their Source, is implied in "for Him." **one Lord**—contrasted with the "lords many" of heathendom (v. 5). Their notions of Godhead were vague : *Lordship* is perfectly realized only in God-Christ (ch. xv. 24, 25). **by whom**—as mediating agent of the Physical and Spiritual Creations (John i. 3 ; Heb. i. 2). **we by him**—as all things are "*of*" the Father as their Source, so they (we believers especially) are restored *to* Him by the new creation (Col. i. 20 ; Rev. xxi. 5). As all things are *by* Christ by creation, so they (we especially) are restored *by* Him by the new creation. **7. Howbeit.** Though to us who "have knowledge" (*vv.* 1, 4-6) all meats are indifferent, yet 'this knowledge is not in all.' St. Paul admitted to the Corinthians that "we all have knowledge" (*v.* 1)—i. e., so far as *theory* goes ; but *practically* some have it defectively. **with conscience**—*the persuasion that idols are real existences.* So C Δ G *f g*, Vulgate. But א A B read συνηθείᾳ. Some Gentile Christians, from old *association* of ideas (or else misdirected *conscience*), when they ate such meats, had a feeling as if the idol were something *real* (*v.* 4), and had changed the meats by the consecration into something either holy or polluted. **unto this hour**—after having embraced Christianity; an implied censure, that they are not farther advanced by this time in Christian "knowledge." **their conscience being weak is defiled**—by eating it 'as a thing offered to idols.' If they ate it unconscious that it had been offered to idols, there would be no defilement of conscience. But conscious of what it was, and not having such knowledge as others boasted of—viz., that an idol is nothing, and can therefore neither pollute nor sanctify meats, they by eating them sin against conscience (cf. Rom. xiv. 15-23). On the ground of Christian expediency, to avoid a stumblingblock to "weak" brethren, the Jerusalem decree forbade partaking of such meats, (though indifferent *in themselves*, Acts xv.) Hence he vindicates it against the asserters of an inexpedient liberty.

8. commendeth. So G *f g*, Vulgate. But א A B

[παραστήσει], 'shall present,' as before a prince. C Δ have 'presents.' A B read 'Neither if we do not eat, are we the better: neither if we eat, are we the worse:' the eaters thus justifying their eating. א Δ G *f g*, Vulgate, read as the English version, wherein St. Paul admits that 'meat neither *presents* us as commended nor as disapproved before God :' it does not affect our religious status (Rom. xiv. 6, 17), but urges that they lose nothing by *not eating;* and at the same time, by thus limiting their liberty, they save the conscience of weak brethren. The "but" (v. 9) confirms A B reading. **9. this liberty of yours**—your watchword. The indifference of meats, which I concede, is just why ye should "take heed" not to tempt weak brethren *to act against conscience* (which constitutes sin, Rom. xiv. 22, 23). **10. if any man**—being weak. **which hast knowledge.** The very knowledge thou pridest thyself on (*v.* 1) will lead him after thy example to do that against his conscience which thou doest without scruple of conscience—viz., to eat meats offered to idols. **conscience of him which is weak**—'*seeing that he is* weak.' **emboldened**—lit., *built up.* You ought to *build up* your brother in good ; but by your example your *building up* is the emboldening him to violate conscience. **11. shall . . . perish.** So G *g*, Vulgate. But א A B C Δ *f* read 'is being destroyed.' A single act, seemingly unimportant, may produce everlasting consequences (Rom. xiv. 23). **for whom** [δι᾽ ὃν] Christ died—implying how precious *He* counted even the weakest ; for whose sake we too ought to be willing to die (1 John iii. 16). Yet professing Christians tempted brethren to their damnation sooner than forego meats for their salvation. It is not true that if *Christ died even for those who perish*, He would have died *in vain* for many. More is involved in redemption than man's salvation: the *character of God*, at once just and loving, is vindicated even in the lost ; for they might have been saved: so even in their case Christ has not died in vain. God's providential mercies are not in vain, though many abuse them. Even the condemned shall manifest God's love, in that they too had the offer of God's mercy. The bitterest ingredient in their cup shall be, they might have been saved, but would not : Christ died to redeem even them (2 Pet. ii. 1). **12. wound their weak conscience**—lit., '*smite* their conscience, being (as yet) *weak*.' It aggravates the cruelty that it is committed on the weak, as if one *struck an invalid.* **against Christ.** Such is the sympathy between Christ and His members (Matt. xxv. 40; Acts ix. 4, 5). **13. meat**—old English for 'food' in general. **make . . . to offend**—Greek, 'is

to offend, I will eat no flesh while the world standeth, lest I make my brother to offend.

9 AM ^aI not an apostle? am I not free? have ^bI not seen Jesus Christ
2 our Lord? are not ye my work in the Lord? If I be not an apostle unto others, yet doubtless I am to you: for ^cthe seal of mine apostleship
3 are ye in the Lord. Mine answer to them that do examine me is this;
4, Have ^dwe not power to eat and to drink? Have we not power to lead
5 about a sister, a ¹wife, as well as other apostles, and *as* ^ethe brethren of
6 the Lord, and ^fCephas? Or I only and Barnabas, ^ghave not we power to forbear working?
7 Who ^hgoeth a warfare any time at his own charges? who ⁱplanteth a vineyard, and eateth not of the fruit thereof? or who feedeth ^ja flock,
8 and eateth not of the milk of the flock? Say I these things as a man?
9 or saith not the law the same also? For it is written in the law of Moses, Thou ^kshalt not muzzle the mouth of the ox that treadeth out
10 the corn. Doth God take care for oxen? Or saith he *it* altogether for our sakes? For our sakes, no doubt, *this* is written: that ^lhe that

A. D. 59.

CHAP. 9.
^a 1 Tim. 2. 7.
  2 Tim. 1.11.
^b Acts 9. 3.
  Acts 18. 9.
^c 2 Cor. 3. 2.
^d 2 Thes. 3. 9.
¹ Or.
  woman.
^e Matt. 13.55.
  Mark 6. 3.
^f Matt. 8. 14.
^g 2 Thes. 3. 8.
^h 2 Cor. 10. 4.
  2 Tim. 4. 7.
ⁱ Deut. 20. 6.
  Pro 27. 18.
^j John 21. 15.
  1 Pet. 5. 2.
^k Deut. 25. 4.
^l 2 Tim. 2. 6.

---

a stumblingblock to.' **no flesh.** To ensure my avoiding flesh offered to idols, I would abstain from *all flesh*, lest I should *be a stumblingblock to* my brother.

CHAP. IX. 1-27.—HE CONFIRMS HIS TEACHING AS TO NOT PUTTING A STUMBLINGBLOCK IN A BROTHER'S WAY (ch. viii. 13) BY HIS OWN EXAMPLE IN NOT USING HIS RIGHTS AS AN APOSTLE, TO WIN MEN TO CHRIST.
1. Am I not an apostle? am I not free? So Δ G *fg.* But א A B, Vulgate, read the order, 'Am I not free? am I not an apostle?' He alludes to ch. viii. 9, "this liberty of yours:" if *you* claim it, I appeal to yourselves, have not *I* also it? For, "am I not an apostle?" I can claim not only Christian, but also apostolic liberty. **have I not seen Jesus?**—*corporeally*, not in mere vision : cf. ch. xv. 8, where he proves the resurrection by actual bodily appearances to Peter, the other apostles, and himself. Cf. Acts ix. 7, 17, the contrast between "the men with him seeing no man," and "Jesus *that appeared unto thee* in the way" to Damascus. His vision of Christ in the temple (Acts xxii. 17) was "in a trance." To be a witness of Christ's resurrection was a function of an apostle (Acts i. 22). A B omit 'Christ.' **ye my work in the Lord**—your conversion is His workmanship (Eph. ii. 10) through my instrumentality (*v.* 2). **2. yet doubtless**—*yet at least* I am such to you. **seal of mine apostleship**—your conversion by my preaching (2 Cor. xii. 12), and your gifts conferred by me (ch. i. 7), vouch for my apostleship, as a seal to a document attests its genuineness (John iii. 33). **3. to them that do examine me**—who call in question mine apostleship. **is this**—viz., that you are the seal of mine apostleship. **4. Have we not power [ἐξουσιαν]**—'right,' lawful power; the same Greek as "liberty" (ch. viii. 9). If *you* claim it, so may *I.* The "we" includes his colleagues. The Greek interrogative [μὴ οὐκ] expresses, 'You surely *wont* say (will you?) that we have *not* the power or right,' &c. **eat and to drink?**—without manual labouring (*vv.* 11, 13, 14). St. Paul's not exercising this right was made a plea for insinuating that he was conscious he was no true apostle (2 Cor. xii. 13-16). **5. lead about a sister, a wife**—'a sister *as a wife;*' "a sister" by faith, which makes all believers brethren and sisters in God: "a wife" by marriage. St. Paul implies he did not exercise his right to marry and "lead about" a believer, for Christian expediency, as well to save the Church the cost of maintaining her in his wide circuits, as also to give himself

more undistractedly to building up the Church of Christ (ch. vii. 26, 32, 35). Contrast the Corinthians' self-pleasing in the exercise of their "liberty" at the cost of destroying, instead of edifying, the Church (ch. viii. 9, 10; *margin*, 11-13). **as other** (Greek, '*the* other') **apostles**—implying that some had used the power which they all had of marrying. We know from Matt. viii. 14 that Cephas or Peter was married. A confutation of St. Peter's self-styled followers, who exclude the clergy from marriage. *Clemens Alexandrinus,* 'Stromata,' vii. § 63, reports that he encouraged his wife, when being led to death, by saying, 'Remember, my dear one, the Lord' (cf. *Eusebius,* 'E. H.' iii. 30). **brethren of the Lord**—held in especial esteem on account of their relationship to Jesus (Matt. xiii. 55; John vii. 5; Acts i. 14; Gal. i. 19)—James, Joses, Simon, and Judas. Probably (according to the Jewish meaning of "brethren") *cousins* of Jesus, sons of Cleopas and Maria, Mary's sister. **Cephas**—singled out as a name carrying weight with one partisan section at Corinth. 'If your favourite leader does so, surely so may I' (ch. i. 12; iii. 22). **6. Barnabas**—long the associate of Paul. He, too, forbore to claim the minister's right of maintenance. St. Paul supported himself by tent-making (Acts xviii. 3; xx. 34; 2 Thess. iii. 8).

7. The minister is spiritually a soldier (2 Tim. ii. 3), a vine-dresser (ch. iii. 6-8; Song i. 6), and a shepherd (1 Pet. v. 2, 4). **of the fruit.** So C. But א A B C Δ G omit "of." **8. as a man**—I speak thus with the sanction of not merely *human judgment,* but the divine law also. **9. ox that treadeth out the corn** (Deut. xxv. 4). In the East they do not, after reaping, carry the sheaves home to barns as we do, but take them to an area in the open air to be threshed by oxen treading them, or else drawing a threshing instrument over them (cf. Mic. iv. 13). **Doth God . . . care for oxen?** [μή.] 'Is it for the oxen that God careth? Surely not.' God does care for the lower animal (Ps. xxxvi. 6; Matt. x. 29), but it is with the ultimate aim of the welfare of *man,* the head of creation. If humane consideration is shown for the lower animal, still more ought it to be for man; the human (spiritual as well as temporal) labourer is worthy of his hire. **10. altogether**—join with "saith." It would be untrue that God saith it *altogether* (in the sense of *solely*) for *our* sakes. But it is true that He *by all means saith* it for our sakes as the ultimate object in the lower world. Else translate 'mainly' or 'especially.' **that—**

ploegheth should plough in hope; and that he that thrasheth in hope
11 should be partaker of his hope. If *ᵐ*we have sown unto you spiritual
12 things, *is it* a great thing if we shall reap your carnal things? If others
be partakers of *this* power over you, *are* not we rather? Nevertheless we
*ⁿ*have not used this power; but suffer all things, lest we should hinder
the gospel of Christ.
13 Do *°*ye not know that they which minister about holy things ²live *of
the things* of the temple? and they which wait at the altar are partakers
14 with the altar? Even so *ᵖ*hath the Lord ordained that they ²which
preach the Gospel should live of the Gospel.
15 But I have used none of these things: neither have I written these
things, that it should be so done unto me: for *it were* better for me to
16 die, than that any man should make my glorying void. For though I
preach the Gospel, I have nothing to glory of: for necessity is laid upon
17 me; yea, woe is unto me, if I preach not the Gospel! For if I do this
thing willingly, I have a reward; but if against my will, a *ʳ*dispensation
18 *of the Gospel* is committed unto me. What is my reward then? *Verily*
that, when I preach the Gospel, I may make the gospel of Christ without
charge, that I abuse not my power in the Gospel.

A. D. 59.

ᵐ Mal 3. ᵏ. 9.
Matt 10 10.
Luke 10. 7.
Rom. 15. 27.
Gal. 6. 6.
Acts 20. 31.
31.
ⁿ 2 Cor. 11 7.
2 Cor. 12, 13,
14.
1 Thes. 2. 6.
9.
° Lev. 6. 16.
Lev. 7. 6, 8.
Num. 5. 9.
Num. 18. 8,
20.
² Or. feed.
ᵖ Luke 10. 7.
² Gal. 6. 6.
1 Tim. 5. 17.
ʳ Gal. 2. 7.
Phil. 1. 17.
Col. 1. 25.

teaching us *that* [ὅτι]. **should plough**—*ought to* plough in hope. The people ought not to let their minister labour without remuneration. **he that thrasheth in hope should be partaker of his hope.** So G *fg*, except "in hope." א A B, Vulgate, Syriac, *Origen*, read 'he that thrasheth (*ought to thrash*) in the hope of partaking' (viz., *of the fruit of his thrashing*). "He that plougheth" is the first planter of a church (cf. ch. iii. 6, 9); "he that thrasheth," the minister who tends a church already planted. **11. we . . . we**—emphatical in the Greek. **your carnal things.** We, who have sown the infinitely more precious treasures of the *spirit*, may at least claim in return the only thing *you* have to give—viz., the goods that nourish the *flesh*. **12. others** —whether true (*v.* 5) or false apostles (2 Cor. xi. 13). **we rather**—considering our greater labours for you (2 Cor. xi. 23). **suffer all things**—without complaining. We *conceal* [στέγομεν], *forbear divulging; hold as a watertight vessel*) any distress we suffer from straitened circumstances: the same Greek, ch. xiii. 7. **lest we . . . hinder . . . gospel** —not to *cause hindrance to* its progress by giving a handle for the imputation of self-seeking, if we received support. The less of encumbrance caused to the Church, and the more of work done, the better for the Gospel cause (2 Tim. ii. 4). **13. minister. about holy things**—the Jewish priests [οἱ τὰ ἱερὰ ἐργαζόμενοι] *who offer sacrifices.* **partakers with the altar**—a part of the victims going to the service of the altar, and the rest being shared by the priests, (Num. xviii. 8, &c.) **14. Even so.** The only inference from this passage is, not that the Christian ministry is sacrificial, as the Jewish priesthood, but simply, that as the latter was supported by the people's contributions, so should the former. The stipends of the clergy were at first from offerings at the Lord's supper. At the love feast preceding it every believer, according to his ability, offered a gift; and when the expense of the table had been defrayed, the bishop laid aside a portion for himself, the presbyters, and deacons; and with the rest relieved widows, orphans, confessors, and the poor, (*Tertullian*, 'Apology,' ch. xxxix.) The stipend was in proportion to the dignity and merits of the bishops, presbyters, and deacons (*Cyprian*, c. iv. ep. 6). **preach the Gospel**—the duty of the Christian minister, in contrast to the *ministering about*

sacrifices (Greek) *and waiting at the altar* of the Jewish priesthood (*v.* 13). If the Lord's supper were a *sacrifice* (as the Mass is supposed to be), this 14th verse would certainly have been worded so, to answer to *v.* 13. The same Lord Christ 'ordains' the ordinances in the Old and in the New Testaments (Matt. x. 10). **15.** Paul's celibacy, and his ability to maintain himself without interrupting his ministry, made that expedient to him which is ordinarily inexpedient—a ministry not supported by the people. What to him was a duty would be the opposite to one to whom God committed a family, without other resources. Under other circumstances he accepted help (Phil. iv. 15, 16). **I have used none of these things**—none of these 'powers' which I might have used (*vv.* 4-6, 12). **neither**—rather, '*yet* I have *not* written. **so done unto me**—lit., *in my case;* as in the case of a soldier, a planter, a shepherd, a ploughman, and a sacrificing priest (*vv.* 7, 10, 13). **make my glorying void**—deprive me of my privilege of preaching without remuneration (2 Cor. xi. 7-10). Rather than hinder the Gospel by giving pretext for a charge of interested motives (2 Cor. xii. 17, 18), St. Paul would "die" of hunger (cf. Abraham's disinterestedness, Gen. xiv. 22, 23). **16. though I** (*if I simply*) **preach . . . I have nothing to glory of**—for the "necessity" laid on me by Christ's commission (Acts xxvi. 16-18) to preach (cf. Jer. xx. 9, and Jonah) does away with "glorying." It is only when I preach *without charge* (*v.* 18) that I have cause for "glorying," since there is no *necessity* laid on me as to *this*: it is my voluntary act for the Gospel's sake. **17.** Translate, 'If [*as is the case:* εἰ πράσσω, *indicative*] I be doing this spontaneously (without remuneration), I have a reward (*v.* 18); but if not spontaneously (not without remuneration), I have a stewardship intrusted to me,' and so have no special claim to glorying or reward for that which 'necessity is laid on me' to do (Luke xvii. 10). **18. What is my reward?** (Greek, *the reward I speak of*)—for preaching, as I do, spontaneously? It is that, by preaching without charge, I do not make my right of charging a hindrance to the Gospel progress. **of Christ.** So G. Omitted in א A B C Δ *f*, Vulgate. **abuse**—'that I use not *to the hindrance of the Gospel* my power.' The "*reward*" ultimately aimed at is the gaining of the more (*v.* 19). It was for this, not to have

19 For though I be free from all *men*, yet have [s] I made myself servant
20 unto all, [t] that I might gain the more. And [u] unto the Jews I became
as a Jew, that I might gain the Jews; to them that are under the law,
21 as under the law, that I might gain them that are under the law; to
[v] them that are without law, as without law, ([w] being not without law to
God, but under the law to Christ,) that I might gain them that are
22 without law. To [x] the weak became I as weak, that I might gain the
weak: I am made all things to all *men*, that I might by all means save
23 some. And this I do for the Gospel's sake, that I might be partaker
thereof with *you*.
24 Know ye not that they which run in a race run all, but one receiveth
25 the prize? So [y] run, that ye may obtain. And every man that [z] striveth
for the mastery is temperate in all things. Now they *do it* to obtain a
26 corruptible crown, but we [a] an incorruptible. I therefore so run, not as

A. D. 59.
[s] Gal. 5. 1*.
[t] Matt. 18.15.
1 Pet. 3. 1.
[u] Acts 16. 3.
Acts 21. 23.
[v] Rom. 2. 12.
Gal. 3. 2.
[w] ch. 7. 22.
[x] Rom. 15. 1.
[y] Gal. 2. 2.
Gal. 5. 7.
Phil. 2. 16.
Heb. 12. 1.
[z] 1 Tim. 6.12.
2 Tim. 2. 5.
[a] Jas. 1. 12.
Rev. 2. 10.

matter for glorying, or 'supererogatory merit,' that he preached without charge.

19. free from all men—*i. e.*, independent of all men. **gain the more**—*i. e.*, the greater number of them ("all men"). "Gain" is appropriate in relation to a "reward;" he therefore repeats it (*vv.* 20-22). **20. I became as a Jew**—in things not defined by the *law*, but by Jewish usage. Not Judaizing in essentials, but in matters where there was no compromise of principle (cf. Acts xvi. 3; xxi. 20-26)—an undesigned coincidence between the history and the epistle: a proof of genuineness. **to them that are under the law, as under the law**—in things defined by *the law;* ceremonies not then repugnant to Christianity. The reason for distinguishing this class from the former is—St. Paul himself belonged *nationally* to "the Jews," but did not *in creed* belong to "them that are under the law." This is confirmed by the reading inserted here by א A B C Δ G *fg*, Vulgate, 'not being (*i. e.*, "not that I am") myself under the law.' **21. To them . . . without-law**—*i. e.*, without *revealed* law: the heathen (cf. Rom. ii. 12, 15). **as without law**—not urging on them the ceremonies and "works of the law," but "the hearing of faith" (Gal. iii. 2); discoursing in their own manner, as at Athens, with arguments from Greek poets (Acts xvii. 28). **not without law to God**—'whilst conforming to others in matters indifferent, being not *without law* towards God, but *responsible to the law* (*lit.*, IN LAW) towards Christ.' The Christian's true position in relation to the world, to himself, and to God. Everything develops itself according to its proper law. So the Christian, though no longer a slave to the letter constraining him from without, is subject to the higher law, the spirit of faith in Christ acting from within as the germ of a new life. *Christ* was responsible to the law for us, so that *we* are no longer responsible to it (Gal. iii. 13, 24), but to Him, as the members to the Head (ch. vii. 22; Rom. viii. 1-4; 1 Pet. ii. 16). In proportion as Christians serve Christ in newness of spirit, they fulfil the righteousness of the law, and are no longer under the law *as an outward letter.* Our old man still needs the law as a rule to convict of sin (Rom. vii. 4 6). To Christ, as man's Head, the Father delegated His authority (John v. 22, 27); whence he substitutes "Christ" for "God"—"not without law to *God*, but under the law to *Christ*." The law of Christ is the law of love, which is the fulfilment of the law (Rom. xiii. 8; Gal. vi. 2: cf. v. 13). **22. gain the weak**—*i. e.*, establish, instead of being a stumblingblock to them (ch. viii. 7; Rom. xiv. 1). *Alford* thinks the "weak" are not Christians at all, for these have been already 'won.' But when "weak" Christians

are by the love of stronger brethren kept from falling, they are rightly said to be 'gained.' **all things to all men**—lit., '*the* all things to *the* all men;' all that is required to all the various classes. *Origen* reads as the English version; but א A B C Δ G omit 'the' before "all things." **by all means . . . some**. The gain of even "*some*" is worth the expenditure of "*all* means." He conformed to the feelings of the several classes, that out of them *all* he might *gain some.* **23. this.** א A B C Δ *fg* read "all things." **partaker thereof** (Greek, '*fellow-partaker*')—of the Gospel blessings promised. **with (you)**—rather 'with *them*;' viz., with those 'gained' by me to the Gospel.

24. Know ye not. The Isthmian games, in which the foot-race was a leading one, were a subject of patriotic pride to the Corinthians in the neighbourhood. These periodical games were to the Greeks rather a passion than an amusement: a suitable image of Christian earnestness. Paul uses the same image, Acts xx. 24—an undesigned coincidence between the history and the epistle: a proof of genuineness. **in a race** [σταδίῳ]—'in a race-course.' **all . . . one.** Although we knew that one only could be saved, it would be well worth our while to run. Not "all" who enter on the Christian race win (ch. x. 1-5). **So run, that ye may obtain**—parenthetically: the words in which the instructors in the exercise schools (gymnasia) and the spectators on the race-course exhorted runners to put forth all exertions. The gymnasium was a prominent feature in every Greek city. Every candidate had to swear that he had been ten months in training, and that he would not violate the regulations (2 Tim. ii. 5: cf. 1 Tim. iv. 7, 8). He lived on a strict diet, refraining from wine and pleasant foods, and enduring cold and heat and laborious discipline. The "prize" awarded by the judge was a chaplet of green leaves; at the Isthmus, of the indigenous pine, for which parsley leaves were temporarily substituted (*v.* 25). The Greek [καταλάβητε] is *fully obtain.* Here is the true scope for 'ambition' (2 Cor. v. 9). It is vain to begin unless we *persevere to the end* (Matt. x. 22; xxiv. 13; Rev. ii. 10). "So" expresses, Run with *such perseverance* in the heavenly course as "all" exhibit in the earthly "race." Run so as not only to receive *salvation*, but a *full reward* (ch. iii. 14, 15; 2 John 8). **25. striveth**—in wrestling: a more severe contest than the foot-race. **is temperate.** So Paul denied himself, in not claiming sustenance, in view of the "reward"—viz., to "gain the more" (*vv.* 18, 19). **corruptible**—*soon withering*, being of fir leaves, from the groves which surrounded the Isthmian race-course. **incorruptible** (1 Pet. i. 4; v. 4; Rev. ii. 10). "Crown" here is not that of a king

308

27 *b*uncertainly; so fight I, not as one that beateth the air: but I keep under my body, and bring *it* into subjection; lest that by any means, when I have preached to others, I myself should be *c*a cast-away.

10 MOREOVER, brethren, I would not that ye should be ignorant, how that all our fathers were under the *a*cloud, and all passed through the

2 *b*sea; and were all baptized unto Moses in the cloud and in the sea;

3, and did all eat the same *c*spiritual meat; and did all drink the same

A. D. 59.

b 2 Cor. 5. 1.
* Jer. 6. 30.
2 Cor. 13. 5.

CHAP. 10.
a Ex. 13. 21.
b Ex. 14. 22.
c Ex. 16. 15.

(a different Greek word, viz., 'diadem'), but a wreath or *garland*. 26. I—return to his main subject, *his own* self-denial, and his motive. run not as uncertainly—not *without definite object* as a runner uncertain of the goal. *Ye* gain no end in entering idol temples or eating idol meats. But *I,* for my part, in all acts, whether in becoming "all things to all men" or in receiving no sustenance from converts, have a definite aim to "gain the more." He who knows what to aim at, and how to aim, looks straight forward to the goal alone, casts away every encumbrance (Heb. xii. 1, 2), is indifferent to what the bystanders say, and is only roused the more by even a fall. not as one that beateth the air—instead of beating the adversary. In the Sciamachia, or *sparring in sham-fight* (cf. ch. xiv. 9), they struck out into the air as if at an adversary. The real adversary is Satan acting through the flesh. 27. keep under [ὑπωπιάζω]— *bruise under the eyes,* so as to render the antagonist powerless: to *chastise* in the most sensitive part (cf. "*mortify* the deeds of the body," Rom. viii. 13; 1 Pet. ii. 11). It is not fasts or macerations of the body which are recommended, but *keeping under* of natural self-seeking; so as, like Paul, to lay ourselves out entirely for the great work. my body—the old man. "My body," so far as the flesh opposes the *spirit* (Gal. v. 17). Men may be severe to their bodies, yet indulge their lust. Ascetic 'neglect of the body' may be all the while a more subtile "satisfying of the flesh" (Col. ii. 23). Unless the soul keep under the body, the body gets above the soul. The body may be a good servant, but is a bad master. bring it into subjection [δουλαγωγῶ]—*as c. slave led captive.* preached— lit., *heralded. Heralds* summoned the candidates for the foot-race into the race-course, and placed the crowns on the conquerors, announcing their names. They proclaimed the laws of the combat, answering to the *preaching* of the apostles. The *Christian* herald is distinguished from the race heralds in being also a *combatant*. a cast-away— losing the prize myself, after having *called* others to the contest: *qualis vita, finis ita. Rejected* by the Judge of the Christian race, notwithstanding having, by my preaching, led others to be accepted (cf. margin, *refuse silver,* Jer. vi. 30; 2 Cor. xiii. 6, "reprobates"). St. Paul implies if such self-denying watchfulness be needed still, with all his labours for others, to make his calling sure, much more is the same needed by the Corinthians, instead of going, as they do, to the extreme limit of Christian liberty. Rather, '*rejected*' *as to the special* '*reward*' of those who "turn many to righteousness" (note, *v.* 24; 1 Thess. ii. 19; Dan. xii. 3). The context (*vv.* 18-23) favours this.

CHAP. X. 1-33.—DANGER OF FELLOWSHIP WITH IDOLATRY ILLUSTRATED IN ISRAEL—SUCH FELLOWSHIP INCOMPATIBLE WITH FELLOWSHIP IN THE LORD'S SUPPER—EVEN LAWFUL THINGS ARE TO BE FOREBORNE, NOT TO HURT WEAK BRETHREN.

1. Moreover [δέ]. So C. But א A B Δ G *f g*, Vulgate, read 'For.' Ye need to exercise self-denying watchfulness, notwithstanding your privileges, lest ye be cast-aways (ch. ix. 24-27). FOR most of the

Israelites, with all their privileges, were cast-aways through want of it. ignorant—with all their boasted "knowledge." our fathers. The Jewish Church is related as parent to the Christian' Church. all. Arrange as the Greek, 'Our fathers were *all* under the *cloud*;' giving the "all" its proper emphasis. Not so much as one of so great a multitude was detained by force or disease (Ps. cv. 37). Five times the "all" is repeated in enumerating the five favours God bestowed on Israel (*vv.* 1-4). Five times, correspondingly, they sinned (*vv.* 6-10). In contrast to the "all" stands "many (rather, 'the most') of them" (*v.* 5). *All* had great privileges, yet *most* were cast-aways through lust. Beware you, having greater privileges, of sharing the same doom through a like sin. Continuing ch. ix. 24, they "run *all,* but *one* receiveth the prize." under the cloud—under the *defence* of the cloud-pillar, veiling them from the Egyptians (Exod. xiii. 21, 22; Ps. cv. 39). passed through the sea—by God's miraculous interposition (Exod. xiv. 29). 2. and—*and so.* baptized unto Moses—the representative of the Old Testament covenant, as Jesus, the Son of God, is of the Gospel covenant (John i. 17; Heb. iii. 5, 6). The people were led to believe in Moses as God's servant by the miracle of the cloud, and by their being conducted safely through the Red Sea. "Baptized unto" him (Exod. xiv. 31) is thus equivalent to '*initiated* into the Mosaic covenant:' introduced into relationship with him as the God-appointed leader. St. Paul's argument is, The Corinthians, it is true, have been "baptized," but so also were the Israelites; if the virtual baptism of the latter availed not to save them from the doom of lust, neither will the actual baptism of the former save them. The symbols also correspond: the cloud and sea consist of water. As these took the Israelites out of sight, then restored them again to view, so the water does to the baptized. The Egyptians represent the death-doomed old man; Israel, the new-born life. "The cloud" (symbol of the Divine presence, Isa. iv. 5) and "the sea" may symbolize the *Spirit* and the *water* respectively (John iii. 5; Acts x. 44-47). Christ is the pillar-cloud that screens us from God's hot wrath. Christ, "the light of the world," is our "pillar of fire" to guide us in this dark world. As the rock, when smitten, sent forth waters, so Christ, once for all smitten, sends forth the waters of the Spirit. As the manna bruised fed Israel, so Christ, when "it pleased the Lord to bruise Him," has become our spiritual food. A proof of inspiration is given in this, that the *historical* Scriptures, without the consciousness even of the authors, are tangible *prophecies,* as in the first germ the future tree is wrapped up. 3 same spiritual meat. As the water from the rock answered to *baptism,* so the manna corresponded to the other of the two Christian sacraments, *the Lord's supper.* St. Paul implies the *importance* attached to the two sacraments by all Christians in those days: an anticipatory protest against those who set them aside. Still, he guards against the other extreme—that the possession of such privileges will ensure salvation. Had there been *seven*

4 ^dspiritual drink; for they drank of that spiritual Rock that [1]followed
5 them; and that Rock was Christ. But with many of them God was not
well pleased: for they were overthrown in the wilderness.
6 Now these things were [2]our examples, to the intent we should not lust
7 after evil things, as they also lusted. Neither be ye idolaters, as *were*
some of them; as it is written, ^eThe people sat down to eat and drink,
8 and rose up to play. Neither let us commit fornication, as some of them
9 committed, and ^ffell in one day three and twenty thousand. Neither let
us tempt Christ, as some ^gof them also tempted, and were destroyed of
10 serpents. Neither murmur ye, as some of them also murmured, and were

A. D. 59.

d Ex. 17. 6.
Num 20.11.
Ps. 78. 15.
1 Or, went
with them.
Deut. 9. 21.
Ps. 105. 41.
2 our
figures.
e Ex. 32. 6.
f Num. 25. 1.
g Ex. 17. 2, 7.

sacraments, as Rome teaches, St. Paul would have alluded to them. He does not mean that *the Israelites and we Christians* have "the same" sacrament; but that *believing and unbelieving* Israelites alike had "the same" spiritual privilege of the manna (cf. *v.* 17). It was "*spiritual* meat" or food, because given by God's Spirit, not by human labour. Gal. iv. 29, "born after the Spirit"—*i. e., supernaturally;* "corn of heaven," Ps. lxxviii. 24; cv. 40. Rather, "spiritual," as *typical* of Christ, the true bread of heaven, John vi. 32 (*Grotius*). Not that the Israelites clearly understood this, but believers among them would feel that the type contained some spiritual truth: their implicit and reverent, though indistinct, faith was counted to them for justification, of which the manna was a sacramental seal. 'They are not to be heard which feign that the old fathers did look only for transitory promises' (Article vii., Church of England: cf. Heb. iv. 2). **4. drink** (Exod. xvii. 6; Num. xx. 8)—the literal water typified, and so is called "*spiritual* drink." **spiritual Rock that followed them.** The tradition of Rabbi Solomon on Num. xx. 2 is, that the rock, or at least the stream from it, followed the Israelites from place to place (cf. Deut. ix. 21). Christ, the "spiritual Rock" (Deut. xxxii. 4, 15, 18, 30, 31, 37; Ps. lxxviii. 20, 25; 1 Pet. ii. 6), 'accompanied them' (Exod. xxxiii. 15). "Followed" implies His *attending on* them *to minister to* them; though mostly going *before* them, He, when occasion required, *followed* "*behind*" (Exod. xiv. 19). He satisfied their bodily thirst whenever they needed it: four occasions are expressly recorded (Exod. xv. 24, 25; xvii. 6; Num. xx. 8; xxi. 16-18). This water symbolized that from the spiritual Rock (cf. John iv. 13, 14; vii. 38: see note, *v.* 3), which believing Israelites drank in types. As by the stream the rock followed them, so by His Spirit Christ is with us to the end of the world. **was**—represented (Matt. xxvi. 26). **5. But**—though they had so many spiritual privileges. **many of them**—rather, 'the majority of them.' All except Joshua and Caleb of the first generation. **God**—whose judgment alone is valid. **not**—in the Greek emphatically beginning the sentence: "Not," as one might naturally expect, 'with the more part of them was,' &c. (Heb. iii. 14-17). **for**—the event shows they pleased not God. **overthrown** [κατεστρώθησαν]—*strewn in heaps.* **in the wilderness**—far from the land of promise.

6. were—Greek, '*came to pass* (*as*).' **our examples**—lit., *types:* prefigurations of what will befall us, if we with all our privileges walk carelessly. There is continuity and unity in God's plan of dealing with the Church in all ages. **lust**—the common fountain of the four offences, and therefore put first (Jas. i. 14, 15: cf. Ps. cvi. 14). A particular lust was that after flesh, when they pined for the fish, leeks, &c., of Egypt, which they had left (Num. xi. 4, 5, 33, 34). These are

not "evil things" in themselves, but they became so to the Israelites when they lusted after what God withheld, and were discontented with what God provided. **7. idolaters.** A case in point. As the Israelites *sat down* (a deliberate act), *ate,* and *drank* at the idol feast to the calves in Horeb, so the Corinthians were in danger of idolatry by a like act, though not professedly worshipping an idol, as the Israelites (Exod. xxxii. 6; ch. viii. 10, 11; x. 14, 20, 21). He passes from the first to the second person, as they alone (not he also) were in danger of idolatry. He resumes the first person appropriately at *v.* 16. **some.** The multitude follow the lead of *some* bad men. **play**—with lascivious dancing, singing, and drumming round the calf (cf. "rejoiced," Acts vii. 41). **8. fornication.** Num. xxv. 1-5 assigns *idolatry* of Baal-peor as the cause; but *fornication* was associated at the idol feast with it, and prompted Israel to it. This harlotry applied to the Corinthians (ch. v. 1, 9; vi. 9, 15, 18; viii. 10). Balaam tempted Israel to both sins (Rev. ii. 14: cf. ch. viii. 7, 9). **three and twenty thousand**—in Num. xxv. 9, "twenty and four thousand." If this were a real discrepancy, it would militate rather against inspiration of the *subject matter* than against *verbal* inspiration. But Moses, in Numbers, includes all who died "in the plague;" St. Paul, all who died "in *one day;*" 1,000 more may have fallen next day; or the real number may have been between 23,000 and 24,000—say, 23,500 or 23,600. When writing generally, where exact figures were not needed, one writer might veraciously give one of the two round numbers near the exact one, and the other writer the other. Whichever be the true way of reconciling the statements, at least they are not irreconcilable. **9. tempt Christ.** So *Irenæus* (264). Δ G *f g*, Vulgate, אBC read 'Lord;' A, from Num. xxi. 5, 'God.' As "Christ" was referred to in one of Israel's five privileges (*v.* 4), so He is mentioned in one of Israel's five corresponding sins. "Christ," or 'Lord' (*i. e.*, the Second Person, Exod. xvii. 2, 7) answers to "God," Num. xxi. 5; so "Christ" must be "God" (cf. Rom. xiv. 11 with Isa. xlv. 22, 23). Israel's complainings were temptings of Christ, the "Angel" of the covenant (Exod. xxiii. 20, 21; xxxii. 34; Isa. lxiii. 9). Though they drank of "that Rock . . . Christ" (*v.* 4), they *put* Him further *to the proof by doubting* could He supply water (Num xx. 3-13). Though eating the meat (manna) that typified Christ, "the bread of life," they cried, "Our soul loatheth this light bread." Being punished by the fiery serpents, they were saved by the brasen serpent, the emblem of *Christ* (cf. John iii. 14; viii. 56; Heb. xi. 26). The Greek [ἐκπειρά-ζωμεν] "tempt" means *try, so as to wear out* by unbelief, Christ's long-suffering (cf. Num. xiv. 22; Ps. xcv. 8, 9). The Corinthians were *provoking God's long-suffering* by verging towards idolatry, through overweening confidence in their knowledge (*v.* 22). **10. some . . . murmured**—upon the

11 destroyed of the destroyer. Now all these things happened unto them for [3] ensamples: and [h] they are written for our admonition, [i] upon whom
12 the ends of the world are come. Wherefore let him that thinketh he standeth take heed lest he fall.
13 There hath no temptation taken you but [4] such as is common to man: but God *is* faithful, [j] who will not suffer you to be tempted above that ye are able; but will with the temptation also [k] make a way to escape, that ye may be able to bear *it*.
14, Wherefore, my dearly beloved, flee from idolatry. I speak as to wise
15, men; judge ye what I say. The [l] cup of blessing which we bless, is it
16 not the communion of the blood of Christ? [m] The bread which we break,
17 is it not the communion of the body of Christ? For [n] we *being* many are one bread, *and* one body: for we are all partakers of that one bread.

A. D. 59.

[3] Or, types.
[h] Rom. 15. 4.
[i] Heb. 10. 25.
[4] Or, moderate.
[j] Ex 13. 17.
2 Pet. 2. 9.
[k] Jer. 29. 11.
Acts 27. 44.
[l] Matt .26.26.
Mark 14.22-24.
Luke 22.19, 20.
[m] Acts 2. 42.
[n] Rom. 12. 5.

---

death of Korah and his company, who themselves were murmurers (Num. xvi. 41, 49). Their murmurs against Moses and Aaron were virtually against God (cf. Exod. xvi. 8). St. Paul glances at the Corinthian murmurs against himself, Christ's apostle. **destroyed.** 14,700 perished. Or the murmuring was that upon the spies' evil report (Num. xiv. 1-37). **the destroyer**—the same God-sent augel as in Exod. xii. 23, and 2 Sam. xxiv. 16. **11. Now all these things . . . ensamples**—resuming *v.* 6. History is a mirror for present times. So Δ G. But ℵ A B C read 'by way of example' [τυπικῶς], 'typically.' **the ends of the world**—*lit.*, 'of the ages.' The New Testament dispensation winds up all former 'ages.' No new dispeusation shall appear till Christ comes as Judge. The "ends" (plural) include various successive periods consummated and merging together (Eph. i. 10: cf. Heb. ix. 26). Our dispensation being the consummation of all that went before, our respousibilities are the greater, and the greater our guilt, if we fall short of our privileges. **12. thinketh he standeth**—viz., "by faith;" in contrast to *v.* 5 (Rom. xi. 20). **fall**—from his place in the Church (cf. *v.* 8, "fell"), both temporally and spiritually (Rom. xiv. 4). Our security as relates to God consists in faith; as relates to ourselves, in fear. **13.** Consolation under temptation; it is such as is "commou to man," or 'such as mau can bear' by God's aid. **faithful** (Ps. cxxv. 3; Isa. xxvii. 3, 8; Rev. iii. 10)—to His covenant with believers (1 Thess. v. 24). To be *led into* temptation is distinct from *running* into it, which would be 'tempting God' (*v.* 9; Matt. iv. 7). **way to escape** (Jer. xxix. 11; 2 Pet. ii. 9). The Greek is, '*the* way of escape:' the appropriate way in each temptation; not immediate, but in due time, after patience has had her perfect work (Jas. i. 2-4, 12). He 'makes' the way of escape simultaneously "with the temptation" which He appoints. He *permits* the exigency, and *provides* the help. **to bear it** [ὑπενεγκεῖν]—*to bear up under it.* Not, he will take it away (2 Cor. xii. 7-9). **14.** Resuming *v.* 7; ch. viii. 9, 10. **flee.** Do not tamper with it by doubtful acts, as eating idol meats on the plea of Christian liberty. Our safety is in *wholly shunning* whatever borders on idolatry (2 Cor. vi. 16, 17). The Holy Spirit presciently warns the Church against the idolatry, subsequently transferred from the idol feast to the Lord's supper, in the figment of transubstantiation. The Lord's supper is here proved to be not a *sacrifice,* but *the feast after the sacrifice:* the "bread" remains so after consecration (*v.* 17; ch. xi. 2-6). **15.** Appeal to their own *judgment* to weigh the argument—viz., That as partaking of the Lord's supper involves a partaking of the Lord himself, and partaking of the Jewish sacrificial meats involved a partaking of the altar, and as the heathens virtually sacrifice to devils, to partake of an idol feast, with belief in idols as entities, is to have fellowship with devils. We cannot divest ourselves of the responsibility of 'judging' for ourselves. The weakness of private judgment is not an argument against its use, but its abuse. We should the more diligently search the infallible Word, with every aid, above all with prayer, for the Spirit's teaching (Acts xvii. 11). If an iuspired apostle not only permits but urges men to *judge* his sayings by Scripture, much more should fallible ministers now do so. **to wise men**—referring ironically to the Corinthian boast of "wisdom" (ch. iv. 10; 2 Cor. xi. 19). Here you have an opportunity of exercising your 'wisdom.' **16. The cup of blessing**—answering to the passover "cup of blessing," over which "blessing" was offered to God. It was in doing so that Christ instituted this part of the Lord's supper (Luke xxii. 17, 20). **we bless**—"we," not merely ministers, but also the congregation. The minister 'blesses' (i. e., *consecrates with blessing*) the cup to be the sign of Christ's blood, and a means of our union with His glorified humanity; not by any priestly transmitted authority, but as representing the congregation, who virtually through him bless the cup. The consecration is the corporate act of the Church. The *joint blessing* by Him and them (not "the cup" itself, which, as also "the bread," in the Greek is accusative), and the consequent *drinking together*, constitute "the communion"—i. e., *joint participation* "of the blood of Christ" (cf. *v.* 18). "Is" in both cases is literal. He who with faith partakes of the cup and the bread, partakes really (because spiritually) of the blood and body of Christ (Eph. v. 30, 32), and of the benefits of His sacrifice on the cross (Heb. xiii. 10). In contrast to this is "fellowship with devils" (*v.* 20). "The cup" (i. e., the wine in the cup), &c., is that whereby, through faith, the participation takes place of the blood, &c. It is the seal, and a means of our living union with our Saviour (John vi. 53, 57). It is not said, 'The cup . . . is *the blood,*' or 'The bread . . . is *the body,*' but 'is the *communion*' (joint-participation of the blood . . . body). If the bread be changed into the body of Christ, where is the sign of the sacrament? Romanists eat Christ '*in remembrance* of Himself.' To drink *blood* would have been an abomination to Jews and Christians alike (Lev. xvii. 11, 12; Acts xv. 29). *Breaking the bread* was part of the consecrating of it; for thus was represented the crucifixion of Christ's body. The specificatiou of both bread and wine disproves the Romish doctrine of concomitancy, aud exclusion of the laity from the cup. **17. one bread**—rather, 'loaf.'

311

18 Behold °Israel after the flesh: ᵖare not they which eat of the sacrifices
19 partakers of the altar? What say I then? that the idol is any thing, or
20 that which is offered in sacrifice to idols is any thing? But *I say*, that
the things which the Gentiles ᵠsacrifice, they sacrifice to devils, and not
to God: and I would not that ye should have fellowship with devils.
21 Ye ʳcannot drink the cup of the Lord, and ˢthe cup of devils: ye cannot
22 be partakers of the Lord's table, and of the table of devils. Do we provoke the Lord to jealousy? are ᵗwe stronger than he?
23 All things are lawful for me, but all things are not expedient: all
24 things are lawful for me, but all things edify not. Let ᵘno man seek
25 his own, but every man another's *wealth*. Whatsoever ᵛis sold in the
26 shambles, *that* eat, asking no question for conscience' sake: for the earth
27 *is* the Lord's, and the fulness thereof. If any of them that believe not
bid you *to a feast*, and ye be disposed to go, ʷwhatsoever is set before
28 you eat, asking no question for conscience' sake. But if any man say
unto you, This is offered in sacrifice unto idols, eat not ˣfor his sake that

A. D. 5⁴.
° Rom. 4. 12
Rom. 9. 3,
8.
1 Cor. 11.18,
22.
Gal. 6. 16.
Eph. 2. 11.
ᵖ Lev. 3. 3.
Lev. 7. 15.
ᵠ Deut. 32.17.
ʳ 2 Cor. 6. 15.
ˢ Deut. 32.38.
ᵗ Job 9. 4.
Job 40. 9-
14.
Eze 22. 14.
ᵘ Rom. 15. 1.
ᵛ 1 Tim. 4. 4.
ʷ Luke 10 7.
ˣ ch. 8. 10.

One loaf alone probably was used in each celebration. (**and**) **one body.** Omit "and:" 'one loaf (that is), one body.' '**We**, *the many* (communicants: so the Greek), are one bread (by partaking of the same loaf, which becomes assimilated to the substance of all; so we become), one body' (with Christ, ch. xii. 12, and with one another). Or, '(as there is) one bread (composed of many separate grains) (so) we **the many are one body**.' **we are all** [οἱ πάντες] —'the whole of us.' 18. **Israel after the flesh**—the literal, as distinguished from the spiritual Israel (Rom. ii. 29; ix. 3; Gal. iv. 29). **partakers of the altar**—so *of God*, whose is the altar: they have fellowship in God and His worship, of which the altar is the symbol (Matt. xxiii. 20, 21). 19. **What say I then?** The inference might be drawn, from the analogies of the Lord's supper and Jewish sacrifices, that an idol is *really what the heathen thought it*, and that in eating idol meats they had fellowship with the god. This verse guards against this: 'What do I mean then? that a thing sacrificed to idols has any real virtue, or that an idol is any real thing?' (A B read in this order: supply '*Nay*'), 'But (I say) that the things which the Gentiles sacrifice, they sacrifice to demons.' St. Paul here introduces a new fact. It is true that an idol has no reality in the heathen's sense; but it has a reality in another sense: heathendom being under Satan's dominion, as "prince of this world," *he* and *his demons* are in fact the powers worshipped by the heathen, whether they are or are not conscious of it (Deut. xxxii. 17, Hebrew, *Sheedim;* Lev. xvii. 7; 2 Chr. xi. 15; Ps. cvi. 37; Rev. ix. 20). 'Devil' is in the Greek restricted to Satan: 'demons' is applied to his subordinate spirits. Fear, rather than love, is the motive of heathen worship: cf. the English word 'panic,' from PAN, whose human form with horns and cloven hoofs gave rise to the vulgar representations of Satan, just as fear is the spirit of Satan and his demons (Jas. ii. 19). 20. **I would not that ye should have fellowship with devils**—by partaking of idol feasts (ch. viii. 10). 21. **Ye cannot,** &c.—really, though ye may outwardly (1 Ki. xviii. 21.) **cup of devils**—in contrast to *the cup of the Lord*. At idol feasts libations were made from the cup to the idol first, then the guests drank; so they had fellowship with the idol. Bread and a cup were used in initiating into the mysteries of Mithras (*Justin Martyr*). **the Lord's table.** The Lord's supper is a feast on a *table*, not a sacrifice on an altar. Our only altar is the Cross, our only sacrifice that of Christ once for all. The Lord's supper stands in the same relation analogically to

Christ's sacrifice as the Jews' sacrificial feasts did to their sacrifices (cf. Mal. i. 7, "altar . . . table of the Lord"), and the heathen idol feasts to theirs (Isa. lxv. 11). Heathen sacrifices were to idol nonentities, behind which Satan lurked. The Jews' sacrifice was a shadow of the substance to come. Our one sacrifice of Christ is the only substantial reality. The partaker of the Jews' sacrificial feast partook rather "of the altar" (*v.* 18) than of GOD; the heathen idol-feaster had fellowship with demons; the communicant in the Lord's supper has in it a symbolic representation of, and a real fellowship in, the body of Christ once sacrificed, and now exalted as the Head of redeemed humanity. 22. **Do we provoke the Lord to jealousy?**—by dividing our fellowship between Him and idols (Ezek. xx. 39). The Greek has 'Or' preceding 'Shall we yield to God's will?' '*Or*' do we wish to provoke Him to assert His power? (Deut. xxxii. 21; Exod. xx. 5.) **are we stronger?**—that we can risk a contest with Him. 23. **All things are lawful for me**, &c. Recurring to the Corinthian plea (ch. vi. 12), he repeats his qualification of it. A B C Δ G *fg*, Vulgate, omit "for me." אּ C have it. **edify** not—*build not up* the spiritual temple, the Church, in faith and love. St. Paul does not appeal to the apostolic decision, Acts xv., but to the broad principle of true Christian freedom, which does not think that, because we *can* use external things, we *must* use them (ch. vi. 12). Their use or non-use should be regulated by regard to general *edification*. 24. (*V.* 33; Rom. xv. 1, 2; ch. xiii. 5.) 25. **shambles** —butchers' stalls. **asking no question**—whether it has been offered to idols or not. **for conscience' sake**—lest, by hearing it had been offered to idols, a needless scruple should arise in your conscience, which, but for your asking, would never have arisen. Or, 'not feeling it necessary for conscience' sake to ask questions.' [μηδέν is subjective.] 26. Ground on which such eating without questioning is justified. The earth and all its contents ("the fulness thereof," Ps. xxiv. 1; l. 12), including all meats, belong to the Lord, and are appointed for our use; where conscience suggests no scruple, all are to be eaten (Rom. xiv. 14, 20; 1 Tim. iv. 4, 5: cf. Acts x. 15). 27. **ye be disposed to go**—tacitly implying they would be safer not to go, yet not forbidding them (*v.* 9). The feast is a general entertainment, at which, however, there might be meat that had been offered to idols. **for conscience' sake** (note, *v.* 25). 28. **if any man**—a weak Christian at table, wishing to warn his brother. **offered in sacrifice unto idols.** So

showed it, and for conscience' sake: for ʸthe earth *is* the Lord's, and the
29 fulness thereof. Conscience, I say, not thine own, but of the other: for
30 *why is my liberty judged of another *man's* conscience? For if I by
⁵grace be a partaker, why am I evil spoken of for that for which I give
31 thanks? Whether ᵃtherefore ye eat, or drink, or whatsoever ye do, do
32 all to the glory of God. Give none offence, neither to the Jews, nor
33 to the ⁶Gentiles, nor to the church of God: even as I please all *men*
in all *things*, not seeking mine own profit, but the *profit* of many,
11 that they may be saved. BE ᵃye followers of me, even as I also *am* of
Christ
2 Now I praise you, brethren, that ye remember me in all things, ᵇand
3 keep the ¹ordinances, as I delivered *them* to you. But I would have you
know, that ᶜthe head of every man is Christ; and the ᵈhead of the
4 woman *is* the man; and ᵉthe head of Christ *is* God. Every man praying
5 or prophesying, having *his* head covered, dishonoureth his head. But

A. D. 59.

ʸ Deut. 10. 14.
ᶻ Rom. 14. 14.
⁵ Or. thanks-giving.
ᵃ Deut. 12. 7 11.
Zech. 7. 6.
⁶ Greeks.

CHAP. 11.
ᵃ 2 Thes. 3. 9.
ᵇ ch 7. 17.
¹ Or.
traditions.
2 Thes. 2. 15.
ᶜ Rom. 14. 9.
Eph. 5. 23.
ᵈ Gen. 3. 16.
ᵉ John 4. 34.

CΔG. But אABH [ἱερόθυτον] omit "unto idols."
At a heathen's table the expression offensive to
him would naturally be avoided. **for conscience'
sake**—not to cause a stumblingblock to thy weak
brother's conscience (ch. viii. 10-12). **for the
earth is the Lord's, &c.** Not in אABCΔGƒg,
Vulgate. **29. Conscience . . . of the other**—the
weak brother (*v.* 28). **for why is my liberty
judged of another man's conscience?** St. Paul
puts himself, as it were, in the position of his
converts. The Greek for "the other" [ἑτέρου]
and "another" [ἄλλης] are distinct. "*The other*"
is *the one with whom St. Paul's and his converts'
concern is:* "*another*" is *any other with whom he
and they have no concern.* If a guest know the
meat to be idol meat, whilst *I* know it not, I have
"liberty" to eat without being condemned by his
"conscience" (*Grotius*). Thus the "for," &c., is
an argument for *v.* 27, "eat, asking no question."
Or, 'Why should I give occasion, by rash use of
my liberty, that another should condemn it'
(*Estius*). Or the words are those of the Corinthian
objector (perhaps quoted by St. Paul from their
letter), 'Why is my liberty judged by another's
conscience?' why should not I be judged only by
my own, and have liberty to do whatever it sanctions? St. Paul replies, *v.* 31, Your doing so
ought always to be limited by regard "to the
glory of God" (*Vatablus*). The first explanation
is simplest: the "for," &c., it refers to "not
thine own" (*i. e.*, 'not *my* own,' in St. Paul's
change to the first person). I am to abstain only
in the case of liability to offend *the other's* conscience; in cases where *my own* has no scruple, I
am not bound, in God's judgment, by *any other*
conscience than my own. **30. For.** אABCΔGƒg
omit "for" [δέ]. **I by grace**—rather, 'with
thankfulness.' **be a partaker**—of the food set
before me. **evil spoken of**—by him who does not
use his liberty, but will eat nothing without
scrupulously questioning whence the meat comes.
give thanks—which consecrates all the Christian's
acts (Rom. xiv. 6; 1 Tim. iv. 3, 4). **31.** Contrast
Zech. vii. 6, worldly men. The godly "eat and
drink," and it is well with him (Jer. xxii. 15, 16).
to the glory of God (Col. iii. 17; 1 Pet. iv. 11)—
which involves regard to the edification of our
neighbour. **32. Give none offence**—in things indifferent; for in essential things affecting doctrine
and practice, even in the smallest *detail*, we must
not swerve from principle, whatever offence result
(Matt. xviii. 7; Acts xxiv. 16; ch. i. 23; Phil. i.
10). **33. I please**—I try to please (Rom. xv. 2;
ch. ix. 19, 22). **not seeking mine own** (*v.* 24).
many—rather, as Greek, 'THE many.'

**CHAP. XI. 1-34.—CENSURE ON DISORDERS IN
THEIR ASSEMBLIES—THEIR WOMEN NOT VEILED
—ABUSES AT THE LOVE FEASTS.**
1. Rather belonging to ch. x. **followers**—
Greek, 'imitators.' **of Christ**—who "pleased not
Himself" (Rom. xv. 3), but gave Himself for us,
laying aside His Divine glory, and dying as man
(Eph. v. 2; Phil. ii. 4, 5). Follow Christ first, and
earthly teachers only so far as they follow Christ.
2. Here the chapter ought to begin. **ye remember me in all things**—in your *general*
practice, though in *particular* instances ye fail.
ordinances [παραδόσεις]—'traditions;' *i. e.,* apostolic directions by word or in writing (*v.* 23; ch.
xv. 3; 2 Thess. ii. 15). The reference here is to
ceremonies; for in *v.* 23, as to the Lord's supper,
which is more than a ceremony, he says not merely,
"I *delivered* unto you," but also, "I have received
of the Lord;" here only, "I delivered them to
you." Romanists argue hence for oral traditions.
The difficulty is to know *what is* a genuine apostolic tradition intended for all ages. Any that
can be *proved* to be such ought to be observed;
any that cannot, ought to be rejected (Rev. xxii.
18). Those preserved in the written Word alone
can be proved to be such. **3.** The Corinthian
women, on the ground of the abolition of distinction of sex in Christ, claimed equality with men,
and, overstepping propriety, came forward to
pray and prophesy without the customary head-
covering. The Gospel did raise women from the
degradation in which they had been sunk, especially in the East. Yet, whilst on a level with
males as to *the offer of, and standing in, grace* (Gal.
iii. 28), their subjection in point of *order, modesty,*
and *seemliness* is to be maintained. St. Paul reproves here their unseemliness as to *dress;* in ch.
xiv. 34, as to *public speaking.* He grounds his
reproof on woman's subjection in the order of
creation. **the head**—an appropriate expression
when he is about to treat of woman's *head-dress.*
of every man is Christ (Eph. v. 23; Col. i. 18).
of the woman is the man (*v.* 8; Gen. iii. 16). **head
of Christ is God.** By Christ's voluntary subordination to the Father He was exalted; so the
woman finds in voluntary subjection to the man
her truest freedom (John xiv. 28; ch. iii. 23; Phil.
ii. 8). 'Since the head is of the same essence as
the body, and God is the head of the Son, the Son
must be of the same essence as the Father' (*S.
Chrysostom*) (Luke iii. 22, 38). 'The woman is of
the essence of the man, not made by him; so the
Son is not made by the Father, but of the Father's
essence' (*Theodoret*, t. iii., p. 171). **4. praying**—
in public (*v.* 17). **prophesying**—preaching in the

313

f every woman that prayeth or prophesieth with *her* head uncovered, dishonoureth her head : for that is even all one as if she were *g* shaven.

6 For if the woman be not covered, let her also be shorn: but if it be *h* a

7 shame for a woman to be shorn or shaven, let her be covered. For a man indeed ought not to cover *his* head, forasmuch as *i* he is the image

8 and glory of God : but the woman is the glory of the man. For the

9 man is not of the woman; but the woman of the man. Neither was

10 the man created for the woman; but the woman for the man. For this cause ought the woman to have ² power on *her* head because of the

11 angels. Nevertheless neither is the man without the woman, neither

A. D. 59.

f Acts 21. 9.
g Deut. 21.12.
h Num. 5. 18.
i Gen 1. 26.
² That is, a covering, in sign that she is under the power of her husband.

Spirit (ch. xii. 10). **having**—*i. e.*, if he were to have—a supposed case, to illustrate the impropriety in the *woman's* case. The Greek custom was for men in worship to be uncovered; the Jews wore the Tallith, or veil, to show reverence and their sense of unworthiness in God's presence (Isa. vi. 2), excepting where (as in Corinth) the Greek custom prevailed. But this passage shows wearing the Tallith was introduced *after apostolic times.* The heathen covered themselves in sacrificing, not to be distracted by outward objects. **dishonoureth his head**—not "Christ" (*v.* 3); but as "head" means before in this verse, *He dishonours his head* (the principal member), he divests himself of his divinely-appointed dignity by wearing a covering —a mark of subjection, making him look downwards instead of upwards to his spiritual Head, Christ. Why, then, ought not man to wear the covering in token of his subjection to Christ, as the woman wears it in token of her subjection to man? Because Christ is not seen, the man is, and visibly represents God (cf. *v.* 7). **5. woman that prayeth or prophesieth.** This instance of women speaking in public worship is extraordinary, and justified only by the miraculous gifts which such women possessed as their credentials. So Anna the prophetess and Priscilla (cf. Acts ii. 18). The ordinary rule to them is silence in public (ch. xiv. 34, 35; 1 Tim. ii. 11, 12). Mental receptivity and activity at home are most accordant with woman's destiny. This passage does not necessarily sanction women speaking in public, even though possessing miraculous gifts; but simply records what took place at Corinth, reserving the censure till ch. xiv. 34, 35. Even those 'prophesying' women were to exercise their gift rather in other times and places than the public congregation. **dishonoureth her head.** In putting away the veil, she puts away the badge of her subjection to man (which is her true 'honour'), and of her connection with Christ, man's Head. Moreover, the *head-covering* was the emblem of maiden *modesty* before man (Gen. xxiv. 65), and *chastity* (Gen. xx. 16). By it unlawful excitement in assemblies is avoided, women not attracting attention. Scripture sanctions not the emancipation of woman from subjection: modesty is her true ornament. Man rules; woman ministers: the respective dress should accord. To *uncover the head* indicated withdrawal from the husband's power; whence a suspected wife had her head *uncovered* by the priest (Num. v. 18). **all one as if . . . shaven.** As woman's hair is given by nature as her covering (*v.* 15), to cut it off like a man would be palpably indecorous; therefore, to put away the head-covering like a man would be similarly indecorous. It is *natural* to her to have long hair for her covering: she ought, therefore, to add the other head-covering, to show that she does of *her own will* that which *nature* teaches she ought to do, in token of her subjection to man. **6.** A woman would not like to be "shorn," or, what is worse, "shaven;" but if

she chooses to be unveiled in front, let her be so also behind—*i. e.*, "shorn." **a shame**—unbecoming (cf. *vv.* 13-15). Thus the shaving of nuns is "a shame." **7-9.** Argument from man's more immediate relation to God, and the woman's to man. **man . . . image and glory of God**—being created in God's "image" *first*, and *directly;* the woman *subsequently*, and *indirectly*, through man's mediation. Man is representative of God's "glory" (this ideal being realized fully in the Son of man, Ps. viii. 4, 5: cf. 2 Cor. viii. 23). Man is both the "image" (*tzelem*), and made in the "likeness" [ὁμοίωσις, *demuth*], of God (cf. Jas. iii. 9). "Image" [εἰκών] alone is applied to the Son of God (Col. i. 15: cf. Heb. i. 3, "express image" [χαρακτήρ], *the impress*). The Divine Son is not merely '*like*' God, He IS God of God, 'of one substance (essence) with the Father' (Nicene Creed). **woman is the glory of the man** —not also '*the image of the man.*' The woman is created in the *image of God* as well as the man (Gen. i. 26, 27). But as the moon in relation to the sun (Gen. xxxvii. 9), so woman shines not so much with light direct from God as with light derived from man—*i. e.*, in her order *in creation*— though *in grace* she comes into *direct* communion with God. Even here much of her knowledge is mediately given her through man, on whom she is dependent. Ministry to man, whom she elevates in his more responsible position, is her "glory." She is more *passive*: he *active.* **8. is . . . of**—*takes her being from* ('out of'). Woman was originally "taken out of man" (cf. Gen. ii. 23). The woman was made by God mediately through man, who was, as it were, a veil between her and God, and therefore should wear the head-covering in public, in acknowledgment of this subordination. The man, being made mediately by God as His glory, has no veil between himself and God. **9.** Neither—rather, 'For also.' *Another argument: the immediate object of woman's creation.* 'The man was not created for the sake of [διὰ, with accusative] the woman, but the woman for the sake of the man' (Gen. ii. 18, 21, 22), as his "help meet." Just as the Church is made for Christ: yet in both the natural and the spiritual creations the bride, whilst made for the bridegroom, in fulfilling that end attains her own true "glory," and brings "shame" and 'dishonour' on herself by departure from it (*vv.* 4, 6). **10. power on her head**—the kerchief: French, 'couvre-chef,' *head-covering, emblem of* "power on her head:" the sign of her being under man, exercising delegated authority. St. Paul had before his mind the root-connection between the Hebrew terms for 'veil' (*Radid*) and subjection (*Radad*). **because of the angels**—who, like the cherubim in the temple, are present at Christian assemblies (cf. Ps. cxxxviii. 1, note), and delight in the orderly subordination of the several worshippers in their respective places—the outward demeanour and dress indicating that inward humility which is most pleasing to their common

12 the woman without the man, in the Lord. For as the woman *is* of the man, even so *is* the man also by the woman; but ʲall things of God.

13   Judge in yourselves: is it comely that a woman pray unto God un-
14 covered? Doth not even nature itself teach you, that, if a man have
15 long hair, it is a shame unto him? But if a woman have long hair, it is a glory to her: for *her* hair is given her for a ³covering.

16   But ᵏif any man seem to be contentious, we have no such custom, neither the churches of God.

17   Now in this that I declare *unto you* I praise *you* not, that ye come
18 together not for the better, but for the worse. For first of all, when ye come together in the church, ˡI hear that there be ⁴divisions
19 among you; and I partly believe it. For ᵐthere must be also ⁵heresies

A. D. 59.
ʲ Pro. 16. 4.
Rom. 11.36.
ch. 8. 6.
Heb. 1. 2.
3.
³ Or. veil.
ᵏ 1 Tim. 6. 4.
ˡ ch. 1. 10.
ch. 3. 3.
ch. 5. 1.
ch. 6. 1.
⁴ Or.
schisms.
ᵐ Matt. 18. 7.
Luke 17. 1.
⁵ Or. sects.

Lord (Eccl. v. 6; ch. iv. 9; Eph. iii. 10). *Chrysostom,* 'Thou standest with angels; thou singest, thou hymnest with them, yet dost thou stand laughing?' *Bengel,* 'As the angels are related to God, so the woman is to man. God's face is uncovered; angels in His presence are veiled (Isa. vi. 2). Man's face is uncovered; woman in his presence is to be veiled. For her not to be so would, by its indecorousness, offend the angels (Matt. xviii. 10, 31). She, by her weakness, specially needs their ministry: she ought to be the more careful not to offend them.' **11.** The one needs the other in sexual relations; and in respect to Christ (" in the Lord "), the man and the woman together (for neither can be dispensed with) realize the ideal of redeemed humanity represented by the Bride, the Church. Christ alone combined the perfections of man and of woman also. He is the Representative Man, having at once man's masculine power and woman's ministering grace. **12.** As woman was formed *out of* man, even so is man born *by means of* woman; but all things (including both man and woman) are *from* God as their source (Rom. xi. 36; 2 Cor. v. 18). They depend each on the other, and both on Him. **13.** Appeal to their own sense of decorum. **a woman pray unto God.** By rejecting the emblem of subjection (the head-covering), she passes at one leap, in praying publicly, beyond both *man* and *angels* (*Bengel*). **14.** The fact that "nature" has provided woman, and not man, with long hair, proves that man was designed to be uncovered, and woman covered. The Nazarite wore long hair lawfully, as part of a vow sanctioned by God (Num. vi. 5: cf. 2 Sam. xiv. 26, and Acts xviii. 18). "Nature" is *God's will impressed on creation;* when He is recognized, Nature's teachings are auxiliary to Revelation. **15. her hair . . . for a covering**—her long hair shows she ought to cover her head as much as possible. The will ought to accord with nature. **16.** A summary by appeal to the universal custom of the churches. **if any man seem**—'*thinks*' (fit) [δοκεῖ] (Matt. iii. 9); if any man *chooses* (still, after all my arguments) to be contentious; if any *thinks* himself *right* in being so. A reproof of the Corinthians' self-sufficiency and disputatiousness (ch. i. 20). **we**—apostles; or, we of the Jewish nation. Jewish women veiled themselves in public, according to *Tertullian.* The former explanation is best, as the Jews are not referred to in the context; but he often refers to himself and his fellow-apostles. "We—us" (ch. iv. 9, 10; x. 5, 6). **no such custom**—as that of women praying uncovered. Not 'that of being contentious.' The Greek [συνήθειαν] implies a *usage* rather than a *mental habit* (John xviii. 39). The usage of true "churches" (plural: not 'the Church,' as an ab-

315

stract entity, but "*the churches,*" as many *independent witnesses*) of God (the churches which God recognizes) is a valid argument as to *external rites,* especially *negatively*—e. g., such rites were not received among them, therefore ought not to be admitted among us; but in *doctrine or essentials* the argument is not valid (ch. vii. 17; xiv. 33). **neither**—nor yet. Catholic usage is not an infallible test of *truth,* but a general test of *decency.* **17. in this**—which follows. **I declare**—rather, 'I enjoin,' as the Greek [παραγγέλλω] is always used. A B C ƒ, Vulgate, read 'this I enjoin (you), not praising (you).' אG g support the received text. **that**—*in that* you, &c. Here he qualifies his praise (v. 2). 'I said I praised you for keeping the ordinances delivered to you; BUT (so the Greek for "now") I must authoritatively enjoin you on a matter in which I praise you not--viz., as to the Lord's supper (v. 23; ch. xiv. 37). **not for the better**—not so as to progress to what is better. **for the worse**—so as to retrograde to what is worse. Holy ordinances, if they do not improve, positively injure. The result of 'coming together' in a carnal spirit must be "condemnation" (v. 34). **18. first of all.** Instead of *secondly,* follows "therefore," v. 20. The "divisions" (Greek, *schisms*) of opinion (ch. i. 10) were the PRIMARY evil, causing, at the Lord's supper, their eating apart from brethren (v. 21)—a *secondary* evil. **in the church**—not the *place* of worship; for *Isidore* of Pelusium denies that there were such places set apart for worship in the apostles' times ('Ep.' 246, 2); but 'in the congregation' met for worship, where especially love, order, and harmony should prevail. The very ordinance instituted for uniting believers was made an occasion of "divisions." **partly**—he excepts the innocent. 'I am loath to believe *all* I hear; but *some* I am forced to believe, whilst my love is unaffected by it.' **19. heresies**—not merely 'schisms,' 'divisions' (v. 18), which are '*recent* dissensions through differences of opinion' (*Augustine*), but also "heresies"—*i. e.,* 'schisms become *inveterate:*' 'sects' (Greek, Acts v. 17; xv. 5). At present there were dissensions at the love feasts; but St. Paul, remembering Jesus' words (Matt. xviii. 7; xxiv. 10, 12; Luke xvii. 1), foresees "there must be (come) also" *matured secessions* of separatists. The "must be" arises not from fatalistic necessity, but from sin necessarily bearing its natural fruits, which he foresees. These are overruled by Providence to the probation of character of both godly and ungodly professors, and to the discipline of the former for glory. There may be *schism* without secession (ch. xii. 21, 25; John vii. 43). "Heresies" had not yet its technical sense, referring to doctrinal errors: it means *confirmed schisms. Augustine's*

among you, ⁿthat they which are approved may be made manifest among you.

20 When ye come together therefore into one place, ⁶*this* is not to eat the
21 Lord's supper. For in eating every one taketh before *other* his own
22 supper: and one is hungry, and ᵒanother is drunken. What! have ye
   not houses to eat and to drink in? or ᵖdespise ye the church of God, and
   shame ⁷ them that have not? What shall I say to you? shall I praise
   you in this? I praise *you* not.
23 For ᑫI have received of the Lord that which also I delivered unto you,
   That the Lord Jesus the *same* night in which he was betrayed took
24 bread: and when he had given thanks, he brake *it*, and said, Take, eat:
   this is my body, which is broken for you: this do ˢ in remembrance of
25 me. After the same manner also *he took* the cup, when he had supped,
   saying, This cup is the ʳ new testament in my blood: this do ye, as oft
26 as ye drink *it*, in remembrance of me. For as often as ye eat this bread,
   and drink this cup, ⁹ ye do show the Lord's death ˢ till he come.

A. D. 59.
ⁿ Luke 2. 35.
⁶ Or. ye cannot eat.
ᵒ Jude 12.
ᵖ Lev. 19. 30.
Ps. 89. 7.
Ps. 9 : 5.
⁷ Or, them that are poor.
Jas. 2. 6.
ᑫ Gal 1. 1.
ˢ Or. for a remembrance.
ʳ Heb. 9. 15.
⁹ Or, show ye.
ˢ Acts 1. 11.
Rev. 1. 7.

rule is a golden one:—'In doubtful questions, liberty; in essentials, unity; in all things, charity.' **that . . . . approved may be made manifest**—through the *disapproved* (reprobates) becoming manifested (Luke ii. 35; 1 John ii. 19). **20. When . . . therefore**—resuming the thread of discourse (v. 18). **this is not to.** *It is not possible* to eat a true Lord's supper where UNITY exists not (ch. x. 17); where each is greedily intent on "HIS OWN SUPPER," and some are excluded altogether, not having been waited for (v. 33); where some are "drunken," others "hungry" (v. 21). The love-feast preceded the Lord's supper (as eating the passover came before the Lord's supper at the first institution of the latter). They ate and drank together earthly, then heavenly food, in token of their unity for time and eternity. It was a club-feast, where each brought his portion, and the rich extra portions for the poor. From it the bread and wine were taken for the Eucharist. It was at it that the excesses took place which made a *true* celebration of the Lord's supper, during or after it, with due discernment of its solemnity, out of the question. Hence the love feasts were afterwards disjoined from the Lord's supper, and in the fourth century forbidden by a council. **21. one taketh before other** —the rich "before" the poor, who had no supper of their own. Instead of 'tarrying for one another' (v. 33; ch. xii. 21, 25). **his own supper** (Phil. iii. 19). "The *Lord's* supper," the spiritual feast, never enters his thoughts. **drunken.** The one has more than is good for him; the other less. **22. What!**—Greek, *For.* It is disgraceful to act so, "for," &c. **houses** (v. 34)—"at home." *There* satisfy your appetite; not in the house of God. **despise ye the church**—*the congregation* mostly composed of the poor, whom "GOD hath chosen," however ye despise them (Jas. ii. 5). **of God**—the true honour of "the Church." **shame them that have not**—viz., *houses* to eat and drink in: who, therefore, ought to have received at the love-feasts from their wealthier brethren (Neh. viii. 10). **I praise you not**—resuming v. 17. **23.** He shows the unworthiness of such conduct from the dignity of the holy supper. **I**—emphatic in the Greek. It is not *my own*, but *the Lord's* institution. **received of the Lord**—by immediate revelation from the risen Saviour (Gal. i. 12: cf. Acts xxii. 17, 18; 2 Cor. xii. 1-4). [ἀπό, here, instead of παρά (commonly used for immediate revelation), is to discriminate between Christ's personal appearance (Acts ix.) and His *revelation by His Spirit.*] The renewal of the institution, by

special revelation to St. Paul, enhances its solemnity. The similarity between St. Luke's and St. Paul's account of it implies that the former drew his information from the apostle, whose companion in travel he was. The undesigned coincidence is a proof of genuineness. **night**—the time for the passover (Exod. xii. 6): the time for the Lord's supper is not fixed. **betrayed.** With the traitor at the table, and though about to receive such injury from man, He gave this last gift, a pledge of His amazing love to man. **24. brake.** The *breaking* of the bread involves its *distribution*, and reproves the Corinthians at the love feast: "every one taketh before other his own supper." **my body, which is broken for you**— "given" (Luke xxii. 19) for [ὑπέρ] you (*in your behalf*), and "broken," to be distributed among you. ℵ A B omit " broken," leaving it to be supplied from "brake." C Δ G support "broken." The Memphitic and Thebaic versions read from Luke, "given." The literal "body" cannot be meant; for Christ was still sensibly present among his disciples. They *could* only have understood Him analogically. As the bread is to your bodily health, so my body is to the believing communicant's spiritual health. "Take, eat," are not in ℵ A B C Δ G: Amiatine, Vulgate, has them. **25. when he had supped**—Greek, 'after the eating of supper;' viz., the passover preceding the Lord's supper. So you Corinthians ought to separate common meals from the Lord's supper. **the new testament**—or "covenant." The cup is the parchment-deed on which my new covenant, or last will, is written and sealed, making over to you all blessings here and hereafter. **in my blood**—ratified by MY blood (Heb. ix. 12). **as oft as** [ὁσάκις ἐάν]—*as many times soever;* for it is an ordinance *often* to be partaken of. **in remembrance of me.** St. Luke expresses this; St. Matthew and St. Mark understand it; St. Paul twice records it. The sacrifices brought *sins* continually to remembrance (Heb. x. 1, 3). The Lord's supper brings to our *remembrance Christ's* sacrifice once for all for the full and final *remission of sins.* Not 'do this for a *memorial* of me,' as if it were a *memorial sacrifice*, which would be *mnemosunon* (Acts x. 4) or *hupomnesin*,—a *reminding* the Father of His Son's sacrifice. Nay, it is for our *remembrance* of it, not to *remind* Him. **26. For**—in proof that the Lord's supper is "in remembrance" of Him. **show**—*announce publicly* [καταγγέλλετε]; not *dramatically represent*, but '*publicly profess* each of you, the Lord died FOR ME' *Wahl*). St. Paul means, not *literal* presence, but *vivid personal appro-*

27 Wherefore ᵗ whosoever shall eat this bread, and drink *this* cup of the
Lord, unworthily, shall be guilty of the body and blood of the Lord.
28 But ᵘ let a man examine himself, and so let him eat of *that* bread, and
29 drink of *that* cup. For he that eateth and drinketh unworthily, eateth
and drinketh ¹⁰ damnation to himself, not discerning the Lord's body.
30 For this cause many *are* weak and sickly among you, and many sleep.
31, For ᵛ if we would judge ourselves, we should not be judged. But when
32 we are judged, ʷ we are chastened of the Lord, that we should not be
33 condemned with the world. Wherefore, my brethren, when ye come
34 together to eat, tarry one for another. And if any man hunger, let him

A. D. 5ᵛ.
ᵗ Num. 9. 10.
John 6. 51.
John 13. 27.
ᵘ 2 Cor. 12. 5.
Gal. 6. 4.
¹⁰ Or. judgment.
Rom. 15. 2.
ᵛ 1 John 1. 9.
ʷ Job 5. 17.
Amos 3. 2.
Heb. 12. 6.

priation by faith of Christ crucified in the Lord's
supper (Eph. v. 30: cf. Gen. ii. 23): realizing that
we ourselves are "members of His body, of His
flesh, and of His bones," ' our sinful bodies made
clean by His body (once for all offered), and our
souls washed through His most precious blood'
('Church of England Prayer Book '). "Show," or
'announce,' applies to *new* things (cf. Exod. xiii.
8). So the Lord's death, and all the saving blessings resulting from it, ought always to be fresh in
our memory (cf. in heaven, Rev. v. 6). That the
Lord's supper is in *remembrance* of Him, implies
that He is bodily absent, though spiritually present; for we cannot ' commemorate' one absent.
Our not only *showing* the Lord's death, but *eating*
and *drinking* the pledges of it, could only be understood by the Jews, accustomed to feasts after
propitiatory sacrifices, as implying our *personal
appropriation* of the benefits of that death. *till
he come*—when there shall be no longer need of
symbols, the body itself being manifested. The
Greek [no, ἄν, before ἔλθῃ] expresses the *certainty*
of His coming. Rome teaches that we eat Christ
present corporally "till He come" corporally!—
a contradiction in terms. The *showbread*, lit.,
bread of the presence, was in the sanctuary, but
not in the Holiest place (Heb. ix. 1-8); so the
Lord's supper shall be superseded in heaven,
the antitype to the Holiest place, by Christ's
own bodily presence: then the wine shall be
drunk "anew" in the Father's kingdom by
Christ and His people together, of which heavenly
banquet the Lord's supper is a spiritual foretaste
(Matt. xxvi. 29; Rev. xix. 9). Meantime, as the
showbread was placed *anew* every Sabbath on
the table before the Lord (Lev. xxiv. 5-8), so the
Lord's death was *shown* (announced *afresh*) at the
Lord's table the first day of every week in the
primitive Church. We are now "priests unto
God" in the dispensation of Christ's spiritual presence, antitypical of the HOLY PLACE: the perfect
dispensation to come when Christ shall come is
antitypical to the HOLIEST PLACE. Christ our
High Priest alone in the flesh as yet has entered
the Heavenly Holiest (Heb. ix. 6, 7; xii. 24); at
his coming, believers too shall enter (Rev. vii. 15;
xxi. 22). The supper joins the consummations of
the Old and New dispensations. The first and
second comings are two phases of *one* coming;
whence the expression is not 'return,' but
"come" (cf., however, John xiv. 3).

27. eat... and drink. So A Δ (*Lachmann* versus
Tischendorf) read. But אBCGƒg, Vulgate, and
Cyprian, read 'or.' Romanists quote this in
favour of communion in one kind. This does not
follow. St. Paul says, Whosoever behaves unworthily, *either* in eating the bread *or* in drinking
the cup, is guilty of the body and blood of Christ.
Impropriety in only *one* vitiates communion in
both. Therefore, in the end of the verse, he says,
"body AND blood." Any who takes the bread
without the wine, *or* the wine without the bread,
"*unworthily*" communicates: so 'is guilty of

Christ's body and blood,' for he disobeys Christ's
command to receive both. If we do not receive
the sacramental symbol of the Lord's death
worthily, we share the guilt of that death (cf.
Heb. vi. 6). *Unworthiness in the person* ought not
to exclude any, but *unworthily communicating*:
however unworthy we be, if we penitently believe
in Christ's meritorious death for us, we worthily
communicate. The 'unworthiness' *primarily*
meant here is that of *unlovingness to brethren*
in the very ordinance which seals love to them as
well as to our common Saviour. **28.** *But—so much
the more;* as the guilt of unworthily receiving
is so great. **examine** [δοκιμαζέτω]—*prove, test*
his own state of mind as to Christ's death, and his
capability of "discerning the Lord's body" (*vv.* 29,
31). Not auricular confession to a priest, but *self*-
examination, is necessary. so—after due self-
examination. **of . . . of** [ἐκ]. In *v.* 27, where the
receiving was *unworthily*, it was, 'eat this bread,
drink this cup' without " of:" the "of" here implies due circumspection. **let him eat.** His self-
examination is not in order that he may stay away,
but that he may eat—*i. e.*, communicate. **29.**
damnation—a stumblingblock to many as to communicating. Translate, ' judgment.' The *judgment*
described (*vv.* 30-32) is temporal. If this failed to
reform, then, and not till then, *eternal judgment*
would ensue. **not discerning**—not discriminatingly
judging: *not distinguishing in judgment* [διακρίνων],
(the sin and its punishment are, by the cognate
words, marked as corresponding) from common
food, the sacramental pledges of the Lord's body.
א A B omit "Lord's " (see *v.* 27). CΔGƒg, Vulgate,
have it. Omitting also "unworthily," with א A B,
translate, ' He that eateth and drinketh, eateth
and drinketh judgment to himself, IF he discern
not THE body" (Heb. x. 29). CΔGƒg, Vulgate,
read "unworthily." The Church is "the body of
Christ" (ch. xii. 27): the Lord's body is *His once
for all sacrificed body*, discerned by the soul in
faithful receiving; not present in the elements
themselves. **30. weak and sickly.** The "weak "
[ἀσθενεῖς] have *naturally* no strength; the "sickly "
[ἄρρωστοι] have *lost their strength* by disease.
sleep—in death: not a violent death; but the
result of sickness, the Lord's chastening for the
individual's salvation, the mind being brought to a
right state on the sick-bed (*v.* 32). **31. If we would
judge ourselves.** א A B Δ G ƒg, Vulgate, read
'But,' not 'For' (which C has). Translate 'if we
discriminatingly judged (the same Greek as " discerning," *v.* 29) ourselves, we should *not have been*
judged' [οὐκ ἄν ἐκρινόμεθα]—i. e., we should have
escaped our present judgments (Job xxxiv. 31).
In order to ' discriminatingly judge the Lord's
body,' we need to 'discriminatingly judge ourselves.' A prescient warning against *priestly*
absolution after auricular confession, as the necessary preliminary to the Lord's supper. **32.**
chastened (Rev. iii. 19). **with the world**—who,
being bastards, are without chastening (Heb. xii.
8). **33. tarry one for another**—in contrast to *v.*

317

eat at home; that ye come not together unto [11] condemnation. And the rest [x] will I set in order when [y] I come.

12 NOW [a] concerning spiritual *gifts*, brethren, I would not have you
2 ignorant. Ye know [b] that ye were Gentiles, carried away unto these
3 dumb idols, even as ye were led. Wherefore I give you to understand, that no man speaking by the Spirit of God calleth Jesus [1] accursed; and *that* no man can say that Jesus is the Lord, but by the Holy Ghost.
4, Now there are diversities of gifts, but the same Spirit. And there
5, are differences of [2] administrations, but the same Lord. And there are
6 diversities of operations, but it is the same God which worketh all in

A. D. 59.

[11] Or. judgment.
[x] Tit. 1. 5.
[y] ch. 4. 19.

CHAP. 12.
[a] ch. 14. 1.
[b] Eph. 2. 11.
[1] Or, anathema.
[2] Or, ministeries.

---

21. Not, 'give a share to one another,' for all the viands brought were *common* property; therefore, they should "tarry" till all met to partake of the common feast of fellowship (*Theophylact*). **34. if any man hunger**—so as not to be able to 'tarry for others,' let him satisfy beforehand his hunger at home (*v. 22*). **the rest**—'the other questions you asked me as to the Lord's supper.' Not other questions in *general;* for he subsequently sets in order other general questions.

CHAP. XII. 1-31.—USE AND ABUSE OF SPIRITUAL GIFTS; ESPECIALLY PROPHESYING AND TONGUES.
This is the *second* subject for correction in the Corinthian assemblies: the '*first*' was discussed, ch. xi. 18-34.
1. spiritual gifts—the signs of the Spirit's efficacious presence in the Church, which is Christ's body; the complement of His incarnation, as the body is the complement of the head. Foremost the *gift of tongues* is referred to here, as being the gift overrated by the self-sufficient, excitable, and loquacious Corinthians. By love pervading the whole, the gifts of the several members, reciprocally complementing each other, tend to perfect the one body of Christ. The ordinary and permanent gifts are comprehended with the extraordinary without distinction, as both alike flow from the indwelling Spirit of life. The extraordinary gift, so far from making professors more peculiarly *saints* than in our day, did not always even *prove* that such persons were saved at all (Matt. vii. 22). They were needed at first—(1.) As a pledge to Christians who had just passed over from Judaism or heathendom, that God was in the Church; (2.) For the propagation of Christianity in the Church; (3.) For edifying the Church. They continued down to the third century, when the Church rose on the decline of heathenism. They were rare after the apostolic age. Now that we have the *whole written* New Testament, which they had not, and Christianity established by miracles, we need no further miracle to attest the truth. So the pillar of cloud which guided the Israelites was withdrawn when they were sufficiently assured of the Divine presence, the manifestation of God's glory being thenceforward enclosed in the Most Holy place. St. Paul sets forth,—I. The unity of the body (*vv.* 1-27). II. The variety of its members and functions (*vv.* 27-30). III. The grand principle for rightly using the gifts —viz., love, (*v.* 31, and ch. xiii.) IV. The comparison of the gifts, (ch. xiv.) **I would not have you ignorant**—with all your boasts of "knowledge." If ignorant now, it will be your own fault, not mine (ch. xiv. 38). **2. (Eph. ii. 11) that ye were.** So B G *f.* But א A C Δ *g*, Vulgate, read 'that WHEN ye were:' thus "ye were" must be supplied. "*Ye were*" blindly "carried away" at the will of your false guides. **these dumb idols**—Greek, '*the* idols which are dumb,' contrasted with the living God, who 'speaks' in the believer by His Spirit

(*v.* 3, &c.): and who then gave "tongues." Their past heathen ignorance of spiritual powers is why they needed instruction as to spiritual gifts, especially as to *the tongues*. When blind, ye went to the *dumb*. **as ye were led.** The Greek is, rather, 'as ye might (happen to) [ἄν] be led.' You had no criterion of truth. The heathen oracles led their votaries at random. **3.** Negative and positive tests of inspiration by the Spirit—the rejection or confession of Jesus' Lordship, not the possession of "tongues" (ch. xiii. 1; 1 John iv. 2; v. 1). St. Paul gives a test of truth against the Gentiles; St. John against the false prophets. **by the Spirit**—Greek, 'IN the Spirit,' that being the power and element *in* which he speaks (Matt. xvi. 17; John xv. 26). **of God . . . Holy.** The same Spirit is called at one time "the Spirit OF GOD," at another, "the HOLY Ghost," or 'Holy Spirit.' Infinite *Holiness* is almost synonymous with *Godhead.* The saying, 'Jesus is accursed' cannot emanate from "the Spirit of God," but from *the evil Spirit.* The saying, 'Jesus is Lord,' cannot emanate from *man's natural spirit*, but from "the Holy Ghost." א A B C read the *nominative*, 'accursed Jesus!' and 'Lord Jesus!' Δ G read the received text. **speaking . . . say.** 'Speak' implies utterance; "say" refers to that which is uttered. Here "say" means a *continued spiritual* and *believing* confession of Him. **Jesus**—not merely the doctrine, but the historical "JESUS" (Rom. x. 9)—that He is the Divine Lord incarnate. **accursed**—as the Jews and Gentiles treated Him (Gal. iii. 13: cf. 'to curse Christ,' in *Pliny's* letter, Ep. x. 97). Not the mere once-execration, but stedfast rejection. The spiritual man feels Him the Source of all blessings (Eph. i. 3): that to be severed from him is to be accursed (Rom. ix. 3). **Lord**—acknowledging himself His servant (Isa. xxvi. 13). "Lord" is the LXX. translation for the incommunicable name JEHOVAH.

4. diversities of gifts—i. e., the one Spirit is refracted into various spiritual endowments peculiar to the several members (*v.* 11): some altogether superhuman, as tongues, healing, &c.; others based on natural capabilities. **same Spirit**—the Holy Trinity: the *Holy* Spirit in this verse; *Christ* in *v.* 5; *the Father* in *v.* 6. "Gifts," "administrations," "operations," respectively correspond to the Divine Tree. *The Spirit* is treated of, *v.* 7, &c.; *the Lord, v.* 12, &c.; *God, v.* 28. Cf. Eph. iv. 4-6. **5, 6.** "Gifts" (*v.* 4), "administrations" (the various *functions* and *services* of those having the gifts: cf. *v.* 28), and "operations" (the *effects* resulting from both) are the same things viewed in a different aspect. They are "gifts" of the same *Spirit of holiness* and *knowledge* (ch. ii. 10); 'ministrations' in the *service* of the same *Lord* of *love*, and "operations" derived from the same source, the omnipotent *Father* (ch. viii. 6), omnipotence. **same Lord**—whom the Spirit glorifies by these *ministrations.* **6. operations**—(cf. *v.* 10.) **same God which worketh**—by His Spirit *working* (*v.* 11). **all**

7 all. But ^cthe manifestation of the Spirit is given to every man to profit
8 withal. For to one is given by the Spirit the word ^dof wisdom; to an-
9 other ^ethe word of knowledge by the same Spirit; to ^fanother faith by
10 the same Spirit; to another ^gthe gifts of healing by the same Spirit; to
^hanother the working of miracles; to another ⁱprophecy; ^jto another
discerning of spirits; to another ^k*divers* kinds of tongues; to another
11 the interpretation of tongues: but all these worketh that one and the
self-same Spirit, ^ldividing to every man severally ^mas he will.
12 For as the body is one, and hath many members, and all the members
13 of that one body, being many, are one body; ⁿso also *is* Christ. For ^oby
one Spirit are we all baptized into one body, ^pwhether *we be* Jews or
³Gentiles, whether *we be* bond or free; and ^qhave been all made to drink
into one Spirit.

A. D. 59.

^c Rom. 12. 6.
^d ch. 2. 6.
^e 2 Cor. 8. 7.
^f Matt. 17.19.
^g Mark 16.18.
^h Gal. 3. 5.
ⁱ Rom. 12. 6.
^j 1 John 4. 1.
^k Acts 2. 4.
^l 2 Cor. 10.13.
^m John 3. 8.
ⁿ Gal. 3. 16.
^o Isa. 44. 3-5.
^p Col. 3. 11.
³ Greeks.
^q John 6. 63.

in all—all of the "gifts" in all the *persons* who possess them. **7. But.** Though all the gifts flow from the one God, Lord, and Spirit, the "manifestation" by which the Spirit, though hidden in Himself, acts, varies in each. **to every man**—*to each* of the church-members *severally*. **to profit withal**—*with a view to the profit* of the whole body. **8-10.** Three *genera* of gifts are distinguished, with their respective *species: allo* marks the species, *hetero* the genera (cf. Greek, ch. xv. 39-41). I. **to one** class [ᾧ μέν] gifts of *intellect*—viz., (1.) wisdom; (2.) **to another** individual [ἄλλῳ], knowledge. II. **to another** [ἑτέρῳ]—to a *distinct class* gifts dependent on a special *faith*—viz., that of miracles (Matt. xvii. 20). (1.) **to another** individual [ἄλλῳ], healings; (2.) Workings of miracles; (3.) Prophecy of future events; (4.) Discerning of spirits—the divinely-given faculty of distinguishing between those really inspired and pretenders. III. **to another** [ἑτέρῳ]—to a *distinct class* gifts referring to the *tongues*. (1.) Divers kinds of tongues; (2.) **to another** individual [ἄλλῳ] interpretation of tongues. The catalogue, *v.* 28, is not meant to harmonize with the one here, though some particulars correspond. The three genera are summarily referred to by single instances in ch. xiii. 8. **by . . . by . . . by.** The first [διά] is, 'by means of,' 'through the operation of;' the second [κατά] is, 'according to' the disposing of (cf. *v.* 11); the third is, 'in'—i. e., *under the influence of* (so Matt. xxii. 43; Luke ii. 27, Greek). **word of wisdom**—ready *utterance of* (for imparting to others, Eph. vi. 19) *wisdom*—viz., NEW revelations of the Divine wisdom in redemption, contrasted with human philosophy (ch. i. 24; ii. 6, 7; Eph. i. 8; iii. 10; Col. ii. 3). **word of knowledge**—ready *utterance,* supernaturally imparted, of truths ALREADY REVEALED (in this it is distinguished from "the word of wisdom"). Cf. ch. xiv. 6, where "revelation" (answering to "wisdom" here) is distinguished from "knowledge." *Wisdom* or *revelation* belonged to "prophets;" *knowledge,* to "teachers." *Wisdom* penetrates deeper than *knowledge.* *Knowledge* relates to things to be done; *wisdom,* to things eternal: hence *wisdom* does not, like *knowledge,* "vanish away" (ch. xiii. 8). **faith**—not of doctrines, but confidence in God, by the impulse of His Spirit, that he would enable them to perform any required miracle (cf. ch. xiii. 2; Mark xi. 23; Jas. v. 15). Its *principle* is the same as that of saving faith—reliance on God; the producing *cause* is the same—a power altogether supernatural (Eph. i. 19, 20). But the *objects* differ respectively. Hence, saving faith does not save by its intrinsic merit, but by the merits of Him who is its object. **healing**—Greek, 'healings:' *different kinds* of disease need *different kinds of healing* (Matt. x. 1). **working of miracles.**

As 'healings' are miracles, those meant must be miracles of extraordinary POWER. Healings might be effected by human skill in course of time; but the raising of the dead, the infliction of death by a word, the innocuous use of poisons, &c., are *miracles of special power* [ἐνεργήματα] (the same Greek as *v.* 6 [δυνάμεων], *energetic operations of powers:* cf. Mark vi. 5; Acts xix. 11). **prophecy**—here not in the wider sense of public teaching by the Spirit (ch. xi. 4, 5; xiv. 1-5), but, as its position between "miracles" and "discerning of spirits" implies, *the inspired disclosure of the future* (Acts xi. 27, 28; xxi. 11; 1 Tim. i. 18). It depends on "faith" (*v.* 9; Rom. xii. 6). The *prophets* ranked next to the *apostles* (*v.* 28; Eph. iii. 5; iv. 11). As *prophecy* is part of the whole scheme of redemption, an inspired insight into the obscurer Scriptures was the necessary preparation for this miraculous foresight of the future. **discerning of spirits**—discerning between the operation of God's Spirit and the evil spirit, or unaided human spirit (Acts v. 1-11; ch. xiv. 29; 1 Tim. iv. 1; 1 John iv. 1). **kinds of tongues**—the power of speaking *various languages* (Acts ii. 8-11); also, a *spiritual language unknown to man, uttered in ecstasy* (ch. xiv. ii. 12). This is a distinct genus (Greek) 'to another and a *different* class.' **interpretation of tongues** (ch. xiv. 13, 26, 27). **11. as he will** (*v.* 18; Heb. ii. 4).

12, 13. Unity, not unvarying uniformity, is the law of God in grace as in nature (Rom. xii. 4, 5). As the body's many members compose an organic whole, and none can be dispensed with, so those variously gifted by the Spirit compose a spiritual organism—the body of Christ—into which all are baptized by the one Spirit. **of that one body.** So CΔ. But אABGg, Vulgate, omit "one." **so also is Christ**—i. e., the whole Christ, *the head and body.* So Ps. xviii. 50, 'His anointed (Messiah or Christ), David (the antitypical David), and his seed.' **by one Spirit are we all baptized**—*lit.,* 'in:' in virtue of; in the sphere or element of. The *designed* effect of baptism realized when not frustrated by man's unfaithfulness. **Gentiles**—lit., *Greeks.* The *Greeks* had a susceptibility for the gift of *tongues* (on which the Corinthians prided themselves), the *Romans* for *practical* gifts, the Jews for *spiritual.* **all made to drink into one Spirit.** אBCΔGfg read 'made to drink one Spirit,' omitting "into" (John vii. 37): an allusion to the Lord's supper (though including all channels of grace: cf. the same Greek verb, ch. iii. 2), as there is to baptism in the beginning of the verse. So the 'spirit, the water, and the blood' (1 John v. 8) combine the two outward signs with the inward things signified, the Spirit's grace, **are . . . have been**—rather, as Greek, 'were . . . were' (Aorists: *past time*).

14, For the body is not one member, but many. If the foot shall say,
15 Because I am not the hand, I am not of the body; is it therefore not of
16 the body? And if the ear shall say, Because I am not the eye, I am not
17 of the body; is it therefore not of the body? If the whole body *were* an
eye, where *were* the hearing? if the whole *were* hearing, where *were*
18 the smelling? But now hath God set the members every one of them in
19 the body, as it hath pleased him. And if they were all one member,
20 where *were* the body? But now *are they* many members, yet but one
21 body. And the eye cannot say unto the hand, I have no need of thee;
22 nor again the head to the feet, I have no need of you. Nay, much more
those members of the body, which seem to be more feeble, are necessary:
23 and those *members* of the body, which we think to be less honourable,
upon these we [4]bestow more abundant honour; and our uncomely
24 *parts* have more abundant comeliness. For our comely *parts* have no
need: but God hath tempered the body together, having given more
25 abundant honour to that *part* which lacked: that there should be no
[5]schism in the body; but *that* the members should have the same care
26 one for another. And whether one member suffer, all the members suffer
with it; or one member be honoured, all the members rejoice with it.
27 Now [v]ye are the body of Christ, and members in particular.
28 And [z]God hath set some in the church, first [t]apostles, secondarily
[u]prophets, thirdly teachers, after that miracles, then gifts of healings,
29 [y]helps, [w]governments, [6]diversities of tongues. *Are* all apostles? *are* all

A. D. 59.
[4] Or. put on.
[5] Or division.
[r] Rom. 12. 5.
Eph. 1. 23.
Eph. 4. 12.
Eph. 5. 23, 30.
Col. 1. 24.
[s] Luke 6. 14.
Acts 13.1.3.
Acts 20. 23.
Rom. 12. 6.
8.
Eph. 2. 20.
Eph. 3. 5.
Eph. 4. 11.
Heb 12. 17, 24.
1 Pet. 5.1,4.
[t] Eph. 2 20
[u] Acts 13. 1.
Rom. 12. 6.
[v] Num.11.17.
[w] Rom. 12. 8.
1 Tim. 5. 17.
Heb. 12. 17.
[6] Or. kinds.
Acts 2.3,11.

14. Translate, 'For the body *also*.' The analogy of the body, not consisting exclusively of one, but of many members, illustrates the mutual dependence of the various members in the one church. Menenius Agrippa's fable of the belly and the members to the seceding commons (*Livy*, ii. 32) was probably familiar to St. Paul's well-stored mind (Acts xvii. 28). But the manifold membership of the one bride, in Song vii. 1-5 (cf. Ps. cxxxix. 16), rather, is the germ of the Spirit-taught truth here set forth. 15. The humble ought not to disparage themselves, or to be disparaged by others more noble (*vv.* 21, 22). foot . . . hand. The humble speaks of the more honourable member which most nearly resembles itself: so the "ear" of the "eye," the more commanding member (Num. x. 31). As in life each compares himself with those whom he approaches nearest, not those far superior. The *foot* and *hand* represent active men; the *ear* and *eye* contemplative men. 17. Superior as the *eye* is, it would not do if *it* were the sole member. 18. now—as the case really is. every one—each severally. 19. where were the body?—which necessarily "hath many members" (*vv.* 12, 14). 20. now—as the case really is: in contrast to the supposition (*v.* 19: cf. *v.* 18). many members—mutually dependent. 21. The higher cannot dispense with the lower. 22. more feeble—more susceptible of injury; *e. g.*, the brain, belly, eye. Their very feebleness, so far from doing away with the need for them, calls forth our greater care for their preservation, as being felt "necessary." 23. less honourable. "We think" the feet and the belly "less honourable," though not really so. bestow . . . honour—*putting* shoes on (*margin*) the feet, and clothes over the belly. uncomely parts—the secret parts. The poorest, though unclad in the rest of the body, cover these. 24. tempered . . . together—by mutual compensation. to that part which lacked—to the less honoured part (*v.* 23). 25. no schism (cf. *v.* 21)—no disunion, referring to the "divisions," ch. xi. 18. care one for another—*in behalf of* one another. 26. And—accordingly. all . . . suffer with it. [s]When a thorn enters the heel, the whole body

feels and is concerned—the back bends, the belly and thighs contract, the hands come forward and draw out the thorn, the head stoops, and the eyes regard the affected member with intense gaze' (*Chrysostom*). 27. members in particular—*i. e.*, severally members of it. Each church is in miniature what the whole aggregate of churches is collectively—"the body of Christ" (cf. ch. iii. 16): its individual components are members, every one in his place.
28. set some in the church—as he has "set the members . . . in the body" (*v.* 18). first apostles—above even the *prophets*. Not merely the *Twelve*, but others; *e. g.*, Barnabas, &c. (Rom. xvi. 7; 2 Cor. viii. 23, Greek.) teachers—of truths already revealed. The *prophets* made new revelations and prophesyings under the Spirit's influence. The teachers had the "word of knowledge," the prophets "the word of wisdom" (*v.* 8). Under "teachers" are included 'evangelists and pastors.' miracles—*lit.*, "powers" (*v.* 10); ranked below "teachers," as *teaching* is more edifying, though less dazzling than working miracles. helps, governments (Greek, *helpings, governings*) — lower and higher departments of 'ministrations' (*v.* 5); as instances of the former, *deacons*, who *helped* in the relief of the poor, and in baptizing and preaching, subordinate to higher ministers (Acts vi. 1-10; viii. 5-17); also others who *helped*, with their time and means, in the Lord's cause (Num. xi. 17: cf. ch. xiii. 3). Americans similarly use "helps" for '*helpers*.' As instances of the latter, *presbyters*, or *bishops*, whose office it was to *govern* the church (1 Tim. v. 17; Heb. xiii. 17, 24). These officers, though now ordinary and permanent, were originally specially endowed with the Spirit for their office; whence they are here classified with other inspired sanctions. Government [κυβερνήσεις] (*guiding the helm* of affairs) being occupied with externals, notwithstanding the outward status it gives, is ranked with the lower functions. Cf. "He that giveth" (answering to "helps"); "he that ruleth" (answering to "governments") (Rom. xii. 8). diversities of tongues (*v.* 10)—"*divers* kinds of tongues." 29. Are all? Surely not.

30 prophets? *are* all teachers? *are* all [7]workers of miracles? have all the gifts of healing? do all speak with tongues? do all interpret?

31 But [x]covet earnestly the best gifts: and yet show I unto you a more

13 excellent way.—THOUGH I speak with the tongues of men and of angels, and have not [a]charity, I am become *as* sounding brass, or a

2 tinkling cymbal.　And though I have *the gift of* [b]prophecy, and understand all mysteries, and all knowledge; and though I have all faith, [c]so that I could remove mountains, and have not charity, I am

3 nothing.　And [d]though I bestow all my goods to feed *the poor*, and though I give my body to be burned, and have not charity, it profiteth me nothing.

4 Charity [e]suffereth long, *and* is kind; charity envieth not; charity

5 [1]vaunteth not itself, is not puffed up, doth not behave itself [f]unseemly,

6 seeketh [g]not her own, is not easily provoked, thinketh no evil; rejoiceth

7 [h]not in iniquity, [i]but rejoiceth [2]in the truth; beareth [j]all things, believeth all things, hopeth all things, endureth all things.

A D. 59.
[7] Or,
　powers.
[x] ch. 11. 1.

CHAP. 13.
[a] Rom. 14.
　1 Tim. 1. 5.
[b] Matt. 7. 22.
　Luke 17. 6.
[d] Matt. 6. 1, 2.
[e] 1 Pet. 4. 8.
[1] Or, is not
　rash.
[f] Phil. 4. 8.
[g] Phil. 2. 4.
[h] Ps. 10. 3.
[i] 2 John 4.
[2] Or, with
　the truth.
[j] Gal. 6. 2.

---

31. covet earnestly [ζηλοῦτε]—'emulously desire;' not with *discontented* 'coveting.' The Spirit 'divides to every man severally *as He will*' (*v.* 11). This does not prevent our *earnestly seeking*, by prayer, watchfulness, and cultivation of our faculties, the *greatest* gifts. *Beza* explains 'highly esteem,' to accord with his distinction (ch. xiv. 1) between '*follow after* charity . . . *zealously esteem* spiritual gifts;' also, with *vv.* 11, 18, the sovereign will of the Spirit precluding us from desiring gifts not vouchsafed to us. But the 'zealous desire' meant is an earnest praying to God for the gifts. **the best gifts.** So Δ G. But אABC read 'the *greatest* gifts. **and yet** [καὶ ἔτι]—'and, *moreover.*' *Besides* recommending zeal for the greatest gifts, I am about to show you in addition something most excellent—*lit.*, 'a way most way-like' to desire, 'the way of love (cf. ch. xiii. 1). This love, or "charity," includes both "faith" and "hope" (ch. xiii. 7); its fruits are the ordinary and permanent fruits of the Spirit (Gal. v. 22-24). Thus, "long-suffering," cf. *v.* 4; "faith," *v.* 7; "joy," *v.* 6; "meekness," *v.* 5; "goodness," *v.* 5; "gentleness" [χρηστότης], *v.* 4; [χρηστεύεται] "is kind." The Holy Spirit creates in the soul love to God, for God's love in Christ to us, and so love to man, especially to the brethren (Rom. v. 5; xv. 30). This is more to be desired than even gifts (Luke x. 20).

CHAP. XIII. 1-13.—CHARITY OR LOVE SUPERIOR TO ALL GIFTS.

The New Testament psalm of love, as the 45th Psalm (see its title) and Canticles in the Old Testament. Whilst Paul's chief theme is *faith*, he handles *love* also with the unction of the beloved disciple.

1. tongues. From these he ascends to "prophecy" (*v.* 2); then to "faith;" then to benevolent and self-sacrificing deeds: a climax. He passes from addressing *them* (ch. xii. 31) to putting the case in *his* own person—"Though *I*," &c. "speak with the tongues"—with the eloquence so much admired at Corinth (*e. g.*, Apollos, Acts xviii. 24: cf. ch. i. 12), and with the command of various languages, which some abused to mere ostentation, (ch. xiv. 2, &c.) **of angels**—higher than "men;" therefore speaking a more exalted language. **charity**—the principal of the ordinary and more important gifts of the Spirit, contrasted with the extraordinary, (ch. xii.) **sounding brass, or a tinkling cymbal**—*sound* without soul: such are "tongues" without *charity*. **cymbal.** Two kinds are noticed, Ps. cl. 5—the loud or *clear*, and the *high sounding:* hand cymbals and finger

cymbals, or castagnets. The sound is sharp and piercing. **2. mysteries** (Rom. xi. 25; xvi. 25). *Mysteries* refer to God's deep counsels heretofore secret, but now revealed; *knowledge*, to truths long known. **faith, so that I could remove mountains** (Matt. xxi. 21)—confidence in God that the miraculous result will surely follow the exercise of the will at the Spirit's secret impulse. Without "love," prophecy, knowledge, and faith are not what they seem (cf. Matt. vii. 22; ch. viii. 1, 2; *v.* 8; Jas. ii. 14), and so fail of the heavenly reward (Matt. vi. 2). Thus St. Paul, who teaches justification by faith only (Gal. ii. 16; iii. 7-14), agrees with St. James, who teaches "by works" (*i. e.*, by LOVE, which is the "spirit" of faith, Jas. ii. 24, 26) a man is justified, and not by faith only." **3. bestow all my goods to feed the poor** [ψωμίσω]—*dole out* (crumble away) *in food* all my goods; one high function of the "helps" (ch. xii. 28). **give my body to be burned**—*lit.*, give up my body *to such a degree* as *that I should be burned.* As the three youths (Dan. iii. 28) "yielded their bodies" (cf. 2 Cor. xii. 15). So C Δ G *f g*, Vulgate. But A B א read [καυχήσωμαι] 'that I may glory' or 'boast.' These acts, when done in love, are most noble. Yet they may be without love: then the "goods" and "body" are given, but not the *soul*, which is the sphere of love. Without the soul, God rejects all else, and so rejects the man (Matt. xvi. 26; Luke ix. 23-25). Men will fight and die for Christianity, but not live in its spirit, which is *love.*

4. suffereth long—under provocations of *evil from* others. The negative side of *love.* **is kind** —the positive; *good to* others. Cf. the features of the "wisdom from above" (Jas. iii. 17). **envieth** The Greek [ζηλοῖ] includes *jealousy.* It is the same as ch. xii. 31, "covet earnestly." **vaunteth not**—ostentatiously, even of gifts which it really possesses [περπερεύεται: from Latin *perperam:* whereas ἀλαζονεύειν is to *boast* of gifts which one does not really possess (Rom. i. 30)]: a rebuke of those at Corinth who used the tongues for mere display. **not puffed up**—with party zeal, as some at Corinth were (ch. iv. 6). **5. not behave itself unseemly**—*is not uncourteous.* **thinketh no evil**—*imputeth not* (Rom. iv. 8; Hebrew, *chashab*) evil; lit., '*the* evil' which actually is there (Prov. x. 12; 1 Pet. iv. 8). Love makes allowances for others, and puts on their acts, as far as truth admits, a charitable construction. Love *doth not take into account* [οὐ λογίζεται] '*the* evil' which another inflicts on her, and so meditates no evil against him. **6. rejoiceth in the truth.** Greek, 'rejoiceth

8   Charity never faileth: but whether *there be* prophecies, they shall fail; whether *there be* tongues, they shall cease; whether *there be* knowledge,
9   it shall vanish away. For [k] we know in part, and we prophesy in part.
10 But [l] when that which is perfect is come, then that which is in part shall
11 be done away. When I was a child, I spake as a child, I understood as a child, I [3] thought as a child; but when I became a man, I put away
12 childish things. For [m] now we see through a glass, [4] darkly; but then [n] face to face: now I know in part; but then shall I know even as also I am known.
13   And now abideth faith, hope, charity, these three; but [o] the greatest of these *is* charity.

A. D. 59.
k ch. 8. 2.
l Isa. 60. 19.
Jer. 31. 34.
3 Or,
reasoned.
m 2 Cor. 3. 18.
2 Cor. 5. 7.
Phil. 3. 12.
4 in a riddle.
n Matt. 18. 10.
1 John 3. 2.
o Matt. 22. 33.

with the truth.' Exults not at unrighteousness perpetrated by others (cf. Gen. ix. 22, 23), but rejoices when the truth (which is on the side of *righteousness*) rejoices: sympathizes with its triumphs (2 John 4). See the opposite, 2 Tim. iii. 8. So the same contrast, Rom. ii. 8. "The truth" is the Gospel truth, the inseparable ally of love (Eph. iv. 15; 3 John 12). The false charity which compromises "the truth" by glossing over "iniquity" is thus condemned (Prov. xvii. 15). **7. beareth all things.** The same Greek as in ch. ix. 12. It *endures without divulging* to the world its distress. Literally, *holding fast*, like a water-tight vessel: the charitable man *contains himself* from giving vent to what selfishness would prompt under personal hardship. **believeth all things**—all that is not palpably false, all that it can with a good conscience believe to the credit of another. Cf. Jas. iii. 17, Greek, '*easily persuaded*.' **hopeth** —what is good of another, even when others have ceased to hope. **endureth**—persecutions in a patient and loving spirit.

8. never faileth—never 'falleth' to the ground (Greek), so as to be out of use: always holds its place. **shall fail . . . vanish away** [καταργη-θήσεται]. The same Greek for both; different from the Greek for "faileth" [πίπτει]. Translate, 'shall be done away with'—*i. e.*, shall be dispensed with at the Lord's coming, superseded by their more perfect analogues; for instance, *knowledge* by *intuition*. Of "tongues," still more temporary, the verb is "shall *cease*." Begun in sin (Gen. xi.), they shall cease with it. A primary fulfilment took place when the Church attained its maturity: then 'tongues ceased,' and 'prophesyings' and "knowledge," as *supernatural* gifts were superseded, as no longer required, when the Scriptures of the New Testament had been collected together. **9, 10. in part**—partially and imperfectly. Cf. a similar contrast to the "perfect man," Eph. iv. 11-13. **that which is in part**—fragmentary and isolated. **11. When I was a child** (ch. iii. 1; xiv. 20). **I spake**—alluding to "tongues." **understood** —'I was minded,' or 'had the sentiments of:' alluding to 'prophecy.' **I thought**—Greek [ἐλογί-ζομην], 'reasoned:' alluding to "knowledge." **but.** So G. But א A B Δ *f* omit it. **when I became a man, I put away**—rather, 'now that I am become a man, I have done away with (the same Greek as in v. 8; see note) the things of the child.' **12. now** [ἄρτι]—in our present state. **see**—appropriate in connection with the "prophets" or *seers* (1 Sam. ix. 9). **through a glass**—i. e., *in a mirror:* the reflection *seeming* behind, so that we see it *through* the mirror. Ancient mirrors were of polished brass or other metals. The contrast is between the inadequate knowledge gained by seeing an object reflected in the dim mirror of the ancients, compared with the perfect idea we have by seeing itself directly. **darkly**—lit., *in enigma.* As a 'mirror' conveys an image to the *eye*, so an

'enigma' to the *ear*. But neither 'eye nor ear' can fully represent (though the believer gets now a revealed glimpse of) "the things which God hath prepared for them that love him" (ch. ii. 9). St. Paul alludes to Num. xii. 8, "not in *dark* speeches;" the LXX., '*enigmas*.' Compared with the *visions* and *dreams* vouchsafed to other pro-phets, God's communications with Moses were 'not in enigmas.' But compared with the intui-tive, direct vision of God hereafter, even the revealed Word is now 'a dark discourse,' shadow-ing forth *by enigma* God's likeness. Cf. 2 Pet. i. 19, where the "light," or 'lamp,' "in a dark place" is contrasted with the "day" dawning (cf. 2 Cor. iii. 18). **then**—"when that which is perfect is come" (*v.* 10). **face to face**—not merely "mouth to mouth" (Num. xii. 8). Gen. xxxii. 30 was a type (John i. 50, 51). **know even as also I am known**—rather [ἐπιγνώσομαι], '*fully* know even as also I am *fully* known.' Then first the saints shall enjoy full mutual recognition—as the disciples recognized Moses and Elijah, whom they had never seen, at the transfiguration. Previously, "sleep in Jesus" implies not unconsciousness, but that the sleeping saints are shut up unto Him in trance-like vision. Now we *are known by*, rather than fully *know*, God (note, ch. viii. 3; Gal. iv. 9). Whatever knowledge God's people have is due to God first knowing them. Hereafter we shall "see Him *as He is*:" here we see Him only *as He is in us* (Olshausen, 1 John iii. 2).

13. And now [νυνὶ]—not the same Greek as "now," *v.* 12. Translate, '*But* now.' As *v.* 8 already showed, "love" extends beyond *this present time;* "now" here expresses not time, but *opposition*, as in ch. v. 11. *Such being the case, that* the three— "prophecy," "tongues," and "knowledge" (speci-mens of the whole cycle)—"fail" (*v.* 8), *there abide* permanently only *these three—faith, hope, charity.* In one sense, *faith* and *hope* shall be done away— faith superseded by sight, and hope by fruition (Rom. viii. 24; 2 Cor. v. 7); and love alone never faileth (*v.* 8). But in another sense, "faith" and "hope," as well as "charity," ABIDE, after the extraordinary gifts have ceased: for those three are *necessary and sufficient for salvation at all times*, whereas the extraordinary are not at all so (cf. "abide," ch. iii. 14). Love is connected specially with the Holy Spirit, the Agent of union between the brethren (Rom. xv. 30; Col. i. 8). *Faith* is towards God. *Hope*, in behalf of ourselves. *Charity* is love to God, creating in us love towards our neighbour. In an unbeliever there is more or less of the three opposites—unbelief, despair, hat~ed. Even hereafter, *faith*, in the sense *trust in God*, "abideth;" also "hope," in the anticipation of ever-new joys in prospect, and ever-increasing blessedness, sure never to be disappointed. Their objects also "abide." Love alone in every sense "abideth:" it presupposes "*faith*," which with-out "love" and its "works" is dead (Gal. v. 6;

322

14 FOLLOW after [a]charity, and [b]desire spiritual *gifts*, [c]but rather that
2 ye may prophesy. For he that [d]speaketh in an *unknown* tongue speaketh not unto men, but unto God: for no man [1]understandeth *him;*
3 howbeit in the spirit he speaketh [e]mysteries. But he that prophesieth
4 [f]speaketh unto men *to* edification, and exhortation, and comfort. He
that speaketh in an *unknown* tongue edifieth himself; but he that pro-
5 phesieth edifieth the church. I would that ye all spake with tongues,
but rather that ye prophesied: for greater *is* he that prophesieth than he
that speaketh with tongues, except he interpret, that the church may
receive edifying.
6   Now, brethren, if I come unto you speaking with tongues, what shall
I profit you, except I shall speak to you either by revelation, or by
7 knowledge, or by prophesying, or by doctrine? And even things without
life giving sound, whether [g]pipe or harp, except they give a distinction
8 in the [2]sounds, how shall it be known what is piped or harped? For if
the trumpet give an uncertain sound, who shall prepare himself to the
9 battle? So likewise ye, except ye utter by the tongue words [3]easy to be
understood, how shall it be known what is spoken? for ye shall speak
10 [h]into the air. There are, it may be, so many kinds of voices in the
11 world, and none of them *is* without signification. Therefore if I
know not the meaning of the voice, I shall be unto him that
speaketh a barbarian, and he that speaketh *shall be* a barbarian unto
me.

A. D. 59.

CHAP. 14.
[a] Lev. 19. 18.
Matt. 22.39.
Mark 12.31.
Rom. -13. 8-
10.
Gal. 5. 14.
Eph. 5. 2.
Col. 3 14.
1 Tim. 1. 5.
Jas 2. 8.
[b] ch 12. 31.
Eph. 1. 3.
[c] Num.11 25.
Rom. 12. 6.
ch. 13. 2. 9.
1 Thes.5.20.
[d] Acts 2. 4.
Acts 10. 46.
Acts 19. 6.
[1] heareth.
Acts 22. 9.
[e] Matt 13 11.
[f] Rom. 15.4.
[g] Job 21. 11,
12.
[2] Or, tunes.
[3] significant.
[h] ch. 9. 26.

Jas. ii. 17-20; and "*hope,*" *v.* 7. **but** |δέ|—rather,
"moreover:" as there is not so strong opposition
between *charity* and the other two, which like it
also "abide." **the greatest.** Greek, 'the greater,'
as compared with the other two.

CHAP. XIV. 1-25.—SUPERIORITY OF PROPHECY
OVER TONGUES.

1. Follow after charity—as your chief aim, seeing it is "the greatest" (ch. xiii. 13). **and desire.**
Translate, 'Yet (as a *secondary* aim) desire
zealously spiritual gifts, with prayer and in submission to the Spirit's will' (ch. xii. 11, 31, note);
not with "envy" (the same Greek, ch. xiii. 4) of
another's gifts. "Follow after" includes *the
activity of the will:* 'desire zealously' implies
entreaty in prayer. **but rather**—*but chiefly* that
ye may prophesy' (speak under inspiration) (Prov.
xxix. 18; Acts xiii. 1; 1 Thess. v. 20), whether as
to future events—i. e., *prophecy*—or explaining
obscure Scriptures, especially the prophetical, or
illustrating questions of Christian doctrine and
practice. Modern *preaching* is its successor, without the inspiration. Desire zealously this (prophecy) *more* than any other spiritual gift, especially
in preference to "tongues," (*v.* 2, &c.) **2. speaketh
. . . unto God** (Rom. viii. 27)—who alone understands *all* languages. **no man understandeth.**
Generally, the few who can interpret tongues are
the exception. **in the spirit**—as opposed to "the
understanding" (*v.* 14). **mysteries**—unintelligible
to the hearers, exciting wonder rather than instructing. Corinth, a mart for merchants from
Asia, Africa, and Europe, would give scope for the
exercise of the gift of tongues; but its legitimate
use was in an audience understanding the tongue
of the speaker, not in mere display. **3. But**—on
the other hand. **edification**—of which the two
species given are "exhortation," to remove *slug-
gishness;* "comfort," to remove *sadness.* Omit
"*to.*" **4. edifieth himself**—as he understands the
meaning of the particular "tongue;" but "the
church," the congregation, does not. **5.** Translate,
'Now I wish you all TO speak with tongues (so
far am I from objecting to tongues), but rather IN

ORDER THAT (as my ulterior, higher wish) ye
should prophesy.' Tongues must therefore mean
languages, not ecstatic unintelligible rhapsodies (as
Neander fancied): for Paul could never 'wish'
for the- latter in their behalf. **greater**—because
more useful. **except he interpret**—the unknown
tongue, 'that the church may receive edifying'
(*building up*).

6. Translate, '*But* now;' seeing there is no edification without interpretation. **revelation . . .
prophesying**—corresponding "revelation" being
the supernatural *unveiling* of divine truths; "prophesying," the open enunciation of such revelations. So "knowledge" corresponds to "doctrine,"
the gift of *teaching* to others our knowledge. As
the former pair refers to *revealed mysteries*, so the
latter pair to the *obvious truths of salvation*, brought
from the common storehouse of believers. **7.**
Translate, '*Even* things without life-giving sound,
whether pipe or harp, if they give not distinction
in (the due interval between) the tones (notes),
how,' &c. [ὅμως: though lifeless, YET they furnish
an illustration: cf. Greek, Gal. iii. 15.] **what is
piped or harped**—i. e., what tune is played on the
pipe or harp. **8.** Translate, 'For if *also:*' an *additional* step in the argument. **uncertain sound**
—without definite meaning. It ought to be so
marked that one succession of notes should summon the soldiers to attack, another to retreat, &c.
9. So likewise ye—who have life, as opposed to
"things without life" (*v.* 7). **by the tongue**—the
language which ye speak in. **ye shall speak**—ye
will be speaking into the air--i. e., *in vain* (ch. ix.
26). **10. it may be**—speaking by conjecture. 'It
may chance' (ch. xv. 37). **so many**—as are enumerated by investigators. (Cf. "so much," for a
definite number left undefined, Acts v. 8.) **kinds
of voices**—of articulate speech: languages [φωνῶν,
distinct from γλωσσῶν, "tongues"]. **without signification.** *None is without its own voice* or meaning *distinct* from the rest. **11.** Therefore—seeing
that none is without meaning. **a barbarian**—*a
foreigner* (Acts xxviii. 2). Not in our deprecatory
sense of the term, but one *speaking a foreign language.*

12   Even so ye, forasmuch as ye are zealous [4]of spiritual *gifts*, seek that ye
13 may excel to the edifying of the church. Wherefore let him that speak-
14 eth in an *unknown* tongue pray that [5]he may interpret. For if I pray in
     an *unknown* tongue, my spirit prayeth, but my understanding is un-
15 fruitful. What is it then? I will pray with the spirit, and I will pray
     with the understanding also; [j]I will sing with the spirit, and I will sing
16 [k]with the understanding also. Else, when thou shalt bless with the
     spirit, how shall he that occupieth the room of the unlearned say [l]Amen
     at thy giving of thanks, seeing he understandeth not what thou sayest?
17, For thou verily givest thanks well, but the other is not edified. I
18, thank my God, I speak with tongues more than ye all: yet in the
19 church I had rather speak five words with my understanding, that *by*
     my voice I might teach others also, than ten thousand words in an
     unknown tongue.
20   Brethren, [m]be not children in understanding: howbeit in malice [n]be
21 ye children, but in understanding be [5]men. In [o]the Law it is [p]written,
     With *men of* other tongues and other lips will I speak unto this people;
22 and yet for all that will they not hear me, saith the Lord. Wherefore
     tongues are for a sign, not to them that believe, but to them that believe

A. D. 59.

[4] of spirits.
   ch. 12. 7, 31.
[i] ch. 12. 10.
[j] John 3. 34.
   25.
   Eph. 5. 19.
   Col. 3. 16.
[k] Ps 47. 7.
   Rom. 12. 1.
[l] ch. 11. 24.
[m] Ps. 119. 99.
   Ps. 131. 2.
   Matt. 11 25
   Rom 16.19
   Heb. 5. 12.
[n] Matt. 18. 3.
   1 Pet. 2. 2.
[5] perfect, or, of a ripe age.
   ch. 2. 6.
   Phil. 3. 19.
[o] John 10. 34.
[p] Isa. 28. 11.

12. zealous—emulously desirous. **of spiritual gifts**—lit., '*spirits*;' *i. e.*, emanations from the one Spirit. **seek that ye may excel to.** Translate, 'seek that ye may *abound in them* to the edifying,' &c. Seek to have not only tongues, but also interpretation and prophecy. **13.** Explain, 'Let him who speaketh with an unknown tongue (*in prayer*) pray with the purpose that he may interpret.' This explanation is needed by the logical connection with "pray in an unknown tongue" (*v.* 14). Though his words be unintelligible, let him in them pray for the gift of interpreting, which will make them "edifying" to "the church" (*v.* 12). It was only when they could interpret that the "understanding" accompanied the "tongue" (*vv.* 15, 19). **14. spirit**—my higher being, the *passive* object of the Holy Spirit's operations, and the instrument of prayer in the unknown tongue; distinguished from the "understanding" [νοῦς], the *active* instrument of thought, which in this case must be "unfruitful" to others, since the vehicle of expression is unintelligible to them. On the distinction of *soul* or *mind* and *spirit*, see Eph. iv. 23; Heb. iv. 12. **15. What is it then?**—What then is my resolve? **and**—rather, 'but.' I will not only pray with my spirit, which (*v.* 14) might leave the understanding unedified, BUT with the understanding also. **pray with the understanding also**—and, by inference, I will keep silence if I cannot pray with the understanding (so as to make myself understood by others). A prescient warning, *mutatis mutandis*, against the Roman and Greek liturgies in dead languages, long since become unintelligible to the masses. When those liturgies were framed originally those languages were *in general* use. **16. Else, when thou.** He changes from the *first* person, as he had just expressed *his own* resolve, "*I* will pray with the understanding" whatever "thou" dost. **bless**—the highest kind of prayer. **occupieth the room of the unlearned** [ἰδιώτου, *a private person*]—one who, whatever other gifts he possess, as wanting the gift of interpretation, is reduced by the unknown tongue spoken to the position of one unlearned. **say Amen.** Prayer is not a vicarious duty done *for* us, as in Rome's masses. We must join *with* the prayers and praises of the congregation, and say aloud our responsive "Amen," as was the usage of the Jewish (Deut. xxvii. 15-26; Neh. viii. 6) and Christian primitive churches

(*Justin Martin*, 'Apol.,' ii. 97). **17. givest thanks.** The synagogue prayers were called 'eulogies,' because to each was joined a *thanksgiving.* Hence Christian prayers also were called *blessings* and *givings of thanks.* This illustrates Col. iv. 2; 1 Thess. v. 17, 18. So the *Kaddisch* and *Keduscha*, the synagogue formulæ of 'hallowing' the Divine 'name' and of prayer for the 'coming of God's kingdom,' answer to the Church's Lord's prayer, repeated often, and made the foundation on which the other prayers are built (*Tertullian*, 'De Oratione'). **18. tongues.** So B. But אAG*fg*, Vulgate, have the singular, 'in a (tongue) foreign.' **19. I had rather.** The Greek more literally expresses, 'I WISH to speak five words with my understanding (rather) than ten thousand words in an unknown tongue:' even the two-thousandth part of ten thousand. The Greek for 'I would rather' would be different. St. Paul would NOT wish *at all* to speak "ten thousand words in an unknown tongue." **20. Brethren**—an appellation to conciliate their favourable attention. **children in understanding** —as preference of gifts abused to non-edification would make you (cf. Matt. x. 16; Rom. xvi. 19; ch. iii. 1; Eph. iv. 14). The Greek [φρεσίν, not elsewhere], "understanding," expresses the will of one's *spirit:* one's *mindedness* (Rom. viii. 6), as the 'heart' is the will of the '*soul.*' **men**—full-grown. Be child-like, not childish. **21. In the Law**—the whole Old Testament, all being the law of God (cf. the Psalms cited as the "Law," John x. 34). The quotation is from Isa. xxviii. 11, 12, where God virtually saith of Israel, 'This people hear me not, though I speak to them in their familiar language: I will therefore **speak** to them in other tongues, those of the foes whom I will send against them; but even then they will not hearken to me;' which St. Paul thus applies, 'Ye see, it is a penalty to be associated with men of a strange tongue, yet ye impose this on the Church by abusing the tongues, instead of using them intelligibly.' They who speak in foreign tongues speak like "children" just "weaned from the milk" (Isa. xxviii. 9), "with stammering lips," unintelligibly to the hearers, appearing ridiculous (Isa. xxviii. 14), or as babbling drunkards (Acts ii. 13) or madmen (*v.* 23). **22.** Thus from Isaiah it appears that "tongues" (uninterpreted) are not a sign for believers (though at the conversion of

not: but prophesying *serveth* not for them that believe not, but for them which believe.

23 If therefore the whole church be come together into one place, and all speak with tongues, and there come in *those that are* unlearned, or un-

24 believers, ^q will they not say that ye are mad? But if all prophesy, and there come in one that believeth not, or *one* unlearned, he is convinced

25 of all, he is judged of all: and thus are the secrets of his heart made manifest: and so falling down on *his* face he will worship God, and report ^r that God is in you of a truth.

26 How is it then, brethren? when ye come together, every one of you hath a psalm, ^s hath a doctrine, hath a tongue, hath a revelation, hath

27 an interpretation. Let ^t all things be done unto edifying. If any man speak in an *unknown* tongue, *let it be* by two, or at the most *by* three,

28 and *that* by course; and let one interpret. But if there be no interpreter, let him keep silence in the church; and let him speak to himself, and to

29 God. Let the prophets speak two or three, and let the other judge. If

30 *any thing* be revealed to another that sitteth by, ^u let the first hold his

31 peace. For ^v ye may all prophesy one by one, that all may learn, and all

A. D. 59.

q Hos. 9. 7.
John 10. 30.
Acts 2. 13.
Acts 26. 24.
r Num. 14. 14
16.
Josb. 2, 9, 10.
Josh. 5. 1.
Isa. 45. 14.
Zech. 8. 23.
s ch. 12. 8, 9.
t Rom. 14. 19.
2 Cor. 12. 19.
2 Cor. 13. 10.
Eph. 4. 12.
2 Thes 5. 11.
u 1 Thes. 5. 19.
v Deut. 33. 10.
Eccl. 12. 9.
Rom. 12. 7.
1 Tim. 2. 7.
2 Tim. 2. 21.

Cornelius and the Gentiles with him, tongues were vouchsafed to confirm their faith), but mainly to *condemn* those who, like Israel, reject the sign and the accompanying message. So the tongues condemned those who rejected the proffered Gospel on Pentecost (Acts ii. 8, contrasted with *v.* 13). Cf. "yet . . . will they not hear me" (*v.* 21); even primitive signs fail to arouse them. 'Sign' is often used for a *condemnatory* sign (Ezek. iv. 3, 4; Matt. xii. 39-42). Since they *will* not understand, they *shall* not understand. **prophesying serveth not for them that believe not, but . . . believe.** It has no effect on *obstinate unbelievers*, like Israel, but on them that are either *in receptivity or, in fact, believers*: it makes believers of those *not wilfully unbelievers* (*vv.* 24, 25; Rom. x. 17), and spiritually nourishes those that already believe.

23. whole . . . all . . . tongues. The more there are assembled, and that speak in unknown tongues, the more will the impression be conveyed to strangers 'coming in' from curiosity ("unbelievers," whether knowing a foreign tongue or not), or even from a better motive ("unlearned," ignorant of foreign tongues), that the *whole* body is a mob of fanatical 'madmen,' and that 'the Church is like the company of Babel builders after the confusion of tongues.' **unlearned—**having some faith, but no gifts. **24. all—**one by one (*v.* 31). **prophesy—**speak by the Spirit intelligibly; not in unintelligible tongues. **one—**singular, implying that *conviction by all* would be produced on *any one* who might happen to enter. In *v.* 23 the plural, "unlearned" or "unbelievers," implying that however many there be, not one will profit by the tongues; yea, their being many would confirm them in rejecting the sign, as many unbelievers together strengthen one another in unbelief: individuals are more easily won. **he—**the "one that believeth not." **convinced—**convicted in conscience (John xvi. 8, 9). **judged—**his secret character is "discerned," viz., the "one unlearned" (cf. ch. ii. 15), who, however unskilled in other tongues, can understand the language that speaks to his heart. **25. and thus—**omitted in ℵ A B Δ G *fg*, Vulgate. **secrets of his heart made manifest.** He sees his inner character opened out by the sword of the Spirit (Heb. iv. 12; Jas. i. 23), the Word of God, in the hand of him who prophesieth (cf. "Nebuchadnezzar," Dan. ii. 30, end, 46, 47). No argument is stronger for the truth

325

than its manifestation of men to themselves. Hence hearers often think the preacher has aimed his sermon particularly at them. **and so—**convicted at last, as was the woman of Samaria by Jesus' unfolding of her to herself (John iv. 19, 29). **and report—**to friends at home, as she did. Rather, 'he will worship God, *announcing*' [*ἀπαγ. γέλλων*], openly avowing, then and there, "that God is in you (dwelling in your souls, John xiv. 23) of a truth," and by implication that the God in you is of a truth the God.

**26-40.—RULES FOR THE EXERCISE OF GIFTS IN THE CONGREGATION.
26. How is it then?** '*What then is* the true rule as to the use of gifts?' Cf. *v.* 15, the same Greek. **hath—**ready beforehand. **a psalm—**inspired by the Spirit, as that of Mary, Zechariah, Simeon, and Anna, (Luke i. and ii.) **a doctrine—**to set forth to the congregation. **a tongue . . . a revelation—**answering to "prophecy." ℵ A B Δ G *fg* transpose the order—"revelation . . . tongue;" "interpretation" properly following "tongue" (*v.* 13). **Let all things be done unto edifying—**the general rule: an answer to the question at the beginning of this verse. Each ought to obey the ordinances of his church, not adverse to Scripture. (See Article XXXIV., 'Church of England Prayer Book.') **27. let it be by two—**at each time: not more than two or three might speak with tongues at each meeting. **by course—**in turns. **let one interpret** —who has the gift of interpreting; and not more than one. **28. let him—**the speaker in unknown tongues. **speak to himself, and to God** (cf. *vv.* 2, 4)—privately, not in hearing of others. **29. two or three—**at one meeting (he does not add "at the most," as in *v.* 27, lest he should seem to 'quench prophesyings,' the most edifying of gifts), and these "one by one," in turns (*vv.* 27, 31). St. Paul gives similar rules to the prophets as he had to those speaking tongues. **judge—**by their power of "discerning spirits" (ch. xii. 10), whether the person prophesying was really under the influence of the Spirit (cf. ch. xii. 3; 1 John iv. 1-3). **30. If any thing—**Greek, '*But if* anything.' **let the first hold his peace—**let him who heretofore spoke, furnished with an ordinary revelation ready beforehand, give place to him who is moved to prophesy by a sudden revelation from the Spirit (*v.* 26; Luke i. 67-79). **31. For ye may—**rather, 'For ye *can* (if you will) all prophesy one by one,' giving way to one another. The

32 may be comforted. And ^w the spirits of the prophets are subject to the
33 prophets. For God is not *the author* of ⁶ confusion, but of peace, ^x as in all churches of the saints.

34   Let ^y your women keep silence in the churches: for it is not permitted unto them to speak; but ^z*they are commanded* to be under
35 obedience, as also saith the ^a Law. And if they will learn any thing, let them ask their husbands at home: for it is a shame for women to speak
36 in the church. What! came the word of ^b God out from you? or came it unto you only?

37   If ^c any man think himself to be a prophet, or spiritual, let him acknowledge that the things that I write unto you are the command-
38 ments of the Lord. But if any man be ignorant, let him be ignorant.
39 Wherefore, brethren, ^d covet to prophesy, and forbid not to speak with
40 tongues. Let all things be done decently and in order.

15   MOREOVER, brethren, I declare unto you the gospel which I preached
2 unto you, which also ye have received, and ^awherein ye stand; by ^bwhich also ye are saved, if ye ¹ keep in memory ²what I preached unto you,

A. D. 59.

^w 1 John 4. 1.
⁶ tumult, or, unquietness.
^x ch. 11. 16.
^y 1 Tim. 2.11.
^z ch. 11. 3.
^a Gen. 3. 16.
^b Isa. 2. 3.
^c Luke 10.16.
    2 Cor. 10. 7.
    1 John 4. 6.
^d ch. 12. 31.
    1 Thes 5.20.

CHAP. 15.
^a Rom. 5. 2.
^b Rom. 1. 16.
¹ Or, hold fast.
² by what speech.

"for" justifies (*v.* 30), "let the first hold his peace." that all may learn, and all may be comforted—that if one prophet do not affect the hearers, another may : so that none may go away unedified. 32. And—following up *v.* 31, 'ye can' (if ye will) restrain yourselves from speaking all together. "*And* the spirits of the prophets"—i. e., their spirits—acted on by the Holy Spirit, are not so hurried away as to cease to be under their own control : they can, if they will, hear others, and not demand that they alone should be heard. 33. In all the churches God is a God of peace (irreconcileable with fanatical disorders); let Him not among you seem to be a God of confusion (cf. ch. xi. 16). Or stop at "peace," and connect, "As in all churches of the saints, let your women keep silence in the churches."
34. (Tim. ii. 11, 12) For women to speak in public would be an act of independence, as if they were not subject to their husbands (cf. ch. xi. 3; Eph. v. 22; Titus ii. 5; 1 Pet. iii. 1). For "under obedience" [ὑποτασσέσθωσαν, as A B א read; or the infinitive, as Δ G *f g,* Vulgate], translate 'in *subjection*' or '*submission,*' as the Greek is translated, Eph. v. 21, 22, 24. the Law—the whole Old Testament here (Gen. iii. 16). 35. Women may say, 'But if we do not understand, may we not "ask" a question publicly, so as to "learn?" Nay, replies Paul : if you want information, "ask" not in public, but "at home;" ask not other men, but 'your own particular [τοὺς ἰδίους] husbands.' shame—indecorous. 36. What!—Greek, 'Or,' Will you obey me? Or, if you set up your judgment above that of other churches, do you pretend that your church is the first FROM which the Gospel came, that you should give law to all others? Or are you the only persons UNTO whom it has come?
37. prophet—the species. spiritual—the genus: spiritually endowed. The followers of Apollos prided themselves as "spiritual" (ch. iii. 1-3). Here one *capable of discerning spirits* is specially meant. things that I write . . . commandments of the Lord (א A B C read the singular, referring to the last commandment alone; viz., that women should be silent in church—'that it is the commandment of the Lord.' The Vulgate supports the received text)—a direct assertion of inspiration. St. Paul's words are Christ's words. St. Paul appeals not merely to one or two, but *to a body of men,* for the reality of three facts about which no body could be mistaken :—(1.) That his influence over them was not due to mere eloquence,

but to the "demonstration of the Spirit and of power;" (2.) That part of this demonstration consisted in imparting miraculous gifts, which they were then exercising so generally as to require to be corrected in the irregular employment of them; (3.) That among these was one which enabled the "prophet," or 'spiritual person,' to decide whether St. Paul's epistle was Scripture or not. He could not have written so unless the facts were *notoriously true;* for he takes them for granted, as consciously known by the whole body of men whom he addresses (*Hinds,* 'On Inspiration'). 38. if any man be ignorant—wilfully; not wishing to recognize my apostolic authority in enjoining these ordinances. let him be ignorant. I leave him to his ignorance; it will be at his own peril—an argument likely to have weight with the Corinthians, who admired "knowledge" so much. 39. covet—earnestly desire with prayer, in submission to God's will. Stronger than "forbid not." He esteemed "prophecy" more highly than "tongues." 40. Let, &c. א A B Δ G *f g,* Vulgate, read '*But* let,' &c., connected with *v.* 39, 'But (whilst *desiring prophecy,* and *not forbidding tongues*) let all things be done decently,' &c. Church government is the best security for Christian liberty (cf. *vv.* 23, 26-33).
    CHAP. XV. 1-58.—THE RESURRECTION PROVED AGAINST ITS DENIERS AT CORINTH.
    Christ's resurrection rests on many eye-witnesses, including St. Paul, and is the great fact preached as the groundwork of the Gospel. They who deny resurrection in general must deny that of Christ; and the consequence will be that Christian preaching and faith are vain. 1. I declare—*lit.,* 'I make known.' It implies some reproach that it should be now necessary to make it known to them afresh, owing to some 'not having the knowledge of God' (*v.* 34: cf. Gal. i. 11). wherein ye stand —ye now take your stand. Your present high standing, if ye suffer not yourselves to fall from it. 2. ye are saved—rather, 'ye are being saved.' if ye keep in memory what I preached unto you. *Bengel,* &c., prefer, 'I declare unto you the Gospel (*v.* 1) in what words I preached it unto you.' St. Paul makes known to them, as if anew, not only the fact of the Gospel, but also *with what arguments* he preached it. Translate, then, 'If ye hold it fast.' I prefer, 'By which ye are saved, if (as I presume is the case, indicative) ye *hold fast* (in memory and personal appropriation [κατέχετε] *with what speech* I preached it unto you.' unless —which is impossible—your faith is vain, in resting

3 unless *ᶜ*ye have believed in vain. For I delivered unto you first of all that which I also received, how that Christ died for our sins *ᵈ*according
4 to the Scriptures; and that he was buried, and that he rose again
5 the third day *ᵉ*according to the Scriptures: and *ᶠ*that he was seen of
6 Cephas, then of *ᵍ*the twelve: after that, he was seen of above five hundred brethren at once; of whom the greater part remain unto this
7 present, but some are fallen asleep. After that, he was seen of James;
8 then of *ʰ*all the apostles. And *ⁱ*last of all he was seen of me also, as of
9 *³*one born out of due time. For I am the least of the apostles, that am not meet to be called an apostle, because *ʲ*I persecuted the church of
10 God. But *ᵏ*by the grace of God I am what I am: and his grace which *was bestowed* upon me was not in vain; but *ˡ*I laboured more abundantly than they all: *ᵐ*yet not I, but the grace of God which was
11 with me. Therefore whether *it were* I or they, so we preach, and so ye believed.

A. D. 59.

ᶜ Gal. 3. 4.
ᵈ Gen. 3. 15.
Ps. 22. 15.
Isa. 53. 5, 6.
Dan. 9. 26.
Zech. 13. 7.
ᵉ Ps. 2. 7.
Ps 16. 10.
ᶠ Luke 24. 34.
ᵍ John 20. 19.
ʰ Acts 1. 3.
ⁱ Acts 9. 4.
³ Or, an abortive.
ʲ Acts 8. 3.
ᵏ Eph. 2. 7.
ˡ 2 Cor. 11. 23.
ᵐ Ps. 115. 1.

on Christ's resurrection as an objective reality. **3. I delivered unto you.** A short summary of articles of faith was probably even then existing (cf. Eph. iv. 4-6; Heb. vi. 1, &c.; 1 John iv. 2); and a profession of it was required of candidates for baptism (Acts viii. 37; Rom. x. 9, 10). **first of all**—*lit.* 'among the foremost points' (Heb. vi. 2). The atonement is, in Paul's view, of primary importance. **which I also received**—from Christ by special revelation (cf. ch. xi. 23). Paul "delivered" what he "received;" not something of his own origination. **died for our sins**—*i. e.*, to atone FOR them, *for* taking away *our sins* (1 John iii. 5). ["For" is here ὑπέρ, 'in behalf of.' So Gal. i. 4; 2 Cor. v. 15; Titus ii. 14: cf. Isa. liii. 5; 1 Pet. ii. 24. Heb. v. 3 has περί, implying that the object is *the centre round which the action concentrates.* Rom. iv. 25 has διά, 'on account of.' In Matt. xx. 28 ἀντί, *instead of,* implying *substitution,* or *vicarious satisfaction* (cf. Greek, Matt. xvii. 27; Luke xi. 11; 1 Cor. xi. 15).] **according to the Scriptures**—which 'cannot be broken.' To deny the resurrection is to renounce the prophetical Scriptures, which it fulfils (Hos. vi. 2). St. Paul puts their testimony before that of the witnesses to Christ's resurrection. So Christ quotes Isa. liii. 12 in Luke xxii. 37 (cf. Ps. xxii. 15, &c.; Dan. ix. 26). **4. buried . . . rose again** (foretold, Isa. liii. 9). At the moment of His death the power of His inextinguishable life exerted itself (Matt. xxvii. 52). The grave was to Him not the receptacle of corruption, but an avenue into life (Acts ii. 26-28). "Rose again"—Greek, 'hath risen;' the state begun, and its consequences continue. **5. seen of Cephas**—Peter (Luke xxiv. 34). **the twelve**—the round number for "the eleven" (Luke xxiv. 33, 36). "The twelve" was their ordinary appellation. Possibly, too, Matthias was present (Acts i. 22, 23). Δ G *fg,* Vulgate, read 'the eleven;' but ℵ A B, "the twelve." **6. five hundred**—probably on the mountain (Thabor, according to tradition) in Galilee, when His most public appearance, according to His special promise, was vouchsafed (Matt. xxvi. 32; xxviii. 7, 10, 16). He 'appointed' this place, remote from Jerusalem, so that believers might assemble there more securely. Such a multitude could not with safety have met in the metropolis after his crucifixion there. The number of disciples (Acts i. 15) at Jerusalem shortly after was *one hundred and twenty,* those in Galilee and elsewhere not being reckoned. Andronicus and Junius were perhaps of the number (Rom. xvi. 7); for they were 'among the apostles,' all witnesses of the resurrection (Acts i. 22). **remain unto this present**—and, therefore, may be sifted

to ascertain the trustworthiness of their testimony. **fallen asleep**—in the sure hope of *awaking* at the resurrection (Acts vii. 60). **7. seen of James**—the less, the brother of our Lord (Gal. i. 19). The Gospel according to the Hebrews (*Jerome,* 'Catalogus Scriptorum Ecclesiasticorum,' p. 170 D.) records that 'James swore he would not eat bread from the hour that he drank the cup of the Lord till he should see Him rising again from the dead.' **all the apostles.** The term includes many others besides "the twelve" (v. 5); perhaps the seventy, (Luke x.) **8. one born out of due time** [τῷ ἐκτρώματι]—'the ONE untimely born' in the family of the apostles. As such a child, though born alive, is yet not of the proper size, and scarcely worthy of the name of man, so "I am *the least* of the apostles," scarcely meet to be called one; a supernumerary taken into the college out of regular course; not led to Christ by gradual instruction, like a natural birth, but by a sudden power, as those prematurely born. Cf. the similar image, and by the same spiritual power (1 Pet. i. 3), "*Begotten again* by the *resurrection* of Jesus." Jesus' appearance on the way to Damascus is the one referred to. **9. least.** 'Paulus' means least. **I persecuted the church of God.** Though God forgave him, Paul could hardly forgive himself for his past sin. **10. by the grace . . . and his grace.** The repetition implies the prominence of God's *grace* in his mind as the sole cause of his marvellous conversion and subsequent labours. Though "not meet to be called an apostle," God's grace has given him the meetness needed for the office (Eph. iii. 8; 1 Tim. i. 15). Translate, 'His grace which was (showed) *towards* [εἰς] me.' **what I am** —occupying the honourable office of an apostle. Contrast the self-sufficient prayer of another Pharisee (Luke xviii. 11). **but I laboured**—by God's grace (Phil. ii. 16). **than they all**—than any of the apostles (v. 7). **grace of God which was with me**—(cf. Mark xvi. 20.) ℵ B Δ G omit "which was." A C read as English version [ἡ σὺν ἐμοί]. *This* reading makes "the grace of God" everything, and Paul nothing, in his 'labours' after conversion. The reading that omits "which was" implies *Paul's co-operation:* still, "not I, but grace," implies that though Paul's human will, when sanctified, concurred *with* God, yet "grace" so preponderated that his co operation is regarded as nothing, and grace as the sole agent (cf. Matt. x. 20; ch. iii. 9; 2 Cor. vi. 1; Phil. ii. 12, 13). **11. whether it were I or they** (the apostles)—who "laboured more abundantly" (v. 10), the subject of our preaching was the truth stated in *vr,* 3, 4.

12 Now if Christ be preached that he rose from the dead, how say some
13 among you that ⁿ there is no resurrection of the dead? But if there be
14 no resurrection of the dead, ^o then is Christ not risen: and if Christ be
15 not risen, then *is* our preaching vain, and your faith *is* also vain. Yea,
and we are found false witnesses of God; because we have testified of
God that he raised up Christ: whom he raised not up, if so be that the
16 dead rise not. For if the dead rise not, then is not Christ raised:
17 and if Christ be not raised, your faith *is* vain; ^p ye are yet in your
18 sins. Then they also which are fallen asleep in Christ are perished.
19 If ^q in this life only we have hope in Christ, we are of all men most
miserable.
20 But now ^r is Christ risen from the dead, *and* become ^s the first-fruits of
21 them that slept. For ^t since by man *came* death, ^u by man *came* also
22 the resurrection of the dead. For as in Adam all die, even so in Christ
23 shall all be made alive. But ^v every man in his own order: Christ the

A. D. 59.

ⁿ Acts 26. 8.
2 Cor. 3. 5.
Col. 1. 23,
29.
2 Tim. 2.17.
^o John 11. 25,
26.
Acts 23. 8.
Rom. 8. 11.
2 Cor. 4. 10.
1 Thes.4.14.
^p Rom. 4. 25.
^q 2 Tim. 3.12.
^r 1 Pet. 1. 3.
^s Acts 26. 23.
^t Rom. 5. 12.
^u John 11. 26.
^a 1 Thes.4.15.

12. if. Since it is an admitted fact that Christ is preached by us eye-witnesses as having risen from the dead, how is it that some of you (whilst admitting Christ's resurrection) deny what is a necessary consequence—viz., the general resurrection? *Christ's* resurrection is said to be "from [ἐκ] the dead:" the *general* resurrection is said to be "the resurrection *of* the dead." **some**—Gentile reasoners (Acts xvii. 32; xxvi. 8) who would not believe it because they did not see "how" it could be (*vv.* 35, 36). They maintained a spiritual resurrection (2 Tim. ii. 17, 18; Rom. vi. 4-6), not corporal, in opposition to Matt. xxii. 23-32. **13.** If there be no general resurrection, which is the consequent, then there can have been no resurrection of Christ, which is the antecedent. The head and the members stand on the same footing (Heb. ii. 17); what does not hold good of them, does not hold good either of Him: His resurrection and theirs are inseparably joined (cf. *vv.* 20 22; John xiv. 19). Christ's resurrection would have been objectless, if it did not entail ours. **14. your faith is also vain** (*v.* 11). The Greek for "vain" here is *empty, unreal* [κενόν]; in *v.* 17 [ματάια], it is *without use, frustrated*. The principal argument of the first preachers of Christianity was, that God had raised Christ from the dead (Acts i. 22; ii. 32; iv. 10, 33; xiii. 37; Rom. i. 4). If this were false, the faith built on it must be false too. **15. testified of God**—*i. e.*, concerning God, or 'against God;' the Greek preposition [κατά], with the genitive, implies, not direct antagonism (as the accusative), but *indirect, to the dishonour of* God: taking His name in vain, invoking it to attest a lie (Exod. xx. 7). If forgery of a king's coin is penal, how much more forgery against the King of kings: miracles are His coin. **if so be**—as they assert. It is not right to "talk deceitfully for" the glory of God (Job xiii. 7). 'Pious frauds' are dishonouring to the God of truth. **16.** The repetition implies the unanswerable force of the argument. **17. vain.** Ye are, if the case be as the sceptics maintain, *frustrated* of all which "your faith" appropriates: ye are still under the everlasting condemnation of your sins (even in the *disembodied* state here referred to), from which Christ's resurrection is our justification (Rom. iv. 25: "saved *by his life*," Rom. v. 10). His death atones for our sin; but we could not have had faith in, and so be saved by, that atonement, but for his resurrection. **18. fallen asleep in Christ**—in communion with Christ as His members. 'In Christ's case the term used is *death*, to assure us of the reality of His suffering; in ours, *sleep*, to give us consolation. In His case, His resurrection having taken place, St. Paul

shrinks not from the term death; in ours, the resurrection being still only a matter of hope, he uses *falling asleep*' (*Photius*, 'Quæstiones Amphilochiæ,' 197). **perished.** Their souls are lost in misery in the unseen world. **19.** If our hopes in Christ were limited to this life only, we should be, of all men, most to be pitied—viz., because, whilst others live unmolested, we are exposed to every trial, and after all are doomed to disappointment in our cherished hope; for our salvation, even of the soul (not merely of the body), hangs on Christ's resurrection, without which His death would not avail us (Eph. i. 19, 20; 1 Pet. i. 3). The heathen are "without hope" (Eph. ii. 12; 1 Thess. iv. 13). We should be even worse, for we should be also without present enjoyment (ch. iv. 9). The immortality of the soul apart from the body is not in Scripture made our hope, but in connection with the raised body.

20. now—as the case really is. **and become.** Omitted in א A B Δ G *f g*, Vulgate. **the first-fruits**—the earliest and most costly, and so consecrated to God; the earnest that the whole resurrection harvest will follow, so that our faith is not vain, nor our hope limited to this life. An appropriate image, for this epistle was written about the passover (ch. v. 7): the day after the passover Sabbath was that for offering the *first-fruits* (Lev. xxiii. 10, 11); the same was the day of Christ's resurrection (Col. i. 18; Rev. i. 5). **21. by man came death, by man came also the resurrection of the dead.** The first-fruits are of the same nature as the ensuing harvest: so Christ, our life, is of the same nature as we men to whom He brings it; just as Adam, the death-bringer by sin, was of the same nature as men on whom he brought it. **22. in Adam all**—in union of nature with Adam, the representative head of mankind in their fall. **in Christ shall all**—in union of nature with Christ, the representative head of mankind in their recovery. The seed of life brought in by Christ is co-extensive with the seed of death brought in by Adam. All sinned in Adam; all rise in Christ, (cf. Rom. v. 12, &c.) **23 But every man in his own order** [τάγματι]—*rank*. The Greek is not abstract, but concrete: image from troops, 'each in his own regiment.' Though all shall rise, not all shall be saved; nay, each shall have his proper place—Christ first (Col. i. 18); after Him the godly who die in Christ (1 Thess. iv. 16), in a separate band from the ungodly; then "the end" —*i. e.*, the resurrection of the rest of the dead. Christian churches, ministers, and individuals, seem about to be judged first "at His coming" (Matt. xxv. 1-30); then "all the nations" (Matt. xxv. 31-46). Christ's own flock shall share His

24 first-fruits; afterward they that are Christ's at his coming. Then *cometh* the end, when he shall have delivered up *w* the kingdom to God, even the Father; when he shall have put down all rule and all authority and
25 power. For he must reign, *x* till he hath put all enemies under his feet.
26, The *y* last enemy *that* shall be destroyed *is* death. For he *z* hath put all
27 things under his feet. But when he saith, All things are put under *him*, *it is* manifest that he is excepted which did put all things under him.
28 And *a* when all things shall be subdued unto him, then *b* shall the Son also himself be subject unto him that put all things under him, that God may be all in all.
29 Else what shall they do which are baptized for the dead, if the dead
30 rise not at all? why are they then baptized for the dead? And *c* why

A. D. 59.

w Dan. 7. 14.
John 17. 2.
2 Cor. 4. 14.
Eph. 5. 27.
x Ps. 110. 1.
Heb. 1. 13.
y Heb 2. 14.
z Matt. 28.18.
1 Pet. 3. 22.
a Matt. 13.41.
Eph. 1. 10.
b John 14 2⁸.
ch. 3. 23.
c 2 Cor. 11 26.

glory "at His coming," which is not to be confounded with "the end," or general judgment (Rev. xx. 4-6, 11-15). The latter is not here discussed, but only the first resurrection—viz., that of those united with Him by justifying faith; not even the judgment of all Christian professors (Matt. xxv. 1-30) at His coming, but only the glory of them "that are Christ's," who alone, in the highest sense, "obtain the resurrection from the dead " (Luke xiv. 14; xx. 35, 36; Phil. iii. 11). Christ's second coming is not a mere *point* of time, but a *period* beginning with the resurrection of the just, and ending with the general judgment. The ground of the universal resurrection (Acts xxiv. 15) is the union of all mankind in nature with Christ, their representative head, who has done away with death, by His death in their stead: the ground of believers' resurrection is not merely this, but their personal union with Him as *their* "Life" (Col. iii. 4), effected *causatively* by the Holy Spirit, *instrumentally* by faith as the *subjective*, and ordinances as the *objective* means. 24. Then [εἶτα]—*after that:* next in the succession of 'orders' or 'ranks.' the end—the general resurrection, final judgment, and consummation (Matt. xxv. 46). delivered up the kingdom to God, even the Father—(cf. John xiii. 3.) *Seemingly* at variance with Dan. vii. 14, "His dominion is an *everlasting* dominion, which *shall not pass away*." *Really,* His giving up the *mediatorial* kingdom to the Father, when the end for which it was established has been accomplished, is in harmony with its continuing everlastingly. The change then to take place shall be in the *manner* of administration, not in the *kingdom* itself: God shall then come into *direct* connection with the earth, instead of *mediatorially,* when Christ shall have fully and finally removed everything that severs the Holy God and a sinful earth (Col. i. 20). The glory of God is the end of Christ's mediatorial office (Phil. ii. 10, 11). His co-equality with the Father is independent of, and prior to, the latter, and shall therefore continue when its function shall have ceased. The Son's power is from the Father, who is not without the Son, but whose power illustrates itself in the Son. Christ's manhood, too, shall everlastingly continue, though, as now, subordinate to the Father. The *throne of the Lamb* (no longer mediatorial), as well as *of God,* shall be in the heavenly city (Rev. xxii. 3). The unity of the Godhead and the unity of the Church shall be simultaneously manifested at Christ's second coming (cf. Zeph. iii. 9; Zech. xiv. 9; John xvii. 21-24). א A B G Δ, Origen, for "*shall have delivered up*" (2 Aorist Subj.), read, '*delivereth* up,' which suits better. It is "when He *shall have* put down all rule," that 'He *delivereth* up the kingdom to *Him who is God and the Father.*' (So the Greek.) put down all rule. The effect produced during the millennary reign

of Himself and His saints (Ps. ii. 6-9; viii. 6; cx. 1), to which passages Paul refers, resting his argument on the words, "all" and "until:" a proof of verbal inspiration of Scripture (cf. Rev. ii. 26, 27). Meanwhile He 'rules in the midst of His enemies' (Ps. cx. 2). He is styled "the King" when He takes His great power (Matt. xxv. 34; Rev. xi. 15, 17). The Greek [καταργήσῃ], "put down," is, '*done away with,*' 'abolish' (2 Tim. i. 10). "All" must be subject to Him, whether hostile powers, as Satan and his angels, or kings and angelic principalities (Eph. i. 21). 25. must —because Scripture foretells it. till—there be no further need of His mediatorial kingdom, its object having been realized. enemies under his feet (Luke xix. 27; Eph. i. 22). 26. shall be— Greek (v. 24), '*is* being done away with' (Rev. xx. 14: cf. i. 18). Christ's victory, already won, is earnest of the final 'abolition' of Death; the abolition *is being effected continuously* up to the consummation (John v. 24; vi. 36). It is to believers especially this applies (*vv.* 55-57); even to unbelievers death is done away with by the general resurrection. Satan brought in *sin,* and *sin death!* So they shall be "destroyed" (*rendered utterly powerless*) in the same order (v. 56; Heb. ii. 14; Rev. xx. 10, 14). 27. all things—including death (cf. Eph. i. 22; Phil. iii. 21; Heb. ii. 8; I Pet. iii. 22). It is said, "*hath* put," for what God has said is as it were already done, so sure is it. Paul here quotes the 8th Psalm in proof of *v.* 24, end, "For (it is written) *He hath put all things,*" &c. under his feet—as His footstool (Ps. cx. 1). In perfect and lasting subjection. when he—viz., God, who by His Spirit inspired the Psalmist. 28. Son also himself be subject—not as creatures are, but as a Son, *voluntarily subordinate* to, though co-equal with the Father. In the mediatorial economy the Son had been in a manner distinct from the Father. Now His kingdom shall merge in the Father's, with whom He is one: not that there is any derogation from His honour; for the Father wills "that all should honour the Son, even as they honour the Father" (John v. 22, 23; Heb. i. 6). God . . . all in all—as Christ is all in all (Col. iii. 11: cf. Zech. xiv. 9). *Then,* and not till then, "*all* things" shall be subject to the Son, and the Son subordinate to the Father, whilst co-equally sharing His glory. Contrast Ps. x. 4; xiv. 1. Even the saints do not fully realize God as their "all" (Ps. lxxiii. 25) now, though desiring it; then each shall feel, *God is my all.*
29. Else—if there be no resurrection. what shall they do?—what profit do they get? baptized for the dead—third person: a class distinct from that in which the apostle places himself—"we" (v. 30): first person. There is no reference to baptizing a living person *in behalf of* a friend who died unbaptized—a heretical practice unknown in the Church before the times of Marcion. *Bengel*

31 stand we in jeopardy every hour? I protest by [4] your rejoicing which I
32 have in Christ Jesus our Lord, [d] I die daily. If [5] after the manner of
men [e] I have fought with beasts at Ephesus, what advantageth it me, if
33 the dead rise not? [f] let us eat and drink; for to-morrow we die. Be not
34 deceived: evil communications corrupt good manners. Awake to righteousness, and sin not; for some have not the knowledge of God: I
speak *this* to your shame.
35   But some *man* will say, How are the dead raised up? and with what

A D. 59.

4 Some read,
 our.
d 2 Cor. 4. 10.
5 Or, to
 speak after
 the man-
 ner of men.
e 2 Cor 1. 8.
f Isa. 22. 13.

---

translates, 'over (immediately upon [ὑπέρ]) the dead'—*i. e.*, who will be gathered to the dead *immediately after* baptism (cf. Job xvii. 1). The fruit they get from their baptism is, that they should be gathered to the dead for ever. Many in the ancient Church put off baptism till near death. But the "for" scarcely bears this meaning in the Greek Testament. Rather, as in Phile. 13, it means, 'baptized *to take the place* of the dead' saints (2 Tim. ii. 2). 'Of what use are fresh witnesses for Christianity, baptized to minister *instead* of those dead?' *Olshausen* takes it, A full number of believers is to be made up before Christ's coming and the resurrection; so every one baptized, by filling up the number, is baptized *for the behoof* of the dead in the Lord (Rev. vi. 10, 11). But the Greek [τί καί before κινδυνεύομεν answering to τί καί before βαπτίζονται] favours the former view, '*Why* are they *then* baptized for the dead? *Why then* (why too) stand we in jeopardy every hour?' Why are they *baptized, filling up the place* of the *martyred dead*, at the risk of sharing the same fate? Why too *stand we in jeopardy* every hour? Probably some symbolical rite of baptism or dedication of themselves to *follow the martyred dead even to death*, grounded on Matt. xx. 22, 23, is alluded to; or, without such rite, "baptized" is used as it is in ch. x. 2. The best punctuation is, 'If the dead rise not at all, why are they then baptized *for them?*' So אAB∆Gfg, Vulgate, read, instead of "for the dead." **30. we**—apostles (*v.* 9; ch. iv. 9). **31. by your** (so אB∆Gfg, Vulgate) **rejoicing**—*by the glorying which I have concerning you*, as the fruit of my labours. A and *Origen* read 'our,' with the same sense. אAB, Vulgate, insert 'brethren' here. ∆Gfg omit it. **I die daily.** This ought to stand first in the sentence, as it is so put prominently in the Greek. I am day by day exposed to and expecting death (2 Cor. iv. 11, 12; i. 8, 9; xi. 23). **32. Punctuate**—"If after the manner of men I have fought with beasts at Ephesus, what advantageth it me? If the dead rise not, let us eat," &c. If '*merely as a man*' (with the mere human hope of the present life; not with the Christian's hope of the future resurrection: answering to "If the dead rise not," the parallel clause in the next sentence) I have fought with beast-like men—Demetrius and his craftsmen. Heraclitus, of Ephesus, had termed his countrymen 'wild beasts' 400 years before. So Epimenides called the Cretians (Titus i. 12). Paul's Roman citizenship exempted him from literal fighting with wild beasts in the arena. He was still at Ephesus (ch. xvi. 8), where his life was daily in danger (2 Cor. i. 8). Though the tumult (Acts xix. 29, 30) had *not yet taken place* (for after it he set out *immediately* for Macedonia), this epistle was written just before it, when the storm was gathering; "many adversaries" (ch. xvi. 9) were already menacing him (cf. Rom. xvi. 4; Acts xviii. 18, 19, 26). **what advantageth it me?**—seeing I have renounced all that, '*as a mere man*,' might compensate me for such sufferings, gain, fame, &c. **let us eat, &c.** Quoted from LXX.

Isa. xxii. 13 describes the reckless indulgence of the despisers of God's call to mourning,—Let us enjoy the good things of life now, for it soon will end. Paul imitates the language of sceptics, to reprove both their theory and practice. 'If men but persuade themselves that they should die like the beasts, they soon will live like beasts too' (*South*). **33. Be not deceived**—as though denial of the resurrection were a mere harmless speculation (ch. vi. 9): nay, association with such unbelievers will corrupt good morals. **evil communications corrupt good manners**—a current saying, from the Thais of Menander, the comic poet, who took it from Euripides (*Socrates*, 'Historia Ecclesiastica,' iii. 16). "Evil communications" refer to intercourse with those who deny the resurrection. Their notion was that the resurrection is merely spiritual, that sin has its seat solely in the body, and will be left behind when the soul leaves it, if, indeed, the soul survive at all. **good**—not only *good-natured*, but *pliant*. Intimacy with the profligate around was apt to corrupt the principles of the Corinthians. **34. Awake**—lit., '*Out of the sleep*' [ἐκνήψατε] of carnal intoxication into which ye are thrown by these sceptics (*v.* 32; Joel i. 5). **to righteousness**—lit., *righteously*, in contrast with "sin" and *corrupt manners* (*v.* 33). **sin not**—in sinful pleasures. The Greek expresses a *continued* abstinence from sin. They who live in sinful pleasures readily persuade themselves of what they wish—viz., that there is to be no resurrection. **some**—the same as in *v.* 12. **have not the knowledge** (lit., *have ignorance*) **of God**—*know not His power* in the resurrection (Matt. xxii. 29). Stronger than, 'are ignorant of God.' Habitual *ignorance: wilful*, positive error, not merely negative, for they prefer to keep, rather than part with, their sins, in order to *know God* (cf. 1 Sam. ii. 12; John vii. 17; 1 Pet. ii. 15). **to your shame**—that you Corinthian Christians, who boast of *knowledge*, should maintain intercourse with those so ignorant of God as to deny the resurrection.

35. How? It is folly to deny a fact of REVELATION because we do not know the "*how.*" Some measure God's power by their intelligence, and won't admit, *even on His assurance*, what they cannot explain. Ezekiel's *answer of faith* to the question is the truly wise one (Ezek. xxxvii. 3). So Jesus argues not on principles of philosophy, but wholly from 'the power of God,' declared by His word (Matt. xix. 26). **come.** The dead are said to *depart*, or be *deceased;* those rising again, to *come.* The objector could not understand *how* the dead rise, and with *what kind of a body* they come. Is it to be the same body? If so, how is this, since the resurrection bodies will not eat or drink, or beget children, as the natural bodies do? Besides, the latter have mouldered into dust. *How*, then, can they rise again? If it be a different body, how can the personal identity be preserved? St. Paul answers, In one sense it will be the same, in another, a distinct body. It will be a body, but a spiritual, not a natural body. **36. fool**—with all thy boasted philosophy (Ps. xiv. 1). **that which thou**—appeal to the objector's *own*

36 body do they come? *Thou* fool, that which thou sowest is not quickened,
37 except it die. And that which thou sowest, thou sowest not that body that shall be, but bare grain, it may chance of wheat, or of some other *grain:*
38 but *ᵍ* God giveth it a body as it hath pleased him, and to every seed his
39 own body. All flesh *is* not the same flesh: but *there is* one *kind of* flesh of men, another flesh of beasts, another of fishes, *and* another of
40 birds. *There are* also celestial bodies, and bodies terrestrial: but the glory of the celestial *is* one, and the *glory* of the terrestrial *is* another.
41 *There is* one glory of the sun, and another glory of the moon, and another glory of the stars: for *one* star differeth from *another* star in glory.
42 So *ʰ* also *is* the resurrection of the dead. It is sown in *ⁱ* corruption; it is
43 raised in incorruption: it *ʲ* is sown in dishonour; it is raised in glory: it is
44 sown in weakness; it is raised in power: it is sown a natural body; it is

A. D 59.

ᵍ Ps. 104. 14.
  ch. 3. 7.
ʰ Gen 1. 11,
  12.
Isa. 61. 11.
Dan. 12. 3.
Matt. 13.43.
Mark 4. 26,
  29.
ⁱ Gen. 3. 19.
Job 17. 14.
Ps. 16. 10.
Ps. 49. 9, 14.
Isa. 38. 17.
Acts 2. 27.
ʲ Phil. 3. 21.

experience: 'The seed which *thou thyself* [σύ] sowest.' St. Paul, in this verse and *v.* 42, answers *v.* 35, "How?" and in *vv.* 37-41 and 43, 'With *what kind* of body?' He converts the very objection (the death of the natural body) into an argument. Death, so far from preventing *quickening*, is the necessary prelude of it, just as the seed "is not quickened" into a new sprout, with increased produce, "except it die" (suffer a dissolution of its previous organization). Christ by His death for us has not reprieved us from death of the life we have from Adam; nay, He permits the law to take its course on our flesh, but brings from Himself new and heavenly life out of death (*v.* 37). **37. not that body that shall be**—but beautiful, and no longer a "*bare* grain," but clothed with blade and ears, yielding many grains, instead of only one. The plant falls back again into the same wheat as its seed: but Paul's comparison of the heavenly body is to the *living plant;* not to the bare *grain* produced subsequently. There is not an identity of all the particles with the old body: for the perpetual transmutation of matter is inconsistent with this. But there is a germ which constitutes the identity of body amidst all outward changes: the outward accretions fall off in its development, whilst the germ remains the same. Every such germ ("seed," *v.* 38) 'shall have its own body,' and be instantly recognized, as each plant now is known from the seed that was sown (see note, ch. vi. 13). So Christ illustrated the truth that His death was the prelude of His putting on His glorified body, which is the ground of the regeneration of the many who believe (John xii. 24). Progress is the law of the spiritual, as of the natural world. Death is the avenue, not to mere *revivification* or *reanimation*, but to *resurrection* and *regeneration* (Matt. xix. 28; Phil. iii. 21). Cf. "*planted*," &c., Rom. vi. 5. **38. as it hath pleased him**—at creation, when He gave *to each of the* (kinds of) *seeds* (so the Greek is for "to every seed") *a body of its own* (Gen. i. 11, "after its kind," suited to its species). So God will give to the blessed at the resurrection *their own body,* such *as pleases Him,* and is suitable to their glorified state: a body peculiar to the individual, substantially the same as that sown. **39-41.** Suitability of bodies, however various, to their species: the flesh of the several species of animals; bodies celestial and terrestrial; the various kinds of light in the sun, moon, and stars. **flesh—animal** organism. Our resurrection bodies shall be really flesh, though glorified and spiritualized; not mere phantoms. So some of the oldest creeds (*Tertullian,* 'De Virg. vel,' c. i.; *Cyril, Ruffinus, Augustine*) expressed it, 'I believe in the resurrection of the *flesh*.' Cf. as to Jesus' own resurrection body, Luke xxiv. 39; John xx. 27; to which *ours shall*

be made like, and therefore shall be *flesh,* but not of animal organism (Phil. iii. 21) and liable to corruption. *V.* 50 implies, it is not "flesh and blood" in the animal sense; for these "shall not inherit the kingdom of God." **not the same**—not of the same nature and excellency. As the kinds of flesh, however widely differing, do not cease to be flesh, so the kinds of bodies, however differing from one another, are still bodies. All this illustrates the difference of the celestial body from its terrestrial seed, whilst substantially identical. **beasts**—quadrupeds. **another of fishes, and another of birds.** So G. But א A B Δ read thus, 'another FLESH of *birds,* and another of *fishes:*' the order of nature. **40. celestial bodies**—not the sun, moon, and stars, which are first introduced *v.* 41, but *the bodies* (organisms) *of angels,* as distinguished from those of earthly creatures. **the glory of the celestial** (Luke ix. 26). **glory of the terrestrial** (Matt. vi. 28, 29; 1 Pet. 1-24). **one . . . another.** The two wholes, celestial and terrestrial bodies, are contrasted by terms [ἑτέρα—ἑτέρα] distinct from those contrasting the individuals classed under them [ἄλλη—ἄλλη]. **41. one glory of the sun, and another of the moon.** The analogy is not to prove different degrees of glory among the blessed (whether this be or not *indirectly* hinted), but this: As the various fountains of *light,* which is so similar in its properties, differ (the sun from the moon, and the moon from the stars; *and even* one star from another, though all seem so much alike); so it is no unreasonable doctrine that *our present bodies* differ much from *our resurrection bodies,* though still continuing *bodies* (cf. the simile, Dan. xii. 3; Matt. xiii. 43). Also that of *seed* in the same parable (Matt. xiii. 24; Gal. vi. 7. 8). **42. sown**—following up the image. A delightful word instead of *burial.* **in corruption**—*liable to corruption:* not merely a prey *when dead* to corruption; as the contrast shows, "raised in incorruption"—i. e., *not liable to corruption.* **43. in dishonour**—answering to "our *vile* body" (Phil. iii. 21); *lit.,* 'our body of humiliation:' liable to various humiliations of disease, injury, and decay. **in glory**—the garment of incorruption (*vv.* 42, 43) like His glorious body, which we shall put on (*vv.* 49, 53; 2 Cor. v. 2-4). **in weakness**—liable to infirmities (2 Cor. xiii. 4). **in power**—answering to a "*spiritual* body" (*v.* 44: cf. Luke i. 17, "spirit and power"). Not liable to the weaknesses of our present bodies (Isa. xxxiii. 24; Rev. xxi. 4). **44. a natural body**—lit., '*an animal* [ψυχικόν] body;' a bodily organism of "flesh and blood" (*v.* 50), to suit the animal soul, which predominates in it. The Holy Spirit *in the spirit* of believers is an earnest of a superior state (Rom. viii. 11): meanwhile *in the body* the animal soul preponderates;

raised a spiritual body. There is a natural body, and there is a spiritual
45 body. And so it is written, The first man [k]Adam was made a living
46 soul; the [l]last Adam *was made* [m]a quickening spirit. Howbeit that
was not first which is spiritual, but that which is natural; and after-
47 ward that which is spiritual. The [n]first man *is* of the earth, [o]earthy;
48 the second man *is* the Lord from [p]heaven. As *is* the earthy, such *are*
they also that are earthy; [q]and as *is* the heavenly, such *are* they also
49 that are heavenly. And [r]as we have borne the image of the earthy, [s]we
shall also bear the image of the heavenly.
50 Now this I say, brethren, that [t]flesh and blood cannot inherit the
51 kingdom of God; neither doth corruption inherit incorruption. Behold,
I show you a mystery; [u]We shall not all sleep, [v]but we shall all be

A. D. 59.

[k] Gen. 2. 7.
[l] Rom. 5. 14.
[m] John 5. 21.
John 6. 33.
[n] John 3. 31.
[o] Gen. 3. 19.
[p] John 3. 13.
[q] Phil. 3. 20.
[r] Gen. 5. 3.
[s] Rom. 8. 29.
Phil. 3. 21.
[t] Matt. 16.17.
[u] 1 Thes. 4.15.
[v] Phil. 3. 21.

hereafter the Spirit shall predominate, and the animal soul be subordinate. **spiritual body**—a body moulded by the Spirit, and its organism not conformed to the lower and animal (Luke xx. 35, 36), but to the higher and spiritual life (cf. ch. ii. 14; 1 Thess. v. 23). **There is, &c.** אABCΔGƒ, Vulgate, 'IF there is a natural (or *animal-souled*) body, there is *also* a spiritual body.' It is no more wonderful that there should be a body fitted to man's future life, in which the spirit preponderates, than that there is (as we all see) one fitted to his present life, in which the animal soul preponderates. Man, standing on the limits of earth and heaven, has a twofold corporeality. **45. so**—in accordance with the distinction between the natural, or *animal-souled*, and the *spiritual* bodies. **it is written** (Gen. ii. 7), "Man became (was made to become) [ἐγένετο εἰς] a living soul"—*i. e.*, endowed with *an animal soul*, the living principle of his body. **the last Adam**—the LAST Head of humanity, who is to be fully manifested *in the last day*, which is *His* day (John vi. 39). He is so called in Job xix. 25 : note there. (Cf. Rom. v. 14.) In contrast to "the last," St. Paul calls "man" "the FIRST Adam." **quickening**—not only living, but *making alive* (John v. 21; vi. 33, 39, 40, 54, 57, 62, 63; xi. 25; Rom. viii. 11; "Christ IS the resurrection and the life;" not merely *gives* them : the gift is not held by the recipient independently of the Giver, but by the believer becoming "one spirit" with Him (Isa. xxvi. 19; ch. vi. 17). As the *animal-souled* body (*v.* 44) is the fruit of our union with the first Adam, an *animal-souled* man, so the *spiritual* body is the fruit of our union with the second Adam, the quickening Spirit (2 Cor. iii. 17). As He became representative of all humanity in His union of the two natures, He exhausted in His own person the sentence of death passed on all, and giveth spiritual and everlasting life to whom He will. **46. afterward.** Adam had "a *living* soul," framed for eternal life by eating the tree of life (Gen. iii. 22) : still, his body was but an *animal-souled*, not a *spiritual* body, such as believers shall have; much less was he a 'life-giving spirit,' as Christ. The natural principle ruled in him. His soul had the germ rather than the fulness of the spirit, such as man shall have when restored, 'body, soul, and spirit,' by the second Adam. As the first and lower Adam came before the second and heavenly Adam, and as we are born naturally before we are in soul born again of the Spirit, so the animal-souled body comes first, and must die before it be changed into the spiritual body—*i. e.*, that in which the spirit predominates over the animal soul. **47. of** (from) **the earth.** Being sprung from the earth, he is "earthy" (Gen. ii. 7; iii. 19)—*i. e.*, not merely earthly or born *upon* the earth, but *terrene*, or *of earth; lit.*, 'of heaped clay' [χοϊκός], and so transitory. Adam means *red earth*. **the Lord.** So C. Omitted in

אABΔGƒg, opposed to "earthy." **from heaven** (John iii. 13, 31)—heavenly and everlasting. Humanity in Christ is generic. In Him man appears in his true ideal, as God originally designed him. Christ is the representative man, the federal head of redeemed man. **48. As is the earthy**—viz., Adam. **they also that are earthy**—all Adam's posterity in their *natural* state (John iii. 6, 7). **the heavenly**—Christ. **they also that are heavenly**—His people in their regenerate state (Phil. iii. 20, 21). As the former precedes the latter state, so the *natural bodies* precede the *spiritual*. **49. as** [καθώς]—'even as' (see Gen. v. 3). **we shall also bear**—wear as a garment. So B. אACΔGƒg, Vulgate, read 'let us also bear' [φορέσωμεν]. It implies the Divine appointment (cf. "must," *v.* 53), and faith assenting to it. An exhortation, yet implying a promise (Rom. viii. 29). The conformity to the image of the heavenly Representative man is to be begun here in our souls, and shall be perfected at the resurrection in both bodies and souls (Rom. viii. 11; 2 Cor. iii. 18). **50. Now this I say**—I concede this much to your objections against the earthly bodies rising again (see notes, *vv.* 37, 39). **flesh and blood**—of the same mortal, corruptible, sin-tainted nature as our (*v.* 39, note, *v.* 44) *animal-souled* bodies. **cannot inherit the kingdom of God.** Therefore the believer acquiesces gladly in the sentence which appoints the death of the present body as the preliminary to the resurrection-body of glory. Hence he "dies daily" to the flesh, as preliminary to his regeneration here and hereafter (John iii. 6; Gal. ii. 20). As being *born of the flesh* constitutes a child of Adam, so being *born of the Spirit*, a child of God. **cannot**—not merely is the change of body *possible*, but *necessary*. The resurrection-body will be still a body, though spiritual, substantially retaining personal identity (note, *v.* 39), even as the glorified soul hereafter will be identical with the regenerated soul here. **the kingdom of God**—which is not animal, but spiritual. *Corruption* doth not *inherit*, though it is the way to *incorruption* (*vv.* 36, 52, 53). **51. Behold**—calling attention to the "mystery" heretofore hidden in God's purposes, but now revealed. **you**—emphatical, 'I *tell* (viz., *by the word of the Lord*, 1 Thess. iv. 15) YOU [ὑμῖν λέγω], who think you have so much knowledge, "a mystery" (cf. Rom. xi. 25) which your reason could never have discovered. אCGg, *Origen*, 2,552 *b c*, Greek MSS. *Didymus*, in *Jerome*, and *Acacius* read, 'We shall all sleep, but we shall not all be changed'—plainly a corrupt reading, inconsistent with 1 Thess. iv. 15, 17, and with the argument here, which is, that a *change* is necessary (*v.* 53). Fear not *death*, as if those found *living* at Christ's coming were to be better off. Nay, *they too* must undergo the great "change." The English version is supported by B, Greek MSS. in *Jerome, Origen*, 1,589ƒ, Syriac and Coptic

52 changed, in a moment, in the twinkling of an eye, at the last trump:
   ^wfor the trumpet shall sound, and the dead shall be raised incorruptible,
53 and we shall be changed. For this corruptible must put on incorruption,
   and ^xthis mortal *must* put on immortality.
54 So when this corruptible shall have put on incorruption, and this mortal
   shall have put on immortality, then shall be brought to pass the saying
55 that is written, Death ^yis swallowed up in victory. O^zdeath, where *is* thy
56 sting? O ⁶grave, where *is* thy victory? The sting of death *is* sin; and
57 ^athe strength of sin *is* the law. But ^bthanks *be* to God, which giveth us
58 ^cthe victory through our Lord Jesus Christ. Therefore, my beloved
   brethren, ^dbe ye stedfast, unmoveable, always abounding in the work of the
   Lord, forasmuch as ye know ^ethat your labour is not in vain in the Lord.
16 NOW concerning ^athe collection for the saints, as I have given order

A. D. 40.

^w Matt. 24. 31.
^x 2 Cor. 5. 4.
^y Isa 25. 8.
Rev 20. 11.
^z Hos 13. 14.
6 Or, hell.
^a Rom. 4. 15.
^b Rom. 7. 25.
^c 1 John 5. 4.
^d 2 Chr. 15. 7.
^e Isa. 3. 10.

CHAP. 16.
^a Acts 11. 29.
Acts 24. 17.
Rom. 15.26.

versions. The Greek is, literally, 'We all shall not sleep, but,' &c. The putting off of the corruptible body for an incorruptible by an instantaneous *change* (like the beautiful butterfly bursting from its larva-envelope into the sunlight) will, in the case of "the quick," be equivalent to *death*, appointed to all men (Heb. ix. 27). Of this Enoch and Elijah are types. The "we" implies that Christians in that age and every successive age since were designed to stand waiting, as if Christ might come in their time, and they be found among "the quick." **52. the last trump**—at the sounding of the trumpet *on the last day* (Matt. xxiv. 31; 1 Thess. iv. 16). Or, the Spirit hints that the other trumpets mentioned subsequently in the Apocalypse shall precede, and that this shall be the *last* (cf. Isa. xxvii. 13; Zech. ix. 14). As the law was given with the sound of a trumpet, so the final judgment according to the law (Heb. xii. 19; cf. Exod. xix. 16). As the Lord ascended "with the sound of a trumpet" (Ps. xlvii. 5), so He shall descend (Rev. xi. 15). The trumpet convoked the people on solemn feasts, especially on the first of the seventh month (the type of the *completion* of time: *seven* indicating *perfection*): on the tenth was the atonement, and on the fifteenth the feast of tabernacles, commemorative of completed salvation out of spiritual Egypt (cf. Ps. l. 1-7; Zech. xiv. 18, 19). Cf., His calling Lazarus from the grave "with a loud voice," John xi. 43, with John v. 25, 28. **the trumpet shall sound, and**—immediately, in consequence. **53. this**—pointing to *his own* and their body. **put on**—as a garment (2 Cor. v. 2, 3). **immortality**—*athanasia*. Here only, besides 1 Tim. vi. 16, the word "immortality" is found (note, *v.* 19). The immortality of the *soul*, distinct from the body, is a notion derived from heathen philosophers. Scripture does not contemplate the anomalous state brought by death as the consummation to be looked for (2 Cor. v. 4), but the resurrection.

54. then—not before. Death has as yet *a sting* even to the believer, in that his *body* is under its power till the resurrection. But then the sting and power of death shall cease for ever. **Death is swallowed up in victory.** Hebrew, Isa. xxv. 8, '*He* (Jehovah) *will swallow up* death in victory'—*i. e.*, *for ever*, in Hebrew idiom (Jer. iii. 5). Christ will swallow it up *so victoriously* that it shall never regain its power (cf. Hos. vi. 2; 2 Cor. v. 4; Heb. ii. 14, 15; Rev. xx. 14; xxi. 4). **55.** From Hos. xiii. 14 substantially, but freely quoted by the warrant of the Spirit. The Hebrew may be translated, 'O death, where are thy plagues? where, O hades, is thy destruction?' The LXX., 'Where is thy victory [δίκη] (lit., *in a lawsuit*), O death? where is thy sting, O hades?' "Sting," the cause, answers to the Hebrew, 'plagues,' the effect.

Appropriate as to the old serpent (Gen. iii.; Num. xxi. 6). Thou who hast stung with plagues others, shalt be stung thyself. "Victory" answers to the Hebrew, 'destruction.' Cf. Isa. xxv. 7, "destroy . . . veil . . . over all nations"—viz., *victoriously destroy* it—and to "in victory" (*v.* 54), which he triumphantly repeats. The "where" implies their past victorious destroying power and sting, now gone for ever; obtained through Satan's triumph over man in Eden, which enlisted God's law on Satan's side against man (Rom. v. 12, 17, 21). The souls in Hades being freed out of it by the resurrection, death's sting and victory are gone. For "O grave" (so C, lit., *Hades;* אBΔG *fg*, Vulgate, *Irenæus, Cyprian*) read "O death," the second time. **56.** If there were no sin, there would be no death. Man's transgression of the law gives death its lawful power. **strength of sin is the law.** Without the law, sin is not discerned or imputed (Rom. iii. 20; iv. 15; v. 13). The law aggravates sin by making its contrariety to God's will apparent. Christ's people are no longer "under the law" (Rom. vi. 14). **57. to God.** The victory was in no way due to ourselves (Ps. xcviii. 1). **giveth**—a present certainty. **the victory**—which death and Hades sought, but which, notwithstanding the opposition of them, the law, and sin, we have gained. The repetition (*vv.* 54, 55) is appropriate to a heart full of the triumph. **58. beloved.** Sound doctrine kindles Christian *love*. Doubters of the resurrection have no motive to zeal in the Lord's work. **stedfast**—not turning aside from the faith *of yourselves*. **unmoveable**—not turned aside *by others* (*v.* 12; Col. i. 23). **the work of the Lord**—the promotion of Christ's kingdom (Phil. ii. 30). **not in vain**—as deniers of the resurrection would make it (*v.* 14, 17). **in the Lord**—applying to the whole sentence and its clauses. Ye, being in the Lord by faith, know that your labour in the Lord (*i. e.*, according to His will) is not to be without its reward in the Lord (through His merits and according to His gracious appointment).

CHAP. XVI. 1-24.—THE COLLECTION FOR THE JUDEAN CHRISTIANS—ST. PAUL'S FUTURE PLANS—HE COMMENDS TO THEM TIMOTHY, APOLLOS, &c.—SALUTATIONS AND CONCLUSION.

1. collection for the saints—at Jerusalem (Rom. xv. 26) and in Judea (Acts xi. 29, 30, xxiv. 17: cf. 2 Cor. viii. 4; ix. 1, 12). He says "saints," rather than 'the poor,' to remind them that in giving, it is to *the Lord's people*, their own *brethren in the faith*. Towards the close of the nation's existence, Judea and Jerusalem were harassed with various troubles, which in part affected the Jewish Christians. The community of goods which existed for a time gave temporary relief, but tended ultimately to impoverish all by para-

2 to the churches of Galatia, even so do ye. Upon [b]the first *day* of the week let every one of you lay by him in store, as *God* hath prospered
3 him, that there be no gatherings when I come. And when I come, [c]whomsoever ye shall approve by *your* letters, them will I send to bring
4 your [1]liberality unto Jerusalem. And if it be meet that I go also, they shall go with me.
5 Now I will come unto you, [d]when I shall pass through Macedonia: for
6 I do pass through Macedonia. And it may be that I will abide, yea,

A. D. 59.
b Pro. 3. 27, 28.
Luke 24. 1.
Acts 20. 7.
Rev. 1. 10.
c 2 Cor. 8. 19.
1 gift.
d Acts 19. 21.
2 Cor. 1. 16.

lyzing individual exertion (Acts ii. 44), and hence was soon discontinued. A beautiful fruit of grace it was, that he who had by persecutions robbed many of their all (Acts xxvi. 10) should be foremost in exertions for their relief. As all Jews contributed a half shekel to the temple, and after its destruction to the Jews residing in Palestine, so Paul urges contributions in support of the Jewish mother church—the more so, that he might show his conflict was with Judaism, not with Jewish Christians. **as I have given**—rather, '*gave* order'—viz., during my journey through Galatia (Acts xviii. 23). The churches of Galatia and Phrygia were the last visited before writing this epistle. He was now at Ephesus, and came thither immediately from visiting them (Acts xviii. 23; xix. 1). That he had not been silent in Galatia on contributions for the poor appears from the hint in his epistle to that church (Gal. ii. 10),—an undesigned coincidence and mark of genuineness. He proposes them as an example to' the Corinthians, the Corinthians to the Macedonians, the Corinthians and Macedonians to the Romans (Rom. xv. 26, 27; 2 Cor. ix. 2). There is great force in example. **2. first day of the week** —already kept sacred by Christians as the day of the Lord's resurrection, the beginning day both of the physical and of the new spiritual creations; it gradually superseded the Jewish seventh day Sabbath (Ps. cxviii. 22-24; John xx. 19, 26; Acts xx. 7; Rev. i. 10). So the beginning of the year was changed from autumn to spring when Israel was brought out of Egypt. Three annual feasts were kept on the FIRST day of the week; the feast of wave offering of the first sheaf, answering to the Lord's resurrection; Pentecost, or the feast of weeks, typical of the fruits of the resurrection in the Christian Church (Lev. xxiii. 11, 15, 16, 36); the feast of tabernacles at harvest, typical of the ingathering of the full number of the elect. Easter was kept as a holy Sabbath (Exod. xii. 16). The Christian Sabbath commemorates the beginnings of the respective works of the Three Divine Persons—*creation, redemption* (the resurrection), and *sanctification* (on Pentecost the Holy Ghost being poured out). Jesus came to fulfil the spirit of the law, not to cancel or lower its standard. The primary object of the Sabbath is *holiness*, not merely *rest:* "Remember that thou keep *holy* the Sabbath day." Cf. Gen. ii. 3, 'God *blessed* and *sanctified* it, because that in it He had rested,' &c. "Remember" implies that it existed *before* the giving of the law from Sinai, and refers to its institution in Paradise (cf. Exod. xvi. 22, 23, 26, 30). "Six days shalt thou labour:" the *spirit* of the command is fulfilled whether the six days' labour be on the last six days or on the first. A perpetual Sabbath would be the highest Christian ideal; but living in a world of business where this is not yet realized, if a law of definite times was necessary in Paradise, it is still more so now. **every one** of you—even those in limited circumstances. **lay by him**—though there be not a weekly *public* collection, each is *privately* to set apart a *definite proportion of his weekly income* for the Lord's cause. The Lord's day, reminding us of His love to us, is the best day for contributing through love to Him. **in store**—abundantly: the earnest of a better store *laid up* for the giver (1 Tim. vi. 19). **as God hath prospered him**—*lit.*, '*whatsoever he may be prospered*,' may *by prosperity have acquired* (Matt. xxv. 15-29; Greek, Acts xi. 29; 2 Cor. viii. 12). **that there be no gatherings when I come**—that they may not *then* have to be made, when our time ought to be employed in directly spiritual things. When men give once for all, not so much is given. But when each *lays by* something every Lord's day, more is collected. **3. approve by your letters**—rather, 'whomsoever ye shall approve, them will I send *with* [διά: cf. Greek, Rom. ii. 27; 2 Cor. ii. 4] letters'—viz., letters (2 Cor. iii. 1) as credentials to several at Jerusalem. There was no need of letters *from them* before Paul's coming, if the persons recommended were *not to be sent off before it*—*lit.*, 'by letters:' abbreviated for, 'I will send, recommending them by letters.' If the English version be retained, the sense will be, 'When I come, I will send those whom by your letters, *then to be given them*, ye shall approve.' **liberality**—lit., *gracious gift* (2 Cor. viii. 4). **4. meet**—'worth while.' If your collections be large enough to be *worth* an apostle's journey (a stimulus to their liberality), I will accompany them *myself*, instead of giving them *letters* credential (*v.* 3: cf. Acts xx. 1-4). **with me**—to guard against all possible suspicion of evil (2 Cor. viii. 4, 19-21).
5-7. His first intention had been (2 Cor. i. 15, 16) to pass through Corinth to Macedonia, and again return to them from Macedonia, and so to Judea; this he had announced in the lost epistle (ch. v. 9); now having laid aside his intention (for which he was charged with levity, 2 Cor. i. 17, &c., whereas it was through lenity, 2 Cor. i. 23; ii. 1), he announces his second plan of 'not seeing them now by the way,' but 'passing through Macedonia' first on his way to them, and then 'tarrying a while,' even 'abiding and wintering with them.' **for I do pass.** 'This is what I at last *resolve upon*' (not as the erroneous subscription represents, as if he was THEN at Philippi, *on his way through* Macedonia: implying that there had been previous communication upon the subject of the journey, and that there had been some indecisiveness in the apostle's plan (*Paley*). In accordance with his second plan, we find him in Macedonia when 2 Corinthians was written (2 Cor. ii. 13; viii. 1; ix. 2, 4), and on his way to Corinth (2 Cor. xii. 14; xiii. 1: cf. Acts xx. 1, 2). "Pass through" is opposed to "abide" (*v.* 6). He was *not yet* in Macedonia (as *v.* 8 shows), but at Ephesus; but he was *thinking* of *passing through* it (not *abiding*, as he proposed to do at Corinth). **6.** He did 'abide, and even winter,' for the three WINTER months in Greece (Corinth) (Acts xx. 3, 6). Paul probably left Corinth about a month before the "days of unleavened bread," the passover (to allow time to touch at Thessalonica and Berea, from which cities two of his companions were; as we read he did at Philippi); thus the three months

334

and winter with you, that ye may *bring me on my journey whither-
7 soever I go. For I will not see you now by the way; but I trust to
8 tarry a while with you, if the Lord permit. But I will tarry at Ephesus
9 until Pentecost. For *f* a great door and effectual is opened unto me, and
g there are many adversaries.
10 Now if Timotheus come, see that he may be with you without fear:
11 for *h* he worketh the work of the Lord, as I also *do.* Let *i* no man therefore despise him: but conduct him forth in peace, that he may come
12 unto me: for I look for him with the brethren. As touching *our* brother
j Apollos, I greatly desired him to come unto you with the brethren: but
his will was not at all to come at this time; but he will come when he
shall have convenient time.

A. D. 59.
* Acts 15. 3.
Acts 17. 15.
Acts 21. 5.
f Acts 14. 27.
2 Cor. 2. 12.
Rev. 3. 8.
g Acts 19. 9.
h Rom. 16.21.
2 Cor. 6. 1.
i 1 Tim. 4. 12.
Tit. 2. 15.
j Acts 18. 24.
ch. 1. 12.
Tit. 3. 13.

at Corinth would be December, January, and February. **ye**—emphatical. **whithersoever I go.** He purposed to go to Judea (2 Cor. i. 16) from Corinth, but his plans were not positively fixed as yet (note, *v.* 4: cf. Acts xix. 21). **7. I will not see you now by the way**—lit., 'I do not wish to see you this time in passing;' *i. e.*, to pay you now what would have to be a merely passing visit, as in the second visit (2 Cor. xii. 14). In contrast to "a while;" i. e., *some time*, as the Greek. **But.** א A B C Δ G *f g*, Vulgate, read "for." **8. at Ephesus**—whence St. Paul writes. Cf. *v.* 19., "Asia," wherein Ephesus was. **until Pentecost.** He seems to have stayed as he here purposes; for, just when the tumult which drove him away broke out, he was already intending to leave Ephesus (Acts xix. 21, 22). Combined with ch. v. 7, 8, this fixes the date of this epistle to a few weeks before Pentecost, very soon after the passover. **9. door** (2 Cor. ii. 12)—an *opening* for extending the Gospel. Wise men watch for, and avail themselves of, *opportunities*. So "*door*" of hope (Hos. ii. 15), "door of faith" (Acts xiv. 27), "an open door" (Rev. iii. 8), "a door of utterance." (Col. iv. 3). "Great"—i. e., *extensive*. "Effectual"—i. e., *opportune for effective working*. **many adversaries** —who would block up the open door, whence my presence is needed to check them. Not here false teachers, but open adversaries—Jews and heathen. After St. Paul, by long-continued labours at Ephesus, had produced effects threatening the gains derived from idolatry, "many adversaries" arose (Acts xix. 9-23). Where great good is, evil is sure to start up its antagonist.

10. Now—rather, *But*. Timothy was not the *bearer* of the epistle: for it would not then be said, 'IF Timothy come.' He must have been *sent* by Paul from Ephesus *before* this epistle was written, to accord with ch. iv. 17-19; yet the passage here implies that St. Paul did not expect him to arrive at Corinth till *after* the letter was received. He tells them how to treat him "if" he should arrive. Acts xix. 21, 22 clears up the difficulty: Timothy, when sent from Ephesus, where this epistle was written, did not proceed direct to Corinth, but *went first to Macedonia;* thus though sent *before* the letter, he might not reach Corinth till *after* it was received in that city. The undesigned coincidence, and the clearing up of the epistle (which does not mention the journey to Macedonia at all) by the history, is a sure mark of genuineness. It is not certain that Timothy actually reached Corinth; for in Acts xix. 22 only *Macedonia* is mentioned; but it does not follow that though Macedonia was the immediate object of his mission, Corinth was not the ultimate object. The 'IF Timothy come,' implies uncertainty. 2 Cor. i. 1 represents him with Paul in *Macedonia;* and 2 Cor. xii. 18, speaking of *Titus* and others sent to Corinth, does not

mention Timothy. But as Timothy is associated with Paul in writing the second epistle, a notice of his own mission in the third person would have been inapposite. The mission of Titus *direct* to Corinth then took place, when it became uncertain whether Timothy could go forward from Macedonia to Corinth, Paul being anxious for *immediate* tidings of the state of the Corinthian church. Titus's presence would thus make amends for the disappointment as to the intended visit of Timothy, and would disarm adversaries of a charge of fickleness in this respect (2 Cor. i. 17; vii. 6, 7). **without fear**—referring to the Corinthians' party violence, and perhaps to a nervous timidity in Timothy (1 Tim. iii. 15; v. 22, 23). His *youth* would add to this, as well as his country, Lystra, despised in refined Corinth. **11. despise.** This charge is not given concerning any other of the messengers whom Paul sent (cf. Ps. cxix., cxli.) He was *young*, younger probably than those usually sent forth (1 Tim. iv. 12); whence St. Paul, apprehending lest he should be exposed to contempt, cautions him, "Let no man despise thy youth." **conduct**—set him on his way with all respect, and with whatever he needs (Titus iii. 13). **in peace** (Acts xv. 33; Heb. xi. 31). "Peace" is the salutation of respect in the East, and so stands for every blessing. Perhaps there is, too, a contrast between "peace" and the "contentions" at Corinth (ch. i. 11). **I look for him.** He and Titus were to meet St. Paul in Troas, whither the apostle purposed proceeding from Ephesus (2 Cor. ii. 12, 13). St. Paul thus claims their respect for Timothy as one whom he felt so necessary to himself as to "look for" him. **with the brethren.** Others besides Erastus accompanied Timothy to Macedonia (cf. *v.* 12; Acts xix. 22). **12. Apollos, I greatly desired him to come unto you.** He says this, lest they should suspect that he from jealousy prevented Apollos's coming to them. Perhaps they expressly requested Apollos to be sent to them. Apollos was not at Ephesus when Paul wrote (cf. *v.* 19 and ch. i. 1). Probably Apollos's unwillingness to go to Corinth at this time was because he did not wish to sanction his name being made a party cry by those Corinthians who admired his oratory (ch. i. 12; iii. 4). St. Paul's freedom from all selfish jealousy led him to urge Apollos to go: he, of course, could not state in his letter particularly these reasons in the existing divisions there. He calls Apollos "brother," to mark the unity between the two. **with the brethren**—who bear this letter (*vv.* 12, 17). Conybeare thinks Titus was one of the bearers (2 Cor. viii. 6, 16-24; xii. 18). **convenient** (*seasonable*) **time.** Apollos did return to Corinth when their divisions were moderated (*Jerome*).

13, 14. Their hopes of salvation ought to depend not on Apollos or any teacher: it rests with themselves. **Watch ye**—for ye are slumbering.

13,   Watch ye, stand fast in the faith, quit you like men, be strong. Let
14 all your things be done with charity.
15   I beseech you, brethren, (ye know the house of Stephanas, that it is
the first-fruits of Achaia, and *that* they have addicted themselves to the
16 ministry of the saints,) that ye submit yourselves unto such, and to every
17 one that helpeth with *us*, and laboureth. I am glad of the coming of
Stephanas and Fortunatus and Achaicus: for *k*that which was lacking
18 on your part they have supplied. For *l*they have refreshed my spirit
and yours: therefore acknowledge ye them that are such.
19   The *m*churches of Asia salute you. Aquila and Priscilla salute you
20 much in the Lord, *n*with the church that is in their house. All the
brethren greet you. Greet ye one another with an holy kiss.
21,   The salutation of *me* Paul with mine own hand. If any man love not
22, the Lord Jesus Christ, *o*let him be Anathema *p*Maran-atha. The grace
23, of our Lord Jesus Christ *be* with you. My love *be* with you all in Christ
24 Jesus. Amen.

The first *epistle* to the Corinthians was written from Philippi by Stephanas, and
Fortunatus, and Achaicus, and Timotheus.

A. D. 59.

k 2 Cor. 11. 9.
Phil. 2. 30.
1 Thes. 3. 6.
Phile. 13.
l Pro. 25. 13.
25.
Rom. 15.32.
2 Cor. 7.6,7.
Phil. 2. 28.
Col. 4. 8.
1 Tim. 3. 6.
3 John 4.
m Acts 16. 6.
Acts 19. 10.
Rev. 1. 4,11.
n Rom. 16. 5.
Phile 2.
o Gal. 1. 8, 9.
Heb. 10. 26.
p Matt. 25.41,
46.
Jude 14, 15.

stand—for ye are tottering. **in the faith**—which
is assailed by some (ch. xv. 1, 2, 12-17). **quit you
like men, be strong**—for ye are effeminate. **Let
all your things be done with charity** (ch. viii. 1;
xiii. 1)—not with strife, as at present.
15. first-fruits of Achaia—the first Achæan converts. Epenetus was the first convert of this
"house," if the received text be right; but oldest
MSS. read *Asia* for *Achaia* in Rom. xvi. 5. The
image is from *first-fruits* offered to the Lord
(Lev. xxiii. 10: cf. ch. xv. 20). This family was
baptized by Paul himself (ch. i. 16). **addicted**
(*set*) **themselves to the ministry of** (*to*) **the
saints**—*voluntarily* (cf. 2 Cor. viii. 4). **16. That
ye.** Translate, 'That ye also'—viz., on your
part . . . in return for their voluntary ministry to you. **helpeth with us**—rather, with
them. **laboureth**—by himself. **17. Fortunatus
and Achaicus**—probably of Stephanas's household.
that which was lacking on your part. So far as
you were unable *yourselves* to '*refresh* my spirit,'
being absent from me, "they have supplied" by
coming to me, and so supplying means of intercourse between you and me. They probably
carried this letter back; see the subscription
below: hence the exhortations *vv.* 16, 18, as though
they would be at Corinth when the epistle arrived.
18. refreshed my spirit and yours. "Yours" will
be refreshed on receiving this letter, by knowing
that 'my spirit is refreshed' by their having
come to me; and (perhaps) by the good report
they give of many of you (ch. i. 4-8; 2 Cor. vii. 13:
cf. Zech. vi. 8). **acknowledge ye them**—by a kind
reception (1 Thess. v. 12). "Know" them in their
true worth, and treat them accordingly.
19. Asia—not all Asia Minor, but *Lydian Asia*
only, of which Ephesus was capital. **much**—with
especial affection. **Aquila and Priscilla** (cf. Acts
xviii. 2; Rom. xvi. 3, 4). Originally driven out of
Italy by Claudius, they had come to Corinth
(whence their salutation of the Corinthians is
appropriate), then had removed with Paul from
Corinth to Ephesus (Acts xviii. 2, 18, 19, 26); here,
as at Rome subsequently, they set up a church
(*assembly of believers*) at their house (Rom. xvi.
3-5). A pattern to Christian husbands and wives.
Their Christian self-devoting love appears where-
ever they were. Even the gifted Apollos, so
highly admired at Corinth, owed much of his
knowledge to them (Acts xviii. 24-26). In *v.* 20,
"All the brethren" (*i. e.*, the whole church) seem
to be distinguished from "the church that is in

their house," which was but a private assembly
out of the general church at Corinth. Rom. xvi.
23 may refer to "the *whole church*" *meeting at the
house of Gaius* (cf. Col. iv. 15). Christ's followers
when dispersed ceased to be a *congregation* (synagogue), but still are a *church*, having the common
union to the same Head by the same faith and
hope. This explains Paul's entering "*into every
house* (viz., to search for the Christians met for
worship there), and haling men and women." **in
the Lord.** They pray for all blessings on you from
the common Lord, the source of every good, IN
whom they and you are one. "In the Lord"
refers to *their union in Christ*, their prayers for one
another's good being in virtue of that union. **20.
holy kiss**—the token of Christians' love ("kiss of
charity," 1 Pet. v. 14), especially at the Lord's
supper (cf. Rom. xvi. 16; 1 Thess. v. 26), in which
all their dissensions would be forgotten.
21. salutation . . . with mine own hand. He
therefore dictated the rest of the epistle. Even
already spurious epistles were circulated (2 Thess.
ii. 2). **22.** A solemn closing warning added *in his
own hand:* as in Eph. vi. 24; Col. iv. 18. **the
Lord**—who ought to be 'loved' above Paul,
Apollos, and all other teachers. Love to one another is to flow from love to Him above all.
Ignatius, 'Epistola ad Romanos,' 7, writes, 'My
love has been crucified' (cf. Song ii. 7). **Jesus
Christ.** So C Δ G *f g*, Vulgate. But omitte l in
א A B. **let him be Anathema**—*accursed* with that
curse which the Jews who call Jesus "accursed"
(ch. xii. 3) are bringing righteously on their own
heads: doomed to Satan's power. So far from
'saluting,' I bid him be *accursed.* **Maran-atha**—
Syriac, *the Lord cometh.* A watchword to urge to
immediate decision for Christ before it is too late;
and preparedness in *love* (1 Thess. iii. 12, 13) for
His coming, as in Phil. iv. 5. **23. The grace, &c.**
This is the salutation meant in *v.* 21; from which
unbelievers (*v.* 22: cf. 2 John x. 11) are excluded.
24. My love, &c. After having administered
severe rebukes, he closes with "love:" his very
rebukes were prompted by *love*, and therefore are
in harmony with the profession here: *love in Christ
Jesus* embraced "*all*" who loved Him.
The subscription represents the epistle as written
from Philippi. V. 8 shows it was written *at
Ephesus. Bengel* conjectures that it was *sent* from
Philippi (*v.* 5), because the deputies of the Corinthians accompanied Paul thither. From Ephesus
there was a road to Corinth above Philippi.

THE SECOND EPISTLE OF PAUL THE APOSTLE TO THE

CORINTHIANS.

1 PAUL, an apostle of Jesus Christ by the will of God, and Timothy *our* brother, unto the church of God which is at Corinth, with *a* all the
2 saints which are in all Achaia: Grace *b be* to you and peace from God our Father, and *from* the Lord Jesus Christ.
3 Blessed *c be* God, even the Father of our Lord Jesus Christ, *d* the
4 Father of mercies, and the God of all comfort; who *e* comforteth us in all our tribulation, that we may be able to comfort them which are in any trouble by the comfort wherewith we ourselves are comforted of
5 God. For as *f* the sufferings of Christ abound in us, so our consolation
6 also aboundeth by Christ. And whether we be afflicted, *g it is* for your consolation and salvation, which ¹ is effectual in the enduring of the same sufferings which we also suffer: or whether we be comforted, *it is*
7 for your consolation and salvation. And our hope of you *is* stedfast,

A. D. 60.

CHAP. 1.
a Col. 1. 2
b Rom. 1. 7.
1 Cor. 1. 3.
Phil. 1. 2.
Col. 1. 2.
c Eph. 1. 3.
1 Pet. 1. 3.
d Ex. 34. 6.
Mic. 7. 13.
e 2 Thes. 2.16.
f Acts 9. 4.
Col. 1. 24.
g ch. 4. 15.
1 Or, is
wrou ht.

CHAP. I. 1-24.—HEADING—ST. PAUL'S CONSOLATIONS IN RECENT TRIALS IN ASIA—HIS SINCERITY TOWARDS THE CORINTHIANS — EXPLANATION OF HIS NOT HAVING PAID HIS PROMISED VISIT.

1. Timothy our brother—perhaps Paul's amanuensis of this epistle. When writing *to* Timothy himself, he calls him "my son" (1 Tim. i. 18); writing *of* him, "brother," &c., and "my beloved son" (I Cor. iv. 17). He had been sent before to Macedonia, and met Paul at Philippi, when the apostle passed over from Troas to Macedonia (cf. ch. ii. 12, 13; notes, 1 Cor. xvi. 10, 11). **in all Achaia**—comprising Hellas and the Peloponnese. The Gentiles and Annæus Gallio, the proconsul (Acts xviii.), strongly testified their disapproval of the accusation brought by the Jews against Paul. Hence the apostle was enabled to labour in the whole province of Achaia with such success as to establish several churches (1 Thess. i. 8; 2 Thess. i. 4), where, writing from Corinth, he speaks of the "churches"—viz., the Corinthian and others also—Athens, Cenchrea, &c. He addresses 'the church in Corinth' *directly*, and all "the saints" in the province *indirectly*. In Gal. i. 2 all the "*churches*" are addressed *directly* in the same circular epistle. Hence here he does not say, *all the churches*, but "all the saints." **3.** This thanksgiving for his late deliverance forms a suitable introduction, conciliating their favourable reception of his reasons for not having fulfilled his promise of visiting them (*vv.* 15-24). **Father of mercies**—*i. e.*, the SOURCE of all mercies (cf. Isa. lxiii. 7; Rom. xii. 1; Jas. i. 17). **comfort**—which flows from His "mercies" experienced. Like a man of faith, he mentions "mercies" and "comfort" before he proceeds to speak of *afflictions* (*vv.* 4, 5, 6). The "tribulation" of believers is not inconsistent with God's mercy, and does not beget in them suspicion of it; nay, they feel that He is "the God of ALL comfort"—*i. e.*, who imparts *the only perfect* comfort *in every instance* (Ps. cxlvi. 3, 5, 8; Jas. v. 11). **4. us**—idiomatic for *me* (1 Thess. ii. 18). **that we may . . . comfort them which are in any trouble.** The Greek is the same as before—"tribulation." Whatever graces God conferred on him, he considered granted, not for himself alone, but that he might have the greater ability to help others. So participation in all

337

man's afflictions qualified Jesus to be man's comforter in them all (Isa. l. 4-6; Heb. iv. 15). **5. sufferings**—in contrast with "salvation" (*v.* 6); as "tribulation" (of mind), with *comfort* or "consolation." **of Christ**—(cf. Col. i. 24.) The *sufferings* endured, whether by Himself or by His Church, with which he identified Himself, are "the sufferings of Christ" (Matt. xxv. 40, 45; Acts ix. 4; 1 John iv. 17-21). Christ calls His people's sufferings His own,—(1.) Because of the sympathy and mystical union between Him and us (Rom. viii. 17; 1 Cor. iv. 10; Heb. ii. 17, 18). Christ's own sufferings are revived in His people's (ch. iv. 10). (2.) They are borne for His sake. (3.) They tend to His glory (Eph. iv. 1; 1 Pet. iv. 14, 16). **abound in us**—Greek, 'abound *unto* us.' The order of the Greek is more forcible than in the English version, 'even so through Christ aboundeth also our comfort.' The *sufferings* (plural) are many, but the *consolation* (though singular) swallows up all. Comfort preponderates in this epistle, as now by the first epistle most of the Corinthians had been much impressed. **6. we be afflicted, it is for your consolation.** Because our afflictions are for the service of the Gospel, *you share in our afflictions, and so in our consolation.* Their hearts were mirrors reflecting the likenesses of each other (Phil. ii. 26, 27) (*Bengel*). Alike the apostle's afflictions and consolations tend, as in him, so in them, by communion with him, to their consolation (*v.* 4; ch. iv. 15). The Greek [θλιβομεθα], "afflicted," is the same as before, and ought to be translated, 'whether we *be in tribulation.*' **which is effectual** —*lit.*, worketh effectually. **in the enduring of the same sufferings which we also suffer**—not *similar* sufferings, but "*the same*;" love for Paul making the Corinthians feel his sufferings their own. א A C, Vulgate, transfer 'which is effectual in enduring the same,' &c., so as to follow the second "consolation," and omit the second "and salvation." The received order is good sense, *Our affliction is for your consolation and salvation, which worketh (or is wrought) effectually in your enduring our sufferings.* B Δ G *fg* support it. *Comfort* is felt in sharing the sufferings of those we love, and "*salvation*"—*i. e.*, edification—is promoted thereby. Here follows, in some oldest MSS. (not as the English version in the beginning of *v.* 7), the clause, 'And our hope is stedfast on knowing, that [h] as ye are partakers of the sufferings, so *shall ye be* also of the consolation.

8   For we would not, brethren, have you ignorant of [i] our trouble which came to us in Asia, that we were pressed out of measure, above strength,

9   insomuch that we despaired even of life: but we had the [2] sentence of death in ourselves, that we should [j] not trust in ourselves, but in God

10   which raiseth the dead: who [k] delivered us from so great a death, and

11   doth deliver: in whom we trust that he will yet deliver *us;* ye also [l] helping together by prayer for us, that [m] for the gift *bestowed* upon us by the means of many persons thanks may be given by many on our behalf.

12   For our rejoicing is this, the testimony of our conscience, that in simplicity [n] and godly sincerity, [o] not with fleshly wisdom, but by the grace of God, we have had our conversation in the world, and more abundantly

13   to you-ward. For we write none other things unto you than what ye read or acknowledge; and I trust ye shall acknowledge even to the

A. D. co.

[h] Rom. 8. 17.
2 Tim. 2.12.
[i] Acts 19. 23.
1 Cor. 16. 9.
[2] Or. answer.
[j] Jer. 17. 5, 7.
Rom. 4. 17-25.
Heb. 11. 19.
[k] 1 Sam. 7.12.
1 Sam. 17. 37.
Job 5.17-22.
2 Pet. 2. 9.
[l] Rom. 15 30.
Phil 1. 19.
Phile 22.
[m] ch. 4. 15.
[n] ch 2. 17.
[o] 1 Cor. 2. 4.

---

your behalf' [ὑπέρ]. א supports the English version. **7. so shall ye be**—rather, 'so *are* ye.' He means there is a community of consolation, as of suffering, between me and you.

8, 9. Referring to the imminent risk of life which he ran in Ephesus (Acts xix. 23, &c.), when the whole multitude were wrought to fury by Demetrius, on the plea of St. Paul having assailed the religion of Diana of Ephesus, and other like dangers. **we had the sentence of death in ourselves**—meaning that *he looked upon himself as condemned to die.* Alford thinks the danger at Ephesus so slight that it cannot be the reference here, without exposing Paul to a charge of cowardice; hence he supposes some deadly *sickness* of Paul (*vv.* 9, 10). But "the sufferings of Christ" (v. 5) would not apply; for *Christ never suffered sickness.* There is little doubt that, had Paul been found by the mob, he would have been torn in pieces: besides, there were other dangers equally distressing—such as "lyings in wait of the Jews" (Acts xx. 19). They, doubtless, had incited the multitude at Ephesus (Acts xix. 9), and were the chief of the "many adversaries," like "(wild) beasts," which he had to fight with (1 Cor. xv. 32; xvi. 9). His weak health combined with this to make him regard himself as all but dead (ch. xi. 29; xii. 10). The very cause of his not having visited Corinth directly, as he had intended, for which he apologizes (*vv.* 15-23), was, that there might be time to see whether the evils arising there, not only from Greek, but from *Jewish* disturbers (ch. xi. 22), would be checked by his first epistle: their not being fully so was what entailed the need of this second epistle. His not specifying this *expressly* is what we might expect in the outset of this letter; towards the close, when he had won their favourable hearing by a kindly tone, he more distinctly refers to Jewish agitators (ch. xi. 22). **above strength**—*i. e.,* ordinary powers of endurance. **despaired**—as far as human help or hope was concerned. But in respect to help from God we were "not in despair" (ch. iv. 8). **9. but**—'yea,' **the** sentence—rather [ἀπόκριμα, not *katakrima*], 'the *answer.*' When I asked myself what must I expect? the answer was "death," Vulgate. *Wahl* supports the English version. **in God which raiseth the dead.** We had so given up all thoughts of life, that our only hope was fixed on the coming resurrection. So in 1 Cor. xv. 22 this hope buoyed him up in contending with foes savage as wild beasts. Here he touches only on the doctrine, taking it for granted that its truth is admitted by the Corinthians, and urging

its bearing on their practice. **10. doth deliver.** So G. But אBC read, 'will deliver'—viz., in *immediately imminent* dangers. 'In whom we trust that He will also (so the Greek) yet deliver us,' refers to God's *continuous* help *hereafter.* **11. helping together by prayer** for us—rather, 'helping together on our behalf by your *supplication*' [δεήσει]. "For us" in the Greek follows "helping together," not "prayer." **that for the gift, &c.**—*lit.,* 'that on the part of many persons the gift (lit., *gift of grace* [χάρισμα]) bestowed *upon us* through (the prayers of) many may be offered thanks for on our behalf.'

12. For. I can confidently expect your prayers for me: "FOR" I walk sincerely towards you. **our rejoicing** [*Kauchesis,* 'our glorying.'] Not that he *boasts* of the testimony of his conscience; nay, this testimony is the thing *in which* his glorying consists. **in simplicity.** So CΔGfg, Vulgate. But א A B, *Origen,* read 'in holiness.' **godly sincerity**—*lit.,* 'sincerity of God;' *i. e.,* sincerity as in the presence of God (1 Cor. v. 8). We glory in this in spite of all our adversities. *Sincerity* [ἐιλικρινεία] implies what bears examination by *sunlight,* and is found *unadulterated* [εἴλη and κρίνω]. He had no selfish aims (as some insinuated) in failing to visit them as he had promised: such aims belonged to his adversaries, not to him (ch. ii. 17). "Fleshly wisdom" suggests insincere courses; but the "grace of God," which influenced him by God's gift (Rom. xii. 3) suggests straightforward, sincere faithfulness to promises (*vv.* 17-20), even as God is faithful to His. The policy which subserves selfish interests, or employs unchristian means, or relies on human aids more than on the Divine Spirit, is "fleshly wisdom." **conversation**—conduct. **in the world** —even in relation to the world, which is full of disingenuousness. **more abundantly to you-ward** (ch. ii. 4). His greater love would manifest his sincerity, especially to them, which his less close connection with *the world* did not admit of his exhibiting towards it. **13. we write none other things** (in this epistle)...than what ye read (in my former epistle (*Bengel*); *present,* because the epistle *continued still* to be read publicly in the church as an inspired apostolic rule). Rather, Paul appeals to their consciousness as witnessing his integrity towards them, in respect to his writing and his acting, 'I write nothing else to you (*to any of you privately*: or else, *I intend by my writing nothing else*) but what ye read openly [ἀναγινώσκετε] in the congregation (1 Thess. v. 27); yea, and what you recognize *inwardly.*' The Greek words for "read"

14 end; as also ye have acknowledged us in part, ^pthat we are your rejoicing, even as ye ^qalso *are* ours in the day of the Lord Jesus.

15 And in this confidence ^rI was minded to come unto you before, that

16 ye might have ^sa second ³benefit; and to pass by you into Macedonia, and ^tto come again out of Macedonia unto you, and of you t: be

17 brought on my way toward Judea. When I therefore was thus minded, did I use lightness? or the things that I purpose, do I purpose ^uaccording to the flesh, that with me there should be yea yea, and nay nay?

18, But *as* God *is* true, our ⁴word toward you was not yea and nay. For

19 ^vthe Son of God, Jesus Christ, who was preached among you by us, *even* by me and ^wSilvanus and Timotheus, was not yea and nay, but in him

20 was yea. For ^xall the promises of God in him *are* yea, and in him

21 Amen, unto the glory of God by us. Now he which stablisheth us with

A. D. 60.

^p ch. 5. 12.
^q Phil. 2. 16.
Phil. 4. 1.
^r 1 Cor. 4. 19.
^s Rom. 1. 11.
³ Or, grace.
^t 1 Cor. 16. 5.
^u ch. 10. 2.
⁴ Or, preaching.
^v Ex. 3. 14.
Mark 1. 1.
Luke 1. 35.
John 7. 58.
^w Acts 18. 5.
^x Rom. 15. 8, 9.

and for "acknowledge" are kindred in sound and root: 'None other things than what ye know *by public reading, or even* (so Greek) *know full well* [ἐπιγινώσκετε] as a fact' (viz., the consistency of my acts with my words: I think exactly as I write). **even to the end**—of my life. Also, to the final consummation, *the day of the Lord* (v. 14, end; 1 Cor. iv. 5). **14. in part.** In contrast to "even to the end;" the testimony *of his life* was not yet completed (*Theophylact*). Rather, "in part"—*i. e.,* some of you, not all (*Grotius*). So in ch. ii. 5; Rom xi. 25. The majority at Corinth had willingly complied with St. Paul's directions in the first epistle; but some were still refractory. Hence arises the difference of tone in different parts of this epistle. (See 'Introduction.') **that** —'because' (*Olshausen*). **your rejoicing**—your subject of *glorying.* **are**—not merely *shall be,* implies the present recognition of one another as a subject of mutual *glorying:* about to be realized in its fulness "in the day (of the coming) of the Lord Jesus."

15. in this confidence—of my character for sincerity being "acknowledged" by you (v. 12-14). **was minded** — I was intending. **before** — "to come unto you before" visiting Macedonia (where he now was). Cf. note, 1 Cor. xvi. 5; also iv. 18; all which imply that the insinuation of some at Corinth, that he would not come at all, rested on his having thus *disappointed* them. His change of intention, and ultimate resolution of going through Macedonia first, took place before his sending Timothy from Ephesus into Macedonia, and therefore (1 Cor. iv. 17) before his writing the first epistle. Cf. Acts xix. 21, 22 (the order there is "Macedonia and Achaia," not *Achaia, Macedonia*); xx. 1, 2. **that ye might have a second benefit**—one in going to, the other in returning from Macedonia. The "benefit" consisted in the *gratification* of having him among them, and receiving spiritual gifts (Rom. i. 11, 12). **16.** This intention of visiting them *on the way* to Macedonia, as well as after having passed through it, must have reached the Corinthians in some way or other—perhaps in the lost epistle (1 Cor. iv. 18; v. 9). The sense comes out more clearly in the Greek order, ' By you to pass into Macedonia, and again from Macedonia to come unto you.' **17. use lightness** — THE levity of which 1 am accused; viz., by promising more than I performed. **or . . . according to the flesh, that with me there should be yea yea, and nay nay?** The "or" expresses a different alternative: Did I act with levity, or (on the other hand) do I purpose what I purpose like fleshly men, so that my "yea" must at all costs, even to the disadvantage of others, be yea, and my "nay" nay? (Matt. xiv. 7. 9.) The

repetition, instead of the single "yea" and "nay," hardly agrees with *Alford's* view, 'What I purpose, do I purpose according to the changeable purposes of the fleshly man, that there may be with me the yea yea, and the nay nay' (*i. e.,* both affirmation and negation concerning the same thing (Matt. v. 37). But Jas. v. 12 proves that the double "yea" here is not equivalent to the single "yea."

18. He adds this lest they might think his DOCTRINE was changeable like his *purposes* (the change in which he admitted in v. 17, whilst denying that it was due to "lightness:" nay, *not* to have changed, where there was good reason, would have been to imitate the *fleshly minded,* who at all costs hold to their purpose). **true**—Greek, 'faithful' (1 Cor. i. 9). **our word**—the *doctrine* we preach. **was not.** So C. But ℵ A B Δ *f g,* read '*is* not.' **yea and nay**—*i. e.,* inconsistent with itself. **19.** Proof of the unchangeableness of the doctrine from the unchangeableness of the subject of it—viz., Jesus Christ. He is called "the Son of God," to show the impossibility of change in One co-equal with God Himself (cf. 1 Sam. xv. 29; Mal. iii. 6). **by me and Silvanus and Timotheus.** The Son of God, though preached by different preachers, proved to be one and the same. *Silvanus* is contracted into *Silas,* Acts xv. 22: cf. 1 Pet. v. 12. **was not yea and nay, but in him was yea** [ἐγένετο—γέγονεν]—'was not made, in our preaching and its results, yea and nay, but *is made* yea in Him'—*i. e.,* is confirmed as true in Him by the Spirit which He has given us in our union with Him (vv. 21, 22), of which Spirit miracles were a subordinate manifestation. Christ preached by us proved to be yea (*i. e.,* fulfilled) *in Christ Himself* (*Bengel*). **20.** Rather, How many soever be the promises of God, in Him is the "yea" ('*faithfulness to His word;*' contrasted with the "yea and nay," v. 19 —*i. e.,* man's *inconstancy to one's word*). **and in him Amen.** ℵ A B C Δ *f g,* Vulgate, read '*wherefore* also *through* Him is the Amen'—i. e., In Him is *faithfulness* ("yea") to His word, 'wherefore *through* Him' is the immutable *verification* of it ("Amen"). As "yea" is His *word,* so "Amen" is His *oath,* which makes our assurance of the fulfilment doubly sure. Cf. "two immutable things" (viz., His word and His oath) in which it was impossible for God to lie (Heb. vi. 18; Rev. iii. 14). All the Old Testament and New Testament promises are secure in their fulfilment for us in Christ. **unto the glory of God by us**—Greek, 'for glory unto God by us' (cf. ch. iv. 15); *i. e.,* by our ministerial labours; by us His promises and His unchangeable faithfulness to them are proclaimed. *Billroth* not so well explains, He sets the "yea"

22 you in Christ, and ^yhath anointed us, *is* God; who ^zhath also sealed us, ^aand given the earnest of the Spirit in our hearts.

23 Moreover I call God for a record upon my soul, ^bthat to spare you I

24 came not as yet unto Corinth. Not for that we have dominion over

2 your faith, but are helpers of your joy: for by ^cfaith ye stand. BUT I determined this with myself, that I ^awould not come again to you in

2 heaviness. For if I make you sorry, who is he then that maketh me

3 glad, but the same which is made sorry by me? And I wrote this same unto you, lest, when I came, I should have sorrow from them of whom I ought to rejoice; ^bhaving confidence in you all, that my

4 joy is *the joy* of you all. For out of much affliction and anguish of heart I wrote unto you with many tears; not ^cthat ye should be grieved,

A. D. 60.
^y 1 John 2.
20, 27.
^z Eph. 1. 13.
Eph. 4. 30.
2 Tim. 2. 19.
Rev. 2. 17.
^a Eph. 1. 14.
^b 1 Cor. 4. 21.
^c Rom. 11. 20.
1 Cor. 15. 1.
CHAP. 2.
^a ch. 12. 20.
^b Gal. 5. 10.
^c ch. 7. 8, 9.

of *verification to all God's promises*, wherefore also through Him the "Amen" *of our announcement of it* is brought about to the glory of God. Where God saith *Yea*, we can only say *Amen* (1 Cor. xiv. 16). **21. stablisheth us with you in Christ**—lit., *into* Christ; *i. e.*, into ever-closer union with Christ. **anointed us.** As "Christ" is the "Anointed," so 'He hath *anointed* [Greek, *chrisas*, akin to *Christos christianoi:* Aorist, *once for all anointed—i. e.*, here in the general sense, *consecrated*, called to the holy office of king and prophet to God (Rev. i. 6); but βεβαιῶν is *stablishing continually*] us, alike ministers and believing people, with the Spirit (1 John ii. 20-27). Hence we become "**a** sweet savour of Christ" (ch. ii. 15). **(is) God; who hath also sealed**—rather put the "*is*" after "God:" 'He which stablisheth us, and hath anointed us, *namely*, God, is He who also hath **sealed us**'—*i. e.*, guaranteed **the** unchangeable truth of our preaching, by giving us His Holy Spirit, the crowning confirmation. A *seal* assures the possession of property to one; "sealed" is the crowning assurance of the Spirit (1 Cor. ix. 2). **the earnest of the Spirit**—*i. e.*, the Spirit as the **earnest** (*i. e.*, money given by a purchaser as a pledge for the full payment of the sum promised). The Holy Spirit is to the believer now as a first instalment to assure him his full inheritance as a son of God shall be his hereafter (Eph. i. 13, 14; Rom. viii. 23): the pledge of the fulfilment of "all the promises" (*v.* 20).

23. Moreover I—Greek, 'But *I* (for my part),' who changed my purpose of coming to you, **in** contrast to GOD who assures us of *His* promises being unchangeably fulfilled (*v.* 20-22). **call God**—the all-knowing One, who avenges wilful unfaithfulness to promises. **for a record upon my soul**—as a witness *to* the secret purposes of my soul, and *against* it, if I lie (Mal. iii. 5) in saying it was not levity, but regard to you, that made me change. **to spare you**—in order not to come in a rebuking spirit, as I should have been obliged if I had come *then.* **I came not as yet** [οὐκέτι—*no longer; i. e.*, I *gave up my purpose of then* visiting Corinth. He wished to give them time for repentance, that he might not have to use severity towards them. Hence he sent Titus before him. Cf. ch. x. 10, 11: his detractors represented him as threatening what he had not courage to perform (1 Cor. iv. 18, 19). **24. Not for that**—*i. e.*, Not that. "*Faith*" is here emphatic. He had "dominion" in *discipline;* but in matters of "*faith*" he was only a '*fellow-helper* of their joy' (viz., in believing: Phil. i. 25). The Greek is, 'Not that we *lord it* over your faith.' This he adds to soften the magisterial tone of *v.* 23. His desire is to cause them not *sorrow* (ch. ii. 1, 2), but "*joy.*" "By faith (Rom. xi. 20) ye stand:" therefore it is that I do not lord over but "help" your faith, the source of all true "joy" (Rom. xv. 13).

CHAP. II. 1-17.—WHY HE HAD NOT VISITED THEM ON HIS WAY TO MACEDONIA—THE INCESTUOUS PERSON OUGHT NOW TO BE FORGIVEN—HIS ANXIETY TO HEAR OF THEIR STATE FROM TITUS—HIS JOY WHEN AT LAST THE GOOD NEWS REACHED HIM.

1. with myself—rather, 'for myself,' to spare myself pain: in contrast to "you" (ch. i. 23: cf. *v.* 2). **not come again to you in heaviness**—'sorrow.' He had *already* paid them *one* visit *in sorrow* since his coming for the first time to Corinth. At that visit he warned them 'he would not spare if he should come again' (notes, ch. xiii. 2: cf. ch. xii. 14; xiii. 1). See 'Introduction' to the first epistle. The "in heaviness" implies *mutual* pain—they grieving him, and he them (cf. *v.* 2 and *v.* 5). In this verse he accounts for having postponed his visit, following up ch. i. 23. **2. For.** Proof that he shrinks from causing them *sorrow* ("heaviness"), **if I.** The "I" is emphatic. Some detractor may say that *this* (*v.* 1) is not my reason for not coming, since I showed no scruple in causing "heaviness" in my first epistle. But I answer, If *I* have been the one to cause you sorrow, my object was that the grieved one (viz., *the Corinthians in general, v.* 3, but with tacit reference to *the incestuous person in particular*) should repent, and so "make me glad." For . . . **who is he then that . . . but the same which is made sorry, &c.** *Present;* not past: the Greek ReflexiveVoice, 'he who *permits himself* to be made sorry.' Returning sensibility is a sign of repentance. (*v.* 7, &c.) Contrast Jer. v. 3. **by** [ἐξ] me—*owing to* me: *his own* sin is the real cause *by* [ὑπό] which he suffers (Jer. ii. 19). **3. I wrote this same unto you**—viz., that I would not come to you *then* (*v.* 1), as, if I were to come then, it would have to be "in heaviness" (causing *sorrow* both to him and them, owing to their impenitent state). He refers to the first epistle (cf. 1 Cor. xvi. 7; iv. 19, 21; v. 2-7, 13). **sorrow from them of whom I ought to rejoice**—i. e., *sorrow* from their impenitence, when he ought, on the contrary, to have *joy* from their penitent obedience. The latter happy effect was produced by the first epistle, whereas the former would have been the result, had he *then* visited them, as he originally proposed. **having confidence . . . that my joy is the joy of you all**—trusting that you, too, would feel there was good ground for deferring my visit, with an ultimate view to our mutual joy. He says "ALL," his charity overlooking, for the moment, the small section of his detractors at Corinth (1 Cor. xiii. 7). **4. So far from my change of purpose being due to "lightness"** (ch. i. 17), I wrote my letter (*v.* 3) "**out of much affliction and anguish**," &c. not **that ye should be grieved.** Translate, 'be made sorry,' to accord with *v.* 2. My ultimate object was not your sorrow, but that through sorrow the transgressors for whom I was so grieved might be

but that ye might know the love which I have more abundantly unto you.

5 But ^d if any have caused grief, he hath not *grieved me, but in part;

6 that I may not overcharge you all. Sufficient to such a man *is* this

7 ¹punishment, which *was inflicted* ᶠof many. So ᵍthat contrariwise ye *ought* rather to forgive *him*, and comfort *him*, lest perhaps such a one

8 should be swallowed up with overmuch sorrow. Wherefore I beseech you

9 that ye would confirm *your* love toward him. For to this end also did I write, that I might know the proof of you, whether ye be obedient in all

10 things. To whom ye forgive any thing, I *forgive* also: for if I forgave any thing, to whom I forgave *it*, for your sakes *forgave I it* ²in the

11 person of Christ; lest ʰSatan should get an advantage of us: for we are not ignorant of his devices.

12 Furthermore, ⁱwhen I came to Troas to *preach* Christ's gospel, and a

A. D. 60.

ᵈ 1 Cor. 5. 1.
ᵉ Gal. 4. 12.
1 Or,
censure.
ᶠ 1 Tim. 5 20.
ᵍ Gal. 6. 1.
Heb. 12. 12.
² Or, in the
sight.
ʰ 1 Chr. 21. 1,
2.
Job 1. 11,
12.
Acts 1. 25.
1 Pet. 5. 8.
ⁱ Acts 16. 8.
Acts 20. 6.

---

led to repentance, and so to joy, redounding both to you and me (*vv.* 2, 3). I made you sorry before going to you, that when I went it might not be necessary. He is easily made sorry who is admonished by a friend himself, weeping (*Bengel*). **that ye might know the love**—of which it is **a** proof to rebuke sins openly and in season (Ps. cxli. 5; Prov. xxvii. 6). **which I have more abundantly unto you**—who have been particularly committed to me by God (Acts xviii. 10; 1 Cor. iv. 15; ix. 2). **5. grief . . . grieved.** Translate as before, "sorrow . . . made sorry." The "any" delicately refers to the incestuous person. **not grieved me, but in part**—he has grieved me only in part (cf. ch. i. 14; Rom. xi. 25)—i. e., *I am not the sole party aggrieved*; most of *you*, also, were aggrieved. Rather punctuate, 'He hath not grieved me (my grief is not the matter for consideration), but *in some measure* (*Fritzsche*) you all, that I may not overcharge you' by (ignoring your grief at the scandal). Or else [πάντας, ὑμᾶς] (*Billroth*), 'but in part (he hath grieved) you, that I may not unduly charge all' with winking at the scandal. Thus, "in part" refers to *the better Corinthians:* others of them were callous (1 Cor. v. 2). **6. Sufficient**—Greek [ἱκανόν], 'a sufficiency' (since he is repenting, *vv.* 2, 7)—without continuing it, so as to drive him to despair (*v.* 7); whereas the object of the punishment was, 'that (his) spirit might be saved.' **to such a man**—implying past estrangement from *such a one* who had caused such grief to the church and scandal to religion (Acts xxii. 22; 1 Cor. v. 5). **this punishment**—his being 'delivered to Satan for the destruction of the flesh:' not only excommunication, but bodily disease (notes, 1 Cor. v. 4, 5). **inflicted of many** —Greek, 'by the majority' of you. Not by an individual priest, as in Rome, nor by the bishops and clergy alone, but by the whole body of the church. **7. with overmuch sorrow**—'with HIS [τῇ] overmuch sorrow.' **8. confirm your love toward him**—giving effect in act to your love; viz., by restoring him to your fellowship, and praying for his recovery from the sickness penally inflicted. **9. For.** Additional reason why they should restore him—viz., as a "proof" of their obedience "in all things;" now in *love*, as previously in *punishing* (*v.* 6), at St. Paul's desire. Besides other reasons for deferring his visit, he wished to make an experiment of their fidelity. Hence he deferred to give, in his first epistle, the *reason* for his change of plan (resolved on before writing it). The full discovery of his motive comes naturally from him now, in the second epistle, after he had seen the success of his measures, but would not have been seasonable before.

All this is as remote as possible from imposture (*Paley*). The interchange of feeling is marked (*v.* 4), "I wrote unto you . . . that *ye* might know the love," &c.: here, "did I write, that *I* might know the proof of *you*." **10.** Another encouragement to their restoring the offender. They may be assured of Paul's apostolic sanction. **for if I forgave any thing, to whom I forgave it.** ℵABCG*fg*,Vulgate, read 'for even what I have forgiven, if I have forgiven any thing.' He uses the perfect tense, as of a thing determined on; as in 1 Cor. v. iii, or as speaking generally: It is **for your sakes** I have forgiven, and do forgive, that the church (of which ye are members) may suffer no hurt by the loss of a soul, and that ye may learn leniency as well as faithfulness. **in the person** [ἐν προσώπῳ] **of Christ**—representing Christ; acting by His authority: answering to 1 Cor. v. **4.** *Wahl* translates, 'in the sight of Christ' [Hebrew, *liphnee:* LXX., ἐν προσώπῳ αυτῶν]; 'before Him' (Prov. viii. 30: cf. Greek, Acts iii. 13). **11.** *Lit.*, 'That we may have no advantage gained over us by Satan'—viz., by letting one member be lost to us through despair, we ourselves furnishing Satan with the weapon, by repulsive harshness to one now penitent. The loss of a single sinner affects all. St. Paul had 'delivered' the offender 'to Satan for the destruction of the flesh, that the spirit might be saved' (1 Cor. v. 5). Satan sought to destroy the spirit also: to let him do so, would be to let him *overreach* us. **not ignorant of his devices.** "Ignorant" and "devices" are akin in sound and root [*noemata agnooumen*]: we are not without *knowledge* of his *knowing* schemes: here to trip up one by excessive grief, as before by licentiousness: to make not only men's lusts, but their very repentance, his instrument of destruction, under the guise of religion (Eph. vi. 11).

12. St. Paul expected to meet Titus at Troas, to receive the tidings as to the effect of his first epistle on the *Corinthians*; but, disappointed in his expectation *there*, he passed on to Macedonia, where he met him at last (ch. vii. 5, 6, 7). The *history* (Acts) does not record his passing through Troas in going from Ephesus *to* Macedonia; but it does in coming *from* that country; also, that he had disciples there (Acts xx. 6, 7), which accords with the *epistle* (ch. ii. 12). An undesigned coincidence, marking genuineness (*Paley*). Doubtless, St. Paul had fixed a time with Titus to meet him at Troas; and had desired him, if detained so as not to be able to be at Troas at that time, to proceed at once to Macedonia, to Philippi, the next station on his own journey. Hence, though a wide door of Christian usefulness opened to Paul at Troas, his eagerness to hear from Titus the tidings from Corinth led him not to stay longer there, when

341

13 door was opened unto me of the Lord, I had no rest in my spirit, because I found not ʲTitus my brother: but taking my leave of them, I went from thence into Macedonia.

14 Now ᵏ thanks *be* unto God, which always causeth us to triumph in Christ, and maketh manifest the savour of his knowledge by us in

15 every place. For we are unto God a sweet savour of Christ, in them that

16 are saved, and in them that perish: to the one *we are* the savour of death unto death; and to the other the savour of life unto life. And

17 who *is* sufficient for these things? For we are not as many, which ³ corrupt the word of God: but as of sincerity, but as of God, in the sight of God speak we ⁴ in Christ.

A. D. 60.
ʲ ch. 8. 6, 16, 23.
ch. 12. 18.
Gal. 2. 1-3.
2 Tim. 4. 10.
Tit. 1. 4.
ᵏ ch. 1. 11.
ch. 8. 16.
Eph. 5. 20.
³ Or, deal deceitfully with.
⁴ Or, of.

the time fixed was past, but he hastened on to Macedonia to meet him there (*Birks*). **to (preach)** —lit., '*for* (unto) the Gospel.' He had been at Troas before; but the vision of a man from Macedonia, inviting him to come over, prevented his remaining there (Acts xvi. 8-12). On his return to Asia, after the longer visit mentioned here, he stayed seven days (Acts xx. 6). **and**—i. e., *though* Paul would, under ordinary circumstances, have gladly stayed in Troas. **a door was opened . . . of the Lord**—Greek, *in* the Lord; *i. e.*, in His work, and by His gracious Providence. **13. no rest in my spirit**—rather, 'no rest *for* my spirit' (Gen. viii. 9). As here his "spirit" had no rest, so in ch. vii. 5, his "flesh." His "spirit"—not from mere human impulse, but under the Holy Spirit—hence concluded that it was not necessary to avail himself of the "door" of usefulness at Troas any longer. **taking my leave of them**—the disciples at Troas.

14. Now—Greek, 'But.' Though we left Troas, disappointed in not meeting Titus there, and in having to leave so soon so wide a door, "thanks be unto God," we were triumphantly blessed in both the good news of you from Titus and in the victories of the Gospel everywhere in our progress. The cause of triumph cannot be restricted (as *Alford*) to the former; for "always," and "in every place," show that the latter also is intended. **causeth us to triumph.** So *Winer.* The Greek *may be*, as in Col. ii. 15, 'maketh us a triumph.' St. Paul regarded himself as a trophy of God's victorious power in Christ. His Almighty conqueror was *leading him about*, through all the world, a sample of His triumphant power at once to subdue and to save. The foe of Christ was now the servant of Christ. As to be led in triumph by man is the most miserable, so to be led in triumph by God is the most glorious lot (*Trench*). Our only true triumphs are God's triumphs over us. His defeats of us are our only true victories (*Alford*). The image is from the triumphal procession of a victorious general. The *additional* idea is included, which distinguishes God's triumph from that of human generals, that the captive is brought into *willing* obedience (ch. x. 5) to Christ, and so *joins in the triumph:* God 'leads him in triumph' as one not merely *triumphed over*, but also as one *triumphing over* God's foes with God (which last will apply to the apostle's triumphant missionary progress under the leading of God). So *Bengel*, '*who shows us in triumph*,' not as conquered, but as the ministers of His victory. Not only the victory, but the open "showing" of it is marked; for there follows, '*who maketh manifest*.' **savour**—retaining the image. As the approach of the triumphal procession was known by the *odour* scattered far and wide by the incense-bearers, so God 'makes manifest by us' (his now at once *triumphed over and triumphing* captives: cf. Greek, Luke v. 10, "catch,"

so as to save alive), the sweet savour of the knowledge of Christ everywhere. As the *triumph* strikes the eyes, so the *savour* the nostrils; thus every sense feels the power of Christ's Gospel. This *manifestation* (a word frequent in his epistles to the Corinthians, cf. 1 Cor. iv. 5) refutes the Corinthian suspicions of his *dishonestly hiding* anything from them (*v.* 17; ch. iv. 2). **15.** The Greek order is, 'For (it is) of Christ (that) we are a sweet savour unto God:' the "for" justifies his previous (*v.* 14), "the savour of HIS (Christ's) knowledge." We not only scatter, but 'we *are* the sweet savour' (Song i. 3: cf. Eph. v. 2, which suggests that the image in "savour" here is not that of incense, but of Christ's sacrifice. God *accepts* (Lev. i. 9-17) my Gospel service in making it known, whether I convince men through His grace or fail through my hearers' fault. **in them that are saved**—rather (not referring to two unalterable states, but to men's different ways of treating the Gospel offer), 'that are *being* saved . . . that are perishing' (note, 1 Cor. i. 18). As the light, though it blinds the weak, is for all that still light; and honey, though it taste bitter to the sick, is in itself still sweet; so the Gospel is of a sweet savour, though many perish through unbelief (*Chrysostom*) (ch. iii. 1; iv. 6). As some of the conquered in a triumph were put to death when the procession reached the capitol, and to them the incense was the "savour of death," whilst to those saved it was the "savour of life," so the Gospel was to the different classes respectively. **16. the savour of [ἐκ, *from*] death unto death . . . of [ἐκ, *from:* א A B C. Δ G *fg*, Vulgate, omit it, as received text, in both places] life unto life**—*an odour* arising *out of death* (an announcement of a *dead* Christ, and a virtually lifeless Gospel, as unbelievers regard our message), *ending* (as the just and natural consequence) *in death* (to the unbelievers); (but to the believer) *an odour* arising *out of life* (*i. e.*, the announcement of a risen and *living* Saviour), *ending in life* (to the believer) (Matt. xxi. 44; Luke ii. 34; John ix. 39). **who is sufficient for these things?**—viz., for diffusing aright the savour of Christ, so diverse in its effects on believers and unbelievers. He here prepares the way for one purpose of his epistle—viz., to vindicate his apostolic mission from the deniers of its sufficiency at Corinth. The Greek order puts prominent the momentous task assigned to him— 'For these things, who is sufficient?' He answers his own question, ch. iii. 5—"Not that we are *sufficient* of ourselves . . . but our *sufficiency* is of God; who also hath made us *able* [ἱκάνωσεν, *sufficient*] ministers," &c. It is not a profession of his insufficiency, through false humility, but of *his sufficiency through God*, as contrasted with those who falsely arrogate it to themselves (*v.* 17). **17. not as many** (ch. xi. 13-18: Phil. ii. 21)—rather, '*the* many;' viz., *the* false teachers (ch. x., xii.; 1 Thess. ii. 3). **which corrupt [καπηλεύοντες]**—

3   DO ^awe begin again to commend ourselves? or need we, as some *others*, epistles ^bof commendation to you, or *letters* of commendation from
2 you? Ye ^care our epistle written in our hearts, known and read of all
3 men: *forasmuch as ye are* manifestly declared to be the epistle of Christ ministered by ^dus, written not with ink, but with the Spirit of the living God; not ^ein tables of stone, but ^fin fleshy tables of the heart.
4, And such trust have we through Christ to God-ward: not ^gthat we
5 are sufficient of ourselves to think any thing as of ourselves; but our

A. D. 60.

CHAP. 3.
^a ch. 5. 12.
^b Acts 18. 27.
^c 1 Cor. 9. 2.
^d 1 Cor. 3. 5.
^e Ex. 24. 12.
^f Ps. 40. 8.
Jer. 31. 33.
^g John 15. 5.

'adulterating, as hucksters do wine for gain' (ch. iv. 2; Isa. i. 22; 2 Pet. ii. 3). **as of sincerity, but as of God**—as becomes one speaking *from* (*out of*) sincerity, as *from* (*i. e.*, with a mission and spiritual life emanating from) God the Father. **in the sight of God**—the Holy Spirit, who hovers over the Church, witnessing and guiding its movements [אABC read κατέναντι for κατενώπιον]. The Trinity is here (cf. Rom. xi. 36). **in Christ**—united to Him in living membership (cf. ch. xii. 19). The *whole* Gospel must be delivered as it is, without concession to men's corruptions, without selfish aims, if it is to be blessed with success (Acts xx. 27).

CHAP. III. 1-18.—THE COMMENDATION TO PROVE GOD'S SANCTION OF HIS MINISTRY HE HAS IN HIS CORINTHIAN CONVERTS—HIS MINISTRY EXCELS THE MOSAIC, AS THE GOSPEL OF LIFE AND LIBERTY EXCELS THE LAW OF CONDEMNATION.

1. Are we beginning (ch. ii. 17) again to recommend ourselves? (ch. v. 12) (as some might say he had done in his first epistle.) **commendation**—recommendation (cf. ch. x. 18). The "some" refers to particular persons of the "many" (ch. ii. 17) teachers who opposed him, and who came to Corinth with letters of recommendation from other churches; and when leaving that city obtained similar letters from the Corinthians to other churches. The 13th canon of the council of Chalcedon (451 A.D.) ordained that 'clergymen coming to a city where they were unknown should not be allowed to officiate without letters commendatory from their own bishop.' The history (Acts xviii. 27) proves the custom here alluded to in the epistle: "When Apollos was disposed to pass into Achaia (Corinth), *the brethren* (of Ephesus) *wrote*, exhorting the disciples to receive him." This was about two years previously, and is probably *one* of the instances to which St. Paul refers, as many at Corinth boasted of being followers of Apollos (1 Cor. i. 12). **2. our epistle** —of recommendation. **written in our hearts**—not borne merely *in the hands*. Though this living epistle be written by affection in my heart, I wish it to be read by all as my recommendation. Your conversion through my instrumentality, and your faith, "known of all men" by report (1 Cor. i. 4-7), is my letter of recommendation (1 Cor. ix. 2). **known and read**—words akin in root, sound, and sense (so ch. i. 13). 'Ye are *known* to be my converts by general knowledge: then *known* more particularly so that my doctrine is *read* in your life.' The handwriting is first "known," then the epistle is "read" (ch. iv. 2; 1 Cor. xiv. 25). There is not so powerful a sermon as a consistent life. The eye of the world takes in more than the ear. Christians' lives are the only religious books the world reads. *Ignatius* ('ad Ephesum,' ch. x.) writes, 'Give unbelievers the chance of believing through you. Consider yourselves employed by God; your lives the language in which He addresses them. Be mild when they are angry; humble when they are haughty; to their blasphemy oppose prayer; to their incon-

sistency, stedfast adherence to your faith.' **3. declared.** The letter is so legible that it can be 'read by all men' (v. 2). Literally, '(Ye) being manifested that ye are an epistle of Christ,' though "*our* epistle" (v. 2), one coming manifestly from Christ, and 'ministered by us'—*i. e.*, carried about and presented by us as its bearers to the world. Christ is the Writer, ye are the letter recommending us. 'What God wished to manifest to all (His Gospel law), He hath written on your hearts: we prepared you to receive the letters, as Moses hewed the stone-tables' (*Chrysostom*). **written not with ink, but with the Spirit of the living God.** St. Paul was the ministering pen, as well as the bearer and presenter of the letter. "Not with ink," in contrast to the letters of commendation which "some" at Corinth (v. 1) used. "Ink" includes all outward materials for writing on, such as the Sinaitic tables of stone. These were not written with ink, but "graven" by "the finger of God" (Exod. xxxi. 18; xxxii. 16). Christ's epistle (his believing members converted by St. Paul) is better: it is written not merely with the *finger*, but with the "*Spirit* of the *living God:*" it is not the "ministration of death," as the law, but of the '*living* Spirit,' that "giveth life" (vv. 6-8). **not in**—not *on* tablets of stone, as the ten commandments (v. 7). **in fleshy tables of the heart.** So Δ *f g*, Vulgate. But אABCG read [καρδίαις] 'On (your) *hearts* (which are) tables of flesh.' Once your hearts were spiritually what the tables of the law were physically—tables of stone; but God has 'taken away the stony heart out of your flesh, and given you a heart of flesh' [*sarkinais*, not *sarkikais; fleshy*, not *fleshly*—*i. e.*, carnal; hence, 'out of your *flesh*'—*i. e.*, your *carnal* nature] (Ezek. xi. 19; xxxvi. 26). Cf. v. 2, As "ye are our epistle written in our hearts," so Christ has first made you 'HIS epistle written with the Spirit in (on) your hearts.' I bear on my heart, as a testimony to all, that which Christ has by His Spirit written in your heart (*Alford*) (cf. Prov. iii. 3; vii. 3; Jer. xxxi. 31-34). This passage (*Paley*) illustrates one peculiarity of St. Paul —viz., his *going off at a word into a parenthetic reflection:* here it is on "epistle." So "savour," ch. ii. 14-17.

4. And—Greek, '*But.*' 'Such confidence, however (viz., of our "sufficiency," vv. 5, 6; ch. ii. 16, to which he reverts after the parenthesis), as ministers of the New Testament, who have a sufficient 'epistle of commendation' in you (vv. 1-3), we have through Christ (not through ourselves: cf. v. 18) toward God' (*i. e.*, in our relation to God, to whom we must render an account of our ministry. Confidence *toward God* is solid, as looking to Him for the strength needed now, and for the reward of grace to be given hereafter. Cf. Acts xxiv. 15. Human confidence is unreal, in that it looks to man for its help and its reward. **5.** The Greek is, 'Not that we are (even yet, after so long experience as ministers) sufficient to think anything OF [ἀφ'] ourselves as (coming) FROM [ἐξ] ourselves; but our sufficiency is (derived) FROM God.' '*From*' more definitely

6 [h] sufficiency *is* of God; who also hath made us able ministers of [i] the new testament; not [j] of the letter, but of the spirit: for [k] the letter
7 killeth, but [l] the spirit [1] giveth life. But if the ministration of death, written *and* engraven in stones, was glorious, so that the children of Israel could not stedfastly behold the face of Moses for the glory of his
8 countenance; which *glory* was to be done away; how shall not [m] the
9 ministration of the spirit be rather glorious? For if the ministration of condemnation *be* glory, much more doth the ministration of [n] righteous-
10 ness exceed in glory. For even that which was made glorious had no
11 glory in this respect, by reason of the glory that excelleth. For if that which is done away *was* glorious, much more that which remaineth *is* glorious.

A. D. 60.

[h] 1 Cor. 15. 10.
Phil 3. 13.
[i] Jer. 31. 31.
Matt. 26. 28.
[j] Rom. 2. 27.
Rom. 7. 6.
[k] Rom. 3. 20.
Gal. 3. 10.
John 6. 61.
Rom. 8. 2.
[l] Or, quick-
eneth.
[m] Gal. 3. 5.
[n] Rom. 1. 17.

refers to the *source* out of which a thing comes; "of" is more general. **to think** [λογίζεσθαι]—to 'reason out' or 'devise' *by our reasonings.* The "we" refers to *ministers* (2 Pet. i. 21). **any** thing—even the least. We cannot expect too little from man, or too much from God. **6. also** —accordingly. **able**—rather, as the Greek is the same as *v.* 5, '*sufficient* as ministers" (Eph. iii. 7; Col. i. 23). **the new testament**—'the new *covenant*' as contrasted with the *Old* (1 Cor. xi. 25; Gal. iv. 24). He reverts here to the contrast between the law on "tables of stone," and that 'written by the Spirit on fleshy tables of the heart' (*v.* 3). **not of the letter**—not of *the mere literal precept,* in which the old law, *as then understood,* consisted. **but of the spirit**—i. e., *the spiritual holiness* which lay under the old law, and which the new covenant brings to light (Matt. v. 17-48), with new *motives* added, and a new *power* of obedience imparted—viz., the Holy Spirit (cf. Rom. vii. 6 with ii. 27, 29). Even in *writing* the *letter* of the New Testament, St. Paul and the other sacred writers were ministers *not of the letter, but of the spirit.* No piety of spirit could exempt a man from the letter of each legal ordinance under the Old Testament; for God had appointed this as the way for a devout Jew to express his mind towards God. Christianity, on the other hand, makes the spirit of outward observances everything, and the letter a secondary consideration (John iv. 24). Still, the moral law of the ten commandments, being written by the finger of God, is as obligatory as ever; but more in the Gospel spirit of "love" than in the letter of a servile obedience, and with a deeper spirituality (Rom. xiii. 9). No literal precepts comprehend the wide range of holiness which LOVE, the work of the Holy Spirit, under the Gospel, suggests to the believer's heart instinctively from the Word understood in its full spirituality. **letter** (the law as an outward ordinance) **killeth**—by bringing home the knowledge of guilt and its punishment, *death* (Rom. iv. 15; vii. 9; Gal. iii. 10, 21). The purer the law, the less is man, without the Spirit, able to keep it: so it is "the ministration of death" (*v.* 7). **spirit giveth life.** The spirit of the Gospel, brought home to the heart by the Holy Spirit, gives new spiritual life (Rom. vi. 4, 11). This 'spirit of life' is for us in Christ Jesus (Rom. viii. 2, 10), who dwells in the believer as a "quickening spirit" (1 Cor. xv. 45). The spiritualism of rationalists admits no 'stereotyped revelation;' only what man's own inner lights, conscience and reason, approve of; thus making the conscience judge of the written Word, whereas the written Word is judge of the conscience (Acts xvii. 11; 1 Pet. iv. 11). True spirituality rests on the whole written Word, applied to the soul by the Holy Spirit, as the only infallible interpreter of its far-reaching spirituality. The *letter* is nothing without the *spirit,* in a subject essentially spiritual: the *spirit* is nothing without the *letter,* in a record substantially historical. **7. the ministration of death**—the legal dispensation, summed up in the decalogue, which denounces *death* for transgression (cf. *v.* 6). **written and engraven in stones.** The dead stones typify the deadness of the people on whose hearts the Spirit did not write the law. There is no "and" in the Greek. 'The ministration of death *in letters,*' which "engraven in stones" explains. So אACG *f,* Vulgate. But BΔ have 'in the letter,' which refers to the preceding *v.* 6, "*the letter* killeth." Even if we read as the English version, 'The ministration of death (written) in letters' alludes plainly to *the* law's *literal precepts* as only bringing the knowledge of sin and "*death*" in contrast to "*the spirit*" in the Gospel bringing us "*life.*" The 'letters' stand in contrast to "the spirit" (*v.* 8). This explains why 'in letters' is used instead of the ordinary 'written and.' **was glorious**—lit., 'was made (invested) *in glory:*' glory was its encompassing atmosphere. **could not stedfastly behold** —'gaze fixedly at' [ἀτενίσαι]. (Exod. xxxiv. 30, "The skin of his face shone; and they were AFRAID *to come nigh him.*") "Could not" therefore means *for* FEAR. The 'glory of Moses' countenance' on Sinai passed away when the occasion was over: a type of the transitory dispensation which he represented (*v.* 11), as contrasted with the permanent Christian dispensation (*v.* 11). **8. shall . . . be**—*i. e.,* shall be found in part now; fully, when the glory of Christ and His saints shall be revealed. **rather glorious**—lit., 'rather (*i. e.,* still more invested) in glory.' **9. ministration of condemnation**—the law regarded in the "letter" which "killeth" (*v.* 6; Rom. vii. 9-11). B *g* read as English version. But ACΔG *f,* Vulgate (oldest MS.), read 'If to the ministration of condemnation there be glory.' **the ministration of righteousness.** The Gospel, which reveals the righteousness of God (Rom. i. 17), imputes righteousness to men through faith in Christ (Rom. iii. 21-28; iv. 3, 22-25), and imparts righteousness by the Spirit (Rom. viii. 1-4). **exceed**—'abound.' **10.** *For even* the ministration of condemnation, the law, *v.* 7 (*which has been glorified* at Sinai in Moses' person), *has* now (English version, less fitly, "*was* made . . . *had*") *lost its glory in this respect by reason of the surpassing glory* (of the Gospel): as the light of the moon fades in presence of the sun. **11. was glorious**—lit., 'was with glory;' or 'marked *by glory*' [διὰ δόξης]. **that which remaineth**—"the *everlasting* gospel" (Rev. xiv. 6). Not 'the ministry,' but the Spirit, and His accompaniments, life and righteousness. **is glorious**—lit., 'is *in* glory.' The [διὰ] 'with' or 'by' is appropriate to that of which the glory was *transient.* 'In' to that of which

12 Seeing then that we have such hope, we use great ² plainness of speech :
13 and not as Moses, ° *which* put a veil over his face, that the children of
Israel could not stedfastly look to the ᴾ end of that which is abolished.
14 But ᑫ their minds were blinded: for until this day remaineth the same
veil untaken away in the reading of the Old Testament; which *veil* is
15 done away in Christ. But even unto this day, when Moses is read, the
16 veil is upon their heart. Nevertheless ʳ when it shall turn to the Lord,
17 ˢthe veil shall be taken away. Now the Lord is that Spirit: and where
18 the Spirit of the Lord *is*, there *is* liberty. But we all, with open face

A. D. 60.

² Or.
boldness.
° Ex. 34. 33.
ᴾ Rom. 10. 4.
Gal. 3. 23.
ᑫ Isa. 6. 10.
John 12. 40.
ʳ Rom. 11.23.
1 Cor. 2. 10.
ˢ Isa. 25. 7.

the glory is permanent. The transient covenant of condemnation had a transient glory: the abiding covenant of justification has an abiding glory. The contrast (*vv.* 10, 11) proves that St. Paul's chief opponents at Corinth were Judaizers. **12. such hope**—of the future glory, which shall result from the ministration of the Gospel (*vv.* 8, 9). **plainness of speech**—openness; without reserve (ch. ii. 17; iv. 2). **13.** We use no disguise, 'as Moses put a veil over his face, that the children of Israel might not look stedfastly upon the end of that which was to be done away,' (*Billroth, Olshausen, Alford, Ellicott, &c.*) The LXX view of Exod. xxxiv. 30-35, is thus adopted by St. Paul, that Moses going in to speak to God *removed the veil till* he came out *and spake to the people;* then *when he had done speaking* he put on the veil, *that they might not look on the end*, or the fading, *of his transitory glory*. But this view does not accord with *v.* 7: the Israelites 'could not look stedfastly on the face of Moses for the glory of his countenance.' Plainly the history (Exod. xxxiv.) implies that Moses' veil was put on *because of* their not having been able to 'look stedfastly at him.' Paul here (*v.* 13) passes from the literal fact to the truth symbolized, the blindness of Jews and Judaizers to the ultimate end of the law: stating that Moses *put on the veil that they might not look stedfastly at* (Christ, Rom. x. 4; the *Spirit, v.* 17) *the end of that* (law in its mere *letter*) *which* (like Moses' glory) *is done away*. Not that *Moses* had this *purpose;* but often God attributes to His prophets the purpose which He has Himself. Because the Jews *would not see*, God judicially gave them up *so as not to see*. They would only see Moses under a legal veil, so that they could not see Christ the end of the mere letter law-veil done away in Him. The glory of Moses' face is antitypically Christ's glory shining behind the veil of legal ordinances (John v. 45-47). The veil, taken off to the believer, is left on to the unbelieving Jew, so that he should not see (Isa. vi. 10; Acts xxviii. 26, 27). He stops short at the letter, not seeing the end. The evangelical glory of the law, like the shining of Moses' face, cannot be borne by a carnal people, and therefore remains veiled to them until the Spirit takes away the veil (*vv.* 14-17). **14-18.** Parenthetical: *of Christians in general*. He resumes *the ministry* (ch. iv. 1). **14. minds** [*noemata*]—'mental perceptions;' 'understandings.' **blinded** — rather [ἐπωρώθη], 'hardened :' the opposite to 'looking stedfastly at the end' of the law (*v.* 13). *The veil on Moses' face* (answering to the mere *letter*) is further typical of *the veil that is on their hearts* through bondage to that letter without the spirit. **untaken away . . . which veil**—rather, 'the same veil . . . remaineth untaken away' [lit., *not unveiled : kalumma mee ana-kaluptomenon*], so that they do not see THAT [ὅτι, *fq.* Vulgate; not ὅ, τι, '*which veil*'] it ("THE OLD TESTAMENT," or covenant of legal ordinances) is done away (*vv.* 7, 11, 13) in Christ; or, as *Bengel, 'because* it is done away in Christ'—i. e., it is not done away *save in Christ:*

the veil *therefore* remains untaken away from them, BECAUSE they will not come to *Christ*, who does away with the law as a mere letter. If they once saw that the law is done away in Him, the veil would be no longer on their hearts in *reading it publicly in their synagogues* [*anagnosei*]: so "read," Acts xv. 21. **15. the veil is**—rather, '*a veil lieth* upon their heart' (their understanding, affected by the corrupt will (John viii. 43; 1 Cor. ii. 14). Cf. as to the Tallith, note, 1 Cor. xi. 4. The veil that lies upon the Old Testament (*v.* 13) really lies upon their own heart: it is their own fault. **16.** Moses took off the veil on going in before the Lord. So as to the Israelites whom Moses represents, 'whensoever their heart (it) *turns* (not as the English version, 'shall turn') to the Lord, the veil is by the very fact (not as the English version, '*shall be*') taken away' [περιαιρεῖται]. Exod. xxxiv. 34 is the allusion. Whenever the Israelites turn to the Lord, who is the Spirit of the law, the veil (like Moses' veil) is taken off their heart in the presence of the Lord: no longer resting on the dead letter, *the veil*, they by the spirit commune with God and with Christ. the inner spirit of the Mosaic covenant (answering to the glory of *Moses' face unveiled* in God's presence). The veil that prevented their seeing that the dead letter of the law is "done away" by its fulfilment in Christ, is itself "taken away." **17. the Lord**—Christ (*vv.* 14, 16; ch. iv. 5). **is that Spirit**—is THE Spirit; viz., *that Spirit* spoken of in *v.* 6, and here resumed after the parenthesis (*vv.* 7-16: Christ is the spirit and "end" of the Old Testament, who giveth life to it, whereas "the letter killeth" (1 Cor. xv. 45; Rev. xix. 10, end). The spirit in the Word and the Spirit of the Lord are related as *effect* and *cause*. The glory behind the veil is the *spirit;* the veil is the *letter*. The Word is a dead letter until Christ's Spirit breathes life into it. The ministry of the spirit includes the law in all its essence. **where the Spirit of the Lord is**—in a man's "heart" (*v.* 15; Rom. viii. 9, 10). **there is liberty** (John viii. 36)— "there," and *there only*. No longer slaves to the letter, which they were whilst the veil was on their heart, they are free to serve God in the spirit, and rejoice in Christ Jesus (Phil. iii. 3); they have no longer the spirit of bondage, but of sonship (Rom. viii. 15; Gal. iv. 7). "Liberty" is opposed to the dead law-letter and to the veil, the badge of slavery; also to the *fear* which the Israelites felt in beholding Moses' *glory unveiled* (Exod. xxxiv. 30; 1 John iv. 18). "The *Spirit*," which "the Lord" bestows, is prominent in the New Testament; the *letter* in the Old Testament. The Christian is made "one spirit" with the Lord (1 Cor. vi. 17). **18. But we all**—Christians, contrasted with the Jews, who have a *veil* on their hearts answering to Moses' veil on his face. He does not resume *ministers* till ch. iv. 1. **with open face**. Translate, 'with *unveiled* face' (the *veil* being removed at conversion), as Moses, unveiled before the Lord, reflected His glory; and as the Old Testament, when the veil is taken off, in its

345

beholding as ^t in a glass the glory of the Lord, ^u are changed into the same image from glory to glory, *even* as ³ by the Spirit of the Lord.

4 THEREFORE, seeing we have this ministry, as we have received
2 mercy, we faint not; but have renounced the hidden things of ¹ dishonesty, not walking in craftiness, nor ^a handling the word of God deceitfully; but by manifestation of the truth commending ourselves to every man's conscience in the sight of God.

3, But if our gospel be hid, ^b it is hid to them that are lost: in whom
4 ^c the god of this world ^d hath blinded the minds of them which believe not, lest the light of the glorious gospel of Christ, ^e who is the image of
5 God, should shine unto them. For we preach not ourselves, but Christ
6 Jesus the Lord; and ^f ourselves your servants for Jesus' sake. For God, who commanded the light to shine out of darkness, ² hath shined in

A. D. 60.
^t ch. 4. 4, 6.
^u John 17.17.
³ Or, of the Lord the Spirit.

CHAP. 4.
¹ shame.
^a 1 Thes. 2. 3.
^b Isa. 6. 9.
^c John 12. 31.
^d Isa. 6. 10.
^e Zech. 13. 7.
^f 1 Cor. 9. 19.
² is he who hath.

Spirit, beneath the letter, reflects plainly the glory of Christ: contrasted with "hid" (ch. iv. 3). **beholding**—'reflecting' [κατοπτριζόμενοι] (*Billroth*). **as in a glass**—a mirror, viz., the Gospel, which reflects the glory of God and Christ (ch. iv. 4; 1 Cor. xiii. 12; Jas. i. 23, 25). **are changed** (*transfigured:* the same word as in Matt. xvii. 2) **into the same image**—that of Christ's glory, spiritually now (Rom. viii. 29 ; 1 John iii. 3) ; an earnest of the bodily change hereafter (Phil. iii. 21). However many they be, believers "*all*" reflect the *same* image, Christ, more or less—a proof of Christianity. **from glory to glory**—from one degree to another. As Moses' face caught a reflection of God's glory from being in His presence, so believers are changed into His image by beholding Him. **even as, &c.**—just such a transformation "*as*" was to be expected, or as proceeds from, 'the Lord the Spirit' [ἀπὸ κυρίου πνεύματος] (*Alford*, v. 17). But the Vulgate supports "the Spirit of the Lord;" the Spirit *glorifies* Christ, and also Christians, by receiving of Christ's and showing it unto them (John xvi. 14: cf. as to hereafter, Ps. xvii. 15; Rom. viii. 11 ; Rev. xxii. 4).

CHAP. IV. 1-18.—His Preaching is Open and Sincere, though to many the Gospel is Hidden; for he preaches Christ, not himself. The human vessel is frail, that God may have the glory; yet, though frail, faith and the hope of future glory sustain him amidst the outward man's decay.

1. Therefore—'for this cause;' because we have the liberty-giving Spirit of the Lord, and with unveiled face behold His glory (ch. iii. 17, 18). **seeing we have this ministry**—"the ministration of the spirit"—of such a spiritual, liberty-giving Gospel: resuming ch. iii. 6, 8. **received mercy**—from God, without desert on our part, in having *this ministry* conferred on us (ch. iii. 5). The sense of "mercy" received from God makes men active for God (1 Tim. i. 11-13). **we faint not**—in boldness of speech and action, and patience in suffering, (*vv.* 2, 8-16, &c.) **2. renounced**—*lit.*, 'bid farewell to.' **of dishonesty**—rather, 'of shame' (Rom. i. 16). Shame would lead to *hiding* (*v.* 3); whereas "we use great plainness of speech" (ch. iii. 12), "by *manifestation* of the truth." We have nothing that needs hiding (cf. ch. iii. 3). He refers to the disingenuous artifices of "many" teachers at Corinth (ch. ii. 17; iii. 1; xi. 13-15). **handling . . . deceitfully**—so 'corrupt' or *adulterate* the "word of God" (ch. ii. 17; cf. 1 Thess. ii. 3, 4). **commending**—recommending ourselves: recurring to ch. iii. 1. **to**—to the verdict of. **every man's conscience** (ch. v. 11)—if only they be candid. Not to men's carnal judgment, as those alluded to, ch. iii. 1. **in the sight of God** (ch. ii. 17; Gal. i. 10).

3. But if—however, even if (as I grant is the case). **hid**—rather (in reference to ch. iii. 13-18) [κεκαλυμμένον], 'veiled.' "Hid" [κέκρυπται] (Col. iii. 3) is said of that withdrawn from view altogether: 'veiled,' of a thing within reach of the eye, but *covered* over so as not to be seen. So Moses' face. **to them**—in the case only of them, for *in itself* the Gospel is plain. **that are lost**—rather, 'that are perishing' (1 Cor. i. 18). So the same cloud that was "light" to the people of God was "darkness" to the Egyptian foes of God (Exod. xiv. 20: cf. ch. ii. 15, 16). Instead of removing the veil that hides Christ's light from their hearts (ch. iii. 15), they draw it closer. **4. in whom**. Translate, 'in whose case.' **god of this world**—only here so called: he is a defaced image of God. The worldly *make him their god* (Phil. iii. 19). He is, *in fact,* 'the prince of the power of the air, *the spirit that ruleth in the children of disobedience*' (Eph. ii. 2). Christ, the God of the world to come, is the perfect image of the Father. **minds**—'understandings;' 'mental perceptions' [*noemata*, as in ch. iii. 14]. **them which believe not**—the same as 'them that are lost' (or 'are perishing') (cf. 2 Thess. ii. 10-12). *South,* 'When the malefactor's eyes are covered, he is not far from his execution' (Esth. vii. 8). Those perishing unbelievers are not merely *veiled,* but blinded (ch. iii. 14; Greek, 'hardened'). **light of the glorious gospel of Christ**. Translate, 'the illumination [*enlightening; photismon;* the *propagation* from those already enlightened to others *of the light*] of the Gospel of the glory of Christ.' 'The glory of Christ' is not a mere *quality* (as "glorious") of the Gospel: it is its *very essence* and *subject-matter.* **image of God** [*eicon*]—implying identity of nature and essence (John i. 18; Col. i. 15; Heb. i. 3). He who desires to see "the glory of God" may see it "in the face of Jesus Christ" (*v.* 6; 1 Tim. vi. 14-16). St. Paul recurs to ch. iii. 18: Christ is "the image of God," into which "same image" we, looking on it in the Gospel mirror, are changed by the Spirit; but this image is not visible to those blinded by Satan (*Alford*). **5. For.** Their blindness is not our fault, as if we sought self in our preaching. **preach . . . Christ Jesus the Lord**—rather, 'Christ *as Lord,* and ourselves as your servants,' &c. "*Lord,*" or *Master,* is the correlative term to "servants." **6. For.** Proof that we are true servants of Jesus unto you; for God imparted to me the heavenly light *that I might impart it to others.* The light that He shed on his path as he went to Damascus suggests the image. **commanded the light**—Greek, 'who by speaking caused light to shine.' So C G *fg,* Vulgate, "light" (Gen. i. 3). But אABΔ read 'who spake, Out of darkness the light *shall* (let the light) shine.'

our hearts, to *give* [g] the light of the knowledge of the glory of God in the face of Jesus Christ.

7 But we have this treasure [h] in earthen vessels, [i] that the excellency of 8 the power may be of God, and not of us. *We are* troubled on every 9 side, yet not distressed; *we are* perplexed, but [3] not in despair; per- 10 secuted, but not forsaken; cast down, but not destroyed; always [j] bearing about in the body the dying of the Lord Jesus, that the life also 11 of Jesus might be made manifest in our body. For we which live are alway delivered unto death for Jesus' sake, that the life also of Jesus might be made manifest in our mortal flesh. 12, So then death worketh in us, but life in you. We having the same 13 spirit of faith, according as it is written, [k] I believed, and therefore

A. D. 60.

[g] Ps. 27. 1.
John 1. 9.
John 8. 12.
1 Pet. 2. 9.
[h] ch. 5. 1.
[i] 1 Cor. 2. 5.
Eph. 1. 19.
[3] Or, not altogether without help, or, means.
[j] Gal. 6. 17.
[k] Ps. 116. 10.

hath shined — rather, as Greek, '*is He who shined;*' Himself our Light and Sun, as well as the Creator of light (Mal. iv. 2; John viii. 12). Regeneration answers to creation. **in our hearts** — in themselves dark. **to give** (that we might give) **the light** — *to others, which is in us* [*pros photismon*] (cf. note, *v.* 4). **the glory of God** — answering to 'the glory of Christ' (note, *v.* 4). **in the face of Jesus Christ.** א C Δ G *fg*, Vulgate, retain "Jesus." A B omit it. Christ is the manifestation of the glory of God, as His image (John xiv. 9); antitypical to the brightness on Moses' "face." The only true and full manifestation of God's brightness and glory is "in the face of Jesus" (Heb. i. 3). **7.** 'Lest any should say, How is it that we enjoy *such unspeakable glory* in a mortal body? he replies, This is one of the most marvellous proofs of God's power, that an earthen vessel could bear such splendour and keep *such a treasure* ("the light of the knowledge of the glory of God")' (*Chrysostom*). The fragile "earthen vessel" is the *body,* the "outward man" (*v.* 16: cf. *v.* 10) liable to afflictions and death. So the light in Gideon's pitchers (Judg. vii. 16-20, 22). The ancients often kept their treasures in vessels of earthenware. 'There are earthen vessels which yet are clean, and golden vessels which are filthy' (*Bengel*). **that the excellency of the power, &c.** — that the *power* of the ministry (the Holy Spirit), in its surpassing "excellency," exhibited in winning souls (1 Cor. ii. 4) and in sustaining us ministers, might be ascribed solely to God. God often allows the vessel to be chipped and broken, that the excellency of the treasure within and of the power may be all His (*vv.* 10, 11; John iii. 30). **may be of God, and not of us** — rather, as Greek, 'may be *God's* (may be seen and thankfully (*v.* 15) acknowledged to *belong* to God), and not (to come) *from* [ἐξ] us.' The power not merely comes *from,* but *belongs* to God continually, and is to be ascribed to him. **8.** [*Thlibomenoi all' ou stenochoroumenoi*] 'BEING hard pressed, yet not reduced to inextricable straits' (nominative to "we have," *v.* 7). **on every side** — Greek, 'in every respect' (cf. *v.* 10, "always"). This verse expresses *inward* distresses, next verse *outward* distresses (ch. vii. 5). The first clause in each member of the series implies the *earthiness of the vessels,* the second clause the *excellency of the power.* **perplexed, but not in despair** [*aporoumenoi ouk exaporoumenoi*] — '*not utterly* perplexed.' As *perplexity* refers to the future, so "troubled" or 'hard pressed' refers to the present. **9. not forsaken** — by God and man. Jesus was forsaken by both: so much do His sufferings exceed those of His people (Matt. xxvii. 46). Lit., *left behind,* as in a race [*enkataleipomenoi*]. **cast down** — or 'struck down:' not only "persecuted" — *i. e., chased* as a deer or bird (1 Sam. xxvi. 20) — but actually *struck* down as with a dart (Heb. xi. 35-38). The [πάντοτε] "always" in this verse means, '*throughout the whole time;*' in *v.* 11 the Greek [ἀεί] is different, and means, '*at every time,* when the occasion occurs.' **10. bearing about in the body the dying of the Lord Jesus** — *i. e.,* having Jesus' (א A B C Δ G, Vulgate, omit "the Lord") continual dying re-enacted in my body: having in it the marks of His sufferings (ch. i. 5), I bear about, wheresoever I go, an image of the Saviour, whose sojourn in the flesh was a continual dying, of which the consummation was His crucifixion (*v.* 11; ch. i. 5: cf. 1 Cor. xv. 31). St. Paul was exposed to more dangers than are recorded in Acts (cf. ch. vii. 5; xi. 26). [*Necrosin*] "The dying" is literally, 'the being made a *corpse.*' Such St. Paul regarded his body, yet a corpse which shares in the life-giving resurrection-power of Christ. **that the life also of Jesus might be made manifest in our body** — rather, 'may be.' "Jesus" is often repeated, as St. Paul, amidst sufferings, peculiarly felt its sweetness. In *v.* 11 the same words occur, with the variation, "in our *mortal flesh.*" The fact of a corpse-like body being sustained amidst such trials manifests that "the (resurrection) life also," as well as the dying "of Jesus," exists in us (Phil. iii. 10). I thus bear about in my own person an image of the risen and *living,* as well as of the suffering Saviour. The "our" is added here to "body," though not in the beginning of the verse. 'For the body is *ours* not so much in death as in life' (*Bengel*). **11. we which live** — in the power of Christ's "life" in us, in our whole man, body as well as spirit (Rom. viii. 10, 11; note, *v.* 10: cf. ch. v. 15). St. Paul regards his preservation amidst so many exposures to "death," by which St. Stephen and St. James were cut off, as a standing miracle (ch. xi. 23). **delivered unto** — not by chance: by the ordering of Providence, who shows 'the excellency of His power' (*v.* 7) in *delivering unto* DEATH His living saints, that He may manifest LIFE also in their dying flesh. "Flesh," the very element of decay (not merely their "body"), is by Him made to manifest *life.* **12.** The "*death*" of Christ, manifested in the continual 'perishing of our outward man' (*v.* 16) works in us, and is the means of working *spiritual* "*life*" in you. The *life* whereof we witness (note, *v.* 11; ch. i. 6, 7) in our dying flesh extends beyond ourselves, by our very dying, to you. **13.** Greek, 'BUT having,' &c. — *i. e.,* notwithstanding our trials, we having, &c. **the same spirit of faith, according as it, &c.** Cf. Rom. viii. 15. The same *living faith* wrought by the Holy Spirit on our "spirit:" stronger than "faith." Though "death worketh in us, but life in you" (*v.* 12), yet, *as we have the same spirit of faith as you,* we therefore (believingly) look for the same immortal *life* as you (*Estius*), and *speak* as we believe. *Alford* not so well: 'The *same* . . . faith *with that described* in Ps. cxvi. 10.' The balance of the sentence requires

14 have I spoken; we also believe, and therefore speak; knowing *that he which raised up the Lord Jesus shall raise up us also by Jesus, and
15 shall present *us* with you. For all things *are* for your sakes, that the abundant grace might through the thanksgiving of many redound to the glory of God.
16 For which cause we faint not; but though our outward man perish,
17 yet the inward *man* is renewed day by day. For our light *m* affliction, which is but for a moment, worketh for us a far more exceeding *and*
18 eternal weight of glory; while we look not at the things which are seen, but at the things which are not seen: for the things which are seen *are* temporal; but the things which are not seen *are* eternal.
5 FOR we know that if *a* our earthly house of *this* tabernacle were dissolved, we have *b* a building of God, an house not made with hands,

A. D. 60.

i ch. 5. 1-4.
Isa 26. 19.
John 11.25.
26.
Rom. 8. 11.
1 Cor. 6. 14.
1 Cor. 15.20.
1.Thes.4.14.
m Ps. 30. 5.
Isa. 54. 8.
Acts 20. 23.

CHAP. 5.
a 2 Pet. 1. 13.
b Phil. 3. 21.
Heb. 11. 10.

the parallelism, 'According to what is written I believed, and therefore have I spoken; we also believe, and therefore speak'—viz., without fear, amidst 'afflictions' and 'deaths' (v. 17). **14.** **Knowing**—by faith (ch. v. 1). **shall raise up us** also—at the resurrection (1 Cor. vi. 13, 14). **by** [διά: so C] **Jesus.** א B Δ G ƒ g, Vulgate, have '*with* [σύν] Jesus.' **present us**—vividly picturing the judgment before the eyes (Jude 24). **with you** (ch. i. 14; 1 Thess. ii. 19, 20; iii. 13). **15. For**—confirming the "with you" (v. 14), and "life . . . worketh in you" (v. 12). **all things**—whether the afflictions and labours of us ministers (vv. 8-11), or your prosperity (v. 12; 1 Cor. iii. 21, 22; iv. 8-13). **for your sakes** (2 Tim. ii. 10). **abundant grace, &c.** — rather, 'that grace (*the* grace which preserves us in trials, and works life in you) being made more abundant by the greater number [*dia tōn pleionōn*] (*of its recipients*, or else *of the intercessors for it*), may *cause the thanksgiving to abound to*,' &c. (*Chrysostom*) (ch. i. 11; ix. 11, 12). Or better, 'that grace, being made the greater *on account of* the thanksgiving [*dia eucharistian*] of *the greater number* (for grace already received), may abound to,' &c. Thus the Greek [περισσεύσῃ] for 'abound' has not to be taken active, but in its ordinary neuter sense. Thanksgiving invites more abundant grace (2 Chr. xx. 19-22; Ps. xviii. 3; l. 23). **16. we faint not**—notwithstanding sufferings. Resuming v. 1. **outward man**—the flesh and all that ministers to the earthly life. **perish**—'is wasting away' by afflictions. **inward man**—our spiritual and true "life," which, even in our mortal bodies (v. 11), 'manifests the life of Jesus.' **is renewed** — 'is being renewed;' viz., with fresh "grace" (v. 15), and "faith" (v. 13), and hope (vv. 17, 18; Rom. xii. 2; Col. iii. 10; Titus iii. 5). **17. which is but for a moment** [τὸ παραυτίκα]— 'which is but *for the present passing moment*.' Cf. Matt. xi. 30; also, "*now for a season* . . . in heaviness" (1 Pet. i. 6). The contrast is between this and the "ETERNAL . . . glory." Also, 'the *lightness* of affliction' ('burden' is not expressed after 'light': the Greek is 'the light of affliction') contrasts beautifully with the '*weight* of the glory.' Hebrew idiom connects *gravity* with glory [*Kabod*]. **worketh**—rather, 'worketh out.' **a far more exceeding and**—'more and more exceedingly' (*Ellicott*) [καθ᾽ ὑπερβολήν εἰς ὑπερβολήν, 'in excess and to excess']. The glory exceeds beyond all measure the affliction. **18. look not at**—as our aim. **things which are seen**—'earthly things' (Phil. iii. 19). We mind not the things seen, whether affliction or refreshment come, so as to be seduced by the latter, or deterred by the former (*Chrysostom*). **things which are not seen** (Heb. xi. 1)—the things which, though not seen

now, shall be so hereafter. **temporal**—rather, '*temporary*,' in contrast to "eternal." The Greek [*proskaira*] is rightly translated in Heb. xi. 25, "the pleasures of sin *for a season*."

CHAP. V. 1-21.—THE HOPE (ch. iv. 17, 18) OF ETERNAL GLORY IN THE RESURRECTION BODY. Hence arises his ambition to be accepted at the Lord's coming judgment. Hence, too, his dealing openly with men, as with God, in preaching: thus giving the Corinthians whereof to boast concerning him against his adversaries. His constraining motive is the transforming love of Christ, by whom God has wrought reconciliation between Himself and men, and has committed to the apostle the ministry of reconciliation. **1. For.** The reason for the statement (ch. iv. 17) that *affliction* leads to *exceeding glory.* **we know**—assuredly (ch. iv. 14; Job xix. 25). **if.** For *all* shall not die; many shall be "changed" without 'dissolution' (1 Cor. xv. 51-53), if this daily *delivering unto death* (ch. iii. 11) should end in actual death. **earthly** [*epigeios*]—not the same as *earthy* (1 Cor. xv. 47): in contrast to "in the heavens." **house of this tabernacle**—rather, 'house of the tabernacle.' "House" expresses more *permanency* than belongs to the body; therefore the qualification, "of this tabernacle" (implying what is *shifting*, not stationary) is added: this tabernacle-like house (cf. Job iv. 19; 2 Pet. i. 13, 14). In the tabernacle in the wilderness, the wooden frame and curtains wore out in time; and when Israel dwelt in Canaan a fixed temple was substituted for it. The temple and the tabernacle in all essentials were one: there were the same ark, the same cloud of glory. Such is the relation between the "earthly" and the resurrection body. The Holy Spirit is enshrined in the believer's body as in a sanctuary (1 Cor. iii. 16). As the ark went first in taking down the tabernacle, so the soul (which, like the ark, is sprinkled with blood of atonement, and is the sacred deposit in the inmost shrine, 2 Tim. i. 12) in the dissolution of the body; next the coverings were removed, answering to the flesh; lastly, the framework and boards, answering to the bones, the last to give way, (Num. iv.) St. Paul, as a *tentmaker*, uses an image from his trade (Acts xviii. 3). **dissolved**—a mild word for the death of believers. **we have** — in *assured* prospect, as certain as if it were in our hands, laid up "in the heavens" for us. The tense is *present* (cf. John iii. 36; vi. 47): not that the dissolution of the earthly, and the having the heavenly habitation, are simultaneous. **a building of God**—Greek, '*from* God.' A solid *building*, not a temporary *tabernacle* or *tent*. "*Our*" body stands in contrast to '*from God*.' Though our present body be also *from God*, yet it is not fresh and perfect from His hands, as our resurrection body shall be, **not**

348

2 eternal in the heavens. For in this ^c we groan, earnestly desiring to be
3 clothed upon with our house which is from heaven: if so be that ^d being
4 clothed we shall not be found naked. For we that are in *this* tabernacle
   do groan, being burdened: not for that we would be unclothed, ^e but
5 clothed upon, that mortality might be swallowed up of life. Now ^f he
   that hath wrought us for the self same thing *is* God, who ^g also hath
6 given unto us the earnest of the Spirit. Therefore *we are* always confident, knowing that, whilst we are at home in the body, we are absent
7, from the Lord: (for ^h we walk by faith, not by sight:) we are confident,
8 *I say*, and ⁱ willing rather to be absent from the body, and to be present
9 with the Lord. Wherefore we ¹ labour, that, whether present or absent,
10 we may be accepted of him. For we must all appear before the judgment

A. D. 60.	
^c Rom 8. 23.	
^d Rev. 3. 18.	
^e 1 Cor 15 53.	
^f Isa. 29. 23.	
^g Rom. 8. 23.	
Eph 1. 14.	
^h Deut 12. 9.	
Rom 8. 21, 25;	
1 Cor.13 12.	
1 Pet. 1. 8.	
ⁱ Phil 1. 23.	
¹ Or, endeavour.	

made with hands—contrasted with houses erected by *man's* hands (1 Cor. xv. 44-49). So Christ's body is designated, as contrasted with the tabernacle reared by Moses (Mark xiv. 58; Heb. ix. 11). Our *resurrection body*, in contrast to the "earthly house of this tabernacle," our present body. The intermediate state is not *directly* taken into account. A comma should separate "eternal" and "in the heavens." **2. For in this**—Greek, 'For *also* in this;' "herein" (ch. viii. 10). *Alford* takes it, 'in this' tabernacle (cf. *v.* 4). But the parallelism is sufficiently exact by making "in this we groan" refer generally to what was just said (*v.* 1)—viz., that we long to have our 'house in the heavens.' "We groan" under the body's weaknesses and mortality. **earnestly desiring to be clothed upon** [Greek middle: *ependusasthai*]—'earnestly *longing* to have ourselves *clothed upon*'—viz., being found *alive* at Christ's coming, so to escape *dissolution* by death (*vv.* 1, 4), and to have our heavenly body put on over the earthly. The groans of the saints prove their longing desire for the heavenly glory—a desire which, as created by God, cannot be doomed to disappointment. **our house.** Different Greek [*oiketerion*] from that in *v.* 1 [*oikia*]. Translate, 'our habitation,' 'our domicile:' it more distinctly refers to the *inhabitant* than the general "house" (*v.* 1) (*Bengel*). **from heaven.** This 'domicile' is "*from heaven*" in its origin; and is to be brought to us by Christ at His coming "from heaven" (1 Thess. iv. 16). Therefore it is not heaven itself. [B Δ G read εἰ περ, *provided that, if so be:* ℵ C, εἰ γε, *seeing that, since.*] Our 'desire' holds good should Christ's coming find us alive. Translate, 'that is [καί], if so be that having had ourselves (already) clothed (with our natural body, cf. *v.* 4), we shall not be found naked' (stripped of it). *Olshausen* takes it improbably, 'having put on *the robe of righteousness.*' **4. For**—resuming *v.* 2. **burdened: not** for that—rather, '*in that* we desire *not* [ἐφ' ᾧ οὐ θέλομεν] to have ourselves unclothed (of our present body), but clothed upon,' or 'over' (with our heavenly body). **that mortality, &c.**—rather, 'that what is mortal [our mortal part: *to thneton*] may be swallowed up of (transformed into) life' (1 Cor. xv. 54). Believers shrink from, not the *consequences*, but the *act* of dying; especially as believing in the possibility of being found alive at the Lord's coming (1 Thess. iv. 15), and of having their mortal body absorbed into the immortal without death. Like Elijah, they wish to have the heavenly body drawn over the mortal body like a garment. Faith does not divest us of natural feeling, but subordinates it to higher feeling. Scripture gives no sanction to the philosophers' contempt for the body. **5. wrought us**—framed us by redemption, justification, and sanctification. **for** (*unto*) **the self-same thing**—viz., unto our mortal part being swallowed up in life (*v.* 4). **who also.** So C. But

ℵ B omit "also:" *inasmuch as* He has given unto us. **earnest of the Spirit** (note, ch. i. 22). It is the Spirit (as "the first-fruits") who creates in us the groaning desire for our coming deliverance and glory (Rom. viii. 23). **6.** Greek, 'Being therefore always confident and knowing,' &c. He intended the verb 'we are willing' ('well content') [εὐδοκοῦμεν] to follow; but digressing on the word "confident" (*vv.* 6, 7), he resumes it in the form of an assertion—'We are confident and well content.' **always** [*pantote*]—under all trials. *Bengel* makes the contrast between "*always* confident" and "confident," especially at the prospect of being "absent from the body," &c. Whilst then being confident *at all times*, yet [δέ, *v.* 8] we are especially confident in the hope of a blessed departure. **whilst we are at home . . . we are absent**—Greek, 'whilst sojourning in our home [*endemountes*] in the body, we are *away from our home* [*ekdemoumen*] in the Lord.' The image from a "house" is retained (cf. Phil. iii. 20; Heb. xi. 13-16; xiii. 14). **7. we walk**—in our Christian course on earth. **by faith** [διὰ πίστεως]—in a medium or *state of* faith. **not by sight** [διὰ εἴδους]—'not by appearance.' Our life is pervaded *by faith in* our immortal hope: not *by* the specious *appearance of* present things (*Tittmann*) (cf. LXX., Num. xii. 8). Ch. iv. 18 confirms the English version (cf. Rom. viii. 24; 1 Cor. xiii. 12, 13). God has appointed in this life faith for our great duty; and in the next, vision for our reward (*South*) (1 Pet. i. 8). **8. willing**—*lit.*, 'well content.' Translate, 'to go from our home [*ekdemesai*] in the body, and to come to our home [*endemesai*] with the Lord.' We prefer to be found alive at the Lord's coming, and to be clothed upon with our heavenly body (*vv.* 2-4). But feeling the sojourn in the body to be a separation from our true home "with the Lord," we prefer even dissolution, so that *in the intermediate disembodied state* we may go to be "with the Lord" (Phil. i. 23). "To depart and be with Christ" (the disembodied state) is distinguished from Christ's coming to take us to *be with Him* in soul and body (1 Thess. iv. 14-17). Perhaps the disembodied spirits of believers have full communion *with Christ* unseen; but not mutual recognition, until clothed with their visible bodies at the resurrection, when they shall recognize Christ's image in each other perfect. **9. Wherefore** —With such a 'confidence' of being blessed, whether we die, or live till Christ's coming. **we labour** [*philotimoumetha*]—'make it our ambition:' the only lawful ambition. **whether present** (with the Lord, *v.* 8) **or absent** (from the Lord's immediate presence). **accepted** [*euarestoi*]—'well-pleasing.' **10. appear** [*phanerothenai*]—'be made manifest;' viz., in our true character. Not 'be judged:' for in one sense the righteous are not judged (1 Cor. vi. 2, 3). So Greek, Col. iii. 4 (cf. 1 Cor. iv. 5). We are at all times 'manifest' to

seat of Christ; *[j]* that every one may receive the things *done* in *his* body, according to that he hath done, whether *it be* good or bad.

11   Knowing therefore the terror of the Lord, we persuade men: but we are made manifest unto God; and I trust also are made manifest in

12 your consciences. For we commend not ourselves again unto you, but give you occasion to glory on our behalf, that ye may have somewhat to

13 *answer* them which glory [2] in appearance, and not in heart. For *[k]* whether we be beside ourselves, *it is* to God; or whether we be sober,

14 *it is* for your cause. For the love of Christ constraineth us; because we

15 thus judge, that if *[l]* one died for all, then were all dead: and *that* he died for all, *[m]* that they which live should not henceforth live unto them-

16 selves, but unto him which died for them, and rose again. Wherefore *[n]* henceforth know we no man after the flesh: yea, though we have

A. D. 60.

[j] 1 Ki. 8. 32.
Job 34. 11.
Ps. 62. 12.
Isa 3. 10.
Matt 16.27.
Rom. 2. 5.
Rev. 22. 12.
[2] in the face.
[k] ch. 11. 1.
[l] Isa. 53. 6.
Matt. 20.28.
Rom. 5. 15.
1 John 2.1,
2.
[m] 1 Pet. 4. 2.
[n] Matt.12.50.

God; *then* we shall be so to the assembled intelligent universe and to ourselves; for the judgment shall be not only in order to assign the everlasting portion to each, but to vindicate God's righteousness, so that it shall be manifest to all His creatures, and even to the sinner himself. **receive—**his reward of grace proportioned to "the things done," &c. (ch. ix. 6-9; 2 John 8): the saved may have a greater or less *reward,* according as he lives to, and labours for, Christ more or less. Hence there is scope for the holy 'ambition' (note, *v.* 9; Heb. vi. 10). This verse guards against supposing that *all* share in the house "from heaven" (*vv.* 1, 2). A searching judgment shall sever the bad from the good, according to their respective deeds (Eph. vi. 8; Col. iii. 25), the *motive* being taken into account, not the mere external act; faith and love to God are the sole motives recognized as sound (Matt. xii. 36, 37; xxv. 35-45). **done in his body.** The Greek may be, 'by the instrumentality of the body' [*dia tou somatos*]; but the English version is legitimate (cf. Greek, Rom. ii. 27). Justice requires that essentially *the same* body, the instrument of the unbelievers' sin, should be the object of punishment. The unbeliever's own sin he shall "receive" as its punishment (Jer. ii. 19): the good deeds of the righteous shall in part be their reward (Isa. iii. 9-11; Rev. xxii. 11-12).

11. terror of the Lord—the coming judgment so terrible to unbelievers (*Estius*). But *Bengel,* 'the fear of the Lord' (ch. vii. 1; Eccl. xii. 13; Acts ix. 31; Rom. iii. 18; Eph. v. 21). **persuade.** Ministers should use the terrors of the Lord to *persuade* men, not to rouse their enmity (Jude 23). *Alford,* "persuade men" by our whole lives—viz., of our integrity as ministers. But this would have been expressed after "persuade" had it been the sense. The connection is: He was accused of seeking to please men, he therefore says (cf. Gal. i. 10), 'It is as knowing the terror (or *fear*) of the Lord that we persuade men; BUT (whether *men* who hear our preaching think us sincere or not) we are made manifest unto God as such (ch. iv. 2); and I trust also in your consciences.' Those so 'manifested' need have no "terror" as to their being 'manifested before the judgment-seat' (*v.* 10). **12. For.** The reason why he leaves the manifestation of his sincerity to their consciences (ch. iii. 1)—viz., his not wishing to "commend" himself again. **occasion to glory** (ch. i. 14)—viz., as to our sincerity. **in appearance**—Greek, 'face' (cf. 1 Sam. xvi. 7). The false teachers gloried in their *personal appearance,* and in external recommendations (ch. xi. 18)—their learning, eloquence, &c.—not in religion of *heart.* Their conscience does not attest their sincerity as mine does (ch. i. 12). **13. be** [*ἐξέστ-*

ημεν]—'have been' in your opinion. The contrast is between the single act (the past tense), 'If we *have ever been* beside ourselves,' and the *habitual* state (the present), 'or whether we *be* sober' [*sophronoumen*]—i. e., *of sound mind*—viz., *in your estimation,* in both cases. **beside ourselves**—the accusation brought by Festus (Acts xxvi. 24). The holy enthusiasm with which he spake of what God effected by his apostolic ministry seemed to many to be *boasting madness.* **sober**—humbling myself before you, not using my apostolic power. **to God . . . for your cause.** The glorifying of his office was not for his own, but for God's glory (ch. iv. 7). The abasing of himself was to meet their infirmity and gain them to Christ (1 Cor. ix. 22). **14. For**—accounting for his being 'beside himself' with enthusiasm: *the love of Christ towards us,* the highest proof of which is His death for us (Rom. v. 6-8), producing in turn love in us to him, and not "terror" (*v.* 11). **constraineth us**—compresses [*συνέχει*] with irresistible power all our energies into one channel (Acts xviii. 5, "pressed in the spirit:" the same Greek). Love is *jealous* of any rival object engrossing the soul (ch. xi. 1-3). **because we thus judge**—*lit.,* (as) 'having judged thus;' a judgment formed at conversion, and ever since regarded as a settled truth. **that if**—i. e., that *since* [*εἰ,* with the indicative]. So C, Vulgate. But א B Δ *fg* omit "if:" 'that one died for all' [*huper,* 'in behalf of all']. The object of His vicarious death was not that He should be by Himself, but have many to live to and with Him (John xii. 24). 'Therefore all (*lit., 'the* all'—viz., for whom He "died") died.' *His* dying is the same as if *they all died.* In their so dying, they died to sin and self, that they might live to God their Redeemer, whose henceforth they are (Rom. vi. 2-11; 1 Cor. vi. 19-20; Gal. ii. 20; Col. iii. 3; 1 Pet. iv. 1-3). **15. they which live**—in the present life (ch. iv. 11) (*Alford*). Rather, who are thus indebted to Him for life of soul as well as body. **died for them.** He does not add, 'rose again for them,' which is not a Pauline phrase. He died *in their stead,* He rose again *for their good,* "for (the manifestation of) their justification" (Rom. iv. 25), and that He might be their Lord (Rom. xiv. 7-9). *Alford* joins "for them" with both "died" and "rose again:" as Christ's death is *our death,* so His resurrection is *our resurrection.* But His *death for us* is *propitiatory* and *vicarious;* His resurrection not so, but *vivifying to us* (Eph. i. 19, 20). Greek, 'who for them died and rose again.' **not henceforth** [*μηκέτι*]—'no longer;' viz., now that His death for them has taken place, and that they know His death saves them from death eternal, and His resurrection brings spiritual and everlasting life to them. **16. Wherefore**—because of our settled *judgment*

known Christ after the flesh, yet [o] now henceforth know we *him* no more.
17 Therefore, if any man *be* in Christ, [3] *he is* a new creature: [p] old things
18 are passed away; behold, all things are become new. And all things
are of God, who hath reconciled us to himself by Jesus Christ, and hath
19 given to us the ministry of reconciliation; to wit, that [q] God was in
Christ, reconciling the world unto himself, not imputing their tres-

A. D. 60.
[o] John 6. 63.
[3] Or, let him be.
[p] Isa. 65. 17. Rev. 21. 5.
[q] Isa. 43. 25.

(*v.* 14). **henceforth**—since our knowing Christ's constraining love (*v.* 14). **know we no man after the flesh**—answering to "old things" (*v.* 17); *i. e.*, according to his mere worldly relations (ch. xi. 18; John viii. 15; Phil. iii. 4): with a view to 'glorying in outward things' (*v.* 12); distinguished from what he is *according to the Spirit*, as a "new creature" (*v.* 17). For instance, the outward distinctions, Jew or Gentile, rich or poor, slave or free, learned or unlearned, are lost sight of in the higher life of those dead in Christ's death and alive with Him in the new life of His resurrection (Gal. ii. 6; iii. 28). **yea, though.** So C. But ℵ B G *g*, Vulgate, read 'if even,' omitting "yea" [δέ, *but*]. **known Christ after the flesh.** Paul when a Jew had looked for a temporal reigning, not a spiritual Messiah. (He says "Christ," not *Jesus:* for he had not known Jesus in the days of His flesh, but had looked for Christ, the Messiah.) When once converted, he no longer "conferred with flesh and blood" (Gal. i. 16). He had this advantage over the Twelve, that as "one born out of due time" he had only known Christ in His heavenly life. To the Twelve it was 'expedient that Christ should go away' that the Comforter should come, and so they might know Christ in the higher spiritual aspect, in His new life-giving power, and not merely in the *carnal* aspect of Him (Rom. vi. 9-11; 1 Cor. xv. 45; 1 Pet. iii. 18; iv. 1. 2). Judaizing Christians prided themselves on the fleshly (ch. xi. 18) advantage of belonging to Israel, the nation of Christ, or on having seen Him in the flesh, and thence claimed superiority over others as having a nearer connection with Him (*v.* 12; ch. x. 7). St. Paul shows the true aim, to know Him spiritually as new creatures (*vv.* 15, 17); outward relations towards Him profit nothing (Luke viii. 19-21; John xvi. 7, 22; Phil. iii. 3-10). This disproves both Romish Mariolatry and transubstantiation. The first verb [οἴδαμεν] ("*know* we no man") means 'we know by the senses as an acquaintance;' the latter [ἐγνώκαμεν] ("known Christ . . . know . . . no more") is to *know mentally*, to estimate. St. Paul's *estimate* of Christ, the expected Messiah, was carnal, but is so now no more. **17. Therefore.** Connected with *v.* 16, 'We know Christ no more after the flesh.' As Christ has entered on His new heavenly life by His resurrection, so all who are "in Christ" (*i. e.*, by faith, as the branch is IN the vine) are new creatures (Rom. vi. 5-11). "New" [*kainé*] implies a new nature quite different from any previously existing: not merely *recent* [*nea*], a different Greek word (Gal. vi. 15). **creature** [*ktisis*]—' creation,' and so the *creature* resulting from it (cf. John iii. 3, 5; Eph. ii. 10; iv. 23; Col. iii. 10, 11). As we are "in Christ," so "God was in Christ" (*v.* 19): hence He is mediator between God and us. **old things**—selfish, carnal views (cf. *v.* 16) of ourselves, of others, and of Christ. **passed away** — spontaneously, like the snow of early spring before the advancing sun. **behold** (Isa. xliii. 19; lxv. 17). **18. all** [THE, Greek] **things**—all our privileges in this new creation (*vv.* 14, 15). **reconciled us** [*katallaxantos*]—*restored us* ("the world," *v.* 19) *to His favour* by satisfying the claims of justice against us. The Aorist implies that the reconciliation is a past accomplished fact. Our position judicially considered in the eye of the law is altered, not as though Christ's mediation made a change in God's character, nor as if the love of God was produced by it: nay, the mediation and sacrifice of Christ were the provision of God's love, not its moving cause (Rom. viii. 32). Christ's blood was the price paid at the expense of God Himself, to reconcile the exercise of mercy with justice, not as separate, but as the eternally harmonious attributes in the same God (Rom. iii. 25, 26). 'Reconcile' is *reciprocally* used as the Hebrew Hithpahel conjugation, *appease*, *obtain the favour of.* Matt. v. 24, "Be reconciled to thy brother"—*i. e.*, take measures that *he* be reconciled to thee, as well as thou to him, as the context proves. [*Diallagethi*, however (Matt. v. 24), implying *mutual* reconciliation, is distinct from *katallassōn* (*v.* 19), which implies the *change* of status wrought in *one* of the two parties.] God reconciles the world to Himself (*v.* 19)—viz., by "not imputing their trespasses unto them." God reconciles the world unto Himself, in the first instance, by satisfying His own justice and righteous enmity against sin (Ps. vii. 11; Isa. xii. 1). Cf. 1 Sam. xxix. 4 [*yithratztzeh zeh el adonaiv*], "Reconcile himself unto his master:" not remove his own anger against his master, but his master's against him (*Archbishop Magee*, 'Atonement'). The reconciling of *men to God* by their laying aside their enmity is the consequence of God laying aside His just enmity against their sin, and follows at *v.* 20. **to us**—ministers (*vv.* 19, 20). **19. God was in Christ, reconciling.** Translate, 'God in (the person of) Christ (*in virtue of Christ's intervention*) was reconciling,' &c. [ἦν καταλλάσσων, the act of reconciliation, is (as the imperfect "was," and the participle "reconciling," imply) simultaneous with the "not imputing their trespasses unto them."] The compound of "was" and "reconciling," instead of the imperfect (Greek), may also imply the *continuous* purpose of God, from before the world, to reconcile to Himself man, whose fall was foreseen. The expression "IN Christ" may imply *additionally* that God was IN Christ (John x. 38; xiv. 10), and so *by* Christ (the God-man) was reconciling, &c. The Greek [*dia*] for "by" or *through* Christ (ℵ B C Δ G *f g*, Vulgate, omit "Jesus"), *v.* 18, is different. "Reconciling" [*katallassōn*] implies 'changing' the judicial status from one of condemnation to one of justification. The *atonement* (*at-one-ment*), or *reconciliation*, is the removal of the bar to peace and acceptance with the holy God, which His righteousness interposed against our sin. The *first* step towards peace between us and God was on God's side (John iii. 16). The *change now* to be effected must be on the part of offending man, God, the offended One, being already reconciled. It is man, not God, who now needs to be reconciled, by laying aside his enmity against God (Rom. v. 10, 11). ('We have *received the atonement*' [*teen katallageen*, 'reconciliation'], cannot mean 'We have received the laying aside of *our own* enmity.') Cf. Rom. iii. 24, 25. **the world**—all men (Col. i. 20; 1 John ii. 2). The *manner* of reconciling is stated—viz., by His 'not imputing their trespasses to men,' but to Christ

passes unto them; and hath [4] committed unto us the word of reconciliation.

20 Now then we are [r] ambassadors for Christ, as though God did beseech
21 *you* by us: we pray *you* in Christ's stead, be ye reconciled to God. For [s] he hath made him *to be* sin for us, who [t] knew no sin; that we might be made [u] the righteousness of God in him.

6 WE then, *as* [a] workers together *with him*, beseech *you* also [o] that
2 ye receive not the grace of God in vain. (For he saith, [c] I have heard thee in a time accepted, and in the day of salvation have I succoured thee: behold, now *is* the accepted time; behold, now *is* the day of salva-
3 tion.) Giving [d] no offence in any thing, that the ministry be not blamed:
4 but in all *things* [1] approving ourselves as [e] the ministers of God, in much
5 patience, in afflictions, in necessities, in distresses, in stripes, in imprison-

A. D. 60.

[4] put in us.
[r] Mal. 2 7.
   Eph. 6. 20.
[s] Isa 53. 6, 9.
[t] Heb. 7. 26.
[u] Jer. 23. 6.

CHAP. 6.
[a] 1 Cor. 3. 9.
   ch. 5. 20.
[b] Heb. 12. 15.
[c] Isa. 49. 8.
[d] 1 Cor. 9. 12,
[1] commend-
   ing.
[e] 1 Cor. 4. 1.

the Sin-bearer (*v.* 21). Where there is a non-imputation of men's sins, there must be an imputation of Christ's righteousness. There is no incongruity that a Father should be offended with that son whom He loveth, and at that time offended when He loveth him. So, though God loved men, yet He was offended with them when they sinned, and gave His Son to suffer for them, that through that Son's obedience He might be reconciled to them (reconcile them to Himself—*i. e.*, restore them WITH JUSTICE to His favour) (*Bishop Pearson*, 'Creed'). **hath committed unto us** [*themenos en hemin*]—'hath put in our hands.' "Us"—*i. e.*, ministers.
20. for Christ . . . in Christ's stead. The Greek of both is the same; 'on Christ's behalf' [*huper*]. **beseech . . . pray**—rather, 'as though God did plead with [παρακαλοῦντος] you . . . beseech' [δεόμεθα]. Such 'beseeching' is uncommon in the case of "ambassadors," who generally stand on their dignity (cf. ch. x. 2; 1 Thess. ii. 6, 7). **be ye reconciled to God.** The English version here inserts "ye," which gives the wrong emphasis. The Greek expresses God was the RECONCILER in Christ . . . let this conciliation have its designed effect. *Be reconciled to God.* Accept the reconciliation already made (*vv.* 18, 19). **21. For.** So C. Omitted in א B Δ G *f g*, Vulgate. The grand reason why they should be reconciled to God—viz., the great atonement in Christ provided by God—is stated without "for" as being part of *the message of reconciliation* (*v.* 19). **he**—God. **sin**—not *a sin offering* [Hebrew, *asham*], which would destroy the antithesis to "righteousness," and would make "sin" be used in different senses in the same sentence; not *a sinful person*, which would be untrue, and would require in the antithesis "righteous men," not "righteousness;" but "sin"—*i. e.*, the representative *guilt-bearer* of the *aggregate sin* of all men past, present, and future. The sin of the world is *one; therefore* the *singular*, not the *plural*, is used; its *manifestations* are manifold (John i. 29: cf. Rom. viii. 3, 4; Gal. iii. 13). **for us**—Greek, 'in our behalf' (cf. John iii. 14). Christ was represented by the *brazen serpent*, the *form*, but not of the *substance*, of the old serpent. At his death on the cross the sin-bearing for us was consummated. **knew no sin**—by personal experience (John viii. 46; Heb. vii. 26; 1 John iii. 5) (*Alford*). **might be made.** Not the same Greek as the previous "made." Rather, 'may become.' **the righteousness of God.** Not merely righteous, but *righteousness* itself; not merely righteousness, but the *righteousness of God*, because Christ is God, and what He is we are (1 John iv. 17), and He is "made of God unto us righteousness." As our sin is made over to Him, so His righteousness to us (in His having fulfilled all the righteousness of the law for us all, as our

representative) (Jer. xxiii. 6; 1 Cor. i. 30); so that God 'imputes not our trespasses to us' (*v.* 19). The innocent was punished voluntarily as if guilty, that the guilty might be gratuitously rewarded as if innocent (1 Pet. ii. 22-24). 'Such are we in the sight of God the Father, as is the very Son of God himself' (*Hooker*). **in him**—in union with Him by faith.
CHAP. VI. 1-18.—HIS APOSTOLIC MINISTRY IS APPROVED BY FAITHFULNESS IN EXHORTATION, IN SUFFERINGS, IN THE FRUITS OF THE HOLY GHOST—HIS LARGENESS OF HEART TO THEM CALLS FOR ENLARGEMENT OF THEIR HEART TO HIM—EXHORTATIONS TO SEPARATION FROM POLLUTION.
1. workers together—with God (Acts xv. 4; 1 Cor. iii. 9). Not only as "ambassadors." He is describing his ministry, not exhorting directly. **you also**—rather, 'WE ALSO (as well as God, ch. v. 20) [*parakaloumen*, ch. v. 20] plead with you:' *vv.* 14, 15, on to ch. vii. 1, is part of this entreaty. **in vain**—by making the grace of God a ground for continuance in sin (*v.* 3). A life of sin makes the word of reconciliation *vain*, so far as the sinner is concerned (Heb. xii. 15; Jude x). "The grace of God" is the "reconciliation" provided by God's love (ch. v. 18, 19: cf. Gal. ii. 2). **2. (For.** God's own promise is the ground of our exhortation. **he saith**—*God the Father* saith to the Son, and so to all believers who are one with Him. **heard thee.** In the eternal purposes of my love I have hearkened to thy prayer for the salvation of thy people (cf. John xvii. 9, 15, 20, 24). **accepted . . . accepted.** The Greek of the latter is more emphatic: 'well-accepted' [*euprosdektos*]. What was "*an accepted* time" [*kairos dektos*] in the prophecy (Isa. xlix. 8; Hebrew, 'in the season of grace') becomes '*the well-accepted* time' in the fulfilment (cf. Ps. lxix. 13). As it is *God's* time of *receiving* sinners, *receive ye* His grace; *accept* (*v.* 1) the word of reconciliation in His *accepted* time. **in the day of salvation)**—'in *a day* of salvation' (Luke iv. 18, 19, 21; xix. 42; Heb. iii. 7). **3.** Resuming the connection, *v.* 1, interrupted by the parenthetical *v.* 2. "Giving no offence" (cf. 1 Cor. x. 32, 33). "approving ourselves," and all the other participles down to *v.* 10, are nominatives to 'we also plead with you' (*v.* 1), showing the pains he took to influence them by example as well as precept. "Offence" would be given if we were without "patience" and the other qualifications which he therefore subjoins (cf. Rom. xiv. 13). **4.** The order of the Greek is, 'In every thing, as God's ministers, recommending ourselves'—*i. e.*, that our hearers may receive favourably our *message*, through our consistency in every respect, not that they may glorify us. Alluding to ch. iii. 1, *We commend ourselves*, not, like them, by word, but by deed. **patience** (ch. xii. 12)

6 ments, [2] in tumults, in labours, in watchings, in fastings; by pureness, by
    knowledge, by long-suffering, by kindness, by the Holy Ghost, by love
7 unfeigned, by the word of truth, by [f] the power of God, by [g] the armour
8 of righteousness on the right hand and on the left, by honour and dis-
    honour, by evil report and good report: as deceivers, and *yet* true;
9 as unknown, and [h] *yet* well known; [i] as dying, and, behold, we live; [j] as
10 chastened, and not killed; as sorrowful, yet alway rejoicing; as poor,
    yet making many rich; as having nothing, and *yet* possessing all things.
11 O *ye* Corinthians, our mouth is open unto you, our heart is enlarged.
12 Ye are not straitened in us, [k] but ye are straitened in your own bowels.
13 Now for a recompence in the same, (I speak as unto *my* children,) be ye
    also enlarged.

A. D. 60.
[2] Or, in toss-
    ings to and
    fro.
[f] Mark 16.20.
    Acts 11. 21.
1 Cor. 2. 4.
Eph 1. 19.
    20.
Heb. 2. 4.
[g] 2 Tim. 4. 7.
[h] ch. 5. 11.
[i] 1 Cor. 4. 9.
[j] Ps. 118. 18.
[k] ch. 12. 15.

first; "pureness" next (v. 6). The heaping together of such varied things implies how inadequate
words are to describe the wide compass of objects.
External afflictions are described as far as "fastings" (v. 5); spiritual advantages as far as "by
the power of God" (v. 7); then come contrasts, in
which the graces conquer the afflictions. Three
triplets of trials exercising "patience" [ὑπομονῇ,
patient endurance] follow it: afflictions [*thlipsesin*,
'tribulations'], necessities, distresses [*stenochoriais*,
'straits']; stripes, imprisonments, tumults; labours,
watchings, fastings. The first triplet expresses
afflictions generally; the second, those arising
from men's violence; the third, those he brought
on himself directly or indirectly. All prove his
right to exhort them authoritatively, and his fitness to be their example. **5. stripes** (ch. xi. 23,
24; Acts xvi. 23). **imprisonments** (ch. xi. 23).
He had been, doubtless, elsewhere imprisoned
besides at Philippi. **tumults** (Acts xiii. 50; xix.
5, 19; xvi. 22; and recently, xix. 23-41). **labours**
—in the cause of Christ (Rom. xvi. 12; ch. xi. 23).
watchings (ch. xi. 27)—sleepless nights. **fastings.**
The context refers to *trials*, not *devotional exercises*. Thus, 'foodlessness' probably is the sense
(cf. 1 Cor. iv. 11; Phil. iv. 12). The usual sense
of the Greek is *fasts* in the strict sense; and in
ch. xi. 27 it is spoken of independently of "hunger
and thirst" (cf. Luke ii. 37; Acts x. 30; xiv. 23).
However, Matt. xv. 32; Mark viii. 3, justify the
rare sense favoured by the context, *foodlessness*.
Gaussen, 'The apostles combine the highest offices
with the humblest exterior: everything in the
Church was cast in the mould of death and resurrection—the cardinal principle throughout Christianity.' **6. By** . . . **by,** &c.—Greek, 'In . . . in,'
&c.; not the instrument, but *the sphere* or *element
in which* his ministry moved. **knowledge**—spiritual; in Gospel mysteries, unattainable by reason
(1 Cor. ii. 6-16; ch. iii. 17, 18). **long-suffering** . . .
kindness—associated with "charity" or "*love*"
(1 Cor. xiii. 4), as here. **by** (Greek, 'in') **the
Holy Ghost**—in virtue of His influences which
produce these graces, "love unfeigned" being the
foremost. **7. By the word of truth, by the
power of God**—rather, 'In . . . in,' &c. As to
"the word of truth," cf. ch. iv. 2; Col. i. 5, and
"the (miraculous) power of God," 1 Cor. ii. 4; ch.
iv. 7. **by the armour** [*dia*]—'through,' or, 'by
means of the armour,' &c. **righteousness**—only
the *breastplate* in Eph. vi. 13-17; here is the *whole*
Christian panoply (cf. ch. x. 4). **on the right
hand and on the left**—*offensive* weapons for the
right hand, *defensive* for the left. He could, in
conscious integrity, attack the bad as well as
defend himself from them. **8.** '*Through glory* and
dishonour'—viz., from *those in authority*—accruing
to us *present;* '*through* evil report and good
report,' from *the multitude*, affecting us *absent*.
By means of [as *dia* means in v. 7] 'glory' and
353

"dishonour," *through* which we pass, we 'approve
ourselves as the ministers of God' (v. 4). It is a
varied and often rough road through which we
pass, but it leads us to victory. *Regarded* "AS
deceivers" by those who, *not knowing* (v. 9), *dishonour* and give us an *evil report;* AS "true," by
those who 'know' (v. 9) us in the real 'glory' of
our ministry. In proportion as the minister has
more or less of *glory* and *good report*, in that
degree has he more or less of *dishonour* and *evil
report*. **9. unknown, and yet well known**—
"unknown" in our true character to, and held
'ignoble' by, those who "evil report" of us;
"well known" to those who hold us in "good
report" (v. 8): above all, "well known" to *God*
(1 Cor. xiii. 12; ch. v. 11; xi. 6). **dying . . . live**
(1 Cor. i. 25; ch. i. 9; iv. 10, 11; x. 1; xi. 23: cf.
note, v. 5). **behold** breaks through the even
tenor of the sentence, and calls attention to
something beyond all expectation. **chastened,
and not killed** (Ps. cxviii. 18). **10.** The "as"
no longer expresses the opinion of adversaries, but
the real state of him and his fellow-labourers.
making many rich—spiritually (1 Cor. i. 5), after
the example of our Lord, who "by His poverty
made many rich" (ch. viii. 9). **having nothing**
[μηδέν, not *ouden*, which is *objective; subjective,
nothing in the opinion of the world*]. The few
earthly goods we have, moreover, we have as
though we had not: as tenants removeable at
will, not owners (1 Cor. vii. 30). **possessing all
things** [*katechontes*]—*holding fast in possession* (cf.
1 Cor. iii. 21, 22). The things of the present and
the future are, in the truest sense, the believer's;
for he possesses them all in Christ, his lasting
possession, though the full *fruition* is reserved for
eternity (Matt. v. 5-10; vi. 33; 1 Tim. iv. 8).
    11. mouth is open unto you. I use no conceal-
ment, as some have insinuated (ch. iv. 2), but all
openness of speech to you as to beloved friends.
Hence he adds, "O ye Corinthians" (cf. Phil. iv. 15).
His *enlargement* of *heart* towards them (ch. vii. 3)
produced, and in turn was promoted by, His *openness of mouth* (Ezek. xxxiii. 22)—*i. e.*, unreserved
expression of his desire to commend himself and
his office to them (vv. 3-10), that they might accept
his message (vv. 1, 2). As an unloving man is
narrow in heart, so the apostle's heart is *enlarged*
by love, so as to have room for all his converts at
Corinth, not only with their graces, but with
their shortcomings (cf. 1 Ki. iv. 29; Ps. cxix. 32;
Isa. lx. 5). Love, like heat, expands. **12.** Any
constraint ye feel is not from want of largeness of
heart on my part towards you, but from want of
it on your part towards me. **not straitened in
us**—*i. e.*, for want of room in our hearts to take
you in. **bowels**—*i. e.*, affections (cf. ch. xii. 15).
13. 'For (as) a recompence of the same kind . . .
be enlarged also yourselves.' 'In the same way'
as my heart is enlarged towards you (v. 11), and

14 Be [l] ye not unequally yoked together with unbelievers: for [m] what
fellowship hath righteousness with unrighteousness? and what com-
15 munion hath light with darkness? and what concord hath Christ with
16 Belial? or what part hath he that believeth with an infidel? and what
agreement hath the temple of God with idols? for [n] ye are the temple of
the living God; as God hath said, [o] I will dwell in them, and walk in
17 *them;* and I will be their God, and they shall be my people. Wherefore [p] come out from among them, and be ye separate, saith the Lord,
18 and touch not the unclean *thing;* and I will receive you, and [q] will be
a Father unto you, and ye shall be my sons and daughters, saith the
Lord Almighty.

7 HAVING [a] therefore these promises, dearly beloved, let us cleanse
ourselves from all filthiness of the flesh and spirit, perfecting holiness in
the fear of God.

2 Receive us; we have wronged no man, we have corrupted no man, we
3 have defrauded no man. I speak not *this* to condemn *you:* for I have

A. D. 60.

[l] Deut. 7. 2, 3.
[m] 1 Sam. 5. 2. Eph. 5. 7.
[n] 1 Pet. 2. 5.
[o] Lev. 26. 12. Jer. 31. 33. Jer. 32. 38. Eze. 11. 20. Eze. 36. 28. Eze. 37. 26. Zech. 8. 8. Zech. 13. 9.
[p] Isa. 52. 11. Rev. 18. 4.
[q] Jer. 31. 1, 9. Rev. 21. 7.

CHAP. 7.
[a] 1 John 3. 3.

as "a recompence" for it (Gal. iv. 12), I ask love for love. **(I speak as unto my children)**—as children would naturally *recompense* their parents' love with similar love.

14. Be ye not—Greek, '*Become* not.' **unequally yoked**—'yoked with one alien in spirit' [ἑτεροζυγοῦντες]. The image is from the symbolical precept, Lev. xix. 19; Deut. xxii. 10: cf. Deut. vii. 3, forbidding marriages with the heathen; also 1 Cor. vii. 39. The believer and unbeliever are utterly *heterogeneous.* Too close intercourse with unbelievers in other relations is included (*v.* 16; 1 Cor. viii. 10). **fellowship** [μετοχή]—*share, participation.* **righteousness**—the state of the believer justified by faith. **unrighteousness**—rather, as elsewhere [*anomia,* lawlessness], 'iniquity:' the state of the unbeliever, the fruit of unbelief. **light**—of which believers are the children (1 Thess. v. 5). **15. Belial.** So B *g,* Vulgate. But C ℵ, '*Beliar.*' Hebrew, '*worthlessness, unprofitableness.*' As Satan is opposed to God, Antichrist to Christ; Belial being here opposed to Christ, must denote all antichristian uncleanness. **he that believeth with an infidel**—'with an unbeliever.' **16. agreement** [*sunkatathesis*]—accordance of sentiments (cf. 1 Ki. xviii. 21; Eph. v. 7, 11). **the temple of God**—*i. e.,* you believers (1 Cor. iii. 16; vi. 19). **with idols**—(cf. Dagon before the ark: 1 Sam. v. 2-4.) **as**—'*even as* God said.' Quotation from Lev. xxvi. 11, 12; Jer. xxxi. 33; xxxii. 38; Ezek. xxxvii. 26, 27: cf. Matt. xxviii. 20; John xiv. 23. **walk in them**—rather, '*among* them.' As "dwell" implies God's *presence,* so "walk," His *operation.* God's dwelling in the saints may be illustrated by its opposite—demoniacal possession of body and soul. **17.** From Isa. lii. 11. Paul, as inspired, gives variations sanctioned by the Holy Spirit. **be ye separate**—'be separated' (Hos. iv. 17). **touch not the** (rather, *any*) **unclean thing** (ch. vii. 1; Mic. ii. 10). *Touching* is more polluting, as implying participation, than seeing. **I will receive you**—'to myself' [εἰσδέξομαι], as persons heretofore out of doors, but now admitted *within* (ch. v. 1-10). Or, as persons heretofore among the enemy, but now received among the Lord's people. With this accords, "come *out from among* them"—viz., *to me.* So Ezek. xx. 41; Zeph. iii. 19. In Isa. lii. 12, *lit.,* The Lord will *gather you up,* as a general *brings up the* 'RERE' of his army, not suffering one straggler to be lost (cf. note there; John xviii. 9). 'The intercourse of believers with the world should resemble that of angels, who, when sent from heaven, discharge their errand with the utmost promptness, and joyfully fly back home to the presence of God' (1 Cor. v. 9, 10; vii. 31). **18.** Translate, 'I will be to you *in the relation of* a Father, and ye shall be *to me in the relation of* sons,' &c. This is a still more endearing relation than (*v.* 16), "I will be their *God,* and they shall be my *people.*" Cf. the promise to Solomon (1 Chr. xxviii. 6; Rev. xxi. 3, 7; Jer. xxxi. 1, 9). **Lord Almighty**—*The Lord the Universal Ruler* (*Pantocrator:* Hebrew, *Shaddai*): only found in Revelation. The greatness of the Promiser enhances the greatness of the promises.

CHAP. VII. 1-16.—SELF-PURIFICATION THE DUTY RESULTING FROM THE FOREGOING—HIS LOVE TO THEM—JOY AT THE GOOD EFFECTS ON THEM OF HIS FORMER EPISTLE AS REPORTED BY TITUS.

1. cleanse ourselves. This concludes the exhortation (ch. vi. 1, 14; 2 Tim. ii. 21; 1 John iii. 3; Rev. xxii. 11), and ought to be attached to ch. vi. **filthiness**—"the unclean thing" (ch. vi. 17). **of the flesh**—for instance, *fornication,* prevalent at Corinth (1 Cor. vi. 15-18). **and spirit**—as *idolatry,* direct or indirect (1 Cor. vi. 9; viii. 1, 7; x. 7, 21, 22). The spirit (Ps. xxxii. 2) receives pollution through the flesh, the instrument of uncleanness. "Flesh and spirit:" the whole man, outward and inward. **perfecting holiness.** *Cleansing away* impurity is a positive step towards holiness (ch. vi. 17). It is not enough to begin: the end crowns the work (Gal. iii. 3; v. 7; Phil. i. 6). **fear of God**—often conjoined with the most glorious promises (ch. v. 11; Heb. iv. 1). **Privilege and promise go hand in hand.**

2. Receive us— with *enlarged* **hearts (ch. vi. 13). we have wronged . . . corrupted . . . defrauded no man** (cf. *v.* 9)—the ground on which he asks their reception of him in their hearts. We *wronged* none by punishing him who did *wrong* (*v.* 12). This he proceeds to treat. We have corrupted none—viz., by beguilements, whilst preaching "another gospel," as the false teachers (ch. xi. 3, 4). This he treats from ch. x. 1. We have defrauded none by 'making a gain' of you (ch. viii. 19, 20; xii. 14-17). This he treats from ch. xii. 13. Modestly he leaves them to supply the *positive* good which he had done; suffering all things himself that they might be benefited (*vv.* 9, 12; ch. xii. 13). **3. In vindicating myself, I do** not accuse you, as though you suspected me of such things (*Menochius*)—as though you were guilty of such things; for I speak only of the false apostles (*Estius*). Rather, 'as though you were ungrateful' (*Beza*). **I have said before**—**in ch.**

4 said before, that ye are in our hearts to die and live with *you*. Great *is* my boldness of speech toward you, great [b]*is* my glorying of you: [c]I am filled with comfort, I am exceeding joyful in all our tribulation.

5   For, [d]when we were come into Macedonia, our flesh had no rest, but we [e]were troubled on every side; without [f]*were* fightings, within *were*

6 fears. Nevertheless [g]God, that comforteth those that are cast down,

7 comforted us by the coming of Titus; and not by his coming only, but by the consolation wherewith he was comforted in you, when he told us your earnest desire, your mourning, your fervent mind toward me; so

8 that I rejoiced the more. For though I made you sorry with a letter, I do not repent, [h]though I did repent: for I perceive that the same epistle

9 hath made you sorry, though *it were* but for a season. Now I rejoice, not that ye were made sorry, but that ye sorrowed to repentance: for ye were made sorry [1]after a godly manner, that ye might receive damage by

10 us in nothing. For [i]godly sorrow worketh repentance to salvation not

11 to be repented of: [j]but the sorrow of the world worketh death. For behold this self-same thing, that ye [k]sorrowed after a godly sort, what

A. D. 60.

[b] 1 Cor. 1. 4.
[c] Rom. 5. 3.
Phil 2. 17.
[d] ch. 2. 13.
[e] ch. 4. 8.
[f] Deut. 32.25.
[g] 2 Thes. 2.16.
[h] Ex. 5. 22,23.
Jer. 20 7-9.
ch. 2. 4.
1 Or,
according
to God.
Isa. 55. 7.
[i] Jer. 31. 18-
20.
Eze. 18. 27-
30.
[j] Matt 27. 4.
[k] Jer. 50 4, 5.
Zech. 12.10

---

vi. 11, 12. **die and live with you**—the height of friendship. I am ready to die and live with and for you (Phil. i. 7, 20, 24; ii. 17, 18: cf. as to Christ, John x. 11). 4. **boldness of speech**—arising from love. But *Olshausen*, 'bold joyful hope' [*parrhesia*] (cf. ch. vi. 11). **glorying of you.** Not only do I speak with unreserved openness *to you*, but I *glory* (boast) *greatly to others in your behalf*, in speaking *of you*. **filled with comfort**—at the report of Titus (*vv.* 6, 7, 9, 13; ch. i. 4). **exceeding joyful**—Greek, I *overabound* with joy. **our tribulation**—described in *v.* 5; also in ch. iv. 7, 8; vi. 4, 5.

5. Greek, 'For also' (For '*even*'). This verse is thus connected with ch. ii. 12, 13, "When I came to Troas . . . I had no rest in my *spirit*:" so '*also*' now, when I came to Macedonia, my "*flesh*" had no rest (he, by the term "flesh" implying here not sin but human weakness, excepts his *spiritual* consolations—from "fightings" with adversaries "without" (1 Cor. v. 12), and from fears for the Corinthian believers "within" the Church, as he knew not what effect his epistle had produced (ch. ii. 12); also fearing "false brethren" (ch. xi. 26). Cf. ch. iv. 8; Deut. xxxii. 25, to which he alludes. 6. Greek order, 'But he that comforteth those cast down [*tapeinous*: those feeling spiritual need] comforted us, even God.' Those of a high spirit are not susceptible of such comfort. The heathen regarded *high spiritedness* [*megalo-psuchon*] as a virtue; Christianity first dignified "lowliness" (Matt. xi. 29). 7. **when he told us**—Greek, 'telling us.' We shared in the comfort Titus felt in recording your desire (*v.* 13). *He* rejoiced in announcing the good news; *we* in hearing it. **earnest desire**—Greek, 'longing desire after' me [*epipothesin*]; both *to see* and *to please me*. **mourning**—over your own remissness in not having immediately punished the sin, (1 Cor. v. 1, &c.) **fervent mind**—Greek, 'zeal' (cf. *v.* 11; John ii. 17). **toward me** [*huper*]—'for my sake.' They *in Paul's behalf* showed the zeal against sin which Paul would have shown had he been present. **rejoiced the more**—more than at the mere coming of Titus; or, 'more than I sorrowed before' (*Olshausen*). 8. **with a letter**—Greek, 'in the letter'; viz., the first epistle. **I do not repent, though I did repent.** Translate, 'I do not *regret* it, though I did *regret* it.' The Greek *regret* [*metamelomai*] and *repent* [*metanoeo*] are distinct. St. Paul was almost regretting, through parental tenderness and doubt of the result, his having by rebukes grieved the Corinthians; but now that he

has learned from Titus the salutary effect produced on them, he no longer regrets it. **for I perceive, &c.**—explanatory of 'I did regret it,' and parenthetical ('for I perceive that *that* epistle did make you sorry, though but for a season') (ch. ii. 2). 9. **Now I rejoice**—Whereas "I did repent," having made you sorry by my letter, I rejoice NOW, not that ye were caused sorrow, but that your sorrow resulted in repentance. **ye sorrowed**—as before, "ye were made sorry." **after a godly manner**—*lit.*, 'according to God,' according to the mind of God; such as leads one to feel the grievousness of sin as being *against God*, and to seek to be made conformable to God (Ps. li. 4; Rom. xiv. 22; 1 Pet. iv. 6). **that**—Greek order, '*to the end that* (cf. ch. xi. 9) ye might in nothing receive damage from us.' This, under God, was my *aim* in 'making you sorry'—viz., that the sorrow, being "after a godly manner," might not "damage," but greatly benefit you (*v.* 10). 10. **worketh . . . worketh.** In the best Greek reading [א B Δ, ἐργάζεται, the first verb: C G, κατεργάζεται], 'worketh (simply) . . . worketh *out*.' "Sorrow" is not repentance, but when "godly," "worketh" it—i. e., *tends to* it (the same Greek; Rom. xiii. 10). The "sorrow of the world" (that felt by the worldly) 'worketh *out*' (Greek), as its *result at last* (note, ch. iv. 17) (eternal) death. **repentance . . . not to be repented of.** There is not in the Greek this play on words, so that the word qualified is not "repentance" merely, but 'repentance unto salvation,' '*never to be regretted*,' however attended with "sorrow" at the time. "*Repentance*" implies *coming to a right mind;* 'regret' implies merely uneasiness of feeling, as the *remorse* of Judas (Matt. xxvii. 3: Greek, 'stricken with remorse;' not as English version, "repented himself"): so that, though always accompanying, is not always accompanied by repentance. "Repentance" removes the impediments to "salvation" (to which "death"—viz., of the soul—is opposed). "The sorrow of the world" is not at the *sin*, but at its *penal consequences;* so that the tears of pain are no sooner dried up, than the pleasures of ungodliness are renewed; also *sorrow such as the world feels* at worldly losses, disappointments, &c. So Pharaoh (Exod. ix. 27, 28-30) and Saul (1 Sam. xv. 23-30). Cf. Isa. ix. 13; Rev. xvi. 10, 11. Contrast David's "godly sorrow" (2 Sam. xii. 13) and St. Peter's (Matt. xxvi. 75). 11. Confirmation of *v.* 10 from the Corinthians' own experience. **carefulness**—solicitude [σπουδήν], 'diligence:' opposed to their past

carefulness it wrought in you, yea, *what* clearing of yourselves, yea, *what* indignation, yea, *what* fear, yea, *what* vehement desire, yea, *what* zeal, yea, *what* revenge! In all *things* ye have approved yourselves to be

12 clear in this matter. Wherefore, though I wrote unto you, *I did it* not for his cause that had done the wrong, nor for his cause that suffered wrong, but that our care for you in the sight of God might appear unto you.

13 Therefore we were comforted in your comfort: yea, and exceedingly the more joyed we for the joy of Titus, because his spirit [1] was refreshed

14 by you all. For if I have boasted any thing to him of you, I am not ashamed; but as we spake all things to you in truth, even so our boast-

15 ing, which *I made* before Titus, is found a truth. And his [2] inward affection is more abundant toward you, whilst he remembereth [m] the

16 obedience of you all, how with fear and trembling ye received him. I rejoice therefore that [n] I have confidence in you in all *things*.

8 MOREOVER, brethren, [1] we do you to wit of the grace of God be-

2 stowed on the churches of Macedonia; how that in a great trial of affliction the abundance of their joy [a] and their deep poverty abounded

A. D. 60.

[i] Rom. 15.32.
1 Cor. 16.18.
2 Tim. 1.16.
Phile. 20.

[2] bowels.
ch. 6. 12.
[m] ch. 2 9.
ch. 10. 5, C.
2 Tim. 3.14.
Phil. 2. 12.
[n] 2 Thes. 3, 4.
Phile. 8, 21.

CHAP. 8.
[1] we must
inform
you.
ch. 7. 16.
[a] Mark 12.44.
Luke 21. 1-
4.
Jas 2. 5.
Rev. 2. 9.

---

negligence. in you—so C G g, Vulgate. But B Δ א omit "in:" 'for you.' yea—not only "carefulness," BUT ALSO [ἀλλά] "clearing of (*apology for*) yourselves"—viz., to me anxiety to show you disapproved of the deed. **indignation**—against the offender. **fear**—of the wrath of God, and of sinning any more (1 Cor. iv. 2, 19-21). **vehement desire**—*longing* for restoration to my favour through amendment [*epipothesin*, as in *v.* 7]. "Fear" is in spite of one's self. '*Longing desire*' is spontaneous, and implies love. "Desire" *for the presence of Paul* is included, as he had given them the hope of it (1 Cor. iv. 19; xvi. 5). **zeal**—for right and for God's honour against wrong. **revenge** [*ekdikesin*]—'exacting of punishment' (1 Cor. v. 2, 3). **In all**—the respects just stated. **clear** [ἀγνούς, *chaste*]—'pure;' viz., from complicity. **approved**—Greek, 'commended yourselves.' Whatever suspicion of complicity rested on you (1 Cor. v. 2, 6) through former remissness, you have cleared off by your present strenuousness in reprobating the deed. **12. though I wrote unto you**—'making you sorry' (*v.* 8). **not for**—*i. e.*, not *so much* for: this was subordinate to my *main* aim, your edification. **his cause that suffered wrong**—the father whose wife the incestuous son had. The father, therefore, was alive. **that our care for you**, &c. So B, Vulgate. But C Δ read 'that YOUR care for US might *be made manifest* (so Greek) unto you,' &c. But the words, 'unto you,' thus would be obscure. *Alford* explains it: 'He wrote in order to bring out *their* zeal on *his* behalf (*i. e.*, to obey his command), and make it manifest *to themselves* in God's sight.' But ch. ii. 4, "I wrote . . . that ye might know the love which *I* have more abundantly *unto you*," accords with the object for which he wrote according to the English version reading here. His writing was not so much for the sake of the individual offender, or the offended, but from his 'earnest care for the welfare of the Church. **13.** א B C Δ G *fg*, Vulgate [δέ after ἐπί, and omitted after περισσοτέρως; and ἡμῶν for ὑμῶν], read, 'Therefore (Greek, '*for this cause*,' because our aim is attained) we *have been* (not "*were*") comforted; yea (Greek, 'but'), in (or [ἐπί], *besides* this) OUR comfort we exceedingly the more joyed for the joy of Titus,' &c. (cf. *v.* 7.) **14. any thing**—*i. e.*, at all. **I am not ashamed**—'put to shame,' viz., by learning from Titus that **you** did not realize the high character I gave of

you. as . . . all things . . . in truth, even so our boasting . . is found a truth—as our speaking *in general* to you was true (ch. i. 18), so our *particular* boasting before Titus *concerning you* is now, by his report, proved to be true (cf. ch. ix. 2). B reads expressly, 'concerning you:' this is the *sense* even if "our" [*hemōn* for *humon*] be read as א Δ G *f g*, Vulgate. As I can boast of not having disappointed you in all things that I spake as a preacher, so you have not disappointed the expectations which I boasted I had concerning you. **15. his inward affection**—*lit.*, bowels (cf. ch. vi. 12; Phil. i. 8; ii. 1). **obedience** (ch. ii. 9). **fear and trembling**—with trembling anxiety to obey my wishes, fearful lest there should be ought in yourselves to offend him and me (*v.* 11: cf. 1 Cor. ii. 3). **16. therefore.** Omitted in א B C Δ G, Vulgate. The conclusion is more emphatical without it. **that I have confidence in you in all things**—Greek, 'that in everything I *am of good courage* in the case of you,' as contrasted with my former misgivings.

CHAP. VIII. 1-24.—COLLECTION FOR THE SAINTS—READINESS OF THE MACEDONIANS A PATTERN TO THE CORINTHIANS—CHRIST THE HIGHEST PATTERN—EACH IS TO GIVE WILLINGLY AFTER HIS ABILITY—TITUS AND TWO OTHERS ARE AGENTS ACCREDITED TO COMPLETE THE COLLECTION.

1. we do you to wit—Greek, 'BUT *we make known to you*:' whilst "I have confidence in you" (ch. vii. 16) I acquaint you with the Macedonians' liberality, which ye ought to imitate. **the grace of God bestowed on** (lit., *in:* in the case of) **the churches of Macedonia.** Their liberality was not of themselves, but of God's *grace* bestowed on them, whereby they became instruments of "grace" to others (*v.* 6, 19). The importance given to the collection arose from St. Paul's engagement (Gal. ii. 10), and chiefly from his hope to conciliate the Judaizing Christians at Jerusalem to himself and to Gentile believers by an act of love on the part of the latter towards their Jewish brethren. **2. trial of affliction**—'in affliction which *tested* them;' *lit.*, 'in a great testing [*dokimee*] of affliction' (Acts xvi. 20, &c.; xvii. 5; 1 Thess. i. 6; ii. 14). **abundance of their joy**—*in giving:* flowing from their possession of the heavenly treasure amidst 'trials,' and going side by side with **their deep poverty**—*lit.*, 'their poverty down to the depth.' Their very 'depth

3 unto the riches of their [2] liberality. For to *their* power, I bear record,
4 yea, and beyond *their* power, *they were* willing of themselves; praying us with much entreaty that we would receive the gift, and *take upon us*
5 [b] the fellowship of the ministering to the saints. And *this they did*, not as we hoped, but first [c] gave their own selves to the Lord, and unto us by
6 the will of God : insomuch that [d] we desired Titus, that as he had begun, so he would also finish in you the same [3] grace also :
7 Therefore, as [e] ye abound in every *thing, in* faith, and utterance, and knowledge, and *in* all diligence, and *in* your love to us, *see* [f] that ye
8 abound in this grace also. I [g] speak not by commandment, but by occasion of the forwardness of others, and to prove the sincerity of your
9 love. For ye know the grace of our Lord Jesus Christ, [h] that, though he was rich, yet for your sakes he became poor, that ye through his poverty
10 might be rich. And herein [i] I give *my* advice : for this is [j] expedient for you, who have begun before, not only to do, but also to be [4] forward a
11 year ago. Now therefore perform the doing *of it;* that as *there was* a readiness to will, so *there may be* a performance also out of that which

A. D. 60.	
[2] simplicity.	
	ch. 9. 11.
[b]	Acts 11. 29.
	Acts 24. 17.
[c]	Matt. 25.40.
	Phil. 4. 18.
	Heb. 13. 16.
[d]	ch. 12. 18.
[3] Or, gift.	
[e]	1 Cor. 1. 5.
	1 Cor. 12.13.
[f]	ch. 9. 8.
[g]	1 Cor. 7. 6.
[h]	Luke 9. 58.
	Phil. 2. 6, 7.
[i]	1 Cor. 7. 25.
[j]	Pro. 19. 17.
	Matt. 10.42.
	Heb. 13. 16.
[4] willing.	
	ch. 9. 2.

of poverty' combined with their "joy" in making them abundantly liberal. A delightful paradox, and triumph, in fact, of spirit over flesh. **abounded unto the riches, &c.**—another beautiful paradox; their *poverty*, instead of producing stinted gifts, "abounded unto the *riches* of their liberality :" margin, 'simplicity :' *singleness of motive to God's glory and man's good enters into the idea : genuine liberality* (cf. Rom. xii. 8, margin ; ch. ix. 11, note, 13 ; Jas. i. 5 ; ii. 5). **3-5. they** (*were*) **willing**—rather supply from *v.* 5, 'According to their power . . . yea, and beyond their power, THEY GAVE,' **of themselves**—not only not being besought, but *voluntarily* beseeching us. **4. that we would receive**—omitted in א B C Δ G *f g*, Vulgate. 'Beseeching of us . . . the grace and fellowship of (*i. e.*, to grant them *the favour of sharing in*) the ministering unto the saints.' The Macedonian contributions must have been from Philippi, because it was the only church that contributed to St. Paul's support (Phil. iv. 10, 15, 16). **5. And (this they did,) not as we hoped.** Translate, 'And not as we hoped (*i. e., far beyond our hopes*), but their own selves gave they first to the Lord and to us ;' "first" not indicating priority of time, but first of all *in importance.* The giving of themselves takes precedency of their other gifts, being the motive which led them to these (Rom. xv. 16). **by the will of God**—not '*according to*,' but '*moved by* the will of God, who made them willing' (Phil. ii. 13). It is therefore called (*v.* 1) "the grace of God." **6. Insomuch that**—As we saw the Macedonians' alacrity in giving, we could not but exhort Titus that, as we collected in Macedonia, so he in Corinth should complete the collection which he had already begun there, lest ye of wealthy Corinth should be outdone in liberality by the poor Macedonians. **as he had begun** [προενήρξατο]—'*previously* begun ;' viz., the collection at Corinth during his former visit. [*Alford* explains προ, *before* the Macedonians had contributed. But *previously* is contrasted with his *subsequently* finishing the collection.] **finish in you the same grace**—complete among you this act of beneficence on your part. **also**—as in other graces ye abound (*v.* 7).
7. Therefore—Greek, '*But*' [*alla*]: I foreknew ye would not disappoint my good opinion of you. '**But as,**' &c. **in faith** (ch. i. 24). **utterance** (note, 1 Cor. i. 5)—not 'doctrine.' **knowledge** (1 Cor. viii. 1). **diligence**—in everything that is good. **your love to us**—*lit.*, 'love from you (*i. e.*, on your part) in us' (*i. e.*, which is felt *in the case*

of us). **8. not by commandment**—'not by way of commandment.' **by occasion of** [*dia* with the genitive, *by means of*, not *on account of*] **the forwardness of others, &c.**—'but by (mention of) the forwardness of others (as an inducement to you), and to prove (*lit.*, proving) the sincerity of your love.' *Bengel*, &c., '*By means of* the forwardness of others, proving the sincerity of your love ALSO.' The former is simpler. **9. ye know the grace**—the gratuitous love whereby the Lord emptied Himself of His heavenly glory (Phil. ii. 6, 7) for your sakes. **became poor.** Yet this is not demanded of you (*v.* 14), but merely that, without impoverishing yourselves, you relieve others with your abundance. If the Lord did so much more, at such a cost, for you ; much more may you do an act of love to your brethren at so little a sacrifice. *Olshausen*, 'As Christ by becoming poor made you rich, *ye can thus bestow of your abundance upon others*, for to this end ye were placed in this condition.' **might be rich**—in heavenly glory, and in all other things that are really good for us (cf. 1 Cor. iii. 21, 22). **10. advice.** Herein he does not disclaim inspiration, but, under the Spirit, states his sentiment or 'judgment' [γνώμην], not a *command*, that so their offering might be free. **this**—my giving an *advice.* **is expedient for you**—it is your own good that ye will thereby promote. **who have begun before**—*seeing that* ye have begun *before ;' i. e.*, already. **not only to do, but also to be forward** (willing)—not only *to do* the outward act of preparing the collection, but also *to be forward* (*heartily-willing*) in doing it. *Bengel*, "Not only to *do*," FOR THE PAST YEAR, "but also to be forward" or *willing* FOR THIS YEAR. But only *one* collection is spoken of throughout, *begun* in Titus's former visit, and now to be *completed*. Something had been done a year before : other texts show the collection was not yet paid (cf. *v.* 11 ; ch. ix. 5, 7). They had *done* so far as to lay by in store : they had not yet *paid in* what was laid by. This agrees exactly with St. Paul's injunction (1 Cor. xvi. 2). **11. perform**—'but now also *complete* the doing' (note, *v.* 10). **a readiness to will**—Greek, '*the* readiness of willing ;' referring to *v.* 10 (Greek for "to be forward," as here, "to will"). **performance**—'completion.' There had been already a *doing* flowing from *willing*, in their laying by in store as God prospered them each first day of the week : that *doing* needed now to be *completed* by their paying in their charity. The godly should show the same zeal to finish as to begin well which the

12 ye have. For *k* if there be first a willing mind, *it is* accepted according
13 to that a man hath, *and* not according to that he hath not. For *I mean*
14 not that other men be eased, and ye burdened; but by an equality, *that*
now at this time your abundance *may be a supply* for their want, that
their abundance also may be *a supply* for your want: that there may
15 be equality: as it is written, *l* He that *had gathered* much had nothing
over; and he that *had gathered* little had no lack.
16 But thanks *be* to God, which put the same earnest care into the heart
17 of Titus for you. For indeed he accepted the exhortation; but being
18 more forward, of his own accord he went unto you. And we have sent
with him *m* the brother, whose praise *is* in the Gospel throughout all the
19 churches; and not *that* only, but who was also chosen *n* of the churches
to travel with us with this *5* grace, which is administered by us *o* to the
20 glory of the same Lord, and *declaration of* your ready mind: avoiding
p this, that no man should blame us in this abundance which is adminis-
21 tered by us: providing *q* for honest things, not only in the sight of the

A. D. 60.

k Ex. 25. 2.
Ex 35. 21.
1 Chr 29. 3.
Mark 12. 43.
44.
Luke 21. 3.
l Ex. 16. 18.
m ch. 12. 18.
n 1 Cor 16. 3.
5 Or, gift.
ch. 9. 8.
o ch. 4. 15.
p Eph. 5. 15.
q Pro 3 4.
Matt. 5. 16.
Matt. 6. 1,
4.
Phil. 4. 8.
1 Thes. 5. 22.
1 Pet. 2. 12.

---

worldly exhibit in their undertakings (Jer. xliv. 25). **12.** For—following up "out of that which ye have" (*v.* 11), and no more. **a willing mind—** Greek, 'the readiness,' viz., to will (*v.* 11). **accepted—**Greek, 'favourably accepted.' **according to that a man hath.** א B Δ G omit [τις] "a man." Translate, 'according to whatsoever IT have:' the *willing mind*, or "readiness" to will, personified (*Alford*, after Vulgate). Better, as *Bengel*, '*He is* accepted according to whatsoever he have' (so ch. ix. 7: cf. as to David, 1 Ki. viii. 18). God judges not according to what a man has not the opportunity to do, but according to what he does when he has it, and what he would do if he had it (cf. Mark xiv. 8, and the widow's mite, Luke xxi. 3, 4). **13.** For—supply from *v.* 8, "I speak." My aim is not that the saints at Jerusalem be relieved at the cost of your being 'distressed' (*lit.*, 'that to others (there should be) relief, to you distress'). "Love thy neighbour *as thyself*," not *more* than thyself. **14. by an equality—***lit.*, out of (from the principle of) equality. **now at this time—**Greek, 'at the present opportune season.' **that their abundance also.** The Greek being distinct from the previous "that," translate, 'in order that'—viz., *at another season*, when your relative circumstances may be reversed. The reference is solely to *temporal* wants and supplies. Those, as *Bengel*, who interpret it of spiritual supplies from the Jews to the Gentiles, forget that Rom. xv. 27 refers to the *past* benefit spiritually which the Jews have conferred on the Gentiles, as a motive to *gratitude* on the part of the latter, not to a *prospective* benefit to be looked for from the former, which the text refers to. **15.** Exod. xvi. 18; LXX. As God gave equal manna to all the Israelites, whether they could gather much or little, so Christians should promote by liberality an equality, so that none should need necessaries whilst others have superfluities. 'Our luxuries should yield to our neighbour's comforts, and our comforts to his necessities' (*J. Howard*). Love creates the only true 'liberty, fraternity, and equality:' the only attainable 'community of goods' without revolution (Acts ii. 44). **16, 17.** Returning to *v.* 6. **for you.** Translate, 'which put the same earnest care for you into the heart of Titus,' as was in myself. My care for you led me to '*desire*' him [*v.* 6, *parakalesai*, and *v.* 17, "*exhortation*," the same Greek]; but Titus had of himself the same care, whence he 'accepted (gladly) my exhortation' (*v.* 17) to go to you (*v.* 6). **being more forward—**more earnest

than to need such exhortation. **of his own accord** —*i. e.*, it is true he has been exhorted by me to go, but he shows that he has anticipated my desires, and already, "of his own accord," was going. **he went—**Greek, 'went forth.' *We* should say, *he is going* forth; but the ancients put the *past* tense in letter-writing, as the things will have been past by the time that the correspondent receives the letter. **18. the brother, whose praise is in the Gospel—**whose praise is known in connection with the Gospel: *Luke* may be meant; not that "the Gospel" refers to his *written* gospel; but the language implies some one well known throughout the churches, and at that time with Paul, as Luke then was (Acts xx. 6). Not a Macedonian, as appears from ch. ix. 4. Of all Paul's "companions in travel" (*v.* 19; Acts xix. 29), St. Luke was the most prominent, having been his companion in preaching at his first entrance into Europe (Acts xvi. 10). The fact that the person referred to was "chosen of the churches" as their trustee to convey, with Paul, the contribution to Jerusalem, implies that he had resided among them some time before: this is true of St. Luke, who, after parting from St. Paul at Philippi (as he marks by the change from "we" to "they," Acts xvi.) six years before, is now again found in his company in Macedonia. In the interim he probably had become so well known that 'his praise was throughout all the churches.' Cf. ch. xii. 18; Phile. 24. He who is faithful in the Gospel will be faithful also in earthly matters. **19. not that only**—not only praised in all the churches. **chosen—**by vote [*cheirotonetheis*]. **of the churches.** Therefore these companions of Paul are called "messengers of the churches" (*v.* 23). **to travel—**to Jerusalem. **with** (B C, Vulgate 'in'—i. e., *in the case of;* א Δ G, "with") **this grace—***gift*.' **to the glory of the same Lord.** So א. But B C Δ G *f g*, Vulgate, omit "same." **(declaration of) your ready mind.** א B C Δ G,Vulgate, read 'our,' not *your*. Connect these clauses with "chosen of the churches to travel with us." The union of the brother with St. Paul in the collection was to guard against suspicions injurious "to the glory" of the Lord. It was also in order *to produce* (not 'to the *declaration* of') a 'readiness' in Paul and the brother for the office which, each by himself, would have been less ready to undertake, for fear of suspicions arising (*v.* 20) as to their mal-administration of the money. **20. Avoiding—** taking precautions against this. **in (the case of)** **this abundance. 21.** The LXX. (Prov. iii. 4;

22 Lord, but also in the sight of men. And we have sent with them our
brother, whom we have oftentimes proved diligent in many things, but
now much more diligent, upon the great confidence which ⁶*I have* in
23 you. Whether *any do enquire* of Titus, *he is* my partner and fellow-
helper concerning you; or our brethren *be enquired of, they are* ^r the
24 messengers of the churches, *and* the glory of Christ. Wherefore show ye
to them, and before the churches, the proof of your love, and of our
boasting on your behalf.

9 FOR as touching ^athe ministering to the saints, it is superfluous for
2 me to write to you. for I know ^b the forwardness of your mind, ^c for
which I boast of you to them of Macedonia, that ^d Achaia was ready a
3 year ago; and your zeal hath provoked very many. Yet ^e have I sent
the brethren, lest our boasting of you should be in vain in this behalf;
4 that, as I said, ye may be ready: lest haply if they of Macedonia come
with me, and find you unprepared, we (that we say not, ye) should be
5 ashamed in this same confident boasting. Therefore I thought it necessary to exhort the brethren, that they would go before unto you, and
make up beforehand your ¹bounty, ²whereof ye had notice before, that
the same might be ready, as *a matter of* bounty, and not as *of* covetousness.

6 But ^f this *I say,* He which soweth sparingly shall reap also sparingly;
7 and he which soweth bountifully shall reap also bountifully. Every man
according as he purposeth in his heart, *so let him give;* ^g not grudgingly,
8 or of necessity: for ^hGod loveth a cheerful giver. And ⁱ God *is* able to

A. D. 60.
⁶ Or, he hath.
^r Phil. 2. 25.
CHAP. 9.
^a Acts 11. 29.
Rom. 15.26.
1 Cor. 16. 1.
Gal. 2. 10.
^b ch. 8. 19.
^c ch. 8. 24.
^d ch. 8. 10.
^e ch. 8. 6. 17.
1 blessing.
Gen. 33. 11.
2 Or, which hath been so much spoken of before.
^f Pro. 11. 24.
Pro. 19. 17.
Pro. 22. 9.
Gal. 6. 7. 9.
^g Deut. 15. 7.
^h Ex. 25. 2.
Ex. 35. 5.
Rom. 12. 8.
ch. 8. 12.
ⁱ Pro. 28. 27.
Phil. 4. 19.

Rom. xii. 17) אBΔGƒg, Vulgate, read 'For we
provide.' But C, "Providing." **honest things—**
'*things honourable.*' **22.** This *second* brother
(*Birks*) was Trophimus; for a Macedonian is not
meant (ch. ix. 4): probably the same as was sent
before with Titus (ch. xii. 18); and therefore sent
from Ephesus,—probably an Ephesian: all this is
true of Trophimus (Acts xx. 4). **oftentimes
proved diligent in many things**—Greek, 'many
times in many things.' **upon the great confidence
which I have in you**—'now more diligent through
the great confidence WHICH HE HAS towards you,
owing to what he heard from Titus concerning
you' (*Alford*). The English version is better, 'We
have sent, &c., *through the confidence* WHICH WE
FEEL *in regard to your liberality.*' **23. fellow-helper
concerning you**—Greek, 'fellow-worker towards
you.' **our brethren**—the two (*vv.* 18, 22). **messengers**—rather, as Greek, 'apostles:' in the less
strict sense (Acts xiv. 14). **of the churches**—sent
by the churches, as we are by the Lord [Phil. ii.
25, *apostolon*]. There was in the synagogue an
officer, "the angel of the church," whence the
title seems derived (cf. Rev. ii. 1). **the glory of
Christ.** Christ's glory is represented by them; so
that whatever treatment ye give them, ye really
give Him (1 Cor. ii. 7; Matt. xxv. 40). **24. show
ye.** So אC. But BΔGƒg read '(continue) *manifesting* [ἐνδεικνύμενοι] to them in the face of the
churches the *manifestation* [*endeixin*] of your
love, and of (the truth of) our boasting on your
behalf.'
CHAP. IX. 1-15.—REASONS FOR HIS SENDING
TITUS—THE GREATER THEIR BOUNTIFULNESS,
THE MORE SHALL BE THE RETURN OF BLESSING
TO THEM AND THANKSGIVING TO GOD.
1. For—connected with ch. viii. 24. 'Show love
to the messengers of the churches; *for*, as concerns
the ministration for the saints, it is superfluous to
write to you, who are so forward already.' **write**
—emphatical. All that I need to do is to *send
brethren* to receive your charity (*v.* 3). **2. ready a
year ago**—to send off the money, owing to the

apostle's exhortation (1 Cor. xvi. 1, 2). **your zeal.**
So אBC. But ΔGƒg,Vulgate, 'the zeal on your
part,' propagated *from you* [ἐξ ὑμῶν] to others.
provoked—*i. e.*, stimulated. **very many** [*tous
pleionas*]—'the greater number,' viz., of the Macedonians. He stimulated the Macedonians by the
example of the Corinthians, and (ch. viii.) the
Corinthians by that of the Macedonians. **3. have
I sent.** We should say, 'I send;' the ancients put
it in *the past,* as it would be by the time that the
letter arrived. **the brethren** (ch. viii. 18, 22)—
Titus and the two others. **should be in vain in
this behalf**—'should be proved futile *in this
particular,*' however true in general (ch. vii. 4).
A tacit compliment, softening the monition. **as I
said**—as I was saying (*v.* 2). **4. if they of Macedonia**—Greek, 'if Macedonians.' **unprepared**—
with your collection: see *v.* 2, "ready" [*pares-
keuastai*], 'prepared.' **we (that we say not, ye)**—
ye would feel more ashamed for yourselves than
we (who boasted of you) would for you. **confident
boasting.** So C. But אBGg, Vulgate, read
'confidence'—viz., in your liberality: no 'boasting.' **5. that they would go before.** Translate,
'that they *should*,' &c. **whereof ye had notice
before** [προκατηγγελμένην]. But אBCΔ,Vulgate,
'promised before;' 'long vouched for *by me* to
the Macedonians' (*v.* 2) (*Bengel*). 'Your promised
bounty' (*Ellicott, &c.*) [*eulogia*]—lit., *blessing*: **it
blesses** both the receiver and the giver (Acts xx.
35). Verbal *blessing* anciently used to accompany
a *gift.* **not as of covetousness**—read [προεπηγ-
γελμένην] which it would be if you gave niggardly.
6. I say—supply the ellipsis, 'But this (is to be
borne in mind)' [*touto de isteon*]. **bountifully**—
lit., '*with,*' or '*in blessings*' [*ep' eulogiais*]: the
word implies a *beneficent spirit in the giver* (*v.* 7,
end), and the *plural,* the *abundance* of the gifts.
'The reaping shall correspond to the proportion
and spirit of the sowing' (*Bengel*). Cf. Ezek.
xxxiv. 26. **7. according as he purposeth in his
heart**—the consent of the free choice [*proairesis*]

make all grace abound toward you; that ye, always having all sufficiency
9 in all *things*, may abound to every good work: (as it is written, *j* He hath
dispersed abroad; he hath given to the poor: his righteousness remaineth
10 for ever. Now he that *k* ministereth seed to the sower, both minister
bread for *your* food, and multiply your seed sown, and increase the fruits
11 of *'*your righteousness;) being enriched in every thing to all *3* bounti-
12 fulness, *m* which causeth through us thanksgiving to God. For the
administration of this service not only supplieth the want of the saints,
13 but is abundant also by many thanksgivings unto God; whiles by the
experiment of this ministration they *n* glorify God for your professed
subjection unto the gospel of Christ, and for *your* liberal distribution
14 *o* unto them, and unto all *men;* and by their prayer for you, which long
15 after you for the exceeding grace of God in you. Thanks *be* unto God
p for his unspeakable gift.
10 NOW *a* I Paul myself beseech you by the meekness and gentleness of
Christ, who *1* in presence *am* base among you, but being absent am bold

A. D. 60.

j Ps. 112. 9.
k Gen. 1. 11.
Isa. 55. 10.
l Hos. 10. 12.
Matt. 6. 1.
3 simplicity,
or, liberal-
ity.
m ch. 4. 15.
n Matt. 5. 16.
o Heb. 13. 16.
p Jas. 1. 17.

CHAP. 10.
a Isa. 42. 2.
Rom. 12. 1.
1 Pet. 2. 23.
1 Or, in out-
ward ap-
pearance.

must accompany the gift. Opposed to "of necessity;" as "grudgingly" is to "a *cheerful* giver"
(Prov. xxii. 9; xi. 25; Isa. xxxii. 8). **8. all grace—**
even in external goods, while ye bestow on others.
that—'in order that.' God's gifts are bestowed
on us, not that we may have them to ourselves, but
may the more 'abound in good works' to others.
sufficiency—so as not to need help of others, having
from God "bread for your food" (*v.* 10). **in all
things** — Greek, 'in everything.' **every good
work—**of charity, which will be "your seed sown"
(*v.* 10). **9. (As it is written—**realizing the highly
blessed character, Ps. cxii. 5, 9. **He—**the "good
man." **dispersed—**as seed sown with full and
open hand, without anxious thought where each
grain may fall. It is implied also that he *has*
always what he may disperse. **the poor.** The
Greek [*penēs*] is here only found in the New Testament, 'one in straitened circumstances, who
earns his bread by labour.' The usual word
[*ptōchos*] means 'one so poor as to live by begging.'
his righteousness—here 'beneficence:' the evidence of being *righteous* before God and man.
Cf. Deut. xxiv. 13; Matt. vi. 1, "alms;" Greek,
'righteousness.' Alms are the poor man's *rightful
due* in God's sight. **remaineth—**unfailing. **10.**
Translate as Isa. lv. 10, 'He that supplieth [*epi-
choregōn*] seed to the sower and bread for food'—
—lit., 'bread for *eating'* [*brōsin*]; cf. spiritually,
John iv. 34. **minister** (and supply) **and increase.**
Optative, '*may* He minister,' &c. So C G.
Rather, future, as א B Δ *f g*, Vulgate, '*Shall*
supply, and multiply, and increase:' implying
certain hope. **your seed—**your means for liberality. **the fruits of your righteousness—**your
acts of charity and the heavenly rewards (Matt.
x. 42). Righteousness shall be itself the reward,
even as it is the thing rewarded (Hos. x. 12; Matt.
v. 6; vi. 33; Gal. vi. 7). **11.** Cf. *v.* 8. **bountifulness** [*haploteta*]—'singleminded liberality' (ch.
viii. 2, note); 'simplicity' (Rom. xii. 8). **causeth
through us—***lit.,* 'worketh through us,' as the
distributors. **thanksgiving—**on the part of the
recipients. **12.** Greek, 'the *ministration* [*diakonia:*
the application to the recipients] of this *public*
service [*leitourgias*, on your part] is not only *still
further* supplying [*προσαναπληροῦσα*] the wants of
the saints (besides the supplies from other quarters), but is abounding also (viz., in respect to
relieving the necessities of others), through (*i. e.,*
in calling forth on the part of the relieved) many
thanksgivings to God' (*Menochius*): cf. "unto
them, and *unto all men*" (*v.* 13). "Thanksgiving,"
in *v.* 11, is singular, referring to that of the Jeru-

salem saints; "thanksgivings," plural (*v.* 12),
include those of the "many" others relieved.
Otherwise, *referring to the Jerusalem saints alone,*
the ministration not only fills up the measure of
their wants, but abounds to *God's* glory in the
thanksgivings it calls forth. God's glory is to be
the ultimate aim of every good work! Therefore
St. Paul himself breaks forth into praise (*v.* 15).
13. by—through. **experiment.** Translate, 'the
experience.' Or, 'the experimental proof [*τῆς
δοκιμῆς*] of your Christian character afforded by
"this ministration." **they—**the recipients. **for
your professed subjection** [*τῇ ὑποταγῇ τῆς
ὁμολογίας*]—'for the subjection of your profession;' *i. e.,* your subjection in accordance with
your profession, in relation to the Gospel precepts,
evinced in acts as well as in profession. **your
liberal distribution—**Greek, 'the liberality of
your contribution to them,' &c. **14.** Translate,
'Themselves also with prayer for you, longing
after you on account of the exceeding grace of
God (resting) upon you.' **15. his unspeakable
gift—**the gift of His own Son, which includes all
other gifts (ch. viii. 9; Rom. viii. 32). If we have
received "His unspeakable gift," what great thing
is it, if we give a few perishing gifts for His sake?
It is this Gift which (the apostle already sees)
ensures the completion of the Corinthians' *gifts.*
    CHAP. X. 1-18.—He Vindicates his Apostolic
Authority against Depreciators of his Personal Appearance—He will make his Power
felt when he comes—He Boasts not, like
them, beyond his Measure.
    1. I Paul myself—no longer "we," "us," "our"
(ch. ix. 11). But (so Greek: *But*, whilst I deal
thus tenderly with you, I can and will exercise
authority) *I* who am represented as "base," &c.
I, the same Paul, *of my own accord,* "exhort"
you *for your sake* [*parakalo*]. As I "beseech you"
[a distinct Greek verb, *deomai: v.* 2] *for my sake.*
Eunnerlie thinks Paul here began to write with
his own hand. His expressing "I Paul myself"
implies condescending tenderness; apostle of the
world though he be, he humbly craves 'as a *personal favour* what is their own interest. **by the
meekness and gentleness of Christ.** He mentions
these graces especially (Ps. xviii. 35; Matt. xi.
29), as for his imitation of them in particular he
was despised. He shows that, though he must
have recourse to more severe measures, he is
naturally inclined to gentle ones, *after Christ's
example.* "Meekness" [*praütēs*] is more in the
mind; "gentleness" [*epieikeia*] in the external
behaviour, and in relation to others, as the *yield-*

2 toward you: but I beseech *you*, *b* that I may not be bold when I am
present with that confidence, wherewith I think to be bold against some,
3 which [2] think of us as if we walked according to the flesh. For though
4 we walk in the flesh, we do not war after the flesh: (for *c* the weapons of
our warfare *are* not carnal, but mighty [3] through God *d* to the pulling
5 down of strong holds;) casting *e* down [4] imaginations, and every high
thing that exalteth itself against the knowledge of God, and bringing
6 into captivity every thought to the obedience of Christ; and *f* having
in a readiness to revenge all disobedience, when *g* your obedience is
fulfilled.
7   Do ye look on things after the outward appearance? *h* If any man
trust to himself that he is Christ's, let him of himself think this again,

A. D. 60.

b 1 Cor. 4. 21.
[2] Or, reckon.
c Eph. 6. 13.
1 Thes. 5. 8.
[3] Or, to God.
d Jer. 1. 10.
e 1 Cor. 1. 19.
1 Cor. 3. 19.
[4] Or, reasonings.
f ch. 13. 2.
g ch. 7. 15.
h 1 Cor. 14. 37.
Gal. 3. 29.
1 John 4. 6.

ingness of a superior to an inferior, the former not insisting on his strict rights (*Trench*). *Bengel*, 'by the meekness and gentleness *derived by me from Christ*,' not from my own nature : he objects to understanding it of *Christ's* meekness and gentleness, since nowhere else is "gentleness" attributed to Him. But though the Greek *word* is not applied to Him, the *idea* is (cf. Isa. xl. 11; Matt: xii. 19, 20). **in presence**—in personal appearance when present with you. **base** [*tapeinos*]—'lowly,' timid, opposed to "bold." "Am" stands here, by ironical concession, for 'am reputed' (cf. *v.* 10). **2. But**—resuming the 'but' (Greek), *v.* 1. **I beseech you**—as I can *beseech* in letters, so I can be severe in presence. **that I may not be**—that I may not *have to be* bold, *fearless* [θαρρῆσαι], &c. **with that confidence**—a soft word for *authoritative sternness.* **I think**—I *reckon* on being bold ('*audacious :*' Paul's adversaries said he would not have the audacity to rebuke them [τολμῆσαι]; a distinct Greek word from "bold" above) against some who *reckon* concerning us as if, &c. The same verb is ironically repeated [*logizomai, logizomenous*]. **as if we walked according to the flesh.** His Corinthian detractors judged of him by themselves, as if he were influenced by fleshly motives, desire of favour, or fear of offending, so as not to exercise his authority. **3. For.** Reason why they should regard him 'beseeching' them (*v.* 2) not to oblige him to have recourse to "bold" exercise of authority. "We walk IN the flesh," and so *in weakness;* but not "ACCORDING TO the flesh" (*v.* 2): though we WALK in it, we do not WAR according to it. A double contrast. They had better not put us to the proof that we neither *walk* nor war according to the flesh. **4.** Confutation of those who propagate their creed by persecution (cf. Luke ix. 54-56). **carnal.** Translate, 'fleshly,' to preserve the allusion to *vv.* 2, 3. **weapons**—for punishing not those without, but offenders in the Church (*v.* 6; 1 Cor. iv. 21; v. 5, 13); viz., boldness of speech, ecclesiastical discipline (*v.* 8; ch. xiii. 10), the Word, the sacraments, and the extraordinary gifts of the Spirit. **mighty through God**—Greek, 'mighty to God;' *i. e.*, before God: *divinely* mighty. The power is not ours, but God's. Cf. 'fair to God'—i. e., *divinely* fair (*margin*, Acts vii. 20). Also ch. ii. 15. 'The efficacy of Christianity proves its truth' (*Bengel*) (2 Tim. i. 7). **pulling down** [*kathairesin*]. The Greek is the same as *v.* 5, "casting down." Cf. Jer. i. 10. **strongholds** (Prov. xxi. 22)—viz., in which sinners entrench themselves against reproof: all that opposes Christ; the learning, eloquence, and philosophical subtleties, the pride of the Corinthians. So Joshua's trumpet-blast cast down Jericho's walls. **5.** ("*We*," *v.* 3) **Casting down imaginations**—a word alluding to 'reckon' (*v.* 2), 'reckonings' [*logismous*], calculating 'reasonings.' Whereas "**thought**" [*noema*] expresses men's own *device*,

intent of living after their own will. **high thing** [*hupsoma*]. So it ought to be translated, Rom. viii. 39: distinct Greek from Eph. iii. 18, "height" [*hupsos*], and Rev. xxi. 16, which belongs to God and heaven, whence we receive nothing hurtful. But "high thing" is not so much "height" as *something made high*, and belongs to those regions of air where the powers of darkness 'exalt themselves' against Christ and us (Eph. ii. 2; vi. 12). **exalteth itself.** 2 Thess. ii. 4 supports the English version [so Vulgate: *epairomenon*,' extollentem se'], rather than it 'lifted up.' Such were the *high towers* of Judaic self-righteousness, philosophic speculations, and rhetorical sophistries, the "knowledge" so much prized by many, which opposed the "knowledge of God" at Corinth. True knowledge makes men humble. Where self is exalted God is not known. Arrange: 'Bringing every thought [i. e., *intent of the mind: noema*] into captivity to the obedience of Christ'—*i. e.*, to obey Christ. The apostle's spiritual warfare (1.) demolishes what is opposed to Christ; (2.) leads captive; (3.) brings into obedience to Christ (Rom. i. 5; xvi. 26). The 'reasonings,' 'imaginations,' are 'cast down.' The 'mental intents,' 'thoughts,' are made willing captives, rendering the voluntary obedience of faith to Christ the conqueror. **6.** Translate, 'Having ourselves (i. e., *being*) in readiness to exact punishment for all disobedience,' &c. **when your obedience, &c.** He charitably assumes that the Corinthian church will act obediently; therefore he says "YOUR obedience." But as some will act otherwise, in order to give all an opportunity of joining the obedient, he waits (not prematurely exacting punishment) until the full number of those who obey Christ has been 'completed,' and the remainder have proved incorrigible. He had acted already so at Corinth (Acts xviii. 6-11: cf. Exod. xxxii. 34; Matt. xiii. 28-30). **7. Do ye regard** mere outward appearance—person, voice, manner, oratory, presence *face to face*, such as they admired in the false teachers, to the disparagement of absent Paul? (*v.* 10; note, ch. v. 12.) Even in *outward bearing* when *present* (in contrast to "by letters," v. 9), I will show you that I more really have the authority of Christ than those who arrogate the title of being peculiarly 'Christ's' (1 Cor. i. 12). *Billroth* objects that what follows—viz., being or not being Christ's—is not a question of *outward appearance.* He translates, 'Behold *what is before your eyes*—viz., what I have done in founding your church' (cf. *v.* 14). But the former interpretation does not make BEING *Christ's* a question of outward appearance, but one EVIDENCED *by* it. **let him of himself think this again.** He may "of himself," without having to be taught it in a more severe manner, by 'thinking again,' reach "this" conclusion, 'that even as,' &c. St. Paul **modestly**

361

8 that, as he *is* Christ's, even so *are* [i] we Christ's. For though I should boast somewhat more of our authority, which the Lord hath given us for

9 edification, and not for your destruction, I should not be ashamed: that

10 I may not seem as if I would terrify you by letters. For *his* letters, [5] say they, *are* weighty and powerful; but [j] *his* bodily presence *is* weak, and

11 *his* [k] speech contemptible. Let such an one think this, that, such as we are in word by letters when we are absent, such *will we be* also in deed

12 when we are present. For [l] we dare not make ourselves of the number, or compare ourselves with some that commend themselves: but they measuring themselves by themselves, and comparing themselves among

13 themselves, [6] are not wise. But we will not boast of things without *our* measure, but according to the measure of the [7] rule which God hath dis-

14 tributed to us, a measure to reach even unto you. For we stretch not ourselves beyond *our measure*, as though we reached not unto you; [m] for

15 we are come as far as to you also in *preaching* the gospel of Christ: not boasting of things without *our* measure, *that is*, [n] of other men's labours; but having hope, when your faith is increased, that we shall be [8] enlarged

A. D. 60.	
[i] ch. 5. 12.	
	ch. 11. 23.
	ch. 12. 11.
	ch. 13. 3.
	1 Cor. 9. 1.
	Gal. 1. 11, 13.
	Gal. 2. 5, 9.
[5] saith he.	
[j] Gal. 4. 13.	
[k] 1 Cor. 1. 17.	
[l] ch. 5. 12.	
[6] Or, understand it not.	
[7] Or, line.	
[m] 1 Cor. 9. 1.	
[n] Rom. 15.20.	
[8] Or, magnified in you.	

demands for himself only an equal place with his spiritual children. **8.** 'For even though I boast somewhat exceedingly (*vv.* 3-6) of our (apostolic) authority (ch. xiii. 10) . . . I shall not be put to shame' (by the fact; my authority shall not be proved abortive by my threats failing to be carried into effect). **for edification, and not for your destruction**—Greek, 'for building up . . . not for . . . CASTING DOWN' [*kathairesin*, as in *v.* 5]; the image of a building. Though we 'cast-down reasonings,' this is not in order to destroy, but to *build up*, by removing hindrances to edification, testing what is unsound, and putting together all that is true in the building (*Chrysostom*). **9.** *Billroth*: 'I say this (that our authority is for your edification, not destruction) lest I should seem to frighten you.' But what St. Paul wished to refute was, not the idea of his severity, but that of *his terrifying only "by letters"* (*v.* 10), and not executing his threats in fact. 'I shall not be shamed by the non-fulfilment of my threats *when present* (*v.* 8), *that I may not seem as if my aim was only to frighten you with threatening letters*' (*v.* 11). **10. letters**—therefore there had been already more *letters* (plural) of St. Paul received by the Corinthians than the one we have—viz., 1 Corinthians. They contained strong reproofs. **say they.** א Δ G *f* read 'says one;' "such an one" (*v.* 11) points to some definite individual. [But B *g*, Vulgate, read 'say they: '*φασιν.*]. Cf. Gal. v. 10: a similar slanderer was in the Galatian church. **weak** (1 Cor. ii. 3; ch. xii. 7). There was nothing of majesty in his manner. He bore himself tremblingly among them,. whereas the false teachers spoke with authoritative bearing. **11. think this**—'consider this.' **12.** 'We do not presume (irony) to judge ourselves among, or in comparison with, some of them that commend themselves.' The charge brought against him of *commending himself* (ch. iii. 1; v. 12) really holds good of the false teachers. The phrase, 'judge ourselves of the number,' is drawn from the testing of athletes and senators, the 'approved' being set on the roll (*Wahl*). **measuring themselves by themselves**—*among* themselves,' to correspond to the previous 'judge ourselves *among* them.' Instead of the public standard, they measure themselves by one made by themselves: they do not compare themselves with others who excel them, but with those like themselves; hence their high self-esteem. The one-eyed is easily king among the blind. **are not wise** [*ou suniasin*, A B C: συνίσασιν, א]—with all their boasted "wisdom" (1 Cor. i. 19-26). **13. not**

boast of things without our measure [*eis ta ametra*]—'to unmeasured bounds.' There is no limit to a man's self-conceit so long as he measures himself by himself (*v.* 13) and his fellows, and not with his superiors. It marks the *personal* character of this epistle that "boast" occurs twenty-nine times in it, and only twenty-six times in all the other epistles. Undeterred by the charge of vanity, he must vindicate his apostolic authority by facts (*Conybeare*). It would be to "boast of things without·our measure" were we to boast of conversions made by "other men's labours" (*v.* 15). **distributed**—assigned. **a measure to reach**—'that, as our measure, we should reach as far as even to you;' not that he meant to go no farther (*v.* 16; Rom. xv. 20-24). St. Paul's "measure" is the *apportionment* of his sphere of Gospel labours *ruled* by God. A 'rule' among the so-called 'apostolic canons' subsequently was, that no bishop should appoint ministers beyond his own limits. At Corinth no minister ought to have been received without St. Paul's sanction, as Corinth was *apportioned* to him by God as *his apostolic sphere.* The epistle here incidentally, and therefore undesignedly, confirms the independent history, the Acts, which represents Corinth as the extreme limit as yet *at which he had stopped*, after he had from Philippi passed southward successively through Amphipolis, Apollonia, Thessalonica, Berea, and Athens (*Paley*). **14.** 'We are not stretching ourselves beyond our measure, as if we should not have come unto you; for as far as even to you have we in fact come in preaching the Gospel.' The fact and the effect produced proves that Corinth is within the measure assigned to me by God. So א Δ G *f g*, Vulgate. But B omits "not;" then read interrogatively, Do we stretch ourselves, &c.? Certainly not. **15.** 'Not boasting to unmeasured bounds of (*lit.*, 'in') other men's labours. **when**—'As your faith goes on increasing' [*αὐξανομένης τῆς πίστεως*]. The cause of his not yet reaching the regions beyond Corinth was the weakness as yet of their faith. He desired not to leave them before the proper time, yet not to put off preaching to others too long. **enlarged by you** [*en humin*]—'in your case.' Our success in your case will be an important step towards further progress beyond (*v.* 16). Calvin makes the balance of the opposite clauses better, 'Having hope that, as your faith *goes on increasing among yourselves* [*en humin*], we may be magnified according to our rule abundantly,' by preaching beyond you: a gain at once to both parties, them

16 by you according to our rule abundantly, to preach the Gospel in the
regions beyond you, *and* not to boast in another man's [9] line of things
17 made ready to our hand. But [o] he that glorieth, let him glory in the
18 Lord. For [p] not he that commendeth himself is approved, but [q] whom
the Lord commendeth.

11 WOULD to God ye could bear with me a little in [a] *my* folly: and
2 indeed [1] bear with me. For I am [b] jealous over you with godly jealousy:
for [c] I have espoused you to one husband, [d] that I may present *you* [e] *as* a
3 chaste virgin to Christ. But I fear, lest by any means, as [f] the serpent
beguiled Eve through his subtilty, so your minds [g] should be corrupted
4 from the simplicity that is in Christ. For if he that cometh preacheth
another Jesus, whom we have not preached, or *if* ye receive another
spirit, which ye have not received, or another gospel, which ye have not
accepted, ye might well bear [2] with *him.*

A. D. 60.

9 Or, rule.
o Isa. 65. 16.
p Pro. 27. 2.
q Rom. 2. 29.

CHAP. 11.
a ch. 5. 13.
1 Or, ye do
  bear with
  me.
b Gal. 4. 17.
c Hos. 2. 19.
d Col. 1. 28.
e Lev. 21. 13.
f Gen. 3. 4.
g Eph. 6. 24.
2 Or, with
  me.

and St. Paul. **according to our rule**—our divinely-assigned sphere of work; for "we stretch not ourselves beyond our measure" (*v.* 14). **abundantly**—Greek, 'unto exceeding abundance,' so as to exceed the limits yet reached (*v.* 16). **16. To**—*i. e., so as to* preach . . . beyond you (and) not to boast, &c. **in another man's line of things made ready to our hand.** Do not connect "line of things," &c.; but 'boast of things,' &c. Arrange, 'Not to boast as to things (already made by the preaching of others) ready to our hand in another man's line' (*i. e.*, within the sphere apportioned by God to another). **17. glorieth.** Translate, to accord with *v.* 16, 'boasteth.' In contrast to his opponents' boasting in another's sphere, St. Paul declares the only true boasting is in the Lord (1 Cor. i. 31; xv. 10). **18. is approved**—stands the test of the final trial [*Dokimos*]: a metaphor from testing metals (Rom. xvi. 10; 1 Cor. xi. 19). On the other hand, those finally rejected by the Lord are termed "*reprobate* silver" (Jer. vi. 30). **whom the Lord commendeth**—to whom the Lord has given, as His "epistle of commendation," the believers whom he was instrumental in converting; as was St. Paul's case (ch. iii. 1-3).

CHAP. XI. 1-33.—THROUGH JEALOUSY OVER THE CORINTHIANS AS TO THE FALSE APOSTLES, HE IS OBLIGED TO COMMEND HIMSELF AS IN MANY RESPECTS SUPERIOR.

1. Would to God—Greek, 'I would that.' **bear with me**—I may not unreasonably ask to be borne with: not so the false apostles (*vv.* 4, 20). my. So א G j g, Vulgate. B Δ omit "my" [τῆς]. **folly.** The Greek is a milder term than "foolishness" (1 Cor. iii. 19; Matt. v. 22; xxv. 2). The [*aphrosune*] "folly" here implies *imprudence;* the Greek [*moria*] "foolishness," includes *perversity* and *wickedness.* **and indeed bear.** A request (so *v.* 16). But the sense favours, 'But indeed ye *do* bear with me:" still I wish you to bear with me further, in entering into self-commendations. **2. For I am jealous.** The justification of his self-commendations, his zealous care lest they fall from Christ, to whom he, as "the friend of the bridegroom" (John iii. 29), has espoused them: in order to lead them back from false apostles to Christ, he is obliged to boast, as the apostle of Christ, in a way which, but for the motive, would be "folly." **godly jealousy**—*lit.,* 'jealousy of God' (cf. ch. i. 12, Greek): a jealousy which has God's honour at heart (1 Ki. xix. 10). **I have espoused you.** St. Paul uses a term [ἡρμοσάμην] applied properly to *the bridegroom,* just as he ascribes to himself "jealousy," a feeling belonging to the husband [the active *hērmosa* would be used of a *father* espousing his daughter to a man]: so entirely does he identify himself with Christ.

to one husband. Those who would attach you to another (1 Cor. i. 12, 13) make you unfaithful to Him. Cf. Isa. liv. 5; lxii. 5; Jer. iii. 1, &c.; Ezek. xvi. 8, &c. **present you as a chaste virgin to Christ**—at His coming, when the heavenly *marriage* shall take place (Matt. xxv. 6; Rev. xix. 7, 9). What St. Paul here says he desires—viz., to "present" the church as "a chaste virgin" to Christ—*Christ Himself* does in the fuller sense. Whatever ministers do effectively, is really done by Christ (Eph. v. 27-32). The *espousals* are going on now. He does not say 'chaste virgins;' for not individuals, but the whole body of believers conjointly constitute the Bride. **3. I fear** (ch. xii. 20)—not inconsistent with love. He feared their yielding character. **subtilty**—the foe of the "simplicity" which is intent on ONE object, Jesus, and seeks none 'other,' and no 'other' and different spirit (*v.* 4); but loves him with tender SINGLENESS OF AFFECTION. Where Eve first gave way was in mentally harbouring for a moment the possibility insinuated by the serpent, of GOD not having her truest interests at heart, and of this 'other' professing friend being more concerned for her than GOD. **corrupted**—so as to lose their virgin purity through seducers (*v.* 4). The same Greek [*noemata*] stands for "minds" as for 'thoughts' (ch. x. 5, note): *intents.* א B Δ *f g,* after "simplicity," add, 'and the purity' or 'chastity' [*hagnotetos:* B, *hagiotetos,* 'the holiness']. **in Christ**—Greek, that is, '*towards* Christ.' **4. if,** &c.—if it were possible, ye might then bear with them (see note, *v.* 1). But there *can be no new gospel:* there is but the *one* which I first preached; therefore it ought not to be 'borne' by you, that the false teachers should supersede me. **he that cometh**—Christ's own title, arrogantly assumed by the false teachers [*ho erchomenos,* Matt. xi. 3, and Heb. x. 37], 'He that is coming.' Perhaps he was leader of the party which assumed peculiarly to be "Christ's" (ch. x: 7; 1 Cor. i. 12). **preacheth . . . receive**—is preaching . . . ye are receiving. **Jesus**—the "Jesus" of Gospel *history.* He does not say "Christ," which refers to the *office.* **another . . . another** [allon—heteron—heteron]—' another Jesus . . . a *different* Spirit . . . a *different* Gospel.' *Another* implies a distinct individual of the same kind; *different* implies one distinct in kind. **spirit . . . received** [*elabete*] . . . **gospel . . . accepted** [*edexasthe*]. The will of man is passive in RECEIVING the "Spirit:" but it is actively concurrent with the will of God (which goes before to give the good will) in ACCEPTING the "Gospel." **ye might well bear with him** [B reads ἀνέχεσθε, 'When any one preaches to you another Jesus, &c., ye bear well with it.'

363

5 For I suppose I was not a whit behind the very chiefest apostles.
6 But though *I be* rude in speech, yet not in ^h knowledge: but we have
7 been throughly made manifest among you in all things. Have I committed an offence ⁱ in abasing myself that ye might be exalted, because I
8 have preached to you the gospel of God freely? I robbed other churches,
9 taking wages *of them,* to do you service. And when I was present with
you, and wanted,^j I was chargeable to no man: for that which was lacking
to me ^k the brethren which came from Macedonia supplied: and in all
things I have kept myself ^l from being burdensome unto you, and *so* will
10 I keep *myself.* As ^m the truth of Christ is in me, ³ no man shall stop me
11 of this boasting in the regions of Achaia. Wherefore? ⁿ because I love
12 you not? God knoweth. But what I do, that I will do, that I ^o may cut
off occasion from them which desire occasion; that wherein they glory
they may be found even as we.

A. D. 60.

^h Eph. 3, 4.
ⁱ Acts 18, 3.
1 Cor. 9, 6.
^j Neh. 5, 15.
Acts 20, 33.
1 Thes. 2, 9.
2 Thes. 3, 8.
^k Phil. 4, 10.
^l ch. 12, 14.
^m Rom. 9, 1.
³ this boast-
ing shall
not be
stopped in
me.
ⁿ ch. 7, 3.
^o 1 Cor. 9, 12.

The 'well' thus is ironical: covert censure. But אΔG *fg*, Vulgate, support the English version read-ing, ἀνείχεσθε]. There would be some excuse for your conduct, though a bad one (for ye ought to give heed to no gospel other than what ye have already heard from me, Gal. i. 6, 7); but the false teachers do not even pretend they have "another Jesus," 'a different Spirit,' and 'a different gos-pel' to bring before you, they merely try to sup-plant me, your accredited Teacher. It therefore is inexcusable that ye not only "bear with" but prefer them.

5. For—my claim is superior to that of the false teachers. "For," &c. So אΔG *fg*, Vulgate. But B reads 'But.' **I suppose**—Greek, 'that I have not been, and am not.' **the very chiefest apostles**—James, Peter, and John, the witnesses of Christ's transfiguration and agony in Gethsemane. Rather, 'those over-much apostles' [*tōn huperlian apostolōn*], those *surpassers of the apostles* in their own esteem. The context does not compare him and the apostles, but him and the false teachers: *v.* 6 also alludes to these: cf. also the parallel, 'false prophets' (note *v.* 13, and ch. xii. 11). **6. rude** [*idiotes*]—'a com-mon man:' 'a laic;' not rhetorically trained. 1 Cor. ii. 1-4, 13; ch. x. 10, 11, shows his *words* were not without *weight*, though his 'speech' was defi-cient in oratorical artifice. 'Yet I am not so in my knowledge' of Gospel mysteries (ch. xii. 1-5; Eph. iii. 1-5). **but** (on the contrary) **we have been throughly made manifest**—read, with אBG, 'we have made (Gospel truths) manifest' [*phan-crosantes*]; so far are we from being 'rude in knowledge.' The English version means, 'Nay,' ye know my *knowledge*, for 'we have been in every thing made manifest in respect to you.' He had not by reserve kept back his "knowledge" in divine mysteries from them (ch. ii. 17; iv. 2; Acts xx. 20, 27). **in all things**—rather 'among all men:' the sense then is, we have in everything manifested the truth among all men with a view to [*eis humas*] your benefit (*Alford*). But the Greek, Phil. iv. 12, 'In each thing and in all things,' sanctions the English version—a clearer sense. *Billroth*, 'In every part' [*en panti*] expresses the *mode* of handling the truths: "in all things" [*en pasin*], the *extent* of the truths handled. **7. Have I** —*lit.,* 'OR have I?' 'Or will you make it an ob-jection that I have preached to you gratuitously?' He leaves their good feeling to answer, that this, so far from being an objection, was a superiority in him above the false apostles (1 Cor. ix. 6-15). **abasing myself**—in my mode of living, earning my maintenance by manual labour—perhaps with slaves as his fellow-labourers (Acts xviii. 3; xx. 34; Phil. iv. 12). **that ye might be exalted**—spiritu-

ally:- that ye might be edified, by my removing every handle of offence in not asking you for the maintenance which is my right. **because**—'in that.' **gospel of God.** "Of God" implies its divine glory. **freely**—'without charge.' **8. I robbed**— *i. e.,* took from them, in order to spare you the cost of my maintenance whilst preaching to you, *e. g.,* the Philippian church (Phil. iv. 15, 16). **wages**— 'subsidy.' **to do you service**—Greek, 'with a view to ministration to you:' cf. 'supplied *in addition,' v.* 9, implying he *brought with him* from the Macedonians supplies towards his mainte-nance at Corinth; and (*v.* 9) *when those resources failed* ("when I wanted"), he received a *new sup-ply* whilst there, from the same. **9. and wanted**— '*though* in want.' **chargeable** [*katenarkesa*]—'bur-densome;' *lit.*, 'to torpify:' so to *oppress:* a Cilician word, natural to Paul of Tarsus in Cilicia (ch. xii. 14, 16). **the brethren which came** [*elthontes:* not *hoi elthontes*]—'the brethren *when they came.'* Perhaps Timotheus and Silas (Acts xvii. 15; xviii. 1, 5). Cf. Phil. iv. 15, 16, which refers to dona-tions received from the Philippians (in Macedonia) at two distinct periods ("once and again")—one at Thessalonica, the other after his departure from Macedonia, when he came into Achaia to Corinth (for he would receive no help from the Corin-thians); and this 'in the beginning of the Gospel'— *i. e.*, at its first preaching in these parts. Thus all three, the two epistles and history, undesignedly coincide: a sure test of genuineness. **supplied** [*prosaneplerosan*]—'supplied in addition;' viz., in addition to their former contributions; or, as *Ben-gel,* in addition to the supply obtained by my own manual labour. **10.** Greek, 'There is (the) truth of Christ in me that,' &c. (Rom. ix. 1). **no man shall stop me of** [*ou phragesetai*]—'this boasting shall not *be shut* (have its mouth stopped) *as regards me.*' Lest they should think his saying he would not ask their help was in anger, he calls it his 'boast.' **11.** Love is often offended at its favours not being accepted, as though the other party wished to be under no obligation to the offerer. **12. I will do**—I will *continue* to decline help. **occasion** [*teen aphormeen*] — 'the *handle,*' viz., of misrepresenting my motives, which would be afforded to detractors, if I accepted help. **that wherein they glory they may be found even as we.** This cannot mean that the false teachers taught gratuitously even as Paul (cf. *v.* 20; 1 Cor. ix. 12). *Olshausen* makes this explain the "occa-sion" which Paul's adversaries sought—viz., that by his accepting maintenance, in receiving which they 'gloried' as an apostolic prerogative, they might be found on a level with him: in spite of their boast of maintenance, and their sneering at him for not accepting it, they would have been

13 For such *are* false apostles, deceitful workers, transforming themselves
14 into the apostles of Christ. And no marvel; for Satan himself is trans-
15 formed into *ᵖ* an angel of light. Therefore *it is* no great thing if his
ministers also be transformed as the ministers of righteousness; whose
ᑫ end shall be according to their works.
16 I say again, Let no man think me a fool: if otherwise, yet as a fool
17 *⁴* receive me, that I may boast myself a little. That which I speak, *ʳ* I
speak *it* not after the Lord, but as it were foolishly, *ˢ* in this confidence
18 of boasting. Seeing *ᵗ* that many glory after the flesh, I will glory also.
19, For ye suffer fools gladly, seeing ye *yourselves* are wise. For ye suffer,
20 *ᵘ* if a man bring you into bondage, if a man devour *you*, if a man take *of*
21 *you*, if a man exalt himself, if a man smite you on the face. I speak as
concerning reproach, *ᵛ* as though we had been weak. Howbeit wherein-
22 soever any is bold, (I speak foolishly,) I am bold also. Are they Hebrews?
ʷ so *am* I. Are they Israelites? so *am* I. Are they the seed of Abra-

A. D. 60.

ᵖ Gal. 1. 8.
Rev. 12. 9.
ᑫ Isa. 9. 14,
15.
Jer. 29. 32.
Matt. 7. 15,
16.
Phil. 3. 19.
⁴ Or, suffer.
ʳ 1 Cor. 7. 6.
ch. 9. 4.
ᵗ Jer. 9. 23,
24.
Phil. 3. 3.
ᵘ Gal. 2. 4.
Gal. 4. 9.
ᵛ ch. 10. 10.
ʷ Acts 22. 3.

glad to have him on the same level of selfishness in this with themselves. But should it not then be 'that *we* may be found even as *they?*' Probably this clause expresses *Paul's* aim—viz., that "wherein they glory (in respect of their receiving apostolic maintenance) they may be found (to say the least, not *superior*, but, through your understanding my disinterestedness in declining it) even AS we," having no cause to glory over us. Cf. *v.* 18, &c.

13. For. Reason why he needs to cut off " occasion " from his detractors. **false apostles.** Those 'overmuch apostles' (note, *v.* 5) are no apostles at all. **deceitful workers**—pretending to be ' workmen' for the Lord, really seeking their own gain. **14. is transformed**—rather, 'transforms himself' (cf. Job i. 6); habitually: the first occasion was in tempting Eve. So in tempting Jesus. " Himself " is emphatical : If their master *himself*, the 'prince of darkness,' the most alien to light, does so, it is less marvellous in his servants (Luke xxii. 53; Eph. vi. 12). **15. no great thing**—no difficult matter. **righteousness**—answering to "light" (*v.* 14) ; the manifestation wherewith God reveals Himself in Christ (Matt. vi. 33 ; Rom. i. 17). **end** —the test, is *the end*, which strips off every specious *form* into which Satan's agents now 'transform' themselves (cf. Phil. iii. 19, 21). **according to their works**—not according to their pretensions.

16. I say again—again, taken up from *v.* 1, the apology for his boasting. **if otherwise**—but if ye will think me a fool. **yet as a fool**—' yet even as a fool receive me;' grant me the indulgent hearing of my " boasting," conceded even to a fool. The Greek [*aphrona*] denotes *one who does not rightly use his mental powers;* not having blame necessarily attached to it : one deceived by foolish vanities, yet boasting himself (*vv.* 17, 19) (*Tittmarsh*). **that I**—Greek, ' that I, *too*—viz., *as well as they*—may boast myself. **17. not after the Lord.** *By inspired guidance* he excepts this 'glorying' from the inspired authoritativeness which belongs to all else that he wrote : even this boasting, though undesirable in itself (Luke xvii. 10), was permitted by the Spirit, taking into account its aim—viz., to draw off the Corinthians from false teachers to the apostle. This passage gives no proof that any Scripture is uninspired. It merely guards against his boasting being made a justification of boasting in general, which (as in the case of the false apostles) is not ordinarily " after the Lord"—*i. e.*, consistent with Christian humility. **foolishly**—Greek, ' in foolishness.' **confidence of boasting** (ch. ix. 4). **18. many** — including the ' false teachers.' **after the flesh**—as fleshly men boast ; viz., of ex-
365

ternal advantages, their birth, doings, &c. (cf. *v.* 22), contrasted with "after the Lord" (*v.* 17). **I will glory also**—*i. e.*, I also will boast of fleshly advantages, to show you that even in these I am not their inferiors, and therefore ought not to be supplanted by them in your esteem : though these are not what I desire to glory in (ch. x. 17). **19. gladly**—willingly. Irony. It is a mark of the wise to bear with fools. A plea why they should " bear with" (the same Greek, *v.* 1) him in his folly —*i. e.*, boasting: ye are, in sooth, so "wise" yourselves (1 Cor. iv. 8, 10) ; his real view of their wisdom was very different (1 Cor. iii. 1-9) ; moreover ye "bear with" the folly of others complacently (*v.* 20). **20. For**—ye may well "bear with" fools; *for* ye even "bear with" oppressors. 'Ye bear with them.' **if a man**—as the false apostles do. **bring you into bondage**—to himself. Translate, ' brings,' for the case is not a supposed case, but a case actually then occurring. Also 'devours' —viz., by exactions (Matt. xxiii. 14)—'takes,' 'exalts,' 'smites,' take *of you.* So the Greek [*lambanei*] for "take" is used for 'take away from' (Rev. vi. 4). *Billroth* translates, as ch. xii. 16, '*catches* you.' **exalt himself**—above you, under the pretext of apostolic dignity. **smite you on the face**—under the pretext of divine zeal. The height of insolence on their part, and of servile endurance on yours (1 Ki. xxii. 24 ; Neh. xiii. 25; Luke xxii. 64; Acts xxiii. 2; 1 Tim. iii. 3). **21. as concerning reproach**—rather, ' by way of *self-disparagement.*' I speak *as though* the allegation were true, that [λέγω ὡς ὅτι] WE ' were weak' when with you, in not, like them, exalting ourselves at your expense (*v.* 20). Irony. *Billroth,* ' By way of reproach (he does not add *to you and your teachers*, leaving their own self-respect to supply the ellipsis), I speak *in consequence of the allegation* that [ὡς ὅτι] we were weak.' But the " reproach" [*atimia*] must refer to *the same person, as the only pronoun expresses*—viz., "WE:" "reproach" is explained by 'we were weak.' The " WE" is contrasted with *the false teachers* who so oppressively displayed their power. Howbeit (we are not really weak ; for) whereinsoever any is bold, &c., I am bold also. **22. Hebrews . . . Israelites . . . the seed of Abraham.** A climax,—"Hebrews" referring to the *language* and *nationality;* "Israelites," to the *theocracy* and *descent from Israel*, the 'prince who prevailed with God' (Rom. ix. 4) ; "the seed of Abraham," to the *claim to a share in the promised* (Gal. iii. 29) *Messiah* (Rom. ix. 7 ; xi. 1). Cf. Phil. iii. 5, "an Hebrew of the Hebrews ;" not an Hellenist or Greek-speaking Jew, but a Hebrew in tongue, sprung

23 ham? so *am* I. Are they ministers of Christ? (I speak as a fool,) I *am*
more: *ˣ*in labours more abundant, *ʸ*in stripes above measure, in prisons
24 more frequent, in deaths oft. Of the Jews five times received I forty
25 *stripes* *ᶻ*save one, thrice was I *ᵃ*beaten with rods, once was *ᵇ*I stoned,
thrice I *ᶜ*suffered shipwreck, a night and a day I have been in the deep;
26 *in* journeyings often, *in* perils of waters, *in* perils of robbers, *ᵈin* perils by
mine own countrymen, *ᵉin* perils by the heathen, *in* perils in the city, *in*
perils in the wilderness, *in* perils in the sea, *in* perils among false breth-
27 ren; in weariness and painfulness, in watchings often, *ᶠ*in hunger and
28 thirst, in fastings often, in cold and nakedness. Besides those things
that are without, that which cometh upon me daily, *ᵍ*the care of all the
churches.
29   Who is weak, and I am not weak? who is offended, and I burn not?
30 If I must needs glory, I will glory of the things which concern mine
31 infirmities. The God and Father of our Lord Jesus Christ, *ʰ*which is
32 blessed for evermore, knoweth that I lie not. In *ⁱ*Damascus the governor

A. D. 60.

ˣ 1 Cor. 15. 10.
ʸ 2 Sam. 7. 14.
Ps. 89. 32.
Acts 9. 16.
ᶻ Deut. 25. 3.
ᵃ Acts 16. 22.
ᵇ Acts 14. 19.
ᶜ Acts 27. 41.
ᵈ Acts 9. 23.
Acts 13. 50.
Acts 14. 5.
Acts 17. 5.
Acts 21. 31.
Acts 28. 10.
ᵉ Acts 19. 23.
ᶠ 1 Cor. 4. 11.
ᵍ Acts 20. 18.
Rom. 1. 14.
ʰ Rom. 9. 5.
ⁱ Acts 9. 24.

from Hebrews (cf. Acts xxii. 3). **23. (I speak as a fool)** [*paraphronōn*]—'I speak as if *beside myself:*' mad, not merely "as a fool." **I am more**—viz., in respect to the credentials and manifestations of my ministry; more self-denying; richer in tokens of God's recognition of my ministry. 1 Cor. xv. 10; B Δ *f*, Vulgate, read the order, 'In prisons above measure [*perissoterōs*], in stripes more abundantly' [*huperballontōs*] (English version, less accurately, 'more frequently'). *Clement* (1st Epistle to Corinthians) describes him as having suffered bonds seven times. **in deaths oft** (ch. iv. 10; Acts ix. 23; xiii. 50; xiv. 5, 6, 19). **24.** Deut. xxv. 3 ordained that not more than forty stripes should be inflicted. To avoid exceeding this number, they gave one short of it—thirteen strokes with a treble lash. This is one of those minute agreements with Jewish usage which a forger would have not been likely to observe. **25.** The beating by Roman magistrates at Philippi (Acts xvi. 23) is the only one recorded in Acts, which does not give a complete biography, but only a sketch of his life in connection with the design of the book —viz., to give an outline of church history from its foundation at Jerusalem to the period of its reaching Rome, the capital of the Gentile world. **once was I stoned** (Acts xiv. 19). **thrice I suffered shipwreck**—before the shipwreck at Melita, (Acts xxvii.) Probably in some of his voyages from Tarsus, where he stayed for some time after his conversion, and from which, as being a seafaring place, he was likely to make missionary voyages to adjoining places (Acts ix. 30; xi. 25; Gal. i. 21). **a night and a day . . . in the deep** —probably swimming, or in an open boat **26. In**— rather 'By:' connected with *v.* 23, but now not with "in," as there, and as in *v.* 27, where again he passes to the idea of surrounding circumstances or environments (*Alford*). **waters** [*potamōn*]— 'rivers'; viz., perils by their flooding, as on the road often traversed by Paul between Jerusalem and Antioch, crossed by the torrents rushing down from Lebanon. **robbers**—perhaps in his journey from Perga to Antioch in Pisidia. Pisidia was notorious for robbers; as indeed were all the mountains that divided the high land of Asia from the sea. **the heathen**—Gentiles. **in the city**— Damascus (Acts ix. 24, 25), Jerusalem (Acts ix. 29), Ephesus (Acts xix. 23). **false brethren** (Gal. ii. 4). **27. fastings**—*voluntary*, to kindle devotions (Acts xiii. 2, 3; xiv. 23; 1 Cor. ix. 27); for they are distinguished from "hunger and thirst" which were *involuntary*. See, however, note, ch. vi. 5. The context refers solely to *hardships*, not to self-imposed devotional mortifications. "Hunger and

thirst" are not 'foodlessness' (as the Greek of "fastings" [*nesteiais*] means), but its consequences. **cold and nakedness** — "cold" resulting from "nakedness" [insufficient clothing: *gumnoteti*], as "hunger and thirst" result from 'foodlessness' (cf. Acts xxviii. 2; Rom. viii. 35). 'When we remember that he who endured all this was a man constantly suffering from infirm health (2 Cor. iv. 7-12; xii. 7-10; Gal. iv. 13, 14), such heroic self-devotion seems almost superhuman' (*Conybeare and Howson*). **28. without.** 'Beside' trials *externally*, there is "that which cometh upon me [lit., *the impetuous concourse to me* of business; *episustasis: so f g*, Vulgate, *a crowd rising up against one again and again, to bear him down*], the care of all the churches" (including those not yet seen in the flesh, Col. ii. 1); an *internal* and more weighty anxiety. But א B Δ G read *epistasis*, 'the pressing inspection that is upon me daily.' *Wahl*, 'Independently of what is BESIDES' [*parektos*]—viz., those other trials *besides* those recounted. But the Vulgate supports the English version. **the care** [*merimna*]—'my *anxious solicitude* for all the churches.'
29. I am not weak—in condescending sympathy with the weak (1 Cor. ix. 22). '*Care* generates sympathy, which causes the minister personally to enter into the feelings of all his people, as if he stood in their position' (*Calvin*). **offended** [*skandalizetai*]—by some *stumblingblock* put in his way by others. The "weak" is liable to be "offended." **I burn not.** The "I" in the Greek is emphatic, but not so in "I am not weak." I not only enter into the feeling of the party offended, but *I* burn with indignation at the offender, as if his cause were my own. Cf. his zeal, 1 Cor. v. 3-5. **30. glory of . . . infirmities.** A striking contrast! *Glorying* in, not power, riches, eloquence, but what others make matter of shame—viz., *infirmities;* for instance, his humbling escape in a basket (*v.* 33), imprisonment, &c. —a character incompatible with an enthusiast (cf. ch. xii. 5, 9, 10). **31.** This solemn *asseveration* refers to what *precedes*, and also what follows, including the revelation, ch. xii., which is in beautiful contrast with the preceding infirmities. The persecution at Damascus was the *first*. He had no human witness of it to adduce, being a fact that happened long before, and was known to few (cf. Gal. i. 20): he therefore subjoins it separately. 'In *Damascus* also, before any of these trials, I had a narrow escape, when the ethnarch guarded the city of the *Damascenes.*' This accounts for the tautology. The *ethnarch* did it to please *the Jews, who,* in Acts ix. 24, are said to have 'watched the

under Aretas the king kept the city of the Damascenes with a garrison, 33 desirous to apprehend me; and through a window in a basket was I let down by the wall, and escaped his hands.

12 IT is not expedient for me doubtless to glory. [1]I will come to visions and revelations of the Lord.

2 I knew a man [a]in Christ above fourteen years ago, (whether in the body, I cannot tell; or whether out of the body, I cannot tell: God 3 knoweth;) such an one [b]caught up to the third heaven. And I knew such a man, (whether in the body, or out of the body, I cannot tell: God 4 knoweth;) how that he was caught up [c]into paradise, and heard unspeakable words, which it is not [2]lawful for a man to utter.

5 Of such an one will I glory: [d]yet of myself I will not glory, but in 6 mine infirmities. For [e]though I would desire to glory, I shall not be a fool; for I will say the truth: but *now* I forbear, lest any man should

A. D. 60.

CHAP. 12.
1 For I will come.
a Isa. 45. 24, 25.
John 6. 56.
John 15. 4.
Rom. 16. 7.
ch 5. 17.
ch. 13. 5.
Gal. 1. 22.
b Acts 22. 17.
c Luke 23. 43.
2 Or, possible.
d ch. 11. 30.
e ch. 10. 8.

---

gates day and night to kill Paul.' **32. governor**—Greek, 'Ethnarch'—a commandant to whom heathen rulers gave authority over the numerous Jews in large cities. He was in this case under Aretas, king of Arabia. Damascus was in a Roman province. But at this time, 38 or 39 A. D., three years after St. Paul's conversion, 36 A. D., Aretas—against whom the emperor Tiberius, as the ally of Herod Antipas, had sent an army under Vitellius—had got possession of Damascus on the death of the emperor, and the consequent interruption of Vitellius's operations. The war of Aretas with Herod arose from the latter having put away, for Herodias, his wife, Aretas's daughter (*Neander*). Rather, it was granted by Caligula (38 A. D.) to Aretas, whose predecessors had possessed it. This is proved by our having no Damascene coins of Caligula or Claudius, though we have of their immediate imperial predecessors and successors (*Alford*).

CHAP. XII. 1-21.—REVELATIONS IN WHICH HE MIGHT GLORY; BUT HE RATHER GLORIES IN INFIRMITIES, AS CALLING FORTH CHRIST'S POWER —SIGNS OF HIS APOSTLESHIP—DISINTERESTEDNESS—NOT THAT HE IS EXCUSING HIMSELF; BUT HE DOES ALL FOR THEIR GOOD, LEST HE SHOULD FIND THEM NOT SUCH AS HE DESIRED, AND SO SHOULD HAVE TO BE SEVERE AT HIS COMING.

1. He illustrates the 'glorying in infirmities' (ch. xi. 30). He gave one instance which might expose him to ridicule (ch. xi. 33): he now gives another, connected with a glorious revelation; but he dwells not on the glory to himself, but on the *infirmity* which followed it, as displaying Christ's power. B G *fg*, Vulgate (C and Vulgate prefix 'if'), read 'I MUST NEEDS [δεῖ for δή, 'doubtless.' א Δ read δέ] boast (or glory), though it be not expedient; but (Δ reads *for:* א B G *fg*, Vulgate, *but)* I will come.' I will take the case of revelations, in which, if anywhere, boasting is harmless. "Visions" refer to things *seen;* "revelations," to things heard (cf. *margin*, 1 Sam. ix. 15) or *revealed* in any way. Of "visions" the signification was not always vouchsafed; in "revelations" there was always an unveiling of truths before hidden (Dan. ii. 19, 31). All parts of Scripture alike are matter of *inspiration*, but not all of *revelation*. There are degrees of revelation, but not of inspiration. **of**—i. e., *from* the Lord; Christ, *v.* 2.

2. *Oida*—'I know;' not "I knew." **a man**—meaning *himself*. He distinguishes between the *rapt and glorified* person of *vv.* 2, 4, and *himself*, the infirmity-laden victim of the "thorn in the flesh" (*v.* 7). Not the glory, but the weakness, belonged to *him*. He did not even know whether he was in or out of the body when the glory was

upon him. His spiritual self was his highest and truest self; the flesh, with its infirmity, his temporary self (Rom. vii. 25). Here, however, the latter is prominent. **in Christ**—a Christian (Rom. xvi. 7). **above**—rather, "fourteen years ago." This epistle was written 55-57 A. D. Fourteen years before will bring the vision to 41-43 A. D., the time of his second visit to Jerusalem (Acts xxii. 17). He had long been intimate with the Corinthians, yet had never mentioned it before: it was not a matter lightly to be spoken of. **I cannot tell**—Greek, 'I know not.' If *in the body*, he must have been caught up bodily; if *out of the body*, his spirit must have been caught up out of the body. At all events, he recognizes the possibility of conscious receptivity in disembodied spirits. **caught up** (Acts viii. 39; x. 10)—"a trance," Greek, *ecstasy*. **to** [ἕως] **the third heaven**—'*even to*,' &c. These *raptures* (plural, "visions," "revelations") had two degrees: first, he was *caught up* "to the third heaven;" thence to "paradise" (v. 4), 'an inner recess of the third heaven' (*Bengel*) (Luke xxiii. 43; Rev. ii. 7). St. Paul was permitted not only to 'hear' the things of paradise, but to *see* also in some degree the things of the third heaven (cf. "visions," *v.* 1). The occurrence TWICE of 'whether in the body, &c., I know not, God knoweth,' may mark two stages in the revelation. 'Ignorance of the *mode* does not set aside the *fact*. Even the apostles were ignorant of many things.' The first heaven is that of the clouds, the *air;* the second, that of the stars, the *sky;* the third is above both, where God's glory continually shines (Eph. iv. 10). **3.** 'I know.' **out of**. So G [*ektos*]. B Δ [*choris*] read 'apart from.' **4. unspeakable**—not in themselves, otherwise Paul could not have heard them; but "which it is not lawful for a man to utter." They were designed for Paul's own consolation, not for communication to others (Exod. xxxiv. 6; Isa. vi. 3). St. Paul had not the power adequately to utter; nor if he had, would he have been permitted; nor would earthly men comprehend them (John iii. 12; 1 Cor. ii. 9). A man may know more than he can speak.

5. of myself—concerning myself. Self is put in the background, except his infirmities. His glorying in his other self, to which the revelations were vouchsafed, was not to give glory to his fleshly self, but to bring out in contrast the "infirmities" of the latter, that Christ might have all the glory. **6. For**—Not but that I might glory as to "myself" (v. 5); 'FOR if I should desire to glory, I shall not be a fool,' for I have good materials for glorying (not mere fleshly advantages, which his adversaries boasted of, and which, when he gloried in (ch. xi.), he termed it "folly:" ch. xi. 1, 16, 17).

367

think of me above that which he seeth me *to be*, or *that* he heareth of me.

7 And lest I should be exalted above measure through the abundance of the revelations, there was given to me a *f* thorn in the flesh, *g* the messenger of Satan to buffet me, lest I should be exalted above measure.

8 For *h* this thing I besought the Lord thrice, that it might depart from

9 me. And he said unto me, *i* My grace is sufficient for thee; for my strength is made perfect in weakness. Most gladly therefore will I rather glory in my infirmities, that *j* the power of Christ may rest upon me.

10 Therefore *k* I take pleasure in infirmities, in reproaches, in necessities, in persecutions, in distresses, for Christ's sake: for *l* when I am weak, then am I strong.

11 I am become a fool in glorying; ye have compelled me: for I ought to have been commended of you; for *m* in nothing am I behind the very

12 chiefest apostles, though I be nothing. Truly *n* the signs of an apostle were wrought among you in all patience, in signs, and wonders, and

A. D. 60.

f Eze 28. 24.
Gal. 4. 13.
g Job 2. 7.
Luke 13.16.
h Deut. 3. 23.
Matt.26.44.
i Eccl. 7. 18.
Isa. 40. 29.
Isa. 41. 10.
1 Cor. 10.13.
Heb. 2. 18.
2 Pet. 2. 9.
j 1 Pet. 4. 14.
k Rom. 5. 3.
ch. 7. 4.
l ch. 13. 4.
m 1 Cor. 3.4-7.
Gal 2. 6.
n Rom. 15.18.
1 Cor. 9. 2.

---

think of me [*logisetai*]—'form his estimate respecting me.' **heareth of me**—Greek, 'heareth [B G א *g*, Vulgate, omit τι, which Δ, received text, have] from me'—viz., in person. If on his healing a cripple (Acts xiv. 12, 13) and shaking off a viper (Acts xxviii.), the people thought him a god, what would they have not done if he had disclosed those revelations? Let each estimate me by 'what he sees' my *present* acts and 'hears' my teaching to be; not by my *past* revelations. They who allow themselves to be thought of too highly defraud themselves of the honour at God's disposal (John v. 44; xii. 43).

7. exalted above measure [*huperairōmai*]—'overmuch uplifted.' How dangerous must self-exaltation be, when even the apostle required so much restraint. **abundance** [*huperbolē*]—'the excess;' exceeding greatness. **given to me**—viz., by God (Job v. 6; Phil. i. 29). **thorn in the flesh** (Num. xxxiii. 55; Ezek. xxviii. 24). Cf. the affliction (Gal. iv. 13, 14). But it rather was one that followed the 'revelation,' something affecting him individually, not as an apostle: causing bodily paroxysms of *pain* (as "thorn" implies), with *shame* ("buffet:" as a *slave*, 1 Pet. ii. 20). **messenger of Satan**—permitted by God to afflict his saints, as Job (Job ii. 7; Luke xiii. 16). to **buffet me**—'that he may buffet me' [*kolaphizee, present*], even now continuously. It was still afflicting him now. After tasting the bliss of good angels, he is now exposed to an evil angel. The chastisement from hell follows the revelation from heaven. As his *sight* and *hearing* had been ravished with heavenly "revelations," so his *touch* is pained with the "thorn in the flesh." **lest I should be** (may be) **exalted above measure.** So B C, Origen, Cyprian, Hilary. But Δ Δ G *fg*, Vulgate, omit it. The repetition may answer to *two* stages of *exaltation*—the third heaven and paradise (if these be distinct). Cf. "Abraham's bosom," Luke xvi. 23, with the heavenly "temple," Rev. iii. 12; vi. 9. **8. For**—'concerning this thing.' **thrice.** To his first and second prayer no answer came. To his third the answer satisfied his faith, and led him to bow his will to God's will. So Paul's master, Jesus, *thrice* prayed on the mount of Olives, in resignation to the Father's will. **the Lord**—Christ. Escape from the cross is not to be sought even indirectly *from Satan* (Luke iv. 7). **9. said**—*lit.*, 'He hath said:' His answer satisfies Paul. **is sufficient.** The trial must endure, but the grace shall also endure and never fail thee (*Alford*) (Deut. xxxiii. 25; 1 Ki. viii. 59, *margin*). The Lord puts the words into Paul's

mouth, that he might say, 'O Lord, thy grace is sufficient for me.' **my strength** [*dunamis*]—'power.' א B Δ G *f g*, Vulgate, omit "my," *power* (viz., God's) being thus put absolutely in contrast to *weakness*. **is made perfect**—has its complete manifestation. **in weakness**—infirmity. Do not ask for exemption from infirmity (*strengthlessness*), FOR my power is perfected in man's 'strengthlessness' [*astheneia*]: thy 'strengthlessness' [the same Greek as *v.* 10, "infirmities," *strengthlessnesses*: *astheneiais*] is the very element in which my 'power' (coincident with "my grace") exhibits itself perfectly. So Paul, instead of desiring the infirmity to "depart," rather *glories in* infirmities, that the power of Christ may rest [*episkenosee*, 'tabernacle upon,' cover all over as with a tabernacle; referring to the shekinah in the temple, the type of believers] (cf. Isa. iv. 5, 6; Greek, John i. 14) upon him. This effect of Christ's assurance on him appears, ch. iv. 7, 16; 1 Cor. ii. 3, 4: cf. 1 Pet. iv. 14. Paul often repeats "weakness," 'infirmity' (chs. xi., xii., and xiii.), as being Christ's word. The Lord more needs our weakness than our strength: our strength is often His rival; our weakness, His servant, drawing on His resources, and showing forth His glory. Man's extremity is God's opportunity; man's security, Satan's opportunity. God's way is not to take His children out of, but to give them strength to bear up against trial (John xvii. 15). **10. take pleasure in.** Too strongly. Rather [*eudoko*], 'I am well-contented in.' **infirmities**—the *genus*. Two pairs of *species* follow, partly from 'Satan's messenger,' partly from men. **reproaches**—'insults.' **when**—in all the cases just specified. **then**—then especially (Isa. xl. 29). **strong**—'powerful' [*dunatos*] in 'the power [*dunamis*] of Christ' (*v.* 9; ch. xiii. 4; Heb. xi. 34).

11. in glorying. Omitted in A B Δ G א *f g*, Vulgate. **ye**—emphatic. 'It is YE who have compelled me; for I ought to have been commended by you,' instead of having to commend myself. **am I behind**—rather [*hustēresa*], 'was I behind' when with you? **the very chiefest**—rather, as in ch. xi. 5, 'those overmuch apostles.' **though I be nothing**—in myself (1 Cor. xv. 9, 10). **12. Truly,** &c. There is understood some such clause as, 'yet I have not been commended by you.' **in all patience** [*hupomenē*] **in signs,** &c. A B Δ G א *f g*, Vulgate, omit "in." "Patience," or *enduring continuance*, is not a "sign," but the element IN which the signs were wrought. Translate, 'IN … patience, BY signs,' &c. His expression is modest, putting himself, the worker, in the background: "were

13 mighty deeds. For °what is it wherein you were inferior to other churches, except *it be* that I ᵖmyself was not burdensome to you? forgive me this wrong.

14 Behold, ᵠthe third time I am ready to come to you; and I will not be burdensome to you: for ʳI seek not yours, but you: ˢfor the children ought not to lay up for the parents, but the parents for the children.

15 And ᵗI will very gladly spend and be spent for ³you; though ᵘthe more abundantly I love you, the less I be loved.

16 But be it so, ᵛI did not burden you: nevertheless, being crafty, I

17 caught you with guile. Did ʷI make a gain of you by any of them

18 whom I sent unto you? I ˣdesired Titus, and with *him* I sent a brother. Did Titus make a gain of you? walked we not in the same spirit? *walked we* not in the same steps?

19 Again, ʸthink ye that we excuse ourselves unto you? ᶻwe speak before God in Christ: ᵃbut *we do* all things, dearly beloved, for your edifying.

20 For I fear, lest, when I come, I shall not find you such as I would, and *that* ᵇI shall be found unto you such as ye would not: lest *there be* debates, envyings, wraths, strifes, backbitings, whisperings, swellings,

A. D. 60.

° 1 Cor. 1. 7.
ᵖ 1 Cor. 9. 12.
ᵠ ch 13. 1.
ʳ Acts 2). 33.
Phil. 4.1,17.
1 Thes. 2. 5,
6, 19, 20.
1 Pet. 5.2,4.
¹ 1 Cor. 4. 14.
ˢ Gal. 4. 19.
Phil. 2. 17.
Col. 1. 24.
1 Thes. 2. 8.
³ your souls.
ᵗ ch. 6. 12.
ᵘ ch. 11. 9.
ʷ ch. 7. 2.
ˣ ch. 8. 6.
ʸ ch 5. 12.
ᶻ Rom. 9. 1.
ch. 11. 31.
ᵃ 1 Cor.10.32.
ᵇ 1 Cor. 4. 21.

wrought," not '*I* wrought.' The first "signs" means the *evidences;* the second, *miracles*. As the *signs* have not been transmitted to us, neither has the apostleship. The apostles have no literal successors (cf. Acts i. 21, 22). **mighty deeds** [*dunamesin*]—works of Divine omnipotence. The silence of the apostles in fourteen epistles, as to miracles, arises from those epistles being hortatory, not controversial. The passing allusions to miracles in seven epistles prove that the writers were not enthusiasts, to whom *miracles* seem the chief thing. *Doctrines* were with them the important matter, save when convincing adversaries. In the seven the mention of miracles is not *obtrusive*, but marked by a calm assurance, as of facts *acknowledged on all hands*, therefore unnecessary to dwell on. This is a stronger proof of their reality than if they were formally asserted. "Signs and wonders" is the regular formula of the Old Testament, which New Testament readers would understand of *supernatural* works. Again, in the gospels the miracles are so inseparably tied up with the history, that you cannot deny the former without denying the latter also. Then you have a greater difficulty than ever —viz. *to account for the rise of Christianity:* so the infidel has something infinitely more difficult to believe than that which he rejects and which the Christian accepts. **13. wherein you were inferior** —*i. e.*, were treated with less consideration by me than other churches. **I myself**—I *made a gain of you* neither *myself*, nor *by* those others *whom I sent*, *Titus*, &c. (*vv.* 17, 18.) **wrong.** His declining support might be regarded as the denial to the Corinthians of a privilege, and a mark of their spiritual inferiority, and of his looking on them with less confidence and love (cf. ch. xi. 9, 11).

14. the third time—(see 'Introduction' to 1 Corinthians.) His *second* visit was probably short (1 Cor. xvi. 7), and attended with humiliation through the scandalous conduct of some (cf. *v.* 21; ch. ii. 1). It was probably paid during his three years' sojourn at Ephesus, from which he could pass so readily by sea to Corinth (cf. ch. i. 15, 16; xiii. 1, 2). The context implies nothing of a *third preparation* to come: but, 'I am coming the third time, and will not burden you with my maintenance this time, any more than I did at my *two previous visits*' (*Alford*). It could be of no moment, in connection with 'I will not burden you,' whether he once or twice was *ready* to go, but whether he had *actually been with them* several

369

times already. **not yours, but you** (Phil. iv. 17). **children . . . parents.** St. Paul, as their spiritual father (1 Cor. iv. 14, 15), does not seek earthly *treasure* from them, but *lays up* the best *treasure* (viz., spiritual) 'for their souls' (*v.* 15). **15. I will very gladly spend**—all I have. **be spent**—all that I am; more than even natural parents do. They 'lay up *treasures* for their children;' but I spend not merely my treasures, but *myself*. **for you**—Greek, 'for your souls,' not for your mere bodies. **the less I be loved.** Love rather descends than ascends. Love to the unwilling only increases distaste: true only of *some* Corinthians. Love him as a true friend who seeks your good more than your good will.

16. I did not burden you. The "I" (Greek) is emphatic. A possible insinuation of the Corinthians is anticipated and refuted. 'You may say, granted that *I* did not burden you *myself*; nevertheless, being crafty, I caught you with guile'— viz., made a gain of you *by means of others* (1 Thess. ii. 3). **17.** Paul's reply: You know well I did not. My associates were as disinterested as myself. An important rule to all who would influence others for good. **18. I desired Titus**— viz., to go unto you. Not the mission (ch. viii. 6, 17, 22), but previous to this epistle; probably that from which he had just returned, announcing to Paul their penitence, (ch. vii. 6, &c.) **a brother** —rather, 'OUR (lit., *the*) brother:' one well known to the Corinthians; probably one of the two (ch. viii. 18, 22). **same spirit**—inwardly. **steps**— outwardly.

19. Again. So C Δ g [πάλιν]: a correction from ch. iii. 1; v. 12. But א A B G f, Vulgate [πάλαι], '*This long time* ye think that we are excusing ourselves unto *you?* (Nay.) It is *before God* that we speak in Christ' (ch. ii. 17). **20. For**—cause why they needed to be thus spoken to "for their edification"—viz., his fear that at his coming he should find them 'not such as he would,' and so be found by them 'such as they would not' like— viz., severe in punishing misconduct. **debates**— 'contentions' [*ereis*], B Δ G *f g*, Vulgate. But א A [*eris*, singular] 'contention.' **envyings.** So א *f g*, Vulgate. But A B Δ G read 'envying.' **strifes** —'intrigues,' 'factious schemes' [*eritheiai*] (*Wahl*). *Ambitious self seeking* [from *erithos*, '*a worker for hire*']. **backbitings, whisperings**—*open* 'slanderings' [*katalaliai*] and 'whispering backbitings' (Rom. i. 29, 30; Gal. v. 20). **swellings**—arrogant

21 tumults: *and* lest, when I come again, my God will ^c humble me among you, and *that* I shall bewail many which have sinned already, and have not repented of the uncleanness, and ^d fornication, and lasciviousness, which they have committed.

13 THIS *is* ^athe third *time* I am coming to you. ^b In the mouth of two
2 or three witnesses shall every word be established. I ^c told you before, and foretell you, as if I were present, the second time; and being absent now I write to them ^d which heretofore have sinned, and to all other, that,
3 if I come again, I will not spare: since ye seek a proof of Christ speaking
4 in ^e me, which to you-ward is not weak, but is mighty ^f in you. For ^g though he was crucified through weakness, yet ^h he liveth by the power of God. For ⁱ we also are weak ¹ in him, but we shall live with him by
5 the power of God toward you. Examine ^j yourselves, whether ye be in the faith; prove your own selves. Know ye not your own selves, ^k how
6 that Jesus Christ is in you, except ye be ^l reprobates? But I trust that

A. D. 60.

^c ch. z. 1, 4.
^d 1 Cor. 5. 1.

CHAP. 13.
^a ch. 12. 14.
^b Num.35.30.
^c ch. 10. 2.
^d ch 12. 21.
^e Matt. 10.20.
^f 1 Cor 9. 2.
^g Phil. 2. 7, 8.
^h Rom. 6. 4.
ⁱ ch. 10. 3, 4.
1 Or. with
him.
^j 1 Cor. 11.28.
^k John 17. 23.
Rom. 8. 10.
^l 1 Cor. 9. 27.

---

elation; puffing up of yourselves (Jude 16; 2 Pet. ii. 18). **21. my God**—implying resignation to the will of God, as being *his* God, however trying the humiliation in store for him. **will humble me.** The indicative implies that it *will actually be so.* The faithful pastor is 'humbled' at, and 'bewails,' the falls of his people, as his own. **sinned already** —before his second visit, in which he had much to rebuke. **uncleanness.** Contempt for authority of pastors tends to unbridled licentiousness (1 Thess. iv. 7).

CHAP. XIII. 1-14.—He threatens a Severe Proof of his Apostolic Authority, but prefers they should spare him the Necessity.

1. This is the third time I am coming to you— not merely *preparing* to come (ch. xii. 14). This proves an *intermediate* visit between the two in Acts xviii. 1, &c.; xx. 2. **In the mouth of two or three witnesses shall every word be established**—quoted from Deut. xix. 15, LXX. 'I will judge, after having tested every statement by examining witnesses.' The apostle, where ordinary testimony was to be had, does not look for an immediate revelation, nor does he order the culprits to be cast out of the church before his arrival. So *Alford, Meyer, Conybeare*, &c. I prefer (with *Chrysostom, Billroth*, &c.) the "two or three witnesses" to mean *his two or three visits*. As surely as a statement supported by two or *three* witnesses is true, so will my present *third* journey bring my threats to realization. **2.** Rather, 'I have already said (at my second visit), and declare (now) beforehand, AS (I did) WHEN I WAS PRESENT THE SECOND TIME, so also (I declare) NOW in my absence (א A B Δ G *f g*, Vulgate, omit the "I write," wrongly in the English version, Greek text) to them which heretofore have sinned (viz., before my second visit, ch. xii. 21), and to all others,' (who have sinned since my second visit, or are in danger of sinning, &c.) 'I have said already' applies chiefly to 'them which have sinned heretofore;' 'I declare' (now) to 'all others' who have sinned since, &c. The English version, "*as if I were* present, the *second* time "— viz., this time—is inconsistent with v. 1, "this is the *third* time I am coming." Paul could not have called the same journey "the second" and "the third time" of his coming. The antithesis between "the second time" and "now" is palpable. **if I come again**—*whensoever I come again* (Acts xx. 2). These were probably the words of his former threat, which he now repeats. **I will not spare**—in contrast to his forbearance towards transgressors at his second visit. **3. Since**—the

reason why he will not spare: since ye challenge me to a "proof" that Christ speaks in me. It would be better if ye would "*prove* your own selves" (*v.* 5). This disproves the assertion that Scripture nowhere asserts the infallibility of its writers when writing it. Christ *spake* through Paul; *lived* in Paul (Gal. ii. 20); *suffered* in Paul (Col. i. 24; Acts ix. 4, 5). **which**—'who' (Christ). **is not weak**—not without power of chastisement *in relation to you*, by me generally, and in this very epistle. **mighty in you**—has given proofs of power in miracles, and in punishing offenders (1 Cor. v. 5). Ye need not put me to the proof. Long ago Christ has exhibited His power by me among you (ch. xii. 12). It is not me, but Christ, whom ye wrong, by derogating from my authority. **4. though.** So A C Vulgate, *Hilary, Origen.* So א B Δ G *f g* omit it. Then translate, 'For He was even crucified,' &c. **through weakness**—Greek, '*from* weakness;' *i. e.*, His assumption of our weakness (susceptibility for suffering) was the necessary condition *from* which the possibility of His crucifixion flowed (Heb. ii. 14; Phil. ii. 7, 8). **by**—Greek, 'from;' 'owing to.' **the power of God** —the Father (Rom. i. 4; vi. 4; Eph. i. 20). **weak in him**—*i. e.*, in virtue of apostolic union with Him, and after His pattern, weakness predominates in us for a time (exhibited in "infirmities" and weak "bodily presence" (ch. x. 10; xii. 5, 9, 10); also in our not putting into immediate exercise our power of punishing, as Christ for a time kept in abeyance His power). **we shall live with him**—not only hereafter, free from present infirmities, in the resurrection (Phil. iii. 21), but presently in the exercise of our apostolic authority against offenders, which flows to us, *in respect to you, from the power of God.* 'With Him'—*i. e.*, even as He now exercises His power in His resurrection life, after His weakness for a time. **5. Examine**—Greek, 'Try yourselves.' **prove your own selves.** This should be your first aim, rather than seeking "a proof of Christ speaking *in me*" (*v.* 3). **your own selves.** If ye try *your own selves* ye will see that Christ is in you (Rom. viii. 10). Finding Christ in yourselves, by faith, ye may believe that He 'speaks in me' (*v.* 3), by whose ministry ye have received this faith. Cf. "we . . . in Him" (*v.* 4). To doubt it would be the sin of Israel, who, after so many experimental proofs of God's presence, still cried (Exod. xvii. 7), "Is the Lord among us or not?" (cf. Mark viii. 11.) **except ye be reprobates.** The Greek softens it, '*somewhat* reprobates' [*adokimoi*]—*i. e.*, not *abiding the "proof"* (alluding to the same word in the context). Image from metals (Jer. vi. 30; Dan.

7 ye shall know that we are not reprobates. Now I pray to God that ye do no evil; not that we should appear approved, but that ye should do
8 that which is honest, though ^m we be as reprobates. For we can do
9 nothing against the truth, but for the truth. For we are glad ⁿ when we are weak, and ye are strong: and this also we wish, *even* ^o your perfec-
10 tion. Therefore I write these things being absent, lest being present ^p I should use sharpness, according to the power which the Lord hath given me to edification, and not to destruction.
11 Finally, brethren, farewell. Be perfect, be of good comfort, ^q be of one mind, live in peace; and the God of love ^r and peace shall be with you.
12, Greet one another with an holy kiss. All the saints salute you. The
14 grace of the Lord Jesus Christ, and the love of God, and the communion of the Holy Ghost, *be* with you all. Amen.

The second *epistle* to the Corinthians was written from Philippi, *a city* of Macedonia, by Titus and Lucas.

A. D 60.

CHAP. 13.
^m 1 Cor. 4. 9,
13.
ch. 6. 9.
ch. 10. 10.
ⁿ 1 Cor. 4. 10.
^o 1 Thes. 3. 10.
2 Tim. 3. 17.
Heb. 6. 1.
^p Tit. 1. 13.
^q Rom. 12.16.
1 Cor. 1. 10.
1 Pet. 3. 8.
^r Rom. 15.33.
1 Thes. 5. 23.
Heb. 13. 20.
1 John 4. 8-
16.

---

v. 27; Rom. i. 28). **6. we are not reprobates**—not *unable to abide the "proof."* "I trust that" your own Christianity will be *known* by you on your proving it ("ye shall *know*," answers to "*know* . . . your own selves," *v.* 5) as "proof" that we are not reprobates, but that 'Christ speaks in me,' without needing a proof from me more trying to yourselves. If ye *know* your own Christianity, ye will not doubt my apostleship, for ye are the fruits of my apostleship. **7. I pray.** אA B Δ G *f g*, Vulgate, read 'we pray.' **not that we should appear approved**—not to gain credit for ourselves by your Christian conduct, but for your good (*Alford*). But the antithesis to "reprobates" suggests supplying the ellipsis: ('therefore our aim is) *not* [ουχ, *objective;* but *μή, subjective,* in the preceding clause] *that* we may appear *approved*,' by your giving us occasion to restrain you when ye do evil; 'but that ye should do what is *right*' (*Kalon*); here not in general, but *right* in relation to his apostolic authority and teaching. **though we be as reprobates**—though we be thereby deprived of occasion for exercising apostolic power (viz., in punishing), and so may appear 'as void of *proof*' of Christ speaking in us. **8.** Our apostolic power is given us only for the furtherance of the truth. Where you are "for the truth," we cannot punish you for the sake of showing our authority (*v.* 10). **9. we are glad**—Greek, 'rejoice.' So far are we from grieving. **when we are weak**—you giving no occasion by disobedience for displaying our power; so we seeming "weak," being compassed with "infirmities" (ch. x. 10; xi. 29, 30). **ye are strong**—"mighty" in faith and the fruits of the Spirit. **and** [δέ]. So C. Not in א A B Δ *f g*, Vulgate. **we wish**—Greek, 'pray for.' **your perfection** [*katartisin*]—'perfect restoration;'

lit., that of a dislocated limb. Cf. *v.* 11, "Be perfect" [*katartizesthe*], a kindred word; also in 1 Cor. i. 10; Eph. iv. 12. **10. Therefore**—because I wish the "sharpness" to be in my *letters* rather than in *deeds.* **edification, and not to destruction**—*for building up . . . not for casting down* [*kathairesin*]. To "use sharpness" seems to be *casting down* rather than *building up;* therefore he prefers not to have to use it.

11. farewell—meaning [*chairete*] also 'rejoice:' thus in bidding farewell he returns to that with which he set out (ch. i. 24; Phil. iv. 4). **Be perfect**—by filling up what is lacking in your Christian character (Eph. iv. 13). **be of good comfort** (ch. i. 6; vii. 8-13; 1 Thess. iv. 18). **14.** The benediction proves the Divine Trinity in unity. "The grace of . . . Christ" comes first, for only by it we come to "the love of God" the Father (John xiv. 6). God was first revealed to man in Christ (John i. 18). The variety in the order of Persons proves that 'in this Trinity none is afore or after other' ('Athanasian Creed'). **communion**—joint fellowship or participation in the same Holy Ghost, which joins in one Catholic Church, His temple, Jews and Gentiles. Whoever has 'the fellowship of the Holy Ghost' has also 'the grace of our Lord Jesus,' and "the love of God," and *vice versâ;* for the three are inseparable, as the three Persons of the Trinity. The doctrine was not revealed fully till Christ came, and the whole scheme of redemption was manifested in Him: we know the Holy Three in One more *in their relations to us* (set forth summarily in this benediction) than in their *mutual relations to one another* (Deut. xxix. 29). **Amen.** So C Δ *f*, Vulgate. Omitted in א A B G *g*. Probably added subsequently for the exigencies of public worship.

GALATIANS.

1 **P**AUL, an apostle, (not of men, neither by man, but *a*by Jesus Christ,
2 and God the Father, who raised him from the dead;) and all the
3 brethren *b* which are with me, *c*unto the churches of Galatia: Grace *d be*
to you and peace from God the Father, and *from* our Lord Jesus Christ,
4 who gave himself for our sins, that he might deliver us from this present

A. D. 58.

CHAP. 1.
a Acts 9. 6.
b Phil. 2. 23.
c 1 Cor. 16. 1.
d 1 Cor. 1. 3.

CHAP. I. 1-24.—SUPERSCRIPTION—GREETINGS—CAUSE OF HIS WRITING, THEIR SPEEDY FALLING AWAY FROM THE GOSPEL HE TAUGHT—DEFENCE OF HIS TEACHING—HIS APOSTOLIC CALL INDEPENDENT OF MAN.

Judaizing teachers persuaded the Galatians that St. Paul had taught them the new religion imperfectly and at second hand; that the founder of their church himself possessed only a deputed commission, the seal of truth and authority being in the apostles at Jerusalem; moreover, that whatever he might profess among them, he had himself at other times, and in other places, given way to the doctrine of circumcision. To refute this, he appeals to the history of his conversion, and to the manner of his conferring with the apostles when he met them at Jerusalem: that so far was his doctrine from being derived from them, or they from exercising any superiority over him, that they had simply assented to what he had already preached among the Gentiles, which preaching was communicated, not by them to him, but by himself to them. Such an apologetic epistle could not be a later forgery, the objections which it meets only coming out incidentally, not being obtruded as they would be by a forger; also being such as could only arise in the earliest age of the Church, when Jerusalem and Judaism still held a prominent place.

1. apostle—here in the highest sense; not as in 2 Cor. viii. 23; Phil. ii. 25; 1 Thess. ii. 6. Rom. xvi. 7 means, 'as being persons who are favourably reported of among the apostles' (*Fritzsche* in *Ellicott*). In the earliest epistles—the two to the Thessalonians—through humility, he uses no title of authority, but associates with him "Silvanus and Timotheus;" yet here, though "brethren" (*v.* 2) are with him, he does not *name* them, but puts his own name and apostleship prominent, evidently because his apostolic commission needs now to be vindicated against deniers. **of** [*apo*]—'from;' the ultimate *origin* from which his mission came; 'not from *men*,' but from Christ and the Father. **by** [*dia*] expresses the mediating agent. Not only was the call *from* God as its source, but '*by* Christ and *His* (*Ellicott*) Father' as the immediate Agent (so entirely are they One, that the *immediate agency* proper to the Son is attributed to both) (cf. Acts xxii. 15; xxvi. 16-18). The laying on of Ananias's hands (Acts ix. 17) is no objection, for that was but a sign of the call, not an assisting cause. So the Holy Ghost calls him (Acts xiii. 2, 3): he was an apostle *before* this *special* mission. **man**—singular, to mark the contrast to "Jesus Christ." The opposition between "Christ" and "man," and his name being put in closest connection with God the Father, imply His Godhead. **raised him from the dead**—implying that though he had not seen Him in His humiliation, as the other apostles (which was made

an objection against him), he had seen and been constituted an apostle *by Him in His resurrection-power* (Matt. xxviii. 18; Rom. i. 4, 5; 1 Cor. ix. 1; xv. 8). Cf. also, as to the ascension, the consequence of the resurrection, and the cause of His giving "apostles," Eph. iv. 11. He rose again, too, for our *justification* (Rom. iv. 25). Thus St. Paul prepares the way for the prominent subject, justification in Christ, not by the law. **2. all the brethren.** I am not alone in my doctrine. All my colleagues in the Gospel work, travelling with me (Acts xix. 29, Gaius and Aristarchus, if the epistle was written at Ephesus; if at Corinth, Acts xx. 4, Sopater, Secundus, Timotheus, Tychicus, Trophimus; some, or all), join with me. Not that these were *joint authors* with St. Paul of the epistle, but joined in the *salutations* and the anti-Judaistic *sentiments*. "All the brethren" accords with a date when he had many travelling companions, he and they having to bear jointly the collection to Jerusalem (*Conybeare*). **the churches.** The epistle, therefore, is encyclical. Pessinus and Ancyra were the principal cities. Doubtless there were many other churches in Galatia (Acts xviii. 23; 1 Cor. xvi. 1). He does not attach any honourable title to the churches here, as elsewhere, being displeased at their Judaizing, (see 1 Cor., 1 Thess., &c.) The first epistle of Peter is addressed to Jewish Christians sojourning in Galatia (1 Pet. i. 1), among other places. The apostle of the circumcision, and the apostle of the uncircumcision, once at issue (ch. ii. 7-15), co-operated to build up the same churches. **3. Grace . . . peace** [*chairis* (God's *gratuitous favour*), akin to *chairein*, 'joy,' the Greek salutation; blended with the Hebrew salutation, *shalom*, "peace," the result of "grace."] **from . . . from.** Omit the second "from." The Greek joins God the Father and our Lord Jesus Christ in closest union, there being but one preposition. As the Father is joined with Christ in the *mediating agency*, so here Christ with the Father as the *ultimate source* [*apo*], usually attributed to the Father. **4. gave himself** (ch. ii. 20)—unto death as an offering. Found only in this and the pastoral epistles (1 Tim. ii. 6). The Greek [*dontos*] is different in Eph. v. 25 [*paredoken*] (note). **for** [*περί*, A אּ Δ G, *Origen;* more used with the thing, *sins;* *ὑπέρ*, *f g*, Vulgate, used with the person, '*in behalf of*' *sinners*, 1 Pet. iii. 18: cf. *Ellicott*] **our sins**—which enslaved us to the present evil world. **deliver us from this** [*ek*]—'*out of* the,' &c. The Father and Son each "deliver us," &c. (Col. i. 13); but the Son, not the Father, "*gave Himself for*" *us* in order to do so, and make us citizens of a better world (Phil. iii. 20). The Galatians, in desiring to return to legal bondage, were renouncing the *deliverance* which Christ wrought for us (ch. iii. 13). "Deliver" [*exaireomai*] is the very word used by the Lord as to His deliverance of

5 evil world, according to the will of God and our Father: to whom *be* glory for ever and ever. Amen.

6 I marvel that ye are so soon removed from him that called you into

7 the grace of Christ unto another gospel: which *e* is not another; but there be some *f* that trouble you, and would pervert the gospel of Christ.

8 But though *g* we, or an angel from heaven, preach any other gospel unto you than that which we have preached unto you, let him be accursed.

A. D. 58.

e Rom. 10. 3.
2 Cor. 11. 4.
f Jer. 23. 26.
Matt. 21. 24.
Acts 13. 10.
Acts 15. 1.
Tit. 1. 10.
g 1 Cor. 16. 22.

Paul himself (Acts xxvi. 17): an undesigned coincidence between St. Paul and Luke, the apostle's companion. **world** [*aionos*]—'age;' *system* or *course* of the world, regarded from a religious point of view. The present *age* opposes the "glory" (*v.* 5) of God, and is under the Evil One. The 'ages of ages' (Greek, *v.* 5), the 'age to come' (Heb. vi. 5), are opposed to the 'present evil age.' **according to the will of God and our Father** [*tou theou kai patros hemōn*]—'of Him who is at once God (the sovereign Creator) and our Father' (John vi. 38, 39; x. 18, end). Without merit of ours. His sovereignty as "GOD," and our filial relation to Him as our "FATHER," ought to keep us from blending our own legal notions (as the Galatians were doing) with His will and plan. This paves the way for his argument. **5. be glory**—rather [*ē* 'be *the* glory;' the glory which is exclusively His (cf. Eph. iii. 21, note).

6. Without the usual thanksgivings for their faith, &c., he vehemently plunges into his subject, zealous for the "glory" of God (*v.* 5), which was being disparaged by the Galatians' falling away from the pure Gospel of the "grace" of God. **I marvel**—implying that he had hoped better things from them; whence his sorrowful surprise at their turning out so different. **so soon**—after my last visit, when I believed you untainted by Judaism. If this epistle was written from Corinth, the interval would be little more than three years from his second visit, which would be "soon" to have fallen away, if they were then apparently sound. Ch. iv. 18, 20 may imply that he saw no symptom of unsoundness *then*, such as he hears of *now*. But the English version is probably not correct there (see note, also 'Introduction'). If from Ephesus, the interval would be not more than one year. I prefer, with *Chrysostom*, to explain "*so soon*" *after* the entry of the Judaizing teachers. So *Ellicott*. *Birks* holds the epistle to have been written from Corinth after his FIRST visit to Galatia; for this agrees best with the "so soon" and ch. iv. 18, "It is good to be zealously affected always in a good thing, and not only when I am present with you." If they had persevered in the faith during three years of his first absence, and only turned aside after his second visit, they could not be charged justly with adhering to the truth only when he was present; for his first absence was longer than both his visits, and they would have obeyed longer in his '*absence*' than in his '*presence*.' But if their decline had begun immediately after he left them, and before his return, the reproof will be just. But see note, ch. iv. 13. **removed** [*metatithesthe*]—'are being removed;' *i. e.*, ye are *suffering yourselves so soon to be removed* by Jewish seducers. Thus he softens the censure by implying that the Galatians were tempted by seducers from without, with whom the chief guilt lay; and the present, 'ye are *being* removed,' implies that their seduction was only in process of being effected, not actually so. *Wahl*, &c., take the Greek as middle voice, 'ye are changing your position'—'shifting your ground.' But thus St. Paul's oblique reference to their misleaders is lost; and Heb. vii. 12 uses

the Greek passively, as here. On the impulsiveness and fickleness of the Gauls, whence the Galatians sprang (another form of Kel-t-s, the progenitors of the Erse, Gauls, and Cymri), see 'Introduction.' **from him that called you**—God the Father (*v.* 15; Rom. viii. 30; 1 Cor. i. 9; ch. v. 8; 1 Thess. ii. 12; v. 24). Calling belongs to the Father; the cause of the calling to the Son. **into**—rather, as Greek, 'IN the grace of Christ;' *in the exercise of it*, as the *element in* which, and the *instrument by* which, God calls us to salvation. 'Immanent [permanently inhering] instrumentality' (*Jelf*). Eph. ii. 13, "made nigh by (Greek, IN) the blood of Christ." (Cf. note, Rom. v. 15; 1 Cor. vii. 15, 'the gift by (Greek, 'in') grace (Greek, '*the* grace') of (the) one man.' "The grace of Christ" is Christ's gratuitously-purchased and bestowed justification. **another** [*heteron*, 'heterogeneous']—'a *different* kind of gospel;' *i. e.*, a *so-called* gospel, different altogether from the only true Gospel. **7. another** [*allo*]—a distinct Greek word from that in *v.* 6. Though I called it a *different* gospel (*v.* 6), there are not many gospels: there is really but *one*, and no *other*. **but** [*ei mē*] —'only that there are some that trouble you,' &c. (ch. v. 10, 12.) All I meant by the 'different gospel' was nothing but a perversion by 'some' of the one Gospel. **would pervert**—Greek, 'wish to pervert.' They could not really pervert the *Gospel*, though they could pervert *Gospel professors* (cf. ch. iv. 9, 17, 21; vi. 12, 13; Col. ii. 18). Though acknowledging Christ, they insisted on circumcision and Jewish ordinances, and professed to rest on the authority of other apostles. Paul recognizes none, save the pure Gospel. **8. But**—however weighty they seem 'who trouble you.' [*kai ean*] 'Even though we'—viz., I and the brethren with me—weighty and many as we are (*vv.* 1, 2). The Greek implies a case *supposed* which never has occurred. **angel**—in which light ye at first received me (cf. 1 Cor. xiii. 1; ch. iv. 14); whose authority is the highest possible next to that of God. A professed revelation, even though seemingly accredited by miracles, is not to be received if it contradict the already existing revelation; for God cannot contradict Himself (Deut. xiii. 1-3; 1 Ki. xiii. 18; Matt. xxiv. 24; 2 Thess. ii. 9). The Judaizers sheltered themselves under the names of the great apostles, James, John, and Peter: 'Do not bring these names up to me; for even if an *angel*,' &c. Not that these apostles really supported the 'Judaizers; but he wishes to show, when the truth is in question, respect of persons is inadmissible. **preach**—*i. e.*, 'should preach.' **any other gospel unto you than**. The Greek [*par' ho euengelisametha*] expresses not only 'any other gospel *different* from what we have preached,' but also 'any gospel BESIDE that which we preached.' This opposes the traditions of Rome, which are at once *besides* and *against* the written Word, our only *attested* rule. The context and argument do not (as *Ellicott* thinks) favour the translation 'against.' Paul just denied not only the existence of a *different* [*heteron*] gospel, but that of *another* [*allo*] gospel. This he enforced by saying, If he or an angel preached aught *beside* what he had preached, let

373

9 As we said before, so say I now again, If any *man* preach any other
10 gospel unto you [h] than that ye have received, let him be accursed. For
[i] do I now [j] persuade men, or God? or [k] do I seek to please men? for if I
yet pleased men, I should not be the servant of Christ.
11 But [l] I certify you, brethren, that the gospel which was preached
12 of me is not after man. For I neither received it of man, neither
13 was I taught *it*, but [m] by the revelation of Jesus Christ. For ye have
heard of my conversation in time past in the Jews' religion, how
that [n] beyond measure I persecuted the church of God, and wasted
14 [o] it: and profited in the Jews' religion above many my [1] equals in
mine own nation, [p] being more exceedingly zealous [q] of the traditions of
my fathers.
15 But when it pleased God, [r] who separated me from my mother's womb,

A. D. 58.

[h] Deut 4. 2. Deut. 12. 32.
[i] 1 Thes. 2. 4.
[j] 1 John 3. 9.
[k] Jas. 4. 4.
[l] 1 Cor. 15. 1.
[m] Eph. 3. 3.
[n] 1 Tim. 1. 13.
[o] Acts 8. 3.
[1] equals in years.
[p] Phil. 3. 6.
[q] Jer. 9. 14. Mark 7. 5.
[r] Isa. 49. 1, 5. Jer. 1. 5.

him be accursed (Rev. xxii. 18). **9. said before**—when visiting you (so "before" means, 2 Cor. xiii. 2: cf. ch. v. 2, 3, 21), 'If any man *preacheth* [εὐαγγελίζεται] unto you any gospel,' &c.: the indicative, not the subjunctive or conditional mood, is used. The *fact* is assumed, not supposed as a contingency, as in *v.* 8, 'should preach.' This implies he had already observed (viz., during his last visit) the machinations of Judaizing teachers; but his *surprise* (*v.* 6) *now* at the Galatians being misled by them, implies that they had not apparently been so *then*. As in *v.* 8, he said, 'which we preached,' so here, with an augmentation of force, 'which ye received'—acknowledging that they had *accepted* it [*parelabete*]. **accursed**—(*anathema*, devoted to death, Lev. xxvii. 28). The opposite appears, ch. vi. 10. **10. For**—accounting for his strong language. **do I now** [*arti*]—resuming the "now" of *v.* 9. 'Am I *now making friends of* men or God?' So [*peitho*] *persuade* means, Acts xii. 20 (*Ellicott*). Is what I have *just now* said a sample of men-pleasing? His adversaries accused him of being an interested flatterer of men, "becoming all things to all men," to make a party for himself; so observing the law among the Jews (for instance, circumcising Timothy), yet persuading the Gentiles to renounce it (ch. v. 11) (really keeping them in a subordinate state, not admitted to full privileges, which the circumcised alone enjoyed). *Neander* explains "now:" 'Once, when a Pharisee, I was actuated only by a regard to human authority (to please men, Luke xvi. 15; John v. 44); but NOW I teach as responsible to God alone' (1 Cor. iv. 3). The "now" answers, I think, to the following "yet" still [ἔτι]. Am I *now still* pleasing men, as I am said to have been heretofore? **for if I yet pleased men.** ℵ A B Δ G *fg*, Vulgate, omit "for." 'If I *were still pleasing* [*ēreskon*] men,' &c. (Luke vi. 26; John xv. 19; 1 Thess. ii. 4; Jas. iv. 4; 1 John iv. 5.) On "yet," cf. ch. v. 11. **servant of Christ**—and so pleasing Him in all things (Titus ii. 9; Col. iii. 22).

11. *The apologetic portion* here begins (*Ellicott*). **I certify**—I make known to you, as to the Gospel which was preached by me, that it is not after [*according to: kata*] man; not *of* [*apo*], *by* [*dia*], or *from* [*para*] man (*vv.* 1, 12). It is not influenced by mere human considerations, as it would be, if of human origin. **brethren.** He not till now calls them so. **12.** Translate, 'For *not even* did *I* (any more than the other apostles) receive it from [*para*, not synonymous with *apo*: *para* implies the more *immediate* source; *apo*, the more *remote*, 1 Cor. xi. 23] man, *nor* was I taught it (by man).' "Received it" implies the absence of labour in acquiring it. "Was I taught it" implies the labour of learning. **by the revelation of Jesus Christ**—'by revelation of (*i.e.*, from) Jesus Christ,' by His revealing it to me. Probably this took place during the three years in part of which he sojourned in Arabia (*vv.* 17, 18), near the scene of giving the law: a fit place for the revelation of Gospel grace, which supersedes the ceremonial law (ch. iv. 25). He, like other Pharisees who embraced Christianity, did not at once recognize its independence of the Mosaic law, but combined both. Ananias, his first instructor, was universally esteemed for legal piety, and was not likely to have taught him to sever Christianity from the law. This severance was partially recognized after the martyrdom of Stephen. St. Paul received it by special revelation (1 Cor. xi. 23; xv. 3; 1 Thess. iv. 15). A vision of the Lord is mentioned (Acts xxii. 18) at his first visit to Jerusalem; but this seems to have been subsequent to the revelation here (cf. *vv.* 15-18), and confined to giving a particular command. The vision, 'fourteen years before' (2 Cor. xii. 1, &c.) was in A.D. 43, still later, six years after his conversion. Thus Paul is an independent witness to the Gospel. Though he received no instruction from the apostles, but from the Holy Ghost, yet when he met them, his gospel exactly agreed with theirs. **13.** I never should have so utterly changed had not God been the Revealer. **For ye have heard**—even before I came among you. **conversation** [*anastrophēn*]—'my former way of life.' **Jews' religion**—'Hebrew' expresses the *language*; 'Jew,' the *nationality*, as distinguished from the Gentiles; 'Israelite' (the highest title), the religious privileges as a member of the theocracy. **the church**—here singular, marking its *unity*, though constituted of many particular churches, under the one Head, Christ. **of God**—added to mark his sinful alienation from God (1 Cor. xi. 22). **wasted**—was laying it waste [*eporthoun*]: the opposite of 'building it up.' **14. profited** [*proekopton*]—'I was becoming a proficient;' 'I made progress.' **above**—beyond. **my equals**—Greek, 'of mine own age.' **traditions of my fathers**—viz., those of the Pharisees, Paul being 'a Pharisee, and son of a Pharisee' (Acts xxiii. 6; xxvi. 5). "MY fathers" shows that it does not mean the traditions *of the nation*.

15. separated [*aphorisas*]—'set me apart' in His electing love (cf. Acts ix. 15; xxii. 14), in order to show in me *His 'pleasure,'* which is the farthest point that any can reach in inquiring the causes of his salvation. The actual 'separating' to the work marked out for him is mentioned Acts xiii. 2; Rom. i. 1. There is an allusion, perhaps by contrast, to the derivation of Pharisee from Hebrew [*pharash*], "separated." I was once a so-called Pharisee or *Separatist;* but God had *separated* me to something far better. **from my mother's womb**—thus merit in me was out of the

16 and called *me* by his grace, to ⁵reveal his Son in me, that I might preach him among the heathen; immediately I conferred not ᵗ with flesh and
17 blood : neither went I up to Jerusalem to them which were apostles before me; but I went into Arabia, and returned again unto Damascus.
18 Then after three years I ²went up to Jerusalem to see Peter, and abode
19 with him fifteen days. But ᵘother of the apostles saw I none, save
20 ᵛJames the Lord's brother. Now the things which I write unto you,

A. D. 58.

⁵ 2 Cor. 4. 6.
ᵗ Matt. 16.17.
1 Cor. 15.50.
2 Or,
returned.
ᵘ 1 Cor. 9. 5.
ᵛ Matt. 13.55.
Mark 6. 3.

question in His call (Ps. xxii. 9; lxxi. 6; Isa. xlix. 1, 5; Jer. i. 5; Luke i. 15; Rom. viii. 30; ix. 11). **called me**—on the way to Damascus, (Acts ix.) The *moving* cause of His call was God's 'good pleasure' [*eudokia*]; the *mediating* cause [*dia*] was His "grace;" the *instrument*. the heaven-sent voice (*Ellicott*). **16. reveal his Son in me**—in my inmost soul, by the Holy Spirit (ch. ii. 20: cf. 2 Cor. iv. 6). The revealing of His Son by me to ' *the Gentiles*' (so translate) was impossible, unless he had first revealed His Son *in me:* this He did at my conversion, but especially at the subsequent revelation from Jesus Christ (*v.* 12), whereby I learnt the Gospel's independence of Mosaic ceremonialism. **that I might preach**—the present [ἐναγγελίζωμαι], which includes 'that I *may* preach Him,' implying an office still *continuing:* the main commission intrusted to him (ch. ii. 7, 9). **immediately**. *From the first* I had no recourse to men. It denotes the sudden fitness of the apostle. So Acts ix. 20, "*straightway* [the same Greek, *eutheōs*] he preached Christ in the synagogues." **I conferred not** [*prosanethemēn*]—' I had not further (viz., in addition to revelation) recourse to . . . for consultation.' The divine revelation was sufficient for me. **flesh and blood** (Matt. xvi. 17)—*weak* man. **17. went I up.** So א A. But B Δ G [*apelthon* for *anēlthon*], 'went away'—viz., from Damascus. **to Jerusalem**—the seat of the apostles. **into Arabia.** This journey (not recorded in Acts) was during his stay at Damascus, called by St. Luke (Acts ix. 23), "many [*hikanai hemerai*, a considerable number of] days." It curiously confirms the taking "many days" to stand for "three years," that the phrase occurs in the same sense (1 Ki. ii. 38, 39). This was a country of the *Gentiles;* here doubtless he preached, as before and after (Acts ix. 20, 22), at Damascus: thus he shows the independence of his apostolic commission. He also here had that comparative retirement needed, after the first fervour of his conversion, to prepare him for the great work before him. Cf. Moses (Acts vii. 29, 30). His familiarity with the scene of the giving of the law, and the meditations and revelations which he had there, appear in ch. iv. 24, 25; Heb. xii. 18: see note, *v.* 12. The Lord from heaven communed with him, as He on earth in the days of His flesh communed with the other apostles. **returned** (back) **again** [*palin hupestrepsa*]. **18. after three years**—from my conversion; as appears by the contrast to "immediately" (*v.* 16). These three years of Paul's direction by God alone answer to the three years (about) of the intercourse of the twelve with Jesus. This is the visit to Jerusalem (Acts ix. 26) at which occurred the vision, Acts xxii. 17, 18. The incident which led to his leaving Damascus (Acts ix. 25; 2 Cor. xi. 33) was not the main *cause* of his going *to Jerusalem.* So that there is no discrepancy in the statement here that he went "to see Peter;" Greek, 'to become personally acquainted with Peter' [*historesai*]; *to visit one important to know.* א A B read 'Cephas,' the name given Peter elsewhere in the epistle, the Hebrew name; as *Peter* is the Greek (John i. 42). Appropriate to the view of him here as the apostle especially of the *Hebrews.* C Δ G *f g*, Vulgate,

read "Peter." Peter himself, in his epistles, uses the Greek, "*Peter*," perhaps to mark his antagonism to the Judaizers who would cling to the Hebraic form. He was prominent among the apostles, though James, as bishop of Jerusalem, had the chief authority there (Matt. xvi. 18). **abode** [*epemeina*]—'tarried.' **fifteen days**—only fifteen days; contrasting with the long period of *three years*, during which, previously, he had exercised an independent commission—a fact proving how little he owed to Peter in regard to apostolical authority or instruction. The plots of Hellenistic Jews prevented him staying longer (Acts ix. 29); also the vision directing him to depart to the Gentiles, for that the people of Jerusalem would not receive his testimony (Acts xxii. 17, 18). **19.** Acts ix. 27, 28. Luke, as a historian, describes more generally what St. Paul, the subject of the history, himself details more particularly. The history speaks of "apostles." St. Paul's mention of a *second* apostle besides Peter reconciles the epistle and the history. At Stephen's martyrdom, and the consequent persecution, the other ten apostles, agreeably to Christ's directions, seem to have *soon* (though not *immediately*, Acts viii. 14) left Jerusalem to preach elsewhere. James remained in charge of the mother church, as its bishop. Peter, the apostle of the circumcision, was present during Paul's fifteen days' stay; but he, too, presently after (Acts ix. 32), went on a circuit through Judea. **James the Lord's brother.** This designation, to distinguish him from James the son of Zebedee, was appropriate whilst that apostle was alive. But before St. Paul's second visit to Jerusalem (Acts xv.; ch. ii. 1) he had been beheaded by Herod (Acts xii. 2). Accordingly, in the subsequent mention of James here (ch. ii. 9, 12), he is not designated by this distinctive epithet: a minute, undesigned coincidence, and proof of genuineness. "Other of the *apostles* . . . save James," implies that *he* was an apostle. James was the Lord's brother, not in our strict sense, but 'cousin,' or 'kinsman' (Matt. xxviii. 10; John xx. 17). His "brethren" are never called 'sons of Joseph' (cf. Ps. lxix. 8, "my mother's children," figurative for *nearest kinsmen*). In John vii. 3, 5, the "brethren" who believed not in Him may mean His *near relations*, not including His two brethren—*i. e.*, relatives (James and Jude) who were among the twelve. *Ellicott* suggests that 'believed' is used there of a *proper, intelligent belief;* as in John vi. 64, 67 it is implied that some disciples, and even the twelve, had not a full belief. Acts i. 14, "His brethren," refers to Simon and Joses, and others (Matt. xiii. 55) of His kinsmen who were not apostles. It is not likely there would be two pairs of brothers named alike, of such eminence as James and Jude: the likelihood is that the apostles James and Jude are also the writers of the epistles and the brethren of Jesus. James and Joses were sons of Alpheus and Mary, sister of the virgin Mary. **20.** Solemn asseveration that his visit was but for fifteen days, and that he saw no apostle save Peter and James. Probably it was reported by Judaizers that he had received a course of instruction from

21 behold, before God, I lie not. Afterwards [w] I came into the regions of
22 Syria and Cilicia; and was unknown by face unto the churches of Judea
23 which were in Christ: but they had heard only, that he which persecuted
24 us in times past now preacheth the faith which once he destroyed. And

2 they glorified God in me. THEN fourteen years after [a] I went up again
2 to Jerusalem with Barnabas, and took Titus with *me* also. And I went
up by [b] revelation, and communicated unto them that gospel which I
preach among the Gentiles, but [1] privately to them which were of reputa-
3 tion, lest by any means [c] I should run, or had run, in vain. But neither
Titus, who was with me, being a Greek, was compelled to be circum-

A. D. 58.
[w] Acts 9. 30.
Acts 11. 25.
CHAP. 2.
[a] Acts 15. 2.
[b] Acts 19. 21.
1 Or,
severally.
[c] Matt. 10.16.
1 Cor. 9. 26.
Phil. 2. 16.
1 Thes. 3. 5.

the apostles in Jerusalem from the first; hence his earnestness in asserting the contrary, to vindicate his apostleship as derived directly from Christ. **21. I came into the regions of Syria and Cilicia**—'preaching the faith' (*v.* 23), and so founding the churches in Syria and Cilicia, which he subsequently confirmed in the faith (Acts xv. 23, 41). His object is to show how *far* he was from where the apostles were: so that they could not have been his teachers. He went first to Cæsarea, the seaport; thence by sea to Tarsus of Cilicia, his native place (Acts ix. 30); thence to Syria; Cilicia having its geographical affinities with Syria rather than with Asia Minor, as the Tarsus mountains separate it from the latter. His placing "Syria" in the order of words before "Cilicia" is due to Antioch being a more important city than Tarsus, as also to his longer stay in the former. Also "Syria and Cilicia," from their connection, became a geographical phrase, the more important being placed first (*Conybeare*). This sea journey accounts for his being "unknown by face unto the churches of Judea" (*v.* 22). He passes by in silence his *second* visit, with alms, to Judea and Jerusalem (Acts xi. 30); doubtless because it, being for a limited and special object, occupied but a few days (Acts xii. 25), as there raged at Jerusalem at the time a persecution in which James, the brother of John, was martyred, and Peter was in prison, and James seems to have been the only apostle present (Acts xii. 17); so it was needless to mention this visit, seeing that he could not at such a time have received the instruction which the Galatians alleged he had derived from the primary fountains of authority —the apostles. **22. So far was I from being a** disciple of the apostles, that I was even *unknown by face in the churches of Judea* (except Jerusalem, Acts ix. 26-29), the chief scene of their labours. **23.** [*Akouontes ēsan*] 'They were hearing:' reports were reaching them from time to time. **he which persecuted us in times past**—Saul's characteristic designation among Christians. **destroyed** [*eporthei*] —'was destroying.' **24. in me**—in my person. 'Learning that the former wolf is now acting the shepherd's part, they received occasion for joyful thanksgiving to God in respect to me' (*Theodoret*). How different *their* spirits from *yours* towards me!

CHAP. II. 1-21.—HIS CO-ORDINATE AUTHORITY AS APOSTLE OF THE CIRCUMCISION RECOGNIZED BY THE APOSTLES—PROVED BY HIS REBUKING PETER FOR TEMPORIZING AT ANTIOCH—INCONSISTENCY OF JUDAIZING WITH JUSTIFICATION BY FAITH.

1. Translate, '*After* [*dia*] fourteen years'—viz., from Paul's conversion inclusive (*Alford*). In the *fourteenth year* from it (*Birks*). The same visit, his *third*, to Jerusalem, as Acts xv. (A. D. 50), when the apostles and church in council decided that Gentile Christians need not be circumcised. His omitting allusion to that decree is—(1.) Because his *design* is to show his own independent apostolic

authority, whence he would not support himself by their decision. Thus general councils are not above apostles. (2.) He argues upon principle, not authoritative decisions. (3.) The decree did not go the length of the position here: the council merely did not impose Mosaic ordinances: the apostle maintains the Mosaic institution itself is at an end. (4.) The Galatians were Judaizing, not because the Jewish law was imposed by the Church as *necessary to Christianity*, but because they thought it necessary to those who aspired to *higher perfection* (ch. iii. 3; iv. 21). The decree would not disprove their view, and therefore would have been useless to quote. St. Paul confutes them far more directly, 'Christ is of *no effect* unto you, whosoever are justified by the law' (ch. v. 4) (*Paley*). **Titus with me also**—specified on account of what follows as to him in *v.* 3. Paul and Barnabas, *and others*, were deputed by the church of Antioch (Acts xv. 2) to consult the apostles and elders at Jerusalem on the circumcision of Gentile Christians. **2. by revelation.** Not to satisfy doubts of my commission, but by divine "revelation," which showed him more than the Church knew of the import of the crisis. Quite consistent with his also being a deputy from the church of Antioch, as Acts xv. 2 states. He by this *revelation* was led to suggest the sending of the deputation. So Peter was led by vision, and at the same time by Cornelius's messengers, to go to Cæsarea, (Acts x.) **I . . . communicated unto them**—*to the Christians at Jerusalem*, the Gospel *in general*, as I preached it. **but privately**—that he and they might decide previously on the principles to be set forward before the public council. The Jerusalem apostles should know beforehand that the *particular doctrine* Paul preached to the Gentiles was the same as theirs, and had received Divine confirmation in the results wrought on the Gentiles. He and Barnabas related to the *multitude*, not the details of doctrine they preached (as Paul did *privately to the apostles*), but only tho general facts and the miracles vouchsafed in *proof of* God's sanctioning their preaching to the Gentiles (Acts xv. 2, 4, 12). **to them which were of reputation**—James, Cephas, and John, and probably some of the "elders" (*vv.* 6, 9). **lest, &c.**—*i. e.*, that they might see that I am not running, and have not run, in vain. Paul does not *himself* fear lest he be running, or had run, in vain; but lest he should, if he gave them no explanation, *seem so to them.* His race was the swift-running proclamation of the Gospel to the Gentiles (cf. "Word . . . have free course"—lit., "run," 2 Thess. iii. 1). His running would have been in vain, had circumcision been necessary, since he did not require it of his converts. **3. But.** So far were they from regarding me as running in vain, that '*not even* Titus who was with me, though he was a Greek (and therefore uncircumcised), was compelled to be circumcised.' The "false brethren," *v.* 4 ("certain of the Pharisees which believed," Acts xv. 5),

4 cised : and that because of false brethren unawares brought in, who came
in privily to spy out our *d* liberty which we have in Christ Jesus, *e* that
5 they might bring us into bondage: to whom we gave place by subjection,
no, not for an hour; that the truth of the Gospel might continue with
6 you. But of those *f* who seemed to be somewhat, whatsoever they were,
it maketh no matter to me : *g* God accepteth no man's person : for they
7 who seemed *to be somewhat* *h* in conference added nothing to me : but
contrariwise, *i* whey they saw that the gospel of the uncircumcision was
j committed unto me, as *the gospel* of the circumcision *was* unto Peter ;
8 (for he that wrought effectually in Peter to the apostleship of the cir-
9 cumcision, *k* the same was mighty in me toward the Gentiles:) and when
James, Cephas, and John, who seemed to be *l* pillars, perceived *m* the grace

A. D. 58.
d ch. 3. 25.
e ch. 4. 3, 9.
f ch. 6. 3.
g Acts 10. 34.
Rom. 2. 11.
h 2 Cor. 12. 11.
i Acts 13. 46.
j 1 Thes. 2. 4.
k Acts 9. 15.
Acts 13. 2.
l Matt. 16. 18.
Rev. 21. 14.
m Rom. 1. 5.
Rom. 12. 3.

demanded his circumcision. The apostles, constrained by the firmness of Paul and Barnabas (*v.*
5), did not insist on his being circumcised. Thus
they sanctioned Paul's course among the Gentiles,
and admitted his independence as an apostle—the
point he desires to set forth here. Timothy, however, being a proselyte of the gate, and son of a
Jewess (Acts xvi. 1), he circumcised (Acts xvi. 3).
Christianity did not interfere with Jewish usages,
regarded merely as social ordinances (though no
longer religiously significant), in the case of Jews
and proselytes, whilst the Jewish polity and
temple stood ; after their overthrow, those usages
necessarily ceased. To insist on Jewish usages for
Gentile converts would have been to make them
essential parts of Christianity. To violate them
abruptly in the case of *Jews* would have been
inconsistent with that charity which (in matters
indifferent) becomes all things to all men, that
by all means it may win some (1 Cor. ix. 22: cf.
Rom. xiv. 1-7, 13-23). Paul brought Titus with
him as a living example of the power of the Gospel
upon uncircumcised heathen. **4. And that**—*i. e.,*
My and their not permitting Titus to be circumcised was not from contempt of circumcision, but
'on account of the false brethren' (Acts xv. 1, 24)
who, had we yielded to their demand, would have
perverted the case into a proof that we deemed circumcision necessary. **unawares**—in an underhand
manner, intrusively [*pareisaktous*] brought in.
who [*hoitines*, being such as] **came in privily**—
stealthily. **to spy out**—as foes in the guise of
friends—wishing to rob us of our liberty—from
the ceremonial yoke. If they had found that we
circumcised Titus through fear of the apostles,
they would have made that a ground for imposing
the legal yoke on the Gentiles. **that they might
bring us into bondage.** The [*katadoulosousin*]
future implies the resulting *certainty* and *continuance* of the bondage: 'that (or *whereby*) they shall
completely [*kata*] enslave us.' **5.** 'To whom not
even for an hour did we yield by subjection.'
Ellicott renders the Greek article ' by yielding THE
subjection they claimed.' We would willingly
have yielded for *love* (*Bengel*) (if no principle
was at issue), but not in the way of *subjection*,
where 'the truth of the Gospel" (*v.* 14; Col. i. 5)
was at stake (viz., the fundamental truth, justification by faith only, without the works of the
law : cf. ch. i. 6). Truth abandons nothing that
belongs to it—admits nothing inconsistent with
it. **might continue** [*permanently: diameinē*] **with
you**—Gentiles. We defended for your sakes your
faith and liberties, which *you* are now renouncing.
6. Greek, 'From those who,' &c. He meant to
add, 'I derived no special advantage;' but he
alters it into "they . . . added nothing to me."
seemed to be somewhat—*i. e.*, not that they
seemed to be what they *were not*, but ' *are reputed
as persons of some consequence.*' **accepteth**—so as

to show partiality: 'respecteth no man's person'
(Eph. vi. 9). **in conference added**—'imparted ;'
the same Greek as ch. i. 16, "I *conferred* not with
flesh and blood." As I *had not recourse for conference* to them at my conversion, so they now did
not *impart in conference* aught additional to me,
above what I already knew by revelation. *Ellicott*
translates in both passages ' addressed.' This
will suit the sense, if there be added, ' addressed
nothing additional (in the way of information) to
me:' not otherwise. [*Emoi*, emphatic : " to ME,"
whatever they might have done *to others.*] This
proves his independence as an apostle. **7. contrariwise.** So far from *adding any* new light to ME,
THEY gave in THEIR adhesion to the new path on
which Barnabas and I, by independent revelation,
had entered—viz., the innovation of preaching
the Gospel without circumcision to the Gentiles.
when they saw—from the effects "wrought" (*v.* 8;
Acts xv. 12). **gospel of the uncircumcision**—*i. e.*,
of the Gentiles, whose circumcision was not to
be required. **was committed unto me**—Greek, 'I
had been permanently intrusted with, &c., as Peter
was with,' &c. **circumcision was unto Peter.**
Peter originally opened the door to the Gentiles
(Acts x. and xv. 7). But in the ultimate apportionment of spheres, *the Jews* were assigned to
him (cf. 1 Pet. i. 1). So Paul wrote to *the Hebrews*
(cf. also Col. iv. 11), though his main work was
among the *Gentiles.* The non-mention of Peter in
the list of names in Rom. xvi. shows that Peter's
residence at Rome, much more primacy, was *then*
unknown. The same appears from the sphere
here assigned to him. **8.** (For—the historical fact
confirms the statement (*v.* 7). **he**—God (1 Cor.
xii. 6 ; Phil. ii. 13). **wrought effectually**—*i. e.*,
made the preached Word efficacious to conversion,
not only by sensible miracles, but by the secret
might of the Holy Ghost. **in Peter.** *Ellicott*
translates ' FOR Peter.' [*en* would be required
before *Petro*, after *energesas* (which is not a pure
compound, there being no form *ergeo*), to admit of
the English version "IN Peter."] **to**—unto; with a
view to. **was mighty.** Translate as before, the
Greek being the same, "wrought effectually." **in
me**—'for (or "in") me *also*.' **9.** James—placed first
in the oldest MSS., before Peter, as being bishop of
Jerusalem ; so presiding at the council, (Acts xv.)
He was called "the Just," from his adherence to
the law ; and was popular among the Jewish
party, though not falling into their extremes ;
whereas Peter was somewhat estranged from them
through his intercourse with Gentile Christians.
To each apostle was assigned the sphere suited to
his temperament ; to St. James, tenacious of the
law, the Jerusalem Jews ; to Peter, who opened
the door to the Gentiles, but was Judaically disposed, the Jews of the dispersion ; to Paul, who,
by the miraculous suddenness of his conversion,
had the whole current of his Jewish prejudices

377

that was given unto me, they gave to me and Barnabas the right hands of fellowship; that we *should go* unto the heathen, and they unto the
10 circumcision. Only *they would* that we should remember the poor; [n] the same which I also was forward to do.
11 But [o] when Peter was come to Antioch, I withstood him to the face,
12 because he was to be blamed. For before that certain came from James, [p] he did eat with the Gentiles: but when they were come, he withdrew and separated himself, fearing them which were of the circumcision.
13 And the other Jews dissembled likewise with him; insomuch that Bar-
14 nabas also was carried away with their dissimulation. But when I saw

A. D 5%.
[n] Acts 11. 30.
Acts 24. 17.
Rom. 18.25, 27.
1 Cor. 16. 2.
Heb. 13. 16.
Jas. 2. 15, 16.
1 John 3. 17.
[o] Acts 15. 35.
[p] Acts 10. 28.

turned into an opposite direction, the Gentiles. The spheres were *geographical*, not personal. For Paul in Gentile lands, though the apostle of the uncircumcision, always preached to the *Jews first*. Not individually, but collectively, the apostles represented Christ, the One Head. The twelve foundation stones of various colours are all joined together to the one great Foundation Stone on which they rest (1· Cor. iii. 11; Rev. xxi. 14, 19, 20). John got an intimation in Jesus' lifetime of the admission of the Gentiles (John xii. 20-24). **seemed**—i. e., *were reputed* (note, *vv.* 2, 6) pillars; *i. e.*, weighty supporters of the Church (cf. Prov. ix. 1; Rev. iii. 12). **perceived the grace that was given unto me** (2 Pet. iii. 15)—the private conference issued in Paul's giving *them* instruction, instead of receiving it from them. Then followed the public conference, (Acts xv.) **gave to me and Barnabas the right hands of fellowship**—recognizing me as a *colleague* in the apostleship, and that the gospel I preached by special revelation to the Gentiles was the same as theirs. Cf. Ezek. xvii. 18. **heathen**—the Gentile lands. **10. remember the poor**—of the *Jewish* Christians in Judea, then distressed. Paul and Barnabas had already done so (Acts xi. 28-30). **I also was forward**—or 'zealous,' (Acts xxiv. 17; Rom. xv. 25; 1 Cor. xvi. 1; 2 Cor. viii., ix.) Paul was zealous for good works, whilst denying justification by them.
11. Peter—'Cephas' in the oldest MSS. Paul's withstanding Peter proves the independence of Paul's apostleship in relation to the other apostles, and upsets Peter's alleged supremacy. The apostles were not always inspired; but were so always in *writing* the Scriptures. If, then, the inspired men who *wrote* them were not at other times infallible, much less were the uninspired men who kept them. The Christian fathers may be trusted generally as witnesses to facts, but not implicitly followed in matters of opinion. **come to Antioch**—then the citadel of the Gentile church, where first the Gospel was preached to *idolatrous Gentiles*, and the name "Christians" was first given (Acts xi. 20, 26). Peter is said to have been subsequently its bishop. Thither Paul and Barnabas went from the Jerusalem council (Acts xv. 30, 35); and Peter soon followed. The question at Antioch was not whether the Gentiles were admissible to the Christian covenant without becoming circumcised—that was the question settled at the Jerusalem council just before—but whether the Gentile Christians were to be admitted to *social intercourse with the Jews* without conforming to the Jewish institution. The Judaizers, soon after the council passed the resolutions recognizing the Gentile Christians, repaired to Antioch, the scene of the gathering in of the Gentiles (Acts xi. 20-26), to witness, what to Jews would look so extraordinary, the receiving of men to communion without circumcision. Regarding the Jerusalem decree with prejudice, they explained away its force; they probably also watched to see whether

the *Jewish* Christians among the Gentiles violated the law, which that decision did not verbally sanction *them*, but only Gentiles, in doing (Acts xv. 19). **to be blamed**—'(self) condemned' [*kategnosmenos*]; his act at one time condemning his contrary acting at another (*Alford*) 'He was condemned by the sounder Christians at Antioch' (*Ellicott*). The English version gives a better reason for Paul's withstanding him (Rev. xxi. 8, so uses perf. passive participle for a verbal in—*teos*). **12. certain**—men: perhaps James's view (in which he was not infallible, any more than Peter) was, that the Jewish converts were to observe Jewish ordinances, from which he had decided the *Gentiles* should be free (Acts xv. 19). But these self-styled delegates from James were perhaps not really from him. Acts xv. 24 favours this: they merely came from the church at Jerusalem under James's bishopric. Still James's leanings were to legalism, which gave him influence with the Jewish party (Acts xxi. 18-26). **eat with the Gentiles**—as in Acts x. 10-20, 48; xi. 3-17; according to the command of the vision. Yet this same Peter, who himself preached the Gospel to the Gentile Cornelius, and so nobly vindicated his eating with them, through fear of man (Prov. xxix. 25) was faithless to his own so distinctly-avowed principles (Acts xv. 7-11). This, too, at Antioch, the stronghold of Christian catholicity, and Paul's centre of missionary enterprise. We recognize the same old nature as led him, after faithfully witnessing for Christ, yet for a brief space to deny him. 'Ever the first to recognize, and the first to draw back from great truths' (*Alford*). An undesigned coincidence between the gospels and the epistle in the consistency of his character. How beautifully misunderstandings of Christians are lost in Christ! In 2 Pet. iii. 15 Peter praises the very epistles of Paul which contained his own condemnation. **but when they were come.** So A C H. But B Δ F G א read 'when (he) came in' —viz., some leader among them: *Origen* says 'James.' **withdrew** [*hupestellen*, imperfect]— 'began to withdraw,' &c.: a *gradual drawing back*. **separated** [*aphorizen*]—*entire severance*. First feelings are sometimes best; second thoughts are not best when prompted by self-seeking and fear. Peter betrays his old character (Matt. xiv. 30). **13. the other** [*hoi loipoi*]—'the rest.' **Jews**—Jewish Christians. **dissembled likewise** [*sunupekrithesan*]—'joined in hypocrisy;' viz., in living as though the law were necessary to perfect justification, through fear of man, though they knew from God their Christian liberty of eating with Gentiles, and had availed themselves of it (Acts xi. 2-17); yea, "rejoiced" (Acts xv. 31) at the Jerusalem decree: so potent is bad example. The case was distinct from 1 Cor. viii.-x.; Rom. xiv. It was not a question of bearing with others' infirmities, but one affecting the essence of the Gospel, whether the Gentiles are compelled "to live as do the Jews," in order to be justified (*v.* 14). **Barnabas also**—'even Barnabas,' one least

378

that they walked not uprightly ^q according to the truth of the Gospel, I
said unto Peter before *them* all, If ^r thou, being a Jew, livest after the
manner of Gentiles, and not as do the Jews, why compellest thou the
Gentiles to live as do the Jews?

15, We ^s *who are* Jews by nature, and not ^t sinners of the Gentiles, know-
16 ing ^u that a man is not justified by the works of the law, but by ^v the
faith of Jesus Christ, even we have believed in Jesus Christ, that we
might be justified by the faith of Christ, and not by the works of the
17 law: for ^w by the works of the law shall no flesh be justified. But if,
while we seek to be justified by Christ, we ourselves also are found sinners,
18 ^x *is* therefore Christ the minister of sin? God forbid. For if I build

A. D. 58.

^q Eccl. 7. 20.
^r Acts 11. 3.
  1 Tim. 5. 20.
^s Acts 15. 10.
^t Matt. 9. 11.
  Eph. 2. 3.
^u Acts 13. 38.
^v Rom. 1. 17.
  Rom. 8. 3.
  Heb. 7. 18.
^w Ps. 143 2.
^x Matt. 1. 21.
  1 John 3. 8.

likely to be so misled, being with Paul in first preaching to the idolatrous Gentiles: showing the power of bad example and numbers. In Antioch, the capital of Gentile Christianity and the centre of Christian missions, the controversy arose, and there it now broke out afresh; here Paul had first to encounter the party that afterwards persecuted him in every scene of his labours (Acts xv. 30-35). **14. walked not uprightly** [*orthopodousin*] —'are not walking with straightforward steps.' Cf. ch. vi. 16. **the truth of the Gospel**—which teaches that justification by legal observances is inconsistent with redemption by Christ. Paul alone maintained the truth against Judaism, as afterwards against heathenism (2 Tim. iv. 16, 17). **Peter**—'Cephas' in the oldest MSS. **before them all** (1 Tim. v. 20). A public scandal could not be privately remedied. **If thou, &c.**—"If thou," though a Jew (and therefore more bound to the law than the Gentiles), livest (habitually from conviction, v. 12; Acts xv. 10, 11) as a Gentile (freely eating of every food, and living as if legal ordinances in no way justify, v. 12) and not as a Jew, *how* is it that (so א A C Δ G *fg*, Vulgate, read for 'why,' which B reads) thou 'art compelling (by thine example) the Gentiles to live as do the Jews?'—lit., *to Judaize; i. e.*, to keep Judaic ceremonies. What was formerly obedience to the law is now mere *Judaism.* Peter's high authority would *constrain* Gentile Christians to regard Judaizing as necessary to all, since Jewish Christians could not consort with Gentiles in communion without it. But how can Peter be said to be *now* 'living as a Gentile?' His doing so was *past* (v. 12). *Archbishop Whately* suggests. 'If thou, Jew as thou art, *hast life* on the same terms as a Gentile, and not by virtue of being a Jew, why dost thou compel the Gentiles to Judaize?' This suggested Peter's own statement immediately after (Acts xv. 11).

15, 16. Connect these verses, and read with most of the oldest MSS., "But," v. 16: 'We (I and thou, Peter) by birth (not by proselytism), Jews, and therefore not sinners (as Jewish language termed the Gentiles) from among the Gentiles, YET' (B C Δ G א read BUT, which A omits) **knowing that, &c.**—even we (resuming the "we" of v. 15, 'we also,' as well as the Gentile sinners; casting away trust in the law) "have believed," &c. **not justified by** [ἐκ, 'from'] **the works of the law** (required by the law)—as the GROUND (cause: source) of justification. **but by** [*ean me dia*]— 'but only (in no other way save) *through* faith *in* Jesus Christ,' as the instrumental MEAN (*Hooker*) which putteth on Christ to justification. **we also**—though being by birth Jews, and subject to the law. **believed in**—so as to be joined into [*eis Christon*]. **Jesus Christ.** In the second case, read with the oldest MSS., 'Christ Jesus,' the *Messiahship* coming into prominence before *Jewish* believers, as "Jesus" does in the first case, the

general proposition. **justified by the faith of Christ** —*i. e.*, by Christ, the object of faith, as the ground of justification. **for** [*dioti:* 'because that'] **by the works of the law shall no flesh be justified**— Greek, 'non-justification is predicated of all flesh' (*Ellicott*). He rests his argument on this axiom in theology (cf. Ps. cxliii. 2). 'Moses and Jesus Christ; The law and the promise; Doing and believing; Works and faith; Wages and the gift; The curse and the blessing—are diametrically opposed' (*Bengel*). The moral law is, in respect to justification, *more legal* than the ceremonial, which was an elementary gospel. So "Sinai" (ch. iv. 24), more famed for the Decalogue than for the ceremonial law, is pre-eminently the type of legal bondage. Thus justification by the law, whether moral or ceremonial, is excluded (Rom. iii. 20). **17. But if** (in your retrograde theory)—seeking to be justified IN [ἐν] (i. e., *in* believing *union with*) Christ (who in the Gospel theory fulfilled the law for us). **we** (you and I) **ourselves also** (as much as the Gentiles) **are found** (in *your* and *my* former communion with Gentiles) **sinners** (such as, from the Jewish stand-point that now we resume, we should be, since we have cast aside the law, an appointed means of justification, thus having put ourselves in the same category as the Gentiles; the opposite of being justified (v. 15). **is therefore Christ the minister of sin?** (cf. 2 Cor.-xi. 15)—are we to admit the conclusion, in this case inevitable, that Christ having failed to justify us by faith, so has become to us the minister of sin, by putting us in the position of "sinners," as the Judaic theory makes us, along with all others "without the law" (Rom. ii. 14; 1 Cor. ix. 21); and with whom, by eating with them, we have identified ourselves? The Christian revolts from so shocking a conclusion. The whole sin lies, not with Christ, but with him who necessitates such a blasphemous inference. By his false theory, though '*seeking* from Christ,' we have not "found" salvation (in contradiction to Christ's own words, Matt. vii. 7), but 'have been ourselves also (after all our seeking, like the Gentiles) *found* (Rom. vii. 10) sinners,' by having entered into communion with Gentiles (v. 12). **18.** Greek, 'For if what things I overthrow (by the faith of Christ), these things I build again (viz., legal righteousness, by subjecting myself to the law), I constitute (*lit.*, I commend) myself a transgressor' (answering to 'we were found sinners'). Instead of commending yourself as you sought (v, 12, end), you merely commend yourself as a transgressor. The "I" is intended for *Peter* to take to himself, as it is *his* case, not Paul's own that is described. A "transgressor" is another word for "sinner" (v. 17), for "sin is the *transgression* of the law." You, Peter, by asserting the law to be obligatory, are proving yourself a "sinner" in having set it aside by living as the Gentiles, and with them. Thus you are debarred by transgression from justification by

19 again the things which I destroyed, I make myself a transgressor. For I
20 ʸ through the law ᶻ am dead to the law, that I might ᵃ live unto God. I
    am ᵇ crucified with Christ: nevertheless I live; yet not I, but Christ
    liveth in me: and the life which I now live in the flesh ᶜ I live by the
21 faith of the Son of God, who loved me, and gave himself for me. I do
    not frustrate the grace of God: for ᵈ if righteousness *come* by the law,
    then Christ is dead in vain.

3   O FOOLISH Galatians, ᵃ who hath bewitched you, that ye should not
    obey the truth, ᵇ before whose eyes Jesus Christ hath been evidently set
2 forth, crucified among you? This only would I learn of you, Received ye

A. D. 58.
ʸ Rom. 8. 2.
ᶻ Rom. 6. 11.
ᵃ Heb 9. 14.
1 Pet. 4. 1.
2, 6.
ᵇ Rom. 6. 6.
ᶜ 2 Cor. 5. 15.
ᵈ Heb. 7. 11.
CHAP. 3.
ᵃ ch. 5. 7.
ᵇ 1 Cor. 1. 23.

the law, and you debar yourself from justification by Christ, since by your theory He becomes a minister of sin. *Ellicott* takes it, 'I demonstrate myself *a transgressor of the law's deeper principles* in reconstructing what I ought from the law itself to perceive is only temporary and preparatory. The Judaizers insisted that whoever keeps not the law is a transgressor; Paul shows, on the contrary, that *he who keeps to the law is a transgressor of the law itself*, as intended to lead to faith in Christ.' The "for I," &c. (*v.* 19), thus is to confirm this assertion. But the correspondence of "I make myself a transgressor" (*v.* 18) to "we are found sinners" (*v.* 17), fixes the former explanation; also the absence of "the law" (*v.* 18), or of any definite equivalent, is against *Ellicott.* 19. Here Paul seems to pass from his *exact words* to Peter, to the *general purport* of his argument. However, his direct address to the Galatians seems not to be resumed till ch. iii. 1, "O foolish Galatians," &c. For—But I am not a "transgressor" by forsaking the law. "God forbid" such premises as would make "Christ the minister of sin" (*v.* 17). "For," &c. Christ, so far from being the minister of sin and death, is righteousness and life in me. I—here emphatical. *Paul himself*, not *Peter*, as in the "I," *v.* 18, enforcing the argument by his personal experience. through the law—my 'schoolmaster to bring me to Christ' (ch. iii. 24): both by its terrors (ch. iii. 13; Rom. iii. 20) driving me to Christ as the refuge from God's wrath against sin, and, when spiritually understood, teaching that itself is not permanent, but must give place to Christ, whom it prefigures as its end (Rom. x. 4); and drawing me to Him by its promises (in the Old Testament prophecies) of a better righteousness, and of God's law written in the heart (Deut. xviii. 15-19; Jer. xxxi. 33; Acts x. 43). am dead to the law [*apethanon*]—'I died to the law,' and so *am* dead to it; *i. e.*, passed from under its power in respect to condemnation (Col. ii. 20; Rom. vii. 1-4, 6); just as a woman, once married and bound to a husband, ceases to be so when death interposes, and may be lawfully married to another. So, by believing union to Christ in His death, we, being considered dead with Him, are severed from the law's power over us (cf. ch. vi. 14; 1 Cor. vii. 39; 1 Pet. ii. 24). *Ellicott*, somewhat differently, 'I, *through the law*, owing to sin (*elicited by the law*, Rom. vii. 8), *was brought under its curse*; but having undergone this sin, and in the person of, Christ (ch. iii. 13; 2 Cor. v. 15), *I died to the law* (not merely as concerns the law, but *as the law required*), being both free from its claims, and having satisfied its curse. live unto God (2 Cor. v. 15; 1 Pet. iv. 1, 2). 20. I am crucified—*lit.*, 'I have been crucified with Christ.' This particularizes the "I am dead" (*v.* 19; Rom. vi. 3 6; Phil. iii. 10). nevertheless I live; yet not I [*Zō de, ouketi ego*]—'nevertheless I live, no longer (indeed) I.' Though crucified, I live, (and this) no longer that old man such as I once was

(cf. Rom. vii. 17). No longer Saul the Jew (ch. v. 24; Col. iii. 11), but "another man" (cf. 1 Sam. x. 6). *Ellicott*, &c., translate, '*And* it is no longer I that live, but Christ that liveth in me.' But the antithesis between "crucified" and "live" requires the translation, "nevertheless." [*Sunestauromai*] 'I am crucified,' answers to [*apethanon*] 'I am dead;' [*zō de*] "nevertheless I live," to [*theo zeso*] "that I might live unto God:" "I" (the old I) is in contrast to "Christ." the life which I now live—contrasted with my life before conversion. in the flesh—my animal life "in the flesh" is not my true life: 'it is but the mask under which lives another—viz., Christ, my true life' (*Luther*); 'Christ and His Spirit dwelling in them as the soul of their souls' (*Hooker*). I live by the faith, &c.—Greek, 'ᴵN faith (viz.), that of (*i. e.*, which rests on) the Son of God.' "In faith" answers by contrast to "in the flesh." *Faith*, not *the flesh*, is the real element in which I live. The phrase, "the Son of God," reminds us that His divine Sonship is the source of His life-giving power (John v. 26). So A C ℵ, Vulgate. But B Δ F G, 'the faith of God and Christ.' loved me —His eternal gratuitous *love* is the link that unites me to the Son of God, and His 'giving Himself for me,' is the strongest proof of that love. 21. I do not frustrate the grace of God—I do not *make* it *void*, as thou, Peter, art doing by Judaizing. In our justification three things go together; on God's part, His *grace;* on Christ's part, the satisfaction of God's justice; on our part, lively faith in Christ's merits, ('Homily on Salvation, I.') for —justifying the strong expression "frustrate." if righteousness [*dikaiosune*]—*justifying* and *sanctifying* (Rom. viii. 2, 3). come by [*dia*] the law. This asserts that the law is not a *medium* of righteousness; ch. iii. 11, that it is not the *sphere* [*en*] of righteousness; ch. iii. 21, that it is not the *origin* [*ek*] (*Ellicott*). is dead in vain [*dorean*]—'Christ died needlessly,' 'without just cause.' Christ's having died shows that the law has no power to justify us; for if the law can justify, the death of Christ is superfluous (*Chrysostom*).

CHAP. III. 1-29.—Reproof of the Galatians for abandoning Faith for Legalism—Justification by Faith—The Law was Subsequent to the Promise—Believers are the Spiritual Seed of Abraham, who was Justified by Faith—The Law our Schoolmaster to bring us to Christ, that we might become Children of God by Faith.

1. foolish [*Anoetoi*]—'unthinking.' They were, like most Kelts, 'acute' [*Themistius*]; but their inconstancy generated *thoughtlessness*. bewitched— fascinated you so that you have lost your wits. that ye should not obey the truth. So C, Vulgate. But ℵ A B Δ G omit it. you—emphatical. 'You, before whose eyes Jesus Christ hath been graphically set forth [*proegraphe*, in *word-painting*; but lexical usage favours "hath been *openly set forth*"] crucified' (so the sense and Greek order). Δ G ƒ g

3 ^cthe Spirit by the works of the law, ^dor by the hearing of faith? Are
4 ye so foolish? ^ehaving begun in the Spirit, are ye now made perfect by
^fthe flesh? Have ^gye suffered ¹so many things in vain? if *it be* yet in
5 vain. He therefore ^hthat ministereth to you the Spirit, and worketh
miracles among you, *doeth he it* by the works of the law, or by the hear-
6 ing of faith? Even as Abraham believed God, and it was ²accounted to
him for righteousness.

7 Know ye therefore that ⁱthey which are of faith, the same are the
8 children of Abraham. And the Scripture, foreseeing that God would
justify the heathen through faith, preached before the Gospel unto
9 Abraham, *saying,* ^jIn thee shall all nations be blessed. So then they
which be of faith are blessed with faithful Abraham.

A. D. 58.

^c Acts 2. 38.
Heb. 6. 4.
^d Rom. 10.16.
^e ch. 4. 9.
^f Heb 7. 16.
^g 2 John 8.
¹ Or, so
great.
^h 2 Cor. 3. 8.
² Or,
imputed.
ⁱ John 8. 39.
Rom. 4. 11.
^j Gen. 12. 3.

have "among you;" join it with "set forth."
א A C B C omit it. The perfect participle implies,
'in His *permanent character* as the crucified.' As
Christ was "crucified," so ye ought to have been
by faith "*crucified* with Christ" "to the law" (ch.
ii. 19, 20). Reference to the "eyes" is appropriate,
as *fascination* was exercised through the eyes.
The sight of Christ crucified ought to have counteracted all fascination. **2.** 'Was it by the works
of the law that ye received the Spirit (manifested
by miracles, *v.* 5; Mark xvi. 17; Heb. ii. 4; and
by spiritual graces, *v.* 14; Gal. iv. 5, 6; Eph. i.
13), or by the hearing of faith?' **only**—'I desire,
omitting other arguments, to rest the question on
this alone:' I who was your *teacher,* desire now to
"learn" this one thing from you. ' Holy' is not
prefixed to "Spirit," because that epithet is joyous
whereas this epistle is stern. **hearing of faith**—
'or, by *faith,* of which you *heard* in preaching.'
Faith consists not in *working,* but in *receiving*
(Rom. x. 16, 17). **3. begun** [*Enarxamenoi*]—after
having taken *the initiatory step in* the Christian
life (Phil. i. 6), which ought to be the pledge of its
completion (cf. Deut. ii. 24, 25, 31). **in the Spirit**
—Not merely was Christ crucified 'graphically
set forth' in my preaching, but also "the Spirit"
confirmed it by imparting His gifts. 'Yet are ye
now *being* made perfect' (Greek)—i. e., *seeking* to
be made perfect with *fleshly, i. e.,* sensuous and
earthly ordinances? (cf. Rom. ii. 28; Phil. iii. 3;
Heb. ix. 10.) Having begun with the Holy Spirit
ruling your spiritual life as its 'essence and active
principle' (*Ellicott*), in contrast to "the flesh," the
element in which the law works (*Alford*). The
Galatians thought that they were going more
deeply into the spirit; for the flesh may be easily
mistaken for the spirit, unless believers maintain a pure faith. **4. Have ye suffered so
many things**—viz., persecution from Jews and
from fellow-countrymen, incited by the Jews:
evidences that ye 'began with the Spirit' (1 Thess.
ii. 13, 14). **in vain** [*ἐικῇ*]—*needlessly;* since ye
might have avoided them by professing Judaism.
Or, shall ye, by falling from grace, lose the reward
promised for your sufferings, so that they shall be
"in vain?" (ch. iv. 11; 1 Cor. xv. 2, 17-19, 29-32;
2 Thess. i. 5-7; 2 John viii.) **yet**—rather, 'if indeed (or *at least*) it be *really* [*ἔιγε καί*] in vain'
(*Ellicott*). Paul mitigates the preceding words.
I will not think that ye will make your sufferings
in vain, but that ye will return from legalism to
grace. **5. He therefore** (resumptive of *v.* 2) **that
ministereth**—'supplieth' [*epichoreyōn*], God (2 Cor.
ix. 10). He who *supplied and supplies* to you the
Spirit. Miracles do not prove grace (Mark ix.
38, 39). He speaks of them as of *unquestioned
notoriety:* an undesigned proof of their genuineness, (cf. 1 Cor. xii.) **worketh miracles** [mighty
powers: *dunameis*] **among you**—rather, 'IN you'
(Matt. xiv. 2; Eph. ii. 2; Phil. ii. 13), at your con-

version and since. **doeth he it by the works of
the law**—*i. e.,* as a *result from* [*ek*] the works of
the law (cf. *v.* 2). This cannot be, because the
law was unknown to you when you received those
gifts of the Spirit. **6.** The answer to *v.* 5 is here
taken for granted, *It was by the hearing of faith:*
following this up, he says, "Even as Abraham
believed," &c. (Gen. xv. 4-6; Rom. iv. 3.) God
supplies unto you the Spirit as the result of faith,
not works, just as Abraham obtained justification
by faith, not by works (*vv.* 6, 8, 16; ch. iv. 22, 26,
28). Where justification is, there the Spirit is, so
that if the former comes *by faith,* the latter must
also. **it**—his believing. **accounted**—'reckoned.'
7. they which are of [from: *ek*] **faith**—as the
source and starting-point of their spiritual life (cf.
Greek, Rom. iii. 26). **the same**—*these, and these
alone,* to the exclusion of all other descendants
of Abraham. **children**—Greek, 'sons' (*v.* 29). **8.
And** [*δέ*]—'Moreover.' **Scripture, foreseeing.**
Scripture is identified with the mind that inspired
it. The promise to Abraham is a Gospel germ developed by St. Paul. In Scripture all points liable
ever to be controverted, are, with prescient wisdom, decided in the appropriate language. **would
justify**—'justifieth.' Present indicative. It is
now, and at all times, God's *one* way of justification. **the heathen**—'the Gentiles,' or 'the nations,' as at the end of the verse. God justifieth
the *Jews* too, 'by faith, not by works.' But he
specifies *the Gentiles,* as it was *their* case that
was in question, the Galatians being Gentiles.
preached before (announced beforehand) **the Gospel**—for the 'promise' was substantially the Gospel by anticipation (cf. John viii. 56; Heb. iv. 2).
'The old fathers did not look only for transitory
promises' ('Article' VII., Church of England).
The Gospel, in its essential germ, is older than
the law, though the development of the former
is subsequent to the latter. **In thee**—not "in thy
seed," a point not here raised; but strictly "in
thee," as father of the faithful (*v.* 9), as well as
(what was the reward of his faith) father of the
promised Seed—viz., Christ (*v.* 16), the Object of
faith (Gen. xxii. 18; Ps. lxxii. 17). **all nations**—
or as above, 'all *the Gentiles*' (Gen. xii. 3; xviii.
18). **be blessed**—an act of grace, not earned by
works. Justification was to Abraham by faith
in the promise, not by works. So to those who
follow Abraham, the father of the faithful, the
blessing—*i. e.,* justification—comes purely by faith
in Him who is the Subject of the promise. **9. they**
—and they alone. **of faith**—(note, *v.* 7.) **with**—
together with. As "IN" regards Abraham as the
spiritual father *in whom,* so "with" regards him
as one *with whom* all believers shall be blessed
(Matt. viii. 11). **faithful**—the point in which
they are 'blessed together with him'—viz., *faith,*
his prominent characteristic, of which the result
is justification.

10 For as many as are of the works of the law are under the curse : for it is written, *k* Cursed *is* every one that continueth not in all things which
11 are written in the book of the law to do them. But that no man is justified by the law in the sight of God, *it is* evident: for, The *l* just
12 shall live by faith. And *m* the law is not of faith: but, The man *n* that
13 doeth them shall live in them. Christ hath redeemed us from the curse of the law, being made a curse for us: for it is written, *o* Cursed *is* every
14 one that hangeth on a tree: that *p* the blessing of Abraham might come on the Gentiles through Jesus Christ; that we might receive the *q* promise of the Spirit through faith.
15 Brethren, I speak after the manner of men; *r* Though *it be* but a man's

A. D. 58.
k Deut. 27.23.
Jer. 11. 3.
l Hab. 2. 4.
Heb. 10. 38.
m Rom. 4. 4.
Rom. 11. 6.
n Lev. 18. 5.
o Deut. 21.23.
p Rom. 4. 9.
q Isa. 32. 15.
Isa. 44. 3.
Eze. 11. 19.
r Heb. 9. 17.

10. Confirmation of *v.* 9. 'They who *depend on* [*ex*] the works of the law' cannot share the blessing, for they are under the curse "written," Deut. xxvii. 26, LXX. PERFECT *obedience* is required by "in all things;" CONTINUAL *obedience* by "continueth." No man renders this (cf. Rom. iii. 19, 20). Paul quotes Scripture to the Jews as conversant with it (cf. epistle to the Hebrews) as *said* or *spoken*, but to the Gentiles as *written.* So Matthew, writing for Jews, quotes it as *said* or *spoken;* Mark and Luke, writing for Gentiles, as *written* (Matt. i. 22; Mark i. 2; Luke ii. 22, 23) (*Townson*). **11. But**—furthermore. **by the law**—Greek, 'IN the law;' *in the sphere of* the law, and *in virtue of* it. The syllogism (*vv.* 11, 12) is, According to Scripture, The just shall live by [*ek*, out of] faith. '*But* the law is not of [*ek*, out of] faith, but of works' (*i. e.*, does not make faith, but working, the conditional ground of justifying). Therefore "in," or, 'by the law, no man is justified (i. e., *shall live*) *before God*'—*at God's tribunal*—whatever the case may be *before men* (Rom. iv. 2)—not even if he could, which he cannot, keep the law, because the Scripture element and conditional mean of justification is *faith* (Rom. i. 17; Hab. ii. 4). *Alford* wrongly translates, 'He who is just by faith shall live.' [*Ho dikaios ek pisteôs zesetai* supports the English version. It would be, if *Alford* were right, *ho ek pisteôs dikaios.*] Also, the contrast would be just between "live *by (of) faith*" (viz., as the ground and source of justification), and "live *in them*"—viz., in his doings (*v.* 12), as the *conditional element wherein* he is justified. **12. And**—'But' [*de*]. **doeth** [*Poiesas*]—'he who *hath done.*' Many depended on the law, although they did not keep it. Without doing, saith Paul, it is of no use to them (Rom. ii. 13, 17, 23; x. 5). **live in them**—as IN the element of *life.* **13.** He breaks away abruptly *from* those who would involve us again in the curse of the *law,* by seeking justification in it, *to* "*Christ.*" The "us" refers primarily to the JEWS, to whom the law principally appertained (cf. ch. iv. 3, 4). But it is not *restricted* to the Jews, for these are the representative people of the world. The curse of the non-fulfilment of the law affects the Gentiles through the Jews; for the law represents that righteousness which God requires of all—which, since the Jews failed to fulfil, the Gentiles must equally fail. *V.* 10, "As many as are of the works of the law are under the curse," refers not to *the Jews only,* but to all, even Gentiles (as the Galatians). The universal law, represented by the Mosaic law, condemned the Gentiles, though with less clear consciousness on their part, (Rom. ii.) God's 'wrath,' revealed by the law of conscience, prepared them for appreciating redemption from the law's curse through Christ. The curse had to be removed from off them as well as the Jews, that the blessing through Abraham might flow to them. "That *we* might

receive the promise of the Spirit" (*v.* 14) refers to both Jews and Gentiles. **redeemed us**—ransomed, *bought us off* from our former bondage (ch. iv. 5), and "the curse" under which all lie who trust to the law for justification. The Gentile Galatians, by putting themselves under it, were involving themselves in the curse from which Christ redeemed the Jews primarily, and through them the Gentiles. The ransom-price was his own precious blood (1 Pet. i. 18, 19; cf. Matt. xx. 28; Acts xx. 28; 1 Cor. vi. 20; vii. 23; 1 Tim. ii. 6; 2 Pet. ii. 1; Rev. v. 9). **being made** [*genomenos*]—'having become.' **a curse for us**—having become what we were, *in our behalf* [*huper hemôn*: Phile. 13 sanctions also 'in our stead'], "a curse," that we might cease to be it. Not merely *accursed,* but *a curse, bearing the curse of the whole human race.* 'He was called a curse for my sake who does away my curse' (*Gregory Nazianzene*). So 2 Cor. v. 21, "*sin* for us;" not *sinful,* but bearing the whole sin of our race, regarded as *one* vast aggregate (see note). 'Anathema' means 'set apart to God's glory,' but to the person's own destruction; "curse" [*Katara*] is an execration. written (Deut. xxi. 23). Christ's bearing the *particular* curse of hanging on the cross is a sample of the *general* curse which He representatively bore. Not that the Jews hanged malefactors; but *after* having put them to death otherwise, to brand some with ignominy, they *hung* the bodies on a piece of *wood,* not on a *tree* [*xulou,* ‮עץ‬] (cf. Gen. xxii. 6), not by the neck, but by the *hands:* such malefactors were accursed (cf. Acts v. 30; x. 39). God's providence ordered it that Jesus should *hang* on the cross by His *hands* and *feet,* so as to be a "curse for us," though that death was not a Jewish mode of execution. The Jews, in contempt, call Him 'the *hanged* one' [*Tolvi*] and Christians, 'worshippers of the hanged one'; and make it their great objection that He died the accursed death (*Trypho,* in *Justin Martyr,* p. 249; 1 Pet. ii. 24). Hung between heaven and earth as though unworthy of either. **14.** Intent of 'Christ becoming a curse for us'—'that unto (*eis*) the Gentiles the blessing of Abraham (i. e. *promised to* Abraham—viz., justification by faith) might come in [*en*] Christ Jesus' (not *in the law*) (cf. *v.* 8). **that we** (Jews and Gentiles alike) **might receive the promise of the Spirit**—the promised Spirit (Joel ii. 28, 29; Luke xxiv. 49). This clause follows not that immediately preceding (for *our receiving the Spirit* is not the result of the *blessing of Abraham coming on the Gentiles*), but "Christ hath redeemed us," &c. **through** faith—not by works. Here he resumes *v.* 2.

15. I speak after the manner of men—I take an illustration from a human transaction of every-day occurrence. As faith is older than the law, so the law cannot set aside the promise. **but a man's covenant**—whose purpose it is far less im-

³ covenant, yet *if it be* confirmed, no man disannulleth, or addeth thereto.
16 Now to Abraham and his seed were the promises made. He saith not,
And to seeds, as of many; but as of one, And to thy seed, which ⁸ is
17 Christ. And this I say, *that* the covenant, that was confirmed before of
God in Christ, the law, ᵗ which was four hundred and thirty years after,
18 cannot disannul, ᵘ that it should make the promise of none effect. For
if ᵛ the inheritance *be* of the law, *it* ʷ *is* no more of promise: but God
gave *it* to Abraham by promise.

A. D 58.

³ Or, testament.
ˢ 1 Cor. 12.12.
ᵗ Ex. 12. 40, 41.
ᵘ Rom. 4. 13, 14.
ᵛ Rom. 8. 17.
ʷ Rom. 4. 14.

portant to maintain. **if it be confirmed**—when once ratified. **no man disannulleth**—'none setteth aside,' not even the author, much less any second party. 'None' who acts in common equity, much less the righteous God. *The law* is, by personification, regarded as a second person, distinct from, and subsequent to, the *promise of God. The promise* is everlasting, and more peculiarly belongs to God. *The law* is as something extraneous, subsequent, exceptional, and temporary (*vv.* 17-19, 21-24). **addeth**—none addeth new conditions, 'making' the covenant "of none effect" (*v.* 17). So legal Judaism could make no alteration in the fundamental relation between God and man, already established by the promises to Abraham; it could not add as a new condition the observance of the law, in which case the fulfilment of the promise would be attached to a condition impossible for man to perform. The "covenant" here is one of free grace—a *promise* afterwards carried into effect in the Gospel. **16.** Parenthetical. **Now** [δέ]. 'This, however, is not a case merely of a *covenant*, but of a *promise;* yea, of *promises:* nor was it made merely to a *man* (*v.* 15), Abraham, but to Christ' (*Ellicott*). The covenant of promise was not 'spoken' [so *errhethesan,* "made"] to Abraham alone, but "to Abraham and his seed;" to the latter especially—namely, Christ (and that which is inseparable from Him, the *literal Israel,* and *the spiritual,* His body, the Church). Christ not having come when the law was given, the covenant could not have been then fulfilled, but awaited the coming of Him—*the Seed, to whom it was spoken.* **promises**—plural, because the same promise was often repeated (Gen. xii. 3, 7; xiii. 15; xv. 5, 18; xvii. 7; xxii. 18), and because it involved both earthly blessings to Abraham's literal children in Canaan, and spiritual and heavenly blessings to his spiritual children; both promised in Christ, 'the Seed' and representative Head of both Israels. [*Zerang sperma is collective:* Abraham's *seed* is 'his posterity (literal and spiritual) viewed as *one organically connected whole*' (*Ellicott*), of whom Christ is the representative Head (cf. Hos. xi. 1 with Matt. ii. 15).] In the spiritual seed there is no distinction of Jew or Greek; but to the literal seed the promises still remain to be fulfilled (Rom. xi. 26). The covenant was not made with "many" seeds (which if there had been, a pretext might exist for supposing there was one seed *before* another *under* the law, and that those sprung from one seed, say the Jewish, are admitted on different terms, with a higher degree of acceptability, than those sprung from the Gentile seed), but with the one seed; therefore, the promise that in Him "all families of the earth shall be blessed" (Gen. xii. 3) joins in this one Seed, Christ, Jew and Gentile, as fellow-heirs on the same terms—viz., by grace through faith; not to some by promise, to others by the law, but to all alike, circumcised and uncircumcised, constituting but one seed in Christ (Rom. iv. 13, 16). But the law contemplates the Jews and Gentiles as distinct seeds. God makes a

covenant, but one of promise; whereas the law is a covenant of works. The law brings in a mediator, a third party (*vv.* 19, 20); God makes His covenant of promise with the *one* Seed, Christ (Gen. xvii. 7), and embraces others only as identified with, and represented by, Christ. The Hebrew noun is collective, and not used in the plural. However many be Abraham's literal and spiritual descendants, they are all included and gathered in the one Christ. **as of . . . as of**—*as speaking of.* **one . . . Christ**—not merely the *individual* man Christ *Jesus,* but "Christ" (without 'Jesus'), including *His people,* who are *part of Himself,* the second Adam, and Head of redeemed humanity. *Vv.* 28, 29 prove this, "Ye are all ONE in Christ Jesus (Jesus is added where *the person* is indicated). And *if* ye be Christ's, then are ye Abraham's SEED, and heirs according to *the promise.*" **17.** **And** (*De*)—'However.' **this I say**—'this is what I mean' by my illustration from 'man's covenants' [λέγω is here *resumed* from *v.* 15]. **confirmed before of God**—'ratified by God' (*v.* 15). **in Christ**—rather, 'unto Christ' (cf. *v.* 16) [*eis Christon*]. So Δ G *f g,* Vulgate. But אA B C omit the words. **the law, which was** [*Gegonōs*]—'which came into existence 430 years after.' In Gen. xv. 13; Acts vii. 6, the round number 400 is given. He does not, as in the case of "the covenant," add 'confirmed *by God*' (John i. 17). The dispensation of "*the promise*" began with the call of Abraham from Ur into Canaan, and ended on the last night of his grandson Jacob's sojourn in Canaan, the *land of promise.* The law dispensation, which 'engenders bondage,' was drawing on from the time of his entrance into Egypt, 'the house of bondage.' It was to Christ in him, as in his grandfather Abraham and his father Isaac, not to them as persons, the promise was spoken. On the day following the last repetition of the promise at Beersheba, Israel passed into Egypt (Gen. xlvi. 1-6). It is from the end, not the beginning, of the dispensation of promise that the 430 years between it and the law are to be counted. At Beersheba Abraham called on the everlasting God, and the well was confirmed to him and his seed as an everlasting possession. Here God appeared to Isaac. Here the blessing was promised Jacob for the last time. The 430 do not include the 215 years in Canaan, if Gen. xv. 13; Exod. xii. 40, 41; Acts vii. 6, be *literally* true. Moreover, '600,000 men' (Exod. xii. 37) imply, with women and children, a population of 2,000,000: 215 years in Egypt would be too short for the increase from 70 (Gen. xlvi. 27), when Jacob entered Egypt, to 2,000,000 at the exodus. The difficulty as to the great length of life (*Ellicott*) thus assigned to the generations between Levi and Moses is cleared up by supposing *omission of links in the genealogy,* as elsewhere in Scripture. **cannot**—Greek, 'doth not disannul.' **make the promise of none effect**—which it would be if the power of conferring the inheritance be transferred from it to the law (Rom. iv. 14). **18. the inheritance**—all the blessings inherited by Abraham's spiritual children, according to the

19 Wherefore then *serveth* the law? ª It was added because of transgressions, till the seed should come to whom the promise was made; *and it*
20 *was* ʸ ordained by angels in the hand of ²a mediator. Now a mediator is not *a mediator* of one; ª but God is one.
21 *Is* the law then against the promises of God? God forbid: for if there had been a law given which could have given life, verily righteous-

A. D. 5⁹.

ª John 15. 22.
1 Tim. 1. 9.
ʸ Acts 7. 53.
Heb. 2. 2.
Ex. 20. 19.
ª Rom. 3. 29.

promise to him and to his seed, Christ, justification and glorification (Rom. viii. 17; 1 Cor. vi. 9; ch. iv. 7). **but God, &c.**—Greek order, 'But to Abraham it was by promise that God hath gratuitously *given* [*kecharistai*] it.' The conclusion is, *Therefore the inheritance is not of, or from, the law.*

19. Wherefore then serveth the law? As it is of no avail for justification, is it either useless, or contrary to the covenant of God? **added**—to the original covenant of promise; not as a *codicil*, but to show man's need: not inconsistent with *v.* 15, "No man . . . addeth thereto;" for there the kind of *addition* meant, and therefore denied, is one that would add *new conditions* inconsistent with the grace of the covenant of promise. The law, though misunderstood by Judaizers as doing so, was really added for a different purpose—viz., 'because of [*tōn parabaseōn charin*, "for the sake of"] the transgressions of it;' *i. e.*, to bring them out into clearer view (Rom. iii. 20; iv. 15; v. 13; vii. 7-9); to make men more conscious of their *sins*, as being *transgressions of the law;* so to make them long for the promised Saviour (cf. *vv.* 23, 24). Not '*to check* transgressions,' for the law rather stimulates the corrupt heart to disobey it (Rom. vii. 13). **till the seed**—*during the period up to the time when* [*achris hou elthē*] *the* seed came. The law was a preparatory dispensation [Rom. v. 20; *pareisēlthen*, 'the law came in *parenthetically*'] intervening between the promise and its fulfilment in Christ. **come**—cf. "faith *came*," *v.* 23. **the promise** (Rom. iv. 21). **ordained** [*diatageis*]—'established.' **by** (through) **angels**—as its mediate ministers. God delegated the law to angels as something rather alien to Him and severe (Acts vii. 53; Heb. ii. 2, 3: cf. Deut. xxxiii. 2; Ps. lxviii. 17). He reserved "the promise" to Himself, dispensing it after His own goodness. **in the hand** [by the ministry; Hebrew, *beyad*] **of a mediator**—viz., Moses. Deut. v. 5, "I stood *between* the Lord and you." Hence the phrase, "By the hand of Moses." In giving the law, the "angels" represented God; Moses, as mediator, represented the people: a *double* mediation; whereas in the promise there was none. Four differences—(1.) The law only *convicted* of transgressions; the promise was of their *removal.* (2.) The law was parenthetical and temporary; the Promised Seed permanently superseded it. The law had angels (3.) and Moses (4.) as its mediators. **20.** 'Now a mediator [*in the essential idea: ho mesites:* the article is generic] cannot be of one (but must be of *two* parties whom he mediates between); but God is one' (not two: His *unity* admits not an intervening party between Him and those to be blessed: as the ONE Sovereign, His own representative, He gives the blessing *directly* by *promise* to Abraham, and, in its fulfilment, to Christ, 'the Seed,' without new conditions, and without a mediator such as the law had). He recognizes no second party (as man) dealing on independent terms with Him through a mediator. The conclusion understood is, *Therefore a mediator cannot appertain to God;* consequently, the law, with its inseparable appendage of a mediator, and two parties to be mediated between in the way of compact, cannot be the normal way of

dealing of God, who acts *singly and directly.* God would bring man into immediate communion, and not have man separated from Him by a mediator, as Israel was by Moses and the legal priesthood (Exod. xix. 12, 13, 17, 21-24; Heb. xii. 19-24). The law that interposed a mediator and conditions between man and God was an exceptional state limited to the Jews, parenthetically preparatory to the Gospel, God's normal dealing, as He dealt with Abraham—viz., *face to face directly,* by *promise* and *grace,* not conditions; *to all nations united* by faith *in the one seed* (Eph. ii. 14, 16, 18); not to one people, to the exclusion of all others from the ONE common Father. It is no objection that the Gospel, too, has a mediator (1 Tim. ii. 5); for Jesus is not a mediator separating the two parties as Moses did, but ONE in nature and office with both *God* and *man* (cf. "God in Christ," *v.* 17), representing the universal manhood (1 Cor. xv. 22, 45, 47), and bearing "all the fulness of the Godhead." Even his mediatorial office is to cease when its purpose of reconciling all things to God shall have been accomplished (1 Cor. xv. 24), and God's ONENESS (Zech. xiv. 9) as 'all in all' shall be fully manifested. Cf. John i. 17, where Moses, the severing mediator of legal conditions, and Jesus, the uniting mediator of grace, are contrasted. The promise is called 'a covenant' (*v.* 17), because settled in the eternal counsels of the triune God, and depending on conditions fulfilled by the Son of God. This covenant was carried out in the *unity* of God, *without a mediator.* It supposes only *one* party (not *two,* as the law): God is that One; Himself, in Christ, being the mediator. St. Paul's argument pre-supposes Christ's Godhead; otherwise He would be a mediator distinct from God, as was Moses, and the argument would fail. The Jews began worship by reciting the *Schemah,* opening thus,—'Jehovah our God is ONE Jehovah;' which words their Rabbis (as Jarchius) interpret as teaching not only the unity of God, but the future *universality of His kingdom* on earth (Zeph. iii. 9). St. Paul (Rom. iii. 30) infers the same truth from the ONENESS of God (cf. Eph. iv. 4-6). He, being one, unites all believers, without distinction, to Himself (*vv.* 8, 16, 28; Eph. i. 10: cf. Heb. ii. 11) in direct communion. The unity of God involves the unity of God's people, and also His dealing directly without intervention of a mediator.

21. "Is the *law* (which involves a mediator) against the promises of God (which are without a mediator, and *rest on God* alone and immediately)? God forbid." **life.** The law, as an externally prescribed rule, can never internally impart spiritual life to men naturally dead in sin, and change the disposition. If what was given were a law able to impart *life,* 'verily (in reality, not in the mere fancy of legalists) righteousness would have been of (resulting *from*) the law' (for where life is, there righteousness, its *condition,* must also be). But the law does not *pretend* to give life, and therefore not righteousness; so there is no opposition between the law and the promise. Righteousness can only come through the promise to Abraham, and through its fulfilment in the Gospel of grace. **22.** But—So far is *righteousness* from being of the law, that, &c., Rom. iii. 20, end.

22 ness should have been by the law. But the Scripture hath concluded all
under sin, that the promise by faith of Jesus Christ might be given to
23 them that believe. But before faith came, we were kept under the law,
24 shut up unto the faith which should afterwards be revealed. Wherefore
b the law was our schoolmaster *to bring us* unto Christ, that *c* we might
be justified by faith.
25 But after that faith is come, we are no longer under a schoolmaster.
26 For ye *d* are all the children of God by faith in Christ Jesus. For as
27 many of you as have been baptized into Christ have put on Christ.
28 There *e* is neither Jew nor Greek, there is neither bond nor free, there is
29 neither male nor female: for ye are all *f* one in Christ Jesus. And *g* if

A. D. 58.
b Matt 5. 17.
c Acts 13. 39.
d John 1. 1°.
John 20. 17.
Rom 8. 14-17.
Phil. 2. 15.
e Rom. 10. 12.
f John 10. 16.
John 17. 21.
g Gen. 21. 10.
Rom. 9. 7.
Heb. 11. 18.

the Scripture—which began to be written just after the promise, at the time when the law was given. The WRITTEN letter of the law was needed to PERMANENTLY convict man of disobedience to God's command. Therefore he says, "the Scripture," not the "law." Cf. *v.* 8. **concluded**—'shut up on every side' under condemnation, as in a prison. Cf. Isa. xxiv. 22. Beautifully contrasted with 'the liberty wherewith Christ makes free,' which follows (ch. iv. 7, 9, 25, 26; v. 1; Isa. lxi. 1). **all** [*Ta panta*]—'the universe of things:' the whole world, man, and all that appertains to him. **under sin** (Rom. iii. 9, 19; xi. 32). **the promise**—*the inheritance promised* (*v.* 18). **by faith of Jesus Christ**—*i. e.*, which is of faith IN Jesus Christ. In contrast to 'of the law' (*v.* 21). **might be given.** The emphasis is on "given:" a free *gift;* not something earned by the works of the law (Rom. vi. 23). **to them that believe**—to them that have the "faith of (in) Jesus Christ." 23. **faith** [*tēn*]—viz., that just mentioned (*v.* 22). **kept** [*ephrouroumetha*]—'kept in ward:' the effect of the 'shutting up' (*v.* 22; ch. iv. 2; Rom. vii. 6; Zech. ix. 12). **under the law**—as a gaoler. **unto**—with a view to the faith, &c. We were constrained to it, so that there remained to us no refuge but faith. Cf. LXX.; Ps. lxxvii.; lxxviii. 50; xxxi. 8. **which should afterwards, &c.**—'afterwards to be revealed.' 24. '*So that* the law hath *proved to be* [*Gegonen*] our schoolmaster ('tutor,' 'pedagogue;' among the Greeks, a faithful servant intrusted with a boy from childhood to puberty, to keep him, *with severe disciplinary strictness*, from evil, physical and moral, in his amusements and studies) to guide us unto Christ,' with whom we are no longer "shut up" in bondage, but are freemen. "Children" (lit., *infants*) need such *tutoring* (ch. iv. 3). The law did so by warnings, threatenings, and convictings of sin. **might be** [*dikaiothomen*]— 'that we *may* be justified by faith;' which we could not be by the law. Meanwhile the law—by outwardly checking the sinful propensity, ever afresh breaking out, and so awakening consciousness of the power of the sinful principle, and hence of the need both of forgiveness of sin and of freedom from its bondage—became our 'schoolmaster to guide us unto Christ.' The *moral* law shows us what we ought to do; so we learn our inability. In the *ceremonial* law we seek, by sacrifices, to answer for our not having done it, but find that dead victims are no satisfaction for the sins of living men, and that outward purifying will not cleanse the soul; that therefore we need an infinitely better sacrifice, the antitype of all the legal sacrifices. Thus delivered up to the *judicial* law, we see the awful doom we deserve: thus the law leads to Christ, with whom we find righteousness and peace. '*Sin, sin!* is the word again and again in the Old Testament. Had it not there for centuries rung in the ear, and fastened on the conscience, the joyful sound, "grace

for grace," would not have been the watchword of the New Testament. This was the end of the whole system of sacrifices' (*Tholuck*.) 25. 'But *now that* faith (which makes the man full-grown) is come,' &c. Moses the lawgiver cannot bring us into the heavenly Canaan, though he can bring us to the border. At that point he is superseded by the true Joshua, who leads the spiritual Israel into their inheritance. The law leads us to Christ; there its office ceases. 26. **children**—no longer *children* in years [*paides*], but [*huioi*], 'sons,' and that, too, not merely sons of Abraham, but *of God*. Fully developed sons. **by faith in Christ** [*Dia tēs pisteōs*]—'through the faith in Christ.' 'Ye all' (Jews and Gentiles alike) are no longer *children* requiring a *tutor*, but SONS walking at liberty. 27. **baptized into** (*into living incorporation with*) **Christ** (Rom. vi. 3; Matt. xxviii. 19: Greek, 'INTO the name'). **have put on Christ**—ye *did, in that act* of being baptized into Christ, clothe yourselves in Christ [*enedusasthe*]. Christ is to you the *toga virilis* (the Roman garment of the full-grown man, assumed when ceasing to be a child) (*Bengel*). By baptism ye have put on Christ; therefore, He being the Son of God, ye become sons by adoption, by virtue of His Sonship by generation. God regards us in Him, as bearing Christ's name and character, rather than our own. Baptism, *where it answers to its ideal*, is not an empty sign, but a means of spiritual transference from legal condemnation to living union with Christ, and sonship to God through Him (Rom. xiii. 14). Christ alone can, by baptizing with His Spirit, make the inward grace correspond to the outward sign. As He promises the blessing in the faithful use of the means, the Church rightly presumes, in charity, that such is the case, nothing appearing to the contrary. 28. There is in [*eni*] this sonship by faith in Christ no class privileged above another, as the Jews under the law were above the Gentiles (Rom. x. 12; 1 Cor. xii. 13; Col. iii. 11). **bond nor free**—Christ belongs by faith to the "bond" as much as to the "free." Notes, 1 Cor. vii. 21, 22; Eph. vi. 8. **neither male nor female**—Greek, 'there is *not* male AND female.' Alterable social distinctions are contrasted by "neither . . . nor:" the unalterable human one of sex, by "and" (Mark x. 6). Male and female form a unity, the one supplementing the other. There is no distinction, spiritually, into male and female. Difference of sex makes no difference in Christian privileges. But under the law the male had great privileges. Males alone had in their body circumcision, the sign of the covenant, (whereas *baptism* applies to male and female alike); they alone were capable of being kings and priests, whereas all of either sex are now "kings and priests unto God" (Rev. i. 6); they had prior right to inheritances. In the resurrection the relation of the sexes shall cease (Luke xx. 35). **one** [*heis*]—'one man:' masculine,

ye *be* Christ's, then are ye Abraham's seed, and *ʰ* heirs according to the promise.

4 NOW I say, *That* the heir, as long as he is a child, differeth nothing
2 from a servant, though he be lord of all; but is under tutors and gover-
3 nors until the time appointed of the father. Even so we, when we were
4 children, were *ᵃ*in bondage under the ¹elements of the world: but *ᵇ*when
the fulness of the time was come, God sent forth his Son, made *ᶜ* of a
5 woman, *ᵈ*made under the law, to *ᵉ*redeem them that were under the law,
6 *ᶠ*that we might receive the adoption of sons. And because ye are sons,

A. D. 58.

ʰ Rom 8. 17.

CHAP. 4.
ᵃ Col. 2. 8.
¹ Or. rudi-
ments.
ᵇ Gen. 40. 10.
ᶜ Gen. 3. 15.
ᵈ Matt. 5. 17.
ᵉ Matt. 20.28.
ᶠ John 1. 12.

not neuter; "one new man" in Christ (Eph. ii.
15). **29. and heirs.** So G. But A B C Δ א *f*, Vulgate, omit "and." Christ is "Abraham's seed:"
ye are "one in Christ" (*v.* 28), and one with
Christ, as having "put on Christ" (*v.* 27); therefore ʏᴇ [*humeis:* emphatic] are "Abraham's seed,"
—tantamount to saying (whence the "and" is
omitted), ye are "heirs according to (in the way
of) the *promise*" (not 'by the *law*,' *v.* 18); for it
was to Abraham's seed that the inheritance was
promised (*v.* 16). Thus he arrives at the truth
which he set out with (*v.* 7). But one "seed" of
a righteous succession. One faultless grain of
human nature was found by God Himself, the
source of a new imperishable seed: "the seed"
(Ps. xxii. 30) who receive from Him a new
nature and name (Gen. iii. 15; Isa. liii. 10, 11;
John xii. 24). In Him David's line becomes
extinct. He died without posterity. But He
lives and shall reign on David's throne. No one
has a legal claim to it but Himself, He being the
only direct representative (Ezek. xxi. 27). His
spiritual seed derive birth from the travail of His
soul, being born again of His Word, the incorruptible seed (John i. 12; Rom. ix. 8; 1 Pet. i.
23).

CHAP. IV. 1-31.—SAME SUBJECT: OUR SUB-
JECTION TO THE LAW ONLY TILL CHRIST CAME
ILLUSTRATED FROM AN HEIR'S SUBJECTION TO
HIS GUARDIAN TILL OF AGE—ST. PAUL'S GOOD-
WILL TO THE GALATIANS SHOULD LEAD THEM TO
THE SAME TO HIM AS THEY HAD FIRST SHOWN—
THEIR DESIRE TO BE UNDER THE LAW SHOWN
BY THE ALLEGORY OF ISAAC AND ISHMAEL TO
BE INCONSISTENT WITH GOSPEL LIBERTY.

1-7. Now I say—a phrase introducing a *continued*
explanatory argument (*Ellicott*). God's sending His
Son to redeem us who were under the law (*v.* 4),
and sending the Spirit of His Son into our hearts
(*v.* 6), confirms the conclusion (ch. iii. 29) that we
are "heirs according to the promise." **the heir**—
not, as in earthly inheritances, the father's death,
but our Father's sovereign will, makes us heirs.
child [*nepios*]—'one under age.' **differeth nothing, &c.**—*i. e.*, has no more freedom than a slave
[*doulou*] not at his own disposal; nay, he is subject to a slave (*v.* 2; ch. iii. 24). **lord of all**—by
title and birthright (cf. 1 Cor. iii. 21, 22). 2.
tutors and governors [*epitropous-oikonomous*]—
rather, '*guardians* (of the person) and *stewards*'
(of the property). So "the law was our schoolmaster" ("tutor," ch. iii. 24). Eliezer (Gen. xv.
2; xxiv. 2). **until the time appointed of the
father**—in His eternal purposes (Eph. i. 9-11).
[*Prothesmia* is a legal term: *a time defined* by law,
or *testamentary disposition*—the term limited for
bringing actions.] 3. **we**—the Jews primarily; in-
clusively the Gentiles also. For the "we" in *v.* 5
plainly refers to *both*. The Jews in their bondage
to Moses' law represented all mankind amenable
to God's universal law of holiness (Rom. ii. 14, 15:
cf. ch. iii. 13, 23, notes). Even the Gentiles were
under "bondage," and in a discipline suitable to
nonage, till Christ came as the Emancipator.

bondage—as 'servants' (*v.* 1). **under the elements** [*stoicheia*] **of the world**—rudimentary
teachings of a non-Christian character: *the elementary lessons of outward things,* such as legal ordinances (*v.* 10; Col. ii. 8, 20; Heb. v. 12). 4. **the
fulness of the time**—viz., 'appointed by the
Father' (*v.* 2). The end of all preparation, the
beginning of all fulfilment, the maturity of man's
spiritual need (note, Eph. i. 10; Acts ii. 1; Ezek.
v. 2). 'The idea is that of a temporal space filled
up by the flowing in of time' (*Ellicott*). 'The
Church has its own ages' (*Bengel*). God does
nothing prematurely, but, foreseeing the end from
the beginning, waits till all is ripe for executing
His purpose. Had Christ come directly after the
fall, the enormity of sin would not have been
realized fully by man, so as to feel his desperate
need of a Saviour. Sin and its deadly fruits were
fully developed. Man's inability to save himself
by the law, whether that of Moses or that of
conscience, was manifested; all the prophecies of
various ages found their common centre in *this*
time; Providence, by various arrangements in the
social, political, and moral world, had fully prepared the way for the Redeemer. God often
permits physical evil long before He teaches the
remedy. The small-pox had long raged before
inoculation and vaccination were discovered.
The honour of God's law required evil to be matured before He revealed the remedy. (Cf. "the
set time," Ps. cii. 13.) **was come** [*elthen*]—'came.'
sent forth [*exapesteilen*]—'*sent forth out of* heaven
from Himself.' The same verb is used of the
Father's sending forth the Spirit (*v.* 6). (Cf. John
viii. 42; Isa. xlviii. 16.) **his** [*ton huion autou*]—
'*His own* Son.' Not *by adoption,* as we are (*v.* 5);
nor merely by the anointing of the Spirit (*v.* 6;
John i. 18). **made of a woman** [*genomenon*]—
'made to be (*born*) of [*ek, from*] a woman,' implying *His true manhood* (cf. 1 Cor. xv. 45). The expression implies God's special interposition in His
birth as man—viz., causing Him to be conceived
by the Holy Ghost. **made under the law**—'made
to be born under the law.' Not merely (as *Alford*)
'born subject to the Law *as a Jew;*' but "made,"
by His Father's appointment and His own free-
will, 'subject to' it, to keep it all, ceremonial and
moral, perfectly for us, as the Representative
Man, and to suffer and exhaust the full penalty
of our whole race's violation of it. Not only very
man, but a true Israelite. This constitutes the
significance of His circumcision, His presentation
in the temple (Luke ii. 21, 22, 27: cf. Matt. v. 17),
and His baptism by John (Matt. iii. 15, "Thus it
becometh us to *fulfil all righteousness*"). 5. **to**—
Greek, '*That He might* redeem' from the law's
bondage as well as *curse.* **them that were under
the law**—primarily the Jews; but as these were
the representative people of the world, *the Gentiles* too (ch. iii. 13). **receive** [*apolabomen*]—implies the *suitableness* of the thing. 'Receive as
something *due*' (as predestined, or laid up for
us by God) (Luke xvi. 25; xxiii. 41; Col. iii. 24;
2 John 8). **adoption** (Rom. viii. 15, 23; ix. 4;

7   God hath sent forth the Spirit of his Son into your hearts, crying, Abba, Father. Wherefore thou art no more a servant, but a son; [g]and if a son, then an heir of God through Christ.

8   Howbeit then, [h]when ye knew not God, ye [i]did service unto them
9   which by nature are no gods. But now, [j]after that ye have known God, or rather are known of God, [k]how turn ye [2]again to the weak and
10   beggarly [3]elements, whereunto ye desire again to be in bondage? Ye

A. D. 58.

[g] Rom. 8. 16.
[h] Eph 2. 12.
[i] Rom. 1 25.
[j] 1 Cor. 8. 3.
[k] ch 3. 3.
[2] Or. back.
[3] Or. rudi-
ments.

Eph. i. 5). There are three stages: (1.) Existing, but not appropriated; (2.) Appropriated through faith in Christ; (3.) Perfected in glory (*Neander*). God makes of sons of men sons of God, as God made of the Son of God the Son of man, (*St. Augustine* on Psalm lii.) **6. because ye are sons, &c.** The spirit of prayer is the fruit of adoption. The Gentile Galatians thought, as the Jews were under the law before their adoption, so they too must first be under the law. St. Paul, by anticipation, meets this objection. *As a proof* 'THAT (*hoti*) ye ARE' really (*Ellicott*) in the free state of SONS of God by faith in Christ (ch. iii. 26); therefore ye need not to be, as children in nonage (*v.* 1), under the tutorship of the law. The Spirit of God's only-begotten Son (which is the Spirit of God: John xiv. 16; Rom. viii. 9), sent from, and leading us to cry to, the Father, attests our sonship by adoption; for the Spirit is the "earnest of our inheritance" (Rom. viii. 15, 16; Eph. i. 14). 'God sent forth (Greek aorist) into OUR (so A א C Δ G *f g*, Vulgate, read; B reads "your") hearts,' &c. (John i. 12; 1 Cor. vi. 19.) As in *v.* 5, he changed from "them," the third person, to "we," the first; so here he changes from "ye," the second person, to 'our,' the first. Thus he identifies their status as Gentiles with that of himself and his believing fellow-countrymen as Jews. Rather (in the usual sense of *hoti*) cf. *Neander's* note on *v.* 5, 'BECAUSE ye *are* sons (already in God's electing love), God sent forth the Spirit of His Son,' &c., manifesting that sonship which He regarded as a *present reality* ("are") because of His *purpose*, even before it was actually fulfilled. So Heb. ii. 13, where "the children" are spoken of as existing in His purpose before their actual existence. **the Spirit of his Son.** By faith ye are one with His Son, so that what is His is yours: His Sonship insures yours; His Spirit insures for you a share in the same. Moreover, as the Spirit of God proceeds from the Father, so the Spirit of the Son proceeds from the Son; so that the Holy Ghost (Nicene Creed) 'proceedeth from the Father and the Son.' The Father was not *begotten*: the Son is *begotten* of the Father: the Holy Ghost *proceedeth* from the Father and the Son. **crying.** The SPIRIT is regarded as the *agent* in praying, the believer as *His organ*. In Rom. viii. 15 "the Spirit of adoption" is said to be that whereby we cry "Abba, Father;" but in Rom. viii. 26 "the SPIRIT ITSELF maketh intercession for us with groanings which cannot be uttered." The believer's prayer is His prayer: hence arises his acceptability with God. **Abba, Father**—the Hebrew says "Abba;" the Greek, "Father" ('*Pater*'): both united in one Sonship and one cry of faith, "Abba, Father." So, 'Even so' ['*Nai*,' Greek, Amen] (Hebrew), both meaning the same (Rev. i. 7). Christ's own cry is the believers' cry. The formula was used in reverent memory of Him who taught us to call God "our Father" (Mark xiv. 36). **7. Wherefore**—conclusion from *vv.* 4-6. **thou**—such an *individual appropriation* of this comforting truth God grants in answer to each who cries "Abba, Father," **heir of God through Christ.** So C Δ *f*.

387

But א A B G, Vulgate, read 'an heir through God.' This combines on man's behalf the whole before-mentioned agency of THE TRINITY: the Father sent His Son and the Spirit; the Son freed us from the law; the Spirit completes our sonship. Thus the redeemed are heirs THROUGH the Triune GOD, not through the law or fleshly descent (*Windischmann* in *Alford*) (ch. iii. 18 confirms this). **heir**—confirming ch. iii. 29 (cf. Rom. viii. 17). Among the Hebrews, '*sons*' by *free women* were heirs (the first-born having double); but not by bond women and Gentiles (Judg. xi. 2). Among the Romans, *male or female* children (ch. iii. 28), natural or *adopted*.

8-11. Howbeit—contrast of their former with their present state. Appeal not to turn back from their privileges as free sons to legal bondage again. **then**—when ye were heathens before your adoption (*v.* 7). **ye knew not God**—not opposed to Rom. i. 21. The heathen *originally knew* God, but *did not choose to retain God in their knowledge*, and so corrupted the original truth. They *might* still *have* known Him, in a measure, from His works; but as a fact they knew him not, so far as His eternity, power as Creator, and holiness, are concerned. **ye did service** [*edouleusate*]—'were *enslaved* to.' **are no gods**—*i. e.*, have no existence in the nature of things, but only in the corrupt imaginations of their worshippers (notes, 1 Cor. viii. 4; x. 19, 20; 2 Chr. xiii. 9). Your "service" was different from that of the Jews, which was a true service. Yet theirs, like yours, was a burdensome yoke; how can ye wish to resume the yoke after that God has transferred you both to a free service? **9. known God, or rather are known of God.** *They* did not first know and love God; but *God* first, in His electing love, knew them, and therefore attracted them to know Him savingly (Matt. vii. 23; 1 Cor. viii. 3; 2 Tim. ii. 19: cf. Exod. xxxiii. 12, 17; John xv. 16; Phil. iii. 12). God's great grace made their fall from it the more heinous. [*Eidotes* (*v.* 8), *gnontes*, and *gnosthentes*: a climax; 'outwardly knew;' 'inwardly having known;' 'having been known by God' in love (2 Cor. v. 6, Greek) (*Olshausen*).] **how**—indignant wonder at such a thing being possible, and even actually occurring (ch. i. 6). **weak**—powerless to *justify*; in contrast to the justifying power of faith (ch. iii. 24: cf. Heb. vii. 18). **beggarly**—contrasted with the *riches* of the believer's inheritance in Christ (Eph. i. 18). The "child" (*v.* 1) is weak, not having attained manhood; "beggarly," not having attained the inheritance. **elements**—'rudiments.' As if a schoolmaster should wish to go back to learn the A B C (*Bengel*). **again . . . again**—two Greek words. "Ye desire again [*beginning afresh: palin, anōthen*] to be in bondage." *Relapsing* to bondage, to *begin anew* its rudiments in the form of Judaism, instead of your former heathenism. The Galatians had never been under the Mosaic yoke; yet they had been under "the elements of the world" (*v.* 3)—the common designation for Jewish and Gentile systems, in contrast to the Gospel (however superior the Jewish was to the Gentile). Both consisted in outward, sensuous worship. Both were in bondage to *the elements*

11 ⁱ observe days, and months, and times, and years. I am afraid of you, lest I have bestowed upon you labour in vain.

12 Brethren, I beseech you, be as ^m I *am;* for I *am* as ye *are:* ye have
13 not injured me at all. Ye know how ⁿ through infirmity of the flesh I
14 preached the Gospel unto you ^o at the first. And my temptation which was in my flesh ye despised not, nor rejected; but received me ^p as an
15 angel of God, *even* ^q as Christ Jesus. ⁴ Where is then the blessedness ye spake of? for I bear you record, that, if *it had been* possible, ye would
16 have plucked out your own eyes, and have given them to me. Am I therefore become your enemy, because I tell you the truth?
17 They ^r zealously affect you, *but* not well; yea, they would exclude

A. D. 58.

i Rom. 14. 5.
Col. 2. 16.
m ch 6. 14.
n 1 Cor. 2. 3.
o ch. 1. 6.
p 2 Sam. 19. 27.
Zech. 12. 8.
q Matt. 10.40.
4 Or, What was then?
r Rom 10. 2.
1 Cor. 11. 2.

of sense, as though these could give justification and sanctification, which the inner spiritual power of God alone could bestow. **ye desire** [*thelete*]—'will.' *Will-worship* is not acceptable to God (Col. ii. 18, 23). **10. Ye observe** [*paratereisthe*]—'Ye *sedulously* observe.' To regard the observance of certain days meritorious as a work is alien to the free spirit of Christianity: not incompatible with observing the Sabbath of the Christian Lord's day as obligatory, though *not as a work* (the Jewish and Gentile error in their observance of days), but as a holy mean appointed by the Lord to the great end, holiness. The whole life alike belongs to the Lord—belongs in the Gospel view—just as the whole world, not the Jews only, belong to Him. But as in paradise, so now one portion of time is needed wherein to draw off the soul more entirely from secular business to God (Col. ii. 16). "Sabbaths, new moons, and set feasts" (1 Chr. xxiii. 31; 2 Chr. xxxi. 3) answer to "days, months, times." "Months," however, may refer to the *first* and *seventh* months, sacred because of the number of feasts. **times** [*kairous*]—'seasons;' viz., the three great feasts, passover, pentecost, and tabernacles. **years**—the Sabbatical year of jubilee was about the time of writing this epistle, A.D. 48 (*Bengel*). **11. lest** [*μήπως*]—'lest, *haply*.' **I have bestowed upon you labour** [*kekopiaka*: indicative]—implying he believed his labour *was actually* vain. My fear is not for my sake, but for yours.

12. be [*become: ginesthe*] **as I am**—'as I, though a zealous Jew by birth (ch. i. 14), in my life among you cast on Jewish habits, so do ye ; for I am become as ye are'—viz., in not observing legal ordinances. 'My laying them aside among Gentiles shows that I regard them as *not at all contributing to justification or sanctification.* Do you regard them in the same light, and act accordingly.' His observing the law among the Jews was not inconsistent with this, for he did so to win them, without compromising principle (1 Cor. ix. 20, 21). But the Galatian Gentiles, by adopting legal ordinances, showed they regarded them as needful for salvation. **ye have not injured me at all**—viz., when I first preached among you, and made myself as you are; viz., living as a Gentile, not as a Jew. *You at that time did me no wrong;* 'ye did not despise my temptation in the flesh' (*v.* 14); nay, you "received me as an angel of God." Then, in *v.* 16, he asks, 'Have I since then become your enemy by telling you the truth?' **13. how through infirmity**—rather [*di' astheneian*], 'yea [δέ], ye know that *because* of an infirmity of *my* flesh I preached,' &c. Some bodily sickness having detained him among them, contrary to his original intention, was the occasion of his preaching the Gospel to them. **at the first** [*to proteron*]—'at the *former* time;' implying that at the time of writing he had been *twice* in Galatia. See 'Introduction;' also *vv.* 15, 16, and ch. v. 21, notes. His sickness was probably the same as the "thorn *in the flesh*"

afterwards, which also was overruled to good (2 Cor. xii. 7, 9, 10), as the "infirmity *of the flesh*" here. **14. my temptation.** א A B Δ G *f g,* Vulgate, read 'your temptation.' My infirmity, which might have been a "temptation" *to you,* ye despised not—*i. e.,* ye were not tempted by it to despise me and my message. *Lachmann,* not so well, connects it with *v.* 13, 'And (ye know) your temptation (*i. e.,* the temptation to which ye were exposed through the infirmity) which was in my flesh. Ye despised not (through *natural* pride), nor rejected (through *spiritual* pride) [*spurned with loathing: exeptusate*], but received me,' &c. "Temptation" may mean 'BODILY TRIALS:' ye, regarding MY trial as your trial, despised it not. **as an angel of God**—as a heaven-sent *messenger* from God: *angel* means messenger (Mal. ii. 7). Cf. the phrase, 2 Sam. xix. 27, a Hebrew one for a person to be received with the highest respect (Zech. xii. 8). An angel is free from the *flesh, infirmity,* and *temptation.* **as Christ**—being representative (Matt. x. 40; 2 Cor. v. 20) of Christ, the Lord of angels. **15. Where, &c.**—*Where* now is to be found your former *felicitation* [*tis—ho makarismos*] of yourselves, on your having among you the *blessing* of my ministry, considering how entirely you have veered about since? [א A B C G *g,* Vulgate, read *pou,* where; Δ, *tis, 'of what value?'*] **ye would have plucked out your own eyes**—the dearest member of the body; so highly did you value me: proverbial for the greatest self-sacrifice (Matt. v. 29). *Conybeare* thinks this particular proverb has reference to a weakness in Paul's *eyes,* connected with a nervous frame, affected by the bright vision (Acts xxii. 11; 2 Cor. xii. 1-7). 'You would have torn out your own eyes to supply the lack of mine.' But there is no 'own' in the Greek. The divine power of Paul's words and works contrasting with his personal feebleness (2 Cor. x. 10), powerfully at first impressed the Galatians, who had all the impulsiveness of the Keltic race. Subsequently they soon changed, with Keltic fickleness. **16.** Translate, 'So then am I become (in your eyes) your enemy *by telling* you the truth?' (ch. ii. 5, 14.) He had not been counted their enemy at his *first* visit: he implies that he had *since then, before* his now writing; so that the occasion of his *telling* them the unwelcome truth must have been at his *second* visit (Acts xviii. 23: see 'Introduction'). The Judaizers designated him 'that enemy' (*Clement,* 'Recogn.' i. 70, 71). The fool and sinner hate, the righteous love, faithful reproof (Ps. cxli. 5; Prov. ix. 8).

17. They—your flatterers: in contrast to Paul, who *tells* them *the truth.* **zealously**—zeal in proselytism characterized Jews and Judaizers (ch. i. 14; Matt. xxiii. 15; Rom. x. 2). **affect you**—*i. e.,* court you (2 Cor. xi. 2). **not well** [*ou kalōs*]—*not in a good way* or for a good end. Neither the *cause* nor the *manner* is what it ought to be. **they would exclude you**—'they wish to shut you

18 [5] you, that ye might affect them. But *it is* good to be zealously affected

19 always in *a good thing*, and not only when I am present with you. My

[*] little children, of whom I travail in birth again until Christ be formed

20 in you, I desire to be present with you now, and to change my voice; for [6] I stand in doubt of you.

21 Tell me, ye that desire to be under the law, do ye not hear the law?

22 For it is written, that Abraham had two sons; [t] the one by a bond maid,

23 [u] the other by a free woman. But he *who was* of the bond woman was [v] born after the flesh; but he of the free woman *was* by promise.

24 Which things are an allegory: for these are the two [7] covenants; the one from the mount [8] Sinai, which gendereth to bondage, which is Agar.

25 For this Agar is mount Sinai in Arabia, and [9] answereth to Jerusalem

A. D. 58.

[5] Or, us.
[*] 1 Cor. 4. 15.
[6] Or, I am perplexed for you.
[t] Gen. 16. 15.
[u] Gen. 21. 2.
[v] Rom. 9. 7, 8.
[7] Or, testaments.
[8] Sina.
[9] Or, is in the same rank with.

out' *from me* (and so from the true Gospel Church, by imposing on you legalism), 'that ye *may zealously court themselves,*' instead of me. **18. good** [*kalon*] **to be zealously affected**—rather, *passive,* to correspond to 'zealously court' (*v.* 17), 'to be zealously courted.' I find no fault with them for zealously courting you, nor with you for *allowing yourselves to be zealously courted;* provided it be 'in a good cause' [*en kalo*] (1 Cor. ix. 20-23). My reason for saying the "not well" (*v.* 17: the same Greek as "good," and 'in a good cause,' *v.* 18), is, that their *zealous courting of you* is not in a good cause. The old interpreters support the English version (cf. ch. i. 14). *Winer,* 'to be reciprocally zealous:' *Bengel,* The *Middle Voice,* 'to kindle zeal by zeal, *you responding to the zeal of your minister.*' **always.** Translate and arrange, '*at all times,* and not only when I am present with you.' I do not desire to have the exclusive privilege of zealously courting you. Others may do so in my absence, if only it be in a good cause (Phil. i. 15-18). **19. My little children** (1 Tim. i. 18; 2 Tim. ii. 1; 1 John ii. 1). My relation to you is not merely that of one *zealously courting* you (*vv.* 17, 18), but that of a *father* to his *children* (1 Cor. iv. 15). **I travail in birth**—*i. e.,* like a mother in pain till her child is born. **again**—a second time. A long-continued travail. The former time was when I was "present with you" (*v.* 18; note, *v.* 13). **Christ be formed in you**—that you may live only Christ, think only Christ (ch. ii. 20; Eph. iii. 17), and glory only in Him. His death, resurrection, and righteousness (Phil. iii. 8-10; Col. i. 27). **20.** [ἤθελον δέ, without ἄν] 'I could indeed wish.' *If circumstances permitted,* I would gladly be with you. **now**—as I was twice already. Speaking face to face is so much more effective towards loving persuasion than writing (2 John 12; 3 John 13). **change my voice**—as a mother (*v.* 19); laying aside the severity heretofore in this epistle: adapting my tone to what I saw in person your case might need. **I stand in doubt of you** [*aporoumai en humin*]—'I am perplexed about you' (lit., *in your case*), viz., how to deal with you, gently or severely, to bring you back to the right path.

21. desire—of your own accord madly courting that which must condemn you. **do ye not hear**—do ye not consider the inner sense of Moses' words? The law itself sends you away from it to Christ. Do ye not *heed* it? Having sufficiently maintained his point by argument, the apostle illustrates it by an allegorical exposition of historical facts. He confutes the Judaizers with their own weapons. But their allegorical interpretations in the synagogues were unauthorized by the Spirit. (Cf. the Jerusalem Talmud, *Succa, cap. Hechalil.*) His allegorical exposition is not the work of fancy, but sanctioned by the Holy Spirit. History, rightly understood, contains in its complicated phenomena

continually-recurring divine laws. The history of the elect people, like their legal ordinances, had, besides the literal, a typical meaning (cf. 1 Cor. x. 1-4; xv. 45, 47; Rev. xi. 8). Just as the extra-ordinarily-born Isaac, the gift of grace according to promise, supplanted, beyond all human calculations, the naturally-born Ishmael, so the new theocratic race, the spiritual seed of Abraham by promise, Gentile as well as Jewish believers, take the place of the natural seed, who imagined that to them exclusively belonged the kingdom of God. **22.** (Gen. xvi. 3-16; xxi. 2.) **Abraham**—whose sons ye wish to be (cf. Rom. ix. 7-9). **a bond maid, the other by a free woman**—Greek, '*the* well-known bond maid . . . *the* free woman.' **23. But.** The two sons, though sprung from a common father, Abraham, were, *notwithstanding,* very different. **after the flesh** (implying *weakness*)—born in the usual course of nature; in contrast to Isaac, born 'by virtue of *the* promise' (Greek), as the efficient cause of Sarah's supernatural pregnancy (Rom. iv. 19). Abraham was to lay aside all confidence in *the flesh* (after which Ishmael was born), and to live by faith alone in *the promise* (according to which Isaac was miraculously born, contrary to all fleshly calculations). **24. Which things** [*hatina*]—*the which* things; all which things; all the circumstances of the history. **are an allegory**—'are allegorical;' *i. e.,* have *another besides the literal* meaning. **these are the two covenants**—'these (women) are (i. e., *mean.* Omit "the," with A B C Δ G. But א has it) two covenants.' As the bondage of the mother determined that of the child, the children of the free covenant of promise, answering to Sarah, are free; the children of the legal covenant of bondage (Hagar) are not so. **one from**—i. e., *taking its* origin *from* mount Sinai. Therefore he is treating of the moral law (ch. iii. 19) chiefly (Heb. xii. 18). Paul was familiar with Sinai in Arabia (ch. i. 17), having gone to that region after his conversion. At the gloomy scene of the giving of the law he learned to appreciate, by contrast, the grace of the Gospel, and so to cast off all past legal dependencies. **which gendereth**—i. e., *bringeth forth children* (doomed) unto bondage, inasmuch as she was a slave herself (cf. Acts iii. 25). **25.** Translate, 'For this *word* [τό], Hagar, is (imports) mount Sinai in Arabia' (*i. e.,* among the Arabians—*in the Arabian tongue*). *Haurat,* the traveller, says that to this day the Arabians call Sinai, 'Hadschar'—i. e., *Hagar,* '*stone.*' Usually called *Dschebel Musa.* Hagar twice fled into Arabia (Gen. xvi. and xxi.): from her the mountain and city took its name, and the people were called Hagarenes. So A B Δ *f.* But א C G read *to gar Sina.* '*for Sinai* is in Arabia' (the home of Hagar's children), instead of *Agar Sina.* Then "the one" (covenant) is nominative to "answereth to." Sinai, with its rugged rocks, far removed from the promised land, well repre-

26 which now is, and is in bondage with her children. But ᵂJerusalem
27 which is above is free, which is the mother of us all. For it is written,
   ˣRejoice, *thou* barren that bearest not; break forth and cry, thou that
   travailest not: for the desolate hath many more children than she which
28 hath an husband. Now we, brethren, as Isaac was, are the ʸchildren of
29 promise. But as then ᶻhe that was born after the flesh persecuted him
30 *that was born* after the Spirit, even so *it is* now. Nevertheless what
   saith ᵃthe Scripture? Cast out the bond woman and her son: for ᵇthe
   son of the bond woman shall not be heir with the son of the free woman.
31 So then, brethren, we are not children of the bond woman, but of the
   free.

5 STAND fast therefore in ᵃthe liberty wherewith Christ hath made us
   free, and be not entangled again with ᵇthe yoke of bondage.

A. D. 58.

ᵂ Isa 2. 2.
Mic. 4. 1, 2.
Heb. 12. 22.
Rev. 3. 12.
Rev. 21. 2.
ˣ Isa. 54. 1.
ʸ Rom. 4. 16.
ᶻ Gen. 21. 9.
ᵃ Gen. 21. 10.
Rom. 11. 7.
ch. 3. 8.
ᵇ John 8 35.

CHAP. 5.
ᵃ John 8. 32.
ᵇ Acts 15. 10.

sents the law, which inspires terror and the spirit of bondage. **and**—moreover [δέ]. **answereth** [*sustoichei*]—'stands in the same rank with,' 'corresponds to,' &c. **Jerusalem which now is**—*i. e.*, the Jerusalem of the Jews, having only a present temporary existence, in contrast with the spiritual Jerusalem of the Gospel, which in germ, under the form of the *promise*, existed ages before, and shall be for ever. **and.** A B C Δ G ℵ read '*for* she is in bondage.' As Hagar was in bondage to her mistress, so Jerusalem that now is, is in bondage to the law, also to the Romans; her civil state corresponding to her spiritual. **26.** This stands instead of the sentence which we should expect, to correspond to v. 24, 'one from mount Sinai.' But *the other covenant* answers to the heavenly Jerusalem above, which is (in the allegory) Sarah. **Jerusalem which is above** (Heb. xii. 22, "the heavenly Jerusalem ")—the centre of the spiritual kingdom, as the old Jerusalem was the centre of Judaism. See note on the distinction between *Hierousâlem* and *Hierosolyma*, Rev. iii. 12; xxi. 2. Here '*the Messianic theocracy*, which before Christ's second appearing is *the Church*, and after it, Christ's kingdom of glory' (*Meyer*). **free**—as Sarah: opposed to "is in bondage" (*v.* 25). **which is**—'in which character she [ἥτις] is.' **mother of us**—viz., *believers* already members of the invisible church hereafter to be *manifested*. **all.** Omitted in ℵ B Δ G *fg*, Vulgate. Supported by A C. **27. For**—proof that 'she is the mother of us' (Isa. liv. 1). **thou barren**—Jerusalem above: the spiritual Gospel Church, the fruit of 'the promise,' answering to *Sarah*, who bore not "after the flesh;" contrasted with the law, answering to *Hagar*, who was fruitful in the course of nature. Isaiah speaks primarily of Israel's restoration after her long calamities; but his language is framed by the Holy Spirit to reach beyond this to the spiritual Zion, including not only the Jews, the natural descendants of Abraham and children of the law, but also the *Gentiles*. The spiritual Jerusalem is regarded as "barren" whilst the law trammelled Israel; for then she had no spiritual children of the Gentiles. **break forth**—into crying. **cry**—shout for joy. **many more.** Translate, as Greek, 'Many are the children of the desolate (the New Testament Church, made up mainly of the Gentiles, *who once had not the promise*, and so without God as her husband), more (the children of both shall be *many*, but those of the desolate *more*) than of her which hath an (Greek, THE) husband' (of whom the other is destitute—viz., the Jewish Church having GOD for her *husband*, Isa. liv. 5; Jer. ii. 2). Numerous as were the children of the legal covenant, those of the Gospel are more so. **28. we.** So A C Δ ℵ, Vulgate. But B G *fg*, 'ye.' "We" better accords

with *vv.* 26, 31. **children of promise**—not children *after the flesh*, but *by virtue of* promise (ch. iii. 18; *vv.* 23, 29, 31). "We . . . *are*" so, and ought to continue so. **29. But**—*But* our being "children of promise" does not exempt us from persecution. **persecuted** [*edioken, used to persecute*]. Ishmael 'mocked' [*tzachaqu*, equivalent in Numbers to *Hagar*] Isaac, which contained the germ and spirit of persecution (Gen. xxi. 9). His mocking was probably directed against Isaac's faith in God's promises. Being the elder by natural birth, he haughtily prided himself above him that was born by promise, as Cain hated Abel's piety. **him that was born after the Spirit.** The language refers primarily to Isaac, born in a spiritual way—viz., by the Spirit-energized promise of God making Sarah, out of the course of nature, fruitful in old age (Rom. iv. 19, 20). But it is so framed as to refer also to believers justified by grace through faith, as opposed to carnal Judaizers and legalists. **even so it is now** (Acts ix. 29; xiii. 45, 49, 50; xiv. 1, 2, 19; xvii. 5, 13; xviii. 5, 6; ch. v. 11; vi. 12, 17). The Jews persecuted Paul, not for preaching Christianity against heathenism, but for preaching it as distinct from Judaism. Except in the two cases of Philippi and Ephesus (where the persons beginning the assault were pecuniarily interested in his expulsion), he was nowhere set upon by Gentiles, unless when stirred up by the Jews. The coincidence between Paul's epistles and Luke's history (the Acts) in this respect is plainly undesigned; and so a proof of genuineness (*Paley*). **30. Nevertheless**—BUT let not believers be disheartened at the prospect of persecution; for "Scripture saith," &c. Gen. xxi. 10, 12, *Sarah's* words confirmed by *God*,—"Shall not be heir with *my son, even with Isaac.*" But what was there said literally is here by inspiration applied in its allegorical import to the New Testament believer, antitypically "the son of the free woman." In John viii. 35, 36, Jesus refers to this. **Cast out**—from the house and inheritance: literally, Ishmael; spiritually, the carnal and legalists. **shall not be heir** [*ou me kleronomesei*]—'*must not (shall in no wise)* be heir.' So Jephthah, Judg. xi. 2. **31. So then** [*ara oun*, G. But ℵ B Δ, *dio*, 'Wherefore.' A C, *hemeis de*, 'But we.' *fg*, Vulgate, *itaque*]—'Wherefore:' the conclusion from what precedes. In ch. iii. 29; iv. 7, it was established that we, New Testament believers, are "heirs." 'Wherefore we are not children of the bond woman (whose son was 'not to be heir,' *v.* 30), but of the free woman' (whose son was, according to Scripture, to be heir). For we are not "cast out" as Ishmael, but accepted as sons.

CHAP. V. 1-26.—PERORATION. STAND FAST IN THE GOSPEL LIBERTY, JUST SET FORTH—BE NOT LED BY JUDAIZERS INTO CIRCUMCISION. OR LAW-

2 Behold, I Paul say unto you, that if *^c* ye be circumcised, Christ shall
3 profit you nothing. For I testify again to every man that is circumcised,
4 *^d* that he is a debtor to do the whole law. Christ *^e* is become of no effect
unto you, whosoever of you are justified by the law; ye *^f* are fallen from
5 grace. For we through the Spirit *^g* wait for the hope of righteousness by
6 faith. For *^h* in Jesus Christ neither circumcision availeth anything, nor
7 uncircumcision; but *ⁱ* faith which worketh by love. Ye *^j* did run well;

A. D. 58.
c Acts 15. 1.
d ch. 3. 10.
e Rom. 9. 31.
f Heb. 12. 15.
g Rom. 8. 24.
h Col. 3. 11.
i 1 Thes. 1. 3.
j 1 Cor. 9. 24.

JUSTIFICATION—YET, THOUGH FREE, SERVE ONE ANOTHER BY LOVE—WALK IN THE SPIRIT, BEARING ITS FRUIT, NOT IN THE WORKS OF THE FLESH.

1. א A B Δ C read no "wherewith." [G, Vulgate, have *ῆ* in the beginning; but the position of *stekete oun* below is against it]. There is no Greek for "in" or "the," as there is in 1 Cor. xvi. 13; Phil. i. 27; iv. 1. '(It is) FOR freedom (that) Christ made us free' (not *for* bondage). 'Stand fast, therefore (this is the order of "therefore" in א A B C Δ G; *stekete oun*), and be not entangled (implying the difficulty of getting free again) again (as when ye were heathen: note, ch. iv. 9) *in a* yoke of bondage' (viz., the law, ch. iv. 24; Acts xv. 10). Cf. v. 13.
2. Behold—*i. e.*, mark what I say. **I Paul.** However you disparage me, I give my personal authority as enough by itself to refute all opposition. **if ye be circumcised**—'if ye still suffer yourselves to be circumcised' (Present, *peritemnēsthe*: implying *continuance*); viz., under the notion of its being necessary to *justification* (*v.* 4; Acts xv. 1). Circumcision is not regarded simply by itself (for, viewed as a *national* rite, it was practised for conciliation's sake by Paul himself, Acts xvi. 3), but as the symbol of *Judaism* and *legalism.* If this be necessary, then the Gospel of grace is at an end. If grace be the way of justification, then Judaism is not. **Christ shall profit you nothing** (ch. ii. 21)—for righteousness of works and justification by faith cannot co-exist. 'He who is circumcised (for justification) is so as fearing the law; he who fears disbelieves the power of grace; and he who disbelieves can profit nothing by that grace which he disbelieves (*Chrysostom*). **3. For** [δέ]—'Yea, not only "Christ shall profit you nothing," BUT you will be debtors to the whole law.' **I testify again to every man**—as well as "unto you" (*v.* 2). **that is circumcised** (present participle)—*allowing himself to be circumcised.* Such a one became a 'proselyte of righteousness.' **the whole law**—impossible for man to keep in part, much less *wholly* (Jas. ii. 10); yet none can be justified by it, unless he keep it *wholly* (ch. iii. 10). **4.** [*Katērgēthēte apo*] (a word frequent in Paul's epistles: only in his companion's gospel (Luke xiii. 7) besides in the New Testament. Its presence, Heb. ii. 14, supports Paul's authorship). 'Ye became void from Christ'—*i. e.*, your connection with Christ became void (*v.* 2). Rom. vii. 2, the same Greek. **whosoever of you are justified**—'are being justified;' *i. e.*, are thinking to be justified. **by the law**—Greek, 'IN the law,' as the element *in* which justification takes place. **fallen** (Aorist, ye fell, the moment ye sought justification by legalism) **from grace**—ye no longer '*stood*' in it (Rom. v. 2). Grace and legal righteousness cannot co-exist (Rom. iv. 4, 5; xi. 6). Christ, by circumcision (Luke ii. 21), undertook to obey all the law, and fulfil all righteousness for us; any, therefore, that now seeks to fulfil it for himself in any degree for justifying righteousness, severs himself from the grace which flows from Christ's fulfilment, and becomes "a debtor to do the whole law" (*v.* 3). The decree of the Jerusalem council said nothing so strong as this: it

merely decided that Gentile Christians were not bound to legal observances. But the Galatians, whilst not pretending to be so *bound*, imagined there was an efficacy in them to merit a higher degree of *perfection* (ch. iii. 3). This accounts for St. Paul not referring to the decree. He took higher ground. The natural mind loves outward fetters, and is apt to forge them for itself, to stand in lieu of holiness of heart. **5. For**—proof of the assertion, "fallen from grace," by contrasting with the *legalists* the Christian's "hope." **through the Spirit** [*Pneumati*]—rather, 'by the Spirit' (the absence of the Greek article does not hinder taking "Spirit," THE HOLY SPIRIT: for *proper names* omit it: the Giver of faith), in opposition to *after the flesh* (ch. iv. 29), or fleshly ways of justification, as circumcision and legal ordinances. "We" is emphatically contrasted with 'whosoever of you would be justified by the law' (*v.* 4). **the hope of righteousness**—'we *assiduously* wait for the (realization of the) hope of righteousness (justification), by [*ek, from*] faith' (the spring of *hope*) (Rom. v. 1, 4, 5; viii. 24, 25), a farther step than "justified;" not only are we this, but "wait for the hope" which is its full consummation. Rom. viii. 24, 25, the same Greek as here [*Elpida apekdechometha*]. "Righteousness," in the sense *justification*, is by the believer once for all already attained; but its consummation above is the object of *hope* to be *waited for:* the "crown of righteousness" (2 Tim. iv. 8); "the hope laid up for you in heaven" (Col. i. 5; 1 Pet. i. 3). Legal justification is only in the *present* (*v.* 4), and in the legalist's *imagination.* Justification by faith is present, and also stretches in sure "hope" on to eternity. Righteousness, now the believer's hidden possession, shall then *shine out* as glory (Matt. xiii. 43; Col. iii. 3, 4). **6. For**—confirming the truth that it is '*from faith*' (*v.* 5) that the 'waiting hope' springs. **in Jesus Christ**—Greek, 'in Christ Jesus.' *In union with Christ* (the ANOINTED)—that is, *Jesus* of Nazareth: the mean of which union is *faith.* **nor uncircumcision**—levelled against those who, being not legalists or Judaizers, think themselves Christians on this ground alone. **faith which worketh** [*energoumene; energetically working*; exhibiting its energy] **by** [*dia*: through] **love.** This corresponds to "a new creature" (ch. vi. 15). Thus in *vv.* 5, 6 are the three, "faith," "hope," and "love" (1 Thess. i. 3; ii. 13). *Love* is not joined with *faith* in justifying, but is the principle of the works which follow after justification by faith. Let not legalists think that the essence of the law is set at nought in justification by faith only. Nay, "all the law is fulfilled in . . . love," the principle on which "faith worketh" (*v.* 14). [*Energeitai* in the New Testament is always used *actively: it puts forth energy from itself:* the force of the middle voice, generally applied to *things: energei* active voice, *persons.*] The Romanist translation is thus untenable, 'which *is made perfect* by love.' Let them then seek "faith" to fulfil the law. Again, let not those who pride themselves on uncircumcision think that, because the law does not justify, they are free to walk after "the flesh" (*v.* 13). Let them seek "love," inseparable from true faith

8 [1] who did hinder you that ye should not obey the truth? This per-
9 suasion *cometh* not of him that calleth you. A little leaven leaveneth
10 the whole lump. I [k] have confidence in you through the Lord, that ye
will be none otherwise minded: but [l] he that troubleth you shall
11 [m] bear his judgment, whosoever he be. And [n] I, brethren, if I yet
preach circumcision, [o] why do I yet suffer persecution? then is [p] the
12 offence of the cross ceased. I [q] would they were even cut off which
trouble you.
13 For, brethren, ye have been called unto liberty; only *use* not liberty

A. D. 58.

[1] Or. who
did drive
you back?
[k] 2 Cor. 8. 22.
[l] ch. 1. 7.
[m] 2 Cor. 10. 6.
[n] ch. 6. 12.
[o] 1 Cor. 15. 30.
[p] 1 Cor. 1. 23.
[q] 1 Cor. 5. 13.

(Jas. ii. 8, 12-22). Love is opposed to the enmities which prevailed (*vv.* 15, 20). The Spirit (*v.* 5) is a Spirit of "faith" and "love" (cf. Rom. xiv. 17; 1 Cor. vii. 19). **7.** [*Etrechete*] 'Ye were running well' in the Gospel race (1 Cor. ix. 24, 26; Phil. iii. 13, 14). **who,** &c.—none whom ye ought to have listened to: the Judaizers (cf. ch. iii. 1). **hinder** [*Enekopsen*, א A B C Δ G: not *anekopsen*, as received text]—'hinder by breaking up a road.' **not obey the** [so C Δ G. But A B א omit "the"] **truth**—not submit yourselves to the Gospel way of justification. **8. This persuasion**—'*The* persuasion;' a play on words akin in sound and in root [*peismone*, *persuasion : peithesthai*, "obey," *v.* 7]. *The readiness to obey* those who oppose *truth*. **cometh not of**—*from* Him, but from the Father of lies. Ye *obey not truth;* ye *are ready to obey* its *hinderers*. *Ellicott* takes *persuasion* as 'the *act* of persuading.' Rather (as the Greek commentators), it is the *state* of being persuaded. The paronomasia favours this. **that calleth you** (*v.* 13; ch. i. 6; Phil. iii. 14; 1 Thess. v. 24). The calling is the rule of the whole race (*Bengel*). **9. A little leaven**—the *false teaching* of the Judaizers. A little legalism, mixed with the Gospel, corrupts its purity. To add ordinances and works in the least degree to justification by faith, is to undermine 'the whole.' So "leaven," *false doctrines* (Matt. xvi. 12: cf. xiii. 33). In 1 Cor. v. 6 it means the corrupting influence of one bad *person;* so *Bengel* refers it here to the person (*vv.* 7, 8, 10) who misled them (Eccl. ix. 18; 1 Cor. xv. 33). False *doctrine* answers better to "persuasion" (*v.* 8). **10.** Greek, 'I (emphatical: "*I on my part*") have confidence IN [*en*] the Lord (the ground of confidence) *with regard to* [*eis*] you (2 Thess. iii. 4), that ye will be none otherwise minded' (than what by this epistle I desire you to be, Phil. iii. 15) [*heterōs*: but here *allo phronein*.] **but he that troubleth you** (Josh. vii. 25; 1 Ki. xviii. 17, 18; Acts xv. 24; ch. i. 7). The article has a selective and definitive force; *the one who, for the time being,* calls forth St. Paul's censure as the troubler (*Ellicott*) (ch. iv. 17). **shall bear**—as a heavy burden. **his**—*the judgment* he deserves; viz., excommunication (*v.* 12): an earnest of God's judgment (Rom. ii. 3). St. Paul distinguishes the case of the seduced, misled through thoughtlessness, who, now that they are set right, he confidently hopes, will return to the right way, from that of the seducer doomed to judgment. **whosoever he be**—whether great (ch. i. 8) or small. **11.** 'If I am still preaching (as I did before conversion) circumcision, why am I still persecuted?' The Judaizing troubler said, 'Paul himself preaches circumcision,' as is shown by his having circumcised Timothy (Acts xvi. 3: cf. xxi. 24). Paul by anticipation meets their objection. As regards myself, the fact that I am still persecuted by the Jews shows that I do *not* preach circumcision; for it is just because I preach Christ crucified, not the Mosaic law, as the sole ground of justification, that they persecute me. If for conciliation he lived as a Jew among Jews, it was in accordance

with his principle (1 Cor. vii. 18, 20; ix. 20). Circumcision or uncircumcision are things indifferent in themselves: their lawfulness or unlawfulness depends on the *animus* of him who used them. The Gentile Galatians' animus in circumcision could only be their supposition that it influenced favourably their standing before God. Paul's living as a Gentile among Gentiles showed that, if he observed Jewish rites, it was not that he thought it meritorious before God, but as a matter indifferent, wherein he might lawfully conform, as a *Jew by birth*, to those with whom he was, in order to put no needless stumblingblock to the Gospel in the way of his countrymen. **then**—presuming I did so, 'then after all,' in that case, the offence of (stumblingblock, 1 Cor. i. 23, occasioned to the Jews by) the cross has become done away' [*katērgētai*]. Thus the Jews' accusation against Stephen was not that he preached Christ crucified, but that "he spake blasphemous words against this holy place and *the law.*" They would have borne the former, if he had mixed with it justification by circumcision and the law, and if he had, through Christianity, brought converts to Judaism. But if justification in any degree depended on legal ordinances, Christ's crucifixion in that degree was unnecessary, and could profit nothing (*vv.* 2. 4). Worldly Wiseman, of the town of Carnal Policy, turns Christian out of the narrow way of the Cross to the house of legality. But the way to it was up a mountain, which, as Christian advanced, threatened to fall on and crush him, amidst lightning flashes from the mountain ('Pilgrim's Progress;' Heb. xii. 18-21). **12. they . . . which trouble you** [*anastatountes*]—*turning upside down* (Acts xvii. 6): setting up what ought to be down, and down what ought to be up: different from [*ho tarassōn*] *v.* 10, 'they who are *subverting* you.' **were even cut off**—rather, 'that they would even *cut themselves* off' from your communion, as a worthless foreskin cast away; even as they desire you to cut off your foreskin (ch. i. 7, 8: cf. Phil. iii. 3) [*apokopsontai:* middle]. *Jerome, Ambrose, Augustine, Chrysostom* explain, 'Would that they would even cut themselves of'—*i. e.,* cut off not merely the foreskin, but the whole member, like the *Galatian* priests of Cybele: if *circumcision* be not enough, then let them have *excision* also: an outburst hardly suitable to the gravity of an apostle, and unsupported by the ancient versions. *Vv.* 9, 10 point to *excommunication* as the judgment threatened against the troublers; and danger of the "leaven" spreading, as the reason for it.

13. Natural transition to the hortatory part. **For**—I wish their excision (*v.* 12): not that I would emancipate you from law; FOR your "liberty" from legalism is quite distinct from fleshly license. YE is emphatical, from its position in the Greek, 'Ye brethren,' &c.; as opposed to those legalists. **unto liberty** [*ep' eleutheria*]—'*for* liberty.' The object *for* which ye were called is liberty. Gospel liberty consists in three

14 for an occasion to the flesh, but by love serve one another. For all the
law is fulfilled in one word, *even* in this, ^r Thou shalt love thy neighbour
15 as thyself. But if ye bite and devour one another, take heed that ye be
not consumed one of another.

16 *This* I say then, ^s Walk in the Spirit, and ² ye shall not fulfil the lust
17 of the flesh. For ^t the flesh lusteth against the Spirit, and the Spirit
against the flesh: and these are contrary the one to the other; so ^u that
18 ye cannot do the things that ye would. But ^v if ye be led by the Spirit,
19 ye are not under the law. Now ^w the works of the flesh are manifest,
20 which are *these;* Adultery, fornication, uncleanness, lasciviousness, idol-

A. D. 58.

^r Lev. 19. 18.
1 Tim. 1. 5.
^s Rom. 6. 12.
² Or, fulfil
not.
^t Rom. 7. 23.
^u Rom. 7. 15.
^v Rom. 6. 14.
1 Pet. 4. 6.
^w 1 Cor. 3. 3.
Eph. 5. 3.
Jas. 3. 14.

things—freedom from the Mosaic yoke, from sin (1 Thess. iv. 7; John viii. 34-36), and from slavish fear. **only, &c.** Translate, 'only turn not *your* [τήν] liberty into an occasion for the flesh.' Do not give the flesh the handle (Rom. vii. 8, "occasion") for indulgence, which it eagerly seeks: do not let it make Christian "liberty" its pretext for indulgence (*vv.* 16, 17; 1 Pet. ii. 16; 2 Pet. ii. 19; Jude 4). **but by love serve one another**—'be servants [be in bondage: *douleuete*] to one another.' If ye must be *servants,* then *be servants to one another in love.* Whilst *free* as to legalism, be *bound* by love [in the abstract, *tēs agapēs:* else '*your* love'] to serve one another (1 Cor. ix. 19). He hints at their unloving strifes springing out of lust of power, which 'is the mother of heresies' (*Chrysostom*). **14. all the law** [*ho pas nomos*]—'the whole law.' *Love to God* is pre-supposed as the root from which *love to our neighbour* springs. In this sense the latter *precept* ('word') is the fulfilling of "*all* the law." Love is "the law of Christ" (ch. vi. 2; Matt. vii. 12, 22, 39, 40; Rom. xiii. 9, 10). **is fulfilled** [Δ G *fg*, Vulgate, *pleroutai*]—'is being fulfilled;' implying the process of fulfilment is *going on.* But א A B C read, 'has been fulfilled [*peplerotai*] permanently and perfectly already (Rom. xiii. 8). The law only united Israelites; the Gospel unites all men, and that in relation to God. **15. bite**—*backbite* the character. **devour**—the substance, by extortion, &c. (Hab. i. 13; Matt. xxiii. 14; 2 Cor. xi. 20.) *Bite*, the act of one enraged: *devour*, of one persevering in malice (*Chrysostom*). **consumed, &c.** Strength of soul, health, character, and resources, are all *consumed* by broils.

16. This I say then—explaining *v.* 13, 'What I mean is this.' **Walk in the Spirit**—'By [*Pneumati*] the (Holy) Spirit' (as your governing principle, rule) (Acts xv. 1; ch. vi. 16; Phil. iii. 16: cf. *vv.* 16-18, 22, 25; ch. vi. 1-8, with Rom. vii. 22; viii. 2, 9, 11). The best way to keep tares out of a bushel is to fill it with wheat. **the flesh**—the natural man, moving in the world of sense and self only. Its manifestations are various (*vv.* 19-21). The spirit and the flesh mutually exclude one another. It is promised, not that we should have no evil lusts, but that we should "not *fulfil*" them. If the spirit in us can be at ease under sin, it is not a spirit that comes from the Holy Spirit. The gentle dove trembles at the sight even of a hawk's feather. **17. For**—the reason why walking by the Spirit will exclude fulfilling the lusts of the flesh; viz., their mutual contrariety. **the Spirit**—not "lusteth," but '*tendeth* (or some such word) against the flesh.' **so that ye cannot do** (so as to be an obstacle to your doing) **the things that ye would.** The Spirit (in the beginning stage of one's repentance) strives against the flesh and its evil influence; the flesh against the Spirit and His good influence; *so that neither the one nor the other can be fully carried out into action.* "But" (*v.* 18) where "the Spirit" prevails, the struggle no longer continues doubtful

(Rom. vii. 15-20). The Greek is, 'that ye may not do whatsoever things ye would.' 'The flesh and Spirit are contrary one to the other,' *so that you must not fulfil what you desire according to the carnal self*, but what the Spirit within you desires (*Neander*). But the antithesis of *v.* 18 ("But," &c.), where the conflict is *decided*, shows, I think, that *v.* 17 contemplates the inability both for fully accomplishing the *good* we "would," owing to the opposition of the *flesh*, and for doing the *evil* our flesh would desire, owing to the opposition of *the Spirit* in the awakened man (such as the Galatians are assumed to be), until we yield ourselves wholly by the Spirit to 'walk by the Spirit' (*vv.* 16, 18). **18.** 'But if ye *are* led (give yourselves up to be led; in contrast to the previous struggle, *v.* 17, the Spirit now prevailing) by the Spirit, ye are not under the law,' because it finds in you no ground of condemnation. For ye are then not working the works of the flesh (*vv.* 16, 19-21), which bring one "under the law" (Rom. vii. 7, 8; viii. 2, 14). Legalism and carnality go together. The 'Spirit makes free from the law of sin and death' (*v.* 23). The law is made for a fleshly man, and fleshly works (1 Tim. i. 9); not for a righteous man (Rom. vi. 14, 15). **19-23.** Confirming *v.* 18 by the contrariety between the works of the flesh and the fruit of the Spirit. **manifest**—the hidden *fleshly* principle betrays itself *palpably* by its works: these leave no doubt whether men "are under the law" or not, as "the fruit of the Spirit" evidences that against it and its bearers "there is no law." **which are these** [*hatina*]—'such as,' for instance, **Adultery.** So C G *fg*: omitted in א A B, Vulgate. **fornication**—a heinous sin in the Christian view; an act indifferent in the pagan (Acts xv. 20). **lasciviousness** [*aselgeia*]—rather, 'wantonness,' petulant insolence: it may display itself in "lasciviousness," but not necessarily (Mark vii. 21, 22, where it is not associated with fleshly lusts) (*Trench*). "Works" (plural) are attributed to the "flesh," because they are not necessarily connected—nay, often mutually at variance—and are man's *doings.* There are four classes: 1. Sensuality; 2. Idolatry (1 Cor. viii. 7); 3. Malice; 4. Excesses (*Winer*). But the "*fruit* of the Spirit" (*v.* 22) is singular; because, however manifold the results, they form one organic whole springing from the Spirit. The results of the flesh are not dignified by the name "fruit;" they are but works (Eph. v. 9, 11). He enumerates those fleshly *works* (committed against our neighbour, against God, and against ourselves) to which the Galatians were most prone (the Kelts have always contentions), and those manifestations of the *fruit* of the Spirit most needed by them (*vv.* 13, 15). "The flesh" does not mean merely *sensuality,* as opposed to *spirituality;* for 'divisions' in the catalogue do not flow from sensuality. The identification of "the natural (Greek, *animal-soulled*) man" with the "carnal" or *fleshly* man (1 Cor. ii. 14), shows that "the flesh" expresses *human nature as estranged from God.* It is proof of our fallen state how much

atry, witchcraft, hatred, variance, emulations, wrath, strife, seditions,
21 heresies, envyings, murders, drunkenness, revellings, and such like : of
the which I tell you before, as I have also told *you* in time past, that
22 *ˣ* they which do such things shall not inherit the kingdom of God.   But
ʸ the fruit of the Spirit is love, joy, peace, long-suffering, *ᶻ* gentleness,
23 goodness, *ᵃ* faith, meekness, temperance : against such there is no law.
24 And they that are Christ's *ᵇ* have crucified the flesh with the *³* affections
25, and lusts.   If we live in the Spirit, let us also walk in the Spirit.   Let
26 us not be desirous of vain-glory, provoking one another, envying one
another.

6   BRETHREN, *¹* if a man be overtaken in a fault, ye *ᵃ* which are spiritual
restore such an one *ᵇ* in the spirit of meekness ; considering thyself, *ᶜ* lest

A. D. 58.

ˣ Rev. 22. 15.
ʸ John 15. 2.
ᶻ Jas. 3. 17.
ᵃ 1 Cor. 13.7.
ᵇ Col. 3. 9.
³ Or,
   passions.

ᶜ CHAP. 6.
1 Or,
  although.
  Jas. 5. 19.
ᵃ 1 Cor. 2.15.
ᵇ 2 Thes.3.15.
ᶜ 1 Cor 7. 5.

richer every vocabulary is in words for sins than in those for graces. St. Paul enumerates *seventeen* (or *sixteen:* note above) "works of the flesh;" only *nine* manifestations of "the fruit of the Spirit" (cf. Eph. iv. 31). **20. witchcraft** — sorcery: prevalent in Asia (Acts xix. 19: cf. Rev. xxi. 8). **hatred** — Greek, 'hatreds.' **emulations** [*zeloi*]. So א C *f g*, Vulgate. In B Δ, singular, 'jealousy:' for one's own advantage. "Envyings" (*v.* 21) are even without advantage to the person. **wrath** [*thumoi :* plural] — 'bursts of passion.' **strife** — rather, 'cabals' [*eritheiai*], derived from *erithos,* 'a worker for hire'], hence *factious practices, party spirit.* **seditions** [*dichostasiai*] — 'dissensions' as to secular matters, or religious matters also (1 Cor. iii. 3). **heresies** — as to sacred things (note, 1 Cor. xi. 19) ; self-constituted *parties* [from *haireo,* to *choose*]. A *schism* is a recent split in a congregation, from a difference in opinion. *Heresy* is a schism become inveterate (*Augustine*). **21. tell you before** — viz., before the event. **I have also told you in time past** — beforehand [*proeipon*], when I was with you. **you** — who, though maintaining justification by the law, are careless about keeping it (Rom. ii. 21, 23). **such** — '*all* such things' [*ta toiauta*]. **things shall not inherit the kingdom of God** (1 Cor. vi. 9, 10 ; Eph. v. 5). **22. love** — the first as well as the last of the band of graces (1 Cor. xiii. 8, 13 ; 2 Pet. i. 7). **joy** (Phil. iv. 4). **peace** — opposed to 'hatred,' 'variance' (*v.* 20). **gentleness** [*chrestotes*] — 'benignity,' 'kindness,' conciliatory to others ; whereas 'goodness,' though *ready to do good,* has not necessarily such *suavity* of manner (*Jerome*). **faith** — 'faithfulness :' opposed to 'heresies' (*Bengel*) (1 Cor. xiii. 7). 'Love believeth all things: *faith* in God's promises, and loving *trust* towards men' (*Ellicott*). 'Trustfulness' (*Conybeare*). **23. meekness** — submissiveness of spirit towards *God and man* (*Ellicott*). **temperance** [*enkrateia*] — *self-restraint* as to one's desires. **against** [*all: τῶν*] such — not *persons,* but *things,* as in *v.* 21. **no law** — confirming *v.* 18 (1 Tim. i. 9, 10). The law commands love (*v.* 14): so far from being "against such." **24. And** — Greek, 'But.' There is no law against love, &c. *But* Christians crucify the flesh, which is contrary to the Spirit, whose fruit love is; therefore they are led by the Spirit, and yield its fruit, and are not under the law. A B C א read 'They that are of Christ Jesus' — *i. e.,* belong to Christ Jesus: 'led by (His) Spirit' (*v.* 18). **have crucified** [aorist, *estaurosan,* '*crucified*'] **the flesh.** They *nailed* it to the cross *once for all* when they became Christ's (Rom. vi. 3, 4). They keep it *now* in a state of crucifixion (Rom. vi. 6); so that the Spirit can produce in them, comparatively uninterrupted by it, "the fruit of the Spirit" (*v.* 22). 'Man, by faith, is dead to the former standing-point of sin, and rises to a new life of communion with Christ (Col. iii. 3). The act by which *they crucified the flesh with*

its lust is already accomplished in principle ; but the outward confirmation of the life must harmonize with the tendency given to the inward life' (*v.* 25) (*Neander*). We are to be executioners of the body of sin, which caused the acting of all cruelties on Christ's body. **with the affections** [*tois pathemasin*] — 'with its passions.' Thus they are dead to the law's condemning power, which is only for the fleshly and their lusts (*v.* 23). **25. in . . . in** — rather, 'If we live (note, *v.* 24) BY the Spirit, let us also walk [*stoichomen: studiously* and with measured step] (*v.* 16; ch. vi. 16) BY the Spirit.' Let our practice correspond to the ideal principle of our spiritual life — viz., our standing by faith as dead to, and severed from, sin and the 'law's condemnation. 'Life by the Spirit' is not an occasional influence, but an abiding state, wherein we are continually alive though sometimes inactive ; not only *live,* but let life put forth *activity.* **26.** 'Let us not BECOME' [*yinōmetha*]. Whilst not asserting that the Galatians are "*vainglorious*" now, he says they are liable to become so. **provoking** [*prokaloumenoi: challenging*] **one ano-ther** — an effect of 'vain-gloriousness' on the *stronger,* as "envying" on the *weaker.* A danger common both to the orthodox and Judaizing Galatians.

CHAP. VI. 1-18. — EXHORTATIONS CONTINUED — TO FORBEARANCE AND HUMILITY — LIBERALITY TO TEACHERS AND IN GENERAL — POSTSCRIPT AND BENEDICTION.

1. Brethren — to conciliate kindly attention. Greek, 'If a man *even* be surprised' (*i. e.,* caught in the very act *before* he could escape) [*kaì prolemphthe:* the *kai* implies that the *pro* is an aggravation, not a palliation, of the offence] (*Ellicott*). Bengel, 'If a man (therefore one claiming the forbearing sympathy of his FELLOW-MEN) even be taken first in a fault *before yourselves.*' If another has *really* been *the first* to offend: for often he who is *first to find fault* is the one who has *first transgressed.* Be taken, the passive, reminds us of the enemy's power and our common infirmity. **a fault** [*paraptomati*] — 'a fall;' such as falling back into legal bondage [*hamartia* is 'sin' *in general*]. Here he warns those who have not so fallen — 'the spiritual' — to be not 'vain-glorious' (ch. v. 26), but forbearing to such (Rom. xv. 1). The *teachers* are mainly addressed, *vv.* 1-5; the *hearers, vv.* 6-10 (*Ellicott*). **restore** [*katartizete*] is used of a dislocated limb, reduced to its place. Such is the tenderness with which we should treat a fallen member in restoring him to a better state. **the spirit of meekness** — a spirit characterized prominently by *meekness,* the work *of the Holy Spirit* in our spirit (ch. v. 23, 25). "Meekness" is that spirit towards God whereby we accept His dealings without disputing; then, towards men, whereby we endure meekly provocations, and do not withdraw from the burdens which their sins impose upon us (*Trench*). **considering thyself** —

2 thou also be tempted. Bear [d]ye one another's burdens, and so fulfil [e]the
3 law of Christ. For [f]if a man think himself to be something, when he [g]is
4 nothing, he deceiveth himself. But [h]let every man prove his own work,
and then shall he have rejoicing in himself alone, and [i]not in another.
5 For [j]every man shall bear his own burden.
6   Let [k]him that is taught in the word communicate unto him that
7 teacheth in all good things. Be [l]not deceived; [m]God is not mocked:
8 for [n]whatsoever a man soweth, that shall he also reap. For [o]he that
soweth to his flesh shall of the flesh reap corruption; but he that
9 soweth to the Spirit shall of the Spirit reap life everlasting. And
[p]let us not be weary in well-doing: for in due season we shall

A. D. 58.

[d] Rom. 15. 1.
[e] John 13. 14.
[f] Rom. 12. 3.
[g] 2 Cor. 3. 5.
[h] 2 Cor 13. 5.
[i] Luke 18. 11.
[j] Rom. 2. 6.
[k] Rom. 15. 27.
[l] 1 Cor. 6. 9.
[m] Job 13. 9.
[n] Luke 16. 25.
[o] Jas. 3. 18.
[p] 2 Thes. 3. 13.

---

transition from the plural to the singular. When congregations are addressed, each should take home the monition *to himself*. **thou also be tempted**—as is likely to happen those who reprove others without meekness (cf. Matt. vii. 2-5; 2 Tim. ii. 25; Jas. ii. 13). The sense of our own weakness should make us indulgent to others. **2.** If ye, legalists, must 'bear burdens,' then (Matt. xxiii. 4) 'bear, not legal (Matt. xxiii. 4), but one another's burdens' (*barē*), 'weights.' Distinguished (*Bengel*) from "burden," *v.* 5 [*phortion*, 'load']. 'Weights' exceed the strength; "burden" is proportioned to the strength. Rather, *Bare* 'weights' is more general, referring to the *community; phortion*, 'a load,' refers to the particular sins of *each*. The *weights* of the infirm, afflicted, and erring are to be shared in by the communion of saints (Rom. xv. 1; 2 Cor. ii. 29); the *burden* of each is to be borne by himself in respect to rendering his account to God (*Ellicott* from *Augustine*). 'Alleviate the soul *weighed down* by the consciousness of *sin*' (*Theodore* of Mopsuestia). **so fulfil.** א A C; or, as B G *fg*, Vulgate, read, 'so ye *will* fulfil' [*anaplerosete*], 'fill up,' 'thoroughly fulfil.' **the law of Christ** —viz., "love," which fulfils the whole law (ch. v. 14). Since ye desire "the law," then fulfil Christ's law, not made up of various observances: its sole "burden" is "love" (John xiii. 34; xv. 12; 1 John iii. 23). Rom. xv. 3 gives Christ as the example. **3.** Self-conceit, the chief hindrance to forbearing sympathy towards our fellow-men, must be laid aside. **something**—possessed of some spiritual pre-eminence, and exempt from the frailty of other men. **when he is nothing**— 'being, after all, nothing' (Rom. xii. 3; 1 Cor. viii. 2). **deceiveth himself** [*phrenapata*]—'he *mentally* deceives himself.' To test his own *work* (his whole course, 1 Pet. i. 17), and judge by it, not by his *mental* fancy, is the remedy (cf. Jas. i. 26). **4. his own work**—not merely his own *opinion* of himself. **have rejoicing in himself alone.** Translate, 'have *his matter for* glorying [*to kauchema*; distinct from *kauchesis*, the *act* of glorying] *in regard to* himself [*eis heauton*] alone, and not *in regard to* the other'—viz., his neighbour —by comparing himself with whom he fancied he has matter for boasting as superior (1 Cor. iv. 5). Not that really a man by looking to "himself alone" is likely to find cause for glorying. Nay, in *v.* 5 he speaks of a "burden," not of matter for glorying, as what really belongs to each. But he refers to *the idea those whom he censures had of themselves:* they *thought* they had cause for 'glorying' in themselves; but it arose **from** self-conceited comparison of themselves **with others,** instead of looking at home. The only **true** glorying is in the Lord, the Giver of a good conscience, through the cross of Christ; and in our weaknesses, which enlist for us His omnipotence (2 Cor. x. 17; xi. 30; xii. 9). **5.** Reason why **a man has**

no ground for claiming superiority in regard to his neighbour (*v.* 4, end). FoR each has his own "burden" ('*load*')—viz., of infirmity: *phortion* is different from *barē*, *v.* 2. This verse does not contradict *v.* 2. There he tells them to bear with others' "burdens" in forbearing sympathy; here, that self examination will make a man to feel he has enough to do to render an account for 'his own load' of sin, without comparing himself boastfully with his neighbour (cf. *v.* 3). Instead of 'thinking himself to be something,' he shall feel his own 'load' of sin: this will lead him to bear sympathetically with his neighbour's weights of infirmity. Æsop says a man carries two bags over his shoulder; the one with his own sins hanging behind, that with his neighbour's sins in front. **6.** One way of bearing others' burdens (*v.* 2), by ministering of **earthly goods to spiritual teachers.** The 'but' in the Greek, beginning this verse, expresses, I said, Each shall bear his own burden; BUT I do not intend that he should not think of others, especially of the wants of his ministers. **communicate unto him**—'impart a share unto his teacher' [*katechounti*]; *him that teacheth catechetically.* **in all good things**—in all the good things *of this life*, according as the case may require (Rom. xv. 27; 1 Cor. ix. 11, 14). **7. God is not mocked.** The Greek [*mukterizetai*] is *to draw up the nostrils in contempt.* God does not suffer Himself to be imposed on by empty words: He will judge according to works, which are seeds sown for an eternity of either joy or woe. Excuses for illiberality in God's cause (*v.* 6) seem valid before men, but are not so before God (Ps. l. 21). **soweth**—especially of his resources (2 Cor. ix. 6). **that**—Greek, 'this,' and nothing else. **reap**—at the harvest, the end of the world (Matt. xiii. 39). **8.** 'He that soweth *unto his own* flesh' [*eis tēn sarka heautou*], with a view to fulfilling its desires. He does not say, '*his* own spirit,' as he does, '*his own* flesh.' For in ourselves we are not spiritual, but carnal. The flesh is essentially *selfish*. **corruption** [*phthoran*]—i. e., *destruction* (Phil. iii. 19). Cf. as to the believer's deliverance from "corruption," Rom. viii. 21. The use of "corruption" implies that *destruction* is not an *arbitrary* punishment of fleshly-mindedness, but its *natural* fruit: the corrupt flesh producing *corruption*, another word for *destruction:* corruption is the fault, and corruption the punishment (note, Rom. vi. 21, 22; 1 Cor. iii. 17; 2 Pet. ii. 12). The future life only expands the seed sown here. Men cannot mock God because they can deceive themselves. They who sow tares cannot reap wheat. They alone reap life eternal who sow to the Spirit (Ps. cxxvi. 6; Prov. xi. 18; xxii. 8; Hos. viii. 7; x. 12; Luke xvi. 25; Rom. viii. 11; Jas. v. 7). **9.** And—Greek, 'But.' It is "life everlasting" to sow unto the Spirit; BUT it must be a *continuous* sowing—we must not "weary" (2 Thess. iii. 13). **in due season**—in its proper season, God's own time (1

10 reap, ^q if we faint not. As ^r we have therefore opportunity, let ^s us do good unto all *men*, especially unto them who are of ^t the household of faith.

11 Ye see how large a letter I have written unto you with mine own
12 hand. As many as desire to make a fair show in the flesh, they constrain you to be circumcised; ^u only lest they should suffer persecution for the
13 cross of Christ. For neither they themselves who are circumcised keep the law; but desire to have you circumcised, that they may glory in
14 your flesh. But God forbid that I should glory, save in the cross of our Lord Jesus Christ, by ² whom the world is crucified unto me, and I unto
15 the world. For in Christ Jesus neither circumcision availeth any thing,
16 nor uncircumcision, but ^v a new creature. And ^w as many as walk

Column marginalia:
A. D. 58.
q Isa. 40. 30.
Matt. 24. 13.
r John 9. 4.
s 1 Tim. 6. 18
t Eph. 2. 19.
u Phil. 3. 18.
2 Or,
whereby.
v 2 Cor. 5. 17.
Eph. 2. 10.
Eph. 4. 24.
w Ps. 73. 1.
Ps. 125. 5.
ch. 3. 7-9.

Tim. vi. 15). **if we faint not** [*me ekluomenoi*]—'be not relaxed.' *Weary* [*ekkakōmen*, C, 'let us not go OUT OF duty's path through *fear*.' But אABΔ, *enkakōmen*, 'let us not *lose heart* IN it'] refers to the *will; faint*, to relaxation of the *power* (Bengel). **10.** *So then* [*ara oun*], *according* (*i. e.*, in proportion) as we have *season* (*i. e.*, opportunity), let us *work* [*ergazometha:* distinct from *poiountes*, 'do,' *v.* 9] *that which is* (in each case) *good'* [*to agathon*]. As thou art able, whilst thou art able, when thou art able (Eccl. ix. 10). We have now the "*season*" for *sowing*, as there will be hereafter the "*due season*" (*v.* 9) for *reaping*. The whole life is the 'seasonable opportunity;' in a narrower sense, there occur in it especially convenient seasons. These are lost in looking for still more convenient seasons (Acts xxiv. 25). We shall not always have the opportunity "we have" now. Satan is sharpened to the greater zeal in evil-doing by the shortness of his time (Rev. xii. 12). Let us be sharpened to the greater zeal in well-doing by the shortness of ours. **them who are of the household** [who peculiarly belong to: *tous oikeious tes pisteōs*] **of faith.** Every right-minded man does well to his own family (1 Tim. v. 8); so believers are to do to the household of faith—*i. e.*, those whom *faith* has made members of "the household of God" (Eph. ii. 19; 1 Tim. iii. 15; 1 Pet. iv. 17).

11. [*Pelikois grammasin*] 'See *in how large letters* I have written.' The Greek is translated "how great," Heb. vii. 4, the only other New Testament passage where it occurs. Owing to his weakness of eyes (ch. iv. 15), he wrote in large letters. So *Jerome*. All the oldest MSS. are written in uncial—*i. e.*, capital letters; the *cursive*, or small letters, being of recent date. St. Paul seems to have had a difficulty in writing, which led him to make the uncial letters larger than ordinary. By these they would know that he WROTE *the whole epistle* with his own hand; as he did also the pastoral epistles, which this epistle resembles in style [*egrapsa:* contrast *graphō*, 2 Thess. iii. 17, present, where he refers only to the closing salutation]. He usually dictated his epistles to an amanuensis, excepting the concluding salutation, which he wrote himself (Rom. xvi. 22; 1 Cor. xvi. 21). This letter he wrote with his own hand, in order that the Galatians may see what a regard he has for them, in contrast to the Judaizing teachers (*v.* 12), who sought only their own ease. If the English version be retained, the words, "how large a letter," will not refer to the length of the epistle *absolutely*, but large for *him* to have written with his own hand. *Neander* explains so, as more appropriate to the earnestness of the apostle and the tone of the epistle: "how *large*" will thus be for 'how *many*.' [But *grammata* nowhere else with St. Paul means "a letter,"

epistole. Grammasin egrapsa is nowhere so used by him (cf. Luke xxiii. 38; 2 Cor. iii. 7).] **12.** Contrast between his zeal in their behalf (*v.* 11) and the zeal for self on the part of the Judaizers. **make a fair show** (2 Cor. v. 12) **in the flesh** —in outward things. **they**—it is 'these who,' &c. **constrain you**—by example (*v.* 13) and importuning. **only lest**—'only that they may not,' &c. (cf. ch. v. 11). **suffer persecution.** They escaped the Jews' bitterness against Christianity, and the offence of Christ's cross, by making the Mosaic law a necessary preliminary; in fact, making Christian converts into Jewish proselytes. **for the cross**—for preaching the doctrine of the cross. **13.** 'For not even do they who are having themselves circumcised [*hoi peritemnomenoi*, אACΔ, Vulgate] keep the law *themselves* (Rom. ii. 17-23), but they wish YOU to be circumcised,' &c. (Matt. xxiii. 4.) They arbitrarily selected circumcision out of the whole law, as though observing it would make up for their non-observance of the rest. **that they may glory in your flesh**—viz., in the outward change (opposed to the *inward, wrought by the* SPIRIT) which they effect in bringing you over to their own Jewish-Christian party. **14.** 'But *as for me* (in opposition to those gloriers "in your flesh," *v.* 13), God forbid [*mē genoito*, far be it] that I,' &c. **in the cross**—the atoning death on the cross; making us dead to self. Cf. Phil. iii. 3, 7, 8 as a specimen of his glorying. The "cross," the object of shame to them and all carnal men, is the great object of glorying to me; for by it, the worst of deaths, Christ has destroyed all kinds of death (*Augustine*). We are to testify the power of Christ's death working in us after the manner of crucifixion (Rom. vi. 5, 6; ch. v. 24). **our.** He reminds them by this pronoun that *they* had a share in the "Lord Jesus Christ" (the full name gives greater solemnity), and therefore ought to glory in Christ's cross as he did. **the world**—'the aim of the old man' (*Calvin*)—inseparably allied to the "flesh" (*v.* 13). Legal and fleshly ordinances are merely outward, and "elements of the world" (ch. iv. 3). **is**—Greek, 'has been crucified to me' (ch. ii. 20). He used "crucified" for "*dead*" with Christ" (Col. ii. 20), to imply his oneness with Christ *crucified* (Phil. iii. 10). **15.** **For**—confirming his *crucifixion to the world* (*v.* 14) by the instance of *circumcision*, which now is become a mere worldly, outward rite. **availeth.** Borrowed from ch. v. 6, Vulgate. But אABCΔ Gfg read 'is.' Not only are they of no *avail*, but they *are nothing.* So far are they from being matter for 'glorying,' that they are 'nothing.' But Christ's cross is 'all in all,' as is subject for glorying, in the "new creature" (Eph. ii. 10, 15, 16). **new creature** (2 Cor. v. 17)—a *transformation by the renewal of the mind* (Rom. xii. 2). **16. as many** —contrasting with the "as many," *v.* 12. **rule**

according to this rule, peace *be* on them, and mercy, and upon the Israel of God.

17 From henceforth let no man trouble me: for *z* I bear in my body the
18 marks of the Lord Jesus.   Brethren, *y* the grace of our Lord Jesus Christ *be* with your spirit.   Amen.

Unto the Galatians, written from Rome.

A. D. 58.

z 2 Cor. 1. 5.
2 Cor. 4. 10.
2 Cor. 9. 23.
Col. 1. 24.
y Rom. 16.24.
2 Cor. 13. 14.
2 Tim. 4. 22.

[*canon*]—*a straight rule*, to detect crookedness; the rule of *faith*. **peace**—from God (Eph. ii. 14-17; vi. 23), the *effect*. **mercy** (Rom. xv. 9)—the *cause*. **Israel of God**—not the Israel after the flesh (1 Cor. x. 18), among whom those teachers wish to enrol you, but the spiritual seed of Abraham by faith (Rom. ii. 28, 29; ch. iii. 9, 29; Phil. iii. 3). The "and" may imply that as the former clause, "as many," &c., refers to Gentile believers, so "the Israel of God" to Jewish believers. But "and" may be explanatory: *even*.

17. let no man trouble me — by opposing, through legalism or licentiousness, my apostolic authority, seeing it is stamped by a sure seal— viz., "I (in contrast to the Judaizing teacher) bear" [*bastazo*, Acts ix. 15; as a badge of honour

from the King of kings]. **the marks**—properly, marks branded on slaves to indicate their owners. So St. Paul's scars, received for Christ, indicate to whom he belongs, and in whose free service he is (2 Cor. xi. 23-25). The Judaizing teachers gloried in the circumcision-mark in the flesh of *their followers;* St. Paul glories in the marks of suffering for Christ on *his own* body (cf. *v.* 14; Col. i. 24). **the Lord.** So אΔG. Omitted in ABC. **18. Brethren.** Place it, as the Greek, *last*, before the "Amen." After much rebuke, he bids them fare-well with the loving expression of *brotherhood* as his parting word (note, ch. i. 6). **be with your spirit**—the spiritual nature, which, I trust, will keep down the *flesh* (1 Thess. v. 23; 2 Tim. iv. 22; Phile. 25).

397

THE EPISTLE OF PAUL THE APOSTLE TO THE

EPHESIANS.

1 PAUL, an apostle of Jesus Christ by the will of God, to the saints
2 which are at Ephesus, ^aand to the faithful in Christ Jesus: Grace ^bbe to you, and peace, from God our Father, and *from* the Lord Jesus Christ.

3 Blessed ^cbe the God and Father of our Lord Jesus Christ, who hath blessed us with all spiritual blessings in heavenly ¹*places* in Christ:
4 according as ^dhe hath chosen us in him ^ebefore the foundation of the world, that we should ^fbe holy and without blame before him in love:
5 having ^gpredestinated us unto ^hthe adoption of children by Jesus Christ
6 to himself, ⁱaccording to the good pleasure of his will, to ^jthe praise

1 PAUL, an apostle of Jesus Christ by the will of God, to the saints
2 which are at Ephesus, [a]and to the faithful in Christ Jesus: Grace [b]be to you, and peace, from God our Father, and *from* the Lord Jesus Christ.

3 Blessed [c]be the God and Father of our Lord Jesus Christ, who hath blessed us with all spiritual blessings in heavenly [1]*places* in Christ:
4 according as [d]he hath chosen us in him [e]before the foundation of the world, that we should [f]be holy and without blame before him in love:
5 having [g]predestinated us unto [h]the adoption of children by Jesus Christ
6 to himself, [i]according to the good pleasure of his will, to [j]the praise

A. D. 64.

CHAP. 1.
[a] Col. 1. 2.
[b] Tit. 1. 4.
[c] Ps. 72. 17.
[1] Or. things.
[d] 1 Pet. 1. 2.
[e] 1 Pet. 1. 20.
[f] Luke 1. 75.
[g] Rom. 8. 29.
[h] John 1. 12.
[i] Luke 12. 32.
[j] Isa 43. 21.

CHAP. I. 1-23.—INSCRIPTION—ORIGIN OF THE CHURCH IN THE FATHER'S ETERNAL COUNSEL AND THE SON'S BLOODSHEDDING—SEALING OF IT BY THE SPIRIT — THANKSGIVING AND PRAYER THAT THEY MAY FULLY KNOW GOD'S GRACIOUS POWER IN CHRIST TOWARDS THE SAINTS.

1. by [*dia*]—'*through* the will of God:' called to the apostleship through that same "will" which originated the Church (*vv.* 5, 9, 11: cf. Gal. i. 4): a cause of thanksgiving to God's grace on his part, and calling for recognition of his authority on theirs. **which are at Ephesus**—see 'Introduction.' **to the saints . . . and to the faithful**—the same persons: Greek, 'to those who are saints, and faithful in Christ Jesus.' The *sanctification* by God is put before man's *faith*. God's grace in the first instance *sanctifies* us (*i. e.*, sets us apart in His eternal purposes as holy unto Himself); and our faith, by God's gift, lays hold of salvation (2 Thess. ii. 13; 1 Pet. i. 2). *Consecration* to God is the idea prominent in "saints." **in Christ**—*in* living *union with* Christ. **2.** (Rom. i. 7; 1 Cor. i. 3; 2 Cor. i. 2; Gal. i. 3.) **Grace**—God's undeserved favour. **peace** —to man, resulting from God's "grace." "Mercy" is added in the epistles to pastors individually (1 Tim. i. 2; 2 Tim. i. 2; Tit. i. 4). **from God our Father, and from the Lord Jesus.** There being but *one preposition*, implies how closely united are the Father and Jesus.

3. The doxologies in the epistles imply real sense of grace experienced by the writers and their readers (1 Pet. i. 3). Verses 3 to 14 set forth summarily the Gospel of the grace of God: the FATHER'S work of love, *v.* 3 (choosing us to *holiness*, *v.* 4; to *sonship*, *v.* 5; to *acceptance*, *v.* 6); the SON'S work of love, *v.* 7 (*redemption; knowledge of the mystery of His will*, *v.* 9; *an inheritance*, *v.* 11); the HOLY SPIRIT'S work of love, *v.* 13 (*sealing; giving an earnest* of the inheritance, *v.* 14). **Blessed** [*Eulogetos*, used only of God: *eulogemenos*, of men] **be the God and Father of . . . Christ**—so the God and Father of us who are in Him (John xx. 17). God is "the God" of the *man* (*v.* 16) Jesus, and "the Father" of the *Divine Word*. [*Eulogesas* (Aorist), '*Blessed* us,' not 'hath blessed us;' the past original counsel of God.] As in creation (Gen. i. 22), so in redemption (Gen. xii. 3; Matt. v. 3-11; xxv. 34) God 'blesses' His children of His grace; not in mere *words*, but in *acts*. Our *blessing Him* is thanksgiving for His grace. **us**—all Christians. **blessings** [*en pasē eulogia pneumatike*]—'with every spirit-bestowed blessing;' '*every possible* blessing for time and eternity which *the Spirit* has to bestow.' Judaism
398

had blessings, but not the blessing of the Spirit. The Trinity appears here, as throughout this epistle. **in heavenly places.** A phrase five times in this epistle, not elsewhere (*v.* 20; ch. ii. 6; iii. 10; vi. 12, *margin*. Our home (Phil. iii. 20), where our hope is (Col. i. 5), and whence the Spirit comes (Heb. vi. 4; John vi. 32). Christ's ascension introduces us into the heavenly places which by our sin were barred against us. Cf. the change made by Christ (Col. i. 20; ch. i. 20). Whilst Christ in the flesh was in the form of a *servant*, God's people could not realize fully their heavenly privileges as *sons*. Now, "our *citizenship* (Greek) is in heaven" (Phil. iii. 20), where our High Priest is ever 'blessing' us. Our "treasures" are there (Matt. vi. 20, 21), our aims and affections (Col. iii. 1, 2), our hope (Col. i. 5; Tit. ii. 13), our inheritance (1 Pet. i. 4). The gift of the Spirit, the source of "spiritual blessings," is by virtue of Jesus having ascended thither (ch. iv. 8). **in Christ**—the centre and source of all blessing. **4. hath chosen us** [*exelexato*]—'*chose* us out for Himself' (viz., *out of* the world, Gal. i. 4): His original choice, spoken of as *past*. **in him.** The repetition of "in Christ" (*v.* 3), implies the paramount importance of the truth that it is *in Him*, by virtue of union to Him, the Second Adam, the Restorer ordained for us from everlasting, the Head of redeemed humanity, believers have all their blessings (ch. iii. 11; 1 Cor. xv. 22). **before the foundation of the world**—in contrast with the temporal election of the Jews. This assumes the eternity of the Son of God (John xvii. 5, 24; 1 Pet. i. 20); as of the election of believers in Him (2 Tim. i. 9; 2 Thess. ii. 13). **that we should be holy.** Positively (Deut. xiv. 2). **without blame.** Negatively (ch. v. 27). **before him.** It is to Him the believer looks, walking as in His presence, before whom he looks to be accepted in the judgment (Col. i. 22: cf. Rev. vii. 15). **in love.** Joined by *Bengel*, *Ellicott*, &c., with *v.* 5, 'in love, having predestinated us,' &c. But the words qualify the whole clause, "that we should be holy . . . before Him." Love, lost to man by the fall, but restored by redemption, is the root, fruit, and sum of all holiness (ch. v. 2; 1 Thess. iii. 12, 13). **5. predestinated**—having respect to the *end* and *means*. We are "chosen" or 'elected' *out of the rest of the world;* "predestinated" *to all things that secure the inheritance* for us (*v.* 11; Rom. viii. 20). [*Proorisas*] "Foreordained" or "predestinated" refers to God's *decree*, which is embodied in God's *election* of us *out* of the mass. **by Jesus** [*dia*] '*through* Jesus.' **to himself**—the Father (Col. i,

of the glory of his grace, wherein ^khe hath made us accepted in the
7 ^lBeloved: in ^mwhom we have redemption through his blood, the forgive-
8 ness of sins, according to ⁿthe riches of his grace; wherein he hath
9 abounded toward us in all wisdom and prudence; having ^omade known
unto us the mystery of his will, according to his good pleasure ^pwhich he
10 hath purposed in himself: that in the dispensation of ^qthe fulness of
times ^rhe might gather together in one all things in Christ, both which

A. D. 64.

k Rom. 3. 24.
l Matt. 17. 5.
m Heb. 9. 12.
n Rom 3. 24.
o Col. 1. 26.
p 2 Tim 1. 9.
q Heb. 9. 10.
r 1 Cor. 3. 22.

20). [*Eis hauton*, rather read *auton*.] 'Adoption . . . *unto* (*into*) Him,' into inward union with God—*i. e.*, so that we should be *partakers of the divine nature* (2 Pet. i. 4). The context favours *Calvin*, &c.: God has regard to *Himself* and the glory of His grace (*vv.* 6, 12, 14) as His ultimate end. He had one only begotten Son, and He was pleased, *for His own glory*, to choose out of a lost world many to become His adopted sons. **the good pleasure of his will**—[Matt. xi. 26, *eudokia*, as here; Luke x. 21.] "The good pleasure of His will" is our utmost limit in searching into the causes of our salvation, or of any of His works (*v.* 9; Job xxxiii. 13). Why needest thou philosophize about an imaginary world of optimism? Thy concern is to take heed that thou be not bad. Nothing in us deserved His love (*vv.* 1, 9, 11) (*Bengel*). 6. (*Vv.* 7, 17, 18.) The grand end of His predestination (Ps. 1. 23)—*i. e.*, that the glory of His grace may be praised by all His creatures. **wherein**. So Δ G C *f g*, Vulgate. But א A B, read [*hēs* for *en hē*], '*which* He graciously bestowed on us.' **us accepted**—a word akin to "grace" [*Charitos, echaritosen*]; 'made us subjects of His grace;' 'graciously accepted us' (Luke i. 28; Rom. iii. 24; v. 15). But see last note. **in the Beloved**—pre-eminently so called (Matt. iii. 17; xvii. 5; John iii. 35; Col. i. 13, *margin*). It is only "IN HIS BELOVED," as our Representative Head, that He loves us (*v.* 3; 1 John iv. 9, 10): in His person and His work, which is identified with His person. **7. In whom**—"the Beloved" (*v.* 6; Rom. iii. 24). **we have**—as a *present* possession. **redemption** [*ten apolutrosin*]—'*our* (lit., *the*) redemption;' THE redemption which is the grand subject of revelation—viz., from the power, guilt, and penalty of sin (Matt. i. 21). If a man were unable to redeem himself from bond-service, his kinsman might redeem him (Lev. xxv. 48). Antitypically the Son of God became the Son of man, that, as our kinsman, He might redeem us (Matt. xx. 28). Another "redemption" follows—viz., that "of the purchased possession" hereafter (*v.* 14). **through his blood** (ch. ii. 13)—as the instrument, the propitiation; i. e., *consideration* (devised by His own love) for which He, who was justly angry (Isa. xii. 1), becomes propitious to us; the *expiation*, the price [*lutron*] paid to divine justice for our sin (Acts xx. 28; Rom. iii. 25; 1 Cor. vi. 20; Col. i. 20; 1 Pet. i. 18, 19). **the forgiveness of sins**—'the remission of our *transgressions*' [*tōn paraptomaton: aphesis*]: not merely [*paresis*: "*pretermission*'] as in Rom. iii. 25. This 'remission,' being the explanation of "redemption," includes not only deliverance from sin's penalty, but from its pollution and enslaving power, negatively; and the reconciliation of an offended God, and a satisfaction unto a just God, positively [*paraptomata* regard *acts* of transgression: *hamartiai* (Col. i. 14), *sins*, as implying a sinful *state*]. **riches of his grace** (ch. ii. 7). Cf. *v.* 18, and ch. iii. 16, "according to the riches of His glory:" so that "grace" is His "glory." **8.** *Ellicott*, 'Which He made to abound towards us" [*hēs eperisseusen*]: the transitive is the more common meaning. **all wisdom and prudence**—"wisdom" in devising the redemption plan; "prudence" in executing it by the means, and in making all

the necessary arrangements of providence for it. St. Paul attributes to the Gospel "all" possible "wisdom and prudence," in opposition to the boasts of wisdom and prudence which unbelieving Jews, heathen philosophers, and false apostles and legalists arrogated for their teachings. "Wisdom" in general: "prudence" [*phronesis*], *intelligence*, the right application of the [*phrēn*] mind, a result of *wisdom* (*Ellicott*): who applies them here to *man* (Col. i. 9), not to God. Christ crucified, though esteemed "foolishness" by the world, is "the *manifold* wisdom of God" (1 Cor. i. 18-30; ch. iii. 10). **9.** Which He 'made to abound toward us' (*v.* 8), *in that He made known* to us—viz., experimentally, in our hearts. **the mystery**—God's purpose of redemption hidden heretofore in His counsels, but now revealed (cf. ch. iii. 4, 9; vi. 19; Rom. xvi. 25; Col. i. 26, 27). This "mystery" is not like the heathen mysteries, imparted only to the initiated few. All Christians are the initiated. Unbelievers alone are the uninitiated. **according to his good pleasure**—the cause why He "made known unto us the mystery"—viz., His own loving "good pleasure" toward us; the *time* and *manner* of His doing so are also according to His good pleasure. **purposed** (*v.* 11) **in himself**—God the Father. *Bengel*, 'in *Him*,' i. e., *Christ*, as *vv.* 3, 4. But "in *Christ*," *v.* 10, immediately after, is inconsistent with His being here meant by the pronoun. **10. in** [*eis*: rather *unto*]—*i. e.*, 'which He purposed in Himself' (*v.* 9), *with a view to* the dispensation of (*i. e.*, the *administration belonging to*) the fulness of the times [*kairōn*, 'fit times;' the moment which *fills up* or *completes* the appointed 'seasons']. More comprehensive than "the fulness of the time" (Gal. iv. 4). The whole Gospel *times* (plural) are meant, with the benefits to the Church *dispensed* in them severally. Cf. "the ages to come" (ch. ii. 7). 'The ends of the ages' (Greek, 1 Cor. x. 11); "the times [*kairoi*, 'seasons'] of the Gentiles" (Luke xxi. 24); "the seasons which the Father hath put in His own power" (Acts i. 7); "the times of restitution of all things, which God hath spoken by the prophets since the world began" (Acts iii. 21). The coming of Jesus at the first advent, "in the fulness of time," was *one* of these "times." The descent of the Holy Ghost, when "Pentecost was *fully come*" (Acts ii. 1), was another. The testimony given by the apostles to Him "in due time" ['in its own seasons:' *kairois idiois*] (1 Tim. ii. 6) was another. The conversion of the Jews, "when the *times* of the Gentiles are fulfilled," the second coming of Christ, the "restitution of all things," the millennial kingdom, the new heaven and earth, shall be severally instances of "the dispensation of the fulness of times"—*i. e.*, "the dispensation of" the Gospel events and benefits belonging to their respective "times," when severally completed. God the Father, according to His own good pleasure, is the Dispenser both of the Gospel benefits and of their several fitting times (Acts i. 7). **gather together in one** [*anakephalaiosasthai*]—'sum up again (in their original unity) for Himself under one head;' 'recapitulate.' The 'good pleasure which He purposed' was 'to sum up all things [*ta panta*: 'THE whole range of things') in

11 are in ²heaven, and which are on earth, *even* in him: in ³whom also we
have obtained an inheritance, being predestinated according to ᵗthe
purpose of him who worketh all things after the counsel of his own will:
12 that ᵘwe should be to the praise of his glory, ᵛwho first ³trusted in
13 Christ. In whom ye also *trusted,* after that ye heard the word of truth,
the gospel of your salvation: in whom also, after that ye believed, ʷye
14 were sealed with that Holy Spirit of promise, which ˣis the earnest of
our inheritance ʸuntil the redemption ᶻof the purchased possession, unto
the praise of his glory.
15 Wherefore I also, after I heard of your faith in the Lord Jesus, and

A. D. 64.

2 the
heavens.
ˢ Rom. 8. 17.
ᵗ Isa. 46. 10.
ᵘ 2 Thes. 2. 13.
ᵛ Jas. 1. 18.
3 Or. hoped.
ʷ Joel 2. 28.
2 Cor. 1. 22.
ˣ 2 Cor. 5. 5.
ʸ Rom. 8. 23.
ᶻ Acts 20. 23.

Christ' [*to Christo:* 'the Christ']. God sums up the whole creation in Christ, the Head of angels, with whom He is linked by His invisible nature; and of men, with whom He is linked by His humanity; of Jews and Gentiles; of the living and the dead (ch. iii. 15); of animate and inanimate creation. Sin has disarranged the creature's relation of subordination to God. God gathers up all in Christ (Col. i. 20). *Alford,* 'The Church is subordinated to Him in conscious and joyful union; those who are not His spiritually in mere subjugation, yet consciously: the inferior creatures unconsciously;—objectively, all are summed up in Him.' 11. In whom—*in union to* whom. obtained an inheritance [*eklerothemen*]—א B, Vulgate, 'We were made to have an inheritance.' Cf. *v.* 18, "*His* inheritance in the saints." As *His* inheritance is *in them,* so *theirs* is *in Him* (Acts xxvi. 18). However, *v.* 12, "that we should BE to . . . His glory," favours *Bengel, Ellicott,* &c., 'We were *made* an inheritance.' So the literal Israel (Deut. iv. 20; ix. 29; xxxii. 9). "Also" does not mean 'we also,' nor as English version, "in whom also;" but, besides His having 'made known to us His will,' we were also 'made His inheritance,' or 'we have also obtained an inheritance:' But A Δ G *f g* read [*eklethemen*] 'we were called,' predestinated (*v.* 5). The foreordination of Israel as the elect nation answers to that of the spiritual Israel—believers—to an eternal inheritance. The "we" means *Jewish* believers (whence Israel's national election is naturally referred to), as contrasted with "you" (*v.* 13), *Gentile* believers. purpose[*prothesin*]—repeated from "purposed" [*proetheto*] (*v.* 9; ch. iii. 11). The Church existed in the mind of God eternally before its creation. counsel of his own will—*v.* 5, "the good pleasure of his will." Not arbitrary caprice, but all-wise "counsel," joined with sovereign will. Cf. his address to the same Ephesians, Acts xx. 27, "all the counsel of God" (Isa. xxviii. 29). Alike in the natural and spiritual creations, God is not constrained by necessity, 'wheresoever counsel is there is election, or else it is vain: where a will, there must be freedom, or else it is weak' (*Pearson*). The *will* is general; the *counsel* its special expression. 12. (*vv.* 6, 14) who first trusted in Christ—rather (we Jewish Christians), 'who have before hoped [*proelpikotas*] in *the* [τῷ] Christ:' who before He came have had our hope in Him (not merely '*towards* Him'), waiting for the consolation of Israel. Cf. Acts xxvi. 6, 7; xxviii. 20; *v.* 18; ch. ii. 12; iv. 4. 13. In whom ye also—ye Gentiles. Supply "trusted" or 'hoped' [the simple verb taken out of the compound *proelpikotas*] from *v.* 12. The priority of us Jews does not exclude you Gentiles from sharing in Christ. *Ellicott,* 'In whom ye too having heard, &c.—in whom (*I say*), having also believed, ye were sealed,' making "were sealed" the verb of the first "ye." But the "also" before "believed" supposes the 'hoped' as having preceded: 'in whom ye too hoped,—in (union to)

400

whom having *also* believed,' (as well as 'hoped, &c.) The Gentiles had a vague *hope* of a Deliverer before Christ's coming (Hagg. ii. 7); a more vivid *hope* when hearing the report of Christ (Matt. xv. 26, 27; Acts xiii. 42, 46); they *believed also* when they "heard" the Gospel "word" preached; then, finally, they were "sealed" by the Spirit: baptism and laying on of hands were the visible signs. the word of truth—the instrument of sanctification and of the new birth (John xvii. 17; 2 Tim. ii. 15; Jas. i. 18). Cf. Col. i. 5, where also, as here, it is connected with 'hope.' Also ch. iv. 21, not mere legal types, but the *truth* (John i. 17). the gospel of —which sets forth "your salvation." sealed—as God's confirmed children (Acts xix. 1-6; Rom. viii. 16, 23, note; 2 Cor. i. 22; 1 John iii. 24). A seal on a document gives validity to the contract in it (John iii. 33; vi. 27: cf. 2 Cor. iii. 3). So the sense of 'the love of God shed abroad in the heart by the Holy Ghost' (Rom. v. 5), and the adoption given through the Spirit at regeneration (Rom. viii. 15, 16), assures believers of God's good-will. The Spirit, like the seal, impresses on the soul the image of our Father. The 'sealing' [*esphragisthete:* aorist] is spoken of as *past* once for all. The witnessing to our hearts that we are the children of God, and heirs (*v.* 11), is the Spirit's *present* testimony, the 'earnest of the (coming) inheritance' (Rom. viii. 16-18). that Holy Spirit of (given by) promise—Greek, 'The Spirit of promise, even the Holy Spirit' (whose essence is holiness, and who therefore imparts it to God's children). The *Spirit promised* in the Old and New Testaments (Joel ii. 28; Zech. xii. 10; John vii. 38, 39). "The word" *promised* the Holy Spirit. Those who believed "the word of truth" were sealed by the Spirit accordingly. 14. earnest—the first instalment paid as a pledge that the rest of the purchased inheritance will follow [*arrhabon*] (Rom. viii. 23); 2 Cor. v. 5): a portion of the purchase-money paid as *earnest.* until—rather, '*unto* [*eis*] the redemption,' &c.: joined thus, "ye were sealed" (*v.* 13) unto; *i. e., for the purpose of, and against,* "the redemption;" viz., not *redemption* in its first stage, made by the blood of Christ securing our *title,* but in its final completion (1 Cor. i. 30), when the *possession* shall be ours, the "redemption of the body," as well as of the soul, from every infirmity (ch. iv. 30). The deliverance of the creature (the whole visible creation) from the bondage of corruption, and from the usurping prince of this world, into the glorious liberty of the children of God (Rom. viii. 21-23; 2 Pet. iii. 13). of the purchased possession [*tēs peripoieseōs:* answering to the Old Testament *segullath, Jehovah,* the *laos periousios* of the LXX.]—God's people *purchased* (acquired) as His *peculiar* possession by Christ's blood (Acts xx. 28). We value highly what we pay dearly for: so God, His church (ch. v. 25, 26; 1 Pet. i. 18; ii. 9; Mal. iii. 17, *margin*). 15. Wherefore—because ye are in Christ sealed by His Spirit (*vv.* 13, 14). I also—on my part, in

16 love unto all the saints, cease not to give thanks for you, making men-
17 tion of you in my prayers; that the God of our Lord Jesus Christ, the Father of glory, *a*may give unto you the spirit of wisdom and revelation
18 *4*in the knowledge of him: the *b*eyes of your understanding being enlightened; that ye may know what is the hope of his calling, and
19 what the riches of the glory of his inheritance in the saints, and what *is* the exceeding greatness of his power to us-ward who believe, *c*according
20 to the working *5*of his mighty power, which he wrought in Christ, when he raised him from the dead, and set *him* at his own right hand in the
21 heavenly *places*, far *d*above all principality, and power, and might, and

A. D. 64.
a Col. 1. 9.
4 Or for the acknow-
ledgment.
b Acts 26. 18.
c Col. 1. 29.
5 Of the
might of
his power.
d Phil. 2. 9.
Col. 2. 10.
Heb. 1. 4.

return for God's so great benefits to *you*. **after** (ever since) **I heard**—not implying that he had only *heard* of their conversion: an argument used by some against the address of this epistle to the Ephesians (note, *v.* 1); but referring to the report he heard, *since* being with them four or five years previously, as to their Christian graces. So in the case of Philemon, his "*beloved fellow-labourer*" (Phile. 4, 5). **your faith** [*tēn kath 'humas pistin*] —'the faith among you;' *i. e.*, which many (not all) of you have. **love** (so Δ G *fg*, Vulgate; but א A B omit) **unto all the saints**—of whatever name, simply because they are saints: a characteristic of true Christianity (ch. vi. 24). '*Faith* and *love* go hand in hand.' *Hope* is added, *v.* 18. **16.** (Col. i. 9) **of you** (so G *fg*, Vulgate: omitted in א A B Δ). Then translate as English version, not as *Alford*, 'making mention of *them*' (your 'faith and love'). **17.** A fit prayer for all. "I also," answering to "ye also," *v.* 13. St. Paul joins his praises and prayers to theirs. **the God of our Lord Jesus**—appropriate title here; as in *vv.* 20-22 he treats of *God's* raising *Jesus* to be Head over all things to the Church. Jesus called the Father "*My* God" (Matt. xxvii. 46; John xx. 17). **the Father of** (whose characteristic is) **glory** (cf. Acts vii. 2)—Father of that infinite glory which shines in the face of Christ; the true Shechinah glory: through whom also 'the glory of the inheritance' (*v.* 18) shall be ours (John xvii. 24; 2 Cor. iii. 7 to iv. 6). **the spirit of wisdom**—whose is infinite wisdom; who works *wisdom in general* in believers (Isa. xi. 2). **and revelation**—whose function it is to *reveal spiritual mysteries* (John xvi. 14, 15; 1 Cor. ii. 10). **in the knowledge** —Greek (see note, 1 Cor. xiii. 12), 'in the *full knowledge* [*epignosei*] of Him'—viz., God (2 Pet. i. 2). **18.** Result of the gift of the Spirit. **understanding.** א A B Δ G *fg*, Vulgate, read 'heart.' Cf. the contrary state of the unbelieving, the *heart* being in fault (ch. iv. 18; Matt. xiii. 15). Translate, 'Having the eyes of your heart enlightened' (Matt. iv. 16; ch. iii. 9, Greek; v. 14): the first effect of the Spirit moving in the new creation, as in the physical creation (Gen. i. 3; 2 Cor. iv. 6). Where spiritual *light* is, there is *life* (John i. 4). The heart is 'the core of life' (*Harless*), the fountain of the thoughts; whence 'the heart' includes the *mind*, as well as the inclinations. Its "eye," or inward vision, both receives and contemplates the light (Matt. vi. 22, 23). The eye is the symbol of intelligence (Ezek. i. 18). **the hope of his calling** —the hope appertaining to, and wrought in, you by the calling wherewith He has called you. **and** (so C: omitted in א A B Δ G *fg*, Vulgate) . . . **riches of the glory** (Col. i. 27). The accumulation marks unspeakable preciousness. **his inheritance in the saints**—the inheritance which He has in store [*estin* being understood] in the case of ('among,' *Ellicott*, Acts xx. 32; xxvi. 18) the saints ('the sphere in which it is found'). Perhaps 'the inheritance which He has in his saints.' (See note,

v. 11; Deut. xxxii. 9). This latter translation would be more certain if the article *tēs* had been before *en tois hagiois*. **19. exceeding**—'surpassing.' **power to us-ward who believe**—the whole working of His grace which He *is* carrying on, and *will* carry on to glory, in us who believe. This is that whereby the "hope" is realized: a climax. The *hope* which the calling awakens; the *glory* of that inheritance to which hope is directed; the *power* that shall bestow (and is bestowing) it (*Ellicott*). By "saints" (*v.* 18), believers are viewed as *absolutely perfected*, and so as being God's inheritance: in this verse, as in the course of *fighting* the good fight. **according to**—what might be expected from [*kata*]. **working** [*energeian*]—'the energizing;' "the effectual working" (ch. iii. 7). The same superhuman power was exerted to make us believe, as was exerted to raise Christ from the dead (*v.* 20). Cf. Phil. iii. 10, "the power of His resurrection" (Col. ii. 12; 1 Pet. i. 3-5). **of his mighty power** [*tou kratous tes ischuos autou*]—'of the strength of His might.' [*Ischus*, 'strength,' is God's *passive* inherent power; *kratos* is His power evinced in *action; '* might' (*Ellicott*).] **20. which**—'working.' **in Christ**—the 'first-fruits' of the resurrection, our Head. **when he raised him**—'in that He (the Father) raised Him.' The raising of Christ is not only an earnest of our bodies being hereafter raised, but has a power in it involving (by virtue of our living union with Him, as members with the Head) the resurrection spiritually of the believer's soul now, consequently of his body hereafter (Rom. vi. 8-11; viii. 11). The Son, too, as God (though not as man), had a share in raising His own human body (John ii. 19; x. 17, 18); also the Holy Spirit (Rom. i. 4; 1 Pet. iii. 18). **set him** [*ekathisen*]—'made Him sit.' The glorious spirits *stand* about the throne, but they do not *sit at God's right hand* (Ps. cx. 1; Heb. i. 13), where He remains till all His enemies have been put under His feet (1 Cor. xv. 24). Being appointed to 'rule in the midst of His enemies' during their rebellion (Ps. cx. 2), He shall resign His commission after their subjection (*Pearson*) (Mark xvi. 19; Heb. i. 3; x. 12); then He, as God-man, shall reign for ever and ever. **in the heavenly places** (*v.* 3; ch. iv. 10). As Christ has a literal body, heaven is not merely a state, but a *place;* and where He is, there His people shall be (John xiv. 3: cf. ch. i. 11; vii. 56). **21.** [*huperano*] 'Far (or high) above all principality [*arches*, rule, 1 Cor. xv. 24], and power [*exousias*] authority, and [*dunameos*] power (Matt. xxviii. 18), and dominion [*kuriotetos*, lordship]' (cf. Phil. ii. 9; Col. i. 16; Heb. vii. 26; 1 Pet. iii. 22). Evil spirits (similarly divided into various ranks, ch. vi. 12), as well as angels of light (ch. iii. 10), and earthly potentates, are included (cf. Rom. viii. 38). Jesus is "King of kings, and Lord of lords" (Rev. xix. 16). The higher is His honour, the greater is that of His people—His members joined to Him, the Head. Philosophizing teachers, of

dominion, and every name that is named, not **only in** this world, but
22 also in that which is to come; and ‘hath put all *things* under his feet,
23 and gave him *f to be* the head over all *things* to the church, which *g* is his
body, the fulness of him that *h* filleth all in all.

2 AND *a* you *hath he quickened*, who were dead in trespasses and sins;
2 wherein *b* in time past ye walked according to the course of this world,
according to the prince of the power of the air, the spirit that now

A. D. 64.	
e Matt. 28. 18.	
f Heb. 2. 7.	
g Rom. 12. 5.	
h John 1. 14.	
CHAP. 2.	
a John 5. 24.	
b 1 John 5. 19.	

the school of Simon Magus, in western Asia, had, according to Irenæus, made much of these various ranks of angels. St. Paul shows that the truest wisdom is to know Christ as reigning above them all. **every name**—every being whatever; "any other creature" (Rom. viii. 38, 39). **in this world** —Greek, ‘*age*;’ *i. e.*, the present *order of things*, wherein sin has place; "things present . . . things to come," **that which is to come**—"the kingdom of God" set up already, but not till hereafter to be fully manifested on earth (Matt. xii. 31, 32). Names which now we know not, but shall know hereafter. We know that the emperor goes before all, though we cannot enumerate all the ministers of his court; so we know that Christ is set above all, although we cannot *name* them all (*Bengel*). **22. put all things under** [*hupetaxen*]—‘put in subjection under’ (Gen. i. 28; Ps. viii. 6; 1 Cor. xv. 27). Not only is He infinitely *exalted* (v. 21), but He has *universal* dominion. The original grant of it to man is realized for him in Christ. **to the church**—for her special advantage. The Greek order is emphatic: ‘ HIM (exalted and supremely glorious as He is) God gave as Head over all things to the Church.’ Had it been any one save HIM, her Head, it would not have been the boon it is. But as *He* is Head over all things who is also her Head, all things are hers (1 Cor. iii. 21-23). He is OVER ("far above") all things; in contrast with "TO *the church*"—viz., *for her advantage.* The former are subject; the latter is joined with Him in His dominion over them. "Head" implies not only His dominion, but our union; therefore, while we look upon Him at God's right hand, we see ourselves in heaven (Rev. iii. 21). For the Head and body are not severed by anything intervening, else the body would cease to be the body, and the Head cease to be the Head (*Chrysostom*). **23. which is** [*hētis*]— *inasmuch as she is.* **his body**—His mystical body. Not merely figurative. He is really, though spiritually, the Church's Head. His life is her life. She shares His crucifixion and His consequent glory. He possesses everything, His fellowship with the Father, His fulness of the Spirit, and His glorified manhood, not merely for Himself, but *for her*, who has a membership of His body, of His flesh, and of His bones (ch. v. 30). **fulness.** The Church is *dwelt in and filled by Christ.* She is *the receptacle*, not of His inherent, but *of His communicated plenitude of gifts and graces.* As His is the "fulness" (John i. 16; Col. i. 19; ii. 9) inherently, so she is His "fulness" by His impartation of it to her, in virtue of her union to Him (ch. v. 18). ‘The *full manifestation* of His being, because penetrated by His life’ (*Conybeare*): the continued revelation of His Divine life in human form; the *fullest representative of His plenitude.* Not the angelic hierarchy, as false teachers taught (Col. ii. 9, 10, 18), but Christ Himself, is the "fulness of the Godhead;" and she represents Him. **filleth all in all.** Christ as Creator, Preserver, and Governor, constituted by God (Col. i. 16, &c.), *fills all* [*ta panta*, א A B Δ G] the universe of things *with all* things, whatever it possesses: [*pleroumenou*] ‘filleth *for Himself.*’

CHAP. II. 1-22.—GOD'S GRACE IN QUICKENING US, ONCE DEAD, THROUGH CHRIST—HIS PURPOSE IN DOING SO—EXHORTATION BASED ON OUR PRIVILEGES AS BUILT TOGETHER, AN HOLY TEMPLE, IN CHRIST, THROUGH THE SPIRIT.

1. And you—you also, among those who have experienced His mighty power in enabling them to believe (ch. i. 19-23). **hath he quickened.** Supplied from the Greek, *v.* 5. **dead**—spiritually (Col. ii. 13). A living corpse: without God's Spirit in the soul; so unable to think, will, or do aught that is holy. **in trespasses and sins**—*in* them, as the element in which the unbeliever is, and through which he is dead to the true life. Sin is the death of the soul (Isa. ix. 2; John v. 25): "dead" (spiritually, 1 Tim. v. 6; ch. iv. 18). Greek, ‘in *your* trespasses,’ &c. ‘Trespass’ [*paraptoma*] expresses a *particular* FALL or LAPSE, such as that whereby Adam fell. ‘Sin’ [*hamartia*] is the *general* term, implying innate *corruption* and ALIENATION from God (lit., *erring from, missing, the rule of truth*), exhibited in *acts* of sin [Greek, *hamartemata*]. *Bengel* refers "trespasses" to the Jews who had the law, yet revolted from it; "sins," to the Gentiles who know not God. **2. the course of this world**—the career (*lit.*, ‘the age:’ cf. Gal. i. 4) or present system of *this* world (1 Cor. ii. 6, 12; iii. 18, 19), as opposed to "the world to come;" not gradually ameliorating, but progressively deteriorating: alien from God, and lying in the wicked one (1 John v. 19). ‘The age’ [*aion*] (something internal and ethical) regulates ‘the world’ [*kosmos*] (something more external). **the prince of the power of the air**— the unseen potentate who lies underneath, guiding "the course of this world" (2 Cor. iv. 4); ranging through the *air*—*i. e.*, the whole region between earth and heaven (cf. Mark iv. 4, "fowls of the air" (Greek, ‘heaven’)—*i. e., v.* 15, "Satan" and his demons). Cf. ch. vi. 12; John xii. 31. Christ's ascension cast Satan out of heaven (Rev. xii. 5, 9, 10, 12, 13, 15, 17), where he had been heretofore, the accuser of the brethren (Job i. 7). No longer able to accuse *in heaven* those justified by Christ, the ascended Saviour (Rom. viii. 33, 34), he assails them on earth with all trials and temptations: ‘we live in an atmosphere poisoned and impregnated with deadly elements; but a mighty purification of the air will be effected by Christ's coming’ (*Auberlen*), for Satan shall be bound (Rev. xx. 2, 3). "The power" is here collectively for the ‘powers of the air;’ in apposition with which ‘powers’ stands "the spirit," taken also collectively: the aggregate of the "seducing spirits" (1 Tim. iv. 1) which ‘work now (*still*, not merely, as in your case, "in time *past*") in the sons of disobedience (a Hebraism: men not merely by accident disobedient, but whose essential characteristic is *disobedience*: cf. Matt. iii. 7), and of which Satan is "the prince." [*Tou pneumatos*] "The spirit" is in apposition, not to *Satan*, "the prince" [*archonta*], but to [*exousias*] ‘*the powers of the air*,’ of which he is prince. The powers of the air are the embodiment of that evil "spirit" which is the ruling principle of unbelievers (Acts xxvi. 18), as opposed to the spirit of the children of God (Luke iv. 33). The potency of that

3 worketh in ^c the children of disobedience : among ^d whom also we all had
our conversation in times past in ^e the lusts of our flesh, fulfilling ¹ the
desires of the flesh and of the mind; ^f and were by nature the children
4 of wrath, even as others. But God, ^g who is rich in mercy, for his great
5 love wherewith he loved us, even when we were dead in sins, hath
6 quickened us together with Christ, (² by grace ye are saved;) and hath
raised *us* up together, and made *us* sit together in heavenly *places* in
7 Christ Jesus: that in the ages to come he might show the exceeding

A. D. 64.

^c Col. 3. 6.
^d Tit. 3. 3.
^e Gal. 5. 16.
1 the wil s.
^f Ps 51. 5.
^g Rom 10.12.
2 Or. by
whose
grace.

"spirit" is shown in the "disobedience" of the former (cf. Deut. xxxii. 20; Isa. xxx. 9; lvii. 4). They disobey the Gospel in faith and practice (2 Thess. i. 8; 1 Cor. ii. 12). But *Ellicott*, 'prince of the *empire* of the air, of the (evil) *principle* that now worketh,' &c. 3. also we—i. e., *we also.* St. Paul joins himself in the same category, passing from the second (*vv.* 1, 2) to the first person. all —Jews and Gentiles. had our conversation— 'our way of life' (2 Cor. i. 12; 1 Pet. i. 18). This [*anestraphemen*] implies an outwardly more *decorous* course than the 'walk' in *gross sins* on the part of the Gentile Ephesians in times past (*v.* 2). Paul and his Jewish countrymen, though outwardly more seemly than the Gentiles (Acts xxvi. 4, 5, 18), had been essentially like them in living to the unrenewed flesh, without the Spirit of God. fulfilling—Greek, 'doing.' mind [*ton dianoiōn*]— 'our thoughts.' *Mental* suggestions and purposes (independent of God); spiritual sins of the intellect; as distinguished from blind impulses of "the flesh," the sensual, worldly principle. and were by nature. He intentionally substitutes 'and we were' for 'and being,' to contrast emphatically his and their *past* state by nature with their present state by grace. Not merely, we had our way of life fulfilling our fleshly desires, *and so being* children of wrath; but *we were by nature* originally "children of wrath," and consequently had our way of life fulfilling our fleshly desires. "Nature" [*phusei*] implies that which has *grown* with our growth, and strengthened with our strength, as distinguished from that wrought on us by mere external influences: what is inherent, not acquired (Job xiv. 4; Ps. li. 5). An incidental proof of original sin. children of wrath —not merely 'sons,' as 'sons [*huiois*] of disobedience' (*v.* 2), but "children" [*tekna*] *by generation*; not merely *by adoption*, as 'sons' might be. The Greek order marks this innate corruption : 'Those who in their (very) nature are children of wrath:' *v.* 5, "grace" is opposed to "nature" here; and *salvation* (implied in *vv.*5, 8, "saved") to "wrath." Cf. Article IX., 'Common Prayer Book.' 'Original, or birth-sin, standeth not in the following of Adam, but is the fault and corruption of the nature of every man naturally engendered of Adam (Christ was *supernaturally* conceived by the Holy Ghost of the virgin), whereby man is very far gone from original righteousness, and is of his own nature inclined to evil; and therefore, in every person born into this world, it deserveth God's wrath and damnation.' St. Paul shows that even the Jews, notwithstanding their birth from Abraham, were naturally children of wrath as the Gentiles, whom the Jews despised for their birth from idolaters (Rom. iii. 9; v. 12-14). '*Wrath* (God's judicial hatred of sin) abideth' on all who disobey the Gospel in faith and practice (John iii. 36). "Children of wrath"—a Hebraism; *i. e.*, essentially *objects of wrath* in our inherent nature, as born in sin. So 'son of death' (*margin*, 2 Sam. xii. 5), "son of perdition" (John xvii. 12; 2 Thess. ii. 3). as others [*hoi loipoi*]—'as the rest' of mankind are (1 Thess. iv. 13). 4. But. Consolatory con-

trast to the universality of men's natural heritage of "wrath." God, who is rich—Greek, '(as) *being* rich in mercy.' for—*i. e.*, 'because of [*dia*] His great love :' the *special* ground of God's saving us; as "rich in mercy" (cf. *v.* 7; ch. i. 7; Rom. ii. 4; x. 12) was the general ground. '*Mercy* takes away misery, *love* confers salvation' (*Bengel*). 5. dead in sins—'dead in *our* [*tois, the*] *trespasses.*' quickened—'vivified' spiritually; by consequence, hereafter, corporally. There must be a spiritual resurrection of the soul before there can be a comfortable resurrection of the body (*Pearson*) (John xi. 25, 26; Rom. viii. 11). together with Christ. The Head being seated at God's right hand, the body also sits there with Him (*Chrysostom*). We are already seated there IN Him ("in Christ Jesus," *v.* 6), and hereafter shall be seated *by* Him: IN Him already as in our Head, which is the ground of our hope; *by* Him hereafter, as by the conferring cause, when hope shall be swallowed up in fruition (*Pearson*). What God wrought in Christ, He wrought (by the very fact) in all united to and one with Christ. (by grace ye are saved) [*sesōsmenoi*]—'ye are in a saved state.' Not merely 'ye are being saved,' but already "passed from death unto life" (John v. 24). Salvation is to the Christian not to be waited for hereafter, but already, in some degree, realized (1 John iii. 14). This parenthetic clause (cf. *v.* 8) is to make them feel what otherwise their remaining corruptions would make them doubt—namely, their present fellowship in the quickening with Christ. Not their works, but God's *grace* throughout, is the sole source of salvation; hence he says "ye," not 'we.' 6. raised us up together—with Christ. The 'raising up' pre-supposes previous quickening of Jesus in the tomb, and of us in the grave of our sins. made us sit together—with Christ; viz., in His ascension. Believers are bodily in heaven in point of right, and virtually so in spirit, and have each their own place assigned there, which in due time they shall take possession of (Phil. iii. 20, 21). He does not say '*on the right hand* of God'—a prerogative peculiar to Christ. They shall share His throne (Rev. iii. 21). in Christ Jesus. Our vital union with Him is the ground of our present spiritual and future bodily resurrection and ascension. "*Christ Jesus*" is the usual phrase in this epistle, in which the *office* of the Anointed Prophet, Priest, and King is prominent; when the Person is prominent, "Jesus Christ" is used. 7. [*endeixetai*] 'That He might show forth (middle reflexive voice: for His own glory, ch. i. 6, 12, 14) in the ages which are coming on'—*i. e.*, the blessed *ages* of the Gospel which supersede 'the *uge* [*aiōna,* "course"] of this world' (*v.* 2), and the past "ages" from which the mystery was hidden (Col. i. 26, 27). These good *ages*, beginning with the first preaching of the Gospel, *and thenceforth continually succeeding one another*, are not consummated till the Lord's coming again (cf. ch. i. 21; Heb. vi. 5). The 'coming on' does not exclude the *time then present*, but implies the ages *following* upon Christ's 'having raised them up together'

8 riches of his grace in *his* kindness toward us through Christ Jesus. For
by grace are ye saved *ʰ*through faith; and that not of yourselves; *ⁱit is*
9, the gift of God : not *ʲ*of works, lest any man should boast. For we are
10 his workmanship, created in Christ Jesus unto good works, *ᵏ*which God
hath before ³ ordained that we should walk in them.
11 Wherefore remember, that ye *being* in time past Gentiles in the flesh,
who are called Uncircumcision by that which is called *ˡ*the Circumcision
12 in the flesh made by hands; that *ᵐ*at that time ye were without Christ,
*ⁿ*being aliens from the commonwealth of Israel, and strangers from *ᵒ*the
covenants of promise, having *ᵖ*no hope, and *q* without God in the world :
13 but *ʳ*now in Christ Jesus ye who sometimes were far off are made nigh by

A. D. 61.	
ʰ Rom. 4. 16.	
ⁱ John 6. 44.	
ʲ Rom. 3. 20.	
ᵏ ch. 1. 4.	
3 Or, pre-pared.	
ˡ Rom 2. 28.	
ᵐ Col. 1. 21.	
ⁿ John 10.16.	
ᵒ Rom 9.4,8.	
ᵖ 1 Thes.4.13.	
q Gal. 4. 8.	
ʳ Gal. 3. 23.	

(*v.* 6). **kindness** [*chrestoteti*]—'benignity.' **through Christ**—Greek, 'in Christ;' as often, to mark that all our blessings centre 'IN HIM' as their source. Hence "Christ" is so often repeated. **8. For**—illustrating 'the exceeding riches of His grace in kindness.' He emphatically recurs to the truth (*v.* 5), 'By grace ye are in a saved state.' **through faith**—the hand which apprehends Christ unto salvation, nerved by the power of Christ's resurrection (ch. i. 19, 20; Phil. iii. 10), whereby we are 'raised together' with him (*v.* 6; Col. ii. 12). A reads 'through your (lit., '*the;*' א B Δ G omit) faith,' which *accepts* "grace." Christ alone is the *meritorious* agent. **and that**—viz., *the act of believing*, or "faith," which might seem to be your own independent act, is not so. **of yourselves** —in contrast to "it is the gift of God" (Phil. i. 29). In saying "through faith," I do not wish to except *faith* from *grace*. 'God justifies the believing man, not for the worthiness of his belief, but for the worthiness of Him in whom he believes'(*Hooker*). The initiation, as well as the increase of faith, is from the Spirit of God; not only by an external proposal of the Word, but by internal illumination in the soul (*Pearson*). Yet "faith" cometh through means—viz., 'hearing the word of God' (Rom. x. 17) and prayer (Luke xi. 13), whilst the blessing is wholly of God (1 Cor. iii. 6, 7). **9. not of works.** This clause stands in contrast to "by grace" (Rom. iv. 4, 5; xi. 6). **lest**—Greek, 'that no man should boast' (Rom. iii. 27; iv. 2). **10. workmanship** [*poiēma*]—'a thing of His making,' 'handiwork.' Here the spiritual creation, not the physical, is referred to (*vv.* 8, 9). **created**—having been created (Ps. cii. 18; Isa. xliii. 21; 2 Cor. v. 5, 17; ch. iv. 24) **unto** [*epi ergois*]—'for good works.' "Good works" cannot be performed until we are new 'created unto' or *for* them. St. Paul never **calls** the works of the law "good works." We are not *saved by*, but *created for*, good works. **before ordained** [*proetoimasen*]—'before made ready' (cf. John v. 36). God marks out for each in His purposes *beforehand* the particular good works, the time, and way, which He sees best. God both makes ready by His providence the opportunities for *the works*, and makes *us* ready for their performance (John xv. 16; 2 Tim. ii. 21). **that we should walk in them**—not 'be saved' by them. Works do not justify, but the justified man works (Gal. v. 22-25).

11. Wherefore—since God has manifested such "grace." The Greek order in א A B Δ, Vulgate, **is**, 'That in time past [*pote, once*] ye,' &c. Such remembrance sharpens gratitude and strengthens faith (*v.* 19) (*Bengel*). **Gentiles in the flesh**—*i. e.*, Gentiles in respect to circumcision. **called Uncircumcision**—who are called (in contempt), *and are*, the Uncircumcision. The Jews were called, but were not truly, the Circumcision: they realized not its spiritual meaning (*Ellicott*). **in the flesh made by hands**—as opposed to the true circum-

cision "of the heart, in the spirit, and not the letter" (Rom. ii. 29): "made without hands, in putting off the body of the sins of the flesh by the circumcision of Christ" (Col. ii. 11; Phil. iii. 2, 3): an external instead of a spiritual process. **12. without Christ** [*chōris*, implying separation of the subject from the object]—'*separate from* Christ:' having no part in Him: far from Him. A different word [*aneu*, implying absence of the object from the subject] would express, 'Christ was not present with you' (*Tittmarsh*). **aliens**—Greek, 'alienated from.' Not merely 'separated from.' The Israelites were cut off from the commonwealth of God, but it was as being self-righteous and unworthy, not as *aliens* and *strangers*. The 'alienated from' takes it for granted that the Gentiles, before they apostatized from the primitive truth, were sharers in light and life (cf. ch. iv. 18, 23). The hope of redemption through Messiah, on their subsequent apostasy, was embodied into a definite spiritual "commonwealth" or *polity*—viz., that "of Israel," from which the Gentiles were alienated. Contrast *v.* 13; ch. iii. 6; iv. 4, 5, with Ps. cxlvii. 20. 'They parted only to unite again (Acts iv. 27) in one act of uttermost rebellion; yet, through redeeming love, to be thereby (*vv.* 15, 16) united in Christ for ever' (*Ellicott*). **covenants of promise**—rather, 'of *the* promise;' viz., "to thee and thy seed will I give this land" (Rom. ix. 4-6; Gal. iii. 16). The plural implies the several renewals of the covenant with Abraham, Isaac, and Jacob (Rom. xv. 8). 'The promise' is singular, to signify that the covenant substantially is the same at all times, only different in its external circumstances (cf. Heb. i. 1, "at sundry times and in divers manners"). **having no** [ME *echontes:* subjective negation: not having, as you would yourselves admit] **hope**— beyond this life (1 Cor. xv. 19). The CONJECTURES of heathen philosophers as to a future life were at best vague, and utterly unsatisfactory. They had no Divine "promise," therefore no sure ground of "hope." Epicurus and Aristotle did not believe in it at all. The Platonists believed the soul passed through perpetual changes,—now happy, then again miserable; the Stoics, that it existed no longer than till the general burning up of all things. **without God** [*atheoi:* objective negation]—'atheists;' *i. e.*, they had not "God" in our sense, the Eternal Being who made and governs all things (cf. Acts xiv. 15); whereas the Jews knew God (cf. also Gal. iv. 8; 1 Thess. iv. 5). So also pantheists are atheists; for an impersonal God is NO GOD—an ideal immortality no immortality. **in the world**—in contrast to belonging to "the commonwealth of Israel:" having their portion and their all in *this godless, secular, ethnic world* (Ps. xvii. 14), from which Christ delivers His people (John xv. 19; xvii. 14; Gal. i. 4). **13. now**—in contrast to "at that time" (*v.* 12). **in Christ Jesus.** Jesus is added (in contrast to *v.* 12.

14 the blood of Christ. For 'he is our peace, who hath made both one, and
15 hath broken down the middle wall of partition *between us;* having abolished 'in his flesh the enmity, *even* the law of commandments *contained* in ordinances; for to make in himself of twain one "new man, *so* making
16 peace; and that he might reconcile both unto God in one body by the
17 cross, having 'slain the enmity ⁴ thereby: and came "and preached peace
18 to you which were afar off, and to them that were nigh. For through him we both have access by one Spirit unto the Father.
19 Now therefore ye are no more strangers and foreigners, but fellow-

A. D. 64.

* Isa. 9. 6, 7.
Eze. 34. 24.
Mic. 5. 5.
‡ Col. 1. 21.
⁵ 2 Cor. 5. 17.
⁶ Rom. 6. 6.
4 Or, in himself.
¹⁰ Isa. 57. 19.
Zech. 9. 10.

"without *Christ*") to mark that they know Christ as the *personal* Saviour, "Jesus." **sometimes**—Greek, 'aforetime.' **far off**—the Jewish description of the Gentiles. Far off from God and from His people (Isa. lvii. 19; Acts ii. 39; *v.* 17). **are**—Greek, 'were.' **by**—Greek, 'in:' *in virtue of your interest in* "the blood of Christ:" IN it as the element of nearness to God, ye were made and are now nigh. In ch. i. 7, where the blood is more directly spoken of as the *instrument*, it is "*through* His blood." **14. he**—Greek, 'Himself,' and none else. **our peace**—not merely 'peacemaker,' but the sole source of our (Jews' and Gentiles' alike) peace with God, so the bond of union between "both" in God. He took both into Himself, and reconciled us to God, by assuming our nature and our penal and legal liabilities (Isa. iv. 5, 6; liii. 5; Mic. v. 5; *v.* 15; Col. i. 20). His title, "Shiloh," means the same (Gen. xlix. 10). **the middle wall of partition** [*mesotoichon tou phragmou*]—'of the partition' or 'fence:' the *middle wall* which *parted* Jew and Gentile. There was a balustrade of stone which separated the court of the Gentiles from the holy place, which it was death for a Gentile to pass. This, though alluded to, was but a symbol of the partition itself—viz., "the enmity" between "*both*" *and God* (*v.* 15), the real cause of separation from God, and so the mediate cause of their separation from one another. Hence there was a twofold wall: one, the inner, severing even the Jewish people from the holy part of the temple where the priests officiated; the other, the outer, separating the Gentile proselytes from the court of the Jews (cf. Ezek. xliv. 7; Acts xxi. 28). This twofold wall represented the Sinaitic law, which *both* severed all men, even the Jews, from access to God (through sin, which is the violation of the law), and also separated the Gentiles from the Jews. As "wall" implies the *strength* of the partition, so 'fence' implies that it was easily removed by God when the due time came. Cf. the rending of the veil at Jesus' death, Heb. x. 20, with Matt. xxvii. 51. 'The temple was a material embodiment of the law; its outward figure a symbol of spiritual distinctions' (*Ellicott*). **15.** Rather, make "enmity" an apposition to "the middle wall of partition." 'Hath broken down the middle wall of partition (not merely, as the English version, "*between us,*" but also *between all men and God)*—to wit, the enmity (resulting *between Jew and Gentile* from the law, and chiefly *between both and God)* (Rom. viii. 7) in His (crucified) flesh; *i. e.*, in virtue of it' (Col. i. 21, 22: cf. Rom. viii. 3; *v.* 16). **the law of commandments contained in** [*ton nomon tōn entolōn en dogmasin*]—'having abolished the law of THE commandments (expressed) in ordinances (in mandatory decrees).' This law was the "partition" which expressed the "enmity" (the "wrath" of God against our sin, and our enmity to Him, *v.* 3) (Rom. iv. 15; *v.* 20; vii. 10, 11; viii. 7). Christ has "abolished" it, so far as its condemning and enmity-creating power is concerned (Col. ii. 14), substituting the law of love, the everlasting spirit

of the law, which flows from realizing in the soul His love in His death for us. Translate, 'That He might make the two (Jews and Gentiles) into one new man.' Not that He might merely reconcile the two to each other, but incorporate the two, reconciled in Him to God, into one new man; the old man, to which both belonged, the enemy of God, having been slain in His flesh on the cross. Observe, ONE new man: believers are all in God's sight one in Christ, as we are but one in Adam (*Alford*). **making peace**—primarily, between all and God; secondarily, between Jews and Gentiles (*v.* 14). This 'peacemaking' precedes its publication (*v.* 17). **16.** Translate, 'Might completely reconcile again both in one body (the Church, ch. iv. 4; Col. iii. 15) unto (their original unity with) God through His cross.' The "reconcile" [*apocatalaxe*], found only here and Col. i. 20, expresses not only a return to favour with one [*catallage*], but so to lay aside enmity that complete amity follows; to pass *from* enmity to *complete reconciliation (Tittmarsh).* **having** (*after He had*) **slain the enmity**—viz., between man and God; and so that between Jew and Gentile, which resulted from it. By His being *slain*, He *slew* it (cf. Heb. ii. 14). **thereby**—Greek, 'therein:' 'in virtue of the cross;' *i. e.*, His crucifixion (Col. ii. 15). **17.** Translate, 'He came (of His free love) and announced glad tidings of [*euengelisato*] peace to the apostles (Luke xxiv. 36; John xx. 19, 21, 26), and by them to others, through His Spirit present in His Church' (John xiv. 18). Acts xxvi. 23 is parallel: after His resurrection 'He showed light to the (Jewish) people ("them that were nigh") and to the Gentiles' ("you which were afar off") by His Spirit in His ministers (cf. 1 Pet. iii. 19). **and to them.** ℵ A B Δ G, *fg*, Vulgate, insert "peace" again: 'And peace to them.' The repetition implies how both alike would dwell again and again upon the welcome word "peace." So Isa. lvii. 19. **18.** Translate, 'For it is through Him (John xiv. 6; Heb. x. 19) that we have our access (Rom. v. 2; ch. iii. 12), both of us, in (*i. e.*, united in; 1 Cor. xii. 13, Greek) one Spirit to the Father;' as our common Father, reconciled to both alike; whence all separation between Jew and Gentile ceases. The *oneness* of 'the Spirit,' as the common element IN which we both have our access (*admission*), entails *oneness* of the body, the Church (*v.* 16). The fact of our *access* proves the reality of our *peace* (*v.* 17) with God through Him. There is allusion to the Introducer in Eastern courts: Jesus is our Bringer to God (1 Pet. iii. 18). The distinctness of persons in the Trinity appears in this verse (marked by the three prepositions, *dia, en, pros*). There are now no sacerdotal priests through whom alone the people can approach God. All alike, people and ministers, can draw nigh *through Christ*, their ever-living Priest. **19. Now therefore**—'accordingly, then' [*ara oun*]. **foreigners** [*paroikoi*]—'sojourners' (Lev. xxii. 10, 11); opposed to 'members of the household,' as "**strangers**" is to 'fellow-citizens' (Phil. iii.

20 citizens with the saints, and of the household of God; and are built
    ^aupon the foundation of the ^yapostles and prophets, Jesus Christ himself
21 being ^zthe chief corner *stone;* in whom all the building, fitly framed
22 together, groweth unto an holy temple in the Lord: in whom ye also are
    builded together for ^aan habitation of God through the Spirit.

3 FOR this cause I Paul, ^athe prisoner of Jesus Christ ^bfor you Gentiles,
2 (if ye have heard of ^cthe dispensation of the grace of God ^dwhich is
3 given me to you-ward: how that by revelation he made known unto
4 me the mystery; (as I wrote ¹afore in few words, whereby, when ye read,
5 ye may understand my knowledge in the mystery of Christ;) which

A. D 64.

^a Matt. 16.18.
^y 1 Cor.12.23.
^z Ps. 118. 22.
^a John :7.23.

CHAP. 3.
^a Acts 21. 33
^b 2 Tim. 2.10.
^c Rom. 1. 5.
^d Acts 9. 15.
¹ Or, a little before.

19, 20, note). **but.** א A B C Δ G *f g*, Vulgate, add 'ye are.' **with the saints**—"the commonwealth of (spiritual) Israel" (*v.* 12). **of God**— THE FATHER, as JESUS CHRIST appears in *v.* 20, and THE SPIRIT in *v.* 22. **20.** [*Epoikodomethentes*, 'built up upon,' &c. ; *having been built up upon:* omit "and are."] Cf. 1 Cor. iii. 11, 12. The same image, in ch. iii. 17, recurs in his address to the *Ephesian* elders (Acts xx. 32), and in his epistle to Timothy at *Ephesus* (1 Tim. iii. 15; 2 Tim. ii. 19), naturally suggested by the splendid temple of Diana. The glory of the Christian temple is internal; not mere idolatrous gaud. The image is appropriate also to the Jew-Christians, as the temple at Jerusalem was the stronghold of Judaism. **foundation of the apostles, &c.**—*i. e.,* upon their preaching (cf. Matt. xvi. 18). Christ Himself, the only Foundation, was the subject of their ministry and spring of their life. As one with Him, His twelve fellow-workers, in a secondary sense, are "foundations" (Rev. xxi. 14). So Christ is THE *living Stone;* believers, *living stones,* by their union with Him (1 Pet. ii. 4, 5). The "prophets" are joined with them; for it is not '*foundations* of the apostles and *the* prophets,' but "*foundation* of the apostles and *prophets.*" For the doctrine of both was *one* (1 Pet. i. 10, 11; Rev. xix. 10). The apostles take the precedence (Luke x. 24). "The prophets" represent the old Jewish dispensation; "the apostles," the new. The "prophets" of the new also are included. *Alford* refers it solely to these. Ch. iii. 5; iv. 11 imply that the New Testament prophets are not excluded; but the apostle's reference to Ps. cxviii. 22, "the head stone of the corner," proves that the Old Testament prophets are prominent. David was a "prophet" (Acts ii. 30). Cf. also Isa. xxviii. 16. Both lean on the earlier prophecy of Jacob (Gen. xlix. 24). The context suits this: Ye were once aliens from the commonwealth *of Israel* (under her *Old Testament prophets*), but now ye are members of the true Israel, built upon the foundation of her New Testament apostles and *Old Testament prophets.* The one Greek article to both implies their close union. St. Paul identifies his teaching with that of Israel's old prophets (Acts xxvi. 22; xxviii. 23). The costly foundation stones of the temple (1 Ki. v. 17) were the type (cf. Jer. li. 26). Christ "Himself," none else, is at once the Corner Stone and the Foundation on which the whole building rests. St. Paul supposes a rock so large and so fashioned as to be both at once supporting the whole as the foundation and in part rising up at the extremities, so that the side walls are united in it as the corner stone (*Zanchius*). *Piazzi Smith* suggests *the topmost angle of the pyramid,* 'HEAD of the corner,' in which all meet (Zech. iv. 7). It is conspicuous; and, coming in men's way, may be stumbled over, as the Jews did at Christ (Ps. cxviii. 22; Matt. xxi. 42; 1 Pet. ii. 6, 7). **21. In whom**—as holding together the whole. **all the** (so A C; but B Δ G א omit *the:* 'every') **building**—*structure.* **fitly framed**—so as exactly to fit together. **growth**

—'is growing' continually. Here an additional thought is added: the Church has the *growth* of a *living organism* besides the solid *increase* of a *building.* Cf. 1 Pet. ii. 5, "*lively* stones . . . built up a spiritual house." Cf. ch. iv. 16; Zech. vi. 12, "the *Branch* shall build the *temple* of the Lord." **holy**—being the "habitation *of God*" (*v.* 22). So 'in the Lord' (Christ) answers to "through (IN) the Spirit" (*v.* 22: cf. ch. iii. 16, 17). Christ is the element in which the Church has its temple-like symmetry and its branch-like growth. **22. are** (being) **builded together . . . through** (Greek, '*in*') **the Spirit**—answering to "in the Lord" (*v.* 21). God, by His Spirit *in* believers, has them for His habitation (1 Cor. iii. 16, 17; vi. 19; 2 Cor. vi. 16).

CHAP. III. 1-21.—HIS APOSTOLIC OFFICE TO MAKE KNOWN THE MYSTERY OF CHRIST BY THE SPIRIT—PRAYER THAT BY THE SAME SPIRIT THEY MAY COMPREHEND CHRIST'S VAST LOVE — DOXOLOGY ENDING THIS DIVISION.

As the first chapter treated of THE FATHER's office; the second, THE SON'S; so this, that of THE SPIRIT.

1. of Jesus Christ—Greek, 'Christ Jesus' (Phile. 13): the *office* is thus prominent; the person in the English version. He marks Jesus' *Messiahship* as the origin of his being a "prisoner," owing to the jealousy of the Jews being roused at his preaching it to the *Gentiles.* My very bonds are profitable "for [*huper*, 'in behalf of'] you Gentiles" (*v.* 13; 2 Tim. ii. 10). He digresses at "For this cause," and does not complete the sentence until *v.* 14, where he resumes, "For this cause" —viz., because I know your call of God (ch. ii. 11-22) to be "fellow-heirs" with the Jews (*v.* 6), "I bow my knees unto" the Father of our common Saviour (*vv.* 14, 15) to confirm you by His Spirit. "I Paul," am the agent employed by the Spirit to enlighten you, having been first enlightened myself by the same Spirit (*vv.* 3-5, 9). **2.** (If—not doubt [*eige*, 'if indeed']: 'assuming (what I know to be the fact, viz.) that ye have heard,' &c. The indicative (Greek) implies: 'seeing that doubtless,' &c. He delicately reminds them of their having heard from himself, and probably from others, the fact (ch. iv. 21: see 'Introduction.' These words do not disprove Paul's personal acquaintance with his readers, or the address of this epistle *to the Ephesians* (cf. Acts xx. 17-24). **the dispensation**—'the office of dispensing, as a steward, the grace of God which was (not "is") given me to you-ward'; viz., to dispense to you. *Ellicott,* 'the dispensation in respect to the grace of God' (the qualifying grace of God for fulfilling my apostleship, ch. i. 10; Col. i. 25). **3. he made known.** א A B C Δ G *f g*, Vulgate, read 'that by way of revelation *was* the mystery (viz., of the admission of the Gentiles, *v.* 6) *made known* [*egnoristhē* for *egnorise*] unto me' (Gal. i. 12; ii. 2). **as** (the *fact,* not the manner) **I wrote afore**—viz., in this epistle (ch. i. 9, 10; ii. 13), the words of which he partly repeats. **4. Whereby**—'according to which,' *writing in brief* (*v.* 3). **understand my**

⁵ in other ages was not made known unto the sons of men, as it is now
6 revealed unto his holy apostles and prophets by the Spirit; that the
Gentiles should be fellow-heirs, and of the same body, ᶠand partakers of
7 his promise in Christ by the Gospel : whereof I was made a minister,
according to the gift of the grace of God given unto me by ᵍthe effectual
8 working of his power. Unto me, who am less than the least of all saints,
is this grace given, that I should preach among the Gentiles ʰ the un-
9 searchable riches of Christ; and to make all *men* see what *is* the fellowship of the mystery, ⁱwhich from the beginning of the world hath been
10 hid in God, ʲwho created all things by Jesus Christ: to ᵏ the intent that
now ˡunto the principalities and powers in heavenly *places* ᵐmight be
11 known by the church the manifold wisdom of God, according to the
12 eternal purpose which he purposed in Christ Jesus our Lord : in whom
we have boldness and access with confidence by the faith of him.

A. D. 64.

ᵉ Acts 10. 28.
ᶠ Gal. 3. 14.
ᵍ Rom. 15.18.
ʰ Ps. 31. 19.
John 1. 16.
Phil. 4. 19.
Col. 1. 27.
ⁱ Matt 13.17.
Luke 10.2ⴑ.
Rom. 16.25.
1 Cor. 2. 7.
ʲ Ps. 33. 6.
John 1. 3.
Col. 1. 16.
ᵏ 1 Pet. 1. 12.
ˡ 1 Pet. 3. 22.
ᵐ 1 Cor. 2. 7.

knowledge [*noesai sunesin*, 'observe my insight :' *sunienai*, to *comprehend* ; *noein*, to *perceive, observe, notice*]. Deep as are the mysteries of this epistle, the way to understand them is to *read* it (2 Tim. iii. 15, 16). By *observing his comprehension* of the mysteries, they, too, will be enabled to comprehend. **the mystery of Christ**—i. e., *Christ Himself*, once hidden, but now revealed as reconciling Jew and Gentile to God, and so to one another (Col. i. 27). **5. in other ages**—Greek, 'generations.' **not made known.** He does not say *revealed*. Making known by *revelation* is the source of making known by preaching (*Bengel*). *Revelation* was vouchsafed to the prophets alone, that they might *make known* the truth so revealed to men in general. **unto the sons of men** [Hebrew, *b'nee Adam*]—men in their birth-state contrasted with the 'holy apostles and prophets,' *holy men of God* (2 Pet. i. 21), illuminated "by the Spirit" (Greek, 'ɪɴ the Spirit :' cf. Rev. i. 10; Matt. xvi. 17). **as.** The call of the Gentiles was known to the Old Testament prophets (Isa. lvi. 6, 7; xlix. 6), but not with the same explicitness (1 Pet. i. 10-12) "AS" it is now known (Acts x. 19, 20; xi. 18-21 ; Luke x. 23, 24 ; 1 John i. 1). They probably did not know that the Gentiles were to be admitted without circumcision, and on a level with the Jews in partaking of the grace of God. The full gift of "the Spirit" was reserved for the New Testament, that Christ might thereby be glorified. "Holy" marks the consecration of *the New Testament* "prophets" (here meant) by the Spirit, compared with which even the Old Testament prophets were but "sons of men" (Ezek. ii. 3). **6.** Translate, 'That the Gentiles *are*,' &c., 'and *fellow-corporate* [*sunsoma*] and *fellow*-partakers of *the* (א A B C Δ, omit 'His') promise (of salvation) *in* (by living union with, and in virtue of the work of) Christ *Jesus* (א A B C, Vulgate) *through* the Gospel.' 'ɪɴ Christ Jesus' they are "fellow-heirs" in the inheritance: "of the same body," under the One Head : in the communion of ᴛʜᴇ ʜᴏʟʏ ꜱᴘɪʀɪᴛ (ch. i. 13 ; Heb. vi. 4). The Trinity is continually prominent in this epistle (ch. ii. 19, 20, 22). **7. Whereof**—'of which' Gospel. **according to**—in consequence of, and in accordance with, "the gift of the grace of God." **given**—'which (gift of grace) was given to me, *according to* [*kata*, as *v.* 20 ; ch. i. 19: as the result of, and in proportion to] the effectual working (Greek, 'energy,' or 'in-working') of His power.' Omnipotence alone could convert the persecutor into the 'minister.' **8. am**—not merely *was* I, but still am the least worthy of so high an office (cf. 1 Tim. i. 15). **least of all saints**—not merely 'of all *apostles*' (1 Cor. xv. 9, 10 ; 2 Cor. xii. 11). **is**—Greek, 'was given.' Δ G *f g*, Vulgate.

But omitted in א A B C. Translate, 'To *announce* to the Gentiles *the glad tidings of* the unsearchable (Job v. 9) riches,' &c. ; viz., of Christ's *grace* (ch. i. 7 ; ii. 7); Rom. xi. 33, as a mine whose treasures can never be fully searched out (*vv.* 18, 19). **9. to make all men see** [*photisai*]—not merely to preach, but, by the Spirit in the Word, 'to *enlighten* all' (ch. i. 18 ; Ps. xviii. 28; Heb. vi. 4). "All" (cf. Col. i. 28). **fellowship.** א A B C Δ G *f g*, Vulgate, read 'economy,' 'dispensation' (cf. Col. i. 25, 26); and note, ch. i. 10, above). 'To make all see God's arrangement ; to *dispense* now (through me and His other *stewards*) what heretofore was a mystery hidden in His counsels.' **from the beginning of the world**—Greek, 'from (the beginning of) the ages' (cf. ch. i. 4 ; Rom. xvi. 25 ; 1 Cor. ii. 7). The "ages" are the vast cycles marked by successive stages of creation and orders of beings. **in God**—'hidden in His counsels' (ch. i. 9). **created all things by Jesus Christ.** God's creation of the world is the foundation of the rest of the "economy," freely dispensed according to His universal power (*Bengel*). As God created "the whole range of things" [*ta panta*], He has an absolute right to adjust all as He will : and so to keep the mystery of world-wide salvation in Christ 'hidden in Himself,' till His own good time for revealing it. א A B C Δ G *f g*, Vulgate, omit "by Jesus Christ." **10.** God's design in giving St. Paul grace to proclaim to the Gentiles the mystery of salvation heretofore hidden. **now**—first : opposed to 'hidden from the beginning of the world' (*v.* 5). **unto the principalities and** (Greek, 'the') **powers**—unto the various orders of *good* angels primarily, who dwell 'in the heavenly places : ' "known" to their adoring joy (1 Tim. iii. 16; 1 Pet. i. 12). Secondarily, unto *evil* angels, who dwell "in heavenly places" in a lower sense—*the air* (cf. ch. ii. 2 with vi. 12). But God's *power*, rather than His "wisdom," is what is "known" unto evil angels, to their dismay (1 Cor. xv. 24 ; Col. ii. 15). **by** (through) **the church**—the 'theatre' for displaying God's wisdom (Luke xv. 10; 1 Cor. iv. 9, Greek): the mirror in which angels contemplate it. Angels are but our "fellow-servants" (Rev. xix. 10). **the manifold wisdom**—which varies the economy as to places, times, and persons (Isa. lv. 8, 9 ; Heb. i. 1), yet makes the various parts to work together to one end (cf. 1 Pet. iv. 10). Man cannot understand it aright till he can survey it as a connected whole (1 Cor. xiii. 12). The call of the Church is no remedial afterthought, but part of the eternal scheme, which, amidst manifold varieties of dispensation, is one in its end. **11. which he purposed**—Greek, '*made* (to be fulfilled) in Christ Jesus' (2 Tim. i. 9). **12.** Translate, '*Our* boldness and *our* access (ch. ii.

407

13 Wherefore I desire that ye faint not at my tribulations for you, which is your glory.

14 For this cause I bow my knees unto the Father of our Lord Jesus
15 Christ, of whom ⁿthe whole family in heaven and earth is named,
16 that he would grant you, ^oaccording to the riches of his glory, ^pto be
17 strengthened with might by his Spirit in ^qthe inner man; that ^rChrist may dwell in your hearts by faith; that ye, being rooted and grounded
18 in love, may be able to comprehend with all saints ^swhat *is* the breadth,
19 and length, and depth, and height; and to know the love of Christ,

A. D. 64.
n Phil. 2. 9.
o Phil 4. 19.
p Job 23. 6.
Ps. 23. 8.
Isa. 40. 29-31.
Col. 1. 11.
q Rom. 7. 22.
r John 14. 23.
1 John 4. 4.
s Rom. 10. 8.

18) *in* confidence *through our* faith *in* Him.' 'THE access' (Greek); the formal *introduction* into a monarch's presence. Esther had access, but not access with confidence (Esth. iv. 16, "So will I go in unto the king: if I perish, I perish"). Three stages: we *believe* God's promises; then conceive confidence; hence follows intrepid *boldness*, so as constantly to draw nigh to God. **13. Wherefore** —since our spiritual privileges are such (*v.* 12), 'I entreat you not to be dispirited' [*enkakein*]: so intimate was their Christian union with him that they were in danger of losing heart at his afflictions, as though their own. **for you**—in your behalf. **which is your glory**—since God loved you so much as both to give His Son for you and to permit His apostles to suffer 'tribulations' (*Chrysostom*) in preaching the Gospel to you Gentiles (note, *v.* 1). My tribulations are your "glory," as your faith is furthered thereby (1 Cor. iv. 10). **14. For this cause**—resuming *v.* 1, "For this cause." Because ye are so loved and favoured by God. **bow my knees**—the proper attitude in prayer. Posture affects the mind, and is therefore not unimportant. See Paul's practice, Acts xx. 36; and that of the Lord Himself, Luke xxii. 41. **unto the Father.** Δ G *f g*, Vulgate, support, but א A B C, *Origen*, omit, "of our Lord Jesus Christ." *V.* 15, 'From whom,' in either case, refers to "the Father" (*Patera*), as "family" (*patria*, akin in etymology) refers to Him. Still, the foundation of sonship is in Jesus Christ. **15. the whole family.** *Middleton, Ellicott*, &c., translate, 'every family'—alluding to the several *families* in heaven and in earth supposed to exist (*Theophylact*)—the apostle thus implying that God, as Father to us His adopted children, is the Prototype of the paternal relation wherever found. But the idea that 'the holy angels are bound up in spiritual *families* or *compaternities*,' is found nowhere else in Scripture. Acts iii. 36, where the article is in most of the oldest MSS. omitted, yet the translation is, "*all the* house of Israel;" also ch. ii. 21, "all *the* building" [*pasa oikodome*: without the article], show that in New Testament Greek the translation is justifiable, '*all the* family,' or "*the whole* family." Nouns referring to what is well known and defined, like proper names, can omit the article. Scripture views angels and men, the saints militant and those with God, as ONE holy family joined under the one Father in Christ, the Mediator between heaven and earth (ch. i. 10; Phil. ii. 10). Hence angels are our "brethren" (Rev. xix. 10), and "sons of God" by creation, as we by adoption (Job xxxviii. 7). The Church is part of the grand family, which comprehends, besides men, the spiritual world, where the archetype, to the realization of which redeemed man is now tending, is already realized. This universal idea of the 'kingdom' of God as one divine community is presented to us in the Lord's prayer. By sin men were estranged, not only from God, but from that higher world in which the kingdom of God is already realized. As Christ, when He reconciled men to God, united them to one another

in a divine community (joined to Himself, the one Head), breaking down the partition wall between Jew and Gentile (ch. ii. 14), so also He joins them in communion with all who have already attained that perfection in the kingdom of God to which the Church on earth is aspiring (Col. i. 20) (*Neander*). **is named**—derive their *origin* and their *name* as sons of our heavenly *Father* [*Patria*, from *Pater*]. To bear God's name is to *belong* to God as *His* peculiar people (Num. vi. 27; Isa. xliii. 7; xliv. 5; Rom. ix. 25, 26). **16. according to**—*i. e.*, in abundance, consonant to the riches of His glory; not "according to" the narrowness of our hearts (ch. i. 7; ii. 7). Col. i. 11, "strengthened with *all* might *according to His glorious power.*" **by**—Greek, '*through* His Spirit.' **in** [*eis*]—'infused *into.*' **the inner man** (2 Cor. iv. 16; ch. iv. 22, 24; 1 Pet. iii. 4). Not predicated of unbelievers, whose inward and outward man alike are carnal. But in believers, the "inner (new) man," their true self, the sphere of regeneration (ch. iv. 24; Col. iii. 10), stands in contrast to their old man, attached to them as a body of death daily being mortified, not their true self. The *spirit* [*pneuma*] is our highest part, linking us to God, the great Spirit; the *soul* [*psuche*] is intermediate between the *body* (with which it is connected by the animal affections) and the *spirit* (with which it is connected by the [*nous*] *intellect, thought*). **17. That**—so that. **dwell** [*katoikesai*]—abidingly (John xiv. 16, 18, 23). Where the Spirit is, there Christ is. **by faith**—Greek, '*through* faith,' which opens the door of the *heart* to Jesus (Rev. iii. 20). It is not enough that He be on the tongue or flit through the brain: the *heart* is His proper seat,—the seat of the *soul* [*psuche*] in respect to the *affections* (*Calvin*). 'You having been rooted and grounded in love' (the state resulting from *Christ's dwelling in the heart*) (cf. *v.* 19), is in the Greek connected with this clause. "Rooted" is an image from a *tree;* "grounded" (Greek, 'founded'), from a *building* (cf. note, ch. ii. 20, 21; Col. i. 23; ii. 7). Contrast Matt. xiii. 6, 21. "Love" (Col. iii. 14; 1 John iv. 7, 8), the first-fruit of the Spirit, flowing from Christ's love realized in the soul, is the basis on which should rest the further comprehension of all the vastness of Christ's love. **18. May be able**—even still further: [*exischusete*] 'May be *fully* able.' **breadth, and length, and depth, and height**—viz., the full dimensions *of the spiritual temple,* answering to "the fulness of God" (*v.* 19), to which the Church, according to its capacity, ought to correspond (cf. ch. iv. 10, 13 as to "the fulness of *Christ*"). The "breadth" implies *Christ's* world-wide love, embracing all men; the "length," its extension through all ages (*v.* 21); the "depth," its profound wisdom, which no creature can fathom (Rom. xi. 33); the "height," its being beyond the reach of any foe to deprive us of it (ch. iv. 8) (*Bengel*). I prefer "the breadth," &c., to refer to *the whole mystery of free salvation in Christ for all, Gentile and Jew alike,* just spoken of (*vv.* 3-9), which he now prays they may comprehend in all

which passeth knowledge, that ye might bc filled *with all the fulness of God.

20 Now unto him that is able to do exceeding abundantly above all that
21 we ask or think, according to the power that worketh in us, unto him
be "glory in the church by Christ Jesus throughout all ages, world
without end. Amen.

4 I THEREFORE, the prisoner ¹of the Lord,) beseech you that "ye
2 walk worthy of the vocation wherewith ye are called, with *b* all lowliness
and meekness, with long-suffering, forbearing one another in love;
3 endeavouring to keep the unity of the Spirit *c* in the bond of peace.
4 *There* *d* *is* one body, and one Spirit, even as ye are called in one hope of

A. D. 64.
t John 1. 18.
Col 2. 9.
u 1 Tim. 1 17.

CHAP. 4.
1 Or, in the Lord.
a Gen. 5. 24.
Acts 9. 31.
Col. 1. 10.
b Gal. 5. 22.
c John 13. 34.
Col 3. 14.
d Rom. 12 5.

---

its vastness. As subsidiary to this, he adds, "and to know *the love of Christ*" (*v.* 19) to us. *Grotius* understands *depth* and *height* of God's goodness raising us from the lowest depression to the greatest height. **19. passeth**—surpasseth. The paradox, "to know . . . which passeth knowledge," implies that by "know" he does not mean that we can *adequately* know: all we know is, that His love exceeds far our knowledge of it; and, with even our fresh accessions of knowledge hereafter, will still exceed them, even as God's power exceeds our thoughts (*v.* 20). "Know" *experimentally* what *intellectually* is beyond our powers of knowing (1 Cor. viii. 2, 3). **filled with**—Greek, 'filled even *unto* all the fulness of God' (the grand goal); *i. e.,* filled, each according to his capacity, with the divine holiness, wisdom, knowledge, and love; *even as God is full,* and as Christ, who dwells in your hearts, hath 'all the fulness cf the Godhead dwelling in Him bodily' (Col. ii. 9).
20. unto him—contrasted with *ourselves* and *our needs.* Translate, 'that is able to do beyond all things exceeding abundantly above what we ask or (even) think.' *Thought* takes a wider range than *prayers.* [*Huper, above,* occurs thrice as often in St. Paul's writings as in all the rest of the New Testament, showing the warm exuberance of Paul's spirit.] **according to the power**—the indwelling Spirit (Rom. viii. 26). He appeals to their and his experience. **21.** Translate, 'Unto Him be *the* glory (*i. e.,* of the gracious dispensation of salvation just spoken of) in the Church (as the theatre for its manifestation, *v.* 10) *in* Christ Jesus (the only element wherein glory is duly given to God, Zech. vi. 13) to all the generations of eternal ages'—*lit.,* 'of the age of the ages.' Eternity, as one grand 'age,' is conceived as consisting of "ages" (these again consisting of 'generations') endlessly succeeding one another.
CHAP. IV. 1-32. *The Practical portion begins here.*—CHRISTIAN DUTIES REST ON CHRISTIAN PRIVILEGES, AS ALL FORM ONE BODY, THOUGH VARYING IN THE GRACES GIVEN TO THE SEVERAL MEMBERS, UNTIL WE COME UNTO A PERFECT MAN IN CHRIST.
1. Greek order, 'I exhort [*parakalo*] you, therefore (seeing that such is your calling of grace, ch. i.; ii.; iii. 1, 14); I, the prisoner *in* the Lord' (*i. e., in the Lord's cause:* in ch. iii. 1, "the prisoner of Jesus," the imprisonment is attributed to *Him* as its author; but here, to *union with* Him). What the world counted ignominy, he counts honour, glorying in his bonds for Christ more than a king in his diadem (*Theodoret*). His bonds enforce his exhortation. **vocation**—translate 'calling,' to accord with "called" (Rom. viii. 28, 30; ch. i. 18; *v.* 4). Col. iii. 15 similarly grounds Christian duties on our "calling." *The exhortations in this part of the epistle rest on realization of the privileges in the former part.* Cf. ch. iv.

32 with ch. i. 7; v. 1 with i. 5; iv. 30 with i. 13; v. 15 with i. 8. **2, 3. lowliness** [in classic Greek, *tapeinophrosune* is *meanness* of *spirit:* the Gospel elevated the word to express a Christian grace]—viz., esteeming ourselves small, as we are so; the thinking truly, and therefore lowlily, of ourselves (*Trench*). **meekness** [*praütēs*]—that spirit in which we accept God's dealings without disputing; also the injuries done by men, patiently, out of the thought that they are permitted by God for the purifying of His people (2 Sam. xvi. 11: cf. Gal. vi. 1; 2 Tim. ii. 25; Titus iii. 2). A *sense of dependence on God* is the groundwork (Matt. xi. 29). It is only the *lowly* heart that is also *meek* (Col. iii. 12, 13). As "lowliness and meekness" answer to "forbearing one another in love" (cf. "love," *vv.* 15, 16), so "long-suffering" ("slow to wrath," Jas. i. 19; forbearance; not immediately punishing a fault) answers to (*v.* 4) "endeavouring [*spoudazontes, 'zealously giving diligence;'* for it needs pains to check the inward feelings when provoked] to keep (maintain) the unity of the Spirit (the unity between men of different tempers, which flows from their having the Spirit, who is Himself "one," *v.* 4) in (united in) the bond of peace" (the "bond" by which "peace" is maintained—viz. "love," Col. iii. 14, 15) (*Bengel*); or, "peace" itself is the "bond" uniting the Church members: the element in which the unity is maintained (*Ellicott*). **4.** In the apostles' creed the article as to THE CHURCH follows that as to THE HOLY GHOST. To the Trinity naturally is annexed the Church, as the house to its tenant, to God His temple, the state to its founder (*Augustine*). There is yet to be a Church, not merely potentially, but actually Catholic: then the Church and the world will be co-extensive. Rome sets up a mere man as a visible head, antedating that consummation which Christ, the true visible Head, at His appearing shall first realize. As the "SPIRIT" is here, so the "LORD" (Jesus), *v.* 5, "GOD the Father," *v.* 6. The Trinity is again set forth. **hope**—associated with "the Spirit," the "earnest of our inheritance" (ch. i. 13, 14). As "faith" is mentioned, *v.* 5, so "hope" here, and "love," *v.* 2. The Holy Spirit, as the common principle of life (ch. ii. 18, 22), gives to the Church its true unity (1 Cor. xii. 13). Outward uniformity is as yet unattainable; but beginning by having one mind, we shall hereafter have "one body." The true "body" of Christ (all believers of every age) is already "one," as joined to the one Head (Rom. xii. 5; Col. i. 24). But its unity is not yet visible, as the Head is not visible; but it shall appear when He shall appear (John xvii. 21-23; Col. iii. 4). Meanwhile the rule is, 'In essentials, unity; in doubtful questions, liberty; in all things, charity.' There is real unity where both go to heaven under different names; none, when with the same name one goes to heaven, the other to hell. Truth is first: those who reach it will reach unity, because

5, your calling; one *[e]* Lord, one faith, *[f]* one baptism, one *[g]* God and Father
6 of all, who *is* above all, and *[h]* through all, and in you all.
7 But unto every one of us is given grace according to the measure of
8 the gift of Christ. Wherefore he saith, *[i]* When he ascended up on high,
9 he led ² captivity captive, and gave gifts unto men. (Now that he
   ascended, what is it but that he also descended first into the lower parts
10 of the earth? He that descended is the same also that ascended up far

A. D. 64.

[e] 1 Cor. 8. 6.
[f] Heb. 6. 6.
[g] Ps. 83. 18.
[h] Rom. 11.36.
[i] Ps. 68. 18.
² Or, a mul-
titude of
captives.

truth is *one*. Those who seek unity at first may purchase it at the sacrifice of truth, and so of the soul itself. **of your calling.** The one "hope" *flowing from* our "calling" is the element "IN" which we were "called." The oneness of the Spirit in the Church—the "one body"—is shown by the oneness of our hope. Instead of privileged classes, as under the law a unity of dispensation is the common privilege of Jew and Gentile alike. Spirituality, universality, and unity were *designed* to characterize the Church: it shall be so at last (Isa. ii. 2-4; xi. 9, 13; Zeph. iii. 9; Zech. xiv. 9). **5.** Similarly "faith" and "baptism" (the sacramental seal of faith) are connected (Mark xvi. 16; Col. ii. 12). "Faith" is not here *that which we believe*, but the act of *believing*, the one mean by which all believers in common apprehend the "one Lord." "Baptism" is the one and only visible sacrament whereby we are once for all united to "one Lord" (Rom. vi. 3; Gal. iii. 27), and *incorporated* into the "one body." Not the Lord's supper, which implies the matured communion of those already incorporate. Baptism, by its *single* celebration and *individual* reference, symbolizes *unity;* the Lord's supper *union* (*Ellicott*). In 1 Cor. x. 17, where a breach of *union* was in question, the latter forms the rallying-point (*Alford*). There is not added, 'One Pope, one council, one form of government.' The Church is one in *unity of faith* (v. 5; Jude 3), *of origination* (ch. ii. 19-21), *of sacraments* (1 Cor. xii. 13; v. 5), *of* "*hope*" (Titus i. 2; v. 4), *of charity* (v. 3); *unity* (*not uniformity*) *of discipline and government:* for where there is no order—no ministry with Christ as the Head—there is no Church (*Pearson*). **6. above** [*epi*]—'*over* all' (Rom. ix. 5). The 'one God over all' (in His sovereignty and His grace) is the crowning apex of unity (ch. ii. 19, end). '*Over, through, in*' express God's threefold relation to his creatures. **through all**—by the mediation of Christ, who 'filleth all things' (ch. i. 22, 23; ii. 20, 21; v. 10), and is "a propitiation" for all men (1 John ii. 2). **in you all**—by His Spirit. אABC, Coptic, omit "you." DG *fg*, Vulgate, both Syriac versions, read 'in *us* all.' The pronoun must be understood (either from the "ye," *v.* 4, or from the "us," *v.* 7); for Scripture proves that the Spirit is not 'in all' men, but only in believers (Rom. viii. 9, 14). God is "Father" both by generation (as Creator) and regeneration (ch. ii. 10; Jas. i. 17, 18; 1 John v. 1).

7. But—though "one" in our common connection with "one Lord," &c., yet 'each' has assigned to him his particular gift (1 Cor. xii. 11) for the good of the whole: none is overlooked; none can be dispensed with for the edifying of the Church (*v.* 12). A motive to unity (*v.* 3). *Translate,* 'unto *each* one of us was *the* grace bestowed at Christ's ascension (*v.* 8) given according to,' &c. **the measure**—*the amount* "of the gift" which Christ gives (Rom. xii. 3, 6). **8. Wherefore**—'for which reason,' viz., to intimate that Christ, the Head, is the author of these different gifts, as an act of His "grace" (*Estius*). **he saith**—God, whose word the Scripture is (Ps. lxviii. 18). **When he ascended**—GOD represented by the ark, which

was being brought up to Zion in triumph by David, after that "the Lord had given him rest round about from all his enemies" (2 Sam. vi.; vii. 1; 1 Chr. xv. 25). St. Paul quotes it of CHRIST ascending to heaven, who is therefore GOD. **captivity**—*i. e.*, a band of captives. In the psalm, the captive foes of David. Antitypically, the foes of Christ the Son of David—Satan, Death, the curse, and Sin (Col. ii. 15; 2 Pet. ii. 4), led in triumphal procession to their ultimate destruction (Rev. xx. 10, 14). **gave gifts unto men**—in the psalm, 'thou hast *received* gifts [בְּ] *among* men;' *i. e., to distribute among* men. As a triumphing conqueror distributes the spoils of foes as donatives among his people, so Christ, after his conquest of the powers of darkness. The impartation of the gifts of the Spirit depended on Christ's ascension (John vii. 39; xiv. 12). Previous gifts of the Spirit were but an earnest of Pentecost (Acts ii. 33). St. Paul stops short in the middle of the verse, not quoting 'that the Lord God might dwell *among them*.' This, though partly fulfilled in Christians being "an habitation of God through the Spirit" (ch. ii. 22), ultimately refers (Ps. lxviii. 16) to 'the Lord dwelling in Zion *for ever;*' the ascension amidst attendant angels having as its counterpart the second advent amidst "thousands of angels" (v. 17), accompanied by the restoration of Israel (v. 22), the destruction of God's enemies, and the resurrection (vv. 20, 21, 23), the conversion of the kingdoms of the world to the Lord at Jerusalem (vv. 29-34). **9. that he ascended.** The psalm's assertion of His *ascent* (assuming Him to be God) implies a previous *descent*, which only holds good of *Christ*, who first descended, then ascended; for the Father does not ascend or descend. Yet the psalm plainly refers to *God* (vv. 8, 17, 18). It must therefore be GOD THE SON (John vi. 33, 62), as Himself declares (John iii. 13). Others, though they did not previously descend, have ascended; none save *Christ* can be referred to in the psalm as having done so, for it is of *God* it speaks. **lower parts of the earth.** The antithesis to "far above all heavens" is *Alford's* argument for this phrase meaning more than the *earth*—viz., the regions *beneath*, even as He ascended not merely to the visible heavens, but "far above" them. Moreover, his design, "that He might fill *all* things" (v. 10, Greek, 'the whole universe of things'), may imply the same; but see note there. Also the leading "captive" of the 'captive band' ("captivity") of Satanic powers may imply that the warfare reached to *their habitation itself* (Ps. lxiii. 9). Christ, as Lord of all, took possession first of the earth and the unseen world beneath it (some conjecture that the region of the lost is in the centre of our globe), then of heaven (Acts ii. 27, 28). All we *surely* know is, that His soul at death descended to *hades; i. e.,* underwent the ordinary condition of departed spirits of men. The leading captive of Satanic powers is not said to be at His descent, but *at His ascension;* so that no argument can be drawn from it for a descent to the abodes of Satan. Acts ii. 27, 28 and Rom. x. 7 favour the view of the reference simply to His descent to

410

11 above all heavens, that he might ³fill all things.) And ʲhe gave some,
apostles; and some, prophets; and some, evangelists; and some, pastors
12 and teachers; for the perfecting of the saints, for the work of the
13 ministry, ᵏfor the edifying of ˡthe body of Christ: till we all come ⁴in
the unity of the faith, ᵐand of the knowledge of the Son of God, unto a
perfect man, unto the measure of the ⁵stature of the fulness of Christ:
14 that we *henceforth* be no more children, tossed to and fro, and carried
about with every ⁿwind of doctrine, by the sleight of men, *and* cunning
15 craftiness, whereby they lie in wait to deceive; but ⁶speaking the truth
in love, may grow up into him in all things, which is the head, *even*

A. D. 64.

³ Or, fulfil
ʲ 1 Cor. 12. 28.
ᵏ 1 Cor 11. 26.
ˡ Col 1 21.
⁴ Or, in o
the unity.
ᵐ Col. 2. 2.
⁵ Or. age.
ⁿ Matt 11. 7.
⁶ Or, being
sincere.
2 Cor. 4. 2.

hades. So *Pearson* 'On Creed' (Phil. ii. 10). **10. the same**—rather [*autos*], HE. **all heavens**—Greek, 'all *the* heavens' (Heb. iv. 4, 14; vii. 26; Greek, 'passed *through* the heavens' to the throne of God itself). **might fill** [πληρώσῃ]—'that He (both) *might*' and 'may fill;' viz., with His divine presence and Spirit, *not with His glorified body.* 'Christ, as God, *is* present *everywhere;* as glorified man, He *can* be present *anywhere'* (*Ellicott*). The attribute of Jehovah (Jer. xxiii. 24). **11.** [*autos*] 'Himself,' by His supreme power. 'It is HE that gave,' &c. (the same One as HE in *v.* 10.) **gave some, apostles.** Their marks were a call from Christ Himself (Gal. i. 1): the working of miracles (2 Cor. xii. 12); the superintendence of the churches in all lands (Matt. xxviii. 19; 2 Cor. xi. 28); chiefly the eye-witnessing of Christ's resurrection (Acts i. 22; 1 Cor. ix. 1). Translate, 'gave some to be apostles, and some to be prophets,' &c. Not only the office, but the men who filled it, were a divine gift. Ministers did not give themselves. Cf. 1 Cor. xii. 10, 28. As the apostles, prophets, and evangelists were special ministers, so "pastors and teachers" are the ordinary ministers of a flock, including, probably, superintending bishops, presbyters (1 Tim. iii. 2, end; Titus i. 9), and deacons. Evangelists were itinerant missionary-preachers, as Philip the deacon (Acts xxi. 8); "pastors and teachers" (2 Tim. iv. 5) were stationary. The *evangelist* founded the Church; the *teacher* built it up in the faith, speaking sometimes in the Spirit, at other times from his own resources. The 'pastor' had the *outward rule* and *guidance* of the Church: the bishop: as *kings* are called 'shepherds' (Isa. xliv. 28, Cyrus; Ezek. xxxiv. 23, David). As to revelation, the evangelist testified infallibly of the past; 'the prophet,' also of the future. The prophet derived all from the Spirit; the evangelist, in the case of the four, recorded facts cognizable to the senses, under the Spirit's guidance. No one church polity, as permanently *unalterable*, is laid down in the New Testament; though the apostolical order of bishops, or presbyters, and deacons, superintended by higher overseers (called bishops after apostolic times), has the sanction of ancient usage. The Old Testament Church was bound to a fixed hierarchy and a ceremonial minutely detailed in the law. In the New Testament the absence of minute directions for church government and ceremonies shows that a fixed model was not designed; the *general* rule is obligatory,—"Let all things be done decently and in order" (cf. Article xxxiv., Church of England); and that a succession of ministers be provided, not self-called, but 'called to the work by men who have public authority given unto them in the congregation, to call and send ministers into the Lord's vineyard"(Article xxiii.,Church of England). That the 'pastors' here are the superintending rulers and bishops or presbyters of the Church is evident from Acts xx. 28; 1 Pet. v. 1, 2, where the *bishops'* and *presbyters'* office is said to be "to feed" the flock. The term 'shepherd,' or 'pastor,' is used of guiding and *governing*, not merely *instructing*, whence it is applied to *kings*, rather than prophets or priests (Jer. xxiii. 4). [Cf. the names of princes compounded of *Pharnas*, Hebrew, 'pastor:' Holo-phernes, Tissa-phernes]. **12. for—with a view to** [*pros*]; the *ultimate aim*. **perfecting**—the [*katartismon*] *correcting* all that is deficient: *instructing* and completing in all parts. Cf. *v.* 13; 2 Cor. xiii. 9. **for**—a different preposition [*eis*]: the *immediate object.* Cf. Rom. xv. 2, "Let every one please his neighbour *for* [*eis*] his good *unto* [*pros*] edification." **of the ministry** [*diaconias*]—of ministration: without the article. The office is stated in this verse. The good aimed at as to the Church (*v.* 13). The way of growth (*vv.* 14, 15, 16). **edifying**—i. e., *building up* as the temple of the Holy Ghost. **13. come in** [*kantantesomen eis*]—rather, 'until we arrive the whole [*hoi pantes*] of us at the unity,'&c. Then the ministry will no longer be needed. **faith, and of the knowledge.** Unity of *faith* is found when all *savingly and fully know* [*epignoseos*] *Christ*, the object of faith, as "the Son of God" (ch. iii. 17, 19; 2 Pet. i. 5). Not even St. Paul thought he had fully "attained" (Phil. iii. 12-14). Amidst the variety of gifts, and the multitude of members, the Church's "faith" is ONE: as contrasted with "children . . . carried about with EVERY WIND OF DOCTRINE" (*v.* 14). **perfect man**—'unto the *full-grown* man' (1 Cor. ii. 6; Phil. iii. 15; Heb. v. 14); *adult maturity*. contrasted with "children" (*v.* 14). Not 'perfect *men;*' for the many members constitute but *one* Church joined to the one Christ. **stature, &c.** The standard ("measure") of spiritual "stature" is "the fulness of Christ;" *i. e.*, which Christ has (ch. i. 23; iii. 19: cf. Gal. iv. 19); that the body should be worthy of the Head, the perfect Christ. **14.** 'To the end that:' the aim of the bestowal of gifts stated negatively, as in *v.* 13 positively. **tossed to and fro**—*inwardly*, even without wind [*kludonizomenoi*]; *like billows of the sea.* Cf. Jas. i. 6. **carried about with every wind**—*from without.* **doctrine** [*didaskalias*]—'teaching.' The various *teachings* are the 'winds' which keep them tossed on a sea of doubts (Heb. xiii. 9: cf. Matt. xi. 7). **by**—Greek, 'in:' expressing 'the evil atmosphere *in* which the varying currents of doctrine exert their force' (*Ellicott*). **sleight**—*lit.*, 'dice-playing.' The player frames his throws so that the numbers may turn up which best suit his purpose. **of men.** Contrasted with *Christ* (*v.* 13). **and**—Greek, 'in.' **cunning craftiness, whereby they lie in wait to deceive** [*panourgia pros tēn methodeian tēs planēs*]— 'craftiness, tending to the methodized system of deceit.' *Bengel* takes 'deceit' for 'the parent of error,' Satan (cf. ch. vi. 11); referring to his concealed mode of acting. **15. speaking the truth** [*aletheuontes*]—'holding' or 'following the truth:' opposed to 'error' or 'deceit' (*v.* 14). **in love**—in contrast to "in craftiness;" spurious professions

411

16 Christ: from °whom the whole body fitly joined together and compacted
by that which every joint supplieth, according to the effectual working
in the measure of every part, maketh increase of the body unto the
edifying of itself in love.

17 This I say therefore, and testify in the Lord, that ye henceforth walk
18 not as other Gentiles walk, in the vanity of their mind, having ᵖthe
understanding darkened, being alienated from the life of God through
the ignorance that is in them, because of the ⁷ blindness of their heart:
19 who ᑫ being past feeling have given themselves over unto lasciviousness,
20 to work all uncleanness with greediness. But ye have not so learned
21 Christ; if so be that ye have heard him, and have been taught by

A. D. 64.

° Col. 2. 19.
ᵖ Isa. 44. 18.
Isa. 46. 5, 8.
Acts 17. 30.
Rom. 1. 21.
Acts 2i. 18.
ch. 2. 12.
Gal. 4. 8.
1 Thes. 4. 5.
⁷ Or.
hardness.
ᑫ Rom 1. 24.
1 Tim. 4. 2.

of love by crafty teachers of error. "Truth" is never to be sacrificed to so-called 'charity;' yet is to be maintained in charity. Truth in word and act, love in manner and spirit (cf. *v.* 21, 24). **grow up**—from the state of "children" to be 'full-grown men.' There is growth only in the spiritually alive, not in the dead. **into him**—so as to be more and more incorporated, and become one with Him. **in all things** [*ta panta*]—'in all *the* elements of our growth' (*Ellicott*). **the head** (ch. i. 22). **16. From whom**—as the Fountain-head of 'making increase.' The energy of vital power varies with the distance from the head (*Ellicott*) (Col. ii. 19). **fitly joined together**—'being fitly framed together,' in *harmony* [*sunarmologoumenon*]; as in ch. ii. 21; all the parts in their proper position, and in mutual relation. **compacted**—in *firm* consolidation. [*Sumbibazomenon* implies the *aggregation; sunarmologoumenon*, the *inter-adaptation* of THE parts (*Ellicott*).] **by that which every joint supplieth** [*dia pasēs aphēs tēs epichoregias*]—'by means of every joint of the supply' (Phil. i. 19). 'By every supplying joint.' The joints are the points of union where the supply of the spiritual gifts from Christ passes to the different members, furnishing the body with the materials of growth. **according to the effectual working** (ch. i. 19; iii. 7)—*of grace*, proportioned to the 'measure of each one part's [B Δ *f g:* but A C, Vulgate, *melous* for *merous:* 'member's'] capability of receiving growth: join this clause with "maketh increase," &c. **maketh increase**—the same Greek as *v.* 15, 'maketh (carrieth on) the *growth* of the body.' The repetition, 'the *body* maketh increase of the *body* unto the edification *of itself*,' implies it is a *living organism* whose growth is due, not to aggregations from *without*, but to vital forces from *within* (*Stier* in *Ellicott*).

17. therefore—resuming the exhortation (*v.* 1), 'I *therefore* beseech you that ye *walk* worthy,' &c. **testify in the Lord**—IN whom (as our element) we discharge our ministry (1 Thess. iv. 1, Greek; Rom. ix. 1). **henceforth walk not** [*meketi*] —'no longer;' resumed from *v.* 14. **other**—Greek, 'the *rest* of the Gentiles.' **in the vanity, &c.**—as their element: opposed to "in the Lord." 'Vanity of mind' (Rom. i. 21) is the *waste* of the rational and moral powers on worthless objects, of which idolatry is a glaring instance. The root of it is departure from the knowledge of the true God (*vv.* 18, 19; 1 Thess. iv. 5). **18.** 'Being darkened in their understanding' [*te dianoia*]; i. e., *intelligence* (cf. ch. v. 8; Acts xxvi. 18; 1 Thess. v. 4, 5: contrast ch. i. 18). **alienated**—this and "darkened" imply that before the fall they (in the person of their first father) had been partakers of *life* and *light*, but had revolted from primitive revelation (cf. ch. ii. 12). **life of God**—the *life* and *light* in Adam before the irruption of death and darkness into human nature; also the life whereby God lives in the regenerate soul (Gal. ii. 20).

'Spiritual life in believers is kindled from the life of God' (*Bengel*). **through** [*dia tēn agnoian*]—'on account of the ignorance;' viz., of God. Wilful ignorance originally, their fathers not 'choosing to retain God in their knowledge:' the beginning point of their misery (Acts xvii. 30; Rom. i. 21, 23, 28; 1 Pet. i. 14). **that is in them**—*deep-seated, indwelling:* the defect of the intellect, owing to the defect of the heart. **because of**—on account of. **blindness** [*porosin*, from *poros*, 'tuffstone']—'hardness,' *lit.*, of the skin, so as not to feel the touch. Hence a soul's *callousness to feeling* (Mark iii. 5). Where there is spiritual "life," there is feeling; where there is not, there is 'hardness.' **19. Who being** [*hoitines*]—*as being persons who: inasmuch as they.* **past feeling**—senseless, shameless, hopeless, with conscience seared: the ultimate result of a long process of 'hardening,' or habit of sin (*v.* 18). Δ G *f g*, Vulgate, read 'being past hope,' *despairing*. A B, *Origen*, support "past feeling," which includes *past hope* (Jer. ii. 25; xviii. 12). **given themselves over.** In Rom. i. 24 it is, "*God* gave them up to uncleanness." Their giving *themselves* to it was punished in kind, *God* judicially giving them up to it by withdrawing His preventing grace: their sin was made their punishment. *They* gave themselves up to the slavery of their lust, to do all its pleasure, as captives who have ceased to strive with the foe: so *God* gave them up to it. **lasciviousness** [*aselgeia*]—'wantonness.' So Rom. xiii. 13; 2 Pet. ii. 18. It does not necessarily include *lasciviousness*, but *incontinent*, reckless readiness for it, and for every self-indulgence. 'The first beginnings of unchastity.' 'Lawless insolence and wanton caprice' (*Trench*). **to work all uncleanness** [*eis ergasian*]—'*with a deliberate view* to the working (as their *business;* not a mere accidental fall into sin) of uncleanness *of every kind*.' **with greediness**—Greek, 'IN greediness.' *Uncleanness* and *greediness* of gain go hand in hand (ch. v. 3, 5; Col. iii. 5); though "greediness" [*pleonexia*] here includes *all* kinds of *self-seeking*. **20. learned Christ** (Phil. iii. 10). To appropriate Christ Himself is the great lesson of the Christian life: this the Ephesians began at their conversion. "Christ," in His *office*, is here the object learned; "Jesus," in His person, in the following verse. **21. If so be that** [*eige*, with indicative]—Assuming what I have no reason to doubt, that, &c. **heard him.** The Him is emphatic: heard *Himself*, not merely *about* Him (John x. 27). **taught by him**—Greek, 'taught IN Him;' *i. e.*, in vital union with Him (Rom. xvi. 7): the further instruction, besides having "*heard* Him" at conversion. **as the truth is, &c.** Connect with "taught:" 'And in Him have been taught, according as is truth in Jesus.' There is no article. "Truth" is truth in its essence and perfection in Jesus; 'if *according as* it is *in Him*, ye have been so taught *in Him:*' in contrast to 'the *vanity* of mind of the Gentiles' (cf. John i. 14, 17; xviii. 37; *v.* 17). **Knowledge**

22 him, as the truth is in Jesus: that ye put off, concerning the former conversation, the old man, which is corrupt according to the deceitful

23 lusts; and ʳbe renewed in the spirit of your mind; and that ye put

24 on the new man, which after God is created in righteousness and ⁸true holiness.

25 Wherefore, putting away lying, speak every man truth with his neighbour: for we are members one of another.

26 Be ye angry, and sin not; let not the sun go down upon your wrath:

27 neither ⁸give place to the devil.

28 Let him that stole steal no more; but rather let him labour, working

A.D. 64.

ʳ Rom. 8. 6.
Rom. 12. 2.
2 Cor. 2. 10, 11.
Col. 3. 10.
1 Pet. 1. 13.
⁸ Or, holiness of truth.
⁹ Acts 5. 3.
Eph. 6. 11.
Jas. 4. 7.

of Christ not accompanied with 'putting off lusts' is not *true*, but spurious. 'What in Jesus is truth, not semblance, is to become truth also in the faithful' (*Olshausen*). Contrast John viii. 44. **22. That ye**—following ye "have been taught" (*v.* 21). **put off**—as an old garment (cf. *v.* 24: Zech. iii. 4; Rom. xiii. 12). **concerning the former conversation**—'in respect to your former way of life.' **the old man**—your old unconverted nature (Rom. vi. 6). **is corrupt** [*phtheiromenon*] **according to the deceitful lusts**—rather, 'which is being corrupted (waxeth corrupt: involving *destruction:* cf. Gal. vi. 8) according to (*i. e.*, as might be expected from) the lusts of Deceit.' *Deceit* is personified: *lusts* (all world and fleshly desires) are its tools. In contrast to 'holiness of *the truth*,' *v.* 24, and '*truth* in Jesus,' *v.* 21: answering to Gentile "*vanity*," *v.* 17. Corruption and destruction are inseparably associated. Man's old-nature lusts are his own executioners, fitting him more and more for eternal corruption. **23. be renewed** [*ananeousthai* implies 'the *continued* renewal in the *youth* of the new man;' but *anakainousthai*, 'renewal *from the old state*'] **in the spirit of your mind**. As there is no Greek for 'in,' as at *v.* 17, translate, '*by* the spirit of your mind;' *i. e.*, *by the Holy Spirit united with your spirit, and influencing your mind* [*nous*] (Rom. xii. 2). The "spirit" of man is only then recognized when it is one spirit with the Lord. The natural or animal [*psuchikoi*] man is described as "having not the Spirit" (Jude 19). Not filling its true function as receptacle of the Holy Spirit, the spirit of the unregenerate is in abeyance (1 Thess. v. 23). **24. put on the new man**—opposed to "the old man," which is to be "put off" (*v.* 22) [*kainon* is different from "re-*new*-ed," *v.* 23]. Put on not merely a *renovated* nature, but the new—*i. e.*, altogether *different*, changed—nature, which redemption contemplates (Col. iii. 9, 10, 12, note). **after God, &c.** Translate, 'which hath been created (once for all [*ktisthenta*] in Christ, ch. ii. 10; so that in each believer this new holy garment has not to be created again, but to be put on) after (the image of) God,' (Gen. i. 27; 1 Pet. i. 15, &c.) God's image, which we lost in the first Adam, is restored to us more gloriously in the second Adam, the image of the invisible God (2 Cor. iv. 4; Col. i. 15; Heb. i. 3). **in righteousness**—"IN" it as the *element* of the renewed man: opposed to "greediness," which *covetously* disregards right (*v.* 19). **true holiness**—opposed to "uncleanness:" Greek, 'piety [*hosiotēs*] *of the truth*;' flowing from following "the truth of God" (Rom. i. 25; iii. 7; xv. 8): opposed to 'the lusts *of deceit*' (Greek, *v.* 22: cf. also *v.* 21, "truth in Jesus"). "Righteousness" relates to our fellow-men, the second table; "holiness" to God, the first table: the religious observance of offices of piety (cf. Luke i. 75). In the parallel (Col. iii. 10) it is "renewed in *knowledge* after the image," &c. As at Colosse the danger was from pretenders to *knowledge*, the true "knowledge" which flows from renewal of the

heart is dwelt on; so at Ephesus, the danger being from the corrupt morals prevalent, the renewal in "holiness," "righteousness," contrasted with Gentile "uncleanness" (*v.* 19), and "greediness," is prominent.

25. Wherefore. From the *general* character of "the new man," there necessarily result the *particular* features which he details. **putting away** [*apothemenoi*]—'having put away' *once for all*. **lying**—'falsehood' in every form [*to pseudos*]; flowing from *selfishness*, the essence of all sin (*Müller*): opposed to "the truth" (*v.* 24); the abstract. 'Speak ye truth each one with his neighbour' is slightly changed from Zech. viii. 16. For "to" Paul has "with," to mark our inner connection *with* one another, as "members *one of another*" (*Stier*). Not merely *of one body*. Union in Christ, the Truth and the Life, instinctively leads Christians to truth towards one another. One member could not injure another without injuring himself, as all have a common spiritual life and interest. **26. Be ye angry, and sin not.** So the LXX. (Ps. iv. 4; see note on *rigzu* there, and Paul's application of it under the Spirit). Should circumstances call for anger on your part, let it be as Christ's (Mark iii. 5), without sin. Natural feelings are not wrong when directed to their legitimate object, and not exceeding due bounds. As in the future literal, so in the present spiritual, resurrection, no essential constituent is removed, but only whatever is a perversion of the original design. Indignation at dishonour to God and wrong to man, as "lying" (*v.* 25), is justifiable anger. *Passion* is sinful (derived from 'passio,' *suffering:* implying that amidst seeming energy, a man is really *passive;* the slave of anger, instead of ruling it). **let not the sun go down upon your wrath**—"wrath" is forbidden; "anger" not so, though, like poison used as medicine, it needs extreme caution. The sense is not, Your *anger* shall not be imputed if you put it away before nightfall; but 'Let no *wrath* (i. e. [*parorgismos*], personal "irritation," "exasperation"), mingle with your "anger," however righteous' (*Trench*). '*Before sunset*' (when the Jewish day began) is proverbial for 'put it away *at once* before *another day begin*' (Deut. xxiv. 15); *also* before you part for the night, perhaps never in this world to meet again. The Pythagoreans, if they had disputes, embraced one another before sunset. So *Jona*, 'Let not night and anger sleep with you, but conciliate the other party, though he have committed the offence.' Let not your 'anger' at another's wickedness verge to hatred. **27. Neither give place (i. e., room) to the devil** (whose name implies he seeks in us *scope to accuse*)—by continuing "wrath." Keeping anger through the dark night is giving place to the prince of darkness (ch. vi. 11, 12).

28. Greek, 'Let the stealing person (whether a bandit, a thief, or one more covert in dishonesty) steal no more.' *Bandits* frequented the mountains near Ephesus. **but rather.** It is not enough to

413

with *his* hands the thing which is good, that he may have [9] to give to him that needeth.

29 Let no corrupt communication proceed out of your mouth, but that which is good [10] to the use of edifying, that it may minister grace unto

30 the hearers. And *[t]* grieve not the Holy Spirit of God, whereby ye are sealed unto the day of redemption.

31 Let all bitterness, and wrath, and anger, and clamour, and evil speak-

32 ing, be put away from you, with all malice: and be ye kind one to another, tender-hearted, forgiving one another, even as God for Christ's

5 sake hath forgiven you. BE *[a]* ye therefore followers of God, as dear chil-

2 dren; and *[b]* walk in love, as Christ also hath loved us, and hath given

A. D. 64.

[9] Or. to distribute.
[10] Or, to edify profitably.
[t] Gen. 6. 3, 6. Isa. 63. 10. Rom. 8. 23.

CHAP. 5.
[a] Matt 5. 45. Luke 6. 36.
[b] John 13. 34.

---

cease from a sin; you must do its opposite. The stealer, when repentant, should labour more than he would be called on to do if he had never stolen. **let him labour.** Theft and idleness go together. **with his hands**—in contrast with his former thievish use of his hands. "His" [A Δ G ℵ *g* read *idiais*, 'his own']: opposed to his past living on the labours of *others'* hands. B, Vulgate, omit it. **the thing which is good**—in contrast with the thing which was evil in his past character. **that he may have to give**—'that he may have *wherewith* to *impart*.' He who has stolen should exercise liberality beyond restoring what he has taken. Christians should make not selfish gain their aim in industry, but honest independence and the acquisition of means of greater usefulness to their fellow-men. So St. Paul himself (Acts xx. 35; 1 Thess. iv. 11; 2 Thess. iii. 8).

29. corrupt [*sapros*]—'insipid;' without ' the salt of grace' (Col. iv. 6); so *worthless*, then becoming *corrupt:* included in "foolish talking" (ch. v. 4). Its opposite is "that which is good to . . . edifying." **communication** — language. **that which, &c.**—Greek, '*whatever* is good.' **use of edifying**—*lit.*, 'for edifying in respect of the need;' according as the occasion and present needs of the hearers require,—now censure, at another time consolation. Even words good in themselves must be introduced seasonably, lest they prove injurious instead of useful. *Trench,* Not vague generalities, which would suit a thousand other cases equally well or ill: our words should be as nails fastened in a sure place, words suiting the present time and the present person, being 'for the edifying of the occasion.' **minister**—Greek, 'give.' The Word 'gives grace (*a blessing: Ellicott*) to the hearers' when God uses it as *His* instrument for that purpose. **30. grieve not**—a touching condescension to human conceptions. Cf. "*vexed*" (Isa. lxiii. 10; Ps. lxxviii. 40); "fretted me" (Ezek. xvi. 43: implying His tender love); and of hardened unbelievers, "resist the Holy Ghost" (Acts vii. 51). *Believers* grieve the *Holy* Spirit by inconsistencies, such as *corrupt* or *worthless conversation*, &c.; implying how far from harmless such ' communications' are: they *grieve* our "Holy" and dearest Friend. This proves His *personality.* To warn us the more, the blessing believers receive from Him follows. **whereby ye are sealed** [*en ho esphragisthete*]—'wherein (or 'IN whom') ye *were* sealed' once for all (*aorist*). As in ch. i. 13, believers are said to be sealed "*in Christ*," so here, in "*the Holy Spirit*," who is one with Christ, and reveals Christ in the soul. It is the *Father* 'BY' whom believers, as well as the Son Himself, were sealed (John vi. 27). The Spirit is itself the *seal* in ch. i. 13. Here the Spirit *is the element* IN *which* the believer is sealed, His gracious influences being the seal. **unto**—kept safely *against* the day (Mal. iii. 17, *margin*) of redemption; viz., of the *completion* of redemption in the deliverance of the

414

body as well as the soul (Luke xxi. 28; Rom. viii. 23; ch. i. 14). **31. bitterness**—both of spirit and of speech: opposed to "kind." **wrath** [*thumos*]—passion for a time: opposed to "tender-hearted." *Bengel* translates *harshness.* **anger** [*orge*]—lasting resentment: opposed to 'forgiving one another.' **clamour**—*Chrysostom,* A horse carrying anger for its rider: 'bridle the horse, and you dismount its rider.' "Bitterness" begets "wrath;" "wrath,): "anger;" "anger," "clamour;" "clamour," the' more chronic "evil-speaking" [*blasphemia*], *revil'ing.* "Malice" is the root of all (Col. iii. [*kakia*; of which *poneria* is the manifestation 'fires fed within, not appearing to bystanders, are the most formidable' (*Chrysostom*). **32. And**—'But.' **be ye**—'become' [*ginesthe*] (Luke vii. 42: Col. iii. 12, 13). **tender-hearted** [*eusplanchnoi*]—with 'bowels of compassion,' Greek (1 Pet. iii. 8). **forgiving one another**—*lit.*, 'yourselves:' in forgiving one another, it is yourselves that you forgive (*Origen*). **even as.** God has shown Himself 'kind, tender-hearted, and forgiving to you;' it is but just that you in turn should be so to your fellow-men, who have not erred against you in the degree that you have against God (Matt. xviii. 33). **God for Christ's sake**—Greek, 'God in Christ' (2 Cor. v. 19). It is *in giving Christ* as a propitiation for our sins that God vouchsafes forgiveness to us. It cost God the death of His Son, as man, to forgive us. It costs us nothing to forgive our fellow-man. **hath forgiven**—Greek, '*forgave* you:' a past fact. God has, *once for all*, forgiven sin in Christ. **you.** So ℵ A G *f g*, Vulgate; against Δ, reading 'us.'

CHAP. V. 1-33.—EXHORTATIONS TO LOVE, AND AGAINST CARNAL LUSTS AND COMMUNICATIONS — CIRCUMSPECTION — REDEEMING THE TIME — FILLED WITH THE SPIRIT—SINGING TO THE LORD WITH THANKFULNESS—DUTY OF WIVES TO HUSBANDS RESTING ON THE CHURCH'S DUTY TO CHRIST.

1. Be ye [*ginesthe*]—'become.' **therefore**—since 'God in Christ forgave you' (ch. iv. 32). **followers**—Greek, 'imitators' of God in "love" (*v.* 2): God's essential character (1 John iv. 16). **as dear children**—Greek, 'as children *beloved;*' to which *v.* 2 refers, "as Christ also hath *loved* us" (1 John iv. 19). 'We are sons of men when we do ill; sons of God when we do well' (*Augustine*) (cf. Matt. v. 44, 48). Sonship infers necessity of *imitation* ('love instinctively prompting to it'), it being vain to assume the title without similitude of the Father (*Pearson*). **2. And**—in proof that you are so. **walk**—resuming ch. iv. 1, "*walk* worthy of the vocation," &c. In this consists the *imitation.* **as Christ also hath loved.** From the love of the Father he passes to that of the Son, in whom God most endearingly manifests His love to us. **us.** ℵ B read 'you:' A Δ G *f g*, Vulgate, "us." **given himself for us** [*paredoken*]—'gave Himself *up*

himself for us an offering and a sacrifice to God ᶜfor a sweet-smelling savour.

3 But fornication, and all uncleanness, or covetousness, let it not be
4 once named among you, as becometh saints; neither filthiness, nor foolish talking, nor jesting, ᵈwhich are not convenient; but rather giving of
5 thanks. For this ye know, that no whoremonger, nor unclean person, nor covetous man, who is an idolater, hath ᵉany inheritance in the king-
6 dom of Christ and of God. Let ᶠno man deceive you with vain words: for because of these things cometh the wrath of God upon the children of
7, ¹disobedience. Be not ye therefore partakers with them. For ᵍye were
8 sometimes darkness, but now ʰ*are ye* light in the Lord: walk as children
9 ⁱof light; (for the fruit of the Spirit *is* in all goodness and righteousness

A. D. 64.

ᶜ Gen. 8. 21.
Lev 1. 9
2 Cor. 2 15.
1 Thes. 4. 3.
ᵈ Rom. 1. 28.
ᵉ Rev 22. 15.
ᶠ Jer. 29. 8.
Matt. 24. 4.
¹ Or,
unbelief.
ᵍ Isa 9. 2.
ʰ John 8. 12.
1 John 2. 9.
ⁱ Luke 16. 8.

(viz., to death, Gal. ii. 20) for [*huper*] us;' i. e., *in our behalf:* vicarious substitution is *indirectly* implied 'in *our* stead.' The offerer and the offering were one and the same (John xv. 13; Rom. v. 8). **offering and a sacrifice.** "Offering" [*prosphora*] expresses *generally* His presenting Himself to the Father, as Representative, undertaking the cause of our lost race (Ps. xl. 6-8), including His *life* of obedience, though not excluding His offering of His body for us [*prosphora*] (Heb. x. 10). Usually an *unbloody offering,* in the limited sense. "Sacrifice" refers to His *death* for us exclusively. Christ is here, from Ps. xl. 6 (quoted in Heb. x. 5), represented as antitype of all the offerings of the law, whether unbloody or bloody, eucharistical or propitiatory. **for a sweet-smelling savour—** Greek, 'for (to be) an odour of a sweet smell;' so that God is well pleased with the offering, and with us for its sake (Lev. i. 9: cf. Phil. iv. 18; Matt. iii. 17; 2 Cor. v. 18, 19; ch. i. 6; Heb. x. 6-17). The ointment compounded of principal spices, poured upon Aaron's head, answers to the various graces which qualified Him to 'offer Himself a sacrifice for a sweet-smelling savour.' Another prophecy by figure was "the sweet savour" (*savour of rest, margin*) which God smelled in Noah's sacrifice (Gen. viii. 21). Again, as what Christ is, believers also are (1 John iv. 17), and ministers are, St. Paul says (2 Cor. ii. 15), "We are unto God a sweet savour of Christ." **3. once named—**'let it not be even [*mēde*] named' (*vv.* 4, 12). Words of evil lead to deeds. "Fornication," so deadly a sin in Christian ethics, was not deemed immoral in heathendom. "Uncleanness" and "covetousness" are resumed from ch. iv. 19. The two are so allied that the Greek for "covetousness" [*pleonexia*] is used sometimes in the Greek fathers for impurity. The common principle is longing to fill one's desire with objects of sense outside of God. 'Not be even named' applies better to impurity than to "covetousness." But the disjunctive "or" marks "covetousness" here as distinct from 'fornication and uncleanness.' **4. filthiness—**in *act* or *gesture.* **foolish talking—**the *talk* of fools: folly and sin together. It [*morologia*] and "filthiness" [*aischrotes*] occur nowhere else in the New Testament. **nor—**rather, 'or' (cf. *v.* 3). (Polished) **jesting** [Greek, '*eutrapelia:*' nowhere else in the New Testament]—that *versatility* which turns about, adapting itself, without regard to principle, to the shifting circumstances of the moment, and the varying moods of those around. Refined 'persiflage' and 'badinage,' for which Ephesus was famed (*Plautus,* 'Miles Gloriosus,' iii. 1, 42-52): so far from being censured, it is thought by the world a pleasant accomplishment. "Filthiness" (cf. Col. iii. 8) refers to the *foulness,* "foolish talking" to the *folly,* "jesting" to the *false refinement* (and *trifling witticism: Tittmann*), of discourse unseasoned with

the salt of grace (*Trench*). **not convenient**—'unseemly;' not such 'as become saints' (*v.* 3). [Rom. i. 28, *mē kathekonta, subjectively,* "not convenient;" here, *ouk anekonta, objectively* so (*Ellicott*).] **rather giving of thanks—**a happy play on sounds: *eucharistia* contrasted with *eutrapedia.* Refined "jesting" sometimes offends the tender feelings of grace; "giving of thanks" gives that real cheerfulness to believers which the worldly try to get from "jesting" (*vv.* 19, 20; Jas. v. 13). **5. this ye know.** א A B Δ G *f g,* Vulgate, read [*iste ginōskontes* for *este gin*] 'this ye surely know:' you are aware, of your own knowledge, that. **covetous . . . idolater** (Col. iii. 5). [א B G *f g,* Vulgate, read *ō, which thing,* for *ōs, who* (A Δ), *whiuh is* (in other words) *an idolater.*] Paul himself had forsaken all for Christ (2 Cor. vi. 10; xi. 27). Covetousness is worship of the creature instead of the Creator—high treason against the King of kings (1 Sam. xv. 23; Matt. vi. 24; Phil. iii. 19; 1 John ii. 15). **hath.** The *present* implies fixed exclusion. It is a settled principle of God's moral government that such a one *hath* not. **of Christ and of God—**rather, as one Greek article includes both, 'of Christ and God,' implying their perfect oneness—consistent only with Christ being God (cf. 2 Thess. i. 12; 1 Tim. v. 21; vi. 13). **6. vain**—unreal words; viz., palliations of "uncleanness" (*vv.* 3, 4; Isa. v. 20) (that it is natural to indulge in love), "covetousness" (that it is useful to society to pursue gain), and "jesting" (that it is witty, and that God will not punish for such things). **because of these things—***uncleanness, covetousness,* &c. (*vv.* 3-5.) **cometh**—not merely, 'shall come.' Is as sure as if *already* come. The principles of God's moral government are *present* and enduring. **children**—rather, '*sons* of disobedience' (ch. ii. 2, 3). The children of 'no faith' in doctrine (Deut. xxxii. 20) are "children of disobedience" in *practice,* having the character of their mother (*Origen*), and so are "children of wrath." **7. Be not—**'Become not' [*ginesthe*]: fall not into association with them. Here fellowship with wicked *workers* is forbidden: in *v.* 11, with their wicked *works.* **8. sometimes—**'once.' Ye ought to have no fellowship with sin, which is darkness, for your state as darkness is now PAST. Stronger than "in darkness" (Rom. ii. 19; vi. 17). **light**—not merely 'enlightened,' but enlightening others (*v.* 13). **in**—in union with the Lord, THE LIGHT: outside of Him all is darkness. **children of light**—not merely 'of the light,' just as "children of disobedience" on the opposite side: those whose characteristic is *light.* Pliny, writing to Trajan, bears unwilling testimony to the extraordinary purity of Christians' lives contrasted with those around them. **9. fruit of the Spirit—**taken from Gal. v. 22. א A B Δ G *f g,* Vulgate, read 'the fruit of THE LIGHT:' in contrast with "the unfruitful works of darkness" (*v.* 11).

10, and truth;) proving [j] what is acceptable unto the Lord. And [k] have no
11 fellowship with the unfruitful works of darkness, but rather [l] reprove
12 *them.* For it is a shame even to speak of those things which are done
13 of them in secret. But [m] all things that are [2] reproved are made manifest
14 by the light: for whatsoever doth make manifest is light. Wherefore
[3] he saith, [n] Awake thou that sleepest, and [o] arise from the dead, and
Christ shall give thee light.
15 See then that ye walk circumspectly, not as fools, but as wise, redeem-
17 ing the time, because the days are evil. Wherefore [p] be ye not unwise,

A. D. 61.	
[j] Phil. 1. 10.	
[k] 1 Cor. 5. 9.	
[l] Lev 19. 17.	
[m] Heb 4. 13.	
[2] Or. dis-	
covered.	
[3] Or. it.	
[n] Iss. 60. 1.	
[o] John 5. 25.	
[p] Col. 4. 5.	

[q] *Walk* as children of light, FOR the fruit of the light (has its sphere: shows itself) in all (kinds of) goodness (opposed to "malice," or *badness*, ch. iv. 31), righteousness (opposed to "covetousness," *v.* 3), and truth' (opposed to "vain words," *v.* 6, and "lying," ch. iv. 25). The good. the right, the true, comprise all morality. **10. Proving** —construed with "walk" (*v.* 8; Rom. xii. 1, 2). As we *prove* a coin by the eye and ear, and by using it; so, by accurate study and experimental trial, we may test 'what is acceptable unto the Lord;' which last is the Christian's one criterion in estimating things. "Light," of which believers are "children," manifests what each thing really is. **11. unfruitful works of darkness.** Sins, being terminated in themselves, are called "works," not 'fruits' (Gal. v. 19, 22). Their only fruit (if the term is to be used) (Deut. xxxii. 32) is "death" (Rom. vi. 21; Gal. vi. 8). Plants cannot bear "fruit" in the absence of light. Sin is "dark-ness;" its parent *the prince of darkness* (ch. vi. 12). Graces, as flourishing in "the light," are repro-ductive, and abound in fruits; which, as har-moniously combining in *one* whole, are singular— "the FRUIT of the Spirit" (*v.* 9). **rather, &c.**— Greek, 'rather, *even* reprove them' (cf. Matt. v. 14-16). Not only 'have no fellowship, but *even* reprove them,' in words (*v.* 13; 1 Cor. xiv. 24; Titus i. 13; ii. 15). Not that we can avoid all intercourse (1 Cor. v. 10), but 'avoid such fellow-ship as will defile you;' just as light, though it touch filth, is not soiled by it; nay, as light *de-tects* it, so 'even *reprove* sin.' **12.** The Greek order is, 'For the things done in secret by them it is a shame even to speak of.' The "for" gives his reason for 'not *naming*' (cf. *v.* 3) *in detail* the works of darkness, whereas he describes definitely (*v.* 9) 'the fruit of the light' (*Bengel*). I think the "for" expresses, Reprove them; for to *speak of* them in detail *without reproving* them is a shame (*v.* 3). Thus 'works of *darkness*' answers to 'things done *in secret*.' And 'even to speak of them' *without reproving* is opposed to 'even reprove them.' **13.** **But**—though 'done in secret.' **that are reproved** —rather [as there is no article before *elenchomena*], 'when they are reproved;' viz., by you (*v.* 11). **whatsoever doth make manifest** [*pan to phane-roumenon*]—rather, 'everything that is (*i. e.*, suf-fers itself to be) made manifest (or 'shone upon;' viz., by your 'reproving,' *v.* 11) is thenceforth no longer "darkness" (*v.* 8), but "light." "Light" can hardly apply, as *Ellicott* thinks [taking *pha-neroumenon* as wholly passive in meaning], to any but those who become *spiritually illumined.* Others may be shone round, but do not become "light." The wicked will not *suffer themselves to be made manifest* by the light, but love darkness. "Light" has no transforming effect on *them* (John iii. 19, 20). But whatsoever suffers itself to be illumined is thenceforth light. You, being light yourselves (*v.* 8), by shedding light, through re-proof, upon some in darkness, will convert them to light. Your consistent lives and faithful re-proofs are your "armour of light" (Rom. xiii. 12)

in assailing the kingdom of darkness. **14. Where-fore**—referring to the whole foregoing argument (*vv.* 8, 11, 13). Since light (spiritual) dispels the pre-existing darkness, He (God) saith, &c. (cf. ch. iv. 8.) **Awake.** אABΔG, *Origen* read [ἔγειρε, for ἔγειραι] 'Up!' 'Rouse thee!' used in stirring men to activity. *A paraphrase* of Isa. lx. 1, 2. The "Christ" shows that Paul, in quoting the prophecy, views it in its *Gospel fulfilment.* As Israel is called on to "awake" from its previous "darkness" and 'death' (Isa. lix. 10; lx. 2), for her Light is come, so the Church, and each indi-vidual, are called to awake: *believers* to "awake" out of *sleep; unbelievers* to "arise" from the *dead* (cf. Matt. xxv. 5; Rom. xiii. 11; 1 Thess. v. 6 with ch. ii. 1). **Christ**—"the true light," "the sun of righteousness." **give thee light** [*epi-phausei*]—'shall shine upon thee' as the sun shines upon those awakened out of sleep, enabling thee, by being "made manifest," to become "light" (*v.* 13); then, being so "enlightened" (ch. i. 18) by 'reproving,' to enlighten others. **15. that** [πῶς]—'see *how* ye walk,' &c.; compris-ing the double idea: 'see *how* ye walk,' and '*that* ye walk circumspectly.' The *manner*, as well as the *act*, is included. See *how* ye are walking, with a view to your *being* circumspect in your walk. Cf. Col. iv. 5, "Walk in *wisdom* (answering to "as wise" here) toward them that are without" (answering to "circumspectly" [*akribōs*]; i. e., *correctly, in relation to unbelievers;* not giving occasion of stumbling, but edifying all by a consistent walk). **not as fools**—'not as unwise' [*asophoi*] **but as wise.** **16. Redeeming the time** (Col. iv. 5) [*exagorazomenoi ton kairon*]—'Buying up for yourselves the seasonable time' (whenever it occurs) of good to yourselves and to others. Buying *off from* the vanities of "them that are without," and of the "unwise" opportunity, each opportunity afforded you for the work of God. *Special seasons for good* occasionally present them-selves, of which believers ought diligently to avail themselves. This constitutes true "wisdom" (*v.* 15). In a larger sense, *the whole season from one's spiritual awakening* is to be "redeemed" from vanity for God (cf. 2 Cor. vi. 2; 1 Pet. iv. 2-4). 'Redeem,' 'buy up' (like buyers on the watch for a favourable market time), implies the precious-ness of the opportune season: a jewel to be bought at any price. Make it your own, as a master will buy, so as to have at command a good servant. Cf. Dan. ii. 8; LXX. [The ἐκ in the compound verb refers to the time or circumstances *out of* which in each case 'the opportune time' is to be bought (*Ellicott*).] **because the days are evil.** The days of life are so (Gal. i. 4) morally beset with evil that we should make the most of each opportunity of good whilst it lasts (ch. vi. 13; Gen. xlvii. 9, Ps. xlix. 5; Eccl. xi. 2; xii. 1; John xii. 35). There are evil days (in persecution, sickness, &c.) when the Christian is laid by, there-fore he needs the more to improve all seasonable times afforded (Amos v. 13). Time generally serves the evil: buy it up for good. **17. Where-**

18 ^q but understanding what ^r the will of the Lord *is*. And be not drunk
19 with wine, wherein is excess; but be filled with the Spirit; speaking to
     yourselves ^s in psalms and hymns and spiritual songs, singing and
20 making melody in your heart to the Lord; giving ^t thanks always for
     all things unto God and the Father in the name of our Lord Jesus
21 Christ; submitting ^u yourselves one to another in the fear of God.
22   Wives, ^v submit yourselves unto your own husbands, as unto the Lord.
23 For the husband is the head of the wife, even as Christ is the head of
24 the church: and he is the saviour of the body. Therefore as the church
     is subject unto Christ, so *let* the wives *be* to their own husbands in every
     thing.

A. D. 64.

q Deut. 4. 6.
  Job 28. 23.
  Rom. 12. 2.
r 1 Thes. 4. 3.
s Col. 3. 16.
  Jas. 5. 13.
t Job 1. 21.
  Ps. 34. 1.
u Phil. 2. 3.
v Gen. 3. 16.
  Col. 3. 18.
  1 Tim. 2. 11.
  12.

---

fore — since ye need to walk circumspectly, choosing the right opportunity of good. **unwise** [*aphrones*]—different Greek from *v.* 15; 'foolish,' 'senseless.' **understanding**—not merely *knowing* as a fact (Luke xii. 47), but *knowing with thoughtful understanding*. **the will of the Lord**—how each opportunity is to be used. The Lord's will ultimately is our "sanctification" (1 Thess. iv. 3); and that "in every thing," meantime, we should "give thanks" (1 Thess. v. 18: cf. above, *v.* 10). **18. wherein**—not in the wine (1 Tim. v. 23), but in 'becoming drunk' with it. **excess** [*asotia*]— 'dissoluteness;' lit., *unsavingness;* unrestrained recklessness. **but be filled with** (*lit.,* IN) **the Spirit.** In *inspiration* the person was "filled" with ecstatic exhilaration, like that caused by wine; hence the two are connected (cf. Acts ii. 13-18). Many prophets—*e. g.*, John Baptist—abstained from wine, in order that the world might distinguish the ecstasy caused by the Spirit from that caused by wine. So in ordinary Christians, the Spirit dwells not in the mind that seeks excitement, but in the well-balanced prayerful mind. Such express their joy, not in drunken or worldly songs, but in Christian hymns of thankfulness. **19.** (Col. iii. 16) **to yourselves.** Hence arose the antiphonal or responsive chanting of which Pliny writes to Trajan: 'They are wont on a fixed day to meet before daylight (to avoid persecution) and to recite a hymn *among themselves by turns*, to Christ as if God.' The Spirit gives true wine a spurious eloquence. **psalms**—generally accompanied by an instrument [Hebrew, *mizmor*]: carefully arranged. **hymns** [*tehillim*]—in direct praise to God (cf. Acts xvi. 25; Jas. v. 13). These are not restricted to church-worship, but are to exhilarate Christians in social meetings. **songs** [*ôdais: shir, joyous*]— the generic term for lyric pieces: "spiritual" marks their being restricted to sacred subjects, praises of God, exhortations, prophecies, &c. Contrast the "songs," Amos viii. 10. **making melody** [*psallontes*]—'playing and singing,' with an instrument. **in your heart**—not merely with the lips (cf. 1 Cor. xiv. 15; Ps. xlvii. 7). The contrast is between the heathen and the Christian practice. Not the drinking songs of heathen feasts, but psalms and hymns; their accompaniment, *not the lyre*, but *the melody of the heart*. **to the Lord.** See *Pliny's* letter, quoted above: 'to *Christ* as God.' **20. thanks always for all things**—even for adversities; also for blessings, unknown as well as known (Col. iii. 17; 1 Thess. v. 18). *Service* and *praise* are the angelical life. **unto** [τῷ: Him who is] **God and the Father**—the Fountain of every blessing in Creation, Providence, Election, and Redemption. **in the name of our Lord Jesus Christ**—by whom all things, even distresses, become ours (Rom. viii. 35-37; 1 Cor. iii. 20-23). **21.** (Phil. ii. 3; 1 Pet. v. 5.) He passes from relations to God to those which concern our fellow-men. **Submitting yourselves.** A *thankful*

spirit towards God (*v.* 20) will be *humble* towards men. **in the fear of God.** א A B, Vulgate, read 'in the fear of CHRIST.' The believer passes from under bondage to the law as a letter to be 'the servant of *Christ*' (1 Cor. vii. 22), which, through instinctive love to Him, is really to be "the Lord's freeman;" for he is "under the law to *Christ*" (1 Cor. ix. 21: cf. John viii. 36). Christ, not the Father (John v. 22), is to be our judge. Thus reverential *fear* of displeasing Him is the motive for discharging relative duties as Christians (2 Cor. v. 11; 1 Pet. ii. 13).
    22. (Ch. vi. 9.) The Church's relation to Christ, in His everlasting purpose, is the archetype of the three greatest earthly relations—husband and wife (*v.* 22-33), parent and child (ch. vi. 1-4), master and servant (ch. vi. 4-9). B and all *Jerome's* Greek MSS. omit "submit yourselves:" supplying it from *v.* 21, 'Ye wives (submitting yourselves) unto your own [*idiois* implying the *legitimacy*, John iv. 18; *exclusiveness*, 1 Cor. vii. 2; and *specialty* of the connection, 1 Cor. xiv. 35 (*Ellicott*)] husbands.' א A, Vulgate, Coptic, read 'Let wives submit themselves' [ὑποτασσέσθωσαν]. Δ supports "submit yourselves." "Your own" is an argument for submissiveness in wives: it is not a stranger, but *your own* husbands, whom you are to submit unto (cf. Gen. iii. 16; 1 Cor. vii. 2; xiv. 34, 35; Col. iii. 18; Titus ii. 5; 1 Pet. iii. 1-7). Those subject ought to submit themselves, whatever their superiors are. "Submit" is used of *wives;* "obey" of *children* (ch. vi. 1) [*hupakouete*], as there is greater equality between wives and husbands than between children and parents. **as unto the Lord**—as unto Christ Himself, whose person the husband represents, the ground of the wife's submission; though that submission is inferior in kind and degree to what she owes Christ (*v.* 24). **23.** (1 Cor. xi. 3.) **even as**—Greek, 'as also.' **and he is.** א A B Δ G *f g*, Vulgate, read 'Himself (being) Saviour,' &c., omitting "and," and "is," which C has. Christ's Headship is united with—nay, gained by—His having SAVED the body in redemption. The being "head" is common to both the husband and Christ: the bodies to which they are so are different. Another particular in which He does not resemble the husband is, HE, and none else [*autos*], is the Saviour of the body. The husband is not saviour of the wife, in which Christ excels; hence "But" (*v.* 24) follows (*Bengel*). **24. Therefore** [*alla*]—"But;" *i. e.*, though the husband be not, as Christ, Saviour of the body (*v.* 23), *nevertheless*, thus far they are one, that the 'subjection' or 'submission' (the same Greek as "submit," *vv.* 21, 22) of the Church to Christ, is the prototype of that of the wife to the husband. **their own.** So A. Not in B Δ G א *f g*. Not needed by the argument. **in every thing**—appertaining to a husband's legitimate authority: "in the Lord" (Col. iii. 18): everything not **contrary to** God.

417

25   Husbands, love your wives, even as Christ also loved the church, and
26 gave himself for it; that he might sanctify and cleanse ^{*w*} it with the
27 washing of water ^{*x*} by the word, that he might present it to himself a
glorious church, not having spot, or wrinkle, or any such thing; but
28 ^{*y*} that it should be holy and without blemish. So ought men to love their
29 wives as their own bodies. He that loveth his wife loveth himself. For
no man ever yet hated his own flesh; but nourisheth and cherisheth it,
30 even as the Lord the church: for ^{*z*} we are members of his body, of his

A. D. 64.

^{*w*} John 3. 5.
Tit. 3. 5.
Heb. 10. 22.
1 John 5. 6.
^{*x*} John 15. 3.
John 17. 17.
^{*y*} 2 Cor. 11. 2.
^{*z*} Rom. 12. 5.
1 Cor. 6. 15.

25. 'Thou hast seen the measure of obedience; now hear the measure of love. Do you wish your wife to obey you, as the Church is to obey Christ? Then have a solicitude for her, as Christ had for the Church (*v.* 23); if it be necessary to give thy life for her, or to endure any other suffering whatever, do not refuse; and if you suffer thus, not even so do you do what Christ has done: for you do so, being already united to her; but He did so for one that treated Him with aversion. As, therefore, He brought to His feet one that even wantonly spurned Him, by much tenderness, not by threats and terror, so do you act towards your wife; and though you see her wayward, you will bring her to your feet by much thoughtfulness, by love, by kindness. For no bond is more sovereign, especially in the case of husband and wife. For one may constrain a servant by fear, though not even he is so to be bound to you. But the companion of your life, the mother of your children, the basis of all your joy, you ought to bind to you, not by fear, but by love' (*Chrysostom*). **gave himself** [*paredōken*]—'gave Himself *up.*' **for it**—'for *her.*' The Church's relation to Christ is the ground of woman's elevation under Christianity to her due social place, from which she was, and is, excluded in heathen lands. **26. sanctify**—*i. e.*, consecrate her to God. Cf. John xvii. 19, 'I *devote* myself as a *holy* sacrifice, that my disciples also may be *devoted as holy* in the truth' (Heb. ii. 11; x. 10, note; xiii. 12). and **cleanse** [*katharisas*, contemporaneous with *hagiasē*] —'cleansing,' without the "and." **with the washing of water** [τῷ λουτρῷ]—'by the *laver* of the water;' viz., the baptismal water. So Titus iii. 5, the only other passage where it occurs in the New Testament. As the bride passed through a purifying bath before marriage, so the Church. He speaks of baptism according to its high *ideal*, as if the inward grace accompanied the outward rite; hence he asserts of baptism whatever is involved in a believing appropriation of the divine truths it symbolizes, and says that Christ by it has purified the Church (1 Pet. iii. 21). **by the word**—'IN [*en*] the word.' Five times in St. Paul's other epistles, and four in Hebrews; always *the word proceeding from God.* To be joined with 'cleansing her.' The Gospel, the "word of faith" (Rom. x. 8, 9, 17), of which confession is made in baptism, and which carries the real cleansing (John xv. 3; xvii. 17), regenerating power (1 Pet. i. 23; iii. 21) (*Alford*). So *Augustine*, 'Tract.,' 80, in John, 'Take away the Word, and what is the water save water? Add the Word to the element, and it becomes a sacrament, being itself as it were the visible Word.' **27. he** [א A B Δ G *f g*, Vulgate, read αὐτός for αὐτήν]—'that He might *Himself* present unto Himself the Church glorious' (the article marks the subject, and its absence the predicate [*endoxon tēn ekklesian*]) ; viz., as a bride (2 Cor. xi. 2). He alone presents her: not paranymphs or attendants: He alone receives her. *Holiness* and *glory* are inseparable. 'Cleansing' is the preliminary to both. *Holiness* is *glory* internal; *glory* is holi-

ness shining out. It is Christ that prepares the Church with the ornaments of grace, for presentation to Himself at His coming again as Bridegroom (Matt. xxv. 1, &c.; Rev. xix. 7; xxi. 2). **not having spot** (Song iv. 7). The visible Church contains clean and unclean together, like Noah's ark; like the wedding room which contained some that had, and others that had not, the wedding garment (Matt. xxii. 10-14: cf. 2 Tim. ii. 20); or as the good and bad fish are in the same net, because the fishermen are unable to know what kind of fish the nets have taken under the waves. Still, the Church is "holy" in her ideal and destination. When the Bridegroom comes, she shall be presented to Him without spot, the evil being cut off from the body for ever (Matt. xiii. 47-50). Not that there are two churches, but one and the same Church in relation to different times—now with good and evil together; hereafter with good alone (*Pearson*). **28.** 'So (*in the same manner* as Christ loves the Church) ought husbands *also* (thus A B Δ G *f g*, Vulgate, read) to love their own (cf. note, *v.* 22) wives as (being) their own bodies.' 'He that loveth his own [*tēn heautou*] wife loveth himself.' For a man's wife is part of his very self. Christ loved the Church, not merely *just as* He loved His own body, but *as being* His own body (*Ellicott*) (*vv.* 30, 32). **29. For.** Grant that a man's wife is himself (*v.* 28), he is sure to love her, "For no man," &c. **his own flesh** (*v.* 31, end)—for "body:" in allusion to Gen. ii. 23. **nourisheth** [*ektrephei*]—'nourisheth it up;' viz., to maturity. Referring to internal sustenance: "cherisheth" [*thalpei*], to clothing and external fostering. Two grounds of love of husbands to wives are mentioned : (1.) Love to one's self, and so to one's wife, who is one's self; (2.) Following Christ's love to the Church (1 Thess. ii. 7). **the Lord.** א A B Δ *f g*, Vulgate, read 'Christ.' Exod. xxi. 10 prescribes three duties to the husband. Two (food and raiment) are alluded to spiritually by "nourisheth and cherisheth;" the third, "duty of marriage," is omitted in consonance with the holy propriety of Scripture: its antitype is, "know the Lord" (Hos. ii. 19, 20). **30. For** [*hoti*]—'Because' (1 Cor. vi. 15). Christ nourisheth and cherisheth the Church, '*Because* we are members of His body (His literal, glorified body), *being* OF [*ek tes sarkos* being formed *out of*] His flesh and of His bones,' not merely of His mystical body, the Church (*Ellicott*) (Gen. ii. 23, 24). Adam's deep sleep, wherein Eve was formed out of his opened side, is emblematic of Christ's death, which was the birth of the Spouse, the Church. John xii. 24; xix. 34, 35, to which fact *vv.* 25, 26, 27 allude, as implying atonement by His *blood*, and sanctification by the "water," answering to that which flowed from His side (cf. John vii. 38, 39; 1 Cor. vi. 11). As Adam gave Eve a new name [*Isha*], "woman," from *Ish*, "man," signifying her formation from him, so Christ, Rev. ii. 17; iii. 12. Gen. ii. 21, 23, 24, puts the *bones* first, because the reference there is to the *natural* structure. But St. Paul is referring to the *flesh of Christ.* It is

31 flesh, and of his bones. For ᵃ this cause shall a man leave his father and mother, and shall be joined unto his wife, and they two shall be
32 one flesh. This is a great mystery: but ᵇ I speak concerning Christ and
33 the church. Nevertheless ᶜ let every one of you in particular so love his wife even as himself; and the wife *see* that she ᵈ reverence *her* husband.

6 CHILDREN, ᵃ obey your parents in the Lord: for this is right.
2 Honour ᵇ thy father and mother; (which is the first commandment with
3 promise;) that it may be well with thee, and thou mayest live long on the earth.

A. D. 64.

ᵃ Gen. 2. 24.
ᵇ Isa. 42. 4, 5.
ᶜ Col. 3. 19.
ᵈ 1 Pet. 3. 6.

CHAP. 6.
ᵃ Pro 23. 22.
ᵇ Ex. 20. 12.
Deut 5. 16.
Deut. 27.16.
Jer ;6. 18.
Matt. 15. 4.

not our bones and flesh, but "*we*," that are *spiritually* propagated (in soul and spirit now, and in the body hereafter, regenerated) from Christ's glorified manhood, which has flesh and bones (Luke xxiv. 39). This existed in God's purpose from everlasting (John vi. 53). A B ℵ, Coptic, omit 'of His flesh and of His bones:' the words perhaps crept into the text, through the *margin*, from Gen. ii. 23; LXX. C Δ G *f g*, *Irenæus*, 294, the old Latin and Vulgate versions, have them. Our real (spiritual) being is as actually 'a true native extract from His own body' (*Hooker*) as was the physical derivation of Eve from Adam. 'Our union with the Deity rests in our mystical union with Christ's humanity, which is *personally* united with His divine nature, which is *essentially* united with God the Father' (*Waterland* in *Ellicott*, who adds, '*in the sacraments* we are made and continued members of Christ's *body*, *of His flesh and of His bones*'). But if *material* sacraments were the *only* means of union with Christ's humanity, what hope would there be for the thief on the cross? What hope for Quakers? **31. For this cause.** The propagation of the Church from Christ, as that of Eve from Adam, is the foundation of the spiritual marriage. The natural marriage, wherein 'a man leaves father and mother (ℵ B Δ G omit "his," which A C support) and is joined [*proskollethesetai: cemented* closely] unto his wife,' is not the principal thing here; but *the spiritual marriage*, on which it rests, whereby Christ left the Father's bosom to woo to Himself the Church out of a lost world (*v.* 32): His earthly mother, *as such*, He holds secondary to His Spiritual Bride (Luke ii. 48, 49; viii. 19-21; xi. 27, 28). He shall again leave His Father's abode to consummate the union (Matt. xxv. 1-10; Rev. xix. 7). This, then, is the first prophecy in Scripture, and 'Adam the first prophet' in typical act (*Jerome* in *Ellicott*). **they two shall be one flesh.** So the Samaritan Pentateuch, the LXX., &c., read (Gen. ii. 24), instead of 'they shall be one flesh.' So Matt. xix. 5. In natural marriage, husband and wife combine to form one perfect human being: the one is the complement of the other. So Christ, as God-man, is pleased to make the Church, the body, a necessary adjunct to Himself, the Head. He is the archetype of the Church, from whom, as the pattern, she is formed. He is her Head, as the husband is of the wife (Rom. vi. 5; 1 Cor. xi. 3; xv. 45). Christ will never allow any power to sever Himself and His bride (Matt. xix. 6; John x. 28, 29; xiii. 1). **32.** [*To musterion-mega estin*] 'This mystery is great.' This *truth, hidden once*, but *now revealed* —viz., Christ's spiritual union with the Church, *mystically represented* by marriage—is of deep import (note, *v.* 30). So "mystery" means a Divine truth not to be discovered save by revelation of God (Rom. xi. 25; 1 Cor. xv. 51). The Vulgate wrongly translates 'This is a great *sacrament*'—the plea of the Romish Church (in spite of

the blunder having been long ago exposed by their own commentators, *Cajetan* and *Estius*) for making marriage a *sacrament*. Not marriage in general, but that of Christ and the Church, is 'the great mystery,' as the words following prove: '*I* (emphatic) say it in regard to [*eis*] Christ and to [*eis*] the Church.' Whereas the words (Gen. ii. 24) refer primarily to literal marriage, *I* quote them *in a higher sense*. **33. Nevertheless.** Not to pursue further the mystical meaning of marriage; 'ye also (as Christ does) severally let each one so love,' &c. The words 'severally each one,' refer to them as *individuals*, contrasted with the previous *col'ective view* of the members as the bride of Christ. **as himself**—*as being one with Himself* (note, *v.* 28). **reverence** [*Phobetai*]—'fear.'

CHAP. VI. 1-24.—DUTIES OF PARENTS AND CHILDREN—MASTERS AND SERVANTS—OUR LIFE A WARFARE—THE SPIRITUAL ARMOUR AGAINST SPIRITUAL FOES—CONCLUSION.
1. obey [*hupakouete*]—stronger than as to wives "submitting," or 'being subject' (ch. v. 21). *Obedience* is unreasoning and implicit; *submission* is the willing *subjection* of an inferior in point of order to one having a right to command. **in the Lord**—join with "obey." ℵ A, Vulgate, support; B Δ G *f g* omit. Both parents and children being Christians, "in the Lord" expresses the *element* in which the obedience has place, and the *motive* to it. In Col. iii. 20 it is, "Children, obey your parents *in all things*." "In the Lord" suggests the limitation of the obedience required (Acts v. 29: cf., on the other hand, the abuse, Mark vii. 11-13). **right**—not merely *becoming*. Even *natural law* requires obedience to them from whom we derive life. **2.** Here the authority of *revealed law* is added. **which is** [ἥτις: *inasmuch as it is*] . . . **promise.** The "promise" is not the *main* motive, but an incidental one. The main motive is, it is God's will (Deut. v. 16, "Honour thy father and thy mother, *as the Lord thy God hath* COMMANDED *thee*"): that it is so, is shown by His accompanying it '*with a* (*en: the first in respect to*) *promise*. **first**—in the decalogue, with a *special* promise.' The promise in the second commandment is *general*. Their duty is more expressly prescribed to children than to parents; for love descends rather than ascends (*Bengel*). This verse proves the law in the New Testament is not abolished. **3. thou mayest live** (lit., *thou shalt*: a lasting and sure effect of obedience) **long on the earth.** In Exod. xx. 12, "long upon *the land which the Lord thy God giveth thee*," which St. Paul adapts to Gospel times by taking away the local reference to Canaan. The godly are equally blessed in every land, as the Jews were in the land which God gave them. This promise is always fulfilled, either literally or by a higher blessing—viz., one spiritual and eternal (Job v. 26; Prov. x. 27). The essence of the law is eternally in force; its accidents alone (applying to Israel) are abolished (Rom. vi. 15).

4 And, ^cye fathers, provoke not your children to wrath: but ^dbring them up in the nurture and admonition of the Lord.

5 Servants, be obedient to them that are *your* masters according to the flesh, with fear and trembling, in singleness of your heart, as unto Christ;

6 not with eye-service, as men-pleasers; but as the servants of Christ,

7 doing the will of God from the heart; with good will doing service, as

8 to the Lord, and not to men: knowing ^ethat whatsoever good thing any man doeth, the same shall he receive of the Lord, whether *he be* bond or free.

9 And, ye ^fmasters, do the same things unto them, ¹forbearing threatening: knowing that ²your Master also is in heaven; neither ^gis there respect of persons with him.

10 Finally, my brethren, be strong in the Lord, and in the power of his

11 might. Put ^hon the whole armour of God, that ye may be able to stand

A. D. 64.
^c Col. 3. 21.
^d Gen. 18. 19.
Deut. 6. 7.
* Rom. 2. 6.
2 Cor. 5. 10.
^f Col. 4. 1.
1 Or, moderating.
Lev. 25. 43.
2 Some read, both your and their Master.
Phil. 2. 10.
^g 1 Pet. 1. 17.
^h Rom. 13.12.
2 Cor. 6. 7.

4. And—superiors *also* have duties to the inferiors. **fathers**—including *mothers.* The fathers are specified, as being the fountains of domestic authority. Fathers are more prone to passion towards their children than mothers, whose fault is rather over-indulgence. **provoke not**—by vexatious commands, unreasonable blame, and uncertain temper (*Alford*). Col. iii. 21, "lest they be discouraged." **nurture**—'discipline;' viz., training by chastening in *act* where needed (Job v. 17; Heb. xii. 7). **admonition** [*nouthesia*]—training by *words* (Deut. vi. 7; Prov. xxii. 6, *margin*, 'catechize'), whether of encouragement, remonstrance, or reproof (*Trench*). Contrast 1 Sam. iii. 13, *margin*. **of the Lord**—such as the Lord approves, and by His Spirit dictates.

5. Servants—lit., 'slaves.' **masters according to the flesh**—in contrast to your heavenly Master (*v.* 4). A consolatory hint that the mastership to which they were subject was but for a time (*Chrysostom*): their real liberty was still their own (1 Cor. vii. 22). **fear and trembling**—not slavish terror, but (1 Cor. ii. 3, note; 2 Cor. vii. 15; Phil. ii. 12) *anxious solicitude to do your duty,* and *fear of displeasing,* as great as is produced in the ordinary slave by "threatening" (*v.* 9). **singleness**—without double-mindedness, hypocrisy, or "eye-service" (*v.* 6), which seeks to satisfy the master's *eye,* but not to make the master's interest at all times the first consideration (1 Chr. xxix. 17; Matt. vi. 22, 23; Luke xi. 34). [*Haplotes*, 'simplicity:' 2 Cor. xi. 3; Rom. xii. 8.] **6.** (Col. iii. 22.) Seeking to please masters only so long as their eyes are on them: as Gehazi was very different in his master's presence from what he was in his absence, (2 Ki. v.) **men-pleasers**—not Christ-pleasers (cf. Gal. i. 10; 1 Thess. ii. 4). **as the servants of Christ**—Christ's 'bond-servants' will not make 'men-pleasing' their aim. **doing the will of God**—the unseen but ever-present Master: the best guarantee for serving faithfully your earthly master alike when present and absent. **from the heart**—lit., *soul* (Ps. cxi. 1; Rom. xiii. 5). **7. good will**—expressing the servant's *feeling* towards his master; as "doing the will of God *from the heart*" (*soul*) expresses the *source* of that feeling (Col. iii. 23)—viz., his having given his 'soul' to "God" to do 'His will.' "Good will" is stated by *Xenophon* ('Economics') to be the slave's principal virtue towards his master; a real regard to his master's interest as his own; a *good will* which not even a master's severity can extinguish. **8. Knowing**—encouraging reason why they were to act so (*Ellicott*). **any man doeth** [*ho ean ti hekastos poiēsē*]—'each man shall have done;' *i. e.,* shall be found at the Lord's coming to have done. **the same**—'this' in full

payment, in heaven's currency. **shall he receive** (back again, as a *deposit:* the appropriative middle [*komisetai*]; 2 Cor. v. 10; Col. iii. 24)—but all of grace (Luke xvii. 10). **bond or free** (1 Cor. vii. 22; xii. 13; Col. iii. 11). Christ will not regard such present distinctions in His future judgment. The slave that has acted faithfully for the Lord's sake, though the master may not repay his faithfulness, shall have the Lord for his Paymaster. The freeman who has done good for the Lord's sake, though man may not reward him, has the Lord for his Debtor (Prov. xix. 17).

9. the same things—*mutatis mutandis.* Show the same regard to God's will, and your servant's well-being, in relation to them, as they ought in relation to you. Love regulates the duties both of servants and masters, as the same light attempers various colours. Equality of nature and faith is superior to distinctions of rank (*Bengel*). Christianity makes all men brothers (cf. Lev. xxv. 42, 43; Deut. xv. 12; Jer. xxxiv. 14, as to how the Hebrews were to treat brethren in service; much more ought Christians to act with love). **threatening** [*tēn*]—'*the* threatening' which masters commonly use. "Masters" [*hoi kurioi*] is not so strong a term as 'despots:' it implies *authority,* not absolute *domination.* **your Master also.** א A B C Δ, Vulgate, read 'the Master both of them and you.' This more forcibly brings out the equality of slaves and masters in the sight of God. *Seneca* says, 'Whatever an inferior dreads from you, this a superior Master threatens yourselves with.' As you treat your servants, so will He treat you. **neither is there respect of persons.** He will not, in judging, acquit thee because thou art a master, or condemn him because he is a servant (Acts x. 34; Rom. ii. 11; Gal. iii. 6; Col. iii. 25; 1 Pet. i. 17). Derived from Deut. x. 17; 2 Chr. xix. 7.

10. my brethren. So C G *g*,Vulgate. But א A B Δ omit. The phrase occurs nowhere else (see, however, *v.* 23): if genuine, it is appropriate in the close of the epistle, where he is urging his fellow-soldiers to the good fight. א A B for 'finally' [*to loipon:* C Δ G] read 'henceforward,' or 'from henceforth' [*tou loipou*] (Gal. vi. 17). **be strong** [*endunamousthe*]—'be strengthened.' **in the power** (in *action*) **of his might** (*passive*)—*Christ's* might (2 Cor. xii. 9): as in ch. i. 19 it is *the Father's.* **11. the whole armour**—"the armour of light" (Rom. xiii. 12) on the right hand and left (2 Cor. vi. 7). The *panoply,* offensive and defensive. An image suggested by the Roman armoury, St. Paul being in Rome. Repeated emphatically *v.* 13. In Rom. xiii. 14 it is, "Put ye on *the Lord Jesus Christ.*" On putting on Him, and the new man in Him, we put on "the armour of light," "the whole armour

420

12 against the wiles of the devil. For we wrestle not against ³flesh and blood, but against ⁱprincipalities, against powers, against ʲthe rulers of the darkness of this world, against ⁴spiritual wickedness in ⁵high *places.*

13 Wherefore take unto you the whole armour of God, that ye may be able

14 to withstand in the evil day, and having done all, to stand. Stand therefore, having your loins girt about with truth, and having on the

15 breastplate of righteousness; and your feet shod with the preparation of

16 the gospel of peace; above all, taking the shield of faith, wherewith ye

A. D. 14.

³ blood and flesh.
ⁱ Rom. 8. 38.
ʲ John 12. 31.
⁴ Or, wicked spirits.
⁵ Or, heavenly.
as ch. 1. 3.

of God." No opening at the head, the feet, the belly, the eye, the ear, or the tongue, is to be given to Satan. Believers have once for all overcome him. On the ground of this fundamental victory already gained, they are ever again to fight against and overcome him, even as they who once die with Christ have continually to mortify their members upon earth (Rom. vi. 2-14; Col. iii. 3, 5). **of God** —*furnished by* God: not our own, else it would not stand (Ps. xxxv. 1-3). Spiritual and mighty through God: not carnal (2 Cor. x. 4). **wiles**— lit., '*schemes sought out; the methodical stratagems*' (cf. 2 Cor. xi. 14). **the devil**—the ruling chief of the foes (*v.* 12) organized into a kingdom of darkness (Matt. xii. 26), opposed to the kingdom of light. **12**. 'For the [*ἡ*] wrestling to us [so א A, Vulgate. But B Δ G *f*, 'to *you*'] ('*the* wrestling' in which we are engaged) is not against flesh,' &c. Not merely against *feeble* man, but against powerful spirits of evil. 'Wrestling,' for it is a hand-to-hand and foot-to-foot personal, individual struggle: to wrestle successfully with Satan, we must wrestle with God in irresistible prayer, like Jacob (Gen. xxxii. 24-29; Hos. xii. 4). Translate, '*the* principalities . . . *the* powers' (ch. i. 21, note; iii. 10; Col. i. 16). The same grades occur in the case of the demons here as in that of the angels there (cf. Rom. viii. 38; 1 Cor. xv. 24; Col. ii. 15). The Ephesians having practised sorcery (Acts xix. 19), he appropriately treats of evil spirits in addressing them. The more any Scripture treats of the kingdom of light, the more clearly does it set forth the kingdom of darkness. Hence, nowhere does the Satanic kingdom come more distinctly into view than in the gospels which treat of Christ, the true Light. **rulers of the darkness of this world** [*tous kosmokratoras tou skotous tou aiōnos toutou*]—'*the world-rulers of the darkness of this age.*' But א A B Δ G *f g*, Vulgate, omit 'of age' [*tou aionos*]. 'Against the world-rulers of this (present) darkness' (ch. ii. 2; v. 8; Luke xxii. 53; Col. i. 13). On 'world-rulers' cf. John xii. 31; xiv. 30; xvi. 11; Luke iv. 6; 2 Cor. iv. 4; 1 John v. 19, Greek, 'lieth in the wicked one.' They rule not merely the disordered world, but the civilized, in so far as it is alienated from God. Though Satan and his demons be 'world-rulers,' they are not rulers of the universe: their usurped rule is soon to cease, when He shall "come whose right it is" (Ezek. xxi. 27). Two cases prove Satan not a subjective fancy: (1.) Christ's temptation; (2.) The entrance of demons into the swine (for these are incapable of such fancies). Satan tries to parody God's working (2 Cor. xi. 13, 14). So when God became incarnate, Satan, by demons, took possession of human bodies. The demoniacally possessed were not peculiarly wicked, but miserable, and so fit subjects for Jesus' pity. St. Paul makes no mention of demoniacal possession: in the time he wrote, it seems to have ceased; it probably lasted only during the Lord's stay on earth, and the foundation of His Church. **spiritual wickedness** [*ta pneumatika tēs ponērias*]—'*the spiritual hosts of wickedness.*' As three clauses describe the *power,*

so this fourth the *wickedness,* of our spiritual foes (Matt. xii. 45). **in high places**—Greek, 'heavenly places:' in ch. ii. 2, "the air," where see note. The alteration to 'in heavenly places,' 'supernal regions,' is to mark the higher range of their powers than ours, they having been, up to the ascension (Rev. xii. 5, 9, 10), dwellers 'in the heavenly places' (Job i. 7), and being now in the regions of the air called the heavens (cf. Luke viii. 5, 12). Pride and presumption are the sins *in heavenly places,* to which especially they tempt (Luke iv. 9-12), being those by which they themselves fell from heavenly places (Isa. xiv. 12-15). Believers have nought to fear, being 'blessed with all spiritual blessings *in the heavenly places*' (ch. i. 3). **13. Wherefore**—since we have such formidable foes. **take** . . . **of God**—not 'make;' God has done that: you have only to 'take up' [*analabete*] and put it on. The Ephesians had myths of gods giving armour to heroes: thus St. Paul's allusion is appropriate. **the evil day**—the day of Satan's special assaults (*vv.* 12, 16; ch. v. 16), and at the dying hour (cf. Rev. iii. 10). Our armour must always be on, to be ready against "the evil day" of especial temptation, which may come at any moment, the war being perpetual (Ps. xli. 1, *margin*). **done all** [*hapanta katergasamenoi*]— 'accomplished all things;' *viz.* necessary to the fight, and becoming a good soldier. **stand.** The repetition in *vv.* 11, 14 shows that *standing*—i. e., *maintaining our ground* during the life-long battle, not yielding or fleeing—is the grand aim. **14. Stand therefore**—ready for battle. 'Having girt about [*perizosamenoi*] your loins with (in: 'en') truth'—i. e., with sincerity, a good conscience (2 Cor. i. 12; 1 Tim. i. 5, 10; iii. 9). 'Truth in Jesus' (ch. iv. 21), experimentally appropriated, is the band that girds up the flowing robes, so that the Christian soldier may be unencumbered for action. So the passover was eaten with the loins girt and the shoes on the feet (Exod. xii. 11 : cf. Isa. v. 27; Luke xii. 35). The girdle kept the armour in its place, and supported the sword. *Faithfulness* (LXX., 'truth') is the girdle of Messiah (Isa. xi. 5): so *truth* of His followers. **having on** [*endusamenoi*]—'having put on.' **breastplate of righteousness** (Isa. lix. 17)—similarly of Messiah. "Righteousness" is joined with "truth," as in ch. v. 9: *righteousness* in works, *truth* in words (1 John iii. 7): Christ's righteousness inwrought in us by the Spirit. "Faith and love"—i. e., faith working righteousness by love—are "the breastplate" in 1 Thess. v. 8. **15.** Translate, 'Having shod your feet' (referring to the military sandals then used). **the preparation** [*etoimasia*]—'the preparedness' or 'readiness (for the good warfare) of' (i. e., *produced by*) the "Gospel" (Ps. x. 17). Preparedness to do and suffer all that God wills, as a Christian soldier. **gospel of peace**—cf. Luke i. 79; Rom. x. 15.) "Peace" within forms a beautiful contrast to the conflict raging without. We maintain peace with God so long as we maintain war with Satan (Isa. xxvi. 3; Phil. iv. 7). **16. Above all** [*epi*] So A

17 shall be able to quench all the fiery darts of the wicked. And take the
helmet of salvation, and the ^k sword of the Spirit, which is the word of
18 God: praying always with all prayer and supplication in the Spirit, and
watching thereunto with all perseverance and ^l supplication for all saints;
19 and for me, that utterance may be given unto me, that I may open my
20 mouth boldly, to make known the mystery of the Gospel, for which I am
an ambassador ⁶ in bonds; that ⁷ therein ^m I may speak boldly, as I ought
to speak.
21 But that ye also may know my affairs, *and* how I do, ⁿ Tychicus, a

A. D. 64.

k Heb. 4. 12.
Rev. 1. 16.
l Phil. 1. 4.
6 Or, in a chain.
Acts 23. 20.
7 Or. thereof.
m 1 Thes. 2. 2.
n Acts 20. 4.
2 Tim. 4.12.

Δ G. 'Over all:' so as to cover all that was put
on before. Three integuments are specified—the
breastplate, girdle, and shoes; two defences—the
helmet and shield; and two offensive weapons—
the sword and the spear (prayer). *Ellicott,* &c.,
'Besides (in addition to) all,' as in Luke iii. 20.
But if it meant this, it would have come *last* in
the list (cf. Col. iii. 14). But א B *f g,* Vulgate,
read [*en*] 'In all (things).' taking [*analabontes*]
—'taking up.' shield—the oblong door-like
[θυρεόν, from *thura*] shield of the Romans, 4
feet long by 2½ feet broad; not the small round
buckler. ye shall be able—not merely '*ye
may.*' The shield of faith will *certainly* in-
tercept, and so 'quench all the fire-tipt [*pepuro-
mena*] darts,' (ancient fire-darts were formed of
cane, with tow and combustibles ignited on the
head, so as to set fire to wood-work, tents, &c.)
of the wicked—'of the EVIL ONE.' Faith conquers (1 Pet. v. 9) his darts of temptation to
wrath, lust, revenge, despair, &c. It overcomes
the world (1 John v. 4), and so the prince of the
world (1 John v. 18). 17. take [*dexasthe*]—different
Greek from *vv.* 13, 16. 'Receive' the helmet
provided by the Lord—viz., "salvation," appropriated already, as 1 Thess. v. 8, "helmet, the
hope of salvation;" not uncertain, but bringing
with it no shame of disappointment. It is subjoined to the shield of faith, as its inseparable
accompaniment (cf. Rom. v. 1, 5). The head was
among the principal parts to be defended, as on it
the deadliest strokes might fall, and it commands
the whole body. The head is the seat of the
mind, which, when it has the sure "hope" of
eternal life, will not receive false doctrine, or give
way to Satan's temptation to *despair.* God, by
this hope, "lifts up the head" (Ps. iii. 3; Luke
xxi. 28). sword of the Spirit—*i. e.,* furnished by
the Spirit, who inspired the writers of the Word
(2 Pet. i. 21). The Gospel word is "the power of
God" to the believer (Rom. i. 16; 1 Cor. i. 18).
The Trinity is implied: the Spirit here; Christ in
"salvation;" and God the Father, *v.* 13 (cf. Heb.
iv. 12; Rev. i. 16; ii. 12). The two-edged sword,
cutting both ways (Ps. xlv. 3, 5), some with conviction and conversion, others with condemnation
(Isa. xi. 4; Rev. xix. 15), is in the *mouth* of Christ
(Isa. xlix. 2), in the *hand* of His saints (Ps. cxlix.
6). Christ's use of it in the temptation is our
pattern how we are to wield it against Satan
(Matt. iv. 4, 7, 10). There is no armour for the
back, but only for the front; we must never turn
our back to the foe (Luke ix. 62); our only safety
is in resisting ceaselessly (Matt. iv. 11; Jas. iv. 7).
18. Praying—joined with the principal verb,
"stand" (*v.* 14). always [*en panti kairo*]—'in
every season:' implying *opportunity* and *exigency:*
the mind being always ready for prayer (Col. iv.
2). St. Paul uses Jesus' very words in Luke xxi.
36 (a gospel which he quotes elsewhere, in undesigned consonance with the account in Acts xvi.
17, of St. Luke being his associate in travel; 1
Cor. xi. 23, &c.; 1 Tim. v. 18: cf. Luke xviii. 1;
Rom. xii. 12; 1 Thess. v. 17). with all—i. e., every

kind of; implying the earnestness of one leaving
nothing untried. prayer [*proseuchēs*]—a sacred
term for *prayer* in general. supplication [*deēseōs*]
—a common term for one kind of prayer (*Harless*);
an imploring request. "Prayer" for obtaining
blessings, "supplication" for averting evil (*Grotius*). in the Spirit—joined with "praying." It
is He *in us,* as the Spirit of adoption, who prays,
and enables us to pray (Rom. viii. 15, 26; Gal. iv.
6; Jude 20). watching—not sleeping (ch. v. 14;
Ps. lxxxviii. 13; Matt. xxvi. 41). So in the
temple a perpetual watch was maintained (cf.
Anna, Luke ii. 37). It was whilst Saul slept
that his spear and cruse were taken. Whilst
Samson slept in Delilah's lap he was shorn of his
locks. Sisera's head was nailed to the ground (a
type of those fastened to earthly things) whilst
sleeping in Jael's tent. Like Jonah sleeping in
the storm, those spiritually asleep shall only
awake to be plunged in destruction. thereunto
—*with a view to prayer* and supplication. with—
Greek, 'in.' *Persevering constancy* [*proskarterēsei*]
and (as a particular instance of it) *supplication* are
to be the element in which watchfulness is to be
exercised, and that supplication is to extend to
others besides yourselves. for all saints—as
none is so perfect as not to need the intercessions of his fellow-Christians. 19. for me—a
different Greek preposition [*huper:* 'on my
behalf' in particular] from that in *v.* 18 [*peri:*
concerning]. that I may open my mouth
boldly [*en anoixei tou stomatos mou en parrhesia
gnorisai*]—'that there may be given to me
"utterance" ('speech') *in the opening of my
mouth* (when I undertake to speak: a formula
in *set and solemn* speech : Job iii. 1; Dan. x. 16;
Matt. v. 2), so as *with boldness to make known,*' &c.
Plainness of speech was the more needed, as the
Gospel is a "mystery" indiscoverable by reason ;
only known by revelation. א A Δ *f,* Vulgate, support " of the Gospel." B G omit. Paul looked for
utterance to be *given* him: he did not depend on
natural or acquired power. The shortest road to
any heart is round by heaven: pray to God to
open the door and to open your mouth, so as to
avail yourself of every opening (Jer. i. 7, 8; Ezek.
iii. 8, 9, 11; 2 Cor. iv. 13). 20. For [*uper*]—'On
behalf of which.' an ambassador in bonds. A
paradox. Ambassadors were inviolable by the
law of nations, and could not, without outrage to
sacred right, be put in chains. Yet Christ's
'ambassador is in *a chain!*' [*en alusei,* singular.]
The Romans used to bind a prisoner to a soldier
by *a single chain,* in a kind of half-free custody.
So Acts xxviii. 16, 20. "Bonds" (plural) is used
when the prisoner's hands or feet were bound together (Acts xxvi. 29: cf. xii. 6). An undesigned
accuracy, marking truth. therein—in making
known the Gospel mystery. as I ought to speak
—qualifying the "boldly" in *v.* 19.
21. that ye also—as I have been discussing
things relating to you, that ye also may know
about me (cf. Col. iv. 7, 8). *Neander* takes it,
'ye also,' as well as the Colossians: presuming

beloved brother and faithful minister in the Lord, shall make known to
22 you all things : whom I have sent unto you for the same purpose, that
ye might know our affairs, and *that* he might comfort your hearts.
23 Peace *be* to the brethren, and love with faith, from God the Father and
24 the Lord Jesus Christ. Grace °*be* with all them that love our Lord Jesus
Christ ⁸ in sincerity. Amen.

Written from Rome unto the Ephesians by Tychicus.

A. D. 61.

° 1 Cor. 16 23.
2 Cor. 13.14.
Col. 4. 8.
⁸ Or. with-
out cor-
ruption.
Tit. 2 7.
Matt. 22.37.

the epistle to Colosse was written *first.* **how I do**
—how I fare. Tychicus—an Asiatic : so a fit
messenger for bearing the respective epistles to
Ephesus and Colosse (Acts xx. 4; 2 Tim. iv. 12;
Titus iii. 12). Tradition states that he became
bishop of Chalcedon. **a**—Greek, '*the* beloved
brother,' &c. **minister**—i. e., *servant.* **in the**
Lord—in the Lord's work. **22. for the same**
purpose—Greek, 'for this very purpose' (Col. iv.
8). **our affairs**—Greek, 'the things concerning
us.'
23. love with [*meta***] faith.** Faith is pre-supposed: he prays that love may *accompany* it (Gal.
v. 6). **24. Grace**—*The* [*η*] grace of God in Christ.
Contrast the malediction on all who love Him
not (1 Cor. xvi. 22). **in sincerity [***en aphtharsia***]**—
'*in incorruption,*' '*in imperishableness,*' 'with an
423

immortal, undecaying love.' Cf. "that which is
not corruptible" (1 Pet. iii. 4). Not fleeting as
earthly love, but spiritual and enduring. Contrast Col. ii. 22, worldly things 'which perish
with the using.' Cf. 1 Cor. ix. 25. 'Purely'
(*Estius*), without the corruption of sin (note, 1 Cor.
iii. 17; 2 Pet. i. 4; Jude 10). He who is good
enough for Christ is good enough for me (*R. Hall*).
The differences on non-essentials among real
Christians show that they are not following one
another like silly sheep, each trusting the one
before him, but independent witnesses. Their
agreement in the main can only be accounted for
by their being all in the right direction (Acts xv.
8, 9; 1 Cor. i. 2; xii. 3). Amen. א A B G omit;
Δ supports. It was added for liturgical purposes.

THE EPISTLE OF PAUL THE APOSTLE TO THE

PHILIPPIANS.

1 PAUL and Timotheus, the servants of Jesus Christ, to all the saints in
Christ Jesus which are at Philippi, with the [1] bishops and deacons:
2 Grace *be* unto you, and peace, from God our Father, and *from* the Lord
Jesus Christ.
3, I *a* thank my God upon every [2] remembrance of you, always in every
4, prayer of mine for you all making request with joy, for *b* your fellowship
5, in the Gospel from the first day until now; being confident of this very

A. D. 64.

CHAP. 1.
[1] Cr. over-
seers.
a Rom. 1. 8.
Col 1. 3.
[2] Or.
mention.
b 2 Cor. 8. 1.

CHAP. I. 1-30.—INSCRIPTION—THANKSGIVING—PRAYERS FOR THE FLOURISHING SPIRITUAL STATE OF THE PHILIPPIANS—HIS OWN IMPRISONMENT AT ROME—RESULTS IN SPREADING THE GOSPEL—EXHORTATION TO CHRISTIAN CONSISTENCY.
1. Timotheus—mentioned as being well known to the Philippians (Acts xvi. 3, 10-12; xix. 22), and now present with Paul. Not that Timothy joined in writing the epistle; for St. Paul presently uses the first person singular, "I," not 'we' (*v.* 3). The mention of Timothy implies merely that he joined in the salutation to them (ch. ii. 19). **servants** [*douli,* 'bond-servants'] **of Jesus Christ**—wholly bound to Him for ever; His property (1 Cor. vii. 22). So Δ G, Vulgate. But א B read the order, 'Christ Jesus.' More special than 'servants of *Jehovah*' (Ps. cxiii. 1). St. Paul does not call himself "an apostle," as in the inscriptions of all the epistles save this, 1 and 2 Thessalonians, and Philemon: the Philippians needed not to be reminded of his apostolic authority. He writes rather in affectionate familiarity. **all** (so *vv.* 4, 7, 8, 25; ch. ii. 17, 26)—comprehensive affection, which would not forget any one among them "all." **saints in Christ**. True saintship depends on living union with Christ. **Philippi**. More memorable as the first city in Europe wherein the Gospel was preached, than for the battle in which Octavius defeated Brutus, whereby the cause of the Roman republic was lost. **bishops**—synonymous with 'presbyters' in the apostolical churches; as appears from the same persons being called "elders of the church" at Ephesus, and "overseers" (Acts xx. 17, 28; Greek, 'bishops,' Titus i. 5: cf. with *v.* 7; 1 Pet. v. 1). This is the earliest epistle where bishops and deacons are mentioned, and the only one where they are separately addressed. This accords with the probable course of events, deduced alike from the letters and history. Whilst the apostles were constantly visiting the churches in person or by messengers, regular pastors would be less needed; but when some were removed by various causes, provision for the permanent order would be needed. Hence the three pastoral letters subsequent to this give instructions as to bishops and deacons. It agrees with this new want of the Church, when other apostles were dead or far away, and Paul long in prison, that bishops and deacons should be prominent for the first time in the opening salutation. The Spirit thus intimated that the churches were to look up to their own pastors, now that the miraculous gifts were passing into God's ordinary providence, and the presence of the inspired apostles, the dispensers of those gifts, was to be withdrawn (*Paley*). 'Presbyter' implied the *age*

and *rank;* 'bishop,' *the duties of the office.* Naturally, when the apostles who had the chief supervision were no more, one among the presbyters presided, with the name 'bishop,' in the restricted and modern sense; just as in the Jewish synagogue one of the elders presided as 'ruler of the synagogue.' The apostle addresses the Church (*i. e.,* the congregation) more directly than its ministers (Col. iv. 17; 1 Thess. v. 12; Heb. xiii. 24; Rev. i. 4, 11). The bishops managed the internal, the deacons the external, affairs of the Church. The plural shows there was more than one bishop or presbyter, and more than one deacon, in the church at Philippi. **2. Grace . . . peace.** The very form of salutation implies the union of Jew, Greek, and Roman. The Greek salutation was 'joy' [*chairein*], akin to the Greek for "grace" [*charis*]. The Roman was "health," intermediate between *grace* and *peace.* The Hebrew was "peace," including both temporal and spiritual prosperity. *Grace* must come first, if we are to have true *peace.* **from . . . from.** The Greek has no second "from;" therefore "God our Father" and "the Lord Jesus Christ" are closely connected.
3. In all his epistles to churches, except Galatians, he thanks or blesses God for their graces. **my God**—appropriating Him (Acts xxvii. 23). [*Epipasē tē mneia,* at all my remembrance of you.] **4. for you all making** [*my: tēn*] **request.** The "all" marks that Paul desires to declare his love for *all* alike, and will not recognize any divisions. "Always," "every," "all," imply exuberance of love. **with joy** — the characteristic feature in this epistle, as *love* in that to the Ephesians (cf. *v.* 18; ch. ii. 2, 19, 28; iii. 1; iv. 1, 4). *Love* and *joy* are the Spirit's two first-fruits. *Joy* gives animation to prayers. There was almost everything in them to give him *joy,* and almost nothing to give him pain. **5.** *Cause* for his 'thanking God' (as *v.* 3 marks the *object* on which his thanks rest, and *v.* 4 *when* he gives thanks). **For your fellowship** (*i. e.,* real spiritual participation) **in** (*lit.,* 'in regard to,' or 'into:' Greek, Matt. xxviii. 19) **the Gospel from the first day** (of your becoming *partakers* in it) **until now** (Acts ii. 42; xvi. 13). Believers *have* the Gospel fellowship of the Son (1 Cor. i. 9) and of the Father (1 John i. 3), by becoming partakers of "the fellowship of the Holy Ghost" (2 Cor. xiii. 14), and *exercise* it by acts of communion, not only the Lord's supper, but holy liberality to brethren and ministers (ch. iv. 10, 15, "*communicated* with me, as concerning giving;" 2 Cor. ix. 13; Gal. vi. 6; Heb. xiii. 16). **6. confident.** Confidence nerves prayers and thanksgivings (*vv.* 3, 4). **this very thing.** What he prays for (*v.* 4) is the very matter of his

6 thing, that he which hath begun *c* a good work in you [3] will perform *it*
7 until the day of Jesus Christ: even as it is meet for me to think this of you all, because [4] I have you in my heart; inasmuch as both in *d* my bonds, and in the defence and confirmation of the Gospel, ye all are
8 [5] partakers of my grace. For God is my record, how greatly I long after
9 you all in the bowels of Jesus Christ. And this I pray, that your love may abound yet more and more in knowledge and *in* all [6] judgment;
10 that ye may [7] approve things that [8] are excellent; that ye may be
11 sincere and without offence till the day of Christ; being filled with the fruits of righteousness, which are by Jesus Christ, unto the glory and praise of God.
12 But I would ye should understand, brethren, that the things *which happened* unto me have fallen out rather unto the furtherance of the
13 Gospel; so that my bonds [9] in Christ are manifest in all [10] the palace,

A. D. 64.
c John 6. 29.
[3] Or, will finish it.
[4] Or, ye have me in your heart.
d Eph. 3. 1.
[5] Or, partakers with me of grace.
[6] Or, sense.
[7] Or, try.
[8] Or, differ.
[9] Or, for Christ.
[10] Or, Cæsar's court.

believing 'confidence' (Mark xi. 24; 1 John v. 14, 15). Hence the answer is sure. **he which hath begun**—God (ch. ii. 13). **a good work.** What God begins, He will finish (1 Sam. iii. 12; 1 Cor. i. 8). Not even men begin a work at random: much more HIS beginning the work is a pledge of its completion (Isa. xxvi. 12). So as to the particular work here, the *perfecting of their fellowship in the Gospel* (v. 5; Ps. xxxvii. 24; lxxxix. 33; cxxxviii. 8; John x. 28, 29; Rom. ii. 7; viii. 29, 35-39; xi. 1, 2; Heb. vi. 17-19; Jas. i. 17; Jude 24). As God cast not off Israel for ever, though chastening them for a time, so He will not cast off the spiritual Israel (Deut. xxxiii. 3; Isa. xxvii. 3; 1 Pet. i. 5). **perform it until** [*epitelesei achris*]—'complete it up to.' **the day of Jesus Christ** (v. 10). The Lord's coming, designed by God in every age to be regarded as near, is to be the goal before believers' minds, rather than their own death. 7. **meet** [*dikaion*]—according to the law of love: 'just.' **to think this**—to have this prayerful confidence: '*to be thus minded*' [*touto phronein*] (*vv.* 4-6). **of you**—lit., '*in behalf of* you;' viz., that God will perfect His own good work of grace in you. **because, &c.** 'Because I have you in my heart (so *v.* 8; not as *margin*), inasmuch as both in my bonds, and in *my* defence and confirmation of the Gospel, you all are fellow-partakers of my grace.' The reason why he cherishes them *in his heart* (2 Cor. iii. 2; vii. 3) is, because they show by their liberality and sufferings for the Gospel that both in his bonds and in his defence and confirmation of the Gospel (such as he was constantly making, Acts xxviii. 17-23, 30; 2 Tim. iv. 16; *vv.* 16, 17 below: his self-defence and confirmation of the Gospel being intimately conjoined, there being but one Greek article to both, *v.* 17), they all are 'fellow-partakers of His grace' (*vv.* 5, 28-30; ch. iv. 15; '*the* [*tēs*] grace' vouchsafed in suffering and efforts for the Gospel). Bonds do not bind love. 8. Confirmation of *v.* 7. **record**—*i. e.*, *witness.* **in the bowels of Jesus Christ**—'Christ Jesus' is the order in א A B Δ G. My *yearning love* [*epipotho*] to you is not only natural affection, but longing for your growth spiritually in Christ. 'Not Paul, but Christ lives in Paul (Gal. ii. 20); Paul is not moved in the bowels (*i. e.*, the tender love, Jer. xxxi. 20) of Paul, but of Jesus Christ' (*Bengel*). All real spiritual love is but a portion of Christ's love, which yearns in all united to him (*Alford*). 9. The subject of his prayer (*v.* 4). **your love**—to Christ, producing love to Paul, Christ's minister, as it does, and also to one another, which it does not as much as it ought (ch. ii. 2; iv. 2). **knowledge** [*epignosei*]—'*full knowledge*' of doctrinal and practical truth. **judgment** [*aisthesei*]—spiritual

perceptiveness or discernment: spiritual sight, hearing, feeling, taste. Christianity is a vigorous plant, not the hot-bed growth of enthusiasm. "IN knowledge," &c., marks the *sphere in* which he prays that their "love" may increase. "Knowledge" and 'perception' guard love from being ill-judged. 10. [*Eisto dokimazein humas*] '*With a view to* your *proving* (and so embracing) *the things that excel*' (Rom. ii. 18); by 'perception' (v. 9), *testing* not merely things not bad, but the best among good things: the things of advanced excellence. Ask as to things, not merely, Is there no harm? but Is there any good? and Which is the best? **sincere** [*eilikrineis;* from a Greek root, *eile krino*]—*examined in the sunlight and found pure* (2 Cor. i. 12; ii. 17). **without offence**—running the Christian race *without stumbling* through temptation in your way (Acts xxiv. 16). **till** [*eis hemeran*]—'unto,' 'against:' so that when the day of Christ comes ye may be found without offence. 11. א A B Δ G *f g* read the singular, 'fruit.' So Gal. v. 22 (see note): regarding the works of righteousness, however manifold, as *one* harmonious whole—"the *fruit* of the Spirit" (Eph. v. 9; Jas. iii. 18; Heb. xii. 11). The 'fruit' is the *product* of "righteousness," which is the *new moral habit*, given along with justification, whereby a man bears fruit (Rom. vi. 13, 22; vii. 4, 5). **which are**—which *is* by [*dia: through*] Jesus Christ. Through His grace to us His Spirit from the Father. 'We are wild and useless olive trees till graffed into Christ, who, by His living root, makes us fruit-bearing branches' (*Calvin*).
12. **understand** [*ginoskein*]—'know.' The Philippians probably feared that his imprisonment would hinder the spreading of the Gospel: he removes this fear. **the things which happened unto me** [*ta kat' eme*]—'the things concerning me.' **rather**—so far is my imprisonment from hindering the Gospel. Faith takes in a favourable light even what seems adverse (*Bengel*) (*vv.* 19, 28; ch. ii. 17). 13. **my bonds in Christ** [*desmous mou phanerous en Christo*]—'so that my bonds *became manifest in Christ;*' *i. e.*, manifest, as endured *in fellowship with Christ*, in Christ's cause. **palace**—lit., 'prætorium;' *i. e.*, the barrack of the prætorian guards attached to Nero's palace, on the Palatine hill at Rome. So "Cæsar's household" is mentioned, ch. iv. 22. The emperor was 'prætor,' or commander-in-chief: so the barrack of his body-guard was the 'prætorium.' The 'ALL the prætorium' implies that the *whole* camp, whether inside or outside the city, is included. The 'camp of the prætorians' was built by Sejanus, near the Viminal gate. Paul seems now not to have been at large *in his own hired house*, chained to a soldier

425

14 and ¹¹ in all other *places;* and many of the brethren in the Lord, waxing
confident by my bonds, are much more bold to speak the word without
15 fear. Some indeed preach Christ even of envy and *ᵉ* strife; and some
16 also of good will: the one preach Christ of contention, not sincerely,
17 supposing to add affliction to my bonds: but the other of love, knowing
18 that I am set for the defence of the Gospel. What then? notwithstanding, every way, whether in pretence, or in truth, Christ is preached; and
19 I therein do rejoice, yea, and will rejoice. For I know that this shall
turn to my salvation *ᶠ* through your prayer, and the supply of *ᵍ* the
20 Spirit of Jesus Christ, according to my earnest expectation and *my* hope,

A. D. 64.

¹¹ Or. to all others.
• Matt. 23. 5.
Rom. 16.17.
1 Cor. 3. 8.
2 Cor.12.20.
Gal. 2. 4.
ch. 2. 2.
Jas 4. 5, 6.
ƒ 2 Cor. 1. 11.
ᵍ Rom. 8. 9.
1 Pet. 1. 11.

(to whom he had been consigned by one of the two prefects of the prætorium, probably Burrus, Acts xxviii. 16, 20, 30, 31), but in strict custody *in the prætorium:* a change which probably took place on Tigellinus becoming prætorian prefect ('Introduction'). **in all other places**—so *Chrysostom.* [*Tois loipois pasin*] 'To all the rest;' *i. e.,* 'manifest to all the other' prætorian soldiers stationed elsewhere, through the instrumentality of the prætorian household guards attached to the emperor's palace, who relieved one another in succession. Paul had been now upwards of two years a prisoner, so that there was time for his cause and the Gospel having become widely known at Rome. **14.** [*Kai tous pleionas tōn adelphōn*] 'And *that* (v. 13) the majority of brethren in the Lord,' &c. "In the Lord," distinguishes them from 'brethren after the flesh,' Jewish fellow-countrymen. *Ellicott,* 'Having in the Lord confidence in my bonds.' Rather, **by my bonds**—encouraged by my patience in bearing my bonds: '*owing to* my bonds' giving a practical testimony to the truth of the Gospel. Ch. ii. 24; Gal. v. 10; 2 Thess. iii. 4, justify connecting, '*having confidence in the Lord.*' "Brethren in the Lord" (Syriac version) would be rather *tōn en kurio adelphōn* than *tōn adelphon en kurio pepoithotas;* also, Paul never joins *en kurio adelphos.* Their *confidence* flows from union *with the Lord.* **much more bold.** Translate as Greek, 'are more abundantly bold' than when I was free. 'In our brethren's person we have the pledge of our own victory' (*Calvin*). **speak the word without fear** (Acts iv. 31). **15.** 'Some indeed *are preaching* Christ even *for* [*dia : on account of:* to gratify] envy; *i. e.,* to carry out the *envy* they felt towards Paul at the success of the Gospel in the capital of the world, owing to his stedfastness in imprisonment: they wished to transfer the credit to themselves. Probably Judaizing teachers (Rom. xiv.; 1 Cor. iii. 10-15; ix. 1, &c. ; 2 Cor. xi. 1-4). **some also of** (*for*) **good will** —answering to "the brethren" (*v.* 14); some being *well disposed* to him. **16, 17.** א A B Δ G, Vulgate, transpose and read, "*These* (last) *indeed out of* love (to Christ and me), knowing (opposed to 'thinking,' below) that I am set (*i. e.,* appointed by God, 1 Thess. iii. 3) for the defence of the Gospel (v. 7). But the others *out of contentiousness* [*eritheias:* 'a factious spirit;' 'cabal;' using unscrupulous means to compass their end] (note, Gal. v. 20) *proclaim* [the Greek is not *kērussousin,* as above, 'preach,' but '*announce,*' 'make known,' *katangellousin*] Christ, not sincerely [answering to 'out of a factious spirit:' *oukh hagnōs*], 'not purely;' not with a pure intention: the Jewish leaven they introduced was in order to *glorify themselves* (Gal. vi. 12, 13: see, however, note, *v.*.18), thinking (but in vain) *to raise up* [so א A B Δ ƒ *g,* Vulgate, *egeirein* for *epipherein*] "affliction to my bonds." Their *thought* was, that, taking the opportunity of my being laid aside, they would exalt themselves **by preaching Judaism,**

and depreciate me, and so add *trouble* to my bonds: they thought that I, like themselves, seek my own glory, and so will be mortified at their success over mine. But "I . . . rejoice" (*v.* 18), so far from being *troubled* at it. [This meaning of *thlipsis* is justified by 2 Cor. ii. 4, though it mostly expresses *outward calamity;* whence *Ellicott* explains 'ill treatment from the Jews and Judaizing Christians.' The former is better sense.] *Ellicott,* to avoid the tautology "of love," "of good will," "of contention," "of envy," translates, 'they *that are* of love (so preach) *because* they know,' &c. : 'but they *that are* of contentiousness, proclaim Christ,' &c. **18. What then?** Things being so, Does this trouble me, as they thought it would? "Notwithstanding" their unkind *thought,* the cause I have at heart is furthered in "every way" of preaching, 'whether in pretence (with a by motive, *v.* 16) or in truth (out of true "love" to Christ, *v.* 17), Christ is *proclaimed;* and therein I do rejoice, yea, and I will rejoice.' *El icott,* 'I *shall* rejoice' when 'this shall turn out to me for salvation' (*v.* 19). These self-seeking teachers 'proclaimed Christ,' not 'another gospel,' as the Judaizers in Galatia (Gal. i. 6-8); though probably having some Jewish leaven (note, *vv.* 15, 16, 17), their *chief* error was their envious *motive,* not so much false doctrine: had there been *vital* error, Paul would not have *rejoiced.* The *proclamation* of CHRIST roused attention, and so was sure to be of service. Paul could thus rejoice at the good result of their bad intentions (Ps. lxxvi. 10; Isa. x. 5, 7). **19. turn to my salvation** [*moi apobesetai eis soterian*]—'turn out to me for salvation.' This proclamation of Christ every way will turn out to *my spiritual good.* Christ, whose interests are mine, being glorified thereby; so the coming of His kingdom being furthered, which will bring completed "SALVATION" (Heb. ix. 28) to me, and to all whose "earnest expectation" (*v.* 20) is that Christ may be magnified in them. So far is their preaching from causing me, as they thought, *tribulation in my bonds* (v. 16). Paul applies to himself (LXX.; Job xiii. 12, 16), 'this shall turn out to my salvation:' a text belonging to all God's people in their tribulation. **through your prayer, and the supply.** The Greek [*dia tēs humōn deeseōs kai epikhoregias*] intimately joins the two nouns by one preposition and one article: 'Through your prayer and (*the consequent*) supply of (*i. e.,* from) the Spirit of Jesus Christ' (obtained for me through your prayer). *Ampleness* is implied in the "supply" and the Giver. **20. According to my earnest expectation** [*apokaradokian*]—'expectation patient and persistent, *with uplifted head* (Luke xxi. 28) *and outstretched neck*' (Rom. viii. 19, the only other place in the New Testament that the word occurs). *Tittmann,* 'Not mere *expectation,* but *the anxious desire of an anticipated prosperous issue in afflictive circumstances.*' The subject of his earnest expectation, which follows, answers to "my salvation" (*v.* 19). **in nothing**

426

that *h* in nothing I shall be ashamed, but *that* with all boldness, as always, *so* now also Christ shall be magnified in my body, whether *it be* by life, or by death.

21, For to me to live *is* Christ, and to die *is* gain. But if I live in the 22 flesh, this *is* the fruit of my labour: yet what I shall choose I wot not. 23 For *i* I am in a strait betwixt two, having a desire to *j* depart, and to 24 be with Christ; which is far better: nevertheless to abide in the flesh *is* 25 more needful for you. And having this confidence, I know that I shall abide and continue with you all for your furtherance and joy of faith; 26 that your rejoicing may be more abundant in Jesus Christ for me by my coming to you again.

27 Only let your conversation be as it becometh the gospel of Christ: that whether I come and see you, or else be absent, I may hear of your affairs, that ye stand fast in one spirit, with one mind striving together for the

A. D. 64.
h Ps. 25. 2.
Ps. 119. 80.
116.
Isa. 45. 17.
Isa. 50. 7.
Isa. 54. 4.
Rom. 5. 5.
Rom. 9. 33.
2 Cor. 7. 14.
i 2 Sam. 21.
14.
1 Chr. 21 13.
Luke 12.50.
2 Cor 5. 8.
j Luke 2. 29,
30.
2 Tim. 4. 6.

I shall be ashamed—in nothing have reason to be ashamed of 'my work for God, or His work in me' (*Alford*). Rather, 'in nothing be *disappointed* in my *hope*, but fully obtain it' (1 John ii. 28: so Rom. ix. 33). Contrast Paul's phrase, "glory", 'boast' [*kaukhasthai*]. **all boldness.** "All" is opposed to "in nothing," as "boldness" is the opposite to "ashamed" (Eph. vi. 19). **so now also**—when "my body" is 'in bonds' (*v.* 17). **Christ** (not Paul) **shall be magnified in my body** —as the theatre of His being magnified (John xxi. 19; Gal. i. 24). **life, or by death.** Whatever be the issue, Christ, and therefore I, must be the gainer. Paul was not omniscient: in the events of things the apostles had the same probation of faith and patience as we. **21. For.** In either event (*v.* 20) I must gain, "For to me," &c. **to live is Christ.** 'Life is but another name for Christ' (*Peile*) (Gal. ii. 20). There *faith* is the prominent idea; here, *works.* Living, in my realization of it, consists only in union with, and *devotion* to, Christ. My whole being and activities are His (*Ellicott*). **to die is gain**—not the act of dying, but, as *to apothanein*, 'to have died,' expresses, *the state after death.* Besides Christ's glorification by my death, which is my primary object (*v.* 20), the change of state caused by death, so far from being a *shame* (*v.* 20) or loss, as my enemies suppose, will be a positive "gain" to me. **22.** 'But if (*since*) to live in the flesh (as opposed to "die", *departing out of the flesh*) (if) this (continuance in life) be the fruit of my labour (*i. e.*, be the necessary condition of fruit from ministerial labour), *then* [*kai*] what I shall choose I know [*gnorizo : discern*] not' (if the choice were given me, both alternatives, being great goods alike). So *Alford* and *Ellicott.* The Greek will bear the English version by an ellipsis, 'If to live in the flesh (be my portion), this (continuing to live) is the fruit of my labour'—*i. e.*, will be the occasion of my bringing in 'fruit of (*from* apostolic) labour.' *Grotius* takes 'the fruit of labour' as an idiom. If I live in the flesh, this is *worth my while*, for thus Christ's interests will be advanced, "For to me to live is Christ" (*v.* 21: cf. ch. ii. 30; Rom. i. 13). The second alternative—viz., dying—is handled, ch. ii. 17, "if I be offered." **23. For.** א A B C Δ *f g*, Vulgate, read 'But.' 'I know not (*v.* 22); BUT am held in a strait betwixt *the* two (viz., "to live" and "to die"), having *the* desire *for* departing [*analusai, to loose* anchor] (2 Tim. iv. 6), and being with Christ; FOR (so A B) it is by far better;' or [*pollo mallon kreisson*] more forcibly, 'by far *the more preferable*:' a double comparative. Therefore the soul is not dormant during its separation from the body. Whilst he regarded the Lord's advent as at all times near, yet his

death before it was a very possible contingency. Eternal life is *initial* here. The *partial* life eternal is in the interval between death and Christ's second advent: the *perfectional*, at that advent (*Bishop Pearson*). To *depart* is better than to remain in the flesh; *to be with Christ is far, far better:* for me personally (a proof that the intermediate state is not one of unconsciousness) (2 Cor. v. 8): a New Testament hope (Heb. xii. 24) (*Bengel*). **24. to abide**—to continue longer. **for you** [*di' humas*] —'for your sake.' To be of service to *you*, I am willing to forego my entrance sooner into blessedness; heaven will not fail to be mine at last. **25.** 'And being confident of this'—viz., that my abiding in the flesh is more necessary on your account. **I know, &c.**—by intimations of the Spirit. *Ellicott* quotes Acts xx. 25 for interpreting "I know," as merely *it is my present feeling;* not any prophetic certitude. But cf. *v.* 38 there. He did not know the issue, as far as *human appearances* were concerned (ch. ii. 23). He doubtless returned from his first captivity to Philippi (Heb. xiii. 19; Phile. 22). **joy of faith** [*charan tes pisteōs*]—joy springing from the faith. 'Joy' is that active emanation of love and thankfulness that forms a spiritual equipoise to 'peace' and 'patience' (*Ellicott*). **26.** 'That your matter of glorying [*kauchema*, not *kauchesis*] may abound in Christ Jesus (the only legitimate *sphere* in which *glorying* has place) in me; *i. e.*, in my case (Gal. i. 24): *in respect to me,* your builder up in the faith, granted to your prayers (*v.* 19) through my presence again among you.' *Alford* makes the 'matter of glorying' *the possession of the Gospel,* or *their being established in the faith* (*Chrysostom*), through Paul, which would be increased by his presence among them. But 'my rejoicing over you' (ch. ii. 16) answers to 'your *rejoicing* in respect to me' here. **27. Only**—Whatever happens as to my coming to you or not, make this your only care. By supposing this or that future contingency, many persuade themselves they will be such as they ought to be, but it is better always, without evasion, to perform present duties under present circumstances (*Bengel*). **let your conversation be** (cf. ch. iii. 20) [*politenesthe*]—'Let your *walk as citizens* (viz., of the heavenly state: 'the city of the living God' Heb. xii. 22; Eph. ii. 19), be,' (Acts xxiii. 1, &c.) **I ... see ... hear**—so *v.* 30. "Hear," in order to take in both alternatives, must include *know.* **your affairs**—your state. **in one spirit**—the fruit of partaking of the Holy Spirit (Eph. iv. 3, 4). **with one mind** [*psuche*]—'soul,' the sphere of the affections: subordinate to the "spirit," man's higher and heavenly nature, whereon the Holy Spirit acts. 'There is sometimes natural antipathies among believers; these are

28 faith of the Gospel; and in nothing *ᵏ* terrified by your adversaries: which is to them an evident token of perdition, but to you of salvation, and
29 that of God. For unto you it is given in the behalf of Christ, not only
30 to believe on him, but also to suffer for his sake; having the same conflict which ye saw in me, *and* now hear *to be* in me.

2 IF *there be* therefore any consolation in Christ, if any comfort of love,
2 if *ᵃ*any fellowship of the Spirit, if any bowels and mercies, fulfil *ᵇ* ye my joy, *ᶜ*that ye be like-minded, having the same love, *being* of one accord,
3 of one mind. Let *ᵈ*nothing *be done* through strife or vain-glory; but
4 *ᵉ*in lowliness of mind let each esteem other better than themselves. Look *ᶠ*not every man on his own things, but every man also on the things of others.
5 Let *ᵍ*this mind be in you, which was also in Christ Jesus: who, *ʰ*being

A. D. 64.
ᵏ Isa. 41. 10.
Matt. 10.28.
Heb. 13. 5.
CHAP. 2.
ᵃ 2 Cor.13.14.
ᵇ John 3. 29.
ᶜ 1 Pet. 3. 8.
ᵈ Jas. 3. 14.
ᵉ 1 Pet. 5. 5.
ᶠ 1 Cor.10.24.
ᵍ John 13. 16.
ʰ Isa. 9. 6.
Zech. 13. 7.
John 1. 1, 2.
John 17. 5.

overcome when there is not only unity of spirit, but also of *soul*' (*Bengel*). **striving together**—with united effort. **28. terrified** [*pturomenoi*]—said of horses suddenly scared: so of sudden *consternation* in general. **by your adversaries: which** (1 Cor. xvi. 9)—'the which': your not being terrified, *seeing it is.* **evident token of perdition**—if they would only perceive it (2 Thess. i. 5). It attests this,—that in contending against you, they are only rushing on their own perdition, not shaking your united faith. **to you of salvation.** א A B read, '**of** *your*' (final: in contrast to their "perdition") **salvation.'** **29. For**—the double favour bestowed on you is a proof that this is an evident token from God of your salvation; '*Because*,' &c. **it is given**—'*as a favour*' [*echaristhē*] or 'gift of grace.' Faith is the gift of God (Eph. ii. 8), not wrought in the soul by the will of man, but by the Holy Ghost (John i. 12, 13). **believe on him.** 'To believe *Him*' would merely mean to believe He speaks the truth. 'To believe *on Him*' [*eis auton pisteuein*] is *to believe in, and trust through,* Him to obtain eternal salvation. *Suffering for Christ* is not only not a mark of God's anger, but *a gift of His grace.* **30. ye saw in me** (Acts xvi. 12, 19, &c.; 1 Thess. ii. 2). I am 'in nothing terrified by mine adversaries' (*v.* 29), so ought not ye. 'Ye saw . . . and . . . hear' answer to 'I come and see you, or else . . . . *hear*' (*v.* 27).

CHAP. II. 1-30.—CONTINUED EXHORTATION— TO UNITY—HUMILITY AFTER CHRIST'S EXAMPLE, WHOSE GLORY FOLLOWED HIS HUMILIATION—TO EARNESTNESS IN SEEKING PERFECTION, THAT THEY MAY BE HIS JOY IN THE DAY OF CHRIST —HIS READINESS TO BE OFFERED NOW BY DEATH, SO AS TO PROMOTE THEIR FAITH—HIS INTENTION TO SEND TIMOTHY—HIS SENDING EPAPHRODITUS MEANTIME.

1. The "therefore" implies that he is here expanding the exhortation (ch. i. 27), "In one spirit, with one mind" (*soul*). *Four influencing motives* in this verse, to inculcate the four Christian duties corresponding respectively (*v.* 2):— 'That ye be *like-minded*, having the same *love*, of one accord, of one mind.' (1.) 'If there be (with you, as I assume) *any consolation in Christ*;' i. e., *any consolation* (but *Ellicott*, to avoid tautology, "comfort" following, translates [*paraklesis*] "exhortation," Rom. xii. 8) *of which Christ is the source*, leading you *to console me* in my afflictions, borne for Christ's sake, ye ought to grant my request, "that ye be like minded" (*Chrysostom*). (2.) 'If there be any comfort of (i. e., flowing from) love,' the adjunct of "consolation in Christ." (3.) 'If any fellowship of (joint participation of) the Spirit' (2 Cor. xiii. 14). As *pagans* meant those who were of one village, and *drank of one fountain*, how much greater is the union which conjoins 428

those who drink of the same Spirit (1 Cor. xii. 4, 13). (4.) 'If any bowels (tender emotions) and mercies' (compassions, Col. iii. 12), the adjuncts of "fellowship of the Spirit." The first and third mark the *objective* sources of the Christian life—Christ and the Spirit; the second and fourth, the *subjective* principle in believers. The opposites of the two pairs into which the four fall are reprobated, *vv.* 3, 4. **2. Fulfil**—i. e., Make full. I have joy in you: *complete* it by that which is still wanting—viz., unity (ch. i. 9). 'What wilt thou (we might suppose them, in hearing his earnest entreaty, to say)? That we release thee from danger? that we relieve thy wants? None of these things' (*Chrysostom*); but **that ye be like-minded** [*to auto phronēte*]—'of the same mind:' more general than the following "of one mind." **having the same love**—disposed to love and be loved. **being of one accord** [*sunpsuchoi*]—'with united *souls.*' This pairs with the following clause:—'With united souls, being of one mind;' as the former two pair together, "that ye be like-minded, having the same love." **3. Let nothing be done.** The italicized words are not in the Greek. Supply the ellipsis from the Greek (*v.* 2) [*phronountes*], '*minding* nothing in the way of strife' ('factious intrigue,' '*contentiousness*,' note, ch. i. 16). It is the *mind* or *thought* which characterizes the action as good or bad before God. **lowliness of mind** [*tapeinophrosune*]. Its *direct* relation is to God alone. Sense of dependence of the creature on the Creator as such places all created beings in this respect on a level. The 'lowly of mind,' as to his spiritual life, is independent of men, while sensible of his continual dependence on God. Still, it INDIRECTLY affects his behaviour towards his fellow-men; for, conscious of entire dependence on God for all his abilities, he will not pride himself on them, or exalt self in his conduct towards others (Eph. iv. 2; Col. iii. 12). *Neander*, 'The thinking lowly of ourselves because we are so.' **let each esteem**— 'esteeming each other superior to *yourselves*' [*huperechontas heautōn*]. Instead of fixing your eyes on those points in which you excel, fix them on those in which your neighbour excels you: this is true "humility" (Rom. xii. 10; Eph. v. 21; 1 Pet. v. 5). **4.** [A B C Δ G, Vulgate, read *hekastoi skopountes-hekastoi;* א, *hekastos skopountes-hekastos.* Elsewhere in the New Testament it is only singular] '*Not looking each of you* (plural) on his own things (i. e., not *having regard* solely to them), but *each of you* on the things of others' also. Cf. *v.* 21; also Paul's own example (ch. i. 24).

5. [א A B C Δ G *f g,* Vulgate, read *phroneite* for *phroneisthe*] 'Have this mind in you,' &c. Pride is the most naked form of selfishness, which is the essence of sin (*Müller*). He does not put

7 in the form of God, thought *it not robbery to be equal with God; but
   *made himself of no reputation, and took upon him the form *of a ser-
8 vant, and *was made in the ¹likeness of men: and being found in fashion
   as a man, he humbled himself, and *became obedient unto death, even
9 the death of the cross. Wherefore God also hath highly exalted him,
10 and given him a name which is above every name: that at the name

A. D. 64.

i John 5. 18.
j Ps. 22. 6.
k Isa. 42. 1.
l John 1. 14.
1 Or, habit.
m Heb. 12. 2.

forward himself (see note, v. 4; ch. i. 24) as an example, but Christ, THE ONE pre-eminently who sought not His own, but "humbled Himself" (v. 8), first, in taking on Him our nature; secondly, in humbling himself further in that nature (Rom. xv. 3). 6. Translate, 'Who *subsisting* [or *existing* —viz., originally: *huparchōn*, not ὤν] in the form of God (God's *essence* is not meant, but His *external self-manifesting characteristics*, the *form* shining forth from His glorious essence. God had infinite beauty in Himself, even without any creature contemplating that beauty: that beauty was "the form of God." As "the *form* of a servant" (v. 7), which is in contrasted opposition to it, takes for granted the *existence* of His human nature, so "the form of God" takes for granted His Divine nature (*Bengel*). Cf. John v. 37; xvii. 5; Col. i. 15, "Who is the IMAGE of the invisible God," at a time *before* "every creature," 2 Cor. iv. 4), *esteemed* (the same Greek [*hegesato*] as in v. 3) His being *on an equality* with God [*to einai isa theō*] no (act of) robbery' or *self-arrogation;* claiming to one's self what does not belong to him. *Ellicott*, &c., translate, 'a thing to be grasped at,' which would require *harpagma*, whereas *harpagmos* means the *act* of seizing. So *harpagmos* means in the only passage where else it occurs (*Plutarch*, 'De Educatione Puerorum,' 120). The same objection lies against *Alford*, 'He regarded not as *self-enrichment* (i. e., an *opportunity for self-exaltation*) His equality with God.' His argument is, that the antithesis (v. 7) requires 'He used His equality with God as *an opportunity, not for self-exaltation,* but for self-abasement.' But the antithesis is not between His *being on an equality with God,* and His *emptying Himself;* for He never emptied Himself of the fulness of His Godhead, or His 'BEING on an *equality with God;*' but between His being "in the FORM (i. e., the glorious self-manifestation) of God," and His 'taking on Him *the form of a servant,*' whereby He in a great measure emptied Himself of His precedent "form" as God. Not 'looking on His own things' (v. 4), He, though existing in the form of God, esteemed it no robbery to be on an equality with God, yet made Himself of no reputation. 'Being on an equality with God' is not identical with 'subsisting in the form of God:' the latter expresses the self-manifesting *characteristics,* majesty and beauty of Deity, which 'He emptied Himself of' to assume "the *form* of a servant;" the former, 'His BEING,' His ESSENTIAL EQUALITY IN ALL RESPECTS with God the Father. A glimpse of Him "in the form of God," previous to His incarnation, was given to Moses (Exod. xxiv. 10, 11), Aaron, &c. 7. made himself of no reputation, and . . . and [*heauton ekenosen morphēn doulou labōn: genomenos*]— 'emptied Himself, *taking* upon Him the form of a servant, (by) *being* made in the likeness of men.' The two latter clauses (there being no "and . . . and" in the Greek) express *in what* Christ's 'emptying of Himself' consists—viz., in 'taking the form of a servant' (note, Heb. x. 5: cf. Exod. xxi. 5, 6; Ps. xl. 6, proving that it was at the time when He assumed a body He took "the form of a servant"); and in order to explain *how* He took "the form of a servant," there is added, by 'being **made** *in the likeness of men*' (an appropriate

phrase: though perfect man, He was not mere man, but *the Word made flesh).* His subjection to the law (Luke ii. 21; Gal. iv. 4) and to His parents (Luke ii. 51); His low state as a carpenter, and carpenter's reputed son (Matt. xiii. 55; Mark vi. 3); His betrayal for the price of a bond-servant (Exod. xxi. 32), and slave-like death, to relieve us from the slavery of sin and death; finally, *His servant-like dependence as man on God,* whilst His divinity was not outwardly manifested (Isa. xlix. 3, 7),—all show His "form as a servant." This proves—(1.) He was in the form of a servant as soon as He was made man. (2.) He was "in the form of God" *before* He was in "the form of a servant." (3.) He did as really subsist "in the form of God," or the self-manifested divine nature, as in "the form of a servant," or in the nature of man. For He was so in the form of God as 'to be on an equality with God:' He therefore could have been none other than God; for God saith, "To whom will ye liken me and make me equal?" (Isa. xlvi. 5) (*Bishop Pearson.*) His *emptying Himself* presupposes His previous *plenitude of Godhead* (John i. 14; Col. i. 19; ii. 9). He remained full of this, yet He bore Himself as if He were empty. 8. being found in fashion as a man—*being already, by His 'emptying Himself,' in the form of a servant,* or likeness of man (Rom. viii. 3). "Found" RECOGNIZED *by men's senses* as really man (cf. Gal. ii. 17). 'He humbled Himself (still further by) *becoming* obedient *even* unto death; and that the death of the cross' [*etapeinosen heauton, genomenos hupekoos mechri thanatou, thanatou de staurou].* "Fashion" expresses that He had the *outward* guise, speech, and demeanour [*schema*]. [*Morphē*] "Form" is more intrinsic and essential. In v. 7 the emphasis is on *Himself* (which stands before the Greek verb): 'He emptied *Himself,*' His *divine self,* viewed in respect to what He had heretofore been. In v. 8 the emphasis is on "*humbled*" (which stands before the Greek "Himself"): He not only 'emptied Himself' of His "form of God" negatively, but submitted to *positive* acts of HUMILIATION. He "became obedient," viz., to God, as His "servant" (Rom. v. 19; Heb. v. 8). Therefore "*God*" "exalted" Him (v. 9), even as it was God to whom He became voluntarily 'obedient' (Matt. xxvi. 39). 'Even unto death,' the climax of His obedience (John x. 18). 9. Wherefore—the just consequence of his self-humiliating obedience (Ps. viii. 5, 6; cx. 1, 7; Matt. xxviii. 18; Luke xxiv. 26; John v. 27; x. 17; Rom. xiv. 9; Eph. i. 20-22; Heb. ii. 9). If we would hereafter be exalted, we too must, after His example, now humble ourselves (vv. 3, 5; ch. iii. 21; 1 Pet. v. 5, 6). Christ emptied Christ; God exalted Christ AS MAN to equality with God (*Bengel*). *As God,* the Son, always had it, at the Ascension He was invested, *as the Son of man,* with all the glory and power of the Godhead. highly exalted [*huper upsosen*]— '*super-eminently* exalted' (Eph. iv. 10) as the Most High. given him [*echarisato*]—'bestowed on Him.' a name [*onoma to huper pan onoma*]—along with the *reality* and majesty. His *revealed* personality, acknowledged by man. which. Translate, (viz.) 'that which is above every name.' The name of humiliation, "JESUS" (v. 10), which is even now in heaven His name of honour (Acts ix. 5) "above,"

429

of Jesus every knee should bow, of *things* in heaven, and *things* in earth,
11 and *things* under the earth; and *ⁿ that* every tongue should confess that
Jesus Christ *is* Lord, to the glory of God the Father.
12 Wherefore, my beloved, as ye have always obeyed, not as in my
presence only, but now much more in my absence, *°* work out your own
13 salvation with fear and trembling: for *ᵖ* it is God which worketh in you
14 both to will and to do of *his* good pleasure. Do all things without
15 murmurings and disputings: that ye may be blameless and *²* harmless,

A. D. 64.

ⁿ John 13.13.
Rom. 19. 4.
° Pro. 10. 16.
Heb. 4. 11.
ᵖ 2 Cor. 3. 5.
Heb. 13. 21.
2 Or,
sincere.
ch. 1. 10.

not only men, but angels (Eph. i. 21). **10. at the name** [*en to onomati*]—"in the name" (Eph. v. 20). **bow** [*kampsē*]—'bend' in worship. Referring to Isa. xlv. 23; quoted also Rom. xiv. 11. To worship "in the name of Jesus" is to worship Jesus *Himself* (cf. *v.* 11; Prov. xviii. 10), or *God in Christ* (Eph. iii. 14). To worship God as manifested in Jesus; to ask God *in the name of Jesus*, "the express image of his person" (John xvi. 23; Heb. i. 3). Cf. "Whosoever shall call upon *the name of the Lord* (i. e., *the Lord in His revealed character*) shall be saved" (Rom. x. 13; 1 Cor. i. 2: cf. 2 Tim. ii. 22; Acts vii. 59; ix. 14, 21; xxii. 16). **of things in heaven.** Angels worship Him not only as God, but as the ascended *God-man*, "Jesus" (Heb. i. 6; 1 Pet. iii. 22). **in earth**—men; among whom he tabernacled for a time. **under the earth**—the dead; among whom he was numbered once (Rom. xiv. 9, 11; Eph. iv. 9, 10; Rev. v. 13). The homage of demons and the lost, being one of fear, not love, hardly suits the sense (Mark iii. 11; Luke viii. 31; Jas. ii. 19; see note, *v.* 11). **11. every tongue**—cf. "every knee" (*v.* 10). *In every way* He shall be acknowledged [*exomologesetai*: 'openly confess'] as Lord (no longer "servant," *v.* 7; Matt. xxviii. 18). As none can fully do so 'but by the Holy Ghost' (1 Cor. xii. 3), the spirits of good men dead must be the class *directly* meant, *v.* 10, "under the earth." **to the glory of God the Father**—the grand end of Christ's mediatorial office and kingdom, which shall cease when this end shall have been fully realized (John v. 19-23, 30; xvii. 1, 4-7; 1 Cor. xv. 24-28). The Father's glory, and the Son's, is inseparable. **12. Wherefore**—seeing that we have in Christ such a specimen of glory resulting from humble '*obedience*' (*v.* 8), see that ye also be "**obedient**" to God; so '*your* salvation' shall follow your obedience. **as** [*kathos*: even as] **ye have always obeyed** —God; as Jesus was "obedient" unto God (note, *v.* 8). **not** [*mē*] **as,** &c.—join with "work out:" "not *as*" a matter to be done "in my presence only, but now much more (with more zeal) in my absence" (because without my support and eye). **work out**—carry out to full perfection [*katergazesthe*] (Rom. vii. 18, 'But how to *work out* that which is good I find not ;' Eph. vi. 13). "Salvation" is 'worked in' (*v.* 13; Eph. i. 20) believers by the Spirit, who enables them through faith to be justified *once for all ;* but it needs, as a progressive work, to be 'worked *out*' by obedience, through the help of the same Spirit, unto perfection (2 Pet. i. 5, 3). The Christian neither, like the formalist, rests in means, without looking to the end, and to the Holy Spirit, who alone can make the means effectual; nor, like the fanatic, hopes to attain the end without the means. **your own**—emphatical. Now that *I* am not present to further your salvation, "work out *your own* salvation" yourselves the more carefully. Think not this work cannot go on because I am absent ; "for (*v.* 13) it is *God* which worketh in you," &c. In this case adopt a rule different from the former (*v.* 4), but resting on the same principle of "lowliness of mind" (*v.* 3); viz. 'look each on *his own*

things,' instead of "disputings" with others (*v.* 14). **salvation**—which is in "Jesus" (*v.* 10), as His name (meaning God-Saviour) implies. **with fear and trembling**—the feeling enjoined on "servants," to accompany their "obedience" (Eph. vi. 5; 1 Cor. ii. 3; 2 Cor. vii. 15). See that, as "servants" to God, after the example of Christ, ye be so 'with the fear and trembling' which becomes servants: not slavish fear, but *trembling anxiety* to please your Holy Master, and to reach *the goal* (1 Cor. ix. 26, 27; Heb. iv. 1), *resulting from distrust of your own sufficiency, and from consciousness that all depends on the power of God,* "who worketh both to will and to do" (Rom. xi. 20; Luke xiii. 34; John vi. 29; 2 Cor. iii. 5). **13. For.** Encouragement to work: "For it is God which worketh in you," always present, though I be absent. Not, 'Work out your own salvation, *though* it is God,' &c., but '*because* it is God which,' &c. The *will*, and the power *to work*, being first instalments of His grace, encourage us to make full proof of, and carry out to the end, the "salvation" which He has first 'worked,' and is still 'working *in*' us, enabling us to 'work it *out*.' 'Our will does nothing thereunto without grace; but grace is inactive without our will' (*Bernard*). Man is, in different senses, entirely active and entirely passive: *God producing all, and we acting all.* It is not that God does some, and we the rest. God does all, and we do all. Thus the same things are represented as from God and from us. God makes a new heart, and we are commanded to make us a new heart; not merely because we must use the means in order to the effect, but the effect itself is our act and our duty (Ezek. xi. 19; xviii. 31; xxxvi. 26) (*Edwards*). The "FOR" is explained by *Wiesinger*, as *enforcing* "Work out your own salvation *with fear,*" &c.: *for* it is not you, but *God* who works in you, to will and work, whereby all *self glorying* is removed (*vv.* 3, 4). **worketh** [*energōn*]—'worketh *effectually.*' We cannot of ourselves embrace the Gospel: the "will" (Ps. cx. 3; 2 Cor. iii. 5) comes solely of God's gift to whom He will (John vi. 44, 65); so also the power "to do" (rather '*to work effectually*' [*to energein: the inward ability showing itself in action*], the same Greek as that for "worketh in") ; *i. e.* effectual perseverance to the end is wholly of God's gift (ch. i. 6; Heb. xiii. 21). Prevenient and co-operating grace. **of his good pleasure** [*huper:* 'in behalf of']—'FOR His good pleasure:' *to carry out* His sovereign gracious purpose towards you (Eph. i. 5, 9). **14. murmurings** [*gongusmōn*]—*secret murmurings* against your fellowmen, arising from selfishness: opposed to the example of Jesus just mentioned (cf. the word, John vii. 12, 13; Acts vi. 1; 1 Pet. iv. 9; Jude 16). **disputings** [*Dialogismoi*]—translated "doubting" in 1 Tim. ii. 8, where see note; but here profitless "disputings" with our fellow-men, in relation to whom we are to be "blameless" (*v.* 15: cf. Mark ix. 33, 34). Disputings flow from "vainglory" (*v.* 3); and abounded among the Aristotelian philosophers in Macedon, where Philippi was. **15. blameless and harmless**—without either the

16 the sons of God, without rebuke, in the midst of a crooked and perverse
nation, among whom [3] ye shine as lights in the world; holding forth the
word of life; that I may rejoice in the day of Christ, that I have not run
in vain, [2] neither laboured in vain.

17 Yea, and if I be [4] offered [r] upon the sacrifice and service of your faith,
18 I joy and rejoice with you all. For the same cause also do ye joy and
rejoice with me.

19 [5] But I trust in the Lord Jesus to send Timotheus [s] shortly unto you,
20 that I also may be of good comfort when I know your state. For I have
21 no man [6] like-minded, who will naturally care for your state. For all
22 seek their own, [t] not the things which are Jesus Christ's. But ye know
the proof of him, that, as a son with the father, he hath served with me

A. D. 64.

[3] Or, shine ye.
Matt. 5. 14.
[2] 1 Cor. 9. 26.
[4] poured forth.
[r] 2 Tim. 4. 6.
[5] Or, Moreover.
[s] 1 Thes. 3. 2.
[6] Or, so dear unto me.
[t] 2 Tim. 3. 2.

repute of, or the inclination to, mischief (*Alford*). Outwardly "blameless;" inwardly "harmless," rather 'pure' [*akeraioi*: from *a*, 'not,' and *kerannumi* "mix," "simple"] (Rom. xvi. 19). **sons** [*tekna*]—"the children of God" (Rom. viii. 14-16). Imitation of our heavenly Father is the instinctive guide to duty as His children, more than any external law (Matt. v. 44, 48). **without rebuke**—'unblameable.' A tacit contrast to Deut. xxxii. 5, "Their *spot* is not *the spot* of His *children*: they are a *perverse* and *crooked* generation" (cf. 1 Pet. ii. 12). [LXX., *tekna mometa, genea skolia kai diestrammenē*.] **ye shine** [*Phainesthe*]—'ye show yourselves' (cf. Matt. v. 14-16; Eph. v. 8-13). **as lights in the world** [*Phostēres*]—'*luminaries*,' as the sun and moon, 'the great lights' in the *material* world. LXX. use the same Greek (Gen. i. 14, 16; note, Rev. xxi. 11). **16. Holding forth** —to them, and so *applying* it [the common meaning of *epechontes*; perhaps here including also 'holding fast']. The image of *light-bearers* or *luminaries* is carried on from *v.* 15. As the heavenly luminaries' *light* develops the *life* of the world, so ye hold forth the light of Christ's "word" (received from me) as the "life" of the Gentiles (John i. 4; 1 John i. 1, 5-7). Christ is "the *Light* of the world" (John viii. 12); believers are 'light-bearers,' reflecting His light. **that I may rejoice in** [*eis kauchema emoi eis hemeran*]—'with a view to (your being) *a subject of rejoicing* to me *against* the day of Christ' (ch. iv. 1; 2 Cor. i. 14; 1 Thess. ii. 19). **that I have not run in vain** (2 Tim. iv. 7)—that it was not in vain that I laboured for your spiritual good.

17. Yea, and if [*Alla ei kai*]—'Yea, if even:' implying the contingency as not unlikely. He had assumed the *possibility* of his being alive at Christ's coming (for in every age Christ designed Christians to stand prepared for His coming as at hand): he here puts a supposition as more likely; viz., his own death before Christ's coming. **I be offered** [*spendomai*]—'I am being poured out' as a *drink offering*. Present, not future, as the danger is threatening him *now*. As in sacrifices drink offerings of wine were 'poured out' to accompany the offerings, so the faith of his Philippian converts is the sacrifice, and *his blood the drink offering* 'poured out' with it (cf. Rom. xv. 16; 2 Tim. iv. 6). The Jewish libation was not poured *upon* the sacrifice, but *around* the altar (Num. xv. 5; xxviii. 7). [Therefore *epi* is 'in': *lit.*, 'unto the sacrifice.'] **service** [*leitourgia*]—'priest's ministration:' carrying out the image. **I . . rejoice**—for myself (ch. i. 21, 23). His expectation of release is fainter than in the epistles to Ephesians, Colossians, and Philemon, written earlier from Rome. The appointment of Tigellinus to be prætorian prefect was probably the cause of this change. See 'Introduction.' **rejoice with you all.** Not 'I *congratulate* you all,' which is against New Testa-

ment Greek usage; but 'I jointly rejoice with you all'—viz., at your "joy of *faith*" (ch. i. 18, 25). For their rejoicing would not be at Paul's *death*: for (cf. ch. i. 22, 24, 25) what he means is, *even his death* will not change his joy at their faith, and with them in their joy of faith. He exhorts them also (*v.* 18) to rejoice and join with him in this their common joy of faith, even in the possible prospect of his martyrdom (ch. i. 21).

19. *V.* 22, "Ye know the proof of him, that . . . . he hath served with me," implies that Timothy had been long with Paul at Philippi. Accordingly, in Acts xvi. 1-4; xvii. 10, 14, we find them *setting out* together from Derbe in Lycaonia, and together again at Berea in Macedonia, near *the conclusion* of St. Paul's missionary journey: an *undesigned* coincidence between the epistle and history: a mark of genuineness (*Paley*). From *vv.* 19-30, it appears Epaphroditus was to set out at once to allay the anxiety of the Philippians on his account, and at the same time bearing the epistle: Timothy was to follow after the apostle's liberation was decided, when they could arrange their plans more definitely as to *where* Timothy should, on his return with tidings from Philippi, meet Paul, who was designing by a wider circuit and slower progress to reach that city. Paul's reason for sending Timothy so soon after having heard of the Philippians from Epaphroditus was that they were now suffering persecutions (ch. i. 28-30); besides, Epaphroditus' delay through sickness on his journey to Rome from Philippi made the tidings he brought to be of less recent date than St. Paul desired. St. Paul himself also hoped to visit them shortly. **But I trust**—Yet my death is by no means certain; yea, 'I *hope* (my hope centres) in the Lord.' **unto you** [not *pros humas*, but *humin*]—'*for* you;' to your satisfaction. **I also**—that not only you 'may be of good *courage*' [*eupsucho*] on hearing of me (*v.* 23), but 'I also, when I know your state.' **20.** His reason for sending Timothy above all others: I have none so [*isopsuchon*] 'like-soulled' with myself as is Timothy (cf. Deut. xiii. 6; Ps. lv. 14): Paul's second self. **naturally** [*gnesiōs*]—'genuinely:' 'with *sincere* solicitude' [*merimnēsei*]. The Spirit of God so changed nature, that to be *natural* was with him to be *spiritual*: a high attainment. **21.** [*Hoi pantes*] '*They* all' (viz., who are now with me, and are eligible for the mission, ch. iv. 21: such Demas, then with him, proved to be, Col. iv. 14: cf. 2 Tim. iv. 10; Phile. 24). **seek their own** —opposed to Paul's precept (*v.* 4; 1 Cor. x. 24, 33; xiii. 5). Ch. i. 16, 17 implies that some of those with Paul at Rome were genuine Christians, though not so self-sacrificing as Timothy. Most help only when Christ's gain is compatible with their own (Judg. v. 17, 23). **22.** Rare praise (Neh. vii. 2). **ye know the proof of him**—*his proved character* (Acts xvi. 1-4, 12). **as a son with the**

23 in the Gospel. Him therefore I hope to send presently, so soon as I shall
24 see how it will go with me. But I trust in the Lord that I also myself shall come shortly.
25   Yet I supposed it necessary to send to you "Epaphroditus, my brother, and companion in labour, and fellow-soldier, but your ^vmessenger, and ^whe
26 that ministered to my wants. For he longed after you all, and was full of
27 heaviness, because that ye had heard that he had been sick. For indeed he was sick nigh unto death: but God had mercy on him; and not on
28 him only, but on me also, lest I should have sorrow upon sorrow. I sent him therefore the more carefully, that, when ye see him again, ye may
29 rejoice, and that I may be the less sorrowful. Receive him therefore in
30 the Lord with all gladness; and ⁷ hold such in reputation: because for the work of Christ he was nigh unto death, not regarding his life, ^x to supply your lack of service toward me.

3 FINALLY, my brethren, rejoice in the Lord. To write the same things to you, to me indeed *is* not grievous, but for you *it is* safe.
2   Beware ^a of dogs, beware of evil workers, ^b beware of the concision.

father—'as a *child to* a father.' **served with me.** When the sentence was to run thus, 'As a child *serveth a father,* so he *served me,*' he changes it to "served *with* me," in modesty; as Christians are not *servants* TO one another, but *servants of God* WITH *one another* (cf. ch. iii. 17). **in the Gospel** [*lis*]—'*unto* the Gospel.' 23. **so soon as I shall see**—lit., *from afar* [*aphido*]. 24. **also myself**—as well as Timothy.

25. **I supposed**—'I thought it necessary.' **to send.** It was properly a *sending* Epaphroditus *back* (ch. iv. 18); but as he came to stay some time with Paul, the word is "send" (cf. *v.* 30). **fellow-soldier**—in the "good fight" (ch. i. 27, 30; 2 Tim. ii. 3; iv. 7). '**My** *brother* in the faith, *fellow-worker* in preaching it, and *fellow-soldier* in maintaining it' (*Ellicott*). **your messenger**—*lit.,* 'apostle.' The "apostles," or "messengers of the *churches*" (Rom. xvi. 7; 2 Cor. viii. 23), were distinct from the "apostles" commissioned *by Christ,* as the twelve and Paul. **ministered to my wants** —by conveying the contributions from Philippi. [*Leitourgon* generally implies the *ministerial office,* but here it has the wider sense.] 26. **For**—reason for thinking it "necessary to send" Epaphroditus: [*Epeide epipothōn ēn*] '*Inasmuch as he was longing* (a continuing state) after you all.' **full of heaviness** [*ademonōn*]—*distracted with heavy grief.* **because that ye had heard that he had been sick** —rather [*ēsthenēsen*], 'that he *was* sick.' He felt how saddened you would be in hearing it; he now is hastening to relieve your minds of the anxiety. 27. Epaphroditus' sickness proves that the apostles had not the *permanent* gift of miracles any more than inspiration: both were vouchsafed only for each occasion, as the Spirit thought fit. **lest I should have sorrow upon sorrow**—viz., the sorrow of losing him by death, besides the sorrow of my imprisonment. Here only a sorrowful tone occurs in this epistle, which generally is most joyous. 28. **the more carefully**—more so than I should have done if ye had not been grieving at his sickness. **I may be the less sorrowful**—as sympathizing in your joy. 29. **Receive him.** There seems something behind respecting him. If extreme affection had been the sole ground of his "heaviness," no such exhortation would have been needed (*Alford*). **in reputation**—'in honour.' 30. **for the work of Christ**—viz., the bringing of a supply to me, the minister of Christ. He was probably in delicate health in setting out from Philippi; but at all hazards he undertook this service of Christian love, which cost him a serious

sickness. **not regarding his life.** אABΔG read [*paraboleusamenos*] 'hazarding,' &c. **to supply your lack of service**—not that they lacked the *will,* but the '*opportunity*' by which to send their accustomed bounty (ch. iv. 10). 'That which ye would have done if you could (but which you could not through absence) he did for you; therefore receive him with all joy' (*Alford*).

CHAP. III. 1-21.—AGAINST JUDAIZERS—HE HAS GREATER CAUSE THAN THEY TO TRUST IN LEGAL RIGHTEOUSNESS, BUT RENOUNCED IT FOR CHRIST'S, IN WHICH HE PRESSES AFTER PERFECTION—AGAINST CARNAL PERSONS—CONTRAST OF THE BELIEVER'S LIFE AND HOPE.

1. **Finally** [*to loipon*]—or (not time, but a transition to another general subject) "Furthermore" (*Bengel*), as in 1 Thess. iv. 1; 'as to what remains,' &c. It often, at the conclusion of epistles, means "finally" (Eph. vi. 10; 2 Thess. iii. 1). But it is not restricted to this, as *Alford* thinks, supposing that Paul used it here intending to close his epistle, but was led by mention of Judaizers into a longer dissertation. **the same things**—concerning 'rejoicing,' the key-note of the epistle: the more remarkable from one writing from prison (ch. i. 18, 25; ii. 17; iv. 4, where cf. "again I say" with "the same things" here). "In the Lord" marks the true sphere of joy, in contrast with "confidence in the flesh," or in any outward matter of boasting (*v.* 3) or carnal joy. **not grievous**—'irksome.' **for you it is safe.** Lest amidst trials (ch. i. 29) you should ever despond, spiritual *joy* is our safety against error (*v.* 2; Neh. viii. 10, end).

2. **Beware** [*blepete*]—'Have your eye on' so as to beware of. Contrast "mark," viz., so as to follow (*v.* 17). **dogs** [*tous kunas*]—'*the* dogs;' viz., those *impure* persons "of whom I have told you often" (*vv.* 18, 19); "the abominable" (cf. Rev. xxi. 8 with xxii. 15; Matt. vii. 6; xv. 26, 27, heathenish in spirit; Titus i. 15, 16): "dogs" in filthiness and snarling (Deut. xxiii. 18; Ps. xxii. 16, 20; lix. 6, 14, 15; 2 Pet. ii. 22). The Jews regarded the Gentiles as "dogs" (Matt. xv. 26); but by their own unbelief they ceased to be the true Israel, and are become "dogs" (cf. Isa. lvi. 10, 11; lxvi. 3). (the) **evil workers** (2 Cor. xi. 13). Not simply 'evil-doers,' but men who 'worked' ostensibly for the Gospel, but really for evil (*v.* 19: cf. Rom. xvi. 18): [*tous kakous ergatas*] 'the evil *workmen; i. e.,* bad *teachers* (cf. 2 Tim. ii. 15). **concision** [*katatomēn*]. Paul digresses at this word. *Circumcision* [*peritomē*] had now lost its

3 For we are ᶜthe circumcision, which worship ᵈGod in the Spirit, and
4 rejoice in Christ Jesus, and have no confidence in the flesh. Though I might also have confidence in the flesh. If any other man thinketh that he
5 hath whereof he might trust in the flesh, I more: circumcised the eighth day, of the stock of Israel, *of* the tribe of Benjamin, an Hebrew of the
6 Hebrews; as touching the law, ᵉa Pharisee; concerning ᶠzeal, ᵍperse- cuting the church; touching the righteousness which is in the law,
7 blameless. But what things were gain to me, those I counted loss for
8 Christ. Yea doubtless, and I count all things *but* loss ʰfor the excel- lency of the knowledge of Christ Jesus my Lord: for whom I have suffered the loss of all things, and do count them *but* dung, that I may
9 win Christ, and be found in him, not ⁱhaving mine own righteousness, which is of the law, but ʲthat which is through the faith of Christ, the

A. D. 64.
ᶜ Deut. 10.16.
  Jer. 4. 4.
ᵈ John 4.23.
  Rom. 7. 6.
  Eph. 6. 18.
ᵉ Act 23. 6.
ᶠ Gal. 1. 13.
ᵍ Acts 8. 3.
ʰ Isa. 53. 11.
  John 17. 3.
ⁱ Ps. 143. 2.
  Isa. 64. 6.
  Rom. 10. 3.
ʲ Rom. 1. 17.
  Gal. 2. 16.
  2 Pet. 1. 1.

spiritual significance, and was to those who rested on it at all for justification a senseless *mutilation.* Christians have the true *circumcision*—viz., of the heart; legalists have only "concision"—i. e., *the cutting off of the flesh.* To make "cuttings in the flesh" was prohibited (Lev. xxi. 5): it was a heathenish practice (1 Ki. xviii. 28): yet this, writes Paul indignantly, is what these *legalists* are virtually doing *in violation of the law.* There is a gradation (*Birks*) in St. Paul's language as to circumcision. In his first discourse (Acts xiii. 39) circumcision is not named, but included in "the law of Moses," which cannot justify. Six or seven years later, in Gal. iii. 3, where first it is named, its inefficiency is maintained against those Gentiles who, beginning in the spirit, thought to be perfected in the flesh. Later, in Rom. ii. 28, 29, he goes further, and claims its substance for every believer, assigning the shadow only to the unbelieving Jew. In Col. ii. 11; iii. 11; also Eph. ii. 11, still later, he expounds the true circumcision as the believer's exclusive privilege. Last of all, here, the very *name* is denied to the legalist: a term of reproach is substituted—"concision." Once obligatory on all the covenant people, then reduced to a national distinction, it was more and more associated with the open hostility of the Jews, and the perverse teaching of false brethren. **3.** 'We are the (real) circumcision' (Rom. ii. 25-29). **worship God in the Spirit.** So C, Vulgate. But אABG read 'worship *by the Spirit of God.*' The Spirit is the influence whereby our religious *service* [*latreia*] is rendered (John iv. 23, 24). Legal worship consisted in outward acts, restricted to certain times and places. Christian worship is *spiritual*, flowing from the inworking Holy Spirit; not restricted to isolated acts, but embracing the whole life (Rom. xii. 1). In the former, men trusted in something human, whether descent from the theocratic nation, or the righteousness of the law, or mortification of "the flesh" (Rom. i. 9). **rejoice** (make our *boast*) **in Christ Jesus**—not in the law. **have no confidence in the flesh**—the outward and earthly, but in the Spirit. **4.** 'Although *I* (emphatical) possess materials of confidence *even in the flesh*' (as well as in Christ); *lit.*, 'I *having*,' &c., but not using. **I more**—I have more 'whereof I might *have confidence* in the flesh.' **5.** In three particulars he 'might have confidence in the flesh:'—(1.) His pure Jewish blood (2 Cor. xi. 22); (2.) His legal preciseness and high status; (3.) His zeal for the law [*peritome octaemeros*]—'being in circumcision an eighth day person;' *i. e.*, not circumcised in later life as a proselyte, but on the eighth day after birth, as the law directed as to Jew-born infants: not after the thirteenth year, as an Ishmaelite. **of the tribe of Benjamin**—son of Rachel,

not of the maid-servant: one of the two tribes that returned from Babylon (Ezra iv. 1). **Hebrew of the Hebrews**—neither one or other parent Gentile. The "Hebrew," wherever he dwelt, retained the *language.* Thus Paul, though settled in Tarsus, a Greek city, calls himself a Hebrew. A 'Grecian,' or Hellenist, is the term used for a *Greek-speaking* Jew (*Trench*). **touching the law**— i. e., as to legal status and strictness. **a Pharisee**—'of the straitest sect' (Acts xxvi. 5). **6. Concerning**—'*As touching* zeal ' (cf. Acts xxii. 3; xxvi. 9). Sad irony. Even in this mournful Judaist zeal, he can, if they will, set himself on a level with them (*Ellicott*) (Gal. i. 14). **blameless** [*genomenos amemptos*, 'one in whom nothing is wanting that can be desired: *amomos*, 'one in whom there is nothing to blame']—'*having become blameless*' as to *ceremonial* righteousness: having attained *in man's eyes* legal perfection. As to holiness *before God*, which is the inner spirit of the law, and which flows from "the righteousness of God by faith," he declares (*vv.* 12-14) that he has *not* attained perfection. **7.** gain [*kerdē*]—'gains:' all possible advantages of outward status which he heretofore enjoyed. **I counted** [*hēgēmai*]—'I *have* counted for Christ's sake loss.' Not plural, as 'gains;' for he counts them all but one great "loss" (Matt. xvi. 26; Luke ix. 25). **8. Yea, doubtless** [*alla men oun* (A adds *ge*) *kai*]—'nay more.' Not only '*have* I counted' *those* things 'loss for Christ's sake, but, moreover, I *even* DO count ALL things but loss,' &c. **for the excellency** [*dia to huperechon*]—'on account of the superexcellency (above them all, including the law) of the knowledge of Christ Jesus.' **my Lord**— believing and loving appropriation (Ps. lxiii. 1; John xx. 28). **for** (the sake of) **whom I have suffered the loss.** Not merely have I "*counted*" them "loss," but "have" actually 'lost them.' **all things** [*ta panta*]—'them all.' The Greek has the article, referring to the preceding "all things." **dung** [*skubala*, from *kusi balein*]—'refuse (excrements, dregs) *cast to the dogs,*' as the derivation expresses. A "loss" is of something having value; but 'refuse' is thrown away as a nuisance. **win**—"gain," as *v.* 7; 1 Tim. vi. 6. A man cannot make other things his "gain," and also 'gain Christ.' He who loses all, and even himself, on account of Christ, gains Christ: Christ is His, and He is Christ's (Song ii. 16; vi. 3; Luke ix. 23, 24; 1 Cor. iii. 21, 23). **9. be found in him** (Eph. ii. 6)— as the element of my life, at His coming again. Once *lost*, I have been "found;" and I hope to be perfectly "found" by Him (Luke xv. 8). **own righteousness, which is of** [*ek, from*: such as I strove after from my own obeying] **the law** (*v.* 6; Rom. x. iii. 5). **righteousness which is of God by faith**—'which is *from* [*ek*] God, (resting) *upon*

433

10 righteousness which is of God by faith; that I may know him, and the power of his resurrection, and ^{k} the fellowship of his sufferings, being
11 made conformable unto his death; if by any means I might ^{l} attain unto the resurrection of the dead.
12 Not as though I had already ^{m} attained, either were already ^{n} perfect; but I follow after, if that I may apprehend that for which also I am
13 apprehended of Christ Jesus. Brethren, I count not myself to have apprehended: but *this* one thing *I do*, forgetting those things which
14 are behind, and reaching ^{o} forth unto those things which are before, I ^{p} press toward the mark for the prize of ^{q} the high calling of God in Christ Jesus.
15 Let us therefore, as many as be ^{r} perfect, ^{s} be thus minded: and if in

A. D. 64.

^{k} Matt. 20.23.
1 Pet. 4. 13.
^{l} Luke 20.35.
Acts 26. 7.
^{m} 1 Tim. 6.12.
^{n} Heb. 12. 23.
^{o} ch. 2. 12.
Heb. 6. 1.
^{p} 2 Tim.4.7,8.
Heb. 12. 1.
^{q} Heb. 3. 1.
^{r} 1 Cor. 2. 6.
1 Cor. 14.20.
^{s} Gal. 5. 10.

[*epi*] faith.' Paul was transported from legal bondage into Christian freedom without gradual transition. Instantaneously opposition to Pharisaic Judaism took the place of opposition to the Gospel. God's providence fitly prepared him for overthrowing legal justification. 'The righteousness of faith,' in Paul's sense, is the righteousness of Christ appropriated by faith, as the *objective* ground of confidence, and also as a new *subjective* principle of life. It includes the essence of a new disposition, and so of *sanctification*, though the two ideas are distinct. It is not any arbitrary act, as if God treated as sinless a man persisting in sin, simply because he believes in Christ; but the *objective* on the part of God corresponds to the *subjective* on the part of man—viz., faith. The realization of the archetype of holiness by Christ is the pledge that this shall be realized in all who are one with Him by faith, and are become the organs of His Spirit. Its germ is imparted in believing, although the fruit of a life perfectly conformed to the Redeemer can here be only gradually developed. **10. That I may know him** —experimentally; not merely know the *doctrine* concerning Him: the aim of the "righteousness" (*v.* 9). This verse resumes and explains "the excellency of the knowledge of Christ" (*v.* 8). Believers are brought, not only to redemption, but to the Redeemer Himself. **the power of** (flowing from) **his resurrection** — assuring believers of justification (Rom. iv. 25; 1 Cor. xv. 17): raising them up spiritually with Him, by virtue of identification with Him in this, as in all the acts of His redeeming work (Rom. vi. 4; Col. ii. 12; iii. 1); and about to raise their bodies with His at His coming (Isa. xxvi. 19; 2 Cor. iv. 10, 11). The Divine Spirit which raised Him from literal death is the same "power" which raises believers from spiritual death (Eph. i. 19, 20), and shall raise their bodies from literal death (Rom. viii. 11). **the fellowship of his sufferings**—by identification with Him in His sufferings and death, *by imputation;* also, in *actually* bearing the cross laid on us, after His example, so 'filling up that which is behind of the afflictions of Christ' (Col. i. 24); and in the *will* to bear aught for His sake (Matt. x. 38; xvi. 24; 2 Tim. ii. 11; 1 Pet. iv. 13). As He bore all our sufferings (Isa. liii. 4), so we participate in His. **conformable unto his death**—'formed to the likeness of His death;' viz., by continued sufferings for His sake, and mortifying the carnal self (Rom. viii. 29; 1 Cor. xv. 31; 2 Cor. iv. 10-12; Gal. ii. 20). **11. If by any means**—not implying uncertainty of the issue, but the earnestness of the struggle (1 Cor. ix. 26, 27), the need of jealous self-watchfulness (1 Cor. x. 12), and indefatigable use of means at all costs. **attain unto the resurrection of the dead.** אABΔ*fg*, Vulgate, read [*tēn exanastasin tēn ek* (for *tōn*) *nekrōn*] 'the resurrection *from* (out of) the dead;' viz., the

first resurrection: that of believers at Christ's coming (1 Cor. xv. 23; 1 Thess. iv. 15; Rev. xx. 5, 6). [*Exanastasis* occurs nowhere else in the New Testament.] 'The power of Christ's resurrection' (Rom. i. 4) ensures the believer's attainment of it (cf. *vv.* 20, 21). Cf. "accounted worthy to *obtain* . . . *the resurrection from the dead*," Luke xx. 35; xiv. 14, "the resurrection of the just." **12.** 'Not *that* I,' &c. (let me not be misunderstood as saying *that,* &c.) **attained**—'obtained;' viz., a perfect knowledge of Christ, the power of His death, the fellowship of His sufferings, and conformity to His death. **either were already perfect**—'or am already (spiritually) *perfected*' [*teteleiōmai*], *crowned* with the garland of victory, my course *completed*, and *perfection absolutely reached.* The image is that of a *race-course* (see 1 Cor. ix. 24; Heb. xii. 23). **I follow after**— 'I press on.' **apprehend . . . apprehended**—'If *so be* that I may *lay hold on* [*Katalabo*] that (viz., the *prize, v.* 14) for obtaining which also *I was laid hold on* by Christ;' viz., at my conversion (Song i. 4; 1 Cor. xiii. 12). **Jesus.** So אA, Vulgate. Omitted in BΔG*fg*. Christ, the Author, is also the Finisher of His people's 'race.' **13. I count not myself**—whatever *others* count as to *themselves.* He who counts himself perfect must deceive himself (1 John i. 8); yet each must *aim* at perfection to be a Christian at all (Matt. v. 48). **forgetting those things which are behind.** *Looking back* ends in *going back:* so Lot's wife (Luke ix. 62; xvii. 32). If we cease pulling the oar against the current, we are carried back. God's word is, "Speak unto the children of Israel, that they go forward" (Exod. xiv. 15). The Bible, as our landmark, shows whether we are progressing or retrograding. **reaching forth** [*epekteinomenos*] —'stretching out after the things in front,' after higher stages of holiness, with hand and foot, like a runner in a race, the body bent forward. Christians are humbled by the contrast between what they are and what they desire to be. The eye reaches before, drawing on the hand; the hand reaches before, drawing on the foot (*Bengel*) (Heb. vi. 1). **14. high calling** [*tēs ano kleseōs*]—'the calling that is *above*' (Gal. iv. 26; Col. iii. 1); the "*heavenly* calling" (Heb. iii. 1). "The prize" is the "crown of righteousness" (2 Tim. iv. 7, 8; Rev. ii. 10, "crown of life;" 1 Pet. v. 4, "a crown of glory that fadeth not 'away.") "The high calling" is not St. Paul's calling as an apostle by God from heaven, but that of *all Christians to salvation in Christ,* which coming from, invites us to, heaven, whither accordingly our minds ought to be uplifted (1 Thess. ii. 12). **15. therefore**—resuming *v.* 3. **perfect**—*full-grown* (no longer 'babes') in the Christian life (*v.* 3, 'worshipping God in the Spirit, having no confidence in the flesh') (1 Cor. ii. 6): established in the things of God; or, one *fully fit for running*

any thing ye be otherwise minded, God shall reveal even this unto you.
16 Nevertheless, whereto we have already attained, let us walk by the same
17 rule, let us mind the same thing. Brethren, be followers together of me,
18 and mark them which walk so as ye *ᵗ*have us for an ensample. (For
      many walk, of whom I have told you often, and now tell you even
19 weeping, *that they are* the enemies of the cross of Christ: whose end *is*
      destruction, whose god *is their* belly, and *whose* glory *is* in their shame,
20 who mind earthly things.) For *ᵘ*our conversation is in heaven; from
21 whence also we *ᵛ*look for the Saviour, the Lord Jesus Christ: who *ʷ*shall
      change our vile body, that it may be fashioned like unto his glorious

A. D. 64.

ᵗ Ps. 37. 37.
  1 Pet 5 3.
ᵘ Col. 3. 1, 3.
ᵛ 1 Cor. 1. 7.
  1 Thes.1 10.
  2 Tim. 4. 8.
  Tit. 2. 13.
ʷ Ps. 17. 15.
  Matt 17. 2.
  1 Cor. 15 43.
  Col. 8. 4.
  1 John 3. 2.

(*Bengel*), observing the *laws* of the course (2 Tim. ii. 5); *sincere* in seeking justification through Christ (Gen. xvii. 1). Though "perfect" in this sense, he was not yet 'made perfect' in the sense of *v.* 12; viz., 'crowned with *complete* victory,' and *absolutely perfect.* thus minded—having the mind described, *vv.* 7-14: renouncing as loss *all* self-dependencies and legal confidences. otherwise minded—deficient somewhat in knowledge of self, and of the entirely gratuitous nature of the Gospel. 'He who thinks he has attained everything, hath nothing' (*Chrysostom*) Some thought to attain *perfection* by the law (Gal iii. 3), who needed the warning, *v.* 2, 'though, on account of their *sincerity*, Paul hopes confidently (as in Gal. v. 10) that God will reveal right-mindedness to them' (ch. i. 9; Eph. i. 17). Paul taught externally: God 'reveals' the truth internally by His Spirit (Matt. xi. 25; xvi. 17; 1 Cor. iii. 6). unto you—who sincerely strive to do God's will (John vii. 17; Eph. i. 17). 16. The expectation of further (*v.* 15), 'revelation' is not to make you less careful in walking according to whatever knowledge and perfection you have already attained. God reveals more to those who walk up to the revelations they already have (Hos. vi. 3). rule, let us mind the same thing. So C Vulgate. Omitted in א A B. Perhaps inserted from Gal. vi. 16 and ch. ii. 2. 'Whereunto we have attained, let us walk on [a military term: *march in order: stoichein*] in the same' (measure of knowledge already attained). 17. be [*ginesthe*, 'become'] followers [*summimetai*]—'imitators together. of me—as I am *of Christ* (1 Cor. xi. 1). Imitate me no farther than as I imitate Christ. *Bengel's* translation better brings out this': 'Become my fellow-imitators *of Christ*;' 'imitators *of Christ together with me*' (note, ch. ii. 22; Eph. v. 1). mark—for imitation, Timothy, Epaphras, and all such. which walk so as [*kathos*] ye have us for an ensample. 'Mark those who are walking *so as* ye have an example in us' (*Ellicott*). I prefer, 'inasmuch as,' instead of "as." The context implies (*vv.* 8, 10, 12, 14) that it is *Christ* who is to be imitated. 18. many walk. Follow not evil-doers, because they are "many" (Exod. xxiii. 2). Their numbers are rather a presumption against their being Christ's "*little* flock" (Luke xii. 32). often. There is need of constant warning. The Lord and His apostles speak more against empty professors (as the Pharisees) than against open scoffers. weeping (Rom. ix. 2). A hard tone in speaking of the inconsistencies of professors is the opposite of Paul's spirit and Jeremiah's (Jer. xiii. 17: cf. Ps. cxix. 136). enemies of the cross of Christ—in *practice*, not in doctrine: practically denying 'that they who are Christ's have crucified the flesh' (Gal. v. 24; vi. 14; Heb. vi. 6; x. 29). 19. end—fixed doom (2 Cor. xi. 15). Contrast Rom. vi. 22. destruction—everlasting, at Christ's coming (ch. i. 28): contrast to "Saviour" (*v* 20). whose god is their belly

(Rom. xvi. 18)—hereafter to be destroyed by; God (1 Cor. vi. 13): in contrast to our "body" (*v.* 21), which *our God*, the Lord Jesus, shall 'fashion like unto His glorious body.' Their belly is now pampered, our body now wasted: then the states of both shall be reversed. glory is in their shame. As "glory" often in the Old Testament means 'god' (Ps. cvi. 20), so here it answers to "whose *god*," in the parallel clause. "Shame" is the Old Testament term contemptuously given to an idol (Judg. vi. 32, *margin*). Hos. iv. 7 seems referred to (cf. Rom. i. 32). Their *glory* is in what is really matter of *shame*—sensuality and carnality. mind earthly things [*ta epigeia phronountes*] (Rom. viii. 5). Contrast *v.* 20; Col. iii. 2 [*ta ano phroneite*], 'Set your *mind* on things above.' The earthly are, like Sisera, nailed to the earth whilst asleep. 20. our conversation—*our life as citizens* [*politeuma*, from *politeuomai*: ch. i. 27; Acts xxiii. 1]. The antithesis to *v.* 19 favours this translation, rather than 'our *citizenship*' [which would be *politeia*], or than 'our *commonwealth*' (*Ellicott*): which last would require 'is heaven' instead of "is IN heaven" (cf. Eph. ii. 6; Gal. iv. 26; Heb. xii. 22; Rev. xxi. 2, 10). We are but *pilgrims* on earth; how *then* should we "mind earthly things?" (Heb. xi. 9, 10, 13-16; Acts xxii. 28: cf. Luke x. 20.) Two circumstances make the frequent use of 'citizenship' (ch. i. 27; iv. 3) an appropriate image in writing to Philippi:—1. It was a Roman colony, possessing, besides local privileges, *Roman citizenship*, of which the people were naturally proud. 2. Paul himself at Philippi had made a remarkable use of his citizenship (Acts xvi. 37-39): a happy illustration of our state absent on earth, but enjoying the protection and civic privileges of heaven. The grand distinction between the worldly and believers is, these alone regard earth as their temporary, heaven as their true and everlasting home. is [*huparchei*]—'has its existence.' in heaven—Greek, 'in the heavens.' look for the Saviour, the Lord Jesus—'We wait for [so *apekdechetai*, *constantly and patiently*, Rom. viii. 19, 23] the Lord Jesus as a (*i. e.*, in the capacity of a) Saviour;' completing "salvation" by redeeming the body (Heb. ix. 28; 1 Cor. i. 7). That He is "the Lord," now exalted above every name, assures our expectation (ch. ii. 9-11). Our High Priest has gone up into the Holy of holies not made with hands, there to atone for us. As the Israelites stood outside the tabernacle, expecting Aaron's return (cf. Luke i. 21), so must we look unto the heavens, expecting Christ thence. 21. [*Metaschematisei to soma tes tapeinoseos*] 'Who shall *transfigure* the body *of our humiliation* (in which our humiliation has place, 2 Cor. iv. 10; 2 Tim. ii. 11, 12: 'not *vile*, nothing that He made is vile' (*Archbishop Whately* on his deathbed), that it may be *conformed* [*summorphon to somati tes doxes*] unto the body *of His glory* (in which His glory is manifested), according to the *effectual working* [*energeian*] whereby,' &c.

body, [x] according to the working whereby he is able even to subdue all
4 things unto himself. THEREFORE, my brethren dearly beloved and
longed for, [a] my joy and crown, so stand fast in the Lord, *my* dearly
beloved.

2 I beseech Euodias, and beseech Syntyche, that they be of the same
3 mind in the Lord. And I entreat thee also, true yoke-fellow, help
those women which laboured with [b] me in the Gospel, with Clement
also, and *with* other my fellow-labourers, whose names *are* in the [c] book
of life.

4, Rejoice in the Lord alway: *and* again I say, Rejoice. Let your
5, moderation be known unto all men. [a] The Lord *is* at hand. Be [e] careful
6 for nothing; but in every thing by prayer and supplication with thanks-

A. D. 64.

[x] Isa. 63. 1.
Matt. 28. 18.

CHAP. 4.
[a] 2 Cor. 1. 14.
1 Thes. 2. 19.
[b] Rom. 16. 3.
ch 1. 27.
[c] Ex. 32. 32.
Ps. 69. 23.
Dan. 12. 1.
[d] Heb. 10. 25,
Jas. 5. 8, 9.
[e] Ps. 55. 22.
Pro. 16. 3.

(Eph. i. 19.) **even**—not only to make *the body*
like His own, but "to subdue *all things*," even
death itself, Satan, and sin. He gave a sample of
the coming *transfiguration* on the mount, (Matt.
xvii. 1, &c.) Not a change of *identity*, but of
fashion or *form* (Ps. xvii. 15; 1 Cor. xv. 26, 51).
Our spiritual resurrection now is the pledge of
our bodily resurrection to glory hereafter (*v.* 20;
Rom. viii. 11). As Christ's glorified body was
essentially identical with His body of humiliation,
so believers' resurrection bodies, being like His,
shall be identical essentially with our present
bodies, yet "spiritual" (1 Cor. xv. 42-44). Our
'hope' is, that Christ, by His rising from the
dead, hath obtained the power, and is become
the pattern, of our resurrection (Mic. ii. 13; Titus
ii. 13).

CHAP. IV. 1-23.—EXHORTATIONS—THANKS
FOR THE SUPPLY FROM PHILIPPI—GREETING—
CLOSING BENEDICTION.

1. 'Wherefore:' since we have such a glorious
hope (ch. iii. 20, 21). **dearly beloved.** Repeated
at the close of the verse, implying that his great
love to them should be a motive to their obedience. **longed for** [*epipothetoi*]—'yearned after'
in your absence (ch. i. 8). **crown**—in the day of
the Lord (ch. ii. 16; 1 Thess. ii. 19). **so**—as I
have admonished you. **stand fast** (ch. i. 27).

2. Euodias and Syntyche were two women at
variance; probably deaconesses or persons of
influence (Acts xvii. 12). He repeats "I beseech,"
as if he would admonish each separately with
impartiality, both being equally to blame. **in the
Lord**—the element of Christian union: for those
"in the Lord" to be at variance is an utter
inconsistency. **3. And.** [א A B Δ G *f g*, Vulgate,
read *Nai:* 'Yea']. **true yoke-fellow**—in the same
Gospel-yoke (Matt. xi. 29, 30: cf. 1 Tim. v. 17, 18):
Luke, who perhaps was at Philippi, as his name
is not among the salutations; or Silas (Acts xv. 40;
xvi. 19, at *Philippi*); or the chief of the bishops
there. Not *Synzygus*, a proper name: 'Who art
truly, as thy name means, a *yoke-fellow.*' **help
those women**—rather [*autais*] 'help *them*;' viz.,
Euodias and Syntyche. 'Co-operate with them'
(*Birks*); or as *Alford*, 'Help toward their reconciliation.' **which laboured with me** [*haitines*]—
'*inasmuch as* they laboured with me:' not without danger (Acts xvi. 19, 20: cf. ch. i. 28). At
Philippi women were the first hearers of the
Gospel, and Lydia the first convert. It is a coincidence which marks genuineness, that in this
epistle alone instructions are given to women who
laboured with Paul in the Gospel. Euodias and
Syntyche were doubtless two of 'the women who
resorted to the river-side, where prayer was wont
to be made' (Acts xvi. 13), and being early converted, would naturally take an active part in
teaching other women called at a later period; of
course, not in public preaching, but in a less

prominent sphere (1 Tim. ii. 11, 12). **Clement**—
bishop of Rome shortly after the death of Paul.
His epistle from the church of Rome to the church
of Corinth is extant. It makes no mention of the
supremacy of the see of Peter. He was the most
eminent of the apostolical fathers. *Alford* thinks
Clement was *a Philippian*, and not necessarily the
Clement bishop of Rome. But *Origen* ('Comment.' John i. 29) identifies the Clement here with
the bishop of Rome. A Christian of Philippi, a
Roman colony, might easily become subsequently
bishop of Rome. **in the book of life**—the register
of those whose ' citizenship is in heaven' (Luke
x. 20; ch. iii. 20). Anciently, free cities had a
roll containing the names of all having the right
of citizenship (Exod. xxxii. 32; Ps. lxix. 28: cf.
Ezek. xiii. 9; Dan. xii. 1; Rev. xx. 12; xxi. 27).

4. alway (Isa. lxi. 10)—even amidst the
afflictions now distressing you (ch i. 23-30).
again—he had already said "Rejoice" (ch. iii. 1).
Joy is the predominant feature of the epistle.
I say—Greek, rather, 'I *will* say.' **5. moderation**
[*to epieikes*, from *eiko*, 'to yield,' whence *yielding-
ness* (*Trench*); or from *eikos*, 'fitting,' whence '*reasonableness of dealing*' (*Alford*)]—considerateness
for others, *not urging one's rights to the uttermost*,
but waiving a part; thereby rectifying the injustices
of justice. The archetype is God, who presses
not the strictness of His law against us (Ps. cxxx.
3, 4), having exacted the fullest payment for us
from our Divine Security. Including *candour* and
kindliness, *joy in the Lord* raises us above rigor-
ism towards others (*v.* 5) and carefulness (*v.* 6) as
to one's own affairs. Sadness produces *moroseness*
towards others—a carking spirit in ourselves. **Let
. . . be known**—*i. e.*, in your conduct to all: let
nothing inconsistent with "moderation" be seen.
Not, Make a *display* of your moderation. Let this
grace "be known" to men in *acts;* let "your
requests be made known unto God" in *words* (*v.* 6).
unto all men—even to the "perverse" (ch. ii. 15),
that so ye may win them. Exercise 'forbearance'
even to persecutors. None is so ungracious as not
to be kindly to some one, from some motive, on
some occasion: the believer is to be so "unto all
men" at all times. **The Lord is at hand.** The
Lord's coming again speedily is the motive to
every Christian grace (Jas. v. 8, 9). Harshness to
others (the opposite of "moderation") would be
taking into our own hands prematurely the Lord's
exclusive prerogative of judging (1 Cor. iv. 5): so
provoking God to judge us by the strict law (Jas.
ii. 12, 13). **6.** [*Merimnate*] 'Be anxious about
nothing' (Matt. vi. 25). Care and prayer are as
mutually opposed as fire and water (*Bengel*). **by
prayer and supplication**—'by your [τῇ: the] prayer
and *your* (*the*) supplication,' as each case requires.
[*Proseuche*] *Prayer* for blessings; the general
term. [*Deesis*] *Supplication* to avert ill; a special
term, *suppliant entreaty* (note, Eph. vi. 18).

436

7 giving let your requests be made known unto God. And *f* the peace of God, which passeth all understanding, shall keep your hearts and minds through Christ Jesus.

8 Finally, brethren, whatsoever things are true, whatsoever things *are* [1] honest, whatsoever things *are* just, whatsoever things *are* pure, whatsoever things *are* lovely, whatsoever things *are* of good report; if *there be*

9 any virtue, and if *there be* any praise, think on these things. Those things, which ye have both learned, and received, and heard, and seen in me, do : and the God of peace shall be with you.

10 But I rejoiced in the Lord greatly, that now at the last *g* your care of me [2] hath flourished again; wherein ye were also careful, but ye lacked

11 opportunity. Not that I speak in respect of want: for I have learned,

12 in whatsoever state I am, *h therewith* to be content. I *i* know both how to be abased, and I know how to abound: every where and in all things I am instructed both to be full and to be hungry, both to abound

13 and to suffer need. I can do all things *j* through Christ which strengtheneth me.

A. D. 64.
f Num. 6. 26.
Job 22. 21.
Ps. 86. 8.
Isa. 26. 3.
John 14. 27.
Rom. 5. 1.
Gal. 5. 22.
Col. 3. 15.
1 Or. venerable.
g 2 Cor. 11. 9.
2 Or. is revived
h 1 Tim. 6. 6.
Heb. 13. 5.
i 1 Cor. 4. 11.
2 Cor. 11. 7. 27.
2 Cor. 12. 7.
j John 15. 5.
2 Cor. 12. 9.

thanksgiving—for every event, prosperity and affliction alike (1 Thess. v. 18; 1 Tim. ii. 1). The Philippians might remember Paul's example at Philippi in the innermost prison (Acts xvi. 25). Thanksgiving gives effect to prayer (2 Chr. xx. 21), and frees from *anxious carefulness*, by making all God's dealings matter for *praise*, not merely for *resignation*, much less *murmuring*. "Peace" is the companion of "thanksgiving" (*v.* 7; Col. iii. 15). **let your requests be made known unto God**—with filial, unreserved confidence; not keeping aught back, as too great or too small to bring before God, though you might feel so as to your fellow-men. So Jacob, fearing Esau (Gen. xxxii. 9-12); Hezekiah, fearing Sennacherib (2 Ki. xix. 14; Ps. xxxvii. 5). **7. And**—the sure consequence of thus laying everything before God in "prayer . . . with thanksgiving." **peace**—dispelling 'anxious care' (*v.* 6). **of God**—coming from and resting in God (John xiv. 27; xvi. 33). **passeth**—*surpasseth* all man's natural powers of understanding it (1 Cor. ii. 9, 10; Eph. iii. 20 : cf. Prov. iii. 17). **shall keep** [*phrourēsei*]—'shall *guard*,' as a well-garrisoned stronghold (Isa. xxvi. 1, 3). The same Greek is used in 1 Pet. i. 5. Peace secure within, whatever outward troubles may besiege. **hearts**—the *seat* of the will and affections. **minds** [*noemata*]—'understandings:' *thoughts* emanating from them. *Heart* has the same relation to *soul* as *mind* [*nous*] to *spirit*. **through**—Greek, '*in* Christ Jesus.' It is in Christ, our fortress (Ps. xviii. 2), that we are 'kept' secure.

8. Summary of exhortations as to relative duties, whether as children or parents, husbands or wives, friends, neighbours, men in the world, &c. **true**—sincere, especially in *words*. **honest** [*semna*]—'seemly' in *bearing* and *action; grave, dignified.* **just**—towards *others*. **pure**—'chaste' [*hagna*] (1 Tim. v. 22), in relation to *ourselves*. **lovely** [*prosphilē*]—loveable (cf. Mark x. 21; Luke vii. 4, 5). **of good report**—referring to the *absent* (ch. i. 27) : "lovely," loveable *face to face:* attracting love. **If there be any virtue**—'whatever virtue there is' (*Alford*). "Virtue," the standing word in heathen ethics, is found once only in St. Paul's epistles, and thrice in St. Peter's (1 Pet. ii. 9; 2 Pet. i. 3, 5); and this in uses different from heathen authors' *excellence*. It is a term earthly and human, as compared with the spiritual graces of Christianity: hence its rarity in the New Testament. Piety and true morality are inseparable. Despise not anything good; only let it keep its due place. **praise**—whatever is *praiseworthy;* not

that man's praise is to be our aim (cf. John xii. 43); but we should live so as to *deserve* it. **think on** [*logizesthe*]—have regard to, so as to "do" these things (*v.* 9) whenever occasion arises. **9. both**—rather, 'the things *also* which ye have *learned*,' &c.; the things which, besides being recommended in *words*, have been *also* recommended *by my example*, carry into practice. **heard, and seen.** These two refer to Paul's *example*, as "learned" and "received" (accepted), to his *teaching*. **and**—'and then,' as the result (*v.* 7). Not only 'the peace of God,' but "the God of peace" Himself, "shall be with you."

10. But [*de*]—transitional conjunction. 'Now' [*ēdē*] is used to pass to another subject. **in the Lord**—the sphere of Christian *joy.* **at the last** [*pote*]—he was expecting their gift, not from selfishness, but as a "fruit" of faith to "abound" to their account (*vv.* 11, 17). Though long in coming, owing to Epaphroditus' sickness and other delays, he does not imply their gift was late. **your care of me hath flourished again** [*anethalete*]—'ye have flourished again (as trees sprouting *again* in spring) in your care for [*huper*] me.' **wherein ye were also careful**—*for* which (reflourishing, viz., the sending of a supply to me) ye were also (all along) careful. **but,** &c.—from want of means or a messenger. Your "lack of service" (ch. ii. 30) was owing to your having "lacked opportunity." **11. I have learned.** The *I* is emphatical. I leave it to others, if they will, to be discontented. *I*, for my part, have learned, by the Holy Spirit's teaching, and the dealings of Providence (Heb. v. 8). **content** [*autarkēs*]—'independent of others, having *sufficiency in one's self.*' Christianity has raised the term above the haughty *self-sufficiency* of heathen stoicism to the *contentment* of the Christian, whose *sufficiency* is not in *self*, but in *God* (2 Cor. iii. 5; 1 Tim. vi. 6, 8; Heb. xiii. 5: cf. Jer. ii. 36; xlv. 5). **12. abased**—in low circumstances (2 Cor. iv. 8; vi. 9, 10). **every where** [*en panti*]—'in every thing.' **instructed** [*memuemai*]—'initiated' in a *secret* teaching, a *mystery* unknown to the world. **13. I can do** (*I have strength for*) **all things** [*panta ischuo*]—not merely 'how to be abased and how to abound.' After special instances, he declares his *universal* power, yet taking no glory to himself. How omnipotent is Christ, who makes His disciples omnipotent in Him! **through Christ** (so C, *Origen*) **which strengtheneth me** [אABΔ*f*, Vulgate, omit "Christ"]—'*in Him* who giveth me *power*' [*endunamounti me*]. IN living union and identification with Him, my power (Gal. ii. 20).

14 Notwithstanding ye have well done that [k] ye did communicate with
15 my affliction. Now, ye Philippians, know also, [l] that in the beginning of
the Gospel, when I departed from Macedonia, [m] no church communicated
16 with me as concerning giving and receiving, but ye only. For even in
17 [n] Thessalonica ye sent once and again unto my necessity. Not because
I desire a gift: but I desire fruit [o] that may abound to your account.
18 But [3] I have all, and abound: I am full, having received [p] of Epaphroditus
the things *which were sent* from you, an odour of a sweet smell, [q] a sacri-
19 fice acceptable, well-pleasing to God. But my God [r] shall supply all
20 your need according to his riches in glory by Christ Jesus. Now unto
God and our Father *be* glory for ever and ever. Amen.
21 Salute every saint in Christ Jesus. The brethren which are with
22 me greet you. All the saints salute you, chiefly they [s] that are of
23 Cesar's household. The grace of our Lord Jesus Christ *be* with you all.
Amen.

It was written to the Philippians from Rome by Epaphroditus.

A. D. 64.

[k] ch. 1. 7.
[l] Acts 11. 15.
[m] 2 Cor. 11. 8.
[n] 2 Thes. 3. 8.
[o] Mic. 7. 1.
John 15. 8, 16.
Rom. 15.28.
[3] Or, I have received all.
[p] ch. 2. 25.
[q] 2 Cor. 9. 12.
Heb. 13. 16.
[r] Ps. 23. 1.
Pro. 8. 21.
2 Cor. 9. 8.
[s] ch. 1. 13.

Cf. 1 Tim. i. 12, whence probably "Christ" was inserted here by transcribers (2 Tim. iv. 17). **14.** He guards against their thinking he thus makes light of their bounty. **ye did communicate with my affliction**—*i. e.*, ye made yourselves *sharers* in my present affliction. What chiefly gives me 'joy' (*v.* 10) in your contribution is, it is a proof of your *sympathy*. **15. Now**—'Moreover' [*de*], 'ye also know' (as well as I do myself). "Ye Philippians" marks his grateful remembrance of *them* in particular as his benefactors. **in the beginning of the Gospel**—dating from the *Philippian* Christian era : at its first preaching at Philippi. **when I departed from Macedonia** (Acts xvii. 14). The Philippians had followed Paul with their bounty when he went on to Corinth. 2 Cor. xi. 8, 9 accords with our passage, the dates assigned to the donation in both agreeing—viz., "in the *beginning* of the Gospel" here, and there at his *first* visit to Corinth (*Paley*). Rather, the supply here is not that received at Corinth, but that sent to him (Acts xvii. 14) previously "in Thessalonica . . . once and again" (*v.* 16) (*Alford*). **as concerning** [*eis logon:* in regard to the account of] **giving and receiving**—in the account between us, the "giving" on your part, the "receiving" on mine ; or rather (cf. *v.* 17), your giving *temporal* gifts and receiving *spiritual* (*Chrysostom*). **ye only.** We are not to wait for others in a good work, saying, 'I will do so when others do it.' We must go forward though *alone*. **16. even in Thessalonica.** "Even" so early as before I left Macedonia, when I had got no further than Thessalonica, ye sent me supplies for my necessities more than once. **17. a gift.** 'It is not that *I seek after the* gift [*to doma*], but *I do seek after the* fruit that *aboundeth* to your account :' the abounding of fruits of your faith to be put down to your account against the day of reward (Heb. vi. 10). **18. But.** Though 'the gift' is not what I 'seek after' (*v.* 17), *yet* I am grateful for it, as ample for all my needs. [*Apecho*] 'I have all' that I want, 'and more than enough ;' *lit.*, 'I abound.' **I am full** [*pepleromai*]—'I am filled full.' **an odour of a sweet smell** (note, Eph. v. 2). The figure is drawn from the sweet-smelling incense burnt with the sacrifices : their gift being in faith, was not so much to Paul as *to God* (Matt. xxv. 40), before whom it came up "for a memorial" (Acts x. 4), sweet-smelling in God's presence (Gen. viii. 21 ; Rev. viii. 3, 4). **sacrifice acceptable** (Heb. xiii. 16). **19. my.** Paul says, "*my God*," to imply that God would reward their bounty to *His servant*, by 'fully supplying' [*plerosei*]—lit., *full to the full*—their every temporal and spiritual "need" (2 Cor. ix. 8), even as they had "fully" supplied his "need" (*vv.* 16, 18). My Master will fully repay you ; I cannot. The Philippians invested their bounty well, since it got them such a return. **according to his riches**—the measure of His supply to you will be the immeasurable "riches of His grace" (Eph. i. 7). **in glory**—the element peculiarly belonging to God, IN which His rich grace operates, and IN which He will 'supply fully all your need.' "Riches," in the New Testament, is always used with the *genitive* of the thing, so is not to be joined to "in glory." **by Christ Jesus**—"IN" [*en*] Christ Jesus, the Mediator of all spiritual blessings. **20. be glory**—not to us, but to Him be '*the* glory' (Greek : implying His exclusive title to the glory) alike of your gift and of His gracious recompense to you.

21. Salute every saint—*individually.* **The brethren which are with me**—perhaps *Jewish* believers (Acts xxviii. 21). I think ch. ii. 20 precludes our thinking of 'closer friends,' 'colleagues in the ministry' (*Alford*) : he had only one close friend with him—viz., Timothy. **greet**—salute you. **22. chiefly** (as being nearest me) **they that are of Cesar's household**—dependents of Nero, probably converted through Paul whilst a prisoner in the prætorian barrack attached to the palace. Philippi was a Roman 'colony ;' hence there might arise a tie between the citizens of the mother city and those of the colony, especially between those of both cities converted by the same apostle and under like circumstances, he having been imprisoned at Philippi as he now is at Rome. **23.** (Gal. vi. 18) **be with you all.** So B C. But אA Δ *fg*, Vulgate, read 'be with your spirit' (the highest of man's three parts, 1 Thess. v. 23). **Amen.** So א A Δ *f*, Vulgate. But B G *g* omit it.

438

THE EPISTLE OF PAUL THE APOSTLE TO THE

COLOSSIANS.

1 PAUL, an apostle of Jesus Christ by the will of God, and Timotheus
2 our brother, to the saints *a* and faithful brethren in Christ which are
at Colosse: Grace *be* unto you, and peace, from God our Father and the
Lord Jesus Christ.
3 We give thanks to God and the Father of our Lord Jesus Christ,
4 praying always for you, since *b* we heard of your faith in Christ Jesus,
5 and of *c* the love *which ye have* to all the saints, for the hope *d* which is
laid up for you in heaven, whereof ye heard before in the word of the
6 truth of the Gospel; which is come unto you, *e* as *it is* in all the world ;
and *f* bringeth forth fruit, as *it doth* also in you, since the day ye
7 heard *of it*, and knew *g* the grace of God in truth: as ye also learned of

A. D. 64.

CHAP. 1.
a Eph. 6. 21.
b Gal. 5. 6.
Eph. 1. 15.
c Heb. 6. 10.
d Matt. 5. 12.
1 Pet. 1. 4.
e Matt. 24. 14.
f John 15. 16.
g Ps. 110. 3.
1 Cor. 15. 10.
Eph 3. 2.
Tit. 2. 11.

CHAP. I. 1-29.—HEADING—INTRODUCTION—
CONFIRMING EPAPHRAS' TEACHING—GLORIES OF
CHRIST—THANKSGIVING AND PRAYER FOR THE
COLOSSIANS—HIS OWN MINISTRY OF THE MYSTERY.
1. Paul, an apostle of Jesus Christ by the
will of God [*dia*]—'*through*,' &c. (note, 1 Cor. i. 1.)
The same designation of himself as in 1 Cor., 2
Cor., Ephes., 2 Tim. The fullest titular distinction is in Gal., where he wished to enforce his
authority. The shortest is in 1 Thess. and 2
Thess., to whom he writes in familiarity: simply
"Paul." Timotheus (notes, 2 Cor. i. 1; Phil. i.
1). He was with Paul when writing in Rome.
He had been Paul's companion in his first tour
through Phrygia, where Colosse was. Hence the
Colossians associated him with Paul in their
affections, and the apostle joins him with himself
in the address. In 1 Cor., Phil., and Phile., Paul
passes to the singular; but here, 2 Cor. i. 3; 1 and
2 Thess., continues the plural. Timothy may
have transcribed the epistle. Neither, probably,
had *seen* the Colossian *church* (cf. ch. ii. 1); but
had seen, during their tour through Phrygia,
individual Colossians—as Epaphras, Philemon,
Archippus, and Apphia (Phile. 2)—who, when
converted, brought the Gospel to their native city.
2. Colosse. So א A G *fg*, Vulgate. But in B,
'Colasse.' As "saints" implies union with God,
so "faithful brethren" union with Christians
(*Bengel*). Here (Rom. i. 7; Eph. i. 1; Phil. i. 1),
Paul does not write to the 'church' expressly,
but to the Christians constituting it. Where he
wishes specially to recommend or praise them for
church unity, he perhaps addresses 'the church.'
and the Lord Jesus Christ. Supported by
א A C G *g*. Omitted by B Δ *f*, Vulgate.
3. Thanksgiving for their 'faith, hope, and
love.' So in the twin epistle sent by the same
bearer, Tychicus (Eph. i. 15, 16). We—I and
Timothy. and the Father. So א A, Vulgate.
But B Δ G omit "and," which possibly crept in
from Eph. i. 3. praying always for you—with
thanksgiving (Phil. iv. 6). 4. Since we heard—
lit., 'Having heard,' &c.: implying that he had
only heard of, and not *seen* them (ch. ii. 1). Cf.
Rom. i. 8, where like language is used of a church
which he had not at the time visited. faith in
Christ [*pistin-en Christo*]—'Christ-centred faith.'
love which ye have to all—the absent as well
as those present (*Ellicott*). 5. For. To be joined
with the words preceding: 'the love which ye
have (*continue having*) to all the saints *because* of
[*dia: on account of*] the hope' (here, *the thing
hoped for*), &c. Hope of eternal life will never be
inactive, but will always produce "love." This
passage is abused by Romanists, as if the hope of
salvation depended upon works. It does not
follow that our *hope* is *founded on* works of *love*
because we are *stimulated* by hope to live well;
since nothing is more effectual for this than the
sense of God's free grace (*Calvin*). Our *hope*
resting on grace, being confident of the heavenly
inheritance *with the saints* (Acts xxvi. 18), leads
us instinctively to *love* them. laid up—a treasure
laid up, set apart, out of danger of being lost
(2 Tim. iv. 8): faith, love, and hope (*vv.* 4, 5), the
sum of Christianity (cf. *v.* 23). in heaven—Greek,
'in the heavens.' whereof ye heard before—
viz., when preached to you. in the word, &c.
That "hope" formed part of "the word of the
truth of (*announced in*) the Gospel" (cf. Eph. i. 13);
i. e., part of the Gospel truth preached unto you.
6. Which is come unto you [*tou parontos eis
humas*]—'Which is *present* (having come) *unto*
you:' which living Gospel word has come to, and
remains with you. (even) as [*kathos*] it is in all
the world—*virtually*, as it was by this time
preached in the leading parts of the world (Rom.
i. 8; x. 18); *potentially*, as Christ's command was
that the Gospel should be preached to all nations
—not limited, as the law was, to the Jews (Matt.
xiii. 38; xxiv. 14; xxviii. 19). So G *fg*, Vulgate.
However, the reading of א A B C Δ omits the following "and" ("*it is*," of the English version, is
not in the original): 'As in all the world it is bringing forth fruit *and growing* [so א A B C Δ G *fg*,
Vulgate, read: *kai auxanomenon*], even as it doth
in you also.' Not that the Gospel has been
preached in all the world, but that it is *bearing
fruits* of righteousness, and (like a tree *growing* at
the same time that it *bears fruit*) *growing in numbers* of its converts in all the world. *Intensively*
within, as well as *extensively* progressing without
(Isa. liv. 2, end; Acts vi. 7; xii. 24; xix. 20).
heard of it—rather, 'heard *it*.' and knew [*epeg-
note*]—'came to know *fully*,' experimentally. the
grace of God (of which the Gospel is the offer,
Titus ii. 11; iii. 4-6) in truth—*i. e.*, in its truth, free
from Judaistic and Gnostic error. 7. As ye also
learned. "Also" is omitted in א A B C Δ G *fg*,
Vulgate. Those inserting it thought that *Paul*
had preached the Gospel to the Colossians *as well*

439

^hEpaphras our dear fellow-servant, who is for you a faithful minister of
8 Christ; who also declared unto us your love in the Spirit.
9 For ⁱthis cause we also, since the day we heard *it*, do not cease to pray
for you, and to desire that ye might be filled with the ^jknowledge of his
10 will in all wisdom and spiritual understanding; that ^kye might walk
worthy of the Lord ^lunto all pleasing, ^mbeing fruitful in every good
11 work, and increasing in the knowledge of God; strengthened with all
might, according to his glorious power, unto all patience and long-suffer-
12 ing ⁿwith joyfulness; giving ^othanks unto the Father, which hath made

A. D. 64.

^h Phile. 23.
ch 4. 12.
ⁱ 1 Cor. 1. 5.
Eph. 1. 16.
^j Rom. 12. 2.
^k 1 Thes.2.12.
^l 1 Thes. 4. 1.
^m John 15. 16.
ⁿ Acts 5. 41.
^o Eph. 5. 20.

as Epaphras; whereas the omission in the oldest MSS. implies that *Epaphras alone* founded the church at Colosse. A Colossian (ch. iv. 12), identified by *Grotius* with Epaphroditus (Phil. ii. 25). of—'*from* Epaphras.' dear—'beloved.' fellow-servant—viz. of Christ. In Phile. 23 he calls him "my fellow-prisoner." Epaphras may have been apprehended for his zealous labours in Asia Minor; but more probably Paul gave him the title as his faithful companion in imprisonment (cf. note, ch. iv. 10). who is for you, &c. [*pistos huper humōn diakonos*]—'who is faithful in your behalf (in behalf of your spiritual good) as a minister of Christ:' hinting that he is one not to be set aside for the new and erroneous teachers (ch. ii.) אABΔGg read 'for us.' C*f*, Vulgate, support the English version. 8. your love (*v.* 4)—"to all the saints." in the Spirit—the element IN which alone true love is found (Rom. xiv. 17; xv. 30), as distinguished from that of those "in the flesh" (Rom. viii. 9). Even they needed to be stirred up to greater love (ch. iii. 12-14). Love is the first-fruit of the Spirit (Gal. v. 22).

9. For this cause (*v.* 8)—as in the games we most urge on those near the victory (*Chrysostom*) (Eph. i. 15). Their progress was *the impelling cause* to Paul's prayer. Unceasing earnestness was its *characteristic* (Eph. i. 16): its *object* was 'that they might be filled,' &c. we also—on our part. heard it (*v.* 4). pray. He states what in *particular* he prays for; as in *v.* 3, *generally* the fact of his praying for them. to desire [*aitoumenoi*: more special than *proseuchomenoi*: Mark xi. 24]—Greek, 'to make request.' might (*may*) be filled—a verb often in this epistle (ch. iv. 12, 17). knowledge [*epignosin*]—'*full* (experimental) knowledge.' Akin to 'knew' (note, *v.* 6). of his will—how ye ought to walk (Eph. v. 17): chiefly that 'mystery of His will, according to His good pleasure which he purposed in Himself: that in the fulness of times He might gather together in one all things in Christ' (Eph. i. 9, 10): God's eternal "will" to reconcile to Himself men by Christ, not by angels, as the false teachers taught (ch. ii. 18) (*Estius*). *Knowledge* was the want among the Colossians, notwithstanding their general excellencies; hence he so often dwells on this (*v.* 28; ch. ii. 2, 3; iii. 10, 16; iv. 5, 6). He less extols *wisdom* to the Corinthians, as "puffed up" with the conceit of knowledge. wisdom—frequent in this epistle, as opposed to the (false) "philosophy" and "show of wisdom' (ch. ii. 8, 23: cf. Eph. i. 8). understanding [*sunesei*]—sagacity to discern what on each occasion is suited to the place and time: its seat is 'the understanding;' *wisdom* is more general, and has its seat in the whole of the faculties of the soul. *Bengel*, 'Wouldst thou know that the matters in the Word of Christ are real? Then never read them for mere knowledge' sake.' Knowledge is to be seasoned with 'spiritual understanding.' *Ellicott* joins 'spiritual (spirit-derived and spirit-characterized) wisdom and understanding' (1 Cor. ii. 13; 2 Cor. i. 12). 10. 'So as to walk,' &c. True knowledge of God's

will is inseparable from walking conformably to it. worthy of the Lord—*Jesus* in Paul's epistles (Eph. iv. 1). unto—so as in every way to be. pleasing (God) [*areskeia*]—'*desire of pleasing*.' being fruitful—'bearing fruit,' as *v.* 6: the *first* manifestation of their walking "worthy of the Lord." The *second* is, "increasing (growing) in the knowledge [*eis tēn epignosin*] of God" (or as אABΔG read [*tē epignosei*] 'growing BY the full knowledge of God"). As the *Gospel Word* (*v.* 6) was said to 'bring forth fruit,' and 'grow' in all the world, even as it did in the Colossians, since the day they *knew* the grace of God, so here Paul prays that they might continue to 'bring forth fruit,' and 'grow' more and more *by the full knowledge* of God (the true means of spiritual growth), the more of that "knowledge" (*v.* 9) was imparted to them. The *third* manifestation of their walk is (*v.* 11), 'Being strengthened,' &c. The *fourth* is (*v.* 12), "Giving thanks," &c. 11. [*En pasē dunamei dunamoumenoi*] 'Being made mighty with (lit., *in*) all (every kind of) might.' according to his glorious power—'according to the power (the characteristic) of His glory:' here appropriate to St. Paul's argument (Eph. i. 19; vi. 10): as its exuberant 'riches' in Eph. iii. 16. The power which characterizes His glory is the *measure of the strength* to be imparted to the Colossians (Rom. vi. 4). unto all patience—so as to attain to all [*hupomonēn*] brave, *patient constancy, perseverance* in the faith, in spite of trials of persecutors and seductions of false teachers. long-suffering [*makrothumian*]—towards those whom one could repel. *Long forbearance* before giving room to passion. "Patience" towards those whom one cannot repel (*Chrysostom*). [*Makrothumia*, towards *persons*: *huponone*, as to things.] Both are ascribed to saints: only *makrothumia* to God (*Trench*). with joyfulness—Paul's own practice in trial (Acts xvi. 25; Rom. v. 3, 11). Joined by *Ellicott* with "giving thanks." 12. *You* (not "*we*," from *v.* 9) 'giving thanks unto the Father.' Note, *v.* 10: this clause is connected with 'That ye may walk' (*v.* 10). unto the Father—of Jesus, and so *our* Father by adoption (Gal. iii. 26; iv. 4, 5, 6). which hath made us meet [*hikanosanti*]—'who *made* us meet, fit, *once for all*' (2 Cor. iii. 6). Not '*is making* us meet' by progressive growth in holiness. The *Spirit's* work is not primarily meant here; but the *Father's* work in putting us by adoption, once for all, in a new standing—viz, *that of children.* The believers meant here were in different stages of progressive sanctification; but in respect to the meetness specified, they all alike had it from *the Father*, in Christ, His Son, being "complete in Him" (ch. ii. 10: cf. John xvii. 17; 1 Cor. i. 30; Jude 1). *Secondarily*, this once-for-all meetness contains the germ of sanctification, developed progressively in the life by the Father's Spirit in the believer. The life of heavenliness is the first stage of heaven itself. There will follow a *personal* meetness for heaven where there is a *judicial* meetness. B prefixes 'Who called and' before 'made us meet' [*kalesanti kai*].

13 us meet to be partakers of the [p] inheritance of the saints in light: who
hath delivered us from [q] the power of darkness, [r] and hath translated
14 *us* into the kingdom of [1] his dear Son: in whom we have redemption
15 through his blood, *even* the forgiveness of sins: who is [s] the image of the
16 invisible God, the [t] first-born of every creature: for [u] by him were all
things created that are in heaven, and that are in earth, visible and invisible, whether *they be* thrones, or dominions, or principalities, or powers:

A. D. 64.

p Eph. 1. 11.
q Heb. 2. 14.
r 2 Pet. 1. 11.
1 the Son of his love.
s John 14. 9.
t Ps. 89. 27.
u John 1. 3.

A C, Vulgate, omit. **to be partakers, &c.** [*eis tēn merida*]—'for the (*our*) portion of the inheritance (Acts xx. 32; xxvi. 18; Eph. i. 11) of the saints in light.' The inheritance is a joint one, of which each saint has his 'portion.' 'Light' (including *knowledge*, *purity*, *love*, and *joy*) begins in the believer here, descending from "the Father of lights" by Jesus, "the true light," and is perfected in the kingdom of light: in antithesis to "darkness" (*v.* 13). It contrasts with the "darkness" of the unconverted state (*v.* 13: cf. 1 Pet. ii. 9). **13. delivered us**—implying that we were *captives.* **from** [*ek*]—'*out of* the power;' out of the sphere in which the power of the prince of darkness is exercised. **darkness**—blindness, hatred, misery (*Bengel*). **translated**—even already (Matt. v. 3): those translated in state are also transformed in character. Satan has an organized dominion, with various orders of evil powers (Eph. ii. 2; vi. 12). But "kingdom" is rarely applied to his usurped rule (Matt. xii. 26): it is generally restricted to the kingdom of God. **his dear Son** [*tou huiou tēs agapēs autou*]—'the Son of His love:' on whom it rests (John xvii. 26; Eph. i. 6): contrast the "darkness," where all is hatred and hateful. **14. we have**—'we are having.' **redemption** [*tēn*]—'the redemption.' **through his blood.** So *Irenæus.* Omitted in ℵ A B C G *g*, Vulgate. Probably inserted from Eph. i. 7. **sins** [*tōn hamartiōn*]—'*our* sins.' The more general term; for which Eph. i. 7 has the special, 'our *transgressions*' [*tōn paraptomatōn*]. **15.** They who have experienced "redemption" (*v.* 14) know Christ in the glorious character here, as above the highest angels for whom the false teachers (ch. ii. 18) claimed worship. Cf. the two other passages as to Christ's person (Eph. i. 20-23; Phil. ii. 6-11). Paul describes Him—(1.) in relation to God and creation (*vv.* 15-17); (2.) in relation to the Church (*vv.* 18-20). The former regards Him as the Creator (*vv.* 15, 16) and Sustainer (*v.* 17) of the natural world; the latter, as the source and stay of the new moral creation. **image**—exact likeness and perfect Representative. Adam was made "in the image of God" (Gen. i. 27). The second Adam perfectly reflected visibly 'the invisible God' (1 Tim. i. 17), whose glories the first Adam only in part represented. "Image" [*eicon*] always supposes a *prototype*, from which it is drawn: the *exact counterpart*, as the reflection of the sun in the water: the child the living image of the parent. "Likeness" [*homoiosis*] implies mere *resemblance*, not the exact *counterpart* and *derivation*; hence it is nowhere applied to the Son, whilst "image" is (cf. 1 Cor. xi. 7 (*Trench*); John i. 18; xiv. 9; 2 Cor. iv. 4; 1 Tim. iii. 16; vi. 16; Heb. i. 3). Before His incarnation He was the image of the invisible God, as the Word (John i. 1-3) by whom God created the worlds, and by whom God appeared to the patriarchs. His *essential* character as *always* "the image of God"—(1.) before the incarnation, (2.) in the days of His flesh, and (3.) now in His glorified state—is, I think, contemplated by "is." **first-born of every creature** (Heb. i. 6)—"the first-begotten:" 'begotten of His Father before all worlds' ('Nicene Creed'). 'God, of the substance of His Father, begotten before the worlds; and man, of the substance of His mother, born in the world' ('Athanasian Creed'). Priority and superlative dignity is implied (Ps. lxxxix. 27). The English version seems to make Christ a creature. Translate [*protokos pasēs ktiseōs*], 'Begotten *before every creature*,' as the context gives the reason why He is so designated: 'For,' &c. (*Trench*), *vv.* 16, 17, "He is *before all things.*" Thus *pasa ktisis* has not to be taken 'the first-begotten *of all creatures*,' but in its strict sense, 'before *every creature*.' "First-begotten" marks at once His eternal *priority* and His condescending to *brotherhood* with us (Rom. viii. 29). "Only-begotten" marks *His relation to the Father* by generation from everlasting. This expression is used by *Origen* (so far is the Greek from favouring Arian views) to mark Christ's *Godhead*, in contrast with His *manhood*, (B. ii., *contra Cels.*) Since He was before "*every creature*" [the genitive of the *point of view*, 'in comparison to' far or *long before*: John i. 15, 30, *prōtosmou*; xv. 18, &c.], He cannot be a *creature* Himself, but the Creator. The Greek is against *Alford's* translation, 'the first-born of *all creation*.' **16. For** [*hoti*]—'because:' the proof that He is not included in the things created, but is the "first-begotten" before "every creature" (*v.* 15); begotten as 'the Son of God's love' (*v.* 13) antecedently to every other emanation; 'because' all other emanations came from Him: whatever was created, *was created by Him.* **by him** [*en*]—'*in* Him:' as the creative centre, the *conditional*, all-including cause, *in* and *on* whom creation rests for its realization: the creation of all things BY *Him* [*di' autou*], as the *mediating cause*, follows. God revealed Himself in the Son, the Word, *before all created existence* (*v.* 15). The Divine Word carries IN *Himself the archetypes of all existences*, so that 'IN *Him* all things in heaven and earth were created.' 'In Him' indicates that the Word is the ideal ground of all existence; "*by* Him," that He is the *instrument* of actually realizing the Divine idea (*Neander*). His essential nature as the Word of the Father is not a mere appendage of His incarnation, but the ground of it. The original relation of the Eternal Word to men 'made in His image' (Gen. i. 27), is the source of His forming, in His incarnation, the new relation whereby He restores them to His lost image. '*In* Him' implies something prior to "by" and "for Him" presently after: the three propositions mark in succession the beginning, the progress, and the end (*Bengel*). The *conditional*, the *mediating*, and the *final* cause. **all things** [*ta panta*]—'*the* universe of things.' The *new creation* is not meant (as Socinians interpret); for *angels*, who are included in the catalogue, were not *new created* by Christ: he does not speak of the new creation till *v.* 18. The creation of 'the things in the *heavens*' (so Greek) includes that of the *heavens themselves*: the former are named, since the inhabitants are more noble than their dwellings. Heaven and earth, and all that is in them (1 Chr. xxix. 11; Neh. ix. 6; Eph. i. 10; Rev. x. 6). **invisible**—the world of spirits. **thrones, or dominions**—*lordships*; the spirits round the

17 all things were created *v* by him, and for him : and *w* he is before all
18 things, and by him all things consist; and he is the head of the body,
the church: who is the beginning, *x* the first-born from the dead; that
2 in all *things* he might have the pre-eminence.
19 For it pleased *the Father* that in him should all fulness dwell;

A. D. 64.

v Rom 11.36.
w John 17. 5.
x Rev. 1. 5.
2 Or, among all.

throne: "thrones" are the greatest; *lordships* the lowest. **principalities, or powers** [*archai, exousiai*]—'*rules* or *authorities:*' the former are stronger than the latter (cf. Eph. i. 21, where the order of angelic ranks is probably descensive, *lordship* being lowest). The latter pair refer to offices *in respect to God's creatures:* 'thrones and dominions,' exalted *relation to God*, they being the *chariots* on which He rides, displaying His glory (Ps. lxviii. 17). **were**—[distinguish the Greek aorist, *ektisthē*, which precedes, from the perfect, *ektistai*, here]—'*have been* created.' In the former the creation was viewed as *a past act at a point of time;* here it is viewed as the *permanent result eternally continuing.* **by him**—the instrumental Agent (John i. 3). **for him**—the grand *End* of creation: the *final* as well as the *efficient* cause (Prov. xvi. 4; Rev. iv. 11). Christ in this has *God's* prerogative (Rom. xi. 36). *Lachmann's* punctuation of *vv.* 15-18 is best, whereby "Who is the image," &c., the "first-born of every creature," (*v.* 15) answers to "who is the beginning, the first-born from the dead" (*v.* 18), the whole forming one sentence with ("All things were created by Him, and for Him: and He is before all things, and by Him all things consist; and He is the Head of the body, the Church") intervening as a parenthesis. Thus Paul puts first *the origination by Him of the natural creation:* secondly, *of the new creation.* The parenthesis falls into four clauses, two and two: the former two support the first assertion, "the first-born of every creature;" the latter two prepare us for "the first-born from the dead:" the former two correspond to the latter two in their form,— "All things by Him . . . and He is," and "by Him all things . . . and He is." **17.** (John viii. 58) 'And *He Himself* [*Autos:* the great HE] is (implying *essential being*) before all things,' in *time*, as well as dignity. Therefore He is *before even time*—i. e., *from eternity* (cf. *v.* 15, note). The contrast is between the things created in time and the Creator *Himself*, before all time. **by him**—Greek, 'IN HIM,' as the *causal* element of their *continuing existence* (*persistence*), besides being the conditional element of their *creation* (*v.* 16) (*Ellicott*). Heb. i. 3, "Upholding all things by the word of His power." **consist** [*sunesteken*]—'subsist" as one integral harmonized *system* or whole (Acts xvii. 28). The Son of God is the *Conserver*, as well as the *Creator*, of all things. *Bengel*, 'All things in Him come together into (and *continue in*) one *system*: the universe found (and retains) its completion in Him.' **18.** Relation of Christ to the Church, the new creation, as its Originator. **he**—emphatical [*Autos*], HIMSELF. Not angels: in opposition to the false doctrine concerning angel-worship, and the power of Œons, imaginary spirit-emanations from God (ch. ii. 10, 18). **head of the body, the church.** The church is His body by virtue of His entering into communion corporeally with human nature (Eph. i. 22; iv. 15, 16). The One who is Head of all things and beings by creation is also, by being "the first-born from the dead," and so the "first-fruits" of the new creation among men, Head of the Church. **who is**—i. e., seeing that He is: this begins a *new paragraph.* As the former paragraph, relating to His originating the *physical* creation, began with "Who is" (*v.* 15), so this, relating to His originat-

ing the new creation, begins with "Who is:" a parenthesis (note, *v.* 16), including from "all things were created by Him" to "Head of the body, the Church:" the last clause prepares the transition to "Who is the beginning," &c. The *head* of kings and high priests was anointed, as the seat of the faculties, the fountain of dignity, and *original* of all the members (according to *Hebrew* etymology, 'Abarbanel,' in *Pearson*, 'Creed,' Article ii., p. 175, note). So Jesus by His unction was designated as the *Head* of the body, the Church. **the beginning**—viz., of the new creation, as of the old (Prov. viii. 22; John i. 1; 2 Cor. v. 17: cf. Rev. i. 8): the beginning of the Church of the first-born (Heb. xii. 23), being Himself "the first-born from [*ek:* not merely *of*] the dead;" He is not called the *first* that rose, but 'the first-begotten *out* of the dead,' rising with a *new birth* into life (Rom. vi. 9; Acts xxvi. 23; iii. 15, 'Prince-leader of life' [*archōgos*, akin to *arche* here]. Christ's primogeniture is threefold: (1.) From eternity the "first-begotten" of the Father (*v.* 15); (2.) The first-born of His mother (Matt. i. 25); (3.) The Head of the Church, mystically begotten of the Father, to a new life, at His resurrection, which is His "regeneration," even as His people's coming resurrection will be their "regeneration" (*i. e.*, the resurrection which, begun in the soul, shall extend to the body and to the whole creation (Matt. xix. 28; Acts xiii. 33; Rom. viii. 11, 21-23; Rev. i. 5). Sonship and resurrection are similarly connected (Luke xx. 36; Rom. i. 4; 1 John iii. 2). Christ by rising from the dead, is the *efficient cause* (1 Cor. xv. 20-23), as having obtained the power; the *exemplary cause*, as being the pattern (Mic. ii. 13; Rom. vi. 5; Phil. iii. 21) of our resurrection: the resurrection of "the Head" involves consequentially that of the members. **that in all things.** He resumes the "all things," *v.* 20. **he might have the pre-eminence** [*genētai en pasin autos proteuōn*]—'He HIMSELF (and none other) *may* become the One holding the first place.' Both ideas are included—priority in *time* and priority in *dignity:* now in the regenerated world, as before in the world of creation (*v.* 15; Ps. lxxxix. 27; John iii. 13).

19. The ellipsis is least by translating (as ch. ii. 9 confirms), 'In Him (Christ) the whole fulness (of the Godhead) was pleased to dwell.' "All the [*tō*] fulness:" whatever divine excellence is in the Father (Eph. iii. 19: cf. John i. 16; iii. 34). The Gnostics used "fulness" for the assemblage of angelic emanations from God. The Spirit presciently by Paul warns the Church that the true "fulness" dwells in Christ alone. This is why Christ takes precedence of every creature (*v.* 15). For two reasons Christ is Lord of the Church: (1.) Because the fulness of the Divine attributes (*v.* 19) dwells in Him according to the Divine "good pleasure," so He has the *power* to govern the universe; (2.) Because (*v.* 20) what He has done for the Church gives Him the *right* to preside over it. **should all fulness dwell**—as in a temple (John i. 14 [*eskenosen*]; ii. 21). *This indwelling Godhead in Christ* is the foundation of the *reconciliation* by Him (*Bengel*). Hence the "and" (*v.* 20) connects as cause and effect the two things. **20.** The order is, 'And through Him (Christ) God (implied in "the fulness") was pleased to

20 and, ³ having made peace through the blood of his cross, by him to reconcile
all things unto himself; by him, *I say*, whether *they be* things in earth,
or things in heaven.

21 And you, that were sometime alienated, and enemies ⁴ in *your* mind by
22 wicked works, yet now hath he reconciled in the body of his flesh through
death, to present you holy and unblameable and unreproveable in his

A. D. 64.

³ Or. making peace
⁴ Or by your mind in wicked works.

reconcile again completely [*apokatallaxai*]; to their original unity (note, Eph. ii. 16) the whole universe of things [*ta panta*] unto Himself (God the Father) [*eis auton*], so as to have reconciled access to Himself (Eph. ii. 16-18), "having made peace through the blood of His (Christ's) cross "—*i. e.*, shed by Christ *on* the cross—the mean of our reconciliation with God. 'God reconciling man to Himself' implies that He takes away by the blood of Jesus the barrier which God's justice interposes against man's being in union with God (cf. note, Rom. v. 10; 2 Cor. v. 18, 19). So the LXX., 1 Sam. xxix. 4 [*en tini diallagesetai houtos to kurio*], "Wherewith should He reconcile himself unto his master ?"—*i. e.*, *reconcile his master* unto him by appeasing his wrath [Hebrew, *yithratztzeh:* 'be reconciled to his master']. So Matt. v. 23, 24. **by him**—through Him (the *mediating cause*): emphatically repeated, to bring the person of Christ, as Head of both the first and the new creations alike, into prominence. **things in earth, or things in heaven.** Good angels do not need reconciliation to God; fallen angels are excluded from it (Jude 6). But redemption has effects on the world of spirits unknown to us. His reconciling *us*, and His reconciling *them*, must be of a different kind, as He took not on Him the nature of angels (Heb. ii. 16), to offer a *propitiation* for them. He being *their* Head as well as *ours*, they are perhaps thereby *brought nearer God*, and put beyond the *possibility of sinning*, and gain *larger views of God's love and wisdom* (Eph. iii. 10). All creation subsists in Christ, and is therefore affected by His propitiation: sinful creation is strictly "reconciled" from its enmity; sinless creation, comparatively distant from His unapproachable purity (Job iv. 18; xv. 15; xxv. 5), is lifted into nearer communion with Him, and in this wider sense is reconciled. Man's fall, following on Satan's, is part of a larger circle of evil; so that the remedy of the former affects the standing of angels, from among whom Satan's host fell. Angels having seen the magnitude of sin, the infinite cost of redemption, the exclusion of the fallen angels from it, and the inability of any creature to stand in his own strength, are *now* put beyond the reach of falling. 'Christ is the Head of *redemption* to man; the Head of *preservation* to angels' (*Bacon*). Satan, when unfallen, may have ruled this earth and the pre-Adamite animal kingdom; hence his malice against man, who succeeded to the lordship of this earth and its animals: hence, too, his assumption of the serpent's form, the subtlest of animals. Luke xix. 38 states "peace in heaven" as the result of finished redemption, as "peace on earth" was the result of its beginning at Jesus' birth (Luke ii. 14; Eph. i. 10, accords). An actual *reconciliation*, or *restoration of peace in heaven*, as well as on earth, is expressed. As long as that blood of reconciliation was not shed, which is opposed (Zech. iii. 8, 9) to Satan's accusations, but was only in promise, Satan could plead his right against men before God day and night (Job i. 6; Rev. xii. 10); hence he was in heaven till the ban on man was broken (cf. Luke x. 18). So here, the world of earth and heaven owe to Christ alone *the restoration of harmony after the conflict, and the subjugation of all things under one Head*

(cf. Heb. xii. 23, 24). Sin introduced discord, not only on earth, but also in heaven, by the fall of demons; it brought into the abodes of holy angels, not positive, yet privative loss, a retardation of their highest development, harmonious gradation, and perfect consummation. Angels were no more able than men, by themselves, to overcome the peace-disturbers, and cast out the devils: it is only "by," or 'through HIM,' and "the blood of HIS cross," that *peace was restored even in heaven:* it is only after Christ has obtained the victory legally that Michael (Rev. xii. 7-10) and his angels can cast out of heaven Satan and his demons (cf. ch. ii. 15). Thus Paul's argument against angel-worship is, that angels themselves wholly depend on Christ, the sole object of worship (*Auberlen*).

21. The Colossians are included in this general reconciliation (ch. ii. 13). **sometime**—'once.' **that were . . . alienated**—a double participle [*ontas apēllotriomenas*] : 'being in a state of *continued alienation;*' objectively *banished from* God, through the barrier which God's justice interposed against your sin; subjectively *estranged* through the alienation of your own wills from God. The former is prominent (cf. Rom. v. 10), the second follows, "enemies in your mind." 'Actual *alienation* makes habitual "enemies"' (Rom. v. 10) (*Bengel*). **in your mind** [*tē dianoia*]—'in your understanding' (Eph. ii. 1-3, 12; iv. 18). **by wicked works** [*en tois ergois tois ponerois*]—'*in your* works that were wicked:' the element in which your *enmity* subsisted. **yet now.** *Notwithstanding* the former alienation, *now* that Christ has come, *God* (the subject, as in *v.* 13) hath *completely reconciled again* (note, *v.* 20). 22. **In the body of his flesh**—the element in which His reconciling sufferings had place. Cf. *v.* 24, "afflictions of Christ *in my flesh*" (1 Pet. ii. 24). Angels, who have not a 'body of flesh,' are not in any way our reconciling mediators, as your false teachers assert, but He, the Lord of angels, who has taken our *flesh*, that *in* it He might atone for our fallen manhood. False spiritualism and ascetic contempt of the body led some to doubt as to even Christ's "flesh" (ch. ii. 23) being the sphere of His atoning work. **through death**—'through *His* [*tou*] death' (which could only take place in a body of flesh like ours, Heb. ii. 14). *Flesh* is the sphere in which His human sufferings could have place (cf. Eph. ii. 15). **to present you** (Eph. v. 27)—the end of His reconciling atonement by death; not that *you* might present *yourselves.* The regenerate derive all their sanctity—imputed, inherent, and actual —from Christ. When we have one of these, we have all. **holy**—positively: in relation to God. **unblameable and unreproveable**—negatively: 'without blemish [as *amomous* is translated as to Jesus our Head, 1 Pet. i. 19] *in one's self.*' *Irreproachable* [*anenkletous: one who gives* no ground for prosecution] *in relation to the world without. Sanctification*, the fruit, is here treated of; *justification* by Christ's reconciliation, the tree, having preceded (Eph. i. 4; Titus ii. 14). Our 'sanctification' is regarded here as *perfect* in Christ, into whom we are grafted at regeneration (1 Pet. i. 2; Jude 1): not merely *progressive*, which is the *gradual development* of the sanctification which

23 sight: if ye continue in the faith grounded and settled, and *be* not moved away from the hope of the Gospel, which ye have heard, *and* which was preached to every creature which is under heaven; whereof I Paul am made a minister.

24 Who now rejoice in my sufferings for you, and fill up ʸ that which is behind of the afflictions of Christ in my flesh for ᶻ his body's sake, which

25 is the church: whereof I am made a minister, according to the dispensation of God which is given to me for you, ⁵ to fulfil the word of God;

26 *even* ᵃ the mystery which hath been hid from ages and from generations,

27 but now is made manifest to his saints: to whom God would make known what *is* the riches of the glory of this mystery among the Gen-

A. D. 64.

ʸ 2 Cor. 1. 5.
2 Cor. 11.23-27.
Phil. 3. 10.
2 Tim. 1. 8.
2 Tim. 2. 10.
ᶻ Eph. 1. 23.
⁵ Or, fully to preach the word of God.
Rom. 15.19.
ᵃ Rom. 16.25.

Christ is made to the believer from the first (1 Cor. i. 30). **in his sight**—in God's sight, at Christ's appearing. **23. If**—'If at least' [*eige*]: not otherwise shall ye be so presented at His appearing (*v.* 22). **grounded** [*tethemeliomenoi*]—'fixed on the (right) *foundation*' (cf. note, Eph. iii. 17; Luke vi. 48, 49). **settled** [*hedraioi*]—'stedfast.' "Grounded" respects the *foundation*; "settled," the believer's internal *stedfastness* (1 Pet. v. 10). [1 Cor. xv. 58, the same, *hedraioi*.] **not moved away**—by the false teachers. **the hope of** (given by) **the Gospel** (Eph. i. 18), **which ye have heard, and which was preached to every creature which is under heaven; whereof I Paul am made a minister.** Three arguments against their being 'moved away from the Gospel:' (1.) Their having heard it when preached; (2.) The universal preaching of it; (3.) Paul's ministry in it. For [*en pasē tē ktisei*] 'in all the creation,' אABCΔG read [*en pasē ktisei*] 'in the hearing of) every creature.' Cf. *vv.* 6, 20; Mark xvi. 15: he implies that the Gospel from which he urges them *not to be moved* has this mark of truth—viz., the universality of its announcement, which accords with Christ's own prophetical command (Matt. xxiv. 14). Not merely '*is being preached*,' but *has been actually preached.* Pliny, not many years subsequently, in his famous letter to the emperor Trajan (B. X., Ep. 97), writes, 'Many of every age, rank, and sex are being brought to trial; for the contagion of that superstition (Christianity) has spread over not only cities, but villages and the country.' "I Paul am" [*egenomēn*] —'*was made* a minister.' The Gospel which ye heard from Epaphras, your "*minister*" (*v.* 7), is the same of which 'I was made a *minister*' (*v.* 25; Eph. iii. 7): if you be moved from it, ye will desert the teaching of Gospel ministers for false teachers. **24. Who.** So ΔGƒ*g*, Vulgate. But ABC omit "who:" 'Now I rejoice.' To enhance Christ's glory as paramount, he mentions his own sufferings for Christ's church. "Now" stands in contrast to '*I was made*,' in the past (*v.* 23). **for** [*huper*] **you**—'on your behalf,' that ye may be confirmed in resting solely on Christ (not on angels) by His glorification in my sufferings (Eph. iii. 1). **fill up** [*autanaplero*]: am filling up with a corresponding supply] **that which is behind** [*ta husteremata*]—'the deficiencies'—all that are lacking of the afflictions of Christ (note, 2 Cor. i. 5). Christ is 'afflicted in all His people's afflictions' (Isa. lxiii. 9). 'The Church is His body, in which He is, dwells, lives, and therefore also suffers' (*Vitringa*). Christ was destined to endure certain afflictions in this figurative body, as well as in His literal; 'that which was behind of these afflictions of *Christ*,' Paul 'filled up.' Christ's *meritorious sufferings in expiation for sin were once for all completely filled up on the cross*, and need not supplementing; but His Church (His second Self) has her complete measure of afflictions fixed, which He regards as

His. The more St. Paul, a member, endured, the less remain for the rest of the Church, the communion of saints giving them an interest in His sufferings (1 Cor. xii. 26). She is afflicted, to promote her completeness in Christ. Not one suffering is lost (Ps. lvi. 8). Rome's inference is utterly false, that the Church has a stock treasury of the merits and satisfactions of Christ and His apostles, out of which she dispenses indulgences: the context has no reference to sufferings in *expiation of sin* and productive of *merit.* Believers should regard their sufferings less in relation to themselves as individuals, and more as *parts of a grand whole*, carrying out God's perfect plan. "In my *flesh*" forms a beautiful contrast to 'His *body* the Church,' and answers to "in the body of His flesh" (*v.* 22; 2 Cor. iv. 11). **25. am**—Greek, 'I *was* made a minister:' resuming *v.* 23, end. There it was *of the Gospel*; here, *of the Church*: to be a minister of the *Church* is to be a minister of *the Gospel.* **dispensation** [*tēn oikonomian*]—the *stewardship* committed to me to dispense in the house of God, the Church, to the whole family of believers: my Master's goods (Luke xii. 42; 1 Cor. iv. 1, 2; ix. 17; Eph. iii. 2). **which is given** [*ten dotheisan*]—'which *was* given.' **for you** [*eis humas*]—with a view to you, Gentiles (*v.* 27; Rom. xv. 16, 19). **to fulfil**—to bring it fully to all: 'to fill up the measures of its foreordained universality' (*Ellicott*): the end of his stewardship. 'The *fulness* of Christ (*v.* 19) and that of the times (Eph. i. 10) required him so to do' (*Bengel*). **26. the mystery** (notes, Eph. i. 9, 10; iii. 5-9)—once hidden, now revealed: redemption for the whole Gentile world as well as for the Jews (*v.* 27). **from ages.** The mystery was hidden ever since the beginning of the "*ages*." The "ages" are the vast temporal periods which have elapsed from the beginning. [Greek, 'Æons:' used by the Gnostics for *angelic beings* emanating from God. The germs of Gnosticism already existed.] The Spirit, by Paul, presciently, in opposition (ch. ii. 18), teaches that the mystery of redemption was hidden in God's purposes in Christ, alike from the *angelic beings* (cf. Eph. iii. 9, 10) of the pre-Adamic "ages," and from the subsequent *human* "generations." [Greek, '*the* ages . . . the generations.' The "from" [*apo*], repeated before 'the generations,' shows that these are distinct from 'the ages,' and do not make them up, as *Ellicott* thinks.] **now** [*nuni*]—the present only; [*nun*, also the past and future]. **made manifest to his saints**—to His apostles and prophets primarily (Eph. iii. 5), and through them to *all* His saints. **27. would** [*ēthelēsen*]—'*willed* to make known.' He resolves all into God's *will*, that man should not glory save in God's grace. **what**—how inexhaustible! **the riches of the glory of this mystery.** He accumulates phrase on phrase to enhance the greatness of the blessing in Christ bestowed by God on the Gentiles (cf. Eph. i. 7;

444

28 tiles; which is Christ [6] in you, the hope of glory: whom we preach, warning every man, and teaching every man in all wisdom; that we may
29 present every man perfect in Christ Jesus: whereunto I also labour, striving according to his working, which worketh in me mightily.

2 FOR I would that ye knew what great [1] conflict I have for you, and *for* them at Laodicea, and *for* as many as have not seen my face in the
2 flesh; that [a] their hearts might be comforted, being knit together in love, and unto all [b] riches of the full assurance of understanding, to the

A.D. 64.

6 Or, among you

CHAP. 2.
1 Or, fear, or. care.
a Isa 40. 1.
2 Cor. 1. 6.
b 2 Pet. 3. 18.

---

iii. 8; ch. ii. 3). "*The glory* of this mystery" is the glory which this once hidden and now revealed truth makes you Gentiles partakers of; partly now, mainly when Christ shall come (Rom. v. 2; viii. 17, 18; Eph. i. 18; ch. iii. 4): for there follows 'Christ in you, the hope of *the* (so Greek) *glory*.' The lower was the degradation of you Gentiles, the higher is the richness of the glory to which the mystery revealed now raises you. You were 'without *Christ*, and having no *hope*' (Eph. ii. 12). Now you have '*Christ in you*, the *hope* of *the* glory' just mentioned. *Alford* translates 'Christ *among* you,' to answer to "this mystery *among* the Gentiles." But the whole clause, "Christ IN you (Eph. iii. 17), the hope of glory," answers to "the riches of the glory of this mystery," and not to the whole sentence, "this mystery *among* the Gentiles." The mystery *made known* 'among you Gentiles' is "Christ *in you* (now, by faith, as your *hidden* life, ch. iii. 3; Gal. ii. 20), the hope of glory" (your *hereafter to be manifested* life). This last antithesis proves it (Rom. v. 2; 1 Cor. ii. 7, 9; 2 Cor. iv. 17). 28. **preach** [*katangellomen*]—'announce.' **warning . . . teaching.** "Warning" leads to *repentance*, refers to *conduct*, and is addressed to the *heart*. "Teaching" leads to *faith*, refers to *doctrines*, and is addressed to the *intellect:* the two heads of evangelical teaching. **every . . . every man**—without distinction of Jew or Gentile, 'great or small (Rom. x. 12, 13). The repeated "every man" teaches ministers to deal with *individual* consciences. **in all wisdom**—with all the wisdom *in our method of teaching* that we possess (*Alford*). But v. 9, and ch. iii. 16, favour *Estius*—the *wisdom communicated to those being taught:* keeping back nothing, but instructing all in the perfect knowledge of the mysteries of faith, the true *wisdom* (cf. 1 Cor. ii. 6, 7; xii. 8; Eph. i. 17). **present**—what Christ does, Paul does (note, *v.* 22): at Christ's coming. **every man.** Paul is zealous lest the false teachers should seduce *one single* soul at Colosse. Each should be zealous for himself and his neighbour. Even one soul is of incalculable value. **perfect in Christ**—the *element in living union with* whom alone each can find *perfection; perfectly instructed* (Eph. iv. 13) in doctrine, and *full grown* in faith and practice. "Jesus" is omitted in אABΔGfg. C, Vulgate, have it. 29. **Whereunto**—viz., 'to present every man perfect in Christ.' **I also labour**—rather, 'I labour also' (2 Cor. vi. 5). I not only 'announce' (*v.* 28) Christ, but I *labour* also. **striving** [*agonizomenos*]—as in the agony of a "conflict" (ch. ii. 1) of spirit (cf. Rom. viii. 26). The same Greek is used of Epaphras (ch. iv. 12). So Jesus in Gethsemane when praying (Luke xxii. 44): so "strive" ('agonize') (Luke xiii. 24). So Jacob "*wrestled*" in prayer (Gen. xxxii. 24-29). Cf. Greek, 'agony,' 'striving earnestness' (1 Thess. ii. 2). **according to his working** [*energeian*]. Paul avows that he has energy to 'strive' in spirit for his converts, so far only as *Christ* energizes in him and by him (Eph. iii. 20; Phil. iv. 13). **mightily** [*en dunamei*]—'in power.'

445

CHAP. II. 1-23.—HIS STRIVINGS FOR THEIR STEDFASTNESS IN CHRIST—FROM WHOM HE WARNS THEM NOT TO BE LED AWAY BY FALSE WISDOM.

1. **For**—in that respect he 'laboured, *striving*' (ch. i. 29). Greek, 'I *wish you to know how* great a *striving* (the same Greek [*agona*] as ch. i. 29; fervent, *anxious prayer*, along with *outward trial*, ch. i. 24; not "striving" with the false teachers, which would have been impossible for him now in prison) I have for you.' **them at Laodicea**—exposed to the same danger from false teachers as the Colossians (cf. ch. iv. 16). This was the cause of his writing to Laodicea as well as to Colosse. Formerly called Diospolis, then Rhoas, finally Laodicea, from Laodice, wife of Antiochus II.: on the river Lycus, 18 miles west of Colosse, 6 miles south of Hierapolis. It suffered an earthquake (A.D. 62) about the date of this epistle; but was restored, so 'rich' was it (Rev. iii. 17), without aid from Rome. **not seen my face in the flesh**—including those in Hierapolis (ch. iv. 13). Paul considered himself a "debtor" to all the Gentiles (Rom. i. 14). His presence ("face") would have been a 'comfort' (*v.* 2; Acts xx. 38): ch. i. 4, 7, 8 shows he had not *seen*, but only *heard of* the Colossians. Hence he 'strives' with God in prayer for them, to make up for his bodily absence (cf. *v.* 5). 2. 'That their hearts *may* be comforted.' The "their," compared with "you" (*v.* 4), proves that in *v.* 1 the words "have not seen my face in the f'esh" is a *general* designation of those for whom Paul declares he has "striving," including the species, 'you (Colossians) and them at Laodicea.' For the prayer 'that *their* hearts may be comforted,' must include the Colossians, for whom he says, 'I have striving.' Thus it is abbreviated for, 'That *your and their* hearts may be comforted' (ch. iv. 8). Not as *Alford*, 'strengthened.' *Comforted* under the trial of false teachings, by knowing that Paul strove in prayer the more fervently, as not present with them; inasmuch as we are more anxious in behalf of absent than present friends; also by being released from doubts, on learning from the apostle that the doctrine which they had heard from Epaphras was true. In writing to churches which he instructed face to face, he enters into details, as a father directing his children. But to those among whom he had not been in person he treats of the general truths of salvation. **being** [*sumbibasthentes:* אABCΔ, for *sumbibasthentōn*]—'*they* being knit together.' The same Greek, Eph. 4. 16, "compacted." **in love**—the element of perfect *knitting together;* the antidote to the schismatical effect of false doctrine; love to God and to one another in Christ. **unto**—the end of their being "knit together." **all** (*the*) **riches of the full assurance** (1 Thess. i. 5; Heb. vi. 11; x. 22)—of *the* (Christian) understanding [*tes plerophorias tes suneseōs*]. The accumulation of phrases, not only "understanding," but "the full assurance of understanding;" not only this, but "the *riches* of," &c.: not only this, but '*all* the riches of,' &c., is to impress them with the momentous im-

acknowledgment of the mystery of God, and of the Father, and of Christ;

3, [2] in whom are hid all the treasures of wisdom and knowledge. And this

4, I say, lest any man should beguile you with enticing words. For though

5 I be absent in the flesh, yet am I with you in the spirit, joying and

6 beholding your order, and the stedfastness of your faith in Christ. As ye

7 have therefore received Christ Jesus the Lord, *so* walk ye in him; rooted and built up in him, and stablished in the faith, as ye have been taught, abounding therein with thanksgiving.

8 Beware [c] lest any man spoil you through philosophy and vain deceit, after [d] the tradition of men, after the [3] rudiments of the world, and not

A. D. 64.

[2] Or,
Wherein.
[c] Song 2. 15.
Jer. 29. 8.
Rom. 16. 17.
Eph. 5. 6.
Heb. 13. 9.
[d] Matt. 15. 2.
[3] Or,
elements.
Gal. 4. 3, 9.

portance of the *assurance* which rests on the Spirit's testimony, not merely the intellect. to—translate 'unto.' **acknowledgment** [*epignosin*] —'the full experimental knowledge: distinct from [*gnosis*] "knowledge," (*v.* 3). They did *acknowledge* the truth : what they wanted was the *full* experimental *knowledge* of it (notes, ch. i. 9, 10 ; Phil. i. 9). **of God, and of the Father, and of Christ.** B omits "and of the Father, and of :" 'of God (viz.) Christ.' "Christ" is in apposition, not to "God," but to "mystery" (ch. i. 27). א A C, Vulgate, read 'of God the Father of Christ.' Δ f, 'of the mystery of God, which (mystery) is Christ.' **3.** Greek order, 'In whom (not as *Alford*, "in which" *mystery :* Christ is Himself the "mystery," *v.* 2 ; 1 Tim. iii. 16) are all the treasures of wisdom and knowledge hidden.' The "all" answers to "all" in *v.* 2 ; as "treasures" answers to "riches :" it is from the *treasures* that *the riches* are derived. "Are" is the predicate : all the treasures ARE in Him ; *hidden* is predicated of the *manner* in which they are in Him. Like a mine of unknown wealth, the *treasures* of wisdom are all in Him, in a *hidden* manner (to which answers "mystery") : not in order to remain so : they only need to be explored to attain 'unto the riches' in them (*v.* 2) : until you press after *the full knowledge* (note, *v.* 2) of them, they remain 'hidden.' They do not immediately thrust themselves before carnal men's eyes, but so lie hidden as to be seen by those alone to whom God gives spiritual eyes. Cf. Matt. xiii. 44, "treasure hid." This sense sets aside *Alford's* objection, that 'the treasures are not hidden, but revealed.' The emphatic reserving of [*apokruphoi*] "hidden" to the end of the sentence, shows it is a second predicate ; not an epithet, 'the *secret treasures* of knowledge.' 'Hidden' answers to "mystery" (*v.* 2), designed by God, if we use our privileges, not to remain *hidden*, but to be revealed (cf. 1 Cor. ii. 7, 8). Still, as the mine is unfathomable, there will, through eternity, be always fresh treasures in Him to be drawn forth inexhaustibly from their hidden state. **wisdom**—*general ;* concerning *experimental* and *practical* truth : whence comes "understanding" (*v.* 2). **knowledge**—theoretical and *intellectual*, in regard to *doctrinal* truth : whence comes 'the full knowledge' (*v.* 2). **4.** And [δέ]—'Now.' Cf. with "lest any man," &c., *vv.* 8, 16, 18. Some blended Judaism with Oriental philosophy, and combined this mixture with Christianity. **enticing words**—plausible, as wearing the guise of *wisdom* and *humility* (*vv.* 18, 23). **5.** For—motive for their not being *beguiled ; i. e.*, regard to his personal authority as though he were present. **joying and** (joying *with you*, inasmuch as) **beholding your order**—your *good order* (cf. "knit together," *v.* 2). as a well-organized body. 'Good order gives stedfastness to a military phalanx : so in the Church, love establishes all things, and there being no schisms' (*Theophilus*) (cf. 1 Cor. xiv. 33, 40). **stedfastness** [*to stereoma*]—'the *solid foundation.*' As "order" expresses the out-

446

ward aspect, so "stedfastness" the inner basis ; not an abstract quality, but the *thing* in the concrete ; their "faith" is *the solid basis* on which rests their firm attitude. **6.** 'As therefore ye received (once for all : ch. i. 7 : *aorist*, from Epaphras) Jesus *the* Christ *as your* Lord (cf. 1 Cor. xii. 3 ; 2 Cor. iv. 5 ; Phil. iii. 8), so walk in Him : as the element of your walk' (Gal. ii. 20). Not merely, "ye received" the doctrine, but "Jesus" Himself (Eph. iv. 20), the essence of faith (John xiv. 21, 23 ; Gal. i. 16). Ye received once for all the Spirit of *life* in Christ : carry that life into your *walk* (Gal. v. 25) : the main scope of the epistle. **7.** (Having been) **Rooted** (Eph. iii. 17). **built up** [*epoikodomeunoi*]—'*being* builded up.' "Rooted" implies their *vitality ;* 'builded up,' massive *solidity.* As in the Song of Solomon, image is added to image, to express varied aspects of Divine truth. Thus 'walking,' a third image (*v.* 6), expresses the thought which "rooted" and "built," though each suggesting a thought peculiar to itself, could not express—viz., onward *motion.* "Rooted" is *past* [*errizomenoi*], implying their first vital grafting "in Him." Builded up is *present*, implying their progressive *increase* in union with Him. Eph. ii. 20 refers to the *Church ;* the passage here to their *individual* edification (Acts xx. 32). (Being) **stablished . . . as** —'even as.' **therein**—in the faith. **with thanksgiving**—to God as the Author of this whole blessing.

8. 'Beware ("Look" well) lest any *shall be* [as I fear there is : the indicative, *estai*] any man (pointing to some known seducer, Gal. i. 7) *leading you* (like others) *away as his spoil* [*humas sulagogōn*] through his philosophy,' &c. The apostle does not condemn *all* philosophy, but '*the* [current : *tēs*] philosophy' (associated inseparably with 'empty deceit,' by one preposition and one article to both) of the Judaic-oriental heretics at Colosse, afterwards developed into Gnosticism. You who may have "the *riches* of the *full* assurance" and "the *treasures* of wisdom" (*vv.* 2, 3, 9) should not suffer yourselves to be led away as a *spoil* by *empty* philosophy (in body, by ritualistic impositions, *vv.* 16, 21, 23 ; in mind, by heresies, *v.* 18). "Riches" are contrasted with spoil ; "full" with "vain," or *empty.* **after**—'according to.' **tradition of men**—opposed to "the fulness of *the Godhead.*" Rabinical traditions (Mark vii. 8). When men could not make revelation even *seem* to tell about deep mysteries which they were curious to pry into, they brought in human philosophy and pretended traditions to help it, as if one should bring a lamp to the sun-dial to find the hour ('Cautions for Times,' p. 85). The false teachers boasted of a higher wisdom, transmitted by tradition among the initiated ; in practice they enjoined asceticism, as though matter and the body were the sources of evil. Phrygia (in which was Colosse) had a propensity for the mystical and magical, which appeared in their worship of Cybele and subsequent Montanism. **rudiments of the world** (note, Gal.

9 after Christ. For ^e in him dwelleth all the fulness of the Godhead bodily.
10 And ^f ye are complete in him, which ^g is the head of all principality and
11 power: in whom also ye are ^h circumcised with the circumcision made
without hands, in putting off the body of the sins of the flesh by the
12 circumcision of Christ: buried ⁱ with him in baptism, wherein also ye are
risen with *him* through ^j the faith of the operation of God, who hath
13 raised him from the dead. And you, being dead in your sins and the
uncircumcision of your flesh, hath he quickened together with him,

A. D. 64.

e Isa. 7. 14.
  Isa. 9 6.
  John 1. 14.
  Rom. 9. 5.
f John 1. 16.
g 1 Pet. 3. 22.
h Jer. 4. 4.
i Rom. 6. 4.
j Eph. 3. 7.

iv. 3)—the elementary lessons "of the (outward) world," such as legal ordinances: our Judaic childhood's lessons (*vv.* 11, 16, 20; Gal. iv. 1-3). 'The *elements* of the world,' in the sense, *what is earthly, carnal, and outward*, are close akin to non-Christian 'rudiments of religion,' Judaical and heathenish. Any return to sensuous services now is essentially "worldly" (Heb. ix. 1). **not after Christ.** Their boasted higher "philosophy" is but human tradition—a cleaving to the worldly, not to Christ. Acknowledging Christ nominally, in spirit they deny him. **9. For**—'Because' all "philosophy" (*v.* 8) not "after Christ" is a delusion; "for in Him (alone) dwelleth" *permanently* [*katoikei*, not merely *paroikei*, sojourneth, *as in a temple*, &c.] **the fulness** (ch. i. 19; John xiv. 10) **of the Godhead.** [Theotes means the ESSENCE of the Godhead; not merely the *divine perfections*, 'theiotes.'] He, as man, was not merely God-like, but GOD. *We* have but an *earnest* of God's Spirit. **bodily**—not as before His incarnation, but "bodily" in Him as the incarnate Word (John i. 14, 18), now glorified (Phil. iii. 21). The Godhead not confined as in a body, but *in bodily fashion.* Believers, by union with Him, partake of His fulness of the Divine nature (note, Eph. iii. 19; 2 Pet. i. 4). **10. And**—And *therefore; And so.* Greek order, 'Ye are in Him (in union with Him) *filled full'* of all you need (John i. 16). Believers receive of the Divine unction flowing down from their Divine Head and High Priest (Ps. cxxxiii. 2). He is *full of the* "fulness" itself; we, *filled* from Him. Therefore ye Colossians need no supplementary sources of grace, such as the false teachers dream of. Christ is 'the Head of all *rule* and *authority*' [*archēs-exousias*] (Eph. i. 21): He, therefore, alone, not these subject 'authorities' also, is to be adored (*v.* 18). **11.** Implying that they did not need, as the Judaizers taught, outward circumcision, since they had already the inward spiritual reality. **are** [*perietmethete*]—' ye *were* (once for all) circumcised (spiritually, at your conversion and baptism, Rom. ii. 28, 29; Phil. iii. 3) with a (so the Greek) circumcision made without hands:' opposed to "the circumcision in the flesh *made by hands*" (Eph. ii. 11; Deut. x. 16; xxx. 6). So Christ's own body, by which the believer is sanctified, is "not made with hands" (Mark xiv. 58; Heb. ix. 11: cf. Dan. ii. 45). **in** (the, *your*) **putting off**—as an old garment (Eph. iv. 22): alluding to *putting off the foreskin* in circumcision. **the body of the sins of the flesh.** So C. But א A B Δ G *f g*, Vulgate, read 'the body of the flesh,' omitting "of the sins;" *i. e.*, "the body" of which the prominent feature is *fleshliness* (cf. Rom. vi. 6, "the body of sin;" viii. 13, where "flesh" and "the body" correspond). This fleshly body, in its *sensuousness*, is put off in baptism, the seal of regeneration, when received in repentance and faith. In circumcision the *foreskin* only was put off; in Christian regeneration 'the (whole) *body* of the flesh' is spiritually put off in its ideal, however imperfectly believers reach that ideal. Cf. ch. i. 22, "The body of His flesh," which is holy, necessitates

those incorporated with Him to put off 'the body of their flesh,' which is corrupt. **by**—Greek, '*in.*' **the circumcision of** (undergone by) **Christ.** Spiritual circumcision is realized in union with Christ, whose "circumcision" implies His having undertaken for us to keep the whole law (Luke ii. 21): identification with Him in all His obedience is the source of our justification and sanctification. *Ellicott*, 'The circumcision *originating from* (imparted in union with) Christ.' The former view better accords with *v.* 12; ch. iii. 1, 3, 4, similarly, makes the believer to have personal fellowship in the several states of Christ—viz., His death, resurrection, and appearing in glory. Nothing was done or suffered by our Mediator but has its counterpart in believers. The first shedding of His blood in circumcision, in fulfilment of the whole law, and the last shedding of it on the cross, vicariously justify, and, by union with Him, sanctify us. But *Pearson*, 'Joshua, the type (not Moses in the wilderness), circumcised the Israelites in Canaan (Josh. v. 2-9), born in the wilderness; the people that came out of Egypt, who were circumcised, having afterwards died in the wilderness. Jesus, the antitype, is the author of the true circumcision; therefore called "the circumcision of Christ." As Joshua was "Moses' minister," so Jesus, "minister of the circumcision for the truth of God" unto the Gentiles (Rom. xv. 8). **12.** '*Having been* buried with Him in your [*tō*] baptism:' coincident in time with the preceding 'ye were circumcised.' Baptism is the burial of the old carnal life, to which immersion symbolically corresponds: in warm climates, where *immersion* is safe, it is the mode most accordant with the significance of the ordinance; but the Spirit of the ordinance is kept by affusion, where immersion would be inconvenient: to insist on literal immersion in all cases would be legal ceremonialism (Rom. vi. 3, 4). **are risen** [*sunēgerthete*]—'*were raised* with Him;' answering to *emerging from* the baptism-water. **through the faith of, &c.** —*through your* faith *in* the operation [*energeias: the effectual working*] of God (so "faith of," *faith in*, Eph. iii. 12; Phil. iii. 9); viz., in raising again Jesus (Rom. iv. 24; x. 9). 'Faith is not the mean by which the grace is wrought, but the mean by which it is *accepted*' (*Waterland*, in *Ellicott*). Eph. i. 19, 20 accords. The same mighty power of God is exercised in raising one spiritually dead to the life of faith as was 'wrought in Christ when God raised Him literally from the dead.' As His resurrection is the ground of the power put forth in our spiritual resurrection now, so it is a pledge of our literal resurrection hereafter (Rom. viii. 11). **13. And you** (like others), being dead—formerly (Eph. ii. 1, 2); even as Christ was dead, before that God raised Him "from the dead" (*v.* 12). **sins**—rather, as at end of this verse, "trespasses," *transgressions* [*paraptomata*], actual *fallings aside*, as that of Adam. **uncircumcision of your flesh**—your not having put off the old fleshly nature (of which the *foreskin* was the visible badge), the foreskin of *original sin*, which now by spiritual circumcision you have put off (Jer. iv. 4). **he** (God)

14 having forgiven you all trespasses; blotting out the hand-writing of ordinances that was against us, which was contrary to us, and took it
15 out of the way, nailing it to his cross; *and,* ᵏhaving spoiled principalities and powers, he made a show of them openly, triumphing over them ⁴in it.
16 Let no man therefore ᶦjudge you ⁵in meat, or in drink, or ⁶in respect
17 of an holyday, or of the new moon, or of the sabbath *days:* which are

A. D. 64.

ᵏ Gen. 3, 15.
⁴ Or, in himself.
ᶦ Rom. 14. 3.
⁵ Or, for eating and drink ng.
⁶ Or, in part.

quickened together with Him—Christ (Rom. viii. 11; Eph. ii. 5). But *Ellicott,* because of *vv.* 14, 15, 'Christ—together with Himself.' What is wrought in Christ, is by the very fact wrought in all one with Him. As Christ's resurrection proved He was delivered from the sin laid on Him, so our spiritual quickening proves we have been forgiven our sins (1 Pet. iii. 22; iv. 1, 2). **forgiven you.** So B (*Lachman: Tischendorff* denies) C, Vulgate. ℵ A Δ G *f g* read 'us,' passing from the Colossians to the general church (ch. i. 14; Eph. i. 7). **all trespasses**—Greek, 'all *our* [*ta*] trespasses:' the cause of 'deadness.' **14. Blotting out** [*exaleipsas*] —'having wiped out:' synchronous with "having forgiven you," (*v.* 13): hereby having *cancelled* the law's indictment. The law (especially the *moral* law, wherein lay the chief difficulty in obeying) is abrogated to the believer, as far as it was a compulsory, accusing code, and as far as "righteousness" and "life" were sought for by it. It can only produce outward works; not inward obedience of the will, which flows from the Holy Spirit in the believer (Gal. ii. 19). **the handwriting of ordinances.** *Alford* [*dogmasin:* dative after the verb contained in *cheiro-graphon:* written] 'IN ordinances' (note, Eph. ii. 15). *Ellicott,* 'the hand-writing (in force) against us BY its *positive decrees*' (Rom. vii. 7, 8): its hostility to us was evinced in these. "The hand-writing" (the Decalogue, *written by the hand of* God) represents *the whole law,* the obligatory bond, under which all lay: the Jews primarily; secondarily, *the world,* of which the Jews were the representative people; in *their* inability to keep the law was involved the inability of the *Gentiles* also, in whose hearts "the work of the law was written" (Rom. ii. 15; iii. 19); as they did not keep this, they were condemned by it. **that was against us, which was contrary to us** [*hupenantion*]—'*adversary* to us:' so in Heb. x. 27. 'Not only was the law *against us* by its demands, but also *an adversary* to us by its accusations' (*Bengel*). *Tittmann* explains, 'having a *latent* contrariety to us:' not *open, designed* hostility, but virtual unintentional opposition through *our* frailty; not through opposition in *the law itself* to our good (Rom. vii. 7-12, 14; 1 Cor. xv. 56; Gal. iii. 21; Heb. x. 3). The "WRITING" "contrary to us" answers to "the *letter* killeth" (note, 2 Cor. iii. 6). **and took it** [*ērken*]—'hath taken it out of the way' (to be no longer a hindrance to us). Christ, by bearing the curse of the broken law, redeemed us from its curse (Gal. iii. 13). Having been punished Himself, He did away with both the sin and the punishment (*Chrysostom*). He included all the law in Himself, so that we being united to Him are united to the law as the law of love written in our hearts. In His person 'nailed to the cross,' the law itself (also the old serpent: John iii. 14; xii. 31, 32) was nailed to it (Rom. iii. 21; vii. 2, 4, 6). One mode of cancelling bonds was by striking a nail through the writing: this existed in Asia (*Grotius*). The bond cancelled was the obligation lying against the Jews as representatives of the world, attested by their *amen,* to keep the whole law under penalty of the curse (Deut. xxvii. 26; Neh. x. 29). **15.** [*Alford* takes *apekdusamenos* as

in ch. iii. 9.] Stripping off from Himself the rules and the authorities: GOD put off from Himself *the angels*—i. e., not employing them to promulgate the Gospel, as He had given the law by their "disposition" (Acts vii. 53; Gal. iii. 19; Heb. ii. 2, 5): God (*stripping off* the mediation of angels, as a kind of veil) manifested Himself without a veil in Jesus. 'THE principalities and THE powers' refer to *v.* 10, Jesus, "the Head of all principality and power," and ch. i. 16. In His sacrifice on the cross, God subjected all the principalities, &c., to Jesus, declaring them powerless as to His work and His people (Eph. i. 21). Paul's argument against those engrafting on Christianity Jewish observances, along with angel-worship, is, whatever part angels had under the law, is now at an end, God having put the legal dispensation itself away. But the context refers to a triumph over *bad angels. Ellicott,* 'Having stripped away from Himself the (hostile) principalities and powers' that sought, in His human nature, to win for themselves a victory. A strained sense. The Greek middle favours 'Having spoiled;' 'having *completely* stripped (of their power) *for Himself*' (cf. Rom. viii. 38, 39; 1 Cor. xv. 24; Eph. vi. 12: especially Matt. xii. 29; Luke xi. 22; Heb. ii. 14; 1 John iii. 8). [So Vulgate, *expolians;* and *Wahl, clavis.*] **made a show of them openly** —at His ascension (notes, Eph. iv. 8: confirming 'Having spoiled.') **openly** [*en parrhesia*]. John vii. 4; xi. 54, supports the English version against *Alford's,* 'in openness of speech;' and *Ellicott's,* 'with boldness.' **in it**—viz., His cross: so the Greek fathers. Many Latins, 'In *Himself,*' Christ. Eph. i. 20; ii. 5, 16 favour the English version. Demons, like other angels, were in heaven up to Christ's ascension, and influenced earth from thence. As heaven was not yet opened to man before Christ (John iii. 13), so it was not yet shut against demons (Job i. 6; ii. 1). But at the ascension Satan and his demons were "judged" and "cast out" by Christ's obedience unto death (John xii. 31; xvi. 11; Rev. xii. 5-10), and the Son of man was raised to the throne of God; thus His resurrection and ascension are an 'open' solemn triumph over the principalities and powers of death. The heathen oracles were silenced soon after Christ's ascension.

16. therefore—because, ye being complete in Christ, God has dispensed with all subordinate means as *essential* to acceptance with Him. **meat, or in drink** [*brosei, posei*]—'eating, drinking' (Rom. xiv. 1-17; 1 Tim. iv. 3). Pay no regard to any who judge you as to legal observances and foods. The Essenes drank water only. **holyday** [*heortēs*]—the greater feasts, yearly. Cf. the three, 1 Chr. xxiii. 31. **new moon**—*monthly.* **the sabbath.** Omit "THE:" not in the Greek (cf. note, Gal. iv. 10). 'SABBATHS' (not 'the Sabbaths') of the day of the atonement and feast of tabernacles end with the Jewish services to which they belonged (Lev. xxiii. 32, 37-39). The *weekly* Sabbath is permanent, having been instituted in Paradise long before the Mosaic law, to commemorate the completion of creation in six days. The typical *Sabbaths* (Heb. iv. 9) must remain till the antitypical *sabbatism* appears. Lev. xxiii. 38

18 a shadow of things to come; but the body *is* of Christ. Let no man beguile you of your reward [7] in a voluntary humility and worshipping of angels, intruding into those things which he hath not seen, vainly puffed 19 up by his fleshly mind, and not holding the Head, from which all the

expressly distinguishes "the Sabbaths of the Lord" from the other Sabbaths. In Rom. xiv. 5, 6 the oldest MSS. omit "He that regardeth not the day, to the Lord he doth not regard it." Some supposed a mystic virtue in the *seventh*-day Sabbath. Others esteemed it indifferent whether it was kept on the seventh or the first day. As the month of Israel's redemption from Egypt became the beginning of months, so the day of Christ's resurrection, which seals our redemption, is made the first-day Sabbath. The reputed epistle of Barnabas, which certainly existed in the second century; *Dionysius* of Corinth, writing to Rome A.D. 170; *Clement* of Alexandria, A.D. 194, speak of the Lord's day Sabbath. The judgment on the Jews for violating the Sabbath was remarkably retributive (2 Chr. xxxvi. 21). The Babylonians carried them captive, 'to fulfil the word of the Lord by Jeremiah, until the land had enjoyed her Sabbaths; for as long as she lay desolate, she kept Sabbath to fulfil *three score and ten years*' (cf. Lev. xxvi. 34-36). There are exactly 70 years of Sabbaths in the 490 from Saul's ascension, B.C. 1095, to B.C. 606, when Nebuchadnezzar carried away Jehoiakim. A *positive* precept is *right because it is commanded*, and ceases to be obligatory when abrogated; a moral precept is *commanded* eternally, *because it is* eternally *right*. If we could keep a perpetual Sabbath, as we shall hereafter, the positive precept, one in each week, would not be needed (Heb. iv. 9, *margin*; Isa. lxvi. 23). But we cannot, since even Adam, in innocence, needed one amidst earthly employments; therefore the Sabbath is still needed, and is linked with the other nine commandments, as obligatory in the Spirit, though the letter has been modified (Rom. xiii. 8-10). The permanent principle is the consecration of one day in seven. The fixing on the *first* day is due to Christ's appearings on that day, and apostolical usage. **17. things to come**—blessings of the Christian covenant. Cf. "ages to come"—*i. e.*, the Gospel dispensation (Eph. ii. 7; Heb. ii. 5, "the world to come"). **the body is of Christ.** The *real substance* (of the blessings 'shadowed' beforehand by the law) belongs to Christ (Heb. viii. 5; x. 1). **18. beguile you of your reward** [*katabrabeueto*]—*lit.*, 'to adjudge a prize out of hostility away from him who deserves it' (*Trench*). This *defrauding of their prize* the Colossians would suffer, by letting any self-constituted *judge* (*i. e.*, false teacher) draw them away from Christ, "the righteous Judge" and Awarder of the prize (Phil. iii. 14; 1 Cor. ix. 25; 2 Tim. iv. 8; Jas. i. 12; 1 Pet. v. 4), to angelworship. **in a voluntary humility** [*thelōn en tapeinophrosunē*]. So[*ethelo-threskeia*]'will-worship and *humility*' [*tapeinophrosunē*] (*v.* 23). Literally, 'delighting in humility' [Hebraism, *chapheetz be*]; *loving* (so the Greek, Mark xii. 38, "*love* to go in long clothing") to indulge *in a humility* of his own imposing: '*a volunteer in humility*' (*Dallæus*). Not as *Alford*, 'Let no one *of purpose* defraud you,' &c. Nor as *Grotius*, 'If he ever so much wish' (to defraud you). For 'wishing' or 'delighting' is one of the series of participles in the same category as 'intruding,' 'puffed up,' 'not holding:' the *self-pleasing* implied stands in happy contrast to the (mock) *humility* with which it is connected. His "humility" (Greek, translates *mind*'), so-called, is a *pleasing of self;* in parallelism to "his fleshly *mind*" (its real name, though he

styles it "humility"), as 'wishing' or 'delighting' is parallel to 'puffed up.' Under pretext of humility, as if they durst not come directly to God and Christ (like modern Rome), they invoked angels, and gave themselves secret names of angels (*Irenæus*, 'Adv. Hær.' i. 31, 32); as Judaizers, they justified this on the ground that the law was given by angels. So *Josephus* (B. I. ii. 8, 7) as to the Essenes. This error continued long in Phrygia (where Colosse and Laodicea were), so that the council of Laodicea (A.D. 360) framed its Thirty-fifth canon against the 'Angelici' (as *Augustine*, 'Hæreses,' 39, calls them), or 'invokers of angels.' As late as *Theodoret* there were oratories to Michael the archangel. The modern Greeks have a legend that Michael opened a chasm to draw off an inundation threatening the Colossian Christians. Once men admit the inferior powers to share invocation with the Supreme, the former gradually engross all serious worship, almost to the exclusion of the latter: thus the heathen, beginning with adding the worship of other deities to the Supreme, ended with ceasing to worship Him at all. Nor does it signify much whether we regard such as directly controlling us (the Pagan view), or as only *influencing* the Supreme in our behalf (Rome's view); because he from whom I expect happiness or misery, becomes the uppermost object in my mind, whether he *give*, or only *procure* it ('Cautions for Times.') Scripture opposes the idea of 'patrons' or 'intercessors' (1 Tim. ii. 5, 6). True humility joins consciousness of personal demerit with a sense of participation in the Divine life through Christ, and in the dignity of our adoption by God. Without this being realized, false self-humiliation results, displaying itself in ceremonies and asceticism (*v.* 23), which after all is but spiritual pride under the guise of humility. Contrast "glorying in the Lord" (1 Cor. i. 31). **intruding into those things which he hath not seen.** So C G *g*, Vulgate, and *Origen*. But א A B Δ *f* and Lucifer omit "not." [*Embateuōn*] 'haughtily treading on [*Erasmus; g, extollens se*] the things which he hath seen:' whether *fancied* visions of angels, or things *actually* seen by him, either of demoniacal origination (1 Sam. xxviii. 11-20) or resulting from natural causation, mistaken as supernatural. Paul, not stopping to discuss the nature of the things so seen, fixes on the radical error, the tendency of such a one to walk by SENSE (viz., what he *haughtily prides himself on having* SEEN), rather than by FAITH in the UNSEEN "Head" (*v.* 19: cf. John xx. 29; 2 Cor. v. 7; Heb. xi. 1). Thus the parallel, "vainly puffed up," explains 'haughtily treading on;' "his fleshly mind" answers to 'the things which he hath seen,' his fleshliness betraying itself in glorying in *what he hath seen*, rather than in the *unseen* objects of *faith*. Cf. 1 Tim. iv. 1, "Some shall depart from the *faith*, giving heed to seducing spirits and doctrines of *demons:*" a warning to spiritualists. **puffed up**—implying that the previous so-called "humility" ('lowliness of *mind*') was really a 'puffing up.' **fleshly mind** — Greek, 'by the *mind* of his own flesh.' How anomalous, that *mind* which ought to govern flesh, is itself sunk under *flesh*. The *flesh*, or sensuous principle, is the fountain whence his *mind* draws its craving after objects of *sight*, instead of, in true *humility* as a member, 'holding fast the (unseen) Head.'

body by joints and bands having nourishment ministered, and knit together, increaseth with the increase of God.

20 Wherefore, if ye be dead with Christ from the [8] rudiments of the world, why, as though living in the world, are ye subject to or-
21, dinances, (touch not; taste not; handle not; which all are to perish
22 with the using;) after the commandments and doctrines of men?
23 which things have indeed a show of wisdom in will - worship and humility, and [9] neglecting of the body; not in any honour to the satisfying of the flesh.

3   IF ye then [a] be risen with Christ, seek those [b] things which are above,

A. D. 64.
[8] Or, elements.
[9] Or, punishing. or, not sparing.
CHAP 3.
[a] Rom. 6 4,5. Gal 2. 19. Eph. 2. 6.
[b] Matt 6. 33.

Fleshliness can assume the spiritual form, pride of asceticism, when its grosser form is suppressed. **19.** ' Not holding *fast* [*kratōn*] the Head.' He who does not hold Christ solely and supremely does not hold Him at all. Want of firm holding to Christ sets him loose to (pry into, and so) ' tread haughtily (pride himself) on things which he hath seen.' Each must hold fast the Head for himself ; not merely be attached to the other members, however high in the body (*Alford*). **all the body**—*i. e.*, all the members (Eph. iv. 16). **joints** [*aphōn*]—the points of union where the supply passes to the different members, furnishing the body with materials of growth. **bands**—the sinews and nerves binding together limb and limb. Faith, love, and peace are the spiritual bands. Cf. *v.* 2 ; ch. iii. 14 ; Eph. iv. 3. **having nourishment ministered** [*epichoregoumenon*]—' receiving *free* and *ample* ministration ' continually : Greek, 2 Pet. i. 5, 8. **knit together**—compacted (Eph. iv. 16) ; firm consolidation. **with the increase of God** —i. e., *wrought by* God, the Author and Sustainer of spiritual life, in union with Christ (1 Cor. iii. 6) ; tending to the honour of God ; worthy of its Author. **20. Wherefore.** So ℵ C. But A B Δ G *f g*, Vulgate, omit "Wherefore." **if ye be dead** [*apethanete*]— ' if ye died (so as to be freed) from,' &c. (cf. Rom. vi. 2, vii. 2, 3 ; Gal. ii. 19). Christ died to the law when He bore its penalty, fulfilling all its claims. Argument from their sharing in Christ's death ; in ch. iii. 1, from their sharing in His resurrection. **rudiments of the world** (*v.* 8)—outward, worldly, legal ordinances. **as though living**—as though not dead to the world (in its non-Christian character), like your crucified Lord, whose death ye were buried (Gal. vi. 14 ; 1 Pet. iv. 1, 2), but *living* in it. **are ye subject to ordinances?**—why do ye submit to ordinances? You are again being made subject to "ordinances," the "hand writing" of which had been 'blotted out' (*v.* 14). **21.** Cf. *v.* 16. Instances of the "ordinances" (*v.* 20) in the words of their imposers. There is an ascending climax of superstitious prohibitions The first [*hapse*] is distinguished from the third [*thiges*] : the former means *close contact* and *retention*, the latter *momentary contact* (cf. 1 Cor vii. 1 ; John xx.17). [*Me mou haptou*] ' Hold me not,' ' Handle not, *neither* taste, *nor even touch*:' referring to eating and drinking.' ' *Handle* (hold) not' nor ' taste' with the *tongue*, 'nor even touch,' however slight the contact. **22. Which**—things, viz., the things handled, touched, and tasted. **are to perish**—'are (constituted by their very nature) for perishing [*phthoran destruction by corruption*] in their using up' [consumption : *apochresei*]. Therefore, they cannot really and lastingly defile (Matt. xv. 17, 18, 1 Cor vi. 13). **after**—according to *v.* 20, 21 All these 'ordinances' are according to human, not Divine, injunction. **doctrines** [*didaskalias*] - 'teachings.' **23.** (All) **Which things** [*hatina*] **have**—Greek, 'are having:' commonly **show**

of wisdom—'the *reputation* [*logon*] of wisdom.' **will-worship**—arbitrarily-invented : *would-be-worship*, devised by *self-will*, not God. So jealous is God of this, that He struck Nadab and Abihu dead for burning strange incense (Lev. x. 1-3). So Uzziah was stricken with leprosy for usurping the priest's office (2 Chr. xxvi. 16-21). Cf. the will-worship of Saul (1 Sam xiii. 8-14), for which he lost his throne. This ' voluntary worship' is the counterpart to "voluntary humility" (*v.* 18): both specious: the former seeming to do even *more* than God requires (as in Rome's dogmas), but really setting aside God's will for man's own: the latter seemingly self-abasing, really proud of man's self-willed "humility ;" whilst foregoing the dignity of direct communion with Christ, the Head, worshipping angels. **neglecting of the body** [*apheidia somatos*]—'not sparing of the body.' This rested on the Oriental theory that matter is the source of evil. This looked plausible (cf. 1 Cor. ix. 27 ; 1 Tim. iv. 8). **not in any honour**—of the body. As " neglecting of the body" describes asceticism *positively*, so this clause *negatively*: not paying any of the "honour" due to the body as redeemed by the blood of Christ. We should have a just estimation of ourselves, not in ourselves, but in Christ (Acts xiii. 46 ; 1 Cor. iii. 21 ; vi. 15 ; vii. 23 ; xii. 23, 24 ; 1 Thess. iv 4). True self-denial regards the spirit, not the forms of self-mortification in ' meats, which profit not those occupied therein' (Heb. xiii. 9), and is consistent with Christian self-respect, the "honour" which belongs to us as dedicated to the Lord. Cf. "vainly," *v.* 18. But *Ellicott*, ' not in any real *value*' [*timē*]. **to the satisfying of the flesh**—the *real* tendency of human ordinances of bodily asceticism, voluntary humility, and will-worship of angels. Whilst seeming to *deny* self and the *body*, they really are *pampering* the *flesh*. Thus " satisfying of the *flesh*" answers to "puffed up by his *fleshly* mind" (*v.* 18) ; so that "flesh" is used for 'the carnal nature,' opposed to the *spiritual :* not in the sense, "body." [*Plēsmonēn*] "Satisfying" implies *satiating to repletion*, or *excess*. "A surfeit to carnal sense in human tradition." (*Hilary the Deacon*, in *Bengel*). Tradition clogs heavenly perceptions. They put away true "honour," to ' *satiate to the full* THE FLESH.' Self-imposed ordinances gratify the flesh (viz., self), even when seeming to mortify it.

CHAP. III. 1-25.—EXHORTATIONS TO HEAVENLY AIMS, NOT EARTHLY, ON THE GROUND OF UNION TO THE RISEN SAVIOUR—TO MORTIFY THE OLD MAN, AND TO PUT ON THE NEW—IN CHARITY, HUMILITY, WORDS OF EDIFICATION, THANKFULNESS—RELATIVE DUTIES.

1. If (Seeing that) **ye then.** In ch. ii. 18, 23 he condemned the "fleshly mind:" in contrast he now says, 'If then ye were once for all raised (Greek, aorist) together with Christ' (viz., at your conversion and baptism, Rom. vi. 4): for death with Him implies also resurrection with Him (ch.

2 where Christ sitteth on the right hand of God. Set your [1] affection on
3 things above, not on things on the earth. For [c] ye are dead, [d] and your
4 life is hid with Christ in God. When [e] Christ, *who is* [f] our life, shall
   appear, then shall ye also appear with him in [g] glory.
5 Mortify therefore your members which are upon the earth; fornication,
   uncleanness, inordinate affection, evil concupiscence, and covetousness,
6 which is idolatry: for which things' sake the wrath of God cometh on
7 the children of disobedience. In the which ye also walked sometime,
8 when ye lived in them. But [h] now ye also put off all these; anger,

A. D. 64.

1 Or, mind.
[c] Gal. 2. 20.
[d] John 3. 16.
  2 Cor. 5. 7.
  Heb. 7. 25.
[e] 1 John 3. 2.
[f] John 11. 25.
1 Tim. 6. 14.
[g] Ps. 17. 15.
1 Cor. 15. 43.
[h] Jas. 1. 21.

---

ii. 20). **seek those things which are above** (Matt. vi. 33; Phil. iii. 20). **sitteth**—'where Christ is, sitting on the right hand of God' (Eph. i. 20): involving 'indisturbance, dominion, and judicature' (*Pearson*). The Head being quickened, the members are so with Him. Where He is, there they must be. The contrast is between the believer's former state, alive to the world, dead to God, and his present state, dead to the world, alive to God; and between the unbeliever's earthly abode and the believer's heavenly abode (1 Cor. xv. 47, 48). We are already seated there *in* Him as our Head; and hereafter shall be seated *by* Him, as the Bestower of bliss. As Elisha (2 Ki. ii. 2) said to Elijah, about to ascend, "As the Lord liveth . . . I will not leave thee:" so we must follow the ascended Saviour with the wings of our meditations and the chariots of our affections. We should trample upon our lusts, that our conversation may correspond to our Saviour's condition; that where the eyes of apostles were forced to leave Him, thither our thoughts may follow Him (Matt. vi. 21; John xii. 32) (*Pearson*). Of ourselves we can no more ascend than a bar of iron lift itself from the earth. But Christ's love is the magnet to draw us up (Eph. ii. 5, 6). The design of the Gospel is not so much to give rules, as to supply *motives* to holiness. 2. [*Ta anō phroneite*] 'Set your *mind* on (stronger than *seek*) the things above, not on the things,' &c. Contrast "who *mind* earthly things," Phil. iii. 19, with 20: Gal. iv. 26. Whatever we make an idol of will either be a cross, if we be believers, or a curse, if unbelievers. 3. (Greek aorist) 'For ye *died* once for all,' in your Head, Christ (Rom. vi. 4, 7, 10), with whom ye are one by faith (ch. ii. 12, 20). Not, Ye must die practically to the world in order to become dead with Christ; but the latter is assumed as *once for all* accomplished by Christ, our Representative, with whom we become identified in regeneration: then, develop this spiritual life in practice. 'No one longs for eternal, incorruptible, and immortal life, unless he be wearied of this temporal, corruptible, and mortal life' (*Augustine*). **your life** (*hath been and*) **is** [*kekruptai:* perfect, expressing the *continuous state* consequent on the previous aorist] **hid** (Ps. lxxxiii. 3)—like a seed buried in the earth (cf. "planted," Rom. vi. 5). Cf. Matt. xiii. 31, 33, "like unto leaven . . . *hid*." As Christ's glory now is hid from the world, so the believer's real inner life, in communion with Him, is hidden with Christ in God (the element and sphere *in* which the life is hid: 'in God,' at whose right hand Christ sitteth, *v*. 1, the express image of His person); but (*v*. 4) when Christ, its Source and Essence, shall manifest Himself in glory, then shall their hidden life be manifest. The Christian's secret communion with God now at times makes itself seen without his intending it (Matt. v. 14, 16); but his full manifestation is at Christ's (Matt. xiii. 43; Rom. viii. 19-23): his manifested life will be the natural development of his present inner life; "glory" will be its prominent characteristic

(1 Cor. xv. 43). 'It is not yet *manifested* what we shall be' (1 John iii. 2; 1 Pet. i. 7). As yet Christians do not always recognize the "life" of one another, and even at times doubt as to their own, (Ps. li.; Rom. vii.) 4. 'When Christ shall *be manifested*, who is our life (John xi. 25; xiv. 19; Gal. ii. 20), then shall ye also with Him *be manifested* in glory' (1 Pet. iv. 13). His non-manifestation is the pretext of unbelievers (2 Pet. iii. 4). The Spirit-imparted life our souls have now in Him shall be extended to our *bodies* (Rom. viii. 11, 17). **then**—and not till then. Those who expect a perfect church before then. The true Church is now militant. Rome errs in trying to set up a church now regnant. The Church shall be visible as perfect and reigning, when Christ shall be visibly manifested as her reigning Head. Rome, ceasing to look for Him in patient faith, has set up a visible mock-head, ante-dating the millennial kingdom. The papacy took to itself by robbery that glory which is an object of hope, and can only be reached by bearing the cross. When the Church became a harlot, she ceased to be a bride going to meet her Bridegroom. Hence the millennial kingdom ceased to be looked for (*Auberlen*). 5. **Mortify** [*nekrosate*]—'make a corpse of.' **therefore** (note, *v*. 3)—follow out to its consequence your *having once for all* died with Christ spiritually at your regeneration, by daily 'deadening your members,' of which, united, "the body of the sins of the flesh" consists (ch. ii. 11): kill the bodily "members," in so far as they are made the fleshly instruments of lust, the deadly foe of your new life (cf. Matt. v. 29, 30; Rom. vi. 19; vii. 5; viii. 13; Gal. v. 24, 25). **upon the earth**—where they find their support (cf. *v*. 2, "things on the earth"). See Eph. v. 3, 4. **inordinate affection** [*pathos*]—'lustful passion.' **evil concupiscence** — more general (*Alford*), the disorder of the *external* senses: 'lustfulness,' *lust within* (*Bengel*). **covetousness** [*tēn pleonexian*]—marked by the article as forming a genus by itself, distinct from the genus containing the various species just enumerated. A self-idolizing, grasping spirit; worse than [*philarguria*] "the love of money" (1 Tim. vi. 10). **which is** [*hetis*]—inasmuch as it is "idolatry." Cf. note, Eph. iv. 19, on its connection with impurity. *Self* and *mammon* are deified in the heart instead of God (Matt. vi. 24; note, Eph. v. 5). 6. (Note, Eph. v. 6.) 7. **walked sometime**—'once.' **when ye lived in them**—as in your very element (before ye became once for all dead with Christ to them): no wonder, then, that ye "*walked*" in them. Contrast '*living* in the Spirit,' and its consequence, '*walking* in the Spirit' (Gal. v. 25). The *living* comes first; the *walking* follows. 8. **But now**—that ye are no longer *living* in them. **ye also**—like other believers: answering to "ye also" (*v*. 7), like other unbelievers formerly. **put off**—imperative. **all these** [*ta panta*]—'the whole of these;' those just enumerated, and those which follow. **anger.**

451

wrath, malice, blasphemy, filthy communication out of your mouth.
9 Lie *not one to another, seeing that ye have put off the old man with
10 his deeds; and have put on the new *man*, which is *ʲrenewed in know-
11 ledge after the image of him that *ᵏcreated him: where there is neither
*ˡGreek nor Jew, circumcision nor uncircumcision, Barbarian, Scythian,
bond *nor* free: *ᵐbut Christ *is* all, and in all.
12 Put on therefore, *ⁿas the elect of God, holy and beloved, *ᵒbowels of
13 mercies, kindness, humbleness of mind, meekness, long-suffering; forbearing one another, and forgiving one another, if any man have a ²quarrel
14 against any: even as Christ forgave you, so also *do* ye. And above all
15 these things *ᵖput on* charity, which is the bond of perfectness. And let

A. D. 64.
i Lev. 19. 11.
Isa. 63. 8.
Jer. 9. 3, 5.
j Rom. 12. 2.
k Eph. 2. 10.
l Gal. 3. 28.
m Eph. 1. 23.
n 1 Pet. 1. 2.
o Gal. 5. 22.
Phil. 2. 1.
2 Or. complaint.
p Rom. 13. 8.

wrath, malice, blasphemy—rather, 'reviling,' 'evil-speaking' (note, Eph. iv. 31). **filthy communication.** The context favours 'foul language,' *abusiveness*, as well as *filthiness*. **9.** (Eph. iv. 22, 25) **put off** [*apekdusamenoi*]—'*wholly* put off.' The conditions into which they had entered rendered a selfish and untruthful life a self-contradiction (*Ellicott*). **the old man**—the unregenerate nature before conversion. **his deeds**—habits of acting (Gal. v. 24). **10. the new man.** [Here *neon* means 'the *recently*-put-on nature at regeneration (note, Eph. iv. 23, 24).] **which is renewed** [*anakainounenon*]—'which is being renewed;' viz., its development into a *perfectly renewed* nature continually progressing, by the Spirit's working (2 Cor. iv. 16; Titus iii. 5). **in knowledge**—rather [*epignosin*], 'unto perfect knowledge' (notes, Eph. i. 17; iv. 13; ch. i. 6, 9, 10; ii. 2). Perfect knowledge of God excludes sin (John xvii. 3). **after the image of him that created him**—viz., created the *new man* (Eph. ii. 10; iv. 23, 24). The new creation is analogous to the first (2 Cor. iv. 6). As man was made in the image of God naturally, so is he now spiritually. But the image of God formed in us by the Spirit is as much more glorious than that borne by Adam, as the Second Man, the Lord from heaven, is more glorious than the first (Gen. i. 26). *Holiness* constitutes our *chief* likeness to God, as originally. Adam, when fallen, begat a son in his own fallen likeness and image (Gen. v. 3). The "image" is claimed for man, 1 Cor. xi. 7; the "likeness," Jas. iii. 9. *Origen* ('Principia,' iii. 6) taught the *image* was something in which all were created, and which continued to man after the fall (Gen. ix. 6). The *likeness* was something *towards* which man was created, that he might strive after and attain it. *Trench* thinks God in the *double* statement in Gen. i. 26 contemplates both man's *first creation* and his being "*renewed* . . . after the image of Him that created him." **11. Where**—'Wherein;' viz., in the sphere of the renewed man. **neither Greek nor Jew, circumcision nor uncircumcision, Barbarian, Scythian, bond nor free.** 'There is *no such thing as* [*ouk eni*] Greek *and* Jew (difference of national privilege), circumcision *and* uncircumcision (difference of legal standing, Gal. vi. 15), bond man, free man (social difference).' The present Church is *called out of the flesh*, and the present *world-course* (Eph. ii. 2), wherein such distinctions exist, to life in the Spirit, and to the future first resurrection; because Satan has such power now over the flesh and the world. At Christ's coming, when Satan shall no longer rule the flesh and the world, the nations in the flesh and the world in millennial felicity shall be willing subjects of Christ and his glorified saints (Dan. vii. 14, 22, 27; Luke xix. 17, 19; Rev. xx. 1-6; iii. 21). Israel in Canaan typified that future state when the Jews, so miraculously preserved distinct in their dispersion, shall be the central Church of

the Christianized world. As Scripture abolishes the religious distinction of Jew and Greek now, so does it expressly foretell that, in the coming new order, Israel shall be first of the Christian nations; not for her own selfish aggrandizement, but for their good, as the medium of blessing to them. Finally, after the millennium, the life that is in Christ transfigures *nature* in the new heaven and the new earth; as, before, it transfigured the spiritual, then the political and social world. **Scythian**—heretofore more barbarian than the barbarians. Though 'bond and free' existed, yet, in relation to Christ, all alike were free, and yet servants of Christ (1 Cor. vii. 22; Gal. iii. 28). **Christ is all**—Christ combines all prerogatives and blessings, and absorbs in Himself all distinctions, being to all alike all they need for justification, sanctification, and glorification (1 Cor. i. 30; iii. 21-23; Gal. ii. 20). **in all**—who believe, without distinction; the sole distinction is, how much each draws from Christ. The unity of the divine life, shared in by all believers, counterbalances differences as great as that between the polished "Greek" and the rude "Scythian." Christianity imparts to the most uncivilized the only spring of sound culture, social and moral. **12. Put on therefore**—As you have put on the new man, put on all its characteristic qualities (*Ellicott*). **the elect of God**—no "the" in Greek (cf. 1 Thess. i. 4). As *chosen out* of darkness: answering to "seeing that ye have *put off* the old man" (*v.* 9). The order is, "elect . . holy . . beloved." *Election* from eternity precedes *sanctification* in time: the *sanctified*, feeling God's *love*, imitate it (*Bengel*). **bowels of mercies.** So B. But א A C G *f g*, Vulgate, read singular, 'mercy.' *Bowels* express yearning compassion, which we feel to act on our inward parts (Gen. xliii. 30; Jer. xxxi. 20; Luke i. 78, *margin*). **humbleness of mind**—true 'lowliness of mind:' thinking lowly, and therefore truly of ourselves; not the mock "humility" of the false teachers (note, Eph. iv. 2, 32; ch. ii. 23). **13. Forbearing**—as to present offences. **forgiving**—as to past. **one another** [*allēlon*] . . . **one another** [*heautois*]—lit., *yourselves: one* Christian "forbearing" *the other*; each "forgiving" all; so doing a benefit redounding to HIMSELF, he being included in the all, Christians being members of each other. **quarrel** [*momphen*] —'cause of complaint.' **Christ**—who had so infinitely greater cause of complaint against us (ch. ii. 13). So C. But A B Δ G *f g*, Vulgate, read 'the Lord.' א, 'God,' from Eph. iv. 32. **14. above** [*epi pasi*]—"over," as in Eph. vi. 16. **charity**—the crowning grace which covers others' sins (1 Pet. iv. 8), must *overlie* all the graces enumerated. **which is**—i. e., *for it is; lit., 'which thing* is.' **bond of** (belonging to) **perfectness**—its distinctive bond: an upper garment, *completing* and keeping together the whole suit, which without it would be loose. Seeming graces, where love is wanting,

q the peace of God rule in your hearts, *r* to the which also ye are called in *s* one body; and be ye thankful.

16   Let *t* the word of Christ dwell in you richly in all wisdom; teaching and admonishing one another in psalms and hymns and spiritual songs,

17   *u* singing with grace *v* in your hearts to the Lord. And *w* whatsoever ye do in word or deed, *do* all in the name of the Lord Jesus, giving *x* thanks to God and the Father by him.

18   Wives, submit yourselves unto your own husbands, as it is fit in the

19   Lord. Husbands, love *your* wives, and be not bitter against them.

20   Children, obey *your* parents in all things: for this is well-pleasing

21   unto the Lord. Fathers, provoke not your children *to anger*, lest they be discouraged.

22   Servants, obey in all things *your* masters according to the flesh; not with eye-service, as men-pleasers; but in singleness of heart, fearing

A. D. 64.

q Ps. 29. 11.
Isa. 26. 3.
John 14. 27.
Rom. 14. 17.
2 Cor. 5. 19-21.
Phil. 4. 7.
r 1 Cor. 7. 15.
s Eph. 2. 16.
Eph. 4. 4.
t Jer. 15. 16.
2 Tim. 3.15-17.
u Eph. 5. 19.
v ch. 4. 6.
w 1 Cor. 10.31.
x Rom. 1. 8.

are hypocrisy. Justification by faith is assumed as already realized (cf. *v.* 12, "elect of God, holy and beloved;" ch. ii. 12); so Rome's plea for justification by works is vain. Love and its works 'perfect'—*i. e., evidence, maturity* of faith (Matt. v. 44, 48, " Love . . . be ye . . . perfect," &c.; Rom. xiii. 8; 1 Cor. xiii.; 1 Tim. i. 5; Jas. ii. 21, 22; 1 John ii. 5; iv. 12). As to "bond," cf. ch. ii. 2, "*knit together* in love;" Eph. iv. 3, "the bond of peace." **15. peace of God.** From Phil. iv. 7. So C. But A B Δ G *j g*, Vulgate, read 'the peace of (coming from) CHRIST.' Therefore Christ is God. Peace was His legacy (John xiv. 27). Peace is peculiarly His to give: following *love* (*v.* 14; Eph. iv. 2, 3). **rule** —'as umpire' [*brabeueto*]: the same Greek verb simple as appears compounded, ch. ii. 18. The false teacher, as a self-constituted *umpire*, defrauds you of your prize; but if the peace of Christ, as umpire, rule in your hearts, your reward is sure. Let it act as umpire when wrong passions arise, and restrain them. Let not them rule, so that you should lose your prize. **in your hearts.** Many have a peaceful look and mouth, whilst war is *in their hearts* (Ps. xxviii. 3; lv. 21). **to the which**—*i. e.,* with a view to which state of Christian peace (Isa. xxvi. 3; 1 Cor. vii. 15). **ye are called** [*kai eklethete*]—'ye were also called:' besides Paul's exhortation, they have *also*, as a motive to "peace," their having been once for all called. (So as to remain) **in one body** (Eph. iv. 4). Its *unity* supposes "peace" among the members. **be** (become) **ye thankful**—for your 'calling.' Thanksgiving is prominent in St. Paul: forty-one times he uses the word. Not to have 'peace ruling in your hearts' would be inconsistent with the 'calling in one body,' and would be practical unthankfulness to God who called us (Eph. v. 4, 19, 20).

16. The form which 'thankfulness' (*v.* 15) ought to take. **Let the word of Christ**—the Gospel *word*, by which ye were called. Having exhorted to thankfulness, he also shows the way. **richly** (ch. ii. 2; Rom. xv. 14) **in all wisdom.** *Alford* joins with "teaching," &c.; for so ch. i. 28 has "teaching in all wisdom:" the two clauses thus correspond, 'In all wisdom teaching,' and 'in grace singing in your hearts' (so Greek order). The participles mark the outgoing in word and deed of 'Christ's word *dwelling within*' (Rom. viii. 11; 2 Tim. i. 5, 14). **and . . . and.** א B C Δ G *f g* read 'psalms, hymns, spiritual songs' (note, Eph. v. 19). In their family circles they were to be so full of the Word of Christ *in the heart* that the mouth should utter hymns of instruction, admonition, and praise (cf. Deut. vi. 7). *Tertullian* ('Apology' 39) records that at the love-feasts [*agapæ*], after the water had been furnished for

the hands, and the lights lit, according as any had remembrance of Scripture, or could compose, he was invited to sing praises to God for the common good. Paul contrasts the songs of Christians at social meetings with the bacchanalian, licentious songs of heathen feasts. Singing formed part of the entertainment at Greek banquets (cf. Jas. v. 13). **with grace** [*en te chariti*]—'IN grace,' the element in which singing is to be: '*the* grace' of the indwelling Spirit. This expresses the seat of true psalmody, whether private or public —viz., the *heart* as well as the voice (cf. *v.* 15); the psalm of love being in the heart before it finds vent by the lips, and even when not actually expressed, as in closet-worship. The Greek order forbids translating, "with grace in your hearts;" rather, 'singing in your hearts.' **to the Lord.** א and the oldest authorities read 'to God.' **17.** Lit., 'And every thing whatsoever ye do . . . do all,' &c.; *words* as well as *deeds*. **in the name of the Lord Jesus**—*as disciples called by His name as His;* seeking so to act as to gain His approval (Rom. xiv. 8; 1 Cor. x. 31; 2 Cor. v. 15; 1 Pet. iv. 11: cf. *v.* 18, and *v.* 11, end). 'In that spiritual element which His name betokens' (*Ellicott*). **God and the Father.** A B C א omit "and," which crept in from Eph. v. 20. **by** (through) **him**—as the channel of His grace to us, and of our thanksgiving to Him (John xiv. 6, end).

18. unto your own husbands. א A B C Δ G *f g*, Vulgate, omit [*idiois*] "own," which crept in from Eph. v. 22. **as it is fit in the Lord** [*anēken*]— '*was* fit,' implying there was at Colosse some failure in this; 'as was your duty as disciples of the Lord.' **19.** (Eph. iv. 31; v. 22-23) **be not bitter** —ill-tempered, provoking. Many polite abroad are rude at home, because they are not afraid there. **20.** (Eph. vi. 1) **obey** [*hupakouo*]—not merely "submit yourselves" to the authority (*v.* 18), as wives ought [*hupotassesthe*], but *obey* the command. **unto the Lord.** א A B C Δ G *f g*, Vulgate, read 'IN the Lord;' *i. e.,* this is acceptable to God when done *in the Lord;* viz., from faith, as disciples in union with the Lord. **21.** '*Irritate* not' [*erethizete*]. So B. But א A C Δ G [*parorgizete*], *provoke to wrath;* perhaps a conformation to Eph. vi. 4. By perpetual fault-finding "children" are [*athumosin*] 'disheartened,' seeing the parents so hard to please. A broken-down spirit is fatal to youth.

22. (Eph. vi. 5, 6) **masters** [*kuriois*]—implying *rule: despotes* would imply *absolute tyranny*. **eye-service**—Greek, 'in eye-services.' To fear God is, when, though none see, we do no *evil;* but if we do, it is not God, but men, whom we fear. **singleness** —without duplicity [*haploteti, 'simplicity'*]. **fearing God.** So C. But א A B Δ G read 'the Lord.'

453

23 God : and whatsoever ye do, do *it* heartily, as to the Lord, and not
24 unto men ; knowing that of the Lord ye shall receive the reward of the
25 inheritance : for ye serve the Lord Christ. But he that doeth wrong
shall receive for the wrong which he hath done ; and there is no respect
of persons.

4 MASTERS, *a* give unto *your* servants that which is just and equal ;
knowing that ye also have a Master in heaven.

2, Continue *b* in prayer, and watch in the same with thanksgiving ; withal
3 *c* praying also for us, that God would *d* open unto us a door of utterance,
4 to speak *e* the mystery of Christ, *f* for which I am also in bonds : that I
may make it manifest, as I ought to speak.

5 Walk *g* in wisdom toward them that are without, redeeming the time.
6 Let your speech *be* alway *h* with grace, seasoned *i* with salt, *j* that ye may
know how ye ought to answer every man.

7 All my state shall Tychicus declare unto you, *who is* a beloved brother,
8 and a faithful minister and fellow-servant in the Lord : whom I have
sent unto you for the same purpose, that he might know your estate,

A. D. 64.

CHAP. 4.
a Lev. 19. 13.
Mal. 3. 5.
Eph. 6. 9.
b Luke 18. 1.
Rom 12.12.
Eph. 6. 18.
1 Thes.5.17.
c Eph. 6. 19.
2 Thes. 3. 1.
d 1 Cor 16. 9.
2 Cor. 2. 12.
e Matt. 13.11.
1 Cor. 4. 1.
f Eph. 6.20.
Phil. 1. 7.
g Eph. 5. 15.
1 Thes.4.12.
h Eccl 10. 12.
i Mark 9. 50.
j 1 Pet. 3. 15.

23. And. Omitted in A B C Δ G*fg*, Vulgate (cf. Eph.
vi. 7, 8). Cf. the same principle in Hezekiah (2
Chr. xxxi. 21 ; Rom. xii. 11). **do, do it.** Distinct
verbs [*polēte, ergazesthe*] ; ‘whatsoever ye *do, work
at* it’ (*labour at* it). **heartily**—not from servile
constraint, but ‘from the soul’ or heart [*ek
psuchēs*]. **24. reward** [*antapodosin*] **of the inheritance**—‘Knowing that it is from the Lord (the
Fountain of reward) ye shall receive the recompence (which will amply amend for your having
no possession, as slaves, now), consisting of the
inheritance’ (a term excluding merit by *works :*
it is all of grace, Rom. iv. 14 ; Gal. iii. 18 ; 1 Pet.
i. 4). **for ye serve.** א A B C Δ, Vulgate, omit
“for.” Translate as Vulgate, ‘serve ye the Lord
Christ’ (cf. *v.* 23 ; 1 Cor. vii. 22, 23). **25. But.**
A B C Δ G*fg*, Vulgate, read ‘For,’ which accords
with ‘serve ye,’ &c. (*v.* 24) : *for* gives a motive for
obeying the precept. Serve ye the Lord Christ ;
leave your wrongs as slaves in His hands to put to
rights : ‘For he (the master) that doeth wrong
shall receive *back* [*komisetai*] *the wrong* which he
hath done (just retribution in kind) ; and there is
no respect of persons’ with the coming Great
Judge. He favours the master no more than the
slave (Rev. vi. 15).

CHAP. IV. 1-18.—EXHORTATIONS TO PRAYER—
WISDOM TOWARDS THE UNCONVERTED—AS TO
THE BEARERS OF THE EPISTLE, TYCHICUS AND
ONESIMUS—CLOSING SALUTATIONS.

1. give [*parechestlie*]—‘afford on your side.’ **equal**
[*tēn isotēta*]. As the slaves owe duties to you, so
you *equally* owe to them duties as masters. Cf.
note, Eph. vi. 9, where the master’s duty *negatively*
is added. *Ellicott*, ‘equity,’ which gives a liberal
interpretation of justice in common matters (Phil.
16). **knowing** (ch. iii. 24) **that ye also**—as well as
they.

2. Continue [*proskartereite*]—‘Continue perseveringly’ (Rom. xii. 12 ; Eph. vi. 18). **in** (*your : tē*)
prayer (1 Pet. iv. 7). **watch in the same**—in
prayer : watching against our natural indolence as
to, and in, prayer. **with** (*lit.*, IN) **thanksgiving**—
for everything, whether joyful or sorrowful, mercies temporal, spiritual, national, family, and
individual (1 Cor. xiv. 17 ; Phil. iv. 6 ; 1 Thess. v.
18). **3. for us**—myself and Timothy (ch. i. 1). **a
door of utterance**—‘a door for *the Word*.’ Not as
in Eph. vi. 19, where “utterance” is his request.
Here *an opportunity for preaching the Word*, by
removal of hindrances (1 Cor. xvi. 9 ; 2 Cor. ii. 12 ;
Phile. 22 ; Rev. iii. 8). **the mystery of Christ**
(ch. i. 27), **for which I am also**—*on account of*

which *I am* (not only “an ambassador,” Eph. vi.
20, but) ALSO (even) in *bonds* (2 Tim. ii. 9). Paul
asks their prayers for a door for the Word being
opened to him, that he might “make it (the
Gospel) manifest,” as he ought. His release from
prison might seem the best means for this. But
Phil. i. 12, 13, written somewhat later, shows that
it could be, and was opened, even whilst he
remained imprisoned.

5. (Notes, Eph. v. 15, 16) **in wisdom**—practical, Christian. **them that are without**—those not
in the Christian brotherhood (1 Cor. v. 12 ; 1 Thess.
iv. 12). The brethren, through love, will make
allowance for indiscretion in a brother ; the world
will make none. Be the more on your guard in
intercourse with the latter. Give no pretext for
unbelief. Contrive all means for their salvation.
redeeming the time (note, Eph. v. 16)—buying
up for yourselves, and *buying off* from worldly
vanities, the *opportunity*, whenever afforded you,
of good to yourselves and others. ‘*Forestall the
opportunity—i. e.*, buy up an article out of the
market, to make the largest profit from it’ (*Conybeare*). **6. with grace**—‘IN grace’ as its element,
investiture (Eph. iv. 29 ; ch. iii. 16). Contrast
those “of the world” who “therefore *speak of* the
world” (1 John iv. 5). Even the smallest leaf of
the believer should be full of the sap of the Holy
Spirit (Jer. xvii. 7, 8) : his conversation cheerful
without levity, serious without gloom. Cf. Luke
iv. 22 ; John vii. 46, Jesus’ speech. **seasoned
with salt**—*i. e.*, the *savour* of fresh spiritual
wisdom and earnestness, excluding all “corrupt
communication,” also tasteless *insipidity* (Matt. v.
13 ; Mark ix. 50 ; Eph. iv. 29). Cf. all the sacrifices *seasoned with salt* (Lev. ii. 13). Not far from
Colosse there was a salt lake : so the image here
is appropriate. **how ye ought to answer** (1 Pet.
iii. 15). This shows the “salt” means mainly
‘*wholesome point and pertinency*’ (*Ellicott*), commending itself to the hearers, to their edification.
every man. EACH is to be answered appropriately to his question, and to the spirit in which he
asks, whether his question be put sincerely or
insincerely, in ignorance or ill will (Prov. xxvi. 5).
So Jesus, Matt. xvi. 1-4 ; xxi. 24-27 ; Paul, Acts
xvii. 22, &c. ; xxiv. 25 ; xxvi.

7. Tychicus (note, Eph. vi. 21). **a beloved
brother**—*the* beloved brother ; the article marks
him as *well-known to them.* Three titles—“beloved brother,” in relation to the Christian community ; “a faithful minister,” in his missionary
services ; “fellow-servant” with the apostle in

9 and comfort your hearts; with [k]Onesimus, a faithful and beloved brother, who is *one* of you. They shall make known unto you all things which *are done* here.

10   Aristarchus [l]my fellow-prisoner saluteth you, and [m]Marcus, sister's son to Barnabas, (touching whom ye received commandments: if he come

11 unto you, receive him;) and Jesus, which is called Justus, who are of the circumcision. These only *are my* fellow-workers unto the kingdom of

12 God, which have been a comfort unto me. Epaphras, [n]who is *one* of you, a servant of Christ, saluteth you, always [1]labouring fervently for you in prayers, that ye may stand [o]perfect and [2]complete in all the will

13 of God. For I bear him record, that he hath a great zeal for you, and

14 them *that are* in Laodicea, and them in Hierapolis. Luke, [p]the beloved physician, and [q]Demas, greet you.

A. D. 64.

[b] Phile. 10.
[i] Acts 19. 29.
Acts 20. 4.
Acts 27. 2.
[m] Acts 15. 37.
2 Tim. 4.11.
[n] ch. 1. 7.
1 Or,
striving.
[o] Matt. 5. 4.
Phil. 3. 15.
Heb. 5. 14.
[2] Or, filled.
[P] Luke 1. 3.
Acts 1. 1.
[q] Phile. 24.

serving the same Master. **that he might** [*may:* γνῶ] **know your estate**—answering to *v. 7.* So C and Vulgate. But ℵ A B Δ G *f g,* 'that YE may know (*gnote*) OUR state.' Perhaps a confirmation to Eph. vi. 22. Paul was the more anxious to know the state of the Colossians, on account of the seductions to which they were exposed from false teachers; owing to which he had " great conflict " for them (ch. ii. 1). **comfort your hearts**— distressed by my imprisonment, as well as by your own trials. 9. **Onesimus**—the slave mentioned in Phile. 10, 16, " a brother beloved:" Paul's son in the faith; therefore sent with Tychicus as his safeguard, and put under the spiritual protection of the whole Colossian Church, as well as of Philemon his master. **a faithful and beloved brother** —'*the* faithful brother,' he being known to the Colossians as slave of Philemon, their fellow-townsman and fellow-Christian. **one of you**— belonging to your city. **They shall make known unto you all** (the) **things.** This repetition of " all " my state shall Tychicus declare unto you," favours the reading in *v.* 8, "that *he* might (may) know your estate." It is unlikely the same thing should be stated *thrice.*

10. Aristarchus—a Macedonian of Thessalonica, dragged into the theatre at Ephesus during the tumult with Gaius, they being "Paul's companions in travel." He accompanied Paul to Asia (Acts xix. 29; xx. 4; xxvii. 2), and subsequently to Rome. He was now at Rome with Paul, as he is here spoken of as Paul's "fellow-prisoner," but in Philemon 24, as Paul's "fellow-labourer;" and *vice versa,* Epaphras in Philemon 23, as his "fellow-prisoner," but here (ch. i. 7) "fellow-servant." *Meyer* conjectures that Paul's friends voluntarily shared his imprisonment by turns, Aristarchus being his fellow-prisoner when he wrote to the Colossians, Epaphras when he wrote to Philemon. [*Sunaichmalotos*] "Fellow-prisoner" is, lit., *fellow-captive;* one taken in warfare, Christians being "fellow-soldiers" (Phil. ii. 25; Phile. 2) whose warfare is "the good fight of faith;" variously represented by tradition as bishop of Apamea, Thessalonica, or one of the seventy disciples. **Marcus**—John Mark (Acts xii. 12, 25), the evangelist, according to tradition. **sister's son**—rather, ' cousin ' or ' kinsman to Barnabas:' who [*anepsios*], being the better known, is introduced to designate Mark. The relationship accounts for Barnabas' selection of Mark as his companion; also for Mark's mother's house at Jerusalem being the place of resort of Christians there. The family belonged to *Cyprus* (Acts iv. 36; xiii. 4, 13); this accounts for Barnabas' choice of Cyprus as the first station on their journey, and for Mark's accompanying them readily so far, it being the country of his family; and for Paul's rejecting him at the second journey for having not gone further

than Perga, in Pamphylia, but thence home to his mother, Mary, at Jerusalem (Matt. x. 37), on the first journey. **touching whom**—viz., Mark. **ye received commandments**—possibly *before* this epistle; or the "commandments" were *verbal* by Tychicus *accompanying this letter,* since the *past* tense was used by the ancients in relation to the time which it would be when the letter was read by the Colossians. Thus (Phile. 19), "I have written," for 'I write.' St. Paul's rejection of him on his second missionary journey, because he had turned back at Perga on the first journey (Acts xiii. 13; xv. 37-39), caused an alienation between himself and Barnabas. Christian love healed the breach: for here he implies his restored confidence in Mark, makes honourable allusion to Barnabas, and desires that those at Colosse, who regarded Mark in consequence of that past error with suspicion, should now "receive" him with kindness. Tradition represents him as first bishop of Alexandria, and martyred there. Colosse is only about 110 miles from Perga, and less than 20 from Pisidia, through which province Paul and Barnabas preached on their return during the same journey. Hence, though Paul had not personally visited the Colossians, they knew of Mark's past unfaithfulness, and needed this recommendation after the temporary cloud on him, so as to receive him as an evangelist. Again, in Paul's last imprisonment, he speaks highly of Mark (2 Tim. iv. 11). **11. Justus**—i. e., *righteous;* a common Jewish name [Hebrew, *tzadik*] (Acts i. 23). **of the circumcision**—Aristarchus, Marcus, and Jesus; therefore Epaphras, Luke, and Demas (*vv.* 12, 14), were *not* of the circumcision. This agrees with Luke's Gentile name (the same as Lucanus), and the Gentile aspect of his gospel. **These only, &c.**— viz., of the Jews. For the Jewish teachers were generally opposed to the apostle of the Gentiles. Epaphras, &c., were also fellow-labourers, but Gentiles. **unto**—i. e., in promoting the Gospel kingdom. **which have been** [*hoitines egenēthēsan*] —'which were *made*' men who proved a comfort to me. [*Paregoria, comfort* in forensic dangers; *paramuthia,* proved in domestic affliction (*Bengel*).] 12. **Christ.** So Δ G *f g.* But ℵ A B C, Vulgate, add 'Jesus.' **labouring fervently** [*agonizomenos*] —'striving earnestly' (as in ch. i. 29; ii. 1), *as in the agony of a contest.* **in** [*his: tais*] **prayers . . . complete.** ℵ A B C Δ G, read 'fully assured' [*peplerophoremenoi* (for *pepleromenoi*), without doubting; 'fully persuaded' (Rom. iv, 21; xiv. 5).] In 'perfect,' he refers to what he has already said, ch. i. 28; ii. 2; iii. 14. Having attained the *full maturity* of a Christian (Eph. iv. 13). **13. a great zeal.** ℵ A B C, Vulgate, have 'much *labour*' [*ponon* for *zelon*]. **for you**—lest you should be seduced (ch. ii. 4). How anxious then you should be for yourselves! **them** , , **in Laodicea** , , , **Hiera-**

15 Salute the brethren which are in Laodicea, and Nymphas, and the
16 church which is in his house. And when ᶜ this epistle is read among
you, cause that it be read also in the church of the Laodiceans; and that
17 ye likewise read the *epistle* from Laodicea. And say to ˢ Archippus,
Take heed to the ᵗ ministry which thou hast received in the Lord, that
thou fulfil it.
18 The salutation by the hand of me Paul. Remember ᵘ my bonds.
Grace *be* with you. Amen.

Written from Rome to the Colossians, by Tychicus and Onesimus.

A. D. 64.
ᶠ 1 Thes.5.27.
ˢ Phile. 2.
ᵗ Acts 1. 17.
Acts 14. 23.
1 Cor. 4. 1.
Eph 4. 11.
1 Tim. 4 6.
2 Tim. 1. 6.
2 Tim. 2. 2.
ᵘ 2 Tim. 1. 8.
Heb. 13. 3.

polis—churches probably founded by Epaphras, as the church in Colosse was. Hierapolis, 20 miles north-west of Colosse, famed for mineral springs and a mephitic cavern, 'Plutonium,' connected with the worship of Cybele. **14. Luke, the beloved physician** (the evangelist)—may have first become connected with Paul in professionally attending on him in the sickness under which he laboured in Phrygia and Galatia (where he was detained by sickness), in the early part of that journey wherein Luke first is found in his company (Acts xvi. 10 : cf. note, Gal. iv. 13). Thus the allusion to his medical profession is appropriate in writing to men of Phrygia. Luke ministered to Paul in his last imprisonment (2 Tim. iv. 11). **Demas**—included among his "fellow-labourers" (Phile. 24) ; afterwards a deserter from him through love of this world (2 Tim. iv. 10). He is last, and alone has no honourable or descriptive epithet. Perhaps, already, his real character was betraying itself.
15. Nymphas—of Laodicea, specified as a person of importance : contracted from Nymphodorus. **church which is in his house.** So ΔG*fg*, Vulgate, read. אAC,'THEIR house.' B,'HER house,' which makes Nymphas a woman. **16. the epistle from Laodicea**—my epistle to the Laodiceans, which you will get *from* them on applying to them. Not that to the Ephesians ; for it is very unlikely Paul should know that his letter to the Ephesians would have reached Laodicea at or near the time of the arrival of his letter to the Colossians. Cf. 1 Cor. v. 9, another epistle not preserved, as not designed by the Holy Spirit for further use than the local and temporary wants of a particular church. See 'Introductions' to the epistles to Ephesians and Colosians. The epistles from the apostles were publicly read in the church assemblies (*Ignatius*, 'ad Ephesum,' xii. ; *Polycarp* 'ad Philippenses,' iii. 11, 12 ; *Clement*, 'ad Corinthios,' i. 47 ; 1 Thess. v. 27 ; Rev. i. 3). Thus, they and the gospels were put on a level with the Old Testament, which were similarly read (Deut. xxxi. 11). It is possible that as the epistle to the Colossians was read to other churches besides Colosse, so the epistle to the Ephesians was read in various churches besides Ephesus ; and that Laodicea, being the last of such churches before Colosse, he might designate the epistle to the Ephesians here as "the epistle *from* Laodicea." But then the epistle to the Ephesians would *precede* that to the Colossians ; whereas the expansion in the former of the precepts in the latter favours the priority of the latter. **17. say to Archippus.** *The Colossians* (not merely the clergy) are directed,—'Speak *ye* to Archippus.' Scripture belongs to the *laity* as well as the clergy : laymen may profitably admonish the clergy in particular cases when they do so in meekness. Archippus was perhaps prevented from going to the church assembly by weak health or age (*Bengel*). "Fulfil" accords with his ministry being near its close (ch. i. 25 : cf. 'Introduction' and note, Phile. 2). However, "fulfil" may mean, as in 2 Tim. iv. 5, "*make full proof of* thy ministry"—a monition perhaps needed by Archippus. **in the Lord**—the element in which every work of the Christian, and especially the minister, is to be done (*v.* 7 ; 1 Cor. vii. 39 ; Phil. iv. 2).
18. St. Paul's autograph salutation (so 1 Cor. xvi. 21 ; note, Gal. vi. 11 : cf. 2 Thess. iii. 17, with ii. 2), attesting that this letter, though written by an amanuensis, is from himself. **Remember my bonds**—already mentioned, *v.* 3, and *v.* 10—an incentive to them to love and pray for him : still more, that they should, in reverential obedience to his monitions, shrink from the false teaching stigmatized, remembering what a conflict (ch. ii. 1) he had in their behalf amidst his *bonds*. 'His bonds moved over the paper as he wrote ; his (right) hand was chained to the (left hand of the) soldier who kept him' (*Alford*). **Grace be with you**—Greek, 'THE grace' which every Christian enjoys in some degree, flowing from God in Christ by the Holy Ghost (Titus iii. 15 ; Heb. xiii. 25).

456

THE FIRST EPISTLE OF PAUL THE APOSTLE TO THE
THESSALONIANS.

1 PAUL, and *a* Silvanus, and Timotheus, unto the church of the Thessa-
lonians *which is* *b* in God the Father and *in* the Lord Jesus Christ:
Grace *be* unto you, and peace, from God our Father, and the Lord Jesus
Christ.

2 We give thanks to God always for you all, making mention of you in
3 our prayers; remembering without ceasing your work of *c* faith, *d* and
labour of love, and patience of hope in our Lord Jesus Christ, in the
4 sight of God and our Father; knowing, brethren [1] beloved, *e* your election
5 of God. For our gospel came not unto you in word only, but also in

A. D. 54.

CHAP. 1.
a 2 Cor. 1. 19.
b John 14. 23.
c John 6. 29.
d Heb. 6. 10.
1 Or beloved
of God,
your
election.
e Col. 3. 12.

CHAP. I. 1-10. — ADDRESS — SALUTATION—
PRAYERFUL THANKSGIVING FOR THEIR FAITH,
HOPE, AND LOVE—THEIR FIRST RECEPTION OF
THE GOSPEL—THEIR GOOD INFLUENCE ON ALL
AROUND.

1. Paul. He does not add "an apostle," &c.,
because in their case, as in that of the Philippians
(note, Phil. i. 1), his apostolic authority needed
not substantiation. He writes familiarly as to
faithful friends, not but that his apostleship was
recognized among them (ch. ii. 6). On the other
hand, in writing to the Galatians, among whom
some called in question his apostleship, he strongly
asserts it in the superscription. An undesigned
propriety, evincing genuineness. **Silvanus** — a
'chief man among his brethren' (Acts xv. 22), a
'prophet' (*v.* 32), and one of the deputies who
carried the decree of the Jerusalem council to
Antioch. His age and position placed him before
"Timothy," then a youth (Acts xvi. 1; 1 Tim. iv.
12). Silvanus (the full form of "Silas") afterwards joined Peter, and is called in 1 Pet. v. 12,
"a faithful brother" (cf. 2 Cor. i. 19). They both
aided in planting the Thessalonian church, and
are therefore included in the address. This, the
first of St. Paul's epistles, being written before
various evils crept into the churches, is without
the censures found in other epistles. So realizing
was their Christian faith that they continually
were looking for the Lord Jesus. **unto the
church.** Not merely, as in the epistles to the
Romans, Ephesians, Colossians, Philippians, "to
the saints," or "the faithful at Thessalonica."
Though they probably had not yet the *final*
church-organization under *permanent* "bishops"
and deacons, which appears in the later epistles
(note Phil. i. 1; 1 and 2 Tim.), yet he designates
them by the honourable term "church," implying
their status as not merely isolated believers, but
a corporate body with spiritual rulers (ch. v. 12;
2 Cor. i. 1; Gal. i. 2). **in**—implying *vital union.*
God the Father — marking that they were no
longer *heathen.* **the Lord Jesus**—marking that
they were not *Jews,* but Christians. **Grace** [*charis,*
including *chairein,* 'joy,' the Greek 'greeting,' Jas.
i. 1] **be unto you, and peace**—may ye have in God
that *favour* and *peace* which men withhold. The
salutation in all the epistles of Paul, except the
three pastoral ones, which have "grace, mercy,
and peace." א A Δ *f,* Vulgate, support; B G *g*
omit "from God our Father and the Lord Jesus
Christ." It may have crept in from 1 Cor. i. 3; 2
Cor. i. 2.

2. (Rom. i. 8; 2 Tim. i. 3) The structure here,
each successive sentence repeating with greater

fulness the preceding, marks Paul's abounding
love and thankfulness: words are heaped on
words, to convey some idea of his exuberant feelings towards his converts. **We—I,** Silvanus, and
Timotheus. Rom. i. 9 has a different order; and so
does not prove *Alford's,* 'Making mention of you
in our *prayers without ceasing*' (*v.* 3). Rather,
"without ceasing," in the third verse, is parallel
to "always," in the second. His '*always* making
mention of them in his prayers' was due to his
'remembering *without ceasing* their work of faith,'
&c. **3. work of faith** —*the working reality of your
faith* (Rom. ii. 15). Not otiose assent, but *realizing, working faith* (Gal. v. 6); not "in word only,"
but in *one* continuous chain of "work" (singular,
not pural, *works*) (*vv.* 5-10; Jas. ii. 22). So 2
Thess. i. 11, "the work of faith:" *its perfected
development* (cf. Jas. i. 4). The other governing
substantives similarly mark the characteristic
manifestation of the grace which follows each in
the genitive. *Faith, love,* and *hope,* the three
great graces (ch. v. 8; 1 Cor. xiii. 13): *faith* producing *love,* and being the foundation of *hope.*
labour of love [*kopou*]—*toil* for others which *love*
prompts us to (ch. ii. 9: Rev. ii. 2). For instances see Acts xx. 35; Rom. xvi, 12. Not here
ministerial labours. Those who shun toil for others
love little (cf. Heb. vi. 10). **patience of hope**—
the *brave, persevering patience* under trials which
characterizes "hope." Rom. xv. 4 shows that
"patience" also nourishes "hope." **hope in our
Lord Jesus**—lit., '*of* our Lord Jesus;' viz., of
His coming (*v.* 10): a hope that looked beyond
all present things. **in the sight of God.** Your
'faith, hope, and love' were not merely such as
pass for genuine *before men,* but "in the sight of
God," the Searcher of hearts. Things are really
what they are before God. *Bengel* takes this
with "remembering." Whenever we *pray* we
remember before God your faith, hope, and love.
Our remembrance is one entertained in His presence, and in which His eye saw no insincerity.
(*Ellicott*). The absence of the article before
emprosthen favours this. But its separation from
"remembering" in the order, and its connection
with "your . . . faith," &c., support the former
view. **and** [*Tou Theou Kaipatros*] (both under one
article)—' in the sight of *Him who is* (at once) *God
and our Father.*' **4 Knowing**—as we know.
The three participles (*vv.* 2, 3, 4) give the *time,
manner,* and *reason* for 'giving thanks' (*v.* 2).
your election of God—rather [*ēgapēmenoi hupo
Theou*], 'beloved by God:' so Rom. i. 7. "Your
election" — *i. e., God elected you,* as individual
believers, to eternal life (Rom. xi. 5, 7; Col. iii. 12;

457

power, and in *f* the Holy Ghost, *g* and in much assurance; as ye *h* know
6 what manner of men we were among you for your sake. And ye became
followers of us, and of the Lord, having received the word in much
7 affliction, with joy of the Holy Ghost: so that ye were ensamples to all
8 that believe in Macedonia and Achaia. For from you *i* sounded out the
word of the Lord not only in Macedonia and Achaia, but also in every
place your faith to God-ward is spread abroad; so that we need not
9 to speak any thing. For they themselves show of us what manner of
entering in we had unto you, and how ye turned to God from idols to
10 serve the living and true God; and to *j* wait for his Son *k* from heaven,

A. D. 54.

f 2 Cor. 6. 6.
g Col 2. 2.
 Heb. 2. 3.
h 2 Thes. 3. 7.
i Rom 10.18.
j Rom. 2. 7.
 Phil 3. 20.
 Tit. 2. 13.
 Heb. 9. 28.
 2 Pet. 3. 12.
 Rev. 1. 7.
k Acts 1. 11.

2 Thess. ii. 13). **5. our gospel**—the gospel we preached. **came** [*egenēthē:* 'proved']—'was made,' by God, its Author. God's having made it in respect to you to be attended with such "power" is the proof that you are 'elect of God' (*v.* 4). **in power**—the Holy Spirit's efficacy clothing us with power (see end of verse; Acts i. 8; iv. 33; vi. 5, 8; 1 Cor. ii. 4) in preaching the Gospel, and making it in you the power of God unto salvation (Rom. i. 16). As "power" produces *faith*, so "the Holy Ghost," *love;* and "much assurance" (Col. ii. 2), *hope* (Heb. vi. 11), resting on faith (Heb. x. 22): *faith, love,* and *hope* (*v.* 3). The "much assurance" is (*Ellicott*) on the part of the *preachers.* But in Col. ii. 2; Heb. vi. 11; x. 22, the only other passages where the noun occurs, it is on the part of *believers:* however cf. Greek 2 Tim. iv. 17. **as ye know**—answering to "knowing;" i. e., *as* WE *know* (*v.* 4) your character as *the elect of God,* so YE *know* ours as *preachers.* **what manner of men we were** [*egenēthēmen*]—'we proved.' **for your sake**—with a view to your best interests: to win and confirm you. Ch. ii. 10-12 shows that, in "what manner of men we were among you," besides *power in preaching,* there is included also Paul's and his fellow-missionaries' *conduct* confirming their preaching: a strong motive to holy circumspection on the Thessalonians' part, so as to win those without (Col. iv. 5: cf. 1 Cor. ix. 19-23). **6. And ye**—answering to "*For our* gospel" (*v.* 5). **followers**—Greek, 'imitators.' The Thessalonians in their turn became "ensamples" (*v.* 7) for others to *imitate.* **of the Lord** —the apostle of the Father: who taught the Word, which he brought from heaven, under adversities (*Bengel*): the point in which they imitated Him and His apostles, *joyful acceptance* and witness for *the word in much affliction:* the second proof of their *election of God* (*v.* 4); *v.* 5 is the first (see note, *v.* 5). **received** [believingly *accepted: dexamenoi;* not merely *paralabontes,* ch. ii. 13] **the word in much affliction** (ch. ii. 14; iii. 2-5; Acts xvii. 5-10). **joy of**—i. e., *wrought by* "the Holy Ghost." "The oil of gladness" wherewith the Son of God was 'anointed above His fellows' (Ps. xlv. 7), is the same with which He, by the Spirit, anoints His fellows too (Isa. lxi. 1, 3; Rom. xiv. 17; 1 John ii. 20, 27). **7. ye were**—'Ye became' [*yenesthai*]. **ensamples** So א A C G *g,* read. B Δ *f,* Vulgate, 'ensample' (singular), the whole church being regarded as *one.* The *Macedonian* church of Philippi was the only one in Europe converted before the Thessalonians (Acts xvi. 12, &c.; ch. ii. 2). Therefore he means their past conduct is an ensample to all believers now; of whom he specifies those "in Macedonia and Achaia," because he was there since the conversion of the Thessalonians, and was now at Corinth in Achaia. "Macedonia" then comprised the whole northern portion of Greece; "Achaia," the southern, including Hellas and the Peloponese. **8. from you sounded out the word of the Lord.**

Not that they actually became missionaries; but by the *report* spread of their "faith" (cf. Rom. i. 8), and by Christian merchants of Thessalonica bearing in various directions "the word of the Lord," they were *virtually* missionaries, recommending the Gospel to all within their influence by word and by example (*v.* 7). "Sounded" [*exēchētai*] is an image from a trumpet filling with its clear-sounding *echo* all the surrounding places. also. א A B C Δ G *f g,* Vulgate, omit. **in every place.** Aquila and Priscilla, who had just come from Rome to Corinth, probably informed Paul of the report of the Thessalonian faith having reached the metropolis of the world (Acts xviii. 2). **to God-ward** —no longer directed to idols. **so that we need not to speak any thing**—to them in praise of your faith; "for (*v.* 9) they themselves" (the people in Macedonia and Achaia) know it already. **9.** Strictly there should follow, 'For they themselves show of YOU,' &c. Instead, he substitutes that which was the instrumental cause of the Thessalonians' conversion. "For they themselves show of US what manner of entering in we had *unto you.*" Cf. *v.* 5, which corresponds to this former clause, as *v.* 6 to the latter, "And how ye turned . . . from idols to serve . . . God," &c. Instead of *our* having "to speak anything" to them (in Macedonia and Achaia) in your praise (*v.* 8), 'they *themselves* (have the start of us in speaking of you, and) report [*apangellousin*] concerning us, what manner of (how effectual an) entrance we had unto you' (*v.* 5; ch. ii. 1). **the living and true God**—as opposed to the *dead* and *false* gods [Acts xiv. 15; 1 Cor. viii. 4; Gal. iv. 8; 1 John v. 20, 21, *elilim*] from which they "turned." Had they been *Jews,* it would have been, 'ye turned to *the Lord'* (Acts ix. 35). In the reading, Acts xvii. 4, "of the *devout Greeks* a great multitude," no mention is made of the conversion of *idolatrous* Gentiles at Thessalonica; but A D *d,* Vulgate, singularly coincides with the statement here: 'Of the devout AND of Greeks (viz., *idolaters*) a great multitude:' so *v.* 17, "the devout"—*i. e.,* Gentile proselytes to Judaism, form a separate class. However, B E א omit 'and.' Luke, even if not stating explicitly the conversion of idolaters at Thessalonica, states what accords with it, the conversion of 'not a few chief women,' and the rising of a tumult instigated indeed by Jews, but carried on by others, which could not have reached such a height if the preaching had not reached the Thessalonian *Gentiles* (Acts xvii. 5-8). **10.** This distinguishes them from the *Jews,* as *v.* 9, from the *idolatrous Gentiles.* To wait for the Lord's coming patiently [*anamenein*] is characteristic of a true believer, and was prominent amidst the graces of the Thessalonians (1 Cor. i. 7, 8). As *joy* is the characteristic feature of the epistle to the Philippians, so *hope,* of this epistle. His *coming* is seldom called His *return* (John xiv. 3); because the two advents are different phases of the same coming. The second coming shall have features

whom he raised from the dead, *even* Jesus, which delivered us from the wrath to come.

2   FOR yourselves, brethren, know our entrance in unto you, that it was

2 not in vain: but even after that we had suffered before, and were shamefully entreated, as ye know, at ^aPhilippi, we were bold in our God ^bto

3 speak unto you the gospel of God with much contention. For our ex-

4 hortation *was* not of deceit, nor of uncleanness, nor in guile: but as ^cwe were allowed of God to ^dbe put in trust with the Gospel, even so we

5 speak; not as pleasing men, but God, which ^etrieth our hearts. For neither at any time used we flattering words, as ye know, nor a cloak of

6 covetousness; God *is* witness: nor ^fof men sought we glory, neither of you, nor *yet* of others, when we might have ¹been burdensome, as the

7 apostles of Christ. But we were gentle among you, even as a nurse

A. D. 54.

CHAP. 2.
^a Acts 16 22.
^b Acts 4. 13,
    20, 31.
Acts 14. 3.
Acts 17. 2.
^c Pro. 4. 1-12.
1 Cor. 4. 15,
    16.
1 Cor. 7. 35.
1 Tim. 1.11.
^d Tit. 1. 3.
^e Pro. 17. 3.
^f John 5. 41.
1 Or, used
authority.

altogether new, so that it will not be a mere repetition of the first, or a mere coming *back.* **his Son . . . raised from the dead**—the grand proof of His Divine *Sonship* (Rom. i. 4). **delivered** [*ton rhuomenon*]—'who *delivereth us.*' Christ hath once for all *redeemed* us: He is '*our Deliverer*' ALWAYS. **wrath to come**—'the wrath which is coming' [present participle, *tēs erchomenēs*]: surely, as the principles of God's moral government are fixed (ch. v. 9; Col. iii. 6): the holy anger of God against sin, which, deeply considered, only serves to evince His love (*Ellicott*).

CHAP. II. 1-20.—HIS MANNER OF PREACHING, AND THEIRS OF RECEIVING, THE GOSPEL—HIS DESIRE TO HAVE RE-VISITED THEM FRUSTRATED BY SATAN.

1. For—confirming ch. i. 9. He discusses the manner of his preaching among them (cf. ch. i. 5 and former part of *v.* 9), from *vv.* 1-12; and the Thessalonians' reception of the word (cf. ch. i. 6, 7, and latter part of *v.* 9), from *vv.* 13-16. **yourselves.** Not only do strangers report it, but *you* know it to be true (*Alford*). **was** [*gegogen*]—rather, 'hath proved:' implying the *permanent* character of his preaching. **not in vain**—Greek, 'not vain;' *i. e.,* 'full of power' (ch. i. 5). **2. even after that we had suffered before**—at Philippi: a circumstance which would have deterred ordinary men from further preaching. **shamefully entreated**—ignominiously scourged (Acts xvi. 22, 23). **bold** (Acts iv. 29; Eph. vi. 20) **in our God.** The ground of our 'boldness in speech'—its element of existence—was our realizing God as "OUR God." **with** (IN) **much contention** [*agōni*]—*conflict* (Col. i. 29; ii. 1). Here *outward* conflict with persecutors, rather than *inward*, was what the missionaries had to endure (Acts xvii. 5, 6; Phil. i. 30). **3. For**—the ground of his 'boldness' (*v.* 2), his freedom from 'deceit [*planē*: imposture, before *men*], uncleanness, and guile' [*dolō*: before *God*, 2 Cor. iv. 2] (cf. 2 Cor. i. 12; ii. 17; Eph. iv. 14): *uncleanness* (towards *one's self*), impure self-seeking in gain (*v.* 5) or lust; such as actuated false teachers (2 Cor. xi. 18; 1 Tim. iii. 8; 2 Pet. ii. 10, 14; Jude 8; Rev. ii. 14, 15). So Simon Magus and Cerinthus. Deceivers do not expose themselves to danger. **exhortation** [*paraclesis*]—'consolation' as well as "exhortation." The same Gospel which exhorts comforts. Its first lesson is peace in believing amidst outward and inward sorrows. It comforts them that mourn (cf. *v.* 11; Isa. lxi. 2, 3; 2 Cor. i. 3, 4). **was** —rather, *is:* St. Paul's habitual preaching. **of . . . of**—*springing from: having its source in.* **4. as**—even as: marking the measure existing between their approval by God to preach and their actual performance of the commission (*Ellicott*). **allowed** [*dedokimasmetha*]—'we have been ap-

proved after trial.' This corresponds to 'God which *trieth* our hearts.' Approval as to sincerity depends solely on the grace of God (Acts ix. 15; 1 Cor. vii. 25; 2 Cor. iii. 5; 1 Tim. i. 11, 12). We are not self-constituted teachers. **not as pleasing** —not as aiming at pleasing men: characteristic of false teachers (Gal. i. 10). **5.** Appeal to their experience of him. **used we flattering words** [*en logo egenēthēmen*]—'came we to be in (use of) language of flattery.' **as ye know.** "Ye know" whether I *flattered* you: as to "covetousness," God, the Judge of hearts, alone can be "witness." Self-interest is the real aim of men-pleasing flattery (Dan. ii. 21). **cloak of**—*i. e.,* any specious guise to cloak "covetousness" [*pleonexias*: cupidity; grasping at more]. **6.** *Lit.,* 'Nor of men seeking glory.' The "of" [ἐξ] here is different from "of" [*apo*] in "of you . . . of others." The former means *originating from;* the latter, *on the part of.* Many teach heretical novelties, though not for gain, yet for "glory." Paul and his associates were free even from this motive (John v. 44). **we might have been burdensome**—*i. e.,* by claiming maintenance (*v.* 9; 2 Cor. xi. 9; xii. 16; 2 Thess. iii. 8). As, however, "glory" precedes, as well as "covetousness," the reference cannot be *restricted* to the latter. Translate, 'when we might have borne heavily upon you,' *with the weight* of self-glorifying *authority,* and *with the burden* of our *sustenance.* Thus the antithesis is appropriate, "But we were *gentle* (the opposite of *pressing weightily*) among you" (*v.* 7). On *weight* being connected with authority, cf. note, 1 Cor. iv. 21; 2 Cor. x. 10. On the other hand, *Ellicott's restriction* [*en barei einai*] to 'we might have used authority,' is against *v.* 9, which uses a kindred word [*epibaresai*] for "chargeable." Twice he received supplies from Philippi at Thessalonica (Phil. iv. 16). **as the** (no "the" in Greek) **apostles** —in the wider sense, including Silvanus and Timothy. **7. we were** [*egenethemen*]—'we were *made*' by God's grace. **gentle** [*ēpioi*] (so A C)— '*mild* in bearing with the faults of others;' gentle (though firm) in reproving (2 Tim. ii. 24). אBΔ G *fg*, Vulgate, read 'we became [*nēpioi*] *little children*' (cf. Matt. xviii. 3, 4). "Gentle" forms a better antithesis to *v.* 6, and harmonizes better with what follows. He would hardly, in the same sentence, compare himself both to the 'little children' and to "a nurse," or 'suckling mother' [*trophos*]. *Gentleness* is the fitting characteristic of *a nurse.* Still, the very *difficulty* renders it unlikely that 'little children' is due to *correctors;* and the weight of authorities is for it (1 Cor. xiv. 20). But the *n* may have been *accidentally* transferred from the end of *egenethemen* to the beginning of *ēpioi.* **among you**—Greek, 'in the midst of you,' laying aside authority: *as one of yourselves,*

459

8 cherisheth her children: so being affectionately desirous of you, we were
willing *g*to have imparted unto you, not the gospel of God only, but
9 also our *h*own souls, because ye were dear unto us. For ye remember,
brethren, our labour and travail: for labouring night and day, because
*i*we would not be chargeable unto any of you, we preached unto you the
10 gospel of God. Ye *are* witnesses, and God *also*, how holily and justly
11 and unblameably we behaved ourselves among you that believe: as ye
know how we exhorted and comforted and charged every one of you, as a
12 father *doth* his children, that *j*ye would walk worthy of God, who hath
called you unto his kingdom and glory.
13 For this cause also thank we God without ceasing, because, when ye
received the word of God which ye heard of us, ye received *it* *k*not *as* the

A. D. 54.

g Rom. 1. 11.
Rom. 15. 29.
h 2 Cor. 12. 15.
i 1 Cor 9. 7, 18.
2 Cor. 11. 9.
j Gal. 5. 16.
Eph. 4. 1.
Col. 1. 10.
1 Pet. 1. 15.
k Matt. 10. 40.
Luke 5. 1.
Rom. 10. 17.
Heb. 4. 12.

her [*ta heautēs*]—'*her own* children' (cf. *v.* 11).
So Gal. iv. 19. How tenderly the mother nurses
her own! **8. So.** '*As* a nurse cherisheth, &c., *so*
we were willing,' &c. (*Alford*). Rather, "So;"
i. e., *seeing that we have such an affection for you.*
being affectionately desirous. [A ℵ B C Δ G read
homeiromenoi for *himeiromenoi*: from *homou eirein*].
Lit., *connecting one's self with another:* closely
attached to. **willing** [*eudokoumen* is stronger]—
'we were *well content:*' 'we would *gladly* have
imparted,' &c., 'even our own *souls*, the centre of
our being, our *lives*' [*psuchas*]; as we showed in
what we endured in giving you the Gospel, (Acts
xvii.). As a nursing mother would impart not
only her milk to her children, but her life for
them, so we not only imparted gladly the spiritual
milk of the Word to you, but risked our lives for
your spiritual nourishment, imitating Him who
laid down His life for His friends, the greatest
proof of love (John xv. 13: cf. the type, 2 Sam.
xxiv. 17). **ye were** [*egenethete*]—'ye were become;'
as our spiritual children. **dear** [*agapetoi*]—'dearly
beloved.' **9.labour and travail** [*kopon*]. "Labour"
means *hardship in bearing;* [*mochthon*] "travail,"
hardship in doing: the former, *toil* with solicitude;
the latter, *weariness* through fatigue (*Grotius*).
Zanchius, the former *spiritual* (ch. iii. 5), the latter
manual, labour. I would translate, 'weariness (so
2 Cor. xi. 27) and toil' [hard labour] from *mogis
megas*, implying the *magnitude* of the obstacles to
be overcome] (*Ellicott*). **for.** Omitted in the oldest
MSS. **labouring** [*ergazomenoi*]—'working;' viz.,
at tent-making (Acts xviii. 3). **night and day.**
The Jews reckoned from sunset to sunset, so that
night is put before day (cf. Acts xx. 31). Their
manual labours for a livelihood had to be not only
by day, but by *night* also, in the intervals between spiritual labours. **because we would not
be chargeable** [*pros to mē epibaresai*]—'*with a view
to* not *burdening* any of' you' (2 Cor. xi. 9, 10).
preached unto you [*eis*]—'*unto and among you.*'
The 'three Sabbaths' mentioned, Acts xvii. 2,
refer merely to the time of his preaching *to the
Jews in the synagogue*. When rejected by them as
a body, after having converted a few, he turned
to the Gentiles: of these (whom he must have
preached to *in a place distinct from the synagogue*)
'a great multitude believed' (Acts xvii. 4, where
A Δ (not ℵ B E) read 'of the devout (proselytes)
AND Greeks a great multitude.' In *v.* 17 "the
devout" are made a distinct class): then after he
had, by labours *among the Gentiles* for some time,
gathered many converts, the Jews, provoked by
his success, assaulted Jason's house, and drove
him away. His receiving "once and again," in
Thessalonica, supplies from Philippi, implies a
longer stay at Thessalonica than three weeks
(Phil. iv. 16). If "and" be omitted (Acts xvii. 4),
the conversion of "devout Greeks" would naturally lead the apostle on to preach to *heathen.* **10.**

Ye are witnesses—as to our outward conduct.
God—as to our inner motives. **holily**—towards
God. **justly**—towards men. **unblameably**—as to
ourselves. **behaved ourselves** [*egenethemen*]—
'were made to be;' viz., by God. **among you
that believe**—*Alford*, '*before* (i. e., in the eyes of)
you that believe:' whatever we seemed to the
unbelieving. As *v.* 9 refers to their outward
occupation, so *v.* 10 to their character among
believers. *Ellicott*, '*to* you that believe:' *for
your interest*. Their being *believers* would enable
them to appreciate his 'behaviour' *in respect to*
them. **11. exhorted and comforted.** *Exhortation*
leads one to do a thing willingly; *consolation*, to
do it joyfully (ch. v. 14). Even in 'exhortation'
[*parakalountes*] there is the additional idea of
comforting and *advocating* one's cause: 'encourag-
ingly exhorted.' Appropriate here, as the Thessalonians were in sorrow, through persecutions,
and also through deaths of friends (ch. iv. 13).
charged—'conjured solemnly' [*marturoumenoi*],
'testifying,' as before God. **every one of you**—
in private, *individually* (Acts xx. 20), as well as
publicly. Marvellous, that in such a multitude
he should not omit one (*Chrysostom*). The minister must not deal merely in generalities, but must
particularize. This special instance illustrated
his general behaviour. **as a father**—with mild
gravity *instructs;* the 'mother' tenderly *nurses*
and *cherishes* (*v.* 7). **his**—'*his own* children.' **12.
worthy of God**—"worthy *of the Lord*" (Col. i. 10);
'worthily *of the saints*' (Rom. xvi. 2, Greek);
". . . *of the Gospel*" (Phil. i. 27); "worthy *of the
vocation* wherewith ye are called" (Eph. iv. 1).
Inconsistency would cause God's name to be
"blasphemed among the Gentiles" (Rom. ii. 24).
[*Tou Theou tou kalountos*] 'Worthy of THE God
who is calling you continually to a worthy walk,
meet for the coming kingdom. So B Δ G *f g*. But
ℵ A, Vulgate, **hath called**. St. Paul always attributes the call to the Father. **his kingdom**—at
the Lord's coming. **glory**—that ye may share His
glory (John xvii. 22; Col. iii. 4).
13. For this cause—seeing ye have had such
teachers (*vv.* 10-12), which involved your responsibility to behave worthily of our teaching, 'we
also (as well as you who have such cause for
thankfulness) thank God without ceasing (ch. i. 2),
that when ye *received* [externally by hearing:
paralabontes] the word of God which ye heard
from us (*lit.*, "God's word of hearing from us,"
Rom. x. 16, 17), ye *accepted* it [internally: *welcomed*
it: *edexasthe*, 2 Cor. viii. 17], not as the word of
men, but, even as it is truly, the word of God.'
Alford omits the "as." But "as" is required by
'even as it is truly.' 'Ye accepted it, not (*as*) the
word of men (which it might have been *supposed*
to be), but (as) the word of God, *even as it really
is*.' The proper object of faith, therefore, is *the
word of God*—at first oral, then, for security

word of men, but, as it is in truth, the word of God, which effectually

14 worketh also in you that believe. For ye, brethren, became followers of the *l*churches of God which in Judea are in Christ Jesus: for *m*ye also have suffered like things of your own countrymen, *n*even as they *have* of

15 the Jews: who both killed the Lord Jesus *o*and their own prophets, and have *2*persecuted us; and they please not God, and are contrary to all

16 men: forbidding *p*us to speak to the Gentiles that they might be saved, *q*to fill up their sins alway: *r*for the wrath is come upon them to the uttermost.

17 But we, brethren, being taken from you for a short time in presence, not in heart, endeavoured the more abundantly to see your face with

18 great desire. Wherefore we would have come unto you, even I Paul,

A. D. 54.

Gal 1. 22.
m Acts 17. 5.
n Heb. 10.33.
o Matt. 5. 12.
Acts 7. 52.
2 Or. chased us out.
p Luke 11.52.
Acts 13. 50.
Acts 14. 19.
Acts 17. 5.
q Gen. 15. 16.
Zech. 5. 6-8.
r Matt. 24. 6.

against error, written (John xx. 30, 31; Rom. xv. 4; Gal. iv. 30). Though it was 'of *us* ye heard' it, it really emanates from "God." Also, that faith is *the gift of Divine grace* is implied in the *thanksgiving*. **effectually worketh also in you that believe.** "Also:" a *further* feature of the heard Word, besides its being "the Word of God"—viz., its 'effectual working.' Besides your accepting it with your hearts, it "also" evidences itself in your lives. It shows its *energy* [*energeitai*] in its practical effects—working in you patient endurance in trial (*v.* 14: cf. Gal. iii. 5; v. 6). **14. For.** Divine *working* (*v.* 13) is most of all seen in affliction. **followers**—Greek, 'imitators.' **in Judea.** The churches in Judea were naturally the patterns to others, having been the first founded, and that on the very scene of Christ's ministry. Reference to them is specially appropriate here, as the Thessalonians, with Paul and Silas, had experienced, in their city, from Jewish persecutions (Acts xvii. 5-9) similar to those which 'the churches in Judea' experienced from Jews in that country. **in Christ Jesus**—not merely 'in God;' for the Jews' synagogues (one of which the Thessalonians were familiar with, Acts xvii. 1) were also *in God*, in contrast to idolaters. The Christian churches alone were not only *in God*, but also *in Christ*. **of your own countrymen**—primarily the Jews at Thessalonica, from whom the persecution originated; also the Gentiles there, instigated by the Jews: thus 'fellow-countrymen' [*Sumphuleton*]: not the *enduring* relation of fellow-citizenship, but sameness of country *for the time being*], including naturalized Jews and native Thessalonians, stand in contrast to the pure "Jews" in Judea (Matt. x. 36). An undesigned coincidence: Paul at this time was suffering persecutions of the Jews at Corinth, whence he writes (Acts xviii. 5, 6, 12); naturally his letter would dwell on Jewish bitterness against Christians. **even as they** (Heb. x. 32-34). There was a *likeness* in respect to *the nation* from which both suffered—viz., Jews, and those *their own countrymen;* in the *cause* for which, and in *the evils* which, they suffered; also in the stedfast *manner* in which they suffered them. Such sameness of fruits, afflictions, and experimental characteristics of believers, in all places and at all times, are a subsidiary evidence of the truth of the Gospel. **15. the Lord Jesus** [*Ton Kurion Jesoun*] —'Jesus THE LORD.' This enhances the enormity of their sin: in killing Jesus they killed the LORD (cf. Acts iii. 14, 15). **their own.** Omitted in א A B Δ G *f g*, Vulgate. **prophets** (Matt. xxi. 33-41; xxiii. 31-37; Luke xiii. 33.) **persecuted us** [*margin, ekdioxanton*]—'by persecution drove us out' (Luke xi. 49). Their killing the prophets and persecuting us refutes the plea of ignorance (Acts iii. 17). **please not God**—are *habitually pursuing a course* not pleasing to God, notwith-

standing their boast of being God's peculiar people, as certainly as, by the universal voice of the world, they are declared to be perversely "contrary to all men." *Josephus*, their own historian ('Apion,' ii. 14), represents one calling them 'atheists and misanthropes, the dullest of barbarians ;' and *Tacitus* ('Histories,' v. 5), 'they have a hostile hatred towards all others.' The *contrariety to all men* here is, *that they* 'forbid us to speak to the Gentiles that they may be saved' (*v.* 16). **16. Forbidding** [*koluonton*]—'hindering us from speaking,' &c. **to fill up their sins alway** —tending thus 'to the [*eis to*] filling up (the full measure of, Gen. xv. 16; Dan. viii. 23; Matt. xxiii. 32) their sins at all times'—i. e., *as at all former times, so now also*. The eternal *purpose* of God developed itself in their wilful, and so judicially-permitted infatuation. Their hindrance of the gospel-preaching to the Gentiles was the last measure added to their continually accumulating iniquity, which made them fully ripe for vengeance. **for**— Greek [δέ], '*but*' they shall proceed no further, for (2 Tim. iii. 8) "the" (foreordered and due) Divine 'wrath *has come upon* (*overtaken unexpectedly ;* the past tense expressing the speedy certainty of the Divinely-destined stroke) them to the uttermost ;' not merely partial, but to its full extent, 'even to the finishing stroke' (*Edmunds*). [א A G, *ephthasen*, completely *past* time. B, *ephthake*, an *act continuing down to the present*: the perfect, which suits well the sense.] The fullest visitation of wrath has already begun. Already, in A. D. 48, a tumult had occurred at the passover in Jerusalem, when about 30,000 were slain: a foretaste of the whole vengeance which speedily followed in the destruction of Jerusalem within fifteen years (Luke xix. 43, 44; xxi. 24). **17. But we**—resumed from *v.* 13: in contrast to *the Jews, vv.* 15, 16. **taken** [*aporphanisthentes*]— 'orphanized (Acts xvii. 7-10) from you,' as parents torn from their children. So "I will not leave you comfortless :" Greek, 'orphanized' (John xiv. 18). **for a short time**—lit., 'for the season of an hour.' 'When severed from you but a very short time (his departure was hasty), we the more abundantly (the shorter was our separation, for the desire of meeting again is more vivid the more recent has been the parting) endeavoured,' &c. (cf. 2 Tim. i. 4.) He does not hereby anticipate a short separation, which would be a false anticipation, for he did not soon revisit them. The Greek *past* participle forbids this view. **18. Wherefore.** [א A B Δ G *f g*, Vulgate read, *dioti* for *dio; Ellicott*, "Wherefore;" but Vulgate 'quoniam,' *seeing that.*] **we would** [*ethelesamen*]—'*we wished*' to come. **even I Paul.** My fellow-missionaries as well as myself intended it. I can answer for *myself* that I intended it more than once. His distinguishing himself here from his fellow-missionaries, whom throughout he associates with himself **in the**

19 once and again; but [s]Satan hindered us. For what *is* our hope, or joy, or crown of [3]rejoicing? *Are* not even ye in the presence of our Lord
20 Jesus Christ at his coming? For ye are our glory and joy.

3 WHEREFORE, when we could no longer forbear, [a]we thought it good
2 to be left at Athens alone, and sent [b]Timotheus, our brother, and minister of God, and our fellow-labourer in the gospel of Christ, to
3 establish you, and to comfort you concerning your faith: that [c]no man should be moved by these afflictions: for yourselves know that [d]we
4 are appointed thereunto. For [e]verily, when we were with you, we told you before that we should suffer tribulation; even as it came to pass,
5 and ye know. For this cause, when I could no longer forbear, I sent to

A. D. 54.

[s] Rom. 1 13.
[3] Or, glory-
ing.

CHAP. 3.
[a] Acts 17. 15.
[b] Rom. 16.21.
2 Cor. 1. 19.
[c] Ps. 112. 6.
Acts 20. 24.
Eph. 3. 13.
[d] John 16. 33.
Acts 9. 16.
[e] Acts 20. 24.

plural, accords with the fact that Silvanus and Timothy stayed at Berea when Paul went on to Athens, where subsequently Timothy joined him, and was thence sent *by Paul alone* to Thessalonica (ch. iii. 1). **Satan hindered us.** On a different occasion 'the Holy Ghost, the Spirit *of Jesus*' (so the oldest MSS.), Acts xvi. 6, 7, forbad them in a missionary design; here it is Satan, acting by wicked men, some of whom had already driven him out of Thessalonica (Acts xvii. 13, 14: cf. John xiii. 27), or else by some more direct 'messenger of Satan—a thorn in the flesh' (2 Cor. xii. 7: cf. xi. 14). The Holy Ghost and the providence of God overruled Satan's opposition to further His own purpose. *We* cannot, in each case, define whence hindrances in good undertakings arise. *Paul*, by inspiration, could say the hindrance was from Satan. [*Enekopsen*, "hindered"—*lit.*, 'to *cut a trench*, or *break up a road*, between one's self and an advancing foe, to prevent his progress;' so Satan opposing the progress of the missionaries. **19. For**—reason for his earnest desire to see them. **Are not even ye?** (The "even," *also*, implies that not *they alone* will be his crown)—our hope, joy, and crown of rejoicing before Jesus when He shall come? (Isa. lxii. 3; 2 Cor. i. 14; Phil. ii. 16; iv. 1.) His "hope," in a lower sense, is that these converts may be found in Christ at His advent (ch. iii. 13). Paul's *chief* "hope" was JESUS CHRIST (1 Tim. i. 1). **in the presence of . . .** Christ. So G. "Christ" is omitted in א A B Δ *f*. **20.** Emphatical repetition. Who but ye and our other converts are our *hope*, &c., *hereafter*, at Christ's coming? For it is *ye* who ARE now *our glory and joy.*

CHAP. III. 1-13. PROOF OF HIS DESIRE AFTER THEM IN HIS HAVING SENT TIMOTHY—HIS JOY AT THE TIDINGS CONCERNING THEIR FAITH AND CHARITY—PRAYERS FOR THEM.

1. Wherefore—because of our earnest love to you (ch. ii. 17-20), and our having been "hindered" going to you, we sent Timothy. **forbear**—'endure' the suspense. [*Stegontes* is said of a watertight vessel.] When we could no longer restrain our yearning, at least to hear of you. **left at Athens** alone. See 'Introduction.' This implies that he sent Timothy *from Athens*, whither the latter had followed him. The determination to send Timothy was that of Paul, Silas, and Timothy, before Paul's leaving Berea (*Alford*): it was carried into effect when Paul reached Athens. Thus the "I" *v.* 5, will express that the *act* of sending Timothy was *Paul's*, whilst the determination that Paul should be left alone at Athens was that of the brethren as well as himself, whence he uses, *v.* 1, "we." The non-mention of Silas at Athens implies that he did not follow Paul to Athens, as was at first intended; but Timothy did. Thus the history, Acts xvii. 14, 15, accords with the epistle. 'Left behind' [*kataleiphthenai*] implies,

that Timothy had been with him *at Athens*. It was an act of self-denial for their sakes that Paul deprived himself of Timothy's presence at Athens, being "left" all "alone" in the midst of philosophic cavillers. But '*we* thought good to be left alone [*monoi*]. We sent Timothy' may mean Paul had another, viz., Silas, with him at Athens. If so, Paul probably sent Silas from Athens on some other mission afterwards, not recorded in the Acts or this epistle; and Silas and Timothy together returned from Macedon to Paul at Corinth (Acts xviii. 1, 5). 2. **minister of God, and our fellow-labourer.** א A, Vulgate, read only "minister of God." Δ G *g*, and 'fellow-labourer of God' (1 Cor. iii. 9; 2 Cor. vi. 1). The English version reading is perhaps compounded of the two other readings. Paul calls Timothy "our *brother*" here; but in 1 Cor. iv. 17, "my *son*." He speaks thus highly of one so lately ordained, both to impress the Thessalonians with respect for the delegate sent to them, and to encourage Timothy, who was apparently of a weakly constitution (1 Tim. iv. 12; v. 23). 'Gospel ministers do the work of God *with* Him, *for* Him, and *under* Him' (*Edmunds*). **establish.** In 2 Thess. iii. 3 GOD is said to "stablish." He is the true stablisher: ministers are His "instruments" (Acts xv. 32). **concerning** (*huper*]—'in behalf of;' i. e., *for the furtherance* of your faith. [*Parakalesai*] "Comfort" includes also 'exhort.' The Thessalonians in their trials needed both (*v.* 3: cf. Acts xiv. 22). 3. **moved**—'shaken.' [*Sainesthai* is said of dogs *wagging* the tail in fawning on one.] *Tittmann* explains, 'That no man should, amidst calamities, be *allured* by the *flattering* hope of a pleasant life to abandon his duty:' 'that no man be cajoled out of his faith.' In affliction, relatives and opponents combine with the ease-loving heart in flatteries which it needs strong faith to overcome. **yourselves know**—by your own experience, and by our words: we always candidly told you so (*v.* 4). None but a religion from God would have held out such a prospect to those who should embrace it, and yet succeed in winning converts. **we**—Christians. **appointed thereunto**—by God's counsel (ch. v. 9). 4. that **we should suffer**—'that we are (sure) to suffer' by the *appointment* of God (*v.* 3). **even as**—'even (exactly) as it *both* came to pass, *and* ye know by experience:' ye know *both* that it came to pass, *and* that we foretold it (cf. John xiii. 19). Prophecy's correspondence to the event confirms faith. 'Forewarned, forearmed' (*Edmunds*). The repetition of "ye know" is an argument that, being forewarned of coming affliction, they should be less readily "moved" by it. 5. For **this cause** —because I know your "tribulation" has actually begun (*v.* 4). **when I** [κάγω]—'when I *also* could no longer contain myself.' **I sent.** Paul was the actual sender; hence the "I." Paul, Silas, and Timothy himself had agreed on the mission already, before Paul went to Athens; hence the

462

know your faith, *f* lest by some means the tempter have tempted you, and *g* our labour be in vain.

6 But *h* now when Timotheus came from you unto us, and brought us good tidings of your faith and charity, and that ye have good remembrance of us always, desiring greatly to see us, *i* as we also *to see* you:

7 therefore, brethren, we were comforted over you in all our affliction and distress by your faith: for now we live, if ye *j* stand fast in the Lord.

8 distress by your faith: for now we live, if ye *j* stand fast in the Lord.

9 For what thanks can we render to God again for you, for all the joy

10 wherewith we joy for your sakes before our God; night *k* and day praying exceedingly that we might see your face, and might perfect that which is lacking in your faith ?

11 Now God himself and our Father, and our Lord Jesus Christ, ¹ direct

12 our way unto you. And the Lord make you to increase and abound in love one toward another, and toward all *men*, even as we *do* toward you :

13 to the end he may stablish your hearts unblameable in holiness before God, even our Father, at the coming of our Lord Jesus Christ *l* with all his saints.

A. D. 54.

f Matt. 4. 3.
1 Cor. 7. 5.
2 Cor. 11. 3.
Gal. 1. 6.
Eph. 4. 14.
Jas. 1 13.
g Gal. 2. 2.
Gal. 4. 14.
Phil. 2. 16.
h Acts 18. 1.
i Phil. 1. 8.
j John 8. 31.
John 15 4.
Phil. 4. 1.
k Acts 26. 7.
2 Tim. 1. 3.
1 Or. guide.
Mark 1. 3.
l Zech. 14. 5.
Jude 14.
Rev 20. 11.

"we" (*v.* 1, note). **to know**—the state of. **your faith**—whether it stood the trial (Col. iv. 8). **lest by some means . . . have tempted you, and our labour be** [*mē pōs epeirasen-kai-genētai*]—the indicative in the former sentence, the subjunctive in the latter. 'To know, *whether haply* (Ellicott, '*lest* haply') the tempter *have* tempted you (the indicative implying such *was* the case), and *lest* (in that case) our labour *may prove* in vain' (Greek, Gal. iv. 11). The *temptation* was a *fact;* Paul's fear was, *lest haply,* by their yielding to it, his labour should prove vain: "vain," so far as *ye* are concerned ; but not as concerns *us*, so far as *we* have sincerely laboured (Isa. xlix. 4; 1 Cor. iii. 8). **6.** Join "now" with 'come:' 'But Timotheus having *just now come*' (*Alford*) (Acts xviii. 5). Paul is therefore writing from Corinth. **your faith and charity** (ch. i. 3)—their faith subsequently increased still more (2 Thess. i. 3). *Faith* was the solid foundation ; *charity* the cement which held together the superstructure of practice. In that *charity* was included their "good (kindly) remembrance" of their teachers. **desiring greatly** [*epipothountes*]—'having a yearning desire for.' **we also**. The desires of loving friends for one another are reciprocal. **7. over you** [*eph 'humin*] —in respect to you. It is a comfort to him who loves to hear that the one beloved knows his love. **in**—notwithstanding "all our distress [*ananke*: *inevitable* trial, '*necessity*] and affliction ;" viz., external trials at Corinth, whence Paul writes (cf. *v.* 6 with Acts xviii. 5, 10). **8. now**—as the case is ; seeing ye stand fast. **we live**—we flourish. It *revives us* in affliction to hear of your stedfastness (Ps. xxii. 26; 3 John 3, 4). **if.** The vivid joy which Paul "now" feels *will continue*, if the Thessalonians continue stedfast. They still needed exhortation (*v.* 10); therefore he subjoins, "if ye," &c. (Phil. iv. 1.) **9. what**—*what sufficient* thanks? **render to God again**—in return for His goodness (Ps. cxvi. 12). **for** [*peri*: *concerning*] **you, for** (on account of) **all the joy**. It was "comfort," *v.* 7, now it is more—viz., *joy*. **for your sakes**— on your account. **before our God**. It is a joy, as in the presence of God, which will bear His searching eye; not self-seeking, but disinterested, sincere, and spiritual (cf. ch. ii. 20; John xv. 11). **10. Night and day** (note, ch. ii. 9). Night is the season for the saints' holiest meditations and prayers (2 Tim. i. 3). **praying**. *What thanks can we render to God*, praying as we do, &c.? [*Deomenoi*, a *beseeching* request.] **exceedingly** [*huperekperissou*]—'*more than exceeding abun-*

dantly' (cf. Eph. iii. 20). **that which is lacking**. Even the Thessalonians in some things needed improvement (Luke xvii. 5). Their doctrinal views as to the nearness of Christ's coming, and the state of those asleep, and their *practice* in some points needed correction (ch. iv. 1-9). Paul's method was to begin by commending what was praiseworthy, then to correct what was amiss: a good pattern to all admonishers.

11. '*May* God Himself, *even* our Father (there being but one article, requires, "He who is at once God and our Father") direct', &c. The "Himself" stands in contrast with "we" (ch. ii. 18): *we* desired to come, but could not through Satan's hindrance ; but if God *Himself* direct our way (as we pray), none can hinder Him. *The unity of the Father and Son* appears here, and in 2 Thess. ii. 16, 17 ; the verb is *singular*, as the subject, the Father and Son, are but *one in essential Being*, not in mere unity of will. Almost all the chapters in both epistles are sealed, each with its own prayer (ch. v. 23; 2 Thess. i. 11; ii. 16; iii. 5, 16) (*Bengel*). St. Paul does not think the issue of a journey an unfit subject for prayer (Rom. i. 10; xv. 32) (*Edmunds*). His prayer, though deferred, in about five years afterwards was fulfilled in his return to Macedonia. **12.** The "you" (Greek) is emphatically put *first*: 'but' (Greek for "and"), what concerns "YOU," whether we come or not, 'may the Lord make you to,' &c. "Increase" or *enlarge* [*pleonasai*] has a *comparative* force: "abound" [*perisseusai*] a *superlative* force, 'make you *full* (supplying) "that which is lacking" (*v.* 10), and even abounding.' "The Lord" may here be the Holy Spirit : so the Three of the Trinity will be appealed to (cf. *v.* 13), as in 2 Thess. iii. 5. So the Holy Ghost is called "the Lord" (2 Cor. iii. 17). "Love" (*brotherly*, towards Christians first, and *philanthropic* towards all men) is the fruit of the Spirit (Gal. v. 22): His office is "to stablish in holiness" (*v.* 13; 1 Pet. i. 2). **13. your hearts** —naturally the spring of unholiness. **before God, even our Father**—rather, 'before Him who is at once God and our Father.' Before not merely men, but Him who is not deceived by the show of holiness—*i. e.*, may your holiness be such as will stand his scrutiny. God will judge by Christ (2 Cor. v. 10; Acts xvii. 31). **coming** [*parousia*]— '*personal* presence.' **with all his saints**—including holy angels, and the holy elect of men (ch. iv. 14; Dan. vii. 10; Zech. xiv. 5; Matt. xv. 31; 2 Thess. i. 7). The saints are "His" (Acts iv. 13). We must have "holiness" if we are to be num-

4 FURTHERMORE then we [1] beseech you, brethren, and [2] exhort *you* by the Lord Jesus, that as ye have received of us how ye ought to walk
2 and *a* to please God, *so* ye would abound more and more. For ye know
3 what commandments we gave you by the Lord Jesus. For this is *b* the will of God, *even* your sanctification, that ye should abstain from forni-
4 cation: that *c* every one of you should know how to possess his vessel in
5 sanctification and honour; not in the lust of concupiscence, even as the
6 Gentiles *d* which know not God: that *e* no *man* go beyond and [3] defraud his brother [4] in *any* matter: because that the Lord *is* the avenger of all
7 such, as we also have forewarned you and testified. For God hath not
8 called us unto uncleanness, but unto holiness. He therefore that [5] despiseth, despiseth not man, but God, who hath also given unto us his Holy Spirit.
9 But as touching brotherly love ye need not that I write unto you; for

A. D. 54.

CHAP. 4.
[1] Or, request.
[2] Or, beseech.
a Col 1. 10.
b Eph. 5. 17.
c Rom. 6. 19.
d Eph. 2. 12.
e Lev. 19. 11.
[3] Or, oppress, or, overreach.
[4] Or, in the matter.
[5] Or, rejecteth.

---

bered with His holy one. [*Hagiotēs* is *holiness* in the *abstract*. *Hagiōsune* is *the state of holiness: hagiasmos*, the *process* of being made holy.] On "unblameable," cf. Rev. xiv. 5. This verse (cf. with *v.* 12) shows "love" is the spring of "holiness" (Matt. v. 44-48; Rom. xiii. 10; Col. iii. 14). God really "stablishes;" Timothy and others are but instruments (*v.* 2) in 'stablishing.'

CHAP. IV. 1-18.—EXHORTATIONS TO CHASTITY —BROTHERLY LOVE—QUIET INDUSTRY—ABSTINENCE FROM UNDUE SORROW FOR DEPARTED FRIENDS, FOR AT CHRIST'S COMING ALL HIS SAINTS SHALL BE GLORIFIED.

1. Furthermore [*loipon*]—' As to what remains.' The transition to the close of his epistles (2 Cor. xiii. 11). then—with a view to the *love* and *holiness* (ch. iii. 12, 13) just prayed for in your behalf, we now give you exhortation. beseech—'ask' as a personal favour [*erōtōmen*]. by—Greek 'IN the Lord Jesus:' in communion with the Lord Jesus, as Christian ministers dealing with Christian people (*Edmunds*) (Eph. iv. 17). as ye have received—when we were with you (ch. ii. 13). how—Greek, the "how;" i. e., *the manner*. walk and (so) to please God—by your walk; in contrast to the Jews, who "please not God" (ch. ii. 15). א A B Δ G *fg*, Vulgate, add here, 'even as also ye do walk' (cf. ch. iv. 10; v. 11). These words, which he could say of them with truth, conciliate a favourable hearing for the precepts which follow. Also, "abound *more and more*," implies there had gone before a recognition of their already in some measure *walking so.* 2. by the Lord Jesus—by His authority, not by our own. He uses the strong term "commandments" [*parangelias*], in writing to this church, not long founded, knowing that they would take in a right spirit this intimation that he spake with Divine authority. He seldom uses the term in writing subsequently, when his authority was established to others. 1 Cor. vii. 10; xii. 17; and 1 Tim. i. 5 (*v.* 18, where the subject accounts for the strong expression) are the exceptions. "The Lord" marks His paramount authority, requiring implicit obedience. 3. For—enforcing the assertion, *v.* 2. Since "this is the will of God," let it be your will also. fornication—not regarded as a sin at all among the heathen, so needing the more to be denounced (Acts xv. 20). 4. know — by moral self-control. how to possess his vessel [*to heautou skeuos ktasthai*]—'how to get for himself *his own* vessel;' i. e., *his own wife*, so as to avoid fornication (*v.* 3; 1 Cor. vii. 2). The emphatical position of 'his own vessel,' for *wife*, in 1 Pet. iii. 7, and in Jewish phraseology, and the correct translation 'get for himself,' all justify this rendering. in sanctification (Rom. vi. 19; 1

Cor. vi. 15, 8). '*His own*' in opposition to dishonouring *his brother* by lusting after *his* wife (*v.* 6). honour (Heb. xiii. 4)—contrasted with "*dishonour* their own bodies" (Rom. i. 24). 5. in the lust [*pathei*]—'passion;' [1] such are unconsciously *passive* slaves of lusts. which know not God— and so know no better. Ignorance of true religion begets unchastity (Eph. iv. 18, 19). A people's morals are like the objects of their worship (Deut. vii. 26; Ps. cxv. 8; Rom. i. 23, 24). 6. go beyond—the bounds appointed by God, as to his brother. First, fornication is forbidden; then a holy use of its natural remedy affirmatively inculcated; lastly, the heinous sin, *adultery*, denounced (*Ellicott*). defraud—'overreach' (*Alford*). in any matter [*en tō pragmati*]—'in *the* matter:' the matter now in question: the conjugal honour of his neighbour (*v.* 4); *v.* 7 confirms this. "Brother" enhances the enormity. It is your Christian *brother* whom you wrong (cf. Prov. vi. 27-33). the Lord—the coming Judge (2 Thess. i. 7, 8). avenger of all such—'concerning all *these things;*' in all such wrongs against a neighbour's conjugal honour. testified [*diemarturametha*]—'solemnly' (*Ellicott*); 'constantly testified' (*Alford*). 7. unto [*epi*]—'for the purpose of.' unto — Greek, 'in.' "Holiness" is the sphere or element in which our calling has place. *Saint* is another name for Christian. 8. despiseth [*ho athetēn*]—'setteth at nought' such duties of his calling (*v.* 7); in relation to his brother (*v.* 6). He who doth so 'sets at nought not man, but God' (Ps. li. 4). As the verb in Luke x. 16; John xii. 48 is used of *rejecting* God's *minister*, it means so here. who hath also given unto us. So A C *fg*, Vulgate. But א B G read 'who *giveth* (present) unto *you*' (not "*us*"). The "also" in א C G *g*, Vulgate. Besides having "called us in holiness" (*v.* 7), He '*also gives* us His Spirit' to realize it. The giving of the Spirit is *continually going on.* his . . . spirit [*To Pneuma autou to hagion*]—' His Spirit, the Holy (one);' emphatically marking "holiness" (*v.* 7) as His Spirit's attribute; and so His Spirit's office to impart to believers. 'Unto you,' as its objects; given *unto, into,* or *within, and among* you (cf. ch. ii. 9; Eph. iv. 30). *Giveth:* sanctification is, not merely once for all completed in the past, but *present* and *progressive.* So the Church of England Catechism, '*sanctifieth* (present) all the elect people of God.' "His:" He gives you that which is essentially identical with Himself, that you should become like Himself (1 Pet. i. 16; 2 Pet. i. 4).

9. brotherly love (Rom. xii. 10; Gal. vi. 10; Heb. xiii. 1; 1 Pet. i. 22; iii. 8; 2 Pet. i. 7)—shown in relieving distressed brethren. A C support 'YE have.' א B Δ G *fg*, Vulgate, read 'WE have.'

10 ye *ᶠ*yourselves are taught of God *ᵍ*to love one another. And indeed ye do it toward all the brethren which are in all Macedonia: but we beseech

11 you, brethren, that ye increase more and more; and that ye study to be quiet, and to do your own business, and to work with your own hands,

12 as we commanded you; that ye may walk honestly toward them that are without, and *that* ye may have lack ⁶ of nothing.

13 But I would not have you to be ignorant, brethren, concerning them which are asleep, that ye sorrow not, even *ʰ* as others which have no hope.

14 For *ⁱ* if we believe that Jesus died and rose again, even so them also

15 which sleep in Jesus will God bring with him. For this we say unto you *ʲ* by the word of the Lord, that we which are alive *and* remain unto the

A.D. 54.
ᶠ Jer. 31. 34. John 6. 45. 1 John 2. 20, 27.
ᵍ John 13. 34.
⁶ Or, of no man.
ʰ Lev. 19. 28. Deut. 14. 1. 2 Sam. 12. 20.
ⁱ 1 Cor. 15. 13.
ʲ 1 Ki. 13. 17.

We need not write, as *ye yourselves* are taught, and that by *God*, in the heart, by the Holy Spirit (John vi. 45; Heb. viii. 11; 1 John ii. 20, 27). Paul indirectly exhorts, whilst formally omitting exhortation. It is so obvious a duty that it will occur to yourselves. Moreover, you will be the more zealous not to fall off from the high character you already have as to it. **to love** [*eis to*]—'with a view to your loving one another.' Divine teachings have their confluence in love (*Bengel*). **10. toward all the brethren which are in all Macedonia.** From one and a half to two years had elapsed between the conversion of the Thessalonians and the writing of this epistle, allowing time for their liberality to their Macedonian brethren. **11. study to be quiet** [*philotimeisthai*]—'*make it your ambition* to be quiet, and to do *your own* business.' In contrast to the world's *ambition* 'to make a great stir,' and the restlessness of fanatical 'busybodies' (2 Thess. iii. 11, 12). **work with your own hands.** B C Δ G *f g*, Vulgate, omit "own" [*idiais*]. A ℵ have it. The Thessalonian converts were, it seems, chiefly of the *working* classes. Their expectation of Christ's immediate coming led some enthusiasts to neglect their daily work, and be dependent on others (end of *v.* 12). The expectation was right so far as that the Church should be always looking for Him; but they were wrong in making it a ground for neglecting daily work. The evil, as it subsequently became worse, is more strongly reproved (2 Thess. iii. 6-12). **12. walk**—a continuous course. **honestly**—in the old English sense, 'becomingly;' as becomes your Christian profession: in contrast to "disorderly" (2 Thess. iii. 6): not bringing discredit on it before the world, as if Christianity led to sloth and poverty (Rom. xiii. 13; 1 Pet. ii. 12). **them that are without**—outside the Christian Church (Mark iv. 11). **have lack of nothing** —not have to beg from others for your wants (cf. Eph. iv. 28). *Ellicott*, with Syriac and Vulgate, 'have need of *no man.*' So far from needing to beg from others, we ought to work, and get the means of supplying the needy. Freedom from pecuniary embarrassment is to be desired by the Christian on account of the liberty which it bestows.

13. The leading topic of Paul's preaching at Thessalonica having been the coming *kingdom* (Acts xvii. 7), some perverted it into a cause for fear as to friends lately deceased, lest these would be excluded from the glory which those found alive alone should share. This error St. Paul corrects (cf. ch. v. 10). **I would not.** A B Δ G ℵ *f g*, Vulgate, have '*we* would not:' Silas, Timothy, and myself desire that ye be not ignorant. **them which are asleep.** So Δ G [*kekoimēmenōn*]. A B ℵ *f g*, Vulgate, read (*present*) 'them which are *sleeping*' [*koimomenōn*]: the same as "the dead in Christ" (*v.* 16), to whose bodies (Dan. xii. 2, not their *souls*; Eccl. xii. 7; 2 Cor. v. 8) death is a

calm and holy sleep, from which the resurrection shall awake them to glory. *Repose, continued existence*, and *awaking* are implied in 'sleep.' 'Cemetery' means *a sleeping-place.* The full glory is not to be realized at death, but at the Lord's coming: one is not to anticipate the other, but all are to be glorified together *then* (Col. iii. 4; Heb. xi. 40). Death affects the individual; the coming of Jesus, the whole Church. At death our souls are invisibly and individually with the Lord; at Christ's coming the Church, with all its members, in body and soul, shall be visibly and collectively with Him. As this is here the consolation to mourning relatives, *the mutual recognition of the saints* at Christ's coming is implied. **that ye sorrow not, even as others** [*hoi loipoi*]—'the rest:' all the world besides Christians. Not natural *mourning* for dead friends is forbidden; for the Lord Jesus and Paul sinlessly gave way to it (John xi. 33, 35; Phil. ii. 27): but sorrow as though there were "no hope," which indeed the heathen had not (Eph. ii. 12). The Christian *hope* is *the resurrection.* Cf. Ps. xvi. 9, 11; xvii. 15; lxxiii. 24; Prov. xiv. 32, show that the Old Testament Church, though not having the hope *so bright* (Isa. xxxviii. 18, 19), yet had this hope. Contrast 'Catullus,' v. 4, 'Once our brief day has set, we sleep one everlasting night.' The sepulchral inscriptions of heathen Thessalonica express this hopeless view. *Æschylus*, 'Eumen.,' 638, 'Of one once dead there is no resurrection.' Whatever glimpses heathen philosophers had of the soul's existence after death, they had none of the body (Acts xvii. 18, 20, 32). **14. For if** (not doubt: the *indicative* follows)—confirmation of *v.* 13, that the removal of *ignorance* as to sleeping believers would remove undue grief respecting them (cf. *v.* 13, "hope"). Our *hope* rests on our *faith* ("if we *believe*"). '*As surely as* we believe that Christ died and rose again (the very doctrine taught at Thessalonica, Acts xvii. 3), *so also* will God bring (not only *raise*, but *bring*) *those laid to sleep* through *Jesus* with Him' (Jesus. The order and balance of the members of the Greek sentence require this translation). Believers are laid in sleep by Jesus (*through Him* death to them is sleep), and so will be brought back from sleep with Jesus in His train when He comes. The reference is not to disembodied souls, but to the sleeping *bodies.* The facts of Christ's experience are repeated in the believer's. He died and then rose; so believers shall die, then rise with Him. In His case *death* is the term (1 Cor. xv. 3, 6, &c.); in their's, *sleep.* His death has taken for them the sting from death. The same hand that shall raise is that which *laid them to sleep.* 'Laid to sleep by Jesus' answers to "dead in Christ" (*v.* 16). **15. by** ('in') **the word of the Lord**—i. e., *in virtue* of a direct revelation from the Lord. So 1 Ki. xx. 35; Hagg. i. 13; 2 Cor. xii. 1; Gal. i. 12; ii. 2. This is the "mystery" once hidden, now

16 coming of the Lord shall not prevent them which are asleep. For *k* the Lord himself shall descend from heaven with a shout, with the voice of the archangel, and with the trump of God: and the dead in Christ shall
17 rise first: then we which are alive *and* remain shall be caught up together with them *l* in the clouds, to meet the Lord in the air: and so
18 *m* shall we ever be with the Lord. Wherefore *7* comfort one another with these words.

5 BUT of *a* the times and the seasons, brethren, ye have no need that I

A. D. 54.

k Matt 24.30.
Acts 1. 11.
l Acts 1. 9.
Rev. 11. 12.
m John 12.26.
John 14. 3.
7 Or, exhort.

CHAP. 5.
a Matt 24. 3.

revealed (1 Cor. xv. 51, 52). **prevent**—i. e., *anticipate.* So far were Christians then from regarding their departed brethren as *anticipating* them in glory, that they needed to be assured that those who remain to the Lord's coming 'will not anticipate them that are asleep.' The "we" means *whichever of us* remain alive (lit., *we, the living, who are being left behind* [*perileipomenoi*]) unto the Lord's coming. The Spirit designed that believers of each successive age should live in continued expectation of the Lord's coming, not knowing but that *they* should be among those found alive (Matt. xxiv. 42). It is a fall from this blessed hope, that *death* is generally looked for rather than the coming of our Lord. Each successive generation represents the generation which shall actually survive till His coming (Matt. xxv. 13; Rom. xiii. 11; 1 Cor. xv. 51; Jas. v. 9; 1 Pet. iv. 5, 6). The Spirit subsequently revealed that which is not inconsistent with the expectation of the Lord's coming at any time—viz., that His coming would not be until there should be a "falling away first" (2 Thess. ii. 2, 3). As symptoms of this soon appeared, none could say but that this precursory event might be realized, and so the Lord come in his day. Each successive revelation fills in the details of the general outline first given. So Paul subsequently, whilst looking mainly for the Lord's coming to clothe him with His body from heaven, looks for going to be with Christ in the meanwhile (2 Cor. v. 1-10; Phil. i. 6, 23; iii. 20, 21; iv. 5). *Edmunds*, 'The "we" is an affectionate identifying of ourselves with our fellows of all ages, as members of the same body, under the same Head, Christ Jesus.' So Ps. lxvi. 6, end; Hos. xii. 4, end. Though neither David nor Hosea was alive at the times referred to, yet each identifies himself with those that were present. **16. himself**—in all the majesty of His personal presence, not by deputy. **descend**—even as He ascended (Acts i. 11). **with**—Greek, 'in:' one concomitant circumstance attending His appearing. **shout** [*keleusmati*]—'signal-shout.' Jesus, as a victorious king, will give the *word of command* to the hosts of heaven in His train for the last onslaught, at His final triumph over sin, death, and Satan (Rev. xix. 11-21), and will call the saints' bodies to life (John v. 28, 29). **the voice of the archangel**—distinct from the 'signal-shout:' Michael perhaps (Jude 9; Rev. xii. 7), to whom especially is committed the guardianship of the people of God (Dan. x. 13). The archangel's voice seconds that of the Lord (Matt. xxv. 6: cf. Heb. ii. 2 with Exod. xx. 1). **trump of God**— which usually accompanied God's manifestation in glory (Exod. xix. 16; Ps. xlvii. 5); here the last of the three accompaniments of His appearing. As the trumpet was used to convene God's people to solemn convocations and to war (Num. x. 2, 10; xxxi. 6), so here it summons God's elect together, preparatory to their glorification with Christ (Ps. l. 1-5; Matt. xxiv. 31; 1 Cor. xv. 52). **shall rise first**—previously to the living being "caught up." The "first" here does not *directly* express the *first* resurrection. as contrasted with that of "the rest

of the dead" (Matt. xiii. 41, 42, 50; 1 Cor. xv. 23, 24; Rev. xx. 5, 6): it simply stands in opposition to "then," *v.* 17. FIRST, "the *dead* in Christ" shall rise, THEN the *living* shall be caught up. The living shall not anticipate the dead saints. The Lord's people alone are spoken of. **17. we which are alive and remain shall be caught up** —after having been "changed in a moment" (1 Cor. xv. 51, 52). Again he says "we," recommending the expression to Christians of all ages, each generation bequeathing to the succeeding one a continually increasing obligation to look for the coming of the Lord (*Edmunds*). If Christ's servants be *secretly* caught up (as some think) *before* the judgments upon the earth, how shall the Gospel be preached up to the end? (Matt. xxiv. 14.) Also, *the gathering of the elect succeeds the great tribulation* through which, though shortened for their sakes (Matt. xxiv. 21, 22, 29, 30), they have to pass: but the elect there are probably *Jews:* the vintage of judgments on apostate Christendom succeeds the harvest of the righteous (Isa. xxvi. 20; lxi. 2; Dan. xii. 1; Zeph. ii. 3; Mal. iv. 1; Rev. xi. 7, 11-15; xiv. 15, 18: see note, Jude 14). **together with them**—all together: the raised dead and changed living forming one joint body. **in the clouds**—Greek, 'in clouds.' The same honour awaits them as their Lord. He was taken in a cloud at His ascension (Acts i. 9), so at His return with clouds (Rev. i. 7) they shall be caught up in clouds, as His and their triumphal chariot (Ps. civ. 3; Dan. vii. 13). *Ellicott* explains, 'robed round by upbearing clouds' ('Aids to Faith'). **in the air** [*eis aera*]—'*into* the air:' caught up *into* the region just above the earth, where shall be the *meeting* (cf. Matt. xxv. 1, 6) between them ascending and their Lord descending. Not that the air is to be their *lasting abode* with Him. When a king enters his city the loyal go forth to meet him, the criminals in confinement await their judge (*Chrysostom*). **and so shall we ever be with** [*σύν*: not merely *in company with*, μετά, but *in coherence with* (*Ellicott*)] **the Lord.** No more parting, no more going out (Rev. iii. 12). His point being established, that the dead in Christ shall have equal advantage with those found alive at Christ's coming, he leaves undefined the other events foretold elsewhere (as not necessary to his discussion)—Christ's reign on earth with His saints (1 Cor. vi. 2, 3), the final judgment, and their glorification in the new heaven and earth. **18. comfort one another**— in your mourning for the dead (*v.* 13).

CHAP. V. 1-28.—SUDDENNESS OF CHRIST'S COMING A MOTIVE FOR WATCHFULNESS—PRECEPTS—PRAYER FOR THEIR BEING FOUND BLAMELESS, BODY, SOUL, AND SPIRIT, AT CHRIST'S COMING—CONCLUSION.

1. times [*chronoi*]—the *general* term for chronological periods in the great cycle of God's scheme of providence and grace. **seasons** [*kairoi*]—the *opportune* times (Dan. vii. 12; Acts i. 7). *Time* denotes quantity; *season*, quality. *Seasons* are parts of *times.* Here, the *times* and *seasons* which bring about the grand consummation at the Lord's

2 write unto you. For yourselves know perfectly, [b] that the day of the
3 Lord so cometh as a thief in the night. For when they shall say, Peace
and safety, then [c] sudden destruction cometh upon them, as travail upon
a woman with child; and they shall not escape.
4 But [d] ye, brethren, are not in darkness, that that day should overtake
5 you as a thief. Ye are all [e] the children of light, and the children of the
6 day: we are not of the night, nor of darkness. Therefore let us not sleep,
7 as *do* others; but let us watch and be sober. For [f] they that sleep sleep
8 in the night; and they that be drunken [g] are drunken in the night. But
let us, who are of the day, be sober, putting [h] on the breastplate of faith
9 and love; and for an helmet the hope of salvation. For [i] God hath not
appointed us to wrath, but to obtain salvation by our Lord Jesus Christ,
10 who died for us, that, whether we wake or sleep, we should live together

A D. 54.

[b] Matt. 25. 13.
Luke 12. 39.
Rev. 3. 3.
Rev. 16. 15.
[c] Isa. 13. 6.
Isa. 30. 13.
Acts 13. 41.
[d] 1 John 2. 8.
[e] Eph. 5. 8.
[f] Luke 21. 34.
[g] Acts 2. 15.
[h] Isa. 59. 17.
Eph. 6. 14.
[i] Rom. 9. 22.
1 Pet. 2. 8.
2 Tim. 2. 19.

coming. **ye have no need**—those who watch need not be told *when* the hour will come, for they are always ready. The Thessalonians 'knew perfectly' [*akribōs*, 'accurately'], by Paul's having told them, and by the Spirit's teaching (2 Thess. ii. 5). **2. as a thief in the night.** The apostles follow their Lord's parable, expressing how His coming shall take men by surprise (Matt. xxiv. 43; 2 Pet. iii. 10). 'The *night* is wherever there is quiet unconcern' (*Bengel*). "At midnight" (perhaps figurative: to some parts of the earth it will be *literal* night), Matt. xxv. 6: cf. Luke xvii. 31, "in that *day*;" 34, "in that *night.*" The thief not only gives no notice of his approach, but takes all precautions to prevent the household knowing of it. So the Lord (Rev. xvi. 15). *Signs* will precede, to confirm the patient hope of the watchful; but the coming itself shall be sudden at last (Matt. xxiv. 32-36). **cometh**—present: expressing its *speedy*, awful *certainty*. **3. they**—the men of the world. Verses 5, 6; ch. iv. 13, "others:" all the rest of the world save Christians. **Peace** (Judg. xviii. 7, 9, 27, 28; Jer. vi. 14; Ezek. xiii. 10). **then**—*at that very moment*, when 'they least expect it.* Cf. Belshazzar, Dan. v. 1-5, 6, 9, 26-28; Herod, Acts xii. 21-23; Luke xxi. 25-35. **cometh upon** [*ephistatai*]—*stands at* their doors "sudden" (not an epithet, but a *secondary predicate of manner*). **as travail.** 'As *the* labour pang' comes in an instant on the woman when otherwise engaged (Ps. xlviii. 6; Isa. xiii. 8). **shall not escape** [*ou mē ekphugōsin*]—'shall not at all escape;' another awful feature of their ruin: there shall be then no possibility of shunning it (Amos ix. 2, 3; Rev. vi. 15, 16).

4. not in darkness—of understanding (*i. e.*, spiritual ignorance), or of the moral nature (*i. e.*, sin) (Eph. iv, 18; 1 John ii. 9). **that** [*hina*]—'in order that:' with God results are all purposed. **that day**—Greek, 'THE day:' the *day* of the Lord (Heb. x. 25), in contrast to "darkness." **overtake**—unexpectedly (cf. John xii. 35). **as a thief.** So א Δ G *f g*, Vulgate. But A B, *kleptas* for *kleptes.* 'As (the daylight overtakes) *thieves*' (Job xxiv. 17). **5.** א A B Δ G *f g*, Vulgate, read 'FOR ye are all,' &c. Ye have no reason for fear, or surprise, by the coming of the day of the Lord: '*For* ye are all sons [*huioi*] of light and sons of day:' a Hebrew idiom: as *sons* resemble their fathers, so you are light (intellectually and morally illuminated in spiritual things) (Luke xvi. 8; John xii. 36). **are not of**—i. e., *belong not to* night nor darkness. The change from "ye" to "we" implies, *Ye* are sons of light, because ye are Christians; and *we*, Christians, are not of night nor darkness. **6. others** [*hoi loipoi*]—'the rest' of the world (ch. iv. 13). "Sleep" here is worldly apathy to spiritual things (Rom. xiii. 11; Eph. v. 14); in *v.* 7, ordi-

nary *sleep;* in *v.* 10, death. **watch**—for Christ's coming [*gregorōmen*]; 'be wakeful.' **be sober**—refraining from carnal indulgences, mental or sensual (cf. Greek, 1 Cor. xv. 34; 2 Tim. ii. 26; 1 Pet. v. 8). **7.** In the literal sense. Night is the time when sleepers sleep, and drinking men are drunk. To sleep by day would imply great indolence; to be drunk by day great shamelessness. In a spiritual sense, 'we Christians profess to be day people, not night people; therefore our work ought to be day work, not night work; or conduct such as will bear the eye of day, and has no need of the veil of night' (*Edmunds*) (*v.* 8). **8. Faith, hope, and love,** the three pre-eminent graces (ch. i. 3; 1 Cor. xiii. 13). We must not only be *awake*, but also *sober;* not only sober, but also *armed;* not only watchful, but guarded. The armour here is only *defensive;* in Eph. vi. 13-17 also offensive. Here our means of being *guarded* against being surprised by the day of the Lord as a thief in the night. The *helmet* and *breastplate* defend the two vital parts, the head and the heart respectively. 'With head and heart right, the whole man is right' (*Edmunds*). The head needs to be kept from error, the heart from sin. For "the breastplate of righteousness" (Eph. vi. 14), we have here "the breastplate of faith and love:" for the righteousness imputed to man for justification is "faith working by love" (Rom. iv. 3, 22-24; Gal. v. 6). *Faith*, as the motive *within*, and *love*, exhibited in outward acts, constitute perfect *righteousness*. In Eph. vi. 17 the helmet is "salvation;" here, "the *hope* of salvation." In one aspect "salvation" is present (John iii. 36; v. 24; 1 John v. 13); in another, it is a matter of *hope* (Rom. viii. 24, 25). Our Head primarily wore the "breastplate of righteousness" and "helmet of salvation," that we might, by union with Him, receive both (Isa. lix. 17). *Hope* keeps the mind from sinking under present trials. **9. For**—the ground of our "hope" (*v.* 8). **appointed us** [*etheto*]—'set' (Acts xiii. 47), in His everlasting purpose of love (ch. iii. 3; 2 Thess. ii. 14; 2 Tim. i. 9). Contrast Rom. ix. 22; Jude 4. **to**—i. e., *unto* wrath. **to obtain** [*peripoiēsin soterias*]—'to the acquisition of salvation:' said (*Bengel*) of one saved out of a general wreck, when all things else are lost: so the elect saved out of the multitude lost (2 Thess. ii. 13, 14). God's 'gracious appointment through Jesus Christ' (Eph. i. 5) precludes our being able to 'acquire' salvation *of ourselves*. Christ 'acquired' [*periepoiēsato*, "purchased"] the Church (and its salvation) with His own blood' (Acts xx. 28): each member is appointed by God to the 'acquiring of salvation.' Primarily, God does the work; in the secondary sense, man does it. **10. dead for us** [*huper*]—'in our behalf.' So that we need

11 with him. Wherefore ¹ comfort yourselves together, and edify one another, even as also ye do.

12 And we beseech you, brethren, ʲ to know them which labour among

13 you, and are over you in the Lord, and admonish you; and to esteem them very highly in love for their work's sake. *And* be at peace among yourselves.

14 Now we ² exhort you, brethren, warn them that are ³ unruly, comfort the feeble-minded, support the weak, be patient toward all *men*.

15 See ᵏ that none render evil for evil unto any *man*; but ever ˡ follow that which is good, both among yourselves, and to all *men*.

16, Rejoice evermore. Pray ᵐ without ceasing. In every thing give

18 thanks: for this is the will of God in Christ Jesus concerning you.

19 Quench ⁿ not the Spirit. Despise ᵒ not prophesyings. Prove ᵖ all

A. D. 54.
¹ Or. exhort.
ʲ Phil. 2. 29.
1 Tim. 5. 17.
Heb. 13. 7.
² Or, beseech.
³ Or, disorderly.
ᵏ Lev. 19. 18.
Pro 20. 22.
ˡ Gal. 6. 10.
ᵐ Luke 18. 1.
ⁿ Eph. 4. 30.
1 Tim. 4. 14.
ᵒ 1 Cor. 14. 1.
ᵖ 1 John 4. 1.

have no doubt of the certainty of our salvation, since Christ has for us satisfied all the demands of justice against us. **whether we wake or sleep** —whether we be found at Christ's coming *alive*, or *in our graves*. **together with him**—rather, '*all* of us *together* should live with Him:' the living not preceding the dead in glorification at His coming (ch. iv. 13; Rom. xiv. 8). **11. comfort yourselves** [*allēlous*]—"one another." Here he reverts to consolation, as in ch. iv. 18. **one another**—Greek, 'edify (ye) one the other;' *lit.*, 'build up' (believers forming the temple of God, 1 Cor. iii. 16); viz., in faith, hope, and love, by discoursing together on such topics as the coming glory of the Lord and His saints (Mal. iii. 16).

12. beseech—"exhort," in *v.* 14; here, "we beseech," as a personal favour (Paul making the cause of the Thessalonian presbyters his own). **know**—to have respect for their office, and treat them accordingly (cf. 1 Cor. xvi. 18) with reverence and liberality in supplying their needs (1 Tim. v. 17). The Thessalonian church being newly planted, the ministers were novices (1 Tim. iii. 6), which may account for the people treating them with less respect. Paul's practice was to ordain elders in every church soon after its establishment (Acts xiv. 23). **them which labour among you, and are over you . . . admonish you.** Not three classes, but one, as there is but one article common to the three (Greek). "Labour" expresses their laborious life: "are over you," their pre-eminence as superintendents ("bishops," i. e., *overseers*, Phil. i. 1; them that have rule over you [*proistamenous*, *leaders*], Heb. xiii. 17; "pastors," Eph. iv. 11): "admonish you," their leading function [*nouthetountas*]; "put in mind:" not arbitrary authority, but gentle, though faithful, admonition (2 Tim. ii. 14, 24, 25; 1 Pet. v. 3). **in the Lord.** Their presidency over you is not in worldly affairs, but in things appertaining to the Lord. **13. very highly** [*huperekperissōs*]—' exceeding abundantly.' **for their work's sake**—the high nature of it alone, the furtherance of your salvation and of the kingdom of Christ, should be a sufficient motive to claim your reverential love. At the same time the term teaches ministers that, whilst claiming the reverence due to their office, it is not a sinecure, but a "work" (cf. "*labour*") even to *weariness* [*kopiōntas*] (*v.* 12). **be at peace among yourselves**—"and" is not in the original. Let there not only be peace between ministers and their flocks, but also no party rivalries among yourselves—one contending in behalf of one favourite minister, another in behalf of another (Mark ix. 50; 1 Cor. i. 12; iv. 6; 2 Cor. xiii. 11). **14. brethren.** This exhortation to "warn" [*noutheteite*; "admonish," as *v.* 12] the unruly (those "disorderly" persons, 2 Thess. iii. 6, 11, who would not work,

through fanatical expectations of Christ's coming, yet expected to be maintained [*ataktous*]: said of soldiers *not remaining in their ranks*, cf. ch. iv. 11; also those insubordinate in discipline, as to those "over" the church, *v.* 12), comfort the *faint-hearted* [*oligopsuchous*: ready to sink 'without hope' in bereavements, ch. iv. 13, and temptations], &c., applies to all clergy and laity alike, though primarily to the clergy (*v.* 12). Not only are they to *be at peace among themselves*, but to promote peace among others. **support** [*antechesthe*]—*lay fast hold on* to support. **the weak**—spiritually. Paul practised what he preached (1 Cor. ix. 22). **be patient toward all** [*makrothumeite*, the opposite of *oxuthumein*]. There is no believer who needs not *long-suffering* (1 Cor. xiii. 4) *patience* to be exercised "toward" him; there is none to whom a believer ought not to show it; many show it more to strangers than to their own families, to the great than to the humble: we ought to show it "toward *all men*" (*Bengel*). Cf. "the long-suffering of our Lord" (2 Cor. x. 1; 2 Pet. iii. 15).

15. Christianity first taught this. The British triad defines three classes: the man of the devil returns evil for good; the man of men returns good for good, evil for evil; the man of God returns good for evil (Rom. xii. 17; 1 Pet. iii. 9). **unto any man**—whether unto a Christian or a heathen, however great the provocation. **follow** —as a matter of earnest pursuit. **good**—that which is *for the good of others*.

16, 17. In order to "rejoice evermore," we must "pray without ceasing." He who thanks God for all things as happening for the best, will have continuous joy (*Theophylact*). Phil. iv. 4, 6, "Rejoice *in the Lord*;" Rom. xiv. 17, "*in the Holy Ghost*" (who is the originating cause, ch. i. 6, as well as the 'sphere of joy:' *faith* lays hold of and keeps it, Phil. i. 25); Rom. xii. 12, "in *hope*;" Acts v. 41, '*in being counted worthy to suffer shame for Christ's name*;' Jas. i. 2, *in falling* "*into divers temptations*." '*Pray* [*adialeiptōs*] *without intermission*:' not allowing prayerless gaps to intervene between the times of prayer. Cherish the spirit of prayer; let devotion be the chief business of life (Eph. vi. 18; Col. iv. 2). **18. In every thing** —even what *seems* adverse; for nothing is *really* so (cf. Rom. viii. 28; Eph. v. 20.) So Christ (Matt. xv. 36; xxvi. 27; Luke x. 21; John xi. 41). **this** —that ye should "in every thing give thanks," "is the will of God in Christ Jesus (the Mediator in whom that will is revealed: cf. Phil. iii. 14) concerning [*towards: eis*] you." *God's will* is the believer's law. Put commas after each of the three precepts (*vv.* 16, 17, 18), making "this" refer to all three.

19. Quench not—The Spirit being a holy *fire*: 'where the Spirit is, He burns' (Matt. iii. 11;

22 things: hold fast that which is good. Abstain *q* from all appearance of evil.

23 And *r* the very God of peace sanctify you wholly: and *I pray God* your whole spirit and soul and body be *s* preserved blameless unto the

24 coming of our Lord Jesus Christ. Faithful *t is* he that calleth you, who also will do *it.*

25 Brethren, pray for us. Greet all the brethren with an holy kiss. I

A. D. 54.

q Ex. 23. 7.
Isa 33. 15.
Matt. 17.26.
Rom. 12.17.
1 Cor. 8. 13.
r Phil. 4. 9.
s 1 Cor. 1. 8.
t 1 Cor.10.13.

Acts ii. 3). Contrast 2 Tim. i. 6 [*anazopurein*], 'rekindle.' Do not throw cold water on those who, under the Spirit's extraordinary inspiration, speak with tongues, reveal mysteries, or pray in the congregation. Enthusiastic statements (perhaps of the nearness of Christ's coming, exaggerating Paul's statement, 2 Thess. ii. 2, "by *spirit*," led some (probably presiding ministers, not always treated with due respect by enthusiasts, *v.* 12), from dread of fanaticism, to discourage the free utterances of those really inspired in the church assembly. On the other hand, the caution, *v.* 21, was needed, not to receive "all" professed revelations without 'proving' them. **20. prophesyings** —whether exercised in *inspired* teaching (as distinguished from [*didache*] 'teaching' under the ordinary influences of grace), or in predicting. 'Despised' by some, as fanatics had brought discredit on all extraordinary manifestations of the Spirit (*v.* 19, note). At Corinth subsequently prophesyings were despised as *beneath tongues*, but are shown by Paul to be a greater gift, though tongues be more showy (1 Cor. xiv. 5). **21, 22.** B Δ G *f q*, Vulgate, insert 'but.' א A C omit it. You ought indeed not to "quench the Spirit" nor "despise prophesyings;" 'but,' at the same time, do not take "all" as genuine which professes to be so; 'prove (test) them all.' Means of testing existed in the Church: some had the "discerning of spirits" (1 Cor. xii. 10; xiv. 29; 1 John iv. 1). Another test, which we also have, is to try the professed revelation whether it accord with Scripture, as the noble Bereans did (Isa. viii. 20; Acts xvii. 11; Gal. i. 8, 9). This negatives Rome's assumption of infallibly laying down the law: the laity have the right of private judgment, and are bound to exercise it in testing every human teaching by Scripture. *Locke*, 'Those who are for laying aside reason in matters of revelation resemble one who should *put out his eyes* to use a *telescope.*' **hold fast . . good.** Join this with the next clause (*v.* 22), not merely with the preceding. As the result of 'proving all things,' especially *prophesyings*, '*hold fast* (Luke viii. 15; 1 Cor. xi. 2; Heb. ii. 1) the good: *hold yourselves aloof from* every *species* of evil.' [*Ellicott:* as the antithesis to "that which is good," and the lexical meaning of *eidous*, 'form,' favour. But see below]. Accept not even a professedly spirit-inspired communication, if at variance with the truth taught you (2 Thess. ii. 2). *Tittmann* supports, 'from every *evil appearance.*' The context refers not to standing aloof from every *evil appearance* IN OURSELVES, but IN OTHERS; for instance, pretended spirit-inspired prophesyings. The Christian often should *not* abstain from what has the "*appearance*" of evil, when really good. Jesus healed on the Sabbath, and ate with publicans— acts which wore the *appearance* of evil, but which were really good. The context favours this sense: However *specious* be such pretended prophets and their "prophesyings," stand aloof from every such appearance when it is evil. [Luke ix. 29 justifies this sense of *eidos* lexically]. **23. And—**'But' [*de*]. **the very God—**rather, 'may the God of peace *Himself*' do for you by *His*

own power what *I* cannot do by all my monitions, nor *you* by all your efforts (Rom. xvi. 20; Heb. xiii. 20). **sanctify you**—for *holiness* is the condition of "peace" (Phil. iv. 6-9). As *peace* is His attribute, so it is His especial gift (John xiv. 27); for which end may He give you *holiness.* **wholly** [*holoteleis*]—(so that you should be) 'perfect in every respect.' **and**—i. e., '*and so* (omit *I pray God:* not in the Greek) may your . . . spirit and soul and body be preserved whole:' a different word from "wholly:" [*holokleron*] 'entire;' with none of the integral parts wanting. [*Teleios* is what has reached its *end*, in respect to *quality; holokleros*, '*complete* in all its parts,' in respect to *quantity*, Jas. i. 4.] It refers to man in his normal integrity: an ideal which shall be attained by the glorified believer. All three—spirit, soul, and body—each in its place, constitute man 'entire.' The "spirit" links man with higher intelligences, and is that highest part receptive of the quickening Holy Spirit (1 Cor. xv. 47). The soul [*psuche*] is intermediate between *body* and *spirit:* it is the sphere of the will and affections. In the unspiritual, the spirit is so sunk under the animal *soul* (which it ought to keep under), that such are 'animal' ('*sensual*,' having merely the *body* of organized matter, and the *soul* the immaterial animating essence), "having *not the Spirit*" (Jude 19: cf. 1 Cor. ii. notes, xv. 44, 46-48; John iii. 6). The unbeliever shall rise with an *animal* (soul-animated) *body*, but not, like the believer, with a *spiritual* (spirit-endued) body like Christ's (Rom. viii. 11). **blameless unto** [*amemptōs*]— 'blamelessly (so as to be in a blameless state) at Christ's coming.' In Hebrew [שלם], "peace" and "wholly" [*holoteleis*] are kindred terms; so the prayer explains "God of peace." *Bengel* takes "wholly" as *collectively—all* the Thessalonians— so that no one should fail; and "whole" *individually—each one entire—*with "spirit and soul and body." The mention of the *body* accords with ch. iv. 16, end. *Trench*, better, "wholly"—*i. e.,* 'having perfectly attained the moral *end;*' viz., to be full-grown in Christ. "Whole," *complete*, with no grace [also *part*] which ought to be in a Christian wanting. **24. Faithful—**to His covenant promises (John x. 27-29; 1 Cor. i. 9, 10; x. 13; Phil. i. 6; 2 Tim. ii. 13). **he that calleth you.** God, the caller of His people, will cause His calling not to fall short of its end. **do it—**preserve and present you blameless at Christ's coming (*v.* 23; Rom. viii. 30; 1 Pet. v. 10). You must not look at the foes before and behind, on the right and the left, but to God's faithfulness to His promises, God's zeal for His honour, and God's love for those whom He calleth.

25. B Δ *f* read 'Pray ye *also* for [*peri, concerning*] us,' even as *we* have been just praying for you (*v.* 23). א A G *g*, Vulgate, omit 'also.' The clergy need much the prayers of their flocks. Paul makes the same request, Rom., Ephes., Phil., Col., Phile., and 2 Cor. Not so 1 and 2 Tim., and Titus, whose intercessions, as his spiritual sons, he was already sure of; nor 1 Cor. and Gal., as these epistles abound in rebuke. **26.** This epistle

⁴charge you by the Lord that this epistle be read unto all the holy brethren.

28   The grace of our Lord Jesus Christ *be* with you. Amen.

The first *epistle* unto the Thessalonians was written from Athens.

A. D. 54.
⁴ Or,
adjure.
2 Thes. 3.
14.

was first handed to *the elders*, who communicated it to "the brethren." In Rom. xvi. 16; 1 Cor. xvi. 20; 2 Cor. xiii. 12, it is, "Greet *one another*." Not able to greet the brethren in person, he begs the elders to do it for him. holy kiss —pure and chaste. "A kiss of charity" (1 Pet. v. 14); 'a kiss of peace' (*Tertullian*, 'De Orat.' c. 14); 'a mystic kiss' (*Clemens Alexandrinus*, 'Pædagogy,' iii. 11); a token of Christian fellowship (cf. Luke vii. 45; Acts xx. 37): not merely a conventional salutation, as in many countries. In the early church the kiss passed through the congregation at the holy communion (*Justin Martyr*, 'Apology,' i. 65; 'Apostolic Constitutions,' ii. 57), the men kissing the men, and the women the women. So in the Syrian church, each takes his neighbour's right hand, and says, 'Peace.' **27. I charge** [*enorkizo*]—'I adjure you.' read **unto all**—viz., publicly in the congregation. The aorist [*anagnosthenai*] implies a single act done at a particular time. The earnestness of his adjuration implies how solemnly important he felt this divinely-inspired message. Also, as this was the FIRST of the New Testament epistles, he gives a solemn charge that its being publicly read should be a sample of what should be done with the others; just as the Pentateuch and the Prophets

were publicly read under the Old Testament, and are still read in the synagogue (Luke iv. 16; Acts xv. 21; 2 Cor. iii. 15; Col. iv. 16). Cf. the same injunction as to the Apocalypse, the LAST of the New Testament canon (Rev. i. 3). The "all" includes women and children, especially those who could not read it themselves (Deut. xxxi. 12; Josh. viii. 33-35). What Paul commands with an adjuration, Rome forbids under a curse (*Bengel*). Though these epistles had difficulties, the laity were all to hear them read (1 Pet. iv. 11; 2 Pet. iii. 16), even the very young (2 Tim. i. 5; iii. 15). "Holy" is omitted before "brethren" in א B Δ G *fg*. A C, Vulgate, support it.

28. (Note, 2 Cor. xiii. 14, which is the longest benediction; as Col. iv. 18; 2 Tim. iv. 22, "Grace be with you," is the shortest) Paul ends as he began (ch. i. 1), with "grace." א A, Vulgate, have, but B Δ G *fg* omit, "Amen:" probably the liturgical response of the church after the public reading of the epistle.

The subscription is comparatively modern. The epistle was not, as it states, written from Athens, but from Corinth; for it is in the names of Silas and Timothy (besides Paul), who did not join the apostle before he reached the latter city (Acts xviii. 5).

470

THE SECOND EPISTLE OF PAUL THE APOSTLE TO THE

THESSALONIANS.

1 PAUL, *a*and Silvanus, and Timotheus, unto the church of the *b*Thes-
2 salonians in God our Father and the Lord Jesus Christ: Grace unto
you, and peace, from God our Father and the Lord Jesus Christ.
3 We are bound to thank God always for you, brethren, as it is meet,
because that your faith *c*groweth exceedingly, and the charity of every
4 one of you all toward each other aboundeth; so that *d*we ourselves glory
in you in the churches of God *e*for your patience and faith *f*in all your
5 persecutions and tribulations that ye endure: *which is* *g*a manifest token
of the righteous judgment of God, that ye may be counted *h*worthy
6 the kingdom of God, for which ye also suffer: seeing *it is* a righteous
thing with God to recompense tribulation to them that trouble you;
7 and to you who are troubled *j*rest with us, when the Lord Jesus shall be

A. D. 54.

CHAP. 1.
a 2 Cor. 1. 19.
b 1 Thes. 1. 1.
c Job 17. 9.
Ps. 84. 7.
d 2 Cor. 7. 14.
e 1 Thes. 1. 3.
f 1 Thes. 2. 14.
g Job 8. 3.
Phil. 1. 28.
h Luke 20, 35.
Rev. 3. 4.
i Rev. 6. 10.
j Rev. 14. 13.

CHAP. I. 1-12.—Address—Salutation—Introduction—Thanksgiving for their Growth
in Faith and Love, and their Patience in
Persecutions: a Token for Good Everlasting
to them, and for Perdition to their Adversaries at Christ's Coming—Prayer for their
Perfection.
1. in God our Father—more endearing than 1
Thess. i. 1, "in God the Father." **2. from** [*apo*,
emanation simply: *para*, from a *personal* source;
2 John 3] **God our Father.** So אAGg, Vulgate.
But BΔ*f* omit "our."
3. We are bound [*opheilomen*]—'We owe it as
a debt' (ch. ii. 13). Their prayer having been
heard (1 Thess. iii. 12), it is a *bounden* return that
they should thank God for it. Paul and his fellow-missionaries practise what they preach (1
Thess. v. 18). In 1 Thess. i. 3 their thanksgiving
was for the Thessalonian 'faith, love, and patience;' here for their *exceeding growth* in *faith*
[*huperauxanei*: 'groweth above measure'], and for
their *charity abounding.* "We are bound"—the
duty of thanksgiving from its *subjective* side, as an
inward conviction. **as it is meet**—from the *objective*, as something answering to the circumstances (*Alford*). The prayer (1 Thess. iii. 12),
"The Lord make you to *abound in love one toward
another*," and the answer, 'The *love* of every one
of you all *toward each other aboundeth*' (cf. 1
Thess. iv. 10). Not merely *general* love, but *individual*; also not shown only to *particular* friends,
but, for Christ's sake, to *all.* **4. glory in you**—
'boast in your case.' Not merely do we hear
others speaking of the Thessalonians' faith, but
we ourselves, who might be expected to be silent
on what redounds to our own praise cannot but
boast of it. In 1 Thess. i. 8 Paul said their faith
was so well known in various places that he
and his fellow-missionaries needed not to speak
of it; here he says, so abounding is their love,
combined with faith and patience, that he and
his fellow-missionaries *themselves* make it their
present glorying in the various churches (now at
Corinth in Achaia, to which church he wrote
subsequently, boasting, in the Lord, of the faith
of the Macedonian churches, 2 Cor. viii. 1; x.
15-17), besides looking forward to glorying thereat
at Christ's coming (1 Thess. ii. 19). **patience.** In
1 Thess. i. 3 "patience *of hope*." Here *hope* is
tacitly supposed as the ground of their brave
patience: *vv.* 5, 7 state the object of their faith—

viz., the kingdom for which they suffer. **tribulations.** The Jews instigated the populace
and the magistrates against Christians (Acts
xvii. 5, 8). **that ye endure**—'are enduring.' **5.
Which.** Your *enduring* tribulations is a 'token of
the (future) righteous judgment of God' at Christ's
coming; your present suffering for Him, and your
adversaries' opposition to Him, is a pledge that
then you will reign, and they perish (2 Tim. ii. 12).
The judgment is even now begun; but its consummation will be then. David (Ps. lxxiii. 1-14)
and Jeremiah (Jer. xii. 1-4) were perplexed at the
wicked prospering and the godly suffering. But
Paul, by the light of the New Testament, makes
this very fact a consolation. It is a *proof* [*endeig-
ma*] of the future judgment, which will set to
rights all present anomalies, by rewarding the
now suffering saint, and punishing the persecutor.
Even now 'the Judge of all the earth does right'
(Gen. xviii. 25); for the godly are in themselves
sinful, and need chastisement. What they suffer
unjustly from men they suffer justly from God:
they have their evil things here, that they may
escape condemnation with the world, and have
their good things hereafter (Luke xvi. 25; 1 Cor.
xi. 32) (*Edmunds*). **that ye may be counted worthy**—the purpose of God's "righteous judgment"
as regards you. **for which**—'*in behalf of* which ye
are also suffering' (cf. Acts v. 41; ix. 16; xiv. 22;
Phil. i. 29). Though men are justified by faith,
they shall be judged "according to their works"
(Rev. xx. 4, 12: cf. 1 Thess. ii. 12; 1 Pet. i. 6, 7).
The "also" implies the connection between *the
suffering for the kingdom* and *being counted worthy*
of it (cf. Rom. viii. 17, 18). **6. Seeing** (that) **it is a
righteous thing**—justifying the assertion that
there is a "*righteous judgment*" (*v.* 5); 'seeing
that [*eiper*, *if, as we all admit: if so be that*] it is a
righteous thing with [*para, Theo:* at the tribunal
of] God.' Our innate feeling of what is just confirms what is revealed. **recompense**—requite *in
kind; viz.,* tribulation to them that trouble you
(*affliction* to those that *afflict* you); and to you who
are *troubled, rest from trouble.* **7. rest**—governed
by "to recompense" (*v.* 6). [*Anesin, relaxation :*
loosening the *tension, epitasis*, which preceded;
relaxing the strings of endurance now so tightly
drawn. *Anapausis,* "rest" (Matt. xi. 28; Rev.
xiv. 13), is *cessation* from labour. *Sabbatismos*
(Heb. iv. 9), 'a keeping of Sabbath.'] **with us**—
viz., Paul, Silas, and Timothy, who are troubled

8 revealed from heaven with ¹his mighty angels, in *ᵏ*flaming fire ²taking vengeance on them *ˡ*that know not God, and that obey not the gospel of
9 our Lord Jesus Christ: who shall be punished with everlasting destruction from the presence of the Lord, and *ᵐ*from the glory of his power;
10 when he shall come to be glorified in his saints, and to be admired in all them that believe, (because our testimony among you was believed,) in that day.
11   Wherefore also we pray always for you, that our God would ³count you worthy of *this* calling, and fulfil all the good pleasure of *his* goodness,
12 and the work of faith with power: that the name of our Lord Jesus

A. D. 54.

1 the angels of his power.
ᵏ Heb 10. 27.
Rev. 21. 8.
2 Or, yielding.
ˡ 1 s. 79. 6.
ᵐ Deut. 33. 2.
Isa 2. 19.
3 Or, vouchsafe.

like yourselves (ch. iii. 2). **when**—not sooner, not later. **the Lord Jesus shall be revealed**—for now He is *hidden*, and our life hidden with Him (Col. iii. 3, 4). **with his mighty angels** (Greek, 'with the angels of His power')—*i. e.*, the ministers by whom He makes His power to be recognized (Matt. xiii. 41, 42). It is not *their*, but 'His might' which is prominent. 8. **In flaming fire**—Greek, 'In (encompassed with) flame of fire.' B Δ G *g*, Vulgate. But א A *f* read, *in fire of flame*. This *flame of fire* accompanied His manifestation in the bush (Exod. iii. 2); also His giving of the law at Sinai (Exod. xix. 18); also it shall accompany His advent (Dan. vii. 9, 10; Mal. iv. 1), symbolizing His own glory and His consuming vengeance against His foes (Heb. x. 27; xii. 29; 2 Pet. iii. 7, 10). **taking**—lit., '*giving*' them, as their portion, "vengeance." **know not God**—the *Gentiles* primarily (Ps. lxxix. 6; Gal. iv. 8; 1 Thess. iv. 5); not those *involuntarily*, but those *wilfully* not knowing Him, as Pharaoh, who might have known God if he would, but boasted, "I know not the Lord" (Exod. v. 2); and as the Thessalonians' persecutors, who might have known God by the preaching of those whom they persecuted. Also all heathens who sin against whatever knowledge of God they have by conscience and from His visible works (Rom. i. 20, 21; ii. 12, 14-16). Secondarily, all who 'profess to know God, but in works deny Him' (Titus i. 16). **obey not the gospel**—primarily the unbelieving *Jews* (Rom. x. 3, 16). The distinct article implying two distinct classes, marks that primarily the former clause refers to the *heathen;* this clause to the Jews. Secondarily, all who obey not the truth (Rom. ii. 8). **Christ.** So א A G *f g*, Vulgate. Omitted in B Δ. 9. **Who** [*hoitines*]—'*persons who*,' &c. **everlasting** [*aionion*]. The oldest Greek commentators, *Theophilus, Theodoret, &c. (Ellicott)*, expound 'eternal,' 'unending,' not in the *qualitative* aspect given by some. **destruction from the presence of the Lord**—the sentence *emanating from Him in person*, sitting as Judge (*Bengel*). But thus "presence of the Lord" would be a circumlocution for *the personal Lord*. Rather, *driving them far from* Him (Matt. xxv. 41; Rev. vi. 16; xii. 14: cf. Isa. ii. 10, 19; 1 Pet. iii. 12). **from the glory of his power**—the *instrument* BY which the sentence is carried into execution (*Edmunds*). But the same preposition [*apo*] must have the same sense in both clauses. Rather, '(driven) FROM the glory of His might:' *the glory emanating from His might* is the sphere wherein the saints shall be '*glorified;*' "*the presence of the Lord*" is the sphere wherein He shall be "*admired* in all them that believe." His *presence* shall be the spring of their blessedness (Ps. xvi. 11; xvii. 15; Matt. xviii. 10; Rev. xxii. 4). Thus *v.* 10 is parallel to and explains this verse. *Cast out from the presence of the Lord* is the sting of *eternal* death; the law of evil left to its unrestricted working, without one counteracting in-

fluence of the presence of God, the Source of all light and holiness (Isa. lxvi. 24; Mark ix. 44). 10. 'When He shall have come.' **glorified in his saints**—as the element and mirror IN which His glory shall shine brightly; not, as in 1 Thess. iii. 13, including *angels*, but only *saints* (Isa. xlix. 3), which involves their being glorified (John xvii. 10, 22). **admired in all them that believed**—Greek, 'them that *believed*.' Once they *believed;* now they *see*. They took His word on trust; now His word is made good, and they need faith no longer. With *wonder* all celestial intelligences (Eph. iii. 10) shall *admire* the Redeemer, because of the glory He has wrought in them that *believed* during their earthly probation. **because, &c.** Supply 'among whom (viz., those who shall be found to have believed) *you*, too, shall be; *because our testimony* (1 Cor. i. 6) *unto* [*epi*: "among"] *you was believed*,' and not rejected, as by those who "obey not the Gospel" (*v.* 8). The early preaching was not abstract discussions, but a *testimony* to facts and truths experimentally known (Luke xxiv. 48; Acts i. 8). *Faith* is (*Bishop Pearson*) 'an assent unto truths, credible upon the testimony of God, delivered unto us by the apostles and prophets' (at first orally, but now in their writings). "Glorified in His saints" reminds us that *holiness* is *glory* in the bud; *glory* is *holiness* developed.
11. Wherefore [*Eis ho*]—'With a view to which;' viz., His glorification in you as His saints. **also.** We not only anticipate generally the coming glorification, but *we also pray concerning* [*peri*] YOU. **our God**—whom we serve. **count you worthy.** The prominent position of "YOU" in the Greek makes it emphatic: May *you* be found among the saints whom God shall count worthy. **of** (this) **calling**—'of the [*tēs*] calling' (Eph. iv. 1) wherewith He hath called you. There is no dignity in us independent of God's calling (2 Tim. i. 9). Here not merely the first actual call, but the whole of God's electing act, originating in His "purpose of grace given us in Christ before the world began," and having its consummation in glory. **all the** [*pasan endokian*]—rather, 'every.' **good pleasure of, &c.**—on the part of God (*Bengel*). **faith**—on your part. **of (his) goodness.** The Greek [*agathōsune*] for *goodness* is never applied to God elsewhere in the New Testament; and there is no "His" in the Greek. But as in the parallel clause, "calling" refers to GOD'S purpose, and as [*eudokia*] "good pleasure" mostly is used of *God* [which is against *Ellicott's* reference of *eudokia* to the Thessalonians' *good pleasure*, Eph. i. 5, 9],—translate, 'fulfil (*His*) *every gracious purpose* of goodness' (on your part)—*i. e.*, fully perfect in you all goodness, according to *His gracious purpose*. Thus, "the *grace* of our God," *v.* 12, corresponds to *God's* "*good pleasure*". here. **the work of faith**—Greek (no article): *faith* manifested by *work*, which is its perfected development (Jas. i. 4; note, 1 Thess. i. 3). Strict parallelism would require "work" to be *God's*, as "good pleasure"

Christ may be glorified in you, and ye in him, according to the grace of our God and the Lord Jesus Christ.

2 NOW we beseech you, brethren, by the coming of our Lord Jesus Christ, [a] and *by* our gathering together unto him, that ye be not soon shaken in mind, or be troubled, neither by spirit, nor by word, nor by letter as from us, as that the day of Christ is at hand. Let no man deceive you by any means: for *that day shall not come*, except [b] there come a falling away first, and [c] that man of sin be revealed, the [d] son of

A. D. 54.

CHAP. 2.
a Matt. 24.31.
  Mark 13.27.
  Eph. 1. 10.
  1 Thes.4.17.
b 1 Tim 4. 1.
c Dan. 7. 25.
  Rev. 13. 11.
d John 17. 12.

---

is. But this may be dispensed with, as 'faith's work' is tacitly understood as really *God's* in and by man (Phil. ii. 13), and so is parallel to *God's* "good pleasure." **with power** — Greek, ' IN power;' i. e., '*powerfully*' (Col. i. 11, 29). **12. the name of our Lord Jesus.** Our Lord Jesus *in His manifested personality* as the God-man. **in you, and ye in him**—reciprocal glorification (cf. Isa. xxviii. 5 with Isa. lxii. 3). **glorified** (John xxi. 19; Gal. i. 24; 1 Pet. iv. 14). The believer's graces redound to Christ's *glory*, and His glory, as Head, reflects glory on them, the members. **according to**—in accordance with the blessed end contemplated by. **the grace of our God, and the Lord Jesus Christ.** The one Greek article to both implies the inseparable oneness of God and the Lord Jesus.

CHAP. II. 1-17.—THEIR ERROR AS TO CHRIST'S IMMEDIATE COMING—THE APOSTASY MUST PRECEDE IT — EXHORTATION TO STEDFASTNESS, INTRODUCED WITH THANKSGIVING FOR THEIR ELECTION BY GOD.

1. Now—'But:' marking the transition from his prayers *for* them to entreaties *to* them. **we beseech you**—affectionate entreaty to win them to the right view, rather than stern reproof. **by** [*huper*]—' with respect to:' as [*huper*] 'of,' 2 Cor. i. 8; Phil. ii. 13—lit., *in behalf of* the true view of Christ's coming, which has been misinterpreted. **our gathering together unto him** — the *final gathering* of the saints to Him at His coming (Matt. xxiv. 31; 1 Thess. iv. 17; Ps. l. 5). [*Episunagoge* is nowhere else found except Heb. x. 25, *the assembling together* of believers for *congregational* worship, which is a pledge of the final assembling never to part.] Then first will believers enjoy mutual recognition. Our instinctive fears of the judgment are dispelled by the thought of being gathered together UNTO HIM ("even as the hen *gathereth* [*episunagei*] her chickens under her wings"), which ensures our safety. **2. soon**—on trifling grounds, readily (Gal. i. 6). **shaken** [*saleuthēnai*]—tossed as ships tossed by an agitated sea (Jas. i. 6, 8, 11; Eph. iv. 14). **in mind** [*apo tou noos*]—*from* your mind; i. e., from your ordinary stedfastness. **or** [*mēde*]—'nor yet.' [A א B Δ G, instead of *mēte*.] **troubled** [*throeisthai*]—*emotional* agitation; as "shaken" to *intellectual*. **by spirit** —by a *person professing* to have the *spirit* of prophecy (1 Cor. xii. 8-10; 1 John iv. 1-3). The Thessalonians were warned (1 Thess. v. 20, 21) to "prove" such professed prophesyings, and "hold fast (only) that which is good." **by word**—*of mouth* (cf. *vv.* 5, 15): some saying alleged to be that of St. Paul, orally communicated. If oral tradition was liable to such perversion in the apostolic age (cf. a similar instance, John xxi. 23), how much more in ours! **by letter as from us**—purporting to be from us, whereas it is a forgery. Hence he gives a test by which to know his genuine letters (ch. iii. 17). **day of Christ.** א A B Δ G *fg*, Vulgate, read 'of *the Lord*.' **is at hand** [*enesteken*]—rather, as in Rom. viii. 38; 1 Cor. iii. 22; Gal. i. 4, '*is present*' [stronger than *ephesteken*, 2 Tim. iv. 6]. **Christ and His apostles**
473

always taught that the Lord's coming *is at hand;* it is not likely that Paul would imply anything contrary: what he denies is, that it is so *immediately imminent*, or *present*, as to justify the neglect of every-day duties. **3. by any means**—Greek, 'in any manner.' Christ (Matt. xxiv. 4) gives the same warning. Paul indicated three ways (*v.* 2) in which they might be deceived (cf. other ways, *v.* 9, and Matt. xxiv. 5, 24). **a falling away** [*hē apostasia*]—'*the* falling away,' or 'apostasy,' of which "I told you" before (*v.* 5), "when I was yet with you," and of which the Lord gave intimation (Matt. xxiv. 10-12; Luke xviii. 8; John v. 43). **that man of sin be revealed**—Greek order, 'and there have been revealed the man of sin.' As Christ was first in *mystery*, and afterwards *revealed;* also as He is now *spiritually* present, and afterwards shall be *revealed personally* (ch. i. 7; 1 Tim. iii. 16); so Antichrist (the term 1 John ii. 18; iv. 3) is first in mystery, and afterwards revealed (*vv.* 7-9). As righteousness found its embodiment in Christ, "the Lord our righteousness," so "sin" shall have its embodiment in "the man of sin." *The hindering* power meanwhile restrains its full manifestation: when that shall be removed, this shall take place. The articles, '*the* apostasy,' and '*the* man of sin,' may refer to their being *well known, as foretold* by Dan. viii. 9-11 (perhaps distinct from "the little horn," Dan. vii. 8, 25, which may refer to the Papacy); xi. 30, the wilful king who "shall exalt and magnify himself above every god, and shall speak marvellous things against the God of gods; neither shall he regard any god." **the son of perdition**—applied to none else besides Judas the traitor (John xvii. 12). The Pope, like Judas, holds a high position in the Church, professing an affectionate reverence for Christ, yet really betraying Him. As 'the lawless one,' he claims supremacy over all law, civil, divine, and that of conscience; with lying signs, and professing to transform a wafer into God. But Rev. xvii. represents apostate Christendom as "a *woman*," the usual emblem of a church. Antichrist is a *man*, seemingly, a *beast* really, and continues only 'a short space:' Christ in person destroys him. But apostate Christendom is destroyed by ten *human* kings, instruments of God's vengeance (Rev. xvii. 16; xviii. 2, 8, 20). Antichrist (the second "beast" coming up out of the earth) shall at first be "like a lamb," whilst he 'speaks as a dragon' (Rev. xiii. 11): ' coming in peaceably and by flatteries,' 'working deceitfully,' but 'his heart shall be against the holy covenant'(Dan. xi. 21, 23, 28, 30). Seeds of the "falling away" soon appeared (1 Tim. iv. 1-3), but the full development and concentration of antichristian elements in one person are still to appear. Contrast the King of Zion's coming as JESUS—(1.) Righteous; (2.) having *salvation;* (3.) *lowly:* whereas Antichrist is—(1.) "The man of (the embodiment of) *sin;*" (2.) the son of *perdition;* (3.) *exalting himself* above all that is worshipped. He is *the son of perdition*, as essentially belonging to, and finally doomed to it (Rev. xvii. 8, 11). As "the *kingdom of heaven*"

4 perdition; who opposeth and *e*exalteth himself above *f* all that is called | A. D. 54.
God, or that is worshipped; so that he as God sitteth in the temple of | *e* Isa. 14. 13.
God, showing himself that he is God. | *f* 1 Cor. 8. 5.

is first brought before us in the abstract, then in the concrete, the *King*, the Lord Jesus; so here, first we have (*v.* 7) "the mystery of *iniquity*" [*anomias*, 'of *lawlessness*']; then 'the *iniquitous one*' [*ho anomos*], 'the *lawless* one' (*v.* 8). Doubtless 'the apostasy' of *Romanism* (the abstract) is the greatest instance of the working of *the mystery of iniquity*; its blasphemous claims for the Pope (the concrete) are forerunners of the final concentration of blasphemy in *the man of sin*, who shall not merely, as the Pope, usurp God's honour as His *vicegerent*, but *oppose* God openly. **4.** (Dan. xi. 36, 37.) The words there as to Antiochus Epiphanes shall receive their exhaustive fulfilment in the man of sin, the New Testament Antichrist. as Antiochus was the Old Testament typical Antichrist. The previous world-kingdoms had each one extraordinary person as its representative head (thus Babylon had Nebuchadnezzar, Dan. ii. 38, end; Medo-Persia, Cyrus; Greece, Alexander, and Antiochus Epiphanes); so the fourth and last world-kingdom, under which we live, shall have one final head, the concentrated embodiment of all the *sin* and *lawless iniquity* in Pagan and Papal Rome. Rome's final phase will probably be an unholy alliance between idolatry and infidelity. **Who opposeth and exalteth himself.** The one Greek article to both [*ho antikeimenos kai huperairomenos*] implies, why he *opposeth himself* is, that he may *exalt himself above* and *against* [*epi-Theon*], &c. *Alford*, absolutely, 'He that withstands (CHRIST)'—*i. e.*, Antichrist (1 John ii. 18), 'the adversary,' instigated by *Satan* (meaning *adversary*, *v.* 9), 'diametrically opposed to Christ' (*Origen*, 'Cels.,' vi. 64). As at the conclusion of the Old Testament, Israel apostate allied itself with the heathen world-power against Jesus (Luke xxiii. 12), and at Thessalonica against His apostles (Acts xvii. 5-9), and was in righteous retribution punished through the world-power itself (Jerusalem being destroyed by Rome, Dan. ix. 26, 27), so the degenerate Church (become an "harlot"), allying itself with the godless world-power (the "beast" of Revelation) against vital religion (*i. e.*, the harlot sitting on the beast), shall be judged by that world-power which shall be finally embodied in Antichrist (Zech. xiii. 8, 9; xiv. 2; Rev. xvii. 1-7, 15-17). In this early epistle the apostate Jewish church as the harlot, and Pagan Rome as the beast, form the historical background on which Paul draws his prophetic sketch of the apostasy. Later, in the pastoral epistles, this prophecy is connected with Gnosticism, which at that time infected the Church. The apostate church is first to be judged by the world-power and its kings (Rev. xvii. 16); afterwards the beasts and their allies (with the personal Antichrist at their head, who rises after the judgment on the harlot, or apostate church) shall be judged by Jesus in person (Rev. xix. 20). Antichristian tendencies produce different Antichrists: these separate Antichrists shall hereafter find their consummation in an individual exceeding them all in intensity of evil (*Auberlen*). Judgment soon overtakes him. He is *a child of death*, immediately after his *ascent as the beast out of the bottomless pit going into perdition* (Rev. xvii. 8, 11). *Idolatry of self, spiritual pride, and rebellion against God* characterize him; as *Christ-worship, humility*, and *dependence on God* characterize Christianity. He does not *feign* (as the "false Christs," Matt. xxiv. 24), but '*opposes*' Christ. [*Antikeimenos:* one

situated on the opposite side: cf. 1 John ii. 22; 2 John 7.] One who, on the destruction of every religion, shall seek to establish his own throne, and for God's truth, 'God is man,' to substitute his own lie, 'Man is God' (*Trench*). **above all** that **is called God** (1 Cor. viii. 5). Pope Clement VI. commanded the angels to admit into Paradise, without the alleged pains of purgatory, certain souls. Still this only foreshadows Antichrist, who will not, as the Pope, act *in God's name*, but *against* God. **or that is worshipped.** Rome here foreruns Antichrist. [*Sebasma* is akin to *Sebastus*, Greek for Augustus, worshipped as the divine vicegerent.] The Papacy rose on the overthrow of *Cesar's* power. Antichrist shall exalt himself above *every* object of worship, whether on earth, as Cesar, or in heaven, as God. The various prefigurations of Antichrist, Mahomet, Rome, Napoleon, and infidel secularism, contain *some*, not *all*, his characteristics. The union of all in some one person shall form THE ANTICHRIST, as the union in one Person, Jesus, of all the types and prophecies constituted THE CHRIST (*Olshausen*). **sitteth in** [*kathisai eis ton naon*: goeth *into*, and *sitteth* in] the **temple of God . . . that he is God.** 'He will reign a time, times, and half a time' (Dan. vii. 25)—*i. e.*, three and a half years—and sit *in the temple at Jerusalem* (Ezek. xxxvii. 26; xli.; xlii.-xliv.); 'then the Lord shall come from heaven and cast him into the lake of fire, and bring to the saints the times of their reigning, the seventh day of hallowed rest, and give to Abraham the promised inheritance' (*Irenæus*, 'Adver. Hær.,' v. 30. 4). **showing himself**—with blasphemous and arrogant DISPLAY (cf. a type, Acts xii. 21-23). The earliest fathers unanimously looked for a personal Antichrist. Two objections exist to Romanism being *the* Antichrist, though Romanism may culminate in him—(1.) So far is Romanism from *opposing all that is called God*, that adoration of gods and lords many (the Virgin Mary and saints) is its leading feature. (2.) The Papacy has existed for more than twelve centuries, and yet Christ is not come; whereas the prophecy regards *the* Antichrist as short-lived, and soon going to perdition through Christ's coming (Rev. xvii. 8, 11). Gregory the Great declared against the patriarch of Constantinople, that whosoever should call himself 'universal bishop' would be 'the forerunner of Antichrist.' The Papacy fulfilled this. The Pope has been called, 'Our Lord God the Pope;' and at his inauguration in St. Peter's, seated in his chair upon the high altar, which is his footstool, he has vividly foreshadowed him who "exalteth himself above all that is called God." An objection to interpreting *the temple of God* here as *the Church* (1 Cor. iii. 16, 17; vi. 19) is, Paul would hardly designate the *apostate* church "the *temple of God*." The local terms point to the *literal* temple. As Messiah was revealed among the Jews at Jerusalem, so anti-Messiah probably shall appear among them when restored to their own land, and after they have rebuilt their *temple at Jerusalem*. Thus Dan. xi. 41, 45 (notes) corresponds, 'He shall enter the glorious land (Judea), and plant the tabernacles of His palaces between the seas in the *glorious holy mountain*;' and then (Dan. xii. 1), 'Michael, the great prince, shall stand up' to deliver God's people (note, Dan. ix. 26, 27). The king of Assyria is type of Antichrist, Isa. xiv. 12-14, "Lucifer," the *light-bearing* "morning star" (a title of Messiah

5 Remember ye not, that, when I was yet with you, I told you these
6 things? And now ye know what ¹withholdeth that he might be revealed
7 in his time. For *ᵍ*the mystery of iniquity doth already work: only he
8 who now letteth *will let*, until he be taken out of the way: and then
  shall that Wicked be revealed, whom *ʰ*the Lord shall consume *ⁱ*with

A. D. 54.
1 Or,
holdeth.
ᵍ 1 John 4. 3.
ʰ Dan. 7. 10.
ⁱ Job 4. 9.

assumed by Antichrist, Rev. xxii. 16): 'I will exalt my throne above the stars of God: I will sit upon the *mount of the congregation* (*i. e.*, God's place of meeting His people; the temple) *in the sides of the north* (the site of *Jerusalem*, Ps. xlviii. 2); I will be like the Most High.' "The temple . . . the holy city" (Matt. iv. 5; Rev. xi. 1, 2). Cf. Ps. lxviii. 18, 29, refer•ng to a period since Christ's ascension not yet fulfilled (Isa. ii. 1-3; Ezek. xl.-xliv.; Zech. xiv. 16-20; Mal. iii. 1). Antichrist possibly shall, the first three and a half years of the prophetical week, keep the covenant, then break it, and usurp divine honours in the midst of the week. He will, 'by flatteries,' bring many, not only Gentiles, but also of 'the tribes' of Israel (so Greek, "kindreds," Rev. xi. 8, 9), to own him as their looked-for Messiah, in the 'city where our Lord was crucified.' "Sitteth" implies his occupying the place of power and majesty; in opposition to Him who sitteth "on the right hand of the Majesty on high" (Heb. i. 3), who shall come to 'sit' where the usurper sat (Matt. xxvi. 64: note, Dan. ix. 27; Rev. xi. 2, 3, 9, 11). Cf. Ezek. xxviii. 2-16 as to Tyre, the type characterized by similar blasphemous arrogance.

5. Remember, &c.—confuting those who suppose Paul erred in his first epistle as to Christ's immediate coming, and now corrects that error. **I told you**—often [*elegon*]: 'I was telling,' or 'used to tell.' **6. now ye know**—by my having told you. The power was one 'known' to the Thessalonians. **what withholdeth**—*holds* him *back*. 'The power that [*to katechon*] keeps in check' the man of sin from his development is *the moral and conservative influence of states* (*Olshausen*): *human polity* as a *coercive* power: "he who now letteth" refers to *those who rule that polity* by which the upbursting of godlessness is kept down (*Alford*). *Legality*, as opposed to 'lawlessness.' The "what withholdeth" is the *general hindrance;* "he who now letteth," *the person in whom that hindrance is summed up.* Romanism, as a forerunner, was kept in check by *the Roman emperor* (the then representative of the coercive power), until Constantine, having removed the seat of empire to Constantinople, the Roman bishop first raised himself to precedency, then to primacy, then to sole empire above the secular power. The historical fact from which Paul starts was probably the emperor Claudius' expulsion of the Jews, the antichristiana dversary in Paul's day, from Rome, thus 'withholding' them in their attacks on Christianity. This suggested the principle about to find its final fulfilment in the removal of *the withholding person* or *authority*, whereupon Antichrist in his worst shape shall arise. **that he might be.** Ye know what keeps him back, in God's purposes, from being sooner manifested—'*in order that* he *may* be revealed in *his own* (Antichrist's proper) time' appointed by God (cf. Dan. xi. 35). This will be when the civil polity derived from the Roman empire, which will b₀ in its last form, divided into ten kingdoms (Rev. xvii. 3, 11-13), shall, with its representative head ("he who now letteth" [*ho katechōn*]: "withholdeth," as in *v.* 6), yield to the prevalent 'lawlessness' of which 'the lawless one' is the embodiment. *The elect Church* and *the Spirit, De Burgh* suggests, are the *withholding* power; but they, to 'the end of the age,' shall never be *wholly*

"taken out of the way" (Matt. xxviii. 20). However, as the testimony of *the elect Church*, and *the Spirit* in her, *hold back* now the apostasy, it is possible that, though a few shall be faithful even then, yet the full energy of the Spirit in *the visible* Church, counteracting the 'working' [*energy: energeitai*] of 'the mystery of lawlessness' by the elect's testimony, shall be so far 'taken out of the way' as to admit the manifestation of 'the lawless one' (Rev. xi. 3-12). The rapture of the elect Church to meet the Lord in the air (Isa. xxvi. 20; 1 Thess. iv. 17) BEFORE Antichrist's brief reign and the great Jewish tribulation, clears away some difficulty. The Thessalonians might easily "know" this through Paul's instruction. **7. the mystery of iniquity**—the counterwork to "the mystery of godliness" (1 Tim. iii. 16). Antichristianity *latently* working, distinguished from its final *open* manifestation. "Mystery" in Scripture means, not what remains a secret, but that which is for a while hidden, but in due time manifested (cf. Eph. iii. 4, 5). Satan will resort to an opposition conformed to Christ's then imminent 'appearing' and 'presence,' and anticipate Him with a last effort for the dominion of the world; just as, at His first advent, Satan openly took possession of men's bodies. "Iniquity" [*anomia*], *lawlessness;* defiant rejection of God's law. Note, *v..* 3: Zech. v. 9, 10, '*Wickedness*' (LXX., the same Greek, 'lawlessness'), embodied there as a woman, answers to "the mystery of iniquity," here embodied in the "man of sin." As the former was banished for ever from the Holy Land to her congenial soil, Babylon, so Iniquity and the Man of sin shall fall before Michael and the Lord, the Deliverer of His people (Dan. xii. 1-3; Zech. xiv. 3-9). Cf. Matt. xii. 43: [*anomian*] xiii. 41: the Jews, dispossessed of the evil spirit, idolatry being cast out through the Babylonian captivity, receive a worse spirit—Christ-opposing self-righteousness. Also, the Christian Church taken possession of by Romish idolatry, then dispossessed of it by the Reformation; then its house 'garnished' by hypocrisy, secularity, and rationalism, but 'swept empty' of living faith; then finally apostatizing and repossessed by the "man of sin," and *outwardly* destroyed for a brief time (though even then Christ shall have witnesses among both Jews (Zech. xiii. 9) and Gentiles (Matt. xxviii. 20), when Christ shall suddenly come (Dan. xi. 32-45; Luke xviii. 7, 8). **already** (3 John ix. 10; Col. ii. 18-23; 1 Tim. iv. 1). Cf. "even now," 1 John ii. 18; iv. 3) as distinguished from 'in his own time' *hereafter*. Antiquity does not justify unscriptural usages or dogma, since these were 'already," in Paul's time, beginning: the written Word is the only sure test. 'Judaism infecting Christianity is the fuel; the mystery of iniquity is the spark.' 'It is one and the same impurity diffusing itself over ages' (*Bengel*). **only he who now letteth**—"*will let*" is not in the Greek. Translate 'only (*i.e.*, the continuance of *the* MYSTERY *of iniquity-working is only*) until he who now *withholdeth* (*v.* 6) be taken out of the way.' Then it will work no longer in *mystery*, but in open manifestation. **8.** 'The lawless one;' the embodiment of all the 'lawlessness' working in "mystery" for ages (*v.* 7): the "man of sin" (*v.* 3). **whom the Lord.** So B. But ℵ A Δ G *fg*, Vulgate read 'the Lord *Jesus*.' How

the spirit of his mouth, and shall destroy ^{j} with the brightness of his
9 coming : *even him,* whose coming is ^{k} after the working of Satan with all
10 power ^{l} and signs and lying wonders, and with all deceivableness of unrighteousness in ^{m} them that perish ; because they received not the love
11 of the truth, that they might be saved. And ^{n} for this cause God shall
12 send them strong delusion, ^{o} that they should believe a lie : that they
all might be damned who believed not the truth, but had pleasure in
unrighteousness.
13 But we are bound to give thanks alway to God for you, brethren
beloved of the Lord, because God hath from the beginning chosen you to

A. D. 54.

^{j} Heb. 10. 27.
^{k} John 8. 41.
Eph. 2. 2.
Rev. 18. 23.
^{l} Deut. 13. 1.
Matt. 24.24.
^{m} 2 Cor 2. 15.
2 Cor. 4. 3.
^{n} 1 Ki 22. 22.
Eze. 14. 9.
^{o} Matt. 21. 5.
1 Tim. 4. 1.

awful that He whose name means *God-Saviour* should be the Destroyer ! But the Church's *salvation* requires her foe's destruction. As Israel's reign in Canaan was ushered in by judgments on the nations for *apostasy* (for the Canaanites originally worshipped the true God : thus Melchizedek, king of Salem, was "priest of the most high God," Gen. xiv. 18, Ammon and Moab came from righteous Lot), so the Son of David's reign in Zion and over the earth shall be preceded by judgments on apostate Christendom. **consume . . . and shall destroy.** So Dan. vii. 26; xi. 45. He shall "consume" [*analoi*, א; *anelei*, B Δ] him by His mere breath (Isa. xi. 4; xxx. 33)—the sentence of judgment being the sharp sword out of His mouth (Rev. xix. 15, 21). Antichrist's manifestation and destruction are declared together: at his height he is nearest his fall, like Herod, his type (Isa. i. 24-27; Acts xii. 20-23). The mere '*manifestation* of Christ's coming' [*epiphaneia tēs parousias*] is enough to "consume" him. He is "cast alive into a lake of fire" (Rev. xix. 20). So the world-kingdom of the beast gives place to that of the Son of man and His saints. [*Katargesei*] 'Destroy,' 'ABOLISH' (the same Greek, 2 Tim. i. 10), means, *render powerless, cause every vestige of him to disappear.* Cf. as to Gog attacking Israel, and utterly destroyed by Jehovah, Ezek. xxxviii.; xxxix. The first outburst or gleam of His presence is enough to *abolish* or *render utterly powerless* Antichrist, as darkness disappears before dawning day. This is for the Church's consolation. Next, his adherents are "slain with the sword out of His mouth." *Bengel's* distinction between 'the appearance of His coming' and the "coming" itself is not justified by 1 Tim. vi. 14; 2 Tim. i. 10; iv. 1, 8; Titus ii. 13, where the same [*epiphaneia*] *appearing* ("brightness") refers to *the coming itself.* "*Manifestation* of His presence" is in awful contrast to the *revelation* of the wicked one. **9. whose coming** [*parousia,* Antichrist's : marking the contrast to the *parousia,* 'personal presence,' of Christ] **is**—in essential character. **after**—*according to* [*kata :* such as might be looked for from] the 'energy' of Satan, as opposed to the Holy Spirit's *energy* in the Church (note, Eph. i. 19). As Christ is to God, so is Antichrist to Satan, his manifested embodiment : Satan works through him (Rev. xiii. 2). **with**—Greek, 'IN :' invested with. **lying wonders**—*lit.,* 'wonders (prodigies) of falsehood.' His 'power, signs, and wonders,' have *falsehood* for their base, essence, and aim (John viii. 44) (*Alford*). Matt. xxiv. 24 shows that the miracles shall be real, though demoniac : such mysterious effects as we read of by the Egyptian sorcerers; not such as Jesus performed in character, power, or aim : for they are against the revealed Word, and therefore not to be accepted as evidences of truth; nay, on the authority of that sure Word, to be rejected as in support of *falsehood* (Deut. xiii. 1-3, 5; Gal. i. 8, 9, Rev. xiii. 11-15; xix. 20). The same three terms occur for *miracles of Jesus,* Acts ii. 22; Heb. ii. 4, showing that as the

Egyptian magician imitated Moses (2 Tim. iii. 1-8), so Antichrist imitates Christ's works as a "sign," or *proof* of divinity. **10. deceivableness** [*apate adikias*]—'deceit of (to promote) unrighteousness' (*v.* 12). **in.** So C. But א A B Δ G *f g*, Vulgate, omit "in." '*Unto* them that *are perishing*' (2 Cor. ii. 15, 16; iv. 3) : victims of him whose name describes his *perishing* nature, "the son of perdition." But *you* need not fear, for (*v.* 13) 'God hath chosen you to *salvation* through *sanctification* of the Spirit and belief.' **because** [*anth' hōn*]—'for that,' 'in requital for which:' in retribution for their having no *love* for the truth which was within their reach (since it was a check on their passions), and for their having pleasure in unrighteousness' (*v.* 12; Rom. i. 18) : they are *lost* because they loved not the truth which would have *saved* them. **received not** [*edexanto*]—'*welcomed not;*' admitted not cordially. **love of the truth**—not merely *truth,* but THE *truth* alone (Jesus), in opposition to Satan's 'lie' (*vv.* 9-11; John viii. 42-44), can *save* (Eph. iv. 21). Not merely must we assent to, but *love,* the truth (Ps. cxix. 97). The Jews rejected Him, coming in His Father's name; they will receive Antichrist, coming in *his own* name (John v. 43). Their sin shall prove their scourge. **11. for this cause**—because "they received not the love of the truth;" the only safeguard against error. **shall send** [*pempei,* 'sends']—'is sending' the "delusion" already. Those who reject the truth, God gives up in righteous judgment to Satan's delusions (Isa. vi. 9, 10; Rom. i. 24-26, 28). They first cast off "the love of the truth," then, given up by God, they settle down into 'believing the lie:' an awful climax (1 Ki. xxii. 22, 23; Job xii. 16; Ezek. xiv. 9; Matt. xxiv. 5, 11; 1 Tim. iv. 1). **strong delusion** [*energeian planēs*]—'*an effectual* (energizing) *working of error,*' answering to the energizing "working of Satan" (*v.* 9), contrasted with the Holy Ghost's 'effectual (energizing) working' in believers (Eph. i. 19). **believe a lie**—Greek, '*the* lie' which Antichrist tells, appealing to his miracles as proofs (*v.* 9). **12. they all might be damned**—Greek, 'that *all,*' &c. : the general proposition which applies specially to Antichrist's adherents. Not all in Rome, or other antichristian systems, shall be damned, but only all "who believed not the truth" *when offered to them,* "but had pleasure in unrighteousness" (Rom. i. 32; ii. 8). Love of *unrighteousness* is the great obstacle to *believing the truth.*

13. But. In delightful contrast to the damnation of the lost (*v.* 12) stands the "salvation" of Paul's converts. **are bound** (ch. i. 3). **thanks . . . to God**—not to ourselves, ministers, nor to you, converts. **beloved of the Lord**—Jesus (Rom. viii. 37; Gal. ii. 20; Eph. v. 2, 25). Elsewhere *God the Father* is said to love us (*v.* 16; John iii. 16; Eph. ii. 4; Col. iii. 12). Therefore Jesus and the Father are one. **from the beginning** (Eph. i. 4: cf. 1 Cor. ii. 7; 2 Tim. i. 9)—in contrast to those that 'worship the beast, whose names are not written

salvation through sanctification of the Spirit and belief of the truth:
14 whereunto he called you by our gospel, to the obtaining of the glory of our Lord Jesus Christ.
15 Therefore, brethren, stand fast, and hold *p* the traditions which ye
16 have been taught, whether by word, or our epistle. Now our Lord Jesus Christ himself, and God, even our Father, which *q* hath loved us, and hath
17 given *us* everlasting consolation and good hope through grace, comfort your hearts, and stablish you in every good word and work.

A. D. 51.

p 1 Cor 11. 2.
ch. 3. 6.
q John 3. 16.
John 13. 1.
John 15. 9.
Rom. 5. 8.
Eph.-2. 4.
1 John 4.10.
Rev. 1. 5.

in the book of life of the Lamb slain from the foundation of the world' (Rev. xiii. 8). א Δ *fg* read [*ap' archēs*] 'from the beginning.' But B G, Vulgate [*aparchēn*], 'as *first-fruit.*' The Thessalonians were among the *first converts* in Europe (cf. Rom. xvi. 5; 1 Cor. xvi. 15; Rev. xiv. 4). In a general sense, in Jas. i. 18. Perhaps so here: as the Thessalonians were not the first believers in Macedonia. **chosen you** [*heilato*] (nowhere else in Paul's epistles)—not the ordinary [*exelexato*] "elected," implying *selection ;* but *taken for Himself,* implying His having *adopted* them in His eternal purpose (LXX. ; Deut. vii. 7 ; x. 15). **through**—Greek, 'IN sanctification :' the element in which the *choice to salvation* had place (cf. 1 Pet. i. 2); in contrast to "unrighteousness," the element in which Antichrist's followers are given over by God to *damnation* (*v.* 12). **of** (wrought by) **the Spirit**—who sanctifies all the elect, first by eternal consecration to perfect holiness in Christ, once for all ; next by progressively imparting it. **belief of the truth**—contrasted with "believed not the truth" (*v.* 12). **14. you.** So א G *g*, Vulgate. But A B Δ *f*, 'us.' **by our gospel** —'*through*' the Gospel which we preach. **to . . . glory**—in *v.* 13, "to salvation ;" *i. e.,* deliverance from all evil, of body and soul (1 Thess. v. 9); here it is to positive good, even "glory," and that "the glory of our Lord Jesus," which believers are privileged to share with Him (John xvii. 22, 24 ; Rom. viii. 17, 29 ; 2 Tim. ii. 10).

15. Therefore. God's sovereign choice, so far from being a ground for inaction, is the strongest incentive to perseverance in action. Cf. the argument (Phil. ii. 12, 13), 'work out *your own* salvation, FOR it is God that worketh in you,' &c. We cannot explain the *theory ;* but to the sincere the *practical* acting is plain. 'Privilege first, duty afterwards' (*Edmunds*). **stand fast**—so as not to be 'shaken or troubled' (*v.* 2). **hold**—so as not to let go. Adding nothing, subtracting nothing (*Bengel*). The Thessalonians had not held fast his oral instructions, but were imposed upon by pretended spirit-revelations, words, and letters, as if from Paul (*v.* 2), that 'the day of the Lord was instantly imminent.' **traditions** — *instructions delivered,* whether orally or in writing (ch. iii. 6 ; 1 Cor. xi. 2, *margin*, 'traditions'). The verb is used by Paul, 1 Cor xi. 23; xv. 3. From the *three* passages in which 'tradition' has a good sense, Rome has argued for her *uninspired* traditions, virtually overriding, whilst held as of co-ordinate authority with, God's Word. She forgets the *ten* passages (Matt. xv. 2, 3, 6 ; Mark vii. 3, 5, 8, 9, 13; Gal. i. 14 ; Col. ii. 8) stigmatizing *man's uninspired* traditions. [*Paradosis* is one of the only two nouns in the 2,000 of the Greek Testament which numerically equals 666, the mark of the beast, Rev. xiii. 18.] *Tradition* is the great corrupter of *doctrine,* as [*euporia*] 'wealth' (the other equivalent of 666) is the corrupter of the Church's practice. Not even the apostles' sayings were all inspired (*e. g.,* Peter's dissimulation, Gal. ii. 11-14), but only when they *claimed* to be so, as in their words afterwards embodied in canonical

writings. Oral inspiration was necessary then, until the canon of the written Word should be complete : they proved their inspiration by miracles in support of the new revelation. This revelation, moreover, accorded with the existing Old Testament—an additional test needed besides miracles (cf. Deut. xiii. 1-6; Acts xvii. 11). When the canon was complete, the infallibility of the living men's inspired sayings was transferred to the written Word, now the sole unerring guide, interpreted by the Holy Spirit. Nothing has come down to us by *ancient* and *universal* tradition save this, *the all-sufficiency of Scripture for salvation.* Therefore, by tradition, we are constrained to cast off all tradition not in, or proveable by, Scripture. The fathers are valuable *witnesses to historical facts,* which give force to the *intimations* of Scripture—such as the Christian Lord's day, the baptism of infants, and the genuineness of the canon. Tradition (in the sense *human testimony*) cannot establish a *doctrine,* but can *authenticate a fact,* such as those mentioned. *Inspired tradition,* in St. Paul's sense, is not a supplementary oral tradition completing *our* written Word, but is the written Word *now* complete ; then, the latter not being complete, the tradition was necessarily in part oral, in part written, and continued so until, the latter being complete before the death of St. John, the last apostle, the former was no longer needed. Scripture is the complete and sufficient rule in all that appertains to making "the man of God *perfect, thoroughly furnished* unto *all* good works" (2 Tim. iii. 16, 17). It is by leaving God-inspired for human traditions that Rome has become the parent of Antichrist. *It is striking that, from this very chapter denouncing Antichrist, she should draw an argument for her "traditions," by which she fosters antichristianity.* Because the apostles' oral word was as trustworthy as their written word, it by no means follows that the oral word of those *not apostles* is as trustworthy as the *written* word of those who were apostles **or** inspired evangelists. No tradition of the apostles, except their written word, can be *proved* genuine on satisfactory evidence. We are no more bound to accept the fathers' interpretations of Scripture, because we accept the Scripture canon on their testimony, than to accept the Jews' interpretation of the Old Testament because we accept the Old Testament canon on their testimony. **our epistle** —as distinguished from the "letter AS from us," (*v.* 2). He means his first epistle to the Thessalonians. **16, 17. himself**—by His own might, contrasted with our feebleness ; ensuring the efficacy of our prayer. Here *our Lord Jesus* stands first; in 1 Thess. iii. 11 "God our Father." By *Christ's* grace we come to the Father's *love* (2 Cor. xiii. 14). **which hath loved us**—in our redemption. Referring both to *our Lord Jesus* (Rom. viii. 37; Gal. ii. 20) and *God our Father* (John iii. 16). **everlasting consolation.** Not transitory, as worldly consolations in trials (Rom. viii. 38, 39). This for all time present, then 'good hope' for the future (*Alford*). **through grace**—Greek, 'IN grace;' to be joined to "hath given." Grace is

3 FINALLY, brethren, pray for us, that the word of the Lord ¹may
2 have *free* course, and be glorified, even as *it is* with you: and that we
may be delivered from ²unreasonable and wicked men: for all *men* have
3 not faith. But the Lord is faithful, who shall stablish you, and ᵃkeep
4 *you* from evil. And we have confidence in the Lord touching you, that
5 ye both do and will do the things which we command you. And ᵇthe
Lord direct your hearts into the love of God, and ³into the patient
waiting for Christ.
6 Now we command you, brethren, in the name of our Lord Jesus
Christ, that ᶜye withdraw yourselves ᵈfrom every brother that walketh
7 disorderly, and not after the tradition which he received of us. For
yourselves know how ye ought to follow us: for we behaved not ourselves
8 disorderly among you; neither did we eat any man's bread for nought;
but ᵉwrought with labour and travail night and day, that we might not

A. D. 54.

CHAP. 3.
¹ may run.
² absurd.
ᵃ John 17.15.
2 Pet. 2. 9.
ᵇ 1 Chr. 29.18.
Matt 22.37.
1 John 4.16.
³ Or, the
patience
of Christ.
ᶜ Rom. 16.17.
2 John 10.
ᵈ 1 Cor. 5. 11.
ᵉ Acts 18. 3.
Acts 20 34.
1 Cor. 4. 12.

---

the element *in* which the gift was made. **comfort**
[*parakalesai*, singular verb, marking that *the*
Son and Father are *one*] **your heart**—unsettled as
you have been through those who announced the
Lord's immediate coming. **good word and work.**
So G *g.* But А ʀ B Δ *f*, Vulgate, invert the order,
'work and word.' *Establishment* in these were
what the young converts needed, not fanatical
teaching (cf. 1 Cor. xv. 58).
CHAP. III. 1-18.—Hᴇ ᴀsᴋs ᴛʜᴇɪʀ Pʀᴀʏᴇʀs—
Hɪs Cᴏɴꜰɪᴅᴇɴᴄᴇ ɪɴ ᴛʜᴇᴍ—Pʀᴀʏᴇʀ ꜰᴏʀ ᴛʜᴇᴍ—
Cʜᴀʀɢᴇs ᴀɢᴀɪɴsᴛ Dɪsᴏʀᴅᴇʀʟʏ Iᴅʟᴇ Cᴏɴᴅᴜᴄᴛ—
Hɪs ᴏᴡɴ Eᴘᴍᴘʟᴇ—Cᴏɴᴄʟᴜᴅɪɴɢ Pʀᴀʏᴇʀ ᴀɴᴅ
Sᴀʟᴜᴛᴀᴛɪᴏɴ.
1. **Finally** [*To loipon*]—'As to what remains.'
pray for us—as I have prayed for you (ch. ii. 16,
17). **may have free course** [*treche*]—'may run,'
without a drag on the wheels of its course. That
the new-creating word may 'run' as "swiftly"
as the creative word at the first (Ps. cxlvii. 15).
The opposite is, the word of God "bound" (2 Tim.
ii. 9). **glorified**—by sinners accepting it (stronger
than in Acts xiii. 48; Gal. i. 23, 24). Contrast
"evil spoken of" (1 Pet. iv. 14). **as it is with you**
(1 Thess. i. 6, 8; iv. 10; v. 11). 2. **that we may**
be delivered from unreasonable [*atopoi*]—men
out of place, inept, out of the way, bad: an undesigned coincidence with Acts xviii. 5-9. Paul was
now at Corinth, where ᴛʜᴇ Jᴇᴡs 'opposed themselves' to his preaching: in answer to his prayers
and those of his converts, 'the Lord, in vision,'
promised exemption from "hurt," and the conversion of "much people." Paul's desire for "deliverance" was in order that it might enable him to
further God's word (Rom. xv. 32). 'The synagogues of the Jews were fountains of persecutions'
(*Tertullian*, 'Gnost. Scorp.' 10). **have not faith**—
Greek, '*the* (Christian) faith:' the only antidote
to what is "unreasonable and wicked." The
Thessalonians, from their ready acceptance of the
Gospel, might think "all" would receive it; but
the Jews were far from having such a readiness to
believe. 3. **faithful**—alluding to "faith" (*v.* 2):
though many will not believe, the Lord (ʀ A C Δ G.
But B, 'God') is still to be believed as to His
promises (1 Thess. v. 24; 2 Tim. ii. 13). *Faith* on
man's part answers to faithfulness on God's part.
stablish you. Though wicked men were assailing
himself, he turns away from asking prayers for ʜɪs
deliverance (*v.* 2: so unselfish was he), to express
his assurance of ᴛʜᴇɪʀ establishment in the faith
and preservation from evil. This assurance exactly
answers to his prayer, ch. ii. 17, "Our Lord . . .
stablish you in every good word and work." So
the Lord's prayer, "Lead us not into temptation,
but *deliver* us *from evil:*" where, as here (in
antithesis to "the Lord") is included, 'from *the*

evil one:' the great hinderer of "every good word
and work." Cf. Matt. xiii. 19; Eph. vi. 16;
1 John v. 18. 4. **And** [*De*]—'Yea.' **we have**
confidence in the Lord—as "faithful" (*v.* 3).
Have confidence in no man when left to himself
(*Bengel*). **that ye both do.** B G (not ʀ A Δ,
Vulgate) insert 'that ye both have done' before,
'and are doing, and will do.' He means the
majority by 'ye;' not *all* (cf. *v.* 11; ch. i. 3; 1 Thess.
iii. 6). 5. **And** [*De*]—'But.' Whilst I am confident
touching you, *yet* may the Lord direct your hearts.
If "the Lord" be here the Holy Ghost (2 Cor. iii.
17), the three Divine Persons occur in this verse.
love of God—love to God (Matt. xxii. 37). **patient**
waiting for Christ [*Tēn hupomonēn tou Christou*]—
'the patience (endurance) *of Christ;*' viz., which
Christ showed (*Alford*) (1 Pet. ii. 21; ch. i. 4;
1 Thess. i. 3). Cf. for the English version, Rev. i.
9; iii. 10. At all events, this grace, "patience,"
is connected (1 Thess. i. 3, 10) with the "hope" of
Christ's coming. Cf. Heb. xii. 1, 2, "Run with
patience (*endurance*) . . . looking unto Jᴇsᴜs . . . who,
for the joy . . . before Him, *endured* the cross:" so
ᴡᴇ are to endure, as looking for the hope to be realized at His coming (Heb. x. 36, 37).
6. He repeats the injunctions, 1 Thess. iv. 11, 12.
we command you. Hereby he puts to a test their
obedience in general, which he had recognized, *v.*
4. **withdraw** [*stellesthai*]—*to furl the sails: to steer*
clear of (cf. *v.* 14). Some had given up labour, as
though the Lord was immediately coming. He
had enjoined mild censure of such in 1 Thess. v.
14, "*Warn* them that are unruly." Now that the
mischief had become more confirmed, he enjoins
stricter discipline—viz., withdrawal from their
company (cf. 1 Cor. v. 5, 11; 2 John 10, 11); not a
formal excommunication, such as was subsequently
passed on more heinous offenders, as in 1 Cor. v.
5; 1 Tim. i. 20. **brother**—professing Christian;
for, in the case of unprofessing heathen, believers
were not to be so strict (1 Cor. v. 10-13). **dis-**
orderly. St. Paul plainly would not have sanctioned the *Order* of Mendicant Friars, who reduce
such a "disorderly," lazy life to a system. **Call**
it not an *Order*, but a *burden* to the community
[*Bengel*, alluding to the *epibarēsai*, *v.* 8, "be
chargeable;" lit., *be a burden*]. **the tradition**—
the *instruction* orally given by him to them (*v.* 10),
and subsequently committed to writing (1 Thess.
iv. 11, 12). **which he received of us.** B G read
'*ye* received.' ʀ A C Δ *f*, '*they* received.' 7. **how**
ye ought to follow us—how ye ought to live so
as *to 'imitate'* (so the Greek) *us* (cf. note, 1 Cor.
xi. 1; 1 Thess. i. 6). 8. **eat any man's bread**—
Greek, 'eat bread *from* any man;' *i. e.*, live at any
one's expense. Contrast *v.* 12, "*eat* ᴛʜᴇɪʀ ᴏᴡɴ
bread." **wrought** (Acts xx. 3⁊. In both epistles

478

9 be chargeable to any of you: not *f* because we have not power, but to
10 make ourselves an *g* ensample unto you to follow us.   For even when we
   were with you, this we commanded you, *h* that if any would not work,
11 neither should he eat.   For we hear that there are some which walk
12 among you *i* disorderly, working not at all, but are busybodies.   Now
   them that are such we command and exhort by our Lord Jesus Christ,
13 *j* that with quietness they work, and eat their own bread.   But ye,
14 brethren, *4* be not weary in well-doing.   And if any man obey not
   our word *5* by this epistle, note that man, and have no company
15 with him, that he may be ashamed.   Yet *k* count *him* not as an
16 enemy, but admonish *him* as a brother.   Now the Lord of peace
   himself give you peace always by all means.   The Lord *be* with
   you all.
17   The salutation of Paul with mine own hand, which is the token in
18 every epistle: so I write.   The grace of our Lord Jesus Christ *be* with
   you all.   Amen.

The second *epistle* to the Thessalonians was written from Athens.

A. D. 54.

f Matt. 10. 10.
1 Cor. 9. 6.
1 Thes 2. 6.
1 Tim. 5. 17.
g 1 Pet. 5. 3.
h Gen 3. 19.
Pro 13. 4.
1 Thes 4. 11.
i Isa. 55. 10.
j Rom. 12. 11.
Eph. 4. 28.
4 Or, faint
not.
5 Or, signify
that man
by an
epistle.
k Lev. 19. 17.
Gal. 6. 1.
1 Thes. 5. 14.

they state they maintained themselves by labour; but in this second epistle they do so to offer an example to the idle; whereas, in the first, their object is to vindicate themselves from imputation of mercenary motives in preaching (1 Thess. ii. 5, 9) (*Edmunds*).   **labour and travail**—'toil and hardship' (note, 1 Thess. ii. 9).   **night and day** —scarcely allowing time for repose.   **chargeable** —Greek, 'burdensome.'   It is at the very time and place of writing these epistles that Paul is said to have *wrought at tent-making* with Aquila: an undesigned coincidence.   9. (1 Cor. ix. 4-6, &c.; Gal. vi. 6.)   **10. For even.**   Translate 'For *also*;' co-ordinate with "For," *v.* 7.   We set you the example, and also gave a 'command.'   **commanded**—Greek imperfect, 'We were commanding:' we kept charging you.   **would not work**— Greek, '*is not willing* to work.'   The argument is, not that such a one is to have his food withdrawn from him by others; but Paul proves from the necessity of *eating* the necessity of *working.*   **11. busybodies.**   In the Greek [*mēden ergazomenous alla periergazomenous*] the similar sounds mark the antithesis, 'Doing none of their own business, yet over busy in that of others.'   Idleness is the parent of busybodies (1 Tim. v. 13).   Contrast 1 Thess. iv. 11.   **12. by** [*dia*].   So C.   But A א B Δ G *f g*, Vulgate, read 'IN the Lord Jesus.'   So the Greek, 1 Thess. iv. 1: the sphere wherein such conduct is appropriate and consistent.   We exhort you as *ministers* IN *Christ*, exhorting our people IN Christ.   **with quietness**— quiet industry; laying aside intermeddling officiousness (*v.* 11).   **their own**—earned by themselves, not another's bread (*n.* 8).   **13. be not weary.**   א A B read [*enkakēsēte*] 'be not cowardly in;' be not wanting in strenuousness in doing well: with patient industry and general consistency.   In contrast to the 'disorderly, not-working busybodies' (*v.* 11: cf. Gal. vi. 9).   **14. note that man**—in your own minds, as one to be avoided (*v.* 6).   **that he may be ashamed** [*entrapē*] —'made to turn and look into himself, and so be put to shame.'   Feeling himself shunned by godly brethren.   **15. admonish him as a brother**—not yet excommunicated (cf. Lev. xix. 17).   Do not shun him in contemptuous silence, but tell him why he is so avoided (Matt. xviii. 15; 1 Thess. v.

14).   **16. Lord of peace**—Jesus Christ.   The same title is given to Him as to the Father (Rom. xv. 33; xvi. 20; 2 Cor. xiii. 11).   An appropriate title here, where the harmony of the Christian community was liable to interruption from the "disorderly" (1 Thess. v. 23; Phil. iv. 7).   Greek, 'give you *the* peace' which it is 'His to give.'   "Peace" outward and inward, with God, with one another, with the world, here and hereafter (Rom. xiv. 17).   Isa. xxvi. 3, 'The deep tranquillity of a soul resting on God' (*Ellicott*).   **always** —not changing with outward circumstances.   **by all means**—Greek, 'in every way.'   [So א B, *tropo.*   But A Δ G *f g*, Vulgate, *topo.*]   'In every place:' thus he prays for their peace *in all times* ('always') *and places.*   **Lord be with you all.**   May He bless you not only with *peace*, but also with His *presence* (Matt. xxviii. 20).   Even the disorderly brethren (cf. *v.* 15, "a brother") are included in this prayer.   **17.** The epistle was written by an amanuensis (perhaps Silas or Timothy), and only the closing salutation, *vv.* 17, 18, by Paul's "own hand" (cf. Rom. xvi. 22; 1 Cor. xvi. 21; Col. iv. 18).   Wherever Paul does not subjoin this autograph salutation, we may presume either he wrote the whole epistle himself (Gal. vi. 11), or deemed formal attestation needless.   **which**—*which* autograph salutation.   **the token**—to distinguish genuine epistles from spurious ones in my name (ch. ii. 2).   **in every epistle.**   Some think he signed his name to every epistle with his own hand; but as there is no trace of this in any MSS. of *all* the epistles, it is more likely that he alludes to *his writing with his own hand in closing every epistle*, even in those epistles (Rom., 2 Cor., Eph., Phil., 1 Thess.) wherein he does not specify his having done so.   **so I write**—so I sign: this is a specimen of my *handwriting*, by which to distinguish my genuine letters from forgeries.   **18.** He closes every epistle by praying for GRACE to "*all*" those whom he addresses, even to those who incurred his reproof: a significant addition to 1 Thess. v. 28.   **Amen.**   So A C Δ G *f g*.   Omitted in א B.   Perhaps the response of the congregation after hearing the epistle read publicly.
   The subscription is spurious, as the epistle was written, not "from Athens," but from *Corinth.*

479

1 PAUL, an apostle of Jesus Christ *a* by the commandment *b* of God our
2 Saviour, and Lord Jesus Christ, *which c is* our hope, unto *d* Timothy,
my own son in the faith: Grace, mercy, *and* peace, from God our Father
and Jesus Christ our Lord.
3 As I besought thee to abide still at Ephesus, *e* when I went into Macedonia, that thou mightest charge some that *f* they teach no other doctrine,
4 neither give heed to fables and endless genealogies, which minister questions, rather than godly edifying which is in faith: *so do.*

A. D. 65.

CHAP. 1.
a Gal. 1. 1.
b ch. 2. 3.
  ch. 4. 10.
c Col. 1. 27.
d Acts 16. 1.
e Acts 20.1,3.
  Phil. 2. 24.
f Gal. 1. 6, 7.

CHAP. I. 1-20.—ADDRESS—PAUL'S DESIGN IN
LEAVING TIMOTHY AT EPHESUS—TO CHECK
FALSE TEACHERS—USE OF THE LAW; HARMON-
IZING WITH THE GOSPEL—GOD'S GRACE IN
CALLING PAUL, ONCE A BLASPHEMER, TO EX-
PERIENCE AND TO PREACH IT—CHARGES.
1. an apostle of Jesus Christ—*belonging to* Him
as His servant. Paul thus designates himself in
an *official* letter; but in a *personal* letter (Phile.
1), "a prisoner of Jesus Christ." by the commandment of God—the authoritative *injunction*
[*epitagon*], as well as commission, of God. In the
earlier epistles, "by the *will* of God." Here the
phrase implies a necessity laid on him to act as an
apostle: not a matter of option. The same expression occurs in the doxology in Rom. xvi. 26. God
our Saviour—the Father (ch. ii. 3; iv. 10; Luke
i. 47; 2 Tim. i. 9; Titus i. 3; ii. 10; iii. 4; Jude
25): a Jewish expression in devotion, from the
Old Testament (cf. Ps. cvi. 21). our hope—the
object, substance, and foundation of our hope
(Col. i. 27; Titus i. 2; ii. 13). 2. my own [*gnesio*]
son—'a *genuine* son' (cf. Acts xvi. 1; 1 Cor. iv.
14-17). See 'Introduction.' mercy. Added, in
addressing Timothy, to the ordinary "Grace unto
you (Rom. i. 7; 1 Cor. i. 3, &c.), and peace." In
Gal. vi. 16 "peace and *mercy*" occur. There are
similarities between the epistle to the Galatians
and the pastoral epistles (see 'Introduction');
perhaps owing to his there, as here, having, as a
leading object, the correction of false teachers,
especially as to the right and wrong use of the *law*
(*v.* 9): also, owing to Galatians and the pastoral
epistles being written by Paul's *own hand.*
"Mercy" is tender grace exercised towards the
miserable, the experience of which in one's own
case especially fits for the MINISTRY. Cf. as to
Paul himself, *vv.* 13, 14, 16; 1 Cor. vii. 25; 2 Cor.
iv. 1; Heb. ii. 17. He did not use "mercy"
as to the churches, because "mercy" in all its
fulness already existed towards them; but in the
case of an individual minister, fresh measures of it
were continually needed. His sense of his need
of "mercy" had deepened the older he grew.
"Grace" refers to men's *sins;* "mercy" to their
misery. God extends His *grace* to men as guilty;
His *mercy* to them as miserable (*Trench*). Jesus
Christ. A Δ G *f g,* Vulgate, read the order,
'Christ Jesus.' In the pastoral epistles "Christ"
is often before "Jesus," to give prominence to the
fulfilment of the Old Testament *Messianic* promises, well-known to Timothy (2 Tim. iii. 15), in
Jesus.
3. Timothy's superintendence of the church at
Ephesus was as temporary overseer, *locum tenens,*
for the apostle. Thus the office at Ephesus and
(Titus i. 5) Crete, in the absence of the presiding

apostle, subsequently became a permanent institution on the removal, by death, of the apostles who
heretofore superintended the churches. The first
title of these overseers was "angels" (Rev. i.
20). As I besought thee to abide. He meant to
add, '*so* I still beseech thee;' but does not complete the sentence until *virtually,* not formally, at
v. 18. at Ephesus. Paul, in Acts xx. 25, declared
to the Ephesian elders, "I *know* that ye all shall
see my face no more." If, then, as the arguments
favour (see 'Introduction'), this epistle was
written subsequently to Paul's first imprisonment,
the meaning of his prophecy was, not that *he*
should never visit *Ephesus* again (which this verse
implies he did), but that '*they all* should see his
face no more.' This verse is hardly compatible
with *Birks's* theory, that Paul did not actually
visit *Ephesus,* though in its immediate neighbourhood (cf. ch. iii. 14; iv. 13). I besought—a mild
word, instead of authoritative command, to
Timothy, as a fellow-helper. some—*slightly* contemptuous (Gal. ii. 12; Jude 4) (*Ellicott*). teach
no other doctrine—than what I have taught (Gal.
i. 6-9). His prophetic bodings years before (Acts
xx. 29, 30) were now being realized (cf. ch. vi. 3).
4. fables — incipient Gnostic legends about the
origin and propagation of angels, as at Colosse
(Col. ii. 18-23). Rather, "Jewish fables" (Titus i.
14). "Profane and old wives' fables" (ch. iv. 7; 2
Tim. iv. 4). genealogies. Not merely genealogies
common among the Jews, tracing their descent
from the patriarchs, which Paul would not class
with "fables," but Gnostic genealogies of spirits
and œons, or emanations (*Alford*). So *Tertullian,*
'Adversus Valentinianos,' ch. iii., and *Irenæus,*
'Præf.' The Judaizers here, whilst maintaining
the obligation of the Mosaic law, joined with it a
theosophic ascetic tendency, pretending to see in
it mysteries deeper than others. The *seeds, not
the full-grown* Gnosticism of the post apostolic age,
then existed. This formed the transition between
Judaism and Gnosticism. "Endless" implies
their tedious unprofitableness (cf. Titus iii. 9).
Scripture opposes to their 'œons' the 'King of
the œons (so Greek, *v.* 17), to whom be glory
throughout the œons of œons.' The *word* 'œons'
was possibly not used in the technical Gnostic
sense as yet; but "the only wise God" (*v.* 17), by
anticipation, confutes subsequent notions in the
Gnostics' own phraseology. questions—of speculation (Acts xxv. 20), not practical; generating
merely curious discussions. which [*haitines*]—
'inasmuch as they' (ch. vi. 4; 2 Tim. ii. 14, 23).
"Vain jangling" (*vv.* 6, 7) of would-be "teachers
of the law." godly edifying. So Δ *f g,* Vulgate.
But A G א read '*the dispensation* [*oikonomian
for oikodomēn*] of God,' the Gospel dispensation

480

5   Now *^g* the end of the commandment is charity *^h* out of a pure heart,
6   and *of* a good conscience, and *of* faith unfeigned : from which some
7   ¹ having swerved have turned aside unto vain jangling ; desiring to be
    teachers of the law ; understanding neither what they say, nor whereof
8   they affirm. But we know that *ⁱ* the law *is* good, if a man use it law-
9   fully ; knowing *^j* this, that the law is not made for a righteous man, but
    ^k for the lawless and disobedient, for the ungodly and for sinners, for
    unholy and profane, for murderers of fathers and murderers of mothers,
10 for man-slayers, for whoremongers, for them that defile themselves with
    mankind, for men-stealers, for liars, for perjured persons, and if there be

A. D. 65.

g Rom. 13. 8.
Gal. 5. 14.
h Ps. 51. 10.
Matt. 12. 35.
2 Tim. 2. 22.
¹ Or, not
aiming at.
i Neh. 9. 13.
Rom. 7. 12.
Gal. 3. 21.
j Gal. 3. 19.
k Rev. 21. 8.

originating from God towards man (1 Cor. ix. 17), which is (has its element) in faith ; not 'questioning' (*v.* 5, end). *Conybeare,* '*the stewardship of God.*' He infers that the false teachers in Ephesus were *presbyters,* which accords with the prophecy, Acts xx. 30 ; 1 Cor. iv. 1, 2. **5. Now**—Greek, 'But,' in contrast to the unedifying doctrine (*vv.* 3, 4). **the end**—the aim. **the commandment** [*parangelias*]—' of the charge :' the same "charge" as *vv.* 3, 18 ; here including *the gospel* 'dispensation of God' (note, *vv.* 4 and 11), the sum and substance of the "charge" (the practical, preceptive teaching) committed to Timothy wherewith to "charge" his flock. **charity**—LOVE : the sum and end of the law and Gospel alike ; that wherein the Gospel fulfils the spirit of the law in its every essential tittle (Rom. xiii. 10). The foundation is *faith* (*v.* 4), the "end" is *love* (*v.* 14 ; Titus iii. 15) ; whereas the '*questions* gender strife' (2 Tim. ii. 23). **out of**—springing as from a fountain. **pure heart**—purified by faith (Luke x. 27 ; Acts xv. 9 ; 2 Tim. ii. 22 ; 1 Pet. i. 22). *The heart,* the centre of the *feelings* and the *imaginations* of the soul. **good conscience**—cleared from guilt by sound faith in Christ (Acts xxiii. 1 ; *v.* 19 ; ch. iii. 9 ; 2 Tim. i. 3 ; 1 Pet. iii. 16, 21 ; Heb. xiii. 18). St. John uses "heart" where Paul uses "conscience." In Paul the understanding is the seat of *conscience,* the *heart* of love (*Bengel*). A good conscience is joined with sound faith ; a bad conscience, with unsound faith (cf. Heb. ix. 9, 14). Conscience is threefold—an exponent of moral law, a judge, and a sentiment (*M'Cosh* in 'Ellicott'). **faith unfeigned**—not hypocritical and unfruitful, but working by love (Gal. v. 6). So "unfeigned" is said of "love," Rom. xii. 9 ; brotherly love, 1 Pet. i. 21 ; the wisdom from above, Jas. iii. 17. Faith is *feigned* where there is not "good conscience." The false teachers drew men off from a loving, working, real faith, to profitless, speculative "questions" (*v.* 4) : they were just the opposite, "of *corrupt* minds," ch. vi. 5 ; "*conscience* seared," ch. iv. 2 ; Titus i. 15, "unbelieving ;" "reprobate concerning the faith," 2 Tim. iii. 8 : cf. Heb. iii. 12. **6. From which**—viz., from a pure heart, good conscience, and faith unfeigned, the well-spring of love. **having swerved** [*astochēsantes*]—'having missed the mark (the "end") to be aimed at ;' viz., "love." Translated "erred," ch. vi. 21 ; 2 Tim. ii. 18. Instead of aiming right, and attaining "love," they "have turned aside (ch. v. 15 ; 2 Tim. iv. 4 ; Heb. xii. 13) unto vainjangling" [*mataiologian,* 'vain talk]' about the law and genealogies (*v.* 7 ; Titus i. 10 ; iii. 9 ; vi. 20). It is the greatest 'vanity' when divine things are not truthfully discussed (Rom. i. 21) (*Bengel*). **7.** Sample of their 'vain talk.' **Desiring**—*would-be* teachers ; not really so. **the law**—the Jewish law (Titus i. 14 ; iii. 9). The Judaizers in the epistles to the Galatians and Romans made the works of the law necessary to justification, in opposition to Gospel grace. The Judaizers here corrupted the law with

"fables" added on to it, subversive of morals as well as truth. Their error was not in maintaining the *obligation* of the law, but in ignorantly *abusing* it by fabulous and immoral interpretations. **neither what they say, nor whereof**—neither understanding *their own* asseverations nor the *object* about which they make them. **8. But**—"*Now* we know" (Rom. iii. 19 ; vii. 14) : as an admitted principle. **law is good**—accordant with God's moral goodness. **if a man**—primarily, *a teacher ;* then, every Christian. **use it lawfully**—in its lawful place in the Gospel economy ; viz., not as a means of a "righteous man" attaining higher perfection than by the Gospel alone (Titus i. 14) (the perverted use to which the false teachers put it, appending fabulous interpretations of it to the Gospel), but to awaken the sense of sin in the ungodly (*vv.* 9, 10 : cf. Rom. vii. 7-12 ; Gal. iii. 21). **9. law is not made** [*keitai: fixed : enacted*] **for a righteous man**—standing by faith in the righteousness of Christ, put *on* him for justification, and put *in* him by the Spirit for sanctification : so not judicially amenable to the law. For *sanctification* the law gives no inward power. *Alford* goes too far in saying the righteous man does 'not morally need the law.' Doubtless, in proportion as he is led by the Spirit, the justified man needs not the outward rule (Rom. vi. 14 ; Gal. v. 18, 23). But as he often gives not himself up wholly to the inward Spirit, he *morally* needs the outward *law* to show him his sin and God's requirements. The reason why the ten commandments have no power to *condemn* the Christian is not that they have no *authority* over him, but because Christ has fulfilled them as our surety (Rom. x. 4). **lawless**—passively. **disobedient**—actively. [*Anupotaktois,* 'not subject,' *insubordinate,* "unruly" (Titus i. 6, 10).] "Lawless and disobedient" are opposers of the *law ;* "ungodly and . . . sinners" [*asebesi kai hamartolois*] are the *irreverent* and *openly sinning* against *God,* from whom the law comes ; sinners against the first and second commandments : "unholy and profane" [*anosiois kai bebēlois*] are the inwardly *impure,* or else *impious,* and those deserving exclusion from the sanctuary, sinners against the *third* and *fourth* commandments ; "murderers [*patroloais, metroloais ;* rather, as *parricide* would be so rare as not to require a special law, *smiters*] of fathers and . . . mothers" (Exod. xxi. 15 ; Lev. xx. 9), against the *fifth* commandment ; 'man-slayers,' against the *sixth* commandment. **10. whoremongers, &c.**—against the seventh commandment. **men-stealers**—*i. e.,* slave-dealers. The worst offence against the eighth commandment. Stealing a man's goods is light compared with stealing a man's liberty. Slavery is not *directly* assailed by Christianity : its aim was not to revolutionize violently the existing order ; but it teaches principles sure to undermine and overthrow slavery wherever Christianity has its natural development (Matt. vii. 12). **liars . . . perjured**—against the ninth commandment.

11 any other thing that is contrary to sound doctrine; according to the glorious gospel of the blessed God, which was committed to my trust.
12 And I thank Christ Jesus our Lord, who hath enabled me, *l* for that he
13 counted me faithful, *m* putting me into the ministry : who *n* was before a blasphemer, and a persecutor, and injurious : but I obtained mercy,
14 because *o* I did *it* ignorantly in unbelief. And the grace of our Lord was
15 exceeding abundant with faith *p* and love which is in Christ Jesus. This *is* a faithful saying, and worthy of all acceptation, that *q* Christ Jesus
16 came into the world to save sinners; of whom I am chief. Howbeit for

A. D. 65.

l 1 Cor 7. 25.
m 2 Cor. 4. 1.
Col. 1. 25.
n Acts 8. 3.
Acts 9. 1.
o Luke 23. 34.
John 9. 39.
p Luke 7. 47.
q Matt 9. 13.
1 John 3. 5.

if there be any other thing, &c.—the tenth commandment in its widest aspect. He does not particularly specify it, his object being to bring out *grosser* forms of transgression ; whereas the tenth is so deeply spiritual that by it the sense of sin, in its subtlest form, "lust" (Rom. vii. 7), was brought home to Paul's own conscience. Paul argues, these *would-be teachers of the law* whilst boasting of a higher perfection through it, really fall down from Gospel elevation to the level of the grossly "lawless," for whom, not for believers, the law was designed. In practice, sticklers for the law, as the means of moral perfection, are most liable to fall from the morality of the law. Gospel grace is the only true means of sanctification as well as justification. **sound** [*hugiainousē*] —*healthy*, spiritually *wholesome* (ch. vi. 3 ; 2 Tim. i. 13 ; iv. 3 ; Titus i. 13 ; ii. 2), as opposed to *diseased, morbid* [*nosōn*, "doting," ch. vi. 4], and "canker" (2 Tim. ii. 17) ; which unhealthy symptoms appearing at the period of the pastoral epistles, cause the use of the terms "sound," 'wholesome' for the first time. **11. According to the glorious gospel** (Rom. ii. 16). The *Christian's freedom from the law as a sanctifier, as well as a justifier* (*vv.* 9, 10), accords with *the Gospel of* (*i. e.*, which manifests) *the glory* [*to euangelion tēs doxēs* : note, 2 Cor. iv. 4] of the blessed God. The Gospel manifests God's "*glory*" (Rom. ix. 23 ; Eph. i. 17 ; iii. 16) in accounting "righteous" the believer, through the righteousness of Christ, without "the law" (*v.* 9) ; and in imparting that righteousness whereby he loathes those sins against which (*vv.* 9, 10) the law is directed. "Blessed" indicates at once *immortality* and *self-derived happiness.* The supremely- "blessed" One is He from whom all our *Gospel blessedness* flows : applied to GOD only here and ch. vi. 15 : appropriate in contrast to the *curse* on those under the law (*v.* 9 ; Gal. iii. 10). **committed to my trust.** The Greek order brings into emphasis *Paul*, 'committed in trust to ME ;' in contrast to the law-teaching which *they* (who had no Gospel-commission) *assumed to themselves* (*vv.* 7, 8 ; Titus i. 3). **12.** The honour of having the Gospel ministry committed to him suggests the digression to what he once was, no better (*v.* 13) than those lawless ones above (*vv.* 9, 10), when the grace of our Lord (*v.* 14) visited him. **And.** So Δ. Omitted in א A G *g*, Vulgate. **I thank** [*charin echo*]—'I have (*i. e.*, feel) gratitude' (1 Cor. xv. 9 ; Eph. iii. 8). Paul can never allude to God's mercy to him without an outburst of thanksgiving. **enabled me, for . . . the ministry** [*endunamosanti*]—' *put power in me.*' Except in Paul's epistles, found nowhere save Acts ix. 22. An undesigned coincidence between Paul and Luke, his companion. Man is by nature "without strength" for good (Rom. v. 6). Conversion confers spiritual power. **for that** (the cause of his 'thanking Christ') he **counted me faithful**—in His predestinating foresight (1 Cor. vii. 25) ; the proof of which is His **putting me into**—rather (1 Thess. v. 9), '*appointing me* (in His sovereign purpose of grace) *unto the* ministry' (Acts xx. 24). *Faithfulness* is the

quality required in stewards (1 Cor. iv. 1, 2). **13. Who was**—'Though I was.' **a blasphemer** (Acts xxvi. 9-11)—towards *God.* **persecutor** (Gal. i. 13) —towards *fellow-men.* **injurious** [*hubristēn*] — '*insolent* outrager.' One who adds insult to injury (Rom. i. 30). [*Uppish* in *myself* : from *huper.*] This threefold relation to *God*, one's *neighbour*, one's *self*, occurs often (*vv.* 5, 9, 14 ; Titus ii. 12). **I obtained mercy** [*ēleēthēn*]—*I was had mercy upon.* God's mercy, and Paul's want of it, are in sharpest contrast (*Ellicott*). The sense of mercy was uppermost in Paul's mind. Those who have most experienced mercy can best show it (Heb. v. 2, 3). **because I did it ignorantly.** His *ignorance* was culpable ; for he might have known, if he had sought aright : but it is less culpable than sinning against light and knowledge. His ignorance gave him no claim on, but put him within the range of, God's mercy. Hence it is Christ's plea (Luke xxiii. 34), and is made by the apostles a mitigating circumstance in the Jews' sin ; opening a door of hope upon repentance ; showing how it was *possible* that such a sinner could be the object of mercy (Acts iii. 17 ; Rom. x. 2). The positive ground of mercy being shown lay solely in the compassion of God (Titus iii. 5). The ground of *ignorance* lay in *unbelief*, which is guilt. But there is a difference between mistaken zeal for the law and wilful striving against the Spirit of God (Matt. xii. 24-32 ; Luke xi. 52). **14. And** [*De*]— 'But.' Not only was *mercy* shown me, *but*, &c. **the grace**—by which 'I was had mercy upon ' (*v.* 13). **was exceeding abundant** [*huperepleonasen*] —' superabounded.' Where sin abounded, grace did much more abound (Rom. v. 20) **with** (*accompanied with*) **faith**—in contrast to "unbelief" (*v.* 13). **love**—in contrast to his cruelty to believers, as "a blasphemer . . . persecutor, and injurious." **which is in Christ**—as its element and its source, whence it flows to us. **15. faithful**—worthy of credit, because "God" who says it "is faithful" to His word (1 Cor. i. 9 ; 1 Thess. v. 24 ; 2 Thess. iii. 3 ; Rev. xxi. 5 ; xxii. 6) : the phrase, *faithful saying*, is peculiar to the pastoral epistles (ch. iv. 9 ; 2 Tim. ii. 11 ; Titus iii. 8). Greek, 'Faithful is the saying.' The New Testament prophets' inspired *sayings* had the same authority as the Old Testament *Scriptures*, and were accepted as axioms among Christians : soon they became embodied in New Testament *Scripture.* John, writing to the same church, Ephesus (one of the seven), records the same expression (Rev. xxi. 5 ; xxii. 6 : cf. 1 Ki. x. 6). **all**—all possible : to be received by all, with all the faculties of the soul, mind, and heart. Paul, unlike the false teachers (*v.* 7), *understands what he says, and whereof he affirms ;* he confutes their abstruse unpractical speculations by the simple, but grand, truth of salvation through Christ (1 Cor. i. 18-28). **acceptation**—*reception* (as of a boon) into the heart, as well as the understanding with all gladness : *faith* welcoming and appropriating the Gospel offer (Acts ii. 41). **Christ**—as promised. **Jesus**—as manifested (*Bengel*). **came into the world**—

this cause I obtained mercy, that in me first Jesus Christ might show forth all long-suffering, for a pattern to them which should hereafter
17 believe on him to life everlasting. Now unto 'the King eternal, ³immortal, invisible, the only wise God, *be* honour and glory for ever and ever. Amen.
18 This charge I commit unto thee, son Timothy, ᵗaccording to the prophecies which went before on thee, that thou by them mightest war a
19 good warfare; holding faith, and a good conscience; which some having
20 put away, concerning faith have made shipwreck: of whom is ᵘHymeneus

A. D. 65.

ʳ Ps. 10. 16.
Ps 45. 1, 6.
Ps: 145. 13.
Dan. 2. 44.
Dan. 7. 14.
Mic. 5. 2.
Matt 6. 13.
ˢ Rom. 1. 23.
ᵗ ch. 4. 14.
ᵘ 2 Tim 2 17.

which was full of sin (John i. 29; xvi. 28; Rom. v. 12; 1 John ii. 2). This implies his pre-existence. **to save sinners**—even notable sinners, like Saul of Tarsus. His instance was unrivalled in the greatness of the sin and of the mercy; that the consenter to Stephen, the proto-martyr's death, should be the successor of the same! "Devout men" carried Stephen to his burial; and "a devout man according to the law," Ananias (Acts viii. 2; xxii. 12), introduced Saul, Stephen's successor, into the Church. **I am**—not merely, 'I *was*' (1 Cor. xv. 9; Eph. iii. 8: cf. Luke xviii. 13). To each believer his own sins always appear greater than those of others, which he never can know as he does his own. **chief**—same Greek as *v.* 16, "first." Translate in both verses, 'foremost.' Where there was mercy for *him* there is mercy for all who will come to Christ (Luke xix. 10). **16.** **Howbeit**—contrasting his own conscious sinfulness with God's gracious mercy to him. **that in me**—in my case. As I was 'foremost' (*v.* 15) in sin, so God has made me the 'foremost' (not "first") sample of *mercy*. **show** — to His own glory [*endeixētai*: middle voice, Eph. ii. 7]. **all long-suffering** [*tēn apasan* —'*the whole* (of His) long-suffering;' viz., in bearing so long with me whilst a persecutor. **a pattern** [*hupotuposin*, 'for an adumbration:' 'for a type-like sample of (for) them,' &c. (1 Cor. x. 6, 11: *tupoi*)]—to assure the greatest sinners that they shall not be rejected in coming to Christ, since even Saul found mercy. No greater long-suffering can be required in the case of any other than was exercised in my case. So David made his own pardon, notwithstanding his great sin, a sample to encourage other sinners to seek pardon (Ps. xxxiii. 5, 6). *Literally,* 'a sketch' or *outline* —the filling up to take place in each man's case. **believe on him**—belief rests ON Him, the only foundation on which faith relies. [*Pisteuein autō* expresses simply *believing Him; p. en auto* involves *union* with Him; *p. eis autōn* (only in John and Peter), a *fuller mystical* union, with the notion of mental motion *towards; p. epi autō, reliance upon; p. epi auton,* mental motion *towards, with a view to reliance on,* Him (*Ellicott*).] **to life everlasting**—the ultimate aim which faith always keeps in view (Titus i. 2). **17.** A suitable conclusion to the beautifully-simple Gospel enunciation, of which his own history is a living pattern. It is from experimental sense of grace that the doxology flows (*Bengel*). **the King eternal**—lit., 'King of the (eternal) ages.' [LXX., *ton aiona, kai ep'aiona, kai eti* (Exod. xv. 18, 'The Lord shall reign *for ages and beyond them'*) (Ps. cxlv. 13, *margin.*)] The "life everlasting" (*v.* 16) suggested 'the King *everlasting.*' It answers to "for ever and ever"—*lit.*, 'to the ages of the ages' (the countless succession of ages made up of ages). **immortal.** So △ *f*, Vulgate. But A G *g* read 'incorruptible' [*aptharto* for *athanato*] (Rom. i. 23). **invisible** (ch. vi. 16; Exod. xxxiii. 20; John i. 18; Col. i. 15; Heb. xi. 27), **the only wise God.** So C. But א A △ G *f g*, Vulgate, omit "wise," which

probably crept in from Rom. xvi. 27 (Jude 25; ch. vi. 15; Ps. lxxxvi. 10; Greek, John v. 44). **honour and glory**—in doxology, only here and Rev. v. 13. **for ever, &c.** The thought of eternity (terrible to unbelievers) is delightful to those assured of grace (*v.* 16) (*Bengel*). **18.** He resumes *v.* 3. The conclusion to the "*As* I besought thee . . . *charge*" (*v.* 3) is here given, not formally, but substantially. **This charge**—viz., 'That thou in them mightest war,' &c.; *i. e.,* fulfil thy Christian and ministerial calling one function of which is to "*charge* some that they teach no other doctrine" (*v.* 3). This verse is the general conclusion; *vv.* 3-11, the direct *charges; vv.* 12-16, Paul's authority; *vv.* 18, 19, the substance of his previous injunctions (*Ellicott*). **I commit** [*paratithemai*]—as a sacred deposit (ch. vi. 20; 2 Tim. ii. 2) for the good of thy hearers. **according to**—in consonance with. **the prophecies which went before on** [*epi:* referring *to*] **thee**— the intimations, given by prophets respecting thy future zeal and success, at thy ordination, ch. iv. 14 (probably by Silas, a companion of Paul and "a prophet," and others; Acts xv. 32). Such prophecies and the good report of Timothy given by the two churches, Lystra (the scene of his conversion) and Iconium, where under the elders he probably had been "messenger of the churches" (2 Cor. viii. 23; Acts xiv. 21, 23; xvi. 2), induced Paul to take him as his companion. Cf. similar prophecies (Acts xiii. 1-3) in connection with laying on of hands; xi. 28; xxi. 10, 11: cf. 1 Cor. xii. 10; xiv. 1; Eph. iv. 11. In Acts xx. 28, it is expressly said, '*the Holy Ghost* had made the Ephesian presbyters overseers.' *Clement* of Rome, 'Epist. ad Corinthios,' states it was the custom of the apostles 'to make trial by the Spirit'—*i. e.,* by the 'power of discerning'—in order to choose overseers and deacons in the several churches. So *Clement* of Alexandria says, as to the churches near Ephesus, that the overseers were marked out for ordination by a revelation of the Holy Ghost to St. John. **by** (Greek, *in*) **them**—arrayed in them as thine armour. **warfare**—not the mere "fight" (ch. vi. 12; 2 Tim. iv. 7), but the *whole campaign* [*tēn kalēn strateian,* 'the good warfare.'] **19. Holding**—Keeping hold of "faith;" and "good conscience" (*v.* 5); not 'putting this away' as "some." The *faith* is the precious liquor; *good conscience,* the clean glass that contains it (*Bengel*). The loss of *good conscience* entails *shipwreck of the faith.* Consciousness of sin (not repented of and forgiven) kills the germ of faith (*Wiesinger*). **which** [*hēn*]—singular; viz., "good conscience;" not "faith" also. **put away** —a wilful act [*apōsamenoi,* 'thrust away.'] They thrust it from them as a troublesome monitor (Acts xiii. 46, Greek). It reluctantly withdraws, extruded by force, when its owner is tired of its importunity, and is resolved to retain his sin at the cost of losing it. One cannot be at once on friendly terms with it and with sin. **made shipwreck.** The *faith* is the vessel in which they had professedly embarked, of which "good conscience"

483

[v]and Alexander; whom I have [w]delivered unto Satan, that they may learn not to blaspheme.

2   I [1]EXHORT therefore, that, first of all, supplications, prayers, inter-
2 cessions, *and* giving of thanks, be made for all men; for [a]kings, and [b]*for* all that are in [2]authority; that we may lead a quiet and peaceable life
3 in all godliness and honesty. For this *is* [c]good and acceptable in the
4 sight of God our Saviour; who will have all men to be saved, and to
5 come unto the knowledge of the truth. For *there is* one God, and one

A. D. 65.

[v] 2 Tim. 4. 14.
[w] Matt 18. 17.

CHAP. 2.
[1] Or. desire.
[a] Jer. 29. 7.
[b] Rom. 13. 1.
[2] Or, emi-
nent place.
[c] Rom. 12. 2.

is the anchor The ancient church often compared the course of faith to navigation. The Greek does not imply that they having once had *faith,* made shipwreck of it, but that they who put away good conscience 'made shipwreck with respect to THE [*tēn*] faith.' 20. Hymeneus—probably the Hymeneus of 2 Tim. ii. 17, 18. Though 'delivered over to Satan' (the lord of all outside the church, Acts xxvi. 18, and the executor of wrath, when judicially allowed by God, ou the disobedient, 1 Cor. v. 5; 2 Cor. xii. 7; Eph. iv. 27), he was restored to the Church subsequently, and again troubled him. Paul, as an apostle, though distant at Rome, pronounced the sentence of excommunication to be executed at Ephesus (Matt. xviii. 17, 18). The sentence operated not only spiritually but physically, sickness, or some such visitation, falling on the excommunicated, in order to bring him to repentance. "Alexander" is probably " the coppersmith" who did St. Paul "much evil" when the latter visited Ephesus. The 'delivering him to Satan' was the consequence of his *withstanding* the apostle (2 Tim. iv. 14, 15): as the sentence on Hymeneus was for his "saying that the resurrection is past already;" his putting away *good conscience,* producing *shipwreck concerning* the FAITH (v. 19). If one's religion better not his morals, his moral deficiencies will corrupt his religion. The rain which falls pure from heaven will not continue pure, if received in an unclean vessel (*Archbishop Whately*). He possibly was the Alexander, *then* a Jew, put forward by the Jews against Paul at the riot in Ephesus (Acts xix. 33). **that they may**—not 'might:' the effect still continues: the sentence is as yet unremoved. **learn** [*paideuthosin*]—' be disciplined;' viz., by *chastisement* and suffering. **blaspheme**—God and Christ, by doings and teachings unworthy of their profession (Rom. ii. 23, 24; Jas. ii. 7). Though the apostles, being infallible, could excommunicate judicially, with bodily inflictions miraculously sent (2 Cor. x. 8), it does not follow that fallible ministers now have any power, save that of excluding from church-fellowship notorious bad livers.

CHAP. II. 1-15.—PUBLIC WORSHIP—INTERCESSIONS FOR ALL MEN, SINCE CHRIST IS A RANSOM FOR ALL—DUTIES OF MEN AND WOMEN RESPECTIVELY IN PUBLIC PRAYER—WOMAN'S SUBJECTION—HER SPHERE OF DUTY.

1. therefore—resuming the general subject (2 Tim. ii. 1). ' What I have therefore to say by way of a *charge* (ch. i. 3, 18), is,' &c. **that, first of all . . . be made.** "First of all," connect with "I exhort." What I *begin with* as of primary importance, &c. As the destruction of Jerusalem drew near, the Jews (including those at Ephesus) dreamed of freedom from every yoke; so virtually "blasphemed" (cf. ch. i. 20) God's name by 'speaking evil of dignities' (ch. vi. 1; 2 Pet. ii. 10; Jude 8). Hence Paul gives prominence to prayer for *all* men, especially for *magistrates* and *kings* (Titus iii. 1-3) (*Olshausen*). Some looked down on all not Christians as doomed to perdition; but Paul says *all men* are to be

prayed for, as Christ died for all (v. 4-6). **supplications** [*deēseis*]—implying *sense of need,* and the suppliant's own *insufficiency.* **prayers** [*proseuchas*] — implying *devotion.* **intercessions** [*enteuxeis*]— *the coming near to God* with child-like confidence, *seeking an audience* in person, generally *in behalf of another.* The accumulation of terms implies prayer in its every form, according to all relations. **thanks**—always to accompany prayer (Phil. iv. 6). **2. for kings**—a confutation of the adversaries who accused Christians of disaffection to the ruling powers (Acts xvii. 7; Rom. xiii. 1-7). **all that are in authority** [*tēn en huperochē*]—' in eminence.' The "quiet" of Christians often more depended on subordinate rulers than on the supreme king. **that we may lead**—that we may be blessed with such good government as to ' pass' [*diagōmen*], &c. The prayers of Christians for the government bring down peace to themselves. **quiet** [*ēremon*]— not troubled *from without.* **peaceable** [*hesuchion*] —'tranquil:' not troubled *from within* (*Olshausen*). ' He is *peaceable* [*hesuchios,* from *hemai, I sit*] who makes no disturbance; he is *quiet* [*ēremos*] who is himself free from disturbance' (*Tittmann*). **in all** —"in all (possible) godliness;" lit., *well-directed reverence* or *worship* [*eusebeia:* but *theosebeia*]; v. 10, "godliness." **honesty** [*semnoteti*]—"gravity" (Titus ii. 2, 7), 'decorum' of conduct. As "godliness" relates *to God,* "gravity" is in relation to men. In the Old Testament the Jews were commanded to pray for their heathen rulers (Ezra vi. 10; Jer. xxix. 7). The Jews, by Augustus' order, offered a lamb daily for the Roman emperor till near the destruction of Jerusalem. The Zealots, instigated by Eleazar, renounced this custom (*Josephus,* 'B. J.' ii. 17), whence the war originated. **3. this**—praying for all men. **acceptable in the sight of God**—not merely *before men,* as if we sought mainly their favour (2 Cor. viii. 21). **our Saviour**—a title appropriate to the subject. "*Our* Saviour God." **4. Who**—seeing He *is willing that all should be saved* (v. 4; Rom. v. 18): we should meet the will of God in behalf of others, by praying for the salvation of all. More would be converted if we prayed more. *Our* Saviour actually saved *us* who believe. ' He is willing that *all* should be saved by believing, even those who do not yet believe (cf. ch. iv. 10; Titus ii. 11). Why multitudes are lost is, they will not come to Him for life (John v. 40) [*ou thelete elthein,* 'ye are *not willing* to come']. St. Paul does not say, ' He wishes *to save* all,' for then He *would* have saved all in fact; but " will have all men to be saved" implies the possibility of man's accepting (through God's prevenient grace) or rejecting it (through man's own perversity). Our prayers ought to include *all,* as God's grace included *all.* **and—for** that purpose. **to come.** They are not forced. **unto the knowledge** [*epignosin*]—'the *full* knowledge' (note, 1 Cor. xiii. 12; Phil. i. 9). **the truth** —the saving truth in and by Jesus (John xvii. 3, 17). **5. For there is one God.** God's *unity* in essence and purpose proves His comprehending all His human children (created in His image) in His offer of grace (cf. the same argument from

6 mediator between God and men, the man Christ Jesus; who gave himself
7 a ransom for all, ³ to be testified *d* in due time. Whereunto I am ordained a preacher, and an apostle, (I speak the truth in Christ, *and* lie not;) a teacher of the Gentiles in faith and verity.
8   I will therefore that men pray * every where, lifting up holy hands,
9 without wrath and doubting. In like manner also, that women adorn themselves in modest apparel, with shamefacedness and sobriety; not
10 with ⁴ broidered hair, or gold, or pearls, or costly array; but (which becometh women professing godliness) with good works.

A. D. 65.

³ Or, a testimony.
1 Cor. 1. 6.
d Gal 4. 4.
* 2 Chr. 33. 11.
Mal. 1. 11.
Luke 23. 42.
John 4. 21.
⁴ Or, plaited.

His unity, Rom. iii. 30; Gal. iii. 20); therefore all are to be prayed for. 'The *universality* of the dispensation is proved by the *unity* of the Dispenser' (*Ellicott*). *V.* 4 is proved from *v.* 5; *v.* 1 from *v.* 4. The *One God* is common to all (Isa. xlv. 22; Acts xvii. 26). The one Mediator is Mediator between God and all potentially (Rom. iii. 29; Eph. iv. 5, 6; Heb. viii. 6; ix. 15; xii. 24). They who have not this one God by the one Mediator have none: *lit.*, a *go-between*. The Greek order is 'one mediator *also* between,' &c. Whilst God will have all men to be saved by knowing God and the Mediator, there is a legitimate order in the exercise of that will wherewith men must receive it. All mankind constitute ONE MAN before God (*Bengel*). **the** (not in the Greek) **man**—rather, "man," generically: not a mere *individual man:* the Second Head of humanity as Mediator, representing in Himself *the whole human race and nature* (cf. Rom. v. 15; 1 Cor. viii. 6; 2 Cor. v. 19; Col. ii. 14). His being "man" was necessary to His being a Mediator, sympathizing with us through experimental knowledge of our nature (Isa. l. 4; Heb. ii. 14; iv. 15). Even in nature, blessings are conveyed to us from God through the mediation of various agents. The effectual intercession of Moses for Israel (Num. xiv.; Deut. ix.); Abraham for Abimelech (Gen. xx. 7); Job for his friends (Job xlii. 10), the mediation being PRESCRIBED *by God* whilst declaring His purpose of forgiveness,—all prefigure the grand mediation for all by the One Mediator. On the other hand, ch. iii. 16 asserts that He was also *God.* **6. gave himself** (Titus ii. 14). Not only the *Father* gave Him for us (John iii. 16), but *the Son* gave Himself (Phil. ii. 5-8). **ransom**—properly of a captive. Man was the slave of Satan, sold under sin. He was unable to ransom himself, because absolute obedience is due to God; therefore no act of ours can satisfy for the least offence. Lev. xxv. 48 allowed one sold captive to be redeemed by one of his brethren. The Son of God therefore became man in order that, as our elder brother, He should redeem us (Matt. xx. 28; Eph. i. 7; 1 Pet. i. 18, 19). [*Antilutron* implies not merely *ransom*, but a *substituted* or *equivalent ransom:* the '*anti*' implying vicarious substitution.] **for** [*huper:* in behalf of] **all**—not merely for a privileged few. Cf. *v.* 1, the argument for *praying in behalf of all.* **to be testified** [*to marturion*]—'the testimony (which was to be testified of, 1 John v. 8-11) in its own due times;' the *seasons* [*kairois idiois*] appointed by God for its being testified of (ch. vi. 15; Titus i. 3)—viz., from the outpouring of the Spirit on the apostles to Christ's second advent. The oneness of the Mediator, involving the universality of redemption (which faith, however, alone appropriates), was the great subject of Christian testimony (*Alford*) (Luke xxiv. 47, 48; 1 Cor. i. 6; ii. 1; 2 Thess. i. 10). **7. Whereunto**—For the giving of which testimony. **I am ordained** [*etethēn*]—'I was set:' same Greek as "putting me," &c. (ch. i. 12.) **preacher** [*kērux*]—'herald' (1 Cor. i. 21;

ix. 27; xv. 11; 2 Tim. i. 11; Titus i. 3). As in ch. i. 16 he proposes *himself* a living *pattern* of the Gospel, so here 'a herald of (it to) the Gentiles' (Gal. ii. 9; Eph. iii. 1-12; Col. i. 23). The universality of his commission is appropriate here, where he would prove that prayers are to be made "for *all* men" (*v.* 1). (**I speak the truth in Christ, and lie not**)—a strong asseveration of his universal commission, exposed as he was to frequent conflict (Rom. xi. 1; 2 Cor. xi. 31). **in faith and verity.** The sphere of his ministry was *the faith*, and (*v.* 4) the *Gospel truth* the subject matter of *the faith* (*Wiesinger*). *Ellicott*, 'Paul's *subjective faith*, which opens out *the objective* doctrinal *truth* (John viii. 31, 32).'

8. I will [*Boulomai*]—I *desire*, active wish: not mere *willingness* [*ethelo*]. **that 'men**—Greek, 'that *the* men,' as distinguished from 'the women,' to whom he has something different to say (*vv.* 9-12; 1 Cor. xi. 4, 5; xiv. 34, 35). The *emphasis* is on the precept of *praying*, resumed from *v.* 1. **every where**—Greek, 'in every place:' viz., of public prayer. Fulfilling Mal. i. 11; Matt. xviii. 20; John iv. 21, 23. **lifting up holy hands.** The early Christians turned up their palms towards heaven, as craving help. 'An oblation to God of the instruments of our necessities' (*Ellicott*). So also Solomon (1 Ki. viii. 22; Ps. cxli. 2). The Jews washed their hands before prayer (Ps. xxvi. 6). St. Paul (cf. Job xvii. 9; Jas. iv. 8) alludes to this: so Isa. i. 15, 16. [*Hosious*] "Holy" means not *profane, untainted with impiety; observing every sacred duty.* The contrite desire to be so is a needful qualification for effectual prayer (Ps. xxiv. 3, 4). **without wrath** [*chōris*]—*putting* it *away* (Matt. v. 23, 24; vi. 15). **doubting** [*dialogismou*]—translated, Phil. ii. 14, 'disputing.' But elsewhere it means *doubting; reasonings* as to whether prayer shall obtain an answer. However, the *verb* means *dispute* (Mark ix. 33, 34). Such things *hinder prayer* (Rom. xiv. 1; 1 Pet. iii. 7: cf. an instance of *doubting* vitiating prayer, 2 Ki. vii. 2; Matt. xiv. 31; Mark xi. 22-24; Jas. i. 6. **9, 10.** The context implies that these directions as to women refer to their deportment *in public worship*, though holding good on *other* occasions also. **in modest apparel**—'in seemly guise' (*Ellicott*). [*Kosmio*, 'orderly,' 'decorous'; *katastole*, 'deportment*' outwardly: '*bearing*,' including, but not restricted to, *apparel.*] Women love fine dress: at Ephesus riches (ch. vi. 17) led some to dress luxuriously. [*Katastēma* (Titus ii. 3), "behaviour," refers to *demeanour.*] **shamefacedness.** *Trench* spells this 'shamefastness' (that which is made *fast* by an honourable *shame*), as 'stedfastness' (cf. *vv.* 11, 12). **sobriety** [*sophrosune*]—'*discretion*,' *'sobermindedness :'* the well-balanced state arising from habitual *self-restraint* (*Ellicott*). **with**—Greek, *in.* **broidered hair**—lit., plaits: probably with the 'gold and pearls' intertwined (1 Pet. iii. 3). Such gaud characterizes the spiritual harlot (Rev. xvii. 4). **10. professing** [*epangellomenais*]—*promising;* engaging to follow. **with** [*dia: through*] **good works.** Their adorning is to be effected *by*

485

11, Let the woman learn in silence with all subjection. But I suffer not
12 a woman to teach, nor to usurp authority over the man, but to be in
13, silence. For Adam was first formed, then Eve. And Adam was not
14, deceived, but the woman being deceived was in the transgression. Not-
15 withstanding she shall be saved in *f* child-bearing, if they continue in
faith and charity and holiness with sobriety

3 THIS *is* a true saying, If a man desire the office of a *a* bishop, he
2 desireth a good work. A bishop then must be blameless, the husband of

A. D. 65.
f Gen. 3. 15,
16.
Isa. 7. 14.
Isa. 9. 6.

CHAP. *3.*
a Acts 20. 28.
Phil. 1. 1.
Tit. 1. 7.
Heb. 12. 15.

---

means of good w**o**rks: not that they are to be clothed *in*, or *with* (*v.* 9) them (Eph. ii. 10). Works, not words in public, is their province (*vv.* 8, 11, 12; 1 Pet. iii. 1). *Works* are often mentioned in the pastoral epistles, to oppose the loose living, combined with loose doctrine, of the false teachers. Everyday duties are honoured with the designation "good works." **11. learn**—not "teach" (*v.* 12). She should not even put questions in the public assembly (1 Cor. xiv. 34, 35). **with all subjection**—not 'usurping authority' (*v.* 12). She might teach, but not in public (Acts xviii. 26). St. Paul probably wrote this from Corinth, where the precept was in force. A canon of the Council of Carthage (A.D. 398) renewed this prohibition. Women might privately teach those of their own sex. **12. usurp authority** [*authentein*]—'to exercise dominion;' *lit.*, 'to be an autocrat:' primarily in *public* ministrations. **13. For**—Reason of the precept: the original order of creation. **Adam was first**—before Eve, who was created *for him* (1 Cor. xi. 8, 9). **formed** [*eplasthē*]—from pre-created matter [Hebrew, *yatzar*]. **14. Adam was not deceived**—*directly*, as Eve was by the serpent, but was *persuaded* by his wife (Gen. iii. 17): *indirectly* deceived. Contrast Gen. iii. 13. Eve says, "The *serpent beguiled* me." Being easily deceived, she easily deceives (2 Cor. xi. 3). Last in being, she was first in sin. The subtle serpent knew she was "the weaker vessel." He therefore tempted her. She yielded to the temptations of sense and the *deceits of Satan;* he, to *conjugal* love. Hence, in the order of God's sentence, the serpent, the prime offender, stands first; the woman, who was deceived, next; the man, persuaded by his wife, last (Gen. iii. 14-19). In Rom. v. 12 Adam is represented as the first transgressor; but there Adam (including Eve) is regarded as head of the sinning race. In Gen. iii. 16 woman's "subjection" (*v.* 11) is represented as the consequence of her "being deceived." So C. But א A Δ G read the compound [*exapatē-theisa* for the simple *apatētheisa*], 'having been *completely deceived*.' Satan *succeeded in deceiving* her. **was in the transgression** [*en parabasei gegonen*]—'*came to be* (became involved) in transgression;' *lit.*, 'going beyond' the positive precept (Rom. iv. 15). **15. be saved in child-bearing** [*dia tēs teknogonias*]—'in (lit., *through*) her (lit., *the*) child-bearing.' *Through* expresses not *the means* of her salvation, but the *circumstances* AMIDST *which* it has place. Thus 1 Cor. iii. 15, "he himself shall be saved; yet so as by (lit., *through*) fire:" in spite of the fiery ordeal which he has to pass *through.* So here, '*In spite of* the child-bearing which she passes *through* (as her portion of the curse, Gen. ñi. 16), she shall be saved.' Moreover, it is *implied* that the very curse will be a condition favourable to her salvation, by her faithfully performing her part in doing and suffering what God has assigned to her—viz., *child-bearing* and home duties, *her* sphere, as distinguished from public teaching, not her's, but *man's* (*vv.* 11, 12). In this home sphere, not ordinarily in public service for the kingdom of

God, she will be saved on the same terms as all others—viz., by living faith. *Ellicott,* 'through THE child-bearing' (Greek), the bearing of the child Jesus. Doubtless this is the ground of women's *child-bearing* becoming to them a blessing instead of a curse; as in the original prophecy (Gen. iii. 15, 16) the promise of "the seed of the woman" (the Saviour), about to bruise the serpent's head, stands in closest connection with the woman's doom to "sorrow" in 'bringing forth children.' Her *child-bearing*, though *in sorrow*, being the function of her sex whereby the Saviour was born, shall be the mean of her salvation. This may be an ulterior reference of the Holy Spirit; but the primary one seems, 'She shall be saved ([though] with child-bearing)'—*i. e.*, though suffering her part of the primeval curse in child-bearing; just as a man shall be saved, though having to bear his part—viz., the sweat of the brow. **if they**—'if *the women* (taken out of "the woman," *v.* 14; put for *the whole sex*) continue' [*meinosin*]; lit., *shall* (be found at the judgment to) *have continued.* **faith and charity**—the essential way to salvation (ch. i. 5). *Faith*, in relation to God; *charity*, to our fellow-man; *sobriety*, to one's self. **holiness**—the normal state of believing (Rom. vi. 22; 1 Thess. iv. 3, 4). **sobriety**—'sobermindedness' (note, *v.* 9, contrasted with the unseemly forwardness reproved, *v.* 11). Mental receptivity, and activity in family life, are the destiny of woman. One reason alleged here is the greater danger of self-deception in the weaker sex, and the errors arising from it, especially in addresses in which sober reflectiveness is least in exercise. The case, Acts xxi. 9, was doubtless in private, not in public.

CHAP. III. 1-16.—RULES FOR BISHOPS AND DEACONS — THE CHURCH, AND THE GOSPEL-MYSTERY REVEALED TO IT, ARE THE END OF ALL SUCH RULES.

1. '**Faithful is the saying.**' A needful preface; for the office of a bishop in Paul's day, being attended with hardship and often persecution, would not seem to the world a desirable and "good work." **desire** [*oregetai*]—'stretch one's self forward to grasp;' *seeks after;* distinct Greek from 'desireth' [*epithumei*]. What one does voluntarily is more esteemed than what he does when asked (1 Cor. xvi. 15): utterly distinct from ambition for office (Jas. iii. 1). **bishop**—overseer: as yet identical with "presbyter" (Acts xx. 17, 28; Titus i. 5-7). Originally *overseers* sent by the Athenian state to subject cities. As the term "bishop" is from the *Greeks*, so "presbyter" from the *Jews* [*Ha-zzqueenim*] (Num. ii. 25). **good** [*kalou: honourable*] **work.** Good men alone are to be entrusted with good work. Not the honour, but the *work*, is the prominent thought (Acts xv. 38; Phil. ii. 30: cf. 2 Tim. iv. 5). He who aims at the office must remember the high qualifications needed for its discharge. **2.** The existence of church organization, presbyters, and presbyteresses at Ephesus is pre-supposed (ch. v. 17, 19). The directions here to Timothy, the apostolic delegate, are as to filling up *vacancies*

one wife, vigilant, sober, [1] of good behaviour, given to hospitality, apt to
3 teach; [2] not given to wine, no striker, not greedy of filthy lucre; but
4 patient, not a brawler, not covetous; one that ruleth well his own
5 house, having his children in subjection with all gravity; (for if a man
know not how to rule his own house, how shall he take care of the
6 church of God?) not a novice, lest being lifted up with pride he fall
7 into the condemnation of the devil. Moreover he must have a good

A. D. 65.

[1] Or, modest.
[2] Or, Not ready to quarrel, and offer wrong, as one in wine.

among the bishops and deacons, or *adding* to their number. *Fresh churches* in the neighbourhood also would require presbyters and deacons. Episcopacy was adopted in apostolic times as the most expedient government, being most like Jewish institutions, and so offering less obstruction through Jewish prejudices to the progress of Christianity. The synagogue was governed by presbyters, "elders" (Acts iv. 8; xxiv. 1), called also *bishops* or *overseers*. Three among them presided as "rulers of the synagogue," answering to modern "bishops" (*Lightfoot*, 'Horæ'); one among them took the lead. *Ambrose* (in 'Amularius de Officiis,' ii. 13, and *Bingham*, 'Eccles. Antiq.,' ii. 11) says, 'Those now called bishops were originally called apostles. But those who ruled the Church after the death of the apostles had not the testimony of miracles, and were in many respects inferior. Therefore they thought it not decent to assume the name of apostles; but dividing the names, they left to *presbyters* that name, and they themselves were called *bishops.*' In the second century no one of the lower order was termed "bishop." In the New Testament there are traces of a superintending president—first an apostle, then an apostolic delegate, as Timothy and Titus, then an angel. "*Presbyter*" expresses the *rank;* "bishop," the *office* or *duties.* Timothy exercised the power at Ephesus which bishops recently exercised. The rule of angel-bishops over dioceses is simply *an apostolic precedent,* like the love-feasts, and kiss of charity, not Divinely and lastingly obligatory. It binds congregations together, instead of being disconnected. When made an absolute law, it tends to spiritual despotism. The authority of a presiding pastor, the consent of presbytery, and that of the people, all combining, is the nearest approach to apostolic usage. Even where there was a real succession of Divine origination, as the Aaronic priesthood, there was no infallibility. For if the disciples had submitted to the visible priesthood, they would have rejected Jesus. **blameless** [*anepilepton*]—'unexceptionable:' giving no *just* handle for blame. **husband of one wife.** Confuting the celibacy of Rome's priesthood. Though the Jews practised polygamy, yet, as he is writing about a Gentile church, and as polygamy was never allowed among even laymen, the ancient interpretation that the prohibition is against polygamy in a candidate-bishop is not correct. It must mean that, though laymen might lawfully marry again, candidates for the episcopate or presbytery were better to be married only *once.* As in ch. v. 9 "wife of one man" implies a woman married but once, so "husband of one wife" must mean the same. The feeling among the Gentiles, as well as Jews (cf. Anna, Luke ii. 36, 37), against a second marriage would, for expediency and conciliation in matters indifferent, not involving compromise of principle, account for Paul's prohibition as to one so prominent as a bishop or a deacon. Hence the stress laid in the context on the *repute* in which the candidate for orders is held among those over whom he is to preside (Titus i. 6). The council of Laodicea and the apostolic canons discountenanced second marriages, especially in candidates for

ordination. Of course, second marriage being *lawful,* the undesirableness holds good only under special circumstances. Also, he who has a wife and virtuous family is to be preferred to a bachelor; for he who is himself bound to discharge the domestic duties will be more attractive to those who have similar ties, for he teaches them not only by precept, but also by example (*vv.* 4, 5). The Jews teach a priest should be neither unmarried nor childless, lest he be unmerciful (*Bengel*). So in the synagogue, 'no one shall offer up prayer in public unless he be married.' (In 'Colbo,' ch. lxv.; *Vitringa*, 'Synagogue.') **vigilant** [*nephalion*]—*sober;* ever on the watch, as sober men alone can be, to foresee what ought to be done (1 Thess. v. 6-8). **sober** [*sophrona*]—soberminded: *discreet.* **of good behaviour** [*kosmion*]—'orderly.' "*Sober*" refers to the inward mind; '*orderly*,' to the *outward* behaviour, tone, look, gait, dress. The new man bears a sacred festival character, incompatible with all disorder, excess, laxity, assumption, harshness, and meanness (Phil. iv. 8) (*Bengel*). **apt to teach** (2 Tim. ii. 24). **3. Not given to wine** [*Mē Paroinon* includes, not indulging in *the brawling* which proceeds from being given to wine. The opposite of *epieikē,* 'patient,' '*forbearing,*' *reasonable* to others (note, Phil. iv. 5)], **no striker**—with either hand or tongue: not as some teachers pretending a holy zeal (2 Cor. xi. 20); answering to "not a brawler" or fighter (cf. 1 Ki. xxii. 24; Neh. xiii. 25; Isa. lviii. 4; Acts xxiii. 2; 2 Tim. ii. 24, 25). **not greedy of filthy lucre.** Omitted in א A Δ *f g,* Vulgate. **not covetous** [*aphilarguron*]—'not a lover of money,' whether he have much or little (Titus i. 7). [*Philarguria* is 'avarice;' *pleonexia,* 'covetousness.'] **4. ruleth** [*proistamenon*]—'presiding over.' **his own house**—children and servants, as contrasted with 'the church (house) of God' (*vv.* 5, 15), which he is to preside over. **having his** (Greek has no *his*) **children** (Titus i. 6). **gravity**—*reverent* propriety. His having *children in subjection to him in all gravity* is a recommendation to him as one likely to rule well the church. **5. For** [*De*]—'But.' **the church.** Perhaps, '*a* church.' [But *Theou* being without the article, justifies its omission before the governing word, *ekklesias.*] How shall he who cannot perform the less function perform the greater? **6. Not a novice**—one just converted. This proves the church of Ephesus was established for some time. The absence of this rule in the epistle to Titus accords with the recent planting of the church at Crete. *Neophite*—lit., *a young plant:* luxuriantly verdant (Rom. vi. 5; xi. 17; 1 Cor. iii. 6). The young convert has not yet been matured by afflictions and temptations. Contrast Acts xxi. 16, "an old disciple." **lifted up with pride** [*tuphotheis*: 'beclouded']—wrapt in smoke; inflated with self-conceit, he cannot see himself or others in the true light (ch. vi. 4; 2 Tim. iii. 4). **condemnation of the devil**—the same condemnation as Satan fell into (*v.* 7; 2 Tim. ii. 26). Pride was Satan's condemnation (Job xxxviii. 15; Isa. xiv. 12-15; John xii. 31; xvi. 11; 2 Pet. ii. 4; Jude 6). It cannot mean condemnation by *the devil.* The devil can bring men into *reproach* (*v.* 7), but not

report of them which are without; lest he fall into reproach and the snare of the devil.

8 Likewise *must* the deacons *be* grave, not double tongued, not given to
9 much wine, not greedy of filthy lucre; holding [b] the mystery of the faith
10 in a pure conscience. And [c] let these also first be proved; then let them
11 use the office of a deacon, being [d] *found* blameless. Even so *must their*
12 wives *be* grave, not [e] slanderers, sober, faithful in all things. Let the
deacons be the husbands of one wife, ruling their children and their own
13 houses well. For they that have [3] used the office of a deacon well purchase to themselves a good degree, and great boldness in the faith which
is in Christ Jesus.

A. D. 65.

[b] 2 John 9, 10.
[c] ch. 5. 22.
1 John 4. 1.
[d] 1 Cor. 1. 8.
Col. 1. 22.
Tit. 1. 6, 7.
[e] Ps. 15. 3.
Ps. 50. 20.
Pro. 10. 18.
Pro. 25. 33.
Jer. 9. 4.
[3] Or, minis-tered.

into *condemnation*, for he does not judge, but is judged (*Bengel*). **7. a good report** — Greek, *testimony*. So Paul was influenced by the good report of Timothy to choose him as his companion (Acts xvi. 2). **of them which are without**—the as yet unconverted Gentiles around (1 Cor. v. 12; Col. iv. 5; 1 Thess. iv. 12), that they may be the more readily won to the Gospel (1 Pet. ii. 12). Not even the former life of a bishop should be open to reproach. **reproach** (*of men*) **and** (*consequently*) **the snare of the devil** (ch. v. 14; vi. 9; 2 Tim. ii. 26). The *reproach* surrounding him for former sins might lead him into *the snare* of becoming as bad as his reputation. Despair of recovering *reputation* might lead into recklessness (Jer. xviii. 12). Only *general* moral qualities are specified, because he presupposes in candidates for a bishopric the special gifts of the Spirit (ch. iv. 14) and faith, which he desires to be evidenced outwardly: also he requires qualifications *in a bishop* not so indispensable in others.

8. deacons. The *singular*, on the other hand, is used of the "bishop" (*v.* 2; Titus i. 7, where "presbyters" (plural) precedes). The deacons were chosen by the people. *Cyprian* ('Epistle,' ii. 5) says that good bishops never departed from the old custom of consulting the people. The deacons answer to the chazzan of the synagogue; the *ministers*, or *subordinate coadjutors* of the presbyter (as Timothy himself was to Paul, ch. iv. 6; Phile. 13; and John Mark, Acts xiii. 5). "Helps," 1 Cor. xii. 28. Their duty was to read the Scriptures in church, to instruct the catechumens, to assist the presbyters at sacraments, to receive oblations, to preach and instruct. As the chazzan covered and uncovered the ark in the synagogue containing the law, so the deacon in the ancient church put the covering on the communion table. (See *Chrysostom*, 19, 'Homily on Acts;' *Theophylact* on Luke xix.; and *Balsaman* on Canon xxii., 'Council of Laodicea.') The appointing of "the seven" in Acts vi., as almoners, does not perhaps describe the *first* appointment of deacons. At least the chazzan previously suggested it. And the *Greek* names of all seven imply that they were to uphold the claims of the *Gentile* widows, those of the *Hebrew widows* being already, it is likely, maintained by *Hebrew deacons*. **double tongued** [*dilogous*]—'of double speech:' saying one thing to one, and another to another (*Theodoret*). The extensive intercourse that deacons would have with members of the church might tempt to such a fault (Prov. xx. 19). **not greedy of filthy** (base) **lucre** —not abusing a spiritual office to subserve covetousness (1 Pet. v. 2). The deacon's office of collecting and distributing alms would render this a necessary qualification. **9. the mystery of the faith.** *Holding the faith*, which to the natural man remains *a mystery*, but which is revealed by the Spirit to them (Rom. xvi. 25; 1 Cor. ii. 7-10)

in a pure conscience (ch. i. 5, 19). ("Pure;" *i. e.*, in which nothing base or foreign is intermixed.) *Ellicott*, 'the mystery which is *the object of faith*.' Though deacons were only occasionally called on to preach (Stephen and Philip preached as *evangelists* rather than as *deacons*), yet, as being officebearers, having much intercourse with all church members, they especially needed to have this characteristic, which all ought to have. **10.** 'And moreover' [*kai-de*] be proved—not by a period of probation, but by searching enquiry by Timothy, the ordaining president (ch. v. 22), then when found 'unaccused' (*anenkletoi*: but *anepileptos*, 'unexceptionable,' *v.* 2: cf. note), 'let them act as deacons.' **11. (their) wives**—rather, 'women;' i. e., *deaconesses*. For there is no reason that special rules should be laid down as to wives of deacons, and not also as to wives of bishops. Moreover, if wives of deacons were meant, there seems no reason for the omission of "their." Also [*hōsautōs*] "even so" ("likewise," *v.* 8; "in like manner," ch. ii. 9) denotes a transition to *another class* of persons. Also the omission of *domestic* duties in their case, though they are specified in the man (*v.* 12). There were doubtless deaconesses at Ephesus, such as Phebe was at Cenchrea (Rom. xvi. 1, "servant;" Greek, *deaconess*), yet no mention is made of them in this epistle, if not here; whereas, if they be meant, ch. iii embraces in due proportion all offices of the church. Naturally, after specifying the deacon's qualifications, Paul passes to those of the deaconess. "Grave" is said of both. "Not slanderers" answers to "not double tongued" in deacons; so Titus ii. 3. "Sober" answers to "not given to much wine" in the deacons (*v.* 8). Thus he requires the same qualifications in deaconesses as in deacons, with such modifications as the difference of sex suggested. *Pliny*, in his letter to Trajan, *calls* them 'female ministers.' **faithful in all things**—of life as well as faith. Trustworthy as to the alms and their other functions; answering to "not greedy of filthy lucre" (*v.* 8) in the deacons. **12. one wife** (note, *v.* 2). **ruling (their) children.** There is no article; 'ruling children' implying he regarded the *having children to rule* as a qualification (*v.* 4; Titus i. 6). **their own houses**—distinguished from "the church of God" (note, *v.* 5). In the deacons, as in the bishops, he mentions the first condition of office rather than the qualifications for its discharge. The practical side of Christianity is most dwelt on in the pastoral epistles, in opposition to heretical teachers; moreover, as miraculous gifts began to be withdrawn, the safest criterion would be the candidate's previous moral character, the disposition and talent for the office being presupposed. So in Acts vi. 3, "Look ye out among you seven men *of honest report*." Less stress is laid on personal dignity in the deacon than in the bishop (notes, cf. *vv.* 2, 3). **13. purchase to them-**

488

14, These things write I unto thee, hoping to come unto thee shortly: but
15 if I tarry long, that thou mayest know how thou oughtest to behave
thyself in the house of God, which is the church of the living God, the
16 pillar and ⁴ ground of the truth. And without controversy great is the
mystery of godliness: ^f God was ⁵ manifest in the flesh, ^g justified in the

A. D. 65.

⁴ Or, stay.
^f Isa. 7. 14.
⁵ mani-
fested.
^g Matt. 3. 16.

---

selves a good degree [*bathmon peripoiountai*]—
'are *acquiring* . . . a . . . *step.*' Not promotion to
the higher office of presbyter. For ambition seems
an unworthy motive to faithfulness for St. Paul
to urge; besides, it would require 'a *better degree.*'
Then the *past* aorist participle, ' they that *used*
the office of deacon well,' implies that the *present*
verb, ' *are acquiring* to themselves boldness,' is
the result of the completed action of using the
diaconate well. Moving upwards in church offices
was as yet unknown (cf. Rom. xii. 7, &c.; 1 Cor.
xii. 4-11). Moreover, there is no connection between a higher church rank and "great boldness."
Therefore, what those who faithfully discharged
the diaconate acquire is ' a good standing place'
(*Alford*) (a well-grounded *hope*) against the day of
judgment (ch. vi. 19 [with *paripoiountai* here : cf
peripoiesin soterias, 1 Thess. v. 9]; 1 Cor. iii. 13, 14;)
(" degree " meaning figuratively *the degree of
worth* which one has obtained in the eye of God,
Wiesinger) ; and boldness (resting on that *standing*)
as well in prayer and in preaching against error
now, as also especially in relation to their coming
Judge, before whom they may be boldly confident
(Acts xxiv. 16; Eph. iii. 12; vi. 19; 1 John ii. 28;
iv. 17; iii. 21; Heb. iv. 16). **in the faith**—Greek,
' in (boldness resting *on*) faith. **which is** (rests) **in
Christ Jesus.**

14. write I unto thee, hoping—*i. e.*, 'though I
hope to come unto thee' (ch. iv. 13). As his
hope was not confident (*v.* 15), he provides for
Timothy's lengthened superintendence by the
preceding rules to guide him. He now gives
general instructions to him as an evangelist
having a "gift" (ch. iv. 14). **shortly** [*tachion*]—
'sooner,' viz., than is pre-supposed in the preceding directions. (See 'Introduction.') This verse
best suits the theory that this epistle was not
written after Paul's visit and departure from
Ephesus (Acts xix. and xx.), when he resolved to
winter at Corinth, after passing the summer in
Macedonia (1 Cor. xvi. 6), but after his first imprisonment at Rome (Acts xxviii.); probably at
Corinth, where he might think of going on to
Epirus before returning to Ephesus (*Birks*). **15.
But if I tarry long**—before coming. **that**—*i. e.*,
I write (*v.* 14) "that thou mayest know," &c. **behave thyself**—in directing the church at Ephesus
(ch. iv. 11). **the house of God**—the Old Testament (Num. xii. 7; Hos. viii. 1) and the New
Testament Church (1 Cor. iii. 16; Eph. ii. 20, 22 ;
Heb. iii. 2, 5, 6 ; x. 21; 1 Pet. iv. 17). **which is**—
i. e., inasmuch as it is. **the church** [*ecclesia*]—'the
congregation,' the communion of saints [Hebrew,
קָהָל]. The fact that thy sphere of office is, ' the
congregation of God' (the ever-living Master of the
house, unlike the *dead* idol Diana, of the Ephesian
temple (2 Tim. ii. 19-21), is the strongest motive
to faithfulness in thy *behaviour as president* of a
department of it. *The living God* contrasts with
the lifeless idol, Diana of Ephesus (1 Thess. i. 9).
He is the fountain of " truth :" the foundation of
our "trust" (ch. iv. 10). Labour for a particular
church is service to the one great house of God,
of which each church is a part, and each Christian
a lively stone (1 Pet. ii. 5). **the pillar and ground**
[*hedraïoma : basis*] **of the truth**—predicated of *the
Church*, not of "the mystery of godliness;" for,

after two weighty predicate substantives, "pillar
and ground," a third, a weaker predicate, and an
adjective, 'confessedly ["without controversy :"
homologoumenōs] great,' would not come. "Pillar" is used metaphorically of the three apostles
on whom, humanly speaking, the Jewish Christian church depended (Gal. ii. 9: cf. Rev. iii. 12).
The Church is "the pillar of the truth," as the
continuance (historically) of the truth rests on it:
it witnesses to and preserves the Word of truth.
He who is of the truth belongs by the very fact to
the Church, for He belongs to Christ, its Head
(John xviii. 37, end). Christ is the alone "ground"
of the truth in the highest sense (1 Cor. iii. 11).
The apostles are 'foundations' in a secondary
sense (Eph. ii. 20; Rev. xxi. 14). The Church
rests on the truth as it is in Christ, not the truth
on the Church. But the truth *as it is in itself* is to
be distinguished from the truth *as it is acknowledged in the world.* The former needs no *pillar*,
but supports itself ; the latter needs the Church
as its pillar—*i. e.*, its human upholder and preserver under God. The importance of Timothy's
commission appears from the excellence of "the
house," and this in opposition to the heresies
which Paul presciently forewarns him of (ch. iv.
1; Matt. xvi. 18; xxviii. 20). Rome falsely claims
the promise. But it is not historical descent that
constitutes a church, but this only, that it upholds *the truth.* The absence of this unchurches
Rome. The "pillar" is the intermediate, the
"ground" (cf. "foundation," 2 Tim. ii. 19) the
ultimate stay of the buildings. It is no objection
that, having called the Church "the house of
God," he now calls it the "pillar ;" for the literal
word "church" immediately precedes the new
metaphors. The *Church*, before regarded as *the
habitation of God*, is now, from a different point of
view, regarded as the *pillar* upholding the truth.
16. And—following up *v.* 15: 'AND (that thou
mayest know how grand is that *truth* which the
Church, like a pillar, upholds) confessedly (by
the universal *confession* of the members of the
Church, which is in this respect "the pillar of
the truth") great is the mystery of godliness:
(viz.) HE WHO [so א A C G, *hos*, for *Theos*, 'God.'
Δ *f g*, Vulgate, read *ho*, '*which* mystery'] was
manifested in (the) flesh, (He who) was justified
in the Spirit,' &c. If Christ were not essentially
superhuman (Titus ii. 13), how could St. Paul declare emphatically that He was *manifested in* (the)
flesh ? (Phil. ii. 7; 1 John i. 2; iii. 5, 8; iv. 2.)
Christ is Himself "the mystery of godliness."
[Hence the neuter, *to musterion*, passes into the
masculine, *hos.*] He who before was hidden 'with
God' was made *manifest* (John i. 1, 14; Rom. xvi.
25, 26; Col. i. 26; 2 Tim. i. 10; Titus ii. 11 ; iii.
4). **the mystery**—the divine scheme embodied in
CHRIST (Col. i. 27), once hidden from, but now
revealed to, believers. There are six New Testament mysteries : (1.) The incarnation here ; (2.) The
mystery of iniquity (2 Thess. ii. 7); (3.) Christ's
marriage to the Church (Eph. v. 32) ; (4.) The
union of Jews and Gentiles in one body (Eph. iii.
4-6); (5.) The final restoration of the Jews ; (6.)
The resurrection of the body (1 Cor. xv. 51). **of
godliness** (note, ch. ii. 10). In opposition to the
ungodliness inseparable from error (*departure from
the faith*, ch. iv. 1, 7 : cf. ch. vi. 3). To the vic-

Spirit, *ᵸ* seen of angels, preached unto the Gentiles, believed on in the world, received up into glory.

4 NOW the Spirit *ᵃ* speaketh expressly, that *ᵇ* in the latter times some shall depart from the faith, giving heed *ᶜ* to seducing spirits, *ᵈ* and doc-
2 trines of devils; speaking lies in hypocrisy; having their conscience
3 seared with a hot iron; forbidding to marry, *and commanding* to ab-

A. D. 65.

ᵸ Matt. 28. 2.

CHAP. 4.
ᵃ John 16.13.
ᵇ 1 Pet. 1. 20.
ᶜ 2 Pet. 2. 1.
ᵈ Dan 11.35.

---

tims of error the "mystery of godliness" (*i. e.*, Christ Himself) remains a *mystery unrevealed* (ch. iv. 2). It is accessible only to "godliness" (ch. iv. 7, 8): in relation to the godly it is termed a "mystery," though *revealed* (1 Cor. ii. 7-14), to imply the unfathomable excellence of Him who is its subject, and who is "wonderful" (Isa. ix. 6; Eph. iii. 18, 19: cf. Eph. v. 32). St. Paul now unfolds this great mystery in detail. Probably some generally-accepted confession or hymn existed in the Church, to which Paul alludes—'*confessedly* great is the mystery,' &c., (to wit,) 'He who was manifested,' &c. (cf. Eph. v. 19; Col. iii. 16; *Pliny*, i. 10, 'Ep.' 97, 'They are wont, on a fixed day, before dawn, to meet and sing a hymn in alternate responses to Christ *as God ;*' and *Eusebius*, 'Ecclesiastical History,' v. 28.) The short unconnected sentences, with words similarly arranged, number of syllables almost equal, and ideas antithetically related, indicate a Christian hymn. The clauses stand in parallelism : each two form a pair, with an antithesis contrasting heaven and earth. The order of this contrast is reversed in each new pair : *flesh* and *spirit*, *angels* and *Gentiles*, *world* and *glory*. The first and the last clause correspond,—'manifested iu the flesh, received up into glory.' justified—evinced to be just (*Ellicott*). Christ, whilst "in the flesh," seemed a mere man in the flesh, and in fact bore man's *sins ;* but having died to sin and risen again, He *gained* for Himself and His people *justifying righteousness* (Isa. l. 8; John xvi. 10; Acts xxii. 14; Rom. iv. 25; vi. 7, 10; Heb. ix. 28; 1 Pet. iii. 18; iv. 1; 1 John ii. 1) (*Bengel*). Rather, as the antithesis requires, He was "justified in the *spirit*" *at the same time* that He was "manifest in the *flesh*"—*i. e.*, vindicated as divine 'in His spirit'—*His higher* spiritual *nature* as man (with which the Godhead inseparably united itself: Mark viii. 12; Luke ii. 40; x. 21; John xi. 33; xiii. 21), in contrast to "in the flesh," *His visible human nature*. So Rom. i. 3, 4, "Made of the seed of David according to the flesh, and *declared to be the Son of God with power*, according to the Spirit of holiness, by the resurrection from the dead." So "justified" means *vindicated in one's true character* (Matt. xi. 19; Luke vii. 35; Rom. iii. 4). His manifestation "in the flesh" exposed Him to *misapprehension*, as though He were nothing more (John vi. 41; vii. 27). His *justification*, or vindication, *in respect to His spirit*, was effected by ALL *that manifested that higher being*, His words (Matt. vii. 29; John vii. 46), His works (John ii. 11; iii. 2), His Father's testimony at His baptism (Matt. iii. 17) and at the transfiguration (Matt. xvii. 5), and especially by His resurrection (Acts xiii. 33). seen of angels. He manifested Himself in His incarnation to their vision: answering to "preached unto [*en: among*] the Gentiles" (Matt. xxviii. 19; Rom. xvi. 25, 26). 'Angels with us saw the Son of God, not having seen Him before' (*Chrysostom*). 'For the invisible nature of the Godhead not even they had seen, but saw Him when He became flesh' (*Theodoret*) (Eph. iii. 8, 10; 1 Pet. i. 12: cf. Col. i. 16, 20). What angels came to know by *seeing*, the nations by *preaching*. He is a new message to the one as to the other: in the wondrous union in His person of things most opposite—heaven and earth—lies "the

mystery" (*Wiesinger*). The contrast is between the *angels*, so *near* the Son of God, the Lord of angels, and *the Gentiles*, so utterly "afar off" (Eph. ii. 17). believed on in the world—which lieth in wickedness (1 John ii. 15; v. 19). Opposed to "glory" (John iii. 16, 17). *Believing* followed His being "preached" (Rom. x. 14). received up into glory—Greek, 'in glory.' 'Received up (*so as now to be*) *in* glory' (Mark xvi. 19; Luke xxiv. 51; Acts i. 11). His reception in heaven answers to His reception on earth by being "believed on."

CHAP. IV. 1-16.—PREDICTION OF A DEPARTURE FROM THE FAITH—TIMOTHY'S DUTY AS TO IT—GENERAL DIRECTIONS.
1. Now — Greek, 'But.' The "mystery of iniquity" here, already working (2 Thess. ii. 7), stands opposed to the "mystery of godliness" (ch. iii. 16). **the Spirit**—in the prophets, then in the Church (resting on the prophecies of the Old Testament, Dan. vii. 25; viii. 23, &c.; xi. 30; as also on those of Jesus, Matt. xxiv. 11-24), and Paul himself, 2 Thess. ii. 3 (with whom accord 2 Pet. iii. 3; 1 John ii. 18; Jude 18). **expressly**—in plain words. Not enigmatically, as some prophecies. **in the latter times**—*following upon the times in which he is now writing*. Not some remote future: times *immediately subsequent*, the beginnings of the apostasy being already discernible (Acts xx. 29); these are the forerunners of "the *last* days" (2 Tim. iii. 1). **depart from the faith**. The apostasy was to be within the Church, the faithful one becoming the harlot. In 2 Thess. ii. 3 (written earlier) the apostasy of the Jews from God (joining the heathen against Christianity) is the groundwork on which the prophecy rises; whereas in the pastoral epistles the prophecy is connected with Gnostic errors, the seeds of which were already sown in the Church (*Auberlen*) (2 Tim. ii. 18). Apollonius Tyanæus, a heretic, came to Ephesus in the lifetime of Timothy. The mediæval apostasy of Romish and Greek superstition is described here (*vv.* 1-3). The last apostasy, of blasphemy and apotheosis of man, is described, 2 Tim. iii. The true "fast" looks to the *spirit ;* the *mode of expression* will vary with persons and circumstances. To fix on *one* mode as *divinely obligatory* is a brand of the apostasy (Isa. lviii. 4-7; Mark ii. 18; Acts xiii. 2; xiv. 23; Rom. xiv. 3, 17; 1 Cor. vii. 5, 25-27; viii. 8). **giving heed** (ch. i. 4; Titus i. 14) **to seducing spirits**—working in heretical teachers. 1 John iv. 2, 3, 6, "the spirit of error," opposed to "the spirit of truth," "the Spirit" which "speaketh" in the true prophets against them. **doctrines of devils** [*didaskaliais daimonion*]—'teachings of (*i. e.*, suggested by; not *concerning*) demons.' Jas. iii. 15, 'wisdom-devilish ; 2 Cor. xi. 15. 2. [*En hupokrisei pseudologon*] 'Through (lit., '*in :*' the element in which the apostasy has place) hypocrisy of lying-speakers:' the means *through* which "some shall (be led to) depart from the faith"—viz., the feigned sanctity of the seducers (cf. Titus i. 10). **having** [*tēn idian: their own*] **their conscience seared**—*i. e.*, "speaking lies" *to others*, to seduce them by a show of sanctity, but all the while having *their own* conscience, &c. Bad consciences have recourse to hypocrisy. As *faith* and a *good conscience*

stain from meats, which God hath created ^e to be received with thanks-
4 giving of them which believe and know the truth. For ^f every creature
of God *is* good, and nothing to be refused, if it be received with thanks-
5 giving: for it is sanctified by the word of God and prayer.
6   If thou put the brethren in remembrance of these things, thou shalt be
a good minister of Jesus Christ, nourished up ^g in the words of faith and
7 of good doctrine, whereunto thou hast attained. But refuse profane and
8 old wives' fables, and exercise thyself *rather* unto godliness. For bodily
exercise profiteth ¹ little; but godliness is profitable unto all things,

A. D. 65.	
^e Gen 1. 29.	
Gen. 9. 3.	
Eccl. 5. 18.	
Acts 10. 13.	
1 Cor. 6. 13.	
^f Tit. 1. 15.	
^g Jer. 15. 16.	
2 Tim. 3. 14.	
1 Or, for a	
little time.	

are joined (ch. i. 5), so *hypocrisy* (i. e., *unbelief*, Matt. xxiv. 5, 51: cf. Luke xii. 46) and a *bad conscience.* "Seared" (*Theodoret*) implies extreme *insensibility;* as cauterizing deadens sensation. Rather [*kekauteriasmenōn*], 'branded' with the consciousness of sins against their better knowledge, like scars burnt in by a branding-iron. Cf. Titus i. 15; iii. 11, "condemned of himself." As a "seal" marks the elect (2 Tim. ii. 19), so 'a brand' the condemned. The image is from branding criminals; consciously-branded slaves of sin. **3.** Sensuality leads to false spiritualism. Their own inward impurity they attribute to the world without; hence their asceticism (Titus i. 14, 15) (*Wiesinger*). By a spurious spiritualism (2 Tim. ii. 18), which made moral perfection consist in abstinence from outward things, they pretended to reach a higher perfection. Matt. xix. 10-12, cf. 1 Cor. vii. 8, 26, 38, gave a seeming handle to their "forbidding marriage" (contrast ch. v. 14): the Old Testament distinction as to clean and unclean, gave a pretext for teaching to "abstain from meats" (cf. Col. ii. 16, 17, 20-23). As these Judaizing Gnostics combined the harlot, or apostate Old Testament church, with the beast (Rev. xvii. 3), or spiritualizing antichristianity, so Rome's Judaizing elements (ch. iv. 3) shall ultimately be combined with the worldly-wise antichristianity of the false prophet or beast (ch. vi. 20, 21; 1 John iv. 1-3; Rev. xiii. 12-15). Austerity gained for them a show of sanctity whilst preaching false doctrine (Col. ii. 8, 23). The Essenes and Therapeutœ already practised false asceticism. Long afterwards, *Eusebius* ('Ecclesiastical History,' iv. 29) quotes *Irenœus* (i. 8), stating that Saturninus, Marcion, and the Encratites, preached abstinence from marriage and animal meats. Paul prophetically warns against notions the seeds of which already were sown (ch. vi. 20; 2 Tim. ii. 17, 18). **to be received** [*eis metalēpsin*]—'to be partaken of.' **of them**—rather, (created) '*for* them,' &c. Though *all* (even the unbelieving, Ps. civ. 14; Matt. v. 45) partake of these foods, 'they which believe' alone fulfil God's design in creation *by partaking of them with thanksgiving;* as opposed to those who *abstain* from, or in partaking of them, do not do so *with thanksgiving.* The unbelieving have not the designed use of such foods by their 'conscience being defiled' (Titus i. 15). The children of God alone "inherit the earth;" for obedience is the necessary qualification (as in the original grant of the earth to Adam). **and know.** Defining who are 'they which believe.' [*Epegnō-kosin*, 'And have *full* knowledge of the truth' (note, Phil. i. 9).] Thus he contradicts the assumption of superior *knowledge* and perfection put forward by the heretics on the ground of abstinence from marriage and meats. "The *truth*" is contrasted with their "*lies*" (*v.* 2). **4, 5.** [*Hoti-gar*] 'Because' (a reason resting on the *objective fact* which Scripture alleges)—"For" (a reason resting on something *subjective* in the *writer's mind*). **every creature of God is good** (Gen. i. 31; Rom. xiv. 14, 20)—a refutation, by anticipation, of the Gnostic

491

opposition to creation: the seeds were now lurking in the Church. Judaism (Acts x. 11-16; 1 Cor. x. 25, 26) was the starting-point of the error as to meats; Oriental Gnosis added new elements. The Gnostic heresy is now extinct: its remains in the celibacy of Rome's priesthood, and its fasts from animal meats, enjoined under the penalty of mortal sin, remain. **if it be received with thanksgiving.** Meats, pure in themselves, become impure by being received with an unthankful mind (Rom. xiv. 6). **5. sanctified**—hallowed: set apart as holy for the use of believing men. By saying grace, separated from "the creature," which is under *the bondage of corruption,* (Rom. viii. 19, &c.) As in the Lord's supper the thanksgiving prayer sanctifies the elements, separating them from their naturally aliën relation to the spiritual world, and transferring them to their true relation to the new life, so in *every* use of the creature, thanksgiving prayer has the same effect (1 Cor. x. 25, 26, 30, 31). Or, *hallowed* from legal, or ascetical supposed, uncleanness. **by the word of God and prayer** [*dia enteuxeōs*]—'through *consecratory* prayer' in its behalf, mainly consisting of "the Word of God." The 'Apostolic Constitutions,' vii. 49, give this ancient grace, almost wholly consisting of Scripture, 'Blessed art thou, O Lord, who feedest me from my youth, who givest food to all flesh: Fill our hearts with joy and gladness, that we, having all sufficiency, may abound unto every good work in Christ Jesus our Lord, through whom glory, honour, and might be to thee for ever. Amen.'

6. If thou put the brethren in remembrance [*hupotithemenos*]—'If thou *suggest to* (bring under the notice of) the brethren,' &c. **these things**—viz., the truths stated in *vv.* 4, 5, in opposition to the errors foretold, *vv.* 1-3. **minister**—'servant.' **nourished up.** The *present* [*entrephomenos*], '*continually being* nourished in' (2 Tim. i. 5; iii. 14, 15). **the words of faith**—Greek, '. . . of *the* faith (cf. *v.* 13). **good doctrine**—'the good *teaching.*' Explanatory of 'the faith:' opposed to the 'teachings of demons' (*v.* 1), which Timothy was to counteract. Cf. "sound doctrine," ch. i. 10; vi. 3; Titus i. 9; ii. 1. **whereunto thou hast attained**—'which thou hast closely *followed* up as a disciple:' traced diligently out. The same Greek, "thou hast fully known," 2 Tim. iii. 10; "having had perfect understanding," Luke i. 3. It is an undesigned coincidence that it is used only by Paul and *Paul's companion,* Luke. **7. refuse**—*have nothing to do with* (2 Tim. ii. 22, 23; Titus iii. 10). (The) **old wives' fables**—which are so current (Titus i. 14): "profane" because leading away from "godliness," *true worship and piety* (ch. i. 4, 7-9; vi. 20; 2 Tim. ii. 16; Titus i. 1, 2). **exercise thyself** [*gumnaze*]—strenuous exertion, as of one training in a *gymnasium.* Contrast 2 Pet. ii. 14. Let thy self-discipline be not in ascetical exercises, as the false teachers (*vv.* 3, 8: cf. Heb. v. 14; xii. 11), but with a view to godliness (ch. vi. 11, 12). Christianity is a discipline as well as a dogma. **8.** (but) **little** [*pros oligon*]

having *h* promise of the life that now is, and of that which is to come.

9, This *is* a faithful saying, and worthy of all acceptation. For therefore

10 we both labour and suffer reproach, because we trust in the living God,

11 *i* who is the Saviour of all men, specially of those that believe. These things command and teach.

12 Let *j* no man despise thy youth; but be thou an example of the believers, in word, in conversation, in charity, in spirit, in faith, in purity.

13 Till I come, give attendance to reading, to exhortation, to doctrine.

A. D. 65.

h Ps. 37. 4.
Ps. 84. 11.
Isa 65. 13.
Matt. 6. 33.
i Ps. 36. 6.
Acts 14. 17.
Acts 17. 25, 28.
j Tit. 2. 15.

—'profiteth to (but) a small extent.' Paul admits that fasting and abstinence from conjugal intercourse for a time, so as to reach the inward man through the outward, do profit slightly (Acts xiii. 3; 1 Cor. vii. 5, 7; ix. 26, 27); but asceticism, dwelling solely on the outward, *v.* 3, is injurious (Col. ii. 23). Timothy seems to have leant to outward self-discipline (cf. ch. v. 23). Paul, whilst not disapproving of this insubordinate proportion, shows the superiority of *godliness,* as profitable not merely 'to a small extent,' but "unto *all* things;" for, having its seat within, it extends thence to the whole outward man for time and eternity (1 Cor. viii. 8). 'He who has *piety* (which is "profitable unto *all* things") wants nothing needful to his well-being, though he be without those helps which, "to a small extent," *bodily exercise* furnishes' (*Calvin*). '*Piety,*' the *end* whereunto "exercise thyself" (*v.* 7), is the essential thing: the means are secondary. Paul *unrestrictedly* condemns asceticism (*vv.* 3-5): how then can he say here, 'it is profitable to some *little* extent:' hence *De Wette* and *Estius* explain, lit., *bodily exercise.* Paul often digresses at a word. So here [*gumnaze*], "exercise thyself" *spiritually* (*v.* 7), may suggest allusion to the temporary use of *bodily* exercise, in order to bring out the all-embracing excellence of *spiritual exercise* unto godliness. **having promise, &c.**—'having (as it has) promise of life—that which now is, and that which is to come:' "life" in its truest sense (2 Tim. i. 1). Length of life so far as is good for the believer; life in its truest enjoyments and employments now, and life blessed and eternal hereafter (Ps. lxxxiv. 11; cxii.; Matt. vi. 33; Mark x. 29, 30; Rom. viii. 28; 1 Cor. iii. 21, 22). Christianity, whilst mainly securing our happiness hereafter, promotes it also here (ch. vi. 6; 2 Pet. i. 3). So it embraces the Old Covenant promises of temporal blessings, with the everlasting ones of the New. Cf. Solomon's prayer and the answer (1 Ki. iii. 7-13). **9.** These 'faithful sayings' (ch. i. 15; iii. 1; 2 Tim. ii. 11) are samples of the prophesyings or inspired utterances of the apostolic Church: *v.* 1 refers to them: they here take the place of Old Testament quotations in the other epistle. This verse confirms *v.* 8, and introduces *v.* 10, which is joined to *v.* 9 by "for." So 2 Tim. ii. 11. Godly men seem to lose in this life; but "God is the *Saviour* specially of those that believe" (*v.* 10), both as to "the life that now is," and as to 'the life to come' (*v.* 8). Mark x. 30 combines and harmonizes 1 Tim. iv. 9 with 2 Tim. iii. 12: "an *hundredfold now in this time* . . . with *persecutions*" (Prov. xi. 4). Mingled blessedness here; unmingled blessedness hereafter. **10. therefore** [*eis touto*]—'with a view to this.' *The reason why* 'we both ("both" is omitted in א A C Δ *f,* Vulgate) labour (amidst hardship) and suffer reproach (so C Δ G *fg,* Vulgate. But א A read [*agonizometha*] (cf. Col. i. 29) "strive"), is *because* we have rested, and do rest our hope [*elpikamen epi*], on the living (and therefore *life-giving, v.* 8) God.' [*Ellicott,* '*Elpizo,* like *pisteuo,* with *en,* expresses hope *laid up in* Christ: with *eis, directed*

492

to Christ: with *epi, leaning on,* as upon a foundation: *epi* with accusative, mental direction *with a view to* reliance.'] **specially of those that believe.** Their "labour and reproach" are not inconsistent with having from the living God, their Saviour, even the present life, much more the life to come. If God is a "Saviour" even of unbelievers (ch. ii. 4; *i. e.,* is *willing* to be so *everlastingly,* and *is temporally here* their *Preserver* and *Benefactor*), much more of believers. So His people are to benefit all, but "specially" the brethren (Gal. vi. 10). He who is the living, is also the loving God. He is the Saviour of all *sufficiently* and *potentially* (ch. i. 15); of believers alone *efficiently* and *effectually.* **11.** These truths, to the exclusion of those useless and even injurious teachings (*vv.* 1-8), whilst weighing well thyself, charge also upon others.

12. Let no man despise thy youth—Act so as to be respected in spite of thy youth (1 Cor. xvi. 11; Titus ii. 15): cf. "youthful," 2 Tim. ii. 22: thy gravity maketh up for thy juvenility. He was but a mere youth when he joined St. Paul (Acts xvi. 1-3). Eleven years had elapsed since. Now, after Paul's first imprisonment, he was still young (about thirty-five probably), especially in comparison with Paul (whose place he was filling), and with elderly presbyters, whom he should "entreat as a father" (ch. v. 1); and in respect to rebuking, exhorting, and ordaining (ch. iii. 1), which ordinarily accord best with an elderly person (ch. v. 19). **be thou an example** [*tupos ginou*]—'become a pattern' (Titus ii. 7): the true way of making men not to despise thy youth. **in word**—in all thou sayest in public and private. **conversation** [*anastrophe*]—'behaviour:' the Old English sense. **in charity . . . faith**—the two cardinal motives of the Christian (Gal. v. 6). א A C Δ G *fg,* Vulgate, omit "in spirit:" perhaps interpolated from 2 Cor. vi. 6. **in purity**—outwardly manifested (ch. v. 22; 2 Cor. vi. 6; Jas. iii. 17; iv. 8; 1 Pet. i. 22). **13. Till I come**—when Timothy's commission would be superseded by the presence of the apostle (ch. i. 3; iii. 14). **reading** [*anagnosei*]—especially in the public congregation. The reading of Scripture was transferred from the Jewish synagogue to the Christian church (Luke iv. 16-20; Acts xiii. 15; xv. 21; 2 Cor. iii. 14). The gospels and epistles being recognized as inspired by those who had the gift of *discerning spirits,* were from the first, according as they were written, read with the Old Testament in the church (1 Thess. v. 21, 27; Col. iv. 16) (*Justin Martyr,* 'Apology,' i. 67). Probably the Spirit intended also to teach that the pastor's Scripture reading in general should be the fountain of all "exhortation" and "doctrine." **exhortation**—addressed to the *feelings* and *will,* with a view to the conduct. **doctrine**—(ministerial) 'teaching.' The three answer respectively to *expository, experimental,* and *doctrinal* preaching. Addressed to *the understanding,* to impart knowledge (ch. vi. 2; Rom. xii. 7, 8). Whether in public or private, *exhortation* and *instruction* should be based on Scripture. **14. Neglect not the gift**—by letting it

14 Neglect ^knot the gift that is in thee, which was given thee ^lby prophecy,
15 ^mwith the laying on of the hands of the presbytery. Meditate upon these things; give thyself wholly to them; that thy profiting may appear
16 ²to all. Take heed unto thyself, and unto the doctrine; continue in them: for in doing this thou shalt both ⁿsave thyself, and them that hear thee.

5 REBUKE ^anot an elder, but entreat *him* as a father; *and* the younger
2 men as brethren; the elder women as mothers; the younger as sisters, with all purity.
3, Honour widows that are widows indeed. But if any widow have
4 children or nephews, let them learn first to show ¹piety at home, and ^bto

A. D. 65.

k 2 Tim. 1. 6.
l ch. 1. 18.
m Acts 6. 6.
2 Or. in all things.
n Eze. 33. 9.

CHAP. 5.
a Lev. 19. 32.
1 Or. kindness.
b Gen. 45. 10.
Matt. 15. 4.

lie unused. **in thee.** In 2 Tim. i. 6 the gift is represented as a *spark* of the Spirit within him, sure to smoulder by neglect, the *stirring up* or keeping in lively exercise of which depends on himself (Matt. xxv. 18, 25, 27, 28). The spiritual gift [*charism*] is that which qualified him for "the work of an evangelist" (Eph. iv. 11; 2 Tim. iv. 5), including perhaps *the discerning of spirits*, needed in ordaining, as overseer. **given thee**—by God (1 Cor. xii. 4, 6). **by prophecy**—*i. e.*, by the Holy Spirit, at his ordination, or else consecration to the see of Ephesus; speaking through the prophets God's will to give him the graces to qualify him for his work (ch. i. 18; Acts xiii. 1-3). **with the laying on of the hands.** So in Joshua's case (Num. xxvii. 18-20; Deut. xxxiv. 9). The gift was connected with the symbolical laying on of hands. [*Meta:* the outward sign of an inward impartation of the Spirit (Acts vi. 6; viii. 17; ix. 17; xiii. 3).] "WITH" implies that *the presbyters'* laying on hands was the *accompaniment* of the conferring of the gift. "BY" [*dia*] (2 Tim. i. 6) implies that *Paul's* laying on hands was the *instrument* of its being conferred. **of the presbytery.** 2 Tim. i. 6 mentions only *the apostle's* laying on of hands. But there his aim is to remind Timothy of the part he took in imparting to Timothy the gift. Here he mentions the fact, consistent with the other, that the neighbouring presbyters joined in the ordination or consecration, he taking the foremost part. Paul, though having the general oversight of the elders everywhere, was an elder himself (1 Pet. v. 1; 2 John 1). The Jewish council was composed of the elders (the presbytery, Luke xxii. 66; Acts xxii. 5) and a presiding Rabbi; so the Christian church was composed of elders and a president (Acts xv. 19, 23). The apostles were presidents in general. As the president of the synagogue was of the same order as his presbyters, so the bishop was of the same as his presbyters. At the ordination of the president there were always three presbyters present to lay on hands; so the early Church canons required three bishops to be present at the consecration of a bishop. As the president of the synagogue, so the bishop of the church alone could ordain, acting as the representative, in the name of the presbytery (*Vitringa*). So, in the Anglican church, the bishop ordains, the presbyters present joining with him in laying on hands. **15. Meditate** [*meleta*]—'*meditate* CAREFULLY *upon*' (Ps. i. 2; cxix. 15: cf. "Isaac," Gen. xxiv. 63). **these things** (*vv.* 12-14). As food would not nourish without digestion, which assimilates it to the substance of the body, so spiritual food, to profit us, needs to be appropriated by prayerful meditation. **give thyself wholly to**—*lit.* 'BE *in* these things;' be wholly absorbed in them. *Entire self-dedication*, as in other pursuits, is the secret of proficiency. There are changes as to all other studies, fashionable to-day, out of fashion to-

morrow; this alone is never obsolete, and sanctifies all other studies. The exercise of the ministry threatens its spirit, unless it be sustained within. **profiting** [*prokope*]—'progress' in the Christian life, and especially towards the ideal of a Christian minister (*v.* 12). **may appear to all**—not for thy glory, but for winning souls (Matt. v. 16). **16. Take heed** [*Epeche*]—'Give heed' (Acts iii. 5); fix attention upon. **thyself, and unto the doctrine**—and unto thy teaching. The pastor's two requisites: his teaching will not avail, unless his life accord with it; his purity of life is not enough, unless he be diligent in teaching (*Calvin*). A summary of *v.* 12. **continue in them** (2 Tim. iii. 14). **in doing this**—not '*by*,' but '*whilst* doing this.' **thou shalt both save thyself, and them**, &c. (Ezek. xxxiii. 9; Jas. v. 20.) In seeking the salvation of others, the minister is promoting his own. He cannot 'give heed unto the teaching' of others, unless he 'give heed unto himself.'

CHAP. V. 1-25.—How TIMOTHY SHOULD DEAL WITH DIFFERENT CLASSES IN THE CHURCH.

1, an elder—*in age; probably not in the ministry;* these latter are not mentioned till *v.* 17. Cf. Acts ii. 17, "your old men:" contrasted with "the younger men." As Timothy was admonished to give no man reason to *despise* his *youth* (ch. iv. 12), so he is told to behave with the modesty which becomes a young man towards his elders. "Rebuke" [*Epiplēxēs*]—'Strike hard upon:' *Rebuke not sharply*; a different word [*epitimēson*] (2 Tim. iv. 2). **entreat** [*parakalei*]—exhort. **as brethren**—therefore equals: not lording it over them (1 Pet. v. 1-3). **2. with all purity.** Respectful treatment of the other sex promotes "purity."

3. Honour—by setting on the church roll as fit objects of charity (*vv.* 9, 17, 18; Acts vi. 1). So "honour" is used for *support*, Matt. xv. 4, 6; Acts xxviii. 10. **widows indeed** (*v.* 16)—really desolate: not like those (*v.* 4) having children or relations answerable for their support, nor like those (*v.* 6) 'who live in pleasure;' but such as, from earthly friendlessness, trust wholly in God, persevere in prayers, and carry out the duties assigned to church widows (*v.* 5). Care for widows was transferred from the Jewish economy to the Christian (Deut. xiv. 29; xvi. 11; xxiv. 17, 19). **4. if any widow**—not "a widow indeed," as having children who ought to support her. **nephews** [*ekgona*] — 'descendants,' or 'grandchildren.' *Nephews* in old English meant *grandchildren* (*Hooker*, 'Ecclesiastical Polity,' v. 20). **let them** —the children and descendants. **learn first**— before calling the church to support them. **to show piety at home**—by sustaining their widowed mother or grandmother. [*Ton idion oikon*, ' . . . towards *their own house*.'] "Piety" means reverential *dutifulness*; the parental relation representing our heavenly Father's relation to us. '*Their*

5, requite their parents: for that is good and acceptable before God. Now she that is a widow indeed, and desolate, trusteth in God, and continueth
6 in supplications and prayers night and day. But she that liveth ² in
7 pleasure is dead while she liveth. And these things give in charge, that
8 they may be blameless. But if any provide not for his own, and specially for those of his own ³ house, he hath denied the faith, and is worse than an infidel.
9 Let not a widow be ⁴ taken into the number under threescore years
10 old, having been the wife of one man, well reported of for good works; if she have brought up children, if she have lodged ᶜ strangers, if she ᵈ have

A. D. 65.
² Or, delicately.
³ Or kindred.
⁴ Or, chosen.
ᶜ Acts 16. 15. Heb. 13. 2. 1 Pet. 4. 9.
ᵈ Gen. 18. 4. Gen. 19. 2. Luke 7. 38. John 13. 5.

own' is opposed to *the church*, to which the widow is comparatively a stranger. She has a claim on *her own*, prior to her claim on the church; let them fulfil this prior claim by sustaining her, and not burdening the church. **parents** [*progonois*]— (living) 'progenitors;' *i. e.*, their mother or grandmother. "Let them learn" implies that some widows had claimed church support, though having children or grandchildren able to support them. **good and.** א A C Δ G *fg*, Vulgate, omit: probably inserted from ch. ii. 3. **5. widow indeed, and** (left) **desolate**—contrasted with her who has children to support her (*v.* 4). **trusteth in God**—Greek, 'hath rested, and doth rest, her hope in God.' This *v.* 5 *adds another* qualification for church maintenance, besides her being "desolate," or without children to support her. She must be not one "that liveth in pleasure" (*v.* 6), but one making God her hope [*epi ton Theon:* note, ch. iv. 10: God is *the aim whereto* her hope is *directed*; whereas, ch. iv. 10, *dative* expresses hope *resting* on God as her *present stay* (*Wiesinger*)], and continuing instantly in prayers. Her destitution of earthly ties leaves her more unencumbered for devoting her days to God (1 Cor. vii. 33, 34). Cf. 'Anna, a widow,' who remained unmarried after her husband's death, and "departed not from the temple, but served God with fastings and prayers night and day" (Luke ii. 36, 37). Such a one is the fittest object for the church's help (*v.* 3); for such a one is helping Christ's Church by her prayers for it. 'Ardour in prayers flows from hoping confidence in God' (*Leo*). **in** [*her: tais*] **supplications and prayers** (notes, Phil. iv. 6; ch. ii. 1) **night and day**—another coincidence with Luke xviii. 7: contrast Satan's accusations "day and night" (Rev. xii. 10). **6. she that liveth in pleasure**—the opposite of the self-denying widow, *v.* 5; therefore one undeserving of church charity. [*He spatalosa* expresses *wanton prodigality*.] The root expresses [*spathao*] *weaving* at a fast rate: so *lavish excess* (note, Jas. v. 5). **dead while she liveth**—dead in the Spirit whilst alive in the flesh (Matt. viii. 22; Eph. iv. 18; v. 14; Rev. iii. 1). **7. these things** (*vv.* 5, 6). **that they may be blameless**—viz., the widows supported by the church. **8. But**—reverting to *v.* 4, 'if any (a general proposition, therefore including *the widow's children* or *grandchildren*) provide not for his own (relations), and especially for those of his own *family*, he hath (practically) denied the faith.' Faith without love and its works is dead. If in any case a duty of love is plain, it is towards one's own relatives. 'Faith does not set aside, but strengthens natural duties.' **worse than an infidel**—because even an infidel is taught by nature to provide for his own relatives, and generally recognizes the duty: the Christian who does not so is worse (Matt. v. 46, 47). He has less excuse with his greater light than the infidel who breaks the laws of nature. The Essenes were forbidden to relieve relatives without

leave of their superiors (*Josephus*, 'B. J.' ii. 8. 6).
9. 'As a widow (*i. e.*, of the ecclesiastical order of *widowhood: a female presbytery*), let none be enrolled (in the catalogue) who is less than sixty years old. These were not *deaconesses*, who were chosen at a younger age (forty was fixed at the council of Chalcedon), and who had virgins (in a later age called *widows*) as well as widows among them, but a band of widows set apart, though not yet formally and finally, to the service of the church. Traces of such a class appear in Acts ix. 41. So Dorcas herself. As it was expedient (note, ch. iii. 2; Titus i. 6) that the presbyter or bishop should have been but once married, so also she. There is a transition to a new subject. The reference cannot be, as in *v.* 3, to *providing church sustenance* for them, for the restriction to widows above sixty would then be harsh, since many might need help at a much earlier age; also the rule that the widow must *not* have been *twice married*, especially since he himself (*v.* 14) enjoins the younger widows to marry again; also that she must have *brought up children*. Moreover, *v.* 10 pre-supposes some competence, at least in past times; so poor widows would be excluded, the very class requiring charity. Also *v.* 11 would then be senseless, for their re marrying would be a benefit, not an injury, to the church, as relieving it of their sustenance. *Tertullian*, 'De velandis Virginibus,' c. 9; *Hermas*, 'Shepherd,' b. i. 2; and *Chrysostom*, 'Homily' 31, mention such an order of ecclesiastical widowhood, each not less than sixty years old, resembling the presbyters in the respect paid to them, and in some of their duties: they ministered with sympathizing counsel to other widows and to orphans—a ministry to which their experimental knowledge of the feelings and sufferings of the bereaved adapted them—and had a general supervision of their sex. *Age* was a requisite in *presbyters*, as it is here stated to have been in *presbyteresses*, with a view to their influence on the younger of their sex. They were supported by the church, but not the only widows so supported (*vv.* 3, 4). Three classes of widows occur,—1. The ordinary widow; 2. The widow indeed—*i̇.e.*, destitute; 3. The presbyteral widow. **wife of one man**—in order not to throw a stumblingblock in the way of Jews and heathen, who regarded with disfavour second marriages (note, ch. iii. 2; Titus i. 6). This is the force of "blameless," giving no offence, even in matters indifferent. **10. for good works**—Greek, 'IN *honourable* works:' the sphere *in* which the good report of her had place (Titus ii. 7). This answers to ch. iii. 7, as to the bishop or presbyter. **if**—if, in addition to being "well reported of," &c. **she have brought up children** —piously, either her own (ch. iii. 4, 12) or those of others, one of the "good works:" a qualification adapting her for ministry to orphan children and to mothers of families. **lodged strangers** (ch. iii.

494

washed the saints' feet, if she have relieved the afflicted, if she have
11 diligently followed every good work. But the younger widows refuse:
for when they have begun to wax wanton against Christ, they will marry;
12, having *e* damnation, because they have cast off their first faith. And
13 *f* withal they learn *to be* idle, wandering about from house to house; and
not only idle, but tattlers also and busybodies, speaking things which they
14 ought not. I *g* will therefore that the younger women marry, bear children, guide the house, *h* give none occasion to the adversary [5] to speak
15, reproachfully. For some are already turned aside after Satan. If *i* any
16 man or woman that believeth have widows, let them relieve them, and
let not the church be charged; that it may relieve them that are widows
indeed.
17   Let *j* the elders that rule well be counted worthy of double honour,
18 especially they who labour in the word and doctrine. For the Scripture

A. D 65.

e Heb. 6. 4, 6.
Heb. 10. 28.
f 2 Thes.3.11.
g 1 Cor. 7. 9.
h Dan. 6. 4
Rom. 14.13.
ch 6. 1.
Tit. 2. 8.
5 for their
railing.
i Gen. 47. 12.
Ruth 2. 18.
Matt. 15. 4.
j Rom. 12. 8.
1 Cor. 9. 10.
Gal. 6. 6
Phil. 2. 29.

2, end; Titus i. 8)—in the case of *presbyters.*
washed the saints' feet—after Jesus' example
(John xiii. 14): a specimen of humbly 'by love
serving one another' (Luke vii. 38; Gal. v. 13).
relieved the afflicted — by pecuniary or other
relief. **followed every good** (1 Thess. v. 15: cf.
instances in Matt. xxv. 35, 36.) **11. younger**—
than sixty years (*v.* 9). **refuse**—to take on the
roll of presbyteress widows. **wax wanton**—'over-
strong' (2 Chr. xxvi. 16). [*Katastreniasosin,* akin
to the Latin *strenuus* like beasts *waxing restive
with over-feeding* (Deut. xxxii. 15).] **against Christ**
—their proper bridegroom. **they will**—Greek,
wish: their *desire* is to marry again. **12. Having**
—*Having* to bear (Gal. v. 10) *judgment* from God
(cf. ch. iii. 6), weighing like a load on them; viz.,
because—rather, *that* (Ellicott). **cast off** their
first faith—viz., pledged to Christ and the Church.
There could be no hardship at sixty or upwards
in not marrying again (end of *v.* 9), for the sake
of serving better the cause of Christ as presbyteresses; though, to ordinary widows, no barrier
existed against re-marriage (1 Cor. vii. 39). This
is distinct from Rome's unnatural vows of celibacy
in young marriageable women. The widow-pres-
byteresses engaged to remain single, not as though
single were holier than married life (Rome's
teaching), but because the interests of Christ made
it desirable (note, ch. iii. 2). They had pledged
"their first faith" to His service as presbyteress
widows: they now wish to transfer their faith to
a husband (cf. 1 Cor. vii. 32, 34). **13. withal**—'at
the same time, moreover.' **learn**—usually in a
good sense. But these women's 'learning' is
idleness, trifling, and *busybodies' tattle.* **wandering**
[*perierchomenai*] — 'going about' ostensibly on
church duties. **from house to house**—of the
church members (2 Tim. iii. 6). 'They carry the
affairs of this house to that, and of that to this:
they tell the affairs of all to all' (*Theophylact*).
tattlers [*phluaroi,* akin to *fluere: fluent*]—'trifling
talkers.' In 3 John 10, "prating." **busybodies**
[*periergoi, meddlers*]—mischievously *busy;* incon-
siderately *curious* (2 Thess. iii. 11). Acts xix. 19,
"curious." *Curiosity* springs from idleness, the
mother of *garrulity* (*Calvin*). **speaking** [*lalousai*]
—not merely '*saying.*' **which they ought not**—
(Titus i. 11.) **14.** younger (women)—rather 'the
younger widows,' as distinguished from *the elder
widows taken on the roll of presbyteresses* (*v.* 9).
The "therefore" means, *seeing that young widows
are exposed to such temptations,* 'I desire,' &c.
Paul here desires re-marriage: above, it was the
widows whose *will* it was to re-marry (*vv.* 11-13).
The precept that they should marry again is not
inconsistent with 1 Cor. vii. 26, 40; for the circumstances were distinct. Here re-marriage is
495

recommended as an antidote to *sexual passion,
idleness,* and the other evils (*vv.* 11-13). Where
there was no tendency to these, marriage again
would not be so requisite: St. Paul speaks of
what is generally desirable when there is danger
of such evils. 'He does not impose *a law,* but
points out *a remedy*' (*Chrysostom*). **bear children**
(ch. ii. 15)—gaining one of the qualifications (*v.* 10)
for being afterwards a presbyteress widow, should
Providence ordain it. **guide** [*oikodespotein*]—
'*rule* the house' in the woman's due place: not
usurping authority over the man (ch. ii. 12). **give
none occasion** [*aphormēn*] — 'starting - point :'
handle of reproach through inconsistent conduct.
the adversary—of Christianity, Jew or Gentile
(Phil. i. 28; Titus ii. 8). Not *Satan,* introduced in
a different relation (*v.* 15). **to speak reproachfully**—*lit.,* 'for the sake of reproach' (ch. iii. 7; vi.
1; Titus ii. 5, 10). If the *handle* were given, *the
adversary* would use it *for the sake of reproach :*
he is eager to exaggerate the faults of a few, and
lay the blame on the whole Church and its doctrines (*Bengel*). **15. For**—*For* in some this result
has already ensued: 'some (widows) are already
turned aside from Christ, the spouse (2 Tim iv. 4),
after Satan,' the seducer (*vv.* 11-13), by sexual
passion, idleness, &c., and so have *given occasion
of reproach* (*v.* 14). **16. If any . . . have widows**
—of his family, however related to him. א A C G *g*
omit "man or," and read, 'If any woman that
believeth.' Δ *f* support received text. He was
speaking of *younger* widows: he now says, If *any
believing young widow* have widows related to her
needing support, let her relieve them, thereby
easing the church of the burden (*vv.* 3, 4) (*there
it was the children* and *grandchildren;* here it is
the young widow,* who, in order to avoid *idleness*
and *wantonness* (Ezek. xvi. 49; *vv.* 11, 13), is to be
diligent in 'relieving the afflicted,' especially
relatives, *widows* like herself (*v.* 10): thus qualifying herself for being afterwards a *widow-presby-
teress*). **let them**—rather 'let him,' or 'her.'
be charged [*bareistho*]—'be *burdened*' with their
support. **widows indeed**—really friendless (*vv.*
3, 4).
17. The transition from the widow - presbyteresses (*v.* 9) to the presbyters is natural. **rule
well** [*proestōtes*]—'preside well,' with wisdom,
ability, and loving faithfulness, over the flock, in
contradistinction to non-ruling presbyters. **be
counted worthy of double honour**—"honour"
expressed by *gifts* (*vv.* 3, 18), and otherwise. If a
presbyter, in virtue of his office, is worthy of
honour, he who *rules well* is *doubly* so (1 Cor. ix.
14; Gal. vi. 6; 1 Thess. v. 12). "Double" is used
for *large, much more* (Rev. xviii. 6). **especially
they who labour in the word and doctrine**—

saith, [k] Thou shalt not muzzle the ox that treadeth out the corn: and, [l] The labourer *is* worthy of his reward.

19   Against an elder receive not an accusation, but [6] before two or three
20 witnesses. Them [m] that sin rebuke before all, that others [n] also may fear.
21 I charge *thee* before God, and the Lord Jesus Christ, and the elect angels, that thou observe these things [7] without preferring one before another, doing nothing by partiality.
22   Lay [o] hands suddenly on no man, neither [p] be partaker of other men's
23 sins: keep thyself pure. Drink no longer water, but use a little wine for thy stomach's sake and thine often infirmities.

A. D. 65.

k Deut. 25. 4.
l Deut.24.14.
  Luke 10. 7.
6 Or. under.
m Tit. 1. 13.
n Deut. 13.11.
7 Or.
  without
  prejudice.
o ch. 4. 14.
p 2 John 11.

'teaching.' Preaching the Word, and instruction, catechetical or otherwise. This implies, that of the *ruling presbyters* there were two kinds—those who *laboured in the Word and teaching*, and those who did not. Lay presbyters have no place here; for both classes mentioned are *ruling* presbyters. A college of presbyters is implied as existing in Ephesus. In ch. iii. their qualifications are mentioned: here the acknowledgments due to them for their services. **18. the Scripture** (Deut. xxv. 4; 1 Cor. ix. 9). The Spirit often designs a fuller meaning under literal precepts. **the ox that treadeth out**—Greek, '*an ox whilst treading,*' &c. Threshing was performed by oxen either by *treading* or by being attached to *a threshing-wain.* **The labourer is worthy of his reward**—or "hire" (Luke x. 7; whereas Matt. x. 10 has "his meat," or 'food.' St. Paul, if, as seems natural, "the Scripture" apply to the second quotation as well as the first, hereby recognizes the gospel of St. Luke, his own helper (whence appears the undesigned appositeness of the quotation), as inspired "*Scripture.*" That gospel was probably in circulation then eight or nine years.

19. Against an elder—a presbyter of the church. **but before two or three witnesses.** A *judicial conviction* was not permitted in Deut. xix. 15, except on the testimony of at least two or three witnesses (cf. Matt. xviii. 16; John viii. 17; 2 Cor. xiii. 1). But Timothy's *entertaining an accusation* against any one is a different case, where the object was not judicially to punish, but to admonish (*vv.* 21, 24). Here he might *ordinarily* entertain it *without the need of more than one witness*, as also Moses' law allowed; but not in the case of an elder, since the more earnest an elder was to *convince gainsayers* (Titus i. 9), the more exposed would he be to vexatious accusations. How important, then, was it, that Timothy should not, without strong testimony, entertain a charge against presbyters, who should, in order to be efficient, be "blameless!" (ch. iii. 2; Titus i. 6.) "Receive" does not include both citation and conviction, but only the former. **20. Them that sin**—*habitually* (present participle), whether presbyters or laymen. **rebuke before all**—by ecclesiastical authority, publicly before the church, it being a case not of mere individual offence, but a public scandal (Matt. xviii. 15-17; 1 Cor. v. 9-13; Eph. v. 11). Not until this "rebuke" was disregarded was the offender excommunicated. **that others also may fear**—offending (Deut. xiii. 11; Acts v. 11). **21. I** (*solemnly*) **charge thee** [*diamarturomai*] (2 Tim. iv. 1). **before**—'*in the presence of* God.' **Lord.** Omitted in א A Δ G *f g,* Vulgate. *God the Father, and Christ the Son,* who will be revealed *with His angels at the last judgment,* will testify against thee, if thou disregardest my injunction. **elect angels**—the objects of Divine *electing* love, in contrast to the *reprobate* angels, "who kept not their first estate" (2 Pet. ii. 4; Jude 6). "Elect" also marks the excellence

of the angels (as God's *chosen* ministers, 'holy angels,' 'angels of light'), and so gives more solemnity to their testimony (*Calvin*) to Paul's adjuration. Angels take part, by action and sympathy, in our affairs (Luke xv. 10; 1 Cor. iv. 9), and will hereafter witness the judgment. **these things**—the injunctions (*vv.* 19, 20). **without preferring one before another** [*prokrimatos*] —'*without prejudice:*' 'judging before' hearing all the facts. There ought to be *judgment*, but not *pre-judging.* (Cf. "suddenly," *v.* 22; also *v.* 24). **partiality**—*in favour of* one, as 'prejudice' is bias *against* one. A Δ read [*prosklēsin*] 'in the way of *summoning* (brethren) *before a* (heathen) *judge.*' But א G *f g,* Vulgate, *Lucifer,* favour [*prosklisin*] "partiality."

22. Lay hands—*i. e.,* ordain (ch. iv. 14; 2 Tim. i. 6; Titus i. 5). The connection is with *v.* 19. The way to guard against scandals in presbyters is, be cautious as to the character of the candidate before ordaining him. This will apply to other church officers also. Thus, this clause refers to *v.* 19, as next clause, "neither be partaker of other men's sins," refers to *v.* 20. *Ellicott* understands it of *receiving back into church fellowship, absolving, by laying hands on those who had been 'rebuked'* (*v.* 20) *and excommunicated* (Matt. xviii. 17). But as in Acts vi. 6; xiii. 3; ch. iv. 14; 2 Tim. i. 6, the laying on of hands is used of *ordination,* and there is no express reference to excommunication and absolution in the context, the ancient interpretation is best. **suddenly**—hastily. *Vv.* 24, 25 show that waiting is salutary. **neither be partaker of other men's sins**—by negligence in ordaining ungodly candidates; so becoming, in some degree, responsible for their sins. Or, there is the same transition from *elders* to *all* who sin, as in *vv.* 19, 20. Be not a partaker in other men's sins by not 'rebuking them that sin before all:' alike those that are candidates for the presbytery, also all "that sin." **keep thyself pure**—"keep THYSELF." (emphatic) *clear* of OTHER men's sin, by not failing to *rebuke them* (*v.* 29). The transition is easy to *v.* 23, concerning Timothy *personally* (cf. also *v.* 24). **23. no longer**—as a habit. This injunction to drink wine occasionally modifies "keep thyself pure." The presbyter and deacon were to be "not given to wine" (ch. iii. 3, 8). Timothy perhaps had a tendency to ascetical strictness (cf. note, ch. iv. 8: cf. the Nazarene vow, Num. vi. 1-4; John Baptist, Luke i. 15; Rom. xiv. 21). Paul modifies the preceding "keep thyself pure." ' Not that I enjoin that purity which consists in asceticism; nay, no longer drink *only* water, but *use a little wine,* as is needed for thy health' (*Ellicott*). The Essenes avoided wine, especially in their weekly festival. *Alford* thus: Timothy was of a feeble frame (note, 1 Cor. xvi. 10, 11), timid as overseer, where vigorous action was needed: hence Paul exhorts him to take means to raise his bodily condition. God commands believers to use all due means for pre-

24   Some men's sins are open beforehand, going before to judgment; and
25 some *men* they follow after. Likewise also ^qthe good works *of some* are
manifest beforehand; and they that are otherwise cannot be hid.

6   LET as many ^aservants as are under the yoke count their own masters
worthy of all honour, ^bthat the name of God and *his* doctrine be not
2 blasphemed. And they that have believing masters, let them not despise
them, ^cbecause they are brethren; but rather do *them* service, because
they are ¹faithful and beloved, partakers of the benefit. These things
teach and exhort.

3   If any man teach otherwise, and consent not to wholesome words, *even*
the words of our Lord Jesus Christ, and to the doctrine which is accord-
4 ing to godliness; he is ²proud, ^dknowing nothing, but ³doting about

A. D. 65.

^q 1 Pet. 3. 8-16.

CHAP. 6.
^a Tit. 2. 9.
^b Gen. 13,8,9.
2 Sam. 12. 14.
Isa. 52. 5.
^c Col. 4. 1.
¹ Or, believing.
² Or, a fool.
^d 1 Cor. 8. 2.
³ Or, sick.

serving health, and condemns, by anticipation, the human traditions which among various sects have denied wine to the faithful.

24. Two kinds of sins,—(1.) Those *palpably notorious* (so *prodēloi*, "open *beforehand;*" Heb. vii. 14, "evident;" lit., '*before' the eyes*) further explained as "going before to judgment;" and (2.) Those which follow after the men ("some men they (*i. e.,* their sins) follow after," as a shadow following the body)—viz., not going beforehand, loudly accusing, but hidden till the judgment: so *v.* 25, *the good works* are of two classes: those *palpably manifest* ('manifest beforehand'), and those "that are otherwise"—*i. e.,* not *palpably manifest.* Both alike "cannot be hid" the former class, the bad and good, are *manifest* already; the latter, in the case of both, are not manifest now, but shall be so *at the last judgment.* **going before to judgment**— as heralds: crying sins, which accuse their perpetrator. The connection is: He had enjoined Timothy (*v.* 20), 'rebuke *them that sin* before all;' and (*v.* 22), "neither be partaker of other men's sins," by ordaining ungodly men; having, by a digression at "keep thyself pure," guarded against an error of Timothy in fancying purity consisted in asceticism, and having exhorted him to use wine for strengthening him, he returns to his being vigorous as an overseer in *rebuking sin,* whether in presbyters or people, and in avoiding participation in men's sins by ordaining ungodly candidates. He says, therefore, there are two classes of *sins,* as there are two classes of *good works*: those palpably *manifest* and those not so; the former are those on which thou shouldest act decidedly at once, when it is needful to rebuke in general, or to ordain ministers in particular: as to the latter, the final *judgment* alone can decide; however hidden now, they "cannot be hid" then. This could only be said of *the final judgment* (1 Cor. iv. 5: therefore, *Alford's* reference to *Timothy's judgment* in choosing elders is wrong): all judgments before then are fallible. Timothy can only be responsible if he connive at *manifest* sins; not that those *that are otherwise* shall escape judgment at last: just as in *good works,* he can only be responsible for taking into account in his judgments those patent to all; not those secret good works which nevertheless will not remain hidden at the final judgment.

CHAP. VI. 1-21. — DISTINCTIONS OF CIVIL RANK—DUTY OF SLAVES, IN OPPOSITION TO THE FALSE TEACHINGS OF GAIN-SEEKERS—TIMOTHY'S PURSUIT IS TO BE GODLINESS, AN EVERLASTING POSSESSION — ADJURATION TO DO SO AGAINST CHRIST'S COMING—CHARGE FOR THE RICH—CONCLUDING EXHORTATION.

1. servants. Explanatory predicate, "Let as many as are under the yoke" (as) slaves (1 Cor. vii. 21; Eph. vi. 5; Col. iii. 22; Titus ii. 9). There was a danger of Christian slaves feeling above
their heathen masters. **their own masters** [*Tous idious despotas: despotes, absolute master* over slaves; *kurios, lord* (used in Paul's other epistles), a milder term.] *Their own* is an argument for submissiveness; it is not *strangers,* but *their own masters* whom they are to respect. **all honour**— *all* possible and fitting *honour;* not merely outward, but inward *honour,* from which flows spontaneously right conduct (note, Eph. v. 22). **that the name of God**—by which Christians are called. **blasphemed.** The heathen would say, What kind of God must be the God of the Christians, when insubordination is the fruit of His worship! (Rom. ii. 24; Titus ii. 5, 10.) **2. And** [*De*]—'But.' The opposition is between Christian slaves *under the yoke* of heathen, and *those that have believing masters* (he does not say "under the yoke" in this case, for service under believers is not a *yoke*). Connect thus, 'Let them (the slaves) not, because they (the masters) are brethren (and so *equals,* masters and slaves alike being Christians), despise (take liberties with) them' (the masters). **but rather, &c.**—but all the more (with the greater good will) do them service, because they (the masters) are faithful (*i. e.,* believers) and beloved (of God) who receive [in the *interchange* of *reciprocal* duties between master and servant: *hoi antilambanomenoi,* the article marking this as the subject, and "faithful and beloved" the predicate] the benefit.' This latter clause is parallel to "because they are brethren;" which proves that "they" refers to *the masters,* not *the servants,* in the common sense of the verb (Luke i. 54; Acts xx. 35), 'who *sedulously labour for* their (masters') benefit.' "Benefit" delicately implies service done with the right *motive,* Christian "good will" (Eph. vi. 7). If the common sense of the verb be urged, explain, 'Because they (the masters) are faithful, &c., who *are sedulously intent* on the *benefiting'* of their servants. But *Porphyry* ('De Abstin.' i. 46) justifies the sense above, which better accords with the context; for otherwise the article, "*the* benefit," will have nothing to explain it; whereas in my explanation "*the* benefit" is *the slaves' service.* **These things teach**—as a matter of *doctrine* (ch. iv. 11; Titus ii. 15). **exhort**—as a matter of *practice.*

3. teach otherwise — than I desire thee to "teach" (v. 2). The Greek indicative implies, he puts not a supposed case, but one actually existing (ch. i. 3, '*every one who teaches* otherwise')— i. e., *heterodoxically.* **consent not** [*proserchetai*]— 'accede not to.' **wholesome**—sound (ch. i. 10). The false teachers' words were *unsound* through profitless science and immorality. **words of our Lord Jesus**—Paul's inspired words are not merely his own, but also *Christ's* words. **4. He is proud** [*tetuphōtai*]—'beclouded;' filled with the fumes of self-conceit (ch. iii, 6), whilst "knowing nothing" —viz., of the doctrine according to godliness (v. 3),

questions and strifes of words, whereof cometh envy, strife, railings, evil
5 surmisings, ⁴perverse disputings of ᵉmen of corrupt minds, and destitute
of the truth, ᶠsupposing that gain is godliness: ᵍfrom such withdraw
thyself.

6, But ʰgodliness with contentment is great gain. For ⁱwe brought
7 nothing into *this* world, *and it is* certain we can carry nothing out.
8, And ʲhaving food and raiment let us be therewith content. But ᵏthey
9 that will be rich fall into temptation and a snare, and *into* many foolish
10 and hurtful lusts, which drown men in destruction and perdition. For
ˡthe love of money is the root of all evil; which while some coveted after,
they have ⁵erred from the faith, and pierced themselves through with
many sorrows.

A. D. 65.

⁴ Or, Gall-
ings one of
another.
ᵉ 2 Tim. 3, 6,
ᶠ Tit. 1. 11.
ᵍ Rom. 16. 7.
ʰ Ps. 37. 16.
ⁱ Job 1. 21.
Ps. 49. 17.
ʲ Gen 28. 20.
ᵏ Pro. 15. 27.
ˡ Ex. 23. 8.
⁵ Or. been
seduced.

though arrogating pre-eminent knowledge (ch. i. 7). **doting about** [*noson*]—'*sick* about;' the opposite of "*wholesome*" (*v.* 3). *Truth* is not the centre *about* which his investigations move, but mere *word-strifes*. **questions**—of controversy. **strifes of words**—rather than *realities* [*logomachies*] (2 Tim. ii. 14). These stand with them instead of "godliness" and "wholesome words" (*v.* 3; ch. i. 4; Titus iii. 9). **evil surmisings**—as to those differing from themselves. **5. Perverse disputings** [*paradiatribai*]—useless disputings. A Δ G א *f g*, Vulgate, read [*diaparatribai*] 'lasting,' 'incessant contests.' "Strifes of words" had already been mentioned, so that he would not be likely to repeat the same idea. **corrupt minds** [*diephtharmenon ton noun*]—'of men corrupted (depraved) in mind.' The source of evil is the perverted 'mind' [*nous*], including the *will* (*v.* 4; 2 Tim. iii. 8; Titus i. 15). **destitute** [*apesteremenon:* judicially deprived of] **of the truth** (Titus i. 14). They had had the truth, but through want of integrity and love of the truth they were misled by a pretended gnosis (knowledge) and higher ascetical holiness, of which they made a trade (*Wiesinger*). **supposing, &c.**—regarding the matter thus, that 'godliness is a means of gain' [*porismon einai tēn eusebeian* the article marks the subject to be *tēn eusebeian*, the predicate *porismon*, distinct from *porisma*, the thing gained, gain]; not "that gain is godliness." **from such withdraw thyself.** Omitted in א Δ G*f g*, Vulgate. The connection with *v.* 6 favours the omission; these words interrupt the connection.

6. But. Though they err, there is a sense in which 'piety is' not merely gain, but "*great gain*:" not the *gaining* which they pursue, which makes men *discontented* with present possessions, and using religion as "a cloak of covetousness" (1 Thess. ii. 5) and *means of earthly gain*, but the *present and eternal gain* which *piety*, whose accompaniment is *contentment*, secures. Timothy possibly shrank from the conflict; whence Paul felt (*v.* 11) that Timothy needed exhortation: cf. also the second epistle. Not merely *contentment* is great gain (a sentiment of *Cicero*, 'Parad.' 6, 'the greatest and surest riches'), but '*piety* with contentment;' for piety not only feels no need of what it has not, but also has that which exalts it above what it has not (*Wiesinger*). [*Autarkeia*, *contentment*, is translated "sufficiency," 2 Cor. ix. 8. But the adjective, Phil. iv. 11, "content," *lit.* 'having a *sufficiency in one's self*' independent of others. 'The Lord supplies his people with what is sufficient. True happiness lies in piety; but this *sufficiency* is thrown into the scale as a kind of overweight' (*Calvin*) (1 Ki. xvii. 1-16; Ps. xxxvii. 19; Isa. xxxiii. 6, 16; Jer. xxxvii. 21). **7. For**—confirming the reasonableness of "contentment." If riches could be gain for the other world, there would be reason for discontent in present poverty.

498

But our real gain must be something not lost, like riches, in leaving the world. **and it is certain.** So C Vulgate. Δ, 'it is true.' But א A G *g* omit "and it is certain;" then translate, 'We brought nothing into the world (to teach us), that neither can we carry anything out' (Job i. 21; Eccl. v. 15). Nature strips man in returning, as in entering (*Seneca*, 'Epist.' 102). Therefore we should have no gain-seeking anxiety, breeding discontent (Matt. vi. 25). **8. And** [*De*]—'But.' In contrast to greedy gain-seekers (*v.* 5). **having**—so long as we have. **food** [*diatrophas*]—food sufficient continually supplied for our wants: we, as believers, shall *have* this. **raiment** [*skepasmata*]—'covering;' perhaps including a *roof to cover us*, as well as clothing. **let us be therewith content**—we shall be sufficiently provided [*arkesthesometha*]. **9. will be rich** [*boulomenoi*]—'wish to be rich;' to have more than "food and raiment;" not merely *willing*, but *resolved*, and earnestly *desiring* riches at any cost (Prov. xxviii. 20, 22). This *wishing* (not the riches themselves) is fatal to "contentment" (*v.* 6). Rich men are not told to cast away, but not to "*trust*" in their riches, and to "do good" with them (*vv.* 17, 18; Ps. lxii. 10). **fall into temptation**—not merely *are exposed to*, but actually "*fall into*" it. This is what we are to pray against, "Lead us not into temptation" (Jas. i. 14); such a one is already in a sinful state, even before any overt act. [*Temptation* and *gain* contain a play on sounds—*Porismus*, *Peirasmus*.] **snare**—a further step downwards; ch. iii. 7, "the snare of the devil." **hurtful** (cf. Eph. iv. 22) **lusts.** With the one evil lust ('*wish* to be rich') many others join themselves: the one is "the root of *all* evil" (*v.* 10). **which** [*haitines*] (hurtful)—'inasmuch as they.' **drown**—an awful descending climax from "fall into." [*Empiptousin:* plunging *into* greed of gain, they are at last inextricably *drowned* by it: the last step in the descent (Jas. i. 15). Translated "sink". (Luke v. 7).] **destruction and perdition** [*olethron-apoleian*]—*destruction* in general (temporal or eternal): *perdition* of body and soul in hell. **10. the love of money**—not the money, but the *love* of it —*wishing to be rich* (*v.* 9)—'is *a* root (not "the root") of all *evils*.' "*The* root" is defensible, as the article of *the Greek predicate* may be omitted. The wealthiest may be rich, not in a bad sense; the poorest may covet to be so. *Love of money* is not the sole root of evils, but a leading "root of bitterness" (Heb. xii. 15); for it 'destroys faith, the root of all good' (*Bengel*); its offshoots are 'temptation, a snare, lusts, destruction, perdition.' **coveted after** [*oregomenoi*]—'*stretching to* reach.' **erred from** [*apeplanēthēsan*]—'have been made to err from the faith' (ch. i. 19; iv. 1). **pierced** (Luke ii. 35) . . . **with many sorrows**—'pains:' the "thorns" (Matt. xiii. 22) which choke the word (Prov. i. 32). *Bengel*, the gnawings of conscience; remorse for wealth badly ac-

11 But thou, ^m O man of God, flee these things; and follow after righ-
12 teousness, godliness, faith, love, patience, meekness. Fight ⁿ the good
fight of faith, lay hold on ^o eternal life, whereunto thou art also called,
13 ^p and hast professed a good profession before many witnesses. I give
thee charge in the sight of God, who ^q quickeneth all things, and *before*
Christ Jesus, ^r who before Pontius Pilate witnessed a good ⁶ confession,
14 that thou keep *this* commandment without spot, unrebukeable, until ^s the
15 appearing of our Lord Jesus Christ: which in his times he shall show,
who is ^t the blessed and only Potentate, ^u the King of kings, and Lord of
16 lords; who ^v only hath immortality, dwelling in the light which no man

A. D. 65.	
^m	Deut. 33. 1.
ⁿ	2 Tim. 4. 7.
^o	Phil 3. 12.
^p	Heb 13. 23.
^q	John 5. 21.
^r	Rev. 1. 5.
⁶	Or. profession.
^s	1 Thes. 3. 13.
^t	ch. 1. 11.
^u	Rev 17. 14.
^v	John 5. 26.

---

quired; harbingers of the future "perdition" (*v.* 9). **11. But thou**—in contrast to the "some" (*v.* 10). **man of God**—who hast God as thy riches (Gen. xv. 1; Ps. xvi. 5; Lam. iii. 24): primarily Timothy as a minister (cf. 2 Pet. i. 21), just as Moses (Deut. xxxiii. 1), Samuel (1 Sam. ix. 6), Elijah, and Elisha; but as the exhortation is as to duties *incumbent on all Christians,* the term applies secondarily to him (so 2 Tim. iii. 17) as a Christian *born of God* (Jas. i. 18; 1 John v. 1), no longer a *man of the world:* raised above earthly things; therefore God's property, not his own, bought with a price, so having parted with all right in himself: Christ's work is *his* great work: he is Christ's living representative. **flee these things**— viz., "the love of money," with its evil results (*vv.* 9, 10). **follow after righteousness** (2 Tim. ii. 22). **godliness**—'piety.' *Righteousness* is in relation to our fellow-man ; "godliness" to God; *faith* is the root of both (note, Titus ii. 12). **love**—by which 'faith worketh :' the cardinal graces. **patience** — *brave, enduring perseverance* amidst trials. **meekness** [*praótes,* or *praütes*]. So C Δ. But א A G read [*praüpatheian*] 'meek-spiritedness'— viz., towards opponents of the Gospel. **12. Fight the good fight**—against Satan, the world, and the flesh. *Birks,* This epistle was written from Corinth, where national games recurred at stated seasons, which accounts for the allusion here, as 1 Cor. ix. 24-26. Contrast "strifes of words" (*v.* 4). Cf. ch. i. 18. The "good profession" is connected with the "good fight" (Ps. lx. 4). **lay hold on eternal life**—the crown or garland (Jas. i. 12; Rev. ii. 10) laid hold of by the winner (2 Tim. iv. 7, 8; Phil. iii. 12-14). [*Agonizou-agona*] 'Strive' with such earnestness in 'the good *strife*' as to "*lay hold on*" the prize, "*eternal life.*" **also** —not in א A Δ G. **professed a good profession**— 'didst confess THE [*ten*] good *confession*'—viz., *the Christian* confession—at thy ordination (whether in general or as overseer at Ephesus): the same occasion as in ch. i. 18; iv. 14; 2 Tim. i. 6. **before many witnesses**—who will testify against thee if thou fall away. **13. in the sight of God**—a far more solemn witness than those "many witnesses" (*v.* 12) before whom Timothy had made profession. **quickeneth all things** [*zoopoiountos*]. So א, Vulgate, 'maketh alive.' But A Δ G [*zoogonountos*], 'preserveth alive;' as in Acts vii. 19: cf. Neh. ix. 6. He urges Timothy to faithfulness by God's power manifested now in *preserving* all things (Matt. x. 29, 30); as in *v.* 14, by its future manifestation at Christ's appearing. The encouragement to "lay hold on eternal life" (*v.* 12) rests in the power of the God of all life, who *keeps* His people unto "eternal life" (1 Pet. i. 5). **witnessed.** It was the Lord's part to *witness,* or *attest* the truth of, Timothy's part to ' *confess* (*v.* 12), *the* good confession ' [*homologia* in both verses]. *The* confession was His *testimony* that He was King, and His kingdom that of *the truth* (*vv.* 12, 15: cf.

Matt. xxvii. 11; John xviii. 36, 37). Christ, in bearing witness to this truth, attested the whole of Christianity. Timothy's *confession* included, therefore, the whole Christian truth. *Ellicott* [*epi*], '*under* Pontius Pilate,' 'the good confession' of Christ's authentication and of Timothy's profession is thus *the Christian confession* generally. So [*epi*] Luke iii. 2, He witnessed before the high priest Caiaphas and the sanhedrim that He is *Messiah, the Son of God;* His confession, which cost Him His life given for us, comprising His (1) *office* and (2) *person* (note, Mark xiv. 61-64). **14. keep this commandment**—Greek, 'the commandment;' *i. e.,* the Gospel rule (John xiii. 34; ch. i. 5; Titus ii. 12; 2 Pet. ii. 21; iii. 2). **without spot, unrebukeable**—agreeing with "thou" [as *aspilon, anepilēpton* are applied in the New Testament only to *persons*]. Keep the commandment; so be without spot, &c. "Pure" (ch. v. 22; Eph. v. 27; Jas. i. 27; 2 Pet. iii. 14). **until the appearing of our Lord Jesus Christ**—*in person* (2 Thess. ii. 8; 2 Tim. iv. 1; Titus ii. 13). Believers then used to set before themselves as a motive the day of Christ as at hand; we, the hour of death. The fact has in all ages of the Church been certain ; the time as uncertain to Paul as it is to us (cf. *v.* 15): the Church's true attitude is, continual expectation of her Lord's return (1 Cor. i. 8; Phil. i. 6, 10). **15. in his times** [*kairois idiois*]—'*His own* (fitting) seasons' (Acts i. 7). The plural implies successive stages in manifesting the kingdom of God, each having its own appropriate time; the regulating principle and knowledge of which rest with the Father (ch. ii. 6; 2 Tim. i. 9; Titus i. 3; Heb. i. 1). **he shall show**—display as a mighty "sign" to men (Matt. xvi. 1) [*deixei*], appropriate to His "APPEARING" [*epiphaneia*], which is stronger than His 'coming,' and implies its *visibility* (cf. Acts iii. 20): "He" is *the Father* (*v.* 16). **blessed**—so about to be the source of *blessing* to His people at Christ's appearing, whence flows their "blessed hope" (Titus ii. 13; ch. i. 11). **only** (John xvii. 3; Rom. xvi. 27; Rev. xv. 4). **King of kings**—elsewhere applied also to Jesus (Rev. i. 5; xvii. 14; xix. 16). **16.** Frequent doxologies occur in the pastoral epistles; the apostle now, in advancing years, realizing more and more God's presence, and instinctively gliding often into language of adoration. **Who only hath immortality**—in His essence: not derived, or at the will of another, as all other immortal beings (*Justin Martyr,* 'Quest. ad Orthod.' 61). As He *hath immortality,* so will He give it to us who believe: to be out of Him is death. It is heathen philosophy that attributes to the soul indestructibility in itself: this is solely of God's gift. As He hath life *in Himself,* so hath He given to the Son to have life *in Himself* (John v. 26). [*Athanatos*] *Immortal* does not occur in the New Testament, but [*aphthartos*] "incorruptible." "Immortality" is found in 1 Cor. xv. 53, 54. **dwelling in the light which no man can approach unto.** After *life* comes *light,* as Dan. ii. 22; John

can approach unto; ^wwhom no man hath seen, nor can see: ^xto whom *be* honour and power everlasting. Amen.

17 Charge them that are rich in this world, that they be not high-minded, nor trust in ⁷uncertain riches, but in the living God, who giveth us

18 richly all things to enjoy; that they do good, that they be rich in good

19 works, ready to distribute, ⁸willing to communicate; laying up in store for themselves a good foundation against the time to come, that they may lay hold on eternal life.

20 O Timothy, keep that which is committed to thy trust, avoiding pro-

A. D. 65.
^w Ex. 33. 20.
Deut. 4. 12.
John 1. 18.
^x Eph. 3. 21.
Rev. 7. 12.
⁷ the uncertainty of riches.
⁸ Or, sociable.

i. 4. That *light* is *unapproachable* to creatures, except so far as they are admitted by Him, and He goes forth to them (*Bengel*). If one cannot gaze stedfastly at the sun, but a small part of creation, by reason of its exceeding heat and power, how much less can mortal gaze at God's inexpressible glory! (*Theophylact,* 'Ad Autolycum:' Ps. civ. 2; 1 John i. 5.) **no man hath seen**—with the bodily eye, nor shall hereafter; with the spiritual eye, though only in part now, the believer shall fully hereafter (Exod. xxxiii. 20; John i. 18; Col. i. 15; Heb. xi. 27; 1 John iv. 12). Still, the saints shall, in some sense, have the blessedness of *seeing* Him face to face in Christ, which is denied to mere *man* (Matt. v. 8; 1 Cor. xiii. 12; Heb. xii. 14; 1 John iii. 2; Rev. xxii. 4).

17. Resuming the subject (*vv.* 5, 10). Ephesus abounded in rich men. The immortality of God, alone rich in glory, and of His people through Him, is opposed to the lust of money (cf. *vv.* 14-16). From those desiring to be rich, he passes to those who *are* rich—1. What ought to be their disposition; 2. And use of their riches; 3. The consequences of so using them. **rich in this world**—contrasted with the rich of the future kingdom, the portion of believers at Christ's "appearing" (*v.* 14). **high-minded**—often characteristic of the rich (see Rom. xii. 16). **trust** [*elpikenai*]—'to have their trust.' **in** [*epi*]—'upon . . . upon.' [א A G Δ have *epi* for *en*]. **uncertain riches** [*ploutou adelotēti*]—'the *uncertainty* of riches.' Riches are not only *uncertain*: *uncertainty* is their very essence. They who rest on riches rest on *uncertainty* itself (Prov. xxiii. 5). Now they belong to one, now to another; that which has many masters is possessed by none (*Theodoret*). **living God.** So Δ. But א A G omit "living." He who trusts in riches renders them the duty he owes to God (*Calvin*). **who giveth** [*parechonti*]—'affordeth.' **richly all things**—temporal and eternal, for body and soul. To be truly rich, seek to be blessed of, and in, God (Prov. x. 22; 2 Pet. i. 3). **to enjoy**—Greek, 'for enjoyment.' Not that the heart may cleave to them as its *trust* (ch. iv. 3). *Enjoyment* consists in giving, not in holding fast. Non-employment should be far removed, as from man, so from his resources (Jas. v. 2, 3) (*Bengel*). Though we have abundance, yet we have no enjoyment of it, save by God's gift (Eccl. vi. 2). **18. do good**—like God Himself (Ps. cxix. 68; Acts xiv. 17) and Christ (Acts x. 38). *Tittmann* translates [*agathoergein*] *to do well;* as to be *beneficent* is a distinct word [*agathopoiein*]. **rich in good works**—so "rich in faith," which produces them (Jas. ii. 5). Contrasted with "rich in this world" (*v.* 17)—*lit.,* 'rich in honourable works.' [Greek, *kalois ergois,* are works *right* in themselves: *agathois,* good to another.] **ready to distribute**—'liberal in distributing:' the heart not cleaving to possessions. **willing to communicate**—to impart a share of goods to others (Gal. vi. 6; Heb. xiii. 16). **19. Laying up in store** [*apothēsaurizontas*]—'therefrom;'

i. e., from their abundance. [*Bengel* makes the *apo* mean laying apart *against a future time,* Matt. vi. 19, 20]. This is a treasure which we act wisely in *laying up in store;* but the wisest thing we can do with earthly treasures is "to distribute," and give others a share (*v.* 18). **good foundation**—the treasure laid up in certainty contrasted with the *uncertainty* of riches (note, ch. iii. 13; Luke vi. 48; 1 Cor. iii. 11). The *sure* reversion of the heavenly inheritance: earthly riches *scattered* in faith lay up in store a *sure increase* of heavenly riches. We gather by scattering (Prov. xi. 24; xiii. 7; Luke xvi. 9). **that . . . eternal life.** א A Δ G *f g,* Vulgate, read [*tēs ontōs* for *aioniou*] 'that which is really life:' joys solid and enduring (Ps. xvi. 11). The life that now is cannot be called so, its goods being unsubstantial, itself a vapour (Jas. iv. 14). In order that ('with their jeet on this foundation,' *De Wette*) 'they may lay hold on that which is life indeed.'

20, 21. Recapitulatory conclusion: the main aim of the epistle summarily stated. **O Timothy.** A personal appeal, marking his affection for Timothy, and his prescience of the coming heresies. **keep**—from spiritual thieves, and from enemies who will, whilst men sleep, sow tares amidst the good seed. **that which is committed to thy trust** [*tēn parathēkēn*]—'the deposit' (ch. i. 18; 2 Tim. i. 12, 14; ii. 2). *The sound doctrine* to be taught; opposed to *the science falsely so called,* leading to *error concerning the faith* (*v.* 21). 'It is not thine: it is another's property with which thou art entrusted: diminish it not at all (*Chrysostom*). 'Entrusted to thee, not found by thee; received, not invented; a matter not of genius, but of teaching; not of private usurpation, but of public tradition; a matter brought to thee, not put forth by thee, in which thou oughtest to be, not an enlarger, but a guardian; not an originator, but a disciple; not leading, but following. "Keep," saith he, 'the deposit;' preserve inviolate the talent of the catholic faith. What has been entrusted to thee, let that same remain with thee; be handed down by thee. Gold thou hast received, gold return. I should grieve if thou shouldest substitute aught else. If for gold thou shouldest substitute lead impudently, or brass fraudulently. I do not want the mere appearance of gold, but its actual reality. Not that there is to be no progress in Christ's Church. Let there be the greatest progress; but then let it be real progress, not a change of the faith. Let the intelligence of the whole Church and its individual members increase exceedingly, provided it be only in its own kind, the doctrine being still the same. Let the religion of the soul resemble the growth of the body, which, though it develops its several parts in the progress of years, yet remains the same essentially' (*Vincentius Lirinensis,* A. D. 434). **avoiding** [*ektrepomenos*]—'turning away from' (cf. 2 Tim. iv. 4). Even as they 'turned away from the truth' (ch. i. 6; v. 15). **profane** (ch. iv. 7; 2 Tim. ii. 16). **vain**—Greek, 'empty:' mere " strifes of words" (*v.* 4)

500

fane *and* vain babblings, and ⁱ oppositions of science falsely so called :
21 which some professing have erred concerning the faith. Grace *be* with
thee. Amen.

The first to Timothy was written from Laodicea, which is the chiefest city of
Phrygia Pacatiana.

A. D. 65.

ⁱ Acts 17. 18-21.
Rom. 1. 22.
1 Cor. 2. 6.
1 Cor. 3. 19.

producing no moral fruit. **oppositions** — *anti-theses.* 'Questions for discussion' (*Wahl.*) *Wiesinger,* not so probably, 'oppositions to sound doctrine.' Germs existed already of the heresy of *dualistic* "*oppositions*"—viz., between the good and evil principle, afterwards developed in Gnosticism. Contrast Paul's just antithesis (ch. iii. 16; vi. 5, 6; 2 Tim. ii. 15-23). **science** (Gnosis) **falsely so called.** Where there is not faith, there is not knowledge (*Chrysostom*). There was a true 'knowledge,' a gift [*charism*] of the Spirit, abused by some (1 Cor. viii. 1; xii. 8; xiv. 6). This gift was counterfeited by false teachers, as if pre-eminently theirs (Col. ii. 8, 18, 23). Hence arose the creeds called *symbols* [*sumbola*]—i. e., *watchwords:* tests whereby the orthodox might distinguish one another from the heretical. Perhaps here, *v.* 20, and 2 Tim. i. 13, 14, imply the existence then of some brief formula of doctrine; if so, we see good reason for its nòt being in Scripture, which is designed not to give dogmatic formularies, but to be the fountain whence they are to be drawn, according to the exigencies of churches and ages. A portion of the so-called Apostles' creed may

501

have had their sanction, and been preserved solely by tradition; but its sole authority to us is its being provable by Scripture. 'The creed, handed down from the apostles, is not written on paper and with ink, but on fleshy tables of the heart,' (*Jerome,* 'Adv. err. Johann. Hieros.,' ch. ix.) Thus, in the creed, contrary to the "oppositions" (the germs of which existed in Paul's latter days) whereby the œons were *set off* in pairs, God is stated to be 'the Father Almighty' (*all-governing*) 'maker of heaven and earth' (*Bishop Hinds*). **21. Which** (falsely-called science) **some professing . . .** erred (note, ch. i. 6)—lit., *missed the mark* (2 Tim. iii. 7, 8). True sagacity is inseparable from faith. 'It is incredible that any forger in the second century should have applied so mild an expression to followers of the Marcionite Gnosis' (*Ellicott*). **Grace**—Greek, '*the* grace,' viz., of God, for which we Christians look, and in which we stand (*Alford.*) **be with thee.** He restricts the salutation to Timothy, as the epistle was not to be read in public (*Bengel*). So Δ *f g,*Vulgate. But א A G *g* read 'be with you.' **Amen.** So C. Omitted in א A G Δ.

TIMOTHY

1 PAUL, an apostle of Jesus Christ by the will of God, according to
2 *a* the promise of life which is in Christ Jesus, to Timothy, *my* dearly
beloved son : Grace, mercy, *and* peace, from God the Father and Christ
Jesus our Lord.
3 I thank God, whom I serve from *my* forefathers with pure conscience,
that without ceasing I have remembrance of thee in my prayers night
4 and day; greatly desiring to see thee, being mindful of thy tears, that I
5 may be filled with joy; when I call to remembrance the unfeigned faith
that is in thee, which dwelt first in thy grandmother Lois, and *b* thy
mother Eunice; and I am persuaded that in thee also.

A. D. 66.

CHAP. 1.
a John 5. 24,
39, 40.
John 6. 40,
54.
John 10. 28.
John 17. 3.
Rom. 5. 21.
Eph. 3. 6.
Tit. 1. 2.
Heb. 9. 15.
b Acts 16. 1.

CHAP. I. 1-18.—ADDRESS—THANKFUL EX-
PRESSION OF LOVE AND DESIRE TO SEE TIMOTHY
—REMEMBRANCE OF HIS FAITH, AND THAT OF
HIS MOTHER AND GRANDMOTHER—EXHORTATION
TO STIR UP THE GIFT IN HIM, AND NOT SHRINK
FROM AFFLICTION, ENFORCED BY THE FREENESS
OF GOD'S GRACE IN OUR CALLING, AND BY THE
APOSTLE'S EXAMPLE—DEFECTION OF MANY—
STEDFASTNESS OF ONESIPHORUS.
1. This epistle is the last testament and swan-
like death-song of Paul (*Bengel*). **according to
the promise of life which is in Christ.** Paul's
apostleship is *in order to carry into effect* this
promise (cf. Titus i. 1, 2). This "promise of life
. . . in Christ" (cf. *v.* 10; ch. ii. 8) was needed to
nerve Timothy to boldness in undertaking the
journey to Rome, which would be attended with
much risk (*v.* 8). **2. my dearly beloved son.** In
1 Tim. i. 2 and Titus i. 4, written earlier, the
expression is (Greek) 'my *genuine* son;' marking
the sincerity of *Timothy:* "my dearly beloved
son" marks the love of *Paul*. *Alford* sees in the
change an altered tone as to Timothy—more of
mere love, less of confidence—as though Paul saw
in him a want of firmness, whence arose the need
of *stirring up* the faith in him (*v.* 6). [This seems
to me not justified by *agapetos*, which implies the
attachment of *reasoning* and *choice*, on the ground
of *merit* in the one "beloved," not merely *instinctive*
love. See *Trench*, 'Synonyms of New Testament.']
3. I thank [*charin echo*]—'I *feel gratitude* to
God.' **whom I serve from my forefathers**—
whose service *handed down from* them I cherish.
He does not mean to put on the same footing the
Jewish and Christian service; but to assert his
own conscientious service of God in the truth
common to Judaism and Christianity, as he had
received it ' from his (immediate) *progenitors*' (not
Abraham, Isaac, &c., whom he calls "the fathers,"
not 'progenitors' [*progonōn*], Rom. ix. 5). The
memory of those gone before, to whom he is about
to be gathered, is now, on the eve of death,
pleasant. He calls to mind the faith of the
mother and grandmother of Timothy: as he walks
in the faith of his forefathers (Acts xxiii. 1; xxiv.
14; xxvi. 6, 7; xxviii. 20), so Timothy should persevere in that of his parent and grandparent.
The Jews who reject Christ forsake the faith of
their forefathers, who looked for Christ; when
they accept Him, the hearts of the children shall
only be returning to the faith of their forefathers
(Mal. iv. 6; Luke i. 17; Rom. xi. 23, 24, 28).
Probably Paul, in his recent defence, dwelt on

this—viz., that he was, in being a Christian,
following his *hereditary faith*. Conscience without
the Word of God is a lamp in which the candle is
apt to go out, or, by its glimmering haze, mislead
(John xvi. 2; Acts xxvi. 9; Titus i. 15). **that**—
rather, '*as* without ceasing I have remembrance
of thee' (cf. Phile. 4). The cause of Paul's thankfulness is, not *that* he remembers Timothy unceasingly in his prayers, but that he calls to
remembrance Timothy's "unfeigned faith" (*v.* 5:
cf. Rom. i. 8, 9). [*ōs* cannot be used for *hoti*.]
night and day (note, 1 Tim. v. 5). **4. desiring**
[*epipothōn*]—'with *yearning* as for one much *missed*.'
mindful of thy tears—under pious feelings.
Wordsworth thinks Timothy's tears were at parting, because of the second arrest of St. Paul (cf.
Acts xx. 37). **that I may be filled with joy**—
joined with "desiring to see thee" (Rom. i. 11, 12;
xv. 32). The "joy" would dispel the "tears."
5. When I call to remembrance, &c. This increased his 'desire to see' Timothy. [C Δ G *fg*,
Vulgate, read *lambanōn*. But א A, *labon*, 'when
I *called* to remembrance:' implying that some
recent incident (perhaps the contrasted cowardice
of the hypocrite Demas, who forsook him) had
reminded him of the sincerity of Timothy's faith.]
'Having received reminding.' [*Anamnesis*, when
one *recalls* to mind something past; *hupomnesis*,
when one *is reminded* by another (2 Pet. iii. 1).]
faith that is in thee [*tēs en soi*]—not merely, as
Alford, 'that *was* in thee.' **which** [*hētis*]—'the
which:' *as being that which in particular*. **dwelt**
[*enōkēsen*]—'made its dwelling' (John xiv. 23).
The past tense implies they were now dead. **first.**
The family pedigree of indwelling faith began *first*
with Lois, the furthest back of Timothy's progenitors whom Paul knew. **mother Eunice—a**
believing Jewess; but his father was a Greek—
i. e., a heathen (Acts xvi. 1). The faith of the one
parent sanctified the child (1 Cor. vii. 14; ch. iii.
15). She was probably converted at Paul's first
visit to Lystra (Acts xiv. 6, 7). It is an undesigned coincidence, and so a mark of truth, that
in Acts xvi. 1, just as here, the belief of the
mother *alone* is mentioned, whilst no notice is
taken of the father (*Paley's* 'Horæ Paulinæ').
and [*de*]—'but;' *i. e.*, notwithstanding appearances (*Alford*). Rather, 'moreover.' The more
persuaded Paul is of Timothy's faith, the more he
exhorts him to stir up the gift of God (*Leo*).
persuaded that—*it dwells* "in thee also." The
faith of his mother and grandmother is the incentive used to stir up his faith.

6　Wherefore I put thee in remembrance that *c* thou stir up the gift of
7　God, which is in thee by the putting on of my hands. For *d* God hath
not given us the spirit of fear; *e* but of power, and of love, and of a
sound mind.
8　Be *f* not thou therefore ashamed of the testimony of our Lord, nor of
me his prisoner : but be thou partaker of the afflictions of the Gospel
9　according to the power of God; who hath saved us, and *g* called *us* with
an holy calling, *h* not according to our works, but *i* according to his own
purpose and grace, which was given us in Christ Jesus *j* before the world
10　began, but *k* is now made manifest by the appearing of our Saviour

A. D. 66.
c 1 Tim. 4. 14.
d Rom. 8. 15.
e Luke 24. 49.
f Mark 8. 38.
Rom. 1. 16.
g 1 Thes. 4. 7.
h Tit. 3. 5.
i Rom. 8. 28.
j Eph. 1. 4.
1 Pet. 1. 20.
k Eph. 1. 9.
Col. 1. 26.

6. Wherefore [*di' hēn aitian*]—'For which cause,' viz., because thou hast inherited, and I am persuaded dost possess, such unfeigned faith. **stir up** [*anazōpurein*]—'kindle up :' *fan into a flame :* the opposite of 'quench,' or *extinguish* (1 Thess. v. 19). Paul does not doubt Timothy's faith; but, just because of his 'persuasion' of its reality, urges him to put it in full exercise. Timothy probably had become dispirited by the long absence and imprisonment of his spiritual father. **gift of God**—the grace received for his ministerial office, either at his original ordination or at his consecration to the superintendency of the Ephesian church, imparting *jearlessness, power, love, and a sound mind* (*v.* 7). **by** [*dia*] **the putting on of my hands.** In 1 Tim. iv. 14 it is [*meta*] "*with* (not *by*) the laying on of the hands *of the presbytery.*" To the apostle, as chief instrument in the ordination and impartation of grace, "BY" is applied ; to the presbytery, as his assistants and concurring participants in ordaining, "with," implying mere *accompaniment,* is applied. So a bishop in our days does the *principal* act ; the presbyters join in laying on hands *with* him. **7. For,** &c.—implying that Timothy needed 'to stir up the gift of God in him,' being constitutionally *timid :* 'For God *did not give* us' [*edōken,* at confirmation, Acts viii. 15-17; and xiii. 3, 4, at ordination], &c. The spirit which He gave us was not the spirit of *cowardice* [*deilias*], which is weakness, but of "power" (exhibited in a fearless "testimony" for Christ, *v.* 8). "Power" invariably accompanies the gift of *the Holy Ghost* (Luke xxiv. 49; Acts i. 8: cf. ch. vi. 6 with *v.* 8). Fear results from "the spirit of bondage" (Rom. viii. 15). Fear *within* exaggerates the causes of fear *without.* 'The spirit of power' is man's spirit dwelt in by the Spirit of God imparting *power;* this "casteth out fear" from ourselves, and stimulates us to cast it out of others (1 John iv. 18). **love**—which moves the believer whilst "speaking the truth " with *power,* when testifying for Christ (*v.* 8), at the same time to do so "in love" (Eph. iv. 15). **a sound mind** [*sophronismou*]—'the bringing of men to a sound mind' (*Wahl*). The Greek admits of the English version, *reflexively,* 'the bringing of *our own* passions under control : self-restraint' (cf. Luke xv. 17; Mark v. 15): a duty to which a young man especially needed to be exhorted to (1 Tim. iv. 12; ch. ii. 22; Titus ii. 4, 6). So Paul urges him (ch. ii. 4) to give up worldly entanglements (Luke viii. 14). These three gifts are preferable to any miraculous powers.

8. therefore—seeing that God hath given us such a spirit; not *fear.* **Be not thou, therefore, ashamed** (at any time) [*mē epaischunthēs*]. The Greek subjunctive, with the negative, implies action *completed at one time,* not *continued,* which the present imperative would express : implying, Timothy had *not yet* evinced such *shame;* still Paul, being deserted by others who once promised fair, and aware of Timothy's constitutional *timidity*

(note, v. 6), felt it necessary to guard him against the possibility of failure in bold confession of Christ. *Shame* (v. 8) is the companion of *fear* (v. 7): if fear be overcome, false shame flees (*Bengel*). Paul himself (*v.* 12), and Onesiphorus (*v.* 16), were instances of fearless profession removing false 'shame.' Contrast sad instances of fear and shame, *v.* 15. **of the testimony of our Lord**—*of giving testimony* in the cause *of our Lord* (Acts i. 8). "Our" connects Timothy and himself in the testimony which both should give for their common Lord. *The testimony which Christ gave before* or *under Pilate* (1 Tim. vi. 12, 13) is an incentive to the believer to *witness a good confession.* **nor of me his prisoner.** The cause of God's servants is that of God Himself (Eph. iv. 1). Timothy might be tempted to be ashamed of one in prison, especially as great risk attended any recognition of Paul. **be thou partaker**—*with me.* **of the Gospel** [*sunkakopatheson tō euangelio*]—'for (suffered *for*) *the Gospel*' (ch. ii. 3-5; Phile. 13). **according to the power of God** —exhibited in having *saved* and *called us* (*v.* 9). God who has done the greater act of power (*i. e.,* saved us) will surely do the less (carry us safe through *afflictions* borne *for the Gospel*). 'Thou hast not to bear these afflictions by thine own power, but by the power of God' (*Chrysostom*). Our readiness to suffer ought to correspond [*be proportionate to: kata*] to the greatness of His power evinced in having "saved us, and called us" (*v.* 9). **9. Who . . . called us**—viz., God the Father (Gal. i. 6). The "saved us" in His purpose of "grace, given us in Christ before the world began," precedes His "calling" us in due time with a call made effective by the Holy Spirit; therefore, "saved us" comes before "called us" (Rom. viii. 28-30). **holy calling**—the actual call *to holiness,* and "the fellowship of His Son" (1 Cor. i. 9; Heb. iii. 1, "heavenly calling :" whereas we were *sinners* and *enemies,* Eph. i. 18; iv. 1). The call comes wholly *from,* and claims us wholly *for,* God. "Holy" implies the believer's *separation* from the world unto God. **not according to**—not having regard to our works in His election and calling (Rom. xi. 11; Eph. ii. 8, 9). **his own purpose.** Salvation originated from *His own purpose* of goodness ; not for works of ours, but wholly of His gratuitous, electing love (*Theodoret* and *Calvin*). **grace which was given us**—in His everlasting purpose, regarded as actually *given.* **in Christ.** Believers are viewed by God as IN HIM, with whom the Father makes the covenant (Eph. i. 4; iii. 11). **before the world began** [*pro chronōn aioniōn*]—'before eternal times :' before times marked by the lapse of unnumbered ages (*Ellicott*). From eternity [*Aionios*]. 'That of which no end is conceived' (*Tittmann*) (1 Cor. ii. 7; Eph. iii. 11). **10. But is now made manifest**—in contrast to its concealment heretofore in God's eternal purpose "before the world began" (*v.* 9; Col. i. 26; Titus i. 2, 3). **appearing** [*epiphaneia*]—Christ's

Jesus Christ, who ¹ hath abolished death, and hath brought life and
11 immortality to light through the Gospel: whereunto I am appointed a
12 preacher, and an apostle, and a teacher of the Gentiles. For the which
cause I also suffer these things: nevertheless I am not ashamed; for I
know whom I have ¹ believed, and am persuaded that he is able to keep
that which I have committed ᵐ unto him against that day.
13 Hold ⁿ fast the ᵒ form of sound words, which ᵖ thou hast heard of
14 me, in faith and love which is in Christ Jesus. That good thing
which was committed unto thee keep by the Holy Ghost which dwelleth
in us.
15 This thou knowest, that all they which are in Asia be turned away
16 from me; of whom are Phygellus and Hermogenes. The Lord ᑫ give
mercy unto the house of Onesiphorus; ʳ for he oft refreshed me, and was

A. D. 66.

ˡ 1 Cor. 15.54,
55.
Heb. 2. 14.
¹ Or.
trusted.
ᵐ 1 Pet. 4. 19.
ⁿ Tit 1. 9.
Heb 10. 23.
Rev. 2. 25.
ᵒ Rom. 2. 20.
Rom. 6. 17.
1 Tim. 1.10.
1 Tim 6. 3.
ᵖ ch. 2. 2.
ᑫ Matt. 5. 7.
ʳ Phile. 7.

whole *manifestation* on earth. **abolished**—'taken away *the power* from' (*Tittmann*). [*Katargesantos*, without the article; 'Having made, as He did, of none effect' (*Ellicott*).] The article before "death" [*ton thanaton*] implies that Christ abolished *death as a principle* (Matt. iv. 16) overshadowing the world' (*Ellicott*), not only in particular instances, but in its essence, as also in all its consequences (John xi. 26; Rom. viii. 2, 38; 1 Cor. xv. 26, 55; Heb. ii. 14). The full abolition shall be at Christ's second coming (Rev. xx. 14). The death of the body meanwhile is but temporary, and is made no account of by Scripture. DEATH seems to me *personified.* Already it is said to be "abolished," because 'the earnest of it was given in Christ's resurrection. This is an appropriate consolation to Paul, soon about to suffer a violent *death* (v. 12). **life**—of the Spirit, acting first on the soul here, about to act on the body also at the resurrection. **immortality** [*aphtharsian*]—'incorruptibility' of the new life, not merely of the raised body (Rom. ii. 7; viii. 11; 1 Pet. i. 4; Rev. xxi. 4). **through**—*brought to light by means of the Gospel: life and immortality,* purposed by God from eternity, but manifested now first to man. Christ, in His resurrection, has given the pledge of His people's final triumph over death through Him. Before the Gospel revelation, man, by the light of nature, at best had but a glimmering idea of a future being of *the soul,* but not the faintest idea of the resurrection of *the body* (Acts xvii. 18, 32). If Christ were not "the life," the dead could never live; if He were not the resurrection, they could never rise; had He not the keys of hell and death (Rev. i. 18), we could never break through the bars of death or gates of hell (*Bishop Pearson*). **11. Whereunto**—For the publication of which gospel. **I am appointed** [*etethēn*]—'I *was* appointed.' **preacher** [*kerux*]—'herald.' **teacher of the Gentiles.** Paul (*vv.* 11, 12) is a pattern for Timothy, as a *public* "preacher," an "apostle" or *missionary,* and a "teacher" *in private.* In 1 Tim. ii. 7 these designations refer to his *dignity;* here, to his *sufferings* which attend his offices, and which Timothy therefore must not be ashamed of. **12. For the which cause**—Because I was appointed a preacher (*vv.* 10, 11). **I also suffer**—besides my *active* work. *Ellicott,* 'I suffer *even* these things:' bonds, &c. (*vv.* 8, 15). **I am not ashamed**—neither be thou (*v.* 8). **for.** Confidence as to the future drives away shame (*Bengel*). **I know**—though the world knows Him not (John x. 14; xvii. 25). **whom**—I know what a *faithful,* promise-keeping God He is (ch. ii. 13). It is not, I know *how,* but WHOM, I have believed: a feeble faith may clasp a strong Saviour. **believed**—put my trust: carrying out the metaphor of a depositor leaving his pledge with one whom He *trusts.* **am persuaded**—

(Rom. viii. 38) **he is able**—in spite of so many foes around me. **that which I have committed unto him** [*tēn paratheken mou*]—'my deposit:' the body, soul, and spirit (1 Thess. v. 23; 1 Pet. iv. 19). So Christ Himself in dying (Luke xxiii. 46). God deposits with us His Word to keep (*vv.* 13, 14) and transmit to others (ch. ii. 2): God commits another deposit to us, which we should commit to His keeping—viz., ourselves and our heavenly portion. *Ellicott,* from *v.* 14; 1 Tim. vi. 20, 'the stewardship committed to me'—viz., of preaching the Gospel. But "keep" applies rather to Paul, the holder, than God, the Giver, of the deposit (cf. also John xvii. 11; 1 Pet. i. 5; Jude 24 [*phulaxai,* as here]). **against that day**—the day of His appearing (*v.* 18; ch. iv. 8). **13. Hold fast the form** [*hupotuposin eche*]—'*Have* (*i. e.,* keep) *the pattern* (1 Tim. i. 16, where only, besides here, the Greek occurs) of sound (*healthy*) words which thou hast heard from me, in faith and love.' "Keep" suits the reference to a *deposit.* The secondary position of the verb forbids our taking it so strongly as "Hold fast." 'Have such a *delineation* drawn from my *sound* words,' in opposition to the *unsound* doctrines so current at Ephesus, '*vividly impressed*' (the verb implies *to make a lively and lasting impress*) on thy mind. **in faith and love**—the element IN which *keeping the pattern of my sound words* is to have place; in it *have the vivid impression* of them as thy *inwardly delineated pattern,* moulding conformably thy outward profession (cf. 1 Tim. iii. 9). **14.** [*Tēn kalēn parathēkēn*]. 'The goodly deposit keep through the Holy Ghost'—viz., 'the sound words which I have committed to thee' (*v.* 13; ch. ii. 2). **in us**—in all believers; also in you and me. Keep the indwelling Spirit, and He will keep for thee from all robbers the deposit of His Word.

15. all they which are in Asia—Proconsular Asia: 'all there *now, when they were in Rome* (not "be," but), turned from me' *then:* "ashamed of my chain," in contrast to Onesiphorus: did not stand with me, but forsook me (ch. iv. 16). Possibly the occasion was at his apprehension in Nicopolis, whither they had escorted him on his way to Rome, but from which they turned back to Asia. An inspiriting call to Timothy, as being his "son" (ch. ii. 1), now in Asia, like Onesiphorus, to make up for their defection, and to come to him (ch. iv. 21). **Phygellus and Hermogenes**—specified, perhaps, as persons from whom such cowardice could least be expected; or, as well known to Timothy, and spoken of in conversations between him and Paul when the latter was in Asia. **16. The Lord give mercy**—as Onesiphorus had showed *mercy.* **the house of Onesiphorus.** He was then absent from Ephesus which accounts

504

17 not ashamed of my chain: but, when he was in Rome, he sought me out
18 very diligently, and found *me*. The Lord grant unto him ^s that he may
find mercy of the Lord ^t in that day: and in how many things he
^u ministered unto me at Ephesus, thou knowest very well.

2 THOU therefore, my son, ^a be strong in the grace that is in Christ
2 Jesus. And the things that thou hast heard of me ¹ among many witnesses, ^b the same commit thou to faithful men, who shall be able to
3 teach others also. Thou therefore endure hardness, as a good soldier of
4 Jesus Christ. No ^c man that warreth entangleth himself with the affairs
of *this* life, that he may please him who hath chosen him to be a soldier.
5 And if a man also strive for masteries, *yet* is he not crowned, except
6 he strive lawfully. ² The husbandman that laboureth must be first
7 partaker of the fruits. Consider what I say; and the Lord give thee
understanding in all things.
8 Remember that Jesus Christ ^d of the seed of David ^e was raised from

A. D. 66.

^s Matt. 25.34.
^t 2 Thes 1.10.
^u Heb. 6. 10.

CHAP. 2.
^a Eph. 6. 10.
1 Or, by.
^b 1 Tim.1. 18.
^c 1 Cor. 9. 25.
2 Or, The husbandman, labouring first, must be partaker of the fruits.
^d Rom. 1. 3,4.
^e 1 Cor. 15. 1.

for the expression (ch. iv. 19). He had not yet returned from his visit at Rome (*v.* 17). His *household* would hardly retain his name after the master was dead. Nowhere has Paul prayers for the dead, which is fatal to the theory that he was dead. God blesses not only the righteous man himself, but all his household: even as a good man's household generally join in his good deeds. **my chain.** Paul, in the second, as in his first imprisonment, was bound by a chain to the soldier who guarded him ('*custodia militaris*'). **17. very diligently** [*spoudaioteron*]—the *more diligently* as I was a prisoner. **found me**—after an anxious search, in a lonely prison. So in turn may he "*find* mercy of the Lord in that day" before the assembled universe. **18. grant unto him**—as well as 'unto his house' (*v.* 16). **of** [*para*]—'from the Lord' is put instead of 'from Himself,' for solemnity and emphasis (2 Thess. iii. 5). **the Lord**—who rewards a kindness done to His disciples as done to Himself (Matt. xxv. 45). **in how many things**—'how many acts of ministry he rendered.' **unto me.** Omitted in א A C Δ G, so that "ministered" includes services *to others* as well as to Paul. **very well** (*Beltion*)—'better' (than I can tell thee, seeing thou art a resident at Ephesus).
CHAP. II. 1-26.—FAITHFULNESS AS A GOOD SOLDIER OF CHRIST—ERRORS TO BE SHUNNED—THE LORD'S SURE FOUNDATION—RIGHT SPIRIT FOR A SERVANT OF CHRIST.
1. Thou therefore—following my example (ch. i. 8, 12), and that of Onesiphorus (ch. i. 16-18), make up by thy stedfastness for the faithlessness of those who forsook me (ch. i. 15). **my son.** Children ought to imitate their father. **be strong** [*endunamou*]—'be inwardly strengthened,' 'be invested with *power:*' an abiding state of power, sure to manifest itself outwardly. **in the grace**—the *element* IN which spiritual strength has place (cf. ch. i. 7). **that is in Christ Jesus**—as its centre and source to those in union with Him. **2. among** [*dia*]—*through* the intervention of many witnesses; viz., the presbyters and others present at his ordination or consecration (1 Tim. iv. 14; vi. 12). **commit**—in trust, as a *deposit* (ch. i. 14). **faithful**—the quality needed by those having a trust committed to them. Faithfulness to the truth is the true apostolic succession (cf. note, 1 Tim. iii 2). **who** [*hoitines*]—'persons *such as* shall: competent to teach (them to) others also.' Thus the way is prepared for inculcating faithful endurance (*vv.* 3-13). As a motive to endurance, thou hast not only to keep the deposit for thyself, but to transmit it unimpaired to others, who in their turn shall fulfil the same office. So far from

505

supporting oral tradition *now*, this teaches how precarious a mode of preserving revealed truth it was, depending, as it did, on the trustworthiness of each individual in the chain of succession (2 Pet. ii. 1). Blessed be God, He *Himself* has given us, before the death of the inspired apostles, *the written Word*, which is exempt from such risk! **3. Thou therefore endure hardness.** א A C Δ G, Vulgate, have no "*Thou therefore*," but 'Endure hardship *with*' (me): share with me in suffering [*sunkakopathēson*, for *su oun kakopathēson*]. **soldier** (1 Cor. ix. 7; 2 Cor. x. 3). A true soldier both *abstains* and *sustains* (*vv.* 3, 4, 22). **4.** 'No one whilst serving as a soldier' [*strateuomenos*]. **the affairs, &c.** [*tais tou biou pragmateiais*]—mercantile, or other than military. [*Zoe* is the opposite of *death, thanatos:* and as sin caused death, where life, *zoe*, is, there sin is not, or ceases to be. So *zoe* is the nobler term in Scripture, expressing holy blessedness and eternal life; *bios*, the present course of life: *zoe*, the life by which we live; *bios*, the life which we live.] **him who hath chosen him**—the general who enlisted him. Paul himself worked at tent-making (Acts xviii. 3). What is prohibited is, not all secular occupation, but the becoming *entangled* or over-engrossed with it. **5. And** [*De*]—'Moreover.' **strive for masteries**—in the great national games of Greece. **yet is he not crowned, except**—even though he conquer. **strive lawfully**—observing the conditions of the contest (keeping within the bounds of the course and stript of his clothes), and also of the preparation for it—viz., as to self-denying diet, anointing, exercise, chastity, &c. (1 Cor. ix. 24-27.) As a *soldier*, the believer is one of *many;* as an *athlete*, he has to wage an *individual* struggle, and that *continually*, bearing the discipline of the *preparation* as well as the *conflict*. **6. must be first** (before all others) **partaker.** The right of *first partaking of the fruits* belongs to him who is not merely a husbandman by profession, but one *labouring:* do not thou relax thy *labours*, as thou wouldest be foremost in the reward (Matt. v. 12). **7.** Consider the scope of the illustrations from the soldier, the athlete, and the husbandman. **and the Lord give thee, &c.** א A C Δ *fg*, Vulgate, read '*for* the Lord *will give* thee,' &c. Thou canst understand my meaning as applying to thyself ministerially; for the Lord will give thee apprehension, when thou seekest it, "in all things." Not intellectual perception, but personal appropriation of the truths metaphorically expressed, was what he needed from the Lord.
8. 'Remember Jesus Christ, as raised from the dead.' Remember Christ in His character as raised, so as to follow Him. As He was raised

9 the dead according *f* to my gospel: wherein I suffer trouble, as an evil-
10 doer, *even* unto bonds; but the word of God is not bound. Therefore I
    endure all things for the elect's sakes, *g* that they may also obtain the
11 salvation which is in Christ Jesus with eternal glory. It *h is* a faithful
12 saying: For *i* if we be dead with *him*, we shall also live with *him:* if *j* we
    suffer, we shall also reign with *him:* *k* if we deny *him*, he also will
13 deny us: if *l* we believe not, *yet* he abideth faithful: *m* he cannot deny
    himself.
14   Of these things put *them* in remembrance, *n* charging *them* before the
    Lord that *o* they strive not about words to no profit, *but* to the sub-
15 verting of the hearers. Study to show thyself approved unto God, a
    workman that needeth not to be ashamed, rightly dividing the word of

A. D. 66.

f Rom. 2. 16.
g 2 Cor. 1. 6.
h 1 Tim. 1.15.
i Rom. 6.5.8.
   2 Cor. 4. 10.
j Rom. 8. 17.
k Matt. 10.33.
   Luke 12. 9.
l Rom. 3. 3.
   Rom. 9. 6.
m Num.23.19.
n 1 Tim. 5.21.
   ch. 4. 1.
o 1 Tim. 1. 4.

after death, so, if thou wouldest share His risen 'life,' thou must share His 'death' (*v.* 11). [The perfect passive participle, *egegermenon*, implies a *permanent character* acquired by *the risen* Saviour, and *our permanent interest in Him as such.*] Christ's resurrection is made prominent, being the truth now assailed (*v.* 18), and the one calculated to stimulate Timothy to share Paul's sufferings for the Gospel's sake (note, *v.* 3). **of the seed of David**—the one and only genealogy (contrasted with the "endless genealogies," 1 Tim. i. 4) worth thinking of, for it proves Jesus to be Messiah, and also the Heir of the throne of David (Jer. xxiii. 5; Matt. xxii. 42-45; John vii. 42). The absence of the Greek article, and this formula, "of the seed of David" (cf. Rom. i. 3, 4), may imply that the words were part of a short creed. In His death He assured us of His humanity; by His resurrection, of His divinity. That He was not crucified for *His own* sin appears from His resurrection; that He was crucified, shows that He bore sin *on*, though not *in*, Him. **my gospel**—that which I always taught. 9. **Wherein**—In proclaiming which Gospel. **I suffer trouble**—'evil.' I am a sufferer of evil as though I were a doer of evil. **bonds** (ch. i. 16). **word of God is not bound.** Though my person is bound, my tongue and pen are not (ch. iv. 17; Acts xxi. 13; xxviii. 31). Rather, he *includes* the freedom of the circulation of the Gospel *by others* (Phil. i. 12). He also hints that Timothy, being free, ought to be the more earnest in circulating it. 10. **Therefore**—in order that the Gospel should be extended; implied in *v.* 9. **endure**—not merely *passively*, but 'I actively with brave patience *endure*,' and 'am ready to endure all things' (Rom. xii. 12; Jas. i. 12). **the elect's**—for the sake of all the members of Christ's spiritual body (Col. i. 24). **they may also**—as well as myself: both God's elect not yet converted and those already so. **salvation . . . glory**—not only *salvation* from wrath, but *glory* in *reigning* with Him (*v.* 12). *Glory* is the full expansion of *salvation* (Acts ii. 47; Rom. viii. 21-24, 30; Heb. ix. 28). So *grace* and *glory* (Ps. lxxxiv. 12). 11. Greek, 'Faithful is the saying;' viz., that 'the elect shall obtain salvation with eternal glory' (*v.* 10). **For**—*For* the fact is so (*v.* 10) that, "if we be dead with Him (the aorist [*sunapethanomen*] implies *a state once for all entered into*, when we took Christ's discipleship, involving a daily cross, 1 Cor. xv. 31; 2 Cor. iv. 10; Phil. iii. 10), we shall also live with Him." The symmetrical form of the "saying" (*vv.* 11-13), and the rhythmical balance of the parallel clauses, make it likely they formed part of a church hymn (note, 1 Tim. iii. 16) or accepted formula, perhaps first uttered by Christian 'prophets' in the public assembly (1 Cor. xiv. 26). 'Faithful is the saying,' the usual formula (cf. 1 Tim. i. 15; iii. 1; iv. 9; Titus iii. 8), favours this. 12. **suffer.** The Greek is the same

as *v.* 10, 'If we endure (with Him),' &c. (Rom. viii. 17). **reign with him**—the peculiar privilege of the elect now suffering with Christ (note, 1 Cor. vi. 2). *Reigning* is something more than bare *salvation* (Rom. v. 17; Rev. i. 6; iii. 21; v. 10; xx. 4, 5). **deny**—*with the mouth*. Denial by deed or by silence is included. "Believe" *with the heart* follows, *v.* 13. Cf. the opposite, "confess with thy mouth" and "believe in thine heart" (Rom. x. 9, 10). **he also will deny us** (Matt. x. 33). 13. **believe not**—'if we are unbelieving' [*apistoumen*]; *continued unbelief:* a farther step than 'denying' (*v.* 12), which might be temporary. He remains *faithful* (Deut. vii. 9, 10). א Δ G (but not C, Vulgate) read '*for*.' He cannot possibly deny Himself. He can do all things consistent with His being God, supremely true, good, and wise. *He* cannot break His word, that He will deny those who deny Him, though *we* break our profession of faith in Him (Rom. iii. 3). Three things are impossible to God—to die, to lie, and to be deceived (*Augustine*, 'Symbolum ad Catechumenos,' i. 1) (Heb. vi. 18). This impossibility is not infirmity, but infinite majesty. Comfort is suggested to believers, that He is faithful to His promises to them; whilst apostates are stripped of their self-deceiving fancy, that because they change, Christ will. 14. **put . . . in remembrance** (Titus iii. 1; 2 Pet. i. 12). **them**—over whom thou presidest (Titus iii. 1). **charging** [*diamarturomenos:* the *dia* implies *interposition of witnesses*]—'testifying solemnly.' **before the Lord** (1 Tim. v. 21). **that they strive not about words**—'not to have a mere *logomachy*' (*vv.* 23, 24; 1 Tim. vi. 4), where vital matters are at stake (*vv.* 17, 18; Acts viii. 15). [A C *fg*, Vulgate, put a stop at "charging them before the Lord," and read the imperative, *Logomachei*, 'Strive not thou about words,' &c. But א Δ G, Syriac, support *logomachein*, as the English version.] **to no profit**—not qualifying "words;" but Greek neuter, in apposition with 'strive about words' '(a thing) profitable for nothing;' the opposite of "meet for the master's use" (*v.* 21). **to** (tending to) **the subverting**—the opposite of 'edifying' (building up) (2 Cor. xiii. 10). 15. **Study** [*Spoudason*]—'Be earnest.' **to show** [*parastesai*]—'present,' as in Rom. xii. 1. **thyself**—as distinguished from those whom Timothy was to charge (*v.* 14). **approved**—tested by trial [*dokimon*]: opposed to "reprobate" [*adokimon:* one who cannot stand the test] (Titus i. 16). **workman**—alluding to Matt. xx. 1, &c.: implying the *laboriousness* of the office (ch. iv. 5). **not to be ashamed**—by his work not being "approved" (Phil. i. 20). Contrast "deceitful workers," 2 Cor. xi. 13. **rightly dividing** [*orthotomounta*]—'rightly handling' (Vulgate); *lit.*, 'cutting straight,' as a road or furrow (*Theodoret*). Or, as a steward (1 Cor. iv. 1) *cutting* and *distributing* bread among

16 truth. But *p* shun profane *and* vain babblings; for they will increase
17 unto more ungodliness. And their word will eat as doth a ³ canker: of
18 whom is *q* Hymeneus and Philetus; who concerning the truth have erred,
saying *r* that the resurrection is past already; and overthrow the faith of
some.
19 Nevertheless *s* the foundation of God standeth ⁴ sure, having this seal,
t The Lord knoweth them that are his. And, Let every one that nameth
20 the name of Christ depart from iniquity. But in a great house there

A. D. 66.

p Tit. 1. 14.
³ Or,
  gangrene.
q 1 Tim. 1.20.
r 1 Cor. 15.12.
s Matt. 24.24.
  Rom. 8. 35.
⁴ Or. steady.
t Nah. 1. 7.

a household (*Vitringa*) (Luke xii. 42). But the "rightly" suits better the former image. LXX., Prov. iii. 6, and xi. 5, use it of 'making one's way:' so here, "the word of truth" is a road to be *laid out straightly:* Timothy must not deviate from this *right line* to the one side or other (Isa. xxx. 21; xl. 3); 'teaching no other doctrine' (1 Tim. i. 3). The same image appears in "increase" (note, *v.* 16). The opposite is 2 Cor. ii. 17, "corrupt the Word of God." **truth**—Greek, '*the* truth' (cf. *v.* 18). **16. shun** [*periistaso*]— 'stand clear of, and superior to.' **vain**—opposed to 'of the truth' (*v.* 15). **babblings** — loud: opposed to the temperate "word" (Titus iii. 9). **increase** [*prokopsousin*]—'advance;' *lit.*, 'strike forward:' an image from pioneers *cutting* away obstacles *before* an advancing army. They pretend *progress;* the only *progress* they *will make* is to greater impiety: the developed evil was as yet *future.* **more ungodliness** — Greek, 'a greater degree of impiety.' **17. will eat** [*nomen hexei*]— 'will have pasture.' Mortification is the image. They pretend to give rich spiritual *pasture* to their disciples: the only *pasture* is that of a spiritual cancer feeding on their vitals. **canker**— a *cancer* or *gangrene.* **Hymeneus** (note, 1 Tim. i. 20). After his excommunication he probably was re-admitted into the church and again troubled it. **18. erred** [*ēstochēsan*]—'missed the aim' (note, 1 Tim. vi. 21). **is past already**—has already taken place. The beginnings of Gnostic heresy already existed. They "wrested" (2 Pet. iii. 16) Paul's words (Rom. vi. 4; Eph. ii. 6; Col. ii. 12), "to their own destruction," as though the resurrection was merely the spiritual raising of souls from the death of sin. Cf. 1 Cor. xv. 12, &c., where he shows all our hopes rest on the literal reality of the resurrection. To believe it past (as the Seleucians or Hermians did, according to *Augustine,* Ep. cxix. 55, 'Ad Januarium,' sec. 4) is really to deny it. **overthrow**—subvert "the foundation" on which alone faith can rest (*v.* 19: cf. Titus i. 11).

19. Nevertheless. Notwithstanding the subversion of *their* faith, 'the firm foundation of (*i. e.*, laid by) *God* standeth' fast [*ho stereos themelios tou Theou hestōken:* the English version would require *ho themelios stereos*]. Taking for granted the *sureness* of the foundation, Paul predicates of it that it 'standeth fast.' The "foundation" here is not "the Church," the "ground" or basement support "of the truth" (1 Tim. iii. 15; as *Alford, Ellicott,* &c.), Christ Himself being the ultimate "foundation" (1 Cor. iii. 11). The Church being the "house" (*v.* 20), can hardly be also "the foundation:" which would make the house to be founded on the house. Rather, "the foundation" is "*the word of truth*" (*v.* 15), "the truth" (*v.* 18); in contrast to Hymeneus and Philetus' "*word,*" which 'eats as a canker' (*v.* 17). They pretend to build up, but really "overthrow," not indeed the word of truth, but "the faith of some" in it (*v.* 18). "Nevertheless, notwithstanding the overthrow of *their* faith, the object of faith, "the word of truth," 'the sure foundation of God stands fast.' The "house" (*v.* 20) is the elect whom "the Lord knoweth" (*acknowledgeth as His,* Matt. vii. 23; John x. 14; 1 Cor. viii. 3), and who persevere to the end, though others 'err concerning the truth' (Matt. xxiv. 24; John x. 28; Rom. viii. 38, 39; 1 John ii. 19). *Bengel* makes "the foundation" *the immoveable faithfulness of God* (to His promises to His elect). Though reprobates 'err concerning the truth' (*v.* 18), and deny *the faith,* God abates not *His faithfulness* (cf. *v.* 13). 'The word of the truth' inseparably *involves God's truthfulness to His Word:* the "foundation" is *primarily* 'the word of the truth,' including, *secondarily,* God's faithfulness to His promises to His own people. Not the word of truth as a bare theory, but as a *surely appropriated foundation* of faith and hope *standeth fast* as the safeguard against error (1 Pet. i. 22-25: contrast Ps. xi. 3; lxxxii. 5). It is the foundation *of God,* not the fiction of man: objective, not merely subjective. **having**—seeing it hath (*Ellicott*). **seal**—*inscription:* indicating *ownership* and *destination.* Inscriptions were often engraven on a "foundation" stone (Rev. xxi. 14) (*Alford*). The "seal" is the token of assurance or security attached to His word of truth ("the foundation of God"), with the legend on one side of its round surface, **The Lord knoweth** [*once for all:* aorist, *egno:* from eternity *knew;* not as if *the Lord* knoweth, but not *man;* for believers *do* know their being His (1 John v. 19; Rom. viii. 16); but the Lord knoweth so as to approve of and *acknowledge.* His *knowing* them as His involves His *making Himself known* to them (John x. 14, 27; Rev. ii. 17; Luke xiii. 25-27). Not God the Creator, but "the Lord," the Redeemer. His knowing is elective (Amos iii. 2); communicative, as it imparts the consciousness of God's recognition to the soul (Ps. xxxi. 7); distinctive (Ps. i. 6) between the godly and the ungodly: the LXX. (Num. xvi. 5), *egnō ho Theos tous ontas autou kai tous hagious,* to which Paul alludes] **them that are his**; on the obverse side, **Let every one that nameth** (as *His* Lord, Ps. xx. 7; Acts xxii. 16; or preacheth in His name, Jer. xx. 9) . . . **Christ depart** [*apostētō*]—'stand aloof.' **from iniquity** (Isa. lii. 11). In both clauses there may be an allusion to Num. xvi. 5, 26, LXX. God's part and man's part: God chooseth and "knoweth" His elect: the inner legend of the seal read by believers—a secret between God and their soul: they in faith, by the Spirit, 'depart from all iniquity:' the outer legend to be read by professors, as a test of sincerity and a warning against self-deception. He cannot be honoured with the name Christian who dishonours, by iniquity, the Author of the name. Blandina's refreshment amidst tortures was, 'I am a Christian, and *with us Christians no evil is done*' (*Eusebius,* 'Ecclesiastical History,' v. 1). Apostasy from the faith is soon followed by iniquity (ch. iii. 2-8, 13). **20. But**—answering the possible objection that thus "iniquity" is said to have place in the Church. **in a great house**—*i. e.,* the professing Church (1 Tim. iii. 15). Paul is

are not only vessels of gold and of silver, but also of wood and of earth;

21 and some to honour, and some to dishonour. If a man therefore purge himself from these, he shall be a vessel unto honour, sanctified, and meet for the master's use, *and* prepared unto every good work.

22 Flee also youthful lusts: but follow righteousness, faith, charity, peace,
23 with them that call on the Lord out of a pure heart. But foolish and
24 unlearned questions avoid, knowing that they do gender strifes. And the servant of the Lord must not strive; but be gentle unto all *men*, apt to
25 teach, [5] patient, in meekness instructing those that oppose themselves; if God peradventure will give them repentance to the acknowledging of
26 the truth; and *that* they may [6] recover themselves out of the snare of the devil, who are [7] taken captive by him at his will.

3 THIS know also, that [a] in the last days perilous times shall come.

A. D. 66.

[5] Or, forbearing.
Eph. 4. 2.
Col. 3. 13.
[6] awake.
Luke 15.17.
1 Cor.15.34.
Eph. 5. 14.
[7] taken alive.

CHAP. 3.
[a] Gen. 49. 1.
Isa. 2. 2.
Jer. 48. 47.
Jude 18.

speaking not of those without, but of the family of God (*Calvin*). So the parable of the sweep net (Matt. xiii. 47-49) gathering together of every kind, good and bad: as the good and bad cannot be distinguished whilst under the waves, but only when brought to shore, so believers and unbelievers continue in the same church, until the judgment makes the everlasting distinction. 'As in Noah's ark there were together the leopard and the kid, the wolf and the lamb, so in the Church the righteous and sinners, vessels of gold and silver, with vessels of wood and earth' (*Jerome*, 'Contra Luciferianos,' 302) (cf. Matt. xx. 16). **vessels of gold and of silver**—precious and able to endure fire. **of wood and of earth**—fragile, and soon burnt (1 Cor. iii. 12-15; xv. 47). **some . . . some**—the former . . . the latter. **to dishonour** (Prov. xvi. 4; Rom. ix. 17-23). **21. If a man therefore purge himself from these** [*Ean tis ekkatharē heauton apo toutōn*]—'If one (*ex. gr.*, thou, Timothy) purify himself (so as to separate) *from among these*' (*vessels* unto dishonour). 'No communion with impugners of fundamentals' (*Ellicott*), as the false teachers. Not, from "profane... babblings" (*v.*16). **sanctified**—set apart as consecrated to the Lord. **and meet**—'serviceable' (ch. iv. 11; Phile. 11); subserving God's [*euchreston*: 'profitable'] glory and their own salvation. א Δ G *f g* omit "and." C, Vulgate, have it. **the master's**—of "the house:" the Lord. Paul was such a vessel: once among those of earth, afterwards he became by grace one of gold. **prepared** (according as opportunities may occur) **unto every good work** (ch. iii. 17; Titus iii. 1). Contrast Titus i. 16. **22. Flee.** There are many lusts from which our safety is in *flight* (Gen. xxxix. 12). Avoid occasions of sin. The abstemious character of Timothy (1 Tim. v. 23) shows that not animal indulgences, but the impetuosity, self-confidence, hastiness, and vain-glory of young men (1 John ii. 14-16), are what *he* is warned against: the Spirit probably intended the warning to include *both* in its application to the Church *in general.* **also**—Greek, 'but:' in contrast to "every good work" (*v.* 21). **youthful.** Timothy was a youth (1 Tim. iv. 12). **righteousness**—the opposite of "iniquity;" *i. e.*, unrighteousness (*v.* 19; cf. 1 Tim. vi. 11). **peace, with**—rather no comma: "*peace with them* that call on the Lord," &c. (Heb. xii. 14). *Love* all men: but *peace* (*spiritual concord*, not mere absence of strife) can only be with those who call on the Lord (Rom. x. 12) sincerely (as contrasted with the false teachers, who had the mere form of godliness, ch. iii. 5, 8; Titus i. 15, 16; Rom. xii. 18). **23.** (Titus iii. 9). **unlearned** [*apaideutous*]—'undisciplined,' 'ignorant,' 'senseless:' not tending to the discipline of faith and morals (Prov. v. 23): in

contrast with "instructing" (*v.* 25), and "wise unto salvation" (ch. iii. 15). **24. not strive.** "The servant of the Lord" must imitate his master in not *striving contentiously*, though uncompromisingly contending for the faith (Jude 3; Matt. xii. 19). **gentle unto all men . . . patient** [*anexikakon*]—'patient of wrongs,' in respect to adversaries: *gentle* in words and demeanour, so as to occasion no evils; *patient*, so as to endure evils. **apt** (ready and skilled) **to teach**—patiently and assiduously, instead of noisily contending. **25.** **instructing** [*paideuonta*]—' disciplining,' *instructing with correction*, which those who deal in '*undisciplined* questions' need (notes, *v.* 23; 1 Tim. i. 20). **those that oppose themselves** [*antidiatithemenous*]—'oppositely affected:' those of a different opinion; not so much definite heretics here (Titus iii. 10) as those unsound about curious questions (1 Tim. vi. 4). **if God peradventure**—at any time: a faint hope [*me pote*]. **repentance**—preliminary to *the full knowledge* [*epignosin*] *of the truth* (1 Tim. ii. 4), their minds being corrupted (ch. iii. 8) and their lives immoral. The spiritual ignorance which prompts such "questions" is moral—has its seat in the *will*, not the intellect (John vii. 17). Therefore "repentance" is their first need. That God alone can "give" (Acts v. 31). **26. recover themselves** [*ananēpsōsin*]—'awake up to soberness;' viz., from the spiritual intoxication whereby they have fallen into "the snare of the devil" (note, 1 Cor. xv. 34). **the snare** (Eph. vi. 11; 1 Tim. iii. 7; vi. 9). **taken captive by him at his will**—*so as to follow the will of* 'THAT' [*ekeinou*] foe. [But *autou* and *ekeinou*, distinct pronouns (cf. ch. iii. 9), stand for "him" and "his;" and the Greek "taken captive," *ezogremenoi*, means not 'captivated *for destruction*,' but '*for being saved alive*,' as in Luke v. 10, 'catch men to life,' *zogrōn*: also there is no article before the Greek participle, which the English version, "who are taken captive," would require.] Translate, 'that they may awake,' &c., being taken as saved captives by him (the servant of the Lord, *v.* 24), so as to follow the will of HIM' ("God," *v.* 25). There are two evils—"the snare" and *sleep*—from which they are delivered: two goods to which they are translated, *awaking* and deliverance. Instead of Satan's thrall comes the free and willing *captivity of obedience* to Christ (2 Cor. x. 5). [*Ezōgrēmenoi*, perfect participle, marks the continuing *state: Zogrethentes* would have expressed the *act.*] God goes before, *giving repentance* (*v.* 25); then the work of His servant follows with success, leading the convert henceforth to live "to the will of God" (Acts xxii. 14; 1 Pet. iv. 2).

CHAP. III. 1-17.—COMING EVIL DAYS—SIGNS ALREADY—CONTRAST IN THE DOCTRINE AND LIFE

2 For men shall be lovers of their own selves, covetous, boasters, proud,
3 blasphemers, *b* disobedient to parents, unthankful, unholy, without natural affection, truce-breakers, ¹false accusers, incontinent, fierce, de-
4 spisers of those that are good, traitors, heady, high-minded, lovers of
5 pleasures more than lovers of God; having a form of godliness, but
6 denying the *c* power thereof: from such turn away. For *d* of this sort are they which creep into houses, and lead captive silly women laden
7 with sins, led away with divers lusts, ever learning, and never able
8 *e* to come to the knowledge of the truth. Now *f* as Jannes and Jambres withstood Moses, so do these also resist the truth: men of corrupt
9 minds, ²reprobate concerning the faith. But they shall proceed no

A D. 61.	
b Rom. 1. 30.	
1 Or, make-bates.	
c Isa. 29. 13. Eze. 33. 10-32.	
1 Tim. 5. 8.	
d Matt. 23. 14.	
e 1 Tim. 2. 4.	
f Ex. 7. 11.	
2 Or, of no judgment. Rom. 1. 28.	

OF PAUL, WHICH TIMOTHY SHOULD FOLLOW, AS EARLY TRAINED IN SCRIPTURE.

The indications of the future increase as we approach the close. After the Gospel doctrines have been put in the clearest light in the epistles, the shadows deepen on the history. The last inspired words of Sts. Paul, Peter, John, and Jude form the prelude to the Apocalypse. The gospels (Acts i. 1) set forth what "Jesus *began* both to do and teach" on earth; the Acts and epistles, what He went on to do and teach from heaven; the Apocalypse is the closing testimony of Jesus, ending with His return from heaven to earth. **1.** **also**—Greek, 'but:' in contrast to *present* evils (ch. ii. 25, 26). **last days**—preceding Christ's second coming (2 Pet. iii. 3; Jude 18). "The *latter* times" (1 Tim. iv. 1) refer to a period not so remote as "the *last* days"—viz., the long mediæval times of Papal and Greek antichristianity. **perilous** [*chalepoi*]—'*difficult*, embarrassing times,' in which it is difficult to know how to meet the dangers, spiritual and temporal. **shall come** [*enstesontai*]—'shall be present unexpectedly.' **2. men**—*generally* [HOI *anthropoi*]; the majority in the professing church. Cf. Rom. i. 29, &c., where much the same sins are attributed to *heathen:* it shall be a relapse into *virtual heathendom*, with its beast-like propensities; whence its symbol is "a beast" (Rev. xiii. 1, 11, 12, &c.; xvii. 3, 8, 11). **lovers of their own selves**—the opposite of 'love:' the root and essence of sin. **covetous** [*philarguroi*]—'money-loving' (the daughter of 'self-love'): distinct from [*pleonektēs:* Eph. v. 5] "covetous" (note, Col. iii. 5). The cognate substantive, 1 Tim. vi. 10, is translated, 'the *love of money* is a root of all evil.' **boasters** [*alazones*]—of having what they have not. **proud** [*huperephanoi*]—overweening, 'haughty,' *showing* themselves *above* their fellows: and so **blasphemers** of their heavenly Father: consequently **disobedient to parents** on earth. The character of the times is even to be gathered from the manners of the young (*Bengel*). **unthankful.** Ingratitude is sure to follow *disobedience to parents.* **unholy** [*anosioi*] (1 Tim. i. 9)—*the inwardly impure;* or else inobservant of the offices of piety. **3. without natural affection** [*astorgoi*]—love between parents and children, and similar relationships. **truce-breakers** [*aspondoi: asunthetoi* would be *truce-breakers*]—rather, as Rom. i. 31, "implacable." **false accusers** (1 Tim. iii. 11). **incontinent, fierce**—at once both soft and hard: *without control over themselves*, and inhuman [*anēmeroi:* 'untamed'] to others. **despisers**, &c.—'*no friends of good*' [*aphilagathoi*]: the opposite of 'a lover of good' (Titus i. 8). **4. Traitors** (Luke vi. 16; xxi. 16)—like Judas. **heady** [*propeteis*]—precipitate in action and passion. **high-minded** [*tetuphomenoi*]—'puffed up' with pride, as with smoke blinding them. **lovers of pleasures . . . God.** Love of pleasure destroys the love and sense of God. **5.**

form [*morphosin*]—the aiming at the intrinsic form [*morphe*]: outward semblance. **denying**—practically and habitually [*ērnēmenoi*]: a continuing *state:* '*having* denied.' **the power** (1 Cor. iv. 20)—the regenerating, sanctifying influence of it. **from such** [*kai toutous*]—'from these in particular,' about to arise, as distinguished from those already existing (ch. ii. 25), of whom there is a hope. The characters here are *types* of the last matured apostasy. **turn away**—implying that some of such characters, forerunners of the last days, were already in the Church. **6. of this sort**—Greek, 'of these' (*v.* 5). **creep into**—stealthily (2 Pet. ii. 1; Jude 4). **laden** [*sesoreumena*]: implying *multitude* and *disorderly confusion: heaped*] **with sins** (Isa. i. 4)—applying to the "silly women" (more easily misled than man, 1 Tim. ii. 14), whose consciences, burdened with sins, are a ready prey to the false teachers who promise relief if they will follow them. A bad conscience leads to shipwreck of faith (1 Tim. i. 19). **divers lusts**—not only animal, but passion for change in doctrine and manner: the running after fashionable men and fashionable tenets, drawing them in opposite directions (*Alford*). **7. Ever learning**—some novelty to suit their own fancies, from mere curiosity and instability, to the disparagement of old truths (Acts xvii. 21). **the knowledge** [*epignōsin*]—'the *perfect* knowledge,' the safeguard against unwarranted novelties. Gnosticism played especially on the credulity of the female sex (*Irenæus*, i. 13. 3; *Epiphanius*, 'Hær.' xxvi. 11): so Jesuitism. **8. Now**—Greek, "But." It is no wonder there should be now such opponents to the truth, for their prototypes existed of old (*Alford*). **Jannes and Jambres**—Egyptian magicians who resisted Moses (Exod. vii. 11, 22). In a point so immaterial, where Scripture had not recorded the names, Paul takes those which Jewish tradition, or more probably history, assigned. *Eusebius* ('Præparatio Evangelica') quotes from *Numenius*, 'Jannes and Jambres were *sacred scribes* (a lower order of priests in Egypt) deemed inferior to none in magic.' Tradition made them to perish in the Red Sea. *Hiller* derives Jannes from the Abyssinian 'trickster,' and Jambres *a juggler. Aan* was the second predecessor of Joseph's Pharaoh. *Ra*, in the ending of Jambres, means the *sun.* The names were known to the Greeks and Romans, independently of St. Paul's mention of them. They probably were in some old chronicle of Israel's history (*Smith*, 'Dictionary of the Bible;' *Pliny*, 'H. N.' xxx. 1; *Apuleius*, 'Apology' 24). **resist** —'withstand,' as before. They tried to rival Moses' miracles. So the false teachers shall exhibit lying wonders in the last days (Matt. xxiv. 24; 2 Thess. ii. 9; Rev. xiii. 14, 15: cf. Acts viii. 9; xiii. 6: xix. 13, 19). **reprobate** (Rom. i. 28)—'not abiding the test:' rejected on being tested (Jer. vi. 30). **9. they shall proceed no further**—

509

further: for their folly shall be manifest unto all *men*, as ^gtheirs also was.

10 But ³thou hast fully known my doctrine, manner of life, purpose, faith,
11 long-suffering, charity, patience, persecutions, afflictions, which came unto me ^hat Antioch, ⁱat Iconium, at Lystra; what persecutions I endured:
12 ^jbut out of *them* all the Lord delivered me. Yea, and ^kall that will live
13 godly in Christ Jesus shall suffer persecution. But evil men and seducers shall wax worse and worse, deceiving, and being deceived.
14 But continue thou in the things which thou hast learned and hast been

A. D. 66.

^g Ex. 8. 18.
³ Or. thou hast been a diligent follower of.
^h Ac's 13. 45.
ⁱ Acts 14. 2.
^j Ps. 34. 19.
^k Acts 14. 22.

though *for a time* (ch. ii. 16) 'they shall [*prokopsousin*] *proceed* (English version, 'increase') unto more ungodliness,' yet there is a *final* limit beyond which they shall not 'proceed further' (Job xxxviii. 11; Rev. xi. 7, 11). The assurance of final victory animates believers for present conflict. They shall "wax worse and worse" *themselves* (v. 13), but shall at last be for ever prevented from seducing *others*. 'Malice proceeds deeper down when it cannot extend itself' (*Bengel*). their folly [*anoia*]—*wicked* senselessness: 'dementation:' *wise* though they think themselves. shall be manifest [*ekdēlos*]—'brought forth from concealment into open day' (1 Cor. iv. 5). as theirs also was—when not only could they no longer rival Moses in sending boils, but the boils fell upon themselves: so as to the lice (Exod. viii. 18; ix. 11).

10. fully known [*parēkolouthēkas*]—'fully followed up;' traced, with a view to following me as thy pattern, so far as I follow Christ. Cf. Greek, Luke i. 3, "*having had perfect understanding of.*" Lois and Eunice would recommend him to *study fully* Paul's Christian course. He was not yet the companion of Paul at the apostle's persecutions in Antioch, Iconium, and Lystra (Acts xiii. 50; xiv. 5, 19), but is first mentioned as such, Acts xvi. 1-3. However, he was 'a disciple' already when introduced in Acts xvi. 1-3. As Paul calls him "my own son in the faith," he must have been converted by the apostle previously: perhaps in the visit to those parts three years before. Hence arose Timothy's knowledge of Paul's persecutions, which were generally spoken of in the churches there at the time of his conversion. The *incidental* allusion to them forms an *undesigned coincidence* between the history and the epistle, indicating genuineness, (*Paley's* 'Hor. Paul.') A forger of epistles from the Acts would never allude to Timothy's *knowledge* of persecutions, when that knowledge is not mentioned in the history, but is only arrived at by indirect inference; also the omission of *Derbe* here minutely agrees with the fact that in Derbe *no persecution* is mentioned in the history, though *Derbe and Lystra* are commonly mentioned together. His reason for mentioning his persecutions before Timothy became his companion, and not those subsequent, was because Timothy being familiar with the latter as an *eye-witness*, Paul needed not to remind him of them, but the former Timothy had *traced up* by information from others. Perhaps St. Paul's sufferings were what first impressed Timothy. If Timothy was converted at Lystra (as seems probable: see 'Introduction'), he may have witnessed the almost-completed martyrdom of Paul (Acts xiv. 19). doctrine—'teaching.' manner of life—'conduct' (1 Cor. iv. 17). purpose [*prothesei*]—elsewhere used of *God's* "purpose;" but here, as in Acts xi. 23, of Paul's 'purpose' of heart in cleaving unto the Lord:' my *set aim* in my apostolic function not selfish gain, but the glory of God. long-suffering—towards adversaries and the false teachers; towards

brethren in bearing their infirmities; towards the unconverted, and the lapsed when penitent (ch. iv. 2; 2 Cor. vi. 6; Gal. v. 22; Eph. iv. 2; Col. iii. 12). charity—*love* to all. patience—'brave endurance:' *patient continuance* in well-doing amidst adversities (v. 11; Rom. ii. 7). **11.** afflictions—'sufferings.' which [*hoia*]—'such as.' at Antioch—of Pisidia (Acts xiii. 14, 50, 51). Iconium (Acts xiv. 1-5). Lystra (Acts xiv. 6, 19). what—how grievous. They 'supposed Paul was dead.' out of them all the Lord delivered me (ch. iv. 17; Ps. xxxiv. 17, 19; 2 Cor. i. 10)—an encouragement to Timothy not to fear persecutions. **12.** Yea, and—an additional consideration. If Timothy *wishes to live godly in Christ*, he must make up his mind to encounter persecution. that will [*hoi thelontes*]—'all whose *will is* (decided) to live,' &c. So far from being a stumblingblock, Timothy should consider persecution a mark of the pious. So Luke xiv. 28, 33, "intending [*thelōn*] to build a tower . . . counteth the cost." live godly in (union with) Christ (Gal. ii. 20; Phil. i. 21). There is no godliness *out of* Christ. The world puts up with the mask of a religion which stops short there; but the piety which derives its vigour directly from Christ is as odious to modern Christians as it was to the ancient Jews (*Bengel*). shall suffer persecution—and will not decline it, (Matt. x. 22; John xv. 20; Gal. v. 11; 1 Thess. iii. 3: cf. Ecclus. ii. 1, &c.) *Bishop Pearson* proves the divine origination of Christianity from its success being inexplicable on the supposition of its human origin. Its doctrine was no way likely to command success. (1.) It condemned all other religions, some established for ages; (2.) It enjoins precepts ungrateful to flesh and blood—mortifying of the flesh, love of enemies, and bearing of the cross; (3.) It enforces these seemingly unreasonable precepts by promises seemingly incredible; not good things such as afford complacency to our senses, but such as cannot be obtained till after this life, and presuppose what seemed impossible, the resurrection; (4.) It predicts to its followers what would keep most men from embracing it, persecutions. **13.** Reason why persecutions must be expected, and these worse and worse as the end approaches. The breach between light and darkness, so far from being healed, shall be widened (*Alford*). seducers [*goetes*]—'conjurers.' Magic prevailed at Ephesus (Acts xix. 19), and had been renounced by many on embracing Christianity; but now, when Paul was writing to Ephesus, symptoms of a return to *conjuring* appeared: an undesigned coincidence. Probably *sorcery* will characterize the final apostasy (Rev. xiii. 15; xviii. 23; xxii. 15). wax worse [*prokopsousin epi*]—'advance in the direction of the worse.' Not contradictory to *v.* 9 (cf. note): there the *diffusion* of the evil was spoken of, here its *intensity* (*Alford*). deceiving, and being deceived. Beginning with deceiving others, they end with being deceived themselves.

14. But continue thou—whatever they do. Resuming the thread (*v.* 10). learned—from me

15 assured of, knowing of whom thou hast learned *them;* and that from a
child thou hast known the holy Scriptures, *l* which are able to make
16 thee wise unto salvation through faith which is in Christ Jesus. All
m Scripture *is* given by inspiration of God, and *is* profitable for doc-
17 trine, for reproof, for correction, for instruction in righteousness: that

A. D. 66.

l Ps. 119. 11.
John 20. 31.
Rom. 10. 17.
m Heb 3. 7.
2 Pet. 1. 20.

---

and thy mother and grandmother (chs. i. 5; ii. 2).
assured of—from Scripture (*v.* 15). **of whom**
[plural, *tinon*]. In ℵ A C G *f g*, 'from what teachers.'
Not only from me, but from Lois and Eunice.
Δ, Vulgate, singular [*tinos*], 'from what person.'
15. from a child [*apo brephous*]—'from *an infant.*'
It is in the tenderest age that the most lasting
impressions of faith may be made. Two grounds
of continuance in the truth : that it was from no
ordinary persons Timothy received it; and not
lately, but from infancy. **holy Scriptures**—the
Old Testament, taught by his *Jewess* mother: an
undesigned coincidence, ch. i. 5; Acts xiv. 1-3.
able—in themselves : though through men's own
fault they often do not *in fact* make men savingly
wise. **wise unto** (attaining) **salvation**—contrast
"folly" (*v.* 9); 'strivings about words,' "profane and vain babblings" (ch. ii. 14, 16). *Wise*
also in extending it to others. **through faith**—
as the *instrument*. Each *knows* divine things
only so far as *his own experience* extends. He
who has not faith has not *wisdom* or *salvation*.
which is in—*i. e.,* rests on Christ Jesus: in the
Old, as in the New Testament (Rev. xix. 10).
16. All Scripture [*pasa graphē*]—'Every Scripture;' *i. e.,* Scripture in its every part. However,
"all Scripture" is a justifiable translation, as the
technical use of "Scripture" is so notorious as
not to need the article (cf. Greek, Eph. iii. 15; ii.
21, in several MSS.). *Graphē* is never used of
any *writings* except the sacred Scriptures. The
position of the two Greek adjectives [*theopneustos
kai ōphelimos*] forbids taking the one as an epithet,
the other as predicate (as *Ellicott*), 'Every Scripture
given by inspiration of God is *also* profitable.'
The adjectives are so closely connected that as
one is a predicate, the other must be so too. This
construction is not, as *Ellicott's,* harsh. [*Theopneustos*] 'God-inspired' is found nowhere else.
Most of the New Testament books were written
when Paul wrote this his latest epistle : so he
includes in 'All Scripture [every portion of the
hiera grammata, "the Holy Scriptures"] is God-
inspired,' not only the *Old Testament,* in which
alone Timothy was taught when a child (*v.* 15),
but the New Testament books, according as they
were recognized in churches, having men gifted
with "discerning of spirits," and so able to distinguish really inspired utterances, persons, and
writings (1 Cor. xii. 10; xiv. 37) from spurious.
'All Scripture is God-inspired, *and therefore* useful :' because *we* see no utility in any portion, it
does not follow it is not God-inspired. It is *useful*
because *God-inspired;* not *God-inspired because*
useful. One reason for the Greek article not
being before "Scripture," may be that, if it had,
it *might* have seemed to limit "Scripture" to the
hiera grammata, "Holy Scriptures" (*v.* 15) *of the
Old Testament,* whereas the assertion is general:
"*all* Scripture" [cf. *pasa prophēteia graphēs,* 2 Pet.
i. 20]. Plenary inspiration of every part of the
Scriptures, as a living organic whole, is here set
forth. The translation, 'all Scripture that is God-
inspired is also useful,' would imply that there is
some *Scripture* which is not God-inspired. But the
exclusive New Testament sense of "Scripture"
forbids this : and who would need to be told that
"all divine Scripture is profitable?" Heb. iv. 13
would then have to be rendered, 'All naked

things are *also* open to the eyes of Him,' &c.: so
also 1 Tim. iv 4 (*Tregelles* 'On Daniel'). *Knapp*
defines inspiration, 'An extraordinary divine
agency upon teachers whilst giving instruction,
whether oral or written, by which they were
taught how and what they should speak or write'
(cf. 2 Sam. xxiii. 1; Acts iv. 25; 2 Pet. i. 21).
The *inspiration* gives God's *sanction* to all the
words of Scripture, though they be the utterances
of the individual writer, and only in special cases
revealed directly (1 Cor. ii. 13). *Inspiration* is
predicated of the *writings,* "All Scripture," not
the persons. The question is not *how* God has
done it: it is as to the *word,* not the *men* who
wrote it. All the sacred writings are everywhere
inspired, though not all alike matter of special
revelation; even the *words* are divinely sanctioned,
as Jesus used them (*ex. gr.,* in the temptation,
and John x. 34, 35) for deciding all questions of
doctrine and practice. There are in Scripture
degrees of *revelation,* but not of *inspiration.* The
sacred writers did not even always know the
full significancy of their own God-inspired words
(1 Pet. i. 10-12). Verbal inspiration is not
mechanical dictation, but 'all Scripture is (so)
inspired by God' that everything in it—its narratives, prophecies, citations, ideas, phrases,
words—are such as He saw fit to be there. The
present condition of the text is no ground against
the *original text* being inspired, but is a reason
why we should use all critical diligence to restore
the original. Inspiration may be accompanied by
revelation or not ; but it is as much needed for
writing *known* doctrines or facts authoritatively
as for communicating *new* truths (*Tregelles*). The
omission of "is," I think, marks that not only
the Scripture *then* existing, but what was *still to
be written till the canon should be completed,* is
included as *God-inspired.* The Old Testament
was the schoolmaster to bring us to Christ; so it
is appropriately designated as "able to make
wise unto salvation :" *wisdom* being appropriated
to a knowledge of the relations between the Old
and New Testaments, and opposed to the sophis-
tical *wisdom* of the false teachers (1 Tim. i. 7, 8).
doctrine — *teaching dogmatic* truths which we
cannot otherwise know. St. Paul so uses the Old
Testament (Rom. i. 17). **reproof** [ℵ A C G read
elegmon for *elenchon* (Δ)]—*confuting* error: including *polemical* divinity. As an example of this
use of the Old Testament, cf. Gal. iii. 6, 13, 16.
'Doctrine and reproof' comprehend *speculative*
divinity. Next follows *practical:* Scripture is
profitable for (1) *correction* [*epanorthosis*], 'setting
one right.' Cf. the Old Testament used for this,
1 Cor. x. 1-10, and *instruction* [*paideian*], 'disciplining,' as a father his child. Note, ch. ii. 25;
Eph. vi. 4; Heb. xii. 5, 11, "training" by instruction, warning, and chastisements. Cf. an example
of this use of the Old Testament, Deut. xiii. 5; 1
Cor. v. 13. The irreverent are 'confuted,' the
frail 'set right' (*Grotius*). Scripture 'teaches'
the ignorant, as the Ethiopian eunuch; 'confutes' the evil, as Elymas; 'sets right' the erring,
as David; 'disciplines' the godly, as Paul's
thorn in the flesh. Thus theology is complete in
Scripture. Since Paul is speaking of Scripture
in general, the only *general* reason why, in order
to *perfecting* the godly (*v.* 17), it should extend to

511

[n] the man of God may be perfect, [4] throughly furnished unto all good works.

4 I CHARGE *thee* therefore before God, and the Lord Jesus Christ, who shall judge the quick and the dead at his appearing and his king-
2 dom; preach the word; be instant in season, out of season; reprove,
3 [a] rebuke, exhort, with [b] all long-suffering and doctrine. For the time will come when they will not endure [c] sound doctrine; but after their own lusts shall they heap to themselves teachers, having itching ears;
4 and they shall turn away *their* ears from the truth, and [d] shall be turned
5 unto fables. But watch thou in all things, endure afflictions, do the work of [e] an evangelist, [1] make full proof of thy ministry.

A. D. 66.
[n] 1 Tim. 6.11.
[4] it. 1. 9
4 Or,
perfected.
ch. 2. 21.

CHAP. 4.
[a] Tit. 1. 13.
[b] 1 Tim. 4.13.
[c] 1 Tim. 1.10.
[d] 1 Tim. 1. 4.
[e] Acts 21. 8.
1 Or, fulfil.

every department of revealed truth, must be that it was intended to be the *complete and sufficient rule.* See Article VI., 'Common Prayer Book.' **in** —'instruction *which is in [tēn en]* righteousness,' as contrasted with the "instruction" in worldly rudiments (Col. ii. 20, 22). **17. man of God** (note, 1 Tim. vi. 11). **perfect, throughly furnished** —'thoroughly perfected' [*artios — exērtismenos*]; *complete* (unmutilated) in the adaptation of parts and aptitude for use: [*teleios*] absolutely *perfect.* If the Scripture be not perfect itself, how can it make the man of God perfect? But he is *perfectly accoutred* out of Scripture for his work, whether as a minister (cf. ch. iv. 2 with ch. iii. 16) or a layman. No oral tradition is needed.

CHAP. IV. 1-22.—Solemn Charge to Timothy to be Zealous, for Times of Apostasy are at Hand, and the Apostle is near his Triumphant End—Request to come and bring Mark, as Luke alone is with Paul, the Others having Gone; also his Cloak and Parchments—Warns Timothy against Alexander—Tells what befell him at his First Defence—Greetings—Benediction.

1. charge [*diamarturomai*] —' adjure.' **therefore.** Omitted in א A C Δ G *fg*,Vulgate. **the Lord Jesus Christ.** א A C Δ G *fg*, Vulgate, read simply 'Christ Jesus.' **shall judge.** His *commission* from God is mentioned (Acts x. 42); his resolution to execute his commission (1 Pet. iv. 5); the execution here. **at his appearing.** So C. But א A Δ G *fg*,Vulgate, read 'and' [*kai ten*], for [*kata ten*], 'at.' '(I charge thee *before God, &c.*), and *by* His appearing.' **and his kingdom**—to be manifested at His appearing, when the saints shall reign with Him. His kingdom is real now, but not visible. It shall then be also VISIBLE (Luke xxii. 18, 30; Rev. i. 7; xi. 15; xix. 6). *Now* He reigns *in the midst of His enemies,* expecting till they shall be overthrown (Ps. cx. 2; Heb. x. 13). *Then* He shall reign with His adversaries prostrate. **2. Preach** [*Kēruxon*]—' Herald.' After "Scripture" (ch. iii. 16) comes 'preaching,' to be based on it. [The term for discourses in the synagogue was *Daraschoth;* the corresponding Greek, *dielegeto* (implying dialectical style, dialogue, and discussion, Acts xvii. 2, 17; xviii. 4, 19), is applied to *discourses* in the Christian Church.) *Justin Martyr* ('Apology' 2) describes public worship: 'On Sunday all meet; the writings of the apostles and prophets are read; then the president delivers a discourse; after this all stand up and pray; then there is offered bread and wine and water; the president likewise prays and gives thanks, and the people solemnly assent, saying, Amen.' The bishops and presbyters had the right to preach; but they sometimes called on deacons, and even laymen. *Eusebius* ('Ecclesiastical History,' vi. 19): in this the church imitated the synagogue (Luke iv. 17-22; Acts xiii. 15, 16). **be instant**— *i. e.,* urgent in thy whole ministry. **in season,**
512

out of season—*i. e.,* at all seasons; whether they regard your speaking as seasonable or unseasonable. It will be "in season" to the willing, "out of season" to the unwilling. 'As the fountains, though none draw from them, still flow on, and the rivers, though none drink of them, still run, so must we do all on our part in speaking, though none give heed to us' (Chrysostom, 'Homily' 30, vol. v., p. 221). There is included the idea of times, whether seasonable or unseasonable, *to Timothy himself:* night as well as day (Acts xx. 31), in danger as well as in safety, in prison as well as when at large, not only in church, but everywhere and on all occasions, whenever and wherever the Lord's work requires it. **reprove**—convict. **with**—Greek, 'IN (the *element* in which the "reproving," &c., ought to have place) all long-suffering (ch. ii. 24, 25; iii. 10) and *teaching.*' Cf. ch. ii. 24, "apt to teach." ["Doctrine" here is *didache;* but in ch. iii. 16, *didascalia. Didache* is the *act; didascalia,* the *substance* or *result* (*Ellicott*).] **3. For**—Make the most of the present time: for the time will come when, &c. **they**—professing Christians. **sound doctrine**—the [*tēs*] sound (note, 1 Tim. i. 10) doctrine [*didascalias*]; viz., of the Gospel. **after their own lusts.** Instead of regarding the will of God, they dislike being interrupted in their selfish [*idias*] lusts by true teachers. **heap**—one on another: an indiscriminate mass : a *rabble* of false teachers. Variety delights itching ears. 'He who despises sound *teaching* leaves sound *teachers;* they seek instructors like themselves' (*Bengel*). It is the corruption of the people that creates priestcraft (Exod. xxxii. 1). **to themselves**—to suit their depraved tastes ['*populus vult decipi, et decipiatur:*' the people wish to be deceived, so let them be deceived (1 Ki. xii. 27-32; Hos. iv. 9).] **itching**—after teachers who give pleasure (Acts xvii. 19-21), and do not offend by truths grating to the ears. They tickle the levity of the multitude (*Cicero*), who come as to a theatre to hear what will delight their ears, not (*Seneca*, 'Ep.' x. 8) what will do them good. 'Itch in the ears is as bad as in any other part of the body, and perhaps worse' (*South*). **4. The ear** brooks not what is opposed to the lusts. **turned** [*ektrapēsontai*] (1 Tim. i. 6). It is a righteous retribution that when men *turn away* (not ignorantly, but wilfully) from the truth, they should be *turned to* fables (Jer. ii. 19). **fables** (1 Tim. i. 4). **5. But . . . thou**—in contrast to the false teachers (ch. iii. 10). I am no longer on the spot to withstand these things: be thou a worthy successor, no longer depending on me for counsel, but swimming without the corks (*Calvin*). **watch** [*nēphe*]—'with the wakefulness of one *sober* **in all things**—on all occasions and under all circumstances (Titus ii. 7). **evangelist**—a missionary bishop or preacher subordinate to the apostles (Acts xvi. 3). **make full proof of**—fulfil all its requirements (Acts xii. 25; Rom. xv. 19; Col. iv. 17.

6 For I am now ready to be offered, and the time of my departure is at
7 hand. I have fought a good fight, I have finished *my* course, I have
8 kept the faith : henceforth there is laid up for me *ᶠ* a crown of righteousness, which the Lord, the righteous Judge, shall give me at that day;
and not to me only, but unto all them also that love his appearing.
9, Do thy diligence to come shortly unto me: for *ᵍ* Demas hath forsaken
10 me, having loved *ʰ* this present world, and is departed unto Thessalonica;
11 Crescens to Galatia, Titus unto Dalmatia. Only Luke is with me.
ⁱ Take Mark, and bring him with thee: for he is profitable to me for the
12 ministry. And *ʲ* Tychicus have I sent to Ephesus. The cloak that I

A. D. 66.

ᶠ Ps. 31. 19.
Ma't 6. 19.
Rev. 2. 10.
ᵍ Col. 4. 14.
Phile 24.
ʰ 1 John 2.
15.
ⁱ Acts 12. 25..
Acts 15 37.
Col. 4. 10.
ʲ Acts 20. 4.
Eph. 6. 12.

6. [*Edē spendomai*] 'For I am already being made a *libation:*' appropriate to the shedding of *his blood.* Every sacrifice had an initiatory libation on the victim's head (note, cf. Phil. ii. 17): answering to Paul's present sufferings. A motive to stimulate Timothy to faithfulness—the imminent departure of Paul: it is the end that crowns the work (*Bengel*). As the time was indicated to Peter, so to Paul (2 Pet. i. 14). my departure [*analuseōs*]—'loosing anchor' (note, Phil. i. 23). *Dissolution.* 7. 'I have striven the good strife of faith' [*egonismai*], includes, besides a *fight,* any competitive *contest—ex. gr.,* the race-course (1 Cor. ix. 24, &c.; Heb. xii. 1, 2; 1 Tim. vi. 12). I have finished my course—realizing his former resolution, Acts xx. 24; Phil. iii. 12-14. kept (*inviolate*) the faith—committed to me as a believer and an apostle (cf. ch. i. 14; Rev. ii. 10; iii. 10). 8. a crown—rather, as Greek, '*the* crown:' not of withering leaves; not awarded by human umpire, nor before human spectators, but angels. The "Henceforth" marks the decisive moment: he regards his state in a threefold aspect :—(1.) The past, *I have fought;* (2.) The immediately present, *there is laid up [reserved; apokeitai] for me;* (3.) The future, *the Lord will give in that day* (*Bengel*). A garland used to be bestowed at the Greek national games on the successful competitor in wrestling, &c. (cf. Jas. i. 12; 1 Pet. v. 4). of righteousness—*in recognition of righteousness* wrought in Paul by God's Spirit: prepared for the righteous: at the same time a crown *which consists in righteousness. Righteousness will be its own reward* (Rev. xxii. 11). Cf. Exod. xxxix. 30. A man is justified gratuitously by Christ's merits through faith; when he is so justified, God accepts his works, and honours them with a reward, not their due, but given of grace. 'So great is God's goodness that He wills that His people's works should be merits, though they are merely his own gifts' ('Ep.' Pope *Celestine I.* 12). give [*apodōsei*] —'award' in righteous requital as 'Judge' (Acts xvii. 31; 2 Cor. v. 10; 2 Thess. i. 6, 7). at that day—not until His appearing (ch. i. 12). The blessed sentence on the "brethren" of the Judge, who sit with Him on His throne, is, in Matt. xxv. 40), taken for granted as *already* awarded, when that affecting those who benefited them is being passed at the general judgment after the millennium (*Bengel*). The elect who reign with Christ in the millennium are fewer than the latter. The *righteous* heavenly Judge stands in contrast to the unrighteous earthly judges who condemned Paul. me—individual appropriation [*ēgapēkosin*]. them also that love—have loved and do love: *habitual* desire for Christ's appearing: the test of *faith* (cf. Heb. ix. 28). They have it not who dread Christ's appearing. A sad contrast, *v.* 10,"*loved* this present world."
9. (*V.* 21; ch. i. 4, 8.) Timothy should come to be a comfort to Paul; also to be strengthened by Paul, for the Gospel work after Paul's decease.

10. Demas—contracted from Demetrius: once a "fellow-labourer" of Paul along with Mark and Luke (Col. iv. 14; Phile. 24). His motive seems to have been love of worldly ease and home comforts [*ton nun aiōna : this present world-course*]: a mournful contrast to "love His appearing," and disinclination to brave danger with Paul (Matt. xiii. 20-22). [*Enkatelipen: left me behind in* my trouble.] *Chrysostom* says Thessalonica was his *home.* Galatia. א C read 'Gaul.' But Δ Δ G *f g,* Vulgate, &c., "Galatia." Titus. He must have therefore left Crete after 'setting in order' the church-affairs there (Titus i. 5). Dalmatia—part of the Roman province Illyricum, on the Adriatic. Paul had written to him (Titus iii. 12) to come in the winter to Nicopolis (in Epirus), intending probably in the spring to preach in the adjoining province of Dalmatia. Titus probably had gone of his own accord thither to carry out the apostle's intention, which was interrupted by his arrest. "Is departed" hardly accords with supposing he was *sent* to Dalmatia by St. Paul. Paul speaks only of his personal attendants having forsaken him: he had still friends among the Roman Christians who visited him (ch. iv. 21), though afraid to stand by him at his trial (*v.* 16). 11. Luke (Col. iv. 14; Phile. 24). He went with Paul on his second missionary journey, Acts xvi. 10; again with him to Asia, xx. 6, and to Jerusalem, xxi. 15; and was with him during his captivity at Cesarea, xxiv. 23; and at Rome, xxviii. 16. Contracted from *Loukanos,* indicating he was a *freedman.* Take [*analabōn*]—'take up' on thy journey (Acts xx. 13, 14). John Mark was probably in, or near, Colosse, as in the epistle to the Colossians (Col. iv. 10), written two years before, he is mentioned as about to visit them. Timothy was now absent from Ephesus, somewhere in the interior of Asia Minor; hence he would be sure to fall in with Mark on his journey. he is profitable to me for the ministry—by his knowledge of Latin, so as to preach at Rome. He was Peter's son by conversion, and was with his spiritual father when 1 Pet. v. 13 was written. He accompanied Paul and his relative (*anepsios*) Barnabas on their first missionary journey (Acts xii. 25). Mark had been under a cloud for having forsaken Paul at a critical moment in his missionary tour (Acts xv. 37-40; xiii. 5, 13), and was the cause of dissension between Paul and Barnabas. Timothy subsequently occupied the same post under Paul. Hence Paul appropriately wipes out the past censure by high praise of Mark, and guards against Timothy's making self-complacent comparisons between himself and Mark, as though superior (cf. Phile. 24). Demas apostatizes. Mark returns to the right way, and is no longer unprofitable, but is profitable for the Gospel ministry (Phile. 11). Egypt and Alexandria were the final field of his labours. 12. And—Greek, 'But.' Thou art to come to me, *but* Tychicus I have sent to Ephesus, to supply Timothy's place

513

left at Troas with Carpus, when thou comest, bring *with thee*, and the books, *but* especially the parchments.

14 Alexander ᵏthe coppersmith did me much evil : ᶦthe Lord reward him
15 according to his works: of whom be thou ware also; for he hath greatly withstood ² our words.

16 At my first answer no man stood with me, but all *men* forsook me :
17 ᵐ*I pray God* that it may not be laid to their charge. Notwithstanding ⁿthe Lord stood with me, and strengthened me; that by me the preaching might be fully known, and *that* all the Gentiles might hear: and I
18 was delivered °out of the mouth of the lion. And ᴾthe Lord shall deliver me from every evil work, and will preserve *me* unto his heavenly kingdom: to whom *be* glory for ever and ever. Amen.

A. D. 66.

ᵏ Acts 19. 33.
1 Tim. 1.20.
ᶦ 2 Sam. 3.39.
Ps. 28. 4.
Rev. 18. 6.
² Or, our preachings.
ᵐ Acts 7. 60.
ⁿ Ps. 109. 31.
Matt 10.19.
° Ps. 22. 21.
2 Pet. 2. 9.
ᴾ Ps. 121. 7.

in presiding over the church there in his absence (cf. Titus iii. 12). *Ellicott* explains, 'I need one profitable for the ministry: I had one in Tychicus (Eph. vi. 21), *but* he is gone.' Tychicus had been already sent, during Paul's first imprisonment, to Asia to comfort the hearts of believers there (Eph. vi. 21; Col. iv. 7). The omission of 'to thee' is against the view that Tychicus bore this epistle. **13. cloak that I left**—probably obliged to leave it in a hurried departure from Troas. **Carpus**—a faithful friend, entrusted with so precious deposits. The mention of his "cloak," so far from being unworthy of inspiration, is a graphic touch which sheds a flood of light on the last scene of Paul, on the confines of two worlds: in this wanting a cloak to cover him from the "winter" cold (cf. *v.* 21), in that covered with the righteousness of saints, 'clothed upon with his house from heaven' (*Gaussen*). So the inner vesture and outer garment of Jesus, Paul's master, suggest most instructive, thought, (John xix.) [*Phelonē*: a long, thick, sleeveless cloak, with only an opening for the head: *the travelling cloak*, Roman, *pœnula*, Grecised. Some explain, a travelling case for clothes or books (*Conybeare*, ii. 499).] **books**—which he was anxious to transmit to the faithful, that they might have the teaching of his writings when he should be gone. **especially the parchments**—containing perhaps some of his inspired epistles. "The books" [*ta biblia*] were written on *papyrus*.

14. Alexander the coppersmith—or 'smith,' some think. Perhaps the same as the Alexander (1 Tim. i. 20; note there) at Ephesus. Excommunicated then, he subsequently was restored, and now vented his malice, because of his excommunition, in accusing Paul before the Roman judges, whether of incendiarism or of introducing a new religion. See 'Introduction.' He may have been the Alexander put forward by the Jews in the tumult at Ephesus (Acts xix. 33, 34). **reward.** A C Δ G א read '*shall* reward' [*apodosei* for *apodōē*]. Personal revenge certainly did not influence the apostle (*v.* 16, end: cf. Ps. cxxxix. 21). **15. withstood** [*anthestē*, G: *antestē*, A C, *past.* But Δ, *withstands*, *anthesteke*] **our words**—the arguments for our common faith. Believers have a common cause.

16. At my first answer—*i. e.*, 'defence' in court: at my first public examination. Timothy knew nothing of this till Paul now informs him. But during his *former* imprisonment at Rome Timothy was with him (Phil. i. 1, 7). He must have been set free before the persecution in A. D. 64, when the Christians were accused of causing the conflagration in Rome; for had he been a prisoner then, he would not have been spared. The tradition (*Eusebius*, ii. 25) that he was finally *beheaded* accords with his not having been put to death in the persecution, A. D. 64, when *burning*

to *death* was the mode of executing the Christians, but subsequently. His "first" trial in his second imprisonment was probably on the charge of complicity in the conflagration: his absence from Rome may have been the ground of his acquittal on that charge. [*Non liquet*] 'Not proven' was the verdict: then followed an adjournment [*ampliatio*], during which he writes: his final condemnation was probably on the charge of introducing a new and unlawful religion into Rome. **stood with me** [*sumparegeneto*]—'came forward with me' as a patron or advocate. **may (it) not be laid to their** (THEIR, emphatical) **charge**—for they were intimidated: *their* drawing back was not from bad disposition so much as fearing: it will be laid to the charge of those who intimidated them. Still Paul, like Stephen, would doubtless have prayed for his persecutors themselves (Acts vii. 60). **17.** the Lord—the more because *men*, even friends (Ps. xxvii. 10), deserted me. **stood with me**—stronger than 'came forward with me' (*v.* 16). **strengthened** [*enedunamōsen*]—'*put strength* within me.' **by me**—'through me:' through my means. One single occasion is often of the greatest moment. **the** (Gospel) **preaching might be fully known** [*plerophorēthē*]—performed (note, *v.* 5). **that all the Gentiles**—present at my trial "might hear" the Gospel. Rome was the capital of the Gentile world, so that a proclamation of the truth to the Romans, in the bar of the highest earthly tribunal, was likely to go forth to the whole Gentile world. **I was delivered out of** [*ek*] **the mouth of the lion**—viz., Satan, the roaring, devouring lion (Luke xxii. 31; 1 Pet. v. 8). I was prevented falling into his snare (ch. ii. 26; Ps. xxii. 21; 2 Pet. ii. 9). *V.* 18 agrees with this interpretation, "the Lord shall *deliver* me *from* [*apo*] *every evil* work"—viz., both from evil and the Evil One, as the Greek of the Lord's Prayer means. The change from [*ek*] "out of" to [*apo*] "from," points to *removal from* all the evil efforts [*ponērou*, expressing *active* wickedness] against him (*Ellicott*). It was not deliverance from Nero (called *the lion*) which he rejoiced in, for he did nor fear *death* (*vv.* 6-8) (and it is doubtful whether Nero was then at Rome), but deliverance from the temptation, through fear, to deny his Lord. *Ellicott*, less appositely, 'from the *greatest danger*' (1 Cor. xv. 31). **18. And the Lord shall.** Hope draws its conclusions from the past to the future (*Bengel*). There is no anticipation of his being delivered out of dangers (*v.* 6), but of his being through them delivered from evil for ever. **will preserve me** [*sosei*]—'will save,' 'bring me safe into.' Jesus is the Lord and Deliverer (Phil. iii. 20; 1 Thess. i. 10). **heavenly kingdom** [*tēn basileian autou tēn epouranion*]—'His kingdom, which is a heavenly one:' *heavenly* now, about hereafter to be *on earth* also, (Rev. xx. and xxi.) **to whom, &c,**—Greek, 'to whom be *the* glory unto the ages

19   Salute ^q Prisca and Aquila, and the household ^r of Onesiphorus.
20   Erastus ^s abode at Corinth: but Trophimus ^t have I left at Miletum sick.
21   Do thy diligence to come before winter.
     Eubulus greeteth thee, and Pudens, and Linus, and Claudia, and all
22   the brethren.   The Lord Jesus Christ *be* with thy spirit.   Grace *be* with
you.   Amen.

The second *epistle* unto Timotheus, ordained the first bishop of the church of the Ephesians, was written from Rome, when Paul was brought before [3] Nero the second time.

A. D. 66.

q Acts 18. 2.
r 2 Tim. 1.16.
s Acts 19. 22.
  Acts 20. 4.
3 Cesar Nero, or, the emperor Nero.

---

of ages.' The very *hope* produces a doxology: how much greater will be the doxology which the *enjoyment* shall produce (*Bengel*).

19. Prisca (Priscilla) **and Aquila**—at Ephesus (Acts xviii. 2, 3, 18; Rom. xvi. 3, 4; 1 Cor. xvi. 19, written from Ephesus, where therefore Aquila and Priscilla must then have been). What a life of holy zeal was theirs, at Corinth, Syria, Ephesus, Rome! **household of Onesiphorus.** If dead at the time, the "household" would not have been called "the household *of Onesiphorus.*" He was probably *absent* (note, ch. i. 16). **20.** To depict his desertion, he informs Timothy that Erastus stayed behind at Corinth, his residence, of which city he was "chamberlain," or city steward and treasurer (Rom. xvi. 23); and Trophimus he left behind at Miletus sick (Acts xx. 4; xxi. 29). Erastus the missionary (Acts xix. 22) can hardly be identical with Erastus the chamberlain, whose office would not admit absence on missionary journeys. This verse is irreconcilable with Paul's present imprisonment being the *first;* for he did not pass by Corinth or Miletus on his way to Rome to be imprisoned for the first time. As Miletus was near Ephesus, there is a presumption that Timothy was *not* at Ephesus when Paul wrote, or he would not need to inform Timothy of Trophimus lying sick in his neighbourhood. However, Trophimus may not have been still at Miletus when Paul wrote, though he had left him there on his way to Rome. Prisca and Aquila were likely to be at *Ephesus* (*v.* 19), and he desires Timothy to *salute them:* so also Onesiphorus' household (ch. i. 18). Paul had not the power of healing at will (Acts xix. 12), but as the Lord allowed him. **21. before winter**—when a voyage, in ancient navigation, would be out of the question: also, Paul would need his "cloak" against the winter (*v.* 13).

Pudens . . . Claudia—afterwards husband and

wife (according to *Martial*, iv. 13; xi, 54): he a Roman knight, she a Briton, surnamed *Rufina*. *Tacitus* ('Agricola,' 14) mentions that territories in South-east Britain were given to a British king, Cogidunus, in reward for his fidelity to Rome, A. D. 52, whilst Claudius was emperor. In 1772 a marble was dug up at Chichester, mentioning Cogidunus with the surname Claudius, added from his patron, the emperor's name; and *Pudens* in connection with Cogidunus, doubtless his father-in-law. His daughter would be Claudia, who was probably sent to Rome for education, as a pledge of the father's fidelity. Here she was under the protection of Pomponia, wife of Aulus Plautius, conqueror of Britain. Pomponia was accused of *foreign superstitions,* A. D. 57 (*Tacitus,* 'Annals,' iii. 32)—probably *Christianity.* She perhaps was the instrument of converting Claudia, who took the name *Rufina* from her, that being a cognomen of the Pomponian gens (cf. Rom. xvi. 13, *Rufus,* a Christian). Pudens in *Martial* and in the Chichester inscription appears as a *pagan.* Perhaps he or his friends concealed his Christianity through fear. Tradition represents *Timothy,* a son of Pudens, as taking part in converting the Britons. **Linus**—put third; therefore not at this time, as afterwards, *bishop.* His name here inserted between Pudens and Claudia implies the two were not yet married. "Eubulus" is identified by some with Aristobulus, who, with his converts, is said to have been the first evangelist of Britain. 'Paul himself,' says *Clement,* 'visited *the farthest west* (perhaps Britain, certainly *Spain*), and was martyred under the rulers at Rome,' who were Nero's vicegerents in his absence from the city. The greetings imply that at Rome, as elsewhere, Timothy gained the affections of those among whom he ministered. **22. Grace be with you**—plural; *i. e.,* thee and the members of the Ephesian and neighbouring churches.

TITUS.

1 PAUL, a servant of God, and an apostle of Jesus Christ, according to the faith of God's elect, *a*and the acknowledging of the truth *b*which
2 is after godliness; ¹in hope of eternal life, which God, that cannot lie,
3 promised *c*before the world began; but hath in due times manifested his word through preaching, which is committed unto me *d*according to the
4 commandment of God our Saviour; to *e*Titus, *mine* own son after the common faith: Grace, mercy, *and* peace, from God the Father and the Lord Jesus Christ our Saviour.
5 For this cause left I thee in Crete, that thou shouldest *f*set in order the things that are ²wanting, and *g*ordain elders in every city, as I had
6 appointed thee: if any be blameless, the husband of one wife, having

A. D. 65.

CHAP. 1.
a 2 Tim. 2. :'5.
b 1 Tim. 6. 3.
1 Or. For.
c 2 Tim. 1. 9.
Rev. 17. 8.
d Acts 9. 15.
e 2 Cor. 2. 13.
Gal 2. 3.
f 1 Cor.11 34.
2 Or. left undone.
g Ac:s 14. 21.

CHAP. I. 1-16.—ADDRESS—FOR WHAT END TITUS WAS LEFT IN CRETE—QUALIFICATIONS FOR ELDERS—GAINSAYERS NEEDING REPROOF.

1. servant of God—not found elsewhere in the same connection. In Rom. i. 1 it is "servant of Jesus Christ" (Gal. i. 10; Phil. i. 1: cf. Acts xvi. 17; Rev. i. 1; xv. 3, Moses). In Rom. i. 1 there follows "called to be an *apostle*." So here the general designation, "*servant* of GOD," is followed by the special 'and further [*de*] *apostle* of *Jesus Christ*.' The expression of his apostolic office answers, in both epistles, to the design, and is a comprehensive index to the contents. The peculiar form here would never have proceeded from a forger. **according to the faith**—'for' [*kata* marks *destination; eis, immediate* purpose; *pros, ultimate* purpose (*Ellicott*)]: *with a view to* subserve the faith, the object of my apostleship (cf. *vv.* 4, 9; Rom. i. 5). **God's elect**—for whose sake we ought to endure all things (2 Tim. ii. 10). This election has its ground, not in any merit of the elected, but in the purpose of God from everlasting (Rom. viii. 30-33; 2 Tim. i. 9: cf. Luke xviii. 7; Eph. i. 4; Col. iii. 12). Acts xiii. 48 shows that the faith of the elect rests on the divine foreordination: they do not become *elect* by their faith, but receive *faith* (Eph. ii. 8), and so become believers, because *elect*. **and the acknowledging of the truth**—'and (for promoting) the *full knowledge* [*epignosin*] of the truth' (Eph. i. 13). **after godliness**—*i. e.*, which *leads to piety:* opposed to the knowledge which has not practical piety for its object (*vv.* 11, 16; 1 Tim. vi. 3). Not *truth* in general, but sanctifying truth, is the aim of Christianity. "Godliness," or 'piety' [*eusebeia*], is a term peculiar to the pastoral epistles; the apostle having in them to combat doctrine tending to 'ungodliness' (2 Tim. ii. 16: cf. ch. ii. 11, 12). **2. In hope of eternal life**. That whereon rests my aim as an apostle to promote *the elect's faith and full knowledge of the truth* is the "hope of eternal life" (ch. ii. 13; iii. 7; Acts xxiii. 6; xxiv. 15; xxviii. 20). **that cannot lie** (Rom. iii. 4; xi. 29; Heb. vi. 18). **promised before the world began** —abbreviated for '*purposed* before the world began [*pro chronōn aioniōn*, "before eternal times"], and *promised* in time,' the promise (Gal. iii. 19) springing from the eternal purpose; as in 2 Tim. i. 9, 10 the *gift* of grace was the result of the eternal *purpose* "before the world began." **3. in due times** [*kairois idiois*]—'in *its* (or *His*) *own seasons:*' the seasons appropriate to, and fixed by God for it (Acts i. 7). **manifested**—implying

516

that the 'promise' (*v.* 2; Gen. iii. 15; Gal. iii. 8) had lain hidden in His eternal purpose heretofore (cf. Rom. xvi. 25, 26; Col. i. 26). **his word**—*i. e.*, "eternal life" (*v.* 2; John. v. 24; vi. 63; xvii. 3, 17). **through preaching**—Greek, '*in* (the Gospel) preaching (cf. 2 Tim. iv. 17), with which I was entrusted.' **according to**—in pursuance of, cf. 1 Tim. i. 1): not by my own impulse. **of God our Saviour** [*tou Soteros hemōn Theou*]—'of our *Saviour God.*' *God* is predicated of *our Saviour*, cf. Luke i. 47; Jude 25. Also Ps. xxiv. 5; Isa. xii. 2; xlv. 15, 21; LXX. [*ho Theos Soter*]. Applied to Jesus, *v.* 4; ch. ii. 13; iii. 6; 2 Tim. i. 10. **4. Titus, mine own son**—'my *genuine* [*gnesio*] child' (1 Tim. i. 2); *i. e.*, converted by my instrumentality (1 Cor. iv. 17; Phile. 10). **after**—a genuine son *in respect to* (in virtue of) the faith *common* to us both; comprising in a common brotherhood Gentiles, as Titus, and Jews, as Paul (2 Pet. i. 1; Jude 3). **mercy.** Omitted in א Δ G *f g*, Vulgate. But A supports it (notes, cf. 1 Tim. 1, 2; 2 Tim. i. 2). Similarities of phrase abound in the pastoral epistles. **the Lord Jesus Christ.** So G Δ (omitting "Christ"). But A C א, Vulgate, omit "Lord." **our Saviour**—found thus added to "Christ" only in Paul's *pastoral epistles* and 2 Pet. i. 1, 11; ii. 20; iii. 18).

5. left I thee—'*behind*' (*Alford*), when I left the island: *not* implying *permanence* of commission (cf. 1 Tim. i. 3) **in Crete**—now Candia. **set in order** [*epidiorthosē*]—'that thou mightest *follow up* (the work begun by me), setting right the things wanting,' which I was unable to complete through the shortness of my stay in Crete. Christianity, doubtless, had long existed there: some Cretians heard Peter's preaching on Pentecost (Acts ii. 11). The number of Jews in Crete was large (*v.* 10); and it is likely that those scattered in the persecution of Stephen (Acts xi. 19) preached to them, as they did to those of Cyprus, &c. Paul also was there on his voyage to Rome (Acts xxvii. 7-12). So the Gospel was sure to reach Crete early. But until Paul's later visit, after his first imprisonment at Rome, the Cretian Christians were without proper church organization. This Paul began, and commissioned (before leaving Crete) Titus to go on with: now he reminds him of that commission. **ordain** [*katastētēs*]— 'constitute.' **in every city** [*katapolin*]—'from city to city.' **as I had appointed thee** [*dietaxamēn*] —"set in order:" 'directed thee:' prescribing the *act*, as also the *manner*, which latter includes the qualifications required in a presbyter. The

7 faithful children, not accused of riot, or unruly. For a bishop must be blameless, *h* as the steward of God; not self-willed, not soon angry, *i* not
8 given to wine, no striker, not given to filthy lucre; but a lover of hospi-
9 tality, a lover of ³ good men, sober, just, holy, temperate; holding fast the faithful word ⁴ as he hath been taught, that he may be able *j* by sound doctrine both to exhort and to convince the gainsayers.
10 For there are many unruly and vain talkers and deceivers, *k* specially
11 they of the circumcision: whose mouths must be stopped, who subvert *l* whole houses, teaching things which they ought not, for filthy lucre's
12 sake. One *m* of themselves, *even* a prophet of their own, said, The Cre-
13 tians *are* alway liars, evil beasts, slow bellies. This witness is true. Wherefore rebuke them sharply, that they may be sound in the faith;

A. D. 65.
h Matt. 24. 45.
1 Cor. 4. 1, 2
i Lev. 10. 9. Pro. 31. 4, 5. Isa. 28. 7.
³ Or. good things.
⁴ Or, in teaching.
j 1 Tim. 1. 10.
k Acts 15. 1.
l Matt. 23. 14.
m Acts 17. 28.

"elders" here are called 'bishops,' *v.* 7. *Elder* marks the *dignity* in relation to the college of presbyters; *bishop*, the *duties* of office in relation to the flock. From the unsound state of the Cretian Christians we see the danger of the want of church government. The appointment of presbyters was designed to check idle *talk*, by setting forth the 'faithful word.' 6. (notes, 1 Tim. iii. 2-4) The thing dwelt on as the requisite in a bishop is a good reputation among those over whom he is to be set. The immorality of the Cretian professors rendered this a necessary requisite in one to be a *reprover:* their unsoundness in doctrine also made needful great stedfastness in the faith (*vv.* 9, 13). **having faithful** (believing) **children.** He who could not bring his children to faith, how shall he bring others? (*Bengel.*) **not accused**—not merely not riotous, but " not (even) accused of riot" [*asotias*]: 'dissolute life' (*Wahl*). **unruly**—*insubordinate:* opposed to "in subjection." 7. **For a bishop must** [*anupotakta*]. The emphasis is on *must.* '' blameless,' for the very idea of a "bishop" (an overseer of the flock: here substituted for 'presbyter,' *v.* 5, to express his *duties*) involves the *necessity* for blamelessness, if he is to influence the flock. *Ellicott* quotes *Bishop Pearson* ('Minor Works,' i. 271-278), that episcopal government was 'sub-apostolis, ab-apostolis, in-apostolis.' **steward of God.** The greater the master the greater the virtues required in His servant (*Bengel*) (1 Tim. iii. 15): the church is God's house, over which the minister is a steward (Heb. iii. 2-6; 1 Pet. iv. 10, 17). Ministers are not merely *church* officers, but *God's* stewards: church government is of divine appointment. **not self-willed** [*authadē*]— 'self - pleasing:' unaccommodating to others. Contrast *v.* 8: so Nabal (1 Sam. xxv.), self-loving, imperious. Such a spirit incapacitates for *leading* a willing flock, instead of *driving.* **not soon angry**—at what one ought not, at those with whom one ought not, and more than they ought. **not given to wine** (notes, 1 Tim. iii. 3, 8). **not given to filthy lucre**—not making the Gospel a means of gain (cf. Gen. xiv. 23, Abraham; 2 Ki. v. 16, Elisha: contrast Acts viii. 18-20): in opposition to those "teaching . . . for filthy lucre's sake" (*v.* 11; 1 Tim. vi. 5; 1 Pet. v. 2). 8. **lover of hospitality**—needed especially in those days (Rom. xii. 13; Heb. xiii. 2; 1 Pet. iv. 9; 3 John 5). Christians travelling from one place to another were received and forwarded on their journey by brethren. **lover of good men** [*philagathon*]—'a lover of (all that is) good,' men or things (Phil. iv. 8, 9). **sober**—towards *one's self* [*sōphrona*]: 'discreet' (note, 1 Tim. ii. 9). **just**- towards *men.* **holy**—pure towards *God* (note, Eph. iv. 24; 1 Thess. ii. 10). **temperate**—'one having his passions, tongue, hand, and eyes at command' (*Chrysostom*): 'continent.' 9. **Holding fast**—firmly to

(cf. Matt. vi. 24; Luke xvi. 13). **the faithful**—true and trustworthy (1 Tim. i. 15). **word as he hath been taught**—'the faithful word (which is) according to the (apostolic) teaching' (cf. 1 Tim. iv. 6, end; 2 Tim. i. 13; iii. 14). **by**—'to exhort *in* [*en*] doctrine (*instruction*) which is sound:' the element in which his *exhorting* is to have place. On "sound" (peculiar to the pastoral epistles), see 1 Tim. i. 10; vi. 3. **convince** [*elenchein*]—'confute' (*v.* 13).
10. **unruly** [*anupotaktoi*]—'insubordinate.' **and.** So Δ G *f g*, Vulgate. Omitted in א A C. 'There are many unruly persons, vain talkers, and deceivers:' "unruly" being predicated of both. **vain talkers**—opposed to "holding fast the faithful word" (*v.* 9). "Vain jangling" (1 Tim. i. 6): "foolish questions . . . unprofitable and vain" (ch. iii. 9). The source of the evil was corrupted Judaism (*v.* 14). There were many Jews in Crete (*Josephus*): so the Jewish leaven remained in some after conversion. (Insinuating) **deceivers**—*lit.*, 'deceivers of minds' [Gal. vi. 3: *phrenapata*]. 11. **mouths must be stopped** [*epistomizein*]—'muzzled,' 'bridled' as an unruly beast (Ps. xxxii. 9). **who** [*hoitines*]—'(seeing they are) such as;' or 'inasmuch as they' (*Ellicott*). **subvert whole houses**—'overthrowing' their "faith" (2 Tim. ii. 18). 'They are the devil's levers by which he subverts the houses of God' (*Theophylact*). **for filthy lucre** (1 Tim. iii. 3, 8; vi. 5). 'The Cretans alone of men consider no gain to be dishonourable' (*Polybius*, 'History,' vi. 46. 3). 12. **One**—Epimenides, priest, bard, and seer of Gnossus, in Crete, about 600 B. C., sent for to purify Athens from the pollution occasioned by Cylon. The words here are probably from his treatise '*concerning oracles.*' Paul also quotes from two other heathen writers, *Aratus* (Acts xvii. 28) and *Menander* (1 Cor. xv. 33), but does not honour them so far as even to mention their names. **of themselves . . . their own**—which enhances his authority as a witness. 'To Cretanise' was proverbial for *to lie*; as 'to Corinthianise' for *to be dissolute.* **alway liars**—not merely *at times*, as every natural man is. Contrast *v.* 2, "God that *cannot* lie." They love "fables" (*v.* 14); even the heathen poets laughed at their lying assertion that they had in their country Jupiter's sepulchre. **evil beasts**—savage, cunning, greedy. Crete was *a country without wild beasts. Epimenides'* sarcasm was, that its human inhabitants supplied their place. **slow bellies**—indolent through pampering their bellies. *They themselves* are called "bellies," for that is the member for which they live (Rom. xvi. 18; Phil. iii. 19). 13. **This witness is** —(though coming from a Cretian) "is true." **sharply**—gentleness would not reclaim so perverse offenders. **that they**—that *those seduced* by the false teachers may be brought back to *soundness* in the faith. Their malady is strifes about words and questions

14 not giving heed to Jewish fables, and commandments [n] of men, that turn
15 from the truth. Unto [o] the pure all things *are* pure: but unto them
that are defiled and unbelieving *is* nothing pure; but even their mind
16 and conscience is defiled. They [p] profess that they know God; but in
works they deny *him*, being abominable, and disobedient, and unto every
good work [5] reprobate.

2, BUT speak thou the things which become [a] sound doctrine: that the
2 aged men be [1] sober, grave, temperate, sound in faith, in charity, in
3 patience. The [b] aged women likewise, that *they be* in behaviour as
becometh [2] holiness, not [3] false accusers, not given to much wine, teachers
4 of good things; that they may teach the young women to be [4] sober, to
5 love their husbands, to love their children, *to be* discreet, chaste, keepers
at home, good, [c] obedient to their own husbands, that the word of God
6 be not blasphemed. Young men likewise exhort to be [5] sober-minded.
7 In all things showing thyself a pattern of good works: in doctrine

A. D. 65.
[n] Isa. 29. 13.
[o] Luke 11.39.
[p] Eze. 33. 31.
[5] Or. void of judgment.

CHAP. 2.
[a] 1 Tim. 6. 3.
[1] Or. vigilant.
[b] 1 Pet. 3. 3.
[2] Or. holy women
[3] Or. make-bates.
[4] Or. wise.
[c] Col. 3. 18.
[5] Or. discreet.

(ch. iii. 9; 1 Tim. vi. 4). **14. Not giving heed to** —viz., "they" (*v.* 13). **Jewish fables** (notes, 1 Tim. i. 4; iv. 7; 2 Tim. iv. 4). These formed the transition to subsequent Gnosticism; as yet the error was but profitless, not tending to godliness, rather than openly opposed to the faith. **commandments of men**—as to *ascetic* abstinence (*v.* 15; Mark vii. 7-9; Col. ii. 16, 20-23; 1 Tim. iv. 3); here resting not on the law, but on men's invention. **that turn from the truth**—whose characteristic is this (2 Tim. iv. 4). **15. all things**—external, "are pure" in themselves; the distinction of *pure* and *impure* is not in the things, but in the disposition of him who uses them: whereas the "commandments of men" (*v.* 14) forbad certain things as if impure intrinsically. "To the pure"—*i. e.*, those purified in heart by *faith* (Acts xv. 9; 1 Tim. iv. 4); all outward things are pure; open to their use. The impurity of the impure is communicated to all outward things that they use. Sin alone touches and defiles the soul (Matt. xxiii. 26; Luke xi. 41). **nothing pure**—either within or without (Rom. xiv. 20, 23). **mind**—their mental sense. **conscience**—their moral consciousness of the conformity or discrepancy between their motives and acts on the one hand, and God's law on the other. A conscience and a mind defiled are the source of the errors opposed in the pastoral epistles (1 Tim. i. 19; iii. 9; vi. 5). **16. They profess**—i. e., *make a profession* acknowledging God. They have *theoretical* knowledge of God, but *practically* know Him not. **deny him** —the opposite of the previous "profess" or 'confess' Him (1 Tim. v. 8; 2 Tim. ii. 12; iii. 5). So often as we are conquered by sins, we deny God (*Jerome*). **abominable**—themselves, though laying such stress on avoiding abomination from outward things (cf. Lev. xi. 10-13; Rom. ii. 22). **disobedient**—to God (ch. iii. 3; Eph. ii. 2; v. 6). **reprobate**—rejected as worthless *when tested* (notes, Rom. i. 28; 1 Cor. ix. 27; 2 Tim. iii. 8).

CHAP. II. 1-15.—How to Exhort various Classes—God's Grace in Christ our Grand Incentive to Live Godly.

1. But . . . thou—in contrast to the reprobate seducers, ch. i. 11, 15, 16. 'He deals more in exhortations, because those intent on useless questions needed chiefly to be recalled to a holy life; for nothing so allays men's wandering curiosity as the being brought to recognize practical duties' (*Calvin*). **speak**—without restraint, with open mouth: contrast ch. i. 11, "mouths must be stopped." **2. sober** [*nephalious*]—'vigilant,' as *sober* men alone can be (1 Tim. iii. 2). But "sober" here answers to "not given to . . . wine" (*v.* 3; ch.

i. 7). **grave**—'dignified.' **temperate** [*sōphronas*]— 'self-restrained,' 'discreet' (ch. i. 8; 1 Tim. ii. 9). **faith, in charity** (love), **in patience**—combined in 1 Tim. vi. 11. "Faith, *hope*, charity" (1 Cor. xiii. 13). "Patience" [*hupomone: brave endurance*] is supported by "hope" (1 Cor. xiii. 7; 1 Thess. i. 3). The grace which especially becomes *old men;* the fruit of ripened experience derived from trials overcome (Rom. v. 3). **3. behaviour** [*katastemati*]—'deportment:' 'the gait, movements, expression of countenance, speech, silence' (*Jerome*). **as becometh holiness** [*hieroprepis*]—'as becometh women consecrated to God' (*Wahl*): Christian women being priestesses unto God (Eph. v. 3; 1 Tim. ii. 10). 'Observant of sacred decorum' (*Bengel*). **not false accusers**—slanderers: a besetting sin of elderly women. **given to much wine**—the besetting sin of the Cretians (ch. i. 12). [*Dedoulomenas*, 'enslaved to much wine.'] Addiction to wine is *slavery* (Rom. vi. 16; 2 Pet. ii. 19). **teachers**—in private: not public (1 Cor. xiv. 34; 1 Tim. ii. 11, 12): influencing for good the younger women by precept and example. **4. teach . . . to be sober** [*sophronizōsin*]—'self-restrained,' 'discreet:' *v.* 2, "temperate" [*sophronas*]. But see note; cf. note, 2 Tim. i. 7. *Ellicott*, 'That they school the young women to be lovers of their husbands,' &c. (the foundation of all domestic happiness). It was judicious that Titus, a young man, should admonish the young women, not directly, but through the elder women. **5. keepers at home** [*oikourous*]—'guardians of the house.' So C H *f g*, Vulgate. But א A Δ G read [*oikourgous*] 'workers at home:' active in household duties (Prov. vii. 11; 1 Tim. v. 13). **good**—kind, *beneficent* (Matt. xx. 15; Rom. v. 7; 1 Pet. ii. 18). Not churlish and niggardly, whilst thrifty as housewives; not harsh to servants. **obedient** [*hupotassomenas*]—"submitting themselves," as in Eph. v. 21-24, notes. **their own**—marking the duty of subjection which they owe them as being *their own* husbands (Col. iii. 18). **blasphemed** —'evil spoken of.' That no reproach may be cast on the Gospel, through the inconsistencies of its professors (*vv.* 8, 10; Rom. ii. 24; 1 Tim. v. 14; vi. 1). **6. Young** [*tous neoterous*]—in contrast to "the aged men" (*v.* 2). 'The younger men.' **sober-minded**—self-restrained. 'Nothing is so hard at this age as to overcome undue pleasures' (*Chrysostom*). **7. In**—*with respect to* all things. **thyself a pattern**—though but a young man. All teaching is useless unless one's example confirm his word. **in doctrine**—*in* thy ministerial *teaching* (showing) *uncorruptness;* i. e., *untainted* sincerity [*aphthorian*, א A Δ, for *adiaphthorian* (C)] (cf. 2

518

8 *showing* uncorruptness, gravity, ᵈsincerity, sound ᵉspeech, that cannot be condemned; ᶠthat he that is of the contrary part may be ashamed, having no evil thing to say of you.'

9   *Exhort* servants to be obedient unto their own masters, *and* to please

10 *them* well in all *things;* not ⁶answering again; not purloining, but showing all good fidelity; that they may adorn the doctrine of God our Saviour in all things.

11 For the grace of God ⁷that bringeth salvation ᵍhath appeared to all

12 men, teaching us that, ʰdenying ungodliness and worldly lusts, we should

13 live soberly, righteously, and godly, in this present world; looking for that blessed hope, and the glorious appearing of the great God and our

A. D. 65.

ᵈ Eph. 6. 24.
ᵉ 1 Tim. 6. 3.
ᶠ Neh. 5. 9.
⁶ Or, gain-
saying.
⁷ Or that
bringeth
salvation
to all men,
hath
appeared.
ᵍ John 1. 9.
ʰ Luke 1. 75.

Cor. xi. 3). As "gravity," &c., refers to Titus' manner (dignified seriousness in delivery), so "uncorruptness" to his *doctrine.* **sincerity** [*aptharsian*]—Δ. But omitted in א A C G, Vulgate. **8. speech**—discourse in public and private. **he that is of the contrary part**—the adversary (ch. i. 9; 2 Tim. ii. 25), whether heathen or Jew. **may be ashamed**—put to confusion by the power of truth and innocence (cf. v. 5, 10; 1 Tim. v. 14; vi. 1). **no evil thing**—*in our acts* or *demeanour.* **of you.** So A. But א C Δ G *f g* read 'of us,' Christians.

9. servants—'slaves.' **to please them well**—*to be complaisant in everything:* to have that zealous desire to gain the master's good-will which anticipates the master's wish, and does even more than is required. The reason for the frequent injunctions to slaves to *subjection* (Eph. vi. 5, &c.; Col. iii. 22; 1 Tim. vi. 1, &c.; 1 Pet. ii. 18) was, that in no rank was there more danger of the *spiritual* equality and freedom of Christians being misunderstood than in that of slaves. It was natural for the slave who became a Christian to forget his place, and put himself on a *social* level with his master. Hence the charge for each to abide in the sphere in which he was when converted (1 Cor. vii. 20-24). **not answering again**—*in contradiction* to the master [*antilegontas*] (*Wahl*). **10. Not purloining** [*nosphizomenous*]—'*Not appropriating*' what does not belong to one. 'Keeping back' dishonestly or deceitfully (Acts v. 2, 3). **showing** —in acts. **all**—all possible, every form of, good; really; not in mere appearance (Eph. vi. 5, 6). 'Heathen do not judge of the Christian's doctrines from these, but from his actions and life' (*Chrysostom*). Men will write, fight, and even die for religion; but how few *live* for it! **God our Saviour** [*Tou Soteros hemōn Theou*]—'of our Saviour God;' *i. e.*, God the Father, the originating Author of salvation (cf. note, 1 Tim. i. 1; ii. 3). God deigns to have His Gospel-doctrine adorned even by slaves, regarded by the world as no better than beasts of burden. 'Though the service be rendered to an earthly master, the honour redounds to God, as the servant's good-will flows from the fear of God' (*Theophylact*). His love in being "our Saviour" is the strongest ground for adorning His doctrine by our lives: the force of "For" in *v.* 11.

11. the grace of God—God's *gratuitous favour* in redemption. **hath appeared** |*epephanē*|—'hath been *made to shine from above*' (Isa. ix. 2; Luke i. 79), 'hath been *manifested*' (ch. iii. 4), after having been long hidden in God's loving counsels (Col. i. 26; 2 Tim. i. 9, 10). The grace of God was embodied in Jesus, "the *brightness* of the Father's glory," the manifested "Sun of righteousness," "the Word made flesh." The Gospel dispensation is "the day" (1 Thess. v. 5, 8: there is a double "appearing," that of "grace," that of "glory," *v.* 13: cf. Rom. xiii. 12). [Translate, *hē*
519

soterios pasin anthropois, 'the grace . . . that *bringeth salvation to all men* hath,' &c., not "appeared to all men:" for "us" follows (1 Tim. ii. 4; iv. 10). Hence God is called "*our Saviour*" (*v.* 10). *Jesus* means the same.] **to all**—cf. the different classes (*vv.* 2-9): even to servants; to us Gentiles, once aliens from God. Hence arises our obligation to all (ch. iii. 2). **12. Teaching** [*paideuousa*]—'disciplining us.' Grace is connected with disciplining chastisements (1 Cor. xi. 32; Heb. xii. 6, 7). Children need disciplining. The *discipline* which grace exercises *teaches* us to *deny worldly lusts, and to live soberly, &c., in this present world* [*aion, course* of things], wherein self-discipline is needed, since its spirit is opposed to God (ch. i. 12, 16; 1 Cor. i. 20; iii. 18, 19): in the coming world we may gratify every desire without need of self-discipline, because all desires there will be conformable to the will of God. **that** [*hina*]—'in order that:' the end of the 'disciplining' is '*in order that* . . . we may live soberly,' &c. This is lost by the *translation*, "*teaching* us." **denying . . . lusts** (Luke ix. 23). The aorist [*arnesamenoi*], 'denying *once for all*.' We deny them when we withhold our consent from them, refuse the delight they suggest, and the act to which they solicit; nay, tear them up by the roots out of our soul (*Bernard*, 'Sermon' 11). **worldly lusts**—the [*tas:* all] lusts of the world (Gal. v. 16; Eph. ii. 3: 1 John ii. 15-17; v. 19). The *world* [*cosmos*] will not come to an end when this present *age* [*æon*] or world-course shall. **live soberly, righteously, and godly**—the *positive* side of the Christian character; as "denying . . . lusts," the *negative.* "Soberly," i. e., *with self-restraint*, in relation to *one's self:* "righteously," or *justly*, towards our *neighbour;* "godly," towards *God* (not merely *amiably* and *justly*, but something higher, with reverential love toward God). These three comprise our 'disciplining' in *faith* and *love*, from which he passes to *hope* (*v.* 13). **13.** (Phil. iii. 20, 21). **Looking for**—with constant *expectation* [*prosdechomenoi*], "waiting for" (Luke ii. 25), and joy (Rom. viii. 19): the antidote to worldly lusts; the stimulus to "live in this present world" conformably to this *expectation.* **that**—Greek, 'the.' **blessed**—bringing blessedness (Rom. iv. 7, 8). **hope**—*i. e.*, object of hope; including *glory, righteousness,* and *resurrection* (Rom. viii. 24; Gal. v. 5; Col. i. 5). **the glorious appearing.** One Greek article connects closely "hope" and "appearing" (the *hope* being about to be realized only at the *appearing* of Christ). '*The* blessed hope *and manifestation* (cf. note, *v.* 11) *of the glory.*' [*Epiphaneian*] 'Manifestation' is translated "brightness," 2 Thess. ii. 8. As His "coming" [*parousia*] expresses the fact, so Epiphany, or 'manifestation,' His personal *visibility* when He shall come. There are two Epiphanies— the one of *grace* (*v.* 11), the other of *glory.* **the great God and our Saviour Jesus** [*Tou megalou*

14 Saviour Jesus Christ: who gave himself for us, that he might redeem us from all iniquity, *i* and purify unto himself *j* a peculiar people, zealous
15 of good works. These things speak, and exhort, and rebuke with all authority. Let no man despise thee.

3 PUT them in mind to be subject to principalities and powers, to obey
2 magistrates, *a* to be ready to every good work, to *b* speak evil of no man,
3 to be no brawlers, *but* gentle, showing all meekness unto all men. For we ourselves also were sometimes foolish, disobedient, deceived, serving divers lusts and pleasures, living in malice and envy, hateful, *and* hating one another.
4 But after that the kindness and *1* love of God our Saviour toward man

A. D. 65.	
i Mal 3. 3.	
Matt. 3. 12.	
Acts. 15. 9.	
Heb. 9. 14.	
Jas. 4. 8.	
j Ex. 15. 16.	
Deut. 7. 6.	
Deut. 14. 2.	
CHAP. 3.	
a Heb. 13. 21.	
b Ex. 20. 16.	
Eph. 4. 31.	
1 Or, pity.	

Theou kai Soteros]. One article combines "God" and "Saviour," which shows that both are predicated of one and the same Being. 'Of Him who is at once the great God and our Saviour.' Also (2.) "appearing" [*Epiphany*] is never by Paul predicated of God the Father (John i. 18), or even of 'His glory' (as *Alford* explains it), but *invariably* of CHRIST's coming, to which (at His first advent, cf. 2 Tim. i. 10) the kindred "appeared" [*epephanee*], *v.* 11, refers (1 Tim. vi. 14, 16; 2 Tim. iv. 1, 8). Also (3.) in the context (*v.* 14) there is no reference to the Father, but to Christ alone; and here there is no occasion for reference to *the Father.* Also (4.) the expression "great God," is uncalled for as to the Father, but is appropriate to Christ, *the glory of His appearing* being contrasted with His humility in "giving Himself for us," as "the true God" is predicated of Christ (1 John v. 20). The phrase occurs nowhere else in the New Testament, but often in the Old. Deut. vii. 21; x. 17, predicated of Jehovah, their manifested Lord, who led the Israelites through the wilderness, the Second Person in the Trinity. Believers now look for the manifestation of His glory, as they shall share in it. Even the Socinian explanation, making "the great God" to be *the Father,* "our Saviour," *the Son,* places God and Christ *on an equal relation to* "the glory" of the future appearing: incompatible with the notion that Christ is not Divine: it would be blasphemy so to couple any created being with God. **14.** **gave himself**—Himself, His whole self, the greatest gift ever given (*Ellicott*) (Gal. i. 4; Eph. v. 25). **for us** [*huper hemōn*]—'in our behalf.' **redeem us** [*lutrosētai*]—'ransom us *from* bondage at *the price* of His precious *blood*' (Eph. i. 7; Matt. xx. 28). An appropriate image in addressing bond servants (*vv.* 9, 10). **from all iniquity** [*anomias*]—'lawlessness,' the essence of sin; viz., 'transgression of the law' (1 John iii. 4), in bondage to which we were till then. The aim of redemption was to redeem us, not merely from the penalty, but the being of iniquity. He reverts to the "teaching," or *disciplining* effect of the grace of God that bringeth salvation (*vv.* 11, 12). **peculiar**—*peculiarly His own,* as Israel was: treasured up as such [*Periousion.* 1 Pet. ii. 9, *laos eis peripoiesin;* Hebrew, *'am segullah,* Exod. xix. 5; Deut. vii. 6; note, Eph. i. 14]. **zealous**—in doing and promoting "good works." **15. with all authority** [*epitages*]—'authoritativeness' (ch. i. 13; Matt. vii. 29, Jesus). **Let no man despise thee.** Speak with such vigour as to command respect (1 Tim. iv. 12): that no one may *think himself above* [*periphroneito*] admonition.

CHAP. III. 1-15.—WHAT TO TEACH CONCERNING CHRISTIANS' BEHAVIOUR TOWARDS THE WORLD—HOW TO TREAT HERETICS—WHEN AND WHERE TITUS IS TO MEET PAUL—SALUTATION—CONCLUSION.

1. Put them in mind—as they are in danger of 520

forgetting their duty, though knowing it. The opposition of Christianity to heathenism, and the Jews' tendency to rebellion against the Roman empire, might lead many in Crete to forget practically the Christian principle recognized in theory, submission to the powers that be. *Diodorus Siculus* mentions the Cretians' insubordination. They had been now 125 years under Roman rule. *Metellus* conquered Crete, B.C. 67. Previously they had a democracy. **principalities . . . powers** [*archais, exousiais*]—'magistracies . . . authorities.' **to be subject**—*willingly* [*hupotassesthai*]. **to obey**—*commands* of 'magistrates' [*peitharchein*], not *spontaneous* obedience. *Willing* obedience is implied in "ready to every good work." Rom. xiii. 3 shows that obedience to the magistracy tends to good, since the magistrate's aim *generally* is to favour the good and punish the bad. Contrast "disobedient," *v.* 3. **2. To speak evil of no man** —especially, not of "dignities." **no brawlers** —not quarrelsome, attacking others. **gentle**—towards those who attack us [*epieikeis*]; considerate; not urging one's rights to the uttermost, but forbearing (note, Phil. iv. 5). Very different from the '*innate* graspingness,' *greediness,* and 'aggression' (*Polybius,* vi. 46. 9) towards others which characterized the Cretians. **showing** [*endeiknumenous: middle*]—'in one's self, evincing in acts.' **all**—all possible. **meekness** (note, 2 Cor. x. 1)—the opposite of passionate severity. **unto all men**—Christian conduct towards *all* men is the proper consequence of the universality of God's grace to all, so often set forth in the pastoral epistles. **3. For.** Our own past sins should lead us to be lenient towards others. 'Despise none, for such wast thou also,' as the penitent said to his fellow-thief, "Dost thou not fear God . . . seeing thou art in the same condemnation." **we**—Christians. **were**—contrast *v.* 4, "But after that," &c.; i. e., *now:* a favourite contrast in Paul's writing, between our *past* state by nature and our *present* state by grace. As God treated us, we ought to treat our neighbour. **sometimes**—*once.* **foolish**—senseless [*anoetoi*] in our course of living. *Irrational.* The exact picture of human life without grace. Grace is the sole remedy (Luke xv. 17). **disobedient**—to God. **deceived** [*planomenoi*]—'out of the way' (Heb. v. 2). **serving** [*douleuontes*]—'in bondage to:' 'serving as slaves.' **divers.** The cloyed appetite craves constant variety. **pleasures**—of the flesh. **malice**—malignity [*kakia, evil habit of mind; poneria,* the *manifestation* of it]. **hateful . . . hating** —correlatives. Provoking the hatred of others by detestable conduct, and in turn hating them.

4. How little reason the Cretian Christians had to be proud of themselves, and despise others (notes, *vv.* 2, 3). It is to the "kindness and love of God," not to their own merits, that they owe salvation. **kindness** [*chrestotōs*]—'goodness,' 'benignity,' which manifests His *grace.* **love . . . toward man** — teaching us to have such "love

5 appeared, not ᶜby works of righteousness which we have done, but
  according to his mercy he saved us, by ᵈthe washing of regeneration,
6 and renewing of the Holy Ghost; which ᵉhe shed on us ²abundantly
7 through Jesus Christ our Saviour; that, being justified by his grace, we
  should be made heirs according to the hope of eternal life.
8   *This is* a faithful saying, and these things I will that thou affirm constantly, that they which have believed in God might be careful to

A. D. 65.

ᶜ Rom. ₃ 20.
   Gal. 2. 16.
ᵈ John 3. 3, 5.
   1 Pet. 3. 21.
ᵉ Eze. 36. 25.
   Joel 2. 23.
   John 1. 16.
2 richly.

toward *man*" [Greek, *philanthropy*] (*v.* 2), even as God had "*toward man*" (ch. ii. 11): opposed to the "hateful and hating" characteristics of unrenewed men, whose wretchedness moved God's *benevolent kindness*. **of God our Saviour** [*tou Soteros hemon Theou*]—'of our Saviour God;' viz., the Father (ch. i. 3), who "saved us" (*v.* 5) "through Jesus Christ our Saviour" (*v.* 6). **appeared**—was manifested. **5. Not by** [*ex*]—'Out of:' 'not as a result *from* works,' &c. **of righteousness** [*tōn en dikaiosune*]—'wrought *in a state of righteousness* (justification); as "deeds . . . wrought *in* God" (John iii. 21). There was wanting in us the element ("righteousness") in which alone righteous works could be done; so necessarily an absence of the works. 'We neither did works of righteousness, nor were saved *in consequence* of them; but His goodness did the whole' (*Theophylact*). **we**—emphatically opposed to "His." **mercy**—the prompting cause of our salvation individually: '*in pursuance of* [*kata*] His mercy.' His *kindness* and *love to man* appeared in redemption once for all wrought for mankind *generally*. *Faith* is pre-supposed as the instrument; our being "saved" is then an *accomplished fact*. *Faith* is not mentioned, but only *God's* part, as Paul's object is not to describe man's new state, but the "mercy" and saving agency of *God* in bringing it about, *independent of any merit on man's part* (note, *v.* 4). **by** [*dia*]—'through:' by means of. **the washing** [*loutrou*]—'the laver;' *i. e.,* the baptismal font. **of regeneration**—*designed* to be the visible mean and seal of regeneration. 'God does not mock us with empty signs, but by His power inwardly makes good what he demonstrates by the outward sign. Wherefore baptism is congruously and truly called *the laver of regeneration*. We must connect the sign and thing signified, so as not to make the sign empty and ineffectual; yet not so honour the sign as to detract from the Holy Spirit what is peculiarly His' (*Calvin*) (1 Pet. iii. 21). Adult candidates are presupposed to have had repentance and faith (for Paul assumes in charity that those addressed are what they profess, though in fact some were not so (1 Cor. vi. 11), in which case baptism would be the visible 'laver of regeneration' to them, 'faith being thereby *confirmed*, and grace *increased*, by virtue of prayer to God,' ('Church of England,' Article XXVII.) Infants are *charitably presumed* to have received a grace in connection with their Christian descent, in answer to the *believing* prayers of their parents or guardians presenting them for baptism, which grace is visibly sealed and increased by baptism. They are *presumed* to be then regenerated, until years of developed consciousness prove whether they have been *actually* so or not. "Born of (from) water and (no 'of' in Greek) the Spirit;" implying the close tie, in the ideal, between the sign and thing signified. The Word is the *remote* and *anterior* instrument of the new birth; baptism, the *proximate* instrument. The Word, the instrument to the *individual*; baptism, in relation to the *society* of Christians. **and renewing**—not '*the laver* ('washing') of renewing,' but "and BY the renewing," &c., following "saved us." To make "renewing of the Holy Ghost" follow 'the laver' would destroy the balance of the clauses and make baptism the seal, not only of *regeneration*, but also of the subsequent *renewing of the Holy Ghost*—i. e., *progressive sanctification*. *Regeneration* is *once for all* done; *renewing* is *daily* proceeding. As "the washing," or 'laver,' is connected with "*regeneration*," so the "renewing of the Holy Ghost" (2 Cor. iv. 16; Rom. xii. 2) is connected with "shed on us abundantly" (*v.* 6). *Conversion* is in the New Testament always used of sinners *turning for the first time to God* (Matt. xiii. 15; Acts iii. 19; xiv. 15; xv. 3, 19; 2 Cor. iii. 16; Jas. v. 20; 1 Pet. ii. 25; except Luke xxii. 32, where it means the *full turning* of Peter again to the Lord after his fall [*epistrepho; strepho*] Matt. xviii. 3). **6. Which**—the Holy Ghost. **he shed** [*execheen*]—'poured out:' not merely *gave* (Acts ii. 17, 18, 33): not only on the church in general, but also "on us" individually. This *pouring out* of the Spirit comprehends the grace received before, in, and subsequently to, baptism. **abundantly** [*plousiōs*]—'richly' (Col. iii. 16). **through Jesus Christ**—the channel of the Holy Ghost. So the Divine Three combine in our salvation. **our Saviour**—immediately, as the Father is immediately. The Father is the Author of salvation, and saves us by Jesus. **7. That, &c.**—the purpose He aimed at in having "saved us" (*v.* 5); viz., 'That having been once for all justified [aorist, *dikaiothentes: accounted righteous* through faith, *the Spirit's work*: sealed at our "regeneration;" followed by daily "renewing of the Holy Ghost"] by His grace (opposed to *works, v.* 5), we should be (not merely saved from the curse of sin, *v.* 3, but) made heirs.' **his grace** [*tē ekeinou chariti*]—'the grace of *the former*;' i. e., *God* (*v.* 4; Rom. v. 15). The Father is the *originating* cause; Christ the *meritorious* cause; the Holy Ghost the *efficient* cause of our justification. **heirs** (Gal. iii. 29) **according to the hope of eternal life.** Ch. i. 2, also the Greek order [*kleronomoi kat' elpida zoes aioniou*], confirms this; i. e., *agreeably to* the hope of eternal life: the eternal inheritance fully satisfying the hope. Gal. iii. 29, "heirs according to the promise" [*kat' epangelian kleronomoi*], justifies this independent use of "heirs" against *Ellicott*, who explains, '*heirs of eternal life*, in the way of hope' (Rom. viii. 24)—i. e., not yet in actual possession. Such a *blessed hope*, once not possessed, leads a Christian to practical holiness and meekness toward others: the lesson needed by the Cretians.
8. Greek, 'Faithful is the saying'—a formula peculiar to the pastoral epistles; here the statement (*vv.* 4-7) as to the gratuitousness of God's gift of salvation, answering to the "Amen" (Rev. iii. 14). **these things, &c.** [*peri toutōn boulomai se diabebaiousthai*]—'concerning these things (the truths dwelt on, *vv.* 4-7) I will that thou *affirm persistently, in order that* they who have *believed* God [*Theo;* but *eiston Theon*, John xiv. 1: 'they who *credit God*' in what He saith, instead of crediting *man's vain talk, v.* 9] may be [*phrontizōsin*] solicitously sedulous (*diligence is necessary*) to be forward in [*proistasthai:* 'to set before themselves so as to sustain'] good works;' no longer applying

maintain good works. These things are good and profitable unto men.

9 But *ᶠ* avoid foolish questions, and genealogies, and contentions, and
10 strivings about the law; for they are unprofitable and vain. A man
11 that is an heretic *ᵍ* after the first and second admonition *ʰ* reject; knowing that he that is such is subverted, and sinneth *ⁱ* being condemned of himself.

12 When I shall send Artemas unto thee, or *ʲ* Tychicus, be diligent to come unto me to Nicopolis: for I have determined there to winter.
13 Bring Zenas the lawyer and *ᵏ* Apollos on their journey diligently, that
14 nothing be wanting unto them. And let ours also learn to ³ maintain
15 good works for necessary uses, that they be *ˡ* not unfruitful. All that are with me salute thee. Greet them that love us in the faith. Grace *be* with you all. Amen.

It was written to Titus, ordained the first bishop of the church of the Cretians, from Nicopolis of Macedonia.

A. D. 65.

ᶠ 1 Tim. 1. 4.
2 Tim. 2,23.
ᵍ 2 Cor. 13 2.
ʰ Matt. 18.17.
2 Tim. 3. 5.
2 John 10.
ⁱ Matt 25.26-28.
Acts 13. 46.
ʲ Acts 20. 4.
2 iTm. 4. 2.
ᵏ Acts 18. 21.
³ Or, profess honest trades.
Eph. 4. 28.
ˡ Col 1. 10.
Phil. 1. 11.

their *care* to "unprofitable" and unpractical speculations (v. 9). **These things**—not 'these (good works) are good,' but, as the antithesis (v. 9) requires, 'these truths' (*vv.* 4-7). **good**—*in themselves,* as well as **profitable unto men. 9. foolish** [*mōras*]—'insipid:' producing no moral fruit. **genealogies**—akin to the "fables" (note, 1 Tim. i. 4). Not so much direct heresy as yet, but profitless discussions about genealogies of æons, &c., which ultimately led to Gnosticism. Synagogue discourses were termed *daraschoth; i.e.,* discussions. Cf. "*disputer* of this world," 1 Cor. i. 20. **strivings about the law**—about "commandments of men," which they sought to confirm by "the law" (ch. i. 14: note, 1 Tim. i. 7); and about the mystical meaning of the various parts of the law in connection with the "genealogies." **avoid** [*periistaso*]—*stand aloof from* (2 Tim. ii. 16). **vain** [*mataioi inanes;* empty of *results:* but *kenos vanus;* empty of *contents*]. **10. heretic.** *Heresy,* originally a *division* resulting from self-will; the individual doing and teaching what he *chose* independently of the church. More aggravated than *schism* (1 Cor. xi. 19; Gal. v. 20): *divisions* on church matters not necessarily fundamental (ch. i. 14; v. 9). In course of time it came to mean 'heresy' in the modern sense, 'the open espousal of fundamental error.' The heretics of Crete were in doctrine followers of their own self-willed questions (v. 9), and immoral in practice. **admonition**—by *word* [*nouthesia;* but *paideia,* by *chastisements*]. **reject** [*paraitou*]—lit., *ask off from:* 'shun.' Not formal excommunication, but 'have nothing more to do with him,' either in admonition or intercourse. **11. Knowing**—by the ill success of your *admonitions.* **is subverted** [*exestraptai*]—'is perverted;' lit., *turned inside out; i. e.,* completely changed for the worse (Deut. xxxii. 20) [*dor tahpukoth*]. **condemned of himself**—continuing the same after frequent admonition, he is self-condemned. When 'he sinneth' he doeth what his own knowledge virtually condemns.

12. When I shall send Artemas unto thee, or Tychicus—to supply thy place in Crete. Artemas. tradition says, subsequently became bishop of Lystra. Tychicus was sent twice by Paul from

Rome to Lesser Asia in his first imprisonment (which shows how well qualified he was to become Titus' successor in Crete) (Eph. vi. 21; Col. iv. 7); and in his second (2 Tim. iv. 12). Tradition makes him subsequently bishop of Chalcedon, in Bithynia. **Nicopolis**—'The city of victory;' called so from the battle of Actium; in Epirus. This epistle was probably written from Corinth in the autumn. Paul purposed a journey through Œtolia and Acarnania into Epirus, and there "to winter." (See 'Introduction' to pastoral epistles.) **13. Bring . . . on their journey**—enable them to proceed by supplying necessaries for their journey. **Zenas**—contracted from Zenodorus. **lawyer** [*nomikon*]—a Jewish scribe,' learned in the Hebrew law, who, when converted, still retained the title. **Apollos**—with Zenas, probably the bearers of this epistle. In 1 Cor. xvi. 12 Apollos is mentioned as purposing to visit Corinth: his now being at Corinth (on the theory of Paul being there when he wrote) accords with this purpose. Crete would be on his way either to Palestine or his native place, Alexandria. Paul and Apollos thus appear in beautiful harmony in that very city where their names had been formerly the watchword of unchristian rivalries. The only pifference had been in their respective modes of teaching, Apollos being more ornate and rhetorical (Acts xviii. 24-28; 1 Cor. iii. 6). It was to avoid this party rivalry that Apollos formerly was unwilling to visit Corinth, though Paul desired him. *Hippolytus* mentions Zenas as one of the seventy, and afterwards bishop of Diospolis. **14. And** [*De: But*] **let ours also**—Not only *thou,* but let others also of 'our' fellow-believers (whom we have won, *Bengel*), at Crete with thee. **for necessary uses** —*to supply the necessary wants* of Christian brethren according as they need in their journeys for the Lord (cf. ch. i. 8). **15. Greet**—'*Salute* them that love us in the sphere of faith.' All at Crete had not this *love* rooted in *faith,* the true bond of fellowship. A salutation peculiar to this epistle. such as no forger would have used. **Grace**—' *The* grace,' viz., *of God.* **with you all.** Not that the epistle is addressed to *all* the Cretian Christians, but Titus would naturally impart it to his flock.

522

THE EPISTLE OF PAUL TO

PHILEMON.

1 PAUL, *a* a prisoner of Jesus Christ, and Timothy *our* brother, unto
2 Philemon our dearly beloved, *b* and fellow-labourer, and to *our*
   beloved Apphia, and Archippus *c* our fellow-soldier, and to the *d* church
3 in thy house : Grace *e* to you, and peace, from God our Father and the
   Lord Jesus Christ.
4 I *f* thank my God, making mention of thee always in my prayers,
5 hearing *g* of thy love and faith, which thou hast toward the Lord Jesus,
6 and toward all saints; that the communication of thy faith may become
   effectual *h* by the acknowledging of every good thing which is in you in
7 Christ Jesus. For we have great joy and consolation in thy love, because
   the bowels of the saints *i* are refreshed by thee, brother.
8   Wherefore, *j* though I might be much bold in Christ to enjoin thee
9 that which is convenient, yet for love's sake I rather beseech *thee*, being
   such an one as Paul the aged, and now also a prisoner of Jesus Christ.

a Eph. 4. 1.
2 Tim. 1. 8.
b Phil. 2. 25.
c Col. 4. 17.
d Rom. 16. 5.
1 Cor. 16. 19.
e Eph. 1. 2.
f 1 Thes. 1. 2.
2 Thes. 1. 3.
Col. 1. 4.
g Eph. 1. 15.
1 John 3. 23.
h Phil. 1. 9.
i 2 Cor. 7. 13.
2 Tim. 1. 16.
j 2 Cor 3. 12.
1 Thes. 2. 6.

1-25. — ADDRESS — THANKSGIVING FOR PHILE-
MON'S LOVE AND FAITH — INTERCESSION FOR
ONESIMUS — CONCLUDING REQUEST — SALUTA-
TIONS.

This epistle affords a specimen of the highest
wisdom as to how Christians ought to manage
social affairs on exalted principles. 1. prisoner
of Jesus Christ—one whom Christ's cause has
made a prisoner (cf. *v.* 13). He does not call himself, as in other epistles, "Paul an apostle:" he
is writing familiarly, not authoritatively. our . . .
fellow-labourer—in building up the church at
Colosse, whilst we were at Ephesus. (See 'Introduction' to Colossians.) 2. Apphia—Latin, 'Appia.'
The wife or some close relative of Philemon. She
and Archippus, if they had not belonged to his
family, would not have been included with
Philemon in the address of a letter on a domestic
matter. Archippus—a minister of the Colossian
church (Col. iv. 17). fellow-soldier (2 Tim. ii. 3).
church in thy house. In the absence of a regular
church building, the houses of particular saints
were used. Observe Paul's tact in associating
with Philemon those associated by kindred or
Christian brotherhood with his *house*, not going
beyond it.

4. always—joined by *Alford* with "I thank my
God." 5. Hearing—the ground of thanksgiving.
It is a delicate mark of authenticity, that he says
"hearing" as to churches and persons whom he
had not seen or *then* visited. Colosse, Philemon's
residence, he had never yet seen. Yet *v.* 19 implies that Philemon was his convert. Philemon,
doubtless, was converted at Ephesus, or some
other place where he met Paul. love and faith.
The theological order is first *faith*, then *love*, the
fruit of faith. But he purposely puts Philemon's
love first, as it is to an act of love he is exhorting
him. toward . . . toward—different Greek:
towards [*pros* in אG; but ACΔ, *eis*] . . . *unto*
[*eis*]. *Towards* implies simply *direction*; *unto*, to
the advantage of. 6. That, &c.—the aim of my
thanksgiving and prayers for thee, *in order that
the*, &c. the communication of thy faith—*the
imparting of it and its fruits* (viz., acts of love, as
Heb. xiii. 16) *to others*: or, *the liberality to others
flowing from thy faith* [so koinōnia, "liberal distribution," 2 Cor. ix. 13. א reads *diaconia* for

koinonia; ministration.] effectual by—Greek,
'IN:' the element *in* which his liberality may be
proved by acts in, &c. acknowledging [*epignosei*]
—'the thorough knowledge;' *i.e.*, the practical
recognition. of every good thing which is in you
—*in thee and the church in thy house*, thine helpers
in good works. Lest Philemon should be over-
praised, St. Paul gives share of the credit to
Philemon's helpers. So אG*g*. But ACΔ*f* read
'in US;' *i.e.*, the practical recognition of every
grace which is in us *Christians*, in so far as we
realize the Christian character. That thy faith
may by acts be proved to be 'a faith which worketh by love.' in Christ Jesus [*eis*]—'*unto* Christ
Jesus;' i.e., *to His glory*. So CΔG. But אA
omit "Jesus." This verse answers to *v.* 5, "thy
love and faith . . . toward all saints." Paul
never ceases to mention him in his prayers, *in
order that* his faith may still further show its
power toward others, by exhibiting every grace
that is in Christians to the glory of Christ. Thus
he paves the way for the request for Onesimus.
7. For—a reason for the prayer, *vv.* 4-6. we have
[*eschomen:* G]—'we had.' But אACG [*eschon*],
I had. joy and consolation—joined in 2 Cor. vii.
4. saints are refreshed by thee—his house was
open to them. brother—put last, to conciliate
his favourable attention to the request which
follows.

8. Wherefore—because of my love, I "*beseech*,"
rather than "enjoin," or *authoritatively command.*
I might . . . enjoin—in virtue of Philemon's
obligation to *obedience* as having been converted
through Paul. in Christ—the element in which
his boldness has place. 9. for love's sake—mine
to thee: in contrast to the "boldness" [*parrhesian*] which I forbear to use (*v.* 8). My "love"
is reciprocal to "thy love" for which thou art so
distinguished (*v.* 7). being such an one—as thou
knowest me to be; viz. *Paul* (the founder of so
many churches, an apostle of Christ, thy father
in the faith) *the aged* (my *age* ought to secure thy
respect for my request), *and now also a prisoner of
Jesus Christ* (the strongest claims I have on thee:
if for no other reason, at least through commiseration gratify me). *Lachmann* better punctuates;
a full stop at "I beseech thee." Connect, "being
such an one . . , I beseech thee for my son," &c.

10 I beseech thee for my son *k* Onesimus, whom *l* I have begotten in my
11 bonds: which in time past was to thee unprofitable, but now profitable
12 to thee and to me: whom I have sent again: thou therefore receive him
13 that is mine own bowels: whom I would have retained with me, that
    m in thy stead he might have ministered unto me in the bonds of the
14 Gospel: but without thy mind would I do nothing; *n* that thy benefit
15 should not be as it were of necessity, but willingly. For *o* perhaps he
    therefore departed for a season, that thou shouldest receive him for ever;
16 not now as a servant, but above a servant, *p* a brother beloved, specially
    to me, but how much more unto thee, both *q* in the flesh, and in the
17 Lord? If thou count me therefore *r* a partner, receive him as myself.
18 If he hath wronged thee, or oweth *thee* ought, put that on mine account.
19 I Paul have written *it* with mine own hand, I will repay *it :* albeit I do
    not say to thee how thou owest unto me even thine own self besides.
20 Yea, brother, let me have joy of thee in the Lord: refresh my bowels
21 in the Lord. Having *s* confidence in thy obedience I wrote unto thee,
22 knowing that thou wilt also do more than I say. But withal prepare me

A. D. 64.

k Col. 4. 9.
l 1 Cor. 4. 15.
Gal. 4. 19.
m 1 Cor. 16. 17.
Phil. 2. 30.
n 1 Chr. 29. 17.
Ps. 110. 3.
2 Cor. 8. 12.
2 Cor. 9. 7.
1 Pet. 5. 2.
o Gen. 45. 5,
8.
Rom. 8. 28.
p Matt. 23. 8.
1 Tim. 6. 2.
q Eph. 6. 5-7.
Col. 3. 22.
r 2 Cor. 8. 23.
s 2 Cor. 2. 3.
2 Cor. 7. 16.
2 Cor. 8. 22.

(*v.* 10.) **10. I beseech thee**—emphatically repeated from *v.* 9. In the Greek "Onesimus" is skilfully put last; the favourable description of him precedes the name that had fallen into so bad repute with Philemon. "I beseech thee for my son, whom I have begotten in my bonds, Onesimus." Scripture does not sanction slavery; yet does not begin a political crusade against it. It sets forth *principles of love* to our fellow-men, sure (as they have done) in due time to undermine and overthrow it, without violently convulsing the existing political fabric, by stirring up slaves against their master. 'By Christianizing the master, the Gospel enfranchises the slave' (*Wordsworth*). **11. Which in time past was to thee unprofitable**—belying his name, Onesimus, which means *profitable.* Not only was he *unprofitable,* but positively injurious, having "wronged" his master. Paul uses a mild expression. **now profitable**—without godliness a man is so in no station. *Profitable* in spiritual as well as in *temporal* things (1 Tim. iv. 8). **12. thou therefore. now receive** [*proslabou*]—C Δ *f*, Vulgate. But א A G omit. Translate then, 'him (I say) that is,' &c. **mine own bowels**—as dear to me as my inmost vitals. Cf. *v.* 17, "as myself." I have for him the intense affection of a parent for a child (Jer. xxxi. 20). **13. I**—emphatical. Since *I* had such implicit trust in him as to desire to keep him with me for his service, *thou* mayest. **I would have retained**—different [*eboulomēn*] from the "would" [*ethelēsa*], *v.* 14; 'I could have *wished,*' 'I was *minded*' here: but 'I was not *willing,*' *v.* 14. **in thy stead**—that he may supply all the services to me which you, if here, would render because of the love you bear to me (*v.* 19). **bonds of the Gospel**—my bonds endure for the Gospel's sake (*v.* 9). **14. without thy mind**—*i. e.,* consent. **should not be as**—'as though a matter of necessity, but of free-will.' Had Paul kept Onesimus, however willing to gratify Paul Philemon might be, he would have no opportunity of *showing* he was so, his leave not having been asked. **15. perhaps**—speaking humanly, yet as believing that God's providence probably (for we cannot dogmatically define God's hidden purposes) overruled the past evil to ultimately greater good to him. This thought would soften Philemon's indignation at Onesimus' past offence. So Joseph in Gen. xlv. 5. **departed** [*echōristhē*]—'was parted from thee:' a softening term for 'ran away,' to mitigate Philemon's wrath. **receive him** [*apechēs*] —'*have him wholly for thyself*' (note, Phil. iv. 18). The same Greek, Matt. vi. 2, 5. **for ever**—

in this life and in that to come (cf. Exod. xxi. 6). Onesimus' absence, however long, was but a short 'hour' [*pros horan*] compared with the everlasting devotion henceforth binding him to his master. **16.** No longer a mere slave (though still that), but above a servant, so that thou shalt have not merely the services of a slave, but higher benefits: a *servant* "in the flesh," he is a *brother* "in the Lord." **beloved, specially to me**—his spiritual father (*v.* 10); who have experienced his faithful attentions. Lest Philemon should dislike Onesimus being called "brother," Paul first recognizes him as a brother, being the spiritual son of the same God. **much more unto thee**—to whom he stands in so much nearer and more lasting relation. **17. a partner**—in the Christian fellowship of faith, hope, and love. **receive him as myself**—resuming "receive him," *v.* 12. But see note there. **18.** '*But* [*de*] if (thou wilt not "receive him" because) he hath wronged thee:' milder than 'robbed thee.' Onesimus confessed some such act to Paul. **put that on mine account**—I am ready to make good the loss to thee, if required. *Vv.* 19, 21 imply that he did not expect Philemon would demand it. **19. with mine own hand**—not employing an amanuensis, as in other epistles: a special compliment of which Philemon ought to show his appreciation by granting Paul's request. Contrast Col. iv. 18. The epistle to the Colossians, accompanying our epistle, had only its "salutation" written by Paul's hand. **albeit &c.** [*hina mē lego*]—'that I may not say,' &c. **thou owest unto me even thine own self**—not merely thy possessions. For to my instrumentality thou owest thy salvation. So the debt which 'he oweth thee,' making myself responsible for it, is cancelled. **20. let me**—'let *me* [emphatic: *ego sou*] have profit [*onaimen,* referring to the name Onesimus, "profitable"] from *thee,* as *thou* shouldest have had from Onesimus:' for 'thou owest thine own self to me.' **in the Lord**—the sphere of *Philemon's* being profitable to Paul. **my bowels**—gratify *my feelings* by granting this. **in the Lord.** א A C Δ G *f g* read '*in Christ.*' The element in which *Paul's* feelings are to be refreshed. The latter clause answers to the former of the verse. **21. Having confidence in thy obedience**—to my apostolic authority, were I to "enjoin" it (*v.* 8), which I do not, preferring to beseech thee for it as a favour (*v.* 9). **thou wilt also do more** —towards Onesimus: hinting at his possible manumission, *besides* being kindly received. **22.** This prospect of Paul's visiting Colosse would

also a lodging: for ^t I trust that ^u through your prayers I shall be given unto you.

23   There salute thee ^vEpaphras, my fellow-prisoner in Christ Jesus; 24, ^wMarcus, ^xAristarchus, ^yDemas, Lucas, ^zmy fellow-labourers. The grace 25 of our Lord Jesus Christ *be* with your spirit. Amen.

Written from Rome to Philemon, by Onesimus a servant.

525

A. D. 64.	
t Phil. 1. 25.	
u 2 Cor. 1. 11.	
v Col 1. 7.	
w Acts 12. 12.	
x Acts 19. 29.	
y Col. 4. 14.	
z 2 Tim. 4. 11.	

secure a kindly reception for Onesimus, as Paul would know in person how he had been treated. **your . . . you**—referring to Philemon, Apphia, Archippus, and the church in Philemon's house. The same expectation is expressed subsequently (Phil. ii. 23, 24).

23. The same persons send salutations in the accompanying epistle, except that 'Jesus Justus' is not mentioned here. **Epaphras, my fellow-prisoner.** He had been sent by the Colossians to enquire after and minister to Paul, and possibly was cast into *prison* by the Roman authorities on suspicion. However, he is not mentioned as a *prisoner* in Col. iv. 12; so "fellow-prisoner" here may mean merely a faithful companion to Paul in *his* imprisonment, putting himself in the position of a prisoner. So "Aristarchus, my fellow-prisoner," Col. iv. 10, may mean. But see note there. *Benson* conjectures that on some *former* occasion these two were Paul's 'fellow-prisoners,' *not at the time.* **25. be with your spirit** (Gal. vi. 18; 2 Tim. iv. 22).

THE EPISTLE OF PAUL THE APOSTLE TO THE

HEBREWS.

1 GOD, who at sundry times and *a*in divers manners spake in time past
2 unto the fathers by the prophets, hath *b*in these last days *c*spoken
unto us by *his* Son, *d*whom he hath appointed heir of all things, by
3 whom also he made the worlds; who being the brightness of *his* glory,
and the express image of his person, and upholding all things by the

A. D. 61.

CHAP. 1.
a Num. 12. 6.
b Gal 4. 4.
c John 1. 17.
d Ps. 2. 8.

CHAP. I. 1-14.—THE HIGHEST OF ALL REVELA-TIONS GIVEN NOW IN THE SON OF GOD, GREATER THAN THE ANGELS—WHO, HAVING COMPLETED REDEMPTION, SITS ENTHRONED AT GOD'S RIGHT HAND.

St. Paul, though not inscribing his name, was well known to those addressed (ch. xiii. 19: see 'Introduction'). In the Pauline method the statement of subject and the division are put before the discussion; at the close, the practical follows the doctrinal portion. The ardour of spirit, as in 1 John, bursting at once into the sub-ject, without prefatory inscription of name and greeting, more effectively strikes the hearers. The date must have been before the temple's destruction, A. D. 70: some time before the mar-tyrdom of Peter, who mentions this epistle of Paul (2 Pet. iii. 15, 16) when many of the first *hearers* of the Lord were dead. **1. at sundry times** [*polumerōs*]—'in many portions.' All was not revealed to each prophet: one received one portion of revelation, another another. To Noah, the quarter of the world to which Messiah should belong was revealed; to Abraham, the nation; to Jacob, the tribe; to David and Isaiah, the family; to Micah, the town; to Daniel, the exact time; to Malachi, the coming of His forerunner; through Jonah, His burial and resurrection, &c. Each only knew in part; Messiah combined and realized all (1 Cor. xiii. 12). **in divers manners**—*e. g.*, internal suggestion, audible voices, Urim and Thummim, dreams, &c. 'In one way He was seen by Abraham, in another by Moses, in another by Elias, in another by Micah, Isaiah, Daniel, and Ezekiel' (*Theodoret*) (cf. Num. xii. 6-8). The Old Testament revelations were fragmentary in sub-stance, manifold in form: the very *multitude* of prophets shows they prophesied only *in part*. In Christ the revelation of God is not in separated colours: He, the pure light, unites in His one person the whole spectrum (*v.* 3). **spake**—the expression usual for a Jew in addressing Jews. So St. Matthew, a Jew writing for Jews, quotes, not by the formula "It is written," but "said," &c. **in time past.** From Malachi, the last Old Testament prophet, for 400 years, there had arisen no prophet, that the Son might be the more an object of expectation (*Bengel*). **As God** (the Father) is introduced as having *spoken* here, so God the Son, ch. ii. 3; God the Holy Ghost, ch. iii. 7. **the fathers**—the Jews of former days (1 Cor. x. 1). **by**—Greek, 'IN.' A mortal king speaks *by*, the King of kings IN, His ambassador. The Son is the last and highest manifestation of God (Matt. xxi. 34, 37): not merely a *measure*, as in the prophets, but the *fulness* of the Spirit of God dwelt in Him bodily (John i. 16; iii. 34; Col. ii. 9). If the Jews boast of their prophets, Jesus is the end of all prophecy (Rev. xix. 10), and of the law (John i. 17; v. 46). **2. in these last days.**

In ℵ A B Δ [*ep' eschatou*], 'at the last part of these days.' The rabbins divided time into 'this age' and the 'age to come' (ch. ii. 5; vi. 5). The days of Messiah were the transition period, or 'last part of these days' (in contrast to "in time past," *v.* 1); the close of the existing, and beginning of the final, dispensation; of which Christ's second coming shall be the consummation. **by his Son**—Greek, 'IN (His) Son' (John xiv. 10): the true 'prophet' of God. 'His majesty is set forth—(1.) *Absolutely*, by "Son," and by three glorious predi-cates, "whom He hath appointed," "by whom also He made the worlds," "who . . . sat down on the right hand of the Majesty on high." Thus His course is described from the beginning of all things down to the goal (*vv.* 2, 3). (2.) *Relatively*, in comparison with the angels, *v.* 4: the *confirma-tion* follows; the name "Son" is proved at *v.* 5; the "heirship," *vv.* 6-9; the "making the worlds," *vv.* 10-12; the "sitting at the right hand" of God, *vv.* 13, 14.' His *heirship* follows His *sonship*, and preceded His *making the worlds* (Prov. viii. 22, 23; Eph. iii. 11). As *the first begotten*, He is heir of the universe (*v.* 6), which He made instrumentally, ch. xi. 3, where "by the word of God" answers to "by whom" (the Son of God) here (John i. 3). Christ was "appointed" (in God's eternal counsel) to creation as an office; the universe so created was assigned to Him as a kingdom. He is "heir of all things" by right of creation, and especially by redemption. The promise to Abraham, that he should be heir of the world, had its fulfilment, and will have it more fully, in Christ (Rom. iv. 13; Gal. iii. 16; iv. 7). **worlds**—the inferior and the superior (Col. i. 16): [*aiōnas*] *ages*, with all things and persons belonging to them: the uni-verse, including all space and ages, and all material and spiritual existences. He not only appointed His Son heir of all things before creation, but *He also* (better than "also He") made by Him the worlds. **3. Who being**—by pre-existent and essential being. **brightness of his glory** [*apaug-asma*]—the *effulgence* of His glory. 'Light of (from) light' ('Nicene Creed'). 'The sun is never seen without effulgence, nor the Father without the Son' (*Theophylact*). It is *because* He is the brightness, &c., and *because* He upholds, &c., that He *sat down on the right hand*, &c. It was a return to His Divine glory (John vi. 62; xvii. 5: cf. 'Wisdom,' vii. 25, 26). **express image**—*char-acter*: 'impress.' But veiled in the flesh.

'The Son of God in glory beams
Too bright for us to scan;
But we can face the light that streams
From the mild Son of man.'

of his person [*hupostaseōs*]—'of His substantial essence.' **upholding all things** [*ta panta*]—'the universe.' Col. i. 15, 17, 20 enumerates the three facts in the same order. **by the word**—therefore

526

word of his power, when he had by himself purged our sins, ^esat down
4 on the right hand of the Majesty on high; being made so much better
than the angels, as ^fhe hath by inheritance obtained a more excellent
name than they.

5 For unto which of the angels said he at any time, ^gThou art my Son,
this day have I begotten thee? And again, ^hI will be to him a Father,
6 and he shall be to me a Son? ⁱAnd again, when he bringeth in ⁱthe
first-begotten into the world, he saith, And ^jlet all the angels of God

A. D. 64.
^e Ps. 110. 1.
^f Phil. 2. 9.
^g Ps. 2. 7.
^h 2 Sam. 7.14.
ⁱ Or. When he bringeth again.
ⁱ Rom. 8. 29.
^j Ps. 97. 7.

the Son of God is a Person; for He has the word (*Bengel*). *His* word is *God's* word (ch. xi. 3). **of his power.** "The word" is the utterance which comes from His (the Son's) power, and gives expression to it. **by himself.** So Δ *f*. Omitted in א A B, Vulgate. **purged** [*katharismon poiēsamenos*] —'*made purification of* our sins.' His atonement covers the guilt of sin. "Our" is omitted in א A B Δ, Vulgate. Sin was *uncleanness* before God: His sacrifice *purges* it away (ch. ix. 13, 14). Our nature, guilt-laden, could not, without our great High Priest's blood of atonement sprinkling the heavenly mercyseat, come into contact with God. *Ebrard*, 'The mediation between man and God, present in the most holy place, was revealed in three forms—(1.) In sacrifices (typical propitiations for guilt); (2.) In the priesthood (the agents of them); (3.) In the Levitical laws of purity (attained by sacrifice *positively*, by avoidance of ceremonial pollution *negatively*, the people being thus admitted into the presence of God without dying) (Lev. xvi.; Deut. v. 26). **sat down on the right hand of the Majesty on high**—fulfilling Ps. cx. 1. This sitting of the Son at God's right hand was by the act of the Father (ch. viii. 1; Eph. i. 20): it never expresses His pre-existing state co-equal with the Father, but always His exalted state as *Son of man* after His sufferings, Mediator for man in the presence of God (Rom. viii. 34): a relation towards God and us about to end when its object shall have been accomplished (1 Cor. xv. 28). **4. Being made so much better** —by His exaltation by the Father (*vv.* 3, 13); in contrast to His being "made . . . lower than the angels" (ch. ii. 9). "Better," *i. e.*, *superior* to. As "being" (*v.* 3) expresses His *essential* being, so "being made" (ch. vii. 26) marks what He *became* in His assumed manhood (Phil. ii. 6-9). His humbled form (at which the Jews stumble) is no objection to His Divine Messiahship. As the law was given by the ministration of angels and Moses, it was inferior to the Gospel given by the Divine Son, who both is (*vv.* 4-14) as God, and has been made, as the exalted Son of man (ch. ii. 5-18), much better than the angels. The manifestations of God by angels (and even by the Angel of the covenant) at different times in the Old Testament, did not bring man and God into personal union, as the manifestation of God in human flesh does. **by inheritance obtained.** He always had the *thing* itself, *sonship*; but *He* 'obtained by inheritance,' according to the Father's promise, the *name* "Son," whereby He is made known to men and angels. He is "the Son of God" in a sense far above that in which angels are "sons of God" (Job i. 6; xxxviii. 7). 'The full glory of the peculiar name, "the Son of God," is unattainable by human thought. All appellations are but fragments of its glory—beams united in it as in a central sun' (Rev. xix. 12) (*Delitzsch*). **5. For.** Substantiating *v.* 4. **unto which.** A frequent argument is derived from the *silence of Scripture* (*v.* 13; ch. ii. 16; vii. 3, 14). **this day have I begotten thee** (Ps. ii. 7). Fulfilled at Christ's resurrection, whereby the Father "de-

clared" His Divine Sonship, heretofore veiled by His humiliation (Acts xiii. 33; Rom. i. 4). Christ has a fourfold right to be "Son of God"—(1.) By *generation*, begotten of God; (2.) By *commission*, sent by God; (3.) By *resurrection*, "the first-begotten of the dead" (cf. Luke xx. 36; Rev. i. 5); (4.) By *actual possession*, as heir of all (*Bishop Pearson*). The Psalm (ii.; lxxxix. 26, 27) applied primarily to Solomon, of whom God promised by Nathan to David, "I will be his Father, and he shall be my son." But as the whole theocracy was of Messianic import, the triumph of David over Hadadezer and neighbouring kings (2 Sam. viii.) typically foreshows God's ultimately subduing all enemies under His Son, whom He sets (Hebrew, *anointed*, Ps. ii. 6) on His "holy hill of Zion," as King of the Jews and of the whole earth, the antitype to Solomon, son of David. "*I* [*ego:* emphatical: the Everlasting Father] have begotten thee this day," the day of thy being *manifested* as My Son, "the first-*begotten* of the dead" (Col. i. 18; Rev. i. 5). He had been always Son, but now first was *manifested* as such in His once humbled, now exalted, manhood united to His Godhead. Not, here, the *eternal* generation of the Son: The everlasting *to-day* in which the Son was begotten by the Father (Prov. xxx. 4; John x. 30, 38; xvi. 28; xvii. 8). The communication of the full Divine essence involves eternal generation; for the Divine essence has no beginning. But a definite point of time is here implied—viz., that of His having entered on the *inheritance* (*v.* 4). The 'bringing the first-begotten into the world' (*v.* 6) is not subsequent, as *Alford* thinks, to *v.* 5, but anterior (cf. Acts ii. 30-35). **6. And** [*De*]—'But.' Not only this, **but** a more decisive proof is Ps. xcvii. 7, which shows that not only at His resurrection, but also in His being *brought into the world* (cf. ch. ix. 11; x. 5), in His incarnation (Luke ii. 9-14), temptation (Matt. iv. 10, 11), resurrection (Matt. xxviii. 2), and second advent in glory, angels were designed by God to be subject to Him. Cf. 1 Tim. iii. 16, "seen of angels:" God manifesting Messiah to be gazed at with adoring love by heavenly intelligences (Eph. iii.; 10; 2 Thess. i. 9, 10; 1 Pet. iii. 22). His Lordship shall be most fully manifested at His second coming (1 Cor. xv. 24, 25; Phil. ii. 9). "Worship Him all ye gods" (Ps. xcvii. 7)—i. e., *exalted beings; LXX.*, '*angels*'), refers to *God;* but the Hebrews generally acknowledged that God would dwell, peculiarly, in Messiah (so as to be, in the Talmud phrase, 'capable of being pointed to with the finger'); so what was said of God was true of Messiah. The 97th Psalm describes such a kingdom as shall be the rejoicing of all nations—viz., those to be called *by Christ*. *Kimchi* says that Psalms 93d to 101st contain in them the mystery of Messiah. God ruled the theocracy in and through him. **the (habitable) world** [*tēn oikoumenēn*]—subject to Christ (ch. ii. 5). As "the first-begotten," He has the rights of *primogeniture* (Rom. viii. 29; Col. i. 15, 16, 18). In Deut. xxxii. 43, the LXX. have [*proskunesatosan autō pantes angeloi*] "Let all the angels of God worship Him;" words

527

7 worship him. And ²of the angels he saith, *ᵏ*Who maketh his angels
8 spirits, and his ministers a flame of fire. But unto the Son *he saith,*
  *ˡ*Thy throne, O God, *is* for ever and ever: a sceptre of ³righteousness *is*
9 the sceptre of thy kingdom. Thou hast loved righteousness, and hated
  iniquity; therefore God, *even* thy God, *ᵐ*hath anointed thee with the
10 oil of gladness above thy fellows. And, *ⁿ*Thou, Lord, in the beginning
  hast laid the foundation of the earth; and the heavens are the works of
11 thine hands: they shall perish; but thou remainest: and they all shall

A. D. 64.	
² unto.	
ᵏ Ps. 104. 4.	
ˡ Ps. 45. 6, 7.	
³ rightness.	
or.	
straight-	
ness.	
ᵐ Isa. 61. 1.	
ⁿ Ps. 102. 25.	

not now in the Hebrew. The LXX. may have been in Paul's mind as to the *form,* but the *substance* is from Ps. xcvii. 7. The type, David, in Ps. lxxxix. 27 (*v.* 5), is called God's *"first-born,* higher than the *kings* of the earth:" so the antitypical first-begotten, the Son of David, is to be worshipped by all inferior *lords,* as *angels* ("gods," Ps. xcvii. 7); for He is "King of kings and Lord of lords" (Rev. xix. 16). The Greek "again" is transposed; not necessarily (cf. *margin*), 'When He *again shall have introduced,*' &c.—viz., at Christ's second coming; for there is no previous mention of a *first* bringing in: "again" is often used in quotations, and may be parenthetical ('that I may again quote Scripture') (cf. Matt. v. 33; Greek, John xii. 39). Still the Second Advent is *included* in the 'bringing in,' accompanied with *angels'* worship of Messiah: to it Ps. xcvii. chiefly refers (Matt. xxiv. 29, 30; 2 Thess. i. 7, 8). His being *brought into the* WORLD [*oikoumene*] as the theatre of His power mainly applies to His Second Advent (*Wahl*). 'When He shall again bring the First-begotten into the world, He shall be deemed worthy of not less honour, for He saith, "Let all the angels," &c. The former *bringing in,* though not expressed, is implied in *vv.* 2, 5. 7. of [*pros tous angelous*]—'in reference TO the angels.' **spirits**—or 'winds.' Who employeth His angels as the winds. His ministers as the lightnings; or, He maketh His angelic ministers the directing powers of winds and flames, when these are required to perform His will. The English version, "maketh His angels *spirits*," means, He maketh them subtle, incorporeal, swift as the wind. So Ps. xviii. 10, "a cherub . . . the wings of the *wind.*" *V.* 14, "ministering *spirits,*" favours the English version. As "spirits" implies the wind-like velocity and subtle nature of the *cherubim,* so "flame of fire" expresses the burning all-consuming devotion of the adoring *seraphim* (meaning 'burning') (Isa. vi. 1). The translation, 'maketh winds His messengers, and a flame of fire His *ministers* (!),' is wrong. In Ps. civ. 3, 4 the subject in each clause comes first, and the attribute predicated of it second; so the article marks "angels" and "ministers" as the *subjects,* and 'winds' and 'flame of fire," predicates [*tous angelous autou pneumata, tous leitourgous autou puros phloga*]. *Schemoth Rabba,* 'God is God of Zebaoth (the heavenly hosts), because, when He pleases, He makes them sit (Judg. vi. 11); stand (Isa. vi. 2); resemble women (Zech. v. 9); men (Gen. xviii. 2); He makes them "spirits," "fire."' "Maketh" implies that, however exalted, they are but creatures (the Son is the Creator, *v.* 10): not *begotten from everlasting,* nor to be *worshipped,* as the Son, Rev. xiv. 7; xxii. 8, 9. 8. O God [*Ho Theos*]. *Grotius,* 'God is Thy throne'—i. e., *God will establish Thy throne.* But nowhere is *God* said to be *Christ's throne.* Heaven, angels, and the righteous are termed God's throne; but Christ sits at God's right hand. The Hebrews, having no vocative form, use the nominative for it. So Targum on Ps. xlv., and Aquila. *Judges* and *angels* (plural) are called *Elohim;* but Elohim,

applied to *one,* expresses GOD alone. The Greek article marks emphasis (Ps. xlv. 6, 7). **for ever . . . righteousness.** *Everlasting duration* and *righteousness* go together, Ps. xlv. 2, 4; lxxxix. 14. **a sceptre of righteousness** [*euthutētos*]—'a rod of rectitude,' or 'straightforwardness.' א A B Δ prefix 'and' (cf. Esth. iv. 11). 9. **iniquity** [*adikian*] —'unrighteousness.' So א A. B Δ read 'lawlessness' [*anomian*]. **therefore**—because God loves righteousness and hates iniquity. **God, even thy God.** Jerome, Augustine, &c., translate (Ps. xlv. 7) 'O God, thy God hath anointed thee,' whereby Christ is addressed as God. This probably the Hebrew there means, and also the Greek here: it is likely the Son is addressed "O God," as in *v.* 8. The *anointing* meant is not that at His baptism, when He solemnly entered on His ministry for us; but that with the "oil of gladness" or 'exulting joy' (*triumph,* the consequence of His manifested *love of righteousness* and *hatred of iniquity*), wherewith, after His triumphant completion of His work, He has been anointed by the Father "above His fellows" (not only above us, the adopted members of God's family, whom 'He is not ashamed to call His brethren;' but above the angels, *partakers* with Him, though infinitely His inferiors, in the holiness and joys of heaven; "sons of God," and angel-"messengers," though subordinate to the Divine Angel-"Messenger of the covenant"). Thus He is antitype to Solomon, 'chosen of all David's sons to sit upon the throne of the kingdom of the Lord over Israel,' even as his father David was chosen before all the house of his father's sons. The image is from the custom of anointing guests at feasts (Ps. xxiii. 5); or rather of anointing kings: not until His ascension did He assume *the kingdom* as Son of man. A fuller accomplishment is yet to be, when He shall be VISIBLY the anointed king over the whole earth (set by the Father) on His holy hill of Zion (Ps. ii. 6, 8). So David, His type, was first anointed at Bethlehem (1 Sam. xvi. 13; Ps. lxxxix. 20); again at Hebron, first over Judah (2 Sam. ii. 4), then over all Israel (2 Sam. v. 3): not till Saul's death did he enter on his actual kingdom; as not till after Christ's death the Father "set Him at His own right hand . . . far above all principality" (Eph. i. 20, 21). The 45th psalm in its first meaning was addressed to Solomon; but the Holy Spirit inspired the writer to use language applying in its fulness to the antitypical Solomon, the true Head of the theocracy. 10. **And.** In another passage He says, **in the beginning.** The LXX. (as in Gen. i. 1) answers by contrast to *the end* implied in "they shall perish," &c. The English version, 'of old:' Hebrew, 'aforetime.' Greek order here (not in LXX.) is, 'Thou in the beginning, Lord,' which throws "Lord" into emphasis. 'Christ is preached even in passages where many might contend that the Father was principally intended' (*Bengel*). **laid the foundation of** [*ethemeliosas*]—*firmly.*' **heavens**—plural: manifold, including various orders of heavenly intelligences (Eph. iv. 10). **works of thine hands**—the heavens, as a hand-woven curtain spread out (Ps. civ. 2). 11. **They.**

12 wax old as doth a garment; and as a vesture shalt thou fold them up, and they shall be changed: but thou art the same, and thy years shall not fail.

13 But to which of the angels said he at any time, °Sit on my right

14 hand, until I make thine enemies thy footstool? Are they not all ministering spirits, sent forth to minister for them who shall be heirs of salvation?

2 THEREFORE we ought to give the more earnest heed to the things

2 which we have heard, lest at any time we should ¹ let *them* slip. For if the word spoken by angels was stedfast, and every transgression and dis-

3 obedience received a just recompence of reward; how shall we escape, if we neglect ª so great salvation; which at the first began to be spoken by the Lord, and was confirmed unto us by them that heard

A. D. 64.

° Ps. 110. 1.
Matt 22.44.
Mark 12. 36.
Luke 20. 42.
Acts 2. 34.
36.
Acts 7. 55.

CHAP. 2.
1 run out as
leaking
vessels.
Hab. 1. 6.
Hab. 2. 16.
ª Isa. 45. 17.
Luke 1. 69.

The earth and the heavens in their present form "shall perish" (ch. xii. 26, 27): not *annihilation;* as in the case of "the world that . . . being over-flowed with water, *perished*" (2 Pet. iii. 6). The covenant of the possession of the earth was renewed with Noah and his seed on the renovated earth. So it shall be after the perishing by fire (2 Pet. iii. 12, 13). remainest—*through [diameneis]* all changes. as doth a garment (Isa. li. 6). 12. vesture [*peribolaion*] — 'an enwrapping cloak.' fold them up. LXX., Ps. cii. 26 [*helixeis*]; but Hebrew, '*change* them.' The Spirit, by Paul, treats the Old Testament with independence of handling, presenting the Divine truth in various aspects; sometimes sanctioning LXX. (cf. Isa. xxxiv. 4; Rev. vi. 14); sometimes the Hebrew; sometimes varying from both. changed—as one lays aside a garment to put on another. thou art the same (Isa. xlvi. 4; Mal. iii. 6). The same in nature, therefore in covenant faithfulness to thy people. shall not fail—Hebrew, 'end.' Israel in Babylon, in Ps. cii., casts her hopes of deliver-ance on Messiah, Israel's unchanging covenant-God.

13. (Ps. cx. 1) The image is from conquerors putting the feet on the necks of the conquered (Josh. x. 24, 25). 14. ministering spirits—*v.* 7, "spirits, and his ministers" Incorporeal *spirits,* as God, but *ministering* to Him as inferiors. sent forth [*apostellomena*]—'being sent forth' *contin-ually,* as their regular service in all ages. to minister [*eis diakonian*]—'unto (*i. e.,* for) ministry.' for them [*dia tous*]—'*for the sake* of them,' &c. Angels are sent forth on *ministrations to God and Christ,* not primarily to men, though *for the good* of 'those who are about to inherit salvation' [*mellontas kleronomein soterian*]: the elect, for whom all things, angels included, work together for good (Rom. viii. 28). Angels' ministrations are not properly *to* men, since the latter cannot command them, though their ministrations *to God* are often *for the good of men.* So the superi-ority of the Son of God to angels is shown. They "all," however various their ranks, *minister;* He is ministered to. They "*stand*" (Luke i. 19) before God, or are "*sent* forth" to execute His commands on behalf of them whom He pleases to save; He *sits* "on the right hand of the Majesty on high" (*vv.* 3, 13). He rules; they serve.

CHAP. II. 1-18.—DANGER OF NEGLECTING SO GREAT SALVATION, FIRST SPOKEN BY CHRIST— TO WHOM, NOT TO ANGELS, THE NEW DISPENSA-TION WAS SUBJECTED—THOUGH FOR A TIME HUMBLED BELOW ANGELS—THIS TOOK PLACE BY DIVINE NECESSITY FOR OUR SALVATION.

1. Therefore—Because Christ the Mediator of the new covenant is so far (ch. i.) above angels, the mediators of the old covenant. the more

earnest [*perissoteros*]—'more abundantly.' heard —spoken by God (ch. i. 2); and the Lord (*v.* 3). let them slip [*pararuomen*]—'flow past them' (ch. iv. 1). 2. (Cf. *v.* 3) Argument *a fortiori.* spoken by angels—the Mosaic law spoken by the ministration of angels (Deut. xxxiii. 2; Ps. lxviii. 17; Acts vii. 53; Gal. iii. 19). When it is said, Exod. xx. 1, "God spake," it means He spake by angels as His mouthpiece, or angels repeating in unison with His voice the decalogue. Whereas the Gospel was first spoken by the Lord alone. was stedfast [*egeneto bebaios*]—'*was made* sted-fast,' or "confirmed:" was enforced by penalties on those violating it. transgression—by doing evil; [*parabasis*] *overstepping* its bounds: a posi-tive violation. disobedience [*parakoe*]—by ne-glecting to do good: a negative violation. recom-pence (Deut. xxxii. 35). 3. we—emphatical: who have received the message of salvation so clearly delivered to us (cf. ch. xii. 25). so great salvation —embodied in Jesus, whose name means *salvation,* not only deliverance from foes and death, and the grant of temporal blessings (which the law promised to the obedient), but also grace of the Spirit, forgiveness of sins, and the promise of glory (*v.* 10). which [*hetis*]—'*inasmuch as being a* salvation *which* began,' &c. spoken by the Lord —not as the law, spoken by angels (*v.* 2). Both law and Gospel came from God; but promulgated by different *instrumentality* (cf. *v.* 5). As the law began with God's writing of the Ten Command-ments, so the Gospel began with the word of the Son of God Himself. His sermon on the mount confirms the law in its far-reaching spirituality, and His life fulfilled it. As the gospels record His actings in person, so the Acts His actings by His Spirit. As the Acts set forth the externals of the Church, so the epistles its internal aspect. Angels recognize Him as "the Lord" (Matt. xxviii. 6; Luke ii. 11). confirmed unto us—not by penalties, as the law, but by spiritual gifts (*v.* 4). by them that heard him (cf. Luke i. 2). Though Paul had an independent revelation of Christ (Gal. i. 16, 17, 19), yet he classes himself with those Jews whom he addresses, "unto us;" for, like them, in many particulars (*ex. gr.,* the agony in Gethsemane, ch. v. 7), he was dependent for autoptic information on the Twelve. So the *discourses* of Jesus—*ex. gr.,* the sermon on the mount, and the first proclamation of the gospel kingdom by the Lord (Matt. iv. 17)—he could only know by report of the twelve: so Christ's saying, Acts xx. 35. Paul mentions what they had *heard,* rather than *seen,* conformably with what he began with (*vv.* 1, 2), "Spake . . . spoken." Appropriately, in his epistles to Gentiles, he dwells on his independent call to the apostleship of the Gentiles; in his epistle to the Hebrews he

529

4 *him;* God also bearing *them* witness, both with signs and wonders, and with divers miracles, and [2] gifts of the Holy Ghost, according to his own will?

5 For unto the angels hath he not put in subjection the world to come,

6 whereof we speak. But one in a certain place testified, saying, [b] What is man, that thou art mindful of him? or the son of man, that thou

7 visitest him? Thou madest him [3] a little lower than the angels: thou crownedst him with glory and honour, and didst set him over the works

8 of thy hands: thou hast put all things in subjection under his feet. For in that he put all in subjection under him, he left nothing *that is* not

A. D. 64.

[2] Or. distributions
1 Cor. 12. 4, 11.
Eph. 4.8,11.
[b] Job 7. 17, 18.
Job 15. 14.
Ps. 8. 4.
[3] Or. a little while inferior to.

appeals to the apostles who had been long with the Lord (cf. Acts i. 21: x. 41): so in his sermon to Jews in Antioch of Pisidia (Acts xiii. 31). 'He only appeals to the testimony of these apostles in general, in order to bring the Hebrews to the Lord alone' (*Bengel*); not to become partizans of particular apostles, as Peter, the apostle of the circumcision, and James, the bishop of Jerusalem. The Hebrews of the *churches of Palestine and Syria* (or those dispersed in Asia Minor (*Bengel*), 1 Pet. i. 1, or in Alexandria) are primarily addressed; for of none so well could it be said, the Gospel was confirmed to them by the immediate hearers of the Lord: the past tense, "was confirmed," implies some time had elapsed since this testification by eye-witnesses. **4. them**—rather, 'God, along with the Lord and His eye-witness, (*v.* 3) bearing witness to *it*;' 'joining in attestation of it.' **signs and wonders**—performed by Christ and His apostles. "Signs" [*sêmeia*] are miracles, or other facts regarded as *proofs* of a divine mission; "wonders" [*terata*] are miracles viewed as prodigies, causing *astonishment* (Acts ii. 22, 33); *powers* [*dunameis*] are miracles viewed as manifestations of superhuman *power*. **divers miracles**—'varied (miraculous) *powers*' (2 Cor. xii. 12) granted to the apostles after the ascension. **gifts, &c.** [*merismois*]—'distributions.' The Holy Spirit was given to Christ without measure (John iii. 34); but to us it is *distributed* in various measures and operations (Rom. xii. 3, 6, &c.; 1 Cor. xii. 4-11). **according to his own will**—God's sovereign will, assigning one gift to one, another to another (Acts v. 32; Eph. i. 5).

5. For—confirming *vv.* 2, 3, that the new covenant was spoken by One higher than the mediators of the old covenant; viz., angels. Greek order, 'Not to angels hath He,' &c. **the world to come.** He *has* subjected to angels (as regards *ministry* only) *the existing world*—the Old Testament dispensation (then still existing in its framework, *v.* 2), the political kingdoms (Dan. iv. 13; x. 13, 20, 21; xii. 1), the natural elements (Rev. ix. 11; xvi. 4), and even individuals (Matt. xviii. 10); but not so "the world to come"—the new dispensation brought in by, and subject to Christ, beginning in grace, to be completed in glory. It is called "to come," as when subjected to Christ by the Divine decree it was as yet future, and is still so to us as to its consummation. The *subjecting* of all things to Christ (Ps. viii.) is still "to come." From the Old Testament standpoint, which looks prophetically forward to the New Testament (and the Old Testament ritual was in force then, and continued till its forcible abrogation by the destruction of Jerusalem), it is "the world to come." Paul, addressing Jews, appropriately calls it so, according to their conventional view of it. We still pray, "Thy kingdom come," for its *manifestation* in glory is yet future. 'This world,' in contrast, expresses the world's present fallen condition (Eph. ii. 2). Believers belong not

to it, but by faith rise in spirit to "the world to come," making it a present, though internal, reality. In the world to come man and the Son of man, man's Head, are to be supreme. Hence greater reverence was paid to angels in the Old Testament than is permitted in the New. For man's nature is exalted in Christ, so that angels are our "fellow-servants" (Rev. xxii. 9). In their ministrations they stand on a different footing towards us from that in the Old Testament. We are "brethren" of Christ; which angels are not (*vv.* 10-12, 16). **6. But**—Not unto *angels* is the Gospel kingdom subjected, "BUT" to MAN. **one ... testified.** The usual way of quoting Scripture to readers familiar with it. Ps. viii. 5-7 praises Jehovah for exalting MAN, so as to subject all God's works on earth to him. This dignity, lost by the first Adam, is realized only in the Son of man, the Representative Man, Head of our redeemed race. In *vv.* 6-8 MAN is spoken of *in general* ("him . . . him . . . his"); then, at *v.* 9, first, JESUS is introduced, fulfilling, as man, all the conditions of the prophecy; Himself through death passing, and so bringing us men, His "brethren," to "glory." **What.** How insignificant in himself, how exalted by God's grace! (cf. Ps. cxliv. 3.) *Enosh* and *Ben-Adam* express *man* and *Son of man* in his weakness: "Son of man" is here *any* and *every child of man*—unlike the lord of creation which he was originally (Gen. i. and ii.), and actually is by title, and shall hereafter fully be in the person of and in union with Jesus, pre-eminently the Son of man (*v.* 9). **art mindful**—as of one absent. **visitest** [*episkeptē*]—*lookest after* him, as one present. **7. a little**—or [מעט] (Hos. i. 4), 'for a little time.' St. Paul's scope is to show Jesus, *the Son of man*, by whom the Gospel comes, *is superior to the angels*, by whom the law was spoken. But it may be objected, Christ was mortal and suffered. True, answers Paul, but that was only 'for a little time,' because our salvation required it. So [*brachu ti*] Acts v. 24. 'Hours on the cross, days of sufferings, years of toil, how little are they all compared with eternity!' (*Bengel.*) **than the angels**—'*than* God [*Elohim*]; *i. e.*, God's abstract qualities, such as' *angels* possess in an inferior form—viz., heavenly, spiritual, incorporeal natures. Man, made for a little lower than angels, has an universal dominion ultimately awaiting him in the man Jesus, Lord of angels. **crownedst him with glory and honour**—as the kingly vicegerent of God over this earth (Gen. i.; ii.; Dan. vii. 27; Rev. v. 10). **and didst set him over the works of thy hands.** Omitted in B Δ; but read by ℵ A C *f*, Vulgate: so Ps. viii. 6. **8.** (1 Cor. xv. 27) **For in that**—*i. e.*, For in that *God saith*, *in the 8th Psalm,* 'He put [*ta panta*] *the* all things (just mentioned) in subjection under him: He left nothing,' &c. As no limitation occurs in the Scripture, the "all things" must include heavenly, as well as earthly things (cf. 1 Cor. iii. 21, 22). **But now**—as things now are, we see not yet *the*

put under him. But now we see not yet all things put under him:
9 but we see Jesus, who was made a little lower than the angels, ⁴ for the
suffering of death crowned with glory and honour; that he by the grace
10 of God should taste death for every man. For ^c it became him, for
whom *are* all things, and by whom *are* all things, in bringing many
sons unto glory, to make the Captain of their salvation ^d perfect through
suffering.
11 For both he that sanctifieth and they who are sanctified *are* all of
12 one: for which cause ^e he is not ashamed to call them brethren, saying,

A. D. 64.

⁴ Or. by.
^c Pro. 16. 4.
Isa. 43. 21.
Luke 24. 46.
^d Matt. 3. 15.
ch. 6. 20.
ch. 12. 2.
^e Matt. 28. 10.
John 20. 17.
Rom 8. 29.

all things put under man. **9. But**—'*But rather,* Him who was made for a little lower than the angels (cf. Luke xxii. 43) we behold (*by faith:* a different verb from "we see" *visibly, v.* 8 [*horomen*], which expresses the impression our eyes *passively* receive from objects; whereas [*blepomen*] "we behold," "look," implies *direction* and *intention,* as of one *deliberately* regarding something, and *mentally perceiving:* so ch. iii. 19; x. 25, Greek)—viz., Jesus, on account of His suffering death, crowned,' &c. He is already so crowned to the eye of faith; hereafter all things shall be subjected to Him visibly. The ground of His exaltation is 'on account of His having suffered death' (Phil. ii. 8, 9; *v.* 10). **that he by the grace of God** (Titus ii. 11; iii. 4). The reading of *Origen,* 'That He *without* (*chŏris* for *chariti God*' (*laying aside His Divinity:* or, for every being *save God;* or perhaps 'apart from God,' forsaken, as the sin-bearer, by the Father on the cross), is not supported by MSS. The "that," &c., is connected with "crowned with glory," &c. His exaltation after sufferings is the *perfecting* of His work (*v.* 10) for us: from it flows the result *that His tasting of death is available* in behalf of *every man.* He is crowned as the Head of our common humanity, presenting His blood as the all-prevailing plea for us. This coronation above makes His death applicable for *every* individual *man* (singular: not merely 'for all men') (ch. iv. 14; ix. 24; 1 John ii. 2). "Taste death" implies personal experimental undergoing it: death of body, and death (spiritually) of soul, in His being forsaken of the Father. 'As a physician first tastes his medicines to encourage his patient to take them, so Christ, when all men feared death, to persuade them to be bold in meeting it, tasted it Himself, though He had no need' (*Chrysostom*) (*vv.* 14, 15). **10. For**—reason why "the grace of God" required that Jesus "should taste death." **it became him.** The scheme of redemption was (not only not derogatory to, but) highly *becoming* God, though unbelief considers it a *disgrace* (*Bengel*). It harmonizes with His love, justice, and wisdom. An answer to Hebrew Christians, whosoever stumbling at Christ *crucified,* and impatient at the delay in the advent of Christ's glory, were in danger of apostasy. The Jerusalem Christians especially were liable to this danger. **for whom**— God the Father (Rom. xi. 36; 1 Cor. viii. 6; Rev. iv. 11). In Col. i. 16 the same is said of Christ. **all things** [*ta panta*]—'*the* universe of things.' "Him, for whom . . . by whom are all things" marks the becomingness of Christ's suffering as the way to being 'perfected' as 'Captain of our salvation,' seeing this is the way that pleased Him whose will and glory are *the end* of all things, and by whose *operation* all things exist. **in bringing** [*agagonta*] — past, 'having brought, as He did;' *in His electing purpose* having determined to bring (cf. note, Gal. iv. 6; Eph. i. 4), which is accomplished in Jesus' being 'perfected through suffering.' **many** (Matt. xx. 28)—"the church" (*v.* 12; ch. xii. 23). **sons**—no longer *children,* as

under the old Testament, but *sons* by adoption (Gal. iv. 3, 5). **unto glory**—to share Christ's (*v.* 9: cf. *v.* 7; John xvii. 10, 22, 24; Rom. viii. 21). Sonship, holiness (*v.* 11), and glory are inseparable. "Suffering," "salvation," and "glory" often go together (2 Tim. ii. 10). *Salvation* presupposes *destruction,* our deliverance from which required Christ's "sufferings." **to make . . . perfect** [*teleiōsai*]—*to consummate:* to bring to consummated glory through sufferings, as the appointed avenue. 'He who suffers for another not only benefits him, but becomes himself the more perfect' (*Chrysostom*). Bringing to the end of troubles, and to the *goal* of glory: a metaphor from contests in the public games (cf. Luke xxiv. 26; John xix. 30 [*tetelestai*]). I prefer, with *Calvin,* 'to perfect as a completed *sacrifice:' legal, official,* not moral, *perfection* is meant: 'to *consecrate* (so the same Greek, ch. vii. 28, *margin*), by His finished expiatory death, as our perfect High Priest, so our "Captain of salvation" (Luke xiii. 32). This agrees with *v.* 11, "He that sanctifieth"—*i. e.,* consecrates them, by being made a consecrated offering for them. So ch. x. 10, 14, 29; John xvii. 19: by perfecting His consecration for them in His death, He perfects their consecration, and so opens access to glory (ch. x. 19-21: ch. v. 9; ix. 9, accords with this sense). **Captain of, &c.** [*Archĕgon*]—*Prince-leader:* as Joshua, not Moses, *led* the people into the Holy land, so our Joshua—Jesus—leads us into the heavenly inheritance (Acts xiii. 39). The same Greek, ch. xii. 2, "*Author* of our faith." Acts iii. 15, "*Prince* of life" (*v.* 31). Preceding by example, as well as the originator of our salvation.

11. he that sanctifieth—Christ, who once for all consecrates His people to God (Jude 1, bringing them nigh as the consequence) and everlasting glory, by having consecrated Himself for them in being made "perfect (as their expiatory sacrifice) through sufferings" (*v.* 10). God, in electing love, through Christ's finished work, *perfectly* sanctifies them to God's service and to heaven *once for all:* then they are *progressively* sanctified by the transforming Spirit. 'Sanctification is glory in embryo: glory is sanctification come to the birth' (*Alford*). **they who are sanctified** [*hoi hagiazomenoi*]— 'they that are being sanctified' (cf. "sanctified," 1 Cor. vii. 14). **of one**—Father, God: not in the sense wherein He is Father of *all* beings, as angels; for these are excluded by the argument, *v.* 16; but as He is Father of His *spiritual human* sons, Christ the elder Brother, and His believing people, the members of the family. This and the following verses justify His having said, "many *sons*" (*v.* 10). "Of one" is not 'of one father, *Adam,*' or 'Abraham,' as *Bengel,* &c.; for the Saviour's participation in the *lowness* of our humanity is not mentioned till *v.* 14, and then as a consequence of what precedes. Moreover, 'sons *of God*' is the dignity obtained by our union with Christ: our *brotherhood* with Him flows from *God* being *His* and *our* Father. Christ's Sonship (by generation) in relation to God is reflected in the sonship (by

f I will declare thy name unto my brethren; in the midst of the church
13 will I sing praise unto thee. And again, *g* I will put my trust in him.
14 And again, *h* Behold I and the children which God hath given me. Forasmuch then as the children are partakers of flesh and blood, he also himself likewise took part of the same; that through death he might
15 destroy him that had the power of death, that is, the devil; and deliver them who *i* through fear of death were all their lifetime subject to bondage.

A. D 64.

f Ps. 22. 22.
g Ps 18. 2.
  Isa. 12. 2.
h Isa 8. 18.
  John 10. 29.
i Ps. 33. 19.
  Luke 1. 74.
  Rom. 8. 7.

adoption) of His brethren. **he is not ashamed** —though being the Son *of God*, since they now by adoption have a like dignity, so that His majesty is not compromised by brotherhood with them (cf. ch. xi. 16). Christianity unites such amazing contrasts as 'our brother and our God.' 'God makes of sons of men sons of God, because God hath made of the Son of God the Son of man,' (*St. Augustine* on Ps. ii.) **12.** Messiah declares the name of the Father, not known fully as Christ's Father, and therefore *their* Father, till after His crucifixion (John xx. 17), among His brethren ("the church," *i. e.*, the congregation), that they in turn may praise Him (Ps. xxii. 22, 23). At *v.* 22, the 22nd Psalm, which begins with Christ's cry, "My God, my God, why hast thou forsaken me?" passes from Christ's sufferings to His triumph, prefigured in the experience of David. **will I sing**—as leader of the choir (Ps. viii. 2). **13. I will put my trust in him**—from LXX. [*pepoithōs esomai ep' autō*], Isa. viii. 17, which immediately precedes "Behold I and the children," &c. The objection is, the following words, "and again," usually introduce a *new* quotation; whereas these two are parts of one passage. However, the two clauses express distinct ideas. "I will put my trust in Him" expresses His *filial* confidence in His Father, to whom He flees in sufferings, and is not disappointed; which His believing brethren imitate, *trusting* solely in the Father through Christ, not in their own merits. 'Christ exhibited this "trust," not for Himself, for He and the Father are one, but for His people' (*v.* 16). Each fresh aid given assured Him, as it does them, of further aid, until the complete victory was obtained over hell (Phil. i. 6) (*Bengel*). **Behold I and the children, &c.** (Isa. viii. 18.) "Sons" (*v.* 10), "brethren" (*v.* 12), "children" imply His right and property in them from everlasting. He calls them "children" of God, though not yet in being, but considered so in His *purpose*; and presents them before the Father, who has given Him them, to be glorified with Himself. Isaiah (meaning 'salvation of Jehovah') typically represented Messiah, at once Father and Son, Isaiah and Immanuel (Isa. ix. 6). Isaiah and his children rely, not like Ahaz and the Jews on the Assyrian king, against the confederacy of Pekah of Israel and Rezin of Syria, but on Jehovah. He then foretells the deliverance of Judah by God, in language realized only in the far greater deliverance wrought by Messiah. Christ, the antitypical Prophet, instead of the human confidences of His age, Himself, and GOD THE FATHER'S *children* (who are therefore *His* children, so antitypical to *Isaiah's*, though regarded also as His "brethren:" cf. Isa. ix. 6, "Father;" and "His *seed*," liii. 10), led by Him, trust wholly in God for salvation. The official words and acts of the prophets find their antitype in the Great Prophet (Rev. xix. 10); as His kingly office is antitypical to that of the theocratic kings, and His priestly office to the Aaronic priesthood. **14.** He who is thus "Captain (prince, *leader*) of their salvation" to the "many sons," by *trusting* and *suffering* like them, must become *man* like them, that His death may avail for them as men.

the children—mentioned, *v.* 13: existing in His eternal purpose, though not in actual being. **are partakers of** [*kekoinōnēken*]—'have (in His purpose) been in common partakers.' **flesh and blood.** א A B C Δ have 'blood and flesh.' The inner element, *blood*, the immediate vehicle of the soul, stands before the palpable element, *flesh*; also, because of *Christ's blood-shedding*, with a view to which He entered into community with our *corporeal* life. "The life of the *flesh* is in the *blood* . . . it is the blood that maketh an atonement for the soul" (Lev. xvii. 11, 14). **likewise** [*paraplesiōs*]—'in a *somewhat* (though not altogether) similar manner.' He, unlike them, was conceived and born not in sin (ch. iv. 15): not *flesh of flesh*, but of the Holy Spirit: not merely man, but taking manhood into union with Godhead: not naturally, but of His own will. [Hence of *men* the word is *kekoinēken*, 'they had the same nature in common;' of Christ, *metesche*, "took part of" in His own peculiar manner. But mainly 'in like manner;' not in *semblance* of a body, as the Docetæ heretics taught.] **took part of**—participated in. The forfeited inheritance (according to Jewish law) was ransomed by the nearest of kin; so Jesus became so to us (*Goel:* at once *kinsman, redeemer, avenger*) by His assumed humanity, in order to be our Redeemer. **that through death** —which He could not have undergone as God, but only by becoming man: not by Almighty power, but '*by His* [*tou*] *death*.' 'Jesus suffering death overcame: Satan wielding death succumbed' (*Bengel*): as David cut off Goliath's head with the giant's own sword, wherewith the latter had won his victories. Coming to redeem mankind, Christ made Himself a sort of hook to destroy the devil; for in Him there was His humanity to attract the devourer, His divinity to pierce, apparent weakness to provoke, hidden power to transfix the hungry ravisher. Latin epigram, 'Mors mortis morti mortem nisi morte tulisset, Æternæ vitæ janua clausa foret'—*Had not Death by death borne to Death the death of Death, the gate of eternal life would be closed.* **destroy** [*katargēsē*]—'render powerless:' deprive of power to hurt His people (Ps. viii. 2). The same verb, 2 Tim. i. 10, "abolished death." Death is not death to believers. Christ plants in them an undying germ of heavenly immortality. **power.** Satan is "strong" (Matt. xii. 29). **of death.** *Death* itself is a *power* which, though originally foreign to human nature, now reigns over it (Rom. v. 12; vi. 9). Satan lurking beneath wields death's *power*, which is manifest. The author of sin is the author of its consequences. Cf. "power of the enemy" (Luke x. 19). God's law (Gen. ii. 17; Rom. vi. 23) makes death the executioner of sin, and man Satan's '*lawful* captive.' Jesus, by dying, has made the dying His own (Rom. xiv. 9), and taken the prey from the mighty ('Wisdom,' ii. 24). **15. fear of death**—even before they experienced its *power*. **all their lifetime.** Such a life can hardly be called life. **subject to bondage** [*enochoi douleias*]—'subjects *of* bondage:' not merely *liable to*, but *enthralled in* it (cf. Rom. viii. 15; Gal. v. 1). Contrast the *glory* of the "sons" (*v.* 10). Christ, by delivering us from

16 For verily ⁵ he took not on *him the nature of* angels; but he took on *him*
17 the seed of Abraham. Wherefore in all things it behoved him to be made like unto *his* brethren, that he might be a merciful and faithful High Priest in things *pertaining* to God, to make reconciliation for the
18 sins of the people. For in that he himself hath suffered, being tempted, he is able to succour them that are tempted.
3 WHEREFORE, holy brethren, partakers of the heavenly calling, con-

A. D. 64.
⁵ he taketh not hold of angels, but of the seed of Abraham he taketh hold

God's curse against our sin, has taken from death all that made it formidable. Death, viewed apart from Christ, can only fill with horror, if the sinner durst think. **16. For verily** [δή που]—' For *as we all* grant.' Paul alludes to Isa. xli. 8; Jer. xxxi. 32, LXX. [*epilabomenou mou tēs cheiros autōn*]. All *Jews* would know that the fact stated as to Messiah was what the prophets led them to expect. **took not on him, &c.**—rather, 'it is not angels that He *is helping* [the present, *epilambanetai*, implies *duration*]; but it is the seed of Abraham that He is *helping:*' lit., *to help by taking one by the hand*, as ch. viii. 9; answering to "succour," *v.* 18; "deliver," *v.* 15. 'Not angels,' who have no flesh and blood, but "the children," who have "flesh and blood," He takes hold of to help by 'Himself taking part of the same' (*v.* 14). Whatever effect Christ's work may have on angels, He is not taking hold of them to help them by suffering in their nature to deliver them from death, as in our case. **seed of Abraham.** He views Christ's redemption (in compliment to the *Hebrews*, and as enough for his purpose) with reference to Abraham's seed, *the Jewish nation.* The Gentiles (*v.* 9, "for every man"), when believers, are also the seed of Abraham spiritually (cf. *v.* 12; Ps. xxii. 22, 25, 27); but *direct* reference to them, such as is in Rom. iv. 11, 12, 16; Gal. iii. 7, 14, 28, 29, would be out of place in his present argument. It is the same argument for Jesus being the Christ which Matthew, writing for Hebrews, uses, tracing His genealogy from Abraham, the father of the Jews, to whom those promises were given on which the Jews especially prided themselves (cf. Rom. ix. 4, 5). **17. Wherefore** [*hothen*]—' Whence.' Found in *Paul's* speech, Acts xxvi. 19. **in all things**—incidental to manhood. *Sin* is not, in man's original constitution, a necessary attendant of manhood, so He had no sin. **it behoved him**—by moral necessity, considering what God's justice and love required of Him as Mediator (cf. ch. v. 3), having voluntarily undertaken to 'help' man (*v.* 16). **his brethren** (*v.* 11) —"the seed of Abraham" (*v.* 16): so also the spiritual seed, His elect out of all mankind. **be** [*genētai*]—'that He might *become* High Priest :' He was *called* so, when 'made perfect by the things which He suffered' (*v.* 10; ch. v. 8-10). He was *made* (*became*) so, when He entered within the veil, from which flows His ever-continuing priestly intercession for us (ch. vi. 20; ix. 24). His death, as man, must first be, that the bringing in of the blood into the heavenly Holy Place might follow, in which consisted the expiation as High Priest. **merciful**—to "the *people*" deserving wrath by "sins." *Mercy* is a priest's prime requisite, since His office is to help the wretched and raise the fallen; such *mercy* is to be found in one who has a fellow-feeling with the afflicted, having been so once Himself (ch. iv. 15): not that the Son of God needed to be taught mercy by suffering; but, in order to save us, He needed to take manhood with all its sorrows, qualifying Himself by experimental suffering with us, to be our sympathizing High Priest in all our sorrows. **faithful**—true to God (ch. iii. 5, 6) and to man (ch. x. 23) in His Mediatorial office. **High Priest**

—which Moses was not, though "faithful" (ch. iii. 2). Only in Ps. cx., Zech. vi. 13, elsewhere, is Christ expressly called a *Priest.* In this epistle alone His *priesthood* is professedly discussed; how necessary, then, this book is to the New Testament. In Ps. cx. and Zech. vi. 13 there is added the *kingdom* of Christ, which elsewhere is spoken of without the *priesthood.* On the cross, whereon as Priest He offered the sacrifice, He had "King" inscribed over Him (*Bengel*). **to make reconciliation for the sins** [*hilaskesthai tas hamartias*]— 'to propitiate (in respect to) the sins :' '*to expiate the sins.*' Strictly Divine *justice* is 'propitiated;' but God's *love* is as much from everlasting as His justice; therefore, lest Christ's sacrifice, or its type, the legal sacrifices, should be thought antecedent to God's grace, neither are said in Scripture to have *propitiated God;* otherwise Christ's sacrifice might be thought to have first induced God to love and pity man, instead of His love having *originated* Christ's sacrifice, whereby Divine justice and Divine love are harmonized. The sinner is brought by that sacrifice into God's favour, which by sin he had forfeited; hence his prayer is, ' God *be propitiated* [*hilastheti*] to me, who am a sinner' (Luke xviii. 13). Sins bring death and the "fear of death" (*v.* 15). He had no sin Himself, and 'made reconciliation for the iniquity' of all (Dan. ix. 24). **of the people**—"the seed of Abraham" (*v.* 16): Israel first, then, through Israel, the believing Gentiles (1 Pet. ii. 10). **18. For**—How His being *made like His brethren in all things* has made Him *a merciful and faithful High Priest* for us (*v.* 17). **in that** [*en ho-autos*]—'*wherein* He suffered Himself, *having been* tempted [*peirastheis*], He is able to succour them *that are being* (now) *tempted* [*peirazomenois*] in the same temptation; and as "He was tempted (tried) in *all* points," He is able (by the power of *sympathy*) to succour us in all possible trials incidental to man (ch. iv. 15; v. 2). He is the antitypical Solomon, having for every grain of Abraham's seed (about to be as the sand for number) "largeness of heart, even as the sand that is on the sea shore" (1 Ki. iv. 29). 'He knows our trials, not only as God, but as man, by experimental feeling.'

CHAP. III. 1-16.—The Son of God greater than Moses, so Unbelief towards Him incurs a Heavier Punishment than befell Unbelieving Israel in the Wilderness.

As Moses especially was the prophet by whom 'God in time past spake to the Fathers' (ch. i. 1), being mediator of the law, Paul shows that, great as was Moses, the Son of God is greater. *Ebrard*, 'The angel of the covenant came in the name of God before Israel; Moses in the name of Israel before God; 'whereas the high priest came *both* in the name of God (bearing the name Jehovah on his forehead) before Israel, and in the name of Israel (bearing the name of the twelve tribes on his breast) before God (Exod. xxviii. 9-29, 36-38). Now Christ is above the angels (chs. i. and ii.), because, (1.) as Son of God He is higher; and (2.) as Son of man, because manhood, though for a time lower than angels, is in Him exalted above them to the lordship of "the world to come," since He is at once Messenger of God to

2 sider the *a* Apostle and High Priest of our profession, Christ Jesus; who was faithful to him that ¹ appointed him, as also *b* Moses *was faithful* in all his house.

3 For this *man* was counted worthy of more glory than Moses, inasmuch as *c* he who hath builded the house hath more honour than the house.

4 For every house is builded by some *man;* but *d* he that built all things *is* God.

5 And Moses verily *was* faithful in all his house, as a servant, *e* for a

6 testimony of those things which were to be spoken after; but Christ as a Son over his own house; whose *f* house are we, *g* if we hold fast the confidence and the rejoicing of the hope firm unto the end.

A. D. 64.

CHAP. 3.
a Matt. 15. 24.
1 Tim. 3. 15.
1 made.
? Sam. 12. 6.
b Num. 12. 7.
c Zech. 6. 12.
Matt. 16. 18.
d Eph. 2. 10.
e Deut. 18. 15.
18. 19.
f Eph. 4. 12.
g Matt. 10. 32.

men, and atoning Priest-Representative of men before God (ch. ii. 17, 18). Parallel with this argument as to His superiority to angels (ch. i. 4) runs that which follows as to His superiority to Moses (ch. iii. 3)—(1.) Because as *Son over the* house He is above the *servant in* the house (*vv.* 5, 6), just as the *angels* were shown to be but *ministering* spirits (ch. i. 14), whereas He is the *Son* (*vv.* 7, 8). (2.) Because the bringing of Israel into the promised rest, not finished by Moses, is accomplished by Him (ch. iv. 1-11) through His being not merely leader and lawgiver as Moses, but also propitiatory High Priest (ch. iv. 14; v. 10). 1. Wherefore [*Hothen*]—'Whence;' i. e., Seeing we have such a sympathizing Helper, you ought to 'contemplate attentively,' fix your mind on Him, so as to profit by the contemplation (ch. xii. 2). [*Katanoēsate*, often used by *Luke, Paul's* companion (Luke xii. 24. 27).] brethren—in Christ, the common bond of union. partakers (*v.* 14; ch. vi. 4). heavenly calling—coming from heaven, and leading to heaven. Phil. iii. 14, "the high calling;" Greek, 'the calling *above.*' the Apostle and High Priest of our profession. One Greek article to both: 'Him *who is at once* Apostle and High Priest'—*Apostle,* as Ambassador (higher than "angel"*-messenger*) sent by the Father (John xx. 21), pleading the cause of *God with us; High Priest,* as pleading *our* cause *with God.* Both His Apostleship and High Priesthood are comprehended in the one title, *Mediator* (*Bengel*). Though "Apostle" is nowhere else applied to Christ, it is appropriate in addressing Hebrews, who used the term of delegates sent by the High Priest to collect the temple tribute from Jews in foreign countries, even as Christ was the Father's Delegate to this world, far off from Him (Matt. xxi. 37). As what applies to Him applies also to His people, the twelve are designated His *apostles,* even as He is the Father's. He is not designated here "angel," in order to distinguish His nature from that of angels mentioned before, though He is "the Angel of the Covenant." The 'legate of the church' (*Sheliach Tsibbur*) offered up prayers in the synagogue in the name and for all. So Jesus, "the Apostle of our profession," is *delegated* to intercede for the Church before the Father. "Of our profession" marks that it is not of the legal ritual, but of our Christian faith, that He is the High Priest. Paul compares Him as an *Apostle* to Moses, as High Priest to Aaron. He alone combines both offices which those two brothers held apart. "Profession" corresponds to God having *spoken* to us by His Son, as Apostle and High Priest. What God proclaims we 'confess.' 2. He first notes the *resemblance* between Moses and Christ, to conciliate the Hebrew Christians, who still entertained a very high opinion of Moses; he afterwards brings forward Christ's superiority. Who was [*onta*]—'being.' He still is faithful, as our mediating High Priest, to the

trust God has assigned Him (ch. ii. 17). So Moses *in* God's *house* (Num. xii. 7). appointed—'*made* Him' HIGH PRIEST: so ch. v. 5; 1 Sam. xii. 6, *margin*; Acts ii. 36: so the Greek fathers. Not as *Ambrose* and the Latins, 'created Him'—*i. e.,* as man, in His incarnation. Moses' likeness to Messiah was foretold by himself (Deut. xviii. 15). Other prophets only *explained Moses,* who was therefore their superior: Christ was *like Moses,* yet superior.

3. For—the reason why they should 'consider' attentively "Christ" (*v.* 1), highly as they regard Moses. was [*ĕxiōtai*]—'has been.' counted worthy of more glory—by God, when He exalted Him to His own right land. The Hebrew Christians admitted this (ch. ɪ. 13). builded the house. 'More honour than the house hath he who *constructed* it' [*kataskeuasas,* instead of "builded," marks that the building meant is not literal, but spiritual—the Church both of the Old and New Testaments; and that the building of such a house includes all the *preparations* of Providence and grace made to furnish it with 'living stones,' and 'servants.' Cf. Exod. i. 21. He who founds a family is said to *build* it [*banah,* whence *Ben,* 'a son']. As Christ the Founder (1 Cor. iii. 9; 1 Pet. ii. 5) is greater than the house so *constructed,* including the servants, He is greater also than Moses, who was but a "servant." Glory results from *honour.* 4. Some one must be the founder of every house: Moses was not the founder, but a portion of the house (but He who established all things, *and therefore* the spiritual house, is God). Christ, being instrumentally the Founder of all things, must be the Founder of the house, so greater than Moses.

5. faithful in all his house—*i. e.,* in all GOD'S house (*v.* 4). servant. Not here [*doulos*] 'slave,' but [*therapōn*] 'a ministering attendant:' free and spontaneous (John viii. 36; xv. 15); marking Moses' high office towards God, though inferior to Christ. Christ was a *servant* (Phil. ii. 7); but He was also the Son, Lord, and Heir of all things. Not so Moses. Christ's service was *assumed* for the economy of salvation; Moses' was so *naturally.* Moses' service could not exceed human bounds: Christ's ministry was unique, capable of being fulfilled by God the Son alone. for a testimony, &c.—that he might, in his typical institutions give 'testimony' to Israel 'of the things' of the gospel 'which were to be spoken afterwards' by Christ (ch. viii. 5; ix. 8, 23; x. 1). 6. But Christ —was and is faithful (*v.* 2). as a Son over his own house—rather, 'over *His* (GOD's, *v.* 4) house:' therefore (as *the inference* from His being one with God) *over His own house.* So ch. x. 21, "having an High Priest over the house of *God.*" Christ enters His Father's house as Master (OVER it), but Moses as servant (IN it, *vv.* 2, 5) (*Chrysostom*). 'An ambassador in the king's absence is distinguished—in the king's presence he falls back

7   Wherefore (as *ʰ*the Holy Ghost saith, To-day *ⁱ*if ye will hear his voice,
8   harden not your hearts, as in the provocation, in the day of temptation
9   in the wilderness; when your fathers tempted me, proved me, and saw
10   my works forty years. Wherefore I was grieved with that generation,
    and said, They do alway err in *their* heart; and they have not known
11   my ways. So I sware in my wrath, ²They shall not enter into my rest.)
12   Take heed, brethren, lest there be in any of you an evil heart of un-
13   belief, in departing from the living God. But exhort one another daily,
    while it is called To-day; lest any of you be hardened through the
14   deceitfulness of sin. For we are made partakers of Christ, if we hold
    the beginning of our confidence stedfast unto the end;

A. D. 64.
ʰ 2 Sam. 23. 2.
Matt. 22. 43.
Mark ⁱ 2. 36.
Acts 1. 16.
Acts 28. 25.
ⁱ Ps. 81 11.
Ps. 95. 7.
Isa. 55. 3.
Matt. 17. 5.
John 5. 25.
2 If they shall enter.

into the multitude' (*Bengel*). **whose house are we**—Paul and His Hebrew readers. So A B C. But Δ *f*, Vulgate, *Lucifer*, '*which* house.' the **rejoicing** [*to kauchema*]—the matter of rejoicing. **of the hope** of *our* hope. Since all our good things lie in hope, we ought so to hold it fast as already to rejoice, as though our hopes were realized (*Chrysostom*). **firm unto the end.** Omitted in B and *Lucifer*. Supported by א A C Δ, Vulgate, *f*.

7. &c. Exhortation, from Ps. xcv., not through unbelief to lose share in the spiritual house. **Wherefore** Seeing we are the house of God if we hold fast our confidence, &c. (*v.* 6.) Jesus is "faithful;" be not ye unfaithful (*vv.* 5, 12). The sentence beginning with "Wherefore," interrupted by the parenthetical confirmation from Ps. xcv., is completed at *v.* 12, "Take heed," &c. **Holy Ghost saith**—by the inspired Psalmist: the words of the latter are the words of God Himself. **To-day**—at length: in David's day, as contrasted with the days of Moses in the wilderness, and the whole time since, during which they rebelled against God's voice (*v.* 8). Each fresh time that the psalm is used in public worship, "to-day" will mean the particular day when used. **hear**—obediently. **his voice**—of grace. **8. Harden not your hearts.** This here only is used of *man's* act: usually of *God's* (Rom. ix. 18). When man is the agent, the phrase usually is "harden his neck," or 'back' (Neh. ix. 17). **provocation . . . temptation**—Massah-meribah, *margin*, 'tentation . . . chiding,' or 'strife' (Exod. xvii. 1-7). Both names refer to the one murmuring of the people against the Lord at Rephidim for want of water. The first offence is the most severely reproved, as it is apt to produce many more. Num. xx. 1-13 and Deut. xxxiii. 8 mention a second, similar, in the wilderness of Sin, near Kadesh, also called Meribah. **in the day**—according to the day of, &c. **9. When** [*Hou*]—'Where;' viz., *in the wilderness.* **your fathers.** The authority of the *ancients* is not conclusive (*Bengel*). **tempted me, proved me.** א A B Δ *f* read [*en dokimasia* for *edokimasan* (C)] 'tempted (me) in the way of testing'—i. e., *putting (me) to the proof* whether I was able and willing to relieve them, not believing that I am so. **saw my works forty years**—they saw, without being led to repentance, my works in affording miraculous help, also in executing vengeance, forty years. The "forty years," joined in the Hebrew and the LXX., and *v.* 17, with "I was grieved," is here joined with they "saw." Both are true: during the same forty years that they were tempting God by unbelief, God was being grieved. The lesson to the Hebrew Christians is, their "to day" is to last only between the first preaching of the Gospel and Jerusalem's impending overthrow—viz., FORTY YEARS; exactly the number of years of Israel's sojourn in the wilderness, until, the full measure of guilt having been filled up, all the

rebels were overthrown. **10. grieved** [*prosochthisa*]—lit., *burdened*, 'displeased.' Cf. "walk contrary," Lev. xxvi. 24, 28. **that generation**—"*that*" (C) implies estrangement. But א B Δ, Vulgate, read 'this.' **said**—"*grieved*" at their first offence. Subsequently, when they hardened their heart in unbelief, He *sware* in His *wrath* (*v.* 11): an ascending gradation (cf. *vv.* 17, 18). **and they have not known** [*autoi de*] — they perceived I was displeased with them, 'yet these very persons' did not a whit the more wish to know my ways (*Bengel*): cf. "but they," Ps. cvi. 43. **not known my ways** — practically and believingly; the "ways" in which I would have had them go, to reach my rest (Exod. xviii. 20). **11.** So [*ὡς*]—'As in conformity with the fact that.' **I sware**—the oath of God preceded the forty years. **not** [*ei*]—'*if* they shall enter, &c. (God do so to me, and more also)' (2 Sam. iii. 35). Greek, Mark viii. 12. **my rest**—Canaan, primarily, their rest after wandering in the wilderness: still, even in it, they never *fully* enjoyed rest; therefore the threat extended further than the exclusion of the unbelieving from the literal land of rest; the rest promised to the believing in its full blessedness was, and is, yet future. Cf. Ps. xxv. 13; xxxvii. 9, 11, 22, 29, and Christ's beatitude, Matt. v. 5. **12. Take heed.** To be joined with "Wherefore," *v.* 7. **lest there be** [*estai*]—'lest there *shall* be;' lest there be, as I fear *there is;* it is not merely a *possible* contingency, there is ground for thinking *it will be so.* **in any**—'in any one of you.' Not merely all ought to be on their guard, but to be so concerned for *each one* as not to suffer any to perish through their negligence (*Calvin*). **heart.** The *heart* is not to be trusted. Cf. *v.* 10. **unbelief** —*faithlessness.* Christ is *faithful;* therefore, saith Paul to the *Hebrews*, we ought not to be *faithless,* as our fathers were under Moses. **departing**—apostatizing. The opposite of "come unto" Him (ch. iv. 16). God punishes apostates in kind. He departs from them—the worst of woes (Hos. ix. 12). **the living God**—the exclusive characteristic of the God of Israel, not like the lifeless gods of the heathen; therefore One whose threats are awful realities. To apostatize from Christ is to apostatize from the living God (ch. ii. 3). **13. one another** [*heautous*]—'yourselves;' let each exhort himself and his neighbour. **daily** [*kath' hekastēn hemeran*]—'on each day.' **while it is called To-day**—whilst the "To-day" of grace lasts (Luke iv. 21): before the day of judgment at Christ's coming (ch. x. 25, 37). To-morrow is the day when idle men work and fools repent. To-morrow is Satan's to-day; he cares not what good resolutions you form, if only you fix them for to-morrow. **lest any of you.** The "you" is emphatic, as distinguished from "your fathers" (*v.* 9). 'That from among you no one (B Δ *f*. But א A C H, Vulgate, "no one from among you") be hardened' (*v.* 8). **deceitfulness**—causing you to 'err in your

15   While it is said, To-day if ye will hear his voice, harden not your
16 hearts, as in the provocation. For *ʲ*some, when they had heard, did
17 provoke: howbeit not all that came out of Egypt by Moses. But with
     whom was he grieved forty years? *was it* not with them that had sinned,
18 *ᵏ* whose carcases fell in the wilderness? And to whom sware he that they
19 should not enter into his rest, but to them that believed not? So we see
     that they could not enter in because of unbelief.

4   LET us therefore fear, lest, a promise being left *us* of entering into his
2   rest, any of you should seem to come short of it. For unto us was the
     Gospel preached, as well as unto them: but ¹ the word preached did not
3   profit them, ² not being mixed with faith in them that heard *it*. For we
     which have believed do enter into rest, as he said, *ᵃ*As I have sworn in
     my wrath, If they shall enter into my rest: although the works were

A D. 64.
ʲ Num. 14. ×,
   4, 11, 24, 30.
Deut. 1. 34,
   36, 33.
ᵏ Num. 26 65.

CHAP. 4.
1 the word
   of hearing.
2 Or, be-
   cause they
   were not
   united by
   faith to.
ᵃ Ps 95. 11.
   ch. 3. 11.

---

heart.' **sin**—unbelief. **14. For,** &c. Enforcing the warning, *v.* 12. **partakers of Christ** (cf. *vv.* 1, 6). So "partakers of the Holy Ghost" (ch. vi. 4). **hold** [*kataschōmen*]—'hold fast.' **the beginning of our confidence** [*hupostaseōs*]—*the substantial confidence* of faith which we have begun (ch. vi. 11; xii. 2). A Christian, so long as he is not *made perfect*, considers himself a *beginner* (*Bengel*). **unto the end**—the coming of Christ (ch. xii. 2). **15. While it is said, To-day** [*En to legesthai*]—*During its being said,* " *To-day* . . . hear his voice." Connect with *v.* 13, "exhort one another," &c.; *v.* 14 being a parenthesis. 'It rests with yourselves that the 95th Psalm be not a mere invitation, but also an actual enjoyment.' **16. For some** —rather, interrogatively, 'For who was it that, when they had heard (referring to "if ye will *hear*," *v.* 15), did provoke (God)?' It might have been objected, that the great blessings which Paul had said Christians enjoy ensure them against apostasy. Nay, he replies, Were not they who were shut out from the Canaan rest the very persons, all of them, who came out of Egypt by God's mighty arm under Moses? Ye need to take heed against unbelief: *for*, was it not because of unbelief that all our fathers were excluded? (Ezek. ii. 3.) "Some," and "not all" (viz., not those under twenty years old, the women, the Levites, Num. i. 47, Joshua, and Caleb), would be a faint statement of his argument, when his object is to show the *universality* of the evil. Not merely *some*, but *all* the Israelites; for the solitary exceptions, Joshua and Caleb, are hardly to be taken into account in so general a statement (Num. xxvi. 64, 65). So *v.* 17, 18 are interrogative: (1.) The beginning of the provocation, soon after the departure from Egypt, is marked in *v.* 16; (2.) The forty years of it in the wilderness, *v.* 17; (3.) The denial of entrance into the land of rest, *v.* 18. Note, cf. 1 Cor. x. 5. **howbeit**—'Nay (why need I put the question), was it not all that came (Paul does not say, *were led*: for they soon ceased to follow God's leading) out of Egypt?' (Exod. xvii. 1, 2.) **by Moses** —as their leader. **17. But** [*De*]—'Moreover;' not in contrast to *v.* 16, but carrying out the same thought. **carcases**—'limbs;' their bodies wasted away limb from limb. [Ps. cxli. 7, *kōla* are the larger limbs; *melē* the smaller.] **18. to them that believed not** [*tois apeithēsasi*]—'to them that *disobeyed*:' *practical* unbelief (Deut. i. 26). **19. they could not enter**—though desiring it.

     CHAP. IV. 1-16—THE PROMISE OF GOD'S REST IS REALIZED THROUGH CHRIST—LET US STRIVE AFTER IT BY HIM, OUR SYMPATHIZING HIGH PRIEST.

     1. Let us therefore fear—not with slavish terror, but godly "fear and trembling" (Phil. ii. 12). Since so many have fallen, *we* have cause to fear

(ch. iii. 17-19). **being left us**—still *remaining* to us after the others have, by neglect, lost it. Or, though the earthly rest has been entered, the promise of the heavenly still *remains*. **his rest**—God's heavenly rest, of which Canaan is the type. "To-day" continues, during which is the danger of failing to reach the *rest*. "To-day," rightly used, terminates in the *rest* which, when once obtained, is never lost (Rev. iii. 12). A foretaste of the rest is given in the inward rest which the believer's soul has in Christ (Matt. xi. 28, 29). **should seem to come short of it** [*husterēkenai*]— 'to be come too late, when the "to-day" is gone (ch. xii. 15; Luke xiii. 25) : 'to *have* come short of it.' The word "seem" mitigates the expression, though not lessening the reality (*Bengel*). Lest there should be any *semblance* of 'falling short. **2. Gospel preached** . . . **unto them**—in type: the earthly Canaan, wherein they failed to realize perfect rest, suggesting that they should look beyond to the heavenly rest, to which *faith* is the avenue, and from which *unbelief* excludes, as it did from the earthly Canaan. **the word preached** [*ho logos tēs akoēs*]—'the word of hearing:' *the word heard by them.* **not being mixed with faith in them that heard.** [So *f*, Syriac, and Lucifer, *sunekramenos:* א, *sunkekerasmenos*]. 'As the word did not unite with the hearers in faith.' The word heard being the food which, as the bread of life (John vi. 33), must pass into flesh and blood, through man's appropriating it in faith. Hearing alone is of as little value as undigested food in a bad stomach (*Tholuck*). [A B C Δ, Vulgate, *sunkekerasmenous*]. 'Unmingled as *they* were (*Greek* accusative, agreeing with "them") in faith with its hearers;' *i. e.* with its *believing, obedient* hearers, as Caleb and Joshua. So "hear" means 'obey,' *v.* 7. The disobedient, instead of being *blended* in 'the same body,' separated themselves as Korah: a tacit reproof to like separatists from the Christian assembling together (ch. x. 25; Jude 19). **3. For**—Justifying his assertion of the need of "faith," *v.* 2. א A C read [*oun*] 'therefore.' **we which have believed**—we who at Christ's coming shall be found to have believed. **do enter** —*i. e.*, are to enter. So B Δ *f* and *Lucifer.* A C read 'let us enter.' **into rest**—'into the [*tēn*] rest' promised in the 95th Psalm. **as he said**— God's saying that *unbelief* excludes, implies that *belief* gains an entrance. What, however, Paul mainly here dwells on in the quotation is, that the promised "*rest*" has not *yet* been entered into. At *v.* 11 he again, as in ch. iii. 12-19 already, takes up *faith* as the indispensable qualification. **although, &c.** Although God finished His works and entered *His* rest from creation long before Moses' time, yet under that leader another rest was promised, which most fell short of through

4 finished from the foundation of the world. For he spake in a certain place of the seventh *day* on this wise, [b] And God did rest the seventh
5 day from all his works. And in this *place* again, If they shall enter
6 into my rest. Seeing therefore it remaineth that some must enter therein, [c] and they to whom [3] it was first preached entered not in because of unbelief—
7 Again, he limiteth a certain day, saying in David, To-day, after so long a time; as it is said, [d] To-day if ye will hear his voice, harden not
8 your hearts. For if [4]Jesus had given them rest, then would he not
9 afterward have spoken of another day. There remaineth therefore a [5]rest
10 to the people of God. For he that is entered into his rest, he also hath ceased from his own works, as God *did* from his.

A. D. 64.

[b] Gen. 2. 2.
Ex. 20. 11.
[c] ch. 3. 19.
[3] Or the gospel was first preached.
[d] Ps 95. 7.
[4] That is, Joshua.
[5] Or keeping of a sabbath.
Isa. 11. 10.
Isa 60. 19.

unbelief; and although the *rest* in Canaan was subsequently attained under Joshua, yet long after, in David's days, God, in the 95th Psalm, still speaks of *the rest of God* as not yet attained. THEREFORE there must be a rest *still future*—viz., that which 'remaineth for the people of God' in heaven (*v.*3-9), when they shall rest from their works, as God did from His (*v.* 10). St. Paul shows that by "my rest" God means a future rest, not *for Himself*, but *for us.* finished [*yenēthentōn*]—'brought into existence.' 4. he spake—God (Gen. ii. 2). God did rest the seventh day—a rest not ending with the seventh day, but beginning then, and still continuing, into which believers enter. God's rest is not a rest necessitated by fatigue, nor consisting in idleness, but that upholding and governing of which creation was the beginning (*Alford*). Hence Moses records the end of each of the first six days, but not of the seventh. 'The day of rest' for the *Sabbath* is taken from 2 Macc. xv. 1 [*he tēs katapauseōs hemera*]. from all his works —Hebrew, Gen. ii. 2, 'from all His *work*.' God's 'work' was *one*, comprehending, however, many "*works*." 5. in this place. In this Psalm, again, it is implied that the rest was even still future. 6. it remaineth—still to be realized. some must enter. The denial of entrance to unbelievers is a virtual promise of entrance to believers. God wishes not His rest to be empty, but furnished with guests (Luke xiv. 23). they to whom it was first preached entered not—'they who first (in Moses' time) had the Gospel preached to them;' viz., in type, note, *v.* 2. unbelief [*apeitheian*]— rather, 'disobedience' (note ch. iii. 18).
7. Again—*Anew* the promise recurs. Greek order, 'He limiteth a certain day, "To-day."' Here Paul interrupts the quotation by, 'In (the Psalm of) David, saying, After so long a time' (after 500 years' possession of Canaan); and resumes it by, 'as it *has been* said *before* (so אA C Δ *f, before,* viz., ch. iii. 7, 15), To-day, if ye hear His voice,' &c. (*Alford*.) 8. Answer to the possible objection to his reasoning—viz., that those brought into Canaan by Joshua (so "Jesus," Acts vii. 45) did enter the *rest* of God. If the rest of God meant Canaan, God would not, after their entrance into that land, have spoken of another (future) day of entering the rest. therefore—because God 'speaks of another day' (note, *v.* 8). 9. remaineth—still to be realized by the "some (who) must enter therein" (*v.* 6); *i. e.*, "the people of God," the true Israel, who enter into *God's rest* ("my rest," *v.* 3). God's rest has a 'sabbatism' (Greek): so also will ours be (*margin*): a home for the exile, a mansion for the pilgrim, a Sabbath for the work-man weary of the world's week-day toil. In time there are many Sabbaths; but then there shall be one perfect and eternal. [The "rest," *v.* 8, is *catapausis;* Hebrew, *Noah;* rest from weariness, as the ark rested on Ararat after its tossings; as

Israel, under Joshua, rested from war in Canaan. *Anesis* (2 Thess. i. 7), *relaxation* from afflictions. *Anapausis,* "rest" given by Jesus now (Matt. xi. 28): but the "rest," *v.* 9, is the nobler (Hebrew) '*Sabbath*' rest; lit.. *cessation* from *work finished* (*v.* 4), as God rested (Rev. xiv. 13; xvi. 17). The two ideas combined give the perfect view of the heavenly Sabbath. *Rest from weariness, sorrow, and sin;* and *rest in the completion of God's new creation* (Rev. xxi. 5). The renovated creation shall share in it; nothing there will be to break the Sabbath of eternity: the Triune God shall rejoice in the work of His hands (Zeph. iii. 17).] Moses, the representative of the law, could not lead Israel into Canaan : the law leads us to Christ; there its office ceases: it is Jesus, the antitype of Joshua, who leads us into the heavenly rest. This verse indirectly establishes the obligation of the Sabbath; for the type continues until the antitype supersedes it: so legal sacrifices continued till the great antitypical sacrifice superseded it. As then the antitypical Sabbath rest will not be till Christ comes to usher us into it, the typical earthly Sabbath must continue till then. The Jews call the future rest the 'day which is all Sabbath.' 10. For—Justifying *v.* 9. he that is entered— whosoever once enters. his rest—God's rest, prepared *by God* for His people (*Estius*). Rather, *the man's* rest; that assigned to him by God. hath ceased [*katepausen,* akin to *katapausis*] (*v.* 3). The aorist is indefinite, '*rests*.' The past tense implies the *certainty* of it, as also that in this life a kind of foretaste in Christ is already given (*Grotius*) (Jer. vi. 16). from his own works —even from those that were good and suitable previously. Labour was followed by rest even in paradise (Gen. ii. 3, 15). The work and sub-sequent rest of God are the archetype to which we should be conformed if we would be supremely happy. The argument is, He who once enters rest, rests from labours; but God's people have not yet rested from them: therefore they have not yet entered the rest; so it must be still future. Alford, 'He that entered into his (Isa. xi. 10; Matt. xxv. 21, 23) rest (viz., *Jesus,* our Forerunner, *v.* 14; ch. vi. 20, in contrast to Joshua the type, who did *not bring* God's people *into* the heavenly rest), He *Himself* (*emphatical*) rested from His works (*v.* 4), as God (did) from *His own* [*idion*] works.' The argument, though generally applying to *any one who has entered his rest,* probably alludes to *Jesus* in particular, the antitypical Joshua, who, having entered His rest at the Ascension, has ceased from His earthly work of redemption, as God on the seventh day rested from physical creation. Not that He has ceased to carry on redemption—nay, He upholds it by His mediation—but He has ceased from those portions of it which constitute the foundation: the sacrifice has been once for all

11　Let us labour therefore to enter into that rest, lest any man fall after
12　the same example of [6]unbelief.　For the word of God *is* '*quick*, and
　　powerful, and sharper than [f]any two-edged sword, piercing even to the
　　dividing asunder of soul and spirit, and of the joints and marrow, and *is*
13　a [g]discerner of the thoughts and intents of the heart.　Neither is there
　　any creature that is not manifest in his sight: but all things *are* naked
　　and opened unto the eyes of him with whom we have to do.
14　Seeing then that we have a great High Priest, that is passed into the

A. D. 64.
[6] Or. dis-
obedience.
[e] Isa 49. 2.
Jer. 23. 29.
[f] Rev. 1. 16.
Rev 2. 16.
[g] 1 Cor. 14. 24,
25.
Eph 5. 13.

accomplished. Cf. as to God's creation, once for all completed and rested from, but now still upheld (note, *v.* 4; 1 Pet iv. 1, 2). **11. Let us . . . therefore**—seeing such a promise is before us. **labour** [*spoudasōmen*]—'strive diligently.' **that rest**—still future and so glorious. Or (cf. *v.* 10), 'that rest into which *Christ* has entered before' (*v.* 14; ch. vi. 20). **fall**—with the soul; not merely the body, as the rebel Israelites fell (ch. iii. 17). **after the same example**—'lest any fall into [*en:* in the sphere of] such *disobedience* [practical *unbelief: apeitheias*] as they gave a sample of' (*Grotius*). The Jews say, 'the parents are a sign (warning) to the sons.' **12. For.** Such *diligent striving* (*v.* 11) is incumbent, FOR we have to do with a God whose "Word," whereby we shall be judged, is heart-searching, and whose eyes are all-seeing (*v.* 13). The qualities attributed to *the word of God* show that it is regarded in its JUDICIAL power, whereby it doomed the disobedient Israelites to exclusion from Canaan, and shall exclude unbelieving Christians from the heavenly rest. The written Word is not the prominent thought, though the passage is often so quoted. Still the Word of God (the same as that preached, **c.** 2), in the broadest sense, is the sword of the Spirit (Eph. vi. 17), with double edge—one edge for convicting and converting believers (*v.* 2), the other for condemning and destroying unbelievers (*v.* 14). Rev. xix. 15 similarly represents the Word's judicial power as a sharp sword going out of Christ's mouth to *smite* the nations (cf. Rev. ii. 12, 16). The same word which saves the faithful (*v.* 2) destroys the disobedient (2 Cor. ii. 15, 16). The personal Word is not here meant: He *is* not the sword, but *has* it. Cf. Josh. v. 13; appropriately Joshua is referred to, *v.* 8. **quick** [*zōn*]—'living:' having living power, as 'the rod of the mouth and the breath of the lips,' with which 'the living God shall smite the earth.' **powerful** [*energēs*]—not only *living,* but *energetically efficacious.* **sharper** [*tomōteros*]—'more cutting.' **two-edged**—sharpened at both edge and back. 'It judges all that is in the heart, for there it passes through, at once *punishing* (unbelievers) and *searching*' (both believers and unbelievers) (*Chrysostom*). *Philo* similarly, 'God passed between the parts of Abraham's sacrifice (Gen. xv. 17) as a "burning lamp," with His Word, the cutter of all things: which sword, sharpened to the utmost, never ceases to divide all sensible things, and even things not perceptible to sense or physically divisible, but perceptible and divisible by the Word.' Paul's early training in the Greek schools of Tarsus and the Hebrew schools at Jerusalem accounts for his acquaintance with Philo's thoughts, which were current among learned Jews everywhere, though Philo belonged to Alexandria. Addressing Jews, he by the Spirit sanctions what was true in their current literature, as he similarly did in addressing Gentiles (Acts xvii. 28). [Traducianists rightly maintain that man's *psychical* nature (*psuche*, soul), moral and intellectual, is transmitted from father to son: original sin would not be, if the soul with its sinful bias were

directly created by God. Creationists are right as to the *pneuma*, that it is not derived by descent, but *created* at birth (John i. 13; iii. 6; Jas. i. 18; 1 John iii. 9; v. 1, 18, 19)]. **piercing** [*diiknoumenos*]—'coming through.' **soul and spirit**—*i. e.*, reaching through even to the separation of the animal *soul,* the lower part of man's incorporeal nature, the seat of animal desires (cf. 1 Cor. ii. 14); 'the natural (animal-*souled*) man' [Jude 19, "sensual," *psuchikoi*]; from the spirit (the higher part, receptive of the Spirit of God, allying man to heavenly being). **and of the joints and marrow**—rather [*achri: reaching even* TO], '*both* [*te kai*] the joints (so as to divide them) and marrow.' Christ "knows what is in man" (John ii. 25): so His word reaches even to the intimate knowledge of man's hidden feelings and thoughts, dividing—i. e., *distinguishing* what is *spiritual* from what is *animal* in him, the *spirit* from the *soul:* so Prov. xx. 27: cf. its effect on Lydia, Acts xvi. 14; and the woman of Samaria, Acts iv. 29. As the knife of the Levitical priest reached to dividing parts closely united, as the *joints,* and penetrated to the innermost parts, as the *marrows* [*muelōn*], so the word of God divides man's closely-joined immaterial parts, soul and spirit, and penetrates to the innermost recesses of them. In א A B C H [f,] Vulgate, there is no 'both' [*te*] before "soul and spirit," as there is in the clause '*both* the joints *and,*' &c.: which makes the latter clause explanatory of the former. "Joints" (metaphorical) answers to "the dividing asunder;" 'marrows,' to "soul and spirit" (especially the latter). It *divides* soul from spirit, and so reaches the "*joints,*" and pierces so as to reach even the *inmost recesses* (the 'marrows') of soul and spirit alike. Soul, as well as spirit, is laid bare and "naked" before God (cf. *v.* 13). 'Moses forms the soul, Christ the spirit. The soul draws with it the body; the spirit draws with it both soul and body' (1 Thess. v. 23) (*Bengel*). The Word's dividing and far penetrating power has both a punitive and a healing effect. **discerner** [*kritikos*]—'*capable of judging.*' **the thoughts**—'the sentiments.' **intents** [*ennoiōn,* from *nous* (*mens*)]—'*mental* cogitations.' [As *enthumeseis,* from *thumos* (*animus*), refers to *the sentiments, feelings,* and *passions,* so *ennoiai* refers to the *intellect.*] **13. creature**—visible or invisible. **in his** (God's) **sight** (*v.* 12). **opened** [*tetrachelismena*]—'thrown on the back, so as to have the neck laid bare,' as a victim with neck exposed for sacrifice. The perfect tense implies this is our *continuous* state in relation to God. 'Show, O man, *shame* and *fear* towards thy God, for no veil, no twisting, bending, colouring, or disguise can cover practical *unbelief*' ('disobedience,' *v.* 11). **14. Seeing then, &c.**—resuming ch. ii. 17. **great** —as being 'the Son of God, higher than the heavens' (ch. vii. 26): the archetype and antitype of the legal high priest. **passed into the heavens** [*dieleluthota tous ouranous*]—'passed *through* the heavens;' viz., those which come between us and God, the aerial heaven, and that above the latter containing the heavenly bodies, the sun, moon,

15 heavens, Jesus the Son of God, let us hold fast *our* profession. For [h] we
have not an high priest which cannot be touched with the feeling of our
infirmities; but [i] was in all points tempted like as *we are,* [j] *yet* without
16 sin. Let us therefore come boldly unto the throne of grace, that we may
obtain mercy, and find grace to help in time of need.

5   FOR every high priest taken from among men is ordained for men in
things *pertaining* to God, [a] that he may offer both gifts and sacrifices for
2 sins: who [1] can have compassion on the ignorant, and on them that are
out of the way; for that he himself also is compassed with infirmity.

A. D. 61.

h Isa. 53. 3.
i Luke 22.28.
j Dan 9. 24.
2 Cor. 5. 21.
1 Pet. 2. 22.

CHAP. 5.
a ch. 8. 3, 4.
1 Or. can
reasonably
bear with.

&c. These heavens were the veil which our High Priest *passed through* into the heaven of heavens, the immediate presence of God; just as the Levitical high priest passed through the veil into the holy of holies. Neither Moses nor even Joshua could bring us into this rest; but Jesus, our Forerunner, already spiritually, hereafter in actual presence, body, soul, and spirit, brings His people into the heavenly rest. Jesus—the antitypical Joshua (*v.* 8). **hold fast**—the opposite of "let . . . slip" (ch. ii. 1) and "fall away" (ch. vi. 6). As the genitive follows, it is, 'let us *take hold* of our profession;' *i. e.,* of faith and hope, the subjects of our profession [*kratomen tes homologias*]. The accusative follows when the sense is "hold fast" (*Tittmann*). **15. For**—The motive to 'holding our profession' (*v.* 14); viz., the sympathy and help we may expect from our High Priest. Though "great" (*v.* 14), He is not above caring for us; nay, being in all points one with us as to manhood, sin only excepted, He sympathizes with us in every temptation. Though exalted to the highest heavens, He has changed His place, not His nature and office, toward us; His condition, not His affection. Cf. Matt. xxvi. 38, "watch with me," showing His desire in His day of suffering for *the sympathy of those whom He loved :* so He now gives His suffering people *His* sympathy. Cf. Aaron, bearing the names of the twelve tribes in the breastplate of judgment on his heart, when he entered into the holy place, for a memorial before the Lord continually (Exod. xxviii. 29). **cannot be touched with the feeling of** [*sumpathesai*]—'cannot sympathize with our *weaknesses,*' physical and moral; not sin, but liability to its assaults. He, though sinless, can sympathize with sinners; His *understanding* more acutely perceived the forms of temptation than we; His *will* repelled them as instantaneously as fire does water cast into it. He experimentally knew what power was needed to overcome. He is capable of sympathizing, for He was at the same time tempted without sin, and yet truly tempted (*Bengel*). In Him alone is an example suited to men of every character and under all circumstances. In sympathy he adapts Himself to each, as if He had not merely taken man's nature in general, but the peculiar nature of that single individual. **like as we are** [*kath' homoioteta*]—'according to (our) similitude.' **without sin** [*choris*]—'*separate* from sin' (ch. vii. 26). [If *aneu* had been used, *sin* would have been regarded as the object absent from Christ, the subject; but *choris* implies that Christ, the *subject,* is regarded separate from sin, the object (*Tittmann*).] Throughout his temptations, in their origin, process, and result, sin had nothing in Him (*Alford*). **16. come**—rather [as *proserchōmetha*], 'approach,' 'draw near.' **boldly** [*meta parrhesias*]—'with confidence,' 'freedom of speech' (Eph. vi. 19). **the throne of grace.** God's throne is become so to us, through the mediation of our High Priest at God's right hand (ch. viii. 1; xii. 2). Pleading Jesus' meritorious death, we shall always find God on a *throne of*

grace. Contrast Job's complaint and Elihu's (Job xxiii. 3-8; xxxiii. 23-28). **obtain** [*labōmen*]—'receive.' **mercy.** 'Compassion,' by its derivation (fellow-feeling from *community* of *suffering*), corresponds to the character of our High Priest (*v.* 15). **find grace**—corresponding to "throne *of grace."* *Mercy* refers to the remission of sins ; *grace,* to the bestowal of spiritual gifts (*Estius*). Cf. "Come unto me . . . and I will give *you* rest" (the rest *received* on first believing). "Take my yoke on you . . . and ye shall *find* rest" (the continuing rest *found* in daily submitting to Christ's easy yoke. The former answers to '*receive* mercy,' the latter to "*find* grace:" Matt. xi. 28, 29). In first *receiving,* we are wholly passive: after having received mercy, our will in *finding* grace is more active. **help** (cf. ch. ii. 18). **in time of need** [*eis eukairon*]—'seasonably:' before we are overwhelmed by temptations, when we most need it; such as is suitable to the time, persons, and end designed (Ps. civ. 27). A supply of grace is in store for believers against all exigencies; but they are only supplied with it according as the need arises. Cf. "in due time." Rom. v. 6.

CHAP. V. 1-14.—CHRIST'S HIGH PRIESTHOOD —NEEDED QUALIFICATIONS—MUST BE MAN— MUST NOT HAVE ASSUMED THE DIGNITY, BUT HAVE BEEN APPOINTED BY GOD—THEIR LOW SPIRITUAL PERCEPTIONS PREVENTS PAUL SAYING ALL HE MIGHT ON CHRIST'S MELCHISEDEC-LIKE PRIESTHOOD.

1. For—Substantiating ch. iv. 15. **every**—*i. e.,* every legitimate high priest; the Levitical; as he is addressing Hebrews, among whom the Levitical priesthood was the legitimate one. Whatever reasons Paul, is excellent in Levitical priests, is also in Christ, besides excellencies not in them. **taken from among men**—not from among angels, who could not have a fellow-feeling with us men. This qualification Christ has, being, like the Levitical priests, *a man* (ch. ii. 14, 16). Being "*from* . . . men," He can be "*for* [*huper :* in behalf of] men." **ordained** [*kathistatai*]—'constituted.' **both gifts**—to be joined with "for sins," as "sacrifices" is (the "both . . . and," in א A C, requires this); therefore not the Hebrew *Mincha, unbloody* offerings, but animal whole burnt offerings, *spontaneously given.* But B Δ *f,* Vulgate, omit "both;" in which reading "gifts" may be the *Mincha,* unbloody offerings. "Sacrifices" are animal sacrifices *due according to the law.* **2. Who can**—'Being one able:' *not pleasing himself* (Rom. xv. 3). **have compassion** [*metriopathein*]—'feel leniently (moderately) towards:' 'to make allowance for:' not showing stern rigour save to the obstinate (ch. x. 28). **ignorant**—sins not committed in resistance of light and knowledge, but as Paul's past sin (1 Tim. i. 13). No sacrifice was appointed for wilful sin committed with a high hand; such were to be put to death: all other sins—viz., ignorances and errors—were confessed and expiated with sacrifices by the high priest. **out of the way**—not deliberately and determinately erring, but deluded through the fraud of Satan

3 And *b* by reason hereof he ought, as for the people, so also for himself, to offer for sins.

4 And *c* no man taketh this honour unto himself, but he that is called

5 of God, as *was* *d* Aaron. So *e* also Christ glorified not himself to be made an High Priest; but he that said unto him, *f* Thou art my Son, to-day

6 have I begotten thee. As he saith also in another *place,* *g* Thou *art* a Priest for ever, after the order of Melchisedec.

7 Who in the days of his flesh, when he had *h* offered up prayers and supplications, with *i* strong crying and tears, unto *j* him that was able to

8 save him from death, and was heard *2* in that he feared : though he were

A. D. 64.

b Lev. 4. 3.
c 1 Sam. 13.9.
d Ex. 28. 1.
e John 8. 54.
   Acts 13. 33.
f Ps. 2. 7.
g Ps. 110. 4.
h John 17. 1.
i Ps. 22. 1.
j Matt. 26.53.
2 Or. for his piety.

and their own carnal frailty. **infirmity**—moral weakness, which, being sinful, and making men capable of sin, requires to be expiated by sacrifices. This "infirmity" Christ had not: He had the "infirmity" of body whereby He was capable of suffering and death. **3. by reason hereof**—'on account of this' infirmity. **he ought . . . also for himself, to offer for sins.** In this our High Priest is superior to the Levitical priest. [The third "for" is *huper,* '*on account* of sins:' not *peri,* as the first two, 'in behalf of.' But א A B C Δ read *peri.*]

4. no man—of any family but Aaron's, according to the Mosaic law, can take the high priesthood. **but he that is called.** So Δ. [But A B C א omit *ho:* 'but when called.'] This verse is quoted by some to prove the need of an apostolic succession of ordination in the Christian ministry; but the reference here is to the *sacerdotal priesthood,* not the Christian *ministry.* The analogy in our Christian dispensation would warn ministers, seeing that God has separated them from the congregation of His people, to bring them near Himself, and to do the service of His house, and to minister (as He separated the Levites, Korah with his company), that, content with this, they should beware of assuming the sacrificial priesthood also, which belongs to Christ alone. The sin of Korah was, not content with the ministry as a Levite, he took the sacerdotal priesthood also. No Christian minister, as such, is ever called *Hiereus*—*i. e.,* sacrificing priest. All Christians, without distinction, whether ministers or people, have a spiritual, not literal, priesthood (1 Pet. ii. 5, 9; Phil. iii. 3; Rev. i. 6; v. 10; xx. 6). The sacrifices which they offer are spiritual, their bodies and the fruit of their lips, praises continually (ch. xiii. 15). Christ alone had a *proper* and *true* sacrifice to offer. The law sacrifices were *typical,* not *metaphorical,* as the Christian's, nor *proper* and *true,* as Christ's. In Roman times the Mosaic restriction of the priesthood to Aaron's family was violated. **5. glorified not himself**—did not assume the glory of the priestly office without the call of God (John viii. 54). **but he that said**—*i. e.,* the Father appointed Him to His glorified priesthood (*v.* 10). This appointment was involved in, and resulted from, His *Sonship,* which qualified Him for it. None else could have fulfilled such an office (ch. x. 5-9). The connection of *Sonship* and *priesthood* is typified in the title [*cohanim*] *priests* being given to David's *sons* (2 Sam. viii. 18). Christ did not constitute *Himself* the Son of God, but was from everlasting the only-begotten *of the Father.* **6. He is here called** "Priest;" in *v.* 5, "High Priest:" a *Priest* absolutely, because He stands alone in that character: "High Priest," in respect of the Aaronic type; also in respect to us, whom by His own access to God He has made priests (*Bengel*). "The *order* of Melchisedec" is explained, ch. vii. 15, "the *similitude* of Melchisedec." Priesthood

is similarly combined with His kingly office in Zech. vi. 13. Melchisedec was at once man, priest, and king. Paul's selecting as the type one not of the stock of Abraham, on which the Jews prided themselves, intimates Messianic catholicity. **7. in the days of his flesh** (ch. ii. 14; x. 20). *Vv.* 7-10 state summarily the subject, to be handled more fully in chs. vii. and viii. **when he had offered**—rather, '*in that He offered.*' His crying and tears were part of the experimental lesson of obedience which He submitted to learn from the Father (when God was qualifying Him for the high priesthood). "Who" is to be construed with "learned (His) obedience;" [*tēn*] *the* obedience which He rendered as the needful qualification for His priesthood. This shows that "Christ glorified not Himself to be made an High Priest" (*v.* 5), but was appointed thereto by the Father. **prayers and supplications**—'*both* prayers and supplications.' In Gethsemane, where He prayed *thrice,* and on the cross, "My God, my God," &c.: probably repeating inwardly *all* the 22nd Psalm. "Prayers" refer to the mind; "supplications" also to the body (viz., the suppliant attitude) (*Bengel*). [*Deēseis,* "prayers," imply *need (dei);* *hiketērias,* "supplications;" *lit.,* an olive branch wrapt in white wool and bands, which suppliants held in their hands to imply they implored help.] **with strong crying and tears.** The "tears" are an additional fact communicated by the inspired apostle, not in the gospels (Matt. xxvi. 37, 39; Mark xiv. 33; Luke xxii. 44, "in an agony He prayed more earnestly . . . His sweat . . . great drops of blood falling down to the ground"). In this, as in other Gospel facts, St. Paul approximates most to St. Luke, his companion in travel. Ps. xxii. 1 ("roaring . . . cry"), 2, 19, 21, 24; lxix. 3, 10, "I *wept.*" **able to save him from death**—Mark xiv. 36, "All things are *possible* unto thee" (John xii. 27). His cry showed entire participation of man's infirmity: His reference of His wish to God's will, His sinless faith and obedience. **heard in that he feared.** There is no intimation in Ps. xxii., or the gospels, that Christ prayed to be saved from mere dying. What He feared was the hiding of the Father's countenance. His holy filial love must rightly have shrunk from this strange and bitterest of trials without impatience. To have been passively content at the approach of such a cloud would have been, not faith, but sin. The cup of death He prayed to be freed from was, not corporal, but spiritual—*i. e.,* the (temporary) separation of His human soul from the light of God's countenance. His prayer was "heard" in His Father's strengthening Him to hold fast His unwavering faith under the trial (*My God, my* God, was still His filial cry, claiming God as *His,* though God hid His face), and soon removing it in answer to His cry during the darkness, "My God, my God," &c. But see below a further explanation. [*Eisakoustheis apo tēs eulabeias*] 'Was heard

9 a Son, yet learned he obedience *k* by the things which he suffered ; and being made perfect, he became the author of eternal salvation unto all
10 them that obey him; called of God an High Priest after *l* the order of Melchisedec.
11   Of whom we have many things to say, and hard to be uttered, seeing
12 ye are dull of hearing. For when for the time ye ought to be teachers, ye have need that one teach you again which *be* the first principles of the oracles of God ; and are become such as have need of milk, and not
13 of strong meat. For every one that useth milk ³ *is* unskilful in the
14 word of righteousness; for he is *m* a babe. But strong meat belongeth to them that are ⁴ of full age, *even* those who by reason ⁵ of use have their senses exercised *n* to discern both good and evil.

A. D. 64.

k Phil 2. 8.
l Matt. 2 32.
   ch. 6. 20.
³ hath no experience.
m 1 Cor 14 20. Eph. 4. 13.
⁴ Or perfect.
⁵ Or. of an habit. or.
p rfection.
n 1 Cor. 2. 14, 15.

from His fear—i. e., so as *to be saved from* His fear. Cf. Ps. xxii. 21, "Save me *from* the lion's mouth (His prayer): thou hast *heard* me *from* the horns of the unicorns." Or what better accords with the strict Greek, '*in consequence of His* REVERENTIAL FEAR'—i. e., in that He *shrank from* separation from the Father's bright presence, yet was *reverentially cautious* not to harbour a shadow of distrust or want of perfect filial love. In the same sense ch. xii. 28, and ch. xi. 7 the verb. The derivation means the *cautious handling* of some precious, yet delicate vessel, which with ruder handling might easily be broken (*Trench*). Cf. Jesus' spirit, "If it be possible . . . *nevertheless not my will, but thy will be done;*" and with *v.* 5, implying *reverent fear:* wherein He showed He had the requisite for the office specified (*v.* 4). *Alford,* 'What is true in the Christian's life, that what we ask from God, though He may not grant in the form we wish, yet He grants in His own, and that a better form, does not hold good in Christ's case; for Christ's real prayer, "Not my will, but thine be done," in consistency with His reverent fear towards the Father, was granted in the very form in which it was expressed, not in another. 8. Though He WAS (a positive fact : not a supposition, as *were* would imply) God's Divine Son (whence, in His agony, He so lovingly and often cried, *Father,* Matt. xxvi. 39), yet He learned *His* obedience, not from His Sonship, but from His sufferings. As the Son, He always obeyed the Father's will ; but *the* special obedience needed to qualify Him as our High Priest, He learned experimentally. Cf. Phil. ii. 6-8, "*equal with God,* but . . . took upon Him the form of a *servant,* and became *obedient* unto death," &c. He was *obedient* before His passion ; but He stooped to a more humiliating and trying form of *obedience* then. [The Greek adage is, *Pathemata, mathemata,* 'sufferings, disciplinings.'] *Praying* and *obeying,* as in Christ's case, ought to go hand in hand. 9. **made perfect**—*perfectly qualified* as Captain of salvation to us: brought to His goal of learning and suffering through death (ch. ii. 10). *Alford,* 'at His resurrection and ascension.' **author** [*aitios*] —'cause.' **eternal salvation**—obtained for us in the *short* 'days of Jesus' flesh' (*v.* 7: cf. *v.* 6, "for ever;" Isa. xlv. 17). **unto all . . . that obey him** As Christ *obeyed* the Father, so must we *obey* Him by faith. 10. [*Prosagoreutheis*] '*Addressed*' (*saluted* by the appellation). Formally recognized by God as High Priest, He was High Priest already *in God's purpose;* but after His passion, when perfected (*v.* 9), He was formally addressed so.
11. Here he digresses to complain of the low attainments of the Palestinian Christians, and to warn them of the danger of falling from light once enjoyed; at the same time encouraging them by God's faithfulness to persevere. At ch. vi. 20 he

resumes the comparison of Christ to Melchisedec. **hard to be uttered** [*dusermēneutos*]—'hard *of interpretation* to speak.' Hard for me to state intelligibly to you, owing to your dulness about spiritual things. Hence, instead of *saying many things,* he writes in comparatively *few words* (ch. xiii. 22). In the ".we," Paul, as usual, includes Timothy in addressing them. **ye are** [*gegonate*] —'ye have *become* dull' [*nothroi,* sluggish]: *once,* when first "enlightened," they were zealous, but had *become* dull. That the Hebrew believers AT JERUSALEM were spiritually dull, and legal in tone, appears from Acts xxi. 20-24, where James and the elders say of the 'thousands of Jews which believe, they are all *zealous of the law:*' that was at Paul's last visit to Jerusalem, after which this epistle was written (*v.* 12, note). 12. **for the time**—considering the long time you have been Christians. Therefore this epistle was not one early written. **which be the first principles** [*ta stoicheia tēs archēs*]—'the *rudiments of the beginning* of,' &c. A Pauline phrase (Gal. iv. 3, 9). Ye need not only to be taught *the first elements,* but also '*which* they be.' They are therefore enumerated, ch. vi. 1, 2. *Alford,* 'That *some one* teach you the rudiments,' [but the position of *tina* favours "which" interrogatively, as the English version, Syriac, Vulgate, &c.] **of the oracles of God**—viz., of the Old Testament. Instead of seeing Christ as the end of the Old Testament, they were relapsing towards Judaism, so as not only not to understand the typical reference to Christ of such an Old Testament personage as Melchisedec, but even more elementary references. **are become**—through indolence. **milk**—such first principles as ch. vi. 1. 2. **strong meat.** *Solid food* is not indispensable for preserving life, but is so for acquiring strength. Especially as the Hebrews so venerated the minute details of the law, the unfolding of the Old Testament types of Christ and His High Priesthood was calculated much to strengthen them in the Christian faith. 13. **useth** [*metechōn*] —'partaketh of.' Even strong men *partake of* milk, but do not make milk their chief, much less their sole, diet. **the word of righteousness**—the Gospel, wherein "is the righteousness of God revealed from faith to faith" (Rom. i. 17); "the ministration of righteousness" (2 Cor. iii. 9). This includes *justification* and sanctification; the first *principles,* as well as the *perfection, of the doctrine of Christ:* the nature of the offices and person of Christ as the true Melchisedec—i. e., "King of *righteousness*" (cf. Matt. iii. 15). 14. **them that are of full age** [*teleiōn*]—'perfect:' akin to "perfection" (ch. vi. 1). **by reason of use** [*hexin*]—'habit.' **senses**—organs of sense. **exercised**—similarly connected with "righteousness" in ch. xii. 11. **to discern both good and evil**—as a child no longer an infant (Isa. vii. 16): able to distinguish between sound and unsound doctrine. The

6 THEREFORE leaving [1] the principles of the doctrine of Christ, let us go on unto perfection; not laying again the foundation of repentance
2 from dead works, and of faith toward God, of *a* the doctrine of baptisms, *b* and of laying on of hands, *c* and of resurrection of the dead, and of
3, eternal judgment. And this will we do, if God permit. For *it is*
4 impossible for those who were once enlightened, and have tasted of the
5 heavenly gift, and were made partakers of the Holy Ghost, and have
6 tasted the good word of God, and the powers of the world to come, if

A. D. 64.

CHAP. 6.
[1] Or, the word of the begin-ning of Christ.
a Acts 19. 4.
b Acts 8. 14.
c Acts 17. 31.

---

mere child puts into its mouth things hurtful and things nutritious, without *discrimination;* not so the adult. Paul warns them against being carried about by strange doctrines through not discriminating (ch. xiii. 9).

CHAP. VI. 1-14.—WARNING AGAINST RETRO-GRADING, WHICH LEADS TO APOSTASY—ENCOUR-AGEMENT TO STEDFASTNESS FROM GOD'S FAITH-FULNESS TO HIS WORD AND OATH.

1. Therefore—Wherefore: seeing that ye ought not to be still 'babes' (ch. v. 11-14). **leaving**—getting further than elementary "principles." 'As in building, one must never leave the foundation; yet to be always labouring in "laying" it would be ridiculous' (*Calvin*). **the principles of the doctrine** [*ton tes arches logon*]—'the word *of* the beginning;' *i. e.,* the discussion of the first principles of Christianity (ch. v. 12). **let us go on** [*pherometha*]—'let us bear ourselves forward:' with active exertion press on. St. Paul classifies himself with his Hebrew learners. Let us together press forward. **perfection**—the matured knowledge of those "of full age" (ch. v. 14) in attainments. **foundation of**—i. e., *consisting in.* **repentance from dead works**—viz., not springing from the *vital* principle of faith and love towards God, so counted, like their doer, *dead* before God. This *repentance from dead works* is therefore paired with "faith toward God." The three pairs of truths enumerated are designedly such as JEWISH be-lievers might have partly known from the Old Testament, but had been taught more clearly as Christians. This accounts for the omission of *distinct* specification of some essential first princi-ples of Christianity. Hence, he mentions "faith toward *God:*" not *explicitly* faith towards Christ (though included). Repentance and faith were the first principles taught under the Gospel. **2. the doctrine of baptisms**—paired with "laying on of hands," as the latter followed Christian baptism, and answers to *confirmation* in Episcopal churches. Jewish believers passed, by an easy transition, from Jewish *baptismal purifications* (ch. ix. 10, "washings"), baptism of proselytes, John's baptism, and legal imposition of hands, to their Christian analogues, *baptism*, and the subsequent *laying on of hands*, accompanied by the Holy Ghost (cf. *v.* 4; Acts viii. 12, 14-17). [*Baptismoi*, plural, including *Jewish* and *Christian baptisms* are to be distinguished from *Baptisma*, singular, *restricted* to Christian baptism.] The six particu-lars specified had been *the Christian Catechism* of the Old Testament. Such Jews who had begun to recognize Jesus as the Christ immediately on the new light being shed on these fundamental particulars were accounted as having the ele-mentary *principles* of Christ's doctrine (*Bengel*). The first and most obvious elementary instruc-tion of Jews, would be *teaching* the typical significance of their own ceremonial law in its Christian fulfilment (*Alford*). **resurrection, &c.**—held already by the Jews from the Old Testament: confirmed with clearer light in Christian "doc-trine." **eternal judgment**—fraught with eternal consequences either of joy or of woe. **3. will we**

do. So אBf, Vulgate, read. But ACΔ, 'let us do.' "This," *i. e.,* 'go on unto perfection.' **if God permit**—for even good resolutions we cannot carry into effect, save through God 'working in us both to will and to do of His good pleasure' (Phil. ii. 13). Without God's blessing, the cultivation of the ground does not succeed (*v.* 7). **4. We must** 'go on towards perfection;' "*For*," if we *fall away*, after having received enlightenment, God will not "permit"—it will be *impossible to renew* us *again to repentance.* But see Luke xviii. 27. **for those**—'in the case of those.' **once enlightened** —once for all illuminated by the Word of God, taught in connection with 'baptism' (to which, in *v.* 2, as once for all done, "once enlightened" here answers) (cf. Eph. v. 26). This passage originated the subsequent application of 'illumina-tion' to baptism. *Illumination* was not supposed inseparably to accompany *baptism*. *Chrysostom* says, 'Heretics have *baptism*, not *illumination:* they are baptized in body, not enlightened in soul: as Simon Magus was baptized, but not illuminated.' That "enlightened" here means *knowledge of the truth* appears from comparing [*photisthentes*] "illuminated," ch. x. 32, with the corresponding *v.* 26, "knowledge of the truth." **tasted** [for themselves: *geusamenous*]. As "enlightened" refers to *sight*, so *taste* follows (1 Pet. ii. 3). **the heavenly gift**—*Christ* given by the Father: re-vealed by the enlightening word: bestowing peace in the remission of sins and the Holy Spirit (John iii. 16; iv. 10; vi. 32; 2 Cor. ix. 15): answering to "baptisms" (*v.* 2: cf. Acts xxii. 16) and "the Son of God" (*v.* 6): distinct from "the Holy Ghost" in the next clause, who also is "the gift of God" (Acts viii. 20). **made partakers of the Holy Ghost**—distinct from, though inseparably connected with, "enlightened," "tasted of the heavenly gift," Christ: answering to "laying on of hands" after baptism, then generally accom-panied with the impartation of *the Holy Ghost* in miraculous gifts. **5. tasted the good word of God**—distinct from "tasted OF (genitive) the heavenly gift." We do not yet enjoy *all* the ful-ness of Christ, but only a taste OF "the heavenly gift;" but believers may taste the *whole* of God's "good word" (accusative) *of promise* already. The promise of Canaan to Israel typified "the good word" of God's promise of the heavenly rest, (ch. iv.) Therefore immediately follows "the powers of the world to come." As 'enlightening' and 'tasting of the heavenly gift,' Christ, the Bread of Life, answers to FAITH, so "made par-takers of the Holy Ghost," to CHARITY, the first fruit of the Spirit; and "tasted the good word of *God*, and the powers of the world to come," to HOPE. Thus the triad of privileges answers to the Trinity—Father, Son, and Spirit—in their respec-tive works towards us. "The world to come" is the Christian dispensation, viewed in its *future glories*, though already begun *in grace.* It stands in contrast to *the course of this world* (Eph. ii. 2), which is disorganized, because God is not its spring of action and end. By faith Christians make the world to come a present reality. "The

they shall fall away, to renew them again unto repentance; *[d]* seeing they
crucify to themselves the Son of God afresh, and put *him* to an open
shame.

7   For the earth, which drinketh in the rain that cometh oft upon it, and
bringeth forth herbs meet for them [2] by whom it is dressed, receiveth

8   blessing from God : but that which beareth thorns and briers *is* rejected,
and *is* nigh unto cursing; whose end *is* to be burned.

9   But, *[e]* beloved, we are persuaded better things of you, and things that

powers" of this new spiritual world, exhibited in outward miracles partly, and then, as now, especially consisting in the Spirit's inward influences, are the fore*taste* of the coming inheritance, and lead the believer to seek to live as the angels, to 'sit with Christ in heavenly places,' to set the affection on things above, and not on things on earth, and to look for Christ's coming. This "world to come" thus corresponds to "resurrection of the dead and . . . eternal judgment" (*v.* 2), the *first* Christian *principles* which the Hebrew believers had been taught by the Christian light thrown back on their Old Testament (note, *vv.* 1, 2). "The world to come," which, as to its "powers," exists already in the redeemed, will pass into a fully realized, manifested fact at Christ's coming (Col. iii. 4). **6. If** [*kai parapesontas*]—'*And* (yet) *have* fallen away' (cf. a less extreme declension, Gal. v. 4). Here a total apostasy is meant. The Hebrews had not yet so fallen away; but he warns them that such would be the end of retrogression, if, instead of 'going on to perfection,' they should need to learn again the first principles (*v.* 1). **to renew them again.** "Once" (*v.* 4) already made anew, now they need 'renewal' over "again." **crucify to themselves**—'*are crucifying* to themselves' Christ, instead of *crucifying the world unto them by the cross of Christ* (Gal. vi. 14). So ch. x. 29. **the Son of God**—His dignity marks the heinousness of their offence. **put him to an open shame** [*paradeigmatizontas*]—'make a public example of' Him, as of a malefactor suspended on a tree. What the carnal Israel did outwardly, those who fall away from light do inwardly: they virtually crucify again the Son of God: 'they tear Him out of their hearts, where He fixed His abode, and exhibit Him to the open scoffs of the world·as something powerless and common' (*Bleek* in *Alford*). The Montanists and Novatians used this passage to justify the lasting exclusion from the Church of the lapsed. The Catholic Church always opposed this, and re-admitted them on repentance, without re-baptism. Persons may be in some sense 'renewed,' yet fall away finally; for "renew . . . again" implies that they have been ONCE RENEWED; but not that 'the elect' can fall away (John x. 28). A *temporary faith* is possible, without one thereby being of the elect (Mark iv. 16, 17; John viii. 31, 35; xv. 2, 5, 6). God's grace is not limited, as if it were "impossible" *for God* to reclaim even such a rebel so as yet to look on Him whom he has pierced. The impossibility rests in their having known in themselves once the power of Christ's sacrifice, yet now rejecting it: there *cannot possibly* be new means for their renewal afresh: the means provided by God's love they now, after experience of them, deliberately and continuously reject: their conscience being seared, "twice dead" (Jude 12), they are past hope, except by a miracle of God's grace. 'It is the curse of evil eternally to propagate evil. The bar to repentance is in the apostate's present attitude towards God, not in his past history, nor in God's attitude towards him. He who abides not in the Christian experi-

543

ences which he had *objectively*, was, at the very time when he had them, not *subjectively* true to them; otherwise, on the principle, "Whosoever hath, to him shall be given, and he shall have more abundance" (Matt. xiii. 12), he would have abided in them, and not have fallen away' (*Tholuck*). Such a one was never a Spirit-led disciple of Christ (Rom. viii. 14-17). The sin against the Holy Ghost, though similar, is not identical with this; for *that* may be committed by those *outside* the church (as in Matt. xii. 24, 31, 32); *this*, only by those *inside*. **7. the earth**—rather (no article), 'land.' **which drinketh in**—not merely receiving it on the surface: those who enjoy, objectively, Christian experiences, in some sense renewed by the Holy Ghost; true of those who persevere, and those who "fall away." **the rain that cometh oft upon it**—not merely falling *over*, or *towards* it, but falling and resting *upon*, so as to *cover* it [the genitive, *ep' autēs*: not the accusative). **The** "oft" implies, on God's part, the riches of abounding grace ('coming' spontaneously and frequently); on the apostate's part, the perversity whereby he does continual despite to the Spirit's oft-repeated motions. Cf. "how *often*," Matt. xxiii. 37. The heavenly rain falls both on the elect and the apostates. **bringeth forth**—the *natural* result of '*having drunk in* the rain.' **meet**—such as the master of the soil wishes. The opposite of "rejected" (*v.* 8). **by whom** [*di' hous*]—rather, '*for* (*i. e.*, on account of) whom;' viz.. the lords of the soil; not the labourers, as the English version—viz., God and Christ (1 Cor. iii. 9). The heart is the earth; man, the dresser; herbs are brought forth meet, not for the dresser, by whom, but for God, the owner, *for* whom, it is dressed. The plural is, *the owners, whoever they may be;* here, *God.* **receiveth** [*metalambanei*]—'partaketh of.' **blessing** — fruitfulness. Contrast God's curse causing unfruitfulness, Gen. iii. 17, 18; spiritually, Jer. xvii. 5-8. **from God.** Man's use of means are vain unless God bless (1 Cor. iii. 6, 7). **8. that which**—rather (Greek, no article), 'but *if it* (the "land," *v.* 7) *bear*' [*ekpherousa*, not so good as *tiktousa*]: "bringeth forth," *v.* 7: said of the good soil. **briers** [*tribolous*]—'thistles.' **rejected**—by God, after having been *tested* [*adokimos*]. *Reprobate.* **nigh unto cursing**—verging to being given up to its own barrenness by God's just curse. "Nigh" softens the severity of "it is impossible," &c. (*vv.* 4, 6). The ground is not yet actually cursed. **whose**—of which (*land*) the end is [*eis kausin*] unto burning, at the last judgment. As the land of Sodom was given to "brimstone, and salt, and *burning*" (Deut. xxix. 23); so as to the ungodly (Matt. iii. 10, 12; vii. 19; xiii. 30; John xv. 6; 2 Pet. iii. 10). Jerusalem, which so resisted the grace of Christ, was then nigh unto cursing, and in a few years was "*burned*." Cf. Matt. xxii. 7, an earnest of a like fate to all abusers of God's grace (ch. x. 26, 27).

9. beloved. Appositely introduced: LOVE prompts me in the strong warnings I have just given; not that I entertain unfavourable thoughts

10 accompany salvation, though we thus speak. For *ʲ* God *is* not unrighteous to forget your work and labour of love, which ye have showed toward his name, in that ye have ministered to the saints, and do minister.

11 And we desire that every one of you do show the same diligence *ᵍ* to

12 the full assurance of hope unto the end : that ye be not slothful, but followers of them who through faith and patience inherit *ʰ* the promises.

13 For when God made promise to Abraham, because he could swear by no

14 greater, he *ⁱ* sware by himself, saying, Surely blessing I will bless thee,

15 and multiplying I will multiply thee. And so, after he had patiently

16 endured, he obtained the promise. For men verily swear by the greater ;

17 and *ʲ* an oath for confirmation *is* to them an end of all strife. Wherein God, willing more abundantly to show unto *ᵏ* the heirs of promise *ˡ* the

A. D. 64.

ʲ Zech 12 10.
Matt. 23. 31, 32.
John 13. 20.
ᵍ Col. 2. 2.
ʰ ch. 10. 36.
ⁱ Gen. 22. 16.
ʲ Ex. 22. 11.
ᵏ Rom. 8. 17.
ch. 11. 9.
ˡ Job 23. 13, 14.
Iss. 14. 24.
Jer. 33. 20, 21, 25, 26.
Rom. 11.29.

of you; nay, I anticipate *better things* of you ('*the things which are better*'); that ye are not *thornbearing, nigh unto cursing*, and doomed *unto burning*, but heirs of *salvation* in accordance with God's faithfulness (*v.* 10). **we are persuaded**—on good grounds : by proofs [*pepeismetha* stronger than *pepoithamen*]. Cf. Rom. xv. 14. A confirmation of the *Pauline* authorship of this epistle. **things that accompany** [*echomena soterias*]—'things that hold by;' *i. e.*, are linked unto salvation (cf. *v.* 19). In opposition to "nigh unto cursing." **though** [*ei kai*]—'if even we thus speak.' 'It is better to make you afraid with words, that ye suffer not in fact' (*Chrysostom*). **10. not unrighteous**—not *unfaithful* to His promise. Not that we have any inherent *right* to *claim* reward; for (1.) a *servant* has no merit, as he only does what is his duty; (2.) our best performances bear no proportion to what we leave undone; (3.) all strength comes from God; but God has *promised of His own grace* to reward His people (already accepted through faith in Christ) for good works : it is *His promise*, not their merits, which would make it *unrighteous* were He not to reward their works. God will be no man's debtor. **your work**—your whole Christian life (John vi. 29). **labour of love.** א A B C Δ *f*, Vulgate, omit "labour of" [*tou kopou*], which crept in from 1 Thess. i. 3. As "love" occurs here, so "hope," *v.* 11; "faith," *v.* 12; as in 1 Cor. xiii. 13 : the *Pauline* triad. By their *love* he sharpens their *hope* and *faith*. **ye have showed**—(cf. ch. x. 32-34.) **toward his name**—your acts *of love* to the saints were done to those who bear His name, and so for His name's sake. The distressed condition of the Palestinian Christians appears from the collection for them (Rom. xv. 26). Though receiving bounty from other churches, therefore not able to minister much by *pecuniary* help, yet those somewhat better off could minister to the greatest sufferers in their church in various ways (cf. Acts ii. 45; iv. 34, 35; 2 Tim. i. 18). St. Paul, as elsewhere, gives them the utmost credit for their graces, whilst delicately hinting the need of perseverance, a lack of which probably began to show itself.

11. And [*De*]—'But.' **desire** [*epithumoumen*]—'*earnestly* desire.' The language of fatherly affection, rather than command. **every one of you**—implying that *all* had not shown the same diligence as some of those whom he praises in *v.* 10. 'He cares alike for great and small, and overlooks none' (*Chrysostom*). 'Every one of them,' even those diligent in showing LOVE (*v.* 10), needed exhortation to show the same diligence, with a view to the full assurance of HOPE unto the end. They needed, besides love, patient perseverance, resting on *hope* and *faith* (ch. x. 36; xiii. 7). Cf. the "full assurance of *faith*" (ch. x. 22; Rom. iv. 21;

1 Thess. i. 5). **unto the end**—the coming of Christ. **12. be not** [*genēsthe*]—'*become* not.' In ch. v. 11, 'ye have become dull [*nothroi*, "*slothful*" *of hearing*];' here he warns them not to become "slothful" *absolutely*—viz., also in mind and deed. He will not become slothful who keeps always *the end* in view: *hope* is the means. **followers** [*mimētai*]—'imitators:' so in Eph. v. 1, Greek; 1 Cor. xi. 1. **patience** [*makrothumia*]—'*long-suffering* endurance.' There is the *long-suffering of love* (1 Cor. xiii. 4), and that of *faith* (*v.* 15). **them who . . . inherit the promises**—not that they *have* actually the *perfect* inheritance, which ch. xi. 13, 39, 40 explicitly denies, though the dead in Christ have, in the disembodied soul, a foretaste of it, but 'them (enumerated in ch. xi.) who in every age have been, are, or shall be, *inheritors* of the promises:' of whom Abraham is an illustrious example (*v.* 13). The *promise* in the Gospel is *singular:* in respect to the patriarchs, *plural* (Gal. iii. 16). For the "promise" is *one* perfect whole in Christ now come: but under the Old Testament *many promises* were given in successive steps and times. The *promise* of salvation in Christ is already realized; the *promises* of the restoration of all things and final glory are yet future. **13. For** —Reasonableness of resting on "the promises" as infallibly sure; *for* they rest on God's oath: instance of Abraham. 'Consolation, by *the oath of God's grace*, to those whom, in ch. iii. and iv., he warned by the *oath* of God's "wrath." The oath of wrath did not primarily extend beyond the wilderness; but the oath of grace is in force for ever' (*Bengel*). **14. multiplying . . . multiply**—Hebraism for *superabundantly multiply.* **thee.** The increase of Abraham's *seed* is virtually an increase of *himself.* Paul's argument refers to Abraham *himself:* therefore he quotes Gen. xxii. 17, "thee," instead of "thy seed." **15. so**—relying on the promise. **16. for confirmation.** Greek order, 'Of all contradiction (among) them an end unto (with a view to) confirmation (of one's solemn covenant : as *God's*) (is) the oath.' So [*antilogia*] 'contradiction,' ch. xii. 3; 'gainsaying,' Jude 11. This shows (1.) an oath is sanctioned even in the Christian dispensation; (2.) the limits to its use are, that it only be employed where it can *put an end to contradiction in disputes*, and *for confirmation* of a solemn promise. **17. Wherein**—i. e., *Which being the case* among men, God, in accommodation to their manner of confirming covenants, superadded to His *word* His *oath :* the "TWO immutable things" (*v.* 18). **willing . . . counsel** [*Boulomenos-boulēs*]—'willing . . . *will*:' the utmost benignity. **more abundantly**—than had He not sworn. His word would have been amply enough; but, to make assurance doubly sure, He [*emesiteusen orko*] 'interposed as Mediator

544

18 immutability of his counsel, ³ confirmed *it* by an oath : that by two immutable things, in which *it was* impossible for God to lie, we might have a strong consolation, who have fled for refuge to lay hold
19 upon the hope ᵐ set before us : which ⁿ *hope* we have as an anchor of the soul, both sure and stedfast, ° and which entereth into that within the
20 veil ; whither the forerunner is for us entered, *even* Jesus, made an High Priest for ever, after the order of Melchisedec.

7 FOR this ᵃ Melchisedec, king of Salem, priest of the most high God, who met Abraham returning from the slaughter of the kings, and blessed

A. D 64.

³ interposed himself by an oath.
ᵐ Isa. 27. 5.
ch. 12. 1.
ⁿ Ps. 130. 7.
° Lev. 16. 15.
ch 9 7.

CHAP. 7.
ᵃ Gen. 14. 18.

with an oath,' coming between Himself and us : as if He were less while He swears, than Himself by whom He swears (for the less usually swear by the greater). Dost thou not yet believe, thou that hearest the promise? (*Bengel.*) **heirs of** (the) **promise**—not only Abraham's literal, but also his spiritual, seed (Gal. iii. 10). **18. impossible . . . to lie**—'*ever* to lie' [*pseusasthai* : the Greek aorist] (*Alford*). His not being able to deny Himself (2 Tim. ii. 13) is a proof, not of weakness, but of strength incomparable. **consolation**—under doubts and fears ; so 'encouragement.' **fled for refuge**—as from a shipwreck ; or, as one fleeing to one of the six cities of refuge. Kedish — i. e., *holy*, implies the holiness of Jesus, our refuge. Shechem—i. e., *shoulder*, the government is upon His shoulder (Isa. ix. 6). Hebron—i. e., *fellowship*: believers are called into His fellowship. Bezer—i. e., a *fortress*: Christ is so to His people. Ramoth—i. e., *high*: Him hath God exalted with His right hand (Acts v. 31). Golan—i. e., *joy*; in Him all the saints glory. **lay hold upon the hope**—i. e., the object of hope, as upon a preservative from sinking: **set before us**—as a prize for which we strive : a new image—viz., the race-course (ch. xii. i. 2). **19.** *Hope* is represented on coins by an *anchor*. **sure and stedfast**—*sure* [*asphalēn*: not disappointing] in respect to *us*: *stedfast* [*bebaian*] in *itself*. Not an *anchor* that will not keep the vessel from tossing ; or unsound or too light (*Theophylact*). **which entereth into that** (*i. e.*, the place) **within** [*to esoteron*] **the veil**. Two images beautifully combined: (1.) The *soul* is *the ship*; the *world*, the *sea*; the *bliss beyond the world*, *the distant coast*; *hope* resting on faith, the *anchor* which prevents the vessel being tossed to and fro ; the *encouraging consolation* through the *promise* and *oath* of God, the cable connecting the ship and anchor. (2.) The world is the fore-court ; heaven, the Holy of holies ; Christ, the High Priest going before us, so as to enable us, after Him, and through Him, to enter within the veil. *Estius*, 'As the anchor does not stay in the waters, but enters the ground hidden beneath, and fastens in it, so hope, our anchor, is not satisfied with merely coming to the vestibule—*i. e.*, with merely earthly and visible goods—but penetrates even to those within the veil, to the Holy of holies, where it lays hold on God Himself, and heavenly goods.' 'Hope, entering within heaven, hath made us already to be in the things promised, even whilst we are still below, and have not yet received them ; such strength hope has, as to make those that are earthly to become heavenly' (*Theophylact*). 'The soul clings, as one in fear of shipwreck, to an anchor, and sees not whither the cable of the anchor runs—where it is fastened ; but she knows that it is fastened behind the veil which hides the future glory ; and that if only she hold on to the anchor, she shall in her time be drawn in where it is, into the Holiest place, by the hand of the Deliverer' (*Ebrard* in *Alford*). **veil**—the *second* veil which shut in the Holiest place. [The *outer*

545

veil was called *kalumma*; the second, or inner veil, *katapetasma*.] **20.** The absence of the Greek article requires (*Alford*) 'Where, AS forerunner in behalf of [*huper*] us, entered Jesus' (*and is now*; implied in the 'where' [*hopou*]: "Whither" is understood, taken out of "where," Whither *Jesus entered*, and *where* He is now). **for us**—implies that it was not for Himself He needed to enter there, but as our High Priest, representing and opening the way to us, by His intercession with the Father, as the Aaronic high priest entered the Holiest once a year to make propitiation for the people. The first-fruits of our nature are ascended : so the rest is sanctified. Christ's ascension is our promotion ; whither the glory of the Head has preceded, thither the hope of the body, too, is called. We ought to keep festal day, since Christ has taken up and set in the heavens the first fruit of our lump, that is, the human flesh (*Chrysostom*). As John Baptist was Christ's forerunner on earth, so Christ is ours in heaven.

CHAP. VII. 1-28.—CHRIST'S HIGH PRIEST-HOOD AFTER THE ORDER OF MELCHISEDEC ABOVE AARON'S.

1. this Melchisedec (ch. vi. 20 ; Ps. cx. 4). The verb does not come till *v.* 3, "abideth." **king . . . priest**. Christ (Zech. vi. 13) unites these offices in their highest sense. **Salem**—Jerusalem ; *i. e., seeing peace* (Ps. lxxvi. 2) ; not the Salem (Gen. xxxiii. 18) which is distinguished by the adjunct, "a city of Shechem." Among the kings conquered by Joshua, no *king of Salem* distinct from *Jerusalem* is mentioned. Adonizedek ('lord of righteousness'), king of Jerusalem, was plainly a successor of *Melchisedec*. "The king's dale" (2 Sam. xviii. 18), identified in Gen. xiv. 17 with Shaveh, is placed by Josephus and tradition near Jerusalem. **the most high God**—called also "Possessor of heaven and earth" (Gen. xiv. 19, 22). This title, "the Most High," handed down by tradition from primitive revelation, appears in the Phœnician [עֶליוֹן] 'Elion,' i. e., *Most High*. It implies that the God whom Melchisedec served is THE TRUE GOD, not one of the gods of the heathen. So in the only other cases in which it is found in the New Testament—viz., the demoniac and the divining damsel confessing other gods are false, and God alone is to be exalted (Mark v. 7 ; Acts xvi. 17). **who met Abraham**—in company with the king of Sodom. **slaughter** [*kopes*]—*defeat* (*Alford*). So Gen. xiv. 17 (cf. 15) may be translated. Arioch, king of Ellasar, lived and reigned after the disaster (*Bengel*). But if Chedorlaomer, Amraphel, and Tidal were slain, though Arioch survived, "*slaughter* of the kings" is correct. **blessed him**. As priest, he first blessed Abraham on God's part ; next, he blessed God on Abraham's part : a reciprocal blessing. Not a mere wish, but authoritative intercession as a priest. The Most High God's prerogative as "Possessor of heaven and earth" is made over to Abraham ; and Abraham's glory from his victory

2 him; to whom also Abraham gave a tenth part of all; first being by interpretation King of righteousness, and after that also King of Salem,

3 which is, King of peace; without father, without mother, ¹without descent, having neither beginning of days, nor end of life; but made like unto the Son of God; abideth a priest continually.

4 Now consider how great this man *was*, unto ᵇwhom even the patriarch

5 Abraham gave the tenth of the spoils. And verily ᶜthey that are of the sons of Levi, who receive the office of the priesthood, have a command-

A. D. 64.

1 without pedigree.
Ex. 6. 18, 20, 27.
1 Chr. 6. 1, 3.
Ps. 110. 4.
ᵇ Gen. 14. 20.
ᶜ Num. 18. 21, 26.

is made over to God: a blessed exchange for Abraham. **2.** gave [*emerisen*]—'apportioned.' **tenth part of all**—viz., the booty. The tithes are closely associated with the priesthood: the mediating priest received them as a pledge of the giver's whole property being God's: as he conveyed God's gifts to man (*v.* 1, "blessed him"), so also man's gifts to God. Melchisedec is a sample how God preserves, amidst apostasy, an elect remnant. The meeting of Melchisedec and Abraham is the link between the two dispensations, the patriarchal (represented by Melchisedec, who was *specially consecrated by God as* KING-PRIEST, the highest form of that primitive system in which each father of a household was its priest) and the Levitical (represented by Abraham, in which the priesthood was limited to one family of one tribe and one nation). The Levitical was parenthetical, severing the kingdom and priesthood; the patriarchal was the forerunner of Christ's, which, like Melchisedec's, *unites the kingship and priesthood*, and is not derived from, or transmitted to, other men; but derived from God, and transmitted to a never-ending perpetuity in Christ. For other points of superiority, see *vv.* 16-21. Melchisedec must have had some special consecration above the other patriarchs, as Abraham, who also exercised the priesthood; else Abraham would not have paid tithe to him as superior: his peculiar function was, by God's special call, KING-*priest*; whereas no other patriarch-priest was also a God-consecrated king. **first being.** The very name suggests a mystical sense (Isa. xxxii. 17). **righteousness**—not merely righteous: so Christ (Jer. xxiii. 6). *Malachi* means *king; Tzedek, righteousness.* **King of Salem.** Even the city he ruled had a typical significance—viz., *peace*. Christ is the true *Prince of peace*. The *peace* which He brings is the fruit of *righteousness* (Isa. xxxii. 17). **3. Without father, &c.**—explained by 'without genealogy' or 'descent' (cf. *v.* 6); *i. e.*, his genealogy is *not known*; whereas a Levitical priest could not dispense with the proof of his descent. **having neither beginning of days, nor end of life**—viz., history not recording his beginning or end, as it has of Aaron. "Days" mean his time of discharging his *function*. So the eternity in Ps. cx. 4 is that of the *priestly office* chiefly. **made like**—not that he was absolutely "like:" *made like*, in the particulars here specified. Nothing is said in Genesis of the end of his priesthood, or of his having had either predecessor or successor, which typically represents Christ's eternal priesthood, without beginning or end. Aaron's *end* is recorded; Melchisedec's, not. "The Son of God" is not said to be made like Melchisedec, but Melchisedec to be "made like unto the Son of God." When *Alford* denies that Melchisedec was made like the Son of God as to *his priesthood*, on the ground that Melchisedec was *prior* to our Lord, he forgets that Christ's eternal priesthood was an archetypal reality *in God's purpose from everlasting*, to which Melchisedec's priesthood was "made like" in time. Cf. ch. viii. 5, where the heavenly things are represented as the *primary*

archetype of the Levitical ordinances. The words, "Without father, &c. . . . beginning of days, nor end . . . abideth . . . continually," belong to Melchisedec only *in respect to his typical priesthood*; in the full sense, they apply to Christ alone. Melchisedec was, in his priesthood, "made like" Christ, as far as the imperfect type could represent the perfect archetype. 'The portrait of a living man can be seen on the canvas, yet the man is very different from his picture.' There is nothing in Gen. xiv. to mark Melchisedec as superhuman: he is classed with the other kings as a living historic personage; not, as *Origen* thought, an angel; nor as the Jews, Shem, son of Noah; nor as *Calmet*, Enoch; nor as the Melchisedekites, the Holy Ghost; nor as others, the Divine Word. He was probably of Shemitic, not Canaanite origin: the last independent representative of the original Shemitic population, which had been vanquished by the Canaanites, Ham's descendants. The greatness of Abraham then lay in *hopes*; of Melchisedec in *present possession*. Melchisedec was the highest and last representative of the Noachic covenant, as Christ was the highest and ever-enduring representative of the Abrahamic. With Melchisedec the priesthood and worship of the true God in Canaan ceased. He was first and last *king-priest* there, till Christ, the antitype; therefore his priesthood is said to last for ever, because it lasts as long as the nature of the thing (viz., his life, and the continuance of God's worship in Canaan) admits. If Melchisedec were literally high priest for ever, then Christ and he would now still be high priests, and we should have two instead of one (!). *Tholuck*, 'Melchisedec remains in so far as the type remains in the antitype, his priesthood, in Christ.' The *father* and *mother* of Melchisedec, as also his children, were not descended from Levi, as the Levitical priests (*v.* 6) were required to be; and are not even mentioned by Moses. The wife of Aaron, Elisheba, the *mother* from whom the Levitical priests spring, is mentioned; as also Sarah, the mother of the Jewish nation itself. As man, Christ had no *father;* as God, no *mother.* **4. consider**—earnestly, not merely *see* [*theoreite: weigh with attentive contemplation*]. **also** [א A C, Vulgate. But B Δ omit *kai*]—'to whom (as his superior) Abraham *even* paid tithe (went so far as to pay tithe) of (consisting of) *the best of the spoils*' [*ek ton akrothinion: from the top of the heap*, from which the general used to take some portion for consecration to God, or for his own use]. Abraham paid 'tithes of ALL;' and these taken out of the topmost and best portion of the whole spoils. **the patriarch**—in the Greek emphatically standing last: and this payer of tithe being no less a personage than "the patriarch," the first forefather and head of our Jewish race (note, *v.* 3, on Melchisedec's superiority as specially-consecrated *king-priest* above other *patriarch-priests*. **5. sons of Levi**—of the family of Aaron, to whom the priesthood was restricted. Tithes originally paid to the whole tribe became at length attached to the priest family. **according to the law—sanc-**

ment to take tithes of the people according to the law, that is, of their
6 brethren, though they come out of the loins of Abraham: but he whose
² descent is not counted from them received tithes of Abraham, and
7 blessed ᵈ him that had the promises. And without all contradiction the
less is blessed of the better.
8 And here men that die receive tithes; but there he *receiveth them*, of
9 ᵉ whom it is witnessed that he liveth. And, as I may so say, Levi also,
10 who receiveth tithes, payed tithes in Abraham. For he was yet in the
loins of his father when Melchisedec met him.
11 If ᶠ therefore perfection were by the Levitical priesthood, (for under it
the people received the law,) what further need *was there* that another
priest should rise after the order of Melchisedec, and not be called after
12 the order of Aaron? For the priesthood being changed, there is made
13 of necessity a change also of the law. For he of whom these things are

A. D. 64.
² Or.
pedigree.
Gen. 12. 2,
3.
ᵈ Gen. 13. 14,
17.
Gen. 17. 4.
Gen. 22. 17.
Acts 3. 25.
Rom. 4. 13.
Gal. 3. 16.
ch. 6. 13.
ch. 11. 17.
ᵉ ch. 5. 6
ch. 6. 20.
ᶠ Gal. 2. 21.
ch. 8. 7.

tioned by Jehovah (ch. ix. 19). **of their brethren, though, &c.** "Though" on a level by common descent from Abraham, they yet pay tithe to the Levites, whose "brethren" they are. Now the Levites are subordinate to the priests; and these again to Abraham, their common progenitor; and Abraham to Melchisedec. "How great" (v. 4), then, must this Melchisedec be in his priesthood, as compared with the Levitical, though the latter received tithes; and how unspeakably great must "the Son of God" be, to whom, as the sacerdotal archetype (in God's purpose), Melchisedec, the type, was made like! Thus compare the "consider" [*theoreite*], v. 4, in the case of Melchisedec, the type, with the "consider" [*katanoesate*: note, ch. iii. 1] in the case of Christ, the archetype. **6. he whose** descent is not counted from them—from "the sons of Levi," as those "who receive the . . . priesthood" (v. 5). This verse explains "without descent" (*genealogy*: cf. v. 3): he who needs not, as the Levitical priests, to trace his genealogy to Levi. **received** [*dedekatoken*]—'hath received tithes.' **blessed**—perfect tense, 'hath blessed:' implying that the significance of the fact *endures* to the present time. **him that had** [*ton echonta*]—'the possessor of the promises' of greatness to himself and his seed, and of possession of Canaan, twice given before Melchisedec's blessing (cf. note, ch. vi. 12): Abraham's peculiar distinction. Paul exalts Abraham in order still more to exalt Melchisedec. As the priests, though above the people (v. 7), whom it was their duty to 'bless,' were yet subordinate to Abraham; and as Abraham was subordinate to Melchisedec, who blessed him, Melchisedec must be much above the Levitical priests. **7.** The principle that the blesser is superior to him whom he blesses, holds good only in a blessing given with divine authority; not merely a prayerful wish, but one divinely efficient, as that of the patriarchs on their children. So Christ's blessing, Luke xxiv. 51; Acts iii. 26. **8.** Second point of superiority: Melchisedec's is an *enduring*, the Levitical a *transitory*, priesthood. As the law was a *parenthesis* between Abraham's dispensation of promise of grace, and its enduring fulfilment at Christ's coming [Rom. v. 20, *pareisēlthen*, 'The law entered as something adscititious and by the way']: so the Levitical priesthood was parenthetical between Melchisedec's typically-enduring priesthood and its antitypical realization in our ever-continuing High Priest, Christ. **here** —in the *Levitical* priesthood, **there** —in the priesthood *after the order of Melchisedec.* To bring out the typical parallel more strongly, Paul substitutes, "He of whom it is witnessed that he liveth," for the more untypical, 'He *who is made like to Him* that liveth.' Melchisedec "liveth"

merely in his *official* capacity, his priesthood being continued in Christ. Christ is, in *His own person*, 'ever living after the power of an endless life' (*vv.* 16, 25). Melchisedec's death not being recorded, is expressed by the positive "liveth," to bring into prominence the antitype, Christ, of whom alone it is fully true, "that He liveth." **9. as I may so say**—to preclude his words being taken in the mere literal sense; *I may say virtually*, Levi, in the person of his father Abraham, acknowledged Melchisedec's superiority, and paid tithes to him. **who receiveth tithes**—(cf. v. 5.) **in Abraham** [*dia*]—through Abraham. "Payed tithes," *lit.*, 'had been tithed.' **10. in the loins of his father**—i. e., *forefather*, Abraham. *Christ* did not pay tithes in Abraham, for He never was in the loins of an earthly father (*Alford*). Though, in respect to His mother, He was 'of the fruit of (David's, and so of) Abraham's loins,' yet, being supernaturally, without human father, conceived, as He is above the natural law of birth, so is He above the law of tithes. Those alone born naturally, and so in sin, needed to pay tithe to the priest, to make propitiation for their sin. Not so Christ, who derived only his flesh, not also the taint of the flesh, from Abraham. *Bengel*, The blessings which Abraham had *before* meeting Melchisedec were the *general* promises, and the special one of a *natural seed*, and so of Levi; but the promises under which *Christ* was comprehended, and the faith for which Abraham was so commended, followed *after* Abraham's meeting Melchisedec, and being *blessed by him:* to which Gen. xv. 1, "*After* these things," calls our attention. This explains why Christ, the supernatural seed, is not included as paying tithes through Abraham to Melchisedec.

11. perfection—'the bringing of man to his highest state, viz., salvation and sanctification.' **under it** [*ep' autē*. א A B C Δ, Vulgate, have *ep' autēs*]—'upon it (i. e., *on the ground of* it as the basis, the priest having to administer the law, Mal. ii. 7) the people (ch. ix. 19, "all the people") hath received the law' [*nenomothetētai* for *nenomothetēto* in A א B C Δ f, Vulgate]. *Perfect*, not aorist: implying the people were *still observing* the law. **what further need** (ch. viii. 7). For God does nothing needless. **another** [*heteron*, not *allon*]—'that a *different* priest (of a different order) should arise' [*anew*, *anistatai*, v. 15]. **not be called** [*legesthai*]—'said;' i. e., that when spoken of in Ps. cx. 4, 'He is not *said* to be (as we should expect, if the Aaronic priesthood was perfect) after the order of Aaron.' **12. For**—The reason for pressing the words "after the order of Melchisedec;" because these presuppose a transference of the priesthood; this carries with it a change

spoken pertaineth to another tribe, of which no man gave attendance at
14 the altar. For *it is* evident that *ᵍ* our Lord sprang out of Judah; of
15 which tribe Moses spake nothing concerning priesthood. And it is yet far
more evident: for that after the similitude of Melchisedec there ariseth
16 another Priest, who is made, not after the law of a carnal commandment,
17 but after the power of an endless life. For he testifieth, *ʰ* Thou *art* a
Priest for ever, after the order of Melchisedec.
18 For there is verily a disannulling of the commandment going before,
19 for *ⁱ* the weakness and unprofitableness thereof. For *ʲ* the law made
nothing perfect; *³* but the bringing in of *ᵏ* a better hope *did:* by the
which *ˡ* we draw nigh unto God.
20 And inasmuch as not without an oath *he was made Priest;* (for those

A. D. 64.

ᵍ Gen. 49. 10.
Isa. 11. 1.
ʰ Ps. 110. 4.
ⁱ Rom. 8. 3.
Gal. 4. 9.
ʲ Acts 13. 39.
Rom. 3. 20.
³ Or, but it
was the
bringing
in.
Gal. 3. 24.
ᵏ ch. 6. 18.
ˡ Rom. 5. 2.

also of the law (which is inseparably bound up with the priesthood: both stand and fall together, *v.* 11). This is Paul's answer to the objection, What need was there of a new covenant? **13.** Confirming his assertion that *a change is made of the law* (*v.* 12), by another fact showing the distinctness of the new priesthood from the Aaronic. **these things** (Ps. cx. 4) **pertaineth** [*metescheken*] —'hath partaken of' (the perfect implies the *continuance still* of His manhood). **another** [*heteras*]—'a *different* tribe' from that of Levi. **14. evident** [*prodelon*]—'manifest before the eyes' as indisputable: a proof that whatever difficulties now appear, *then* Christ's genealogy laboured under none. **our Lord**—the only place where this now common title occurs without "Jesus," or "Christ," except 2 Pet. iii. 15. **sprang** [*anatetalken*] —as a plant and a branch. **Judah** (Gen. xlix. 10; Luke i. 27, 39 (Hebron of Judah, where *Lightfoot* thinks Jesus was conceived); ii. 4, 5; Rev. v. 5). **of which tribe . . . priesthood** [*eis hēn phulēn*]—'*in respect to* which tribe Moses spake nothing concerning *priests*' (so א A B C Δ, Vulgate [*hiereēn* for *hierosunes*]; "spake nothing" to imply that priests were to be taken from it). **15, 16.** Another proof that the law (economy) is changed; as Christ is appointed Priest, 'not according to the law of a carnal commandment;' one in which a *carnal succession* was required, as in the Levitical priesthood; but 'according to the power of an *indissoluble* [*akatalutou*] life.' The argument, and Melchisedec's priesthood "*for ever*," in antithesis to the Levitical priesthood *not continuing in one person, through the fleeting mortality of the flesh,* require this view. Ps. cx. appoints Him "for ever" (*v.* 17). In contrast to the *carnal succession through death* stands "the power" of Christ to overcome death (Rom. i. 4; 2 Cor. xiii. 4). Not conformably to a *statute* is Christ appointed, but according to an inward *living power:* that derived from the Father, whose eternal Spirit dwelt in Him in all the fulness (ch. ix. 14; John iii. 34). **it**—the change of the economy (*vv.* 12, 18). **far more** [*perissoteron*]—'more abundantly.' **for that** [*ei*] —'since.' **after the similitude of Melchisedec**— in that it is "for ever:" "after the order of Melchisedec" (ch. v. 10). The "order" cannot mean a *series of priests,* for Melchisedec neither received his priesthood from, nor transmitted it to, any other mere man: it must mean 'answering to the *office* of Melchisedec.' **another** [*heteros*]— 'a different.' **16. carnal . . . endless**—mutually contrasted. As "form" and "power," 2 Tim. iii. 5; so here "the law" and "power," cf. Rom. viii. 3, "the law . . . was *weak* through the flesh;" and *v.* 18, "weakness." "The law" is here not the law in general (which in its *moral* essence is "spiritual" (Rom. vii. 14), but the *ceremonial statute* as to the priesthood. "Carnal," as being *temporary,* is contrasted with "endless:" "com-

mandment," with "life." The *law* can give a *commandment,* but not *life* (*v.* 19; Gal. iii. 21). But our High Priest, by His inherent "power," has in Him 'life for ever' (ch. vii. 25; John v. 26). In the power of His resurrection life, not of His earthly life, Christ officiates as a Priest. **17. For**—Proving His *life* "endless" (*v.* 16). א A B Δ read [*martureitai*], '*He is testified of,* that Thou art,' &c. **18. there is** [*ginetai*]—'there takes place,' according to Ps. cx. 4. **disannulling**—a repealing. **of the commandment**—ordaining the Levitical priesthood. And, as the Levitical priesthood and the law are inseparable, a repealing of the law also (note, *v.* 11). **going before**—the legal ordinance giving place to the Christian, the antitypical and permanent end of the former. **weakness and unprofitableness**—opposite of "power" (*v.* 16). **19. For, &c.**—Justifying his calling the law *weak* and *unprofitable* (*v.* 18). The law would not bring men to justification or sanctification before God, which is the 'perfection' that we need in order to be accepted of Him, and which we have in Christ. **nothing**—not merely 'no one,' but "nothing." The law brought nothing to its perfected end: everything in it was introductory to its Christian antitype, which realizes the perfection contemplated. Cf. "unprofitableness," *v.* 19. **did**— rather [as the correspondence of *men* and *de* requires], connect with *v.* 18, 'There takes place (by virtue of Ps. cx. 4) a repealing of the commandment on the one hand (*men*), but [*de:* on the other] *a* bringing in *afterwards* [*epeisagoge* expresses a bringing in of something *over and above* the law: a *superinducing of something new,* and better than the good things of the pre-existing law (*Wahl*)] of a better hope;' not one weak and unprofitable, but (as the Christian dispensation is called) "everlasting," "true," "the second," "more excellent," "different," "living," "new," "to come," "perfect." Cf. ch. viii. 6: bringing us *near to God,* now in spirit; hereafter, both in spirit and in body. (For the law made nothing perfect) is a parenthesis. **we draw nigh unto God**—the token of 'perfection.' *Weakness* is the opposite of this filial confidence of access. The access through the legal sacrifices was only symbolical and through a priest; that through Christ is immediate, perfect, and spiritual. **20.** Another superiority of Christ's Melchisedec-like priesthood: the *oath of God* gave a solemn weight to it which was not in the law-priesthood, not so confirmed. **he was made Priest**—rather supply from *v.* 22, which completes the sentence begun in this verse, *v.* 21 being a parenthesis, 'Inasmuch as not without an oath, *He was made surety of the testament* (for, &c.), of so much better a testament hath Jesus been made the surety.' **21.** Greek order, 'For they indeed (the existing legal priests) without the (solemn) *promise on*

priests were made [4]without an oath; but this with an oath by him that said unto him, [m]The Lord sware and will not repent, Thou *art* a Priest
22 for ever after the order of Melchisedec:) by so much was Jesus made a surety of a better testament.
23 And they truly were many priests, because they were not suffered to
24 continue by reason of death: but this *man*, because he [n]continueth ever,
25 hath [5]an unchangeable priesthood. Wherefore he is able also to save them to [6]the uttermost that come unto God by him, seeing he ever liveth [o]to make intercession for them.
26 For such an High Priest became us, *who is* holy, harmless, undefiled,
27 separate from sinners, and made higher than the heavens; who needeth

A. D. 64.

[4] Or. without swearing of an oath.
[m] Ps. 110. 4.
[n] Isa 9. 6. 7.
[5] Or, which passeth not from one to another.
[6] Or. evermore.
[o] Rom. 8. 34.

oath [*horkomosias*] are priests made' (*Tittmann*). by him—by God. unto him—the Lord, the Son of God (Ps. cx. 1). not repent—never change His purpose. after the order of Melchisedec—So A Δ *f.* Omitted in ℵ B C, Vulgate. 22. surety [*enguos*]—ensuring in His own person the certainty of the covenant to us, by becoming responsible for our guilt, by sealing the covenant with His blood, and by being openly acknowledged as our triumphant Saviour by the Father, who raised Him from the dead. Thus he is at once God's surety for man and man's surety for God: so Mediator between God and man (ch. viii. 6). better (ch. viii. 6; xiii. 20)—'everlasting.' testament [*diathēkēs*]—'covenant.' The term implies that it is *appointed* by God, and comprises the relations partly of a *covenant*, partly of a *testament* —(1.) The appointment made without the concurrence of a second party, of somewhat concerning that party: a last will. So in ch. ix. 16, 17. (2.) A mutual agreement in which both parties consent.
23. Another superiority: the Levitical priests were *many*, as death caused the need of continually new ones being appointed in succession. Christ dies not; so hath a priesthood which passes not from one to another. were [*eisin hiereis gegonotes*]—'are priests made.' The present shows the Levitical priesthood was still existing. many—one after another: opposed to His "*unchangeable* (intransmissible) priesthood" (*v.* 24).· not suffered to continue [*koluesthai paramenein*]—'hindered from *permanently* continuing' *in the priesthood*. 24. he [*ho de*]—emphatic. So in Ps. cx. 4, "THOU art a *priest ;*" singular, not *priests*, 'many.' continueth [*menei*]—not the compound, as in *v.* 23. 'Remaineth'—viz., *in life.* unchangeable [*aparabaton echei tēn hierosunēn*]—'hath His priesthood *intransmissible: not passing from one to another*.' Therefore no so-called apostolic succession of priests are His vicegerents. The Jewish priests had *successors* in office, because 'they could not continue by reason of death.' But this man, because He liveth ever, hath no successor in office, not even Peter (1 Pet. v. 1). [In the dialogue of Minucius Felix, Cœcilius charges the Christians with having no altar—'Cur nullas aras habent. Nulla templa? Nulla nota simulacra.' Octavius, the Christian, replies—'Delubra et aras non habemus.'] 25. Wherefore [*Hothen*] — 'Whence:' inasmuch as 'He remaineth *for ever*.' also—as a natural consequence from the last, at the same time *a new and higher* thing (*Alford*). save—JESUS (*v.* 22), meaning *Saviour*. to the uttermost [*eis to panteles*] —perfectly, so that nothing should ever after be wanting. It means 'in any wise' (Luke xiii. 11). come unto God—by faith. by him [*di' autou*]— *through Him* as their mediating Priest, instead of through the Levitical priests. seeing he ever liveth—resuming "He continueth ever," *v.* 24; therefore "He is able... to the uttermost;" never,

like the Levitical priest, prevented by *death*, for "He ever liveth" (*v.* 23). to make intercession. There was the one *offering* on earth once for all. But the *intercession* for us in the heavens (*v.* 26) is ever continuing: whence it follows that we can never be separated from the love of God in Christ (Rom. viii. 26, 34, 39). He *intercedes* specially for those who come unto God through Him; not for the unbelieving world (John xvii. 9). As samples of His intercession, cf. Isa. lxii. 1; lxiii. 11; Zech. i. 12, 14; Ps. lxix. 6, 7. 'By an humble omnipotency (for it was by His *humiliation* that He obtained *all power*), or omnipotent humility, appearing in the presence, and presenting His postulations at the throne of God' (*Bishop Pearson*). He was not only the offering, but the priest who offered it. Therefore, He is also an intercessor: His intercession being founded on His voluntary offering of Himself without spot to God. We are not only in virtue of His sacrifice forgiven, but in virtue of the intercession admitted to favour (*Archbishop Magee*). John xvi. 26 is no contradiction. He does not "pray [rather *ask*, *erotēso;* the asking of an *equal*] the Father," as though the Father were unwilling; but *meets the Father in behalf of man* [*entunchanei*] as Mediator in whom the Father is well pleased with man. There was a "perpetual incense before the Lord" (Exod. xxx. 8) unseen by the people, burnt by the high priest: so Christ's hidden ever-continuing life of intercession.
26. such—as is above described. A B Δ read 'also.' 'For to US (as *sinners :* emphatical) there was *also* becoming (besides His other excellencies) such as High Priest.' ℵ C *f*, Vulgate, omit it. holy [*hosios*]—*pious* [*hagios* would imply *holy* by *consecration*] towards *God:* perfectly answering God's will in reverent piety (Ps. xvi. 10) [*chasid*]. harmless [*akakos*]—'free from evil,' in *Himself.* undefiled [*amiantos*] — by stain from others, in relation to *men*. The high priest for seven days before the Atonement abstained from intercourse with his family (Talmud). Temptation left no trace of evil in Jesus. separate [*kechorismenos*]—'separated from sinners,' in His heavenly state as our High Priest, after having been *parted from the earth*, as the Levitical high priest was separated from the people in the sanctuary (whence he was not to go out) (Lev. xxi. 12). Though justifying through faith the ungodly, He hath no contact with them *as such*. Lifted above our sinful community, being "made higher than the heavens," at the same time that He makes believers *as such* "to sit together (with Him) in heavenly places" (Eph. ii. 6). So Moses *on the mount*, alone with God, was separated from and above the people (Job xxii. 12). made. Jesus WAS higher before (John xvii. 5), and as the *God*-MAN was *made* so by the Father after His humiliation (cf. ch. i. 4). higher than the heavens—for 'He passed *through* (Greek) the heavens' (ch. iv. 14).

not daily, as those high priests, to offer up sacrifice, *p* first for his own sins, *q* and then for the people's: for this *r* he did once, when he offered
28 up himself. For the law maketh *s* men high priests which have infirmity; but the word of the oath, which was since the law, *maketh* the Son, *t* who is *7* consecrated for evermore.

8 NOW of the things which we have spoken *this is* the sum: We have such an High Priest, *a* who is set on the right hand of the throne of the
2 Majesty in the heavens; a minister *1* of the sanctuary, and of the *b* true tabernacle, which the Lord pitched, and not man.
3 For every high priest is ordained to offer gifts and sacrifices: where-
4 fore *it* *c* *is* of necessity that this man have somewhat also to offer. For if he were on earth he should not be a priest, seeing that *2* there are

A. D. 64.
p Lev. 9. 7.
q Lev. 16. 15.
r Rom. 6. 10.
s ch. 5. 1, 2.
t ch 2. 10.
7 perfected.
CHAP. 8.
a Eph. 1. 20.
Col 3 1.
1 Or, of holy things.
b ch. 9. 11.
2 Or, they are priests.

27. daily—'day by day.' The priests *daily* offered sacrifices (ch. ix. 6; x. 11; Exod. xxix. 38-42). The high priests took part in these daily-offered sacrifices only on festival days; but as they represented the whole priesthood, the daily offerings are attributed unto them: their exclusive function was to offer the atonement "once every year" (ch. ix. 7), and "year by year continually" (ch. x. 1). The "daily" strictly belongs to *Christ*, "who needeth not daily, as those high priests (*year by year*, and their subordinate priests daily), to offer,' &c. **offer up** [*anapherein* is peculiarly used of *sacrifices for sin*]. The high priest's double offering on the day of atonement, the bullock for himself, and the goat for the people's sins, had its counterpart in the TWO lambs offered daily by the ordinary priests. But *Philo*, The priests offered the lambs for the people, the flour for themselves. **this he did**—not 'died first for His own sins and then the people's,' but 'offered up sacrifice' *for the people's* only. He needeth not to offer (1.) daily; nor (2.) to offer for His own sins also: for He offered Himself once a spotless sacrifice (*v.* 26; ch. iv. 15). The sinless alone could offer for the sinful. **once** [*ephapax*]—'once for all.' The sufficiency of the *one* sacrifice to atone for *all* sins *for ever*, resulted from its absolute spotlessness. **28. For**—Reason for the difference (*v.* 27) between His one sacrifice and their oft-repeated sacrifices; viz., because of his freedom from the sinful *infirmity* to which they are subject; *He needed not, as they, to offer* FOR HIS OWN SIN; and being now 'perfected for evermore,' *He needs not to* REPEAT *His sacrifice.* **the word**—"the word" confirmed by "the oath." **which**—*oath* was after the law, viz., in Ps. cx. 4, abrogating the law-priesthood. **the Son**—contrasted with "men." **consecrated** [margin: *teteleiomenon*] (ch. ii. 10; v. 9, notes). Opposed to 'having infirmity.' 'Perfected' by His once for all completed sacrifice, and consequent consecration and exaltation to the right hand of the Father, exempt from all human infirmity, *having no further righteousness to fulfil to qualify Him as our High Priest for ever.* The fall of the temple annihilates man's priesthood: the temple of stone gives way to the temple of the Spirit.

CHAP. VIII. 1-13.—CHRIST, HIGH PRIEST IN THE TRUE SANCTUARY, SUPERSEDING THE LEVITICAL PRIESTHOOD—THE NEW RENDERS OBSOLETE THE OLD COVENANT.

1. the sum [*kephalaion*]—'the principal point;' the participle is present, not *past*, which would be required for the English version. 'The chief point in ("in the case of" [*epi*]: so ch. ix. 10, 15, 17) the things which are being spoken.' **such**—so transcendently pre-eminent; viz., in that "He is set on the right hand of," &c. Infinitely above all other priests in this one grand respect, He exercises His priesthood IN HEAVEN, not in the

earthly 'holiest place.' The Levitical high priests, even when they entered the holiest once a year, only STOOD for a *brief space before the symbol* of God's throne; but Jesus SITS on *the throne* of the Divine Majesty in the heaven itself, and this *for ever* (ch. x. 11, 12). **2. minister** [*leitourgos*]—implies *priestly ministry* in the temple; **the sanctuary** [*tōn hagiōn*]—'the holy places;' the heavenly Holy of holies. **the true** —the archetypal and antitypical contrasted with the typical and symbolical (ch. ix. 24). [*Alethinos* is opposed to that which does not fulfil its idea; for instance, a *type*; *alethēs*, to that which is untrue, as a *lie.* The measure of *alethes* is reality; that of *alethinos*, ideality. In *alethes* the idea corresponds to the thing; in *alethinos*, the thing to the idea (*Kahnis* in *Alford*).] **tabernacle** (ch. ix. 11). Through *His glorified body* as the "tabernacle," Christ passes into the heavenly "Holy of holies," the immediate presence of God, where He intercedes for us. This tabernacle in which God dwells is where God in Christ meets us who are "members of His body." This tabernacle answers to the heavenly Jerusalem, where God's *visible* presence is to be manifested to His perfected saints and angels, united in Christ the Head; in contradistinction to His *invisible* presence in the Holy of holies, unapproachable save to Christ. John i. 14, "Word ... dwelt among us" [*eskenōsen*]: 'tabernacled.' **pitched** [*epēxen*]—'fixed' firmly. **not man**—as Moses (*v.* 5).

3. For—Reason for calling Him "minister of the sanctuary" (*v.* 2). **somewhat.** He does not offer again His *once for all* completed sacrifice. But as the high priest did not enter the holy place *without blood*, so Christ has entered the heavenly Holy place *with His own blood*, as the oblation which He has to offer before God. That "blood of sprinkling" is in heaven; and is thence made effectual to sprinkle believers as the end of their election (1 Pet. i. 2). 'Consecrate' as a priest, is literally to *fill the hand*, implying that an offering is given into the priest's hands, which he is to present to God. **4.** Christ's priestly office is exercised in heaven, not earth; in the power of His resurrection life, not His earthly life. **For.** א A B Δ read [*men oun*] 'accordingly then.' **if, &c.**—'if He were on earth He would *not even* [*oude*] be a priest' (cf. ch. vii. 13, 14); therefore, certainly, could not exercise the high priest's function in the earthly Holy of holies. **seeing that there are**—now (the temple service not yet being set aside, as it was on the destruction of Jerusalem) 'those (א A B Δ, Vulgate, omit "priests") who offer *the* (appointed) gifts [*ta dora*] according to the law.' *Therefore, His sacerdotal 'ministry' must be* "*in the heavens,*" *not on earth* (*v.* 1). I conceive that the denial of Christ's priesthood *on earth* does not extend to the sacrifice on the cross, which *He offered as a priest on*

5 priests that offer gifts according to the law: who serve unto the example *^c*and shadow of heavenly things, as Moses was admonished of God when he was about to make the tabernacle: *^d*for, See, saith he, *that* thou make all things according to the pattern showed to thee in the mount.

6 But now *^e*hath he obtained a more excellent ministry, by how much also he is the Mediator of a better ³covenant, which was established upon better promises.

7 For if that first *covenant* had been faultless, then should no place have 8 been sought for the second. For, finding fault with them, he saith, *^f*Behold, the days come, saith the Lord, when I will make a new cove-

9 nant with the house of Israel and with the house of Judah: not according to the covenant that I made with their fathers in the day when I took them by the hand to lead them out of the land of Egypt; because they continued not in my covenant, and I regarded them not, saith the Lord.

A. D. 64.

^c Col. z. 17.
ch. 9. 9, 23.
ch. 10. 1.
^d Ex. 25. 40.
Ex. 26. 30.
Ex. 27. 8.
1 Chr.28.12,
19.
Acts 7. 44.
Num. 8. 4.
^e 2 Cor. 3. 6.
ch. 7. 22.
³ Or, testa-
ment.
^f Jer. 23. 5, 7.
Jer. 30. 3.
Jer. 31. 31.

earth; but only to the *crowning* work of His priesthood—the *bringing of the blood into the Holy of holies*, which He could not have done in the *earthly* Holy of holies, not being an Aaronic priest. The *place* (the heavenly Holy of holies) was as essential to the atonement as the *oblation* (the blood). The body was burnt without the gate; but the sanctification was effected by the high priest presenting the blood within the sanctuary. If on earth He would not be a priest *in the sense of the law of Moses* ("according to the law"). **5.** Who [*hoitines*]—*Being persons who.* **serve unto,the example**—not '*after* the example,' as *Bengel;* but as ch. xiii. 10, 'serve (the tabernacle, which is but) *the outline* and shadow.' [*Hupodeigmati*, "example," is the *sketch* or *suggestive representation* of the heavenly sanctuary— the antitypical reality and primary archetype.] "The mount" answers to *heaven*, ch. xii. 22. **admonished** [*kechrēmatistai*]— expresses *divine responses* and **commands. to make** [*epitelein*]— *perfectly.* **See**—Accurately observe, that thou mayest make, &c. **saith he**—God. **the pattern** [*tupon*]—An accurate representation, in vision to Moses, of the heavenly sanctuary. The earthly tabernacle was copy of a copy, which accurately represented the grand archetypal original in heaven (Exod. xxv. 40). **6. now**—not *time;* 'as it is.' **more excellent ministry**—than any earthly. **by how much** [*hoso*]—in proportion as. **Mediator** —coming between us and God, to carry into effect God's covenant with us. "The messenger (angel) of the covenant." **which** [*hētis*]—*as being one which,* &c. **established** [*nenomothetētai*] — 'has been enacted as a law.' So Rom. iii. 27 ; viii. 2 ; ix. 31, apply "law" to the Gospel covenant. For the Gospel is founded on the *law*, in spirit and essence. **upon**—resting upon. **better promises** (*vv.* 10, 11). The Old Testament promises were mainly of earthly, the New Testament of heavenly blessings : the exact fulfilment of the earthly was a pledge of the fulfilment of the heavenly. 'Like a physician who prescribes a certain diet, and then, when the patient is beginning to recover, changes it, permitting what he before forbade; or as a teacher gives his pupil an elementary lesson, preparatory to leading him to a higher stage:' so *Rabbi Albo*, in 'Ikkarim.' Jer. vii. 21, 22 shows that God's design in the old covenant ritual was that it should be pedagogical, as a schoolmaster preparing for Christ.

7. Same reasonings as in ch. vii. 11. **faultless** —perfect in its parts, so as *not to be found fault with* as wanting anything which ought to be there: answering all purposes of a law. The law in its *morality* was *blameless* [*amomos*]; but *in saving us* defective, and so not *faultless* [*amemptos*].

should **no place have been sought**—as it has to be now, and as it is in the prophecy, *vv.* 8-11. The old covenant would have anticipated all man's wants, so as to give no occasion for *seeking* something more perfectly adequate. Cf. on "place . . . sought," ch. xii. 17. **8. finding fault with them**—the people of the old covenant not made "faultless" by it (*v.* 7); whose *disregard* of God's covenant made Him to '*regard* them *not*' (*v.* 9). The law is not *in itself* blamed, but *the people* who observed it not. **he saith** (Jer. xxxi. 31-34: cf. Ezek. xi. 19 ; xxxvi. 25-27). At Rama, the headquarters of Nebuzaradan, whither the captives of Jerusalem had been led, Jeremiah uttered this prophecy of Israel's restoration under another David, whereby Rachel, wailing for her lost children, shall be comforted : in part fulfilled at the restoration under Zerubbabel; more fully to be hereafter at Israel's return to their own land ; spiritually fulfilled in the Gospel, whereby God forgives absolutely His people's sins, and writes His law, by His Spirit, on the hearts of believers— the true Israel. *^f*This prophecy forms the third part of the third trilogy of the three great trilogies into which Jeremiah's prophecies may be divided : Jer. xxi.-xxv., against the shepherds of the people; xxvi.-xxix., against the false prophets ; xxx. and xxxi., the book of restoration' (*Delitzsch* in *Alford*). **Behold, the days come**—the formula introducing a Messianic prophecy. **make** [*sunteleso*]—' perfect,' 'consummate.' Appropriate to the new covenant which perfected what the old could not (cf. end of *v.* 9 with end of *v.* 10). **Israel** . . . **Judah**—therefore, the ten tribes, as well as Judah, share in the new covenant. As both shared the exile, so both shall share the literal and spiritual restoration. **9. Not according to**—Very different from, and far superior to, the old covenant, which only 'worked wrath' (Rom. iv. 15) through man's 'not regarding' it. The new covenant enables us to obey, by the Spirit's impulse producing love because of the forgiveness of our sins. **made with** —Greek, 'to :' the Israelites being only *recipients*, not co-agents (*Alford*) with God. [*Diatheke* does not, like 'covenant,' *sunthece*, imply *reciprocity :* but a *legal disposition, dispensation*, the gift of God *to* man ; not a compact *between* God and man.] **I took them by the hand**—as a father takes his child to support and guide his steps. 'There are three periods—(1.) That of the promise; (2.) Of pedagogical instruction ; (3.) Of fulfilment' (*Bengel*). The second, the pedagogical pupilage, began at the exodus. **I regarded them not.** The English version (Jer. xxxi. 32) translates, "although *I was an husband unto* them." St. Paul's translation here is supported by the LXX, Syriac, and *Gesenius*, and accords with the kindred

551

10 For this *is* the covenant that I will make with the house of Israel after those days, saith the Lord ; I will ⁴ put my laws into their mind, and write them ⁵ in their hearts; and ^g I will be to them a God, and they

11 shall be to me a people : and ^h they shall not teach every man his neighbour, and every man his brother, saying, Know the Lord: for all shall

12 know me, from the least to the greatest. For I will be merciful to their unrighteousness, and their sins and their iniquities will I remember no more.

13 In that he saith, A new *covenant*, he hath made the first old. Now that which decayeth and waxeth old *is* ready to vanish away.

9 THEN verily the first *covenant* had also ¹ ordinances of divine service,
2 and ^a a worldly sanctuary. For ^b there was a tabernacle made ; the first,

A. D. 64.
4 give.
5 Or, upon.
g Gen. 17. 7, 8.
Jer. 24. 7.
Eze 37. 27.
Zech. 8. 8.
h Isa. 54. 13.
John 6. 45.
1 John 2 27.
CHAP. 9.
1 Or, ceremonies.
a Ex. 25. 8.
b Ex. 26. 1.

Arabic. The Hebrews *regarded not* God : so God, in righteous retribution, *regarded* them *not*. *Schelling* observes—The law was in fact the mere *ideal* of a religious constitution : in *practice* the Jews were throughout, before the captivity, more or less polytheists, except under David, and the first years of Solomon (the type of Messiah's reign). After the return from Babylon to idolatry there succeeded what was not much better, formalism and hypocrisy (Matt. xii. 43). The law was—(1.) A typical picture, tracing out the features of the glorious Gospel to be revealed ; (2.) It had a delegated virtue from the Gospel, which ceased when the Gospel came. 10. make with—'make *unto*.' Israel—comprising the before disunited (*v.* 8) ten-tribes kingdom and that of Judah. They are united in the spiritual Israel, the elect Church now : they shall be so in the literal restored kingdom of Israel to come. I will put [*didous*]— '(I) giving.' This is the first of the "better promises" (*v.* 6). mind—their intelligent faculty. in [*epi*]—'ON their hearts.' Not on tables of stone, as the law (2 Cor. iii. 3). write [*epigrapso*] —'inscribe.' I will be to them [*eis theon :* ch. i. 5 : *for*] a God, &c. Fulfilled first in the outward kingdom (Lev. xxvi. 12) ; next, in the inward Gospel kingdom (2 Cor. vi. 16) ; thirdly, in the kingdom at once outward and inward, the spiritual being manifested outwardly (Rev. xxi. 3). Cf. a similar progression as to the priesthood—(1.) Exod. xix. 6 ; (2.) 1 Pet. ii. 5 ; (3.) Isa. lxi. 6 ; Rev. i. 6. This progressive advance in the significance of the Old Testament institutions, &c. (*Tholuck*), shows the *transparency* and prophetic character throughout the whole. 11. Second, of the "better promises" (*v.* 6). they shall not— 'have to teach.' his neighbour. So Vulgate [*plesion*]. But א A B Δ *f* [*politēn*], 'his (fellow) *citizen*.' brother—a closer and more endearing relation than *fellow-citizen*. from the least to the greatest—Greek, 'from the little one to the great one' (Zech. xii. 8). Under the old covenant, the priest's lips were to keep knowledge ; at his mouth the people were to seek the law : under the new, the Holy Spirit teaches every believer. Not that the mutual teaching of brethren is excluded whilst the covenant is being promulgated ; but when once the Holy Spirit shall have imparted remission of their sins and inward sanctification, there shall be no further need of man teaching his fellowman. Cf. 1 Thess. iv. 9 ; v. 1 : an earnest of that perfect state. On the way to it every man should teach his neighbour. 'The teaching is not hard, because grace renders all teachable ; for it is not the ministry of the letter, but of the spirit (2 Cor. iii. 6). The believer's stedfastness does not depend on *authority* of human teachers. God Himself teaches' (*Bengel*). The New Testament is shorter than the Old, because, instead of *letter details*, it gives the all-embracing *principles* of the

spiritual law written on the conscience, leading to instinctive obedience in outward details. None save the Lord can teach effectually. "Know the Lord." 12. For, &c.—The *third* of "the better promises " (*v.* 6). *Forgiveness of sins* is the root of this new state of inward knowledge of the Lord. Sin being abolished, sinners obtain grace. I will be merciful [*hileōs*]—'propitious ;' the Hebrew 'salach' is always used to God only in relation to men. and their iniquities. So A Δ *f*. Not in B א, Vulgate, Syriac, Coptic (perhaps from ch. x. 17). remember no more—contrast the law (ch. x. 3).

13. he—God. made the first old (at the time of speaking the prophecy)—'antiquated the first covenant.' From the time of God's mention of a NEW covenant (since God's words are all realities), the *first* covenant was ever dwindling away, until its complete abolition on the introduction of the Gospel. Both cannot exist side by side. Verbal inspiration is proved in Paul's argument turning wholly on the one word "NEW," which occurs but once in the Old Testament. that which decayeth [*to palaioumenon*]—'that which is being antiquated:' growing *out of date* (at the time when Jeremiah spake). waxeth old [*geraskon*]—with senile *decrepitude*. For in Paul's time the new had set aside the old covenant. [*Kaine*] *New* (Testament) implies that it is *of a different kind*, and *supersedes the old*: not merely *recent* [*nea*] (cf. Hos. iii. 4, 5).

CHAP. IX. 1-28.—INFERIORITY OF THE OLD TO THE NEW COVENANT IN THE ACCESS TO GOD— THE BLOOD OF BULLS AND GOATS OF NO REAL AVAIL—THE BLOOD OF CHRIST ALL SUFFICIENT TO PURGE AWAY SIN, WHENCE FLOWS OUR HOPE OF HIS APPEARING AGAIN FOR PERFECT SALVATION.

1. Then verily [*men oun*]—'Accordingly then.' Resuming ch. viii. 5. In accordance with the command to Moses, "the first covenant had," &c. had—not 'has ;' for as a *covenant* it no longer existed, though its rites continued till the destruction of Jerusalem. ordinances—of divine institution. service [*latreias*]—worship. a worldly sanctuary [*to hagion* (the article marking the subject), *kosmikon* (the *predicate*)]—'its (lit., *the*) sanctuary worldly,' mundane : consisting of elements of the visible world. Contrasted with the *heavenly sanctuary*. Cf. *vv.* 11, 12, "not of this building;" *v.* 24. Material, outward, perishing (however precious) ; also defective religiously. In *vv.* 2-5 *the* "*worldly sanctuary*" is discussed ; in *v.* 6, &c., the "ordinances of . . . service." The outer tabernacle signified *this world;* the Holy of holies, *heaven*. *Josephus* calls the outer, divided into *two* parts, 'a secular, common place,' answering to 'the earth and sea ;' the inner holiest place, the *third* part, appropriated to God, not accessible to men. *Worldliness* is the root of sensuous ritualism.

wherein *was* the candlestick, and the ^ctable, and the showbread; which
3 is called ²the Sanctuary. And ^dafter the second veil, the tabernacle
4 which is called the Holiest of all; which had the golden censer, and the
ark of the covenant overlaid round about with gold, wherein *was* ^ethe
golden pot that had manna, ^fand Aaron's rod that budded, and ^g the
5 tables of the covenant; and ^h over it the cherubim of glory shadowing
the mercyseat; of which we cannot now speak particularly.

A. D. 64.

^c Lev. 24. 5.
² Or holy.
^d Ex. 40. 3.
^e Ex 16. 33.
^f Num 17.10.
^g Ex 25. 16.
Deut. 10. 2.
^h Lev. 16. 2.

The modern mass-idol would be too monstrous for any to believe in, were it not decked in worldly finery. 2. Defining the "worldly sanctuary." made [*kateskeuasthē*]—built and furnished. the first—the anterior tabernacle. candlestick, and the table—typifying *light* and *life* (Exod. xxv. 23-39). The candlestick consisted of a shaft and six branches of gold, seven in all; the bowls made like almonds, with a knop and flower in one branch. It was carried in Vespasian's triumph: the figure is to be seen on Titus' arch at Rome. The *table* [*shulchan hapanim:* 'the show-table,' Num. iv. 7] of shittim wood, covered with gold, was for the showbread [*hē prothesis tōn artōn*]— 'the setting forth of the loaves;' *i. e.*, the loaves set forth: Hebrew [*lechem panim*], 'bread of the faces,' or 'presence;' and 'bread *of ordering*' (1 Chr. ix. 32) [מערכת]: that bread through participation of which God's *face* or *person* is seen: *spiritual food*, the means of having *life* in *seeing* God. Christ is the antitypical "bread of life" (John vi. 27-63), 'the express image of God's person,' in whom we see God, and, as the communion of saints, have everlasting nourishment (Lev. xxiv. 7, 8). In the *outer* holy place: so the Eucharist continues *until* our entrance into the heavenly *Holy of holies* (1 Cor. xi. 26). which, &c.—'which (tabernacle) is called the holy place,' as distinguished from 'the Holy of holies.' 3. And [*De*]— 'But.' after—behind: within. second veil. There were two curtains; one before the Holy of holies [*cataj etasma*] here alluded to, the other before the tabernacle door [*calumma*]. called—as opposed to 'the true.' 4. golden censer [*thumiaterion*]—must not be translated 'altar of incense,' for *it* was in the outer holy place, not in "the Holiest" place; but es in Ezek. viii. 11, "censer." So Vulgate and Syriac. This GOLDEN censer was only used on the day of atonement (other censers on other days), and is associated with *the holiest place*, as being taken into it on that anniversary by the high priest. "Which had" does not mean that the golden censer was deposited there, for then the high priest would have had to go in and bring it out before burning incense in it; but that the golden censer was one of the articles *belonging to* the yearly service in the holiest place. He virtually supposes (without specifying) the 'altar of incense' in the anterior holy place, by mentioning *the golden censer* filled with incense from it: the incense answers to *the prayers of the saints;* the altar, though outside, is connected with the holiest place (*standing close by the second veil, directly before the ark of the covenant*), even as we find an antitypical altar in heaven (Rev. viii. 3). The rending of the veil by Christ has brought the antitypes to the altar, candlestick, and showbread of the anterior holy place into the holiest place, heaven. In 1 Ki. vi. 22 [*asher laddebir*] the altar is said to belong to the oracle, or holiest place (cf. Exod. xxx. 6). ark—of shittim wood; *i. e.*, acacia. Not in the second temple, but in its stead was a stone basement ('the stone of foundation') three fingers high. [*Aron*, from *arah*, to collect, a *repository:* its lid, the Greek *hilasterion*, the mercyseat, was the meeting place of God and man. *Theebah*, the ark of Noah; and that of Moses,

when exposed in the Nile.] pot—"golden," added in the LXX.; sanctioned by Paul. manna—an omer, each man's daily portion. 1 Ki. viii. 9 states there was nothing in the ark of Solomon's temple save the two stone tables of the law put in by Moses. But the expression that there was nothing THEN therein save the two tables, leaves the inference that *formerly* there were the other things mentioned by the rabbis and by Paul, the pot of manna (the memorial of God's providential care of Israel) and the rod of Aaron (the memorial of the lawful priesthood, Num. xvii. 3, 5, 7, 10). Perhaps these were lost when the ark was in the hands of the Philistines. "Before the Lord" (Exod. xvi. 32-36), and "before the Testimony," or covenant expressed in the two tables (Num. xvii. 10), thus mean 'IN the ark.' 'In,' however, may refer to appendages [as the Hebrew, קל] *attached to* the ark, as the book of the law put '*in the side* of the ark;' so the golden jewels offered by the Philistines (1 Sam. vi. 8). tables of the covenant (Deut. ix. 9; x. 2). The purpose of the ark was to guard the sacred deposit; the sanctity attached to it symbolizing the religious observance due to the decalogue. The manna within typifies Jesus, "the hidden manna" of the believer (John vi. 31-35; Col. ii. 3; Rev. ii. 17). 5. over it—over "the ark of the covenant." cherubim—representing the ruling powers by which God acts in the moral and natural world (note, Ezek. i. 6; x. 1): sometimes the ministering *angels;* mostly *the elect redeemed*, by whom God shall rule the world and set forth His manifold wisdom: redeemed humanity, combining in and with itself the highest forms of subordinate creaturely life. They stand on the mercyseat, and *on that ground* become the habitation of God, from which His glory is to shine upon the world. They expressly say, Rev. v. 8-10, "Thou . . . hast *redeemed us:*" there distinguished *from the angels*, and associated with the elders. They were of one piece with the mercyseat, even as the Church is one with Christ: their sole standing is on the blood-sprinkled mercyseat; they gaze down at it as the redeemed shall for ever; the "habitation of God through the Spirit." of glory. The *cherubim* were *bearers* of the divine glory (the "*chariot* of the cherubims," 1 Chr. xxviii. 18; Ps. lxviii. 17; Ezek. i.); whence, perhaps, they derive their name [from *rakab, to carry;* by transposition]. The shechinah cloud of *glory* between the cherubim over the mercyseat, the lid of the ark, represented Jehovah. The twelve loaves of showbread represent the twelve tribes, *presented as a consecrated community* before God; just as in the Lord's supper believers, the spiritual Israel, all partaking of the one spiritual bread, and becoming one bread and one body in Christ, present themselves before the Lord as consecrated to Him (1 Cor. x. 16, 17); the oil and light, the pure knowledge of the Lord, in which the covenant people shine (the *seven* (lights) implying perfection); the ark of the covenant, God's Old Testament kingdom, God dwelling among His own; the ten commandments in the ark, the law as the basis of union between God and man; the mercyseat covering the law, and sprinkled with

6   Now when these things were thus ordained, *the priests went always 7 into the first tabernacle, accomplishing the service *of God :* but into the second *went* the high priest alone *once every year, not without blood, 8 which he offered for himself, and *for* the errors of the people : the *Holy Ghost this signifying, that the *way into the holiest of all was not yet 9 made manifest, while as the first tabernacle was yet standing : which *was* a figure for the time then present, in which were offered both gifts and sacrifices, *that could not make him that did the service perfect, as 10 pertaining to the conscience ; *which stood* only in *meats and drinks, and °divers washings, *and carnal *ordinances, imposed *on them* until the time of reformation. 11   But Christ being come an High Priest of *good things to come, *by a

A. D. 64.
i Num. 28. 3.
j Ex. 30. 10.
k ch. 10. 19.
l John 14. 6.
ch. 4. 15, 16.
m Gal. 3. 21.
n Rom. 14.17.
o Num. 19. 7.
p Eph. 2. 15.
3 Or, rites, or, ceremonies.
q ch. 10. 1.
r ch. 8. 2.

the blood of atonement for the people's collective sin, represents God's mercy in Christ stronger than the law ; the cherubim, the redeemed creation personified, looking down on the mercyseat, where God's mercy and God's law are set forth as the basis of creation and redemption. **mercyseat** [*hilasterion*]—'the propitiatory ;' the golden cover of the ark, on which was sprinkled the blood of the propitiatory sacrifice on the day of atonement ; the footstool of Jehovah ; the meeting-place of Him and His people. **we cannot**—conveniently. Besides what met the eye in the sanctuary, there were spiritual realities symbolized which it would take too long to detail, our chief subject being the *priesthood* and the *sacrifices.* "Which" refers not merely to the cherubim, but to *all* the contents of the sanctuary (*vv.* 2-5).

6. The use made of the sanctuary by the high priest on the anniversary of atonement. The tabernacle is described according to *the original design,* not as the temple of Herod, its continuation, actually was. **ordained**—arranged. **went**—'enter,' present. **always**—twice every day, for the morning and evening care of the lamps and offering of incense (Exod. xxx. 7, 8). **7. once every year**—the tenth day of the seventh month. "Once" means *on the one occasion only.* The two, or possibly more, entrances within the veil on that one day were regarded as parts of one whole. **not without blood** (ch. viii. 3). **offered** —'offers.' **errors** [*agnoematōn*] — 'ignorances:' 'inadvertent errors.' They might have known, as the law was clearly promulged : they were bound to study it: so their *ignorance* was culpable (cf. Acts iii. 17; Eph. iv. 18; 1 Pet. i. 14). Though one's ignorance mitigate one's punishment (Luke xii. 48), it does not wholly exempt from punishment. **8. The Holy Ghost.** *Moses* did not comprehend the typical meaning (1 Pet. i. 11, 12). **signifying**—by the typical exclusion of all from the holiest, save the high priest once a year. **the holiest of all**—heaven, the antitype. **the first** (anterior) **tabernacle** — representing the whole Levitical system. *While as yet 'has a standing'* [*echousēs stasin ;* i. e., *has continuance*], *the way to heaven* (the antitypical "holiest place") *is not yet made manifest* (cf. ch. x. 19, 20). The Old Testament economy is represented by the holy place; the New Testament by the Holy of holies. Redemption by Christ has opened the Holy of holies (access to heaven by *faith,* ch. iv. 16; vii. 19, 25; x. 19, 22: by *sight* hereafter, Isa. xxxiii. 24; Rev. xi. 19; xxi. 2, 3) to all mankind. "Not yet" [*mē pō*] refers to the *mind of the Spirit ;* the Spirit intimating that men should *not think* the way was yet opened (*Tittmann*) [*ou po* would deny the *fact* objectively; *me po* denies subjectively]. **9. Which** [*Hētis*]—'The which ;' viz., anterior tabernacle: 'inasmuch as it *is*,' not 'was.' **figure**—'parable :' *a parable setting forth of the*

character of the Old Testament. **for the time then present**—rather, '*in reference to the (now) existing time.*' *The temple worship* belonged to the Old Testament, but *continued still in Paul's time.* In contrast to the 'existing time' stands "the time of reformation" (the New Testament; *v.* 10), which to believers was already existing. So 'the age *to come*' is applied to the Gospel, because it was *present only to believers,* and its fulness even to them is still *to come* (cf. *v.* 11). **in which**—*tabernacle,* not *time* [*kath' hēn,* for *hon* in אABΔ, Vulgate]; or, 'according to which' *parabolic representation.* **were** [*prospherontai*]—'are offered.' **gifts**—unbloody oblations. **could not**—Greek, 'cannot.' **make him that did** (does) **the service**—any worshipper. [*Latreuonta, serving God,* the duty of all men ; not *leitourgounta,* performing a *ministerial office*]. **perfect**—perfectly remove the sense of guilt, and sanctify inwardly through love. **as pertaining to the conscience**—'in respect to the (moral-religious) consciousness.' They can only reach the outward flesh (*vv.* 10, 13, 14). **10. Which**—sacrifices. **stood** [*epi bromasi*]—consisted in (*Alford*); or, *have attached to them* only what appertains to the use of foods, &c. The latter go *side by side with* the sacrifices (*Tholuck*) (cf. Col. ii. 16). **drinks** (Lev. x. 9; xi. 4). **and carnal ordinances.** א A, Syriac and Coptic, omit "and" [*dikaiomata,* for *kai dikaiomasi* of C]. "Ordinances" stand in apposition to "sacrifices," *v.* 9. *Carnal* (affecting only the *flesh*) is opposed to *spiritual.* Contrast "flesh" with "conscience," *vv.* 13, 14. **imposed**—as a burden (Acts xv. 10, 28) continually pressing heavy. **until the time of reformation** [*kairou diorthoseōs*]—'the *season* of *rectification,*' when the reality should supersede the type (ch. viii. 8-12: cf. "better," *v.* 23).

11. **But**—in contrast to "*could not* make . . . perfect" (*v.* 9). **Christ**—of whom all the prophets foretold : not "Jesus." From whom the *rectification* (*v.* 10) emanates, which frees from the yoke of carnal ordinances, being realized gradually now, to be so perfectly in the consummation of 'the age (world) to come.' "Christ . . . High Priest," answers to Lev. iv. 5, "the *priest* that is *anointed.*" **an**—having come forward (cf. [*heko*] ch. x. 7: here [*paragenomenos*] vividly presenting Him before us) *as* High Priest. The Levitical priests must retire. Just as on the day of atonement no work was done, no sacrifice offered, or priest allowed to be in the tabernacle while the high priest went into the holiest place to make atonement (Lev. xvi. 17, 29), so not our righteousness, nor any other priest's sacrifice, but Christ alone atones ; as the high priest before offering incense had on common garments of a priest, but after it wore his holy garments of "glory and beauty" (Exod. xviii. 29-40 ; Lev. xvi. 29), in entering the holiest, so Christ entered heaven in His glorified body. **good things to come** [*tōn*]—*the* "good things to

554

greater and more perfect tabernacle, not made with hands, that is to say,
12 not of this building; neither by the blood of goats and calves, but *by his
own blood he entered in ^tonce into the holy place, having ^uobtained eternal
13 redemption *for us.* For if ^vthe blood of bulls and of goats, and ^wthe
ashes of an heifer sprinkling the unclean, sanctifieth to the purifying of
14 the flesh; how much more ^xshall the blood of Christ, ^ywho through the
eternal Spirit offered ^zhimself without ⁴spot to God, purge your conscience from dead works to serve the living God!

A. D. 64.

^s Rev. 1. 5.
^t Zech. 3. 9.
^u Dan. 9. 24.
^v Lev. 16. 14.
^w Num. 19. 2.
^x 1 John 1. 7.
^y Rom. 1. 4.
^z Eph 2. 5.
⁴ Or, fault.

come," ch. x. 1; "better promises," ch. viii. 6; "eternal inheritance," *v.* 15; 1 Pet. i. 4; "things hoped for," ch. xi. 1. **by a . . . tabernacle**—joined with "He entered." *'Through the greater tabernacle.'* As the Jewish high priest passed *through* the anterior tabernacle into the Holiest, so Christ passed through *heaven* into the inner abode of the unapproachable God (note, ch. iv. 14). But "the tabernacle" is also *the glorified body of Christ* (note ch. viii. 2), "not of this building" (not of the natural *'creation,* but of the spiritual and heavenly, *the new creation'*), the Head of the mystical body, the Church. *Through* this glorified body He passed into the heavenly Holiest (*v.* 24), the immaterial presence of God, where He intercedes for us. *His glorified body,* as the meeting-place of God and all Christ's redeemed, and the angels, answers to the *heavens* through which He passed. His *body* is opposed to the *tabernacle,* as His blood to the blood of goats, &c. **greater**—contrasted with the small dimensions of the earthly tabernacle. **more perfect**—effective in giving pardon, peace, sanctification, and closest communion with God (cf. *v.* 9; ch. x. 1). **not made with hands**—but by the Lord Himself (ch. viii. 2). **12. Neither**—Nor yet. **by**—through: as the means of His approach. **goats . . . calves.** Not a bullock, such as the Levitical high priest offered for himself, and a goat for the people, on the day of atonement (Lev. xvi. 6, 15), *year by year* (whence the plural, *goats . . . calves*). Besides the goat offered for the people, the blood of which was sprinkled before the mercyseat, the high priest led forth a second—viz., the scape-goat: over its head he confessed the people's sins, and sent it as the sin-bearer into the wilderness, implying that the atonement by the goat sin offering consisted in the transfer of the people's sins on the goat, and their consequent removal out of sight. The translation of sins on the victim, usual in other expiatory sacrifices, being omitted in the case of the slain goat, but employed in the case of the goat sent away, proved the two goats were regarded as *one* offering (*Archbishop Magee*). Christ's *death* is symbolized by the slain goat: His *resurrection to life* by the living goat. Modern Jews substitute a *cock* for the goat as an expiation; the sins of the offerers being transferred to the entrails, and exposed on the house-top for the birds to carry out of sight, as the scapegoat did; the Hebrew for *man* and *cock* being similar [*yebher*] (*Buxtorf*). **by**—through: the key unlocking the heavenly Holy of holies to Him [*dia tou idiou haimatos*] 'through THE blood of His own' (cf. *v.* 23). **once** [*ephapax*]—"once for all." **having obtained**—*thereby* [*heuramenos*] 'found for Himself:' a thing of insuperable difficulty, save to Divine omnipotence, self-devoting zeal, and love (ch. v. 7). **eternal.** The entrance of our Redeemer, *once for all,* into the heavenly Holiest, secures *eternal* redemption to us; whereas the Jewish high priest's entrance was repeated year by year, and the effect temporary and partial {cf. Matt. xx. 28; Eph. i. 7; Col. i. 14; 1 Tim. ii. 5; Titus ii. 14; 1 Pet. i. 19).

13-28. PROOF OF THE "ETERNAL REDEMPTION" (*v.* 12).—His blood, offered by Himself, purifies not only outwardly, as the Levitical sacrifices on the day of atonement, but inwardly unto the service of the living God (*vv.* 13, 14). His death inaugurates the new covenant, and the heavenly sanctuary (*vv.* 15-23). His entrance into the true Holy of holies consummates His once-for-all offered sacrifice of atonement (*vv.* 24-26); His re-appearance alone remains to complete our redemption (*vv.* 27, 28). **13. if**—as we know is the case: the indicative. Argument from the less to the greater. If the blood of mere brutes could purify, in however small a degree, how much more shall inward purification, and complete and eternal salvation, be wrought by the blood of Christ, in whom dwelt all the fulness of the Godhead? **ashes of an heifer** (Num. xix. 16-18). The type is full of comfort. The water of separation, made of the ashes of the red heifer, removed ceremonial defilement whenever incurred *by contact with the dead.* As she was slain without the camp, so Christ (cf. ch. xiii. 11; Num. xix. 3, 4). The ashes were laid by for constant use; so Christ's blood, once for all shed, continually cleanses. In our wilderness journey we are continually defiled by contact with the spiritually dead, and with dead works, and need continual application to the life-giving cleansing blood, whereby we are afresh restored to peace and living communion with God in the heavenly Holy place. **the unclean** [*kekoinomenous*]—'those defiled' on any occasion. **purifying** [*katharotēta*]—'purity.' **the flesh**—their intrinsic effect extended no further. The law had a carnal and a spiritual aspect: *carnal,* as an instrument of the Hebrew polity, God, their King, accepting, in minor offences, expiatory victims instead of the sinner, otherwise doomed; spiritual, as *the shadow of good things to come* (ch. x. 1). The spiritual Israelite derived, in these legal rites, spiritual blessings not flowing from them, but from the Antitype. Ceremonial sacrifices released from *temporal penalties* and *ceremonial disqualifications:* Christ's sacrifice releases from *everlasting penalties* (*v.* 12) and *moral impurities of conscience* disqualifying from access to God (*v.* 14). The purification of the *flesh* (the outward man) was by "sprinkling;" the *washing* followed by inseparable connection (Num. xix. 19). So *justification* is followed by *renewing.* **14. offered himself.** The voluntariness of the offering gives it its efficacy. He "through the eternal Spirit"—*i. e.,* His Divine Spirit (Rom. i. 4, in contrast to His "flesh," *v.* 3; *His Godhead,* 1 Tim. iii. 16; 1 Pet. iii. 18), giving free consent to the act—offered Himself. "God is love:" so the Godhead in Him was the impulse to the self-sacrifice. The animals offered had no *spirit* to consent in the sacrifice: they were offered *according to the law:* they had a life neither enduring nor of intrinsic efficacy. But He from eternity, with *His Divine and everlasting Spirit,* concurred with the Father's will of redemption by Him. His offering began on the altar of the cross, and was completed in His entering the Holiest

15　And [a] for this cause he is the Mediator of the new testament, [b] that by means of death, for the redemption of the transgressions *that were* under the first testament, they [c] which are called might receive the promise of
16　eternal inheritance.　For where a testament *is*, there must also of necessity [5] be the death of the testator.　For a testament *is* of force after

A. D. 64.

[a] 1 Tim. 2. 5.
[b] Rom. 3. 25.
[c] ch. 3. 1.
[5] Or, be brought in.

with His blood.　The *eternity* of His Divine Spirit gives *eternal* (*v.* 12; ch. vii. 16, 25 : cf. *v.* 15) efficacy to His offering, so that not even God's infinite justice has any exception to take against it.　It was 'through His most burning love flowing from His eternal Spirit,' that He offered Himself (*Œcolampadius*).　So א A B.　But C Δ *f.* Vulgate [*hagiou* for *aioniou*], '*Holy* Spirit' (Isa. xi. 2 ; lxi. 1; Luke i. 35; iv. 14 ; John iii. 34).　Christ offered Himself not merely in figure, but really and spiritually for man's spiritual life.　The outward bloodshedding is subordinate to the inward offering which preceded it (ch. x. 7; John xvii. 19). **without spot** — the animal victims were without *outward* blemish: Christ on the cross was a victim *inwardly* and *essentially* stainless (1 Pet. i. 19). **purge**—purify from fear, guilt, alienation from Him, and selfishness, the source of *dead works* (*vv.* 22, 23). **your.** So א, Vulgate.　But A Δ *f*, 'our.' **conscience**—religious *consciousness.* **dead works.**　All works done in the natural state before justification, however life-like they look, are *dead* in the sight of "the living God ;" for they come not from living faith in, and love to, Him (ch. xi. 6).　As contact with a dead body defiled ceremonially (cf. "ashes . . . sprinkling the unclean," *v.* 13), so dead works defile the spiritual consciousness. **to**—*so as to* [*eis to*] **serve.**　The ceremonially unclean could not *serve God* in the outward communion of His people: the unrenewed cannot serve God in spiritual communion.　A dead animal offered to God would have been an insult (cf. Mal. i. 8), much more for one not justified by Christ's blood to offer dead works.　But those purified by Christ's blood in *living* faith serve (Rom. xii. 1), and shall more fully serve, God (Rev. xxii. 3). **living God**—requiring living spiritual service (John iv. 24).

15. for this cause—the all-cleansing power of His blood fits Him to be Mediator of the new covenant (ch. viii. 6), securing forgiveness for the sins not covered by the former imperfect covenant, and also an eternal inheritance to the called. **by means of death** [*thanatou genomenou*]—'death having taken place.'　At the moment that His death took place, 'the called received the (*fulfilment of the*) promise' (ch. vi. 15; Luke xxiv. 49; Acts i. 4): His death divides the Old from the New Testament.　The "called" are the elect "heirs," "partakers of the heavenly calling" (ch. iii. 1). **redemption of the transgressions that were under the first testament**—the transgressions of *all men* from Adam to Christ, first against the primitive revelation, then against the revelations to the patriarchs, then against the law given to Israel, the representative people of the world.　The "first testament" includes the whole period from Adam to Christ, not merely that of the covenant with Israel, which was a concentrated representation of *the former covenant made with mankind by sacrifice*.　Before the *inheritance by the New Testament* [for here the "INHERITANCE," resulting from Christ's "death," requires *diatheke* to be testament, as it was before *covenant*] could come in, there must be *redemption* of (*i. e.*, deliverance from the penalties incurred by) the *transgressions* committed *under the first testament*, for the propitiatory sacrifices reached only as far as removing outward defilement.　But

in order to obtain the inheritance which is a reality there must be a real propitiation, since God could not enter into covenant-relation with us so long as sins were unexpiated (Rom. iii. 24, 25. **might** [*labosin*]—'*may* receive,' which previously they could not (ch. xi. 39, 40). **the promise** —to Abraham.　**16.** An axiomatic truth ; "*a* (not 'the ') testament."　The testator must die before his *testament* takes effect (*v.* 17) [a common meaning of *diathece*].　So Luke xxii. 29, "I appoint [by testamentary disposition : the cognate *diatithemai*] unto you a kingdom," &c.　The need of death before the testamentary appointment takes effect holds good only in Christ's relation as MAN to us. be [*pheresthai*]—'be borne ;' 'be involved in the case ;' or else, 'be brought forward in court,' to give effect to the will.　[This sense (*testament*) here does not exclude other secondary senses of *diathece* in the New Testament—(1.) A *covenant* between *two* parties ; (2.) An arrangement made by *God alone* in relation to us.　Thus, Matt. xxvi. 28, "blood of the *covenant :*" for a *testament* does not require *blood* shedding.　Cf. Exod. xxiv. 8, *covenant*, which Christ quotes, though probably He *included* "testament" also under *diathece*, as this designation strictly applies to the new dispensation, and is applicable to the old also, not in itself, but viewed as typifying the new.]　Moses speaks of the same thing as Paul.　Moses, by "covenant," means one giving the heavenly *inheritance* (typified by Canaan) after the testator's death, which he represented by the sprinkling of blood.　Paul, by "testament," means one having *conditions*, and so being a *covenant* (*Poli*, 'Synopsis'): the conditions are fulfilled by Christ, not by us ; we must indeed *believe* ; but even this God works in His people.　*Tholuck*, ' *covenant* . . . covenant . . .' . mediating victim :' the *masculine* used of the victim regarded as mediator of the covenant: especially as in the new covenant a MAN (Christ) was the victim.　The covenanting parties used to pass between the divided parts of the sacrificed animal ; but, without reference to this, the need of a *sacrifice* for establishing a covenant suffices.　Others consider that the death of the victim represented the death of both parties as *unalterably bound to the covenant*.　So in the redemption covenant, Jesus' death symbolized the death of God (?) in the person of the mediating victim, and also the death of man.　But it is not, 'there must be the death of *both parties* making the covenant,' but singular, 'of *Him* who made [aorist, *diathemenou :* not "of Him *making*"] the testament.'　Also, it is "death," not 'sacrifice' or 'slaying.'　The death is supposed *past :* the fact of the death is *brought* forward to give effect to the will.　These requisites of a testament concur—1. A testator ; 2. Heir ; 3. Goods ; 4. The testator's death ; 5. The fact of the death *brought forward*.　In Matt. xxvi. 28, two other requisites appear: *witnesses*, the disciples ; *a seal*, the sacrament of the Lord's supper, the sign of His *blood* wherewith the testament is sealed.　The *heir* is ordinarily the *successor* of him who dies, and so ceases to have possession.　But Christ comes to life again, and is Himself (including all that He had), in the power of His now endless life, His people's inheritance; in *His* being Heir (ch. i. 2), *they* are heirs.　**17.** **after** [*epi*]—'over ;' we say 'upon the death of

men are dead : otherwise it is of no strength at all while the testator liveth.

18   Whereupon *d* neither the first *testament* was [6] dedicated without blood.

19   For when Moses had spoken every precept to all the people according to the law, he took the blood of calves and of goats, with *e* water, and [7] scarlet wool, and hyssop, and sprinkled both the book, and all the

20   people, saying, *f* This *is* the blood of the testament which God hath

21   enjoined unto you.   Moreover *g* he sprinkled likewise with blood both

22   the tabernacle and all the vessels of the ministry.   And almost all things are by the law purged with blood; and *h* without shedding of blood is no remission.

23   *It was* therefore necessary that *i* the patterns of things in the heavens

A. D. 64.

d Ex. 24. 6.
[6] Or,
  purified.
e Ex. 21. 5-8.
  Lev. 14. 4.
  Lev. 16, 14,
  15, 18.
[7] Or, purple.
f Ex. 24. 8.
  Matt. 26.28.
g Ex. 29. 12.
  Lev. 8. 15.
h Lev. 17. 11.
i ch. 8. 5

the testator.' The Greek hardly sanctions *Tholuck*, 'on the condition that slain sacrifices be there.' otherwise [*epei mē pote ischuei*]—'seeing that it is never availing'(*Alford*). *Lachmann*, with an interrogation, 'Since, is it ever in force (surely not) while the testator liveth?'

18. Whereupon [*Hothen*]—'Whence.' Since the old dispensation also had its testamentary aspect. **the first testament**—not that the old dispensation, *regarded by itself*, is a *testament*, but it is so as the *typical representative of the new*, which is more strictly a *Testament*. **dedicated** [*enkekainistai*]—'inaugurated.' The Old Testament formally began on that day. **19. For**—Confirming *v.* 18. **spoken every precept ... according to the law**—adhering to every ordinance (Eph. ii. 15). Cf. "Moses told *all the words of the Lord, and all the judgments;* and *all the people* answered," &c. **the blood of calves** [*tōn*]—'the calves,' those sacrificed by the "young men" sent by Moses to do so (Exod. xxiv. 3, 5). The "peace offerings" were "of oxen" (LXX. [*moscharia*], 'little calves'), and the "burnt offerings" were probably (though this is not specified), as on the day of atonement, *goats*. The law of Exodus sanctioned formally many sacrificial practices handed down from the primitive revelation. **with water**—prescribed not in Exod. xxiv., but in other purifications, as *ex. gr.*, of the leper, and the water of separation, which contained the ashes of the red heifer. **scarlet wool, and hyssop**—ordinarily used for purification. *Scarlet* or *crimson*, resembling blood: thought to be a peculiarly deep dye, whence it typified sin (note, Isa. i. 18). So Jesus wore a scarlet robe, emblem of the deep dyed sins He bore *on* Him, though He had none *in* Him. Wool was used as retaining water; the hyssop, as a tufty plant (wrapt round with the scarlet wool) for sprinkling it. The wool was also a symbol of purity. The *hyssopus officinalis* grows on walls, with small lancet-formed woolly leaves an inch long, with blue and white flowers, and a knotty stalk about a foot high. **sprinkled . . . the book** —out of which he read "every precept:" not mentioned in Exod. xxiv. 7. Hence *Bengel*, 'And (having taken) the book itself (so Exod. xxiv. 7), he both sprinkled all the people, and (*v.* 21) moreover [*kai de*] sprinkled the tabernacle.' The 'itself' expressing that the testament was more important than that blood. The double exhibition, of the blood and of the book, thus constituted the 'dedication' (*v.* 18). But the "and" [*kai*] before "sprinkled" is thus superfluous; whereas in the English version it regularly follows [*te*] "both." Paul, by inspiration, supplies the particular specified here. The sprinkling of the *roll* [*biblion*] of the testament, as well as the people, implies that neither can *the law* be fulfilled nor the people purged from sins, save by the sprinkling

of Christ's blood (1 Pet. i. 2). Cf. *v.* 23, which shows that there is something antitypical to the Bible in heaven (cf. Rev. xx. 12). 'Itself' distinguishes *the book* from the 'precepts' in it which he 'spake.' **20.** Exod. xxiv. 8, "*Behold* the blood of the covenant, which *the Lord* has made with you." The change accords with Christ's inauguration of the New Testament, recorded Luke xxii. 20, "This cup (is) the New Testament in my blood, which is shed for you;" the only Gospel in which the "is" has to be supplied, as here. Luke was *Paul's* companion, whence the correspondence. **testament** (note, *vv.* 16, 17). Christ has sealed it with His *blood*, of which the Lord's supper is the sacramental sign. The testator was represented by the animals slain in the old dispensation. In both dispensations the inheritance was bequeathed : in the new, by One who has come in person and died : in the old, by the same one, only typically present. See *Alford's* excellent note. **enjoined** (me to ratify) **unto** (in relation to) **you**— me to ratify *in relation to you*. In the old dispensation the condition on the people's part is implied in Exod. xxiv. 8, "(Lord . . . made with you) *concerning all these words*." Paul omits this, as he includes the fulfilment of obedience to "all these words" as part of God's promise in the new covenant (ch. viii. 8, 10, 12), whereby Christ fulfils all for our justification, and will enable us by His Spirit in us to fulfil all in our now progressive and finally complete sanctification. **21.** The *sprinkling of the tabernacle with blood* is added by inspiration. Exod. xxx. 25-30 ; xl. 9, 10, mentions only Moses' anointing the tabernacle and its vessels. Lev. viii. 10, 15, 30 mentions sprinkling of blood upon Aaron and his garments, upon his sons, and upon the altar, as well as the anointing; so we may infer, as *Josephus* has stated, that the tabernacle and its vessels were sprinkled with blood as well as anointed. Lev. xvii. 16, 19, 20, 33 favours this. The tabernacle and its contents needed atonement (2 Chr. xxix. 21). **22. almost all things**—under the old dispensation. The exceptions are Exod. xix. 10 ; Lev. xv. 5, &c. ; xvi. 26, 28 ; xxii. 6 ; Num. xxxi. 22-24. **without** [*choris*]—'apart from.' **shedding of blood**—in the slaughter of the victim. The *pouring out the blood on the altar* subsequently is the main part of the sacrifice (Lev. xvii. 11), and could not have place apart from the previous *shedding of* the blood in slaying. **is** [*ginetai*]—'takes place.' **remission**—of sins: a favourite expression of Luke, Paul's companion. Properly used of remitting debts (Matt. vi. 12; xviii. 27, 32) : our sins are debts. Cf. Lev. v. 11-13, an exception because of poverty, confirming the general rule.

23. patterns [*hupodeigmata*]—'the suggestive representations:' the typical copies (note, ch. viii. 5). **things in the heavens**—the heavenly taber-

should be purified with these; but the heavenly things themselves with
24 better sacrifices than these. For *ʲ*Christ is not entered into the holy
places made with hands, *which are* the figures of the true; but into
25 heaven itself, now *ᵏ*to appear in the presence of God for us: nor yet that
he should offer himself often, as the high priest entereth into the holy
26 place every year with blood of others; for then must he often have
suffered since the foundation of the world: but now once *ˡ*in the end of
the world hath he appeared to put away sin by the sacrifice of himself.
27 And as it is appointed unto men once to die, but after this the judg-

A. D. 65.

ʲ ch. 6. 20.
ᵏ Rom. 8. 34.
  ch. 7. 25.
  1 John 2. 1.
ˡ 1 Cor. 10. 11.
  Gal. 4. 4.
  Eph. 1. 10.
  ch. 7. 27.
  ch. 10. 10.
  1 Pet. 3. 18.

nacle and its contents. **purified with these**—with the blood of bulls and goats. **heavenly things themselves**—the archetypes. Man's sin introduced disorder into the relations of God and His holy angels in respect to man. The *purification* removes this element of disorder, and changes God's wrath against man in heaven (designed to be the place of God's grace to men and angels) into reconciliation. Cf. "peace in heaven," Luke xix. 38. 'The uncreated heaven of God, though in itself untroubled light, yet needed a purification, in so far as the light of love was obscured by the fire of wrath against sinful man' (*Delitzsch* in *Alford*). Contrast Rev. xii. 7-10. Christ's atonement had the effect also of casting Satan out of heaven (Luke x. 18; John xii. 31: cf. ch. ii. 14). Christ's body, the true tabernacle (notes, ch. viii. 2; ix. 11), as bearing our imputed sin (2 Cor. v. 21), was consecrated (John xvii. 17, 19) by the shedding of His blood, to be the meeting-place of God and man. **sacrifices.** The plural is used in the general proposition, though strictly referring to the *one* sacrifice of Christ. Paul implies that it, by its matchless excellency, is equivalent to the Levitical many sacrifices. It, though one, is manifold in its applicability to many. **24.** Resumption of the thought, "He entered in once into the holy place," *v.* 12. He has, in *vv.* 13, 14, expanded "by His own blood," *v.* 12; and in *vv.* 15-23 enlarged on *v.* 11, "an High Priest of good things to come." **not entered into the holy places made with hands**—as was the Holy of holies in the earthly tabernacle (note, *v.* 11). **figures**—copies "of the true" holiest, heaven, the archetype (ch. viii. 5). **into heaven itself**—the immediate presence of God beyond all the created heavens *through* which Jesus passed (note, ch. iv. 14; 1 Tim. vi. 16). **now**—ever since His ascension (cf. *v.* 26). **to appear**—TO PRESENT HIMSELF *visibly* [*emphanisthēnai*]: 'to be manifested.' Mere man may have a vision through a veil, as Moses had (Exod. xxxiii. 18, 20-23). Christ alone beholds, and is beheld by, the Father without a veil. **in the presence of God**—'*to the face* of God.' Cf., as to the saints hereafter, Rev. xxii. 4, and the earnest, 2 Cor. iii. 18. Aaron, the high priest *for* the people, stood *before the ark*, and only saw the *cloud*, the symbol of God's glory (Exod. xxviii. 30). Christ appears before God Himself. **for us**—in our behalf as Advocate and Intercessor (ch. vii. 25; Rom. viii. 34; 1 John ii. 1). It is enough that Jesus *shows Himself for us* to the Father: the sight satisfies God in our behalf. He brings before the face of God no offering which, as only sufficing for a time, needs renewal; but He is in person, by the eternal Spirit in Him, our eternally-present offering before God. **25. Nor yet** (did He enter heaven) **that.** Another superiority of Christ. His sacrifice needs not, as the Levitical sacrifices did, to be repeated. His purpose in entering the true sanctuary is not *that He may offer* [*prospherē*: subjunctive] *Himself often*; i. e., *present Himself* **as** the offering *in the presence of God*, **as the high priest does the blood**

(Paul uses the *present*, as the legal service was then existing, year by year, on the day of atonement, entering the Holy of holies. **with**—Greek, 'in.' **blood of others**—*not his own*, as Christ did. **26. then**—in that case. **must he often have suffered** [*edei pollakis pathein*]—'it would have been necessary for Him often to suffer.' In order to "offer" (*v.* 25) Himself often before God in the heavenly holiest, like the high priests, He would have had, and would have often to suffer. His *oblation* of Himself before God was once for all (i. e., the bringing in of His blood into the heavenly Holy of holies); therefore the preliminary *suffering* was once for all. **since the foundation of the world.** The continued sins of men, down from creation, would entail a continual suffering on earth, and consequent oblation of His blood in the heavenly holiest, if the one oblation "in the fulness of time" were not sufficient. 'Philo de Mon.,' p. 637, 'The high priest of the Hebrews offered sacrifices for the whole human race.' 'If there had been greater efficacy in the repetition of the oblation, Christ would have been sent immediately after the foundation of the world to suffer, and offer Himself at successive periods, or at least at the jubilees' (*Grotius*). **now**—as the case is. **once**—for all: without need of renewal. Rome's UNBLOODY sacrifice in the mass contradicts her assertion that the *blood* of Christ is in the wine, and also that the mass is propitiatory; for, if *unbloody*, it cannot be *propitiatory*; for *without shedding of blood there is no remission* (*v.* 22). Moreover, "*once*" for all here, and in *v.* 28, and ch. x. 10, 12, disproves her view that there is a continually-repeated offering of Christ in the Eucharist. The offering of Christ was once done, that it might be thought of for ever (note, cf. ch. x. 12). **in the end of the world** [*sunteleia ton aiōnon*]—'at the consummation of the ages:' the winding up of all the previous ages, to be followed by a new age, ch. i. 1, 2: *the last age*, beyond which no further is to be expected before Christ's speedy second coming, the complement of the first, 1 Cor. x. 11: Matt. xxviii. 20, 'the consummation of *the age*' (singular). Cf. "the fulness of times" (*seasons*), Eph. i. 10. **appeared** [*pephanerotai*]—'been manifested' on earth (1 Tim. iii. 16; 1 Pet. i. 20). [The English version has confounded, *v.* 24, *emphanisthenai*; *v.* 26, *pephanerotai*; *v.* 28, *ophthesetai*. But in *v.* 24 it is 'to present Himself' *before God in the heavenly sanctuary*: in *v.* 26, 'been manifested' *on earth*; in *v.* 28, 'shall be seen' by all, and especially believers.] **put away** [*athetesin*]—abolish: doing away sin's power, as well as the guilt and penalty, so that it should be powerless to condemn; as also its yoke, so that believers shall at last sin no more. **sin**—singular: all the sins of men of every age are *one mass* laid on Christ. He hath not only atoned for *actual sins*, but destroyed *sin itself*. John i. 29, "Behold the Lamb of God, which taketh away the *sin* (not merely *the sins*: singular) of the world." **by** (through) **the sacrifice of himself**—not by "blood *of others*" (*v.* 25). **27. as** [*kath' hoson*]—inasmuch

28 ment; so ^m Christ was once ⁿ offered to bear the sins of many: and unto them that look for him shall he appear the second time without sin unto salvation.

10 FOR the law having ^a a shadow of good things to come, *and* not the very image of the things, can never with those sacrifices which they offered year by year continually make the comers thereunto perfect.

2 For then ¹ would they not have ceased to be offered? because that the worshippers once purged should have had no more conscience of sins.

3 But in those *sacrifices there is* a remembrance again *made* of sins every year.

A. D. 64.
^m Rom. 6. 10.
ⁿ 1 Pet. 2. 24.

CHAP. 10.
^a Col 2. 17.
1 Or, they would have ceased to be offered, because, etc.

---

as. it is appointed [*apokeitai*]—'it is *laid up* (as our appointed lot)' (Col. i. 5). "Appointed" [Hebrew, *Seth*], in the case of man, answers to 'anointed' in the case of Jesus; therefore the "Christ" is the title here. The history of *man* and that of *the Son of man* strictly correspond. The two most solemn facts of our being are connected with the two most gracious truths of our dispensation, our death and judgment answering in parallelism to Christ's first coming to die for us, and His second coming to consummate our salvation. **once**—no more. **after this the judgment** —viz., at Christ's appearing, to which, in *v.* 28, "judgment" in this verse is parallel. Not 'after this comes the heavenly glory.' The intermediate state is a joyous, or else agonizing *expectation* of "judgment;" after the judgment comes the full and final joy, or else woe. **28. Christ**—Greek, 'THE Christ:' the representative MAN; representing all men, as the first Adam did. **once offered** —not "often" (*v.* 25); just as "men," of whom He is the Head, are appointed *once* to die. He did not need to die again and suffer for each individual, or each successive generation; for He represents *all* of every age, and therefore once for all exhausted the penalty incurred by all. He was offered by the Father, His own "eternal Spirit" (*v.* 14) concurring; as Abraham spared not Isaac, but offered him, the son unresistingly submitting to the father's will, (Gen. xxii.) **to bear the sins**—from Isa. liii. 12, "He bare the sin of many"—viz., *on Himself:* so "bear," Lev. xxiv. 15; Num. v. 31; xiv. 34: [*anenenkein*] *to bear up* (1 Pet. ii. 24). 'Our sins were laid on Him. When, therefore, He was lifted up on the cross, He *bare up* our sins along with Him' (*Bengel*). **many**—not opposed to *all*, but to *few*. He, *the One*, was offered for *many*, and that *once for all* (cf. Matt. xx. 28). **look for him** [*apekdechomenois*] —*with waiting expectation even unto the end* (Rom. viii. 19, 23; 1 Cor. i. 7, which see). **appear**—'be seen.' No longer in the alien "form of a servant," but in His own proper glory. **without** [*choris*] —apart from, separate from "sin" (Rom. vi. 10). Not bearing the sin of many *on* Him as at His first coming (even then there was no sin *in* Him). That sin has been once for all taken away, so as to need no repetition of His sin offering (*v.* 26; 1 Pet. iv. 1, 2). At His second coming He shall have no more to do with sin. **unto salvation** —to bring in completed salvation; redeeming the body now subject to the bondage of corruption. Hence, in Phil. iii. 20, "we look for THE SAVIOUR" (note, 1 Cor. i. 30). *Note,* Christ's *prophetical* office, as the *Divine Teacher,* was prominent during His earthly ministry; His *priestly* is now from His first to His second coming; His *kingly* shall be fully manifested at His second coming.

CHAP. X. 1-39.—CONCLUSION OF THE ARGUMENT. THE RECURRING LAW-SACRIFICES CANNOT PERFECT THE WORSHIPPER, BUT CHRIST'S ONCE-FOR-ALL OFFERING CAN.

Instead of the daily ministry of priests, Christ's service is perfected by the one sacrifice, whence He now sits on God's right hand as Priest-King, until all His foes shall be subdued unto Him. Thus the new covenant (ch. viii. 8-12) is inaugurated, whereby the law is written on the heart, so that an offering for sin is needed no more. Wherefore we ought to draw near the Holiest in firm faith and love: fearful of the awful results of apostasy; looking for the recompense at Christ's coming. **1.** Previously the *oneness* of Christ's offering was shown: now is shown its *perfection,* contrasted with the law-sacrifices. **having**—inasmuch as it has but 'the shadow, not the very image;' *i. e.,* exact likeness, reality, such as the Gospel has. The "image" [*eikona*] is *the archetype* (cf. ch. ix. 24) of those heavenly verities of which the law furnished but *a shadowy outline.* The law is the primer, teaching the elements of Christianity by object-lessons (cf. 2 Cor. iii. 13, 14, 18). As Christ is '*the express image* (*character*) of the Father's person' (ch. i. 3), so the Gospel is the very realization to us of *the* heavenly *archetype,* of which the law was drawn as a sketch, or outline copy (ch. viii. 5). The law was a continual acted prophecy, showing the divine design that its counterparts should come, and proving their truth when they came. Thus the imperfect and continued sacrifices before Christ foreshowed, and now prove the reality of Christ's one perfect antitypical expiation. **good things to come** (ch. ix. 11)—belonging to 'the world (age) to come.' *Good things* in part made present by faith, and to be fully realized hereafter in perfect enjoyment. 'As Christ's Church on earth is a prediction of the future life, so the Old Testament economy is a prediction of the Christian Church' (*Lessing*). In relation to the law's temporal goods, the Gospel's spiritual and eternal goods are "good things *to come.*" Col. ii. 17, calls legal ordinances 'the shadow,' and Christ "the body." **never** [*oude-pote*]—at any time (*v.* 11). **with those sacrifices** [*tais autais*]—'with *the same* sacrifices.' **year by year**—referring to the whole sentence, not merely to "which they (the priests) offered" [*prospher-ousin,* 'offer']. *The law year by year, by the repetition of the same sacrifices, testifies its inability to perfect the worshippers*—viz., on the YEARLY *day of atonement.* The "*daily*" sacrifices are referred to, *v.* 11. **continually** [*eis to dienekes*]—'continuously.' Implying they offer a toilsome and ineffectual '*continuous*' *round* of the 'same' atonement sacrifices "year by year." **comers there-unto**—the worshippers (the whole people) *coming to God* in the person of their representative, the high priest. **perfect**—fully meet man's needs as to justification and sanctification (note, ch. ix. 9). **2. For**—if the law could have perfected the worshippers. **they**—the sacrifices. **once purged** —IF *once for all cleansed* (ch. vii. 27). **conscience** —*consciousness* of sins (ch. ix. 9). **3. But**—So far from *those sacrifices* purging from consciousness of

4 For ^b*it is* not possible that the blood of bulls and of goats should take
5 away sins. Wherefore, when he cometh into the world, he saith, ^cSacrifice
6 and offering thou wouldest not, but a body ² hast thou prepared me: in
7 burnt offerings and *sacrifices* for sin thou hast had no pleasure. Then
said I, Lo, I come (in the volume of the book it is written of me.) to do

A D 61.
b Mic. 6. 6.
c Ps. 40. 6.
2 Or, thou hast fitted me.

sins (*v.* 2). **in, &c.**—in the fact of their being offered, and during the offering. Contrast *v.* 17. **a remembrance**—*a recalling to mind* by the high priest's confession, on the day of atonement, of the sins of each past year and of all former years, proving that the sacrifices of former years were not felt by men's consciences to have fully atoned for sins; in fact, the expiation and remission were only legal and typical (*v.* 4, 11). There was no true atonement till Christ died: the repeated sacrifices kept vividly before believers the promised Redeemer, through whom alone their consciences had peace. The Gospel remission is so complete, that sins are 'remembered no more' (*v.* 17) by God. It is unbelief to "forget" this once for all purgation, and to fear because of 'former sins' (2 Pet. i. 9). The believer, once for all *bathed* [*leloumenos*], needs only to "wash" [*nipsasthai*] his hands and "feet" of soils, daily contracted, in Christ's blood (John xiii. 10).

4. For—Reason why, necessarily, there is a continually-recurring 'remembrance of sins' in legal sacrifices (*v.* 3). *Typically,* "the blood of bulls," &c., had power; but it was only in virtue of the one antitypical sacrifice of Christ: they had no power *in themselves;* they were not the instrument of vicarious atonement, but an exhibition of the need of it, suggesting to believing Israelites the sure hope of coming redemption, according to God's promise. **take away** [*aphairein*]—'take *off.*' [*Perielein, v.* 11, is stronger: 'take away *utterly.*'] The blood of *brutes* could not take away the sin of *man.* A MAN must do that (notes, ch. ix. 12-14). **5.** Christ's voluntary self-offering, in contrast to those inefficient sacrifices, fulfils perfectly "the will of God" as to redemption, by completely atoning 'for (our) sins.' **Wherefore**—seeing that a nobler than animal sacrifices was needed. **when he cometh**—'coming.' The time referred to is *before* (or *just at*) His entrance into the world, when the inefficiency of animal sacrifices for expiation had been proved (*Tholuck*). [*Ethelēsas-katērtiso* are past: 'sacrifice, &c., thou *didst* not wish, but a body thou *didst* prepare for me;' but *hēko,* present perfect, 'Lo, *I am come:*' to harmonize these times. refer 'am come' to *His actual arrival in the world,* or *incarnation,* the *past* tenses to God's *purpose* from eternity, regarded as if already fulfilled.] 'A body thou didst prepare in thy eternal counsel.' This is more likely than explaining, with *Alford,* 'coming into the world,' as *entering on His public ministry.* David, in Ps. xl. (here quoted), reviews his past troubles and God's having delivered him, and his consequent desire to render willing obedience to God as more acceptable than sacrifices; but the Spirit puts into his mouth language finding its *full* realization only in the Divine Son of David. 'The more any son of man approaches the incarnate Son of God in office, or spiritual experience, the more may his holy breathings in the power of Christ's Spirit be taken as utterances of Christ Himself. Of all men, the prophet-king of Israel foreshadowed Him the most' (*Alford*). **a body hast thou prepared me**—'thou didst *fit* for me a body.' 'In thy counsels *thou didst determine to make for me a body,* to be a sacrificial victim' (*Wahl*). In the Hebrew, Ps. xl. 6, it is "mine ears hast thou opened," or 'dug.'
560

Perhaps this alludes to *boring the ear of a slave who volunteers to remain under his master when he might be free.* Christ's assuming a *body,* in order to die the death of a slave (ch. ii. 14), was a voluntary submission to God's service, like that of a slave suffering his ear to be bored by his master. His *willing obedience to the Father's will* is what gave especial virtue to His sacrifice for man (*vv.* 7, 9, 10). The *fitting of a body* for Him is not with a view to His incarnation merely, but to His expiatory *sacrifice* (*v.* 10), as the *contrast to* "sacrifice and offering" requires: cf. also Rom. vii. 4; Eph. ii. 16; Col. i. 22. More probably 'opened mine ears,' means *opened mine inward ear,* to be obedient to what God wills me to do—viz., to assume the body He has prepared for my sacrifice. So Job, margin, xxxiii. 16; xxxvi. 10 (doubtless the boring of a slave's *ear* symbolized *such willing obedience*); Isa. l. 5, "The Lord God hath opened mine ear" —*i. e.,* made me *obediently* attentive as a slave to his master. Others, 'Mine ears hast thou digged,' or '*fashioned;*' not with allusion to Exod. xxi. 6, but to the true office of the ear—a willing, submissive *attention to God's voice.* The forming of the ear implies the preparation of the body; this secondary idea, really in the Hebrew, though less prominent, is the one which Paul uses for his argument. As He obediently assumed the body prepared by the Father, in which to make His self-sacrifice, so ought we *present our bodies a living sacrifice* (Rom. xii. 1). **6. burnt offerings** [*holokautomata*]—'*whole* burnt offerings.' **thou hast had no pleasure**—God had pleasure in [*eudokesas,* 'was *well pleased* with'] them, in so far as they were in obedience to His positive Old Testament command, but *not as having intrinsic efficacy to atone for sin,* such as Christ's sacrifice had. Contrast Matt. iii. 17. **7. I come** [*hēko*]—'I am come' (note v. 5). 'Here we have the creed of Jesus: "*I am come* to fulfil the law, Matt. v. 17; to preach, Mark i. 38; to call sinners to repentance, Luke v. 32; to send a sword, and to set men at variance, Matt. x. 34, 35; to do the will of Him that sent me, John vi. 38, 39 (Ps. xl. 7, 8); I am sent to the lost sheep of the house of Israel, Matt. xv. 24; for judgment, John ix. 39; that they might have life, and might have it more abundantly, John x. 10; to seek and to save that which was lost, Matt. xviii. 11; Luke xix. 10: cf. 1 Tim. i. 15; to save men's lives, Luke ix. 56; to send fire on the earth, Luke xii. 49; to minister, Matt. xx. 28; as 'the Light,' John xii. 46; to bear witness unto the truth, John xviii. 37." See, reader, that thy Saviour obtain His aim in thy case. Do thou for thy part say, why thou art come here? Dost thou, also, do the will of God? From what time? in what way?' (*Bengel*). When the two goats on the day of atonement were presented before the Lord, that goat was to be offered as a sin offering on which the lot of the Lord should fall; that lot was lifted up on high in the high priest's hand, and then laid upon the head of the goat which was to die; so the *hand* of God *determined* all that was done to Christ (Acts iv. 28). Besides the covenant of God with man through Christ's blood, there was another made by the Father with the Son from eternity. The condition was, "If He shall make His soul an offering for sin, He shall see His seed," &c. (Isa. liii. 10.) The Son accepted it, "Lo, I

8 thy will, O God. Above when he said. Sacrifice and offering and burnt offerings and *offering* for sin thou wouldest not, neither hadst pleasure
9 *therein;* which are offered by the law; then said he, Lo, I come to do thy will, O God. He taketh away the first, that he may establish the
10 second. By ^d the which will we are sanctified through the offering of the body of Jesus Christ once *for all.*
11 And every priest standeth ^e daily ministering and offering oftentimes
12 the same sacrifices, which can never take away sins: but ^f this man, after he had offered one sacrifice for sins for ever, sat down on the right hand
13 of God; from henceforth expecting ^g till his enemies be made his foot-

A. D. 64.

^d Zech. 13. 1.
John 17.19.
John 19. 34.
ch. 13. 12.
^e Num. 23. 3.
ch 7. 27.
^f Col. 3. 1.
ch. 1. 3.
^g Ps. 110. 1.
Acts 2. 35.
1 Cor. 15.25.
ch. 1. 13.

come to do thy will, O God" (*Bishop Pearson*). Oblation, intercession, and benediction, are His three priestly offices. **in the volume, &c.**—*lit.*, the roll: the parchment MS. wrapped round a cylinder headed with knobs. Here, the Scripture meant is the 40th Psalm. 'By this very passage "written of me," I undertake to do thy will (to die for the sins of the world, that all who believe may be saved, *v.* 6, by my death).' This is Messiah's written contract (cf. Neh. ix. 38) to be our surety. So complete is the inspiration of all that is written, so great the authority of the Psalms, that David's words are Christ's words. **8. he**—Christ. **sacrifice, &c.** אA C Δ *f*, Vulgate, read '*sacrifices* and *offerings*' (plural). This verse combines the two clauses quoted distinctly, *vv.* 5, 6, in contrast to Christ's sacrifice with which God was well pleased. **9. Then said he**—'*At that very time* (viz., when speaking by David's mouth in the 40th Psalm) He hath said.' The rejection of the legal sacrifices involves Jesus' voluntary offer to make the self sacrifice with which God is well pleased (for, indeed, it was God's own "will" that He *came to do* in offering it: so that *this* sacrifice could not but be well pleasing to God). **taketh away** [*anairei*]—'sets aside the first;' viz., the legal system of "sacrifices," which God wills not. **the second**—'the will of God' (*vv.* 7, 9) that Christ should redeem us by His self-sacrifice. **10. By**—IN. So "in" and "through" occur in the same sentence, 1 Pet. i. 22; also 1 Pet. i. 5, Greek. The 'IN (fulfilment of) which will' (cf. the use of IN, Eph. i. 6) expresses the *originating* cause; "THROUGH the offering . . . of Christ," the *instrumental* or *mediatory* cause. Redemption flows from 'the will' of God the Father, as the First cause, who decreed redemption from before the foundation of the world. The "will" [*thelema*] is His *absolute sovereign will.* His 'good will' [*eudokia*] is a particular aspect of it. **are sanctified**—once for all, as our *permanent state* [*hegiasmenoi*]. It is the finished work of Christ in having sanctified us (*i. e.*, translated us from unholy alienation into a state of *consecration* to God, having "no more conscience of sins," *v.* 2) once for all, not gradual sanctification, which is referred to. **the body**—prepared for Him by the Father (*v.* 5). As the atonement, or reconciliation, is by the blood of Christ (Lev. xvii. 11), so our *sanctification* (consecration to God, holiness, and eternal bliss) is by the *body* of Christ (Col. i. 22). 'Common Prayer Communion Service,' 'that our sinful bodies may be *made clean by His body*, and our souls washed through His most precious blood.' **once for all** (*vv.* 12, 14; ch. vii. 27; ix. 12, 26, 28).
11. And. A new contrast: the frequent repetition of the sacrifices. **priest.** So א Δ *f*, Vulgate. But A C, 'high priest.' Though he did not in person stand "daily" offering sacrifices, he did so by the subordinate priests of whom, as of all Israel, he was the representative. So "daily" of

the high priests, ch. vii. 27. **standeth**—the attitude of one ministering: in contrast to (Christ) "*sat down* on the right hand of God" (*v.* 12): the posture of one ministered to as a king. **which** [*haitines*]—'the which;' *i. e.*, of such a kind as. **take away**—utterly [*perielein: strip off all round*]. Legal sacrifices could scarcely, *in part*, produce the sense of forgiveness (note, *v.* 4); but could never *entirely* strip off guilt. **12. this man**—emphatic (ch. ni. 3). **for ever**—join with "offered one sacrifice;" viz., the efficacy of which endures for ever [*eis to dienekes: continuously*] (cf. *v.* 14). The mass, which professes to be the frequent repetition of one and the same sacrifice of Christ's body, is hence disproved. For not only is Christ's body one, but also *His offering is one*, and *past* [*prosenenkas: aorist*, not action continued down to the present, as the perfect], and *inseparable from His suffering* (ch. ix. 26). The mass is as opposed to St. Paul's view of Christ's ONE finished sacrifice, as the Jewish sacrifices would be now. A repetition would imply that the once for-all offering was *imperfect*, and so would be dishonouring to it (*vv.* 2, 18). *V.* 14, on the contrary, says, "He hath PERFECTED FOR EVER them that are sanctified." If Christ offered Himself at the last supper, then He offered Himself again on the cross, and there would be *two* offerings; but Paul says there was only *one, once for all* (note, ch. ix. 26). Usage in this epistle puts [*eis to dienekes*] "for ever" *after*, not *before*, that which it qualifies (*vv.* 1, 14; ch. vii. 3). Also, "one sacrifice . . . for ever," stands in contrast to "oftentimes the same sacrifices" (*v.* 11). Also, 1 Cor. xv. 23-25, 28, agrees with *vv.* 12, 13; not joining, as *Alford*, "for ever" with "sat down;" for Jesus is to *give up* the Mediatorial throne 'when all things shall be subdued unto Him,' and not to sit on it *for ever*. Lev. xvi. 17 (cf. ch. iv. 13-31) shows that on the day of atonement none but the high priest could offer a sin offering for the people, until he came out of the Holiest, having finished his? Christ, our High Priest, having gone within the heavenly veil, and not yet come out, precludes any other from priestly ministry during our whole dispensation, which is our day of atonement and year of jubilee (Lev. xxv. 9). His ascension into heaven is necessary to His priesthood: 'if on earth, He would not be a priest;' much less are His disciples (Heb. viii. 4). **13. expecting** [*ekdechomenos*]—the Son '*awaiting*' the fulfilment of the Divine promise (Ps. cx. 1) till the Father shall 'send Him forth to triumph over all His foes.' He is now *sitting* at rest (*v.* 12), invisibly reigning, having His foes *virtually*, by right of His death, subject. This is a necessary preliminary to His coming forth to His visibly manifested kingdom and conquest over his foes. He is, by His Spirit and His providence, now subjecting them in part, The subjection *fully* shall be at His second advent, and from that time to the general judgment (Rev. xix., xx.); then comes the subjection of Himself, *as*

14 stool. For by one offering he hath perfected for ever them that are sanctified.

15 Whereof [h] the Holy Ghost also is a witness to us: for after that he had

16 said before, This [i] *is* the covenant that I will make with them after those days, saith the Lord, I will put my laws into their hearts, and in

17 their minds will I write them; [3] and their sins and iniquities will I

18 remember no more. Now where remission of these *is, there is* no more offering for sin.

19 Having therefore, brethren, [4] boldness to enter into the holiest by the

20 blood of Jesus, by [j] a new and living way, which he hath [5] consecrated

21 for us, through the veil, that is to say, his flesh; and *having* an High

A. D. 64.

h 2 Pet. 1. 21.
f Jer. 31. 33.
3 Some copies have. Then he said. And their.
4 Or. liberty.
j John 10. 9. John 14. 6. ch 9. 8.
5 Or. new made.

Head of the Church, to the Father (the *Mediatorial* economy ceasing when its end shall have been accomplished), that God may be all in all. Eastern conquerors used to tread on the necks of the vanquished, as Joshua did to the five kings. So Christ's absolute conquest is symbolized. his enemies — Satan and Death, whose strength consists in 'sin:' this being taken away (*v.* 12), their power is taken away; their destruction necessarily follows. be made his footstool—*lit.*, 'be put footstool of His feet.' 14. For. The sacrifice being "for ever" in its efficacy (*v.* 12) needs no renewal. "For," &c. them that are sanctified [*hagiazomenous*]—'them that *are being* sanctified.' The sanctification (consecration to God) of the elect (1 Pet. i. 2) is perfect in Christ once for all (note, *v.* 10). (Contrast the law, ch. vii. 19; ix. 9; x. 1.) The development of that sanctification is progressive.

15. [Δέ] 'Moreover.' is a witness—of the truth I am setting forth. The Father's witness, ch. v. 5, 6; the Son's, ch. x. 5; now that of the Holy Spirit, called accordingly "the Spirit of grace," *v.* 29. The testimony of all Three confirms *v.* 18. for after that he had said, &c. The conclusion to the sentence is *v.* 17, '*After* He had said before, This is the covenant that I will make with them (*with the house of Israel*, ch. viii. 10, also with the spiritual Israel), &c., saith the Lord, I will put [*didous, giving :* referring to the *giving* of the law; not now as then, *into the hands*, but *giving*] my laws into their hearts (*mind*, ch. viii. 10), and in their minds (*hearts*, ch. viii. 10) I will *inscribe* [*epigrapso*] them (here he omits the addition in ch. viii. 10, 11, *I will be to them a God*, &c., *and they shall not teach every man his neighbour*, &c.), and (i. e., *after having said the foregoing*, HE ADDS) their sins, &c., will I remember no more.' The object of the quotation is to prove that, there being *in the Gospel covenant* "REMISSION of sins" (*v.* 17), *there is no more need of a sacrifice for sins*. The object of the same quotation in ch. viii. 8-13 is to show that, there being a "NEW covenant," *the old is antiquated*. 18. where remission of these is—as there is under the Gospel covenant (*v.* 17). 'Here ends the finale (ch. x. 1-18) of the tripartite arrangement (ch. vii. 1-25; vii. 26— ix. 12; ix. 13—x. 18) of the middle portion of the epistle. Its great theme was Christ, a High Priest for ever after the order of Melchisedec. What it is to be this is set forth, ch. vii. 1-25, as contrasted with the Aaronic order. That Christ, however, as High Priest, is Aaron's antitype in the true holy place, by virtue of His self-sacrifice on earth, and Mediator of a better covenant, whose essence the old only typified, we learn, ch. vii. 26—ix. 12. And that Christ's self-sacrifice, offered through the eternal Spirit, is of everlasting power, as contrasted with the unavailing cycle of legal offerings, is established in the third part, ch. ix. 13—x. 18; the first half of this last portion, ch. ix. 13-28,

showing that both our present possession of salvation and our future completion of it are as certain as that He is with God, ruling as a Priest and reigning as a King, once more to appear, no more as bearer of our sins, but in glory as Judge. The second half, ch. x. 1-18, reiterating the main position, the High Priesthood of Christ, grounded on His offering of Himself, its kingly character, its eternal accomplishment of its end, confirmed by Ps. xl. and cx., and Jer. xxxi.' (*Delitzsch* in *Alford*).

19. Here begins the third and last division of the epistle: *our duty now whilst waiting for the Lord's second advent*. Resumption and expansion of the exhortation (ch. iv. 14-16: cf. *vv.* 22, 23 here) wherewith he closed the first part of the epistle, and prepared the way for his doctrinal argument, beginning ch. vii. 1. boldness [*parrhesian*]—of speech, 'free confidence,' grounded on the consciousness that our sins are forgiven. to enter [*eis ten eisodon*]—'*unto* the entering.' by [*en*]—'in :' it is *in* the blood of Jesus that our boldness is grounded. Cf. Eph. iii. 12. It is *His* having once for all entered as our Forerunner (ch. vi. 20) and High Priest (*v.* 21), making atonement for us with His blood continually there (ch. xii. 24) before God, that gives *us* confident access. No priestly caste now mediates between the sinner and his Judge. We may come with loving confidence, not slavish fear, directly through Christ, the only mediating Priest. The minister is not officially nearer God than the layman; nor can the latter serve God at a distance, or by deputy, as the natural man likes. Each must come for himself; all are accepted when they come by the new and living way opened by Christ. Thus all Christians are, as to access directly to God, virtually high priests (Rev. i. 6). They draw nigh in and through Christ, the only proper High Priest (ch. vii. 25). 20. which. The antecedent is 'the entering;' not, as the English version, "way." Translate, 'which (entering) He has consecrated (not as though already existing, but *has* INAUGURATED *as a new thing* [*enekainisen*]: note, ch. ix. 18) for us (as) a new [*prosphaton, recent:* recently opened, Rom. xvi. 25, 26] and living way' (not the lifeless way through the law offering of blood of *dead* victims, but *vital*, and of perpetual efficacy, because the *living* and *life-giving* Saviour is that *way*. It is a *living hope*, producing not *dead*, but *living* works). Christ, the first-fruits of our nature, has ascended: the rest is sanctified thereby. 'Christ's ascension is our promotion; whither the glory of the Head hath preceded, thither the hope of the body is called' (*Leo*). the veil. As the *veil* had to be passed *through* to enter the holiest, so the human suffering *flesh* (ch. v. 7) of Christ's humanity (which veiled His Godhead) had to be passed through by Him in entering the heavenly Holiest for us; in putting off His *rent flesh*, the temple veil, its type, was simultaneously rent from top

562

22 Priest *k* over the house of God; let us draw near with a true heart, *l* in
full assurance of faith, having our hearts sprinkled from an evil con-
23 science, and our *m* bodies washed with pure water. Let us hold fast the
profession of *our* faith without wavering; for *n* he *is* faithful that pro-
24 mised; and let us consider one another to provoke unto love and to
25 good works: not *o* forsaking the assembling of ourselves together, as the
manner of some *is;* but exhorting *one another:* and *p* so much the more
as ye see *q* the day approaching.
26 For *r* if we sin wilfully *s* after that we have received the knowledge of

A. D. 64.

k 1 Tim. 3.15.
l Jas. 1. 6.
m Eze. 36. 25.
2 Cor. 7. 1.
n 1 Cor. 1. 9.
o Acts 2. 42.
p Rom. 13.11.
q 2 Pet. 3. 9.
r Num. 15.30.
s 2 Pet. 2. 20.

to bottom (Matt. xxvii. 51). Not His *body*, but His suffering *flesh*, was the veil: His body was the temple (John ii. 19). **21. high priest** [*hierea megan*]. A different term [*archiereus*] is used always in this epistle for "high priest." Translate, 'A *Great* Priest:' one at once King and "Priest upon His throne" (Zech. vi. 13): a royal Priest, and a priestly King. **house of God**—the spiritual house, the *Church*, made up of believers, whose home is *heaven*, where Jesus, their Head, now is (ch. xii. 22, 23). Thus *heaven* is included, as well as the *Church*, whose home it is. **22.** (Ch. iv. 16; vii. 19) **with a true heart**—without hypocrisy: 'in truth, and with a perfect heart;' thoroughly imbued with "the truth" (v. 26). **full assurance** (ch. vi. 11)—with no doubt as to our acceptance when coming to God by the blood of Christ. As "*faith*" occurs here, so '*hope*' and "*love*," vv. 23, 24. **sprinkled from**—i. e., *so as to be cleansed from*. **evil conscience**—a consciousness of guilt unatoned for, and uncleansed away (v. 2; ch. ix. 9). Legal purifications, with blood of animal victims and with water, could only cleanse the *flesh* (ch. ix. 13, 21). Christ's blood purifies our *hearts* and consciences as well as our 'body.' The Aaronic priest, in entering the holy place, washed with *water* (ch. ix. 19) in the brazen laver. Believers, as priests to God, are once for all washed in BODY at baptism. As we have an immaterial and a material nature, the cleansing of both is expressed by "hearts" and 'body'—the inner and the outer—so the whole man. The baptism of body, however, is not mere putting away of material filth, nor an act operating by intrinsic efficacy, but the sacramental seal, applied to the outer man, of a spiritual washing (1 Pet. iii. 21). 'Body' (not merely "flesh," the *carnal* part, as 2 Cor. vii. 1) includes the *whole* material man, which needs cleansing, being redeemed, as well as the soul. The body, once polluted with sin, is washed, so as to be fitted, like and by Christ's holy body, to be spiritually a pure and living offering. On "pure water," the symbol of consecration and sanctification, cf. Ezek. xxxvi. 25; John xix. 34; 1 Cor. vi. 11; 1 John v. 6. The perfects, 'having . . . hearts *sprinkled* . . . body [*to sōma*] *washed*,' implying a *continuing state* by a once-for-all-accomplished act—viz., our justification by faith through Christ's blood, and consecration to God, sealed sacramentally by the baptism of our body. **23.** (Ch. iii. 6, 14; iv. 14.) **profession** [*homologian*]—'confession,' **our faith** [*tēs elpidos*]—'OUR HOPE;' which is indeed *faith* exercised as to the future inheritance. *Hope* rests on faith; at the same time quickens *faith*, and is the ground of bold *confession* (1 Pet. iii. 15). *Hope* is similarly (v. 22) connected with *purification* (1 John iii. 3). **without wavering**—without declension "stedfast unto the end." **he**—God is faithful to His promises (ch. vi. 17, 18; xi. 11; xii. 26, 28; 1 Cor. i. 9; x. 13; 1 Thess. v. 24; 2 Thess. iii. 3: also Christ's promise, John xii. 26), but man is often unfaithful to his duties. **24.** As elsewhere, *love* follows *faith* and *hope:* the Pauline tr_ad of

graces. **consider** [*katanoomen*]—with the mind attentively fixed on "one another" (note, ch. iii. 1), contemplating considerately the characters and wants of our brethren, so as to render mutual help. Cf. Ps. xli. 1; ch. xii. 15, "(*All*) looking diligently lest *any* . . . fail of.the grace of God." **to provoke** [*eis paroxusmon*]—'*with a view to* PROVOKING unto love,' instead of to hatred, as is too often the case. The only right 'provocation' (Eph. iv. 26): once St. Paul forgot his own rule [Acts xv. 39: *paroxusmos*, "contention"]. **25. assembling of ourselves together** [*episunagoge*]—is only found here and 2 Thess. ii. 1 (the gathering together of the elect to Christ at His coming, Matt. xxiv. 31). The assembling of ourselves for Christian communion is an earnest of our being gathered together to Him at His appearing. Union is strength: continual assemblings beget and foster *love*, and give opportunities for 'provoking to good works,' by "exhorting one another" (ch. iii. 13). *Ignatius*, 'When ye frequently and in numbers meet together, the powers of Satan are overthrown, and his mischief is neutralized by your likemindedness in the faith.' To neglect such assemblings might end in apostasy. [He avoids *sunagoge*, as suggesting the Jewish *synagogue* meetings (cf. Rev. ii. 9).] **as the manner of some is** [*ethos*]—*custom*. This gentle expression proves he is not as yet speaking of *apostasy*. **the day approaching.** This shortest designation of the Lord's coming occurs only in 1 Cor. iii. 13: confirming the Pauline authorship of this epistle. The Church being in all ages uncertain how soon Christ is coming, *the day* is, in each age, practically always near; whence believers are called on always to be watching for it as nigh at hand. The Hebrews were now living close upon one great type and foretaste of it—the destruction of Jerusalem (Matt. xxiv.), 'the bloody and fiery dawn of the great day, the day of days, the ending day of all days, the settling day of all days, the day of the promotion of time into eternity, the day which, for the Church, breaks off the night of the present world' (*Delitzsch* in *Alford*). **26.** Cf. ch. vi. 4, &c. There the warning was, that if there be not diligence in *progressing*, a falling off, and then an apostasy, will ensue: here it is, if there be lukewarmness in Christian *communion*, apostasy ensues. **if we sin** [*hekousiōs hamartanontōn:* present participle]—if we at that day be found *sinning; i. e.*, not isolated acts, but in a *state* of sin (*Alford*): sin against not only the *law*, but the whole Gospel economy (vv. 28, 29). **wilfully**—presumptuously; 'willingly.' After receiving '*full knowledge* [*epignosin:* cf. 1 Tim. ii. 4] of the truth,' by having been "enlightened," and having "tasted" a measure even of "the Holy Ghost" (the Spirit of truth, John xiv. 17; and "the Spirit of grace," v. 29), to *fall away* ("sin," ch. iii. 12, 17: cf. ch. vi. 6) to Judaism or infidelity is not an *ignorance* or error ("*out of the way*," ch. v. 2: the result) of infirmity, but a *deliberate sinning* against the Spirit: a consciousness of

27 the truth, there remaineth no more sacrifice for sins, but a certain fearful looking for of judgment and *t* fiery indignation, which shall devour the
28 adversaries. He that despised Moses' law died without mercy under two
29 or three witnesses: of how much sorer punishment, suppose ye, shall he be thought worthy, who hath trodden under foot the Son of God, and *u* hath counted the blood of the covenant, wherewith he was sanctified, an
30 unholy thing, *v* and hath done despite unto the Spirit of grace? For we know him that hath said, Vengeance *w* belongeth unto me, I will recompense, saith the Lord. And again, *x* The Lord shall judge his people.
31 It *y* is a fearful thing to fall into the hands of the living God.
32 But *z* call to remembrance the former days, in which, after ye were
33 illuminated, ye endured *a* a great fight of afflictions; partly, whilst ye were made a gazing-stock both by reproaches and afflictions; and partly,
34 whilst *b* ye became companions of them that were so used. For ye had compassion of me in my bonds, and *c* took joyfully the spoiling of your

A. D. 64.

t Eze. 36. 5.
u 1 Cor ii.29.
v Matt 12.31
w Deut 32.35.
Ps. 94. 1.
x Deut. 32.36.
Ps 50. 4.
Ps. 96. 13.
y Isa. 33. 14.
Luke 12. 5.
Luke 21.11.
z Gal. 3. 4.
2 John 8.
a Col. 2. 1.
b Phil. 1. 7.
Phil. 4. 14.
c Matt. 5. 12.
Acts 5. 41.

Gospel obligations not only was, but *is* present: a sinning presumptuously and perseveringly against Christ's redemption *for* us, and the Spirit of grace pleading *in* us. 'He only who stands high can fall low. A vivid apprehension of good is necessary in order to be thoroughly wicked; hence man can be more reprobate than beasts, and apostate angels than apostate man' (*Tholuck*). **remaineth no more sacrifice**—for there is but ONE sacrifice that can atone for sin: they, after having fully known it, deliberately reject it. 27. **a certain**—an indescribable. The indefiniteness, as of something *peculiar*, makes the description the more terrible [cf. *tina*, Jas. i. 18]. **looking for** [*ekdoche*]—'expectation.' *Alford* strangely translates 'reception.' the classic sense. Contrast Christ's "expecting" [the kindred verb, *ekdechomenos*] (v. 13) and Abraham's '*looking for* a city which hath foundations,' which refutes *Alford*. **fiery indignation**—*lit.*, 'zeal of fire.' Fire is personified: zeal of Him who is "a consuming fire" (Isa. lix. 17, 18). **devour**—present: continually. **28.** Cf. ch. ii. 2, 3; xii. 25. **despised** [*athetesas*]—utterly and heinously *set aside*, not merely in minor detail, but *the whole law*, as by idolatry (Deut. xvii. 2-7). So *apostasy* answers to such utter violation of the old covenant. **died** [*apothneskei*]—'dies:' the normal punishment then still in force. **without mercy** [*oiktirmōn*]—*mercies*: removed out of the pale of mitigation or respite. **under**—on the evidence of. **29. sorer** [*cheironos timōrias*]—'*worse vengeance*' than any temporal punishment. **suppose ye**—an appeal to the Hebrews' conscience. **thought worthy**—by God at the judgment. **trodden under foot the Son of God**—and so God Himself, who 'glorified His *Son* as an High Priest;' by 'wilful' apostasy (ch. v. 5; vi. 6). **wherewith he was sanctified**—for Christ died even for him (2 Pet. ii. 1). "Sanctified," in the full sense belongs only to the saved elect; but in some sense it belongs also to those who have gone far in Christian experience, yet fall away at last. **an unholy thing** [*koinon*]—'common:' opposed to "sanctified:" as if Christ were a common man, and so, in claiming to be God, guilty of blasphemy, and deserving to die! **done despite unto** [*enubrisas*]—'insulted,' repelling *in fact;* as 'blasphemy,' in *words* (Mark iii. 29). 'Of the Jews who became Christians and relapsed into Judaism, we find from the history of Uriel Acosta that a blasphemy was required against Christ. They applied to Him epithets used against Moloch, "the adulterous branch," &c. In their prayer Olenu they spit whilst they mention His name' (*Tholuck*). **the Spirit of** (that confers) **grace.** 'He who does not accept the benefit insults the Bestower. He hath

made thee a son: wilt thou become a slave? He has come to take up His abode with thee; but thou admittest evil into thyself' (*Chrysostom*). 'For him who profanes the Christ *without him*, and blasphemes the Christ *within him*, there is subjectively no renewal, and objectively no new *sacrifice for sins* (v. 26; ch. vi. 6)' (*Tholuck*). **30. him**—who utters no empty threats. **Vengeance belongeth unto me**—'To me belongeth vengeance:' exactly according with *Paul's* quotation, Rom. xii. 19. **Lord shall judge his people**—in grace, or else anger, as each deserves: here, "judge" so as to punish the reprobate; there (Deut. xxxii. 35, 36), "judge" so as to interpose in behalf of His people. **31. fearful thing to fall into the hands.** It is good, like David, *to fall into the hands of God* rather than man, with filial *faith* in one's father's love, though God *chastises* (2 Sam. xxiv. 14). 'It is fearful' to fall into His hands as a presumptuous sinner doomed to His just vengeance as judge (v. 27). **living God**—therefore able to punish for ever (Matt. x. 28).

32. As previously He warned them by the awful end of apostates, so here he stirs them up by the remembrance of their own faith, patience, and self-sacrificing love. So Rev. ii. 3, 4. **call to remembrance**—habitually: the present tense. **illuminated**—"enlightened:" come to "the (full) knowledge of the truth" (v. 26), in connection with baptism (note, ch. vi. 4). In spiritual baptism, Christ, "the Light," is put on. 'On the one hand, we are not to sever the sign and the grace, where the sacrament truly answers its design; on the other, the glass is not to be mistaken for the liquor, nor the sheath for the sword' (*Bengel*). **fight of**—i. e., *consisting of* afflictions. **33.** The persecutions referred to were probably endured by the Hebrew Christians at their first conversion, not only in Palestine, but also in Rome and elsewhere, the Jews inciting the populace and the Roman authorities against Christians. **gazing-stock**—as in a *theatre* [*theatrizomenoi*], often used as the place of punishment in the presence of assembled multitudes. Acts xix. 29; 1 Cor. iv. 9, 'Made a *theatrical* spectacle [*theatron*] to the world.' **ye became**—of your own accord: attesting your sympathy with suffering brethren. **companions of**—sharers in affliction with [*koinonoi*]. **34. ye had compassion of me in my bonds.** So א. But A Δ, Vulgate, omit "me," and read [*desmiois* for *desmois*], 'Ye both sympathized with *those in bonds* (answering to the last clause of v. 33: cf. ch. xiii. 3, 23; vi. 10), and accepted [*prosedexasthe*, as in ch. xi. 35] with joy (Jas. i. 2; as exercising faith and other graces, Rom. v. 3; and the pledge of coming glory, Matt. v. 12) the plundering of *your*

goods, knowing [6] in yourselves that ye have in heaven a better and an
35 enduring substance. Cast not away therefore your confidence, which
hath great recompence of reward.

36 For [d] ye have need of patience, that, after ye have done the will of
37 God, [e] ye might receive the promise. For yet a little while, and he
38 that shall come will come, and will not tarry. Now the just shall live
by faith: but if *any man* draw back, my soul shall have no pleasure in
39 him. But we are not of them who draw back unto perdition, but of
them that believe to the saving of the soul.

11 NOW faith is the [1] substance of things hoped for, the evidence of
2 things not seen. For by it the elders obtained a good report.

A. D. 64.

[6] Or. that ye
have in
your-
selves, or,
for your-
selves.
[d] Luke 21.19.
[e] Col. 3. 24.

CHAP. 11.
[1] Or,
ground, or,
confi-
dence.

(*own*) goods' [*tōn humōn*, answering to the first clause of *v.* 33]. in yourselves. א A, Vulgate, omit "in:" 'knowing that ye have *yourselves.*' Δ, 'for yourselves.' in heaven. So C. But א A Δ *f*, Vulgate, omit. better—a heavenly (ch. xi. 16). enduring—not liable to *spoiling.* substance —possession: peculiarly our own, unless we *cast away* our birthright. 35. Consequent exhortation to confidence and endurance, as Christ is soon coming. Cast not away. They now have "confidence," and it will not withdraw of itself, unless they 'cast it away' wilfully (cf. ch. iii. 14). which [*hetis*]—inasmuch as it. hath—present: it is as certain as if you had it in hand (*v.* 37). It *hath* in reversion. recompence of reward—of grace, not debt: of a kind which no mercenary self-seeker would seek: holiness will be its own reward; self-devotion for Christ will be its own rich recompence (note, ch. ii. 2; xi. 26).

36. patience [*hupomonēs*]—'enduring perseverance.' The kindred verb in the LXX., Hab. ii. 3, is translated '*wait for* it' (cf. Jas. v. 7). after ye have done the will of God—'that whereas ye have done the will of God' hitherto (*vv.* 32-35), ye may show also *persevering endurance*, and so "receive" the promised reward—eternal bliss commensurate with our work of faith and love (ch. vi. 10-12): not only *do*, but also *suffer* (1 Pet. iv. 19). God first uses the *active* talents of His servants; then polishes the other side of the stone, making the *passive* graces shine—*patience, meekness*, &c. It may be also [*hina poiēsantes komisesthe*] 'that ye may do the will of God, and receive,' &c. (*Alford.*) "Patience" is a further persevering doing of 'God's will,' otherwise it would be no real grace (Matt. vii. 21). We should look not merely for individual bliss at death, but for the general consummation of the bliss of all saints in body and soul. 37. Encouragement to enduring perseverance, by consideration of the shortness of the time till Christ shall come, and God's rejection of him that draws back, from Hab. ii. 3, 4. a little while (John xvi. 16). he that shall come—*lit.*, 'the Comer.' In Habakkuk it is *the vision* about to come. *Christ*, the grand subject of all prophetical vision, is made by Paul, under inspiration, the ultimate subject of the Spirit's prophecy by Habakkuk, in its exhaustive fulfilment. 38. just. א A, Vulgate, read 'MY just man.' God is the speaker—'He who is just in my sight.' *Bengel*, with Δ *f*, 'The just shall live by MY *faith.*' So the Hebrew, Hab. ii. 4, *lit.*, 'The just shall live by the faith *of Him*'—viz., *Christ*, the final subject of "the vision," who 'will not lie;' *i. e.*, disappoint. Here not merely the *beginning*, as in Gal. iii. 11, but the *continuance* of the spiritual *life* of the justified man is referred to, as opposed to apostasy. In Rom. i. 17 the *righteousness* or *justice of God* in the Gospel plan is what is dwelt on; so the emphasis falls on "just." In Gal. iii. 11 the emphasis is on "faith" as the means of *justification.* Here,

the emphasis is on "live." As the justified man receives first spiritual life by faith, so it is *by faith* that he *shall* continue to *live* (Luke iv. 4). Faith here is that fully-developed living trust in the unseen (ch. xi. 1) Saviour, which keeps men stedfast amidst persecutions and temptations (*vv.* 34-36). but—Greek, 'and.' if any man draw back. The Greek admits *Alford's*, 'if *he* (the just man) draw back.' This would not disprove the final perseverance of saints: for 'the just man' in this latter clause would mean one seemingly, and in part really, though not savingly, "just;" as in Ezek. xviii. 24, 26. In the Hebrew this latter half stands first. Therefore 'and' (not "but"), in Paul, merely joins his two quotations: the 'drawer back' answering to the 'lifted-up soul' must, if Paul follows Habakkuk (ch. ii. 4, note), be distinct from "the just;" for the former stands first, and refers to the Chaldean, or else the *unbelieving* Jews. "Behold, his soul which is lifted up is not upright in him." Habakkuk states the *cause* of drawing back: *a soul lifted up* by prosperity, like the Chaldean, in self-inflated unbelief setting itself up against God. Paul, by the Spirit, states the effect: it *draws back*. What in Habakkuk is, "his soul . . . is not upright in him," is in Paul, "my soul shall have no pleasure in him." Habakkuk states the *cause*, Paul the *effect:* He who is not right in his own soul does not stand right with God; God has no pleasure in him. *Bengel* translates Habakkuk, 'His soul is not upright in *respect to him*'—viz., Christ, the subject of "the vision;" i. e., *Christ has no pleasure in him* (cf. ch. xii. 25). Every flower in spring is not a fruit in autumn. 39. A Pauline elegant turning-off from denunciatory warnings to charitable hopes (2 Thess. ii. 13). saving of the soul [*peripoiēsin*] —'acquisition (or *obtaining*) of the soul.' The kindred verb is applied to Christ's *acquiring* the Church as the *purchase* of his blood (Acts xx. 28). If we *acquire* our soul's salvation, it is through Him who has obtained it for us by His blood-shedding. 'The unbeliever *loses his soul;* for not being God's, neither is he his own (cf. Matt. xvi. 26 with Luke ix. 25): faith saves the soul by linking it to God' (*Delitzsch* in *Alford*).

CHAP. XI. 1-40. — DEFINITION OF FAITH — EXAMPLES FROM THE OLD COVENANT FOR PERSEVERANCE IN FAITH.

1. faith—in its widest sense: not restricted to *faith* in the Gospel. Not a *definition* of faith in its whole nature, but a *description* of its characteristics in relation to Paul's exhortation to perseverance (ch. x. 39). substance, &c.—it *substantiates* God's promises, the fulfilment of which we hope for, making them present realities to us. [However, *hupostasis* is *translated* in ch. iii. 14, 'confidence.'] So *Alford*. *Thomas Magister*, like our version, 'The whole thing is virtually contained in the first principle; now the *first commencement* of the things hoped for is in us through the assent

3   Through faith we understand that the worlds ^a were framed by the word of God; so that things which are seen were not made of things which do appear.

4   By faith ^b Abel offered unto God a more excellent sacrifice than Cain,

A. D. 64.

a John 1. 3.
b Gen. 4. 4.
1 John 3.11,
12.

of faith, which virtually contains all the things hoped for' (cf. note, ch. vi. 5). Through faith, the future object of Christian hope, *in its beginning*, is already substantiated (*v.* 6). *Hugo de St. Victor* distinguished *faith* from *hope*. By *faith* we are sure of eternal things that they ARE; by *hope* we are confident that WE SHALL HAVE them. Hope presupposes faith (Rom. viii. 25). **evidence** [*elenchos*]—'demonstration:' convincing proof to the believer; the soul thereby seeing what the eye cannot see. **things not seen**—the whole invisible spiritual world. 'Eternal life is promised to us, but it is when we are dead; we are told of a blessed resurrection, but meanwhile we moulder in the dust; we are declared to be justified, and sin dwells in us; we hear that we are blessed, meantime we are overwhelmed in miseries; we are promised abundance of all goods, but we still endure hunger and thirst; God declares He will immediately come to our help, but He seems deaf to our cries. What should we do if we had not *faith* and *hope* to lean on, and if our mind did not emerge amidst the darkness above the world by the shining of the Word and Spirit of God?' (*Calvin*.) Faith is an assent unto truths credible upon the testimony of God (not on their intrinsic *reasonableness*), delivered unto us in the writings of the apostles and prophets. Christ's ascension is the cause; His absence the crown of our faith (*Bishop Pearson*). Faith believes what it sees not; for if thou seest, there is no faith, the Lord has gone away so as not to be seen: He is hidden, that He may be believed; the yearning desire by faith after Him who is unseen is the preparation of a heavenly mansion for us; when He shall be seen, it shall be given to us as the reward of faith (*Augustine*). As revelation deals with invisible things exclusively, faith is the faculty needed by us. By faith we venture our eternal interests on the bare Word of God: this is altogether reasonable. **2. For**—Faith is all this; for, &c. **by**—Greek, 'in this,' as their element. **the elders**—not merely [*hoi archaioi*] *the ancients*, as though solely of the past; nay, they belong to one and the same blessed family as ourselves (*vv.* 39, 40). "*The* elders" whom we all revere so highly for their faith and practice: a title of honour, as 'the fathers.' 'Paul shows how to seek in all its fulness, under the veil of history, the essential substance of the doctrine sometimes briefly indicated' (*Bengel*). **obtained a good report**—Greek, 'were testified of;' viz., favourably (cf. ch. vii. 8): a phrase of Luke, *Paul's* companion. Not only men, but God, gave testimony to their faith (*vv.* 4, 5, 39). Thus they, having first received the witness of God, then being testified of themselves, have become "witnesses" to all others (ch. xii. 1). The earlier elders had their patience exercised for a long life: those later, in sharper afflictions. Many things which they hoped for, and did not see, subsequently were conspicuously seen, the event confirming faith (*Bengel*). **3. we understand**—we perceive with our spiritual intelligence the world's creation by God, though we see neither Him nor the act as described, Gen. i. The natural world could not, without revelation, teach us this, though it confirms it when apprehended by faith (Rom. i. 20). Adam is passed over here as to faith, being the first who brought sin on us all; though it does not follow that he did not repent and believe the promise.

worlds—*lit.*, 'ages:' all that exists in time and space, visible and invisible, present and eternal. **framed** [*katērtisthai*]—'fitly formed;' including the creation of the single parts, their harmonious organization, and the continual providence which maintains the whole throughout all ages. As creation is the foundation and a specimen of the whole Divine economy, so faith in creation is the foundation and a specimen of all faith (*Bengel*). **by the word of God**—not the *personal* Word [*logos*, John i. 1] here, but *the spoken word* [*rhema*], though by the instrumentality of the personal Word (ch. i. 2). **not made, &c.**—Greek, 'so that not [*mē*, the subjective negative, *not* as one might think] out of things which appear hath that which is seen been made:' not as in all things reproduced from previously-existing and visible materials; for instance, the plant from the seed, the animal from the parent, &c., has the visible world sprung into being from apparent materials. *Bengel* explains by distinguishing "appear"—i. e., *begin to be seen* (viz., at creation) from *that which is seen* as already in existence; 'so that the things seen were not made of things which appear'— i. e., which *began to appear to us in the act of creation*. We were not spectators of creation: it is by faith we perceive it (Job xxxviii. 4).

4. more excellent sacrifice—because in *faith*. Now *faith* must have some *revelation of God* on which it fastens. The revelation was doubtless God's command to sacrifice *animals* ('the firstlings of the flock'), in token of the forfeiture of men's life by sin, and as a type of the promised bruiser of the serpent's head (Gen. iii. 15), Himself to be bruised as the one sacrifice: this command is implied in God's having made coats of skin for Adam and Eve (Gen. iii. 21); for these must have been taken from animals slain *in sacrifice*, as it was not for *food* they were slain, animal food not being permitted till after the flood: nor for *clothing*, as clothes might have been made of the fleeces without the needless cruelty of killing the animal; but a coat of skin put on Adam from a sacrificed animal typified the covering or atonement [*kaphar*] (*atone* means to *cover*) resulting from Christ's sacrifice. [*Pleiona* is well rendered by *Wickcliffe*, 'a *much more* sacrifice.'] A fuller sacrifice, which partook more largely of the true virtue of sacrifice (*Archbishop Magee*). It was not intrinsic merit in 'the firstling of the flock' above "the fruit of the ground." It was God's appointment that gave it all its excellency; if it had not been so, it would have been presumptuous *will-worship* (Col. ii. 23), and taking of a life which man had no right over before the flood (Gen. ix. 2-4). The sacrifice was probably a holocaust, and the sign of the Divine acceptance was its consumption by fire (Gen. xv. 17). Hence, 'to accept' a burnt offering is in Hebrew 'to turn it to ashes' (*margin*, Ps. xx. 3). A flame perhaps issued from the shechinah or cherubim, east of Eden ("the presence of the Lord," Gen. iv. 16), where the first sacrifices were offered. Cain, in unbelieving self-righteousness, presented merely a *thank-offering*, not like Abel, feeling his need of the propitiatory sacrifice appointed for sin. God "had respect (first) unto Abel and (then) to his offering" (Gen. iv. 4). Faith causes the person to be accepted, then his offering. Even an animal sacrifice, though of God's appointment, would not have been accepted had it not been in faith. God

by which he obtained witness that he was righteous, God testifying of his gifts: and by it he, being dead, [2] yet speaketh.

5   By faith [c] Enoch was translated that he should not see death; and was not found, because God had translated him: for before his translation he had this testimony, that he pleased God. But [d] without faith *it is* impossible to please *him:* for he that cometh to God must believe that he is, and *that* he is a rewarder of them that diligently seek him.

7   By faith [e] Noah, being warned of God of things not seen as yet, [3] moved with fear, prepared an ark to the saving of his house; by the which he condemned the world, and became heir of [f] the righteousness which is by faith.

8   By faith Abraham, when he was called to go out into a place which he should after receive for an inheritance, obeyed; and he went out, not

9 knowing whither he went. By faith he sojourned in the land of promise, as *in* a strange country, dwelling in [g] tabernacles with Isaac and Jacob,

10 the heirs with him of the same promise: for he looked for a city which

Right margin references:

A. D. 64.
[2] Or, is yet spoken of.
[c] Gen 5. 22, 24.
Matt. 23. 35.
Luke 3. 37.
Jude 14.
[d] Num 14.11.
Num. 20. 12.
Ps. 78. 22, 32.
Ps 106. 21.
John 3. 18, 36.
[e] Gen. 6. 13.
[3] Or, being wary.
[f] Rom. 3. 22.
Phil. 3. 9.
[g] Gen. 12. 8.

---

testifying—by fire. his gifts—the common term for *sacrifices*, implying they must be freely *given*. by it—by faith exhibited in his sacrifice. dead, yet speaketh—His *blood crying from the ground to God* shows how precious, because of his "faith," he was still in God's sight (Gen. iv. 10; Ps. cxvi. 15; Rev. vi. 10). So he becomes a witness to us of faith's blessed effects.

5. *Faith* was the ground of his *pleasing God;* his *pleasing God* was the ground of his *translation.* translated (Gen. v. 22, 24)—implying a *sudden* removal [*metetethē*] (Gal. i. 6) from mortality, without death, to immortality: such a CHANGE as shall pass over the living at Christ's coming (1 Cor. xv. 51, 52). had (has had) this testimony—viz., of Scripture. [*Memarturetai* (perfect: 'he has been testified of')] implies that this testimony continues still.] pleased God. So LXX. translate for "walked with God," Gen. v. 22, 24. 6. without [*chōris*]—'*apart from* faith:' if one be destitute of faith (cf. Rom. xiv. 23). to please. Translate, as *Alford* [*euarestesai*, the aorist], 'It is impossible to please God *at all*' (Rom. viii. 8). 'Works done before the grace of Christ are not pleasant to God, forasmuch as they spring not of faith in Jesus Christ; yea, rather, for that they are not done as God hath willed them to be done, we doubt not but they have the nature of sin' (Article XIII., 'Book of Common Prayer'). Works not rooted in God are splendid sins (*Augustine*). he that cometh to God—as a worshipper (ch. vii. 19). must believe—*once for all* [*pisteusai*, Greek aorist]. that he is—IS: the self-existing Jehovah (contrasted with all so-called gods, Gal. iv. 8), the source of all being, though he sees Him not (*v.* 1), being "invisible" (*v.* 27). So Enoch: this implies that he had not been favoured with *visible* appearances of God; yet he *believed* in God's *being* and *moral government*, as the Rewarder of His diligent worshippers, in opposition to antediluvian scepticism. Also Moses was not so favoured before he left Egypt the first time (*v.* 27); still he believed. and . . . is—a different Greek verb from "is" [*ginetai: proves to be*]. rewarder—awarder of reward. So God proved to be to Enoch. The reward is *God Himself* diligently 'sought' and "walked with" in partial communion here, fully enjoyed hereafter. Cf. Gen. xv. 1. of them—and them only. diligently seek [*ekzetousin*]—'seek out' God. Cf. "seek *early*" (Prov. viii. 17). Not only "ask" and "seek," but "knock," Matt. vii. 7: cf. xi. 12; Luke xiii. 24, "strive" [*agonizesthe*], as in an agony of contest.

7. warned of God [*chrematistheis*] (ch. viii. 5)—

'admonished of God.' moved with fear—not slavish fear, but, as in ch. v. 7 [*eulabetheis*], *reverential fear:* opposed to the world's sneering disbelief of the revelation, and self-deceiving security. Join "by faith" with "prepared an ark" (1 Pet. iii. 20). by the which—faith. condemned the world—for since he believed and was saved, so might they: their condemnation by God is by his case shown to be just. righteousness which is by [*kata:* according to] faith. A Pauline thought. Noah is first called "righteous" in Gen. vi. 9. Christ calls Abel so, Matt. xxiii. 35. Cf. Ezek. xiv. 14, 20; 2 Pet. ii. 5, "a preacher of righteousness." Paul makes *faith* the principle and ground of his righteousness. heir—the privilege of sonship, which flows from faith (Rom. viii. 17; Gal. iii. 29; iv. 7).

8. From the antediluvian saints he passes to the patriarchs of Israel, to whom "the promises" belonged. called—by God (Gen. xii. 1). So א. But A Δ, Vulgate [*ὁ*], read, 'He that is called Abraham,' his name being changed from Abram to Abraham, when God made with him and his seed a covenant, sealed by circumcision, many years after his call out of Ur. 'Abraham (*father of nations*, Gen. xvii. 5; his becoming which was the object of God's bringing him out of Ur) obeyed (*the command of God:* to be understood), *so as to go out,* &c. which he should after receive. He had not fully received even this promise when he went out, for it was not *explicitly* given till he had reached Canaan (Gen. xii. 1, 6, 7). When the promise was given him the Canaanite was still in the land, and himself a stranger. It is in the new heaven and new earth that he shall receive his personal inheritance; so believers sojourn on earth as strangers, whilst the ungodly and Satan lord it here; but at Christ's coming that same earth, the scene of the believer's conflict, shall be the inheritance of Christ and His saints. 9. sojourned—as a 'stranger and pilgrim.' in [*eis gēn*]—he went *into* it, and sojourned there. as in a strange country—*not belonging to him,* but to others [*allotrian*] (Acts vii. 5, 6). dwelling in tabernacles—*tents:* as *sojourners* do: moving from place to place, having no fixed possession. In contrast to the abiding "city" (*v.* 10). with. Their dwelling being the same, proves their faith was the same. They all alike were content to wait for their good things hereafter (Luke xvi. 25). Jacob was fifteen years old at Abraham's death. heirs with him of the same promise—Isaac did not inherit it from Abraham, nor Jacob from Isaac, but they all from God directly, as "fellow-

11 hath foundations, *h* whose builder and maker *is* God. Through faith also
i Sara herself received strength to conceive seed, and *j* was delivered of a
child when she was past age, because she judged him faithful who had
12 promised. Therefore sprang there even of one, and *k* him as good as
dead, *so many* as the stars of the sky in multitude, and, as the sand
which is by the sea-shore, innumerable.

13   These all died *4* in faith, not having received the promises, *l* but having
seen them afar off, and were persuaded of *them*, and embraced *them*,
14 and *m* confessed that they were strangers and pilgrims on the earth. For
they that say such things *n* declare plainly that they seek a country.
15 And truly, if they had been mindful of that *country* from whence
they came out, they might have had opportunity to have returned :
16 but now they desire a better *country*, that is, an heavenly : wherefore
God is not ashamed *o* to be called their God ; for *p* he hath prepared for
them a city.

A. D. 64.

h Isa. 14. 32.
2 Cor. 5. 1.
Rev. 21. 2.
i Gen. 17. 19.
j Luke 1. 38.
k Rom 4. 19.
4 according
to faith.
l Gen. 49. 10.
John 8. 56.
1 Pet. 1. 10-
12.
m Gen. 47. 9.
n Rom 8. 23-
25.
ch. 13. 14.
o Ex. 3. 6, 15.
p Phil. 3. 20.

heirs." In ch. vi. 12, 15, 17, "the promise"
means *the thing promised*, as in part *already
attained ;* but here "the promise" is of something
future. See, however, note, ch. vi. 12. **10. looked
for** [*exedecheto*]—'he was expecting;' waiting for
with eager expectation (Rom. viii. 19). a—Greek,
'*the* city,' &c. Cf. Ps. cxxii. Worldly Enoch,
son of the murderer Cain, was the first to build
his *city* here : the godly patriarchs waited for their
city hereafter (*v.* 16 ; ch. xii. 22 ; xiii. 14). **foundations**—Greek, '*the* foundations' which the *tents*
had not, nor even men's present cities have. **whose
builder and maker** [*technites, demiourgos*: 'artificer and architect'] (Eph. i. 4, 11). The city is
worthy of its *Framer* and *Builder* (cf. *v.* 16 ; ch.
viii. 2). Cf. 'found,' note, ch. ix. 12. **11. also
Sara herself**—though the weaker vessel, and at
first doubting, **was delivered of a child.** So C.
[But A Δ א *f*, Vulgate, omit *eteken :* then translate,
'and that when she was past age' (Rom. iv. 19).]
she judged him faithful who had promised—she
ceased to doubt, being instructed by the angel
that it was no jest, but serious earnest. **12. as
good as dead** [*nenekromenou*]—'deadened :' no
longer having, as in youth, energetic powers.
stars . . . sand (Gen. xxii. 17).
13. Characteristic excellences of the patriarch's
faith. **These all**—beginning with "Abraham"
(*v.* 8) : to whom *the promises were made* (Gal. iii.
16 : cf. the end of *v.* 13 and in *v.* 15) (*Alford*). But
the "ALL" must include Abel, Enoch, and Noah.
Now as these did not receive the promise of entering Canaan, *some other promise made in the first
ages*, and repeated, must be meant—viz., the promise of a Redeemer to Adam (Gen. iii. 15). Thus
the promises cannot have been merely temporal ;
for Abel and Enoch received no temporal promise
(*Archbishop Magee*). This promise of eternal redemption is the essence of the promises to Abraham. **died in faith**—as *believers*, waiting for, not
seeing as yet, their promised good things. They
were true to *faith* even unto, and especially in,
their dying hour (cf. *v.* 20). **not having received**
—this constituted their "faith." If they had
"received" THE THING PROMISED ("the promises," plural : the promise *often renewed*), it
would have been *sight*, not *faith*. **seen them afar
off** (John viii. 56). Christ, as the Word, was
preached to the Old Testament believers, and so
became the seed of life to their souls, as He is to
ours. **and were persuaded of them.** א A Δ *f*,
Vulgate, omit. **embraced them**—as though not
"afar off," but within reach, so as to clasp them
in their embrace. *Trench* denies that the Old
Testament believers *embraced* them, for they only
saw them *afar off*: he translates 'saluted (greeted)

them,' as the homeward bound mariner, recognizing from afar the well-known promontories of his
native land. Jacob's, "I have waited for thy
salvation, O Lord," Gen. xlix. 18, is such a
greeting of salvation from afar (*Delitzsch*). **confessed that they were strangers**—so Abraham
to the children of Heth, Gen. xxiii. 4 ; and Jacob
to Pharaoh, Gen. xlvii. 9; Ps. cxix. 19. Believers
sit loose to earthly things. *Citizens of the world*
do not confess themselves "strangers on the earth."
pilgrims [*parepidemoi*]—'temporary (lit., *by the
way*) sojourners.' **on the earth**—contrasted with
"an heavenly" country (*v.* 16 ; ch. x. 34 ; Ps. cxix.
54 ; Phil. iii. 20). 'Whosoever professes he has a
Father in heaven, confesses himself a stranger on
earth ; hence there is in the heart an ardent
longing, like that of a child among strangers, in
want and grief, far from his fatherland' (*Luther*).
'Like ships in seas, while *in, above* the world.'
14. For—Proof that "faith" (*v.* 13) actuated them.
declare plainly [*emphanizousin*]—make it evident. **seek** [*epizetousin*]—'seek *after :*' implying
towards what their desires ever tend. **a country**
[*patrida*]—'a fatherland.' In confessing themselves *strangers* here, they evidently regard not
this as their fatherland, but seek after a better.
15. As Abraham, had he desired to leave his
pilgrim life in Canaan, and resume his former
fixed habitation in Ur, among the worldly, had
ample opportunities to have done so, so spiritually, all believers who came out from the world
to become God's people might, if so minded,
have easily gone back. **16.** Proving that the old
fathers did not 'look only for transitory promises' (Article VII., 'Book of Common Prayer').
now—as the case is. **is not ashamed**—Greek
adds, '*of them.*' Not merely once did God call
Himself *their God*, but He IS NOW not ashamed
to have Himself called so, they being *alive* with
Him where He is. For, by the law, God cannot
come into contact with anything dead. None
remained dead in Christ's presence (Luke xx. 37,
38). The Lord of heaven and earth, when asked,
What is thy name ? said, omitting all His other
titles, "I am the God of Abraham, and the God
of Isaac, and the God of Jacob" (*Theodoret*). Not
only is He *not ashamed*, but *glories* in the relation
to His people. "Wherefore" does not mean that
God's *good pleasure* is the meritorious, but *gracious*, consequence of their obedience (which last is
the work of His Spirit in them). He first so
"called" Himself, then they so called Him. **for**
—proof of His being "*their* God ;" viz., "He hath
prepared (in His eternal counsels, Matt. xx. 23 ;
xxv. 34, and by the progressive acts of redemption, John xiv. 2) for them a city," that where He

17   By faith ^qAbraham, when he was tried, offered up Isaac: and he that
18 had received the promises ^roffered up his only-begotten *son,* ⁵of whom it
19 was said, ^sThat in Isaac shall thy seed be called: accounting that God
    was able to raise *him* up, even from the dead; from whence also he
    received him in a figure.
20   By faith ^tIsaac blessed Jacob and Esau concerning things to come.
21 By faith Jacob, when he was a-dying, blessed ^uboth the sons of Joseph;
22 and worshipped, ^u*leaning* upon the top of his staff. By faith ^wJoseph,
    when he died, ⁶made mention of the departing of the children of Israel;
    and gave commandment concerning his bones.

A. D. 64.

^q Gen. 22. 1.
^r Jas. 2, 21.
⁵ Or, To.
^s Gen. 21. 12.
^t Gen. 27. 27.
^u Gen. 48. 5.
^u Gen 47. 31.
^w Gen. 50. 24.
Ex. 13. 19.
⁶ Or, remembered.

---

reigns their yearning *desires* shall not be disappointed (*vv.* 14, 16). **a city.** Cf. its garniture by God, Rev. xxi. 10-27.

17. tried [*peirazomenos*]—'tempted,' as in Gen. xxii. 1. *Put to the proof* of his faith. Not that God 'tempts' *to sin*, but in the sense *proves* (Jas. i. 13-15). **offered up** [*prosenēnochen*]—'hath offered up,' as if the work and its praise were yet enduring (*Alford*). In intention he did sacrifice Isaac; in actual fact he "offered" him, as far as the presentation to God is concerned. **and—and so. he that had received** [*anadexamenos*]—'accepted;' i. e., *welcomed* by faith : not merely "had the promises," as ch. vii. 6. The difficulty to faith was, that in Isaac's posterity the promises were to be fulfilled. How could this be if Isaac were sacrificed? **offered up** [*prosepheren*]—'was offering up :' was in the act of offering. **his only-begotten son** (cf. Gen. xxii. 2). *Eusebius* ('Præparatio Evangelica,' i. 10 and iv. 16) has preserved a fragment of a Greek translation of Sanchoniatho, which mentions a mystical sacrifice of the Phœnicians, wherein a prince in royal robes was the offerer, and his only son the victim: evidently a tradition derived from Abraham's offering, handed down through Esau or Edom, Isaac's son. Isaac was Abraham's "only-begotten son" in respect of Sarah and the promises; he sent away his other sons by other wives (Gen. xxv. 6). Abraham is a type of the Father not sparing His only-begotten Son to fulfil the Divine purpose of love. God allowed no human sacrifices, though He claimed the first-born of Israel as His (cf. 2 Ki. iii. 27). **18. Of whom**—'He (*Abraham*, not Isaac) TO whom it was said' (*Alford*). But ch. i. 7 uses the same [*pros*] 'unto' for 'in respect to,' or "of," as the English version. This verse defines "only-begotten son," *v.* 17. **in Isaac shall thy seed be called** (Gen. xxi. 12). The posterity of Isaac alone shall be accounted the seed of Abraham, which is heir of the promises (Rom. ix. 7). **19.** Faith answered the objections which reason brought against God's command to offer Isaac, by suggesting that what God promised He both can and will perform, however impossible it seem (Rom. iv. 20, 21). **able to raise him**—rather, general, 'able to raise from the dead.' Cf. Rom. iv. 17. The quickening of Sarah's dead womb suggested that God can raise even the dead, though no instance had as yet occurred. **he received him in a figure**—Greek, 'in a parable.' *Alford*, 'Received him back, risen from that death which he had undergone under *the figure of the ram*.' Rather (*Gregory* of Nyssa), the *figure* is the representation which the scene gave to Abraham of Christ in His death (typified by Isaac's offering in intention, and the ram's actual substitution, answering to Christ's vicarious death), and in His resurrection (typified by Abraham's receiving him back from the jaws of death : cf. 2 Cor. i. 9, 10); as on the day of atonement the slain goat and the scape-goat together formed one joint rite, representing Christ's death and resurrec-

tion. It was then that Abraham saw Christ's day (John viii. 56). 'From which state (viz., that of the dead) he received him back *in the way of* [so *en* is used, ch. iv. 11] *a type of the resurrection in Christ.*'

20. Jacob is put before Esau, as heir of the chief, viz., the *spiritual*, blessing. (even) **concerning things to come** [*kai*]—as if they were present: not only concerning things actually present. **21. both the sons**—Greek, '*each* of the sons' (Gen. xlvii. 29; xlviii. 8-20, 22). He could not distinguish Joseph's sons by sight, yet *he did by faith*, transposing his hands intentionally, so as to lay his right hand on the younger, Ephraim, whose posterity was to be greater than that of Manasseh. He also adopted these grandchildren as his own sons, having transferred the primogeniture to Joseph. **and worshipped, &c.** This did not take place in connection with the foregoing, but before it, when Jacob made Joseph swear that he would bury him with his fathers in Canaan, not in Egypt. The assurance that Joseph would do so filled him with pious gratitude to God, which he expressed by raising himself on his bed to an attitude of *worship*. His faith, as Joseph's (*v.* 22), consisted in his so confidently anticipating the fulfilment of God's promise of Canaan to his descendants, as to desire to be buried there as his proper possession. **leaning upon the top of his staff**—Gen. xlvii. 31, Hebrew and English version, 'upon the bed's head.' The LXX. translate as Paul. *Jerome* reprobates the notion that Jacob *worshipped the top of Joseph's staff*, having on it an image of Joseph's power—i. e., bowed in recognition of the future sovereignty of his son's tribe : the father bowing to the son ! The Hebrew sets it aside : *the bed* is alluded to afterwards (Gen. xlviii. 2; xlix. 33). Probably Jacob turned himself in *bed* so as to have his face towards the pillow, Isa. xxxviii. 2 (there are no *bedsteads* in the East). Paul, by adopting the LXX. version, brings out, under the Spirit, *an additional fact*—viz., that the aged patriarch used *his own* (not Joseph's) *staff* to lean on in worshipping on his bed. *The staff* was the *emblem of his pilgrim state* on his way to his heavenly city (*vv.* 13, 14), wherein God had so wonderfully supported him. Gen. xxxii. 10, "With my *staff* I passed over Jordan, and now I am become," &c. (cf. Exod. xii. 11; Mark vi. 8.) So (1 Ki. i. 47) David 'bowed on his bed,' in adoring thanksgiving for God's favour to his son, before death. St. Paul omits the chief blessing of Jacob's twelve sons, because 'he plucks only the flowers by his way, and leaves the whole meadow full to his readers' (*Delitzsch* in *Alford*). **22. when he died**—'when dying.' **the departing** —'the exodus' (Gen. l. 24, 25). Joseph's eminent position in Egypt did not make him regard it as his home: in faith he looked to God's promise of Canaan, and desired that his bones should rest there: testifying thus—(1.) That he had no doubt of his posterity obtaining it; (2.) That he believed

23 By faith *Moses, when he was born, was hid three months of his parents, because they saw *he was* a proper child; and they were not
24 afraid of the king's *y* commandment. By faith Moses, when he was come
25 to years, refused to be called the son of Pharaoh's daughter; choosing *z* rather to suffer affliction with the people of God, than to enjoy the
26 pleasures of sin for a season; esteeming the reproach *7* of Christ greater riches than the treasures in Egypt: for he had respect unto the recom-
27 pence of the reward. By faith *a* he forsook Egypt, not fearing the wrath
28 of the king: for he endured, as seeing him who is invisible. Through faith *b* he kept the passover, and the sprinkling of blood, lest he that destroyed the first-born should touch them.
29 By faith they passed through the Red sea as by dry *land:* which the Egyptians assaying to do were drowned.
30 By faith *c* the walls of Jericho fell down, after they were compassed about seven days.

A. D. 64.
z Ex. 2. 2.
Acts 7. 20.
y Ex. 1. 16.
Ps. 56. 4.
Ps. 118. 6.
Isa. 8. 12,
13.
z Ps. 84. 10.
Matt. 5. 10-
12.
2 Cor. 4. 17.
Col. 1. 24.
7 Or. for
Christ.
Acts 9. 4.
a Ex. 10. 29.
Ex. 12. 37.
b Ex. 12. 21.
c Josh. 6. 20.

in the resurrection of the body, and its enjoyment of the heavenly Canaan. His wish was fulfilled (Josh. xxiv. 32; Acts vii. 16).
23. parents. So the LXX.—viz., Amram and Jochebed (Num. xxvi. 59); but Exod. ii. 2 mentions the mother alone. Doubtless Amram sanctioned all she did: secrecy being their object, he did not appear prominent. **a proper child** [*asteion to paidion*]—'comely.' Acts vii. 20, Greek, 'fair to God.' His parents' faith in saving him must have had some Divine revelation to rest on, which marked their "exceeding fair" babe as designed for a great work. His *beauty* was 'the sign' appointed to assure their faith. **the king's commandment**—to slay all the males (Exod. i. 22). **24.** So far from *faith* being opposed to *Moses*, he was an eminent example of it (*Bengel*). **refused**—in believing self-denial, when he might have succeeded to the throne of Egypt. Thermutis, Pharaoh's daughter, adopted him (*Josephus*), with the king's consent. *Josephus* states that, when a child, he threw on the ground the diadem put on him in jest: a presage of his subsequent rejection of Thermutis' adoption. Faith made him to prefer the adoption of the King of kings, unseen, and to choose (*vv.* 25, 26) things the last which flesh and blood relish. *Piazzi Smyth* says, 'Rameses Sesostris, reigning at Thebes, condemned his daughter Thuoris to sacrifice herself for his ambition. Her exile at the delta was providentially overruled to Moses' preservation. He was offered the crown if he would acknowledge himself her son. The monuments show what unbounded wealth and power he rejected for conscience' sake. Settos II., a profligate, ascended the throne in Moses' place, and perished in the Red Sea.' **25.** Balancing the best of the world with the worst of religion, he 'chose' the latter, with deliberate resolution, not hasty impulse. He was forty years old when the judgment is matured. **for a season.** If the world has 'pleasure' [*apolausin:* 'enjoyment'] to offer, it is but *for a season.* If religion bring with it "affliction," it too is but for a season: its 'pleasures are for evermore' (Ps. xvi. 11). **26. the reproach of Christ**—which, falling on the Church, Christ regards as His own. Israel typified Christ: Israel's sufferings were Christ's (cf. 2 Cor. i. 5; Col. i. 24). As uncircumcision was Egypt's *reproach,* so circumcision was the badge of Israel's expectation of Christ, which Moses cherished, and which the Gentiles reproached Israel for. Christ's people's reproach will ere long be their great glory (Isa. xxv. 8). **had respect unto** [*apeblepen*]—'*turning his eyes from* other considerations, *he fixed them on the* (eternal) recompense' (*vv.* 39, 40). **27. not fearing the wrath of the king.** But in

Exod. ii. 14, 15, "Moses feared . . . and fled from the face of Pharaoh." He was *afraid*, and fled, when to have stayed would have been to tempt Providence, and *to sacrifice his being Israel's future deliverer according to the Divine intimations:* his great aim (note, v. 23). He *did not fear the king* so as to neglect duty, and not return when God called him. It was *in spite of the king's prohibition he left Egypt,* not fearing the consequences likely to overtake him if he should be caught. If he had stayed as adopted son of Pharaoh's daughter, his slaughter of the Egyptian would have been connived at: his resolution to take his portion with oppressed Israel, which he could not, had he stayed, was the motive of his flight, and constituted the "faith" of this act. The exodus of Moses with Israel cannot be meant; for it was made, not in defiance, but by the desire, of the king. Besides, the chronological order would be broken, the next particular specified, viz., the *passover,* having taken place *before the exodus.* It is Moses' *personal* history and faith which are here described. The faith of the people is not introduced till v. 29. **endured**—stedfast in faith amidst trials. He fled, *not so much from fear of Pharaoh,* as from disappointment at not having been able to inspire Israel with those hopes for which he had sacrificed all earthly prospects. This accounts for his strange despondency when commissioned by God to arouse the people (Exod. iii. 15; iv. 1, 10-12). **seeing him who is invisible**—as though he had to do only with God, ever before him by faith, though *invisible* to the bodily eye (Rom. i. 20; 1 Tim. i. 17; vi. 16): he feared not the wrath of *visible* man (v. 1; Luke xii. 4, 5). **28. kept** [*pepoieken*]—'*hath* kept;' the passover being, in Paul's day, still observed. His *faith* here was in the invisible God's promise that the destroying angel should *pass over,* and not *touch* the inmates of the blood-sprinkled houses (Exod. xii. 23). **the first-born** [*ta prototoka:* neuter]—both of man and beast.
29. they—Moses and Israel. **Red sea**—named from Edom (meaning *red*), whose country adjoined it. **which . . . assaying to do** [*hēs peiran labontes*]—'of which (Red sea) the Egyptians having made 'experiment.' *Rash presumption* mistaken by many for *faith:* with similar presumption many rush into eternity. The same thing done by the believer and by the unbeliever is not the same thing. What was *faith* in Israel was *presumption* in the Egyptians. **were drowned** [*katepothesan*]—'were swallowed up.' They sank in the sands as much as in the waves. Cf. Exod. xv. 12, "The *earth swallowed* them."
30. Trumpets, though one were to sound for ten

570

31   By faith *d* the harlot Rahab perished not with them *8* that believed not, when she had received the spies with peace.

32   And what shall I more say? for the time would fail me to tell *e* of Gedeon, and *of f* Barak, and *g of* Samson, and *of k* Jephthae; *of i* David

33   also, and *j* Samuel, and *of* the prophets: who through faith subdued kingdoms, wrought righteousness, obtained promises, stopped *k* the mouths

34   of lions, quenched *l* the violence of fire, escaped the *m* edge of the sword, *n* out of weakness were made strong, waxed valiant in fight, turned *o* to

35   flight the armies of the aliens. Women *p* received their dead raised to life again: and others were tortured, not accepting deliverance; that

36   they might obtain a better resurrection: and others had trial of *cruel* mockings and scourgings, yea, moreover of bonds and imprisonment:

37   they were stoned, they were sawn asunder, were tempted, were slain with the sword: they wandered about in sheep-skins and goat-skins;

A. D. 64.

d Jas. 2. 25.
8 Or, that were disobedient.
e Judg. 6. 11.
f Judg. 4. 6.
g Judg 13.24.
h Judg. 11. 1.
i 1 Sam. 16 1.
j 1 Sam. 1.20.
k Dan. 6. 22.
l Dan. 3. 25.
m 1 Sam. 20.1.
8 2 Ki. 20. 7.
o 1 Sam. 14.
13.
p 1 Ki. 17. 22.

---

thousand years, cannot throw down walls; but *faith* can do all things (*Chrysostom*). **seven days** —whereas sieges often lasted for years.

31. Rahab showed her "faith" in her confession (Josh. ii. 9, 11). **the harlot**—her former life adds to the marvel of her repentance, faith, and preservation (Matt. xxi. 31, 32). **believed not** [*apeithesasin*]—'were disobedient;' viz., to God's will, manifested by miracles wrought in behalf of Israel (Josh. ii. 8-11). **received**—in her house. **with peace**—so that they had nothing to fear in her house. Paul, quoting the same examples (*vv.* 17, 31) for *faith* as Jas. ii. 21, 25 (see notes) does for justification by *works* evidentially, shows that, in maintaining justification by faith alone, he means not dead faith, but "faith" which *worketh* by "love" (Gal. v. 6).

32. the time—suitable for an epistle. He accumulates some out of many examples. **Gedeon**—put before Barak, not chronologically, but as more celebrated. Samson for the same reason is put before Jephthae. The mention of Jephthae's "faith" makes it unlikely he sacrificed his daughter's *life* for a rash vow. David, the warrior-king and prophet, forms the transition from warrior-chiefs to the "prophets," of whom "Samuel" is the first. **33. subdued kingdoms**—as *David did* (2 Sam. viii. 1, &c.): also Gedeon subdued Midian, (Judg. vii.) **wrought righteousness**—as *Samuel* did (1 Sam. viii. 9; xii. 3-23; xv. 33; David, 2 Sam. viii. 15). **obtained promises**—the prophets (v. 32); through them the promises were given (cf. Dan. ix. 21) (*Bengel*). Rather, 'obtained the fulfilment of promises' previously the object of their *faith* (Josh. xxi. 45; 1 Ki. viii. 56). Not "*the* promises," which are still future (*vv.* 13, 39). **stopped the mouths of lions** (Dan. vi. 22, 23)—'because he *believed* in his God.' Samson (Judg. xiv. 6), David (1 Sam. xvii. 34-37), Benaiah (2 Sam. xxiii. 20). **34. Quenched the violence of fire** (Dan. iii. 27). Not merely 'the fire,' but 'the *power* of the fire;' the last miracles of the Old Testament. So the martyrs of the reformation, though not escaping *the fire*, were delivered from its *power* lastingly to hurt them. **escaped . . . sword.** So Jephthah (Judg. xii. 3); and David escaped Saul's sword (1 Sam. xviii. 11; xix. 10-12); Elijah (1 Ki. xix. 1, &c.), Elisha (2 Ki. vi. 14). **out of weakness were made strong** — Samson (Judg. xvi. 28; xv. 19), Hezekiah, (Isa. xxxvii. and xxxviii.) Milton says, 'The martyrs shook the powers of darkness with the irresistible power of weakness.' **valiant in fight**—Barak (Judg. iv. 14, 15). The Maccabees, sons of Matthias, Judas, Jonathan, and Simon delivered the Jews from their cruel oppressor, Antiochus of Syria. **armies** [*parembolas*]—*camps:* referring

to Judg. vii. 21. Or else the Maccabees having put to flight Syrian and other foes. **35. Women received their dead raised**—the widow of Zarephath. The Shunammite, (2 Ki. iv.) [So C. But א A Δ *f*, read *gunaikas* for *gunaikes*—'they received women of aliens (connect *allotriōn* with *gunaikas*) by raising their dead' (*anastaseōs*, the verbal noun, thus governing *nekrous*) (1 Ki. xvii. 24).] Through raising the widow's son, Elijah *took* her into the fellowship of faith, an *alien* though she was before. Christ, Luke iv. 26, especially notices that Elijah was sent to an alien from Israel, a woman of Sarepta. Elijah's faith appeared in that, at God's command, he went to a Gentile city (contrary to Jewish prejudices), and, as the fruit of faith, not only raised her dead son, but *received* her as a convert into the family of God. [So *elabon*, 2 Cor. xii. 16.] **and** [*de*]—'but:' in contrast to those raised again to life. **tortured** [*etumpanisthesan*]—'broken on the wheel.' The sufferer was stretched on an instrument like a drumhead, and scourged to death. **not accepting deliverance** — when offered. So the seven brothers (2 Macc. vii. 9, 11, 14, 29, 36); and Eleazar (2 Macc. vi. 18-21, 28, 30), 'Though I might have been delivered from death, I endure these severe pains, being beaten.' **a better resurrection**—than the resurrection which their foes could give them by delivering them from death (Dan. xii. 2; Luke xx. 35; Phil. iii. 11). The fourth of the brethren (referring to Dan. xii. 2) said to King Antiochus, 'To be put to death by men is to be chosen to look onward for the hopes which are of God, to be raised up again by Him; but for thee there is no resurrection to life.' The writer of 2 Maccabees *expressly disclaims inspiration;* so that Paul's allusion to it cannot sanction the Apocrypha as inspired. In quoting Daniel, he quotes a book *claiming inspiration*, and so tacitly sanctions that claim. **36. others**—of a *different* class: confessors for the truth [*heteroi;* but in *v.* 35, *alloi*]. **trial**—testing their *faith*. **imprisonment**—as Hanani (2 Chr. xvi. 10), imprisoned by Asa. Micaiah, the son of Imlah, by Ahab (1 Ki. xxii. 26, 27). **37. stoned**—as Zechariah, son of Jehoiada (2 Chr. xxiv. 20-22; Matt. xxiii. 35). **sawn asunder**—as Isaiah was said to have been by Manasseh; but see 'Introduction to Isaiah.' **tempted**—*by their foes*, in the midst of tortures, to renounce their faith: the most bitter aggravation. Or, *by those of their own household*, as Job was (*Estius*); or by the fiery darts of Satan, as Jesus in his last trials (*Glassius*). Probably it included all three; in every possible way, by friends, foes, human and Satanic agents, by caresses and afflictions, words and deeds, to forsake God, but in vain, through the power of faith. **sword** [*en phono machairēs apethanon*]—

38 being destitute, afflicted, tormented; (of whom the world was not worthy:) they wandered in deserts, and *in* mountains, and *q in* dens and caves of the earth.

39 And these all, having obtained a good report through faith, received

40 not the promise; God having [9]provided some better thing for us, that they without us should not be made *r*perfect.

12 WHEREFORE, seeing we also are compassed about with so great a cloud of witnesses, let us lay aside every weight, and the sin which doth so easily beset *us*, and let us run with patience the race that is set before

A. D. 64.

q 1 Sam 22. 1.
1 Sam. 23.
16. 19.
1 Sam. 24.1.
1 Ki. 17. 3.
1 Ki. 18. 4.
1 Ki. 19. 9.
9 Or,
foreseen.
r Rom. 11 26.
Rev. 6. 11.

'they died in the murder of the sword.' In *v.* 34, the contrary: "they escaped the edge of the sword." Both are marvellous effects of faith. It accomplishes great things, and suffers great things, without counting it suffering (*Chrysostom*). Urijah was so slain by Jehoiakim (Jer. xxvi. 23); and *the prophets* in Israel. **in sheep-skins**—as Elijah (1 Ki. xix. 10, 13, LXX.): *white*, as the "goat-skins" were *black* (cf. Zech. xiii. 4). **tormented** [*kakouchoumenoi*]—'in evil state.' **38. Of whom the world was not worthy**—So far from their being unworthy of living in the world, as their exile in desert, &c., might imply. The world, in shutting them out, shut out from itself a source of blessing; such as Joseph proved to Potiphar and Jacob to Laban (Gen. xxx. 27; xxxix. 5). In condemning them, the world condemned itself. **caves** [*opais*]—'chinks.' Palestine, from its hilly character, abounds in *fissures* and caves, affording shelter to the persecuted, as the fifty hid by Obadiah and Elijah (1 Ki. xviii. 4, 13; xix. 8, 13); Mattathias and his sons (1 Macc. ii. 28, 29); Judas Maccabeus (2 Macc. v. 27).

39. having obtained a good report — 'borne witness of.' *Though* they were so, yet they "received not the promise"—*i. e.*, the consummation of "salvation" *promised* at Christ's coming again (ch. ix. 15, 28): 'the eternal inheritance.' Abraham *obtained* the thing *promised* (ch. vi. 15) *in part*—viz., blessedness *in soul* after death by faith in Christ about to come. 'It is probable that some accumulation of blessedness was added to holy souls when Christ came and fulfilled all things: as at His burial many rose from the dead, who doubtless ascended to heaven with Him' (*Flacius* in *Bengel*) (note, Eph. iv. 8). The *perfecting* of believers in *title* and as to *conscience* took place, once for all, at Christ's death, through His being made thereby *perfect* as Saviour. Their *perfecting in soul* ever since has taken place at their death. The final perfecting will not take place till Christ's coming. **40. provided**—with Divine forethought from eternity (cf. Gen. xxii. 8, 14). **some better thing for us** (ch. vii. 19)—than they had here. They had not in this world, 'apart from us' [*choris hemon,* "without us"—*i. e.*, they had to wait for us], the revelation of the promised salvation actually accomplished, as we now have it in Christ: their souls probably attained an increase of *heavenly* bliss on the death and ascension of Christ: they shall not attain the full *glory in body and soul* (the regeneration of the creature) until the full number of the elect (including us with them) is completed (1 Thess. iv. 15, 17): all together, no one preceding the other. *Chrysostom*, &c., restricted *v.* 39, 40 to this last truth. 'You, Hebrews, may more easily exercise patience than Old Testament believers: *they* had much longer to wait, and are still waiting, until the elect are all gathered in: *you* have not to wait for them' (*Estius*). I think his object is to warn Hebrew Christians against relapsing into *Judaism.* Though the Old Testament worthies attained such eminence by faith, they are not above us in privileges, but the reverse. It is not *we* who are perfected *with them*, but *they with us*. They *waited* for His coming: we enjoy Him, having come (ch. i. 1; ii. 3). Christ's death, the means of *perfecting* what the Jewish *law could not*, was reserved for our time. Cf. ch. xii. 2, '*perfecter* (Greek) of our faith,' and *v.* 23, end: however, see note there. Ch. ix. 12: the blood of Christ, brought into the heavenly holy place by Him, first opened an entrance into heaven (cf. John iii. 13). Still the fathers were in blessedness by faith in the Saviour to come at death (ch. vi. 15; Luke xvi. 22).

CHAP. XII. 1-29.—EXHORTATION TO FOLLOW THE WITNESSES JUST MENTIONED—NOT TO FAINT IN TRIALS—TO REMOVE ALL BITTER ROOTS—FOR WE ARE UNDER, NOT A LAW OF TERROR, BUT THE GOSPEL OF GRACE, TO DESPISE WHICH WILL BRING HEAVIER PENALTIES, IN PROPORTION TO OUR GREATER PRIVILEGES.

1. we also—as well as those, *v.* 11. **are compassed about**—'have so great a cloud (a numberless multitude *above* us, like a cloud, "holy and pellucid," *Clemens Alexandrinus*) of witnesses surrounding us:' an image from a 'race,' well understood even in Palestine from its contact with the Græco-Macedonian empire and its national games. The "witnesses" answer to the spectators pressing round to see the competitors for the prize (Phil. iii. 14). Those 'witnessed of' (ch. xi. 5, 39) become in turn "witnesses" in a twofold way,— (1.) *Attesting by their own case the faithfulness of God to His people* (ch. vi. 12), some of them *martyrs;* (2.) *Witnessing our struggle of faith.* This second sense, though agreeing with the *image*, is not *positively* and *directly* sustained by Scripture. It gives vividness to the image: as the crowd of spectators gave additional spirit to the combatants, so the *cloud of witnesses,* who have themselves been in the same contest, ought to increase our earnestness, testifying, as they do, to God's faithfulness. **weight** [Hebrew, *kabeed*, 'rich :' Gen. xiii. 2 is, lit., *weighty*]—as corporeal unwieldiness was, through disciplinary diet, laid aside by candidates for the prize, so carnal and worldly lusts, and all, from without or within, that would impede the heavenly runner, are the spiritual *weight* to be laid aside. [*Onkon*] 'Encumbrance,' *superfluous weight:* the lust of the flesh, lust of the eye, and pride of life: even harmless and otherwise useful things which would retard us (Mark ix. 42-48: x. 50: cf. Eph. iv. 22; Col. iii. 9, 10). **the sin which doth so easily beset** (stands around) **us** [*tēn euperistaton hamartian*]—*sinful propensity* (*Luther*), 'which always so clings to us:' 'surrounding us, ever present and ready' (*Wahl*): not primarily "*the sin*," &c., but *sin* in general, with special reference to 'apostasy,' against which he already warned them—the besetting sin of the Hebrews, UNBELIEF, to which they might *gradually* give way. **with patience** [*di' hupomones*]—'in persevering endurance' (ch.

2 us, looking [a] unto Jesus the [1] author and finisher of *our* faith; [b] who for the joy that was set before him endured the cross, despising the shame, [c] and is set down at the right hand of the throne of God.

3 For [d] consider him that endured such contradiction of sinners against

4 himself, lest [e] ye be wearied and faint in your minds. Ye have not yet

5 resisted unto blood, striving against sin. And ye have forgotten the exhortation which speaketh unto you as unto children, My [f] son, despise not thou the chastening of the Lord, nor faint when thou art rebuked of

6 him: for [g] whom the Lord loveth he chasteneth, and scourgeth every son

7 whom he receiveth. If ye endure chastening, God dealeth with you as

8 with sons; for what son is he whom the father chasteneth not? But if ye be without chastisement, whereof [h] all are partakers, then are ye bastards, and not sons.

9 Furthermore we have had fathers of our flesh which corrected *us*, and we gave *them* reverence: shall we not much rather be in subjection unto

A. D. 61.

CHAP. 12.
[a] Isa. 8. 17.
Zech. 12. 10.
2 Cor. 3. 18.
[1] Or,
beginner.
[b] Luke 21. 26.
Phil 2. 8.
1 Pet 1. 11.
[e] Ps. 110. 1.
ch. 1. 3.
ch. 8. 1.
[d] John 15. 20.
[e] Gal. 6. 9.
[f] Job 5. 17.
[g] Ps. 94. 12.
Jas. 1. 12
[h] Ps. 73. 14.

x. 36: cf. 1 Cor. ix. 24, 25). **2. Looking unto** [*aphorontes*]—'from afar' (note, ch. xi. 26); *fixing the eyes upon* Jesus seated on the throne of God. **author** — 'Prince-leader.' [*Archēgon*] "Captain (of salvation)," ch. ii. 10; "Prince (of life)," Acts iii. 15. Going before us as Originator of our faith, and the Leader whose matchless example we are to follow always. The examples of faith in ch. xi. are to be followed only so far as they followed Christ (ch. xi. 26; xiii. 8: cf. 1 Cor. xi. 1). On His "faith," cf. ch. ii. 13; iii. 2. **finisher** [*teleiotēn*]—'perfecter' (ch. xi. 40). **of our faith**—Greek, 'of *the* faith,' including both *His* faith (as exhibited in what follows) and *ours*. He fulfilled the ideal of faith, and so, both as a vicarious offering and an example, He is the object of faith. **for the joy that was set before him**—viz., of presently after *sitting down at the right hand of the throne of God* as a Prince and Saviour, to give repentance and remission of sins. The coming joy disarmed of its sting the present pain. **cross** . . . **shame**—the great stumblingblock to the Hebrews. 'Despised'—*i. e.*, disregarded. **3. For**—justifying his exhortation, "Looking unto Jesus." **consider** [*analogisasthe*]—by comparison with yourselves. **contradiction**—unbelief: every kind of opposition (Acts xxviii. 19). **sinners.** *Sin* assails us. Not *sin*, but *sinners*, contradicted Christ (*Bengel*). **be wearied and faint** [*kamēte ekluomenoi*]—'lest ye weary fainting,' &c. Cf. Isa. xlix. 4, 5, a specimen of Jesus' not being *wearied out* by the *contradiction* and strange unbelief of those among whom He *laboured*, preaching and exhibiting miracles by His inherent power, as none else could do. **4. not yet resisted unto blood**—image from *pugilism*, as from a *race;* both taken from the national Greek games. Ye have suffered the loss of *goods*, and *been a gazingstock both by reproaches and afflictions* (ch. x. 33, 34: ye have not shed your *blood*, note, ch. xiii. 7). 'The athlete who hath seen his own *blood*, and though cast down by his opponent, does not let his spirits be cast down, who, as often as he falls, rises the more determined, goes to the encounter with great hope' (*Seneca*). **against sin**—personified as an adversary; whether within, leading you to *spare* your blood, or in your adversaries, leading them to *shed* it, if they cannot, through your faithfulness, induce you to apostatize. **5. forgotten** [*eklelēsthe*]—utterly (cf. *vv.* 15-17): *some* had utterly forgotten God's word. His *exhortation* ought to have more effect on you than the cheers of the spectators have on the competitors in the games. **which** [*hētis*]—'such as:' 'the which.' **speaketh unto you** [*dialegetai*]—as in a *dialogue:* God's loving condescension (cf. Isa. i. 18). **despise**

not [*oligorei*]—'do not *hold of little account.*' Betraying *contumacious unbelief* (ch. iii. 12), as "faint" implies a broken-down, *desponding spirit.* "Chastening" [*discipline: paideia*] is to be borne with "subjection" (*v.* 9); 'rebuke' [more severe: *elenchomenos*], with *endurance* (*v.* 7). 'Some in adversity kick against God's will, others despond: neither is to be done by the child of God. Such adverse things occur only by the decree of God in kindness—viz., to remove defilements adhering to the believer, and to exercise patience' (*Grotius*). **6.** (Rev. iii. 19) **and** [*de*]—'yea, and:' an additional circumstance. **scourgeth** —which draws forth "blood" (*v.* 4). **receiveth**— accepts as a son "in whom He *delighteth*" (Prov. iii. 12). **7.** In *vv.* 7, 8 the need of "chastening;" in *v.* 9 the duty of those to whom it is administered. **If.** אΑΔ*f*, Vulgate, read [*eis* for *ei*] 'With a view to chastening (*i. e.*, since God's chastisement is with a view to disciplinary amelioration), endure patiently.' **dealeth with you** [*prospheretai*]— 'beareth Himself toward you' in the very act of chastening. **what son is he**—in ordinary life? Much more God as to His sons (Isa. xlviii. 10; Acts xiv. 22). The most eminent saints were the most afflicted. God leads them by a way they know not (Isa. xlii. 16). We too much look at trial by itself, instead of in connection with the whole plan of our salvation; as if a traveller were to complain of the roughness of one turn, without considering that it led him into green pastures, on the direct road to the city of habitation. The New Testament alone uses the Greek 'education' [*paideia*] to express 'discipline' of a *child* by a wise father. **8. if ye be without** [*choris*]—wishing to be *removed from it.* **all**—all *sons*: all the worthies in ch. 11: all the *witnesses, v.* 1. **are** [*gegonasi*]—'*have been made* partakers.' **then are ye bastards**—of whose education their fathers take no care; whereas every right-minded father is concerned for the moral well-being of his legitimate son. 'Since, then, not to be chastised is a mark of bastardy, we ought to rejoice in chastisement, as a mark of our genuine sonship' (*Chrysostom*). **9. fathers of our flesh which corrected us** [*tous pateras paideutas*]—' we had the fathers of our flesh as correctors.' **Father of spirits**—contrasted with *fathers of our flesh.* 'Generation by men is carnal, by God spiritual.' As "Father of spirits," He is both the Originator and the Providential, Gracious Sustainer of animal and spiritual life. Cf. "and LIVE"—viz., spiritually and eternally: not *die*, the penalty of filial insubordination (Deut. xxi. 18; *v.* 10, end; 2 Pet. i. 4). God is a Spirit, and the Creator of spirits like Himself; men are

10 the Father of spirits, and live? For they verily for a few days chastened *us* [2] after their own pleasure; but he for *our* profit, [i] that *we* might be
11 partakers of his holiness. Now no chastening for the present seemeth to be joyous, but grievous: nevertheless afterward it yieldeth [j] the peaceable fruit of righteousness unto them which are exercised thereby.
12 Wherefore [k] lift up the hands which hang down, and the feeble knees;
13 and make [3] straight paths for your feet, lest that which is lame be turned
14 out of the way; [l] but let it rather be healed. Follow peace with all *men*,
15 and holiness, without which no man shall see the Lord: looking diligently lest any man [4] fail of the grace of God; lest any root of bitter-

A. D. 64.
2 Or. as seemed good, or, meet to them.
i Lev. 19. 2.
j Jas 3. 15.
k Job 4. 3, 4.
3 Or. even.
l Gal 6. 1.
4 Or. fall from.

---

but flesh, and the progenitors of flesh (John iii. 6). Jesus, our pattern, "learned obedience" experimentally by suffering (ch. v. 8). **10.** Wherein the chastisement of our heavenly Father is preferable to that of earthly fathers. **for a few days** [*pros oligas hemeras*]—*with a view to* our well-being in *the few days* of earthly life. **after their own pleasure** [*kata to dokoun autois*]—'according to what seemed fit to themselves.' Their rule of chastening is their own often-erring judgment or caprice. The two defects of human education are —(1.) An undue view to the interests of our *short* earthly term of *days;* (2.) The absence in parents of our heavenly Father's unerring wisdom. 'They err at one time in severity, at another in indulgence (1 Sam. iii. 13; Eph. vi. 4), and do not so much chasten as THINK they chasten' (*Bengel*). **that we might be partakers of his holiness**— holy as He is holy (John xv. 2; 1 Pet. i. 15, 16). To become *holy* like God is to be educated for passing *eternity* with God (*v.* 14; 2 Pet. i. 4). So 'partaking of God's holiness' contrasts with the "few days" of this life for which earthly fathers generally educate their sons. **11. joyous, but grievous**—Greek, 'matter of joy . . . of grief.' The objection that chastening is grievous is anticipated. It only 'seems' so to those being chastened, whose judgments are confused by present pain. Its ultimate *fruit* amply compensates for temporary pain. The real object of chastening is not that fathers find pleasure in children's pain. Gratified wishes would often be real curses (Ps. cvi. 15). **afterward**—the time often when God works. **fruit of righteousness.** *Righteousness* (springing from faith) is the *fruit* which chastening, the tree, yields (Phil. i. 11). "Peaceable" (cf. Isa. xxxii. 17; xxxiii. 20, 21; lvii. 2); in contrast to the conflict by which it is won. As the olive garland, emblem of *peace* as well as *victory*, was put on the victor's brow in the games. **exercised thereby**—as athletes trained for a contest. *Chastisement* is the *exercise* to give experience, and make the spiritual combatant victorious (Rom. v. 3). 'Happy the servant for whose improvement his Lord is earnest, with whom He deigns to be angry, whom He does not deceive by dissembling admonition'(*Tertullian,* 'De Pat.' c. 11). **12.** He addresses them as runners, pugilists, warriors (*Chrysostom*). **Wherefore** — resumed from *v.* 1. **lift up** [*anorthosate,* 'erect ']. In Isa. xxxv. 3, 4, it is, "*Strengthen* ye the weak hands." The *hand* is the symbol of strength. **feeble** [*paralelumena*]—'paralyzed:' used only by Luke, *Paul's* companion. The exhortation has three parts: the first relates to *ourselves, vv.* 12, 13; the second, to *others, v.* 14, "peace with all men;" the third, to *God,* "holiness, without which," &c.: the first is referred to in *v.* 15, "lest any man fail of the grace of God;" the second, in "lest any root of bitterness," &c.; the third in *v.* 16, "Lest there be any . . . profane person," &c. This threefold relation often occurs in *Paul's* epistles.

Note, Titus ii. 12. The Greek *active*, not the middle, requires the sense, Lift up not only *your* own hands and knees, but also those *of your brethren* (cf. *v.* 15). **13.** From Prov. iv. 26, LXX., 'Make straight paths for thy feet;' *i. e.,* a straight road to joy and grace (*vv.* 1, 2, 15). Cease to "halt" (as the "*lame*") between Judaism and Christianity (*Bengel*). "Paths" [*trochias*]—'*wheel tracks.*' Let your walk be so firm and unanimous in the right direction, that a plain "highway" may be established for those who follow you (Isa. xxxv. 8) (*Alford*). **that which is lame**—those "weak in the faith" (Rom. xiv. 1), having Judaizing prejudices. **be turned out of the way** (Prov. iv. 27)—and so missing the way, lose the prize (*v.* 1). **rather be healed.** Proper exercise contributes to *health;* walking straight onward in the right way tends to *healing.* **14. Follow peace with all**—with the brethren especially (Rom. xiv. 19), that so the "lame" among them be not "turned out of the way" (*v.* 13), and that no one of them "fail of the grace of God" (*v.* 15). **holiness** [*hagiasmon:* 'sanctification']—distinct from God's "holiness" [*hagiotes*] (*v.* 10), which is absolute, and which we are to put on, becoming "holy as He is holy," by *sanctification.* Whilst 'following peace with all men,' we are not so to please them as to make God's will and our sanctification secondary: this latter must be our first aim (Gal. i. 10). **without** [*choris: apart from*] **which no man shall see the Lord**—*as a son;* in heavenly glory (Rev. xxii. 3, 4). In the East, none but great favourites are admitted to see the king (cf. 2 Sam. xiv. 24). The Lord being pure, none but the pure shall see him (Matt. v. 8). Without holiness in them, they could not enjoy Him who is holiness itself (Zech. xiv. 20; 1 John iii. 2, 3; Eph. v. 5). Contrast *v.* 16 (cf. 1 Thess. iv. 3). *All* (Matt. xxiv. 30; Rev. i. 7) shall see the Lord as a *Judge;* not as their lasting portion, which is meant here. [*Opsetai* does not denote the mere action of seeing, but the seer's state of mind to which the object is presented: so in Matt. v. 8, they shall *truly comprehend* God (*Tittmann*).] None but the holy could *appreciate* the holy God: none else, therefore, shall abide in His presence. 'The bad shall only see Him as *Son of man* (cf. Rev. i. 13 with 7; and Matt. xxiv. 30; Acts i. 11; xvii. 31): it will be in the glory in which He shall judge, not in the lowliness in which He was judged. *His form as God,* wherein He is equal to the Father, without doubt the ungodly shall not see; for only "the pure in heart shall see God"' (*Augustine*). 'He shall come to judge, who stood before a judge: in the form in which He was judged, that they may see Him whom they pierced: He who was before hidden shall come manifested in power: He shall condemn the real culprits, who was Himself falsely made a culprit.' **15. lest any man fail** [*husteron*]—'lest any (viz., through sloth in running) *failing* (*falling short*) of the grace of God . . . *trouble you.*' The image is

16 ness springing up trouble *you*, and thereby many be defiled; lest there *be* any fornicator, or profane person, as Esau, *^m*who for one morsel of meat
17 sold his birthright. For ye know how that afterward, when he *ⁿ*would have inherited the blessing, he was rejected: for he found no ⁵place of repentance, though he sought it carefully with tears.
18   For ye are not come unto *^o*the mount that might be touched, and that
19 burned with fire, nor unto blackness, and darkness, and tempest, and the sound of a trumpet, and the voice of words; which *voice* they that heard
20 entreated *^p*that the word should not be spoken to them any more: (for they could not endure that which was commanded, And if so much as a beast touch the mountain, it shall be stoned, or thrust through with a
21 dart: and so terrible was the sight, *that* Moses said, I exceedingly fear

A. D. 64.

^m Gen. 25. 33.
ⁿ Gen. 27. 34.
⁵ Or, way to change his mind.
^o Ex. 19. 12. Ex. 20 18. Deut. 5, 11. Rom. 6. 14. Rom. 8. 15.
2 Tim. 1. 7.
^p Ex. 20. 19. Deut. 5. 24. Deut. 18.16.

from travellers, one of whom lags behind, and so never reaches the end of the labourious journey (*Chrysostom*). **root of bitterness.** A *bitter* root might possibly bring forth sweet fruits; a root whose *essence* is "*bitterness*," never could. Paul refers to Deut. xxix. 18. [*Bleek* infers from *enochle* of Alexandrine MS. being here, not *en chole* of Vatican MS., that *Paul used the Alexandrine text of the* LXX. (cf. Acts viii. 23). Every *person* (cf. *v.* 16) and every *principle* so radically corrupt as to spread corruption around. **many** [*hoi polloi*]— '*the* many;' *i. e.*, the whole congregation. So long as it is under the earth it cannot be remedied, but when it 'springs up,' it must be dealt with boldly. Still remember the caution (Matt. xiii. 26-30) as to rooting out *persons*. No such danger can arise in rooting out bad *principles*. **16. fornicator** (ch. xiii. 4; 1 Cor. x. 8). **or profane.** *Fornication* is nearly akin to gluttony, Esau's sin. He *profanely* cast away his spiritual privilege for the gratification of his palate. Gen. xxv. 34 graphically portrays his reckless, self-indulgent levity. An example well fitted to strike horror into those Hebrews, whosoever, like Esau, were only sons of Isaac according to the flesh (*Bengel*). **for one morsel.** The smallness of the inducement aggravates the guilt of casting away eternity for a trifle, so far is it from being a claim for mercy (cf. Gen. iii. 6). *One* act has often the greatest power for good or for evil. So the cases of Reuben and Saul, for evil (Gen. xlix. 4; 1 Chr. v. 1; 1 Sam. xiij. 12-14); for good, Abraham and Phinehas (Gen. xii. 1, &c.; xv. 5, 6; Num. xxv. 6-15). **his birthright**—his own (so אAC read, intensifying the suicidal guilt of the act) rights of primogeniture [*ta prototokia heautou* for *autou* in CΔ], involving the privilege of being ancestor of the promised seed, and heir of the promises in Him. The Hebrews had, as Christians, the spiritual rights of primogeniture (cf. *v.* 23): they must exercise holy self-control, if they wish not, like Esau, to forfeit them. **17. afterward** [*kai*] — '*even* afterward.' He despised his birthright; accordingly *also* he was despised, when he wished to have the blessing. As in the believer's case, so in the unbeliever's, there is an "afterward" coming, when the believer shall look on his past griefs, and the unbeliever on his past joys, in a very different light from that in which they were respectively viewed at the time. Cf. "nevertheless *afterward*," &c., *v.* 11, with it here. Cf. "the cool of the day," Gen. iii. 8, with 6. **when he would**—*wished* to have. 'He that will not when he may, when he will, shall have nay' (Prov. i. 24-30; Luke xiii. 28, 34, 35; xix. 42, 44). **he was rejected** [*apedokimasthe*, '*as reprobate*']—not as to every blessing; only that which would have followed the primogeniture. **he found no place of repentance.** The *cause* put for the *effect*, "repentance" for the object which Esau aimed at—viz., *the change of his*
575

father's bestowal of the chief *blessing on Jacob.* Had he *sought* real *repentance with tears*, he would have *found* it (Matt. vii. 7). But he did not find it, because this was not what he sought. What proves his *tears* were not those of one seeking *repentance* is, immediately after he was foiled in his desire, he resolved to murder Jacob! He shed tears, not for sin, but for suffering the penalty of it. His were tears of vain remorse, not repentance. 'Before, he might have had the blessing without tears; afterwards, however many he shed, he was rejected. The most hardened shed tears at times; when they repent not then, they hardly ever do afterwards' (*Bengel*). *Alford*, '*He found no way, by repenting, to repair*' (i. e., to regain the lost blessing. 'No place for *changing* HIS FATHER'S *mind*' is a harsh interpretation. The "repentance" sought is *Esau's* own; but referring to the *real object* he sought, viz., the reversal of his forfeiture of the blessing. *Profane* despisers cast away grace, and, when overtaken by judgment, *seek repentance* (i. e., in *their* view of it, *escape from the penalty* of their sin), but in vain. Cf. "afterward," Matt. xxv. 11, 12. Tears are no proof of real repentance (1 Sam. xxiv. 16, 17: contrast Ps. lvi. 8). **it**—*the blessing*, the real object of Esau, though ostensibly seeking "repentance."
18. For—The fact that we are not under the law, but under the glorious privileges of the Gospel is why especially the Hebrew Christians should 'look diligently,' &c. (*vv.* 15, 16). **are not come** [*proseleluthate*]—'have not come near to.' Alluding to Deut. iv. 11, "Ye *came near* . . . and the mountain burned with fire . . . clouds, and thick darkness." 'In your *coming near unto God*, it has not been to,' &c. **the mount.** אAC, Vulgate, omit "the mount." "The mount" must be supplied from *v.* 22. **that might be touched**—palpable and material. Moses alone was allowed to touch it (Exod. xix. 12, 13). The Hebrews drew near to the material Sinai with material bodies; we to the spiritual mount in the spirit. The "darkness" was that of the clouds hanging round the mount; the "tempest" accompanied the thunder. **19. trumpet**—to rouse attention, and herald God's approach (Exod. xix. 16). **entreated that the word should not be spoken** [*prostethēnai*]—'that speech should not be *added* to them;' not that they refused the Word of God, but they wished that God should not Himself speak, but employ Moses as His mediating spokesman. "The voice of words" was the decalogue, spoken by God—a voice issued forth without *any* form being seen: after which "He *added* no more" (Deut. v. 22). **20. that which was commanded** [*to diastellomenon*]—viz., 'the (stern) interdict.' **And, &c.**—'*Even* if a beast (much more a man) touch,' &c. **or thrust through with a dart.** Omitted in אACΔf, Vulgate. The *full* interdict (Exod. xix. 12, 13) is abbreviated; the beast alone

22 and quake:) but ye are come ^q unto mount Sion, and ^runto the city of
the living God, the heavenly Jerusalem, ^sand to an innumerable company
23 of angels, to the general assembly and church of the first-born, which are
⁶written in heaven, and to God the Judge of all, and to the spirits of
24 just men ^tmade perfect, and to Jesus the Mediator of the new ⁷covenant,
and to the blood of sprinkling, that speaketh better things than *that*
of Abel.

A. D. 64.

q Gal. 4. 26.
r Phil. 3. 20.
s Ps. 68. 17.
6 Or,
enrolled.
t Phil 3. 12.
7 Or, testament.

being put for ' whether man or beast:' the *stoning*, which applies to *human* offenders, alone being specified ; the beast's punishment—viz., the being *thrust through with a dart*—being understood. 21. **the sight** [*to phantazomenon*]—the *vision* of God's majesty. **quake** [*entromos*]—' I am in trembling:' " fear " affected his *mind* ; ' trembling' his body. Moses in Exodus does not use these words. But Paul, by inspiration, supplies (cf. Acts xx. 35 ; 2 Tim. iii. 8) this detail. Deut. ix. 19, LXX., has like words of Moses, after breaking the two tables, through fear of God's anger at the people's sin in making the golden calves. He similarly ' feared' in hearing the ten commandments spoken by Jehovah. 22. **are come** [*proseleluthate*]—' have come near unto' (cf. Deut. iv. 11). Not merely ye *shall*, but *ye have already come*. **mount Sion** —antitypical Sion, of which the spiritual church (whose first foundation was laid in literal Zion, John xii. 15 ; 1 Pet. ii. 6) is the earnest, and of which the restored literal Jerusalem shall be the earthly representative, to be succeeded by the everlasting " new Jerusalem, coming down from God out of heaven" (Rev. xxi. 2-27 : cf. ch. xi. 10). **22, 23. to an innumerable company of angels, to the general assembly and church.** After the *city* of God, mention of its citizens follows. Believers being like the angels (Job i. 6 ; xxxviii. 7), " sons of God," adopted into God's great and blessed family, are their ' equals' (Luke xx. 36). For the full manifestation of this we pray (Matt. vi. 10). The English version is opposed—(1.) By " and " beginning each new member of the whole sentence ; (2.) " General assembly and church" form a tautology ; (3.) " General assembly," or ' *festal* (jubilant) full assembly' (such as the celebrated Olympic games, with joyous singing, &c.), applies better to the *angels*, ever hymning God's praises, than to the Church, of which a considerable part is militant on earth. Translate, ' To myriads (ten thousands, cf. Deut. xxxiii. 2 ; Ps. lxviii. 17 ; Dan. vii. 10 ; Jude 14; namely), the festal assembly of angels, and the church of the first-born.' Angels and saints together constitute the *ten thousands*. Cf. "*all* angels," " *all* nations" (Matt. xxv. 31, 32). Messiah is pre-eminently "the First-born," or " First-begotten" (ch. i. 6): all believers become so by adoption. Cf. the type, Num. iii. 12, 45, 50. As the kingly and priestly succession was in the first-born, and Israel was God's "first-born" (Exod. iv. 22: cf. xiii. 2 ; xix. 6), a "kingdom of priests" to God (Exod. xix. 6), so believers (Rev. i. 6). **written in heaven**—enrolled as citizens there. *All* who at the coming of " God the Judge of all" (which clause naturally follows) shall be found "written" *in the Lamb's book of life* (Rev. xxi. 27). Though fighting the good fight on earth, still, in your destiny and life of *faith*, which substantiates things hoped for, ye *are* already members of the heavenly citizenship. *Alford* wrongly restricts 'the church of the first-born written in heaven' to *those militant on earth ;* rather, *all* who *at the Judge's* coming shall be found written in heaven (the true patent of heavenly nobility; contrast "written in the earth," Jer. xvii. 13, and Esau's profane sale of his birthright, *v.* 16); believers from the beginning to the end of the world

form *one* church, to which the Hebrews were already come. The *first-born* of Israel were " written" in a roll (Num. iii. 40). **the spirits of just men made perfect**—at the resurrection, when the "JUDGE" shall appear, and perfect believers' bliss by uniting the glorified *body* with the *spirit:* the New Testament hope (Rom. viii. 20-23 ; 1 Thess. iv. 16). The place of this clause *after* " the JUDGE OF ALL " is my objection to *Alford's* explanation, the souls of the just *in their separate state perfected.* Cf. (note) ch. xi. 39, 40: those heretofore *spirits*, but now to be *perfected* by being clothed upon with the body. Still, "*spirits* of just men made perfect" may favour the reference to the *spirits* in their separate state, whose *perfecting* by earthly trials is completed. In no other passage are *the just* said to be *perfected* before the resurrection and the completion of the number of the elect (Rev. vi. 11); therefore, '*spirits* of the just' may be used to express *the just whose predominant element in their perfected state shall be Spirit.* So *spirit* is used of *a man in the body under the influence of the Spirit*, not the *flesh* (John iii. 6). In the resurrection *bodies* of the saints the *spirit* shall preponderate over the *animal soul* (note, 1 Cor. xv. 44). Others think Christ at His ascension carried the redeemed church from the paradise of Sheol or Hades to the paradise of the third or highest heaven (Matt. xxvii. 52, 53; Rom. x. 6, 7 ; Eph. iv. 9 ; 1 Pet. iii. 18, 20). **24. new** —not the usual [*kaine*]: the Christian covenant (ch. ix. 15): *new*, as *different from*, and superseding the *old ;* but [*nea*] recent, having the *freshness* of *youth*, as opposed to *age*. The mention of Jesus, *the Perfecter* of our faith (*v.* 2), Himself *perfected* through sufferings in His resurrection and ascension (ch. ii. 10; v. 9), is suggested by the mention of " the just *made perfect*" at their resurrection (cf. ch. vii. 22). "Jesus" stands here as the *person* realized as our loving Friend ; not merely in His *official* character as the *Christ*. **and to the blood of sprinkling**—enumerated distinct from "Jesus." *Bengel* argues: His blood was entirely ' poured out' by various ways. His bloody sweat, the crown of thorns, the scourging, the nails, and after death the spear, just as the blood was entirely poured out and extravasated from the animal sacrifices. It was *incorruptible* (1 Pet. i. 18, 19). No scripture states it was again put into the Lord's body. At His ascension, as our High Priest, He entered the heavenly holiest ' BY His own blood ' (not *after* shedding his blood, nor *with* the blood in His body, but), carrying it separately (cf. the type, ch. ix. 7, 12, 25; xiii. 11): not merely by the efficacy of His blood, but ' by *His own proper* blood' (ch. ix. 12): not MATERIAL blood, but " the blood of Christ, who through the eternal Spirit offered Himself without spot unto God" (ch. ix. 14). So in ch. x. 29, *the Son of God* and *the blood of the covenant wherewith* (the professor) *was sanctified* are separate. Also in ch. xiii. 12, 20; also cf. ch. x. 19 with 21. So in the Lord's Supper (1 Cor. x. 16; xi. 24-26) *the body* and *blood* are separately represented. The blood itself continues still in heaven before God, the perpetual ransom-price of ' the eternal covenant' (ch. xiii.

25   See that ye refuse not him that speaketh: for if they escaped not who
refused him ᵘthat spake on earth, much more *shall not* we *escape* if we
26 turn away from him that *speaketh* from heaven: whose ᵛvoice then shook
the earth; but now he hath promised, saying, ʷYet once more I shake
27 not the earth only, but also heaven. And this *word,* Yet once more,
signifieth ˣthe removing of those things that ⁸are shaken, as of things
that are made, that those things which cannot be shaken may remain.
28 Wherefore, we receiving a kingdom which cannot be moved, ⁹let us have

A. D. 64.

ᵘ Num. 16.
ᵛ Ex 19. 13.
ʷ Hag 2. 6.
ˣ Ps 102. 26.
Matt 24. 35.
⁸ Or, may be shaken.
⁹ Or, let us hold fast.

20). Once for all Christ sprinkled the blood peculiarly for us at his ascension (ch. ix. 12). But
it is called "the blood of sprinkling" on account
also of its continued use in heaven, and in the
consciences of the saints on earth (Isa. lii. 15;
ch. ix. 14; x. 22). This sprinkling is analogous to
the sprinkled blood of the passover. Cf. Rev. v.
6, "In the midst of the throne, a Lamb, *as it had
been slain.*" His glorified body does not require
circulation of blood. His blood introduced into
heaven took away the dragon's right to accuse.
Thus Rome's theory of *concomitancy* of the blood
with the body, the excuse for giving only the
bread to the laity, falls to the ground. The mention of "the blood of sprinkling" naturally follows
the mention of the "covenant," which could not be
consecrated without *blood* (ch. ix. 18, 22). **speaketh
better things than that of Abel**—viz., than the
sprinkling [אΑϹΔ read the article *masculine,
ton* (not *to*), which refers to "sprinkling," not to
"blood, *neuter*] of blood by Abel in his sacrifice
spake. This comparison between *two things of the
same kind* (viz., Christ's sacrifice and Abel's), is
more natural than between two things different
in kind and in results (viz., Christ's sacrifice and
Abel's own blood (*Alford*) which was not a sacrifice at all) (cf. ch. xi. 4; Gen. iv. 4). This accords
with the whole epistle (*vv.* 18-22), which is to show
the superiority of Christ's New Testament sacrifice
to the Old Testament sacrifices (of which Abel's
is the first; it, moreover, was testified to by God
as acceptable above Cain's) (cf. chs. ix. and x.)
"Better" implies superiority to something *good;*
but Abel's *own* blood was not at all good for the
purpose efficaciously wrought by Christ's blood,
nay, it cried for vengeance (cf. *Magee*, 'Atonement'). This is the objection to *Bengel's* view, that
"the blood of Abel" is put for *all* the blood shed
on earth crying for vengeance, and increasing the
other cries raised by sin, counteracted by Christ's
blood calmly speaking in heaven for us, and from
heaven to us. To deny that Christ's atonement
is a propitiation overthrows Christ's priesthood,
makes the Mosaic sacrifices an unmeaning mum-
mery, and Cain's sacrifice as good as that of Abel.

25. refuse not—through unbelief. As the *blood
of sprinkling speaks* to God *for* us (v. 24), so God
also *speaks* to us (ch. i. 1, 2). His word now pre-
ludes the last 'shaking' of all things, v. 27. The
same word which is heard in the Gospel *from
heaven* will shake *heaven and earth, v.* 26. **who
refused him** [*paraitēsamenoi*, without *hoi*]—'declining as they did.' Their submissive entreaty
that the word should not be spoken by God any
more (*v.* 19), covered over refractory hearts, as
their subsequent deeds showed (ch. iii. 16). **that
spake** [*ton chrematizonta*]—*with oracular warnings
His Divine will.* **if we turn away** [*hoi apostre-
phomenoi*]—'we who turn away;' greater refrac-
toriness than "refused" or 'declined.' **him that
speaketh from heaven**—God, by His Son in the
Gospel, speaking from His heavenly throne.
Hence Christ's frequent mention of 'the kingdom
of the heavens' (Greek, Matt. iv. 17). In giving
the law, God spake on earth (viz., mount Sinai)

by angels (ch. ii. 2: cf. ch. i. 2). In Exod. xx. 22,
"I talked with you *from heaven;*" not the highest
heavens (as here), but the visible heavens, the
clouds, are meant, out of which God proclaimed
the law. **26. then shook**—when He gave the
law. **now**—under the Gospel. **promised.** His
coming to break up the present order of things is
to the ungodly a terror, to the godly a *promise,*
the fulfilment of which they look for with joyful
hope. **Yet once more**—Notes, Hagg. ii. 6, 21, 22,
both which passages are condensed into one here.
The shaking began at His first coming: it will be
completed at His second coming, prodigies in
nature accompanying the overthrow of all kingdoms that oppose the Messiah. [עוֹד אַחַת מְעַט הִיא]
'It is yet one little'—*i. e.,* a single brief space till
the series of movements begins, ending in Messiah's
advent. Not merely the earth, as at the Sinaitic
covenant, but heaven also, is to be shaken. The
two advents of the Messiah are regarded as one,
the complete shaking belonging to the second, of
which the presage was given in the shakings at the
first; the convulsions connected with the overthrow of Jerusalem shadowing forth those about
to be at the overthrow of all the God-opposed
kingdoms by the coming Messiah. **27. this word,
Yet once more**—So Paul, by the Spirit, sanctions
the LXX. [*eti hapax*] (Hagg: ii. 6), giving an additional feature to the Hebrew (English version),
not merely that it shall be *in a little while,* but
that it is to be "*once* more." The stress is on
"ONCE." *Once for all and for ever.* 'In saying
"once more," the Spirit implies that something
else shall be which is to remain, no more to be
changed, for the *once* is inclusive—i. e., *not many
times' (Estius).* **those things that are shaken**—
heaven and earth. As the shaking is to be *total,*
so shall the removal be, making way for the better
things that are unremovable. Cf. the Jewish
economy (type of the present order of things) giving
way to the new and abiding covenant, the forerunner of the everlasting state. **as of things that
are made**—viz., of this present *visible creation* (cf.
2 Cor. v. 1 and ch. ix. 11), 'made with hands
. . . of this creation'—*i. e.,* things so *made* at
creation that they would not remain of themselves. The new abiding heaven and earth are
also *made,* but of a higher nature than material
creation, and partaking of the Divine nature of
Him who is *not made:* so, as linked with the uncreated God, they are not of the same class as the
things made. The things *made* in the former sense
do *not remain;* the things of the new heaven and
earth, like the uncreated God, "shall REMAIN
before God" (Isa. lxvi. 22). The spirit, the seed
of the new being, not only of the believer's soul,
but also of the future body, is an *uncreated* and
immortal principle. **28. receiving**—as we do, in
sure hope, also in possession of the Spirit, the first-
fruits (Rom. viii. 23; Eph. i. 13). **let us have
grace** [*echomen charin*]—'thankfulness' (*Alford*
after *Chrysostom*). But (1.) this, though classical
Greek, is not Paul's phraseology. (2.) 'To God'
would then have been added. (3.) "Whereby
we may serve God" suits "grace" (*i. e.,* the work

grace, whereby we may serve God acceptably with reverence and godly
29 fear: for our God *is* a consuming fire.

13 LET brotherly love continue. Be ^anot forgetful to entertain strangers:
2, for thereby ^b some have entertained angels unawares. Remember ^c them
3 that are in bonds, as bound with them; *and* them which suffer adversity,
4 as being yourselves also in the body. Marriage *is* honourable in all, and
the bed undefiled: but whoremongers and adulterers God will judge.
5 *Let your* conversation *be* without covetousness; *and be* content with such
things as ye have: for he hath said, ^d I will never leave thee, nor forsake
6 thee. So that we may boldly say, ^e The Lord *is* my helper, and I will
not fear what man shall do unto me.
7 Remember them which ¹ have the rule over you, who have spoken unto
you the word of God; whose faith follow, considering the end of *their*
8 conversation; Jesus Christ ^f the same yesterday, and to-day, and for ever.
9 Be not carried about with divers and strange doctrines. For *it is* a good

A. D. 64.

CHAP. 13.
^a Matt. 25.35.
^b Gen. 18. 3.
  Gen. 19. 2.
^c Matt. 25.36.
  Rom. 12.15.
  1 Cor.12.26.
^d Gen. 28. 15.
  Ps. 37. 25.
^e Ps. 27. 1.
  Ps. 118. 6.
1 Or, are the guides.
^f John 8. 58.
1 Cor. 1. 24.
Eph. 4. 5.
ch .1. 12.
Rev. 1. 4.

of the Spirit, producing faith exhibited in *serving God*), but does not suit 'thankfulness.' **acceptably** [*euarestōs*]—'well-pleasingly.' **reverence and godly fear** [so C, *aidous kai eulabeias*: but א A C Δ, *eulabeias kai deous*]—'*reverent caution*' (note, ch. v. 7: lest we should offend God, who is of purer eyes than to behold iniquity) '*and fear*' (lest we should bring destruction on ourselves). **29.** [*kai gar*] 'For even;' 'For also:' an *additional* incentive to diligence. From Deut. iv. 24. **our God**—in whom *we hope*, is also to be *feared*. He is *love*, yet He has also *wrath* against sin (ch. x. 27, 31).

CHAP. XIII. 1-25.—EXHORTATION TO GRACES, ESPECIALLY CONSTANCY IN FOLLOWING JESUS AMIDST REPROACHES—CONCLUSION—PIECES OF INTELLIGENCE—SALUTATIONS.

1. brotherly love—a distinct manifestation of "charity" (2 Pet. i. 7). The church of Jerusalem, to which in part this epistle was addressed, was distinguished by this grace (Acts ii. 45; iv. 34, 35; xi. 29, 30: cf. ch. vi. 10; x. 32-34; xii. 12, 13). **continue**—*charity* will itself *continue*. See that it *continue with you* (1 Cor. xiii. 8). **2.** Two manifestations of "brotherly love"—*hospitality* and *care for those in bonds*. **Be not forgetful.** They all recognized the duty, but might forget to act on it (*vv.* 3, 7, 16). The enemies of Christianity themselves noticed this virtue among Christians (*Julian*, 'Ep.' 49), **entertained angels unawares** —Abraham and Lot (Gen. xviii. 2; xix. 1). To obviate the natural distrust of strangers, Paul says an unknown guest may be better than he looks: he may be found as much a *messenger* of God for good as the angels (whose name means *messenger*) are; nay more, if a Christian, he represents Christ. There is ʒ play on the same Greek [*epilanthanesthe-elathon*]: let *not* the duty of *hospitality to strangers escape* you; for, by *entertaining strangers*, it has *escaped* the entertainers that they were entertaining angels. *Not unconscious* of the duty, they have *unconsciously* brought on themselves the blessing. **3. Remember**—in prayer and acts of kindness. **bound with them**—by the unity of the members under one Head (1 Cor. xii. 26). **suffer adversity** [*kakouchoumenōn*]—'are in evil state.' **being yourselves also in the body**—so liable to the adversities incident to the body, which ought to dispose you the more to sympathize with them, not knowing how soon your turn of suffering may come. 'One experiences adversity almost his whole life, as Jacob; another in youth, as Joseph; another in manhood, as Job; another in old age' (*Bengel*). **4. is.** Translate, 'Let marriage be *treated* as honourable;' as *v.* 5 is an exhortation. **in all**—'among all.' "To avoid for-

nication, let EVERY MAN have his own wife" (1 Cor. vii. 2). Judaism and Gnosticism soon after disparaged marriage. Paphnutius, in the council of Nice, quoted this verse to justify the married state. If one does not himself marry, he should not prevent others. Romanists translate, 'in all *things*,' as in *v.* 18. But the contrast to "*whoremongers* and *adulterers*" in the parallel clause requires the "in all" in this clause to refer to *persons*. **the bed undefiled** [*hē koitē amiantos* requires "undefiled" to be a *predicate*, not an epithet]—'and let the bed *be* undefiled.' **God will judge.** Most whoremongers escape human tribunals; but God takes cognizance of those whom man does not punish. Gay immoralities will be regarded very differently from what they are now. **5. conversation** [*ho tropos*]—'manner of life.' Lust and lucre follow one another as closely akin, both seducing the heart from the Creator to the creature. **such things as ye have** [*tois parousin*]—'present things' (Phil. iv. 11). **I will never leave thee, nor forsake thee**—so to Jacob, Gen. xxviii. 15; to Israel, Deut. xxxi. 6, 8; to Joshua, Josh. i. 5; to Solomon, 1 Chr. xxviii. 20. It is a Divine adage. What was said to them extends to us. He will neither withdraw His *presence* ("never leave") nor His *help* ("nor forsake thee") (*Bengel*). **6. may** [*ωστε θαρροῦντας λέγειν*]—rather, confidence actually realized, 'so that we confidently *say*' (Ps. lvi. 4, 11; cxviii. 6). Both the Hebrew (Ps. cxviii. 6) and the Greek [*ti poiesei*: not *poiesē*] require 'And (so) I will not fear: what (then) shall man do unto me?'

7. Remember—so as to imitate: not to *invoke*, as Rome teaches. **have the rule**—rather [*tōn hēgoumenon humōn*], 'those who (*were*) your (spiritual) *leaders*.' **who** [*hoitines*]—'*as being persons who*.' **have spoken** [*elalēsan*]—'spake' during their lifetime. This epistle was among those later written, when many heads of the Jerusalem church had passed away. **whose faith**—even unto death: probably by martyrdom, as in the instances of *faith* in ch. xi. 35. Stephen, James the brother of our Lord and bishop of Jerusalem, as well as James the brother of John (Acts xii. 2), in the *Palestinian* church, suffered martyrdom. **considering** [*anatheorountes*]—'looking up to:' 'contemplating all over,' as an artist would a model. **the end**—the *exit*, *issue*. [*Ekbasin* expresses a *way of escape* (1 Cor. x. 13): such is *death* to the martyr (Isa. lvii. 1).] **of their conversation** [*anastrophes*]—'manner of life;' 'walk' (Gal. i. 13; Eph. iv. 22; 1 Tim. iv. 12; Jas. iii. 13). *Considering* how their *walk* and its *end* (their death by martyrdom) evidenced the power of "faith," (ch. xi.) **9.** This verse is not in apposition with "the

thing that the heart be established with grace; not with meats, which
10 have not profited them that have been occupied therein. We ^{g} have an
altar, whereof they have no right to eat which serve the tabernacle.
11　For ^{h} the bodies of those beasts, whose blood is brought into the sanc-
12 tuary by the high priest for sin, are burnt without the camp. Wherefore Jesus also, that he might sanctify the people with his own blood,
13 suffered 'without the gate. Let us go forth therefore unto him without

A. D. 64.

^{g} 1 Cor. 9. 13.
1 Cor. 10. 18.
^{h} Ex. 29. 14.
Lev 4. 11.
Lev. 6. 30.
Lev. 9. 11.
^{i} John 19. 17.
Acts 7. 58.

end of their conversation" (v. 7), but forms the transition, Greek order: 'Jesus Christ, yesterday and to-day (is) the same, and (shall be the same) unto the ages' (i. e., unto all ages). The *Jesus Christ* (the full name marks with affectionate solemnity His *person* and His *office*) who supported your spiritual *rulers* through life unto their *end* "yesterday" (in times past), being at once 'the Author and the Finisher of their faith' (ch. xii. 2), remains still the same Jesus Christ "to-day," ready to help you also, if you too walk by "faith." Cf. "this same Jesus," Acts i. 11. He who *yesterday* (the past time) suffered and died is *to-day* in glory (Rev. i. 18). 'As night comes between yesterday and to-day, yet is itself swallowed up by *yesterday* and *to-day*; so the glory of Jesus Christ which was of yesterday, and that which is to-day, was not so interrupted by His *suffering* as not to continue the same. He is the same *yesterday*, before He came into the world, and *to-day*, in heaven: *yesterday* in the time of our predecessors, and *to-day* in our age' (*Bengel*). So the doctrine is the *same*, not variable: the transition from *v*. 7 to *v*. 9. He is always "the same" (ch. i. 12); the same in the Old and New Testaments. **about** [*peripheresthe*]. א A C Δ, Vulgate, read [*parapheresthe*] 'carried *aside*'—viz., cf. Eph. iv. 14. **divers** [*poikilais*]—differing from the one faith in the same Jesus Christ, as taught by them who had the rule over you (v. 7). **strange**—foreign to the truth. **established with grace; not with meats**—not with Jewish distinctions between clean and unclean meats, to which ascetic Judaizers added the rejection of some meats and the use of others: noticed also by *Paul* in 1 Cor. viii. 8, 13; vi. 13. Rom. xiv. 17, an exact parallel: some of the "divers and strange doctrines." Christ's body offered once for us is our true spiritual 'meat' to "eat" (v. 10), "the stay and the staff . . . of bread" (Isa. iii. 1), the mean of all "grace." **which have not profited**—'in which they who walked were not profited' as to justification and perfect cleansing of the conscience. Cf. on "walked," Acts xxi. 21—viz., with superstitious scrupulosity, as though God's true worship consisted in legal observances. **10.** Christianity and Judaism are so totally distinct that 'they who serve the (Jewish) tabernacle' have no right to eat our spiritual meat—viz., the Jewish priests, and those who follow their guidance in serving ceremonial ordinance. He says, "serve *the tabernacle*;" not 'serve IN' it: servile worship. Contrast Phil. iii. 3. **an altar**—Christ's cross, whereon His body was offered. The Lord's table represents the cross, as the bread and wine represent the sacrifice offered on it. Our meat which we by faith spiritually eat is the flesh of Christ, in contrast to typical "meats." The two cannot be combined (Gal. v. 2). *Bishop Waldegrave* explains the "altar," Christ's *Godhead*, on which He offered His *manhood;* for (1.) "The altar . . . sanctifieth the gift" (Matt. xxiii. 19); (2.) Prevents the sacrifice being consumed, as the manhood would have been by God's judicial wrath but for the Godhead. Neither holds good of the *cross*, contact with which involved a curse. Rather, Christ, at once the *Altar*, the *Sacrifice*, and the *Priest*. "We

have" Him by faith: so need no further sacrifice or sacrificial "meats" (note, Rev. vi. 9). That not a literal eating of the sacrifice of Christ is meant in the Lord's supper, but a spiritual, appears from comparing v. 9 with v. 10, "with GRACE, NOT with MEATS." As the sacerdotal priest's duty was to 'wait at the altar,' so the Christian minister's is to "preach the Gospel" (1 Cor. ix. 13, 14).
11, 12. As "the bodies of those beasts, whose blood is brought into the sanctuary by, &c., are burnt without the camp," so "Jesus also, that, &c., suffered *without the gate*" of *ceremonial Judaism*, of which His crucifixion outside the gate of Jerusalem is a type. **For**—Reason why they who serve the tabernacle are excluded from share in Christ, because their religion is mainly concerned with "meats" (v. 9); but His sacrifice is not like those sacrifices in which they have meats, but answers to one 'wholly burnt' [*katakaietai*] 'burnt down,' which consequently *they could not eat of:* Lev. vi. 30, "No sin offering, whereof any of the blood is brought into the tabernacle of the congregation to reconcile withal in the holy place, shall be eaten; it shall be burnt in the fire." The sin offerings are twofold—the *outward*, whose blood was sprinkled on the outward altar, and of whose bodies the priests might eat; and the *inward*, the reverse. Not "we," but "*have*" and "*eat*," are emphatical in the Greek. We have the benefit of Christ's *sin offering*, not by literal *eating;* for His offering is one of a kind which "they who serve the tabernacle" have no right to "*eat*" (literally)—*i. e.*, a *burnt offering: v*. 11, "for the bodies, &c., are *burnt* without the camp" (Col. ii. 16). The sin offering, the fullest representative of Christ's atonement, has no eating of meats. On the Hebrews' own ground, Paul shows the heart must be established with grace, not *meats, v*. 9. Our eating of Christ's flesh is *figurative* of spiritual realities, as the *sacrifice* of "praise" and 'doing good' is figurative (vv. 15, 16). "We have an altar" cannot mean that Paul speaks *as a Jew* of the *temple altar;* for, after having proved the Jewish sacrifices were superseded by Christ's one sacrifice, he never would identify himself with his countrymen in retaining the superseded altar. **the sanctuary**—*the Holy of holies*, into which the blood of the sin offering was brought on the day of atonement. **without the camp**—in which were the tabernacle, Levitical priests, and legal worshippers, during Israel's journey through the wilderness; replaced afterwards by Jerusalem (containing the temple), outside of whose walls Jesus was crucified. **Wherefore Jesus**—That the Antitype might fulfil the type. **sanctify.** Though not brought into the temple "sanctuary" (v. 11), His blood has been brought into the heavenly, and 'sanctifies the people' (ch. ii. 11, 17), by cleansing them from sin, and consecrating them to God. **his own**—not blood of animals. **without the gate**—of Jerusalem; as if unworthy of the society of the covenant-people. The fiery ordeal of His *suffering* answers to the *burning* of the victim; thereby His fleshly life was completely destroyed, as their bodies were: the second part of His offering was His carrying His blood into the heavenly Holiest before God at His ascension,

14 the camp, bearing [j]his reproach. For [k]here have we no continuing
15 city, but we seek one to come. By him therefore let us offer [l]the sacrifice of praise to God continually, that is, the fruit of *our* lips [2]giving thanks to his name.
16   But to do good and to communicate forget not; for with such sacrifices
17 God is well pleased. Obey them that [3]have the rule over you, and submit yourselves: [m]for they watch for your souls, as they that must give account, that they may do it with joy, and not with grief: for that
18 *is* unprofitable for you. Pray for us: for we trust we have a good

A. D. 64.

[j] 1 Pet. 4. 14.
[k] Mic. 2. 10.
[l] Lev. 7. 12.
Ps. 50. 14.
Eph. 5. 19.
[2] confessing to.
[3] Or. guide.
[m] Eze. 3. 17
Eze. 33. 2, 7.

to be a perpetual atonement for sin. **13. therefore**—breathes deliberate fortitude (*Bengel*). **without the camp**—'outside the legal polity' (*Theodoret*) of Judaism (cf. *v.* 11). 'Faith considers Jerusalem as a *camp*, not a *city*.' The reason is given *v.* 14 (*Bengel*). He contrasts with the earthly sanctuary (ch. viii. 5), which the Jews "serve," the altar in heaven which "we have," but which Judaizers "have no right to." As Jesus suffered without the gate, so spiritually must those who belong to Him withdraw from the earthly Jerusalem and its sanctuary, as from this world in general, of which it is the representative: ch. ix. 1, "a worldly sanctuary." We must leave all sacerdotal ritualism and sensuous worship to offer spiritual sacrifices at the spiritual altar (Christ) which we carry with us everywhere (Ezek. xi. 16, end). Referring to Exod. xxxiii. 7, when the tabernacle was moved *without the camp*, then polluted by the people's idolatry of the golden calves, so that "every one which sought the Lord went out unto *the tabernacle of the congregation* (as Moses called it), which was without the camp:" **a** lively type of what the Hebrews should do—viz., come out of the carnal worship of earthly Jerusalem to worship God in Christ in spirit (2 Cor. v. 16), since here we have "no continuing city," *v.* 14. **bearing**—as Simon of Cyrene. **his reproach**—that which He bare, and all His people bear with Him. **14. here**—on earth. Those who clung to the earthly sanctuary represent all who cling to this earth. The earthly Jerusalem proved to be no "abiding city," having been destroyed shortly after: with it fell the Jewish civil and religious polity: a type of the whole earthly order of things soon to perish. **one to come** (ch. ii. 5; xi. 10, 14, 16; xii. 22; Phil. iii. 20). **15.** As the "altar" was mentioned, *v.* 10, so the "sacrifice" here (cf. 1 Pet. ii. 5—viz., *praise* and *doing good, v.* 16). Cf. Ps. cxix. 108; Rom. xii. 1. **By him**—as Mediator of our prayers and praises (John xiv. 13, 14); not by Jewish observances (Ps. l. 14, 23; lxix. 30, 31; cvii. 22; cxvi. 17). The rabbis had an old saying, 'At a future time all sacrifices shall cease, but praises shall not.' **praise**—for salvation. **continually**—not merely at fixed seasons, as those on which the legal sacrifices were offered, but all our life long. **fruit of our lips** (Isa. lvii. 19; Hos. xiv. 2). **giving thanks** [*homologountōn*] (our lips)—'confessing.' *Bengel*, The Hebrew [*Todah*] is beautifully emphatic: literally *acknowledyment* or *confession.* In praising a creature, we may easily exceed the truth; but in praising God, we have only to go on *confessing* what He really is to us. Hence it is impossible to exceed the truth: here is *genuine* praise.
16. But—But the sacrifice of praise with the lips (*v.* 15) is not enough; there must be also *doing good* and communicating (*i. e.*, imparting of your means, Gal. vi. 6) to the needy. **with such**—not mere ritualistic sacrifices. **17. Obey them that have the rule over you** (cf. *vv.* 7, 24). This threefold mention of *rulers* is peculiar to this epistle. In others, Paul includes the *rulers* in his

exhortations. Here, the address is to the *general body of the Church*, as distinguished from the *rulers*, to whom they are charged to yield reverent submission. This is just what might be expected when the apostle of the Gentiles was writing to the *Palestine Christians*, among whom James and the eleven had exercised immediate authority. It was important he should not seem to interfere with their guides, but rather strengthen their hands: he claims no authority directly or indirectly over these rulers (*Birks*). "Remember" deceased rulers (*v.* 7); "obey" your living rulers: not only *obey* where no sacrifice of self is required, and where you are *persuaded* they are right [so *peithesthe:* "obey"], but [*hupeikete*] "*submit*" with dutiful *yielding* when your natural judgment and will are averse. **they** [*autoi*]—on their part: as they do their part, so do you yours. So Paul, 1 Thess. v. 12, 13. **watch** [*agrupnousin*]—'are vigilant.' **for** [*huper*]—'in behalf of.' **must give account**—the strongest stimulus to *watchfulness* (Mark xiii. 34-37). *Chrysostom* ('De Sacerdotio,' b. vi.), 'The fear of this threat continually agitates my soul.' **do it**—"watch for your souls." It is a perilous responsibility for one to have to give account for others, who is not sufficient for his own (*Estius*, from *Aquinas*). I wonder whether it be possible that any rulers should be saved (*Chrysostom*). Cf. Paul's address to the elders, Acts xx. 28; 1 Cor. iv. 1-5, where also he connects ministers' responsibility with the account to be hereafter given (cf. 1 Pet. v. 4). **with joy**—at your obedience: anticipating, too, that you shall be their "joy" in the day of giving account (Phil. iv. 1). **not with grief**—at your disobedience: apprehending also that you may be among the lost, instead of being their crown of rejoicing. In giving account, the stewards are liable to blame if aught be lost to the Master. 'Mitigate their toil by every attention, that with alacrity, rather than grief, they may fulfil their duty, arduous enough in itself, even though no unpleasantness be added on your part' (*Grotius*). **that.** *Grief* in your pastors is *unprofitable for you*, for it weakens their spiritual power. 'The *groans* [*stenazontes:* 'grief'] of other creatures are heard; how much more of pastors!' (*Bengel*): God may avenge on you their 'groaning.' If they must render God an account of their negligence, so must you for your ingratitude (*Grotius*). **18. Pray for us.** Paul usually requests the church's intercessions in closing his epistles, as he begins with assuring them of his having them at heart in his prayers (but in this epistle not till *vv.* 20, 21) (Rom. xv. 30). "Us" includes himself and his companions; he passes to himself alone, *v.* 19. **we trust we have a good conscience**—in spite of former jealousies, and the charges of my Jewish enemies at Jerusalem, which are the occasion of my imprisonment at Rome. In refutation of the Jews' aspersions, he asserts in the same language his own *conscientiousness* before God and man, Acts xxiii. 1-3; xxiv. 16, 20, 21 (so that his reply to Ananias was not mere impatience; for it was a prophecy which he was inspired to

19 conscience, in all things willing to live honestly. But I beseech *you* the
rather to do this, that I may be restored to you the sooner.
20 Now the God of peace, that brought again from the dead our Lord
Jesus, [n]that great Shepherd of the sheep, [o]through the blood of the
21 everlasting [4]covenant, make you perfect in every good work to do his
will, [5]working in you that which is well-pleasing in his sight, through
Jesus Christ; [p]to whom *be* glory for ever and ever. Amen.
22 And I beseech you, brethren, suffer the word of exhortation: for I have
written a letter unto you in few words.
23 Know ye that [q]*our* brother Timothy is [r]set at liberty; with whom, if
24 he come shortly, I will see you. Salute all them that have the rule over
25 you, and all the saints. They of Italy salute you. Grace *be* with you
all. Amen.

Written to the Hebrews from Italy by Timothy.

A. D. 64.
[n] Isa 40. 11. Eze 34. 23. Eze. 37. 24. John 10. 11.
[o] Zech. 9. 11. Matt. 26. 28. Luke 22. 20.
[4] Or, testament.
[5] Or, doing.
[p] Gal. 1. 5.
[q] Acts 16 1-3. 1 Thes. 3. 2.
[r] 1 Tim 6. 12. 2 Tim. 1. 8. Phile. 1.

utter, and which was fulfilled soon after). "We trust" [*pepoithamen*], C, Vulgate. But [*peithometha*] 'we are persuaded,' in A C Δ. Good conscience produces confidence, where the Holy Spirit rules (Rom. ix. 1). **honestly** [*kalōs*]—'in a *good* way.' The same Greek as "*good* (right) conscience:" lit., *rightly*. **19. the rather** [*perissoterōs*]—'*I the more abundantly* beseech you.' **to do this**—to pray for me. **that I may be restored to you** (Phile. 22). It is here first he mentions himself so unobtrusively as not to prejudice his Hebrew readers against him, which they would have been had he commenced this, as other epistles, with authoritatively announcing his name and apostolic commission.

20. *Concluding Prayer.* **God of peace.** So Paul, Rom. xv. 33; xvi. 20; 2 Cor. xiii. 11; Phil. iv. 9; 1 Thess. v. 23; 2 Thess. iii. 16. Judaizing was calculated to sow seeds of discord, disobedience to pastors (*v.* 17), and alienation towards Paul. *The God of peace*, by giving unity of doctrine, will unite in mutual love. **brought again from the dead** [*anagagon*]—'brought up,' &c.: God brought up the Shepherd; the Shepherd shall bring the flock. Here only he mentions the resurrection. He would not conclude without the connecting link between the two truths discussed—the *one perfect sacrifice* and the *continual priestly intercession*—the depth of His humiliation and the height of His glory—the "altar" of the cross and the ascension to the heavenly Holy of holies. **Lord Jesus**—the title marking His *person* and His *Lordship*. But *v.* 21, "through Jesus *Christ*." His *office*, as *Anointed* of the Spirit, making Him the medium of communicating the Spirit to us, the unction flowing down from the Head on the members (cf. Acts ii. 36). **great** (ch. iv. 14). **Shepherd of the sheep**—a title familiar to Hebrew readers, from their Old Testament (Isa. xl. 11; lxiii. 11 [*ton poimena tōn probatōn*]; LXX.): primarily *Moses*, antitypically *Christ*; already compared ch. iii. 2-7. The transition is natural from earthly pastors (*v.* 17) to the Chief Pastor, as in 1 Pet. v. 1-4. Cf. Ezek. xxxiv. 23 and Jesus' words, John x. 2, 11, 14. **through the blood**—'in:' *in virtue of* the blood (ch. ii. 9). The "blood" was seal of the everlasting covenant between the Father and Son (ch. x. 29); *in virtue of the Son's blood*, first Christ was raised (Phil. ii. 6-10), then Christ's people shall be so (Zech. ix. 11, referred to here: Acts xx. 28). **everlasting**—its *everlastingness* necessitated the resurrection. "The blood of the everlasting covenant" is a summary retrospect of the epistle (cf. ch. ix. 12). **21. Make you perfect**—properly healing a rent [*katartisai*]: *join you together in perfect harmony* (*Bengel*). **to do his will, working in you** [*poiōn*] (ch. x. 36)—*doing* in you. Whatever good we *do*, God *does* in us (Phil. ii. 13). **well-pleasing in his sight** (Isa. liii. 10; Eph. v. 10). **through Jesus Christ**—'God *doing* in you that, &c., *through Jesus Christ*' (Phil. i. 11). **to whom.** He closes, as he began (ch. i.), with glory to Christ.

22. suffer the word. The Hebrews not being the section assigned to Paul (but the Gentiles), he uses gentle entreaty rather than authoritative command. **few words**—compared with what might be said on so important a subject. *Few*, in an epistle more a *treatise* than an epistle (cf. 1 Pet. v. 12). On the seeming inconsistency with Gal. vi. 11, cf. note.

23. our brother Timothy. So Paul, 1 Cor. iv. 17; 2 Cor. i. 1; Col. i. 1; 1 Thess. iii. 2. **is set at liberty**—from prison. So Aristarchus was imprisoned with Paul. Timothy probably, after sharing Paul's imprisonment, was set free by the death of Nero. *Birks* translates [*apolelumenon*] 'sent away'—viz., on a mission to Greece, as Paul promised (Phil. ii. 19). However, *some* previous detention is implied before his being *let go* to Philippi. Paul, though at large, was still *in Italy*, whence he sends salutations of Italian Christians (*v.* 24), waiting for Timothy to join him, so as to start for Jerusalem. We know from 1 Tim. i. 3, he and Timothy were together at Ephesus after his departing from Italy eastward. He probably left Timothy there and went to Philippi, as he had promised. Paul implies, that if Timothy shall not *come shortly*, he will start on his journey to the Hebrews at once. **24. all.** The Scriptures are for *all*, young and old; not merely for ministers. Cf. the different classes addressed—"wives," Eph. v. 22; "little children," 1 John ii. 18; "all," 1 Pet. iii. 8; v. 5. He says "all;" for the Hebrews were not all in one place, though the Jerusalem Hebrews are chiefly addressed. **They of Italy**—not merely the brethren at Rome, but of other places in Italy. **25.** *Paul's* characteristic salutation in every one of his other thirteen epistles, as he says himself, 1 Cor. xvi. 21, 23; Col. iv. 18; 2 Thess. iii. 17, 18. It is found in no epistle written by any other apostle in Paul's lifetime, being known to be his badge. It is used in Rev. xxii. 21 subsequently, and in *Clement* of Rome. Greek, '*The* grace (viz., of our Lord Jesus Christ) be with you all.'

THE GENERAL EPISTLE OF

JAMES.

1 JAMES, *a* a servant of God and of the Lord Jesus Christ, *b* to the twelve
tribes which *c* are scattered abroad, greeting.
2 My brethren, count it all joy when ye fall into divers temptations;
3, knowing *this*, that the trying of your faith worketh patience. But let
4 patience have *her* perfect work, that ye may be perfect and entire,
wanting nothing.
5 If *d* any of you lack wisdom, *e* let him ask of God, that giveth to all
6 *men* liberally, and upbraideth not; and *f* it shall be given him. But *g* let
him ask in faith, nothing wavering. For he that wavereth is like a
7 wave of the sea driven with the wind and tossed. For let not that man

A. D. 60.

CHAP. 1.
a Matt. 10. 3.
Gal. 1. 19.
Gal. 2. 9.
b Acts 26. 7.
c John 7. 35.
Acts 2 5.
d 1 Ki. 3. 9.
e John 15. 7.
f Jer. 29. 12.
g 1 Tim. 2. 8.

CHAP. I. 1-27.—INSCRIPTION: ON HEARING, SPEAKING, AND WRATH. The last subject is discussed in ch. iii. 13; iv. 7.

1. James— an apostle of the circumcision, with Peter and John; James in Jerusalem, Palestine, and Syria; Peter in Babylon and the East; John in Ephesus and Asia Minor. St. Peter addresses the dispersed *Jews of Pontus, Galatia, Cappadocia;* St. James, the *Israelites of the twelve tribes scattered abroad.* **servant of God**— not that he was not an *apostle;* for Paul, an apostle, also calls himself so; but as addressing the Israelites generally, including indirectly the unbelieving, he in humility omits "apostle:" so Paul in writing to the Hebrews; similarly Jude, an apostle, in his general epistle. **Jesus Christ** — not mentioned again, save in ch. ii. 1: not at all in his speeches (Acts xv. 14, 15, and xxi. 20, 21), lest his introducing the name oftener should seem to arise from vanity, he being "the Lord's brother" (*Bengel*). His teaching being practical, rather than doctrinal, required less express mention of Christ. **scattered abroad** [*tais en tē diaspora*]—'*which are in the dispersion.*' The dispersion of the Israelites, and their connection with Jerusalem as a centre of religion, was a divinely-ordered means of propagating Christianity. The pilgrim troops of the law became caravans of the Gospel (*Wordsworth*). **greeting**—in no other Christian letter but in James and the Jerusalem Synod's epistle to the Gentile churches: an undesigned coincidence and mark of genuineness. [*Chairein*, "greeting," is akin to *charan*, "joy," to which they are exhorted amidst distresses from poverty and consequent oppression: cf. Rom. xv. 26.]

2. My brethren—often in St. James, marking community of nation and of faith. **all joy**—cause for the highest joy (*Grotius*). Nothing but joy. Count *all* "divers temptations" to be *each* matter of *joy* (*Bengel*). **fall into**—unexpectedly, so as to be *encompassed by* them [*peripēsete*]. **temptations** —not allurements to sin, but *trials* which test and purify the Christian character. Some to whom St. James writes were "sick," or otherwise "afflicted" (ch. v. 13). Every possible trial to the child of God is a masterpiece of strategy of the Captain of his salvation for his good. **3. the trying** [*to dokimion*]—the *testing* or *proving* of your faith—viz., by "divers temptations." Cf. Rom. v. 3, "*tribulation* worketh patience; and patience, experience" [*dokime*, akin to *dokimion*: there *experience;* here the "trying" or *testing* whence experience flows]. **patience** [*hupomone*]—'*persevering endurance*' (cf. Luke viii. 15). **4. Let** endurance have a perfect *work* (taken out of "*worketh* patience" or endurance); *i. e.,* have its *full effect,* by showing perfect endurance—viz., joy in the cross (*Menochius*), and enduring to the end (Matt. x. 22) (*Calvin*). **ye may be perfect**— fully developed in all the attributes of a Christian. "Joy" is an essential of the "perfect work" of probation. 'If *God's* teaching by patience have had a perfect work in you, *you* are perfect' (*Alford*). **entire** [*holokleroi*]—with all *its parts complete, wanting no integral part:* 1 Thess. v. 23, "your whole (*lit.,* 'entire') spirit and soul and body:" as "perfect" implies *without a blemish in its parts.*

5. Greek, 'BUT (as this *perfect entireness* is no easy attainment) if any,' &c. **lack**—rather, as the Greek is repeated, after St. James's manner, from *v.* 4, "*wanting* nothing." 'If any of you *want* wisdom,' whereby to "count it all joy when ye fall into divers temptations," and "let patience have her perfect work." This "wisdom" is shown in its effects, ch. iii. 17. The highest wisdom governs patience alike in poverty and riches (*vv.* 9, 10). **ask** (ch. iv. 2). **liberally** [*haplōs*]—*with simplicity* (Rom. xii. 8). God gives without adding aught to take from the graciousness of the gift (*Alford*). God requires the same 'simplicity' in His children ("eye . . . single," Matt. vi. 22: *lit., simple*). **upbraideth not**—an illustration of *simply.* God gives to the suppliant without upbraiding him with past ingratitude, or future abuse of God's goodness. The Jews pray, 'Let me not have need of the gifts of men, whose gifts are few, but their upbraidings manifold; but give me out of thy large hand.' Cf. Solomon's prayer for "wisdom," and God's gift above what he asked, though God foresaw his future abuse of it would deserve very differently. St. James has before his eye the sermon on the mount (see 'Introduction'). God hears every true prayer, and grants either the thing asked or something better: as a good physician consults his patient's good, better by denying what the latter asks, not for his good, than by conceding a temporary gratification to his hurt. **6. ask in faith**—*i. e.,* the persuasion that God can and will give. St. James begins and ends with *faith.* In the middle of the epistle he removes hindrances to faith, and shows its true character (*Bengel*). **wavering** [*diakrinomenos*]—between belief and unbelief. Cf. the Israelites who seemed to believe in God's power, but leant to unbelief by 'limiting' it (Ps. lxxviii. 41). Contrast Acts x. 20; Rom. iv. 20 ("*staggered not* . . . through unbelief;" lit., '*wavered not*') (1 Tim. ii. 8). **like a wave of the sea** (Isa. lvii. 20; Eph. iv. 14) [*klu-*

8 think that he shall receive any thing of the Lord. A double-minded man *is* unstable in all his ways.

9, Let the brother of low degree [1]rejoice in that he is exalted; but the
10 rich, in that he is made low: because as the flower of the grass he shall
11 pass away. For the sun is no sooner risen with a burning heat, but it withereth the grass, and the flower thereof falleth, and the grace of the fashion of it perisheth: so also shall the rich man fade away in his ways.

12 Blessed [h]*is* the man that endureth temptation: for when he is tried, he shall receive [i]the crown of life, which the Lord hath promised to
13 them that love him. Let no man say when he is tempted, I am tempted of God: for God cannot be tempted with [2]evil, neither tempteth he any
14 man; but every man is tempted, when he is drawn away of his own lust,
15 and enticed. Then, when lust hath conceived, it bringeth forth sin; and sin, when it is finished, bringeth forth death.

A. D. 60.
1 Or. glory.
[h] Job 5. 17.
Ps. 94. 12.
Pro. 3. 11, 12.
Heb. 6. 15.
Heb. 10. 32.
Heb. 12. 5.
Rev. 3. 19.
[i] Matt 25.34.
Luke 22.28-30.
1 Cor. 9. 25.
2 Tim. 4. 8.
ch 2. 5.
1 Pet. 5. 4.
Rev. 2. 10.
2 Or, evils.

donizomenoi, like a wave]—'tossed to and fro with every *wind*.' **driven with the wind**—from without. **tossed**—from within, by its own instability (*Bengel*). At one time cast on the shore of faith and hope, at another rolled back into unbelief; at one time raised to the height of worldly pride, at another tossed in the sands of despair (*Weisinger*). **7. For**—Resumed from *v.* 6. **that man**—such a wavering self-deceiver. **think.** Real *faith* is something more than a mere [*oiestho*] *surmise*. **any thing.** He does receive many things from God, food, raiment, &c., but these are the general gifts of His providence. Of the things specially granted in answer to prayer, the waverer shall not receive "any thing," much less wisdom. **8. double-minded** [*dipsuchos*]—*double-soulled :* the one soul directed towards God, the other to something else. The words in this *v.* 8 are in apposition with "that man," *v.* 7: thus the "is," which is not in the original, needs not to be supplied. "A man double-minded, unstable in all his ways!" [*Dipsuchos* is found here and ch. iv. 8, for the first time in Greek.] Not a *hypocrite*, but a *fickle,* "wavering" man (*v.* 6): opposed to *the single eye* (Matt. vi. 22).

9, 10. *But* "let the brother," &c.—*i. e.,* the best remedy against *double-mindedness* is that Christian *simplicity* of spirit whereby the "brother," low in outward circumstances, may "rejoice (answering to *v.* 2) in that he is exalted"—viz., by being accounted a son and heir of God, his very sufferings being a pledge of his coming crown (*v.* 12); and the rich may rejoice "in that he is made low," by being stripped of his goods for Christ's sake (*Menochius*); or, in that he is made, by sanctified trials, lowly in spirit (*Gomarus*). The design is to reduce all things to an equable footing (ch. ii. 1; v. 13). The "low," rather than the "rich," is termed "the brother" (*Bengel*). So far as one is merely "rich" in worldly goods, "he shall pass away;" in so far as his predominant character is that of a "brother," he "abideth for ever" (1 John ii. 17). This view meets all *Alford's* objections to regarding "the rich" here as a "brother" at all. **11.** From Isa. xl. 6-8. **heat** [*tō kausōni*]—'the *hot wind*' from the (east or) south, which scorches vegetation (Luke xii. 55). The "burning heat" of the sun is not at its *rising,* but at noon; whereas the scorching [*Kadim*] wind is often at sunrise (Jonah iv. 8) (*Middleton,* Greek article). Matt. xx. 12 uses *the Greek* for "heat." Isa. xl. 7, "*bloweth* upon it," answers to 'the hot *wind*.' **grace of the fashion** [*prosopou*]—*of the external appearance.* **in his ways** [*poreiais*]—the simple word, and that, in the plural, usually ascribed to the rich **man**, instead of [*euporia*] 'wealth,' to mark his care-attended "ways" of

securing wealth. Cf. "ways," *paths* [*hodois*], v. 8. **12. Blessed**—Cf. the beatitudes in the sermon on the mount (Matt. v. 4, 10, 11). **endureth temptation**—not the 'falling into,' but the *enduring* of, temptation (Matt. xxiv. 13) is cause for "joy" (*v.* 2; Job v. 17). **when he is tried** [*dokimos genomenos*] — *when he has become approved,* having passed through the "trying" [*dokimion*] (*v.* 3), victorious through "faith." **the crown** [*stephanon,* not *diadema :* the garland of victory]. Heb. xii. 1 answers *Alford's* objection to a *Gentile* custom being alluded to in addressing *Jews.* In this case a *kingly* crown accompanies the *victor's* crown [Rev. ii. 10; xiv. 14; Ps. xxi. 3, LXX., *stephanon*]. The unfading "crown of life" beautifully contrasts with "the flower of the grass," *v.* 10, "fade away," *v.* 11 [*maranthesetai*]. **of life**—lit., *the* life, the only true, highest, and eternal life. **the Lord.** So C. Not in א A B. The believer's heart fills up the omission. The 'faithful one who promised' (Heb. x. 23). **to them that love him** (2 Tim. iv. 8). Love produces persevering *endurance* amidst sufferings: by this we attest our love. **13. when he is tempted**—by *solicitation to evil.* Heretofore the "temptation" was *by afflictions.* Let no one fancy God lays upon him an inevitable necessity of sinning. God does not send trials to make you worse, but better (*vv.* 16, 17). Therefore do not sink under the pressure (1 Cor. x. 13). **of God**—by agency proceeding *from God* [*apo Theou*]: indirect agency. **cannot be tempted with evil, &c.**—'neither do our sins tempt God to entice us to worse, nor does He tempt any *of His own accord*' [*autos*]: nay, *v.* 18, "*Of His own will* begat He us" *to holiness:* so far is he from tempting us *of His own will* (*Bengel*). God is said (Gen. xxii. 1) to have "tempted Abraham;" but there the *tempting* is *trying* or *proving; not seducement. Alford* [*apeirastos kakōn*], 'God is *unversed* in evil.' But ecclesiastical Greek often uses words in new senses, as the exigencies of the new truths required. **14.** Every man when tempted is so through being drawn away of [*hy: hupo ;* the *source,* rather than the agent] his own lust. The cause of sin is in ourselves. Satan's suggestions do not endanger us before they are made *our own.* Each has *his own peculiar* [*tēs idias*] lust, arising from his own temperament. Lust flows from original birth-sin in man, inherited from Adam. **drawn away**—the *beginning* step: drawn away from truth and virtue. **enticed** [*deleazomenos*]—*taken with a bait* as fish. The *further progress*: the man *allowing himself* (middle voice) *to be enticed.* "Lust" is personified as the harlot that allures man. **15.** The guilty union is committed

16, Do not err, my beloved brethren. Every good gift and every perfect
17 gift is from above, and cometh down from the Father of lights, *j* with
18 whom is no variableness, neither shadow of turning. Of *k* his own will
begat he us with the word of truth, that we should be a kind of first-fruits
l of his creatures.

19 Wherefore, my beloved brethren, let every man be swift to hear, slow
20 to speak, slow to wrath: for the wrath of man worketh not the righ-
21 teousness of God. Wherefore lay apart all filthiness and superfluity of
naughtiness, and receive with meekness the ingrafted word, *m* which is
able to save your souls.

A. D. 60.

j Num 23.19.
Mal 3. 6.
k John 1. 13.
1 (or. 4. 15.
l Jer. 2. 3.
Rev 14. 4.
m Acts 13. 26.
Rom 1. 16.
1 Cor 15. 2.
Eph. 1. 13.
Titus 2. 11.
Heb. 2. 3.

by the will embracing the temptress. "Lust," the harlot, then 'brings forth sin,' that to which the temptation inclines. Then *the particular sin* [*he hamartia*], 'when completed, brings forth death,' with which it was all along pregnant (*Alford*). "Death" stands in striking contrast to the "crown of *life*" (*v.* 12), which "patience" brings when it has its "perfect work" (*v. 4*). He who fights Satan with Satan's own weapons must not wonder if he be overmatched. Nip sin in the bud of lust.

16. Do not err in attributing to God temptation to evil; nay, "every good," all that is good on earth, comes from God. 17. gift . . . gift [*dosis —dorema, dosis: the act of giving;* the gift in its *initiatory* stage ; *dorema, the thing given, the boon, when perfected*]. As the "good gift" contrasts with "sin" in its initiatory stage (*r.* 15), so the 'perfect boon' contrasts with "sin when it is finished," bringing forth *death* (2 Pet. i. 3). from above (cf. ch. iii. 15.) Father of lights—Creator *of the lights in heaven* (cf. Job xxxviii. 28 (*Alford*); Gen. iv. 20, 21). So reference to *changes in the light of the heavenly bodies* follows. Also, Father of the spiritual lights in the kingdom of grace and glory. Heb. xii. 9 typified by the supernatural lights on the high priest's breastplate, the Urim. As "God is light, and in Him is no darkness at all" (1 John i. 5), He cannot in any way be Author of sin (*v.* 13), which is darkness (John iii. 19). no variableness, neither shadow of turning (Mal. iii. 6). No alternations of light and shadow, such as the physical "lights," and even the spiritual lights, are liable to. "Shadow of turning" [*tropēs aposkiasma*]—the *shadow-mark* cast *from* a heavenly body in its *turning* or revolution; *e. g.*, when the moon is eclipsed by the earth, and the sun by the moon. *Bengel* makes a climax, 'no variation (in the *understanding:* answering to "every good gift")—not even the shadow of a turning' (in the *will:* answering to "every *perfect* gift"). 18. (John i. 13.) The believer's regeneration is the highest example of every good proceeding from God. Of his own will [*Bouletheis*]—Of His good pleasure (proving it is God's essential nature to do good, not evil), not induced by any external cause. begat he us [*apekuesen*]—spiritually : a once-for-all accomplished act (1 Pet. i. 3, 23). In contrast to "sin bringeth . . . forth [*apokuei*] *death*" (*v.* 15). *Life* follows naturally *light* (*v.* 17). word of truth—the Gospel. The objective mean, as *faith* is the appropriating mean, of regeneration by the Holy Spirit, the efficient agent. a kind of first-fruits—Christ is, as to the resurrection, "the first-fruits " (1 Cor xv. 20, 23): believers, as to regeneration, are *a kind of* first-fruits (as the first-born of man, cattle, and fruits were consecrated in Israel to God)—*i. e.*, the first of God's regenerated creatures, the pledge of the ultimate regeneration of the creation. Rom. viii. 19, 23, where the Spirit, the Agent of the believer's regeneration, is termed "the first-fruits "—*i. e.*, the earnest that the regeneration begun in the soul shall at last

extend to the body, and to the lower creation. Of all God's visible creatures, believers are the noblest, and, like the legal "first-fruits," sanctify the rest ; therefore they are much 'tried' now.

19. Wherefore--as your evil is of yourselves, but your good from God. A B C, Vulgate, read [*ἴστε* for *ὥστε*] 'YE KNOW IT (so Eph. v. 5; Heb. xii. 17): BUT let every man be [א, *isto*, "let every man know it, and consequently be] swift to hear," the word of truth' (*vv.* 18, 21). The true method of hearing is treated in *vv.* 21-27 and ch. ii. slow to speak (Prov. x. 19 ; xvii. 27, 28 ; Eccl. v. 2)—a good way of escaping one temptation arising from ourselves (*v.* 13). Slow to speak authoritatively as a 'master' of others (cf. ch. iii. 1): a Jewish fault: slow to speak hasty things of God, as *v.* 13. Two ears are given to us, the Rabbis observe, but only one tongue : the ears are exposed, the tongue is walled in behind the teeth. slow to wrath (ch. iii. 13, 14 ; iv. 5.)—slow in becoming heated by debate: another Jewish fault (Rom. ii. 8), to which much *speaking* tends. *Tittmann*, Not "wrath ' is meant, but *indignant fretfulness* under the calamities to which human life is exposed : this accords with "divers temptations," *v.* 2. Hastiness of temper hinders hearing God's word: so Naaman, 2 Ki. v. 11 ; Luke iv. 28. 20. Man's angry zeal in debating, as if jealous for the honour of God, is far from working that which is really righteousness in God's sight. True "righteousness is sown in peace," not in wrath (ch. iii. 18). א A B read [*ergazetai*] 'worketh'—i. e., *practiseth* not: instead of 'worketh out' [*katergaxetai*], *produceth* not. 21. lay apart—*once for all* [*apothemenoi:* aorist]: as a filthy garment (cf. Joshua's, Zech. iii. 3, 5; Rev. vii. 14). "Filthiness" is cleansed away by hearing the word (John xv. 3). superfluity of naughtiness—*excess* (as the *intemperate* spirit of "wrath," *vv.* 19, 20), arising from *malice* (*evil disposition* towards one another) (1 Pet. ii. 1). So Eph. iv. 31 ; Col. iii. 8. Superfluous excess in *speaking* is reprobated as 'coming *of evil,*' in the sermon on the mount (Matt. v. 37), on which this epistle comments. with meekness—towards one another: the opposite to "wrath" (*v.* 20): "as new born babes" (1 Pet. ii. 2). *Meekness* includes also a childlike, *humble,* as well as uncontentious spirit (Ps. xxv. 9; xlv. 4; Isa. lxvi. 2; Matt. v. 5; xi. 28-30 ; xviii. 3, 4: contrast Rom. ii. 8). On "receive," cf. the ground receiving seed, Mark iv. 20. Cf. Acts xvii. 11; 1 Thess. i. 6, with 2 Thess. ii. 13. engrafted word—the Gospel *engrafted* by the Holy Spirit into living incorporation with the believer, as the fruitful shoot is with the wild stock on which it is engrafted. The law came only from without, and admonished man of his duty. The Gospel is *engrafted* inwardly, and so fulfils the law's ultimate design (Deut. vi. 6 ; xi. 18 ; Ps. cxix. 11). able to save—a strong incentive to correct our dulness: that word which we hear so carelessly is able (instrumentally) to save us (*Calvin*). souls—your true selves, for the "body" is liable to sickness and death ; but the

22 But be ye doers of the word, and not hearers only, deceiving your own
23 selves. For [n]if any be a hearer of the word, and not a doer, he is like
24 unto a man beholding his natural face in a glass: for he beholdeth
himself, and goeth his way, and straightway forgetteth what manner of
25 man he was. But [o]whoso looketh into the perfect law of liberty, and
continueth *therein*, he being not a forgetful hearer, but a doer of the
work, [p]this man shall be blessed in his [3]deed.
26 If any man among you seem to be religious, and bridleth not his
27 tongue, but deceiveth his own heart, this man's religion *is* vain. Pure
religion and undefiled before God and the Father is this, [q]To visit the
fatherless and widows in their affliction, [r]*and* to keep himself unspotted
from the world.
2 MY brethren, have not the faith of our Lord Jesus Christ, [a]*the Lord*

A. D. 60.

n Jer. 44. 16. Eze. 33. 31. Matt. 7. 26. Luke 6. 47.
o 2 Cor. 3. 18.
p John 13.17.
3 Or, doing
q Isa. 1. 16. 1 Tim. 1. 5.
r Ps. 19 11. Rom 12. 2.

CHAP 2.
a Acts 7. 2. 1 Cor. 2. 8. Phil. 2. 9.

soul being now saved, both soul and body at last shall be so (ch. v. 15, 20).

22. Qualification of "be swift to *hear*." **be ye doers of the word, and not hearers only**—not merely '*do*,' but '*be doers*' systematically and continually, as your regular business. St. James again refers to the sermon on the mount (Matt. vii. 21-29). **deceiving your own selves** [*paralogizomenoi*]—by the logical fallacy that the mere hearing is all that is needed. **23. For**—the logical self deceit (*v.* 22) illustrated. The true disciple, say the Rabbis, learns that he may do, not that he may merely know or teach. **his natural face** [*to prosopon tēs geneseōs*]—*the countenance of* his birth: that he was born with. As a man beholds his *natural* face in a mirror, so the hearer perceives his *moral* visage in God's Word. This faithful portraiture of man's soul in Scripture is strong proof of its truth. In it we see mirrored God's glory as well as our natural vileness. **24. beholdeth** [*katenoesen-apeleluthen*]—'he *contemplated* himself and *hath gone* his way;' *i. e.*, no sooner has he contemplated his image than he goes his way (*v.* 11). 'Contemplate' answers to hearing; "goeth his way," to relaxing the attention after hearing—letting the mind go elsewhere, and the interest pass away; then *forgetfulness* follows (*Alford*) (cf. Ezek. xxxiii. 31). 'Contemplate' here, and *v.* 23, implies that, though cursory, yet some knowledge of one's self, for the time, is imparted in hearing (1 Cor. xiv. 24). **and . . . and**—the repetition expresses hastiness joined with levity (*Bengel*). **forgetteth what manner of man he was**—in the mirror. Forgetfulness is no excuse (*v.* 25; 2 Pet. i. 9). **25. looketh into** [*parakupsas*]—*stoopeth down to take a close look.* Peers into: stronger than "beholdeth" (*v.* 24). A blessed curiosity if efficacious in bearing fruit (*Bengel*). **perfect law of liberty**—the Gospel-rule of life, perfect and perfecting (shown in the sermon on the mount, Matt. v. 48): making us truly walk at liberty (Ps. cxix. 32, 45). Christians should aim at a higher standard than was generally understood under the law. The *principle* of love takes the place of the letter of the law, so that by the Spirit they are free from the yoke of sin, obeying by spontaneous instinct (ch. ii. 8, 10, 12; John viii. 31-36; xv. 14, 15: cf. 1 Cor. vii. 22; Gal. v. 1, 13; 1 Pet. ii. 16). The law is thus *not made void*, but *fulfilled.* **continueth therein**—contrast "goeth his way," *v.* 24: continueth both *looking into* God's Word and doing its precepts. **doer of the work**—rather, 'of work:' an actual worker. **blessed in his deed** [*poiesei*]—'in his *doing*:' the very doing is blessedness (Ps. xix. 11).

26, 27. An example of *doing work.* **26. religious . . . religion** [*threskos—threskeia*]—express the *external service of religion*, 'godliness' being the internal soul. James, as president of the council at Jerusalem (Acts xv. 13-21), had decided against ritualism. So here he adds, Instead of Judaic ceremonialism, true service is (1.) active, (2.) passive piety. 'If any *think himself* [*dokei*] *to be* religious—i. e., *observant of religious offices*—let him know these consist not so much in outward observances as in *acts* of mercy and in *practical* piety (Mic. vi. 7, 8), *visiting the fatherless*, &c., and *keeping one's self unspotted from the world*' (Matt. xxiii. 23). St. James does not mean that these *offices* are the essentials or sum total of religion; but that, whereas the law service was merely ceremonial, the very *services* of the Gospel consist in mercy and holiness (*Trench*). The Greek is only found in Acts xxvi. 5; Col. ii. 18. **bridleth not his tongue.** Discretion in speech is better than fluency (cf. ch. iii. 2, 3). Cf. Ps. xxxix. 1. God alone can give it. St. James, in treating of the law, notices this sin. For they who are free from grosser sins, and even bear the show of sanctity, often exalt themselves by detracting others, under pretence of zeal, whilst their real motive is love of evil-speaking (*Calvin*). **heart**—it and the tongue act and re-act on one another. **27. Pure religion and undefiled** [*kathara*]. "Pure" is that love which has in it *no foreign admixture*—self-deceit and hypocrisy: [*amiantos*] "undefiled" is the means of its being "pure" (*Tittmann*). "Pure" expresses the *positive*, "undefiled" the *negative* side of religious service: as *visiting the fatherless*, &c., is the active, *keeping himself unspotted from the world* the passive side of religious duty. This is the nobler shape that our religious exercises take, instead of the ceremonial offices of the law. **before God and the Father** [*to Theo kai patri*]—'before Him who is (our) God and Father.' If we would be like 'our Father,' it is not by fasting, &c., for He does none of these things, but in being 'merciful, as our Father is merciful' (*Chrysostom*). **visit**—in sympathy and kind offices. **the fatherless**—whose "Father" is God (Ps. lxviii. 5): peculiarly helpless. **and**—not in the Greek, so close is the connection between works of mercy to others, and the maintenance of personal unworldliness: no copula is needed. Religion in its rise interests us about *ourselves*; in its progress, about our *fellow-creatures*; in its highest stage, about the honour of *God.* **keep himself**—with jealous watchfulness, at the same time praying as depending on God as alone able to keep us (John xvii. 15; Jude 24).

CHAP. II. 1-26.—RESPECT OF PERSONS—UNWORKING FAITH SAVES NO MAN.

1-13. Illustrating "the perfect law of liberty" (ch. i. 25) in one instance of a sin against it; concluding with reference to that law (*vv.* 12, 13). **1. brethren**—the equality of Christians as "breth-

	A. D. 60.

2 of glory, with *b*respect of persons. For if there come unto your ¹assembly a man with a gold ring, in goodly apparel, and there come in also a poor
3 man in vile raiment; and ye have respect to him that weareth the gay clothing, and say unto him, Sit thou here ²in a good place; and say to
4 the poor, Stand thou there, or sit here under my footstool: are ye not then partial in yourselves, and are become judges of evil thoughts?
5 Hearken, my beloved brethren, *c*Hath not God chosen the poor of this world rich in faith, and heirs of ³the kingdom *d*which he hath promised
6 to them that love him? But ye have despised the poor. Do not rich
7 men oppress you, and draw you before the judgment seats? Do not they

Marginal references
b Lev. 19.15.
Deut. 1.17.
Deut.16.19.
1 synagogue.
² Or, well,
or. seemly.
c John 7. 48.
³ Or, that.
d Ex. 20. 6.
1 Sam. 2.30.
Pro. 8. 17.
Matt. 5. 3.

ren" forms the groundwork of the admonition. **the faith of . . . Christ.** St. James grounds Christian practice on *Christian faith.* **the Lord of glory.** So 1 Cor. ii. 8. As believers, rich and poor, derive their glory from union with Him, "the Lord of glory," not from external advantages, the sin in question is peculiarly inconsistent with His "faith." *Bengel,* without ellipsis of *the Lord,* makes "glory" in apposition with Christ, who is THE GLORY (Luke ii. 32): the true shechinah of the temple (Rom. ix. 4). Christ's glory resting on the poor believer should make him be regarded as highly by "brethren" as his richer brother; nay, more so, if the poor has more of Christ's spirit than the rich. **with respect of persons** [*prosōpolempsiais*]—'*in respectings* of persons;' *in* partial preferences of persons in various ways. **2. if there come** [*ean eiselthē*]. **assembly** — lit., *synagogue:* this the latest honourable, and the only *Christian,* use of the term in the New Testament occurs in St. James, the apostle who maintained to the latest the bonds between the Jewish synagogue and the Christian church. Soon the continued resistance of the truth by the Jews led Christians to leave the term to them exclusively (Rev. iii. 9). 'Synagogue,' an *assembly* or congregation not necessarily united by any common tie. 'Church,' a people bound together by mutual ties, whether assembled or not. From St. James's Hebrew tendencies, and from the Jewish Christians retaining Jewish forms, 'synagogue' is used here instead of the Christian 'church' [*ecclesia,* derived from *ekkalein,* implying union of its members in spiritual bonds, independent of space, and *called out* into separation from the world]: an undesigned coincidence and mark of truth. People in the Jewish synagogue sat according to rank, those of the same trade together. The introduction of this custom into Christian worship is reprobated by St. James. Christian churches were built like synagogues, the holy table in the east end, as the ark had been: the *desk* and *pulpit* were the chief articles of furniture in both. This shows the error of comparing the church to the temple, and the ministry to the priesthood: the temple is represented by the whole body of worshippers; the church building was on the model of the synagogue (*Vitringa,*'Synagogue'). If, as at Berea, the greater part were converted, the synagogue with its officers became the Christian church. If, as at Thessalonica, the majority of the synagogue rejected the Gospel, the apostle withdrew with the minority into the neighbouring house of a convert, a Jason or a Justus, and there continued the Sabbath reading of the Old Testament with a Christian exposition (Rom. xvi. 5; Col. iv. 15). When, as at Corinth, the ruler of the synagogue was converted, he naturally became president or bishop, as tradition records Crispus became. From the synagogue came the ecclesiastical, but unclassical, sense of "presbytery" (Luke xxii. 26: cf. with 1 Tim. iv. 14: also "angel," Rev. i. 20; ii. 1;

"shepherd" or "pastor," Eph. iv. 11; 1 Pet. v. 2; "Amen," 1 Cor. xiv. 16) (*Justin,*'Apol.,' 67). Also the discipline, Matt. xviii. 17; excommunication, 1 Cor. v. 4; the collection of alms, 1 Cor. xvi. 2. The love-feast was late on Saturday, the Sabbath evening: when the Eucharist was separated from it, and administered on the following morning, the Lord's day became established as holy: so *Pliny's* letter to Trajan recognizes it. **goodly apparel . . . gay clothing** (*apparel:* the same Greek). **have respect to him,** &c.—though ye know not who he is: perhaps a heathen. The deacons used to direct to a seat the members of the congregation (*Clement,* 'Constitut.' ii. 57, 58). **unto him.** Not in A B C ℵ, Vulgate. "Thou" is demonstratively emphatic. **here**—near the speaker. **there**—far from the good seats. **under my footstool**—on the ground, down by my footstool. The poor must either *stand,* or if he sit, *sit* low down. The speaker has a footstool as well as a good seat. **4. Are ye not then partial** [*ou diekrithete*]—*Have ye not drawn* (unbelieving) *distinctions* (preferring one to another.) So Jude 22. But see note. **in yourselves**—according to your carnal inclination (*Grotius*). **are become judges of evil thoughts** [*kritai*]—"judges" and [*diekrithēte*] 'partial' are akin. Translate,'*Do ye not partially judge between men, and are become evilly-thinking judges'* (distinction - makers) (Mark vii. 21). The "evil thoughts" are in the judges themselves (Luke xviii. 6): Greek, 'judge of injustice," "unjust judge." *Alford,* 'Did ye not (by such distinctions) *doubt'* (for *faith* is inconsistent with distinctions between rich and poor). So the Greek means, Matt. xxi. 21; Acts x. 20; Rom. iv. 20. [*V.* 1 shows that *diekrithete* must comprehend '*unbelieving* distinction-making.' As it implies the *process;* so *kritai* the definite *result: the diakrisis* (so Acts xv. 9 uses the *active*) precedes the *krisis.* The same play on the kindred words occurs Rom. xiv. 10, 23. The blame of being a judge, when one ought to be an obeyer, of the law, occurs ch. iv. 11.] **5. Hearken.** St. James *brings to trial* the self-constituted "judges" (*v.* 4). **poor of this world.** ℵ B read [*tō kosmō*] 'those poor *in respect to the* world.' In contrast to 1 Tim. vi. 17. Not of course *all* the poor; but they, *as a class,* furnish more believers than the rich. The rich, if a believer, renounces riches as his portion; the poor, if an unbeliever, neglects what is the peculiar advantage of poverty (Matt. v. 3; 1 Cor. i. 26, 27, 28). **rich in faith**—*their* riches consist *in faith* (Luke xii. 21; 1 Tim. vi. 18; Rev. ii. 9: cf. 2 Cor. viii. 9). Christ's poverty is the source of the believer's riches. **kingdom . . . promised** (Luke xii. 32; 1 Cor. ii. 9; 2 Tim. iv. 8). **6.** The world's judgment of the poor contrasted with God's. **ye** —from whom better things might have been expected: no marvel that men of the world do so. **despised the poor** [*ētimasate*]—'*dishonoured* those whom God honours, so inverting the order of God' (*Calvin*). **rich**—as a class. **oppress** [*katadunasteuousin*]—'*abuse their power against* you.' **draw**

8 blaspheme that worthy name by the which ye are called? If ye fulfil
the royal law according to the scripture, *^e*Thou shalt love thy neighbour
9 as thyself, ye do well: but if ye have respect to persons, ye commit sin,
and are convinced of the law as transgressors.
10 For whosoever shall keep the whole law, and yet offend in one *point,*
11 he *^f*is guilty of all. For *⁴*he that said, *^g*Do not commit adultery, said
also, Do not kill. Now if thou commit no adultery, yet if thou kill,
thou art become a transgressor of the law.
12 So speak ye, and so do, as they that shall be judged by the law of
13 liberty. For he shall have judgment without mercy that hath showed
no mercy; and mercy *⁵*rejoiceth against judgment.
14 What *doth it* profit, my brethren, though a man say he hath faith,

Marginal references
A. D. 60.
^e Lev. 19. 18.
Matt 22.39.
^f Deut. 27.26.
Matt. 5. 19.
Gal. 3. 10.
⁴ Or. that law which said.
^g Ex. 20. 13.
Deut. 5. 18.
Matt. 5. 27, 28.
⁵ Or. glorieth.

you—is it not *they* [*kai autoi helkousin*: *those very persons* whom ye partially prefer, *vv.* 1-4] that *drag you*? (viz., with violence) (*Alford.*) before the **judgment seats**—instituting persecutions for religion, as well as oppressive lawsuits, against you. 7. 'Is it not they [*autoi*] that blaspheme,' &c., as in *v.* 6? Rich heathen must be meant; none others would directly blaspheme the name of Christ. *Indirectly,* rich Christians may be meant, who, by inconsistency, *caused* His name *to be blasphemed:* so Ezek. xxxvi. 21, 22; Rom. ii. 24. There were few rich Jewish Christians at Jerusalem (Rom. xv. 26). They who dishonour God by wilful sin 'take (or *bear*) the Lord's name in vain' (cf. Prov. xxx. 9 with Exod. xx. 7). **that worthy name** (Ps. lii. 9; liv. 6)—which ye pray may be "hallowed" (Matt. vi. 9), " by the which ye are called" [*to epiklethen eph' humas*]: *which was called upon you* (cf. Gen. xlviii. 16; Isa. iv. 1, *margin:* Acts xv. 17), so that at your baptism '*into* the name' (Greek, Matt. xxviii. 19) of Christ, ye became Christ's people (1 Cor. iii. 23). 8. [*Ei mentoi*] 'If, *however* (in the honour you pay the rich), ye are fulfilling the royal law,' &c., not depreciating the poor, but only honouring each according to his due, my censure does not apply; but respect of persons is a breach of it' (*Alford* after *Estius*). I prefer, 'If *in very deed, on the one hand,* ye fulfil the royal law, &c., ye do well; *but* if, *on the other,* ye respect persons, ye *practise* sin.' The Jewish Christians boasted of the "law" (Acts xv. 1; xxi. 18-24; Rom. ii. 17; Gal. ii. 12). To this the 'indeed' alludes. '(Ye rest in the law): If *indeed* (then) ye fulfil it, ye do well; but if,' &c. **royal**—the law that is king of all laws, as He is King of kings: the sum of the ten commandments. The great King is love: His law is the royal law of love. He 'is no respecter of persons;' to respect persons is at variance with Him and His law. The law is the "whole;" the particular "scripture" (Lev. xix. 18) quoted is a part. To break a part is to break the whole (*v.* 10). **ye do well**—being 'blessed in your deed,' as doers, not forgetful hearers (ch. i. 25). 9. *Respect of persons* violates the command to *love all alike* "as thyself.' **ye commit** [*ergazesthe: work*] **sin**—referring to Matt. vii. 23, as ch. i. 22. Your *works* are sin, however ye in words boast of the law (note, *v.* 8). **convinced**—*Old English* for 'convicted.' **as transgressors**—not merely of some particular command, but of the whole.
10. א B C, Vulgate, read 'Whosoever *shall have* kept [*tērēsē*] the whole law, and yet *shall have offended* [*ptaisē, stumbled:* not so strong as "fall," Rom. xi. 11] in one (point: the *respecting of persons*), is (hereby) become guilty of all.' The law is one seamless garment, which is rent if you but rend a part; or a musical harmony, spoiled if there be one discordant note (*Tirinus*); or a golden chain, whose completeness is broken if you break

one link (*Gataker*). You break *the whole law,* though not the whole of the law, because you offend against *love,* the fulfilling of the law. If any part of a man be leprous, the whole man is judged a leper. God requires perfect, not partial obedience. We are not to choose parts of the law to keep, which suit our whim, whilst we neglect others. Any sin brings death: not that all sins are equal as *acts,* but all alike betray a *state* of natural alienation from God. 11. He is One who gave the whole law; therefore they who violate His will in one point, violate it all (*Bengel*). The law and its Author have a complete unity. **adultery . . . kill**—selected as the most glaring violations of duty towards one's neighbour.
12. Summing up the previous reasonings. **speak**—referring back to ch. i. 19, 26: the fuller discussion is given, ch. iii. **judged by the law of liberty** (ch. i. 25)—*i. e.,* the Gospel law of love; not a law of external constraint, but of *free* instinctive inclination. The law of liberty frees us from the curse of the law, that henceforth we should be free to love and obey willingly (Rom. viii. 2-4). If we will not in turn practise love to our neighbour, that law of grace condemns us more heavily than the old law, which spake nothing but wrath to him who offended in the least (*v.* 13). Cf. Matt. xviii. 32-35; John xii. 48; Rev. vi. 16, "wrath of the (merciful) Lamb." 13. The converse of Matt. v. 7, '*The* [*hē*] judgment (which is coming on all) shall be without mercy to him who showed no mercy.' "Mercy" here corresponds to "love," *v.* 8. **mercy rejoiceth against judgment.** Mercy, so far from fearing judgment as to its followers, *glorifieth against* it, knowing that it cannot condemn them. Not that *their* mercy is the ground of their acquittal, but *God's* mercy in Christ towards them, producing mercy on their part towards their fellow-men, makes them to *triumph over judgment,* which all otherwise deserve.
14. St. James, passing from the particular "mercy" or "love" violated by "respect of persons," notwithstanding profession of the "faith of our Lord Jesus" (*v.* 1), combats the Jewish tendency (transplanted into Christianity) to substitute a lifeless acquaintance with the letter of the law for change of heart to holiness, as if justification could be thereby attained (Rom. ii. 3, 13, 23). It seems likely that St. James had seen St. Paul's epistles, for he uses the same phrases and examples (cf. *vv.* 21, 23, 25 with Rom. iv. 3; Heb. xi. 17, 31; and *vv.* 14, 24 with Rom. iii. 28; Gal. ii. 16). At all events, the Holy Spirit by St. James combats, not St. Paul, but those who abuse St. Paul's doctrine. The teaching of both alike is inspired, and to be received without wresting of words; but each has a different class to deal with: St. Paul, self-justiciaries; St. James, advocates of a mere notional faith. St. Paul urged as strongly

15 and have not works? can faith save him? If a brother or sister be
16 naked, and destitute of daily food, and one of you say unto them,
Depart in peace, be *ye* warmed and filled; notwithstanding ye give
them not those things which are needful to the body; what *doth it*
17, profit? Even so faith, if it hath not works, is dead, being ⁶ alone. Yea,
18 a man may say, Thou hast faith, and I have works: show me thy faith
19 ⁷ without thy works, and I will show thee my faith by my works. Thou
believest that there is one God; thou doest well: ʰ the devils also believe,
20 and tremble. But wilt thou know, O vain man, that faith ⁱ without
21 works is dead? Was not Abraham our father justified by works, ʲ when

A. D. 60.
⁶ by itself.
⁷ Some copies read, by thy works.
ʰ Matt. 8. 29.
   Mark 1. 24.
   Mark 5. 7.
   Luke 4. 34.
   Acts 16. 17.
ⁱ Gal 5. 6.
ʲ Gen 22. 9.

as St. James the need of works as evidences of faith, especially in the later epistles, when many were abusing the doctrine of faith (Titus ii. 14; iii. 8). 'Believing and doing are blood relatives' (*Rutherford*). **though a man say**—not 'if a man have faith', but if "a man *say* [*legē, allege*] he hath faith;" referring to a mere *profession* of faith, such as was usually made at baptism. Simon Magus so "*believed* and was baptized," and yet had "neither part nor lot in this matter," for his "heart," as his words and works evinced, was not right in the sight of God. The illustration (*v.* 16) proves the emphasis on "say;" if "one of you *say*" *the words* to a naked brother [*eipē*, referring to the *words; legē*, to the *sentiment*] 'Be ye warmed, notwithstanding ye give not those things needful.' The inoperative *profession* of sympathy answers to the inoperative *profession* of faith. **can faith save him?**—rather, 'can such a faith (lit., *the faith*) save him?' the empty boast contrasted with true fruit-producing faith. So that which self-deceivers claim is called "wisdom," though not true wisdom (ch. iii. 15). The "him" also is emphatic; the particular man who professes faith without having works to evidence its vitality. **15.** Greek, '*But* if,' &c., taking up the argument against one who 'said he had faith, yet had not works.' **a brother, &c.**—a *fellow-Christian*, whom we are specially bound to help, independent of our general obligation to help all fellow-creatures. **be** [*huparchosin:* denoting a *condition* in which one is *supposed* to be: *eimi*, simply to be]—'*be found*.' **16.** Passive sentimental impressions from sights of woe not carried out into active habits only harden the heart. **one of you**—St. James brings home the case individually. **Depart in peace**—as if all their wants were satisfied by the mere words. The same words in the mouth of Christ, whose faith they said they had, were accompanied by deeds of love. **be ye warmed**—with clothing, instead of being as heretofore "naked" (Job xxxi. 20; *v.* 15). **filled**—instead of being "destitute of food" (Matt. xv. 37). **what doth it profit?**—concluding as at the beginning, *v.* 14. Just retribution: kind professions unaccompanied with corresponding acts, as they are of no "profit" to the needy object, so are of no profit to the professor. So faith consisting in mere profession is unacceptable to God, the object of faith, and profitless to the professor. **17. faith . . . being alone.** *Alford* joins, '*is* dead *in itself*.' *Bengel*, 'If the works which living faith produces have no existence, it is a proof that faith *itself* (lit., *in itself*) has no existence, is *dead*.' "Faith" is said to be 'dead *in itself*,' because when it has works it is *alive*, not *in its works*, but in *itself*. The English version does not mean that faith can exist "alone" (*i. e.*, severed from works), but, Even so *presumed* faith, if it have not works, is dead, being by itself —*i. e.*, severed from charity; just as the body would be "dead" if severed from the spirit (*v.* 26). So *Estius*. **18.** '*But* some one *will* say' [*all' erei* 588

tis: erein expresses the *mind* of the speaker], continuing the argument from *vv.* 14, 16. One may [*legē*] *allege* he has faith,·though he have not works. Suppose one were to *say* [*eipē*] *the words* to a naked brother, 'Be warmed,' without giving him clothing. '*But* some one (entertaining right views) will *object* [*erei*] against the "say" of the professor, &c. **show me thy faith without thy works**—if thou canst; but thou canst not SHOW—i. e., *evidence*—thy alleged (*v.* 14) faith without works. "Show" does not mean *prove*, but *exhibit* to me. Faith is unseen save by God. To *show* faith to man, works in some form are needed: we are justified judicially by God (Rom. viii. 33), meritoriously by Christ (Isa. liii. 11; Rom. v. 19), mediately by faith (Rom. v. 1), evidentially by works. The question is not as to the *ground* on which believers are justified, but as to the *demonstration* of their faith: so Gen. xxii. 1, it is written, God did *tempt* Abraham—*i. e.*, put to the *test of demonstration* his faith, not for the satisfaction of God, who knew it well, but of men. The offering of Isaac (*v.* 21) formed no *ground* of his justification; for *he was justified previously* on his simple *believing* in the promise of spiritual heirs, numerous as the stars (Gen. xv. 6). That justification was *showed* by his offering Isaac forty years after. That work of faith *demonstrated*, but did not contribute to his justification. The tree *shows* its life by fruits, but was alive before either fruits or even leaves appeared. **19. Thou**—emphatic. Thou self-deceiving claimant to faith without works. **that there is one God** [*ho Theos estin heis*]—'that God is one:' God's *existence* is also asserted. The fundamental article of Jews and Christians alike; the point of faith on which especially the former boasted themselves, as distinguishing them from the Gentiles; hence adduced by St. James here. **thou doest well.** But unless thy faith goes farther than an assent to this truth, 'the *demons* ("devil" is restricted to *Satan*, their head) believe' in common with thee, 'and (so far from being saved by such a faith) shudder' [*phrissousin*] (Matt. viii. 29; Luke iv. 34; 2 Pet. ii. 4; Jude 6; Rev. xx. 10). Their faith only adds to their torment at having to meet Him who is to consign them to their just doom: so thine (Heb. x. 26, 27), not the faith of love, but fear, that hath torment (1 John iv. 18). **20. wilt** [*theleis*] **thou know.** "Vain" men are not *willing* to know, since they have no wish to *do* the will of God (John vii. 17). St. James beseeches such a one to lay aside his *unwillingness* to know, and as the preliminary step to be willing to do. **vain**—who deceivest thyself with a delusive hope, resting on unreal faith. **without works** [*choris tōn ergōn*]—*separate from the works* which flow from real faith. **is dead** [so א A. But B C, Vulgate, read *arge* for *nekra*]—'is idle;' *i. e.*, unavailing for salvation. **21. Abraham our father justified by works**—*evidentially before men* (note, *v.* 18). In *v.* 23 St. James, like St. Paul, recognizes that it was his *faith* that was counted

22 he had offered Isaac his son upon the altar? [8] Seest thou how faith
23 wrought with his works, and by works was faith made perfect? And the
scripture was fulfilled which saith, [k] Abraham believed God, and it was
imputed unto him for righteousness: and he was called [l] the Friend of
24 God. Ye see then how that by works a man is justified, and not by
25 faith only. Likewise also, [m] was not Rahab the harlot justified by works,
when she had received the messengers, and had sent *them* out another
26 way? For as the body without the [9] spirit is dead, so faith without works
is dead also.

3 MY brethren, [a] be not many masters, knowing [b] that we shall receive

A. D. 60.
[8] Or. Thou seest.
[k] Gen. 15. 6. Rom. 4. 3.
[l] 2 Chr. 20. 7. Isa 41. 8.
[m] Josh. 2. 1.
[9] Or. breath.
CHAP. 3.
[a] Matt. 23. 8.
[b] Luke 6. 37.

to Abraham for righteousness in his justification before God. **when he had offered** [anenenkas]— 'when he offered;' *i. e.*, brought as an offering. **22. how** [hoti]— *that.* In the two clauses, emphasize "faith" in the former, and "works" in the latter, to see the sense (*Bengel*). **faith wrought** [sunergei: *was working*] **with his works**—for it was *by faith* he offered his son. **by works was faith made perfect**—not *vivified*, but attained its *consummated development* [eteleiothe]. So 2 Cor. xii. 9, "my strength is *made perfect* in weakness"—i. e., *exerts itself perfectly; shows* how great it is: so 1 John iv. 17; Heb. ii. 10; v. 9. The germ, from the first, contains the full-grown tree; but its perfection is not attained till it is developed. So ch. i. 4, "Let patience have her *perfect work*, that ye may be *perfect*"—i. e., *fully developed* in the *exhibition* of Christian character. *Alford*, 'Received its realization.' So Phil. ii. 12, "*Work out* your own salvation:" salvation was already in germ theirs in free justification through faith. It needed to be *worked out* to developed perfection in their life. **23. scripture was fulfilled**—Gen. xv. 6, quoted by St. Paul, as realized in Abraham's justification by *faith;* by St. James, as realized subsequently in Abraham's *work* of offering Isaac, which, he says, *justified* him. Plainly St. James means by *works* the same thing as St. Paul means by *faith;* only he speaks of faith in its manifested development; St. Paul speaks of it in its germ. Abraham's offering of Isaac was not a mere act of obedience, but an act of faith. Isaac was the subject of God's promises, that in him Abraham's seed should be called. The same God calls on Abraham to slay the subject of His own promise, when as yet there was no seed in whom those predictions could be realized. St. James's saying that Abraham was justified by *such* a work, is equivalent to saying, as St. Paul, that he was justified by faith; for it was *faith expressed in action,* as in other cases faith is expressed in *words.* St. Paul states as the mean of salvation faith *expressed.* St. Paul opposes *self-righteousness;* St. James, *unrighteousness.* The "scripture" would not be fulfilled, as St. James says it was, but contradicted, by any interpretation which makes man's *works* justify him before God: for that scripture makes no mention of works at all, but says that Abraham's *belief* was counted to him for righteousness. God, in the first instance, 'justifies the *ungodly*' through faith; subsequently the believer is justified *before the world* as righteous through faith manifested in words and works (cf. Matt. xxv. 35-37, "the righteous," 40). Greek, '*But* Abraham believed,' &c. **and he was called the Friend of God**—He was not so *called* in his lifetime, though he *was* so from the time of his justification; but he was *called* so, when recognized as such by all, because of his works of faith. 'He was the *friend* (active), the *lover of God*, as to his works; and (passive) *loved by God* as to his justification by works. Both senses are united' (John xv. 14, 589

15) (*Bengel*). **24. justified, and not by faith only** —i. e., by 'faith *severed from* works,' its proper fruits (note, v. 20). Faith, to justify, must, from the first, include obedience in germ (to be developed subsequently), though the former alone is the ground of justification. The scion must be grafted on the stock, that it may live; it must bring forth fruit, to prove that it does live. **25.** Rahab's act was such that it cannot be quoted to prove justification by works as such. She *believed* assuredly what her other countrymen disbelieved, and this in the face of every improbability that an unwarlike few would conquer well-armed numbers. In this belief she hid the spies at the risk of her life. Hence Heb. xi. 31 names this as an example of *faith*, rather than of obedience. "By faith the harlot Rahab perished not with them that *believed* not." If an instance of obedience were wanting, St. Paul and St. James would hardly have quoted a woman of previously *bad character*, rather than the many moral and pious patriarchs. But as an example of *grace* justifying men through an *operative*, as opposed to a mere verbal *faith*, none could be more suitable than a saved "harlot." As Abraham was an instance of an illustrious man, the father of the Jews, so Rahab is quoted as a woman, one of abandoned character, and a Gentile, showing that justifying faith has been manifested in those of every class. The nature of the works alleged is such as to prove that St. James uses them only as *evidences of faith*, contrasted with a mere verbal profession: not works of charity and piety, but works the value of which consisted solely in their being proofs of faith: they were *faith expressed in act*, synonymous with *faith* itself. The consequent is put for the antecedent. We are justified by works because we are justified by faith, which always works. Our justification by works is the fruit and natural necessary development of our justification once for all by faith. So Rom. i. 17, "the righteousness of God revealed *from faith to faith*." **messengers**—spies. **had received ... had sent** [dexamene-ekbalousa] — 'received ... thrust them forth' (in haste and fear) (*Alford*). **by another way**—from that whereby they entered her house; viz., through the window of her house on the wall, and thence to the mountain. **26.** Faith is a spiritual thing: works material. Hence we might expect *faith* to answer to the *spirit: works* to the *body.* But St. James reverses this. He therefore does not mean that *faith* answers to the body; but the FORM *of faith* without *the working reality* answers to the *body* without the *animating spirit.* It does not follow that *living faith* derives its life from works, as the body derives its life from the animating spirit. Faith apart from [choris] the spirit of faith, which is LOVE (and love evidences itself in *works*), is dead, according to *St. Paul* also, 1 Cor. xiii. 2.

CHAP. III. 1-18.—DANGER OF EAGERNESS TO TEACH, AND AN UNBRIDLED TONGUE—TRUE

2 the greater [1]condemnation. For ^cin many things we offend all. ^dIf any man offend not in word, ^ethe same *is* a perfect man, *and* able also to
3 bridle the whole body. Behold, we put bits in the horses' mouths, that
4 they may obey us; and we turn about their whole body. Behold also the ships, which though *they be* so great, and *are* driven of fierce winds, yet are they turned about with a very small helm, whithersoever the
5 governor listeth. Even so the tongue is a little member, and boasteth
6 great things. Behold how great [2]a matter a little fire kindleth! And the tongue *is* a fire, a world of iniquity: so is the tongue among our members, that ^fit defileth the whole body, and setteth on fire the [3]course
7 of nature; and it is set on fire of hell. For every [4]kind of beasts, and of birds, and of serpents, and of things in the sea, is tamed, and hath
8 been tamed of [5]mankind: but the tongue can no man tame; *it is* an
9 unruly evil, full of deadly poison. Therewith bless we God, even the Father; and therewith curse we men, which are ^gmade after the simili-
10 tude of God. Out of the same mouth proceedeth blessing and cursing.

A. D. 60.

1 Or, judgment.
c 1 Ki. 8. 46.
  Pro 20. 9.
  Eccl. 7. 20
  1 John 1. 8.
d 1 Pet. 3. 10.
e Matt. 12 37.
2 Or, wood.
f Matt.15.11.
  Mark 7. 15,
  20, 23.
3 wheel.
4 nature.
5 nature of man.
g Gen. 1. 26.
  Gen. 5. 1.
  Gen. 9. 6.
  1 Cor. 11. 7.

WISDOM SHOWN BY UNCONTENTIOUS MEEKNESS.

1. be not [*ginesthe*] — *become not:* taking the office too hastily, of your own accord. **many.** The office is noble; but few are fit for it. Few govern the tongue well (*v.* 2); only such are fit for the office; therefore 'teachers' ought not to be many. **masters** [*didaskaloi*] — 'teachers.' The Jews were prone to this presumption. The idea that faith without works (ch. ii.) is all that is required, prompted "many" to set up as 'teachers,' as in all ages of the Church. At first all were allowed to teach in turns. Even their inspired gifts did not prevent liability to abuse; much more so when self-constituted teachers have no such gifts. **knowing** — as all might know. **we shall receive the greater condemnation.** St. James, in a humble spirit, includes himself: if *we* teachers abuse the office, we shall receive greater condemnation than mere hearers (cf. Luke xii. 42-46). *Calvin* also translates "masters" — *i. e.,* self-constituted *censors* of others. So ch. iv. 12. **2. all** [*hapantes*] — 'all without exception;' even the apostles. **offend not** [*ptaiei*] — **stumbleth** not: *slips* not in word: in which one especially tried who sets up as a 'teacher.' **3. Behold.** So C. But א A B, Vulgate [*ei de*], 'But if;' "What if" (Rom. ix. 22): there being understood, Should we not similarly bridle our tongue? (Ps. xxxix. 1.) Others explain, *Now whensoever* (in the case) of horses. So the position of "horses" in the Greek, we put *the customary* [*tous*] bits into their mouths that they may obey us; we turn about *also* their whole body. So *man* turns about his whole body with the little tongue. 'The same applies to the pen, the substitute for the tongue' (*Bengel*). **4.** Not only animals, but *even* ships. **the governor** [*he orme tou euthunontos*] — *the impulse of the steersman,* answering to the feeling which moves the tongue. **5. boasteth great things.** What the careless think 'little,' is often of great moment (*Bengel*). "A world," "the course of nature," "hell" (*v.* 6), show how great mischief the little tongue's great words produce. **how great a matter** [material for burning: *fuel.* Alford, 'forest:' *hulēn*] **a little fire kindleth.** א B C, Vulgate, read [*hēlikon*] '*how great* a fire kindleth how great a matter.' **6.** [*He glossa pur ho kosmos tes adikias:* 'the tongue, that world of iniquity, is **a** fire.'] As man's little world is an image of the greater, the universe, so the tongue is an image of the former (*Bengel*). Omitted in א A B C, Vulgate. **is** [*kathistatai*]. 'The tongue *is constituted,* among the members, the one which defileth, &c. — viz., as fire defiles with its

smoke. **course of nature** [*ton trochon tes geneseos*] — 'the cycle of creation.' **setteth on fire ... is set on fire** — habitually, continually. Whilst a man inflames others, he passes out of his own power, being consumed in the flame himself. **of hell** — Greek, 'Gehenna:' here only and Matt. v. 22. St. James has much in common with the sermon on the mount (Prov. xvi. 27). **7. every kind** [*phusis*] — "nature." **of beasts** — *i. e.,* quadrupeds of every disposition; distinguished from the three other classes, 'birds,' creeping things [*herpetōn :* not merely "serpents"] and things in the sea. **is tamed, and hath been** — is continually being tamed, and hath been so long ago. **of mankind** [*tē phusei tē anthropinē*] — 'by the nature of man:' man's characteristic nature taming that of the inferior animals. The Greek may imply, 'Hath been brought into tame subjection TO the nature of men.' So it shall be in the millennial world: even now man, by gentle firmness, may tame and even elevate the lower animal's nature. **8. no man** — lit., *no one of men:* neither can a man control his neighbour's, nor even his own tongue. Hence the truth of *v.* 2 appears. **unruly evil** [*akatastaton,* akin to *akatastasia, v.* 16] — *unstable, unquiet,* and *incapable of restraint.* Nay, though nature has hedged it in with a double barrier, the lips and teeth, it bursts forth to assail and ruin men (*Estius*). **deadly** [*thanatephorou*] — *death-bearing.* **9. God.** א A B C read 'Lord' [*ton kurion kai patera*]; 'Him who is Lord and Father.' The uncommon application of 'Lord' to the Father doubtless caused the change to "God" (ch i. 27). But as Messiah is called "Father" (Isa. ix. 6), so the Father is called the Son's title, 'Lord:' showing the unity of the Godhead. "Father" implies His *paternal* love; 'Lord,' His *dominion.* **men, which** — not 'men, *who*;' what is meant is not particular men, but men *generically* (*Alford*). **are made after the similitude of God.** Though in a great measure man has lost God's *likeness,* in which he was originally made, yet enough still remains to show what once it was, and what in regenerated and restored man it shall be. We ought to reverence this remnant and earnest of what man shall be in ourselves and in others. 'Absalom has fallen from his father's favour; but the people still recognize him to be the king's son' (*Bengel*). Man resembles the Son of man, "the express image of his person" (Heb. i. 3: cf. Gen. i. 26; 1 John iv. 20). In Gen. i. 26 "image" [*eicon*] and "likeness" [*homoiosis*] are distinct: "image," according to the Alexandrians, was something *in* which men were created, common to all,

11 My brethren, these things ought not so to be. Doth a fountain send
12 forth at the same [6] place sweet *water* and bitter? Can the fig tree, my
 brethren, bear olive berries? either a vine, figs? so *can* no fountain both
 yield salt water and fresh.
13 Who [h] *is* a wise man and endued with knowledge among you? let him
 show out of a good conversation his works with meekness of wisdom.
14 But if ye have [i] bitter envying and strife in your hearts, glory not, and
15 lie not against the truth. This [j] wisdom descendeth not from above,
16 but *is* earthly, [7] sensual, devilish. For [k] where envying and strife *is*,
17 there *is* [8] confusion and every evil work. But [l] the wisdom that is from
 above is first pure, then peaceable, gentle, *and* easy to be entreated, full
 of mercy and good fruits, [9] without partiality, [m] and without hypocrisy.

A D
6 Or. hole.
h Gal. 6. 4.
i Rom. 13.13.
j Phil 3. 19.
7 Or. natural. Jude 19.
k 1 Cor. 3. 3.
8 tumult, or, unquietness.
l 1 Cor 2. 6.
9 Or, without wrangling.
m 1 Pet. 1. 22.

and continuing after the fall, while the "likeness" was something *toward* which man was created, to strive and attain it: the former marks man's physical and intellectual, the latter his moral preeminence. 10. The tongue (*Æsop*) is at once the best and the worst of things. A man with the same breath blows hot and cold. 'Life and death are in the power of the tongue' (cf. Ps. lxii. 4). brethren—a mild appeal to their consciences by their *brotherhood* in Christ. ought not so to be —themselves may understand that such conduct deserves severe reprobation. 11. fountain—the *heart:* as the *aperture* [so *opēs*, 'place'] of the fountain represents the *mouth*. The image is appropriate to the scene of the epistle, Palestine, wherein salt and bitter springs are found. Though "sweet" springs are sometimes found near, yet "sweet and bitter" (water) do not flow 'at the same *aperture*.' Grace can make the mouth that 'sent forth the bitter' once, send forth the sweet: as the wood (typical of Christ's cross) changed Marah's bitter water into sweet. 12. Transition from the mouth to the heart. Can the fig tree, &c.—an *impossibility:* as in *v.* 10, it "*ought* not so to be." St. James does not, as Matt. vii. 16, 17, ask, "Do men gather figs of *thistles?*" His argument is, No tree "can" former bring forth *fruit inconsistent with its nature*, as, *e. g.*, the fig tree, olive berries: so if a man speaks bitterly, and afterwards good words, the latter must be so only seemingly, and in hypocrisy: they *can not* be real. so can no fountain both yield salt water and fresh. א A B C read [*oute halukon gluku poiēsai hudōr*] 'neither can a salt (water spring) yield fresh.' So the mouth that emits cursing cannot really emit also blessing.
13. Who—(cf. Ps. xxxiv. 12, 13.) All wish to appear "wise:" few are so. show—'by works,' not merely by profession (ch. ii. 18). out of a good conversation his works—by *general* 'good conduct' [*anastrophes*] manifested in *particular* "works." "Wisdom" and "knowledge," without these being 'shown,' are as dead as faith without works (*Alford*). with meekness of wisdom— with the meekness inseparable from true *wisdom*. 14. if ye have—*as is the case* (Greek indicative). bitter (Eph. iv. 31). envying [*zelon*]—*zeal:* generous *emulation* is not condemned, but "bitter" (*Bengel*). strife [*eritheian*]—'*rivalry:' cabal, faction* (note, Gal. v. 20). in your hearts—from which flow words and deeds, as from a fountain. glory not, and lie not against the truth. To *boast of wisdom* which your lives evince not, is virtually lying against the Gospel truth. Ver. 15; ch. i. 18, "the word of truth." Rom. ii. 17, 23, warns such "contentious" Jewish Christians. 15. This wisdom—in which ye "glory," as if "wise" (*vv.* 13, 14). descendeth not from above —'*is not one descending,*' &c.: "from the Father of lights" (true illumination) (ch. i. 17), through

"the Spirit of truth" (John xv. 26). earthly— opposed to *heavenly:* what is IN the earth. Distinct from "earthy" (1 Cor. xv. 47): what is OF the earth. sensual [*psuchike*]—*animal-like;* the wisdom of the "natural" [*psuchikos*] (1 Cor. ii. 14) man, not born again of God: "having not the Spirit" (Jude 19). devilish — originating from "hell" (*v.* 6): not from God, the Giver of true wisdom (ch. i. 5): its character accords with its origin. Earthly, sensual, and devilish answer to man's three spiritual foes, the world, the flesh, and the devil. 16. envying—Greek, 'zeal,' '*emulation*' (note, *v.* 14; Rom. xiii. 13). 'The envious man stands in his own light. He thinks his candle cannot shine in presence of another's sun. He aims directly at men, obliquely at God, who makes men to differ.' confusion [*akatastasia*] (note, *v.* 8)—*tumultuous anarchy;* both in society ("commotions," Luke xxi. 9; "tumults," 2 Cor. vi. 5) and in the individual; in contrast to the "peaceable" composure of true "wisdom" (*v.* 17). St. James does not honour such effects of earthly wisdom with the name "fruit," as in the case of the wisdom from above. Ver. 18: cf. Gal. v. 19- 22, "*works* of the flesh . . . *fruit* of the Spirit." 17. first pure [*hagne*]—'clean' from all that is "earthly, sensual (animal), devilish" (*v.* 15). This is '*first of all*' before "peaceable," because there is an unholy peace with the world, which makes no distinction between clean and unclean. Cf. "undefiled" and "unspotted from the world," ch. i. 27; iv. 4, 8; 1 Pet. i. 22, "*purified* your souls" [*hēgnikotes*]. Ministers must not preach before a purifying change of heart, "Peace" (Ezek. xiii. 10, 19). *Seven* (the perfect number) characteristics of true wisdom are enumerated. *Purity* (*sanctity*) is put first, because it has respect both to God and ourselves: the six that follow regard our fellowmen. Our first concern is to have in ourselves sanctity; our second, to be at peace with men. gentle [*epieikēs*]—'forbearing:' making allowance for others: lenient as to the DUTIES they owe us. easy to be entreated [*eupeithēs*]—*easily persuaded;* not harsh as to a neighbour's FAULTS. full of mercy—as to a neighbour's MISERIES. full of mercy and good fruits—contrasted with "every evil work" (*v.* 16). without partiality—recurring to the warning against "respect to persons" (ch. ii. 1, 4, Greek, 9). *Alford* translates [*adiakritos:* cf. Greek, ch. i. 6], '*without doubting.*' But thus there would be an epithet referring to *one's self* amidst those referring to one's conduct towards others. without hypocrisy. Not as *Alford*, from ch. i. 22, 26, 'Without deceiving yourselves' with the name without the reality of religion. For it must refer, like the other six epithets, to our relations to others: our peaceableness and mercy must be 'without dissimulation.' 18. 'The peaceable fruit of righteousness.' *Righteousness* is itself the true wisdom. As in the case of the earthly wis-

18 And [n]the fruit of righteousness is sown in peace of them that make
    peace.

4   FROM whence *come* wars and [1]fightings among you? *come they* not
2 hence, *even* of your [2]lusts that war in your members? Ye lust, and have
    not: ye [3]kill, and desire to have, and cannot obtain: ye fight and war,
3 yet ye have not, because ye [a]ask not. Ye [b]ask, and receive not, [c]because
    ye ask amiss, that ye may consume *it* upon your [4]lusts.
4   Ye adulterers and adulteresses, know ye not that the friendship of
    the world is enmity with God? whosoever therefore will be a friend of
5 the world is the enemy of God. Do ye think that the Scripture saith in
6 vain, The spirit that dwelleth in us lusteth [5]to envy? But he giveth
    more grace. Wherefore he saith, God resisteth the proud, but giveth

Marginal notes:

A. D. 60.
[n] Matt. 5 9.
CHAP. 4.
[1] Or, brawlings.
[2] Or, pleasures.
[3] Or, envy.
[a] Ps 10. 4.
[b] Job 27. 9.
[c] Ps. 66. 18.
[4] Or, pleasures.
[5] O enviously.

---

dom, after the description came its *results:* so in the case of the heavenly wisdom. There the results were present; here, future. **fruit ... sown** —(cf. Ps. xcvii. 11; Isa. lxi. 3.) The seed whose "fruit," "righteousness," shall be ultimately reaped, is now "sown in peace." "Righteousness," now in germ, when developed as "fruit," shall be itself the everlasting *reward* of the righteous. As 'sowing in peace' (cf. Prov. xi. 18; Hos. x. 12; 1 Cor. xv. 43; Gal. vi. 8) produces the "fruit of righteousness," so, conversely, "the work" and "effect of righteousness" is "peace" (Isa. xxxii. 17). **of them that make peace**—*by* (implying also that it is *for* them *to* their good) them that work peace. They, and they alone, are "blessed" (Matt. v. 9). "Peacemakers," not merely reconcile others, but *work* (cultivate) peace. Those wise towards God, whilst peaceable and tolerant towards their neighbours, make it their chief concern to sow righteousness, not cloaking, but reproving, sins with such moderation as to be the physicians, rather than the executioners, of sinners (*Calvin*).

CHAP. IV. 1-17.—FIGHTINGS AND THEIR SOURCE —WORLDLY LUSTS—UNCHARITABLE JUDGMENTS, AND PRESUMPTUOUS RECKONING ON THE FUTURE.

1. whence. The cause of quarrels is often sought in external circumstances: internal lusts are the true origin. **wars, &c.**—contrast the "peace" of heavenly wisdom. "Fightings," the active carrying on of wars. אBC have a second "whence" before "fightings." Tumults marked the era before the destruction of Jerusalem. St. James alludes to these. The members are the seat of war; thence it passes to conflict between man and man, nation and nation. **come they not, &c.**—an appeal to their consciences. **lusts** [*hedonōn*]—*pleasures* which your lusts prompt you to "desire" (note, *v.* 2) at the cost of your neighbour: hence flow "fightings." **that war** [*strateuomenōn*]—'*campaign, as soldiers,*' against the interests of your fellow-men, whilst lusting to advance self. But whilst warring thus against others, they war against the soul of the man himself, and against the Spirit; therefore they must be 'mortified' by the Christian (Col. iii. 5). **2. Ye lust** [*epithumeite*] —a different word from *v.* 1; ye *set your mind* or heart *on* an object. **have not.** Desire does not ensure possession. For this "ye kill" (not as *margin*, without authority, 'envy'). Not probably in a literal sense, but 'kill and envy' [*zeloute*]— i. e., *harass and oppress* through envy (*Drusius*). Cf. Zech. xi. 5, *through envy, hate* and desire to get out of your way; so are 'murderers' in God's eyes (*Estius*). If literal murder (*Alford*) were meant, it would not occur so early in the series; nor had Christians as yet reached so open criminality. In the Spirit's application to all ages, literal *killing* is included, from the desire to possess: so David and Ahab. There is a climax:

'ye desire,' individual lust for an object; 'ye kill and envy,' the feeling and action of individuals against individuals; "ye fight and war," the action of many against many. **ye have not, because ye ask not.** God promises to those who pray, not fight. The petition of the lustful, murderous, and contentious is not recognized by God as *prayer*. If ye prayed, there would be no "wars and fightings." This last clause answers the question, *v.* 1. **3.** Some are supposed to object, But we do "ask" (cf. *v.* 2). St. James replies, It is not enough to ask for good things, but we must ask with a good spirit. "Ye ask amiss, that ye may consume *it* (your object) upon (lit., *in*) your lusts" (lit., *pleasures*): not that ye may have the things you need for the service of God. Contrast ch. i. 5 with Matt. vi. 31, 32. If ye prayed aright, all your proper wants would be supplied: the improper cravings which produce "fightings" would cease. Even believers' prayers are often best answered when their desires are most thwarted.

4. אAB omit "adulterers and" (which C has): read simply, 'Ye adulteresses.' God is the rightful husband; the men of the world are collectively one *adulteress*; individually, *adulteresses.* **the world**—in so far as men's motives and acts are alien to God; *e. g.*, selfish "lusts" (*v.* 3), covetous and ambitious "wars" (*v.* 1). **enmity**— not merely 'inimical,' but enmity itself (cf. 1 John ii. 15). **whosoever therefore will be** [*hos ean oun boulēthe*]—'shall be *resolved* to be.' Whether he succeed or not, if his *wish* be to be friend of the world, he *renders himself*, is constituted [*kathistatai*] by the very fact, 'the enemy of God.' Contrast ch. ii. 23. **5. in vain**—no Scripture can be so. The quotation, as in Eph. v. 14, seems not so much from a particular passage, as gathered under inspiration from the general tenor of the Old and New Testaments (Num. xi. 29; LXX., Ps. lxii. 10 [*me epipotheite*], 'lust not on robbery;' Prov. xxi. 10; Gal. v. 17). **spirit that dwelleth in us.** אB [*katokisen*] read 'that God *made to dwell* in us' (viz., at Pentecost). 'Does the (Holy) Spirit that (God) hath placed in us lust [*epipothei*] to (towards) envy?' (viz., as ye do in your worldly "fightings.") Certainly not: ye are walking in the flesh, not in the Spirit, whilst ye *lust with envy* against one another. The friendship of the world breeds *envy;* the Spirit produces very different fruit. [*Alford* attributes *pros phthonon* to the Holy Spirit: 'The Spirit *jealously desires* us for His own.' *Katokēsen* would mean, 'The (natural) spirit that hath its dwelling in us lusts with (*pros: towards*) envy.'] Ye lust; and because ye have not what ye lust after (*vv.* 1, 2), ye envy your neighbour who has: so the *spirit of envy* leads you to "fight." St. James refers to ch. iii. 14, 16. **6. But**—*Nay rather.* **he**—God. **giveth more grace**—ever increasing, the farther ye depart from

	A. D. 60.

7 grace unto the humble. Submit yourselves therefore to God. Resist
8 *a* the devil, and he will flee from you. Draw *e* nigh to God, and he will
draw nigh to you. Cleanse *your* hands, *ye* sinners; and purify *your*
9 hearts, *ye* double-minded. Be afflicted, and mourn, and weep: let your
10 laughter be turned to mourning, and *your* joy to heaviness. Humble
yourselves in the sight of the Lord, and he shall lift you up.
11 Speak not evil one of another, brethren. He that speaketh evil of *his*
brother, and judgeth his brother, speaketh evil of the law, and judgeth
the law: but if thou judge the law, thou art not a doer of the law, but a
12 judge. There is one lawgiver, *f* who is able to save and to destroy: who
art thou that judgest another?
13 Go to now, ye that say, To-day or to-morrow we will go into such a
14 city, and continue there *c* year, and buy and sell, and get gain: whereas
ye know not what *shall be* on the morrow. For what *is* your life? *6* It is
even a vapour, that appeareth for a little time, and then vanisheth away.
15 For that ye *ought* to say, If the Lord will, we shall live, and do this, or

Marginal references (A. D. 60):
d Matt. 4. 3.
Luke 4. 2.
Eph 4. 27.
Eph. 6. 11,
12.
1 Pet 5. 9.
Rev. 12. 9,
11.
e Gen. 18. 23.
2 Chr. 15. 2.
Ps. 73. 28.
Ps. 115. 18.
Isa 29. 13.
Isa. 55. 6, 7.
Hos 6. 1, 2.
Zech. 1. 3,
Mal 3. 7.
f Matt 10. 28.
6 Or, For it
is.

"envy" (*Bengel*). **he saith.** The same God who causes His Spirit to dwell in believers (*v.* 5) also speaks in Scripture. The quotation is probably from Prov. iii. 34; as Prov. xxi. 10 was generally referred to in *v.* 5. In Hebrew it is 'scorneth the scorners'—viz., those who think 'Scripture speaketh in vain.' **resisteth** [*antitassetai*]—*setteth Himself in array against;* even as they, like Pharaoh, set themselves against Him. God repays sinners in their own coin. 'Pride' is the mother of "envy" (*v.* 5): it is peculiarly satanic, for by it Satan fell. **the proud** [*huperephanois*]—one who *shows himself above* his fellows, and so lifts himself against God. **the humble**—the unenvious, uncovetous, unambitious as to the world. Contrast *v.* 4. 7. **Submit yourselves therefore to God**—so ye shall be among "the humble" (*v.* 6; also *v.* 10; 1 Pet. v. 6). **Resist the devil.** Under his banner *pride* and *envy* are enlisted: "resist" (stand against) these his temptations. Faith, prayers, and heavenly wisdom are the weapons of resistance. "Submit," as a good *soldier* puts himself in subjection to his captain. **he will flee** —a promise of God: he shall flee worsted, as he did from Christ. 8. **Draw nigh to God**—so "cleave unto Him" (Deut. xxx. 20); viz., by prayerfully (*vv.* 2, 3) 'resisting Satan,' who opposes our access to God. **he will draw nigh**—propitious. **Cleanse your hands**—the outward instruments of action. None but the clean-handed can ascend into the hill of the Lord (justified through Christ, who alone, being perfectly so, 'ascended' thither) (Ps. xxiv. 3, 4). **purify your hearts** [*hagnisate*]— *make chaste* of spiritual *adultery* (*v.* 4; *i. e.,* worldliness) *your hearts,* the inward source of all impurity. **double-minded**—divided between God and the world: at fault in *heart;* the *sinner* in his *hands* likewise. 9. **Be afflicted, &c.** [*talaiporesate*] —*endure misery; i. e.,* mourn over your wretchedness through sin. *Repent with deep sorrow* instead of "laughter." A blessed *mourning.* Contrast Isa. xxii. 12, 13; Luke vi. 25. In ch. v. 1, "howl" for the *doom of the impenitent*—viz., at the coming destruction of Jerusalem. **heaviness** [*katēpheian*] —*falling of the countenance:* casting down of the eyes. 10. **in the sight of the Lord**—as continually in the presence of Him who alone is to be exalted: the truest incentive to *humility.* The tree, to grow upwards, must strike its roots downwards; so man, to be exalted, must have his mind deep-rooted in humility. In 1 Pet. v. 6, "Humble yourselves . . . *under the mighty hand of God*"—viz., in His providential dealings: a distinct thought. **lift you up** —partly in this world, fully in that to come.

593

11. (Ch. iii.) *Evil speaking* flows from the same spirit of exalting self at the expense of one's neighbour as caused the "fightings" reprobated, *v.* 1. [*Me katalaleite: Speak not against one* another.] **brethren.** Such depreciatory speaking of one another is peculiarly unbecoming in *brethren.* **speaketh evil of the law**—for the law. "Love thy neighbour as thyself" (ch. ii. 8), condemns evil speaking. He who superciliously condemns others' acts and words which do not please him, aiming at the reputation of sanctity, puts his own moroseness in the place of the law (*Calvin*); as though the law could not perform its own office of *judging,* but he must pounce upon it (*Bengel*). This is the last mention of the law. Here the moral law applied in its spiritual fulness by Christ: "the law of liberty." **if thou judge the law, thou art not a doer . . . but a judge.** Our Christian calling is to be *doers* of the law. But in judging our brother, we *judge the law,* which commands us to love our brother. 12. **There is one lawgiver.** א A B, Vulgate, 'and judge' [*ho nomothetes kai krites*], 'There is one (alone) who is (at once) Lawgiver and Judge; (namely), He who is able to save and destroy.' God alone is Lawgiver, *and therefore* Judge, since it is He alone who can execute His judgments: our inability in this shows our presumption in trying to be judges. **who art thou, &c.** The order is emphatic, 'But (in א A B, Vulgate) thou, who art thou that,' &c. How rashly arrogant in judging thy fellows, and wresting from God the office which belongs to Him over thee and THEM alike. **another.** א A B, Vulgate, read 'thy neighbour.' 13. **Go to now**—'Come now:' to excite attention. **ye that say**—'*boasting* of the morrow.' **To-day or to-morrow**—as if ye had the free choice of either day as a certainty. So א B, Vulgate. But A, 'To day *and* to-morrow.' **such a city**—lit., *this the city. This city here.* **continue there a year**—spend a year. They imply that when this year is out, they purpose settling plans for years to come. **buy and sell.** Their plans are all worldly. 14. **what** [*poia*]—'*of what nature* is your life?'—*i. e.,* how evanescent. **It is even.** B reads 'For ye are.' A reads 'For it shall be' (*vv.* 13-15). The former expresses, 'Ye yourselves are transitory:' so everything of yours partakes of the same transitoriness. **and then vanisheth away**—afterwards vanishing as it came [*epeita kai aphanizomene*]; *afterwards* (as it appeared) *so vanishing* (*Alford*).

15. *Literally,* 'instead of your saying,' &c. **we shall live.** 'We shall *both* live *and* do,' &c. The boaster spoke as if *life* and the particular

16 that. But now ye rejoice in your boastings: all such rejoicing is evil.
17 Therefore ^g to him that knoweth to do good, and doeth *it* not, to him it is sin.

5 GO to now, *ye* rich men, weep and howl for your miseries that shall
2 come upon *you.* Your riches are corrupted, and your garments are
3 moth-eaten. Your gold and silver is cankered; and the rust of them shall be a witness against you, and shall eat your flesh as it were fire.
4 Ye ^a have heaped treasure together for the last days. Behold, ^b the hire of the labourers which have reaped down your fields, which is of you kept back by fraud, crieth; and ^c the cries of them which have reaped
5 are entered into the ears of the Lord of sabaoth. Ye have lived in pleasure on the earth, and been wanton; ye have nourished your hearts,
6 as in a day of slaughter. Ye have condemned *and* killed the just; *and* he doth not resist you.
7 ¹ Be patient therefore, brethren, unto the coming of the Lord. Be-

A. D 60.
^g Luke 12.47.
John 9. 41.
John 15.22.
Rom 1. 20.
Rom 2. 17.
CHAP. 5.
^a Rom. 2. 5.
^b Lev 19 13.
Job 24. 10.
Jer. 22. 13.
Mal. 3. 5.
^c Deut. 24.15.
Job 31. 28.
1 Or, Be long patient, or, Suffer with long patience.

action were in their power; whereas both depend entirely on the will of the Lord. **16. now**—*as it is.* **rejoice in your boastings**—ye boast in your arrogant presumptions that the future is certain to you (*v.* 13). **rejoicing** [*kauchesis*]—boasting. **17.** The general principle is here stated: knowledge without practice is imputed to a man as presumptuous sin. St. James reverts to ch. i. 22-24. Nothing more injures the soul than wasted impressions. Feelings exhaust themselves and evaporate, if not embodied in practice. As we will not act except we feel, so, if we will not act out our feelings, we shall soon cease to feel.

CHAP. V. 1-20.—WOES COMING ON THE WICKED RICH—BELIEVERS SHOULD BE PATIENT UNTO THE LORD'S COMING—EXHORTATIONS.

1. Go to now—Come now: to call solemn attention. **ye rich**—who neglect the true enjoyment of riches, which consists in doing good. St. James intends this address to rich Jewish unbelievers, not so much for themselves as for the saints, that they may bear with patience the violence of the rich (*v.* 7), knowing that God will speedily avenge them. **miseries that shall come** [*eperchomenais*]—'that are coming upon you' unexpectedly and swiftly; viz. (*v.* 7), primarily, at the destruction of Jerusalem; finally, at the Lord's visible coming to judge the world. **2. corrupted**—*about to be destroyed* through God's curse for your oppression, whereby your riches are accumulated (*v.* 4). *Calvin*, Your riches *perish*, without being of use either to others or even yourselves; for instance, your garments are moth-eaten in your chests. Referring to Matt. vi. 19, 20. **3. is cankered**—rusted through. **rust ... witness against you**—in the day of judgment; viz., that your riches were of no profit, lying unemployed, so contracting rust. **shall eat your flesh.** The rust which once eat your riches shall then gnaw your conscience, accompanied with punishment which shall prey upon your bodies for ever. **as ... fire**—not with the slow process of *rusting*, but with the swiftness of *fire.* **for the last days**—ye have heaped together, not treasures, as ye suppose (cf. Luke xii. 19), but wrath *against* the last days. Rather, '*In* the last days (before the coming judgment) ye laid up treasure' to no profit, instead of seeking salvation (see note, *v.* 5). **4. Behold**—calling attention to their sin crying for judgment. **of you kept back.** Not as *Alford*, 'crieth out *from* you.' The 'keeping back of the hire' was, *on the part* OF the rich, a virtual "*fraud,*" because the poor workmen were not immediately paid. The phrase is 'kept back *of* you;' implying *virtual*, rather than overt, fraud. St. James refers

to Deut. xxiv. 14, 15. Many sins "cry" to heaven for vengeance which men take no account of, as unchastity and injustice (*Bengel*). Sins peculiarly offensive to God "cry" to Him. The rich ought to have given freely to the poor: their not doing so was sin. A still greater sin was not paying their debts. Their greatest sin was not paying the poor, whose wages is their all. **cries of them**—a double cry: both that of the hire and that of the labourers hired. **the Lord of sabaoth.** Here only in the New Testament. In Rom. ix. 29 it is a quotation. Suited to the Jewish tone of the epistle. It reminds the rich, who think the poor have no protector, that the Lord of the whole hosts in heaven is avenger of the latter. He is the "coming Lord" Jesus (*v.* 7). **5.** 'Ye have luxuriated . . . and wantoned.' [*Etruphesate, luxurious effeminacy; espatalesate, wantonness* and *prodigality.*] Their luxury was at the expense of the defrauded poor (*v.* 4). **on the earth**—the same earth, the scene of your wantonness, shall be that of the judgment coming on you: instead of earthly delights, ye shall have punishments. **nourished your hearts**—*i. e.,* glutted your bodies like beasts to your heart's desire: ye live to eat, not eat to live. **as in a day of slaughter.** So C. But א A B, Vulgate, omit "as." Ye are beasts which eat to their heart's content *on* the day of their slaughter, unconscious it is near. The phrase answers to "the last days," *v.* 3, which favours there, "in," not "for." **6. Ye have condemned . . . the just.** The aorist [*katedikasate*], 'Ye are *wont* to condemn, &c., the just.' Their condemnation of Christ, "the Just" (Acts iii. 14; vii. 52; xxii. 14), is the *prominent* thought. All the innocent blood shed is *included,* the Holy Spirit comprehending St. James himself, called "the just," slain in a tumult. See 'Introduction.' Cf. the "righteous (*just*) man," *v.* 16. The righteousness of Jesus and His people peculiarly provokes the ungodly great of the world. **he doth not resist you.** The very patience of the just is abused as an incentive to bold persecution, as if sinners may do as they please with impunity. God doth 'resist [*antitassetai,* as here] the proud' (ch. iv. 6); but Jesus, as man, "opened not His mouth:" so His people are meek under persecution. The just seem destitute of help: none dares *resist* you, oppressors. But the day will come when God will resist [*antitassetai, set Himself in array against*] His people's foes.

7. Be patient therefore—As judgment is so near (*vv.* 1, 3), ye can afford to be "long-suffering" [*makrothumesate*], after the example of the *un-resisting just one* (*v.* 6). **brethren**—contrasted with

hold, the husbandman waiteth for the precious fruit of the earth, and hath long patience for it, until he receive *d* the early and latter rain.

8 Be ye also patient; stablish your hearts: for *e* the coming of the Lord draweth nigh.

9 *2* Grudge not one against another, brethren, lest ye be condemned :

10 behold, the Judge *f* standeth before the door. Take, *g* my brethren, the prophets, who have spoken in the name of the Lord, for an example of

11 suffering affliction, and of patience. Behold, we count them happy which endure. Ye have heard of *h* the patience of Job, and have seen *i* the end of the Lord; that *j* the Lord is very pitiful, and of tender mercy.

12 But above all things, my brethren, swear *k* not, neither by heaven, neither by the earth, neither by any other oath: but let your yea be yea; and *your* nay, nay; lest ye fall into condemnation.

13 Is any among you afflicted? let him pray. Is any merry? let him sing

14 psalms. Is any sick among you? let him call for the *l* elders of the church; and let them pray over him, *m* anointing him with oil in the name

A. D. 60.

d Deut 11. 14
e Phil. 4. 5.
2 Or, Groan.
or. Grieve not
f Matt. 24. 33
g Matt. 5. 12
h Job 1. 21.
i Job 42. 10.
j Ex 34. 6.
Num. 14. 18.
1 Chr. 21. 13.
Ps. 25. 6, 7.
Dan. 9. 9.
Luke 6. 36.
Rom. 2, 4.
k Matt. 5. 34.
l 1 Tim. 5. 17.
1 Pet. 5. 1.
m Mark 6. 13.
Mark 16. 14.

the "rich" oppressors, *vv.* 1-6. **unto the coming of the Lord**—when the trial of *long-suffering waiting* shall cease. **husbandman waiteth for** —*i. e.*, amidst toils and delays, through hope of the harvest. Its 'preciousness' (cf. Ps. cxxvi. 6, "precious seed") will amply compensate for all the past. Cf. Gal. vi. 8, 9. **hath long patience** (*suffering*) **for it**—'over it,' *in respect to* it. **until he receive** — 'until *it* receive' (*Alford*). The receiving of the early and latter rains is not the object of his hope, but *the harvest*, to which those rains are the preliminary. The early rain fell at sowing time, about November or December; the latter rain, about March or April, to mature the grain for harvest. The latter rain that shall precede the spiritual harvest will probably be another Pentecost-like effusion of the Holy Ghost (Heb. ii. 23, 28-32). **8. patient**—'*long-suffering*.' **coming . . . draweth nigh** [*ēngiken*]—*hath and is drawn nigh:* a settled state (1 Pet. iv. 7). We are to live in a continued expectancy of the Lord's coming as *always* nigh. Nothing can more 'stablish the heart' amidst troubles than His coming realized as at hand.

9. Grudge not [*stenazete*]—'Murmur not;' *lit.*, 'groan :' a half-suppressed murmur of impatience and harsh judgment. Having enjoined long-suffering in bearing wrongs from the wicked, he now enjoins a forbearing spirit as to offences from brethren. Christians who bear the former patiently, sometimes are impatient at the latter, though less grievous. **lest ye be condemned.** ℵ A B, Vulgate [*krithete*], 'judged,' referring to Matt. vii. 1. To 'murmur against one another' is virtually to *judge*, and so become liable to be *judged*. **Judge standeth before the door**—referring to Matt. xxiv. 33. It ought to be translated here, as there, 'doors,' plural. The phrase means 'is near at hand;' (Gen. iv. 7, which the Targums of Jonathan and Jerusalem explain, 'thy sin is reserved *unto the judgment of the world to come:*' cf. "the everlasting doors," Ps. xxiv. 7, whence He shall come forth). The Lord's coming to destroy Jerusalem primarily; ultimately, His coming visibly to judgment. **10. the prophets**—especially persecuted, therefore especially 'blessed.' **example of suffering affliction** [*kakopatheias*]— 'of evil treatment.' **patience** [*makrothumias*]— 'long-suffering.' **11. count them happy** (Matt. v. 10). **which endure.** ℵ A B, Vulgate [*hupomeinantas*], 'which *endured*' trials in *past* days, like the prophets and Job. Such, not those who 'lived in pleasure and wantonness on the earth'

(*v.* 5), are "happy." **patience** [*hupomonen*]— 'endurance:' answering to [*hupomeinantas*] "endure." Distinct from [*makrothumia*] "patience" (*v.* 10): *long-suffering.* He reverts to the subject, ch. i. 3. **Job.** He was therefore a real, not an imaginary person; otherwise his case would not be an example at all. Though he showed impatience, he always returned to committing himself wholly to God, and at last showed a perfect spirit of enduring submission. **and have seen** (with your mental eyes). So ℵ [*eidete*]. But A B [*idete*], 'see also,' &c. **the end of the Lord**—which the Lord gave. If Job had much to "endure," remember also Job's happy "end." Hence learn, though much tried, to 'endure to the end.' **that**—or [*hoti*] 'for.' **pitiful, and of tender mercy** [*polusplanchnos* refers to the *feeling; oiktirmōn,* to *acts*). His *pity* is shown in not laying on the *patient endurer* more trials than he is able to bear; His *mercy*, in giving a happy end to them (*Bengel*). God sees graces beneath, where we see only the surface imperfections: He takes into account the severity of His people's trials.

12. But above all—as swearing is utterly alien to Christian 'endurance.' **swear not**—through impatience, to which trials may tempt you (*vv.* 10, 11). In contrast stands the proper use of the tongue (*v.* 13). Referring to Matt. v. 34, &c. **let your yea be yea**—do not use oaths in everyday conversation : let a simple affirmative or denial be enough to establish your word. **condemnation**— *judgment* of "the Judge" who "standeth before the door" (*v.* 9).

13. afflicted [*kakopathei*]—'evil treated :' "suffering affliction" (*v.* 10). **let him pray**—not "swear" in rash impatience. **merry**—in mind. **sing psalms**—of praise, as St. Paul and Silas did in prison. **14. let him call for the elders**—not some *one*, as Romanists interpret it, to justify their *extreme unction*. The prayers of the elders over the sick would be much the same as though the whole church which they represent should pray (*Bengel*). **anointing him with oil.** The usage which Christ committed to His apostles was afterwards continued with laying on of hands, as a token of the highest faculty of medicine in the Church; as we find in 1 Cor. vi. 2 the Church's. highest judicial function. Now that miraculous healing is withdrawn, to use the sign where the reality is wanting, would be unmeaning superstition. Cf. other apostolic usages, now discontinued, 1 Cor. xi. 4-15; xvi. 20. 'Let them use

595

15 of the Lord: and the prayer of faith shall save the sick, and the Lord shall raise him up; [n]and if he have committed sins, they shall be forgiven
16 him. Confess *your* faults one to another, and pray one for another, that ye may be healed. The [o]effectual fervent prayer of a righteous man
17 availeth much. Elias was a man subject to like passions as we are, and [p]he prayed [3]earnestly that it might not rain; and it rained not on the
18 earth by the space of three years and six months. And he prayed again, and the heaven gave rain, and the earth brought forth her fruit.
19 Brethren, if any of you do err from the truth, and one convert him;
20 let him know, that he which converteth the sinner from the error of his way shall [q]save a soul from death, and [r]shall hide a multitude of sins.

A. D. 60.

[n] Isa 33. 21.
Matt. 9. 2.
[o] Gen. 20. 17.
Num. 11. 2.
Deut. 9. 18.
Josh. 10.12.
[p] 1 Ki. 17. 1.
[3] Or. in prayer.
[q] 1 Tim 4.16.
[r] Ps. 32. 1.
Ps 51. 9.
Pro 10. 12.

oil who can by their prayers obtain recovery for the sick; let those who cannot do this, abstain from the empty sign' (*Whittaker*). Romish extreme unction is administered to those *whose life is despaired of*, to heal the *soul*: St. James's unction was to heal the *body*. Cardinal Cajetan ('Commentary') admits that St. James cannot refer to extreme unction. Oil among the Jews (see Talmud, *Jerusalem* and *Babylon*) was used as a curative agent (Luke x. 34). It was also a sign of Divine grace. Hence it was an appropriate sign in miraculous cures. **in the name of the Lord**—by whom alone the miracle was performed: men were but the instruments. **15. prayer.** He does not say *the oil* shall save: it is but the symbol. **save**—not, as Rome says, "*save*" *the soul*, but "the sick;" as the words, "the Lord shall raise him up," prove. So [*sesoke*] 'made (thee) *whole*,' Matt. ix. 21, 22. **and if he have committed sins** —for not all who are sick are so because of special sins. Here it is one visited with sickness for special sins (1 Cor. xi. 30-32). **have committed** [*ē pepoiēkōs*]—*be* in a state of *having committed* sins; *i. e.*, be under their consequences. **they**—or *it: his having committed sins* shall be forgiven him. The connection of sin and sickness appears in Isa. xxxiii. 24; Matt. ix. 2-5; John v. 14. The absolution of the sick in the Church of England refers to sins which the sick man confesses (*v.* 16) and repents of, whereby *outward scandal* has been given to the Church; not to sins in their relation to God, the only Judge. **16.** ℵ A B, Vulgate, read 'Confess, THEREFORE,' &c.: not only in sickness, but universally. **faults** [*ta paraptomata*]—your *falls*, in relation to one another. ℵ A B, Vulgate, read [*hamartias*] *sins*. Matt. v. 23, 24; Luke xvii. 4 illustrate the precept. **one to another**—not to the priest, as Rome insists. The Church of England *recommends* in certain cases. Rome *compels* confession in all cases. Confession is desirable in case of (1.) *wrong* done to a neighbour; (2.) when, under a troubled conscience, we ask *counsel* of a godly minister or friend how to obtain God's forgiveness and strength to sin no more, or when we desire their intercessory prayers ("pray one for another"): 'confession may be made to any who can pray' (*Bengel*); (3.) *open confession* of sin before the church, in token of penitence. Not *auricular*. **that ye may be healed**—of bodily sicknesses: also that, if your sickness be the punishment of sin, the latter being forgiven on intercessory prayer, "ye may be healed" of the former: also, that ye may be healed spiritually. **effectual** [*energoumenē*]—intense: not "wavering" (ch. i. 6) (*Beza*). 'When *energized*' by the Spirit, as those were who performed miracles (*Hammond*). This suits the Greek collocation and the sense.

A righteous man's prayer is always heard in some form; his *particular* request for another's *healing* will be granted when energized by *a special charism of the Spirit*. *Alford*, 'Availeth much *in its working*.' The "righteous" himself shuns "sins" or "faults," showing his faith by works (ch. ii. 18). **17. Elias was a man subject to like passions as we.** It cannot be said that he was so raised above us as to afford no example to common mortals. **prayed earnestly**—lit., *prayed with prayer:* Hebraism for *intensely* (cf. Luke xxii. 15). *Alford* is wrong in saying Elias's prayer that it might not rain 'is not even hinted at in the Old Testament.' In 1 Ki. xvii. 1 it is plainly implied, "As the Lord God of Israel liveth, *before whom I stand*, there shall not be dew nor rain these years, but *according to my word*." His prophecy of the fact was according to a divine intimation given to him in answer to prayer. In jealousy for God's honour (1 Ki. xix. 10), being of one mind with God in abhorrence of apostasy, he prayed that the national idolatry should be punished with a national judgment, drought, if haply it might bring them to repent: on Israel's profession of repentance he prayed for the removal of it, as is implied in 1 Ki. xviii. 39-42: cf. Luke iv. 25. **three years, &c.**— Cf. 1 Ki. xviii. 1, "the third year;" viz., from Elijah's going to Zarephath (1 Ki. xvii. 9): the prophecy (*v.* 1) was probably about five or six months previously. **18. prayed again, and**—i.e., *and so*. Mark the connection between the prayer and its accomplishment. **her fruit**—her usual due fruit, heretofore withheld for sin. Three and a half years is the time also that the two witnesses prophesy who "have power to shut heaven that it rain not" (Rev. xi. 3, 6).

19. The blessing of reclaiming an erring sinner by mutual counsel and intercessory prayer (*v.* 16). **do err** [*planēthē*]—'be led astray.' **the truth**— the Gospel. **one** [*tis*]—'any.' *Every one* ought to seek the salvation of *every one* (*Bengel*). **20. Let him** (the converter) **know**—for his encouragement. **shall save**—future. The salvation of the converted shall be manifested hereafter. **shall hide a multitude of sins**—not his own, but *of the converted* [*kalupsei* (active voice) requires this]. Prov. x. 12 (cf. note) refers to charity 'covering' the sins of others *before men;* St. James to one's effecting by another's conversion that that other's sins be covered *before God*—viz. (Ps. xxxii. 1), by making the convert partaker in Christ's atonement for the remission of all sins. Though this hiding of sins was included in "shall save," St. James expresses it to mark the greatness of the blessing conferred on the penitent through the converter's instrumentality, and so incite others to the same good deed.

PETER.

1 PETER, an apostle of Jesus Christ, to the strangers *a*scattered through-
2 out Pontus, Galatia, Cappadocia, Asia, and Bithynia, elect *b*according
to the foreknowledge of God the Father, *c*through sanctification of the
Spirit, unto obedience and *d*sprinkling of the blood of Jesus Christ:
Grace unto you, and peace, be multiplied.

A. D. 60.

CHAP. 1.
a John 7. 35.
b Rom. 8. 29.
c 2 Thes. 2. 13.
d Heb. 12. 24.

CHAP. I. 1-25.—ADDRESS TO THE ELECTED OF
THE GODHEAD—THANKSGIVING FOR THE LIVING
HOPE TO WHICH WE ARE BEGOTTEN, PRODUCING
JOY AMIDST SUFFERINGS—THIS SALVATION OF
DEEPEST INTEREST TO PROPHETS AND TO ANGELS
—ITS COSTLY PRICE A MOTIVE TO HOLINESS AND
LOVE, AS WE ARE BORN AGAIN OF GOD'S EVER-
ABIDING WORD.

1. Peter—Greek of Cephas, *man of rock.* **an
apostle of Jesus Christ.** 'He who preaches otherwise than as a messenger of Christ, is not to be
heard: if he preach as such, then it is all one as if
Christ spake in thy presence' (*Luther*). **to the
strangers scattered** [*parepidemois diasporas*]—
'sojourners *of the dispersion:*' only in John vii. 35
and Jas. i. 1; LXX.; Ps. cxlvii. 2, "the outcasts of
Israel:" the designation particular to *the Jews*
dispersed throughout the world ever since the
Babylonian captivity. These he, as apostle of the
circumcision, primarily addresses, but not in the
temporal sense only: their temporal condition is a
shadow of their spiritual calling to be *strangers*
and pilgrims on earth, looking for the heavenly
Jerusalem as their home (Heb. xi. 8-10). So the
Gentile Christians are included secondarily, as
having the same high calling. Ch. i. 14; ii. 10; iv.
3, plainly refer to Christian *Gentiles* (cf. *v.* 17).
Christians, if they rightly consider their calling,
must never settle here, but feel themselves *travellers.* As the Jews in their *dispersion* diffused
through the nations the knowledge of the one God,
preparatory to Christ's first advent, so Christians,
by their dispersion among the unconverted, diffuse
the knowledge of Christ, preparatory to His second
advent. "The children of God scattered abroad"
constitute one whole in Christ, who "gathers them
together in one," now partially and in spirit,
hereafter perfectly and visibly. "Elect" (Greek
order) comes before "strangers:" *elect,* in relation
to heaven; *strangers,* in relation to earth. The
election is that of individuals to eternal life by
God's sovereign grace, as the sequel shows. While
each is certified of his own election by the Spirit,
he receives no assurance concerning others; nor
are we to be too inquisitive (John xxi. 21, 22).
Peter numbers them among the *elect,* as they
carried the appearance of being regenerated. He
calls the whole Church by the designation belonging
only to the better portion (*Calvin*). The election
to *hearing,* and that to *eternal life,* are distinct.
Realization of our election is a strong motive to
holiness. The minister invites all; in the elect
alone the preaching takes effect. As the chief
fruit of exhortations redounds to them, Peter at
the outset addresses *them.* *Steiger* translates, To
'the elect pilgrims who form the dispersion in
Pontus,' &c. The *order* of the provinces is that
in which they would be viewed by one writing
from the East from *Babylon* (ch. v. 13); from
north-east southwards to Galatia, south-east to

Cappadocia, then Asia, and back to Bithynia,
west of Pontus. Contrast the order, Acts ii. 9.
He now was ministering to those same peoples as
he preached to on Pentecost: "Parthians, Medes,
Elamites, dwellers in Mesopotamia and Judea"—
i. e., the Jews now subject to the Parthians, whose
capital was *Babylon,* where he laboured in person;
"dwellers in Cappadocia, Pontus, Asia, Phrygia,
Pamphylia," the Asiatic dispersion derived from
Babylon, whom he ministers to by letter. **2. foreknowledge**—*foreordaining* love (*v.* 20) inseparable
from God's *foreknowledge,* the origin *from* which,
and pattern *according to* which, election takes place.
Acts ii. 23, and Rom. xi. 2, prove "foreknowledge"
to be *foreordination.* God's *foreknowledge* is not
the perception of any ground of action out of Himself; still, in it liberty is comprehended, and all
absolute constraint debarred (*Anselm* in *Steiger*).
For so the Son of God was 'foreknown' (Greek
for "foreordained," *v.* 20) to be the sacrificial
Lamb; not without His will, but His will resting
in the will of the Father. This includes self-
conscious action—nay, even cheerful acquiescence.
The Scriptural "know" includes *approval* and
acknowledging as one's own. The Hebrew marks
the oneness of *loving* and *choosing* by having one
word for both [*Bachar*] [LXX., *hairetizo*]. Peter
descends from God's eternal 'election,' through
the *new birth,* to believers' "sanctification," that
from this he may again raise them through consideration of their *new birth* to a 'living hope'
of the heavenly "inheritance" (*Heidegger*). The
divine three are introduced in their respective
functions in redemption. **through**—Greek, 'in':
the element in which we are elected. 'Election'
realizes itself 'IN' their sanctification. Believers
are "sanctified through the offering of Christ once
for all" (Heb. x. 10). 'Thou must believe that
thou art holy; not, however, through thine own
piety, but through the blood of Christ' (*Luther*).
The true sanctification of the Spirit is to obey the
Gospel, to trust in Christ (*Bullinger*). **sanctification**—the Spirit's setting apart of the saint as
consecrated to God. The execution of God's *choice*
(Gal. i. 4). God the Father gives us salvation by
gratuitous election: the Son earns it by His blood-
shedding: the Holy Spirit applies the Son's merits
to the soul by the Gospel word (*Calvin*). Cf. Num.
vi. 24-26, the Old Testament triune blessing. **unto
obedience**—the *end aimed at* by God as respects
us, the *obedience* which consists in, and that which
flows from, faith: "obeying the truth through the
Spirit" (*v.* 22; Rom. i. 5). **sprinkling, &c.** Not
justification through the atonement once for all,
which is expressed in the previous clauses, but (as
the order proves) *the daily sprinkling by Christ's
blood, cleansing from all sin,* which is the privilege
of one already justified and "walking in the light"
(1 John i. 7; John xiii. 10). **Grace**—the source of
"peace." **be multiplied**—(Dan. iv. 1.) 'Ye have

3   Blessed *be* the God and Father of our Lord Jesus Christ, which according to his [1]abundant mercy *[c]*hath begotten us again unto a lively hope,
4 by *[f]*the resurrection of Jesus Christ from the dead, to an inheritance incorruptible, and undefiled, and that fadeth not away, reserved in
5 heaven [2]for you, who *[g]*are kept by the power of God through faith unto

A D. (0.

[1] much.
[c] Jas. 1. 18.
[f] 1 Thes. 4.14.
[2] Or, for us.
[g] John 0. 28.

peace and grace, but still not in perfection: ye must go on increasing until the old Adam be dead' (*Luther*).

3. He begins, like Paul, in opening his epistles, with giving thanks to God for the great salvation: he looks forward (1.) into the future (*vv.* 3-9); (2.) backward into the past (*vv.* 10-12) (*Alford*). **Blessed**—absolutely, *His blessedness being self-derived,* and our blessing Him being only an ascription to Him of what is His own. [*Eulogetos* in the New Testament is restricted to God; *eulogemenos* (*blessed with blessing from without*) is said of man, and even of the Messiah as man (Matt. xxi. 9; xxv. 34: cf. John xii. 13; Luke i. 28, 42); *Barak,* lit., *to kneel.*] To bless any, without reference to God as the original source of blessing, is idolatry (Ps. ciii. 22; Rev. v. 12). **Father.** This whole epistle accords with the Lord's prayer: "Father," ch. i. 3, 14, 17, 23; ii. 2; "our," ch. i. 4, end; "in heaven," ch. i. 4; "hallowed be thy name," ch. i. 15, 16; iii. 15; "thy kingdom come," ch. ii. 9; "thy will be done," ch. ii. 15; iii. 17; iv. 2, 19; "daily bread," ch. v. 7; "forgiveness of sins," ch. iv. 8, 1; "temptation," ch. iv. 12; "deliverance," ch. iv. 18 (*Bengel*): cf. ch. iii. 7, and iv. 7, for allusions to *prayer.* **abundant** [*polu*]—'much.' That God's "mercy" should reach *us* guilty enemies, proves its fullness. "Mercy" met our *misery,* "grace" our *guilt.* **begotten us again**—of the *Spirit* by the *Word* (*v.* 23); children of wrath, naturally *dead* in sins. **unto**—so that we have. **lively** [*zōsan*]— 'living.' It has in itself, gives, and looks for, *life* (*De Wette*). *Living* is a favourite expression of St. Peter (*v.* 23; ch. ii. 4, 5). He delights in contemplating *life* overcoming death. *Faith* and *love* follow *hope* (*vv.* 8, 21, 22). "(Unto) a lively hope" is explained by "(to) an inheritance incorruptible . . . fadeth not away," and "(unto) salvation . . . ready to be revealed in the last time." Join [*elpida zosan di' anastaseos*] 'unto a hope *living* (possessing vitality) *through* the resurrection of Jesus Christ.' Faith, the subjective means of the soul's spiritual resurrection, is wrought by the same power whereby Christ was raised (Eph. xix. 20). Baptism is an objective means (ch. iii. 21). Its moral fruit is a new life. The connection of our sonship with the resurrection appears in Luke xx. 36; Acts xiii. 33. Christ's resurrection is—(1.) the efficient cause of ours (1 Cor. xv. 22); (2.) the exemplary cause: all the saints shall rise after the similitude of His resurrection (Phil. iii. 21). Our "hope" is, Christ rising ordained the power, and is the pattern of the believer's resurrection. The soul, born again from nature into grace, is also born again unto the life of glory. Matt. xix. 28, "The *regeneration,* when the Son of man shall sit in the throne of His glory;" the resurrection of our bodies is a coming out of the womb of the earth, a nativity into an immortal life (*Bishop Pearson*). Our private adoption is now (Gal. iv. 6); our public, at the coming resurrection. The four causes of salvation are—(1.) the primary, God's mercy; (2.) the proximate, Christ's death and resurrection; (3.) the formal, our regeneration; (4.) the final, our eternal bliss. John is the disciple of *love;* Paul, of *faith;* Peter, of *hope.* Hence Peter, most of all the apostles, urges the resurrection of Christ: an undesigned coinci-

dence between the history and the epistle (cf. 'Introduction'), so a proof of genuineness. Christ's resurrection was the occasion of his own restoration by Christ after his fall (Mark xvi. 7). **4. To an inheritance**—the object of "hope" (*v.* 3); therefore not a *dead,* but a '*living*' hope. The inheritance is the believer's already by title, being actually assigned; the entrance on its possession is future, a hoped-for certainty. Being "begotten again" as a "son," he is an "heir," as earthly fathers *beget* children to *inherit* their goods. The inheritance is "salvation" (*vv.* 5, 9); "the grace to be brought at the revelation of Christ" (*v.* 13; ch. v. 4). **incorruptible**—not having the germs of death. Negations of the imperfections here are the chief means of conveying to us a conception of the things which "have not entered into the heart of man," our faculties now being inadequate to comprehend them. Peter, impulsive and susceptible of outward impressions, was more likely to feel painfully the deep-seated *corruption* lurking under the loveliest of earthly things, and dooming them to speedy decay. **undefiled**—not stained as earthly goods by sin, either in acquiring or using them; unsusceptible of stain. 'The rich man is either dishonest himself, or the heir of a dishonest man' (*Jerome*). Even Israel's inheritance was *defiled* by sin. Defilement intrudes on our holy things now; whereas God's service ought to be undefiled. **that fadeth not away.** Contrast *v.* 24. Even the delicate bloom of the heavenly inheritance continues *unfading.* 'In *substance* incorruptible; in *purity* undefiled; in *beauty* unfading' (*Alford*). **reserved**—*kept up* (Col. i. 5; 2 Tim. iv. 8); perfect [*tetērēmenēn*], an *abiding state;* 'which has been and is reserved.' The inheritance is beyond risk, out of Satan's reach, though we for whom it is reserved are still amidst dangers. If we are believers, we too (*v.* 5), as well as the inheritance, are "kept" (John xvii. 12). **in heaven**—Greek, 'in the heavens,' where it can neither be destroyed nor plundered. St. Peter remembers Jesus' sermon on the mount (Matt. vi. 20). Though *now* laid up in *heaven,* it shall *hereafter* be on *earth* also. **for you.** It is secure not only in itself from misfortune, but also from alienation; no other can receive it in your stead. He had said US (*v.* 3), he now turns to the elect, to encourage them. א A C, Vulgate, "you;" B, 'us.' **5. kept** [*phrouroumenous*]—'who are being guarded.' He answers the objection, Of what use is it that salvation is "reserved" for us in heaven, as in a secure haven, when we are tossed in the world as on a troubled sea, amidst a thousand wrecks? (*Calvin*). As the inheritance is "kept" (*v.* 4) safely "in heaven," so must we be 'guarded' in the world to be sure of reaching it. This defines the "you," *v.* 4. The inheritance belongs only to those who "endure unto the end," 'guarded' "IN [*en*] the power of God through *faith.*" Contrast Luke viii. 13. 'It is God's *guarding power* which saves us from our enemies. It is His *long-suffering* which saves us from ourselves' (*Bengel*). Jude 1; Phil. i. 6; iv. 7, "keep" [*phrouresei*], "guard," as here. This guarding is effected by God's "power," the efficient cause; "through faith," on man's part, the effective means. The believer lives spiritually *in* God, in virtue of His power; and God lives in him. "In" marks that

6 salvation ready to be revealed in the last time: wherein [h] ye greatly rejoice, though now for a season, if need be, ye are in heaviness through
7 manifold temptations; that the trial of your faith, being much more precious than of gold that perisheth, though [i] it be tried with fire, might be found unto praise and honour and glory at the appearing of Jesus
8 Christ: whom [j] having not seen, ye love; [k] in whom, though now ye see *him* not, yet believing, ye rejoice with joy unspeakable and full of glory:
9 receiving the end of your faith, *even* the salvation of *your* souls.
10 Of [l] which salvation the prophets have enquired and searched dili-
11 gently, who prophesied of the grace *that should come* unto you: searching

A. D. 60.

[h] Matt. 5. 12.
Rom. 12. 12.
[i] Ps. 66. 10.
Isa. 48. 10.
[j] John 20. 29.
1 John 4. 20.
[k] John 20. 29.
2 Cor. 5. 7.
[l] Gen. 49. 10.
Dan. 2. 44.
Hag. 2. 7.
Zech. 6. 12.

the cause is inherent in God, working organically through them with living influence, so that the means exist also in the cause. The power of God which guards the believer is no force working upon him from without with mechanical necessity, but God's spiritual power in which he lives, and with whose spirit he is clothed (1 Chr. xii. 18; Hagg. i. 13). It comes down on, then dwells in, him, even as he is in it (*Steiger*). None is being guarded by the power of God unto salvation, if not walking by faith. Neither speculative knowledge nor works of seeming charity avail, severed from *faith:* through faith salvation is both received and kept. **unto salvation**—the end of the new birth; not merely accomplished for us in title by Christ, and made over to us on believing, but *manifested, and finally completed* (Heb. ix. 28). **ready to be revealed**—when Christ shall be revealed. The preparations have been long going on: "all things are now *ready:*" salvation is accomplished, and only waits the Lord's time to be manifested: He "is ready to judge" (ch. iv. 5). **last time**—closing the day of grace: the day of judgment, redemption, restitution of all things, and perdition of the ungodly. **6. Wherein**—in which salvation. **greatly rejoice** [*agalliasthe*]—'exult with joy.' *Salvation* is realized by faith (*v.* 9), as so actually present as to cause exulting joy in spite of afflictions. **for a season** [*oligon*]—'for a little.' **if need be**—'*since* (God sees) *it is needed*' for His glory and our salvation. God sends affliction on His people only where there is need (Job v. 6). One need not lay a cross on himself, but only "take up" that which God imposes ("his cross"). 2 Tim. iii. 12 is not to be pressed too far. Not every believer, nor every sinner, is afflicted. Some falsely think that notwithstanding our forgiveness in Christ, an expiation of sin by suffering is still needed. **ye are in heaviness** [*lupēthentes*]—'ye were grieved.' The 'grieved' is *past;* the 'exulting joy' present: because the realized joy of coming salvation makes *present* grief seem a thing of the *past.* At the first shock ye *were grieved*, but now *by anticipation ye rejoice.* **through**—'IN:' the element in which the grief has place. **manifold**—of various kinds (ch. iv. 12, 13). **temptations**—'trials' testing faith. **7.** Aim of the "temptations." **trial** [*dokimion*]—*testing.* That your *faith so proved* 'may be found (aorist, *heurethē: once for all*, as the result of being proved) unto (eventuating in) praise,' to be bestowed by the Judge. **than of gold**—rather 'than gold.' **though** [*de*]—'which perisheth, YET is tried with fire.' If gold, though perishing (*v.* 18), is yet tried with fire, to remove dross and test genuineness, how much more does your faith, which shall never perish, need to pass through a fiery trial to remove defects, and test its genuineness and preciousness? **glory.** "Honour" is not so strong as "glory." "Praise" is in *words;* "honour" in deeds; *honorary reward.* **appearing**—as in *v.* 13, "revelation of Jesus." Then shall take place also the revelation of the sons of God (Rom.

viii. 19), "manifestation" [*apokalupim*], "revelation" (1 John iii. 2, Greek, 'manifested). **8.** **having not seen, ye love**—in other cases *knowledge* of the person produces *love.* They are more "blessed that have not seen, yet have believed," than they who believed because they saw (John xx. 29). On Peter's love to Jesus, cf. John xxi. 15-17. Though the apostles had seen, they now ceased to know Him after the flesh (2 Cor. v. 16). **in whom**—connected with "believing:" the result is, "ye rejoice." **now**—*in the present state*, contrasted with the *future*, when believers "shall see His face."—(1 Cor. ii. 9.) **full of glory** [*dedoxasmene*]—'glorified.' A joy already *encompassed with glory.* The "glory" is partly in possession, through the presence of "the Lord of glory" in the soul; partly in assured anticipation. The Christian's *joy* accompanies *love* to Jesus: its ground is *faith;* it is not therefore either self-seeking or self-sufficient' (*Steiger*). **9.** **Receiving**—in sure anticipation—**the end of your faith**—*i. e.*, its crowning consummation, finally-completed "salvation" (Peter confirms Paul's teaching, *justification by faith*); also receiving *now* the title, and the first-fruits. In *v.* 10, "salvation" is represented as *already present*, whereas "the prophets" had it not so. It must, therefore, in this verse refer to present. *Deliverance from wrath:* believers even now "receive salvation," though its full "revelation" is future. **of your souls.** The immortal *soul* was lost, so "salvation" primarily concerns it; the *body* shall share in redemption hereafter; the believer's *soul* is *saved already.*

10. The magnitude of this "salvation" is proved by the earnestness with which "prophets," and even "angels," searched into it. From the beginning of the world it has been testified to by the Holy Spirit. **prophets**—"(*the*) prophets" generally (including the Old Testament *inspired* authors). **enquired** [*exezetesan*]—perseveringly. Much more is manifested to us than by diligent enquiry the prophets attained. Still, it is not said they searched *after*, but '*concerning*' [*peri*] it. They were already certain of redemption coming. They did not *see*, but *desired* to see, the same Christ whom we fully see in spirit. 'As Simeon was anxiously desiring, and found peace only when he saw Christ, so the Old Testament saints only saw Christ hidden, and as it were absent—not in power and grace, but not yet manifested in the flesh' (*Calvin*). The prophets, *as private individuals*, had to reflect on the far-reaching sense of their own prophecies. Their words, *in their public function*, were not so much their own as the Spirit's, speaking by and in them: thus Caiaphas, John xi. 49-52,—a testimony to verbal inspiration. The *words* of the inspired authors are God's, expressing the mind of the Spirit; the writers themselves searched into the words, to fathom the precious meaning, even as believing readers did. "Searched" [*exēreunesan*] implies they had determinate marks to go by. **the grace (that**

599

what, or what manner of time, [m]the Spirit of Christ which was in them did signify, when it testified beforehand [n]the sufferings of Christ, and the
12 glory that should follow. Unto [o]whom it was revealed, that not unto [p]themselves, but unto us, they did minister the things which are now reported unto you by them that have preached the Gospel unto you with [q]the Holy Ghost sent down from heaven; [r]which things the angels desire to look into.
13 Wherefore gird up the loins of your mind, be sober, and hope [3]to the end for the grace that is to be brought unto you at [s]the revelation of
14 Jesus Christ: as obedient children, not fashioning yourselves according

A. D. 60.	
[m] Rom. 8 9.	
Gal. 4. 6.	
ch. 3. 19.	
[n] Ps. 22. 6.	
Isa. 53. 3.	
Dan 9. 26.	
[o] Dan 12. 9.	
[p] Heb 11. 39.	
[q] Acts 2. 4.	
[r] Ex 25. 20.	
[3] perfectly.	
[s] Luke 17. 30.	

should come) unto you—that of the New Testament; an earnest of "the grace" of perfected "salvation" 'to be brought at the (second) revelation of Christ.' Old Testament believers also possessed the grace of God; but it was as children in their nonage, so as to be like servants; we enjoy the full privilege of adult sons. **11. what** [*eis tina*]—'in reference to what;' the *time* absolutely; *what* was to be the era of Messiah's coming. **what manner of time**—what *features* should characterize the time of His coming. "Or" implies that some prophets, when not permitted to discover the exact *time*, searched into its *characteristics*. [*Kairon:* "time," *season*, the fit epoch in God's purposes.] **Spirit of Christ . . in them**—(Acts xvi. 7; in ℵ A B D E, 'the Spirit of Jesus;' Rev. xix. 10.) So *Justin Martyr*, 'Jesus was He who communed with Moses, Abraham, and the patriarchs.' *Clemens Alexandrinus* calls Him 'the Prophet of prophets, and Lord of all the prophetical spirit.' **did signify** [*edēlou*]—'did intimate.' **of** [*ta eis Christon pathemata*]—'the sufferings appointed *unto*,' or *foretold, in regard to Christ, the anointed* Mediator, whose *sufferings* are the price of our "salvation" (*vv.* 9, 10); the channel of "the grace that should come unto you." **the glory** [*doxas*]—'glories,' viz., of His resurrection, His ascension, His coming kingdom, the consequence of the sufferings. **that should follow** [*meta tauta*]—'after these sufferings' (ch. iii. 18-22; v. 1). Since "the Spirit of Christ" is the *Spirit* of God, Christ is God. Because the Son of God was to become our Christ, He manifested Himself, and the Father through Him, in the Old Testament, and by the Holy Spirit eternally proceeding from the Father and Himself, spake in the prophets. **12.** Not only was the future revealed to them, but also that these revelations were given them mainly, not for themselves, but for our good. This only quickened them in testifying in the Spirit for the partial good of believers of their own generation, and for the full benefit of believers in Gospel times. (Contrast Rev. xxii. 10.) This was "revealed" to them, lest they should be disheartened in not discovering, with all their *enquiry and search*, the full particulars of the coming "salvation." To Daniel (Dan. ix. 25, 26) the "time" was revealed. *Our* immense privileges, thus brought forth by contrast with theirs (notwithstanding that they had the great honour of Christ's Spirit speaking in them), is an incentive to greater earnestness than even they manifested, (*v.* 13, &c.) **us.** [So B; but ℵ A C, Vulgate, read "you," as in *v.* 10.] *We*, Christians, may understand the prophecies, by the Spirit's aid, in their important part—viz., so far as they have been already fulfilled. **with (in) the Holy Ghost sent down**—on Pentecost. [So ℵ C; but A B, Vulgate, Hilary, omit *en—i. e.*, 'in,' then translate 'by.'] The evangelists, speaking by the Holy Spirit, were infallible witnesses. "The Spirit of Christ" was in the prophets also (*v.* 11),

but not manifestly, as in the Christian Church's first preachers, "SENT down from heaven." How favoured are we in being ministered to, as to "salvation," by prophets and apostles, these now announcing the same things actually fulfilled which those foretold! **which things**—'the things now reported unto you' by the evangelistic preachers: 'Christ's sufferings and the glory that should follow' (*vv.* 11, 12). **angels**—higher than the prophets (*v.* 10). Angels have not, any more than ourselves, INTUITIVE knowledge of redemption. **to look into** [*parakupsai*]—to bend over, so as to look deeply into and see to the bottom (note, Jas. i. 25). As the cherubim bent down to the mercy-seat, the emblem of redemption, in the holiest, so the angels intently gaze, desiring to fathom the depths of 'the great mystery of godliness: God manifest in the flesh, justified in the Spirit, *seen of angels*' (1 Tim. iii. 16). Their 'ministry for the heirs of salvation' makes them wish to penetrate this mystery, as reflecting such glory on the love, justice, wisdom, and power of their and our Lord. They can know it only through the manifestation in the Church, as they personally have no direct share in it. 'Angels have only the contrast between good and evil, without conversion from sin to righteousness: witnessing such conversion in the Church, they long to penetrate the knowledge of the means whereby it is brought about' (*Hofman* in *Alford*). **13. Wherefore.** Seeing that the prophets ministered unto you in these high Gospel privileges which they did not themselves, though 'searching,' fully share in, and seeing that even angels "desire to look into" them, how earnest and watchful you ought to be! **gird up the loins.** Christ's own words (Luke xii. 35): an image from the Israelites eating the passover with the loose outer robe girded up about the waist with a girdle, as for a journey. Workmen, pilgrims, runners, wrestlers, warriors (all types of the Christian), so gird themselves up, both to prevent the garment impeding motion, and to brace up the body for action. The believer is to have his mind collected, and always ready for Christ's coming. *Sobriety*—i. e., *self-restraint*, lest one be overcome by the allurements of the world and sense, and enduring waiting *hope* for Christ's revelation, are the true 'girding up the loins of the mind.' **to the end** [*teleiōs*]—'perfectly,' so that there be nothing deficient in your hope; no *casting away of confidence*. Still, there is an allusion to the "end" (*v.* 9). Hope so *perfectly* as to reach *the end* [*telos*] of your faith and hope—viz., 'the grace that is being brought unto you in [*pheromenēn en*] the revelation of Christ.' As *grace* shall then be *perjected*, so do you *hope perfectly* (*v.* 3). Christ's two appearances are but different stages of the ONE great revelation, comprising the New Testament from beginning to end. **14.** From *sobriety of spirit* and *endurance of hope*, he passes to *obedience, holiness*, and *reverential fear*. As—their present character

15 to the former lusts in your ignorance : but as he which hath called you
16 is holy, so be ye holy in all manner of conversation ; because it is written,
  t Be ye holy ; for I am holy.
17   And if ye call on the Father, who without respect of persons judgeth
  according to every man's work, pass the time of your *u* sojourning *here* in
18 fear : forasmuch as ye know that ye were not redeemed with corruptible
  things, *as* silver and gold, from your vain conversation *v* received by tra-

A. D. 60.

t Lev. 11. 44.
Jer. 19. 2.
Amos 3. 3.
u 2 Cor 5. 6.
Heb. 11. 13.
Heb. 12. 28.
v Eze. 20. 18.
ch. 4. 3.

as "born again" (*vv.* 3, 23). **obedient** [Greek, 'children of obedience']—of whom *obedience* is the characteristic, as a child is of the same nature as the father. (Contrast Eph. v. 6: cf. *v.* 17.) Having the obedience of *faith* (*v.* 22) and *practice* (*vv.* 16, 18). 'Faith is the highest obedience,' because discharged to the highest command' (*Luther*). **fashioning** [*suschematizomenoi*]—*fashion* [*schema*] is fleeting, and on the surface. The 'form' [*morphe*]*,* or *conformation* in the New Testament, is something deeper and more essential. **the former lusts** in—characteristic of your state of ignorance of God : true of Jews and Gentiles. The sanctification is first described negatively (*v.* 14, putting off the old man, even in outward *fashion*, as well as in inward *conformation*), then positively (*v.* 15, putting on the new man : cf. Eph. iv. 22, 24). "Lusts" flow from original birth-sin (inherited from Adam, who by self-willed desire brought sin into the world), the *lust* which, ever since man has been alienated from God, seeks to fill up with earthly things the emptiness of his being. The manifold forms which the mother-lust assumes are *lusts*. In the *new man* of the regenerate, which constitutes his truest self, 'sin' no longer exists ; but in the flesh, or old man, it does (1 John iii. 9). Hence arises the conflict through life, wherein the new man in the main prevails, and at last completely. But the natural man knows only the combat of his lusts with one another, or with the law, without power to conquer them. **15.** [*Kata ton Kalesanta*] 'But (rather) after the pattern of Him who hath called you (whose characteristic is that He is) holy, be [*become: genethete*] yourselves also holy.' God is our model. God's *calling* is a frequently-urged motive. 'Let the acts of the offspring indicate likeness to the Father' (*Augustine*). **conversation** [*anastrophe*]—deportment, course of life: distinct from, but reflecting, one's internal nature. Christians are holy unto God by *consecration ;* they must be so also in *outward walk and behaviour.* **16.** *Scripture* is the source of all authority in questions of doctrine and practice. **Be ye holy ; for I am.** It is ME you have to do with. Ye are mine. We are too prone to have respect unto men (*Calvin*). As I am the fountain of holiness, being holy in my *essence*, be ye zealous to *partake* of holiness, that ye may be as I am (*Didymus*). The creature is holy only in so far as it is sanctified by God. God, in giving the command, is willing to give also the power to obey, through the sanctifying Spirit (*v.* 2).
 17. *if*—i.e., '*seeing that* ye call on ;' for all the regenerate pray as *children* of God, "Our *Father*," &c. **the Father** [*Patera epikaleisthe ton krinonta*] —'call upon *as Father* Him who without acceptance of persons (Acts x. 34, not accepting the Jew above the Gentile ; 2 Chr. xix. 7, a judge not biassed by respect of persons) judgeth,' &c. The Father judgeth by His Son, His Representative, exercising His delegated authority (John v. 22). This marks the unity of the Trinity. **work.** Each man's *work* is *one* whole, whether good or bad. The particular works of each are manifestations of his general life-work, whether it be of faith and

love, whereby alone we please God and escape condemnation. **pass** [*anastraphete*] —'conduct yourselves during.' **sojourning.** The state of the Jews in their *dispersion* typifies the *sojourner-like* state of believers in this world, away from our fatherland. **fear** — reverential, not slavish. He who is your Father is also your Judge : this may well inspire reverential fear. *Theophylact,* A double fear is mentioned : (1.) *elementary*, causing one to become serious ; (2.) *perfective*, the motive by which Peter urges them as sons of God to be obedient. *Fear* is not opposed to *assurance*, but to carnal *security :* producing *vigilant caution* lest we offend God and backslide. '*Fear* and *hope* flow from the same fountain : *fear* prevents our falling away from *hope*' (*Bengel*). Though *love* has no *fear* IN it, yet our present imperfect love needs fear to go ALONG WITH it as a subordinate principle. This fear drowns all other fears. The believer fears God, so has none else to fear. Not to fear God is the greatest baseness. The martyrs' more than human courage flowed from this. **18.** Another motive to reverential *fear* (*v.* 17) of displeasing God,—the consideration of the costly price of our redemption from sin. It is *we* who are bought by the blood of Christ, not heaven : heaven is the "inheritance" (*v.* 4) given to us as sons, by the promise of God. **redeemed.** Gold and silver being corruptible themselves, and so of little value, can free no one from spiritual and bodily corruption. Contrast *v.* 19, Christ's "*precious* blood." The Israelites were ransomed with half a shekel each, which went towards purchasing the *lamb* for the daily sacrifice (Exod. xxx. 12-16 : cf. Num. iii. 44-51). But the Lamb who redeems the spiritual Israelites does so 'without money or price' (Isa. lv. 1). Devoted by sin to God's justice, the church of the first-born is redeemed from sin and the curse with Christ's precious blood. In Matt. xx. 28 ; 1 Tim. ii. 6 ; Titus ii. 14 ; Rev. v. 9, the idea is that of *substitution*, the giving of one for another by way of ransom or equivalent. Man is 'sold under sin' as a slave ; shut up under condemnation. The ransom was, therefore, paid to the righteously incensed Judge, and accepted as a vicarious satisfaction for our sin, inasmuch as it was His own love, as well as righteousness, which appointed it. An Israelite sold as a bond-servant for debt might be redeemed by one of his brethren. As, therefore, we could not redeem ourselves, Christ assumed our nature to become our Brother, and so our God or Redeemer. Holiness is the natural fruit of redemption "from our vain conversation ;" for He *by* whom we are redeemed is also He *for* whom we are redeemed. 'Without the righteous abolition of the curse, either there could be found no deliverance, or the grace and righteousness of God must have come in collision' (*Steiger*) ; but now Christ having borne the curse of our sin, frees from it those who are made God's children by His Spirit. **corruptible.** Cf. *vv.* 7, 23. **silver and (or) gold.** Cf. Peter's own words, Acts iii. 6 : an undesigned coincidence. **vain**—self-deceiving, promising good which it does not perform. (Cf. the heathen, Acts xiv. 15 ; Rom. i. 21 ; Eph. iv. 17 ; human philoso-

19 dition from your fathers; but *with the precious blood of Christ, as *of
20 a lamb without blemish and without spot: who *verily was foreordained
before the foundation of the world, but was manifest *in these last
21 times for you, who by him do believe in God, that raised him up from
the dead, and *gave him glory; that your faith and hope might be
in God.
22 Seeing ye have purified your souls in obeying the truth through the
Spirit unto unfeigned love of the brethren, *see that ye* love one another
23 with a pure heart fervently: being *born again, not of corruptible seed,
but of incorruptible, by *the word of God, which liveth and abideth for

A. D. 60.

w Rev. 5. 9.
x Ex. 12. 5.
    John 1. 29.
y 2 Tim. 1. 9.
    Tit. 1. 2. 3.
    Rev. 13. 8.
z Gal. 4. 4.
a Phil 2. 9.
b John 1. 13.
    John 3. 5.
    1 John 3. 9.
c Jas. 1. 18.

---

phers, 1 Cor. iii. 20; the disobedient Jews, Jer. iv. 14.) **conversation**—course of life. To know our sin we must know its cost. **received by tradition from your fathers.** 'Human piety is a vain blasphemy, the greatest sin that man can commit' (*Luther*). There is only one *Father* to be imitated (*v.* 17: cf. Matt. xxiii. 9). **19. precious** — of inestimable value. Greek order, 'With precious blood, as of a lamb without blemish (*in itself*) and without spot (*contracted from others*), [even the blood] of Christ.' Though very man, He remained pure *in Himself* ("without blemish"), and uninfected by any impression of sin *from without* ("without spot"), which would have unfitted Him for being our atoning Redeemer: so the passover lamb; so too, the Church, the Bride, by union with Him. As Israel's redemption from Egypt required the blood of the paschal lamb, so our redemption from the curse required the blood of Christ; "foreordained" (*v.* 20) from eternity, as the passover lamb was taken up on the tenth day of the month. **20.** God's eternal foreordination of Christ's redeeming sacrifice, and completion of it *in these last times for us*, are an additional obligation to our maintaining a holy walk. Peter's language in the history corresponds (Acts ii. 23), "*foreknowledge:*" here, *lit.*, "*foreknown:*" an undesigned coincidence and mark of genuineness. Redemption was no after-thought remedy of an unforeseen evil. God's *foreordaining* of the Redeemer refutes the slander that, on the Christian theory, there are 4,000 years of nothing but an incensed God. God *chose us in Christ before the foundation of the world* (Eph. i. 4). **manifest**—in the fulness of the time. He existed from eternity before. **in these last times** (1 Cor. x. 11). This last dispensation, made up of "times" marked by great changes, still retaining a general unity, stretches from Christ's ascension to His coming to judgment. **21. by** (through) **him.** Cf. "the *faith* which is *by Him*" (Acts iii. 16); His Spirit, obtained for us in His resurrection and ascension, enabling us to believe. This excludes all who do not 'by Him believe in God,' and includes all that do. *To believe* IN [*eis Theon*] *God* expresses *internal* trust: 'going INTO, and cleaving to Him, incorporated into His members. By this faith the ungodly is justified; *thenceforth* faith itself begins to work by love' (*P. Lombard*). To *believe* ON [*epi Theon*, or *Theo*, or dative] *God* expresses confidence, reposing ON God. "Faith IN [*en*] His blood" (Rom. iii. 25) implies that His blood is the element IN which faith has its abiding place. Cf. Acts xx. 21, "Repentance toward [*eis*, turning *towards* and *going into*] God and faith toward [*eis*, 'into'] Christ:" where, as there is but one article to both, "repentance" and "faith" are joined as one truth. Where *repentance* is, there *faith* is. When one knows God the Father, then he must know the Son by whom alone we come to the Father: the only living way to God is through Christ's sacrifice. **that raised him**—the ground of "believing:" (1.) because by it God declared

His acceptance of Him as our righteous substitute; (2.) by it and His glorification He received power, viz., the Holy Spirit, to impart to His elect "faith:" the same power enabling us to believe as raised Him from the dead (Eph. i. 19, 20). Our faith must not only be IN, but BY and THROUGH Christ. 'Since in Christ's resurrection our salvation is grounded, *there* "faith" and "hope" find their stay' (*Calvin*). **that your faith and hope might be** [or, *so that*—*are: hōste einai*] **in God**—the *object* and the *effect* of *God's raising Christ:* an indirect exhortation. Your *faith* flows from His *resurrection;* your *hope* from God's having 'given Him *glory*' (cf. *v.* 11). So Peter, in Acts ii. 32, 33; v. 31; x. 40, makes Christ's being raised *by God* the foundation of faith. Apart from Christ we could have only *feared,* not *believed* and *hoped* in, God. Cf. *vv.* 3, 7-9, 13, on *hope* with *faith; love* is introduced, *v.* 22. Faith and hope in Christ, so far from drawing *from,* draws *to,* God: for He is God: otherwise by believing in Him we should incur the curse (Jer. xvii. 5). **22. purified** [*hegnikotes:* made chaste] . . . **in obeying the truth**—'in *your* (*the*) obedience of (i. e., *to*) the truth' (the Gospel way of salvation); *i. e.,* in your *believing. Faith* purifies the heart by implanting the only pure motive, love to God (Acts xv. 9; Rom. i. 5). **through the Spirit.** Omitted in א A B C. The Holy Spirit bestows the obedience of faith (*v.* 2; 1 Cor. xii. 3). **unto**—*with a view to:* the proper result of faith. 'For what end must we lead a pure life? That we may thereby be saved? No: but that we may serve our neighbour' (*Luther*). **unfeigned**—(ch. ii. 1, 2.) **love of the brethren**—*i. e.,* Christians; distinct from common *love.* 'The Christian loves primarily those in Christ; secondarily, all who might be in Christ—viz., all men, as Christ died for all, and as he hopes that they, too, may become Christian brethren' (*Steiger*). Bengel: here, as in 2 Pet. i. 5, 7, 'brotherly love' is preceded by the purifying graces, "*faith,* knowledge, godliness," &c. Love to the brethren evidences our regeneration and justification. **love one another.** When the *purifying by faith into love of the brethren* has formed the *habit,* the *act* follows, so that "love" is at once *habit* and *act.* **with a pure heart.** So א. But A B read, '(love) from the heart.' **fervently** [*ektenōs*]—'intensely:' with all powers *on the stretch* (ch. iv. 8; Acts xxvi. 7). **23.** Christian brotherhood flows from new birth of an imperishable seed, God's abiding word; the consideration urged to lead us to *brotherly love.* As natural relationship begets natural affection, so spiritual relationship spiritual, and therefore abiding love, even as the *seed* from which it springs is abiding, not transitory, as earthly things. **of . . . of . . . by.** "The word of God" is not the material of the spiritual new birth, but its mean. By means of the *word* the man receives the incorruptible *seed, the Holy Spirit,* and so becomes "born again:" John iii. 3-5, "Born *of*

24 ever. [4] For all flesh *is* as grass, and all the glory of man as the flower
25 of grass. The grass withereth, and the flower thereof falleth away: but
[d] the word of the Lord endureth for ever. And this is the word which
2 by the Gospel is preached unto you. WHEREFORE, laying aside all
malice, and all guile, and hypocrisies, and envies, and all evil speakings,
2 as [a] new-born babes, desire the sincere milk [b] of the word, that ye may
3 grow thereby: if so be ye have [c] tasted that the Lord *is* gracious.

A. D. 60.

[4] Or, For
that.
[d] Isa. 40. 8.

CHAP. 2.
[a] Matt. 18. 3.
[b] 1 Cor. 3. 2.
[c] Heb. 6. 5.

---

water and the Spirit," where, there being but one Greek article to the two nouns, *the* close connection of the sign and the grace signified is implied. The *word* is the remote and anterior instrument; *baptism,* the proximate and *sacramental* instrument. The word is the instrument in relation to the individual; baptism, in relation to the Church (Jas. i. 18). We are born again *of the Spirit,* yet not without means, but by the word of God. The word is not the begetting principle, but that by which it works: the vehicle of the germinating power (*Alford*). **which liveth and abideth for ever.** The Bible is a living organism, not a haphazard collection of fragments: its parts have a mutual relation and a special function, subordinate to the design of the whole. It is because the Spirit of God accompanies it that the word carries the germ of life. They who are born again *live and abide for ever,* in contrast to those who sow to the flesh (Gal. vi. 8). 'The Gospel bears incorruptible fruits, not dead works, because it is itself incorruptible' (*Bengel*). The word is an eternal power. For though the speech vanishes, there remains the kernel, the truth comprehended in the voice. This sinks into the heart, and is living—yea, is God Himself. So God to Moses, Exod. iv. 12, "I will be with thy mouth" (*Luther*). 'The *gospel* shall never cease, though its ministry shall' (*Calov*). The abiding *resurrection-glory* is connected with our *regeneration* by the Spirit. Regeneration, beginning with renewing man's *soul* at the resurrection, passes on to the *body,* then to the world of nature. 24. Scripture proof that the word of God lives for ever, in contrast to man's frailty. If ye were born again of flesh, corruptible seed, ye must perish again as grass; but now that from which you derive life remains eternally, and so will render you eternal. **flesh**—man's earthly nature. **of man.** A B C, Vulgate, read 'of it' (*i. e.,* of the flesh); א, 'of him.' "The glory"—*i. e.,* the wisdom, strength, riches, learning, honour, beauty, art, virtue, and righteousness of *the* NATURAL man ("flesh"),—all are transitory (John iii. 6); not OF MAN absolutely; for the glory of *man, in his true ideal* realized in the believer, is eternal. **withereth** [aorist: *exeranthē*]—*i. e.,* is withered as a thing of the *past.* So [*exepesen*] '*fell* away'—*i. e.,* is fallen away: it no sooner is, than it is gone. **thereof.** Omitted in A B א. "The grass" is the *flesh:* "the flower," its *glory.* **25.** (Ps. cxix. 89.) **the word . . . is** (rather, *was*) **preached** [*euangelisthen*] **unto you.** That is eternal which is born of incorruptible seed (*v.* 24); but ye have received this, viz., the word (*v.* 25); therefore ye are born for eternity, and so are bound to live for eternity (*vv.* 22, 23). Ye have not far to look for the word; it is the Gospel glad tidings *which was preached to you* by our brother Paul. See 'Introduction,' showing Peter addresses some of the same churches as Paul wrote to.

CHAP. II. 1-25.—EXHORTATIONS—TO GUILE-LESS FEEDING ON THE WORD BY THE SENSE OF THEIR PRIVILEGES AS NEW-BORN BABES—LIVING STONES IN THE SPIRITUAL TEMPLE, BUILT ON CHRIST THE CHIEF CORNER STONE; ROYAL PRIESTS; IN CONTRAST TO THEIR FORMER STATE—

603

ALSO TO ABSTINENCE FROM FLESHLY LUSTS, AND TO WALK WORTHILY IN ALL RELATIONS OF LIFE, SO THAT THE WORLD WHICH OPPOSES THEM MAY GLORIFY GOD IN SEEING THEIR GOOD WORKS—CHRIST THE GRAND PATTERN IN PATIENCE UNDER SUFFERING FOR WELL-DOING.

1. laying aside—once for all. So [*apothemenoi*] aorist, as a garment *put off.* The exhortation applies to Christians alone: in none else is the new nature existing which, as "the inner man" (Eph. iii. 16), can more and more cast off the old as an outward thing. To unbelievers the exhortation is that *inwardly,* in the *nous* (mind), they must become changed [*meta-noeisthai: repent*] (*Steiger*). 'Therefore' resumes ch. i. 22. Seeing that ye are born again of incorruptible seed, be not again entangled in evil, which 'is an acting in contrariety to the being formed in us' (*Theophylact*). "Malice," &c., are utterly inconsistent with "love of the brethren," unto which ye have "purified your souls" (ch. i. 22). The vices here are those which offend against the BROTHERLY LOVE inculcated above. Each succeeding one springs out of that which immediately precedes, so as to form a *genealogy* of sins against love. Out of *malice* springs *guile;* out of *guile, hypocrisies* (pretending to be what we are not; not showing what we really are: the opposite of 'love unfeigned," "without dissimulation"); out of *hypocrisies, envies* of those to whom we play the hypocrite; out of *envies, evil speaking. Guile* is the permanent *disposition; hypocrisies,* acts flowing from it. The guileless knows no envy. Cf. *v.* 2, "sincere" [*adolon*], 'guileless.' '*Malice* delights in another's hurt; *envy* pines at another's good; *guile* imparts duplicity to the heart; *hypocrisy* (flattery), duplicity to the tongue; *evil speakings* wound another's character' (*Augustine*). **2. new-born babes**—altogether without "guile" (*v.* 1; Rev. xiv. 5); in a specially tender relation to God (Isa. xl. 11). The childlike spirit is indispensable if we would enter heaven. "Milk" is here not elementary truths, as in 1 Cor. iii. 2; Heb. v. 12, 13; but in contrast to "guile," &c. (*v.* 1); the simple *Christian doctrine* relished by the childlike spirit. The same "word of grace" which is the instrument in regeneration, is that also of *building up.* 'The mother of the child is also its natural nurse' (*Steiger*). The babe, instead of chemically analyzing, instinctively feeds on the milk; our part is not self-sufficient questionings, but simply receiving the truth in the love of it (Matt. xi. 25). **desire** [*epipothesate*]—'have a yearning for,' or 'longing after,' natural to the regenerate; 'for as no one needs to teach new-born babes what food to take, knowing instinctively that a table is provided for them in their mother's breast,' so the believer of himself thirsts after the word of God, (Ps. cxix.) **of the word** [*logikon*]—not as *Alford,* 'spiritual;' nor "reasonable," as Rom. xii. 1: *logos* in Scripture means, not the *reason,* but the WORD; the context requires so here: *logikos* follows the meaning of *logos,* 'word.' Jas. i. 21, "*Lay apart* all filthiness, &c., and receive with meekness *the engrafted* WORD,*" confirms the English version here. **sincere** —'guileless.' *Irenæus* says, 'Heretics mix chalk

4   To whom coming, *as unto* a living stone, disallowed indeed of men, but
5 chosen of God, *and* precious, ye ^{*d*}also, as lively stones, ¹are built up a
    spiritual house, ^{*e*}an holy priesthood, to offer up ^{*f*}spiritual sacrifices,
6 acceptable to God by Jesus Christ. Wherefore also it is contained in
    the Scripture, ^{*g*}Behold, I lay in Sion a chief corner stone, elect, precious :
7 and he that believeth on him shall not be confounded. Unto you there-
    fore which believe *he is* precious : ²but unto them which be disobedient,

A. D. 60.
d Eph 2. 21.
1 Or. be ye bu'lt.
e Isa. 66 21.
f Hos. 14. 2.
g Isa. 28. 16.
2 Or. an honour.

---

with the milk.' "The" implies that, besides *the well known pure milk*, there is no other unadulterated doctrine : *the* Gospel alone can make us *guileless* (*v.* 1). **grow.** א A B C, Vulgate, read, 'grow *unto salvation.*' Being BORN *again*, we are also to *grow unto* (perfected) *salvation*, the end of our growth. 'Growth is the measure of that, not only rescue from destruction, but positive blessedness, implied in *salvation*' (*Alford*). **thereby**—Greek, 'IN it :' fed *on it : in its strength* (Acts xi. 14). 'The word is to be desired with appetite as the cause of life, swallowed in the hearing, chewed as cud is, by rumination with the understanding, and digested by faith' (*Tertullian*). 3. Peter alludes to Ps. xxxiv. 8. The first *tastes* of God's goodness are afterwards followed by fuller experiences. A taste whets the appetite (*Bengel*). **gracious** [*Chrestos*]—*benignant*, kind ; as God is revealed in Christ, "the Lord." We who are born again, ought so to be *kind* to the brethren (ch. i. 22). 'Whosoever has not tasted the word, to him it is not sweet ; but to them who have experienced it, who with the heart believe, "Christ has been sent *for me* and is become *my own : my* miseries are His, and His *life* mine," it tastes sweet' (*Luther*).

4. coming—*drawing near* [*proserchomenoi*] (Heb. x. 22) by faith continually ; present : not having come once for all at conversion. **stone.** Peter (i. e., *a stone*, named so by Christ) desires that all similarly should be *living stones* BUILT ON CHRIST, THE TRUE FOUNDATION-STONE : cf. his speech in Acts iv. 11 : an undesigned coincidence and mark of genuineness. The Spirit foreseeing the Romanist perversion of Matt. xvi. 18 (cf. *v.* 16, "Son of the LIVING God," which coincides with "LIVING stone" here), presciently makes Peter himself refute it. He herein confirms Paul (1 Cor. iii. 11). Omit *as unto.* Christ is positively the "living stone :" *living*, as having life in Himself, and as raised from the dead to live evermore (Rev. i. 18), after His rejection by men ; so the source of life to us. Like no earthly *rock*, He lives and gives life. Cf. 1 Cor. x. 4, and the type, Exod. xvii. 6 ; Num. xx. 11. **disallowed** [*apodedokimasmenon*]—reprobated ; referred to also by Christ, Matt. xxi. 42 ; also by Paul : cf. Isa. viii. 14 ; Luke ii. 34. **chosen of God** [*para*]—'with (*in the presence and judgment of*) God elect' (*v.* 6). Many are alienated from the Gospel because it is rejected by most men. Peter answers that, though rejected by men, Christ is the *stone* of salvation honoured by God (cf. Gen. xlix. 24, end). **5. Ye also, as lively stones**—partaking of the name and life which is in "THE LIVING STONE" (*v.* 4). Many names which pre-eminently belong to Christ are assigned to Christians in a lower sense. He is "THE Son," "High Priest," "King," "Lamb :" they, "sons," "priests," "kings," "lambs." So the Shulamite from Solomon (Song vi. 13) (*Bengel*). **are built up** [*oikodomeisthe*]—'are being built up,' as Eph. ii. 22. Not as *Alford*, 'Be ye built up.' Peter grounds his exhortations, *vv.* 2, 11, &c., on their consciousness of being *living stones in the course of being built up into a spiritual house* (i. e., the temple of the Spirit). **priesthood.** Christians

are at once the *temple* and the *priests* [*hieron* (*the sacred place*) expresses *the whole building*, including the courts wherein the sacrifice *was killed ;* and *naos* (*the dwelling*, viz., of God), *the inner shrine* wherein God peculiarly manifested Himself : where, in the Holiest, the *blood* of the sacrifice was presented before Him]. All believers alike, not merely ministers, are now the dwelling of God [and are called *naos*, not *hieron*], and priests unto God (Rev. i. 6). The minister is not, like the Jewish priest [*hiereus*], nearer God than the people, but merely for order's sake leads their spiritual services. *Priest* is the abbreviation of *presbyter*, not corresponding to the Aaronic *priest* [*hiereus*], who offered *literal* sacrifices. Christ is the only literal *Hiereus-priest* in the New Testament : through Him alone we may always draw near to God. Cf. *v.* 9, "a royal priesthood." The Spirit never applies *hiereus, sacerdotal* priest, to Gospel ministers. **spiritual sacrifices**—not the literal one of the mass, as Rome's self-styled disciples of Peter teach. Cf. .Isa. lvi. 7, with "*acceptable* to God" here ; xix. 21 ; Ps. iv. 5 ; l. 14 ; li. 17, 19 ; Hos. xiv. 2 ; Phil. iv. 18. 'The foremost of spiritual sacrifices is the oblation of ourselves (Rom. xii. 1). For never can we offer anything to God until we have offered ourselves (2 Cor. viii. 5). Then follow prayers, giving of thanks, alms-deeds, and all exercises of piety' (*Calvin*). Christian houses of worship are never called temples, because the *temple* was for *sacrifice*, which has no place in the Christian dispensation ; the Christian "temple" is *the congregation of spiritual worshippers.* The synagogue (where reading of Scripture and prayer constituted the worship) was the model of the Christian house of worship (note, Jas. ii. 2 ; Acts xv. 21). Our sacrifices are prayer, praise, and self-denying services to Christ (*v.* 9, end). **by Jesus Christ**—as our mediating High Priest before God. Connect with "offer up." Christ is *precious* Himself, and makes us *accepted* (*Bengel*). As the temple, so the priesthood, is built on Christ (*vv.* 4, 5) (*Beza*). Imperfect as are our services, we are not with unbelieving timidity, or refined self-righteousness, to doubt their acceptance THROUGH CHRIST. After extolling the dignity of Christians, he goes back to CHRIST, its sole source. **6. Wherefore also.** א A B C, Vulgate, read [*dioti*], 'Because that.' The statement above is so, '*because* it is contained in Scripture.' **Behold**—calling universal attention to the glorious announcement of His eternal counsel. **elect**—so believers (*v.* 9). **precious.** In Hebrew, Isa. xxviii. 16, 'a corner stone of preciousness.' Cf. note there. So *v.* 7. **confounded.** Same Greek as Rom. ix. 33 (Peter confirming Paul). See 'Introduction ;' Rom. x. 11, "ashamed." In Isa. xxviii. 16, "make haste"—*i. e.*, flee in panic, covered with the *shame* of *confounded* hopes. **7.** Application of the same Scripture to the believer ; then to the unbeliever. On the Gospel's opposite effects on different classes, cf. John ix. 39 ; 2 Cor. ii. 15, 16. **precious** [*he time*] —"THE PRECIOUSNESS" (*v.* 6). To you believers belongs *the preciousness* of Christ just mentioned. **disobedient**—to the faith ; so disobedient in prac-

h the stone which the builders disallowed, the same is made the head of
8 the corner, and *i* a stone of stumbling, and a rock of offence, *even to them*
which stumble at the word, being disobedient; *j* whereunto also they
9 were appointed. But ye *are* *k* a chosen generation, *l* a royal priesthood,
m an holy nation, [3] a peculiar people; that ye should show forth the
[4] praises of him who hath called you out of darkness into his marvellous
10 light: which *n* in time past *were* not a people, but *are* now the people of
God: which had not obtained mercy, but now have obtained mercy.
11 Dearly beloved, I beseech *you* as strangers and pilgrims, abstain from
12 fleshly lusts, which war against the soul; having your conversation honest

A. D. 60.

h Ps. 118. : 2.
i Isa 8. .4.
j Rom 9. 22.
k Deut. 10. 15.
l Ex 19 5.
m John 17 19.
[3] Or a J ur-chased people.
[4] Ur. virtues.
n Hos. 2. 23.

tice. **the stone which,** &c., **head of the corner** —(Ps. cxviii. 22.) Those who rejected the STONE were all the while, in spite of themselves, contributing to its becoming Head of the corner. The same Gospel magnet has two poles—one repulsive, the other attractive. **8. stone of stumbling,** &c. —from Isa. viii. 14. Not merely they *stumbled*, in the sense that their prejudices were offended, but that they suffered the *judicial punishment* of their rejection of the Messiah: they hurt themselves in stumbling over the corner stone (cf. Jer. xiii. 16; Dan. xi. 19). **at the word**—join 'being disobedient to the word:' so ch. iii. 1; iv. 17. **whereunto**—to penal *stumbling;* the judicial punishment of unbelief. **also**—an additional thought; not that God ordains to *sin*, but they are given up to "the fruit of *their own* ways" according to God's eternal counsel. The moral ordering of the world is altogether of God. God appoints the ungodly to be *given up unto their own reprobate mind* and its necessary penalty. **were appointed** [*etethesan*]—'set,' answers to "*I* lay,' 'set' (*v.* 6). God is said to *appoint* Christ and the elect (directly). Unbelievers are *appointed* (God acting less directly in the appointment of the sinner's awful course) (*Bengel*). God ordains the wicked to punishment, not to crime (*J. Cappel*). "Appointed" (not here 'FORE-ordained') refers, not to God's eternal counsel so directly as to His penal justice. Through the same Christ whom sinners rejected, they shall be rejected; unlike believers, they are *appointed unto wrath*, as FITTED for it (Rom. ix. 22). The lost shall lay all the blame on their own perversity, not on God's decree; the saved shall ascribe all the merit to God's electing grace. **9.** Contrast the privileges and destinies of believers. **chosen**—'elect' of God, even as Christ your Lord is (*v.* 6). **generation.** Believers are one in spiritual *origin and kindred*, as distinguished from the world. **royal** —kingly. Believers, like Christ, the antitypical Melchisedec, are *a body of priest-kings.* Israel spiritually was designed to be the same among the nations of the earth. The full realization of this, both to the literal and the spiritual Israel, is as yet future (Isa. lxi. 6; lxvi. 21). **holy nation**—antitypical to Israel. We must be singular, if we would be holy; consistent, if we would be useful. **peculiar people** [*laos eis peripoiesin*]—'a people *for an acquisition;*' i. e., whom God chose to be *peculiarly His:* Acts xx. 28, "purchased;" lit., *acquired.* God's "*peculiar treasure*" (Exod. xix. 5). **show forth** [*exangeilēte*]—*published abroad.* Not *their own* praises, but *His.* They have no reason to magnify themselves above others; for once they had been in the same darkness, and only through God's grace had been brought to the light which they must henceforth *show forth* to others. **praises** [*aretas*]—'virtues,' 'excellences:' His glory, *mercy* (*v.* 10), *goodness* (Greek, *v.* 3; Num. xiv. 17, 18; Isa. lxiii. 7): applied to believers (2 Pet. i. 3, 5). **out of darkness**—heathen, and even

Jewish, ignorance, sin, misery; so out of the dominion of the prince of darkness. **marvellous.** Peter still has in his mind Ps. cxviii. 23; note, *v.* 7. **light.** It is called "His"—*i. e.*, God's. Only the (spiritual) *light* is created by God, not *darkness*. In Isa. xlv. 7, it is physical darkness and evil, not moral, that God is said to *create :* the punishment of sin, not sin itself. Peter, with characteristic boldness, brands as *darkness* what all the world calls *light;* reason, without the Holy Spirit, in spite of its vaunted power, is spiritual darkness. 'It cannot apprehend what faith is: there it is stark blind; it gropes as one without eyesight, stumbling from one thing to another, and knows not what it does' (*Luther*). **10.** From Hos. i. 9, 10; ii. 23. Peter plainly confirms Paul, who quotes the passage as implying the call of the Gentiles to become spiritually what Israel had been literally, "the people of God" (Rom. ix. 25). Primarily, the prophecy refers to literal Israel, hereafter to be fully what in their best days they were only partially,—God's people. **not obtained mercy** [*ēleēmenoi—eleēthentes*]. Formerly 'not in a state of being compassionated, but now *once for all* compassionated.' It was God's *mercy*, not their merits, which made the blessed change : this ought to kindle lively *gratitude*, to be shown with their life as well as their lips.

11. As heretofore he exhorted them to walk worthily of their calling, in contrast to their former walk, so now he exhorts them to glorify God before unbelievers. **Dearly beloved.** He gains their attention by assuring them of his love. **strangers and pilgrims**—(ch. i. 17.) [*Paroikous—parepidemous*, sojourners, having a *house* in a city, without the rights of *citizenship:* a picture of the Christian's position on earth; *and pilgrims*, staying for a time in a foreign land.] *Flacius:* (1.) Purify your souls (*a*) as *strangers* on earth, who must not allow yourselves to be kept back by earthly lusts; and (*b*) because these lusts war against the soul. (2.) Walk piously among unbelievers (*a*) that they may cease to calumniate Christians, and (*b*) be themselves converted. **fleshly lusts**—enumerated in Gal. v. 19, &c. Not only gross animal appetites, but all the workings of the unrenewed mind. **which** [*haitines*]—'*the* which;' *i. e.*, inasmuch as they "war," &c. They not only impede, but assail. **the soul**—*i. e.*, the regenerated soul, such as those addressed. The believer is besieged by sinful lusts. Like Samson in Delilah's lap, the moment that he gives way to fleshly lusts, he has the locks of his strength shorn, and ceases to maintain that spiritual separation from the world and the flesh of which the Nazarite vow was the type. **12. conversation**—'conduct.' In two things 'pilgrims' ought to bear themselves well: —(1.) The *conduct*, as subjects (*v.* 13), servants (*v.* 18), wives (ch. iii. 1), husbands (ch. iii. 7), and under all circumstances (*v.* 8); (2.) *Confession* of the faith (ch. iii. 15, 16). Both derived from the *will of God.* Our conversation should correspond

among the Gentiles; that, [5]whereas they speak against you as evil doers, they may by *your* good works, which they shall behold, glorify God [o]in the day of visitation.

13 Submit [p]yourselves to every ordinance of man for the Lord's sake:

14 whether it be to the king, as supreme; or unto governors, as unto them that are sent by him for the punishment of evil doers, and for the praise

15 of them that do well. For so is the will of God, that with well doing ye

16 may put to silence the ignorance of foolish men: as free, and not [6]using *your* liberty for a cloak of maliciousness, but as the servants of God.

A. D 60.

[5] Or, wherein.
[o] Luke 19.44.
[p] Pro. 17. 11.
Pro. 21. 21.
Jer. 29. 7.
Matt. 22.21.
Mark 12.17.
Luke 20.21.
[6] having

to our Saviour's condition : this is in heaven, so ought that to be. **honest**—becoming (ch. iii. 16). Contrast ch. i. 18, end. A good walk does not make us pious : we must first be pious by believing before we can lead a good course. Faith first receives from God, then love gives to our neighbour (*Luther*). **whereas they speak against you—now** (*v.* 15); they may at some time *hereafter* glorify God. [*En ho* may be, ' *Wherein* they speak against you, &c., that (*therein*) they may, by your good works, which *on a closer inspection they shall behold* (the strict sense of *epopteuontes :* so ch. iii. 2: as opposed to their "*ignorance*" (*v.* 15), of the true character of Christianity by judging on hearsay), glorify God.'] The very works 'which, on careful consideration, must move the heathen to praise God, are at first the object of raillery' (*Steiger*). **evil doers.** Because as Christians they could not conform to heathenish customs, they were accused of disobedience to legal authority ; to rebut this charge, they are told to *submit to every ordinance of man* (not sinful). 'Others *narrowly look at* the actions of the righteous' (*Bengel*). *Tertullian* contrasts the early Christians and the heathen. These delighted in the bloody gladiatorial spectacles of the amphitheatre ; whereas a Christian was excommunicated if he went to it at all. No Christian was found in prison for crime, but only for the faith. The heathen excluded slaves from some of their religious services ; Christians had some of their presbyters of slaves. Slavery silently and gradually disappeared by the power of the Christian law of love: "Whatsoever ye would that men should do to you, do ye even so to them." When the Pagans deserted their nearest relatives in a plague, Christians ministered to the sick. When Gentiles left their dead unburied after the battle, and cast their wounded into the streets, the disciples hastened to relieve the suffering. *Justin Martyr*, 'We formerly rejoiced in fornication. now we welcome chastity alone ; then we loved the procuring of goods and money more than anything else, now we bring all we have to a common fund, and share it with every one who needs. We who hated one another, now pray for our enemies, and try to persuade those who unjustly hate us to become, by living according to Christ, sharers of the hope of obtaining the same blessings with us from God the ruler of all.' *Merivale* assigns four causes of the conversion of the Roman empire :—1. Fulfilled prophecies and miracles ; 2. Sense of sin and need on the part of the heathen ; 3. The holy example of primitive Christians ; 4. Its final temporal successes. **glorify** —forming a high estimate of Him whom Christians worship, from the exemplary conduct of Christians themselves. We must do good, not with a view to *our own* glory, but to that of *God.* **the day of visitation**—when God shall *visit* them *in grace* (Luke xix. 44).

13. every ordinance of man—'every human institution' (*Alford*) ; [*Ktisei*] 'every human *creation.*' For though of Divine appointment, yet in the mode and exercise of authority, earthly gover-

nors are human institutions, being *of men*, and *in relation to men.* The apostle speaks as one raised above human things. But lest they should think themselves raised by faith above human authorities, he tells them, *submit yourselves for the sake of Christ,* who desires you to be subject, and once was subject to earthly rulers Himself, though having all things subject to Him, and whose honour is at stake in you, His earthly representatives (cf. Rom. xiii. 5). **king.** The Roman emperor was 'supreme' in the Roman provinces to which this epistle was addressed. Jewish zealots refused obedience. 'If "the king" command one thing, and the "governor sent by him" another, we ought rather to obey the superior' (*Augustine* in *Grotius*). Scripture prescribes nothing upon forms of government, but subjects Christians to that everywhere subsisting, without entering into the question of *right* (thus the Roman emperors had by force seized supreme authority, and Rome had, by unjustifiable means, made herself mistress of Asia): because the *de facto* governors have not been made by chance, but by the providence of God. **14. governors**—subordinate to the emperor ; delegated by Cæsar to preside over provinces. **for the punishment.** No tyranny ever has been so unprincipled that some equity was not maintained in it : however corrupt a government be, God never suffers it to be so much so as not to be better than anarchy (*Calvin*). Although bad kings often oppress, yet that is scarcely ever done by public authority (and it is of public authority that Peter speaks), save under the mask of right. Tyranny harasses many, but anarchy overwhelms the whole state (*Horneius*). The only justifiable exception is where obedience to the earthly king involves disobedience to the King of kings. **praise of them that do well.** Every government recognizes the excellence of Christian subjects. Thus *Pliny*, in his letter to the Emperor Trajan : 'I have found in them nothing else save a perverse and extravagant superstition.' This recognition in the long run mitigates persecution (ch. iii. 13). **15.** Ground of directing them to *submit themselves* (*v.* 13). **put to silence** [*phimoun*]—'muzzle,' 'stop the mouth.' **ignorance**—spiritual : not having "the knowledge of God," therefore misconstruing His children's acts : influenced by appearances, ever ready to open their mouths, rather than their eyes and ears. Their *ignorance* should move the believer's pity, not anger. They judge of things which they are incapable of judging, through unbelief (*v.* 12). Maintain such a walk that they shall have no charge against you, except touching your faith ; so their minds shall be favourably disposed towards Christianity. **16. As free**—from sin, and to duty: 'the Lord's freemen' (1 Cor. vii. 22), connected with *v.* 15, *doing well as* being *free.* "Well doing" (*v.* 15) is the natural fruit of being Christ's *freemen,* made free by "the truth" 'from sin's bondage. Duty is enforced to guard against licentiousness ; but the *way* is by love and the holy instincts of Christian liberty. We have given *principles*, not *details.* **not using** [*me hos*

17 ⁷Honour all *men*. Love the brotherhood. Fear God. Honour the king.

18 Servants, *be* subject to *your* masters with all fear; not only to the

19 good and gentle, but also to the froward. For this *is* ⁸thankworthy, if a

20 man for conscience toward God endure grief, suffering wrongfully. For what glory *is it*, if, when ye be buffeted for your faults, ye shall take it patiently? but if, when ye do well, and suffer *for it,* ye take it patiently,

21 this *is* ⁹acceptable with God. For even hereunto were ye called; because Christ also suffered ¹⁰for us, leaving us an example, that ye should follow

22 his steps: who ᵠdid no sin, neither was guile found in his mouth: who,

23 ʳwhen he was reviled, reviled not again; when he suffered, he threatened

24 not; but ¹¹committed *himself* to him that judgeth righteously: who his own self bare our sins in his own body ¹²on the tree, that we, being dead

A. D 60.
⁷ Or, Esteem
⁸ Or. thank. Luke 6. 32.
⁹ Or. thank.
¹⁰Some read, for you.
ᵠ Isa. 53. 9. John 8. 46.
ʳ Isa 53. 7. John 8. 48.
¹¹Or, committed his cause.
¹³Or. to.

epikalumma echontes tēs kakias ten eleutherian]— 'not *as having* your liberty for a veil (cloak) of *badness*, but as the servants of God:' therefore bound to *submit to every ordinance of man* (v. 13) which is of God's appointment. **17. Honour all men**—*according to the honour due in each case.* Equals have a respect due to them. Christ has dignified our humanity by assuming it; therefore we should honour our common humanity, even in the humblest. [*Pantas timēsate*, aorist,—'*In every case render promptly* every man's due' (*Alford*). *Basilea timate*, present,—*habitually* honour the king.] The first is the general precept; the three following are its divisions. **Love** [*aga-pate*, present]—*habitually* love, with the congenial affection you ought to feel to brethren, besides general *love* to all men. **Fear God. Honour the king**. The king is to be *honoured;* God alone, in the highest sense, *feared*.

18. Servants [*oiketai*]—'household servants:' not [*douloi*] 'slaves;' including *freedmen* remaining in their master's house. *Masters* were not commonly Christians: he therefore mentions only *servants'* duties. These were often persecuted by unbelieving masters. Peter's object is to teach them *submission*, whatever the master's character be. Paul not having this design, includes *masters'* duties. **be subject** [*hupotassomenoi*]—*being subject:* a particular instance of the general exhortation, *vv*. 11, 12, of which the first particular precept is *v*. 13. The general exhortation is taken up again, *v*. 16; and so, *v*. 18, 'being subject,' is joined to the imperatives, "abstain," "submit yourselves," "honour all men." **with**—Greek, 'IN.' all—all possible: under all circumstances. **fear**—the awe of one subject. God is its ultimate object: *fear* "for the Lord's sake" (*v*. 13), not merely slavish fear of masters. **good**—kind. **gentle**—indulgent towards errors [*epieikesin*]; yielding, not exacting all which justice might demand. **froward**—perverse. Those bound to obey must not make the disposition of the superior the measure of their obligations. **19.** Reason for subjection even to froward masters. **thankworthy** [*charis*]—(Luke vi. 33.) A course out of the common: especially *praiseworthy* before God: not as Rome, *earning merit;* so a work of supererogation (cf. *v*. 20). **for conscience toward God** [*suneidēsin Theou*]—'consciousness of God:' conscientious regard to God, more than men. **endure** [*hupopherei*]—*bear up under*. **grief** [*lupas*]—'griefs.' **20. what** [*Poion*]—'what kind of.' **glory**—*merit*. **buffeted**—*this is*. So א C, Vulgate; but A B read 'for.' Then, 'but if when . . . ye take it patiently (it is a glory): *for* this is,' &c. **acceptable** [*charis*]—'thankworthy.' as *v*. 19. **21.** Christ's example a proof of *v*. 20, end. **hereunto**—to the patient endurance of unmerited

suffering (ch. iii. 9). Christ is an example to servants, having been in "the form of a servant" (Phil. ii. 7). **called**—with a heavenly calling, though slaves. **for us**—the highest exemplification of 'doing well' (*v*. 20). Ye must patiently suffer, being innocent, as Christ innocently suffered (not for Himself, but *for us*). א A B C, for "us . . . us," read, 'you . . . you.' Christ's sufferings, whilst they are an example, were primarily sufferings "*for us*," a consideration which imposes an ever-lasting obligation on us to please Him. **leaving**—*behind* [*hupolimpanōn*]—on His departure to the Father. **an example** [*hupogrammon*]—a *writing copy* set by masters for their pupils. Christ's precepts were the *transcript* of His life. Peter *graphically* sets before servants features suited to their case. **follow**—*close upon* [*epakolouthēsēte*]. **his steps**—*footsteps:* of His *patience*, combined with *innocence*. **22.** Christ's *well doing* (*v*. 20), though *suffering*. **did** [*aorist*]—'Never in a single instance' (*Alford*), from Isa. liii. 9, end, LXX. **neither**—nor yet. Sinlessness of *mouth* is a mark of *perfection* (Jas. iii. 2). *Guile* is a common fault of servants. On Christ's sinlessness, cf. 2 Cor. v. 21; Heb. vii. 26. **23.** Servants are apt to 'answer again' (Titus ii. 9). *Threats* of Divine judgment against oppressors are often used by those who have no other arms. Christ, who could have threatened with truth, never did so. **committed himself**—*His cause*, as man in His suffering: cf. Jer. xi. 20; Isa. liii. 8. Cf. Rom. xii. 19, on our corresponding duty. Leave your case in His hands: not to make Him executioner of your revenge, but praying for enemies. God's *righteous judgment* gives tranquillity to the oppressed. **24. his own self**—there being *none other* who could have done it. His *voluntary* undertaking of redemption is implied. The Greek puts in contrast OUR, and HIS OWN SELF, to mark *His substitution for us*. **bare** [*anēnenken*]—*carried and offered up:* a sacrificial term. Isa. liii. 11, 12, where *bearing on Himself* is the prominent idea; here *offering in sacrifice* is combined with it. So v. 5, if He were *only* an *example*, the effect of His sacrifice would only be to His successors: there would be no retrospective efficacy to those who lived in Old Testament times. **our sins**. In *offering in sacrifice* His body, Christ offered in it our sins' *guilt* upon the cross, as upon God's altar, that it might be expiated in Him, and so taken away from us (cf. Isa. liii. 10). Peter means by "bare" what the Syriac expresses by two words, *to bear*, and *to offer*:—(1.) He hath *borne* our sins laid upon Him (viz., their guilt, curse, and punishment); (2.) He hath so borne them that He *offered* them along with Himself on the altar. He refers to the bullocks and goats upon which sins were first laid, and which were then *offered* thus laden (*Vitringa*).

to sins, should live unto righteousness: *by whose stripes ye were healed.
25 For *ye were as sheep going astray; but are now returned *unto the Shepherd and Bishop of your souls.

3 LIKEWISE, ye wives, *be* in subjection to your own husbands; that, if any obey not the word, [a]they also may without the word [b]be won by the
2 conversation of the wives; while they behold your chaste conversation
3 *coupled* with fear. Whose [c]adorning let it not be that outward *adorning* of plaiting the hair, and of wearing of gold, or of putting on of apparel;
4 but *let it be* [d]the hidden man of the heart, in that which is not corruptible, *even the ornament* of a meek and quiet spirit, which is in the sight
5 of God of great price. For after this manner in the old time the holy

A. D. 60.

* Isa. 53. 5.
‡ Eze. 34. 6.
* Eze. 37. 21.
John 10. 11.

CHAP. 3
a 1 Cor. 7. 16.
b Matt. 18. 15.
c 1 Cor. 9. 19.
d Isa. 3. 16-24.
d Ps 45. 13.
Rom. 2 29.

Sin among Semitic nations is considered as a burden lying upon the sinner (*Gesenius*). **on the tree** —the cross, the proper place for the Curse-bearer. This curse stuck to Him until it was legally (through His death as the guilt-bearer) destroyed in His body: thus the handwriting of the bond against us is cancelled (Col. ii. 14). [*Epi to xulon:* He took them *to* the tree and offered them *on* it.] **that we, being dead to sins**—the effect of His death to 'sin' in the aggregate, and to all particular "sins"—viz., that we should be as entirely *delivered from* them as a slave that is *dead* is delivered from service to his master [*apogenomenoi*]. This is our spiritual *standing* through faith by virtue of Christ's death: our *actual* mortification of *sins* is in proportion to the degree of our being made conformable to His death. 'That we should *die to the sins* whose collected guilt Christ carried away in His death, and so LIVE TO THE RIGHTEOUSNESS (cf. Isa. liii. 11), the gracious relation to God which He has brought in' (*Steiger*). **by whose stripes** [*molopi*]—stripe. **ye were healed**—a paradox, yet true. 'Ye servants (cf. *v.* 20) often bear *the stripe;* but it is not more than He bore: learn from Him patience in wrongful sufferings.' Cf. Paul at Philippi (Acts xvi. 23-25). **25. For**—why they need *healing* (v. 24). **now**—that the atonement for all has been made, the foundation is laid for *individual conversion:* so '*ye have become converted* to,' &c. **Shepherd and Bishop.** The designation of the Church's *pastors* and *elders* belongs in its fullest sense to the great Head, "the good Shepherd." As the "*bishop*" oversees (as *episkopos* means), so "the *eyes of the Lord are over* the righteous" (ch. iii. 12). He gives us His Spirit, feeding and guiding us by His Word. "Shepherd" [*Parnas*] often applied to *kings:* of the compound *Pharna*bazus.

CHAP. III. 1-22.—RELATIVE DUTIES—HUSBANDS AND WIVES—EXHORTATIONS TO LOVE AND FORBEARANCE—RIGHT CONDUCT UNDER PERSECUTIONS FOR RIGHTEOUSNESS' SAKE, AFTER CHRIST'S EXAMPLE, WHOSE DEATH RESULTED IN QUICKENING TO US THROUGH HIS BEING QUICKENED AGAIN, OF WHICH BAPTISM IS THE SACRAMENTAL SEAL.

1. Likewise [*Homoiōs*]—'in like manner.' as 'servants' (cf. the reason of the woman's subjection, 1 Cor. xi. 8-10; 1 Tim. ii. 11-14). **your own** —enforcing the obligation: it is not strangers ye are required to *be subject to.* [Every time that obedience is enjoined upon *wives* to husband, *idios*, 'one's own peculiarly,' is used, whilst *men's* wives are designated only by *heautōn*, 'of themselves.'] Feeling the need of leaning on one stronger, the wife (especially if joined to an *unbeliever*) might be tempted, though only spiritually, to enter into that relation with another in which she ought to stand to *her own* spouse (1 Cor. xiv. 34, 35). An attachment to the teacher might spring up, which, without being adultery,

would still weaken in its spiritual basis the married relation (*Steiger*). **that (even), if**—*even if* you have a husband that obeys not the word (*i. e.,* an unbeliever). **without the word**—*independently of hearing the word preached*, the usual way of faith. But *Bengel*, 'without word'—*i. e., without direct* gospel *discourse* of the wives, 'they may (א A B C, SHALL, which marks the almost objective *certainty* of the result) be won' indirectly. 'Unspoken acting is more powerful than unperformed speaking' (*Œcumenius*). 'A soul converted is *gained* to itself, to the pastor, wife, or husband, who sought it, and to Christ; added to His treasury who thought not His own precious blood too dear to lay out for this gain' (*Leighton*). 'The discreet wife would choose first of all to persuade her husband to share with her in the things which lead to blessedness; but if this be impossible, let her alone diligently press after virtue, in all things obeying him so as to do nothing against his will, except such things as are essential to salvation' (*Clemens Alexandrinus*). **2. behold**—on narrowly looking into it [*epopteusantes*]. **chaste**—free from all impurity. **fear**—*reverential*, towards your husbands. Scrupulously pure; not the noisy ambitiousness of worldly women. **3.** 'To whom let there belong (viz., as their ornament) not the outward adornment (usual in the sex which first, by the fall, brought in the need of covering: note, ch. v. 5) of, &c., but,' &c. **plaiting** —artificial, to attract admiration. **wearing** [*peritheseos*]—'putting round,' viz., the head, as a diadem: the arm, as a bracelet: the finger, as rings. **apparel**—showy and costly. 'Have the blush of modesty instead of paint, and moral worth and discretion instead of gold and emeralds' (*Melissa*). **4. But**—Rather. The 'outward adornment' of jewellery, &c., is forbidden, in so far as a woman loves such things, not in so far as she uses them from a sense of propriety. Singularity comes from pride, and throws needless hindrances to religion in the way of others. Under costly attire there may be a humble mind. 'Great is he who uses his earthenware as if it were plate; not less great is he who uses his silver as if it were earthenware' (*Seneca*). **hidden**—*inner* man, which the Christian instinctively *hides* from public view **of the heart**—*consisting in the heart* adorned by the Spirit. This 'inner man of the heart' is subject of the verb "be" (*v.* 3): 'of whom let the hidden man be'—viz., the adornment. **in that**— consisting *in that* as its element. **not corruptible** —transitory, not tainted with corruption, as earthly adornments. **meek and quiet**—*meek* [*hesuchiou*]; not creating disturbances; *quiet* [*praeos*], bearing tranquilly the disturbances caused by others. *Meek* in feelings; *quiet* in words, countenance, actions (*Bengel*). **in the sight of God**— who looks to inward, not merely outward things. **of great price**—the results of redemption should correspond to its costly price (ch. i. 19). **5. after**

women also, who trusted in God, adorned themselves, being in subjection
6 unto their own husbands: even as Sara obeyed Abraham, calling him
‘lord: whose ¹daughters ye are as long as ye do well, and are not afraid
with, any amazement.

7 Likewise, ye husbands, dwell with *them* according to knowledge, giving
honour unto the wife, as unto the weaker vessel, and as being heirs together of the grace of life; ʲthat your prayers be not hindered.

8 Finally, *be ye* all of one mind, having compassion one of another, ²love
9 as brethren, *be* pitiful, *be* courteous: not rendering evil for evil, or railing
for railing: but contrariwise blessing; knowing that ye are thereunto
10 called, ᵍthat ye should inherit a blessing. For ʰhe that will love life,
and see good days, let him refrain his tongue from evil, and his lips that
11 they speak no guile: let him eschew evil, and do good; let him seek
12 peace, and ensue it. For the eyes of the Lord *are* over the righteous,
ⁱand his ears *are open* unto their prayers: but the face of the Lord *is*
13 ³against them that do evil. And ʲwho *is* he that will harm you, if ye be
14 followers of that which is good? But ᵏand if ye suffer for righteousness’

A. D. 60.

ᶜ Gen 18. 12.
¹ children,
ᶠ Job 42. 8.
Matt 5. 23,
24.
Matt 18.19.
Rom 8. 25,
27.
Eph. 4. 30.
Eph. 6. 18.
² Or, loving
to the
brethren.
ᵍ Matt. 25.31,
ʰ Ps. 34. 12.
ⁱ John 9. 31.
Jas. 5. 16.
³ upon.
ʲ Pro. 16. 7.
Rom. 8. 23.
ᵏ Matt. 5. 10.

this manner—with the *ornament of a meek and quiet spirit* (cf. the portrait of the godly wife, Prov. xxxi. 10-31). **trusted** [*elpizousai eis Theon*]. "Holy" is explained by ‘*hoped in* (so as to be *united to*) God.’ Hope in God is the spring of holiness. **in subjection**—their ornament consisted in subordination. Vanity was forbidden (v. 3), as contrary to female *subjection*. **6. Sara** —an example of *faith*. **calling him lord**—(Gen. xviii. 12.) **ye are** [*egenethete*]—‘ye have become:’ "children" of Abraham and Sara by *faith*, whereas ye were Gentile aliens from the covenant. **afraid with any amazement** [*ptoesin*]—‘fluttering alarm.’ *Act well, and be not thrown into panic*, as weak females are apt to be, by opposition from without. *Bengel*, ‘Not afraid or *any fluttering terror* from without’ (vv. 13-16). LXX. [*ptoesin*] (Prov. iii. 25) was probably in Peter’s mind. Anger assails men ; *fear*, women. You need fear no man in doing right : not thrown into fluttering agitation by any sudden outbreak of an unbelieving husband’s temper, whilst you *do well.*

7. dwell [*sunoikountes*]—‘dwelling:’ connected with the verb, ch. ii. 17, "Honour all." **knowledge**—Christian : appreciating the due relation of the sexes in God’s design : acting with tenderness and forbearance accordingly : *with wise consideration.* **giving honour unto the wife**—rather, ‘dwelling according to knowledge with the female [*gunaikeio*, adjective] as the weaker vessel (note, 1 Thes. iv. 4. Both husband and wife are *vessels* in God’s hand, of God’s making, to fulfil His gracious purposes. Both weak, the woman the *weaker*. Sense of his own weakness, and that she, like himself, is God’s *vessel*, ought to lead him to act with tender and wise consideration towards her, the *weaker fabric*) ; (*assigning* [*aponemontes*], *apportioning*) honour as being also (besides being man and wife) heirs together,’ &c.; or as C B, Vulgate, read, ‘as to those who are also (besides being your wives) fellow-heirs.’ (The reason why the man should dwell considerately *with the wife* is, because she is *the weaker vessel;* the reason why he should *give honour* to her is, because *God gives honour to both* as fellow-heirs : cf. the same argument, v. 9.) He does not take into account the case of an *unbelieving* wife, as she might yet believe. **grace of life**—God’s *gracious gift of life* (ch. i. 4, 13). **that your prayers be not hindered** —by dissensions, which prevent *united* prayer, on which depends the blessing.

8. *General* summary of relative duty, after the

particular duties from ch. ii. 18. **of one mind**— as to the faith. **having compassion one of another** [*sumpatheis*]—‘sympathizing’ in the joy and sorrow of others. **love as brethren** [*philadelphoi*]—‘loving the brethren.’ **pitiful**—towards the afflicted. **courteous** [*philophrones*]—friendly-minded : Christian politeness : not the world’s tinsel : stamped with *unfeigned love* on one side, and *humility* on the other. א A B C, Vulgate, read [*tapeinophrones*], ‘humble-minded.’ It differs from ‘humble,’ in that it marks a *conscious effort* to be truly so. **9. evil**—in deed. **railing**—in word. **blessing**—your revilers [*eulogountes*, participle, not a noun]. **knowing that.** א A B C, Vulgate, read merely, ‘because.’ **are** [*eklethete*] —‘*were* called.’ **inherit a blessing**—not only passive, but active : receiving blessing from God by faith, and in turn blessing others from love (*Gerhard* in *Alford*). ‘It is not in order to inherit a blessing that we must bless, but because our portion is blessing.’ No *railing* can harm you (v. 13). Imitate God who *blesses* you. The first-fruits of His *blessing* for eternity are enjoyed by the righteous even now (v. 10) (*Bengel*). **10. will love** [*thelōn*]—‘wishes to love.’ He who *loves life* (present and eternal), and *desires to continue to do so*, not involving himself in troubles which make this life a burden, and involve forfeit of eternal life. Peter confirms v. 9 by Ps. xxxiv. 12 16. **refrain** [*pausato*]—‘cause to cease;’ implying that our inclination and custom is to speak evil. ‘Men think they would be exposed to the wantonness of enemies if they did not vindicate their rights. But the Spirit promises a life of blessedness to those alone who are patient of evils’ (*Calvin*). **evil . . . guile.** First he warns against sins of *tongue*, evil and double-tongued speaking ; next, against *acts* of injury to one’s neighbour. **11.** In A B C, Vulgate [*de*], ‘*Moreover* (besides his *words*, in *acts*) let him.’ **eschew**—‘turn from.’ **ensue**—*pursue* as hard to attain, and fleeing from one in this troublesome world. **12. For,** &c. Ground of the promised life of blessedness to the meek (v. 10). **ears . . . unto their prayers**—(1 John v. 14, 15.) **face . . . against.** The Lord’s *eyes* imply *favourable* regard (Deut. xi. 12) ; His *face upon* (not "against") them that do evil, implies that He narrowly observes, so as not to let them *really* hurt His people (cf. v. 13). **13. who . . . will harm you.** This fearless confidence in God’s protection Christ in His sufferings realized (Isa. l. 9) ; so His members (Rom. viii. 33-39). **if ye be** [*genēsthe*]—‘if ye have *become*.’ **followers** [*mimē-*

609

sake, happy *are ye:* and [l]be not afraid of their terror, neither be troubled;
15 but sanctify the Lord God in your hearts: and [m]*be* ready always to *give*
an answer to every man that asketh you a reason of the hope that is in
16 you with meekness and [4]fear; having a good conscience; that, whereas
they speak evil of you, as of evil doers, they may be ashamed that falsely
17 accuse your good conversation in Christ. For *it is* better, if the will of
God be so, that ye [n]suffer for well doing, than for evil doing.
18 For Christ also hath once suffered for sins, the just for the unjust, that
he might bring us to God, being put to death [o]in the flesh, but [p]quick-
19 ened by the Spirit: by [q]which also he went and preached unto the spirits

A. D. 60

[l] Isa. 8. 12.
Jer. 1. 8.
[m] Col. 4. 6.
2 Tim. 2..25.
[4] Or,
reverence.
[n] 2 Tim. 3. 12.
[o] Col 1. 21.
[p] Rom. 1. 4.
Rom 8. 11.
[q] Gen. 6. 3.
ch. 1. 11. 12.

tai]. א A B C, Vulgate, read [*zelotai*] "zealous of" (Titus ii. 14). **good.** 'Who will do you *evil* [*Kakōsōn*], if ye be zealous of *good?*' **14. But and if**—'But *if even.*' The promises of *this* life extend only so far as is expedient for us : a qualification to the promise (*v.* 10). 'If even ye should *suffer:*' a milder word than *harm.* **for righteousness**—'not the suffering, but the cause for which one suffers, makes the martyr' (*Augustine*). **happy.** Not even can *suffering* take away your *blessedness,* but promotes it (cf. Mark x. 30). **and** [*de*]—'but.' Do not impair your blessing (*v.* 9) by *fearing* man's *terror* in adversity. Lit., 'Be not terrified with their terror,' which they try to strike into you, and which strikes themselves in adversity. Quoted from Isa. viii. 12, 13. He that fears God has none else to fear. **neither be troubled**—the threat of the law (Lev. xxvi. 36; Deut. xxviii. 65, 66) ; the Gospel gives a heart assured of God's favour, and therefore unruffled amidst adversities. Not only be not *afraid,* but not even *agitated.* **15. sanctify**—*honour as holy,* enshrining *in your hearts.* So the Lord's prayer, Matt. vi. 9. God's holiness is glorified by our hearts being the dwelling place of His Spirit. **the Lord God.** א A B C, Vulgate, read *Christ.* [*Kurion ton Christon*] 'Sanctify *Christ as Lord.*' and [*de*]—'but,' 'moreover.' *Besides* inward sanctification of God *in the heart, be also ready always to give,* &c. So A B; but א C, Vulgate, omit *de*]. **answer**—apologetic: defending your faith. **to every man that asketh you.** The last words limit the "always." Not to a railer; but to every one who enquires honestly. **a reason**—a reasonable account. This refutes Rome's 'I believe it, because the Church believes it.' Credulity is believing without, faith is believing on, evidence. There is no repose for reason but in faith. This verse does not impose an obligation to bring a learned and logical proof of revelation. But as believers deny themselves, crucify the world, and brave persecution, they must be buoyed up by some strong 'hope:' men of the world, having no such hope, are moved by curiosity to *ask* the secret of it; the believer must be *ready* to give an *experimental account* 'how this hope arose in him, what it contains, on what it rests' (*Steiger*). **with.** א A B C, Vulgate, read '*but* with.' Be ready, *but* with 'meekness:' not with self-sufficiency (*v.* 4). The most effective way. **fear**—due respect towards man, and reverence towards God; His cause does not need hot temper to uphold it. **16. Having a good conscience**—the spring of *readiness to give account* of our *hope.* *Hope* and *good conscience* go together, Acts xxiv. 15, 16. Profession without practice has no weight. But those who *have a good conscience* can afford to give an account of their hope 'with meekness.' **whereas**—(ch. ii. 12.) **falsely accuse** [*epereazontes*]—malice shown in deeds as well as words; "despitefully use," Matt. v. 44; Luke vi. 28. **conversation**—conduct. **in Christ** —the element of your life as Christians : it defines '**good.**' It is your good walk *as Christians,* not as citizens, that calls forth malice (ch. iv. 4, 5, 14). **17. better.** Say not, I would not bear it so ill if I deserved it. It is *better* that you do not deserve it, that doing well, yet being spok enagainst, you may prove yourself a true Christian (*Gerhard*). **if the will of God be so.** [Optative *theloi* is in א A B C, 'if the will of God should will it so.'] Those who honour God's will as their highest law (ch. ii. 15) have the comfort to know that suffering is God's appointment (ch. iv. 19). Our will does not wish it. **18.** Confirmation of *v.* 17, by the glorious results of Christ's suffering innocently. **For**—"Because." That is "better," *v.* 17, by which we are rendered more like Christ in death and life: for His death brought the best issue to Himself and to us (*Bengel*). **Christ**—the Anointed *Holy* One of God: the *Holy* suffered for *sins,* the *Just* for the *unjust.* **also**—as well as yourselves (*v.* 17). Cf. ch. ii. 21: there His suffering was made an example to us; here, a proof of the blessedness of suffering for well doing. **once**—for all : never again to suffer. It is "better" for us also once to suffer with Christ, than for ever without Christ (*Bengel*). We now are suffering our "once;" it will soon be a thing of the past: a bright consolation. **for sins** —as though He had Himself committed them. He incurred death by His "confession" (1 Tim. vi. 13); as we are called on to 'give an answer to him that asketh a reason of our hope.' This was "well doing" in its highest manifestation. As He suffered, "the Just," so we ought willingly suffer "*for righteousness*' sake" (*vv.* 12, 14, 17). **that he might bring us to God**—us, "the unjust," justified together with Himself in His ascension to the right hand of God (*v.* 22). Thus Christ's death draws *men to Him* (John xii. 32); spiritually now, in our *access into the Holiest,* opened by Christ's ascension; literally hereafter. "Bring us" by the same humiliation and exaltation through which Himself passed. The several steps of Christ's progress are trodden over again by His people, they being one with Him (ch. iv. 1-3). "To God" [*Theo,* dative, implying more than *pros Theon*]— viz., that *God wishes* it (*Bengel*). **put to death**— the means of *bringing us to God.* **in the flesh**— i. e., *in respect to* the life of *flesh.* **quickened by the Spirit.** א A B C, *Origen,* omit the article. Translate, as the antithesis to "*in* the flesh" requires, 'IN spirit;' *i. e.,* in respect to His Spirit. "Put to death" in that *mode of life;* "quickened" in this. Not that His Spirit ever died and was *quickened* again; but whereas He had lived like mortal men in the flesh, He *began to live a spiritual* "resurrection" (*v.* 21) *life,* whereby He has power to bring us to God. Two explanations of *vv.* 18; 19, are possible: (1.) 'Quickened in Spirit,' *i. e., immediately* on His release from the "flesh," the energy of His undying spirit-life was "quickened" by the Father into new modes of action, viz., 'in the Spirit He *went* down (as subsequently He *went* up to heaven, *v.* 22; the same [*poreutheis*]) and heralded [not *salvation,* as *Alford,* contrary to

20 'in prison; which sometime were disobedient, when once the long-suffering of God waited in the days of Noah, while the ark ⁸ was a-preparing,
21 wherein few, that is, eight souls were saved by water. The like figure

A. D. 60

ʳ Isa. 42. 7.

ˢ Heb. 11. 7.

Scripture, which everywhere represents man's state after death irreversible. Nor is mention made of *conversion* of the spirits in prison. Note, *v.* 20. Nor is the phrase here 'preached *the Gospel'* [*euangelizo*], but *heralded* [*ekeruxe*]; simply *made announcement* of His finished work (so [*kerussein*] Mark i. 45, "publish"); confirming Enoch and Noah's testimony; thereby declaring the condemnation of the diluvian unbelievers, and the salvation of Noah and believers (*Birks* thinks Christ announced His finished work to those who repented when the flood suddenly came, but who were shut out from the ark): a sample of the opposite effects of the word preached on *all* unbelievers and believers respectively; also a consolation to those whom Peter addresses, in their sufferings from unbelievers. This case is selected for the sake of "baptism," its 'antitype' (*v.* 21), which seals believers as separated from the doomed world] to the spirits (His *Spirit* speaking to the *spirits*) in prison (in Hades or Sheol, awaiting the judgment, 2 Pet. ii. 4, which were of old disobedient when,' &c. (2.) The strongest argument for (1.) is the position of "sometime," "*of old*," connected with "disobedient;" whereas if the *preaching* were long past, we should expect "sometime" to be joined to "went and preached." But this transposition may express that *their disobedience preceded His preaching.* The participle expresses the reason of His *preaching*, '*inasmuch as* they were sometime disobedient' (cf. ch. iv. 6). Also "went" seemingly is a *personal* going, as in *v.* 22, not merely *in spirit.* But see below. The objections are, "quickened" must refer to Christ's *body* (cf. *v.* 21, end); for as His *Spirit* never ceased to live, it could not be "quickened." Cf. John v. 21; Rom. viii. 11, &c., where "quicken" is used of the *bodily* resurrection. Also, not His *Spirit*, but His *soul*, went to Hades. His Spirit, commended at death to His Father, was forthwith "in Paradise." The theory (1.) would thus require that His descent to the spirits in prison should be *after* His resurrection! Cf. Eph. iv. 9, 10, which makes the *descent* precede the *ascent.* Scripture elsewhere is silent about such a heralding, though probably Christ's death had immediate effects on the state of both the godly and the ungodly in Hades: the souls of the godly, perhaps, then were, as some fathers thought, translated to God's immediate presence; sheol was divided into Paradise and Gehenna (Ps. xvi. 10; Luke xvi. 22-26; xxiii. 43). The way into the heavenly Holiest was not made manifest whilst the Levitical dispensation stood, nor until Christ the Forerunner ascended into heaven (Rom. x. 6, 7; Eph. iv. 9; Heb. ix. 8; xi. 40; Matt. xxvii. 51-53; John iii. 13; Col. i. 18). But *prison* is always in a *bad* sense in Scripture: so that good spirits cannot be meant *here.* "Paradise," and "Abraham's bosom," the abode of good spirits in Old Testament times, are separated by a wide gulf from Gehenna, and cannot be "prison." Cf. 2 Cor. xii. 2, 4, where "paradise" and the "third heaven" correspond. Also, Why should the antediluvian unbelievers in particular be selected as objects of His preaching in Hades? Explain: Quickened *in spirit*, in which (as distinguished from *in person;* "in which," *i.e., in spirit*, obviating the misconception that "went" implies a *personal going*) He went (in the person of Noah, "a preacher of righteousness," 2 Pet. ii. 5. *Alford's note* (Eph. ii. 17) is the best reply to his argument from "went," that a *local* going to

Hades *in person* is meant. As 'He CAME and preached peace' *by His Spirit* in the apostles after His death and ascension, so before His incarnation He preached in Spirit through Noah to the antediluvians (John xiv. 18, 28; Acts xxvi. 23); "Christ should show" [*katangellein*], '*announce* light to the Gentiles') and preached unto the spirits in prison, *i.e.*, the antediluvians, whose bodies seemed free, but their spirits were in prison, shut up in the earth as one great condemned cell (parallel to Isa. xxiv. 22, 23), 'upon the earth . . . they shall be gathered together as *prisoners* gathered in the pit, and shall be shut up *in the prison,'* &c. (just as the fallen angels are judicially regarded as "in chains of darkness," though for a time at large on the earth, 2 Pet. ii. 4), where *v.* 18 has an allusion to the flood, "the *windows from on high* are open" (cf. Gen. vii. 11); from this prison the only way of escape was that preached by Christ in Noah. Christ, who in our times came in the flesh, in Noah's days preached *in Spirit* by Noah to the spirits then in prison (Isa. lxi. 1, end, "The Spirit of the Lord God hath sent me to *proclaim* the opening of the *prison* to them that are bound"). So in ch. i. 11, "the Spirit of Christ" 'testified in the prophets.' His 'Spirit strove' with the antediluvian men, but did not continue to do so, because man was "flesh," and suffered it to quench the Spirit (Gen. vi. 3): so now they are "spirits in prison." Then His preaching had little success; now that He is gone to heaven (*v.* 22) the Spirit's power in Him is infinite, owing to the resurrection. To share in this His resurrection power of the Spirit of life, they must be willing to suffer in the *flesh.* They have a double motive to this set before them:—(1.) Christ's example of the blessed effect of voluntary suffering in the flesh; (2.) Christ's accession of power *now*, as compared with then (Matt. xxviii. 18). As Christ suffered even to death by enemies, and was afterwards quickened in virtue of His "Spirit" (or Divine nature, Rom. i. 3, 4; 1 Cor. xv. 45; 2 Cor. xiii. 4), which henceforth evinced its full energy, the first result of which was the raising of His body (*v.* 21, end) from the prison of the grave and His soul from Hades, so the same Spirit of Christ enabled Noah, amidst reproach, to preach to the disobedient spirits fast bound in wrath. That Spirit in you can enable you also to suffer patiently now, looking for the resurrection-deliverance. Be not afraid of suffering from well doing, for *death in the flesh leads to life in the Spirit* (cf. ch. ii. 19-24; iii. 17). 20. **when once the long suffering of God waited in the days of Noah.** א A B C, Vulgate, read [*apexedecheto* (omitting *hapax*, "once")] '*was continuing* to wait on' (if haply men in the 120 years of grace would repent) until the *end* of His waiting came in their death by the flood. This refutes *Alford's* second day of grace given in Hades. Noah's days are selected, as the ark and the destroying flood answer respectively to "baptism" and the coming destruction of unbelievers by fire. Be not shaken in spirit by the majority hardening themselves against Christ's grace now: it was still more so at the flood, when all but "eight" perished through unbelief. **while the ark was a-preparing**—(Heb. xi. 7.) A long period of God's 'long-suffering and waiting,' which rendered the world's unbelief the more inexcusable. **wherein** [*eis hen*]—'(by having entered) *into* which.' **few**—so now. **eight**—seven (the sacred number) with ungodly Ham. **souls**—

whereunto *even* baptism doth also now save us (not the putting away of the filth of the flesh, but the answer of a good conscience toward God,)

22 by the resurrection of Jesus Christ: who is gone into heaven, and *'*is on the right hand of God; angels and authorities and powers being made subject unto him.

4 FORASMUCH then as Christ hath suffered for us in the flesh, arm yourselves likewise with the same mind: for he *"*that hath suffered in

2 the flesh hath ceased from sin; that he no longer should live the rest of

3 *his* time in the flesh to the lusts of men, but to the will of God. For the time past of *our* life may suffice us to have wrought the will of the Gen-

A. D. 60.

t Ps 110. 1.
Rom. 8. 34.
Eph. 1. 20.
Col. 3. 1.
Heb 1. 3.

CHAP. 4.

a Rom. 6. 2,
7.
Gal. 5. 24.
Col. 3. 5.
ch. 3. 18.

used in *living* persons; why should not "spirits" also? Noah preached to their ears, but Christ *in spirit*, to their *spirits*, or spiritual natures. **saved by water.** The same water which drowned the unbelieving buoyed up the ark in which the eight were saved. Others, 'were brought safe *through* the water' [*di*'*hudatos*]. The sense may be as in 1 Cor. iii. 15, 'they were safely preserved *though having to be in the water*' (cf. *dia* with genitive, 'spite of,' Rom. ii. 27). **21. whereunto.** A B C, Vulgate, read [ὅ for ῷ] 'which'—lit., 'which (viz., water, in general; being) the antitype (of the water of the flood) is now saving (the salvation being not yet fully realized, cf. 1 Cor. x. 1, 2, 5; Jude 5; *puts into a state of salvation*) us also (so B C; but א A, Vulgate, read '*You also;*' as well as Noah and his party), to wit, baptism.' Water saved Noah, not of itself, but by sustaining the ark built in *faith* on God's word: it was to him *the sign and mean of a regeneration* of the earth. It betokened a *death* to be brought safe through, preliminary to a *resurrection*. Perishing humanity is the old man; Noah and the saved the new-born creature: the water that separated the two answers to baptism (Rom. vi. 3, 4). The flood was for Noah a baptism, as the passage through the Red Sea for the Israelites. By the flood he and his family were transferred from the old world to the new; from immediate destruction to lengthened probation; from the companionship of the wicked to communion with God; from severing all bonds between the creature and the Creator to the privileges of the covenant: so we by spiritual baptism. As there was a Ham who forfeited the privileges, so many now. The antitypical water, viz., baptism, saves you also, not of itself, but the spiritual thing conjoined with it, repentance and faith, of which it is the seal, as Peter explains. Cf. the union of the sign and thing signified, John iii. 5; Eph. v. 26; Titus iii. 5: cf. 1 John v. 6. **not the, &c.**—"Flesh" is emphatic. "Not the putting away of the filth of *the flesh*" (as by a mere water-baptism, unaccompanied with the Spirit's baptism, cf. Eph. ii. 11), but of the soul. The ark (Christ and His Spirit-filled Church), not the water, is the instrument of salvation: the water only flowed round the ark; so not the mere water-baptism, but water when accompanied with the Spirit. **answer** [*eperotēma*]—'interrogation,' viz., of candidates for baptism (Acts viii. 37); eliciting confession of faith "toward God," and renunciation of Satan (*Augustine*, 'Ad Catechumenos,' b. iv.; *Cyprian*, Ep. vii., 'Ad Rogation'), which, when flowing from "a good conscience," assure one of being "saved." *Lit.*, 'a good conscience's *interrogation* (including the satisfactory *answer*) toward God.' Metonymy: a conscience that can bear *interrogation* in relation to the all-seeing God, and can *answer*, it is good and cleansed (Heb. ix. 14; x. 22). I prefer this to (*Wahl, Alford*, &c.) '*enquiry* of a good conscience *after God:*' none of the parallels alleged, not even

2 Sam. xi. 7, LXX., is strictly in point. Byzantine Greek idiom (whereby the term meant—(1.) The question; (2.) the stipulation; (3.) the engagement), easily flowing from the usage in Peter, confirms the former. **by the resurrection of Jesus**—joined with 'saves:' in so far as baptism applies the power of Christ's resurrection. As Christ's death unto sin is the source of the believer's death unto, and so deliverance from, sin's penalty and power, so His resurrection-life is the source of the believer's new spiritual life. **22.** (Ps. cx. 1; Rom. viii. 34, 38; 1 Cor. xv. 24; Eph. i. 21; iii. 10; Col. ii. 10-15.) The fruit of His patience in voluntarily - endured, undeserved, sufferings: a pattern to us (*vv.* 17, 18). **gone** (Luke xxiv. 51)—proving His literal ascension. *Lit.*, 'Is on the right hand of God, *having gone* into heaven.' Vulgate and Latin fathers add the benefit of Christ's sitting on God's right hand, 'Who is on the right hand of God, *having swallowed up death, that we may become heirs of everlasting life;*' involving for us A DEATHLESS LIFE. The Greek MSS. reject the words. Cf. *Peter's* speeches, Acts ii. 32-35; iii. 21, 26; x. 40, 42. An undesigned coincidence and proof of genuineness.

CHAP. IV. 1-19.—LIKE THE RISEN CHRIST, BELIEVERS HENCEFORTH HAVE NO MORE TO DO WITH SIN. AS THE END IS NEAR, CULTIVATE SELF - RESTRAINT, WATCHFUL PRAYERFULNESS, CHARITY, HOSPITALITY, SCRIPTURAL SPEECH, MINISTERING TO ONE ANOTHER OF YOUR SEVERAL GIFTS TO THE GLORY OF GOD—REJOICING PATIENCE UNDER SUFFERING.

1. suffered. א, 'died' [*apothanontos*]. **for us.** Supported by א ('you') A; but B C, Vulgate, omit. **in the flesh**—in His body of humiliation. **arm**—(Eph. vi. 11, 13.) **the same mind**—of suffering with patient willingness what God *wills*. **he that hath suffered**—a thing now *past* [*pathōn*]: Christ first, and in His person the believer: a general proposition. **hath ceased** [*pepautai*]—'has been made to cease;' *i. e.*, has obtained by His past and completed suffering *a cessation from sin*, which heretofore lay on him (Rom. vi. 6-11, especially 7). The Christian is by faith one with Christ: as Christ by death is judicially freed from sin, so the Christian who has in the person of Christ died has no more to do with it judicially, and ought to have no more to do with it actually. "The flesh" is the sphere in which sin has place. **2. That he, &c.** 'That he (the believer, who has once for all obtained cessation from sin by suffering, in the person of Christ, viz, in virtue of his union with the crucified Christ) should no longer live the rest of his time in the flesh to the lusts of men, but to the will of God.' '*Rest of his time in the flesh*' (the Greek has 'in' here, not in v. 1 as to Christ) proves that the reference is not to Christ, but to the believer, whose *remaining time in the flesh* for glorifying God is short (v. 3). Not as *Alford*, '*Arm yourselves* . . . with a view no longer to live the rest of *your* time.' **3. may suffice**—'is

tiles, when we walked in lasciviousness, lusts, excess of wine, revellings,
4 banquetings, and abominable idolatries: wherein they think it strange
that ye run not with *them* to the same excess of riot, speaking evil of
5 *you*: who shall give account to him that is ready [b]to judge the quick and
6 the dead. For, for this cause [c]was the Gospel preached also to them that
are dead, that they might be judged according to men in the flesh, but
live according to God in the spirit.
7 But [d]the end of all things is at hand: be ye therefore sober, and watch
8 unto prayer. And above all things have fervent charity among your-
9 selves: for [e]charity [1]shall cover the multitude of sins. Use hospitality

A. D. 60.

[b] Acts 10. 42.
Acts 17. 31.
Rom. 14.10.
[c] ch. 3. 19.
[d] Matt 24.13.
Rom. 13.12.
Phil. 4. 5.
Heb. 10. 25.
[e] Pro. 10. 12.
1 Cor. 13. 7.
Jas 5. 20.
1 Or. will.

sufficient.' Peter takes the lowest ground: for not even the past time ought to have been wasted in lust; but since you cannot recall it, at least lay out the future to better account. **us.** Omitted in A B C, Vulgate; ℵ has 'you.' **wrought** [*kateirgasthai*]—'wrought out.' **Gentiles**—heathen: which many of you were. **when, &c.** [*peporeumenous*]—'walking as ye have done in *lasciviousness*' (*Alford*) [*aselgeiais* means *petulant, wantonness*]; unbridled conduct: not merely filthy lust. **excess of wine** [*oinophlugiais*]—'wine-bibbings.' **abominable** [*athemitois*]—'*lawless* idolatries,' violating God's sacred *law*: not that *all* Peter's readers (note. ch. i. 1) *walked* in these, but many, viz., the Gentile portion. **4. Wherein**—in respect to which abandonment of your former *walk* (v. 3). **run not with them**—eagerly, in troops (*Bengel*). **excess** [*anachusin*]—*profusion*; sink: stagnant water after an inundation. **riot**—profligacy. **speaking evil**—charging you with pride, singularity, hypocrisy, and secret crimes (2 Pet. ii. 2). However, there is no Greek "of you;" simply 'blaspheming.' It seems always used, either directly or indirectly, of *impious reviling against God, Christ, the Holy Spirit*, or the Christian religion; not merely against men as such (Greek, v. 14). **5.** They who call you to account falsely shall have to give account of themselves for this evil-speaking (Jude 15). and be condemned justly. **ready**—speedily (v. 7; 2 Pet. iii. 10). **6. For**—reason for v. 5, "judge the *dead*." **gospel preached also to . . . dead**—as well as to them now living, and to them that shall be found alive at the Judge's coming. "Dead" must be taken in the literal sense, as v. 5, which refutes the explanation "dead" *in sins*. Moreover, the absence of the article does not restrict "dead" to particular dead persons, for there is no article in v. 5 also, where "the dead" is universal in meaning. The sense seems, Peter, representing the attitude of the Church in every age expecting Christ at any moment, says, The Judge is ready to judge the quick and dead—*the dead*, I say, *for* they, too, in their lifetime, had the Gospel preached to them, that so they may be judged at last as those living now (and those who shall be alive when Christ comes), viz., 'men in the flesh,' and that they may, having escaped condemnation by embracing the Gospel so preached, live unto God in the spirit (though death has passed over their flesh: Luke xx. 38), thus being made like Christ in death and in life (note, ch. iii. 18). He says, "live," not "made alive;" for they are supposed to have been already "quickened together with Christ" (Eph. ii. 5). This is parallel to ch. iii. 19: cf. note. The Gospel, substantially, was "preached" to the Old Testament Church; though not so fully as to us. It is no objection that the Gospel was not preached to *all* that shall be found dead at Christ's coming. For Peter is plainly referring only to those within reach of the Gospel, or who might have known God through His ministers in Old and New Testament times. Peter, like Paul (1 Thess. iv. 15), argues that those

found *living* at Christ's coming shall have no advantage above the *dead* who shall then be raised, since the latter *live unto*, or 'according to,' *God*, already in His purpose. *Alford* is wrong, 'that they might be judged according to men as regards the flesh'—i. e., *be in the state of the completed sentence on sin*, which is *death after the flesh*. For "judged" cannot have a different meaning here from "judge" in v. 5. "Live according to God" means, 'live a life *such as God lives*'—divine: contrasted with "according to men in the flesh"—i. e., such as men live in the flesh.

7. Resuming v. 5. **the end of all things**—therefore also of the wantonness (vv. 3, 4) of the wicked, and of the sufferings of the righteous. The nearness is not that of *time*, but that *before the Lord;* as he explains, 2 Pet. iii. 8, 9, to guard against misapprehension, and defends God from the charge of procrastination. We live in the last dispensation, not like the Jews under the Old Testament. The Lord will come as a thief: He is "ready" (v. 5) to judge the world at any moment: it is only God's long-suffering, that the Gospel may be preached as a witness to all nations, that lengthens out the time which is with Him still as nothing. **sober** [*sophronesate*]—'self-restrained.' The opposite duties to the sins, v. 3, are inculcated. "Sober," the opposite of "lasciviousness" (v. 3). **watch** [*nepsate*]—'be soberly vigilant;' not intoxicated with worldly cares and pleasures. Temperance promotes *wakefulness;* both promote prayer. Drink makes drowsy; drowsiness prevents prayer. **prayer**—Greek, 'prayers:' the end for which we should exercise vigilance. **8. above all things**—not that "charity" is above "prayer," but *love* is the animating spirit, without which other duties are dead. [*Tēn eis heautous agapēn ektenē*, 'Have your mutual (lit., *towards yourselves*) love intense.'] He presupposes its existence: he urges them to make it more fervent. **charity shall cover the multitude of sins.** So ℵ; but A B, Vulgate, 'covereth.' From Prov. x. 12: cf. xvii. 9. 'Covereth,' so as not harshly to condemn or expose; but to bear the other's burdens, forgiving and forgetting offences. Perhaps the *additional* idea is included. By prayer for them, *love tries to have them covered by God;* so being the instrument of converting sinners, 'covereth a (not "the") multitude of sins;' the former idea from Proverbs is *prominent*. It is not, as Rome teaches, 'covereth' *his own* sins; then the Greek middle would be used; and Prov. x. 12: xvii. 9, support the Protestant view. 'As God with His love covers my sins if I believe, so must I *cover my neighbour's*' (*Luther*). Cf. the conduct of Shem and Japheth (Gen. ix. 23), in contrast to Ham's exposure of his father's shame. We ought to cover others' sins only where love itself does not require the contrary. **9.** (Rom. xii. 13; Heb. xiii. 2.) Not the spurious hospitality which passes current in the world; but entertaining those *needing* it; especially those exiled for the faith, as representatives of Christ; and all hospitality to whomsoever

10 one to another without *f* grudging. As *g* every man hath received the gift, *even so* minister the same one to another, as good stewards of the
11 manifold grace of God. If *k* any man speak, *let him speak* as the oracles of God; if any man minister, *let him do it* as of the ability which God giveth: that *i* God in all things may be glorified through Jesus Christ; *j* to whom be praise and dominion for ever and ever. Amen.
12   Beloved, think it not strange concerning the fiery trial which is to try
13 you, as though some strange thing happened unto you: but rejoice, inasmuch as *k* ye are partakers of Christ's sufferings; that, when his glory
14 shall be revealed, ye may be glad also with exceeding joy. If *l* ye be reproached for the name of Christ, happy *are ye;* for *m* the Spirit of glory and of God resteth upon you: on their part he is evil spoken of, but on
15 your part he is glorified. But let none of you suffer as a murderer, or *as* a thief, or *as* an evil doer, or *as* a busybody in other men's matters.
16 Yet if *any man suffer* as a Christian, let him not be ashamed; but *n* let

A. D. 60.

f 2 Cor. 9. 7.
g 1 Cor. 4. 7.
h Jer 23. 22.
i Eph 5. 20.
ch 2. 5.
j 1 Tim. 6.16.
ch 5. 11.
Rev. 1. 6.
k Rom. 8. 17.
2 Cor. 1. 7.
Rev 1. 9.
l Matt. 5. 11.
2 Cor. 12.10.
Jas. 1. 12.
ch 2. 19,20.
m Matt 10.20.
2 Cor. 12. 9.
n Acts 5. 41.

exercised, from Christian love. **without grudging** [*gongusmou*]—'murmuring' (Rom. xii. 8); openhearted sincerity, cordiality. Not secretly speaking against the person whom we entertain, or upbraiding him with the favour we have conferred. **10. every**—'even as *each* received,' in whatever degree, and of whatever kind. The Spirit's *gifts* [*charisma*, '*a gift of grace*'—i. e., *gratuitous*] are the common property of the Christian community, each being but a steward for edifying the whole; not receiving the gift merely for himself. **minister the same**—not discontentedly envying or disparaging *the gift of another*. **one to another**—Greek as *v.* 8, 'towards yourselves:' all form one body; in seeking the good of other members they are promoting the good of *themselves*. **stewards**— (Matt. xxv. 15, &c.; Luke xix. 13-26.) **11. If any man speak**—viz., as a prophet, or divinely-taught *teacher* in the church assembly. **the**—no article: 'as oracles of God.' This may be due to "God" having no article, it being a principle, when a governed noun omits the article, that the governing noun shall omit it too. In Acts vii. 38 the article is wanting: thus, "as *the* oracles of God," *the Old Testament* may be right; so Rom. xii. 6. But the context suits better, 'Let him speak as (becomes one speaking) *oracles* OF GOD.' His divinely-inspired words are *not his own*, but *God's*; as a *steward* (*v.* 10) having them committed to him, he ought so to speak them. Jesus was the pattern (Matt. vii. 29; John xii. 49; xiv. 10: cf. 2 Cor. ii. 17). Note, the very term restricted elsewhere (Acts vii. 38; Rom. iii. 2; Heb. v. 12) to the *Old Testament* writings, is here predicated of the inspired *words* (the substance of which was afterwards *written*) of the *New Testament* prophets. **minister**—in *acts:* the other sphere of spiritual activity besides *speaking*. **as of**—'out of' the store of his '*strength*' [*ischuos*, *physical:* for outward service; not moral and intellectual 'ability:' so Mark xii. 30]. **giveth** [*choregei*]—'supplieth:' said of a *Choragus*, who *supplied* the chorus with necessaries for performing their several parts. **that God in all things may be glorified**—the end of all a Christian's acts. **through Jesus Christ** —the Mediator through whom all blessings come down to us, and all our praises ascend to God. Through Christ alone can God be glorified in us, our sayings, and doings. **to whom**—Christ. **be**—'is.' **for ever and ever**—'unto the ages of the ages.'
12. strange—they might *think it strange* that God should allow his chosen children to be sore tried. **fiery trial**—like the fire by which metals are tested and their dross removed. The Greek adds 'in the case.' **which is to try you**—Greek,

'which is taking place for a trial to you.' Instead of its '*happening* to you' as some strange *chance*, it 'is taking place' with the gracious *design* of trying you: a consolatory reflection. **13. inasmuch as.** א A B read [*katho*] 'in proportion as ye by suffering are partakers of Christ's sufferings—i. e., by faith enter willingly into realizing fellowship with them. **with exceeding joy** [*agalliomenoi*] — 'exulting joy:' now ye *rejoice* amidst sufferings; then ye shall EXULT for ever free from sufferings (ch. i. 6, 8). If we will not bear suffering for Christ now, we must bear eternal sufferings hereafter. **14. for**—'IN the name of Christ;' viz., *as Christians* (*v.* 16; ch. iii. 14, above; Mark ix. 41), '*in my name*, because *ye belong to Christ.'* *V.* 15, 'as a murderer, thief,' &c., stands in contrast. Let your suffering be *on account of Christ*, not on account of evil doing (ch. ii. 20). **reproached.** *Reproach* affects noble minds more than loss of goods, or even bodily sufferings. **the Spirit . . . upon you**—the same as rested on Christ (Luke iv. 18). "The Spirit of glory" is *His* Spirit, for He is the "Lord *of glory*" (Jas. ii. 1). Believers may well overcome '*reproach*' (cf. Heb. xi. 26), since "the Spirit of *glory*" rests upon them, as upon Him. *Reproach* cannot prevent their happiness, because they retain before God their *glory* entire, as having the Spirit, with whom *glory* is inseparably joined (*Calvin*). א A add, 'and of His power;' B C omit. **and of God** [*kai to tou Theou*]—'and *the* (Spirit) of God:' *the Spirit of glory (i. e.*, Christ's Spirit) is also *the Spirit of God*. **on their part he is evil spoken of, but on your part he is glorified.** So the oldest Vulgate, Thebaic, and Cyprian; omitted in א A B, Syriac, and Coptic versions, &c. "Evil spoken of"—*lit.,* 'blasphemed.' Not merely do they '*speak against you*,' as ch. iii. 16, but *blasphemously mock Christ* and Christianity. **15. But**—'For.' 'Reproached *in the name of Christ*,' I say (*v.* 14), 'FOR let none,' &c. **as . . . as . . . as . . . as.** The *as* twice in italics is not in the Greek. The second Greek "as" distinguishes the class "busybody in other men's matters" from the previous delinquents. Christians, from mistaken zeal, under the plea of faithfulness, might make themselves judges of the acts of unbelievers. [*Allotriepiskopos*, 'a bishop in what is (not his own, but) another's province; an allusion to the existing *bishops* of the Church; a self constituted overseer in others' concerns.] **16. a Christian**—the name given first at Antioch (Acts xi. 26; xxvi. 27, 28); the only three places where the term occurs. At first believers had no distinctive name, but were called among themselves "brethren," "disciples," 'those of the way' (Acts vi. 1, 3; ix. 2), "saints" (Rom. i. 7); by the

17 him glorify God on this behalf. For the time *is come* [o] that judgment
must begin at the house of God: and [p] if *it* first *begin* at us, [q] what shall
18 the end *be* of them that obey not the gospel of God? And [r] if the righteous scarcely be saved, where shall the ungodly and the sinner appear?
19 Wherefore let them that suffer according to the will of God commit
the keeping of their souls *to him* in well doing, as unto a faithful
Creator.

5 THE elders which are among you I exhort, who am also [a] an elder,
and [b] a witness of the sufferings of Christ, and also [c] a partaker of the
2 glory that shall be revealed: feed the flock of God [1] which is among you,

A. D. 60.

[o] Isa 10. 12.
[p] Luke 23.31.
[q] Luke 10.12.
[r] Pro. 11 31.

CHAP. 5.
[a] Phile. 9.
[b] Luke 24.48.
[c] Rom. 8. 17.
[1] Or, as much as in you is.

Jews (who denied that Jesus was the *Christ*, and so would never originate '*Christian*' in contempt), 'Nazarenes.' At Antioch, where first *idolatrous* Gentiles (Cornelius, Acts x., was not an idolater, but a proselyte) were converted, and wide missionary work began, they could be no longer looked on as a *Jewish* sect; so *the Gentiles*, perhaps first, designated them by the new name, 'Christians.' [But *Chrematizo* is always used of a *Divine utterance:* so Acts xi. 26 probably means, the name was given by *Divine appointment*, rather than by the nicknaming wit for which the people of Antioch were notorious.] The new name marked a new epoch in the Church's development—viz., its missions to the Gentiles. The date of this epistle must have been when this had become the generally recognized designation *among Gentiles* (for its common use among believers was not till subsequently)—an undesigned proof that the New Testament was composed when it professes, and when the name exposed one to reproach and suffering, though not yet to *systematic* persecution. **let him not be ashamed** —though the world is ashamed of shame. To suffer for one's faults is no honour (*v.* 15; ch. ii. 20)—for Christ, is no *shame* (*v.* 14; ch. iii. 14). **but let him glorify God**—not merely glory in persecution. Peter might have said, 'but let him esteem it an honour;' but the honour is to be given *to God*, who counts him worthy of it, involving exemption from the coming judgments on the ungodly. **on this behalf.** ℵ A B, Vulgate, read 'in this *name*'—*i. e.*, in suffering for such a name. **17.** Another consolation. All must pass under God's judgment: God's own household first, their chastisement being here, for which they glorify Him as a proof of their membership in His family, and a pledge of their escape from the end of those whom the last judgment shall find disobedient to the Gospel. **the time** [*ho kairos*]—'fit time.' **judgment must begin at the house of God**—the Church of living believers. Peter has in mind Ezek. ix. 6: cf. Jer. xxv. 29; Amos iii. 2. Judgment is already begun—the Gospel, as a "two-edged sword," having the double effect of saving some and condemning others—and shall be consummated at the last. God limits the destroyer's temporarily permitted power over His people. **if . . . at us, what shall the end be of them, &c.** If even the godly have chastening judgments now, how much more shall the ungodly be doomed to damnatory judgments at last! **gospel of God**—the God who is to judge them. **18. scarcely** (cf. 1 Cor. iii. 15, end)—having to pass through trying chastisements, as David did for sin. "The righteous" man has trial, but the issue is certain, and the entrance into the kingdom *abundant* at last. The "scarcely" marks *the severity of the ordeal*, and the unlikelihood (in a human point of view) of the righteous sustaining it; but the righteousness of Christ, and God's everlasting covenant, make it sure. **ungodly**—without regard for God: negative. **sinner**—loving sin: positive: the same man is at once God-forgetting and sin-loving. **appear**—in judgment. **19.** Conclusion from *vv.* 17, 18. Since the godly know that their sufferings are *by God's will*, for their good (*v.* 17), to chasten them that they may not perish with the world, they ought to trust God cheerfully amidst sufferings, persevering *in well doing.* **let them**—Greek, 'let them *also*,' as well as those not suffering. Not only in ordinary circumstances, but *also* in *suffering*, *let* believers *commit*, &c. (cf. note, ch. iii. 14). **according to the will of God**—(note, ch. iii. 17.) **in well doing** —B ℵ; but A, Vulgate, read '*well doings*' (contrast ill doings, *v.* 15). Our committing of ourselves to God is to be, not in indolent quietism, but accompanied with active *well doings.* **faithful**—to His covenant promises. **Creator**—who is therefore our Almighty Preserver. He, not we, must *keep* our souls. Sin destroyed the spiritual relation between us and the Creator, leaving that only of government. Faith restores it: the believer, living to *the will of God* (ch. iv. 2), rests implicitly on his *Creator's* faithfulness.

CHAP. V. 1-14.—EXHORTATIONS TO ELDERS, JUNIORS, AND ALL—PARTING PRAYER—CONCLUSION.

1. elders—alike in office and age (*v.* 5). **I . . . also an elder.** To put one's self on a level with those we exhort gives weight to exhortations (cf. 2 John 1). Peter, in humility, for the Gospel's sake, does not put forward his *apostleship*, wherein he *presided over the elders.* In this the apostles have no successors, for 'the signs of an apostle' have not been transmitted. The presidents over the presbyters and deacons, by whatever name designated, *angel, bishop*, or *moderator*, &c., though *of the same* ORDER *as the presbyters*, yet have virtually succeeded to a superintendency *analogous* to that exercised by the apostles (this priority existed from the earliest times after the apostles) (*Tertullian*); just as the Jewish synagogue (the model which the Church followed) was governed by a council of presbyters, presided over by one of themselves, "the chief ruler of the synagogue," (cf. *Vitringa*, 'Synagogue,' part ii., chs. iii. and vii.) **witness**—an *eye-witness* of Christ's sufferings; so qualified to exhort you to believing patience in *suffering for well doing* after His example (ch. ii. 20). This explains the 'therefore' in ℵ A B, 'I therefore exhort,' resuming ch. iv. 19. His higher dignity as an *apostle* is delicately implied, as *eye-witnessing* was a necessary qualification for apostleship (cf. Peter's own speeches, Acts i. 21, 22; ii. 32; x. 39). **also**—the righteous recompense corresponding to the sufferings. **partaker of the glory**—according to Christ's promise; an earnest was given in the transfiguration. **2. Feed** [*Poimanate*]—'Tend as a shepherd,' by discipline and doctrine. Lead, feed, heed; by prayer, exhortation, government, example. The *dignity* is marked by "*elder;*" the *duties*, to *tend* or *oversee*, by

taking the oversight *thereof,* not by constraint, but willingly; not for
3 filthy lucre, but of a ready mind; neither as [2]being lords over [d]*God's*
4 heritage, but being ensamples to the flock. And when [e]the chief Shepherd shall appear, ye shall receive a crown of glory that fadeth not
away.
5 Likewise, ye younger, submit yourselves unto the elder. Yea, [f]all *of*
you be subject one to another, and be clothed with humility: for God
6 resisteth the proud, and giveth [g]grace to the humble. Humble yourselves therefore under the mighty hand of God, that he may exalt you in
7 due time: casting [h]all your care upon him; for he careth for you.

A. D. 60.

[2] Or, over-
ruling
Eze. 31. 4.
Matt. 20 25.
[d] Ps. 74. 2.
[e] Heb. 13. 20.
[f] Eph. 5. 21.
[g] Isa. 66. 2.
[h] Ps. 37. 5.
Ps. 55. 22.
Matt. 6. 25.
Luke 12.11.

"*bishop.*" Peter has in mind Christ's injunction [*Poimaine—boske*]: "Feed (*tend*) my sheep . . . Feed (*pasture*) my lambs" (John xxi. 16). He invites the elders to share the same duty (cf. Acts xx. 28). The flock is Christ's. **which is among you.** Whilst having a concern for *all,* your special duty is to feed that portion *which is among you.* **oversight**—'bishopric;' duty of overseer. **not by constraint.** Necessity is laid upon them; but willingness prevents it being felt, both in under-taking and fulfilling the duty (*Bengel*). 'He is a true minister of the counsel of God who doeth and teacheth the things of the Lord; not accounted righteous because he is a presbyter, but, because righteous, chosen into the presbytery' (*Clemens Alexandrinus*). **willingly.** א A, Vulgate, Syriac, and Coptic, add [*Kata Theon*], 'as God would have it done' (Rom. viii. 27). **not for filthy lucre** —(Isa. lvi. 11; Titus i. 7.) **of a ready mind**—promptly, heartily, without selfish gain-seeking, as the Israelites gave their services *willing-heartedly* to the sanctuary (Exod. xxxv. 5, 21, 22, 29). **3. being lords** [*katakurieuontes*]—'lording it' with despotic pride (2 Cor. i. 24). **God's heritage** [*tōn klerōn*]—'the inheritances;' *i. e.,* the *portions* of the Church committed severally to your charge (*Bengel*); explained by "the flock." However, in *v. 2,* "flock *of God* which is among you," answers to "(*God's*) heritages" (*the sheep* which are *God's* portion and inheritance, Deut. xxxii. 9). *Your* assuming *lordship* would be to usurp *God's.* The Church, *as one whole,* is God's heritage or *flock* (singular). Regarded as to its *component parts,* divided among several pastors, it is plural, 'heritages.' Cf. Acts i. 17, 25. Greek, the 'parts' are still *God's heritages. Bernard* of Clairvaux wrote to *Pope Eugene,* 'Peter could not give thee what he had not: what he had he gave: the *care* over the Church, not *dominion.*' "Lot" for "inheritance" came from the division of Canaan into allotments. The whole land was God's: each one's portion was from God. **being** [*ginomenoi*]—'becoming.' **ensamples**—the most effective recommendation of precept (1 Tim. iv. 12; Titus ii. 7). 'A monstrosity it is to see the highest rank joined with the lowest life, a grandiloquent tongue with a lazy life, much talking with no fruit' (*Bernard*). **4. And**—*And so:* as the result of "being ensamples" (*v.* 3). **chief Shepherd**—Christ's peculiar title, not Peter's or the pope's. **when . . . shall appear**—'be manifested' (Col. iii. 4). Faith serves the Lord while still unseen. **crown** [*stephanos*]—a garland of *victory;* in the Grecian games woven of ivy, parsley, myrtle, olive, or oak. *Our* crown is distinguished from *theirs* in that it "fadeth not away," as theirs soon did. "The crown *of life.*" Not a *kingly* "crown" [*diadema*], exclusively attributed to the Lord Jesus (Rev. xix. 12). **glory** [*tes*]—'*the* glory,' viz., *to be* then *revealed* (v. 1; ch. iv. 13). **that fadeth not away**—Greek, 'amarantine' (cf. ch. i. 4).

5. ye younger. The *deacons* were originally

younger men, the *presbyters* older : subsequently, as presbyter expressed the *office* of church ruler or teacher, so *neoteros* means not *young men* in age, but *subordinate ministers* of the Church. So Christ uses "younger" (Luke xxii. 26); for He explains it by "he that doth serve" [*ho diakonōn*], *he that ministereth as a deacon;* as He explains "the greatest" by "he that is chief" [*ho hegoumenos*]. 'He that *ruleth*' applied to the *bishops* or *presbyters* (Heb. xiii. 7, 17, 24). So "the young men" (Acts v. 6, 10) are the deacons of the church of Jerusalem, of whom, as all Hebrews, the Hellenistic Christians subsequently complained as neg-lecting their Grecian widows, whence arese the appointment of seven others, Hellenistic deacons. So Peter, having exhorted the *presbyters* not to lord it over those committed to them, adds, 'Likewise, ye younger'—*i. e.,* subordinate ministers—'submit cheerfully to the elders' (*Mosheim*). There is no Scripture sanction for "younger" meaning *laymen* (as *Alford* explains) : this sense is probably of later date. The "*all* of you" that follows refers to the *congregation* generally; it is likely that, like Paul (Eph. iv. 11-13), Peter notices, previous to the general congregation, the *subordinate ministers* as well as the *presbyters,* writing as he did to the same region (Ephesus), to confirm the teaching of the apostle of the Gentiles. **Yea**—to sum up all my exhortations. **be subject.** Omitted in א A B, Vulgate; but *Tischendorf* quotes B for it. Then 'gird (ch. i. 13; iv. 1) fast on humility (lowliness of mind) to one another.' [*Enkombosasthe*], 'Tie on with a fast knot' (*Wahl*). Or, '*gird on* humility as *the slave dress*' [*encomboma*]: as the Lord girded Himself with a towel to perform a servile office of humble love, washing His disciples' feet,—a scene in which Peter played an important part, so that he would naturally have it before his mind. Cf. similarly *v.* 2, with John xxi. 15-17. Clothing was the original badge of man's sin and shame. Pride caused the need of clothing, and pride still reigns in dress; the Christian clothes himself in humility (ch. iii. 3, 4). God provides the robe of Christ's righteousness, to receive which man must strip off pride. **God resisteth the proud**—quoted, as Jas. iv. 6, from Prov. iii. 34. Peter gives James's epistle inspired sanction. Cf. *v.* 9, with Jas. iv. 6, 7. Other sins flee from God : pride alone opposeth itself to God ; therefore God also in turn *opposes Himself to* the proud (*Gerhard* in *Alford*). Humility is the vessel of all graces (*Augustine*). **6. under the mighty hand**—afflicting you (ch. iii. 15) : 'accept' His chastisements ; turn to Him that smiteth you (Isa. ix. 13). He depresses the proud and exalts the humble. **in due time**—wait patiently His own fit time. So א B ; but A, Vulgate, read :In the season of (His) visitation' in mercy. **7. Casting**—once *for all* [*epiripsantes,* aorist]. **care** [*merimnan*]—'anxiety ;' advantage from *humbling ourselves under God's hand* (v. 6), confident reliance on His goodness, and exemption from care. **careth**

8   Be sober, be vigilant; because your adversary the [i]devil, as a roaring
9 lion, walketh about, seeking whom he may devour: whom resist stedfast
in the faith, knowing that the same afflictions are accomplished in your
brethren that are in the world.

10   But the God of all grace, who hath called us unto his eternal glory by
Christ Jesus, after that ye have suffered a while, make you perfect, stab-
11 lish, strengthen, settle *you*. To him *be* glory and dominion for ever and
ever. Amen.

12   By [j]Silvanus, a faithful brother unto you, as I suppose, I have [k]written
briefly, exhorting, and testifying that this is the true grace of God

A. D. 10
[i] Matt. 4. 1, 11.
Matt. 13.39.
Matt 25.41.
John 8. 44.
Eph. 4. 27.
Eph. 6. 12.
Jas. 4. 7.
[j] 2 Cor. 1. 19.
1 Thes. 1. 2.
2 Thes 1. 1.
[k] Heb. 13. 22.

for you [*peri*]—'*respecting* you.' Care is a burden which faith casts off the man on his God. Cf. Ps. xxii. 10; xxxvii. 5; lv. 22; Phil. iv. 6. "Careth" [*melei*]—not so strong as the previous 'anxiety.' **8.** Peter has in mind Christ's warning to *watch* against *Satan*, from forgetting which he fell (Luke xxii. 31). **Be sober.** "Care" will intoxicate the soul; therefore be sober—*i. e.*, self-restrained. Yet, lest this freedom from *care* should lead to false security, **be vigilant**—against "your adversary." Let this be your "care." God provides, therefore be not *anxious.* The devil seeks, therefore watch (*Bengel*). **because.** So C, Vulgate; omitted in א A B,Vulgate. The broken sentences are fervid and forcible. **adversary** [*antidikos*]—*opponent in a court of justice* (Zech. iii. 1). "Satan" means *opponent.* "Devil," *accuser* (Rev. xii. 10). "The enemy" (Matt. xiii. 39). "A murderer from the beginning" (John viii. 44). He counteracts the Gospel. "The tempter." **roaring lion**—implying his insatiable hunger for prey. Through man's sin he got God's justice on his side against us; but Christ, our Advocate, by fulfilling all the demands of justice for us, has made our redemption altogether consistent with justice. **walketh about**—(Job i. 7; ii. 2.) So his children *cannot rest* (Isa. lvii. 20). Evil spirits are (2 Pet. ii. 4; Jude 6) already "in chains of darkness"—*i. e.*, this is their doom *finally:* a doom already begun in part; though for a time they are permitted to roam in the world (of which Satan is prince), especially in the dark air that surrounds the earth (Eph. ii. 2). Hence, perhaps, arises miasma of the air, as physical and moral evil are closely connected. **devour**—with worldly "care" (*v.* 7), so as finally to destroy. Cf. Rev. xii. 15, 16. **9.**—(Luke iv. 13; Eph. vi. 11-17; Jas. iv. 7.) **stedfast** —(cf. 2 Pet. i. 12, end.) Satan's power exists only against the unbelieving: the faithful he cannot touch (1 John v. 18). Faith gives strength to prayer, the instrument against the foe, (Jas. i. 6, &c.) **knowing**, &c.—'encouragement not to faint in afflictions:' your brethren have the same common lot of Christians (1 Cor. x. 13). It is a sign of God's favour, rather than displeasure, that Satan is allowed to harass you, as he did Job. **are**—*are being accomplished* according to God's appointment. **in the world**—lying in the wicked one, therefore the scene of "tribulation" (John xvi. 33).

10. Assurance that God will "perfect" His work of "grace" in them, after they have undergone the preliminary suffering. **But**—only do you watch and resist the foe: God will perform the rest (*Bengel*). **of all grace**—(cf. ch. iv. 10.) To God, as it ssource, all grace is to be referred: He in grace completes what in grace He began. He from the first 'called you (so א A B) unto (with a view to) glory.' He will not let His purpose fall short of completion (1 Sam. iii. 12). If He does so in punishing, much more in grace. The four are fitly conjoined: the *call;* the *glory* to which we are called; the *way* (*suffering*); the ground of the

calling, viz., *the grace of God in* [en] *Christ.* Christ is He *in virtue of,* and *in union with,* whom believers are called to glory. The opposite is "in the world" (*v.* 9). **after that ye have suffered.** *Suffering,* as a preliminary to *glory,* was contemplated in God's *calling.* **a while**—short and inconsiderable, as compared with the *glory.* **perfect,** &c. א A B, Vulgate; Coptic versions read '*Shall Himself* perfect (so that there shall be nothing *defective* in you), stablish, strengthen.' **settle.** So א; but A B omit "settle" [*themeliosai*—*sei*]: *fix on a foundation.* The climax requires rather a verb of *completing* the work of grace, than *founding* it. Though you are called on to *watch* and *resist* the foe, God *Himself* [*autos*] must do all in and through you. The same God who begins must *Himself* complete the work. [*Stērixei*] "**Stablish**" (so as to be "stedfast in the faith," *v.* 9) is the same as "strengthen," Luke xxii. 32. Peter has in mind Christ's charge. His exhortation accords with his name (Matt. xvi. 18). "Stablish," not to waver. "Strengthen" *with might in the inner man by His Spirit,* against the foe (Eph. iii. 16). **11. To him**—alone: not to ourselves. Cf. "Himself," note, *v.* 10. **glory and.** So א; omitted in A B, Vulgate. **dominion** [*to kratos*]—'*the* might' shown in 'perfecting,' &c., you, *v.* 10.

12. Silvanus—*Silas,* the companion of Paul and Timothy: a suitable messenger by whom to confirm *Paul's* doctrine of 'the true grace of God' in the same churches (cf. 2 Pet. iii. 16). We never meet with Silvanus as Paul's companion after Paul's last journey to Jerusalem. His connection with Peter was subsequent. **as I suppose.** Silvanus, perhaps, stood in a close relation to the churches in Asia, having taken the oversight of them after Paul's departure, and afterwards went to Peter, by whom he is now sent back to them with this epistle. He did not *know,* by observation, *Silvanus's faithfulness to them;* he therefore says, 'faithful to *you,* as I suppose,' from the accounts I hear: not expressing doubt. But *Birks,* 'The seeming uncertainty is not as to Silvanus's *faithfulness,* which is strongly marked by the article [*tou* in א A; B omits], but as to whether he or some other would prove to be the bearer of the letter, addressed as it was to five provinces, *all* of which Silvanus might not reach: 'By Silvanus, that faithful brother, as I *expect,* I have written to you.' **briefly**—Greek, 'in few (words),' as compared with the importance of the subject (Heb. xiii. 22). **exhorting**—not so much formally *teaching,* which could not be done in so 'few words.' **testifying** —*in confirmation* [so *epimarturōn*] of that truth which ye have already heard from Paul and Silas (1 John ii. 27). **that this**—of which I have just written, and Paul before testified (whose testimony, now that he was no longer in those regions, was called in question by some: cf. 2 Pet. i. 12; iii. 15, 16); 'the present truth'—viz., the grace formerly promised by the prophets, and *now* manifested to you. "Grace" is the key-note of

13 wherein ye stand. The *church that is* at ¹Babylon, elected together with
14 *you*, saluteth you; and *so doth* ᵐ Marcus my son. Greet ye one another
with a kiss of charity. Peace *be* with you all that are in Christ Jesus.
Amen.

Paul's doctrine, which Peter confirms (Eph. ii. 5, 8). Their sufferings for the Gospel made them to need some confirmation of the truth, that they should not fall back from it. **wherein ye stand.** ℵ A B read imperatively *'stand ye'* [*eis hen*]—*'into which* (having been already admitted, ch. i. 8, 21; ii. 7, 9, 10) stand (therein).' Peter has in mind Paul (Rom. v. 2; 1 Cor. xv. 1). 'The grace wherein we stand must be true, and our standing in it true also' (*Bengel*). Cf. *Steiger*, 'He began with grace (ch. i. 2), he finishes with grace, he has besprinkled the middle with grace, that in every part he might teach that the Church is saved only by grace.' **13. The . . . at Babylon.** *Alford* and *Bengel*, 'She that is elected together with you in Babylon,' viz., *Peter's wife*, whom he *led about* in his missionary journeys (cf. ch. iii. 7). But why she should be called 'elected together with you *in Babylon*,' as if there were no Christian woman in Babylon besides, is inexplicable. The sense is clear: 'that portion of *the whole dispersion* (ch. i. 1, Greek), the church of Christianized Jews, with Gentile converts, which resides in Babylon.' As Peter and John were closely associated, Peter addresses the church in John's province, Asia, and closes with 'your *co-elect* sister church at *Babylon* saluteth you.' John similarly addresses the "elect lady"—i. e., *the church in Babylon*—and closes with 'the children of thine elect sister (the Asiatic church) greet thee' (cf. 'Introduction,' 2 John). 'Mark, *who is in the peace of a son to me*' (cf. Acts xii. 12 on Peter's connection with Mark); whence the mention of him with *the church* at Babylon, in which he laboured under Peter before he went to Alexandria, is natural. *Papias* reports from the presbyter John (b. iii., 39), that Mark was interpreter of Peter, recording in his gospel the facts related to him by Peter. Silvanus or Silas had been substituted for John Mark, as Paul's companion, because of Mark's temporary unfaithfulness (Acts xv. 37-40). But now Mark restored is associated with Silvanus, Paul's companion, in Peter's esteem, as Mark was already reinstated in Paul's esteem. That Mark had a spiritual connection with the Asiatic churches which Peter addresses, and so naturally salutes them, appears from Col. iv. 10; 2 Tim. iv. 11. **"Babylon"**—the Chaldean Babylon on the

Euphrates. See 'Introduction,' ON THE PLACE OF WRITING, in proof that *Rome* is not meant. How unlikely that in a *friendly salutation* the enigmatical title of Rome given in *prophecy* (John, Rev. xvii. 5) should be used! Babylon was the centre from which the Asiatic *dispersion* whom Peter addresses was derived. *Philo*, 'Legat. ad Caium,' sec. 36, and *Josephus*, 'Antiquities,' xv., 22; xxiii. 12, inform us that Babylon contained many Jews in the apostolic age, whereas those at Rome were comparatively few—about 8,000 (*Josephus*, xvii. 11)—so it would naturally be visited by the apostle of the circumcision. It was the headquarters of those whom he had so successfully addressed on Pentecost (Acts ii. 9)—Jewish 'Parthians, dwellers in Mesopotamia' (the Parthians were then masters of Mesopotamian Babylon); these he ministered to *in person*. His other hearers—the Jewish 'dwellers in Cappadocia, Pontus, Asia, Phrygia, Pamphylia'—he now ministers to by letter. The earliest authority for Peter's martyrdom *at Rome* is *Dionysius*, bishop of Corinth, in the latter half of the second century. The desirableness of representing Peter and Paul, the two leading apostles, as together founding the church of the metropolis probably originated the tradition. *Clement* of Rome ('1 Epistola ad Corinthios,' secs. 4, 5), often quoted for, is really against it. He mentions Paul and Peter together, but makes it as a *distinguishing* circumstance of Paul that he preached both in the East and West, implying that Peter never was in the West. 2 Pet. i. 14, "I must *shortly* put off this tabernacle," implies his martyrdom was near; yet he makes no allusion to Rome, or to any intention of visiting it. **14. kiss of charity** (Rom. xvi. 16, "an *holy* kiss")—token of love to God and the brethren. *Love* and *holiness* are inseparable (cf. Acts xx. 37). **peace**—Peter's closing salutation; as Paul's is, "Grace be with you," accompanied with "peace be to the brethren." "Peace" (flowing from *salvation*) was Christ's own salutation after the resurrection: from Him Peter derives it. **be with you all that are in Christ.** [ℵ adds, A B omit, "Jesus."] In Eph. vi. 24, addressed to the same region, the same limitation of the salutation occurs, whence Peter adopts it. Contrast "be *with you all*," Rom. xvi. 24; 1 Cor. xvi. 23.

PETER.

1 SIMON PETER, a servant and an apostle of Jesus Christ, to them that have obtained ^alike precious faith with us through the righteousness
2 ¹of God and our Saviour Jesus Christ: grace and peace be multiplied unto you through the knowledge of God, and of Jesus our Lord,
3 According as his divine power hath given unto us all things that *pertain* unto life and godliness, ^b through the knowledge of him ^cthat hath
4 called us ²to glory and virtue: whereby ^d are given unto us exceeding great and precious promises: that by these ye might be ^e partakers of the divine nature, having escaped the corruption that is in the world through
5 lust. And besides this, giving all diligence, add to your faith virtue;

A. D. 66.

CHAP. 1.
^a Acts 11. 17.
Eph 4. 5.
1 of our God
and
Saviour.
^b John 17. 3.
^c 1 John 2. 20,
27.
2 Or, by.
^d 2 Cor. 7. 1.
^e 2 Cor. 3. 18.

CHAP. I. 1-21.—ADDRESS—EXHORTATION TO ALL GRACES, AS GOD HAS GIVEN US, IN THE KNOWLEDGE OF CHRIST, ALL THINGS PERTAINING TO LIFE—TESTIMONY OF APOSTLES AND PROPHETS TO THE POWER AND COMING OF CHRIST.
1. Simon. So B, Greek form; in א A, 'Symeon' (Hebrew, *i. e., hearing*), as Acts xv. 14. His mention of his original name accords with the design here, to warn against the coming false teachers, by setting forth the true "knowledge" of Christ on the testimony of the *original apostolic eyewitnesses* like himself. This was not required in the first epistle. **servant**—'slave:' so Paul, Rom. i. 1. **to them, &c.** He addresses a wider range of readers (*all* believers) than in the first epistle, but includes *especially* those therein addressed, as ch. iii. 1 proves. **obtained**—by grace [*lachousi*]; applied by *Peter* to receiving of the apostleship *by allotment* (Acts i. 17; Luke i. 9). They did not acquire it: Divine election is as independent of man's control as the *lot* which is cast forth. **like precious**—'equally precious' to those who believe, though not having seen Christ, as to Peter and those who have seen Him. For it lays hold of the same "exceeding great and *precious* promises," and the same "righteousness of God our Saviour." "The *common salvation*," Jude 3. "Precious" is applied by St. Peter to "faith" and its "trial," 1 Pet. i. 7; to "Christ," 1 Pet. ii. 7; it is "blood," 1 Pet. i. 19; God's "promises," ch. i. 4. **with us**—apostles and eyewitnesses (*v.* 18). Though enforcing his exhortation by his *apostleship*, he puts himself, as to "the faith," on a level with all believers. The degree of faith varies in different believers; but as *to its objects*, justification, sanctification, and future glorification, it is common to all. Christ is to all believers "made of God wisdom, righteousness, sanctification, and redemption." **through** [*en*]—'IN.' The one article to both nouns requires, "the righteousness of *Him who is* (at once) *our God and* (our) Saviour." Peter, confirming Paul's testimony to the same churches, adopts Paul's inspired phraseology. The Gospel plan sets forth *God's righteousness*, which is Christ's righteousness, in the brightest light. This passage establishes the imputation to us of the righteousness *of Christ*. Cf. Isa. xlii. 21; Jer. xxiii. 6; Rom. iii. 22; iv. 6; x. 4; 1 Cor. i. 30. Faith has its sphere IN it as its element: God is in redemption "righteous," and at the same time a "Saviour" (cf. Isa. xlv. 21, end). **2. Grace and peace**—(1 Pet. i. 2.) **through** [*en*]—'in:' the sphere IN which alone *grace* and *peace* can be multiplied. **knowledge** [*epignosei*]—'*full* knowledge.' of God, and of Jesus our Lord. The *Father* is here meant by "God," but the *Son* in *v.* 1. How entirely *one* the Father and Son are! (John xiv. 7-11.) The prominent object is 'the knowledge *of Jesus our Lord*' (a rare phrase); only secondarily of the Father through Him (*v.* 8; ch. ii. 20; iii. 18).
3. According as. '*As* He hath given us ALL things needful for life and godliness, (so) do you give ALL diligence,' &c. The oil and flame are given wholly by God's grace, and 'taken' by believers: their part is to 'trim their lamps,' (cf. *vv.* 3, 4, with 5, &c.) **life and godliness.** Spiritual *life* must exist first, before there can be *godliness. Knowledge of God* experimentally is *life* (John xvii. 3). The child must have vital breath, then cry to, and walk in the ways of, his father. It is not by *godliness* we obtain *life*, but by *life, godliness.* To *life* stands opposed *corruption;* to *godliness, lust* (*v.* 4). **called us**—(*v.* 10, "calling") (1 Pet. ii. 9.) **to glory and virtue** [*dia*]—'*through* (His) glory.' So B; but א A C, Vulgate [*idia doxe*], '*by His own* glory and excellency,' which characterize 'His divine power.' "Virtue," the standing word in heathen ethics, is found only once in Paul (Phil. iv. 8), and in Peter in a distinct sense from classic usage. It is a term too earthly for expressing the gifts of the Spirit (*Trench*, 'Synonyms'). **4. Whereby**—By which *glory* and *virtue:* His *glory* making the "promises" *exceeding great;* His *virtue* making them "precious" (*Bengel*). *Precious promises* are the object of *precious faith.* **given.** The *promises* themselves are a *gift;* for they are as sure as if fulfilled. **by these** —*promises.* They even now have a sanctifying effect, assimilating the believer to God. Still more so when *fulfilled.* **might** [*genesthe*]—'that ye MAY become partakers,' now in part, hereafter perfectly (1 John iii. 2). **of the divine nature**—not God's essence, but His *holiness,* including His "glory" and "virtue" (*v.* 3): opposite to 'corruption through lust.' Sanctification is the imparting of *God Himself* by the Holy Spirit in the soul. We by faith partake also of the material nature of Jesus (Eph. v. 30). The "Divine *power*" enables us to be partakers of the "Divine *nature.*" **escaped the corruption**—which involves in itself *destruction* of soul and body. (On "escaped," as from a condemned cell, cf. Gen. xix. 17; Col. i. 13; ch. ii. 18-20.) **through** [*en*]—'IN.' 'The corruption in the world' has its seat, not so much in the surrounding elements, as in the "lust" of men's hearts. **5. And besides this** [*auto de touto,* א B C (A, *autoi de, yourselves also*)]—'And for this

6 ᶠand to virtue knowledge; and to knowledge temperance; and to tem-
7 perance patience; and to patience godliness; and to godliness brotherly
8 kindness; and ᵍto brotherly kindness charity. For if these things be in
   you, and abound, they make *you that ye shall* neither *be* ³barren nor
9 unfruitful in the knowledge of our Lord Jesus Christ. But he that lacketh these things ʰis blind, and cannot see afar off, and hath forgotten
·10 that he was ⁱpurged from his old sins. Wherefore the rather, brethren,
   give diligence ʲto make your calling and election sure: for if ye do these
11 things, ye shall never fall: for ᵏ so an entrance shall be ministered unto

A. D. 66.

ᶠ 1 Pet 3. 7.
ch. 3. 18.
ᵍ Gal. 6. 10.
1 John 4.21.
³ idle.
ʰ 1 John 2. 9.
ⁱ Eph. 5. 26.
Heb. 9. 14.
ʲ 1 John 3.19.
ᵏ 2 Tim. 4. 8.

very reason,' viz., 'seeing that His Divine power hath given all things that pertain to life and godliness' (v. 3). **giving** [*pareisenenkantes*]—*introducing*, side by side with God's *gift*, on your part, "diligence" (cf. 2 Cor. vii. 11 ; v. 10; ch. iii. 14). **all**—*possible*. **add** [*epichoregesate*]—'minister additionally,' or *abundantly* (cf. 2 Cor. ix. 10): said of one who *supplied* all the equipments of a chorus. So 'there will be *ministered abundantly unto you an entrance into the everlasting kingdom'* (v. 11). **to** [*en*]—'IN;' *in* the possession of *your faith, minister virtue.* Their *faith* answering to "knowledge of Him" (v. 3), is presupposed as God's gift (v. 3 ; Eph. ii. 8), and not required to be *ministered* by *us. In* its exercise, *virtue* is to be, moreover, ministered. Each grace being assumed, becomes the stepping-stone to the succeeding grace : the latter in turn completes the former. *Faith* leads the band, *love* brings up the rear (*Bengel*). The fruits of *faith* are *seven*—the perfect number. **virtue**—moral excellency; manly energy answering to the *virtue* (energetic excellency) of God (v. 3). Courage is needed to be a Christian (cf. Josh. xxiii. 6 ; x. 24). **and to** [*en*]—'IN;' 'and in the exercise of your virtue knowledge,' viz., practical discrimination of good and evil : perceiving what is the will of God in each detail. **6.** [*En*—*enkratian*], 'And *in* your knowledge *self-control.*' In the exercise of *knowledge*, or discernment of God's will, let there be practical *self-control* as to one's lusts. Incontinence weakens, self-control imparts strength (*Bengel*). 'And in your self-control *persevering endurance* [*hupomone*] amidst sufferings,' so much dwelt on in 1 Pet. ii., iii., and iv. 'And in your endurance godliness.' It is not to be mere stoicism, but united to piety as its source. **7.** 'And in your godliness brotherly-kindness;' not suffering your piety to be morose and sullen, but kind to the brethren. 'And in your brotherly-kindness love'—viz., to *all* men, even to enemies. From *brotherly-kindness* towards *believers*, we are to go forward to *love* to *all* men. (Cf. 1 Thess. iii. 12.) So *charity* completes the choir of graces in Col. iii. 14. In retrograde order, he who has *love* will exercise *brotherly-kindness ;* he who has *brotherly-kindness* will feel *godliness* needful ; the *godly* will mix nothing stoical with *patience ;* to the patient, *temperance* is easy ; the temperate weighs things well, so has *knowledge ;* knowledge guards against sudden impulse carrying away its *virtue* (*Bengel*). **8. be** [*huparchonta*, א B C ; *paronta, present*, A, Vulgate]—'subsist ;' *i. e.*, supposing these things to have an actual *subsistence* in you : "be" would express the mere fact. **abound** [*pleonazonta*]—*more than in others*. **make** [*kathistesin*]—'constitute you,' by the very fact of possessing these graces. **barren**—'inactive,' as a field lying *unworked* [*argous*], so *useless*. **unfruitful in** [*eis*]—'. . . *in respect to,'* &c. 'The *full knowledge* [*epignosin*] of Christ' is the goal towards which all these races tend. As their *subsisting* constitutes us *not barren*, so their *abounding* constitutes

us *not unfruitful*, in respect to it. It is through *doing* His will, and so becoming like Him, that we grow in *knowing* Him (John vii. 17). **9. But** [*Gar*]—'For.' Confirming the need of these graces (*vv.* 5-8) by the fatal consequences of wanting them. **he that lacketh**—Greek, 'he to whom these are not present.' **blind**—as to unseen spiritual realities. **and cannot see afar off**—explaining "blind." He *closes his eyes* [*muopazōn*], unable to see distant objects—viz., heavenly things—and fixes his gaze on present earthly things, which alone he can see. *Wilfulness* in the blindness is implied in 'closing the eyes,' which constitutes its culpability : rebelling against the light shining around him. **forgotten** [*lēthēn labōn*]—'contracted forgetfulness :' wilful obliviousness. **that he was purged.** The present sense of one's sins having been once for all forgiven, is the stimulus to every grace (Ps. cxxx. 4). This once for all cleansing of believers *at their new birth* is taught symbolically by Christ (John xiii. 10) [*Leloumenos*—*nipsasthai*], 'He that has been *bathed* (once for all) needeth not save to *wash* his feet (of the soils contracted in the daily walk), but is clean every whit (in Christ our righteousness).' 'Once purged (with Christ's blood), we should have no more consciousness of sin' (as condemning us, Heb. x. 2, 17), because of God's promise. Baptism sacramentally seals this. **10. Wherefore**—seeing the blessed consequence of having, and the evil effects of not having, these graces (*vv.* 8, 9). **the rather**—the more earnestly. **brethren.** The term, which only here he addresses to them, marks his affection, which constrains him so earnestly to urge them. **to make** [*poieisthai, middle*]—'to make *so far as it depends on you.*' "To make" absolutely is God's part : in the active. **your calling and election sure**—by '*ministering additionally in your faith virtue, and in your virtue knowledge*,' &c. God must work all these graces in us, yet not so that we should be *machines*, but *willing instruments* in His hands, in making His election of us 'secure.' א A, Vulgate, add, *dia tōn kalōn humōn ergōn ;* B C omit. The *ensuring* of our *election* is spoken of not as to God, whose counsel is stedfast, but as to *our part*. There is no uncertainty on His, but on ours the only security is our *faith* in His promise and the fruits of the Spirit (*vv.* 5-7, 11). Peter subjoins *election to calling*, because the *calling* is the effect and proof of God's *election*, which goes before, and is the main thing (Rom. viii. 28, 30, 33, where God's 'elect' are those '*predestinated*,' and election is "His *purpose*," *according to* which He "called" them). We know His *calling* before His *election ;* therefore *calling* is put first. **fall** [*ptaisēte*]—'*stumble*' finally (Rom. xi. 11). Metaphor from a race (1 Cor. ix. 24). **11. an** [*he*]—'the entrance' which ye look for. **ministered**—the same verb as *v.* 5. *Minister* in your faith virtue and the other graces, so shall there be *ministered to you* the entrance into heaven, where these graces shine most brightly. The reward of grace hereafter shall correspond to the work of grace here.

you abundantly into the everlasting kingdom of our Lord and Saviour Jesus Christ.

12 Wherefore I will not be negligent to put you always in remembrance of these things, though ye know *them,* and be established in the present

13 truth. Yea, I think it meet, as long as I am in this tabernacle, to stir

14 you up by putting *you* in remembrance; knowing *ᴵ* that shortly I must put off *this* my tabernacle, even as *ᵐ* our Lord Jesus Christ hath showed

15 me. Moreover I will endeavour that ye may be able after my decease to have these things always in remembrance.

16 For we have not followed cunningly devised fables, when we made known unto you the power and coming of our Lord Jesus Christ, but

17 were *ⁿ* eye-witnesses of his majesty. For he received from God the Father honour and glory, when there came such a voice to him from the excellent glory, This *ᵒ* is my beloved Son, in whom I am well pleased.

18 And this voice which came from heaven we heard, when we were with him in *ᵖ* the holy mount.

A. D. 66.

ᴵ Deut. 4. 21.
22.
Deut 31 14.
Josh 23 11.
1 Ki. 2. 2.
3.
Acts 20 23.
1 Tim 4 6.
ᵐ John 21.18.
ⁿ Matt. 7. 1.
Mark 9. 2.
Luke 9. 2ª.
ᵒ Matt. 3. 17.
Matt. 17. 5.
Mark 1. 11.
Mark 9. 7.
Luke 3. 22.
Luke 9. 35.
ᵖ Ex. 3. 5.
Josh. 5. 15.

---

abundantly [*plousiōs*]—'richly.' So "abound," *v.* 8. If these graces *abound* in you, you shall have your entrance into heaven, not merely "scarcely" (as 1 Pet. iv. 18), nor "so as by fire" (1 Cor. iii. 15), like one escaping with life after having lost all his goods, but in triumph, without 'stumbling and *falling.*'

12. Wherefore—as these graces are so necessary to your abundant entrance into Christ's kingdom (*vv.* 10, 11). **I will not be negligent.** א A B C, Vulgate, read [*Mellēso*] '*I will be about* always to put you in remembrance' (an accumulated future): I will regard you as always needing to be reminded (cf. *v.* 15). **always**—why he writes the second epistle so soon after the first: *there is likely to be* more and more need of admonition on account of the increasing corruption (ch. ii. 1, 2). **in the present truth**—*the Gospel truth:* formerly promised to Old Testament believers as *about to be,* now in the New Testament *actually* with, and in, believers, so that they are "established" in it as a "*present*" reality. Its importance renders frequent monitions never superfluous (cf. Rom. xv. 14, 15). **13. Yea** [*de*]—"But;" though "you know" the truth (*v.* 12). **this tabernacle**—soon to be taken down (2 Cor. v. 1): I therefore need *to make the most of my short time* for the good of Christ's Church. The zeal of Satan against it, the more intense *as his time is short,* ought to stimulate Christians (Rev. xii. 12). **by**—"IN" (cf. ch. iii. 1). **14. shortly I must put off** [*apothesis*]. 'The putting off (as a garment) of my tabernacle is speedy:' a *soon approaching,* also a *sudden,* death. Christ's words (John xxi. 18, 19), 'When thou art old,' &c., were the ground of his "knowing," now that he was old, that his foretold martyrdom was near. Cf. Paul, 2 Tim. iv. 6. Though a violent death, he calls it a 'departure' (*v.* 15: cf. Acts vii. 60). **15. endeavour**—'use my *diligence*' [*spoudaso*], as *v.* 10, the field in which my *diligence* has scope. Peter fulfils Christ's charge, "Feed my sheep." **that ye may be able**—by this written epistle; perhaps also by St. Mark's gospel, which Peter superintended. **decease**—'departure.' The very word [*exodus*] used in the transfiguration, Moses and Elias conversing about Christ's *decease* (*found nowhere else in the New Testament,* but Heb. xi. 22, 'the *departing* of Israel' out of Egypt, to which the saints' deliverance from the bondage of corruption answers). "Tabernacle" also is found here, as well as there (Luke ix. 31, 33): an undesigned coincidence, confirming Peter's authorship. **always** [*hekastote*]—'on each occasion;' as occasion may require. **to have . . . in remembrance** [*tēn*

toutōn mnemēn poieisthai]—'to exercise remembrance of,' as of precious truths. Not merely 'to remember' as things we care not about. **16. For**—reason why he is so earnest that the remembrance of these things be continued after his death. **followed**—*out* in detail [*exakolouthē-santes*]. **cunningly devised**—'devised by (*man's*) *wisdom*' [*sesophismenois:* 'sophisticated'], as distinguished from what *the Holy Ghost* teaches (cf. 1 Cor. ii. 13). Cf. also ch. ii. 3, "feigned words." **fables**—as heathen mythologies, and subsequent Gnostic 'fables and genealogies,' of which the germs already existed in Judaism, combined with Oriental philosophy in Asia Minor. The Spirit's precautionary protest against the rationalistic mythical theory of the Gospel. **when we made known unto you.** Not that Peter himself had *personally* taught the churches in Pontus, Galatia, &c.; but he was one of the apostles whose testimony was borne to *the Church in general,* to whom this epistle is addressed, (ch. i. 1, *including,* but not *restricted* to, as 1 Peter, the churches in Pontus, &c.) **power**—the opposite of "fables:" cf. the contrast of "word" and "power," 1 Cor. iv. 20. A specimen of His *power* was given at the transfiguration; also of His "*coming*" again, and its attendant glory. [*Parousia*] "Coming" is always used of His *second* advent. A refutation of the scoffers (ch. iii. 4): I, James, and John, saw with our own eyes a sample of His coming glory. **were** [*genethentes*]—'were made.' **eye-witnesses.** As initiated spectators of mysteries [*epoptai*], we were admitted into His innermost secrets, viz., at the transfiguration. **his** [*tes ekeinou*]—THAT great ONE's majesty. **17. received . . . honour**—in the *voice* that spake to Him. **glory**—in the *light* which shone round Him: answering to the *Shechinah* glory in the *Tabernacle.* **came** [*enechtheisēs*]—'was borne:' only in 1 Pet. i. 13: the argument against this second epistle, from its dissimilarity of style, as compared with 1 Peter, is not well founded. **from the excellent glory** [*hupo tēs megaloprepous doxēs*]—'BY (*i. e.,* uttered by) the magnificent glory' (*i. e.,* by *God:* as His manifested presence is called by the Hebrews 'the Glory:' cf. "His Excellency," Deut. xxxiii. 26; Ps. xxi. 5). **in whom** [*eis hon*]—'*in regard to* whom' (accusative); but Matt. xvii. 5, "in whom" [*en ho*] centres my good pleasure. Peter omits, as not required by his purpose, "hear Him," showing his independence in his inspired testimony. **I am**—aorist [*eudokesa*]: 'My good pleasure *rested* (from eternity).' **18. which came**—'we heard borne from heaven.' **we**—

19　We have also a more sure *q*word of prophecy; whereunto ye do well
that ye take heed, as unto a light that shineth in a dark place, until the
20　day dawn, and *r*the day-star arise in your hearts: knowing this first, that
21　*s*no prophecy of the Scripture is of any private interpretation.　For *t*the
prophecy came not *4*in old time by the will of man; but holy men of
God spake *as they were* moved by the Holy Ghost.

A. D. 66.

q Isa. 8. 20.
r 2 Cor. 4. 4.
s Rom. 12. 6.
t 2 Tim 3.16.
4 Or. at any
time.

James, and John, and myself. **holy mount**—as
the transfiguration mount came to be regarded as
the scene of Christ's divine glory.

19. We—all believers. **a more sure** [*echomen
bebaioteron ton prophetikon logon*]—'we have *the*
word of prophecy more sure' (confirmed); become
a firmer ground of confidence.　Previously we
knew its *sureness* by faith; through that visible
specimen of its future fulfilment, assurance is
made *doubly sure:* so that, even after Peter and
the other apostles are dead, those whom he addresses will feel sure that they have "not followed
cunningly devised fables."　Prophecy assures us
that Christ's *sufferings*, now past, are to be followed by Christ's *glory*, to come.　The transfiguration gives a pledge to make faith still stronger,
that "the day" of His glory will "dawn" ere
long.　He does not mean that the "word of prophecy," or Scripture, is surer than *the voice of God*
at the transfiguration.　The fulfilment of *prophecy*
so far in Christ's history makes *us* the *surer* of
what is yet to be fulfilled—His consummated
glory.　The word was the 'lamp [*luchno*, "light"]
heeded' by Old Testament believers, until a gleam
of the "day dawn" was given at Christ's first
coming, especially in His transfiguration.　So the
word is *a lamp* to us still, until "the day" burst
forth fully at the second coming of "the Sun of
righteousness."　*The day*, when it dawns upon
you, makes *sure* the fact that you saw correctly,
though indistinctly, the objects revealed by *the
lamp*.　**whereunto**—to which *word of prophecy:*
primarily the Old Testament (and the New Testament, so far as it was then written) in Peter's
day; now also in our day the whole New Testament, which, though brighter than the Old
Testament (cf. 1 John ii. 8, end), is but a *lamp*
even still, as compared with the brightness of the
eternal day (cf. ch. iii. 2).　Oral teachings and
traditions are to be tested by the written word
(Acts xvii. 11).　**dark** [*auchmero*, squalid]—without water, or light.　Such spiritually is the world
without, and the smaller world (microcosm) within, the natural heart.　Cf. "*dry* places," Luke xi.
24 (viz., unwatered by the Spirit), through which
the unclean spirit goeth.　**dawn**—bursting *through*
the darkness. **and**—*and* so; viz., by this sample
of Christ's glory in His humiliation (John i. 14),
and earnest of His coming glory in His exaltation.　**day-star** [*phosphoros*]—"the morning star"
(Rev. xxii. 16); the Lord Jesus.　**in your hearts.**
Christ's *arising in the heart*, by His Spirit giving
full assurance, creates spiritually full day, the
means to which is prayerfully *giving heed to the
word*.　This is associated with *the day of the Lord*
—being the earnest of it.　Even our *hearts* shall
not *fully* realize Christ in all His glory and felt
presence, until He shall come (Isa. lxvi. 14, 15;
Mal. iv. 2).　However, *Tregelles's* punctuation is
best, 'Whereunto ye do well to take heed (as unto
a light shining in a dark place, until the day
have dawned, and the morning star arisen) in
your hearts.'　For the day has already dawned
in the believer's heart; what he waits for is, its
visible manifestation at Christ's coming.　**20.**
'Forasmuch as ye know this' (1 Pet. i. 18). **first**
—the *foremost* consideration in studying pro-
phecy; a *first principle*, never to be lost sight

of. **is** [*ginetai*]—'proves to be.' No prophecy is
found to be the result of "private (the individual
writer's uninspired) *interpretation*" (solution), and
so *origination*. [*Epilusis* does not mean in itself
origination, but that which the sacred writer
could not always *interpret;* though, being the
speaker or writer (1 Pet. i. 10-12), was plainly not
of his own, but of God's *disclosure, origination*,
and *inspiration*, as Peter proceeds to add, " But
holy men . . . spake (and afterwards *wrote*) . . .
moved by the Holy Ghost:" a reason why ye
should 'give' all "heed" to it.]　The parallelism
to *v.* 16 shows that "*private interpretation*," contrasted with "moved by the Holy Ghost," answers to 'fables *devised by* (human) *wisdom*,'
contrasted with "we were eye-witnesses of *His
majesty*," &c., attested by the 'voice from God.'
The words of the prophetical (so of all) Scripture
writers were not mere words *of the individuals*,
therefore to be *interpreted by them*, but of "the
Holy Ghost," by whom they were "moved."
" Private" is explained (*v.* 21) "by the will of
man " (viz., the individual writer).　In a secondary sense, as the word is the *Holy Spirit's*, it
cannot be *interpreted* by its *readers* (any more
than by its *writers*) by their *private* human
powers, but by the teaching of the Holy Ghost
(John xvi. 14); for it was by the Holy Ghost that
its speakers and writers were "moved." [*Idias*,
" private," is not opposed to the *Catholic Church's*
interpretation (as Rome argues), but to the Holy
Ghost's motion.]　It is not by individual wisdom,
but by the Holy Ghost, the Bible's Author, that
any can interpret it.　No Scripture is an isolated
composition of the individual man, but part of
an organic whole, to be solved by comparison with
the rest of the Spirit-inspired Word.　'He who
is the Author of Scripture is its Supreme Interpreter' (*Gerhard*).　*Alford*, 'Springs not out of
human interpretation'—*i. e.*, is not a prognostica-
tion by a man, *knowing what he means* when he
utters it, but, &c. (John xi. 49-52.)　Rightly: except that the verb is, *Doth prove to be*.　It not
being of private interpretation, you must '*give
heed*' to it, looking for the *Spirit's* illumination
"in your hearts " (notes, *v.* 19).　**21. came not in
old time** [*ou enecthē pote*]—' was never at any time
borne' (to us). **by the will of man**—alone (Jer.
xxiii. 26: cf. ch. iii. 5, "willingly ").　**holy men of
God.** ℵA, Vulgate; but BC, 'men FROM God;'
emissaries from God.　"Holy," because they had
the Holy Ghost. **moved** [*pheromenoi*]—' borne'
(along), as by a mighty wind: Acts ii. 2,
'*rushing* [*pheromenēs*] wind:' rapt out of themselves; still not in fanatical excitement (1 Cor.
xiv. 32).　[Hebrew, *nabi*, 'prophet,' meant an interpreter of God.　He, as *God's spokesman, interpreted* not his own "private" will or thought, but
God's.]　'Man *of the Spirit*' (margin, Hos. ix. 7;
Neh. ix. 30, margin).　'Seer,' on the other hand,
refers to the *mode of receiving* the communications
from God, rather than to the *utterance* of them to
others.　"Spake" implies that, both in its original *oral* announcement and now even in *writing*,
it has been always *the living voice* of God *speaking*
to us through His inspired servants.　'Borne
along' forms a beautiful antithesis to 'was borne.'
They were passive, yet not mere mechanical in-

2 BUT [a]there were false prophets also among the people, even as [b]there shall be false teachers among you, who privily shall bring in damnable heresies, even denying the Lord [c]that bought them, and bring upon

2 themselves swift destruction. And many shall follow their [1]pernicious

3 ways; by reason of whom the way of truth shall be evil spoken of. And through covetousness shall they with feigned words make merchandise of you: whose judgment now of a long time lingereth not, and their damnation slumbereth not.

4 For if God spared not [d]the angels [e]that sinned, but [f]cast *them* down to hell, and delivered *them* into chains of darkness, to be reserved unto

5 judgment; and spared not the old world, but saved Noah, [g]the eighth *person*, a preacher of righteousness, bringing in the flood upon the world

6 of the ungodly; and [h]turning the cities of Sodom and Gomorrha into ashes condemned *them* with an overthrow, making *them* an ensample unto

7 those that after should live ungodly; and delivered just Lot, vexed with

A. D. 66.

CHAP. 2.
[a] Deut. 13. 1.
[b] Matt. 21. 11.
[c] Heb. 10. 29.
1 Or lascivious ways, as some copies read.
[d] Job 4. 18. Jude 6.
[e] John 8. 44.
[f] Luke 8. 31. Rev. 20. 2, 3
[g] Gen. 7. 1.
[h] Gen. 19 24.

struments. The *Old Testament* prophets primarily; including also *all* the inspired penmen, whether of the New or Old Testament (ch. iii. 2).

CHAP. II. 1-22.—FALSE TEACHERS TO ARISE— THEIR BAD PRACTICES AND SURE DESTRUCTION, FROM WHICH THE GODLY SHALL BE DELIVERED, AS LOT WAS.

1. But—in contrast to the prophets "moved by the Holy Ghost" (ch. i. 21). **also**—as well as the true prophets (ch. i. 19-21). Paul had already testified the entrance of false prophets into the same churches (Acts xx. 29, 30). **among the people**—Israel. He is writing to believing *Israelites* primarily (note, 1 Pet. i. 1). Such a 'false prophet' was Balaam (v. 15). **there shall be**—already symptoms were appearing (vv. 9-22; Jude 4-13). **false teachers** [*pseudodidaskaloi*]—teachers of falsehood. In contrast to the true teachers, whom his readers are to give heed to (ch. iii. 2). **who**—*such as* [*hoitines*], 'the which' shall. **privily**—not at first openly and directly, but *by the way*, bringing in error *by the side* of the truth [*pareisaxousin*]. Rome objects, Protestantism cannot point out the exact date of the beginnings of the false doctrines superadded to the original truth; we answer, Peter foretells that the first introduction of them would be stealthy and unobserved (Jude 4). **damnable** [*apōleias*]—'of destruction;' entailing destruction (Phil. iii. 19) on all following them. **heresies**—*self-chosen* doctrines, not emanating from God (cf. "will-worship," Col. ii. 23). **even** —going *even* to such a length as to *deny* both in teaching and practice. Peter knew, by bitter repentance, what a fearful thing it is to *deny* the Lord (Luke xxii. 61, 62). **denying**—Him whom, above all, they ought to *confess*. **Lord** [*despotēn*]—'Master and Owner' (cf. Jude 4). Whom the true doctrine teaches to be· their OWNER *by* right of purchase. 'Denying Him who bought them, that He should be thereby their Master. Even the ungodly were "bought" by His "precious blood." It shall be their bitterest self-reproach in hell, that, as far as Christ's redemption was concerned, they might have been saved. The denial of His *propitiatory* sacrifice is included (cf. 1 John iv. 3). **bring upon themselves**—(cf. 'God *bringing in* the flood *upon* the world,' v. 5). Man brings upon himself the vengeance which God brings upon him. **swift**— swiftly descending: as the Lord's coming shall be. As the ground swallowed up Korah and Dathan, and "they went down *quick* (alive) into the pit." Cf. Jude 11. **2. follow** [*exakolouthesou-*

sin]—out. **pernicious ways** [*apoleiais*]. א A B C, Vulgate, read [*aselgeiais*] 'licentiousnesses' (Jude 4). False doctrine and immoral practice go together (vv. 18, 19). **by reason of** [*di' hous*]—'on account of whom,' viz., the followers of the false teachers. **the way of truth shall be evil spoken of**—'blasphemed' by those without, who lay on Christianity itself the blame of its professors' evil practice. Contrast 1 Pet. ii. 12. **3. through** [*en*] —'in covetousness' as their element (v. 14, end: contrast 2 Cor. xi. 20; xii. 17). **of a long time**— in God's eternal purpose. "*Before of old*," Jude 4. **lingereth not** [*argei*]—though sinners think it lingers. 'Is not idle' (Eccl. viii. 11, 12). **damnation** [*apoleia*]—'destruction' (note, v. 1). Personified. **slumbereth not**—though sinners *slumber*.

4. if. The consequent member of the sentence is virtually contained in v. 9. If God in past time has punished the ungodly and saved His people, He will be sure to do so also in our days (cf. end of v. 3). **angels**—the highest of intelligent creatures (cf. Jude 6), yet not spared when they sinned. **hell** [*Tartarosas*]—'Tartarus:' nowhere else in New Testament or LXX.: equivalent to *Geenna*. Not inconsistent with 1 Pet. v. 8: though their final doom is *hell*, for a time they are permitted to roam beyond it in 'the darkness of this world.' Slaves of *Tartarus* ('the abyss,' or "deep," Luke viii. 31; "the bottomless pit," Rev. ix. 11) may come upon earth. Step by step they are given to Tartarus, until at last they shall be wholly bound to it. **delivered**—as the judge delivers the condemned prisoner to the officers (Rev. xx. 2). **into chains.** א A B C read [*seirois*] 'dens' (*Alford*). This, however, may, in Hellenistic Greek, be equivalent to [*seirais*] "chains" (cf. Jude 6). They are "reserved" unto hell's "mist of darkness" as their final "judgment." Meanwhile their exclusion from the light of heaven is begun. Satan and his demons are free to hurt us only to the length of their chain, like a chained dog. "Darkness" is their 'chain.' So the ungodly were virtually 'in prison,' though at large on the earth, from the moment that God's sentence went forth, though not executed till 120 years after (1 Pet. iii. 19). **5. eighth**—*i. e.*, Noah and seven others. Contrasted with the densely peopled "world of the ungodly." **preacher**—not only "righteous" himself (cf. v. 8), but also "a preacher of righteousness:" adduced against the *licentiousness* of the false teachers (v. 2), who have no prospect but destruction, even as it overtook the ungodly in Noah's days. **6. with**—'TO over-throw' (*Alford*). **ensample**—'of (the fate that should befall) those who in after time should live

8 the filthy conversation of the wicked; (for that righteous man dwelling among them, in seeing and hearing, vexed *his* righteous soul from day to
9 day with *their* unlawful deeds;) the ⁱLord knoweth how to deliver the godly out of temptations, and to reserve the unjust unto the day of judg-
10 ment to be punished: but chiefly them that walk after the flesh in the lust of uncleanness, and despise ²government.

Presumptuous *are they*, self-willed,. they are not afraid to speak evil of
11 dignities: whereas ʲangels, which are greater in power and might, bring
12 not railing accusation ³against them before the Lord. But these, ᵏas natural brute beasts, made to be taken and destroyed, speak evil of the things that they understand not; and shall utterly perish in their own
13 corruption; and ˡshall receive the reward of unrighteousness, *as* they that count it pleasure ᵐto riot in the day time. Spots *they are* and blemishes, sporting themselves with their own deceivings while they ⁿfeast
14 with you; having eyes full of ⁴adultery, and that cannot cease from sin; beguiling unstable souls: an heart they have exercised with covetous
15 practices; cursed children: which have forsaken the right way, and are

A. D. 66.	
ⁱ Ps. 34. 17.	
1 Cor.10.13.	
² Or, dominion.	
ʲ Jude 9.	
³ Some read, against themselves.	
ᵏ Jer. 12. 3. Jude 10.	
ˡ Isa. 3. 11. Rom. 2, 8, 9. Phil. 3. 19. 2 Tim. 4.14.	
ᵐ Rom. 13.13.	
ⁿ 1 Cor. 11.20, 21.	
⁴ an adulteress.	

ungodly' (cf. Jude 7). **7. filthy conversation** [*en aselgeia anastrophes*]—'behaviour in licentiousness' (Gen. xix. 5). **the wicked** [*athesmōn*]—'lawless:' who set at defiance the *laws* of nature, man, and God. The Lord reminds us of Lot's faithfulness, not of his sin in the cave: so in Rahab's case. 8. **vexed** [*ebasanizen*]—'tormented.' **9. knoweth how.** He is at no loss for means, even when men see no escape. **out of**—not actually *from.* **temptations**—trial. **to be punished** [*kolazomenous*]—'being punished:' as the fallen angels (*v.* 4) under sentence, awaiting its final execution. Sin is already its own penalty: hell will be its full development. **10. chiefly**—they *especially* will be punished (Jude 8). **after**—following after. **lust of uncleanness** [*miasmou*]—*defilement.* **government** [*kuriotetos*]—"dominion" (Jude 8).

Presumptuous [*tolmetai*]. *Self-will* begets *presumption: presumptuously* 'daring.' **are not afraid**—though so insignificant in *might.* [*Ou tremousin*, 'tremble not' (Jude 8, end).] **speak evil of**—Greek, 'blaspheme.' **dignities** [*doxas*]—'glories.' **11. which are** — though they are. **greater** — than these blasphemers. Jude instances Michael. **railing accusation** — Greek, 'blaspheming judgment' (Jude 9). **against them**—against "dignities" (for instance, the fallen angels). **before the Lord**—in the presence of *the Judge* they reverently abstain from judgment (*Bengel*). So ℵBC; but A, Vulgate, omit. How great is the dignity of the saints who, as Christ's assessors, shall hereafter judge angels! Meanwhile, *railing judgments*, though true, *against dignities*, being uttered irreverently, are of the nature of 'blasphemies' (1 Cor. iv. 4, 5). If superior angels dare not, as in the presence of God, speak evil even of bad angels, how awful the presumption of those who speak evil of good "dignities!" (Num. xii. 8; xvi. 2, 3, Korah, &c.; 2 Sam. xvi. 7, 8, Shimei; Jude 11.) The angels who sinned still retain the impress of majesty. Satan is still "a strong man:" "prince of this world." Under him are "principalities, powers, rulers of the darkness of this world." We are to avoid irreverence as to them, on account of God: a warning to those who use Satan's name in blasphemy. 'When the ungodly curseth Satan, he curseth his own soul,' 12. (Jude 10, 19.) **But**—in contrast to the "angels" (*v.* 11). **natural . . . made.** Transposed in ℵABC. 'Born natural'—*i.e.,* born *in their very nature* as irrational animals, **to be taken and destroyed** (Greek, 'unto capture

and destruction' [*phthoran, corruption*], note, Gal. vi. 8: cf. below). **brute** [*aloga*]—'irrational.' In contrast to *angels* that 'excel in strength.' **beasts** [*zoa*]—'animals' (cf. Ps. xlix. 20). **speak evil of**—'*in the case of* things which they understand not.' Cf. presumption, the parent of subsequent Gnostic error, producing an opposite, though kindred error—'the worshipping of good angels' (Col. ii. 18, "*intruding into those things which he hath not seen*"). **shall utterly perish**—lit., '*shall be corrupted* in their own *corruption*' (Jude 10). [*Phthora* is both *corruption*, the seed, and *destruction*, the developed fruit.] **13. receive** [*komioumenoi*]—'shall *carry off* as their due.' **reward of** —i.e., *for* their "unrighteousness" (*Alford*). Also, *unrighteousness* shall be its own *reward* (Rev. xxii. 11). "Wages of unrighteousness" (*v.* 15) has a different sense. *The earthly gain gotten by* "unrighteousness" in the day time; Greek, 'counting the luxury which is in the day time (not restricted to *night*, as ordinary revelling. Or, Vulgate, "the luxury which is comprised in *a day.*" So Heb. xi. 25, and xii. 16, Esau) to be pleasure,' *i. e.,* their chief good. **Spots**—*in themselves.* **blemishes**—disgraces: bringing *blame* [*momoi*] on the Church and Christianity. **sporting themseves** [*entruphontes*]—'luxuriating.' **with**—'ɪɴ.' **deceivings** —or passively, 'deceits:' *luxuries gotten by deceit* (cf. Matt. xiii. 22; Eph. iv. 22). Whilst deceiving others, they are deceived themselves (cf. Phil. iii. 19). "Their own," in opposition to "you." 'Whilst partaking of the *love-feast* with *you*,' they are 'luxuriating in *their own* deceivings' or 'deceits' (to which answers Jude 12, end. Peter presents the positive side, Jude the negative. 'Feeding themselves *without fear*'). So ℵC; but B, Vulgate, Syriac, and Sahidic versions (as Jude) [*agapais*], 'in their own love-feasts.' 'Their own' will imply, they make the *love-feasts* subserve *their own* self-indulgent purposes. **14. full of adultery**, B C [*moichalidos*], 'an adulteress,' as though they carried about adulteresses always in their eyes—the avenue of lust (*Horneius*). *Bengel*, 'the *adulteress* who fills their eyes is alluring desire' [ℵ A, *moichalias*]. **that cannot cease**—'that cannot *be made to cease* from sin.' [*Akatapaustous*, ℵ C; *akatapastous* (an Hellenistic form, from *pazo*, the same as *pauomai*, A B).] **beguiling** [*deleazontes*]--'laying baits for.' **unstable**—not firmly established in faith. **heart**—not only the *eyes*, the channel, but the *heart*, the fountain-head of lust (Job xxxi. 7, "Mine *heart* walked after mine *eyes*"). **covetous practices.**

624

gone astray, following the way [o] of Balaam *the son* of Bosor, who loved
16 the wages of unrighteousness; but was rebuked for his iniquity: the
dumb ass speaking with man's voice forbade the madness of the prophet.
17 These are wells without water, clouds that are carried with a tempest; to
whom the mist of darkness is reserved for ever.
18 For when they speak great swelling *words* of vanity, they allure through
the lusts of the flesh, *through much* wantonness, those that [p] were [5] clean
19 escaped from them who live in error. While they promise them [q] liberty,
they themselves are [r] the servants of corruption: for of whom a man is
20 overcome, of the same is he brought in bondage. For [s] if, after they
[t] have escaped the pollutions of the world through the knowledge of the
Lord and Saviour Jesus Christ, they are again entangled therein, and
21 overcome, the latter end is worse with them than the beginning. For
[u] it had been better for them not to have known the way of righteousness,
than, after they have known *it*, to turn from the holy commandment
22 delivered unto them. But it is happened unto them according to the
true proverb, [v] The dog *is* turned to his own vomit again; and the sow
that was washed to her wallowing in the mire.

3 THIS second epistle, beloved, I now write unto you; in *both* which [a] I

A. D. 66.

[o] Num 22. Rev. 2. 14.
[p] Acts 2. 40. ch. 1. 4.
[5] Or, for a little, or, a while, as some read.
[q] Gal. 5. 13.
[r] John 8. 34. Rom. 6. 16.
[s] Matt. 12. 45. Luke 11. 26. Heb. 6. 4. Heb. 10. 26, 27.
[t] ch. 1. 4.
[u] Luke 12. 47. John 9. 41.
[v] Pro. 26. 11.

CHAP. 3.
[a] 2 Tim. 1. 6. ch. 1. 13-15.

So B; but ℵ A C, Vulgate, singular, 'covetousness.' **cursed children**—Greek, 'children of (*i. e.*, devoted to) curse.' *Cursing* and *covetousness*, as in Balaam's case, often go together. The curse he designed for Israel fell on Israel's foes and himself. True believers *bless*, and curse not, so *are blessed*. **15. have.** Some seducers are spoken of as *already come*, others as *yet to come*. **following**—out, Greek. **the way**—(Num. xxii. 5, 23, 32; Isa. lvi. 11.) **son of Bosor**—the same as *Beor*. This form was adopted because the kindred *Basar* means *flesh*. Balaam is justly termed *son of carnality*, as covetous, and enticer of Israel to lust. **loved the wages of unrighteousness**—and therefore wished (in order to gain them from Balak) to curse Israel, whom God blessed, and at last gave the hellish counsel, that the only way to bring God's curse on Israel was to entice them to *fleshly lust* and *idolatry*, which go together. **16. was rebuked** [*elenxin eschen*]—'had a *conviction*:' an *exposure* of his specious wickedness on being *tested* (from *elencho*, to *convict on testing*). **his** [*idias*]—*his own* beast convicted him of *his own* iniquity. **dumb** [*aphonon phone*]—'*voiceless* speaking *in* man's *voice*:' marking the marvellous miracle. **ass** [*hupozugion*]—'beast of burden.' The ass was most used in riding in Palestine. **forbade.** It was not the *words* of the ass (for it merely deprecated his beating it), but *the miraculous fact of its speaking at all*, which *withstood* Balaam's perversity. Indirectly the ass, directly the angel, *rebuked* his worse than asinine obstinacy. The ass *turned aside* at the sight of the angel; but Balaam, after God had said, 'Thou shalt not go,' persevered in wishing to go for gain. Thus the ass, *in act*, *forbade* his madness. How awful a contrast—a *dumb beast* forbidding an *inspired prophet!* **17. wells**—"clouds," in Jude 12, 13, both *promising* (cf. *v.* 19) water, but yielding none. So their "great swelling words" are found, on trial, to be but "vanity" (*v.* 18). **clouds.** ℵ A B C read [*homichlai*] 'mists:' *dark*, not bright as "clouds" often are; whence the latter is applied to the saints: fit emblem of the children of darkness. "Clouds" is inserted from Jude 12, where it is appropriate—"clouds . . . without water" (promising what they do not perform); not here. **mist** [*zophos*]—*blackness*: 'the *chilling horror* accompanying *darkness*' (*Bengel*).

18. allure [*deleazousin*]—'lay baits for.' **through**—'IN:' the *lusts of the flesh* being the element IN which they lay their baits. **much wantonness** [*aselgeiais*]—'by licentiousnesses,' the bait which they lay. **clean escaped** [*ontōs*]—'*really*,' ℵ; but A B C, Vulgate [*oligōs*], 'scarcely,' or 'for a little time:' scarcely have they escaped from them who live in error (the ungodly world), when they are allured by these seducers into sin again (*v.* 20). **19. promise them liberty**—instances of their "great swelling words" (*v.* 18). The *liberty* which they propose is such as fears not Satan, nor loathes the flesh. Pauline language, adopted by Peter: cf. John viii. 34; Rom. vi. 16-22; viii. 15, 21; Gal. v. 1, 13: cf. 1 Pet. ii. 16, note; cf. ch. iii. 15. **corruption**—note, *v.* 12. **of whom**—'by whatever . . . by the same,' &c. **20. after they**—*the seducers* 'themselves' *have escaped* (*v.* 19; note, Heb. vi. 4 6). **pollutions**—which bring "corruption" (*v.* 19). **through**—'IN.' **knowledge** [*epignosei*]—'full knowledge.' **the Lord and Saviour Jesus Christ**—designating in full the great and gracious One from whom they fall. **latter end is worse . . . than the beginning.** Peter remembers Christ (Luke xi. 26). "Worse" stands opposed to "better" (*v.* 21). **21. the way of righteousness**—"the way of truth" (*v.* 2): "the knowledge of the Lord and Saviour." **turn**—*back again* [*eis ta opiso*], ℵ A, Vulgate; omitted in B C. **from the holy commandment**—the Gospel, which enjoins *holiness*: in opposition to their *corruption* [*hagias*]. Not that it makes holy, but because it ought to be kept *inviolate*. **delivered**—once for all. **22. But.** You need not wonder; for *dogs* and *swine* they were before, and dogs and swine they will continue (Prov. xxvi. 11). They 'scarcely' (*v.* 18) have escaped from their filthy folly, when they again are entangled in it. Then they seduce others who have in like manner 'for a little time escaped from them that live in error' (*v.* 18). Peter quoted Proverbs in his first epistle (ch. i. 7; ii. 17; iv. 8, 18): another proof that both epistles come from the same writer.

CHAP. III. 1-18.—SURENESS OF CHRIST'S COMING—ITS ACCOMPANIMENTS—DECLARED IN OPPOSITION TO COMING SCOFFERS—GOD'S LONG-SUFFERING A MOTIVE TO REPENTANCE, AS PAUL'S EPISTLES SET FORTH—CONCLUDING EXHORTATION TO GROWTH IN KNOWLEDGE OF CHRIST.

1. now. 'This now a second epistle I write.' Therefore he had lately written the former epistle.

2 stir up your pure minds by way of remembrance; that ye may be mindful of the words which were spoken before by the holy prophets, *b* and of the
3 commandment of us the apostles of the Lord and Saviour: knowing *c* this first, that there shall come in the last days scoffers, *d* walking after their
4 own lusts, and saying, *e* Where is the promise of his coming? for since the fathers fell asleep, all things continue as *they were* from the beginning of the creation.
5 For this they willingly are ignorant of, that *f* by the word of God the heavens were of old, and the earth ¹ standing out of the water and in the
6 water: whereby *g* the world that then was, being overflowed with water,
7 perished: but the heavens and the earth which are now, by the same word are kept in store, reserved unto *h* fire against the day of judgment and perdition of ungodly men.
8 But, beloved, be not ignorant of this one thing, that one day *is* with

A. D. 66.
b Jude 17.
c 1 Tim. 4. 1.
d ch. 2. 10.
e Isa 5. 19.
Jer 17 15.
Eze 12 22.
f Gen 1. 6.
Ps 33. 6.
Heb. 11 3.
¹ consisting.
Col 1. 17.
g Gen. 7. 11, 21-23.
ch. 2. 5.
h Matt. 25.41.
2 Thes. 1. 8.
Heb 1. 11.

The seven Catholic epistles were written by James, John, and Jude, shortly before their deaths: whilst having the prospect of being for some time alive, they felt writing less necessary (*Bengel*). **unto you.** The second epistle, though more general in its address, *included* especially the same persons as the first was addressed to. **pure** [*eilikrine*]—'pure when examined by sunlight:' *adulterated with no error.* Opposite to Eph. iv. 18. *Alford*, The mind, in relation to the outer world, being turned to God (the *Sun* of the soul), and not obscured by fleshly regards. **by way of** [*en*]—'*in putting you in remembrance*' (ch. i. 12, 13). Ye already *know* (*v.* 3): it is only needed that I *remind* you (Jude 5). **2. prophets**—of the Old Testament. **of us.** Vulgate reads, 'and of the commandment of the Lord and Saviour (declared) by YOUR apostles' (so Rom. xi. 13)—the apostles *who live among you at present*, in contrast to the *Old Testament* "prophets." **3. Knowing this first**—from the apostles. **shall come.** Their very *scoffing* shall confirm the prediction. **scoffers.** א A B C, Vulgate, add, '(scoffers) *in* (*i. e.*, with) *scoffing*' [*en empaigmone*] (Rev. xiv. 2, end). **walking after their own lusts**—(ch. ii. 10; Jude 16, 18): their sole law, unrestrained by revereuce for God. **4.** (Cf. Ps. x. 11; lxxiii. 11.) Presumptuous scepticism and lawless lust, setting nature and its laws above the God of nature and revelation, and arguing from the continuity of nature's phenomena that there can be no interruption to them, was the sin of the antediluvians, and shall be that of the scoffers in the last days. **Where**—implying it would have taken place before this, if ever it was to take place, but that it never will. **the promise** —which you, believers, are so continually looking for (*v.* 13). **his**—*Christ's:* the subject of prophecy from the earliest days. **the fathers**—to whom *the promise* was made, who rested all their hopes on it. **all things**—in the *natural world:* sceptics look not beyond this. **as they were**—*continue* as we see them to continue. From the time of the promise of Christ's coming as King being given to the fathers, down to the present, all things have continued, *as now*, from "the beginning of *creation.*" The "scoffers" are not atheists, nor do they maintain that the world existed from eternity. They recognize a God, but not the God *of revelation.* They reason from seeming delay against the fulfilment of God's word.
5. Refutation of their scoffing from Scripture history. **willingly**—wilfully: they do not *wish* to know. Their ignorance is voluntary. **are ignorant of**—in contrast to *v.* 8, "be not ignorant of this." [*Lanthanei-lanthaneto*, 'This escapes THEIR notice (sagacious philosophers though they think themselves): let this not escape YOURS.']

They shut their eyes to the Scripture record of creation and the deluge: the latter is parallel to the coming judgment by fire; as Peter remembered Jesus' words (Luke xvii. 26, 27). **by the word of God**—not by a fortuitous concurrence of atoms (*Alford*). **of old**—'from of old:' from the first beginning. A confutation of their objection, 'all things continue as they were FROM THE BEGINNING OF CREATION.' Before the flood, the same objection to the possibility of it might have been as plausibly urged. The heavens (sky) and earth have been FROM OF OLD, how unlikely that they should not *continue* so? But the flood came in spite of their reasonings; so will the conflagration of the earth come in spite of the "scoffers" of the last days, changing the whole order of things (the "world" [*kosmos*], 'order'), and introducing the new heavens and earth (*v.* 13). **earth standing out of** [*sunestōsa*]—'consisting of,' 'formed out of the water.' The waters under the firmament were at creation gathered together into one place, and the dry land emerged *out of*, and above them. **in** [*di' hudatos*]—'*by means of* the water,' as an instrument (along with *fire*), in the changes wrought on the earth's surface, to prepare it for man. *Held together* BY *the water.* The earth arose *out of* the water *by the efficacy of the water* itself (*Tittmann*). *Berosus*, the Chaldean, records the tradition in Babylon of a great flood under Xisuthrus, who built the ark. So the Egyptian and Hindu monuments. The Chinese record a great flood under the emperor Yao. So the Greeks, under Deucalion and Pyrrha. The beginning of established government is referred by the Greeks to Minos; by the Hindus to Menu; the Assyrian Ninus; the Egyptian first mortal king, Menes: all have the root MEN, which appears in Nimrod. **6.** Whereby [*Di' hōn*]—(plural). *By means of which* heavens and earth (in respect to the WATERS which flowed together *from both*) *the then world perished* (*i. e.*, in respect to its *occupants*, men and animals, and its existing *order:* not *was annihilated*): for in the flood "the fountains of the great deep were broken up" from *the earth* (1.) below, and "the windows of *heaven*" (2.) above "were opened." The earth was deluged by that water *out of* which it had originally risen. **7.** (Cf. Job xxviii. 5, end.) **which are now**—'the postdiluvian world.' In contrast to "that *then was*," *v.* 6. **the same.** So A B, Vulgate; but א C read 'His' (God's). **kept in store**—'treasured up.' **reserved**—"kept." It is only God's *keeping* which holds together the present state of things till His time for ending it.
8. be not ignorant—as those scoffers (*v.* 5). Besides the refutation (*vv.* 5-7) drawn from the deluge, he adds another (addressed more to be-

9 the Lord as a thousand years, and *ⁱ* a thousand years as one day. The
ʲ Lord is not slack concerning his promise, as some men count slackness;
but is *ᵏ* long-suffering to us-ward, not *ˡ* willing that any should perish,
10 but *ᵐ* that all should come to repentance. But *ⁿ* the day of the Lord will
come as a thief in the night; in the which *ᵒ* the heavens shall pass away
with a great noise, and the elements shall melt with fervent heat, the
earth also and the works that are therein shall be burnt up.
11   *Seeing* then *that* all these things shall be dissolved, what manner *of*
12 *persons* ought ye to be in *all* holy conversation and godliness, looking for
and ² hasting unto the coming of the day of God, wherein the heavens
being on fire shall *ᵖ* be dissolved, and the elements shall *�q* melt with fer-
13 vent heat? Nevertheless we, according to his promise, look for *ʳ* new
heavens and a new earth, wherein dwelleth righteousness.

A D 66.
ⁱ Ps. 90. 4.
ʲ Hab 2. 3.
Heb 10 37.
ᵏ Isa 3 . 19.
ˡ Eze. 18. 23.
Eze 3 . 11.
ᵐ Rom. 2. 4.
ⁿ Matt. 24 43.
ᵒ Matt. 24. 35.
Rev 20 11.
2 Or. hasting
the
coming.
ᵖ Is. 20. 3.
q Mic. 1. 4.
ʳ Isa. 65. 17.

lievers)—God's delay in fulfilling His promise is not, like men's delays, owing to inability or fickleness in keeping His word, but through "longsuffering." **this one thing**—as the consideration *of chief importance* (Luke x. 42). **one day . . . thousand years.** Ps. xc. 4, Moses says, Thy *eternity*, knowing no distinction between a *thousand* years and a *day*, is the refuge of us creatures of a day. Peter views God's eternity in relation to the last day. It seems to us short-lived beings long in coming; but *with the Lord* the interval is irrespective of the idea of long or short. His eternity exceeds all measures of time. To His Divine knowledge future things are present. His power requires not long delays for performing His work. His long-suffering excludes men's impatient expectation. He can do the work of a thousand years in one day: so in *v.* 9, He has always the power to fulfil His "promise." **thousand years as one day.** No delay is long to God: as to a man of countless riches, a thousand guineas are as a single penny. God's œconologe (*eternal-ages*-measurer) differs wholly from man's horologe (*hour*-glass). His gnomon (dial-pointer) shows all the hours at once in the greatest activity and in perfect repose. To Him the hours pass neither more slowly nor more quickly than befits His economy. There is nothing to make Him need to hasten or delay the end. "With the Lord" (Ps. xc. 4) silences all objections, on the ground of man's incapability of understanding this (*Bengel*). **9. slack**—tardy, *late*, as though the due time were already come. (Heb. x. 37, "Will not *tarry*.") **his promise**—which scoffers cavil at (*v.* 4). It shall be surely fulfilled (*v.* 13). **some**—the "scoffers." **count**—the delay to result from "slackness." **long-suffering**—waiting until the full number of those appointed to "salvation" (*v.* 15) shall be completed. **to us-ward.** א A, Vulgate, have [*di' humas*] 'for your sake;' B C, 'towards you' [*eis humas*]. **any**—not desiring that any, even the scoffers, should perish, which would result if He did not give space for repentance. **come**—'*go and be received* to repentance' [*choresai*, go and find *room* for repentance] (cf. Greek, Mark ii. 2; John viii. 37). **10. The certainty, suddenness, and concomitants**, of the coming of the day of the Lord. *Faber* argues that the millennium, &c., must *precede* Christ's literal coming; not *follow* it. But "the day of the Lord" comprehends the whole series of events, beginning with the premillennial advent, and ending with the destruction of the wicked, final conflagration, and general judgment (which last intervenes between the conflagration and the renovation of the earth). **will come.** But (notwithstanding the mockers, and the delay) *come and be present* the day of the Lord SHALL. **as a thief.** Peter repeats his Lord's image (Luke xii. 39, 41) in the conversation in

which he took a part: so also Paul (1 Thess. **v.** 2) and John (Rev. iii. 3; xvi. 15). **the heavens**—which the scoffers say shall "continue" as they are (*v.* 4; Matt. xxiv. 35; Rev. xxi. 1). **with a great noise** [*roizēdon*]—a noise like a *whizzing* arrow, or the crash of devouring flame. **elements**—*the world's component materials* (*Wahl*). As "the works" in the earth are distinguished from "the earth," so by "elements" after "the heavens," *Bengel* explains 'the works therein'—viz., *the sun, moon, and stars* (as *Theophilus* of Antioch, pp. 22, 148, 228; and *Justin Martyr*, 'Apology,' ii., 44, use *stoicheia*). Rather, as "elements" is not so used in Scripture Greek, *the component materials* of "the heavens," including the *heavenly bodies* (mentioned in the world's destruction, as in its creation): it clearly belongs to "the heavens," not to "the earth," &c. **melt**—be dissolved, as in *v.* 11. **the works . . . therein**—of nature and of art.

11. then. So א A, Vulgate; but B C substitute (*houtōs*) 'thus' for "then:" a happy refutation of the 'thus' of the scoffers, *v.* 4, "AS they were." **shall be** [*luomenōn*]—'*are being* (in God's appointment, soon to be fulfilled) dissolved;' implying *the certainty*, as though actually present. **what manner of persons**—how watchful, prayerful, zealous! **to be**—not mere existence [*einai*], but [*huparchein*] a *state* in which one is supposed to be (*Tittmann*). What man ye ought to be found, when the event comes! This is "the holy commandment" (*v.* 2; ch. ii. 21). **conversation and godliness** [*anastrophais, eusebeiais*]—*behaviours* (towards men), *pieties* (towards God), in their *manifold* manifestations. **12. hasting unto**—*with the utmost eagerness* praying for, and contemplating, the Saviour as at hand. The Greek *may* mean 'hastening *onward* the day of God;' not that God's time is changeable, but God appoints *us* as instruments of accomplishing those events which must be first before the day can come. By praying for His coming, furthering the preaching of the Gospel for a witness to all nations, and bringing in those whom 'the long-suffering of God' waits to save, we *hasten the coming of the day of God.* [*Speudo* is always in New Testament neuter, not active; but the LXX. use it *actively*.] *Christ* says, "Surely I come quickly. Amen." Our part is to *speed* this consummation by praying, "Even so, come, Lord Jesus." **the coming** [*tēn parousian*]—'personal *presence*;' usually, of the Saviour. **the day of God.** God has given many myriads of days to *men*: one shall be the "day of God" Himself. **wherein**—rather (*di' hēn*), 'on account of (*owing to*) which' day. **heavens**—the upper and lower regions of the sky. **melt.** Our igneous rocks show they were once liquid. **13. Nevertheless**—in contrast to the destructive effects of the day of God stand its constructive effects. As the flood was the earth's baptism, eventuating in its renovation

14 Wherefore, beloved, seeing that ye look for such things, be diligent
15 that ye may be found of him in peace, without spot, and blameless. And account *that* ⁸ the long-suffering of our Lord *is* salvation; even as our beloved brother Paul also, according to the wisdom given unto him, hath
16 written unto you; as also in all *his* epistles, ᵗ speaking in them of these things; in which are some things hard to be understood, which they that are unlearned and unstable wrest, as *they do* also the other scriptures, unto their own destruction.
17 Ye therefore, beloved, seeing ye know *these things* before, ᵘ beware lest ye also, being led away with the error of the wicked, fall from your
18 own stedfastness: but grow in grace, and *in* the knowledge of our Lord and Saviour Jesus Christ. To him *be* glory both now and for ever. Amen.

A. D 66.

ˢ Rom 2. 4.
1 Tim. 1.16.
1 Pet. 3. 20.
ᵗ Rom. 8, 19.
1 Cor.15 24.
1 Thes. 4.
15.
ᵘ Matt 7. 15.
Matt. 1ᵢ. 6,
11.
Eph 4. 14.
Phil. 3. 2.
Col 2. 8.
2 Tim 4.15.

and partial deliverance from 'the curse,' so its baptism with fire shall purify it, to be the renovated abode of regenerated man, wholly freed from the curse. **his promise**—(Isa. lxv. 17; lxvi. 22.) "We" is not emphatical. **new heavens**—new atmospheric, surrounding the renovated earth. **righteousness**—*dwelleth* in that world as its home, all pollutions having been removed; all other enjoyments are the accidents; *righteousness* is the essence of heavenly enjoyment. **14. that ye may be found of him** [*auto*]—'in His sight' (*Alford*): at His coming *in person.* **in peace** —towards God, your own consciences, and your fellow-men, and as its consequence eterna l*blessedness:* 'the God of peace' will effect this for you. **without spot**—at the coming marriage feast of the Lamb: in contrast to ch. ii. 13, "Spots they are and blemishes . . . while they feast," not having on the King's pure wedding garment. **blameless** —(1 Cor. i. 8; 1 Thess. v. 23.) **15. account that the long-suffering . . . is salvation**—is designed for the salvation of those yet to be gathered in: whereas those scoffers 'count it (the result of) slackness' on the Lord's part (*v.* 9). **our beloved brother Paul**—beautiful love and humility. Peter praises the very epistles which contain his condemnation (Gal. ii. 9-14): a practical exhibition of *v.* 14, "in peace." **according to the wisdom given unto him**—Paul's own language (1 Cor. iii. 10, "*According to the* grace of God which is *given unto* me, as a *wise* master-builder"). Inspired wisdom "GIVEN" him, not acquired in human schools. **hath written** [*eyrapsen*, aorist]—'wrote;' a thing wholly *past:* Paul was either dead or had ceased to minister to them. **unto you**—*Galatians,* Ephesians, *Colossians;* the same whom Peter addresses. Col. iii. 4 refers to *Christ's second coming.* The epistle to the Hebrews, too (addressed not only to the Palestinian, but secondarily to the Hebrew Christians everywhere), may be referred to, as Peter primarily addresses in both epistles the *Hebrew* Christians of the dispersion (note, 1 Pet. i. 1). Heb. ix. 27, 28; x. 25, 37, 'speak of these things' (*v.* 16) which Peter has been handling—viz., the coming of the day of the Lord; delayed through His "long-suffering," yet near and sudden. **16. also in all his epistles.** Rom. ii. 4 is similar to *v.* 15, beginning. The Pauline epistles were by this time the *common* property of all the churches. The "all" implies they were now completed. The Lord's coming is handled, 1 Thess. iv. 13—v. 11: cf. *v.* 10. Peter distinguishes Paul's epistle, or epistles, "TO YOU," from "*all* his (*other*) epistles," showing that definite churches, or particular classes of believers, are meant by "you." **in which**—*epistles.* [ℵ A B read the feminine relative (*hais*); not as C (*hois*), 'in which *things.*'] **some things hard to be understood**—viz., concerning Christ's coming, the man of sin, and the apostasy, previously. 'Paul seemed thereby to delay Christ's coming to a longer period

than the other apostles, whence some doubted it altogether' (*Bengel*). Though there be some things hard to be understood, there are enough besides plain, easy, and sufficient for perfecting the man of God (2 Tim. iii. 16, 17). 'There is scarce anything drawn from the obscure places, but the same in other places may be found most plain' (*Augustine*). It is our own prejudice, foolish expectations, and carnal fancies, that make Scripture difficult (*Jeremy Taylor*). **unlearned**—not those wanting *human* learning, but *lacking the learning imparted by the Spirit.* The humanly *learned* have been often deficient in spiritual learning, and originated most heresies. Cf. 2 Tim. ii. 23, a different word, "unlearned" [*apaideutous*], 'untutored.' When religion is studied as a science, nothing is more abstruse; when studied to know and practise our duty, nothing is easier. **unstable**—not established in what they have learned; shaken by every difficulty; who, in perplexing texts, instead of comparing them with other Scriptures, waiting until God by His Spirit make them plain, hastily adopt distorted views. **wrest**—strain and twist [*streblousin*], as with a *hand-screw,* what is straight in itself: *e. g.*, 2 Tim. ii. 18. **other scriptures.** Paul's epistles were by this time recognized in the Church as 'scripture:' a term never applied, in any of the fifty places where it occurs, save to the Old and New Testament writings. Men in each church having *discernments of spirits,* would have prevented any uninspired writing from being put on a par with the Old Testament word of God; the apostles' lives were providentially prolonged,—Paul's and Peter's at least to thirty-four years after Christ's resurrection; John's, to thirty years later; so that fraud in the canon is out of question. The first three gospels and Acts are included in "the other scriptures;" perhaps all the New Testament books, save John and Revelation, written later. **unto their own destruction**—not through Paul's fault (ch. ii. 1). **17. Ye**—warned by the case of those "unlearned and unstable" persons (*v.* 16). **know . . . before** —the event. **led away with**—the term, as Peter remembers, used by Paul of Barnabas's being 'carried' [*sunapēchthē*] (Gal. ii. 13), *led away with,* Peter and the other Jews in their hypocrisy. **wicked** [*athesmōn*]—'lawless,' as ch. ii. 7. **fall from**—*grace* (Gal. v. 4): the true source of "stedfastness" or *stability* in contrast with the "unstable" (*v.* 16): "established" (ch. i. 12): all kindred terms (Jude 20, 21). **18. grow**—not only do not "fall from" (*v.* 17), but *grow onward:* the secret of not going backward (Eph. iv. 15). (the) **grace, and . . . knowledge** of . . . **Christ**—*the grace* of which *Christ* is the author; *the knowledge* of which *Christ* is the object. **for ever** [*eis hemeran aiōnos*]—'to the day of eternity:' the day that has no end; "the day of the Lord," beginning with the Lord's coming.

JOHN.

1 THAT ^awhich was from the beginning, which we have heard, which we
have seen with our eyes, ^bwhich we have looked upon, and ^cour
2 hands have handled, of the ^dWord of life; (for ^ethe life ^fwas manifested,
and we have seen it, ^gand bear witness, and show unto you that eternal
3 life ^hwhich was with the Father, and was manifested unto us;) that which
we have seen and heard declare we unto you, that ye also may have fellowship with us: and truly ⁱour fellowship is with the Father, and with
4 his Son Jesus Christ. And these things write we unto you, that your
joy may be full.
5 This then is the message which we have heard of him, and declare

A. D. 90.

CHAP. 1.
^a Mic 5. 2.
John 1. 1.
Rev. 1. 6.
^b 2 Pet. 1. 16.
^c Luke 24. 39.
^d Rev. 19. 13.
^e John 1. 4.
^f Rom. 16.26.
^g John 21, 24.
^h John 1. 1,2.
ⁱ John 17. 21.

CHAP. I. 1-10.—THE WRITER'S AUTHORITY AS AN EYE-WITNESS TO THE GOSPEL FACTS, HAVING SEEN, HEARD, AND HANDLED HIM WHO WAS FROM THE BEGINNING—OBJECT IN WRITING—MESSAGE—IF WE WOULD HAVE FELLOWSHIP WITH HIM, WE MUST WALK IN LIGHT, AS HE IS LIGHT.
1. Instead of a formal, John adopts a virtual, address (cf. v. 4). To wish joy to the reader was the ancient address. The sentence begun, v. 1, is broken off by the parenthetic v. 2, and is resumed at v. 3, with the repetition of words from v. 1. That which was—essentially (not 'began to be') [een, not egeneto]; before He was manifested (v. 2): answering to "Him that is from the beginning" (ch. ii. 13); so John's gospel, i. 1; Prov. viii. 23. we—apostles. heard . . . seen . . . looked upon . . . handled. A gradation. Seeing is a more convincing proof than hearing of; handling, than even seeing. "Have heard . . . have seen" [Heorakamen] (perfects), as a possession still abiding with us; but [etheasametha] "looked upon" (without "have:" not perfect, as of a continuing thing, but aorist, past time), whilst Christ the incarnate Word was still with us. "Seen," viz., His glory, as revealed in the transfiguration and in His miracles; and His passion and death, in a real body of flesh and blood. "Looked upon" as a wondrous spectacle, stedfastly, deeply, contemplatively. Appropriate to John's contemplative character. "Hands have handled" [epselaphesan]—Thomas and the other disciples, on distinct occasions, after the resurrection. John himself had leant on Jesus' breast at the last supper. Contrast the wisest of the heathen feeling after (the same Greek, Acts xvii. 27: cf. Rom. x. 8, 9), groping after WITH THE HANDS, if haply they might find God. This proves against Socinians; he is speaking of the personal incarnate Word, not of Christ's teaching from the beginning of His official life. of [peri]—'concerning;' following "heard." "Heard" is the verb most applying to the purpose of the epistle—viz., the truth which John had heard concerning the Word of life; i. e., (Christ) the Word who is the life—viz. from Christ Himself; all Christ's teachings about Himself. Therefore he puts 'concerning' before "the Word of life," which is inapplicable to any of the verbs except "heard;" also "heard" is the only verb which he resumes at v. 5. 2. the life—Jesus, "the Word of life." was manifested—previously having been "with the Father." show [apangellomen]—as v. 3, "declare" (cf. v. 5). The general term: write is the particular (v. 4). that eternal life [tēn zoen

ten aionion]—'the life which is eternal.' As the epistle begins, so it ends with "eternal life," which we shall ever enjoy with, and in, Him, 'the eternal life.' which [hetis]—'the which;' inasmuch as it was with the Father "from the beginning" (cf. v. 1; John i. 1). This proves the distinctness of the First and Second Persons. 3. That which we have seen and heard—resumed from v. 1, where the sentence was interrupted by v. 2, a parenthesis. declare we unto you. אABC add also: unto you also who have not seen or heard Him. that ye also may have fellowship with us—that ye also who have not seen, may have the fellowship with us which we who have seen enjoy. What that fellowship consists in he states: "Our fellowship is with the Father and with His Son." Faith realizes the unseen as spiritually visible. Not till by faith we too have seen, do we know all the excellency of the true Solomon (1 Ki. x. 6, 7). We are "partakers of the Divine nature" (2 Pet. i. 4). We know God only by fellowship with Him. He may thus be known, but not comprehended. The repetition of "with" [meta] before the "Son" distinguishes the persons, whilst the fellowship with both Father and Son implies their unity. It is not added, 'and with the Holy Ghost;' for it is by the Holy Spirit of the Father and Son in us that we have fellowship with the Father and Son (cf. ch. iii. 24). Believers enjoy the fellowship OF, but not WITH, the Holy Ghost. 'Through Christ God closes up the chasm that separated Him from the human race, and imparts Himself to them in the communion of the Divine life' (Neander). 4. these things—and none other: this whole epistle. write we unto you. אB have [hēmeis] "we" for [humin] "unto you." Thus the antithesis is between "we" (apostles and eye-witnesses) and "your" (A C). We write thus, that your joy may be full. But Bא, Vulgate, read 'OUR joy. In this case, for antithesis' sake, I prefer "unto you," in the former clause. 'We write unto you that OUR joy over you may be filled full' [pepleromene], by your being brought into fellowship with the Father and the Son. (Cf. John iv. 36, end; Phil. ii. 2, 16; iv. 1; 2 John 8.) John xv. 11; xvi. 24, make "YOUR" the probable reading; for John often repeats the language of his beloved Lord. So 2 John 12, "your" in most of oldest MSS. Christ Himself is the source, object, and centre of His people's joy (cf. v. 3, end). It is in fellowship with Him that we have joy, the fruit of faith (Rom. v. 11). 5. First division of the body of the epistle (cf. 'Introduction'). declare [anangellomen] — 'an-

629

6 unto you, that God *ʲ* is light, and in him is no darkness at all. If we say that we have fellowship with him, and walk in darkness, we lie, and
7 do not the truth: but if we walk in the light, as he is in the light, we have fellowship one with another, and the blood of Jesus Christ his Son cleanseth us from all sin.
8   If *ᵏ* we say that we have no sin, we deceive ourselves, and the truth is
9 not in us. If *ˡ* we confess our sins, he is faithful and just to forgive us *our*
10 sins, and to cleanse us from all unrighteousness. If we say that we have not sinned, we make him a liar, and his word is not in us.

A. D. 90.

ʲ John 1. 9
John 8. 12.
John 9. 5.
John 12. 35.
Rev. 1. 5.
ᵏ 1 Ki 8. 46.
Eccl 7. 20.
Jas. 3 2.
ˡ Lev. 26. 40-42.

nounce;' report in turn: different from *v.* 3. As the Son announced the message heard from the Father as His apostle (John xv. 15; Heb. iii. 1), so the Son's apostles announce what they have heard from the Son. John nowhere uses 'gospel;' but the *witness* or *testimony, the word, the truth:* here the *message.* **God is light.** What light is in the natural world, that God, the source of even material light, is in the spiritual—the fountain of wisdom, purity, beauty, joy, and glory. As all material life and growth depend on *light,* so all spiritual life and growth depend on GOD. As God here, so Christ, in ch. ii. 8, is called "the true light." **no darkness at all.** Strong negation [*skotia ouk estin oudemia:* 'no, not even one speck of darkness']; no ignorance, error, untruthfulness, sin, death. John heard this from Christ, not only in express, but in acted, words—viz., His whole manifestation in the flesh as "the brightness of the Father's *glory.*" Christ Himself was the embodiment of "the message," representing fully in all His sayings, doings, and sufferings. Him who is LIGHT. **6. have fellowship with him** (*v.* 3)— the essence of the Christian life. **walk**—in inward and outward action. **in darkness** (Greek, 'in *the* darkness')—opposed to "the light" (cf. ch. ii. 8, 11). **lie**—(ch. ii. 4.) **do not**—in *practice,* whatever we *say.* **the truth**—(Eph. iv. 21; John iii. 21.) **7.** (Eph. v. 8, 11-14.) **we walk.** 'God IS (*essentially,* in His very nature, as "light," *v.* 5) in the light.' WALKING *in the light,* the element in which God IS, is the test of fellowship with Him. Christ, like us, *walked* in the light (ch. ii. 6). *Alford,* 'Walking in the light, as He is in the light, is no mere imitation of God, but *an identity in the essential element* of our daily walk with the essential element of God's being.' **we have fellowship one with another**—and of course *with God* (understood from *v.* 6), without having fellowship with whom there can be no Christian fellowship one with another (cf. *v.* 3). To believe, with John, is eternal life; to love, is blessedness; to serve, is usefulness. **and**—as the result of 'walking in the light, as He is in the light.' **the blood of Jesus . . . cleanseth us from all sin**—daily contracted through the weakness of the flesh, and the power of Satan and the world. He is speaking, not of justification through His blood once for all, but of *present sanctification* ("cleanseth"), which the believer, *walking in the light,* and having *fellowship with God and the saints,* enjoys as his privilege. Cf. John xiii. 10, 'He that has been *bathed* [*leloumenos*] needeth not save to *wash* [*nipsasthai*] his feet, but is clean every whit.' Cf. *v.* 9, "*cleanse* us from all unrighteousness:" a further step besides '*forgiving* us our sins.' Christ's blood is the mean whereby, being already justified, and in fellowship with God, we become gradually *clean* from all sin which would mar fellowship with God. Faith applies the cleansing, purifying blood. א B C omit "Christ;" A retains it.

8. *Confession of sins* flows from 'walking in the

630

light' (*v.* 7). 'If thou shalt confess thyself a sinner, the *truth* is in thee; for the *truth* is *light.* Not yet has thy life become perfectly light, as sins are still in thee; yet thou hast already begun to be illuminated, because there is in thee confession of sins' (*Augustine*). **that we have no sin.** "HAVE," not 'have had,' must refer, not to the past life whilst unconverted, but to the *present* state, wherein believers *have sin* even still. "Sin" is singular; "(confess our) *sins,*" *v.* 9, plural. *Sin* means the *corruption of the old man* still in us, and the *stain* created by actual *sins* flowing from that old nature. To confess our need of cleansing from *present sin* is essential to 'walking in the light;' so far is the presence of sin incompatible with our *in the main* 'walking in light.' But the believer hates, confesses, and longs to be delivered from all sin, which is *darkness.* 'They who defend their sins will see in the great day whether their sins can defend them.' **deceive ourselves**—not God (Gal. vi. 7): we only make ourselves to err. **the truth**—(ch. ii. 4.) True faith. 'The truth respecting God's holiness and our sinfulness, the first spark of light in us, has no place in us' (*Alford*). **9. confess**—with the lips, from a contrite heart; involving confession to our fellow-men of offences against them. **he—God. faithful**—to His own promises: 'true' to His word. **just.** Not merely the mercy, but the *justice* of God is set forth in the redemption of the penitent believer in Christ. God's promises of mercy, to which He is *faithful,* harmonize with His *justice* (Rom. iii. 25, 26). **to** [*hina*]—'*in order that.*' His *forgiving us our sins and cleansing us* from, &c., further the *ends* of His eternal *faithfulness and justice.* **forgive**—remitting the *guilt.* **cleanse**—purify from filthiness. Henceforth we more and more become free from the presence of sin through the Spirit of sanctification (cf. Heb. ix. 14; above, note, *v.* 7). **unrighteousness**—offensive to Him who 'is just.' Called "sin," *v.* 7, because "sin is the transgression of the law," and the law is the expression of God's *righteousness;* so sin is *unrighteousness.* **10.** Parallel to *v.* 8. **we have not sinned**—commission of actual *sins,* even after regeneration and conversion; whereas in *v.* 8, "we *have no sin,*" refers to present GUILT, remaining (until cleansed) from *actual sins* committed, and to the SIN of our old nature still adhering to us. The perfect "have . . . sinned" brings down the commission of sins to the present time: not merely sins *before,* but *since, conversion.* **we make him a liar**—a gradation: *v.* 6, "we lie;" *v.* 8, "we deceive ourselves;" worst of all, "we make Him a liar," by denying His Word that all are sinners (cf. ch. v. 10). **his word is not in us.** "His word," "the truth" (*v.* 8), accuses us truly; by denying it we drive it from our hearts (cf. John v. 38). Our rejection of it, as to our being sinners, involves our rejection of His word and will revealed in the Law and Gospel *as a whole;* for these throughout rest on the fact that *we have sinned,* and *have sin.*

2   MY little children, these things write I unto you, that ye sin not. And if any man sin, [a]we have an advocate with the Father, Jesus Christ

2   the righteous: and [b]he is the propitiation for our sins; and not for ours only, but [c]also for *the sins of* the whole world.

3   And hereby we do know that we know him, if we keep his command-

4   ments.   He that saith, I know him, and keepeth not his commandments,

5   is a liar, and the truth is not in him.   But whoso [d]keepeth his word, in him verily is the love of God perfected: hereby know we that we are in

6   him.   He [e]that saith he abideth in him ought himself [f]also so to walk, even as he walked.

A. D. 90.

CHAP. 2.
[a] Rom. 8. 34.
1 Tim. 2. 5.
Heb. 7. 24.
[b] Rom 3. 25.
ch. 1. 10.
[c] John 1. 29.
John 4. 42.
ch. 4. 14.
[d] Tit. 2. 11.
[e] John 15. 4.
[f] Matt 11. 29.

CHAP. II. 1-29.—CHRIST'S ADVOCACY IS OUR ANTIDOTE TO SIN, IF WE WALK IN THE LIGHT; FOR TO KNOW GOD, WE MUST KEEP HIS COMMANDMENTS, AND LOVE THE BRETHREN; NOT LOVE THE WORLD, NOR GIVE HEED TO ANTICHRISTS, AGAINST WHOM OUR SAFETY IS THROUGH THE INWARD ANOINTING OF GOD, TO ABIDE IN GOD : SO AT CHRIST'S COMING WE SHALL NOT BE ASHAMED.

1.—(ch. v. 18.)   **My little children** [*Teknia*]—the diminutive expresses the tender affection of an aged pastor and spiritual father. *My own dear children,* i. e., sons and daughters (note, *v.* 12). **these things**—(ch. i. 6-10.)   My purpose in writing so is, not that you should abuse them as a license to sin; on the contrary, 'in order that ye may not sin at all' (the aorist [*hamartete*] implying the absence, not only of the habit, but of *single acts* of sin, *Alford*).   To "walk in the light" (ch. i. 5-7), the first step is *confession of sin* (ch. i. 9), the next (ch. ii. 1), that we should *forsake all sin.* The Divine purpose aims either to prevent the commission of, or to destroy, sin (*Bengel*). **And**—*Furthermore,* "if any man sin," let him, whilst loathing and condemning it, not fear to go at once to God, the Judge, confessing it; for "we have an Advocate with Him." He is speaking of a BELIEVER'S *occasional* sins of infirmity through Satan's fraud. The "we" immediately after implies that *we all* are *liable,* though not necessarily constrained, to sin. **we have an advocate**—God's family blessing: other blessings He grants to good and bad alike; but justification, sanctification, *continued* intercession (contrast Luke xxiii. 34, *for enemies*), and peace, He grants to *His children alone.* **advocate** [*paraclete*]—the same term as is applied to the Holy Ghost, the 'other Comforter:' showing the unity of the Second and Third Persons. Christ is the Intercessor *for us* above; in His absence, here below, the Holy Ghost is the 'other' Intercessor *in us* (Rom. viii. 26). Christ's *advocacy* is inseparable from the Holy Spirit's working in us, as the spirit of intercessory prayer. **righteous**—as our "Advocate" is not a mere suppliant. He pleads for us on the ground of *justice,* as well as mercy. Though He can say nothing good *of* us, He can say much *for* us. On HIS *righteousness,* obedience to the law, and endurance of its full penalty for us, He grounds His claim for our acquittal. The sense is, 'in that He is *righteous:*' in contrast to our *sin* ("if any man *sin*"). The Father, by raising Him from the dead, and setting Him at His own right hand, has once for all accepted Christ's claim for us. Therefore the accuser's charges against God's children are vain (Ps. cix. 6, 31; Rev. xii. 10). 'The righteousness of Christ stands on our side; for God's righteousness is, in Christ, ours,' (*Luther*) (Zech. iii. 1, &c.)   **2. And he** [*Autos*]—'And Himself.' He is our all-prevailing Advocate, because He is *Himself* 'the propitiation:' *abstract,* as in 1 Cor. i. 30: He is to us *all that is needed for* '*propitiation* in behalf of [*hilasmos peri*] our sins:'

the *propitiatory sacrifice,* provided by the Father's love, removing the estrangement, appeasing God's righteous wrath against the sinner. 'There is no incongruity that a father should be *offended* with that son whom he loveth, and at that time offended with him, when he *loveth* him' (*Bishop Pearson*). [The only other New Testament passage where *hilasmos* occurs, is ch. iv. 10: it answers in LXX. to Hebrew *caphar,* to *effect an atonement* or *reconciliation* with God; in Ezek. xliv. 27, to the sin-*offering;* in Rom. iii. 25 (*hilasterion*), it is a "propitiatory"—*i. e.,* the mercy-seat, or lid of the ark whereon God, represented by the Shekinah glory above it, met His people, represented by the high priest who sprinkled the blood of the sacrifice on it.] **and** [*de*]—'yet.'   **ours**—believers: not *Jews,* in contrast to Gentiles; for he is not writing to Jews (ch. v. 21).   **also for the sins of the whole world.**   Christ's *advocacy* is limited to *believers* (*v.* 1; ch. i. 7): His *propitiation* extends as widely as *sin:* note, 2 Pet. ii. 1, "the *whole* world" cannot be restricted to the *believing* portion (cf. ch. iv. 14 and ch. v. 19). 'Thou, too, art part of the world: thine heart cannot think, The Lord died for Peter and Paul, but not for me' (*Luther*).

3. hereby [*en touto*]—'in this.' 'It is *herein* only that we know (present) that we have knowledge of (perfect: once-for-all obtained and continuing *knowledge of*) Him' (*vv.* 4, 13, 14). Tokens whereby to discern grace are frequent in this epistle. The Gnostics, by the Spirit's prescient forewarning, are refuted, who boasted of *knowledge,* but set aside *obedience.* "Know Him," viz., as "the righteous" (*vv.* 1, 29): our "Advocate and Intercessor." **keep**—John's favourite word, instead of *do* [*tērōmen*], *to guard,* and *keep safe* as a precious thing; observing so as to keep.   So Christ Himself (John xv. 10).   Not faultless conformity, but hearty acceptance of, and willing subjection to, God's whole revealed will. **commandments** [*entolas*]—*injunctions* of faith, love, and obedience. John uses 'the law' to express, not the rule of Christian obedience, but the Mosaic law. **4. I know**—'I *have knowledge of* (perfect) Him' (cf. ch. i. 8). **5.** Not merely repeating the proposition, *v.* 3, or asserting the opposite alternative to *v.* 4, but expanding the "know Him" of *v.* 3 into "in Him verily (not vain boasting) is the love of (i. e., towards) God perfected," and "we are in Him." *Love* here answers to *knowledge* in *v.* 3. In proportion as we *love* God, we *know* Him: until our *love* and *knowledge* shall attain their full maturity of perfection. **his word.** *His word* is one (note, ch. i. 5), comprising His "*commandments,*" which are many (*v.* 3). **hereby**—in our progressing towards this ideal of perfected love and obedience. There is a gradation: *v.* 3, "*know* Him;" *v.* 5, "we *are in* Him;" *v.* 6, "*abideth* in Him:" respectively, *knowledge, fellowship, abiding constancy* (*Bengel*). **6. abideth**—a condition lasting, without intermission and end.   **He that saith . . . ought.**   So that his deeds may be consistent with his words. **even as he.**   Believers readily supply the name,

7   Brethren, [g] I write no new commandment unto you, but an old commandment which [h] ye had from the beginning. The old commandment
8 is the word which ye have heard from the beginning. Again, [i] a new commandment I write unto you, which thing is true in him and in you:
9 [j] because the darkness is past, and the [k] true light now shineth. He that saith he is in the light, and hateth his brother, is in darkness even until
10 now. He that loveth his brother abideth in the light, and [l] there is none
11 [1] occasion of stumbling in him: but he that hateth his brother is in darkness, and [m] walketh in darkness, and knoweth not whither he goeth, because that darkness hath blinded his eyes.
12   I write unto you, little children, because your sins are forgiven you
13 for his name's sake. I write unto you, fathers, because ye have known

A. D. 90.

[g] 2 John 5.
[h] ch 3. 11.
[i] John 13.34.
[j] Rom 13.12.
[j] Eph. 5. 8.
1 Thes 5. 5
[k] John 1. 9.
John 8. 12.
John 12. 35.
[i] 2 Pet 1. 19.
1 scandal.
[m] John 12. 35
[n] Luke 24.47.
Acts 4. 12.

their hearts being full of Him (cf. John xx. 15). "Even as He walked" when on earth, especially as to *love*. John delights in referring to Christ as the model man: "even as He," &c. 'It is not Christ's walking on the sea, but His ordinary walk, we are called on to imitate' (*Luther*).
7. Brethren. ℵ A B C, Vulgate, read 'Beloved,' appropriate to the subject, *love*. **no new commandment** — *love*, the principle of walking *as Christ walked* (*v.* 6), and that commandment, of which exemplification is given, *vv.* 9, 10, *the love of brethren*. **ye had from the beginning** — from the time ye first heard the Gospel word. **8. a new commandment.** It was "old," in that *Christians as such had heard it from the first;* but "new" [*kaine*, not *nea: new and different* from the *old* legal precept], in that it was first *clearly* promulgated with Christianity: though the inner *spirit* of the law was *love* even to enemies, yet it was enveloped in some bitter precepts, which caused it to be temporarily almost unrecognized. Christianity first put *love to brethren* on the new and highest MOTIVE, instinctive love to Him who first loved us, constraining us to love all, even enemies, thereby walking in the steps of Him who loved us when enemies. So Jesus calls it "new," John xiii. 34, 35: "Love one another, *as I have loved you*" (the new motive), xv. 12. **which thing is true in him and in you.** '*In Christ* all things are always true, and were so from the beginning; but *in Christ and in us* conjointly *the commandment* (the love of brethren) *is then true* when we acknowledge the truth which is *in Him*, and have the same flourishing *in us*' (*Bengel, Alford*). Which thing (*the fact that the commandment is a new one*) is true in the case of Him and of you, because the darkness is *passing away* in the case of you, and the true light is now shining, and began to shine ever since He came into the world, bringing this commandment. I prefer, The *new commandment* finds its *truth* in its practical *realization* in the walk of Christians in union with Christ. Cf. "verily," *v.* 5. John iv. 42; vi. 55, "indeed." The repetition, "in Him and *in* you," not "in Him and you," implies that the love-commandment finds its realization *separately:* first "*in Him*," and then "*in us*," in so far as we now "also walk even as He walked;" yet it finds its realization also *conjointly*, by the two being united in one sentence, even as it is by the love-commandment having been first fulfilled *in Him*, that it is also now fulfilled *in us*, through His Spirit in us: cf. a similar case, John xx. 17, "*My* Father and *your* Father:" by virtue of His being "*My* Father," He is also *your* Father. **darkness is past** — rather, as *v.* 17, 'is passing away.' It shall not be wholly "past" until 'the Sun of righteousness" shall arise *visibly:* "the light is shining" *already*, though partially until the day bursts forth. **9.** There is no mean between *light*

and *darkness, love* and *hatred, life* and *death, God* and the *world:* wherever spiritual *life* is, however weak, there *darkness* and *death* no longer reign, *love* supplants *hatred*. Luke ix. 50 holds good: wherever *life* is not, there *death, darkness*, the *flesh*, the *world*, and *hatred*, however hidden from man's observation, prevail. Luke xi. 23 holds good: 'where love is not, there hatred is; for the heart cannot remain a void' (*Bengel*). **in the light** — as his proper element. **his brother** — his neighbour, especially the Christian brotherhood. The title *brother* is a reason why *love* should be exercised. **even until now** — notwithstanding that 'the true light already has begun to shine' (*v.* 8). **10.** Abiding in *love* is *abiding in the light; for* Gospel light not only illumines the understanding, but warms the heart. **none occasion of stumbling** — in contrast to *v.* 11. 'In him who loves there is neither blindness nor *occasion of stumbling* (to himself): in him who does not love, there is both. He who hates his brother stumbles against himself and everything within and without: he who loves has an unimpeded path' (*Bengel*). John has in mind Jesus' words, John xi. 9, 10. 'The light and the darkness are within; admitted into us by the eye, whose singleness fills the whole body with light' (*Alford*). **11. is in darkness, and walketh.** "Is" marks his continuing STATE: he has never come out of 'the darkness:' "walketh" marks his OUTWARD COURSE. **whither [pou]** — where: including not only the destination *to which*, but the way *whereby*. **hath blinded** — aorist, "blinded" of old. Darkness not only surrounds, but blinds him, and that a blindness of long standing.
12. little children [*teknia*] — 'little *sons;*' 'dear sons and daughters:' not the same as *v.* 13 [*paidia*], "little *children*," 'infants' (in age and standing). He calls ALL to whom he writes, 'little *sons*' (*v.* 1, Greek; *v.* 28; iii. 18; iv. 4; v. 21); but only in *vv.* 13 and 18 he uses "little children." Our Lord, whose spirit John so deeply drank into, used to His disciples (John xiii. 33), 'little sons' — *dear sons and daughters;* but in John xxi. 5, "little children." It is an undesigned coincidence with the epistle, that in John's gospel similarly the classification, 'lambs, sheep, sheep' [in A C, not ℵ B D, *arnia probata probatia*] occurs. **are forgiven** [*apheōntai*] — 'have been, and are forgiven you.' ALL God's *sons and daughters* [*teknia*], not merely the *paidia*] enjoy this privilege. **13, 14.** All three classes are first addressed in the present, "I write;" then in the aorist [*egrapsa*], 'I wrote.' Moreover, in ℵ A B C, in the end of *v.* 13, 'I wrote,' not "I write." Two classes, "fathers" and "young men," are addressed with the same words each time (except that the address to the *young men* has an addition, expressing the source of their victory); but the 'little sons' and "little children' are differently addressed, as 'little sons' includes all three classes. **have known — and do**

him °*that is* from the beginning. I write unto you, young men, because
ye have overcome the wicked one. I write unto you, little children,
14 because ye have known the Father. I have written unto you, fathers,
because ye have known him *that is* from the beginning. I have written
unto you, young men, because ᴾ ye are strong, and the ᑫ word of God
abideth in you, and ye have overcome the wicked one.

15   Love not the world, neither the things *that are* in the world. ʳ If any
16 man love the world, the love of the Father is not in him. For all that *is*
in the world, the lust of the flesh, ˢ and the lust of the eyes, and the pride
17 of life, is not of the Father, but is of the world. And the world passeth

A. D. 90.

° ch. 1. 1.
ᴾ Eph. 6. 10.
   Phil. 4. 13.
   Col 1. 11.
ᑫ 2 Tim. 2. 1.
ᑫ Ps. 119. 11.
   Jer. 31. 33.
   John 8. 31.
ʳ Matt. 6. 24.
   Gal. 1. 10.
   Jas. 4. 4.
ˢ Eccl. 5. 11.

know: so the perfect means. The 'I wrote' refers not to a former epistle, but to this. It was an idiom to put the *past*, regarding the time from the *reader's* point of view: when he should receive the epistle the writing would be *past*. When he uses "I write," he speaks from *his own* point of view. **him that is from the beginning**—Christ: 'that which was from the beginning.' **overcome**. The *fathers*, appropriately to their age, are characterized by *knowledge*. The *young men*, appropriately to theirs, by activity in conflict. The *fathers*, too, have *conquered*; but now their active service is past, and they and *the children* alike are characterized by *knowing* (the *fathers* know *Christ*, 'Him that was from the beginning;' *the children* know the Father). The first thing that the *little children* realize is that God is their *Father;* answering in the parallel clause to 'little sons . . . ' your sins are forgiven you for His name's sake'—the universal privilege of *all* those really dear *sons* of God. Thus this latter includes *all*, whereas the former refers to those especially in the *first* stage of spiritual life, "little children." Of course these can only know *the Father* as theirs through *the Son* (Matt. xi. 27). It is beautiful to see how the *fathers* are characterized as reverting to the first great truth of spiritual childhood, the ripest fruit of advanced experience, the *knowledge of him that was from the beginning* (twice, *vv.* 13, 14). Many of them had probably known *Jesus* in person, as well as by faith. **young men . . . strong**—*made* so *out of* natural *weakness*, hence enabled to *overcome* 'the strong man armed,' through Him that is 'stronger' (Heb. xi. 34). Faith is the victory that overcomes the world. "Overcome" is peculiarly John's term, adopted from his loved Lord (John xvi. 33). It occurs sixteen times in the Apocalypse, six times in the first epistle, only thrice in the rest of the New Testament. In order to overcome the world on the ground of the blood of the Saviour, we must be willing, like Christ, to part with whatever of the world belongs to us: whence immediately after 'ye have overcome (and are overcoming: perfect) the wicked one (the prince of the world),' it is added, "Love not the world, neither the things . . . in the world." **and**, &c.—the secret of the young men's *strength:* the Gospel *word* clothed with living power by the Spirit who *abideth* permanently in them. This is "the sword of the Spirit" wielded in prayerful waiting on God. Contrast the mere physical strength of young men, Isa. xl. 30, 31. *Oral teaching* prepared them for the profitable use of *the word* when *written.* 'Antichrist cannot endanger you (*v.* 18), nor Satan tear from you *the word of God.*' **the wicked one**—who, as "prince of this world," enthrals it (*vv.* 15-17; ch. v. 19, Greek, "the wicked one"), especially the young. Christ came to destroy him (ch. iii. 8). Believers achieve the first conquest over him when they pass from darkness to light; but afterwards they need to maintain a continual *keeping* of themselves from his assaults, looking to God,

by whom alone they are *kept* safe. *Bengel* thinks John refers to the remarkable constancy exhibited by youths in Domitian's persecution. Also to the young man whom John, after his return from Patmos, led, with loving persuasion, to repentance. This youth had been commended by John, in one of his apostolic tours, as a promising disciple to the overseers of the Church: he had been, therefore, carefully watched up to baptism. But afterwards, relying too much on baptismal grace, he joined evil associates, and fell from step to step down, till he became a captain of robbers. When John, some years after, revisited that church, and heard of it, he hastened to the retreat of the robbers, suffered himself to be seized, and taken into the captain's presence. The youth, stung by conscience, fled away from the venerable apostle. Full of love, the aged father ran after him, called on him to take courage, and announced to him forgiveness of his sins in the name of Christ. The youth was recovered to Christianity, and induced many of his bad associates to repent and believe (*Clemens Alexandrinus*, 'Quis dives salvus?' c. iv., 2).

15. Love not the world—that *lieth in the wicked one* (ch. v. 19), whom ye young men *have overcome.* Having once for all, through *faith*, *overcome* the *world* (ch. iv. 4; v. 4), keep your conquest by not loving "the world" in its state as *fallen from God.* "God loved (with *compassion*) the world." We should feel the same love for the fallen world; but we are *not* to *love* the world with *congeniality* and *sympathy* in its alienation from God. We cannot have *this* love for the God-estranged world, and yet have also "the love of the Father" in us. neither [*mēde*]—'nor yet.' A man might deny in general that he *loved the world*, whilst keenly following THE THINGS IN IT—its riches, honours, or pleasures; this clause prevents him escaping conviction. **any man.** Therefore the warning, though primarily addressed to the young, applies to *all.* **love of**—i. e., *towards* "the Father." The two, God and the (sinful) world, are so opposed, that both cannot be congenially loved at once. **16. all that is in the world**—can be classed under one or other of the three. **lust of the flesh**—i. e., which has its seat in our lower animal nature. Satan tried this temptation first on Christ (Luke iv. 3). Youth is especially liable to fleshly lusts. **lust of the eyes**—the avenue through which outward things of the world, riches, pomp, and beauty, inflame us. Satan tried this temptation on Christ when he showed Him the kingdoms of the world in a moment. By lust of the eyes David (2.Sam. xi. 2) and Achan fell (Josh. vii. 21). Cf. Ps. cxix. 37; Job's resolve, xxxi. 1; Matt. v. 28. The only good of riches to the possessor is beholding them with the *eyes.* Cf. Luke xiv. 18, "I must go and SEE it." **pride of life** [*alazoneia*]—*arrogant assumption:* vainglorious display. *Pride* was that whereby Satan fell, and forms the link between the two foes, the *world* (answering to the *lust of the eyes*) and the *devil* (the lust of the *flesh* is

away, and the lust thereof: but he that doeth the will of God *abideth for ever.

18 Little children, "it is the last time: and as ye have heard "that antichrist shall come, "even now are there many antichrists; whereby we
19 know that it is the last time. They went out from us, but they were not of us; for *if they had been of us, they would *no doubt* have continued with us: but *they went out*, that *they might be made manifest that they
20 were not all of us. But *ye have an unction *from the Holy One, and

A. D. 90.

t Ps. 125. 1.
u Heb 1. 2.
v 2 Thes 2. 3.
w Matt 21. 5.
x Matt 24 21.
y 1 Cor.11.19.
z Isa. 41. 3
2 Cor 1. 21.
a Mark 1. 24.

the third foe). Satan tried this temptation against Christ on the temple-pinnacle, that, in spiritual *presumption*, on the ground of His Father's care, He should cast Himself down. The same three foes appear in the three classes of soil on which the Divine seed falls: The wayside hearers, *the devil;* the thorns, *the world;* the rocky under soil, *the flesh.* The world's *anti-trinity*, the "lust of the flesh, the lust of the eyes, and the pride of life," similarly is presented in Satan's temptation of Eve: 'When she saw that the tree was good for *food*, pleasant to the *eyes*, and a tree to be desired to make one *wise*' (one manifestation of "the pride of life," desire to know above what God has revealed, Col. ii. 8; pride of unsanctified knowledge).   **of** — does not spring *from* "the Father" (as the "little children," *v.* 13). He who is born *of* God alone turns *to* God; he who is of the world turns to the world; the sources of love to God and love to the world are irreconcilably distinct.   **17. the world**—with all who are of the world worldly.   **passeth away** [*paragetai*]—'is passing away' even now.   **the lust** [of life]—in its threefold manifestation (*v.* 16).   **he that doeth the will of God**—not his own *fleshly* will, or that of the *world*, but that of God (*vv.* 3-6), especially as to *love*.   **abideth for ever**—'even as God abideth for ever' (with whom the godly is one, cf. Ps. lv. 19): a true *comment*, which *Cyprian* and *Lucifer* added to the *text* without support of Greek MSS. In contrast to the three *passing* lusts of the world, the doer of God's will has three *abiding* goods, "riches, honour, and life" (Prov. xxii. 4).

18. Little children—in age. Same Greek as *v.* 13. After the *fathers* and *young men* were gone, "the last time" with its "many antichrists" was about to come suddenly on *the children.* 'In this *last hour* we all still live.' Each successive age has had some signs of "the last time" which precedes Christ's coming, in order to keep the Church in continual waiting for the Lord. 1 Cor. x. 11, "the ends of the world"—i. e., *the last dispensation.* The connection with *vv.* 15-17 is, There are coming those seducers who are of the world (ch. iv. 5), and would tempt you to go out from us (*v.* 19) and deny Christ (*v.* 22).   **as ye have heard**—from the apostles (*e. g.*, 2 Thess. ii. 3-10; and in the reign of Ephesus, Acts xx. 29, 30).   **shall come**—'cometh' out of his own place. *Antichrist* is interpreted— (1.) a false Christ (Matt. xxiv. 5, 24); a *vice-Christ*, '*instead* of Christ;' (2.) an *adversary* of Christ, '*against* Christ.' As John never uses *pseudo-Christ* for *antichrist*, he probably means an *adversary of Christ*, claiming what belongs to Christ, wishing to *substitute himself for Christ* as the supreme object of worship. He *denies the Son*, not merely acts in the name of the Son. 2 Thess. ii. 4, "Who *opposeth* himself [ANTI-*keimenos*] [to] all that is called God." For God's great truth, 'God is man,' he substitutes his own lie,' man is God' (*Trench*).   **are there** [*gegonasin*]—'there have begun to be.' These "many antichrists" answer to "the mystery of lawlessness doth already work" (2 Thess. ii. 7). The antichristian *principle* appeared then, as now, in evil men, teachings, and

writings; still "THE antichrist" means a hostile *person*, even as 'THE Christ' is a personal Saviour. As "cometh" is used of Christ, so of antichrist, the embodiment of all the antichristian features of those "many antichrists" which have been his forerunners. John uses the singular of him. No other New Testament writer uses the term. He answers to "the little horn having the eyes of a man, and speaking great things" (Dan. vii. 8, 20); "the man of sin, son of perdition" (2 Thess. ii.); "the beast ascending out of the bottomless pit," *i. e.*, the beast healed of its deadly wound (Rev. xi. 7; xvii. 8), rather, "the false prophet," the same as "the second beast coming up out of the earth" (Rev. xiii. 3, 11-18; xvi. 13).   **19. out from us**—from our Christian communion. Not necessarily a formal secession; thus Rome has spiritually *gone out*, though formally still of the Christian Church.   **not of us**—by spiritual fellowship (ch. i. 3): 'like bad humours in the body of Christ: when they are vomited out, the body is relieved; it is still under treatment, and has not yet attained the perfect soundness which it shall have only at the resurrection' (*Augustine*, 'Ep. John, Tract,' 3, 4).   **they would . . . have continued**—implying the indefectibility of grace in the elect. 'Where God's call is effectual, there will be sure perseverance' (*Calvin*). No fatal, but a 'voluntary necessity' (*Didymus*), causes men to remain, or else go from the body of Christ. 'We are among the members, or else among the bad humours. It is of his own will that each is either an antichrist, or in Christ' (*Augustine*). God's eternal election harmonizes in a way *inexplicable to us*, with man's free agency. It is men's own *evil* will that chooses hell; it is God's sovereign grace that draws any to heaven. To God the latter shall ascribe wholly their salvation; the former shall reproach themselves alone, not God's decree, with their condemnation (ch. iii. 9; v. 18).   **that they were not all of us.** This would imply that *some of the antichrists are of us!* Translate, "That all (who are among us) ARE not of us." Cf. 1 Cor. xi. 19. Such occasions test who are, and who are not, the Lord's people.   **20. But**— Greek, 'And.' He states the means which believers have to withstand *antichrists* (*v.* 18), viz., the *chrism* [*chrisma*: a play upon similar sounds] or '*anointing unguent*,' the Holy Spirit (plainly mentioned further on, in John's style, ch. iii. 24; iv. 13; v. 6), which *they* ("ye," in contrast to those apostates, *v.* 19) have from *Christ* (John i. 33; iii. 34; xv. 26; xvi. 14): "the righteous" (*v.* 1), "pure" (ch. iii. 3), "the Holy One" (Acts iii. 14) "of God" (Mark i. 24). Those anointed of God in *Christ* alone can resist those anointed with Satan's spirit, *antichrists*, who would sever them from the Father and the Son. Believers have the anointing Spirit from *the Father*, as well as from the Son; even as the Son is anointed therewith by the Father. Hence the Spirit is the token that we are in the Father and in the Son; without it one is none of Christ's. The material unguent of costliest ingredients, poured on the head of priests and kings, typified this spiritual unguent, derived from Christ, the Head, to us, His members. We have

21 *b* ye know all things. I have not written unto you because ye know not
22 the truth, but because ye know it, and that no lie is of the truth. Who
is a liar but he that denieth that Jesus is the Christ? he is antichrist,
23 that denieth the Father and the Son. Whosoever denieth the Son, the
same hath not the Father: [*but*] *c he that acknowledgeth the Son hath the
Father also.*
24   Let that therefore abide in you, which ye *d* have heard from the
beginning. If that which ye have heard from the beginning shall remain
25 in you, *e* ye also shall continue in the Son, and in the Father. And *f* this
26 is the promise that he hath promised us, *even* eternal life. These *things*
27 have I written unto you concerning them that seduce you. But the
anointing which ye have received of him abideth in you, and ye *g* need
not that any man teach you: but as the same anointing *h* teacheth you
of all things, and is truth, and is no lie, and even as it hath taught you,
ye shall abide in *2* him.
28   And now, little children, abide in him; that, when he shall appear,
we may have confidence, and not be ashamed before him at his coming.
29 If *e* ye know that he is righteous, *3* ye know that every one that doeth

A. D. 90.

b John 10. 4,
5.
John 14. 23.
John 16. 13.
c John 14. 7.
d 2 John 6.
e John 14 29.
John 15. 9.
10.
John 17. 21-
24.
ch. 1. 3.
f John 17. 3.
g Jer 31. 33.
John 14.26.
John 16. 13.
Heb. 8. 10.
h John 16. 13.
2 Or. it.
i Acts 2 14.
3 Or. know
ye

no share in *Jesus,* except we become truly *Christians,* being in *Christ,* anointed with that unction from the Holy One. The Spirit poured on the Head is by Him diffused through the members. 'We all are the body of *Christ,* because we all are anointed; we all in Him are both *Christ's* and *Christ,* because in some measure the whole *Christ* is Head and body.' and—therefore. **ye know all things**—needful for acting against antichrist's seductions, and for Christian life. In whatever measure one hath *the Spirit* (no more and no less), he knows all needful things. **21. because ye know it, and that, &c.** Ye not *only* know the truth (concerning the Son and the Father, *v.* 13), but also can detect a lie as opposed to the truth. For right is index of itself and of what is crooked (*Estius*). *Alford,* 'Because we know it, and *because* no lie is of the truth' ('every lie is excluded from being of the truth'), I therefore wrote (in this epistle) to point out the lie and liars. **22. a.** 'Who is the [*ho*] liar?' guilty of *the* lie just mentioned (*v.* 21). **that Jesus is the Christ**—the central truth. **he is antichrist**—'*the* antichrist:' not, however, here *personal; the ideal of antichrist* is he "that denieth the Father and the Son." To deny the latter is virtually to deny the former. Again, to deny that Jesus is the Christ, or that He is the Son of God, or that He came in the flesh, invalidates the whole (Matt. xi. 27). **23.** 'Every one who denieth the Son, hath not the Father either' (ch. iv. 2, 3); 'inasmuch as God hath given Himself to us wholly to be enjoyed in Christ' (*Calvin*). **he *that acknowledgeth the Son hath the Father also.*** These words ought not to be in italics, for א A B C, Vulgate, *Origen, Cyprian, Hilary,* have them. **hath**—in abiding possession as his 'portion;' by personal 'fellowship.' **acknowledgeth**—by open confession. **24. Let that**—truth respecting the Father and the Son, as a seed not merely dropped in, but having taken root (ch. iii. 9). **ye**—standing emphatically at the beginning of the Greek sentence. Yᴇ, therefore, *acknowledge the Son,* so shall ye *have the Father also* (*v.* 23). **from the beginning** —of the Gospel being preached to you. **remain** —'abide.' **ye also**—in your turn: distinguished from 'that which ye have heard,' the seed *abiding in you.* Cf. *v.* 27, "the anointing . . . *abideth in you* . . . ye shall *abide in Him.*" Having taken into us the living seed of truth concerning the Father and the Son, we become transformed into the likeness of Him whose seed we have. **25.**

this is the promise. *Eternal life* shall be the permanent consummation of *abiding in the Son and in the Father* (*v.* 24). **he** [*autos*]—'Himself,' "the Son" (cf. ch. i. 1). **promised**—(John iii. 15, 36; vi. 40, 47, 57; xvii. 2, 3.) **26. These things**—(*vv.* 18-25.) **have I written**—resumed from *vv.* 21 and 14. **seduce you**—try to lead you into error. **27. But**—Greek, 'And you (contrasting believers with the *seducers: and you* stands prominent, the construction of the sentence following being altered, no verb agreeing with "and you" until "need not") . . . the anointing,' &c. (resumed from *v.* 20). **received of him**—(John i. 16.) So 2 Cor. ii. 15. **abideth in you.** He tacitly admonishes them to say to seducers, 'The anointing abideth in us: we do not need a teacher (for we have the Holy Spirit as our teacher, Jer. xxxi. 34; John vi. 45; xvi. 13): it teaches us the truth: in it we will abide' (*Bengel*). **and**—and therefore. God is sufficient for those taught of Him: they are independent of others, though, of course, not declining the counsel of faithful ministers. 'Mutual communication is not set aside, but approved of, in the case of partakers of the anointing in one body' (*Bengel*). **the same anointing**—which ye once for all received, and which still abides in you. **of**—'concerning.' **all things**—essential to salvation: the point under discussion. Not that the believer is infallible; for none here receive the Spirit in its fulness, but only the measure needful for keeping him from soul-destroying error. So the Church, though having the Spirit in her, is not infallible (for fallible members can never make one infallible whole), but is kept from ever wholly losing everywhere the saving truth. **no lie—as** antichristian teaching. **ye shall abide in him** (*v.* 24, end)—even as 'the anointing abideth in you.' The oldest MSS. read the imperative, '*abide* in Him.' **28. little children** [*teknia*]—'little sons,' as *v.* 12: believers of every stage. **abide in him**— Christ. John, as a loving *father,* repeats his monition. **when** [*ean*]—'if.' The uncertainty is not as to the fact, but *the time.* **appear**—'be manifested.' **we**—both writer and readers. **ashamed before him** [*apo*]—'*from* Him,' shrink *from Him* ashamed. Contrast "boldness in the day of judgment," ch. iv. 17: cf. ch. iii. 21; v. 14. In the Apocalypse (written subsequently) Christ's coming appears at a greater distance. **29.** *Heading of the second division of the epistle:*—'God is righteous, therefore every one that doeth righteous-*

3 righteousness is born of him. BEHOLD what manner of love the Father hath bestowed upon us, that *ᵃ*we should be called the sons of God!
2 therefore the world knoweth us not, *ᵇ*because it knew him not. Beloved, now are we the sons of God; and *ᶜ*it doth not yet appear what we shall be: but we know that, when he shall appear, *ᵈ*we shall be like him; for *ᵉ*we shall see him as he is.
3   And every man that hath this hope in him purifieth himself, even as

A. D. 90.

CHAP. 3.
ᵃ John 1. 12.
ᵇ John 15. 18.
ᶜ 1 Cor. 2. 9.
ᵈ Ps 17. 15.
ᵉ Job 19. 26.
Ps. 16. 11.
Matt. 5. 8.

ness is born of Him.' Love is the grand principle of "righteousness" selected for discussion, ch. ii. 29—iii. 3. **29. If ye know** [*Eidēte*—*ginosketē*—'If ye *are aware* (are in possession of the knowledge) . . . *ye discern* also that,' &c. Ye are *aware* that *God* (both "the Father," *of* whom the believer *is born*, end of this verse, and ch. iii. 1; and "the Son," *vv.* 1, 23) *is righteous;* ye must thereby *perceive* also the consequence of that truth—viz., 'that every one that doeth righteousness (and he alone: *the* righteousness such as the righteous God approves) is born of Him.' The righteous begetteth the righteous. We are never said to be *born* again *of Christ*, but of *God*, with whom Christ is one. *Hollaz* in *Alford* defines *the righteousness of God:* 'The Divine energy by whose power God wills and does all things conformable to His eternal law, prescribes suitable laws to His creatures, fulfils His promises to men, rewards the good, and punishes the ungodly.' **doeth.** 'For the graces are practical, and have their being in being exercised: for when they have ceased to act, or are only about to act, they have not even being' (*Œcumenius*). 'God is righteous, therefore the *source* of righteousness: when a man doeth righteousness, we know that he has acquired by new birth that righteousness which he had not by nature. We argue from his *doing righteousness* to his being *born of God.* The error of Pelagians is to conclude that *doing righteousness* is a condition of *becoming* a child of God' (*Alford*). Cf. Luke vii. 47, 50: her much love *evinced* that her sins *were already* forgiven; not, were the *condition* of her sins being forgiven.

CHAP. III. 1-24.—MARKS OF THE CHILDREN OF GOD AND THE CHILDREN OF THE DEVIL— BROTHERLY LOVE THE ESSENCE OF RIGHTEOUSNESS.
1. Behold—calling attention to something wonderful, little as the world sees to admire. This verse is connected with ch. ii. 29. All our *doing* of *righteousness* is a mere sign that God, of His matchless love, has adopted us as children: it does not save us, but indicates that we are saved of His grace. **what manner of**—how surpassingly gracious on His part, how precious to us! **love . . . bestowed.** He does not say that God hath given us some gift, but *love itself*, the fountain of all blessings; not for our works, but of His grace (*Luther*). **that** [*hina*]—resulting in. The *effect aimed at* in the bestowal of His love is, 'that we should be called children of God.' **should be called**—should have such a glorious *title* (imaginary as it seems to the world), along with the glorious *reality.* With God *to call* is to *make really.* Who so great as God? What nearer relationship than that of *sons?* א A B C, Vulgate, add, 'And we ARE so' really. **therefore**—because 'we are (really) so.' so.' —the children, like the Father. **it knew him not** —viz., the Father. 'If they who regard not God hold thee in any account, feel alarmed about thy state' (*Bengel*). Contrast ch. v. 1. The world's whole course is one great act of non-recognition of God. **2. Beloved**—by the Father, therefore by me. **now**—in contrast to "not yet." We *already* are sons, though unrecognized as such by the world, and (as the consequence) we look for the

manifestation of our sonship, which *not yet* has taken place. **doth not yet appear** [*ephanerothē*] —'it hath not yet (*at any time*, aorist) been manifested what we shall be,' what glory we shall attain by virtue of our sonship. "What" suggests a something inconceivably glorious. **but**—omitted in א A B. Its insertion gives a wrong antithesis. Not, '*We do not yet know manifestly* what, &c., *but* we know,' &c. Rather, the manifestation *to the world* of what we shall be has not yet taken place. *We know* (in general, with *well-assured knowledge*) [*oidamen*] that when [*ean*] ('if' expressing no doubt of the fact, but only as to the time: also implying that on the coming preliminary fact, the consequence follows, Mal. i. 6; John xiv. 3) He (not 'it,' viz., that which is not yet manifested, *Alford*) shall be manifested (*v.* 5; ch. ii. 28), we shall be like Him (Christ: sons substantially resemble their father: Christ, whom we shall be like, is 'the express image of the Father's person:' so in resembling Christ we shall resemble the Father). We *wait for the manifestation* (Rom. viii. 19, *the apocalypse:* applied also to Christ's own manifestation) *of the sons of God.* After natural birth, the new birth into the life of grace is needed; to be followed by the new birth into the life of glory: the two alike are 'the regeneration' (Matt. xix. 28). The resurrection of our bodies is a coming out of the womb of the earth: being born into another life. Our first temptation was that we should be like God in knowledge: by that we fell; but raised by Christ, we become truly like Him, by knowing Him as we are known, and seeing Him as He is (*Pearson*, 'Creed'). As the first immortality, which Adam lost, was *to be able not to die*, so the last shall be *not to be able to die.* As man's first free choice was to be able not to sin, so our last shall be not to be able to sin (*Augustine*, 'Civit. Dei,' b. xxii., c. 30). The devil fell by aspiring to God's *power;* man, by aspiring to His *knowledge;* but aspiring after God's *goodness*, we shall ever grow in His likeness. The transition from *God* to "He," "Him," referring to Christ (who alone is said in Scripture to be *manifested*, not the Father, John i. 18), implies the unity of the Father and the Son. **for, &c.** Continual beholding generates likeness (2 Cor. iii. 18); as the face of the moon, being always turned towards the sun, reflects its glory. **see him**—not in His innermost Godhead, but as manifested in Christ. None but the pure can see the infinitely Pure One (Matt. v. 8; Heb. xii. 14; Rev. i. 7; xxii. 4). In all these passages [*opsomai*], not the action of seeing, but the state of him to whose eye or mind the object is presented; hence the verb is always in the middle, or reflexive voice, to *perceive*, *inwardly appreciate* (*Tittmann*). Our spiritual bodies will recognize spiritual beings hereafter, as our natural bodies do natural objects.
3. this hope—of being hereafter "like Him." Answering to "we *know*" (*v.* 2); so far from it being a vague, uncertain hope. *Faith, love*, and *hope*, concur (*vv.* 11, 23). **in** [*epi*]—'resting *upon* Him:' on His promises. **purifieth himself**—by Christ's Spirit in him (John xv. 3, 5, end). One's justification through faith is presupposed (Acts

4 he is pure. Whosoever committeth sin transgresseth also the law: for
5 sin is the transgression of the law. And ye know that he was manifested
6 to *ᶠ* take away our sins; and *ᵍ* in him is no sin. Whosoever abideth in
him sinneth not: whosoever sinneth hath not seen him neither known
him.

7   Little children, let no man deceive you: he *ʰ* that doeth righteousness
8 is righteous, even as he is righteous. He *ⁱ* that committeth sin is of the
devil; for the devil sinneth from the beginning. For this purpose the
Son of God was manifested, *ʲ* that he might destroy the works of the
9 devil. Whosoever *ᵏ* is born of God doth not commit sin; for *ˡ* his seed
remaineth in him: and he cannot sin, because he is born of God.

A. D. 90

ᶠ Iss 53. 4.
Matt 1. 21.
Heb. 1. 3.
ᵍ 2 Cor 5. 21.
ʰ Eze. 18. 5.
Rom 2. 13.
ⁱ Matt 13.39
John 8 44.
ʲ Gen. 3. 15.
Luke 10.18.
John 16.11.
ᵏ ch 5. 18.
ˡ 1 Pet. 1. 23.

xv. 9). **as he is pure** [*hagnos*]—unsullied with
uncleanness. The Second Person, by whom both
the Law and Gospel were given. **4.** Sin is incompatible with birth from God (*vv.* 1-3). John
often sets forth the truth *negatively*, which he
before set forth *positively*. He had shown birth
from God involves self-purification; he now shows
where sin—*i. e.*, absence of self-purification—is,
there is no birth from God. **4. Whosoever** [*Pas
ho*]—'*Every one* who,' &c. **committeth sin**—in
contrast to *v.* 3, "every man that hath this hope
in him purifieth himself" (cf. *v.* 7). **transgresseth
also the law** [*poiei ten anomian*]—'committeth
transgression of law.' God's law of purity; so
shows he has no such hope of being hereafter pure
as God is pure; therefore, that he is not born of
God. **for** [*kai*]—'and.' **sin is the transgression
of the law**—definition of *sin*. The Greek (א A C;
but B [*hamartia*], without *he*) having the article to
both, implies they are convertible terms. "Sin"
[*hamartia*] is *a missing of the mark*, God's will to
be ever aimed at. (Rom. iii. 20, "By the law is
the knowledge of sin.") The crookedness of a line
is shown by juxtaposition with a straight ruler.
5. Additional proof of the incompatibility of sin
and sonship: the very object of Christ's manifestation in the flesh was *to take away* (by one act)
entirely [aorist, *ἄρῃ*] all sins, as the scape-goat did
typically. **and**—another proof. **in him is no sin**
—not 'was,' but 'is,' as *v.* 7, "He *is* righteous,"
and *v.* 3. Therefore we are to be so. **6.** Christ's
entire separation from sin implies that those in
Him must also be separate from it. **abideth in
him**—as the branch in the vine, by vital union,
living by His life. **sinneth not.** So far as he
abides in Christ, he is free from all sin. The
ideal of the Christian. The life of sin and the life
of God exclude one another, as darkness and light.
In matter of *fact*, believers do fall into sins (ch. i.
8 10; ii. 1, 2); but all sins are alien from the life
of God, and need Christ's cleansing blood, without
application to which the life of God could not be
maintained. He sinneth not so long as he abideth
in Christ. He that falls into sin is a man: he that
boasts of sin is a devil: he that grieves at sin is a
saint (*Fuller*). **whosoever sinneth hath not seen
him** [*heōraken*]—'has not seen, and does not see
Him.' The *ideal* of Christian intuitive knowledge
is presented, John x. 4. All sin is at variance
with the notion of one regenerated. Not 'whosoever is betrayed into sins has never seen, nor
known' God; but *in so far* as sin exists, *in that
degree* spiritual intuition of God doth not exist in
him. **neither**—'not even.' To *see* spiritually is
a further step than *to know;* for by *knowing* we
come to *seeing* by vivid, experimental realization.
7. The same truth, with the addition that he
who sins is, so far as he sins, "of the devil." **let
no man deceive you — as** antinomians would.
righteousness—'*the* righteousness' of Christ or
God. **he that doeth . . . is righteous.** Not his

doing makes him *righteous*, but his *being righteous*
(justified by the righteousness of God in Christ,
Rom. x. 3-10) makes him to do *righteousness:* an
inversion common in familiar language, logical in
reality, though not in form, as in Luke vii. 47;
John viii. 47. Works do not justify, but the justified man works. We infer from his *doing righteousness* that he is already *righteous* (i. e., has the
true and only principle of *doing righteousness*—
viz., *faith*), and is therefore *born of God* (*v.* 9);
just as we say, The tree that bears good fruit is a
good tree, and has a living root: not that the fruit
makes the tree and its root good, but *shows* that
they are so. **he**—Christ. **8. He that committeth
sin is of the devil**—in contrast to "he that doeth
righteousness" (*v.* 7). He is *a son of the devil*
(*v.* 10; John viii. 44). John does not say, 'born
of the devil,' as he does 'born of God;' for 'the
devil neither creates nor begets; but whoever
imitates the devil becomes his child by imitation,
not by proper birth' (*Augustine*, 'Tract.,' iv. 10).
From the devil there is not generation, but corruption (*Bengel*). **sinneth from the beginning**—
from the time that sin began; that he became
what he is, the devil. He kept his first estate
only a short time after his creation (*Bengel*).
Since the fall of man (at the beginning of *our
world*) *the devil is* (*ever*) *sinning* (he has sinned
from the beginning, is the cause of all sins, and
still *goes on sinning*). As author of sin, and
prince of this world, he has never ceased to
seduce man to sin (*Luecke*). **destroy** [*lusē*]—
break up and do away with: bruising and crushing
the serpent's head. **works of the devil**—sin, and
its awful consequences. Christians cannot do that
which Christ came to destroy. **9. Whosoever is
born of God**—'every one that is begotten of God.'
doth not commit sin—his higher nature, as begotten of God, doth not sin. *To be begotten of
God*, and *to sin*, are states mutually excluding
each other. In so far as one sins, he makes it
doubtful whether he be *born of God*. **his seed**—
God's living Word, made by the Holy Spirit the
seed in us of a new life: the continual mean of
sanctification. **remaineth**—abideth in Him (note,
v. 6; John v. 38). Not contradictory to ch. i. 8, 9.
The regenerate show the utter incompatibility of
sin with *regeneration*, by at once cleansing away
every sin into which their old nature betrays
them, in the blood of Christ. **cannot sin, because he is born of God**—'because it is *of God*
that *he is born*' (cf. the Greek order with that of
the same words in the beginning of the verse):
not 'because he *was* born of God' [*gegennetai*,
perfect; *present* in meaning, not aorist]: not, Because a man *was once for all born of God* he never
afterwards can sin; but, Because he is born of God,
the seed abiding now in Him, he cannot sin; so
long as it energetically abides, sin can have no
place. Cf. Gen. xxxix. 9, Joseph, "How CAN I do
this great . . . sin against God?" The principle

10 In this the children of God are manifest, and the children of the devil:

Whosoever doeth not righteousness is not of God, neither he that lov-
11 eth not his brother. For this is the [1]message that ye heard from the
12 beginning, [m]that we should love one another. Not as [n]Cain, *who* was of that wicked one, and slew his brother. And wherefore slew he him?
13 because his own works were evil, and his brother's righteous. Marvel
14 not, my brethren, if the world hate you. We know that we have passed from death unto life because we love the brethren. He that loveth not
15 *his* brother abideth in death. Whosoever [o]hateth his brother is a murderer: and ye know that [p]no murderer hath eternal life abiding in him.
16 Hereby [q]perceive we the love *of God*, because he laid down his life for
17 us: and we ought to lay down *our* lives for the brethren. But [r]whoso hath this world's good, and seeth his brother have need, and shutteth up his bowels *of compassion* from him, how dwelleth the love of God in him?

A. D. 90.
[1] Or. command-ment.
[m] John 13. 34, 35.
John 15.12.
Gal. 6. 2.
Eph 5 2.
[n] Gen. 1. 4.
[o] Matt. 5. 21.
ch 4. 20.
[p] Gal. 5. 21.
Rev. 21. 8.
[q] John 3. 16.
Rom. 5. 8.
Eph. 5. 2,
25.
[r] Deut. 15. 7.
Luke 3. 11.

within is at utter variance with sin, and gives a hatred for all sin, and an unceasing desire to resist it. 'The child of God receives wounds daily, and never throws away his arms, or makes peace with his deadly foe' (*Luther*). The exceptional sins of the regenerate are owing to the new life being suffered to lie dormant, and to the sword of the Spirit not being drawn instantly.' Sin is ever active, but no longer reigns. The believer's *normal* direction is against sin ; the law of God after the inward man is the *ruling* principle of his true self, though the old nature, not yet *fully* deadened, rebels. Contrast ch. v. 18 with John viii. 34: cf. Ps. xviii. 22, 23; xxxii. 2; cxix. 113, 176. The magnetic needle, the nature of which is always to point to the pole, is easily turned aside, but always re-seeks it. **children of the devil**—(note, *v.* 8; Acts xiii. 10.) There is no middle class between them and the children of God.

doeth not righteousness. Contrast ch. ii. 29. **he that loveth not his brother** (ch. iv. 8)—a particular instance of *love*, which is the sum of all righteousness, and the token (not loud professions, and even seemingly good works) that distinguishes God's children from the devil's. **11. the message** [*angelia*]—'announcement,' as of something good; not a mere *command*, as the law. The Gospel *message* of Him who loved us, announced by His servants, is, that we *love*—not here all mankind, but our *brethren* in Christ, children of the same family of God, of whom we have been born anew. **12. who** — not in the Greek. **of that wicked one**—'*evil* one :' corresponding to "because his own works were *evil*." Cf. *v.* 8, "of the devil," in contrast to "of God," *v.* 10. **slew he him ? because his own works were evil, and his brother's righteous**—through envy and hatred of his brother's piety, for which God accepted Abel's, but rejected Cain's offering. Enmity from the first existed between the seed of the woman and that of the serpent. **13. Marvel not.** The marvel would be if the world loved you. **the world**— whom Cain represents (*v.* 12). **hate you**—as Cain hated his own brother, to the extent of murdering him. The world feels its bad works tacitly reproved by good works. **14. We** — emphatical : hated as we are by the world, *we* know (as an assured fact) what it knows not. **passed** [*metalebekamen*]—*changed our state* (Col. i. 13). **from death unto life** [*ek tou—eis tēn*]—'*out of the* death (which enthrals the unregenerate) *into the* life' (of the regenerate). A palpable coincidence, the beloved disciple adopting his Lord's words (John v. 24, end). **because we love the brethren**—the

ground, not of *passing over out of death into life*, but of our *knowing* that we have. *Love* is the *evidence* of our justification and regeneration, not the *cause.* 'Let each go to his own heart : if he find there love to the brethren, let him feel assured he has passed from death unto life. Let him not mind that his glory is only hidden: when the Lord shall come he shall appear in glory. He has vital energy, but it is still winter: the root has vigour, but the branches are dry: within there is vigorous marrow, within are leaves, within fruits ; but they must wait for summer' (*Augustine*). **He that loveth not.** אAB, Vulgate, omit "his brother" (C), which makes the statement general. **abideth**—still. **in death**— 'in *the* (spiritual) death' (ending in eternal death), the state of all by nature. His want of *love* evidences that no saving change has passed over him. **15. hateth** — "loveth not," *v.* 14 : there is no medium. 'Love and hatred, like light and darkness, life and death, necessarily replace, as well as exclude, one another' (*Alford*). **is a murderer**— because indulging that passion, which, if followed to its natural consequences, would make him one. 'Verse 16 desires us to lay down our lives for the brethren ; *duels* require one (awful to say !) to risk *his own* life, rather than not deprive *another* of life' (*Bengel*). God regards the inward disposition as tantamount to the outward act which would flow from it. Whomsoever one hates, one wishes dead. **hath**—such a one still "abideth in death." Not his *future* state, but his *present* is referred to. He who hates (*i. e.*, loveth not) his brother (*v.* 14) cannot, in his present state, have eternal life abiding in him.

16. What true *love to the brethren* is, is illustrated by Christ's to us. **Hereby**—'herein.' **the love of God.** "Of God" is not in the original. Translate, 'We arrive at the knowledge of LOVE;' we apprehend *what true love is.* **he**—Christ. **and we**—on our part, if necessary for the glory of God, the good of the Church, or the salvation of a brother. **lives.** Christ laid down His one *life* for us all : we ought to lay down our *lives* severally for the lives of the brethren ; if not actually, at least virtually, by giving our time, care, prayers, substance: '*Non nobis, sed omnibus.*' Our life ought not to be dearer to us than God's own Son was to Him. The apostles and martyrs acted on this principle. **17. this world's good** [*bion*]—'livelihood' or substance. If we ought to lay down our *lives* for the brethren (*v.* 16), how much more our *substance?* **seeth**—not *casually*, but deliberately *contemplates as a spectator* [*theorē*]. **shutteth up his bowels of compassion**—momentarily opened by the *spectacle* of

18 My little children, let us not love in word, neither in tongue; but in deed, and in truth.

19 And hereby we know [s]that we are of the truth, and shall [2]assure our

20 hearts before him. For if our heart condemn us, God is greater than our

21 heart, and knoweth all things. Beloved, [t]if our heart condemn us not,

22 [u]*then* have we confidence toward God. And [v]whatsoever we ask, we receive of him, because we keep his commandments, [w]and do those

23 things that are pleasing in his sight. And this is his commandment,

A. D. 90.

[s] John 18. 37.
[2] p'rsuade
[t] Job 22. 26.
[u] Heb. 10. 22.
[v] I's. 34. 15.
    Matt. 21.22.
[u] Mark 11.24.
    John 14.13.
[w] John 8. 29.

---

his brother's need. 'The bowels' mean *the inward parts,* the seat of compassion. **how.** *How* is it possible that "the love of (i. e., *to*) God dwelleth (*abideth*) in him?" Our superfluities should yield to the necessities—our comforts, and even necessaries, in some measure, to the extreme wants—of our brethren. 'Faith gives Christ to me; love flowing from faith gives me to my neighbour.' **18.** When the venerable John could no longer walk to the meetings of the Church, but was borne thither by his disciples, he always uttered the same address; that one commandment which he received from Christ, comprising all the rest, the distinctive feature of the new covenant, "My little children, love one another." When the brethren asked why he always repeated the same thing, he replied, 'Because it is the commandment of the Lord, and if this one be attained, it is enough' (*Jerome*). **in word**—'*with* word . . . *with* tongue, but *in* deed and truth.'

19. hereby—'herein;' in *loving in deed and truth* (*v.* 18). **we know.** א A B C have 'we shall know,' viz., if we fulfil the command (*v.* 18). **of the truth**—real disciples of, belonging to, *the truth,* as it is in Jesus: begotten of God with the word of truth (Jas. i. 18). Having *the truth* radically, we shall not love merely *in word and tongue* (*v.* 18). **assure**—*persuade,* so as to cease to condemn us; satisfy the doubts of our consciences as to whether we be accepted *before God* or not (cf. Acts xii. 20, "*having made* Blastus . . . *their friend,*" 'persuaded'). The "heart," the seat of the feelings, is our inward *judge;* the *conscience,* as witness, acts either as our justifying advocate, or our condemning accuser, even now. John nowhere (save John viii. 9, rejected by the oldest MSS.) uses *conscience.* Peter and Paul alone use it. **before him**—in the sight of Him, the omniscient Searcher of *hearts. Assurance* is the designed experience and privilege of the believer. **20.** *Bengel* takes this as consoling the believer whom his *heart condemns;* who therefore, like Peter, appeals from conscience to Him who is *greater than conscience,* "Lord, thou *knowest all things:* thou knowest that I love thee." Peter's conscience, though condemning him of his denial of the Lord, assured him of His *love;* but fearing the possibility, owing to his fall, of deceiving himself, he appeals to the all-knowing God (John xxi. 17): so Paul, 1 Cor. iv. 3, 4). So, *if our heart condemn us of sin in general,* yet if we have the one sign of sonship, *love,* we may still *assure our hearts,* knowing *that God is greater than our heart, and knoweth all things.* But *Alford* objects, Thus *hoti* is translated 'because' in the beginning, and '(we know) *that*' in the middle of the verse. If the verse were consolatory, it probably would have been, 'Because EVEN if our heart condemn us,' &c. Translate, '*Because* (the reason why it was stated in *v.* 19 to be so important to "assure our hearts before Him") if our heart condemn [*kataginoskē*] ('*know* [aught] *against* us:' in contrast to 'we shall *know* that we are of the truth') us (it is) *because* God is greater than our heart, and knoweth all things.' If our heart judges us unfavourably, we

may be sure that He, knowing more than our heart knows, judges us more unfavourably still (*Alford*). Cf. the ellipsis, 1 Cor. xiv. 27; 2 Cor. i. 6; viii. 23. The condemning testimony of conscience is not alone, but is the echo of the voice of Him who is greater, and knoweth all things. Our hypocrisy in *loving by word and tongue,* not *in deed and truth,* does not escape even conscience, though knowing but little, how much less God who knows all things? I prefer the consolatory view. For [*peisomen*] 'we shall *assure* our hearts' (note, *v.* 19), is *gain over,* so as to be stilled, implying a previous *self-condemnation by the heart* (*v.* 20), which is *got over* by the consolatory thought, 'God is greater than my heart,' which condemns (*knows against*) me: God '*knows* all things' [*ginoskei,* not *kataginoskei,* '*condemns*'], therefore knows my *love* and desire to serve Him; knows my *frame,* so as to pity my weakness (Ps. ciii. 13, 14). This *gaining over* of the heart to peace is not so advanced experience as *having* CONFIDENCE *towards God,* which flows from a *heart condemning us not.* The first 'because' applies to the two alternatives (*vv.* 20, 21), giving the ground of saying, that *having love we shall gain over,* or *assure our minds before Him* (*v.* 19): the second 'because' applies to the first alone—viz., *if our heart condemn us.* When he reaches the second alternative (*v.* 21), he states it independently of the former 'because,' which connected it with *v.* 19, inasmuch as CONFIDENCE *toward God* is a farther stage than *persuading our hearts,* though always preceded by it. **21. Beloved.** There is no *But* contrasting the two cases, *vv.* 20, 21, because "Beloved" sufficiently marks the transition to the case of walking in full confidence of *love* (*v.* 18). The two results of being able to "assure our hearts before Him" (*v.* 19), and of 'our heart condemning us not' (of insincerity as to *the truth* in general, and LOVE in particular), are—(1.) confidence toward God; (2.) a sure answer to prayer. John does not mean that all whose heart does not condemn them are therefore safe before God; for some have their conscience seared, others are ignorant of the truth: it is not *sincerity,* but *sincerity in the truth,* which saves men. Christians are meant: knowing Christ's precepts, and testing themselves by them. **22. we receive**—according to His promise (Matt. vii. 8). Believers, as such, ask what is in accordance with God's will; or if they ask what God wills not, they bow their will to God's; so God grants them either their request or something better. **because we keep his commandments**—(cf. Ps. xxxiv. 15; lxvi. 18; cxlv. 18, 19.) Not that our merits earn a hearing, but our works of faith being the fruit of *His* Spirit in us, are 'pleasing in God's sight; and our prayers being the voice of the same Spirit in us (Rom. viii. 26), necessarily are answered by Him. **23.** God's commandments summed up in the one Gospel commandment. **this is his commandment**—*singular:* for *faith* and *love* are not *separate* commandments, but indissolubly one. We cannot truly *love* one another without *faith* in Christ, nor truly believe in Him

That we should believe on the name of his Son Jesus Christ, and love
24 one another, as he gave us commandment. And he that keepeth his
commandments *[x]*dwelleth in him, and he in him. And *[y]*hereby we know
that he abideth in us, by the Spirit which he hath given us.

4 BELOVED, *[a]*believe not every spirit, but try the spirits whether they
are of God; because *[b]*many false prophets are gone out into the world.
2 Hereby know ye the Spirit of God: Every *[c]*spirit that confesseth that
3 Jesus Christ is come in the flesh is of God: and *[d]*every spirit that confesseth not that Jesus Christ is come in the flesh is not of God: and this
is that *spirit* of antichrist, whereof ye have heard that it should come;
and even now already is it in the world.

4 Ye are of God, little children, and have overcome them; because greater
5 is he that is in you, than *[e]*he that is in the world. They *[f]*are of the
world: therefore speak they of the world, and *[g]*the world heareth them.
6 We are of God: *[h]*he that knoweth God heareth us; he that is not of
God heareth not us. Hereby know we *[i]*the spirit of truth, and the spirit
of error.

7 Beloved, let us love one another: for love is of God; and every one

A.D. 90

[x] John 17.21.
[y] Eze 37.27.
Rom 8.9.

CHAP. 4.
[a] Jer. 29.8.
[b] Matt. 24.5.
[c] 1 Cor. 12 3.
ch. 5 1.
[d] ch. 2. 22.
2 John 7.
[e] John 12. 31.
John 14. 30.
John 16. 11.
[f] John 3. 31.
[g] John 15. 19.
John 17. 14.
[h] John 8. 47.
John 10. 27.
John 13. 20.
John 18 37.
[i] Isa. 8. 20.
John 14. 17.

---

without love. **believe**—*once for all* [aorist, *pis-teusomen*, B; but אAC, *pisteuomen*, '*continually* believe]. **on the name of his Son**—all that is revealed in the Gospel concerning Him, and on Himself, in His person, offices, and atoning work. **as he**—*Jesus*. 24. **dwelleth in him.** The believer dwelleth in Christ. **and he in him**—Christ in the believer. Reciprocity. 'The key-note of the epistle, *abide in Him*, with which the former part concluded' (ch. ii. 28) (*Alford*). **hereby**—'herein we (believers) know that He abideth in us, viz., from (the presence in us of) the Spirit.' This prepares, by mention of the true Spirit, for the transition to false "spirits," ch. iv. 1-6; after which he returns again to *love*.

CHAP. IV. 1-21.—TEST OF FALSE PROPHETS—LOVE THE TEST OF BIRTH FROM GOD, AND THE FRUIT OF KNOWING HIS GREAT LOVE IN CHRIST TO US.

1. Beloved—the affectionate address wherewith he calls attention to an important subject. **every spirit**—in the person of a prophet. The Spirit of truth, and that of error, speak by men's spirits as their organs. There is but one Spirit of truth, and one of antichrist. **try**—by the tests (*vv.* 2, 3). All are to do so: not merely ecclesiastics. Even an angel's message should be tested by the Word of God; much more men's teachings, however holy the teachers seem (Gal. i. 8). **because, &c.**—reason why we must *test* the spirits. **many false prophets**—not in the sense 'foretellers,' but organs of the spirit that inspires them, *teaching* error: 'many antichrists.' **are gone out**—as if from God. **into the world**—said alike of good and bad prophets (2 John 7). The world is easily seduced (*vv.* 4, 5). 2. 'Herein' **know ... Spirit of God**—whether He be, or not, in those professing to be moved by Him. **Every spirit**—i.e., *Every teacher* claiming inspiration by THE HOLY SPIRIT. **confesseth**—the truth is taken for granted. Man is required to *confess* it openly, as in teaching. **Jesus Christ is come in the flesh**—a twofold truth confessed: that *Jesus is the Christ;* and that *He is come* [*eleluthota*, perfect; not a mere past historical fact, but *present*, and *continuing* in its blessed effects] *in the flesh* ('invested with flesh;' not with a *seeming* humanity, as the Docetæ afterwards taught). He therefore was previously something far above flesh. His *flesh* implies His *death* for us; for only by assuming flesh could He die (as God He could not, Heb. ii. 9, 16),

and His death implies His LOVE for us (John xv. 13). To deny the reality of *His flesh* is to deny His *love*, and so cast away the root which produces true love on the believer's part (*vv.* 9-11, 19). Rome, by the doctrine of the Virgin's immaculate conception, denies Christ's proper humanity. 3. **confesseth not that Jesus Christ is come in the flesh.** So א, *Cyprian, Polycarp, Irenæus* (iii. 8). *Lucifer, Irenæus, Origen,* on Matt. xxv. 14, and Vulgate, read, 'Every spirit which destroys (*sets aside*, or *does away with*) Jesus Christ.' AB read only, 'Every spirit that confesseth not (*i. e.*, refuses to confess) Jesus' (in His person, His offices, and divinity). **ye have heard**—from your Christian teachers. **already is it in the world**—in the person of *false prophets* (*v.* 1).

4. Ye—emphatical. YE who confess Jesus: in contrast to 'them,' the false teachers. **overcome** (ch. v. 4, 5)—instead of being 'overcome, and brought into (spiritual) bondage' by them (John x. 5, 8; 2 Pet. ii. 19). **he that is in you**—*God, of* whom ye are. **he that is in the world**—the spirit of antichrist, Satan, "the prince of this world." **5. of the world**—they derive their spirit and teaching from the world: 'unregenerate human nature, ruled over and possessed by Satan' (*Alford*). **speak they of the world**—they draw their conversation from the life, opinions, and feelings of the world. **the world heareth them**—(John xv. 18, 19.) *The world loves its own.* 6. **We**—*true teachers* of Christ; in contrast to *them.* **are of God**—and therefore *speak of God;* in contrast to 'speak of the world,' *v.* 5. **knoweth God**—as his Father, being a child "*of God*" (ch. ii. 13). **heareth us**—(cf. John xviii. 37.) Hereby (*vv.* 2-6)—by their confessing, or not confessing, Jesus: by the reception given us respectively by those who know God, and by those who are of the world, and not of God. **spirit of truth**—*the Spirit* coming from God and teaching *truth.* **spirit of error**—*the spirit* coming from Satan, and seducing into *error.*

7. Resumption of the main theme (ch. ii. 29). *Love*, the sum of *righteousness*, is the test of being *born of God.* Love flows from a sense of God's love. *V.* 9 resumes ch. iii. 16; *v.* 13 resumes ch. iii. 24. At the same time, *vv.* 7-21 are connected with the preceding context, *v.* 2 setting forth *Christ's incarnation, the great proof of God's love* (*v.* 10). **Beloved**—appropriate to his subject, "**love.**" **love.** *All* love is *from God*, its fountain;

8 that loveth is born of God, and knoweth God. He that loveth not
9 knoweth not God; for *j* God is love. In this was manifested the love of
God toward us, because that God sent his only-begotten Son into the
10 world, that we might live through him. Herein is love, *k* not that we
loved God, but that he loved us, and sent his Son *to be* the propitiation
11 for our sins. Beloved, if God so loved us, we ought also to love one
12 another. No *l* man hath seen God at any time. If we love one another,
13 God dwelleth in us, and his love is perfected in us. Hereby *m* know we
that we dwell in him, and he in us, because he hath given us of his
Spirit.
14 And *n* we have seen and do testify that the *o* Father sent the Son *to be*
15 the Saviour of the world. Whosoever *p* shall confess that Jesus is the
16 Son of God, God dwelleth in him, and he in God. And we have known
and believed the love that God hath to us. God is love; and he that
17 dwelleth in love dwelleth in God, and God in him. Herein is *l* our love
made perfect, that we *q* may have boldness in the day of judgment : *r* be-
18 cause as he is, so are we in this world. There is no fear in love; but

A. D. 90.

j Ex 31. 6,
7.
Ps. 86. 5, 15.
Mic 7. 18.
2 Cor. 13. 11.
k John 15. 16.
Tit. 3. 4.
l Ex. 33. 20.
John 1. 18.
1 Tim. 6.
16.
m John 14. 20.
n John l. 14.
o John 3. 17.
p Rom. 10. 9.
1 love with
us.
q Jas. 2. 13.
ch. 2. 28.
ch. 3. 19.
r ch. 3. 3.

especially its great embodiment, God manifest in the flesh. The *Father* also is *love* (*v.* 8). The *Holy Ghost* sheds *love* as its first-*fruit* abroad in the heart (Rom. v. 5). **knoweth God**—spiritually, experimentally, habitually. **8. knoweth not** [*egno*, aorist]—not only *knoweth* not now, but never *has once for all known* God. **God is love.** There is no article to *love*, but to *God ;* therefore we cannot translate, *Love is God.* God is essentially LOVE : not merely *loving ;* for then John's argument would fall : for the conclusion from the premises then would be, *This man is not loving ; God is ; therefore he knoweth not God* IN SO FAR AS GOD IS LOVING : still he might know Him in His *other* attributes. But when we take *love* as God's *essence,* the argument holds : *This man doth not love ; therefore knows not love : God is essentially love ; therefore he knows not God.* **9. toward us** [*en hemin*]—'in our case.' **sent** [*apestalken*]—'*hath* sent.' **into the world**—therefore the Son existed before. Otherwise, too, He could not have been our *life* (*v.* 9), our "*propitiation*" (*v.* 10), our "Saviour" (*v.* 14). It is the grand *proof* of God's love, His having sent *His only-begotten Son that we might live through Him, the Life,* who has redeemed our forfeited life : it is also the grand *motive* to our mutual love. **10. Herein is love**—*love* in the abstract, in its highest ideal, is herein. The love was all on God's side, none on ours. **not that we loved God**—though so altogether worthy of love. **he loved us**—though so altogether unworthy of love. [*Egapesamen,* the aorist, Not that we *did* any act of love *at any time* to God, but that He *did* the act of love to us in sending Christ.] **11.** God's love to us the grand motive for love to one another (ch. iii. 16). **if**—as we all admit. **we ought also** —as *born of God,* and therefore resembling our Father, who is love. In proportion as we appreciate God's love to us, we love Him and also *the brethren,* children (by regeneration) of the same Father, representatives of the unseen God. **12.** *God,* whom *no man hath seen at any time,* appoints His children the *visible* recipients of our outward kindness, flowing from love to Himself, '*whom not* having *seen,* we love' (1 Pet. i. 8 : cf. note, *vv.* 11, 19, 20). Thus *v.* 12 explains why, instead (in *v.* 11) of saying, 'If God so loved us, we ought also to love *God,*' he said, "We ought also to love *one another.*" **If we love one another, God dwelleth in us**—for God is love. It must have been from Him dwelling in us that we drew the love we bear to the brethren (*vv.* 8, 16 : discussed, *vv.* 13-16). **his love**—rather, 'love of (*i. e.,* to) Him,' evinced

by love to His representatives, our brethren. **is perfected in us.** (Discussed, *vv.* 17-19.) Cf. ch. ii. 5, "Is perfected ;" *i. e.,* attains its maturity. **13.** 'Herein.' The token vouchsafed to us of God's dwelling (*abiding*) in us, though we see Him not, is that He hath given us "of His Spirit" (ch. iii. 24). Where the Spirit is, there God is. ONE Spirit dwells in the Church : each believer receives a measure "of" that Spirit in the proportion God thinks fit (1 Cor. xii. 11). *Love* is His first-fruit (Gal. v. 22). In Jesus alone the Spirit dwells without measure (John iii. 34). **14. And we**—primarily, *we apostles,* Christ's appointed eye-witnesses to testify to the facts concerning Him. The internal evidence of the indwelling Spirit (*v.* 13) is corroborated by external evidence of the eye-witnesses to the fact of the Father having "sent the Son to be the Saviour of the world." **seen** [*tetheametha*]—'contemplated ;' 'attentively beheld' (note, ch. i. 1). **sent**—'*hath* sent :' not entirely past (aorist), but one *of which the effects continue* (perfect). **15. shall confess**—once for all (aorist). **that Jesus is the Son of God** —and therefore "the Saviour of the world" (*v.* 14). **16. And we**—*John and his readers* (not as *v.* 14, *the apostles* only). **known and believed.** True faith is a faith of *knowledge* and experience : true *knowledge* is a knowledge of *faith* (*Luecke*). **to us** [*en hēmin*]—'in our case' (note, *v.* 9). **dwelleth**—'abideth' (cf. *v.* 7). **17.** (Cf. ch. iii. 19-21.) **our love** [*he agape meth' hēmōn*]. 'LOVE is made perfect (in its relations) *with us.*' Love dwelling *in us* advances to its consummation 'with us ;' *i. e.,* as it is concerned *with us.* (Luke i. 58, "showed great mercy upon (*with*) her ;" 2 John 2.) **boldness**—'confidence' [*parrhesian*] : parallel to ch. iii. 21 ; opposite to "fear," *v.* 18. *Herein* is love perfected, viz., *in God dwelling in us, and our dwelling in God* (*v.* 16), involving as its *result,* 'that we can have *confidence* (*boldness*) in the day of judgment' (so terrible to other men, Acts xxiv. 25). **because, &c.** The ground of our 'confidence' is, '*because* even as He (Christ) is, we also are in this world' (He will not, in that day, condemn those *like Himself*) : we are *righteous* as He is righteous, especially in that which is the sum of righteousness, *love* (ch. iii. 14). Christ IS righteous, and *love* itself, in heaven : so are we, His members, still "in this world." Our oneness with Him even *now* in His exaltation (Eph. ii. 6), so that all that belongs to Him of righteousness, &c., belongs to us by perfect imputation, and progressive impartation, is the ground of our *love*

perfect love casteth out fear: because fear hath torment. He that fear-
19 eth is not made perfect in love. We love him, because he first loved us.
20 If a man say, I love God, and hateth his brother, he is a liar: for he that
loveth not his brother whom he hath seen, how can he love God whom he
21 hath not seen? And *this commandment have we from him, That he who
loveth God love his brother also.

5 WHOSOEVER *believeth that *Jesus is the Christ is born of God:
*and every one that loveth him that begat loveth him also that is be-
2 gotten of him. By this we know that we love the children of God, when
3 we love God, and keep his commandments. For *this is the love of God,
that we keep his commandments: and *his commandments are not griev-
4 ous. For *whatsoever is born of God overcometh the world: and this is

A. D. 90.
* John 3. 34.
CHAP. 5.
* Matt. 16. 16.
John 1. 12.
ch 2. 22, 31.
* ch. 2. 22.
ch. 3. 9.
ch. 4. 7.
* John 15. 23
* John 14, 15.
2 John 6.
* Mic. 6. 8.
Matt. 11. 30
* John 16 33

being *perfected, so that we can have confidence in the day of judgment. We are in, not of, this world.* **18.** *Fear* has no place in *love.* **Bold confidence (v. 17),** based on *love,* cannot co-exist with *fear.* *Love,* which, when *perfected,* gives *bold confidence,* casts out *fear* (cf. Heb. ii. 14, 15). Christ's propitiatory death was designed to *deliver* from this *bondage of fear,* but [*alla*] —'on the contrary.' **fear hath torment** [*kolasin*] —*punishment.* Fear is always revolving the punishment deserved; and, by anticipation (through consciousness of deserving it), has even now its foretaste. *Perfect love* is incompatible with self-punishing *fear.* *Fear* of offending God differs from slavish fear of consciously-deserved punishment: the latter is natural to us all, until *love* casts it out. 'Men's states vary: one is without fear and love; another, with fear without love; another, with fear and love; another, without fear with love' (*Bengel*). **19. him.** Omitted in A B: א has 'God.' '*We* (emphatical, on our part) love (in general. *Him, the brethren,* and *our fellow-men*), because He (emphatical: answering to 'WE;' *because it was He who*) first loved us, in sending His Son (aorist of a definite act at one time). He was the first to love us: this thought ought to create in us *love casting out fear* (v. 18). **20. loveth not his brother whom he hath seen, how can he love God whom he hath not seen?** It is easier for us, influenced as we are by sense, to love one within the range of our senses, than One unseen, appreciable only by faith.' 'Nature is prior to grace: we by nature love things seen before things unseen' (*Estius*). *The eyes are our leaders in love.* 'Seeing is its incentive' (*Œcumenius*). If we do not love *the brethren,* God's visible representatives, how can we love the invisible One, *whose children they are?* Man's true ideal (as made in God's image), lost in Adam, is realized in Christ, in whom God is revealed as He is, and man as he ought to be. Till Christ came we had lost the knowledge of MAN as well as of GOD. Thus, by faith in Christ, we learn to love both the true God and the true man: so to love the brethren as bearing His image. "Hath seen:" and continually sees. **21.** Besides the argument (v. 20) from men's common feeling, he adds a stronger from God's express *commandment* (Matt. xxii. 39). He who loves will do what the object of His love wishes. **he who loveth God**—he who wishes to be regarded as loving Him.

CHAP. V. 1-21.—THE BRETHREN ESPECIALLY TO BE LOVED (ch. iv. 21)—OBEDIENCE, THE TEST OF LOVE, EASY THROUGH FAITH, WHICH OVER-COMES THE WORLD—LAST SECTION—THE SPIRIT'S WITNESS TO THE BELIEVER'S SPIRITUAL LIFE—TRUTHS REPEATED—FAREWELL WARNING.

1. Why our "brother" (ch. iv. 21) is entitled to such *love,* viz., because he is 'begotten of God:' so, if we want to show love to *God,* we must show

it to God's representative. **Whosoever** [*Pas ho*]— 'Every one that.' He could not be our "Jesus" (God-Saviour) unless He were "the Christ;" for He could not reveal the way of salvation except He were a *prophet:* He could not work it out except He were a *priest:* He could not confer it upon us except He were a *king.* He could not be *prophet, priest,* and *king,* except He were the Christ (*Pearson* 'On the Creed'). **born**—"begotten," as in end of the verse. Christ is the "only-begotten Son" by *generation:* we become begotten sons of God by *regeneration* and adoption. Parallel to John iii. 3, 5. **every one that loveth him that begat**—sincerely; not in mere profession (ch. iv. 20). **loveth him also that is begotten**—'his brethren' (ch. iv. 21). **2. By**—'IN this.' As *love to the brethren* is the test of our *love to God,* so *love to God* (tested by 'keeping His commandments') is, conversely, the only basis of real *love to our brother.* **we know.** John means not the *outward* criteria of genuine brotherly love, but the *inward* criteria, *consciousness of love to God,* manifested in heartily keeping His commandments. When we have this inwardly-and-outwardly-confirmed *love to God,* we *know* that we truly *love the children of God.* '*Love to one's brother* is prior in the order of nature (note, ch. iv. 20); *love to God* is so in the order of grace (ch. v. 2). At one time the former is more known, at another the latter, according as the mind is more occupied with human relations, or with what concerns the Divine honour' (*Estius*). True *love* is referred to God as its first object. Previously John urged the effect; now he urges the cause. For he wishes us so to cultivate mutual love, as that *God* should always be placed first (*Calvin*). **3. this is**—the *love* of God consists in this. **not grievous**—as many think them. It is 'the way of the transgressor' that "is hard" (Prov. xiii. 15). What makes them to the regenerate "not grievous" is *faith* (v. 4). In proportion as faith is strong, the grievousness of God's commandments to the rebellious flesh is 'overcome.' The reason why believers feel any irksomeness in God's commandments is, they do not realize fully by faith their spiritual privileges. **4. For**—(note, v. 3.) Reason why "His commandments are not grievous." Though there is a conflict in keeping them, the issue for all and each of the regenerate is victory over every opposing influence: meanwhile present *joy* in keeping them makes them "not grievous" (Ps. cxix. 77, 92, 111, 174). **whatsoever** [*pam to*]—'*all* that is begotten of God.' The neuter expresses *the universal whole,* or *aggregate of the regenerate,* regarded as one body (John iii. 6; vi. 37, 39). *Bengel* remarks, that in Jesus' discourses, whatever the Father has given Him is called, in the singular neuter, *all* whatsoever; those who come to the *Son* are described in the masculine plural, *they all,* or singular, *every one.* The Father has given the whole mass to the Son,

5 the victory that overcometh the world, *even* our faith. Who is he that overcometh the world, but *g*he that believeth that Jesus is the Son of God?

6   This is he that came *h*by water and blood, *even* Jesus Christ; not by water only, but by water and blood. And *i*it is the Spirit that beareth

7 witness, because the Spirit is truth. For there *j*are three that bear record in heaven, the Father, *k*the Word, and the Holy Ghost: *l*and these three

8 are one. And there are three that bear witness in earth, the spirit, and the water, and the blood: and these three agree in one.

A. D. ſ0.

g 1 Cor. 1. 57.
h John 19 34.
i John 15 23.
j Isa 18 16.
j Hag 2. 5, 7.
1 Cor. 12. 4-6.
k John 1. 1.
Rev 9 13.
l Deut. 6. 4.

that all may be *one* whole : that *universal* whole the Son singly evolves, in execution of the Divine plan. overcometh—habitually. **the world**—all that is opposed to keeping God's commandments, or draws us off from God, in this world, including our *flesh*, on which the *world's* blandishments or threats act ; also including Satan, *the prince of this world.* **this is the victory that overcometh** [aorist, *nikesasa*]—'that *overcomes* (has once for all overcome) the world : ' the *victory* (where *faith* is) is *already obtained* (ch. ii. 13 ; iv. 4). **5. Who**—else, "but he that believeth that Jesus is the Son of God :" "the Christ" (*v.* 1)? Confirming, by a question defying contradiction, *v.* 4, that *the victory* which overcomes the world is *faith* (Rom. viii. 33-35). For it is by *believing* that we are made one with *Jesus the Son of God*, partaking of *His victory over the world*, and having in us One greater than he who is in the world (ch. iv. 4). 'Survey the world, and show me even one of whom it can be affirmed that he overcomes the world, who is not a Christian' (*Episcopius* in *Alford*).

6. This—the Person mentioned, *v.* 5 : *Jesus.* **he that came by water and blood**—"by water," when His ministry was inaugurated by baptism in Jordan, and He received the Father's testimony to His Messiahship and Divine *Sonship.* Cf. *v.* 5, with John i. 33, 34, and *v.* 8, below. Corresponding is *the baptism of water and the Spirit*, which He instituted as a standing seal of initiatory incorporation with Him (John iii. 5). **"And blood."** He came by "the blood of His cross" (so "by," Heb. ix. 12, i. e., *with*)—a fact *seen* and solemnly *witnessed to* by John. 'These two past facts in the Lord's life are this abiding *testimony* to us, by the permanent application to us of their cleansing and atoning power' (*Alford*). **Jesus Christ**—not a mere appellation, but a solemn assertion of the Lord's Person and Messiahship. **not by.** [Greek, 'not IN *the* water only, but IN *the* water and IN (B; but א omits) *the* blood,'] As "*by*" [*dia*] implies the mean *through*, or *with*, which He came, so '*in*,' the element in which He came. 'The' implies their being *the well-known* symbols. John Baptist came only baptizing with water ; therefore was not the *Messiah.* Jesus came first to undergo Himself the double baptism of water and blood, then to baptize us with the Spirit-cleansing, of which *water* is the sacramental seal, and with His atoning *blood*, the efficacy of which, once-for-all shed, is perpetual ; and therefore is *the Messiah.* It was His shed *blood* which gave *water-baptism* its spiritual significance. We are baptized *into His death :* the grand point of union between us and Him, and, through Him, between us and God. **it is the Spirit, &c.** *The Holy Spirit* is an additional witness (*v.* 7), besides the *water* and the *blood*, to Jesus' *Sonship* and *Messiahship.* The Spirit attested these at Jesus' baptism, by descending on Him, and throughout His ministry, by enabling Him to speak and do what man never could have spoken or done. It is the abiding Spirit that beareth witness of Christ,—in the inspired New Testament, and in the hearts of believers, and in the spiritual reception of baptism and the Lord's Supper. **because the Spirit is truth.** It is His essential *truth* which gives His witness such infallible authority. **7. three.** Two or three witnesses were required by law to constitute adequate testimony. The only Greek MSS., *in any form*, which support the words, "in heaven, the Father, the Word, and the Holy Ghost, and these three are one : and there are three that bear witness in earth," are the Montfortianus of Dublin, copied from the *modern* Latin Vulgate ; the Revianus, copied from the Complutensian Polyglot ; a MS. at Naples, with the words added in the margin by a recent hand ; Ottobonianus, 298, of the fifteenth century, the Greek of which is a *translation* of the accompanying Latin. All the old versions omit the words. The oldest MSS. of the Vulgate omit them, the earliest Vulgate MS. which has them being Wizanburgensis, 99, of the eighth century. A Scholium quoted in Matthæi shows that the words did not arise from fraud ; for all Greek MSS. ("there are *three* that bear record"), the Scholiast notices, have "three," *masculine*, because the three things (*the Spirit, the water*, and *the blood*) are SYMBOLS OF THE TRINITY. To this *Cyprian*, 196, refers : 'Of the *Father, Son*, and *Holy Spirit*, it is written, "*And these* three are one"' (a unity). There must be some mystical truth implied in "*three*" [*hoi treis*] twice in the *masculine*, though the antecedents, 'Spirit, water, and blood,' are *neuter.* That THE TRINITY was meant is a natural inference : the triad specified pointing to a still higher Trinity ; as is plain also from *v.* 9, "the witness of God," referring to the *Trinity*, alluded to in 'the Spirit, water, and blood.' It was therefore first written as a *marginal* comment to complete the sense ; then, as early, at least, as the eighth century, was introduced into the *text* of the Latin Vulgate. The testimony, however, could only be borne *on earth* to men, not *in heaven.* The marginal comment that inserted "in heaven" was inappropriate. It is *on earth* that the context requires the witness of the three—*the Spirit, the water*, and *the blood*—to be borne : mystically setting forth the Divine *triune* witnesses—the Father, the Spirit, and the Son. *Luecke* notices as internal evidence against the words, John never uses "the Father" and "the Word" as correlates, but, like other New Testament writers, associates "the Son" with "the Father," and always refers "the Word" to 'God' as its correlate, not "the Father." *Vigilius*, at the end of the fifth century, first quotes the disputed words as in the text. The *term* 'Trinity' occurs first in the third century in *Tertullian*, 'adversus Praxean,' 3. **8. agree in one** [*eis to hen asin*]—'tend unto one result :' their agreeing testimony to Jesus' Sonship and Messiahship they give by the sacramental grace in *water-baptism*, received by the penitent believer through His atoning *blood*, and through His inwardly witnessing *Spirit* (*v.* 10) ; answering to the testimony given to *Jesus*' Sonship and Messiahship by His

9   If we receive *ᵐ* the witness of men, the witness of God is greater : *ⁿ* for
10 this is the witness of God which he hath testified of his Son. He that
believeth on the Son of God hath *°* the witness in himself : he that believeth not God *ᵖ* hath made him a liar; because he believeth not the
11 record that God gave of his Son. And this is the record, that God
12 hath given to us eternal life, and *ᵠ* this life is in his Son. He *ʳ* that
hath the Son hath life; *and* he that hath not the Son of God hath
not life.
13   These *ˢ* things have I written unto you that believe on the name of
the Son of God, *ᵗ* that ye may know that ye have eternal life, and that
14 ye may believe on the name of the Son of God. And this is the confidence that we have ¹ in him, that, if we ask any thing according to his
15 will, he heareth us. And if we know that he hear us, what soever we ask,
we know that we have the petitions that we desired of him.

A. D. 90.

ᵐ John 3 32.
John 8. 17,
18.
ⁿ Matt 3. 16.
° Rom. 8. 16.
Gal. 4. 6.
ᵖ John 3. 33.
ᵠ John 1. 4.
ʳ John 5. 24.
Heb 3. 14.
ch. 2. 23,
24.
ˢ John 20. 31.
ᵗ ch 1. 1, 2.
1 Ur.
concerning
him.

baptism, His crucifixion, and the Spirit's manifestations in Him (note, *v.* 6). It was by *coming by
water* (*i. e.*, His baptism in Jordan) that Jesus was
solemnly inaugurated in office, and revealed as
Messiah. This must have been peculiarly important in John's estimation, as he was first led to
Christ by the Baptist's testimony. By Christ's
baptism then, by His redeeming *blood*-shedding,
and by what the Spirit of God, whose witness is
infallible, effected, and still effects, by Him, the
Spirit, the *water,* and the *blood* unite, as the
threefold witness, to verify His Divine Messiahship (*Neander*).
9. If, &c. We do *accept* (and rightly) the witness
of veracious men, fallible though they be; much
more ought we to accept *the* infallible witness of
God (the Father). 'The testimony of the Father
is the basis of that of the Word and of the Holy
Spirit ; just as the testimony of *the Spirit* is the
basis of the testimony of *the water* and the *blood'*
(*Bengel*). **for.** This principle applies in the present case, FOR, &c. **which.** In א A B, Vulgate,
' *Because* He hath given testimony concerning His
Son.' What that testimony is, we find in *vv.* 1, 5,
10, 11. **10. hath the witness**—of God ; which
[*Theou*] A, Vulgate, have; but א B omit; by His
Spirit (*v.* 8). **in himself**—God's Spirit dwelling in
him ; *witnessing* that "Jesus is the Lord" (1 Cor.
xii. 3), "the Christ," "the Son of God" (*vv.* 1, 5).
The Spirit's witness *in* the believer *himself* to his
Sonship is not expressed, but follows from his
believing the witness of God to Jesus' Divine Sonship. **believeth not God** [*pisteuōn to Theo*]—
credits not His *witness.* So B א ; but Λ, Vulgate
[*huio*], 'the Son.' **made him a liar**—a consequence
which virtual and even avowed unbelievers may
well startle back from as fearful blasphemy (ch. i.
10). **believeth not the record** [*eis ten marturian*]
—' IN the *witness.*' Refusal to *credit* God's testimony is involved in refusing *to believe* IN (to rest
one's trust in) Jesus Christ (*v.* 10) [*eis ton huion*],
the object of it. ' Divine *faith* is an assent to
something as *credible* upon God's testimony.
This is the highest *faith ;* because the object hath
the highest credibility, because grounded upon
God's testimony, which is infallible' (*Pearson* 'On
Creed'). **gave**—'hath testified, and now testifies.' **of**—concerning. **11. hath given**—aorist,
' gave,' once for all. Not only ' *promised* ' it. **life
is in his Son**—essentially (John i. 4; xi. 25; xiv.
6); bodily (Col. ii. 9); operatively (2 Tim. i. 10)
(*Lange*). It is in the second Adam, the Son of
God, that this *life* is secured to us, which, if left
to depend on us, we should lose, like the first
Adam. **12. the Son hath life**—' THE life.' *Bengel,*
The verse has two clauses : in the former the Son
is mentioned without "of God," for believers

know *the Son ;* in the second, the addition "of
God" is made, that unbelievers may know what
a serious thing it is not to have Him. In the
former, "has" bears the emphasis ; in the second,
life. To *have the Son* is to be able to say as the
bride, "I am my Beloved's, and *my Beloved is
mine.*" By *faith* the regenerate HAVE Christ as a
present possession, and in Him *have life* in its germ
now, and shall have life in its fully developed
manifestation hereafter. *Eternal life* here is (1.)
initial ; an earnest of that which is to follow ; in
the intermediate state (2.) *partial,* belonging but
to a part of man, though his nobler part, the soul
separated from the body ; at the resurrection (3.)
perfectional. This *life* is not only *natural,* consisting of union of soul and body (as that of the reprobate in eternal pain, which is rather *death* eternal,
not *life*), but also *spiritual,* the union of the soul to
God, and supremely *blessed* for ever (for *life* implies
happiness) (*Pearson* 'On Creed').
13. These things—this epistle. He, in closing
his gospel (John xx. 30, 31), wrote similarly,
stating his purpose in having written. In ch. i.
4, he states the object of this epistle "that your
joy may be full." To "*know that we have eternal
life*" is the sure way to 'joy in God.' A B א,
Vulgate, read, 'These things have I written unto
you (omitting *that believe on the name of the Son of
God*) that ye may know that ye have eternal life
(cf. *v.* 11), THOSE (of you I mean) WHO believe (not,
and that ye may believe) on the name of the Son of
God.' [B א read *tois pisteuousin* ; but A C, Vulgate, *hoi pisteuontes.*] The English version means,
'that ye may *continue* to believe,' &c. (cf. *v.* 12).
14. the confidence [*parrhesia*]—"boldness" (ch.
iv. 17) in prayer, from *knowing that we have eternal
life* (*v.* 13 ; ch. iii. 19-22). **according to his will**—
which is the believer's will, and therefore no
restraint to his prayers. In so far as God's will
is not ours, we are not abiding in faith, and our
prayers are not accepted. *Alford,* If we *knew*
God's will, and *submitted* to it heartily, it would
be impossible for us to ask anything for the spirit
or the body which He should not perform : it is
this ideal state which the apostle has in view. It
is the *Spirit* who teaches us inwardly, and Himself in us asks according to the will of God. **15.
hear**—' that He *heareth* us.' **we have the petitions that we desired of him**—as present possessions, each thing *whatsoever we ask from Him.*
Not one of our *past* prayers offered in faith,
according to His will, is lost. Like Hannah, we
can rejoice over them as granted even beforehand ;
and recognize the event when it comes to pass, as
not from chance, but obtained by past prayers (1
Sam. i. 18, 27). Cf. Jehoshaphat's confidence in
the issue of his prayers, so much so that he ap-

16　　If any man see his brother sin a sin *which is* not unto death, he shall ask, and he ^ushall give him life for them that sin not unto death.

17　^vThere is a sin unto death: I ^wdo not say that he shall pray for it.　All unrighteousness is sin: and there is a sin not unto death.

18　　We know that whosoever is born of God sinneth not; but he that is begotten of God keepeth himself, and that wicked one toucheth him not.

19　*And* we know that we are of God, and the ^xwhole world lieth in wicked-

20　ness.　And we know that the Son of God is come, and ^yhath given us an understanding, ^zthat we may know him that is true; and we are in him

A D. 90.

^u Job 42. 8.
^v Matt 19.31.
Mark 3 29.
Luke 12 10.
^w Jer. 7. 16.
Jer. 14. 11.
John 17. 9.
^x Gal. 1. 4.
^y Luke 24.45.
^z John 17. 3.

---

pointed singers to praise the Lord beforehand (2 Chr. xx. 21, 22).

16. If any man see—on any particular occasion [*idē*, aorist]. **his brother**—a fellow - Christian. **sin**—in the act, and continuing in the sin: present. **not unto death**—provided it is *not unto death.* **he shall give.** The *asker* shall be the means, by intercessory prayer, of *God giving* life to the sinning brother. Kindly reproof ought to accompany intercessions. *Life* was being forfeited by the sinning brother, when the believer's intercession obtained its restoration. **for them, &c.** Resuming the proviso, 'shall give life,' I say, *to* —*i. e.*, obtain life '*for* (in the case of) them that sin not unto death.' **I do not say that he shall pray for it.** [*Erotēsē*, "pray," means a REQUEST as of one on an equality, or at least on terms of familiarity, with him from whom the favour is sought.] 'The Christian intercessor shall not assume the authority which would be implied in making *request* for a sinner who has sinned the sin unto death (1 Sam. xv. 35; xvi. 1; Mark iii. 29), that it might be forgiven him' (*Trench*, 'Synonyms of the New Testament'). Cf. Deut. iii. 26. [*Aiteo*, 'ask,' implies the humble petition of an inferior: our Lord never uses it, but always uses *erotao*, 'request.'] Martha, from ignorance, once uses "ask" in His case (John xi. 22). 'Asking,' for a brother sinner not unto death, is a humble petition in consonance with God's will. To 'request' for a sin unto death (*intercede authoritatively for it,* as though we were more merciful than God) savours of presumption; prescribing to God in what lies out of the bounds of brotherly yearning (because one sinning unto death is thereby demonstrated not to be truly a brother, ch. ii. 19), how He shall inflict and withhold His righteous judgments. Jesus Himself intercedes, not for the world which hardens itself in unbelief, but for those given to Him out of the world (John xvii. 9). **17.** Every "unrighteousness (even that of believers, cf. ch. i. 9; iii. 4: coming short of *right*) is sin;" (but) not every sin is that unto death. **there is a sin not unto death**—in the case of which believers may intercede. *Death* and *life* stand in correlative opposition (*vv.* 11-13). *The sin unto death* must be one tending 'towards' [*pros*], so resulting in, *death. Alford* makes it an appreciable ACT, *the denying Jesus to be the Christ, the Son of God* (in contrast to confessing it, *vv.* 1, 5; ch. ii. 19, 22; iv. 2, 3; v. 10). Such wilful deniers of Christ are not to be received into one's house, or wished "God speed" (2 John 10, 11). Still, the *state* of apostasy accompanying the *act* is included—a 'state of soul in which faith, love, and hope, the new life, is extinguished. The chief commandment is *faith* and *love*, which imply *life.* Therefore the chief sin is that by which faith and love are destroyed, *death.* As long as it is not *evident* ("see," *v.* 16) that it is a sin unto death, it is lawful to pray. But when it is a palpable rejection of grace, and the man puts from him life, how can others procure for him life?' Contrast Jas. v. 14-18. Cf. Matt. xii. 31, 32, as to

the obstinate rejection of the Holy Ghost's plain testimony to the Divine Messiah. Jesus, on the Cross, pleaded only for those who KNEW NOT *what they were doing* in crucifying Him; not for those wilfully resisting grace (Luke xxiii. 34). If we *pray for* the impenitent, it must be with humble submission to God's will; not with the intercessory *request* which we should offer for *a* brother when erring.

18. (Ch. iii. 9.) **We know.** Thrice repeated (*vv.* 19, 20), to enforce the three truths which the words preface, as matters of the brethren's joint experimental knowledge. This *v.* 18 warns against abusing *vv.* 16, 17, as warranting carnal security. **whosoever**—'every one who,' &c. Not only advanced believers, but *every one* who is born again, "sinneth not." **he that is begotten** [*gennetheis*, aorist]—was (once for all) "begotten of God;" in the beginning it is perfect, "is begotten" [*gegenemenos*], as a *continuing* state. **keepeth himself.** Vulgate, 'The having been begotten of God [*generatio Dei*] keepeth HIM;' so B [*auton*]: 'He having been begotten of God, *it* (the divine generation implied in the nominative pendent) keepeth him.' So ch. iii. 9, "his seed remaineth in him." But א A read [*heauton*] 'himself,' as the English version. God's working by His Spirit, and man's working under that Spirit as a responsible agent, often occurs. That *God* must *keep* us, if we are to *keep ourselves* from evil, is certain. Cf. John xvii. 15; 1 Pet. i. 5. **that wicked one toucheth him not**—so as to hurt him. In so far as he realizes his regeneration-life, the prince of this world *hath nothing in him* to fasten his deadly temptations on, as in Christ's case (John xiv. 30). His Divine regeneration severed once for all his connection with the prince of this world. **19. world lieth in wickedness** [*en to ponero*]—rather, 'lieth in *the wicked one*,' as *v.* 18; ch. ii. 13, 14: cf. ch. iv. 4; John xvii. 14, 15; *i. e.*, in the power of, and abiding in, the wicked one, as its lord and resting-place. Cf. "abideth in death," ch. iii. 14: contrast *v.* 20, "we are in Him that is true." The believer is delivered out of his power; the whole world *lieth* helpless still in it, including the wise, great, respectable—all who are not by vital union in Christ. 20. Summary of our Christian privileges. **is come** [*hēkei*]—*is present, having come.* 'HE IS HERE—all is full of Him—His incarnation, work, abiding presence, is to us a living fact' (*Alford*). **given us an understanding.** Christ's office is to give the spiritual understanding to discern the things of God. **that we may know.** א A read [*ginōskomen* for *ginōskōmen*], '(So) that *we know.*' **him that is true**—God, as opposed to every *idol* (*v.* 21). Jesus, by his oneness with God, is also 'He that is true' (Rev. iii. 7). **even**—'we are in the true' God, *by virtue of being* "in His Son Jesus Christ." **This is the true God.** '*This* Jesus Christ (the last-named Person) is the true God' (identifying Him with the Father in being "the only true God," John xvii. 3). **and eternal life**—predicated of the Son of God: *Alford*, wrongly, 'He was *the life*; but not *eternal life*.' The

that is true, *even* in his Son Jesus Christ. This ᵃis the true God, and eternal life.

21   Little children, ᵇkeep yourselves from idols.   Amen.

A. D. 90.

ᵃ Isa 9, 6.
ᵇ 1 Cor. 0.14.

Father is *eternal life* as its *source;* the Son also is that *eternal life manifested*, as the very passage (ch. i. 2) which *Alford* quotes proves against him (cf. *vv.* 11, 13). It is as *Mediator of* ETERNAL LIFE *to us* that Christ is here contemplated. 'The true God and eternal life is this' Jesus Christ; *i. e.*, in believing in Him, we believe in the true God, and have eternal life. This prepares the way for warning against *false* gods (*v.* 21). Jesus Christ is the only 'express image of God's person' sanctioned, the only true manifestation of God. All other representations of God are forbidden as *idols.* Thus the epistle closes as it began (ch. i. 1, 2).

21. Affectionate parting caution. **from idols**— Christians were everywhere surrounded by *idolaters* with whom it was impossible to avoid intercourse. Hence the need of being on their guard against any indirect compromise or communion with idolatry. Some at Pergamos, in the region whence John wrote, fell into the snare of eating things sacrificed to idols (Rev. ii. 14). The moment we cease to abide "in Him that is true (by abiding) in Jesus Christ," we become part of 'the world that lieth in the wicked one,' given up to *spiritual*, if not in all places *literal*, *idolatry* (Eph. v. 5; Col. iii. 5).

THE SECOND EPISTLE OF

JOHN.

1 THE ᵃelder unto the elect lady and her children, ᵇwhom I love in the truth; and not I only, but also all they that have known
2 'the truth; for the truth's sake, which dwelleth in us, and shall be
3 with us for ever. Grace ¹be with you, mercy, *and* peace, from God the Father, and from the Lord Jesus Christ, the Son of the Father, in truth and love.
4   I rejoiced greatly that I found of thy children ᵈwalking in truth, as
5 we have received a commandment from the Father. And now I beseech thee, lady, ᵉnot as though I wrote a new commandment unto thee, but

A. D 90.

ᵃ 1 Pet 5. 1.
ᵇ 1 John 3. 18.
ᶜ John 8. 32. 2 Thes. 2. 13. 1 Tim 2. 4.
¹ shall be.
ᵈ 3 John 3.
ᵉ 1 John 2 7, 8.

1-13.— ADDRESS — GREETING — THANKSGIVING FOR THE ELECT LADY'S FAITHFULNESS IN THE TRUTH — ENJOINS LOVE — WARNS AGAINST DECEIVERS, LEST WE LOSE OUR REWARD—CONCLUSION.

1. The elder. In a familiar letter John gives himself a less authoritative designation than "apostle:" so 1 Pet. v. 1. **lady.** *Bengel* takes *Kyria* as a proper name; the Hebrew 'Martha.' Being a person of influence, "deceivers" (*v.* 7) were insinuating themselves into her family to seduce her and her children from the faith (*Tirinus*); whence John felt it necessary to write, warning her. (But see 'Introduction,' and 1 Pet. v. 13.) A *church*, probably that at Babylon, was intended. 'Church' is derived from *Kuriake*, akin to *Kuria*; which, among the Romans and Athenians, means *ecclesia*—the term appropriated to *the church assembly.* **love in the truth.** Christian *love* rests on the Christian *truth* (*v.* 3, end). Not merely 'I love *in truth,*' but "I love in THE truth." **all**—all Christians form one fellowship, rejoicing in one another's spiritual prosperity. 'The communion of love is as wide as the communion of faith' (*Alford*). **2. For the truth's sake**—joined with "I love," *v.* 1. 'They who love *in* the truth, also love *on account of* the truth.' **dwelleth in us, and shall be with us for ever**—in consonance with Christ's promise, John xiv. 16, 17. **3. Grace be with you.** So B, Vulgate; but ℵ has 'us' for *you. Lit.*, 'Grace *shall*

be with us;' *i. e.*, with both *you and me*. A prayer, besides a confident affirmation. **Grace . . . mercy . . . peace.** "*Grace*" covers men's sins; "mercy," their *miseries. Grace* must first do away with guilt before misery can be relieved by *mercy.* Therefore *grace* stands before *mercy. Peace* is the result of both; therefore stands third. Casting all our care on the Lord, with thanksgiving, maintains this peace (Phil. iv. 6, 7). **the Lord.** So ℵ; but A B, Vulgate, omit. John never elsewhere uses this title in his epistles, but "the Son of God." **in truth and love**—the element in which alone *grace, mercy*, and *peace* have place. He mentions *truth* in *v.* 4; *love*, in *v.* 5. Paul uses FAITH and *love* (1 Tim. i. 14); for *faith* and *truth* are close akin. **4. I found**—probably in one of his tours of superintendence. See 'Introduction,' and *v.* 12; 3 John 10, 14. **of thy children**—some, in truth; *i. e.*, in *the* Gospel truth. **as**—even as. 'The Father's commandment' is the standard of "the truth." **5. I beseech** [*Erōtō*]—rather (cf. note, 1 John v. 16), 'I request thee,' implying some *authority*. **not . . . new commandment.** It was *old*, in that Christians heard it from the first in the Gospel: *new*, in that love now rests on the new principle of filial imitation of God, who first loved us, and gave Jesus to die for us; and also in that love is now set forth with greater clearness than in the Old Testament. Love fulfils both tables of the Law, and is the end of Law and Gos-

6 that which we had from the beginning, [f] that we love one another. And [g] this is love, that we walk after his commandments. This is the commandment, That, [h] as ye have heard from the beginning, ye should walk in it.

7 For many deceivers are entered into the world, who confess not that Jesus Christ is come in the flesh. This is a deceiver and an antichrist.

8 Look to yourselves, that we lose not those things which we have [2] wrought,

9 but that we receive a full reward. Whosoever transgresseth, and abideth not in the doctrine of Christ, hath not God. He that abideth in the

10 doctrine of Christ, he hath both the Father and the Son. If there come any unto you, and bring not this doctrine, receive him not into *your*

11 house, neither bid him God speed: for he that biddeth him God speed is partaker of his evil deeds.

12 Having many things to write unto you, I would not *write* with paper

A. D. 90.

[f] John 15. 2.
[g] John 14. 15, 21.
Rom. 13. 8.
1 John 5. 3.
[h] 1 John 2. 24.

[2] Or, gained: Some copies read, which ye have gained but that ye receive, etc.

pel alike (cf. note, 1 John ii. 7, 8). **that we.** St. John already had love: he urges her to join him in the same grace. This verse, I think, decides that a *church*, not an *individual lady*, is meant. For a man to urge a woman ("THEE," not *thee and thy children*) that he and she should *love one another*, is hardly apostolic, however pure may be the love enjoined: all is clear 'if the lady' represent a *church*. **6.** 'Love is the fulfilling of the law,' and the fulfilling of the law is the test of love. **This is the commandment**—viz., *love*, in which all other commandments are summed up.

7. As *love* and *truth* go hand in hand (*vv.* 3, 4), he gives warning against teachers of untruth. **For**—reason why he dwelt on *truth*, and on *love*, which manifests itself in keeping God's commandments (*v.* 6). **many**—(1 John ii. 18; iv. 1.) **are entered.** B; but ℵ A, Vulgate, *Irenæus*, 207, read [*exēlthan*], 'are *gone forth*;' viz., from us. **confess not that Jesus . . . in the flesh**—the token of antichrist. **is come** [*erchomenon*]—'coming.' He who denies (as these deceivers did) Christ's *coming* in the flesh, denies the *possibility* of the incarnation; he who denies that He *has* come, denies its *actuality* (Neander). I think 'coming' implies *both* the first and the second advent of Christ. He is often elsewhere called *the Coming One* [*ho erchomenos*] (Matt. xi. 3; Heb. x. 37). The denial of the reality of His incarnation, at His first coming, and of His personal advent again, constitutes antichrist. 'The world *turns away* from Christ, busily intent upon its own husks; but to OPPOSE Christ is of the leaven of Satan' (*Bengel*). **This is a** [*ho*]—'This (such a one as described) is *the* deceiver and *the* antichrist.' The *many* who in a degree fulfil the character, forerun the final antichrist, who shall concentrate in himself all the features of previous antichristian systems. **8. Look to yourselves**—amidst the wide-spread deception, so many being led astray. So Christ's warning, Matt. xxiv. 4, 5, 24. **we lose not . . . we receive.** ℵ A B, Vulgate, read, 'that YE lose not, but that YE receive.' **which we have wrought.** So B. ℵ A, Vulgate, *Irenæus, Lucifer*, read, 'which YE have wrought.' "*We*" being the more difficult reading, is less likely to have been a transcriber's alteration. Look that ye lose not the believing state of "truth and love," which WE (as God's workmen, 2 Cor. vi. 1; 2 Tim. ii. 15) were the instruments of working in you. **a full reward**—of grace, not debt: consummated glory. If 'which YE have wrought' be read, the reward is that of their "work (of faith) and labour of love." There are degrees of heavenly reward proportioned to the capability of receiving heavenly blessedness. Each vessel of glory hanging on Jesus shall be full. But the larger the vessel, the greater will be its capacity for heavenly bliss (Isa. xxii. 24). He who with one pound made ten, received authority over ten cities; he who made five pounds, received five cities: each in proportion to his capacity of rule, and his faithfulness (Luke xix. 15-19; 1 Cor. xv. 41). 'There is no half reward. It is either lost altogether or received *in full: full* communion with God' (*Bengel*). No service of minister or people shall fail of its reward. **9.** The *loss* (*v.* 8) is explained: the *not having God*, which results from *abiding not in the doctrine of Christ.* **transgresseth.** ℵ A B, Vulgate, read [*proagōn* for *parabainōn*], 'every one who *takes the lead:*' sets up as a teacher; lit., *leads on before* (cf. John x. 4; 3 John 9). **hath not God** —(1 John ii. 23; v. 15.) The second "of Christ" is omitted in ℵ A B, Vulgate. he—*He alone*. **10. If there come any**—as a teacher or brother: indicative, not subjunctive: implying that such persons *do actually*, and *are sure to come:* when any comes, as there will. True love is combined with hearty separation from all that is false, whether persons or doctrines. Misbelief destroys faith, the source of love, so love itself: therefore love abhors it as overthrowing Christianity, the centre of love's affection. **receive him not . . . neither bid him God speed.** This is not said of those always aliens from the Church, but of those who wish to be esteemed brethren, and subvert true doctrine (*Grotius*). The greeting forbidden in the case of such is that *usual among Christian brethren:* not a mere formality, but a token of *Christian brotherhood.* **11.** By wishing a false brother *joy* [*chairein*], "God speed," you imply that he is capable of good speed and *joy*, and that you wish him it whilst opposing Christ; so you identify yourself as 'having communion with [*koinōnei*] his evil deeds.' We cannot have communion with saints and with antichrist at once. Here we see John's naturally fiery zeal directed to a right end (Luke ix. 54). *Polycarp*, disciple of John, told contemporaries of *Irenæus*, who narrates it on their authority, that once when John was about to bathe, and heard that Cerinthus, the heretic, was within, he retired with abhorrence, exclaiming, Surely the house will fall in ruins since the enemy of the truth is there!

12. I would not write. A heart full of love pours itself out more freely face to face than by letter. **paper**—of Egyptian papyrus. Pens were then reeds split. **ink**—made of soot and water, thickened with gum. Parchment was used for permanent MSS., in which the epistles were preserved. Writing *tablets* were used merely for temporary purposes, as slates. **face to face**—*lit.,* 'mouth to mouth.' **full** [*pepleromene*]—'filled full.' Your joy will be complete in hearing from

and ink: but I trust to come unto you, and speak ³face to face, that our joy may be full.

13   The children of thy elect sister greet thee.   Amen.

A. D. 90.

³ mouth to mouth.

me in person the joyful Gospel truths which I now defer communicating till I see you. In 1 John i. 4, his writing was for the same purpose.

13. *Alford*, The non-mention of the "lady" herself seems to favour the hypothesis that a *church* is meant.

THE THIRD EPISTLE OF

JOHN.

1 THE elder unto the ᵃwell-beloved Gaius, whom I love ¹in the truth.

2   Beloved, I ²wish above all things that thou mayest prosper and be

3 in health, even as thy soul prospereth.   For I rejoiced greatly when the brethren came and testified of the truth that is in thee, even as ᵇthou

4 walkest in the truth.   I have no greater joy than to hear that my ᶜchil-

5 dren walk in truth.   Beloved, thou ᵈdoest faithfully whatsoever thou

6 doest to the brethren, and to strangers: which have borne witness of thy charity before the church: whom if thou bring forward on their journey

7 ³after a godly sort, thou shalt do well: because that for his name's sake

8 they went forth, ᵉtaking nothing of the Gentiles.   We therefore ought to receive such, that we might be fellow-helpers to the truth.

9   I wrote unto the church : but Diotrephes, who loveth to have the pre-

A. D. 60.

ᵃ Acts 19. 29.
Acts 20. 4.
Rom. 16.23.
1 Cor. 1. 14.
1 Or. truly.
² Or, pr y.
ᵇ 2 John ¹.
ᶜ 1 Cor 4. 15.
Phile. 10.
ᵈ Luke 2.42.
³ worthy of God
ᵉ 1 Cor. 9. 1 ,
15.

1-14.—ADDRESS—WISH FOR GAIUS' PROSPERITY —JOY AT HIS WALKING IN THE TRUTH—HOSPI-TALITY TO THE BRETHREN AND STRANGERS, THE FRUIT OF LOVE—DIOTREPHES' OPPOSITION AND AMBITION—PRAISE OF DEMETRIUS—CONCLUSION. **1. I**—*I* personally, for my part.   On Gaius, or Caius, see 'Introduction.' **love in the truth**—(2 John 1.)   "Beloved" is repeated often, indicating strong affection (*vv.* 1, 2, 5, 11). **2. above all things** [*peri*] — '*concerning* all things.' *Alford, in all respects. Wahl* justifies the English version (cf. 1 Pet. iv. 8).   Since his *soul's prosperity* is presupposed, "above all things" does not imply that John wishes Gaius' bodily prosper-ity above that of his soul, but as the *first* object to be desired *next after spiritual health.*   I know you are prospering in your soul.   I wish you similar prosperity in your body.   Perhaps John had heard from the brethren (*v.* 3) that Caius was in bad health, and was tried in other ways (*v.* 10), to which the wish refers.   **prosper**—in general.   **be in health**—in particular.   **3. testified of the truth that is in thee**—'to thy truth:' thy share of that truth in which thou walkest (*Alford*).   **even as** thou—in contrast to Diotrephes (*v.* 9).   **4. my children**—members of the Church: confirming the view that the *elect lady* (2 John 1) is a church. **5. faithfully**—an act becoming a faithful man. **whatsoever thou doest** [*ergazē*]—distinct from the former [*poieis*] ."doest."   Translate, 'workest :' whatsoever work of love thou dost perform.   So Matt. xxvi. 10.   **and to strangers.**   A ℵ B C have [*touto* for *eis tous*], 'and that (*i. e.*, and those brethren) strangers.'   The fact of the brethren whom thou didst entertain being "strangers" en-hances the love manifested in the act.   This favours Gaius of Corinth (Rom. xvi. 23) being the

Gaius of this epistle.   **6. borne witness of thy charity before** (in the presence of) **the church**—to stimulate others by the good example.   The brethren so entertained by Caius were missionary evangelists (*v.* 7).   Probably, in narrating their missionary labours "before the church" where John was, they incidentally mentioned the loving hospitality of Caius.   **bring forward on their journey**—'if thou (*continue to*) forward on their journey,' by giving them provisions for the way. **after a godly sort** [*axiōs Theou*]—'in a manner worthy of God,' whose ambassadors they are, and whose servant thou art.   He who honours God's missionaries (*v.* 7), honours God.   **7. his name's sake** — Christ's.   **went forth** — as missionaries. **taking nothing**—refusing to *receive* aught as pay, or maintenance, though justly entitled to it : as Paul at Corinth and at Thessalonica (1 Cor. ix. 12, 15 ; 1 Thess. ii. 6, 9).   **Gentiles.**   As Caius was a *Gentile* convert, "the Gentiles" must mean the *converts just made from the heathen*, the Gentiles to whom they had *gone forth*.   It would have been inexpedient to have taken aught [*meden* implies, not that they *got* nothing, though they desired it ; but, of *their own choice*, they *took nothing* from the infant Gentile churches]: the case was different in receiving hospitality from Caius.   **8. We**—in contradistinction to "the Gentiles" (*v.* 7).   **there-fore**—as they take nothing from the Gentiles **receive.**   ℵ A B C read, 'take up.'   As they *take* nothing from the Gentiles, we ought to *take up* their support.   **fellow-helpers**—with them.   **to the truth**—i. e., *to promote* the truth. **9. I wrote.**   ℵ A B add [*ti*], 'something :' *a com-munication*, probably as to *receiving the brethren* with brotherly love (*vv.* 8, 10).   That epistle was not designed by the Spirit for the universal

10 eminence among them, receiveth us not. Wherefore, if I come, I will remember his deeds which he doeth, prating against us with malicious words; and not content therewith, neither doth he himself receive the brethren, and forbiddeth them that would, and casteth *them* out of the
11 church. Beloved, *f* follow not that which is evil, but that which is good. *g* He that doeth good is of God: but he that doeth evil hath not seen God.
12 Demetrius *h* hath good report of all *men*, and of the truth itself: yea, and we *also* bear record; *i* and ye know that our record is true.
13 I had many things to write, but I will not with ink and pen write
14 unto thee: but I trust I shall shortly see thee, and we shall speak ⁴ face to face. Peace *be* to thee. *Our* friends salute thee. Greet the friends by name.

A D 90.
f Ex. 23. 3.
Ps. :7. 27.
Isa. 1. 16. 17.
John *'*0 27.
1 Cor. 4. 16.
1 Cor. 11. 1.
g 1 John 2. 29.
1 John 3. 6.
h 1 Thes. 4. 12.
1 Tim 3 7.
i John :1 21.
4 mouth to mouth.

Church, else it would have been preserved. **unto the church**—to which Caius belongs. **loveth . . . pre-eminence**—through ambition. Evidently occupying a high place in that church: a Judaizer, and so opposed to the missionaries who preached the doctrines of grace to the Gentiles (*v.* 10). **among them**—*over* the members. **receiveth us not**—virtually, by not *receiving* with love the brethren whom he recommended (cf. Matt. x. 40). **10. if I come**—(*v.* 14.) **I will remember** [*hupomneso*]—'I will bring to mind' before all, by stigmatizing and punishing. **prating** — with silly tattle. **neither doth he himself receive the brethren** — with hospitality: the missionaries. **forbiddeth them that would** — receive them. **casteth them**—those that would receive the brethren, by excommunication from the Church, which his influence (*v.* 9) in it enabled him to do. *Neander* thinks that the missionaries were JEWS; whence it is said in their praise they *took nothing from* THE GENTILES: in contrast to other Jewish missionaries who abused ministers' rights of maintenance elsewhere (2 Cor. xi. 22; Phil. iii. 2, 5, 19). In the Gentile churches there existed an ultra-Pauline party of anti-Jewish tendency, forerunners of Marcion. Diotrephes stood at the head of this party, which, as well as his domineering spirit, may account for his hostility to the missionaries, and to the apostle John, who had, by love, tried to harmonize the various elements in the Asiatic churches. At a later period Marcion,

we know, attached himself to Paul alone, and paid no deference to John's authority. **11. follow not that which is evil**—as Diotrephes. **but . . . good**—as Demetrius (*v.* 12). **is of God**—born of God, who is good. **hath not seen God**—spiritually. **12. Demetrius**—a hospitable presbyter in the place; or else one of the missionary strangers who bore the letter. **of all men**—who have opportunity of knowing his character. **of the truth itself.** The Gospel standard of *truth* witnesses that he walks conformably to it, in real love, hospitality to the brethren (in contrast to Diotrephes), &c. Cf. John iii. 21. **we also**—besides the testimony of "all men," and of "the truth itself." **ye know.** אABC*d*, Vulgate, read, 'thou knowest.' **13. I will not** [*thelo*]—'I *wish* not . . . to write' more. **14. face to face**—'mouth to mouth.' **Peace** —inward of conscience; fraternal of friendship; supernal of glory (*Lyra*). **friends.** Seldom in the New Testament, as it is absorbed in the higher title, 'brother, brethren.' Still, Christ recognizes the relation of *friend* (John xv. 13-15; Jas. ii. 23), based on the highest grounds—obedience from love, entailing the highest privileges—admission to the intimacy of the holy God and sympathizing Saviour: so Christians have "friends" in Christ. In a friendly letter, mention of "friends" appropriately occurs. **by name**—no less than if their names were written (*Bengel*).

THE GENERAL EPISTLE OF

JUDE.

1 JUDE, the servant of Jesus Christ, *a* and brother of James, to them that are sanctified by God the Father, and *b* preserved in Jesus Christ, *and*
2 called : Mercy unto you, and peace, and love, be multiplied.

A. D 66.
a Luke 6. 16.
b John 17. 11.

1-25.—ADDRESS—GREETING—OBJECT IN WRITING—WARNING AGAINST SEDUCERS IN DOCTRINE AND PRACTICE FROM GOD'S VENGEANCE ON APOSTATES, ISRAEL, THE FALLEN ANGELS, SODOM—DESCRIPTION OF THESE BAD MEN, IN CONTRAST TO MICHAEL—LIKE CAIN, BALAAM, AND CORE—ENOCH'S PROPHECY AS TO THEM—THE APOSTLES' FOREWARNING — CONCLUDING EXHORTATION TO PRESERVE THEIR OWN FAITH, AND TRY TO SAVE OTHERS—DOXOLOGY.

1. servant of Jesus Christ—as His minister and apostle. **brother of James**—more widely known as bishop of Jerusalem and "brother of the Lord" (*i. e.*, either *cousin*, or stepbrother, being son of Joseph by a former marriage. Ancient traditions universally agree that Mary, Jesus' mother, continued perpetually a virgin). Jude therefore calls himself modestly "brother of James." See 'Introduction.' **to them . . . sanctified by** (*in*) **God the Father.** A B א, Vulgate, *Origen*, *Lucifer*, read

3   Beloved, when I gave all diligence to write unto you *c* of the common salvation, it was needful for me to write unto you, and exhort *you* that ye should earnestly contend for the faith which was once delivered unto
4 the saints. For there are certain men crept in unawares, *d* who were before of old ordained to this condemnation, ungodly men, turning *e* the grace of our God into lasciviousness, and *j* denying the only Lord God, and our Lord Jesus Christ.
5   I will therefore put you in remembrance, though ye once knew this, how that the Lord, having saved the people out of the land of Egypt,
6 afterward *g* destroyed them that believed not. And *h* the angels which kept not their *i* first estate, but left their own habitation, he hath reserved

A. D. 66.

c Tit. i. 4.
d Rom 9 2.
   1 Pet 2. 5.
e Tit. 2. 11.
j 2 Pet. 2. 1.
   1 John 2
   22.
g Num 14.29
h Matt 8. 29.
   John 8. 44.
   2 Pet 2. 4.
i Or, p inci-
   pality

[*ĕgapēmenois*], 'beloved,' for *sanctified*. If the English version be read, cf. Col. i. 12; 1 Pet. i. 2. [*En.*] Not "by," but 'in.' The Father's *love* is the element IN which they are 'beloved.' The conclusion, *v.* 21, corresponds: "Keep yourselves *in* the love of God" (cf. 2 Thess. ii. 13). **preserved in**—'kept.' Not "in," but as *Greek*, 'FOR Jesus Christ.' 'Kept *continually*' (so the *perfect* means) 'by God the Father for Jesus Christ,' against the day of His coming. Jude, beforehand, mentions the source and guarantee for the final accomplishment of believers' salvation, lest they should be disheartened by the evils which he announces (*Bengel*). **and called**—predicated of 'them that are beloved in God the Father, and preserved for Jesus Christ: who are called.' God's effectual *calling*, in exercise of His Divine prerogative, guarantees their eternal safety. **2.** Mercy—in a time of wretchedness. Therefore *mercy* stands first: of *Christ* (*v.* 21). **peace**—in the *Holy Ghost* (*v.* 20). **love**—of *God* (*v.* 21). The three answer to the Trinity. **be multiplied**—in and towards you. **3.** Design .of the epistle (cf. *vv.* 20, 21). **all diligence**—(2 Pet. i. 5.) As the minister is to give *all diligence* to admonish, so the people should give *all diligence* to have all Christian graces, and make their calling sure. **the common salvation**—wrought by Christ. Note, "LIKE precious faith," 2 Pet. i. 1. This *community* of *faith*, and of its object, *salvation*, forms the ground of appeals to common hopes and fears. **it was needful for me** [*ananken eschon grapsai*]—'I felt it necessary to write (*at once*: aorist: the preceding *present* infinitive, "to write" [*graphein*], expresses *writing* generally), exhorting you.' The reason why he felt it necessary 'to write *with exhortation*,' he states, *v.* 4, "For there are certain men crept in," &c. Having intended to write generally of *the common salvation*, he found it necessary, from existing evils, to write specially, that they should *contend for the faith against* those evils. **earnestly contend**—(cf. Phil. i. 27.) *once* [*hapax*]—'*once for all* delivered,' &c. No other faith is to supersede it. A strong argument for resisting heretical innovators (*v.* 4). Believers, like Nehemiah's workmen, with one hand "build themselves up in their most holy faith," with the other "contend earnestly for the faith" against its foes. **the saints**—all Christians, *holy*, *i. e.*, consecrated to God, by their calling, in God's design. **4.** certain men—disparagement. **crept in unawares**—stealthily, (note, 2 Pet. ii. 1, "*privily*," &c.) **before . . ordained**—'fore-written;' viz., in Peter's prophecy (*vv.* 17, 18), and in Paul's (1 Tim. iv. 1; 2 Tim. iii. 1), and by implication in the judgments upon apostate angels, the disobedient Israelites, Sodom and Gomorrha, Balaam and Core—all *written* "for an example" (*vv.* 7 and 5, 6, 11). God's eternal character as Punisher of sin, set forth in Scripture "of old," is the ground on which such apostate characters are ordained to condemnation. Scrip-

ture reflects God's "book of life" in which believers are "written among the living" (Isa. iv. 3; Phil. iv. 3). 'Fore-written' is applied also, in Rom. xv. 4, to the things in Scripture. Scripture mirrors forth God's character from everlasting—the ground of His decrees from everlasting. *Bengel* makes it abbreviated for, 'They were *of old foretold* by Enoch (*v.* 14, who did not write), and afterwards noted by the *written* Word.' **to this condemnation.** Jude graphically puts their judgment before the eyes, "THIS." Enoch's prophecy comprises the "ungodly" of the last days before Christ's second coming, as well as their forerunners, the "ungodly men" before the flood—the type of the last judgment (Matt. xxiv. 37-39; 2 Pet. iii. 3-7). The disposition and the doom of both correspond. **the grace of our God**—a phrase for the Gospel, especially sweet to believers who appropriate God in Christ as "*our* God;" so rendering the more odious the perversity of those who turn Gospel grace into a ground of licentiousness, as if exemption from the law gave a license to sin. **denying the only Lord God.** א A B C omit "God." [*Ton monon despoten, kai Kurion*, 'the only Master;' here, *Jesus Christ*, who is at once '*Master*' and 'Lord.'] So 2 Pet. ii. 1, note. By virtue of Christ's oneness with the Father, He also is termed "the ONLY" God and 'MASTER.' 'Master' implies God's *absolute ownership*, to dispose of His creatures as He likes. **5.** (Heb. iii. 16—iv. 13.) **therefore.** [*Oun*, C, *Lucifer*; but A B, Vulgate, read, 'but:' in contrast to the ungodly, *v.* 4.] **though ye once** —'I wish to remind you, *as knowing* ALL (viz., *that I am referring to*. So א A B, Vulgate, Coptic) *once for all*' [*hapax*]. *As* already they know all the facts, he needs only to 'remind' them. **the Lord.** So א ; but A B, Vulgate, read, 'Jesus,' the true Joshua, *God-Saviour*. So "Christ" (1 Cor. x. 4) accompanied the Israelites in the wilderness: "Jesus" is one with the Divine angel of the covenant (Exod. xxiii. 20-23; xxxii. 34; xxxiii. 2, 14), the God of the Israelite theocracy. **saved**—brought into a state of safety. **afterward** [*to deuteron*]—'secondly, destroyed them that believed not:' contrasted with His *in the first instance* having *saved* them (cf. 1 Cor. ix. 26, 27). **6.** (2 Pet. ii. 4.) **kept not their first estate.** Vulgate [*heauton archen*], 'their own *principality*,' which the fact of angels being elsewhere called "principalities" favours: 'their own' implies that, not content with the *dignity* once for all assigned to them under the Son of God, they aspired higher. *Alford* thinks Gen. vi. 2 is alluded to; not the fall of the devil and his angels, as he thinks "giving themselves over to fornication" (*v.* 7) proves. [Cf. *ton homoion tropon toutois*, 'in like manner *to these*'—viz., to the angels (*v.* 6).] It is more natural to take "sons of God" (Gen. vi. 2) of the Sethites, than of angels, who, as 'spirits,' do not

in everlasting chains, under darkness, *unto the judgment of the great
7 day.   Even as *Sodom and Gomorrha, and the cities about them, in like
manner giving themselves over to fornication, and going after ²strange
flesh, are set forth for an example, suffering the vengeance of eternal
fire.
8   Likewise also these *filthy* dreamers defile the flesh, despise dominiun,
9 and *speak evil of dignities.   Yet *Michael the archangel, when contending with the devil, he disputed about the *body of Moses, *durst

A. D. (6.
* Rev. ：0 10.
j Gen 19. 24.
   Deut. 29.23.
₂ other
   Rom. 1. 27.
* Ex. 2. 28.
i Dan. 10. 13.
ᵐ Deut. 34. 6.
ⁿ 2 Pet 2. 11.

seem capable of carnal connection. The parallel,
2 Pet. ii. 4, plainly refers to the fall of the apostate
angels. 'In like manner *to these*,' *v.* 7, refers to
the inhabitants of Sodom and Gomorrha, "the
cities about them" sinning "in like manner" as
they did (*Estius*). Even if 'these,' *v.* 7, refer to
the angels, 'in like manner as these' will mean,
not that the angels carnally *fornicated* with the
daughters of men, but that their ambition, whereby
their affections went *away from* God and they fell,
is a sin of like kind spiritually as Sodom's going
away from God's order of nature after strange
flesh; the sin of the apostate angels after their kind
is analogous to that of the Sodomites after their
kind. Cf. the somewhat similar connection of
whoremongers and *covetousness* (Eph. v. 5). The
apocryphal book of Enoch interprets Gen. vi. 2,
as *Alford*. But though Jude accords with it in
some particulars, it does not follow that he
accords with it in all. The Hebrews name the
fallen angels Aza and Azael. **left**—of their own
accord. **their own** [*to idion*]—'their proper.'
habitation—Heaven, all bright and glorious, opposed to the "*darkness*" to which they now are
doomed. Their ambitious designs seem to have
had a peculiar connection with this earth, of
which Satan before his fall was probably God's
vicegerent: whence arises his subsequent connection with it as, first, the Tempter, then "the prince
of this world." **reserved.** As there is evident
reference to *their* having "*kept not* their first
estate," translate, 'He hath *kept*' [the same Greek,
tetereken]. Retributive justice. He hath kept
them *in His purpose:* that is their sure doom. As
yet, Satan and his demons roam at large on the
earth. An earnest of their doom is their having
been cast out of heaven; already restricted to
'the darkness of this present world,' the 'air'
that surrounds the earth, their peculiar element.
They lurk in places of gloom, looking forward with
agonizing fear to their final torment in the bottomless pit. Not literal chains and darkness, but
figurative in this present world, where, with restricted powers and liberties, shut out from
heaven, they, like condemned prisoners, await
their doom. Even now, as chained dogs, they
can go no farther than the length of their chain.
everlasting. [Lest any doubt whether *aionios*
mean 'eternal,' here *aidios*, from *aei*, always is
used, which can only mean *everlasting*.] 7. **Even
as** [*ôs*] *Alford*, '(I wish to remind you, *v.* 5)
that,' &c. **Sodom**, &c.—(2 Pet. ii. 6.) **giving
themselves over to fornication**—*extraordinarily;*
i. e., *out* of the order of nature [*ekporneusasai*].
On 'in like manner *to them*,' cf. note, *v.* 6. Cf.,
on spiritual fornication, Ps. lxxiii. 27, end. **going
after strange flesh** [*apelthousai*]—*departing from*
the course of nature, and *going after* that which
is unnatural. In later times most enlightened
heathens indulged in the sin of Sodom without
compunction. **are set forth**—be ore our eyes.
suffering—*to this present time lying under* the ashes
of volcanic fires at the Dead sea. **the vengeance**
[*diken*]—'righteous retribution.' **eternal fire**—the
lasting marks of the fire that consumed the cities

irreparably is a type of *the eternal fire* to which
the inhabitants have been consigned. *Bengel*
translates, '*Suffering (the) punishment* (which they
endure) as a *sample of the eternal fire* which shall
consume the wicked.' Ezek. xvi. 53-55, shows
that Sodom's punishment, as a nation, is *not eternal.*
   8. **also** [*homiōs mentoi*]—'in like manner nevertheless' (notwithstanding these warning examples)
(*Alford*). **these filthy dreamers.** The Greek has
not "*filthy.*" The clause, 'these men in their
dreamings' belongs to all the verbs, "defile," &c.;
"despise," &c.; "speak evil," &c. All sinners are
spiritually asleep; their carnal activity is as it
were a *dream* (1 Thess. v. 6, 7). Their *speaking
evil of dignities* is because they are *dreaming*, and
know not what they are speaking evil of (*v.* 10). 'As
a man dreaming thinks he is seeing and hearing
many things, so the natural man's lusts are
agitated by joy, distress, fear, and other passions.
But he knows not self-command. Hence, though
he bring into play all the powers of reason, he
cannot conceive the true liberty which the sons of
light, who are awake and in the daylight, enjoy'
(*Bengel*). **defile the flesh**—(*v.* 7.) **dominion**—
'lordship.' **dignities**—'glories.' Earthly and
heavenly. 9. **Michael the archangel**—nowhere
in Scripture plural, 'archangels;' but ONE,
"archangel." The only other New Testament
passage where it occurs is 1 Thess. iv. 16, where
Christ is distinguished from the archangel, with
whose voice He shall descend to raise the dead:
therefore Christ is not Michael. The name means,
Who is like God. In Dan. x. 13, he is called "One
(margin, *the first*) of the chief princes." He is
champion of Israel. In Rev. xii. 7, the conflict
between Michael and Satan is again alluded to,
disputed [*diakrinomenos*]—*debated in controversy*.
shows it was a judicial contest. **about the body of
Moses**—his literal body. Satan, having the power
of death, opposed the raising of it again (or else its
being kept from corruption: cf. Deut. xxxiv. 6), on
the ground of Moses' sin at Meribah, and his murder of the Egyptian. That Moses' body was raised,
appears from his presence with Elijah and Jesus
(who were in the body) at the transfiguration: the
sample and earnest of the coming resurrection-
kingdom, to be ushered in by Michael's standing
up for God's people (Dan. xii. 1, 2). Thus in each
dispensation a pledge of the future resurrection
was given: Enoch in the patriarchal dispensation,
Moses in the Levitical, Elijah in the prophetical,
Jesus, the first-fruits, in the Christian. It is noteworthy that the same rebuke was used by the
Angel of the Lord, or Jehovah the Second Person,
in pleading for Joshua, the representative of the
Jewish church, against Satan, in Zech. iii. 2;
whence some think that also here "the body of
Moses" means the Jewish church accused by
Satan, before God, for its filthiness; on which
ground he demands that Divine justice should
take its course against Israel, but is rebuked by
the Lord, who has 'chosen Jerusalem:' thus, as
"the body of Christ" is *the Christian church*, so
"**the body of Moses**" is the Jewish church. But

not bring against him a railing accusation, but said, °The Lord rebuke

10 thee. But these speak evil of those things which they know not: but what they know naturally, as brute beasts, in those things they corrupt

11 themselves. Woe unto them! for they have gone in the way *P*of Cain, and *q*ran greedily after the error of Balaam for reward, and perished *r* in the gainsaying of Core.

12 These are spots in your *s*feasts of charity, when they feast with you, feeding themselves without fear: clouds *they are* without water, carried about *t*of winds; trees whose fruit withereth, without fruit, twice dead,

13 plucked up by the roots; raging *u*waves of the sea, foaming out their own shame; wandering stars, to whom is reserved the blackness of darkness for ever.

14 And Enoch also, *v*the seventh from Adam, prophesied of these, saying,

A.D 6.

° 1 Chr. 12. 17.
Isa 37. 3. 4.
Zech 3 2.
P Gen 4. 5.
1 John 3. 12.
q Num. 22. 7.
Num. 31. 6.
Deut. 23. 4.
Josh 24. 9.
2 Pet 2. 15.
r Num 16. 1.
s 1 Cor 11 21.
t Eph. 4. 14.
u Isa. 57. 20.
v Gen 5. 18.

---

the literal body is here meant (though, secondarily, the Jewish church is typified by Moses' body, as it was there represented by Joshua the High Priest); and Michael, whose connection is so close with Jehovah-Messiah, and with Israel, naturally uses the same language as his Lord. As Satan (*adversary* in court) or the Devil (*accuser*) accuses the Church collectively, and 'the brethren' individually, so Christ pleads for us as our Advocate (1 John ii. 1). Israel's, and all believers' full justification, and the accuser's being 'rebuked' finally, is yet future. *Josephus* ('Antiquities,' iv., 8) states that God hid Moses' body, lest, if exposed to view, it should have been idolized. Jude adopts this account from the apocryphal 'assumption of Moses' (as *Origen, concerning* 'Principalities,' iii., 2, thinks), or else from the ancient tradition on which that work was founded. Jude, as inspired, could distinguish how much of the tradition was true, how much false. *We* have no such means of distinguishing, therefore can be sure of no tradition, save that which is in the *written Word.* **durst not**—from reverence for Satan's former *dignity* (v. 8). **railing accusation** [*krisin blasphemias*]—'judgment of blasphemy,' *evil speaking.* Peter said, angels do not, to avenge themselves, rail at dignities, though ungodly, when they have to contend with them: Jude says, that the archangel Michael himself did not rail even when he fought with the Devil, the prince of evil spirits—not from fear of him, but reverence of God, whose delegated power in this world Satan once had, and even in some degree still has. **10.** (2 Pet. ii. 12.) **those things which** [*hosa*]—'*as many things soever* as they *understand not*,' viz., things of the spiritual world. **but what they know naturally.** Connect, 'as many things as naturally (by blind instinct) as the unreasoning [*aloga*] animals, they know,' &c. The former "know" [*oidasin*] implies deeper knowledge; the latter "know" [*epistantai*], perception by the 'animal senses and faculties.' **11. Woe.** Note, 2 Pet. ii. 14, "*cursed* children." **Cain**—the murderer: the root of whose sin was hatred and envy of the godly; the sin of these seducers. **ran greedily** [*exechuthesan*]—'have been poured forth' like a torrent bursting its banks. Reckless of the cost, the loss of God's favour and heaven, on they rush after gain like Balaam. **perished in the gainsaying of Core**—(note, v. 12.) In reading of Korah perishing by gainsaying, we read also of these perishing through the same: for the same seed bears the same harvest.

12. spots. So 2 Pet. ii. 13 [*spiloi*; here, *spilades*], which, in secular writers, means *rocks*, viz., on which the Christian *love-feasts* were in danger of shipwreck]. A B C read [*hoi*] emphatically, 'THE rocks.' The reference to "clouds ... winds ...

waves," accords with *rocks.* Vulgate, misled by the similar word, translates, "spots." Cf., however, v. 23, which favours the English version. A C, to make Jude say the same as Peter, read, 'deceivings' [*apatais*] for 'love-feasts' [*agapais*]; but א B, Vulgate, support 'love-feasts.' The love-feast accompanied the Lord's Supper (1 Cor. xi., end). Korah the Levite, not satisfied with his *ministry*, aspired to the *sacrificing priesthood* also: so ministers in the Lord's Supper, seeking to make it a *sacrifice*, and themselves *sacrificing* priests, usurp the function of our only Christian sacerdotal *Priest*, Christ Jesus. Let them beware of Korah's doom! **feeding themselves** [*poimainontes*]—'pasturing themselves.' What they look to is *tending themselves*, not the flock: they are 'pastors,' but it is to "themselves." **without fear.** Join, not as the English version, but with 'feast.' Sacred feasts especially ought to be celebrated *with fear.* Feasting is not faulty in itself (*Bengel*), but needs to be accompanied with *fear* of forgetting God, as Job (ch. i. 5) in his sons' feasts. **clouds**—from which one would expect refreshing rain; but "without water" (2 Pet. ii. 17): professors without practice. **carried about.** So Vulgate, probably from Eph. iv. 14; but א A B C [*parapheromenai*], 'carried aside;' *i. e.*, out of the right course. **trees whose fruit withereth** [*phthinoporina*]—'trees of the late (*waning*) autumn,' viz., when there are no longer leaves or fruits on the trees (*Bengel*), &c. **without fruit**—*without good fruit* of knowledge and practice; sometimes what is positively *bad.* **twice dead**—first, when they cast their leaves in autumn, and seem dead during winter *dead*, but revive again in spring; secondly, when they are "plucked up by the roots." So these apostates, once dead in unbelief, then, in respect to profession, raised from the death of sin to the life of righteousness, but now having become *dead again* by apostasy, so *hopelessly dead.* A climax. Not only *without leaves*, like *trees* in late autumn, but *without fruit;* not only so, but *dead twice;* to crown all, "plucked up by the roots." **13. Raging**—wild. Jude has in mind Isa. lvii. 20. **shame** [*aischunas*]—plural, 'shames' (cf. Phil. iii. 19). **wandering stars**—instead of moving on in a regular orbit, as lights to the world, bursting forth like erratic comets, or rather fiery meteors, with a strange glare, then doomed to fall back again into black gloom.

14. See 'Introduction,' on the source whence Jude derived this prophecy. The Holy Spirit, by Jude, sealed the truth of this much of the matter in the book of Enoch, though probably that book, as well as Jude, derived it from tradition (cf. note, v. 9). So facts unrecorded in the Old Testament are referred to by St. Paul, 2 Tim. iii. 8; Gal. iii. 19; Heb. xi. 24. There are

15 Behold, the ^wLord cometh with ten thousand of his saints, to execute judgment upon all, and to convince all that are ungody among them of all their ungodly deeds which they have ungodly committed, and of all their hard *speeches* which ungodly sinners have spoken against him.

16 These are murmurers, complainers, walking after their own lusts; and their mouth speaketh great swelling *words*, having ^xmen's persons in admiration because of advantage.

17 But, beloved, remember ye the words which were spoken before of the

18 apostles of our Lord Jesus Christ; how that they told you there should be mockers in the last time, who should walk after their own ungodly lusts.

19 These be they ^ywho separate themselves, sensual, having not the Spirit.

A. D 66.

^w Deut. 33. 2.
Dan. 7. 10.
Zech. 14. 5.
Matt. 25. 31.
Heb. 11. 5.
Rev. 1. 7.
^x Pro. 28. 21.
Jas. 2. 1, 9.
^y Pro. 18. 1.
Eze. 14. 7.
Hos 4. 14.
Hos. 9. 10.
Heb. 10. 25.

reasons for thinking the book of Enoch, in the form now extant, copied from Jude, rather than *vice versâ*. From the first, prophecy hastened towards its consummation. The earliest prophecies of the Redeemer dwell on His second coming in glory, rather than His first coming in lowliness (cf. Gen. iii. 15, with Rom. xvi. 20). Enoch, in his translation without death, illustrated that which he all his life preached to the unbelieving world—the Lord's certain coming, and the resurrection of the dead—as the antidote to their sceptical, self-wise confidence in nature's permanence. **And** [*de kai*]—'Moreover, also Enoch,' &c. **seventh from Adam.** Jude intimates the earliness of the prophecy. In Enoch, freedom from death and the sacred number are combined; for every seventh object is most valued. Note, "of old," *v.* 4. There were only *five* fathers between Enoch and Adam. The *seventh* from Adam prophesied the things which shall close the *seventh age* of the world (*Bengel*). **of these**—in relation to these. His reference was not to the antediluvians alone, but to *all* the ungodly (*v.* 15). His prophecy applied primarily to the flood, ultimately to the final judgment. **cometh** [*ēlthen*]—'came.' Prophecy regards the future as certain as if *past*. Many harmonize with this the distinct statement that the Lord shall come, and His *elect* be caught up to meet Him *in the air* (1 Thess. iv. 17), by supposing that His coming in the air to take (Zeph. ii. 3) them out of the last tribulation shall precede by some interval His coming *with them* to Mount Olivet (Zech. xiv. 45; Rev. xix. 14) to save *the elect Jews*. Cf. Isa. xxvi. 20; lxi. 3; John xiv. 3; Rev. iii. 10. Still, the saints must be for a time in the little horn's hands (Dan. vii. 25-27); but the little horn may be Rome; not the last antichrist. Matt. xxiv. 22-24, 31, refers to the elect *Jews* (the looking for "Christ" only can apply to the *Jews*, not to the Gentiles, Jer. xxx. 7). The Jews, like Noah in the deluge, shall be in the tribulation, but saved out of it (Isa. lv. 9). The elect Church, like Enoch, shall be caught up and transfigured *before* the tribulation (2 Cor. iv. 14; 1 Thess. v. 9; especially Luke xxi. 28, 35, 36). The warning to *all on the face of the whole earth* to *watch*, for the day is coming "as a snare," would be hardly appropriate, if the Jews' reception of antichrist were to precede the coming; for then the coming day would be *announced* by the precursory antichrist. **saints**—holy angels (cf. Deut. xxxii. 2; Dan. vii. 10; Zech. xiv. 5; Matt. xxv. 31). **15.** Enoch's prophecy is in Hebrew poetic parallelism, the oldest specimen extant. Some think Lamech's speech, which is in poetic parallelism, was composed in mockery of Enoch's; as Enoch foretold Jehovah's coming to judgment, so Lamech presumes on impunity in polygamy and murder (as Cain the murderer seemed to escape). **convince**—convict. **hard**

speeches—noticed in *vv.* 8, 10, 16; Mal. iii. 13, 14: contrast 16, 17. **ungodly sinners**—not merely *sinners*, but [*asebeis*] *despisers of God: impious.* **against him.** They who speak against God's children speak *against* God *Himself*. **16.** **murmurers**—*muttering murmurs* against God's ordinances and ministers in church and state. Cf. *v.* 8, 15. **complainers**—never satisfied with their lot (Num. xi. 1: cf. the penalty, Deut. xxviii. 47, 48). **walking after their own lusts**—(*v.* 18.) The secret of *murmuring* and *complaining* is the restless insatiability of desires. **great swelling words** —(2 Pet. ii. 18.) **men's persons**—mere outward rank. **because of advantage**—for the sake of what they gain from them. Whilst they *talk great swelling words*, they are really mean and fawning towards those of wealth.

17. But, beloved—in contrast to those reprobates, *v.* 20, again. **remember.** His readers had been contemporaries of the apostles: for Peter uses the same formula in reminding the contemporaries of himself and the other apostles. **spoken before**—already before now. **the apostles**—Peter (notes, 2 Pet. iii. 2, 3), and Paul before Peter (Acts xx. 29; 1 Tim. iv. 1; 2 Tim. iii. 1). Jude includes himself among *the apostles*; for in *v.* 18 he says, "they told **you**," not *us* [*elagon*], 'used to tell you.' Jude's readers were contemporaries of the apostles who *used to tell* them. **18. mockers.** In 2 Pet. iii. 3 [*empaiktai*, the same Greek], 'scoffers:' nowhere else in the New Testament. 2 Pet. iii. 2, 3 is referred to: for Jude quotes the very words of *Peter* as those which *the apostles* used to speak to his (Jude's) readers. **walk after their own ungodly lusts**— *lit.*, 'according to their own lusts *of ungodlinesses*.' **19. These be they**—showing their characters are such as Peter and Paul foretold. **separate themselves**—from church communion *in its vital reality;* outwardly they took part in church ordinances (*v.* 12). א A, Vulgate, omit "themselves;" then "separate" means cast-out members of the church by excommunication (Isa. lxv. 5; lxvi. 5; Luke vi. 22; John ix. 34; 3 John 10). Or else understand "themselves;" which is read in B C. Arrogant setting up of themselves, as having peculiar sanctity, wisdom, and doctrine. **sensual** [*psuchikoi*]—'animal-souled,' opposed to *spiritual*, 'having the spirit;' translated "the *natural* man," 1 Cor. ii. 14. In man's threefold nature—*body, soul, and spirit*—the due state in God's design is, that "the spirit," the recipient of the Holy Spirit uniting man to God, should be first, and should rule the soul, which stands intermediate between *the body* and *spirit;* but in the *animal*, or *natural* man, the spirit is subservient to the animal-soul, which is earthly in its aims. The 'carnal' sink lower; for in these *the flesh*, the lowest and corrupt element of man's bodily nature, reigns paramount. **having not the Spirit.** In the animal or natural man, *the spirit, his*

653

20 But ye, beloved, *building up yourselves on your most holy faith,
21 praying *a* in the Holy Ghost, keep yourselves in the love of God, looking
22 for the mercy of our Lord Jesus Christ unto eternal life. And of some
23 have compassion, making a difference: and others *b* save with fear, *c* pulling *them* out of the fire; hating even the *d* garment spotted by the flesh.
24 Now *e* unto him that is able to keep you from falling, and *f* to present
25 *you* faultless before the presence of his glory with exceeding joy, to *g* the only wise God our Saviour, *be* glory and majesty, dominion and power, both now and ever. Amen.

A. D. 66.
a Col 2. 7.
1 Tim. 1. 4.
a Rom 8. 26.
Eph. 6. 18.
b Rom. 11.14.
1 Tim 4.16.
c Amos 4. 11.
d Zech. 3. 4,
5
e Eph. 3. 20.
f Col. 1. 22.
g 1 Tim. 1. 17.

higher part, which ought to be the seat of the Holy Spirit, is not so; therefore, his spirit not being in its normal state, he is said *not to have the spirit* (cf. John iii. 5, 6). In completed redemption the parts of redeemed man shall be in their due relation; in the ungodly, *the soul,* severed from *the spirit,* shall have for ever animal life, without union to God and heaven—a living death.
20. Resuming *v.* 17. **building up yourselves**—opposite to "separate themselves" (*v.* 19); as "in the Holy Ghost" is opposed to "having not the Spirit." **on** -- as *on* a foundation. *Building on* THE FAITH is building on *Christ,* its object. **praying in the Holy Ghost**—(Rom. viii. 26.) The Holy Spirit teaches *what we* are to pray for, and *how.* None can pray aright save by being *in the Spirit*—*i.e.,* in the elements of His influence. *Chrysostom* mentions among the Spirit's gifts at the beginning of the New Testament, that *of prayer,* bestowed on some, who prayed in the name of the rest, and taught others to pray. Their prayers so conceived, and often used, were preserved among Christians; and out of them forms were framed. Such is the origin of liturgies (*Hammond*). 21. In *vv.* 20, 21, Jude combines the Father, Son, and Holy Ghost: *faith, hope,* and *love.* **Keep yourselves**—not in your own strength, but "in the love of God;" i. e., *God's love to you* and all believers: the only guarantee for their being *kept* safe. Man needs to watch; but cannot *keep* himself, unless God in His love keep him. **looking for**—in hope. **the mercy of our Lord Jesus Christ**—to be fully manifested at His coming. *Mercy* is usually attributed to the Father: here to the Son; so entirely one are they. 22. None but those who 'keep themselves' are likely to "save" others. **have compassion.** So א B read; but A C, Vulgate, &c. [*elenchete*], 'reprove to their conviction;' 'confute,' so as to convince. **making a difference.** א A B C, Vulgate, Syriac, Coptic, read the accusative for the nominative [*diakrinomenous* for *diakrinomenoi*], 'when separating themselves' (*Wahl*), *v.* 19; or 'when contending with you,' as *v.* 9. 23. **save with fear.** A B א, Vulgate, have, after 'snatching them out of the fire' (with which cf. Amos iv. 11; Zech. iii. 2; 1 Cor. iii. 15: a most narrow escape), a THIRD class, 'and others compassionate (not in C) with (IN) fear.' Three kinds of patients require three kinds of treatment. Ministers and Christians "save" those whom they are the instruments of

saving. [*Sozete,* "save," is present; therefore meaning, 'try to save.'] Jude already (*v.* 9) referred to the passage, Zech. iii. 1-3. The three classes are—(1.) those who *contend with you* (accusative in oldest MSS.), whom *convict;* (2.) those as brands already in *the fire,* of which hell fire is the consummation: these *try to save by snatching out;* (3.) those who are objects of *compassion,* whom accordingly *compassionate* and help, but let not pity degenerate into connivance at their error. Your "compassion" is to be accompanied "with fear" of being defiled by them. **hating.** *Hatred* has its legitimate field of exercise. Sin is the only thing which God hates; so ought we. **even the garment**—proverbial: avoiding the least contact with sin; hating that which borders on it. As *garments* of the apostles wrought good in healing (Acts xix. 12: cf. the woman with an issue of blood, Matt. ix. 20, 21), so the *garment* of sinners metaphorically; *i. e.,* anything brought into contact with their pollution is to be avoided. Cf. as to leprosy and other defilements, Lev. xiii. 52-57; xv. 4-17. Any one touching the garments of those so defiled was excluded, until purified, from religious and civil communion with the sanctified people of Israel. Christians who received at baptism the white garment, in token of purity, are not to defile it by any approach to defiled things. 24. Concluding doxology. **Now**—'But.' **you.** So א C, Vulgate; 'us,' A: B in *Tischendorf,* 'them.' *You* is in contradistinction to those *ungodly men* above. **keep you from falling** [*phulaxai aptaistous*]—'guard . . . (so as to be) *without falling,*' or *stumbling.* **faultless** [*amomous*]—'blameless.' **before the presence of his glory**—i. e., *before Himself,* when He shall be revealed in *glory.* **with exceeding joy** [*en agalliasei*]—'with exultation,' as of those who *leap* for joy. **25. To the only wise God our Saviour.** א A B C, Vulgate, add, 'through Jesus Christ our Lord.' The transcribers, fancying that "Saviour" applied to Christ alone, omitted the words. To the only God (the Father) who is our Saviour through (*i. e.,* by the mediation of) Jesus Christ our Lord. **dominion** [*kratos*]—'might.' **power**—*authority* [*exousia*]; *legitimate power.* א A B C, Vulgate, add, 'before all the age' [*pro pantos tou aionos*], before all time *past;* '*and* now,' as to the present; 'and to all the ages,' i. e., *for ever,* as to the time to come.

THE REVELATION

OF S. JOHN THE DIVINE.

1 THE Revelation of Jesus Christ, *a*which God gave unto him, to show unto his servants things which must shortly come to pass; and *b*he
2 sent and signified *it* by his angel unto his servant John: who bare record of the word of God, and of the testimony of Jesus Christ, and of all things
3 *c*that he saw. Blessed *d*is he that readeth, and they that hear the words of this prophecy, and keep those things which are written therein: for the time is at hand.
4 JOHN to the seven churches which are in Asia: Grace be unto you, and

A. D. 96.

CHAP. 1.
a John 12.49.
b Dan 8. 16.
Dan. 9. 21.
ch. 22 6, 16.
e 1 John 1. 1.
d Pro 8. 34.
Luke 11.28.
ch. 22. 7.

CHAP. I. 1-20.—TITLE—SOURCE AND OBJECT OF THIS REVELATION—BLESSING ON THE READER AND KEEPER OF IT, AS THE TIME IS NEAR—INSCRIPTION TO THE SEVEN CHURCHES—APOSTOLIC GREETING—KEY-NOTE, "BEHOLD HE COMETH" (cf. the close, ch. xxii. 20, "Surely I come quickly")—INTRODUCTORY VISION OF THE SON OF MAN IN GLORY, AMIDST THE SEVEN CANDLESTICKS, WITH SEVEN STARS IN HIS RIGHT HAND.
1. Revelation — Apocalypse: *unveiling* those things which had been veiled. A *manifesto* of Christ's kingdom. The Church's travelling manual for the Gentile Christian times. Not a *detailed history*, but a representation of the great epochs and powers in developing the kingdom of God in relation to the world. The Church-*historical* view goes counter to the great principle, that Scripture interprets itself. Revelation is to teach us to understand the times, not the times to interpret the Apocalypse, although a reflex influence is exerted here, understood by the prudent (*Auberlen*). The book is in a series of parallel groups, not in chronological succession. Still there is an organic historical development of the kingdom of God. In this book all the other books of the Bible meet: in it is the consummation of all previous prophecy. Daniel foretells as to Christ and the Roman destruction of Jerusalem, and the last antichrist. But John's Revelation fills up the intermediate period, and describes the millennium and final state beyond antichrist. Daniel, as a godly statesman, views God's people in relation to *the four world-kingdoms*. John, as an apostle, views history from the *Christian Church* aspect. *Apocalypse* is applied to no Old Testament book. Daniel is the nearest approach to it; but what Daniel was told to *seal* and *shut up till the time of the end* (Dan. xii. 4), St. John (ch. xxii. 10), now that *the time is at hand* (*v.* 3), is directed to *reveal*. **of** (*i. e.,* from) Jesus Christ. Jesus Christ, not John, is the Author of the Apocalypse. The title ought to be, 'The Revelation of Jesus Christ according to John;' not 'of John.' Cf. His promise, John xv. 15; xvi. 13, end. The gospels record His first advent in the flesh; the Acts, His coming in the Spirit; the epistles are the inspired comment on them. The Apocalypse is of His second advent, and the preliminary events. **which God gave unto him.** The Father reveals Himself in and by His Son. **to show.** So ch. xxii. 6. Revelation comprises, in a perfect compendium, things close at hand, far off, and between; great and little; destroying and saving; prophecies of l and new, long and short; mutually involving and evolving one another: so that in no book more than in this would the addition, or taking away,

of a single word or clause (ch. xxii. 18, 19), have the effect of marring the sense (*Bengel*). **his servants**—not merely to "His servant John" (cf. ch. xxii. 3). **shortly** — 'speedily;' 'in' or 'with speed.' Cf. *v.* 3; ch. xxii. 6, 7. Not, according to man's computation, near; but "shortly" corrects our estimate of worldly periods. Though a "thousand years" (ch. xx.), at least, are included, the time is *at hand* (Luke xviii. 8). Israel's praiseworthy, but premature, eagerness for the predicted end, prophecy restrains, (cf. Dan. ix.) The Gentile church needs to be roused from her tendency to make this transitory world her home, by the nearness of Christ's advent. Revelation saith, "the time is at hand." On the other hand, the succession of seals, &c., shows that many events must first elapse. **he** — Jesus Christ, by His angel, joined with "sent." The angel does not 'signify things' until ch. xvii. 1; xix. 9, 10: cf. ch. xxii. 16. Previously John receives information from others. Jesus Christ opens the Revelation, *vv.* 10, 11; ch. iv. 1: in ch. vi. 1, one of the four living creatures acts as his informant; in ch. vii. 13, one of the elders; in ch. x. 8, 9, the Lord and His angel, who stood on the sea and earth. Only at ch. xvii. 1 does the one angel stand by him (cf. Dan. viii. 16; ix. 21; Zech. i. 19). **2. bare record of**—'testified the Word of God:' this book. John's testimony from God: "the words of this prophecy" (*v.* 3). Instead of '*testifies*,' the ancients in letters use the past tense. **the testimony of Jesus**—'the Spirit of prophecy' (ch. xix. 10). **and of all things that.** ℵ A C, Vulgate, omit "and." 'As many things as he saw,' in apposition with "the Word of God, and the testimony of Jesus Christ." **3. he that readeth, and they that hear** [*ho anaginôskôn*]— the *public reader* in church assemblies, and *his hearers*. Firstly, he by whom John sent the book, from Patmos to the seven churches, read it publicly. A special *blessing* attends him who *reads* or *hears* the apocalyptic "prophecy" with a view to *keeping* the things (as *one* article combines 'they that hear and keep:' not two classes, but only one—'they who not only hear, but also keep those things,' Rom. ii. 13): even though he find not the key, he finds a stimulus to faith, hope, and patient waiting for Christ. "Prophecy" relates to the human medium inspired—here John; "Revelation," to the Divine Being who reveals His will—here Christ. God gave the Revelation to Jesus: He, by His angel, revealed it to John, to make it known to the Church.
4. John—the apostle. None but he (supposing the writer honest) would sign himself nakedly without addition. As sole surviving representative of the apostles and eye-witnesses of the Lord,

peace, from him *e* which is, and *f* which was, and which is to come; and
5 *g* from the seven Spirits which are before his throne; and from Jesus
Christ, *h who is* the faithful Witness, *and* the *i* first-begotten of the dead,
and *j* the Prince of the kings of the earth. Unto *k* him that loved us,
6 *l* and washed us from our sins in his own blood, and hath made us kings
and priests unto God and his Father; to him *be* glory and dominion
for ever and ever. Amen.

A. D 96.
e Ex. 3. 14.
f John 1. 1.
g Zech 3 9.
h John 8. 14.
i Col. 1. 18.
j Eph. 1. 20.
k John 13 34.
l Heb 9 14.

he needed no designation save his name to be recognized. **seven churches**—not that there were not more churches in that region, but *seven* expresses *totality*. These *seven* represent the universal Church of all times and places. See *Trench's* 'Epistles to Seven Churches,' note, ch. i. 20, on *seven*. It is the *number* signifying God's covenant relation to mankind, especially to the Church. Thus, the *seventh* day, Sabbath, Gen. ii. 3; Ezek. xx. 12. Circumcision, sign of the covenant, after *seven* days, Gen. xvii. 12. Sacrifices, Num. xxiii. 1, 14, 29; 2 Chr. xxix. 21. Cf. God's directions, Josh. vi. 4, 15, 16; 2 Ki. v. 10. The feasts by *sevens* of time, Deut. xv. 1; xvi. 9, 13, 15. It is a combination of *three*—the Divine number (the Trinity: the thrice Holy, Isa. vi. 3; the blessing, Num. vi. 24-26)—and *four:* the organized world in its extension (thus the *four* elements, *four* seasons, *four* winds, *four* corners or quarters of the earth, *four* living creatures, emblems of redeemed creaturely life, Ezek. i. 5, 6; ch. iv. 6, with *four* faces and *four* wings each; the *four* beasts, and *four* metals, representing the four world-empires, Dan. ii. 32, 33; vii. 3; the *four*-sided Gospel, designed for all quarters; the sheet tied at *four* corners, Acts x. 11; the *four* horns—the world's forces against the Church, Zech. i. 18). In the Apocalypse, where God's covenant reaches its consummation, appropriately *seven* recurs more frequently than elsewhere. **Asia**—proconsular, governed by a Roman proconsul: Phrygia, Mysia, Caria, and Lydia: the kingdom which Attalus III. bequeathed to Rome. **Grace . . . peace**—Paul's apostolical greeting. In his pastoral epistles, 'mercy' in addition: so John 2. **him which is . . . was . . . is to come**—a periphrasis for the incommunicable name JEHOVAH, the self-existing, unchangeable. ['Aπὸ ὁ ὢν καὶ ὁ ἦν καὶ ὁ ἐρχόμενος.] The indeclinability implies His unchangeableness. Perhaps 'He which is to come' is used instead of 'He that shall be,' because Revelation's grand theme is the Lord's *coming* (v. 7). Still, THE FATHER (v. 5) is here meant. But so one are the Father and Son, that the designation, "which is to come," peculiar to Christ, is used here of the Father. **the seven Spirits which are before his throne** [א A read τῶν for ἅ ἐστιν]—*lit.*, 'in the presence of.' The Holy Spirit in His sevenfold (*i. e.*, perfect and universal) energy. Corresponding to "the *seven* churches." One in His essence, manifold in His influences. The *seven* eyes resting on the stone laid by Jehovah (Zech. iii. 9; ch. v. 6). Four is the number of the creature world (cf. the fourfold cherubim); *seven*, that of God's revelation. **5. the faithful Witness**—of the truth concerning Himself and His mission as Prophet, Priest, and King Saviour. 'All things that He heard of the Father, he faithfully made known to His disciples. Also, He taught the way of God in truth, and cared not for man, nor regarded the persons of men. Also, the truth which He taught in words He confirmed by miracles. Also, the Father's testimony to Himself He denied not even in death. Lastly, He will give true testimony of the works of good and bad at the judgment day' (*Richard* of St. Victor). The Greek nominative, "the faithful Witness," stands majestically prominent, in apposi-

tion to the genitive, "Jesus Christ." **the first-begotten of the dead**—(Col. i. 18.) Lazarus rose, to die again; Christ, to die no more. The image is not that the grave was the womb of His resurrection-birth (*Alford*), but as Acts xiii. 33; Rom. i. 4, Christ's resurrection is the event which fulfilled Ps. ii. 7, "This day (at the resurrection) have I *begotten* thee." Then His Divine Sonship as the God-man was openly attested by the Father. So our resurrection, and our manifested sonship, are connected. Hence "regeneration" is used of our *resurrection-state* at the restitution of all things (Matt. xix. 28; Luke xx. 36; 1 John iii. 2; Rom. viii. 11, 19, 23). **the Prince** [*Archōn*]—ruler. kingship of the world which the Tempter offered to Jesus on condition of doing homage, and so shunning the Cross, He has obtained by the Cross. "The kings of the earth" conspired against the Lord's Anointed; these He shall break in pieces (Ps. ii. 2, 9). Those wise in time, who kiss the Son, shall *bring their glory* unto Him at His manifestation as King of kings, after having destroyed His foes. **Unto him that loved us.** א A C read [*agapōnti*], '*loveth* us.' His ever-continuing character is, *He loveth*, and ever shall love, us. His love rests evermore on His people. **washed us.** א A C read [*lusanti*], '*loosed* (as from a bond) us:' so *Andreas* and *Primasius*. B, the Vulgate, and Coptic, read "washed," perhaps from ch. vii. 14. 'Loosed us in (virtue of) His blood,' being the *harder* reading, is less likely to come from the transcribers. The reference is to [*lutron*] the 'ransom' paid for our release (Matt. xx. 28). "Washed" refers to the priests, before putting on the holy garments and ministering, *washing* themselves: so believers, as '*priests* unto God,' must be *washed* in Christ's blood from every stain before they can serve God now, or minister as dispensers of blessing to the subject nations in the millennial kingdom, or minister before God in heaven. **6. And hath made** [B, *poiesanti*; A C א, *Kai epoiēsen*]—'And (He) made.' **us kings.** א A C, Vulgate, read, 'a kingdom;' A, 'for us;' B א, Vulgate, Syriac, and Coptic, 'us,' accusative: 'He made us (to be) a kingdom, (namely) priests,' &c. Omit "and" before 'priests,' with all oldest authorities. So Exod. xix. 6; 1 Pet. ii. 9, "a royal priesthood." The saints shall constitute a *kingdom* of God (ch. v. 10); sharing His King-Priest throne in the millennial kingdom (ch. iii. 21). The emphasis thus falls on *kingdom*. This book lays prominent stress on the saints' *kingdom*. They are kings *because they are priests:* the priesthood is the continuous ground of their kingship; kings in relation to man, priests in relation to God, serving day and night in His temple (ch. v. 10; vii. 15). The priest-kings shall rule, not in mechanical externalism, but in virtue of what they are, by the power of attraction and conviction overcoming the heart (*Auberlen*). **priests**—having pre-eminently near access to the king. David's sons were priests [*Kohanim*] (2 Sam. viii. 18). The distinction of *priests* and people, nearer and more remote from God, shall cease; all shall have nearest access. All persons and things shall be holy to the Lord. **God and his Father.** There is one article to both; 'unto Him who is at once God

656

7 Behold, ^mhe cometh with clouds; and every eye shall see him, and ⁿthey *also* which pierced him: and all kindreds of the earth shall wail
8 because of him. Even so, Amen. I ^oam Alpha and Omega, the beginning and the ending, saith the Lord, which is, and which was, and which is to come, the Almighty.
9 I John, who also am your brother, and companion in tribulation, ^pand in the kingdom and patience of Jesus Christ, was in the isle that is called
10 Patmos, for the word of God, and for the testimony of Jesus Christ. I ^qwas in the Spirit on ^rthe Lord's day, and heard behind me a great voice,

A. D. 90.
^m Dan. 7. 13.
ⁿ Zech. 12. 10.
John 19. 37.
^o Isa. 41. 4.
Isa. 43. 10.
^p Rom 8. 17.
^q Acts 10. 10.
^r John 20. 26.
Acts 20. 7.
1 Cor. 16. 2.

and His Father.' **glory and dominion**—'*the* glory and *the might*' [*to kratos*]. The threefold doxology occurs, ch. iv. 9, 11: fourfold, Jude 25; ch. v. 13: sevenfold, 1 Chr. xxix. 11; ch. vii. 12. Doxology occupies the prominent place above; prayer, below. If we thought of *God's glory* first (as in the Lord's prayer), and the secondary place to our needs, we should please God and gain our petitions better. **for ever and ever** [*eis tous aionas tōn aionon*; א C, Vulgate: *t. aiōnōn* A omits]—'unto the ages.'
7. **with clouds**—'*the* clouds,' viz., of heaven. "A cloud received Him out of their sight" at His ascension (Acts i. 9): which resembles the manner of His coming again (Acts i. 11). Clouds are symbols of *wrath* to sinners. **every eye**—His coming shall be a visible appearing. **shall see.** Because they do not now *see*, they will not believe. Contrast John xx. 29. **they also**—*in particular* [*hoitines*]: 'whosoever.' At His pre-millennial advent *the Jews* shall "look upon Him whom they pierced," and mourn *in repentance*, saying, "Blessed is He that cometh in the name of the Lord." Secondarily, and *chiefly*, at the general judgment all the ungodly who *actually*, or *virtually* by their sins, pierced Him, shall tremblingly see [*opsetai* implies a vision *realized inwardly*] Him. St. John is the only evangelist who records Christ's *piercing*. This allusion identifies the author of the Apocalypse. The reality of Christ's humanity and death is proved by His *piercing*: the *water and blood* from His side were the antitype to the Levitical waters of cleansing and blood-offerings. **all kindreds . . . shall wail**—the unconverted at the general judgment: at His pre-millennial advent, the antichristian confederacy (Zech. xii. 3-6, 9; xiv. 1-4; Matt. xxiv. 30) [*hai phulai tes ges*]: 'all *the tribes* of the *land*,' or 'the earth.' See the limitation to "all," ch. xiii. 8. Even the godly, whilst rejoicing in His love, shall feel penitential sorrow at their sins, which shall all be manifested. **because of** [*epi*]—'*at*,' or '*in regard to* Him.' **Even so, Amen**—God's seal of His word: to which corresponds the believer's prayer, ch. xxii. 20. The [*nai*] "even so" is Greek; "Amen," Hebrew. To both Gentiles and Jews His promises and threats are unchangeable. 8. 'I am *the* Alpha and *the* Omega'—the first and last letters of the alphabet. God in Christ comprises all between, as well as first and last. **the beginning and the ending.** Omitted in א A B C, though in the Vulgate and Coptic. Transcribers probably inserted it from ch. xxi. 6. In Christ, Genesis, the Alpha of Scripture, and Revelation, the Omega, meet; the last presenting man and God reconciled in Paradise, as the first presented man at the beginning innocent and in God's favour in Paradise. Accomplishing *finally* what I *begin*. Always the same: before the dragon, the beast, false prophet, and all foes. Anticipatory consolation under the Church's coming trials. **the Lord.** א A B C read, 'the Lord God.' **Almighty** —Hebrew, *Shaddai* and *Jehovah Sabaoth*; i. e., of hosts: commanding all the powers in heaven and earth, so able to overcome all our foes. Often in

Revelation, but nowhere else in the New Testament, save 2 Cor. vi. 18, quoted from Isaiah.
9. **I John**—so 'I Daniel' (ch. vii. 28; ix. 2; x. 2). One of many resemblances between the Old and the New Testament apocalyptic seers. No other Scripture writer uses the phrase. **also.** א A B C omit "also." In his gospel and epistles he mentions not his *name*, though describing himself as "the disciple whom Jesus loved." Here, with similar humility, he mentions his name, but not his apostleship. **companion** [*sunkoinonos*]—'fellow-partaker in *the* tribulation;' which is preliminary to 'the kingdom.' It must be borne with 'persevering endurance.' א A B C omit "in the" before "kingdom." All three are inseparable: joined by one article: *the tribulation, kingdom, and endurance*. **patience** [*hupomone*]—'persevering endurance' (Acts xiv. 22): 'the queen of graces' (virtues) (*Chrysostom*). **of.** א C, Vulgate, read 'IN Jesus;' A, 'in Christ;' B, 'in Christ Jesus.' It is IN Him that believers have the right to the *kingdom*, and spiritual strength to *endure* perseveringly for it. **was** [*egenomēn*]—'came to be.' **in . . . Patmos**—now Patmo, or Palmosa. See 'Introduction' on John's exile to it under Domitian, from which he was released under Nerva. Restricted to a small spot on earth, he is admitted into the wide heaven and its secrets. Thus John drank of Christ's cup, and was baptized with His baptism (Matt. xx. 22). **for** [*dia*]—'on account of the Word of God and testimony.' A C *h*, Vulgate, omit the second "for," thus joining closely "the Word of God" and "testimony of Jesus." But א B read it. א A C, Vulgate, omit "Christ." The Apocalypse has been always appreciated most in adversity. Thus the Asiatic church, from the flourishing times of Constantine, less estimated it. The African church being more exposed to the Cross, made much of it (*Bengel*). 10. **I was**—'I came to be:' 'I became.' **in the Spirit**—in a state of ecstasy: the outer world shut out: the inner spirit, being taken possession of by God's Spirit, establishing an immediate connection with the invisible world. Whilst the *prophet* 'speaks' in the Spirit, the apocalyptic seer *is* in the Spirit wholly. The spirit alone (which connects us with God) is active, or recipient, in the apocalyptic state. With Christ this being "in the Spirit" was not the exception, but invariable. **on the Lord's day.** Though forcibly detained from church communion with the brethren on "the Lord's day," the weekly commemoration of the resurrection, John was enjoying spiritual communion. The earliest mention of *the term*. But the consecration of the day to worship, almsgiving, and the Lord's supper, is implied, Acts xx. 7; 1 Cor. xvi. 2: cf. John xx. 19-26. It corresponds to "the Lord's supper," 1 Cor. xi. 20. *Ignatius* alludes to "the Lord's day" ('Ad Magnes,' ix.), and *Irenæus*, in the 'Quæsts. ad Orthod.,' cxv. (in *Justin Martyr*). *Justin Martyr*, 'Apology,' ii., 98, &c., 'On Sunday we hold our joint meeting: for the first day is that on which God, having removed darkness, made the world, and Jesus Christ our Saviour rose from the dead.

11 as of a trumpet, saying, I am Alpha and Omega, the first and the last: and, What thou seest, write in a book, and send *it* unto the seven churches which are in Asia; unto Ephesus, and unto Smyrna, and unto Pergamos, and unto Thyatira, and unto Sardis, and unto Philadelphia, and unto Laodicea.

12 And I turned to see the voice that spake with me. And being turned

13 [s] I saw seven golden candlesticks; and in the midst of the seven candlesticks [t] *one* like unto the Son of man, clothed [u] with a garment down to

A. D. 96.

[s] Ex. 25. 37.
Zech 4. 2.
[t] Eze 1. 26, 28.
Dan. 7. 13.
Phil 2. 7, 8.
Heb. 2. 14.
ch 14. 14.
[u] Dan. 0 5.

On the day before Saturday they crucified Him; on the day after Saturday, Sunday, having appeared to His apostles, He taught.' To it *Pliny* refers ('Ep.,' xcvii., b. x.): 'The Christians, on a *fixed day*, before dawn, meet and sing a hymn to Christ as God,' &c. *Tertullian*, 'De Coron.,' iii., 'On the Lord's day we deem it wrong to fast.' *Melito*, bishop of Sardis (second century), wrote a book *on the Lord's day* ('Eusebius,' iv., 26). Also *Dionysius* of Corinth (A.D. 170), in *Eusebius*, 'Ecclesiastical History,' iv., 23, 8; *Clement* of Alexandrinus (A. D. 194), 'Stromata,' v. and vii., 12; *Origen*, 'C. Cels.,' viii., 22. Rom. xiv. 5, 6, refers not to the Sabbath, but to days of Jewish observance: "He that regardeth not the day, to the Lord he doth not regard it," is not in א A B C Δ G ƒ *g*, Vulgate. The theory that *the day of Christ's second coming* is meant, is untenable. 'The day of the Lord' is different from [*he kuriake hemera*] "the Lord's (an adjective) day," which in the ancient Church always designates Sunday, though possibly the two shall coincide (at least in parts of the earth), whence a tradition is in *Jerome*, on Matt. xxv., that the Lord's coming was expected on the Paschal Lord's day. The visions of the Apocalypse, seals, trumpets, and vials, &c., are grouped in *sevens*, and naturally begin on the first day of the seven, the birthday of the Church, whose future they set forth (*Wordsworth*). **great voice**—summoning solemn attention: Greek order, א C *h*, Vulgate, 'I heard behind me a voice great (loud) as (that) of a trumpet.' The trumpet summoned to religious feasts, accompanying God's revelation of Himself. **11. I am Alpha and Omega, the first and the last: and.** B א A C, Vulgate, omit all this clause. **write in a book.** To this *book*, having such an origin, and to the other books of Scripture, who gives their due weight, preferring them to the *many books* of the world? (*Bengel*.) **seven churches.** As there were many other churches in Proconsular Asia (*e. g.*, Miletus, Magnesia, Tralles) besides, *seven* is fixed upon because of its mystical signification, *totality* and *universality*. "Which are in Asia" is rejected by א A B C, *Cyprian*, Vulgate, and Syriac. Coptic has it. These seven are representative churches; as a complex whole, ideally complete, embodying the spiritual characteristics of the Church, whether as faithful or unfaithful, in all ages. Those selected are not taken at random, but have a many-sided completeness. Thus, we have Smyrna, a church exposed to persecutions unto death; on the other hand, Sardis, having a high *name* for spiritual *life*, *yet dead*. Laodicea, in its own estimate, *rich*, *needing nothing*, with ample talents, yet *lukewarm*; on the other hand, Philadelphia, with but *little strength*, yet *keeping* Christ's *word*: so an *open door* of usefulness *set before* it by Christ Himself. Ephesus, intolerant of *evil* and *false apostles*, yet having *left its first love*; on the other hand, Thyatira, abounding in *works*, *love*, *service*, *and faith*, yet *suffering* the false *prophetess* to *seduce* many. Again, Ephesus in conflict with false freedom—*i. e.*, fleshly licentiousness (the Nicolaitanes); so Pergamos in conflict with

Balaam-like tempters to fornication and *idol meats;* on the other side, Philadelphia, in conflict with the Jewish synagogue—*i. e.*, legal bondage. Finally, Sardis and Laodicea, without opposition to call forth spiritual energies: a dangerous position, considering man's natural indolence. In the historic interpretation, Ephesus ('the beloved' or 'desired') (*Stier*) represents the waning of the apostolic age. Smyrna ('myrrh,' bitter, yet costly perfume), the martyr period of the Decian and Diocletian age. Pergamos (a 'castle'), the church in earthly power and decreasing spirituality, from Constantine's time until the seventh century. Thyatira ('unwearied about sacrifices'), the apostate church in the first half of the middle ages; like "Jezebel," keen about its *sacrifice* of the mass, and slaying God's witnesses. Sardis, from the twelfth century to the Reformation. Philadelphia ('brotherly love'), the first century of the Reformation. Laodicea, the Reformed church after its first zeal cooled. **12. see the voice**—i. e., *ascertain* from whom the *voice* proceeded. **that** [*hetis*]—'of what kind it was *which*.' The voice of God the Father, as at Christ's baptism and transfiguration, so here in presenting Christ as our High Priest. **spake.** א B C, Vulgate, *h*, *Irenæus*, read, 'was speaking.' **being**—'having turned.' **seven golden candlesticks**—'lamp-stands' (*Kelly*). The stand holding the lamp. In Exod. xxv. 31, 32, the seven are united in ONE candlestick—*i. e.*, SIX arms and a central shaft: so Zech. iv. 2, 11. Here the seven are *separate*, typifying the entire Church, but now no longer as the *one* Jewish Church (represented by the *one* sevenfold candlestick), restricted to one outward unity and place. The several churches are mutually independent as to external ceremonies and government (provided all things are done to edification, and 'schisms' or needless separations are avoided), yet one in the unity of the Spirit and the Headship of Christ. The candlestick is not light, but bears light, holding forth light around. The light the Church bears is the Lord's, not her own (Phil. ii. 15, 16). His glory is the end of her light (Matt. v. 16). The candlestick stood in the Holy Place, type of the Church on earth, as the Holiest was type of the Church in heaven. The Holy Place's only light was from the candlestick, daylight being excluded: so the Lord God is the Church's only light (cf. Rev. xxi. 23): the light of grace, not nature. "Golden" symbolizes the greatest *preciousness* and *sacredness*. In the Zend Avesta, "golden" is synonymous with heavenly or divine (*Trench*). **13.** His glorified form could be recognized by John, who saw it at the transfiguration. **in the midst**—implying Christ's presence and ceaseless activity *in the midst* of His people *on earth*. In ch. iv., appearing *in heaven*, His insignia undergo a corresponding change; even there the rainbow reminds us of His everlasting covenant. **seven.** Omitted in A C; so א B. **Son of man.** The form which John had seen enduring the agony of Gethsemane, and the shame of Calvary, he now sees glorified. His glory as *Son of man* (not merely *Son of God*) is the

14 the foot, and girt about the paps with a golden girdle. His head and
 ᵛhis hairs *were* white like wool, as white as snow; and *ʷ*his eyes *were* as
15 a flame of fire; and *ˣ*his feet like unto fine brass, as if they burned in a
16 furnace; *ʸ*and his voice as the sound of many waters. And he had in
 his right hand seven stars; and *ᶻ*out of his mouth went a sharp two-edged
 sword; *ᵃ*and his countenance *was* as the sun shineth in his strength.
17 And *ᵇ*when I saw him, I fell at his feet as dead. And *ᶜ*he laid his right
 hand upon me, saying unto me, Fear not; *ᵈ*I am the first and the last:
18 *I ᵉam* he that liveth, and was dead; and, behold, I am alive for ever-
19 more, Amen; and *ᶠ*have the keys of hell and of death. Write the things

A D 96.

ᵛ Dan. 7. 9.
ʷ ch 2. 18.
ʷ Eze 1. 7.
ʸ Eze 43. 2.
ᶻ Isa. 49. 2.
ᵃ Acts 26. 13.
ᵇ Eze. 1. 28.
ᶜ Dan. 8 18.
ᵈ Isa 41 4.
 Isa. 44 6.
ᵉ Rom 6. 9.
ᶠ Ps. 68 20.

fruit of His humiliation. **down to the foot**—marking high rank. The garment and girdle are emblems of His *priesthood.* Cf. Exod. xxviii. 2, 4 [the same word in the LXX. as here; *podere*], 31, 42; xxxix. 27-29; LXX. Aaron's robe and girdle were "for glory and beauty," combining the insignia of royalty and priesthood, characteristic of Christ's king priesthood "after the order of Melchisedec." His being *in the midst of the candlesticks* (only seen in the *temple*), shows it is as *king-priest* He is so attired. This priesthood He has exercised since His ascension; and therefore wears its emblems. As Aaron put on the holy white linen tunic [*chetoneth*], for making the atonement, then assumed his usual 'golden vestments,' when he came forth from the sanctuary to bless the people (Lev. xvi. 4, 23, 24), so when Christ shall come again, He shall appear in similar attire of 'beauty and glory' (margin, Isa. iv. 2). The angels are attired like their Lord (Ezek. ix. 2, 11; Dan. x. 5; ch. xv. 6). The ordinary girding for active work was at *the loins;* but *Josephus* ('Antiquities,' iii., 7, 2) tells us the Levitical priests were girt higher, about the *paps,* appropriate to calm, majestic movement. The girdle bracing the frame symbolizes collected powers. *Righteousness* and *faithfulness* are Christ's girdle (Isa. xi. 5). The high priest's girdle was only interwoven with gold, but Christ's all of gold: the antitype exceeds the type. **14.** Greek, 'But.' **like wool**—Greek, 'like *white* wool.' The *colour* is the point of comparison: signifying lovely *purity.* So in Isa. i. 18. Not *age;* for hoary hairs indicate decay. Still, He is "the ancient of days" (Dan. vii. 9). **eyes were as a flame**—all-searching, penetrating like fire; also, *consuming* indignation against sin, especially at His coming "in flaming fire, taking vengeance" on all the ungodly. Confirmed by Rev. xix. 11, 12. **15. fine brass** ['*chalcolibanus,*' derived by some from the Greek, *brass* and *frankincense:* by Bochart, from *brass,* and Hebrew, *libben,* to whiten *brass*]—having in the furnace reached a *white* heat: so "burnished (*glowing*) brass" (Ezek. i. 7; Rev. x. 1). Translate, '*glowing* brass, as if they had been made redhot in a furnace.' The feet of the priests were bare in ministering in the sanctuary. So our great High Priest. **voice as . . . many waters**—(Ezek. xliii. 2; in Dan. x. 6, "like the voice of *a multitude*"). As the bridegroom's voice, so the bride's, ch. xiv. 2; xix. 6; Ezek. i. 24, the cherubim, or redeemed creation. His voice here refers to its terribleness to His foes. Contrast Song ii. 8; v. 2: cf. Rev. iii. 20. **16. he had**—'having.' St. John takes up the description, irrespective of the construction, *with separate strokes of the pencil* (*Alford*). **in his right hand seven stars**—(v. 20; ch. ii. 1; iii. 1.) He holds them as a star-studded "crown of glory," or "royal diadem," in His hand: so Isa. lxii. 3, as their Possessor and Upholder. **out of his mouth went**—'going forth;' not wielded in the hand. His WORD, the sword of His Spirit, is omnipotent in executing His will

against sinners. Its reproving, punishing, rather than its converting power, is here prominent. Still, as He encourages the churches, as well as threatens, its saving power is not excluded. Its *two* edges (back and front) imply its double efficacy, condemning some, converting others. *Tertullian* ('Adv. Jud.') explains them *the Old and the New Testament. Richard* of St. Victor, 'the Old Testament cutting externally our *carnal,* the New Testament internally our *spiritual,* sins.' **sword** [*Romphaia,* the Thracian long, heavy broadsword]—six times in Revelation, once elsewhere in the New Testament, viz., Luke ii. 35. **sun shineth in his strength**—in unclouded power. So shall the righteous shine, reflecting the image of the Sun of righteousness. *Trench* remarks, This description, sublime as a purely mental conception, would be intolerable if we gave it outward embodiment. With the Greeks, æsthetical taste was the first consideration, to which all others must give way. With the Hebrews, the full representation ideally of the religious reality was paramount, that representation being designed to remain a purely mental conception. This exalting of the essence above the form marks their deeper religious earnestness. **17.** So fallen is man, that God's manifestation of His presence overwhelms him. **laid his right hand upon me** —so Jesus at the transfiguration to the three prostrate disciples, of whom John was one, saying, "Be not afraid." The 'touch' of His hand imparted strength (Dan. viii. 18; x. 10; Matt. viii. 3, 15; ix. 29). **unto me.** Omitted in א A C *h,* Vulgate. **the first and the last**—(Isa. xli. 4; xliv. 6; xlviii. 12.) From eternity, and to eternity: 'First by creation, the Last by retribution: First, because before me there was no God; Last, because after me there shall be no other: First, because from me are all things; Last, because to me all things return' (*Richard* of St. Victor). **18.** Greek, 'And THE LIVING ONE:' connected with *v.* 17. **and was** [*egenomēn*]—'and (yet) I *became* dead.' **alive for evermore**—'living unto the ages of ages:' not merely '*I live,*' but I have, and am the Source of, life to my people. 'To Him belongs *absolute* being, contrasted with the creature's *relative* being: others may *share,* He only *hath* immortality; *being in essence, not by participation, immortal*' (*Theodoret*). B reads "Amen;" א A C, Vulgate, Coptic, omit it. His having passed through death as one of us, and now living in the infinite plenitude of life, reassures us, since through Him death is the gate of resurrection to eternal life. **have the keys of hell**—'Hades;' Hebrew, 'Sheol.' "Hell," in the sense of the *place of torment,* answers to *Gehenna.* I can release from *the unseen world of spirits* and from DEATH whom I will. א A B C transpose thus, 'Death and Hades.' Death (which came by sin, robbing man of his immortal birthright, Rom. v. 12) peoples Hades; therefore should stand first. *Keys* are emblems of authority, opening and shutting at will 'the gates of Hades' (Ps. ix. 13, 14; Isa.

which thou hast seen, and the things which are, and the things which
20 shall be hereafter; the mystery of the seven stars which thou sawest in
my right hand, and the seven golden candlesticks. The seven stars are
g the angels of the seven churches; and the *h* seven candlesticks which
thou sawest are the seven churches.

2   UNTO the angel of the church of *a* Ephesus write; These things saith
b he that holdeth the seven stars in his right hand, who walketh in the
2 midst of the seven golden candlesticks; I *c* know thy works, and thy
labour, and thy patience, and how thou canst not bear them which are
evil: and thou *d* hast tried them *e* which say they are apostles, and are

A D. 96.	
g Mal 2. 7.	
h Zech 4. 2.	
Matt 5. 15.	
Phil 2. 15.	
CHAP. 2.	
a Acts 19.	
b ch. 1. 16.	
c Ps 1. 6.	
Matt 7. 23.	
d 1 John 4. 1.	
e 2 Pet 2. 1.	

xxxviii. 10; Matt. xvi. 18). **19.** A B C ℵ read, 'Write *therefore*' (since I, "the First and the Last," have the keys of death, and vouchsafe this vision for the comfort and warning of the Church). **things which are.** "The things which thou hast seen" are those in this chapter (cf. *v.* 11); "the things which are," the present state of the churches when John was writing (ch. ii. and iii.); "the things which shall be hereafter," the things symbolically represented concerning the future, (chs. iv.-xxii.) *Alford,* '*What* things they *signify;*' but the antithesis, next clause, forbids this, 'the things which are about to come to pass hereafter.' The *plural* [*eisin*] "are," instead of the usual Greek *singular,* is owing to *churches* and *persons* being meant by "the *things* which are." **20. in** [*epi,* ℵ B C]—'*upon* my right hand;' but A [*en*], 'in.' **the mystery . . . candlesticks**—in apposition to, and explaining, "the things which thou hast seen," governed by "Write." *Mystery,* the hidden truth veiled under this symbol, now revealed: its correlative is *revelation. Stars* symbolize lordship (Num. xxiv. 17: cf. Dan. xii. 3, of faithful teachers; ch. viii. 10; xii. 4; Jude 13). **angels.** Not as *Origen,* 'Homily xiii. on Luke; xx. on Numbers,' the guardian angels of the churches, as individuals have their guardian angels. For how could heavenly angels be charged with the delinquencies charged against these angels? If a man be meant (as the Old Testament analogy favours, Hagg. i. 13, "the Lord's Messenger (*angel*) in the Lord's message;" Mal. ii. 7; iii. 1), *the bishop,* or superintendent pastor, must be 'the angel.' For whereas there were many presbyters in the larger churches (as, *e. g.,* Ephesus, Smyrna, &c.), there was but *one* angel, whom the Chief Shepherd and Bishop of souls holds responsible for the church under him. *Angel,* designating an office, may be in accordance with Revelation's enigmatic symbolism, transferred from the heavenly to the earthly ministers of Jehovah: reminding them that, like the angels above, they below should fulfil God's mission zealously and efficiently. "Thy will be done on earth, as it is in heaven!" The term is more probably from the synagogue. Note 2 Cor. viii. 23. The 'legate of the church' [*scheliach tsibbur,* answering to *angel* or *apostle*] recited the prayers in the name of the congregation. The president of the synagogue was legate *ex officio.*
CHAP. II. 1-29. — EPISTLES TO EPHESUS, SMYRNA, PERGAMOS, THYATIRA.
Each of the seven commences with, "I know thy works." Each contains a promise, "To him that overcometh." Each ends with "He that hath an ear, let him hear what the Spirit saith unto the churches." The title of our Lord in each accords with the address, and is mainly taken from the imagery of the vision, ch. i. Each of the addresses has a threat or a promise, and most have both. Their order seems ecclesiastical, civil, and geographical: Ephesus first, as the Asiatic metropolis

(termed 'the light' and the 'first city of Asia')' nearest to Patmos, where John received the epistle to the seven churches; also being that church with which John was especially connected; then the churches on the west of Asia; then those in the interior. Smyrna and Philadelphia, the most afflicted, alone receive unmixed praise. Sardis and Laodicea, the most wealthy, receive almost solely censure. In Ephesus, Pergamos, and Thyatira, there are some things to praise, others to condemn—the latter preponderating in Ephesus, the former in Pergamos and Thyatira. The different states of different churches, in all times and places, are portrayed, and they are suitably encouraged or warned. **1. Ephesus**—famed for the temple of Diana, one of the seven world-wonders. For three years Paul laboured there. He subsequently ordained Timothy superintending overseer or bishop: probably his charge was but temporary. The praise and blame accord with *Timothy's* character. The zeal against self-styled apostles and the Nicolaitanes, the unwearied labour, and the declension from first love, are not inapplicable: the promise, *v.* 7, accords with 2 Tim. ii. 4 6. Paul's death, and the charge in the pastoral epistles to Timothy, may have changed his position from *superintendent of many churches* to *bishop* of *Ephesus.* He was but thirty-five when the pastoral epistles were addressed to him. Now he was advanced in years. But all this is conjecture. St. John, towards the close of life, took Ephesus as the centre from which he superintended the province. **holdeth** [*kratōn*]—'holdeth fast in His grasp,' as *v.* 25; ch. iii. 11: cf. John x. 28, 29. Christ's title as 'holding fast the seven stars (ch. i. 16: only, for *having* is substituted *holding fast*), and walking in the midst of the seven candlesticks,' accords with the introduction, ch. i. 16, 20. *Walking* expresses His unwearied activity in the Church, guarding her from internal and external evils, as the high priest moved to and fro in the sanctuary. **2. I know thy works**—His omniscience. Not merely 'thy professions, desires, good resolutions' (ch. xiv. 13, end). **thy labour.** A C omit "thy;" ℵ B support it. [*Kopon* means 'labour *unto weariness.*'] **patience**—persevering *endurance.* **bear** [*bastasai*]—*evil men:* the Ephesian church regarded as an intolerable *burden.* We are to '*bear* (same Greek, Gal. vi. 2) burdens' of *weak* brethren; but not of *false brethren.* **tried** [*epeirasas*]—by experiment; not [*dokimazete*] 'test,' as 1 John iv. 1. The apostolical churches had the miraculous gift of *discerning spirits.* So (Acts xx. 28-30) Paul presciently warned the *Ephesian* elders of the coming false teachers, and warned Timothy at Ephesus. Tertullian ('De Baptism.,' 17) and *Jerome* ('In Catal. Vir. Illustr. in Luca,' 7) record of John, that when a professedly canonical history of St. Paul's acts had been composed by a presbyter of Ephesus, John convicted the author and condemned the work. So once he would not remain under the same roof as Cerinthus the heretic. **say**

3 not, and hast found them liars: and hast borne, and hast patience, and
4 for my name's sake hast laboured, and hast not *f* fainted.   Nevertheless
I have *somewhat* against thee, because thou hast left thy first love.
5 Remember therefore from whence thou art fallen, and repent, and do the
first works; *g* or else I will come unto thee quickly, and will remove thy
6 candlestick out of his place, except thou repent.   But this thou hast,
that thou hatest the deeds of the Nicolaitanes, which I also hate.
7 He *h* that hath an ear, let him hear what the Spirit saith unto the
churches; To him that overcometh will I give *i* to eat of *j* the tree of life,
which is in the midst of the paradise of God.

A. D. 96.

f Gal. 6. 9.
Heb. 12. 3,
5.
v Matt 21.41.
Matt 24.48-
51.
Mark 12. 9.
ch. 3. 3.
h Matt 11.15.
ch. 13. 9.
i ch. 22.
j Gen. 2. 9.

they are apostles—probably Judaizers. *Ignatius* ('Ad Ephesum,' 6) says, 'Onesimus praises exceedingly your good discipline, that no heresy dwells among you;' and ('Ad Ephesum,' 9), 'Ye did not permit those having evil doctrine to sow their seed, but closed your ears.' **3. borne . . . patience.** א A B C, Vulgate, transpose. 'Thou hast borne' my reproach (א adds 'all afflictions' [*thlipsis pasas*]), but 'canst not bear the evil' (*v.* 2). A beautiful antithesis. **and . . . hast laboured, and hast not fainted.** א B [*ekopiasas*] A C *h*, Vulgate, read [*ouk kekopiakas*], 'and . . . hast not laboured;' omitting 'and hast fainted.' The difficulty which the received text tried to obviate was the seeming contradiction, 'I know thy *labour* . . . and thou hast *not laboured.*' What is meant is, 'thou hast not been *wearied out* with labour.' **4. somewhat . . . because**—rather, 'I have against thee (this) *that*,' &c. Not a mere "somewhat:" it is everything. How characteristic of our gracious Lord, that He puts foremost all He can find to approve, and only afterwards notes the shortcomings! **left thy first love**—to Christ. Cf. 1 Tim. v. 12. See their first *love*, Eph. i. 15. This epistle was written under Domitian, thirty years since Paul had written to them. Their warmth had given place to lifeless orthodoxy. Cf. Paul's view of faith so-called without love, 1 Cor. xiii. 2. **5. whence**—from what a height. **do the first works**—which flowed from thy *first love.* Not merely 'feel thy first feelings,' but do works flowing from the same principle as formerly (Gal. v. 6). **I will come**—'I am coming' in special judgment on thee. **quickly.** So B; omitted in א A C, Vulgate, Coptic versions. **remove thy candlestick out of his place**—"remove" the Church from Ephesus elsewhere. 'Removal of the candlestick, not extinction of the candle, is threatened here; judgment for some, the occasion of mercy for others. The seat of the Church has been changed; the Church itself survives. What the East lost, the West has gained. One who lately visited Ephesus found only three Christians, and these so ignorant as scarcely to have heard the names of St. Paul or St. John' (*Trench*). **6. But.** How graciously He returns to praise for our consolation, and as an example to *us*, that we should show, when we reprove, we have more pleasure in praising than fault-finding. **hatest the deeds**—I ate men's evil *deeds*, not the men. **Nicolaitanes.** *Irenæus* ('Hæreses,' i. 26, 3) and *Tertullian* ('Præscriptione Hæreticorum,' 46) suppose followers of Nicolas, one of *the seven* (Acts vi. 3, 5), as there was a Judas among the twelve. They, *Clemens Alexandrinus* ('Stromata,' ii. 20; iii. 4) and *Epiphanius* ('Hæreses,' 25), confound the later Gnostic Nicolaitanes, followers of one Nicolas, with those of Revelation. *Michaelis's* view is: Nicolas (*conqueror of the people*) is the Greek of Balaam, from Hebrew Belang Am, *Destroyer of the people.* Revelation abounds in duplicate Hebrew and Greek names: Apollyon, Abaddon; Devil, Satan; Yea [*Nai*], Amen. The name, like other names,

Egypt, Babylon, Sodom, is symbolic. Cf. *vv.* 14, 15, which shows the true sense; not a sect, but professing Christians who, like Balaam, introduced a false freedom—*i. e.*, licentiousness; a reaction from Judaism, the first danger to the Church, combated in the council of Jerusalem, which, whilst releasing Gentile converts from legal bondage, required their abstinence from idol meats, and concomitant "fornication;" also in the epistle to Galatians. These Nicolaitanes, or followers of Balaam, as Christ designates them by a name expressing their true character, abused Paul's doctrine of the grace of God into a plea for lasciviousness (2 Pet. ii. 15, 16, 19; Jude, 4, 11, who both describe such seducers as followers of *Balaam*). They persuaded many to escape obloquy, by yielding in what was a test of faithfulness, *the eating of idol meats:* going further, they joined in the *fornication* of the idol feasts, as permitted by Christ's 'law of liberty.' Thus the 'love-feasts' were made like heathen orgies (Jude 12).

7. He that hath an ear. This clause precedes the promise in the first three addresses, succeeds to it in the last four. Thus the promises are enclosed on both sides with the precept urging the deepest attention to most momentous truths. Every man "hath an ear" naturally; he alone will be able to hear spiritually to whom God has given "the hearing ear;" whose 'ear God hath wakened' and "opened" (Isa. l. 4). Cf. 'faith, the ears of the soul' (*Clemens Alexandrinus*). **the Spirit saith**—what *Christ* saith; so one are the Second and Third Persons. **unto the churches**—not merely to the particular, but to the universal, Church. **give . . . the tree of life.** The promise corresponds to the faithfulness. They who refrain from Nicolaitane indulgences (*v.* 6) and idol meats (*vv.* 14, 15) shall eat of meat infinitely superior—viz., the fruit of the tree of life, and the hidden manna (*v.* 17). **overcometh**—in John's gospel (ch. xvi. 33) and first epistle (ch. ii. 13, 14; v. 4, 5) an object follows—viz., 'the world,' 'the wicked one.' Here, where the final issue is spoken of, *the conqueror* is named absolutely. Paul uses a similar image, 1 Cor. ix. 24, 25; 2 Tim. ii. 5; not the same as John's, except Rom. xii. 21. **will I give**—as Judge. The tree of life in Paradise, lost by the fall, is restored by the Redeemer. Cf. Prov. iii. 18; xi. 30; xiii. 12; xv. 4; prophetically, ch. xxii. 2, 14; Ezek. xlvii. 12: cf. John vi. 51. These introductory addresses are linked closely to the body of Revelation. Thus, *the tree of life* here, with ch. xxii. 2; deliverance from *the second death* (ch. ii. 11), with ch. xx. 14; xxi. 8; *the new name* (ch. ii. 17), with ch. xiv. 1; *power over the nations* (*v.* 26), with ch. xx. 4; *the morning star* (ch. ii. 28), with ch. xxii. 16; *the white raiment* (ch. iii. 5), with ch. iv. 4; xvi. 15; *the name in the book of life* (ch. iii. 5), with ch. xiii. 8; xx. 15; *the new Jerusalem* and its citizenship (ch. iii. 12), with ch. xxi. 10. **in the midst of the paradise.** א A B C *h*, Vulgate, omit "the midst of." In Gen. ii.

8   And unto the angel of the church in Smyrna write; These things saith
9 *ᵏ*the First and the Last, which was dead, and is alive; I know thy works, and tribulation, and poverty, (but thou art *ˡ*rich,) and *I know* the blasphemy of *ᵐ*them which say they are Jews, and are not, but *are* the
10 synagogue of Satan. Fear *ⁿ*none of those things which thou shalt suffer: behold, the devil shall cast *some* of you into prison, that ye may be tried; and ye shall have tribulation ten days: *º*be thou faithful unto death, and I will give thee *ᵖ*a crown of life.
11 He *�q*that hath an ear, let him hear what the Spirit saith unto the churches; He that overcometh shall not be hurt of the *ʳ*second death.

A. D. 96.

k ch 1 8.
l Luke 12.21.
  1 Tim. 6 18.
  Jas 2. 5.
m Rom. 2. 17.
n Matt.10 *º*2.
  Isa. 41. 10,
  14.
o Matt.24.13.
p Jas. 1. 12,
q ch 13. 9.
r ch. 20. 14.

9, appropriate; for there were *other* trees in the garden, but not *in the midst* of it. Here *the tree of life* is simply *in the paradise;* for no other tree is mentioned in it. In ch. xxii. 2, the tree of life is '*in the midst* of the street of Jerusalem;' from this the clause was inserted here. *Paradise* (Persian), originally any garden of delight: then specially Eden: then the temporary abode of pious souls: then "the paradise *of God*," the third heaven, the immediate presence of God (2 Cor. xii. 4). **of God**—(Ezek. xxviii. 13.) א A C; but B, Vulgate, Syriac, Coptic, and *Cyprian*, 'MY God,' as ch. iii. 12. So Christ calls God "*My* God and your God" (John xx. 17: cf. Eph. i. 17). God is *our* God, as being peculiarly *Christ's* God. The main bliss of Paradise is, it is the Paradise *of God: God* dwells there (ch. xxi. 3). We lost in Adam the paradise of man; we gain in Christ the paradise of God. We were driven out of that: we 'go no more out' of this.

8. Smyrna—in Ionia, north of Ephesus. *Polycarp*, martyred in 168 A. D., eighty-six years after conversion, was bishop: probably "the angel of the church in Smyrna." The allusions to persecutions unto death, accord with this view. *Ignatius* ('Martyrium Ignatii,' iii.), on his way to martyrdom in Rome, wrote to *Polycarp*, then (108 A. D.) bishop of Smyrna. If his bishopric commenced ten or twelve years earlier, the dates will harmonize. *Tertullian* ('Præscriptione Hæreticorum,' xxxii.) and *Irenæus*, who talked with *Polycarp* in youth, tell us, *Polycarp* was consecrated by St. John. **the First and the Last, which was dead, and is alive**—attributes of Christ most calculated to comfort Smyrna under its persecution: resumed from ch. i. 17, 18. As death was to Him the gate to life eternal, so it is to them (*vv.* 10, 11). **9. thy works, and**—so א B; but A C, Vulgate, and Coptic, omit. **tribulation**—owing to persecution. **poverty**—owing to 'spoiling of their goods.' **but thou art rich**—in grace. Contrast Laodicea, *rich* in the world's eyes, *poor* before God. 'There are both poor rich-men, and rich poor-men in God's sight' (*Trench*). **blasphemy of them**—blasphemous calumny of thee *arising from* them, &c. **say they are Jews, and are not**—Jews by national descent, not spiritually of "the true circumcision." The Jews blaspheme Christ as 'the hanged one.' As elsewhere, so at Smyrna, they bitterly opposed Christianity; at *Polycarp's* martyrdom they joined the heathens in clamouring for his being cast to the lions; and when there was an obstacle to this, for his being burnt alive; with their own hands they carried logs for the pile. **synagogue of Satan.** Only once is "synagogue" in the New Testament used of the Christian assembly, and that by the apostle who longest maintained the union of the Church and Jewish synagogue (margin, Jas. ii. 2). As the Jews opposed Christianity, and it more and more rooted itself in the Gentile world, "synagogue" was left altogether to the former, and Christians appropriated the honourable term

"Church:" contrast an earlier time, when the Jewish theocracy was "the church in the wilderness" (Acts vii. 38). Cf. Num. xvi. 3; xx. 4, "congregation *of the Lord*." The *Jews,* who might have been "the Church of God," had now, by their opposition, become the "synagogue of Satan." So 'the throne of Satan' (*v.* 13) represents the *heathen's* opposition; "the depths of Satan" (*v.* 24), the opposition of *heretics.* **10. none.** So א, Vulgate, Syriac; but A B C, Coptic, 'Fear *not* those things,' &c. 'The Captain of our salvation never keeps back what faithful witnesses for Him may have to bear: never entices recruits by promising they shall find all things easy and pleasant' (*Trench*). **devil**—'the accuser,' acting through Jewish *accusers,* against Christ and His people. The conflict is not with mere flesh and blood, but with the rulers of the darkness of this world. **tried** [*peirasthete*]—with *temptation.* The same event is often both a *temptation* from the devil, and a *trial* from God—God sifting the man to separate his chaff from his wheat, the devil sifting him in hope that nothing but chaff will be found in him (*Trench*). **ten days**—not the ten persecutions from Nero to Diocletian. *Lyra* explains *ten years* on the year-day principle. The *shortness* of the persecution is made the ground of consolation. The time of trial shall be short, the joy for ever. Cf. "ten days" for a short time, Gen. xxiv. 55; Num. xi. 19. *Ten* is the number of the world-powers hostile to the Church: cf. the beast's *ten* horns, ch. xiii. 1. **unto death**—so as even to die for my sake. **crown of life**—(Jas. i. 12; 2 Tim. iv. 8, "of righteousness;" 1 Pet. v. 4, "of glory.") The *crown* is the *garland* of a *conqueror,* or one *rejoicing,* or at a *feast;* but *diadem* is the mark of a KING.

11. shall not be hurt—'shall not by any means be hurt.' **the second death**—'the lake of fire.' 'The death in life of the lost, contrasted with the life in death of the saved' (*Trench*). "The second death" is peculiar to the Apocalypse. What matter about the first, which sooner or later must come, if we escape *the second death.* 'They who die that death shall be *hurt* by it. If it were annihilation, so a conclusion of their torments, it would be no way hurtful, but highly beneficial to them. But the living torments are the second death' (*Bishop Pearson*). Smyrna (*myrrh*) yielded its sweet perfume in being bruised to death. Myrrh was used in embalming dead bodies (John xix. 39): was an ingredient in the holy anointing oil (Exod. xxx. 23): a perfume of the heavenly Bridegroom (Ps. xlv. 8), and of the bride (Song iii. 6). 'Affliction, like it, is *bitter,* but *salutary;* preserving the elect from *corruption, seasoning* for immortality, giving scope for the *fragrantly-breathing* Christian virtues' (*Vitringa*). *Polycarp's* words to his heathen judges, refusing to recant, were, 'Fourscore and six years have I served the Lord, and He never wronged me: how then can I blaspheme my King and Saviour?' Smyrna's

662

12 And to the angel of the church in Pergamos write; These things saith
13 he *which hath* *the sharp sword with two edges; I know thy works, and where thou dwellest, *even* where Satan's seat *is:* and thou holdest fast my name, and hast not denied my faith, even in those days wherein Antipas *was* my faithful martyr, who was slain among you, where "Satan
14 dwelleth. But I have a few things against thee, because thou hast there them that hold the doctrine of *Balaam, who taught Balac to cast a stumblingblock before the children of Israel, *to eat things sacrificed
15 unto idols, *and to commit fornication. So hast thou also them that
16 hold the doctrine of the Nicolaitanes, which thing I hate. Repent; or else I will come unto thee quickly, and *will fight against them with the sword of my mouth.
17 He that hath an ear, let him hear what the Spirit saith unto the churches; To him that overcometh will I give to eat of the hidden manna,

A. D .96.
* Isa 11. 4.
Heb 4. 12.
ch 1. 16.
ch 19. 15,
21.
* Josh. 5. 13.
" Lev 17. 7.
Deut 32 16,
17.
* Num. 25. 1.
Num.31.16,
2 Pet. 2. 15.
Jude 11.
* Acts 15. 29.
* 1 Cor. 6. 13.
* Isa 11. 4.
2 Thes. 2. 8.

faithfulness is rewarded by its candlestick not having been removed (*v.* 5): Christianity has never wholly left it: whence the Turks call it 'Infidel Smyrna.'

12. *Trench* prefers *Pergamus,* or *Pergamum:* on the river Caïcus. Capital of Attalus the Second's kingdom, bequeathed by him to the Romans, B.C. 133. Famous for its library, founded by Eumenes (197-159), and destroyed by Caliph Omar. Parchment—i. e., *Pergemena charta*—was here discovered for book purposes. Also, famous for the magnificent temple of Esculapius, the healing god (*Tacitus,* 'Annals,' iii., 63). **he which hath the sharp sword with two edges**—His address having a twofold bearing, a searching power to convict and convert some (*vv.* 13, 17), and to condemn others (*vv.* 14-16, especially *v.* 16: cf. note, ch. i. 16). **13. I know thy works.** So B; but א A C, Vulgate, Coptic, omit. **Satan's seat**—rather, all through Revelation, "throne." Satan, in impious mimicry of God's heavenly throne, sets up his earthly throne (ch. iv. 2). Esculapius was worshipped there under the serpent form. Satan, the old servant, as instigator (cf. *v.* 10) of devotees of Esculapius, and, through them, of the supreme magistracy at Pergamos, persecuted one of the Lord's people (Antipas) to death. This address is an anticipatory preface to ch. xii. 1-17, notes. **even in those days.** So A C; but א B omit "even." **wherein.** So B; but א A C, Vulgate, Coptic, omit: then translate, 'in the days of Antipas, my faithful witness.' So א B; but A C read, 'My witness, MY faithful one.' Another form for Antipater. *Simeon Metaphrastes* has a legendary story, that Antipas, in Domitian's persecution, was shut up in a redhot brazen bull, and ended his life in thanksgivings and prayers. *Hengstenberg* makes the name symbolical, meaning one standing out 'against all' for Christ. **14. few**—in comparison of *many* tokens of thy faithfulness. **hold the doctrine** (teaching) **of Balaam**—that which he "taught Balac." Cf. "the counsel of Balaam," Num. xxxi. 16. *Balac* is dative, whence *Bengel,* 'taught (the Moabites) for (*i. e.*, to please) Balac.' But though in Numbers it is not expressly said he taught *Balac,* yet there is nothing inconsistent with his having done so; *Josephus* ('Antiquities,' iv., 6, 6) says he did. The dative is a Hebraism for the accusative. **stumblingblock**—*lit.*, that part of a trap on which the bait was laid, and which, when touched, caused the trap to close on its prey: then any entanglement (*Trench*). **children**—'*sons* of Israel.' **eat things sacrificed unto idols**—common to the Israelites and the Nicolaitanes. He does not add what was peculiar to the Israelites—viz., that they *sacrificed* to idols. The temptation to eat idol meats was peculiarly

strong to the Gentile converts. Not to do so involved almost a withdrawal from any social meal with the heathen. For idol meats, after a part had been offered in sacrifice, were generally on the heathen entertainer's table; so much so, that 'to kill' [*thuein*] meant originally 'to sacrifice.' Hence arose the decree of the council of Jerusalem forbidding such meats: subsequently some at Corinth ate *knowingly* such meats, on the ground that the idol is nothing; others tortured themselves with scruples, lest *unknowingly* they should eat them, in getting meat from the market, or in a heathen friend's house (1 Cor. viii. and x. 25-33). **fornication**—often connected with idolatry. **15. thou**—'so THOU also hast,' &c. As Balac and the Moabites of old had Balaam's followers literally, *so hast thou also them that hold the* same Balaamite or *Nicolaitane doctrine* spiritually. Literal eating of idol meats and fornication in Pergamos were accompanied by spiritual idolatry and fornication. So *Trench.* I prefer, "THOU *also*," as well as Ephesus ("in like manner" as Ephesus), hast ... Nicolaitanes, with this important difference, Ephesus *hates* and casts them out, THOU '*hast* (retainest) *them.*' **doctrine**—*teaching* (note, *v.* 6): tempting God's people to idolatry. **which thing I hate.** It is sin not to hate what God hates. Ephesus (*v.* 6) had this superiority to Pergamos. But A B C א, Vulgate, Syriac, read, instead of [*ho miso*] 'which I hate' [*homoiōs*], 'IN LIKE MANNER.' **16.** A B C read, 'Repent, *therefore*' [*oun*]; א *h,* Vulgate, Syriac, omit 'therefore.' Not only the Nicolaitanes, but all Pergamos, is called on to repent of not having *hated* the Nicolaitane teaching and practice. Contrast Acts xx. 26. **I will come**—I am come. **fight against** (war with) **them**—the Nicolaitanes primarily: including *chastisement of the* whole church at Pergamos: cf. "unto THEE," **with the sword of my mouth**—from ch. i. 16; but with an allusion to the angel of the Lord confronting with a drawn *sword* Balaam on his way to curse Israel: an earnest of *the sword* by which he and the seduced Israelites fell (Num. xxv. 5; xxxi. 8). The spiritual Balaamites are to be smitten with the Lord's spiritual sword, the word of His mouth (Isa. xi. 4).

17. to eat. Omitted in א A B C, Vulgate, Coptic. **the hidden manna**—Israel's heavenly food, in contrast to the idol meats (*v.* 14). A pot of manna was laid up in the Holy Place 'before the testimony.' The allusion is to this: also to the Lord's discourse (John vi. 31-35). 'The manna which is hidden.' As the manna hidden in the sanctuary was by Divine power preserved uncorrupt, so Christ, in His incorruptible body, is hidden in heaven until His appearing (Acts iii. 21). Christ is the manna "hidden" from the world, but re-

and will give him a white stone, and in the stone [a] new name written, which no man knoweth saving he that receiveth *it.*

18 And unto the angel of the church in Thyatira write; These things saith the Son of God, [o] who hath his eyes like unto a flame of fire, and

19 his feet *are* like fine brass; I know thy works, and charity, and service, and faith, and thy patience, and thy works; and the last *to be* more than

20 the first. Notwithstanding I have a few things against thee, because thou sufferest that woman [b] Jezebel, which calleth herself a prophetess, to

A. D. 96.

[a] Isa 56 4.
Isa. 65. 15.
ch. 3. 12.
ch. 19. 12.
13.
[o] ch. 1. 14.
[b] 1 Ki. 16. 31.
1 Ki. 18. 4.
13.

vealed to the believer, who has already a foretaste of His preciousness. Cf. Christ's own hidden food on earth (Job xxiii. 12; John iv. 32, 34). The full manifestation shall be at His coming. Believers are now hidden, even as their meat is (Ps. lxxxiii. 3; Col. iii. 3). Like the incorruptible manna in the sanctuary, the spiritual feast, offered to all who reject the world's dainties for Christ, is everlasting: an incorruptible body and life in Christ at the resurrection. **white stone . . . new name . . . no man knoweth saving he,** &c. *Trench, White* is the livery of heaven. "New" [*kainon*] implies something *altogether renewed*. The white stone is a glistering diamond, the Urim borne by the high priest within the *choschen* or breastplate of judgment, with the twelve tribes' names on the twelve precious stones, next the heart. The word *Urim* means light, answering to *white.* None but the high priest knew the name written upon it: probably the incommunicable name, "Jehovah." The high priest consulted it in some divinely-appointed way for direction from God when needful. The priest-judges of Egypt wore suspended an image of *Truth* or *Justice.* Thmei or Themis, answering to the Thummim [*aletheia* in LXX.]: the closed eyes of Thmei answer to Deut. xxxiii. 9. So answering to the Urim, the Egyptian priest wore in his breastplate the Scarabæus of precious stone, symbol of *light.* The high priest gazing on the gems symbolizing Light and Truth, and on the holy name Jehovah, became entranced, and so was enabled to give responses to those consulting God (cf. 1 Sam. xiv. 19). Ps. xliii. 3 is a worshipper's echo of the high priest's prayer. *Now,* the priest's peculiar treasure, consultation of God's light and truth, belongs to all believers, as spiritual priests (*Smith,* 'Dictionary of the Bible'). The "new name" is *Christ's* (cf. ch. iii. 12): some new revelation of Himself hereafter to be imparted to His people, which they alone are capable of receiving. The connection with the "hidden manna" is thus clear, as *the high priest* alone had access to the 'manna hidden' in the sanctuary. What believers had to contend against at Pergamos was *idol meats* and *fornication,* put in their way by Balaamites. As Phinehas was rewarded with 'an everlasting priesthood' for his zeal against these sins to which the Old Testament Balaam seduced Israel, so the heavenly high priesthood is the reward promised to those zealous against the New Testament Balaamites tempting Christ's people. **receiveth it**—viz., "the stone:" not the "new name:" which is *Christ's* new character as the glorified Son of man; not the believer's own new name. See above. The 'name that no man knew but Christ Himself' (cf. ch. iii. 12, end, with ch. xix. 12), He shall hereafter reveal to His people.

18. Thyatira — in Lydia, south of Pergamos. Lydia, the purple seller of this city, converted at Philippi, a Macedonian city (with which Thyatira, as being a Macedonian colony, had naturally much intercourse), was probably the instrument of first carrying the Gospel to her native town. John follows the geographical order; for Thyatira lay a

little to the left of the road from Pergamos to Sardis (*Strabo,* xiii., 4). **Son of God . . . eyes like . . . fire . . . feet are like fine brass**—or 'glowing brass' (resumed from ch. i. 14, 15). Again, His attributes accord with His address. "Son of God" is, from Ps. ii. 7, 9, referred to in *v.* 27. 'Eyes like flame,' &c., answers to *v.* 23, "I am He which searcheth the reins and hearts." "Feet are like fine brass" answers to *v.* 27, "as the vessels of a potter shall they be broken to shivers," He *treading* them *to pieces.* **19.** A B C, Vulgate, transpose, and read, 'faith and service.' The four are subordinate to "thy works:" 'I know thy works, *even* the love and the faith (forming one pair, as "faith works by love," Gal. v. 6), and the service (*ministration* to suffering members, and to all in spiritual or temporal need), and the persevering endurance of (*i. e.,* shown by) thee.' As *love* is inward, so *service* outward. Similarly, *faith* and persevering *endurance* (Rom. ii. 7) are connected. **and thy works; and the last.** Omit the second "and," with A B C א, Vulgate, 'And (I know) thy works which are last (to be) more in number than the first;' realizing 1 Thess. iv. 1: the converse of Matt. xii. 45; 2 Pet. ii. 20. Instead of retrograding from "first works" and "first love," as Ephesus, Thyatira's *last works* exceeded her *first* (*vv.* 4, 5). **20. a few things.** So oldest Vulgate; omitted in A B C: 'I have against thee *that,*' &c. א has 'much' [*polu*]. **sufferest** [*eas;* but א A B C read, *apheis,* 'lettest alone']. **that woman.** So א C, Vulgate; but A B, 'THY wife.' The symbolical Jezebel was to Thyatira what Jezebel, Ahab's 'wife,' was to him. Some self-styled prophetess (or, as the feminine in Hebrew often *collectively* expresses a multitude, *a set of false prophets*), as closely attached to the church of Thyatira as a *wife* is to a husband, and as powerfully influencing for evil that church as Jezebel did Ahab. As Balaam, in Israel's early history, so Jezebel, daughter of Eth-baal, king of Sidon (1 Ki. xvi. 31), formerly priest of Astarte, and murderer of his predecessor on the throne (*Josephus,* 'Contra Apion,' i., 18), was the great seducer in Israel's later history. Like her father, she was swift to shed blood. Wholly given to Baal-worship, like Eth-baal, whose name expresses his idolatry, she, with her strong will, seduced the weak Ahab and Israel beyond the calf-worship (a worship of the true God under the cherub-ox form; *i. e.,* a violation of the second commandment) to that of Baal (a violation of the first also). She was herself a priestess and prophetess of Baal. Cf. 2 Ki. ix. 22, 30, "*whoredoms* of . . . Jezebel and her *witchcrafts*" (impurity was part of the worship of the Phœnician Astarte, or Venus). Her spiritual counterpart at Thyatira lured God's "servants" by pretended inspiration to the same libertinism, fornication, and idol meats, as the Balaamites and Nicolaitanes (*vv.* 6, 14, 15). By false spiritualism these led their victims into gross carnality, as though things done in the flesh were outside the man, and therefore indifferent. 'The deeper the Church penetrated into heathenism, the more she became heathenish. This prepares us for

teach and to seduce my servants to commit fornication, and to eat things

21 sacrificed unto idols. And I gave her space ^c to repent of her fornica-

22 tion; and she repented not. Behold, I will cast her into a bed, and them that commit adultery with her into great tribulation, except they

23 repent of their deeds. And I will kill her children with death; and all the churches shall know that ^dI am he which searcheth the reins and hearts: and ^eI will give unto every one of you according to your works.

24 But unto you I say, and unto the rest in Thyatira, as many as have not this doctrine, and which have not known ^f the depths of Satan, as they

25 speak; ^gI will put upon you none other burden. But that which ye have *already* hold fast till I come.

26 And he that overcometh, and keepeth my ^hworks unto the end, ⁱ to

27 him will I give power over the nations: and ^j he shall rule them with a

A.D. 96
^c Rom. 2. 4.
^d 1 Sam 16.7.
1 Chr. 28. 9.
1 Chr 29.17.
Ps. 7. 9.
^e Ps. 62. 12.
Matt.16.27.
2 Cor. 5. 10.
^f 2 Cor. 2. 11.
^g Acts 15 28.
^h John 6. 29.
ⁱ Matt.19.28.
Luke 22.29.
1 Cor 6. 3.
^j Ps. 2. 8, 9.
Ps. 49. 14.

"harlot" and "Babylon," applied to her afterwards' (*Auberlen*). **to teach and to seduce.** So Vulgate; but א A B C, 'and she teaches and seduces' [*plana*, 'deceives']. 'Thyatira was just the reverse of Ephesus. There, zeal for orthodoxy, but little love; here, activity of faith and love, but insufficient zeal for discipline and doctrine: a patience of error even where there was not a participation in it' (*Trench*). **21. space**—'time.' **of her fornication; and she repented not.** א omits "and she repented not;" A reads, 'she *willed* not;' B C, Vulgate, 'she *willeth* not *to repent of* [*ek, out of*] (i.e., so as to come out of) *her fornication.*' A transition from *literal* to *spiritual* fornication (cf. *v.* 22). Jehovah's covenant relation to the Old Testament Church being regarded as a marriage, any transgression against it was *fornication*, or *adultery* (Isa. liv. 5). **22. Behold**—calling attention to her awful doom. **I will**—present, 'I cast her.' **a bed.** The bed of her sin shall be her bed of anguish. Perhaps a pestilence was to be sent. Or the bed of the grave, and the hell beyond, where the worm dieth not. **them that commit adultery with her**—spiritually: including both the *idol meats* and *fornication*. "With [*meta*] her" implies *participation* in her adulteries—viz., by *suffering* her (*v.* 20), or *letting* her *alone*, virtually encouraging her. Her punishment is distinct from theirs: she is to be cast into a *bed*, and her *children* to be *killed*; whilst those who partake in her sin, by tolerating her, are to be cast into *great tribulation*. **except they repent** [*metanoesosin*]—aorist, "repent" *at once*: shall have repented by the time limited in my purpose. **their deeds.** So A, Cyprian; but א B C, Vulgate, Coptic, Syriac, 'her.' God's true servants, who, by connivance, incur the guilt of *her deeds*, are distinguished from her. **23. her children**—(Isa. lvii. 3; Ezek. xxiii. 45, 47.) Her proper adherents: not those who *suffer*, but those who are begotten of, her. A distinct class from those, *v.* 22 (cf. note there), whose sin was that only of connivance. **kill . . . with death**—which overtook the literal Jezebel's votaries of Baal, and Ahab's sons (1 Ki. xviii. 40; 2 Ki. x. 6, 7, 24, 25). A Hebraism for *slay with sure and awful death:* so 'dying, die' (Gen. ii. 17). Not "die the common death of all men" (Num. xvi. 29). **all the churches shall know.** These addresses are for the Catholic Church of all ages and places. So palpably shall God's hand be seen in the judgment on Thyatira, that the whole Church shall recognize it. **I am he**—strongly emphatical: 'it is *I* am He who,' &c. **searcheth . . . hearts**—God's peculiar attribute is given to Christ. The "reins" are the seat of the desires; the "heart," that of the thoughts. [*Ereunōn*, "searcheth:" accurately following up all tracks and windings.] **unto every one of you**—'unto you, to each,' &c. **according to**

your works—to be judged, not according to the act as it appears to man, but with reference to *faith* and *love*, the only motives which God accepts. **24. you . . . and unto the rest.** A B C omit "and," 'unto you, the rest.' א [*en*], '*among* the rest.' **as many as have not**—not only do not *hold*, but are free from contact with. **and which.** א A B C omit "and," 'whosoever.' **the depths.** These false prophets boasted of their *knowledge of the deep things of God:* pretensions subsequently expressed by their arrogant title, *Gnostics* ('full of knowledge'). The Spirit declares their so-called "depths" (of knowledge) to be really "depths *of Satan;*" just as *v.* 9, He says, instead of 'the synagogue *of God*,' "the synagogue *of Satan.*" *Hengstenberg* thinks the teachers professed to fathom the *depths of Satan*, giving loose rein to fleshly lusts, without harm. They who think to fight Satan with his own weapons find him more than a match for them. "As they speak," *i.e.*, 'as they call them,' coming after not only "depths," but "depths of Satan," favours this. The sin of Adam was a desire to know EVIL *as well as good:* so those who professed to know "the depths of Satan." It is the prerogative of God alone to know evil fully, without being hurt by it. **I will put.** So א B; but A C have, 'I put,' or 'cast.' **none other burden**—save abstinence from, and protestation against, these abominations: no "depths" beyond your reach, such as they teach; the old faith and rule once for all delivered to the saints. Exaggerating Paul's doctrine of grace without the law for justification and sanctification, the seducers rejected the law as an intolerable "burden." But it is a 'light' burden. In Acts xv. 28, 29, "burden," as here, is used of abstinence from fornication and idol meats: to this the Lord refers. **25. that which ye have already**—(Jude 3, end.) **hold fast**—do not let go from your grasp, however they try to wrest it from you. **till I come**—when your conflict with evil will end [*achris hou an hēxo*, implies *uncertainty* when He shall come].

26. And—implying the close connection of the promise with the exhortation, *v.* 25. **and keepeth**—'and he that keepeth :' alluding, as in *v.* 24, to Acts xv. 28, 29, end. **my works**—in contrast to 'her (or *their*) works' (*v.* 22). The works which I command, the fruit of my Spirit. **unto the end** —(Matt. xxiv. 13.) The image is from the race, wherein it is not enough to enter the lists: the runner must persevere *to the end*. **give power** [*exousian*]—'authority.' **over the nations.** At Christ's coming, the saints shall possess the kingdom "under the whole heaven" (Dan. vii. 27): therefore over this earth (cf. Luke xix. 17). **27. rule** [*poimanei*]—'rule as a shepherd.' In Ps. ii: 9 it is, "Thou shalt *break* them with a rod of iron."

665

rod of iron; as the vessels of a potter shall they be broken to shivers:
28 even as I received of my Father. And I will give him ᵏthe morning
29 star. He that hath an ear, let him hear what the Spirit saith unto the
churches.

3 AND unto the angel of the church in Sardis write; These things saith
he that hath the seven Spirits of God, and the seven stars; I know thy
2 works, that thou hast a name that thou livest, ᵃand art dead. Be watchful, and strengthen the things which remain, that are ready to die: for
3 I have not found thy works perfect before God. Remember therefore
how thou hast received and heard; and hold fast, and repent. ᵇIf there-

A. D. 96.

ᵏ 2 Pet 1. 19.
ch. 22. 16.

CHAP. 3.
ᵃ Luke 15. 24, 32.
Eph. 2. 1.
Col 2. 13.
1 Tim. 5. 6.
Jas. 2. 26.
Jude 12.
ᵇ Luke 12 39.

The LXX., pointing the Hebrew differently, read as Revelation. The English version of Ps. ii. 9 (note) is right, as the parallel, "dash in pieces," proves. But the Spirit sanctions the *additional* thought, that the Lord shall mingle mercy to some with judgment on others: beginning by destroying antichristian foes. He shall reign in love over the rest. 'Christ shall rule them with a *sceptre* of iron, to make them capable of being ruled with a sceptre of gold: severity first, that grace may come after' (*Trench*, who translates 'SCEPTRE' for "rod," as in Heb. i. 8). 'Shepherd' is used, in Jer. vi. 3, of *hostile rulers;* so Zech. xi. 16. As severity is prominent, 'rule as a shepherd' is used thus: He who would have shepherded them with a pastoral rod, shall, because of their hardened unbelief, shepherd them with a rod of iron. **shall they be broken.** So B, Vulgate, Syriac, Coptic versions read; but A C, 'as the vessels of a potter *are* broken to shivers.' *A potter's vessel dashed to pieces*, because of its failing to answer its maker's design, is the image for God's sovereign power to give reprobates to destruction, not by caprice, but in His righteous judgment (Rom. xi. 21, 22). The saints shall be in Christ's victorious 'armies' when He shall inflict the last decisive blow, and afterwards shall reign with Him, (chs. xix. and xx.) Having by faith "overcome the world," they shall also rule the world. **even as I**—'as *I* also have received of (from) my Father,' in Ps. ii. 7-9. Jesus refused to receive the kingdom without the Cross at Satan's hands: He would receive it from the Father alone, who appointed the Cross, the path to the crown. As the Father has given the authority to me over the heathen and uttermost parts of the earth, so I impart a share to my victorious disciple. **28. the morning star**—i. e., *Myself* (ch. xxii. 16): so that, reflecting my brightness, He shall shine like me, the morning star, and share my *kingly glory* (of which a *star* is the symbol, Num. xxiv. 17; Matt. ii. 2). Cf. *v.* 17, 'I will give him the hidden manna,' i. e., *Myself* (John vi. 31-33).

CHAP. III. 1-22.—EPISTLES TO SARDIS, PHILADELPHIA, AND LAODICEA.
1. Sardis—the ancient capital of Lydia, the kingdom of wealthy Crœsus, on the river Pactolus. The address is full of rebuke: not in vain; for Melito, bishop of Sardis in the second century, was eminent for piety. He visited Palestine to assure himself and his flock as to the Old Testament canon, and wrote an epistle on the subject (*Eusebius*, iv., 26); also a commentary on the Apocalypse, (*Eusebius*, iv., 26; *Jerome*, 'Catalogus Scriptorum Ecclesiasticorum,' xxiv.) **he that hath the seven Spirits of God**—i. e., the fulness of the Spirit (John iii. 34; ch. i. 4; iv. 5; v. 6: cf. Zech. iii. 9; iv. 10), proving His Godhead. Implying His infinite power by the Spirit to convict of sin and of a hollow profession. **and the seven stars**—(ch. i. 16, 20.) His *having the seven stars*, or presiding ministers, flows from His *having the seven*

Spirits, or the fulness of the Holy Spirit. The human ministry is the fruit of Christ's sending the gifts of the Spirit. *Stars* imply brilliancy; the fulness of the Spirit, and of brilliant light in Him, form a contrast to the formality which He reproves. **name . . livest . . . dead**—(1 Tim. v. 6; 2 Tim. iii. 5; Titus i. 16: cf. Eph. ii. 1, 5; v. 14.) Sardis was *famed* among the churches for spiritual *vitality;* yet He who sees not as man seeth, pronounces her *dead:* how great searchings of heart should her case create among even the best! Laodicea deceived herself as to her state (*v.* 17); but she is not mentioned as having a high *name* among the churches, as Sardis. **2. Be** [*ginou*]—'Become' what thou art not, 'watchful' [*gregoron*], 'waking.' **the things which remain**—those thy remaining few graces, which, in thy spiritual slumber, are not yet extinct (*Alford*). Hardly 'the PERSONS that are not yet dead, but *ready to die;*' for *v.* 4 implies that the "few" faithful at Sardis were not "ready to die," but full of life. **are.** ℵ A C, Vulgate, Coptic, Syriac, read, 'were ready' [*emellon*], 'were about to die,' at the time when you "strengthen" them. 'Thou art dead,' *v.* 1, is therefore to be taken with limitation; for those must have some life who can *strengthen the things that remain.* **perfect** [*pepleromena*]—'filled up in full complement:' 'complete.' Wanting in living faith as the motive of works. **before God** —'in the sight of God.' ℵ A B C, Vulgate, Syriac, Coptic, read, 'in the sight of MY God:' Christ's judgment is the Father's. In the sight of men, Sardis had 'a name of living :' 'so many and so great are the obligations of pastors, that he who would fulfil even a third of them, would be esteemed holy by men; whereas, if content with that alone, he would be sure not to escape hell' (*Juan D'Avila*). Note, in Sardis and Laodicea, alone of the seven, we read of no conflict with foes within or without. Not that either had renounced *apparent* opposition to the world; but neither had the faithfulness to witness for God by word and example, so as to 'torment them that dwelt on the earth' (ch. xi. 10). **3. how thou hast received** —(Col. ii. 6; 1 Thess. iv. 1; 1 Tim. vi. 20.) Sardis is to "remember," not *how* joyfully she had received the Gospel, but how the precious deposit was committed to her originally, so that she could not say she had not "received" it. Not aorist (as ch. ii. 4, Ephesus, "Thou *didst leave* thy first love"), but "thou hast received" (perfect), and still hast, the deposit of doctrine. 'Keep' [*terei*], "hold fast." Observe the commandment thou hast received. **heard**—(aorist), 'didst hear,' viz., when the Gospel was committed to thee. *Trench* explains "how," *with what demonstration of the Spirit* from Christ's ambassadors the truth came to you, and how heartily you at first received it. *Bengel*, 'Regard to her former *character* (how it once stood) ought to guard Sardis against the future *hour*, whatsoever it shall be, proving fatal to her.' But thus the same exhortation would be addressed to Sardis

fore thou shalt not watch, I will come on thee as a thief, and thou shalt
4 not know what hour I will come upon thee. Thou hast *c*a few names even in Sardis which have not *d*defiled their garments; and they shall walk with me *e*in white: for they are worthy.
5 He that overcometh, the same shall be clothed in white raiment; and I will *f*not blot out his name out of the book *g*of life, but *h*I will confess
6 his name before my Father, and before his angels. He that hath an ear, let him hear what the Spirit saith unto the churches.
7 And to the angel of the church in Philadelphia write; These things

A. D. 96.

c Acts 1. 15.
d Isa 52. 1.
Isa. 61.3,10.
Jude 23.
e ch. 7. 9, 13.
f Ex. 32. 32.
Ps. 69. 28.
g Phil. 4. 3.
ch. 21. 27.
h Matt. 10.32.

as to Ephesus. **If therefore**—seeing thou art so warned; if, nevertheless, &c. **come on thee as a thief**—in judgment on thee as a church; as stealthily and unexpectedly shall be my second coming, as *the thief* gives no notice of his approach. Christ, in language which in its full sense describes His second coming, describes His coming with judgments on churches and states (as Jerusalem, Matt. xxiv.); these judgments being anticipatory earnests of that great last coming. 'The last day is hidden from us, that every day may be observed by us' (*Augustine*). Twice Christ spake the same words (Matt. xxiv. 42, 43; Luke xii. 39, 40); which so deeply sank in the mind of the apostles, that they often repeat them (1 Thess. v. 2, 4, 6; 2 Pet. iii. 10; ch. xvi. 15). The Greek proverb, 'the feet of the avenging deities are shod with wool,' expresses the noiseless approach and nearness of Divine judgments, when they are supposed far off (*Trench*). **4.** א A B C,Vulgate, prefix 'nevertheless' (notwithstanding thy spiritual deadness), and omit "even." **names**—persons *named* in the book of life (*v.* 5), known by the Lord as His own (John x. 3). These had the reality corresponding to their name; not a *name* among men as *living*, whilst really *dead* (*v.* 1). The gracious Lord does not overlook exceptional saints among unreal professors. **not defiled their garments**—their Christian profession, of which baptism is the initiatory seal, whence the candidates used in the ancient Church to be arrayed in white. Cf. Eph. v. 27, and ch. xix. 8, as to the "fine linen, clean and white, the righteousness of the saints," in which it shall be granted to the Church to be arrayed; and "the wedding garment." Meanwhile she is not to sully her profession with defilement of flesh or spirit, but to 'keep her garments,' for no defilement shall enter the heavenly city. Not that any keep themselves here wholly undefiled; but, as compared with hollow professors, the godly *keep themselves unspotted from the world;* and when they contract defilement, they wash it away, so as to have "robes white in the blood of the Lamb" (ch. vii. 14). Not 'stain' [*miainein*], but 'defile,' besmear [*molunein*] (Song v. 3). **they shall walk with me in white.** The reward accords with the character of those rewarded: keeping their *garments undefiled* through the blood of the Lamb now, they shall *walk with Him in white* hereafter. On "with me," cf. Luke xxiii. 43; John xvii. 24. "Walk" implies spiritual life; for only the living walk: also liberty, for it is only the free who walk at large. The grace of flowing garments is seen to best advantage when the person 'walks:' so the graces of the saint shall appear fully when he shall *serve* the Lord perfectly hereafter (ch. xxii. 3). they are **worthy**—with worthiness (not their own, but that) which Christ has put on them (ch. vii. 14; Ezek. xvi. 14). Grace is glory in the bud. 'The *worthiness* denotes a congruity between the saints' *state of grace* on earth, and that of *glory*, which the Lord has appointed for them, and is estimated by the law itself of grace' (*Vitringa*). Contrast Acts xiii. 46.

5. the same—'THIS man;' he alone. So B; but א A C,Vulgate, Coptic, Syriac, 'shall THUS be clothed,' &c. **white**—glittering, dazzling white. Cf. Matt. xiii. 43. The body transfigured into the likeness of Christ's, and emitting light reflected from Him, is probably the "white raiment." **raiment**—'garments.' "He that overcometh" shall receive the same reward as they who "have not defiled their garments" (*v.* 4): the two are identical. **I will not** [*ou me*]—'I will not by any means.' **blot out his name out of the book of life**—of the heavenly city. A register of citizens was kept in ancient states: the names of the dead were erased. So those who have a *name that they live and are dead* (*v.* 1), are blotted out of God's roll of the heavenly citizens; not that in God's electing decree they ever were there. But those having a high name for piety would be supposed to be in it, and were, as to privileges, actually among those in the way of salvation; these privileges, however, and the fact that they once might have been saved, shall not avail them. As to the *book of life*, cf. Exod. xxxii. 32; Ps. lxix. 28; Dan. xii. 1; ch. xiii. 8; xvii. 8. Many are enrolled among the *called* to salvation, who shall not be among *the chosen* at last. The pale of salvation is wider than that of election. Election is fixed. Salvation is open to all, and is pending (humanly speaking) in the case of those mentioned here. Ch. xx. 15; xxi. 27, exhibit the book of the elect alone, after the erasure of the others. **before ... before**—'in the presence of.' Cf. the same promise, Matt. x. 32, 33; Luke xii. 8, 9. He omits 'in heaven,' because there is, now that He is in heaven, no contrast between the Father *in heaven* and the Son *on earth.* He sets His seal from heaven upon many of His words uttered on earth (*Trench*). An undesigned coincidence, proving that these epistles are, in words as well as substance, Christ's own; not even tinged with John's style, such as it appears in his gospel and epistles. The coincidence is mainly with the three other gospels, not John's, which makes it more markedly undesigned. So also "He that hath an ear, let him hear," is not repeated from John's gospel, but from the Lord's own words in the three synoptic gospels (Matt. xi. 15; xiii. 9; Mark iv. 9, 23; vii. 16; Luke viii. 8; xiv. 35). **6.** Note, ch. ii. 7.
7. Philadelphia—in Lydia, twenty-eight miles south-east of Sardis, built by Attalus Philadelphus, king of Pergamus, who died 138 A. D. It was nearly destroyed by an earthquake in the reign of Tiberius (*Tacitus*, 'Annals,' ii., 47). The connection of this church with Jews causes the address to have an Old Testament colouring in the images. It and Smyrna alone of the seven, the most afflicted, receive unmixed praise. **he that is holy**—as in the Old Testament, "*the Holy One* of Israel." Jesus and the God of the Old Testament are one. God alone is absolutely holy [*hagios*, separate from evil, perfectly hating it]. In contrast to "the synagogue of Satan" (*v.* 9). **true** [*alethinos*]—VERY God, as distinguished from false gods, and from all who *say that they are* what

saith he ⁱ that is holy, ʲ he that is true, he that hath ᵏ the key of David, ˡ he that openeth, and no man shutteth; ᵐ and shutteth, and no man
8 openeth; I know thy works: behold, I have set before thee ⁿ an open door, and no man can shut it: for thou hast a little strength, and hast
9 kept my word, and hast not denied my name. Behold, I will make them of the synagogue of Satan, which say they are Jews, and are not, but do lie; behold, ° I will make them to come and worship before thy feet, and
10 to know that I have loved thee. Because thou hast kept the word of my patience, ᵖ I also will keep thee from the hour of temptation, which shall
11 come upon all the world, to try them that dwell upon the earth. Behold, I come quickly: hold that fast which thou hast, that no man take thy crown.

A. D 96.

ⁱ Isa. 6. 3.
Acts 3. 14.
Heb. 7. 26.
ʲ John 14. 6.
1 John 5.
20.
ᵏ Isa. 22. 22.
Luke 1 32.
ch. 1. 18.
ˡ Matt.16.19.
ᵐ Job 12. 14.
ⁿ 2 Cor. 2. 12.
° Isa. 49. 23.
Isa. 60. 14.
ᵖ 2 Pet. 2. 9.

they are not (*v.* 9); real, genuine. He *perfectly realizes* all that is involved in the names, GOD, *Light* (1 John ii. 8), *Bread*, the *Vine* (John vi. 32; xv. 1), as distinguished from typical, partial, imperfect realizations of the idea. His nature answers to His name (John xvii. 3; 1 Thess. i. 9). [*Alethes*, on the other hand, is *truth-speaking, truth-loving* (John iii. 33; Titus i. 2).] **he that hath the key of David**—antitype of Eliakim, to whom the "key"—emblem of authority 'over the house of David'—was transferred from Shebna, who was removed from the office of chamberlain or treasurer, as unworthy of it. Christ, the Heir of the throne of David, shall supplant all less worthy stewards who abuse their trust in God's spiritual house, and 'shall reign over the house of Jacob,' literal and spiritual (Luke i. 32, 33) 'for ever,' "as a Son over His own house" (Heb. iii. 2.6). It rests with Christ to open or shut the heavenly palace, deciding who is, and who is not, to be admitted. He also opens or shuts the prison, *having the keys of hell* (*the grave*) *and death* (ch. i. 18). The power of the keys was given to Peter and the other apostles only when, and in so far as, Christ made him and them infallible. Whatever degrees of this power may have been committed to ministers, the supreme power belongs to Christ alone. Thus Peter rightly opened the Gospel door to the Gentiles (Acts x.; xi. 17, 18; especially xiv. 27). But he wrongly tried to shut it again (Gal. ii. 11-18). Eliakim had 'the key of the house of David laid upon his shoulder.' Christ, the antitypical David, Himself has the key of supreme 'government upon His shoulder' (Isa. ix. 6). His attribute accords with His promise. Though "the synagogue of Satan," false Jews (*v.* 9), try to "shut" the "door" which I 'set open before thee,' "no man can shut it" (*v.* 8). **shutteth.** So Vulgate and Syriac; but ℵ A B C, Coptic, *Origen*, 'shall shut.' **and no man openeth.** B ℵ, Coptic version, *Origen*, 'shall open;' A C, Vulgate, "openeth." **8. I have set**—'given;' my gracious *gift* to thee. **open door**—for spiritual usefulness. The *opening of a door* by Him to the Philadelphian church accords with His having "the key of David." **and.** A B C, *Origen*, '*which* no man can shut.' **for**—'because.' **a little.** This gives the idea that Christ sets before Philadelphia an open door, because she has *some little* strength: rather, He does so because she has '*but little* strength:' consciously weak herself, she is the fitter object for God's power to rest on (*Aquinas*), that Christ may have all the glory (2 Cor. xii. 9, 10). **and hast kept**—*and* so, the *littleness of thy strength* leading thee to rest wholly on My great power, *thou didst keep my word*. *Grotius* explains "little strength," that she had a church *small in numbers and external resources*: 'of small account in the eyes of men' (*Trench*). Aorist, 'Thou didst

668

not deny my name,' on some particular occasion, when thy faithfulness was put to the test. **9. I will make**—present, 'I make;' 'I give' (note, *v.* 8). The promise to Philadelphia is larger than to Smyrna. To Smyrna it was that "the synagogue of Satan" should not prevail against the faithful in her; to Philadelphia, that she should even win over some of "the synagogue of Satan" to *fall on their faces and confess God is in her of a truth* (1 Cor. xiv. 25). Translate, '(some) of the synagogue.' For until Christ shall come, when *all* Israel shall be saved, there is but "a remnant" being gathered out of her "according to the election of grace" (Rom. xi. 5). This shows how Christ set before her an "open door"—some of her greatest adversaries, the Jews, being brought to the obedience of faith. Their *worshipping before her feet* expresses the converts' willingness to take the lowest place in the Church, doing servile honour to those whom once they persecuted, rather than dwell with the ungodly (Ps. lxxxiv. 10). So the Philippian gaoler before Paul. **10. patience.** 'The word of my persevering endurance' is *my Gospel word*, which teaches it in expectation of my coming (ch. i. 9). *My endurance* is the endurance which I require and I practise. Christ Himself now *endures*, *patiently* waiting until the usurper be cast out, and all "His enemies be made His footstool." So, too, His Church, for the joy before her of sharing His coming kingdom, *endures patiently*. Hence (*v.* 11) follows, "Behold, I come quickly." **I also.** The reward is in kind: 'because thou didst keep,' &c., 'I also (on my side) will keep thee,' &c. **from** [*ek*, not *apo*]—'(so as to deliver thee) *out of*,' not to exempt *from* temptation. **the hour of** (the) **temptation**—the appointed *season* of affliction (Deut. iv. 34, the plagues are called "the temptations of Egypt"): *the* sore temptation coming on: the great tribulation before Christ's second coming. **to try them that dwell upon the earth**—of earth, earthy (ch. viii. 13). "Dwell" implies their *home* is earth, not heaven. *All mankind, except the elect* (ch. xiii. 8, 14). The temptation brings out the fidelity of those *kept* by Christ, and hardens the reprobates (ch. ix. 20, 21; xvi. 11, 21). The persecutions which befell Philadelphia shortly after, were the earnest of the great tribulation before Christ's coming, to which the Church's attention in all ages is directed. **11.** Behold. Omitted by ℵ A B C, Vulgate, Coptic, Syriac. **I come quickly**—the great incentive to faithfulness, and the consolation under trials. **that fast which thou hast** —"the word of my patience" (*v.* 10), just commended to them for keeping: involving with it the attaining of the kingdom. This they would lose if they exchanged consistency and suffering for compromise and ease. **that no man take thy crown**—that no tempter cause thee to lose what

	A. D. 96.

12   Him that overcometh will I make *q* a pillar in the temple of my God, and he shall go no more out: and *r* I will write upon him the name of my God, and the name of the city of my God, *which is* *s* new Jerusalem, which cometh down out of heaven from my God; and *t* *I will write upon*

13 *him* my new name. He that hath an ear, let him hear what the Spirit saith unto the churches.

14   And unto the angel of the church *1* of the Laodiceans write; These things saith the *u* Amen, the faithful and true *v* Witness, *w* the beginning

15 of the creation of God; I know thy works, that thou art neither cold nor

q Gal. 2. 9.
r ch. 14. 1.
s Gal 4. 26.
t ch. 22. 4.
1 Or, in Laodicea.
u 2 Cor. 1. 20.
v Isa. 55. 4.
w Pro. 8. 22. John 1.

otherwise thou wouldst receive: not that the tempter would secure it for himself (Col. ii. 18).

12. pillar in the temple. In one sense there shall be 'no temple' in the heavenly city, because there shall be no distinction of things sacred and secular; for all shall be holy to the Lord. The city shall be one great temple, in which the saints shall be not merely *stones*, as in the spiritual temple on earth, but eminent as *pillars:* immovably firm (unlike Philadelphia, the city so often shaken by earthquakes, *Strabo*, xii. and xiii.), like the colossal pillars before Solomon's temple, Boaz (*i. e.*, 'in it is strength') and Jachin ('it shall be established'). Those pillars were outside, these shall be within the temple. **my God**—(note, ch. ii. 7.) **go no more out** [*ou me eti*]—*never more at all*. As the elect angels are beyond possibility of falling, being under 'the blessed necessity of goodness,' so shall the saints be priests for ever unto God (ch. i. 6). The door shall once for all shut safely in for ever the elect, and shut out the lost (Matt. xxv. 10; John viii. 35: cf. Isa. xxii. 23, the type, Eliakim). 'Who would not yearn for that city out of which no friend departs, into which no enemy enters?' (*Augustine*.) **write upon him the name of my God**—belonging to God in a peculiar sense (ch. vii. 3; ix. 4; xiv. 1; especially xxii. 4), therefore secure. As the golden plate on the high priest's forehead bare Jehovah's name, "Holiness to the Lord" (Exod. xxviii. 36-38), so the saints in their royal priesthood shall bear His name openly, as consecrated to Him. Cf. its caricature in the brand on the forehead of the beast's followers (ch. xiii. 16, 17), and on the harlot (ch. xvii. 5: cf. ch. xx. 4). **name of the city of my God**—as one of its citizens (ch. xxi. 2, 3, 10), briefly alluded to by anticipation here. The full description forms the appropriate close of the book. The saints' citizenship is now hidden, then it shall be manifested: he shall have *the right to enter in through the gates into the city* (ch. xxii. 14)—the city which Abraham *looked for* (Heb. xi. 10). **new** [*kaines*]. Not the old Jerusalem, once "the holy city," but having forfeited the name. [*Nea* would express that it had *recently come* into existence; *kaine*, that which is *new and different*, superseding the worn-out old Jerusalem and its polity (Heb. viii. 13).] 'John, in the gospel, applies to the old city the Greek, *Hierosolyma;* but in the Apocalypse, always, to the heavenly city, the Hebrew, *Hierousalem*. The Hebrew is the original and holier name; the Greek, the recent secular one' (*Bengel*). **my new name**—at present incommunicable: only known to God; to be hereafter revealed as the believer's own in union with God in Christ. Christ's name written on him denotes he shall be *wholly Christ's*. *New* also relates to Christ, who shall assume a *new* character (answering to His "new name"), taking with His saints a kingdom; not what He had with the Father before the worlds, but that earned by His humiliation as Son of man. *Gibbon* (' Decline and Fall,' ch. lxiv.) gives an unwilling testimony to the fulfilment of prophecy as to Philadelphia tem-

porally: 'Among the Greek churches of Asia, Philadelphia is still erect—a *column* in a scene of ruins; a pleasing example that the paths of honour and safety may sometimes be the same.' (Note, ch. ii. 7.)

14. Laodiceans—in the south-west of Phrygia, on the river Lycus, not far from Colosse, lying between it and Philadelphia: destroyed by an earthquake, 62 A. D.; rebuilt by its wealthy citizens without the help of the state (*Tacitus*, 'Annals,' xiv., 27). This wealth (arising from the excellence of its wools) led to a self-satisfied, lukewarm state in spiritual things, as *v*. 17. describes. Note on Col. iv. 16, on the epistle thought to have been written to the Laodiceans by Paul. The church in later times was flourishing; for one of the councils at which the canon of Scripture was determined was held in Laodicea, in 361 A. D. Hardly a Christian is now to be found near its site. **the Amen**—(Isa. lxv. 16, Hebrew, 'Bless Himself in the God of *Amen* . . . swear by the God of *Amen;*' 2 Cor. i. 20.) He who not only says, but is, *the Truth*. The saints used *Amen* at the end of prayer, or the Word of God; none, save the Son of God, ever said, 'Amen, I say unto you:' it is language peculiar to God, who avers *by Himself*. The New Testament 'Amen, I say unto you,' is equivalent to the Old Testament formula '*As I live*, saith Jehovah.' In St. John's gospel alone He uses the double "Amen" (John i. 52; iii. 3, &c.): English version, "Verily, verily." The title harmonizes with the address. His unchanging faithfulness as "the Amen" contrasts with Laodicea's wavering—"neither hot nor cold" (*v.* 16). The angel of Laodicea has, with probability, been conjectured to be Archippus, to whom, thirty years previously, Paul had given a needed monition to diligence in his ministry (Col. iv. 17). So the 'Apostolic Constitutions,' viii., 46, name him as first bishop of Laodicea: supposed to be the son of Philemon (Phile. 2). **faithful and true Witness.** "The Amen" expresses the truth of His promises; "the true Witness," the genuineness of His revelations of heavenly things which He has seen and testifies (John iii. 11, 12). "Faithful," *i. e.*, trustworthy (2 Tim. ii. 11, 13). "True" is here [*alethinos*] not truth-speaking [*alethes*], but 'perfectly realizing all that is comprehended in "*Witness*"' (1 Tim. vi. 13). Three things are necessary: (I.) to have seen with His own eyes; (2.) to be competent to relate it; (3.) to be willing truthfully to do so. In Christ all these conditions meet (*Trench*). **beginning of the creation of God**—not He whom God created first, but as in Col. i. 15-18 (note), the *Beginner* of all creation: its originating instrument. All creation would not be represented adoring Him, if He were but one of themselves (ch. v. 8, 11, 13). His being the Creator is a guarantee for His *faithfulness* as 'the Witness and Amen.' **15. neither cold**—antithesis to "hot" [*zestos, boiling* ("fervent," Acts xviii. 25; Rom. xii. 11: cf. Song viii. 6; Luke xxiv. 32), requires that "cold" should mean more than negatively *cold;* positively, *icy cold:* never yet warmed l

16 hot: I would thou wert cold or hot. So then because thou art luke-
17 warm, and neither cold nor hot, I will spue thee out of my mouth. Because thou sayest, *ˣ*I am rich, and increased with goods, and have need
of nothing; and knowest not that thou art wretched, and miserable, and
18 poor, and blind, and naked: I counsel thee *ʸ*to buy of me gold tried in
the fire, that thou mayest be rich; *ᶻ*and white raiment, that thou mayest
be clothed, and *that* the shame of thy nakedness do not appear; and
19 anoint thine eyes with eye-salve, that thou mayest see. As *ᵃ*many as
20 I love, I rebuke and chasten: be zealous therefore, and repent. Be-

A. D 96.

ˣ Hos 12, 8.
1 C r 4. 8.
ʸ Isa. 55, 1.
Matt. 13, 44.
Matt 25. 9.
ᶻ 2 Cor 5. 3.
ᵃ Job 5. 17.
Pro 3. 11.
Heb. 12, 5,
6.

The Laodiceans were *cold* comparatively, not as the world outside, and those who never belonged to the Church. The lukewarm state, if the transitional stage to a warmer, is desirable (for a little religion, if real, is better than none); but fatal when an abiding condition, for it is mistaken for a safe state (*v.* 17). Hence Christ desires that they were cold rather than *lukewarm;* for there would not be the same 'danger of mixed motive and disregarded principle' (*Alford*). There is more hope of the *cold—i. e.,* those of the world not yet warmed by the Gospel call; for, when called, they may become fervent Christians: as the once-cold publicans, Zaccheus and Matthew. But the *lukewarm* has been within reach of the holy fire, without being kindled into *fervour;* having religion enough to lull the conscience in security, not enough to save the soul: as the *halters between two opinions* in Israel (1 Ki. xviii. 21: cf. 2 Ki. xvii. 41; Ezek. xx. 39; Matt. vi. 24). **16. neither cold nor hot.** So A, Vulgate; but א B C, Syriac, Coptic, transpose, 'hot nor cold.' The adjectives are in the *masculine,* agreeing with *the angel;* not with the Church (feminine). The Lord addresses the angel as representing the Church. The chief minister is answerable for his flock, if he had not faithfully warned it. **I will** [*mello*]—' I am about to;' I have it in my mind: implying graciously the possibility of the threat not being executed, if only they repent at once. His dealing towards them will depend on theirs towards Him. **spue thee out of my mouth**—reject with righteous loathing, as Canaan spued out its inhabitants for their abominations (Lev. xviii. 28). Physicians used *lukewarm* water to cause *vomiting. Cold* and *hot* drinks were common at feasts: never *lukewarm.* There were hot and cold springs near Laodicea. **17.** A lukewarm state generates fatal self-sufficiency (note, *v.* 15). **thou sayest**—mentally, if not in words. **increased with goods** [*peplouteka*]—'have become enriched:' self-praise in self-acquired riches. Alluding to Hos. xii. 8. The riches on which they prided themselves were spiritual; their spiritual self-sufficiency ("I have need of nothing") was fostered by worldly wealth; as *poverty of spirit* is fostered by *poverty* in worldly riches. Cf. Matt. v. 3, with Luke vi. 20. **knowest not that thou**—in particular, above all others. **art wretched**—'art *the* wretched one.' **miserable.** So א C; but A B prefix 'the.' [*Ho eleeinos,* 'the pitiable:' especially to be pitied.] How different Christ's estimate from men's own estimate of themselves! **blind.** Laodicea boasted of a deeper than common *insight* into Divine things. Not absolutely *blind:* else *eye-salve* would have been of no avail, but comparatively. **18.** Gentle, loving irony. Take *my advice,* thou who fanciest thou 'needest none.' Not only art thou not in need of nothing, but in need of the commonest necessaries. He graciously stoops to their modes of thought. Thou art ready to listen to any *counsel* how to *buy* to advantage: then, listen to mine (for I am "*Counsellor,*" Isa. ix. 6), "buy of ME" (*in whom,* according to Paul's epistle to the neigh-

bouring Colosse, intended for the Laodiceans also, Col. ii. 1, 3; iv. 16, *are hidden all the treasures of wisdom and knowledge*). "Buy:" not that we can, by any merit of ours, *purchase* God's free gift; nay, the purchase money consists in renouncing all self-righteousness (*v.* 17). "Buy" at the cost of thy self-sufficiency (so Phil. iii. 7, 8), and of all things, however dear, that would prevent *receiving* Christ's salvation as a *free gift—e. g.,* self and worldly desires. Cf. Isa. lv. 1. **of me**—the source of "unsearchable riches" (Eph. iii. 8). Laodicea had extensive money transactions (*Cicero*). **gold tried in** [*pepuromenon*]—'*fired from* the fire;' *i. e.,* fresh *from* the furnace which proved its purity; retaining its gloss. Sterling spiritual wealth, contrasted with its counterfeit, in which Laodicea boasted. Having this *gold,* she will be no longer *poor* (*v.* 17). **mayest be rich** —'enriched.' **white raiment**—'garments.' Laodicea's wools were famous. Christ offers infinitely whiter raiments. As "gold tried in the fire" expresses *faith* tested by fiery trials, so "white raiment" *Christ's righteousness* imputed to the believer in justification, imparted in sanctification. **appear**—' be manifested' at the day when every one without the wedding garment shall be discovered. To strip, in the East, implies putting to open shame. So to clothe with fine apparel is the image of doing honour. Man can discover his shame; God alone can cover it, so that his nakedness shall not be manifested at last (Gen. iii. 7, 21; Col. iii. 10-14). Blessed is he whose sin is so *covered* (Ps. xxxii. 1). The hypocrite's shame may be manifested now, it must be so then. **anoint . . . with eye-salve.** א A C [*enchrisai*], '(buy of me) eye-salve (collyrium, a roll of ointment) *to anoint* thine eyes.' Christ, the Anointed, has for Laodicea an ointment far more precious than all the costly unguents of the East (John ix. 6; 1 John ii. 20, 27). The *eye* is the conscience or inner light of the mind. According as it is sound and 'single' [*haplous,* 'simple'], or otherwise, the man sees spiritually, or does not (Matt. vi. 22). The Holy Spirit's unction, like ancient eye-salves, first smarts with conviction of sin, then heals: He opens our eyes first to our wretchedness, then to the Saviour's preciousness. The most sunken churches of the seven, Sardis and Laodicea, are those in which there were no opponents from without nor heresies from within. The Church owes much to God's providence, which makes internal and external foes, in spite of themselves, to promote His cause, by calling forth her energies in contending for the faith once delivered to the saints. Peace is dearly bought at the cost of spiritual stagnation, where there is not interest enough felt in religion to contend about it at all. **19.** (Prov. iii. 11, 12.) So Manasses (2 Chr. xxxiii. 11-13). **As many. All.** 'And shalt thou be an exception? If excepted from the scourge, thou art excepted from the number of the sons' (*Augustine*). An encouragement to Laodicea not to despair, but to regard the rebuke as a token for good, if she profit by it. **I love** [*philo*]—gratuitous

hold, [b]I stand at the door and knock: if [c]any man hear my voice, and open the door, [d]I will come in to him, and will sup with him, and he with me.

21   To him that overcometh [e]will I grant to sit with me in my throne, even as I also overcame, and am set down with my Father in his throne.

22 He that hath an ear, let him hear what the Spirit saith unto the churches.

A. D. 96

[b] Song 5. 2.
Isa 1. 18.
[c] Luke 12 37.
[d] John 14.23.
[e] Matt. 19.28.
1 Cor. 6. 2.
2 Tim. 2 12.
ch. 2. 26.

affection, independent of grounds for esteem in the object loved. But Philadelphia (*v.* 9), "I have loved thee" [*egapesa*] with love of *esteem,* founded on the judgment. Note my 'English Gnomon' of *Bengel,* John xxi. 15-17. **I rebuke.** "**I**" stands first emphatically. *I* in my dealings, so unlike man's, *rebuke all whom I love.* [*Elencho* is the same verb as in John xvi. 8, '(the Holy Ghost) will *convince* (rebuke to conviction) the world of sin.'] **chasten**—'chastise' [*paideuo:* in classical Greek, to *instruct;* in the New Testament, to *instruct by chastisement* (Heb. xii. 5, 6)]. David was *rebuked unto conviction* when he cried, "I have sinned against the Lord:" the *chastening* followed, when his child was taken (2 Sam. xii. 13, 14). In Divine *chastening,* the sinner at once winces under the rod and learns righteousness. **be zealous**—habitually. [Present, *zeleue: a lifelong course of zeal,* opposite of "lukewarm."] The alliteration marks this: Laodicea had not been "hot" [*zestos*], she is therefore urged to "be zealous" [*zeleue*]: both are from the same [*zeo, to boil*]. **repent** [*metanoeson,* aorist]—of an act to be done *once for all,* and *at once.* 20. **stand**—waiting in wonderful condescension and long-suffering. **knock**—a further manifestation of His loving desire for our salvation. Himself "the door" (John x. 7), who bids us "knock," that it may be "opened unto" us (Matt. vii. 7), is first Himself to knock at the door of our hearts. If He did not knock first, we should never come to knock at His door. Song v. 2, 4-6, is plainly alluded to; the Spirit here sealing the canonicity of that mystical book. The spiritual state of the bride there, between *waking* and *sleeping,* slow to open the door to her Divine lover, answers to the *lukewarm* Laodicea. 'Love towards men emptied God; for He does not remain in His place and call to Him the servant whom He loved, but comes down Himself to seek him; He who is all-rich arrives at the lodging of the pauper, with His own voice intimates His yearning love, seeks a similar return, withdraws not when disowned, is not impatient at insult, and when persecuted still waits at the doors' (*Nicolaus Cabasilas* in *Trench*). **if any man hear**—for man is not compelled; Christ *knocks,* but does not break open the door, though the violent take heaven by force of prayer (Matt. xi. 12). Whosoever hears, does so not of himself, but by the *drawings* of God's grace (John vi. 44): *repentance* is Christ's gift (Acts v. 31). He *draws,* not drags. The Sun of righteousness, the moment *the door* is opened, pours in His light, which could not previously find entrance. **my voice.** He appeals to the sinner not only with His hand (His providence) *knocking,* but with His *voice* (His word: or rather, His Spirit applying to man's spirit the lessons to be drawn from His providences and His word). If we disregard His knocking at our door now, He will disregard our knocking at His door hereafter. As to His second coming, He is even now *at the door* (Jas. v. 9); we know not how soon He may *knock;* we should always be ready to *open to Him immediately.* **I will come in to him**—as I did to Zaccheus. **sup with him, and he with me.** Delightful reciprocity. Cf. John vi. 56, end. Ordinarily, the admitted guest sups with the

admitter: here the Divine guest becomes Himself the host, for He is the bread of life, and Giver of the marriage feast. Here again He alludes to Song ii. 3; iv. 16, where the Bride invites Him to *eat pleasant fruits,* even as He first prepared a feast for her: "His fruit was sweet to my taste." Cf. the same interchange, John xxi. 9-13, the feast being made up of the viands Jesus brought, and those the disciples brought. The consummation of this blessed intercommunion shall be at the Marriage Supper of the Lamb, of which the Lord's Supper is the foretaste.

21. sit with me in my throne—(Matt. xix. 28; xx. 23; John xvii. 22, 24; 2 Tim. ii. 12; ch. ii. 26, 27; xx. 6.) He whom Christ just before threatened to *spue out of His mouth,* is now offered a *seat with Him on His throne!* 'The highest place is within reach of the lowest: the faintest spark of grace may be fanned into the mightiest flame' (*Trench*). **even as I also.** Two thrones are mentioned: (1.) His Father's, upon which He has sat since His ascension, after victory over death, sin, the world: upon this none can sit save God, and the God-man Christ Jesus, for it is the incommunicable prerogative of God; (2.) the throne peculiarly *His* as the once humbled and then glorified *Son of man,* to be set up over the whole earth (heretofore usurped by Satan) at His coming again: in this the *victorious* saints shall share (1 Cor. vi. 2). The transfigured elect shall with Christ judge and reign over the nations in the flesh, and Israel foremost of them: ministering blessings to them, as angels were the Lord's mediators of blessing and administrators of government in setting up His throne in Israel at Sinai. This privilege belongs exclusively to the present time whilst Satan reigns, when alone there is scope for conflict and *victory* (2 Tim. ii. 11, 12). When Satan shall be bound (ch. xx. 4) there shall be no longer scope, for all on earth shall know the Lord, from the least to the greatest. This, the crowning promise, at the end of all the seven addresses, gathers all in one. It forms the link to the next part, where the Lamb is seated *on His Father's throne* (ch. iv. 2, 3; v. 5, 6). The Eastern throne is broader than ours, admitting others besides the chief in the centre. *Trench,* The order of the promises corresponds to the unfolding of the kingdom of God from its first beginnings on earth to its consummation in heaven. To the faithful at Ephesus—(1.) *the tree of life in the paradise of God* (ch. ii. 7), answering to Gen. ii. (2.) Sin entered the world, and death by sin: to the faithful at Smyrna it is promised they *shall not be hurt by the second death* (ch. ii. 11). The promise of the *hidden manna* (ch. ii. 17) to Pergamos (3.) answers to the Mosaic period, the Church in the wilderness. (4.) That to Thyatira, triumph *over the nations* (ch. ii. 26, 27), consummates the kingdom, answering to the prophetic type, David and Solomon's *power over the nations.* The seven fall into two groups, *four* and three, as the Lord's prayer, three and four. The last three pass from earth to heaven; the Church contemplated as triumphant, with its steps from glory to glory. (5.) Christ promises to the believer of Sardis not to blot his name out of the book of life, but to confess him before His Father and the angels at

4   AFTER this I looked, and, behold, a door *was* opened in heaven: and the first voice which I heard *was* as it were of a trumpet talking with me; which said, Come up hither, and I will show thee things which must be hereafter.

2   And immediately *^a*I was in the Spirit: and, behold, *^b*a throne was set

3 in heaven, and *one* sat on the throne. And he that sat was to look upon like a jasper and a sardine stone: *^c*and *there was* a rainbow round about

4 the throne, in sight like unto an emerald. And round about the throne *were* four and twenty seats: and upon the seats I saw four and twenty elders sitting, clothed in white raiment; and they had on their heads

A. D. 96

CHAP. 4.
^a Eze 3. 12.
ch 1. 10.
ch. 17. 3.
ch 21. 10.
^b Isa 6. 1.
Jer. 17. 12.
Eze 10. 1.
Dan. 7. 9.
^c Gen. 9. 13.
Isa. 54. 9.
Eze. 1. 21.

the judgment day, and clothe him with a glorified body of dazzling whiteness (*vv.* 4, 5). To believers at Philadelphia, (6.) that they shall be citizens, fixed as immoveable pillars in the new Jerusalem, where city and temple are one (*v.* 12). Here not only individual salvation is promised, as in Sardis, but also privileges, in the blessed communion of the Church triumphant. (7.) Lastly, to the faithful of Laodicea is given the crowning promise, a seat with Christ on His throne, even as He sits with His Father on His Father's throne (*v.* 21).

CHAP. IV. 1-11.—GOD'S THRONE IN HEAVEN—THE FOUR AND TWENTY ELDERS—THE FOUR LIVING CREATURES.

Here begins Revelation proper; first, chs. iv. and v. set forth the heavenly scenery of the succeeding visions, and God on His throne, the *covenant God of His Church*, revealing them to His apostle through Christ. The first great portion comprises the opening of the seals and the sounding of the trumpets, (chs. iv.-xi.) As the communication respecting the seven churches opened with a suitable vision of the Lord Jesus as Head of the Church, so this part opens with a vision suitable to the matter to be revealed. The scene passes from earth to *heaven*. **1. After this**—'After these things,' marking the next vision in the succession: the transition from "the things which are" (ch. i. 19) in John's time, the existing state of the seven churches (type of the church in general), to "the things which shall be hereafter," in relation to the time when John wrote. **I looked** [*eidon*]—'I saw' in vision: not, I directed my *look* that way. **was**—not in the Greek. **opened**—'standing open:' not that John saw it being opened. Cf. Ezek. i. 1; Matt. iii. 16; Acts vii. 56; x. 11. But, in those visions, the heavens opened, disclosing visions to those below. Here heaven, the temple of God, remains closed to those on earth; but John is transported in vision through an open door up into heaven, whence he can see things passing on earth or in heaven, according as the several visions require. **the first voice which I heard**—the voice which I heard at first (ch. i. 10). **was as it were.** Omit *was*. **Come up hither**—through the 'open door.' **be**—come to pass. **hereafter**—'after these things:' after the present time (ch. i. 19).

2. And. Omitted in א A B, Vulgate, Syriac. **I was**—'I became in the Spirit' (note, ch. i. 10); rapt in vision into the heavenly world. **was set** —not *was placed*, but *was situated* [*ekeito*]. **one sat on the throne**—the Eternal Father: the Creator (*v.* 11: cf. *v.* 8, with ch. i. 4): the Father, 'which is, and was, and is to come.' When the Son, "the Lamb," is introduced (ch. v. 5-9), a *new song* is sung which distinguishes *the Sitter on the throne* from *the Lamb;* and *v.* 13, "Unto Him that sitteth upon the throne, and unto the Lamb." So in Dan. vii. 13, the *Son of man* brought before *the Ancient of days* is distinguished from Him. The Father in essence is invisible, but at times is

represented assuming a visible form. **3. was.** So Vulgate, Coptic; omitted in א A B. **to look upon**—'in sight.' **jasper.** From ch. xxi. 11, where it is called *most precious*, which the *jasper* was not. *Ebrard* infers it was a diamond. Ordinarily, the *jasper* is a stone of various wavy colours, somewhat transparent. In ch. xxi. 11 it represents crystalline brightness. The *sardine*, our cornelian, or else a fiery red. As the brightness represents God's holiness, so the fiery red His just wrath. The same union of white brightness and fiery redness appears in Ezek. i. 4; viii. 2; Dan. vii. 9; ch. i. 14; x. 1. **rainbow round about the throne** —a complete circle (type of God's perfection and eternity: not a half-circle, as the earthly rainbow) surrounding the throne vertically. Its various colours, which combined form one pure ray, symbolize the various aspects of God's providences uniting in one harmonious whole. Here, however, predominant among the prismatic colours is green, the most refreshing to look upon, symbolizing God's consolatory promises in Christ to His people amidst judgments on His foes. The rainbow was the token of God's covenant with all flesh, and His people in particular. Hereby God renewed the grant originally made to the first man. As the rainbow was reflected on the waters of the world's ruin, and is seen only when a cloud is over the earth, so another deluge, of fire, shall precede the 'new heavens and earth' granted to redeemed man, as the earth after the flood was restored to Noah. The Lord on His throne, whence (*v.* 5) proceed "lightnings and thunderings," shall issue the commission to rid the earth of its oppressors; but amidst judgment, when other men's hearts fail for fear, the believer shall be reassured by the rainbow, the covenant token, round the throne (*De Burgh*). The heavenly bow speaks of the shipwreck of the world through sin; also of calm sunshine after the storm. The *cloud* is the token of God's presence—in the tabernacle Holiest Place; on mount Sinai at the giving of the law; at the ascension (Acts i. 9); at His coming again (ch. i. 7). **4. seats**—rather, 'thrones;' of course lower than the grand central *throne*. So ch. xvi. 10, 'the *throne* of the beast,' in hellish parody of God's throne. **four and twenty elders.** B, '*the* (well-known) twenty and four (or, א A, "twenty-four") elders' (*Alford*). But *Tregelles*, 'upon the twenty-four thrones (*I saw*: omitted in A B, Vulgate) elders sitting:' more probable, as *the twenty-four elders* were not mentioned before, whereas *the twenty-four thrones* were. Not angels, for they have *white robes* and *crowns* of victory, implying a conflict and endurance—"Thou hast *redeemed us*" (ch. v. 9); but the *Heads* of the *Old* and *New* Testament churches—the Twelve Patriarchs (cf. ch. vii. 5-8), not in their personal, but their representative character, and Twelve Apostles. So ch. xv. 3, "the song of *Moses* and of the *Lamb:*" the double constituents of the Church, the Old and the New Testament. "Elders" is the term for

5 crowns of gold. And out of the throne proceeded lightnings and thunderings and voices: ^dand *there were* seven lamps of fire burning before
6 the throne, which are the seven Spirits of God. And before the throne *there was* a ^esea of glass like unto crystal: ^fand in the midst of the throne, and round about the throne, *were* four beasts, full of eyes before
7 and behind. And ^gthe first beast *was* like a lion, and the second beast like a calf, and the third beast had a face as a man, and the fourth beast
8 *was* like a flying eagle. And the four beasts had each of them six ^hwings about *him;* and *they were* full of eyes within:
And ¹they rest not day and night, saying, Holy, holy, holy, Lord God
9 Almighty, which was, and is, and is to come. And when those beasts

A. D. 96.
d Ex. 37. 23.
2 Chr. 4. 10.
Eze. 1. 13.
Zech. 4. 2.
e Ex 33. 8.
1 Ki. 7. 23,
ch. 15. 2.
f Eze. 1. 5.
g Num. 2. 2.
Eze. 10. 14.
h Isa. 6. 2.
1 they have
no rest.

the ministry, both of the Old and New Testament, the Jewish and the Catholic Church. The tabernacle was a "pattern" of the heavenly antitype (Heb. viii. 5; ix. 24); the Holy Place a figure of HEAVEN. Jehovah's throne is represented by the mercyseat with the Shechinah cloud over it. 'The seven lamps of fire before the throne' (*v.* 5) are antitypical to the seven-branched candlestick before the Holiest Place—emblem of the manifold Spirit of God. 'The sea of glass' (*v.* 6) corresponds to the molten sea before the sanctuary, wherein the priests washed before entering on holy service: so here in connection with the redeemed "priests unto God" (note, ch. xv. 2). The 'four living creatures' (*vv.* 6, 7) answer to the cherubim over the mercyseat. So the twenty-four throned and crowned elders are typified by the chiefs of the twenty-four courses of priests, '*governors* of the sanctuary, and governors of God' (1 Chr. xxiv. 5; xxv. 31). 5. proceeded — 'proceed.' thunderings and voices. א A B, Vulgate, transpose, 'voices and thunderings.' Cf., at the giving of the law, Exod. xix. 16. 'The *thunderings* express God's threats against the ungodly; there are voices in them (ch. x. 3): *i.e.*, not only does He threaten generally, but predicts *special* judgments' (*Grotius*). seven lamps . . . seven Spirits—the Holy Spirit in His sevenfold operation, as the light-and-life-giver (cf. ch. i. 4; v. 6, *seven eyes* . . . *the seven Spirits of God;* xxi. 23; Ps. cxix. 105) and fiery purifier of the godly, and consumer of the ungodly (Matt. iii. 11). 6. א A B, Vulgate, Coptic, Syriac, read, '*As it were* a sea of glass.' like unto crystal—not imperfectly transparent as the ancient glass, but like rock crystal. Contrast the turbid "many waters" on which the harlot "sitteth," (ch. xvii.) Cf. Job xxxvii. 18. Primarily, the pure ether which separates God's throne from all things before it, symbolizing the 'purity, calmness, and majesty of God's rule' (*Alford*). But see the analogue in the temple, the molten sea *before* the sanctuary (note, *v.* 4). There is in it depth and transparency, but not the fluidity and instability of the natural sea (cf. ch. xxi. 1). It stands solid and clear. God's *judgments* are "a great deep" (Ps. xxxvi. 6). In ch. xv. 2, it is a "sea of glass mingled with *fire*." There is symbolized the purificatory baptism with water and the Spirit, of all made "kings and priests unto God." In ch. xv. 2, the baptism with trial is meant. Through both all the king-priests have to pass in coming to God. His *judgments*, which overwhelm the ungodly, they stand firmly upon, able, like Christ, to walk on the sea as if solid glass. round about the throne—one in the midst of each side of the throne. four beasts—rather, 'living creatures' [*zoa*]: "beasts," ch. xiii. 1, 11, is different [*therion*]: symbol of the carnal man, who, by rebellion, loses his true glory, as lord, under God, of the lower creatures: degraded to the level of the *beast*. 7. calf—'a steer' (*Al-*

673

ford). [The LXX. often use *moschos* for an *ox*, (Exod. xxii. 1; xxix. 10, &c.)] as a man. A, Vulgate, Coptic, have 'as of a man;' א, 'as like a man.' 8. about him [*kuklothen*]—'round about him.' *Alford* connects with the following: 'All round and within (their wings) they are [so A B א, Vulgate, *gemousin* for *gemonta*] full of eyes.' St. John shows, the six wings in each did not interfere with what he before declared—viz., that they were "full of eyes before and behind." The eyes were *round* the outside of each wing, and up the *inside* of each when half expanded, and of the part of body in that inward recess. rest not—'have no rest.' How awfully different the reason why the worshippers of the beast 'have no rest day nor night:' 'their torment for ever and ever' (ch. xiv. 11). Holy, holy, holy—the 'tris-hagion' of the Greek liturgies. Isa. vi. 3; also Ps. xcix. 3, 5, 9: He is praised as "holy"—(1.) for His majesty (*v.* 1), about to display itself; (2.) His justice (*v.* 4) now displaying itself; (3.) His mercy (*vv.* 6-8) displayed in time past. So here, "holy," as He "who was;" "holy," as He "who is;" "holy," as He "who is to come." He showed Himself an object of holy worship in the past creation of all things: more fully He shows Himself so in governing all: He will, in the highest degree, show Himself so in the consummation of all things. 'Of (from) Him, through Him, and to Him, are all things: to whom be glory for ever. Amen' (Rom. xi. 36). In Isa. vi. 3 there is added, "the whole EARTH is full of His glory." But in Revelation this is deferred until the glory of THE LORD fills *the earth*, His enemies having been destroyed (*Bengel*). Almighty—answering to "Lord of hosts" (Sabaoth). The cherubim here have *six* wings, like the seraphim in Isa. vi.; whereas the cherubim in Ezek. i. 6 had *four* each. They have the same name—'living creatures.' Whereas in Ezekiel each living creature has all four faces, here the four are distributed, one to each (note, Ezek. i. 6). The four *living creatures* answer by contrast to the four world-powers, represented by four *beasts*. The fathers identify them with the four gospels—Matthew, the lion; Mark, the ox; Luke, the man; John, the eagle. The symbols express not the personal character of the evangelists, but the manifold aspect of *Christ*, presented by them respectively, in relation to the world (*four* signifying world-wide extension, *e. g.*, the four quarters of the world): the lion, *royalty*, as Matthew gives prominence to this; the ox, *laborious endurance*, Christ's characteristic in Mark; man, *brotherly sympathy* with our whole race, Christ's feature in Luke; the eagle, *soaring majesty*, prominent in John's description of Christ as the Divine Word. Here the context best accords with the *four living creatures* representing the *redeemed election-Church* ministering as king-priests to God; and media of blessing to the redeemed earth, with its nations and

give glory and honour and thanks to him that sat on the throne, who
10 liveth for ever and ever, the four and twenty elders fall down before him
that sat on the throne, and worship him that liveth for ever and ever,
11 and cast their crowns before the throne, saying, Thou art worthy, O Lord,
to receive glory and honour and power: for thou hast created all things,
and for thy pleasure they are and were created.

5 AND I saw in the right hand of him that sat on the throne ^a a book
2 written within and on the back side, sealed ^b with seven seals. And I
saw a strong angel proclaiming with a loud voice, Who is worthy to open

A. D. 96.

CHAP. 5.
^a Isa 34. 16.
Eze. 2. 9.
ch. 10. 2, 8.
ch 20. 12.
^b Isa. 8. 16.
Isa. 29. 11.
Dan. 8. 23.
Dan. 12. 4.
ch. 6. 1.

animal creation, in which *man* stands at the head; *the lion* at the head of wild beasts; *the ox*, of tame beasts; *the eagle*, of birds and of creatures of the waters. Cf. ch. v. 8-10; ch. xx. 4, the partakers with Christ of the first resurrection, who with Him *reign* over the redeemed nations which are in the flesh. Cf. as to the happy subjection of the animal world, Isa. xi. 6-8; lxv. 25; Ezek. xxxiv. 25; Hos. ii. 18. Jewish tradition says, the 'four standards' under which Israel encamped in the wilderness—to the east Judah, to the north Dan, to the west Ephraim, to the south Reuben—were respectively a *lion, eagle, ox*, and *a man;* in the midst was the tabernacle containing the Shechinah, symbol of the Divine presence: 'the picture of that blessed period when—the earth being fitted for being the kingdom of the Father—the court of heaven will be transferred hither, the "tabernacle of God shall be with men" (ch. xxi. 3), and the whole world be subject to a never-ending theocracy' (cf. *De Burgh*, 'Revelation'). Christ is the perfect realization of the ideal of man: Christ is presented in His fourfold aspect in the four gospels. The redeemed election-church, realizing in and through Christ (with whom she shall reign) the ideal of man, shall combine similarly human perfections, having a fourfold aspect :—(1.) Kingly righteousness with hatred of evil, answering to the 'lion springing terribly on the victim;' (2.) laborious diligence in duty, the 'ox bound to the soil;' (3.) human sympathy, the 'man;' (4.) contemplation of heavenly truth, the 'eagle.' As high-soaring intelligence forms the contrasted complement to practical labour, so holy judgment against evil forms the contrasted complement to human sympathy. In Isa. vi. 2 we read, " Each had six wings: with twain he covered his face (in *reverence*, not presuming to look up, Luke xviii. 13), with twain his feet (in humility, as not worthy to stand before God), and with twain he did fly (ready to do instantly God's command). 9. The ground of praise is God's *eternity, power*, and *glory* manifested in creating all things for His pleasure. Creation is the foundation of all God's other acts of power, wisdom, love, and therefore forms the first theme of thanksgivings. The four living creatures take the lead of the twenty-four elders, both in this anthem and that *new song* which follows, on the ground of their redemption (ch. v. 8-10). **9. when**—*i. e.*, whensoever. A simultaneous giving of glory by the living creatures and the elders. **give**. 'Shall give' in A; but B ℵ [*dososin*], 'shall have given.' **for ever and ever**—Greek, 'unto the ages of the ages.' **10. fall**—immediately. '*Shall* fall down:' this ascription of praise *shall be* repeated onward to eternity. So '*shall* worship . . . *shall* cast their crowns,' in acknowledgment that they owe their *crowns* (not kingly *diadems*, but *crowns* of conquerors) wholly to Him. **11. O Lord.** A B ℵ, Vulgate, Syriac, add, 'and our God.' 'Our' by creation, especially by redemption. B, Syriac, insert, 'the Holy One.' **glory, &c.**—'*the* glory, *the* honour, *the*

674

power.' **thou**—emphatical : 'it is THOU who didst create.' **all things**—'*the* all things :' the universe. **for** [*dia to thelema*]—'on account of :' 'for the sake of thy pleasure.' It was *because of thy will,* that 'they were' (so A, Vulgate, Syriac, Coptic, instead of "are." B, 'they were *not*, and were created,' out of nothing)—i. e., *were existing*, contrasted with their previous non-existence. With God, to *will* is to effect. So in Gen. i. 3, "Let there be light, and there was light" [*yehi or vayehi or*], expressive tautology, the same word, tense, and letters for "let there be" and "there was :" simultaneity and identity of the will and the effect. *D. Longinus* ('On the Sublime,' sec. 9), a heathen, praises this description of God's power by 'the lawgiver of the Jews, no ordinary man,' as one worthy of the theme. **were created**—aorist : by thy definite act at a definite time.

CHAP. V. 1-14.—THE BOOK WITH SEVEN SEALS —NONE WORTHY TO OPEN IT BUT THE LAMB—HE TAKES IT AMIDST PRAISES OF THE REDEEMED, AND OF THE WHOLE HEAVENLY HOST.

1. in [*epi*]—'(lying) *upon* the right hand,' &c.: upon His open right hand lay the book. On God's part there was no withholding of His future purposes in the book: the obstacle to unsealing it is stated, *v.* 3 (*Alford*). **book**—rather, as the ancient form of books, and the *writing on the back side* require, 'a roll.' The *writing on the back* implies completeness, so that nothing needs to be added (ch. xxii. 18). The roll, '*the title deed of man's inheritance*' (*De Burgh*), redeemed by Christ (cf. Jer. xxxii. 11-14), contains the successive steps by which He shall recover from its usurper possession of the kingdom already 'purchased' for Himself and His elect. However, no portion of the roll is *unfolded* and *read;* simply the *seals* are successively *opened;* giving final access to its contents as a perfect whole, when the events symbolized by the seals shall have been past; then Eph. iii. 10 shall receive its *complete* accomplishment, and the Lamb reveal God's providential plans in redemption in their manifold beauties: a theme for all-satisfying and adoring praise through eternity. The opening of the seals means the successive steps by which God in Christ clears the way for the final reading of the book at the visible setting up of Christ's kingdom. Cf., at the grand consummation, ch. xx. 12; xxii. 19. None is worthy to do so save the Lamb; for He alone has redeemed man's forfeited inheritance, of which *the book is the title deed*. The question (*v.* 2) is not, Who should reveal the destinies of the Church (this any inspired prophet might do)? but, Who has the WORTH *to give man a new title to his lost inheritance?* (*De Burgh*.) **sealed with seven seals** [*katesphragismenon*]—'sealed up,' &c. *Seven* (divided into four, the world-wide number, and three, the Divine) often recurs, expressing *completeness*. Thus, the *seven seals*, representing all power given to the Lamb; the *seven trumpets*, by which the world-kingdoms are overthrown, and the Lamb's kingdom ushered in; and the *seven vials*, by which the beast's kingdom is destroyed.

3 the book, and to loose the seals thereof? And ^cno man in heaven, nor in earth, neither under the earth, was able to open the book, neither to
4 look thereon. And I wept much, because no man was found worthy to
5 open and to read the book, neither to look thereon. And one of the elders saith unto me, Weep not: behold, ^dthe Lion of the tribe of Juda, ^ethe Root of David, hath ^fprevailed to open the book, and to loose the seven seals thereof.
6 And I beheld, and, lo, in the midst of the throne and of the four beasts, and in the midst of the elders, stood a ^gLamb as it had been slain, having seven horns and seven ^heyes, which are ⁱthe seven Spirits
7 of God sent forth into all the earth. And he came and took the book out of the right hand of him that sat upon the throne.
8 And when he had taken the book, the four beasts and four *and* twenty elders fell down before the Lamb, having every one of them ^jharps, and
9 golden vials full of ¹odours, ^kwhich are the prayers of saints. And ^lthey sung a new song, saying, Thou ^mart worthy to take the book, and

---

A. D. 96.

^c John 1. 18.
^d Gen. 49. 9.
    Heb. 7. 14.
^e Isa. 11.
    Rom. 5. 12.
^f Heb. 2. 10.
    Heb 7. 25.
^g Isa. 53. 7.
    John 1. 29.
^h Zech. 3. 9.
    Zech. 4. 10.
ⁱ ch. 4. 5.
^j ch. 14. 2.
    ch. 15. 2.
¹ Or,
    incense.
^k Ps. 141. 2.
    ch. 8. 3, 4.
^l Ps. 40. 3.
^m ch. 4. 11.

---

2. strong—(Ps. ciii. 20.) His voice penetrated heaven, earth, and hades (ch. x. 1-3). **3. no man**—'no one.' Not merely *no man*, but also *no one* of all created beings. **in earth**—'upon the earth.' **under the earth**—viz., in hades. **look thereon** —upon the contents, so as to read them. **4. and to read**. B, ℵ, Vulgate, *Origen, Cyprian, Hilary* omit. *To read* would be awkward between 'to open the book' and "to look thereon." St. John, having been promised a revelation of "things which must be hereafter," *weeps* at his earnest desire being frustrated. He is a pattern to all, as an eager, teachable learner of the Apocalypse. **5. one of**—'one from among.' The 'elder' is, according to some (in Lyra), Matthew. With this accords the description, "the *Lion*, which is of the tribe of Juda, the Root of David:" the royal, David-descended, lion-aspect of Christ being prominent in Matthew, whence the lion among the fourfold cherubim is assigned to him. *Gerhard* thought Jacob meant, and that he was one of those who rose with Christ and ascended to heaven (Matt. xxvii. 52, 53): cf. his words, "Judah is a LION'S whelp," &c. The elders round God's throne know better than John, still in the flesh, Christ's far-reaching power. **Root of David** —(Isa. xi. 1, 10.) Not merely 'a sucker from David's ancient root' (as *Alford*), but also Himself the root and origin of David. Cf. these two brought together, Matt. xxii. 42-45. Hence He is not merely *Son of David*, but also *David* (Ezek. xxxiv. 23, 24; xxxvii. 24, 25). He is at once "the branch" and "the root" of David, David's Son and David's Lord, the *Lamb* slain, therefore the *Lion* of Juda: about to reign over Israel, and thence over the whole earth. **prevailed**—'conquered' absolutely, as ch. iii. 21: His past *victory* over all the powers of darkness entitles Him to open the book. **to open**. So A, Vulgate, Coptic, *Origen;* but B, 'he that openeth'—i. e., whose office is to open.
6. And I beheld, and, lo. So Vulgate; but A omits "And I beheld;" B, *Cyprian*, &c., omit "and, lo." **in the midst of the throne**—not *on* the throne (cf. *v.* 7), but in the midst of the company (ch. iv. 4) "round about the throne." **Lamb** [*arnion*]—in Revelation exclusively, except John xxi. 15: expressing *endearment;* the endearing relation which Christ bears to us: the consequence of His previous relation as the *sacrificial Lamb* [*amnos*]. So our relation to Him: He the *precious Lamb*, we His *dear lambs*, one with Him. [*Bengel* thinks *arnion* implies, *taking the lead of the flock*. Another object of the form *arnion*, the

Lamb, is to mark the contrast to *therion*, the Beast. Elsewhere *amnos* is found, the *paschal, sacrificial Lamb* (Isa. liii. 7; LXX.; John i. 29, 36; Acts viii. 32; 1 Pet. i. 19).] Christ is "the Lion," yet "the Lamb" (*v.* 5): combining opposites. **as it had been slain**—bearing marks of His past death-wounds: *standing*, though bearing the marks of one *slain*. In the midst of heavenly glory, Christ crucified is still prominent. **seven horns**—i. e., *perfect might;* "seven," *perfection;* "horns," *might*. In contrast to the *horns* of the antichristian world-powers, (Dan. vii. 7, 20; viii. 3; Zech. i. 19, 21; ch. xvii. 3, &c.) **seven eyes ... the seven Spirits ... sent forth**. So ℵ [*apestalmena*]; A [*apestalmenoi*]; but B [*apostellomena*], 'being sent forth.' As the *seven lamps* before the throne represent the Spirit *immanent* in the Godhead, so the *seven eyes* of the Lamb represent the same sevenfold Spirit *profluent* from the incarnate Redeemer in world-wide energy. "Sent forth" [*apestalmenoi*] is akin to *apostles*, whose labours for Christ throughout the world flowed from His Spirit's impulse. If the present be read, those labours are regarded as *continually going on* unto the end. "Eyes" symbolize His all-watchful providence for His Church, and against her foes (Zech. iv. 10). **7.** The book lay on the open hand of Him that sat on the throne, for any to take who was found worthy (*Alford*). The Lamb takes it from the Father in token of formal investiture into His universal and everlasting dominion as Son of man. This introductory vision presents, in summary, the consummation to which all the events in the seals, trumpets, and vials converge—viz., the setting up of Christ's kingdom visibly. Prophecy ever hurries to the grand crisis, and dwells on intermediate events only in their typical relation to, and representation of, the end. **8. had taken**—'took.' **fell down before the Lamb**—who shares worship and the throne with the Father. **harps**—A B, Syriac, Coptic, read, 'a harp:' a guitar, played with the hand or a quill. **vials**—'bowls:' censers. **odours**—'incense.' **prayers of saints**—as the angel offers them (ch. viii. 3), with incense (cf. Ps. cxli. 2): not the least sanction to Rome's dogma of praying to saints. Though *they* be employed by God in some way unknown to us to present our prayers (nothing is said of their *interceding* for us), yet *we* are told to pray only to Him (ch. xix. 10; xxii. 8, 9). *Their own* employment is praise (whence they all have *harps*): ours is prayer. **9. sung**—'sing:' their blessed occupation continually. The theme *re-*

675

to open the seals thereof: for thou wast slain, and [n]hast redeemed us to
God by thy blood [o]out of every kindred, and tongue, and people, and
10 nation; and [p]hast made us unto our God kings and priests: and we shall
11 reign on the earth. And I beheld, and I heard the voice of many angels
round about the throne and the beasts and the elders: and the number
of them was [q]ten thousand times ten thousand, and thousands of thou-
12 sands; saying with a loud voice, Worthy is the Lamb that was slain to
receive power, and riches, and wisdom, and strength, and honour, and
13 glory, and blessing. And [r]every creature which is in heaven, and on the
earth, and under the earth, and such as are in the sea, and all that are
in them, heard I saying, [s]Blessing, and honour, and glory, and power, *be*
unto him that sitteth upon the throne, [t]and unto the Lamb, for ever and
14 ever. And the four beasts said, Amen. And the four *and* twenty elders
fell down and worshipped him that liveth for ever and ever.
6　　AND I saw when the Lamb opened one of the seals; and I heard, as

A D 96.

[n] Matt. 26 28.
Acts 0. 28.
Rom. 3. 21-
26.
Heb 9. 12.
2 Pet. 2. 1.
1 John 1. 7.
[o] Dan. 4. 1.
Dan. 6. 25.
[p] Ex. 19. 6.
[q] Deut. 33. 2.
Ps. 68. 17.
Dan. 7. 10.
Heb. 12. 22.
[r] Phil. 2. 10.
[s] 1 Chr. 29.11.
Eph. 3. 21.
[t] John 5. 23.

demption is ever new, suggesting fresh thoughts of
praise, embodied in "new song." us to God. So
א B, Coptic, Vulgate, *Cyprian*. But A omits "us."
out of—the present *election-church* gathered *out of*
the world; distinguished from the peoples gathered
to Christ as subjects of a *world-wide* conversion of
all nations. kindred, and tongue, and people, and
nation. *Four* marks world-wide extension: the
four quarters of the world. [*Phules*, "kindred,"
'*tribe*.'] This and [*laos*] "people" are usually restricted to *Israel*: "tongue" and "nation" to the
Gentiles (ch. vii. 9; xi. 9; xiii. 7, the oldest reading;
xiv. 6), marking the election-church gathered
from Jews and Gentiles. In ch. x. 11, for 'tribes,'
we find among the four "kings:" in xvii. 15,
"multitudes." 10. made us—A B א, Vulgate,
Syriac, Coptic, read 'them.' The Hebrew, third
person for the first, has a graphic relation to *the
redeemed*, also a more modest sound than *us*,
priests (*Bengel*). unto our God. So B א; but A
omits. kings. So B; but A א, Vulgate, Coptic,
Cyprian, 'a kingdom.' א reads also 'a priesthood'
for *priests*. They who cast their crowns before
the throne do not call themselves *kings* before the
great *King* (ch. iv. 10, 11); though their priestly
access has such dignity, that their reigning on
earth cannot exceed it. So in ch. xx. 6, they are
not called "kings" (*Bengel*). we shall reign on the
earth—a new feature added to ch. i. 6. א,Vulgate,
Coptic, read, '*they* shall reign.' A B read, '*they
reign;*' which *Alford* explains of the Church EVEN
NOW, in Christ her Head, reigning on the earth:
'all things are being put under her feet, as under
His; her kingly office is asserted, even in the
midst of persecution.' But even '*they reign*' is
the prophetical present for the future: the seer
being transported into the future when the full
number of the redeemed (represented by the *four
living creatures*) shall be complete, and the visible
kingdom begins. The saints do spiritually reign
now; but certainly not as they shall when the
prince of this world shall be bound (notes, ch. xx.
2-6). So far from *reigning on the earth* now, they
are "made as the filth of the world and the offscouring of all things" (1 Cor. iv. 8-13). In ch. xi.
15, 18, the locality and time of the kingdom are
marked. *Kelly* translates, 'reign *over* the earth'
[*epi tees gees*]; justified by LXX. (Judg. ix. 8;
Matt. ii. 22). The elders, though ruling *over the
earth*, shall not necessarily remain *on* the earth.
The English version is grammatically possible
(ch. iii. 10). 'The elders were *meek* (Matt. v. 5);
but the flock of the meek is much larger' (*Bengel*).
11. I beheld—the angels forming the outer circle;
the Church, the object of redemption, the inner
circle nearest the throne. The heavenly hosts

around gaze with intense adoration at this crowning of God's love, wisdom, and power. ten thousand times ten thousand—'myriads of myriads.'
12. to receive (the) power. The remaining six (the
whole being *seven*, implying *perfection*) are under
the one Greek article, before "power," as they
form *one* complete aggregate belonging to God and
His coequal, the Lamb. Cf. ch. vii. 12, where
each of all seven has the article. riches—spiritual
and earthly. blessing—ascribed praise: the *will*
on the creature's part, though unaccompanied by
the *power*, to return blessing for blessing conferred
(*Alford*). 13. The universal chorus of creation,
the outermost circles as well as the inner (of saints
and angels), winds up the doxology. The *full*
accomplishment is to be when Christ takes His
great power and reigns visibly. every creature
—(Ps. ciii. 22.) under the earth—the departed
spirits in Hades. such as are. So B, Vulgate;
but A א omit. in the sea [*epi*]—'*upon* the sea:'
the sea animals regarded as on the surface (*Alford*). א [*ta en te thalasse*], 'those *in* the sea.' all
that are in them. So A א, 'all (things)' [*panta*].
B, Vulgate, 'I heard *all* [masculine: *pantas*] saying' [*legontas*]: the harmonious concert of all in
the four quarters of the universe. Blessing, &c.—
'*the* blessing, *the* honour, and *the* glory, and *the*
might to the ages of the ages.' The *fourfold* ascription indicates *world-wide* universality. 14. said.
So A א,Vulgate, Syriac, read; but B, Coptic, read
[*legonta*], '(I heard) *saying*.' Amen. So A; but B,
'*the* (accustomed) Amen.' As in ch. iv. 11, the
four and twenty elders asserted God's worthiness
to receive the glory, as having *created all things*,
so here the four living creatures ratify by their
"Amen" the whole *creation's* ascription of the
glory to Him. four and twenty. Omitted in A B
א. him that liveth for ever and ever. Omitted in
A B C א; inserted from ch. iv. 9. There, where
the thanksgiving is *expressed*, the words are appropriate; here less so, as their worship is silent prostration. "Worshipped" (God and the Lamb).
So ch. xi. 1, "worship" absolutely.

CHAP. VI. 1-17.—OPENING OF THE FIRST SIX
OF THE SEVEN SEALS.
Note, ch. v. 1. *Mede, Fleming, Newton*, &c.,
hold that all these seals are fulfilled, the sixth by
the overthrow of Paganism and establishment of
Christianity under Constantine's edict, 313 A.D.
But, in the full sense at least, the sixth seal is
future, to be realized at the coming again of Christ.
The objection to the seals having been finally and
exhaustively fulfilled (though particular events
may be partial fulfilments typical of the final
one), is that, if so, they ought to furnish (as the
destruction of Jerusalem, according to Christ's

it were the noise of thunder, one of the four beasts saying, Come and see.
2 And I saw, and behold *ᵃ*a white horse: and *ᵇ*he that sat on him had a bow; *ᶜ*and a crown was given unto him: and he went forth conquering, and to conquer.
3 And when he had opened the second seal, I heard the second beast
4 say, Come and see. And *ᵈ*there went out another horse *that was* red: and *power* was given to him that sat thereon to take peace from the earth, and that they should kill one another: and there was given unto him a great sword.
5 And when he had opened the third seal, I heard the third beast say, Come and see. And I beheld, and lo a *ᵉ*black horse: and he that sat on
6 him had a pair of balances in his hand. And I heard a voice in the midst of the four beasts say, ¹A measure of wheat for a penny, and three measures of barley for a penny; and *ᶠsee* thou hurt not the oil and the wine.

A. D. 96.

CHAP. 6.
ᵃ Zech. 6. 3.
ᵇ Ps. 45. 4, 5.
ᶜ ch. 14. 14.
ᵈ Zech. 6. 2.
ᵉ Zech. 6. 2.
¹ The word Chœnix signifieth a measure containing one wine quart, and the twelfth part of a quart.
ᶠ ch. 9. 4.

prophecy, does) external evidence of revelation. But they cannot be used for this, as hardly two interpreters of this school agree on what events constitute the fulfilment. Probably, not isolated facts, but *classes* of events preparing for Christ's coming kingdom, are intended. The first horse marks *conquests;* the second, third, and fourth horses mark civil wars, scarcity, and mortality. The fifth seal marks even persecutions of Christians overruled to Christ's final triumph. The four living creatures severally cry at the opening of the first four seals, " Come;" which divides the *seven,* as often, into *four* and *three.*

1. **one of the seals.** א A B C, Vulgate, Syriac, read, ' one of the *seven* seals.' **noise.** A B C read this [*phone,* or *phonei*] nominative, or dative, not the genitive: 'I heard one from among the four living creatures saying, as (it were) *the voice* (or, *as with the voice*) of thunder' [א, *phonēn*]. The first living creature was like a *lion* (ch. iv. 7): his voice corresponds to the lion-like boldness with which, in successive revivals, the faithful have *testified for Christ,* and especially before His coming shall testify. Rather, their earnestness in praying for *Christ's coming.* **Come and see.** So א B [*ide*]; but A C, Vulgate, reject it. *Alford* objects to "Come and see," 'Whither was John to come? Separated by the glassy sea from the throne, was he to cross it?' Contrast the expression, ch. x. 8. It is more probably the cry of the redeemed to the Redeemer, "Come," deliver the groaning creature from the bondage of corruption [*erchou* echoing His *erchomai*]. Thus *v.* 2 answers the cry, 'went (lit., *came*) forth,' corresponding to "Come." "Come" (*Grotius*) is the living creature's address to John, *calling his earnest attention.* "Come" can hardly mean this. Cf. the only other places of its occurrence in Revelation (ch. xxii. 17) [*elthe, v.* 20, *erchou*]. If the four living creatures represent the four gospels, "Come" will be their invitation to every one (for their address is not necessarily to *John*) to *accept* Christ's salvation whilst there is time, as the opening of the seals marks a progressive step towards the end. Judgments are foretold as accompanying the *preaching of the Gospel as a witness to all nations* (Matt. xxiv. 6-14; ch. xiv. 6-11, to which the invitation, "Come," is parallel. The opening of the four first seals is followed by judgments preparatory for His coming. At the opening of the fifth, the martyrs above express the same (cf. Zech. i. 10; *vv.* 9, 10). At the opening of the sixth, the Lord's coming is ushered in with terrors to the ungodly. At the seventh, the consummation is reached (ch. xi. 15). 2. *Christ,* whether in person or by His angel, preparatory to His coming again, as appears from ch. xix. 11, 12. **bow**—(Ps. xlv. 4, 5.) **crown**

[*stephanos*]—the wreath of a *conqueror;* also implied by His *white horse,* white being the emblem of victory. In ch. xix. 11, 12, the last step in His victorious progress: accordingly there He wears *many diadems* [*diademata;* not merely *stephanoi,* wreaths], personally attended by the hosts of heaven. Cf. Zech. i. and vi.; especially *v.* 10 below, with Zech. i. 12: cf. the colours of the four horses. The black is not in Zechariah. **and to** (that He should) **conquer**—to gain a lasting victory. All four seals usher in *judgments* on the earth, as the power which opposes the reign of Himself and His Church. This, rather than conversion, is meant, though, secondarily, the elect will be gathered out through His Word and His judgments.
3. **and see.** Omitted in A B C, Vulgate. **4. red** —the colour of *blood.* The colour of each horse answers to the mission of the rider. Cf. Matt. x. 34-36. The *white* horse of the Conqueror is soon followed, through man's perversion of the Gospel, by the *red* horse of bloodshed: this is overruled to the clearing away of the obstacles to Christ's coming kingdom. The patient *ox* is the emblem of the second *living creature,* who, at the opening of this seal, saith, "Come." The saints, amidst judgments on the earth, in patience 'endure to the end.' **that they should kill** [*sphaxosin,* א B ; but A C, *sphaxousin,* indicative future]—'that they may, *as they shall,* kill one another.'
5. and see. So B [*ide* for *blepe*]; but A C, Vulgate, omit. **black**—implying *sadness* and *want.* **had**—'having.' **a pair of balances**—symbol of scarcity: bread being doled out by weight. **6. a voice.** So B; but א A C read, '*as it were* a voice.' The voice is heard 'in the midst of the four living creatures' (as Jehovah in the Shechinah cloud manifested His presence between the cherubim); because it is only in connection with His redeemed that God mitigates His judgments on the earth. **A measure**— 'A chœnix.' Whilst making food scarce, do not make it so much so that a chœnix (a day's provision of wheat, variously estimated at two or three pints) shall not be got "for a penny" [*denarius,* eight-and-a-half-pence of our money: probably the day's wages of the labourer]. *Famine* generally follows the *sword.* Ordinarily, from sixteen to twenty measures were given for a denarius. A spiritual famine may be included (Amos viii. 11). The "Come" of this third seal is said by the third of the four living creatures, whose likeness is *a man:* indicative of human sympathy for the sufferers. God in it tempers judgment with mercy. Cf. Matt. xxiv. 7, which foretells the very calamities in these seals: *nation rising against nation* (the sword), *famines, pestilences* (v. 8), and *earthquakes* (v. 12). **three mea-**

7 And when he had opened the fourth seal, I heard the voice of the
8 fourth beast say, Come and see. And I looked, and behold a pale horse:
and his name that sat on him was Death, and Hell followed with him.
And power was given [2]unto them over the fourth part of the earth, [g]to
kill with sword, and with hunger, and with death, [h]and with the beasts
of the earth.

9 And when he had opened the fifth seal, I saw under [i]the altar [j]the
souls of them that were slain for the word of God, and for [k]the testi-
10 mony which they held: and they cried with a loud voice, saying, [l]How
long, O Lord, holy and true, dost thou not judge and avenge our blood
11 on them that dwell on the earth? And white robes were given unto
every one of them; and it was said unto them, that [m]they should rest

A.D 96

2 Or. to him.
g Eze. 14. 21.
h Lev. 26. 22.
i Lev 4. 7.
Phil. 2. 17.
ch. 8. 3.
ch. 9. 13.
j ch 20. 4.
k 2 Tim. 1. 8.
ch 12. 17.
l Gen 4. 10.
Zech 1. 12.
m Heb 11. 40.
ch. 14. 13.

sures of barley for a penny—the cheaper and less nutritious grain, bought by the labourer who could not buy wheat for his family with his day's wages —a denarius—but barley. see thou hurt not the oil and the wine—luxuries rather than necessaries. The oil and wine were to be spared for refreshment of the sufferers.

7. and see. Supported by B; omitted by A C, Vulgate. The *fourth living creature*, "like a flying eagle," introduces this seal: high-soaring intelligence, and judgment, swooping down on the ungodly, as the king of birds on his prey. 8. pale [*chloros*]. Death — personified. Hell — *Hades*. unto them—*Death* and *Hades*. So A א C; but B, Vulgate, read, 'to him.' fourth part of the earth —his portion, as one of the first four seals, being a *fourth*. with ... with ... with—IN [*en*]. death —pestilence (cf. Ezek. xiv. 21, with God's four judgments here—the *sword, famine, pestilence*, and *wild beasts: famine* resulting from the *sword*; *pestilence* from *famine*; and *beasts* multiplying by the consequent depopulation). with the beasts [*hupo*] —*by*: direct agency. These four seals are marked off from the three last by the four living creatures introducing them with "Come." The calamities indicated are not restricted to one time, but extend through the whole of church history to the coming of Christ, before which last great day of the Lord they shall reach their height. The first seal is the summary—Christ going forth on His *white* horse (as in ch. xix. 11), *conquering*, till all enemies are subdued (Ps. cx. 1); with a view to which the subsequent judgments accompany the *preaching of the Gospel, for a witness to all nations.*

9. The three last seals relate to the invisible, as the first four to the visible world; the fifth, to the martyrs who died as believers; the sixth, to those who died, or shall be found at Christ's coming, unbelievers—viz., "the kings ... great men ... bond man ... free man;" the seventh, to the silence in heaven. The scene changes from earth to heaven; so that interpretations which make these three last consecutive to the first four are doubtful. I saw—in spirit. Souls are not naturally visible. under the altar. As the blood of sacrificial victims on the altar was poured *at the bottom of the altar*, so the souls of those sacrificed for Christ's testimony are symbolically represented *under the altar* in heaven; for 'the life (animal *soul*) is in the *blood*,' and blood is often represented as crying for vengeance (Gen. iv. 10). The altar in heaven, antitypical to the altar of sacrifice, is Christ crucified (Heb. xiii. 10). As 'the altar sanctifies the gift,' so Christ alone makes our obedience, and even our sacrifice of life for the truth, acceptable to God. The sacrificial altar was not in the sanctuary, but outside; so Christ's literal sacrifice, and the figurative sacrifice of the

martyrs, took place, not in the heavenly sanctuary, but outside, here on earth. The only altar in heaven is that antitypical to the temple-altar of incense. The *blood* of the martyrs cries from the earth under Christ's cross, whereon they may be considered virtually to have been sacrificed: their *souls* cry from under the altar of incense, which is Christ in heaven, by whom alone the incense of praise is accepted before God. They are *under* Christ, in His immediate presence; shut up unto Him in joyful expectancy, until He come to raise the sleeping dead. Cf. the language, 2 Macc. vii. 36, as indicating Jewish opinion. 'Our brethren who have now suffered a short pain are dead *under God's covenant* [*hupo diatheken theou*] of everlasting life.' testimony which they held—*i. e.*, bore, as committed to them. Cf. ch. xii. 17, "*have* (hold) the testimony of Jesus." 10. How long? [*Heōs pote*]—'Until when?' As in the parable, the woman (the Church) *cries day and night* to the unjust judge for justice against her adversary always oppressing her (cf. ch. xii. 10); so the elect (not only on earth, but *under Christ's covering*, in His presence in Paradise) *cry day and night* to God, who will assuredly, in His own time, avenge His and their cause, "though He bear *long* with them" (Luke xviii. 1-8). This need not be *restricted* to particular martyrdoms, but receives partial fulfilments, until the last exhaustive fulfilment before Christ's coming. So as to the other events foretold here. The glory even of those in Paradise shall only be complete when Christ's and the Church's foes are cast out, and the earth become Christ's kingdom at His coming to raise the sleeping, and transfigure the living, saints. Lord [*ho Despotes*]—"Master;" implying He has them, their foes, and all creatures, as absolutely at His disposal as a master has his *slaves*; hence (*v.* 11) "*fellow-servants*," or *fellow-slaves*, follows. holy— '*the Holy One.*' avenge—'exact vengeance for our blood.' on—'*from* them.' that dwell on the earth — the ungodly, of earth, earthy; distinguished from the Church, whose home and heart are even now in heaven. 11. white robes. So Vulgate; but A B C א read, 'a white robe was given.' every one of them. B omits; A C א read, 'unto them, unto each;' *i. e.*, unto them severally. Though their joint cry for the riddance of the earth from the ungodly is not yet granted, it will be so in due time; meanwhile, *individually* they receive the white robe, indicative of light, joy, and triumph over their foes; even as the Captain of their salvation goes forth on a *white* horse, *conquering and to conquer*: also of sanctity through Christ. *Maimonides* says that the Jews arrayed priests, when approved of, *in white robes*. They are admitted among the blessed, who, as spotless priests, minister unto God and the Lamb. should. So א C; but A B, '*shall* rest.' a little

678

yet for a little season, until their fellow-servants also and their brethren,
that should be killed as they *were,* should be fulfilled.
12 And I beheld when he had opened the sixth seal; [n]and, lo, there was
a great earthquake; and [o]the sun became black as sackcloth of hair, and
13 the moon became as blood; and the stars of heaven fell unto the earth,
even as a fig tree casteth her [3]untimely figs, when she is shaken of a
14 mighty wind. And [p]the heaven departed as a scroll when it is rolled
together; and every mountain [q]and island were moved out of their places.
15 And the kings of the earth, and the great men, and the rich men, and
the chief captains, and the mighty men, and every bond man, and every
free man, [r]hid themselves in the dens and in the rocks of the moun-
16 tains; and said to the mountains and rocks, Fall on us, and hide us
from the face of him that sitteth on the throne, and from the wrath of
17 the Lamb: for [s]the great day of his wrath is come; [t]and who shall be able
to stand?
7 AND after these things I saw four angels [a]standing on the four corners

A. D. 96.

[n] ch. 16. 18.
[o] Joel 2. 10.
Joel 3. 15.
Matt. 24. 29.
Acts 2 20.
[3] Or, green figs.
[p] Ps. 102. 26.
Isa. 34. 4.
Heb 1. 12.
[q] Jer. 3. 23.
Jer. 4. 24.
[r] Isa. 2. 19.
[s] Isa. 13. 6.
Zeph. 1. 14.
[t] Ps. 76. 7.

CHAP. 7.
[a] Ps. 34. 7.
Heb. 1. 14.

season. So א A C; but B omits "little." Even if omitted, the "season" is short compared with eternity. *Bengel* fancifully made a *season* [*chronus*] to be $1{,}111\frac{1}{9}$ years, and a *time* (ch. xii. 12, 14) [*kairos*], a fifth of a *season—i. e.,* $222\frac{2}{9}$ years. The only distinction is, a *season* [*chronus*] is an aggregate of *times*. [*Kairos,* a specific time, so of short duration.] As to their *rest,* cf. ch. xiv. 13 [the same *anapauomai*]; Isa. lvii. 2; Dan. xii. 13; LXX. **until their . . . brethren . . . be fulfilled**—until their full number shall have been completed. The number of the elect is definite; perhaps to fill up that of the fallen angels. The *full* blessedness of all the saints shall be simultaneous (1 Thess. iv. 15; Heb. xi. 40; xii. 23). The earlier shall not anticipate the later. A C read, 'shall have been accomplished;' B א, 'shall have accomplished (their course).'

12. As *vv.* 4, 6-8, the sword, famine, and pestilence, answer to Matt. xxiv. 6, 7; *vv.* 9, 10, as to martyrdoms, answer to Matt. xxiv. 9, 10: so this passage, *vv.* 12-17, answers to Matt. xxiv. 29, 30, *the portents* of the immediate coming of the day of the Lord; *not the coming itself,* until the elect are sealed, and the judgments invoked by the martyrs descend on the earth, the sea, and the trees, (ch. vii.) **and, lo.** So A; but B C א omit "lo." **earthquake**—'shaking' of *the heavens,* the sea, and the dry land: the shaking of these mutable things, the necessary preliminary to setting up those *things which cannot be shaken* (Heb. xii. 26-28). One of the *catchwords* (*Wordsworth*) connecting the sixth seal with the sixth trumpet (ch. xi. 13) and the seventh vial (ch. xvi. 17-21); also the seventh seal (ch. viii. 5). **sackcloth**—made of the "hair" of Cilician goats: 'cilicium,' or Cilician cloth, used for tents, &c. Paul, a Cilician, made such tents (Acts xviii. 3). **moon.** א A B C *h,* Vulgate, read, 'the whole' or 'full moon:' not merely the crescent. **as blood**—(Joel ii. 31.) **13. stars . . . fell . . . as a fig tree casteth her untimely figs**—(Isa. xxxiv. 4; Nah. iii. 12.) The Church shall be then ripe for glorification, the antichristian world for destruction; accompanied with mighty phenomena in nature. As to the stars falling to the earth, Scripture describes phenomena as they appear to the spectator, not in scientific language: science itself has often to do the same. Yet, whilst adapting itself to ordinary men, Scripture drops hints which anticipate modern discoveries. **14. departed** [*apechoristhe*]—'*was separated from*' its place: 'made to depart.' Not as *Alford,* 'parted *asunder;*' on the contrary, it was rolled *together* as an open scroll is rolled up and laid aside. There is no 'asunder one from another,' as in Acts xv. 39. **mountain . . . moved out of their places**—(Ps. cxxi. 1, margin; Jer. iii. 23; iv. 24; Nah. i. 5). This disruption shall be the precursor of the new earth, as the pre-Adamic convulsions prepared it for its present occupants. **15. kings . . . hid themselves.** Where was now the spirit of those whom the world so greatly feared? (*Bengel.*) **great men**—high officers of state. **rich men . . . chief captains.** א A B C *h,* Vulgate, 'chief captains . . . rich men.' **mighty** [*dunatoi*]. א A B C read [*ischuroi*], 'strong' physically (Ps. xxxiii. 16). **in** [*eis*]—ran *into,* so as to *hide themselves* in. **dens**—'caves.' **16. from the face**—(Ps. xxxiv. 16: cf. Hos. x. 8; Luke xxiii. 30.) **17.** 'The day, the great (day).' After the Lord has exhausted all His ordinary judgments—the sword, famine, pestilence, and wild beasts, and still sinners are impenitent—*the last great day* of the Lord itself shall come. Matt. xxiv. (note, *v.* 12, above) forms a perfect parallelism to the six seals, not only in the events, but the order: *v.* 3, the first seal; *v.* 6, the second; *v.* 7, the third; *v.* 8, end, the fourth; *v.* 9, the fifth; the persecutions, abounding iniquity, and consequent judgments, accompanied with Gospel-preaching to all nations as a "testimony," are detailed *vv.* 9-28; *v.* 29, the sixth. **to stand**—justified, not condemned, before the Judge. Thus the sixth seal brings us close to the Lord's coming. The ungodly 'tribes of the earth' tremble at the signs of His immediate approach. Before He actually inflicts the blow, "the elect" must be 'gathered' out.

CHAP. VII. 1-17.—Sealing of the Elect of Israel—The Countless Multitudes of the Gentile Elect.

1. And. So B, Syriac; but A C, Vulgate, Coptic, omit. **after these things.** A B C א, Coptic, read, 'after this.' The two visions come in as an episode *after* the sixth seal, before the seventh. Though "Israel" may elsewhere designate the spiritual Israel, "the elect (church)" here, where the several names of the tribes are specified, these can only have the literal meaning. The second advent will be the time of *the restoration of the kingdom to Israel* (Acts i. 6, 7), when *the times of the Gentiles shall have been fulfilled* (Luke xxi. 24), and the Jews shall say, "Blessed is He that cometh in the name of the Lord" (Matt. xxiii. 39). During the Lord's absence, the Jews have had no existence as a nation. As Revelation is the Book of the Second Advent, God's favour restored to Israel naturally has place among the events that

of the earth, *b* holding the four winds of the earth, that *c* the wind should not blow on the earth, nor on the sea, nor on any tree.

2 And I saw another angel ascending from the east, having the seal of the living God: and he cried with a loud voice to the four angels, to

3 whom it was given to hurt the earth and the sea, saying, *d* Hurt not the earth, neither the sea, nor the trees, till we have sealed *e* the servants of our God in *f* their foreheads.

4 And *g* I heard the number of them which were sealed : *and there were* sealed an *h* hundred *and* forty *and* four thousand of all the tribes of the

5 children of Israel. Of the tribe of Juda *were* sealed twelve thousand. Of the tribe of Reuben *were* sealed twelve thousand. Of the tribe of Gad

6 *were* sealed twelve thousand. Of the tribe of Aser *were* sealed twelve thousand. Of the tribe of Nephthalim *were* sealed twelve thousand.

7 Of the tribe of Manasses *were* sealed twelve thousand. Of the tribe of Simeon *were* sealed twelve thousand. Of the tribe of Levi *were* sealed twelve thousand. Of the tribe of Issachar *were* sealed twelve thousand.

8 Of the tribe of Zabulon *were* sealed twelve thousand. Of the tribe of Joseph *were* sealed twelve thousand. Of the tribe of Benjamin *were* sealed twelve thousand.

A. D. 96.
b Isa 27. 8.
Jer 49 36.
Dan 7. 2.
Jon. 1. 4.
c Ex 15. 10.
Ps 1:7. 18.
ch. 9. 4.
d Matt. 21.21,
31.
ch. 6. 6.
ch 9. 4.
e Eze. 9. 4.
Eph. 4. 30.
2 Tim. 2.
19.
ch 14. 1.
f ch. 13. 16.
ch 14. 1.
ch. 22. 4.
g ch. 9. 16.
h Gen. 15 5.
Isa 4. 2, 3.
Rom. 9. 27.
ch. 14. 1.

usher it in. earth . . . sea . . . tree. The judgments on these are in answer to the martyrs' prayer under the *fifth* seal (ch. v. 10). Cf. the same under the *fifth* trumpet, the sealed being exempt (ch. ix. 4). on any tree—'*against* any tree' [*epi ti dendron*], but '*on* the earth' [*epi tees gees*].
2. from the east—'the rising of the sun:' the quarter from which God's glory manifests itself. 3. Hurt not—by letting loose destructive winds. till we have sealed the servants of our God—parallel to Matt. xxiv. 31. God's love is such that He *cannot do anything* in judgment till His people are secured (Gen. xix. 22). Israel, just before the Lord's coming, shall be re-embodied as a nation; for its tribes are specified (Joseph, however, substituted for Dan: whether because antichrist is to come from Dan, or Dan is to be his tool [*Arethas*, tenth century], cf. Gen. xlix. 17; Jer. viii. 16; Amos viii. 14, as there was a Judas among the Twelve. Out of these tribes *a believing remnant* will be preserved from the judgments which destroy the antichristian confederacy (ch. vi. 12-17), and *shall be transfigured with the elect of all nations*—viz., 144,000 (or whatever is meant by the symbolical number), who shall faithfully resist the seductions of antichrist, while the rest, restored to Palestine in unbelief, are his dupes, and at last his victims. Previously to the Lord's judgments on antichrist, His hosts shall destroy *two-thirds* of the nation, *one-third* escaping. By the Spirit's operation through affliction, this remnant, turning to the Lord, shall form the nucleus on earth of the Israelite nation that is thenceforth to stand at the head of the millennial nations. Israel's spiritual resurrection shall be as "life from the dead" to all nations (Rom. xi. 15). As now a regeneration goes on of individuals, so there shall then be a regeneration of nations, in connection with Christ's coming. Matt. xxiv. 34, 35, "this generation (the Jewish nation) shall not pass till all these things be fulfilled:" Israel can no more *pass away* before Christ's advent, than Christ's own *words* can *pass away*. So Zech. xiii. 1, 2, 8, 9; xiv. 2-4, 9-21: cf. ch. xii. 2-14. So Ezek. viii. 17, 18; ix. 1-7, especially *v.* 4. Cf. also Ezek. x. 2, with ch. viii. 5, where the final judgments fall on the earth, with the same accompaniment, *the fire of the altar cast into the earth*, including the *fire scattered over the city.* So ch. xiv. 1, the same

144,000 appears on Zion with the Father's name in their forehead; at the close of the section, chs. xii., xiii., xiv., concerning the Church and her foes. The saints are not exempt from trial: *v.* 14 apparently disproves the theory that the elect shall be caught up *before* the great tribulation (notes, 1 Thess. iv. 17; Jude 14); but their trials are distinct from the *destroying* judgments that follow on the world: from these they are exempted, as Israel was from Egypt's plagues, especially from the last, the Israelite doors having the blood-mark seal. foreheads—the conspicuous, noblest part of man's body: whereon the helmet, "the hope of salvation," is worn.
4. *Twelve* is the number of the tribes, appropriate to *the Church:* three by four: three, the *Divine*, multiplied by four, the number for *world-wide extension.* Twelve by twelve, *fixity and completeness;* taken a thousandfold in 144,000. A *thousand* implies *the world perfectly pervaded by the Divine;* for it is *ten*, the world number, raised to the power of *three*, the number of God. of all the tribes—'out of every tribe:' not 144,000 of each, but the aggregate of the 12,000 *from every tribe.* children—'*sons* of Israel.' Ch. iii. 12; xxi. 12, are no objection to the literal Israel being meant; for, in consummated glory, still the Church will be that "built on the foundation of the (*Twelve*) apostles (Israelites), Jesus Christ (an Israelite) being the chief corner-stone." Gentile believers shall have *the name Jerusalem written on them*, as having the heavenly citizenship antitypical to the literal Jerusalem. 5. Judah (*praise*) stands first, as Jesus' tribe. Benjamin, the youngest, is last; with him is associated second last, Joseph. Reuben, as first-born, comes next after Judah, to whom it gave place, having by sin lost primogeniture right. Another reason (note, *v.* 3) for the omission of Dan is, its having been the first to lapse into idolatry (Judg. xviii.); for which "Ephraim" also (cf. Judg. xvii.; Hos. iv. 17) is omitted, and Joseph substituted. Long before, the Hebrews say (*Grotius*), it was reduced to the one family of Hussim, which perished subsequently in the wars before Ezra's time. Hence it is omitted, 1 Chr. iv. 8. Dan's small numbers are joined to Naphtali's, whose brother he was by the same mother (*Bengel*). The twelve times 12,000 sealed ones of Israel, who resist antichrist's idolatry, are the nucleus of transfigured

9   After this I beheld, and, lo, *i* a great multitude, which no man could number, *j* of all nations, and kindreds, and people, and tongues, stood before the throne, and before the Lamb, *k* clothed with white robes, and
10 palms in their hands; and cried with a loud voice, saying, Salvation *l* to
11 our God *m* which sitteth upon the throne, and unto the Lamb. And *n* all the angels stood round about the throne, and *about* the elders, and the four beasts, and fell before the throne on their faces, and worshipped
12 God, saying, *o* Amen : Blessing, and glory, and wisdom, and thanksgiving, and honour, and power, and might, *be* unto our God for ever and ever. Amen.
13 And one of the elders answered, saying unto me, What are these which
14 are arrayed in white robes? and whence came they? And I said unto him, Sir, thou knowest. And he said to me, *p* These are they which came out of great tribulation, and have *q* washed their robes, and made them
15 white in the blood of the Lamb. Therefore are they before the throne of God, and serve him day and night in his temple: and he that sitteth

A. D. 96.

i Gen. 12. 3.
Gen. 22. 17.
Gen 49. 10.
Isa. 2. 2, 3.
Isa. 43. 6.
j ch. 5. 9.
k ch. 3. 5.
l Ps 3. 8.
Isa. 43. 11.
Jer. 3. 23.
Hos. 13. 4.
m ch. 5. 13.
n ch. 4. 6.
o ch 5. 13.
p Acts 11. 22.
q Isa 1. 18.
Zec'. 3. 3.
Heb 9. 14.
1 John 1. 7.
ch. 1. 5.

humanity (*Auberlen*), to which the elect are joined, "a multitude which no man could number," *v.* 9 (the church of Jews and Gentiles indiscriminately, in which the Gentiles are predominant, Luke xxi. 24. "Tribes" ('kindreds') implies that *believing Israelites* are in this *countless multitude*). Both are in heaven, yet ruling over the earth, as ministers of blessing to its inhabitants; whilst upon earth the world of nations is added to the kingdom of Israel. The twelve apostles stand at the head of the whole. The upper and the lower congregation, though distinct, are intimately associated. **9. no man**—'no one.' **of all nations**—'OUT OF *every nation*.' The human race is *one nation* by origin, but afterwards separated itself into *tribes*, *peoples*, and *tongues;* hence, the one singular stands first, followed by the three plurals. **kindreds**—'tribes.' **people**—'peoples.' The 'firstfruits unto the Lamb,' the 144,000 (ch. xiv. 1-4) of Israel, are followed by a copious harvest of all nations, an election *out of* the Gentiles, as the 144,000 are an election out of Israel (note, *v.* 3). **white robes**—(note, ch. vi. 11 ; also ch. iii. 5, 18; iv. 4.) **palms in their hands**—antitype to Christ's entry into Jerusalem amidst the palm-bearing multitude. This shall be just when He is about to come visibly and take possession of His kingdom. The *palm branch* is the symbol of joy and triumph : used at the feast of tabernacles, on the fifteenth day of the seventh month, when they kept feast to God in thanksgiving for the ingathered fruits. The antitype shall be the completed harvest of the elect here described. Cf. Zech. xiv. 16; the *earthly* feast of tabernacles will be renewed, in commemoration of Israel's preservation in her long wilderness-like sojourn among the nations from which she shall have been delivered, just as the original feast commemorated her dwelling for forty years in tabernacles in the wilderness. **10. cried.** 'Cry' in א A B C, Vulgate, Syriac, Coptic. It is their continuing, ceaseless employment. **Salvation**—'THE salvation :' all the praise of our salvation be ascribed to our God. At the Lord's entry into Jerusalem, the type, *salvation* was the cry of the palm-bearing multitudes. *Hosanna* means *save us now*, from Ps. cxviii. 14, 15, 22, 25, 26, where the same connection occurs between *salvation*, *tabernacles*, of the righteous, and the cry of the whole Jewish nation at Christ's coming, "Blessed be He that cometh in the name of the Lord." **11.** The angels, as in ch. v. 11, take up the anthem. There it was "*many* angels;" here, "*all* the angels" **stood**—

'were standing.' **12.** '*The* blessing, *the* glory, *the* wisdom, *the* thanksgiving, *the* honour, *the* power. *the* might (*sevenfold* doxology, implying its completeness), *unto the ages of the ages.*'
  13. answered—to my thoughts: asked the question naturally arising in John's mind from what went before. One of the twenty-four elders, representing the Old and New Testament ministry, appropriately is interpreter of this vision of the glorified Church. **What, &c.** 'These which are arrayed in white robes, WHO are they?' **14. Sir**—'Lord.' א B C, Vulgate, Syriac, Coptic, *Cyprian*, read, 'My Lord.' A omits 'My.' **thou knowest** —from Ezek. xxxvii. 3. Comparatively ignorant ourselves, we ought to look upwards for Divine knowledge. **came**—'come:' implying, they are *just come.* **great tribulation** [*tēs thlipseōs tēs megalēs*]—'THE great tribulation:' 'the tribulation, the great one,' to which the martyrs were exposed under the fifth seal ; which, Christ says, is to precede His coming (Matt. xxiv. 21, 29, 30, "*great tribulation*, such as was not since the beginning of. the world "), followed by the same signs as the sixth seal : cf. Dan. xii. 1: the climax including all *the tribulation* which saints of all ages have passed through. This ch. vii. recapitulates the vision of the six seals, ch. vi. filling up the outline there in what affects the faithful. There, however, their number was waiting to be completed ; here it is completed ; they are taken out of the earth before the judgments on the antichristian apostasy: with their Lord, they, and all His faithful witnesses of past ages, wait for His and their coming to be glorified and reign together. Meanwhile, in contrast with their previous sufferings, they are exempt from the hunger, thirst, and scorching heats of their earthly life (*v.* 16), and are refreshed by the Lamb of God Himself (*v.* 17 ; ch. xiv. 1-4, 13): an earnest of the post-millennial final state (ch. xxi. 4-6; xxii. 1-5). **washed their robes . . . white in the blood of the Lamb**—(Isa. i. 18; Heb. ix. 14; 1 John i. 7; ch. i. 5: cf. Isa. lxi. 10; Zech. iii. 3-5.) Faith applies to the heart the purifying blood ; once for all for justification, continually throughout life for sanctification. **15. Therefore**—because they are washed white: for without it they could never enter God's holy heaven: ch. xxii. 14, 'Blessed are those who *wash their robes* (the true reading), that they may have right to the tree of life' (Eph. v. 26, 27 ; ch. xxi. 27). **before**—'in the presence of.' Matt. v. 8; 1 Cor. xiii. 12, "face to face." **throne . . .** temple—connected, because we can approach the heavenly *King* only through *priestly mediation;*

6 on the throne shall ^r dwell among them. They ^s shall hunger no more, neither thirst any more; ^t neither shall the sun light on them, nor any

17 heat. For the Lamb which is in the midst of the throne ^u shall feed them, and shall lead them unto living fountains of water; and ^v God shall wipe away all tears from their eyes.

8 AND when he had opened the seventh seal, there was silence in heaven about the space of half an hour.

2 And ^a I saw the seven angels which stood before God; ^b and to them

3 were given seven trumpets. And another ^c angel came and stood at the altar, having a golden censer; and there was given unto ̦him much ^d incense, that he should ¹ offer *it* with the prayers of all saints upon the

A. D 6.

^r Isa 4. 5, 6.
^s Isa 49. 10.
^t Ps. 1 !1. 6.
^u Ps. 23. 1.
^v Isa. 25. 8.

CHAP. 8.
^a Matt.18.10.
^b 2 Chr.23,25.
^c Acts 7. 30.
^d Eph. 5. 2.
¹ Or, add it to the prayers.

---

therefore Christ is at once King and Priest on His throne (Zech. vi. 13). **day and night**—*i. e.*, perpetually: as those approved as priests by the Sanhedrim, clothed in white, kept by turns a perpetual watch in the temple at Jerusalem (cf. the singers, 1 Chr. ix. 33; Ps. cxxxiv. 1). Strictly 'there is no night' there (ch. xxii. 5). **in his temple**—the heavenly analogue to His temple on earth; strictly there is "no temple therein" (ch. xxi. 22), 'God and the Lamb are the temple' filling the whole, so that there is no distinction of sacred and secular places: the city is the temple, and the temple the city. Cf. ch. iv. 8, &c. **shall dwell among them**—rather [*scenosei ep' autous*], 'shall be the tabernacle over them' (cf. Lev. xxvi. 11; ch. xxi. 3; especially Isa. iv. 5, 6; viii. 14; xxv. 4; Ezek. xxxvii. 27). His *dwelling among them* is a secondary truth, besides His being their *covert.* When once He *tabernacled among us* as *the Word made flesh* (John i. 14), He was in lowliness; then He shall be in great glory. **16.** (Isa. xlix. 10.) **hunger no more**—as here. **thirst any more**—(John iv. 13.) **the sun**—scorching in the East; symbolically, the sun of persecution (Matt. xiii. 6, 21). **light**—'by no means at all . . . light' (fall), &c. **heat**—as the sirocco. **17. in the midst of the throne**—*i. e.*, in the middle point in front of the throne (ch. v. 6). **feed** [*poimanei*]—'tend as a shepherd.' **living fountains of water.** ℵ A B, Vulgate, *Cyprian*, read (eternal) '*life's* fountains of waters.'

CHAP. VIII. 1-13.—SEVENTH SEAL—PREPARATION FOR THE SEVEN TRUMPETS—THE FOUR FIRST, AND CONSEQUENT PLAGUES.

1. was—'began to be.' **silence in heaven about . . . half an hour.** The last seal being opened, the book of God's plan of redemption is opened for the Lamb to read to the blessed ones. The *half-hour's silence* contrasts with the loud anthem of *the great multitude*, taken up by *angels* (ch. vii. 9-11). It is the solemn introduction to the eternal Sabbath-rest, commencing with the Lamb's reading the book, heretofore sealed, which we cannot know till then. In ch. x. 4, similarly at the eve of the sounding of the seventh trumpet, when the seven thunders uttered their voices, John is forbidden to write them. The seventh trumpet (ch. xi. 15-19) winds up God's vast plan of providence and grace, just as the seventh seal does. So the seventh vial (ch. xvi. 17). Not that the seven seals, seven trumpets, and seven vials, though parallel, are repetitions. They each trace the Divine action up to the grand consummation in which they all meet, under a different aspect. *Thunders, lightnings, an earthquake,* and *voices,* close the seven thunders and the seven seals alike (cf. *v.* 5 with ch. xi. 19). Cf. at the seventh vial (ch. xvi. 18). The *half-hour silence* is GIVEN TO JOHN between the preceding vision and the following one: it is, on one hand, the solemn introduction to the eternal sabbatism following the

seventh seal; on the other, the silence during the incense accompanied prayers which usher in the first of the seven trumpets (*vv.* 3-5). In the Jewish temple, musical instruments and singing resounded during the whole offering of sacrifices, which formed the first part of the service. But at the offering of incense solemn silence was kept (Ps. lxii. 1, "My soul *waiteth* upon God;" margin, 'is silent;' lxv. 1, margin), the people praying secretly. The *half-hour* stillness implies, too, the adoring expectation with which the blessed spirits and angels await the unfolding of God's judgments. A *short* space; for even an *hour* is so used (ch. xvii. 12; xviii. 10, 19).

2. the seven angels. Cf. the apocryphal Tobit, xii. 15, 'I am Raphael, one of the seven holy angels which present the prayers of the saints, and go in and out before the glory of the Holy One.' Cf. Luke i. 19. **stood**—'stand.' **seven trumpets.** These come in whilst the martyrs *rest until their fellow-servants also, that should be killed as they were, should be fulfilled:* for it is *the inhabiters of the earth* on whom the judgments fall, as the martyrs prayed that they should (ch. vi. 10). *All* the ungodly, not merely one portion, are meant; all opponents to the kingdom of Christ and His saints, as is proved by ch. xi. 15, 18, at the close of the seven trumpets. Revelation becomes more special only as it advances, (ch. xiii.; xvi. 10; xvii.; xviii.) By the seven trumpets the world-kingdoms are overturned to make way for Christ's universal kingdom. A *martial* instrument. *War* is the general feature of this group of judgments. The first four are connected; and the last three, which alone have *Woe, woe, woe* (*vv.* 7-13). **3. another angel**—not Christ; for He, in Revelation, is always designated by His proper title. Doubtless, He is the only High Priest, the Angel of the covenant, standing before the golden altar of incense, and, as Mediator, offering up His people's prayers, acceptable before God through the incense of His merit (Mal. i. 11). Here the angel acts as a *ministering spirit,* just as the twenty-four elders *have vials full of odours,* or incense—*the prayers of saints*—which they present before the Lamb (ch. v. 8). How precisely their ministry, in perfuming the prayers of the saints, and offering them on the altar of incense (which also Christ is, Heb. xiii. 10), is exercised, we know not, but we do know they are not to be prayed to (ch. xix. 2). If we send an offering to the king, the king's messenger is not to appropriate what is due to the king alone. **there was given unto him.** The angel does not provide the incense: it is *given to him* by Christ, whose meritorious obedience and death are the incense rendering the saints' prayers well-pleasing to God. Not the saints give the angel the incense; nor are their prayers identified with it; nor do they offer their prayers to him. Christ alone is the Mediator through and to whom prayer is to be offered. **offer it with the prayers**

4 ^egolden altar which was before the throne. And ^fthe smoke of the incense, *which came* with the prayers of the saints, ascended up before
5 God out of the angel's hand. And the angel took the censer, and filled it with fire of the altar, and cast *it* ²into the earth: and ^gthere were voices, and thunderings, and lightnings, ^hand an earthquake.
6 And the seven angels which had the seven trumpets prepared themselves to sound.
7 The first angel sounded, ⁱand there followed hail and fire mingled with blood, and they were ^jcast upon the earth: and the third part ^kof trees was burnt up, and all green grass was burnt up.
8 And the second angel sounded, and as it were a great mountain burning with fire was cast into the sea: and the third part of the sea ^lbecame
9 blood; and the third part of the creatures which were in the sea, and had life, died; and the third part of the ships were destroyed.
10 And the third angel sounded, and there fell a great star from heaven, burning as it were a lamp, and it fell upon the third part of the rivers,
11 and upon the fountains of waters: and the name of the star is called Wormwood: ^mand the third part of the waters became wormwood; and many men died of the waters, because they were made bitter.
12 And ⁿthe fourth angel sounded, and the third part of the sun was

A. D. 96.
^e Ex. 30. 1.
^f Ps 141. 2.
² Cr. upon.
^g 2 Sam. 22. 7-9
Ps 1?. 1?.
Isa. 30. 0.
Heb. 12. 18, 19.
ch. 11. 19.
ch. 16. 18.
^h 2 Sam. 22.8.
1 Ki. 19. 11.
Acts 4. 31.
ⁱ Eze. 38. 22.
^j ch 16. 2.
^k Isa. 2. 13.
ch. 9. 4.
^l Ex 7. 17.
Eze 14. 19.
^m Ex. 15. 23.
Jer 9. 15.
Jer. 23. 15.
ⁿ Isa. 13. 10.
Amos 8. 9.

[*dosē proseuchais*]—'*give* it TO the prayers,' so rendering them a *sweet-smelling savour* to God. Christ's merits alone can *incense* our prayers, though the angelic ministry be employed to attach this incense to the prayers. The saint's praying on earth, and the angel's incensing in heaven, are simultaneous. **all saints**—both those in the heavenly rest and those militant on earth. The martyrs' cry is the foremost (ch. vi. 10), and brings down the ensuing judgments. **golden altar**—antitype to the earthly: Christ (Heb. xiii. 10; ch. vi. 9). **4. the smoke . . . which came with the prayers . . . ascended up**—rather, 'the smoke of the incense FOR (or *given* TO: understood from *v.* 3) the prayers of the saints ascended up, out of the angel's hand, in the presence of God.' The angel merely burns the incense given him by Christ the High Priest, so that its smoke blends with the saints' ascending prayers. The saints themselves are priests; the angels in this priestly ministration are but *their fellow-servants* (ch. xix. 10). **5. cast it** into (*unto*) **the earth.** The hot coals off the altar cast on the earth, symbolize God's fiery judgments about to descend on the Church's foes in answer to the saints' incense-perfumed prayers, which just ascended before God (cf. ch. vi. 10). How marvellous the power of prayers! **there were—**'ensued.' **voices, and thunderings, &c.** אB place "voices" after "thunderings;" A places it after "lightnings."
6. sound—blow the trumpets.
7. The common feature of the first four trumpets is, the judgments affect *natural objects,* accessories of life—the earth, trees, grass, sea, rivers, fountains, light of the sun, moon, and stars. The last three, the *woe-trumpets* (*v.* 13), affect men with pain, death, and hell. The language is from the plagues of Egypt, five or six out of the ten exactly corresponding: the *hail, fire,* WATER *turned to blood, darkness, locusts,* perhaps the *death* (Exod. vii. 19; ix. 24; x. 12, 21; ch. ix. 18). Judicial retribution in kind characterizes the four first—those elements which were abused punishing their abusers. **mingled with.** A B א, Vulgate, read, 'IN blood.' So in the second and third vials (ch. xvi. 3, 4). **upon the earth**—'*unto* the earth.' A B א, Vulgate, Syriac, add, 'and the third of the earth was burnt up.' So under the third trumpet, the *third* of the rivers is affected; also,

under the sixth trumpet, the *third* part of men are killed. In Zech. xiii. 8, 9, this tripartite division appears—two parts killed, a third preserved. Here *vice versâ*—two-thirds escape, one-third is smitten. Fire was the predominant element. **all green grass**—no longer a third, but *all* is *burnt up.*
8. as it were—not literally: a *mountain-like* burning mass: in allusion to Jer. li. 25; Amos vii. 4. **third part of the sea became blood.** In the parallel second vial, the *whole* sea becomes *blood.* The overthrow of Jericho (type of the antichristian Babylon), after which Israel under Joshua (*Jesus*) took possession of Canaan (type of Christ's and His people's kingdom), is perhaps alluded to in the SEVEN *trumpets,* which end in the overthrow of Christ's foes, and the setting up of His kingdom. On the *seventh* day, at the *seventh* time, when the *seven* priests blew the *seven* rams' horn trumpets, the people shouted, and the walls fell flat; then ensued the *blood*-shedding of the foe. A mountain-like fiery mass would not naturally change water into blood; nor would the third of ships be destroyed. Symbolical interpreters take *ships* here to be *churches.* For [*ploiŏn*] "ships" is in the gospels the term for the apostolic vessel in which Christ taught. The first churches were in the shape of an inverted ship; and [*diephtharesan*] *destroyed* is used of heretical *corruptings* (1 Tim. vi. 5).
10. a lamp—*a torch.* **11.** Symbolizers interpret the *star fallen from heaven* a chief minister (*Arius,* &c., or some future false teacher) falling from his high place, and instead of shining with heavenly light as a *star,* becoming a torch lit with earthly fire and smouldering with smoke. *Wormwood,* though medicinal, if used as ordinary water, would not only be disagreeable, but also fatal; so 'heretical wormwood changes the sweet Siloas of Scripture into deadly Marahs' (*Wordsworth*). Contrast the converse change of Marah water into sweet, (Exod. xv. 23, &c.) *Alford* instances the conversion of water into *fire-water*—*ardent* spirits—which may destroy a third of the ungodly in the latter days.
12. third part—not *total* obscuration, as in the sixth seal (ch. vi. 12, 13). This, therefore, comes between the prayers of the martyrs under the fifth seal, and the last overwhelming judgments on the

smitten, and the third part of the moon, and the third part of the stars; so as the third part of them was darkened, and the day shone not for a third part of it, and the night likewise.

13 And I beheld, and heard an angel flying through the midst of heaven, saying with a loud voice, Woe, woe, woe to the inhabiters of the earth, by reason of the other voices of the trumpet of the three angels, which are yet to sound!

9 AND the fifth angel sounded, *a* and I saw a star fall from heaven unto 2 the earth: and to him was given the key of *b* the bottomless pit. And he opened the bottomless pit; and there arose *c* a smoke out of the pit, as the smoke of a great furnace; and the sun and the air were darkened 3 by reason of the smoke of the pit. And there came out of the smoke locusts upon *d* the earth: and unto them was given power, as the scor-4 pions of the earth have power. And it was commanded them *e* that they should not hurt *f* the grass of the earth, neither any green thing, neither any tree; but only those men which have not *g* the seal of God in their 5 foreheads. And to them it was given that they should not kill them, *h* but that they should be tormented five months: and their torment *was* 6 as the torment of a scorpion, when he striketh a man. And in those days *i* shall men seek death, and shall not find it; and shall desire to die, and 7 death shall flee from them. And *j* the shapes of the locusts *were* like unto horses prepared unto battle; and *k* on their heads *were* as it were crowns 8 like gold, *l* and their faces *were* as the faces of men. And they had hair

A. D. 96.

CHAP. 9.
a Luke 10.13.
2 Thes. 2.
3-9.
2 Tim. 3. 1-
5
b Luke 8. 31.
ch 17. 8.
ch. 20. 1.
c Joel 2. 2,
10.
d Ex. 10. 4.
e ch. 6. 6.
f ch. 8. 7.
g Ex 12. 23.
Eze. 9 4.
ch. 7. 3.
ch. 14. 1.
h ch 11. 7.
i Job 3. 20-
2 .
Job 7. 15.
Isa. 2. 19.
Hos 10. 8.
Luke 23.29.
ch. 6. 16.
j Joel 2. 4.
k Nah 3. 17.
l Dan. 7. 8.

ungodly under the sixth, just before Christ's coming. **the night likewise**—withdrew a third of the light which the bright Eastern moon and stars ordinarily afford.

13. an angel. א A B, Vulgate, Syriac, Coptic, read, for "angel," 'an eagle:' symbol of judgment descending like the king of birds pouncing on the prey. Alluding to Matt. xxiv. 28. Cf. this fourth trumpet and the flying *eagle* with the fourth seal introduced by the fourth living creature: "like a flying eagle," ch. iv. 7; vi. 7, 8: the aspect of Jesus presented by the fourth evangelist. *John* is compared in the cherubim, by primitive interpretation, to a flying eagle: *Christ's divine majesty* is set forth in the Gospel, His *judicial visitations* in the Revelation, of John. Contrast "another angel" (*messenger*) with "the everlasting gospel," ch. xiv. 6. **through the midst of heaven**—'in the mid-heaven,' at the *meridian:* where the eagle is conspicuous to all. **the inhabiters of the earth**—the "men of the world," whose 'portion is in this life' (Ps. xvii. 14); upon whom the martyrs had prayed that their blood might be avenged (ch. vi. 10). Not for personal revenge, but zeal for the honour of God against the foes of God and His Church (Ps. cxxxix. 21, 22). **the other**—'*the remaining* voices.'

CHAP. IX. 1-21.—Fifth Trumpet—The Fallen Star Opens the Abyss whence Issue Locusts—Sixth Trumpet—Four Angels at the Euphrates Loosed.

1. The last three trumpets of the seven are called, from ch. viii. 13, *the woe-trumpets.* **fall**—'fallen.' When John saw it, it was not *falling,* but had *fallen* already. This is a link joining this fifth trumpet with ch. xii. 8, 9, 12, 'Woe to the *inhabiters of the earth* . . . for the *devil* is *come down,*' &c. Cf. Isa. xiv. 12. **the bottomless pit**—'the pit of the abyss:' *the mouth of the hell* to which Satan and his demons are doomed. **3. upon**—'unto.' **as the scorpions of the earth**—contrasted with the "locusts" *from hell,* not "of the earth." **have power**—viz., to sting. **4. not hurt the grass . . . neither any green thing, neither any tree**—on which they ordinarily prey. There-

fore not natural locusts. Their instinct is supernaturally restrained to mark the judgment as Divine. **those men which**—'*the* men whosoever.' **in**—'*upon* their forehead.' Thus this fifth trumpet is proved to follow the *sealing* in ch. vii., under the sixth seal. None of the saints are hurt by these locusts; not true of the saints in Mohammed's attack, who is supposed to be meant by the locusts; for many believers fell in the Mohammedan invasions of Christendom. **5. they . . . they.** The first "they" is *the locusts;* the second, the *un-sealed.* **five months**—the ordinary time during which locusts continue their ravages (*Elliott*); 150 *prophetical days, i.e.,* years, from 612 A.D., when Mohammed opened his mission, to 762 A.D., when the Caliphate was moved to Bagdad. **their torment**—the torment of the sufferers. This and *v.* 6 cannot refer to an invading army; for it would *kill,* not merely *torment.* **6. shall desire** [*epithume-sousin*]—set their mind on. **shall flee.** So B, Vulgate, Syriac, Coptie [א, φυγη]; but A, '*fleeth,*' viz., continually. In ch. vi. 16, at a later stage of God's judgments, the ungodly seek annihilation, not from the torment of suffering, but from fear of the Lamb, before whom they have to stand. **7. prepared unto battle**—'war.' Note, Joel ii. 4, where the resemblance of locusts to horses is traced: the plates of a horse armed for battle represent the outer shell of the locust. **crowns**—(Nah. iii. 17.) *Elliott,* The *turbans* of Mohammedans. But how could turbans be "like gold"? The correspondences are—1. The Turks came from the Euphrates. 2. Their cavalry was countless. 3. The breastplates of fire answer to the rich colours (scarlet, blue, yellow) of the Ottoman attire. 4. Out of the horses' mouths fire and smoke, the Turkish artillery. 5. The Turkish standard, the horse tails. 6. The period: an hour, day, month, year; 396 years, 118 days, the time between the going forth of Thogrul Beg, Jan. 18, 1057, and the fall of Constantinople, May 29, 1453. The serpent-like stinging tails answer to Mohammedanism supplanting Christianity. *Alford,* The head of the locusts actually ends in a crown-shaped fillet, resembling gold. **as the faces of men.** "As" seems

684

9 as the hair of women, and ^mtheir teeth were as *the teeth* of lions. And they had breastplates, as it were breastplates of iron; and the sound of their wings *was* as the sound of chariots of many horses running to battle.

10 And they had tails like unto scorpions, and there were stings in their

11 tails: and their power *was* to hurt men five months. And ⁿthey had a king over them, *which is* the angel of the bottomless pit, whose name in the Hebrew tongue *is* Abaddon, but in the Greek tongue hath *his* name ¹Apollyon.

12 One ^owoe is past; *and,* behold, there come two woes more hereafter.

13 And the sixth angel sounded, and I heard a voice from the four horns

14 of the golden altar which is before God, saying to the sixth angel which had the trumpet, Loose the four angels which are bound ^pin the great

15 river Euphrates. And the four angels were loosed, which were prepared ²for an hour, and a day, and a month, and a year, for to slay the third

16 part of men. And ^qthe number of the army ^rof the horsemen *were* two

17 hundred thousand thousand: ^sand I heard the number of them. And thus I saw the horses in the vision, and them that sat on them, having

A. D. 96.
^m Ps. 57. 4.
Joel 1. 6.
ⁿ John 12.31.
John 11.30.
Eph. 2. 2.
2 Thes. 2. 3.
10.
1 That is to
say, a
destroyer.
John 8. 44.
^o ch. 8. 13.
^p Gen. 2. 14.
2 Sam. 8. 3.
Jer. 51. 63.
ch. 16. 12.
² Or, at.
^q Ps. 6^l. 17.
Dan. 7. 10.
^r Eze. 38. 4.
^s ch. 7. 4.

to imply the locusts do not mean *men*. Still they must be supernatural; for locusts do not sting *men* (*v.* 5). **8. hair of women**—long and flowing. Sign of a half-civilized race (1 Cor. xi. 14, 15). An Arabic proverb compares the antlers of locusts to the hair of girls. *Ewald* understands the hair on the legs or bodies of the locusts: cf. "rough caterpillars" (Jer. li. 27). **as the teeth of lions**—(Joel i. 6.) **9. as it were breastplates of iron**—not the thorax of the natural locust. **as . . . chariots**—(Joel ii. 5-7.) **battle**—'war.' **10. tails like unto scorpions**—*the tails* of scorpions. **and there were stings.** A B ℵ, Syriac, Coptic, read, 'and (they have) stings: and in their tails (is) their power (lit., *authority*) [*exousia*] to hurt,' &c. **11. And.** So Syriac; but A B ℵ omit "and." **had**—'have.' **a king . . . which is the angel.** So A ℵ read the article before "angel." Translate, 'They have as king over them *the* angel,' &c.: Satan (cf. *v.* 1). B omits the article, 'They have as king *an* angel,' &c.: some chief demon under Satan. I prefer, from *v.* 1, the former. **bottomless pit**—'abyss.' **Abaddon**—i.e., *destruction* (Job xxvi. 6; Prov. xxvii. 20). The locusts are supernatural—Satan's instruments to torment, yet not kill, the ungodly. As in the case of godly Job, Satan was allowed to torment with elephantiasis, but not to touch *life*. In *v.* 20, these two woe-trumpets are called "plagues." *Andreas* of Cesarea, A. D. 500, held that the locusts mean *evil spirits*, permitted to come on earth and afflict men with various plagues. **12. '*The* one woe.' hereafter**—'after these things.' These *locusts from the abyss* are probably judgments to fall on the ungodly immediately before Christ's second advent. None of the interpretations which regard them as past are satisfactory. Joel i. 2-7; ii. 1-11, is parallel, and refers (ii. 11) to THE DAY OF THE LORD GREAT AND VERY TERRIBLE; *v.* 10 gives the portents accompanying the Lord's coming, *the earth quaking, the heavens trembling, the sun, moon, and stars withdrawing their shining; vv.* 18, 31, 32, point to the immediately succeeding deliverance of Jerusalem : cf. Joel iii. 11-17, the previous last conflict in the valley of Jehoshaphat, and God's dwelling thenceforth in Zion, blessing Judah. *De Burgh* confines the locust-judgment to *the Israelite land*, as the sealed in ch. vii. are Israelites : not that there are not others sealed as elect in *the earth;* but that, the judgment being confined to *Palestine*, the sealed of *Israel alone* needed to be expressly excepted from the visitation. He translates through-

out ' THE LAND ' (*i. e.,* of Israel and Judah), instead of ' the earth.' **13. a voice**—'*one* voice.' **from**—'out of.' **the four horns.** So B, *Cyprian;* but A, Vulgate (*Amiatinus* MS.), Coptic, Syriac, omit "four." The *four* horns together uttered their voice, not diverse, but *one*. God's revelation (*e. g.*, the Gospel), though in its aspects *fourfold* (expressing *world-wide* extension : whence the evangelists are *four*), still has one and the same voice. However, from the parallelism of this sixth trumpet to the fifth seal (ch. vi. 9, 10), the martyrs' cry for avenging their blood from the altar reaching its consummation under the sixth seal and sixth trumpet, I prefer understanding this *cry from the four corners of the altars*, to mean the saints' cry from the four quarters of the world, *incensed* by the angel, ascending to God from the golden altar of incense, and bringing down fiery judgments. ℵ omits the clause, ' one from the four horns.' **14. in** [*epi to potamo*]—'ON,' or 'AT, the great river.' **Euphrates** (cf. ch. xvi. 12)—whereat Babylon, the ancient foe of God's people, was situated. Again, whether from the literal Euphrates (the boundary between Israel and the great world-kingdom), or from spiritual Babylon (*the apostate church*, especially ROME), four angelic ministers of God's judgments shall go forth, assembling horsemen throughout the four quarters of the earth, to slay a third of men. The brunt shall be on Palestine. **15. were** —'which had been prepared.' **for an hour, &c.** —rather, as Greek, 'for (*i. e.*, against) THE hour, and day, and month, and year,' viz., appointed by God. The article [*teen*], once only before all the periods, implies that the hour in the day, and the day in the month, and the month in the year, and the year itself, had been definitely fixed by God. The article would have been omitted had a sum total of periods been specified—viz., 391 years and one month (from A. D. 1281, when the Turks first conquered the Christians, to 1672, their last conquest, since which their empire has declined). **slay**—not merely "hurt" (*v.* 10), as in the fifth trumpet. **third part**—(note, ch. viii. 7-12.) **of men**—of *earthly* men (ch. viii. 13), as distinguished from God's sealed people (of which the sealed of Israel, ch. vii., form the nucleus). **16.** Cf. with these 200,000,000, Ps. lxviii. 17; Dan. vii. 10. The hosts are evidently, from their numbers and appearance (*v.* 17), not merely *human*, but *infernal*, though constrained to work out God's will (cf. *vv.* 1, 2). **and I heard.** A B ℵ, Vulgate, Syriac, Coptic, *Cyprian,* omit "and." **17. thus—as fol-**

breastplates of fire, and of jacinth, and brimstone: and *the heads of the horses *were* as the heads of lions; and out of their mouths issued fire and

18 smoke and brimstone. By these three was the third part of men killed, by the fire, and by the smoke, and by the brimstone, which issued out of

19 their mouths. For their power is in their mouth, and in their tails: *for their tails *were* like unto serpents, and had heads, and with them they do

20 hurt. And the rest of the men, which were not killed by these plagues, *yet repented not of the works of their hands, that they should not *wor-ship devils, *and idols of gold, and silver, and brass, and stone, and of

21 wood: which neither can see, nor hear, nor walk: neither repented they of their murders, nor of their sorceries, nor of their fornication, nor of their thefts.

10 AND I saw another mighty angel come down from heaven, clothed with a cloud; *and a rainbow *was* upon his head, and *his face *was* as it

2 were the sun, and his *feet as pillars of fire: and he had in his hand a little book open: *and he set his right foot upon the sea, and *his* left

3 *foot* on the earth, and cried with a loud voice, as *when* a lion roareth:

A. D. 96.

t 1 Chr 12. 8.
Isa. 5. 28.
u Isa 9 15.
v Deut 31 29.
2 Chr 23. 22.
Jer. 5. 3.
w Lev. 17. 7.
Deut. 32. 17.
Ps. 106. 37.
Isa. 2. 8.
Jer. 44. 8.
x Ps. 115. 4.
Isa. 41. 7.
Dan. 5. 23.
Acts 17. 29.

CHAP. 10.
a Eze 1. 28.
b Matt. 17. 2.
ch. 1. 16.
c ch. 1. 15.
d Matt 28. 18.

lows. **of fire**—the *fiery colour* of the breastplates answering to the *fire* issuing out of their mouths. **of jacinth**—*of hyacinth colour:* answering to our *dark-blue iris:* their *dark-dull-coloured* breast-plates correspond to the *smoke* out of their mouths. **brimstone**—*sulphur-coloured:* answering to the *brimstone out of their mouths.* **18. By these three.** A B C א read [*apo* for *hupo*], 'From:' the *direc-tion* whence the slaughter came; not direct in-strumentality, as "by" implies. A B C א add 'plagues' after "three." **by the fire** [*ek*]—'owing *to* the fire.' **19. their.** B C א read, 'the power *of the horses;*' A [*topōn*], 'of the places.' **in their mouth**—whence *issued* the *fire, smoke, and brim-stone* (v. 17). Considering the parallelism of this sixth trumpet to the sixth seal, probably events are intended immediately preceding the Lord's coming. "The false prophet" (Isa. ix. 15), or second beast, having a lamb's horns, but speaking as *the dragon,* who supports by lying miracles the final antichrist, seems intended. Mohammed is a forerunner of him, not the exhaus-tive fulfiller of the prophecy. Satan will, towards the end, bring out all the powers of hell for the last conflict (note, "devils," *v.* 20: cf. *vv.* 1, 2, 17, 18). **with them**—the serpent heads with venomous fangs. **hurt** [*adikousin*]—'do wrong,' 'injury.' **20. the rest of the men**—*i. e.,* the ungodly. **yet.** So A, Vulgate, Syriac, Coptic; B א read, 'did *not* even repeat of,' so as to give up "the works," &c. Like Pharaoh hardening his heart against repent-ance, notwithstanding the plagues. **of their hands** —(Deut. xxxi. 29.) Especially the idols *made by their hands.* Cf. ch. xiii. 14, 15; xix. 20. **that they should not.** So B; but A C א, 'shall not:' a prophecy of *certainty* that it shall be so. **devils**— 'demons:' which lurk beneath idols (1 Cor. x. 20). **21. sorceries**—witchcrafts by means of *drugs* [*pharmakeion*]. A work of the unrenewed flesh (Gal. v. 20), the sin of the heathen: to be repeated by apostate Christians in the last days (ch. xxii. 15). The heathen who shall reject the proffered Gospel and cling to fleshly lusts, and apostate Christians who shall relapse into the same, shall share the same terrible judgments. The worship of images was established in the East in 842 A. D. **fornication**—singular. The other sins (plural) are perpetrated at intervals: those lacking purity in-dulge in *one* perpetual fornication (*Bengel*).

CHAP. X. 1-11.—THE LITTLE BOOK.
As there was an episode between the sixth and seventh seals, so there is one (ch. x. 1-11) after the sixth, introductory to the seventh trumpet (ch.

xi. 15, the grand consummation). The Church and her fortunes are the subject: as the judg-ments on the unbelieving *inhabiters of the earth* (ch. viii. 13) were the subject of the fifth and sixth woe-trumpets. Ch. vi. 11 is referred to, *v.* 6: the martyrs crying to be avenged were told they must 'rest yet for a little *time.*' In *v.* 6, they are assured 'there should be no longer (any interval of) time;' but (*v.* 7) *at the trumpet sounding of the seventh angel, the mystery of God* (His mighty plan here-tofore hidden, but then to be revealed) *shall be finished.* The *little open book* (*vv.* 2, 9, 10) is given to John by the angel with a charge (*v.* 11) that he *must prophesy again concerning* [*epi*] *peoples, nations, tongues, and kings* (ch. xi.), only in so far as these affect ISRAEL AND THE CHURCH, the main object of the prophecy. **1. another mighty angel** —as distinguished from the *mighty angel* who asked as to the former more comprehensive book (ch. v. 2), "Who is worthy to open the book?" **clothed with a cloud**—emblem of God coming in judgment (ch. i. 7). **a.** A B C א read, 'the:' re-ferring to *the rainbow,* in ch. iv. 3. **rainbow was upon his head**—emblem of covenant-mercy to God's people, amidst judgment on God's foes (note, ch. iv. 3). **face was as . . . the sun**—(ch. i. 16; xviii. 1.) **feet as pillars of fire**—(Ezek. i. 7; ch. i. 15.) The angel, as representative, reflects Christ's glory, and bears the insignia attributed in ch. i. 15, 16; iv. 3, to Christ Himself. The *pillar of fire* by night led Israel through the wilderness: the symbol of God's presence. **2. he had**—'hav-ing.' **in his hand**—in his left hand: as in *v.* 5 (note), *he lifts up his right hand to heaven.* **a little book**—a roll, *little* in comparison with the "book" (ch. v. 1) which contained the *whole* vast scheme of God's purposes, not to be read till the consummation. The *less book* contained only a portion which John was now to make his own (*vv.* 9, 11), then to use in prophesying to others. The New Testament begins with "book" [*biblus*], of which the "little book" [*biblaridion*] is the diminutive, the Bible in miniature. **upon the sea . . . earth.** Though the beast with seven heads is to arise out of the *sea* (ch. xiii. 1), and the beast with two horns like a lamb (ch. xiii. 11) out of the *earth,* yet it is but for a time, and that *time shall no longer be* (*vv.* 6, 7), when once *the seventh trumpet is to sound.* The angel with his right foot on the sea and his left on the earth, claims both as God's, and as soon to be cleared of the usurper and his followers. **3. as . . . lion.** Christ, whom the angel represents, is often so symbolized (ch. v.

4 and when he had cried, seven *thunders uttered their voices. And when the seven thunders had uttered their voices, I was about to write: and I heard a voice from heaven saying unto me, *Seal up those things which
5 the seven thunders uttered, and write them not. And the angel which I saw stand upon the sea and upon the earth lifted up his hand to heaven,
6 and sware by him that *liveth for ever and ever, who created heaven, and the things that therein are, and the earth, and the things that therein are, and the sea, and the things which are therein, *that there should be
7 time no longer: but *in the days of the voice of the seventh angel, when he shall begin to sound, the mystery of God should be finished, as he hath declared to his servants the prophets.
8   And the voice which I heard from heaven spake unto me again, and said, Go *and* take the little book which is open in the hand of the angel
9 which standeth upon the sea and upon the earth. And I went unto the angel, and said unto him, Give me the little book. And he said unto me, *Take *it*, and eat it up; and it shall make thy belly bitter, but it
10 shall be in thy mouth *sweet as honey. And I took the little book out of

A D 96
* ch. 8. 5.
ch 14. 2.
ch 15. 1. 7.
f Deut. 29. 29.
Isa. 8. 16.
Isa. 29. 11.
Dan. 8. 26.
Dan. 12. 4.
g Jer. 10 10.
ch. 1. 18.
ch. 4. 9.
h Dan. 12 7.
ch. 16. 17.
i ch. 11. 15.
j Job 23. 12.
Jer. 15. 16.
Eze. 2. 8.
Eze 3. 1.
Col. 3. 16.
k Ps. 19. 10.
Ps. 104. 31.

5). **seven thunders**—'*the* seven thunders.' Being part of the apocalyptic symbolism, they have the article as *well known*. *Thunderings* marked the opening of the seventh seal (ch. viii. 1, 5): so at the seventh vial (ch. xvi. 17, 18). *Wordsworth* calls this *the prophetic use of the article: 'the* thunders, of which more hereafter.' Their full meaning shall be only known at the grand consummation marked by the seventh seal, the seventh trumpet (ch. xi. 19), and the seventh vial. **uttered their**—'*spake their own* voices:' peculiarly *their own*, not now revealed. Cf. the *seven voices* of Jehovah, Ps. xxix. 4. **when.** So A C, Vulgate; but א, 'whatsoever things.' **uttered their voices.** A B C א omit 'their voices.' 'Had spoken.' **unto me.** Omitted by A B C א, Syriac. **Seal up**—the opposite to ch. xxii. 10. Though at *the time of the end* the things *sealed* in Daniel's time were to be revealed, yet not so the voices of these thunders. Though heard by John, they were not to be imparted to others in this book: so terrible are they that God in mercy withholds them, since "sufficient unto the day is the evil thereof." The godly are kept from morbid ponderings over the evil to come, and the ungodly not driven by despair into utter recklessness. *Alford* adds another aim, 'godly fear.' Besides the terrors foretold, there are others unutterable and more horrifying in the background. **5. lifted up his hand.** So A, Vulgate; but B C א, Syriac, Coptic, 'his *right* hand.' It was customary to lift up the hand towards heaven, appealing to the God of truth, in a solemn oath: an allusion to Dan. xii. Cf. *vv.* 4-6, end, with Dan. xii. 4, 7, 9. But there the angel clothed in linen, standing upon the waters, sware 'a time, times, and a half' were to interpose before the consummation: here the angel with his left foot on the earth, and his right upon the sea, swears *there shall be time no longer.* There he lifted up both hands to heaven; here he has *the little book* now *open* (in Daniel *the book* is *sealed*) *in his* left *hand* (*v.* 2), and he *lifts up* only *his right to heaven*. **6. liveth for ever and ever**—'unto the ages of the ages.' **created heaven ... earth ... sea,** &c. This detailed designation of the Creator is appropriate to the subject of the angel's oath—viz., the consummating of the mystery of God (*v.* 7), which can surely be brought to pass by the same Almighty power that created all things, and by none else. **that there should be time no longer**—'that time (*i. e.*, an interval) no longer shall be.' The martyrs shall have no longer to wait for the accomplishment of their

prayers for the purgation of the earth by judgments to remove their and God's foes from it (ch. vi. 11). The appointed *time* of delay is at an end [the same Greek as ch. vi. 11, *chronus*]. Not, time shall end and eternity begin. **7. But.** 'There shall be no longer time (*v.* 6, delay), *but* in the days of the voice of the seventh angel, when he is about to sound his trumpet [*mellē salpizein*], then (*also* [*kai*] often introduces the consequent member of a sentence) the mystery of God is finished' [aorist, *etelesthe*]: the prophet regarding the future as certain as if past. So A C א, Coptic; B, the future [*telesthee*], 'should be finished' (cf. ch. xi. 15-18). Sweet consolation to the waiting saints! **the mystery of God**—the theme of the "little book;" so of the remainder of the Apocalypse: a grand contrast to the 'mystery of iniquity—Babylon' (ch. xvii. 5). The mystery of redemption, once hidden in God's secret counsels, dimly shadowed forth in types and prophecies, but now more and more clearly revealed according as the Gospel kingdom develops itself, up to its fullest consummation. Finally, His servants shall praise Him fully for the glorious consummation, in taking to Himself and His saints the kingdom so long usurped by Satan and the ungodly. This verse is an anticipation of ch. xi. 15-18. **declared** [*euēngelisen*: the glad tidings] **to.** "The mystery of God" is the *Gospel*. The office of the *prophets* is to receive *the glad tidings* from God, in order to *declare* them to others. The final consummation of "the Gospel" is their great theme (cf. Gal. iii. 8). **8. spake ... and said.** So Syriac and Coptic; but א A B C, '(I heard) again speaking with me, and saying' [*lalousan ... legousan*]. **little book.** So א and B; but A C, 'the book.' **9.** 'I went *away.*' John leaves heaven, his standing-point heretofore, to be near the angel standing on the earth and sea. **Give.** א A B C, Vulgate, Syriac, read the infinitive, 'Telling him *to* give.' **eat it up**—appropriate its contents so entirely that they become assimilated with thyself (as food), so as to impart them the more vividly to others. His finding the roll sweet to the taste is because, divesting himself of carnal feeling, he regarded God's will as always agreeable, however bitter might be the message. Cf. Ps. xl. 8, margin: Christ's inner appropriation of God's Word. **thy belly bitter**—parallel to Ezek. ii. 10. **as honey**— (Ps. xix. 10; cxix. 103.) Honey, sweet to the mouth, sometimes turns into bile in the stomach. The thought that God would be glorified (ch. xi.

the angel's hand, and ate it up; and it was in my mouth sweet as honey:

11 and as soon as I had eaten it, my belly was bitter. And he said unto me, Thou must prophesy again before many peoples, and nations, and tongues, and kings.

11 AND there was given me *a* reed like unto a rod: and the angel stood, saying, Rise, *b* and measure the temple of God, and the altar, and them

2 that worship therein. But *c* the court which is without the temple ¹leave out, and measure it not; for *d* it is given unto the Gentiles: and the holy city shall they *e* tread under foot *f* forty *and* two months.

A. D. 96.

CHAP. 11.
a Eze 40. 3.
Zech. 2. 1.
b Num 23 18.
c Eze. 40. 17.
1 cast out.
d Ps. 9. 1.
Luke 21.24.
e Dan. 8. 10.
f ch. 13. 5.

3-6, 11-18) gave him sweet pleasure. Afterwards the *belly*, or natural feeling, was embittered with grief at the coming persecutions of the Church (ch. xi. 7-10: cf. John xvi. 1, 2). The revelation of futurity is *sweet* at first, but *bitter* to our natural man, when we learn the cross to be borne before the crown. John was grieved at the coming apostasy and the sufferings of the Church from antichrist. **10. the little book.** So A C; but B א, Vulgate, 'the book.' **was bitter**—'embittered.' **11. he said.** A B א, Vulgate, read, '*they say* unto me:' indefinite for 'it was said unto me.' **Thou must**—as the servant of God, bound to prophesy at His command. **again**—as thou didst already in the previous part of this book. **before**—rather [*epi laois*], '*concerning* many peoples,' in their relation to the Church. The eating of the book, as in Ezekiel's case, marks John's inauguration to a fresh stage in his prophetical office—viz., revealing the things which befall the holy city and the Church of God—the subject of the rest of the book.

CHAP. XI. 1-19.—MEASUREMENT OF THE TEMPLE—THE TWO WITNESSES—THEIR DEATH, RESURRECTION, ASCENSION—THE EARTHQUAKE—THIRD WOE—THE SEVENTH TRUMPET USHERS IN CHRIST'S KINGDOM—THANKSGIVING OF THE TWENTY-FOUR ELDERS.

This ch. xi. is a compendious summary of, and introduction to, the detailed prophecies of the same events to come, in chs. xii.-xx. Hence occur *anticipatory* allusions to subsequent prophecies (cf. *v.* 7, "the beast that ascendeth out of the bottomless pit" (not mentioned before), with the detailed accounts, ch. xiii. 1, 11; xvii. 8; also *v.* 8, "the great city," with ch. xiv. 8; xvii. 1, 5; xviii. 10).

1. and the angel stood. So B, Syriac; omitted in A א, Vulgate, Coptic. If it be omitted, *the reed* will agree with "saying." So *Wordsworth.* The *canon* [from *kaneh*, "a reed"] of Scripture, the measuring *reed* of the Church, our rule of faith, *speaks.* So ch. xvi. 7, *the altar* is personified *speaking* (cf. note). The Spirit speaks in the canon. (John it was who completed the canon.) So *Victorinus.* **like unto a rod**—*straight; of iron* (ch. ii. 27), unbending, destroying all error, that 'cannot be broken' (Heb. i. 8, "a rod," or 'sceptre of straightness,' margin). Added to guard against the *reed* being thought to be one 'shaken by the wind.' In the abrupt style of the Apocalypse, "saying" may be indefinite for '*one said.*' *Wordsworth's* view agrees with the Greek. So *Andreas* of Cesarea, in the end of the fifth century (note, *vv.* 3, 4). **the temple** [*naon*, distinguished from *hieron*, or temple in general]—the Holy Place, '*the sanctuary.*' **the altar**—of incense, for it alone was in *the sanctuary.* The measurement of the Holy Place seems to stand parallel to the sealing of the elect of Israel under the sixth seal. It implies, there shall be always an inner true Church, however the outer courts of hollow profession, without self-dedication, be desecrated. God's elect are symbolized by the sanctuary at

Jerusalem (1 Cor. iii. 16, 17, where the same [*naos*] occurs for "temple" as here). Literal Israel in Jerusalem, with the temple restored (Ezek. xl. 3, 5, where also the temple is measured with the measuring reed; xli.-xliv.), shall stand at the head of the elect Church. The measuring implies at once the exact proportions of the temple to be restored, and the definite completeness (not one wanting) of the numbers of the Israelite and of the Gentile elections. The literal temple at Jerusalem shall be typical forerunner of the heavenly Jerusalem, in which there shall be all temple—*no* portion exclusively *temple.* John's accurately distinguishing in subsequent chapters between God's servants and those who bear the mark of the beast, is the way whereby he fulfils the direction given him *to measure the temple.* The fact that the *temple* is distinguished from *them that worship therein*, favours the view that the spiritual temple —the Jewish and Christian Church—is not exclusively meant, but that the literal temple is also meant. It shall be rebuilt on the return of the Jews to their land. Antichrist shall there put forward his blasphemous claims. The sealed elect of Israel—the head of the elect Church—alone shall refuse his claims. These shall constitute the true sanctuary, here measured—*i. e.,* accurately marked, and kept by God —whereas the rest shall yield to his pretensions. *Wordsworth* objects, that in the twenty-five passages of Acts, wherein the Jewish temple is mentioned, it is called *hieron*, not *naos;* so in the apostolic epistles; but this is simply because no occasion for mentioning the literal *Holy Place* [*naos*] occurs in Acts and the epistles; indeed, in Acts vii. 48, there does occur *naos*, indirectly referring to the Jerusalem temple *Holy Place.* John ii. 20 uses *naos* of the Jerusalem temple. In addressing Gentile Christians, to whom the literal *temple* was not familiar, it was to be expected *naos* should not be in the literal, but the spiritual, sense. In *v.* 19, *naos* is used in a *local* sense: cf. also ch. xiv. 15, 17; xv. 5, 8. **2. But—'And.' the court ... without**—all outside *the Holy Place* (*v.* 1). **leave out**—of thy measurement; 'cast out;' reckon as unhallowed. **it**—emphatical. *It* is not to be measured; whereas the Holy Place is. **given**—by God's appointment. **unto the Gentiles.** In the wider sense, ' the times of the Gentiles' are meant; wherein Jerusalem is 'trodden down of the Gentiles,' as Luke xxi. 24 proves; for the same word is used here [*patein*]. Cf. also Ps. lxxix. 1; Isa. lxiii. 18. **forty and two months**—(ch. xiii. 5.) The same period as Daniel's (Dan. vii. 25 ; xii. 7) "time, times, and an half " (*v.* 3, and ch. xii. 6, 14, the woman a fugitive in the wilderness "a thousand two hundred and three-score days"). In the wider sense, we may adopt the year-day theory of 1,260 years (on which, and the papal rule of 1,260 years, see notes, Dan. vii. 25 ; viii. 14; xii. 11), or rather, regard the 2,300 days (Dan. viii. 14), 1,335 days (Dan. xii. 11, 12), 1,290 days, and 1,260 days, as symbolical of the long Gentile times, dating from the subversion of the Jewish theocracy at the Babylonian captivity

3   And I will give *power* unto my *g* two witnesses, *h* and they shall prophesy *i* a thousand two hundred *and* threescore days, clothed in sackcloth.
4   These are the *j* two olive trees, and the two candlesticks standing before
5   the God of the earth.   And if any man will hurt them, fire proceedeth

A. D. 96.

g ch. 20, 4.
h ch. 19. 10.
i ch. 12. 6.
j Ps. 52. 8.

(the *kingdom* having been never since restored to Israel), or from the last destruction of Jerusalem under Titus, and extending to the restoration of the theocracy at the coming of Him "whose right it is" (Ezek. xxi. 27). The different epochs marked will not be cleared up till the grand consummation; but, meanwhile, our privilege urges us to investigate them. Some one of the epochs assigned may be right, but as yet it is uncertain. The times of the Gentile monarchies during Israel's *seven times'* (Lev. xxvi. 18, 21, 24) punishment will probably, in the narrower sense (*v.* 2), be succeeded by the restricted times of antichrist's tyranny in the Holy Land. The long papal misrule may be followed by the short time of the man of sin, who shall concentrate in himself all the apostasy, persecution, and evil of the forerunning antichrists—Antiochus, Mohammed, Popery—just before Christ's advent. His time shall be THE RECAPITULATION and *open* consummation of the "*mystery* of iniquity" (so long leavening the world). Witnessing churches may be followed by witnessing individuals—the former occupying the longer, the latter the shorter period. The *three and a half* (1,260 days—three and a half years of 360 days each), during which the two witnesses prophesy in sackcloth, is the sacred *seven* halved, implying the antichristian world-power's time is broken at best. It answers to the *three and a half* years of Christ's witness for the truth, when the Jews, His own people, disowned, and the God-opposed world-power crucified Him (note, Dan. ix. 27). The three and a half marks the time in which the earthly rules over the heavenly kingdom. It was the duration of Antiochus' treading down the temple, and persecuting faithful Israelites. The world-power's times never reach the sacred fulness of seven times 360—*i. e.*, 2,520, though they approach it in 2,300 (Dan. viii. 14). The forty-two months answer to Israel's forty-two sojournings (Num. xxxiii. 1-50) in the wilderness, contrasted with the Sabbatic rest in Canaan: reminding the Church that here, in the world-wilderness, she cannot look for her Sabbatic rest. Also, three and a half years was the period of the heaven being shut up, and of consequent famine in Elias' time. Three and a half represented to the Church the toil, pilgrimage, persecution.

3. **I will give power**—or *commission*. There is no "power" in the Greek. **my two witnesses**—'*the* two witnesses of me.' The article implies the two were well known. **prophesy**—preach under the Spirit's inspiration, denouncing judgments against the apostate. They are symbolized as "the two olive trees," "the two candlesticks standing before the God of the earth." The reference is to Zech. iv. 3, 12, 14, where *two individuals*, 'the two anointed ones,' are meant—Joshua and Zerubbabel, who ministered to the Jewish Church—as the two olive trees emptied the oil out of themselves into the bowl of the candlestick. So in the final apostasy, God will raise up two inspired witnesses to minister encouragement to the afflicted, though sealed; remnant. As *two* candlesticks are mentioned, *v.* 4, but only *one* in Zech. iv., the twofold Church, Jewish and Gentile, may be meant by the two candlesticks represented by the two witnesses; just as in ch. vii., there are described first the sealed of Israel, then those of all nations. But see note, *v.* 4. The actions of the two witnesses are just those of Moses when witnessing for God against Pharaoh (the type of antichrist, the last and greatest foe of Israel), *turning the waters into blood*, and *smiting* with *plagues*, and of Elijah (the witness for God in Israel's almost universal apostasy), a remnant of 7,000, however, being left, as the 144,000 sealed (ch. vii.), causing *fire* by his word to *devour the enemy*, and *shutting heaven, so that it rained not* for *three years and six months*—the very time (1,260 days) during which the two witnesses prophesy. Moreover, "witness" and "prophesy" are usually applied to *individuals*, not to abstractions (cf. Ps. lii. 8). *De Burgh* thinks Elijah and Moses will again appear, as Mal. iv. 5, 6, may imply (cf. Matt. xvii. 11; Acts iii. 21). Moses and Elijah appeared with Christ at the transfiguration, which foreshadowed His millennial kingdom. As to Moses, cf. Deut. xxxiv. 5, 6; Jude 9. Elias's genius and procedure bear the same relation to Christ's second coming that John the Baptist's did to the first (*Bengel*). Many of the early Church thought the two witnesses Enoch and Elijah. This would avoid the difficulty of the dying a *second* time; for these have never yet died. Still, the *turning the water to blood, and the plagues* (*v.* 6), apply best to *Moses* (cf. ch. xv. 3, "the song of *Moses*"). The transfiguration-glory of Moses and Elias was not their permanent resurrection-state, which shall not be till Christ shall glorify His saints, for He has precedence before all in rising. An objection to this interpretation is, that those blessed servants of God would have to submit to death (*vv.* 7, 8), and this in Moses' case a *second* time, which Heb. ix. 27 denies. See note, Zech. iv. 11, 12, on the two witnesses, answering to "the two olive trees." The two olive trees are channels of the oil feeding the Church, and symbols of peace. The Holy Spirit is the oil in them. Christ's witnesses, in remarkable times of the Church, have appeared in pairs: as Moses and Aaron, the inspired civil and religious authorities; Caleb and Joshua; Ezekiel the priest, and Daniel the prophet; Zerubbabel and Joshua. **in sackcloth**—the garment of prophets, especially when calling people to mortification of their sins, and to repentance. Their exterior aspect accorded with their teachings: so Elijah, and John who came in his spirit and power. The *sackcloth* is a catchword, linking this episode, under the sixth trumpet, with the *sun black as sackcloth* (in righteous retribution on the apostates who rejected God's witnesses under the sixth seal (ch. vi. 12). **4. standing before** (in the presence of) **the God of the earth.** א A B C, Vulgate, Syriac, Coptic, *Andreas*, read 'Lord' for "God;" so Zech. iv. 14. Ministering to (Luke i. 19) Him who, though now so widely disowned on *earth*, is its rightful King, and shall at last be openly recognized as such (*v.* 15). The article "the" implies allusion to Zech. iv. 10, 14. They are "the two candlesticks; not the Church, the *one* candlestick, but its representative *light-bearers* [Phil. ii. 15, *phosteres*], ministering for its encouragement amidst apostasy. *Wordsworth's* view is, *the two witnesses, the olive trees*, are THE TWO TESTAMENTS ministering *testimony* to the Church of the old dispensation, as well as to that of the new, which explains the two witnesses being called also *the two candlesticks* (the Old and New Testament Churches: the candlestick in Zech. iv. is but *one*, as there was then but one

out of their mouth, and devoureth their enemies: *k* and if any man will
6 hurt them, he must in this manner be killed. These *l* have power to shut
heaven, that it rain not in the days of their prophecy: and *m* have power
over waters to turn them to blood, and to smite the earth with all plagues,
as often as they will.

7 And when they *n* shall have finished their testimony, *o* the beast that
ascendeth out of the bottomless *p* pit shall make war against them, and
8 shall overcome them, and kill them. And their dead bodies *shall lie* in
the street of *q* the great city, which spiritually is called Sodom and Egypt,
where *r* also our Lord was crucified.

9 And *s* they of the people, and kindreds, and tongues, and nations,
shall see their dead bodies three days and an half, *t* and shall not suffer
10 their dead bodies to be put in graves. And *u* they that dwell upon the
earth shall rejoice over them, and make merry, and shall send gifts one

A. D. 96.

k Num 16. 29.
l 1 Ki. 17. 1.
  Jas. 5. 16.
  17.
m Ex 7. 19.
n Luke 13. 32.
o ch. 13. 1.
p Dan. 7. 21.
  Zech. 14. 2.
q ch 14. 8.
  ch 17. 1, 5.
r Heb 13. 12.
s ch. 18. 24.
  ch. 17. 15.
t Ps. 79. 2, 3.
u ch. 12. 12.
  ch. 13. 8.

Testament, and one Church—the Jewish). The Church in both dispensations has light, not in herself, but from the Spirit, through the witness of the twofold Word, the two olive trees (cf. note, *v.* 1). *The reed,* the Scripture *canon,* the measure of the Church: so *Primasius X.,* p. 314. The two witnesses preach in sackcloth, marking the ignominious treatment which the Word, like Christ Himself, receives from the world. So the twenty-four elders represent the ministers of the two dispensations by the double twelve. But *v.* 7 proves that primarily the two testaments cannot be meant; for these shall not be "killed," or "have finished their testimony," till the world is finished. **5. will hurt**—'*desires* to hurt them.' **fire .. devoureth** — (cf. Jer. v. 14; xxiii. 29.) **out of their mouth.** God makes their inspired denunciations of judgment to come to pass and *devour* their enemies. **if any man will hurt them**—repeated, to mark the *certainty* of the accomplishment. **in this manner**—in like manner as he tries to hurt them (cf. ch. xiii. 10). Retribution in kind. **6. These have power** [*exousian*]—'authorized power.' **it rain not** [*huetos brechee*]—'rain, shower not,' '*moisten* not' (the earth). **smite . . . with all plagues**—'with *(in)* every plague.' **7. finished their testimony.** The same verb is used of Paul's ending his ministry by a violent death (2 Tim. iv. 7). **the beast that ascendeth out of the bottomless pit**—'*the wild beast . . . the abyss.*' This beast was not mentioned before, yet is introduced as "*the* beast." John, viewing revelation as a whole, mentions objects to be described hereafter by himself (ch. xvii. 8: cf. Dan. vii. 11): a proof of the unity that pervades Scripture. **make war against them.** So Dan. vii. 21; *the little horn* among the ten on the *fourth* beast: ch. xi. 31, the wilful king, answering to 'the little horn' of the *third* beast; ch. viii. 9, 23-25: *the earth-sprung beast;* ch. xiii. 11, note: seeming to be the '*beast from the bottomless pit,*' or *abyss,* which is distinct from "the sea" (*v.* 1; Dan. vii. 3). **8. dead bodies.** So א, Vulgate, Syriac, *Andreas;* but A B C, Coptic, read singular, 'dead body.' The two fallen in one cause are considered *one.* **the great city**—*eight* times elsewhere used of Babylon (ch. xiv. 8; xvi. 19; xvii. 18; xviii. 10, 16, 18, 19, 21). In ch. xxi. 10 (*the new Jerusalem*), the oldest MSS. omit "the great" before *city;* so it forms no exception. The reference is, by anticipation, to mystical Babylon. **which**—'the which.' **spiritually**—in a spiritual sense. **Sodom**—the term applied by Isa. i. 10 to apostate Jerusalem (cf. Ezek. xvi. 48). **Egypt**—leaning on which was the Jews' besetting sin. **where . . . Lord was crucified.** This identifies the city as Jerusalem, though the Lord was crucified *outside.*

Eusebius mentions that the scene of Christ's crucifixion was enclosed within the city by Constantine: so it will be at the time of slaying the witnesses. The Beast (*e.g.,* Napoleon and France) has been long struggling for a footing in Palestine: after his ascent from the bottomless pit he struggles more (*Bengel*). One of the Napoleonic dynasty may obtain that footing, and even be regarded as Messiah by the Jews, in virtue of restoring them to their own land; and so may prove the last antichrist. The difficulty is, How can Jerusalem be "the great city," *i. e.,* Babylon? By becoming the world's capital of idolatrous apostasy, such as Babylon, and then Rome, has been; just as she is called also "Sodom and Egypt," also our. A B C, *Origen, Andreas,* &c., read, 'also *their.*' Where *their Lord also,* as well as they, was slain. Cf. ch. xviii. 24, where *the blood of* ALL *slain on earth* is said to be found IN BABYLON; as in Matt. xxiii. 35, 'upon the Jews and JERUSALEM' (cf. *vv.* 37, 38) shall 'come ALL the righteous blood shed upon earth.' Jerusalem shall be the last capital of the world-apostasy, and so receive the last and worst visitation of all the judgments ever inflicted on the apostate world, the earnest of which was given in the Roman destruction of Jerusalem. In the church-historical sense, the Church being the sanctuary, all outside is the world, the great city, wherein all the martyrdoms of saints have taken place. *Babylon* marks its idolatry, *Egypt* its tyranny, *Sodom* its desperate corruption, *Jerusalem* its pretensions to sanctity, because of spiritual privileges, whilst being the murderer of Christ in the person of His members. True of Rome. In the special sense, *Jerusalem* is (Heb. xiii. 12-14) the world-city from which believers were then to go forth to "seek one to come." **9. they**—rather, '*(some)* of the peoples.' **kindreds**—'tribes:' all save the elect; or, *some of the peoples,* &c., may be *those of the nations,* &c., who *at the time shall hold possession of Palestine and Jerusalem.* **shall see.** So Vulgate, Syriac, Coptic; but א A B C, *Andreas,* present [*blepousin*], 'look upon.' Prophetic present. **dead bodies.** So Vulgate, Syriac, *Andreas;* but א A B C, Coptic, singular, as *v.* 8, 'dead body.' Three and a half days answer to the three and a half years (notes, *vv.* 2, 3); half of seven, the perfect number. **shall not suffer.** So B, Syriac, Coptic, *Andreas;* but A C א, Vulgate, 'do not suffer.' **in graves.** So Vulgate, *Primasius;* but א B C, Syriac, Coptic, *Andreas,* singular, 'into a sepulchre,' a *monument.* In righteous retribution, *the flesh* of the antichristian hosts is not buried, but given to *all the fowls in mid-heaven* to eat (ch. xix. 17, 18, 21). **10. they that dwell upon the earth**—citizens belonging to

690

to another; because these two prophets tormented them that dwelt on the earth.

11 And after three days and an half ᵛ the Spirit of life from God entered into them, and they stood upon their feet; and great fear fell upon them

12 which saw them. And they heard a great voice from heaven saying unto them, Come up hither. And ʷ they ascended up to heaven ˣ in a cloud;

13 and their enemies beheld them. And the same hour was there a great earthquake, ʸ and the tenth part of the city fell, and in the earthquake were slain ² of men seven thousand: and the remnant were affrighted, and gave glory to the God of heaven.

14 The second woe is past; *and*, behold, the third woe cometh quickly.

A. D. 96.

ᵛ Gen 2. 7.
Eze. 37. 5, 14.
Rom. 8. 2.
ʷ 2 Ki. 2. 1.
Isa. 14. 13.
Acts 1. 9.
ˣ Isa 60 8.
Acts 1. 9.
ʸ ch. 16. 19.
² names of men.
ch. 3. 4.

---

earth, not to heaven (ch. iii. 10; viii. 13; xii. 12; xiii. 8). **shall.** So Vulgate, Syriac, Coptic; but א A B C, present: cf. note, v. 9. **rejoice over them.** The antichristianity of the last days shall probably be under the name of philosophical enlightenment, really man's deification of himself. Fanaticism shall lead antichrist's followers to exult in having silenced in death their Christian rebukers. Like her Lord, the Church will have her dark passion-week, followed by bright resurrection-morn. It is a historical coincidence that, at the fifth Lateran council, May 5, 1514, no witness (not even the Moravians who were summoned) testified for the truth, as Huss and *Jerome* did at Constance. An orator, mounting the tribunal before the representatives of Papal Christendom, said, 'There is no reclamant, no opponent.' *Luther*, on October 31, 1517, exactly three and a half years afterwards, posted up his famous theses on the church at Wittenberg. The objection is, the years are 365, not 360 days; so two and a half days are deficient: still the coincidence is curious. **send gifts one to another**—as was usual at a joyous festival. **tormented them**—viz., with the plagues (*vv.* 5, 6); also, by their testimony against the earthly.

11. 'After *the* three days,' &c. **the Spirit of life**—which breathed *life* into Israel's dry bones (Ezek. xxxvii. 10, 11, notes). Both passages are connected with *Israel's* restoration to national and religious life. Cf. Hos. vi. 2, Ephraim says, 'After two days will He revive us: in the *third day* He will *raise* us *up*, and we shall *live* in His sight.' **into.** So B א, Vulgate [*eis*]; but A [*en autois*], '(so as to be) IN them.' **stood upon their feet**—the very words, Ezek. xxxvii. 10, which proves the allusion to be to *Israel's* resurrection, in contrast to 'the times of the Gentiles' wherein these 'tread under foot the holy city.' **great fear** —as fell on the soldiers guarding Christ's tomb at His resurrection (Matt. xxviii. 4), when also there was a great earthquake (v. 2). **saw** [*theorountas*]—'beheld.' **12. they.** So א A C, Vulgate; but B, Coptic, Syriac, *Andreas*, 'I heard.' **a cloud**—'the cloud:' possibly the generic expression for what we are familiar with, '*the* clouds.' I prefer taking the article as definitely, alluding to THE cloud which received Jesus at His ascension, Acts i. 9 (where there is no article, there being no allusion to a previous cloud, as here). As they resembled Him in their three and a half years' witnessing, their three and a half days' lying in death (though not for exactly the same time, nor put in a tomb as He was), so also in their ascension: which is the translation and transfiguration of the sealed of Israel (ch. vii.), and the elect of all nations, caught up out of the reach of the antichristian foe. In ch. xiv. 14, 15, 16, He sits on a *white cloud*. **their enemies beheld them**—openly convicted by God for unbelief and persecution of His servants: unlike Elijah's ascension, in the sight of friends only. The Church caught up to meet the Lord in the air, and transfigured in body, is justified by her Lord before the world, even as the man-child (Jesus) was "caught up unto God and His throne" from before *the dragon standing ready to devour the woman's child as soon as born* (ch. xii. 4, 5). **13.** 'In that same (lit., *the*) hour.' **great earthquake**—answering to the "great earthquake" under the sixth seal, at the approach of the Lord (ch. vi. 12). Christ was delivered unto His enemies on the fifth day of the week, on the *sixth* was crucified, and on the Sabbath rested: so under the sixth seal and sixth trumpet the Church's last suffering, begun under the fifth seal and trumpet, is to be consummated, before she enters on her seventh day of eternal Sabbath. *Six* expresses the world-power's height, at the same time verges on *seven*, the Divine number, when its utter destruction takes place. Cf. 666, ch. xiii. 18. **tenth part of the city fell**—"the great city" (ch. xvi. 19; Zech. xiv. 2). Ten is the number of the *world-kingdoms* (ch. xvii. 10-12), the *beast's horns* (ch. xiii. 1), and the dragon's (ch. xii. 3). In the church-historical view, one of the ten apostate world-kingdoms falls. In the narrower view a tenth of *Jerusalem* under antichrist falls: nine-tenths remain, and become, when purified, the centre of Christ's earthly kingdom. **of men**— 'names of men:' men as accurately enumerated as if their names were given. **seven thousand.** Elliott, *seven chiliads* or provinces, the seven Dutch united provinces lost to the papacy; and 'names of men,' titles of dignity, duchies, lordships, &c. Rather, *seven thousand* combines the perfect and comprehensive numbers, *seven* and *thousand*, implying the *full and complete* destruction of the impenitent. **the remnant**—the Israelite inhabitants not slain. Their conversion forms a blessed contrast to ch. xvi. 9; and ch. ix. 20, 21. These (Zech. xii. 10-14; xiii. 1) become in the flesh loyal *subjects* of Christ reigning over the earth with His transfigured saints. **gave glory to the God of heaven**—which, whilst apostates, worshipping the beast's image, they had not done. "God of heaven:" the apostates of the last days, in selfwise enlightenment, recognize no *heavenly* power; only the earth's natural forces which come under their observation. His receiving up into *heaven* the two witnesses who had *power* whilst on earth *to shut heaven* from raining (v. 6), constrained His and their enemies witnessing it, to acknowledge *the God of heaven* to be *God of the earth* (v. 4). As He declared Himself *God of the earth* by His two witnesses, so now He proves Himself *God of heaven* also.

14. The second woe—under the sixth trumpet, ch. ix. 12-21; including also ch. xi. 1-13: *Woe* to the world, joy to the faithful, as *their redemption draweth nigh*. **the third woe cometh quickly**—not mentioned in detail, until there is given a sketch

15 And the seventh angel sounded; and there *were great voices in heaven, saying, The kingdoms of this world are become *the kingdoms* of our Lord, and of his Christ; *a*and he shall reign for ever and ever.

16 And the four and twenty elders which sat before God on their seats,
17 fell upon their faces, and worshipped God, saying, We give thee thanks, O Lord God Almighty, which art, and wast, and art to come; because
18 thou hast taken to thee thy great power, and hast reigned. And the nations were angry, and thy wrath is come, *b*and the time of the dead, that they should be judged, and that thou shouldest give reward unto thy servants the prophets, and to the saints, and them that fear thy name, small and great; and shouldest destroy them which *3* destroy the earth.

19 And the temple of God was opened in heaven, and there was *c*seen in his temple the ark of his testament: and there were lightnings, and voices, and thunderings, and an earthquake, and great hail.

A. D. 96.

* Isa. 27. 13.
a Dan. 2. 44.
Dan. 4. 3, 34.
Mic. 4. 7.
Luke 1. 33.
b Dan. 7. 9.
Ac s 10. 42.
2 Tim. 4. 1.
1 Pet. 4 5.
ch 6. 10.
3 Or.
corrupt.
c Ex. 25. 21, 22.
Num. 3. 5.
Num. 10.23.
Heb. 9. 4-3.

of the origination, suffering, and faithfulness of the Church in apostasy and persecution. Instead of the third woe, the grand consummation is summarily noticed—the thanksgiving of the twenty-four elders in heaven for the establishment of *Christ's kingdom on earth*, attended with the *destruction of the destroyers of the earth*.

15. sounded — with his trumpet: 'the LAST trumpet.' *Six* is close to *seven*, but does not reach it. The world-judgments are complete in *six;* but by the *seven*, the world-kingdoms become Christ's. *Six* marks the world given over to judgment. It is half of *twelve*, the Church's number, as three and a half is half of seven, the Divine number. [*Bengel* thinks the angel Gabriel, compounded of *El*, GOD, and *Geber*, MIGHTY MAN (ch. x. 1).] Gabriel appropriately announced to Mary the advent of the *mighty God-man* (Isa. ix. 6: cf. the *man-child's* birth which follows, ch. xii. 1-6), to which this forms the transition, though the seventh trumpet in time is subsequent, being the consummation of the historical episode, (chs. xii. and xiii.) The seventh trumpet, like the seventh seal and seventh vial, being the consummation, is accompanied differently from the preceding six: not the consequences on earth, but those IN HEAVEN, are described, the *great voices and thanksgiving of the twenty-four elders in heaven*, as the *half-hour's silence in heaven* at the seventh seal, and *the voice out of the temple in heaven*, "*It is done*," at the seventh vial. Parallel to Dan. ii. 44, 'the God *of heaven* shall set up a *kingdom*, which shall break to pieces all these *kingdoms*, and it shall stand for ever:' the setting up of *heaven's* sovereignty over the earth visibly, which, heretofore invisibly exercised, was rejected by earthly rulers. There will then be no beast in opposition to the woman. Poetry, art, science, and social life will be at once worldly and Christian. **kingdoms.** א A B C, Vulgate, singular, 'the *kingdom* (sovereignty) *of* (over) the world is our Lord's, and His Christ's.' The *kingdoms* of the world give way to Christ's *kingdom of* (over) *the world*. The earth-kingdoms are many: His shall be *one*. "Christ," *the Anointed*, here, where His *kingdom* is mentioned, is appropriately for the first time used in Revelation: for it is equivalent to KING. Though priests and prophets also were *anointed*, yet it is peculiarly applied to Him as *King*, insomuch that "the Lord's anointed" is His title, in places where He is distinguished from the priests. The glorified Son of man shall rule mankind by His transfigured Church in heaven, and by His people Israel on earth: Israel shall be priestly mediator of blessings to the world, realiz-

ing them first herself (Exod. xix. 6). **he**—not emphatical. **shall reign for ever and ever**—'unto the ages of the ages.' Here begins the millennial reign, the consummation of "the mystery of God" (ch. x. 7).

16. before God. So A C, Vulgate, Coptic; B, Syriac, read, 'before *the throne of* God.' **seats**—'thrones.' **17. thanks**—for the answer to our prayers (ch. vi. 10, 11), in *destroying them which destroyed the earth* (v. 18), preparing the way for the kingdom of thyself and thy saints. **and art to come.** Omitted in א A B C, Vulgate, Syriac, *Cyprian, Andreas*. The consummation having come, they do not address him as when it was still future. Cf. *v.* 18, "is come." From the seventh trumpet He is to His people JAH, the ever-present Lord WHO IS, rather than JEHOVAH, 'who is, was, and *is to come*.' **taken to thee thy great power.** "To thee" not in the Greek. Christ *takes* the kingdom as His own of *right* (Ezek. xxi. 27). **18. the nations were angry**—alluding to Ps. xcix. 1 [cf. note, *Ragaz*]; LXX., 'The Lord is become King: let the peoples become wroth ;' rage combined with *alarm* (Exod. xv. 14 ; 2 Ki. xix. 26-28). Translate, 'the nations were wroth, and thy wrath is come.' How impotent is man's wrath side by side with that of Omnipotence! **dead... be judged.** Therefore this seventh trumpet is at the end of all things, when the judgment on Christ's foes, and reward of His servants, long prayed for, shall take place. **the prophets**—for instance, the two *prophesying witnesses* (v. 3), and those who showed them kindness for Christ's sake. Jesus shall effect by His presence what we have looked for long, but vainly, in His absence. **destroy them which destroy the earth**—retribution in kind (cf. ch. xvi. 6; Luke xix. 27 ; Dan. vii. 14-18, notes). **19.** A similar conclusion to the seventh seal, ch. viii. 5, and to the seventh vial, ch. xvi. 18. Thus, the seven seals, seven trumpets, and seven vials, are not consecutive, but parallel, ending in the same consummation. They, from distinct standpoints, unfold God's plans for bringing about the grand end, under three aspects, mutually complementing each other. **the temple**—the *Holy Place* [*naos*]; not the whole *temple* [*hieron*]. **opened in heaven.** So B א; but A C read the article, 'the temple of God, *which is* in heaven, was opened.' **the ark of his testament**—'His *covenant*.' As in *v.* 1, the earthly sanctuary was *measured*, so here its heavenly antitype, and the antitype above to the *ark of the covenant* in the Holiest below, are seen, the pledge of God's faithfulness to His covenant in saving His people, and punishing their

12 AND there appeared a great ¹ wonder in heaven; a ᵃwoman clothed with the sun, and the moon under her feet, and upon her head a crown
2 of twelve stars: and she being with child cried, travailing ᵇin birth, and pained to be delivered.
3 And there appeared another ² wonder in heaven; and behold ᶜa great red dragon, having seven heads and ten horns, and seven crowns upon

A. D. 96.

CHAP. 12.
¹ Or, s'gn.
ᵃ Isa. (0 19.
ᵇ Isa. 6·. 7.
² (r. sign.
ᶜ ch. 17. 3.

enemies. A fit close to the trumpet-judgments, and an introduction to the episode (chs. xii. and xiii.) as to His faithfulness to His Church. First, His secret place (Ps. xxvii. 5) is open for the assurance of His people; thence proceed His judgments in their behalf (ch. xiv. 15, 17; xv. 5; xvi. 7, 17), which the great company in heaven laud as "true and righteous." Parallel to the scene at the heavenly altar closing the seals and opening the trumpets (ch. viii. 3), and at the close of the episode (chs. xii. and xv.), and opening of the vials (ch. xv. 7, 8). Note, opening of ch. xii.

CHAP. XII. 1-17.—THE WOMAN—HER CHILD—THE PERSECUTING DRAGON.

1. This episode (chs. xii.-xv.) *details* the persecution of Israel and the elect by the beast, *summarily* noticed in ch. xi. 7-10, and the triumph of the faithful and torment of the unfaithful. So also chs. xvi.-xx. detail the judgment on the beast, &c., summarily noticed in ch. xi. 13, 18. The beast (*v.* 3, &c.) is shown to be the instrument in the hand of a greater power of darkness, Satan. The period of ch. xi. is that also in which the events of chs. xii. and xiii. take place, viz., 1,260 days (*vv.* 6, 14; ch. xiii. 5: cf. ch. xi. 2, 3). wonder [*semeion*]—'sign:' significant of momentous truths. in heaven—not merely the sky, but the *heaven* just mentioned, ch. xi. 19: cf. *vv.* 7-9. woman clothed with the sun ... moon under her feet—Israel first, then the Gentile Church: clothed with Christ, 'the Sun of righteousness.' "Fair as the moon, clear as the sun" (Song vi. 10). Clothed with the Sun, the Church is bearer of Divine light in the world. So the seven churches (*i. e.*, the Church universal, the woman) are represented as light-bearing *candlesticks*, (ch. i.) The *moon*, though above the sea and earth, is connected with them, and is earthly: *sea, earth*, and *moon* represent the worldly element, in opposition to the kingdom of God—heaven, the sun. The moon cannot change darkness into day: she represents the world-religion in relation to the supernatural world. The Church has the moon under her feet; but the stars, heavenly lights, on her head. Satan directs his efforts against the stars, *the angels of the churches*, hereafter to shine for ever (ch. i. 20). Or, the twelve stars are *Israel's twelve tribes* (*Auberlen*). The allusions to *Israel* accord with this (cf. ch. xi. 19). The ark, lost at the Babylonian captivity, and never since found, is seen in the 'temple of God opened in heaven,' signifying that God enters again into covenant with His ancient people. The woman cannot mean, literally, the virgin mother of Jesus; for she did not flee into the wilderness and stay there for 1,260 days, whilst the dragon persecuted the remnant of her seed (*vv.* 13-17) (*De Burgh*). The *sun, moon,* and *twelve stars*, symbolize Jacob, Leah, or Rachel, and the twelve patriarchs, *i. e.*, THE JEWISH CHURCH: secondarily, THE CHURCH UNIVERSAL, of which Christ is ideally the Son, as 'seed of the woman;' having *under her feet*, in subordination, the ever-changing moon, with its borrowed light, *the Jewish dispensation*, now in a position of inferiority and become "worldly" (Heb. ix. 1), though supporting the woman (the moon symbolizes also the changeful things of this world): having *on her head the crown of twelve stars*, the twelve apostles, related

closely to Israel's twelve tribes. The Church, in passing over into the Gentile world, is (1.) persecuted; (2.) then seduced, as heathenism reacts on her. This is the key to the symbolic woman, beast, harlot, and false prophet. *Woman* and *beast* form the same contrast as *the Son of man* and the *beasts* in Daniel. As the Son of man comes *from heaven*, so the woman is seen *in heaven* (*v.* 1). The two beasts arise respectively *out of the sea* (cf. Dan. vii. 3) and *the earth* (ch. xiii. 1, 11): their origin is not of heaven, but of earth earthy. Daniel beholds the heavenly Bridegroom coming visibly to reign. John sees the woman, the Bride, whose calling is heavenly, in the world, before the Lord's coming again. The characteristic of woman, in contradistinction to man, is being subject; surrendering herself, as receptive. This is man's relation to God, to be subject to, and receive from, God. Autonomy reverses man's relation to God. Woman-like receptivity constitutes *faith*. By it the *individual* becomes a child of God: the children *collectively* (humanity, so far as it yields itself to God) are "the woman." Christ, the Son of the woman, is (*v.* 5) emphatically "the MAN-child" [*huios arrheen*, 'male-child']. Though born of a woman, and so 'Son of man,' under the law, for man's sake, He is also, as male-child, the Son of God, so HUSBAND of the Church. All who have their life in themselves severed from Him, the source of life, standing in their own strength, sink to the level of senseless *beasts*. The woman designates the kingdom of God; the beast, the kingdom of the world. The woman, of whom Jesus was born, represents *the Old Testament congregation;* the woman's travail-pains (*v.* 2), Old Testament believers' longings for the promised Redeemer. Cf. Isa. ix. 6. As new Jerusalem ('the woman,' or "wife," ch. xxi. 2, 9-12), with its twelve gates, is the transfigured Church, so the woman with the twelve stars is the Church militant. 2. pained—'tormented' [*basanizomene*]. De Burgh explains this, the bringing in of the first-begotten into the world AGAIN, when Israel shall at last welcome Him, and 'the man-child shall rule all nations with the rod of iron.' But there is a contrast between the *painful travailing* of the woman and Christ's second coming to the Jewish Church. Isa. lxvi. 7, 8, "*Before she travailed*, she brought forth . . . a MAN-CHILD"—*i. e., without travail-pangs*, she receives (at His second advent), as born to her, Messiah and a numerous seed.

3. appeared—'was seen.' wonder—'sign.' red. So A א, Vulgate [*purrhos*]; but B C, Coptic [*puros*], 'of fire.' The *colour* implies the dragon's fiery rage as a *murderer from the beginning*. His representative, *the beast*, corresponds, *having seven heads and ten horns*, (the number of horns on the fourth beast, Dan. vii.) But in ch. xiii. 1, *ten* crowns are on the *ten horns* (for, before the end, the fourth empire is divided into *ten* kingdoms); here, *seven* crowns ['diadems,' not *stephanoi*, 'wreaths'] are *upon his seven heads*. In Dan. vii., the antichristian powers, up to Christ's second coming, are represented by four beasts, having among them *seven* heads—*i. e.*, the first, second, and fourth beasts having *one* head each; the third, *four* heads. His universal dominion as prince of this fallen world is implied by the *seven diadems* (contrast

693

4 his heads. And *d* his tail drew the third part of the *e* stars of heaven, *f* and did cast them to the earth: and the dragon stood before the woman which was ready to be delivered, *g* for to devour her child as soon as it

5 was born. And she brought forth a man-child, who *h* was to rule all nations with a rod of iron: and her child was caught up unto God, and

6 *to* his throne. And the woman fled into the wilderness, where she hath a place prepared of God, that they should feed her there *i* a thousand two hundred *and* threescore days.

A. D. 96.

d ch. 9. 10.
e ch 17. 18.
f Dan. 8. 10.
g Ex 1. 16.
1 Pet 5. 8.
h Ps. 2. 9.
ch 2. 27.
ch. 19. 15.
i ch. 11. 3.

the 'many diadems on Christ's head,' ch. xix. 12, when coming to destroy him and his), caricaturing the *seven* spirits of God. His worldly instruments of power are the *ten horns*, ten being the world-number. The ten horns, among which *subsequently* arose the little horn, seem earlier in the fourth kingdom; and the little horn, which plucks up three, the temporal papacy. The ten crowned horns, which receive power *with the beast*, are at the close of the fourth kingdom. The little horn '*wears out* the saints' for "a time, and times, and the dividing of time;" but the beast's reign with the ten kings is but "one hour" (cf. Dan. vii. 7, 8, 20, 21, 22, 24, 25, 26, with Rev. xvii. 12, 13, 16, 17). 'The judgment takes away the little horn's dominion, consumes and destroys it unto the end' by a lengthened process; but 'the beast is (summarily) slain, and his body given to the burning flame' (cf. Rev. xix. 20, 21). It marks his self-contradictions that he and the beast bear both *seven* (the Divine) and *ten* (the world-number). **4. drew**—present, 'drags down.' His *dragging down the stars* with *his tail* (lashed back and forward in fury), implies his persuading to apostatize, and become earthy, those angels and once eminent human teachers who formerly were heavenly (cf. *v.* 1; Isa. xiv. 12; ch. i. 20). *Elliott* makes Licinius, who upheld heathenism ruling in the East, a third of the empire, to answer to the "third part of the stars," under Satan's influence, and Constantine, the Christian emperor, to be the man-child caught up to the imperial throne, which, as son of the Church, he held as the Lord's throne. But Satan did not draw Licinius and the third of the empire from the stars of heaven to the earth. **stood**—'stands' [*hesteken*]. **ready to be delivered**—'about to bring forth.' **for to devour,** &c.—'that when she brought forth he might devour her child.' So his agent Pharaoh (a name common to all the Egyptian kings, meaning *crocodile*, like the dragon, and an Egyptian idol) was ready to devour Israel's *males* at the nation's birth. The antitypical Israel, Jesus, when born, was sought for destruction by Herod, who slew all the *males* at Bethlehem. **5. man-child**—a son, a male.' Cf. notes, *vv.* 1, 2. **rule** [*poimainein*]—'tend as a shepherd' (note, ch. ii. 27). **rod of iron**—for long-continued obstinacy, until they submitted themselves to obedience (*Bengel*): Ps. ii. 9, which proves the Lord Jesus to be meant. Any interpretation which ignores this must be wrong. The *male son's* birth cannot be the Christian *state* triumphing over heathenism under Constantine, which was not a divine child of the woman, but had many worldly elements. *The ascending of the witnesses to heaven* (ch. xi. 12) answers to Christ's own ascension, "caught up unto God, and unto His throne:" also His ruling the nations with a rod of iron is to be shared in by believers. What took place primarily in the Divine Son of the woman shall take place in those who are one with Him, the sealed of Israel (ch. vii.), and the elect of all nations, to be translated and to reign with Him over the earth at His appearing. **6. woman fled.** Mary's flight with

694

Jesus into Egypt is a type. **where she hath.** So C, Vulgate; but א A B add, 'there.' **a place**—that portion of the world which received Christianity professedly, mainly the fourth kingdom, having its seat in modern Babylon, Rome, implying that *all* the heathen would not be Christianized in the present order of things. **prepared of God** [*apo*]—'*from:*' 'on the part of God.' Not by human caprice, but by the fore-determined counsel of God, the *woman*, the Church, *fled into the wilderness.* **they should feed her**—'nourish her.' Indefinite for 'she should be fed.' The heathen world, *the wilderness*, could not nourish her, but only afford an outward shelter. Here, as in Dan. iv. 26, the third person plural refers to *the heavenly powers*, who minister from God *nourishment* to the Church. As Israel had its time of first bridal love, on first going out of Egypt into the wilderness, so the Church's *wilderness*-time of *first love* was the apostolic age, when separate from the *Egypt* of this world, having no city here, but seeking one to come; having only a *place in the wilderness prepared of God* (*vv.* 6, 14). The harlot takes the world-city as her own, as Cain the first builder of a *city*, whereas the believing patriarchs lived in *tents*. Then apostate Israel was the harlot (Isa. i. 21), and the young Christian Church the woman; soon spiritual fornication crept in, and the Church (ch. xvii.) is no longer *the woman*, but *the harlot*, the *great Babylon*, which, however, has in it hidden the true people of God (ch. xviii. 4). The deeper the Church penetrated into heathendom, the more herself became heathenish. Instead of overcoming, she was overcome by the world (*Auberlen*). *The woman* is 'the one inseparable Church of the Old and New Testament' (*Hengstenberg*), the stock of the Christian Church being Israel (Christ and His apostles being Jews), on which Gentile believers have been *graffed*, and into which Israel, on her conversion, shall be graffed, as into *her own olive tree* (Rom. xi. 17-24). During the church-historic period, or 'times of the Gentiles,' wherein 'Jerusalem is trodden down of the Gentiles,' there is no believing Jewish Church; therefore, only the Christian Church can be "the woman." There is meant, however, secondarily, the preservation of the Jews during this church-historic period, that Israel, once "the woman," and of whom the *man-child* was born, may become so again at the close of the Gentile times, and stand at the head of the two elections, literal and spiritual Israel, the church elected from Jews and Gentiles without distinction. Ezek. xx. 35, 36, "I will bring you into *the wilderness of the people* (*peoples*), and there will I plead with you . . . like as I pleaded with your fathers in the wilderness of Egypt" (note there): not a *wilderness* locally, but spiritually a *state of discipline and trial* among Gentile "*peoples*," during the long Gentile times, and finally consummated in the last unparalleled trouble under antichrist, in which the sealed remnant (ch. vii.) who constitute "the woman," are nevertheless preserved "from the face of the serpent" (*v.* 14). **thousand two hundred and threescore days**—

7   And there was war in heaven: [j] Michael and his angels fought against
8 the [k] dragon; and the dragon fought and his angels, and prevailed not;
9 neither was their place found any more in heaven. And [l] the great
dragon was cast out, that [m] old serpent, called the Devil, and Satan,
which deceiveth the whole world: he [n] was cast out into the earth, and
10 his angels were cast out with him. And I heard a loud voice saying in
heaven, [o] Now is come salvation, and strength, and the kingdom of our
God, and the power of his Christ: for the accuser of our brethren is cast

A. D. 96.

[j] Dan 10. 13.
Dan. 12. 1.
[k] ch. 20. 2.
[l] Luke 10.18.
[m] Gen. 3. 1.
[n] John 12.3L.
ch. 9. 1.
[o] ch. 11. 15.
ch. 19. 1.

---

anticipatory of *v.* 14, where the persecution which caused her to flee is mentioned in its place: ch. xiii. gives the details. It is evident that Revelation should pass from Christ's birth to the last antichrist, without notice of the long intervening church-historical period. Still, the history of Gentile nations in the Old Testament is only noticed in connection with Jewish history; in the New Testament, it is accordingly to be expected that the history of the world-nations should be noticed only in connection with that of the literal or the spiritual Israel, the Church. Probably the 1,260 days, representing this long interval, are RECAPITULATED on a shorter scale analogically during antichrist's short reign. They are equivalent to three and a half years, which, as half of the divine *seven*, symbolize the world's seeming victory over the Church. As they include the *times* of *Jerusalem's being trodden of the Gentiles*, they must be much longer than 1,260 years, for above five and a half centuries more than 1,260 years have elapsed since Jerusalem fell.

7. In Job i. and ii., Satan presents himself among the sons of God, before God in heaven, as accuser of the saints; again, in Zech. iii. 1, 2. But at Christ's coming as our Redeemer, he *fell from heaven*, especially when Christ suffered, rose, and ascended to heaven. Christ appearing before God as our Advocate (Heb. ix. 24), Satan, the accusing adversary, could no longer appear against us, but was *cast out judicially* (Rom. viii. 33, 34). He and his angels range through the air and the earth, during the interval between the ascension and the second advent, about to be cast hence also, and bound in hell. That "heaven" here does not mean the air, but the abode of angels, appears from 1 Ki. xxii. 19-22; *vv.* 9, 10, 12. **there was** [*egeneto*]—'there came to pass.' **war in heaven**—a seeming contradiction in terms, yet true! Contrast the blessed result of Christ's triumph, Luke xix. 38, "peace in heaven." Col. i. 20, "to *reconcile* all things . . . whether . . . in earth, or . . . *in heaven.*" **Michael and his angels . . . the dragon . . . and his angels.** It was fitting that as the rebellion arose from unfaithful angels and their leader, so they should be overcome by faithful angels and their archangel, in heaven. On earth they are fittingly to be overcome, as represented by the beast and false prophet, by the Son of man and His human saints (ch. xix. 14-21). The conflict on earth, as in Dan. x., has its correspondent conflict of angels in heaven. Michael is peculiarly the prince, angel, of Israel. The conflict in heaven, though judicially decided already against Satan from the time of Christ's ascension, receives its completion in the judgment to be executed by the angels who cast out Satan. From Christ's ascension he has no standing-ground against the believing elect. Luke x. 18, "I beheld (in the earnest of the future fulfilment given in the demons' subjection to the disciples) Satan as lightning fall from heaven." As Michael fought with Satan about the body of the mediator of the old covenant (Jude 9), so now the Mediator of the new covenant, by offering His sinless body in

sacrifice, arms Michael with power to complete the victory. That Satan is not yet *finally*, but only judicially, cast out of heaven, appears from Eph. vi. 12, "spiritual wickedness in high (*heavenly*) places." This is the primary church-historical sense. Through Israel's unbelief, in the ulterior sense, Satan the accuser has ground against the elect nation. At the eve of her restoration, his standing-ground in heaven against her shall be taken from him, 'the Lord that hath chosen Jerusalem' *rebuking*, and casting him from heaven for ever by Michael. In Zech. iii. 1-9, similarly, Joshua the high priest represents Israel, and Satan, standing at God's right hand as adversary, resists Israel's justification. Not till then fully (*v.* 10, "NOW," &c.) shall ALL *things be reconciled unto Christ* IN HEAVEN (Col. i. 20), and there shall be *peace in heaven* (Luke xix. 38). **against.** אA B C read, 'with.' **8. prevailed not.** So א B C, Vulgate; but A, Coptic, read, '*He* prevailed not.' **neither.** א A B C read, 'not even' [*oude*]: a climax. Not only did they not prevail, but *not even their place was found any more in heaven.* There are four gradations in Satan's ever deeper downfall. (1.) He is deprived of his heavenly excellency, though having still access to heaven as man's accuser, up to Christ's ascension. As heaven was not fully yet opened to man (John iii. 13), so it was not yet shut against Satan. The old dispensation could not overcome him. (2.) From Christ to the millennium, he is judicially cast out as accuser of the elect, and shortly before the millennium loses his standing against Israel, and has expulsion fully executed on him and his by Michael. His rage on earth becomes the greater, his power being concentrated on it, towards the end, when "he knoweth that he hath but a short time" (*v.* 12). (3.) He is bound during the millennium (ch. xx. 1-3). (4.) Having been loosed for a while, he is cast for ever into the lake of fire. **9. that old serpent**—(Gen. iii. 1, 4.) As *destroyer*, he is a "roaring *lion:*" as *deceiver*, a "serpent." **Devil**—Greek for 'accuser,' 'slanderer.' **Satan**—Hebrew for *adversary*, especially in a court of justice. The twofold designation marks the twofold objects of his accusations and temptations—the elect, Gentiles and Jews. **world** [*oikoumenen*]—'habitable world.' **10. Now.** *Now* that Satan is cast out of heaven. Primarily at Jesus' resurrection and ascension: Jesus' rise is Satan's fall. Matt. xxviii. 18, "All power [*exousia*, 'authority,' as here] is given unto me in heaven and in earth:" connected with *v.* 5, "her child was *caught up unto God and to His throne.*" In the ulterior sense, just before Christ's coming, when Israel shall be restored as mother-church of Christendom, Satan, who resisted her restoration on the ground of her unworthiness, is cast out by Michael, (note, *v.* 7). This is preliminary to the glorious event similarly expressed (ch. xi. 15), "The kingdom of this world is become (the very word here [*egeneto*], 'is come') our Lord's and His Christ's:" Israel resuming her place. **salvation**, &c.—'*the* salvation (viz., fully, finally, Heb. ix. 28: cf. Luke iii. 6; hence, not till *now* do the blessed raise the

695

11 down, *P* which accused them before our God day and night. And *Q* they
overcome him by the blood of the Lamb, and by the word of their testi-
12 mony; *r* and they loved not their lives unto the death. Therefore
rejoice, *ye* heavens, and ye that dwell in them. *s* Woe to the inhabiters
of the earth and of the sea! for the devil is come down unto you, having
great wrath, *t* because he knoweth that he hath but a short time.
13   And when the dragon saw that he was cast unto the earth, he perse-
14 cuted the woman which brought forth the man-*child*. And *u* to the
woman were given two wings of a great eagle, that she might fly into
v the wilderness, into her place, where she is nourished *w* for a time, and

A. D. 96.

P Job 1. 9.
Job 2. 5.
Zech. 3. 1.
Q Rom. 8. 37.
Rom. 16 20.
Heb. 2 14.
r Luke 14.26.
s ch 8. 13.
t ch 10. 6.
u Ex. 19. 4.
v ch. 17. 3.
w Dan. 7. 25.

fullest hallelujah for *salvation* to the Lamb, ch. vii.
10; xix. 1), *the power [dunamis],* and *the authority
[exousia: legitimate]* of His Christ.' **accused them
before our God day and night**—hence the need
that the oppressed Church, *God's own elect* (the
widow, Luke xviii. 1-7, *continually coming,* so as
even to *weary* the unjust judge), should *cry day
and night unto Him.* **11.** they—in particular;
emphatic, 'they alone.' **overcame**—(Rom. viii.
33, 34, 37; xvi. 20.) **him**—(1 John ii. 14, 15.) It is
the same *victory* over Satan and the world which
John's gospel describes in the life of Jesus, his
epistle in each believer's life, and his apocalypse
in the life of the Church. **by** [*dia to haima :*
accusative, not genitive, as "by" would require:
cf. Heb. ix. 12]—'*on account of* (on the ground of)
the blood of the Lamb :' by virtue of its having
been shed. Had it not been shed, Satan's accusations would have been unanswerable : that blood
meets every charge. *Schöttgen* mentions the Rabbinical tradition that Satan accuses men all days
of the year, except the day of atonement. *Tittmann* less probably takes [*dia*] *out of regard to :* the
blood of the Lamb *induced* them to undertake the
contest *for the sake of* it. **by** (on account of) the
word of their testimony. On the ground of their
faithful testimony they are constituted victors.
It evinced their victory. Hereby they confess
themselves worshippers of the slain Lamb, and
overcome the beast, Satan's representative : an
anticipation of ch. xv. 2 (cf. ch. xiii. 15, 16). **unto**
[*achri*]—'even as far as.' They carried their not-
love of life *as far as even unto* death. **12.** Therefore—because Satan is cast out of heaven (*v.* 9).
dwell—'tabernacle.' Not only angels and souls of
the just with God, but also the faithful militant on
earth, who already in spirit 'tabernacle in heaven,'
having their home and citizenship there, *rejoice*
that Satan is cast out of their home. 'Tabernacle'
marks that, though still on earth, they in spirit
are hidden "in the secret of God's *tabernacle*" (Ps.
xxvii. 5). They belong not to the world, and
therefore exult in judgment having been passed
on the prince of this world. **the inhabiters of.**
So *Andreas;* but א A B C omit. The words,
probably, came from ch. viii. 13. **is come down**—
rather [*catebee*], 'is *gone* down:' John regarding
heaven as his standing-point, whence he looks down
on the earth. **unto you**—*earth and sea,* with your
inhabiters : those who lean upon, and essentially
belong to, *earth* (contrast John iii. 7, margin, with
John iii. 31; viii. 23; Phil. iii. 19, end; 1 John iv.
5) and its *sea*-like politics (Isa. lvii. 20). Furious
at his expulsion from heaven, knowing his time on
earth is short until he be cast down lower, when
Christ shall set up *His* kingdom (ch. xx. 1, 2), Satan
concentrates all his power to destroy as many souls
as he can. Though no longer able to accuse the elect
in heaven, he can tempt and persecute on earth.
The more light becomes victorious, the more
violent become the powers of darkness : at the last
crisis, antichrist will manifest himself with an

intensity of iniquity greater than ever. **short time**
—'season' [*kairon*]: *opportunity* for assaults.
13. Resuming from *v.* 6 the thread of discourse,
interrupted by the episode, *vv.* 7-12 (the ground in
the invisible world of the corresponding conflict
between light and darkness on earth): this verse
accounts for her *flight into the wilderness* (*v.* 6).
14. were given—by God's appointment, not human
chances (Acts ix. 11). **two**—'*the* two wings of *the*
great eagle.' Alluding to Exod. xix. 4: therefore
the Old Testament Church, as well as the New, is
included in "the woman." All believers (Isa. xl.
30, 31). *The great eagle* is the world-power; in
Ezek. xvii. 3, 7, *Babylon* and *Egypt;* in early
church-history, *Rome,* whose standard was the
eagle, turned by God's providence from being
hostile into a protector of the Christian Church.
As "wings" express remote parts, the *two* wings
may here mean *the east and west divisions of the
Roman empire.* **wilderness**—the land of the Gentiles ; in contrast to Canaan, the *pleasant* and
glorious land. God dwells there ; demons (the
rulers of the heathen world, 1 Cor. x. 20 ; ch. ix.
20), in the wilderness. Hence Babylon is called
the desert of the sea, Isa. xxi. 1-10 (referred to in
ch. xiv. 8 ; xviii. 2). Heathendom, being without
God, is essentially a desolate *wilderness* (Jer. xvii.
6). Thus, the woman's flight into the wilderness
is the passing of the kingdom of God from the
Jews to the Gentiles (typified by Mary's flight
with her child from Judea into Egypt). The eagle-
flight is from Egypt into the wilderness. *Egypt*
here is virtually (ch. xi. 8) Jerusalem become
spiritually so by *crucifying our Lord* (Heb. xiii. 13,
14). Out of her the New Testament Church flees,
as the Old out of the literal Egypt ; and as the
true Church subsequently is to flee out of Babylon
(the woman become an harlot, the Church apostate)
(*Auberlen*). **her place**—the seat of the then world-
empire, Rome. Acts describes the Church's passing from Jerusalem to Rome. The Roman protection was the eagle-wing which shielded Paul, the
instrument of this transmigration, from Jewish
opponents stirring up the heathen mobs. By
degrees the Church gained "her place" until,
under Constantine, the empire became Christian.
Still, this church-historical period is regarded as a
wilderness-time, wherein she is in part protected,
in part oppressed, by the world-power, until just
before the end of the world-power's enmity under
Satan shall break out against her worse than ever.
As Israel was in the wilderness forty years, and
had forty-two stages in her journey, so the Church
for *forty-two* months, three and a half *times* [*seasons,*
used for *years* in Hellenistic Greek (*Mœris,* the
Atticist), *kairous*], or 1,260 days (*v.* 6) between the
overthrow of Jerusalem and Christ's coming again,
shall be a wilderness-sojourner before she reaches
her millennial rest (answering to Canaan). Besides this church-historical fulfilment, there may
be an ulterior narrower fulfilment in the restoration of Israel to Palestine, antichrist for seven

15 times, and half a time, from the face of the serpent. And the serpent ^x cast out of his mouth water as a flood after the woman, that he might
16 cause her to be carried away of the flood. And the earth helped the woman; and the earth opened her mouth, and swallowed up the flood
17 which the dragon cast out of his mouth. And the dragon was wroth with the woman, ^y and went to make war with the remnant of her seed, which keep the commandments of God, and have ^z the testimony of Jesus Christ.
13 AND I stood upon the sand of the sea, and saw ^a a beast rise up out of the sea, having seven heads and ten horns, and upon his horns ten crowns,

A. D. 96.

^x Ps. 18 4.
Ps. 65 7.
Ps. 93 3, 4.
Isa. 8. 2.
Isa 29. 2.
Isa 59. 19.
^y Gen. 3. 15.
^z ch 1. 2, 9.

CHAP. 13.
^a Dan. 7. 2,
7.

times (short periods analogical to the longer) having power there, for three and a half times keeping covenant with the Jews, then breaking it in the midst of the week, and the mass fleeing by a second exodus into the wilderness, whilst a *remnant* remains exposed to fearful persecution (the "144,000 sealed of Israel," ch. vii. 7, and ch. xiv. 1, *standing with the Lamb*, after the conflict is over, *on mount Zion:* "the first-fruits" of a large company to be gathered to Him) (*De Burgh*). These *details* are conjectural: cf. the parallel, Dan. vii. 25. In Dan. xii. 1, 7, the subject is Israel's calamity. That several times do not necessarily mean seven years, in which each day is a year, *i. c.*, 2,520 years, appears from Nebuchadnezzar, *seven times* (Dan. iv. 23), answering to antichrist, the beast's duration. **15. flood**—'river,' (cf. Exod. ii. 3; Matt. ii. 20; especially Exod. xiv.) The *flood* is the Germanic tribes which, pouring on Rome, threatened Christianity. But *the earth helped the woman, by swallowing up the flood: earth*, contradistinguished from water, is the world consolidated. The German masses were brought under the influence of Roman *civilization* and Christianity (*Auberlen*). It includes, generally, the help given by earthly powers (those least likely, led by God's overruling Providence) to the Church against persecutions and heresies by which she has been at various times assailed. **17. wroth with**—'*at.*' went—'*away.*' **the remnant of her seed**—distinct in some sense from the woman. Satan's first effort was to root out the Christian Church as a visible profession of Christianity. Foiled in this, he *wars* (ch. xi. 7; xiii. 7) against the invisible Church, "those who keep the commandments of God, and have the testimony of Jesus" (A B C omit "Christ"). These are "the remnant," or *rest of her seed*, as distinguished from her seed, "the man-child" (*v.* 5), and from mere professors. The Church in her beauty (Israel at the head of Christendom, one perfect Church) is not to be manifested till Christ comes: so we now await the *manifestation of the sons of God.* Unable to destroy the Church as a whole, Satan directs his enmity against true Christians, the elect *remnant;* the others he leaves unmolested.

CHAP. XIII. 1-18.—**The Beast that Came out of the Sea**—**The Second out of the Earth, Exercising the Power of the First, and Causing the Earth to Worship him.**
1. I stood. So B, Coptic; but א A C, Vulgate, Syriac, '*He* stood.' Standing on the sand of the *sea*, Satan gave his power to the beast rising out of the sea. **upon the sand of the sea**—whence could be seen *the four winds striving upon the great sea* (Dan. vii. 2). **beast**—'wild beast.' Man becomes "brutish" (Jer. x. 14), severed from God, the archetype, in whose image he was made, which ideal is realized by the man Christ Jesus. Hence, the world-powers seeking their own glory, not God's, are *beasts;* Nebuchadnezzar, when in self-deification he forgot that "the most High

697

ruleth in the kingdom of men," was driven among the beasts. In Dan. vii. there are *four;* here the *one* expresses the sum total of the God-opposed world-power in its universal development, not restricted to one manifestation, Rome. This first beast expresses the world-power attacking the Church from without; the second, a revival of, and minister to, the first, the world-power as *the false prophet* corrupting the Church from within. **out of the sea** (Dan. vii. 3; note, ch. viii. 8)—out of the troubled waves of *peoples, multitudes, nations, and tongues* (ch. xvii. 15). The *earth* (*v.* 11) means the ordered world of nations, with its civilization. **seven heads and ten horns.** א A B C transpose, 'ten horns and seven heads.' The ten horns are now put first (contrast ch. xii. 3), because they are crowned. They shall not be so till the close of the fourth kingdom (the Roman), which continues until the fifth, Christ's, shall supplant it: this last stage is marked by the *ten toes* (five on one foot, five on the other) of the image, Dan. ii. The *seven* implies the world-power assuming Godhead, and caricaturing the *seven* spirits of God; its God-opposed character is detected by *ten* accompanying the *seven.* Dragon and beast both bear crowns—the former on the heads, the latter on the horns (ch. xii. 3; *v.* 1). Both heads and horns refer to kingdoms: in ch. xvii. 7, 10, 12, "kings" represent kingdoms whose heads they are. The *seven* kings—the great powers of the world—are distinguished from the *ten*, represented by the horns (simply "kings," ch. xvii. 12). *The ten* mean the last phase of the world-power, the fourth kingdom divided into *ten parts.* They are connected with the *seventh head* (ch. xvii. 12), and are yet future (*Auberlen*). The mistake of those who interpret the beast Rome exclusively, and the *ten horns* kingdoms which took the place of Rome in Europe, is, the fourth kingdom in the image has TWO legs, the eastern as well as the western empire: the ten toes are not upon one foot (the west), but on the two (east and west) together. If the ten kingdoms were those which sprang up on the overthrow of Rome, the ten would be known; whereas twenty-eight different lists are given, making in all sixty-five kingdoms! (*Tyso* in *De Burgh.*) The seven heads are the seven world-monarchies—Egypt, Assyria, Babylon, Persia, Greece, Rome, the Germanic empire. Under the last we live (*Auberlen*); it devolved on Napoleon, after Francis, Emperor of Germany and King of Rome, resigned the title in 1806. *Faber* explains *the healing of the deadly wound* to be the revival of the Napoleonic dynasty after its overthrow at Waterloo. That secular dynasty, in alliance with the ecclesiastical papacy, "the eighth head," yet "of the seven" (ch. xvii. 11), will temporarily triumph over the saints, until destroyed in Armageddon, (ch. xix.) A Napoleon thus would be the antichrist, restoring the Jews to Palestine, accepted as their Messiah, and afterwards fearfully opposing them. But the mention of the

2 and upon his heads the ¹ name of blasphemy. And ᵇthe beast which I saw was like unto a leopard, and his feet were as *the feet* of a bear, and his mouth as the mouth of a lion: and ᶜthe dragon gave him his power,
3 and his seat, and great authority. And I saw one of his heads as it were ²wounded to death; and his deadly wound was healed: and ᵈall the
4 world wondered after the beast. And they worshipped the dragon which gave power unto the beast: and they worshipped the beast, saying, ᵉWho
5 *is* like unto the beast? who is able to make war with him? And there was given unto him ᶠa mouth speaking great things and blasphemies;
6 and power was given unto him ³to continue ᵍforty *and* two months. And

A. D 9⸗.	
¹ Or, names.	
ᵇ Dan 7. 6.	
ᶜ ch. 12. 9.	
² slain.	
ᵈ 2 Thes. 2 3.	
ᵉ ch 1⸗. 18.	
ᶠ Dan 7 -25.	
Dan 11. 3⁶.	
³ Or. to make war.	
ᵍ ch 11 ⸗.	
ch 12. 6.	

leopard, bear, and *lion*, answering to the *first three* kingdoms (Dan. vii. 4-6), and the little horn of Dan. viii., and "wilful king," ch. xi., arising out of the third, make it likely that the antichrist about to oppress Israel is to arise from the east, the Greek empire, rather than the west: Gog, Meshech, and Tubal (Ezek. xxxviii., notes). The sea-beast comprises both the east and west: the earth-beast comes from the east. crowns—'diadems.' name of blasphemy. So א C, Coptic, *Andreas;* but A B, Vulgate, 'names,' &c.—viz., a name on each of the heads; blasphemously arrogating attributes of God (note, ch. xvii. 3). A characteristic of the wilful king (Dan. xi. 36; 2 Thess. ii. 4). 2. leopard . . . bear . . . lion. This beast unites in itself the God-opposed characteristics of the three preceding. It rises up out *of the sea,* as Daniel's four, and has *ten horns,* as Daniel's fourth beast, *and seven heads,* as Daniel's four beasts had in all—viz., one on the first, one on the second, four on the third, and one on the fourth. Thus it represents *the world-power* (represented by *four*) of *all times and places,* as opposed to God: just as the *woman* is the Church of all ages. The beast is vicar of Satan, who similarly has *seven heads* and *ten horns:* implying his *universal power in all ages.* Satan as a serpent is archetype of beast nature (ch. xii. 9): his *seven heads* represent 'Satan's power on earth collectively' (*Auberlen*). The third kingdom, the leopard (Dan. vii. 4-6), here *first,* including the former two, the bear and lion in reverse order, was the parent of Antiochus's blasphemy. Christianity gave its idolatry the deadly wound: and in it were the seven churches of Asia, to which Revelation is addressed. Its apostasy to picture-worship, mariolatry, and adoration of the eucharist, healed the wound. Dan. viii. and xi. imply, from it shall come Israel's antichrist. 3. one of—'from among.' wounded . . . healed. Thrice emphatically (*vv.* 12, 14): cf. ch. xvii. 8, 11, "the beast that *was, and is not, and shall ascend* out of the bottomless pit" (*v.* 11 below): the Germanic empire, the seventh head (revived in antichrist *the eighth*), future in John's time (ch. xvii. 10). Contrast Nebuchadnezzar, humbled from self-deifying pride, and converted from *beast*-like character to MAN's form and true position towards God: symbolized by his *eagle-wings plucked,* and himself made stand upon his feet as a *man* (Dan. vii. 4). Here, the *beast's* head is not changed into human, but receives a deadly wound—*i. e.,* the world-kingdom does not turn to God, but for a time its God-opposed character remains paralyzed ('as it were slain:' marking the beast's outward resemblance to the Lamb 'as it were slain,' notes, ch. v. 6: cf. the second beast's resemblance to the *Lamb, v.* 11). Though seemingly *slain* [*esphagmenēn*, 'wounded'], it remains the beast still, to rise again in another form (*v.* 11). The six first heads were heathenish—Egypt, Assyria, Babylon, Persia, Greece, Rome; the seventh

world - power (the German hordes pouring on Christianized Rome, including the Greek third empire, and so the two former), whereby Satan hoped to stifle Christianity (ch. xi. 15, 16), became Christianized (the beast's, *as it were, deadly wound: slain,* and *it is not,* ch. xvii. 11). Its *ascent out of the bottomless pit* answers to the *healing of its deadly wound* (ch. xvii. 8). No change is noticed in Daniel as effected by Christianity upon the fourth kingdom. The beast, *healed* of its *wound,* returns from, not only the *sea,* but the *bottomless pit,* whence it draws new strength of hell (*vv.* 3, 11, 12, 14; ch. xi. 7; xvii. 8). [It was *antitheos:* it now is *antichristos.*] Cf. the *seven evil spirits* taken into the temporarily dispossessed, and *the last state worse than the first,* Matt. xii. 43-45. A worse heathenism breaks in upon the Christianized world, more devilish than that of the first beast's heads. The latter was apostasy only from the revelation of God in nature and conscience; this is from God's revelation of love in His Son. It culminates in antichrist, the man of sin, son of perdition (cf. ch. xvii. 11): 2 Thess. ii. 3: cf. 2 Tim. iii. 1-4, the *characteristics of old heathenism* (Rom. i. 29-32) (*Auberlen*). More than one wound is meant: *e. g.,* that under Constantine (when the worship of the emperor's image fell before Christianity), followed by healing, when image-worship and the Romish and Greek Catholic errors were introduced (Dan. vii. 8, 11, 24, 25; 1 Tim. iv. 1-3); again, that at the Reformation, followed by the *form of godliness without the power,* to end in the last apostasy, the second beast (*v.* 11), antichrist (the wilful king of the third kingdom, Dan. viii. 11, 12; xi. 36), the same seventh world-power in another form (2 Tim. iii. 1-9). wondered after—followed with wondering gaze. 4. which gave. So B; but א A B C, Vulgate, Syriac, *Andreas,* '*because* he gave.' power—'*the authority:*' its authority. Who is like unto the beast? the language appropriated to *God,* Exod. xv. 11 (whence [from the initials *Mi Camocah Baelin Jehovah*] the Maccabees took their name: the opponents of the Old Testament antichrist, Dan. viii. and xi., Antiochus; Ps. xxxv. 10; lxxi. 19; cxiii. 5; Mic. vii. 18: *blasphemously* (*vv.* 1, 5) assigned to the beast: a parody of "Michael" (cf. ch. xii. 7), 'Who is like unto God?' 5. blasphemies. So א C, *Andreas;* B, 'blasphemy;' A, 'blasphemous things' (cf. Dan. vii. 8, 11, 25). The "mouth" answers to both *Antiochus Epiphanes' three and a half years* of blasphemy against God's "tabernacle," suspending the daily sacrifice (notes, Dan. viii.), and to the little horn of *the fourth* kingdom, the papacy in its forty-two prophetical months, as also the great sacerdotalist pretensions of the *Greek eastern* (*third kingdom*) patriarchate in the same period. power—'authority:' *legitimate* [*exousia*]. א omits. to continue—'to act,' 'work' [*poiesai*]. B, "to make *war*" (cf. *v.* 4); but A C, Vulgate, Syriac, *Andreas,* omit "war;" א

he opened his mouth in blasphemy against God, to blaspheme his name,
7 [h] and his tabernacle, and them that dwell in heaven. And it was given unto him [i] to make war with the saints, and to overcome them : and power
8 was given him over all kindreds, and tongues, and nations. And all that dwell upon the earth shall worship him, [j] whose names are not written in
9 the book of life of the Lamb [k] slain from the foundation of the world. If
10 any man have an ear, let him hear. He [l] that leadeth into captivity shall go into captivity : [m] he that killeth with the sword must be killed with the sword. Here [n] is the patience and the faith of the saints.
11 And I beheld another beast coming up out of the earth ; and he had
12 two horns like a lamb, and he spake as a dragon. And he exerciseth all the power of the first beast before him, and causeth the earth and them which dwell therein to worship the first beast, whose deadly wound was

A. D 96.

[h] John i. 14.
Col 2. 9.
[i] Dan 7. 21.
[j] Ex. 3 '. 33.
Dan 12. 1.
Phil 4. 3
ch. 21. 27.
[k] John i. 29.
36.
Eph. 1. 4.
1 Pet 1. 19.
ch 5. 6-13.
[l] Isa. 33. 1.
[m] Gen. 9. 6.
Matt. 26. 52.
[n] ch 14. 12.

has, 'to do *what he wills*' [*ho thelei*] (Dan. xi. 36; xii. 7). **forty and two months**—(notes, ch. xi. 2, 3; xii. 6.) **6. opened his mouth**—the formula of a set speech, or series of speeches. *Vv.* 6, 7 expand *v.* 5. **blasphemy.** So B, *Andreas*; but א A C, 'blasphemies.' **and them.** So Vulgate, Coptic, *Andreas, Primasius*, read ; A C א omit "and :" 'them that dwell [*skenountas : tabernacle*] in heaven ;' not only angels, and departed souls of the righteous, but believers on earth, having their citizenship in heaven, whose life is hidden from the antichristian persecutor in *the secret of God's tabernacle* (Ps. xxvii. 5; note, ch. xii. 12; margin, John iii. 7). **7. power**—'authority.' **all kindreds, and tongues, and nations**—'every tribe . . . tongue . . . nation.' A B C א, Vulgate, Syriac, *Andreas, Primasius*, add, 'and people,' after 'tribe.' **8. all that dwell upon the earth**—of earth earthy : in contrast to 'them that dwell in heaven.' **whose names are not written.** So א; but A B C, Syriac, Coptic, *Andreas*, read singular, '(every one) whose [*hou :* but א B, *hon*, plural] *name* is not written.' **Lamb slain from the foundation of the world.** The Greek order favours this. He was *slain* in the Father's eternal counsels : cf. 1 Pet. i. 19, 20. Otherwise, 'written from the foundation of the world in the book of life of the Lamb slain.' So ch. xvii. 8. 'As He was "the Lamb slain from the foundation of the world," so all (previous sacrificial) atonements were only effectual by His blood' (*Bishop Pearson*). **9.** Christ's monition calling solemn attention (Matt. xiii. 9, 43). **10. He that leadeth into captivity.** A B C, Vulgate, read, 'if any one (be) for captivity.' **shall go into captivity**—present, 'goeth into captivity.' A, Vulgate ; Jer. xv. 2 is alluded to : א B C read simply, 'he goeth away,' and omit "into captivity." **he that killeth with the sword must be killed with the sword.** So א; but B C, Vulgate, 'shall kill ;' A omits "must :" 'if any (be) for being killed, (it must be) that he be killed.' As of old, so those to be persecuted by the beast have their trials severally appointed by God's fixed counsel. א B C reading is, a warning to persecutors that they shall be punished in kind. **Here**—*Herein:* in bearing their appointed sufferings lies the *persevering endurance of the saints.* This is to be the watchword of the elect during this period. The first beast is to be met by *patience* and *faith* (v. 10) ; the second by true *wisdom* (v. 18; ch. xvi. 13 ; xix. 20; xx. 10).

11. another beast—"the false prophet" (ch. xvi. 13; xix. 20; xx. 10). **out of the earth**—society civilized and consolidated, still, with all its culture, of earth earthy : as distinguished from 'the sea,' the agitations of peoples, out of which the world-power and its kingdoms have emerged. '*The sacerdotal persecuting power, Pagan and Christian:* the pagan priesthood making an image of the

emperors, which they compelled Christians to worship, and working wonders by magic ; the Romish priesthood, inheritor of pagan rites, images, and superstitions, lamb-like in Christian professions, dragon-like in word and act' (*Alford*, from the Spanish Jesuit *Lacunza*, or *Ben Ezra*). As the first beast was like the Lamb in being, *as it were, wounded to death*, so the second is like the Lamb in having *two lamb-like horns* (its essential difference is marked by its having TWO, the Lamb SEVEN, ch. v. 6). The paganism of the world-power, seeming wounded to death by Christianity, revives. The harlot-apostasy of the Church answers to the healing of the wound. When she has been eaten by the beast and burned with fire (ch. xvii. 16), the second beast (antichrist) brings back the first beast's paganism, recommending it by a spiritual form and earthly culture. Matt. xxiv. 11, 24, "*Many* false prophets shall rise :" ushering in "*the* false prophet." This antichrist has both the mouth of blasphemy (v. 5) of the little horn of the third kingdom (Dan. viii. 11, 12, 23-25; xi. 36), and also "the eyes of man" of the little horn of the fourth kingdom (Dan. vii. 8). "The eyes of man" symbolize intellectual culture and spiritual pretensions, characteristic of "the false prophet" (vv. 13-15; ch. xvi. 14). The first beast is political ; the second spiritual, the power of ideas (the favourite term in the French school) : humanity substituted for the Son of man, antichrist for Christ. Lawless democracy [*anomia*] (2 Thess. ii. 7, 8), ever since the 1789 revolution, has been preparing the way for the lawless one. Both alike are *beasts*, from below, not from above; faithful allies, worldly *antichristian wisdom* serving worldly *God-opposing power:* both "*lion*" and "*dragon*" (vv. 2, 11): might and cunning. The dragon gives his power to the first beast, his spirit to the second, so that it *speaks as a dragon.* The second, arising *out of the earth*, is in ch. xi. 7, and xvii. 8, said to *ascend out of the bottomless pit:* its *earthy* culture only intensifies its *infernal* character, the pretence to rationalistic philosophy (as in the primeval temptation, Gen. iii. 5, 7, "their EYES were opened") veiling the *deification of nature, self, and man.* Hence spring Idealism, Materialism, Pautheism, Atheism. The fourth kingdom little horn, the papacy's claim to the double power, secular and spiritual, is the immediate forerunner of the twofold beast in its final state, that *out of the sea*, ministered to by that *out of the earth*, or *bottomless pit. Primasius* of Adrumetum (sixth century), 'He feigns to be a lamb, that he may assail the Lamb—the body of Christ.' **12. power**—'authority.' **before him**—'in his presence;' as ministering to him. The non-existence of the beast (ch. xvii. 8) embraces the Germanic and Greek Christian period. **which dwell therein**—the earthly-minded. The Church becomes the *harlot;* the

13 healed. And ° he doeth great wonders, ᵖ so that he maketh fire come
14 down from heaven on the earth in the sight of men, and deceiveth them
that dwell on the earth by *the means of* those miracles which he had
power to do in the sight of the beast; saying to them that dwell on the
earth, that they should make an image to the beast, which had the wound
15 by a sword, and �q did live. And he had power to give ⁴ life unto the
image of the beast, that the image of the beast should both speak, and
ʳ cause that as many as would not worship the image of the beast should
16 be killed. And he caused all, both small and great, rich and poor, free
and bond, ⁵ to receive a mark in their right hand, or in their foreheads:
17 and that no man might buy or sell, save he that had the mark, ˢ or the

A. D. 91.

° Deut. 13. 1.
Matt 24.24.
2 Thes 2 9.
ch 16. 14.
ᵖ 1 Ki. 18. 38.
2. Ki. 1. 10,
12.
q 2 Ki 20. 7.
⁴ breath.
ʳ ch. 20. 4.
⁵ to give
them.
ˢ ch. 14. 11.

world's power, the antichristian *beast;* the world's wisdom, *the false prophet.* Christ's three offices are perverted: the first beast is the false *kingship;* the harlot, the false *priesthood;* the second beast, the false *prophet.* The beast is the *bodily,* the false prophet the *intellectual,* the harlot the *spiritual* power of antichristianity (*Auberlen*). The *Old Testament Church* stood under the beast, the heathen world-power: *the Middle Ages Church* under the harlot: *in modern times* the false prophet predominates. But in the last days all three shall *co-operate; the false prophet causes men to worship the beast, and the beast carries the harlot,* (ch. xvii.) These three are reducible to two: *the apostate church* and *the apostate world, pseudo-christianity* and *antichristianity,* the harlot and the beast; for the false prophet is also a beast; and the two beasts, different manifestations of the same beast-like principle, are finally judged together, whereas separate judgment falls first on the harlot (*Auberlen*). **deadly wound**—'wound of death.' **13. wonders**—'signs.' **so that**—so *great* that. **maketh fire**—'maketh even fire.' The very miracle which the two witnesses, and Elijah long ago, performed: this the beast from the bottomless pit, or false prophet, mimics. Not tricks, but miracles by demon aid, like those of the Egyptian magicians, calculated to deceive: wrought "after the working (*energy*) of Satan" (2 Thess. ii. 9). Probably this second beast answers to "the little horn," the 'wilful king' of Dan. viii. 9-12, 23-25; xi. 21-38; the antichrist that oppresses *Israel,* from the third ingdom: as the first beast represents the God-opposed world-power, generally comprising Antiochus's blasphemies in the third kingdom, and the sacerdotal pretensions of the Eastern patriarchate, and the Romish little horn of Dan. vii. 7, 8, 11, 24-26, that oppressed Gentile believers, of the *fourth* kingdom. As Dan. vii. is *Chaldaic,* so with Dan. viii. begins the Hebrew portion. The little horn of the third kingdom, whose forerunner was Antiochus, is probably the pseudo-Messiah or false prophet which "shall come in his own name" (Dan. viii.; xi.; John v. 43), received by, and then tearing, the Jews (Zech. xi. 16); after that the apostate churches, Roman and Greek (the harlot), shall have been divested of all traces of their *Christianity* (answering to the *humanity* of the harlot). Hence follow the 144,000 on *Zion* (ch. xiv. 1; xv. 3): probably *Israelites.* The little horn, in Dan. vii. 8, 11, 25, 26, is distinct from the beast: the horn (the papal kingdom) is *judged* and *his dominion taken away,* simultaneous with judgment on the whore, or *whole* apostate church, stripped naked, eaten, and burnt by the beast (ch. xvii. 16); the *beast's* (antichrist's) body is given by the *Lord in person to the burning flame* (ch. xix. 16-20). Antichrist's persecutions, though primarily falling on Israel, will also secondarily fall on Gentile believers. For the seven Asiatic Gentile churches addressed are urged to obtain the king-

dom through suffering and keeping Christ's Word in the hour of universal temptation (ch. iii. 10). **14. deceiveth them that dwell on the earth**—tho earthly-minded. Even a miracle is not enough to warrant belief in a professed revelation, unless in harmony with God's already-revealed will (Deut. xiii. 1-5; Matt. xxiv. 24). **by the means of those miracles**—rather [*dia ta semeia*], 'on account of those miracles.' **which he had power to do**—'which were given him to do,' **in the sight of the beast**—(*v.* 12.) **which.** So א; but A B C read, 'who:' a personal antichrist. **had.** So B, *Andreas;* but A א C, Vulgate, read, 'hath.' **15. he had power**—'it was given to him.' **to give life**—'breath,' 'spirit.' **image.** Nebuchadnezzar set up in Dura a golden *image* to be worshipped, probably of himself; for his dream had been interpreted, "Thou art this head of gold." The three Hebrews who refused to worship it were cast into a burning furnace. Typifying the last apostasy. *Pliny,* in his letter to Trajan, states that he punished Christians who would not worship the emperor's *image* with incense. So Julian, the apostate, set up his image with idols in the Forum, that the Christians, in doing reverence to it, might seem to worship the idols. So Charlemagne's image was set up; and the Pope *adored* the new emperor (*Dupin,* vol. vi., p. 126). Napoleon, Charlemagne's successor, designed, after he had first lowered the Pope by removing him to Fontainbleau, then to 'make an idol of him' (*Memorial de Sainte Helene*): he would, through the Pope's influence, have directed the religious as well as the political world. Antichrist will realize the project, becoming the beast supported by the false prophet (some infidel supplanter of the papacy, under a spiritual guise, after the harlot, or apostate church, has been judged by the beast, ch. xvii. 16); he then might have his image set up as a test of secular and spiritual allegiance. **speak.** 'False doctrine will give a spiritual appearance to the foolish apotheosis of the creaturely personified by antichrist' (*Auberlen*). *Jerome,* on Dan. vii., says, Antichrist shall be 'a man in whom the whole of Satan shall dwell bodily.' Rome's *speaking* images, and winking pictures of the Virgin Mary, are an earnest of the demoniacal miracles of the false prophet in making the beast's image to speak. **16. to receive a mark**—'that they should give them a mark:' such as masters stamp on their slaves. Soldiers punctured their arms with marks of the general under whom they served. Votaries of idols branded themselves with the idol's symbol. Antiochus Epiphanes branded the Jews with the ivy leaf, the symbol of Bacchus (2 Macc. vi. 7; 3 Macc. ii. 29). Contrast God's *seal* and *name in the foreheads of His servants* (Gal. vi. 17; ch. vii. 3; xiv. 1; xxii. 4). The mark in the right hand and forehead implies prostration of *body* and *intellect* to the beast. 'In *the forehead* for profession; in the *hand* for work and service'

18 name of the beast, *or the number of his name. Here "is wisdom.
Let him that hath understanding count the number of the beast: for
it is the number of a man; and his number *is* Six hundred threescore
and six.

14 AND I looked, and, lo, a "Lamb stood on the mount Sion, and with

A. D. 91.
*ch. 15. 2.
" Ps. 107. 43.

CHAP. 14.
" John 1. 29.

(*Augustine*). **17. And.** So A B,Vulgate; but א C,
Irenæus, 316, Coptic, Syriac, omit it. **might buy**
—'may be able to buy.' **the mark, or the name**
—*Greek*, 'the mark, the name of the beast.' The
mark may be, as in sealing the saints, not visible,
but symbolical of allegiance. So the sign of the
cross. The Pope's interdict has often shut out the
excommunicate from social intercourse. Under
antichrist this shall reach its worst form. **number of his name**—implying that the name has
numerical meaning. **18. wisdom.** Spiritual *wisdom* is needed to solve the *mystery* of iniquity, and
not be beguiled by it. **count . . . for**—implying
the possibility of our counting the beast's number.
the number of a man — *i. e.*, counted as men
generally count. So ch. xxi. 17. The number of
a *man*, not of *God;* he shall extol himself above
the Godhead, as the MAN *of sin* (*Aquinas*). Though
it imitates the Divine name, it is only *human.*
six hundred threescore and six. A, Vulgate, write
the numbers in full; B, merely the three letters
standing for numbers, *Ch, X, St.* C reads 616;
Irenæus, 328, disciple of Polycarp, John's disciple,
maintained 666, which he thought to be contained
in the Greek, Lateinos (L, 30; A, 1; T, 300; E, 5;
I, 10; N, 50; O, 70; S, 200): or else *Teitan.* Latin is
the language of Rome in all official acts: the forced
unity of language in ritual being the counterfeit
and premature anticipation of real unity, only to
be realized at Christ's coming, when all the earth
shall "in a pure language . . . serve the Lord with
one consent" (Zeph. iii. 9). The last antichrist
will have a close connection with his Romish predecessor, and will arrogate all Rome's pretensions,
besides others. The Hebrew letters of Balaam
amount to 666 (*Bunsen*): a type of the *false prophet*,
whose characteristic will be spiritual knowledge
perverted to Satanic ends. Ch. ii. 14 favours
this: also, the fact that the antichrist here has
been shown primarily to oppress the Hebrews.
Six is the world-number: in 666, in units, tens,
and hundreds. It is next to the sacred *seven*,
which it mimics (*v.* 1), but severed from it by an
impassable gulf. The wounding to death of the
seventh head leaves the beast's world-number *six*
disclosed. It is that *of the world given over to
judgment:* hence there is a pause between the
sixth and seventh seals, the sixth and seventh
trumpets. The judgments on the world are complete in *six:* by the fulfilment of *seven*, the kingdoms of the world become Christ's. As *twelve* is
the number of the Church, so six, its half, symbolizes the world-kingdom broken. The raising of
the six to tens and hundreds indicates that the
beast, notwithstanding his progression to higher
powers, can only rise to greater ripeness for judgment. Thus 666, the judged world-power, contrasts with the 144,000 sealed and transfigured
ones (the Church-number, twelve, squared and
multiplied by 1,000, the number symbolizing the
world pervaded by God; ten, the world-number,
raised to the power of three, the number of God)
(*Auberlen*). The *mark* [*charagma*] and *name* are
the same. The first two radicals of *Christ, Ch*
and *R*, are the first two of *charagma*, the imperial
monogram of Christian Rome. Antichrist, personating Christ, adopts a symbol like, but not
agreeing with, Christ's monogram, *Ch, X, St:*
whereas the radicals in 'Christ' are *Ch, R, St.*
701

Papal Rome has substituted *the Keys* for *the Cross.*
So on the papal *coinage* (the *image* of power, Matt.
xxii. 20). In 'Christ,' *Ch R* represent *seven* hundred, the perfect number. The *Ch, X, St* represent an imperfect number, a triple *falling away*
(apostasy) from *septenary* perfection (*Wordsworth*).
A friend, E. L. Garbett, has calculated the numerical value of 3,000 nouns in the Greek Testament,
and found just two represent 666 [*paradosis*, 'tradition,' the great engine of *doctrinal* corruption; and
euporia, 'wealth,' that of *practice*]. *Euporia* occurs
only once (Acts xix. 25): in *Ephesus, one of the
seven towns addressed in Revelation.* The only un-
contradicted entry of 666 is (1 Ki. x. 14; 2 Chr. ix.
13) the 666 talents of gold that came in yearly to
Solomon, and which were among the corrupting
influences that misled him. The two horns of the
earth beast represent the two phases of idolatry
which ever corrupt the Church, literal and spiritual, image-worship and covetousness (Ps. xvii. 14;
xlix. 12, 20; Col. iii. 5). The seven heads of the
first, the sea-beast, are the totality of capital sins
(ch. xxi. 8; xxii. 15), the "mountains" which lift
themselves up against God (ch. xvii. 9). Idolatry
is the wounded and revived head. *Gold, silver,
brass*, the materials of the first three empires in
Nebuchadnezzar's image, and the medium of
wealth, have in the fourth kingdom *iron* added, as
the prominent metal of civilization. The children
of Adonikam (Ezra ii. 13) are 666, but in Neh. vii.
18, 667: x. 15. Adonijah rose against the Lord's
anointed, and so is a type of antichrist: his name
is changed into a curse, Adonikam. The forehead
is the seat of avowed *intention*. The *act* and the
intention are the two ways of worshipping the
beast (*v.* 16). The heart-worship of money bearing
"the image" of the world-power (Luke xx. 24)
fulfils *vv.* 15-17. E. L. Garbett takes *v.* 5, 'Power
was given to IT (*the mouth*) to work forty-two
months:' the mouth is not yet given. He quotes
Pelletan ('Profession of Faith in the Nineteenth
Century'), wherein *wealth* is addressed, 'Divine
Son—Messiah—Redeemer—dumb confidant of God
—begotten by mysterious conception, who hast
saved man from misery, redeemed the world,' &c.
E. L. Garbett denies the identity of the *scarlet-
coloured* beast (ch. xvii. 3) and the *leopard-like*
beast here (*v.* 2).
  CHAP. XIV. 1-20.—THE LAMB ON ZION WITH
THE 144,000—THEIR SONG—THE GOSPEL PRO-
CLAIMED BEFORE THE END BY ONE ANGEL; THE
FALL OF BABYLON BY ANOTHER; THE DOOM OF
THE BEAST-WORSHIPPERS BY A THIRD—BLESSED-
NESS OF THE DEAD IN THE LORD—THE HARVEST
—VINTAGE.
  In contrast to the beast, false prophet, and
apostate church (implied in the healing of the
wound that had been inflicted on idolatry by
the Sword of the Spirit, ch. xiii. 3, 14): introductory to the judgments about to descend
on them and the world (*vv.* 8-11, anticipatory of
ch. xviii. 2-6; xix. 20) stand the redeemed,
'the divine kernel of humanity' (*Auberlen*).
Chs. xiv.-xvi. describe the preparations for
Messianic judgment. As ch. xiv. begins with *the
144,000 of Israel* (cf. ch. vii. 4-8), no longer exposed
to trial as then, but triumphant, 'the first-fruits,'
and then follow the general Gentile 'harvest' of
redeemed; so ch. xv. combines with Israel those

him an hundred forty *and* four thousand, ^bhaving his Father's name

2 written in their foreheads. And I heard a voice from heaven, as the voice of many waters, and as the voice of a great thunder: and I heard

3 the voice of harpers harping with their harps: and they sung as it were a new song before the throne, and before the four beasts, and the elders: and no man could learn that song but the hundred *and* forty *and*

4 four thousand, which were redeemed from the earth. These are they which were not defiled with women; ^cfor they are virgins. These are they which follow the Lamb whithersoever he goeth. These ¹were redeemed from among men, ^d*being* the first-fruits unto God and to the

5 Lamb. And ^ein their mouth was found no guile: for ^fthey are without fault before the throne of God.

6 And I saw another angel fly in the midst of heaven, ^ghaving the ever-

A. D. 96.
^b Luke 12. 8.
ch 7. 3.
^c Ps 45. 14.
Matt. 25. 1.
1 Cor. 7. 25.
2 Cor. 11. 2.
¹ were
bought.
^d Jas. 1. 18.
^e Ps. 32. 2.
Zeph. 3. 13.
^f Eph. 5. 27.
Jude 24.
^g Matt. 28.19.
Eph. 3. 9.
Tit. 1. 2.

who have *overcome* from among the Gentiles (cf. ch. vii. 9-17, with ch. xv. 1-5): the two classes of elect form together the whole company of transfigured saints who reign with Christ.

1. a. א A B C, Coptic, *Origen*, read, '*the* Lamb.' **Lamb stood on . . . Sion**—having left His position "in the midst of the throne," now taking His stand *on Sion*. **his Father's name.** א A B C read, '*His name and* His Father's name.' **in** [*epi*] —'upon.' God's and Christ's *name* here answers to the *seal* "upon their foreheads" in ch. vii. 3. As the 144,000 of Israel are "the first-fruits" (*v.* 4), so "the harvest" (*v.* 15) is the general assembly of Gentile saints to be translated by Christ as His first act in assuming His kingdom, prior to judgment (ch. xvi., the seven last vials) on the antichristian world, in executing which His saints shall share. As Noah and Lot were taken seasonably out of the *judgment*, but exposed to the *trial* till the last moment (*De Burgh*), so those who reign with Christ first suffer with Him—delivered out of the *judgments*, but not out of the *trials*. True Israelites cannot join in the idolatry of the beast any more than true Christians. The common affliction will draw closely together, in opposing the beast's worship, the Old Testament and New Testament people of God. Thus the way is paved for Israel's conversion. This last *scattering of the holy people's power* leads them, under the Spirit, to hail Messiah. "Blessed is He that cometh in the name of the Lord." **2. from**—'out of.' **voice of many waters.** As is the voice of Himself (ch. i. 15), such also is the voice of His people. **I heard the voice of harpers.** א A B C, *Origen*, read, 'the voice which I heard (was) as of harpers.' **3. sung**—'sing.' **as it were** [ὡς]. So A C, Vulgate. It is AS IT WERE a *new song:* for it is, in truth, as old as God's eternal purpose. But א B, Syriac, Coptic, *Origen, Andreas*, omit. **new song**—(ch. v. 9, 10.) The song is that of victory after conflict with the dragon, beast, and false prophet: never sung before; for such a conflict was never fought before. Till now Christ's kingdom on earth was usurped. They sing the new song in anticipation of His taking possession of His blood-bought kingdom with His saints. **four beasts**—'four living creatures.' The harpers and singers include the 144,000 (cf. ch. xv. 2, 3, where the same act is attributed to *the general company of saints*). Not as *Alford*, 'the harpers and song are in heaven, the 144,000 on earth.' Still, the 144,000 here are distinguished from the four living creatures, which represent the elect Church: as though the latter had the priority in heaven. **redeemed** [*eegorasmenoi*]—'purchased.' Not even the angels can learn that song; for they know not *experimentally* what it is to have 'come out of the great tribulation, and washed their robes white in

the blood of the Lamb' (ch. vii. 14). **4. virgins**—spiritually (Matt. xxv. 1): in contrast to the apostate church, Babylon (v. 8), 'a harlot' (ch. xvii. 1-5; Isa. i. 21). Contrast 2 Cor. xi. 2; Eph. v. 25-27. Their not being *defiled with women* means they were not led astray from Christian faithfulness by the spiritual 'harlot.' **follow the Lamb whithersoever he goeth**—in glory being especially near His person: the fitting reward of their following Him so fully on earth. **redeemed**—'purchased.' **being the**—rather, '*as a* first-fruit.' Not merely in the sense in which *all* believers are so (Jas. i. 18), but Israel's 144,000 elect are the first-fruit; the Gentile elect, of "every nation, kindred, tongue, and people," who refuse to worship the beast, are the *harvest:* in a further sense, the whole transfigured and translated Church, which reigns with Christ at His coming, is the *first-fruit*, and the consequent *universal* ingathering of Israel and the nations, ending in the last judgment, is the full harvest. **5. guile.** So *Andreas;* but א A B C, *Origen, Andreas*, in other copies, read, 'falsehood.' Cf. Ps. xxxii. 2; Isa. liii. 9; John i. 47. **for.** So א B, Syriac, Coptic, *Origen, Andreas;* but A C, Vulgate, omit. **without fault** [*amomoi*]—'blameless;' in sincere fidelity to Him. Not in themselves, but on the ground of His righteousness in whom alone they trusted, and whom they faithfully served by His Spirit in them (Ps. xv. 1, 2: cf. v. 1, 'stood on mount Sion'). **before the throne of God.** So oldest Vulgate; but א A B C, Syriac, Coptic, *Origen, Andreas*, omit.

6. Relating to the Gentile world, as the former verses related to Israel. Before the *end* the Gospel is to be preached for a WITNESS *unto all nations* (Matt. xxiv. 14); not that all shall be converted, but all shall have the opportunity given them of deciding whether they will be for Christ or antichrist. Those thus *preached* to are 'they that dwell (so A, Coptic, Syriac; but א B C, *Origen*, Vulgate, *Cyprian*, 312, 'SIT:' cf. Matt. iv. 16; Luke i. 79; having their *settled* home) on the earth,' being of the earth earthy. This last season of grace is given, if yet they may repent, before "judgment" (*v.* 7) descends: if not, they will be left without excuse, as the world which resisted the preaching of Noah in the 120 years, 'whilst the long-suffering of God waited.' 'So the prophets gave the people a last opportunity of repentance before the Babylonian destruction of Jerusalem, and our Lord and His apostles before the Roman destruction of the holy city' (*Auberlen*). "Unto" [*epi* in א A C; not in B]—*lit.*, 'upon,' 'over,' or 'in respect to' (Mark ix. 12; Heb. vii. 13). So also "TO every nation" [*epi* in א A B C, Vulgate, Syriac, *Origen, Andreas, Cyprian*]. This hints that the Gospel, though diffused *over* the globe, shall come savingly only *unto* the elect. The world

lasting gospel to preach unto them that dwell on the earth, and to every

7 nation, and kindred, and tongue, and people, saying with a loud voice, Fear God, and give glory to him; for the hour of his judgment is come: [h]and worship him that made heaven, and earth, and the sea, and the fountains of waters.

8 And there followed another angel, saying, [i]Babylon is fallen, is fallen, that great city, because she made all nations drink of the wine of the wrath of her fornication.

9 And the third angel followed them, saying with a loud voice, If any man worship the beast and his image, and receive *his* mark in his fore-

10 head, or in his hand, the same [j]shall drink of the wine of the wrath of God, which is poured out without mixture into the cup of his indignation; and he shall be tormented with fire and brimstone in the presence

11 of the holy angels, and in the presence of the Lamb: and [k]the smoke of their torment ascendeth up for ever and ever: and they have no rest day nor night, who worship the beast and his image, and whosoever receiveth the mark of his name.

12 Here [l]is the patience of the saints: here *are* [m]they that keep the com-

13 mandments of God, and the faith of Jesus. And I heard a voice from heaven saying unto me, Write, [n]Blessed *are* the dead [o]which die in

A. D. 96.

[h] Ex 20. 11.
Ps 33. 6.
Ps. 95. 5.
Ps. 124. 8.
Ps. 146. 5.
Neh. 9. 6.
Acts 14. 15.
Acts 17. 21.
[i] Isa. 21. 9.
Jer. 51. 8.
ch. 16. 19.
ch 17. 5.
ch. 18. 2.
[j] Ps. 75. 8.
Isa. 51. 17.
Jer. 25. 15.
[k] Isa. 34. 10.
[l] ch. 13. 10.
[m] ch. 12. 17.
[n] Eccl. 4. 1, 2.
ch. 20. 6.
[o] 1 (or 15.18.
1 Thes. 4.
16.

will not be evangelized till Christ comes; meanwhile God's purpose is 'to take out of the Gentiles a people for His name' (Acts xv. 14), as witnesses of the effectual working of the Spirit during the counter-working of "the mystery of iniquity." **everlasting gospel**—the *glad tidings* of the *everlasting* kingdom of Christ, about to ensue immediately after "judgment" on antichrist, announced as imminent in *v.* 7. As the former angel "flying through the midst of heaven" (ch. viii. 13) announced "woe," so this angel "flying in the midst of heaven" announces *joy*. The three angels making this last Gospel proclamation—the fall of Babylon (*v.* 8); the harlot, and judgment on the beast-worshippers (*vv.* 9-11); the voice from heaven respecting the blessed dead (*v.* 13); the vision of the Son of man on the cloud (*v.* 11); the harvest (*v.* 15); and the vintage (*v.* 18)—form the summary, amplified in the rest of the book. **7. Fear God**—forerunner to embracing the *love* of God in *the Gospel*. Repentance accompanies faith. **give glory to him**—not to the beast (cf. Jer. xiii. 16; ch. xiii. 4). **the hour** (the *definite time*) **of his judgment.** "Judgment," not general, but that upon Babylon, the beast, and his worshippers (*vv.* 8-12). **worship him that made heaven**—not antichrist, who "sitteth in the temple of God, showing himself that he is God" (cf. Acts xiv. 15). **sea . . . fountains**—distinguished in ch. viii. 8, 10. **8. another.** So Vulgate; but ℵ A B, Syriac, *Andreas*, 'another, a second angel.' **Babylon**—here first: *the harlot*, the apostate church: distinct from the beast: judged separately. **is fallen.** Anticipation of ch. xviii. 2. A, Vulgate, Syriac, *Andreas*, support the second "is fallen;" B C, Coptic, omit. **that great city.** A B C, Vulgate, Syriac, Coptic, omit "city." 'Babylon the great.' The ulterior fulfilment of Isa. xxi. 9. **because.** So *Andreas*; but A C, Vulgate, Syriac, read, 'which;' B, Coptic, omit. 'Which' gives the *reason* of her fall. **all nations.** A B C, 'all the nations.' **the wine of the wrath of her fornication**—*the wine of* God's *wrath*, the consequence *of her fornication*. As she made the nations drunk with her fornication, so she herself shall be made drunk with God's wrath. **9.** A B C, *Andreas*, read, 'another, a third angel.' Cf. ch. xiii. 15, 16. **10. The same**—'he also,' as the just, inevitable retribution (Ps. lxxv. 8).

without mixture. Wine was so commonly *mixed* with water, that to *mix* wine is used for to *pour out* wine. This wine of God's wrath is *undiluted :* no drop of water to cool its heat. Nought of grace or hope blended with it. God's threat may well raise us above fear of man's threats. This *unmixed* cup is already *mingled* for Satan and the beast's followers. **indignation**—*wrath* [*orges*], '*abiding.*' But "wrath" above [*thumou*] is *boiling indignation*, from [*thuo*] a root *to boil :* temporary ebullition of anger [*Ammonius : orge*], accompanied with a purpose of vengeance (*Origen*, 'On Psalm ii. 5'). **tormented . . . in the presence of the holy angels**—(Ps. xlix. 14; lviii. 10; cxxxix. 21; Isa. lxvi. 24.) God's enemies are regarded by saints as their enemies; and when the day of probation is past, their mind shall be so entirely one with God's, that they shall rejoice in witnessing God's righteousness judicially vindicated in sinners' punishment. **11. for ever and ever**—'unto ages of ages.' **no rest day nor night.** Contrast the same said of the four living creatures in heaven. "They rest not day and night, saying, Holy, holy, holy," &c. : yet they do "rest" in another sense: they rest from sin, sorrow, weariness, weakness, trial, and temptation (*v.* 13): the lost have no rest from sin, Satan, terror, torment, and remorse. The mediæval idea of devils tormenting men, and men blaspheming God for ever, is unscriptural. Every word of rebellion shall be eternally silenced, every act of evil repressed (cf. Matt. xxii. 12).

12. Here, &c. Resumed from ch. xiii. 10 (note). In the fiery persecution which awaits all who will not worship the beast, the *faith* and *patience* of the followers of *God and Jesus* shall be proved. **patience** [*hupomene*]—*persevering endurance.* The second "here" is omitted in ℵ A B C, Vulgate, Syriac, Coptic, *Primasius*. 'Here is the endurance of the saints, who keep,' &c. **the faith of** (exercised towards) **Jesus. 13.** Encouragement to those persecuted under the beast. **unto me.** Omitted in ℵ A B C, Vulgate, Syriac, Coptic. **Write**—on record for ever. **Blessed**—in *resting from their toils*, and, in the case of the saints, persecuted by the beast, in *resting from persecutions.* Their *blessedness* is now "from henceforth"—*i. e.,* FROM THIS TIME, when judgment on the beast and the harvest-gathering of the

the Lord [2]from henceforth: Yea, saith the Spirit, that [p]they may rest
from their labours; and their works do follow them.
14 And I looked, and behold a white cloud, and upon the cloud *one* sat
like unto [q]the Son of man, having on his head a golden crown, and in
15 his hand a sharp sickle. And another angel came out of the temple,
crying with a loud voice to him that sat on the cloud, [r]Thrust in thy
sickle, and reap: for the time is come for thee to reap; for the harvest
16 [s]of the earth is [3]ripe. And he that sat on the cloud thrust in his
sickle on the earth; and the earth was reaped.
17 And another angel came out of the temple which is in heaven, he also
18 having a sharp sickle. And another angel came out from the altar,
[t]which had power over fire; and cried with a loud cry to him that had
the sharp sickle, saying, [u]Thrust in thy sharp sickle, and gather the clus-
19 ters of the vine of the earth; for her grapes are fully ripe. And the angel
thrust in his sickle into the earth, and gathered the vine of the earth,
20 and cast *it* into [v]the great wine-press of the wrath of God. And [w]the
wine-press was trodden without [x]the city, and blood came out of the
wine-press, even unto the horse-bridles, by the space of a thousand *and*
six hundred furlongs.

15 AND I saw another sign in heaven, great and marvellous, [a]seven
angels having the seven last plagues; for [b]in them is filled up the wrath
of God.

A. D. 96.

2 Or, from henceforth saith the Spirit, Yea.
p Isa 57. 1, 2. 2 Thes. 1. 7. Heb. 4. 9.
q Eze. 1. 26. Dan. 7. 13. ch 1. 13.
r Joel 3. 13. Matt. 13.39.
s Jer. 51. 33. ch. 13. 12.
3 Or, dried.
t ch. 16. 8.
u Joel 3. 13.
v ch. 19. 15.
w Isa 63. 3. Lam. 1 15.
x Heb 13. 12. ch. 11 8.

CHAP. 15.
a ch. 16. 1. ch. 21. 9.
b ch. 14. 10.

elect are imminent. The time so longed for by former martyrs is now all but come: the full number of their fellow-servants is on the verge of completion: they have no longer to "*rest* (ch. vi. 10, 11, as here, *anapausis*) yet for a little season;" their eternal *cessation* from toils (2 Thess. i. 7 [*anesis*], relaxation after hardships. Heb. iv. 9, 10, *sabbatism of rest;* and God's *complete rest* [*catapausis*, akin to *anapausis*] is at hand now. They are *blessed* in being called to *the marriage supper of the Lamb* (ch. xix. 9), and having *part* IN THE *first resurrection* (ch. x . 6), and *right to the tree of life* (ch. xxii. 14). In *vv.* 14-16, follows *why* they are "blessed" *now* in particular—viz., *the Son of man on the cloud* is just coming to gather them in as *the harvest* ripe for His garner. **Yea, saith the Spirit.** The Father's words (the "voice from heaven") are echoed back by the Spirit (speaking in the Word, ch. ii. 7; xxii. 17; and in the saints, 2 Cor. v. 5; 1 Pet. iv. 14). All 'God's promises in Christ are yea' (2 Cor. i. 20). **that they may.** א A B C [*anapausontai*] (future indicative). They are blessed, *in that they* SHALL *rest from their toils* (so the Greek). **and** [*de*]. So B, *Andreas;* but א A C, Vulgate, Syriac, read, 'for.' They rest from toils, *because* their time for toil is past: they enter the *blessed rest, because* of their faith evinced by works, which 'follow WITH [*meta*] them.' In the coming judgment every man shall be 'judged according to his works.' His works do not go before the believer, nor even by his side, but *follow*, at the same time that they go *with*, him as a proof that he is Christ's.

14. one sat—'one sitting' [*cathemenon homoion* in א A B C, Vulgate, Coptic]. **crown** [*stephanon*] —*garland* of victory; not His *diadem* as King. The victory is described, ch. xix. 11-21. **15. Thrust in**—'Send.' The angel does not command the "Son of man" (*v.* 14), but, as messenger, announces to the Son the will of *God the Father*, in whose hands are *the times and the seasons.* **thy sickle**—(Mark iv. 29, where also He '*sendeth* the sickle.') The Son sends His sickle-bearing angel to reap *the righteous.* **harvest.** By the *harvest*-reaping the elect righteous are gathered; by the *vintage*, the antichristian offenders are removed out of the earth—the scene of Christ's coming kingdom (Matt. xiii. 41-43). The Son of man Himself, with a golden crown, is introduced in the *harvest*-gathering of the elect, a mere angel in the *vintage* (*vv.* 18-20). **is ripe**—'is dried:' all the bitter elements removed. Ripe for glory (Job v. 26). **16. thrust in**—'cast.'

17. out of the temple . . . in heaven—(ch. xi. 10.) **18. from the altar**—upon which were offered the incense-accompanied prayers of all saints, which bring down in answer God's fiery judgment on the Church's foes, the *fire* being *taken from the altar and cast upon the earth* (ch. vi. 9-11; viii. 3-5). **fully ripe**—for punishment [*eekmasen*]: 'come to their acmé' (Gen. xv. 16). **19.** "**The vine**" is the subject of judgment, because its grapes are not what God looked for after careful culture, but "wild grapes" (Isa. v. 4). Apostate Christendom, not heathendom, which has not heard of Christ, is the object of judgment. Cf. the emblem, Isa. lxiii. 2, 3; Joel iii. 12, 13; ch. xix. 15. **20. without the city**—Jerusalem. The scene of blood-shedding of. Christ and His people shall be also the scene of God's vengeance on the antichristian foe (ch. xix. 14). **blood**—the red wine. The slaughter of apostates is here meant, not their eternal punishment. **even unto the horse-bridles**—of the avenging "armies of heaven" (ch. ix. 16; xix. 14). **by the space of a thousand and six hundred furlongs**—'1,600 furlongs *off*' (*W. Kelly*). 1,600—a square number: 4 by 4 by 100. The *four* quarters—north, south, east, and west—of the Holy Land, or else of the world (the universality of the world-wide destruction being indicated). It does not exactly answer to the length of Palestine, as given by *Jerome*—160 Roman miles. *Bengel* thinks the valley of Kedron, between Jerusalem and the mount of Olives, is meant, its torrent being about to be discoloured with blood for 1,600 furlongs. This accords with Joel's prophecy, that the *valley of Jehoshaphat* is to be the scene of overthrow of the antichristian foes.

CHAP. XV. 1-8.—THE SEVEN LAST VIALS—SONG OF THE VICTORS OVER THE BEAST.

1. the seven last plagues—'seven plagues the

2 And I saw as it were ^ca sea of ^dglass mingled with fire; and them that had gotten the victory over the beast, ^eand over his image, and over his mark, *and* over the number of his name, stand on the sea of glass, having
3 the harps of God. And they sing ^fthe song of Moses the servant of God, and the song of the Lamb, saying, ^gGreat and marvellous *are* thy works, Lord God Almighty; just ^hand true *are* thy ways, thou King of ¹saints.
4 Who ⁱshall not fear thee, O Lord, and glorify thy name? for *thou* only *art* holy: for all nations shall come and worship before thee; for thy judgments are made manifest.

A. D 96.

^c ch. 4. 6.
^d Matt. 3. 11.
^e ch 13. 15.
^f Ex 15. 1.
^g Deut. 32. 4.
^h Hos. 14. 9.
¹ Or,
nations,
or, ages.
ⁱ Ex. 15. 14.

last.' **is filled up**—'was consummated:' prophetical past for the future, the future being to God as though past, so sure of accomplishment is His word. This is the summary of the vision that follows: the angels do not actually receive the vials till *v.* 7; but here, by anticipation, they are spoken of as *having* them. There are no more plagues until the Lord's coming in judgment. The destruction of Babylon (ch. xviii.) is the last: then (in ch. xix.) He appears.

2. **sea of glass**—answering to the molten sea or great brasen laver between the tabernacle of the congregation and the altar, for purifying the priests: typifying the baptism with water and the Spirit of all made kings and priests unto God. **mingled with fire**—answering to the *baptism with fire, i. e.,* fiery trial (Matt. xx. 23), as well as with the Holy Ghost, which Christ's people undergo to purify them, as gold loses its dross in the furnace. **them that had gotten the victory over**—'those (coming) off from (conflict with) the beast conquerors.' **over the number of his name.** א A B C, Vulgate, Syriac, and Coptic, omit "over his mark." *The mark* is the *number of his name* which the faithful refused to receive, and so were victorious over it. **stand on the sea of glass.** *Alford,* 'on (the shore of) the sea:' *at* the sea. [So *epi,* with the accusative, is used for *at,* ch. iii. 20. 'Standing' implies *rest; epi,* with the accusative, *motion towards.*] Thus the meaning is, having come TO the sea, and now *standing* AT it. In Matt. xiv. 26, where Christ walks *on* the sea, oldest MSS. have the genitive, not the accusative. Allusion is made to Israel standing *on the shore at the Red Sea,* after passing victoriously through it, when the Lord had destroyed the Egyptian foe (type of antichrist) in it. Moses' and Israel's song of triumph (Exod. xv. 1) has its antitype in the saints' 'song of Moses and the Lamb' (*v.* 3: cf. Isa. ii. 15). Still, "on the sea" is consistent with Greek; *Cyprian* and Vulgate support it: the sense is, As the sea typifies the troubled state out of which the beast arose, and is to be no more in the blessed world (ch. xxi. 1), so the victorious saints stand *on* it, *under their feet* (as the *woman* had the *moon,* ch. xii. 1, note); now no longer treacherous, wherein the feet sink, but solid like glass, as it was under the feet of Christ, whose triumph the saints now share. Firm footing amidst apparent instability is represented. They stand, not merely as victorious Israel *at* the Red Sea, and as John *upon* [*epi* with accusative] the sand of the shore (ch. xiii. 1), but *upon the sea* itself, now firm, and reflecting their glory as glass: past conduct shedding the brighter lustre on their present triumph. The happiness is heightened by retrospect of danger through which they have passed. So ch. vii. 14, 15. **harps of God**—in the hands of these heavenly *virgins* (ch. xiv. 4), infinitely surpassing the timbrels of Miriam and the Israelitesses. **3. the song of Moses . . . and . . . the Lamb.** The New Testament song which the Lamb shall lead, "the Captain of our salvation" (as Moses was leader of Israel), and in which those who conquer through Him (Rom. viii. 37) join (ch. xii. 11), is antitype to the triumphant Old Testament song of Moses and Israel at the Red Sea, (Exod. xv.) The Old and New Testament churches are essentially one in conflicts and triumphs. The two appear joined in this phrase, as in the "twenty-four elders." Isa. xii. foretells the song of the redeemed (Israel foremost) after the antitypical exodus and deliverance *at the Egyptian sea.* The passage through the Red Sea under the pillar of cloud was Israel's baptism, to which the believer's baptism in trials corresponds (1 Cor. x. 1). The elect after their *trials* (especially those from the beast) shall be taken up before the vials of *wrath* be poured on the beast and his kingdom. So Noah and his family were taken out of the doomed world before the deluge; Lot out of Sodom before its destruction; the Christians escaped by a special interposition of Providence to Pella, before the destruction of Jerusalem. As the pillar of *cloud* and *fire* interposed between Israel and the Egyptian foe, so that Israel safely landed on the opposite shore before the Egyptians were destroyed, so the Lord, coming with *clouds* and in flaming *fire,* shall first catch up His elect people "in the clouds to meet Him in the air," then shall with fire destroy the enemy. The Lamb leads the song in honour of the Father amidst the great congregation (Ps. xxii. 25). This is the "new song," ch. xiv. 3. The singular victors are the 144,000 of Israel, "the first-fruits," and the "harvest" of the Gentiles. **servant of God**—(Exod. xiv. 31; Num. xii. 7.) The Lamb is more: He is the SON (Heb. iii. 5, 6). **Great and marvellous are thy works, &c.** Part of Moses' last song. God's vindication of His justice, that He may be glorified, is His grand end. Hence His servants again and again dwell upon this (ch. xiv. 7; xix. 2; Prov. xvi. 4; Jer. x. 10; Dan. iv. 37). Especially at the judgment (Ps. l. 1-6; cxlv. 17). **saints.** A B, Coptic, *Cyprian,* read, 'of the NATIONS;' א C, 'of the ages;' so Vulgate and Syriac. The point at issue in the Lord's controversy with the earth is, whether He, or Satan's minion, the beast, is 'King of the nations;' here, at the eve of judgments descending on the kingdom of the beast, the transfigured saints hail Him as 'King of the nations' (Ezek. xxi. 27). **4. Who shall not**—'Who is there but must fear thee?' Cf. Moses' song, Exod. xv. 14-16, on the fear which God's judgments strike into the foe. **thee.** So א, Syriac; but A B C, Vulgate, *Cyprian,* reject "thee." **all nations shall come.** Alluding to Ps. xxii. 27-31: cf. Isa. lxvi. 23; Jer. xvi. 19. The conversion of *all nations* shall be when Christ shall come, and not till then; the first moving cause will be Christ's *manifested judgments* preparing all hearts for receiving Christ's mercy. He shall effect by His presence what we have in vain tried to effect in His absence. The present preaching of the Gospel is gathering out the elect remnant; meanwhile "the mystery of iniquity" is at work, and will at last come to its crisis: then shall judgment descend on the apostates at *the harvest-end of this age* (Matt. xiii. 39, 40), when the tares

5   And after that I looked, and, *ʲ*behold, the temple of the tabernacle of
6 the testimony in heaven was opened: and the seven angels came out of
the temple, having the seven plagues, clothed in *ᵏ*pure and white linen,
7 and having their breasts girded with golden girdles. And *ˡ*one of the
four beasts gave unto the seven angels seven golden vials full of the wrath
8 of God, who liveth for ever and ever. And *ᵐ*the temple was filled with
smoke from *ⁿ*the glory of God, and from his power; and no man was able
to enter into the temple, till the seven plagues of the seven angels were
fulfilled.

16   AND I heard a great voice out of the temple saying to the seven
angels, Go your ways, and pour out the vials of the wrath of God upon
the earth.

2   And the first went, and poured out his vial *ᵃ*upon the earth; and
*ᵇ*there fell a noisome and grievous sore upon the men which *ᶜ*had the
mark of the beast, and *upon* them which worshipped his image.

3   And the second angel poured out his vial upon the sea; and *ᵈ*it
became as the blood of a dead *man:* *ᵉ*and every living soul died in
the sea.

A. D. 96.

ʲ Num. 1. 50.
ch. 11. 19.
ᵏ Ex. 23. 6.
Eze. 44. 17.
ˡ ch. 4. 6.
ᵐ Ex. 40. 34.
1 Ki. 8. 10.
2 Chr 5. 14.
Isa. 6. 4.
ⁿ 2 Thes. 1.
9.

CHAP. 16.
ᵃ ch. 8. 7.
ᵇ Ex. 9. 9.
Deut. 7. 15.
Deut. 28-27.
1 Sam. 5. 6.
9.
2 Chr. 21. 15.
ᶜ ch. 13. 16.
ᵈ Ex. 7. 17.
ᵉ ch. 8. 9.

shall be cleared out of the earth, which thenceforward becomes Messiah's kingdom. The confederacy of apostates against Christ becomes,
when overthrown with fearful judgments, the very
means, in God's overruling providence, of preparing the nations not joined in the antichristian
league to submit themselves to Him. **judgments**
—'righteousnesses.' **are**—'were:' the prophetical
past for the immediate future.
  5. So ch. xi. 19: cf. ch. xvi. 17. 'The tabernacle of the testimony' appropriately comes to
view, where God's faithfulness in avenging His
people with judgments on their foes is set forth. We
need a glimpse within the Holy Place to "understand" (Dan x. 14) the secret spring and the end
of God's righteous dealings. **behold.** So Vulgate;
but omitted by א A B C, Syriac, *Andreas*. **6.**
having. So א B; but A C, 'who have:' not that
they had them yet (cf. *v.* 7), but by anticipation
described according to their office. **linen.** So B
א, 'linens;' but A C, Vulgate, *lithon*], 'a stone.'
The principle, that the harder reading is least
likely to be an interpolation, favours 'a stone pure
(*and* is omitted in א A B C, *Andreas*) brilliant'
[*lampron*], probably the diamond (cf. Acts i. 10;
x. 30). **golden girdles**—resembling the Lord (ch.
i. 13). **7. one of the four beasts**—'living creatures.' The presentation of the vials to the angels
by one of their living creatures implies the
Church's ministry as medium for manifesting to
angels the glories of redemption (Eph. iii. 10).
vials—'bowls:' a broad shallow cup. The breadth
in their upper part would cause their woe-contents
to pour out *all at once*, with overwhelming suddenness. **full of the wrath.** How sweetly the *vials*
full of odours—i. e., incense-perfumed prayers of
saints—contrast (ch. viii. 3, 4). **8. temple was filled**
(Isa. vi. 4: cf. Exod. xl. 34; 2 Chr. v. 14)—
the earthly temple, of which this is antitype.
the glory of God, and . . . power—then fully
manifested. **no man was able to enter into the**
temple—because of God's manifested glory and
power during these judgments.
  CHAP. XVI. 1-21.—SEVEN VIALS AND CONSE-
QUENT PLAGUES.
  The trumpets shook the world-kingdoms in a
longer process: the vials swiftly and suddenly
overthrow the kingdom of the beast, who invested
himself with the world-kingdom. The Egyptian
plagues were inflicted with but a month between
them severally (*Bengel*, referring to Seder Olam).

As Moses took ashes from an earthly furnace
(Exod. ix. 8), so angels, as priestly ministers in
the heavenly temple, take holy fire in sacred vials
from the heavenly altar, to pour down (cf. ch. viii.
5). The same heavenly altar which would have
kindled sweet incense of prayer, bringing down
blessing upon earth, by man's sin kindles the
fiery descending curse. Just as the Nile, ordinarily the source of Egypt's fertility, became blood
and a curse through Egypt's sin.
  1. a great voice—viz., God's. These seven
vials (the detailed expansion of *the vintage*, ch.
xiv. 18-20) being 'the last,' must be just when the
beast's power has expired (whence reference is
made in them all to the beast's worshippers as
objects of the judgments), close to the coming of
the Son of man. The first four are distinguished
from the last three, as in the case of the seven
seals and seven trumpets. The first four are
general—affecting the earth, sea, springs, and sun:
not merely a portion of these natural bodies, as
the trumpets, but the whole; the last three are
particular—affecting the throne of the beast, the
Euphrates, and the grand consummation. Some
of these judgments are given in detail, chs.
xvii.-xx. **out of the temple.** B, Syriac, omit;
but א A C, Vulgate, *Andreas*, support. **the vials.**
So Syriac, Coptic; but א A B C, Vulgate, *Andreas*,
read, 'the *seven* vials.' **upon**—'unto.'
  2. went—'away.' **poured out.** So the angel
cast fire into the earth previous to the series of
trumpets (ch. viii. 5). **upon.** So Coptic; but
A B C, Vulgate, Syriac, read, 'into.' **sore upon**
the men—antitype to the sixth Egyptian plague.
"Noisome"—'evil' (cf. Deut. xxviii, 27, 35). [*Hel-*
kos is used in LXX., as here.] The reason why
the sixth Egyptian plague is *first* here, is because
it was directed against the Egyptian magicians,
Jannes and Jambres, so that they could not stand
before Moses; so here the plague is upon those
who, in the beast-worship, practised sorcery. As
they submitted to the mark of the beast, so they
must bear the mark of the avenging God. Contrast Ezek. ix. 4, 6; ch. vii. 3. "Grievous"—distressing. **which had the mark of the beast.**
Therefore this first vial is subsequent to the
beast's rule.
  3. angel. So B, *Andreas;* but A C, Vulgate,
omit. **upon**—'into.' **became as the blood**—answering to another Egyptian plague. **of a dead**
man—putrefying. **living soul.** So א B, *Andreas:*

4 And the third angel poured out his vial upon the rivers and fountains
5 of waters; and they became blood. And I heard the angel of the waters
say, Thou *f* art righteous, O Lord, which *g* art, and wast, and shalt be,
6 because thou hast judged thus: for *h* they have shed the blood of saints
and prophets, *i* and thou hast given them blood to drink; for they are
7 worthy. And I heard another out of the altar say, Even so, Lord God
Almighty, *j* true and righteous *are* thy judgments.
8 And the fourth angel poured out his vial upon the sun; and power
9 was given unto him to scorch men with fire. And men were [1] scorched
with great heat, and blasphemed the name of God, which hath power
over these plagues: and *k* they repented not to give him glory.
10 And the fifth angel poured out his vial upon *l* the seat of the beast;
and his kingdom was full of darkness; and they gnawed their tongues for
11 pain, and blasphemed the God of heaven because of their pains and their
sores, and repented not of their deeds.
12 And the sixth angel poured out his vial *m* upon the great river
Euphrates; and *n* the water thereof was dried up, that *o* the way of the
13 kings of the east might be prepared. And I saw three unclean *p* spirits

A. D. 96.

f Ps. 97. 2.
g ch. 1. 4, 8.
ch. 4. 8.
ch. 11. 17.
h Matt. 23.34.
i Isa. 49. 16.
j ch. 13 10.
ch. 14. 10.
ch. 19. 2.
[1] Or,
burned.
k 2 Chr 28.22.
Isa. 8. 21.
Jer. 5. 3.
Dan. 5. 22.
l ch. 13. 2.
m ch. 9. 14.
n Jer. 50. 38.
Jer. 51. 36.
o Isa. 41. 2.
25.
p 1 John 4. 1.

but A C, Syriac, 'soul of life' (cf. Gen. i. 30; vii. 21, 22). **in the sea.** So B, *Andreas;* but A C, Syriac, 'as respects the things in the sea.'
4. (Exod. vii. 20.) **angel.** So Syriac, Coptic, *Andreas;* but א A B C, Vulgate, omit it. **5. angel of** (presiding over) **the waters. O Lord.** Omitted by א A B C, Vulgate, Syriac, Coptic, *Andreas.* **and shalt be.** א A B C, Vulgate, *Andreas,* for this clause, read, '(which art and wast) *holy*' [*hosios* for *ho esomenos*]. The Lord is no longer He that *shall be,* for He *is come* in vengeance; therefore the third of the three clauses, ch. i. 4, 8; iv. 8, is here, and in ch. xi. 17, omitted. **judged thus**—'these things.' 'Thou didst inflict this judgment.' **6.** (Gen. ix. 6; Isa. xlix. 26; ch. xi. 18, end.) Anticipation of ch. xviii. 20, 24: cf. **xiii. 15. For.** A B C, *Andreas,* omit: א, 'of which (blood) they are worthy.' **7. another out of.** Omitted in א A C, Syriac, Coptic. 'I heard **the altar** (personified) saying.' On it the prayers of saints are presented before God: beneath it are the martyrs' souls crying for vengeance on the foes of God.
8. angel. So א, Coptic, *Andreas;* but A B C, Vulgate, Syriac, omit. **upon.** Not as *vv.* 2, 3, 'into.' **sun.** Whereas by the fourth trumpet the sun is darkened (ch. viii. 12) in a third part, here, by the fourth vial, the sun's bright scorching power is intensified. **power was given unto him** —rather, 'unto *it:*' the sun. **men**—'the men;' those who had the mark of the beast (*v.* 2). **9. men** —'*the* men.' **repented not to give him glory**—(ch. ix. 20.) Affliction, if it does not melt, hardens. Cf. the better result on others (ch. xi. 13; xiv. 7; xv. 4).
10. angel So Coptic, *Andreas;* omitted by א A B C, Vulgate, Syriac. **seat**—'*throne* of the beast:' set up in arrogant mimicry of God's: the dragon gave his throne to the beast (ch. xiii. 2). **darkness**—parallel to the Egyptian plague. Pharaoh being type of antichrist (cf. ch. xv. 2, 3, notes: cf. the fifth trumpet, ch. ix. 2). **gnawed their tongues for pain**—'*owing to the* pain' of the previous plagues, rendered more appalling by the darkness. Or, as 'gnashing of teeth' is one of hell's accompaniments, so this 'gnawing of their tongues' is through rage at the baffling of their hopes and overthrow of their kingdom. They meditate revenge, but are impotent to effect it; hence their frenzy. Those in anguish, mental and bodily, bite their lips and tongues. **11. sores.** Therefore each fresh plague was accompanied with

the preceding plagues: there was an accumulation, not a mere succession, of plagues. **repented not** —(cf. *v.* 9.)
12. angel. So Coptic, *Andreas;* but א A B C, Vulgate, Syriac, omit. **kings of the east**—'the kings who are from the rising of the sun.' So *the Euphrates* is referred to in the sixth trumpet. The drying up of the *Euphrates* is figurative, as *Babylon* itself, situated on it, is undoubtedly so, ch. xvii. 5. The waters of the Euphrates (cf. Isa. viii. 7, 8) are spiritual Babylon's, the apostate church's spiritual and temporal powers. The drying up of Babylon's waters answers to the ten kings' stripping, eating, and burning the whore. The phrase 'way prepared for' is applied to *the Lord's coming* (Isa. xl. 3; Matt. iii. 3; Luke i. 76). He shall come *from the east* (Matt. xxiv. 27; Ezek. xliii. 2, "the glory of the God of Israel came *from the way of the east*"): not alone, for His elect transfigured saints of Israel and the Gentiles accompany Him, "*kings* and priests unto God" (ch. i. 6). As the antichristian ten *kings* accompany the beast, so the saints accompany as *kings* the *King of kings* to the last decisive conflict. *De Burgh,* &c., take it of *the Jews,* also designed to be *a kingdom of priests to God* on earth. They shall, doubtless, become priest-kings in the flesh to the nations in the flesh at His coming. Abraham from the east (if Isa. xli. 2, 8, 9 refers to him, and not Cyrus), conquering the Chaldean kings, is a type of Israel's victorious restoration to the priest-kingdom. Israel's exodus after the last Egyptian plagues typifies Israel's restoration, after the spiritual Babylon, the apostate Church, has been smitten. Israel's promotion to the priest-kingdom after Pharaoh's downfall, at the Lord's descent at Sinai to establish the theocracy, typifies the restored kingdom of Israel at the Lord's more glorious descent, when antichrist shall be destroyed utterly. Thus Israel secondarily may be meant by "the kings from the east," who shall accompany the "King of kings," returning "from the way of the east" to reign over His ancient people. As to the *drying up* again of the *waters* opposing His people's assuming the kingdom, cf. Isa. x. 26; xi. 11, 15: Zech. x. 9-11. Israel (Gen. xxxii. 28) implies a *prince with God* (cf. Mic. iv. 8). *Durham,* 200 years ago, interpreted the drying up of the Euphrates the wasting away of the Turkish power, which has heretofore held Palestine, so the way being prepared for Israel's restoration. But as *Babylon* is the apostate church, not Moham-

707

like frogs *come* out of the mouth of the ⁹dragon, and out of the mouth
14 of the beast, and out of the mouth of the false prophet.   For ʳthey are
the spirits of devils, working ˢmiracles, *which* go forth unto the kings of
the earth ᵗand of the whole world, to gather them to the ᵘbattle of that
15 great day of God Almighty.   Behold, ᵛI come as a thief.   Blessed *is* he
that watcheth, and keepeth his garments, ʷlest he walk naked, and they
16 see his shame.   And he gathered them together into a place called in the
Hebrew tongue Armageddon.
17   And the seventh angel poured out his vial into the air; and there
came a great voice out of the temple of heaven, from the throne, saying,
18 ˣIt is done.   And there were voices, and thunders, and lightnings; and

A. D. 96.

⁹ ch. 12 3.
ʳ 1 Tim. 4. 1.
  Jas. 3. 15.
ˢ 2 Thes. 2.
  9
ᵗ Luke 2. 1.
ᵘ ch. 20. 8.
ᵛ Matt 24 43.
  1 Thes 5.
  2.
2 Pet. 3. 10.
ʷ 2 Cor. 5 3.
ˣ ch. 21 6.

medanism, the drying up of the Euphrates (an-swering to Cyrus's overthrow of Babylon by marching into it through the dry channel of the Euphrates) must answer to the draining off of the apostate church's resources, the Roman and Greek apostasies having been heretofore the greatest bar-riers, by idolatries and persecutions, in the way of Israel's restoration and conversion. The earthly *kings of the earth* (v. 14) stand in contrast to the *kings from the east*, who are heavenly. **13. un-clean spirits like frogs**—antitype to the frogs sent on Egypt. The '*unclean spirit*' in the land (Palestine) is foretold, Zech. xiii. 2, in connection with idolatrous *prophets*. Beginning with in-fidelity, as to Christ's coming in the flesh, men shall end in gross idolatry of the beast, the incar-nation of all that is self-deifying and God-opposed in the world-powers of all ages. Having rejected Him that came in the Father's name, they shall worship one that comes in his own (John v. 43), really the devil's representative. As frogs croak by night in marshes, so these unclean spirits in dark error teach lies amidst the mire of filthy lusts. They talk of *liberty* (2 Pet. ii. 19), not Gospel liberty, but license for lust. There being *three*, as also *seven*, in the last and worst state of the Jewish nation (Matt. xii. 45), implies a parody of the two divine numbers, *three* of the Trinity, and *seven* of the Holy Spirit (ch. i. 4). *Three frogs* were the original arms of France, the centre of infidelity, socialism, and false spiritualism. א A B read, '*as it were* frogs,' instead of "*like* frogs." The unclean spirit out of the mouth of *the dragon* symbolizes proud infidelity opposing God and Christ. That out of *the beast's* mouth is the spirit of the world, which in politics, whether lawless democracy or despotism, sets man above God. That out of the mouth of *the false prophet* is lying spiritualism, which shall take the place of the superseded harlot. **the dragon**—Satan, who *gives his power and throne* (ch. xiii. 2) *to the beast.* **false prophet**—distinct from the harlot, the apostate church (of which Rome is the chief, though not sole, representative)' (ch. xvii. 1-3, 16); identical with *the second beast:* compare ch. xix. 20 with ch. xiii. 13; ultimately consigned to the lake of fire with the first beast; also the dragon a little later (ch. xx. 10). The dragon, beast, and false prophet, "the mystery of iniquity," form a blasphemous antitrinity, counterfeit of "the mys-tery of godliness," God manifest in Christ, wit-nessed to by the Spirit. The dragon personates the Father, assigning his authority to his representa-tive, the beast, as the Father assigns His to the Son. They are accordingly jointly worshipped : cf. as to the Father and Son, John v. 23: as the ten-horned beast has its ten horns crowned with *diadems* (ch. xiii. 1), so Christ has on His head *many diadems* (ch. xix. 12). Whilst the false pro-phet, like the Holy Ghost, speaks not of himself, but tells all men to worship the beast, and con-

firms his testimony by *miracles*, as the Holy Ghost attested Christ's divine mission. **14. devils**—'de-mons.' **working miracles**—'signs.' **go forth unto** [*epi*]—'for,' *i. e.*, to tempt them to the battle with Christ. **the kings of the earth and.** א A B, Syriac, *Andreas*, omit "of the earth and." [*Oikou-menes*], 'Kings of the whole habitable world,' 'of this world,' in contrast to "the kings of (from) the east" (the sunrising); v. 12, the saints to whom Christ *has appointed a kingdom* (Luke xxii. 29), "children of light." God, in permitting Satan's *miracles*, as in the Egyptian magicians His instru-ments in hardening Pharaoh's heart, gives the reprobate up to judicial delusion preparatory to their destruction (1 Ki. xxii. 22). As Aaron's rod was changed into a serpent, so were those of the Egyptian magicians. Aaron turned the water into blood ; so did the magicians. Aaron brought up frogs; so did the magicians. With the *frogs* their power ceased. So, whatever is antitypical to this, will be the last effort of the dragon, beast, and false prophet. **battle**—'war :' the final conflict for the kingship of the world (ch. xix. 17-21). **15.** The gathering of the world-kings with the beast against the Lamb presages Christ's coming; therefore He here gives the charge to be watching for His com-ing, clothed in the garments of justification and sanctification. **thief**—(Matt. xxiv. 43 ; 2 Pet. iii. 10.) **they**—saints and angels. **shame**—'unseem-liness' [*aschemosunee*, 1 Cor. xiii. 5; different from ch. iii. 18, *aischunee*]. **16. he**—rather, 'they (the three unclean spirits) gathered them together.' "He" (if retained) will refer to *God* giving them over to the delusion of the three unclean spirits, or else *the sixth angel* (v. 12). **Armageddon**—*Har*, a mountain, and *Megiddo*, in Manasseh of Galilee, the scene of overthrow of the Canaanite kings by God's miraculous interposition under Deborah and Barak; the great plain of Esdraelon. Josiah, too, as *ally of Babylon*, was defeated and slain at Megiddo ; and the mourning of the Jews just be-fore God shall interpose for them against all nations confederate against Jerusalem, is com-pared to the mourning for Josiah at Megiddo (Zech. xii. 11). [Megiddo comes from *gadad*, 'cut off'—i. e., *slaughter*. Cf. Joel iii. 2, 12, 14, where " the valley of Jehoshaphat" (*i. e.*, 'judgment of God') is mentioned as the scene of God's ven-geance on the God-opposing foe. Probably some great plain, antitypical to the valleys of Megiddo and Jehoshaphat, will be the scene.] **17. angel.** So *Andreas;* but א A B, Vulgate, Syriac, omit. **into.** So *Andreas* [*eis*]; but א A B, 'upon' [*epi*]. **great.** So א B, Vulgate, Syriac, Coptic, *Andreas;* but A omits. **of heaven.** So B, *Andreas;* but א A, Vulgate, Syriac, Coptic, omit. **It is done** [*Gegonen*]—' It is come to pass.' God's voice as to the consummation, as Jesus' voice on the Cross, when the expiation was com-pleted, "It is finished" [*Tetelestai*]. **18. voices, and thunders, and lightnings.** A has the order,

there was a great earthquake, ^ysuch as was not since men were upon
19 the earth, so mighty an earthquake, *and* so great. And ^zthe great
city was divided into three parts, and the cities of the nations fell: and
great Babylon ^acame in remembrance before God, ^bto give unto her the
20 cup of the wine of the fierceness of his wrath. And ^cevery island fled
21 away, and the mountains were not found. And ^dthere fell upon men a
great hail out of heaven, *every stone* about the weight of a talent: and
men blasphemed God because of the plague of the hail; for the plague
thereof was exceeding great.

17 AND there came ^aone of the seven angels which had the seven vials,
and talked with me, saying unto me, Come hither: I will show unto thee
2 the judgment of ^bthe great whore that ^csitteth upon many waters: with
whom the kings of the earth have committed fornication, and ^dthe inhabitants of the earth have been made drunk with the wine of her forni-
3 cation. So he carried me away in the spirit into the ^ewilderness: and I
saw a woman sit upon ^fa scarlet-coloured beast, full ^gof names of blas-

A. D. 96.	
^y Dan. 12. 1.	
^z ch. 14. 8.	
^a ch. 18.5.	
^b Isa 51. 17.	
Jer. 25. 15, 16.	
^c ch. 6. 14.	
^d ch. 11. 19.	
CHAP. 17.	
^a ch. 21. 9.	
^b Nah. 3. 4.	
2 Tim. 3. 1-6.	
2 Tim. 4. 3.	
^c Jer 51. 13.	
^d Jer. 51. 7.	
^e ch. 12. 6.	
^f ch. 12, 3.	
^g ch. 13. 1.	

'lightnings . . . voices . . . thunders.' The same
close as that of the seven seals and seven thunders; with the difference, that they do not merely
form the conclusion, but introduce the consequence, of the last vial—viz., the destruction of
Babylon, then of the antichristian armies. **earthquake**—often preceded by a lurid air, such as
would result from the vial poured upon it. **men
were.** So ℵ B, Vulgate, Syriac, *Andreas;* but A,
Coptic, read, 'a man was.' **so mighty**—'such.'
19. the great city—capital of the apostate church,
spiritual Babylon (of which Rome is the representative). The city, in ch. xi. 8 (note), is distinct
—viz., Jerusalem under antichrist (*the beast*, distinct from *the harlot*, or apostate church). Cf.
Zech. xiii. 8, 9, as to *Jerusalem*, "two parts shall
die, but the *third* shall be left." In ch. xi. 13,
only a *tenth* falls of Jerusalem; whereas here the
city (Babylon) 'became into three parts' by the
earthquake. Panslavism, Pantentonism, and Pan
latinism are the three divisions into which Christendom tends, the precursory sign of Babylon's
fall. **cities of the nations**—other great cities in
league with spiritual Babylon. **great Babylon
came in remembrance**—'Babylon the great was
remembered' (ch. xviii. 5). Now the last call to
escape from Babylon is given to God's people in
her (ch. xviii. 4). **fierceness**—the *boiling over* of
His wrath [*thumou orgees*] (note, ch. xiv. 10). **20.**
Parallel to ch. vi. 14-17; by anticipation descriptive of the last judgment. **the mountains**—
'there was found no mountains.' **21. fell**—
'descends.' **upon men**—'*the* men.' **men**—not
those struck who died, but the rest. Unlike the
result in Jerusalem (ch. xi. 13), where "the remnant were affrighted, and gave glory to the God of
heaven." **was**—'is.'

CHAP. XVII. 1-18.—THE HARLOT BABYLON'S
GAUD—THE BEAST SHE RIDES, HAVING SEVEN
HEADS AND TEN HORNS, THE INSTRUMENT OF
JUDGMENT ON HER.
As ch. xvi. 12 stated generally the vial judgment on *the harlot*, Babylon's power, so chs. xvii.
and xviii. give it in detail: so ch. xix. details the
judgment on the *beast* and the *false prophet*, summarily noticed, ch. xvi. 13-15, before the Lord's
coming.
1. unto me. ℵ A B, Vulgate, Syriac, Coptic,
omit. **many.** So ℵ A; but B, '*the* many waters'
(Jer. li. 13): *v.* 15, below, explains. The whore is
the church apostate, as *the woman* (ch. xii.) is *the
Church whilst faithful.* Satan having failed by
violence, succeeds in seducing her by the world's
allurements: unlike her Lord, she was overcome
709

(Luke iv. 6-8): hence she is seen *sitting on the
scarlet beast,* no longer the wife, but the harlot; no
longer Jerusalem, but spiritually Sodom (ch. xi.
8). **2. drunk with**—'owing to.' It cannot be
pagan, but papal, Rome, if a particular seat of
error be meant; but I think that the judgment
(ch. xviii. 2) and the spiritual fornication (ch. xviii.
3), though culminating in Rome, are not restricted to it, but comprise the whole apostate
church—Roman, Greek, and even Protestant—in so
far as it is seduced from its "first love" (ch. ii. 4)
to Christ, the heavenly Bridegroom, and gives its
affections to worldly idols. *E. L. Garrett's* explanation of 666 (ch. xiii. 8) holds good of the *whole* visible
Church in yielding to the number of the beast's
name, except the elect. The *woman* (ch. xii. 1) is
God's congregation in its purity under the Old and
New Testament, and appears again as Bride of the
Lamb, the transfigured Church prepared for the
marriage feast. The woman, the invisible Church,
is latent in the apostate church, the Church militant; the Bride is the Church triumphant. **3. the
wilderness.** Contrast her in ch. xii. 6, 14, having *a
place in the wilderness*-world, not a home; a sojourner, looking for the city to come. Now, on
the contrary, she is contented to have her portion in this moral wilderness. **upon a scarlet-
coloured beast.** The same as ch. xiii. 1: there
described as here, 'having seven heads and ten
horns (betraying that he is representative of the
dragon, ch. xii. 3), and upon his heads name of
blasphemy:' cf. also *vv.* 12-14, below, with ch.
xix. 19, 20, and ch. xvii. 13, 14, 16. Rome, resting
on the world-power, and ruling it by the claim of
supremacy, is her chief, though not exclusive,
representative. As the dragon is fiery-*red*, so the
beast is blood-red; implying *blood-guiltiness*, and
deep dyed sin. The *scarlet* is also symbol of kingship. **full**—all over: not merely "on his heads,"
as in ch. xiii. 1; for its opposition to God now
develops itself in all its intensity. Under the
harlot's superintendence, the world-power puts
forth blasphemous pretensions worse than in
pagan days. So the pope is placed by the
cardinal *in God's* (so-called) *temple on the altar to
sit there,* and the cardinals *kiss the feet* of the pope.
This ceremony is called, in Romish writers, *the
adoration* ('Histoire de Clergè Amsterd.,' 1716;
and *Lettenburgh's* 'Notitia Curiæ Romanæ,' 1683,
p. 125; *Heidegger,* 'Myst. Bab.,' i., 511, 514, 536). A
papal coin ('Numismata Pontificum,' Paris, 1679,
p. 5) has the *blasphemous* legend, 'Quem creant,
adorant.' [*Kneeling* and *kissing* are the worship
meant by *proskunein*: nine times used of the rival

4 phemy, having seven heads and ten horns. And the woman [h] was arrayed in purple and scarlet colour, and [1] decked with gold, and precious stones, and pearls, [i] having a golden cup in her hand full of abominations and

5 filthiness of her fornication: and upon her forehead *was* a name written, [j] MYSTERY, BABYLON THE GREAT, THE MOTHER OF [2] HAR-

6 LOTS AND ABOMINATIONS OF THE EARTH. And I saw the

A. D. 96.

h ch. 18. 12.
1 gilded.
i Jer 51. 7
j 2 Thes. 2 7.
2 Or, forni-
cations.

of God.] *Abomination* is the scriptural term for idol, or creature worshipped with the homage due to the Creator. Still, there is some check on the world-power whilst ridden by the harlot: the consummated antichrist will be when, having destroyed her, the beast shall be revealed as the concentration of all self-deifying God-opposed principles which have appeared in various forms and degrees heretofore. 'The Church has gained outward recognition by leaning on the world-power, which in its turn uses the Church for its own objects: such is Christendom ripe for judgment' (*Auberlen*). The seven heads in the view of many are Rome's seven successive governments: kings, consuls, dictators, decemvirs, military tribunes, emperors, the German emperors (*Wordsworth*), of whom Napoleon is the successor (*v.* 11). See, rather, notes, *vv.* 9, 10. The crowns on the ten horns (ch. xiii. 1) have disappeared: perhaps an indication that the ten kingdoms into which the Germanic-Sclavonic world (*the old Roman empire*, the East as well as the West, the two legs of the image with five toes on each) is to be divided will lose their monarchical form in the end (*Auberlen*); but *v.* 12 seems to imply crowned *kings*. 4. Scarlet is the colour reserved for popes and cardinals. Paul II. made it penal for any but cardinals to wear scarlet hats: cf. 'Cœremoniale Rom.,' iii., sec. 5, c. 5. This book was compiled more than 340 years ago by *Marcellus*, a Romish archbishop, and dedicated to Leo X. In it are enumerated five articles of dress, all *scarlet;* a vest studded with *pearls.* The pope's mitre is of *gold* and *precious stones.* The very characteristics outwardly which Revelation thrice assigns to the harlot or Babylon. *Joachim*, an abbot from Calabria, A. D. 1200, when asked by Richard of England, who summoned him to Palestine, concerning antichrist, replied that ' he was born long ago at Rome, and is now exalting himself above all that is called God.' *Roger Hoveden* (' Angl. Chron.,' i., 2) wrote, ' The harlot arrayed in gold is the Church of Rome.' Whenever and wherever the Church, instead of being "clothed (as ch. xii. 1) with the sun" of heaven, is arrayed in earthly gauds, compromising the truth of God through fear, or flattery, of the world's power, science, or wealth, she becomes *the harlot seated on the beast*, and doomed in righteous retribution to be *judged by the beast* (*v.* 16). Soon, like the Jews of the apostles' time leagued with heathen Rome, she becomes persecutor of the saints (*v.* 6). Instead of drinking her Lord's "cup" of suffering, she has "a cup full of abominations." Rome, in medals, represents herself holding *a cup* with the self-condemning inscription, '*Sedet super universum.*' Meanwhile the world-power gives up its hostility, and accepts Christianity externally: the beast gives up its God-opposed character, the woman gives up her divine one. They meet half-way by mutual concessions: Christianity becomes worldly, the world Christianized. The gainer is the world, the loser the Church. The beast receives a *deadly wound* (ch. xiii. 3), but is not really transfigured: he will return worse than ever (*vv.* 11-14). The Lord alone by His coming can make the kingdoms of this world His kingdoms. The "purple" is badge of empire: as in mockery it was put on

our Lord. decked — 'gilded.' stones — 'stone.' filthiness. א A B, *Andreas*, read, 'the filthy (impure) things.' 5. upon her forehead ... name—as harlots had. What a contrast to "HOLINESS TO THE LORD," inscribed on the mitre on the high priest's *forehead.* mystery—a spiritual fact heretofore hidden, incapable of discovery by reason, but now revealed. As the union of Christ and the Church is a 'great mystery' (a momentous spiritual truth, once hidden, now revealed, Eph. v. 31, 32), so the Church, by conformity to the world, becoming a harlot, is a counter "mystery." As iniquity in the harlot is a leaven working in "*mystery*"—i. e., latently (' the *mystery* of iniquity')—so, when she is destroyed, the iniquity shall be *revealed* in *the man of iniquity*, the open embodiment of all previous evil (2 Thess. ii. 7, 8). Contrast the "mystery of God" and "godliness," ch. x. 7 ; 1 Tim. iii. 16. Rome crucified Christ; destroyed Jerusalem and scattered the Jews; persecuted the early Christians in pagan times, and Protestant Christians in papal times ; and probably shall be restored to its pristine grandeur, as under the Cæsars, just before the burning of the harlot and of itself with her. So *Hippolytus* ('De Antichristo,' in the second century) thought. Popery cannot be at once the '*mystery* of iniquity' and the *manifested* antichrist. Probably it will compromise for political power (*v.* 3) the Christianity still in its creed, and thus prepare for antichrist's manifestation. The name Babylon given in the image, Dan. ii., to the *head*, is here given to the harlot. This connects her with the fourth kingdom, Rome, the last part of the image. Benedict XIII., in his indiction for a jubilee, A. D. 1725, called Rome '*mother* of all believers, and mistress of all churches' (harlots like herself). [The correspondence of syllables and accents is striking: *Hè pórne kaì tò theríon; Hé númphe kaì tò arníon.* The whore and the beast; the Bride and the Lamb.] OF HARLOTS—'of *the* harlots and of *the* abominations.' Not merely Rome, but Christendom, as a whole, as Israel, as a whole (Isa. i. 21), has become a harlot. The invisible Church of believers is hidden in the visible. The lines which separate harlot and woman are not denominational, but can only be spiritually discerned. If Rome were the *only* Babylon, much of the spiritual profit of Revelation would be lost to us; but the harlot "sitteth upon many waters" (*v.* 1), and "ALL nations have drunk of the wine of her fornication" (*v.* 2; ch. xviii. 3; "the earth," ch. xix. 2). External extensiveness over the world, and internal conformity to it—worldliness in extent and contents—is symbolized by the world-city's name, "Babylon." As the sun shines on all the earth, thus the woman clothed with the sun is to let her light penetrate to the uttermost parts. But she, in externally Christianizing the world, permits herself to be seduced by it: thus her catholicity is not that of the *Jerusalem* we look for ("the MOTHER of us all," Isa. ii. 2-4; Gal. iv. 26; ch. xxi. 2), but that of *Babylon*, the world-wide harlot city! [As Babylon was destroyed, and the Jews restored to Jerusalem, by Cyrus, so our Cyrus (Persian, the *sun*), the Sun of righteousness, shall bring Israel, literal and spiritual, to the holy Jerusalem at His coming.

woman drunken with the blood of the saints, and with the blood of *k*the martyrs of Jesus: and when I saw her, I wondered with great admiration.

7 And the angel said unto me, Wherefore didst thou marvel? I will tell thee the mystery of the woman, and of the beast that carrieth her, which hath the seven heads and ten horns.

8 The beast that thou sawest was, and is not; and *l*shall ascend out of the bottomless pit, and go into perdition: and they that dwell on the earth shall wonder, (whose names were not written in the book of life from the *m*foundation of the world,) when they behold the beast that was, and is not, and yet is.

9 And *n* here *is* the mind which hath wisdom. *o*The seven heads are 10 seven mountains, on which the woman sitteth. And there are seven

A. D. 96.

k Acts 22. 20.
ch. 2. 13.
ch 6. 9.
ch 12. 11.
l ch. 11. 7.
ch. 13. 1.
m Matt. 25. 34.
John 17. 24.
Acts 15. 18.
Eph 1. 4.
n Dan. 12, 4.
Hos. 4. 9.
Matt. 13. 11.
Matt. 24. 15.
ch .13. 18.
o ch. 13. 1.

Babylon and Jerusalem are the two opposite poles of the spiritual world.] Still, Rome is not accidentally, but in its very PRINCIPLE, a harlot, metropolis of whoredom, "the mother of harlots;" whereas the Evangelical Protestant Church is, in her principle, a chaste woman: the Reformation was the woman's protest against the harlot. The spirit of heathen Rome had, before the Reformation, changed the Church in the West into a *Church-State*, Rome; and in the East, into a *State-Church*, fettered by the world-power, having its centre in Byzantium. The Roman and Greek churches have thus fallen from the spiritual essence of the Gospel into the elements of the world (*Auberlen*). Cf. the woman "Wickedness" or 'lawlessness,' '*iniquity*' (Zech. v. 7, 8, 11), carried to *Babylon:* cf. "the mystery of iniquity," 'the man of sin,' 'that *wicked* one,' lit., '*the lawless one*' (2 Thess. ii. 7, 8; also Matt. xxiv. 12). 6. **martyrs** — witnesses. **I wondered with great admiration**—wonder. John did not *admire* her. Elsewhere (ch. xiii. 3; *v.* 8), all the earthly-minded *wonder* in admiration of the beast. Here only is John's *wonder* called forth: not the *beast*, but the woman sunken into the harlot, the Church become a world-loving apostate, moves his astonishment at so awful a change. That the world should be beastly is natural; but that the faithful bride should become the whore is monstrous, and excites the same amazement in him as Israel's like transformation excited in Isaiah and Jeremiah. "Horrible thing" (Jer. ii. 20, 21; xxiii. 14) answers to "abominations" here. '*Corruptio optimi pessima:*' when the Church falls, she sinks lower than the godless world, in proportion as her right place is higher than the world. In *v.* 3, "woman" has not the article, '*the* woman,' as if before mentioned: for though identical in one sense with the *woman* (ch. xii.), in another she is not. The elect never become apostates, but remain as *the* true *woman* invisibly in the *harlot;* yet Christendom, regarded as *woman*, has apostatized from its first *faith*. **8. beast . . . was, and is not**—(cf. *v.* 11.) The time when the beast "is not" is during 'the deadly wound' (ch. xiii.): the time of *the seventh head's* Christianity, when its beast-like character was suspended temporarily. The *healing of its wound* answers to its *ascending out of the bottomless pit.* The antichristian world-power returns worse than ever, with Satanic powers from hell (ch. xi. 7), not merely from *the sea* of convulsed nations (ch. xiii. 1). Christian civilization smites the beast but for a time: the *deadly wound* is always connected with its being *healed* up, the non-existence of the beast with its reappearance. Daniel does not even notice any change in the world-power effected by Christianity. We are endangered on one side by the harlot's spurious

Christianity, on the other by the beast's open anti-Christianity: the third class is Christ's 'little flock.' go. So א B, Vulgate, *Andreas*, read future; but A, *Irenæus*, 'goeth.' **into perdition**. The continuance of this revived seventh (*i. e.*, the eighth) head is short: it is therefore called 'the son of perdition,' essentially doomed to it immediately after his appearance. **names were**. So ℣, Vulgate, *Andreas;* but A B, Syriac, Coptic, singular, 'name is.' **written in**—'*upon*.' **which**—rather, 'when they behold the beast *that* it was,' &c. So Vulgate. **was, and is not, and yet is**. A B, *Andreas*, read, '. . . and shall come' (*lit.*, 'be present' [*parestai*]). The *tetragrammaton*, or sacred four letters in *Jehovah*, 'who is, was, and is to come,' the believer's worship, has its counterpart in the beast 'who was, and is not, and shall be present,' the object of the earth's worship (*Bengel*). They exult with *wonder* that the beast, which seemed to have received its death-blow from Christianity, *is on the eve of reviving* with greater power than ever on the ruins of that religion which tormented them (ch. xi. 10). **9.** Cf. ch. xiii. 18; Dan. xii. 10. Spiritual discernment is needed to understand the symbolical prophecy. **seven heads are seven mountains.** The connection between *mountains* and *kings* must be deeper than the outward fact to which allusion is made, that Rome (the then world-city) is on seven hills [whence she observed a *Septimontium*, the feast of the seven-hilled city (*Plutarch*); and on imperial coins she is represented as a *woman seated on seven hills*—Coin of Vespasian, 'Roman Coins,' p. 310; *Ackerman*, i., p. 87]. The seven heads can hardly be at once seven *kings* or kingdoms (*v.* 10), and seven geographical *mountains*. But, as the *head* is prominent in the body, so the *mountain* in the land. Like 'sea,' 'earth,' "waters . . . peoples" (*v.* 15), so "mountains" have a symbolical meaning, viz., prominent seats of power. Especially such as oppose the cause of God (Ps. lxviii. 16, 17; Isa. xl. 4; xli. 15; xlix. 11; Ezek. xxxv. 2); Babylon geographically in a *plain*, spiritually is "a destroying *mountain*" (Jer. li. 25), in majestic contrast to which stands mount Zion, "the mountain of the Lord's house" (Isa. ii. 2); ch. xxi. 10, "a great and high mountain . . . that great city, the holy Jerusalem." So in Dan. ii. 35, the *stone* becomes a *mountain*—Messiah's universal kingdom supplanting the world-kingdoms. As nature shadows forth spiritual realities, so seven-hilled Rome is *a* representative of the seven-headed world-power, of which the dragon is the prince. The "seven kings" are hereby distinguished from the "ten kings" (*v.* 12): the former are what the latter are not, "mountains," great seats of the world-power. The seven universal God-opposed monarchies are Egypt (the first

kings: five are fallen, and one is, *and* the other is not yet come; and
11 when he cometh, he must continue a short space. And the beast that
was, and is not, even he is the eighth, and is of the seven, and goeth into
perdition.
12 And *ᵖ* the ten horns which thou sawest, are ten kings, which have
received no kingdom as yet; but receive power as kings one hour with
the beast.

A. D. 96.

P Dan. 2. 40.
Dan. 7. 20.
Dan. 8. 20,
24.
Zech. 1. 18.
21.
ch. 12. 3.
ch. 13. 1.

world-power arrayed against God's people), Assyria, Babylon, Greece, Medo-Persia, Rome, the Germanic Sclavonic empire (the *clay* of the fourth kingdom mixed with its iron in Nebuchadnezzar's image, a *fifth* material, Dan. ii. 33, 34, 42, 43, symbolizing this last head). These seven might accord with the seven heads in Dan. vii. 4-7, *one* head on the first beast (Babylon), *one* on the second (Medo-Persia), *four* on the third (Greece; viz., Egypt, Syria, Thrace with Bithynia, and Greece with Macedon); but Egypt and Greece are in both lists. Syria answers to Assyria (from which 'Syria' is abbreviated), and Thrace with Bithynia answers to the Gothic-Germanic-Sclavonic hordes which, pouring on Rome from the North, founded the Germanic-Sclavonic empire. *The woman sitting on the seven* implies the Old and New Testament Church conforming to, and resting on, the world-power, the seven world-kingdoms. Abraham and Isaac dissembling as to their wives, through fear of kings of Egypt, foreshadowed this. Cf. Ezek. xvi. and xxiii., on Israel's whoredoms with Egypt, Assyria, Babylon; Matt. vi. 24; xxiv. 10-12, 23-26; Col. iii. 5, on the New Testament Church's harlotry—viz., distrust, hatred, treachery, party divisions, false doctrine. **10. there are**—or, 'they (the seven heads) are seven kings.' They are "mountains" (*v.* 9) in relation to the woman who sits on them; "kings" in relation to the beast of which they are heads. **five . . . one**—'the five . . . the one:' the first five are *fallen* (applicable not to *forms of government*, but to once powerful empires: Egypt (Ezek. xxix., xxx.), Assyria, Nineveh (Nah. iii. 1-19), Babylon (Jer. l. and li.), Medo-Persia (Dan. viii. 3-7, 20-22; x. 13; xi. 2), Greece (Dan. xi. 4). *Rome* was 'the one' existing in St. John's days. "Kings" stand for *kingdoms*, because these are represented in character by some one head, as Babylon by Nebuchadnezzar, Medo-Persia by Cyrus, Greece by Alexander, &c. But *Elliott*, The seventh short-lived ruling head, next after the sixth in John's time, with the Asiatic DIADEM (cf. *v.* 1), not the Roman *laurel* crown, is the new quadripartite headship, instituted by Diocletian, which was *short-lived*, falling after thirty years by Constantine's victory. The new head, out of the cicatrice of the old amputated seventh, is heathenish, though professedly Christian, the eighth, yet one of the seven in character, the second beast, the papacy with its two lamb-horns, the secular and the regular clergy(?). **the other is not yet come**. Not as *Alford*, the *Christian* empire *beginning with Constantine*; but the *Germanic-Sclavonic* empire *beginning* and continuing beast-like, *i.e.*, HEATHEN for only "a short space." The time when "it is not" (*v.* 11), is whilst it is "wounded to death" with the "deadly wound" (ch. xiii. 3). The Christianization of the northern hordes which descended on Rome is the *wound* to the beast, answering to the *earth swallowing up the flood* (heathen tribes) sent by the dragon to drown the woman (ch. xii. 15, 16). The emphasis is on "a *short* space" (first in the Greek); not on (as *Alford*) "he must continue." The external Christianization (whilst the beast's wound continues) has lasted more than fourteen centuries, since Constantine. Rome and the Greek

churches partially healed the wound by restoring image-worship. **11. beast that . . . is not**—his beastly character being kept down by outward Christianization of the state until he starts to life again as "the eighth" king, his 'wound being healed' (ch. xiii. 3), antichrist manifested in fullest opposition to God. HE [*autos*] is emphatical. *He*, pre-eminently: to whom the ten kings or kingdoms "give their power and strength" (*vv.* 12, 13, 17). That a *personal* antichrist will head the antichristian kingdom, is likely, from the analogy of Antiochus Epiphanes, the Old Testament antichrist, "the little horn" (Dan. viii. 9-12); "the son of perdition" (2 Thess. ii. 3-8), answers to 'goeth into perdition,' and is applied to an individual, Judas, in the only other passage where it occurs (John xvii. 12). He is a child of destruction, and has but a little time ascended out of the bottomless pit, when he 'goes into perdition' (*vv.* 8, 11). 'Whilst the Church passes through death of the flesh to glory of the Spirit, the beast passes through glory of the flesh to death' (*Auberlen*). **is of the seven**—'springs *out of* the seven.' The eighth is not merely one *of* the seven restored, but a new power proceeding *out of* the seven. At the same time, there are not *eight*, but only *seven* heads, for the eighth is the embodiment of all the God-opposed features of the seven. In the birth-pangs which prepare the 'regeneration,' there are *wars, earthquakes*, and *disturbances* (*Auberlen*), wherein antichrist takes his rise ("sea," ch. xiii. 1; Mark xiii. 8; Luke xxi. 9-11, 25, 26). He does not *fall* like the other seven (*v.* 10), but is *destroyed, going to* his own *perdition*, by the Lord in person. **12. ten kings . . . received no kingdom as yet; but receive power as kings . . . with the beast.** Hence, and from *vv.* 14, 16, it seems that these ten kings or kingdoms are to be *contemporaries with the beast* in its last or eighth form, viz., antichrist. Cf. Dan. ii. 34, 44, "the stone smote the image upon *his feet*"—i. e., upon the *ten* toes, which are, in *vv.* 41-44, interpreted "*kings*." The ten kingdoms are not, therefore, ten which arose in the overthrow of Rome (heathen), but are to rise out of the last state of the fourth kingdom under the eighth head. Three of the former ten, the fourth kingdom's little horn, the papacy, starting *subsequently*, absorbed Dan. vii. 8. But *the last ten* of the fourth kingdom, the 'ten toes,' shall tread down the earth as ten *simultaneous* kingdoms, subordinate to the beast. *Alford* observes, "*as* kings" implies that they reserve their kingly rights and *name* in giving "their power and strength unto the beast" (*v.* 13; note, *v.* 3). **one hour**—a definite short *time*, during which "the devil is come down to the inhabiters of the earth and of the sea, having great wrath, because he knoweth that he hath but a *short time*' (ch. xii. 12). Probably the three and a half years (ch. xi. 2, 3; xiii. 5). Antichrist exists long before Babylon's fall; but it is only then he obtains the vassalage of the ten kings. He first imposes on the Jews as Messiah, then persecutes those who refuse his blasphemous pretensions. Not until the sixth vial, in the latter part of his reign, does he associate the ten kings with him in war with the Lamb, having gained them over by the spirits of devils working

13   These have ^q one mind, and shall give their power and strength unto
14 the beast. These ^r shall make war with the Lamb, and the Lamb shall overcome them : ^s for he is Lord of lords, and King of kings: and ^t they that are with him *are* called, and chosen, and faithful.
15   And he saith unto me, ^u The waters which thou sawest, where the whore sitteth, ^v are peoples, and multitudes, and nations, and tongues.
16 And the ten horns which thou sawest upon the beast, ^w these shall hate the whore, and shall make her desolate ^x and naked, and shall eat her
17 flesh, and ^y burn her with fire. For ^z God hath put in their hearts to fulfil his will, and to agree, and give their kingdom unto the beast, ^a until the words of God shall be fulfilled.
18   And the woman which thou sawest ^b is that great city, ^c which reigneth over the kings of the earth.

A. D. 96.

q Rom. ъ. 7.
r ch 16. 14.
s Dent 10.17.
1 Tim 6.15.
t Jer. 50. 44.
1 Pet. 2. 9.
u Isa. 8. 7.
v ch 13. 7.
w Jer. 50. 41.
x Eze. 16. 37-44.
y ch. 19. 8.
z Rom. 1. 26.
a ch. 10. 7.
b ch. 16. 19.
c ch. 12. 4.

miracles. His connection with Israel appears from his sitting "in the temple of God" (2 Thess. ii. 4), the antitypical "abomination of desolation standing in the Holy Place" (Dan. ix. 27; xii. 11; Matt. xxiv. 15), "in the city where our Lord was crucified" (ch. xi. 8). *Irenæus* ('Hær.,' v., 25) and *St. Cyril* of Jerusalem ('Ruffinus Hist.,' x., 37) prophesied that antichrist should have his seat at Jerusalem, and restore the kingdom of the Jews. Julian the apostate took part with the Jews, and aided in building their temple, herein being antichrist's forerunner. **13. one mind** [*gnomen*]—one *sentiment*. **shall give.** So Coptic; but א A B, Syriac, 'give.' **strength**—'authority.' They become his dependent allies (*v.* 14). Thus antichrist claims to be *king of kings*. Scarcely has he made his claim when *the* KING OF KINGS appears and destroys him as in a moment. **14. These shall make war with the Lamb**—in league with the beast: a summary anticipation of ch. xix. 19 : not till they have first executed judgment on the harlot (*vv.* 15, 16). **Lord of lords**, &c. Anticipating ch. xix. 16. **are** —not in the Greek. 'And they that are with Him, called, chosen, and faithful (shall overcome them—viz., the beast and his allied kings).' These have been with Christ in heaven, but now appear with Him. **15. waters ... where the whore sitteth**—(Isa. viii. 7; *v.* 1.) In impious parody of Jehovah, who 'sitteth upon the flood' (*Alford*). Contrast the "many waters," ch. xix. 6, "Alleluia." The 'peoples,' &c., mark the universality of the Church's spiritual fornication. The 'tongues' remind us of Babel, the confusion of *tongues*, the beginning of Babylon, and of idolatrous apostasy after the flood, as the tower was doubtless dedicated to the deified heavens. Thus, Babylon is the harlot's appropriate name. The pope, as her chief representative, claims a double supremacy over all *peoples*, typified by the "two swords" (Luke xxii. 38); according to Boniface VIII., in the Bull, '*Unam Sanctum*,' and represented by the two keys—viz., spiritual, as the universal bishop, whence he is crowned with the mitre; and temporal, whence he is also crowned with the tiara, in token of imperial supremacy. Contrast with the pope's *diadems* the 'many diadems' of Him who alone, and of right, shall exercise the twofold dominion (ch. xix. 12). **16. upon the beast.** א A B, Vulgate, Syriac, read, '*and* the beast.' **shall make her desolate**—having first dismounted her from her seat (*v.* 3). **naked**—stripped of all her gaud (*v.* 4). As Jerusalem used the world-power to crucify her Saviour, and then was destroyed by that very power, Rome, so the Church, having apostatized to the world, shall have judgment executed on her by the world-power, the beast and his allies. These afterwards shall have judg-

ment executed on them by Christ Himself. So Israel leaning on Egypt, a broken reed, is pierced by it, then Egypt itself is punished. So Israel's whoredom with Assyria and Babylon was punished by the Assyrian and Babylonian captivities. So the Church going a whoring after the world, as if it were the reality, instead of witnessing against its apostasy, is false to its profession : being no longer a reality herself, she is judged by that world which for a time used her to further its ends, whilst all the while 'hating' Christ's unworldly religion, but which now no longer wants her aid. **eat her flesh**—plural, 'masses of flesh ;' *i. e.*, 'carnal possessions;' implying the *gross carnalities* into which she is sunk. The judgment on the harlot is again and again described : first, by an "angel having great power" (ch. xviii. 1), then by "another voice from heaven" (ch. xviii. 4-20), then by "a mighty angel" (ch. xviii. 21-24), then by the jubilant voice of much people in heaven (ch. xix. 2). Cf. Ezek. xvi. 37-44, originally Israel; further applicable to the New Testament Church when fallen into spiritual fornication. On "eat . . . flesh," for *prey upon one's property, character,* and *person,* cf. Ps. xiv. 4; xxvii. 2; Jer. x. 25; Mic. iii. 3. The first Napoleon's edict at Rome, in 1809, confiscating the papal dominions, and lately the severance of large portions of territory from the pope's sway, for union to the kingdom of Italy, through Louis Napoleon, are a first instalment of the whore's complete destruction. "Her flesh" points to her temporal resources, as distinguished from 'herself.' How striking a retribution, that having obtained her first temporal dominions, the exarchate of Ravenna, the kingdom of the Lombards, and the state of Rome, by recognizing the *usurper* Pepin as lawful king of France, she should be stripped of her dominions by another usurper of France, the Napoleonic dynasty ! After temporal sovereignty and possessions shall be lost to the apostate church, she may prove to be the "false prophet," combining with the beast and dragon. The Reformation saved Christianity from the infidelity with which it was threatened under Pope Leo. **burn her with fire** —the legal punishment of abominable fornication (Lev. xx. 14; xxi. 9). **17. hath put**—prophetical past for the future. **fulfil**—'do,' 'accomplish.' [*Poiesai* is distinct from 'fulfilled,' *telesthesontai,* below.] **his will**—*His purpose;* whilst they think only of doing their own. **to agree**—*lit.,* 'to do one purpose.' So א B; A, Vulgate, omit this clause. **the words of God** [*ta rhemata*]—foretelling the beast's rise and downfall [*hoi logoi* in א A B, *Andreas*]. Not mere utterances, but the efficient *words* of Him who is *the Word* [*logos*]. **fulfilled**—(ch. x. 7.) **18. reigneth**—'*hath kingship* over the kings.' The harlot cannot be a mere *city*, but in a spirit-

713

18 AND after these things I saw another angel come down from heaven,
2 having great power; *ᵃ*and the earth was lightened with his glory. And
he cried mightily with a strong voice, saying, *ᵇ*Babylon the great is fallen,
is fallen, and *ᶜ*is become the habitation of devils, and the hold of every
3 foul spirit, and *ᵈ*a cage of every unclean and hateful bird. For all
nations have drunk of the wine of the wrath of her fornication, and the
kings of the earth have committed fornication with her, and the merchants of the earth are waxed rich through the ¹abundance of her
delicacies.
4 And I heard another voice from heaven, saying, *ᵉ*Come out of her, my
people, that ye be not partakers of her sins, and that ye receive not of her
5 plagues: for *ᶠ*her sins have reached unto heaven, and God hath remem-
6 bered her iniquities. Reward *ᵍ*her even as she rewarded you, and double
unto her double according to her works: in the cup which she hath filled
7 fill to her double. How *ʰ*much she hath glorified herself, and lived
deliciously, so much torment and sorrow give her: for she saith in her
8 heart, I sit a *ⁱ*queen, and am no widow, and shall see no sorrow. There-

A. D. 96.

CHAP. 18.
ᵃ Eze. 43. 2.
2 Thes. 2.
3-:2.
ᵇ Isa. 13. 19.
Isa. 21 .9.
Jer. 51. 8.
ᶜ Isa 34. 14.
Jer. 50. 39.
ᵈ Isa. 14. 23.
Mark 5.2, 3.
1 Or, power.
ᵉ Gen. 19. 12.
Isa. 48. 10.
Isa 52. 11.
ᶠ Gen. 18. :0.
Jon. 1. 2.
ᵍ Ps. 137. 8.
Jer 50. 15.
ʰ Eze. 28. 2.
ⁱ Isa. 47. 7, 8.

ual sense (ch. xi. 8). Also the beast cannot represent a spiritual power, but a world-power. Now the harlot is ripe for judgment. Ch. xviii. details it.

CHAP. XVIII. 1-24.—BABYLON'S FALL—GOD'S PEOPLE CALLED OUT OF HER—KINGS AND MERCHANTS OF THE EARTH MOURN, WHILST SAINTS REJOICE AT HER FALL.

1. And. So Vulgate, *Andreas;* but א A B, Syriac, Coptic, omit "and." **power**—'authority.' **lightened**—'illumined.' **with**—'owing to.' **2. mightily** . . . **strong.** א A B, Vulgate, Syriac, and Coptic, read [*en ischura phone*], 'with (*lit.,* IN) a mighty voice.' **is fallen, is fallen.** So A, Vulgate, Syriac, *Andreas;* but א B, Coptic, omit the second "is fallen" (Isa. xxi. 9; Jer. li. 8). This is prophetical of her fall, still future, as v. 4 proves. **devils**—'demons.' **the hold**—a prison. **3. drunk**—ch. xiv. 8, 10, from which "the wine" may be interpolated. They have *drunk of her fornication:* the consequence will be *wrath* to themselves. So Vulgate; but א A B C, read [*peptokasin* for *pepokasin*], '(owing to the wrath of her fornication all nations) have *fallen.*' The harder, so the more probable, reading. As the nations 'have *fallen*' through her, so she, in retribution, "is fallen" herself (v. 2). Before the beast slays the two witnesses (ch. xi.), then the beast is destroyed. **the wine.** So א B, Syriac, Coptic; but A C, Vulgate, omit. **abundance**—'power,' resources. **delicacies** [*strenous*]. Note, 1 Tim. v. 11, where the verb "wax wanton" is akin to the noun. 'Resources of'—*i. e.,* subserving 'wanton luxury.' Reference is not to earthly, but spiritual wares, indulgencies, idolatries, superstitions, worldly compromises, wherewith the apostate church has made *merchandise* of men. This applies especially to Rome and the Greek apostasy; but even Protestant churches are not guiltless. The *principle* of Evangelical Protestantism is pure: the *principle* of Rome and the Greek churches is not so.

4. Come out of her, my people. From Jer. l. 8; li. 6, 45. Even in Rome, God has a people; but they are in great danger: their safety is in coming out of her at once. So in every world-conforming church there are some of God's true Church, who must come out. Especially at the eve of God's judgment on apostate Christendom: as Lot was warned to come out of Sodom before its destruction, and Israel, to come from about Dathan's tents. So the first Christians came out of Jerusalem, when apostate Judah was judged.

'State and Church are precious gifts of God. But the State being desecrated to a different end from what God designed—viz., to govern for, and under, God—becomes *beast*-like; the Church apostatizing becomes the *harlot.* The woman is the kernel; beast and harlot are the shell: whenever the kernel is mature, the shell is thrown away' (*Auberlen*). 'The harlot is every church that has not Christ's mind. Christendom, divided into many sects, is Babylon—*i. e.,* confusion. In all Christendom the true Jesus-congregation, the woman clothed with the sun, lives and is hidden. Corrupt, lifeless Christendom, is the harlot, whose aim is the pleasure of the flesh, governed by the spirit of nature and the world' (*Hahn* in *Auberlen*). The first justification of the woman is in her being called out of Babylon, the harlot, at the culmination of Babylon's sin, when judgment is to fall: for apostate Christendom is not to be converted, but destroyed. Secondly, she has to pass through an ordeal of persecution from the beast, which purifies her for the transfiguration-glory at Christ's coming (Luke xxi. 28; xxii. 28, 29; ch. xx. 4). **be not partakers**—'have no *fellowship with* her sins.' **that ye receive not of her plagues**—as Lot's wife, by lingering too near the polluted city. **5. her sins**—as a great heap. **reached**—'so far as to *cleave* unto' [*ekollethesan,* א A B C, for *eekolouthesan*]. **6.** Addressed to the executioners of God's wrath. **Reward**—'repay.' **she rewarded.** The English Version adds "you;" but א A B C, Vulgate, Syriac, Coptic, omit it. She had not *rewarded* the world-power for some injury which it inflicted on her, but had *given* it that which was its *due*—viz., spiritual delusions—because it did not like to retain God in its knowledge; her principle was [*populus vult decipi, et decipiatur*], 'the people like to be deceived, so let them be deceived.' **double**—of sorrow. Contrast the *double* of joy which Jerusalem shall receive for past suffering (Isa. lxi. 7; Zech. ix. 12): even as she received *double* punishment for her sins (Isa. xl. 2). **unto her.** So Syriac, Coptic, *Andreas:* א A B C omit. **in the cup**—(v. 3; ch. xiv. 8; xvii. 4.) **filled**—'mixed.' **fill to her double**—of the Lord's wrath. **7. How much**—*i. e.,* in proportion as. **lived deliciously**—luxuriously (note, v. 3). **sorrow** [*penthos*]—'mourning,' as for a dead husband. **I sit.** So Vulgate; but א A B C prefix 'that.' **I** . . . **am no widow**—for the world-power is my husband. **and shall see no sorrow**—'mourning.' 'I am (*long*) seated . . . I am no widow . . . I *shall* see no sorrow,' marks her unfore shall her plagues come in one day, death, and mourning, and famine; and she shall be utterly burned with fire: ^jfor strong *is* the Lord God who judgeth her.

9 And ^kthe kings of the earth, who have committed fornication and lived deliciously with her, ^lshall bewail her, and lament for her, when they

10 shall see the smoke of her burning, standing afar off for the fear of her torment, saying, ^mAlas, alas, that great city Babylon, that mighty city! for in one hour is thy judgment come.

11 And ⁿthe merchants of the earth shall weep and mourn over her; for

12 no man buyeth their merchandise any more; the merchandise of gold, and silver, and precious stones, and of pearls, and fine linen, and purple, and silk, and scarlet, and all ²thyine wood, and all manner vessels of ivory, and all manner vessels of most precious wood, and of brass, and iron, and

13 marble, and cinnamon, and odours, and ointments, and frankincense, and wine, and oil, and fine flour, and wheat, and beasts, and sheep, and horses,

14 and chariots, and ³slaves, and ^osouls of men. And the fruits that thy

A. D. 96.

j Job 9. 19.
Ps 62. 11.
Isa. 27. 1.
Jer. 50. 34.
1 Cor. 10. 22.
ch. 11. 17.
k Eze. 26. 16.
ch. 17. 2.
l Ps. 58. 10.
Jer 50. 46.
Eze. 26. 16,
17.
Dan. 4. 14.
m Isa. 21. 9.
ch 14. 8.
n Eze. 27. 27.
2 Or, sweet
3 Or. bodies.
o Eze. 27. 13.
2 Pet. 2. 3.

---

concerned security as to the past, present, and future (*Bengel*). I shall never have to mourn as one bereft of husband. Babylon was queen of the East; so Rome is queen of the West: called on imperial coins 'the *eternal* city.' *Ammian Marcellin* says (ch. xv. 7), 'Babylon is a former Rome, and (papal) Rome a latter Babylon. Rome is a daughter of Babylon: by her, as by her mother, God has subdued the world under one sway' (*St. Augustine*). As the Jews' restoration did not take place till Babylon's fall, so (*R. Kimchi* on Obadiah) 'when Rome (Edom) shall be devastated, there shall be redemption to Israel.' Romish idolatries are stumblingblocks to the Jews' acceptance of Christianity. **8. death**—on herself, formerly (*v.* 7) secure even from the death of her husband. **mourning**—instead of her feasting. **famine**—instead of her *luxurious delicacies* (*vv.* 3, 7). **fire**—(note, ch. xvii. 16.) Literal fire may burn literal Rome, which is in the midst of volcanic agencies. As the ground was cursed for Adam's sin, and under Noah was sunk beneath the flood, and Sodom was burned with fire, so may Rome be. But as the harlot is mystical (the whole faithless Church), the *burning* is mainly mystical: utter destruction and removal. Rome will rise to power just before her fall. The carnal, faithless, worldly elements in all churches—Roman, Greek, and Protestant—tend towards one centre, preparing for the last form of the beast, antichrist. The Pharisees were mostly sound in creed, yet judgment fell on them as on the unsound Sadducees and half-heathenish Samaritans. So faithless and adulterous Protestant churches will not escape for soundness of creed. **the Lord.** So א B C, Syriac, *Andreas*; but A, Vulgate, omit. 'Strong;' as God's name [EL] means. **judgeth.** But א A B C read, past [*krinas*], 'who *judged* her:' prophetical past for future. The charge in *v.* 4, to *come out of her*, implies the judgment was not yet executed. **9. lived deliciously**—luxuriated. The faithless church, instead of reproving, connived at the world's self-indulgent luxury, and sanctioned it by her practice. Contrast the world's *rejoicing* over the two witnesses' dead bodies (ch. xi. 10) who had tormented it by faithfulness, with its *lamentations* over the harlot who made the way to heaven smooth, and was a useful tool in controlling subjects. Men's carnal mind relishes the apostate church, which gives an opiate to conscience and virtual license to lusts. **bewail her.** א A B C, Syriac, Coptic, *Cyprian*, omit "her." **10.** God's judgments inspire fear in the worldly, but of short duration; for kings and great men soon

join the beast, in its last, worst shape, as open antichrist, claiming all the harlot claimed in blasphemous pretensions, and more: so making up to them for the loss of the harlot. **mighty.** *Rome*, in Greek, means *strength*. **11. shall.** So B; but א A C read, present, 'weep and mourn.' **merchandise**—'cargo' in *ships*: shiplading (cf. *v.* 17). Rome was not commercial, and is not likely, from her position, to be so. The *merchandise* must be spiritual, as the harlot is not literal. She did not witness against carnal luxury and pleasure-seeking—the source of *merchants*' gains—but conformed to them (*v.* 7). She cared not for the sheep, but for the wool. Professing Christian merchants lived as if this world were the reality, not heaven, unscrupulous as to the means of gain. Cf. Zech. v. 4-11 (notes), the judgment on mystical *Babylon's* merchants for unjust gain. All the merchandise here occurs repeatedly in the 'Roman Ceremonial.' **12.** Note ch. xvii. 4. **stones**—Greek, 'stone . . . pearl.' **fine linen.** A B C read [*bussinou* for *bussow*], 'fine linen manufacture' [א, plural, *bussinōn*]: the manufacture for which *Egypt* (type of the apostate church, ch. xi. 8) was famed. Contrast 'the fine linen' (Ezek. xvi. 10) put on Israel, and on the New Testament Church (ch. xix. 8), the Bride, by God (Ps. cxxxii. 9). **thyine wood**—the *citrus* of the Romans; found in Mauretania: probably the *Callitris quadrivalvis*, or *thuia articulata*. *Pliny* says there was a mania for tables of this wood. When Roman ladies were upbraided by their husbands for extravagance in pearls, they retorted the men's fondness for thyine tables. **all manner vessels**—'every vessel;' 'furniture.' **13. cinnamon**—designed by God for better purposes: an ingredient in the holy anointing oil: a plant in the garden of the Beloved (Song iv. 14); but desecrated to vile uses by the adulteress (Prov. vii. 17). **odours**—of incense. א A C, Vulgate, Syriac, prefix, 'and amomum' (a precious hair ointment from an Asiatic shrub). **ointments**—'ointment.' **frankincense.** Contrast the "incense" which God loves (Ps. cxli. 2; Mal. i. 11). **fine flour** [*semidalin*]—the *similago* of the Latins (*Alford*). **beasts**—of burden. **slaves**—'bodies.' **souls of men**—(Ezek. xxvii. 13.) Said of *slaves*. Appropriate 'to the harlot, apostate Christendom, especially Rome, which so often *enslaved* both *bodies* and *souls*. Though Christianity does not *directly* forbid slavery, which might then have incited a slave-revolt, it virtually condemns it. Popery derived its greatest gains from masses for *the souls of men* after death, and from indulgences purchased from

soul lusted after are departed from thee, and all things which were dainty and goodly are departed from thee, and thou shalt find them no more
15 at all.   The merchants of these things, which were made rich by her,
16 shall stand afar·off for the fear of her torment, weeping and wailing, and saying, Alas, alas, that great city, that was clothed in fine linen, and purple, and scarlet, and decked with gold, and precious stones, and pearls!
17 for in one hour so great riches is come to nought.

And [p] every shipmaster, and all the company in ships, and sailors, and
18 as many as trade by sea, stood afar off, and [q]cried when they saw the smoke of her burning, saying, What *city is* like unto this great city!
19 And [r] they cast dust on their heads, and cried, weeping and wailing, saying, Alas, alas, that great city, wherein were made rich all that had ships in the sea by reason of her costliness! for in one hour is she made desolate.
20 Rejoice [s] over her, *thou* heaven, and *ye* holy apostles and prophets; for [t] God hath avenged you on her.
21 And a mighty angel took up a stone like a great millstone, and cast *it* into the sea, saying, [u]Thus with violence shall that great city Babylon
22 be thrown down, and shall be found no more at all.   And [v] the voice of harpers, and musicians, and of pipers, and trumpeters, shall be heard no more at all in thee; and no craftsman, of whatsoever craft *he be*, shall be found any more in thee; and the sound of a millstone shall be heard no
23 more at all in thee; and the light of a candle shall shine no more at all

A. D. 96.
[p] Isa. 23. 14.
Eze. 27. 29.
[q] Eze. 27. 30, 31.
[r] Josh. 7. 6.
1 Sam. 4.12.
Job 2. 12.
[s] Judg 5. 31.
Ps. 48. 11.
Ps 58. 10.
Ps. 96. 11-13.
Fro 11.10.
Jer. 51. 47, 48.
ch 19. 1-3.
[t] Deut 32.42.
Ps. 18. 47.
Isa. 26 21.
Luke 11.49.
[u] Ex. 15. 5.
Neh. 9. 11.
Jer 51. 63, 64.
[v] Isa. 21. 8.
Jer. 7. 34.
Jer. 16. 9.
Jer 25. 10.
Eze 26 13.

the papal chancery by rich merchants in various countries, to be retailed at a profit (*Mosheim*, iii., 95, 96). **14.** Direct address to Babylon. **the fruits that thy soul lusted after**—'thy autumn-ripe fruit of the eager desire of the soul.' **dainty** —'fat;' 'sumptuous' in food. **goodly**—'splendid' in dress and equipage. **departed.** But א A B C, Vulgate, Syriac, Coptic, read, 'perished.' **thou shalt.** א A C, Vulgate, Syriac, read, '*they* (men) *shall* no more find them at all.' **15. of these things**—of the things mentioned. *vv.* 12, 13. **which** —'*who.*' **made rich by**—'derived riches *from* her.' **stand afar off for the fear**—(cf. *v.* 10.) **wailing**— 'mourning.' The reaction in Reformed churches towards the Romish and Greek apostasies is a fulfilment of this. **16. And.** So Vulgate, *Andreas*; but א A B C omit. **decked**—'gilded.' **stones . . . pearls**—'stone . . . pearl.' B, *Andreas*, read "pearls;' but A א C, 'pearl.' **17. is come to nought**—'is desolated.'

shipmaster—'pilot.' **all the company in ships.** א A C, Vulgate, Syriac, read, 'every one who saileth to a place' (B has '. . . to *the* place'): *every voyager.* *Vessels* were freighted with pilgrims to various shrines, so that in one month (A. D. 1300) 200,000 pilgrims were counted in Rome (*D'Aubigne*, 'Reformation'): a gain, not only to the papal see, but to *shipmasters, merchants,* &c. These are not restricted to literal 'shipmasters,' &c., but mainly refer to all who share in the spiritual traffic of apostate Christendom. **18. when they saw**—[*horontes*; but א A B C, *Andreas, blepontes,* 'looking at :' *blepo* is to *use the eyes,* to *look :* the act of seeing, without thought of the object seen: *horao* refers to the thing *seen* or presented to the eye (*Tittmann*)]. **smoke.** So B C; but A, Vulgate, place.' **What city is like?** Cf. the similar boast as to *the beast,* ch. xiii. 4: so closely do the harlot and beast approximate. Contrast its attribution to God, to whom alone it is due, by *His* servants (Exod. xv. 11). *Martial* says of Rome, 'Nothing is equal to her;' *Athenæus,* 'She is the world's epitome.' **19. wailing**—'mourning.' **that had ships.** A B א C read, 'that had *their* ships; lit.,

'*the* ships.' **costliness**—costly treasures: abstract for concrete.

20. holy apostles. So C; but א A B, Vulgate, Syriac, Coptic, *Andreas,* 'ye *saints and ye apostles.*' **avenged you on her**—'judged your judgment on (exacting it *from*) her.' 'Heaven more rejoices at the harlot's downfall than at that of the two beasts. For the most heinous of sins is that of those who know God's word of grace and keep it not. The worldliness of the Church is the most worldly of all worldliness. Hence Babylon has not only Israel's sins, but also those of the heathen. John dwells longer on the abominations and judgments of the harlot than of the beast. "Harlot" describes the false church's essential character. She retains human shape, as *woman*—does not become a beast—has the form of godliness, but denies its power. Her rightful Husband, Jehovah-Christ, and the goods of His house, are no longer her all, but she runs after the visible and vain things of the world. The fullest form of whoredom is where the Church wishes to be a worldly power, makes flesh her arm, uses unholy means for holy ends, spreads her dominion by sword or money, fascinates men by sensuous ritualism, becomes "mistress of ceremonies" to the dignitaries of the world, flatters prince or people, and, like Israel, seeks help of one world-power against danger threatening from another' (*Auberlen*). *Judgment,* therefore, *begins with* the harlot, as in privileges the *house of God* (1 Pet. iv. 17).

21. a—'one.' **millstone.** Cf. the judgment on Egypt at the Red Sea (Exod. xv. 5, 10; Neh. ix. 11), and the doom of Babylon, the world-power (Jer. li. 63, 64). **with violence**—'with impetus.' This prophecy is regarded as still to be fulfilled. **22. pipers**—flute-players. "Musicians," painters, sculptors: desecrated art to lend fascination to the sensuous worship of corrupt Christendom. **craftsman**—artisan. **23.** A blessed contrast is ch. xxii. 5, "They need *no candle* (Babylon shall *no more* have even *the light of a candle*); . . . for the Lord God giveth them light." **candle**—'lamp.' **bridegroom**

in thee; *"*and the voice of the bridegroom and of the bride shall be heard
no more at all in thee: for *ˣ*thy merchants were the great men of the
24 earth; *ʸ*for by thy sorceries were all nations deceived. And in her was
found the blood of prophets, and of saints, and of all that *ᶻ*were slain upon
the earth.

19 AND after these things I heard a great voice of much people in heaven,
saying, Alleluia! *ᵃ*Salvation, and glory, and honour, and power, unto the
2 Lord our God: for true and righteous *are* his judgments; for he hath
judged the great whore, which did corrupt the earth with her fornication,
3 and hath avenged *ᵇ*the blood of his servants at her hand. And again
4 they said, Alleluia! *ᶜ*And her smoke rose up for ever and ever. And
*ᵈ*the four and twenty elders, and the four beasts, fell down and worshipped
5 God that sat on the throne, saying, *ᵉ*Amen, Alleluia! And a voice came
out of the throne, saying, *ᶠ*Praise our God, all ye his servants, and ye
that fear him, both small and great.
6 And *ᵍ*I heard as it were the voice of a great multitude, and as the
voice of many waters, and as the voice of mighty thunderings, saying,
7 Alleluia! for the Lord God omnipotent reigneth. Let us be *ʰ*glad and

A. D. 96.

ʷ Jer. 33. 11.
ˣ Isa 23 8.
ʸ 2 Ki. 9. 22.
Nah 3. 4.
ᶻ Jer 51. 49.

CHAP. 19.
ᵃ ch. 4. 11.
ch. 7. 10
ch. 12 10
ᵇ Deut. 32. 43.
ch 6. 10
ch. 18. 20.
ᶜ Isa 34 10.
ch 14. 11.
ᵈ ch 4. 4, 6,
10
ᵉ Neh. 5. 13.
Neh. 8 6.
ᶠ Ps. 134. 1.
Ps. 135. 1.
ᵍ Eze. 1. 24.
ʰ Isa. 44. 23.

... **bride ... no more . . . in thee.** Contrast the
heavenly city, with *Bridegroom, Bride* and *marriage supper* (Isa. lxii. 4, 5; ch. xix. 7, 9; xxi. 2,
9). **thy merchants were.** So א B C; but A omits
the Greek article before "merchants:" 'the great
men of, &c., were thy merchants.' **sorceries**—
'sorcery.' **24.** Applied by Christ (Matt. xxiii. 35)
to apostate Jerusalem, which proves that not
merely literal Rome, and the Romish Church
(though the *chief* representative), but the WHOLE
faithless church of both Old and New Testament
is Babylon the harlot; just as the whole Church
is 'the woman' (ch. xii. 1). *Aringhus* in *Bengel*
says, Pagan Rome was the *general shambles* for
slaying Jesus' sheep. *Frederick Seyler* calculates
that papal Rome, between A. D. 1540 and 1580,
slew more than 900,000 Protestants. Three reasons for the harlot's downfall are given: (1.) The
worldly greatness of her *merchants*, due to traffic in
spiritual things. (2.) Her *sorceries*, or juggling
tricks, in which the false prophet, ministering to
the beast in its last form, shall exceed her. Cf.
"sorcerers" (ch. xxi. 8; xxii. 15), specially doomed
to the lake of fire. (3.) Her persecution of (Old
Testament) "prophets" and (New Testament)
"saints."

CHAP. XIX. 1-21.—CHURCH'S THANKSGIVING
IN HEAVEN FOR JUDGMENT ON THE HARLOT—
MARRIAGE OF THE LAMB—THE SUPPER—BRIDE'S
PREPARATION—JOHN FORBIDDEN TO WORSHIP
THE ANGEL—THE LORD AND HIS HOSTS COME
FORTH—BEAST AND FALSE PROPHET CAST INTO
THE LAKE OF FIRE—THE KINGS AND THEIR
FOLLOWERS SLAIN BY THE SWORD OUT OF CHRIST'S
MOUTH.

1. As in the opening of the prophecy (ch. iv. 8; v.
9, &c.), so now, at one of the closing events in the
vision, the judgment on the harlot (described, ch.
xviii.), there is a song of praise in heaven to God:
cf. ch. vii. 10, &c., towards the close of the seals,
and ch. xi. 15-18, at the close of the trumpets;
ch. xv. 3, at the saints' victory over the beast.
And. So *Andreas;* but א A B C, Vulgate, Syriac,
Coptic, omit. **a great voice.** א A B C, Vulgate,
Coptic, *Andreas*, read, 'as *it were* a great voice.'
What a contrast to the lamentations, ch. xviii.!
Cf. Jer. li. 48. The *great* manifestation of God's
power in destroying Babylon calls forth a *great
voice* of praise *in heaven.* **people**—'multitude.'
Alleluia—'Praise ye JAH:' here first in Revelation,
whence *Elliott* infers the *Jews* bear a prominent
part. JAH is not a contraction of JEHOVAH, as it
sometimes occurs with the latter. It means 'He
who IS:' Jehovah, 'He who will be, is, and was.'
It implies God experienced a PRESENT help; so
that 'Hallelujah,' says *Kimchi*, is found first in
Psalms *on the destruction of the ungodly.* 'Hallelu-
Jah' occurs *four* times here. Cf. Ps. cxlix. 4-9,
plainly parallel, identical in many phrases, as well
as the general idea. Israel, especially, will join in
the Halleluia, when 'her warfare is accomplished'
and her foe destroyed. **Salvation**—*'The* salvation
. . . the glory . . . the power.' **and honour.** So
Coptic; but א A B C, Syriac, omit. **unto the
Lord our God.** So *Andreas;* but א A B C, Coptic,
read, '(Is) of (belongs to) our God.' **2. which did
corrupt the earth**—'*used* to corrupt' continually.
'Instead of opposing, she promoted the sinful
decay of the world by her earthliness, allowing the
salt to lose its savour' (*Auberlen*). **avenged**—
'exacted in retribution.' Application of the principle (Gen. ix. 5). **blood of his servants**—literally
shed by the Old and the New Testament apostate
church; also virtually, by all who, though called
Christians, hate or love not the brethren of Christ,
but shrink from the reproach of the cross, and
show unkindness to those who bear it. **3. again**
—'a second time.' **rose up**—'goeth up.' **for ever
and ever**—'to the ages of the ages.' **4. beasts**—
'living creatures.' **sat**—'sitteth.' **5. out of [*apo*]**
—'out from the throne' in A B C. **Praise our
God.** Cf. the solemn praise by the Levites (1
Chr. xvi. 36; xxiii. 5): the house of God was consequently filled' with the Divine glory (2 Chr. v.
13). **both**—omitted in א A B C, Vulgate, Coptic,
Syriac: '*the* small and *the* great.'

6. many waters. Contrast the "many waters"
on which the whore sitteth (ch. xvii. 1). This
verse is the hearty response to the stirring call,
'Halleluia! Praise our God,' &c. (*vv.* 4, 5). **the
Lord God omnipotent**—'*the* Omnipotent.' **reigneth**—*reigned:* hence *reigneth once for all.* His
reign is a fact established. Babylon, the harlot,
was one great hindrance to His reign being recognized. Her overthrow clears the way for His
advent to reign: not merely Rome, but all Christendom, in so far as it compromised Christ for the
world, is comprehended in the 'harlot.' The beast
hardly arises when he at once "goeth into perdition;' so Christ is considered as already reigning,
so soon does His advent follow the judgment on
the harlot. **7. glad ... rejoice**—'rejoice ...

rejoice, and give honour to him: for ‡ the marriage of the Lamb is come,

8 and his wife hath made herself ready. And ʲ to her was granted that she should be arrayed in fine linen, clean and ¹white: for ᵏ the fine linen is

9 the righteousness of saints. And he saith unto me, Write, ˡ Blessed *are* they which are called unto the marriage supper of the Lamb. And he

10 saith unto me, These are the true sayings of God. And ᵐ I fell at his feet to worship him. And he said unto me, ⁿ See *thou do it* not: I am thy fellow-servant, and of thy brethren °that have the testimony of Jesus: worship God: for the testimony of Jesus is the spirit of prophecy.

11 And I saw heaven opened, and behold a white horse; and he that sat upon him *was* called ᵖFaithful and True; and ᵠin righteousness he doth

A. D. 96.

‡ Matt. 22. 2.
  Matt 25.10.
ʲ Ps. 45. 13.
¹ Or, bright.
ᵏ Ps 132. 9.
ˡ Luke 14.15.
ᵐ ch 22. 8.
ⁿ Acts 10. 26.
  Acts 14. 14.
° 1 John 5.10.
ᵖ John 14. 6.
  ch. 3. 14.
ᵠ Isa 11. 4.

exult.' **give.** So B א, *Andreas;* but A, 'we *will* give.' 'Glory'—'*the* glory.' **the marriage of the Lamb is come.** The *full, final* consummation is at ch. xxi. 2-9, &c. Previously there must be the beast's overthrow, &c., at the Lord's coming, the binding of Satan, the millennial reign, the loosing of Satan, his last overthrow, and the general judgment. The elect Church, the heavenly Bride, soon after the destruction of the harlot, is transfigured at the Lord's coming, and joins in His triumph over the beast. On the emblem of the heavenly Bridegroom and Bride, cf. Matt. xxii. 2; xxv. 6, 10; 2 Cor. xi. 2. Perfect union with Himself, and participation in His holiness, joy, glory, and kingdom, are included in this symbol (cf. Song). Besides the *heavenly* Bride, the transfigured, translated, and risen Church, reigning *over* the earth with Christ, there is also the *earthly* bride, Israel, in the flesh, never yet *divorced*, though for a time separated, from her Divine Husband, who shall then be re-united to the Lord, and be mother-church of the millennial earth, Christianized through her, (Isa. l. 1; liv.; lx.-lxii.; lxv.) Scripture restricts the language of marriage-love to *the Bride*, the Church *as a whole. Individuals*, in relation to Christ, ought not to adopt it, as Rome does as to her nuns. Individually, believers are *guests;* collectively, they constitute *the Bride.* The harlot divides her affections among many; the Bride gives hers exclusively to Christ. **8. granted.** Though in one sense *she* 'made herself ready,' by the Spirit's work in her, putting on "the wedding garment," yet, in the fullest sense, not she, but her Lord, makes her ready, by '*granting* to her that she be arrayed in fine linen.' It is He who, by *giving Himself for* her, *presents her to Himself a glorious Church, not having spot, but holy and without blemish* (Eph. v. 5-27). He *sanctifies* her, naturally vile and without beauty, *with the washing of water by the Word,* and *puts His own comeliness on her.* **clean and white.** So *Andreas;* but א A B transpose, 'bright and pure:' brilliantly *splendid* and *spotless* as the Bride herself. **righteousness**—'righteousnesses:' distributively. *Each* saint must have righteousness; not merely be justified, as if it belonged to the Church *in the aggregate.* The saints together have *righteousness:* Christ is *accounted* "the Lord our righteousness" to each on believing, the robe being made *white in the blood of the Lamb.* The righteousness of the saint is not *inherent*, but *imputed.* If it were otherwise, Christ would be merely enabling the sinner to justify himself. Rom. v. 18, 19, is decisive. Cf. 'Article XI.,' Church of England. The justification already given in title and unseen possession, is now GIVEN the saints *in manifestation*—they openly *walk with Christ in white.* This, rather than their primary justification on earth, is the reference here. Their justification before the world, which persecuted them, contrasts with the

judgment on the harlot. 'Now that the harlot has fallen, the woman triumphs' (*Auberlen*). Contrast with the Bride's [*bussinon*, not the *linon* of the angels, ch. xv. 6] *pure fine linen* (indicating simplicity and purity), the harlot's (ch. xvii. 4; xviii. 16) tawdry ornamentation. Babylon, the apostate church, is antithesis to new Jerusalem, the transfigured Church. The woman (ch. xii.), the harlot (ch. xvii.), the Bride (ch. xix.), are the Church's three aspects. **9. he**—God by His angel *saith unto me.* **called**—effectually. The "unto" [*eis*], 'into,' expresses this: not merely invited *to* [*epi*], but made *partakers of* (cf. 1 Cor. i. 9). **marriage supper** — 'the supper of the marriage.' Typified by the Lord's supper. **true** [*alethinoi*]—'genuine;' veritable; which shall surely be fulfilled—viz., all the previous revelations. **10. at**—'before.' John's intending to worship the angel, as in ch. xxii. 8, who revealed the coming glory, is the involuntary impulse of adoring joy at so blessed a prospect. It forms a contrast to the sorrowful *wonder* with which he looked on the Church as the harlot (ch. xvii. 6). How corrupt is our fallen nature, that even John, an apostle, should have all but fallen into "voluntary humility and worshipping of angels" (Col. ii. 18), which Paul warns against! **and of thy brethren**—i. e., *a fellow-servant* of thy brethren. **have the testimony of Jesus**—(note, ch. xii. 17.) **the testimony of**—i. e., *respecting* Jesus. **is the spirit of prophecy**—emanates from the same spirit of prophecy in you as in myself. We angels, and you apostles, alike bear testimony concerning Jesus by the same Spirit, who enables me to show you these revelations, and you to record them: wherefore we are *fellow-servants*—not I your lord to be worshipped. Cf. ch. xxii. 9, 'I am fellow-servant of thee and of thy brethren *the prophets;*' whence the "FOR the testimony," &c., here may give the reason for his adding, 'and fellow-servant of thy brethren that have the testimony of Jesus.' I mean, *of the prophets;* 'for it is of *Jesus* that thy brethren, *the prophets,* testify by the Spirit in them.' A condemnation of Romish invocation of saints, as if they were our superiors.

11. behold a white horse; and he that sat upon him. Identical with ch. vi. 2. He comes forth "conquering and to conquer." Compare the *ass*-colt on which He rode into Jerusalem. The *horse* was used for war: here He is going forth to war with the beast. The *ass*, for peace. His riding on it into Jerusalem is an earnest of His reign in Jerusalem over the earth, as *Prince of peace,* after all hostile powers have been overthrown. When the security of the world-power and the distress of the people of God have reached their highest, the Lord Jesus shall appear from heaven to end the whole world-course, and establish His kingdom of glory. He comes to judge with vengeance the world-power, and bring to the Church redemption, transfiguration, and power over the

12 judge and make war. His eyes *were* as a flame of fire, and on his head *were* many crowns; and he had a ʳname written that no man knew but
13 he himself: and ˢhe *was* clothed with a vesture dipped in blood: and his
14 name is called The ᵗWord of God. And the armies *which were* in heaven followed him upon white horses, ᵘclothed in fine linen, white and clean.
15 And ᵛout of his mouth goeth a sharp sword, that with it he should smite the nations: and ᵂhe shall rule them with a rod of iron: and ˣhe tread-
16 eth the wine-press of the fierceness and wrath of Almighty God. And he hath on *his* vesture and on his thigh a name written, ʸKING OF KINGS, AND LORD OF LORDS.
17 And I saw an angel standing in the sun; and he cried with a loud voice, saying to all the fowls that fly in the midst of heaven, ᶻCome and
18 gather yourselves together unto the supper of the great God; that ye may eat the flesh of kings, and the flesh of captains, and the flesh of mighty

A. D 9⁴.

ʳ Isa 9. 6.
ˢ Isa 6³. 2, 3.
ᵗ John 1. 1.
   1 John 5. 7.
ᵘ Matt. 28. 3.
ᵛ Isa 11. 4.
   2 Thes. 2. 8.
   ch. 1. 16.
ᵂ Ps. 2. 9.
   ch. 2. 27.
   ch. 12. 5.
ˣ Isa 63. 3.
ʸ Ps 72.
   Dan. 2. 7.
   1 Tim. 6.15.
   ch 17. 14.
ᶻ Eze. 39. 17.

world. Distinguish this *coming* (Matt. xxiv. 27, 29, 37, 39 [*parousia*]) from *the end*, or final judgment (Matt. xxv. 31; 1 Cor. xv. 24). Powerful natural phenomena shall accompany His advent (*Auberlen*). **12.** Identifying Him with the Son of man (ch. i. 14). **many crowns**—'diadems:' not merely [*stephanoi*] garlands of victory, but crowns, as KING OF KINGS. Christ's diadem comprises all diadems of the earth and of heavenly powers. Contrast the papal tiara of *three diadems*. Cf. also the little horn (antichrist) that overcomes the *three* horns or kingdoms, Dan. vii. 8, 24 (*the Papacy?* which, as a temporal kingdom, was made up of *three* kingdoms — the exarchate of Ravenna, the kingdom of the Lombards, and the state of Rome, obtained by Pope Zachary and Stephen II. from Pepin, the usurper of France). Also, the *seven crowns* (diadems) *on the seven heads of the dragon* (ch. xii. 3), and *ten diadems on the ten heads of the beast.* These usurpers claim the diadems belonging to Christ. **he had a name written.** B, Syriac, insert, 'He had *names written*, and a name written,' &c. *The names of the dominion which each diadem indicated were written* on them severally. But א A, Vulgate, *Origen, Cyprian,* omit. **that no man knew but he himself**—(Judg. xiii. 18; 1 Cor. ii. 9, 11; 1 John iii. 2.) The same is said of the "new name" of believers, ch. ii. 17. In all respects the disciple is like his Lord. The Lord's "new name" is to be theirs, "in their foreheads" (ch. iii. 12; xiv. 1; xxii. 4); therefore His as yet *unknown* name also is written on His forehead: as the high priest had "Holiness to the Lord" inscribed on the mitre on his brow. John saw it as "written," but *knew not* its meaning. A name which, in all its glorious significancy, can be only understood when the union of His saints with Him, and their joint triumph and reign, shall be perfectly manifested. **13. vesture dipped in blood**—(Isa. lxiii. 2: cf. *v.* 15, end.) The *blood* there is not His own, but that of His foes. Here the blood on His "vesture," reminding us of *His own blood*, shed for even the ungodly who trample on it, prefigures the shedding of *their* blood in retribution; not that of the godly, as the harlot and beast shed, but of the blood-stained ungodly, including them both. **The Word of God**—who made the world, is He who, under the same character, shall make it anew. *Son of God* is applicable, in a lower sense, also to His people; but "the Word of God" indicates His incommunicable Godhead, which, joined to His manhood, He shall manifest in glory. 'The Bride does not fear the Bridegroom: love casteth out fear: she welcomes Him: she cannot be happy but at His side. The Lamb

(*v.* 9) is the symbol of His gentleness. Even a little child, instead of being scared by a lamb, caresses it. There is nothing to make us afraid of God but sin: and Jesus is the *Lamb of God that taketh away the sin of the world.* What a fearful contrast is the aspect He will wear towards His enemies! Not as the Bridegroom and Lamb, but as the Judge and Warrior stained in the blood of His enemies.' **14. the armies . . . in heaven**—(cf. ch. xiv. 20.) The glorified saints whom God "will bring with" Christ at His advent: both the living transfigured, and those raised and meeting the Lord in the air (1 Thess. iv.: cf. ch. xvii. 14); also "His mighty angels" (2 Thess. i. 7). **white and** (so א, *Origen, Andreas*) **clean**—'pure.' A B, Vulgate, Syriac, *Cyprian,* omit "and." **15. out of his mouth . . . sword**—(ch. i. 16; ii. 12, 16.) Here in *avenging* power; 2 Thess. ii. 8, "consume with the Spirit *of His mouth*" (Isa. xi. 4, to which there is allusion); not in its converting efficacy (Eph. vi. 17; Heb. iv. 12, 13, where the sword-like Word's judicial keenness is included). The Father commits the judgment to the Son (John v. 22). **he shall rule.** HE is emphatical: none other; in contrast to the usurpers who misruled on earth. [*Poimanei*, 'tend as a shepherd.'] He who would have *shepherded* them with pastoral rod and golden sceptre of His love, shall dash them in pieces as refractory rebels, with "a rod of iron." **treadeth the wine-press**—(Isa. lxiii. 3.) **of the fierceness and wrath.** So *Andreas;* but א A B, Vulgate, Coptic, *Origen,* 'of the fierceness (*boiling indignation*) of the wrath,' omitting "and." **Almighty.** Christ's wrath against His foes will be executed with the resources of omnipotence. **16.** 'His name written on His vesture and thigh' was partly on the vesture, partly on the thigh itself, where, in an equestrian figure, the robe drops. The *thigh* was touched in taking an oath, as the seat of *strength:* it symbolizes Christ's humanity, as, sprung from the *loins* of David, according to His covenant, and now the glorified "Son of man." His incommunicable Divine name, "which no man knew," is on His head, *v.* 12 (*Menochius*). KING OF KINGS. Contrast ch. xvii. 14, 17, the beast being in usurpation a *king of kings,* the ten kings delivering their kingdom to him.

17. an—'one.' **in the sun**—conspicuous in sight of the whole world. **to all the fowls**—(Ezek. xxxix. 17-20.) **and gather yourselves.** א A B, Vulgate, Syriac, Coptic, *Andreas,* read, 'be gathered,' omitting "and." **of the great God.** א A B, Vulgate, Syriac, Coptic, *Andreas,* 'the great supper (banquet) of God.' **18.** Contrast *vv.* 17, 18, with *the marriage-supper of the Lamb* (*v.* 9). **captains**—'captains of thousands.' The "kings"

men, and the flesh of horses, and of them that sit on them, and the flesh of all *men*, *both* free and bond, both small and great.

19 And ^aI saw the beast, and the kings of the earth, and their armies, gathered together to make war against him that sat on the horse, and
20 against his army. And the beast was taken, and with him the false prophet that wrought miracles before him, with which he deceived them that had received the mark of the beast, and them that worshipped his image. These ^bboth were cast alive into a lake of fire burning with brimstone.
21 And the remnant were slain with the sword of him that sat upon the horse, which *sword* proceeded out of his mouth: and all the fowls were filled with their flesh.

20 AND I saw an angel come down from heaven, ^ahaving the key of the
2 bottomless pit and a great chain in his hand. And he laid hold on ^bthe dragon, that old serpent, which is the Devil, and Satan, and bound him
3 a thousand years, and cast him into the bottomless pit, and shut him up, and ^cset a seal upon him, that ^dhe should deceive the nations no more,

A. D. 96.

^a Eze. 38. ⊢.
Dan 7. 21.
ch. 13. 1.
ch 16. 16.
^b Ɵan. 7. 11.
Dan. 11. 45.
ch. '0. 0.

CHAP. 20.
^a Luke 8. 31.
ch. 1. 18.
ch. 9. 1.
^b z Pet 2. 4.
Jude 6.
ch 12. 9
^c Dan 6. 17.
^d Matt 21.21.
ch. 12. 9.
ch. 13. 14.
ch. 16. 14.

are "the ten" who "give their power unto the beast." **free and bond**—ch. vi. 15: xiii. 16, 'receiving the mark of the beast.' The repetition of *flesh* (plural, *masses of flesh*) five times, marks the gross *carnality* of the beast's followers. Again, the giving of their flesh to the fowls to eat, is a righteous retribution for their not suffering *the dead bodies of* Christ's *witnesses to be put in graves* (ch. xi. 9).

19. gathered together—at Armageddon, under the sixth vial. For "*their* armies," in א B, *Andreas*, there is '*His* armies' in A. **war**. So *Andreas;* but א A B, '*the* war'—viz., that foretold, ch. xvi. 14; xvii. 4. **20. and with him, &c.** So א; but A, 'and those with him;' B, 'and the false prophet who was with him.' **miracles**—'*the* miracles' ('signs') recorded already (ch. xiii. 14) as wrought by *the second beast* in sight of *the first beast*. Therefore the *second beast* is *the false prophet*. Many represent the first beast the secular, the second the ecclesiastical, power of Rome; and think the change of title for the latter, from the 'other beast' to the "false prophet," is because, by the judgment on the harlot, the ecclesiastical power will then retain nothing save the power to deceive. I think the false prophet will succeed to the spiritual pretensions of the papacy; whilst the beast, in its last form, as the fully-revealed antichrist, will be the secular embodiment of the fourth world-kingdom, Rome, in its last intensified opposition to God. Cf. Ezek. xxxviii. and xxxix.; Dan. ii. 34, 35, 44; xi. 44, 45; xii. 1; Joel iii. 9-17; Zech. xii.-xiv. Daniel (chs. vii. and viii.) does not mention the second beast, but "the little horn" with "the eyes of a man"—*i. e.*, spiritual and intellectual culture. This is expressed by the apocalyptic "false prophet," embodying man's unsanctified knowledge, derived from the old serpent. The first beast is political, the second is spiritual. Both are *beasts*—antichristian wisdom serving antichristian power—both lion and serpent. As God's moral government requires that "judgment should begin at the house of God," executed on the harlot, the faithless Church, by the world-power with which she intrigued, so also that the world-power, after being God's instrument of punishment, should itself be punished. As the harlot is judged by the beast and the ten kings, so these are destroyed by the Lord in person. So Zech. i.: cf. ch. ii. Jeremiah, after denouncing Jerusalem's judgment by Babylon, ends with denouncing Babylon's own. In the interval between judgment on the harlot, and the Lord's destruction of the beast, &c., earthly mindedness

will culminate, and antichristianity triumph, for its short three and a half days whilst the two witnesses lie dead. Then shall the Church be ripe for glorification, the antichristian world for destruction. The world, at its highest development of material and spiritual power, is but a decorated carcase round which the eagles gather. Antichrist and his kings, in their blindness, imagine they can war against the King of heaven with earthly hosts: betraying the extreme folly of Babylonian confusion. The Lord's appearance, without actual encounter, shows antichrist his nothingness. Cf. the effect of Jesus' appearance even in His humiliation, John xviii. 6 (*Auberlen*). **had received**—'received,' *once for all*. **them that worshipped**—'them worshipping:' not an act *once for all*, as "received," but *in the habit of* 'worshipping.' **These both were cast alive into a lake**—'*the* lake of fire,' Gehenna. Satan is subsequently cast in, at the close of the outbreak, after the millennium (ch. xx. 10). Then death and hell, with those not found at the general judgment "written in the book of life:" this constitutes "the second death." "Alive"—a living death; not annihilation. 'Their worm dieth not, their fire is not quenched' (Mark ix. 44, 46, 48). **21. the remnant**—'the rest;' *i. e.*, 'the kings and their armies' (*v.* 19), one indiscriminate mass. A solemn confirmation of Ps. ii. 10.

CHAP. XX. 1-15.—SATAN BOUND—THE FIRST-RISEN SAINTS' REIGN WITH CHRIST, A THOUSAND YEARS—SATAN LOOSED, GATHERS THE NATIONS, GOG AND MAGOG, ROUND THE SAINTS' CAMP—CONSIGNED TO THE LAKE OF FIRE—GENERAL RESURRECTION—LAST JUDGMENT.

1. The destruction of his representatives, the beast and the false prophet, to whom he gave his *power*, *throne*, and *authority*, is followed by the binding of Satan himself a thousand years. **the key of the bottomless pit**—transferred from Satan's hands, heretofore permitted to use it in letting loose plagues on the earth: he is now to feel himself the torment which he inflicted on men: his full torment is not until he is cast into "the lake of fire" (*v.* 10). **2. that old**—ancient (ch. xii. 9). **thousand years**. As *seven* implies universality, so a *thousand* implies *perfection*, whether in good or evil, (*Aquinas*, on ch. xi.) *Thousand* symbolizes the world is perfectly pervaded by the Divine: since *thousand* is *ten*, the number of the world, raised to the *third* power, the number of God (*Auberlen*). It may denote *literally* a *thousand years*. **3. shut him.** א A B, Vulgate, Syriac, *Andreas*, omit "him." **set a seal upon him** [*epano*]—

till the thousand years should be fulfilled: and after that he must be loosed a little season.

4 And I saw *e*thrones, and they sat upon them, and *f*judgment was given unto them: and *I saw* *g*the souls of them that were beheaded for the witness of Jesus, and for the word of God, and *h*which had not worshipped the beast, neither his image, neither had received *his* mark upon their foreheads, or in their hands; and they lived and *i*reigned with Christ a

5 thousand years. But the rest of the dead lived not again until the thou-

6 sand years were finished. This *is* the first resurrection. Blessed and

A. D 96.

* Dan. 7.
Matt. 19.2t.
Luke 22.30.
f 1 Cor. 6. 2,3.
g Mal. 4. 5.
ch. 6. 9.
h ch 13. 12.
i Rom. 8. 17.
2 Tim 2.12.
ch. 5 9, 10.

sealed up the door of the abyss '*over*' his head. A surer seal than his seal over Jesus in Joseph's tomb burst on the resurrection morn. Satan's binding at this juncture is not arbitrary, but the necessary consequence of the events, ch. xix. 20; just as Satan's being cast out of heaven, where he was previously accuser of the brethren, was the legitimate judgment passed on him through the death, resurrection, and ascension of Christ (ch. xii. 7-10). Satan imagined he had overcome Christ on Golgotha; but the Lord in death overcame him, and, by His ascension as our righteous Advocate, cast out the accuser from heaven. Time was given him on earth to make the beast and harlot powerful, then to concentrate all his power in antichrist. The antichristian kingdom, his last effort, being destroyed by Christ's mere appearing, his power on earth is at an end. He thought to destroy God's people by persecutions (just as previously to destroy Christ); but the Church is not destroyed from the earth, but raised to rule over it; and Satan himself is shut up for a thousand years in the 'abyss' ("bottomless pit"), preparatory to the "lake of fire," his final doom. As before he ceased, by Christ's ascension, to be accuser in heaven, so during the millennium he ceases to be seducer and persecutor on earth. As long as he rules in the darkness of the world, we live in an atmosphere impregnated with deadly elements. A mighty purification will be effected by Christ's coming. Though sin will not be abolished—for men will still be in the flesh (Isa. lxv. 20)—sin will no longer be a universal power, for the flesh is no longer seduced by Satan. He will not be, as now, 'the god and prince of the world;' nor will the world 'lie in the wicked one:' the flesh will become ever more overcome. Christ will reign with His transfigured saints over men in the flesh (*Auberlen*). The nations in the millennium will be prepared for a higher state, as Adam in Paradise, supposing he had lived in an unfallen state. Cf. ch. xxi., notes, at beginning. This will be the *manifestation* of "the world to come," already set up invisibly in the saints, amidst "this world" (2 Cor. iv. 4; Heb. ii. 5; v. 5). The rabbis thought, as the world was created in six days, and on the *seventh* God rested, so there would be six millenaries, followed by a Sabbatical millennium. Of seven years, every seventh is the year of remission: so of the seven thousand of the world, the seventh millenary shall be the millenary of remission. A tradition in the house of Elias, A. D. 200, states, the world is to endure 6,000 years: 2,000 before the law, 2,000 under the law, and 2,000 under Messiah. Cf. note and margin, Heb. iv. 9; ch, xiv. 13. *Papias, Justin Martyr, Irenæus, Cyprian*, expected a millennial kingdom on earth: not till millennial views degenerated into carnalism was this doctrine abandoned. **that he should deceive.** So A; א, 'shall;' but B, '*that he deceive*' [*plana*, for *planeesee*]. **and.** So Coptic, *Andreas*; but א A B, Vulgate, omit "and."

4. they sat—the twelve apostles, and the saints in general. **judgment was given unto them**

(note, Dan. vii. 22)—the office of judging, (2 Cor. v.) Though having to stand before the judgment seat of Christ (2 Cor. v. 10), yet they 'do not come into judgment (condemnation), but have already passed from death unto life' (John v. 24). **souls.** This term is made a plea for denying the literal first resurrection, as if the life and reign of souls were raised in this life from the death of sin by vivifying faith. But "souls" expresses their *disembodied* state (cf. ch. vi. 9) at first; "and they lived" implies their *coming to life in the body again*, so as to be *seen* by John, as *v.* 5, "This is the first resurrection," proves: for as "the rest of the dead lived not (again) until," &c., must refer to the *bodily* general resurrection, so must *the first resurrection* refer to the body. If the first resurrection be not corporeal, then the saints do not rise at all; for they do not rise with "the rest of the dead." This also accords with 1 Cor. xv. 23. Cf. Ps. xlix. 11-15. "Souls" is in counting used for *persons* (Acts xxvii. 37; 1 Pet. iii. 20: cf. LXX.; Lev. xxii. 4): 'a dead body.' **beheaded** [*pepelekismenōn*]—'smitten with an axe:' a *Roman* punishment, though crucifixion, casting to beasts, and burning, were the common modes. The guillotine, in revolutionary France, still continued in imperial France, is a revival of the capital punishment of imperial Rome. Paul was *beheaded*, and shall share *the first resurrection*, in accordance with his prayer that he 'might attain unto *the resurrection from out of the rest of the dead*' [*exanastasis*] (Phil. iii. 11). **for . . . for** [*dia*]—'on account of.' **and which**—'and the *which:*' and prominent among this class (the beheaded), *such as* did not worship the beast, &c. So ch. i. 7. The *extent* of the first resurrection is not spoken of here. In 1 Cor. xv. 23, 51; 1 Thess. iv. 14, we find, all "in Christ" shall share in it. John himself was not "beheaded;" yet who doubts he shall share in it? The martyrs are put first, because most like Jesus in suffering and death, therefore nearest Him in life and reign; for Christ implies there are relative degrees and places of honour in His kingdom, the highest being for those who drink His cup of suffering (Matt. xx. 22, 23; Luke xxii. 28-30). Next, those who have not bowed to the world-power, but looked to the things unseen and eternal. **neither**—'not yet.' **foreheads . . . hands**—'forehead ... hand.' **reigned with Christ**—over the earth. **5. But.** B, Coptic, *Andreas*, 'and;' A, Vulgate, omit. **again.** A B, Vulgate, Coptic, *Andreas*, omit. *Lived* is used for *lived again*, as in ch. ii. 8. John saw them not only when restored, but in the act of reviving (*Bengel*). **first resurrection**—'the resurrection of the just' (Luke xiv. 14). Earth is not yet transfigured, so cannot be meet for the transfigured saints; but *from heaven* they with Christ rule the earth, there being a much freer communion of the heavenly and earthly churches (a type of which is seen in the forty days during which the risen Saviour appeared to His disciples); they know no higher joy than to lead their brethren on earth to the same salvation as they share themselves. The millennial reign on earth

holy *is* he that hath part in the first resurrection: on such the *ʲ* second death hath no power, but they shall be priests *ᵏ* of God and of Christ, and shall reign with him a thousand years.

does not rest on an isolated passage, but all Old Testament prophecy goes on the same view (cf. Isa. iv. 3; xi. 9; xxxv. 8). Jesus, whilst opposing the Jews' expectation of a carnal kingdom, confirms the Old Testament view of a coming earthly Jewish kingdom of glory: beginning from within, and spreading now spiritually, the kingdom of God shall manifest itself outwardly at Christ's coming again. The papacy is a blasphemous anticipation of the visible Headship which Christ shall then assume. It is reigning as kings without Christ (1 Cor. iv. 8; *Irenæus*, v., 36, 1; xxxv., 1, 2; *Justin Martyr*, 'Dial.,' li., 80). *Melito* and *Tertullian* ('Adv. Marcion'), in the age next after John, held that Jerusalem will be rebuilt, and the saints enjoy the sight of the Lord in various degrees in the holy city for a thousand years, and in heaven; and that this is part of the entireness of sound Christian faith. 'When Christianity became a worldly power under Constantine, the future hope was weakened by joy over present success' (*Bengel*). Becoming a harlot, the Church ceased to be a bride going to meet her Bridegroom. The rights which the harlot usurped shall be exercised in holiness by the Bride. They are "kings" because "priests" (*v.* 6; ch. i. 6; v. 10); their priesthood unto God and Christ (ch. vii. 15) is the ground of their kingship towards men. Men will be willing subjects of the transfigured priest-kings, in the day of the Lord's power. Their power is that of attraction, winning the heart; not counteracted by devil or beast. Church and State shall be co-extensive. Man, created 'to have dominion over the earth,' is to rejoice over *his* world with unmixed joy. St. John saith that instead of the devil, the transfigured Church—Daniel, that instead of the heathenish beast, the holy Israel—shall rule (*Auberlen*). **6. Blessed**—(cf. ch. xiv. 13; xix. 9.) **on such the second death hath no power**—even as it has none on Christ now risen. **priests of God.** Apostate Christendom being destroyed, and the believing Church translated, there will remain Israel and the heathen, the majority of men then alive, who, not having come into contact with the Gospel, have not been guilty of rejecting it. These will be subjects of a general conversion (ch. xi. 15). "The veil" shall be taken off Israel first, then from off "all people" (Isa. xxv. 7). The glories attending Christ's appearing, the destruction of antichrist, transfiguration of the Church, and binding of Satan, will prepare the nations for embracing the Gospel. As *individual* regeneration goes on now, so a "regeneration" of *nations* then. Israel, as a nation, shall be 'born at once—in one day' (Isa. lxvi. 8). As *the Church* begins at Christ's ascension, so the *kingdom* at His second advent. The humiliation of civilized nations will be, that nations which they despise—Jews and barbarians, the negro descendants of Ham, under the curse of Noah, Kush, and Sheba—shall supplant them, (cf. Deut. xxxii. 21; Rom. x. 19; xi. 20, &c.) Since the Jews' rejection, revelation has been silent. Both Old and New Testaments are written by Jews. If revelation is to recommence in the millennial kingdom, converted Israel must head humanity. Jews and Gentiles stand on an equal footing, as both alike needing mercy; but as regards God's instrumentalities for establishing His kingdom on earth, Israel is His chosen people. The Israelite priest-kings on earth are what the transfigured priest-kings are in heaven, A blessed

chain of giving and receiving—God, Christ, the transfigured Bride, the Church, Israel, the world of nations. A new time of revelation will begin by the outpouring of the Spirit (Zech. xii. 10). Ezekiel (xxxix. 29; xl. 48), son of a priest, sets forth Israel's priestly character; Daniel, the statesman, its kingly; Jeremiah (xxxiii. 17-21), both its priestly and kingly. In the Old Testament, Israel's national life was religious in an external legalism. The New Testament Church insists on inward renewal, but leaves outward manifestations free. But in the millennial kingdom, all spheres of life shall be Christianized from within outwardly. The Mosaic ceremonial corresponds to Israel's priestly office; the civil law to its kingly office. The Gentile Church, adopting the moral law, exercises the prophetic office by the Word working inwardly. But when the royal and the priestly office shall be revived, then—the *principles* of the epistle to the Hebrews remaining—the ceremonial and civil law also will develop its spiritual depths in Divine worship (cf. Matt. v. 17-19). Now is the time of preaching; then the time of *liturgy* of "the great congregation" shall come. Our present defective governments shall give place to perfect rule in Church and State. Under the Old Testament the Jews exclusively, in the New Testament the Gentiles chiefly, enjoy salvation; in the millennium both Jews and Gentiles united, under the first-born brother, Israel, walk in the light of God, realizing the full life of humanity. The human race is not an aggregate of individuals and nationalities, but *an organic whole*, laid down once for all (Gen. ix. 25-27; x. 1, 5, 18, 25, 32; Deut. xxxii. 8, declares that from the first the division of the nations was made with relation to Israel). Hence arises the importance of the Old Testament to the Church. Three grand groups—Hamites, Japhethites, and Shemites—correspond respectively to man's three fundamental elements—body, soul, and spirit. The flower of Shem, the representative of *spiritual* life, is Israel: as the flower of Israel is He in whom all mankind is summed up, the second Adam (Gen. xii. 1-3), Israel is mediator of Divine revelations for all times. Even nature and the animal-world will share in the millennial blessedness (Isa. lxv. 20-25). As sin loses its power, decay and death will decrease (*Auberlen*). Earthly and heavenly glories shall be united in the twofold election. Elect Israel in the flesh shall stand at the head of the earthly; the elect spiritual Church, the Bride, in the heavenly. These elections are not merely for the good of the elect, but for those to whom they minister. The heavenly Church is elected, not merely to salvation, but to rule in love, and minister blessings over the earth, as king-priests. The glory of the transfigured shall be a blessing to men in the flesh; as at the transfiguration the three earthly disciples enjoyed the glory of Jesus, and of Moses and Elias, so that Peter exclaimed, "It is good for us to be here:" 2 Pet. i. 16-18 makes the transfiguration the earnest of Christ's coming in glory. The privilege of "our high *calling* in Christ" is limited to the present time of Satan's reign; when he is bound, there will be no scope for suffering for, and so afterwards *reigning* with, Him (ch. iii. 21: cf. note, 1 Cor. vi. 2). None are saved in the present age, in the Christian pale, who shall not also reign with Christ, the preliminary to which is suffering with Christ now. If we fail to gain the crown, we

7   And when the thousand years are expired, Satan shall be loosed out
8 of his prison, and shall *l* go out to deceive the nations which are in the
four quarters of the earth, *m* Gog and Magog, *n* to gather them together
9 to battle: the number of whom *is* as the sand of the sea. And *o* they
went up on the breadth of the earth, and compassed the camp of the
saints about, and the beloved city: and fire came down from God out of
10 heaven, and devoured them. And the devil, that deceived them, was
cast into the lake of fire and brimstone, where the beast and the false
prophet *are,* and shall be tormented day and night for ever and ever.
11   And I saw a great white throne, and him that sat on it, from whose
face *p* the earth and the heaven fled away; *q* and there was found no place
12 for them. And *r* I saw the dead, small and great, stand before God:
s and the books were opened; and *t* another book was opened, which is

A. D. 96.

l Job 1. 7.
1 Pet. 5. 8.
m Eze. 38.
Eze. 39.
n ch. 16. 14.
o Isa 8. 8.
p 2 Pet 3. 7.
q Dan 2. 35.
r John 5. 22.
2 Cor. 5.
1 Thes. 4.
15, 17.
s Dan. 7. 10.
t Ps. 69. 28
Dan. 12. 1.
Phil. 4. 3.

lose all—'*the gift of grace* as well as the *reward of service*' (De Burgh).

7. expired—'finished.' **8.** quarters—'corners.' **Gog and Magog**—(notes, Ezek. xxxviii., xxxix.) Magog represents northern nations of Japheth's posterity, whose ideal head is Gog (Gen. x. 2). A has but one article to "Gog and Magog," whereby the prince and the people are closely connected; B reads the second article before Magog. *Hiller* ('Onomasticon') explains both as *lofty, elevated.* **to battle**—'to *the* war,' in א A B; but *Andreas* omits 'the.' **9. on the breadth of the earth**—completely overspreading it. Perhaps translate, '. . . of the (holy) *land.*' **the camp of the saints . . . and the beloved city**—the camp of the saints encircling *the beloved city,* Jerusalem (Ecclus. xxiv. 11). Contrast "hateful" in Babylon, (ch. xviii. 2; '*Jacob,* the beloved,' Deut. xxxii. 15; LXX.) Ezekiel's prophecy of Gog and Magog refers to the attack on Israel *before* the millennium; but this attack is *after* the millennium; so that "Gog and Magog" represent the final adversaries led by Satan. Ezekiel's Gog and Magog come from *the north,* but those here 'from the four corners of the earth.' *Gog* is by some connected with a Hebrew root, 'covered.' **from God.** So B, Vulgate, Syriac, Coptic, *Andreas;* but A omits. Even during the millennium there is a separation between heaven and earth, humanity transfigured and humanity in the flesh. Hence an apostasy can take place at its close. In the judgment on this the world of nature is destroyed and renewed, as the world of history was before the millennium: it is only then that the new heaven and new earth are perfected. The *millennial* heaven and earth, connected but separate, are but a foretaste of this everlasting state, when the upper and lower congregations shall be no longer separate, and new Jerusalem shall descend from God out of heaven. Man's birth-sin, the flesh, shall be the only influence during the millennium to prevent the saving of all souls. When this time of grace shall end, no other shall succeed. For what can move him in whom the Church's visible glory, whilst evil is restrained, evokes no longing for communion with the Church's King? As the history of nations ended with the manifestation of the Church in glory, so that of mankind in general shall end with the separation of the just from the wicked (*v.* 12) (Auberlen). **10. that deceived**—'that deceiveth,' &c. **lake of fire**—his final doom: as "the bottomless pit" (*v.* 1) was his temporary prison. **where.** So א, Coptic; but A B, Vulgate, Syriac, 'where *also.*' **the beast and the false prophet are**—(ch. xix. 20.) **day and night**—*without intermission* (ch. xxii. 5), such as now night interposes between day and day. The same phrase is used of the eternal state of the blessed (ch. iv. 8). As the bliss is

eternal, so the woe must be. As the beast and the false prophet led the former conspiracy against Christ and His people, so Satan in person heads the last. Satan shall be permitted to enter this paradise regained, to show the security of believers, unlike the first Adam, whom Satan robbed of paradise; and shall, like Pharaoh at the Red Sea, receive in this last attempt his final doom, for ever and ever—'to the ages of the ages.'

11. great—in contrast to the "thrones" (*v.* 4), **white**—emblem of purity and justice. **him that sat on it**—the Son, to whom 'the Father hath committed all judgment,' God in Christ, *i. e.,* the Father represented by the Son, before whose judgment-seat we must all stand. The Son's mediatorial reign is to prepare the kingdom for the Father's acceptance, which having done, He shall give it up to the Father, 'that God may be all in all,' coming into direct communion with His creatures, without a Mediator's intervention, for the first time since the fall. Christ's *Prophetical* mediation was prominent in His earthly ministry; His Priestly is prominent now in heaven between His first and second advents; His Kingly shall be so during the millennium and at the general judgment. **earth and . . . heaven fled away.** The final conflagration precedes the general judgment, followed by the new heaven and new earth, (ch. xxi.) **12. the dead**—'the rest of the dead' who did not share the first resurrection, and those who died during the millennium. **small and great.** B, '*the* small and *the* great.' A א, Vulgate, Syriac, *Andreas,* 'the (א has 'both' for 'the') great and the small' (ch. vi. 15). The wicked who died from Adam to Christ's second advent, and all the righteous and wicked who died during and after the millennium, shall then be judged. The transfigured godly, who reigned with Christ during it, shall also be present, not to have their portion assigned (for that was fixed long before, John v, 24), but to have it *confirmed* for ever, and that God's righteousness may be vindicated in both the saved and the lost, before an assembled universe. Cf. "We must ALL appear," &c. (Rom. xiv. 10; 2 Cor. v. 10). The saints having been pronounced just by Christ out of "the book of life," shall be assessors of the Judge, Cf. Matt. xxv. 31, 32, 40, "*these* my brethren." God's omniscience will not allow the least to escape: His omnipotence the mightiest must obey. The *living* are not mentioned: as these shall probably first (before the destruction of the ungodly, *v.* 9) be transfigured, and caught up with the saints long previously transfigured; and though present for confirmation of their justification by the Judge, shall not then first have their eternal state assigned, but sit as Christ's assessors. **the books . . . opened**—(Dan. vii. 10.) The books of God's remembrance, of evil

723

the book of life: and the dead were judged out of those things which
13 were written in the books, "according to their works. And the sea gave
up the dead which were in it; and death and ¹ hell delivered up the dead
which were in them: and they were judged every man according to their
14 works. And ʸdeath and hell were cast into the lake of fire. This is the
15 second death. And whosoever was not found written in the book of life
was cast into the lake of fire.

21 AND "I saw a new heaven and a new earth: for the first heaven and
2 the first earth were passed away; and there was no more ᵇsea. And I

A. D. 96.	
" Jer. 17. 10	
Matt. 16. 27.	
Rom. 2. 6.	
¹ Or, the grave.	
ʸ 1 Cor 15. 26.	
CHAP. 21.	
" Isa. 65. 17.	
Isa. 66. 22.	
ᵇ Isa. 57. 20.	

and good (Ps. lvi. 8; cxxxix. 4; Mal. iii. 16): Conscience (Rom. ii. 15, 16), Christ's Word (John xii. 48), the Law (Gal. iii. 10), God's eternal counsel (Ps. cxxxix. 16). **book of life**—(Exod. xxxii. 32, 33; Ps. lxix. 28; Dan. xii. 1; Phil. iv. 3; ch. iii. 5; xiii. 8; xxi. 27.) Besides the general book of all, there is a special book for believers, in which their names are written, not for their works, but for Christ's work *for*, and *in*, them: '*the Lamb's* book of life.' Electing grace has singled them out from the mass. **according to their works.** We are justified *by* faith, judged *according to* (not *by*) our works. The general judgment is designed for the final vindication of *God's righteousness* before the universe, which in this chequered dispensation, though really ruling, has been less manifest. *Faith* is appreciable by God and the believer alone (ch. ii. 17). *Works* are appreciable by all. These, then, are the evidential test to decide men's eternal state, showing that God's government is altogether righteous. **13. death and hell**—Hades. The essential identity of the dying and risen body is shown; for the *sea* and *grave* give up *their dead*. The body that sinned or served God shall, in righteous retribution, be the body also that shall suffer, or be rewarded. The "sea" may have a symbolical (*Cluver* from *Augustine*) meaning, as in ch. viii. 8; xii. 12; xiii. 1; xviii. 17, 19. But the literal sense holds good: all the different regions, wherein men's bodies and souls were, gave them up. **14.** Death and Hades personified, cast into the lake of fire, express that Christ and His people shall never more die, or be disembodied spirits. The yawning, craving Sheol, that can never be satisfied, is abolished. "In Christ ALL shall be made alive" (Rom. xiv. 9; 1 Cor. xv. 22). The dark ABYSS and *the first death* are destroyed, and the "LAKE (not an *abyss* or *sea*) of fire," surrounded on all sides by Immanuel's land, substituted: wherein *the second death* is, admitting of no rebellion of thought, word, or deed against God, but a deep everlasting woe, shame, and irreversible separation from the saints, though in their presence and that of God. No empire of evil shall be tolerated, rivalling in extent and continuance the empire of the holy and loving God. Satan's power of rebellion must cease: for Death being the *last* enemy destroyed, Satan too is so (Hos. xiii. 14; 1 John iii. 8). The continual spectacle (ch. xiv. 10) of what the creature is in itself, vanity and shame (Dan. xii. 2), will be one means of retaining the unfallen, ransomed universe, in its only true position of safety, humble dependence on Jehovah: it will eternally show how the God of love repels the spirits in which pride and selfishness reign. Matt. xxvi. 24; Mark xiv. 21, both hint [*kalon*] that eternal *forfeiture of* HONOUR is the doom of the lost (*Birks*). **This is the second death**—"the lake of fire" is added in א A B, *Andreas*. In hell the ancient form of death, one of the enemies destroyed by Christ, shall not continue, but a death far different reigns there, '*everlasting* destruction from the presence of the Lord:' an abiding testimony of Christ's victory. **15.** The bliss of the righteous is not here specified,

as it commenced *before* the final judgment. Cf., however, Matt. xxv. 34, 41, 46.

CHAP. XXI. 1-27.—New Heaven and Earth—New Jerusalem out of Heaven.

The remaining two chapters describe the eternal and consummated kingdom of God on the new earth. As the world of nations is pervaded by Divine influence in the millennium, so that of nature shall be, not annihilated, but transfigured, in the subsequent eternal state. The earth was cursed for man, but is redeemed by the second Adam. *Now* is the Church; in the millennium shall be the kingdom; after that shall be the new world, wherein God shall be all in all. The "day of the Lord" and conflagration of the earth are, in 2 Pet. iii., spoken of together, from which many argue against a millennial interval between His coming and the general conflagration, preparatory to the new earth; but "day" is used often of a period comprising events closely connected, as are the Lord's second advent, the millennium, and the general conflagration and judgment. Cf. Gen. ii. 4, "day." Man's *soul* is redeemed by spiritual regeneration now; man's *body* shall be so at the resurrection; man's *dwelling-place*, his inheritance, the earth, shall be so at the creation of the new heaven and earth, which shall exceed the first paradise, as much as the second Adam exceeds in glory the first Adam before the fall, and as man regenerated in body and soul shall exceed man at creation. Isaiah (lxv. 17) mentions the "new heaven and new earth" in the beginning of the millennium; St. John, at its close: because Isaiah takes the beginning to be a pledge of the completion. God's works are progressive. The millennium, in which sin and death are much restricted, is the transition state from the old to the new earth. The millennium is the age of regeneration. The final age shall be wholly free from sin and death. The millennial earth will not be the dwelling, but the *kingdom*, of the transfigured saints: they shall be "the new Jerusalem" on the new earth subsequently. **1. the first**—the former. **passed away.** In א A B, 'were departed' [*apeelthon*, not *pareelthe*]. **was**—'is:' graphically setting it before our eyes. **no more sea**—the type of perpetual unrest (Isa. lvii. 20; Mark iv. 39). Hence our Lord 'rebukes' it as an unruly hostile troubler of His people. It symbolized the political tumults out of which "the beast" arose (ch. xiii. 1). As the physical corresponds to the spiritual world, so the absence of *sea*, after the earth's metamorphosis by *fire*, answers to the unruffled peace which shall prevail. The *sea*, though severing lands, is now, by God's eliciting good from evil, made the medium of their communication, through navigation. Then man shall possess powers which shall make the *sea* no longer necessary, but a hindrance: a perfect state. A "river" and "water" are mentioned, ch. xxii. 1, 2, probably literal (*i. e.*, with such changes of the natural properties as correspond analogically to man's own transfigured body), as well as symbolical. The sea was once the element

John saw *c* the holy city, new Jerusalem, coming down from God out of
3 heaven, prepared *d* as a bride adorned for her husband. And I heard a
great voice out of heaven, saying, Behold, *e* the tabernacle of God *is* with
men, and he will dwell with them, and they shall be his people, and God
4 himself shall be with them, *and be* their God. And *f* God shall wipe away
all tears from their eyes; and *g* there shall be no more death, *h* neither
sorrow, nor crying, neither shall there be any more pain: for the former
things are passed away.
5 And *i* he that sat upon the throne said, Behold, *j* I make all things
new. And he said unto me, Write: for these words are true and faithful.
6 And he said unto me, It is done. I am Alpha and Omega, the beginning
and the end. *k* I will give unto him that is athirst of the fountain of the
7 water of life freely. He that *l* overcometh shall inherit [1] all things; and
8 *m* I will be his God, and he shall be my son. But *n* the fearful, and unbelieving, and the abominable, and murderers, and whoremongers, and

A. D 96.

c Isa 52. 1.
Gal. 4. 26.
Heb 11. 10.
d Isa. 54 5.
Isa 61. 10.
e Lev. 26. 11.
Eze 43. 7.
f Isa 25. 8.
g 1 Cor.15 26.
h Isa. 35 10.
i ch 4. 2, 9.
j Isa. 43. 19.
k Isa 12. 3.
l Rom. 8. 17.
1 Or these
things
m Zech. 8. 8
n 1 Cor 6. 9.

of the world's destruction, and is still death to thousands; whence, at the general judgment, it is specially said, "the *sea* gave up her dead." Then it shall cease to destroy or disturb: removed on account of its past destruction. **2. And I** John. "John" is omitted in א A B, Vulgate, Syriac, Coptic, *Andreas;* also "I" is not emphatical. The insertion of "I John" would interfere with the close connection between "the new heaven and earth," *v.* 1, and the "new Jerusalem." **Jerusalem . . . out of heaven**—(Gal. iv. 26; Heb. xi. 10; xii. 22; xiii. 14; ch. iii. 12.) The *descent* of the new Jerusalem *out of heaven* is distinct from the *earthly* Jerusalem, in which Israel in the flesh shall dwell during the millennium, and follows on the "new heaven and earth." [John in his gospel always writes *Hierosoluma* of the old city; in the apocalypse, always *Hierousaleem* of the heavenly city (ch. iii. 12). *Hierousaleem* is Hebrew, the original, holy appellation. *Hierosoluma* is the common Greek, in a political sense.] St. Paul observes the same distinction when refuting Judaism (Gal. iv. 26: cf. ch. i. 17, 18; ii. 1; Heb. xii. 22); not so in the epistles to Romans and Corinthians (*Bengel*). **bride**—made up of the citizens of "the holy city." There is no longer merely a paradise, as in Eden (there is that also, ch. ii. 7), a mere garden, but now *the city of God* on earth, costlier and statelier, at the same time the result of labour such as had not to be expended by man in dressing the garden of Eden. "The lively stones" were in time laboriously chiselled into shape, after the pattern of "the chief corner stone," to prepare them for the place which they shall everlastingly fill in the heavenly Jerusalem. **3. out of heaven.** So B, Coptic, *Andreas;* but א A, Vulgate, 'out of the throne.' **the tabernacle** —alluding to that in the wilderness (wherein many signs of His presence were given): of which this is the antitype, having previously been in heaven (ch. xi. 19; also xiii. 6; xv. 5). Cf. the contrast in Heb. ix. 23, 24, between "the patterns" and "the heavenly things themselves;" "the figures" and "the true." The earnest of the heavenly tabernacle is afforded in the Jerusalem temple of the millennium, (Ezek. xl., &c.) **dwell** (tabernacle) **with them.** The same Greek as is used of the Divine Son '*tabernacling* among us' (John i. 14). Then He was in the weakness of the *flesh:* at the new creation He shall tabernacle among us in the glory of His manifested Godhead (ch. xxii. 4). **they**—*in particular,* emphatical. **his people.** א A, 'His *peoples:*' 'the nations of the saved' peculiarly His, as Israel was designed to be; B, Vulgate, Syriac, Coptic, "His *people*." **God himself . . . with them**—realizing fully His name Im-

manuel. **4. all tears**—'every tear.' **no more death**—'death shall be no more:' not the millennium, for in this there is *death* (Isa. lxv. 20; 1 Cor. xv. 26, 54, "the *last* enemy . . . destroyed is *death*," ch. xx. 14, *after* the millennium). **sorrow** —'mourning.' **passed away**—'departed,' as *v.* 1. **5. sat**—'sitteth.' **all things new**—not recent, but *changed from the old* [*kaina,* not *nea*]. An earnest of this regeneration of nature is given already in the regenerate soul. **unto me.** So א, Coptic, *Andreas;* but A B, Vulgate, Syriac, omit. **true and faithful.** So *Andreas;* but א A B, Vulgate, Syriac, Coptic, transpose, 'faithful and true' (*genuine*). **6. It is done**—*come to pass.* The same Greek as ch. xvi. 17. So Vulgate; but A, 'they (*these words, v.* 5) are come to pass.' All is as sure as if actually fulfilled; for it rests on God's unchanging word. When the consummation shall be, God shall rejoice over His work, as at the first creation God *saw everything that He had made, and behold it was very good.* **Alpha and Omega.** In A B, '*the* Alpha . . . *the* Omega' (ch. i. 8). **give unto . . . athirst . . . water of life** —(Isa. xii. 3; lv. 1; John iv. 13, 14; vii. 37, 38; ch. xxii. 17): added lest any should despair of attaining this exceeding weight of glory. *Now* we may drink of the stream, *then* we shall drink at the *Fountain.* **freely**—'gratuitously;' the same [*dorean*] as is translated, "(They hated me) without a cause" (John xv. 25). As *gratuitous* as was man's hatred of God, so *gratuitous* is God's love to man: there was every cause in Christ why man should love, yet man hated Him; there was every cause in man why (humanly speaking) God should hate, yet God loved man. Even in heaven, our drinking at the Fountain shall be God's *gratuitous* gift. **7. He that overcometh.** Another aspect of the believer's life: conflict with sin, Satan, and the world. *Thirsting* for salvation is the beginning of faith, and continues for ever (as a relish for Divine joys) characteristic of the believer. In a different sense, the believer 'shall never thirst.' **inherit all things**—(1 Cor. iii. 21-23.) א A B, Vulgate, *Cyprian,* read, '*these* things:' the blessings described. **I will be his God**—'to him a God;' *i. e.,* all that is implied of blessing in "God.' **he shall be my son**—emphatical: *He,* in a peculiar sense, above others: 'shall be to *me* a son,' fully realizing the promise made to Solomon, son of David, and antitypically to the Divine Son of David. **8. the fearful** [*deilois*]—'the cowardly,' who do not *quit themselves like men,* so as to "overcome" in the good fight (1 Cor. xvi. 13); who have the spirit of slavish 'fear,' not love, towards God; and through fear of man, are not bold for God, or 'draw back' (cf. *v.* 27; ch. xxii. 15). **unbelieving**

725

sorcerers, and idolaters, and all liars, shall have their part in the lake
which burneth with fire and brimstone: which is the second death.
9 And there came unto me one of the seven angels, which had the seven
vials full of the seven last plagues, and talked with me, saying, Come
10 hither, I will show thee the bride, the Lamb's wife. And he carried me
away in the spirit to a great and high mountain, and showed me [o] that
11 great city, the holy Jerusalem, descending out of heaven from God, having
the glory of God: and her light *was* like unto a stone most precious, even
12 like a jasper stone, clear as crystal; and had a wall great and high, *and*
had twelve gates, and at the gates twelve angels, and names written
thereon, which are *the names* of the twelve tribes of the children of Israel:
13 on the east, three gates; on the north, three gates; on the south, three
14 gates; and on the west, three gates. And the wall of the city had twelve
foundations, and [p] in them the names of the twelve apostles of the Lamb.
15 And he that talked with me [q] had a golden reed to measure the city, and
16 the gates thereof, and the wall thereof. And the city lieth four-square,
and the length is as large as the breadth. And he measured the city
with the reed, twelve thousand furlongs. The length, and the breadth,

A. D 96.

[o] Eze. 48. 15-22

[p] Matt. 10. 2-4. Matt. 16 18. 1 Cor. 3. 10, 11. Gal. 2. 9. Eph. 2. 20. Eph. 3. 5. Eph. 4. 11. Jude 17. ch. 18. 20.

[q] Isa 8. 10. Isa. 28. 17. Eze. 40. 3. Eze 41. 1. Eze. 42. 15, 20. Eze. 47. 3. Zech 2. 1. ch. 11. 1, 2.

—'faithless.' **abominable**—having drunk the harlot's 'cup of abominations.' **sorcerers**—one characteristic of antichrist's time. As Bar-jesus withstood Paul, so 'the false prophet,' antichrist, the minister of the world-power, shall oppose the witnesses in the last days (Acts xiii. 6-8). **all liars**—'all *the* liars:' cf. 1 Tim. iv. 1, 2, where *lying*, and dealings with *spirits* and *demons*, are made features of 'the latter times.' **second death**—ch. xx. 14: "*everlasting* destruction," 2 Thess. i. 9; Mark ix. 44, 46, 48.

9. The angel who showed John *Babylon, the harlot*, appropriately shows him, in contrast, *new Jerusalem, the Bride* (ch. xvii. 1-5). The angel is the one that had the seven last plagues, to show that the ultimate blessedness of the Church is one end of the Divine judgments on her foes. **unto me.** א A B, Vulgate, omit. **the Lamb's wife**—in contrast to her *who sat on many waters* (ch. xvii. 1); *i. e.*, intrigued with many peoples of the world, instead of giving her undivided affections, as the Bride, to the Lamb. **10.** The words correspond to ch. xvii. 3, to heighten the contrast of the Bride and the harlot. **mountain**—(cf. Ezek. xl. 2.) **that great.** Omitted in א A B, Vulgate, Syriac, Coptic. 'The holy city Jerusalem.' A perfect cube: the complete elect Church. **descending.** Even in the millennium the earth will not be a suitable abode for transfigured saints, who therefore shall reign in heaven over the earth. But after the millennium and judgment, they shall *descend* from heaven to dwell on an earth renewed, and assimilated to heaven itself. "From God," implies, 'we (the city) are God's building' (1 Cor. iii. 9). **11. Having the glory of God**—not merely the Shechinah, but God Himself, as her glory, dwelling in the midst of her. Cf. the type, earthly Jerusalem in the millennium (Zech. ii. 5: cf. *v.* 23, below). **her light** [*phoster*]—'light-giver:' properly applied to the sky's light-giving *luminaries* (note, Phil. ii. 15, its only other occurrence). "And," before "her light," is omitted in א A B, Vulgate. **even like**—'as it were.' **jasper**—representing *watery crystalline brightness.* **12. And.** א A B omit. Ezek. xlviii. 30-35, similarly, which implies that the millennial Jerusalem shall have its antitype in the heavenly Jerusalem descending on the finally-regenerated earth. **wall great and high**—the security of the Church. Also, the exclusion of the ungodly. **twelve angels**—guards of the twelve gates: an additional emblem of perfect security; whilst the gates being never shut (*v.* 25), imply perfect liberty and peace. Also, angels shall be brethren of the heavenly citizens. **names of the twelve tribes.** The inscription of the names on the gates implies that none but spiritual Israel, God's elect, shall enter. As the millennium, wherein *literal* Israel *in the flesh* shall be mother church, is antitype to the Old Testament *earthly* theocracy in Canaan, so the *heavenly* Jerusalem is the consummation antitypical to the *spiritual* Israel, the elect Jews and Gentiles being now gathered out: as spiritual Israel now is an advance upon the previous literal Israel, so the heavenly Jerusalem shall be much in advance of the millennial Jerusalem. **13. on the north . . . on the south.** א A B, Vulgate, Syriac, Coptic, read, '*and* on the north *and* on the *south*.' In Ezek. xlviii. 32, Joseph, Benjamin, Dan (for which Manasseh is substituted in ch. vii. 6), are on the east; Reuben, Judah, Levi, on the *north;* Simeon, Issachar, Zebulun, on the *south;* Gad, Asher, Naphtali, on the *west.* In Num. ii., Judah, Issachar, Zebulun, are on the east; Reuben, Simeon, Gad, on the south; Ephraim, Manasseh, Benjamin, on the *west;* Dan, Asher, Naphtali, on the *north.* **14. twelve foundations.** Joshua, the type of Jesus, chose twelve of the people to carry stones over Jordan, as Jesus chose twelve apostles to be foundations of the heavenly city, Himself being the chief corner-stone. Peter is not the only apostolic rock on whose preaching Christ builds His Church. Christ is the true Foundation: the twelve are foundations only in their apostolic testimony concerning Him. Though Paul was an apostle, besides the twelve, yet the mystical twelve representing the Church is retained—viz., three, the Divine, multiplied by four, the world-number. **in them** (so Vulgate) **the names, &c.** As architects inscribe their names on their great works, so the apostles shall be held in everlasting remembrance. א A B, Syriac, Coptic, *Andreas*, read, 'upon them.' These also insert "twelve" before "names." **15. had a golden reed.** So Coptic; but א A B, Vulgate, Syriac, read, 'had (as) *a measure* a golden reed.' In ch. xi. 2, the non-measuring of the outer courts of the temple implied its being given up to secular desecration. Here, the city being measured implies the entire consecration of every part, brought up to the exact standard of God's requirements; also God's guardianship henceforth of even the most minute parts of His Holy City from evil. **16. twelve thousand furlongs**—'*to* 12,000 *stadia*:'

17 and the height of it are equal. And he measured the wall thereof, an
hundred *and* forty *and* four cubits, *according to* the measure of a man,
18 that is, of the angel. And the building of the wall of it was *of* jasper:
19 and the city *was* pure gold, like unto clear glass. And 'the foundations
of the wall of the city *were* garnished with all manner of precious stones.
The first foundation *was* jasper; the second, sapphire; the third, a chal-
20 cedony; the fourth, an emerald; the fifth, sardonyx; the sixth, sardius;
the seventh, chrysolite; the eighth, beryl; the ninth, a topaz; the tenth,
21 a chrysoprasus; the eleventh, a jacinth; the twelfth, an amethyst. And
the twelve gates *were* twelve pearls; every several gate was of one pearl:
⁴and the street of the city *was* pure gold, as it were transparent glass.
22 And ⁴I saw no temple therein: for the Lord God Almighty and the Lamb
23 are the temple of it. And ⁴the city had no need of the sun, neither of
the moon, to shine in it: for the glory of God did lighten it, and the
24 Lamb *is* the light thereof. And ⁵the nations of them which are saved
shall walk in the light of it: and the kings of the earth do bring their
25 glory and honour into it. And the gates of it shall not be shut at all
26 by day: for ⁵there shall be no night there. And they shall bring the
27 glory and honour of the nations into it. And ⁵there shall in no wise
enter into it any thing that defileth, neither *whatsoever* worketh abomination or *maketh* a lie; but they which are written in the Lamb's ⁵book
of life.

22 AND he showed me ⁴a pure river of water of life, clear as crystal,

A. D 96.
ʳ Isa. 54. 11.
⁴ ch 22. 2.
ᵗ 1 Ki. 6. 27.
Isa. 66. 1.
John 4. 23.
1 Cor.13.12.
1 Cor.15.28.
ᵘ Isa. 24. 2?.
Isa. 60. 19.
ᵛ Isa 60. 3.
Isa 66. 12.
ʷ Isa. 60. 20.
Isa 35. 8.
Isa 52. 1.
Joel 3. 17.
ch. 22. 14,
15.
ʸ Ps 69. 28.
Dan. 12. 1.
ch. 4. 3.
ch. 3. 5.
ch. 13. 8.
CHAP. 22.
ᵃ Ps. 36. 8.
Eze. 47. 1.
Zech. 14. 8.
John 7. 38,
39.

1,000 furlongs being the space between the several
twelve gates. *Bengel* makes the length of *each
side* of the city 12,000 *stadia.* The stupendous
height, length, and breadth being exactly alike,
imply its faultless symmetry, transcending in
glory all our most glowing conceptions. **17. hundred and forty and four cubits**—twelve times
twelve: the Church-number squared. The wall is
far beneath the height of the city. **measure of a
man, that is, of the angel.** The ordinary measure
used by *men* is the measure here used by the *angel*, distinct from 'the measure of the sanctuary.'
Men shall then be *equal to the angels.* **18. the
building**—'the structure' (*Tregelles*) [*endomeesis*].
gold, like unto clear glass—ideal gold, transparent as no gold is (*Alford*). Excellencies will be
combined, now incompatible. **19. And.** So Syriac,
Coptic, *Andreas*; but A B, Vulgate, omit. Cf. *v.*
14; also Isa. liv. 11. **all manner of precious
stones.** Contrast ch. xviii. 12, as to Babylon.
These constituted the "foundations." **chalcedony**
—agate from Chalcedon: semi-opaque, sky-blue,
with stripes of other colours (*Alford*). **20. sardonyx**—having the redness of cornelian, and the
whiteness of onyx. **sardius**—(note, ch. iv. 3.)
chrysolite—described by *Pliny* as transparent,
and of a golden brightness, like topaz; different
from our pale green crystallized *chrysolite.* **beryl**
—sea-green. **topaz.** *Pliny* (xxxvii., 32) makes it
green and transparent, like our chrysolite. **chrysoprasus**—somewhat pale, having the purple of
the amethyst (*Pliny*, xxxvii., 20, 21). **jacinth.**
The violet brightness in the amethyst is diluted
in the jacinth (*Pliny*, xxxvii., 41). **21. every
several**—'each one severally.' **22. no temple . . .
God . . . the temple.** As God now dwells in the
spiritual Church, His "temple" [*naos*, shrine] (1
Cor. iii. 17: vi. 19), so the Church perfected shall
dwell in Him as her "temple" [*naos*]. As the
Church was "His sanctuary" (Ps. cxiv. 2), so He
is to be theirs. Means of grace cease when the
end of grace is come. Church ordinances give
place to the God of ordinances. Uninterrupted,
immediate communion with Him and the Lamb
(cf. John iv. 23) supersedes intervening ordinances.

23. **in it.** So Vulgate; but א A B, *Andreas,*
'(shine) *on* it,' or, 'for her.' **the light**—'the
lamp' (Isa. lx. 19, 20). The direct light of God
and the Lamb shall make the saints independent
of God's creatures, the sun and moon. **24. of them
. . . saved . . . in.** א A B, Vulgate, Coptic, *Andreas,* '(the nations shall walk) *by means of* [*dia
photos*] her light;' omitting "of them which are
saved." Her brightness supplies them with light.
the kings of the earth—who once sought only
their own glory, being converted, in the new
Jerusalem bring their glory to lay it down at the
feet of their God and Lord. **and honour.** So B,
Vulgate, Syriac; but א A omit. **25. not be shut
. . . by day**—therefore never; for it shall *always*
be day. Gates are usually shut by night; but in
it shall be no night. There shall be continual
free ingress; so that all which is blessed may be
brought into it. So in the millennial type. **26.**
All that was truly glorious in the earth and its
converted nations is gathered into it. Whilst all
are *one*, there are various orders among the redeemed, analogous to the *nations* on earth constituting one great human family, and to the various
orders of angels. Still, the Bride, the transfigured
Church, that reigned above during the millennium, and descended after it on the new earth, as
its "holy Jerusalem," is probably the prominent
centre, and the nations (saved in the millennium?)
partake of her blessedness (*v.* 24, note), 'walking
in *her* light,' and 'healed' by 'the leaves of the
tree of life.' Dwelt in by Jehovah, she will be the
medium of blessings to the new earth (cf. Luke
xix. 17, 19). **27. any thing that defileth** [*koi-
noun*]. א A B read [*koinon*], 'anything *unclean.*'
in the Lamb's book of life—(note, ch. xx. 12, 15.)
As the filth of old Jerusalem was carried outside
the walls and burnt, so nothing defiled shall enter
the heavenly city, but be burnt *outside* (cf. ch.
xxii. 15). The apostle of love, who shows us the
glories of the heavenly city, is he also who speaks
plainly of the terrors of hell.

CHAP. XXII. 1-21.—RIVER OF LIFE—TREE
OF LIFE — OTHER BLESSEDNESSES OF THE RE-
DEEMED — JOHN FORBIDDEN TO WORSHIP THE

2 proceeding out of the throne of God and of the Lamb. In the midst of
the street of it, and on either side of the river, *was there* the *b*tree of life,
which bare twelve *manner of* fruits, *and* yielded her fruit every month:
3 and the leaves of the tree *were* *c*for the healing of the nations. And
*d*there shall be no more curse: but the *e*throne of God and of the Lamb
4 shall be in it; and his servants shall serve him: and *f*they shall see his
5 face; and his name *shall be* in their foreheads. And there shall
be no night there; and they need no candle, neither light of the sun;

A. D. 68

b Gen. 2. 9.
ch. 2. 7.
c ch 21. 24.
d Zech 14.11.
ch. 21. 4
e Eze. 48. 35.
f Matt. 5. ».
1 Cor 13 12.
1 John 3. 2.

ANGEL—NEARNESS OF CHRIST'S COMING TO FIX
MEN'S ETERNAL STATE—TESTIMONY OF JESUS,
HIS SPIRIT, AND THE BRIDE—ANY ADDITION
OR SUBTRACTION SHALL BE ETERNALLY PUN-
ISHED—CLOSING BENEDICTION.
  1. pure. א A B, Vulgate, *Hilary*, 22, omit.
water of life—infinitely superior to the typical
waters in Paradise (Gen. ii. 10-14), and even to
those figurative ones in millennial Jerusalem
(Ezek. xlvii. 1-12; Zech. xiv. 8), as matured
fruit is superior to the flower. The millenniald
waters represent full Gospel grace; these of
new Jerusalem represent Gospel glory. Their
continuous flow from God, the Fountain of life,
symbolizes the uninterrupted life derived by the
saints, ever fresh, from Him: fulness of joy, as
well as perpetual vitality. Like pure crystal, free
from every taint (cf. ch. iv. 6). clear—'bright.'
2. The unity of Scripture is, say the Fathers, a
ring, an unbroken circle, returning into itself.
Between the events of Genesis and those of the
Apocalypse, at least 6,000 or 7,000 years intervene; and between Moses, the first writer, and
John, the last, abou t 1,500 years. As at the be
ginning, man and his wife are presented in innocence in Eden, so at the close, the second Adam,
the Lord from heaven, appears with His Bride, the
Church, in a better paradise, amidst better waters
(*v.* 1). street of it—of the city. on either side
of the river. [For the second *enteuthen,* A B,
Coptic, Syriac, read, *ekeithen.*] The sense is the
same: cf. Greek, John xix. 18. The trees were
on each side, in the middle of the space between
the street and the river. The antitype exceeds
the type: in the first paradise was only *one* tree;
now there are '*very many* trees *at the bank of the
river, on one side and the other.*' Supposing but
one tree, we should either, as *Mede,* suppose that
[*plateia*] street is a *plain* washed on both sides by
the river (as the first paradise was washed on one
side by the Tigris, on the other by the Euphrates),
aud that in the midst of the plain, which itself is
in the midst of the river's branches, stood the
tree. 'In the midst of the street (plain) *itself,* and
of the river (having two branches, flowing on this
and on that side), was there the tree of life.' Or
else (*Durham*), *the tree* was in the midst of the
river, and extending its branches to both banks.
But cf. Ezek. xlvii. 12, the millennial type, which
shows several trees of one kind, all termed "the
tree of life." Death reigns now because of sin:
even in the millennial earth, sin, and therefore
death, though limited, shall not altogether cease.
But in the final heavenly city on earth, sin and
death utterly cease. yielded her fruit every
month—'according to each month:' each month
had its proper fruit; as different seasons now
marked have their own productions: only then,
unlike now, there shall be *no season without its
fruit*—an endless variety, answering to *twelve,*
symbolical of the world-wide Church (notes, ch.
xii. 1; xxi. 14). *Archbishop Whately* thought the
tree of lif was among those of which Adam *freely*
ate (Gen. ii. 9, 16, 17), and that his continuance in
immoriality was dependent on his *continuing* to

eat of it: having forfeited it, he became liable to
death; still, the effects of having eaten of it for a
time appeared in the longevity of the patriarchs.
God could undoubtedly endue a tree with medicinal powers. But Gen. iii. 22 implies, *man had
not yet taken of the tree,* and that if he had, he
would have lived for ever, which, in his fallen
state, would have been the greatest curse. leaves
. . . for the healing—(Ezek. xlvii. 9, 12.) The
leaves shall be *health-giving,* not healing, 'but
securing them against sicknesses; whilst 'the
fruit shall be for meat.' In the millennium (Ezek.
xlvii., and ch. xx.), the Church shall give the
Gospel-tree to the nations outside Israel and the
Church: so shall heal their spiritual malady; but
in the *final, perfect* new Jerusalem here, the state
of all is eternally fixed: no saving process goes on
any longer (cf. *vv.* 11, 15). The "nations" (ch. xxi.
24) are those which long before—viz., in the millennium (ch. xi. 15)—became the Lord's. 3. no
more curse—of which the earnest shall be given
in the millennium (Zech. xiv. 11). God can only
dwell where the curse and its cause—the cursed
thing, sin (Josh. vii. 12)—are removed. So there
follows, 'but the throne of God and of the Lamb
(who redeemed us from the curse, Gal. iii. 10, 13)
shall be in it.' Cf. in the millennium (Ezek.
xlviii. 35). serve him—with *worship* (ch. vii. 15)
and active ministrations, as the angels whom they
resemble (Ps. ciii. 20, 21; Luke xx. 35, 36; *v.* 9).
The sabbatism of heaven, as that of earth, is kept
as much by working mercy and holiness as by
direct worship (John v. 17; Rom. xii. 1). No
separation shall be there between things secular
and divine (ch. xxi. 22). 4. see his face—revealed
in Divine glory *in Christ Jesus.* They shall know
Him with intuitive knowledge, *even as they are
known by Him* (1 Cor. xiii. 9-12): face to face. Cf.
1 Tim. vi. 16, with John xiv. 9. God the Father
can only be seen in Christ. in—'*on* their foreheads.' Not only shall they personally, in secret
(ch. iii. 17), know their sonship, but shall be
known as sons of God to all citizens of new Jerusalem; so that the free flow of mutual love among
Christ's family members will not be checked by
suspicion, as here. 5. there. So *Andreas;* but
א A B, Vulgate, Syriac, 'there shall be no night
any longer' [*eti* for *ekei*]. Moses tells of paradise lost; John, paradise regained. "In the
beginning God created the heaven and the
earth:" so 'Jesus, a new heaven and a new earth.'
Satan, the old serpent, victorious at the beginning;
Satan cast into the lake of fire at the close. Then
the curse (Gen. iii. 17): now "no more curse"
(*v.* 3). Then *death:* now "no more death" (ch.
xxi. 4). Then exclusion from the tree of life:
now its restoration (ch. ii. 7). Night appointed,
Gen. i. 5: "no night there" twice repeated (ch.
xxi. 5; *v.* 5): neither literal nor figurative toil,
ignorance, sorrow. they need. So א; but A,
Vulgate, Coptic, future, 'they *shall* not have
need;' B, '(there shall be) no need.' candle—
'lamp.' א A, Vulgate, Syriac, Coptic, insert,
'light (*of a candle,* or *lamp*);' B omits. of the
sun. So א; but A B omits. giveth . . . light—

728

for [g] the Lord God giveth them light: and [h] they shall reign for ever and ever.

6 And he said unto me, These sayings *are* faithful and true: and the [i] Lord God of the holy prophets sent his angel to show unto his servants

7 the things which must shortly be done. Behold, I come quickly: blessed *is* he that keepeth the sayings of the prophecy of this book.

8 And I John saw these things, and heard *them*. And when I had heard and seen, I fell down to worship before the feet of the angel which showed

9 me these things. Then saith he unto me, See *thou do it* not: for I am thy fellow-servant, and of thy brethren the prophets, and of them which keep the sayings of this book: worship God.

10 And [j] he saith unto me, Seal not the sayings of the prophecy of this

11 book; for the time is at hand. He [k] that is unjust, let him be unjust still: and he which is filthy, let him be filthy still: and he that is righteous, let him be righteous still: and he that is holy, let him be holy still.

12 And, behold, I come quickly; and my reward [l] *is* with me, to give every

13 man according as his work shall be. I [m] am Alpha and Omega, the be-

A. D. 96.

[g] Ps. 36. 9.
Ps. 84. 11.
[h] Dan. 7. 18, 27.
Rom. 5. 17.
2 Tim. 2.12.
1 Pet. 1. 3, 4
ch. 3. 21.
ch. 11. 15.
[i] Heb. 1. 1.
[j] Dan. 8. 26.
Dan. 12.4,9.
ch. 10. 4.
[k] Eze. 3. 27.
2 Tim. 3. 13.
[l] Isa. 40 10.
Matt. 16.27.
Rom. 2. 6-11.
Rom. 14.12.
[m] Isa. 44. 6.

'illumines.' So Vulgate, Syriac; but א B A, '*shall give light.*' **them.** So B, *Andreas;* but א A, '*upon* them.' **reign**—with a glory transcending that of their reign in heaven with Christ over the millennial nations (ch. xx. 4, 6): that reign was but for a time—" a thousand years:" this is ' unto the ages of the ages.'

6. These sayings are ... true—thrice. ch. xix. 9; xxi. 5. For we are slow to believe God is as good as He is. The news seems to us, habituated to this fallen world, too good to be true (*Nangle*). No dreams of a visionary, but realities of God's sure Word. **holy.** So *Andreas;* but א A B, Vulgate, Syriac, Coptic, '(the Lord God of the) *spirits* (of the prophets):' who with His Spirit inspired their spirits to prophesy. There is one Spirit; but individual prophets, according to the measure given them (1 Cor. xii. 4-11), had their own spirits, of which God is the Lord (*Bengel*) (1 Pet. i. 11; 2 Pet. i. 21). **be done**—'come to pass.' **7.** 'And' omitted in Coptic, *Andreas;* inserted by A B, Vulgate, Syriac. **blessed**—(ch. i. 3.)

8. Both here and in ch. xix. 9, 10, the apostle's falling at the angel's feet is preceded by a glorious promise to the Church, and the assurance, 'These are the true sayings of God,' and that those are "blessed" who keep them. Rapturous gratitude and adoration, at the prospect of the Church's glory, transport him out of himself, to fall into an unjustifiable act. Contrast his opposite feeling at the Church's deep fall (*Auberlen*) (ch. xvii. 6, note; xix. 9, 10). **saw ... and heard.** So א; but A B, Vulgate, Syriac, transpose, ' I John (was he) who heard and saw these things.' In ch. xix. 10, it is, " I fell before his feet to worship *him ;*" here, " I fell down to worship (God?) *before the feet* of the angel." It seems unlikely that John, once reproved, would fall into the same error again. Probably John intended to worship [*proskunesis,* a lower worship than *latreia*] *the angel* (ch. xix. 10), but now only *at his feet* intends to worship (God). The angel does not even permit this. **9.** *Lit.,* ' See not:' the abrupt phrase marking the angel's abhorrence of being worshipped, however indirectly. Contrast the fallen angel's temptation to Jesus, " Fall down and worship me" (Matt. iv. 9). **for.** א A B, Vulgate, Syriac, Coptic, *Andreas, Cyprian,* omit " for," suiting the abrupt earnestness of the angel's prohibition of an act derogatory to God. **and of**—" and (the fellow-servant) of thy brethren."

10. Seal not. But in Dan. xii. 4, 9 (cf. viii. 26),

" seal the book," for the vision shall be 'for many days.' The fulfilment of Daniel's prophecy was distant, that of John's is near. The New Testament is the time of the fulfilment. The Gentile church, for which John wrote, needs more to be impressed with the shortness of the period, as it is inclined to conform to the world, and forget the Lord's coming. The Revelation pointed to Christ's coming as distant, for it foretold the succession of seven seals, trumpets, and vials; on the other hand, it proclaims, "Behold, I come quickly." So Christ marked many events to intervene before His coming, yet saith, "Behold, I come quickly," because our right attitude is continual prayerful watching for His coming (Matt. xxv. 6, 13, 19; Mark xiii. 32-37 (*Auberlen*): cf. ch. i. 3). **11. unjust**—'unrighteous:' towards one's fellow-men: opposed to "righteous," below. [*Ho adikon adikesato,* 'he that *doeth unjustly,* let him *do unjustly* still.'] **filthy**—in one's own soul before God: opposed to "holy," consecrated to God as pure. A omits "he which is filthy, let him be filthy still;" but א B support it. In the letter of the Vienne and Lyons Martyrs (in *Eusebius*), in the second century, it is, ' he that is *lawless* [*anomos*], let him be lawless; and he that is righteous, let him be righteous [*dikaiotheto,* "be justified"] still.' No MS. is so old. א A B, Vulgate, Syriac, Coptic, *Andreas, Cyprian,* read, 'let him do righteousness' (1 John ii. 29; iii. 7). The punishment of sin is sin, the reward of holiness is holiness. Eternal punishment is not an arbitrary law, a necessary result from the very nature of things, as the fruit from the bud. No worse punishment can God lay on ungodly men than to give them up to themselves. The solemn lesson is, Be converted now in your short time (*v.* 10, end), before " I come" (*vv.* 7, 12), else you must remain unconverted for ever. Sin in the eternal world will be left to its own consequences: holiness in germ will develop itself into perfect holiness, which is happiness. **12. And.** א A B, Vulgate, Syriac, Coptic, *Cyprian,* omit. **behold, I come quickly**—(cf. *v.* 7.) **my reward is with me**—(Isa. xl. 10; lxii. 11.) **to give**—'to award.' **every man**—'to *each.*' **shall be.** So B in *Mai;* but B in *Tischendorf,* and A א, Syriac, 'is.' **13. I am Alpha**—' *the* Alpha and the Omega.' א A B, Vulgate, Syriac, *Origen, Cyprian,* transpose, ' the first and the last, the beginning and the end.' Cf. ch. i. 8, 17; xxi. 6. At the winding up of the whole Revelation, the Lord Jesus announces

729

14 ginning and the end, the first and the last. Blessed *[n] are* they that do
his commandments, that they may have right to the tree of life, and may
15 enter in through the gates into the city. For without *are* dogs, and sorcerers, and whoremongers, and murderers, and idolaters, and whosoever
16 loveth and maketh a lie. I *[o]* Jesus have sent mine angel to testify unto
you these things in the churches. I am *[p]* the root and the offspring of
David, *and [q]* the bright and morning star.
17 And the Spirit and the bride say, Come. And let him that heareth
say, Come. *[r]* And let him that is athirst come. And whosoever will let
him take the water of life freely.
18 For I testify unto every man that heareth the words of the prophecy
of this book, If *[s]* any man shall add unto these things, God shall add
19 unto him the plagues that are written in this book: and if any man shall
take away from the words of the book of this prophecy, God *[t]* shall take
away his part [1] out of the book of life, and out of the holy city, and *from*
the things which are written in this book.
20 He which testifieth these things saith, Surely *[u]* I come quickly. Amen.

A. D. 96.

[n] Ps. 106. 3, 5.
Ps. 119. 1, 6.
Isa. 56. 1, *.
Dan. 12. 12.
John 14. 15.
[o] 1 Pet. 3. 2 .
[p] Isa. 11. 1.
Jer. 23. 5,
6.
[q] Num. 24.17.
Zech. 6. 12.
[r] Isa. 55. 1.
John 7. 37.
[s] Deut 4. 2.
Deut. 12 32.
Pro. 30. 6.
[t] Ex. 32. : 3.
[1] Or, from
the tree of
life
[u] Heb 9. 23.

Himself the One *before and after whom there is no God.* **14. do his commandments.** So B, Syriac, Coptic, *Cyprian;* but A א, Vulgate, read, '(blessed are they that) *wash their robes'*—viz., *in the blood of the Lamb* (cf. ch. vii. 14). This takes away pretext for the notion of salvation by works. But the English reading is compatible with salvation by grace : for God's first grand Gospel "commandment" is to believe on Jesus (John vi. 28, 29; 1 John iii. 23). Our "right" to [*exousia, privilege over*] the tree of life is due to, not our doings, but what He has done for us. The *privilege* is founded on, not merits, but God's grace. **through—***by* the gates.' **15. For.** So Coptic ; but א A B, *Hippolytus, Andreas, Cyprian,* omit. **dogs**—'the dogs :' the impure, filthy (*v.* 11 : cf. Phil. iii. 2). **maketh**—including 'whosoever *practiseth* a lie' (*W. Kelly*). **16. mine angel**—Jesus is Lord of the angels. **unto you**—ministers and people in the seven representative churches, and, through you, to Christians of all times and places. **root . . . offspring of David.** Appropriate here where assuring His Church of "the sure mercies of David," to Israel first, and through Israel to the Gentiles. *Root* of David, as Jehovah: offspring of David as man. David's Lord, yet David's son (Matt. xxii. 42-45). **the . . . morning star**—ushering in the day of grace in the beginning of this dispensation, and the everlasting day of glory at its close.
17. Reply of the spiritual Church to Christ (*vv.* 7, 12, 16). **the Spirit**—in the churches and the prophets. **the bride.** Not here "wife," as that title applies to her only when the elect shall have been completed. The *invitation,* "Let him that is athirst come," only holds good whilst the Church is but an affianced *Bride,* not the actually wedded *wife.* "Come" is the prayer of the Spirit in the Church and in believers. in reply to Christ's "I come quickly," crying, Even so, "Come" (*vv.* 7, 12); *v.* 20 confirms this. The whole question of your salvation hinges on your being able to hear with joy Christ's "I come," and to reply, "Come" (*Bengel*). Come to glorify the Bride. **let him that heareth**—*i. e.,* let him that heareth the Spirit and Bride saying to the Lord Jesus, "Come," become part of the Bride by faith, and so say with her to Jesus, "Come." Or "heareth" means 'obeyeth :' for until one has *obeyed* the Gospel call, he cannot pray to Jesus, "Come ;" so "hear," John x. 16; ch. i. 3. Let him that obeys Jesus' voice (*v.* 16) join in praying, "Come." Cf.

ch. vi. 1, note, 10. In the view which makes "Come" an invitation to sinners, this clause urges those who hear savingly the invitation to address it to others, as did Andrew and Philip after they had obeyed Jesus' invitation, "Come" (John i. 41, 45). **let him that is athirst come.** As the Bride prays to Jesus, "Come," so she urges all, whosoever *thirst* for participation in the redemption-glory at *His coming to us,* to COME *to Him* in the meantime, and drink of the living waters, the earnest of "the water of life, clear as crystal, proceeding out of the throne of God and of the Lamb" (*v.* 1), in the regenerated heaven and earth. **And.** So Syriac ; but א A B, Vulgate, Coptic, omit "And." **whosoever will**—*i. e.,* is desirous. A descending climax : Let him that *heareth* savingly Christ's voice pray individually, as the Bride does collectively, "Come, Lord Jesus" (*v.* 20). Let him who, though not yet having *heard* unto salvation, nor able to join in the prayer, 'Lord Jesus, come,' still *thirsts* for it. *come* to Christ. Whosoever is even *willing,* though his desires do not yet amount to *thirsting,* let him take the water of life freely—*i. e.,* gratuitously.
18. For. א A B, Vulgate, *Andreas,* read, "I," emphatical. "*I* testify." **unto these things.** A B, *Andreas,* read [*ep' auta* for *pros tauta*], 'unto them.' **add . . . add**—retribution in kind. **19. book.** A B א, Vulgate, Syriac, Coptic, read, 'take away his part (*i. e.,* portion) from the *tree* of life :' *i. e.,* exclude him from the tree of life. **and from the things.** So Vulgate ; but A B א, Syriac, Coptic, *Andreas,* omit "and :" then, "which are writ ten in this book" refers to 'the holy city and the tree of life.' As in the beginning (ch. i. 3), a blessing was promised to the obedient student, so now, at the close, a curse is denounced against those who add to or take from the book.
20. Amen. Even so, come. The Song of Solomon (viii. 14) closes with the same yearning prayer. A B א omit "Even so" [*nai*]. Translate, 'So be it (but א omits *Amen* also), come, Lord Jesus :' joining "Amen," or 'So be it,' not with Christ's saying (for He calls Himself the "Amen" at the beginning of sentences. rather than make it a confirmation at the end), but with St. John's reply. Christ's "I come," and St. John's "Come," are almost coincident : so truly does the believer reflect the mind of his Lord. **21. our.** So Vulgate, Syriac, Coptic ; but A B א omit. **Christ.** So B, Vulgate, Syriac, Coptic, *Andreas ;* but A א omit. **with you all.** B has 'with all the saints.'

21 Even so, come, Lord Jesus. ^{*v*}The grace of our Lord Jesus Christ *be* with you all. Amen.

A. D. 96.

v Rom. 16. 20.

A, Vulgate, has 'with all.' א has 'with the saints.' This closing benediction — Paul's mark in his epistles—was, after Paul's death, taken up by John. The Old Testament ended with a " curse " from *the law;* the New Testament ends with a blessing from the Lord Jesus. **Amen.** So B א, *Andreas.* A, Vulgate Fuldensis, omit.

May the blessed Lord, who has caused all holy Scriptures to be written for our learning, bless this humble effort to make Scripture expound itself, sanctifying it as an instrument towards the conversion of sinners and the edification of saints, to the glory of His great name and the hastening of His kingdom. Amen.

731